The New Unger's Bible Dictionary

Merrill F. Unger

R. K. HARRISON
EDITOR

Howard F. Vos   Cyril J. Barber
CONTRIBUTING EDITORS

MOODY
PUBLISHERS
THE NAME YOU CAN TRUST

Scripture taken from the *New American Standard Bible*,
© 1960, 1962, 1963, 1968, 1971, 1972, 1973, 1975,
1977 by The Lockman Foundation. Used by
permission.
Scripture taken from *The Holy Bible: New International
Version.* © Copyright 1973, 1978, 1984 by the
International Bible Society. Used by permission of
Zondervan Bible Publishers.

Library of Congress Cataloging-in-
Publication Data
Unger, Merrill Frederick, 1909—
    The new Unger's Bible dictionary / Merrill F.
Unger; R. K. Harrison, editor; Howard F. Vos and
Cyril J. Barber, contributing editors. — Rev. and
updated ed.
    p. cm.
    Revision of: Unger's Bible dictionary. 3rd ed. ©
1966.
    ISBN-10: 0-8024-9066-2
    ISBN-13: 978-0-8024-9066-7
    1. Bible—Dictionaries I. Harrison, R. K. (Roland
Kenneth) II. Vos, Howard Frederic, 1925— . III.
Barber, Cyril J. IV. Unger, Merrill Frederick, 1909—
Bible dictionary. V. Title.
BS440.U5 1988
220. 3—dc19   88-9189
                                        CIP

Design copyright © 2005 Lion Hudson plc/
Tim Dowley & Peter Wyart trading as Three's
Company

Worldwide co-edition organised and produced by
Lion Hudson plc
Wilkinson House
Jordan Hill Road
Oxford OX2 8DR
England
Tel: +44 (0) 1865 302750
Fax +44 (0) 1865 302757
email: coed@lionhudson.com
www.lionhudson.com

Printed in Singapore
5 6 14 13 12

Since 1894, Moody Publishers has been dedicated
to equip and motivate people to advance the cause
of Christ by publishing evangelical Christian
literature and other media for all ages around the
world. Because we are a ministry of the Moody
Bible Institute of Chicago, a portion of the proceeds
from the sale of this book go to train the next
generation of Christian leaders.

If we may serve you in any way in your spiritual
journey toward understanding Christ and the
Christian life, please contact us at:
www.moodypublishers.com

Preface

Throughout the history of Christendom there have arisen persons who, by their spiritual insight, intellectual learning, and disciplined dedication of their time and talents to the work of the gospel of Christ, have enriched their own and successive generations in many matters pertaining to the Word of God.

Merrill F. Unger was one of these giants of the Faith. He was a distinguished scholar who received a doctorate in Semitics from Johns Hopkins University; he manifested the sympathies and insights of a conscientious pastor during an influential period of his ministry; his gifts as an instructive, persuasive teacher earned him lasting admiration at Dallas Theological Seminary and beyond, while his reputation as an informed and perceptive Bible student was enhanced by the many books and articles that he wrote, reflecting his wide theological interests and stimulating the reader to further investigation. But above all Dr. Unger was a man of explicit Christian faith. He stated his views clearly and unequivocally, but with a charity that leavened any possible differences of opinion. In whatever he undertook he endeavored to present the centrality of Jesus Christ as Savior and Lord of human life, and at a time when many were questioning some of the basic tenets of Christianity, he remained true to the Faith once delivered to the saints.

His *Bible Dictionary* was one of his outstanding works, revealing as it did the breadth of mind of its compiler. To be invited to revise the work of such an outstanding author was at once daunting, yet gratifying. The passing of time had brought many new insights and discoveries to bear upon biblical knowledge, and it therefore seemed only proper to try to accommodate such information to this popular and well-used *Bible Dictionary*. Nevertheless one approached the prospect of revision with considerable diffidence. What was gratifying about the task was the knowledge that the new information, combined with an attractive physical format, would bring the fruits of Dr. Unger's learning to another generation by extending significantly the life of the original book. Every attempt, however, has been made to preserve all that was distinctive about it, including Dr. Unger's "early" chronology for Old Testament history, his system of cross-referencing and his eschatology.

This revision has been enhanced by the labors of others, including Dr. Howard F. Vos (The King's College), who supplied much new material pertaining to archaeology and geography; Dr. Cyril J. Barber (Insight for Living, and the Simon Greenleaf School of Law), who prepared new bibliographies throughout; and Dr. Eugene H. Merrill (Dallas Theological Seminary), who provided the new entry terms and cross references pertaining to the *New International Version*.

It is hoped that this revised edition of a favorite text will continue to provide an important resource for biblical study, and that the deeply spiritual ideals which Dr. Unger cherished may abound to the glory of Christ, our Savior and Lord.

R. K. Harrison

Preface to the First Edition

In 1900 Charles Randall Barnes edited a *Bible Encyclopaedia* that was the work of a number of distinguished scholars of that day and appeared in both a two-volume and a three-volume edition. In 1913 this work was issued in a single volume, which was identical in content with the earlier *Encyclopaedia* except that a short archaeological supplement by Melvin Grove Kyle was added. This edition was entitled *The People's Bible Encyclopaedia.*

The present dictionary is based upon this earlier *Bible Encyclopaedia.* However, it has been revised and rewritten in the light of the latest historical, archaeological, and linguistic discoveries in Bible lands.

Only because of the drastic nature of the revision and rewriting of this earlier work and in acquiescence to the definite desires of the publisher did the writer consent to the title, *Unger's Bible Dictionary.* In doing so, he has no intention of detracting from the credit due earlier scholars; nor does he have any thought of diminishing his great obligation to them. Rather, he fully confesses his deep indebtedness to those whose labors preceded his.

Where new articles of any length have been added or older entries retained but completely revised, they are usually appended by the editor's initials. Large numbers of entries, however, that have to a great extent been rewritten have not been initialed, and this is likewise the case with many completely rewritten shorter articles.

In addition to *Barnes' Bible Encyclopaedia*, the editor acknowledges his heavy indebtedness to practically all of the standard Bible Dictionaries. Especially useful have been [Sir William] Smith's *Dictionary of the Bible* (edited by James Hackett), Peloubet's, Davis's, Davis's revised by Gehman, and Harper's.

Useful, too, have been *Encyclopaedia Biblica, The Jewish Encyclopaedia, The International Standard Bible Encyclopaedia*, Hasting's *Encyclopaedia of Religion and Ethics*, Hasting's *Dictionary of the Bible, and The New Schaff-Herzog Encyclopaedia of Religious Knowledge.*

Scientific periodicals have been consulted throughout, particularly the *Biblical Archaeologist, The Bulletin of the American Schools of Oriental Research, The Annual of the American Schools of Oriental Research, The Journal of Biblical Literature, Archiv für Orientforschung, Revue Biblique, The Bulletin of the John Rylands Library, The American Journal of Semitic Languages and Literatures, Revue d'Assyriologie, Palästina Jahrbuch, Zeitschrift für Assyriologie*, and *Zeitschrift des Deutschen Palästina-Vereins.*

In the preparation of this work the editor has made extensive use of the labors of contemporary scholars, in particular the published works of the following: Professor William Foxwell Albright, of the Johns Hopkins University, under whose stimulating guidance the author spent three years of study and research; the late professor James H. Breasted and Professor A. T. Olmstead, both of the University of Chicago; Professor Millar Burrows of Yale University; Dr. G. Ernest Wright of McCormick Seminary, Chicago; Dr. Nelson Glueck of the Hebrew Union College, Cincinnati; Eleazar L. Sukenik of the Museum of

Jewish Antiquities, Jerusalem; and Professor H. L. Ginsberg of the Jewish Theological Seminary of New York.

Although the editor is indebted to many authors and publishers, special thanks is due to The Johns Hopkins Press and the Muhlenberg Press for permission to use brief quotations from the writings of W. F. Albright; the University of Chicago Press for permission to quote from D. D. Luckenbill's *Ancient Records of Assyria and Babylonia*, vols. I and 2; the Westminster Press for brief quotations from the *Westminster Historical Atlas to the Bible*, by George Ernest Wright and Floyd Filson; Harper & Brothers, Publishers, for short references from the *Encyclopaedia of Bible Life*, by Madeline S. Miller and J. Lane Miller, and especially for many adaptations and for lengthy quotations from approximately fifty articles in the *Harper's Bible Dictionary*, by Madeline S. Miller and J. Lane Miller; Princeton University Press for brief excerpts from Jack Finegan's *Light from the Ancient Past* and J. B. Pritchard's *Ancient Near Eastern Texts*; and Thomas Nelson & Sons and the Division of Christian Education of the National Council of Churches for brief quotations from the *Revised Standard Version*. Special acknowledgment is given Dr. A. Henry Detweiler, President of the American Schools of Oriental Research, for permission to quote briefly from the *Bulletin*, the *Annuals*, and the *Biblical Archaeologist*.

This dictionary, which is actually a one Bible encyclopaedia, has aimed at clarity, conciseness, and biblical relevancy.

To achieve clarity and simplicity, longer articles have been outlined in bold type, so that a busy reader can more readily locate what he or she is looking for without having to read through an entire article. Hebrew and Greek words have been transliterated for the convenience of lay readers, and full pronunciation of all proper names and places has been given. Mere technical discussions and impractical theorizings have been bypassed.

To achieve conciseness and biblical relevancy the dictionary has omitted subjects that do not have a direct bearing upon the Bible. The goal has been to provide a readily usable handbook for the help of Bible teachers and Christian workers in general.

Duplication has been avoided by a system of cross references. In addition, consecutive study of particular subjects has been facilitated by subgroupings under general topics—such as the Animal Kingdom, Dress, False Gods (but listed under Gods, False), Festivals, Handicrafts, Metrology (weights, measures, coinage), the Mineral Kingdom, and the Vegetable Kingdom. This arrangement enables the reader with ease to gain a comprehensive knowledge of a particular subject, if he or she so desires.

Four emphases characterize this dictionary. First, the *archaeological*. The latest contributions of scientific biblical archaeology have been collated to expand and illustrate Bible backgrounds, customs, and history. Second, the *historical-geographical*. The facts of the history and geography of ancient Near Eastern lands as they bear upon the Bible are copiously drawn upon to make the Old and New Testament live. Third, the *biographical*. Bible characters are presented in consecutive narrative form, and events in their lives are connected with the history, geography, and archaeology of Palestine and the ancient Near East. Fourth, the *doctrinal*. Important biblical doctrines are presented—yet not as held by any one group, but as subscribed to by the various segments of the church as a whole.

In matters of chronology the editor employs an early (c. 1440 B.C.) date for the Exodus and posits an extended period of c. 1400–1020 B.C. for the period of the Judges. On the other hand, he is fully aware of the present trend of modern scholarship to place the Exodus much later (not before c. 1280 B.C.) and thereby practically to telescope the era of the Judges. The editor feels this practice of late-dating in Israel's early history is so seriously out of focus with biblical chronology that he has been unable conscientiously to subscribe to it in a work aimed at being not only accurate scientifically but sound theologically and biblically. However, after the period of Saul (c. 1020 B.C.), the author follows substantially the results of the chronological researches of Albright, Kugler, Vogelstein, Thiele, Begrich, and others in a period where archaeological synchronisms are more specific and incontrovertible.

The editor is especially grateful to Dr. Howard Vos, professor at the Moody Bible Institute, Chicago, for invaluable editorial assistance; and to Mr. Kenneth Taylor and the Moody Press staff for their efficiency in the publication of the work.

Merrill F. Unger, 1957

editor feels this practice of late-dating in Israel's early history is so seriously out of focus with biblical chronology that he has been unable conscientiously to subscribe to it in a work aimed at being not only accurate scientifically but sound theologically and biblically. However, after the period of Saul (c. 1020 B.C.), the author follows substantially the results of the chronological researches of Albright, Kugler, Vogelstein, Thiele, Begrich, and others in a period where archaeological synchronisms are more specific and incontrovertible.

The editor is especially grateful to Dr. Howard Vos, professor at the Moody Bible Institute, Chicago, for invaluable editorial assistance and to Mr. Kenneth Taylor and the Moody Press staff for their efficiency in the publication of the work.

Merrill F. Unger, 1957

Acknowledgments

Photographs

Bible Scene: pp. 3, 29 left, 160, 163, 247, 299, 303 top, 396, 535, 642, 876, 878, 1191, 1233, 1235, 1290

Church's Ministry to the Jews: pp. 266, 303 bottom, 1199

Tim Dowley: pp. 13, 22, 48 top, 58, 93, 96, 97, 98, 99, 101, 106, 122, 123, 161, 164, 167, 191, 202, 209, 225, 263, 272, 291, 294, 336, 339 top, 356, 362, 363, 367, 387, 392, 432, 442, 451, 453, 467, 469, 491, 505, 533, 548, 554, 558, 594, 603, 604 bottom, 619, 645, 655, 672, 673, 675, 676, 677, 679, 692, 704, 707, 709, 712, 723, 738, 757, 789, 798, 814, 826, 831, 833, 854, 891, 902, 906, 907, 909, 913, 944, 958, 995, 1011, 1013, 1018, 1021, 1022, 1023, 1024, 1039, 1050, 1063, 1082, 1086, 1090, 1091, 1098, 1115, 1116, 1149, 1154, 1155, 1170, 1174, 1175, 1192, 1193, 1200, 1207, 1214, 1218, 1221, 1222, 1228, 1230, 1237, 1247, 1249, 1254, 1256, 1263, 1266, 1270, 1271, 1272, 1278 top, 1279, 1294, 1326, 1337, 1338, 1345, 1353 top, 1358, 1361, 1363, 1365, 1389, 1391

Israel Government Press Office: pp. 83, 113, 184, 238, 318, 328, 341, 407, 408, 414, 418, 460 top, 470, 472, 478, 479, 537, 689, 744, 766, 794, 819, 938 bottom, 1059, 1113, 1118, 1146, 1257, 1318, 1325, 1353 bottom, 1392

Greek Tourist Board: p. 1002

Hanan Isaachar: pp. 48 bottom, 758

Jamie Simson: pp. 910, 1321

Jordan Tourist Office: p. 1180

Peter Stibbons: pp. 132, 460 bottom

Unique Image: pp. 183, 753

Peter Wyart: pp. i, 9, 20, 26, 29 right, 34, 42, 84, 90, 104, 114, 115, 119, 148, 153, 165, 179, 180, 188, 193, 200, 213, 222, 264, 273, 278, 303, 316, 337, 339 bottom, 352, 353, 366, 368, 374, 406, 422, 424, 431, 439, 446, 455, 457, 465, 476 both, 484, 515, 516, 517, 531, 542, 556, 568, 571, 604 top, 626, 652, 678, 743, 760, 790, 808, 813, 816, 829, 851, 856, 885, 892, 895, 917, 918, 919, 936, 937, 938 top, 941, 945, 948, 949, 952, 953, 959, 985, 986, 1014, 1019, 1060, 1065, 1084, 1130, 1131, 1132, 1148, 1156, 1173, 1183, 1186, 1188, 1204, 1205, 1253, 1261, 1269, 1278 bottom, 1298, 1332, 1360, 1362, 1364

Illustrations

Frank Baber: pp. 35, 1029

Shirley Bellwood: p. 1034

Peter Dennis: pp. 292, 1141, 1144, 1145

Pam Glover: pp. 64, 65

Jeremy Gower: pp. 134 bottom, 214, 592, 911, 1126, 1208, 1357

Alan Harris: pp. 316, 1103

James MacDonald: pp. 134 top, 486, 1140, 1320, 1327, 1329, 1330, 1331, 1333, 1334, 1335, 1336, 1339, 1340, 1341

National Tourist Office of Greece: p. 1002

Alan Parry: pp. 2, 107, 177, 322, 323, 437, 528, 530, 587, 759, 894, 1030, 1037, 1105, 1242 bottom, 1243 bottom, 1277, 1376

Richard Scott: pp. 95, 220, 588, 882, 915, 926, 1138, 1242 top

Paul Wyart: p. 593

Using This Book

In general, after each entry word there appears a set of parentheses enclosing the English pronunciation (roman type) or the Hebrew or Greek transliteration (*italic* type), followed by the meaning of the Hebrew or Greek term (set within quotation marks). Text material follows, persons or places with the same name being listed successively by number, or, in some instances, listed in successive entries. Scripture quotations are from the *New American Standard Bible*, unless stated otherwise; readings from the King James Version and the *New International Version* are also cited. Contributors or revisers are indicated by capital initials. The bibliographies that follow the articles are arranged by date, the earliest listed first. Initial reference to a journal is given in full, but succeeding references are abbreviated.

Zoological and Botanical Classifications

Animals and plants mentioned in the articles Animal Kingdom and Vegetable Kingdom are frequently identified by standard zoological or botanical classifications. Genus and species are given in Latin, followed in many cases by an abbreviation of the name of the person who proposed the classification names. After the first use, the genus name is also abbreviated. Thus, the genus (initial capital) and species (lower case) of two species of mustard first named by the botanist Carolus Linnaeus are listed as *Sinapsis arvensis,* L, and *S. alba,* L.

Contributors

Contributors to the 1957 edition of the *Dictionary* in addition to Merrill F. Unger included pastors (S. L. Bowman, E. McChesney, and A. H. Tuttle), academicians (H. A. Butz, W. Haskell [then of Yale University], D. S. Martin [then of Barnard College, New York City], J. F. McCurdy [Toronto, Canada], and the Assyrian scholar R. W. Rogers), and a medical doctor (George E. Post [then of Beirut, Syria]). Contributors to the present revision in addition to the general editor, R. K. Harrison (Toronto, Canada), include Howard F. Vos (The Kings College, New York), Cyril J. Barber (Insight for Living, Fullerton, California, and the Simon Greenleaf School of Law, Anaheim, California), and Eugene H. Merrill (Dallas Theological Seminary).

Pronunciation Guides

Pronunciation guides are given in roman type. The long vowels are marked, indicated by the macron or the circumflex. The accent mark (') indicates the syllable receiving the primary stress. The pronunciation system is English as opposed to Hebrew.

ā	late	î	pier
ê	obey	ō	oat
ē	eve	ū	fuse
ī	line		

Hebrew Transliteration

The transliteration system used in this Dictionary is that followed in *Theological Wordbook of the Old Testament,* edited by R. Laird Harris, Gleason L. Archer, Jr., and Bruce K. Waltke (Chicago: Moody, 1980).

Consonants

'Aleph	א	'
Beth	ב or כ	b
Gimel	ג or ג	g
Daleth	ד or ך	d
He (pronounced *hay*)	ה or ה (final consonantal ה)	h
Waw	ו	w
Zayin	ז	z
Heth (or Het)	ח	ḥ
Teth	ט	ṭ
Yodh (or Yod)	י	y
Kaph	כ כ or ך	k
Lamedh	ל	l
Mem	מ or ם	m
Nun (pronounced *noon*)	נ or ן	n
Samekh	ס	s
'Ayin	ע	'
Pe (pronounced *pay*)	פ פ or ף	p
Tsadhe	צ or ץ	ṣ
Qoph (English q, but not qu)	ק	q
Resh	ר	r
Sin (pronounced *seen*)	שׂ	ś
Shin (pronounced *sheen*)	שׁ	sh
Taw	ת or ת	t

Full Vowels and Their Pronounciation Following "M"

Pathah	_	a	מַ	ma as in man
Qameṣ	ָ	ā	מָ	mā as in ma
Final Qameṣ with vocalic He	ה,	â	מָה	mâ as in ma
Hiriq	.	i	מִ	mi as in pin
Hiriq with Yodh	ִי	î	מִי	mî as ee in seen
Seghol	ֶ	e	מֶ	me as in met
Sere	ֵ	ē	מֵ	mē as ay in may
Sere with Yodh	ֵי	ê	מֵי	mê as ay in may
Qameṣ-Hatuph (in closed syllable)	ָ	o	מָ	mo as au in naught

Holem		ō	מֹ	mō as in mole
Holem with Waw	וֹ	ô	מוֹ	mô in mole
Qibbuṣ (short in closed syllable)		ū	מֻ	mū oo in nook
Shureq (always with Waw)	וּ	û	מוּ	mû as oo in fool

Vowels and Silent Consonants

Qameṣ with final consonantal He	הָ	āh	מָה	māh
Qameṣ with final vocalic 'Aleph	אָ	ā'	מָא	mā'
Sere with final vocalic He	הֵ	ēh	מֵה	mēh
Seghol with final vocalic He	הֶ	eh	מֶה	meh

Half-vowels (all pronounced "o")

Shewa		ᵉ	מְ	mᵉ
Hateph-pathah		ă	מֲ	mă
Hateph-seghol		ĕ	מֱ	mĕ
Hateph-qames		ŏ	מֳ	mŏ

Greek Transliteration

Alpha	α	a	Nu	ν	n
Beta	β	b	Xi	ξ	x
Gamma	γ	g	Omicron	o	o
Delta	δ	d	Pi	π	p
Epsilon	ε	e	Rho	ρ	r
Zeta	ζ	z	Sigma	σ, ς	s
Eta	η	e	Tau	τ	t
Theta	θ	th	Upsilon	υ	u (y)
Iota	ι	i	Phi	φ	ph
Kappa	κ	k	Chi	χ	ch
Lambda	λ	l	Psi	Ψ	ps
Mu	μ	m	Omega	Ω	o

Diphthongs

$\alpha\iota$	ai
$\varepsilon\iota$	ei
$o\iota$	oi
$\nu\iota$	yi
$\alpha\upsilon$	ay
$\varepsilon\upsilon$	ey
$\eta\upsilon$	ēu
$o\upsilon$	oy

Breathing Marks

᾿ clear breathing mark

῾ harsh breathing mark

h as in ᾿υπερ (hyper)

Abbreviations

General

A.D.	*anno domini* (in the year of our Lord)
Against Apion	*Flavius Josephus Against Apion* (Josephus)
Ant.	*Antiquities of the Jews* (Josephus)
A.U.C.	*ab urbe condita* (from the founding of the city [Rome])
Arab.	Arabic
Aram.	Aramaic
Akkad.	Akkadian
B.C.	Before Christ
c.	*circa* (about)
cf.	*confer* (compare)
chap(s).	chapter(s)
Com.	*Commentary*
Delitzsch	*See* Keil and Delitzsch
E	east
e.g.	*exempli gratia* (for example)
et al.	*et alii* (and others)
f., ff.	following
Gk.	Greek
Heb.	Hebrew
ibid.	*ibidem* (in the same place)
id.	*idem* (the same)
Keil	*See* Keil and Delitzsch
Keil, *Arch.*	Johann Karl Friedrich Keil, *Manual of Biblical Archaeology* (1888)
K. & D.	*See* Keil and Delitzsch
Keil and Delitzsch	Johann Karl Friedrich Keil and Franz Julius Delitzsch, *Old Testament Commentaries* (1875)
KJV	King James Version
Lat.	Latin
LXX	Septuagint
marg.	margin, marginal reading
MT	Masoretic Text
MS, MSS	manuscript(s)
N	north
NASB	*New American Standard Bible*
NIV	*New International Version*
NKJV	*New King James Version*
NT, N.T.	New Testament
OT, O.T.	Old Testament
p., pp.	page(s)
Pers.	Persian
pl.	plural
RSV	*Revised Standard Version*
RV	*Revised Version*

S	south
sing.	singular
Syr.	Syriac
v., vv.	verse(s)
W	west
Wars	*The Wars of the Jews* (Josephus)

Contributors

C.J.B.	Cyril J. Barber	J.F.M.	J. F. McCurdy
S.L.B.	S. L. Bowman	E.H.M.	Eugene H. Merrill
H.A.B.	H. A. Butz	G.E.P.	George E. Post
R.K.H.	R. K. Harrison	R.W.R.	R. W. Rogers
W.H.	W. Haskell	A.H.T.	A. H. Tuttle
D.S.M.	D. S. Martin	M.F.U.	Merrill F. Unger
E.MCC.	E. McChesney	H.F.V.	Howard F. Vos

Old Testament Books

Gen.	1 Kings	Eccles.	Obad.
Ex.	2 Kings	Song of Sol.	Jonah
Lev.	1 Chron.	Isa.	Mic.
Num.	2 Chron.	Jer.	Nah.
Deut.	Ezra	Lam.	Hab.
Josh.	Neh.	Ezek.	Zeph.
Judg.	Esther	Dan.	Hag.
Ruth	Job	Hos.	Zech.
1 Sam.	Ps.	Joel	Mal.
2 Sam.	Prov.	Amos	

New Testament Books

Matt.	2 Cor.	1 Tim.	2 Pet.
Mark	Gal.	2 Tim.	1 John
Luke	Eph.	Titus	2 John
John	Phil.	Philem.	3 John
Acts	Col.	Heb.	Jude
Rom.	1 Thess.	James	Rev.
1 Cor.	2 Thess.	1 Pet.	

Apocryphal Books

1 Esd. (1 Esdras)
2 Esd. (2 Esdras)
Tobit (Tobit)
Judith (Judith)
Rest of Esther (The Rest of Esther)

Wisd. of Sol. (The Wisdom of Solomon)
Ecclus. (Ecclesiasticus)

Baruch (Baruch)
Song of Children (Song of the Three Holy Children)

Susanna (Susanna)
Bel and Dragon (Bel and the Dragon)
Prayer (Prayer of Manasses)
1 Macc. (1 Maccabees)
2 Macc. (2 Maccabees)

AARON (ār'un; Heb. derivation uncertain). The son of Amram the Levite and Jochebed (Ex. 6:20) and the first high priest of Israel. Third in line of descent from Levi, he was the brother of Moses and his senior by three years, although he was younger than his sister *Miriam* (which see). His wife was Elisheba, the daughter of Amminadab, by whom he had four sons: Nadab, Abihu, Eleazar, and Ithamar (6:23).

Moses' Assistant. He was eloquent of speech and divinely appointed to be Moses' mouthpiece (prophet). God specifically told Moses that Aaron would be his spokesman and that "he shall be as a mouth for you, and you shall be as God to him" (Ex. 4:16). Together with Moses he withstood Pharaoh and saw the deliverance of the Israelites from Egypt by great signs and miracles. In the battle with Amalek, Aaron and Hur supported Moses' arms, which held the official rod, the uplifting of which brought victory to Israel. When Moses went up to Mt. Sinai to receive the tables of the law (24:12), Aaron and his sons, Nadab and Abihu, and the seventy elders accompanied him part of the way, being granted a glimpse of the divine presence (24:1-11). While Moses was on the mountain, Aaron in a moment of weakness and under pressure from the people made a golden image of a male calf as a visible symbol of Jehovah (32:4). The choice of this animal was doubtless suggested by the vigor and strength symbolized by it and by the people's recollection of bull worship in Egypt.

High Priest. In the divine institution of the priesthood Aaron was appointed high (Heb. "great") priest, and his sons and descendants priests. The tribe of Levi was consecrated as the priestly caste. After the Tabernacle was erected according to the divine plan and the ritual established (Ex. 24:12-31; 18; 35:1–40:38), Aaron and his sons were solemnly consecrated to their priestly office by Moses (Lev. 8:6) about 1440 B.C.

(cf. 1 Kings 6:1). Tragedy overtook the family shortly thereafter, when Nadab and Abihu, his elder sons, died because they conducted the worship improperly (Lev. 10:1-2).

The elaborate description of the high priest's garments of glory and beauty (Ex. 28:2), including the jeweled ephod, turban, and crown, is not an interpolation from a later period. Archaeology has shown that in the Desert of Sinai at Serabit el-Khadem turquoise and copper were being mined for Egyptian craftsmen at this early period. The jewels of silver and gold that the Israelites obtained from the Egyptians (11:2) are illustrated from ancient times. Artistic gold and jeweled ornaments were recovered from the ruins of Sumerian Ur over a millennium before the Mosaic period, and there is nothing in the furnishing of the Tabernacle or the clothing of the high priest that would be out of keeping with the artistic accomplishments of contemporary craftsmen.

In his invidious conduct against Moses (Num. 12:1-15) the same weak side of Aaron's character appears as in the incident of the golden calf. In the conspiracy formed against Aaron and Moses led by Korah, a Levite, and Dathan and Abiram, Reubenites, the destruction of the conspirators by the hand of God resulted in the vindication of the Aaronic priesthood (chap. 16). An added attestation of Aaron's divine priestly appointment was the budding of his rod, which was preserved for "a sign against the rebels" (17:10). Aaron shared Moses' sin at Meribah (20:8-13, 24) and consequently was not allowed to enter the Promised Land, dying soon after (20:22-29) on Mt. Hor at the borders of Edom.

Type of Christ. In Scripture typology Aaron is a figure of Christ, our High Priest (Ex. 28:1), who executes His priestly office after the Aaronic pattern (Heb. 9). This type is seen (1) in Aaron's offering sacrifice; (2) in his being anointed with

1

Jewish high priest

oil by *pouring* (Ex. 29:7; Lev. 8:12), prefiguring our Lord's measureless anointing with the Holy Spirit (John 3:34); and (3) in his bearing the names of the Israelite tribes upon his breast and shoulders, thus presenting them perpetually before God as our Lord bears our cause before the Father (John 17; Heb. 7:25). Aaron entered into the Holy Place on the Day of Atonement (Lev. 16) as Christ has entered "heaven itself, now to appear in the presence of God for us" (Heb. 9:24).

BIBLIOGRAPHY: H. W. Soltau, *The Tabernacle, the Priesthood and the Offerings* (1884); H. G. Judge, *Journal of Theological Studies* 7 (1956): 70ff.; R. H. Mount, Jr., *The Law Prophesied* (1963), pp. 156-65; R. L. Honeycutt, *Review and Expositor* 74 (1977): 523-36.

AAR'ONITE. Descendants of Aaron, and therefore priests, who to the number of 3,700 fighting men under Jehoiada joined David at Hebron (1 Chron. 12:27). Later we find that their leader was Zadok (27:17).

AB (āb). Babylonian name of the fifth ecclesiastical and the eleventh civil month of the Jewish year. It was introduced after the Babylonian captivity, and is not mentioned in Scripture, in which it is known as the *fifth* month (Num. 33:38), i.e., July-August.

AB (āb; "father"). The first member of several Hebrew compound names, e.g., Absalom.

ABAD'DON (a-bad'don; Gk. *Abaddon,* "destruction"). The angel of the bottomless pit (Rev. 9:11), and corresponding to Apollyon, "destroyer." The word *abaddon* means destruction (Job 31:12), or the place of destruction, i.e., Hades or the region of the dead (Job 26:6; 28:22; Prov. 15:11).

ABAG'THA (a-bag'tha). One of the seven chief eunuchs of Xerxes who were commanded by the king to bring Queen Vashti into the royal presence (Esther 1:10), 483 B.C.

ABA'NA. *See* Abanah.

ABA'NAH (a-bā'na). One of the rivers of Damascus (2 Kings 5:12; marg., *Amanah;* Gk. *Chrysorrhoas,* "golden river"). It is, no doubt, the present Barada, about fifteen miles NW of Damascus, and has its source in the Anti-Lebanon Mts. and flows through the city of Damascus; thence after fifty miles it is lost in the marshy lake Bahret el-Kibliyeh. It was one of the rivers that Naaman would have washed in rather than the Jordan River.

BIBLIOGRAPHY: D. Baly, *The Geography of the Bible* (1957), pp. 109ff.

AB'ARIM (ab'ā-rîm; "regions beyond"). A mountain chain SE of the Dead Sea, at the N end of which stands Mt. Nebo (Deut. 32:49). It also featured an elevated outcrop (Heb. *happisgâ*) from which Moses viewed the Promised Land (3:27). Israel had an encampment in the mountains of Abarim (Num. 33:47-48).

Aaron's tomb in the mountains of Edom

AB'BA (ab'a). A customary title of God in prayer (Mark 14:36; Rom. 8:15; Gal. 4:6). It was in common use in the mixed Aram. dialect of Palestine and was used by children in addressing their father. It answers to our "papa." The right to call God "Father" in a special and appropriative sense pertains to all who have received the testimony of the Spirit to their forgiveness. *See* Adoption.

BIBLIOGRAPHY: N. Turner, *Christian Words* (1980), p. 1.

AB'DA (ab'dā; "the servant," i.e., "of God").

1. The father of Adoniram, who was "over the men subject to forced labor" under Solomon (1 Kings 4:6), about 960 B.C.

2. The son of Shammua, and a Levite of the family of Jeduthun, resident in Jerusalem after the Exile (Neh. 11:17), 444 B.C. Elsewhere (1 Chron. 9:16) he is called Obadiah the son of Shemaiah.

AB'DEEL (ab'dē-ēl; "servant of God"). The father of Shelemaiah, one of those appointed to seize Jeremiah (Jer. 36:26), before 606 B.C.

AB'DI (ab'dī; "my servant").

1. A Levite and the grandfather of Ethan, and one of the singers appointed by David for the sacred service (1 Chron. 6:44).

2. A Levite, in the reign of Hezekiah, father of Kish (2 Chron. 29:12).

3. A son of Elam who put away his Gentile wife after the return from Babylon (Ezra 10:26), 456 B.C.

AB'DIEL (ab'di-ēl; "servant of God"). Son of Guni and father of Ahi, one of the Gadites resident in Gilead (1 Chron. 5:15).

AB'DON (ab'dōn; "servile").

1. The son of Hillel, a Pirathonite, of the tribe of Ephraim. He ruled Israel for eight years, about 1120-1112 B.C. The only other fact respecting him is that he had forty sons and thirty grandsons, who rode on young asses—a mark of their consequence before the introduction of the horse into Israel. Upon his death he was buried in Pirathon (Judg. 12:13-15), a place probably six miles WSW of Shechem.

2. A son of Shashak and one of the chief Benjamites dwelling in Jerusalem (1 Chron. 8:23), before 1200 B.C.

3. The firstborn of Gibeon (or, as in NIV, Jeiel), a Benjamite resident at Jerusalem (1 Chron. 8:30; 9:36), ancestor of King Saul.

4. The son of Micah, and one of those sent by King Josiah to Huldah to inquire concerning the recently discovered books (2 Chron. 34:20), about 624 B.C. In 2 Kings 22:12 he is called Achbor (or Acbor).

5. A Levitical city of Asher, about nine miles NE of Acco (Josh. 21:30; 1 Chron. 6:74).

ABED'NEGO (a-bēd'ne-gō; "servant of Nego or Nebo"). The Babylonian god of wisdom, connected with the planet Mercury. Abednego was the Aram. name given by the king of Babylon's officer to Azariah, one of the three Jewish youths who, with Daniel, were selected by Ashpenaz (master of the eunuchs) to be educated in the language and wisdom of the Chaldeans (Dan. 1:3-7). Abednego and his friends Shadrach and Meshach were cast into the fiery furnace for refusing to worship the golden statue set up by Nebuchadnezzar, but

were miraculously delivered (chap. 3), about 603 B.C. The Heb. name *Azariah* means "Jehovah has helped." The folly of trying to change inward character by an outward name is hereby illustrated. A tyrant may change the name but not the nature of one true to God.   M.F.U.

A'BEL (ā'bēl; Heb. *hebel,* "breath"). Probably applied to the younger son of Adam and Eve anticipatively because of the brevity of his life, being slain by his elder brother, Cain. Abel, a shepherd and a righteous man (Matt. 23:35; 1 John 3:12), speaks of a regenerate believer. Cain, the farmer, on the other hand, well illustrates the unregenerate natural man, whose worship was destitute of any adequate sense of sin or need of atonement, and who offered the works of his hands instead of faith as a basis of acceptance with God. Abel by contrast "brought of the firstlings of his flock and of their fat portions" (Gen. 4:4) and shed atoning blood (Heb. 9:22). By this act he confessed his sense of sin and need of atonement and exercised faith in the interposition of a coming Substitute (Gen. 3:15; Heb. 11:4) instead of presenting the works of his hands as a ground for acceptance with God.   M.F.U.

A'BEL (Heb. *'ābēl,* "watercourse").

1. A word used as a prefix in a number of cases (2 Sam. 20:14, 18). *See* Abel-beth-maachah.

2. A great stone (1 Sam. 6:18) near Beth-shemesh, upon which the Philistines set the Ark when they returned it to Israel.

Abel Beth-Maachah

A'BEL-BETH-MA'ACHAH, or **Abel Beth Maacah, Abel Bethmaachah** (NIV; ā'bel-beth-mā'a-kā; "brook [?] of the house of oppression," 2 Sam. 20:14-15; 1 Kings 15:20; 2 Kings 15:29). A place in the north of Palestine, identified with Abil el-Qamh, twelve miles N of Lake Huleh. In 2 Sam. 20:14, 18, it is called simply Abel. It was a place of importance, a metropolis, and called a "mother in Israel" (20:19). It was besieged by Joab, Ben-hadad, and Tiglath-pileser (20:14; 1 Kings 15:20; 2 Kings 15:29).

A'BEL-KERA'MIM (ā'bel-keramim), or **Abel Keramim** (NIV). A place E of the Jordan to which Jephthah pursued the Ammonites (Judg. 11:33), and possibly now represented by a ruin bearing the name of Biet el-kerm—"house of the vine" —to the N of Kerak. Its location cannot be definitely determined.

A'BEL-MA'IM (ā'bel-mā'im; "water brook" [?]), or **Abel Maim** (NIV). Either the name by which Abel-beth-maachah is called in 2 Chron. 16:4 or the name of a nearby city.

A'BEL-MEHO'LAH (ā'bel-me-hō'lā; "watercourse of dancing"), or **Abel Meholah** (NIV). A place in the Jordan Valley and the home of Elisha (1 Kings 19:16; Judg. 7:22). It was in the tribe of Issachar. Identified by Nelson Glueck with Tell el-Maqlub (see *The River Jordan*, pp. 166-74), but by others with Tell Abu Sifri, a neighboring site.

A'BEL-MIZ'RAIM (ā'bel-miz'ra-im; "mourning of Egypt"), or **Abel Mizraim** (NIV). The scene of the lament of Egypt over Jacob (Gen. 50:11); the name the Canaanites gave to the "threshing floor of Atad" in Transjordan.

A'BEL-SHIT'TIM (ā'bel-shit'tim; "watercourse of acacias"), or **Abel Shittim** (NIV). The last halting place of Israel during the Exodus (Num. 33:49). Identified with Khirbet Kefrein or Abila in the plains of Moab opposite Jericho, the acacias still fringe the upper terraces of the Jordan with green. Near Mt. Peor at Shittim in the shade of the acacia groves, Israel was lured into the licentious rites of Baal worship (Num. 25:1; Josh. 2:1; Mic. 6:5), resulting in the death of twenty-four thousand by plague.

A'BEZ (ā'bez). In the KJV, the same as Ebez (so NIV), a town in Issachar (Josh. 19:20).

A'BI (ā'bī; "my father"). The daughter of Zechariah and mother of King Hezekiah (2 Kings 18:2). The fuller form of the name, Abijah, is given in 2 Chron. 29:1, NASB, and in 2 Kings 18:2, NIV.

A'BI (ăbī; an old construct form of "father of"). Forms the first part of several Heb. proper names.

ABI'A. *See* Abijah.

ABI'AH. *See* Abijah.

A'BI-AL'BON (a'bī-al'bôn; "valiant"). One of David's mighty men (2 Sam. 23:31), called in the parallel passage (1 Chron. 11:32) by the equivalent name *Abiel* (which see).

ABI'ASAPH (a-bī'a-saf; "my father has gathered"). The last mentioned (Ex. 6:24) of the sons of Korah, the Levite. His identity with *Ebiasaph* (which see) (1 Chron. 6:23, 37) is a matter of much uncertainty and difference of opinion. The probability is that they are the same person.

ABI'ATHAR (a-bī'a-thar; "the father is preeminent"). A high priest and fourth in descent from Eli, who alone of the sons of the high priest Ahimelech escaped death when Saul, in revenge for aid given to David, attempted to wipe out this entire line of priests (1 Sam. 22). Fleeing to David, Abiathar inquired of the Lord for him in the fierce struggle with Saul (23:9-10; 30:7) and became David's lifelong friend. When David became king, he appointed Abiathar high priest (1 Chron. 15:11). David did not depose Zadok, whom Saul had appointed after Ahimelech's decease. Both appointments accordingly stood, and Zadok and Abiathar constituted a double high priesthood (1 Kings 4:4). They jointly superintended the transfer of the Ark to Jerusalem (1 Chron. 15:11). During Absalom's rebellion Abiathar remained loyal to David (2 Sam. 15:24). However, he adhered to Adonijah when the latter attempted to gain the royal succession at David's death, while Zadok cast his lot with Solomon (1 Kings 1:19). For this unwise move Solomon banished Abiathar to Anathoth, deposing him from his office (2:26-27) and confining the high-priestly succession to Zadok of the elder line of Aaron's sons. In this manner the rule of Eli's house terminated in fulfillment of prophecy (1 Sam. 2:31-35).

The reference to Ahimelech, the son of Abiathar, as priest with Zadok (2 Sam. 8:17) is most unusual and is regarded by many as a simple copyist's error, in which the names of the father and the son were accidentally transposed. But this solution of the difficulty is unlikely since the references to Ahimelech, the son of Abiathar, as priest are so clear that a mistake is not easily explained (1 Chron. 18:16, LXX; 24:3, 6, 31). The best explanation seems to be that the reference is to Ahimelech, who was a son of Abiathar (2 Sam. 8:17; 1 Chron. 18:16; 24:3, 6, 31). He should not be confused with his grandfather. (*See* Ahimelech, no. 2.) The reference to Abiathar in Mark 2:26 as high priest at Nob (instead of his father Ahimelech, as recounted in 1 Sam. 21:1) is to be explained under the supposition either that our Lord used the name of the more famous priest of the two, who, though not then actually high priest, was at the Tabernacle at the time alluded to, or that the son acted as coadjutor to his father as Eli's sons apparently did (4:4).

M.F.U.; R.K.H.

BIBLIOGRAPHY: H. G. Judge, *Journal of Theological Studies* 7 (1956): 70ff.

A'BIB (ā'bib; "an ear of corn"). The month the Hebrews were divinely directed to make the first of the year as a memorial of their deliverance from Egypt (Ex. 12:1-2; 13:4). The Passover and the feast of unleavened bread occurred in it, and it marked the beginning of the barley harvest. On the tenth day the Passover lamb was selected and on the fourteenth day was slain and eaten. On the fifteenth day the Jews began harvesting by gathering a sheaf of the barley firstfruits and on the sixteenth day offered it (Lev. 23:4-14). The slaying of the lamb was typical of the death of Christ, the feast of unleavened bread of the believer's separated walk, while the waving of the sheaf of firstfruits spoke of the resurrection of Christ. The Jewish months were lunar and do not exactly correspond to ours, which are fixed. Abib corresponds to March-April, and its name was changed to *Nisan* (which see) after the Exile (Neh. 2:1; Esther 3:7).   M.F.U.

ABI′DA (a-bi′da; "father of knowledge," i.e., "knowing"). The fourth of the five sons of Midian, the son of Abraham by Keturah (Gen. 25:4; 1 Chron. 1:33).

ABI′DAN (a-bi′dan; "father is judge"). The son of Gideoni and head of the tribe of Benjamin (Num. 1:11; 2:22; 10:24; cf. 7:60, 65).

A′BIEL (a′bi-el; "God is my father").
1. A Benjamite, son of Zeror (1 Sam. 9:1) and father of Ner (14:51), who was the grandfather of King Saul (1 Chron. 8:33, 9:39). In 1 Sam. 9:1 the phrase "son of Abiel" should be "grandson of Abiel."
2. One of David's mighty men (1 Chron. 11:32). He is the same as Abi-albon (or Abi-Albon, NIV), the Arbathite (2 Sam. 23:31), about 1000 B.C.

ABIE′ZER (a′bi-ē′zer; "father of help").
1. The second son of Hammoleketh, sister of Gilead and granddaughter of Manasseh (1 Chron. 7:17-18). He was the founder of the family to which Gideon belonged, and which bore his name as a patronymic (Josh. 17:2; Judg. 6:34); before 1170 B.C. He is elsewhere called Iezer, and his descendants Iezerites (Num. 26:30).
2. The Anathothite, one of David's thirty chief warriors (2 Sam. 23:27). Abiezer commanded the ninth division of the army (1 Chron. 27:12), 1000 B.C.
3. Another name for Bukki's father *Abishua* (which see; the term Abiezar appears in Josephus *Ant.* 5.11.5.).

ABI′EZRITE (a-bi′ez-rīt; "father of the Ezrite"). A patronymic designation of the descendants of Abiezer (Judg. 6:11, 24; 8:32).

AB′IGAIL (ab′i-gāl; "my father rejoices").
1. The wife of *Nabal* (which see), a sheep master of Carmel (1 Sam. 25:3), about 1000 B.C. In sheep-shearing time David sent some of his young men to Nabal for a present, which was insolently refused. David was greatly enraged and set out with four hundred men to avenge the insult. Abigail, having been informed of her husband's conduct and the impending danger, went to meet David with an abundant supply of bread, grain, and wine. She prayed for David's forbear-

ance, arguing from Nabal's character (v. 25), the leadings of God by which David had been kept from murder by her coming to meet him, and the fact that God is the avenger of the wicked (v. 26). David was mollified by Abigail's tact and beauty, and he recalled his vow. Returning home, Abigail found her husband intoxicated and told him nothing of her conduct and his danger until morning. The information produced so great a shock that "his heart died within him so that he became as stone" (v. 37), and he died about ten days after. Abigail became David's wife and shared his varying fortunes, dwelling at Gath (27:3), being among the captives taken by the Amalekites from Ziklag (30:5), and accompanying her husband to Hebron when he was anointed king (2 Sam. 2:2). She bore David a son named Chileab (3:3; Kileab, NIV), also called Daniel (1 Chron. 3:1).
2. A daughter of Nahash (Jesse) and sister of David, and wife of Jether, or Ithra, an Ishmaelite, by whom she had Amasa (2 Sam. 17:25; 1 Chron. 2:16-17).

BIBLIOGRAPHY: C. E. Macartney, *Ancient Wives and Modern Husbands* (1934), pp. 123-40; id., *Great Women of the Bible* (1942), pp. 105-20; C. J. and A. A. Barber, *You Can Have a Happy Marriage* (1984), pp. 81-93.

AB′IHAIL (ab′i-hāl; "father of might").
1. The father of Zuriel and chief of the Levitical family of Merari when Moses numbered the Levites at Sinai (Num. 3:35), c. 1440 B.C.
2. The wife of Abishur (of the family of Jerahmeel) and the mother of Ahban and Molid (1 Chron. 2:29).
3. The son of Huri and one of the chiefs of the family of Gad, who settled in Bashan (1 Chron. 5:14).
4. The "daughter," i.e., descendant, of Eliab, David's oldest brother and second wife of Rehoboam. She could hardly have been the daughter of Eliab, as David, his youngest brother, was thirty years old when he began to reign, some eighty years before her marriage (2 Chron. 11:18).
5. The father of Esther and uncle of Mordecai (Esther 2:15; 9:29), c. 500 B.C.

ABI′HU (a-bi′hū; "He [God] is my father"). One of Aaron's sons, who with his brother Nadab offered "strange [i.e., "unauthorized," as in NIV] fire before the Lord, which He had not commanded them" (Lev. 10:1). As a result both priests were struck dead by the divine Presence manifested in fire (v. 2). The sin of Nadab and Abihu, illustrative of the sin of a believer unto physical death (1 Cor. 5:5; 1 John 5:16), was in acting in the things of God without first seeking the mind of God. It was "will worship" (cf. Col. 2:23). Supernatural fire from the divine Presence had kindled the natural fire that burned upon the altar of burnt offering. It was the priests' duty to keep this fire burning continuously. No command, however, had been given as to how the incense should be kindled

5

(Lev. 16:12). Not waiting for instruction concerning taking the sacred fire from the brazen altar, but taking common fire that they themselves had kindled, they lighted the incense on the golden altar. This flagrant sacrilege at the commencement of a new dispensation (the legal) had to be divinely punished to serve as a warning, as the sin of Ananias and Sapphira at the beginning of the NT church age was similarly severely dealt with (Acts 5:1-11). Aaron's disobedient sons seem, moreover, to have committed their serious trespass under the influence of wine (cf. Lev. 10:8-9). The true source of exhilaration for the genuine spiritual priest is not wine, with its attendant temptations and perils, but the Holy Spirit (Eph. 5:18).   M.F.U.

ABI'HUD (a-bi'hud; "father of renown"). One of the sons of Bela, the son of Benjamin (1 Chron. 8:3).

ABI'JAH (a-bi'jā; "God is my father" or "daddy").

1. A son of Jeroboam I, king of Israel. On his falling ill Jeroboam secretly sought help from the God whom he had openly forsaken. He sent his wife, disguised and bearing a present of bread and honey, to Ahijah, the prophet, who was at Shiloh. The prophet was blind but had been warned by God of her coming. He revealed to her that, though the child was to die, yet because there was found in Abijah only, of all the house of Jeroboam, "something good . . . toward the Lord," he only, of all that house, should come to his grave in peace and be mourned in Israel (1 Kings 14:14). The queen returned home, and the child died as she crossed the threshold. "And all Israel buried him and mourned for him" (1 Kings 14:18), about 922 B.C.

2. The second king of Judah, the son of Rehoboam and grandson of Solomon (1 Chron. 3:10). He is called Abijam in 1 Kings 14:31; 15:1-8 (though Abijah throughout in NIV).

Two names are given for his mother. In 1 Kings 15:2 we read, "His mother's name was Maacah the daughter of Abishalom" (cf. 2 Chron. 11:20, 22); but in 2 Chron. 13:2 it is written, "His mother's name was Micaiah [or Maacah in NIV], the daughter of Uriel of Gibeah." The solution of the difficulty probably is that the mother of Abijah had two names, and that Abishalom was her grandfather.

Abijah began to reign 913 B.C., in the eighteenth year of Jeroboam, king of Israel, and reigned three years. Considering the separation of the ten tribes of Israel as rebellion, Abijah made a vigorous attempt to bring them back to their allegiance. He marched with four hundred thousand men against Jeroboam, who met him with eight hundred thousand men. In Mt. Ephraim he addressed a speech to Jeroboam and the opposing army, in which he advocated a theocratic institution, referred to the beginning of the rebellion, showed the folly of opposing God's kingdom, and concluded with urging Israel not to fight against God. His view of the political position of the ten tribes with respect to Judah, though erroneous, was such as a king of Judah would be likely to take. He gained a signal victory over Jeroboam, who lost five hundred thousand men, and though he did not bring Israel to their former allegiance, he took Bethel, Jeshanah, and Ephraim (Ephron, NIV), with their dependent towns, from them, and Jeroboam never again warred with him (2 Chron. 13:1-20). He imitated his father's sins (1 Kings 15:3) and had fourteen wives, by whom he had twenty-two sons and sixteen daughters (2 Chron. 13:21). He was succeeded by his son Asa (14:1).

3. The second son of Samuel, appointed with Joel, his elder brother, judge of Beersheba by his father. The brothers "turned aside after dishonest gain and took bribes and perverted justice" (1 Sam. 8:3). By reason of their conduct Israel demanded of Samuel a king (8:2, 6; 1 Chron. 6:28), before 1030 B.C.

4. The wife of Hezron and mother of Ashhur (1 Chron. 2:24).

5. One of the sons of Becher (or Beker, NIV), the son of Benjamin (1 Chron. 7:8).

6. One of the descendants of Eleazar, the son of Aaron, and chief of one of the twenty-four divisions or orders into which the whole body of the priesthood was divided by David (1 Chron. 24:10). Of these the division of Abijah was the eighth; 1000 B.C.

7. The daughter of Zechariah and mother of King Hezekiah (2 Chron. 29:1) and, consequently, the wife of Ahaz. She is also called Abi (2 Kings 18:2); before 719 B.C.

8. One of the priests, probably, who affixed their signatures to the covenant made with God by Nehemiah (Neh. 10:7). He seems to be the same (notwithstanding the great age this implies) who returned from Babylon with Zerubbabel (12:4), and who had a son Zichri (12:17; Zicri, NIV); 445 B.C.

BIBLIOGRAPHY: C. F. Keil, *The Books of Kings* (1950), pp. 217ff.; W. F. Albright, *The Biblical Period from Abraham to Ezra* (1963), pp. 60f.; E. R. Thiele, *Mysterious Numbers of the Hebrew Kings* (1983), pp. 34, 81.

ABI'JAM (a-bi'jam; "father of the sea"). The name always given in the book of Kings to the king of Judah (1 Kings 14:31; 15:1, 7-8); elsewhere called Abijah (*see* NIV, however, where Abijah is used consistently). First Kings 14:1 refers to another person. *Abijam* is probably a clerical error, some manuscripts giving *Abijah*.

ABILE'NE (ab-i-lē'ne; Gk. *Abilēnē*, so called from its capital, Abila, which probably in turn was derived from Heb. *'ābēl*, "watercourse"). A tetrarchy on the eastern slope of Lebanon, governed in the fifteenth year of Tiberius by Lysanias (Luke 3:1). Abila lay on the Barada (Abana) some fourteen miles NW of Damascus, where the modern village of Suk Wadi Barada now stands. Tradition, in naming the spot as the location of the tomb of Abel, the first martyr, is the result of confusing Abel, properly Heb. *hebel*, with *'ābēl*, "a watercourse." Latin inscriptions found here mentioning repairs to the local road by the "Abileni" and having reference to the sixteenth legion, identify the place. Archaeological remains cover two small hills —Tell Abil and Tell umm el-Amad—and include a temple, a theater, and a basilica.   M.F.U.

ABIM'AEL (a-bim'ā-ēl; "my father is God" [?]). One of the sons of Joktan, in Arabia (Gen. 10:28; 1 Chron. 1:22). He has been supposed to be the founder of an Arabian tribe called Maël.

ABIM'ELECH (a-bim'e-lek; "my father is king," or "royal father"). Probably a general title of royalty, as *Pharaoh* among the Egyptians.

1. The Philistine king of Gerar in the time of Abraham (Gen. 20:1-16), about 2086 B.C. After the destruction of Sodom, Abraham moved into his territory and remained some time at Gerar. Abimelech took Sarah, whom Abraham had announced to be his sister, into his harem, being either charmed with her beauty or desirous of allying himself with Abraham. God appeared to Abimelech in a dream and threatened him with death on account of Sarah, because she was married. Abimelech, who had not yet come near her, excused himself on the ground that he supposed Sarah to be Abraham's sister. That Abimelech, in taking Sarah, should have supposed that he was acting "in the integrity of my heart and the innocence of my hands" (20:5) is accounted for by considering the customs of that day. The next morning Abimelech obeyed the divine command and restored Sarah to Abraham, providing him with a liberal present of cattle and servants and offering him settlement in any part of the country. He also gave him a thousand pieces of silver as, according to some, an atoning or vindicating present. Others think that the money was to procure a veil for Sarah to conceal her beauty, that she might not be coveted for her beauty. Thus she was "cleared" for not having worn a veil, which as a married woman, according to the custom of the country, she ought to have done. Some years after, Abimelech, accompanied by Phichol (or Phicol, NIV), "the commander of his army" (21:22), went to Beer-sheba to make a covenant with Abraham, which is the first league on record. Abimelech restored a well that had been dug by Abraham but seized by the herdsmen of Abimelech without his knowledge (21:22-34).

2. Another king of Gerar in the time of Isaac (Gen. 26:1-31), about 1986 B.C. Supposed to have been the son of the preceding Abimelech. Isaac sought refuge with Abimelech from famine and dwelt at Gerar. Having the same fear concerning his wife, Rebekah, as his father entertained respecting Sarah, he reported her to be his sister. Abimelech discovered the untruthfulness of Isaac's statement (v. 8), whereupon he reproved him for what he had said and forbade any of his people to touch Rebekah on pain of death. The agricultural operations of Isaac in Gerar were highly successful, returning him in one year a hundredfold. He also claimed his proprietary right to the soil by reopening the wells dug by his father. The digging of wells, according to the custom of those times, gave one a right to the soil. His success made the Philistines envious, so that even Abimelech requested him to depart, fearing his power. Isaac complied, and encamped in the open country ("the valley of Gerar," v. 17). In this valley he opened the old wells of Abraham's time, and his people dug three new ones. But Abimelech's herdsmen contended concerning two of these, and the patriarch moved to so great a distance that there was no dispute respecting the third. Afterward Abimelech visited Isaac at Beersheba and desired to make a covenant of peace with him. Isaac referred to the hostility that the Philistines had shown, to which Abimelech replied that they not strike him, i.e., drive him away by force, but let him depart in peace, and he closed by recognizing Isaac as being one blessed of God (vv. 27-29). Isaac entertained Abimelech and his companions with a feast, contracted the desired covenant with them, and dismissed them in peace (vv. 30-31). *See also* Gerar.

3. King of Shechem (Judg. 9). After Gideon's death Abimelech (Judg. 9:1-5), son of Jerubbaal (Jerub-Baal, NIV), formed a conspiracy with his mother's family, who seem to have had considerable influence in Shechem. The argument used was the advantage of the rule of one person to that of seventy. He also reminded them that he was one of themselves. Thus influenced, the Shechemites furnished him with money out of the treasure of Baal-berith, with which Abimelech hired desperate men and, returning to Ophrah with them, killed all his brothers save Jotham, the youngest, who hid himself.

At a general assemblage of the men of *Shechem* (which see) and the house of *Millo* (which see) Abimelech was declared king, c. 1108-1105 B.C. When Jotham was told of the election of Abimelech he went to the top of Mt. Gerizim, where the Shechemites were assembled for some public purpose, perhaps to inaugurate Abimelech (Kitto), and rebuked them in his famous parable of the trees choosing a king (Judg. 9:6-21).

Judgment against Abimelech was not long delayed, for in three years "God sent an evil spirit between" him "and the men of Shechem," and they "dealt treacherously with Abimelech" (9:23). They caused ambushes to be laid in the mountains and robbed all that passed. The design was, probably, to bring the government into discredit by allowing such lawlessness, or to waylay

Abimelech himself. The insurgents found a leader in *Gaal* (which see), the son of Ebed, who, while they were cursing Abimelech in the excitement of a village feast to Baal, called upon them to revolt from Abimelech and declared that he would dethrone him. He then challenged the king to battle (9:25-29).

Zebul, the ruler of Shechem, sent word to Abimelech of the revolt and requested him to place himself in ambush that night and be prepared to surprise Gaal in the morning. As was expected, Gaal started out in the morning, was met and defeated by Abimelech, and prevented by Zebul from entering the city. The next day, when the people went out into the field, possibly to continue their vine dressing, Abimelech and two companies of troops killed them. At the same time his remaining company seized the city gates. After fighting against the city all day he took it, destroyed it utterly, and strewed it with salt (9:30-45).

When the leaders of Shechem, who took refuge in the city's tower, heard of the fate of the city they went to the temple of *Baal-berith* (which see; El-Berith, NIV). Their purpose in so doing was evidently not to defend themselves, but to seek safety at the sanctuary of their god from the vengeance of Abimelech. When he heard of this, Abimelech went with his men to Mt. Zalmon and brought from there branches of trees. These were piled against the building and set on fire. The building was consumed with all its occupants, about one thousand men and women (9:46-49).

At last the fate predicted by Jotham (9:20) overtook Abimelech. He went from Shechem to Thebez, besieged the town, and took it. This town possessed a strong tower, and in this the inhabitants took refuge. When Abimelech approached the door to set it on fire a woman threw a piece of millstone (the upper millstone) upon him, crushing his skull. Seeing that he was mortally wounded, he called upon his armor-bearer to thrust him through with a sword, lest it should be said, "A woman slew him" (v. 54). After Abimelech's death his army was dissolved. "Thus God repaid the wickedness of Abimelech, which he had done to his father, in killing his seventy brothers" (v. 56).

4. The son of Abiathar and high priest in the time of David (1 Chron. 18:16). The name is probably an error of transcription for "Ahimelech," as in NIV (2 Sam. 8:17).

5. In the title of Ps. 34 the name *Abimelech* is interchanged for that of *Achish* (which see), king of Gath, to whom David fled for refuge from Saul (1 Sam. 21:10).

BIBLIOGRAPHY: J. J. Wood, *Distressing Days of the Judges* (1975), pp. 227-29, 234-52; F. J. Delitzsch, *A New Commentary on Genesis* (1978), 2:65-72, 80-84; G. Bush, *Notes on Genesis* (1981), 1:335-46, 360-64.

ABIN'ADAB (a-bin'a-dab; "father is noble").

1. A Levite of Kiriath-jearim (or Kiriath Jearim, NIV) in whose house the Ark was deposited after it was returned by the Philistines (1 Sam. 7:1; 2 Sam. 6:3-4; 1 Chron. 13:7); before 1030 B.C.

2. The second of the eight sons of Jesse (1 Sam. 17:13; 1 Chron. 2:13) and one of the three who followed Saul to the campaign against the Philistines in which Goliath defied Israel (1 Sam. 17:13).

3. One of the four sons of King Saul (1 Chron. 8:33; 9:39; 10:2). He was slain by the Philistines in the battle of Gilboa (1 Sam. 31:2; 1 Chron. 10:2), c. 1004 B.C. His name appears as Ishvi in the list in 1 Sam. 14:49.

4. The father of one of Solomon's purveyors (or, rather, Ben-Abinadab is to be regarded as the name of the purveyor himself) who presided over the district of Dor and married Taphath, the daughter of Solomon (1 Kings 4:11); after 960 B.C.

ABIN'OAM (a-bin'ō-am; "father of pleasantness"). The father of Barak, the judge (Judg. 4:6, 12; 5:1, 12), about 1190 B.C.

ABI'RAM (a-bi'ram; "exalted father").

1. One of the sons of Eliab, a Reubenite, who with his brother Dathan, and with On, of the same tribe, joined Korah, a Levite, in conspiracy against Moses and Aaron, about 1430 B.C. He and the other conspirators were destroyed by an earthquake (Num. 16:1-33; 26:9-10; Deut. 11:6). *See* Korah.

2. The eldest son of Hiel, the Bethelite, who died prematurely (for such is the evident import of the statement) for the presumption or ignorance of his father, in fulfillment of the doom pronounced upon the posterity of him who should undertake to rebuild Jericho (1 Kings 16:34). Perhaps what is really involved in the prophecy and its fulfillment is infant sacrifice. It was a common practice of Canaanites to make a sacrifice of an infant and bury it in the foundation of a structure in order to placate a god and assure divine blessing on a people or a project. For prophecy, *see* Josh. 6:26.

AB'ISHAG (ab'i-shag; "father of error"). A beautiful young woman of Shunem, in the tribe of Issachar, who was selected by the servants of David to minister to him in his old age (1 Kings 1:3-4), 965 B.C. She became his wife, but the marriage was never consummated (1:4). Soon after David's death Adonijah sought, through the intercession of Bathsheba, Solomon's mother, the hand of Abishag. But as the control and possession of the harem of the deceased king were associated with rights and privileges peculiarly regal, Solomon supposed this demand to be part of a conspiracy against the throne. Adonijah was therefore put to death. (2:17-25). *See* Adonijah.

ABISH'AI (a-bish'a-ī; "father of a gift"). A son of

Zeruiah, sister of David (by an unknown father), and brother to Joab and Asahel (1 Chron. 2:16). The first we learn of Abishai is his volunteering to accompany David to the camp of Saul, about 1006 B.C. The two went down by night and found Saul and his people asleep. Abishai begged of David that he might slay Saul with his spear, which was stuck in the ground near his head (1 Sam. 26:6-12). With his brother Joab, Abishai pursued after Abner (who had just slain Asahel) until sundown, and until they had reached the hill of Ammah (2 Sam. 2:24) and aided in the treacherous assassination of Abner (3:30). In the war against Hanun, undertaken by David to punish the Ammonites for insulting his messengers, Abishai, as second in command, fought the army of the Ammonites before the gates of Rabbah and drove them headlong into the city (2 Sam. 10:10, 14; 1 Chron. 19:11, 15). The same impetuous zeal and regard for David that he showed in the night adventure to Saul's camp Abishai manifested in his desire to slay Shimei, when the latter cursed David (2 Sam. 16:9, 11; 19:21). When the king fled beyond Jordan, Abishai remained faithful to David and was entrusted with the command of one of the three divisions of the army that crushed the rebellion (18:2, 12), 967 B.C.

In the revolt of Sheba the Benjamite, David ordered Amasa to muster the forces of Judah in three days. His tardiness compelled David to again have recourse to the sons of Zeruiah, and Abishai was appointed to pursue Sheba, which he did (accompanied by Joab), leading the Cherethites (or Kerethites, NIV), the Pelethites, and all the mighty men (2 Sam. 20:4-10). Later, when David's life was imperiled by Ishbi-benob (or Ishbi-Benob, NIV), Abishai came to his help and slew the giant (21:15-17). He was chief of the three "mighty men" (23:8) who performed the chivalrous exploit of breaking through the host of the Philistines, to procure David a draught of water from the well of his native Bethlehem (23:14-17). Among the exploits of this hero it is mentioned (23:18) that he withstood three hundred men and slew them with his spear, but the occasion of this adventure, and the time and manner of his death, are equally unknown.

In 2 Sam. 8:13, the victory over the Edomites in the Valley of Salt is ascribed to David, but in 1 Chron. 18:12, to Abishai. It is hence probable that the victory was actually gained by Abishai but is ascribed to David as king and commander.

ABISH'ALOM (a-bish'a-lom). A fuller form (1 Kings 15:2, 10) of the name *Absalom* (which see).

ABISH'UA (a-bish'ū-a; "father of salvation").

1. The son of Phinehas (grandson of Aaron), and fourth high priest of the Jews (1 Chron. 6:4-5, 50; Ezra 7:5).

2. One of the sons of Bela, the son of Benjamin (1 Chron. 8:4); possibly the same as Jerimoth (7:7).

AB'ISHUR (ab'i-shūr; "my father is a wall," i.e., "stronghold," or perhaps "mason"). The second son of Shammai, of the tribe of Judah. He was the husband of Abihail, and father of two sons, Ahban and Molid (1 Chron. 2:28-29).

AB'ITAL (ab'i-tal, "father of the dew," i.e., "fresh"). The fifth wife of David and mother of Shephatiah, who was born in Hebron (2 Sam. 3:4; 1 Chron. 3:3).

AB'ITUB (ab'i-tūb; "father of goodness," i.e., "good"). A son of Shaharaim, a Benjamite, by his wife Hushim, in Moab (1 Chron. 8:11).

ABI'UD (a-bi'ūd). A Gk. form (Matt. 1:13) of *Abihud* (which see). The great-great-grandson of Zerubbabel and father of Eliakim, among the paternal ancestry of Jesus (Matt. 1:13). He is probably the same as Judah, son of Joanna, and father of Joseph in the maternal line (Luke 3:26), and also as Obadiah, son of Arnan and father of Shechaniah (or Shecaniah, NIV) in 1 Chron. 3:21.

ABLUTION. A ceremonial washing, it might be of the person (or part thereof), clothing, vessels, or furniture, as a symbol of purification.

Ceremonial hand-washing

1. Cleansing from the taint of an inferior condition preparatory to initiation into a higher one. Of this sort was the washing with water of Aaron and his sons before they were invested with the priestly robes and anointed with the holy oil (Ex. 29:4; Lev. 8:6). The same is doubtless true of the ablution of persons and clothing that was required of the Israelites as a preparation to their receiving the law from Sinai (Ex. 19:10-15).

2. Preparation for a special act of religious service. Before they entered into the service of the Tabernacle the priests were required, under penalty of death, to wash their hands and feet. For this purpose a large basin of water always stood in readiness (Ex. 30:18-21; Lev. 16). The Egyptian priests carried the practice to a burden-

some extent. Herodotus tells us (2. 37) that they shaved their bodies every third day and that no insect or other filth might be upon them when they served the gods. The Muslim law requires ablution before each of the five daily prayers, permitting it to be performed with sand when water is not to be had, as in the desert.

3. Purification from actual defilement. Eleven species of uncleanness of this nature are recognized by the Mosaic law (Lev. 12-15), the purification for which ceased at the end of a prescribed period, provided the unclean person then washed his body and his clothes. In a few cases, such as leprosy and the defilement caused by touching a dead body, he remained unclean seven days. The Jews afterward introduced many other causes of defilement, being equaled, however, by the Muslims.

4. Declaration of freedom from guilt of a particular action. An instance of this is the expiation for the murder of a man by unknown hands, when the elders of the nearest village washed their hands over a slain heifer, saying, "Our hands have not shed this blood, nor did our eyes see it" (Deut. 21:1-9). The Pharisees carried the practice of ablution to such excess, from the affectation of purity while the heart was left unclean, that our Lord severely rebuked them for their hypocrisy (Matt. 23:25).

All these practices come under the head of purification from uncleanness; the acts involved were made so numerous that persons of the stricter sect could scarcely move without contracting some involuntary pollution. Therefore, they never entered their houses without ablution, from the strong probability that they had unknowingly contracted some defilement on the streets. They were especially careful never to eat without washing their hands (Mark 7:1-5). A distinction must be made between this ceremonial washing and ordinary cleansing of the hands as a matter of decency. When the charge was made against our Lord's disciples that they ate with unwashed hands, it was not meant that they did not wash their hands at all, but that they did not do it ceremonially.

These ceremonial washings were prescribed with such minute details as to be not only burdensome but sometimes impossible. Before the ceremony one had to decide the kind of food to be partaken of—whether it was prepared first-fruits, common food, or holy, i.e., sacrificial food. "The water was poured on both hands, which must be free from anything covering them, such as gravel, mortar, etc. The hands were lifted up, so as to make the water run to the wrist, in order to insure that the whole hand was washed and that the water polluted by the hand did not again run down the fingers. Similarly, each hand was rubbed with the other (the fist), provided the hand that rubbed had been affused; otherwise the rubbing might be done against the head, or even against a wall. But there was one point on which special stress was laid. In the 'first affusion,' which was all that originally was required when the hands were not Levitically 'defiled,' the water had to run down to the wrist. If the water remained short of the wrist, the hands were not clean. Accordingly, the words of St. Mark can only mean that the Pharisees eat not 'except they wash their hands to the wrist.' If the hands were 'defiled' two affusions were required: the first to remove the defilement, and the second to wash away the waters that had contracted the defilement of the hands. Accordingly, on the affusion of the first waters the hands were elevated, and the water made to run down at the wrist, while at the second waters the hands were depressed, so that the water might run off by the finger joints and tips" (Edersheim, *Life and Times of Jesus*, 2:11).

BIBLIOGRAPHY: A. Edersheim, *Life and Times of Jesus the Messiah* (1956), 2:11; R. deVaux, *Ancient Israel: Its Life and Institutions* (1961), pp. 460-61.

AB'NER (ab'ner; "my father is Ner" [?]). The son of Ner and uncle of Saul (being the brother of his father, Kish).

Under Saul. Abner was a renowned warrior and the commander in chief of the army of Saul (1 Sam. 14:50), 1030 B.C. He was the person who conducted David into the presence of Saul after the death of Goliath (17:57). He was doubtless held in high esteem by Saul, and with David and Jonathan sat at the king's table (20:25). He accompanied Saul to Hachilah (Hakilah, NIV) in his pursuit of David, who sarcastically reproached him for not guarding his master more securely (26:1, 5, 15).

Under Ish-bosheth. After the death of Saul, 1004 B.C., Abner, taking advantage of the feeling entertained in the other tribes against Judah, took Ish-bosheth, a surviving son of Saul, to Mahanaim, proclaimed him king, and ruled in his name. This happened five years after Saul's death, the intervening time being probably occupied in recovering land from the Philistines and in gaining influence with the other tribes. Desultory warfare was kept up for two years between the armies of David and Ish-bosheth. The only engagement of which we have an account is the battle of Gibeah, Joab and Abner commanding the opposing forces.

Slays Asahel. Abner was beaten and fled for his life but was pursued by Asahel (brother of Joab and Abishai). Not wishing to have a blood feud with Joab (for according to usage, Joab would become the avenger of his brother Asahel, in case he was slain), Abner begged Asahel to cease following him and pursue someone else. Asahel refused, and Abner thrust him through with a back stroke of his spear. The pursuit was kept up by Joab and Abishai until sunset, when a conference of the leaders was held, and Joab sounded the trumpet of recall. Abner withdrew to Mahanaim and Joab to Hebron (2 Sam. 2:8-30).

Breaks with Ish-bosheth. At last Abner took a step that was so presumptuous and significant of his consciousness of power that even the feebler Ish-bosheth protested. It was the exclusive right of the successor to the throne to cohabit with the concubines of the deceased king. Yet Abner took to his own harem Rizpah, one of Saul's concubines. The rebuke of Ish-bosheth so greatly enraged Abner that he declared his purpose of abandoning the house of Saul and allying himself with David (2 Sam. 3:6-9). To excuse his conduct he asserted that he was aware of the divine purpose concerning David.

Joins David. Abner made overtures through messengers to David, who required, as a preliminary, the restoration of his wife, Michal, who had been given to Paltiel by Saul. Abner made a tour among the elders of Israel and Benjamin, advocating the cause of David. He then went in person to David, who showed him great attention and respect, giving him and the twenty men accompanying him a feast. In return Abner promised to gather all Israel to the standard of David and was then dismissed in peace (2 Sam. 3:9-22).

Slain by Joab. Joab, returning from Hebron from a military expedition and fearing the influence of such a man as Abner, resolved to avenge his brother's death. Unknown to the king, but doubtless in his name, he sent messengers after Abner to call him back. Drawing Abner aside under the pretence of private conversation, he struck him under the fifth rib so that he died (2 Sam. 3:26-30). Abner was buried at Hebron with the honors due to a prince and chieftain, David himself following the bier (vv. 31-32). David's lamentation over Abner exonerated him in public opinion from any blame, and his declaration to his servants (3:38-39) showed that he could properly estimate the character even of an enemy and that he would have punished his murderer had he the power to do so.

ABOMINATION (Heb. *piggûl,* "filth," Lev. 7:18; *shiqqûṣ,* "unclean," Deut. 29:17, etc., *sheqeṣ,* "rejected," Lev. 7:21, etc.; *tô'ēbâ,* "causing abhorrence," Gen. 43:32; Gk. *bdelugma,* Matt. 24:15, etc.). This word is used to denote that which is particularly offensive to the moral sense, the religious feeling, or the natural inclination of the soul. Israel became an abomination ("stench," NIV) to the Philistines because of the antipathy caused by war (1 Sam. 13:4); David, for his distressed condition, was an abomination ("repulsive," NIV) to his friends (Ps. 88:8).

The practices of sin—such as the swellings of pride, lips of falsehood, the sacrifices of the wicked, and the foul rites of idolatry—are stigmatized as abominations (Prov. 6:16; 12:22; 15:8; Jer. 6:15; "detestable" in Prov., "loathsome" in Jer., NIV).

There are some peculiar applications of the term, to which attention is called:

1. "The Egyptians could not eat bread with the Hebrews, for that is loathsome [*tô'ēbâ;* "detestable," NIV] to the Egyptians" (Gen. 43:32). The explanation probably is that the Egyptians thought themselves ceremonially defiled if they ate with strangers. The primary reason may have been that the cow was the most sacred animal to the Egyptians, and the eating of it was obnoxious to them; whereas it was eaten and sacrificed by the Jews and most other nations. The Jews themselves, in later times, considered it unlawful to eat or drink with foreigners in their houses, or even to enter their dwellings (John 18:28; Acts 10:28; 11:3).

2. Joseph told his brothers to answer when questioned by Pharaoh, "Your servants have been keepers of livestock from our youth even until now, both we and our fathers." Joseph adds as a reason for giving this statement, "That you may live in the land of Goshen; for every shepherd is loathsome ["detestable," NIV] to the Egyptians" (Gen. 46:34). The origin of this feeling is nowhere given either in sacred or secular history, but the fact is beyond dispute, being amply attested by the evidence of the monuments, on which shepherds are always represented in a low and degrading attitude.

3. When Pharaoh told the Israelites to sacrifice to "your God" without going to the desert, Moses replied, "It is not right to do so, for we shall sacrifice to the Lord our God what is an abomination to the Egyptians. If we sacrifice what is an abomination ["detestable," NIV] to the Egyptians before their eyes, will they not then stone us?" (Ex. 8:26). Some think the abomination to consist in the sacrifice of the cow. Others (K. & D., *Com.,* ad loc.) think that "the Israelites would not carry out the rigid regulations observed by the Egyptians with regard to the cleanness of the sacrificial animals, and in fact would not observe the sacrificial rites of the Egyptians at all." The Egyptians would, doubtless, consider this a manifestation of contempt for themselves and their gods, and this would so enrage them that they would stone the Israelites.

BIBLIOGRAPHY: R. L. Harris, ed., *Theological Wordbook of the Old Testament* (1980), 2:955, 976.

ABOMINATION OF DESOLATION. Interpreted by premillennialists as the idolatrous image to be set up by the final Antichrist (the "beast," or "man of lawlessness" of 2 Thess. 2:3-4) in the restored Temple at Jerusalem in the latter half of Daniel's seventieth week (Dan. 9:27; 12:11). For the first part of the three and one-half days (years) of the prophetic week of years, the Antichrist keeps his covenant with the Jews. At the beginning of the last half of the week he breaks it (Zech. 11:16-17), compelling the Jews to worship his image. This is "the abomination (idol) of the desolator" or "the idol that causes desolation" (cf. Dan. 11:31; 12:11), inaugurating the period of "Jacob's trouble" (Jer. 30:7), a time of terrible suffering to Palestinian Jews of the end time, of which our Lord spoke (Matt. 24:15). In Dan. 11:31 the reference is to the act of Antiochus Epiphanes, prototype of the final Antichrist, who, in June 168 B.C. desecrated the Temple at Jerusalem. He built an altar to Jupiter Olympus on the altar of burnt offering, dedicated the Temple to this heathen deity, and offered swine's flesh. Premillennialists maintain that neither Antiochus Epiphanes nor the Romans under Titus in A.D. 70 exhausted Daniel's prophecy, which still awaits fulfillment. Amillennial interpretation, however, sees a fulfillment in the advance of the Romans against Jerusalem in A.D. 70 with their image-crowned standards, which were regarded as idols by the Jews.

BIBLIOGRAPHY: D. Daube, *The New Testament and Rabbinic Judaism* (1956), pp. 418-37; L. Gaston, *No Stone on Another* (1970); J. F. Walvoord, *Daniel: Key to Prophetic Revelation* (1971), pp. 235-37; G. R. Beasley-Murray, *New International Dictionary of New Testament Theology* (1975), 1:74-75.

A'BRAHAM (ā'bra-ham; "father of a multitude"). Up to Gen. 17:5, also in 1 Chron. 1:27; Neh. 9:7, he is uniformly called Abram, "high father." The name *Abram*—Abu-ramu, "the exalted father"—is found in early Babylonian contracts.

Family. Abraham was a native of Chaldea, and descendant in the ninth generation from Shem, the son of Noah. His father's name was Terah, and he was born in Ur, 2161 B.C. (Gen. 11:27).

Personal History. The life of Abraham, from his call to his death, consists of four periods, the commencement of each of which is marked by a divine revelation of sufficient importance to constitute a distinct epoch.

The First Period. The call and Abraham's journey to Canaan, to Egypt, and back again to Canaan occurred during this period.

Moves to Haran. When Abraham was about seventy years of age he, with his father, Terah, his nephew Lot, and his wife Sarah, went to live in Haran (Gen. 11:27-31). The reason for this movement is given in Acts 7:2-3: "The God of glory appeared to our father Abraham when he was in Mesopotamia, before he lived in Haran, and said to him, 'Depart from your country and your relatives, and come into the land that I will show you.'"

Departs from Haran. At the death of his father the call to Abraham was renewed. "Now the Lord said to Abram, 'Go forth from your country, and from your relatives and from your father's house, to the land which I will show you'" (Gen. 12:1). A condition was annexed to the call that he should separate from his father's house and leave his native land. He left his brother Nahor's family (who had also come to Haran, cf. Gen. 22:20, 23;

24:29; and 27:43) and departed, taking with him Lot, probably regarded as his heir (Josephus *Ant.* 1.7.1), and all his substance, to go "not knowing where he was going" (Heb. 11:8). Genesis 12:5 states that Abraham "set out for the land of Canaan," but Heb. 11:8 states that "he went out, not knowing where he was going." At first the name of the country was not revealed to him. It is designated simply as a "land which I will show you" (Gen. 12:1). But even if the name *Canaan* had been mentioned at the onset, it might still be true that he went forth "not knowing where he was going." For, in those days of slow transit, imperfect communication, and meager geographical knowledge, the mere name of a country several hundred miles distant would convey almost no idea of the country itself (Haley).

ABRAHAM'S MIGRATION FROM UR TO HARAN AND HEBRON

Arrival in Canaan. He traveled until he came into the land of Canaan, and there he formed his first encampment beside the oak of Moreh, between the mountains of Ebal and Gerizim, where his strong faith was rewarded by the second promise that his seed should possess this land. Abraham built "an altar there to the Lord who had appeared to him" (12:6-7). It is probable that the Canaanites were jealous of Abraham, and that he therefore soon removed to the mountainous district between Bethel and Ai, where he also built an altar to Jehovah.

In Egypt. He still moved southward until, at length, compelled by a famine, he went into Egypt. Fearing that the beauty of Sarah would tempt the Egyptians and endanger his life, he caused her to pass for his sister, which was partly true, for she was his half sister, having the same father but a different mother (Gen. 20:12). Sarah was taken to the royal harem, and Abraham was loaded with valuable gifts which he did not deserve, that could not be refused without an insult to the king. Warned of his mistake, Pharaoh summoned Abraham, and indignantly rebuked him for his subterfuge. He then dismissed Abraham, who went out of Egypt, taking his wife and Lot and his great wealth with him (Gen. 12).

Return to Canaan. Having reached his former encampment between Bethel and Ai, he again established the worship of Jehovah (Gen. 13:3-4). The increased wealth of Abraham and Lot became the cause of their separation. The country did not furnish sufficient pasture for the flocks and herds of both Abraham and Lot, and dissensions arose between their herdsmen. In order to avoid strife and consequent weakness before their enemies, Abraham proposed that they occupy different districts. He gave the choice of locality to Lot, who selected the plain of the Jordan and pitched his tent there. The childless Abraham was rewarded with a third blessing, in which God reiterated His promise to give him the land and a posterity as numerous as the dust of the earth. Then Abraham moved his tent, dwelt in Mamre, near Hebron, and built an altar (Gen. 13).

Rescue of Lot. Lot was now involved in danger. The five cities of the plain had become tributary to Chedorlaomer (Kedorlaomer, NIV), king of Elam. In the thirteenth year of their subjection they revolted, and Chedorlaomer (Kedorlaomer) marched against them with three allied kings. The kings of Sodom and Gomorrah fell, their cities were spoiled, and Lot and his goods were carried off (Gen. 14:1-12). Word was brought to Abraham, who immediately armed his dependents, 318 men, and with his Amorite allies overtook and defeated them at Dan, near the springs of Jordan. Abraham and his men pursued them as far as the neighborhood of Damascus and then returned with Lot and all the men and goods that had been taken away, about 2080 B.C.

Meeting with Melchizedek. Arriving at Salem on their return, they were met by *Melchizedek* (which see), king of Salem, and "priest of God Most High," who brought him refreshments. He also blessed Abraham in the name of the most high God, and Abraham presented him with a tenth of the spoils. By strict right, founded on the war usages still subsisting in Arabia, Abraham had a claim to all the recovered goods. The king of Sodom recognized this right, but Abraham refused to accept anything, even from a thread to a shoe latchet, lest any should say, "I have made Abram rich" (Gen. 14:17-24).

The Second Period. The promise of a lineal heir and the conclusion of the covenant (Gen. 15-16) took place in this period.

Vision of Abraham. Soon after this Abraham's faith was rewarded and encouraged by a distinct and detailed repetition of former promises and by a solemn covenant contracted between himself and God. He was told, and he believed, that his seed should be as numerous as the stars of heaven, that his posterity should grow up into a nation under foreign bondage, and that after four hundred years they should come up and possess the land in which he sojourned (Gen. 15).

Birth of Ishmael. Abraham had lived ten years in Canaan, and still he had no child. Sarah, now seventy-five years of age, followed contemporary custom and allowed Abraham to take Hagar, her Egyptian handmaid, who bore him Ishmael (Gen. 16), 2075 B.C.

The Third Period. The establishment of the covenant, the change of Abraham's name, and the appointment of the covenant sign of circumcision (Gen. 17-21) occurred during this period.

Change of Name. Thirteen more years passed, and Abraham reached his ninety-ninth year. God appeared to him and favored him with still more explicit declarations of His purpose. He changed his name from Abram to Abraham, renewed His covenant, and in token of it commanded that he and the males of his company should receive circumcision. Abraham was assured that Sarah, then ninety years old, should in a year become the mother of Isaac, the heir of the special promises. Abraham wavered in faith and prayed for Ishmael, whom God promised abundantly to bless, but declared that He would establish his covenant with Isaac.

Circumcision. That very day Abraham, his son Ishmael, and all the males of his household were circumcised (Gen. 17).

Visit of Angels. Abraham was favored, shortly after, with another interview with God. Sitting in his tent door under the oaks of Mamre he saw three travelers approaching and offered them his hospitality. They assented, and partook of the fare provided, Abraham standing in respectful attendance, according to oriental custom. These three persons were, doubtless, the "Angel of Jehovah" and two attending angels. The promise of a son by Sarah was renewed, and her incredulity rebuked. The strangers continued their journey, Abraham walking some way with them.

Bedouin tent

Destruction of Sodom. The Lord revealed to him the coming judgment upon Sodom and Gomorrah; and then followed that wondrous pleading in behalf of the cities (Gen. 18). Abraham rose early the next morning to see the fate of the cities and saw their smoke rising "up as the smoke of a furnace" (19:27-29), 2063 B.C.

Sarah Taken by Abimelech. After this Abraham journeyed southward, and dwelt between Kadesh and Shur, and sojourned in Gerar. Abimelech, king of Gerar, sent for and took Sarah, but was warned of God in a dream and sent her back the next morning to Abraham, whom he reproved for the deceit he had employed. He was healed in answer to Abraham's prayer (Gen. 20).

Isaac Born. At length, when Abraham was one hundred years old, and Sarah ninety, the long-promised heir was born, 2061 B.C. The altered position of Ishmael in the family excited the ill will of himself and his mother. This was so apparent in the mocking behavior of Ishmael at the weaning of Isaac that Sarah insisted that he and Hagar should be sent away, to which Abraham reluctantly consented. Abraham, after settling a dispute concerning a well taken by Abimelech's servants, made a treaty with him (Gen. 21).

The Fourth Period. In this period occurred the test of Abraham's faith and his final years.

Abraham's Great Trial (Gen. 22–25:11), 2036 B.C. When Isaac was nearly grown (twenty-five years old, says Josephus *Ant.* 1.13.2) God subjected Abraham to a terrible trial of his faith and obedience. He commanded him to go to Mt. Moriah (perhaps where the Temple afterward stood) and there offer up Isaac, whose death would nullify all his hopes and the promises. Probably human sacrifices already existed, and therefore the peculiar trial lay in the singular position of Isaac and the improbability of his being replaced. Abraham decided to obey, because "he considered that God is able to raise men even from the dead" (Heb. 11:19). Assisted by his two servants, he made preparations for the journey and started early the next morning. On the third day he saw the place and told his servants that he and his son would proceed on farther to worship, then return. Upon Isaac's asking, "Where is the lamb for the burnt offering?" Abraham replied, "God will provide for Himself the lamb." The altar was built and Isaac placed upon it. The uplifted hand of the father was arrested by the angel of Jehovah, and a ram caught in the thicket was substituted for Isaac. Abraham called the name of the place Jehovah-jireh, "The Lord Will Provide." The promises formerly made to Abraham were then confirmed in the most solemn manner. Abraham returned to his young men and with them went to Beersheba and dwelt there (Gen. 22:1-19).

Some have found it difficult to reconcile God's command to sacrifice Isaac with His prohibition of human sacrifices (Lev. 18:21; 20:2). We answer, "God's design was not to secure a certain *outward act,* but a certain *state of mind,* a willingness to give up the beloved object to Jehovah" (Haley). "The divine command was given in such a form that Abraham could not understand it in any other way than as requiring an outward

burnt offering, because there was no other way in which Abraham could accomplish the complete surrender of Isaac than by an actual preparation for really offering the desired sacrifice" (K. & D., *Com.*). Moreover, any criticism of Abraham's sacrifice of his son must be modified by his evident belief in God's ability to raise that son from the dead.

Death of Sarah. The next event recorded in Abraham's life is the death of Sarah, 127 years of age, at or near *Hebron* (which see). Abraham purchased from Ephron the Hittite the cave of *Machpelah* (which see), the field in which it stood, and all the trees in the field, and there he buried Sarah (Gen. 23).

Marriage of Isaac. His next care was to procure a suitable wife for Isaac. He commissioned his eldest servant to go to Haran, where Nahor had settled, and get a wife for his son from his own family. The servant went and, directed by God, chose Rebekah, the daughter of Bethuel son of Nahor. In due time he returned, and Rebekah was installed in Sarah's tent (Gen. 24). Some time after Abraham took another wife, Keturah, by whom he had several children. These, together with Ishmael, seem to have been portioned off by their father in his lifetime and sent away to the E, that they might not interfere with Isaac.

Death. Abraham died when he was 175 years old and was buried by Isaac and Ishmael in the cave of Machpelah (Gen. 25), 1986 B.C.

Man of Faith. The spiritual experience of Abraham was marked by four far-reaching crises in which his faith was tested, and which, in each case, called forth the surrender of something naturally most dear to him: first, his giving up country and kindred (Gen. 12:1); second, his breaking off with his nephew, Lot, particularly close to Abraham by virtue of kinship as a fellow believer and possible heir (Gen. 13:1-18); third, the abandonment of his own cherished plans for Ishmael and his being called upon to center his hope in the promise of the birth of Isaac (Gen. 17:17-18); fourth, the supreme test of his mature life of faith in his willingness to offer up Isaac, his only son, whom he loved passionately and in whom all his expectations centered (Gen. 22:1-19; Heb. 11:17-18).

Man of Covenant Promise. As a friend of God and a man who implicitly trusted the divine promises, Abraham was the recipient of an important covenant involving not only himself, but his posterity, natural as well as spiritual. The Abrahamic covenant as originally given (Gen. 12:1-4) and reaffirmed (Gen. 13:14-17; 15:1-7; 17:1-8), contains the following elements: (1) "I will make you a great nation," fulfilled: (a) in a natural posterity, "as the dust of the earth," the Hebrew people (13:16, John 8:37), (b) in a spiritual progeny (John 8:39; Rom. 4:16; Gal. 3:6-7, 29), comprising all persons of faith, whether Jew or Gentile, (c) in the descendants of Ishmael

(Gen. 17:18-20). (2) "I will bless you," fulfilled in a double sense: (a) temporally (Gen. 13:14-18; 15:18) and (b) spiritually (Gen. 15:6; John 8:56). (3) "And make your name great." In three great world religions —Judaism, Islam, and Christianity—Abraham is revered as one of the eminent men of all time. (4) "And so you shall be a blessing." By his personal example of faith and that faith as manifested in his descendants, Abraham has been a worldwide blessing. (5) "I will bless those who bless you, and the one who curses you I will curse." This has been remarkably fulfilled in the Jewish dispersion. Nations who have persecuted the Jews have fared ill, and those who have protected them have prospered. Prophecy, both fulfilled and unfulfilled, substantiates this principle (Deut. 30:7; Mic. 5:7-9; Hag. 2:22; Zech. 14:1-3; Jer. 50:11-18; 51:24-36; Ezek. 25:2; 26:2-3). (6) "In you all the families of the earth shall be blessed." This is the great messianic promise fulfilled in Abraham's descendant, Christ (John 8:56-58; Gal. 3:16).

Abraham and Archaeology. Archaeological evidence related to the time of Abraham has been found in Mesopotamia and Palestine.

Life in Ur. The biblical chronology would place Abraham's birth in lower Mesopotamia about 2161 B.C. According to one chronology, he lived there under the new Sumero-Akkadian empire of Ur Nammu, the founder of the famous Third Dynasty of Ur (c. 2135-2035 B.C.), who took the title of "King of Sumer and Akkad," and whose mightiest work was the erection of the great ziggurat (temple tower) at Ur. Abraham left "Ur of the Chaldeans" (Gen. 11:31) when it was entering the heyday of its commercial and political prestige. According to the new minimal chronology, Abraham was born in Ur and left it during the period when the hated Guti ruled the land (2180-2070 B.C.). He then left Haran for Canaan about the time Ur entered her golden age (Ur III period). The new chronology dates Ur III 2070-1960 B.C. It was the appearance of "the God of glory" to him "when he was in Mesopotamia, before he lived in Haran" (Acts 7:2) that enabled Abraham to leave a famous center of wealth and culture for an unknown destination. In addition to a lucrative woolen trade, Ur was the center of numerous other industries that centered about the worship of the moon god Sin (Nannar) and his consort Nin-gal. The great temples and ziggurat of this deity made Ur a mecca for thousands of pilgrims. The far-flung commercial ventures of Ur gave her so much economic power in Mesopotamia that she virtually controlled the region. The total population of the city-state at that time has been estimated at 360,000.

At Haran. The town of Haran (Gen. 11:31; 12:5) in NW Mesopotamia to which Abram migrated on his way to Canaan is still in existence on the Balikh River sixty miles W of Tell Halaf. It was a flourishing city in the nineteenth and eighteenth centuries B.C., as is known from frequent references to it in cuneiform sources (Assyr. *Harranu,* "road"). It was on the great east-west trade route, and like Ur, it was the seat of the worship of the moon god. Whether Terah chose Haran as a place to settle because he had not made a clean break with the idolatry of his youth, or perhaps for commercial reasons, can only be surmised. The city of Nahor, which was Rebekah's home (Gen. 24:10) is also attested by the Mari Tablets, discovered in 1935 and belonging to the eighteenth century B.C. Evidence of Hebrew occupation of this region also appears in names of Abraham's forefathers, which correspond to the names of towns near Haran: Serug (Assyr. *Sarugi*) and Terah (*Til Turakhi,* "Mound of Terah") in Assyrian times. Other immediate ancestors of Abraham listed in Gen. 11:10-30 have left their trace in this territory called Padan-Aram (Paddan Aram, NIV; Aram. "field or plain of Aram," Gen. 25:20; 28:2-7). Reu corresponds to later names of towns in the Middle Euphrates Valley, and Peleg recalls later Paliga on the Euphrates just above the mouth of the Habur River.

In Canaan. After the death of Terah, Abraham left Haran and came into Canaan (Gen. 12:4-5). Archaeological and historical studies show that in Palestine and much of Syria deurbanization had set in as early as the twenty-fourth century B.C. and certainly characterized the land during the period 2200-2000 B.C. Newer discoveries indicate that this abandonment of towns resulted not from invasion but from a significant shift to drier conditions combined with a greatly weakened economy and disruption of trade systems. After 2000 B.C. reurbanization of Palestine gradually occurred once more, but the central and southern hill country of Palestine continued to be rather thinly settled even after the rapid growth of urbanization elsewhere. Thus the patriarchal period in Palestine fits admirably into what is now known of the historical context. No great cities or city-states could have confronted the patriarch. And when reurbanization occurred, it was less pronounced in the central and southern hill country, where the patriarchs spent most of their time.

The places that appear in connection with the movements of the patriarchs are not the sites of later periods, such as Mizpah or Gibeah, but include Shechem, Bethel, Dothan, Gerar, and Jerusalem (Salem)—all known by means of exploration and excavation to have been inhabited in the patriarchial age. The five cities of the plain of the Jordan (Gen. 13-14) that appear prominently in the story of Abraham and Lot, namely, Sodom, Gomorrah, Admah, Zeboiim, and Zoar also belong to this early period (c. 2065 B.C.), being located at the southern end of the Dead Sea. This area "full of tar pits" (Gen. 14:10) was overwhelmed by a catastrophe of fire, which with the salt and sulphur of the region, doubtless accompanied by earthquakes common in this area of the Arabah, was the natural aspect of the supernatural destruction of the cities of the plain. These cities are now probably under the slowly rising waters at the southern end of the Dead Sea. The account of Lot's wife turned into a pillar of salt is reminiscent of the great salt mass, five miles long, stretching N and S at the SW end of the Dead Sea.

Clash with the Mesopotamian Kings. The fourteenth chapter of Genesis is the pivotal passage in the patriarchal narratives from a historical point of view. Although archaeology has not yet furnished a link to tie it into the general context of ancient Near Eastern history, evidence is continually increasing of its historical character, which used to be almost universally denied by critics. A remarkable fact about this chapter, demonstrating its great age and authenticity, is its use of archaic words and place names, often appended with a scribal explanation to make them comprehensible to a later generation when the name had changed. Examples are "Bela (that is, Zoar)" in v. 2; "the vale of Siddim (that is, the Salt Sea)" in v. 3; "En-mishpat (that is, Kadesh)" in v. 7; "the valley of Shaveh (that is, the King's Valley)" in v. 17. Interesting examples of the confirmation of place names occur in the reference to Ashteroth-karnaim and Ham (Gen. 14:5). These two cities, mentioned in the invasion of Chedorlaomer and the kings with him, have both been shown to have been occupied at this early period, as archaeological examination of their sites has demonstrated. Ham was first surmised to be identical with a modern place by the same name in eastern Gilead, and examination of the site by A. Jirku and W. F. Albright (1925 and 1929) disclosed a small but ancient mound going back to the Bronze Age. Thutmose III lists the place among his conquests in the early fifteenth century B.C. Archaeology has likewise confirmed the general line of march followed by the invading kings, later known as "The King's Highway."

Added Archaeological Light. The site of Nuzi near modern Kirkuk (excavated between 1925 and 1941) dates from the fifteenth century B.C. and has yielded several thousand tablets illustrating vividly adoption (cf. Gen. 15:2), marriage laws (cf. Gen. 16:1-16), rights of primogeniture (Gen. 25:27-34), the teraphim (Gen. 31:34), and other customs and practices appearing in the life of Abraham and the Hebrew patriarchs. Also the discoveries at *Mari* (which see), a site near modern Abou Kemal on the Middle Euphrates, since 1933 have shed a great deal of indirect light on the age of Abraham. Moreover, the name *Abraham* (not of course the biblical character) has been found in Mesopotamia in the second millennium B.C., showing that it was actually a name in use at an early date. Certain radical literary critics such as J. L. Thompson (*The Historicity of the*

Patriarchal Narratives [1974]) and J. Van Seters (*Abraham in History and Tradition* [1975]) have dismissed the validity of Early and Middle Bronze Age archaeology for the dating of Abraham. Van Seters actually proposed locating the patriarch about 600 B.C., but Near Eastern history simply does not support such a late date. Additional archaeological evidence to that inadequately "disproved" or suppressed by Thompson and Van Seters supports a much earlier date than they propose through the use of literary critical methods. *See* Sacrifice, Human.   H.R.H; H.F.V.; R.K.H.

BIBLIOGRAPHY: J. O. Dykes, *Abraham the Friend of God* (1877); H. G. Thomkins, *Abraham and His Age* (1897); W. H. Thomson, *Life and Times of the Patriarchs* (1912); H. H. Rowley, *Recent Discovery and the Patriarchal Age* (1949); F. B. Meyer, *Abraham: The Obedience of Faith* (1953); A. Edersheim, *Bible History* (1954), 1:51-106; J. Finegan, *Light from the Ancient Past* (1959), pp. 66-73, 145f., 179, 461, 466, 480f., 490, 497f.; C. F. Pfeiffer, *The Patriarchal Age* (1961); K. A. Kitchen, *Ancient Orient and Old Testament* (1966); A. C. Swindell, *Expository Times* 87 (1975): 50-53; D. J. Wiseman, *Bibliotheca Sacra* 134 (1977): 123-30; F. J. Delitzsch, *A New Commentary on Genesis* (1978), 1:364–2:112; G. Bush, *Notes on Genesis* (1981), 1:188–2:58.

ABRAHAM'S BOSOM. The phrase "to be in one's bosom" applies to the person who so reclines at the table that his head is brought almost into the bosom of the one sitting next above him. To be in Abraham's bosom signified to occupy the seat next to Abraham, i.e., to enjoy felicity with Abraham. Jesus, accommodating His speech to the Jews, describes the condition of Lazarus after death by this figure (Luke 16:22-23). "Abraham's bosom" is also an expression of the Talmud for the state of bliss after death. Father Abraham was, to the Israelites, in the corrupt times of their later superstitions, almost what the virgin Mary is to the Roman church. He was constantly invoked as though he could hear the prayers of his descendants, wherever they were; and he was pictured standing at the gate of paradise to receive and embrace his children as they entered, and the whole family of his faithful descendants was gathered to his arms.

A'BRAM (ā'bram; "high father"). The original name (Gen. 17:5) of Abraham.

ABRO'NAH (ab-rō'na; "passage"). The thirtieth station of the Israelites on their way from Egypt to Canaan (Num. 33:34-35). Since it lay near Ezion-geber on the W as they left Jotbathah, it was probably in the plain "Kâ'a en-Năkb," immediately opposite the pass of the same name at the head of the Elamitic branch of the Red Sea. In the KJV this term is rendered Ebronah.

AB'SALOM (ab'sa-lom; "father of peace"). The third son of David, and his only one by Maacah, the daughter of Talmai, king of Geshur (2 Sam. 3:3), born about 1000 B.C. He was known for his personal beauty—"In all Israel was no one as handsome as Absalom" (2 Sam. 14:25). Though his hair was doubtless very heavy, and thus was considered beautiful, the weight given, two hundred shekels, is too much and is evidently a scribal error (K. & D., *Com.;* 2 Sam. 14:26).

Avenges Tamar. Absalom's sister, Tamar, became the object of the lustful desire of Amnon, her half brother, David's eldest son, and was violated by him (2 Sam. 13:1-18). According to Eastern notions the duty of avenging his sister's wrong fell upon Absalom. He therefore took Tamar and kept her secluded in his own house, saying nothing to Amnon "either good or bad." After two years had passed he found an opportunity for revenge. He then invited all his brothers, including Amnon, to a great sheep-shearing at Baal-hazor, and, to lull suspicion, requested the presence of his father also. Amid the mirth of the feast, while they were warm with wine, the servants of Absalom, at a preconcerted signal, fell upon Amnon and killed him (13:23-29). Absalom fled to his grandfather Talmai and remained there three years (vv. 37-38).

Return to Jerusalem. David, yearning for his exiled son Absalom (v. 39), yielded easily to the scheme of Joab and permitted Absalom to return to Jerusalem, but not to appear before him. Absalom lived for two whole years in Jerusalem, and then sent for Joab, who refused to see him until Absalom ordered his servants to burn Joab's barley field. Then Joab secured an interview for him with the king (2 Sam. 14).

Preparations for Revolt. But Absalom proved himself false and faithless. He secretly plotted a revolt, winning over the people by his handsomeness and charisma and by the magnificence of his trappings, riding in a chariot with fifty outriders. He also fostered the discontent of the people by insinuations against his father's justice. Other causes, doubtless, were favorable for Absalom: the affair of Bathsheba, the probable disaffection of Judah for being merged in one common Israel, and less attention on the part of David, because of his age, to individual complaints (2 Sam. 15:1-6).

Revolt. When the plot was ripe, Absalom obtained leave to go to Hebron, to pay a vow that he had made at Geshur in case he should be permitted to return to Jerusalem. (The reference in 2 Sam. 15:7 to "forty years" is a scribal error, for David reigned but forty years in all [1 Kings 2:11], and he certainly had reigned many years before Absalom's rebellion. The Syr. and Arab. versions read "four years," and with this Josephus and NIV agree.) Absalom had sent spies throughout all the tribes of Israel, summoning those favorable to his cause to assemble at Hebron, where he went attended by two hundred unsuspecting adherents (2 Sam. 15:7-11). His next step was to send for Ahithophel, David's counselor, and secure his approval and advice

(15:12), Ahithophel being an oracle in Israel (16:23).

Entry into Jerusalem. When David heard the sad tidings of revolt he at once prepared for flight and, leaving Jerusalem, went to Mahanaim, beyond the Jordan (2 Sam. 15:13-17). Absalom now entered Jerusalem (15:37) and, through the advice of Ahithophel, publicly took possession of the portion of his father's harem left in the city. The motive in this latter act was to gain the more unreserved support of the people, from the assurance that any reconcilement between Absalom and his father would thereafter be impossible (16:20-22). Absalom had already met Hushai, who had been sent to join him by David, that he might be instrumental in thwarting the counsels of Ahithophel (15:33-37; 16:16-19). A council of war was held to consider the course to be pursued against David. Ahithophel advised the immediate pursuit and death of the king—that one death would close the war. Hushai, to gain time for David, urged the king's skill and bravery, the number and might of his warriors, and the possibility and disastrous consequences of defeat, and he advised a general gathering against David and the total annihilation of him and his followers. The advice was accepted by Absalom. Information was secretly sent to David, who then went beyond Jordan and there collected a force sufficient to oppose Absalom (17:1-14, 21-24).

Anointed King. Absalom was formally anointed king (2 Sam. 19:10), appointed Amasa captain of his host, and crossed over Jordan in pursuit of his father (17:25-26). A battle was fought in the wood of Ephraim. The army of Absalom was defeated, twenty thousand were slain, and a still greater number perished in the defiles of the forest.

Death. Absalom fled on a swift mule, and as he was riding through the forest, his "head" became wedged between two branches. When he raised his hands to try to dislodge himself, he let go of the bridle and the unrestrained mule kept going. More than likely Absalom was riding without a saddle, and he simply slipped off the animal's back and hung suspended in midair. The text does not say he was caught by his hair; the historian Josephus stated that. He probably had a helmet over his hair on this occasion; so his hair would not have caught in the branches. Joab, being informed of what had happened to Absalom, hastened to the spot and killed him, notwithstanding David's request that he should be spared. The body was taken down and cast into a pit, over which the people raised a great heap of stones as a mark of abhorrence, a burial that the historian contrasts with the splendid monument prepared by Absalom for himself in the "King's Valley" (2 Sam. 18:1-18), about 967 B.C. The so-called tomb of Absalom that stands today in the Valley of the Kidron can have no connection with the monument Absalom erected for himself; it probably dates to the first century A.D. Absalom had three sons and one daughter, the latter named Tamar (14:27), who alone survived him (18:18) and became the mother of Maacah, the wife of Rehoboam (2 Chron. 11:20-21).

H.F.V.

BIBLIOGRAPHY: C. E. Macartney, *Chariots of Fire* (1951), pp. 93-103; R. N. Whybray, *The Succession Narrative: A Study of 2 Sam. 9-20* (1968); W. G. Blaikie, *The Second Book of Samuel* (1978); R. Battenhouse, *Christianity and Literature* 31, no. 3 (1982): 53-57; L. Rost, *The Succession to the Throne of David* (1982).

ABSTINENCE. A general term signifying to refrain from something or some action. In the ecclesiastical sense it means the refraining from certain kinds of food or drink on certain days.

Jewish. The first mention of abstinence in Scripture is found in Gen. 9:4, where the use of blood was forbidden to Noah. The next is in Gen. 32:32: "Therefore, to this day the sons of Israel do not eat the sinew of the hip which is on the socket of the thigh, because he touched the socket of Jacob's thigh in the sinew of the hip." The law confirmed abstinence from blood (Lev. 3:17) and the use even of lawful animals if the manner of their death rendered it likely that they were not properly bled (Ex. 22:31; Deut. 14:21). Whole classes of animals that might not be eaten are given in Lev. 11. *See* Animal: clean and unclean. Certain parts of lawful animals, as being sacred to the altar, were forbidden, namely, the caul (or fat covering the liver), the kidneys and the fat upon them, the fat covering the entrails, and also the "entire fat tail" (Lev. 3:9-11). Everything consecrated to idols was also interdicted (Ex. 34:15). While engaged in their official duties, the priests were commanded to abstain from wine and strong drink (Lev. 10:9), and the Nazirites had to abstain from strong drink and the use of grapes during the whole time of their separation (Num. 6:3). The *Rechabites* (which see) voluntarily assumed a constant abstinence from wine (Jer. 35:6). The *Essenes* (which see), a Jewish sect, were stringent in their abstinence, refusing all pleasant food, eating nothing but coarse bread and drinking only water, while some abstained from all food until evening.

Christian. Some among the early Christian converts thought themselves bound by Mosaic regulations respecting food, and abstained from flesh sacrificed to idols and from animals accounted unclean by the law. Others considered this a weakness, and boasted of the freedom with which Christ had set them free. Paul discusses this matter in Rom. 14:1-3 and 1 Cor. 8 and teaches that everyone is at liberty to act according to his own conscience, but that the stronger should refrain from that which might prove a stumbling block to his weaker brother. In 1 Tim. 4:3-4 he reproves certain persons who forbid marriage and enjoin abstinence from meats. The council of the apostles at Jerusalem limited enforced abstinence upon the converts to that of meats offered to idols, blood, and "things strangled" (Acts 15:29).

In the early church catechumens were required, according to Cyril and Jerome, to observe a season of abstinence and prayer for forty days; according to others, twenty days. Superstitious abstinence on the part of the clergy was considered a crime, and if that abstinence arose from the notion that any creature of God was not good they were liable to be deposed from office. Strict observance of the church fasts was enjoined.

ABYSS' (à-bĭs'; Gk. *hēabussos*). In the NT the abyss is the abode of the imprisoned demons (Rev. 9:1-21). At least many of the demons whom Jesus expelled in His earthly ministry were commanded to return to the abyss (cf. Luke 8:31), but these evil spirits dreaded to go there before their predetermined time. Myriads of demons will be let loose during the period of Tribulation to energize age-end apostasy and revolt against God and His Christ, but will be shut up again in this prison together with Satan at the second advent of Christ (20:1-3). The abyss is therefore to be distinguished from *sheol* (hell) or *hades* (which see). This "unseen world" is revealed as the place of departed human spirits between death and the resurrection (Matt. 11:23; 16:18; Luke 10:15; Rev. 1:18; 20:13-14). It is also to be distinguished from "tartarus," the "prison abode of fallen angels" (cf. 2 Pet. 2:4) and "the lake of fire" (Rev. 19:20; 20:10; 21:8), or the eternal abode of all wicked, unrepentant creatures, including Satan, angels, and men. The LXX renders Heb. *tᵉhôm*, "the primeval ocean" (Gen. 1:2; Ps. 24:2, etc.) as "abyss." In classical Gk. the word *abussos* is always an adjective meaning "very deep" ("bottomless") or "unfathomable" ("boundless"). *See* Hell; Lake of Fire.

ACACIA, ACCACIA. *See* Vegetable Kingdom: Acacia.

AC'BOR. *See* Achbor.

AC'CAD or **Akkad** (ăk'ăd). An ancient center of Hamitic imperial power founded by Nimrod (Gen. 10:10). The *city* is evidently Agade, which Sargon I brought into great prominence as the capital of his far-flung Semitic empire, which dominated the Mesopotamian world from about 2360 to 2180 B.C. The location of Accad cannot presently be identified, but it must be in the vicinity of Babylon, perhaps N of it. The *country* was named after its capital and embraces the stoneless alluvial plain of southern Babylonia N of *Sumer* (which see). The term "the land of Shinar," in which the world's first imperial power developed embracing "Babel [Babylon, NIV] and Erech [Uruk] and Accad and Calneh" (Gen. 10:10), is descriptive of the entire alluvial plain of Babylonia between the Tigris and the Euphrates, in approximately the last two hundred miles

18

of the course of those great rivers as they flowed in ancient times. In the cuneiform inscriptions the region is divided into a northern part called Accad (Akkad), in which Babel (Babylon) and the city of Accad (Agade) were situated; and a southern part called Sumer, in which Erech (ancient Uruk, modern Warka) was located. At Uruk the first sacred temple tower (Babylonian, ziggurat) was found, as well as evidence of the first cylinder seals (Finegan, *Light from the Ancient Past,* pp. 19-23). The inhabitants of this region were originally non-Semitic Sumerians, who racially must have been of Hamitic origin, according to Gen. 10:8-10, and who were the inventors of cuneiform writing and the cultural precursors of their later conquerors, the Babylonian Semites. The city of Accad (Agade) disappeared in ancient times and by Assyrian times was utterly unknown.   M.F.U.; H.F.V.

BIBLIOGRAPHY: H. Frankfort, *The Art and Architecture of the Ancient Orient* (1954), pp. 41-46; J. Finegan, *Light from the Ancient Past* (1959), pp. 19-23; C. J. Gadd, "The Dynasty of Agade and the Gutian Invasion," *The Cambridge Ancient History,* rev. ed. (1963), 1:xix.

ACCEPT, ACCEPTABLE, ACCEPTED (Heb. *rāṣâ,* "to take pleasure in"; Gk. *dechomai,* "to take with the hand," i.e., "to receive with hospitality"). *To accept* is to receive with pleasure and kindness (Gen. 32:20) and is the opposite of *to reject,* which is a direct refusal with disapprobation (Jer. 6:30; 7:29). An *accepted* or *acceptable time* (Ps. 69:13; 2 Cor. 6:2) is the time of favor, a favorable opportunity. Luke 4:24 means that no prophet is welcomed or appreciated favorably in his own country.

Acceptance also means that relation to God in which He is well-pleased with His children, for by children of God only is it enjoyed. In Acts 10:35 we learn that "in every nation the man who fears Him and does what is right, is welcome to Him."

The Christian scheme bases acceptance by God on justification. Paul in Eph. 1:6 refers to the grace of God, "which He freely bestowed on us in the Beloved." In Christ only are we acceptable to God. Out of Him we are sinners and subjects of wrath.

The Calvinist teaches that the sins that are pardoned in justification include all sins, past, present, and future, and that God will not deal with the believer according to his transgressions; whereas the Arminian holds that the state of acceptance can be maintained only by perpetually believing in and appropriating to himself the atoning merits of Jesus, and obediently keeping God's holy commandments.

ACCESS TO GOD (Gk. *prosagōgē,* "act of moving to"). That friendly relation with God whereby we are acceptable to Him and have assurance that He is favorably disposed toward us (Rom. 5:2; Eph. 2:18; 3:12). In substance it is not different from the "peace of God," i.e., the peaceful rela-

tion of believers toward God, brought about through Christ's death. By the continuous power and efficiency of His atoning act, Jesus is the constant Bringer to the Father. Access means the obtaining of a hearing with God, and if a hearing, the securing in some form an answer to our requests. The apostle John (1 John 5:14-15) says: "This is the confidence which we have before Him, that, if we ask anything according to His will, He hears us. And if we know that He hears us in whatever we ask, we know that we have the requests which we have asked from Him." Here we learn that access to God involves asking according to His will. A child has right of access to his father. Such right and privilege are granted to, and should be enjoyed by, every child of God. We must not infer that our access is cut off if we do not realize direct answers to some of our requests, but we must believe that God always hears His children and does the best things for them.

AC'CO (ăc'kō). A town on the Mediterranean coast, thirty miles S of Tyre, and ten from Mt. Carmel (Judg. 1:31). It was known to the ancient Greeks and Romans as Ptolemais, from Ptolemy the king of Egypt, who rebuilt it in 100 B.C. During the Middle Ages it was called Acra, and subsequently called St. Jean d'Acre. Paul visited this place (Acts 21:7). The original site is a mound called Tell-el-Fukhar, located one mile E of the present city.

Archaeological activity at Acre has concentrated on Crusader structures under the present city. In 1955 the Israel Department of Antiquities cleared the refectory of the Knights of St. John, and in 1956 and from 1959 to 1962 the Department of Antiquities and the National Parks Authority cleared a hospital and chapel of the order.

Other finds in the town include sections of the wall of the Hellenistic city (10-15 feet thick), and a glass furnace and temple dating to the same period. In 1976 Moshe Dothan worked at the harbor area where he uncovered a large tower and defensive wall of the Hellenistic town of Ptolemais. *See* Ptolemais.   H.F.V.

ACCOUNTABILITY. Not a Bible word but an abstract term for that return for his talents and opportunities that every soul must make to God day by day, and especially at the judgment, as we are taught in Matt. 12:36, Rom. 4:10, Heb. 13:17, and 1 Pet. 4:5. It is a well-established doctrine of Holy Scripture, attested to by human consciousness, that we are free moral agents, entirely dependent upon our Creator for our existence and maintenance, and rightly answerable to Him for our conduct; and that God consequently has a right to our perfect obedience and service. It is accordingly easy for us to feel that He is justified in calling us to a strict reckoning for all He has entrusted us with. Disabled by our fall into sin, gracious strength has been provided for us in the atonement, so that we are without excuse if we fail to do God's will.

ACCURSED. *See* Anathema; Oath.

ACCUSER (Heb. *shāpaṭ* "judge"; *śāṭān* "adversary"; in the NT, Gk. *katēgoros,* "prosecutor").

1. One who has a cause or matter of contention; the accuser, opponent, or plaintiff in any suit (Judg. 12:2; Matt. 5:25; Luke 12:58).

2. In Scripture, in a general sense, an adversary or enemy (Luke 18:3; 1 Pet. 5:8). In the latter passage reference is made to the old Jewish teaching that Satan was the accuser of men before God (Job 1:6-11; Rev. 12:10). *See* Adversary.

ACEL'DAMA (a-sel'dā-mä; ASV and NIV, Akeldama). Called at present "Hak ed-damm," it signifies "Field of Blood" (Matt. 27:8; Acts 1:18-19), now at the E end and on the southern slope of the valley of Hinnom. The tradition that fixes this spot reaches back to the age of Jerome. Once the tradition was that the soil of this spot, a deep pit or cellar, was believed to have the power of consuming dead bodies in the space of twenty-four hours, so that whole shiploads of it are said to have been carried away in A.D. 1218, in order to cover the famous Campo Santo in Pisa.

Aceldama, the field of blood

ACHAI'A (a-kā'ya). The name once applied to the NW portion of the Peloponnesus and afterward applied to the entire Peloponnesus, called now the Morea. It was one of the two provinces, of which Macedonia was the other, into which the Romans divided Greece (27 B.C.). It was under a proconsular government at the time when Luke wrote the Acts, so that the title given to Gallio, "proconsul," was proper (Acts 18:12), A.D. 51 or 52.

ACHA'ICUS (a-kā'i-kus; "an Achaean"). A Christian of Corinth who had rendered Paul personal aid, and by him was kindly commended to the Corinthian church (1 Cor. 16:17), A.D. 54.

A'CHAN (ā'kan; "troublesome"). A son of Carmi, of the tribe of Judah; called also Achar (1 Chron. 2:7).

Achan's Sin. By one incident of his life Achan attained a disgraceful notoriety. Before Jericho was taken, the city was put under that awful ban whereby all the inhabitants (excepting Rahab and her family) were consigned to destruction, all the combustible goods to be burned, and the metals consecrated to God (Deut. 7:16, 23-26; Josh. 6:17-19). After Jericho fell (1400 B.C.) the whole nation kept the vow, with the exception of Achan. His covetousness made him unfaithful, and, the opportunity presenting, he took a "beautiful mantle from Shinar [or Babylonia, NIV] and two hundred shekels of silver and a bar of gold fifty shekels in weight" (7:21).

Result of Achan's Sin. Ai had been visited by spies, who declared that it could easily be taken. An expedition of three thousand men sent against the city was repulsed, and they returned to Joshua, who inquired of the Lord concerning the cause of the disaster. The answer was that "Israel has sinned,... they have even taken some of the things under the ban and have both stolen and deceived" (Josh. 7:11). This was the reason for Israel's defeat, and Joshua was commanded to sanctify the people and on the morrow to cast lots for the offender. Achan was chosen and, being exhorted by Joshua, made a confession of his guilt, which was verified by the finding of the spoil in his tent.

Objection has been urged against the use of the lot to discover the guilty party. We answer that the decision by lot, when ordered by God, involved no chance but was under His special direction, as is evident from the expressions "which the Lord takes" (Josh. 7:14), and "the lot is cast into the lap, but its every decision is from the Lord" (Prov. 16:33).

Achan's Punishment. Achan was conveyed with his family, property, and spoils to the valley (afterward called Achor, "trouble," or "disaster" as in NIV), where they "stoned them with stones; and they burned them with fire" (Josh. 7:25).

The severity of the punishment of Achan, as regards his family, has excited considerable comment. Some vindicate it by saying that Achan by his sin had fallen under the ban pronounced against Jericho and was exposed to the same punishment as a town that had fallen away into idolatry (Deut. 13:16-17); others believe that the family of Achan were aware of his crime and therefore were deserving of a share in his punishment (K. & D., *Com.*); others, again, consider it as the result of one of those sudden impulses of indiscriminate popular vengeance to which the Jewish people were exceedingly prone (Kitto). The real explanation is evidently to be found in the fact that the iniquity of the inhabitants of Canaan was now "complete" (cf. Gen. 15:16), and God's righteous wrath was poured out upon them.

BIBLIOGRAPHY: J. R. Porter, *Vetus Testamentum* 15 (1965): 367-73; J. Kitto, *Daily Bible Illustrations* (1981), 1: 540-42.

A'CHAR (ā'kār; "trouble"). Another form of the name *Achan* (which see), and given to that person in 1 Chron. 2:7.

ACH'BOR (ak'bor; "mouse"), or **Acbor** (NIV).
1. The father of Baal-hanan, the seventh Edomite king, mentioned in Gen. 36:38-39.
2. The son of Micaiah and one of the courtiers whom Josiah sent to Huldah to inquire about the course to be pursued respecting the newly discovered book of the law (2 Kings 22:12, 14), 624 B.C. In the parallel passage (2 Chron. 34:20) he is called Abdon the son of Micah. He is doubtless the same person whose son, Elnathan, was courtier of Jehoiakim (Jer. 26:22; 36:12).

A'CHIM (ā'kim; perhaps the same word as Jachin, "whom God makes firm"), or **Akim** (NIV). The son of Zadok and father of Eliud, among the paternal ancestors of Christ (Matt. 1:14), after 410 B.C.

A'CHISH (ā'kish). Probably a general title of royalty, like *Abimelech* (which see), another Philistine kingly name, with which, indeed, it is interchanged in the title of Ps. 34.
1. A Philistine king of Gath with whom David sought refuge from Saul (1 Sam. 21:10-15). The servants of Achish soon recognized David as the successful champion of Israel against Goliath, and he escaped only by pretending madness, "well knowing that the insane were held inviolable, as smitten but protected by the Deity" (De Rothschild, *Hist. of Israel*). This is undoubtedly the same King Achish to whom David again returned. Achish received him kindly, probably considering their common enmity against Saul as a strong bond of union. After living for a while at Gath, David received from Achish the town of Ziklag for a possession (27:2-6). He made numerous forays against the neighboring nomads, which activity he persuaded Achish was as much in his interest as his own (27:8-12). Achish still had great confidence in David, and he proposed making him chief of his bodyguard (28:1-2). He took David and his men with him when he went up to the battle that sealed the fate of Saul but was led to dismiss them by the jealousy and opposition of the Philistine leaders. Thus David was spared from participating in the battle (29:2-11), about 999 B.C.
2. Another king of Gath, the son of Maacah, to whom two servants of Shimei fled. Shimei went to reclaim them, and thus, by leaving Jerusalem, broke his parole and met his death (1 Kings 2:39-40), 957 B.C.

ACH'METHA (ak'mē-tha; "a station, fortress"). The capital of Media. The classical name is Ecbatana, modern Hamadân, high in the Zagros Mountains, about 180 miles WSW of Tehran. Cyrus II, the Great, founder of the Persian Empire (died 530 B.C.) held his court here during the summer. It is stated (Ezra 6:2) that here was found in the palace a scroll upon which was the decree of Cyrus for the rebuilding of the Temple at Jerusalem. A considerable amount of Persian treasure has been unearthed at Achmetha, often by illegal diggers. Much of it has found its way to the Archaeological Museum in Tehran. The Iranian Archaeological Service has begun clearing old buildings on the mounds at the city's northern outskirts, but so far scientific excavations are only in their infancy. Excavations at the NE corner of Hamadan have uncovered remains of walls and foundations of the palaces of Median and Persian kings.   H.F.V.

A'CHOR (ā'kôr; "trouble"). A place SW of Jericho; now identified with the el-Buqei'ah plain near Qumran. Its name resulted from the sin and consequent punishment of Achan (Josh. 7:24-26). The term "valley of Achor" was proverbial, and the expression of the prophet (Hos. 2:15), "the valley of Achor, a door of hope," is suggestive of the good results of discipline.

ACH'SA (ak'sā), or **Acsah** (NIV). A less correct mode (1 Chron. 2:49) of anglicizing the name *Achsah* (which see).

ACH'SAH (ak'sāh; "anklet"), or **Acsah** (NIV). The name of Caleb's daughter (1 Chron. 2:49). Caleb offered her in marriage to the man who should capture the city of Debir, c. 1362 B.C. His own nephew, Othniel, won the prize. On her way to her future home Achsah asked of her father an addition to her dower of lands. She received the valley full of springs situated near Debir. Her request was probably secured the more readily as it was considered ungracious to refuse a daughter under such circumstances (Josh. 15:16-17; Judg. 1:12-13).

ACH'SHAPH (ak'shaf; "sorcery"), or **Acshaph** (NIV). Identified with Tell Kîsân. It belonged to Asher (Josh. 19:25).

ACH'ZIB (ak'zib; "falsehood, deceit"), or **Aczib** (NIV). A town of Asher (Josh. 19:29; Judg. 1:31), identical with ez-Zib, about ten miles N of Accho. The town of the same name in Judah (Josh. 15:44; Mic. 1:14) is probably the same as Chezib (Gen. 38:5).

ACRE (Heb. *ṣemed,* "a yoke"). Given as the translation of the Heb. word that is used as a measure of land, i.e., so much as a yoke of oxen can plow in a day (1 Sam. 14:14; Isa. 5:10).

ACROP'OLIS (a-crop'o-lis). A fortified hill overlooking many Greco-Roman cities. When the apostle Paul visited Athens, the most famous center of art and culture in Greece, the acropolis was adorned with splendid temples. The renowned sculptor Phidias, who died about 432 B.C., made a colossal statue of Athena Promachos, the goddess who fights in front, which was erected on the acropolis. Then the magnificent Parthenon was built, housing a great gold and ivory statue of Athena by Phidias. Later, the stately entrance, the Propylaea, was completed, as were the beautiful temples, the Erechtheum and the shrine of Athena Nike, the goddess of victory. Paul in his second missionary journey visited other cities with a fortified acropolis, such as Philippi and Corinth. But at Athens "his spirit was being provoked within him as he was beholding the city full of idols" (Acts 17:16).   M.F.U.

The Acropolis at Athens

ACROSTIC. An ode in which the first, the first and last, or certain other letters of the lines taken in order, spell a name or sentence. They are not found in this form in the Bible.

In the poetical parts of the OT are what may be called alphabetical acrostics: e.g., Ps. 119 has as many stanzas or strophes as there are letters in the Hebrew alphabet. Each strophe has eight lines, each beginning with the same letter, the first eight lines beginning with Aleph, the next with Beth, and so on. In Bibles the divisions of Ps. 119 are sometimes indicated by the placement of the Heb. character and its name immediately above the successive sections of the psalm. Thus "א Aleph" appears before vv. 1-8, "ב Beth" before vv. 9-16, and "ג Gimmel" before vv. 17-24, the process continuing through the last letter, ת (Tav), which marks the close of the psalm, vv. 169-76. Psalms 25 and 34 have one verse to each letter in its order. In others, as Pss. 111 and 112, each verse is divided into two parts following the alphabet. The Lamentations of Jeremiah are mostly acrostic, and the last chapter of Proverbs has the initial letters of its last twenty-two verses in alphabetical order.

In ecclesiastical history the term *acrostic* is used to describe a mode of performing the psalmody of the ancient church. A precentor began a verse and the people joined him at the close. It was then much used for hymns, as follows:

> J esus, who for me hast borne
> E very sorrow, pain, and scorn,
> S tanding at man's judgment seat,
> U njust judgment there to meet:
> S ave me by thy mercy sweet, etc.

The acrostic was also commonly used for epitaphs. But the most famous of all ancient acrostics is the one used by ancient Christians as a secret symbol of faith. This is the Gk. word *ichthus*, "fish," formed from the initial letters of five titles of our Lord, "Jesus Christ, God's Son, Savior."

$$\begin{array}{ll} \mathrm{I} & \eta\sigma o\tilde{v}\varsigma \\ \mathrm{X} & \rho\iota\sigma\tau\grave{o}\varsigma \\ \Theta & \varepsilon o v \\ \mathrm{Y} & \iota\grave{o}\varsigma \\ \Sigma & \omega\tau\acute{\eta}\rho \end{array}$$

ACSAH. *See* Achsa; Achsah.

ACSHAPH. *See* Achshaph.

ACTS, BOOK OF. The fifth book of the NT.
    The Name. Commonly called "The Acts of the Apostles," a more accurate title would be "The Acts of the Holy Spirit," since He fills the scene. As the presence of the Son, exalting and manifesting the Father, is the central theme of the four gospels, the presence of the Holy Spirit, who came at Pentecost (Acts 2), magnifying and revealing the risen and ascended Son, is the underlying truth of the Acts.
    The Date. The book was probably written about A.D. 63 or a little later, since it concludes with the account of Paul's earliest ministry in Rome.
    The Author. Luke, the "beloved physician," who also wrote the gospel of Luke (Acts 1:1), was the author. Both the gospel and the Acts are addressed to "most excellent Theophilus," who was evidently a distinguished Gentile. The numerous "we" sections (16:10-17; 20:5–21:18; 27:1–28:16) indicate where Luke joined Paul as a fellow traveler.
    The Theme. Acts is the continuation of the account of Christianity begun in the gospel of Luke. In the "first account" Luke relates what Jesus "began to do and teach" and catalogs in the Acts what Jesus continued to do and teach through the Holy Spirit sent down from heaven. The book, accordingly, records the ascension and promised return of the risen Lord (Acts 1); the advent of the Spirit and the first historical occurrence of the baptism of the Spirit (Acts 2; cf. 1:5 with 11:16); with the consequent formation of the church as the mystical Body of Christ (1 Cor. 12:13). It also recounts Peter's use of the keys of the kingdom of the heavens in opening gospel opportunity for this age to Jew (Acts 2), Samaritan (Acts 8), and Gentile (Acts 10). It describes

Paul's conversion and the extension of Christianity through him to the "remotest part of the earth."

The Content. The book is arranged about the threefold outline given in 1:8:

I. The apostles as witnesses "in Jerusalem" (1:1–8:3)

II. "In all Judea and Samaria" (8:4–12:24)

III. Paul as a witness "even to the remotest part of the earth" (12:25–28:31)

Acts and Archaeology. Researches have greatly strengthened the historical credibility of the Acts. Early in this century William M. Ramsay pioneered in NT archaeology, especially as it bore on the accuracy of Luke's narratives. Among the more useful of his voluminous works is *The Bearing of Recent Discovery on the Trustworthiness of the New Testament.* Subsequently, A. T. Robertson made an important contribution with his *Luke the Historian in the Light of Historical Research.* In 1981 Jack Finegan published the second volume of his *The Archeology of the New Testament,* which bears particularly on the narrative of Acts. A multitude of excavations and explorations has now been conducted at places mentioned in the book of Acts. Reference to some of this activity is included in the articles on those places appearing in this dictionary.

Besides being accurate in detail, Luke gives a remarkably vivid account of many phases of first-century life in the Mediterranean world, for example, the philosophical inquisitiveness of the Athenians (Acts 17:17-18) and the commercial monopoly of the silversmiths at the temple of Artemis in Ephesus (19:24-34). His picture of modes of travel of the day is far clearer than that set forth in the *Odyssey.* Whether on land by foot or horse (23:24, 32) or chariot (8:27-38), or on sea by coastal freighter (21:1-3; 27:1-5), Luke's account is filled with local color. The story of the wreck of Paul's ship is the most exciting and dramatic narrative of sea adventure in ancient literature (Acts 27-28).   M.F.U.; H.F.V.

BIBLIOGRAPHY: H. B. Hackett, *A Commentary in the Acts of the Apostles* (1851); C. J. Vaughan, *The Church of the First Days,* 3 vols. (1864); R. B. Rackham, *The Acts of the Apostles* (1904); F. J. Foakes-Jackson and K. Lake, *The Beginnings of Christianity,* 5 vols. (1920-33); G. C. Morgan, *Acts of the Apostles* (1924); F. F. Bruce, *Commentary on the Book of Acts,* New International Commentary on the New Testament (1954); W. M. Ramsay, *Pictures of the Apostolic Church* (1959); C. K. Barrett, *Luke the Historian in Recent Study* (1961); G. Ogg, *Odyssey of Paul* (1968); A. Ehrhardt, *The Acts of the Apostles* (1969); E. Haenchen, *The Acts of the Apostles* (1971); W. W. Gasque, *A History of the Criticism of the Acts of the Apostles* (1975); E. F. Harrison, *Acts: The Expanding Church* (1976); P. J. Gloag, *The Acts of the Apostles,* 2 vols. (1979); I. H. Marshall, *The Acts of the Apostles,* Tyndale New Testament Commentaries (1980).

ACZIB. *See* Achzib.

ADADAH' (a-da-dah'). A city in the southern part of Judah (Josh. 15:22).

A'DAH (ā'dā; "adornment").

1. One of the two wives of Lamech and the mother of Jabal and Jubal (Gen. 4:19-23).

2. Daughter of Elon the Hittite, the first of the three wives of Esau, and the mother of Eliphaz (Gen. 36:2, 4, 10, 12, 16). She is elsewhere (26:34) called Basemath.

ADA'IAH (ād-ā'yā; "whom Jehovah adorns").

1. A native of Boscath (Bozkath, in the valley of Judah, Josh. 15:39), and father of Jedidah, the mother of Josiah, king of Judah (2 Kings 22:1), the latter born 632 B.C.

2. The son of Ethni and the father of Zerah, of the Levitical family of Gershom, in the ancestry of Asaph, the celebrated musician (1 Chron. 6:41). Probably the same as Iddo (v. 21).

3. A son of Shimei and one of the chief Benjamites living in Jerusalem before the captivity (1 Chron. 8:21), before 586 B.C.

4. A priest, son of Jeroham, who, after the return from Babylon, was employed in the work of the sanctuary (1 Chron. 9:12; Neh. 11:12).

5. The father of Maaseiah, one of the "captains of hundreds" during the protectorate of Jehoiada (2 Chron. 23:1).

6. A "son of Bani" and an Israelite who divorced his Gentile wife after the captivity (Ezra 10:29).

7. Another of the sons of Bani (probably not the same Bani as in no. 6) who put away his Gentile wife (Ezra 10:39).

8. The son of Joiarib and the father of Hazaiah, of the tribe of Judah (Neh. 11:5), some of whose posterity dwelt in Jerusalem after the captivity, 445 B.C.

ADALIA (a-da'li-a). The fifth son of *Haman* (which see), a Persian ruler under Ahasuerus (Esther 9:8).   E.H.M.

AD'AM (Heb. *'ādām,* "red"; hence *'ădāmâ,* "the ground"). The first man and "son of God" (Luke 3:38) by special creation. The name that God gave him (Gen. 5:2) is founded upon the earthly side of his being: Adam from *'ădāmâ,* earth, the earthly element, to guard him from self-exaltation; not from the red color of his body, since this is not a distinctive characteristic of man, but common to him and to many other creatures.

Creation. In the first nine chapters of Genesis there appear to be three distinct histories relating more or less to the life of Adam. The first (1:1–2:3) records the creation; the second (2:4–4:26) gives an account of paradise, the original sin of man, and the immediate posterity of Adam; the third (5:1–9:29) contains mainly the history of Noah, referring to Adam and his descendants principally in relation to that patriarch. "The Lord God formed man of dust from the ground, and breathed into his nostrils the breath of life; and man became a living being" (2:7).

In Eden. God gave him dominion over all the lower creatures (Gen. 1:26), and placed him in Eden that he might cultivate it and enjoy its fruits (2:15-16). The beasts of the field and the birds of the air were brought to Adam, who examined them and gave them names. This examination gave him an opportunity to develop his intellectual capacity and also led to this result, that there was not found a helper suitable for man.

Creation of Eve. "So the Lord God caused a deep sleep to fall upon the man, and he slept; then He took one of his ribs, and closed up the flesh at that place. And the Lord God fashioned into a woman the rib which He had taken from the man" (2:21). The design of God in the creation of the woman was perceived by Adam when she was brought to him by God: "This is now bone of my bones, and flesh of my flesh; she shall be called Woman, because she was taken out of Man" (Gen. 2:21-23). Thus Adam was given charge of the earth and its inhabitants and was endowed with everything requisite for the development of his nature and the fulfillment of his destiny. In the fruit of the trees he found sustenance; in the tree of life, preservation from death; in the tree of knowledge, a positive law for the training of his moral nature; in the care of the garden, exercise of his physical strength; in the animal and vegetable kingdoms, a capacious region for the development of his intellect; and in the woman, a suitable companion and helper. The first man was a true man, with the powers of a man and the innocence of a child.

Fall. But Eve, having been beguiled by the tempter to eat of the forbidden fruit, persuaded her husband to do the same. When called to judgment before God, Adam blamed his wife, who in turn blamed the tempter. God punished the tempter by degradation and dread, the woman by painful travail and submission (*see* Eve), and the man by a life of labor. With the loss of innocence came a feeling of shame, and they sought to hide their nakedness with leaves, but were afterward taught by God to make clothing from the skins of animals. Adam and Eve were expelled from the garden, at the eastern side of which cherubim and a sword of flame turning every way were placed. The object of these was to guard the way of the *Tree of Life* (which see), and prevent Adam's return to it (Gen. 3).

Subsequent History. It is not known how long Adam lived in Eden, and therefore we cannot determine the length of his life after the expulsion. Shortly after leaving Eden, Eve gave birth to Cain (Gen. 4:1). Scripture gives the names of only three sons of Adam — Cain, Abel, and Seth —but contains an allusion (5:4) to "other sons and daughters."

Figurative. Paul declares that Adam was a figure of Christ, "a type of Him who was to come"

(Rom. 5:14); hence our Lord is sometimes called the *second Adam*. This typical relation stands sometimes in likeness, sometimes in contrast. In *likeness,* Adam was formed immediately by God, as was the human nature of Christ; in each the nature was holy; both were invested with dominion over the earth and its creatures (see Ps. 8). In contrast, Adam and Christ were each a federal head to the whole race of mankind, but the one was the fountain of sin and death, the other of righteousness and life (Rom. 5:14-19); Adam communicated a living soul to all his posterity, Christ is a "life-giving spirit" to restore life and immortality to them (1 Cor. 15:45).

Chronology. The opening chapters of the Bible leave both the date of the creation of the world and of man an open question. Genesis 1:1 places the origin of the universe in the dateless past. Man's appearance upon the earth is set forth as the result of a direct creative act of God, which took place at least over 4,000 years B.C. and perhaps as early as 7,000 or 10,000 years B.C., "which is more in the spirit of the Biblical record than either Ussher's compressed chronology or the evolutionist's greatly expanded ages" (Laird Harris, "The Date of the Flood and the Age of Man," *Bible Today* 37, no. 9 [Sept. 1943]: 570). Byron Nelson, a conservative, argues for a still greater antiquity for man (*Before Abraham, Prehistoric Man in Biblical Light* [1948], p. 95). In dealing with the genealogies of Gen. 5-11 it must be remembered that they are not exhaustive or complete and most certainly are abbreviated. B. B. Warfield demonstrated long ago that there are gaps in biblical genealogies (Ex. 6:16-24, Ezra 7:1-5, Matt. 1:1-17; *see* "The Antiquity and Unity of the Human Race," *Studies in Theology* [1932], pp. 235-58).

Furthermore, Semitic idiom dealing with "beget," "begotten," "father" and "son," and so on, differs strikingly from our usage, and thus "son" may be an actual son, a grandson, a great-grandson, or even, in the case of royalty, no blood relation at all. To employ the genealogical lists of Genesis to calculate the creation of man about 4004 B.C., as Archbishop Ussher has done, is not only unwarranted from the text of Scripture, but is incontrovertibly disproved by the well-attested facts of archaeology.   M.F.U.

BIBLIOGRAPHY: K. Barth, *Christ and Adam: Man and Humanity in Romans 5* (1956); P. Ramsey, *Moravian Theological Seminary Bulletin* (1960): 35-60; C. K. Barrett, *From First Adam to Last* (1962); A. C. Custance, *Genesis and Early Man* (1975); id., *Man in Adam and in Christ* (1975).

ADAM. A town near the Jordan, and beside Zaretan (Josh. 3:16; Zarethan, NIV). It is identified with Tell ed-Damieh on the E bank of the river, near the mouth of the Jabbok and eighteen miles above Jericho. Here the waters miraculously rose in a heap while the Israelites crossed the Jordan River.

AD'AMAH (ad'ā-mä; "earth, ground"). A fenced city of Naphtali (Josh. 19:36). The modern Tell ed-Damiyeh.

ADAMANT. *See* Mineral Kingdom: Diamond.

AD'AMI (ad'ā-mī; "pertaining to [red] earth, earthy"). A place in Palestine near the border of Naphtali, now identified with Khirbet Damiyeh.

ADA'MI. *See* Adami-nekeb.

ADA'MI-NE'KEB (adā'mī-ne'keb; "a hollow, narrow passage"). A town on the border of Naphtali (Josh. 19:33), halfway between Tiberias and Mt. Tabor.

A'DAR (a'där; from Akkad. *adaru, addaru,* probably "dark" or "cloudy"). A later name of the twelfth month of the Jewish year borrowed by the Jews from the Babylonian calendar during the Exile. It extended from the new moon of February to that of March (Ezra 6:15; Esther 3:7, 13; 9:15). *See* Time. For the city, *see* Hazaraddar.

ADBEEL (ad'bēl). The third son of *Ishmael* (which see) (Gen. 25:13; 1 Chron. 1:29). E.H.M.

AD'DAN (ad'dän). Another form (Ezra 2:59) of the name (Neh. 7:61) *Addon* (which see).

AD'DAR (ad'där; "threshing floor," or "wide, open place"). A son of Bela and grandson of Benjamin (1 Chron. 8:3), elsewhere (Gen. 46:21) called Ard. For the city, *see* Hazaraddar.

AD'DER (ad'der). The rendering in the KJV of four Heb. words, each of which probably signifies some kind of venomous serpent. *See* Animal Kingdom: Serpent.

AD'DI (ad'dī; "ornament"). The son of Cosam and father of Melchi (Melki, NIV) in the maternal ancestry of Jesus (Luke 3:28).

AD'DON (ad'don). The name of the second of three persons (Neh. 7:61) who, when they returned from the captivity to Palestine, were unable to "show their fathers' houses or their descendants, whether they were of Israel," 536 B.C. In Ezra 2:59, this person is called Addan.

ADER. *See* Eder.

A'DIEL (a'dī-el; "ornament of God").
1. One of the family heads of the tribe of Simeon, who seem to have dispossessed the aborigines of Gedor (1 Chron. 4:36).
2. A priest and the son of Jahzerah and father of Maasai, which last was active in reconstructing the Temple after the captivity (1 Chron. 9:12), 563 B.C.
3. The father of Azmaveth, the treasurer under David (1 Chron. 27:25).

A'DIN (a'din; "effeminate" [?]).
1. The head of one of the Israelite families, of which a large number returned with Zerubbabel to Jerusalem from Babylon, 536 B.C. The number

is given in Ezra 2:15 as 454; in Neh. 7:20 as 655, the discrepancy being occasioned by an error in the hundreds and the including or excluding of himself. Fifty more of the family returned (with Ebed, the son of Jonathan) under Ezra (Ezra 8:6), 457 B.C.
2. One of those who sealed the covenant made by Nehemiah and the people after their return to Jerusalem (Neh. 10:16), about 445 B.C.

AD'INA (ad'ī-na; "slender, delicate" [?]). The son of Shiza, a Reubenite, and captain of thirty of his tribesmen, Adina was one of David's mighty men (1 Chron. 11:42), before 1000 B.C.

AD'INO (ad'ī-nō; "slender as a spear" [?]). The name given in 2 Sam. 23:8 (but lacking in the NIV) as one of David's mighty men. Much difference of opinion respecting it exists. Some think the passage has been corrupted. It is clear that these words "Adino the Eznite" are not proper names, although their grammatical construction is not easy. See also the parallel passage (1 Chron. 11:11).

ADITHA'IM (ad-i-thā'im). A place in Palestine, but location unknown (Josh. 15:36).

ADJURATION (Heb. *'ālâ,* in Hiphel, "to cause to swear," in 1 Kings 8:31; 2 Chron. 6:22, "to make swear"; Gk. *exorkidzō,* "to exact an oath").
1. An act or appeal whereby a person in authority imposes upon another the obligation of speaking or acting as if under the solemnity of an oath (1 Kings 22:16; 2 Chron. 18:15). In the NT we have an example of this where the high priest calls upon Jesus to avow His character as the Messiah (Matt. 26:63; cf. Mark 5:7). Such an oath, although imposed upon one without his consent, was binding in the highest degree; and when it was connected with a question, it made an answer compulsory.
2. In Acts 19:13, the term occurs with reference to the expulsion of demons.
3. In the Roman Catholic church, the use of the name of God, or of some holy thing, to induce one to do what is required of him.

AD'LAI (ad'lā-i). The father of Shaphat, a chief herdsman under David (1 Chron. 27:29), after 1000 B.C.

AD'MAH (ad'mah; "red earth"). A city in the Siddim Valley (cf. Gen. 10:19; 14:1-3), destroyed with Sodom (19:24; Deut. 29:23). Supposed by some to be identical with Adam of Josh. 3:16.

AD'MATHA (ad'mā-thä; perhaps "earthly, dark-colored"). The third named of the princes or courtiers of Ahasuerus (or Xerxes, NIV; Esther 1:14).

ADMINISTRATION (Gk. *diakonia,* "service"). In the NT it signifies "to relieve," "to minister," as in 2 Cor. 8:19-20.

AD'NA (ad'nä; "pleasure").

1. An Israelite of the family of Pahath-moab, who divorced his Gentile wife after the captivity (Ezra 10:30).

2. A chief priest, son of Harim, and contemporary with Joiakim (Neh. 12:15), about 536 B.C.

AD'NAH (ad'nāh; "pleasure").

1. One of the captains of the tribe of Manasseh who joined David at Ziklag (1 Chron. 12:20), before 1000 B.C.

2. A warrior of the tribe of Judah and principal general under Jehoshaphat (2 Chron. 17:14), about 872-852 B.C.

ADO'NI-BE'ZEK (a-dō'nī-be'zek; "lord of Bezek"). King or lord of Bezek, a city of the Canaanites. He had subdued seventy of the petty kings around him and, after having cut off their thumbs and great toes, compelled them to gather their food under his table. At the head of the Canaanites and Perizzites he opposed the men of Judah and Simeon and, being defeated, was served in the same manner as he had treated his own captives; about 1375 B.C. He died of his wounds at Jerusalem, where he was carried by his captors (Judg. 1:5-7).

BIBLIOGRAPHY: C. E. Macartney, *Chariots of Fire* (1951), pp. 76-84; A. E. Cundall, *Judges,* Tyndale Old Testament Commentaries (1968), pp. 51-54.

ADONI'JAH (a-dō-nī'jāh; "my lord is Jehovah").

1. The fourth son of David and second by Haggith, born in Hebron while his father reigned over Judah only (2 Sam. 3:4); about 1003 B.C. According to oriental usages Adonijah might

The Kidron Valley

have considered his claim superior to that of his eldest brother, Amnon, who was born while his father was in a private station; but not to that of Absalom, who was not only his elder brother, and born while his father was a king, but was of royal descent on the side of his mother. When Amnon and Absalom were dead, Adonijah became heir apparent to the throne, but this order had been set aside in favor of Solomon, who was born while his father was king over *all* Israel.

Adonijah aspired to the throne, prepared a guard of chariots and horsemen and fifty foot runners, and gained over to his side Joab and Abiathar, the priest. He was also a man of handsome appearance and likely to win the people. Waiting until David seemed to be at the point of death, he called around him his brothers (excepting Solomon) and other influential men and was proclaimed king at Zoheleth by the spring of En-rogel at the S end of the Kidron Valley. The plot was defeated by the prompt action of the aged king, who, through the influence of Nathan and Bathsheba, caused Solomon to be proclaimed king and to be anointed by Zadok, the priest, at the Spring Gihon, a few hundred yards N of En-rogel.

Adonijah fled for refuge to the altar, which he refused to leave until pardoned by Solomon. He received pardon but was told that a future attempt of the same kind would be fatal (1 Kings 1:5-53).

Some time after David's death he covertly asserted his claim in asking for *Abishag* (which see) the virgin widow of his father in marriage. Adonijah was immediately put to death by the order of Solomon (1 Kings 2:23-25), about 960 B.C. The execution of Adonijah by Solomon must not be judged by the standards of the present day. According to the custom of Eastern princes a thousand years before Christ, Solomon would probably have slain all his brothers upon ascending the throne, whereas we learn of the death of Adonijah alone, and that only after his second treasonable attempt.

2. One of the Levites sent by King Jehoshaphat to assist in teaching the law to the people of Judah (2 Chron. 17:8), after 875 B.C.

3. A chief Israelite after the captivity (Neh. 10:16), probably the same elsewhere (Ezra 2:13; 8:13; Neh. 7:18) called *Adonikam* (which see).

ADONI'KAM, (a-dōn-ī-kam; "my Lord has risen"). One whose descendants, to the number of 666, returned to Jerusalem with Zerubbabel (Ezra 2:13), 536 B.C. He himself is included in Neh. 7:18. Somewhat later, three of his immediate descendants, with sixty male followers, came with Ezra (Ezra 8:13), 458 B.C. He appears (from the identity of the associated names) to have been the Adonijah who joined in the religious covenant of Nehemiah (Neh. 10:16).

ADONI′RAM (ă-dō-nī′răm; "high lord"). The son of Abda, and receiver-general of the imposts in the reigns of David, Solomon, and Rehoboam (1 Kings 4:6). During his extended term of office he rendered both himself and the tribute so odious to the people, in sustaining the immense public works of Solomon, that when Rehoboam rashly sent him to enforce the collection of the taxes the exasperated populace rose upon him and stoned him to death. This was the signal for the revolt under Jeroboam (1 Kings 12:18), 922 B.C. Adoniram is called, by contraction, Adoram (2 Sam. 20:24; 1 Kings 12:18) and Hadoram (2 Chron. 10:18).

ADO′NI-ZE′DEK (a-dō′nī-ze′dek; "just lord"). The king of Jerusalem when the Israelites invaded Palestine (Josh. 10:1), about 1400 B.C. After Jericho and Ai were taken and the Gibeonites had succeeded in forming a treaty with the Israelites, Adoni-zedek induced the Amorite kings of Hebron, Jarmuth, Lachish, and Eglon to join him in a confederacy against the enemy. They began operations by besieging the Gibeonites, who sent to Joshua for help. Joshua marched all night from Gilgal and, falling unexpectedly upon the besiegers, put them to flight. The five kings took refuge in a cave at Makkedah but were detected, and the cave's mouth was closed by placing huge stones against it. When the Israelites returned from the pursuit the cave was opened and the kings taken out. The chief men of Israel then set their feet upon the necks of the prostrate monarchs —an ancient mark of triumph. The five kings were then slain, and their bodies hung on trees until evening, when, as the law forbade a longer exposure of the dead (Deut. 21:23), they were taken down and cast into the cave. The mouth of the cave was filled up with large stones, which remained long after (Josh. 10:1-27). In considering the severe treatment of these kings we must remember that the war was one of extermination and that the treatment of the Jews was neither better nor worse than those of the people with whom they fought.

ADOPTION (Gk. *huiothesia*, the "placing" as a "son"). The admission of a person to some or all of the privileges of natural kinship. As the practice of adoption was confined almost exclusively to sons—the case of Esther being an exception —it probably had its origin in the natural desire for male offspring. This would be especially true where force, rather than well-observed laws, decided the possession of estates.

Hebrew. Abraham speaks of Eliezer (Gen. 15:3), a house-born slave, as his heir, having probably adopted him as his son. Jacob adopted his grandsons Ephraim and Manasseh, and counted them as his sons (48:6), thus enabling him to bestow through them a double portion upon his favorite son Joseph. Sometimes a man without a son would marry his daughter to a freed slave, the children then being accounted her father's; or the husband himself would be adopted as a son (1 Chron. 2:34). Most of the early instances of adoption mentioned in the Bible were the acts of women who, because of barrenness, gave their female slaves to their husbands with the intention of adopting any children they might have. Thus Sarah gave Hagar to Abraham, and the son (Ishmael) was considered the child of Abraham and Sarah (Gen. 16:1-15). The childless Rachel gave her maid, Bilhah, to her husband (30:1-7) and was imitated by Leah (30:9-13). In such cases the sons were regarded as fully equal in the right of heritage with those by the legitimate wife.

Roman. Adoption was a familiar social phenomenon, and its initial ceremonies and incidents occupied a large and important place in their laws. By adoption an entire stranger in blood became a member of the family in a higher sense than some of the family kin, emancipated sons, or descendants through females. Such a one assumed the family name, engaged in its sacrificial rites, and became, not by sufferance or at will, but to all intents and purposes, a member of the house of his adoption. The tie thus formed could only be broken through the ceremony of emancipation, and formed as complete a barrier to intermarriage as relationship by blood. At Rome there were two kinds of adoption, both requiring the adopter to be a male and childless: *arrogatio* and adoption proper. The former could only take place where the person to be adopted was independent (*sui juris*) and his adopter had no prospect of male offspring. The adopted one became, in the eyes of the law, a new creature. He was born again into a new family. This custom was doubtless referred to by Paul (Rom. 8:14-16).

The ceremony of adoption took place in the presence of seven witnesses. The fictitious sale and resale, and the final "vindication" or claim, were accompanied by the legal formula, and might mean the sale of a son into slavery or his adoption into a new family, according to the words used. The touch of the *festuca* or ceremonial wand might be accompanied by the formula, "I claim this man as my son," or "I claim this man as my slave." It was the function of the witnesses, upon occasion, to testify that the transaction was in truth the adoption of the child.

Greek. In Athens adoption took place either in the lifetime of the adopter or by will; or if a man died childless and intestate, the state interfered to bring into his house the man next entitled by the Attic law of inheritance, as heir and adopted son. If there were daughters, one of them was usually betrothed to the adopted son. If after that a male heir was born, he and the adopted son had equal rights.

ADOPTION (Theological). This term as used in

a theological sense commonly denotes that act of God by which He restores penitent and believing men to their privileges as members of the divine family and makes them heirs of heaven.

1. Theology owes its use of the word *adoption* in this way to the apostle Paul. He is the only Scripture writer who employs the term thus translated. The passages in Paul's writings in which the doctrine of adoption is stated in connection with the use of that term are Rom. 8:15-17; Gal. 4:4-6; Eph. 1:5. These are not by any means, however, the only passages in his writings in which the essential thought is plainly declared (2 Cor. 6:18). And more generally speaking this may be said to be one of the doctrines upon which the NT lays special stress. That we who have forfeited and lost our place and privileges as children of God may be fully reinstated therein was one of the great teachings of Jesus Christ. For that the parable of the prodigal son was spoken.

Taking the Scripture teachings as a whole, adoption, it appears, while not the same as our justification, is necessarily connected with it, as forgiveness would be empty without restoration to the privileges forfeited by sin. Adoption and regeneration are two phases of the same fact, regeneration meaning the reproduction of the filial character, and adoption the restoration of the filial privilege. *See* Justification; Regeneration.

Adoption is a word of *position* rather than *relationship*. The believer's relation to God as a child results from the new birth (John 1:12-13), whereas adoption is the divine act whereby one who is already a child is, through redemption from the law, placed in the position of an *adult son* (Gal. 4:1-5).

2. The word *adoption* is also used by the apostle Paul with reference to the full and final outcome of salvation, the complete "revealing of the sons of God" and perfect investiture with all their heavenly privileges, for which Christians must wait. So he writes of waiting "for the revealing of the sons of God" and "waiting eagerly for our adoption as sons, the redemption of our body" (Rom. 8:19, 23).

3. Another use of this word by the same apostle is in Rom. 9:4, where he speaks of the Israelites "to whom belongs the adoption." By this is meant the special place that was given to Israel among the nations as the chosen people of God.

BIBLIOGRAPHY: A. H. Strong, *Systematic Theology* (1907), p. 857; L. S. Chafer, *Systematic Theology* (1948), 3:242, 243; 7:9-11; J. B. Lightfoot, *St. Paul's Epistle to the Galatians* (1966), pp. 168-69; C. E. B. Cranfield, *A Critical and Exegetical Commentary on the Epistle to the Romans*, International Critical Commentary (1975), 1:396-98; F. F. Bruce, *Epistle to the Galatians*, New International Greek Testament Commentary (1982), pp. 196-98.

ADORA'IM (a-dō-rā'im). A town, doubtless in the SW of Judah, since it is enumerated among the cities fortified by Rehoboam (2 Chron. 11:9). It is met with in 1 Macc. 13:20 as an Edomite city, "Adora," and so also frequently in Josephus. It was taken by Hyrcanus. Robinson has identified it with the present Dûra, a village about five miles to the W of Hebron.

ADO'RAM (a-dō'ram). An officer in charge of the forced labor (2 Sam. 20:24; 1 Kings 12:18), elsewhere called *Adoniram* (which see).

ADORATION. In its true sense, the act of paying honor to a divine being. In the Scriptures various forms of adoration are mentioned; e.g., putting off the shoes (Ex. 3:5; Josh. 5:15), bowing the knee (Gen. 41:43), falling prostrate (43:26; Dan. 2:46), and kissing (Luke 7:38). The passage "If I have looked at the sun when it shone, or the moon going in splendor, and my heart became secretly enticed, and my hand threw a kiss from my mouth, that too would have been an iniquity calling for judgment" (Job 31:26-28) clearly intimates that kissing the hand was considered an overt act of worship in the East. In the same manner respect was shown to kings and other persons of exalted station. "Put your hand over your mouth" (Job 21:5; 29:9; Ps. 39:9) implied the highest degree of reverence and submission.

ADORN (Gk. *kosmeō*, "to ornament"). To embellish with honor, gain; followed by a participle designating the act by which the honor is gained (Titus 2:10; 1 Pet. 3:5).

ADRAM'MELECH (a-dram'mel-ek; "splendor of the king" [?]).

1. A son of Sennacherib, king of Assyria. The king was dwelling at Nineveh after his disastrous expedition against Hezekiah. While worshiping his god in the house of Nisroch, Sennacherib was murdered by Adrammelech and his brother Sharezer, 681 B.C. Having accomplished the crime, the two brothers fled into the land of Ararat (2 Kings 19:37; Isa. 37:38).

2. The name of a Sepharvite god (2 Kings 17:31). *See* Gods, False.

ADRAMYT'TIUM (a-dra-mit'ti-um; "the mansion of death"). A seaport of Mysia, in Asia Minor (Acts 27:2-5), whence Paul sailed in an Alexandrian ship to Italy. The site is known today as Karatash, and a nearby town is named Edremit.

R.K.H.

A'DRIA (a'dri-a). Called the "Adriatic Sea" in the NASB and NIV (Acts 27:27). It is the modern Gulf of Venice, the *Mare Supernum* of the Romans, as distinguished from the *Mare Inferum* or the Tyrrhenian Sea. It probably derived its name from Adria, a city in Istria.

A'DRIEL (a'dri-ēl; "God is my help"). A son of Barzillai the Meholathite. Saul gave to him in marriage his daughter Merab, who had been

Adramyttium

The Judean wilderness near Adullam, where David hid

promised to David (1 Sam. 18:17-19). His five sons were among the seven descendants of Saul whom David surrendered to the Gibeonites (2 Sam. 21:8) in satisfaction for the endeavors of Saul to extirpate them, although a league had been made between them and the Israelites (Josh. 9:15).

ADUL'LAM (a-dūl'lam). A town SW of Jerusalem about midway to Lachish and 4½ miles NE of Beit Jibrin; now identified as Tell esh-Sheikh Madhkur. It first appears as the resident city of a Canaanite king (Josh. 12:15; 15:35) but is most famous for its cave in which David hid as a fugitive from Saul (1 Sam. 22:1; 2 Chron. 11:7).

ADUL'LAMITE (a-dul'la-mīt). An inhabitant (Gen. 38:1, 12, 20) of *Adullam* (which see).

ADULTERY. In Jewish thought adultery was seen as the willful violation of the marriage contract by either of the parties through sexual intercourse with a third party. The divine provision was that the husband and wife should become "one flesh," each being held sacred to the other. Jesus taught: "Have you not read, that He who created them from the beginning made them male and female . . . . and the two shall become one flesh." When the Pharisees, with the apparent hope of eliciting some modification in favor of the husband, put the question, "Why then did Moses command to give her a certificate and divorce her?" Jesus replied, "Because of your hardness of heart, Moses permitted you to divorce your wives; but from the beginning it has not been this way . . . . whoever divorces his wife, except for immorality, and marries another commits adultery" (Matt. 19:3-9). In perfect accord with this also is the teaching of the apostle Paul (Eph. 5:25-33; 1 Cor. 7:1-13; 1 Tim. 3:12). It will

be seen that according to the fundamental law it is adultery for the man as well as the woman to have a sexual relationship with a person other than the legal spouse. In ancient times, however, exception was made among the nations generally in favor of the man. He might have more wives than one or have intercourse with a person not espoused or married to him without being considered an adulterer. Adultery was sexual intercourse with the married wife, or what was equivalent, the betrothed bride of another man, for this act exposed the husband to the danger of having a spurious offspring imposed upon him. In the seventh commandment (Ex. 20:14) all manner of lewdness or unchastity in act or thought seems to be meant (Matt. 5:28).

The Roman law appears to have made the same distinction as the Hebrew between the unfaithfulness of the husband and wife, by defining adultery to be the violation of another man's bed. The infidelity of the husband did not constitute adultery. The Greeks held substantially the same view.

Trial of Adultery. A man suspecting his wife of adultery, not having detected her in the act, or having no witness to prove her supposed guilt, brought her to the priest that she might be sub-

29

mitted to the ordeal prescribed in Num. 5:11-31. *See* Jealousy, Offering of.

When adultery ceased to be a capital crime, as it doubtless did, this trial probably fell into disuse. No instance of the ordeal being undergone is given in Scripture, and it appears to have been finally abrogated about forty years before the destruction of Jerusalem. The reason given for this is that the men were at that time so generally adulterous that God would not fulfill the imprecations of the ordeal oath upon the wife.

Penalties. The Mosaic law assigned the punishment of death to adultery (Lev. 20:10) but did not state the mode of its infliction. From various passages of Scripture (e.g., Ezek. 16:38, 40; John 8:5) we infer that it was by stoning. When the adulteress was a slave the guilty parties were scourged, the blows not to exceed forty; the adulterer was to offer a trespass offering (a ram) to be offered by the priest (Lev. 19:20-22). Death does not appear to have been inflicted, perhaps by reason of guilt on the part of those administering the law (John 8:9-11). We find no record in the OT of a woman taken in adultery being put to death. The usual remedy seems to have been a divorce, in which the woman lost her dower and right of maintenance, thus avoiding public scandal. The expression "to disgrace her" (Matt. 1:19) probably means to bring the matter before the local Sanhedrin, the usual course.

The Roman civil law looked upon adultery as "the violation of another man's bed," and thus the husband's incontinence could not constitute the offense. The punishment was left to the husband and parents of the adulteress, who under the old law suffered death. The most usual punishment of the man was mutilation, castration, and cutting off the nose and ears. Other punishments were banishment, heavy fines, burning at the stake, and drowning. Among the Greeks and other ancient nations the adulterer might lose eye, nose, or ear. Among savage nations of the present time the punishment is generally severe. The Muslim code pronounces it a capital offense.

Spiritual. In the symbolical language of the OT adultery means idolatry and apostasy from the worship of Jehovah (Jer. 3:8-9; Ezek. 16:32; 23:37; Rev. 2:22). This figure resulted from the sort of married relationship, the solemn engagement between Jehovah and Israel (Jer. 2:2; 3:14; 13:27; 31:32; Hos. 8:9). Our Lord used similar language when He charged Israel with being an "adulterous generation" (Matt. 12:39; 16:4; Mark 8:38), meaning a faithless and unholy generation. An "adulterous" church or city is an apostate one (cf. Isa. 1:21; Jer. 3:6-9; Ezek. 16:22; 23:7).

Ecclesiastical. The following views prevailed in the early church:

1. Under Justinian the wife was regarded as the real criminal, and her paramour as a mere ac-

complice. This view seems to have been held during the whole early Christian period. Gregory of Nyssa makes a distinction between fornication and adultery. A canon of Basle furnishes this definition: "We name him who cohabits with another woman (not his own wife) an adulterer." Ambrose says: "All unchaste intercourse is adultery; what is illicit for the woman is illicit for the man." Gregory Nazianzen argues that the man should not be left free to sin while the woman is restrained. Chrysostom says: "It is commonly called adultery when a man wrongs a married woman. I, however, affirm it of a married man who sins with the unmarried." Jerome contends that 1 Cor. 6:16 applies equally to both sexes.

2. A convicted adulterer cannot receive orders. An adulterer or adulteress must undergo seven years' penance. A presbyter so offending is to be excommunicated and brought to penance. The layman whose wife is guilty cannot receive orders, and if already ordained must put her away under pain of deprivation. An unchaste wife must be divorced, but not the husband, even if adulterous. The adulterer must undergo fifteen years of penitence but only seven for unchastity. Two conclusions were drawn by canonists and divines: (1) divorce, except for adultery, is adultery; (2) to retain an adulterous wife is adultery. A woman must not leave her husband for blows, waste of dower, unchastity, nor even disbelief (1 Cor. 7:16), under penalty of adultery. An offending wife is an adulteress and must be divorced, but not so the husband. The Catholic church holds that marriage is not and ought not to be dissolved by the adultery of either party (Council of Trent, sess. xxiv, can. 7).

3. The following are treated as guilty of actual adultery: a man marrying a betrothed maiden; a girl seduced marrying someone other than her seducer; consecrated virgins who sin, and their paramours; a Christian marrying a Jew or an idolater.

BIBLIOGRAPHY: E. Neufeld, *Ancient Hebrew Marriage Laws* (1944), pp. 163-75; L. M. Epstein, *Sex Laws and Customs in Judaism* (1948), pp. 194-215; R. de Vaux, *Ancient Israel: Its Life and Institutions* (1961), pp. 36-37, 158-59; M. Fishbane, *Hebrew Union College Annual* 45 (1974): 25-45; P. Davies, *Christian Century* 95 (1978): 360-63; Z. C. Hodges, *Bibliotheca Sacra* 136 (1979): 318-32; M. Lamm, *The Jewish Way in Love and Marriage* (1980), pp. 41-48, 76-79.

ADUM'MIM (a-dum'im; "red" or "bloody"). A place on the road from Jerusalem to Jericho (Josh. 15:7; 18:17) and supposed to be the scene of the Good Samaritan's rescue of the man who fell among thieves. It has the modern name of Tal 'at ed-Damm ("ascent of blood").

ADVENT, SECOND. *See* Millennium.

ADVERSARY. In its general meaning refers to an enemy, as in the expression "The Lord takes vengeance on His adversaries" (Nah. 1:2). Frequently it is derived from Heb. *ṣûr*, "to bind"; in 1 Sam. 2:10, *rîb*, "to strive." In the NT we have *antikeimenos, hupenantios,* "one who opposes"; and *antidikos,* "opponent in law." In Isa. 50:8 the expression *Baal mispāṭ,* means "he who has a judicial cause or lawsuit against me"; just as in Roman law *dominus lilit* is distinguished from the procurator, i.e., from the person who represents him in court (Delitzsch, *Com.*). Specifically (Heb. *śāṭān*) the devil, as the general enemy of mankind (1 Pet. 5:8).

ADVOCATE (Gk. *paraklētos,* "paraclete"). One who pleads the cause of another. The term is applied by Jesus to the Holy Spirit (John 14:16; 15:26; 16:7), where it is rendered Helper; and by John to Christ Himself (1 John 2:1). The word *advocate* (Lat. *advocatus*) might designate a consulting lawyer or one who presents his client's case in open court; or one who, in times of trial or hardship, sympathizes with the afflicted and administers suitable direction and support. *See also* Helper; Holy Spirit.

AENE'AS (e-nē'as). A paralytic of Lydda cured by Peter (Acts 9:33-34).

AE'NON (ē'non; "springs"). The place "near Salim" where John baptized (John 3:23). Site uncertain.

AE'ON (ē'on; Gk. *aiōn,* "age"). A human lifetime, life itself (according to Homer, Herodotus, and others); an unbroken age, perpetuity of time, eternity. With this signification the Hebrew and rabbinic idea of the word *'ōlām,* "concealed," combines in the biblical and ecclesiastical writers. Hence in the NT *aeon* is used in the following ways:

1. In the phrases *eis tōn aiōna,* i.e., *forever* (John 6:51, 58; 14:16; Heb. 5:6; 6:20; Jude 13; with a negative, *never* (John 4:14; 8:51; 10:28; 11:26); *unto the ages,* i.e., *as long as time shall be, forever* (Luke 1:33; Rom. 1:25; 9:5; 11:36). In the expression *unto the ages of the ages* (Gal. 1:5; 2 Tim. 4:18; 1 Pet. 4:11; Rev. 1:6, 18) the endless future is divided up into various periods, the shorter of which are comprehended in the longer. *From the age* is used in the sense of *from the most ancient time, from of old* (Luke 1:70; Acts 3:21; 15:18).

2. As the Jews distinguished the time before the Messiah and the time after the Messiah, so most of the NT writers distinguish *this age* (and similar expressions), the time before the appointed return or truly messianic advent of Christ, and *aiōn mellōn, the future age* (Matt. 12:32; Eph. 1:21) or Millennium.

Figurative. The container is used for the contained, and *hoi aiōnes* denotes "the worlds," the universe, i.e., the aggregate of things contained in time (Heb. 11:3; cf. 1:2).

AFFLICTION (usually Heb. *'ōnê,* "depressed";

Gk. *thlipsis,* "pressure"). Other Heb. and Gk. words are used, and if they were all literally rendered we should have iniquity, straitness, lowered, evil, breach, suffering. This last word expresses its meaning in common use. The English word comes from the Lat. *adflictus,* a striking, as one thing against another; pain; grief; distress of body or mind.

Respecting the well-known and often quoted passage which begins "For momentary, light affliction is producing for us" (2 Cor. 4:17), we quote from Meyer, *Com.,* Notes by American Editor: "The Revision of 1881 gives this weighty and impressive verse in a rendering which is exact, and yet faithful to our Engish idiom. The verse contains the whole philosophy of the Christian view of affliction. It does not deny the reality of earthly sorrows or underrate their power, as did the Stoics; but after allowing them all their force, calmly says that they dwindle into insignificance when compared with the exceeding and eternal glory to which they lead. But this applies only to believers, as appears by the next verse, 'while we look,' etc. Afflictions have a salutary operation, provided that we look at the things which are eternal."

AFTERNOON (Heb. *neṭôt hayyôm,* "the day's declining," Judg. 19:8). According to the Jewish reckoning, the fifth of the six divisions of the day. *See* Time.

AG'ABUS (ag'a-bus). A prophet, supposed to have been one of the seventy disciples of Christ. He came with others from Jerusalem to Antioch while Paul and Barnabas were there and predicted an approaching famine, which actually occurred the following year. The expression "all over the world" (Acts 11:28) was probably used in a national sense, and by it Judea was doubtless meant, and the words must be understood to apply to that famine which, in the fourth year of Claudius, spread throughout Palestine. The poor Jews in general were then relieved by the queen of Adiabne, who sent to Egypt to purchase corn for them (Josephus *Ant.* 20.2.5; 5.2). For the relief of the Christians in Judea contributions were raised by their brethren in Antioch and taken to Jerusalem by Paul and Barnabas (Acts 11:28-30). Many years after, this same Agabus met Paul at Caesarea and warned him of the sufferings that awaited him if he continued his journey to Jerusalem (21:10-12). Agabus took Paul's belt and fastened it around his own hands and feet and said, "This is what the Holy Spirit says: 'In this way the Jews at Jerusalem will bind the man who owns this belt and deliver him into the hands of the Gentiles.' "

A'GAG (ā'gag). Probably a common name of all the Amalekite kings, like *pharaoh* in Egypt.

1. The king, apparently, of one of the hostile neighboring nations at the time of the Exodus,

31

1441 B.C. He is referred to by Balaam (Num. 24:7) in a manner implying that the king of the Amalekites was, then at least, a great monarch, and his people a greater people, than is commonly imagined.

2. The king of the Amalekites, who, being taken prisoner by Saul, was spared by him, contrary to the solemn vow of devotion to destruction whereby the nation, as such, had of old precluded itself from giving any quarter to that people (Ex. 17:14; Deut. 25:19). When Samuel came to the camp of Saul he chided him, told him of his rejection, and ordered Agag to be brought to him. Agag came "cheerfully," i.e., in a joyous state of mind, thinking that his life would still be spared (K. & D., *Com.*). But the prophet ordered him to be cut in pieces, and in the expression which he employed—"As your sword has made women childless, so shall your mother be childless among women"—indicates that, apart from the obligations of the vow, some such example of retributive justice was intended as had been exercised in the case of *Adoni-bezek* (which see). Perhaps Agag had treated prisoners in the same way he was now treated by Samuel (1 Sam. 15:8-33), about 1020 B.C.

A'GAGITE (ā'ga-gīt). Found (Esther 3:1, 10; 8:3, 5; 9:24) in connection with Haman, the enemy of Mordecai. Josephus (*Ant.* 11.6.5) explains it as a synonym of Amalek, and so it possibly was.

AG'APE (ag'a-pē), pl. **Agapae** (Gk. *agapē,* "love"). A simple meal of brotherly love celebrated daily in the apostolic times in connection with the Eucharist, the two being spoken of together as the Lord's Supper. At this meal the Christians, in connection with their common Redeemer, ignored all distinctions of rank, wealth, and culture, and met as members of one family. At the feast the bishop (or presbyter) presided, the food having been prepared at home, or at the place of meeting, according to circumstances. Before eating, the guests washed their hands, prayer was offered, and the Scriptures were read. After the meal a collection was taken for widows and orphans, the kiss of charity was given, and communications from other congregations were read and answered.

The Agape was never enjoined by divine command, and gradually, losing its peculiar feature of childlike unity, it led to all sorts of abuses, such as we find rebuked by the apostle Paul. Another cause for its discontinuance was that the Third Council of Carthage (A.D. 391) decreed that the Eucharist should be taken while fasting. Later several councils forbade its being held in the church buildings. Vestiges of the practice remained as late as the Council of Basle, in the fifteenth century. *See* Lord's Supper.

Apparently the Lord's Supper and the Agape were originally one (1 Cor. 11:17-34). The common conservative view unites a simple repast

with the Lord's Supper on the general plan of the Last Supper. A. Arnold maintains this view and traces the beginning of the separation of the two in the *Didache* 9.11 (cf. *Didascalia Apostolorum, Martyrdom of Polycarp* 18; Justin Martyr *Apologia* 65-67; A. Arnold, *Der Ursprung des christlichen Abendmahls,* 1937). The view that the Lord's Supper was once connected with the Agape was taken by J. F. Keating at the beginning of the century. Following the conservative view, Keating maintained that the excesses narrated in the Pauline epistles were the first reasons for the gradual separation of the Lord's Supper and the Agape Feast (*The Agape,* 1901). The thesis that the Lord's Supper constituted the sacramental portion of a meal, which was later differentiated from the common repast, was espoused by J. Hoffmann (*Das Abendmahl im Urchristentum,* 1903). Both Keating's and Hoffmann's views clashed with the view of a number of German scholars of the nineteenth century that the Agape meal was first, and the Lord's Supper grew out of this common repast. Pierre Batiffol, on the other hand, was of the opinion that the Agape was connected with the Lord's Supper only by way of excess (*Etudes,* 1907). E. Baumgartner likewise distinguished between the Agape and the Supper. The results of his research were that the Lord's Supper was a midnight or early Sunday morning ritual and that the Agape was a separate Sunday evening function going back to ancient Jewish practices (cf. E. Baumgartner, *Eucharistie und Agape im Urchristentum,* 1901). A. J. McLean (*Encyclopaedia of Religion and Ethics,* 1908) posited a Jewish pagan origin of the Agape. This view is reflected in R. L. Cole (*Love-Feasts,* 1916). Another scholar who saw a Jewish origin for the Agape was W. O. E. Oesterley in his *The Jewish Background of the Christian Liturgy,* 1925. Hans Lietzmann, while positing a Jewish influence, sees less of this than Oesterley or Baumgartner. Karl Voelker argues a Gnostic beginning in the latter part of the second century (*Mysterium und Agape,* 1927). The Agape was related to the funeral banquet by H. Leclercq (*Catholic Encyclopedia,* 1907). *See also* G. Kittel and G. Friedrich, eds., *Theological Dictionary of the New Testament* (1966-1976), vol. 1, s.v. "agape."　　　　　　　　　　　　　　　　　M.F.U.

BIBLIOGRAPHY: J. H. Kelly, *Love Feasts* (1916); R. C. Trench, *Synonyms of the New Testament* (1948), pp. 41-44; W. Barclay, *More New Testament Words* (1958), pp. 11-23; N. Turner, *Christian Words* (1980), pp. 261-66.

A'GAR. *See* Hagar.

AGATE. *See* Mineral Kingdom.

AG'EE (ag'ē; "fugitive"). A Hararite, father of Shammah, who was one of David's chief warriors (2 Sam. 23:11).

AGONY (Gk. *agōnia,* "struggle"). Used both in

classical and NT Gk. of severe mental struggles and emotions; our *anguish*. The Gk. word is used in the NT only by Luke (22:44) to describe the fearful struggle through which our Lord passed in the Garden of Gethsemane. The circumstances of this mysterious transaction are recorded in Matt. 26:36-46; Mark 14:32-42; and Heb. 5:7-8. Luke alone notices the agony, the bloody sweat, and the appearance of the strengthening angel. All agree that He prayed for the removal of "this cup" and are careful to note that He qualified this petition by a preference of His Father's will to His own. The question is, What did He mean by "this cup"? What was the cause of this sorrow unto death?

In answer we quote Edersheim: "Not fear, either of bodily or mental suffering: but death. Man's nature, created of God immortal, shrinks (by the law of its nature) from the dissolution of the bond that binds body to soul. Yet to fallen man death is not by any means fully death, for he is born with the taste of it in his soul. Not so Christ. It was the unfallen Man dying; it was He, who had no experience of it, tasting death, and that not for Himself but for every man, emptying the cup to its bitter dregs. It was the Christ undergoing death by man and for man; the incarnate God, the God-man, submitting Himself vicariously to the deepest humiliation, and paying the utmost penalty: death—all death. No one could know what death was (not dying, which men dread, but Christ dreaded not); no one could taste its bitterness as He. His going into death was His final conflict with Satan for man, and on his behalf. By submitting to it He took away the power of death. He disarmed Death by burying his shaft in His own heart. And beyond this lies the deep, unutterable mystery of Christ bearing the penalty due to our sin, bearing our death, bearing the penalty of the broken law, the accumulated guilt of humanity, and the holy wrath of the righteous Judge upon them" (*Life of Jesus*, 2:538-39).

AG'ORA (ag'o-ra). The marketplace or public square of a Greek city, where men assembled to debate or transact civic business. In the agora at Athens the apostle Paul met daily and disputed with those who were there (Acts 17:17). The Athenian marketplace has been completely excavated by the American School of Classical Studies (in the 1930s and to completion since 1946). Remains of this famous area include the round *Tholos*, where standard measures and weights were kept; the *Metroon*, where archives were deposited; the *Bouleuterion* or council chamber; and several stoas (including the great Stoa of Attalos). The entire complex of agora structures was dominated by the temple of Hephaisteion, the god of metal craftsmen. In addition to buildings many small finds have been made such as Mycaenean urns (fourteenth cen-

tury B.C.), ostraca, pottery, jewelry, and *objets d'art*. Paul was also familiar with the agora at Corinth and other Greek cities. The Greek agora corresponds to the forum of Roman cities.

M.F.U.

AGRAPHA (Gk. *agraphos*, "unwritten"). A term applied to the sayings of our Lord not recorded in the gospels. Naturally, there would be many of these, and this fact is recorded (John 21:25). The sources of our knowledge of these sayings are fivefold.

1. The first and surest is to be found in the books of the NT itself. An unquestionable example is given in Acts 20:35: "Remember the words of the Lord Jesus, that He Himself said, 'It is more blessed to give than to receive.' " Mayor, in his comments on James 1:12, "He will receive the crown of life, which the Lord has promised to those who love Him," thinks these words a semiquotation of some saying of Christ.

2. The next source, both in amount and authority, is supplied by some manuscripts of the NT, among them the well-known addition in *Codex Bezae* to Luke 6:4. "On the same day, beholding one working on the Sabbath, He said unto him. 'Man, if thou knowest what thou doest, blessed art thou; but if thou knowest not, accursed art thou and a transgressor of the law.' "

3. Quotations in early Christian writers and in lost gospels. The quotations of these sayings ceased almost entirely after the fourth century, when the current gospel text had won its way to acceptance. Of these unrecorded sayings Resch has collected 74 that he regards as genuine, and 103 apocryphal. In the main, these sayings neither have historical settings nor do they affect the truth of our Lord's life. They do, however, often illustrate His teaching and express it perhaps in a terser, more remarkable form than is found elsewhere. The following are two of the most remarkable of these sayings: "He that is near me is near the fire; he that is far from me is far from the kingdom"; "that which is weak shall be saved by that which is strong."

4. "The Logia, or Sayings of our Lord," found in Oxyrhynchus, 120 miles S of Cairo, Egypt, by B. F. Grenfell and Arthur S. Hunt, 1896.

Logion 1. ". . . and then shalt thou see clearly to cast out the mote that is in the brother's eye."

Logion 2. "Jesus saith, Except ye fast to the world, ye shall in no wise find the kingdom of God; and except ye keep the sabbath, ye shall not see the Father."

Logion 3. "Jesus saith, I stood in the midst of the world, and in the flesh was I seen of them, and I found all men drunken, and none found I athirst among them; and my soul grieveth over the sons of men, because they are blind in their heart. . . ."

Logion 4. Undecipherable.

Logion 5. "Jesus saith, Wherever there are . . .

and there is one . . . alone, I am with him. Raise the stone and there thou shalt find me; cleave the wood, and there am I."

Logion 6. "Jesus saith, A prophet is not acceptable in his own country, neither doth a physician work cures upon them that know him."

Logion 7. "Jesus saith, A city built upon the top of a high hill, and stablished, can neither fall nor be hid."

Logion 8. Undecipherable.

5. Near Nag Hammadi in Upper Egypt about 1945 a Gnostic library of thirteen volumes was found. In volume 3 appears *The Gospel According to Thomas,* a Coptic text that dates to the fourth or fifth century and is a translation or adaptation of a Gk. text that must have been produced in the second century A.D. This work has numerous sayings attributed to Christ but bearing a Gnostic bias.   H.F.V.

BIBLIOGRAPHY: D. S. Margoliouth, *Expository Times* 5 (1893): 59, 107, 177; M. R. James, *The Apocryphal New Testament* (1924), pp. 33-37.

AGRICULTURE. The cultivation of the soil dates back to Adam, to whom God assigned the occupation of cultivating and keeping the garden (Gen. 2:15). We are told that "Cain was a tiller of the ground" (4:2). The ancestors of the Hebrews in Mesopotamia followed pastoral pursuits, which were kept up by Abraham, Isaac, and Jacob, whose sons settled as shepherds on the fruitful pasturelands of Goshen (chap. 47). During their four hundred years' residence in Egypt the Israelites engaged in the pursuit of agriculture (Deut. 11:10), so that they were prepared to make the cultivation of the soil their principal employment, and in this sense the Mosaic state was founded on agriculture. As the soil could not be alienated, but reverted to the owner in the year of Jubilee, each family had a stake in the soil, and its culture was held in high esteem (1 Sam. 11:5; 1 Kings 19:19; 2 Chron. 26:10). As the pastoral life of Israel had kept it from mixture and local attachment, especially while in Egypt, so agriculture in Canaan tended to check a nomadic life of plunder.

Irrigation. In all countries climate and soil have much to do with the methods of agriculture and sorts of crops. In Eastern countries generally, the heat and dryness of the greater portion of the year make irrigation by canals and aqueducts indispensable. This is true to a considerable extent of Palestine, although its rains are more frequent than in Egypt or Assyria. There is reference, however, to natural irrigation by conduits *palegê-mayim,* "water-partings, canals" (Job 38:25; Prov. 21:1). These were well known to the Israelites in Egypt (Deut. 11:10).

Care of Soil. The several portions of the land were carefully marked off (1 Sam. 114:14; Prov. 22:28); divided for the various products of the soil (Isa. 28:25); secured against injury from wild

Plowing

animals by hedges and walls (Isa. 5:5; Num. 22:24); and the soil fertilized by manuring (Ps. 83:10). The preparation of manure from straw trodden in the manure pile appears from Isa. 25:10. The dung, the carcasses, and the blood of animals were used to enrich the soil (2 Kings 9:37; Ps. 83:10; Jer. 9:22). Salt, either by itself or mixed in the manure pile in order to promote putrefaction, is specifically mentioned as a compost (Matt. 5:13; Luke 14:34-35). The land was burned over to destroy the seed of noxious herbs (Prov. 24:31; Isa. 32:13) and was then enriched with ashes. The cultivation of hillsides in terraces cannot be proved from any clear statement of Scripture, but the nature of its soil makes it necessary. Terraces are still seen on the mountain slopes, rising above one another, frequently to the number of sixty or eighty, and on them fields, gardens, and plantations.

The soil was broken up by the *plow* (which see), a crude affair, probably similar to those used in Egypt. Early in the year the ground was cleared

Winnowing fork

of stones and thorns (Isa. 5:2), sowing or gathering from among thorns being a proverb for slovenly husbandry (Job 5:5; Prov. 24:30-31). New land was plowed a second time. The plow was followed by men using hoes to break the clods (Isa. 28:24), but in later times a harrow was employed. This appears to have been then, as now, merely a thick block of wood pressed down by the weight of a stone or a man (Job 39:10; Isa. 28:24). The seed appears to have been sowed and harrowed at the same time, although sometimes the seed was plowed in by a cross furrow.

Crops. The principal crops of Palestine were, undoubtedly, wheat and barley, from which was derived the common bread of the country. Mention is also made of spelt, millet, lentils, flax, cucumbers, melons, beans, cummin, and so forth. Hay was not in use, and, therefore, barley with chopped straw was fed to cattle (Gen. 24:25, 32; Judg. 19:19).

The sowing began after the feast of Tabernacles (the end of October and in November), in the time when the autumn rains come gradually, thus leaving the farmer time to sow his wheat and barley. Summer fruits (millet, beans, and so forth) were sown in January and February. Harvest began with barley (2 Sam. 21:9; Ruth 2:23), which ripens in Palestine from two to three weeks before wheat, and was begun by law on the 16th Nisan with the presentation of the first barley sheaf. Lentils were ready at the same time as barley. Then came wheat and spelt, so that the

chief part of the grain harvest closed about Pentecost.

The OT gives little information regarding the cultivation of flax and cotton. The Israelites probably learned the working of these in Egypt (Ex. 9:31), and they seem to have grown them in Palestine, for according to Hos. 2:9 and Prov. 31:13, flax and wool were to be found in every house. Cotton must have been introduced into Israel shortly after the captivity (c. 525 B.C.) and into Assyria and Egypt about 700 B.C., and cultivated early by the Israelites, for in 1 Chron. 4:21 among the ancient households of Judah is named a family of workers in linen.

Harvest. Grain was cut with a sickle (Deut. 16:9). The reapers lived on parched grain and bread dipped in vinegar (Ruth 2:14). It is probable, however, that the modern custom of pulling up by the roots prevailed to a considerable extent in ancient times. This was done to save all the straw, as it grew very short. When cut it was gathered on the arms (Ps. 129:7), bound in sheaves, and laid in heaps (Song of Sol. 7:2; Ruth 3:7) to be threshed. Threshing floors were placed in the open air, leveled and tramped hard, generally on elevated ground, so that in winnowing the wind might carry away the chaff (Hos. 13:3; Jer. 4:11). Threshing was done by oxen driven over the grain to tread out the kernels with their hoofs (Hos. 10:11); by machines made either of planks with stones or bits of iron fastened to the lower surface to make it rough, and rendered heavy by

Harvesting grain

35

some weight upon it; or by small wagons with low cylindrical wheels like saws (Isa. 28:27; 41:15).

Flails were used for threshing tender cereals or small quantities of grain (Ruth 2:17; Isa. 28:27). Winnowing was done with a broad shovel or a wooden fork with bent prongs. The mass of chaff, straw, and grain was thrown against the wind so that the chaff might be blown away. This was usually done in the evening, when there was generally a breeze (Ruth 3:2; see Jer. 4:11; 51:2). The chaff and stubble were burned (Isa. 5:24; Matt. 3:12). Finally, the grain was sifted (Amos 9:9).

Israel owed its possession of Palestine and its fertility to Jehovah; hence its cultivation was put under obedience to the Lord's commands. The Sabbath rest was to be observed (Lev. 19:3), for the soil was to lie fallow in the sabbatic (25:3-5) and jubilee years (25:11). The Israelites were forbidden to yoke an ox and donkey together (Deut. 22:10), the one being a clean and the other an unclean animal; to sow with mingled seed (Lev. 19:19; Deut. 22:9); or to sow moistened seed on which the carcass of an unclean animal had fallen (Lev. 11:37-38). The corners of the fields were not reaped, and the gleanings of the fields were left for the poor (19:9; Deut. 24:19; cf. Ruth 2:2).

Israelites passing along in the path were allowed to pluck the heads of ripened grain left in the field (Deut. 23:25; Matt. 12:1; Luke 6:1). The firstfruits of all kinds of planting belonged to Jehovah, in recognition of His being the giver of all good things. The fruit of the orchard the first three years was considered uncircumcised (unclean) and not to be eaten. All of the fourth year's yield was consecrated to Jehovah. The first eating by men was to be that of the fifth year (Lev. 19:23-25). For cultivation of the vine and the olive, see under respective words.

BIBLIOGRAPHY: N. Glueck, *Rivers in the Desert* (1959); J. Pedersen, *Israel, Its Life and Culture* (1959), 3-4:376-465; D. Baly, *Geographical Companion to the Bible* (1963); F. Schwanitz, *The Origin of Cultivated Plants* (1966); N. Glueck, *The Other Side of Jordan* (1970), pp. 40-58, 138-244.

AGRIP′PA (a-grip′a). The name of two members of the Herodian family. *See* Herod.

AGUE. *See* Diseases: Fever.

A′GUR (a′gūr; "gathered"). The author of the sayings contained in Prov. 30, which the inscription describes as being composed of the precepts delivered by "Agur the son of Jakeh." Beyond this, everything that has been stated of him, and of the time in which he lived, is pure conjecture.

AH- ("brother of"). The former part of many Heb. words, signifying relationship or property.

A′HAB (ā′hab; "father's brother"). The name of two biblical personages.

1. The son of the seventh king of Israel, Omri, and second of the dynasty of Omri. He succeeded

his father in the thirty-eighth year of Asa, king of Judah, and reigned twenty-two years in Samaria, 874-853 B.C. His wife was Jezebel, a heathen princess, daughter of Ethbaal, king of Sidon.

Jezebel was a decided and energetic character, and soon acquired complete control over her husband, so that he eventually established the worship of the Phoenician idols, and especially of the storm god Baal-Melcarth. Ahab built him a temple and an altar in Samaria and made a grove for the impure orgies of the goddess Asherah (1 Kings 16:29-33). So strong was the tide of corruption that it appeared as if the knowledge of the true God would be lost among the Israelites. But a man suited to this emergency was raised up in the person of Elijah (chap. 18), who opposed the royal power and succeeded in retaining many of his countrymen in the worship of the true God. *See* Elijah.

Ahab had a taste for splendid architecture, which he indulged by building an ivory house and several cities (22:39). He erected his royal residence at Jezreel, in the Plain of Esdraelon, still keeping Samaria as capital of his kingdom.

Refused a neighboring vineyard, which he desired to add to his pleasure grounds, Ahab, through the influence of Jezebel, caused its proprietor, Naboth, to be put to death on a false charge of blasphemy. For this crime Elijah prophesied the total extinction of the house of Ahab. The execution of the sentence was delayed in consequence of Ahab's repentance (1 Kings 21).

Ahab undertook three campaigns against Ben-hadad I, king of Damascus, two defensive and one offensive. In the first, Ben-hadad had laid siege to Samaria, and Ahab, encouraged by God's prophets, made a sudden attack upon him while at a banquet and totally routed the Syrians. Ben-hadad was again defeated the next year by Ahab, who spared his life and released him on the condition of restoring the cities of Israel he had held and of allowing Ahab certain commercial and political privileges (1 Kings 20:34). For three years Ahab enjoyed peace, when, with Jehoshaphat, king of Judah, he attacked Ramoth-gilead. Micaiah told Ahab that the expedition would fail. The prophet was imprisoned for giving this warning, but Ahab was so impressed that he took the precaution of disguising himself when he went into battle.

He was slain by a man who "drew a bow at random," and although he stayed up in his chariot for a time he died at evening, and his army was dispersed (1 Kings 22). When he was brought to be buried in Samaria the dogs licked up his blood as a servant was washing his chariot, thus fulfilling the prophecy of Elijah (21:19).

Ahab appears prominently on the Assyrian monuments of the great conqueror Shalmaneser III (859-824 B.C.). The Monolith Inscription, now in the British Museum, recounts the clash of

Assyrian arms in 853 B.C. with a Syrian coalition of kings at Qarqar N of Hamath, a fortress guarding the approaches to all lower Syria. Conspicuously mentioned among those who successfully withstood Assyria's advance is "Ahab, the Israelite." The Israelite ruler's prominence is indicated by the large number of chariots he is said to have thrown into the battle—2,000 as compared with the next largest number of 1,200 supplied by Hadadezer of Damascus. Ahab ran a close race with the Damascene state as heading the foremost power in central and lower Syria in the middle of the ninth century B.C., as is represented by the Bible and proved by the monuments.

M.F.U.

2. A false prophet who deceived the Israelites at Babylon and was threatened by Jeremiah, who foretold that he should be put to death by the king of Babylon in the presence of those whom he had beguiled, and that in following times it should become a common malediction to say, "May the Lord make you like Zedekiah and like Ahab, whom the king of Babylon roasted in the fire" (Jer. 29:21-22).

AHAR'AH (a-har'āh). The third son of Benjamin (1 Chron. 8:1). Elsewhere he is called Ehi (Gen. 46:21), Ahiram (Num. 26:38), and Aher (1 Chron. 7:12).

AHAR'HEL (a-har'hel). A son of Harum whose families are named among the lineage of Koz, a descendant of Judah (1 Chron. 4:8).

AHAS'BAI (a-has'bī). A Maacathite and the father of Eliphelet, one of David's warriors (2 Sam. 23:34). In 1 Chron. 11:35, he is apparently called *Ur* (which see).

AHASUE'RUS (a-haz-ū-ē'rus). The Heb. form of the name representing the Persian Khshayarsha of which the Gk. form is Xerxes (so NIV), and appearing as the title of two Median and Persian monarchs mentioned in the Bible.

1. The Persian king mentioned in the book of Esther and in Ezra 4:6. He is probably identical with Xerxes, whose regal state and affairs tally with all that is here said of Ahasuerus. His kingdom was extensive, extending from India to Ethiopia (Esther 1:1).

In the third year of his reign he made a sumptuous banquet for his nobility. On that occasion, being partially intoxicated, he ordered Vashti, his wife, to be brought before him, that he might exhibit her beauty to his courtiers. She, however, refused to appear, for it was contrary to Persian etiquette as well as to female propriety. Thereupon Ahasuerus indignantly divorced her and published a royal decree asserting the superiority of husbands over their wives.

In the seventh year of his reign (2:16) he married Esther, the beautiful Jewess, who, however, concealed her parentage. His prime minister, Haman, was enraged with Mordecai, the Jew, because he did not give him reverence and, in the twelfth year of the king's reign, offered him ten thousand talents of silver for the privilege of ordering a general massacre of the Jews in the kingdom on an appointed day. The king refused the money but granted the request. Couriers were dispatched to the most distant parts of the realm to order the execution of the decree. Mordecai immediately sent word to Esther of the impending danger and through her intercession the decree was so far annulled as to empower the Jews to defend themselves against their enemies. Ahasuerus disgraced and hanged Haman and his ten sons (7:10; 9:14) and made Mordecai his prime minister (10:3).

Xerxes (486-465 B.C.), the son of Darius I the Great, is undoubtedly the Ahasuerus of the book of Esther and in Ezra 4:6. The third year of his reign in which he held a great feast and assembly at Susa (Shushan), the palace, corresponds identically to the third year of the reign of Xerxes when he arranged the Grecian war. In the seventh year of his reign Xerxes returned defeated from Greece and consoled himself in the pleasures of his palace. It was then that Ahasuerus sought "beautiful young virgins" and replaced Vashti by marrying Esther. An important historical inscription of Xerxes discovered at Persepolis lists the numerous subject nations over which he ruled, and fully corroborates Esther 1:1, that he ruled "from India to Ethiopia."

The palace of Darius, Persepolis

2. The father of Darius the Mede (Dan. 9:1). It is generally agreed that the person referred to here is the Astyages of secular history, but some identify him with Cyaxares.

BIBLIOGRAPHY: A. T. Olmstead, *History of the Persian Empire* (1948); H. H. Rowley, *Darius the Mede and the Four World Empires in the Book of Daniel* (1953); J. C. Whitcomb, Jr., *Darius the Mede* (1959); R. C. Zaehner, *The Dawn and Twilight of Zoroastrianism* (1961); A. R. Burn, *Persia and the Greeks* (1962); R. N. Frye, *Heritage of Persia* (1966).

AHA'VA (a-hā'va). The river itself or a place beside the river, where the Jewish exiles who were to return from Babylon to Jerusalem gathered (Ezra 8:21).

A'HAZ (ā'haz; "possessor").

1. The twelfth king of the separate kingdom of Judah, being the son and successor of Jotham. He reigned sixteen years (according to some authorities, two years as viceroy), 735-715 B.C.

In 2 Kings 16:2 the age of Ahaz, at his accession, is given as twenty years. This probably refers to some earlier viceroyship, otherwise he would have been only eleven years old at the birth of his son Hezekiah (cf. 2 Kings 16:2, 20; 18:2). In the latter passage his age is given as twenty-five years.

At the time of his accession, Pekah, king of Israel, and Rezin, king of Syria, were in league against Judah. They proceeded to lay siege to Jerusalem, intending to place on the throne Ben-Tabeel, probably a Syrian noble (Isa. 7:6). Isaiah hastened to announce to him the destruction of the allied monarchs, who failed in their attack upon Jerusalem, although they inflicted serious damage on him elsewhere. Rezin, king of Syria, captured Elath (2 Kings 16:6); Zichri, an Ephraimite, slew the king's son, the ruler of his house, and his prime minister; and Pekah, king of Israel, gained a great advantage over him in a battle in Judah, killing 120,000 men and taking captive 200,000 of his people. These, however, were returned through the remonstrance of the prophet Oded (2 Chron. 28:3-15).

In his extremity Ahaz applied to Tiglath-pileser, king of Assyria, for assistance, who freed him from his most formidable enemies by invading Syria, taking Damascus, and killing Rezin. He purchased this help at great cost, becoming tributary to Tiglath-pileser. He sent him the treasures of the Temple and of his own palace, and even appeared before him at Damascus as his vassal.

While he was there his idolatrous propensities induced him to take the pattern of a heathen altar and have one like it built in Jerusalem. Upon his return he offered upon the altar, closed the Temple, removed its sacred utensils, and raised shrines to heathen deities everywhere.

He died unlamented, and his body was not deposited in the sacred sepulchers (vv. 16-27).

In an inscription of the famous Assyrian emperor Tiglath-pileser III (744-727 B.C.), referred to as Pul (Pulu) in 2 Kings 15:19, occurs the name of Ahaz. In an account of the payment of tribute by various vassal states of Syria-Palestine including the kings of Hamath, Arvad, Moab, Gaza, Ashkelon, Edom, and others, occurs "Iauhazi [Jehoahaz, i.e., Ahaz] of Judah." Tribute is mentioned as consisting of "gold, silver, lead, iron, tin, brightly colored woolen garments, linen, the purple garments of their lands . . . all kinds of costly things, the products of the sea and the dry land . . . the royal treasure, horses, mules, broken to the yoke . . . (D. D. Luckenbill, *Ancient Records of Assyria and Babylonia*, vol. 1, sec. 801).   M.F.U.

2. A great-grandson of Jonathan, son of King Saul, being one of the four sons of Micah and the father of Jehoaddah or Jarah (1 Chron. 8:35-36; 9:42; in the NIV Jarah is replaced by Jadah).

AHAZI'AH (ā-ha-zī'a; "has grasped Jehovah").

1. The son of Ahab, king of Israel, whom he succeeded in every sense, being as completely under the control of Jezebel and idolatry as was his father (1 Kings 22:51-53). He was the ninth king of Israel and reigned two years, 853-852 B.C. The single most public event of his reign was the revolt of the vassal king of the Moabites, who took the opportunity of the defeat and death of Ahab to discontinue the tribute that he had paid to the Israelites, consisting of one hundred thousand lambs and as many rams with their wool (2 Kings 1:1; 3:4-5). Ahaziah became a party with Jehoshaphat to revive the maritime traffic of the Red Sea. Because of this alliance God was displeased with Jehoshaphat and the vessels were destroyed (2 Chron. 20:35-37). Soon after Ahaziah was injured by falling from the roof gallery of his palace in Samaria (the "lattice" of the text probably meaning a balustrade to keep persons from falling). He sent to inquire of Baal-zebub, the idol of Ekron, what should be the result of his injury. But the messengers were met and sent back by Elijah, who announced that he should rise no more from the bed upon which he lay (2 Kings 1:2-4). He died shortly after and was succeeded by his brother Jehoram (1:17; 3:1).

2. The son of Jehoram by Athaliah and sixth king of Judah, 841 B.C. He is also called Jehoahaz (2 Chron. 21:17; 25:23) and Azariah (22:6). He followed the example of his father-in-law, Ahab, and was given to idolatry (2 Kings, 8:25-27; 2 Chron. 22:1-4). He joined his uncle, Joram, of Israel, in an expedition against Hazael, king of Syria, which proved disastrous. The king of Israel was wounded, and Ahaziah visited him in Jezreel. During this visit Jehu was secretly anointed king of Israel and conspired against Joram. The two kings rode out in their chariots to meet Jehu, and when Joram was shot through the heart Ahaziah attempted to escape but was pursued as far as the pass of Gur and, being mortally wounded there, only had strength to reach Megiddo, where he died. His body was conveyed by his servants to Jerusalem for burial (2 Kings 9:1-28).

AH'BAN (a'bän; "brother of the wise"). The first named of the two sons of Abishur by Abihail, of the descendants of Judah (1 Chron. 2:29).

A'HER (a'hēr; "another"). A descendant of Benjamin (1 Chron. 7:12); probably the same person as Ahiram (Num. 26:38).

A'HI (a'hī; "brotherly").

1. A son of Abdiel, and head of the tribe of Gad, resident in Bashan (1 Chron. 5:15).

2. The first named of the four sons of Shemer

(Shomer, NIV), a leader of the tribe of Asher (1 Chron. 7:34).

AHI'AH (a-hī'a; "little brother"). Another mode of anglicizing the name of Ahijah. The term is variously rendered in the KJV, NIV, and NASB. In 1 Sam. 14:3, 18; 1 Kings 4:3; and 1 Chron. 8:7, the term is given as Ahiah in the KJV and *Ahijah* (which see) in the NASB and NIV. In Neh. 10:26, where the term refers to one of those who subscribed the covenant, drawn up by Nehemiah, to serve the Lord, 445 B.C., the KJV renders Ahijah and the NASB and NIV render Ahiah.

AHI'AM (a-hī'am; perhaps for *Achiab'*, "father's brother"). A son of Sharar, the Hararite, and one of David's thirty heroes (2 Sam. 23:33; 1 Chron. 11:35), 1000 B.C.

AHI'AN (a-hī'an; "brotherly"). The first named of the four sons of Shemidah, of the tribe of Manasseh (1 Chron. 7:19).

AHIE'ZER (a-hī-ē'zēr; "brother of help," i.e., "helpful").

1. The son of Ammishaddai and the head of the tribe of Dan when the people were numbered at Sinai (Num. 1:12), about 1438 B.C. He made an offering for the service of the Tabernacle, like the other leaders (Num. 7:66).

2. The chief of the Benjamite warriors who joined David at Ziklag (1 Chron. 12:3), before 1000 B.C.

AHI'HUD. The English form of two similar Heb. names.

1. Heb. *'Ăhîhûd,* "brother of renown," refers to the son of Shelomi and head of the tribe of Asher (Num. 34:27). He was one of those appointed by Moses to oversee the partition of Canaan, about 1401 B.C.

2. Heb. *'Ăhîhud,* "brother of a riddle," i.e., "mysterious," refers to the second named of the two later sons of Ehud, the son of Benjamin (1 Chron. 8:7).

AHI'JAH (à-hī-jā; "brother of Jehovah").

1. The son of Phinehas's son Ahitub, and high priest in the reign of Saul (1 Sam. 14:3, 18), about 1020 B.C. He is here described as "the priest of the Lord at Shiloh [and] wearing an ephod." In 14:18 it appears that the Ark was under his care. There is some difficulty in reconciling this with the statement in 1 Chron. 13:3 that they did not seek the Ark in the days of Saul. Some avoid the difficulty by inserting "ephod" for "ark" (K. & D., *Com.*, ad loc.); others, by interpreting *ark,* in this case, to mean a chest for carrying the ephod. Others apply the expression only to all the latter years of the reign of Saul, when we know that the priestly establishment was at Nob and not at Kiriath-jearim, where the Ark was. But probably the last time that Ahijah inquired of the Lord before the Ark was on the occasion related in 1 Sam. 14:36, when Saul marred his victory

over the Philistines by a rash oath, which nearly cost Jonathan his life. But it seems God returned no answer in consequence of Saul's curse. If, as is commonly supposed, Ahijah is the same person as Ahimelech (cf. 1 Sam. 14:3; 22:16; 24:3), this failure to obtain an answer may have led to an estrangement between the king and the high priest, and predisposed the king to suspect Ahimelech's loyalty and to take that terrible revenge upon him for his favor to David. Gesenius supposes (*Thesaurus Heb.,* p. 65) that Ahimelech may have been a brother to Ahijah, and that they officiated simultaneously, the one at Gibeah, or Kiriath-jearim, and the other at Nob.

2. Son of Shisha and a secretary of King Solomon (1 Kings 4:3), about 960 B.C.

3. A prophet of Shiloh (1 Kings 14:2) and hence called the Shilonite (11:29). There are two remarkable prophecies of Ahijah extant. The one in 1 Kings 11:31-40 is addressed to Jeroboam, about 940 B.C. In this he foretold the rending of the kingdom of Solomon in punishment for his idolatries and the transference of ten tribes after his death to Jeroboam. Solomon, hearing of this prophecy, sought to kill Jeroboam, who fled to Shishak, king of Egypt, and remained there until Solomon's death. The other prophecy (1 Kings 14:6-16) was delivered to the wife of Jeroboam, who came to him in disguise to inquire concerning the king's son, who was sick. In this he foretold the death of the son, the destruction of Jeroboam's house on account of the images he had set up, and the captivity of Israel. In 2 Chron. 9:29 reference is made to a record of the events of Solomon's reign contained in the "prophecy of Ahijah the Shilonite."

4. An Israelite of the tribe of Issachar and the father of Baasha, king of Israel (1 Kings 15:27), before 911 B.C.

5. The last named of the five sons of Jerahmeel by his first wife (1 Chron. 2:25).

6. One of the sons of Bela, son of Benjamin (1 Chron. 8:7), elsewhere (v. 4) called *Ahoah* (which see).

7. A Pelonite, one of David's famous heroes (1 Chron. 11:36), apparently the same called *Eliam* (which see), the son of Ahithophel the Gilonite in the parallel passage (2 Sam. 23.34).

8. A Levite appointed, in the arrangement by David, over the sacred treasure of dedicated gifts at the Temple (1 Chron. 26:20; see marg.), 1000 B.C.

9. In the KJV of Neh. 10:26, one of those who subscribed the covenant, drawn up by Nehemiah, to serve the Lord. Rendered Ahiah in the NASB and NIV.

BIBLIOGRAPHY: W. F. Albright, *Archaeology and the Religion of Israel* (1956), pp. 201ff.

AHI'KAM (a-hī'kam; "my brother has risen"). One of the four persons sent by King Josiah to inquire of the prophetess Huldah concerning the proper course to be pursued in relation to the acknowledged violations of the newly discovered book of the law (2 Kings 22:12-14; 2 Chron. 34:20-22), 624 B.C. He afterward protected the prophet Jeremiah from the persecuting jury of Jehoiakim (Jer. 26:24), about 609 B.C. His son, Gedaliah, showed Jeremiah a like kindness (Jer. 39:14). He was the son of Shaphan and the father of Gedaliah, who was appointed over Judea after the capture of Jerusalem by the Babylonians (2 Kings 25:22; Jer. 40:5-16).

AHI'LUD (a-hī'lud; "brother's child"). The father of Jehoshaphat, recorder under David and Solomon (2 Sam. 8:16; 20:24; 2 Kings 4:3), and also of Baana, one of Solomon's deputies (1 Kings 4:12), 960 B.C.

AHIM'AAZ (a-him'a-az; "brother of anger").

1. The father of Ahinoam, wife of King Saul (1 Sam. 14:50), about 1020 B.C.

2. The son and successor of Zadok (1 Chron. 6:8, 53) in the high priesthood. When Absalom revolted, David refused to allow the Ark to be removed from Jerusalem, believing that God would bring him back to the city. The high priests, Zadok and Abiathar, necessarily remained in attendance upon it; but their sons, Ahimaaz and Jonathan, concealed themselves outside the city to be in readiness to relate to David any important movements and designs of Absalom that they might receive from within. When, therefore, Hushai informed the priests that Absalom had preferred his own counsel to that of Ahithophel, they sent word to Ahimaaz and Jonathan by a girl, doubtless to avoid suspicion. A lad saw the transaction and informed Absalom, who dispatched servants after them. They were hid by a woman in a dry well, the mouth of which was covered and strewn over with grain. She told the pursuers that the messengers had passed on in haste, and when all was safe she released them, and they made their way to David (2 Sam. 15:24-27; 17:15-22), 967 B.C. After the death of Absalom, Ahimaaz prevailed upon Joab to let him run after the Cushite who had been sent to inform David. He outstripped him, being doubtless swift of foot and taking another route, and proceeded to break the news gently to David, telling him at first only of the victory. While he spoke the Cushite entered and bluntly revealed the truth. The estimate in which he was held by David is shown in his answer to the watchman who announced his coming: "This is a good man and comes with good news" (2 Sam. 18:19-32).

3. Solomon's deputy in Naphtali, who married Basemath, daughter of Solomon (1 Kings 4:15), about 950 B.C.

AHI'MAN (a-hī'man; "generous" [?]).

1. One of the three famous giants of the race of Anak, who dwelt at Hebron when the Hebrew spies explored the land (Num. 13:22), about 1440 B.C., and who (or their descendants) were afterward expelled by Caleb (Josh. 15:14) and eventually slain by the Judaites (Judg. 1:10).

2. A Levite who was one of the gatekeepers of the Temple (1 Chron. 9:17).

AHIM'ELECH (a-him'e-lek; "brother of the king").

1. High priest of the Jews and the son of Ahitub (1 Sam. 22:11) and father of Abiathar (v. 20); he was probably the same as *Ahijah* (which see). He was a descendant of the line of Ithamar through Eli (1 Chron. 24:3, 6; Josephus *Ant.* 5.11.5; 8.1.3). When David fled from Saul (about 1010 B.C.) he went to Nob, where the Tabernacle then was. His unexpected appearance alarmed Ahimelech, whose anxious inquiry was answered by David's falsehood, "The king has commissioned me with a matter" (1 Sam. 21:2). Under this pretext Ahimelech was induced to give him bread and the sword of Goliath (21:3-9). A servant of Saul, Doeg, an Edomite, witnessed the transaction, and informed King Saul, who immediately sent for Ahimelech and the other priests then at Nob, and charged them with treason. But they declared their ignorance of any hostile designs on the part of David. This, however, availed them nothing, for the king ordered his guards to slay them. Upon their refusing to do so he commanded Doeg, who slew the priests, eighty-five in number. He then marched to Nob and put to the sword everything it contained (1 Sam. 22:9-20). The only priest that escaped was Abiathar, Ahimelech's son, who fled to David, and who afterward became high priest (23:6; 30:7). The names in 2 Sam. 8:17 and 1 Chron. 24:6 are commonly regarded as having been transposed by a copyist. (But *see* the article Abiathar and also no. 2, below, for another explanation.)

2. A son of Abiathar (2 Sam. 8:17; 1 Chron. 18:16; 24:3, 6, 31).

3. A Hittite, one of David's warriors, whom David invited to accompany him at night into the camp of Saul in the wilderness of Ziph; but Abishai alone seems to have gone with him (1 Sam. 26:6-7), about 1010 B.C.

AHI'MOTH (a-hī'mōth). One of the sons of Elkanah, a Levite (1 Chron. 6:25). In v. 26 he is called Nahath.

AHIN'ADAB (a-hin'a-dab; "noble brother"). Son of Iddo, and one of the twelve deputies of Solomon. His district was Mahanaim, the southern half of the region beyond Jordan (1 Kings 4:14), about 950 B.C.

AHIN'OAM (a-hin'ō-am; "my brother is pleasantness").

1. The daughter of Ahimaaz and the wife of King Saul (1 Sam. 14:50), about 1020 B.C.

2. A Jezreelitess and one of David's wives taken before he was king (1 Sam. 25:43), 1004 B.C. She

and his other wife, Abigail, lived with him at the court of Achish (27:3). They were taken prisoners by the Amalekites when they plundered Ziklag (30:5) but were rescued by David (v. 18). She went with him to Hebron and resided with him while he remained there as king of Judah (2 Sam. 2:2). She was mother of his eldest son, Amnon (3:2).

AHI'O (a-hī'ō; "brotherly").

1. One of the sons of the Levite Abinadab, to whom, with his brother, was entrusted the care of the Ark when David first attempted to move it to Jerusalem. Ahio probably guided the oxen, while his brother Uzzah walked by the cart (2 Sam. 6:3-4; 1 Chron. 13:7), 992 B.C.

2. A Benjamite, one of the sons of Beriah (1 Chron. 8:14).

3. One of the sons of Jeiel, a Gibeonite, by Maacah (1 Chron. 8:31; 9:37).

AHI'RA (a-hī'ra). The son of Enan and the leader of the tribe of Naphtali (Num. 2:29). He was appointed as "head man" of his tribe to assist Moses in numbering the people (1:15) and made his contribution to the sacred service on the twelfth day of offering (7:78, 83; 10:27), c. 1440 B.C.

AHI'RAM (a-hī'ram).

1. A son of Benjamin (Num. 26:38).

2. A Phoenician king of Gebal (later Byblos) whose magnificent sarcophagus inscribed with Phoenician writing (c. eleventh century B.C.) was recovered and forms an important link in the development of the Phoenician alphabet. The sarcophagus and jewels of Ahiram are in the National Museum at Beirut. Ahiram of Byblos, however, is not to be identified with Hiram of Tyre, Solomon's ally, although the names are evidently identical, and they lived perhaps contemporaneously.   M.F.U.

AHI'RAMITE (a-hī'ra-mīt). A descendant (Num. 26:38) of the Benjamite *Ahiram* (which see).

AHIS'AMACH (a-his'a-mach; "my brother helps"). Father of one of the famous workers upon the Tabernacle, Oholiab, the Danite (Ex. 31:6; 35:34; 38:23), c. 1440 B.C.

AHISH'AHAR (a-hish'a-har; "brother of the dawn"). A warrior, last named of the sons of Bilhan, of the tribe of Benjamin (1 Chron. 7:10).

AHI'SHAR (a-hī'shar; "my brother has sung"). The officer who was "over the household" of Solomon (1 Kings 4:6), i.e., steward, or governor of the palace, a place of great importance and influence in the East, 960 B.C.

AHITH'OPHEL (a-hith'o-fel; "brother of folly"). A counselor of David whose wisdom was so highly esteemed that his advice had the authority of a divine word (2 Sam. 16:23). Absalom, when he revolted, sent to Ahithophel, who was at Giloh,

his native city, and secured his support. He perhaps thought to wield a greater sway under the prince than he had done under David, and he also resented David's conduct to his granddaughter, Bathsheba (cf. 2 Sam. 11:3 with 23:34). When David heard of Ahithophel's defection, he prayed that God would turn his counsel to "foolishness" (doubtless alluding to his name) and induced Hushai, his friend, to go over to Absalom to defeat the counsels of this now dangerous enemy (15:31-37). Ahithophel's advice to Absalom was to show that the breach between him and his father was irreparable by publicly taking possession of the royal harem (16:20-23). He also recommended immediate pursuit of David and would probably have succeeded had not Hushai's plausible advice been accepted by the council. When Ahithophel saw that his counsel was rejected for that of Hushai, the far-seeing man gave up the cause of Absalom for lost; and he returned to his home in Giloh, hanged himself, and was buried in the grave of his father (17:1-23), 967 B.C.

BIBLIOGRAPHY: W. G. Blaikie, *David, King of Israel* (1981), pp. 279-83; F. W. Krummacher, *David the King of Israel* (1983), pp. 422-27.

AHI'TUB (a-hī'tūb; "good brother").

1. The son of Phinehas and grandson of Eli. He probably succeeded the latter in the high priesthood, his father being slain in battle, 1050 B.C. He was succeeded by his son Ahijah, or Ahimelech (1 Sam. 14:3; 22:9, 11, 20).

2. The son of Amariah and father of Zadok, who was made high priest by Saul after the death of Ahimelech (2 Sam. 8:17; 1 Chron. 6:7). It is not probable that this Ahitub was ever high priest. The coincidence of the names (1 Chron. 6:8, 11, 12) would lead us to infer that by the Ahitub found therein is meant Azariah (2 Chron. 31:10). Of the Ahitub mentioned in 1 Chron. 9:11 and Neh. 11:11 nothing definite is known, save that he was "leader of the house of God" (11:11).

AH'LAB (ah'lāb; "fertile"). A town of Asher, whose inhabitants the Israelites were unable to expel (Judg. 1:31). It has not been identified successfully.

AH'LAI (a'lī; "Oh that!").

1. The "son" of Sheshan, a descendant of Judah (1 Chron. 2:31). In v. 34 we read that Sheshan had "no sons, only daughters," that he gave his Egyptian servant, Jarha, his daughter to be his wife, and that this daughter bore a son named Attai (vv. 34-35). Some suppose Ahlai to be the name of Jarha's wife, but the masculine form of the word and the use of Ahlai (1 Chron. 2:31; 11:41) for a man is adverse to this conclusion. Others suppose Ahlai to be a clerical error for Attai; still others believe that Ahlai was a name given to Jarha on his incorporation into the family of Sheshan; some conjecture that Ahlai was a

son of Shesan, born after the marriage of his daughter.

2. The father of one of David's "valiant men" (1 Chron. 11:41), about 995 B.C.

AHO'AH (a-hō'ah; "brotherly"). The son of Bela, the son of Benjamin (1 Chron. 8:4); called also Ahijah (v. 7) and perhaps Iri (7:7), probably about 1600 B.C. It is probably he whose descendants are called Ahohites (2 Sam. 23:9, 28).

AHO'HITE (a-hō'hīt). A patronymic applied to Dodo, or Dodai, one of the captains under Solomon (1 Chron. 27:4). His son Eleazar was one of David's three chief warriors (2 Sam. 23:9; 1 Chron. 11:12); and Zalmon, or Ilai, was another bodyguard (2 Sam. 23:28; 1 Chron. 11:29); probably from their descent from *Ahoah* (which see).

AHO'LAH. See Oholah.

AHO'LIAB. See Oholiab.

AHOL'IBAH. See Oholibah.

AHOLIBA'MAH. See Oholibamah.

AHU'MAI (a-hū'mī; "brother of water"). The son of Jahath, a descendant of Judah, and of the family of the Zorathites (1 Chron. 4:2).

AHU'ZZAM (a-hū'zam; "their possession"). The first named of the four sons of Ashhur ("father of Tekoa") by one of his wives, Naarah; of the tribe of Judah (1 Chron. 4:6).

AHUZ'ZATH (a-hūz'zath; "possession"). One of the friends (perhaps "favorite") of the Philistine king Abimelech, who accompanied him on his visit to Isaac (Gen. 26:26), about 2040 B.C.

AH'ZAI (ah'zī; perhaps a prolonged form of Ahaz, "possessor," or contracted form of Ahaziah, "whom Jehovah holds"). A grandson of Immer and one whose descendants dwelt in Jerusalem after the return from Babylon (Neh. 11:13). Gesenius thinks he is the same with *Jahzerah* (which see), who is made the grandson of Immer (1 Chron. 9:12).

A'I (ā'ī; KJV Hai, "the Ruin"). A city near Bethel where Abraham sojourned upon his arrival in Canaan (Gen. 12:8) and which the conquering Israelites under Joshua are said to have destroyed (Josh. 7:2-5; 8:1-29). The site is commonly identified with Et-Tell, 1½ miles from Bethel and excavated in 1933-35 by Judith Marquet-Krause. The diggings revealed an occupational gap in the history of the mound from 2200 B.C. till after 1200 B.C., so that if Ai is represented by Et-Tell, there was nothing but a ruin there when Joshua and the Israelites are said to have destroyed it. Some critics, like Martin Noth, dismiss the biblical story as an etiological legend, which supposedly explains how the place came to be in ruins and to be called "Ruin," the meaning of Ai in Heb. (*Palaestina Jahrbuch* [1938]: 7-20). Others, such as W. F. Albright (*Bull. Am. Schs.* 74: 16ff.),

assume that the narrative of Josh. 8 originally referred to the destruction of Bethel in the thirteenth century B.C. but that the etiological interest in the ruins of Ai caused the story to be attached to this site instead of Bethel. But this explanation, besides being objectionable in reflecting upon the historicity of the biblical account, is extremely unlikely because the biblical narrative carefully distinguishes between the two cities (Josh. 8:12), and there is not the slightest evidence of any destruction of Bethel at this time (c. 1401 B.C.). More reasonable is the explanation of Hugues Vincent (*Revue Biblique* [1937]: 231-66) that the inhabitants of Ai had merely a military outpost at Ai of such modest proportions and temporary nature that it left no remains to give a clue of its existence to the archaeologist, although the narrative clearly indicates an inhabited city.

Remains of ancient walls at Et-Tell, ancient Ai

To deal with the continuing problem of Ai, Professor Joseph A. Callaway of Southern Baptist Theological Seminary, in cooperation with several other institutions, conducted five major archaeological expeditions at Et-Tell (1964, 1966, 1968, 1969, 1970) and two small digs (1971-72). Excavation revealed that the earliest village at the site dated to about 3100 B.C. This was rebuilt several times until its destruction and abandonment about 2200 B.C. A small village was built on the site about 1200 B.C. and lasted until the final abandonment of the place in about 1050 B.C. Callaway tended to assume that Et-Tell was Ai, but there is no solid evidence for the identification; scholars such as J. Simon have argued against the identification. D. Livingston (*Westminster Theological Journal* 33 [1970]: 20-44) suggested that the true site of Ai lay to the SE near a hill named Et-Tawil, but further work at the site is necessary to confirm this suggestion.

M.F.U.; H.F.V.

BIBLIOGRAPHY: W. F. Albright, *Annual of the American Schools of Oriental Research* 4 (1924): 141-49; id., *Bulletin of the American Schools of Oriental Research* 74 (1939): 11-23; J. A. Callaway, *Pottery from the Tombs at Ai (et Tell)* (1964); id., *BASOR* 178 (1965):

13-40; id., *BASOR* 183 (1966): 12-19: R. Amiran, *Israel Exploration Journal* 17 (1967): 185-86; J. A. Callaway, *Journal of Biblical Literature* 87 (1968): 312-20; id., *BASOR* 199 (1969): 2-16; id., *BASOR* 200 (1970): 7-31; id., *BASOR* 201 (1971): 9-19; F. M. Cross and D. N. Freedman, *BASOR* 201 (1971): 19-22; Y. Aharoni, *IEJ* 21 (1971): 130-35; J. A. Callaway, *Biblical Archaeologist* 39 (1976): 18-30; Z. Zevit, *Biblical Archaeologist Review* 11, no. 2 (1985): 58-69; J. A. Callaway, *BAR* 11, no. 2 (1985): 68-69.

AI'AH (ā-ī'āh; "a cry," often "hawk").
1. The first named of the two sons of Zibeon the Horite (Gen. 36:24; 1 Chron. 1:40), or rather Hivite (Gen. 36:2).
2. The father of Rizpah, Saul's concubine (2 Sam. 3:7; 21:8, 10-11), about 1053 B.C.

AI'ATH (ā-ī'āth; Isa. 10:28). Another form of the city *Ai* (which see).

AI'JA (ā-ī'ja; Neh. 11:31). Another form of *Ai* (which see).

AI'JALON (ā'ja-lon; "place of deer" or "gazelles").
1. A Levitical city of Dan (Josh. 19:42); a city of refuge (Josh. 21:24; 1 Sam. 14:31; 1 Chron. 6:69). It was with reference to the valley named after this town that Joshua said, "O sun, stand still at Gibeon, and O moon in the valley of Aijalon" (Josh. 10:12). Aijalon is the modern Yalo, fourteen miles from Jerusalem, N of the Jaffa road and mentioned as Aialuna in the Amarna Letters.
2. A city in the tribe of Zebulun (Judg. 12:12). Elon, the judge, was buried there. The modern site is uncertain.

BIBLIOGRAPHY: F.-M. Abel, *Géographie de la Palestine* (1938), 2:241; Y. Aharoni, *The Land of the Bible* (1967), pp. 311-55.

AI'JELETH HASHSHA'HAR. Occurs in the title of Ps. 22; it is probably the name of the tune to which the psalm was set.

A'IN (ā'in). Literally, an eye, and also, in the simple but vivid imagery of the East, a spring or natural burst of living water, always to be distinguished from the well or tank of artificial formation, which is designated by the words *Beer* and *Bor.* The term *Ain* most frequently occurs in combination with other words to form the names of definite localities, as Engedi, En-gannim, and so forth. It occurs alone in two cases:
1. One of the landmarks on the eastern boundary of Palestine, as described by Moses (Num. 34:11). It is probably 'Ain el-'Azy, the main source of the Orontes, a spring remarkable for its force and magnitude.
2. One of the southernmost cities of Judah (Josh. 15:32), afterward allotted to Simeon (Josh. 19:7; 1 Chron. 4:32) and given to the priests (Josh. 21:16). In the list of priests' cities in 1 Chron. 6:59 Ashan takes the place of Ain.

AIR (Gk. *aēr*, "the air," particularly the lower

and denser, as distinguished from the higher and rarer, *ho aithēr*, "ether"). The atmospheric region (Acts 22:23; 1 Thess. 4:17; Rev. 9:2; 16:17). In Eph. 2:2 "the prince of the power of the air" is the devil, the prince of the demons that fill the realm of the air. It is not to be considered as equivalent to *darkness* (Gk. *skotos*). "Beating the air" (1 Cor. 9:26) refers to boxers who miss their aim, and means "to contend in vain." "Speaking into the air" (1 Cor. 14:9, i.e., without effect) is used of those who speak what is not understood by their hearers.

A'JAH. Another form of *Aiah* (which see).

AJ'ALON. Another form of *Aijalon* (which see).

A'KAN (ā'kan; "twisted"). The last named of the three sons of Ezer, the son of Seir, the Horite (Gen. 36:27), called also (1 Chron. 1:42) Jaakan.

AKELDAMA. *See* Aceldama.

AKIM. *See* Achim.

AKKAD. *See* Accad.

AK'KUB (ak'kūb; "pursuer").
1. The fourth named of the seven sons of Elioenai, or Esli, a descendant of David (1 Chron. 3:24).
2. One of the Levitical gatekeepers of the Temple after the captivity (1 Chron. 9:17; Neh. 11:19; 12:25), 536 B.C. Perhaps the same who assisted Ezra in expounding the law to the people (8:7). His descendants appear to have succeeded to the office (Ezra 2:42).
3. The head of one of the families of Temple servants that returned from Babylon (Ezra 2:45), 536 B.C.

AKRAB'BIM (a-krab'bim; "scorpions"). A place, as the name suggests, which abounded in scorpions; it is located where the country ascends from the neighborhood of the southern end of the Dead Sea to the level of Palestine, and is called the ascent of Akrabbim (Num. 34:4).

AKRAB'BIM, ASCENT OF (a-krab'bim; "steep of scorpions," i.e., "scorpion hill"). A pass in the SE border of Palestine (Num. 34:4; Josh. 15:3). It is identified with the steep pass of es Sufah.

ALABASTER. *See* Mineral Kingdom.

AL'AMETH. Another form of *Alemeth* (which see).

ALAM'MELECH. Another form of *Allammelech* (which see).

AL'AMOTH (al'a'mōth). A musical term (1 Chron. 15:20; title of Ps. 46).

ALARM (Heb. *terû'â*, "a loud noise" or "shout"). The peculiar sound of the silver trumpet of the Hebrews, giving them signals while on their journey (Lev. 23:24; 25:9; Num. 10:5-6; 29:1). In times of peace, when the people or rulers were to be assembled together, the trumpet was blown softly. When the camps were to move forward, or the people march to war, it was sounded with a deeper note. A war note, or call to arms, or other public emergency (Jer. 4:19; 49:2).

AL'EMETH (al'e-meth; "covering").

1. The last named of the nine sons of Becher (Beker, NIV), the son of Benjamin (1 Chron. 7:8).

2. The first named of the sons of Jehoaddah, or Jarah, the son of Ahaz, of the posterity of Saul (1 Chron. 8:36; 9:42), about 1030 B.C.

A'LEPH (א) (ā'lef; "ox"). The first letter of the Heb. alphabet, corresponding to Gk. *alpha* (α), cf. English "a." But Heb. aleph is a consonant and has no representative in English. It is transliterated by the apostrophe ('). This letter heads Ps. 119, each of the first eight verses beginning with aleph in the Heb.

ALERT (Gk. *grēgoreō*, to "keep awake," to "watch"). To take care lest some destructive calamity suddenly overtake one (Matt. 24:42; 25:13; Mark 13:35; Rev. 16:15, "stay awake"), or lest one fall into sin (1 Cor. 16:13; 1 Thess. 5:6; 1 Pet. 5:8). To keep alert (Col. 4:2) is to employ to most punctilious care.

ALEXAN'DER (ăl-ĕx-ăn'dēr; "man-defender").

1. A man, whose father, Simon, a Cyrenian Jew, was compelled to bear the cross of Jesus (Mark 15:21).

2. A kinsman, probably of the high priest, and one of the chief men in Jerusalem, present at the examination of Peter and John before the Sanhedrin for the cure of the lame man (Acts 4:6), A.D. 30.

3. A Jew of Ephesus, known only from the part he took in the uproar about Artemis, which was raised there by the preaching of Paul (Acts 19:33), A.D. 58. He was probably put forward by the Jews to defend them from any connection with the Christians. His appeal to them for opportunity was in vain; an uproar followed for two hours.

4. A coppersmith or brazier, who, with Hymenaeus and others, apostatized (1 Tim. 1:20). It is not certain, but not at all improbable, that he is the same person as the one mentioned in 2 Tim. 4:14, who seems to have opposed and hindered Paul.

ALEXAN'DRIA. A celebrated city and seaport of Egypt situated on a narrow stretch of land between Lake Mareotis and the Mediterranean, fourteen miles from the Canopic mouth of the Nile. It was named for Alexander the Great, who founded it in 331 B.C. The long, narrow island of Pharos was formed into a breakwater to the port by joining the middle of the island to the mainland by means of a mole, seven stadia in length, and hence called the Hepta-stadium. Upon the island of Pharos the famous lighthouse, which

Alexander called after his friend Hephaestion, was constructed, but it was not finished until the reign of Ptolemy Philadelphus, 284-246 B.C.

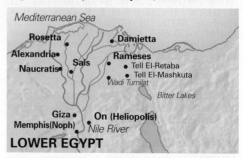

LOWER EGYPT

The most famous of all the public buildings planned by Ptolemy Soter were a library and museum, or college of philosophy, the professors of which were supported out of the public income. The library soon became the largest in the world, numbering over a half million volumes in the second century B.C.

Alexandria is not named in the OT and only incidentally in the NT (Acts 6:9; 18:24; 27:6; 28:11), and yet it is very important to the history of the Jews. There the Gk. translation of the OT called the Septuagint (LXX) was produced during the third and second centuries B.C. In the third century A.D. the city became an important center of Christianity as a result of the work of Clement and Origen. During the fourth century both the heretical leader Arius and the great orthodox theologian Athanasius came from Alexandria. It was also a great center for the production of copies of Scripture, and several early NT manuscripts evidently were produced there; e.g., Codex Alexandrinus (A).   H.F.V.

BIBLIOGRAPHY: V. Tcherikover, *Hellenistic Civilization and the Jews* (1961), pp. 320-28, 409-15; E. Badian, *Studies in Greek and Roman History* (1964), pp. 179-91.

ALEXAN'DRIAN. An inhabitant of Alexandria in Egypt, particularly a Jewish resident there (Acts 6:9; 18:24). The Jews, being highly valued as citizens, were encouraged to settle in the city and were admitted into the first of its three classes of citizens, having equal rights with the Greek inhabitants. In the reign of Tiberius (A.D. 16), the Jews in Alexandria numbered about one-third of the population. Nothwithstanding many persecutions and massacres, they continued to form a large proportion of the population and retained their civil rights until A.D. 415, when forty thousand of them were expelled at the instigation of Cyril, the Christian patriarch. They recovered their strength and appear to have been numerous at the time of the Muslim conquest.

ALGUM TREE, ALMUG TREE, ALGUMWOOD. *See* Vegetable Kingdom: Algum Tree.

ALI'AH (a-lī'ah). A less correct form of *Alvah*

(which see). The second named of the chiefs of Edom, descended from Esau (1 Chron. 1:51).

ALI'AN (a-lī'an). A less correct form of the name *Alvan* (which see). This person is the first named of the five sons of Shobal, a descendant of Seir (1 Chron. 1:40), about 1853 B.C.

ALIEN (Heb. *gēr,* lit., "stranger"; Gk. *allotrios,* "belonging to another," i.e., "foreign"). A foreigner, or person born in another country, and thus not entitled to the rights of citizenship in the country in which he lives (Deut. 14:21; Ps. 69:8). *See* Foreigner.

A LITTLE WAY. "Some distance," NASB. *See* Metrology: Linear Measures.

ALLAM'MELECH (a-lam'me-lek; "oak of [the] king"). A town in the territory of Asher (Josh. 19:26).

ALLEGORY (Gk. *allegoreō*). The term occurs only once (Gal. 4:24), "This is allegorically speaking," NASB; "these things are an allegory," KJV; "these things may be taken figuratively," NIV. "To allegorize" means to express or explain one thing under the image of another. "St. Paul is here declaring, under the influence of the Holy Spirit, that the passage he has cited has a second and deeper meaning than it appears to have: that it has that meaning, then, is a positive, objective, and indisputable truth" (Ellicott, *Com.*). To say that a history is allegorized is quite different from saying that it is allegory itself. "As Hagar bore children to bondage, so does the Sinaitic covenant produce sons under circumcisional bondage to the heavy ritual" (Whedon, *Com.*). Dean Trench says, "The allegory needs not, as the parable, an interpretation to be brought to it from without, since it contains its interpretation within itself." The real object of the allegory is to convey a moral truth. Every allegory is a kind of parable, containing a statement of a few simple facts followed by the explanation or allegorical interpretation (Luke 8:5-15). The allegories found in Scripture are its parabolical representation, such as, in the OT, Song of Sol., Pss. 45, 80, Isa. 5:1-7, and in the NT the parables of our Lord.

In early times there was an allegorical mode of interpreting the historical portions of the OT, which reached its climax in the writings and school of Origen. It assumed a double or threefold sense of the Scriptures, an obvious literal sense, and a hidden spiritual sense, both being intended by the author. Thus the book of Joshua has been treated as an allegory of the soul's victory over sin and self. The allegorical interpretation of the Bible arose among the Alexandrian Jews in their attempt to reconcile the Mosaic account with Greek philosophy. Thus the four rivers of paradise were seen as Plato's four cardinal virtues, and Adam as the lower, sensuous man, and so forth. The early Christian church received al-

legorical interpretation also from the Jews of Alexandria, wishing to reconcile Christianity with Greek thought. Origen taught a threefold sense of Scripture, corresponding to man's body, soul, and spirit. As we come to the Middle Ages, four senses were found in Scripture: historical, allegorical, moral, and anagogical; e.g., Jerusalem is, *literally,* a city of Palestine; *allegorically,* the church; *morally,* the believing soul; *anagogically,* the heavenly Jerusalem.

Swedenborg held that "all and every part of Scripture, even the most minute, not excepting the smallest jot or tittle, signify and involve spiritual and celestial things" (*Arcana Coelestia.* 2). This mode of interpreting Scripture is fascinating and yet dangerous, because there is a temptation to read into the word one's imaginings and not to be content with its plain and simple teachings.

BIBLIOGRAPHY: R. M. Grant, *A Short History of the Interpretation of the Bible* (1948); J. F. Walvoord, ed., *Inspiration and Interpretation* (1957); R. P. C. Hanson, *Allegory and Event* (1959); F. W. Farrar, *History of Interpretation* (1961).

ALLELUIA. A Gk. form of *Hallelujah* (which see).

ALLIANCE. The political or social relations formed between nations by treaty. In Scripture such compacts are known as leagues, covenants, treaties, and so forth. In this article we treat them only as related to the Israelites.

Pre-Mosaic. The patriarchs entered into international relations with the peoples of Canaan for their subsistence in the land of promise, not yet given in actual possession. Abraham was allied with some of the Canaanite princes (Gen. 14:13), and he also entered into an alliance with Abimelech the Philistine king (21:22-24, 32), which was renewed by his son (26:27).

Mosaic. Israel, as the covenant people of Jehovah, was to hold itself aloof from heathen influences and idolaters; and, therefore, when they settled in Palestine, alliance with such nations was strongly prohibited (Lev. 18:3-4; 20:23-24). The Israelites' country and occupation protected them from mixing with peoples that would have endangered their nationality and mission. But it was by no means intended that they should live without any dealings with other nations; rather they were to cultivate friendly relations with them and seek their good. The Mosaic legislation taught Israel to love and respect strangers (Ex. 22:21; 23:9; Lev. 19:33-34; Deut. 10:18-19). The law commanded Israel to root out the nations of Canaan because of their abominations and to make no covenant with them (Ex. 23:32-33; 34:12-16; Deut. 7:1-4); also the Amalekites were to be destroyed (Ex. 17:14, 16; Deut. 25:17-19) because of their cruel attack upon the Israelites. Yet it forbade them to make war upon the other peoples, the Edomites, Ammonites, and Moabites, or to conquer their land (Deut. 2:4-5, 9, 19).

The law, therefore, was not opposed to Israel's forming friendly and peaceful relations with other peoples, nor was it opposed to Israel's maintaining peace with them by covenants and treaties.

In Later Times. When the commonwealth of Israel was fully established in Canaan, formal alliances sprang up between it and other nations. Thus David entered into friendly relations with Hiram, king of Tyre (2 Sam. 5:11), and with King Hanun, the Ammonite (10:2); and Solomon made a treaty with Hiram to furnish materials and workmen for the Temple (1 Kings 5:2). In neither case was their theocratic standing falsified or endangered. Solomon also entered into treaty relations with a pharaoh, by which he secured the monopoly of trade in horses and other products (10:28-29). We find Asa, when at war with Baasha, king of Israel, sending an embassy to Ben-hadad, king of Syria, reminding him of a league existing between Israel and Judah (2 Chron. 16:2-3), which ceased in Jehu's reign. When Pekah, king of Israel, with Rezin, king of Syria, laid siege to Jerusalem, Ahaz formed a league with Tiglath-pileser, king of Assyria (2 Kings 16:5-10). Later we find the kings of Judah alternately allying themselves with Egypt and Assyria, according as the one or other of these powers was most likely to aid them.

The prophets, however, rightly denounced the treaties by which Israel, distrusting the help of its God, sought to find support from the invasion of nations by allowing themselves to become entangled in idolatrous practices and licentious habits (Ezek. 16:20-43; Hos. 5).

Respecting the rites by which treaties were ratified, *see* Covenants.

BIBLIOGRAPHY: D. J. M. McCarthy, *Analecta Biblica* 21a (1978): 368.

AL'LON (al'lon; "an oak").

1. The expression in the KJV of Josh. 19:33, "from Allon to Zaanannim," is more correctly rendered in the NASB, "from the oak in Zaanannim" (cf. NIV, "the large tree"), which served as a landmark.

2. The son of Jedaiah and father of Shiphi, a chief Simeonite, of the family of those who expelled the Hamites from the valley of Gedor (1 Chron. 4:37).

AL'LON-BAC'UTH (al'lon-bak'ūth; "oak of weeping"). A landmark consisting of a tree marking the spot where Deborah, Rebekah's nurse, was buried (Gen. 35:8).

ALMIGHTY. The word used in the OT as the translation of the Heb. *shadday*, "mighty," as, "I am God Almighty" (Gen. 17:1). In the NT it is the word for the Gk. *pantokratōr*, "all-powerful."

ALMO'DAD (al-mō'dad). The son of Joktan, of the family of Shem (Gen. 10-26; 1 Chron. 1:20).

He is said to have been the founder of an Arabian tribe, the locality of which is unknown.

AL'MON (al'mōn; "hidden"). The last named of the four priestly cities of Benjamin (Josh. 21:18; Allemeth, 1 Chron. 6:60). It is identified with the mound of Khirbet 'Almit between Geba and Anathoth.

ALMOND. *See* Vegetable Kingdom.

ALMOND BLOSSOMS (Heb. *shāqad*, "the awakening one," probably from its early blossoming). Cups "shaped like almond blossoms" or flowers are referred to in the NASB and NIV of Ex. 25:33-34; 37:19-20 in connection with the design of the golden lampstand in the Tabernacle. The KJV renders "almond." *See* Tabernacle of Israel.

For the almond as a plant, *see* Vegetable Kingdom.

AL'MON-DIBLATHA'IM (al'mon-dib-lā-tha'-im). The fifty-first station of the Israelites in the wilderness E of the Dead Sea (Num. 33:46-47). Perhaps the same with Beth-diblathaim (Jer. 48:22) and Diblah (Ezek 6:14). Identified with Deleilat el-Gharbiyeh, a town commanding three roads, 2½ miles NE of Libb.

ALMS, ALMSDEEDS (Gk. *eleēmosunē*, "beneficence," or "benefaction" itself). In Heb. *ṣedāqâ*, "righteousness," is the usual equivalent for *alms* (Ps. 24:5; Prov. 10:2; 11:4; Mic. 6:5). The word *alms* is not found in the OT but is met with frequently in the Apocrypha. The great antiquity of almsgiving is shown in Job 29:13-17.

Jewish Almsgiving. The general distribution of property in Israel, and the precautions taken to prevent the alienation of inheritances on the one hand, as well as the undue accumulation of wealth on the other, with the promised blessing of Jehovah in case of obedience, tended to make extreme poverty rare. Still there would arise cases of need. Moses imposed for all time the obligation "Therefore I command you, saying, 'You shall freely open your hand to your brother, to your needy and poor in your land' " (Deut. 15:11). Specific provisions were made for the regular distribution of alms on a large scale among the poorer members of the commonwealth—the Sabbatical year—"so that the needy of your people may eat" (Ex. 23:11); the gleanings of field and fruit and the forgotten sheaf (Lev. 23:22; Deut. 24:19-22); the tithings laid up in store every third year for the Levite, the stranger, the fatherless, and the widow (Deut. 14:28-29); the freeing at Jubilee of the poor (Lev. 25:39-54); the law giving the poor the right to enter a field or vineyard and satisfy hunger (Deut. 23:24-25); interest forbidden on loans to the poor (Ex. 22:25; Lev. 25:35-36); the command to entertain at the annual festivals the Levite, stranger, orphan, and poor (Deut. 16:11-14). It is only as we remember these laws that we can understand the expression *righteousness,* which the OT uses to express the idea of charity (Deut. 24:13; Prov. 10:2; 11:4). Literally meaning "right" or "acts of right," or "justice," *ṣᵉdāqâ* came to mean "charity," because according to the Mosaic law the poor had an inalienable right to certain produce of the soil. Hence it does not exactly correspond to our term *alms* but occupies a midway position between deeds of right and love.

Naturally, almsgiving came to be considered a virtue (Ezek. 18:7, 9; Prov. 19:17), and a violation of the statutes regarding it a heinous sin (Isa. 58:6-7). Among the later Jews poverty became quite prevalent, owing to foreign dominion and the oppression of wealthy Israelites. The Mosaic statutes were changed to meet the increasing claims upon the charity and benevolence of the community. Two collections were ordered: (1) a daily collection of food (Heb. *tamhû,* "alms for the dish") distributed every morning and (2) a weekly collection of money (*quppâ,* "alms for the box") distributed weekly. There was also a chamber in the Temple where alms were deposited for the poor of good families who did not wish to receive charity openly.

Almsgiving came to be associated with merit and was looked upon as a means of conciliating God's favor and warding off evil (Dan. 4:27). It was among the essential virtues of the godly (Isa. 58:4-7; Ezek. 18:7, 9; Amos 2:6-7). To be reduced to soliciting alms was regarded as a curse from God, and Judaism gave no encouragement to begging as a sacred calling.

Christian. Almsgiving was noticed by Jesus in His warning against following the example of those who gave "to be noticed by" men. He urged His followers to give without ostentation, looking to God alone for reward (Matt. 6:1-4). The Christian spirit of caring for the needy is forcibly expressed (1 John 3:17). Christianity does not encourage indolence and consequent poverty (2 Thess. 3:10), and yet it is emphatic in insisting upon the general duty of ministering to those in distress (Luke 3:11; 6:30; 12:33; Acts 9:36; 10:2, 4). The disposition of the giver is of more account than the amount of the gift (Mark 12:41-44; 2 Cor. 8:12; *see also* Acts 11:29; Rom. 12:13; Eph. 4:28; 1 Tim. 6:18; Heb. 13:16).

BIBLIOGRAPHY: R. deVaux, *Ancient Israel: Its Life and Institutions* (1961), pp. 72-76, 514ff.; J. Lawson, *Theological and Historical Introduction, to the Apostolic Fathers* (1961); R. Bultmann, ελεημοσυνη, *Theological Dictionary of the New Testament* (1964), 2:77-487; D. Seccombe, *Journal of Theological Studies* 29 (1978): 140-43.

ALMUG TREE, ALMUGWOOD. *See* Vegetable Kingdom: Algum Tree.

ALOE, ALOES. *See* Vegetable Kingdom.

A'LOTH. *See* Bealoth.

AL'PHA AND O'MEGA (A, Ω) (Gk. *alpha, ōmega*). The first and last letters of the Gk. alphabet, used to express the eternity of God (Rev. 1:8; 21:6; 22:13; *see also* Isa. 44:6).

The early Christians frequently placed the letters A, *alpha,* and Ω, *omega,* on either side of the cruciform monogram, formed from the letters X, *chi,* and P, *rho,* the first two letters of the name Christ, in Gk. ΧΡΙΣΤΟΣ.

ALPHAE'US (al-fē'us).
1. The putative father of James the Less (Matt. 10:3; Mark 3:18; Luke 6:15; Acts 1:13) and husband of that Mary who, with the mother of Jesus and others, was standing by the cross during the crucifixion (John 19:25). By comparing John 19:25 with Luke 24:18 and Matt. 10:3, it appears that Alphaeus is the Gk., and Cleopas or Clopas, the Heb. or Syr., name of the same person.
2. In the KJV and NIV, the father of the evangelist Levi, or Matthew (Mark 2:14). Rendered Alpheus in the NASB.

ALPHE'US (al-fē'us). The father of the evangelist Levi, or Matthew (Mark 2:14).

ALTAR (from Lat. *altus,* "high"; *ara,* "elevation"; Heb. *mizbēaḥ;* Gk. *thusiastērion,* "place of sacrifice").
Early. The altar was originally a simple elevation made of earth, rough stones, or turf. The altars for constant use, especially in temple service, were generally of stone, though they might be of other materials. Thus, in Greece, several were built of the ashes of burnt offerings, as that of Zeus at Olympia; and one at Delos made of goats' horns. The probability is that some of the ancient monuments of unhewn stones, usually thought to be Druidical remains, were derived from altars of primitive times, as *cromlechs,* in the form of a table, one large stone being supported in a horizontal position upon other stones.

Another form of altar was a heap of small stones with a large, flat stone placed upon its top. Many of these *cairns* still remain. In some instances, as at Stonehenge, a circle of stones encloses a central one, somewhat similar in construction to those found in Persia. Two pictures discovered at Herculaneum represent sacred Egyptian ceremonies, probably in honor of Isis. The altars in these pictures have at each corner a rising, which continues square to about one-half its height, gradually sloping off to an edge or point. These are, no doubt, the "horns" of the altar (Ex. 27:2).

Heathen altars generally faced the E, standing one behind the other, and so placed that the images of the gods appeared behind them. Upon them were carved the name of the deity or some appropriate symbols. They were of two kinds, higher and lower: the higher for the celestial gods, and called by the Romans *altaria;* the lower

Israelite altar, after repairs, showing its four horns

for terrestrial deities, and called *arae*. There was a third kind of altar, *anclabris*, or *enclabris*, a sort of table on which the sacrificial utensils were placed and the entrails of victims laid. The *mensa sacra* was a table on which incense was sometimes presented and offerings not intended to be burned. Some altars, as well as temples, were dedicated to more than one god; we even read of some being dedicated to all the gods.

Hebrew. The first altar on record is the one built by Noah after leaving the ark (Gen. 8:20). Mention is made of altars erected by Abraham (12:7; 13:4; 22:9), by Isaac (26:25), by Jacob (33:20; 35:1, 3), and by Moses (Ex. 17:15; 20:24-26). In the Tabernacle and Temple two altars were erected, the one for sacrifices and the other for incense.

The Altar of Burnt Offering (Heb. *mizbah hā'ōlâ*, Ex. 30:28; "bronze altar," *mizbah hannᵉhōshet*, Ex. 39:39; "table of the Lord," Mal. 1:7, 12). This altar differed in construction, etc., at different times.

In the Tabernacle (Ex. 27:1-8). Here the altar was a hollow square, five cubits in length and breadth and three cubits high, and was made of acacia wood overlaid with bronze (probably copper). The corners terminated in *horns* (which see). The altar had a grating, which projected through openings on two sides, and had four rings fastened to it for the poles with which the altar was carried. These poles were made of the same materials as the altar. The priests were forbidden to go up to the altar by steps (20:26); the earth was probably raised about the altar to enable them to serve easily.

The utensils for the altar (Ex. 27:3), made of bronze (copper), were *ash pans; shovels,* for cleaning the altar; *basins,* for receiving the blood to be sprinkled on the altar; *flesh hooks,* i.e., large *forks,* to handle the pieces of flesh; *fire pans* (38:3), *snuffers* (25:38). According to Lev. 6:13, the fire on this altar was never to be allowed to go out.

In Solomon's Temple. In adapting the instru-

ments of worship to the larger proportions of the Temple, the altar of burnt offering was, naturally, increased in size. It became now a square of twenty cubits, with a height of ten cubits (2 Chron. 4:1), made of bronze (copper). This is the altar that was restored by Asa (15:8), removed by Ahaz, probably to make room for the one erected after a model seen by him in Damascus (2 Kings 16:14); "cleansed" by Hezekiah (2 Chron. 29:18); and rebuilt by Manasseh (33:16).

In the Second Temple. This altar was erected before the Temple (Ezra 3:3, 6), and on the place occupied by the former (Josephus *Ant.* 11.4.1). It was probably made of unhewn stone (Ex. 20:25), for in the account of the Temple service by Judas Maccabaeus it is said, "They took whole stones according to the law, and built a new altar according to the former" (1 Macc. 4:47).

In Herod's Temple. According to Josephus, this altar was a square whose sides were fifty cubits each, with a height of fifteen cubits. It had corners like horns, "and the passage up to it was by [a gradual rise from the south]. It was formed without any iron tool, nor did any iron tool so much as touch it at any time" (*Wars* 5.5.6). According to the Mishna, it was a square thirty-two cubits at the base, and decreasing at intervals until it was twenty-four cubits. The Mishna states, according to Josephus, that the stones were unhewn, and whitewashed every year at the Passover and the feast of Tabernacles. A pipe connected with the SW horn conveyed the blood of victims by a subterranean passage to the Kidron.

Altar of Incense (Heb. *mizbēah miqṭar qᵉṭōret,* "altar of incensing of incense," cf. Ex. 30:1; called also the "golden altar," *mizbah hazzāhāb,* cf. Ex. 39:38; Num. 4:11).

Replica of the Altar of Incense

In the Tabernacle. This would seem to be the "altar . . . of wood," further described as "the table that is before the Lord" (Ezek. 41:22). It was made of acacia wood overlaid with gold, and was one cubit square, with a height of two cubits having horns of the same materials (Lev. 4:7). Running around the sides near the top was a border of gold, beneath which were rings for the staves of acacia wood covered with gold, "with which to carry it" (Ex. 30:1-5). Its place was in front of the veil, midway between the walls (Lev. 16:12; Ex. 30:6). In Ex. 40:5 Moses was commanded to place this altar "before the ark of the testimony," and in Heb. 9:4 it is enumerated among the articles within the second veil, i.e., in the Holy of Holies. The meaning, probably, is that the great typical and symbolical importance of this altar associated it with the Holy of Holies.

In Solomon's Temple. In the Temple Solomon built this altar was similar but made of cedar (1 Kings 6:20; 7:48; 1 Chron. 28:18). Upon this altar incense was burned every morning and evening (Ex. 30:7-8), and the blood of atonement was sprinkled upon it (v. 10). Being placed immediately before the throne of Jehovah (Ark of the Covenant), it was the symbol of believing and acceptable prayer.

This is the only altar that appears in the heavenly Temple (Isa. 6:6; Rev. 8:3). It was the altar at which Zacharias was ministering when the angel appeared to him (Luke 1:11).

Other Altars. Mention is made in Isa. 65:3 of "burning incense on bricks," which may have reference to a Babylonian custom of burning incense on bricks covered with magical formulas or cuneiform inscriptions. An Assyrian-Damascene altar erected by Ahaz from a model seen by him in Damascus is referred to in 2 Kings 16:10-13. In Acts 17:23 Paul observes that he has "found an altar [dedicated] 'TO AN UNKNOWN GOD.'" Reliable authorities assure us that there were several altars in Athens with this inscription. Meyer (*Com.*, ad loc.) says, with reference to the meaning of this inscription, "On important occasions, when the reference to a god known by name was wanting, as in public calamities of which no definite god could be assigned as the author, in order to honor or propitiate the god concerned by sacrifice, without lighting on a wrong one, altars were erected which destined and designated the unknown god."

Typology of the Hebrew Altars. The altar of burnt offering (bronze altar) is commonly thought to be a type of the cross upon which Christ, our whole burnt offering (Lev. 1:1-17), offered Himself without blemish unto God (Heb. 9:14), the brass speaking of divine judgment as in the bronze serpent (Num. 21:9; John 3:14; 12:31-33). The altar of incense is a type of Christ our Intercessor (John 17:1-16; Heb. 7:25), through whom our prayers and praises ascend to God (Heb. 13:15; Rev. 8:3-4) and, in turn, pic-

tures the believer-priest's sacrifice of praise and worship (Heb. 13:15).

BIBLIOGRAPHY: R. deVaux, *Ancient Israel: Its Life and Institutions* (1961), pp. 406-14; N. H. Snaith, *Vetus Testamentum* 28 (1978): 330-35; Y. Yadin, *Bulletin of the American Schools of Oriental Research* 222 (1976): 5-17.

AL-TAS'CHITH. See Al-tashheth.

AL-TASH'HETH (al-tash'heth). A term found in the titles of Pss. 57, 58, 59, 75.

A'LUSH (a'lūsh). The place of encampment of Israel in the desert, next to Rephidim, where there was no water (Num. 33:13-14).

AL'VAH (al'vā). The second named of the Edomite chieftains descended from Esau (Gen. 36:40). The name is translated Aliah in some versions of 1 Chron. 1:51.

AL'VAN (al'vān; "tall"). The first named of the five sons of Shobal, the Horite, of Mt. Seir (Gen. 36:23); called also Alian in some versions (1 Chron. 1:40).

A'MAD (ā'mad; "station" [?]). A town near the border of Asher (Josh. 19:26); not identified.

A'MAL (ā'mal; "toil"). The last named of the four sons of Helem, of the tribe of Asher (1 Chron. 7:35).

AM'ALEK (am'a-lek). The son of Eliphaz (the firstborn of Esau) by his concubine, Timna (Gen. 36:12; 1 Chron. 1:36), and chieftain of an Edomite tribe (Gen. 36:16). This tribe was probably not the same as the Amalekites so often mentioned in Scriptures, for Moses speaks of the Amalekites long before this Amalek was born (Gen. 14:7). See Amalekites.

AM'ALEKITES (am'a-lek-īts; also "Amalek, Amalekite"). An ancient race whose history is thus summed up by Balaam (Num. 24:20): "Amalek was the first of the nations, but his end shall be destruction." Although this people is prominent in the OT, archaeology has as yet revealed nothing concerning them.

In Abraham's time we find the Amalekites SW of the Dead Sea (Gen. 14:7). In the time of Moses they occupied all the desert of *et Tih* to the borders of Egypt, and most of the Sinaitic peninsula, with the S country of Palestine. There was also a "hill country of the Amalekites" in Ephraim (Judg. 12:15). Two routes lay through the land of Amalek, one by the Isthmus of Suez to Egypt, the other by the Aelanitic arm of the Red Sea (i.e., the Gulf of Akabah). It has been thought that the expedition noted in Gen. 14 may have been connected with the opening of the latter route.

According to the view that we have taken, Amalek, the "son" of Esau (Gen. 36:12, 16) may have been progenitor of a tribe that was merged with the original Amalekites so as to form part of the great Amalekite race, or he may have taken his name from some connection with the Amalekites, possible as Scipio won his name Africanus, or it may have been a mere coincidence. Historical accounts of Amalekites in southern Arabia will then refer to a time subsequent to their dispossession by the Israelites.

Some have supposed that all the Amalekites were descended from Amalek, "son" of Esau. In that case the language of Gen. 14:7 would mean what was "all the country of the Amalekites."

The Amalekites were always bitter foes of Israel, sometimes alone, sometimes in conjunction with other tribes. Their first attack was made in time of distress at Rephidim. They were doomed to utter destruction; but though they suffered heavily, especially at the hands of Saul and David, the sentence was so imperfectly executed that there was a remnant to be smitten in the days of Hezekiah (1 Chron. 4:43). This is their last appearance in Bible history. In the Sinaitic peninsula are massive stone buildings averaging seven feet high by eight feet diameter inside, which may perhaps be remains of the Amalekites.

BIBLIOGRAPHY: G. A. Smith, *The Historical Geography of the Holy Land* (1896), p. 282; D. Baly, *The Geography of the Bible* (1957), p. 159; D. J. Wiseman, ed., *Peoples of Old Testament Times* (1973), pp. 125, 232.

A'MAM (a'mam). A city in the S of Judah (Josh. 15:26), probably in the tract afterward assigned to Simeon (19:1-9).

AMA'NA (ā-man'a; "fixed"). A mountain (Song of Sol. 4:8), part of Anti-Libanus, from which the waters of Abana flow.

AMA'NAH (a-mā'na; "constant"). In the NASB of 2 Kings 5:12, the marg. reading of *Abanah* (which see). The KJV and NIV render Abana.

AMARANTHINE (Gk. *amarantinos*, "unfading"). The original of KJV "that fadeth not away" (1 Pet. 5:4; cf. 1:4, Gk. *amarantos*), and "meaning *composed of amaranth,* a flower so called because it never withers or fades, and when plucked off revives if moistened with water; hence it is a symbol of perpetuity and immortality."

AMARI'AH (am-a-rī'a; "said [i.e, promised] by Jehovah").

1. A person mentioned in 1 Chron. 6:7, 52, in the list of the descendants of Aaron by his eldest son, Eleazar, as the son of Meraioth and father of Ahitub, 1440 B.C. There is no means of determining whether Amariah was ever high priest, but it is probable that he was the last of the high priests of Eleazar's line prior to its transfer to the line of Ithamar in the person of *Eli* (which see). Josephus calls him Arophaeus and says he lived in private, the pontificate being at the time in the family of Ithamar.

2. A high priest at a later date (probably 740 B.C.), son of another Azariah and father of another Ahitub (1 Chron. 6:11; Ezra 7:3).

3. A Levite, second son of Hebron and grandson of Kohath and of the lineage of Moses (1 Chron. 23:19; 24:23).

4. A chief priest active in the reforms instituted by King Jehoshaphat (2 Chron. 19:11), 873-849 B.C.

5. One of the Levites appointed by Hezekiah to superintend the distribution of the Temple dues among the sacerdotal cities (2 Chron. 31:15), 726 B.C.

6. A Jew, son of Bani, who divorced his Gentile wife, whom he had married after the return from Babylon (Ezra 10:42), 456 B.C.

7. One of the priests who returned from Babylon with Zerubbabel (Neh. 11:4), 536 B.C.; and probably the same person who years after (445 B.C.) sealed the covenant with Nehemiah (10:3). He appears to have been identical with the chief priest, the father of Jehohanan (12:13).

8. The son of Shephatiah and father of Zechariah. His descendant Athaiah was one of the Judahite residents in Jerusalem after the captivity (Neh. 11:4), 445 B.C.

9. The great-grandfather of the prophet Zephaniah (Zeph. 1:1).

AMARNA, EL- ("city of the horizon"). The modern name of ancient Akhetaton, the capital city of Amenhotep IV (Akhnaton), who reigned c. 1387-1366 B.C. At this place, located some 190 miles S of present-day Cairo, a peasant woman in 1887 accidentally discovered some three hundred clay tablets in Akkadian cuneiform, the *lingua franca* of the fifteenth and fourteenth centuries B.C. These constituted the diplomatic correspondence of petty Canaanite princelings with their Egyptian overlords Amenophis III and Amenophis IV (Akhnaton) in the first half of the fourteenth century B.C. Although many difficulties of interpretation remain, this earliest known international diplomatic correspondence seems to portray the general situation in Palestine during the Israelite invasion under Joshua. This is to be expected if the early date of the Exodus (c. 1440) and of the conquest (c. 1440) is accepted; moreover, the evidence in the letters of a large number of city-states owing allegiance to Egypt and yet free to form alliances to deal with local problems tallies with indications in the Joshua narrative. The Habiru, who appear prominently in the letters of Abdi-Hiba, governor of Jerusalem, to Akhnaton asking for Egyptian troops to stem off these invaders, were once thought to have been the invading Hebrews under Joshua. The linguistic equation making *Habiru* equal to *Hebrew* is no longer accepted by scholars.   R.K.H,; H.F.V.

BIBLIOGRAPHY: J. Blaikie, *The Amarna Age* (1926); H. Frankfort, *The City of Akhenaten* (1933); W. C. Hayes, *The Scepter of Egypt* (1959), 2:280-325; W. F. Albright, *Yahweh and the Gods of Canaan* (1968), pp. 73-91; P. Artzi, *Orientalia* 36 (1967): 432; C. F. Pfeiffer, *Tell el Amarna and the Bible* (1963); R. Silverberg, *The Rebel*

Amarna papyrus

AM'ASA (am'a-sa; "burden").

1. The son of Abigail, a sister of King David, by Jether, or *Jithra* (which see), an Ishmaelite (2 Sam. 17:25; 1 Kings 2:5, 32; 1 Chron. 2:17). His paternity probably led David to neglect him in comparison with the more honored sons of David's other sister, Zeruiah. He joined Absalom in his rebellion and was appointed by him commander in chief in the place of Joab, by whom he was totally defeated in the forest of Ephraim (2 Sam. 18:6-7). Afterward David gave him command of his army in place of Joab, who had incurred displeasure by his overbearing conduct and his slaying of Absalom (19:13), after 1000 B.C. On the breaking out of Sheba's rebellion, Amasa was so tardy in his movements (probably from the reluctance of the troops to follow him) that David dispatched Abishai with the household troops in pursuit of Sheba, and Joab joined his brother as a volunteer. Amasa overtook them at the great stone of Gibeon, and Joab, while in the act of saluting him, struck and killed him with his sword, thus ridding himself of a dangerous rival. Joab continued the pursuit of Sheba and, by his popularity with the army, prevented David from removing him from command or calling him to account for his bloody deed (2 Sam. 20:4-13). Whether Amasa be identical with the Amasai who is mentioned among David's commanders (1 Chron. 12:18) is uncertain.

2. A son of Hadlai and chief of Ephraim, who with others vehemently and successfully resisted the retention as prisoners the persons whom Pekah, king of Israel, had taken captive in a campaign against Ahaz, king of Judah (2 Chron. 28:12), about 735 B.C.

AMAS'AI (a-mas'ā-ī; "burden bearer").

1. A Levite, son of Elkanah, and father of Mahath, of the ancestry of Samuel (1 Chron. 6:25, 35).

2. One of the chief captains of Judah who, with a considerable body of men from Judah and Benjamin, joined David while an outlaw at Ziklag. He, with others, was made captain of David's band (1 Chron. 12:18), about 1015 B.C. This is the Amasai who is supposed by some to be identical with Amasa.

3. One of the priests appointed to precede the Ark with blowing of trumpets on its removal from

the house of Obed-edom to Jerusalem (1 Chron. 15:24).

4. Another Levite, and father of the Mahath who assisted Hezekiah in restoring the worship of God and was active in cleansing the Temple (2 Chron. 29:12), 726 B.C.

AMASH'AI. *See* Amashsai.

AMASH'SAI (a-mash'sā-ī; probably an incorrect form of the name *Amasai*). The son of Azarel, and one of the priests appointed by Nehemiah to reside at Jerusalem and do the work of the Temple (Neh. 11:13), 445 B.C.

AMASI'AH (am-a-sī'ā; "burden of Jehovah"). The son of Zichri, a chieftain of Judah, who volunteered to assist King Jehoshaphat in his religious reform, with 200,000 chosen troops (2 Chron. 17:16), 872 B.C.

AMAZI'AH (am-a-zī'ā; "Jehovah is mighty").

1. The son and successor of Jehoash, or Joash, and the ninth ruler of Judah. He ascended the throne at the age of twenty-five and reigned twenty-nine years (2 Kings, 14:1-2; 2 Chron. 25:1), 796-767 B.C. He began his reign by killing the persons who had murdered his father but spared their children according to the Mosaic injunction (Deut. 24:16). In the twelfth year of his reign he prepared a great expedition for the recovery of Edom, which had revolted from Jehoram. He raised a large army (300,000) of his own and increased it by hiring 100,000 Israelites, the first example of a mercenary army that occurs in the history of the Jews. At the command of the prophet he dismissed these mercenaries, who returned in anger and sacked several of the cities of Judah. The obedience of Amaziah was rewarded by a great victory over the Edomites, ten thousand of whom were slain in battle and ten thousand more dashed to pieces from the rocks of Sela, which Amaziah took and called Joktheel. Among the spoil that he took were the idols of Mt. Seir, in the worship of which Amaziah allowed himself to be engaged. Then began his disasters. A prophet was sent to reprove him, and he resented his faithful admonition. The prophet then foretold his downfall. Urged by arrogance or provoked by the conduct of the disbanded mercenaries, he sent a challenge to the king of Israel to meet him in battle. The king returned him a scornful reply through a parable and advised him to remain at home. Amaziah, still belligerent, was met by Jehoash and by him defeated, taken prisoner, and brought to Jerusalem, his own metropolis. The N city wall was broken down, the Temple and palace despoiled, and hostages taken. Amaziah was allowed to remain on the throne and survived about fifteen years, when a conspiracy was formed against him and he was slain at Lachish. His body was brought "on horses" to Jerusalem and buried in the royal sepulcher (2 Kings 14:1-20; 2 Chron. 25:2-28).

2. The father of Joshah, one of the Simeonite chiefs who expelled the Amalekites from the valley of Gedor in the time of Hezekiah (1 Chron. 4:34), after 726 B.C.

3. The son of Hilkiah and father of Hashabiah, a Levite of the ancestry of Ethan, a singer of the Temple (1 Chron. 6:45), considerably before 1000 B.C.

4. The priest of the golden calves at Bethel in the time of Jeroboam II, c. 793-753 B.C. He complained to the king of Amos's prophecies of coming evil and urged the prophet to withdraw into the kingdom of Judah and prophesy there. Amos in reply told him of the severe degradation his family should undergo in the approaching captivity of the Northern Kingdom (Amos 7:10-17), c. 770 B.C.

AMBASSADOR (Heb. *ṣîr,* one who goes on an "errand"; *lûṣ,* "interpreter"; *mal'āk,* "messenger"). The isolated position of ancient Israel rendered comparatively unnecessary the employment of ambassadors, although examples are afforded of the employment of such functionaries. They do not seem to have known of "ministers resident" at a foreign court, all the embassies of which we read being "extraordinary." David sent ambassadors to Hanun, king of the Ammonites, to congratulate him upon his accession to the throne (2 Sam. 10:2), and Hiram sent them to Solomon for a like purpose (1 Kings 5:1). Toi, king of Hamath, sent his son Joram to David "to greet him and bless him" after his victory over Hadadezer (2 Sam. 8:10). Ambassadors were also sent to protest against a wrong (Judg. 11:12), to solicit favors (Num. 20:14), and to contract aliances (Josh. 9:3-6).

Ambassadors were not considered as representing the *person* of the sovereign according to present thought, but rather as distinguished and privileged messengers, and their dignity was rather that of heralds (2 Sam. 10:1-5). More frequent mention is made of them after Israel came to have relations with Syria, Babylon, etc. They were usually men of high rank. The word occurs once in the NT (2 Cor. 5:20, Gk. *presbeuō,* to be a "senior").

AMBER. *See* article Glowing Metal.

AMBUSH (Heb. *'ārab,* to "lie in wait"). A lying in wait and concealment to attack by surprise. Joshua, at the capture of Ai, shows himself to have been skilled in this method of warfare (Josh. 8). The attempt on the part of Abimelech to surprise Shechem (Judg. 9:30-35) appears to have been unskillful.

AMEN (Heb. *'āmēn;* Gk. *amēn,* "true, faithful"). A word used to affirm and confirm a statement. Strictly an adjective, meaning *firm,* metaphorically *faithful,* it came to be used as an adverb by which something is asserted or confirmed. Used at the beginning of a sentence, it emphasizes

what is about to be said. It is frequently so employed by our Lord and is translated "truly." It is often used to confirm the words of another and adds the wish for success to another's vows and predictions. "The repetition of the word employed by John alone in his gospel (twenty-five times) has the force of a superlative, *most assuredly"* (Grimm, *Gk. Lex.,* s.v.).

Among the Jews the liturgical use of the word is illustrated by the response of the woman in the trial by the water of jealousy (Num. 5:22), by that of the people at Mt. Ebal (Deut. 27:15-26; cf. Neh 5:13; see also 1 Chron. 16:36). It was a custom, which passed over from the synagogues into the Christian assemblies, that when he who had read or discoursed had offered up a solemn prayer to God the others in attendance responded *Amen,* and thus made the substance of what was uttered their own (1 Cor. 14:16). Several of the church Fathers refer to this custom, and Jerome says that at the conclusion of public prayer the united voice of the people sounded like the fall of water or the noise of thunder.

AMETHYST. *See* Mineral Kingdom.

A'MI (a'mī). One of the servants of Solomon whose descendants went up from Babylon (Ezra 2:57). In Neh. 7:59 he is called Amon.

AMIABLE (Heb. *yādîd,* "loved"). The word occurs only in Ps. 84:1, KJV, "How amiable are thy tabernacles." In 127:2 it is rendered "beloved." Its plural form, signifying "delights," is found in the title to Ps. 45, "A song of *love."*

AMIN'ADAB. A Gk. form (Matt 1:4; Luke 3:33, KJV) of *Amminadab* (which see).

AMIT'TAI (a-mit'ī; "true"). A native of Gathhepher, of the tribe of Zebulun, and father of the prophet Jonah (2 Kings 14:25; Jonah 1:1), c. 800 B.C.

AM'MAH (am'mā; Heb. *'ammâ,* a "cubit"). The place reached by Joab and Abishai at sundown in their pursuit of Abner (2 Sam. 2:24).

AM'MI (am'ī; i.e., as explained in the marg. of the KJV, "my people"). A figurative name applied to the kingdom of Israel in token of God's reconciliation with them, in contrast with the equally significant name Lo-ammi given by the prophet Hosea to his second son by Gomer, the daughter of Diblaim (Hos. 1-9). In the same manner Ruhamah contrasts with Lo-ruhamah.

AM'MIEL (am'i-el; "people of God").

1. The son of Gemalli, of the tribe of Dan, one of the twelve spies sent by Moses to explore the land of Canaan (Num. 13:12), c. 1439 B.C. He was, of course, one of the ten who perished by the plague for their "very bad report" (Num. 14:37).

2. The father of Machir of Lo-debar, who entertained Mephibosheth until he was befriended by David (2 Sam. 9:4-5; 17:27), before 1000 B.C.

3. The father of Bathsheba, wife of Uriah and afterward of David (1 Chron. 3:5), before 1030 B.C. In 2 Sam. 11:3 he is called *Eliam* (which see), by the transposition of the first and last syllables.

4. The sixth son of Obed-edom, and one of the gatekeepers of the Temple (1 Chron. 26:5), about 955 B.C.

AMMI'HUD (am-mi'hud; "people of glory").

1. An Ephraimite, whose son Elishama was appointed head of the tribe at the time of the Exodus (Num. 1:10; 2:18; 7:48, 53; 10:22; 1 Chron. 7:26), before 1210 B.C.

2. The father of Samuel who was the Simeonite leader appointed for the division of the Promised Land (Num. 34:20), before 1452 B.C.

3. A man of the tribe of Naphtali, whose son Pedahel was head of the tribe and was appointed for the division of the land (Num. 34:28), before 1452 B.C.

4. The father of Talmai, king of Geshur, to whom Absalom fled after his murder of Amnon (2 Sam. 13:37), before 1030 B.C.

5. The son of Omri and descendant of Pharez, and father of Uthai, who was one of the first to live at Jerusalem on the return from Babylon (1 Chron. 9:4), before 536 B.C.

AMMIN'ADAB (am-min'ā-dab; "people of liberality").

1. Son of Ram (Aram, KJV of Matt. 1:4) and father of Nahshon (Naason, KJV of Luke 3:32) who was head of the tribe of Judah at the first numbering of Israel in the second year of the Exodus (Num. 1:7; 2:3), about 1440 B.C. He was the fourth in descent from Judah, the sixth in ascent from David (Ruth 4:19-20; 1 Chron. 2:10), and one of the ancestors of Jesus Christ (Matt. 1:4; Luke 3:33; KJV renders Aminadab. He is probably the same Amminadab whose daughter Elisheba was married to Aaron (Ex. 6:23).

2. A son of Kohath, the second son of Levi (1 Chron. 6:22). In vv. 2 and 18 he seems to be called *Izhar* (which see).

3. A Levite of the sons of Uzziel, who, with 112 of his relatives was appointed by David to assist in bringing up the Ark to Jerusalem (1 Chron. 15:10-11), 1000 B.C.

AMMIN'ADIB (am-min'ā-dib; another form of Amminadab, mentioned in the margin of Song of Sol. 6:12). A person whose chariots were proverbial for their swiftness from which he appears to have been, like Jehu, one of the most celebrated charioteers of his day.

AMMISHAD'DAI (am-mi-shad'dā-ī; "people of the Almighty"). The father of Ahiezer, head of the tribe of Dan at the time of the Exodus (Num. 1:12; 2:25; 7:66, 71; 10:25), before 1440 B.C.

AMMIZ'ABAD (am-miz'ā-bad; "people of endowment"). The son and subaltern of Benaiah, who was David's captain of the host commanding

in the third month (1 Chron. 27:6), 1000 B.C.

AM'MON (am'mon; "inbred," another form of *Ben-ammi,* which see). The son of Lot by his youngest daughter (Gen. 19:38), about 2000 B.C. His descendants were called Ammonites (Deut. 2:20), sons of Ammon (Gen. 19:38), and sometimes simply Ammon (Neh. 13:23).

AM'MONITES (am'mon-īts). A nomadic race descended from Lot's youngest daughter, as the more civilized Moabites were from the elder one (Gen. 19:36-38). The two tribes were so connected that their names seem sometimes to have been used interchangeably (cf. Deut. 23:3 with Num. 22:2-7; Num. 21:29 with Judg. 11:24; and Judg. 11:13 with Num. 21:26).

Ammon, having dispossessed the Zamzummim (Deut. 2:19-21), dwelt E and N of Moab, from the Arnon to the Jabbok; "Sihon, king of the Amorites" having just before the Exodus taken the land between these streams from "the former king of Moab" (Num. 21:26), "from the wilderness as far as Jordan" (Judg. 11:22), and thus crowded Ammon eastward into the desert.

Although the Israelites were forbidden to molest the Ammonites, Ammon was often in league with other nations against Israel, such as with Moab (Deut. 23:3-4); with Moab and Amalek (Judg. 3:12-13), with the Syrians (2 Sam. 10:1-19), with Gebal and Amalek (Ps. 83:7), and was almost always hostile, both before and after the captivity (Neh. 4:3, etc.; *see also* Judith, chaps. 5-7; 1 Macc. 6:30-43), till all were swallowed up by Rome. In the time of Justin Martyr (about A.D. 150) the Ammonites were quite numerous, but in the time of Origen (about A.D. 186-254) they were merged with the Arabs.

The Ammonites were governed by a king (1 Sam. 12:12). The national deity was Molech (1 Kings 11:7), often called Milcom (1 Kings 11:5, 33). The capital was Rabbah, or Rabbath Ammon, for a while called Philadelphia from Ptolemy Philadelphus, but now called Amman.

The Ammonites seem to have furnished a small contingent to the Syrian confederacy against Shalmaneser II (854 B.C.), and Budnilu of Ammon was among the twelve kings of the Hatti and of the seacoast who sent ambassadors to Esarhaddon at Nineveh (671 B.C.).

The Ammonite names in the Bible show that the language was akin to that of the Hebrews.

Solomon set an example in marrying Ammonite women, Rehoboam's mother being Naamah, an Ammonitess (1 Kings 14:31), which example Israel was too ready to imitate (Neh. 13:23).

The doom of desolation prophesied against Ammon (Ezek. 25:5, 10; Zeph. 2:9) has been literally fulfilled. "Nothing but ruins are found here by the amazed explorer. Not an inhabited village remains, and not an Ammonite exists on the face of the earth" (Thomson, *Land and Book,* 3:622).

BIBLIOGRAPHY: Y. Aharoni, *Israel Exploration Journal* 1 (1950): 219-22; N. Avigad, *IEJ* 2 (1952): 163-64; G. L. Harding, *The Antiquities of Jordan* (1959); J. B. Hennessey, *Palestine Exploration Quarterly* 98 (1966): 155-62; S. H. Horn, *Bulletin of the American Schools of Oriental Research* 193 (1969): 2-19; N. Glueck, *The Other Side of Jordan* (1970).

AM'NON (am'non; "faithful").

1. The eldest son of David by Ahinoam, the Jezreelitess, born in Hebron (2 Sam. 3:2; 1 Chron. 3:1), before 1000 B.C. By the advice and assistance of Jonadab he violated his half sister Tamar, which her brother Absalom avenged two years after by causing him to be assassinated (2 Sam. 13).

2. The first named of the four sons of Shimon, or Shammai, of the children of Ezra, the descendant of Judah (1 Chron. 4:20).

AMOK (A-mok'). One of the priests who returned from exile in Babylonia with Zerubbabel (Neh. 12:7, 20).   E.H.M.

A'MOMUM (a'mō-mum). The Gk. word *ammōmon* occurs only in Rev. 18:13, where it is rendered "spice" (see marg.). It is, however, the name of a plant. *See* Vegetable Kingdom.

A'MON (ā'mon; "faithful").

1. The governor of "the city" (probably Samaria) in the time of Ahab, who was charged to keep Micaiah till the king should return from the siege of Ramoth-gilead (1 Kings 22:26; 2 Chron. 18:25), 850 B.C.

2. The fifteenth king of Judah, who succeeded his father, Manasseh, at the age of twenty-two (642 B.C.) and reigned two years. He followed Manasseh's idolatries without sharing his repentance. When he fell victim to a court conspiracy, the people avenged his death by slaying the conspirators and placing upon the throne his son Josiah, age eight. Amon was buried with his father in the garden of Uzza (2 Kings 21:19-26; 2 Chron. 33:20-25).

3. The head, or ancestor, of one of the families of the Temple servants who returned from Babylon with Zerubbabel after the captivity (Neh. 7:59), before 536 B.C.

4. An Egyptian deity (Amon, "the hidden one"). *See* Gods, False: Amon.

AM'ORITES (am'o-rīts; Heb. always singular, used collectively, *hā'ĕmōrî*, "the Amorite"). A tribe descended from Canaan (Gen. 10:16) and one of the seven whose lands were given to Israel (Deut. 7:1; cf. Gen. 15:16). "The Amorite" means literally "the Westerner," whence the name Amorites is generally supposed to mean "western highlanders" (cf. Num. 13:29; Deut. 1:7-20; Josh. 10:6), or "tall ones" (cf. Amos 2:9; *see also* Num. 13:33; Deut. 2:10).

The Amorites were so prominent that their name seems sometimes to be used for Canaanites in general (e.g., Josh. 24:8), and in the Amarna Letters Amurri is the name for Palestine-Phoenicia.

In Abraham's day the Amorites lived W of the Dead Sea, in Hazazon-tamar (Gen. 14:7), "that is Engedi" (2 Chron. 20:2), now Ain Jidi, and about Hebron (Gen. 14:13, cf. 13:18). The Israelites found E of the Jordan two Amorite kingdoms: that of Sihon, which lay along the Jordan from the Arnon (Wadi Mojib) to the Jabbok (Wadi Zerka), and from the Jordan to the desert (Judg. 11:21-22); and that of Og, king of Bashan, from the valley of Arnon to Mt. Hermon (Jebel esh Sheik) (Deut. 3:4, 8-9).

As Sihon and Og attempted to act on the offensive, Israel immediately possessed their territories (Deut. 3:8-10). The Israelites' next collision with the Amorites was with the anti-Gibeonite confederacy of the five Amorite kings of Jerusalem, Hebron, Jarmuth, Lachish, and Eglon (Josh. 10:1-43). Amorites also appear in the northern confederacy that was vanquished near the waters of Merom (11:1-14). This was the last hostile stand of the Amorites. In the days of Samuel they were at peace with Israel (1 Sam. 7:14). Solomon levied on the remnant of the Amorites and of the other Canaanite nations a tribute of bond service (1 Kings 9:20-21). The other notices of the Amorites after Solomon's day are mere historical reminiscences.

The Akkadians called the Amorites Amurru, and in the third millennium B.C. Syria-Palestine was called "the land of the Amorites." The First Dynasty of Babylon (c. 1830-1550 B.C.) was Amorite, and its most important king, Hammurabi the Great (1728-1686 B.C.), conquered the Amorite capital *Mari* (which see; the site is known today as Tell Hariri) on the Middle Euphrates near present-day Abou Kemal. The dynasty of Babylon fell when the Hittites sacked Babylon c. 1550. Thousands of clay tablets from the archives of an Amorite king at Mari are now in the Louvre Museum in Paris as the result of the excavations of that ancient Amorite center since 1933 by André Parrot. From the palace archives of Zimri-Lim, the last king of Mari, more than 20,000 tablets were recovered, a large number representing diplomatic correspondence of this king with his own ambassadors and with the great Hammurabi himself. The Mari Letters shed remarkable light on the customs recounted in the patriarchal narratives of Genesis.

See also Mari.

BIBLIOGRAPHY: A. Clay, *The Empire of the Amorites* (1919); E. Dhorme, *Revue Biblique* 37 (1928): 161-80; W. F. Albright, *From Stone Age to Christianity* (1957); K. M. Kenyon, *Amorites and Canaanites* (1966); J. van Seters, *Vetus Testamentum* 22 (1972): 64-81.

A'MOS (ā'mos; "burden").

1. One of the twelve minor prophets and a native of Tekoa, a town about six miles S of Bethlehem. He belonged to the shepherds there

and was not trained in any school of the prophets. Yet, without dedicating himself to the calling of a prophet, he was called by the Lord to prophesy concerning Israel in the reigns of Uzziah, king of Judah, and Jeroboam, king of Israel, c. 786-746 B.C., two years before the earthquake (Amos 1:1), about 763 B.C. The exact date of his appearing, or the length of his ministry, cannot be given. The two kingdoms were at the summit of their prosperity. Idleness, luxury, and oppression were general, and idolatry prevalent. It was at such a time as this that the plain shepherd of Tekoa was sent into Israel and prophesied at Bethel. This is almost a solitary instance of a prophet's being sent from Judah into Israel and, doubtless, attracted considerable attention. His prophetic utterances were directed against Judah as well as Israel, and closed with promises of divine mercy and returning favor to the chosen race. He was charged with a conspiracy against Jeroboam, the king, and threatened by Amaziah, the high priest of Bethel. After fulfilling his mission he probably returned to Judah. The time and manner of his death are unknown.

2. The ninth in the line of ascent from Christ, being the son of Nahum and father of Mattathias (Luke 3:25), about 400 B.C.

AMOS, BOOK OF. The second quarter of the eighth century B.C. in which Amos prophesied was one of great wealth and corruption. As a result of Jeroboam II's successes against the Moabites and the Aramaeans, the borders of the Northern Kingdom reached their widest extent since the Solomonic era (2 Kings 14:25; Amos 6:14). Fiery denunciation of the luxurious living, idolatry, and moral depravity of Israel were the subject of the rustic prophet from the mountaintop Judean village of Tekoa. But beyond the warning of judgment and final captivity upon the backslidden people, the prophet catches a magnificent glimpse of the yet-future millennial kingdom (9:11-15).

Contents. The book itself falls into three divisions: Part I. Judgments upon surrounding nations—Damascus, Philistia, Phoenicia, Edom, Ammon, Moab (1:1–2:3)—and upon Judah (2:4-5) and Israel herself (2:6-16). Part II. Divine indictment of the whole family of Jacob (3:1–9:10), including three denunciatory sermons (3:1–6:14) and five symbolic visions (7:1–9:10). Part III. Future kingdom blessing of restored Israel (9:11-15), embracing the Messiah's return and the establishment of the earthly messianic reign (9:11-12), millennial prosperity (9:13), and a restored Jewish nation (9:14-15).

Authenticity. The divine authority of the prophecy is corroborated by the NT. Stephen, in his speech before the Sanhedrin (Acts 7:42-43), quotes Amos 5:25-27. James, addressing the Jerusalem Council (Acts 15:16), cites Amos 9:11.

Criticism. Nearly all critics except the ultra-

radical concede the substantial integrity of the prophecy, except for 1:9-10; 1:11-12; 2:4-5; three doxologies 4:13; 5:8; 9:5-6; and the messianic-millennial passage 9:11-15. The assumptions under which these passages are commonly regarded as later additions (glosses), however, are the result of erroneous theories of the development of Israel's religion. Oesterley and Robinson, for example, regard 9:11-12 as exilic, because it envisions the Tabernacle of David as having fallen (*Introduction to the Books of the O.T.* [1934], p. 366). But A. Bentzen (*Introduction to the O.T.* [1949], 2:142) is correct in showing that Amos saw David's house as fallen "because it had lost the position which it had occupied in David's own time, not as a consequence of the events of 587, which he had not seen."

BIBLIOGRAPHY: J. D. W. Watts, *Vision and Prophecy in Amos* (1955); A. S. Kapelrud, *Central Ideas in Amos* (1961); E. B. Pusey, *The Minor Prophets* (1961), 1:232-341; J. K. Howard, *Amos Among the Prophets* (1968); R. K. Harrison, *Introduction to the Old Testament* (1970), pp. 883-97; R. S. Cripps, *Critical and Exegetical Commentary on Amos* (1981); F. A. Tatford, *The Minor Prophets* (1982), 1:1:1-39; J. M. Boice, *The Minor Prophets* (1983), 1:133-86; F. E. Gaebelein, ed., *Expositor's Bible Commentary* (1985), 7:269-331.

A'MOZ (ā'moz; "strong"). The father of the prophet Isaiah (2 Kings 19:2; Isa. 1:1), before 738 B.C. According to rabbinical tradition, he was also the brother of King Amaziah, and a prophet; but of this there is no proof.

AMPHIP'OLIS (am-fip'o-lis; "a city surrounded," so called because the Strymon flowed round it). A city of Macedonia through which Paul and Silas passed on their way from Philippi to Thessalonica (Acts 17:1). It was about thirty-three miles from Philippi. The Greek Archaeological Service excavated S of the acropolis of Amphipolis in 1920, uncovering the foundations of an early Christian basilica, and subsequently worked on the site of the necropolis, about a mile NW of the ancient town. The "Lion of Amphipolis," erected in the early part of the fourth century B.C. to

River Strymon, Macedonia, near Amphipolis

commemorate some unknown victory, was also turned up by the excavators and has been properly mounted once more along the main highway near the town.   H.F.V.

AM'PLIAS. *See* Ampliatus.

AMPLIATUS (am'pli-a-tus). A Christian at Rome, mentioned by Paul as one whom he particularly loved (Rom. 16:8; KJV renders Amplias), A.D. 60.

AM'RAM (am'ram; "high people").

1. The first named of the sons of Kohath, a Levite. He married his father's sister Jochebed, and by her became the father of Miriam, Aaron, and Moses (Ex. 6:18, 20; Num. 26:59). He died at 137, probably before the Exodus.

2. One of the sons of Bani, who, after the return from Babylon, separated from his Gentile wife (Ezra 10:34), 456 B.C.

3. A son of Dishon, properly known as *Hemdan* (which see). He is incorrectly given as Amram in the KJV of 1 Chron. 1:41 ("Hamran," NASB).

AM'RAMITES (am'ram-īts). Descendants (Num. 3:27; 1 Chron. 26:23) of Amram, no. 1.

AM'RAPHEL (am'ra-fel). A king of Shinar, the alluvial lowland of southern Babylonia, and an ally of Chedorlaomer in the invasion of the W in the time of Abraham, c. 2080 B.C., and formerly generally identified with Hammurabi the Great of the First Dynasty of Babylon (c. 1728-1689). This Amraphel-Hammurabi equation always was difficult linguistically but is now also disproved chronologically.   M.F.U.

AMULET (Heb. *leḥāshîm*, "charms"; Isa. 3:20, KJV, "earrings"). A supposed preservative against sickness, accident, witchcraft, and evil spirits or demons. Amulets consisted of precious stones, gems, gold, and sometimes of parchment written over with some inscription. They have been widely used from antiquity and are still worn in many parts of the world. They were often worn as *earrings* (which see), as the centerpiece of a necklace, and among the Egyptians frequently consisted of the emblems of various deities. Among the Arabs the figure of an open hand is used, as well as that of a serpent. *See also* Dress.

Egyptian amulet

Amulets formed part of the trappings that Jacob commanded his household to put away (Gen. 35:4). The most fanciful and superstitious notions have prevailed respecting the marvelous powers of gems. The gem appropriate for a particular month was worn as an amulet during the month and was supposed to exert mysterious control in reference to beauty, health, riches, and so forth. One's person and house were thought to be protected from malignant influences by holy inscriptions placed upon the door. The existence of such a custom is implied in the attempt of Moses to turn them to a proper use by directing that certain passages of the law should be employed (Ex. 13:9, 16; Deut. 6:9; 11:18), "to look at and remember all the commandments of the Lord, so as to do them" (Num. 15:39). Such written scrolls afterward degenerated into instruments of superstition among the Jews, so that "there was hardly any people . . . that more used or were more fond of amulets, charms, mutterings, exorcisms, and all kinds of enchantments" (Lightfoot, *Horae Heb.*, Matt. 24:24). These amulets consisted of little roots, parts of animals, or, more commonly, bits of paper or parchment upon which were written words or characters, and were supposed to have magical power to protect from evil spirits. One of the most frequent of the latter was the cabalistic hexagonal figure known as "the shield of David," and "the seal of Solomon."

Many of the Christians of the first century wore amulets marked with a fish as a symbol of the Redeemer, or the pentangle, consisting of three triangles intersected and made of five lines, which could be so set forth with the body of man as to touch and point out the places where our Savior was wounded. Among the Gnostics Abraxas gems were used. At a later period ribbons with sentences of Scripture written on them were hung about the neck. The Council of Trullo ordered the makers of all amulets to be excommunicated and deemed the wearers of them guilty of heathen superstition. *See* Teraphim.

AM'ZI (am'zī; "strong").

1. Son of Bani, of the family of Merari, and in the ancestry of Ethan, who was appointed one of the leaders of the Temple music (1 Chron. 6:46).

2. Son of Zechariah and ancestor of Adaiah, who was actively engaged in the building of the second Temple (Neh. 11:12), before 445 B.C.

A'NAB (ā'nab; "grapes"). A place upon the mountains of Judah from which Joshua expelled the Anakim (Num. 13:33; Josh. 11:21; 15:50); now bearing the same name Khirbet 'Anab; about thirteen miles SW of Hebron.

ANAGOGICAL. The spiritual method of biblical interpretation relating to the eternal glory of the believer to which its teachings are supposed to lead; thus the rest of the Sabbath, in an *anagogi-*

cal sense, signifies the repose of the saints in heaven.

A'NAH (a'nāh; "answer"). The son of Zibeon and grandson of Seir. His daughter Oholibamah is the second named of Esau's wives (Gen. 36:2, 14, 25). An Anah is mentioned in 36:20 as one of the sons of Seir and head of an Edomite tribe. Both passages probably refer to the same person, the word *sons* being used in v. 20 in the larger sense of descendants. While feeding his father's donkeys in the desert, he discovered warm springs, from which circumstance he probably obtained the name Beeri, "the man of the wells" (cf. Gen. 26:34; 36:24).

ANA'HARATH (a-nā'ha-rath; "gorge"). A town within Issachar (Josh. 19:19). Now identified with 'En-na'ûrah.

ANAI'AH (a-nī'a; "Jah has answered"). One of the persons (probably priests) who stood at the right hand of Ezra while he read the law to the people (Neh. 8:4), and perhaps the same as one of the leaders of the people who joined Nehemiah in a sacred covenant (10:22), 445 B.C.

A'NAK (ā'nak; "long-necked," i.e., "a giant"). The son of Arba, the founder of Kiriath-arba. He was the progenitor of a race of giants called Anakim. These Anakim were a terror to the children of Israel (Num. 13:22, 28) but were driven out by Caleb, who came into possession of Hebron (Josh. 15:13-14).

ANAKIM. *See* Giant.

ANALOGY (Gk. *analogia,* "proportion").

Works of God. As applied to these, *analogy* generally leads to the conclusion that (1) a part of a system of which he is the author must, in respect of its leading principles, be similar to the whole of that system; (2) the work of an intelligent and moral being must bear in all its lineaments traces of the character of its author; (3) the revelation of God in Scriptures is in all respects agreeable to what we know of God from the works of nature and the order of the world.

Analogy of Faith. This phrase is derived from the words of the apostle Paul (Rom. 12:6), "If prophecy, according to the proportion of his faith," and signifies the harmony of the different parts of Scripture. The parts of Scripture must be explained according to the tenor of the whole, not bringing any one part so conspicuously into view as to obscure or contradict others. Thus, for example, the exaggerated teaching respecting the dignity of the virgin Mary's relation to our Lord has tended to obscure the doctrines relating to our Lord as the only Mediator. The better to follow the analogy of the faith, one should study the Scriptures with a love of truth for its own sake and not with the purpose of finding proof for opinions already formed.

AN'AMIM (an'a-mim). Descendants of Mizraim (Gen. 10:13; 1 Chron. 1:11) and an Egyptian tribe of which nothing is known.

ANAMITES (NIV). The same as Anamim.

ANAM'MELECH. *See* Gods, False.

A'NAN (ā'nan; a "cloud"). One of the chief Israelites who sealed the covenant on the return from Babylon (Neh. 10:26), 445 B.C.

ANA'NI (a-nā'ni; "cloudy"). The last named of the seven sons of Elioenai, a descendant of David, after the captivity (1 Chron. 3:24), about 400 B.C.

ANANI'AH (an-a-nī'a; "protected by Jehovah").

1. The father of Maaseiah and grandfather of Azariah. The latter repaired a portion of the wall of Jerusalem after the return from exile (Neh. 3:23), about 445 B.C.

2. The name of a town in Benjamin, mentioned as inhabited after the captivity (Neh. 11:32), perhaps Bethany, E of Jerusalem.

ANANI'AS (an-a-nī'as; of Heb. Ananiah, "protected by Jehovah").

1. A member of the early Christian church at Jerusalem, who, conspiring with his wife, Sapphira, to deceive and defraud the brethren, was overtaken by sudden death and immediately buried (Acts 5:1-5). The members of the Jerusalem church had a common fund, which was divided by the apostles among the poor. Those who carried into full effect the principle that "not one of them claimed that anything belonging to him was his own" sold their lands and houses and laid the price at the apostles' feet (4:32, 34-35). One Joseph, surnamed Barnabas, had done this and, it would seem, had received hearty commendation for it. Probably incited by this and desirous of applause, Ananias and his wife, Sapphira, sold a possession and brought the pretended price to the apostle. Either their covetousness or fear of want influenced them to keep back part of the price—an acted lie. Peter was moved by the Spirit to uncover the deceit; instead of extenuating it because the lie had not been uttered, he passed on all such prevarication the awful sentence, "You have not lied to men, but to God" (5:4). Upon hearing these words Ananias "fell down and breathed his last" and was carried out and buried by the young men present (5:5-6). *See* Sapphira. The apparent undue severity of the punishment meted out upon Ananias and Sapphira is to be explained as "a sin leading to [physical] death" (1 John 5:16). It was an offense that involved being given over to Satan "for the destruction of his flesh, that his spirit may be saved in the day of the Lord Jesus" (1 Cor. 5:5). The ushering in of a new era at Pentecost necessitated that offenders against divine dealing in grace might be made a public example, such as Nadab and Abihu (Lev. 10:1-10) were made a similar warning when they

disregarded God's commands at the beginning of the legal age.

The expression "All things were common property to them" (Acts 4:32) should not imply that the first Christians adopted a form of modern Communism, divesting themselves of individual property, and throwing all they had and earned into a common stock. They had a common fund, but that it was not binding upon all to contribute everything to it is evident from what Peter said to Ananias—that he might have kept the land if he had chosen or even have used its price after it was sold. The principle universally accepted was that none should want while any of their brethren had the means of helping them. By becoming Christians the Jewish converts suffered the loss of all things unless they had property independent of the will, favor, or patronage of others, and the proportion of these was few. So deep an offense against Jewish prejudices cast them loose from Jewish charities and involved loss of employment to such as were traders and dismissal from their employments to such as were workmen and servants, producing a state of destitution that rendered extraordinary exertions necessary on the part of the more prosperous brethren. This is illustrated and proved by what we actually see in operation at this day in Jerusalem.

2. A devout and honored Christian of Damascus, to whom the Lord appeared in a vision and

Model of the Jerusalem Temple, where the high priest Ananias officiated

bade him go to a street called Straight and inquire at the house of Judas for Saul of Tarsus (Acts 9:10-11). Ananias at first hesitated because of his knowledge of Saul's former character and conduct. But assured of Saul's conversion and God's purpose concerning him, he consented. He "departed and entered the house, and after laying his hands on him said, 'Brother Saul, the Lord Jesus, who appeared to you on the road by which you were coming, has sent me so that you may regain your sight, and be filled with the Holy Spirit.' And immediately there fell from his eyes something like scales"; and, recovering his sight which he had lost when the Lord appeared to him on the way to Damascus, Paul, the new convert, arose, was baptized, and preached Jesus in the synagogues (Acts 9:17-20; 22:12-16), A.D. 35 or 36. Tradition makes Ananias to have been afterward bishop of Damascus and to have suffered martyrdom.

3. The high priest before whom Paul was brought previous to being taken to Felix (Acts 23). He was made high priest by Herod, king of Chalcis, who for this purpose removed Joseph, the son of Camydus (Josephus *Ant.* 20.5.2). Being implicated in the quarrels of the Jews and the Samaritans, he with others went to Rome to answer for his conduct before Claudius Caesar (20.6.2). The emperor decided in favor of the accused party, and Ananias returned with credit and remained in office until Agrippa gave it to Ismael (20.8.8). When Paul appeared before Ananias he made the declaration "I have lived my life with a perfectly good conscience before God up to this day" (Acts 23:1). Thereupon the high priest ordered the apostle to be struck in the face. Paul, indignant at so unprovoked an assault, replied, "God is going to strike you, you whitewashed wall." Being asked, "Do you revile God's high priest?" Paul said, "I was not aware, brethren, that he was high priest," perhaps having overlooked in his warmth the honor due him in his official station (Acts 23:2-5). A plot having been formed against Paul, he was sent by Claudius Lysias to Felix, whither he was followed by Ananias (accompanied by the orator Tertullus), who appeared against him (23:23–24:1). Ananias was deposed shortly before Felix quitted his government, and was finally assassinated (Josephus *Wars* 2.17.9), 67 B.C.

BIBLIOGRAPHY: D. E. Hiebert, *Personalities Around Paul* (1973), pp. 125-30.

'ANAT. *See* Gods, False.

A'NATH (a'nath; an "answer," i.e., to prayer).

1. The father of Shamgar, the third of the judges of Israel after the death of Joshua (Judg. 3:31; 5:6). Perhaps 1250 B.C.

2. 'Anat (Anath, ā'năt), a N Semitic goddess, now well known from the religious epic literature discovered as Ras Shamra (ancient Ugarit) from

1929 to 1937. *See also* Gods, False: 'Anat; Asherah; Ashtoreth.

ANATHEMA (Gk. *anathema*, a "thing laid by"). A votive offering consecrated to a god and hung up in the temple. When used in this general sense, as it often is by classical writers, it is written with a long *ē*, *anathēma* (Luke 21:5, "gifts"). The form *anathema* and its special meaning seem to be peculiar to the Hellenistic dialect, probably from the use made of the word by the Greek Jews. In the LXX anathema is generally the translation of the Heb. word *ḥerem*, to "consecrate." The following are its uses:

Old Testament. A type of *vow* (which see) by which persons and things were irrevocably and irredeemably devoted to the Lord (Lev. 27; Num. 21:2) and in such a way that the persons devoted had to be put to death, while the things fell to the sanctuary or to the priests. But inasmuch as the deliberate killing of anyone, even a slave, was treated as a punishable offense (Ex. 21:20), it is evident that the pronouncing of the anathema could not be left to the pleasure of any individual, since it might be used for impious purposes. The anathema, being a manifestation of the judicial holiness of God, realizing itself in executing righteous judgment upon men, assumed the character of a theocratic penalty. It could, therefore, be inflicted only by God or by the divinely appointed authorities, acting with a view to the glory of God and the upholding and edifying of His kingdom.

It was sometimes a command and not a vow. The only instance in which the anathema is expressly enjoined in the law is the command against those who served other gods (Ex. 22:20), even against whole cities. In such cases the men and cattle were ordered to be put to death by the sword and the houses with their contents to be burned (Deut. 13:12-17). This was carried out, especially in the case of the Canaanites (20:17-18), but in all its severity against Jericho alone (Josh. 6:17-18). In the case of the other cities, only the inhabitants were put to death, the cities themselves being spared (Josh. 10:28-42). Often the cattle were spared and with the rest of the spoil divided among the soldiers (Deut. 2:34-35; 3:6-7; Josh. 8:21-22, 27; 11:11-12, 14). In case anyone retained a part of that which had been anathematized for his own use, he brought upon himself the anathema of death (6:18; 7:11-12; cf. Deut. 13:17).

Among the Later Jews. In later years the ban of the synagogue was the excommunication or exclusion of a Jew (usually for heresy or blasphemy) from the synagogue and the congregation or from familiar communication with other Jews. This modification of the anathema owes its origin to Ezra 10:8, where the *ḥerem* consisted in the anathematizing of the man's entire possessions and the exclusion of the anathematized individual from the congregation. The later rabbinical writers mention three degrees of *anathema:* (1) *Niddu'i*, "separation," a temporary suspension from ecclesiastical privileges, which might be pronounced for twenty-four reasons. It lasted thirty days and was pronounced without a curse. The person thus anathematized could enter the Temple only on the left hand, the usual way of departure; if he died while under anathema there was no mourning for him, and a stone on his coffin denoted that he was separated from his people and deserved stoning. (2) *Ḥerem*, "curse." This was pronounced upon the individual who did not repent at the expiration of thirty days by an assemblage of at least ten persons and was accompanied with curses. The person so excommunicated was cut off from all social and religious privileges; it was unlawful to eat or drink with him (1 Cor. 5:11). The anathema could be removed by three common persons or by one person of dignity. (3) Upon the still impenitent person was inflicted the severer punishment of *shammata'*, "imprecation," a solemn act of expulsion from the congregation, accompanied with fearful curses, including the giving up of the individual to the judgment of God and to final perdition.

In the New Testament. From the above we are prepared to find that the *anathema* of the NT always implies execration but do not think that the word was employed in the sense of technical excommunication either from the Jewish or Christian church. It occurs only five or six times.

In Acts 23:12 it is recorded that certain Jews "bound themselves under an oath" (lit., anathematized themselves) "that they would neither eat nor drink until they had killed Paul." The probability seems to be that these persons looked upon Paul as unworthy of life and considered it their religious duty to bring about his death. They therefore *anathematized*, i.e., devoted themselves to destruction, if they drew back from their purpose.

When Peter was charged the third time with being a follower of Jesus he began "to *curse* and swear" (Matt. 26:74, i.e., "anathematize"). This is thought by some to be a vulgar oath; by others, an imprecation he called down upon himself in case he should be found telling an untruth.

In Rom. 9:3 Paul writes, "I could wish that I myself were accursed [*anathema*], separated from Christ." We have no means of knowing exactly what the apostle intended to be understood by the above expression. From the words "accursed . . . from Christ" we are hardly warranted in believing that he referred to either (1) the OT *anathema* or (2) the ban of the synagogue. Nor does it seem to refer to sudden death or a judicial act of the Christian church. Meyer (*Com.*, ad loc.) observes, "Paul sees those who belong to the fellowship of his people advancing to ruin through their unbelief; therefore he would fain wish that *he himself* were a curse offering, if by means of this sacrifice of his *own self* he could only save the beloved *brethren.*" Much of the difficulty of understanding this passage would be obviated if we remember that the apostle does not give expression to a decision formally reached, but rather to a sentiment stirred within him by an unutterable sorrow. He "could wish himself accursed, if the purport of the wish could be realized to the advantage of the Israelites" (Meyer, *Com.*).

"Let him be accursed" (Gal. 1:8-9) has the probable meaning of, "Let him be execrable and anathema."

"No one speaking by the Spirit of God says, 'Jesus is accursed'" (*anathema,* 1 Cor. 12:3) means, doubtless, the act of any private individual who execrated Christ and accounted Him accursed. The thought appears to be that those who speak by the Spirit do not *execrate* Jesus, but *confess Him as Lord.*

In 1 Cor. 16:22 we find the expression "Let him be accursed. Maranatha." In this the apostle announces his accord with the will of God, that those who are destitute of love to Jesus should be doomed to final perdition. *Maranatha* is the Aram. phrase for "the Lord comes" and seems to be used in this connection to indicate that the fulfillment of such punishment will be associated with His coming.

Roman Catholic View. "The Church has used the phrase *'anathema sit'* from the earliest times with reference to those whom she excludes from her communion, either because of moral offenses or because they persist in heresy. In pronouncing anathema against willful heretics the Church does but declare that they are excluded from her communion, and that they must, if they continue obstinate, perish eternally" (*Cath Dict.*).

BIBLIOGRAPHY: N. H. Snaith, *The Distinctive Ideas of the Old Testament* (1944).

ANATHEMATA (from *anatithēmi,* "to lay up"). In general the term was applied to all kinds of ornaments in churches, these things having been set apart to the service of God. In Luke 21:5 the word is thus used for the gifts and ornaments of the Temple. In a stricter sense the word is used to denote memorials of great favors that men had received from God. Very early a custom, still existing, sprang up of anyone receiving a signal cure presenting to the church what was called his *ectypoma,* or figure of the member cured, in gold or silver. Anathemata is also a term used to designate the coverings of the altar.

AN'ATHOTH (an'a-thōth; "answers," i.e., to prayer).

1. One of the sons of Becher, the son of Benjamin (1 Chron. 7:8), B.C.

2. One of the chief Israelites who sealed the covenant after the return from Babylon (Neh. 10:19), about 445 B.C.

3. A town in the tribe of Benjamin belonging to the priests, also a city of refuge (Josh. 21:18; Jer. 1:1). It is chiefly noted as the birthplace of the prophet Jeremiah, and also his residence (Jer. 1:1; 11:21-23; 29:27). It was a walled town of some strength, seated on a broad ridge of hills and overlooking the valley of the Jordan and the northern part of the Dead Sea. It was three miles NE of Jerusalem. Modern research identifies the present Anata with Anathoth, an hour and a quarter distant from Jerusalem, containing about one hundred inhabitants. *See* 2 Sam. 23:27; 1 Chron. 12:3; Ezra 2:23; Neh. 7:27.

ANCHOR (Gk. *ankura*). Very naturally the anchor has been in use from the earliest times. In the heroic times of the Greeks large stones called *eunai* were used for anchors. The anchors used by the Romans were usually of iron and in shape resembled the modern anchor. The scriptural mention of the use of anchors is in Acts 27:29-30, 40. From this passage it would seem that anchors were used at both the stern and bow of vessels.

Figurative. In Heb. 6:19 the *anchor* is used metaphorically for a spiritual support in times of trial, in which sense it is still frequently employed. In the early church it was also used with reference to the persecutions which threatened the ship of the church. In some cases, above the transverse bar of the anchor stands the letter E, probably an abbreviation of *Elpis,* "hope." Sometimes the anchor was associated with the *fish,* the symbol of the Savior, the union of the two symbols expressing "hope in Jesus Christ."

ANCIENT OF DAYS (Aram. "advanced in days"). An expression applied to Jehovah in a vision of Daniel (7:9, 13, 22). "When Daniel represents the true God as an aged man, he does so not in contrast with the recent gods of the heathen which Antiochus Epiphanes wished to introduce, or specially with reference to new gods; for God is not called the old God, but appears only as an old man, because age inspires veneration and conveys the impression of majesty. This impression is heightened by the robe with which He is covered, and by the appearance of the hair of His head, and also by the flames of fire which are seen to go forth from His throne" (Keil, *Com.,* ad loc.).

ANCIENTS (Heb. *zāqēn,* "old"). The *aged* either decrepit or vigorous (Gen. 18:12-13; 19:31; 24:1, etc.); *elders,* i.e., chief men, magistrates (Isa. 3:14; 24:23; Jer. 19:1; Ezek. 7:26; 8:11-12). *See* Elders.

AN'DREW. (Gk. *Andreas,* "manly"). A native of the city of Bethsaida in Galilee (John 1:44), the son of John (21:15) and brother of Simon Peter (Matt. 4:18; 10:2; John 1:40).

Receives Christ. At first a disciple of John the Baptist, Andrew was led to receive Jesus when John pointed Him out as "the Lamb of God" (John 1:36-40). He then brought his brother Simon to the Master, telling him that he had "found the Messiah" (v. 41). They both returned to their occupation as fishermen on the Sea of Galilee and remained there until, after John the Baptist's imprisonment, they were called by Jesus to follow Him (Matt. 4:18-20; Mark 1:14-18).

As Apostle. Further mention of him in the gospels includes his being ordained as one of the twelve (Matt. 10:2; Mark 3:18; Luke 6:14); his calling the attention of our Lord to the lad with the loaves and fishes at the feeding of the five thousand (John 6:8-9); his introducing to Jesus certain Greeks who desired to see Him (12:20-22); and his asking, along with his brother Simon and the two sons of Zebedee, for a further explanation of what the Master had said in reference to the destruction of the Temple (Mark 13:3-4). He was one of those who, after the ascension, continued at Jerusalem in the "upper room" (Acts 1:13). Scripture relates nothing of him beyond these scattered notices.

Traditions. The traditions about him are various. Eusebius makes him preach in Scythia; Jerome and Theodoret in Achaia (Greece); Nicephorus in Asia Minor and Thrace. It is supposed that he founded a church in Constantinople and ordained *Stachys* (which see), named by Paul (Rom. 16:9), as its first bishop. At length, tradition states, he came to Patrae, a city of Achaia, where Aegeas, the proconsul, enraged that he persisted in preaching, commanded him to join in sacrificing to the heathen gods, and upon the apostle's refusal ordered him to be severely scourged and then crucified. To make his death more lingering, he was fastened to the cross, not with nails, but with cords. Having hung two days, praising God, and exhorting the spectators to embrace, or adhere to, the faith, he is said to have expired on November 30, but in what year is uncertain. The cross is stated to have been of the form called *Crux decussata*, and commonly known as "St. Andrew's cross, ✖." Some ancient writers speak of an apocryphal Acts of Andrew.

BIBLIOGRAPHY: J. R. Harris, *The Twelve Apostles* (1927), pp. 1-139; E. A. T. W. Budge, *The Contendings of the Apostles* (1935), pp. 137-85; G. H. Dalman, *Sacred Sites and Ways* (1935), pp. 161-63; P. M. Peterson, *Andrew, Brother of Simon Peter* (1958); W. Barclay, *The Master's Men* (1959), pp. 40-46; J. D. Jones, *The Apostles of Christ* (1982), pp. 87-108.

ANDRONI'CUS (an-dro-nī'kus; "man-conquering"). A Jewish Christian, kinsman and fellow prisoner of Paul. He was converted before Paul and was of note among the apostles (Rom. 16:7), A.D. 60. According to Hippolytus, he became bishop of Pannonia; according to Dorotheus, of Spain.

A'NEM (a'nem; "two fountains"). A Levitical city in Issachar, assigned to the Gershomites (1 Chron. 6:73). It is called En-gannim (Josh. 19:21; 21:29).

A'NER (a'nēr).

1. A Canaanite chief near Hebron who, with Eschol and Mamre, was confederate with Abraham. He joined in pursuit of Chedorlaomer and shared in the spoil, not following the example of Abraham (Gen. 14:13, 24), about 2060 B.C.

2. A Levitical city assigned to the Kohathites and situated in Manasseh, W of the Jordan (1 Chron. 6:70). It is called Taanach (Josh. 21:25).

AN'ETHOTITE (an'e-tho-tīt). Also Anetothite, less correct forms of anglicizing the word *Anathothite*. See Anathoth.

ANGEL (Heb. *mal'āk;* Gk. *angelos,* both meaning "messenger"). In some cases the word is applied to human beings (Mal. 2:7; Rev. 1:20) or even figuratively to impersonal agents (Ex. 14:19; 2 Sam. 24:16-17; Ps. 104:4). The connection must determine its force. In its most common use in Scripture the word nevertheless designates certain spiritual and superhuman beings who are introduced to us as messengers of God. There are but few books of the Bible—such as Ruth, Nehemiah, Esther, the epistles of John, and James —that make no mention of angels.

With respect to their existence and nature, we find the Scriptures presenting the same progress and development as with many other subjects of revelation. Thus it is that the doctrine of angels becomes more distinct in the later periods of Jewish history and is more full and significant in the NT writings. Angels appear most frequently and conspicuously in connection with the coming and ministry of our Lord. His words concerning the angels are of unmistakable meaning and value. According to His teaching they are personal, sinless, immortal beings, existing in great number, and in close relation not only with individual men but also with the history of God's kingdom (Matt. 13:39; 18:10; 22:30; 25:31; 26:53; Luke 15:10; 16:22).

There is harmony between the teachings of our Lord upon this subject and those of the apostles and other Scripture writers. Many questions that may be raised can receive no answer whatever from the Scriptures. Of the history of the angels we can know but little. It is clear that Satan and the fallen angels (demons) were created sinless and later fell (Isa. 14:12-15; Rev. 12:3-4). Some of their number "did not keep their own domain" but fell under divine displeasure and are reserved "for the judgment of the great day" (Jude 6).

Aside from the teachings of Scripture there is nothing irrational, but quite the opposite, in believing in the existence of creatures superior to man in intelligence, as there are many inferior. But we depend wholly upon the Scriptures for our knowledge. The denial of the existence of angels, as that of a personal devil and demons, springs from the materialistic, unbelieving spirit, which in its most terrible form denies the existence of God.

The revelations of Scripture concerning angels are few, but nevertheless have great value:

1. They furnish a necessary safeguard against narrowness of thought as to the extent and variety of the creations of God.

2. They help us in acquiring the proper conception of Christ, who is above the angels, and the object of angelic worship.

3. They give a wonderful attractiveness to our conception of that unseen world to which we are hastening.

4. They set before us an example of joyous and perfect fulfillment of God's will. "Thy will be done in earth as it is in heaven," i.e., by the angels.

5. They put to shame the horrible indifference of multitudes of mankind with respect to the great work of conversion. "There is joy in the presence of the angels of God over one sinner who repents" (Luke 15:10).

6. They broaden our view of the manifold mercies of God, whose angels are "sent out to render service for the sake of those who will inherit salvation" (Heb. 1:14; cf. 12:22).

7. They remind us of our high rank as human beings, and our exalted destiny as Christians. We, who are made but "a little lower than the angels" (KJV, Ps. 8:5; NASB, "lower than God") may become "like angels in heaven" (Matt. 22:30).

BIBLIOGRAPHY: L. S. Chafer, *Systematic Theology* (1948), 4:5, 411-16; 7:13-15; H. Lockyer, *The Mystery and Ministry of Angels* (1958); A. C. Gaebelein, *The Angels of God* (1969).

ANGELS, FALLEN. Besides the good, elect, and unfallen angels two classes of fallen angels exist:

1. The angels who are unimprisoned and follow Satan as their leader. These apparently are identical with the *demons* (which see). During the Great Tribulation war will ensue between "Michael and his angels" and "the dragon and his angels" (Rev. 12:7). The dragon will be cast out of the heavenlies upon the earth and his angels with him (12:8-9). These are remanded to the abyss at the second coming of Christ (20:1-3) and consigned to the lake of fire after their final postmillennial revolt (Matt. 25:41; Rev. 20:10).

2. The angels who are imprisoned are the more wicked spirits that did not maintain their original estate "but abandoned their proper abode," being "kept in eternal bonds under darkness" awaiting judgment (Jude 6; 2 Pet. 2:4; 1 Cor. 6:3). Many Bible teachers hold that they include the fallen angels that cohabited with mortal women (Gen. 6:1-2) and were imprisoned in the nether world as a special punishment for their crime of breaking through God-ordained orders of being.

M.F.U.

ANGER. The emotion of instant displeasure and indignation arising from the feeling of injury done or intended, or from the discovery of offense against law.

The anger attributed to God in the NT is that part of God that stands opposed to man's disobedience, obstinacy (especially in resisting the gospel), and sin, and manifests itself in punishing the same.

Anger is not evil per se, being, as love, an original susceptibility of our nature. If anger were in itself sinful, how could God Himself be angry? Paul commands the Ephesians (Eph. 4:26) that when angry they are not to sin. "Paul does not forbid the being angry in itself, and could not forbid it, because there is a *holy* anger, which is the 'spur to virtue,' as there is also a *divine* anger; . . . but the being angry is to be *without* sin" (Meyer, *Com.*, ad loc.).

Anger is sinful when it rises too soon, without reflection; when the injury that awakens it is only apparent; when it is disproportionate to the offense; when it is transferred from the guilty to the innocent; when it is too long protracted and becomes revengeful (Matt. 5:22; Eph. 4:26; Col. 3:8).

ANGLE. See Fishhook.

ANIAM (a-nī'am). The fourth named of the four sons of Shemidah, of the tribe of Manasseh (1 Chron. 7:19).   E.H.M.

A'NIM (a'nim; "fountains"). A city in the mountains of Judah (Josh. 15:50), ten miles SW of Hebron, and probably the same as the present Khirbet Ghuwein et Tahta.

ANIMAL. An organized living body, endowed with sensation. In the Heb. there are several terms rendered "creature," "living thing," "cattle,"and so forth. The animals in Lev. 11 are divided into four classes: (1) larger terrestrial animals (v. 2); (2) aquatic animals (vv. 9-10); (3) birds (vv. 13-19); (4) smaller animals (vv. 20, 29, 41); and these classes were again distinguished into clean, i.e., eatable, and into unclean, whose flesh was not to be eaten (cf. Lev. 11 and Deut. 14:1-20). The larger terrestrial animals were, moreover, in the OT separated into cattle, i.e., tame domestic animals, and into beasts of the field or wild beasts.

Clean and Unclean. The distinction between clean and unclean animals goes back to the time of primeval man (Gen. 7:2; 8:20), but it did not originate in a dualistic view of creation. According to Bible teaching all the creatures of the earth were created good and pure, as creations of the holy God (1:31). Impurity entered into creation through man's Fall; and the irrational creature, although not affected by sin, suffered under its consequences. From the lists (Lev. 11:1-31, 46-47; Deut. 14:1-20), the clean animals (i.e., such as could be eaten) were ruminant quadrupeds, which parted the hoof, were cloven-footed, and chewed the cud; aquatic animals with fins and scales; all birds except the nineteen species named; flying insects, having two long legs for leaping, such as the grasshopper.

For Sacrifice. Sacrifices were of (1) the beef kind —a cow, bull, or calf; the ox, having been mutilated, could not have been offered (Lev. 22:24); (2) the goat kind—a he-goat, a she-goat, or a kid; (3) the sheep kind—an ewe, ram, or lamb. *See* Sacrifice.

These regulations would seem to have been abrogated by our Lord, when He taught that inward purity was the great essential (Matt. 15:11, 17-20). In his vision Peter was taught the essential cleanliness of all God's creatures (Acts 10:11-16).

Paul speaks decidedly upon this point (Rom. 14; Col. 2:16; Titus 1:15), and yet the apostolic council at Jerusalem placed things "strangled" and "blood" along with things "contaminated by idols and from fornication," on the list of things prohibited (Acts 15:20).

BIBLIOGRAPHY: F. S. Bodenheimer, *Animal and Man in Bible Lands* (1960); F. E. Zeuner, *A History of Domesticated Animals* (1963); V. Møller-Christensen and K. E. Jordt Jørgensten, *Encyclopedia of Bible Creatures* (1965); G. Cansdale, *Animals of the Bible Lands* (1970); W. W. Ferguson, *Living Animals of the Bible* (1972).

ANIMAL KINGDOM. The proportion of animals mentioned in the Bible compared with the total number found in Bible lands is far larger than that which occurs in the case of plants. There are 38 mammals, out of perhaps 130, 34 birds out of about 350, 11 reptiles out of nearly 100, and one amphibian out of a considerable number indigenous to these lands. It is a notable fact that not a single species of fish is mentioned by name. Of insects there are 16, out of a number not as yet satisfactorily settled. Scorpions and spiders are mentioned generically. The number of species is considerable. Four only of the large number of mollusks and only one of the worms are specifically named. Coral and sponge are the generic representations of their respective orders. Few even of the mammals, except the domestic animals, are specific. Most of them are generic or family names, to which is often appended "after his kind."

Adder. *See* Serpent.

Ant. There are large numbers of species of ants in the East, and innumerable hosts of them make their nests beside the threshing floors and wherever their favorite food is found. In every country in the world the ant is proverbial for *industry*, so there has never been any controversy with regard to the passage in Prov. 6:6, "Go to the ant, O sluggard." The habits of the ants of cool climates and of those of the tropical and semitropical countries differ so much that considerable controversy has arisen as to the *wisdom* and *foresight* of this insect. Some cite 30:25: "The ants are not a strong folk, but they prepare their food in the summer." There are, however, certain facts in regard to the ants of the Holy Land that settle this controversy in favor of the rigid ac-

curacy of the author of the Proverbs: (1) The ants of these countries lay up vast stores of grain in their nests. (2) To facilitate this act of providence they place their nests as near as possible to the places where grain is threshed or stored. (3) They certainly eat this grain during the winter season. (4) They encourage certain insects that secrete sweet juices to consort with them and collect and store their eggs with their own, that they may have them at hand for future use when they shall have hatched.

Antelope. An animal referred to in Heb. as *te'ô* in the NASB and NIV of Deut. 14:5 and Isa. 51:20. In the Gk. versions and the Vulg. the word is translated generally oryx (*Antilope leucoryx*). This animal is characterized by long, slender, cone-shaped horns and is white with a conspicuous tuft of black hair under its throat. Its habitat is Upper Egypt, Arabia, and Syria. The Targums, however, rendered the Heb. word "wild ox" (so also the RV) but probably had in mind the bubale (*Antilope bubalis*) of Arabia and Egypt, classified by Arabs with wild oxen.   M.F.U.

See also Ibex.

Ape (Heb. *qôp,* "monkey"). We have no hint as to the kinds of apes that were brought by the merchant navies of Solomon and Hiram, but it is probable that they were numerous. They are distributed in considerable numbers throughout all the countries bordering on the Mediterranean, though they are not indigenous to any except the United Arab Emirates and Gibraltar. The Heb. word *qôp* (Akkad. *uqûpu,* and Sanskrit *kapi*) is rendered "ape" and probably includes apes that are tailless and monkeys that possess tails. If they came from India, they were a species of tailed monkey, common to the area and worshiped there.

Arrowsnake. *See* Serpent.

Asp. *See* Serpent.

Ass. *See* Donkey.

Baboons. *See* Peacocks.

Badger (Heb. *tahash*). *See* Porpoise. The *badger* of the KJV is not the same as the *rock badger* of the NASB, which replaces the KJV *coney.*

Bald Locust. *See* Locust.

Bat (Heb. *'ăṭallēp*). The Hebrew idea of a bat was "a fowl that creeps, going upon all fours." It was unclean (Lev. 11:19). It is in reality a mammal and not a bird at all; its wings are membranous and destitute of feathers. It lives in caverns, tombs, or ruins (Isa. 2:19-21). The bat is a voracious destroyer of fruit, making it necessary for those who try to raise it in the neighborhood of cities to cover the clusters, or even the whole tree, with a net. There are about fifteen species of bats in the Holy Land.

Bear. The bear is now a somewhat rare animal in Syria, being confined to the higher regions of Lebanon, Anti-Lebanon, and Amanus, and found sparingly in the wilder portions of Bashan, Gilead, and Moab. It is rarely or never seen now in

Animal Kingdom

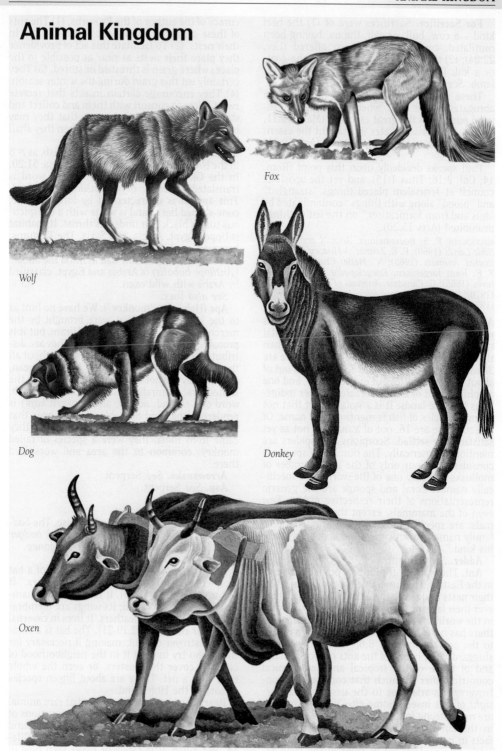

Fox

Wolf

Dog

Donkey

Oxen

Sparrows

Eagle

Dove

Raven

Serpent

Scorpion

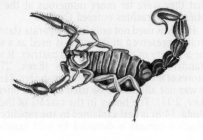

western Palestine. It is known in science as *Ursus Syriacus,* Ehr. and differs from the brown bear of Europe by its grayish fur. It was once abundant in Palestine (1 Sam. 17:36; 2 Kings 2:24). The Scripture alludes to the cunning of the bear (Lam. 3:10), to the ferocity of the she bear robbed of her cubs (2 Sam. 17:8; Prov. 17:12; Hos. 13:8), to the danger of the bear to man (1 Sam. 17:34, 36; Amos 5:19). The bear feeds principally on roots, fruits, and other vegetable products but does not fail to avail itself of the chance to devour any animal that may come in its way. Hence the significance of the picture of the peaceful reign of Christ (Isa. 11:7).

Beast. In the Bible, used in three distinctive ways:

1. Of a mammal, not man, as distinguished from creeping things and birds of the heavens (Gen. 1:29-30). Wild beasts in Scripture are differentiated from domesticated animals (Lev. 26:22; Isa. 13:21-22; Jer. 50:39; Mark 1:13).

2. Of the inferior animals, including birds and reptiles, as differentiated from human beings (Ps. 147:9-10; Eccles. 3:19; Acts 28:5).

3. Figuratively, of a fierce, destructive political power, as for example, the four successive world powers—Babylon, Media-Persia, Greece, and Rome of Dan. 7:1-7. In Rev. 13:1-10 the composite beast represents the final Antichrist, whereas a beast with lamb's horns portrays the false prophet of the end times (13:11-18). Unregenerate man's (i.e., Gentile) civilization and government in its *outward* manifestation is brilliant and dazzling (cf. the shining metallic colossus of Dan. 2:31-45), but internally it is evil and cruel, like so many wild beasts (7:1-7).   M.F.U.

See also Behemoth; Wild Beasts.

Bees. In the Holy Land, although bees occasionally make their hives in trees, as in other countries (1 Sam. 14:25-26), they generally resort to clefts in the rocks, almost always inaccessible to man. There are several allusions to the rocky homes of the bees (Deut. 32:13; Ps. 81:16). They are especially abundant in the wilderness of Judea (Matt. 3:4), and they resent with great fury any interference by man with their retreats (Deut. 1:44; Ps. 118:12).

The number of wild bees at present in Palestine would not justify the expression "a land flowing with milk and honey." It is, however, probable that they were far more numerous at the time when the Israelites entered Canaan.

Honey is used not only in its separate state, but fruit is preserved in it, and it is used as a sauce for a variety of confections and pastries. It was a standard article of commerce (Ezek. 27:17). Stores of it were collected at Mizpah (Jer. 41:6-8). It was not allowed to be used in burnt offerings (Lev. 2:11). The honey in the carcass of the lion (Judg. 14:8) is best explained by the rapidity with which a carcass is denuded by wild beasts and

ants in this hot climate and then dried in the blazing sun.

According to the author of Proverbs (24:13), it is good to eat honey but (25:16, 27) not to indulge to surfeit. Other references to honey convey various moral lessons (Ezek. 3:3; Ps. 19:10; Prov. 16:24).

Beetle. *See* Cricket; Locust.

Beeves. *See* Cattle; Ox.

Behemoth (be-hē'mōth; "colossal beast"). The plural of the Heb. word for beast, used in Job 40:15-24 of the hippopotamus, only excelled by "leviathan." The description of the behemoth is the climax of the passage begun in chap. 38 and carried upward until it culminates in the exclamation at the end of chap. 41: "He looks on everything that is high; he is king over all the sons of pride" (41:34). The hippopotamus is a pachyderm, the largest except for the elephant and the rhinoceros, amphibious in habits, living on vegetable food, and corresponding well with the description in Job 40. It is found in the upper Nile and was common in the lower in ancient times. It may have been found in the Jordan (40:23), although poetic license would make it quite possible that the mention of that river should have reference only to its aquatic habits and its courage, not to its geographical range. Indeed, "a river" of the first member of the parallelism can only mean the Nile, and the mention of the Jordan in the second would seem to be simply to strengthen the hyperbole.

Bird. A number of Heb. words are rendered bird, as *barbūr, 'ôp, ṣippôr.* However, the *barbūr* is the lark-heeled cuckoo, a delicacy served on Solomon's table (1 Kings 4:23). *See* Cock. The *'ôp* is a generic word for bird. The *ṣippôr* is the lowly sparrow.

In the NT "birds" (KJV, "fowls") is the rendering most frequently of Gk. *ta peteina.*

1. Birds were divided into *clean* and *unclean,* the latter including the carrion birds, fish hunters, and some others, as the hoopoe. Domestic fowl are mentioned, but it is nowhere said that they were eaten. It is, nevertheless, extremely probable that they were so used.

2. The allusions to birds' nests in the Bible are frequent and forcible. They were made in the sanctuary (Ps. 84:3), rocks (Job 39:27; cf. Num. 24:21; Jer. 49:16), trees (Ps. 104:17; Jer. 22:23; Ezek. 31:6). Nests were concealed in ruins (Isa. 34:15) and holes (Jer. 48:28). The NT nests (Matt. 8:20; Luke 9:58) were mere roosts.

3. Eggs are frequently alluded to (Deut. 22:6; Job 39:14; Isa. 10:14). They were well-known articles of food (Luke 11:12).

4. Migration of birds (Song of Sol. 2:11-12; Jer. 8:7), their singing (Eccles. 12:4; Ps. 104:12), flight (Ex. 19:4), care of young (Deut. 32:11-12), voracity (Matt. 13:4), and many other characteristics are alluded to.

Bittern. A KJV term replaced in the NASB by *Hedgehog* (which see).

Black Kite. *See* Kite.

Boar. *See* Swine.

Bull, Bullock. *See* Ox.

Buzzard (Heb. *'ozniyyâ;* the "fish eagle," *Pandion halioetus,* L; KJV, "osprey"; NIV "black vulture"). An unclean bird (Lev. 11:13; Deut. 14:12) that fishes along the coasts of the Holy Land and in Hûleh.

Calf. *See* Ox.

Camel (Heb. *gāmāl;* Gk. *kamēlos*). One of the most useful of the domestic animals of the East. With the exception of the elephant it is the largest animal used by man. It is often eight feet or more in height and possesses great strength and endurance. It has a broad foot, which enables it to walk over sandy wastes without sinking deeply beneath the surface. It has a provision in its stomach that enables it to store enough water to travel for days without drinking. It is capable of subsisting on the coarsest and bitterest of herbage and can take into its horny mouth the most obdurate thorns, which it grinds up with its powerful teeth and digests with its ostrich-like stomach. To offset its great height it is formed to kneel, so that it can be loaded as easily as a donkey and then rise with its burden of five hundred pounds and plod on through the hottest day and the most inhospitable waste of the deserts, in which it finds its congenial home. The hump on its back is not only a help to retaining its pack saddle but also a storehouse of fat, in reserve against its long fasts. The flesh, although forbidden to the Israelites, is eaten by the Arabs and sold in the markets of all oriental cities. Its skin is used in making sandals and its hair in the weaving of the coarse cloth of which their tents and outer garments are made. Its milk and the products made from it are a prime element in the diet of the Bedouin.

The allusions to the camel in the Scripture are so numerous that it is unnecessary to point them out.

Archaeological discoveries show the effective domestication of the camel at least as early as 1200-1000 B.C., so that swarms of camel-riding Midianites in Gideon's time (c. 1155-1148 B.C.), as recounted in Judg. 6-7, and later the wealthy camel caravan of Solomon's royal visitor the queen of Sheba (1 Kings 10:1-2), about 950 B.C., offer no difficulties historically. Apparently the earliest known art depiction of a Near-Eastern camel (one-humped) is a late Hurrian work from Tell Halaf, now in the Walters Art Gallery of Baltimore, dating about 1,000 B.C. However, references to domesticated camels in Abraham's time (c. 2000 B.C.) have been set aside by such writers as T. E. Peet, *Egypt and the Old Testament* (1924) p. 60, R. Pfeiffer, *Introduction to the O.T.* (1941), p. 154, and others. This idea seems to be presumptuous in the light of such evidence

as camel statuettes, bones, and other references that appear in archaeological materials beginning about 3,000 B.C. (cf. J. P. Free, "Abraham's Camels," *Journal of Near Eastern Studies* [July 1944]: 187-93). Free's research concerned the use of camels in Egypt. In recent years numerous indications of the domestication and use of camels in Mesopotamia and Syria during the patriarchal period have come to light. K. A. Kitchen has collected some of this information (see *Ancient Orient and Old Testament* [1966], pp. 79-80; "Camel," *Illustrated Bible Dictionary* [1980], 1:228-30). H.F.V.

Since wild camels were known from earliest times, there is no credible reason why such an indispensable animal in desert and semi-arid lands should not have been sporadically domesticated in patriarchal times and even earlier. Large scale domestication after the twelfth century B.C., however, greatly expanded desert trade as a result of the advantages of camel nomadism over donkey nomadism, enabling camel traders to travel much greater distances on this animal specially adapted to desert conditions.

Figurative. In two passages (Matt. 19:24; 23:24) the size of the camel is made the basis of comparison. There is not a particle of evidence in favor of the statement that the needle's eye, in the former passage, refers to the smaller gate cut through the panel of the city gates of the East or that such a gate is, or ever was, called a needle's eye. The whole force of the comparison in both passages is found in the hyperbole. Moreover, no camel could ever be forced through one of these small gates.

See also the bibliography that follows the last entry under Animal Kingdom.

Cankerworm. *See* Locust.

Carrion Vulture. *See* Vulture.

Cat. The cat is not alluded to in the Bible except in the Apocrypha (Epistle of Jer. 21). It is not mentioned in classical authors except when treating Egyptian history. This seems the stranger as there are two species of wild cats in Palestine, and the domestic cat is exceedingly common now all through the East.

Caterpillar. *See* Locust.

Cattle (the rendering of several Heb. and Gk. words). Cattle were of prime importance to the Hebrews, whose first employment was the care of flocks and herds. On their arrival in Egypt they were assigned to the land of Goshen, on account of its pastoral facilities. They then became herdsmen and shepherds to Pharaoh. One of the words, *miqneh,* translated "cattle," signifies "possessions." It includes horned cattle, horses, donkeys, sheep, and goats. The specific word for animals of the bovine species, and for sheep and goats, is also occasionally rendered cattle. Also *behēmâ,* which means, primarily, "beast" in general.

Chameleon (Heb. *kōaḥ,* KJV; but Heb. *tinshe-*

met, NASB, NIV). There is no possibility of determining with certainty the animal intended by this Heb. word in the list of creeping things (Lev. 11:30). It was probably a lizard and more likely to have been the *Nile monitor* than the *chameleon.* The NASB renders it *land crocodile;* the NIV, *monitor lizard.* The Nile monitor attains a length of five to six feet, and the chameleon four to five. On the authority of the LXX and the Vulg. the KJV has rendered it "chameleon."

On the other hand the NASB and NIV have rendered *tinshemet,* at the end of the verse, "chameleon," instead of "mole" of the KJV. This is based on the fact that *tinshemet* is derived from a root signifying "to breathe" and that the ancients believed that the chameleon *lived on air.* This somewhat fanciful idea is hardly probable enough to do away with the authority of the LXX and the Vulg., which render the word "mole." The reference, however, is not to the true mole but to the mole rat, *Spalax typhlus,* which is abundant in Bible lands. If the above views are correct, chameleon should be dropped from the biblical fauna.

Chamois. *See* Mountain Sheep.

Chicken. *See* Cock.

Chicks. *See* Cock.

Cock. The only mention of domestic fowl in the OT is in connection with the daily provision for Solomon's table (1 Kings 4:23). The Heb. word *barbūr* has been rendered "swans," "geese," "guinea fowls," "capons," and "fatted fish," as well as the "fatted fowl" of the KJV and the RV. However, the delicacy referred to is the lark-heeled cuckoo (*Centropus aegyptius Shelley*), a dainty morsel even to the present day in Italy and Greece.

In the NT the cock crowing is mentioned as a measure of time in connection with Peter's denial of Christ (Matt. 26:34, 74; Mark 14:30; Luke 22:34; John 18:27). Cocks are not regular in their times of crowing, sometimes crowing twice, and at other times irregularly through the night or before the dawn (Mark 13:35).

The *hen* is alluded to but once in the Scripture (Luke 13:34).

Cockatrice. A KJV term appearing in Isa. 11:8; 14:29; 59:5; Jer. 8:17. *See* Serpent.

Cockow, Cuckoo. *See* Sea Gull.

Colt. *See* Donkey; Horse.

Coney. *See* Rock Badger.

Coral (Heb. *rā'mâ,* "high" in value). It is uncertain what substance is intended by the word *rā'môt,* rendered "coral" by the KJV, NASB, and NIV. As coral, however, is a precious commodity, and highly suitable for the requirements of the only two passages in which the word occurs, we may rest contented with this translation (Job 28:18; Ezek. 27:16). This substance is the skeleton of microscopic zoophytes. It is of a great variety of colors, shapes, and consistency, the most valuable being red. Many of the branches of

coral are extremely beautiful. The Red Sea was probably named on account of the red coral growing in its waters. The best coral is brought from Persia and the Red Sea, but a good quality is also found in the Mediterranean. Fine specimens of the best colors may bring $50 an ounce. Coral was highly valued among the ancients and the Arabs for making beads and other ornaments.

Cormorant. In the list of unclean birds (Lev. 11:17; Deut. 14:17) the word *cormorant* is probably the correct rendering of the Heb. *shālāk.* It is abundant in the Holy Land, and it is a large black bird that subsists by fishing. Its scientific name is *Phalacrocorax carbo.* In the KJV the term *cormorant* appears also in Isa. 34:11; Zeph. 2:14, but in those verses it should be *pelican,* that being the true rendering of the Heb. original, *qā'at,* "vomiting." *See* Pelican.

Cow. *See* Ox.

Crane. The word occurs twice in the KJV (Isa. 38:14; Jer. 8:7) and once in the NASB (Isa. 38:14) and should be rendered "twittering," or "twitterer," as applied to the swallow or some similar bird. Notwithstanding the opinion of the KJV, the RV, and the NASB, we think that the crane ought to be dropped from the list of biblical birds.

Creeping Locust. *See* Locust.

Cricket. The rendering of the NASB, NIV, and RV, of the Heb. word *ḥargōl* in Lev. 11:22. This is the corrected translation of "beetle" of the KJV. The word *cricket* also appears in NASB Deut. 28:42, but as the rendering of a different Heb. word, which the KJV renders *"locust"* (which see). The creature referred to belongs with the locust and the grasshopper, since it is winged and leaps rather than creeps. The chief leaping insects belong to three families of *Orthoptera* (the grasshoppers, the locusts, and the crickets); the *ḥargōl* undoubtedly belongs to one of the three, though to which now cannot be determined. The KJV rendering of *ḥargōl* by "beetle" does not take into account that the most typical species of the *Coleoptera* (beetle order) do not leap.

Crocodile (marg. Job 41:1). A well-known saurian, found in ancient times in Lower as well as Upper Egypt but now confined to the upper waters of the Nile. It was probably abundant in the Kishon in Bible days. It is said to be still found there. It is the creature intended by "monster" (Ezek. 29:3; 32:2).

See also Chameleon; Dragon; Jackal; Leviathan.

Cuckoo, Cuckow. *See* Sea Gull.

Deer. An animal, *Cervus dama,* L., once found in Palestine but now probably extinct S of Amanus. The KJV translates Heb. *'ayyāl* as "hart," whereas the NASB and NIV translate it as "deer" (Deut. 12:15, 22; 14:5; 15:22; 1 Kings 4:23; Ps. 42:1; Isa. 35:6), "young stag" (Song of Sol. 2:9, 17; 8:14), and "bucks," or "deer" (Lam. 1:6) in the NASB and NIV respectively.

The "fallow deer" in the KJV of Deut. 14:5;

1 Kings 4:23 is a mistranslation of Heb. *yaḥmûr.* It is correctly rendered "roebuck" in the NASB and NIV.

The female deer, or hind (Heb. *'ayalâh*), appears always as "hind" in the KJV. In the NASB it is rendered by "hind" (2 Sam. 22:34; Ps. 18:33; Prov. 5:19; Song of Sol. 2:7; 3:5), "doe" (Gen. 49:21; Jer. 14:5), and "deer" (Job. 39:1; Ps. 29:9). In the NIV it is rendered "deer" (2 Sam. 22:34; Ps. 18:33; Prov. 5:19), "doe" (Gen. 49:21; Job 39:1; Prov. 5:19; Jer. 14:5), and "gazelle" (Song of Sol. 2:7; 3:5).

See also Doe for a reference to the female mountain goat.

Desert Owl. *See* Owl; Peacocks.

Doe. In one place (Prov. 5:19; Heb. *ya'ālā;* KJV, "roe") doe should be *wild she-goat.* Elsewhere it refers to the female *deer* (which see). KJV "roe" is normally rendered *"gazelle"* (which see) in the NASB. *See* Goat, Wild.

Dog (Heb. *keleb;* Gk. *kuōn,* "dog"). The dog referred to in the Scriptures is invariably the unclean animal so familiar in the streets of all oriental cities. He is a cowardly, lazy, despised creature. He eats garbage, dead animals (Ex. 22:31), human flesh (1 Kings 14:11), and blood (22:38). His is the lowest type of vileness (2 Sam. 3:8; Isa. 66:3). Dogs wander through the streets (Ps. 59:6, 14). With all their cowardice they are treacherous and violent (22:16, 20). The only good thing said of them is that they watch the flocks (Job 30:1; Isa. 56:10-11). Christ compares the Gentiles to them (Matt. 15:26), and those who are shut out of heaven are called dogs (Rev. 22:15). The price of a dog (Deut. 23:18) probably refers to sodomy. The return of a fool to his folly is compared to one of the most disgusting of the many filthy habits of the dog (Prov. 26:11; 2 Pet. 2:22).

Doleful Creatures. A KJV term that appears in Isa. 13:21; the NASB and NIV render "owl," with a marginal reading in NASB of "howling creatures." The point of the allusion is the fact that such creatures resort to ruins and deserted dwellings, and it indicates the desolation that has overtaken them.

Donkey (Heb. *ḥamôr,* the "male donkey"; *'ātôn,* "female donkey"; Gk. *onos,* "donkey"; *hupozugion,* "under the yoke"). The donkey is one of the earliest and most frequently mentioned animals alluded to in the Bible. They are spoken of in connection with the history of Pharaoh (Gen. 12:16), Abraham (22:3), Jacob (32:5), Moses (Ex. 4:20), Balaam (Num. 22:21-33), and in fact most of the notable persons mentioned in the OT. There was nothing in any sense degrading in the idea of riding on a donkey, as might perhaps be inferred from Zech. 9:9 (cf. Matt. 21:7). It was the sign of the peaceful mission of Christ. Kings, high priests, judges, and the richest people of ancient and modern times have ridden on donkeys. Many of the donkeys of Da-

mascus, Baghdad, Aleppo, Cairo, Cyprus, and other parts of the East are beautiful animals, easy in gait, and perfectly surefooted. They often cost high prices and are adorned with magnificent trappings.

They have also been used from earliest times as beasts of burden. Special breeds of them are raised for this purpose. Some of them are small and cheap, whereas others are but little smaller than a mule and carry burdens of greater weight in proportion to their size than any other animal. The pack saddle differs according to the use to which it is put. The familiar crosstree is employed for firewood. Abraham doubtless loaded the wood for the sacrifice in this way (Gen. 22:3). When sheaves of grain are to be loaded a kind of cradle is suspended to this or to the flat saddle. This latter, called in Arabic a *jebâl,* is composed of an under layer of thick felt and an upper of strong haircloth, with a padding between, about six inches in thickness, of straw or sedges. This saddle is flat on top and bent down over each side of the animal, so as to protect his ribs from the pressure of the load. Over such a saddle as this, sacks of grain or cut straw are thrown and tied fast by a rope passing under the breast. The sons of Jacob probably used this sort (42:26-27). If sand is to be carried, small panniers are slung over the saddle, and hang down on either side without touching the body. If bread or other provisions, not liable to be injured by pressure, are taken, larger panniers are used. In something similar to this Jesse and Abigail may have sent their presents (1 Sam. 16:20; 25:18). If fruit is to be carried, two boxes are slung in a similar manner. Children are often carried in this way in larger boxes. Probably Moses' wife sat on a *jebâl,* with her children in boxes on either side of her, when going down to Egypt (Ex. 4:20). Sacks of grain or straw are often slung across the bare back of a donkey.

Donkeys were also used for plowing (Isa. 30:24; 32:20).

The Israelites were not allowed to yoke an ox and a donkey together (Deut. 22:10). They were not allowed to eat its flesh, yet in the stress of hunger during the siege of Samaria they violated this law (2 Kings 6:25).

The *female donkey* is the one intended in a number of places not indicated in our translations (Num. 22:21-33; 1 Sam. 9:3; 2 Kings 4:22, 24). David had an officer to take care of his *female donkeys* (1 Chron. 27:30).

Donkey colts (Gen. 49:11) are also called *foals* (Job 11:12), *young donkeys* (Isa. 30:6), and *colt* (Zech. 9:9). They are all translated from the same Heb. word, *'ayir.*

Wild donkeys are frequently mentioned, two Heb. words (*pere',* "running" wild; *'ārôd,* "lonesome") being so translated. Both are found together in one parallelism (Job 39:5) but rendered by the single expression "wild donkey." We have no means of knowing whether they refer to the same or different species. The wild donkey is found in the deserts nearest to Palestine.

Dove. (Heb. *yōnâ;* Gk. *peristera*). Four species of wild pigeons are found in Bible lands, the *ring dove,* or *wood pigeon,* the *stock dove,* the *rock dove,* and the *ash-rumped rock dove.* They are all known by the Arab. name of *hamâm.* They make their nests in the clefts and holes of the rocks (Song of Sol. 2:14; Jer. 48:28; Ezek. 7:16). They also nest in trees. They are unresisting (Matt. 10:16) and therefore suitable for sacrifice (Gen. 15:9; Lev. 12:6-8; Mark 11:15; Luke 2:24; John 2:14-16). They are timid (Hos. 11:11); they fly great distances in their migrations (Ps. 55:6-8); they are gentle (Song of Sol. 1:15; 4:1; etc.). Therefore a dove was the form in which the Holy Spirit descended on Jesus Christ (Matt. 3:16). *See* Turtle, Turtledove.

Wild doves are numerous in some parts of the Holy Land. There are also vast numbers of tame pigeons in all the cities and villages. They have been kept from the earliest times. Being acceptable for sacrifices, they were also clean and used as food.

Dove's Dung. Several theories have been formulated to explain the difficulty in regard to this material as an article of food (2 Kings 6:25): (1) That it was a kind of plant, such as one known by that name to the Arabs. But it is unlikely that any plant would have been found in any quantity in a place in the last extremity of famine. (2) That it was in reality dung but used as a fertilizer, to promote the quick growth of vegetables for food. This is fanciful and not supported by the context. (3) That the people, in the depth of their despair and starvation, actually ate this disgusting material. This seems the most probable view and is supported by the fact that a similar occurrence took place in the English army in 1316.

Dragon (Heb. *tannîm*). The word *dragon* (Heb. *tannîm*; Gk. *drakōn*) appears much more frequently in the KJV than in the NASB and NIV, where it is sometimes replaced by the word *jackal* from Heb. *tan* (*see also* Whale, for another translation of *tan* and *tannîm*).

In the NASB the word appears three times in the OT: in connection with *Leviathan* (which see; Isa. 27:1); as an example of the strength of the Lord, who "pierced the dragon" (51:9); and as the name of a spring (Nah. 2:3). It does not appear at all in the NIV in the OT. In the NT (Rev. 12:3-4, 7, 9, 13, 16, 17; 13:2, 4, 11; 16:13; 20:2) it refers to a *mythical monster,* which is variously described and figured in the legends of all nations. This monster is used as a lively figure of *Satan* (which see).

In the KJV OT "dragon" is used with several meanings:

1. In connection with *desert animals* and in those cases best translated by "wolf," although the NASB and NIV use "jackal" repeatedly (Job 30:29; Ps. 44:19; Isa. 13:22; 34:13; 35:7; 43:20; Jer. 9:11; 10:22; 14:6; 49:33; 51:34, 37). The feminine form, Heb. *tannâ,* is found in Mal. 1:3.

2. As a reference to a *sea monster* (Pss. 74:13; 148:7, which give "sea monster," or "sea creature," in the NASB and NIV; Isa. 27:1, which renders "dragon" in both the NASB and KJV but "monster of the sea" in NIV).

3. As a reference to *serpents,* even of the smaller sorts (cf. KJV, NASB, and NIV of Deut. 32:33; Ps. 91:13; *see also* Ex. 7:9-10, 12).

4. As a reference to a *crocodile* or *monster* (cf. KJV, NASB, and NIV of Jer. 51:34; Ezek. 29:3; 32:2).

Dromedary. The references to the dromedary in the KJV of Isa. 60:6; Jer. 2:23 should be rendered "young camel" (Heb. *bikrâ;* cf. NASB and NIV readings). In the NASB of 1 Kings 4:28; Esther 8:10, the Heb. terms are given as "swift steeds" and "steeds." The NIV renders "horses" and "fast horses." *See also* Camel.

The dromedary is the Arabian camel (*Camelus dromedarius*) and is native to India, the Near East, and the northern part of Africa. It has one large hump on the back, unlike the Bactrian camel (*C. bactrianus*), which has two.

Eagle. The word *eagle* in the KJV includes both the *eagles* proper and the *vultures.* There are no less than four of the former and eight of the latter in the Holy Land. The most common of the vultures are the *griffon* and the *Egyptian vulture,* commonly known as *Pharaoh's chicken.* Of the eagles the most common is the *short-toed eagle, Circoetus Gallicus,* Gmel. All of these birds are swift (Deut. 28:49), soar high (Prov. 23:5), nest in inaccessible rocks (Job 39:27-30), and sight their prey from afar (Job 39:29). Besides the above references the habits of eagles and vultures are alluded to in numerous passages (Num. 24:21; Job 9:26; Prov. 30:17-19; Jer. 49:16; Ezek. 17:3; Obad. 4; Hab. 1:8; Matt. 24:28; Luke 17:37). The tenderness of the eagle to its young is also graphically set forth (Ex. 19:4; Deut. 32:11), and its great age is noted (Ps. 103:5, Isa. 40:31).

See also the bibliography that follows the last entry under Animal Kingdom.

Eagle Owl. *See* Owl.

Eggs. *See* Bird.

Elephant. An animal whose tusks furnished ivory (1 Kings 10:22, KJV marg. 2 Chron., 9:21, marg.). The animal is mentioned in 1 Macc. 1:17; 3:34 in connection with its later use in war, each beast being manipulated by an Indian driver and supporting on its broad back a tower from which as many as four soldiers fought (1 Macc. 6:37, where 32 is obviously erroneous). Before combat, elephants were often inflamed by the smell or taste of wine (1 Macc. 6:34; 3 Macc. 5:2). Two extant species of this huge animal are the *Elephas indicus* (Indian elephant) and the *Elephas africanus* (African variety), with several other types now extinct.

Ewe. *See* Sheep.

Falcon. A "bird of prey" known for its keen eyesight (Job 28:7). *See also* Kite; Vulture.

Fallow Deer. *See* Roebuck.

Ferret. *See* Gecko.

Fish. The Gk. language has more than four hundred names of fish. The Heb., as we have it in the Bible, has not even one. Nevertheless, fish are mentioned frequently in the Scriptures. They are classified as *clean,* having fins and scales, and *unclean,* those not so furnished. Whales, seals, dugongs, and other creatures, now known to be lung breathers, were regarded by the Hebrews as fish. There are forty-five species in the inland waters and large numbers in the Mediterranean Sea. Dagon, the god of the Philistines, had a man's body and a fish's tail. There are many allusions to fishing in the Bible.

Flea (Heb. *par'ōsh*). A most annoying and unfortunately common insect in the East. David compares himself to a flea in order to discredit Saul (1 Sam. 24:14). The similar reference (1 Sam. 26:20) is considered by some as an error in the text.

Fly (Heb. *zᵉbûb*). The immense number of flies in the East is one of its most striking characteristics. The number of species is also large. The Heb. *zᵉbûb,* which is part of the name of the god of Ekron, Baal-zebub, is generic, but as the housefly is the most familiar representative it would be most frequently thought of in connection with this name. It is uncertain whether the plague of flies, *'ārōb,* refers to the swarming of a single species (NASB, Ps. 78:45, "swarms of flies") or a multiplication of such noxious insects (KJV, "divers sorts of flies"). "Devoured them" can hardly mean ate them up bodily, nor bit them, but destroyed their food and overwhelmed them with their nastiness.

Foal. *See* Donkey; Horse.

Fowl. *See* Bird.

Fox. In several places it is uncertain whether Heb. *shû'āl;* Gk. *alōpēs,* signifies "fox" or "jackal" (Lam. 5:18; Ezek. 13:4; Song of Sol. 2:15). In others it doubtless means "jackals" (Judg. 15:4; Ps. 63:10). The difficulty in regard to the number of jackals that Samson turned loose into the fields of the Philistines disappears if we consider that he probably collected them, doubtless with the aid of his companions, over a wide district of the Philistine plain, and set them loose in pairs, at perhaps as many as 150 centers, so as to burn up as much as possible of the "shocks and the standing grain, along with the vineyards and groves" (Judg. 15:5). In only one place is it more probable that fox is intended (Neh. 4:3); Gk. *alōpēs* in the NT can mean nothing but "fox." The Syrian fox is identical with the common European fox, *Vulpes vulgaris,* L.

Frog (Heb. *ṣᵉpardēa').* The frog of the Egyptian plague (Ex. 8:2-14) is *Rana esculenta,* L., an amphibian, common everywhere in Egypt and the Holy Land (*see* Wisd. of Sol. 19:10).

Gazelle. The correct rendering of *ṣᵉbî* ("beauty"), translated "roe" and "roebuck" in the KJV (Deut. 12:15, 22; 14:5; 15:22; 2 Sam. 2:18; 1 Kings 4:23; 1 Chron. 12:8; Prov. 6:5; Song of Sol. 2:7, 9, 17; 3:5; 4:5; 7:3; 8:14; Isa. 13:14). Note that "fallow deer," Heb. *yaḥmûr,* in the KJV of Deut. 14:5; 1 Kings 4:23, is properly "roebuck" and is so translated in the NASB ("roedeer" in NIV of Deut. 14:5). The gazelle is the smallest of the antelopes in the Holy Land. It is abundant in the wildest portions of the country, and its beauty and speed are often alluded to in sacred and profane poetry. Its scientific name is *Gazella Dorcas,* L.

See also Deer.

Gecko (Heb. *'ănāqâ,* "wail," NASB and NIV, Lev. 11:30, for KJV, "ferret"). This lizard is named from the plaintive wail that it emits. Its scientific name is *Ptyodactylus Hasselquistii,* Schneid. It is frequently found in houses. It runs with great rapidity and clings to walls and ceilings by the suckers with which its feet are furnished. It is in no way probable that the Heb. original of this word signifies the "ferret," which is a weasel-like animal in modern times kept for hunting rabbits and rats.

Gier Eagle. A KJV term of indefinite meaning, referring to the soaring of birds of prey. For KJV "gier eagle" (Heb. *rāḥām*), Deut. 14:17, the NASB renders "carrion vulture," and the NIV, "osprey." *See* Vulture for a discussion of Heb. *peres,* rendered "gier eagle" in the RV but "vulture" in the NASB.

Glede. An old name for *kite* (which see). The NASB and NIV of Deut. 14:3 render "red kite" in place of KJV "glede."

Gnat (Gk. *kōnōps*). The wine gnat or midge used in fermenting and evaporating wine. Gnats or mosquitoes are irritating pests in all parts of the East and are common in the low-lying marshy lands of Palestine and Egypt. The term may refer to any small bloodsucking insect and the more minute creatures, whether bloodsuckers or not, which torment man and beast.

Figurative. Among the Jews, the custom of filtering wine was founded on the prohibition of "winged insects" being used for food, excepting *saltatorii* (see Lev. 11:22-23).

The saying of our Lord "You blind guides, who strain out a gnat and swallow a camel" (Matt. 23:24) was doubtless taken from this custom. The contrast between the *smallest insect* and the *largest animal* is used to illustrate the inconsistency of those who are superstitiously anxious in avoiding small faults, yet do not scruple to commit the greatest sins.

Gnawing Locust. *See* Locust.

Goat (Heb. *'aqqô,* "slender"; *yā'ēl,* "climbing"; *'ēz,* "strong"; *'attûd,* "prepared," and so "leader"; *śā'îr,* "shaggy"; Gk. *eriphion, tragos*). An animal often associated with sheep and mentioned with them in many places in Scripture, once in sharp contrast (Matt. 25:32-33). Owing to the unlovely disposition of the goat it was used less often for ordinary sacrifices. Nevertheless it was an allowable animal (Lev. 3:12; 4:24; 9:15; 10:16; chap. 16, passim; Num. 15:27; 28:22). Goats were only second in importance to sheep as a source and investment of wealth.

Figurative. In Matt. 25:32-33, sheep and goats are used to represent the righteous and the wicked respectively. "The wicked are here conceived of under the figure of *goats,* not on account of the wantonness and stench of the latter (Grotius), or in consequence of their stubbornness (Lange), but generally because these animals were considered to be comparatively worthless (Luke 15:29); and hence, in v. 33, we have the diminutive *ta 'eriphia* for the purpose of expressing contempt" (Meyer, *Com.* on Matt. 25:32-33).

See also Gods, False: Shaggy Goat; Wild Goat.

Goat, Wild. *See* Wild Goat.

Grasshopper. *See* Locust.

Great Lizard (NASB, RV, Lev. 11:29; KJV, "tortoise"). The Heb. *ṣāb* is the cognate of the Arab. *dabb,* which is the term applied to the *land monitor, Psammosaurus scincus,* an animal often six feet long, and to another lizard, *Uromastyx spinipes,* which attains a length of two feet, and has a short rounded head, and a tail surrounded by rings of spines. Although there are *land* and *sea tortoises* in the Holy Land and its adjacent sea, *ṣāb* does not refer to any of them; hence the NASB and NIV translation, "great lizard."

See also Lizard.

Great Owl. *See* Owl.

Greyhound, a translation of Heb. *zarzîr matnayim,* "girt in the loins" (Prov. 30:31, marg.). The greyhound, portrayed on Assyrian monuments, may be intended. The word, on the other hand, may denote the "war-horse" (RV marg.), decorated with trappings around the loins, or the starling, as the cognate word in Arab., Syr., and postbiblical Heb. suggests. The NASB renders "the strutting cock."　　　　　　　　　M.F.U.

Hare. *See* Rabbit.

Hart. *See* Deer.

Hawk (Heb. *nēṣ,* Lev. 11:16; Deut. 14:15; Job 39:26; *taḥmās,* Lev. 11:16; Deut. 14:15). There are eighteen species of the hawk "in its kind," ranging in size from the little sparrow hawk to the buzzard. These are exclusive of the kites and gledes. *See also* Night Hawk.

Hawk, Night. *See* Night Hawk.

He Ass. *See* Donkey.

Hedgehog. A hedgehog may be "any of a genus *Erinaceus* of Old World nocturnal insectivorous mammals having both hair and spines that they present outwardly by rolling themselves up," or it may be "any of several spiny mammals (as a porcupine)" (Webster's). NASB *hedgehog* (Isa. 34:11) replaces KJV *bittern,* but the modern *bit-*

tern refers to a type of *heron* (which see). The NIV reads "owl," or "screech owl."

Heifer. *See* Ox.

Hen. *See* Cock.

Heron. There are six species of herons in the Holy Land. As the Heb. *ănāphâ* (Lev. 11:19; Deut. 14:18) is associated with the stork and accompanied by the qualifying phrase "in their kinds," it is reasonable to accept "heron" rather than *eagle, parrot, swallow,* or *ibis,* all of which have been suggested in its place.

Hind. Another word used for female *deer* (which see).

Hippopotamus. *See* Behemoth.

Honey. *See* Bee.

Hoopoe. Probably the correct translation of Heb. *dûkîpat,* Lev. 11:19; Deut. 14:18; KJV, "lapwing." It is a migratory bird, *Upupa epops,* L., which spends the summer in the Holy Land and the winter in more southerly districts. Its head is often figured on the Egyptian monuments. If it is the bird intended by *dûkîpat,* it was unclean.

Hornet (Heb. *ṣir'â,* "stinging"). An insect with a formidable sting. It is found in considerable abundance in the Holy Land. Commentators are at variance as to whether the intention of the passages in which it is mentioned (Ex. 23:28; Deut. 7:20; Josh. 24:12) is literal or figurative. There are several species of hornets in the Holy Land.

Horse. Indo-European nomads E of the Black Sea domesticated the horse early. War horses and horse-drawn chariots were introduced in Asia Minor and Syria between 1900 and 1800 B.C., and the patriarchal narratives make mention of horses at the time of Jacob (Gen. 49:17). The horse was found in Egypt, where it was introduced by the Hyksos, who began to infiltrate as early as about 1900 B.C. When the Exodus took place (c. 1440 B.C.) Pharaoh's pursuing army was furnished with horses and chariots (Ex. 14:9; 15:19). Horses were also found in the host of Sisera at the time of Deborah (c. 1195-1155 B.C.; Judg. 4-5).　　　　　　　　　　　M.F.U.

The Hebrews were at first forbidden to retain the horses they captured (Deut. 17:16) and accordingly disabled most of those which they took (Josh. 11:4-9). But they soon ceased to regard this restriction and accumulated large studs of cavalry and chariot horses, mostly from Egypt and Assyria. Solomon had twelve thousand cavalry and four thousand chariot horses. Riding a horse was usually a sign of military rank. Many high functionaries, however, rode donkeys, mules, and camels. For a more detailed discussion of the horse, *see* articles Horse; Horses, Horsemen. For the use of the term *horses* in Esther 8:10 (NIV), *see* Dromedary.

Horseleech. *See* Leech.

Howler. *See* Owl, no. 3.

Hyena (Heb. *ṣabûa',* "speckled"). The hyena is

common throughout the Holy Land and would be one of the beasts of the field to devour the carrion (cf. NASB and NIV, Isa. 13:22). The place name Zeboim (1 Sam. 13:18; Neh. 11:34) means "hyena." It may be referred to in the "beasts" of KJV Isa. 3:18. *See* Jackal.   R.K.H.

Ibex (Heb. *dîshôn*, "leaper"; KJV, "pygarg"). Probably the *addax, Antilope addax,* Licht., an animal found in the Syrian and Arabian deserts (but note that in the NASB and NIV of Deut. 14:5 "antelope" is distinct from the ibex and replaces KJV "wild ox"). The ibex is mentioned in only one of the two lists of clean animals (Deut. 14:5). There seems to be no authority for KJV marg., "bison." *See also* Antelope.

Jackal (NASB, Heb. *tan*, "monster"; KJV, Heb. *tannîm,* "monster"). In the NASB and NIV "jackal" from Heb. *tan* sometimes appears in place of KJV "dragon" or "sea monster," from Heb. *tannîm* (Job 30:29; Ps. 44:19; Isa. 13:22; 34:13; 35:7; 43:20; Jer. 9:11; 10:22; 14:6; 49:33; 51:37; Mic. 1:8). *See* Dragon. It would be better rendered *wolf* (which see). In the RV the marg. reading for Jer. 14:6 is "crocodile," whereas "jackal" is the reading in the NKJV and NIV of the verse. We believe this also should be rendered "wolf." On the other hand "wild beasts of the islands" (KJV, Jer. 50:39) should be "jackals," and is so rendered in the NASB. The NIV renders "hyenas" here. "Jackal" should in some cases be substituted for "fox," as the translation of *shû'āl. See* Fox. The jackal, a familiar nocturnal animal with a peculiar howl, feeds on live prey and carrion. *See also* Owl, no. 8.

Kid. *See* Goat.

Kine. *See* Ox.

Kite. A bird of prey belonging to the falcon family with long pointed wings and forked tail. Kites are of various sorts (Deut. 14:13). The black kite appears in Palestine in March and feeds on offal. The word *kite* in the RV renders Heb. *dā'â* and *dayyâ* (Lev. 11:14; Deut. 14:13; in KJV "vulture") and twice this name is employed in the KJV to render *'ayyâ* (Lev. 11:14; Deut. 14:13; in NASB, "falcon"; in NIV, "black kite"). *See also* Gier Eagle; Glede; Vulture.   M.F.U.

Lamb. *See* Sheep.

Land Crocodile. *See* Chameleon.

Lapwing. *See* Hoopoe.

Leech (Heb. *'alûqâ,* "sucking," Prov. 30:15). Either one of the leeches, *Hirudo medicinalis,* Sav., or *Hoemopis sanguisorba,* Sav., found in stagnant waters throughout the land.

Leopard (Heb. *nāmēr,* "spotted"; Gk. *pardalis, Felis leopardus,* L.) a wily, active, ferocious beast (Isa. 11:6; Jer. 5:6; Dan. 7:6; Hab. 1:8; Rev. 13:2). Next to the bear it is the largest of the existing carnivora in the Holy Land. It has a beautiful spotted skin (Jer. 13:23), which is highly admired and is used for rugs and saddle covers; one is sometimes hung over the back by religious mendicants. The *cheetah* or *hunting leopard, Felis*

jubata, Schreb., is probably included under the Heb. generic name *nāmēr.*

Leviathan (Heb. *liwᵉyātān*). A word signifying an animal writhing or gathering itself into folds; used for the "crocodile" (Job 3:8, "Leviathan," NASB, NIV, but "their mourning," KJV; 41:1, "leviathan," or "Leviathan," NASB, NIV, KVJ, with marg. "crocodile," NASB, NIV; also Ps. 74:14); for a "serpent" (Isa. 27:1); for some "sea monster" (Ps. 104:26), possibly the whale. However, leviathan may be purely a mythical concept adapted to biblical usage (as dragon used to prefigure Satan). Since the discovery of the Ras Shamra religious texts in Syria on the site of ancient Ugarit, it has become evident that there is a parallel between the seven-headed Canaanite monster Lotan of prevailing mythology, 1700-1400 B.C., and the biblical leviathan. Isaiah seems to employ this ancient mythological idea of the destroyed leviathan poetically (Isa. 27:1) to symbolize the Judgment Day when God will triumph over the threatening evil of this world system.

Lice. Notwithstanding the authority of the RV (marg., Ex. 8:16; Ps. 105:31) "sandflies" or "fleas" for Heb. *kēn* and its derivatives, and the NASB and NIV rendering "gnats," the weight of evidence is in favor of the KJV translation "lice." These filthy insects are an endemic pest of the first magnitude in the East. What it must have been when they became universal is beyond the power of our imagination to conceive. The Muslims shave their heads and use means to cause hair to fall out by the roots in other parts of their bodies to escape this pest. This is the inheritance of an ancient custom of the Egyptian priests and other inhabitants.

Lion. The well-known king of beasts, formerly abundant in Palestine (Judg. 14:5; 1 Sam. 17:34; 2 Kings 17:25; Jer. 49:19, etc.) and not extinct there until the end of the twelfth century. Seven words, *'aryēh, kᵉpîr, gûr, lābî, layish, shahal,* and *shāhāh,* are used to denote the lion in general or at different ages and in different states. Four words *shā'ag, nā'ar, nāham,* and *hagâ,* express his voice in varying moods, as the "roar," "yell," or "growl." Six words denote his attitudes and movements in quest of prey, *rābaṣ, shāhah, yāshab, 'ārab, rāmaś, zinnēq,* as "prowling," "crouching," and "ambushing."

Figurative. The Scriptures abound in allusions to the strength, courage, cruelty, and rapacity of this beast. His royal attributes made him an emblem of Christ (Rev. 5:5).

Little Owl. *See* Owl.

Lizard (Heb. *lᵉṭa'â*), a family term, occurring in a list (Lev. 11:30) of six, all of which are rendered by names denoting lizards. A considerable number of the lizard family are found in the Holy Land, and several of them are common about houses, especially the *wall lizard, Zootica muralis,* Laur.; the *sand lizard, Lacerta agilis,* L.; and the *green lizard, L. viridis,* L.

See also Chameleon; Gecko; Great Lizard; Mole.

Lizard, Great. *See* Great Lizard.

Locust (Heb. *'arbeh,* generic term). The devastations that the locust is capable of producing made it a fitting instrument of one of the ten memorable plagues of Egypt. Two species, *Aedipoda migratoria* and *Acridium peregrinum,* are the most common. They are always to be found in the southeastern deserts but, from time to time, multiply in vast numbers and spread over the whole country, carrying ruin and despair everywhere. The poetical and prophetical books abound in vivid descriptions of their destructiveness and the powerlessness of man to resist them. Eight Heb. words seem to refer to locusts, some of them probably to various stages in their development. It is, however, impossible to determine the exact meaning of each. Locusts were undoubtedly eaten (Matt. 3:4).

Jahn (*Biblical Archaeology,* sec. 23, s.v.) gives a vivid description of locusts: "Vast bodies of migrating locusts, called by the orientals the armies of God, lay waste the country. They observe as regular order, when they march, as an army. At evening they descend from their flight, and form, as it were, their camps. In the morning, when the sun has risen considerably, they ascend again, if they do not find food, and fly in the direction of the wind (Prov. 30:27; Nah. 3:16-17). They go in immense numbers (Jer. 46:23), and occupy a space of ten or twelve miles in length, and four or five in breadth, and are so deep that the sun cannot penetrate through them; so that they convert the day into night, and bring a temporary darkness on the land (Ex. 10:14-15; Joel 2:2, 10). The sound of their wings is terrible (Joel 2:5). When they descend upon the earth, they cover a vast track a foot and a half high; if the air is cold and moist, or if they be wet with the dew, they remain . . . till they are dried and warmed by the sun (Nah. 3:17). Nothing stops them. They fill the ditches which are dug to stop them with their bodies, and extinguish by their numbers the fires which are kindled. They pass over walls and enter the doors and windows of houses (Joel 2:7-9). They devour everything which is green, strip off the bark of trees, and even break them to pieces by their weight (Ex. 10:12-19; Joel 1:4, 7, 10, 12, 16, 18, 20; 2:3)."

The *palmerworm* (Heb. *gāzām,* "devouring") does not appear in the NASB or NIV but is instead rendered as "gnawing locust," or "locust swarm" (Joel 1:4; 2:25) or "caterpillar" (Amos 4:9). Nor does *cankerworm* appear, being replaced by "creeping locust," or "young locust" (Joel 1:4; 2:25). The *bald locust* of KJV Lev. 11:22 is replaced in the NASB by "devastating locust," and by the NIV as "katydid." The *cricket* appears in the NASB for Deut. 28:42 and Lev. 11:22 but as the translation of two separate Heb. terms (rendered as "locust" in Deut. 28:42 and "beetle" in

Lev. 11:22). The NIV translates "cricket" in Lev. 11:22 but "swarms of locusts" in Deut. 28:42. *See also* Cricket.

Locusts, grasshoppers, and *caterpillars* appear in the KJV, NASB, and NIV, but the relationship of these terms to one another and to the underlying Heb. is complex, as a study of concordances for the KJV, NASB, and NIV readily indicates.

See also the bibliography that appears at the end of the article on the Animal Kingdom.

Mice. *See* Mouse.

Migration of Birds. *See* Birds.

Mole. No true mole exists in the Holy Land. The mole rat, *Spalax typhlus,* Pall., may be the animal intended by Heb. *tinshemet* (Lev. 11:30, NASB and NIV, "chameleon," which see).

Another Heb. term, *ḥepōr pērôt,* is translated "moles" in Isa. 2:20. It would perhaps better be translated "burrowing rats," or "mice," being understood as generic for all the numerous burrowers found in waste places. The mole rat is a rodent (which is the NIV translation), whereas the mole is one of the insectivora, which comprise the *shrews, hedgehogs,* and *moles.*

A third Heb. word, *ḥōled,* is translated "mole" in the NASB of Lev. 11:29, and "weasel" in the KJV and NIV of that verse. The cognative Arab. of the term, *huld,* refers to the *mole rat, Spalax typhus,* and the term must be understood in a family sense for all the *Mustelidoe,* as the *marten, ichneumon, genet,* and *polecat.*

Monitor Lizard. *See* Chameleon.

Moth. Several species of the family *Tineidae* that infest woolen goods and furs. It is almost impossible to guard against them in the Eastern climate. The people wrap up their carpets and clothes with pepper grains, tobacco, pride of India leaves, and other substances. The scriptural and apocryphal allusions to moths are a significant reference to their subtle and noxious abilities (Job 4:19; Hos. 5:12; Matt. 6:19-20; Luke 12:33; Sir. 19:3; 42:13).

Mountain Sheep (Heb. *zemer;* KJV, "chamois"). The mountain sheep was almost certainly known to the Israelites by its Heb. name *zemer.* It was within the reach of them, as it was spoken of as an animal they might eat. The mountain sheep of Egypt and Arabia is known as the *aoudad* and the *kebsh.* It is probable that it was abundant in the Sinai, where it is to be found even now. It is distinguished from the other animals of its group by the long hair on its throat and breast, extending like a ruffle to its foreknee. Its horns resemble those of the *beden,* or *mountain goat.*

Mouse. The number of species of mouselike animals in the Holy Land is about forty. Probably all of them are included in the generic prohibition (Lev. 11:29). One species was eaten by the rebellious Israelites, along with swine's flesh (Isa. 66:17). We cannot be sure what species it was. It may have been the *hamster,* which is said to be eaten by the Arabs.

Mule. Mules were not allowed according to the Mosaic law (Lev. 19:19). Yet they were used early in the period of the kings (2 Sam. 13:29; 18:9; 1 Kings 1:33, etc.). They were imported from Beth-togarmah (Ezek. 27:14). The Heb. term *pered* undoubtedly refers to the mule.

Nest. *See* Bird.

Night Creature. *See* Owl, no. 3.

Night Hawk. The Heb. *tahmās* is uncertain in meaning. Some have rendered it "ostrich," others "owl." As the owl is mentioned in the list (Lev. 11:16; Deut. 14:15), and at least one other word exists for the ostrich, the RV has done well in transliterating in the marg. "tahmas," with the gloss "of uncertain meaning." *See also* Hawk; Owl.

Night Monster. *See* Owl.

Onycha (on'ī-ka), a substance mentioned as an ingredient of the holy perfume (Ex. 30:34). It is the operculum of shells of Strombi and is prepared for use by roasting, which evolves the oil on which its aromatic properties depend.

Osprey. *See* Buzzard; Gier Eagle; Vulture, no. 4.

Ossifrage. *See* Vulture.

Ostrich (Heb. *renānim*, "birds of piercing cries," Job 39:13, NASB and NIV; elsewhere *ya'ănâ*). The KJV translates *ya'ănâ* or *bat ya'ănâ* as "owl," sometimes with a marginal reading "ostrich." The RV, NASB, and NIV correctly and uniformly render it "ostrich." The ostrich is a well-known bird, found in the deserts of Africa and Arabia. Its renown for voracity is due to the large size of the pebbles, bits of glass, or other objects that it swallows, as fowls swallow gravel, to assist in the subdivision of their food in the gizzard. The female ostrich makes a shallow nest and lays so many eggs that some of them are left uncovered and therefore not incubated. She does, however, cover most of them with sand and, while leaving them to the influence of the sun's rays by day, incubates them by night. The ostrich, when pursued, runs against the wind and in large circles, a fact that enables the hunter to lie in wait for it and thus partially neutralize the advantage of its great speed. It is not true that it hides its head in the sand on the approach of danger. When compared with some other birds, as the partridge, noted for their cunning in concealing their eggs and young and escaping from their enemies, the ostrich, which runs away from eggs and chicks in the frantic desire to escape by its great speed, seems open to the charge of stupidity (Job 39:14-17).

Ostrich plumes graced ancient royal courts as fans. An ivory-handled fan of King Tutankhamen still retains its lovely ostrich plumes in the National Museum at Cairo after more than three thousand years. *See also* Owl.

Owl. The rendering of several Heb. words of which perhaps only two actually refer to this broad-headed, large-eyed bird.

1. Heb. *bat ya'ănâ* (Lev. 11:16; Deut. 14:15; Isa. 13:21; 34:13; 43:20; Jer. 50:39; Mic. 1:8) is certainly the *ostrich* (which see), and is so rendered in the NASB. The NIV translates "owl" in all these passages.

2. Heb. *lîlît* (Isa. 34:14) is a nocturnal specter or more precisely a night demon, not a "screech owl" (KJV). NASB reads "night monster," and the NIV, "night creature."

3. Heb. *qippôz* (Isa. 34:15) is perhaps the dart snake (RV), not the "great owl" (KJV). The NASB reads "tree snake," and NIV, "owl."

4. Heb. *tinshemet* (Lev. 11:18) is rendered "swan" (KJV and Vulg.), "water hen" (RSV), or "white owl" (NASB and NIV). *See also* Swan. Note that in Lev. 11:30 *tinshemet* is translated "mole" in the KJV and "chameleon" in the NASB and NIV.

5. Heb. *yanshôp* (Lev. 11:17; Deut. 14:16; Isa. 34:11) is rendered "ibis" (LXX and Vulg.), "owl" (Targums and Peshitta), and "great owl" (KJV, NASB, and NIV). The species may, however, be the Egyptian eagle owl (*Bubo ascalaphus*), living in caves and ruins about Beersheba and Petra.

6. Heb. *kôs*, "a cup" (Lev. 11:17; Deut. 14:16; Ps. 102:6). The Heb. term is rendered "little owl" (NASB, NIV, and KJV), "owl of the waste places" (NASB), and "owl of the desert" (KJV). The reference is probably to the little owl, *Athene glaux*, commonly seen in Palestine at twilight. The Athenians considered this bird wise and associated it with their patron deity, stamping its image on their silver money.

7. Heb. *tahmās* is rendered "owl" in the NASB and "night hawk" in the KJV.

8. Heb. *ōah*, a "howler" (Isa. 13:21, marg., "Ochim") is rendered "doleful creatures" in the KJV but "owl" in the NASB, and "jackals" in the NIV.

Ox.

1. The translation of Heb. *shôr*. The cognate Arab. *thaur* (Gk. *tauros;* Lat. *taurus*) refer to the male. *Shôr*, however, is generic for both sexes and all ages. Though generally translated "ox," it is sometimes rendered "bull."

2. **Cow.** The rendering of Heb. *bāqār*, which is also generic for bovines; *beqarâ*, with the feminine ending, signifies the "cow."

3. **Bull.** The equivalent of Heb. *par*, or *pār*. The feminine *pārâ* is once used (Num. 19:2) for "heifer." Sometimes the term *'abbîr*, "strong one," is used metaphorically for "bull" (Ps. 22:12; Isa. 34:7), but it is also used in the same sense for "horse" (Jer. 8:16; 47:3).

4. **Calf, Heifer.** The rendering of Heb. *'ēgel* and *'eglâ*. Once "heifer" is used as the equivalent of *pārâ* (Num. 19:2).

5. **Wild Ox.** The translation of Heb. *teô* (Deut. 14:5, KJV). **Wild Bull** is the rendering of Heb. *tô'* (Isa. 51:20, KJV). The NASB, NIV, and RV correctly render *"antelope"* (which see). "Unicorn" of the KJV is rendered "wild ox" in NASB, NIV,

and RV (Num. 23:22; 24:8; Job 39:9-10; Ps. 29:6; 92:10). *See also* Wild Ox.   M.F.U.

Ox, Wild. *See* Wild Ox, below.

Palmerworm. *See* Locust.

Partridge (Heb. *gōrē*, a "caller," from its "cry"). There are two species of partridges in the Holy Land, *Caccabis chukar,* C. R. Gray, the *red-legged partridge,* and *Ammoperdix Heyi,* Temm., the *sand partridge.* The former is generally found in the middle and upper mountain regions and the Syrian desert. The latter is peculiar to the Dead Sea and Jordan Valley. This may be the one alluded to by David (1 Sam. 26:20). The passage Jer. 17:11, in which RV has adopted the KJV marginal rendering, "gathereth young which she hath not brought forth," is obscure. It may refer to pirating a nest, after the manner of the cuckoo, or decoying away the chicks of another bird. Although no modern authority has witnessed such theft, some of the ancients believed that the partridge was guilty of it.

Peacocks. In one place where KJV has given "peacock" (Job 39:13) the original is Heb. *r^enānâ,* which is undoubtedly a name for the ostrich, as in NASB, NKJV, and NIV. In the other two passages where "peacocks" occurs in NASB, KJV, and RV (1 Kings 10:22; 2 Chron. 9:21), the reference is unquestionably to this lordly bird. The Heb. *tŭkkî* survives in a similar word *tokei,* which is the Tamil name of the bird. Since it is now known that the words for the ivory and apes that Solomon imported are of Indian origin, the equation *tŭkkî = "peacock"* may be defended as it finds a satisfactory origin in Malabar *togai, toghai* (Old Tamil *tokei, togu*), a peacock. The peacock (*Pavo cristatus*) is native to India where it is unmolested and common. However, another rendering of *tŭkkî* is possible as a result of evidence from Egypt, where it may be equated with *t.ky* (monkey), the letter *t* (feminine particle) indicating two varieties of monkeys. This interpretation would suggest an African origin of the animal as well as an African location for the enigmatic Ophir. Thus the NIV renders it "baboon" in 1 Kings 10:22 and 2 Chron. 9:21.

Pelican. Probably the correct translation of Heb. *qā'at,* "the vomiter." The NIV renders it "desert owl!" throughout. It was an unclean bird (Lev. 11:18; Deut. 14:17). It was found in desolate places (Ps. 102:6) and ruins (Isa. 34:11; Zeph. 2:14, KJV, "cormorant," marg., "pelican"). Two species are found in the Holy Land, *Pelecanus onocrotalus,* L. and *P. crispus,* Brush. The pelican lives on fish that it catches with its long beak and stores in the capacious pouch beneath it. When gorged with food it flies away to some lonely place and, pressing its pouch against its breast, stands in this attitude for hours or days, until it is hungry again, when it resumes its fishing. If *qā'at* does in fact refer to the pelican, this attitude would well suit the melancholy inactivity to which David alludes when comparing himself with the "pelican of the wilderness."

Pigeon. *See* Dove.

Porpoise. (Heb. *tahash*). This member of the dolphin family occurs in the coastal waters of Africa and Asia. Although its skin has been suggested as suitable for an outer covering of the Tabernacle (Ex. 25:5; 26:14; NIV, "sea cows"), this is actually incorrect. Dolphins have fins, but they do not have scales, and therefore they would be abhorrent and unclean to the Israelites (Lev. 11:10). It is thus inconceivable that the skin from such unclean carcasses should adorn Israel's most holy shrine. The identity of the *tahash* is unknown, and to argue from the cognate Arab. *tuhas* to an identification with the dugong or any other marine mammal that would have been ceremonially unclean for the Hebrews is therefore fruitless.   R.K.H.

Pygarg. *See* Ibex.

Quail (Heb. *śelāw*). A heavy-bodied, terrestrial bird, *Coturnix vulgaris,* L., more or less resident in Egypt and the Holy Land, but also passing through them on its migrations northward in March and southward in September. The quails pass over narrow portions of the sea but arrive greatly exhausted. Many of them perish in transit. Those which the Israelites captured (Ex. 16:13; Num. 11:31-32) were on their way N. Tristram has pointed out their course up the Red Sea, across the mouth of the Gulf of Akabah and Suez, to the Sinaitic peninsula, and so blown by a sea wind over the camp of the Israelites.

Rabbit (Heb. *arnebet,* Lev. 11:6; Deut. 14:7). A rodent of which there are four species in the Holy Land, of which *Lepus Syriacus,* Hempr. et Ehr., is generally diffused. The others, *L. Sinaiticus,* Hempr. et Ehr., *L. Aegyptius,* Geoffr., and *L. Isabellinus,* Rüpp., are desert species.

Ram. *See* Sheep.

Raven. The raven, *Corvus corax,* L., is the first bird named (Gen. 8:7). It feeds in part on seeds and fruit. To this fact our Savior alludes (Luke 12:24; Gk. *korax*). It also captures small creatures alive, but it loves carrion (Prov. 30:17) and so was unclean. Orientals, as well as occidentals, look upon it as a bird of evil omen (Isa. 34:11). The Heb. word *'ōrēb,* of which raven is the translation, doubtless includes the *crows, jays,* and *choughs,* as is implied in the expression "in its kind" (Lev. 11:15; Deut. 14:14).

Rock Badger (Heb. *shāpān*). A small pachydermatous animal, with teeth and feet resembling those of the hippopotamus. It is as large as a rabbit, but is not to be confused with the rabbit of England. Common in Sinai, around the Dead Sea area and in N Palestine, it is called a "coney" in KJV. It has a plump body and short ears and tail. Its scientific name is *Hyrax Syriacus.* It does not really chew the cud but has a motion of the jaws that resembles that function. If it had a divided hoof, it would undoubtedly have been admitted into the list of animals allowed to the Hebrews for food (Lev. 11:5; Deut. 14:7).

The rock badger lives in holes and clefts of the rocks (Ps. 104:18). It is found throughout the whole length of Sinai, Palestine, and Lebanon.

In the NASB "rock badger" replaces KJV "coney" and is to be distinguished from KJV "badger," rendered "porpoise" in the NASB.

Roe. *See* Doe; Gazelle; Roebuck. The NIV retains "coney" in all three texts.

Roebuck. A term appearing in the KJV, NIV, and NASB, though of different Heb. words. Except in the case of Prov. 5:19, where "roe" of the KJV refers to Heb. *ya'ălâ* and is more properly translated "doe" (so NASB and NIV), KJV "roe" and "roebuck" are mistranslations of Heb. *ṣebî,* which signifies the *gazelle* (which see). In the NASB and NIV "roebuck," *Cervus capreolus,* L., is the proper translation of Heb. *yaḥmûr* (Deut. 14:5; 1 Kings 4:23; KJV wrongly, "fallow deer"). The roebuck must have been abundant in the days of Solomon. It is now found on rare occasion in northern Galilee and Carmel and in the woods of Gilead. It is still known E of the Jordan.

Roedeer. *See* Gazelle.

Sand Flies. *See* Lice.

Sand Lizard. *See* Snail; Lizard.

Satyr. The equivalent of *śā'îr,* which means a "he-goat," and is usually so translated; in NASB it is translated "shaggy goats" (marg., "goat demons"; Isa. 13:21), or in 34:14, "hairy goat." The NIV translates "wild goats" in both passages. The same word is rendered in KJV (Lev. 17:7; 2 Chron. 11:15) "devils," RV, "he-goats," marg., "satyrs." Grotesque creatures, half man and half goat, figure in the Greek and Roman mythologies under the name of *satyrs* and *fauns,* but the OT representations are rather demonic conceptions. *See also* Gods, False: Shaggy Goat.

Scorpion. A generic term for about a dozen species of the *Arachnidoe,* which inhabit the Holy Land. The poison is in the sting at the end of the tail. The scorpion is an emblem of torture and wrath. Some of the species of southern Palestine are six inches long.

Screech Owl. *See* Owl.

Sea Gull (Heb. *shāḥap*; KJV, "cuckoo"; Lev. 11:16; Deut. 14:15). The Heb. term can refer to gulls, terns, and petrels, all of which are common on the seashore and lakes of Palestine. It was listed among the unclean birds (Lev. 11:16; Deut. 14:15).

Sea Cows. *See* Porpoise.

Sea Monster. *See* Dragon; Whale.

Serpent. It is impossible to unravel the tangle in which the translators, ancient and modern, have involved the eight words used in the Heb. for serpents. Only one of them (Heb. *shepîpôn*) can be identified with any degree of certainty. This is in all probability *Cerastes Hasselquistii,* Strauch, the "horned cerastes" of the desert. It is reasonably probable that *peten* refers to the

"cobra." *Ṣepa'* and *ṣip'onî* and *'ep'eh* are uncertain. Heb. *tannîm* is usually translated "dragon," and if it refers to a snake in the story of the controversy between Moses and Pharaoh we have no means of guessing the species. Heb. *nāḥāsh* is a general term, corresponding exactly to the English "serpent" or "snake." Heb. *sārap* means "fiery" and is therefore only a term to characterize the venomousness of the unknown species intended.

The serpents of Egypt, Sinai, and the Holy Land are numerous. Of the venomous ones the principal are *Daboia zanthina,* Gray, *Cerastes Hasselquistii,* Strauch, *Naja haje,* L., *Echis arenicola,* Boie, *Vipera Euphratica,* Martin, and *V. ammodytes,* L. The English names of snakes mentioned are "adder," "arrowsnake," "asp," "basilisk" (fictitious), "cockatrice" (fictitious), "fiery flying serpent," "viper," and the generic term "serpent." Besides these the following terms are used: "crooked," "crossing like a bar," "fleeing," "gliding," "piercing," "swift," "winding," as adjectives to the serpent, but seeming to refer to the "crocodile" under the name "leviathan" (Isa. 27:1).

Almost all the allusions to the serpent in the Scriptures are to its malignity and venom. Probably the Hebrews regarded most or all snakes as poisonous. Only once (Matt. 10:16) is there a doubtful commendation of the serpent on account of its wisdom. Its habits, even to being oviparous (Isa. 59:5), were minutely noted. The devil is the "old serpent."

See also Dragon.

She Ass. *See* Donkey.

Sheep. The rendering of several Heb. and Gk. words. This animal is mentioned about five hundred times in the Bible. The broadtailed variety is the one which is, and probably has been from ancient times, the one raised in the East. Allusion is made to its fat tail ("rump," KJV; Ex. 29:22; Lev. 3:9; NASB, NKJV, NIV, "fat tail"). The number of sheep raised in ancient times was prodigious. We read of the tribute of 200,000 fleeces from the king of Moab (2 Kings 3:4). Reuben took 250,000 sheep from the children of Ishmael (1 Chron. 5:21). Lambs were offered in immense numbers in sacrifice, usually males, in one case a female (Lev. 14:10). Solomon offered 120,000 on occasion of the consecration of the Temple (1 Kings 8:63). Sheeps' milk and wool were and are of immense importance for food and clothing and as articles of commerce. Rams' skins were used in the structure of the Tabernacle.

Shepherds in Bible lands have the same personal knowledge and exhaustive care of their flocks as in ancient times. Their offices were chosen as emblems of those of Christ and His ministers in the care of the believers committed to their charge.

The interest of the sheep to Christians culminates in the fact that Christ is the atoning, illuminating, life-giving, reigning Lamb of God.

She Goat. *See* Goat.

Skink. *See* Snail.

Slug. *See* Snail.

Snail. The Heb. word *ḥōmeṭ*, rendered (KJV, Lev. 11:30) "snail," is generic for "lizard" (NASB, "sand reptile;" RV, "sand lizard," which rendering is, however, only conjectural); NIV, "skink." Another word, *shablûl* (Ps. 58:8), is probably generic for "snail," although neither the LXX nor Vulg. supports the rendering. The NIV identifies it as "slug." The surface of rocks, walls, and tree trunks in this land is often covered with a thin film, looking like a coating of collodion or gelatin. This is caused by the passing and repassing of snails, which always leave a slimy track behind them. This is the "melting" of the snail, alluded to in the above passage. If a snail remains attached to a place in the hot sun it will dry up and be stuck fast to its resting place by this thick mucilaginous fluid. The number of species of snails in Bible lands is large.

Sow. *See* Swine.

Sparrow. One rendering of Heb. *ṣippôr*, which, like *'ûsfur* in Arab., is generic for small birds. *Ṣippôr* is more frequently rendered "bird" and "fowl." The NT *strouthion* probably refers to the house sparrow (Matt. 10:29; Luke 12:6-7).

Speckled Bird. *See* Hyena.

Spider. Two Heb. words are translated by KJV "spider."

1. Heb. *śemāmît* (Prov. 30:28), from a root signifying "to be poisonous." The NASB and NIV give "lizard." Both the spider and several varieties of lizards frequent houses.

2. Heb. *'akkābîsh* (Job 8:14; Isa. 59:5) is generic for "spiders," of which there are a large number in the Holy Land.

Sponge (Gk. *spongos*). A porous body, produced in the sea, composed of tubules and cells and lined with an amoeboid substance. The vital action of these protozoa keeps up a steady circulation of water through the channels. Commercial sponges consist only of the skeleton, out of which the lining and investing amoeboid substance has been cleaned. The only mention of the sponge is in connection with the crucifixion of our Savior (Matt. 27:48; etc.).

Stork (Heb. *ḥăsîdâ*). Two species, *Ciconia alba* L., the *white stork,* and *C. nigra,* L., the *black stork,* are found in the Holy Land. It was an unclean bird. Although its usual nesting place is in ruins, it also, especially the black species, resorts to trees (Ps. 104:17). It is a migratory bird, going to northern Europe in the summer, flying high in the heaven (Jer. 8:7), and making a rushing noise ("the wind in their wings," Zech. 5:9). Their affection for their young is proverbial.

Swallow. The only Heb. words properly translated "swallow" are *deôr* (Ps. 84:3; Prov. 26:2) and *sûs* (Isa. 38:14). The NIV translates *sûs* "swift" in Isa. 38:14. In the latter *'agûr* signifies

"twitterer" instead of "swallow," as in KJV, or "crane," as in RV. The *swallows, swifts,* and *martins* are numerous in Bible lands. Their shrill cries, as they skim the ground and sweep through the air with incredible rapidity, are among the most characteristic features of oriental towns.

Swan. A KJV term. It appears there as the rendering of Heb. *tinshemet* (Lev. 11:18; Deut. 14:16; RV, "horned owl," marg., "swan"; NASB and NIV, "white owl"). The Heb. would refer to the *purple gallinule, Porphyrio coeruleus,* Vandelli, or one of the *ibises, Ibis religiosa,* L., or *I. falcinella,* L., and not to the *swan,* which is hardly found in the Holy Land and would not have been regarded as unclean. *See* Chameleon; Owl for other renderings of Heb. *tinshemet.*

Swarming Locust. *See* Locust.

Swift. *See* Swallow.

Swine (Heb. *ḥăzîr;* Gk. *choiros*). The hog is regarded by Muslims with no less loathing than by Jews. Many oriental Christians share this feeling, while others raise swine and eat freely of its flesh. The Jews in Christ's time had come to ignore their own law on this subject (Matt. 8:30-34), as had some of their ancestors who ate pork (Isa. 66:17).

Tortoise. *See* Lizard, Great.

Tree Snake. *See* Owl; Snake.

Turtle, Turtledove (Heb. *tôr*), one of the best-known birds of the Holy Land. It was used by the poor for sacrifices (Lev. 5:11; etc.). Its peculiar note and gentle disposition (Ps. 74:19) made it a type of Christ. There are three species in the Holy Land, *Turtur auritus,* L., the *common turtledove; T. risorius,* L., the *collared turtledove;* and *T. Senegalensis,* L., the *palm* or *Egyptian turtle.*

Unicorn. *See* Wild Ox.

Viper. *See* Serpent.

Vulture. Several vultures are referred to in Scripture, the Heb. or Gk. being rendered by various English terms.

1. Heb. *'ayyâ* is given as "kite" (Lev. 11:14; Deut. 14:13) or "red kite" (Deut. 14:13) in the NASB and NIV. The KJV rendering is "vulture" (for "kite") and "glede" (for "red kite").

2. Heb. *dayyâ* appears in Isa. 34:15 as "hawks" in the NASB, "falcons" in the NIV, and "vultures" in the KJV. It is present also in the KJV of Deut. 14:15 ("vultures") but not in the NASB, which uses Heb. *dā'â* ("kite") instead.

3. Heb. *'ayyâ* appears in Lev. 11:14; Deut. 14:13; and Job 28:7. In Lev. 11:14 and Deut. 14:13 the Heb. term is rendered "falcon" in the NASB and NIV and "kite" in the KJV. In the passage in Job "falcon" appears in the NASB and NIV and "vulture" in the KJV.

4. Heb. *rāḥām* is rendered "carrion vulture" in the NASB and "osprey" in the NIV of Lev. 11:18 and Deut. 14:17, but "gier eagle" in the KJV of those verses. The Heb. term refers to *Pharaoh's chicken, Neophron Percnopterus,* Sav.

5. Heb. *peres,* the *lamergeier, Gypoetus barbatus,* L., is the "ossifrage" of KJV Lev. 11:13 and Deut. 14:12, but "vulture" in the NASB and NIV. This bird is the largest of the vultures in the Holy Land. As it is a familiar bird in Europe, its habits are well known. It kills its prey but also does not disdain carrion. Hence it is unclean (Lev. 11:13; Deut. 14:12). The RV renders "gier eagle."

6. Gk. *aetos* is given as "vultures" in the NASB of Matt. 24:28 and Luke 17:37, but as "eagles" in the KJV.

See also Buzzard; Eagle.

Wasp. The reference in an apocryphal passage, the only place in which this insect is mentioned (Wisd. of Sol. 12:8), is doubtless to the common *yellow jacket, Vespa vulgaris,* L. It is very common throughout the Holy Land, especially so in the vineyards during vintage, about the grape presses, and about the fruit shops in towns.

Weasel. *See* Mole.

Whale (Heb. *tan,* or *tannîm;* a "monster"). The "great whales" (KJV, Gen. 1:21; NASB, "sea monsters"; Job 7:12; Ezek. 32:2) are to be understood as all aquatic creatures not considered fish. Jonah's whale (*kētos,* Matt. 12:40, from the LXX, Jonah 1:17) was a "great fish." It might have been a *spermaceti whale,* had one wandered into the Mediterranean, or a *large shark,* of which that sea contains many large enough to have swallowed Jonah.

White Owl. *See* Owl.

Wild Ass. *See* Donkey.

Wild Beasts. The significance of beasts in many places, and of wild beasts in all, has to do with beasts of prey. The context will always settle the meaning. There are no longer any lions in Syria and Palestine. They were, however, numerous in Bible times. Bears are still found in considerable numbers in Anti-Lebanon, and a few still linger in Lebanon. They become more abundant in Amanus and the Taurus. Wolves are common throughout. Leopards are occasionally seen in Lebanon, more freqently in Anti-Lebanon and E of the Jordan, and in the neighborhood of the Dead Sea. Jackals are common everywhere. Foxes are also numerous. Hyenas haunt ruins and waste places. Badgers, martens, polecats, mongooses, and genets are also found. Among the wild beasts that are not carnivorous are the deer, the gazelle, the antelope, wild donkey, the beden (wild goat), and swine.

Hunting, except for deer and gazelles, is not common. A few bears are shot every year. Wolves are killed by the shepherds. Foxes are occasionally trapped or shot. Hyenas are caught in steel traps or shot, and rarely a leopard is killed in the more lonely parts of the mountains. Rabbits are shot in the winter and brought to the markets of the large cities. The allusions to wild beasts in the Bible are numerous (2 Kings 14:9; Job 39:15; Ps. 80:13; Hos. 13:8; etc.).

Wild Donkey. *See* Donkey.

Wild Goat. A graceful animal, *Capra beden,* L., with semicircular horns two and a half to three feet long. It is found in the more inaccessible mountains and deserts. Of the two Heb. words *ya'ălâ* and *'aqqô* (Deut. 14:5), the first certainly, and the second probably, refer to this species. *See also* Satyr.

Wild Ox (Heb. *re'êm,* KJV, "unicorn"). Probably *Bos primigenius,* L., the true "auerochs." This animal is now extinct but certainly existed in Germany in the time of Caesar and probably did not become extinct in Europe until the Middle Ages. Caesar describes it as immense in size, of great strength (cf. Num. 23:22; 24:8), speed (Ps. 29:6), and ferocity, untamable (Job 39:9-10), associated with bulls (Isa. 34:7; KJV marg., "rhinoceroses") (*Coes., Bell. Gall.,* iv, 29). It cannot be the Arab. *ri'm,* which is doubtless *Antilope leucoryx* (*see* Antelope), nor *Bison bonasus,* which is called by the modern Germans "auerochs," but which is an animal with short horns, quite unsuitable for "horns of the unicorns" (KJV, Ps. 22:21). Still less can it be the intention to speak of a fictitious creature like the traditional *unicorn,* with the single horn springing from the center of the forehead. The *re'êm* had more than one horn (Deut. 33:17). The Heb. word most certainly denotes the "wild ox," for the cognate word in Akkad. *rimu* has this meaning. Representations of it by ancient Assyrian artists picture it as the aurochs. Tiglath-pileser 1 (c. 1115-1102 B.C.) hunted it as game in Hittite country in the Lebanon Mountains. It became extinct early in Syria-Palestine, and its name transferred to its descendant, the common ox. But the extinct species was notorious for its flatter forehead, colossal strength and ferocity, and its powerful horns of double curvature. Tristram offered independent corroboration of its previous occurrence in the Lebanon Mountains by recovering its teeth in the bone caves of the region.   M.F.U.

Wolf (Heb. *ze'êb;* Gk. *lukos*). We believe it also to be the proper rendering of *tannîm,* translated, KJV, "dragons"; NASB, NIV, "jackals" (Job 30:29; Ps. 44:19; Isa. 13:22; 34:13; 43:20; Jer. 9:11; 10:22; 14:6); RV marg., "the crocodile" (49:33; 51:37; Mic. 1:8). The wolf is the terror of sheep but usually flees from the shepherd. Wolves are numerous in all the sheep walks of this land. The emblematic references to the ferocity and bloodthirstiness of the wolf are numerous and forcible (Isa. 65:25; Matt. 7:15; 10:16).

Worm. The only worms alluded to in Scripture are the *larvae of insects,* such as the *grub of the moth* (Isa. 51:8); *rimmâ, maggots* bred in decaying *vegetable* and *animal* substances (Ex. 16:24; Job 7:5, etc.), and *tôlā'îm,* also *maggots* similar to the last. *Tôla'* and *tôla'at,* from the same root, refer to the *cochineal insect. Earthworms* are not mentioned in the Bible. The *worms* that devoured Herod (Acts 12:23) were *maggots,* bred in a wound or sore or, more probably, intestinal worms.

BIBLIOGRAPHY: *Camel:* W. F. Albright, *Archaeology of Palestine* (1954), pp. 206ff.; S. F. Bodenheimer, *Animals and Man in Bible Lands* (1960); J. P. Free, *Archaeology and Bible History* (1964), pp. 54-55, 169-71.

Eagle: A. Parmelee, *All the Birds of the Bible* (1959); F. S. Bodenheimer, *Animal and Man in Bible Lands* (1960); G. S. Crandall, *Animals of the Bible* (1970).

Horse: V. Møller-Christensen and K. Jørgensen, *Encyclopedia of Bible Creatures* (1965); G. S. Crandall, *Animals of Bible Lands* (1970).

Locust: H. B. Tristram, *The Natural History of the Bible* (1898), pp. 306-18; J. D. Whiting, *National Geographic Magazine* 28 (December 1915): 512-50; T. Chapelle and D. Chapelle, *National Geographic Magazine* 103 (April 1953); 545-62; R. A. M. Conley, *National Geographic Magazine* 136 (August 1969): 202-27.

ANIMAL, WORSHIP OF. This is of great antiquity, its origin involved in much obscurity. Zoolatria (animal worship) is said to have been introduced into Egypt under the Second Dynasty (c. 2750 B.C.). The gods of the Egyptian, Indian, Greek, and Teutonic mythologies were the "powers" of nature; the principal sacred animals and reptiles were worshiped as their incarnations or servants. Many of them were carefully tended while living and when dead were buried with great pomp. To cause the death of any of these creatures by design was punishable with death; if anyone caused the death of a cat, hawk, or ibis, with or without intent, he had to die.

The Israelites often degraded themselves by an imitation of this kind of worship (Ex. 32), for which they were severely punished.

ANISE. *See* Vegetable Kingdom: Dill.

ANKLET (Heb. *'ekes,* KJV, "tinkling ornaments"). The ornament mentioned in the description given of female attire (Isa. 3:18). It was a ring of gold, silver, or ivory worn around the ankles. The anklet was widely used by the ancients, nor has its use ceased in the East. The Egyptian monuments show them to have been worn by both sexes. The practice was forbidden in the Koran (24:31), though the prohibition may refer rather to the small bells worn around the ankles, especially by dancing girls. *See also* "ankle chains" in the article Dress.

AN'NA (an'a). The Gk. form of Hannah, the prophetess, and daughter of Phanuel, of the tribe of Asher. Married in early life, after seven years she lost her husband. From that time she devoted herself to attendance upon the Temple services and probably by reason of her great piety was allowed to reside in one of the chambers of the women's court. Anna was eighty-four years old when the infant Jesus was presented to the Lord. Entering as Simeon was thanking God, Anna also broke forth in praise for the fulfillment of the divine promises (Luke 2:36).

ANNALS (an'nals). *See* Chronicles.

AN'NAS (an'as; a contracted form of Ananias). A high priest of the Jews. Josephus calls him Ananus, the son of Seth. He was first appointed high priest by Quirinius, proconsul of Syria, about A.D. 7 but was removed after seven years (Kitto says fifteen years) by Valerius Gratus, procurator of Judea (Josephus *Ant.* 18.2.1-2). Annas is mentioned in Luke 3:2 as being high priest *along with* Caiaphas. Our Lord's first hearing was before Annas (John 18:13), who sent Him bound to Caiaphas (v. 24). In Acts 4:6 he is plainly called high priest. He had four sons who filled that office, besides his son-in-law, Caiaphas. There have been several theories advanced to reconcile the application of high priest to Annas and Caiaphas at the same time. Kitto thinks that Annas was regarded as being high priest *jure divino* and having authority in spiritual matters, whereas Caiaphas was the pontiff recognized by the government. The probability is that his great age, abilities, and influence, and his being the father-in-law of Caiaphas made him practically the high priest, although his son-in-law held the office.

BIBLIOGRAPHY: F. Josephus *Ant.* 18.2.1-2; 20.9.1; A. Edersheim, *Sketches of Jewish Social Life in the Days of Christ* (1961), pp. 239-48; E. Schürer, *A History of the Jewish People in the Time of Jesus Christ* (1973-79), 2:184-236, 404-14.

ANOINTING. Anointing the body with oil was an ancient and widespread custom common among Egyptians, Hebrews, and inhabitants of the Far East, as well as among Greeks and Romans. The purpose was, doubtless, to keep the skin supple and to moderate the evaporation that is so great in hot climates. In Scripture the usual Heb. word for anointing is *māshah;* the Gk. term is *chriō,* to "rub." *See* the second article Anointing (below).

Cleansing. The allusions to anointing as part of ordinary washing are numerous, both in the OT and NT (Ruth 3:3); as expressive of joy (Ps. 23:5; Heb. 1:9); its disuse indicative of grief (2 Sam. 14:2; Ps. 92:10; Dan. 10:3). It was reckoned among the civilities extended to guests (Luke 7:46), although the ointments used on such occasions seem to have been perfumes rather than oils. It was also used medicinally (Isa. 1:6; Mark 6:13; James 5:14). *See* Oil.

The practice of anointing the bodies of the dead is referred to in Mark 14:8 and Luke 23:56. This ceremony was performed after the washing of the body and was doubtless intended to check decay. *See* Embalming.

Consecration. The first instance of the religious use of oil is the anointing of the stone by Jacob (Gen. 28:18; 35:14), evidently designed to be a formal consecration of the stone, or spot, to a sacred purpose. Under the Mosaic law persons and things set apart for sacred purposes were

80

anointed with the "holy anointing oil" (Ex. 30:23-25, 30-33). *See* Priesthood, Hebrew.

Coronation. It was a custom among the Jews to anoint with oil those set apart as kings, which custom was adopted by the Christian church.

Figurative. The anointing with oil was a symbol of endowment with the Spirit of God (1 Sam. 10:1, 6; 16:13; Isa. 61:1) for the duties of the office to which a person was consecrated (Lev. 8). *See* King; Priest.

ANOINTING (Gk. *chrisma,* "ointment," "anointing"). The gift of the Holy Spirit as an efficient aid in getting a knowledge of the truth (1 John 2:20). Not that the work of Jesus was imperfect, but the Spirit helps us to understand the truth He taught and thus to glorify Him (John 16:14) in whom the full revelation of God had been given (v. 15).

ANSWER (Heb. *'ānâ,* to "testify," Gk. *apokrinomai,* to "respond"). In Scripture this term has other meanings than the usual one of "reply."

1. Miriam is said to have "answered," i.e., taken up the strain of victory sung by Moses and the men (Ex. 15:21; *see* 1 Sam. 18:7; 29:5; cf. Num. 21:17).

2. To respond to requests or entreaties (1 Sam. 4:17; Ps. 3:4; 18:41; 27:7); to announce future events (1 Sam. 14:37; 28:6).

3. In a forensic sense: of a judge investigating (Acts 24:25) or giving sentence (Ex. 23:2); of a witness answering inquiries of a judge, hence *to testify, bear witness* (Deut. 19:16; Job 16:8); to accuse or defend in court (Deut. 31:21; Gen. 30:33).

4. To "answer" is also used for the commencement of a discourse when no reply to any question or objection is expected (Job 3:2; Song of Sol. 2:10; Matt. 11:25; 12:38; etc.).

ANT. *See* Animal Kingdom.

ANTEDILUVIANS. The people who lived before the Flood. Of this period we have little authentic information (Gen. 4:16–6:8), although additional knowledge may be gathered from the history of Noah and the first men after the Deluge. In Scripture we find few indications of savagery among these people, and it need not be held that they gradually civilized themselves.

It is the opinion of some that the antediluvians were acquainted with astronomy, from the fact that the ages of Seth and his descendants were recorded (Gen. 5:6-32); and they appear to have been familiar with botany, from the mention of the vine, olive, etc. (6:14; 8:11); mineralogy (2:12); music (4:21); architecture, from the fact that Cain built a city (4:17); metallurgy, so far as forging and tempering are concerned (4:22). Agriculture was evidently the first employment of Adam (2:15; 3:17-18); afterward of Cain (4:2) and of Noah, who planted a vineyard (9:20). The slight intimations to be found respecting *government* favor the notion that the particular governments were patriarchal and subject to general theocratic control. Respecting *religion,* sacrifices are mentioned (4:4); some think that the Sabbath was observed; mention is made that "men began to call upon the name of the Lord" (4:26). We have here an account of the commencement of that worship of God that consists in prayer, praise, and thanksgiving, or in the acknowledgment and celebration of the mercy and help of Jehovah. Noah seemed to have been familiar with the distinction between clean and unclean beasts (Gen. 7:2).

ANTELOPE. *See* Animal Kingdom.

ANTHOTHIJAH (an-thō-thī'jah). The ninth son of Shashak, a Benjamite (1 Chron. 8:24). E.H.M.

ANTHROPOPATHISM (from Gk. *anthropatheia,* "with human feelings"), the attributing of human emotions, such as anger, grief, joy, etc., to God. Traces of this are found in Scripture (Gen. 6:6; 8:21; 11:5, and many other passages). If we understand such expressions to be the imperfect approximating expression of eternal truth, then they become the means of a better knowledge of God.

ANTICHRIST (Gk. *antichristos,* "against Christ"; some, "instead of Christ"). A word used only by the apostle John (epistles 1 and 2).

Meaning. The Gk. preposition *anti* in composition sometimes denotes substitution, taking the place of another; hence, "false Christ." The connection in which the word is used appears to import opposition, covert rather than avowed, with a professed friendliness.

Antichrists. John seems to make a distinction between "antichrist" and "antichrists" (1 John 2:18), for he declares that "even now many *antichrists* have arisen," but "that *antichrist* is coming." An antichrist is one who opposes Christ, whether he opposes the doctrine of His deity or His humanity; or whether he sets himself against Him in respect to His *priestly* office, by substituting other methods of atoning for sin and finding acceptance with God; His *kingly* office, by claiming authority to exact laws in His church contrary to His laws or to dispense with His commandments; or his *prophetical* office, by claiming authority to add to, alter, or take away from the revelation that He has given in His holy Word. This is agreeable to the description of an antichrist (2:22; 4:3; 2 John 7). In a general sense an antichrist is a person who is opposed to the authority of Christ as head of the church and creation.

The Antichrist. From early times the opinion has prevailed that the antichrists referred to were the forerunners of an evil rather than the evil itself. Some individual would arise who, by way of eminence, would be fitly called the Antichrist;

and who, before being destroyed by Christ, would utter horrid blasphemies against the Most High and practice great enormities upon the saints. This view is scriptural and came from connecting the passages in John's epistles with the descriptions in Daniel and the Apocalypse of the great God-opposing power that would persecute the saints of the Most High; and of the apostle Paul's "man of lawlessness" (2 Thess. 2:3-10).

See also our Lord's own prediction respecting the last age of the world (Matt. 24:24) and the description of such an Antichrist (Rev. 13:1-8).

Identification. Early Christians looked for Antichrist as a person and not a polity or system. The general opinion of those who closely followed the Scriptures was that he would be a man in whom Satan would dwell utterly and bodily, and who would be armed with satanic and demonic powers. In the OT he is prefigured under the "king of Babylon" (Isa. 14:4); the little "horn" (Dan. 7:8; 8:9); the king "insolent and skilled in intrigue" (8:23); "the prince who is to come" (9:26); the willful king (11:36). In the NT he is called "the man of lawlessness," "the son of destruction" (2 Thess. 2:3-8); "antichrist" (1 John 2:18); and "the beast" (Rev. 13:1-10). This sinister, demon-inspired leader will rise to dominate the world in the end-time, persecute the saints, seek to destroy the Jew and banish the name of God and His Christ from the earth, and thus take over. This would mean the thwarting of God's plan for the messianic millennial kingdom, which involves the restoration of Israel (Acts 1:6) and universal peace. He is destroyed by the second advent of Christ (Rev. 19:11-16), who sets up the earthly kingdom (Rev. 20:1-3). This is the premillennial view. Amillennialism rejects an earthly kingdom in favor of Christ's ushering in the eternal state, rather than His establishing another era in time. Views that identify the Antichrist with Muhammad (Innocent III in 1213) or with the papal church (Protestantism) can scarcely be called scriptural.

BIBLIOGRAPHY: J. Eadie, *Commentary on the Epistles to the Thessalonians* (1877), pp. 330-70; J. D. Pentecost, *Things to Come* (1961), pp. 337-39; J. F. Walvoord, *The Revelation of Jesus Christ* (1966), pp. 197-212; W. K. Price, *The Coming Antichrist* (1974); A. W. Pink, *The Antichrist* (1979).

ANTICHRISTIANISM. A convenient term used to designate in a collective manner the various forms of hostility to Christianity. It is equivalent to the "spirit of the antichrist" (1 John 4:3). It was this that Enoch and Noah denounced in their preaching (Jude 14; 2 Pet. 2:5-7) and that "tormented" the righteous soul of Lot. It is the mind "hostile toward God" and opposed to Him (Rom. 8:7); the "mystery of lawlessness" foreseen by Paul (2 Thess. 2:7). Since the days of persecution it has been chiefly confined to intellectual modes of opposition, known as Infidelity, Deism, Rationalism, etc.

AN'TIOCH (an'ti-ok, from Antiochus, a Syrian king).

1. In Syria, on the left bank of the Orontes, 16½ miles from the Mediterranean and three hundred miles N of Jerusalem, between the Lebanon and Taurus mountain ranges. It was founded about 300 B.C. by Seleucus Nicator and called Epidaphne (near Daphne), or "on the Orontes," to distinguish it from fifteen other Antiochs. The city was destroyed several times by earthquakes, one of which, A.D. 526, killed 250,000 persons. It was luxurious. Its main street, four miles in length, was lined with magnificent mansions. It was highly cultured, but its social life was debased, sensual, and shocking. Jews formed a large portion of the population, having been brought there by Seleucus Nicator. It became the third city in the Roman Empire, having a population of 500,000. Pompey made it the seat of the legate of Syria, 64 B.C., and a free city.

Antioch was associated early with Christian effort. It was there that the persecuted disciples fled after the demise of Stephen (Acts 11:19-20). The name *Christian* was first applied to followers of Jesus there, and all three of Paul's missionary journeys began in Antioch. The most flourishing period in the history of the Christian church in Antioch was in the time of Chrysostom, who was born there in 347. In 635 it was taken by Muslim Arabs, by the Turks in 1084, and by Crusaders in 1098. It gradually declined under early Arab and Ottoman rule, but modern Turkish Antakya is a growing city in excess of 75,000 inhabitants.

Princeton University and the National Museum of France excavated at Antioch for six seasons during the years 1932-39. A street plan of a large part of the ancient city has been established; and numerous significant mosaic pavements were uncovered in churches, villas, and other public buildings of the city. A few of them may be seen in the Louvre in Paris, and there is a significant collection in the Antakya museum.

The Chalice of Antioch is a controversial art object found at Antioch in 1910 and now in the Metropolitan Museum of Art in New York. The chalice is of two parts: a plain inner cup of silver, about seven and a half inches high and six inches in diameter, and an outer gilded silver holder with twelve figures displayed on the outside. Much has been written about the chalice, and it has even been identified as the Holy Grail used by Christ at the Last Supper. Perhaps the best that can be said about this chalice is that it is an early piece of Christian art of some century later than the first and that Christ or some of the disciples may be intended by the artistic representations.

2. Antioch in Pisidia, also founded by Seleucus I Nicator (312-280 B.C.), was a commercial center commanding the great trade route between Ephesus and the Cilician Gates. Paul's success here is recounted in Acts 13:14-52, and he revisited this important city on his first missionary tour

(14:21). A University of Michigan team under the direction of David Robinson excavated at Antioch in 1924. They were able to show that life at Antioch in Paul's day centered on two paved squares, the Square of Tiberius (built during the emperor's reign, A.D. 14-37) and the Square of Augustus (constructed just before the birth of Christ). From the lower square, twelve steps some seventy feet long led into the Square of Augustus through a magnificent triple-arched gateway. The squares were at least partly faced with shops and houses. Unfortunately, nearly all the stone uncovered by excavators has been carried off by local inhabitants; so the ancient magnificence of the place can only be imagined today.   H.F.V.

BIBLIOGRAPHY: *Pisidian Antioch:* W. M. Ramsay, *The Cities of St. Paul* (1907), pp. 245-314; id., *The Bearing of Recent Discovery on the Trustworthiness of the New Testament* (1915), pp. 353-69; id., *Historical Geography of Asia Minor* (1972), pp. 47, 57, 85, 453.

Syrian Antioch: G. Downey, *A History of Antioch in Syria from Seleucus to the Arab Conquest* (1961).

AN'TIPAS (an'ti-pas).

1. Herod Antipas was the son of Herod the Great by Malthace, a Samaritan. Of his father's dominions he inherited Galilee and Perea. He was the Herod who executed John the Baptist. *See* Herod.

2. A "faithful" martyr mentioned in Rev. 2:13, A.D. before 100. He is said to have been one of our Savior's first disciples and a bishop of Pergamum, and to have been put to death in a tumult there by the priests of Aesculapius, who had a celebrated health center and temple in that city.

AN'TIPA'TER. The father of Herod the Great. *See* Herod.

ANTIP'ATRIS (an-tip'a-tris; "instead of his father"). A city built by Herod the Great in honor of his father, Antipater. It is the modern Ras-el-Ain. It lay on the road built by the Romans, leading from Caesarea to Jerusalem, thirty-eight miles from the former place. Paul was taken to it by night as a prisoner (Acts 23:31). In OT times it was called *Aphek* (which see).

Definitive excavations at the site began in 1972 under the auspices of Tel Aviv University and the municipality of Peta Tikva, with the cooperation of New Orleans Baptist Theological Seminary and with Moshe Kochavi and George Kelm as directors. In the several seasons of excavation that have been conducted since, discoveries have been made that date to periods extending from about 3000 B.C. to the sixteenth century A.D. Typical Philistine pottery was uncovered in the eleventh-century B.C. level, when Philistines used the site as a base of operations for the battle in which they succeeded in taking the Ark (1 Sam. 4:1, 11). Of special interest are findings in the level dating to the reign of Herod the Great. The main street

Antipatris fortress

Modern building on the site of the Antonia fortress

ditions, Apelles was one of the seventy disciples and bishop either of Smyrna or Heracleia. The Greeks observe this festival on October 31.

A'PHEK (a'fek; "strength, fortress").

1. A city mentioned in Josh. 13:4, apparently N of Sidon and accordingly commonly identified with Afga, ancient Aphaca, some twenty-three miles N of Beirut.

2. Aphek (Aphik) was also an Asherite city not conquered by the Israelites (Josh. 19:30; Judg. 1:31). A. Alt located it at Tell Kurdaneh about six miles SE of Acco (Ptolemais).

3. A town in the plain of Sharon about eleven miles NE of Joppa (modern Ras el-Ain). It was evidently here the Philistines camped on their way to Shiloh to attack Israel at Ebenezer (1 Sam. 4:1). *See also* Antipatris.

Remains of ancient aqueduct, Pisidian Antioch

was twenty-six feet wide; its center was paved with diagonally laid flagstones. Shops, workshops, and elevated sidewalks flanked both sides of the street. Dominating the site today is a Turkish fort built in 1571.   H.F.V.

ANTITYPE (Gk. *antitupon,* a "counterpart"; Heb. 9:24). That which is represented or prefigured by a type. The type may be considered a rough draft, while the antitype is the perfect image. The type is a figure, and antitype is the reality that the type prefigured, as Christ is the antitype of the Paschal Lamb.

ANTO'NIA (an-tō'ni-a). A strong fortress built and named by Herod in honor of Antonius, or Mark Antony, situated to the NW of the Temple area in Jerusalem, partly surrounded by a deep ditch 165 feet wide. It was garrisoned with Roman soldiers, whose watchfulness preserved order in the Temple courts. Spoken of as the barracks (Acts 21:37), here Paul made an address (22:1-21). Herod constructed a secret passage from the fortress to the Temple.

APE. *See* Animal Kingdom.

APEL'LES (a-pel'ēz). A Christian in Rome, whom Paul salutes in his epistle to the church there (Rom. 16:10) and calls "approved in Christ," A.D. 60. According to the old church tra-

Model of Antonia fortress, Jerusalem

4. A town beyond the Jordan about four miles E of the Sea of Galilee on the highway between Damascus and the plain of Esdraelon, fortress city of Bethshan, modern Afik (Fik). Cf. 1 Kings 20:26, 30; 2 Kings 13:17. However, another village between Shunem and Jezreel seems required by the narratives of the Philistine wars in 1 Sam. 28:4; 29:1, 11; 31:1.   M.F.U.

BIBLIOGRAPHY: Y. Aharoni, *The Archaeology of the Land of*

Israel (1978), pp. 57, 71, 95-99, 119; id., *The Land of the Bible* (1979), pp. 109ff.

APHE′KAH (a-fē′ka; "fortress"). A city in the hill country of Judah (Josh. 15:53). Its site has not been discovered.

APHI′AH (a-fī′a). The father of Becorath, a Benjamite and ancestor of Saul (1 Sam. 9:1).

A′PHIK. *See* Aphek, no. 2.

APOCRYPHA. The name given by Jerome to a number of books that in the LXX are placed among the canonical books of the Bible but which, for evident reasons, do not belong to the sacred canon. The term itself, a Gk. adjective in the neuter plural (from *apokruphos,* "hidden, concealed") denotes strictly "things concealed." But almost certainly the noun *biblia* is understood, so that the real implication of the expression is "apocryphal books" or "writings."

Old Testament Apocrypha. In its *final* quasi-technical meaning of "noncanonical," in common use since the Reformation, the term specifically refers to the fourteen books written after the OT canon was closed and which, being the least remote from the canonical books, laid strongest claim to canonicity. The OT apocryphal books have an unquestioned historical and literary value but have been rejected as inspired for the following reasons:

1. They abound in historical and geographical inaccuracies and anachronisms.

2. They teach doctrines that are false and foster practices that are at variance with inspired Scripture.

3. They resort to literary types and display an artificiality of subject matter and styling out of keeping with inspired Scripture.

4. They lack the distinctive elements that give genuine Scripture its divine character, such as prophetic power and poetic and religious feeling.

The OT apocryphal books are fourteen in number, classified as follows:

Didactic or Wisdom Literature (2 books).

The Wisdom of Solomon. This is an ethical treatise in commendation of wisdom and righteousness and a denunciation of iniquity and idolatry, written under the name of Solomon. The writer wrote in Gk. and was apparently an Alexandrian Jew who seems to have lived between 150 B.C. and 50 B.C. Swete calls this work "the solitary survival from the wreck of the earlier works of the philosophical school at Alexandria which culminated in Philo, the contemporary of our Lord."

Ecclesiasticus. Called also *The Wisdom of Jesus, Son of Sirach.* This long and valuable ethical treatise contains an extensive range of instruction in general morality and practical godliness. It follows the model of Proverbs, Ecclesiastes, and Job. It was written originally in Heb. about 180 B.C. and translated into Gk. about

132 B.C. by a grandson of the original author. About two-thirds of the Heb. is now extant.

Historical Literature (3 books).

First Esdras. Esdras is the Gk. for Ezra. The book narrates in Gk. the declension and fall of Judah from Josiah's reign, the destruction of Jerusalem, the Babylonian Exile, the return of the exiles, and the share taken by Ezra in the restored community. The book consists of an independent and somewhat free version of portions of 2 Chronicles and Ezra-Nehemiah broken by an extended context that has no parallel in the Heb. Bible (1 Esdras 3:1–5:6). Swete calls this "perhaps the most interesting of the contributions made by the Greek Bible to the legendary history of the captivity and the return" (*Introduction to the O.T. in Gk.* [1902], p. 266).

First Maccabees. This valuable historical treatise covers a period of about forty years from the accession of Antiochus Epiphanes (175 B.C.) to the death of Simon Maccabees (135 B.C. or a little later). The book is of first-rate importance as a source for the interbiblical period and gives a full and worthy account of the important Maccabean wars and the noble struggle for Jewish independence.

Second Maccabees. This much less historically accurate book covers a part of the same period as the first (175-160 B.C.) but offers a striking contrast to it. Swete (op. cit., p. 378) calls it "a partially independent but rhetorical and inaccurate and, to some extent, a mythical panegyric of patriotic revolt."

Religious Romance (2 books).

Tobit. This is a tale of a pious Naphtalite named Tobit, who has a son named Tobias. The father loses his eyesight. The son is dispatched to obtain payment of a debt to a certain Rages in Media. On the way an angel guides him to Ecbatana, where he makes a romantic marriage with a widow who still remained a virgin despite the fact that she had been married to seven husbands, all of whom had been killed by a demon named Asmodeus on their marriage day. Encouraged by the angel to become the eighth husband, Tobias escapes death by burning the inner parts of a fish, the smoke of which exorcises the evil spirit. Thereupon he cures his father's blindness by anointing the sightless eyes with the gall of the fish that had already proved so efficacious. The book was probably written as moral fiction toward the close of the third century B.C.

Judith. Judith, a rich, beautiful, and devout Jewish widow, is the heroine of the romance with a pseudo-historical background. At the time of the Babylonian invasion of Judah she disguises herself as a traitoress and succeeds in beguiling and slaying the Babylonian general Holofernes, thus saving her city. The narrative is apparently intended as religious fiction. It is immoral, since it teaches that the end justifies the means. The book dates from Maccabean times and was almost certainly written in Heb. according to R. H. Ottley (*Handbook to the Septuagint* [1929], p. 138).

Prophetic Literature (2 books).

Baruch (with *The Epistle of Jeremiah*). This consists of prayers and confessions of Jews in exile with promises of restoration reportedly written by Baruch, the scribe, in imitation of Jeremiah's language and style. The first five chapters are made nominally to emanate from Baruch, while the sixth was entitled *The Epistle of Jeremy,* i.e., Jeremiah. Although Baruch and the epistle appear in lists that otherwise rigorously excluded noncanonical books, this work never was included in the Heb. Scriptures and is unquestionably uncanonical.

Second Esdras. This is a religious treatise, apocalyptic in character. Chapters 3-14 purport to record seven revelations granted to Ezra in Babylon, several of which took the form of visions. The book, according to Ottley, is supposed to have been written about A.D. 100. The RV contains seventy additional verses in chap. 7 that were discovered in 1875.

Legendary Additions (5 books).

Prayer of Manasses. This is supposed to be a deeply penitential prayer of Manasseh, the wicked king of Judah, when he was carried away as a prisoner to Babylon by the Assyrians. It was thought to follow 2 Chron. 33:18-19, which outlines Manasseh's wicked reign and his repentance. Its date is uncertain.

The Rest of Esther. Composed in Gk., this writing consists of passages that were interpolated throughout the canonical Esther of the LXX in the form of visions, letters, and prayers intended to explain supposed difficulties and show the hand of God in the narrative.

Song of the Three Hebrew Children. This, the first of three unauthenticated additions to the canonical book of Daniel, was inserted after 3:23, and consists of a petition of Azariah in the furnace and an account of the miraculous deliverance, together with an ode of praise of the three.

The History of Susanna. This amplification of the book of Daniel is in the form of a religious romance, narrating how the godly wife of a wealthy Jew in Babylon is exonerated of the false charges of two immoral men through the agency of Daniel's wisdom. In the LXX the narrative is placed before the book of Daniel; in the Vulg. it is placed as Dan. 13.

Bel and the Dragon. This final spurious addition to Daniel tells in melodramatic fashion how Daniel destroys two objects of Babylonian worship, Bel and the Dragon, and escapes from the lion's den.

New Testament Apocrypha. The apocryphal books of the NT, unlike those of the OT, have never claimed the faith of the Christian church, except in a few isolated instances. There are more than one hundred of them, and it is doubtful whether one of them appeared before the second century of our era. Most of them portray a much later date. They are valuable as an indication of the growth of thought and the rise of heresy in the age just subsequent to that of the apostles. None of them ever received the sanction of any ecclesiastical council.

BIBLIOGRAPHY: R. H. Charles, *Apocrypha and Pseudepigrapha of the Old Testament,* 2 vols. (1913); id., *Religious Development Between the Testaments* (1914); M. R. James, *The Apocryphal New Testament* (1950); B. M. Metzger, *Introduction to the Apocrypha* (1957); E. Hennecke, *New Testament Apocrypha,* ed. W. Schnelmelcher, 2 vols. (1963); R. K. Harrison, *Introduction to the Old Testament* (1969), pp. 1173-78; J. H. Charlesworth, ed., *The Old Testament Pseudepigrapha,* in process (1983-1985).

APOLLO'NIA (ap-o-lō'ni-a; Gk. "belonging to Apollo"). The name of several towns in the Mediterranean world, so called in honor of the Greek sun-god, Apollo. Paul visited the famous biblical city by this name on his second missionary journey (Acts 17:1). It was located on the well-known Roman road called the Egnatian Way, twenty-eight miles W of Amphipolis in Macedonia.

M.F.U.

APOL'LOS (a-pol'los). A learned, "eloquent" Jew of Alexandria, well acquainted with the Scriptures and the Jewish religion (Acts 18:24). About A.D. 56 he came to Ephesus, where he began to teach in the synagogue "the things concerning Jesus, being acquainted only with the baptism of John" (v. 25). Here he met Aquila and Priscilla, who "explained to him the way of God more accurately," and Apollos preached Christ with great zeal and power (v. 26). After this he preached in Achaia and especially at Corinth (18:27-28; 19:1), having been recommended by the brethren in Ephesus (18:27). On his arrival at Corinth he was useful in watering the seed that Paul had sown (1 Cor. 3:6). Many of the Corinthians became so attached to him that a schism was produced in the church, some saying, "I am of Paul"; others, "I am of Apollos" (3:4-7). That this party feeling was not encouraged by Apollos is evident from the manner in which Paul speaks of him and his unwillingness to return to Corinth (1 Cor. 16:12). Apollos was, doubtless, at this time with Paul in Ephesus. Paul again mentions Apollos kindly in Titus 3:13 and recommends him and Zenas the lawyer to the attention of Titus, knowing that they planned to visit Crete, where Titus was. Jerome thinks that Apollos remained there until he heard that the divisions in the church at Corinth had been healed by Paul's letter and then returned and became bishop of that city. Other authorities make him bishop of Duras, of Colophon, of Iconium (in Phrygia), and of Caesarea.

BIBLIOGRAPHY: H. M. Seekings, *Men of the Pauline Circle* (1914), pp. 107-14; A. C. McGiffert, *History of Christianity in the Apostolic Age* (1951), pp. 290-94; D. E. Hiebert, *Personalities Around Paul* (1973), pp. 21-32.

APOL'LYON (a-pol'yun; "destroyer"). The Gk. equivalent (Rev. 9:11) of *Abaddon* (which see).

APOSTASY. A "falling away." The common classical use of the word has to do with a political defection (Gen. 14:4, LXX; 2 Chron. 13:6, LXX; Acts 5:37). In the NT its more usual meaning is that of a religious defection (21:21; 1 Tim. 4:1; Heb. 3:12). This is called "apostasy from the faith" (*apostasia a fide*): a secession from the church, and a disowning of the name of Christ. Some of its peculiar characteristics are mentioned, such as seducing spirits, doctrines of demons, hypocritical lying, a seared conscience, forbidding of marriage and of meats, a form of godliness without the power (1 Tim. 4:1; 2 Tim. 3:5). The grave nature of apostasy is shown by such passages as Heb. 10:26-29, 2 Pet. 2:15-21, and John 15:22. Apostasy as the act of a professed Christian, who knowingly and deliberately rejects revealed truth regarding the deity of Christ (1 John 4:1-3) and redemption through His atoning sacrifice (Phil. 3:18; 2 Pet. 2:1) is different from error, which may be the result of ignorance (Acts 19:1-6), or heresy, which may be the result of falling into the snare of Satan (2 Tim. 2:25-26). Both error and heresy may accordingly be consistent with true faith. On the other hand, apostasy departs from the faith but not from the outward profession of it (2 Tim. 3:5). Apostasy, whether among the angels (Isa. 14:12-14; Ezek. 28:15; Jude 6), in Israel (Isa. 1:1-6; 5:5-7), or in the church (Rev. 3:14-16) is irremediable and awaits judgment. Mankind's apostasy in Adam (Gen. 3:6-7) is curable only through the sacrifice of Christ. Apostates apparently can only be professors and not actual possessors of true salvation, otherwise their defection would incur severe chastening or, if this failed to restore them, untimely (physical) death (1 Cor. 5:5; 11:32; 1 John 5:16).   M.F.U.

APOSTLE (Gk. *apostolos,* a "delegate"). One sent with a special message or commission. In this sense the word is used in the LXX (1 Kings 14:6; Isa. 18:2), and in the NT: John 13:16, "Neither is one *who is sent* [apostle] greater than the one who sent him"; 2 Cor. 8:23; Phil. 2:25, where persons sent out by churches on special errands are called their *apostles,* or messengers. In Heb. 3:1 Jesus is called "the *Apostle* and High Priest of our confession."

Hebrew. The Jews, it is said, called the collector of the half shekel, which every Israelite paid annually to the Temple, an *apostle;* also those who carried about encyclical letters from their rulers. Paul may have used the word in this sense when he declared himself "an apostle, not sent from men, nor through the agency of man" (Gal. 1:1), plainly indicating that his commission was directly from Christ. (*See also* Rom. 1:1; 1 Cor. 15:1.)

Christian. The official name of those twelve of the disciples chosen by our Lord to be with Him during His ministry and to whom He entrusted the organization of His church. These He chose early in His ministry and ordained "that they might be with Him." The number *twelve* was, doubtless, with reference to the twelve tribes of Israel and was fixed, so that the apostles were often called simply "the twelve" (Matt. 26:14; John 6:67; 20:24; 1 Cor. 15:5). Their names were (1) Simon Peter (Cephas, Barjona); (2) Andrew; (3) John; (4) Philip; (5) James; (6) Bartholomew (perhaps same as Nathanael); (7) Thomas (Didymus); (8) Matthew (Levi); (9) Simon the Zealot; (10) Jude (Thaddaeus); (11) James the Less; (12) Judas Iscariot. The original qualification of an apostle, as stated by Peter (Acts 1:21-22), was that he should have been personally acquainted with our Lord's ministry, from His baptism by John to His ascension. By this close personal relation with Him they were peculiarly fitted to give testimony to the facts of redemption. Shortly after their ordination "He gave to them authority over unclean spirits, to cast them out, and to heal every kind of disease and every kind of sickness"; "and sent them out in pairs" to preach (Matt. 10:1-6; Mark 3:14; 6:17; Luke 6:1, 13; 9:1). They accompanied our Lord on His journeys, saw His wonderful works, heard His discourses to the people (Matt. 5:1; Luke 6:13-49) and those addressed to the learned Jews (Matt. 19:3-12; Luke 10:25-37). They sometimes worked miracles (Mark 6:13; Luke 9:6) and sometimes attempted to do so without success (Matt. 17:16). They recognized Jesus as "the Christ of God" (16:16; Luke 9:20) and ascribed supernatural power to Him (9:54), but did not have a high understanding of His spiritual mission (Matt. 15:16; 16:22; 17:20; Luke 9:54; 24:25; John 16:12) and acknowledged the weakness of their faith (Luke 17:5). Jesus taught them to understand the spiritual meaning of His parables (Mark 4:10-34; Luke 8:9-18), and yet when He was removed from the earth their knowledge of His kingdom was limited (Luke 24:21; John 16:12). Apparently loyal at heart, when He was arrested they all forsook Him and fled (Matt. 26:56). Before His death our Lord promised to the apostles the Holy Spirit, to fit them to be founders and rulers of the Christian church (John 14:16-17, 26; 15:26-27; 16:7-15), and after His resurrection He confirmed their call and commissioned them to "preach the gospel to all creation" (John 20:21-23; Matt. 28:18-20; Mark 16:15). Shortly after Christ's ascension they, under divine guidance, chose Matthias to be the successor of Judas Iscariot (Acts 1:26). On the Day of Pentecost the Holy Spirit descended upon the church (Acts 2), and the apostles became altogether different men, testifying with power of the life and death and resurrection of Jesus (Luke 24:48; Acts 1:22; 2:32; 3:15; 5:32; 13:31). Their first work was the building up of the church in Jerusalem (Acts 3-7), and then they carried the gospel into Samaria (Acts 8:5-25). With this ends the first period of the apostles' ministry, with its center at Jerusalem and Peter as its prominent figure. In this age Peter represents Jewish Christianity, Paul Gentile Christianity, and John the union of the two. The center of the second period of the apostolic agency is Antioch, where a church was soon built up, consisting of Jews and Gentiles. Of this and the subsequent period Paul was the central figure and labored with the other apostles (Acts 11:19-30; 13:1-5). In the third period the twelve almost entirely disappear from the sacred narrative, and we have only bits of personal history, which will be found under their respective names.

The Apostolic Office. As regards the apostolic office, it seems to have been preeminently that of founding the churches and upholding them by supernatural power specially bestowed for that purpose. It ceased, as a matter of course, with its first holders, all continuation of it, from the very conditions of its existence (cf. 1 Cor. 9:1), being impossible. The bishops of the ancient churches coexisted with, and did not in any sense succeed, the apostles, and when it is claimed for bishops or any church officers that they are their successors it can be understood only chronologically and not officially.

In a lower sense the term *apostle* was applied to all the more eminent Christian teachers, e.g., to Andronicus and Junias (Rom. 16:7).

BIBLIOGRAPHY: E. D. Burton, *A Critical and Exegetical Commentary on the Epistle to the Galatians*, International Critical Commentary (1920), Appendix 1; A. von Schlatter, *The Church in the New Testament Period* (1955); L. L. Morris, *Ministers of God* (1964), pp. 39-61; W. Schmitherals, *The Office of Apostle in the Early Church* (1969); C. K. Barrett, *Signs of an Apostle* (1970).

APOSTOLIC, APOSTOLICAL. Belonging or relating to or traceable to the apostles, such as apostolical age, apostolical doctrine, etc. The title, as one of honor, and likely also implying authority, has been falsely assumed in various ways. The pretended succession of bishops in some churches is called apostolical succession. So the Roman church calls itself the apostolical church, and the see of Rome the apostolical see, the bishop of Rome styling himself apostolical bishop. In the early church all bishops' sees were called *apostolical,* but at length some of the popes declared that the title "apostolical" was their right as successors of the apostle Peter, and the Council of Rheims (1049) declared the pope to be the sole apostolical primate of the universal church.

APOSTOLIC AGE. That period of church history covering the time between the Day of Pentecost and the death of John, the last apostle. The apostolic age lasted as long as the churches were under the immediate guidance of an apostle. The

arrangements made by the apostles can be ascribed to our Lord so far as relates to the principle but not to the details of execution. The form of worship seems to have been simple, much being left to the choice of individuals and churches. Its principal features, however, with regard to the Sabbath, church festivals, and the sacraments were fixed. There were many pious customs among these Christians, partly new and partly derived from Judaism. The apostolic age is commonly divided into three periods: (1) From Pentecost until the second appearance of Paul (about A.D. 41). (2) Until the death of Paul (about 67). (3) The Johannine period (about 100).

BIBLIOGRAPHY: P. Schaff, *The History of the Apostolic Church* (1853); A. C. McGiffert, *History of Christianity in the Apostolic Age* (1897); W. M. Ramsay, *St. Paul the Traveller and Roman Citizen* (1949); F. F. Bruce, *The Spreading Flame* (1953); E. M. Blaiklock, *Century of the New Testament* (1962); B. I. Reike, *New Testament Era* (1968).

APOSTOLIC COUNCIL. The assembly of the apostles and elders, held in Jerusalem (A.D. 50), an account of which is given in Acts 15. At Antioch, under the labors of Paul and Barnabas, many uncircumcised persons had been gathered into the church. Some Jewish Christians on a visit from Jerusalem contended that circumcision was necessary to salvation. Paul and Barnabas, with others, were deputed to lay the matter before a general meeting of the church in Jerusalem.

A preliminary meeting appears to have been held, at which some converts from among the Pharisees showed such opposition (Acts 15:5-6; Gal. 2) that it was thought best to submit the matter to the whole body. After much dispute Peter told of his experience with Cornelius and was followed by Barnabas and Paul, who told of their great success among the Gentiles. Then James, as president of the council, summed up the debate and pronounced in favor of releasing Gentile converts from the necessity of circumcision and other observances of the Mosaic ceremonial law. The conclusion being agreed upon, a letter was drawn up and sent to Antioch by two delegates chosen to accompany Paul and Barnabas (see Acts 15:22-30ff.). When read at Antioch, the letter gave great cheer to the Gentile converts.

APOTHECARY. See Handicrafts: Perfumer; Oil and Ointment; Perfume.

AP'PAIM (ap'pa-yim; "nostrils"). The second named of the sons of Nadab and the father of Ishi, of the posterity of Jerahmeel, of the tribe of Judah (1 Chron. 2:30).

APPAREL (Heb. *beged,* "dress," or some form of Aram. *lᵉbish,* "clothing"). See Dress.

APPEAL (Gk. *epikaleomai,* to "invoke" for aid, Acts 25:11-12, 21, 25).

Jewish. In patriarchal times the head of the

tribe administered justice, and, having no superior, there was no appeal from his decisions. In the condemnation of Tamar (Gen. 38:24) Judah exercised this power over the women of his family. Had the case been between man and man it would, doubtless, have been referred to Jacob. After the Exodus, Moses at first adjudged all cases himself, but at the suggestion of Jethro he arranged for a number of inferior judges, with evident right of appeal to himself (Ex. 18:13, 26). Later on the judges of the different towns were to bring all difficult cases that they were unable to decide before the Levitical priests and judges at the place of the sanctuary for a final decision (Deut. 17:8-11).

According to the above regulation the appeal lay in the time of the Judges to the judge (Judg. 4:5) and under the monarchy to the king, who appears to have designated certain persons to inquire into the facts of the case and record his decision (2 Sam. 15:3). Jehoshaphat delegated his judicial authority to a court permanently established for the purpose (2 Chron. 19:8). These courts were reestablished by Ezra (Ezra 7:25). After the institution of the Sanhedrin the final appeal lay to them.

Roman. A Roman citizen under the Republic had the right to appeal in criminal cases from the decision of a magistrate to the people, and as the emperor succeeded to the power of the people there was an appeal to him in the last resort. The apostle Paul, as a Roman citizen, exercised a right of appeal from the jurisdiction of the local court at Jerusalem to the emperor (Acts 25:11). But as no decision had been given there could be no appeal, properly speaking, in his case; the language used (25:9) implies the right on the part of the accused of electing either to be tried by the provincial magistrate or by the emperor. Since the procedure in the Jewish courts at that period was of a mixed and undefined character, the Roman and Jewish authorities coexisting and carrying on the course of justice between them, Paul availed himself of his undoubted privilege to be tried by the pure Roman law.

Ecclesiastical. In the early church all ecclesiastical matters were determined by the bishop with his court, an appeal being allowed to the provincial synod. Appeal to the pope was first formally recognized by the Council of Sardica (A.D. 343), where it was agreed that a condemned bishop had the right of appeal to the pope, who should either confirm the verdict of the synod or appoint new judges. The decision of the council was not at first generally accepted, yet within the next half century the opinion prevailed that in all important cases an appeal could be made not only by a bishop but by anyone aggrieved. Thus it came to pass that during the medieval period the pope became, *ex officio,* the ecclesiastical judge of highest resort for all the nations whose churches acknowledged obedience to him. The

first instance in England of an appeal occurred in the reign of Stephen, but the concession was withdrawn under Henry II when one of the Constitutions of Clarendon decided that no appeals should be made to the pope without the king's consent. In Germany the first reaction against papal usurpation appeared in the "Golden Bull," which forbade appeals to Rome from a civil court. The *Concordatum Constant* (1418) and the decree of the thirty-first sitting of the Council of Basel, determined that appeals to the pope should not be decided in Rome by the *curia* but by *judices in partubis,* chosen first by provincial or diocesan synods, and afterward by the bishops and chapters. The following is from the *Catholic Dictionary* (s. v.): "*The object* of appeals is the redress of injustice, whether knowingly or ignorantly committed. Appeal can be made from any judge recognizing a superior; thus no appeal is possible in secular matters from the decision of the sovereign power, or the highest secular tribunal, in any country; for these, in such matters, recognize no superior. There can be no appeal from the pope, for he, as the vicar of Christ, recognizes no superior on earth. . . . Nor can an appeal be made from a general council legitimately convened and approved, because it, being in union with the Roman pontiff who approved it, represents the whole Church, from the sentence of which there can be no appeal." In the Methodist, the Presbyterian, and most of the Protestant churches the right of appeal is recognized and modes of procedure provided for in their various books of discipline.

APPEARANCE. A term usually applied to the interviews granted to the disciples by Jesus after His resurrection. From the several accounts we see that our Lord's body had undergone a change, having extraordinary powers of locomotion, of becoming invisible and visible at pleasure, while it still retained characteristics of matter and was capable of taking food in the ordinary way. The following appearances are recorded: to Mary Magdalene (Mark 16:9-10; John 20:11-18); to other women (Matt. 28:9-10); to Simon Peter (Luke 24:34; 1 Cor. 15:5); to the two going to Emmaus (Luke 24:13-31); to the apostles (Mark 16:14; John 20:19); to apostles, including Thomas (20:26-29); to seven disciples at the Sea of Galilee (21:1-14); to five hundred (1 Cor. 15:6); to James, then to all apostles, giving them a commission (Luke 24:44-49; Acts 1:3-8); at the ascension (Mark 16:19-20; Luke 24:50-53; Acts 1:9-12).

APPEARING of our Lord (1 Tim. 6:14; 2 Tim. 1:10; 4:1, 8; etc.). *See* Millennium.

APPHIA (af'i-a). The name of a woman affectionately saluted by Paul (A.D. 64) as a Christian at Colossae (Philem. 2), supposed by Chrysostom and Theodoret to have been the wife of Philemon, with whom, according to tradition, she suffered martyrdom. *See* Philemon.

BIBLIOGRAPHY: J. B. Lightfoot, *St. Paul's Epistles to the Colossians and Philemon* (1968), pp. 304-6.

The Appian Way, Rome

AP'PII FO'RUM (ap-ī-ī fō'rum). The marketplace of Appius. A town or station located forty miles from Rome, upon the Appian Way, over which Paul passed on his way to the capital (Acts 28:15). Three Inns was a village about ten miles nearer Rome. Scholars now locate the town about three miles from modern Cisterna. "Taverns" almost certainly denotes inns for travelers in this instance.

APPIUS (ap'pi-us). *See* Appii Forum.

APPLE. *See* Vegetable Kingdom.

APRON. *See* Dress.

A'QABA (a'ka-ba), **Gulf of.** The northern arm of the Red Sea, at the head of which lay Solomon's seaport of *Ezion-geber* (which see; 1 Kings 9:26).

AQUEDUCT (ak'wē-duct). *See* Conduit.

AQ'UILA (ak'wi-la; "eagle"). A Jew and a native of Pontus, and by occupation a tentmaker. Fleeing from Rome in consequence of an order of Claudius commanding all Jews to leave that city, he went to Corinth, where he was living when Paul found him, and, being of the same handicraft, lived with him. Some time after, being opposed by the Jews and perhaps to remove any obstacle to his acceptance by the Gentiles, Paul left the house of Aquila and dwelt with one Titius Justus. It is not certain when Aquila and his wife, Priscilla, were converted to Christianity, but it was before Paul left Corinth, for they accompanied him to Ephesus. While there they instructed Apollos in "the way of God more accurately" (Acts 18) and appear to have been zealous promoters of the Christian cause in that city (1 Cor. 16:19). At the time of Paul's writing to Corinth, Aquila and his wife were still at Ephesus (16:19), but in Rom. 16:3-5 we find them again at Rome and their house a place of assemblage for Christians. Some years after they appear to have returned to Ephesus, for Paul sends salutations to them during his second imprisonment at Rome (2 Tim. 4:19), as being with Timothy. Nothing further concerning them is known.

BIBLIOGRAPHY: H. C. Lees, *St. Paul's Friends* (1918), pp. 47-67; D. E. Hiebert, *Personalities Around Paul* (1973), pp. 33-45; C. J. and A. A. Barber, *You Can Have a Happy Marriage* (1974), pp. 159-71.

AR (ar; "city"). The same as Ar Moab (Num. 21:15, 28; Deut. 2:9, 18, 29), on the border of the Arnon (Num. 22:36).

A'RA (a'ra). The last named of the three sons of Jether, of the tribe of Asher (1 Chron. 7:38).

A'RAB (a'rab; "ambush"). A city in the mountains of Judah, and given to that tribe (Josh. 15:52). It is located at modern er-Rabiyeh, a ruin E of Dumah.

AR'ABAH (ar'a-bā; "desert," Josh. 18:18). *The Arabah* (KJV, "the plain") is applied (Deut. 1:1; 2:8; 3:17; 4:49; Josh. 3:16; 12:1, 3; 2 Kings 14:25; Amos 6:14) to the valley between the Dead Sea and the Gulf of Aqaba. The valley is about one hundred miles in length and is somewhat wider in the N than in the S. The southern third of the Arabah is only about six miles wide and is formed by Nubian sandstone on the W and granite on the E. The valley floor rises to its highest point, 650 feet above sea level, in about the middle of the Arabah and then descends to the Gulf of Aqaba. Everywhere the Arabah is desert, though there are several wadi bottoms in the northern Arabah. Some oases stand there today, and in Nabatean times these were marked by forts and cultivated fields. About a quarter of the way down the Arabah from the Dead Sea were the copper mines of Punon (modern Feinan), a source of Edomite and Nabatean wealth. Here water was available, which made it possible to work the mines.

H.F.V.

BIBLIOGRAPHY: D. Baly, *Geography of the Bible* (1957), pp. 198-216; N. Glueck, *Rivers in the Desert* (1959), pp. 153-63.

The reddish cliffs in the Arabah Valley known as Solomon's Pillars

ARA'BIA (a-rā'bi-a; "desert"). In the Bible Arabia does not denote the whole peninsula between the Red Sea and the Persian Gulf, but only the northern part contiguous to Palestine (Isa. 21:13; Jer. 25:24; Ezek. 27:21); and in the same manner "the Arab" (Isa. 13:20; Jer. 3:2) does not denote the Arab in general, but only the inhabitant of the northern region. Only in the later books of the OT, as, for instance, 2 Chron. 21:16, where the Arabians are spoken of together with the Ethiopians, or in Neh. 2:19; 6:1, and in the NT (Acts 2:11; Gal. 1:17; 4:25) does the name seem to have obtained a more general signification.

Arabia is an area of about one million square miles, with just over twenty-four million inhabitants. It is the world's largest peninsula, consisting of a desert area close to one-third the size of the United States. Its ancient divisions were Arabia Petraea (the NW section, including the Sinai, which became a Roman province), Arabia Felix (the main part of the peninsula), and Arabia Deserta (the northern part between Syria and Mesopotamia). The political divisions of this area today are Saudi Arabia, North Yemen, South Yemen, Oman, Kuwait, United Arab Emirates, Qatar, and Bahrain.

The part of Arabia that holds special interest for the Bible student is the SW region, from which the queen of Sheba came to see Solomon. This area derived much of its wealth and significance from its position on the trade routes between Ethiopia and lands to the N. In fact, it has been suggested that the queen of Sheba made the long journey to see Solomon not primarily because of his wisdom or even his wealth but because the activities of his merchant marine were cutting into her sphere of mercantile influence.

Sometime during the second millennium B.C. Semitic tribes from the N came into the area of Yemen and established settlements that later were to become the kingdoms of Saba' (Sheba),

Ma'in (Minaeans) and Qataban. Excavations in the area have been few. The first excavations in the region of Saba' were conducted by C. Rathjens and H. von Wissman in 1928. Among other things, they found a temple dedicated to the sun-goddess about fourteen miles NNW of San'a and in use for several centuries B.C. An American expedition in 1951-52 found an eighth-century B.C. temple SE of Marib. They recovered more than three hundred Sabean texts at the site. The Americans also worked at Timna', capital of the Qatabanian kingdom, and its necropolis. They investigated the remains in the nearby Wadi Beihan of an irrigation system dated to about 1500 B.C. Although some approach to a pottery chronology of the region has now been developed, nothing has been found that throws much light on the civilization of the region in the days of Solomon in the tenth century B.C.   H.F.V.

BIBLIOGRAPHY: J. A. Montgomery, *Arabia and the Bible* (1934); S. Moscati, *Ancient Semitic Civilizations* (1957), pp. 181-207; P. K. Hitti, *History of the Arabs* (1970); W. S. LaSor, *International Standard Bible Encyclopedia* (1979) 1: 220-26.

A'RAD (a'rad; "fugitive").

1. In the KJV of Num. 21:1, "king Arad" should read "king of Arad."

2. One of the "sons" of Beriah, of the tribe of Benjamin (1 Chron. 8:15).

3. A Canaanite city on the southernmost borders of Palestine, whose inhabitants drove back the Israelites while trying to enter Canaan from Kadesh (Num. 21:1; 33:40) but were finally subdued by Joshua (Josh. 12:14; Judg. 1:16). It lay about seventeen miles S of Hebron and is now called Tell Arad.

Yohanan Aharoni and Ruth Amiran excavated at Arad from 1962 to 1967 and since 1971 on behalf of the Hebrew University, the Israel Department of Antiquities, and the Israel Exploration Society. They found that a Canaanite village existed there from about 3200 to 2900 B.C. and was followed by a city of some twenty-two acres surrounded by a stone wall dating from 2900 to 2700. Thereafter the site was unoccupied until the eleventh century. A strong citadel was built there in the tenth century, probably in Solomon's reign. Of special interest is the Israelite temple built inside the tenth-century citadel and measuring sixty-five by forty-five feet. Apparently this was destroyed during King Josiah's reform in the seventh century B.C. Since Tell Arad was uninhabited during the days of Moses and Joshua, that Arad must be located elsewhere. That there were two Arads is supported by the fact that Pharaoh Shishak of Egypt in 926 claimed to have captured two Arads in the Negev: Arad the Great and Arad of the House of Yeroham.   H.F.V.

A'RAH (a'rā; "wayfaring").

1. The first named of the three sons of Ulla, of the tribe of Asher (1 Chron. 7:39).

2. An Israelite, whose posterity (variously stated as 775 and 652 in number) returned from Babylon with Zerubbabel (Ezra 2:5; Neh. 7:10), 536 B.C. He is probably the same as the Arah whose son, Shecaniah, was father-in-law of Tobiah (6:18).

A'RAM (a'ram). A son of Shem, progenitor of the Aramaean peoples (Gen. 10:22-23), who spread widely in Syria and Mesopotamia from the Lebanon Mountains. to beyond the Euphrates and from the Taurus Range on the N to Damascus and northern Palestine on the S. Contacts of the Aramaeans in the Balikh-Habur region ("Paddan-aram," Gen. 28:5) with the Hebrews go back to the patriarchal age (31:47, marg.). The maternal ancestry of Jacob's children was Aramaic (Deut. 26:5). During the long period of Israel's sojourn in Egypt, their wanderings in the Sinaitic Wilderness, and the extended period of the Judges in Canaan, the Aramaeans were multiplying and extending in every direction, particularly southward. At the time of Saul (c. 1020 B.C.), Aramaic expansion was beginning to clash with Israelite strength, and by this time several Aramaean districts appear prominently in the OT narratives.

Aram-Naharaim, "Aram of the (Two) Rivers," was the country between the Tigris and Euphrates (Gk., Mesopotamia), or more probably the territory between the Euphrates and the Habur. This was the region of Haran where the Aramaeans had settled in patriarchal times, where Abraham sojourned, and from which Aramaean power spread.

Aram-Damascus emerged from a petty S Syrian state when a man named Rezon seized the city at the time David conquered Zobah (1 Kings 11:23-24) and founded a strong Aramaean kingdom there. This power was the inveterate foe of the Northern Kingdom for more than a century and a half under such powerful Aramaean rulers as Hezion, Tabrimmon, the Ben-hadads, Hazael, and Rezon. The Aramaic kingdom of Damascus did not come to an end until destroyed by Assyria in 732 B.C.

Aram-Zobah was a powerful Aramaean kingdom that flourished N of Hamath and reached its zenith under Saul and the early years of David's reign. David conquered it and incorporated it into his realm (2 Sam. 8; cf. vv. 10, 12-13, marg.).

Aram-Maachah was an Aramaean principality that lay E of the Jordan near Mt. Hermon (Josh. 12:5; 13:11) and extended at least as far W as the Jordan. *See also* Maachah, no. 3.

Geshur was a small Aramaic principality E of the Jordan and the Sea of Galilee and S of Maachah within Manasseh's territory (Deut. 3:14; 2 Sam. 13:37; 15:8).

Aram-Beth-rehob is in the general vicinity of Geshur. If identical with the place mentioned in Num. 13:21 and Judg. 13:28, it was near Maacah and Dan.

Tob was an Aramaic principality E of the Jordan and is probably identifiable with et-Taiyibeh, ten miles S of Gadara. It was there that Hanun, king of Ammon, drew soldiers to war against David (2 Sam. 10:6). David was bound to clash with these Aramaean kingdoms at his back door. He conquered them and incorporated them into his kingdom, making possible the empire of Solomon.

BIBLIOGRAPHY: Merrill F. Unger, *Israel and the Aramaeans of Damascus* (1957).

ARAMA'IC (ar-a-mā'ik). A NW Semitic dialect. It was formerly inaccurately called Chaldee (Chaldaic) because it was spoken by the Chaldeans of the book of Daniel (2:4-7:28). But since the Chaldeans are known to have generally spoken Akkad., the term Chaldee has been abandoned. Numerous references to the Aramaeans (*Arimi, Ahlâme*) occur in Assyrian records from the fourteenth century B.C. onward. Monumental inscriptions in Aram. also are found, such as the votive stela of Ben-hadad II set up about 850 B.C. and discovered in 1941 just N of Aleppo in Syria. These monuments inscribed in Aram. extend into the Persian Period, when Aram. became the lingua franca of all SW Asia as the result of the traffic of Aramaean merchants; business documents, weights, measures, etc., are found in Aram. dating in the eighth to the fifth century B.C. The main source of Aram., however, is the deposit of Aram. papyri from Elephantine in Upper Egypt dating from 500 to 400 B.C. (*see* article Amarna, el-).

Our Lord spoke Galilean Aram., and Aram. portions of the OT include Dan. 2:4–7:28; Ezra 4:8–6:18; 7:12-26; Jer. 10:11 (gloss?). The Greeks called Aram *Syria;* consequently the language is called "Syriac" (Dan. 2:4, KJV). This designation is now confined to the Aram. dialect spoken at Edessa, which became the language of the Christian churches of Syria and Mesopotamia.

ARAN (a'ran). The second son of Dishan, a descendant of Seir the Horite (Gen. 36:28; 1 Chron. 1:42).   E.H.M.

AR'ARAT (ar'a-rat; Gen. 8:4; Jer. 51:27). This name, applied to the country between the Tigris and the Caucasus Mountains, known as Armenia and called in the Assyrian inscription Urartu, came to apply to the mountain range there. The highest of these mountains, Ağri Dağ, on the Russian border in eastern Turkey, is usually seized on as the place where Noah's ark landed because it is the highest mountain (16,946 feet) in the chain and in the entire Near East. But ancient traditions point to at least six other landing places, and it is not possible to be dogmatic about the site. Numerous expeditions have explored the traditional Mt. Ararat, without any definitive results. The Mesopotamian flood account says that its flood hero landed on Mt. Nisir, usually identified with Pir Omar Gudrum, a nine-thousand-foot peak considerably S of the Ararat chain and about four hundred miles N of the Persian Gulf and E of the Tigris River.

H.F.V.

ARAU'NAH (a-rā'na). A Jebusite who had a threshing floor on Mt. Moriah, which he sold to David as a site for an altar to Jehovah. The angel of pestilence, sent to punish King David for taking a census of the people, was stayed in the work of death near this plot of ground. When David desired to purchase it, Aruanah liberally offered the ground to him as a free gift. David insisted upon paying for it, giving him, according to 2 Sam. 24:24, fifty shekels of silver and, according to 1 Chron. 21:25, six hundred shekels of gold. (Many efforts have been made to reconcile this difference, some saying that the fifty shekels were given for the oxen and the six hundred shekels for the land; others, that the fifty shekels were for the threshing floor and oxen and the six hundred shekels for additional ground.)

This land was the site of the Temple (2 Chron. 3:1). Araunah's name is sometimes written Ornan. *See* Chronicles.

AR'BA (ar'ba; "four"). A giant, father of Anak. From him Hebron derived its early name of Kiriath-arba, i.e., "city of Arba" (Gen. 35:37; Josh. 14:15; 15:13; 21:11).

AR'BITE (ar'bīt). Paarai the Arbite was one of David's guards (2 Sam. 23:35). The word signifies a native of Arab in the hill country of Judah. In 1 Chron. 11:37 the name is given as Naarai.

ARCHAEOLOGY (Gk. *archaiologia,* "science of ancient things"). General archaeology is a study based on the excavation, decipherment, and critical evaluation of records of the ancient past.

Biblical Archaeology. Biblical archaeology is a more restricted field than general archaeology and deals with the excavation, decipherment, and critical evaluation of ancient records of the past that touch either directly or indirectly upon the Bible and its message.

Interest and Importance. Biblical archaeology, shedding light upon the historical background and the contemporary life out of which the Holy Scriptures came and illuminating and illustrating its pages with its truly remarkable discoveries, borrows much of the great interest that is attached to it from its connection with the Bible. It is accordingly attracting larger and larger numbers of enthusiastic investigators, students, and Bible readers in general. In fact, no field of research offers greater challenge and promise than biblical (particularly OT) archaeology. This appears from the simple fact that up to about 1800 exceedingly little was known of OT times except what appeared on the pages of the

Scriptures themselves or what happened to be preserved in the writings of classical antiquity. This was considerable for the NT era but was practically nil insofar as the OT was concerned, since Greek and Latin historians cataloged little information prior to 400 B.C. As a consequence, knowledge of the OT period was confined to the Bible itself, and this, from the point of view of contemporary history, was sparse indeed. The result was that before the advent of modern archaeology at about 1800, there was practically nothing available to illustrate OT history and literature.

Discoveries. Modern archaeology may be said to have had its beginning in 1798 when the rich antiquities of the Nile Valley were opened up to scientific study by Napoleon's expedition. Toward the middle of the next century the treasures of Assyria and Babylonia were uncovered as a result of the work of Paul Botta, A. H. Layard, H. C. Rawlinson, and others. With the decipherment of the Rosetta Stone, which unlocked Egyptian hieroglyphics, and the reading of the Behistun Inscription, which furnished the key to Assyrian and Babylonian cuneiform, a vast mass of material bearing on the OT was released. The finding of the Moabite Stone in 1868 created a veritable sensation because of its close connection with OT history, and it aroused widespread enthusiasm in Palestinian excavations.

Excavations at the Forum, Rome

However, many of the most notable discoveries affecting the Bible (particularly the OT) were not made until within aproximately the last eighty years, such as the Code of Hammurabi (1901), the Elephantine Papyri (1903), the Hittite Monuments at Boghazkeui (1906), the tomb of Tutankhamen (1922), the sarcophagus of Ahiram of

Byblus (1923), the Ras Shamra religious epic literature (1929-37), the Mari Letters and the Lachish Ostraca (1935-38), the Dead Sea Scrolls (1947-67), and the remarkable finds at Ebla (since 1964). The discoveries at Ebla (Tell Mardikh) in Syria have demonstrated a well-developed written language c. 2500 B.C., but the interpretation of these tablets is controversial.

Contributions. Although archaeological findings in the hands of the purely technical scholar, who has little proper understanding or appreciation of the unique message and meaning of the Bible, are continually in peril of being misinterpreted and misapplied and made the basis of unsound theories, archaeology in the hands of the scientist who is at the same time a devout believer yields vast and far-reaching results for good. Legitimately handled, the contributions of archaeology to biblical studies are tremendous.

Archaeology Authenticates the Bible. Although there is genuine benefit of archaeological research in Bible lands, especially in dealing with extreme liberalism and the many vagaries of higher criticism, yet its subordinate nature appears from several considerations. In the first place, the Bible does not need to be "proved" either by archaeology, geology, or any other science. As God's revelation to man, its own message and meaning, its own claims of inspiration and internal evidence, its own fruits and results in the life of humanity are its best proof of authenticity. It demonstrates itself to be what it claims to be to those who *believe* its message. Since God has made the realization of the spiritual life dependent on faith and not sight (2 Cor. 5:7; Heb. 11:6), whatever contributions archaeology or any other science might make in attesting to the reliability of the Bible can never supplant faith. Scientific authentication may act as a help to faith, but God has established simple trust that honors Him as the medium of receiving His salvation and understanding His revealed ways with man. Despite the truth of these facts, archaeology has an important role in authenticating the Bible both generally and specifically. Generally, scientific archaeology has exploded many extreme theories and false assumptions that used to be paraded in scholarly circles as settled facts. No longer can higher criticism dismiss the Hebrew patriarchs as mere legendary figures, or deny that Moses could write, or assert that the Mosaic legislation is completely anachronistic for such an early age. These and other extreme opinions have been shown to be completely untenable by archaeological research. Other examples of general confirmation of the Bible are the results of excavations at Jerusalem, Gibeah of Saul, Megiddo, Samaria, and numerous other Palestinian cities. Cases of specific confirmation, although of course less numerous, are striking. The historicity of Belshazzar (Dan. 5), the authentication of the name *Sargon* (Isa.

20:1), and the corroboration of Jehoiachin's captivity in Babylon (2 Kings 25:27-30) by the actual finding of the name of the king on cuneiform tablets there, are but a few examples of specific attestations.

Archaeology Illustrates and Explains the Bible. This is by far the most important contribution of archaeological research in Bible lands, and its ramifications are practically endless. It is no exaggeration to say that insofar as its background is concerned, the Bible is a whole new book as a result of the marvelous contributions of archaeology toward illuminating and illustrating it. Examples are numberless. Whether it is the longevity of the antediluvian patriarchs, Abraham's hometown of Ur, the conquest of Jericho, Jeroboam's golden calves at Bethel, Jonah's preaching in Nineveh, the Temple of Herod, the ministry of Paul in Ephesus, everywhere archaeology sheds light on the sacred page and makes its message and meaning more understandable to our present day.

Archaeology Supplements the Bible. The human authors of the Bible, writing under divine inspiration, were not interested in profane history, geography, ethnology, and other fields of human knowledge, except incidentally as they chanced to touch upon the history of redemption. It is, therefore, natural from the modern scholar's view that there should be great gaps in the Bible in these branches of learning; whereas from the divine side and insofar as the spiritual comprehension of the divine message is concerned, there was no need for further knowledge of these and kindred subjects. Yet from a human standpoint light from these spheres of research is of incalculable value in extending biblical horizons, increasing knowledge of biblical backgrounds, and giving a fuller comprehension of the message of the Bible. Examples of supplementation are numerous, such as the destruction of Shiloh, which is nowhere recounted in Scripture but is assumed by Jeremiah (Jer. 7:12-15; 26:6-7). Excavations at the site of Israel's ancient sanctuary by the Danish Expedition uncovered pottery and other evidence showing that this destruction took place 1050 B.C., presumably at the hands of the Philistines (see H. Kjaer, *Journal of Palestine Oriental Society* [1930]: 87-114). Other examples occur in excavations at Bethshan, the Esdraelon fortress, destroyed not long after Shiloh, and evidently at the hands of David as a punishment for the ignominious treatment of the deceased king Saul (1 Sam. 31:10, 12; 2 Sam. 21:12). Striking supplementation is common in the Assyrian period. The Israelite kings Omri, Ahab, Jehu, Menahem, and Hoshea and the Judean kings Ahaz, Hezekiah, Manasseh, Josiah, and Jehoiachin are all much better known by the supplementary material gleaned from the cuneiform records of the great Assyrian emperors Shalmaneser III, Tiglath-pileser III, Sargon II,

Sennacherib, Esarhaddon, and Ashurbanipal. Archaeology has thus yielded momentous results up to the present and gives fair promise of even greater contributions in the future as research in Bible lands progresses.   M.F.U.

BIBLIOGRAPHY: M. Avi-Yonah and E. Stern, eds., *Encyclopedia of Archaeological Excavations in the Holy Land,* 4 vols. (1975-78); H. F. Vos, *Archaeology in Bible Lands* (1977); E. M. Blaiklock and R. K. Harrison, eds., *New International Dictionary of Biblical Archaeology* (1983). For additional information see *The Minister's Library* (1985), pp. 109-16.

ARCHANGEL. See Michael.

ARCHELA'US (ar-ki-lā'us; "ruler of the people"). Son of Herod the Great by a Samaritan woman, Malthace (Josephus *Wars* 1.28.4), and brought up, with his brother Antipas, at Rome (Josephus *Wars* 1.31.1). Upon his father's death, Caesar divided his kingdom, giving to Archelaus (4 B.C.) Edom, Judea, and Samaria, with the important cities Caesarea, Sebaste, Joppa, and Jerusalem. His share of the kingdom brought him a yearly income of six hundred talents. He was made ethnarch, with promise of becoming king if he ruled virtuously (Josephus *Ant.* 17.11.4). After Herod's death, and previous to going to Rome to receive the government, Archelaus ordered his soldiers to attack the Jews, who were becoming tumultuous, at the Temple. The attack resulted in the death of about three thousand Jews. On his going to Rome the Jews sent a deputation of the principal citizens protesting against his cruelty and asking to be permitted to live according to their own laws, under a Roman governor. Some have thought that our Lord alludes to this circumstance in Luke 19:21-27. Archelaus returned to Judea, and, under pretense that he had countenanced the seditions against him, he deprived Joazar of the high priesthood and gave that dignity to his brother Eleazar. He governed Judea with so much violence that in the tenth (ninth according to Dio Cassius) year of his reign he was dethroned, deprived of his property, and banished to Vienna, in Gaul (Josephus *Ant.* 17.13.2). His cruelty was manifested toward Samaritans as well as Jews. The parents of our Lord turned aside, from fear of him, on their way back from Egypt and went to Nazareth in Galilee, in the domain of his more gentle brother Antipas (Matt. 2:22). *See also* article Herod.

ARCHERS (Heb. *qashshāt,* "bowman," Gen. 21:20; *ba'al hēṣ,* "arrow man," Gen. 49:23; *'ĕnôsh baqqeshet,* "bowman," 1 Sam. 31:3; also "shooter with the bow," 1 Chron. 10:3; "one bending the bow," Jer. 51:3). The bow and arrow are weapons of ancient origin (Gen. 48:22; 49:24; cf. Gen. 9:14-15). Archers were numerous among the Hebrews, especially in the tribes of Benjamin and Ephraim (Ps. 76:3; 1 Chron. 8:40; 2 Chron. 14:8; 17:17). Archers are frequently found on Egyptian monuments and Assyrian sculptures.

Reference is made to the Philistine archers in 1 Sam. 31:3, and the Persians were famous for their archers (Isa. 13:18; Jer. 49:35; 50:29). *See* Armor.

Israelite archer

ARCHIP'PUS (ar-kip'us; "master of the horse"). A Christian minister at Colossae, to whom Paul sends a salutation, calling him "our fellow soldier" (Philem. 2), and whom he exhorts to increased activity (Col. 4:17), A.D. 61. In the epistle to Philemon he is addressed jointly with Philemon and Apphia, from which it has been inferred that he was a member of Philemon's family. Tradition states that he was one of Jesus' seventy disciples and suffered martyrdom at Chonae, near Laodicea.

ARCHITECTURE. Today hundreds of architectural works built in Bible times and known to Bible characters have been dug up and may now be seen. However, the architectural beauty that the Hebrews knew was largely the result of Egyptian, Babylonian, Assyrian, Phoenician, Greek, or Roman influence.

Egyptian. Egyptian art and architecture were splendid almost from the time of Menes of the First Dynasty, c. 2900-2700 B.C. Abraham, Jacob, and their descendants gazed upon the gigantic pyramids that were already centuries old by Abraham's time (c. 2000 B.C.) and belong to the Old Kingdom (Dynasties III-VI), c. 2700-2200 B.C. Djoser, first king of the Third Dynasty, had an architect who constructed for him the famous Step Pyramid at Saqqara. Khufu, founder of the

Pyramids at Gizeh

Fourth Dynasty, built the greatest of the pyramids at Gizeh, whose base covers thirteen acres, required 2,300,000 2½-ton blocks of yellow limestone to erect, and towered originally 481 feet in height. Khafre, the successor of Khufu, built the even more spectacular Second Pyramid at Gizeh, 447½ feet high. Khafre himself is represented in the head of the Sphinx, which stands to the E of the Second Pyramid and which was carved out of a spur of natural rock and built up with blocks of stone at the same time the pyramid of Khafre was constructed. Kings of the Fifth and Sixth Dynasties carved the famous pyramid texts on the walls of the inner chambers of their pyramids. Remarkable temples, tombs, etc., were part of Egypt's long and brilliant history. But in the New Kingdom (Dynasties XVIII-XX), c. 1570-1150 B.C., when Egypt ruled the East, many architectural wonders appeared such as the exquisite Mortuary temple of Queen Hatshepsut (c. 1520 B.C.) at Deir-el-Bahri, near Thebes, a beautiful structure of white limestone built in colonnaded terraces. Another outstanding builder was Rameses II (c. 1301-1234 B.C.). His mortuary temple, the Ramesseum at Thebes, is exquisite. Moreover, he added to the temple at Luxor and constructed the enormous hypostyle hall of the Kar-

Layard excavates ancient Nineveh

nak temple, consisting of 134 tremendous columns the highest of which rose seventy feet in the air; this hall was part of the largest temple ever built by man. At Abu Simbel above the First Cataract of the Nile, Rameses II hewed out a complete temple in the sandstone cliff overlooking the Nile and carved four great statues of himself from the rock in front of it.

Mesopotamian. The OT refers a number of times to palaces and other types of Mesopotamian architecture (Isa. 39:7; 2 Kings 20:18). At Erech (Uruk, Warka, Gen. 10:10), some fifty miles NW of Ur, the Deutsche Orientgesellschaft under Adolph Koldewey discovered (besides the first cylinder seals and earliest known writing) monumental architecture including temples, remains of the huge mud-brick Tower of Eanna (c. 2500 B.C.) and first evidences of the Babylonian stage tower, or ziggurat (cf. Gen. 11:1-6). At ancient Ur (Abraham's birthplace) in numerous campaigns Sir Leonard Woolley recovered abundant evidences of Sumerian art, complexes of temples, palaces, city streets, and the remains of one of the best-preserved ancient ziggurats (cf. 11:28, 31; 15:7; Neh. 9:7). At Asshur on the Tigris River S of Nineveh, the German expedition under Walter Andrae before World War I uncovered an archaic temple of Ishtar, a fine temple of Asshur (native god of Assyria), stout city walls, gates, and landmarks revealing the architectural splendor of the ancient city going back to c. 3000 B.C. At Babylon on the Euphrates N of Kish a German expedition under Robert Koldewey laid bare the magnificent ancient city of Nebuchadnezzar and an utterly bewildering group of palaces, public buildings, famous streets, including the Processional, temples, and a tower identified by many as the tower of Babel (Gen. 10:10; 11:9; 2 Kings 17:24, 30; etc.). At Calah (Nimrud, Gen. 10:10), some twenty miles SE of Nineveh, Austin Layard, and later M. E. L. Mallowan, found palaces of Assyrian kings of the eighth century B.C. with man-headed lions and colossal reliefs. At ancient Kish, some eight miles E of Babylon, the Oxford University and the Field Museum of Natural History expedition located an ancient palace of the kings of Kish and a temple of Ishtar. At Nineveh, on the Upper Tigris N of Asshur, A. H. Layard, M. E. Mallowan, H. Rassam, and others recovered remains of ornate Assyrian palaces, including the magnificent palace of Sennacherib (c. 704-681 B.C.) containing no less than seventy-one rooms with almost ten thousand feet of walls lined with sculptured slabs. Besides this, Nineveh yielded the superb library of Ashurbanipal (669-633 B.C.; cf. Gen. 10:11-12; 2 Kings 19:36; Isa. 37:37; Jonah 1:2; Nah. 1:1–3:19; Matt. 12:41). At Khorsabad (Dur Sharrukin) Paul Emile Botta dug up the famous palace of Sargon II (721-705 B.C.) containing splendid reliefs and enameled tile paintings. At Mari (Tell el Hariri), on the Middle Euphrates near Abou Kemal, the Musée du Louvre under André Parrot uncovered a huge palace of Amorite rulers, a temple of Ishtar, and a ziggurat. The palace at Mari is most notable, being a tremendous structure covering more than fifteen acres, with royal apartments, offices, school for scribes, etc., besides containing archives yielding twenty thousand clay tablets.

Persian. The most impressive evidence of the height to which Persian art and architecture attained is furnished by the ruins of Persepolis, twenty-five miles SW of Pasargadae. The magnificent complex at Persepolis was especially the creation of Darius I the Great (522-486 B.C.). Archaeological excavations at Persepolis by the Oriental Institute of the University of Chicago, under the direction of Ernst Herzfeld and Erich Schmidt, have uncovered ruins that are mute but eloquent testimony to the splendor that was ancient Persia's. Among the famous buildings are the palace of Darius (known as the Tachara), the Tripylon (reception hall), the Apadana (the huge audience hall of Darius and Xerxes), the Hall of One Hundred Columns, the Gate of Xerxes, with colossal bulls guarding it as in Assyrian palaces, the Harem of Darius and Xerxes, the residence of Xerxes (486-465 B.C.), and the royal treasury, which contains fine reliefs of Darius and Xerxes like those in the Tripylon,

Susa (Shushan, KJV, Neh. 1:1; Esther 1:2) in

ancient Elam, excavated by a French expedition under Jacques de Morgan, revealed the palace of Darius I, enlarged and beautified by later kings, as its greatest monument of the Persian period. Panels of beautifully colored glazed brick decorated the interior of the palace, many of the designs being executed in relief, including winged bulls, winged griffins, and the famous spearmen of the guard.

Greek. The architectural glory of Greece is best illustrated by *Athens* (which see). In the fifth century B.C. the ancient hill became a religious center with superb temples, the most important of which were dedicated to Athena, the city's patron goddess. Outstripping all were the world-famous architectural wonders of the Erechtheum, the Parthenon, and the temple of the Wingless Victory Famous structures located elsewhere in Athens were the Odeion (Music Hall), the Stoa of Eumenes II, the Theseion, the temple of Zeus, and the marketplace (*see* agora). Besides extensively excavating at Athens, the American School of Classical Studies has conducted thirty seasons of work at Corinth, uncovering a vast agora, a theater, temple of Apollo, the Sanctuary of Aesculapius, a basilica, and other buildings. The following Greek orders of architecture appear:

Doric. The Doric column consists of: (1) The

The Parthenon, Athens

The Temple of Apollo at Corinth

97

shaft, which increases in diameter almost invisibly up to about one-quarter of its height and diminishes slightly after that point. It has no base, but rests immediately on the stylobate. It is surrounded by semicircular flutings meeting each other at a sharp angle. (2) The capital, consisting of three parts: the *hypotrachelion,* or neck of the column, a continuation of the shaft but separated by an indentation from the other drums; the *echinus,* a circular molding, or cushion, which widens greatly toward the top; the *abax,* or *abacus,* a square slab supporting the architrave, or *epistylion.* The architrave is the quadrangular stone reaching from pillar to pillar. Above this is the frieze (*zophoros*), surmounted by the cornice.

The style known as the Tuscan is a degenerate form of the Doric. The column has a smooth shaft, tapering up to three-quarters of its lower dimensions. Its base consists of two parts, a circular plinth and a cushion of equal height.

Ionic. This column is loftier than the Doric; the enlargement of the lower part is less than the Doric, the distance between the columns is greater, and the flutings deeper and separated by flat surfaces. The Ionic column has a base consisting of a square slab and several cushionlike supports separated by grooves. The capital again is more artistically developed, resembling a ram's horn or scroll, while the architrave is divided into three bands, projecting one above the other, and upon it rises, in an uninterrupted surface, the frieze, adorned with reliefs along its whole length, and, finally, the cornice is composed of different parts.

Columns of the Theseum, Athens

Corinthian. The base and shaft are identical with the Ionic, but the capital takes the form of an open *calix* formed of acanthus leaves, from between which grow stalks with small leaves, rounded into the form of volutes. On this rests a small *abacus* widening toward the top, and on this rests the entablature, its style borrowed from the Ionic order.

Etruscan and Roman. The Etruscans united wonderful activity and inventiveness with a passion for covering their buildings with rich ornamental carvings. Almost none of their temples remain, for they built the upper parts of wood; but we have evidences of their activity in walls and tombs. Some old gateways, such as those at Volterra and Perugia, exhibit the true *arch* of wedge-shaped stones. The most imposing monument of ancient Italian arch-building is to be seen in the sewers of Rome, laid in the sixth century B.C.

The Roman architects kept alive the Etruscan method of building the arch, which they developed and completed by the invention of the *cross arch* and the *dome.* With the arch they combined, as a decorative element, the columns of the Greek order. They also introduced building with brick. A vigorous advance was made from the opening of the third century B.C., when the Romans began making great military roads and aqueducts.

Vespasian's Arch, Rome

In the last decades of the Republic, simplicity gradually disappeared, and a princely pomp was displayed in public and private buildings; witness the first stone theater erected by Pompey as early as 55 B.C. All that had gone before was eclipsed by the works undertaken by Caesar—the theater, the amphitheater, circus, Basilica Iulia, and the Forum Caesaris. These were finished by Augustus, under whom Roman architecture seems to have reached its culminating point. The greatest monument of that age, and one of the loftiest creations of Roman art in general, is the Pantheon, built by Agrippa. Of the luxurious grandeur of private buildings we have ocular proof in the dwelling houses of Pompeii, a paltry country town in comparison with Rome. The progress made under the Flavian emperors is evidenced by Vespasian's amphitheater (the Coliseum), the baths of Titus, and his triumphal arch. All previous forums were surpassed in size and splendor when Trajan's architect, Apollodorus of Damascus, raised the Forum Traianum, with its huge Basilica Ulpia and the still surviving Column of Trajan.

The Colosseum in Rome

Hebrew. The Israelites of the patriarchal period were shepherds and, by habit, dwellers in tents. They accordingly had originally no architecture. It was likely in connection with Egypt that the Hebrews first became builders of cities, being compelled to labor in the vast building enterprises of the pharaohs. From the time of their entrance into Canaan they became dwellers in towns and houses of stone (Lev. 14;34; 1 Kings 7:1-8), which, however, in most cases were not built by themselves (Deut. 6:10; Num. 13:19).

Early Hebrew Architecture. Hebrew architecture, in the proper sense of the word, did not exist until the time of the kings. Evidently few if any Israelites before the time of Saul had either time or money to indulge in architectural fancies. However, Israel's first king (c. 1020-1000 B.C.) made attempts in this direction as revealed by his fortress city at Gibeah (Tell el Ful), excavated by W. F. Albright (1922 and 1933). But the principal buildings from Saul's era, with massive stone construction and deep walls, were like a dungeon rather than a royal residence in comparison to the Canaanite masonry with which Solomon later graced Jerusalem. "Saul was only a rustic chieftain, as far as architecture and the amenities of life were concerned" (W. F. Albright, *From the Stone Age to Christianity* [1940], p. 224). Moreover, what was true of Saul was in a general way culturally true of all the Israelite tribes up to the efflorescence of industry and the arts and sciences in the prosperous Davidic-Solomonic era. Israelite poverty and rusticity of life in the premonarchic period have been fully demonstrated by Palestinian excavation.

Architecture Under David and Solomon. David, as a result of rapid conquest, soon had wealth and some leisure to think about building. His first "palace" at Hebron, where he reigned seven years, was perhaps just a flat-roofed stone house, but when he captured the Jebusite stronghold, he built himself "a house of cedar" (2 Sam. 7:2) in the SE corner of what became Jerusalem. He also began to fortify and build the city itself. But the peaceful reign and vast wealth of his son Solomon gave great impulse to architecture and development. For his palace and the magnificent Temple that he constructed, Solomon drew heavily upon Phoenician skill. It is now known that the plan of the latter edifice was characteristically Phoenician, which was to be expected, since it was built by a Tyrian architect (1 Kings 7:13-15). Similar ground plans of sanctuaries of the general period 1200-900 B.C. have been excavated in northern Syria at Tell Tainat in 1936 by the University of Chicago, and the findings have demonstrated that the specifications of the Solomonic structure are pre-Greek and authentic for the tenth century B.C. The pillars, Jachin and Boaz (gigantic cressets or fire altars), the proto-Aeolic pilaster, the motifs of lilies, palmettes, and cherubim, and the furnishings are all authentically early and show Phoenician or early Semitic genuineness. Archaeological excavations at Megiddo, Hazor, and Gezer give evidence of Solomon's building operations there of "chariot cities" (1 Kings 4:26; 10:26).

Later Hebrew Architecture. Other kings of Israel and Judah recorded as builders were Asa (1 Kings 15:23), Baasha (15:17), Omri (16:23-24), and Ahab (16:33) (confirmed by the excavations at Samaria), Hezekiah (2 Chron. 32:29; confirmed by the *Siloam Inscription*; which see) and Jehoahaz (Jer. 22:14). After the captivity, the poverty of the Jewish community made only modest repairs of walls and construction of a Temple possible (Ezra 3:8; 5:8; Neh. 2:8). Later the reigns of Herod and his successor were especially remarkable for their architectural works—the Temple (Matt. 24:1-2), Samaria (Sebaste), Caesarea, etc., all of which show heavy Greco-Roman influence.

Christian. The early Christians held their services in synagogues, private houses, the fields, the catacombs —indeed, wherever opportunity afforded. As early as in the third century buildings erected by them existed, but they were neither substantial nor costly. Christian architecture did not become an art until the time of Constantine, when it appeared in two entirely different forms, the *Basilican* and the *Byzantine*.

Basilican. When Christianity became the religion of the state and ancient basilicas, or halls of justice, were turned into churches, this style became prevalent throughout the Western countries and lasted until the eleventh century. The lower floor was used by the men, and the galleries reserved for the women. Specimens of this style of architecture still existing and in good repair are S. Paolo fuori le mura, S. Clemente in Rome, S. Apollinaire in Classe in Ravenna, etc.

Byzantine. The principal feature of this style is the dome, which was frequently used in Roman tombs. In Persia the problem was first solved by placing the cupola on a square substructure, forming an octagon in the interior of the square by means of a huge pillar in each angle. The Latin cross was abandoned for the Greek cross, whose branches are of equal length. The objection to images obliged the architects to seek some means other than sculpture for enriching the churches, hence the profusion of mosaic work. The masterpieces of this style are St. Mark's at Venice, St. Vitale at Ravenna, and St. Sophia at Constantinople. Still later the Greek cross was combined with the square, and the number of cupolas was increased to nine—one at the end of each arm, one over the crossing, and one in each corner of the square.

Romanesque. This resulted from a union of the two previous styles, the basilica and the dome. The ground plan and the interior and exterior of the old basilica were materially changed. An important feature was the transept, with fixed proportions, the cross being invariably produced by repeating the square, chosen as a unit, three times to the W, and one time respectively to the N, E, and S. Other features were apses for the side altars; the raised choir, to allow for the crypt; a belfry, first one and, as an independent building, then two, and connected with the western termination of the building; small arched galleries running a round parts or the whole of the church within and without. The exterior was covered with numerous well-disposed arches, pilasters, and other ornaments, and the richly decorated doorways and windows drew the eye to the central part of the facade. The result was that the whole external had a dignity not to be found in any other style of church architecture. Among the finest examples of this style are the cathedrals

of Pisa, Vercelli, Parma, Modena, and Lucca (in Italy), of Worms, Bonn, Mayence, and St. Gereon and St. Apostoli in Cologne. To this style belong the peculiar churches and round towers of Ireland, and the round tower of Newport, R.I.

Gothic. This style retains the ground plan and general arrangement of the Romanesque but substitutes the pointed for the round arch. The pointed arch was probably brought to Europe by the Crusaders from Asia, where it was used by the Muslims. The use of the pointed arch requires, for harmony, a corresponding upward tendency in all parts of the structure and, by obliterating the idea of a mechanical contrivance, produces the impression of organic growth. This style arose in the twelfth century, reaching its culmination in the thirteenth, which is known as the "golden period of Gothic architecture." The earliest fully developed example of this style is the cathedral of St. Denis, consecrated in 1144. In northern France it is seen in highest perfection in the cathedrals of Notre Dame, Paris (1163-1312), Chartres (1195-1260), Rheims (begun 1212), and Amiens (1220-1288). In England examples are seen at Canterbury (1174), Westminster Abbey, London (1245-69), Salisbury (1220-58), and Exeter (1327-69).

Renaissance. The Gothic style had never taken such deep root in Italy as in the other countries of Europe. The revival of classical studies resulted in a return to classical forms of architecture. It began with eclecticism, the adoption of the round arch, the cupola, the column in its classical proportions and signification. It ended, however, in servile copying of ancient temples. The chief monument of this style is St. Peter's at Rome.

Respecting modern architecture it can be said that it is marked by no style such as is followed by all builders of the period. Sometimes there is a mixing together of several styles, sometimes a renunciation of style altogether.   M.F.U.

BIBLIOGRAPHY: A. Badawy, *A History of Egyptian Architecture* (1954); H. Frankfort, *The Art and Architecture of the Ancient World* (1954); W. F. Albright, *Archaeology of Palestine* (1956); id., *From Stone Age to Christianity* (1957); K. M. Kenyon, *Archaeology in the Holy Land* (1960); R. deVaux, *Ancient Israel: Its Life and Institutions* (1961); A. Badawy, *Ancient Egyptian Architectural Design* (1965).

ARC'TURUS. *See* Bear.

ARD (ard). *See* Ardite.

ARD'ITE (ard'īt). A descendant of Ard, or Addar, the grandson of Benjamin (Num. 26:40).

AR'DON (ar'don). The last named of the three sons of Caleb, but whether by Azubah or Jerioth is uncertain (1 Chron. 2:18).

ARE'LI (a-rē'li). The last named of the seven sons of Gad, and founder of the family of Arelites (Gen. 46:16; Num. 26:17).

ARE'LITES (a-rē'līts; Heb. same as Areli, Num. 26:17). The descendants of *Areli* (which see), the last of the seven sons of Gad (Gen. 46:16).

AREOP'AGITE (ar-e-op'a-gīt; Acts 17:34). A member of the court of *Areopagus* (which see).

AREOP'AGUS (ar-e-op'a-gus). The Hill of Ares, the Greek god of war, equivalent to Roman Mars. Mars' Hill is thus the Lat. form of Areopagus. It is the name of a bare rocky place, some 377 feet high, immediately NW of the acropolis of Athens and separated from it by a narrow declivity. Steps cut in the rock lead to the summit, where benches, rough and rock hewn, can still be seen. In ancient times the Areopagus court assembled at this spot. The word *Areopagus* in Acts 17:19, 22 may refer either to the hill or to the court that met there. In either case, Paul's speech was in all likelihood on this hill as the customary meeting place of the court. This court was composed of city fathers and in early times exercised supreme authority in political as well as religious matters. Although largely a criminal court in the age of Pericles, in Roman times it had reverted once more to interest in educational and religious matters. It is quite understandable, therefore, that this court took hold of Paul and brought him to its judges in session, saying, "May we know what this new teaching is which you are proclaiming?" (Acts 17:19). The Areopagus court, it is true, met at intervals in the Stoa Basileios, or Royal Stoa. If this happened to be the case when Paul was in Athens, then the famous apostle gave his address (Acts 17:22-31) in the stoa. This stoa was excavated at the N end of the agora in the 1960s.

The city of Athens with the Areopagus in the foreground

AR'ETAS (ar'ĭ-tas). A name common to many of the kings of Arabia Petrea; the fourth king of that name was the father-in-law of *Herod Antipas* (which see). Herod afterward married the wife of his brother Philip, and in consequence of this the daughter of Aretas returned to her father. Enraged at the conduct of Herod, Aretas instituted hostilities against him and destroyed his army. When complaint was made to the emperor Tiberius, he sent Vitellius to punish Aretas; but while on the march he received news of the death of Tiberius, and the Roman army was withdrawn. It is probable that Caligula gave Damascus to Aretas as a free gift (A.D. 38), and he is mentioned as the king of that city who tried to arrest the apostle Paul (2 Cor. 11:32).

AR'GOB (ar'gob).

1. Either an accomplice of Pekah in the murder of Pekahiah, or, with Arieh, a prince of Pekahiah, whose influence Pekah feared and whom he therefore slew with the king (2 Kings 15:25), 759 B.C.

2. An elevated district or tableland in Bashan, an island in form, some twenty by thirty miles in extent; elsewhere (Luke 3:1) called Trachonitis. It was allotted to the half tribe of Manasseh. The statement (Deut. 3:4) of there being sixty cities in this region is confirmed by recent discoveries. "The sixty walled cities are still traceable in a space of three hundred and eight square miles. The architecture is ponderous and massive: solid walls, four feet thick, and stones on one another without cement; the roofs, enormous slabs of basaltic rock like iron; the doors and gates are of stone eighteen inches thick, secured by ponderous bars. The land bears still the appearance of having been called 'the land of giants under the giant Og' " (Porter, *Giant Cities of Bashan*).

ARID'AI (a-rid'a-ī). The ninth of the ten sons of Haman, slain by the Jews in Babylonia (Esther 9:9).

ARID'ATHA (a-rid'a-tha). The sixth son of Haman, slain by the Jews (Esther 9:8).

ARI'EH (ar-ya'; "the lion"). Either one of the accomplices of Pekah in his conspiracy against Pekahiah, king of Israel, or one of the princes of Pekahiah, who was put to death with him (2 Kings 15:25), 737 B.C.

AR'IEL (ar'i-el; "lion of God"). One of the "leading men" sent by Ezra to Iddo at Casiphia to bring ministers for the house of God to go with the people to Jerusalem (Ezra 8:16-17), about 457 B.C.

In commenting upon Isa. 29:1-11, Delitzsch understands Ariel to mean the "hearth of God," as a figurative name given to Jerusalem. He argues this from the fact of Ezekiel's giving (43:15-16, marg.) this name to the altar of burnt offering in the new Temple, and that Isaiah could not say anything more characteristic of Jerusalem than that Jehovah had a fire and a hearth there (31:9, "furnace"). "By the fact that David fixed his headquarters in Jerusalem, and then brought the sacred ark thither, Jerusalem became a hearth of God."

ARIMATHEA (a-ri-ma-thî-a). The birthplace and

sepulcher of Joseph in Judea. Here the body of Jesus was buried (Matt. 27:57; Mark 15:43; Luke 23:51; John 19:38). G. Dalman, *Sacred Sites and Ways* (1935) identifies it with the present Rentis (Jerome, Remphtis), once most probably Ramathaim, which was the home of Samuel, situated NW of Jerusalem in the hill country of Ephraim.

AR'IOCH (ar'i-ok). Perhaps Sumerian *êri-aku,* "servant of the moon god."

1. The king of Ellasar (Larsa, Senkereh, a city-state in S Babylonia), who was in alliance with Chedorlaomer in his invasion of the Jordan Valley (Gen. 14:1, 9). Some connect this name with Warad-Sin (c. 1836-1824 B.C.) or Rim-Sin (c. 1824-1763 B.C.), sons of Kudur-Mabug of Larsa. The chronology of this era, however, has not been definitely established. The events of Gen. 14 date c. 2080 B.C. in the biblical chronological notices of Abraham's life.

2. Captain of the royal guard at Babylon under Nebuchadnezzar II (c. 605-562 B.C.). The name is perhaps the title of the official who, with others in authority, had power to execute sentences of death (Dan. 2:14-15, 24).

ARIS'AI (a-ris'ī). The eighth of the ten sons of Haman, slain by the Jews in Babylonia (Esther 9:9), about 480 B.C.

ARISTAR'CHUS (a-ris-tar'kus; "the best ruler"). A native of Thessalonica and a faithful adherent of the apostle Paul in his labors. He became the companion of Paul on his third missionary tour, accompanying him to Ephesus, where he was seized and nearly killed in the tumult raised by the silversmiths under Demetrius (Acts 19:29), A.D. 59. He left that city accompanying Paul to Greece, then to Asia (20:4), and subsequently to Rome (27:2), to which he was sent as a prisoner, or he became one while there (Philem. 24), for Paul calls him his "fellow prisoner" (Col. 4:10). Tradition makes him to have suffered martyrdom in the time of Nero.

ARISTOBU'LUS (a-ris-to-bū'lus; "best counselor"). A person to whose household at Rome Paul sends salutation (Rom. 16:10), A.D. 60. Tradition represents him as a brother of Barnabas, ordained a bishop by Barnabas or Paul, and as laboring and dying in Britain. Ramsay (*St. Paul the Traveller,* p. 353) identifies Aristobulus as a son of Herod the Great.

ARK. The name given to three vessels mentioned in the Bible.

Noah's Ark (Heb. *tēbâ,* a "chest"). The vessel in which Noah and his family were saved during the Deluge. It was made of gopher (i.e., cypress) wood, which on account of its lightness and durability was employed by the Phoenicians for shipbuilding. A covering of pitch (bitumen) was laid on the inside and outside to make it watertight and, perhaps, as a protection against marine animals. The ark consisted of a number of "nests," or small compartments, arranged in three tiers, one above another—"with lower, second, and third decks" (Gen. 6:14-16).

The ark was three hundred cubits long, fifty broad, and thirty high; and appears to have been built in the form of a chest, with flat bottom and flat (or slightly sloping) roof, being intended not for sailing but merely to float upon the water. Light and air were furnished through a window, the construction of which we do not have sufficient data to form an intelligent idea. The phrase "finish it a cubit from the top" seems to imply either that it was a cubit wide and ran the whole length of the ark, or that it was placed within a cubit of the roof. The most probable conclusion is that the window was on the side. Some place the window on the roof, covering it with transparent (or translucent) material. The ark had a door in the side.

In addition to Noah and his family, eight persons in all (Gen. 7:7; 2 Pet. 2:5), one pair of all "unclean" animals, seven pairs of all that were "clean," and seven pairs of birds, with a contingent of "everything that creeps on the ground," were to be sheltered in the ark. As to the possibility of housing the animals, we must consider the extent of the Flood, etc. *See* Flood.

The Ark of Bulrushes (Heb. same as above). In Ex. 2:3 (KJV) it is recorded that when the mother of Moses could no longer hide him, she placed him among the reeds of the Nile in an ark (boat or "basket," NASB) of bulrushes, daubed with slime and pitch. This ark was made from the papyrus reed, which grows in the marshy places of Egypt. Pliny says that "from the plant itself they *weave* boats; and boats of this material were noted for their swiftness." They are alluded to in Isa. 18:2.

Sargon of Akkad, founder of a Semitic Empire in Babylonia c. 2400-2200 B.C., was similarly set afloat and rescued from death.

Ark of the Covenant (Heb. *'arôn,* the common name for a "chest" or "coffer").

Names. It was called the "ark of the covenant" (Num. 10:33; Deut. 31:26; Heb. 9:4; etc.), because in it were deposited the two tablets of stone upon which were written the Ten Commandments, the terms of God's covenant with Israel; "the ark of the testimony" (Ex. 25:16, 22), the commandments being God's testimony respecting His own holiness, and the people's sin; "the ark of God" (1 Sam. 3:3; 4:11), as the throne of the divine presence. For full description, *see* Tabernacle.

History. The history of the Ark is in accordance with its intensely moral character. As the symbol of the Lord's presence, it was borne by the priests in advance of the host (Num. 10:33; Deut. 1:33; see also Ps. 132:8). At its presence the waters of the Jordan separated; only when it was carried to the farther shore did the waters resume their

Replica of the Ark of the Covenant

usual course (Josh. 3:11-17; 4:7, 11, 18). The Ark was carried about Jericho at the time of its downfall (6:4-12). Very naturally, the neighboring nations, ignorant of spiritual worship, looked upon the Ark as the god of Israel (1 Sam. 4:6-7), a delusion that may have been strengthened by the figures of the cherubim upon it.

The Ark remained at Shiloh until the time of Eli, when it was carried along with the army, in the hope that it would secure victory for the Israelites against the Philistines. The latter were not only victorious but also captured the Ark (1 Sam. 4:3-11); but they were glad to return it after seven months (5:7). It was taken to Kiriath-jearim (7:2), where it remained until the time of David. Its removal to Jerusalem was delayed three months by the death of Uzzah while carelessly handling it. Meanwhile it rested in the house of Obed-edom, from which it was taken, with greatest rejoicing, to Mt. Zion (2 Sam. 6:1-19).

When the Temple was completed, the Ark was deposited in the sanctuary (1 Kings 8:6-9). In 2 Chron. 35:3 the Levites were directed to restore it to the Holy Place. It may have been moved to make room for the "carved image" that Manasseh placed "in the house of God" (33:7), or possibly on account of the purification and repairs of the Temple by Josiah. When the Temple was destroyed by the Babylonians the Ark was probably removed or destroyed (2 Esd. 10:21-22). Sacred chests were in use among other peoples of antiquity, and served as receptacles for the idol, or the symbol of the idol, and for sacred relics.

BIBLIOGRAPHY: *Noah's Ark:* A Heidel, *Gilgamesh Epic and Other Old Testament Parallels* (1946); J. C. Whitcomb, Jr., and H. M. Morris, *The Genesis Flood* (1962); J. W. Montgomery, *The Quest for Noah's Ark* (1972); J. Dillow, *The Waters Above* (1981).

Ark of Bulrushes: M. Jastrow, Jr., *Jewish Encyclopedia* (1946), 2: 578-79.
Ark of the Covenant: J. Morgenstern, *Hebrew Union College Annual* 17 (1942-43): 153-266; id., *The Ark, the Ephod, and the Tent of Meeting* (1945); F. M. Cross, *Biblical Archaeologist* 10 (1947): 45-68; R. E. Hough, *The Ministry of the Glory Cloud* (1955); E. Nielsen, *Supplements to Vetus Testamentum* 7 (1960): 61-74; J. B. Payne, *Theology of the Older Testament* (1962); M. H. Woudstra, *The Ark of the Covenant from Conquest to Kingship* (1965).

ARK'ITE (ark'īt). Of Gen. 10:17; 1 Chron. 1:15, represents the inhabitants of present-day Tell Arka, some eighty miles N of Sidon at the foot of Lebanon. Arkantu, mentioned by the great Egyptian conqueror Thutmose III (fifteenth century B.C.) is evidently the same place. It was called Irkata in the Amarna Letters and was taken by Tiglath-pileser III of Assyria in 738 B.C.

ARM. The common instrument of strength and agency, the *arm* is often used in Scripture as the emblem of power. The "arm" of God is only another expression for His might (Ps. 89:13; Isa. 53:1). Hence "an outstretched arm," and "the Lord has bared His holy arm," signifies His power and promptness to protect or punish (Ex. 6:6; Deut. 4:34; Isa. 52:10), a figure taken from the attitude of ancient warriors.

ARMAGED'DON (ar-ma-ged'on; Gk. *Armageddon,* from Heb. *har Megiddô,* "hill or city of Megiddo," Rev. 16:16, see marg.). Megiddo occupied a marked position on the southern rim of the plain of *Esdraelon* (which see), the great battlefield of Palestine. It was famous for two great victories: of Barak over the Canaanites (Judg. 4:15) and of Gideon over the Midianites (chap. 7); and for two great disasters: the deaths of Saul (1 Sam. 31:8) and Josiah (2 Kings 23:29-30; 2 Chron. 35:22). Armageddon became a poetical expression for terrible and final conflict.

To John the Revelator the ancient plain of Megiddo, the battleground of the centuries, furnished a type of the great battle in which the Lord, at His advent of glory, will deliver the Jewish remnant besieged by the Gentile world powers under the Beast (Rev. 13:1-10) and the false prophet (13:11-18). Apparently the besieging hosts, whose advance upon Jerusalem is typically set forth in Isa. 10:28-32 and who are demon-energized (Rev. 16:13-16; Zech. 12:1-9), have retreated to Megiddo after the events of Zech. 14:2. There their decimation commences and is completed in Moab and Edom (Isa. 63:1-3). This last grand battle of "the times of the Gentiles" and of this present age finds fulfillment in the striking-stone prophecy of Dan. 2:35 and ushers in "the day of the Lord," when God actively and visibly manifests His glorious power to the discomfiture and utter destruction of His enemies.

BIBLIOGRAPHY: J. D. Pentecost, *Things to Come* (1964), pp. 340-63; J. F. Walvoord and J. E. Walvoord, *Armageddon: Oil and the Middle East* (1974).

ARME'NIA (ar-mē'ni-a). Heb. *'ărārāt,* for Akkad. *Urartu,* which occurs frequently in the Assyrian monuments. Sennacherib's sons escaped there after murdering their father (2 Kings 19:37). On one of the mountains of this region the ark of Noah rested (Gen. 8:4). The country extends from the Black Sea to the Caspian Sea and from the Caucasus Mountains to the Taurus Mountains. It was N of the Assyrian Empire.

ARMLET. This word is not used in the KJV or NASB, being rendered in 2 Sam. 1:10 by the expression, "the bracelet which was on his arm." It does appear in the NIV in Num. 31:50. *See* Bracelet.

ARMO'NI (ar-mō'ni). The first named of the two sons of Saul by Rizpah, who were given up by David to be hanged by the Gibeonites. He was slain with six of his brothers in the beginning of the barley harvest (2 Sam. 21:8-14).

ARMOR, ARMS. The weapons of the nations mentioned in the Bible were essentially the same, with modifications according to age and country. Offensive weapons (arms) included the battle-axe, sword, spear, bow and arrow, sling, and battering ram. Defensive weapons (armor) included the shield, helmet, breastplate, greaves, and girdle.

Offensive Weapons.

Battle-axe and Mace. The most primitive of weapons were the club and the throwing bat. The *club* at first consisted of a heavy piece of wood, of various shapes, used in hand-to-hand fighting. The "mace" (Heb. *barzel*) was of wood bound with bronze, about two and one-half feet long, with an angular piece of metal projecting from the handle, perhaps intended as a guard. At the striking end it was sometimes furnished with a ball. Maces were borne by the heavy infantry, and each charioteer was furnished with one. The Egyptian *battle-axe* was about two or two and one-half feet long, with a single blade secured by bronze pins and the handle bound in that part to prevent splitting. The blade was shaped like the segment of a circle and made of bronze or iron. The *poleaxe* was about three feet in length, with a large metal ball, to which the blade was fixed. Allusions to these weapons are supposed to occur in Ps. 2:9; 35:3; Prov. 25:18. The *throwstick* is the same weapon seen figured on Egyptian and Assyrian monuments. "Axes" (Ezek. 26:9), literally *irons,* is used figuratively for weapons or instruments of war.

Sword (Heb. *ḥereb*). The Egyptian sword was short and straight, from two and one-half to three feet in length, usually double-edged and tapering to a point, and was used to cut and thrust. The king's sword was worn in his girdle and was frequently surmounted by one or two heads of a hawk, the symbol of the sun. The sword thus worn was really a *dagger,* a common

Egyptian weapon. It was from seven to ten inches in length, tapering gradually to a point, the blade, made of bronze, being thicker in the middle than at the edges. Assyrian swords were often richly decorated, the hilt embossed with lions' heads so arranged as to form both handle and crossbar. The sword of the Greeks and Romans generally had a straight two-edged blade, rather broad, and of nearly equal width from hilt to point. It was worn on the left side.

Stone carving of Roman arms and armor, Ephesus.

The sword of the Hebrew resembled that of other oriental nations and appears to have been short. That of Ehud was only a cubit (from eighteen to twenty-two inches) long. It was carried in a sheath held by the girdle (1 Sam. 17:39; 2 Sam. 20:8); hence the expression "to gird one's self" with a sword means to commence war; and "to loose the sword," to finish it (1 Kings 20:11).

Figurative. The sword itself is the symbol of war and slaughter (Lev. 26:25; Isa. 34:5, etc.), of divine judgment (Deut. 32:41; Ps. 17:13; Jer. 12:12; Rev. 1:16), and of power and authority (Rom. 13:4). The Word of God is called "the sword of the Spirit" (Eph. 6:17). The sword is used in Scripture as illustrative of the Word of God (Eph. 6:17; Heb. 4:12); Christ (Isa. 49:2; Rev. 1:16); the justice of God (Deut. 32:41; Zech. 13:7); the protection of God (Deut. 33:29); severe calamities (Ezek. 5:2, 17; 14:17; 21:9); deep mental affliction (Luke 2:35); the wicked (Ps. 17:13); their tongue (57:4; 64:3; Prov. 12:18); their persecuting spirit (Ps. 37:14); their end (Prov. 5:4); false witnesses (25:18); judicial authority (Rom. 13:4). *Drawing of sword* is figurative of war and destruction (Lev. 26:33; Ezek. 21:3-5); *sheathing it,* of peace and friendship (Jer. 47:6); *living by it,* of plunder (Gen. 27:40); *not departing,* of perpetual calamity (2 Sam. 12:10).

The Spear, Javelin, Dart. The *spear* is a weapon common to all nations of antiquity. That of the Egyptians was of wood, from five to six feet long, with the head of bronze or iron, usually with a double edge like that of the Greeks. The *javelin* was similar to the spear, but lighter and shorter, the upper extremity of the shaft terminating with a bronze knob surmounted by a ball. It was sometimes used as a spear for thrusting, and sometimes it was darted, the knob of the extremity keeping it from escaping the warrior's hand. The spear of the Assyrian infantry was short, scarcely exceeding the height of a man; that of the cavalry was longer. Several kinds of spears are mentioned in Scripture, but how the several terms used are to be understood is somewhat uncertain. (1) The *ḥănît,* a "spear" of the largest kind, was the weapon of Goliath (1 Sam. 17:7, 45; 2 Sam. 21:19; 1 Chron. 20:5) and also of other giants (2 Sam. 23:21; 1 Chron. 11:23) and mighty warriors (2 Sam. 2:23; 23:18; 1 Chron. 11:11, 20). It was the habitual companion of King Saul, and it was this heavy weapon, not the lighter "javelin," that he cast at David (1 Sam. 18:10-11; 19:9-10) and at Jonathan (20:33). (2) Apparently lighter than the preceding was the *kîdôn* ("javelin"). When not in action, the *javelin* was carried on the back of the warrior (1 Sam. 17:6, KJV, "target"). (3) Another kind of spear was *rōmaḥ.* In the historical books it occurs in Num. 25:7 and 1 Kings 18:28 and frequently in the later books, as in 1 Chron. 12:8 ("buckler," KJV); 2 Chron. 11:12. (4) The *shelah* was probably a lighter missile, or "dart" (see KJV, 2 Chron. 23:10; 32:5, "darts"; Neh. 4:17, 23, see marg.; Job 33:18; 36:12; Joel 2:8). (5) *shēbeṭ,* a "rod," or "staff," is used only once to denote a weapon (2 Sam. 18:14).

Figurative. The spear is used figuratively of the bitterness of the wicked (Ps. 57:4); the instruments and effects of God's wrath (Hab. 3:11).

Bow and Arrow. The bow was the principal weapon of offense among the Egyptians, Assyrians, and Hebrews. That of the Egyptians was a round piece of wood, from five to five and one-half feet long, either straight or bending in the middle when unstrung. The string was made of hide, catgut, or string. The Assyrian archer was equipped in all respects as the Egyptian, the bow being either long and slightly curved or short and almost angular. Among the Hebrews the bow (Heb. *qeshet*) and arrow (*hēṣ*) are met with early in their history, both for the chase (Gen. 21:20; 27:3) and war (48:22). In later times archers accompanied the armies of the Philistines (1 Sam. 31:3; 1 Chron. 10:3) and of the Syrians (1 Kings 22:34). Among the Hebrews captains high in rank (2 Kings 9:24), and even kings' sons (1 Sam. 18:4), carried the bow and were expert in its use (2 Sam. 1:22). The tribe of Benjamin seems to have been especially addicted to archery (1 Chron. 8:40; 12:2; 2 Chron. 14:8; 17:17); but there were also bowmen among Reuben, Gad, Manasseh (1 Chron. 5:18), and Ephraim (Ps. 78:9). Of the form of the bow we can gather almost nothing. It seems to have been bent by the aid of the foot (1 Chron. 5:18; 8:40; 2 Chron.

14:8; Ps. 7:12; Isa. 5:28; etc.). Bows of bronze are mentioned as if specially strong (2 Sam. 22:35; Job 20:24). It is possible that in 1 Chron. 12:2 a kind of bow for shooting bullets or stones is alluded to (Wisd. of Sol. 5:22, "stone-bow"). The arrows were carried in quivers (Heb. *ṭelî*) hung on the shoulder or at the left side. They were probably of reed and mostly tipped with flint points; others were of wood tipped with metal, about thirty inches long and winged with three rows of feathers. They were sometimes poisoned (Job 6:4) or tipped with combustible materials ("flaming missiles," *those set on fire,* Eph. 6:16).

Figurative. This word is frequently used as the symbol of *calamity* or *disease* sent by God (Job 6:4; 34:6, marg.; Ps. 38:2), the metaphor deriving propriety and force from the popular belief that all diseases were immediate and special inflictions from heaven. Lightning is described as the arrows of God (18:14; 144:6; Hab. 3:11). "The arrow that flies by day" (Ps. 91:5) denotes some sudden danger. The *arrow* is also figurative of anything injurious, as a deceitful tongue (Jer. 9:8), a bitter word (Ps. 64:3), a false witness (Prov. 25:18). A good use of "arrow" is in Ps. 127:4-5, where children are compared to "arrows in the hand of a warrior"; i.e., instruments of power and action. The word is also used to denote the efficiency of God's Word (45:5). The "bow of battle" is figurative for weapons of war and military power (Zech. 9:10; 10:4).

The Sling (Heb. *qela').* This may be justly reckoned as among the most ancient instruments of warfare (Job 41:28). This weapon was common among the Egyptians, Assyrians, and Hebrews. Later the Greek and Roman armies contained large numbers of slingers. The weapon was simple, being made of a couple of strings of sinew, leather, or rope, with a leather receptacle in the middle to receive the stone. After being swung once or twice around the head it was discharged by letting go of one of the strings. Besides stones, plummets of lead shaped like an acorn were used and could be thrown to the distance of six hundred feet. The stones were selected for their smoothness (1 Sam. 17:40) and were considered as munitions of war. In action they were either carried in a bag (17:40) or lay in a heap at the feet of the slinger. Among the Hebrews the Benjamites were especially expert slingers (Judg. 20:16; cf. 1 Chron. 12:2).

Figurative. The rejection of one by Jehovah is represented by the expression "the lives of your enemies He will sling out as from the hollow of a sling" (1 Sam. 25:29); in Zechariah (9:15) sling stones represent the enemies of God.

Engine, Battering Ram. Two machines are in view. (1) Heb. *hishshābôn,* "contrivance." The engines that went by this name (2 Chron. 26:15) were the *balista,* used for throwing stones, and the *catapulta,* for arrows, an enormous stationary bow. Both of these engines were of various throwing power, stones being thrown weighing from fifty to three hundred pounds. Darts varied from small beams to large arrows, and their range exceeded one-quarter mile. All these engines were constructed on the principle of the string, the bow, or spring. (2) Heb. $m^e\dot{h}\hat{\imath}$, "stroke," Ezek. 26:9, the battering ram, so rendered, 4:2; 21:22; Heb. *kar*, "butting." This instrument was well known both to the Egyptians and the Assyrians. The ram was a simple machine consisting of a metal head affixed to a beam, which might be long enough to need one or two hundred men to lift and impel it. When it was still heavier it was hung in a movable tower and became a wonderful engine of war. Its object was to make a breach in the wall of a beleaguered town. *See also* Chariot.

Defensive Weapons.

The Shield. The ancient soldier's chief defense, his shield, was various in form and material. The shield of the Egyptian was about one-half his height and generally about twice as high as broad. It was probably formed of a wooden frame covered with rawhide, having the hair outward, with one or more rims of metal and metal studs. Its form resembled a funeral tablet, circular at the top and square at the base. A rare form of Egyptian shield was of extraordinary size and pointed at the top. The shields of the Assyrians in the more ancient bas-reliefs are both circular and oblong, sometimes of gold and silver, but more frequently of wickerwork covered with hides. The shield in a siege covered the soldier's whole person and at the top had a curved point or a square projection like a roof at right angles with the body of the shield. This was to defend the combatants against missiles thrown from the walls.

Shield is the rendering of the following words, of which the first two are the most frequent and important: (1) Heb. *ṣinnâ*, "protection." This shield was large enough to cover the whole body (Pss. 5:12; 91:4). When not engaged in conflict it was carried by the shield bearer (1 Sam. 17:7, 41). The word is used with "spear" as a formula for weapons generally (1 Chron. 12:24; 2 Chron. 11:12). (2) Heb. *māgēn*. This was smaller, a buckler or target, probably for hand-to-hand fighting. The difference in size between this and the above-mentioned shield is evident from 1 Kings 10:16-17; 2 Chron. 9:15-16, where twice as much gold is named as being used for the latter as for the former. This shield is usually coupled with light weapons, as the bow (14:8) and darts (32:5, KJV). (3) Heb. *shelet*. The form of this shield is not well known. Although by some it is translated "quiver," and by others "weapons" generally, it is evident that *shield* is proper by comparing 2 Kings 11:10 with 2 Chron. 23:9; 2 Sam. 8:7; 1 Chron. 18:7-8. The *sōḥērâ*, "buckler," is found only in Ps. 91:4, KJV, and is used poetically. (4) Finally, we have the Gk. *thureos* (Eph. 6:16), a large oblong or square shield. The ordinary

shield among the Hebrews consisted of a wooden frame covered with leather and could be easily burned (Ezek. 39:9). Some shields were covered with brass or copper and when shone upon by the sun caused the redness mentioned in Nah. 2:3. Shields were rubbed with oil to render the leather smooth and slippery and to prevent its being injured by the wet (2 Sam. 1:21-22; Isa. 21:5), as well as to keep the metal from rusting. Except in actual conflict, the shield was kept covered (22:6). The golden shields mentioned in connection with the equipment of armies (1 Macc. 6:39) were most probably only gilt; on the contrary, those of the generals of Hadadezer (2 Sam. 8:7) and those Solomon made (1 Kings 10:16-17; 14:26) are to be regarded as ornamental pieces of massive gold, such as were later sent to Rome as gifts (1 Macc. 14:24; 15:18). Bronze shields also occur only in connection with leaders and royal guards (1 Sam. 17:6; 1 Kings 14:27).

A Roman shield

Figurative. The shield is illustrative of God's protection (Gen. 15:1; Deut. 33:29; 2 Sam. 22:3; Pss. 3:3; 5:12; 28:7; 33:20; 59:11; 84:9, 11; 115:9-11; 119:114; 144:2); truth of God (91:4); salvation of God (2 Sam. 22:36; Ps. 18:35); of faith (Eph. 6:16).

The Helmet. The helmet of the Egyptians was usually of quilted linen cloth that served as an effectual protection to the head, without the inconvenience of metal in a hot climate. The Assyrian helmet assumed different shapes in different ages, but its earliest form was a cap of iron terminating in a point and sometimes furnished with flaps, covered with metal scales, protecting the ears and neck and falling over the shoulders.

We find several references to the "helmet" (Heb. *kôba'*) as being in use among the Hebrews. They seem to have been commonly of bronze (1 Sam. 17:38).

Figurative. In Isa. 59:17 Jehovah is represented as arming Himself for the defense of man, and among other articles He puts on is "a helmet of salvation," seeming to teach that salvation is the crowning act of God. The helmet as a part of the Christian's armor represents salvation (Eph. 6:17), "the hope" of salvation (1 Thess. 5:8).

Roman soldiers

The Breastplate, or Cuirass. The earliest material used to protect the body was probably the skins of beasts, which were soon abandoned for coats of mail. The cuirass of the Egyptians consisted of about eleven horizontal rows of metal plates, well secured by brass pins, with narrower rows forming a protection for the throat and neck. Each plate, or scale, was about an inch in width. In length the cuirass may have been a little less than two and one-half feet, covering the thigh nearly to the knee; in order to prevent its pressing too heavily on the shoulder it was bound with a girdle about the waist. Usually, however, that part of the body below the girdle was protected by a kind of kilt, detached from the girdle. Such was the covering of the heavy-armed troops. With the light-armed infantry, and, indeed, among the Asiatic nations in general, the quilted linen cuirass was in much demand.

The Assyrians used coats of scale armor and embroidered tunics, both of felt and leather. Among the Hebrews we have two types of protective garment for the torso. (1) The *breastplate* (Heb. *shiryôn,* "glittering") is enumerated in the description of the arms of Goliath, "scale armor,"

literally, a "*breastplate* of scales" (1 Sam. 17:5), and further (v. 38), where *shiryôn* alone is rendered "armor." It may be noticed that this passage contains the most complete inventory of the dress of a warrior to be found in the whole of the sacred history. *Shiryôn* also occurs in 1 Kings 22:34 and 2 Chron. 18:33. The last passage is obscure; the meaning is probably "between the joints of the breastplate." (2) The *tahrā'* is mentioned but twice—in reference to the gown of the high priest (Ex. 28:32; 39:23). Like the English "habergeon," it was probably a quilted shirt or doublet put on over the head.

Figurative. Being an efficient means of protection for the body, it is used metaphorically for *defense:* "the breastplate of righteousness" (Eph. 6:14) and "the breastplate of faith and love" (1 Thess. 5:8).

Greaves (Heb. *miṣḥâ,* lit., "a facing"). Coverings for the leg, made of brass and widely known among the ancients, are mentioned only in the case of Goliath (1 Sam. 17:6), and the warrior's "boot" (Heb. *se'ôn*), a sort of half boot made of leather, studded with strong nails, only in Isa. 9:5 (lit., "every shoe"). We infer, therefore, that they did not belong to the common armor of the Hebrews.

Girdle (Heb. *'ēzôr*). The sword was suspended from the girdle, and the girdle is frequently mentioned among the articles of military dress (Job 12:18; Eph. 6:14). It was of leather, studded with metal plates. When the armor was light the girdle was broad and girt about the hips; otherwise it supported the sword scarfwise from the shoulder. *See* Girdle.

ARMOR BEARER (Heb. *nāśa' kelî,* "one carrying weapons"). A person selected by prominent officers to bear their armor, to stand by them in danger, and to carry out their orders, somewhat as adjutants in modern service (Judg. 9:54; 1 Sam. 14:6; 16:21; 31:4).

ARMORER. *See* Handicrafts.

ARMORY. The place in which armor was deposited. In Neh. 3:19 mention is made of "the armory at the Angle" in Jerusalem; probably the arsenal, which Hezekiah showed with so much pride to the Babylonian ambassadors (Isa. 39:2, Heb. *nesheq*). A poetical allusion is made to armory in Song of Sol. 4:4, see marg. (Heb. *talpîyyâ*). In Jer. 50:25 God is said to have "opened His armory" (Heb. *'ôṣār*).

BIBLIOGRAPHY: R. deVaux, *Ancient Israel: Its Life and Institutions* (1961), pp. 213-46; Y. Yadin, *The Art of Warfare in Bible Lands,* 2 vols. (1963).

ARMY. The English term is represented in Scriptures by several Heb. and Gk. names.

Jewish. Although Israel was not to be a conquering people, yet it had to defend itself against hostile attacks, at first in the wilderness and afterward in the Promised Land. Hence Israel marched out of Egypt (Ex. 12:41; 13:18), as the host of Jehovah, armed. As such, the people were arranged according to their tribes and divisions of tribes (Num. 1-4), and every man above twenty years of age was enrolled for military service (1:2-19; 26:2) with the exception of the Levites (2:33). Up to what age military duty lasted is not given. Josephus states (*Ant.* 3.12.4) that it was to the fiftieth year.

In time of war the number of fighting men needed was collected from the different tribes under the direction of inspectors (Heb. *shōterîm,* Deut. 20:5; 2 Kings 25:19), by whom also the commanders were appointed (Deut. 20:9). The principle on which these levies were made is not known to us. The law provided that anyone having built a new house not yet consecrated, having planted a vineyard and not having as yet enjoyed its fruit, or having betrothed but not yet married a wife should not go to battle (20:5-7). The faint-hearted were also dismissed, in order that they not discourage their brethren (20:8). The army thus constituted was divided into companies of thousands, hundreds, and fifties under their respective officers (Num. 31:14), and still further into families (2:34; 2 Chron. 25:5; 26:12); each father's house probably formed a detachment, led by the most valiant among them. The provisioning of the army was laid on each tribe (Judg. 20:10; 1 Sam. 17:17-18). From the time of Moses to that of David the army of Israel consisted of foot soldiers (15:4), and from the time Israel entered into Canaan until the establishment of the kingdom little progress was made in military affairs.

Soon after the establishment of the kingdom a standing army was set up, the nucleus of which was the band of three thousand men selected by Saul (1 Sam. 13:2; 24:2) and to which he constantly added men (14:52). Before David became king he had a band of six hundred men, gathered in his wars with Saul (23:13, 25:13), from whom his most noted captains were chosen (2 Sam. 23:8-11, 18-39). To these he added the Cherethites and Pelethites (8:18; 15:18; 20:7). Moreover, he organized a national militia in twelve divisions, each consisting of 24,000, and responsible for a month's service every year (1 Chron. 27:1). At the head of the army when in active service was a commander in chief ("captain of his army," 1 Sam. 14:50).

The army hitherto had consisted entirely of infantry (1 Sam. 4:10; 15:4), the use of horses having been prohibited (Deut. 17:16). David had reserved a hundred chariots from the spoil of the Syrians (2 Sam. 8:4), which probably served as the foundation of the force that Solomon enlarged through his alliance with Egypt (1 Kings 10:26, 28-29).

The army, with the exception of a regularly maintained bodyguard (1 Kings 14:28; 2 Kings 11:4, 11), was, strictly speaking, only a national militia, not in constant service but in time of peace at home engaged in agriculture, and without pay. Even in war their pay probably consisted only of supplies and a fixed portion of the spoil. These arrangements were kept up by his successors, and by some of them the military power was greatly strengthened by foot and horse (2 Chron. 14:8; 17:14; 25:5; etc.). Sometimes foreign troops were hired as auxiliaries (25:6).

With regard to the arrangement and maneuvering of the army in the field, little is known. A division into three bodies is frequently mentioned (Judg. 7:16; 9:43; 1 Sam. 11:11). Jehoshaphat divided his army into five bodies but retained the threefold principle of division, the heavy-armed troops of Judah being considered the proper army and the two divisions of light-armed men of the tribe of Benjamin an appendage (2 Chron. 17:14-18). It is difficult to ascertain the numerical strength of the Jewish army, the numbers given in the text being manifestly corrupted. The discipline and arrangement of the army was gradually assimilated to that of the Romans, and the titles of officers borrowed from it.

Roman. The Roman army was divided into legions, the number of soldiers in a legion varying at different times; but its full strength was to be 6,000. These legions were commanded by six tribuni ("commander," Acts 21:31), who commanded by turns. The tenth part of a legion, containing six hundred men, was called a *cohors,* ("cohort," Acts 10:1); the cohort was divided into three maniples, and the maniple into two *centuries,* originally containing one hundred men but later varying according to the strength of the legion. These centuries were under the command of centurions (10:1, 22; Matt. 8:5; 27:54). There were in addition to the legionary cohorts independent cohorts of volunteers. One of these was called the Italian (Acts 10:1), consisting of volunteers from Italy. There is a cohort named Augustus (Acts 27:1), which Meyer (*Com.,* ad loc.) thinks to mean "the imperial cohort, one of the five cohorts stationed at Caesarea, and regarded as bodyguard of the emperor, employed here on special service affecting the emperor."

See War.

BIBLIOGRAPHY: Y. Yadin, *The Art of Warfare in Bible Lands* (1963); G. R. Watson, *The Roman Soldier* (1969); G. Webster, *Roman Imperial Army* (1969).

AR'NAN (ar'nan; Heb. from Arab., "quick, lively"). Probably the great-grandson of Zerubbabel, in the line of David's descendants (1 Chron. 3:21); perhaps the same as Joanan (Luke 3:27), an ancestor of Jesus.

AR'NON (ar'non; "rushing torrent"). A river rising in the mountains of Gilead, E of the Jordan, and reaching the Dead Sea through a stony and precipitous chasm of red and yellow sandstone. "The name is also applied to the valley, or valleys, now known as 'Wady Mojib,' an enormous trench across the plateau of Moab. It is about seventeen hundred feet deep, and two miles broad from edge to edge of the cliffs which bound it, but the floor of the valley over which the stream winds is only forty yards wide. About thirteen miles from the Dead Sea the trench divides into two branches, one running NE, the other SSE, and each of them again dividing into two. . . . Properly all the country from Jabbok to Arnon belonged northward to Ammon, southward to Moab. But shortly before Israel's arrival, *Sihon* (which see), an Amorite king from western Palestine, had crossed the Jordan and, driving Moab southward over Arnon and Ammon eastward to the sources of the Jabbok, had founded a kingdom for himself between the two rivers" (Smith, *Hist. Geog.,* p. 558). Afterward it was taken possession of by Israel on its way to Palestine, and Arnon became the boundary between Israel and Moab (Num. 21:13, 26; Josh. 12:1; Judg. 11:22; Isa. 16:2; Jer. 48:20).

A'ROD (a'rod; "humpbacked"). The sixth son of Gad (Num. 26:17), whose descendants were called Arodites, about 1700 B.C. He is called Arodi (Gen. 46:16).

AR'ODI, A'RODITE. See Arod.

AR'OER (ar'ō-er; "nudity").
 1. A town on the northern bank of the Arnon (Deut. 2:36; 3:12; 4:48; Josh. 12:2; 13:9, 16; Judg. 11:26, 33; 1 Chron. 5:8). As the southernmost town of Israel E of the Jordan, it has been called "the Beersheba of the East." It was fortified by Mesha as mentioned on the *Moabite Stone* (which see). Now called Arair, thirteen miles E of the Dead Sea.
 2. A town built by the Gadites (Num. 32:34; Josh. 13:25; 2 Sam. 24:5), connected with the history of Jephthah.
 3. A city twelve miles SE of Beersheba, associated with David and his warriors (1 Sam. 30:26-28; 1 Chron. 11:44), now called Ararah.

AR'OERITE (ar'ō-er-īt). An inhabitant of *Aroer* (which see above; no. 3), probably in the tribe of Judah (1 Chron. 11:44).

AROMA. A term used in several ways in Scripture.
 1. Sweet smell (Heb. *nîḥôaḥ;* "restful," Lev. 26:31; "fragrant incense," Dan 2:46).
 2. In the general sense of *fragrance* (which see), as from *spices* (which see), *see* 2 Chron. 16:14; Esther 2:12; Jer. 34:5; John 12:3. In Phil. 4:18 the expression is "a fragrant aroma." The word "savor(s)" (Heb. *rêaḥ,* "odor") is used in some versions to describe the pleasing effect that sacrifices offered according to ritual requirements had upon Jehovah (Ex. 29:18; Lev. 1:9, 13, 17; etc., but contrast Jer. 48:11).
 Figurative. The rendering of the Gk. *mōrainō,*

"is more flat or tasteless." In 2 Cor. 2:14, 16 (Gk. *osmē*), "the knowledge of God" is symbolized as "an odor that God everywhere makes manifest through the apostolic working, inasmuch as He by that means brings to pass that the knowledge of Christ everywhere exhibits and communicates its nature and efficacy" (Meyer, *Com.,* ad loc.). Christ's sacrifice is described as a "fragrant aroma" to God, and one that we are to imitate (Eph. 5:2). R.K.H.

ARPACH'SHAD (ar-pax'shad). The first postdiluvian patriarch, son of Shem, and father of Shelah, born two years after the Deluge and died aged four hundred thirty-eight years (Gen. 11:10-13; 1 Chron. 1:17-18). Arpachshad has been frequently identified with the mountainous country on the Upper Zab River N and NE of Nineveh, the Arrapachitis of the Greek geographers.

AR'PAD (ar'pad). Rendered Ar'phad (ar'fad) twice in the KJV, Arpad is identified as Tell Erfad, twenty-five miles N of Aleppo. Arpad was a place of considerable importance in Assyrian times, being overrun by Adadnirari in 806 B.C., Ashurninari in 754 B.C., besieged and captured by Tiglath-pileser (742-740 B.C.), and included in an uprising that was suppressed by Sargon in 720 B.C. It is commonly associated with the city-state of Hamath in OT references, being not far distant (2 Kings 18:34; 19:13; Isa. 10:9; 36:19; 37:13). Arpad was excavated by the Czechoslovakian archaeologist Hrozny in 1924, and a British team has been working there since 1960.

ARPHAX'AD. See Arpachshad.

ARROGANT, ARROGANCE.
 1. Gk. *huperogkos,* a "swelling," "immoderate, extravagant," as in "arrogant words" (2 Pet. 2:18; Jude 16).
 2. Gk. *phusiōsis,* a "puffing up of soul," "loftiness, pride" (2 Cor. 12:20).

ARROW. See Armor: Bow and Arrow.

ARROWSNAKE. *See* Animal Kingdom: Serpent.

ARSENAL (ar'se-nal). *See* Armory.

ARTAXERXES (ar-ta-zerk'sez).
 Artaxerxes I Longimanus, who reigned over Persia forty years, 464-424 B.C. In the seventh year of his reign he commissioned Ezra to return to Jerusalem, granting large privileges to him and those accompanying him (Ezra 7:11-26), 457 B.C. About thirteen years later (445 B.C.) he granted permission to Nehemiah to assume control of the civil affairs at Jerusalem (Neh. 2:1-8).

AR'TEMAS (ar'ti-mas, contraction of Gk. *Artemidoros,* "gift of Artemis," i.e., Diana).
 1. The name of a disciple mentioned in connection with Tychicus, one of whom Paul wished to send into Crete to supply the place of Titus when he invited the latter to visit him at Nicopolis

(Titus 3:12), A.D. 65. Traditionally, he was bishop of Lystra.

2. *See* Gods, False: Artemis.

ARTEMIS. One of the Greek goddesses, a huntress. The Roman name and KJV rendering is Diana. *See* Gods, False.

ARTILLERY (Heb. *kelî,* "prepared"). Used in the KJV of 1 Sam. 20:40 to refer to Jonathan's weapons (cf. NASB).

ARTISAN (Heb. *ḥōrēsh,* or *ḥārāsh).* A fabricator of any material, such as a carpenter, smith, or engraver (Isa. 3:3). *See also* Handicrafts.

ARTS. *See* Handicrafts.

AR'UBBOTH (ar'u-both); a city or district. Mentioned (1 Kings 4:10) as the district belonging to the son of Hesed. Probably to be identified with Arrabeh near Dothan.

ARU'MAH (a-ru'ma; "height"). A place in the neighborhood of Shechem where Abimelech, the son of Gideon, dwelt (Judg. 9:41).

AR'VAD (ar'vad). A rocky island off the coast of Syria, two miles from the shore, and peopled by marines and soldiers (Ezek. 27:8, 11). It is modern Ruad, a little more than two miles from the shore to the S of Tartus. On that small island are Phoenician remains; there "the family" of the Arvadites settled.

AR'VADITE (ar'va-dīt; Gen. 10:18; 1 Chron. 1:16). An inhabitant of the island of Aradus, or *Arvad* (which see). The Arvadites were descended from the sons of Canaan (Gen. 10:18). They appear to have been in some dependence upon Tyre, as we find them furnishing a contingent of mariners to that city (Ezek. 27:8, 11). They took their full share in Phoenician maritime affairs, particularly after Tyre and Sidon fell under the dominion of the Greco-Syrian kings.

AR'ZA (ar'za; "earthiness"). A steward over the house of Elah, king of Israel, in whose house, at Tirzah, Zimri, the captain of half of his chariots, conspired against *Elah* (which see), and killed him during a drunken debauch (1 Kings 16:8-10).

A'SA (ā'sa; "healing"). Cf. Arab. *'asa,* "to heal"; Aram. *'assâ,* a "physician."

1. The son and successor of Abijah, king of Judah, who reigned forty-one years, c. 910-869 B.C. On assuming the reins of government, Asa was conspicuous for his support of the worship of God and opposition to idolatry. Even his grandmother Maacah was deposed from the rank of "queen mother" because she had set up an idol, which Asa overthrew and burned by the brook Kidron (1 Kings 15:13). Still, the old hill sanctuaries were retained as places of worship. He placed in the Temple gifts dedicated by his father and rich offerings of his own, and renewed

the altar, which had apparently been desecrated (2 Chron. 15:8).

The first ten years of his reign his kingdom enjoyed peace, which Asa utilized in fortifying his frontier cities and raising an army, which numbered at the beginning of hostilities 580,000 men (2 Chron. 14:8), though this number has been thought an exaggeration of the copyist. In the eleventh year of his reign Zerah, the Ethiopian, invaded Judah with an army of a million men. Asa besought God for help and, marching against Zerah, met and defeated him at Mareshah. He returned to Jerusalem with the spoil of the cities around Gerar and with innumerable sheep and cattle (14:9-5). The prophet Azariah met Asa on his return and encouraged him and the people to continue their trust in God.

Asa carried on his reforms; a gathering of the people was held at Jerusalem, sacrifices were offered, and a covenant was made with Jehovah. To these ceremonies there came many from the kingdom of Israel, believing that God was with Asa (2 Chron. 15). In the thirty-sixth year (according to some the twenty-sixth) of his reign hostilities were begun by Baasha, king of Israel, who fortified Ramah to prevent his subjects from going over to Asa.

The good king then committed the great error of his life. He resorted to an alliance with Ben-hadad I, of Damascus, purchasing his assistance with treasures from the Temple and the king's house. Ben-hadad made a diversion in Asa's favor by invading northern Israel, whereupon Baasha left Ramah. Asa took the material found there and built Geba and Mizpah. His lack of faith was reproved by the seer Hanani, who told him that he had lost the honor of conquering the Syrians because of this alliance, and also prophesied war for the rest of his days. Asa, angered at Hanani, put him in prison and oppressed some of the people at the same time (2 Chron. 16:1-10).

Sickness and Death. In the thirty-ninth year of his reign he was afflicted with a disease in his feet and "did not seek the Lord," but depended upon the physicians. The disease proved fatal in the forty-first year of his reign. He died greatly beloved and was honored with a magnificent burial (2 Chron. 16:12-14).

2. A Levite, son of Elkanah and father of Berechiah, who resided in one of the villages of the Netophathites after the return from Babylon (1 Chron. 9:16), after 536 B.C.

AS'AHEL (as'a-hel; "God's creature").

1. The son of David's sister, Zeruiah, and brother of Joab and Abishai (2 Sam. 2:18; 1 Chron. 2:16). He was an early adherent of David, being one of the famous thirty (2 Sam. 23:24) and, with his son Zebadiah, was commander of the fourth division of the royal army (1 Chron. 27:7). He was renowned for his swiftness of foot, and after the battle of Gibeon he pursued and

overtook Abner, who reluctantly, and in order to save his own life, slew Asahel with a back thrust of his spear (2 Sam. 2:18-23), about 1000 B.C. Joab, to revenge Asahel's death, slew Abner some years after at Hebron (3:26-27).

2. One of the Levites sent by Jehoshaphat into Judah to teach the law of the Lord (2 Chron. 17:8), after 875 B.C.

3. One of the Levites appointed by Hezekiah as overseer of the contributions to the house of the Lord (2 Chron. 31:13), about 700 B.C.

4. The father of Jonathan, who was one of the elders that assisted Ezra in putting away the foreign wives of the Jews on the return from Babylon (Ezra 10:15), 457 B.C.

ASAI'AH (a-sa-ī'a; "whom Jehovah made).

1. An officer of Josiah who was sent with others to consult Huldah the prophetess concerning the book of the law found in the Temple (2 Kings 22:12-14; 2 Chron. 34:20), 624 B.C. His name is given as Asahiah in the KJV of 2 Kings 22:12-4.

2. A leader of one of the families of the tribe of Simeon who, in the time of Hezekiah, drove out the Hamite shepherds from the rich pastures near Gedor (1 Chron. 4:36), about 700 B.C.

3. The son of Haggiah (1 Chron. 6:30) and head of the 220 Levites of the family of Merari, appointed by David to remove the Ark from the house of Obed-edom (1 Chron. 15:6, 11), after 1000 B.C.

4. The "first-born" of the Shilonites who returned to Jerusalem after the captivity (1 Chron. 9:5), about 536 B.C.

ASAHI'AH. *See* Asaiah.

A'SAPH (a-saf; "collector").

1. The father (or ancestor) of Joah, who was "recorder" in the time of Hezekiah (2 Kings 18:18, 37; Isa. 36:3, 22), about 710 B.C.

2. A Levite, son of Berechiah, of the family of Gershom (1 Chron. 6:39; 15:17), eminent as a musician and appointed by David to preside over the sacred choral services (16:5), after 1000 B.C. The "sons of Asaph" are afterward mentioned as musicians of the Temple (1 Chron. 25:1-2; 2 Chron. 20:14, and elsewhere), and this office appears to have been made hereditary in the family (1 Chron. 25:1-2). Asaph was celebrated in later times as a prophet and "seer" (2 Chron. 29:30; Neh. 12:46), and the titles of twelve of the psalms (50, 73-83) bear his name, though in some of these (74, 75, 79) the "sons of Asaph" rather than Asaph himself should be understood, as matters of late occurrence are referred to (Kitto, s. v.).

3. A "keeper of the king's forest," probably in Lebanon. Nehemiah requested Artaxerxes to give him an order on Asaph for timber to be used in the rebuilding of the Temple (Neh. 2:8), about 445 B.C.

ASAR'EL (a-sar'el). The last named of the four

sons of Jehallelel, of the tribe of Judah (1 Chron. 4:16).

ASARE'LAH. *See* Ashare'lah.

ASCENSION OF CHRIST. His glorious withdrawal, as to His bodily presence, from the earth; and entrance, as the God-man and mediatorial King, into heaven.

The Fact. The ascension was from the Mount of Olives forty days after the resurrection. (1) Predicted in Pss. 68:18; 110:1; then interpreted (Eph. 4:8-10; Heb. 1:13); also by Christ Himself (John 6:62; 20:17). (2) Recorded (Mark 16:19; Luke 24:50-51; Acts 1:9-11). (3) Recognized by the apostle John (passages above cited) and by other NT writers who based doctrines upon it (2 Cor. 13:4; Eph. 2:6; 4:8-10; 1 Pet. 3:22; 1 Tim. 3:16; Heb. 1:13; 6:20). (4) Certified by the disciples who were eyewitnesses, by the words of the two angels, by Stephen and Paul and John, who saw Christ in His ascended state (Acts 1:9-11; 7:55-56; 9:3-5; Rev. 1:9-18). (5) Demonstrated by the descent of the Holy Spirit on the Day of Pentecost (Matt. 3:11; Luke 24:49; Acts 2:1-4, 33) and by the manifold gifts bestowed by the ascended Lord upon His church (Eph. 4:11-12).

Doctrinal and Ethical Significance. The visible ascension of Christ was the necessary sequel and seal of His resurrection (Rom. 6:9). It was the appropriate connecting link between His humiliation and glorification (Phil. 2:5-11). As consequences of the ascension the NT writers particularly note: (1) The removal of His bodily, but not His spiritual, presence from the earth; Christ "has passed through the heavens," but invisibly He is always near at hand (Heb. 4:14; Matt. 28:20; Acts 23:11; 2 Tim. 4:17). (2) The investiture of Christ with power and dominion in heaven and earth. He is "at the right hand of the throne of God" (Matt. 28:18; Phil. 2:10; Heb. 12:2). (3) The perpetual intercession of Christ, as our great High Priest (Rom. 8:34; Heb. 5:10; 7:25). (4) The sending forth of the Holy Spirit, and the bestowal of other gifts upon the church (Acts 2:33; Eph. 4:11-12).

Of practical import, accordingly, the ascension of Christ is closely related to the peace and sanctification and hope of believers. (1) He is their heavenly Advocate (1 John 2:1). (2) He is still interceding for their perfection (John 17:20-24). (3) They are then encouraged to fidelity and to confident prayer (Heb. 4:14-16). (4) He powerfully attracts them to things above (Col. 3:1-4). (5) He has gone to prepare a place for them (John 14:2). (6) He awaits His perfect triumph over all His foes (Heb. 10:13). (7) He shall come again to judge the world (Acts 1:11; Matt. 25:31-32).

BIBLIOGRAPHY: H. B. Swete, *The Ascended Christ* (1911); C. F. D. Moule, *Expository Times* 68 (1957): 205-9; W. J. Sparrow-Simpson, *Our Lord's Resurrection* (1964); id., *The Resurrection and the Christian* (1968);

W. Milligan, *The Ascension of Christ* (1980); P. Toon, *The Ascension of Our Lord* (1984).

ASCENTS, SONG OF ("song of steps"). A title given to each of the fifteen psalms from 120 to 134. Four of them are attributed to David, one is ascribed to the pen of Solomon, and the other ten give no indication of their author.

The opinion held by Rosenmüller, Herder, and others is that some of the psalms were written before the Babylonian captivity, some by exiles returning to Palestine, and a few at a later date; but that all were incorporated into one collection because they had one and the same character. With respect to the term rendered in the NASB and NIV "ascents" (KJV, "degrees"), a great diversity of opinion prevails among biblical critics. According to some it refers to the melody to which the psalm was to be chanted. Others, including Gesenius, derive the word from the poetical composition of the song and from the circumstance that the concluding words of the preceding sentence are often repeated at the commencement of the next verse (cf. 121:4-5, and 124:1-2 and 3-4).

A good instance of the "step" style is found in the KJV rendering of Ps. 121: "I will lift up mine eyes unto the hills, from whence cometh *my help. My help* cometh from the Lord, which made heaven and earth."

Iben-Ezra quotes an ancient authority that maintains that the ascents or degrees allude to the fifteen steps which, in the Temple of Jerusalem, led from the court of the women to that of the men, and on each of which steps one of the fifteen songs of ascents was chanted. The generally accredited opinion, however, is that they were pilgrim songs sung by the people as they went up to Jerusalem.

BIBLIOGRAPHY: S. Cox, *The Pilgrim Psalms* (1983).

AS'ENATH (as'e-nath; "who belongs to Neith," i.e., the Egyptian Minerva). The daughter of Potipherah, priest of On, whom the king of Egypt gave in marriage to Joseph (Gen. 41:45), 1715 B.C. She became the mother of Ephraim and Manasseh (46:20). Beyond this nothing is known concerning her.

ASH. *See* Vegetable Kingdom: Fir.

A'SHAN (a'shan; "smoke"). A Levitical city (1 Chron. 6:59) in the low country of Judah, assigned first to Judah (Josh. 15:42) and again to Simeon (19:7; 1 Chron. 4:32; this last passage giving it as a priests' village). Ain instead of Ashan is used in Josh. 21:16. Ashan is identified with Khirbet Ashan about five miles NW of Beersheba.

ASHARE'LAH (ash-a-re'la). One of the sons of the Levite Asaph, who was appointed by David to be in charge of the Temple music (1 Chron. 25:2). He is probably the same as Jesharelah

(1 Chron. 25:14) and, if so, was in the seventh of the (twenty-four) divisions, after 1000 B.C.

ASH'BEA (ash'be-a). In the KJV, the head of a family mentioned as working in fine linen (1 Chron. 4:21). The NASB and NIV interpret the Heb. to be part of the name of a village, *Beth-ash-bea* (which see).

ASH'BEL (ash'bel). The second son of Benjamin (Gen. 46:21; 1 Chron. 8:1). His descendants were called Ashbelites (Num. 26:38).

ASH'BELITE. *See* Ashbel.

ASHCHE'NAZ (ash-ke'-nas). *See* Ashkenaz.

ASH'DOD (ash'dod). One of the five principal cities of the Philistines. Together with Gaza, Gath, Ekron, and Ashkelon it formed what is known as the Philistine Pentapolis. These cities were at the zenith of their power at the time of Saul (c. 1020 B.C.) and continued to be important after the ascendancy of the Hebrew monarchy under the Davidic dynasty (c. 1000-587 B.C.). Ashdod was situated between Ashkelon, a seaport, and Ekron, inland on the caravan route E to Lydda and W to Joppa. Sargon besieged and took the city (Isa. 20:1) despite its commanding position on a hill, which made it the envy of Israel. The Ark of God was carried by the Philistines to Ashdod after their victory at Ebenezer (c. 1050 B.C.) and carried into the temple of Dagon, an ancient Canaanite deity associated with agriculture, who was worshiped there (1 Sam. 5). It was later carried to Gath and Ekron with similar disastrous results as at Ashdod. Mentioned some twenty-one times in the OT, its palaces and temples (Amos 3:9) preserve its memory as a city of importance. Nehemiah in his day protested against Israelite men marrying wives from Ashdod and rearing children who could not speak "the language of Judah" (Neh. 13:23-25).

A joint expedition of the Pittsburgh Carnegie Museum, the Pittsburgh Theological Seminary, and the Israel Department of Antiquities excavated Ashdod in 1962, 1963, 1965, and from 1968 to 1972. M. Dothan served as director of excavations. The site encompasses an acropolis of about seventeen acres and a lower city of perhaps ninety acres. Excavations revealed twenty-two strata of settlement extending from the seventeenth century B.C. to the Byzantine period. A fragment of a basalt stela of Sargon II came to light, mentioning some of his conquests and confirming the fact that Sargon took the town (Isa. 20:1). The excavators also uncovered evidence of Hezekiah's conquest and learned that the Philistines took the city early in the twelfth century B.C.   H.F.V

BIBLIOGRAPHY: J. B. Pritchard, *Ancient Near Eastern Texts* (1969), pp. 284, 286-88; M. Dothan, *New Directions in Biblical Archaeology*, ed. D. N. Freedman and J. C. Greenfield (1971), pp. 17-27; id., *Israel Exploration Journal* 23 (1973): 2-17; Y. Aharoni, *The Archaeology of the Land of Israel* (1982), pp. 184-88, 196ff., 270-71.

Aerial view of Ashdod

ASH'DODITES (ash'do-dīts; Josh. 13:3; Neh. 4:7). Inhabitants of *Ashdod* (which see).

ASH'DOTHITES. *See* Ashdodites.

ASH'ER (ash'er; "happiness"). The eighth son of Jacob and second of Zilpah, the maid of Leah (Gen. 30:13).

Personal History. Of this we have no record.

The Tribe of Asher. Asher had four sons and one daughter. Upon quitting Egypt the tribe numbered 41,500, ranking *ninth*; and at the second census the number had increased to 53,400 men of war, ranking *fifth* in population.

Position. During the march through the desert Asher's place was between Dan and Naphtali, on the N side of the Tabernacle (Num. 2:27).

Territory. The general position of the tribe was on the seashore from Carmel northward, with Manasseh on the S, Zebulun and Issachar on the SE, and Naphtali on the NE. The boundaries and towns are given in Josh. 19:24-31; 17:10-11; Judg. 1:31-32.

Subsequent History. The richness of the soil and the tribe's proximity to the Phoenicians may have contributed to its degeneracy (Judg. 1:31; 5:17). In the reign of David the tribe had become so insignificant that its name is altogether omitted from the list of the chief rulers (1 Chron.

27:16-22). With the exception of Simeon, Asher is the only tribe W of the Jordan that furnished no judge or hero to the nation. Anna, daughter of Phanuel, who was of the tribe of Asher, as a prophetess and a godly woman, recognized the infant Jesus as the Messiah (Luke 2:36-38).

ASHE'RAH (a-she'ra). A Canaanite goddess appearing as "Lady of the Sea" in the Ras Shamra literature of the fourteenth century B.C. *See* Gods, False.

ASH'ERITES (ash'er-its). Descendants of *Asher* (which see) and members of his tribe (Judg. 1:32).

ASHES.

1. The ashes on the altar of burnt offering were removed each morning by a priest clad in linen (his official dress) and were then carried by him, attired in unofficial dress, to a clean place outside the camp (Lev. 6:10-11). According to the Mishna, the priest who was to remove the ashes was chosen by lot. The ashes of the red heifer (*see* Purification) had the ceremonial efficacy of purifying the unclean (Heb. 9:13) but of polluting the clean.

Figurative. It has been the custom in all ages to burn captured cities; and so, to *reduce a place to ashes* is a well-understood expression for effecting a complete destruction (Ezek. 28:18; 2 Pet. 2:6). A frequent figurative employment of the word is derived from the practice of sitting among ashes, or scattering them upon one's person, as a symbol of grief and mourning (Job 2:8; 42:6; Isa. 58:5; Jer. 6:26; Matt. 11:21; etc.). In Ezek. 27:30 it is declared of the mourning Tyrians that "they will wallow in the ashes," expressive of great and bitter lamentation. *Eating* ashes is expressive of the deepest misery and degradation (Ps. 102:9; Isa. 44:20). Ashes are also used to represent things easily scattered, perishable, and, therefore, worthless. Thus Abraham speaks of himself as "dust and ashes" (Gen. 18:27), and to the righteous the wicked are said to be "ashes under the soles of your feet" (Mal. 4:3).

2. The early Christians naturally adopted a ceremony that had acquired so much significance. Tertullian speaks of the "substitution of sackcloth and ashes for a man's usual habit" as a regular ceremony of public confession and penance in the second century. Penitents under excommunication used to sprinkle ashes upon their heads and, standing at the doors of the churches, ask the prayers of those entering, that they might be readmitted to Communion.

ASH'HUR (ash'hur). A posthumous son of Hezron (grandson of Judah, Gen. 46:12), by his wife Abijah (1 Chron. 2:24). He had two wives, Helah and Naarah, each of whom bore him several sons (1 Chron. 4:5), and through these he is called the "father" (founder) of Tekoa, which appears to have been the place of their eventual settlement.

ASH'IMA (ash'i-ma). The god of the people of Hamath (2 Kings 17:30). *See* Gods, False.

ASH'KELON (ash'ke-lon; Askalon, Askelon, Ascalon in NT times). One of the five principal cities of Philistia, located on the fertile Maritime Plain some dozen miles N of Gaza. It probably derived its name from the *escallot* (scallion) that grew there. It has been excavated and shows stratigraphic layers of occupation from late Arab at the summit, through the Crusader and NT periods down to an early Canaanite town that came to an end around 2000 B.C. In Samson's time Philistines occupied it (Judg. 14:19). Both Zephaniah (2:4) and Zechariah (9:5) foretold its destruction. Ashkelon was Herod the Great's birthplace and the residence of his sister Salome. Conseqently, he took an interest in the place, beautifying it with impressive colonnaded courts. The site was prominent in the period of the Crusades, but its chief interest is in the biblical period. David mentions the city in his lament over Saul and Jonathan (2 Sam. 1:20). Excavations at the 160-acre site were carried on in 1920 and 1921 by W. J. Phythian-Adams and John Garstang on behalf of the Palestine Exploration Fund. Among other things, the excavators found Hyksos fortifications and a council house (110 meters long) dating to the Roman period. In 1967 V. Tsaferis uncovered a Christian basilica with a mosaic pavement.   H.F.V.

BIBLIOGRAPHY: Y. Aharoni, *The Archaeology of the Land of Israel* (1982), pp. 183-86.

Ruins at the coastal city of Ashkelon

ASH'KELONITE (ash'ke-lon-īt). The designation (Josh. 13:3) of an inhabitant of *Ashkelon* (which see).

ASHKENAZ' (ash-ke-nas'). The first named of the sons of Gomer son of Japheth (Gen. 10:3) and equivalent to Assyr. *Ashkuz*, "the Scythians" (W. F. Albright, *O.T. Commentary* [1948], p. 138). In the time of Jeremiah they dwelt in the neighborhood of Ararat and Minni (the Mannai of the Assyrian inscriptions) SE of Lake Van. They were rude and retarded in civilization and peri-

odically overran extensive territory, so that their name came to be tantamount to barbarians.
                                                    M.F.U.

ASH'NAH (ash'na). The name of two cities, both in the tribe of Judah (Josh. 15:33, 43). Neither of them has been positively identified.

ASH'PENAZ (ash'pe-naz). The chief of the officials (or eunuchs, Dan. 1:3, see marg.), a chamberlain of Nebuchadnezzar, after 604 B.C., who was commanded to select certain Jewish captives to be instructed in the "literature and language of the Chaldeans" (1:4). Among those he selected were Daniel and his three companions, Hananiah, Mishael, and Azariah, whose Heb. names he changed to Babylonian (1:7). The request of Daniel, that he might not be compelled to eat the provisions sent from the king's table, filled Ashpenaz with apprehension. But God had brought Daniel into favor with Ashpenaz, and he did not use constraint toward him, and this kindness the prophet gratefully records (1:16).

ASH'RIEL. *See* Asriel.

ASH'TAROTH (ash'ta-rōth).
 1. An ancient city of Bashan, E of the Jordan (Deut. 1:4; Josh. 9:10; 12:4; 3:12, 31) in the half tribe of Manasseh. The inhabitants, including King Og, were giants. The town was the seat of the lewd worship of Astarte and was the capital of Og. By the time of Israel's entrance into the land, the iniquity of the inhabitants was full (Gen. 15:16), and God commanded the conquering Israelites to utterly exterminate them (Deut. 3:2-6). The site of the ancient city is identified with Tell Ashtarab, twenty-one miles E of the Sea of Galilee, the hill being surrounded by a well-watered plain.
 2. The plural form of the god Ashtoreth (Astarte). *See* Gods, False.   M.F.U.

BIBLIOGRAPHY: Y. Aharoni, *The Land of the Bible* (1979), pp. 114-16, 120, 140-46, 156ff.

ASH'TEROTH KAR'NAIM (ash'te-rōth kar-na'-im; "Ashteroth of the two horns," Gen. 14:5). This was probably distinct from Ashtaroth. The Rephaim dwelt in Ashteroth Karnaim, a place probably at or near Tell 'Ashtarah. There was a temple there, dedicated to the principal female divinity of the Phoenicians; both the city, in later Hebrew times called Carnaim, and the temple are mentioned in Maccabees, and the reference seems to be the same place.

ASH'UR. *See* Ash'hur.

ASH'TORETH. One of the names of a Sidonian goddess. *See* Gods, False.

ASHURBAN'IPAL (a-shūr-ban'i-pal; Assyr. "Ashur creates a son"). Called also *Osnappar* (which see; the name is sometimes given as Asnappar), Ashurbanipal was the grandson of Sennacherib (705-681 B.C.), and the last great Assyrian monarch (669-626 B.C.). His father was the famous Esarhaddon. He is renowned as a scholar and a protector of literature and art. His great library, excavated at Nineveh, has yielded a large quantity of cuneiform literature, numbering about 22,000 religious, literary, and scientific texts. This vast corpus of material furnishes one of the main sources of information extant for the reconstruction of the history and civilization of ancient Assyria. Texts giving the ancient Babylonian versions of the creation and the Flood found in the Nineveh beautified by this king have shed light on the account of these events recorded in Genesis. Ashurbanipal was on the throne of Assyria during a large part of Manasseh's long and wicked reign in Judah (c. 696-642 B.C.). The narrative of 2 Chron. 33 relates how Manasseh was deported to Babylon by the Assyrians (Esarhaddon or Ashurbanipal?). The authenticity of this event is supported by the fact that Assyrian kings of this period did spend part of their time in Babylon.   M.F.U.

BIBLIOGRAPHY: J. B. Pritchard, ed., *Ancient Near Eastern Texts* (1969), pp. 101ff.

Relief of Ashurbanipal on campaign

ASHURI (a-shū'ri). The name of a people in the Transjordan over whom Ish-bosheth was made king following Saul's death (2 Sam. 2:9). E.H.M.

ASHURNA'SIRPAL II (a-shūr-na'zir-pal; 883-859 B.C.). A ruthless conqueror who brought the Assyrian Empire to a place of dread power in all SW Asia. He built up a fighting machine that overran vast sections of the Near Eastern world. He is notorious for his barbarous cruelty. The final edition of his annals was inscribed on the pavement slabs on the entrance of the temple of Ninurta in Calah, an ancient and ruined city (cf. Gen. 10:11; now the Mound of Nimrud) where A. H. Layard began his Assyrian excavations in 1845. At the very beginning the palace of Ashurnasirpal was uncovered. In a nearby small temple a half-life-size statue of the king was found. Inscribed on it was the claim that he had conquered the whole region from the Tigris to the Great Sea (Mediterranean). M. E. L. Mallowan excavated at the site again in 1949 and 1950, concentrating once more at Ashurnasirpal's palace, a new southeastern wing of which was found and excavated.   H.F.V.

Relief of Ashurnasirpal from Nimrud

ASHVATH (ash'vath). The third son of Japhlet of the tribe of Asher (1 Chron. 7:33).

A'SIA (ā'sha). A name of doubtful origin that, as a designation along with Europe and Africa, came into use in the fifth century B.C. The Scriptures do not mention Asia as a whole, the several references being to separate nations or parts of the continent. In the NT the word is used in this narrower sense, sometimes for Asia Minor and sometimes for proconsular Asia, the latter of which included Phrygia, Mysia, Caria, and Lydia. Proconsular Asia was governed by a propraetor until the emperor Augustus made it a proconsular province. J. Strong (*Cyclopedia*) thinks "Asia" denotes all of Asia Minor in Acts 19:26-27; 21:27;

24:18; 27:2; and that proconsular Asia is referred to in 2:9; 6:9; 16:6; 19:10, 22; 20:4, 16, 18; Rom. 16:5; 1 Cor. 16:19; 2 Cor. 1:8; 2 Tim. 1:15; 1 Pet. 1:1; and contained the seven churches of the Apocalypse (Rev. 1:4, 11). Luke appears to have used the term *Asia* in a still more restricted sense, counting Phrygia and Mysia as provinces distinct from Asia (Acts 2:9-10; 16:6-7).

BIBLIOGRAPHY: A. H. M. Jones, *The Cities of the Eastern Roman Province* (1937), pp. 28-95; O. R. Gurney, *The Hittites* (1952); S. Lloyd, *Early Anatolia* (1956); E. M. Blaiklock, *Cities of the New Testament* (1965); B. Levick, *Roman Colonies in Southern Asia Minor* (1967); W. M. Ramsay, *The Historical Geography of Asia Minor* (1972).

A'SIA, CHURCHES OF. See under their respective names.

ASIARCHS (ā'si-arks; "rulers of Asia," Acts 19:31). The ten superintendents of the public games and religious rites of proconsular Asia, who celebrated at their own expense the games in honor of the gods and emperor. Each city annually, about the time of the autumnal equinox, delegated one of its citizens with a view to this office; out of the entire number ten were elected by the assembly of deputies, and one of the ten, perhaps chosen by the proconsul, presided. It has been disputed whether only the president or the whole of the ten bore the title *asiarch*. From 19:31 it would appear that all bore the title and also that through courtesy it was extended to those who had held the office previously.

A'SIEL (a'si-el; "created by God"). The father of Seraiah, and progenitor of one of the Simeonite leaders that expelled the Hamites from the valley of Gedor in the time of Hezekiah (1 Chron. 4:35), before 715 B.C.

AS'KELON. See Ashkelon.

AS'NAH (as'na). The head of one of the families of the Temple servants (KJV, Nethinim) that returned from the Babylonian captivity with Zerubbabel (Ezra 2:50), about 536 B.C.

ASNAPPER. See Ashurbanipal; Osnapper.

ASP. See Animal Kingdom: Serpent.

ASPALATHUS. See Vegetable Kingdom.

ASPATHA (Aspatha'). The third son of Homan, a ruler of Persia under Ahasuerus (Xerxes, NIV; Esther 9:7).   E.H.M.

ASPHALT. Asphalt was extensively procured from the Dead Sea in ancient times, which was one of the major sources of this building material. The Nabataeans controlled the Dead Sea bitumen industry in the Greco-Roman period (Diodorus Siculus *Historia* 2. 48; 19. 98-100); F. R. Clapp, "Geology and Bitumen of the Dead Sea Area, Palestine and Transjordan," *American Association of Petroleum Geologists* 20, no. 7

(1936): 901; *The Biblical Archaeologist* 22, no. 2 (1959): 40-48. See Mineral Kingdom: Tar.

AS'RIEL (as-ri-el'). The head of a family that belonged to the half tribe of Manasseh (Num. 26:31; Josh. 17:2; 1 Chron. 7:14).

ASS. See Animal Kingdom: Donkey.

ASSEMBLY. The term used for several Heb. words, elsewhere translated *"Congregation"* (which see). It is also the representative of the following: (1) *'aṣārâ*, a "coming together," especially for a *festal* occasion (Lev. 23:36; Num. 29:35; Deut. 16:8). (2) *miqrā'*, something "called," a public meeting (Isa. 1:13; 4:5). (3) "general assembly" (Gk. *panēguris*, "a festal gathering of all the people" (Heb. 12:23), commonly believed to be the same as the church. (4) *ekklēsia*, a term in use among the Greeks from the time of Thucydides for "an assemblage of the people for the purpose of deliberating" (Acts 19:39).

ASSEMBLY, MOUNT OF (Heb. *har mô'ēd*). A mountain in the farthest N referred to in Isa. 14:13 in connection with the fall of Satan (Lucifer). The reference is illustrated by the common concept among the Babylonians that the gods assembled on a mountain of the N. Some suppose that Mt. Moriah as the site of the Temple is intended, but Zion was neither a northern point of the earth nor was it situated on the N of Jerusalem. "The prophet makes the king of Babylon speak after the general notion of his people, who placed the seat of the Deity on the summit of the northern mountains, which were lost in the clouds" (Delitzsch, *Com.*).

AS'SHUR (ash-ur; a "step"). The second named of the sons of Shem (Gen. 10:22; 1 Chron. 1:17). His descendants peopled the land of Assyria. The name also appears in the KJV of Gen. 10:11, but the verse should be rendered, "From that land he went forth into Assyria" (so NASB and NIV).

AS'SIR (as'sir; "prisoner").
1. A Levite, son of Korah (Ex. 6:24; 1 Chron. 6:22). His descendants constituted one of the Korhite families.
2. Son of Ebiasaph, great-grandson of the preceding, and father of Tahath (1 Chron. 6:23, 37). There is some suspicion, however, that the name here has crept in by repetition from the preceding.
3. In the KJV of 1 Chron. 3:17, the son of Jeconiah, a descendant of David. The NASB and NIV render "Jeconiah, the prisoner," referring to the captivity of that prince in Babylon.

ASSOCIATE. The rendering of Heb. *'āmît*, "neighbor," in that remarkable passage "Awake, O sword, against My Shepherd, and against the man, My Associate" (Zech. 13:7). The expression "man, who is my nearest one" implies much more than unity or community of vocation, or that he had to feed the flock as Jehovah. The idea of nearest one (or associate) involves not only similarity in vocation, but community of physical or spiritual descent, according to which He whom God calls His neighbor cannot be a mere man but can only be one who participates in the divine nature or is essentially divine. This passage is quoted and applied to Himself by our Lord (Matt. 26:31).

AS'SOS (as'os). A seaport town in Mysia, on the northern shore of the Gulf of Adramyttium and about thirty miles from Troas by sea, opposite Lesbos. Paul came to it on foot from Troas to embark for Mitylene (Acts 20:13-14). Assos was excavated by an American expedition directed by J. T. Clarke and F. H. Bacon (1881-83). At the site may be seen remains of a city wall (fourth century B.C.), a temple of Athena (sixth century B.C.), an agora (third-second century B.C.), a gymnasium (second century B.C.), and a theater (third century B.C.).

ASSURANCE. A term brought into theology from the Scriptures, sometimes used broadly by theologians as referring to certitude respecting the validity of Christian revelation; most commonly employed to denote the firm persuasion of one's own salvation. The latter must of course include the former. In experience the two are closely connected. In both senses assurance is a product of the Holy Spirit (Col. 2:2; Heb. 6:11; 10:22). *See also* other passages expressing "confidence," "boldness."

As to the assurance of personal salvation it must be emphasized that this must not be confused with the eternal security of a genuine believer. The latter is a fact due to God's faithfulness whether it is realized by the believer or not, whereas the former is that which one believes is true respecting himself at any given moment.

1. Assurance has been held, chiefly by Calvinists, to relate not only to present but also to final salvation. This is the logical outcome of the doctrine of unconditional election. It must stand or fall with that doctrine. Others, who regard mankind as in a state of probation, limit the assurance to present acceptance with God.

2. Is assurance the common privilege of believers? This the doctrine of the Roman Catholic church answers in the negative "since no one can certainly and infallibly know that he has obtained the grace of God" (Council of Trent, sess. 6, chap. 9, "De Justificatione"). Luther and Melanchthon and many other Reformers held strongly to the affirmative and even made assurance the criterion of saving faith. Calvinistic doctrine has regarded assurance (implying not only present but also final salvation) as a special gift of grace possessed by relatively few believers, though, theoretically at least, within the privilege and duty of all. Methodist theology has given strong

emphasis to assurance as the common privilege of all who truly believe in Christ, presenting not the doubting and desponding type but the confident and joyous type of religious experience as the one that is normal and scriptural.

3. As to whether assurance is of the essence of, or a necessary element in, saving faith the first Protestant Confession (Augsburg) held that it is involved therein in accordance with Luther's declaration that "he who hath not assurance spews faith out." Other and later utterances of the Reformed doctrine discriminated between the act of justifying and saving faith and the assurance that comes as its result. The Westminster Assembly was the first Protestant synod, however, that formally declared assurance not to be of the essence of saving faith. Wesley, although seeming at times to teach the opposite view, nevertheless clearly held and taught that assurance is not involved in justifying faith or necessarily connected with it. "The assertion, 'Justifying faith is a sense of pardon,' " he says, "is contrary to reason; it is flatly absurd. For, how can a sense of pardon be the condition of our receiving it?" For a most discriminating presentation of his views as to the relation of assurance to faith, see his *Works,* 11:109-10.

4. As to the grounds of assurance, opinions have also varied, especially as to their order and relative importance. Calvinists are rather disposed to lay stress upon the external grounds of confidence instead of those that are internal; i.e., the truths and promises of Scripture are dwelt upon more largely and strongly than the fruits of the Spirit and the "witness of the Spirit." Wesley and other Methodist theologians emphasize chiefly the "witness of the Spirit," though they by no means undervalue the confidence that comes from the recognition of the validity of the truth and promises of God and that which comes from finding in one's self the graces that surely proclaim the fact of personal salvation. The "witness of the Spirit" brings faith to its full development, so that, uplifted to a joyous experience of the new life, we become possessed more abundantly of the fruits of the Spirit, and the faith in God's Word that was intellectual, rational, and dim or wavering becomes spiritual, living, and certain. Thus is realized "the full assurance of faith" and "of hope" and "understanding." *See* Westminster Con., art. 18, "Of the Assurance of Grace and Salvation"; Hodge's *Systematic Theology;* Pope's *Compendium of Christian Theology;* Dorner's *System of Christian Doctrines,* introductory chapter, "The Doctrine of Faith"; Watson's *Theological Institutes;* Wesley's "Works," especially sermon on "The Witness of the Spirit"; Chamberlayne's *Saving Faith;* L. S. Chafer, *Systematic Theology,* 7:21-24.

BIBLIOGRAPHY: J. M. Boice, *Foundations of the Christian Faith* (1986), pp. 410, 431-40, 453-54; J. Calvin, *Theological Treatises,* Library of Christian Classics (1954),

22:22, 104, 423f.; J. Miley, *Systematic Theology* (1894), 2:340-52; C. C. Ryrie, *Basic Theology* (1986), pp. 328-29, 381; W. H. G. Thomas, *Principles of Theology* (1930), pp. 381-87; R. Watson, *Theological Institutes* (n.d.), 2:270.

ASSYR'IA (a-sir'I-ya). The name of a country and the mighty empire that dominated the ancient biblical world from the ninth to the seventh century B.C.

The Land. Assyria lay along the middle Tigris between the Kurdish Taurus Mountains and Jebel Hamrin and formed an area about the size of the state of Connecticut. On the W bank of the Tigris lay a single plain, while on the E bank the country was divided into three sections: the area between the mountains and the Great Zab, the sector between the Great and Lesser Zab rivers, and the region between the Lesser Zab and the mountain Jebel Hamrin. The land is fertile and undulating and has enough rainfall to support dry farming. Assyria had abundant supplies of limestone and alabaster and some marble.

The major cities were Ashur on the W bank of the Tigris and Arrapkha, Erbil, Nineveh, and Calah to the E of the Tigris. Most of the population lived in country towns. In time the Assyrians were able to build a sizable empire that stretched from Egypt on the W to Persia on the E and from the Persian Gulf on the S to Anatolia on the N.

THE ASSYRIAN EMPIRE
c. 640 B.C.

CILICIA   ASSYRIA MEDIA
            Nineveh•• Calah
            Ashur •
                   •Arrapkha
Mediterranean Damascus
Sea   • Euphrates River   Tigris River
                               • Babylon
         ISRAEL
         •Samaria
         •Jerusalem
EGYPT
            ARABIA
                               Persian
                               Gulf
    Red Sea

The People. The people who inhabited Assyria belonged to the great Semitic race. They had come originally, so it appears, from Babylonia to settle as colonists. They were not a pure race, for there had already been an intermixture of blood with the Sumerian people, who were the original inhabitants of the land. After this immigration the Babylonians continued the process of intermixture with successive invading peoples from Elam, Arabia, and elsewhere, but the Assyrians intermarried little with neighboring peoples and held it a subject for much boasting that they were

of purer blood than the Babylonians. However, during the height of the Assyrian Empire (c. 725-635), the Assyrians deported large numbers of people from conquered lands and settled them in their homeland, with the result that by the fall of Nineveh in 612 the population of Assyria was greatly diluted. In stature the Assyrians were of average modern European height and were well built. Their complexion was dark, the nose prominent, the hair, eyebrows, and beard thick and bushy. They were apparently of cheerful disposition, given to mirth and feasting, but of implacable cruelty. The pages of history are nowhere more bloody than in the records of their wars. It may be argued, however, that the Assyrians were not much more cruel than other peoples of the ancient Near East but merely kept better records. As cases in point, Egyptian monuments occasionally show mounds of body parts, demonstrating that the Egyptians mutilated their enemies; and even the Hebrews were known to have hacked away at those whom they had vanquished (e.g., 1 Sam. 18:25, 27).

Language and Literature. The language of Assyria was closely akin to that of Babylonia and may properly be regarded as practically the same language. It belongs to the Semitic family of languages and is, therefore, akin to Arab., Aramaean, and Heb. Unlike these three kindred languages, the Assyrian never developed an alphabet, though it did develop a few alphabetic characters. During its entire history the Assyrian language was prevailingly ideographic and syllabic. It expressed words by means of signs that represented the *idea;* thus there was a single sign for *sun,* another for *city,* another for *wood,* another for *hand.* These are called ideograms and originated in considerable measure out of pictures, or pictographs, of the objects themselves. But besides these ideograms the language also possessed numerous syllabic signs such as *ab, ib, ub, ba, bi, bu.* By means of these, words could be spelled out. Clumsy though this appears to be, the Assyrians were able to develop it far enough to make it a wonderfully accurate and sufficiently flexible tool. The materials on which they wrote were clay and stone, the use of which had come from Babylonia. In writing upon stone the characters were chiseled deeply into the surface, in regular lines, sometimes over raised figures of gods or kings. Writings thus executed were of monumental character and could not be used for business or literary purposes. The great bulk of Assyrian literature has come down to us upon clay and not upon stone. The clay tablets, as they are called, vary greatly in size. Some are shaped like pillows, two inches in length by an inch and a quarter in width. Others are flat and sometimes reach sixteen inches in length by nine or ten inches in width. The clay is also sometimes shaped like barrels, varying in height from five to nine inches, or like cylinders or prisms, which are found sometimes sixteen inches in height. When the soft clay had been formed into one of these shapes, the characters were formed by pressing into the surface a small metallic tool with a triangularly pointed end. Each pressure formed a wedge-shaped, or cuneiform, depression, and by repeated indentations the characters were made. On these clay tablets the Assyrians wrote a varied literature. We now have in our possession vast stores of this literature, representing widely differing phases. There are historical inscriptions, narrating in annalistic form the deeds of Assyrian monarchs; public documents, royal and private letters and dispatches; lists of taxes; innumerable business documents, such as receipts and bills of sale; religious documents, such as hymns, prayers, incantations, and lists of omens; linguistic documents, such as lists of signs and of words with explanations; astronomical lists of eclipses and the like; tables of square and cube roots; and medical treatises and lists of recipes for the healing of disease. Only a small part of this vast literature has been published in facsimile or made accessible in translations in European languages. When they are made thus accessible they will give an insight into the whole life of these people such as we are able to obtain of very few peoples of antiquity.

Religion. The people of Assyria derived their religious ideas from Babylonia and during all their history had constant contact with the mother country in this matter, as in others. The faith was polytheistic and never shows in any text yet found any approach to monotheism. The god who stood at the head of the Assyrian pantheon was the great god Ashur, always honored as the divine founder of the nation. After him and below him were the gods Anu, Bel, and Ea, the middle of whom, under slightly varying names and with changes of titles, was worshiped in Babylonia and even far westward among other Semitic peoples. Besides this great triad, there was another consisting of the moon god Sin, the sun-god Shamash, whose name appears in royal names so frequently, and Ishtar, the goddess of the crescent moon and the queen of the stars, though her place in this triad is often taken by Ramman, the "thunderer," god of rain, of tempests, and of storms. These gods are invoked in phrases that seem to raise each in turn to a position of supremacy over the others. Early students of religious texts sometimes mistakenly supposed that these ascriptions of praise and honor were in reality tokens of monotheism. This is now well known to be a false inference. Monotheism was unknown, henotheism seems at times to have been reached, but polytheism was the prevailing, as it was always the popular, belief. Besides these great triads of gods there were large numbers of minor deities, as well as countless spirits of heaven, earth, and sea. *See* Nergal.

The religious ceremonies of the Assyrians, with their sacrifices morning and evening and their offerings of wine, milk, honey, and cakes, was similar to that of Babylonia but is not yet satisfactorily known, save in outline.

Archaeology. It is clear that the origin of the Assyrian commonwealth is to be found among Babylonian colonists (Gen. 10:11). Archaeology also points to this fact, and the Assyrians themselves looked back to Babylonia as the motherland.

A full account of Assyrian archaeology would fill volumes. There is room here for only a few brief references. Paul Emil Botta began the archaeological history of Assyria in 1842 with significant success at Khorsabad, capital of Sargon II; Victor Place succeeded him there (1851-55). Austen Henry Layard launched English excavations in Assyria, making significant finds at biblical Calah (1846-47) and at Calah and Nineveh (1849-51). At the latter he uncovered much of the great palace of Sennacherib. Layard's associate, Hormuzd Rassam, continued work at Nineveh (1852-54) and had the good fortune to locate Ashurbanipal's palace and the major part of his library. M. E. L. Mallowan led a British School of Archaeology dig at Calah from 1949 to 1961, completing the excavation of Ashurnasirpal's palace and excavating the great fort of Shalmaneser III. R. Campbell Thompson's work at Nineveh (1927-32) was especially responsible for bringing order out of the chronology of the site and establishing the history from its destruction in 612 B.C. back almost to 5000 B.C. Edward Chiera and Henri Frankfort led a University of Chicago excavation at Khorsabad (1929-36) and reexamined the entire palace area and the city. André Parrot of the Louvre excavated at Mari in the middle Euphrates (1933 to 1939 and 1951-56), finding the great royal palace and the archive of more than twenty thousand cuneiform tablets, providing contextual information for biblical studies. And an American Schools of Oriental Research excavation at Nuzi in northeastern Iraq (1925-31) likewise recovered some twenty thousand cuneiform tablets that throw light on patriarchal customs.

Relief depicting Assyrians riding horses and camels

History. Under Shamshi-Adad I (c. 1748-1716 B.C.) Assyria began to spread as a great city-state, with strong fortifications and a splendid temple to house its national god, Ashur. As the political powers of Babylonia declined, Assyria entered its Old Kingdom period, c. 1700 to 1100 B.C. By the fourteenth century B.C. Assyria had risen to a position of power comparable to Egypt on the Nile and the Hittite Empire in Asia Minor. Among the Amarna Tablets is a letter written by Ashur-uballit ("Ashur has given life," c. 1362-1327) to Amenhotep IV of Egypt, in which the Assyrian monarch speaks as a royal equal. With Tiglath-pileser I (c. 1114-1076) Assyria entered the period of empire, extending from c. 1100 to 633 B.C. This great conqueror was able to push Assyrian power westward to the Mediterranean Sea and northward to the region of Lake Van and the mountains of Armenia. The next two centuries, however, marked a period of retrogression for Assyria until the rise of Ashurnasirpal II (883-859) who made his land a formidable fighting machine and who swept everything before his ruthless cruelty, as his annals tell. His son Shalmaneser III (858-824) inherited his father's gigantic fighting machine and conducted numerous campaigns against Syria-Palestine, in one of which he fought against Ahab of Israel at Qarqar on the Orontes River in 853 B.C. and in another received tribute from "Jehu, son of Omri." Shalmaneser III called himself "the mighty king, king of the universe, the king without a rival, the autocrat, the powerful one of the four regions of the world, who shatters the might of the princes of the whole world, who has smashed all of his foes as pots" (D. D. Luckenbill, *Ancient Records of Assyria and Babylonia,* vol. 1, sec. 674). Despite his boasts Shalmaneser III died amid revolts that his son Shamsi-Adad V (823-811) also had to face. Adad-nirari III (810-783) kept Assyrian power aggressive, but under Shalmaneser IV (782-773), Ashur-dan III (772-755), and Ashur-nirari V (754-745) declension set in. Then the throne was seized by a great warrior and statesman, Tiglath-pileser III, who assumed the name of the illustrious conqueror Tiglath-pileser I of the eleventh century B.C. and brought back the empire to its glory, even conquering Babylon, where he was known as Pulu (cf. 2 Kings 15:19). This great warrior overran Israel, took tribute from Menahem, and transported his conquered peoples to distant sections of his empire. Soon after the death of Tiglath-pileser, Hoshea of Israel attempted to revolt against Assyria. The new emperor, Shalmaneser V (726-722), thereupon laid siege to the Israelite capital of Samaria. Before the fall of the city had been fully consummated a new leader had seized the reins of power. He was Sharrukin II or Sargon II (721-705), whose new regime was inaugurated by the fall of the city. Sargon is mentioned but once in Scripture (Isa. 20:1), but as the result of the excavation of

his splendid palace at Dur Sharrukin, or Khorsabad, he is now one of the best known of Assyrian emperors. In 704 B.C. he was succeeded by his son Sennacherib, who ruled Assyria until 681 B.C. and was succeeded in turn by his son Esarhaddon (680-669), one of the greatest Assyrian conquerors. He added Egypt to the empire. Esarhaddon's son, Ashurbanipal (668-633), also campaigned in Egypt and seems to have been a great warrior; but he is especially known for his cultural interests. The great royal library, in existence at least since 700 B.C., was especially his creation. He sent scribes all over Mesopotamia to copy texts on a variety of subjects. After Esarhaddon, the Assyrian stranglehold on the ancient world began to give way. In the intervening years till 612 B.C., when Nineveh fell and Assyrian civilization was suddenly snuffed out, there were several undistinguished rulers. The neo-Babylonian Empire arose on the ruins of Assyria, and a new historical epoch dawned.   H.F.V.

BIBLIOGRAPHY: S. A. Pallis, *The Antiquity of Iraq* (1956); D. J. Wiseman, *The Vassal Treaties of Esarhaddon* (1959); H. W. F. Saggs, *The Greatness That Was Babylon* (1962); A. L. Oppenheim, *Ancient Mesopotamia* (1964); D. J. Wiseman, ed., *Peoples of Old Testament Times* (1973), pp. 156-78; H. W. F. Saggs, *The Might That Was Assyria* (1984).

ASTARTE. The Gk. name for Ashtoreth. *See* Gods, False: Asherah; Ashtoreth.

AS'TAROTH. *See* Gods, False: Asherah; Ashtoreth.

ASTROLOGER. *See* articles Astrology; Magic: Various Forms.

ASTROLOGY. The ancient art of divination by consulting the planets and stars, which until Kepler's time was inextricably bound up with astronomy. The practice consists in consulting the heavenly bodies, particularly the signs of the zodiac in relation to observed human events, and making deductions and predictions on this basis. This largely unscientific practice is nevertheless an important divinatory practice still in vogue in modern Western civilization —as is evidenced by horoscopes printed regularly in metropolitan newspapers, the existence of popular astrology magazines having large circulation, and astrological services available for those who refuse to make important decisions without first consulting the stars (*see* Astrologers; Divination, Diviners under Magic: Various Forms).   M.F.U.

BIBLIOGRAPHY: R. C. Thompson, *Reports of the Magicians and Astrologers of Nineveh and Babylon* (1897); F. Cumont, *Astrology and Religion Among the Greeks and Romans* (1912); L. MacNeice, *Astrology* (1964); R. Gleadow, *The Origin of the Zodiac* (1969).

ASTRONOMY (Gk. *astronomia,* "laws of the stars"). This science probably owes its origin to the Chaldeans, there being evidence that they had conducted astronomical observations from remote antiquity. Callisthenes sent to his uncle, Aristotle, a number of these observations, of which the oldest must have dated back to the middle of 2300 B.C. "The Chaldean priests had been accustomed from an early date to record on their clay tablets the aspect of the heavens and the changes which took place in them night after night, the appearance of the constellations, their comparative brilliance, the precise moments of their rising and setting and culmination, together with the more or less rapid movements of the planets, and their motions toward or from one another." They discovered the revolution and eclipses of the moon and frequently predicted with success eclipses of the sun (Maspero, *Dawn of Civilization,* p. 775).

The astronomy of China and India dates back to an early period, for we read of two Chinese astronomers, Ho and Hi, being put to death for failing to announce a solar eclipse that took place in 2169 B.C.

The Hebrews do not appear to have devoted much attention to astronomy, perhaps because *astrology,* highly esteemed among the neighboring nations (Isa. 47:9, 12-13; Jer. 27:9; Dan. 2), was interdicted by the law (Deut. 18:10-11). And yet we find as early as the book of Job that the constellations were distinguished and designated by peculiar and appropriate names (Job 9:9; 38:31; also Isa. 13:10; Amos 5:8).

BIBLIOGRAPHY: R. deVaux, *Ancient Israel: Its Life and Institutions* (1961), pp. 178-94; A. Duveen and L. Motz, *Essentials of Astronomy* (1966).

ASYLUM (Heb. *miqlāṭ*). A place of safety where even a criminal might be free from violence from the avenger.

Ancient. From Ex. 21:14; 1 Kings 1:50, we see that the Hebrews, in common with many other nations, held that the altar, as God's abode, afforded protection to those whose lives were in danger. By the law, however, the place of expiation for sins of weakness (Lev. 4:2; 5:15-18; Num. 15:27-31) was prevented from being abused by being made a place of refuge for criminals deserving of death. The Mosaic law also provided *cities of refuge* (which see). Among the Greeks and Romans, the right of asylum pertained to altars, temples, and all holy shrines. These sanctuaries were exceptionally numerous in Asia. During the time of the Roman Empire the statues of the emperors were used as refuges against momentary acts of violence. Armies in the field used the eagles of the legions for the same purpose.

Christian. In the Christian church the right of asylum was retained and extended from the altar to all ecclesiastical buildings. By act of Theodosius II (A.D. 431), not only the church was to be considered sacred but also the *atrium,* the garden, bath, and cells. Many abuses crept in, until the custom has either become extinct or greatly reformed.

ASYN'CRITUS (a-sing'kri-tus; "incomparable"). The name of a Christian at Rome to whom Paul sends salutation (Rom. 16:14), A.D. 60.

A'TAD (Heb. *'āṭād,* "a thorn"). It is uncertain whether Atad is the name of a person or a descriptive appellation given to a "thorny" locality. At the threshing floor of Atad, the sons of Jacob and the Egyptians who accompanied them "lamented there with a very great and sorrowful lamentation" for Jacob seven days (Gen. 50:10-11), c. 1871 B.C.

AT'ARAH (Heb. *'aṭārâ,* a "crown"). The second wife of Jerahmeel of the tribe of Judah, and mother of Onam (1 Chron. 2:26).

ATAR'GATIS (a-tar'ga-tis). A Syrian divinity. *See* Gods, False.   M.F.U.

AT'AROTH (Heb. *'aṭārôt,* "crowns").

1. A city near Gilead, E of Jordan, in a fertile grazing district (Num. 32:3). Rebuilt by the Gadites (v. 34).

2. A city on the border of Ephraim and Benjamin, called Ataroth-addar (Josh. 18:13).

3. "Ataroth of the house of Joab," in the tribe of Judah, a city founded by the descendants of Salma (1 Chron. 2:54, KJV; NASB and NIV render "Atroth-beth-joab").

ATER (a'ter).

1. The name of a man ninety of whose descendants returned from exile in Babylon (Ezra 2:16; Neh. 7:21; 10:17).

2. The name of a man whose sons were Levitical gatekeepers in the Temple of Zerubbabel following the Exile (Ezra 2:42; Neh. 7:45).   E.H.M.

A'THACH (a'thak). A city in Judah to which David sent a present of the spoils recovered from the Amalekites who had sacked Ziklag (1 Sam. 30:30). Its site is Khirbet Attir near Enrimmon.

ATHA'IAH (ath-a'ya; perhaps the same as Asaiah). A son of Uzziah, of the tribe of Judah, who dwelt in Jerusalem after the return from Babylon (Neh. 11:4), 445 B.C.

ATHALI'AH (a-tha-lī'ah).

1. The daughter of Ahab, king of Israel, doubtless by his wife Jezebel. She is called (2 Chron. 22:2) the granddaughter of Omri, who was father of Ahab. She was married to Jehoram, king of Judah, who "walked in the way of the kings of Israel, just as the house of Ahab did," no doubt owing to her influence (2 Chron. 21:6). After the death of Jehoram, Ahaziah came to the throne, and he also walked in the way of Ahab's house, following the wicked counsel of his mother (22:2-3).

Ahaziah reigned one year and was slain by Jehu, whereupon Athaliah resolved to seat herself upon the throne of David. She caused all the male members of the royal family to be put to death, only Joash, the son of Ahaziah, escaping (2 Kings

11:1-2), 841 B.C. Athaliah usurped the throne for six years, 841-835 B.C. Joash, in the meantime, had been concealed in the Temple by his aunt, Jehosheba the wife of Jehoiada the high priest. In the seventh year, Jehoiada resolved to produce the young prince, and, arrangements having been made for defense in case of necessity, Joash was declared king. Athaliah, who was probably worshiping in the house of Baal, was aroused by the shouts of the people and went to the Temple, where her cry of "treason" only secured her own arrest. She was taken beyond the sacred precincts of the Temple and put to death. The only other recorded victim of this revolution was Mattan, the priest of Baal (11:16-18; 2 Chron. 23:14-17).

2. One of the sons of Jeroham, and head of the tribe of Benjamin, who dwelt at Jerusalem (1 Chron. 8:26).

3. The father of Jeshaiah, who was one of the "sons" of Elam that returned with seventy dependents from Babylon under Ezra (Ezra 8:7), about 457 B.C.

BIBLIOGRAPHY: T. Kirk and G. Rawlinson, *Studies in the Books of Kings,* 2 vols. in 1 (1983), 2:101ff.

ATHARIM (a'tha-rim). A place whose precise location is unknown, but somewhere between Mt. Hor and Arad (Num. 21:1).   E.H.M.

ATHEISM (Gk. *atheos,* "without God"). The denial of the existence of God. The term has always been applied according to the popular conception of God. Thus the Greeks considered a man *atheos,* "atheist," when he denied the existence of the gods recognized by the state. The pagans called Christians atheists because they would not acknowledge the heathen gods and worship them. In the theological controversies of the early church the opposite parties not infrequently called each other atheists.

The question may be fairly asked, Is true atheism or antitheism possible to the human mind? And the answer must be finally given that it is not. If we appeal to Scripture, and such an appeal should be allowed, we find that through the whole book there is no single allusion to men from whose mind the thought of God is erased. The Bible demonstrates everything about the Deity but His existence. It never descends to argue with an atheist. If it recognizes a man who is a disbeliever in God, it counts him a "fool" (Ps. 53:1). "In Eph. 2:12 the expression, *atheoi en tō kosmō,* 'without God in the world,' the word *atheoi,* 'godless,' may be taken either with the active, neuter, or passive reference, i.e., either denying, ignorant of, or *forsaken* by God. The last meaning seems best to suit the passive tenor of the passage and to enhance the dreariness and gloom of the picture" (Ellicott, *Com.,* ad loc.).

Atheism proper has mostly sprung from moral causes, and denotes a system of thought that the healthiest instinct of mankind has always abhorred. Even among the heathen the denial of the existence of the gods was proscribed and punished.

ATH'ENS (ath'enz). A city named after the patron goddess Athena, and the capital of the important Greek state of Attica, which became the cultural center of the ancient pre-Christian world. It grew up around the 512-foot-high Acropolis and was connected with its seaport Piraeus by long walls in the days of its glory. Tradition carries the fortunes of the city back beyond the time of the Trojan War in the thirteenth century B.C.

Greek figures used as columns in this temple in Athens

After a great victory over the Persians at Marathon in 490 B.C. and at Salamis in 480 B.C., the Athenians were able to establish a small empire, with Athens as its capital and a substantial fleet as its protector. In the age of Pericles, an enlightened leader, art, literature, drama, and architecture flourished. But before the death of this great leader the Peloponnesian War broke out (431 B.C.), eventuating in the surrender of Athens to Sparta in 404 B.C. Thereafter the city passed through many vicissitudes politically, but the culture and intellectual preeminence of its inhabitants gave them prestige despite varying political fortunes. Four great systems of philosophy flourished there—Platonic, Peripatetic, Epicurean, and Stoic—attracting students from all over the ancient world.

The city was captured by the Romans in 146 B.C. and was under Roman rule when Paul came as a visitor (Acts 17:15). The remark of the sacred historian concerning the inquisitive nature of the Athenians (17:21) is attested by the voice of antiquity. For instance, Demosthenes rebuked his countrymen for their love of constantly going about in the marketplace, asking one another, "What news?" The apostle Paul's remark upon the "religious" character of the Athenians (17:22) is likewise confirmed by the ancient writers. Thus Pausanias and Philostratus, second-century A.D. writers, record altars dedicated to "the unknown god" as existing along the four-mile road from the port Piraeus to the city and elsewhere in the city itself (cf. v. 23). Pausanias, moreover, says the Athenians surpassed all other states in the attention that they paid to the worship of gods. Hence the city was crowded in every direction with temples, altars, and other sacred buildings. Among pagan temples still standing in the city are the Hephaistion, overlooking the marketplace (*agora;* which see), the temple of Zeus, and overtopping all, the architectural splendors of the *Acropolis* (which see)—the temple of the Wingless Victory, the Erechtheum, and the superb Parthenon. The American School of Classical Studies has excavated the agora and outlined the streets and buildings with which Pericles, Phidias, Plato, and Paul were familiar.

The Acropolis, Athens

Mars' Hill or the Areopagus was at the W approach to the Acropolis. Here Paul preached the gospel of redemption through Christ to the devotees of three current philosophies—Platonism, Stoicism, and Epicureanism. The apostle argued against polytheism and offered salvation in the name of the one God manifested in Christ. Dionysius, an Areopagite, and a few others were converted (17:34), but Paul did not succeed in establishing a church at Athens, as at Corinth, Thessalonica, Philippi, Colossae, and Ephesus.

It was in Athens that Paul manifested evidence of his Hellenistic culture by familiarly quoting a verse taken from an invocation to Zeus, written by a minor Cilician poet, Aratus (312-245 B.C.). Doubtless while in the city the great missionary saw the music hall or Odeion of Pericles (cf. 1 Cor. 13:1) and the great Tower and Waterclock of Andronicus (cf. 5:16). Likewise he may have visited the *keramikos,* or pottery-making section of the city, which was famous (cf. Rom. 9:21).

Archaeological work in Athens has been extensive. The American School of Classical Studies excavated the agora from 1931 to 1940, from 1946 to 1960, and in the late 1960s. A few hundred feet E of the Greek agora lay the Roman market, built by Julius and Augustus Caesar. Here the Greek Archaeological Society worked intermittently from 1890 until 1931. Greek archaeologists also dug the whole Acropolis area down to bedrock in 1884-91, and the American School of Classical Studies excavated the N slope of the Acropolis in 1931-39. The Greek Archaeological Society worked at the Temple of Zeus in 1886-1901, and the German School conducted a new excavation there in 1922-23.   H.F.V.

BIBLIOGRAPHY: I. T. Hill, *Ancient City of Athens* (1953); O. Broneer, *Biblical Archaeologist* 21, no. 1 (1958): 1-28; R. E. Wycherley, *The Stones of Athens* (1978).

ATHLAI (ath'lī). A son of Bebai who put away his Gentile wife after the return from Babylon (Ezra 10:28).   E.H.M.

ATONEMENT (Heb. *kaphar,* to "cover, cancel"; Gk. *katallagē,* "exchange, reconciliation").

Definition. In accordance with the force of these terms of Scripture the atonement is the covering over of sin, the reconciliation between God and man, accomplished by the Lord Jesus Christ. It is that special result of Christ's sacrificial sufferings and death by virtue of which all who exercise proper penitence and faith receive forgiveness of their sins and obtain peace.

Scripture Doctrine—Terms and Methods. In addition to the terms named above there are other words used in the Scriptures that express the idea of atonement or throw special light upon its meaning. Of these may be here cited (1) *hilaskomai,* translated (Heb. 2:17; Rom. 3:25; 1 John 2:2; 4:10) to "make propitiation"; (2) *lutron,* translated "ransom," "redemption" (Matt. 20:28; Mark 10:45; Luke 2:38; Heb. 9:12). By such words and in such passages as these the doctrine is taught that Christ died to effect reconciliation between God and man, to propitiate the divine favor on behalf of sinful men, and to redeem or ransom men from the penalties and the dominion of their sins.

There are also forms of expression in which the idea of substitution, that Christ stands as our substitute in the economy of divine grace, appear with marked emphasis (Rom. 5:6-8; 1 Cor. 15:3; 2 Cor. 5:21; Gal. 3:13; Titus 2:14; 1 Pet. 2:24; 3:18).

The divinely appointed sacrifices of the OT dispensation are also full of significance, embracing as they did special offerings or sacrifices for sin. The uniform teaching of the NT is that these were typical of the sacrifice that Christ made of Himself for the sins of the world.

Summary. Although the Scriptures do not give a philosophical theory or explanation of the atonement, nor perhaps furnish us with data altogether sufficient for such a theory, they still give much information. (1) The Scriptures reveal the atonement to us as an accomplished and completed fact (Heb. 9:13-26). (2) They represent this fact as necessary to human salvation (Luke 24:41-47; Acts 4:12). (3) Although the whole earthly life of Christ contained an atoning and even sacrificial element, the virtue of the atonement is to be found chiefly in His sacrificial death, thus His death was indispensable (John 3:14-15). (4) In the atoning death of Christ was exhibited not only the holy wrath of God against sin but quite as much the love of God toward sinful men (Rom. 3:25-26; 5:6-8; John 3:16). (5) The gracious divine purpose realized in the atonement was wrought into the creation of man. Redemption was in the thought and plan of the Creator so that man, falling, fell into the arms of divine mercy. The Lamb of God was in the fore-knowledge of God slain from the foundation of the world (Rev. 13:8; 1 Pet. 1:19-20). (6) The atonement is not limited but universal in the extent of its gracious provisions (Heb. 2:9; 1 Tim. 2:5-6; 4:10; Rom. 5:18; 2 Cor. 5:14-15). (7) The universality of the atonement does not lead to universal salvation. The greater offer of salvation may be, and often is, rejected, and when the rejection is final the atonement avails nothing for the sinner (Mark 16:16; John 3:36; Heb. 10:26-29). (8) The atonement is the actual objective ground of forgiveness of sins and acceptance with God for all penitent believers (John 3:16; Acts 2:38; Eph. 1:7; Col. 1:14).

Theological Treatment. This branch of the subject calls for two classes of statements: (1) as to the history of the doctrine; (2) as to the theological views most generally held at the present time.

History. During the early centuries of the history of the church, and particularly prior to the Nicene Council (A.D. 325), Christian theology simply reflected, in the main, the teaching of the NT upon this subject. The attention of theologians was concentrated upon the Person of Christ. There was but little speculation as to the method of the atonement or the exact ground of its necessity. That the sacrifice of Christ was vicarious, that He suffered in the stead of men, was, however, an idea constantly held; that these sufferings were necessary to meet the require-

ment of divine righteousness was sometimes declared with emphasis. A fanciful notion, it is true, began to appear at that early period, a notion that afterward obtained some measure of prominence. Christ was regarded as a ransom paid to the devil to redeem men who by their sin had come under the dominion of the devil. This was taught by Origen (A.D. 230) and more emphatically by Gregory of Nyssa (A.D. 370). This view has also, but incorrectly, been attributed to Irenaeus (A.D. 180). Captious critics and infidels have often cited this incident in the history of theology in order to bring all theology into ridicule and contempt. But it is to be remembered that this phase of doctrine was always met with the strongest denial and opposition, as by Athanasius (A.D. 370) and Gregory of Nazianzum (A.D. 390). It was never the accepted doctrine of the Christian church.

Anselm. Prominent in the history of the doctrine of the atonement must stand the name of Anselm, A.D. 1100. In his book *Cur Deus Homo* he brings out most clearly and emphatically the idea of the atonement as satisfaction to divine majesty. He viewed the necessity of atonement as entirely in the justice of God. He made this term "satisfaction," it has been said, "a watchword for all future time." It is certain that what is known as the *satisfaction* theory of the atonement will ever stand associated with his name, although his satisfaction theory is not quite the same as that of the Reformers.

Abelard. Chief among the opponents of Anselm was Abelard, A.D. 1141. He referred the atonement wholly to the love of God and taught that there could be nothing in the divine essence that required satisfaction for sin. The death of Christ upon the cross was solely an exhibition of divine love. The effect is moral only. It is intended to subdue the hearts of sinful men, to lead them to repentance and devotion to Christ. Thus Abelard stands as the father of what is known as the *moral influence* theory.

Grotius. An epoch in the history of the doctrine was reached when Grotius, A.D. 1617, wrote his *Defensio fidei Cathol. de Satisfactione*. He wrote in refutation of the teaching of Socinus, who denied the vicarious character of Christ's death and the need of any reconciliation of God with man. Grotius held fast to the vicariousness of Christ's sufferings and used the term *satisfaction*. But in his view it was a satisfaction to the requirements of moral government and not to the justice that inheres in God Himself. The necessity of the atonement, accordingly, he found not in the nature of God but in the nature of the divine government. The purpose of the atonement is to make it possible to exercise mercy toward fallen and sinful men, and at the same time maintain the dignity of the law, the honor of the Lawgiver, and protect the moral interests of the universe. Grotius thus founded what is known as the *rectoral* or *governmental* theory.

The doctrines of Anselm, Abelard, and Grotius represent the principal tendencies of thought and discussion throughout the whole history of the doctrine. Under the treatment of various theologians these doctrines received modification more or less important, but in their leading principles these three forms of teaching have been the most prominent in the theology of the Christian church.

Modern Views. Aside from the opinion of rationalists and semirationalists, who wholly or in part reject the authority of Scripture and accordingly attach but slight if any importance to Scripture teaching concerning the atonement, the three theories prominent in the past are still the prominent theories of the present. With various shadings and modifications and attempts at interblending, they embody in the main the thinking of modern times upon this subject.

It should be said, however, that the moral influence theory has never obtained formal or general acceptance in any evangelical communion. It has justly been regarded as falling far short of adequately representing the teaching of Scripture. It contains some measure of truth but leaves out the truth most essential: that of real, objective atonement. It reduces the atonement to an object lesson.

The thought of the Christian church of today is divided in its adherence between the satisfaction and governmental theories, these theories appearing in various forms. But no one of these views is free from grave logical objections if held too rigidly and exclusively. Thus the satisfaction theory, if held in the sense that Christ actually bore the punishment for the sins of men, or that He literally, according to the figure of Anselm, paid the debt of human transgressors after the manner of a commercial transaction, must lead logically to one or the other of two extremes—either that of a limited atonement or that of universalism. It tends also to antinomianism, to say nothing of other objections often raised. The governmental theory, held alone and too boldly, loses sight of the fact that the divine government must be a reflection of the divine nature and that what is required by that government must be required also by some quality inherent in God. Further, this theory, if not guarded strongly, and by bringing in, in some form, the idea of satisfaction to divine justice, reduces the death of Christ to a great moral spectacle. It becomes, in fact, another moral influence theory.

A strong tendency, accordingly, of the present day is to seek some way of mediating between or of uniting the elements of truth found in these various theories. It is certain that the Scriptures do represent the death of Christ as a most affecting manifestation of the love of God. It is certain also that His death is represented as sacrificial and required by the justice of God. And it is equally true that it is often viewed in its relations to divine law and the moral economy that God has established. And if the earnest attempts of devout thinkers do not succeed wholly in penetrating the mystery of the cross and in bringing the exact meaning of Christ's death within the compass of their definitions, still it is held as beyond all question that the atonement wrought by Christ is a fundamental fact in human salvation, a real "covering" for sin, the divinely appointed measure for "reconciliation" between God and man.

Extent of Atonement. The extent of atonement is much less discussed than formerly. Many Calvinists have departed from the view they once strenuously held, that the atonement was for the elect only.

BIBLIOGRAPHY: G. Aulen, *Christus Victor* (1935); L. S. Chafer, *Systematic Theology* (1950), 3:135-64; 7:25-27; L. L. Morris, *The Apostolic Preaching of the Cross* (1955); K. Barth, *Church Dogmatics* (1961), 4:1-3; H. P. Liddon, *Divinity of Our Lord and Saviour Jesus Christ* (1978), pp. 480ff.; J. Denney, *The Death of Christ* (1982).

ATONEMENT, DAY OF. *See* Festivals.

AT'ROTH (Num. 32:35). *See* Atroph-shophan.

ATROTH BETH JOAB. *See* Ataroth.

A'TROPH-SHO'PHAN (a'trōth-shō'fan). A town in Gad, listed between Aroer and Jazer (Num. 32:35).

AT'TAI (a'tā-ī).

1. The son of a daughter of Sheshan, of the tribe of Judah, by his Egyptian servant, Jarha. He was the father of Nathan (1 Chron. 2:35-36).

2. One of David's mighty men, of the tribe of Gad, who joined David at Ziklag, where he had fled from Saul (1 Chron. 12:11).

3. The second of the four sons of King Rehoboam, by his second wife, Maacah, the daughter of Absalom (2 Chron. 11:20).

ATTALI'A (at-a-lī'a). A seaport on the coast of Pamphylia, at the mouth of the river Cattarrhactes. The town was named after its founder, Attalus Philadelphus, king of Pergamos, 159-138 B.C. Paul and Barnabas stopped there on the way to Antioch (Acts 14:25). Its name in the twelfth century appears to have been Satalia; it still exists, under the name of Adalia.

ATTIRE. *See* Dress.

ATTITUDE. *See* Prayer; Salutation.

AUGUSTUS (aw-gus'tus). The imperial title assumed by Octavius, successor of Julius Caesar. He was born 63 B.C. and was principally educated by his great-uncle, Julius Caesar, who made him his heir. After the death of Caesar, he acquired such influence that Antony and Lepidus took him into their triumvirate. Afterward he shared the empire with Antony and attained supreme power after the battle of Actium, 31 B.C., being saluted imperator by the Senate, who conferred on him the title Augustus in 27 B.C. He forgave Herod, who had espoused the cause of Antony, and even increased his power. After the death of Herod, 4 B.C., his dominions were divided among his sons by Augustus, almost in exact accordance with his will. Augustus was emperor at the birth and during half the lifetime of our Lord, and his name occurs (Luke 2:1) in the NT as the emperor who ordered the enrollment in consequence of which Joseph and Mary went to Bethlehem, the place where the Messiah was to be born.

Augustus brought order and prosperity to the Roman Empire after the long period of civil war, and for his successes he was worshiped in many places. With him began the emperor cult, and Herod the Great built temples to the divine Augustus at Caesarea and Samaria; both of these have been excavated. Augustus was worshiped in Ephesus too, and a great lintel with an inscription to the divine Augustus has been excavated there and reerected over the gate to the Greek agora. Paul would have seen it and passed under it often as he ministered in the city for most of three years on his third missionary journey. *See also* Acts 25:21, 25; 27:1.   H.F.V.

BIBLIOGRAPHY: J. Buchan, *Augustus* (1937); M. Grant, *The Twelve Caesars* (1975).

AUNT (Heb. *dôdâ,* "loving"). A father's sister (Ex. 6:20); also an uncle's wife (Lev. 18:14; 20:20).

AUTHORITY. The power or right to perform certain acts without impediment. It is based upon some form of law, whether divine, civil, or moral. Supreme authority is God's alone (Rom. 13:1), hence all human authority is derived.

There is no specific Heb. word for authority, but *rebôt* (Prov. 29:2) and *tōqep* (Esther 9:29) are rendered in this way by some versions. The Gk. word *exousia* furnishes the NT basis of authority, along with such words as *dunamis* ("power"), *epitage* ("command"), *dunastes* (Acts 8:27), and *authenteo* (1 Tim. 2:12).

God's authority is unconditional and absolute (Ps. 29:10; Isa. 40), making Him supreme over nature and human history alike. From this intrinsic authority comes that of governments (Rom. 13:1-7), employers (Eph. 6:5-9), parents (Eph. 6:1-4), church elders (Heb. 13:7, 17), and others in positions of power. Similarly the angels function under divine authority (Luke 1:19-20), and evil spirits are also subject to God's power (Eph. 6:11-12).

Because Jesus was God, His authority was not merely derived from the Father but was also intrinsic. His power knew no limitations (Matt. 28:18) and was the ground of His commissions to His disciples (Mark 6:7; John 20:22). A preeminent source of derived authority is the Scriptures, inspired by God Himself (2 Tim. 3:16; 2 Pet. 1:20-21) and therefore by His supreme au-

thority. For this reason believers are required to obey them.

The general purpose of authority is to promote order in human society, and its highest use is an altruistic one, as Christ stated (Luke 22:26-27). Christians are given the authority to become children of God (John 1:12) and have the right to pursue certain forms of behavior (1 Cor. 6:12). Ultimately all derived authority will revert to God, who bestowed it (1 Cor. 15:24-28).   R.K.H.

A'VA. *See* Avva; Ivvah.

AVE MARIA (a'vä ma-rē'a; "Hail Mary").

1. The words of the angel Gabriel to the virgin Mary, when announcing the incarnation (Luke 1:28), as rendered by the Vulg.

2. The familiar prayer, or form of devotion, in the Roman Catholic church, called also the "Angelical Salutation." It consists of three parts: (1) the salutation of Gabriel, *Ave* (Maria) *gratia plena Dominus tecum; benedicta tu in mulieribus;* (2) the words of Elizabeth to Mary, *et benedictus fructus ventris tui;* (3) an addition made by the church, *Sancta Maria, Mater Dei, ora pro nobis peccatoribus nunc et in hora mortis nostrae.* The whole Ave Maria, as it now stands, is ordered in the breviary of Pius V (1568) to be used daily before each canonical hour and after compline; i.e., the last of the seven canonical hours (*Cath. Dict.,* s. v.).

A'VEN (a'ven; "nothingness, vanity," an "idol").

1. The popular name of Heliopolis, in Lower Egypt, probably selected intentionally in the sense of an idol city (Ezek. 30:17, marg.) because On-Heliopolis was from time immemorial one of the principal seats of the Egyptian worship of the sun and possessed a celebrated temple of the sun and a numerous and learned priesthood.

2. The "high places of Aven" are the buildings connected with the image worship at Bethel, which were to be utterly ruined (Hos. 10:8).

3. Mentioned as "the valley of Aven" (Amos 1:5) and thought by some to be the same as the plain of *Baalbek* (which see), an early center of Baal worship. Others, however, connect the place with Awaniyek near Jerud on the road to Palmyra.

AVENGE, AVENGER. These words are often used in the sense of to avenge a wrong, or the one who brings punishment (*see* Blood, Avenger of). This is the meaning in Num. 35:19-27; 2 Sam. 14:11; Ps. 79:10; Jer. 15:15. The civil magistrate is called by Paul "a minister of God, an avenger who brings wrath upon the one who practices evil" (Rom. 13:4); while in 2 Cor. 7:11 the apostle recognizes as a prominent virtue of the church in Corinth its zeal in avenging wrong, i.e., *disciplinary zeal* against the incestuous person. He writes the church (2 Cor. 10:6) that he is "ready to punish all disobedience, when your obedience is complete." *How* he intends to execute this vengeance he does not tell; he might do it by excommunication, by giving the intruders over to the power of Satan (1 Cor. 5:5), or by the exercise of his miraculous apostolic power. Revenge, or vengeance, is attributed to God in two remarkable passages (Deut. 32:41-43; Nah. 1:2), in which Jehovah is represented as bringing certain punishment upon the wicked. The ordinary understanding of *revenge* is quite different from the above, and implies a vindictive feeling against the offender. It differs from *resentment,* which rises up in the mind immediately upon being injured; for revenge may wait years after the offense is committed. In this vindictive sense we have scriptural instances (Jer. 20:10; Ezek. 25:15). This sort of revenge is forbidden by the command to love our enemies and to return good for evil.

AVENGER OF BLOOD. *See* Blood, Avenger of.

A'VIM. *See* Avvim.

A'VITH (a'vith). A city of the Edomites, capital of King Hadad before there were kings in Israel (Gen. 36:35; 1 Chron. 1:46).

AV'VA (av'va, 2 Kings 17:24; "Ava," KJV), or Iv'vah (Iv'vah, 2 Kings 18:34; 19:13; "Ivah," KJV). Identified with Tell Kafr 'Ayah on the Orontes SW of Homs.

AV'VIM (av'vim), or **Av'vites.**
1. A people among the early inhabitants of Palestine, whom we meet in the SW corner of the seacoast where they may have made their way northward from the desert. The only notice of them that has come down to us is contained in a remarkable fragment of primeval history preserved in Deut. 2:23. Here we see them dwelling in the villages in the S part of the Shefelah, or great western lowland, "as far as Gaza." In these rich possessions they were attacked by the invading Philistines, "the Caphtorim which came forth from Caphtor," and who "destroyed them and lived in their place" and then appear to have pushed them farther N. Possibly a trace of their existence is to be found in the town "Avvim" that occurs among the cities of Benjamin (Josh. 18:23). It is a curious fact that both the LXX and Jerome identified the Avvim with the Hivites, and also that the town of ha-Avvim was in the actual district of the Hivites (9:7, 17; cf. 18:22-27).
2. The people of Avva, among the colonists who were sent by the king of Assyria to reinhabit the depopulated cities of Israel (2 Kings 17:31). They were idolaters, worshiping gods called Nibhaz and Tartak. *See* Avva.

AVVITES. *See* Avvim.

AWL (Heb. *marṣēa',* from a verb signifying "to bore"). A boring instrument, probably of the simplest kind, and similar to those in familiar use at the present time. It occurs twice in the Scriptures (Ex. 21:6; Deut. 15:17).

AXE, AX. The rendering of several original words:
1. Heb. *garzen* ("cut"). This appears to have consisted of a head of iron (Isa. 10:34), fastened with thongs or otherwise, upon a handle of wood, and so liable to slip off (Deut. 19:5; 2 Kings 6:5). It was used for felling trees (Deut. 20:19) and for shaping timber, perhaps like the modern adze.
2. Heb. *ḥereb,* usually rendered "sword," is used of other cutting instruments; once rendered "axes" (Ezek. 26:9); probably a pickaxe as it says "with his axes he will break down your towers."
3. Heb. *kashshîl* occurs only in Ps. 74:6 and appears to have been a later word denoting a "large axe" (rendered "hammer," NASB, see marg.).
4. Heb. *magzērâ,* "iron cutting tools" (K. & D., *Com.,* on 2 Sam. 12:31).
5. Heb. *ma'aṣād,* "hewing" instrument, rendered "cutting tool" (Isa. 44:12; Jer. 10:3). Some axes were shaped like chisels fastened to a handle. This may have been the instrument named in Jeremiah; but as Isaiah (44:12) refers to the work of a blacksmith, this instrument was probably a chisel for cutting iron on the anvil.
6. Heb. *qardōm* is the most common name for axe or hatchet. This is the tool referred to in Judg. 9:48; 1 Sam. 13:20-21; Ps. 74:5; Jer. 46:22, and was used extensively for felling trees.
7. The Gk. word for axe is *axine* (Matt. 3:10; Luke 3:9).

Figurative. The axe is used in Scripture as a symbol of divine judgment. John the Baptist, referring probably to the excision of the Jewish people, says, "And the axe is already laid at the root of the trees" (Matt. 3:10). This denotes that it had already been stuck into the tree prior to felling it. The axe was also used as a symbol of human instrument, e.g., "Is the axe to boast itself over the one who chops with it?" (Isa. 10:15), i.e., Shall the king of Assyria boast himself against God?

AXE HEAD (Heb. *barzel*). In 2 Kings 6:5 the term is literally "iron," but as an axe is certainly intended, the passage shows that the axe heads among the Hebrews were of iron. Those found in Egypt are of bronze, such as was anciently used, but they have made them also of iron, the latter having been consumed through corrosion. The Iron Age began in 1200 B.C.

AXLE. The term occurs only in 1 Kings 7:32-33, as the translation of *yād,* "hand," the whole phrase being the "hands of the wheels."

A'YIN (a'yin; in the KJV A'in, Heb. *'ayin,* an "eye", a "spring").
1. The sixteenth letter of the Heb. alphabet (ע). It heads the sixteenth section of Ps. 119, in which

passage (vv. 121-28) each verse begins with this letter in the original.

2. A place near Riblah in northern Palestine (Num. 34:11).

3. A place near Rimmon (Josh. 15:32).

AYYAH (ay'yah). A city with its suburbs that lay within the territory of the tribe of Ephraim (1 Chron. 7:28).   E.H.M.

A'ZAL. *See* A'zel.

AZALI'AH (az-a-lī'a; "reserved by Jehovah"). The son of Meshullam and father of Shaphan the scribe. The latter was sent with others by Josiah to repair the Temple (2 Kings 22:3; 2 Chron. 34:8), about 624 B.C.

AZANI'AH (az-a-nī'a; "whom Jehovah hears"). The father of Jeshua, who was one of the Levites that subscribed the sacred covenant after the Exile (Neh. 10:9), 445 B.C.

AZA'REL (a-za'rel; "God has helped"; KJV Azareel).

1. One of the Korhites who joined David at Ziklag (1 Chron. 12:6), before 1000 B.C.

2. The head of the eleventh division of the musicians of the Temple (1 Chron. 25:18), about 1000 B.C. Called Uzziel in v. 4.

3. The son of Jeroham, and prince of the tribe of Dan when David numbered the people (1 Chron. 27:22).

4. An Israelite, descendant of Bani, who renounced his Gentile wife after the return from Babylon (Ezra 10:41).

5. The son of Ahzai and father of Amashsai, who was one of the chiefs of 128 mighty men who served at the Temple under the supervision of Zabdiel on the restoration from Babylon (Neh. 11:13-14). He is probably the same as one of the first company of priests who were appointed with Ezra to make the circuit of the newly completed walls with trumpets in their hands (Neh. 12:36).

AZARI'AH (az-a-rī'a; "helped by Jehovah"). A common name in Heb., and especially in the families of the priests of the line of Eleazar, whose name has precisely the same meaning as Azariah. It is nearly identical and is often confused with Ezra, as well as with Zeraiah and Seraiah.

1. A son or descendant of Zadok, the high priest in the time of David, and one of Solomon's princes (1 Kings 4:2), 960 B.C. He is probably the same as no. 6 below.

2. A son of Nathan, and captain of King Solomon's guards or "deputies" (1 Kings 4:5).

3. Son and successor of Amaziah, king of Judah (2 Kings 14:21; 15:1-7; 1 Chron. 3:12), more frequently called *Uzziah* (which see).

4. Son of Ethan and great-grandson of Judah (1 Chron. 2:8).

5. The son of Jehu and father of Helez, of the tribe of Judah (1 Chron. 2:38-39).

6. A high priest, son of Ahimaaz and grandson of Zadok (1 Chron. 6:9), whom he seems to have immediately succeeded (1 Kings 4:2). He is probably the same as no. 1 above.

7. The son of Johanan and father of Amariah, a high priest (1 Chron. 6:10-11). He was probably high priest in the reigns of Abijah and Asa, as his son Amariah was in the days of Jehoshaphat.

8. The son of Hilkiah and father of Seraiah. The last high priest before the captivity (1 Chron. 6:13-14; 9:11; Ezra 7:1).

9. A Levite, son of Zephaniah and father of Joel (1 Chron. 6:36). In v. 24 he is called Uzziah. It appears from 2 Chron. 29:12 that his son Joel lived under Hezekiah and was engaged in the cleansing of the Temple.

10. The prophet who met King Asa on his return from a victory over Zerah the Ethiopian (2 Chron. 15:1, where he is called the son of Obed). He exhorted Asa to put away idolatry and restore the altar of God before the porch of the Temple. A national reformation followed, participated in by representatives out of all Israel.

11. Two sons of King Jehoshaphat (2 Chron. 21:2), 875 B.C. M'Clintock and Strong (s. v.) conjecture that there is a repetition of name and that there was but one son of that name. The NIV reads the second of these as Azariahu.

12. A clerical error (2 Chron. 22:6, see marg.), for *Ahaziah* (which see), king of Judah.

13. A son of Jeroham, one of the "captains" who assisted Jehoiada in restoring the worship of the Temple, opposing Athaliah and placing Joash on the throne (2 Chron. 23:1).

14. The son of Obed, another of the "captains" who assisted in the same enterprise (2 Chron. 23:1).

15. High priest in the reign of Uzziah. When the king, elated by his success, "entered the temple of the Lord to burn incense," Azariah went in after him, accompanied by eighty of his brethren, and withstood him (2 Chron. 26:16-20).

16. Son of Johanan, and one of the heads of the tribe of Ephraim. One of those who protested against enslaving their captive brethren taken in the invasion of Judah by Pekah (2 Chron. 28:12-13).

17. A Merarite, son of Jehallelel, who was one of those who cleansed the Temple in the time of Hezekiah (2 Chron. 29:12).

18. A high priest in the time of Hezekiah (2 Chron. 31:10, 13), 719 B.C. He appears to have cooperated zealously with the king in that thorough purification of the Temple and restoration of the Temple services that were such conspicuous features of his reign.

19. The father of Amariah, and an ancestor of Ezra (Ezra 7:3).

20. Son of Maaseiah, who repaired part of the wall of Jerusalem (Neh. 3:23-24). He was one of the Levites who assisted Ezra in explaining the law (8:7), sealed the covenant with Nehemiah

(10:2), and assisted at the dedication of the city wall (12:33).

21. One of the nobles who returned from Babylon with Zerubbabel (Neh. 7:7). Called Seraiah in Ezra 2:2.

22. One of the "arrogant men" who rebuked Jeremiah for advising the people that remained in Palestine after their brethren had been taken to Babylon not to go down into Egypt, and who took the prophet himself and Baruch with them to that country (Jer. 43:2-7).

23. The Heb. name of *Abed-nego* (which see), one of Daniel's three friends who were cast into the fiery furnace (Dan. 1:7).

A'ZAZ (a'zaz; "strong"). A Reubenite, the son of Shema and father of Bela (1 Chron. 5:8).

AZA'ZEL (azā'zel; Heb. *'ăzā'zēl*, likely for *'ăzāl-zēl*, i.e., "an entire removal"; Arab. *'azala,* "remove"). The Heb. term is translated (Lev. 16:8, 10, 26) "scapegoat." It is a word of doubtful interpretation and has been variously understood.

1. By some it is thought to be the name of the goat sent into the desert. The objection to this is that in vv. 10, 26 the Azazel clearly seems to be that *for* or *to* which the goat is let loose.

2. Others have taken Azazel for the name of the place to which the goat was sent. Some of the Jewish writers consider that it denotes the height from which the goat was thrown; whereas others regard the word as meaning "desert places."

3. Many believe Azazel to be a personal being, either a spirit, a demon, or Satan himself. The Cabalists teach that in order to satisfy this evil being and to save Israel from his snares, God sends him the goat burdened with all the "iniquities and transgressions" of His people once a year. But we think it entirely improbable that Moses under divine guidance would cause Israel to recognize a demon whose claims on the people were to be met by the bribe of a sin-laden goat.

4. The most probable rendering of Azazel is "complete sending away," i.e., solitude. The rendering then of the passage would be "the one for Jehovah, and the other for an utter removal." *See* Atonement, Day of; Scapegoat.

AZAZI'AH (a-za-zī'a; "strengthened by Jehovah").

1. One of the Levites who were appointed to play the lyre in the service of the Tabernacle at the time when the Ark was brought up from Obed-edom (1 Chron. 15:21), about 991 B.C.

2. The father of Hoshea, who was prince of the tribe of Ephraim when David numbered the people (1 Chron. 27:20), after 1000 B.C.

3. One of those who had charge of the Temple offerings in the time of Hezekiah (2 Chron. 31:13), 726 B.C.

AZ'BUK (az'būk). The father of Nehemiah, who was ruler of half of the district of Beth-zur, and

who repaired part of the wall after the return from Babylon (Neh. 3:16), before 445 B.C.

AZE'KAH (a-zē'ka; "tilled"). A town in the plain of Judah (Josh. 15:35; 1 Sam. 17:1), with suburban villages (Neh. 11:30), and a place of considerable strength (Jer. 34:7). The confederated Amorite kings were defeated here by Joshua, and their army destroyed by an extraordinary shower of hailstones (Josh. 10:10-11). Joshua's pursuit of the Canaanites after the battle of Beth-horon extended to Azekah; between it and Socoh the Philistines encamped before the battle between David and Goliath (1 Sam. 17:1). It was fortified by Rehoboam (2 Chron. 11:9), was still standing at the time of the invasion of the kings of Babylon (Jer. 34:7), and was one of the places reoccupied by the Jews on their return from captivity (Neh. 11:30).

A'ZEL (a'zel).

1. The son of Eleasah, of the descendants of King Saul (1 Chron. 8:37-38; 9:43).

2. A place, evidently in the neighborhood of Jerusalem and probably E of the Mount of Olives (Zech. 14:5). Its site has not been identified, but the LXX rendering "Iasol" suggests Wadi Yasūl, a tributary of the Kidron.

A'ZEM. *See* Ezem.

AZ'GAD (az'gad; "strong in fortune"). An Israelite whose descendants, to the number of 1,222 (2,322 according to Neh. 7:17), returned from Babylon with Zerubbabel (Ezra 2:12). A second detachment of 110, with Johanan at their head, accompanied Ezra (Ezra 8:12). Probably the Azgad of Neh. 10:15 is the same person, some of whose descendants joined in the covenant with Nehemiah.

A'ZIEL (a'zī-el). A shortened form (1 Chron. 15:20) for *Jaaziel* (which see), in v. 18.

AZI'ZA (a-zi'za; "strong"). An Israelite, descendant of Zattu, who, after his return from Babylon, divorced the Gentile wife he had married (Ezra 10:27), 456 B.C.

AZMA'VETH (ăz-má'vĕth; "strong as death").

1. A Barhumite (or Baharumite), one of David's thirty warriors (2 Sam. 23:31; 1 Chron. 11:33), and father of two of his famous slingers (12:3), about 1000 B.C.

2. The second of the three sons of Jehoaddah (1 Chron. 8:36), or Jarah (9:42), a descendant of Jonathan, after 1030 B.C.

3. Son of Adiel, and in charge of the storehouses of David (1 Chron. 27:25), about 1000 B.C.

4. A village of Judah or Benjamin (Neh. 12:29), called (7:28) Beth-azmaveth. It was occupied by Jews who returned with Ezra from Babylon. The notices of it seem to point to some locality in the northern environs of Jerusalem.

AZ'MON (az'mon; "bonelike"). A place on the

southern border of Palestine, between Hazarad-dar and the "brook of Egypt" (Num. 34:4-5; Josh. 15:4).

AZ'NOTH-TABOR (az'noth-tā'bor; "tops of Tabor"). A town in the W of Naphtali, between the Jordan and Hukkok (Josh. 19:34). Perhaps Amm Jebeil near Mt. Tabor.

A'ZOR (a'zor). The son of Eliakim and father of Zadok, in the paternal ancestry of Christ (Matt. 1:13).

AZO'TUS (a-zō'tus). The Grecized form (Acts 8:40) of *Ashdod* (which see).

AZ'RIEL (az'ri-el; "help of God").
1. A mighty man of valor, and one of the heads of the half tribe of Manasseh beyond the Jordan who were taken into captivity by the king of Assyria as a punishment for their national idolatry (1 Chron. 5:24), about 740 B.C.
2. The father of Jeremoth, who was ruler of the tribe of Naphtali under David (1 Chron. 27:19), about 1000 B.C.
3. The father of Seraiah, who with others was appointed by King Jehoiakim to apprehend Baruch the scribe and Jeremiah for sending him a threatening prophecy (Jer. 36:26), 606 B.C.

AZ'RIKAM (az'ri-kam; "help" against "the enemy," or "my help arises").
1. The last named of the three sons of Neariah, a descendant of Zerubbabel (1 Chron. 3:23), about 404 B.C. He is perhaps the same as *Azor* (which see).
2. The first of the six sons of Azel, of the tribe of Benjamin (1 Chron. 8:38; 9:44).
3. A Levite, son of Hashabiah and father of

Hasshub (1 Chron. 9:14; Neh. 11:15), before 536 B.C.
4. The governor of the king's house in the time of Ahaz, slain by Zichri, a mighty man of Ephraim (2 Chron. 28:7), 741 B.C.

AZU'BAH (a-zū'ba; "forsaken").
1. The daughter of Shilhi and mother of King Jehoshaphat (1 Kings 22:42; 2 Chron. 20:31), before 875 B.C.
2. The wife of Caleb, the son of Hezron (1 Chron. 2:18-19), about 1471 B.C. *See* Jerioth.

A'ZUR. *See* Azzur.

AZ'ZAH (az'zah; the "strong"). The more correct English form (Deut. 2:23; 1 Kings 4:24; Jer. 25:20) of *Gaza* (which see). The latter is the form given in the NASB and NIV.

AZ'ZAN (az'zan). The father of Paltiel, leader of the tribe of Issachar, and commissioner from that tribe in the dividing of Canaan (Num. 34:26), c. 1370 B.C.

AZ'ZUR (az'zur; "helper"; sometimes Azur, KJV).
1. One of the chief Israelites who signed the covenant with Nehemiah on the return from Babylon (Neh. 10:17), 445 B.C.
2. The father of Hananiah of Gibeon, the latter of whom was the prophet who falsely encouraged King Zedekiah against the Babylonians (Jer. 28:1), about 596 B.C.
3. The father of Jaazaniah, who was one of the men whom the prophet Ezekiel saw in a vision devising false schemes of safety for Jerusalem (Ezek. 11:1), 594 B.C.

B

BA'AL (bā'al; Heb. *ba'al,* "lord, possessor").

1. A common name for god among the Phoenicians; also the name of their chief male god. *See* Gods, False.

2. The word is used of the master of a house (Ex. 22:7; Judg. 19:22), of a landowner (Job 31:39), of an owner of cattle (Ex. 21:28; Isa. 1:3), and so on. The word is often used as a prefix to names of towns and men, e.g., Baal-gad, Baal-hanan.

3. A Reubenite, son of Reaiah. His son Beerah was among the captives carried away by *Tiglath-pileser* (which see; 1 Chron. 5:5-6), before 740 B.C.

4. The fourth named of the sons of Jeiel, the founder of Gibeon, by his wife Maacah (1 Chron. 8:29-30; 9:35-36).

5. The name of a place (1 Chron. 4:33), elsewhere called *Baalath-beer* (which see).

BIBLIOGRAPHY: A. S. Kapelrud, *Baal and the Ras Shamra Texts* (1952); J. Gray, *The Canaanites* (1956); W. F. Albright, *Yahweh and the Gods of Canaan* (1968); G. R. Driver and J. C. L. Gibson, *Canaanite Myths and Legends* (1978).

BA'ALAH (bā'a-lā; "mistress").

1. A city on the northern border of the tribe of Judah (Josh. 15:10), one of the religious sanctuaries of the ancient Gibeonites, as it appears (15:9) that Baalah and Kiriath-jearim were applicable to the same place. See 1 Chron. 13:6.

2. A city on the S of Judah (Josh. 15:29). Called Balah (19:3); also Bilhah (1 Chron. 4:29).

3. A mountain on the NW boundary of Judah, between Shikkeron and Jabneel (Josh. 15:11), usually regarded as the same as Mt. Jearim.

BA'ALATH (bā'a-lath; "mistress"). A town of the tribe of Dan (Josh. 19:44); supposed to be the place fortified by Solomon (1 Kings 9:18; 2 Chron. 8:6).

BA'ALATH-BE'ER (bā'a-lath be'er; "mistress of

the well"). A city of Simeon (Josh. 19:8). Probably the same as Baal (1 Chron. 4:33). Doubtless identical with Ramah of the Negev (Josh. 19:8). It is also the same as the *Bealoth* (which see) of Judah (15:24).

BA'ALBEK (bā'al-bek; Gk. Heliopolis, "city of the sun," but distinct from three other sites whose names also have reference to the sun: *Beth-shemesh,* no. 4; the *City of Destruction* [Ir-hahares, KJV]; and *On* [all which see]). A popular ancient center of the worship of Baal in the region between Lebanon and Anti-Lebanon or "Hollow-Syria." Later called Heliopolis when the Greeks associated Helios with Baal. It is fifty-three miles E of Beirut and is to be distinguished from a city in Egypt, *On* (which see), that is also sometimes called Heliopolis. The site may be identical with Baal-gad "in the valley of Lebanon at the foot of Mount Hermon" (Josh. 11:17). Greek architectural skill and Rome's resources were lavished on Baalbek and its immense and beautiful temples. The temple complex was probably begun as early as the reign of Augustus (27 B.C.-A.D. 14), and construction continued there for a couple of centuries.

A worshiper entered the acropolis area through a tower-flanked propylaea 165 feet wide, passed through a hexagonal court and a great altar court, and finally ascended a magnificent stairway to the temple of Jupiter. Six of its Corinthian columns still stand to a height of 65 feet, tallest in the Greco-Roman world. Adjacent to the temple of Jupiter on the south and at a lower level is the temple of Bacchus with a peristyle of 46 columns 57 feet high. Beautifully preserved, it is the best surviving example of a Roman temple interior. East of the acropolis was a round temple, probably erected to Venus, constructed about A.D. 250. A German archaeological team began serious work at the site in 1900, and French and Lebanese efforts continued there intermittently until hostilities forced termination in 1975. The Baalbek complex is the most magnificent example of pagan worship and architecture in the Middle East.   M.F.U.; H.F.V.

Temple at Baalbek

BIBLIOGRAPHY: F. Ragette, *Baalbek* (1980).

BA'AL-BE'RITH (bā'al-be-rith'). A god worshiped in Shechem. *See* Gods, False.

BA'ALE-JU'DAH (bā'a-le jū'da; "lords of Judah"). A city of Judah from which David brought the Ark into Jerusalem (2 Sam. 6:2). Probably the same as *Baalah*, no. 1 (which see); so also NIV.

BA'AL-GAD (bā'al gad; "lord of fortune"). A Canaanite city (Josh. 11:17; 12:7) at the foot of Mt. Hermon, hence called Baal-hermon (Judg. 3:3; 1 Chron. 5:23). Location uncertain.

BA'AL-HA'MON (bā'al ha'mon; "lord of the multitude"). The place where Solomon had a vineyard (Song of Sol. 8:11), which he let out to "caretakers." Location is unknown.

BA'AL-HA'NAN (bā'al ha'non; "lord of grace").

1. An early king of Edom, son of Achbor, successor of Shaul, and succeeded by Hadar (Gen. 36:38-39; 1 Chron. 1:49-50).

2. A Gederite, David's overseer of "the olive and sycamore trees in the Shephelah" (1 Chron. 27:28), after 1000 B.C.

BA'AL-HA'ZOR (bā'al-ha'zor; "having a village"). A place near Ephraim where Absalom had a sheep farm and where he murdered Amnon (2 Sam. 13:23). Probably the same as Hazor (Neh. 11:33), now Tell 'Asar.

BA'AL-HER'MON (bā'al her'mon; "lord of Hermon").

1. A city of Ephraim near Mt. Hermon (1 Chron. 5:23). Probably identical with Baal-gad (Josh. 11:17).

2. A mountain E of Lebanon (Judg. 3:3), from which the Israelites were unable to expel the Hivites. "*Baal-hermon* is only another name for *Baal-gad,* the present *Banjas,* under the Hermon (see Josh. 13:5)" (K. & D., *Com.*).

BA'ALI (bā'a-lî; "my master"). "You will call Me Ishi / And will no longer call Me Baali" (Hos. 2:16). The meaning is that Israel will enter into right relation with God, in which she will look toward Him as her husband (Ishi) and not merely as Baal, "owner, master." Calling or naming is a designation of the nature or the true relation of a person or thing. Israel calls God her husband when she stands in the right relation to Him, when she acknowledges, reveres, and loves Him, as He has revealed Himself, i.e., as the only true God. On the other hand, she calls Him Baal when she places the true God on the level of the Baals, either by worshiping other gods along with Jehovah or by obliterating the essential distinction between Jehovah and the Baals.

BA'ALIM (bā'al-im). The plural of Baal. *See* Gods, False.

BA'ALIS (bā'a-lis; "in exultation"). King of the Ammonites about the time of the Babylonian captivity, whom Johanan reported to Gedaliah, the viceroy, as having sent Ishmael to slay him (Jer. 40:13-14), 588 B.C.

BA'AL-ME'ON (bā'al-me-on'; "lord of the dwelling"). One of the towns rebuilt by the Reubenites and their names changed (Num. 32:38). Baalmeon ("Beon," v. 3; "Beth-meon," Jer. 48:23; and "Beth-baal-meon," Josh. 13:17) is to be located at Ma'in nine miles E of the Dead Sea.

BA'AL-PE'OR (bā'al-pe'or). A god of the Moabites. *See* Gods, False.

BA'AL-PERA'ZIM (bā'al-per-a'zim; "possessor of breaches"). Called Mt. Perazim (Isa. 28:21), in central Palestine. Location unknown. Here David fought the Philistines (2 Sam. 5:20; 1 Chron. 14:11). The place and the circumstances appear to be again alluded to in Isa. 28:21, where it is called Mt. Perazim.

BA'AL-SHAL'ISHA (bā'al-shal'i-sha; "lord of Shalisha"). A place of Ephraim, not far W of Gilgal (2 Kings 4:38, 42). From this place a man brought provisions for Elisha.

BA'AL-TA'MAR (bā'al-tā'mar; "lord of the palm

trees"). One of the groves of Baal. Probably the palm tree of Deborah (Judg. 4:5), in the tribe of Benjamin near Gibeah of Saul (20:33). The notices seem to correspond to the present ruined site Erhah, about three miles NE of Jerusalem.

BA'AL-ZEBUB' (bā'al-ze-bub'). The god of the Philistines at Ekron. *See* Gods, False.

BA'AL-ZE'PHON (bā'al-ze'fon; "Baal of winter, or north"). A place belonging to Egypt on the border of the Red Sea (Ex. 14:2; Num. 33:7), mentioned in connection with Pi-hahiroth, on the journey of the Israelites. It must have been a well-known place, inasmuch as it is always mentioned to indicate the location of Pi-hahiroth, but its present location is unknown.

BA'ANA (bā'a-na).
1. The son of Ahilud, one of Solomon's twelve deputies, whose district comprised Taanach, Megiddo, and all Beth-shean, with the adjacent region (1 Kings 4:12), 960 B.C.
2. The son of Hushai and also a deputy of King Solomon. His district was in Asher and Bealoth (1 Kings 4:16), 960 B.C.
3. The father of Zadok, which latter person assisted in rebuilding the walls of Jerusalem under Nehemiah (Neh. 3:4), 445 B.C.

BA'ANAH (bā'a-na). Another form of *Baana* (which see).
1. A son of Rimmon, the Beerothite. He, with his brother Rechab, slew Ish-bosheth while he lay in his bed and took the head to David in Hebron. For this David caused them to be put to death, their hands and feet to be cut off, and their bodies, thus mutilated, hung up over the pool at Hebron (2 Sam. 4:2-12), about 992 B.C.
2. A Netophathite, father of Heleb, or Heled, who was one of David's mighty men (2 Sam. 23:29; 1 Chron. 11:30), about 1000 B.C.

BA'ARA (bā'a-ra). One of the wives of Shaharaim, of the tribe of Benjamin (1 Chron. 8:8). In v. 9, she is called Hodesh.

BAASE'IAH (bā'a-se'ya). A Gershonite Levite, son of Malchijah and father of Michael, in the lineage of Asaph the singer (1 Chron. 6:40), before 1000 B.C.

BA'ASHA (bā'a-sha). The third sovereign of the separate kingdom of Israel and the founder of its Second Dynasty. He reigned c. 908-866 B.C. Baasha was the son of Ahijah, of the tribe of Issachar, and conspired against King Nadab, the son of Jeroboam (when he was besieging the Philistine town of Gibbethon), and killed him and his whole family (1 Kings 15:27-28). He was probably of humble origin, as the prophet Jehu says, "I exalted you from the dust" (16:2). In matters of religion his reign was no improvement on that of Jeroboam, and he was chiefly remarkable for his hostility to Judah. He built Ramah "in order to

prevent anyone from going out or coming in to Asa king of Judah" (15:17). He was compelled to desist by the unexpected alliance of Asa with Ben-hadad I of Damascus. Baasha died in the twenty-fourth year of his reign and was honorably buried in Tirzah, which he had made his capital (15:33; 16:6). For his idolatries the prophet Jehu declared to him the determination of God to exterminate his family, which was accomplished by Zimri in the days of his son Elah (1 Kings 16:10-13).

BABBLER. The KJV rendering (Eccles. 10:11) of the Heb. *ba'al lāshôn*, "master of the tongue." The word is understood by some as "charmer" (NASB); by others as "slanderer." Paul was called a "babbler" (Acts 17:18, Gk. *spermologos*, "seed picker," as the crow), probably with a twofold meaning: from the manner in which that bird feeds, a "parasite," and from its chattering voice.

BA'BEL, TOWER OF. The building that the Babel builders intended to construct and that became the symbol of their God-defying disobedience and pride (Gen. 11:1-9). This structure is adequately illustrated by a characteristic Mesopotamian building called the ziggurat. The Assyro-Babylonian word *zigguratu* denotes a sacred temple tower and means a "pinnacle" or "mountaintop." The Babylonian ziggurat was a gigantic artificial mound of sun-dried bricks. The oldest extant ziggurat is that at ancient Uruk, biblical Erech (Gen. 10:10), modern Warka. This ancient temple tower dates from the latter part of the fourth millennium B.C. Nothing in the biblical narrative indicates that the so-called Tower of Babel was a temple tower or ziggurat. It is simply called a tower (*migdāl*). It seems clear that the Tower of Babel was the first structure of this sort ever attempted, and if later towers have any connection with the Tower of Babel, they are to be thought of as descendants of it. Ziggurats were consecrated to the guardian deity of the city. At Ur, the birthplace of Abraham, the god was Nanna, and his holy shrine was set on the topmost stage. At Borsippa (Birs-Nimrûd), some ten miles SW of Babylon, Nebo, the god of knowledge and literature, was the divinity. These ancient ziggurats were built in steplike stages. The highest one was seven stories, although the common height was three stories. The ziggurat at Uruk was a vast mass of clay stamped down hard and buttressed on the outside with layers of brick and bitumen. Similar structures at Ur, Babylon, Borsippa, and other Mesopotamian cities illustrate the words of 11:3-4: "Come, let us make bricks and burn them thoroughly. And they used brick for stone, and they used tar for mortar. And they said, 'Come, let us build for ourselves a city, and a tower whose top will reach into heaven, and let us make for ourselves a name; lest we be scattered abroad over the face of the whole earth.'" Also illustrated is a salient difference between the building materials of the stoneless alluvial plain of Babylonia and those of Palestine and Egypt. In the building of the tower sun-dried bricks were used for stone, and tar (bitumen, or "slime," KJV), which was abundant in the general regions of Babylon, was used for mortar (cf. 11:3). Ruins of more than two dozen ziggurats may be seen in Mesopotamia.

The Tower of Babel may have looked like this ziggurat

The original Tower of Babel was probably constructed prior to 4000 B.C. when the arts and sciences had developed to such a degree as to contemplate building a city, and especially a tower "whose top will reach into heaven" (11:4). This phrase is not mere hyperbole but an expression of pride and rebellion manifested by the Babel builders. Both Assyrian and Babylonian kings greatly prided themselves upon the height of their temples and boasted of having their tops as high as heaven.

BIBLIOGRAPHY: A. Parrot, *Tower of Babel* (1955).

BABOONS. *See* Animal Kingdom: Peacocks.

BAB'YLON (bab'i-lon). An ancient city-state in the plain of Shinar, derived from Hurrian *papil.*

Name. The name is derived by the Hebrews from the root *bālal* ("to confound") and has reference to the confusion of tongues at the Tower (Gen. 11:9). Thus the biblical writer refutes any God-honoring connotation of the name. The biblical account ascribes the founding of the ancient prehistoric city of Babylon to the descendants of Cush and the followers of Nimrod (10:8-10). This statement distinguishes the people who founded the city (evidently the Sumerians) from the Semitic-Babylonians who afterward possessed it.

Beginnings. The beginnings of the city of Babylon are unknown to us except for the biblical passage mentioned earlier (Gen. 10:10). About 1830 B.C. the city began its rise to prominence. In the ensuing struggle with surrounding city-states, Babylon conquered Larsa and the First Dynasty of Babylon was established. Such kings

as Sumu-abu, Sumla-el, Sabum, Apel-Sin, and Sin-mu-ballit ruled. Then the great *Hammurabi* (which see), ascended the throne about 1728-1686, and conquered not only all of S Babylonia but extended his conquests as far N as Mari. At this famous city on the middle Euphrates, André Parrot, excavating for the Musée du Louvre (1933ff.), unearthed thousands of cuneiform tablets, a vast royal palace, a temple of Ishtar, and a ziggurat.

The city of Babylon did not reach the height of its glory, however, until the reign of Nebuchadnezzar II (605-562 B.C.). Nebuchadnezzar made the city splendid, and the king's own inscriptions are concerned largely with his vast building operations. Babylon was excavated thoroughly by the Deutsche Orientgesellschaft under the direction of Robert Koldewey, 1899 to 1917 (cf. *Das wieder erstehende Babylon,* 4th ed. [1925]). Nebuchadnezzar's brilliant city included vast fortifications, famous streets such as the Processional, canals, temples, and palaces. The Ishtar Gate led through the double wall of fortifications and was adorned with rows of bulls and dragons in colored enameled brick. Nebuchadnezzar's throne room was likewise adorned with enameled bricks. The tall ziggurat was rebuilt. This, Herodotus said, rose to a height of eight stages. Near at hand was Esagila ("whose housetop is lofty"), the temple of Marduk or Bel, which the king restored. Not far distant were the "hanging gardens," which to the Greeks were one of the seven wonders of the world. How well the words of Dan. 4:30 fit this ambitious builder: "Is this not Babylon the great, which I myself have built as a royal residence by the might of my power and for the glory of my majesty?"

Restoration of Babylon

The splendid Babylonian Empire of Nebuchadnezzar was destined soon to fall. He was succeeded on the throne by Amel-Marduk (561-560), the

Evil-merodach of 2 Kings 25:27. This man was murdered by his brother-in-law, Nergal-shar-usur (559-556), whose son ruled only a few months and was succeeded by one of the conspirators, who did away with him. A noble named Nabunaid, or Nabonidus, then ruled, together with his son Belshazzar (555-539; see Dan. 5); Nabonidus was the last king of the neo-Babylonian Empire. On October 12, 539 B.C., Babylon fell to Cyrus of Persia, and from that time on the decay of the city began. Xerxes plundered it. Alexander the Great thought to restore its great temple, in ruins in his day, but was deterred by the prohibitive cost. During the period of Alexander's successors the area decayed rapidly and soon became a desert. From the days of Seleucus Nicator (312-280 B.C.), who built the rival city of Seleucia on the Tigris, queenly Babylon never revived.

Size and Appearance. Herodotus says the city was in the form of a square, 120 stades (13 miles, 1,385 yards) on each side. It had two walls, inner and outer. The vast space within the walls was laid out in streets at right angles to each other, lined with houses three to four stories in height. He lists the following chief public buildings: the temple of Bel, consisting of a tower in the shape of a pyramid, more than eight stories, topped with a sanctuary; the palace of the king; the bridge across the Euphrates connecting the eastern and western sections of the city. Herodotus described the city as overwhelming in its size (1.178-86). The next Greek writers whose records are important are Ctesias and Diodorus Siculus (2.7-8). According to them the city was much smaller than Herodotus had represented, its circuit being 360 stades (41 miles, 6 yards). To the bridge of Herodotus, Diodorus has added a tunnel under the river and describes the hanging gardens of Nebuchadnezzar as rising in terraces, which supported full grown trees. Hebrew accounts represent the city as great in size, beauty, and strength; in this they were amply sustained by the inscriptions and excavations. As a matter of fact, excavations show that Babylon was smaller than ancient Greek writers said. The wall was about eleven miles long and eighty-five feet thick and was protected by a moat filled with water from the Euphrates. Actually the wall was double: the outer wall was twenty-five feet thick and the inner one twenty-three feet thick with an intervening space filled with rubble. Watchtowers stood sixty-five feet apart on the walls. Eight or nine gates pierced the wall. The population of greater Babylon (the walled city and its suburbs) in Nebuchadnezzar's day has been estimated at about a half million.

The Figurative Meaning. In the prophetical writings, when the actual city is not meant, the illustration is to the "confusion" into which the whole social order of the world has fallen under Gentile world domination (Luke 21:24; Rev. 6:16). The divine order is given in Isa. 11, that is, Israel in her own land the center of divine government of the world and the medium of the divine blessing, with Gentile nations blessed when associated with Israel. Anything else is politically mere "babel." In the NT Babylon prefigures apostate Christendom, that is, ecclesiastical Babylon, the great harlot (Rev. 17:5-18). It also prefigures political Babylon (17:15-18), which destroys ecclesiastical Babylon. The power of political Babylon is destroyed by the glorious second advent of Christ (Rev. 16:19; 18:2-21).

M.F.U.; H.F.V.

BIBLIOGRAPHY: D. J. Wiseman, *Chronicles of the Chaldean Kings* (1956); A. Parrot, *Babylon and the Old Testament* (1958); H. W. F. Saggs, *The Greatness That Was Babylon* (1962); J. G. Macqueen, *Babylon* (1964); W. G. Lambert, *Peoples of Old Testament Times*, ed. D. J. Wiseman (1973); J. Oates, *Babylon* (1979).

BABYLO'NIA (bab-i-lō'ni-a). The eastern end of the Fertile Crescent, which had Babylon for its capital, called Shinar (Gen. 10:10; 11:2; Isa. 11:11), and land of the Chaldeans (Jer. 24:5; Ezek. 12:13).

Principal Cities. The region anciently comprised Sumer and Akkad. Akkad was the northern region of the lower alluvial plain of the Tigris-Euphrates, in which were Babylon, Borsippa, Kish, Kuthah, Sippar, and Agade (Accad). Principal towns of Sumer were Nippur, Lagash, Umma, Larsa, Uruk (Erech, Gen. 10:10), Ur (Abraham's city), and Eridu.

Geography. The two great rivers Tigris and Euphrates, which have their source in the mountains of Armenia, have built up the alluvial plain of lower Babylonia. The old standard view subscribed to in most textbooks is that the rivers gradually pushed the coastline of the Persian Gulf ever southward. In fact, the entire area below Babylon is supposed to have been formed in that way. Presumably, the Tigris and Euphrates did not join in earlier days but flowed as separate streams into the gulf. On the basis of newer studies in geology, however, this view is being seriously questioned. It is argued that, although the rivers bring down much silt, some 90 percent apparently is deposited before reaching the gulf. But the rise of the land level has not been marked in this area. So the theory has been advanced that the Tigris and Euphrates drop their sediment in a slowly subsiding basin. The gradual sinking of the land level supposedly has prevented the land elevation or the coastline from changing significantly since Old Testament times, and the two Mesopotamian rivers are now believed always to have flowed into the gulf as a single stream. Although many geologists have followed the new theories, archaeologists have not been so quick to do so, and further study is necessary in order to solve this knotty problem.

In any case, Babylonia is a flat and stoneless alluvial plain without mineral or timber resources. This fertile plain, irrigated by the Tigris and Euphrates rivers, became the cradle of civilization. In this lower part of Mesopotamia, some fifty-five miles S of present Baghdad, there once stood on the banks of the Euphrates a city bearing the proud name of Bab-ilu, "gate of god," or Babylon. Although the history of the lower valley does not begin with this city, Babylon became prominent early, and its name is attached primarily to this region that is now known familiarly as Babylonia.

Early Inhabitants. People called Sumerians preceded the Semites in lower Babylonia as far as the biblical reports are concerned. They seem to have been "Hamitic" (Gen. 10:8-10), but scholars profess ignorance of their race and origin. They probably entered the plain of Shinar around 4000 B.C. and developed a high civilization. Their accomplishments included development of the wedge-shaped cuneiform script. They were polytheistic. Originally each city-state had its own

gods or goddesses, but eventually a triad pantheon developed: Anu (sky), Enlil (atmosphere and earth), and Ea (waters).

Earliest History. As the marshes dried up and areas of solid land appeared in lower Babylonia, civilization began. The earliest known culture is dubbed Obeid, the name being derived from Tell el-Obeid, a small mound 4½ miles NW of the more famous site of Ur. The culture, characterized by a definite style of pottery, is also known from the remains of other sites, including Ur. At Warka, the site of ancient Erech or Uruk, some 35 miles up the Euphrates valley from Tell el-Obeid, appears the second culture of ancient Babylonia. It probably dates from the middle of the fourth millennium B.C. At Warka another distinctive form of pottery was found, as well as the oldest ziggurat (*see* Babel, Tower of), the first cylinder seals, and the beginnings of writing. A further period in the early history of Mesopota-

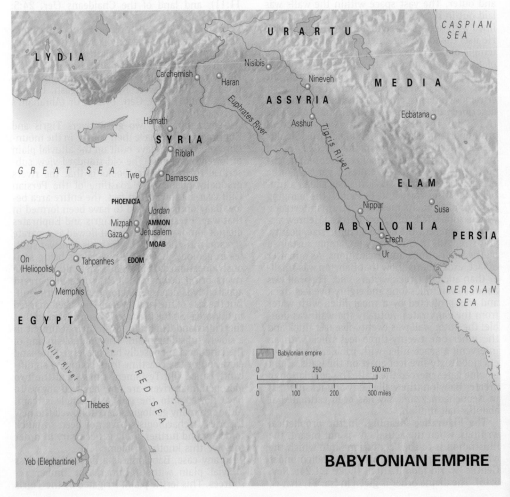

BABYLONIAN EMPIRE

mia is known from the findings at Jemdet Nasr, a site in the Mesopotamian valley near Babylon. This culture with its characteristic pottery dates around 3200-2800 B.C. Its bronze tools indicate the beginning of the Bronze Age in Mesopotamia. During this period the important cities of Shuruppak (Fara), Eshnunna (Tell Asmar), and Kish were founded.

Early Dynastic Period, about 2800-2360 B.C. During this period dynasties of kings appear at Kish, Uruk, Ur, Awan, Hamazi, Adab, and Mari. Among the rulers in the First Dynasty of Kish was Etana, "a shepherd, the one who to heaven ascended." The next dynasty is described as centering at the temple precinct of E-Anna, where the city of Uruk was subsequently built. Twelve kings were said to have reigned here for 2,310 years including Gilgamesh, the epic hero. Excavations at Tell Asmar (ancient Eshnunna) reveal the art and religion of the middle phase of the Early Dynastic Period. The First Dynasty of Ur indicates the last and culminating phase of the Dynastic Period. The Sumerian King List (Thorkild Jacobsen, *The Sumerian King List, Assyriological Studies* [1939]) states that "Uruk was smitten with weapons; its kingship to Ur was carried. In Ur Mes-Anne-Pada became king and reigned 80 years." Four kings are mentioned as reigning 177 years. Then "Ur was smitten with weapons." The high degree of culture that obtained under the First Dynasty of Ur is revealed in the famous royal cemetery uncovered there by C. Leonard Woolley. These tombs, dating around 2500 B.C., revealed a highly developed culture. Another dynasty flourishing during the last phase of the Early Dynastic Period was that established by Ur-Nanshe at Lagash (Al Hiba) about fifty miles N of Ur. Reference is made in the inscriptions of Ur Nanshe to extensive building operations, including construction of temples and digging of canals. A later ruler named Eannatum claimed victories over Umma, Uruk, Ur, Kish, and Mari. His battle against Umma is portrayed on the Stela of the Vultures. Subsequently Lagash fell again to Umma. The new conqueror was Lugalzagesi, who was governor of Umma. This conqueror ultimately became king of Uruk and Ur and was one of the most powerful figures in Sumerian history. His quarter-century reign constituted the Third Dynasty of Uruk. His armies marched to the Mediterranean Sea.

The Old Akkadian Period, about 2360-2180 B.C. Meanwhile the Semites were increasing in power in Babylonia under the leadership of the mighty Sargon, who was of humble origin and had been placed in an ark of bulrushes like Moses. He built up a far-flung empire and was succeeded by Rimush, Manishtusu, Sargon's grandson, whose victory stela was discovered at Susa. But Naram-Sin's sprawling empire, extending from central Persia to the Mediterranean and NE Arabia to the Taurus Mountains, lasted only through

the reign of his son Sharkalisharri. Then Caucasian people, the Gutians, overran Babylonia.

The Neo-Sumerian Period, about 2070-1960 B.C. When Gutian power declined, a Sumerian governor of Lagash, named Gudea, came to power. He is represented by numerous statues. Gudea built a famous temple, bringing cedar wood for it all the way from the Amanus Mountains of northern Syria, part of the same general range as the Lebanon, from which Solomon more than a millennium later was to cut cedar trees for the Temple at Jerusalem (1 Kings 5:6). With the downfall of the Gutians the powerful Third Dynasty of Ur also arose in splendor under the leadership of Ur-Nammu, who took the new title of "king of Sumer and Akkad" and who erected a mighty ziggurat at Ur. He was succeeded by Shulgi, Amar-Sin, Shu-Sin, and Ibbi-Sin.

The Isin-Larsa Period, about 1960-1830 B.C. Elamites sacked Ur and carried off Ibbi-Sin. Amorites from Mari and elsewhere settled at Isin and Larsa. An Elamite ruler came into power at Eshnunna. Isin and Larsa were the two powerful competitive city-states during this period.

Old Babylonian Period, about 1830-1550 B.C. This was the period of the ascendancy of *Babylon* (which see), particularly under the great *Hammurabi* (which see). Excavations at the brilliant city of Mari on the middle Euphrates have shed great light on this era. The Code of Hammurabi, discovered at Susa in 1901, was subsequently carried from Babylon and belongs to the period around 1700 B.C. It was during this time also that the famous epic of creation called *Enuma elish* assumed the form in which it was current for the next millennium. The discoveries at Nuzi, an ancient Hurrian center about twelve miles NW of modern Kirkuk, illuminated this period and especially the earlier patriarchal period.

Kassite Invasion, about 1550-1158 B.C. The Kassites, who had been invading the land from the highlands to the E and NE for a number of centuries, made themselves masters of the country. Finally Tukulti-Ninurta, king of Assyria (1244-1208 B.C.), invaded Babylonia and ruled for seven years before being expelled.

Dynasty II of Isin. With the fall of the Kassites a new dynasty arose in Babylonia, Dynasty II of Isin. The kings were all native Babylonians, among them Nebuchadnezzar I (1126-1105). He defeated the Elamites and the Hittites but was routed by the Assyrians. This dynasty came to an end in 1027 B.C.

Later History. About 1100-900 B.C. Aramaic tribes began invading Babylonia, and Assyria began to interfere in Babylonian affairs. *Tiglath-pileser III* (which see; 729 B.C.; his name is given as "Pul" in 2 Kings 15:19) became king of Babylon. In 689 the city revolted against Sennacherib, who sacked and burned it to the ground. It was rebuilt by Esarhaddon and remained a part of Assyria until 625 B.C.

Neo-Chaldean Empire, 605-539 B.C. The new nation, the Chaldeans, under Merodach-baladan, who proclaimed himself king of Babylon (721), sent an embassy to Hezekiah, king of Judah, but was defeated by Sennacherib in 703. In 625 B.C. Nabopolassar became king of the Chaldeans and founded the neo-Babylonian or Chaldean Empire; with Cyaxares, king of the Medes, he destroyed Nineveh in 612. His son Nebuchadnezzar defeated Neco of Egypt at Carchemish in 605. Now in control of all SW Asia, Nebuchadnezzar (605-562) entered his long and brilliant reign, destroying Jerusalem and making Babylon one of the most splendid of ancient cities. He was succeeded by his son Amel-Marduk (561-560). The latter was assassinated, and Neriglissar (559-556) succeeded to the throne. Neriglissar's son reigned for nine months after Neriglissar's death and was also assassinated in 556. Then a Babylonian noble, Nabonidus, came to the throne; he appointed his son *Belshazzar* as coregent (which see). In 539 B.C. Gobryas, one of Cyrus's generals, took Babylon, which remained under Persian rule, 539-332 B.C. Alexander the Great controlled Babylon until 323. The Seleucids established their dynasty in Babylon in 311 B.C. and in 275 removed the inhabitants of Babylon to Seleucia on the Tigris; with that event the history of Babylon ended.   M.F.U.; H.F.V.

BABYLONISH GARMENT. *See* Beautiful Mantle from Shinar.

BA'CA (ba'ka; "balsam tree" or "weeping"). An unidentified valley in Palestine (Ps. 84:6). It was possibly an imaginary poetical name, not intended to describe an actual location but to stand for any experience of drought (cf. Arab. *baka'a,* "to be sparsely watered") in contrast to a well-watered experience ("who passing through the valley of Baca, make it a *well,*" KJV, italics added); or it may refer to an experience of "weeping" with a play upon the Heb. word *bākâ* ("to weep"). If it actually refers to a place, it was likely so named from the balsam trees in it, which exude a tearlike gum (cf. the valley of Rephaim, 2 Sam. 5:22-23, where such trees were found).   M.F.U.

BACKBITE. *See* Slander.

BACKSLIDING. In the Heb. the idea is of "going back" (*sûg,* "backsliding," Prov. 14:14), "being stubborn or refractory like a heifer" (*sōrēr;* Hos. 4:16, KJV; NASB, "stubborn") and "turning back" (*meshûbâ;* Jer. 3:6, 8, 11-12, 14, 22; 8:5; 31:22; all KJV; NASB reads, "faithless" or "turned away") to the old life of sin and idolatry. In the NT backsliding is set forth as involving a change of the believer's *state* before God but not of his *standing.* The former is variable and depends upon daily contact with Christ, "if we walk in the light" (1 John 1:7) and many other factors of the spiritual life. *Standing,* by contrast, refers to the believer's position "in Christ," which is grounded in the unchangeable and perfect work of Christ for the believer, whereas *state* describes the changing and imperfect condition of his soul from moment to moment as affected by backsliding on the one hand or spiritual progress on the other. Faith in Christ secures standing (John 1:12; Rom. 5:1-2; 8:17; Eph. 1:3, 6; Col. 2:10; Heb. 10:19; etc.), but observance of all the laws of the spiritual life alone assures protection against backsliding. Compare 1 Cor. 1:2-9 (standing) with 1 Cor. 1:11; 3:1-4; 4:18; 5:2 (state). Backsliding not only results in a changed state or experience but involves corrective chastening (Heb. 12:6; 1 Cor. 11:31), loss of rewards and fellowship (2 Cor. 5:10; 1 John 3:10), curtailment of usefulness, and in extreme cases physical death (1 Cor. 5:5; 1 John 5:16) that the "spirit may be saved in the day of the Lord Jesus." Those who hold that one may fall from grace teach that backsliding may become complete, rather than partial, and that the individual must then be converted a second time.   M.F.U.

BADGER. *See* Animal Kingdom: Porpoise.

BAGPIPE. *See* Music.

BAGS. Bags made of leather or woven materials were in common use in Bible lands to hold money—lumps of gold or silver in most ancient times (Prov. 7:20; Isa. 46:6) and, after the Persian period, minted coins. Water or wine bags were manufactured from skins of animals. The shepherd's bag contained a heterogeneous assortment ranging from sling stones to food (1 Sam. 17:40). In Luke 12:33 Jesus referred to the common wallet for traveling (cf. 10:4; 22:35-36).   M.F.U.

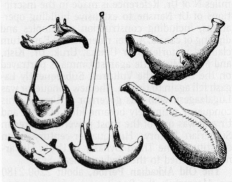

Sheepskin bag

BAHA'RUMITE (ba-ha'rû-mīt). A native of *Bahurim* (which see). An epithet applied to Azmaveth, one of David's warriors (1 Chron. 11:33); called Barhumite in 2 Sam. 23:31.

BAHU'RIM (ba-hur'im; "young men"). A town of Judah on the road from Jerusalem to the Jordan, E of Olivet (2 Sam. 3:16). David had trouble here with Shimei, and his spies hid here (16:5; 17:18). Azmaveth is the only other native of this place, except Shimei, mentioned in Scripture (23:31; 1 Chron. 11:33). It is identified with Râs et-Tmîm, just E of Mt. Scopus, near Jerusalem.

BAIL. See Surety.

BA'JITH (ba'jith; "house"). In the KJV, supposed to be a city in Moab where there may have been a celebrated idol temple; by others the Heb. is rendered "temple house" (Isa. 15:2) or, as in NASB and NIV, just "temple."

BAKBAK'KAR (bak-bak'ar; "searcher"). One of the Levites inhabiting the villages of the Netophathites, after the return from Babylon (1 Chron. 9:15), about 536 B.C.

BAK'BUK (bak'buk; a "bottle"). The head of one of the families of the Temple servants that returned from Babylon with Zerubbabel (Ezra 2:51; Neh. 7:53), about 536 B.C.

BAKBUKI'AH (bak-bu-kī'a). A Levite, "second among his brethren," who dwelt at Jerusalem on the return from Babylon (Neh. 11:17). He was also employed on the watches and was a gatekeeper (12:9, 25), about 536 B.C.

BAKE, BAKING. See Bread.

BAKER. See Handicrafts.

BA'LAAM (bā-lam). A heathen diviner who lived at Pethor, which is said, in Deut. 23:4, to have been a city of Mesopotamia. Although doubtless belonging to the Midianites (Num. 31:8), he possessed some knowledge of the true God and acknowledged that his superior powers as poet and prophet were derived from God and were His gift. His fame was great, and he became conceited and covetous. The Israelites having encamped in the plain of Moab (1401 B.C.), Balak, the king of Moab, entered into a league with the Midianites against them and sent messengers to Balaam "with the fees for divination in their hand" (22:5-7). Balaam seems to have had some misgivings as to the lawfulness of their request, for he invited them to remain overnight, that he might know how God would regard it. These misgivings were confirmed by the express prohibition of God upon his journey. Balaam informed the messengers of God's answer, and they returned to Balak. A still more honorable embassy was sent to Balaam, with promises of reward and great honor. He replied that he could not be tempted by reward but would speak what God should reveal. He requested them to remain for the night, that he might know what more the Lord would say to him. His importunity secured for him permission to accompany Balak's messengers with the divine injunction to speak as God should dictate. In the morning Balaam proceeded with the princes of Moab. But "God was angry because he was going, and the angel of the Lord took his stand in the

way as an adversary against him" (22:22). Though Balaam did not see the angel, the donkey that he rode was aware of his presence. At first it turned into the field; again, in its terror, it pressed against the wall, squeezing Balaam's foot; upon the third appearance of the angel, there being no way of escape, it fell down. This greatly enraged Balaam, who struck it with a stick, whereupon the donkey questioned Balaam as to the cause of the beating. He soon became aware of the presence of the angel, who accused him of perverseness. Balaam offered to return; the angel, however, told him to go on but to speak only as God should tell him. Meeting Balak, he announced to him his purpose of saying only what the Lord should reveal. According to his direction seven altars were prepared, upon each of which Balak and Balaam offered a bull and a ram. Three times Balaam tried to speak against Israel, but his utterances were overruled by God, so that instead of cursings there were blessings and magnificent prophecies, reaching forward until they told of "a star" coming "forth from Jacob" (24:17). Balaam is accused by Moses of seducing the Israelites to commit fornication (31:16). The effect of this is recorded in chap. 25. A battle was fought afterward with the Midianites, in which Balaam sided with them and was slain (Num. 31:8).

Typical. The "error of Balaam" (Jude 11) was the diviner-prophet's mistake in concluding on the basis of natural morality that God *must* righteously curse the nation Israel, seeing the evil in it. He was ignorant of the higher morality of the cross, through which God enforces the awful sanctions of His law, at the same time manifesting His grace, so that He can be just and the justifier of a believing sinner. The "way of Balaam" (2 Pet. 2:15) is the covetous conduct of the typical hireling prophet, solicitous only to commercialize His gift. The "teaching of Balaam" (Rev. 2:14) was the teaching of the mercenary seer to abandon godly separation and a pilgrim character in favor of worldly conformity. Balaam taught Balak to corrupt the people who could not be cursed (Num. 31:15-16; 22:5-6; 23:8) by seducing them to marry Moabite women and commit spiritual adultery (James 4:4). Balaam as a prophet offers the strange spectacle of a prophet-diviner—a mixture of paganistic ritual with a true, though blurred, knowledge of the true God.

M.F.U.

BIBLIOGRAPHY: E. W. Hengstenberg, *Dissertation on the Genuineness of Daniel and the Integrity of Zechariah; and a Dissertation on the History and Prophecies of Balaam* (1848), pp. 337-569; S. Cox, *Balaam, an Exposition and a Study* (1884); E. J. Young, *My Servants the Prophets* (1955), pp. 20-29.

BAL'ADAN (bal'a-dan; Akkad. "[He] Marduk has given a son").

A shortened form of Merodach-Baladan (Babylonian: Marduk-apla-iddina) or Berodach-Baladan, king of Babylon twice (721-710 and 703) in the time of Hezekiah, king of Judah (2 Kings 20:12; Isa. 39:1). He was a powerful Chaldean leader who was able to keep the Assyrians at bay for a few years but was ultimately destroyed by them.   H.F.V.

BA'LAH (bā'la; to "decay"). A city in Simeon (Josh. 19:3), or Baalah (15:29).

BA'LAK (bā'lak; "destroyer, emptier"). The son of Zippor, the king of the Moabites (Num. 22:2, 4). He was so terrified at the approach of the victorious army of the Israelites, who, in their passage through the desert had encamped near the confines of his territory, that he appealed to Balaam to curse them, about 1400 B.C. His designs being frustrated in this direction, he acted upon Balaam's suggestion and seduced the Israelites to commit fornication (25:1; Rev. 2:14).

BALANCES (Heb. *mō'znayim,* i.e., "two scales"). That these were known to the early Hebrews and in common use is evident from the frequent reference to them in the OT (Lev. 19:36; Job 6:2; 31:6, "scales"; Hos. 12:7; etc.). The probability is that the Hebrews used the common balances of Egypt. They were not essentially different from the balances now in use. Sometimes they were suspended by a ring, and in other cases the crossbeams turned upon a pin at the summit of an upright pole, each end of the arm terminating in a hook, to which the precious metal to be weighed was attached in small bags.

Balance, from an Egyptian tomb

Figurative. In a figurative sense the balance is employed in Scripture as an emblem of justice and fair dealing (Job 31:6; Ps. 62:9; Prov. 11:1). A balance or scale used in connection with the sale of bread or fruit by weight is the symbol of

scarcity (Rev. 6:5; see also Lev. 26:26; Ezek. 4:16-17).

BALD LOCUST. *See* Animal Kingdom: Locust.

BALDNESS. In Scripture baldness is mentioned as a defect, interfering with personal beauty; and the more naturally so, as the hair was frequently allowed to grow with peculiar luxuriance as an ornament. Natural baldness appears to have been uncommon and is alluded to as a mark of squalor and misery (Isa. 3:24; 15:2; Jer. 47:5). The address to Elisha, "Go up, you baldhead" (2 Kings 2:23), may mean that his scoffers referred to his age only. Baldness was expressly distinguished from leprosy but had certain points of contact with it (Lev. 13:40-44). Artificial baldness was a mark of mourning (Jer. 16:6; Ezek. 7:18; Amos 8:10) and was forbidden to the Israelites on the ground of their being a holy people (Deut. 14:1-2); it was a punishment inflicted upon captives (21:12). The priests were forbidden to make their heads bald or to shave off the corners of their beards (Lev. 21:5; Ezek. 44:20). The Jewish interpretation of this injunction excluded a bald priest from ministering at the altar, although baldness is not mentioned as a disqualification (Lev. 21:17-20). Baldness by shaving marked the conclusion of a Nazirite's vow (Num. 6:9, 18).

BALM. *See* Vegetable Kingdom.

BALSAM TREE. *See* Vegetable Kingdom.

BA'MAH (ba'ma; "height"). A high place where idols were worshiped. The word appears in its Heb. form only in Ezek. 20:29, where in the first part of the verse it is translated "high place." By some the name is supposed to refer to some particular spot. Keil (*Com.,* ad loc.) says that the word "is to be taken collectively and that the use of the singular is to be explained from the antithesis to the one divinely appointed Holy Place in the temple, and not from any allusion to one particular *bamah* of peculiar distinction."

BA'MOTH (ba'mōth; "heights"). The forty-seventh station of the Israelites (Num. 21:19-20) in the country of the Moabites, and probably the same as *Bamoth-baal* (which see).

BA'MOTH-BA'AL (ba'moth-bā'al; "heights of Baal"). A place E of the Jordan, beside the river Arnon (Josh. 13:17). In the RV at Num. 21:28, called "the high places of Arnon." Bamoth-baal is called Beth-bamoth on the *Moabite Stone* (line 27, which see), and is located somewhere near Mt. Nebo.

BAN. *See* Devote, Devoted.

BAND. The representative of several Heb. and Gk. words, especially of *speira,* a "cohort." *See* Army.

BANGLES. *See* Anklets.

BA'NI (ba-ni; "built").

1. A Gadite, one of David's mighty men (2 Sam. 23:36), about 1000 B.C.

2. A Levite, son of Shemer and father of Amzi, a descendant of Merari (1 Chron. 6:46).

3. A descendant of Perez and father of Imri, one of whose descendants returned from Babylon (1 Chron. 9:4) long before 536 B.C.

4. One whose "sons" (descendants or retainers), to the number of 642, returned from Babylon with Zerubbabel (Ezra 2:10). He is elsewhere (Neh. 7:15) called Binnui. He is probably the one mentioned (10:14) as having sealed the covenant.

5. The name of Bani is given (Ezra 10:29, 34, 38) three times as one who, either himself or his descendants, had taken strange wives after the captivity.

6. A Levite whose son, Rehum, repaired a portion of the wall of Jerusalem (Neh. 3:17). Apparently the same Bani was among those who were conspicuous in all the reforms on the return from Babylon (8:7; 9:4; 10:13). He had another son named Uzzi, who was appointed overseer of the Levites at Jerusalem; his own father's name was Hashabiah (Neh. 11:22).

BANISH (Heb. *nādaḥ*, to "cast out," 2 Sam. 14:13-14); **Banishment** (Heb. *maddûaḥ*, "causes of banishment," Lam. 2:14, KJV, but NASB, "oracles," marg., "burdens"; Aram. *sherōshî*, "rooting out," Ezra 7:26, NASB, marg.). Banishment was not a punishment prescribed by the Mosaic law but was adopted, together with the forfeiture of property, by the Jews after the captivity. It also existed among the Romans, together with another form of exile called *disportatio,* which was a punishment of great severity. The person banished forfeited his estate and was transported to some island named by the emperor, there to be kept in perpetual confinement (see Smith, *Dict. of Classical Antiquity,* s.v. "Banishment"). Thus the apostle John was banished to the island of Patmos (Rev. 1:9).

BANK. In Scripture the term *bank* does not designate a financial institution for the custody of money but rather a "table" or "counter" (Gk. *trapeza*) at which a money changer stood or sat, exchanging coins (Matt. 21:12; Mark 11:15; John 2:15). In Luke 19:23, however, the word apparently approximates "bank" in the modern sense of the word. In the simple pastoral-agricultural economy of the OT era, loaning money among the Hebrews was not viewed favorably (Ex. 22:25; Lev. 25:37). In the NT period, however, not only was money lent between friends, but money lending was a lucrative business. The banker presided at his table (Luke 19:23) and loaned funds to others in pledge of mortgage (cf. Neh. 5:3-4). Exchanging money from one denomination to another, as shekels for the half shekel for the Temple tax, or current coins for foreign money, such as the Hebrew shekel for the Roman denari-

us or Greek drachma, was a profitable branch of the ancient banking business.   M.F.U.

BANNER (Heb. *'ôt*). A more literal rendering of this word is "sign" (Num. 2:2, see marg.), denoting the standard of each tribe and one that is different from the *degel,* the banner of these tribes together.

BIBLIOGRAPHY: J. Pedersen, *Israel, Its Life and Culture* (1959), 3-4:1-13; R. deVaux, *Ancient Israel: Its Life and Institutions* (1961), pp. 227-29.

BANQUET (generally Heb. *mishteh,* "drinking"). Feasts are common in the Scripture narratives, and hospitality has always characterized life in Bible lands.

Relief of feast scene from Nineveh

Occasions. Besides being a part of the religious observance of the great festivals, banquets or feasts were given on great family occasions, such as a birthday (Gen. 40:20; Matt. 14:6), the weaning of a son and heir (Gen. 21:8), a marriage (29:22; Judg. 14:10; Esther 2:18; Matt. 22:2-4), the separation and reunion of friends (Gen. 31:27, 54), a burial (2 Sam. 3:35; Jer. 16:7; Hos. 9:4), a sheep-shearing (1 Sam. 25:2, 8, 36; 2 Sam. 13:23-29).

Time. The usual time for holding the banquet was toward evening, corresponding to the dinners of modern times. To begin early was a mark of excess (Isa. 5:11; Eccles. 10:16). These festivals were often continued for seven days, especially wedding banquets (Judg. 14:12); but if the bride was a widow, three days formed the limit.

Invitations. Invitations were sent out through servants (Prov. 9:2-3; Matt. 22:3-4, 8-9) some time previous to the banquet; and a later announcement informed the expected guests that the arrangements were complete and their presence was looked for (22:4; Luke 14:7). This after-summons was sent only to those who had accepted the previous invitation, and to violate that acceptance for trivial reasons could only be viewed as a gross insult.

Etiquette. At a small entrance door a servant received the tablets or cards of the guests, who were then conducted into the receiving room. After the whole company had arrived, the master of the house shut the door with his own hands, a signal that no others were to be admitted (Luke 13:25; Matt. 25:10). The guests were kissed upon their arrival (Tobit 7:6; Luke 7:45); their feet washed (7:44), a custom common in ancient Greece and still found in Palestine; the hair and beard anointed (Ps. 23:5; Amos 6:6); and their places assigned them according to rank (1 Sam. 9:22; Luke 14:8; Mark 12:39). In some cases each guest was furnished with a magnificent garment of a light and showy color and richly embroidered, to be worn during the banquet (Eccles. 9:8; Rev. 3:4-5). The refusal of such a mark of respect implied a contempt for the host and his entertainment that could not fail to provoke resentment (Matt. 22:11).

Fare. In general the feasts of the Israelites were simple; but, no doubt, under the kings, with growing prosperity and luxury, riotous banquets were not unknown. Particularly choice dishes were set before the guest intended to be specially honored (1 Sam. 9:24), sometimes a double (1:5) and even fivefold portion (Gen. 43:34). In addition to a great variety of foods, wine was used, often drugged with spices (Prov. 9:2; Song of Sol. 8:2); the banquets frequently degenerated into drinking bouts (Isa. 5:12; Amos 6:6).

The Jews of the OT appear to have used a common table for all the guests, although persons of high official position were honored with a separate table. In some cases a ceremonial separation prevailed, as at Joseph's entertainment of his brothers (Gen. 43:32). In early times *sitting* was the usual posture (1 Sam. 16:11; 20:5, 18); but later they adopted the luxurious practice of *reclining* upon couches (Luke 7:37-38; John 12:2-3).

In the houses of the common people the women and children also took part in the feast (1 Sam. 1:4; John 12:3), the separation of the women not being a Jewish custom.

Diversion. At private banquets the master of the house presided and did the honors of the occasion, but in large and mixed companies it was the ancient custom to choose a "headwaiter" (John 2:8). This functionary performed the office of chairman in preserving order and also took upon himself the general management of the festivities. The guests were entertained with exhibitions of music, singers, dancers, riddles, jesting, and merriment (Wisd. of Sol. 2:7; 2 Sam. 19:35; Isa. 5:12; 25:6; Judg. 14:12; Neh. 8:10; Amos 6:5-6; Luke 15:25). *See* Festivals; Food.

BIBLIOGRAPHY: A. C. Bouquet, *Everyday Life in New Testament Times* (1954), pp. 66-79.

BAPTISM. The application of water as a rite of purification or initiation; a Christian sacrament. *See* Sacraments.

The word *baptism* is the English form of the Gk. *baptismos*. The verb from which this noun is derived — *baptizo*—is held by some scholars to mean "to dip, immerse." But this meaning is held by others to be not the most exact or common but rather a meaning that is secondary or derived. By the latter it is claimed that all the term necessarily implies is that the element employed in baptism is in close contact with the

person or object baptized. The Gk. prepositions *en* and *eis* have played a prominent part in discussions respecting the mode of baptism.

The scope of this article is limited mainly to Christian baptism, but as preliminary to this brief mention is made of Jewish baptism, John's baptism, the baptism of Jesus, and the baptism of Christ's disciples:

Jewish Baptism. Baptisms, or ceremonial purifications, were common among the Jews. Not only priests and other persons but also clothing, utensils, and articles of furniture were thus ceremonially cleansed (Lev. 8:6; Ex. 19:10-14; Mark 7:3-4; Heb. 9:10).

John's Baptism. The baptism of John was not Christian, but Jewish. It was, however, especially a baptism "for repentance." The only faith that it expressed concerning Christ was that His coming was close at hand. Those who confessed and repented of their sins and were baptized by John were thus obedient to his call to "make ready the way of the Lord" (Matt. 3:3).

Because the disciples Paul met at Ephesus (Acts 19:1-7) were "acquainted only with the baptism of John" (18:25), i.e., were ignorant of the Christian message and the baptism of the Holy Spirit, save as a prophesied event (19:4), they did not "receive the Holy Spirit, when [they] believed" (19:2). They had heard only John's message and received only John's baptism, which were introductory and merely preparatory. Faith in them could not bring the free gift of the Holy Spirit. The moment they heard and believed the new message of a crucified, risen, and ascended Savior, they received the blessing of that message—the gift of the Holy Spirit, which included His baptizing ministry.

Baptism of Jesus. The baptism that Jesus received from John was unique in its significance and purpose. It could not be like that which John administered to others, for Jesus did not make confession; He had no occasion to repent. Neither was it Christian baptism, the significance of which we shall consider later. Jesus Himself declared the main purpose and meaning of this event in His words "It is fitting for us to fulfill all righteousness" (Matt. 3:15). It was an act of ceremonial righteousness appropriate to His public entrance upon His mission as the Christ, which included His threefold office of Prophet, Priest, and King, especially the second, for the essence of His redemptive work lies in His consecration as a Priest, the Great High Priest. In this office He offered not "the blood of goats and bulls," but Himself to put away sin (Heb. 9:13-26). It is this consecration to His redemptive priesthood that comes into clearest view in His baptism in the Jordan. By "fulfilling all righteousness" our Lord meant the righteousness of obedience to the Mosaic law. The Levitical law required all priests to be consecrated when they began to be about thirty years of age (Num. 4:3; Luke 3:23). The consecration was twofold—first the washing (baptism), then the anointing (Ex. 29:4-7; Lev. 8:6-36). When John on the Jordan's bank "washed" (baptized) Jesus, the heavens were opened, and the Holy Spirit came upon Him. This was the priestly anointing of Him who was not only a Priest by divine appointment but an eternal Priest (Ps. 110:4) who was thus divinely consecrated for the work of redemption (Matt. 3:16; Acts 4:27; 10:38).

Baptism of Christ's Disciples. That Christ Himself baptized His disciples is a matter, to say the least, involved in doubt. Although it is probable that at the beginning of His ministry our Lord baptized those who believed in Him, He not long afterward delegated this work to His disciples (John 4:1-2). The office of Christ was and is to baptize with the Holy Spirit. His disciples administered the symbolical baptism, He that which is real (Matt. 3:11).

Christian Baptism. This may be considered under two heads: Baptist and non-Baptist views.

Baptist Views. Christian baptism is the immersion of a believer in water as a sign of his previous entrance into the communion of Christ's death, burial, and resurrection. In other words, baptism is a token of the regenerated soul's union with Christ.

Obligation. Baptism is an ordinance instituted by Christ (Matt. 28:19; Mark 16:16), practiced by the apostles (Acts 2:38), submitted to by members of NT churches (Rom. 6:3-5; Col. 2:11-12), and subsequently practiced as a rite in Christian churches. No church hierarchy has the right to modify or dispense with this command of Christ because only the local church (no other visible church of Christ is known in the NT, and it is purely an executive, not a legislative body.

Significance. Symbolizing regeneration through union with Christ, baptism portrays not only Christ's death and resurrection and their purpose in atoning for sin in delivering sinners from sin's penalty and power, but also betokens the accomplishment of that purpose in the person baptized (Rom. 6:3-5; Gal. 3:27; Col. 3:3). By that external rite the believer professes his death to sin and resurrection to spiritual life. He also gives witness to the method by which God's purpose has been wrought for him, namely, by union with Christ. The rite sets forth the fact that the believer has received Christ and in faith given himself to Him (Rom. 6:5; Col. 2:12).

Proper Subjects of Baptism. Only those who give credible evidence of regeneration, and who thus by faith have entered into the communion of Christ's death and resurrection, are considered proper candidates for the rite. Biblical authority for this view is given in the command of Christ that those are to be baptized who have previously been made disciples (Matt. 28:19; Acts 2:41), or previously repented and believed (2:37-38; 8:12; 18:8). It is also proved from the nature of the

church as a company of regenerated believers (John 3:5; Rom. 6:13) and the symbolism of the ordinance itself (Acts 10:47; Rom. 6:2-5; Gal. 3:26-27). Since it is intended only for the regenerate, baptism can never be the means of regeneration. It is the appointed sign, but never the condition, of forgiveness of sins.

Mode. This is immersion only as confirmed from the meaning of the original Gk. word *baptizo* in Greek writers and church Fathers, and in the NT. Immersion was a doctrine and practice of the Greek church.

Administration. Many Baptists, and others practicing believer's baptism, require the rite to be performed properly as a prerequisite to membership in the local church and participation in the Lord's Supper.

Non-Baptist Views. The views of other Christian groups on the subject of baptism vary from those like most Quakers, who deny the present-day validity of the rite at all, to Roman Catholics and others who attach to it regenerating efficacy.

Obligation. Most Christians believe that the rite, in one form or another, for one purpose or another, is permanently obligatory and rests upon Christ's command (Matt. 28:19) and the practice of the early church.

Significance. The Roman Catholic and the Greek Orthodox churches, most Lutheran bodies, and many in the Church of England and the Protestant Episcopal church hold that baptism is the direct instrument of regeneration. Roman Catholics subscribe so strongly to this view that, accordingly, they also hold that all adults or infants who die unbaptized are excluded from heaven. Many evangelical churches believe that baptism is not only the rite of initiation into the church of Christ but a sign and seal of divine grace symbolizing spiritual cleansing or purification (Acts 22:16; Rom. 6:4-11; Titus 3:5). For example, the Westminster Confession, art. 28, says: "Baptism is a sacrament of the New Testament, ordained by Jesus Christ, not only for the solemn admission of the party baptized into the visible Church, but also to be unto him a sign and seal of the covenant of grace of his ingrafting into Christ, of regeneration, of remission of sins, and of his giving up unto God through Jesus Christ, to walk in newness of life; which sacrament is, by Christ's own appointment, to be continued in His Church until the end of the world." As circumcision was the sign and seal of the Abrahamic covenant and practiced under the Mosaic covenant, so baptism is construed as the sign and seal of the New Covenant of the gospel. Baptism, under the new economy, takes the place of circumcision under the old (Col. 2:10-12).

Proper Subjects of Baptism. In contrast to those holding Baptist views that exclude all except adult believers from the rite, many believe it should be administered to children who have believing parents or sponsors to care for their Christian nurture. This is contended to be scriptural since Paul expressly teaches that believers in Christ are under the gracious provisions of the covenant that God made with Abraham (Gal. 3:15-29). Under the Abrahamic covenant circumcision was administered to children as a sign of their participation in the relation in which their parents stood to God. It is contended that children of Christian parentage have a similar right to the ordinance, which is construed as having replaced circumcision.

Mode. Non-Baptists deny that immersion is the only valid mode of baptism and admit sprinkling, pouring, and immersion as legitimate. All that is held essential is the application of water "in the name of the Father, and of the Son, and of the Holy Ghost."

Administration. The administration of baptism is commonly regarded as exclusively a prerogative of the ministerial office. The wise and proper observance of church order has deemed this necessary, although in extreme cases it is held that a layman (or even a laywoman) can perform the rite. The same view is held among Lutherans and others who hold strongly to the doctrine of baptismal regeneration.

BIBLIOGRAPHY: K. Barth, *The Teaching of the Church Regarding Baptism* (1948); O. Cullmann, *Baptism in the New Testament* (1959); J. Warns, *Baptism* (1958); J. Jeremias, *Infant Baptism in the First Four Centuries* (1960); R. E. O. White, *The Biblical Doctrine of Initiation* (1960); G. R. Beasley-Murray, *Baptism in the New Testament* (1962); K. Aland, *Did the Early Church Baptize Infants?* (1963); T. J. Conant, *The Meaning and Use of BAPTIZEIN* (1977).

BAPTISM FOR THE DEAD (1 Cor. 15:29). Of this difficult passage there are many expositions, a few of which we present:

1. The Cerinthians, the Marcionites, and other heretics had a custom supposed to be referred to by the apostle. Persons who had been baptized had themselves baptized again for the benefit of people who had died *unbaptized* but *already believing,* in the persuasion that this would be counted to them as their own baptism. From this the apostle drew an argument to prove their belief in the resurrection. Meyer (*Com.,* ad loc.) believes that this is the practice to which the apostle refers. " 'For the benefit of the dead' remains the right interpretation."

2. Chrysostom believed the apostle referred to the profession of faith in baptism, part of which was, "I believe in the resurrection of the dead." The meaning, then, would be, "If there is no resurrection of the dead, why, then, art thou baptized for the dead, i.e., the body?" Whedon (*Com.,* ad loc.) holds to this interpretation and says: "The apostolic Christians were baptized into the faith of the resurrection of the dead, and thereby they were sponsors *in behalf of* the dead, that the dead should rise."

3. Another interpretation, that of Spanheim, considers "the dead" to be martyrs and other believers who, by firmness and cheerful hope of resurrection, have given in death a worthy example, by which others were also inspired to receive baptism. This interpretation, however, may perhaps also be improved if *Christ* is considered as prominently referred to among those deceased, by virtue of whose resurrection all His followers expect to be likewise raised.

4. Olshausen takes the meaning of the passage to be that "all who are converted to the Church are baptized *for the good* of the dead, as it requires a certain number (Rom. 11:12-25), a 'fullness' of believers, before the resurrection can take place."

5. "Over the graves of the martyrs." Vossius adopted this interpretation, but it is unlikely that this custom should have prevailed in the days of Paul.

BAPTISM OF FIRE. It is clear from the immediate context of this reference (Matt. 3:9-12; Luke 3:16-17) and from the general testimony of Scripture, that this baptism of fire is connected with judgment at the second advent of Christ as the baptism with the Holy Spirit (Acts 1:5 with 11:16) is connected with grace flowing from the death, resurrection, and ascension of Christ at His first advent. As John F. Walvoord correctly observes, "While the Church Age is introduced with a baptism of the Spirit, the Kingdom Age is to be introduced with a baptism of fire" (*Doct. of the Holy Spirit* [1943], p. 165). At first glance it might seem singular that John the Baptist should speak of the first and second advents in such intimate connection, but he is merely expressing himself as many of the OT prophets do, who often envision the Lord's first and second comings in a blended view and speak of both in the same clause (cf. Isa. 61:1-2 with Luke 4:16-21). Though some expositors, as Plumptre, have attempted to find a fulfillment of the baptism with fire in the "tongues as of fire" (Acts 2:3), and others have construed it as a description of the baptizing work of the Holy Spirit as an experience to be sought in this age, a kind of "second Pentecost," these interpretations are manifestly erroneous. It is not scriptural to pray for a baptism with fire; there is no such baptism now, for the believer has been graciously delivered from wrath by the blood of Christ.   M.F.U.

BAPTISM OF JE'SUS. *See* Baptism: Baptism of Jesus.

BAPTISM OF THE SPIRIT. This momentous spiritual operation is set forth in the NT as the basis of all the believer's positions and possessions "in Christ" (Eph. 1:3; Col. 2:10; 3:1-4; etc.). The operation is prophetic in the gospels (Matt. 3:11; Mark 1:8; Luke 3:16-17; John 1:33-34, where Christ is the baptizer), historic in the Acts (cf. 1:5 with 11:16), and doctrinal in the epistles (1 Cor. 12:13, where the Spirit is named specifically as the agent; Rom. 6:3-4; Gal. 3:26-27; Col. 2:9-12; Eph. 4:5). The Spirit's baptizing work, placing the believer "in Christ," occurred initially at Pentecost at the advent of the Spirit, who baptized believing Jews "into Christ." In Acts 8, Samaritans were baptized in this way for the first time; in chap. 10, Gentiles likewise were so baptized, at which point the normal agency of the Spirit as baptizer was attained. According to the clear teaching of the epistles, every believer is baptized by the Spirit into Christ the moment he is regenerated. He is also simultaneously indwelt by the Spirit and sealed eternally, with the privilege of being filled with the Spirit, as the conditions for filling are met. No subject in all the range of biblical theology is so neglected, on one hand, or misunderstood and abused, on the other, as this. The baptism of the Spirit is widely confused with regeneration and with the indwelling, sealing, and filling ministries of the Spirit, as well as with water baptism and a so-called "second blessing."   M.F.U.; R.K.H.

BIBLIOGRAPHY: J. D. G. Dunn, *Baptism in the Holy Spirit* (1970); M. F. Unger, *Baptizing Work of the Holy Spirit* (1974); R. E. O. White, *Evangelical Dictionary of Theology.*

BAR. A word with various meanings. (1) A bar, *crossbar* passing along the sides and rear of the *Tabernacle* (which see), through rings attached to each board, and thus holding the boards together (Ex. 26:26-29). (2) A bar or *bolt* for fastening a gate or door (Judg. 16:3; Neh. 3:3, 6, 13-15). The word is used figuratively of a rock in the sea (Jonah 2:6), the bank or shore of the sea (Job 38:10, NASB, "bolt"), of strong fortifications and impediments (Isa. 45:2; Amos 1:5).

BAR- (Aram., "son"). A patronymic sign, used like Ben, which had the same meaning. Ben, however, prevails in the pure Heb. names of the OT, and Bar in those of the NT, because bar was much more used in the Aram. and Syr. languages.

BARAB'BAS (bar-ab'as; Gk. *barabbas*, for Aram. *bar'abbā'*, "son of the father," or "Abba"). A robber who had committed murder in an insurrection (Mark 15:7; Luke 23:19) in Jerusalem and was lying in prison at the time of the trial of Jesus before Pilate, A.D. 29. The latter, in his anxiety to save Jesus, proposed to release Him to the people, in accordance with their demand that he should release one prisoner to them at the Passover. Barabbas was guilty of the crimes of murder and sedition, making him liable to both Roman and Jewish law. But the Jews were so bent on the death of Jesus that of the two they preferred pardoning this double criminal (Matt. 27:20; Mark 15:11; Luke 23:18; John 18:40). "And wishing to satisfy the multitude, Pilate released Bar-

abbas for them, and after having Jesus scourged, he delivered Him over to be crucified" (Mark 15:15).

BAR'ACHEL (bar'a-kel; "God has blessed"). The father of Elihu the Buzite, one of four persons who visited Job in his affliction (Job 32:2, 6).

BARACHI'AH. *See* Berechiah.

BARACHI'AS. *See* Berechiah; Zechariah.

BA'RAH. *See* Beth-barah.

BAR'AK (bār'ak; "lightning"). The son of Abinoam of Kedesh, a city of refuge in the tribe of Naphtali (Judg. 4:6). He was summoned by the prophetess Deborah to take the field against the army of the Canaanitish king, Jabin, commanded by Sisera, with a force of ten thousand men from the tribes of Naphtali and Zebulun. He was further instructed to proceed to Mt. Tabor, for Jehovah would draw Sisera and his host to meet him at the river Kishon and deliver him into his hand. Barak consented only on the condition that Deborah would go with him, which she readily promised. Sisera, being informed of Barak's movements, proceeded against him with his whole army, including nine hundred chariots. At a signal given by the prophetess, the little army, seizing the opportunity of a providential storm, boldly rushed down the hill and utterly routed the host of the Canaanites. The victory was decisive: Harosheth-hagoyim was taken, Sisera murdered, and Jabin ruined (chap. 4), between 1195 and 1155 B.C. The victory was celebrated by a beautiful hymn of praise composed by Barak in conjunction with Deborah (chap. 5). Barak appears in the list of the faithful of the OT (Heb. 11:32).

BIBLIOGRAPHY: J. Kitto, *Daily Bible Illustrations* (1981), 1:457-63.

BARAKEL. *See* Barachel.

BARBARIAN (Gk. *barbaros*, "rude"). Originally the term was the Gk. epithet for a people speaking any language other than Gk. After the Persian wars it began to carry with it associations of hatred and to imply vulgarity and lack of culture. The Romans were originally included by the Greeks under the name *barbaroi*, but after the conquest of Greece and the transference of Greek art and culture to Rome, the Romans took the same position as the Greeks before them and designated as barbarians all who in language and manners differed from the Greco-Roman world. The word *barbarian* is applied in the NT, but not reproachfully, to the inhabitants of Malta (Acts 28:4, see marg.), who were of Phoenician or Punic origin, and to those nations that had indeed some refinement of manners but not the opportunity of becoming Christians, such as the Scythians (Col. 3:11). The phrase "Greeks and . . . barbarians" (Rom. 1:14) means "all peoples."

BARBER (Heb. *gallāb*). Occurs but once in the

Scriptures (Ezek. 5:1); but, inasmuch as great attention was paid to the hair and beard among the ancients, the barber must have been a well-known tradesman. *See* Hair.

BAREFOOT (Heb. *yāḥēf,* "unshod," Jer. 2:25). In the East great importance was attached to the clothing, and feelings respecting it were peculiarly sensitive, so that a person was looked upon as stripped and naked if he only removed an outer garment. To go "barefoot" was an indication of great distress (Isa. 20:2-4; 2 Sam. 15:30). Persons were also accustomed to removing their shoes when coming to places accounted holy (Ex. 3:5).

BARHU'MITE (bar-hū'mīt). A transposed form (2 Sam. 23:31) of the Gentile name *Baharumite* (which see).

BARIAH (ba-rī'ah). The third son of Shemaiah, a royal descendant of David (1 Chron. 3:22).

BAR-JE'SUS (bar-jî'sus; "son of Joshua"). Otherwise called *Elymas* (which see), a demonized sorcerer-magician who withstood Barnabas and Paul (Acts 13:6-12).

BARJO'NA (bar-jō'na; "son of Jonah"). The patronymic of the apostle Peter (Matt. 16:17; cf. John 1:42).

BAR'KOS (bar'kos). The head of one of the families of Temple servants that returned from the captivity with Zerubbabel (Ezra 2:53; Neh. 7:55), 536 B.C.

BARLEY. *See* Vegetable Kingdom.

BAR'NABAS (bar'na-bas; Gk. from Aram. *barnᵉbû'â,* "son of prophecy," especially as it is manifested in exhortation and comfort). The name given by the apostles to Joseph (Acts 4:36), probably on account of his eminence as a Christian teacher.

Charity. Barnabas was a native of Cyprus and a Levite by extraction. Possessing land, he generously disposed of it for the benefit of the Christian community and laid the money at the apostles' feet (Acts 4:36-37). As this transaction occurred soon after the Day of Pentecost, he must have been an early convert to Christianity.

Associated with Paul. When Paul made his first appearance in Jerusalem, Barnabas brought him to the apostles and attested to his sincerity (Acts 9:27). Word being brought to Jerusalem of the revival at Antioch, Barnabas (who is described as "a good man, and full of the Holy Spirit and of faith," 11:24) was sent to make inquiry. Finding the work to be genuine, he labored among them for a time; fresh converts were added to the church through his personal efforts. He then went to Tarsus to obtain the assistance of Saul, who returned with him to Antioch, where they labored for a whole year (11:19-26). In anticipation of the famine predicted by Agabus, the Christians at Antioch made a contribution for their poor brethren at Jerusalem and sent it by the hands of Barnabas and Saul (11:27-30), A.D. 44. They, however, speedily returned, bringing with them John Mark, a nephew of the former (12:25).

First Missionary Journey. By divine direction (Acts 13:2) they were separated to the office of missionaries and as such visited Cyprus and some of the principal cities in Asia Minor (13:14). At Lystra, because of a miracle performed by Paul, they were taken for gods, the people calling Barnabas Zeus (14:8-12). Returning to Antioch, they found the peace of the church disturbed by a certain sect from Judea, who insisted upon the Gentile converts being circumcised. Paul and Barnabas, with others, were sent to Jerusalem to consult with the apostles and elders. They returned to communicate the result of the conference, accompanied by Judas and Silas (15:1-32).

Second Missionary Journey. As they prepared for a second missionary journey, a dispute arose between Paul and Barnabas on account of John Mark. Barnabas determined to take Mark with them; Paul was not sure that they should. The contention became so sharp that they separated, Barnabas with Mark going to Cyprus, while Paul and Silas went through Syria and Cilicia (Acts 15:36-41). At this point Barnabas disappears from the record of the Acts. Several times he is mentioned in the writings of Paul, but nothing special is noted save that Barnabas was at one time led away by Judaizing zealots. All else is a matter of inference.

BIBLIOGRAPHY: J. S. Howson, *The Companions of St. Paul* (n.d.), pp. 7-27; H. S. Seekings, *Men of the Pauline Circle* (1914), pp. 33-39; W. S. LaSor, *Great Personalities of the New Testament* (1961), pp. 118-27; D. E. Hiebert, *Personalities Around Paul* (1973), pp. 46-62.

BARREL. The English term *barrel,* from Heb. *kad,* appears only in the KJV. In the NASB it is replaced by *bowl* (marg., lit. "pitcher," 1 Kings 17:12, 14, 16) and *pitcher* (1 Kings 18:33). The NIV renders it "jar" (1 Kings 17:12, 14, 16; 18:33) consistently. *See* Bowl; Pitcher.

BARREN (Heb. *'āqār,* when spoken of persons). Barrenness, in the East, was looked upon as a ground of great reproach as well as a punishment from God (1 Sam. 1:6; Isa. 47:9; 49:21; Luke 1:7, 25; etc.). Instances of childless wives are found in Gen. 11:30; 25:21; 29:31; Judg. 13:2-3; and Luke 1:7, 36. Certain marriages were forbidden by Moses and were visited with barrenness (Lev. 20:20-21). The reproach attached to barrenness, especially among the Hebrews, was doubtless due to the constant expectation of the Messiah and the hope cherished by every woman that she might be the mother of the promised Seed. In order to avoid the disgrace of barrenness, women gave their handmaidens to their husbands, regarding the children born under such circumstances as their own (Gen. 16:2; 30:3).

146

BARSAB'BAS (bar-sab'as; "son of Sabas"). A surname.

1. Of Joseph, a disciple who was nominated along with Matthias to succeed Judas Iscariot in the apostleship (Acts 1:23).

2. Of Judas, who, with Silas, was sent to Antioch in the company of Paul and Barnabas (Acts 15:22).

BARTHOL'OMEW (bar-thol'o-mū; "son of Tolmai"). One of the twelve apostles of Jesus, and generally supposed to have been the same person who in John's gospel is called Nathanael.

Name and Family. In the first three gospels (Matt. 10:3; Mark 3:18; Luke 6:14) Philip and Bartholomew are constantly named together, whereas Nathanael is not mentioned. In the fourth gospel Philip and Nathanael are similarly combined, but nothing is said of Bartholomew. Nathanael must therefore be considered his real name, whereas Bartholomew merely expresses his filial relation (Kitto).

Personal History. If this may be taken as true, he was born in Cana of Galilee (John 21:2). Philip, having accepted Jesus, told Bartholomew that he had "found Him of whom Moses in the Law and also the Prophets wrote, Jesus of Nazareth." To his question, "Can any good thing come out of Nazareth?" Philip replied, "Come and see." His fastidious reluctance was soon dispelled. Jesus, as He saw him coming to Him, uttered the eulogy "Behold an Israelite, indeed, in whom is no guile!" (John 1:45-47). He was appointed with the other apostles (Matt. 10:3; Mark 3:18; Luke 6:14), was one of the disciples to whom the Lord appeared after the resurrection (John 21:2), was a witness of the ascension, and returned with the other apostles to Jerusalem (Acts 1:4, 12-13). Tradition only speaks of his subsequent history. He is said to have preached the gospel in India (probably Arabia Felix); others say in Armenia, and report him to have been flayed alive there, then crucified with his head downward.

Character. Nathanael "seems to have been one of those calm, retiring souls whose whole sphere of existence lies not here, but 'where, beyond these voices, there is peace.' It was a life of which the world sees nothing, because it was 'hid with Christ in God' " (Farrar).

BIBLIOGRAPHY: D. Browne, *Expository Times* 38 (1927): 286; R. B. Y. Scott, *Expository Times* 38 (1927): 93-94; W. Barclay, *The Master's Men* (1959), pp. 102-13; J. D. Jones, *The Apostles of Christ* (1982), pp. 130-49.

BARTIMAE'US (bar-ti-mā'us; "son of Timaeus"). A blind beggar of Jericho who sat by the wayside begging as our Lord went out of the city on His last journey to Jerusalem (Mark 10:46). Hearing that Jesus was passing, he cried for mercy, and in answer to his faith he was miraculously cured and "began following Him on the road" (v. 52).

BA'RUCH (ba'ruk; "blessed").

1. The son of Zabbai. He repaired (445 B.C.) that part of the wall of Jerusalem between the Angle of Zion and the house of Eliashib the high priest (Neh. 3:20) and joined in Nehemiah's covenant (10:6).

2. Son of Col-hozeh, a descendant of Perez, a son of Judah. His son Maaseiah dwelt in Jerusalem after the captivity (Neh. 11:5).

3. Son of Neriah and brother of Seraiah, who held an honorable office in Zedekiah's court (Jer. 32:12; 36:4; 51:59). Baruch was the faithful friend and scribe of Jeremiah. In the fourth year of King Jehoiakim (about 604 B.C.), Baruch was directed to write all the prophecies delivered by Jeremiah and read them to the people. This he did in the "Lord's house" both that and the succeeding year. He afterward read them privately to the king's counselors, telling them that he had received them through the prophet's dictation. The king, when the roll was brought to him, cut it and threw it into the fire. He ordered the arrest of Jeremiah and Baruch, but they could not be found. Baruch wrote another roll, including all that was in the former and an additional prediction of the ruin of Jehoiakim and his house (chap. 36). Terrified by the threats in the prophetic roll, he received the assurance that he should be spared from the calamities that would befall Judah (chap. 45). During the siege of Jerusalem Jeremiah purchased the territory of Hanamel and deposited the deed with Baruch (32:12), 590 B.C. Baruch was accused of influencing Jeremiah in favor of the Chaldeans (Jer. 43:3; cf. 37:13), and he was thrown into prison with the prophet, where he remained until the capture of Jerusalem (Josephus *Ant.* 10.9.1). By the permission of Nebuchadnezzar he lived with Jeremiah at Mizpah but was afterward forced to go to Egypt (Jer. 43:6-7). Nothing certain is known of the close of his life. According to one tradition, he went to Babylon upon the death of Jeremiah, where he died, the twelfth year after the destruction of Jerusalem. There are two apocryphal books that purport to be the productions of Baruch.

BIBLIOGRAPHY: S. Cox, *The Expositor* (1896), 2:192-216.

BARZIL'LAI (bar-zil'î; "of iron").

1. A wealthy and aged Gileadite of Rogelim, who showed great hospitality to David when he fled beyond the Jordan from his son Absalom, c. 967 B.C. He sent in a liberal supply of provisions, beds, and other conveniences for the use of the king's followers (2 Sam. 17:27-29). On the king's triumphant return Barzillai accompanied him over the Jordan but declined on account of his age (being eighty years old), and perhaps from a feeling of independence, to proceed to Jerusalem and end his days at court. He, however, recommended his son Chimham to the royal favor (19:31-39). On his deathbed David recalled this

kindness and commended Barzillai's children to the care of Solomon (1 Kings 2:7).

2. A Meholathite, father of Adriel, who was the husband of Mereb, Saul's daughter (2 Sam. 21:8), before 1021 B.C.

3. A priest who married a descendant of Barzillai (no. 1) and assumed the same name. His genealogy became so confused that his descendants, on the return from captivity, were set aside as unfit for the priesthood (Ezra 2:61; Neh. 7:63-64), before 536 B.C.

BASE′MATH (bas′e-math; "fragrance").

1. A daughter of Ishmael, the last married of the three wives of Esau (Gen. 36:3-4, 13), from whose son Reuel four tribes of the Edomites were descended. When first mentioned she is called Mahalath (28:9), while, on the other hand, the name Basemath is given in the narrative (26:34) to another of Esau's wives, the daughter of Elon the Hittite. It may have been the original name of one and the name given to the other upon her marriage, for as a rule, the women received new names when they were married.

2. A daughter of Solomon who became the wife of Ahimaaz, one of the king's deputies (1 Kings 4:15), about 965 B.C.

BA′SHAN (bā′shan). This territory extended from Gilead in the S to Hermon on the N, and

Bathing: The Pool of Siloam, Jerusalem

from the Jordan to Salecah, the present Salkhat, on the E, and included Edrei (Deut. 3:10; Josh. 9:10), Ashtaroth (Deut. 1:4; Josh. 9:10; etc.), the present Tell-Ashtur, and Golan (Deut. 4:43; Josh. 20:8; 21:27). Golan, one of its cities, was a city of refuge. Its productiveness was noted in the OT (Ps. 22:12; Jer. 50:19). The western part is exceedingly fertile today. On the E rise the Hauran Mountains to a height of six thousand feet. It was noted for its fine breed of cattle (Deut. 32:14; Ezek. 39:18). The cities are described by Moses as "cities fortified with high walls, gates and bars" (Deut. 3:5). The inhabitants were giantlike men who were called Rephaim in the era of Abraham (Gen. 14:5).

Some of the deserted towns are as perfect as when inhabited. When Israel entered Canaan, Argob, a province of Basham, contained sixty fenced cities (Deut. 3:4-5; 1 Kings 4:13). After the Exile Bashan was divided into four districts: Gaulonitis, or Jaulan, the western; Auranitis, or Hauran (Ezek. 47:16); Argob, or Trachonitis; and Batanaea, now Ard-el-Bathanyeh.

BA′SHAN, MOUNTAIN OF. In Ps. 68:15 the poet says, "A mountain of God is the mountain of Bashan;/A mountain of many peaks is the mountain of Bashan." "This epithet, not applicable to the long, level edge of the tableland, might refer either to the lofty triple summits of Hermon, or to the many broken cones that are scattered across Bashan, and so greatly differ in their volcanic form from the softer, less imposing heights of western Palestine" (Smith, *Hist. Geog.*, p. 550).

BA′SHAN-HA′VVOTH-JA′IR (bā-shan-ha′voth-jā′re; "The Bashan of the villages of Jair"). The name given by Jair to the places he had conquered in Bashan (Deut. 3:14, KJV). It contained sixty cities with walls and bronze gates (Josh. 13:30; 1 Kings 4:13). In Num. 32:41 it is called Havvoth-jair, which is the correct name (NASB; NIV; also KJV, but with only one "v"). The NASB correctly translates Deut. 3:14: ". . . Jair called it, that is, Bashan, after his own name, Havvoth-jair, as it is to this day."

BASH′EMATH. *See* Basemath.

BASIN. This word is used for dishes, containers, and bowls of various descriptions. (1) A large bowl, Heb. *mizrāq*, was a part of the furnishing of the Tabernacle and the Temple, particularly in service at the altar of burnt offering (Num. 4:14) to hold the grain offering (7:13) and to receive sacrificial blood (Zech. 9:15; 14:20). It was commonly made of gold or silver, sometimes of bronze (Ex. 27:3; Num. 7:84). In inordinate reveling, wine is said to be drunk from such bowls (Amos 6:6). (2) A smaller vessel, Heb. *'aggān*, was a vessel for washing, a laver (Ex. 24:6). It was also a wine cup (Isa. 22:24; Song of Sol. 7:2, translated "goblet"). *See* Laver. (3) A shallow vessel, Heb. *sap.* Such basins were of several types: utensils for holding the animal's blood (Ex. 12:22; Jer. 52:19), containers for the oil for the sacred candlestick (1 Kings 7:50), basins for domestic purposes (2 Sam. 17:28), and cups for drinking (Zech. 12:2). The basin from which our Lord washed the disciples' feet (John 13:5) was called a *niptēr* signifying, evidently, a utensil for washing. *See* Bowl; Cup.   M.F.U.

BASKET. No fewer than five common Heb. words are used to denote baskets or containers of different sizes, shapes, and construction. Ancient art reliefs and sculptures and the etymological meaning of the words used show that the baskets were frequently woven or made of fiber from leaves of the palm tree or rushes, leaves, and twigs. Some were used especially for holding bread (Gen. 40:16-18; Ex. 29:3, 23; Lev. 8:2, 26, 31; Num. 6:15, 17, 19). Egyptian bread baskets appear on ancient tombs. Baskets were also used in gathering grapes (Jer. 6:9, KJV) and carrying fruit (Amos 8:1-2). In Egypt heavy burdens such as grain were carried in large baskets swung from a pole hung on the shoulders. In the NT baskets are described as sometimes large enough to hold a man. Paul was lowered from the wall of Damascus in such a hamper (2 Cor. 11:33).   M.F.U.

BAS'MATH. *See* Basemath.

BASTARD. The word occurs in the KJV in Deut. 23:2 and Zech. 9:6 (NASB, see Zech. 9:6, marg.). Its etymology is obscure, but it appears to denote anyone to whose birth a serious stain is attached. The rabbis applied the term not to any illegitimate offspring but to the issue of any connection within the degrees prohibited by the law (*see* Marriage). A very probable conjecture is that which applies the term to the offspring of heathen prostitutes in the neighborhood of Palestine who were priestesses of a sort to the Syrian goddess Astarte. In Zech. 9:6, the word is, doubtless, used in the sense of *foreigner* (so NIV; the NASB reads "mongrel"), expressing the deep degradation of Philistia in being conquered by other people.

1. Persons of illegitimate birth among the Jews had no claim to a share in the paternal inheritance or to the proper filial treatment of children of the family. This is what is referred to in Heb. 12:8, where a contrast is drawn between the treatment that God's true children might expect, as compared with that given to such as are not so related to Him but are "illegitimate."

2. Persons of illegitimate birth are forbidden by the canon law from receiving any of the minor orders without a dispensation from the bishop; nor can they in the Latin church be admitted to holy orders or to benefices with cure of souls, except by a dispensation from the pope. In the Church of England a bastard cannot be admitted

to orders without a dispensation from the sovereign or archbiship.

BAT. *See* Animal Kingdom.

BATH. *See* Metrology: Liquid Measures of Capacity.

BATHE, BATHING (Heb. *rāḥaṣ*). The hot climate of the East, with its abundant dust, made bathing a constant necessity for the preservation and invigoration of health. This natural necessity was greatly furthered among the Israelites by the religious purifications enjoined by the law. For although these precepts had the higher object of teaching personal purity, they could not fail to intensify the instinct of cleanliness and to make frequent washing and bathing an indispensable arrangement of life.

The Israelites, from early times, were accustomed not only to wash the hands and feet before eating but also to bathe the body when about to visit a superior (Ruth 3:3), after mourning, which always implied defilement (2 Sam. 12:20), but especially before any religious service (Gen. 35:2; Ex. 19:10; Josh. 3:5; 1 Sam. 16:5), that they might appear clean before God. The high priest at his inauguration (Lev. 8:6) and on the day of atonement before each act of propitiation (16:4, 24) was also to bathe. Snow water was used to cleanse the body or lye was put into the water (Job 9:30), also bran, according to the Mishna. Bathing in running water (Lev. 15:13) or in rivers (2 Kings 5:10; Ex. 2:5) was especially favored. Baths were placed in the courts of private houses (2 Sam. 11:2; Susanna 15). In the later Temple there were bathrooms over the chambers for the use of the priests. The "pools," such as those of Siloam and Hezekiah (2 Kings 20:20; Neh. 3:15-16; Isa. 22:11; John 9:7), were public baths by NT times, no doubt introduced in imitation of a Roman and Greek custom.

BATHSHEBA (bath-she'ba; "daughter of the oath"). Daughter of Eliam (2 Sam. 11:3), or Ammiel (1 Chron. 3:5), the granddaughter of Ahithophel (2 Sam. 23:34) and wife of Uriah. She had illicit intercourse with David while her husband was absent at the siege of Rabbah, about 980 B.C. Uriah was slain by a contrivance of David, and after a period of mourning for her husband Bathsheba was legally married to the king (11:3-27). The child that was the fruit of her adulterous intercourse with David died, but she became the mother of four sons—Solomon, Shimea (Shammua), Shobab, and Nathan (2 Sam. 5:14; 1 Chron. 3:5). When Adonijah attempted to set aside in his own favor the succession promised to Solomon, Bathsheba was employed by Nathan the prophet to inform the king of the conspiracy and received from him an answer favorable to Solomon (1 Kings 1:11-31). After the accession of Solomon she, as queen-mother, requested permission of her son for Adonijah to take in marriage Abishag the Shunammite (2:21). The request was refused and became the occasion of the execution of Adonijah (2:24-25).

BIBLIOGRAPHY: W. G. Blaikie, *David, King of Israel* (1981), pp. 219-39; C. J. and A. A. Barber, *You Can Have a Happy Marriage* (1984), pp. 95-106.

BATH'-SHUA (bath-shu'a). A variation of the name *Bathsheba* (which see), the mother of Solomon (1 Chron. 3:5). *See also* Shua.

BATTERING-RAM. *See* Armor.

BATTLE. *See* War.

BATTLE-AXE. *See* Armor.

BATTLE-BOW. *See* Armor.

BATTLEMENT. A wall or lattice surrounding the flat roofs of an Eastern house, regarded as a protection against accidents (Deut. 22:8; "parapet," NASB, NIV). The term may also refer to the parapet of a city wall (Jer. 5:10; but *see* NASB and NIV, which read "branches"). *Battlement* appears in the KJV, NASB, and NIV, but not in the same verses.

BAV'VAI (bav'ī). A son of Henadad, and ruler of the half part of Keilah. He repaired a portion of the wall of Jerusalem on the return from Babylon (Neh. 3:18), 445 B.C.

BAY (Heb. *lāshôn,* "tongue"). The cove of the Dead Sea, at the mouth of the Jordan (Josh. 15:5; 18:19) and also of the southern extremity of the same sea (15:2). The same term is used (in the original) with reference to the forked mouths of the Nile ("the *tongue* of the Sea of Egypt," Isa. 11:15).

BAY. The color, according to the RV, of one of the spans of horses in the vision of Zechariah (6:3, 7). It is the rendering of *strong* (NASB). Keil and Delitzsch translate "speckled, powerful horses" (*Com.,* ad loc.).

BAY TREE. *See* Vegetable Kingdom.

BAZ'LITH (baz'lith). The head of one of the families of the Temple servants that returned to Jerusalem from the Exile (Neh. 7:54). He is called Bazluth in Ezra 2:52. The NIV renders Bazluth in both passages.

BAZ'LUTH (baz'luth). Another form of *Bazlith* (which see).

BDELLIUM. *See* Mineral Kingdom.

BEACH (Gk. *aigialos*). A shore, on which the waves *dash* (Matt. 13:2, 48; John 21:4; Acts 21:5; 27:39-40). *See also* Seashore, Seacoast.

BEALI'AH (bē-a-li'a; "whose Lord is Jehovah"). One of the Benjamite heroes who went over to David at Ziklag (1 Chron. 12:5), before 1000 B.C.

BE'ALOTH (bē'a-lōth).

1. A town in the southern part of Judah, i.e.,

in Simeon (Josh. 15:24), probably the same as Baalath-beer (19:8).

2. A district in Asher of which Baanah was deputy (1 Kings 4:16); NIV *Aloth* (which see).

BEAM. *See* Log.

BEAN. *See* Vegetable Kingdom.

BEAR (KJV, "Arcturus"). A part of the constellation Bootes and one of the three most brilliant stars of the Southern Hemisphere in line with the tail of Ursa Major, "the Great Bear." *See* Job 9:9; 38:32. For the animal, *see* Animal Kingdom.

BEARD. *See* Hair.

BEAST. *See* Animal Kingdom.

Figurative. In a figurative or symbolical sense, the term frequently occurs in Scripture and generally refers to the sensual and groveling or ferocious and brutal natures properly belonging to the brute creation. The psalmist speaks of himself as being "like a beast" before God, while giving way to merely sensuous considerations (Ps. 73:22). The word is sometimes used figuratively of brutal men. Hence the phrase "I fought with wild beasts at Ephesus" (1 Cor. 15:32, cf. Acts 19:29) is a figurative description of a *fight with strong and exasperated enemies.* For a similar use of the word see Eccles. 3:18; 2 Pet. 2:12; Jude 10.

A wild beast is the symbol of selfish, tyrannical monarchies. The four beasts in Dan. 7:3, 17, 23, represent four kingdoms (Ezek. 34:28; Jer. 12:9).

In the Apocalypse the Beast obviously means a worldly power whose rising out of the sea indicates that it owes its origin to the commotions of the people (Rev. 13:1; 15:2; 17:8).

The "four beasts" (Gk. *zōa,* "living creatures," not *thêrion,* "beast" in the strict sense) of the KJV of Rev. 4:6 should be rendered "four living ones" or "four living creatures" (so NASB and NIV). *See* Cherub, Cherubim.

BEATING. A punishment in universal use throughout the East. It appears to be designated by the Heb. phrase "rod of discipline," *shebeṭ mûsār* (Prov. 22:15). Beating with rods ("scourging," Matt. 27:26; "chastising," Deut. 22:18) was established by law and was quite common among the Jews (Prov. 10:13; 26:3). The person to be punished was extended upon the ground and blows, not exceeding forty, were applied to his back in the presence of a judge (Deut. 25:2-3). Among the Egyptians, ancient and modern, minor offenses were generally punished with the stick, and persons who refused to pay taxes were frequently brought to terms by a vigorous use of the stick. Superintendents were wont to stimulate laborers by the persuasive powers of the rod. The punishment was inflicted on both sexes. *See* Punishments.

BEAUTIFUL MANTLE FROM SHINAR (Heb.,

"cloak of Shinar [or Babylon]"). An ample robe with figures of men and animals either embroidered or interwoven in the fashion for which the Babylonians were noted. It came to mean a valuable piece of clothing in general (Josh. 7:21).

BEAUTIFUL TREES (Heb. *'ēṣ hādār,* "trees of ornament"). The Israelites were directed to take "the foliage of beautiful trees, palm branches and boughs of leafy trees and willows of the brook; and . . . rejoice before the Lord your God for seven days," i.e., to carry them about in festive procession (Lev. 23:40). This was to be done on the first day of the feast of Booths (*see* Festivals) in memory of their having dwelt in booths. The expression "beautiful trees" probably included not only the orange and citron, which were placed in gardens for ornament rather than for use, but also myrtles, olive trees, and others that had beauty or pleasant odor.

BEB'AI (be'baī).

1. The head of one of the families that returned with Zerubbabel from Babylon (about 536 B.C.) to the number of 623 (Ezra 2:11) or 628 (Neh. 7:16). At a later period 28 more, under Zechariah, returned with Ezra (Ezra 8:11), about 457 B.C. Several of his sons were among those who had taken foreign wives (10:28).

2. The name of one who sealed the covenant with Nehemiah (Neh. 10:15), 445 B.C.

BE'CHER (be'ker; "firstborn," or "a young camel," cf. Arab. *bakr,* "young camel").

1. The second son of Benjamin, according to the list of both in Gen. 46:21 and 1 Chron. 7:6 but omitted in 8:1. Some suppose that the word "first-born" in the latter passage is a corruption of Becher; others, that Becher in the two passages above is a corruption of the word signifying "first-born." Yet 7:8 gives Becher as a person and names his sons. He was one of the sons of Benjamin that came down to Egypt with Jacob, being one of the fourteen descendants of Rachel who settled there. At the numbering of the Israelites in the plain of Moab (Num. 26) there is no family named after him. But there is a Becher and a family of Becherites among the sons of Ephraim. This has given rise to the supposition that the slaughter of the sons of Ephraim by the men of Gath had sadly thinned the house of Ephraim of its males, and that Becher, or his heir, married an Ephraimitish heiress, a daughter of Shuthelah (1 Chron. 7:20-21), and so his house was reckoned in the house of Ephraim.

2. Son of Ephraim; called Bered (1 Chron. 7:20); his posterity were called Becherites (Num. 26:35). He is probably the same as the preceding.

BECO'RATH (be-ko'rath; "firstborn"). The son of Aphiah, of the tribe of Benjamin, one of the ancestors of King Saul (1 Sam. 9:1), long before 1030 B.C.

BED. A common article of domestic furniture. In the ancient Near East, however, the poor and travelers often slept on the ground, using their outer garment as a covering (Gen. 28:11; Ex. 22:26-27). Sometimes a bed might be no more than a mat of rough material easily carried about (Matt. 9:6), but regular beds raised above the ground to protect from dampness and drafts were in existence early (Deut. 3:11). The wealthy of Amos's day in the eighth century B.C. had beds of ivory (Amos 6:4) and expensive coverings and cushions (3:12). Beds of the wealthy often had a canopy. The Jewish bed may be described in five principal parts: (1) *Mattress.* A mere matter of one or more garments. (2) *Covering.* A finer garment than used for the mattress. In summer, a thin blanket or an outer garment worn by day (1 Sam. 19:13) was sufficient. Hence the Mosaic law provided that this garment should not be kept in pledge after sunset, that the poor might not be without his covering (Deut. 24:13). (3) *Pillow,* mentioned in 1 Sam. 19:13 (NASB, "quilt"; NIV, "garment"), apparently a material woven of goat's hair with which persons in the East covered the head and face while sleeping. (4) *The Bedstead.* This was not always necessary. The divan or platform along the side or end of an oriental room serving as a support for the bed with a frame seems implied in such references as 2 Sam. 3:31; 2 Kings 4:10; Esther 1:6. (5) *Ornamental Portions.* These consisted of pillows, a canopy, ivory carvings, and probably mosaic work, purple, and fine linen (Esther 1:6; Song of Sol. 3:9-10; Amos 6:4).   M.F.U.

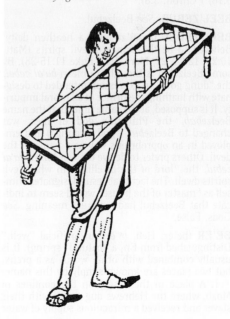

Man carrying his bed

BE'DAD (be'dad; "separation"). The father of Hadad, a king in Edom (Gen. 36:35; 1 Chron. 1:46).

BE'DAN (be'dan).

1. The name of a judge of Israel, not found in Judges but only in 1 Sam. 12:11. It is difficult to identify him with any of the judges mentioned elsewhere, but it is probable that *Bedan* is a contracted form for the name of the Judge *Abdon* (which see). The NIV identifies Bedan with *Barak* (which see).

2. The son of Ulam, the great-grandson of Manasseh (1 Chron. 7:17).

BEDCHAMBER. *See* Bedroom.

BEDE'IAH (be-de'ya). One of the family of Bani who divorced his Gentile wife on the return from Babylon (Ezra 10:35), 456 B.C.

BEDROOM (Heb. *ḥădar hammiṭṭôt,* "room of beds," 2 Kings 11:2; 2 Chron. 22:11; *ḥădar mishkāb,* "sleeping room," Ex. 8:3; 2 Sam. 4:7; 2 Kings 6:12). The "bedroom" in the Temple where Joash was hidden was probably a room used for storing beds (2 Kings 11:2; 2 Chron. 22:11). The position of the bedroom in the most remote and secret parts of the palace seems marked in the passages Ex. 8:3; 2 Kings 6:12.

BEDSTEAD. *See* Bed.

BEE. *See* Animal Kingdom.

BEELI'ADA (be-el-i'a-da; "Baal has known"). One of David's sons, born in Jerusalem (1 Chron. 14:7), after 1000 B.C. He is called Eliada (2 Sam. 5:16; 1 Chron. 3:8).

BEEL'ZEBUB. *See* Beelzebul.

BEEL'ZEBUL (be-el'ze-bul), a heathen deity. Believed to be the prince of evil spirits (Matt. 10:25; 12:24, 27; Mark 3:22; Luke 11:15-28). By some Beelzebul is thought to mean *ba'al zebel,* the "dung god," an expression intended to designate with loathing the prince of all moral impurity. It is supposed, at the same time, that the name Beelze*bub,* the Philistine god of flies, was changed to Beelze*bul* ("god of dung") and employed in an opprobrious way as a name of the devil. Others prefer to derive the word from *ba'al zebul,* the "lord of the dwelling" in which evil spirits dwell. The fact that Jesus designates Himself as "master of the house" would seem to indicate that Beelzebul had a similar meaning. *See* Gods, False.

BE'ER (be'er; Heb. *be'ēr,* an artificial "well." Distinguished from En, a "natural" spring). It is usually combined with other words as a prefix, but two places are known simply by this name:

1. A place in the desert on the confines of Moab, where the Hebrews dug a well with their staves and received a miraculous supply of water (Num. 21:16-18). It is probably the same as Beer-elim (Isa. 15:8).

2. A town in Judah to which Jotham fled for fear of Abimelech (Judg. 9:21), probably about eight Roman miles N of Eleutheropolis, the present el Bireth, near the mouth of the Wadi es Surâr.

BEE'RA (be-er'a; a "well"). The last given of the sons of Zophah, a descendant of Asher (1 Chron. 7:37).

BEE'RAH (be-er'a; a "well"). The son of Baal, a prince of the tribe of Reuben, carried into captivity by the Assyrian Tiglath-pileser (1 Chron. 5:6).

BE'ER-E'LIM (be'er-e'lim; "well of heroes"). A spot named in Isa. 15:8 as around the "territory of Moab," probably the S, Eglaim being on the N end of the Dead Sea. It seems to be the same as Beer (Num. 21:16).

BEE'RI (be-er-i; "of a fountain," or "well").

1. A Hittite, and father of Judith, a wife of Esau (Gen. 26:34), about 1950 B.C.

2. The father of the prophet Hosea (Hos. 1:1), before 748 B.C.

BE'ER-LAHAI'-ROI (be'er-la-hī'roi; "the well of him that liveth and seeth me," or "the well of the vision of life"). The fountain between Kadesh and Bered, near which the Lord found Hagar (Gen. 16:7, 14). In 24:62; 25:11 the KJV has "the well Lahai-roi."

BEE'ROTH (be-e'roth; "wells").

1. One of the four cities of the Hivites who made a covenant with Joshua (Josh. 9:17). Beeroth was allotted to Benjamin (18:25), in whose possession it continued at the time of David, the murderers of Ish-bosheth belonging to it (2 Sam. 4:2). Beeroth, with Chephirah and Kiriath-jearim, is in the list of those who returned from Babylon (Ezra 2:25; Neh. 7:29).

2. Beeroth of the children of Jaakan is named (Num. 33:31-32; Deut. 10:6) as a place through which the Israelites passed twice in the desert, their twenty-seventh and thirty-third station on their way from Egypt to Canaan, probably in the valley of the Arabah.

BEE'ROTHITE (be-e'ro-thīt). An inhabitant of *Beeroth* (which see) of Benjamin (2 Sam. 4:2; 23:37).

BE'ERSHEBA (be'er-she'ba; "well of the oath," or "of seven"). A city in the southern part of Palestine, about midway between the Mediterranean Sea and the southern end of the Dead Sea. It received its name because of the digging of the well and making of a covenant between Abraham and Abimelech (Gen. 21:31). It was a favorite residence of Abraham and Isaac (26:33). The latter was living there when Esau sold his birthright to Jacob, and from the encampment around the wells Jacob started on his journey to Mesopotamia. He halted there to offer sacrifice to "the God of his father" on his way to Egypt (46:1). Beersheba was allotted to Simeon (1 Chron. 4:28), and Samuel's sons were appointed deputy judges for the southernmost districts in Beersheba (1 Sam. 8:2). Elijah fled to Beersheba, which was still a refuge in the eighth century, and frequented even by northern Israel (Amos 5:5; 8:14). The expression "from Dan to Beersheba" was a formula for the whole land. During the separation of the kingdoms the formula became "from Geba to Beersheba," or "from Beersheba to Mount Ephraim." After the Exile, Beersheba was again peopled by Jews, and the formula ran "from Beersheba as far as the valley of Hinnom" (Neh. 11:30).

Well at Beersheba

The biblical town of Beersheba has been located at Tel es-Saba (Tell Beersheba), about two miles NE of the modern city. Yohanan Aharoni directed a Tel Aviv University excavation there from 1969 to 1976. He discovered that the town had a Hebrew foundation, built in the twelfth and eleventh centuries B.C. Apparently unwalled, it probably was the place where the sons of Samuel judged the people (1 Sam. 8:2). Beersheba was fortified with a twelve-foot-thick wall in the tenth century. At that time the enclosed area was a little less than three acres in size. Aharoni found nothing at Tell Beersheba dating to the patriarchal period, and he concluded that patriarchal Beersheba was located near the valley and the wells, probably at Bir es-Saba, within the area of modern Beersheba.   H.F.V.

BIBLIOGRAPHY: M. Avi-Yonah, *Encyclopedia of Archaeological Excavations in the Holy Land* (1975), 1:160-68.

BE-ESHTE′RAH (be′esh-te′ra). One of the two Levitical cities allotted to the Gershonites, out of the tribe of Manasseh beyond the Jordan (Josh. 21:27). In the parallel list (1 Chron. 6:71) Ashtaroth is given; and Be-eshterah is only a contracted form of Beth-Ashtaroth, the "temple of Ashtoreth."

BEETLE. *See* Animal Kingdom: Cricket.

BEEVES. *See* Animal Kingdom: Cattle; Ox.

BEGGAR (Heb. *'ebyôn*, "destitute," 1 Sam. 2:8, NASB, "needy"; Gk. *ptōchos*, Luke 16:20, 22; Gal. 4:9; elsewhere "poor"). A beggar, whose regular business it was to solicit alms publicly or to go promiscuously from door to door as understood by us, was unknown to the Pentateuchal legislation. The poor were allowed privileges by the Mosaic law, and indeed the Hebrew could not be an absolute pauper. His land was inalienable, except for a certain period; then it reverted to him or his posterity, and if this resource was insufficient he could pledge the services of himself and family for a valuable sum. In the song of Hannah (1 Sam. 2:8-9), however, beggars are spoken of, and beggary is predicted of the posterity of the wicked, while it was promised not to be the portion of the seed of the righteous (Pss. 37:25; 109:10). In the NT we read of beggars that were blind, diseased, and maimed seeking alms at the doors of the rich, by the waysides, and before the gate of the Temple (Mark 10:46; Luke 16:20-21; Acts 3:2).

BEGINNING (Heb. *rē'shît*, "first"). "In the beginning" (Gen. 1:1) is used in an absolute sense. However, the "beginning" of John 1:1 used of Christ, the Logos, antedates that of Gen. 1:1 and refers to the eternal preexistence of the Son. Genesis 1:1 merely gives the commencement of the physical universe and time. The "beginning" of 1 John 1:1 evidently refers to the commencement of Christ's public ministry.

Our Lord is called "the Beginning" (Gk. *archē*) by both Paul and John (Col. 1:18; Rev. 1:8; 3:14), and it is interesting to note that the Greek philosophers expressed the First Cause of all things by the same name.

BEHEAD. *See* Punishment.

BEHEMOTH (be-he′mōth). *See* Animal Kingdom.

BEINGS, LIVING. A term appearing frequently in the NASB (Ezek. 1:5-25; 3:13; 10:15, 17, 20; Rev. 4:6). The KJV renders "living creatures." *See* Cherub, Cherubim.

BEKA, BE′KAH (bē′kà). An early Jewish weight and coin, being half a shekel. *See* Metrology: Measures of Weight; Measures of Value, or Money.

BEKER, BEKERITE. *See* Becher.

BEL. The national god of Babylonia. *See* Gods, False.

BE′LA, BE′LAH (be′la; "swallowed").

1. A king of Edom, the son of Beor, and a native of the city of Dinhabah (Gen. 36:32-33; 1 Chron. 1:43). From the name of his father, Beor, we may infer that he was a Chaldean by birth and reigned

in Edom by conquest. He may have been contemporary with Moses and Balaam.

2. The eldest son of Benjamin (Gen. 46:21; 1 Chron. 7:6-7; 8:3), about 1640 B.C. From him came the family of the Belaites (Num. 26:38).

3. A son of Azaz, a Reubenite (1 Chron. 5:8), "who lived in Aroer, even to Nebo and Baal-meon."

4. Another name (Gen. 14:2, 8) for the city of *Zoar* (which see).

BE'LAITE (be'la-īt). The patronymic (Num. 26:38) of the descendants of *Bela,* no. 2 (which see).

BE'LIAL (be'li-al; "worthlessness, wickedness"). Belial is often used in the KJV as if it were a proper name, but beyond question it should not be regarded in the OT as such, its meaning being "worthlessness," and hence "recklessness, lawlessness." The expression "son" or "man of Belial" must be understood as meaning simply a worthless, lawless fellow (Deut. 13:13, KJV; Judg. 19:22; 20:13, see marg.; etc.).

In the NT the term appears (in the best manuscripts) in the form *Belias,* and not *Belial,* as given in the KJV. The term, as used in 2 Cor. 6:15, is generally understood as applied to Satan, as the personification of all that is bad.

Belial occurs only once in the NASB and NIV (2 Cor. 6:15). Elsewhere in those translations the Heb. terms rendered "sons [or children] of Belial" in the KJV are given as "worthless men," "worthless fellows," or "wicked men," often with a marginal reading, "lit., sons of Belial."

BELIEVE. "To remain steadfast" (Heb. *'āman,* Gen. 15:6; Ex. 4:1; Num. 14:11; etc.). "To be persuaded" of God's revealed truth (Gk. *peithomai,* Acts 17:4; 27:11; 28:24). "To adhere to, rely on" God's promises (Gk. *pisteuō,* Matt. 8:13; Mark 5:36; John 3:16; etc.). Although belief as mere credence or confidence is exceedingly common and often the result of ignorance or deception and not grounded in facts of knowledge or truth, yet in a scriptural sense faith in its larger usage represents four principal ideas. The first is personal confidence in God; second, a creedal or doctrinal concept of the essential body of revealed truth (Luke 18:8; 1 Cor. 16:13; 2 Cor. 13:5, Col. 1:23; 2:7; Titus 1:13; Jude 3); third, faithfulness as an evidence or fruit of the believer's trust in God (Gal. 5:22-23); fourth, a designation for Christ as the object of faith (3:23-25). As personal confidence in God, it is of immense importance to clearly distinguish three features of faith:

Saving faith is inward confidence in God's promises and provisions in Christ for the salvation of sinners. It leads one to trust solely in the Person and work of the Savior Jesus Christ (John 3:16; 5:24; Eph. 2:8-10). Such faith gives the believer an unchangeable and unforfeitable *posi-*

tion described in innumerable passages as being "in Christ" (Rom. 8:1; Eph. 1:3; etc.).

Sanctifying faith comprehends *knowledge* of and *trust* in our *position* "in Christ" (Rom. 6:1-10), so that one has experiential *possession* of Christ (Rom. 6:11). Compare Eph. 1-3, setting forth the believer's position, with Eph. 4-6, his experience of that position. Sanctifying or sustaining faith appropriates the power of God for conforming one's position in Christ to one's enjoyment of the blessings of that position, but in no sense is it to be confused with saving faith, which results in that position. *All* believers have a *position* of sanctification (cf. 1 Cor. 1:2 with 3:1-3; 5:5), are "saints," and by faith are to realize that position in practice in living a saintly life (Eph. 4:1; Col. 3:1-4). All believers who have exercised "saving faith" in Christ *are* what they are "in Him," whether or not they ever realize it. The difference is that when they realize it and in faith act upon it, they begin to enjoy the benefits of it in daily living.

Serving faith, acts upon the truth of divinely bestowed spiritual gifts and maintains confidence in all the details of divine enablement and appointments for service. "The faith which you have, have as your own conviction before God" (Rom. 14:22). This faith is accordingly a personal, individual matter. *See also* Faith.   M.F.U.

BIBLIOGRAPHY: N. Turner, *Christian Words* (1980), pp. 153-58.

BELIEVERS (Gk. *pistoi*). A term applied to Christian converts (Acts 5:14; 1 Tim. 4:12). It signifies those who have exercised saving faith in the Person and work of Jesus Christ and who, as a result, have obtained a position that is denoted by the oft-recurring phrase in the NT "in Christ" (Rom. 8:1; 1 Cor. 1:2; Eph. 1:3; etc.). This "in Christ" position wrought by the baptizing work of the Holy Spirit (6:3-4; 1 Cor. 12:13; Gal. 3:27; Col. 2:9-12) is the basis of all the believer's spiritual possessions. The NT presents Christian obligation as living in accordance with this position (Eph. 4:1; Rom. 6:11). The NT, therefore, presents the believer's position as unchangeable and unforfeitable as a result of the efficacy of Christ's atoning work and God's faithfulness.
     M.F.U.

BELL (Heb. *pa'amôn,* something "struck," Ex. 28:33-34; 39:25-26; *meşillâ,* "tinkling," Zech. 14:20). The bell is closely allied to the cymbal. The indentation of cymbals would be found to add to their vibrating power and sonority, and as this indentation became exaggerated nothing would be more probable than that they should eventually be formed into half-globes. This form is found in Roman and Greek sculpture. The most ancient bells yet discovered consist of a plate of metal, bent round and rudely riveted where the edges meet. Such were in use among the Assyrians and ancient Chinese.

1. Small golden bells were attached to the lower part of the blue robe (robe of the ephod) that formed part of the official dress of the high priest. These may have been partly for ornament but partly also for use, to ring as often as the high priest moved, so as to announce his approach and departure (Ex. 28:33-35).

2. In Isa. 3:16-18 reference is made to little tinkling bells (NASB, "bangles"; NIV, "ornaments") that are worn to this day by women upon their wrists and ankles to attract attention and gain admiration.

3. "Bells of the horses" (Zech. 14:20) were probably concave pieces or plates of brass, that were sometimes attached to horses for the sake of ornament. These by their tinkling served to enliven the animals, and in the caravans served the purpose of our modern sheep bells. In the passage referred to the motto "Holy to the Lord," which the high priest wore upon his turban and that was also inscribed upon the bells of horses, predicted the coming of a millennial age when all things, even to the lowest, should be sanctified to God.

BELLOWS ("blower"). The term *bellows* appears in Jer. 6:29 only, though other passages that speak of blowing the fire (Isa. 54:16; Ezek. 22:21) may refer to them; but as wood was the common fuel in ancient times, and kindles readily, a fan would generally be sufficient. Bellows seem to have been of great antiquity in Egypt, and were used at the forge or furnace. They were worked by the foot of the operator pressing alternately upon two skins till they were empty and pulling up each empty skin with a string held in his hand. The earliest specimens seem to have been simply of reed tipped with a metal point where it came in contact with the fire.

Egyptian bellows

BELLY (Heb. usually *beṭen*, "hollow"; Gk. *koilia;* also Heb. *mē'îm;* Gk. *gaster,* especially the "bowels"). Among the Hebrews and most ancient nations the belly was regarded as the seat of the carnal affections, as being, according to their view, that which first partakes of sensual pleasures (Titus 1:12; Phil. 3:19; Rom. 16:18).

Figurative. It is used figuratively for the heart, the innermost recesses of the soul (Prov. 18:8; 20:27; 26:22). The "belly of hell" (KJV; NASB, "depth of Sheol"; NIV, "depths of the grave"), literally, "out of the womb of the nether world," is a strong phrase to express Jonah's dreadful condition in the deep (Jonah 2:2).

BELOMANCY. Divination by arrows. *See* Magic.

BELSHAZ'ZAR (Bel-shuz'er; Akkad. Bel-shar-uṣur, "Bel has protected the king"). The eldest son and coregent of Nabonidus (539 B.C.), the last sovereign of the neo-Babylonian Empire. The following passage explicitly states that before Nabonidus started on his expedition to Tema in Arabia he entrusted actual kingship to Belshazzar: "He entrusted a campaign to his eldest, first-born son; the troops of the land he sent with him. He freed his hand, he entrusted the kingship to him. Then he himself undertook a distant campaign. The power of the land of Akkad advanced with him; towards Tema in the midst of the Westland he set his face. . . . He himself established his dwelling in Tema. . . . That city he made glorious. . . . They made it like a palace of Babylon. . . ." The Babylonian records indicate that Belshazzar became coregent in the third year of Nabonidus's reign (553 B.C.) and continued in that capacity until the fall of Babylon (539 B.C.). The Nabunaid Chronicle states that in the seventh, ninth, tenth, and eleventh years "the king was in the city of Tema. The son of the king, the princes and the troops were in the land of Akkad (Babylonia)." During Nabonidus's absence in Tema, the Nabunaid Chronicle explicitly indicates that the New Year's Festival was not celebrated but that it was observed in the seventeenth year upon the king's return home. Accordingly, it is evident that Belshazzar actually exercised the coregency in Babylon and that the Babylonian records in a remarkable manner supplement the biblical notices (Dan. 5; 7:1; 8:1). The book of Daniel is thus not in error in representing Belshazzar as the last king of Babylon, as negative criticism once believed, nor can it be said to be wrong in calling Belshazzar the son of Nebuchadnezzar (Dan. 5:2). Apparently Belshazzar was lineally related to Nebuchadnezzar because his mother, Nitrocris, seems to have been Nebuchadnezzar's daughter. Moreover, "son of " in Semitic usage is equivalent to "successor of "; so one could properly be called a son of even if not in lineal descent (cf. R. P. Dougherty, *Nabonidus and Belshazzar,* [1929]). In the Assyrian records Jehu is called "the son of Omri"; actually Jehu was only a royal successor with no lineal relation at all.							M.F.U.; H.F.V.

BIBLIOGRAPHY: R. P. Dougherty, *Nabonidus and Belshazzar* (1929).

BELT. *See* Dress.

BELTESHAZ'ZAR (bel-te-shaz'er; Akkad.

"Balaṭ-su-uṣur (Bel), protect his life"). The Babylonian name given to the prophet Daniel (Dan. 1:7). *See* Daniel.

BEN ("son"). A Levite "of the second rank," one of the porters appointed by David to the service of the Ark (1 Chron. 15:18), 988 B.C.

BEN (Heb. *ben*, "son of"). Often used as a prefix to proper names in Scripture, the following word being either a proper name, an appellative, or geographical location, or even a number expressing age. Thus, a "son of twenty years" would mean twenty years old. Hadadezer Ben-rehob (cf. 2 Sam. 8:3) would mean Hadadezer of Beth-rehob, born or brought up in that place. A "son of valor" (Heb. *ben ḥayil*, cf. Deut. 3:18) would mean a valorous one. "Son of " may, of course, mean a lineal father-son relationship, as the term is used today (Gen. 4:25), or contrary to our usage may mean to bear a more remote descendant as a grandchild (46:24; 2 Kings 9:2, 20) or a great-grandchild (Gen. 46:18). The Israelites were known as "the sons of Jacob" (or Israel) for centuries after the death of the patriarch (Mal. 3:6). The seventy souls that "came from the loins of Jacob" (Ex. 1:5) included grandchildren. Usage extends to tribes or countries (Gen. 10:20-22) or even to a nonblood relation. Jehu, a usurper and founder of a new dynasty in Israel, and with no blood relationship whatever to the house of Omri, is nevertheless called "the son of Omri" in the Black Obelisk of Shalmaneser III of Assyria (D. D. Luckenbill, *Ancient Records of Assyria and Babylonia*, 1:590).   M.F.U.

BENA'IAH (be-na'ya; "built by Jehovah").

1. The son of Jehoiada the chief priest (1 Chron. 27:5), and a native of Kabzeel (2 Sam. 23:20; 1 Chron. 11:22). He was placed by David (11:25) over his bodyguard of Cherethites and Pelethites (2 Sam. 8:18; 20:23; 1 Kings 1:38; 1 Chron. 18:17), and given a position above "the thirty" but not included among the first three of the "mighty men" (2 Sam. 23:22-23; 1 Chron. 11:24-25; 27:6). He was a valiant man, and his exploits against man and beast that gave him rank are recorded in 2 Sam. 23:21; 1 Chron. 11:22. He was captain of the host for the third month (27:5). Benaiah remained faithful to Solomon during Adonijah's attempt on the crown (1 Kings 1:8-10). Acting under Solomon's orders he killed Joab and was appointed to fill his position as commander of the army (2:33-35; 4:4), c. 938 B.C. Jehoiada, the son of Benaiah, succeeded Ahithophel as counselor to the king according to 1 Chron. 27:34. This is possibly a copyist's mistake for "Benaiah the son of Jehoiada."

2. A man of Pirathon, of the tribe of Ephraim, one of David's thirty mighty men (2 Sam. 23:30; 1 Chron. 11:31) and the captain of the host for the eleventh month (1 Chron. 27:14), 1000 B.C.

3. One of the leaders of the families of Simeon,

who dispossessed the Amalekites from the pasture grounds of Gedor (1 Chron. 4:36), about 715 B.C.

4. A Levite in the time of David who played with "harps tuned to alamoth" at the removal of the Ark (1 Chron. 15:18, 20; 16:5), about 990 B.C.

5. A priest appointed to blow the trumpet before the Ark when David caused it to be moved to Jerusalem (1 Chron. 15:24; 16:6), about 990 B.C.

6. A Levite of the sons of Asaph, the son of Jeiel and grandfather of Jahaziel, who was sent by God to encourage the army of Jehoshaphat against the Moabites (2 Chron. 20:14), about 875 B.C.

7. A Levite in the time of Hezekiah who was one of the overseers of the offerings to the Temple (2 Chron. 31:13), 726 B.C.

8-11. Four Jews who had taken Gentile wives after the return from Babylon, 456 B.C. They were respectively of the "sons" of Parosh (Ezra 10:25), Pahath-moab (v. 30), Bani (v. 34), and Nebo (v. 43).

12. The father of Pelatiah, who was one of the "leaders of the people" in the time of Ezekiel (Ezek. 11:1), before 592 B.C.

BEN-ABIN'ADAB (ben-a-bin'a-dab). One of Solomon's district governors, who ruled over the district of Dor (1 Kings 4:11).

BEN-AM'MI (ben-am'i; "son of my kindred"). A son of Lot by his youngest daughter. He was the progenitor of the Ammonites (Gen. 19:38), twentieth century B.C.

BENCH. *See* Deck of Boxwood.

BEN-DE'KAR (ben-de'kar; "stab"). The father of Solomon's deputy in the second royal district, lying in the western part of the hill country of Judah and Benjamin, Shaalbim, and Beth-shemesh (1 Kings 4:9), before 960 B.C.

BEN-DE'KER. *See* Ben-Dekar.

BEN'E-BE'RAK (ben'e-be'rak; "sons of lightning"). One of the cities of Dan (Josh. 19:45), the present Ibn Abrak, four miles E of Joppa. Sennacherib mentions it as one of the cities besieged and taken by him.

BENEDICTION. An essential form of public worship was the priestly benediction, the form of which is prescribed in the law, "The Lord bless you, and keep you;/The Lord make his face shine on you,/And be gracious to you;/The Lord lift up His countenance on you,/And give you peace" (Num. 6:24-26), the promise being added that God would fulfill the words of the blessing. This blessing was pronounced by the priest after every morning and evening sacrifice with uplifted hands, as recorded of Aaron (Lev. 9:22). The people responded by uttering an amen. This blessing was also regularly pronounced at the close of the service in the synagogues. The Levites appear also to have had the power of giving the blessing

(2 Chron. 30:27), and the same privilege was accorded the king, as the viceroy of the Most High (2 Sam. 6:18; 1 Kings 8:55). Our Lord is spoken of as blessing little children (Mark 10:16; Luke 24:50), besides the blessing on the occasion of the institution of the Eucharist (Matt. 26:26).

BEN'E-JA'AKAN (ben'e-ja'a-kan; "children of Jaakan"). A tribe that gave its name to certain wells in the desert that formed one of the halting places of the Israelites on their journey to Canaan (Num. 33:31-32). *"Bene-Jaakan* is simply an abbreviation of *Beeroth-bene-Jaakan,* wells of the children of *Jaakan.* Now if the children of Jaakan were the same as the Horite family of *Jakan* mentioned in Gen. 36:27, the wells of *Jaakan* would have to be sought for on the mountains that bound the *Arabah"* (K. & D., *Com.,* ad loc.).

BENE-KEDEM. *See* East, Sons of.

BENEVOLENCE, DUE (Gk. *hē opheilomenē eunoia,* NASB, "fulfill his duty"). In the KJV, a euphemism for marital duty (1 Cor. 7:3).

BEN-GEB'ER (ben-geb'er). Solomon's district officer over the Transjordanian district of *Ramoth-Gilead* (which see; 1 Kings 4:13).

BEN-HA'DAD (ben-hā'dad). The Heb. form of Aram. Bar-hadad, "son of the god Hadad."
    1. The Early Kings of Damascus. The succession of Syrian kings who reigned at Damascus and elevated the city-state to the height of its power. Under them it became the inveterate foe of Israel for a full century and a half after 925 B.C. Biblical reference to the Ben-hadads has been remarkably illuminated by archaeology as a result of the discovery of the inscribed stela of Ben-hadad I, recovered in N Syria in 1940. This important royal inscription in general confirms the order of early Syrian rulers as given in 1 Kings 15:18, where Ben-hadad is said to be the "son of Tabrimmon, the son of Hezion, king of Abram, who lived in Damascus." According to W. F. Albright's rendering of the Ben-hadad monument, with the somewhat precarious restoration of the partly undecipherable portion, the sequence is identical: "Bir-hadad, son of Tabramman, son of Hadyan, king of Aram" (cf. *Bulletin of the American Schools of Oriental Research* 87 [Oct. 1942]: 23-29; 90 [Apr. 1943]: 32-34). Bir-hadad is equivalent to Bar-hadad (Heb. Ben-hadad), and Tab-ramman and Hadyan are equatable with Heb. Tabrimmon and Hezion. The correct name of the first king of Damascus has been corroborated by archaeological evidence, but the identity of Rezon who seized Damascus during Solomon's reign and apparently ruled there (11:23-25) is still unsolved. Is Hezion the same as Rezon? If so, then the form Rezon is secondary and may be regarded as a corruption of Hezion. If this is not the case, which apparently is unlikely, Rezon must be excluded from the dynastic list of 15:18, which is improbable since he was ostensibly the founder of the powerful Damascene state.
    2. Ben-hadad I. By the time Ben-hadad entered into the succession of Syrian kings somewhere around 890 B.C., Syria had become the strongest state in this region of W Asia and was ready to seize any opportunity to increase its territories. Such an occasion offered itself when the hard-pressed Asa, king of Judah (c. 917-876 B.C.), sent an urgent appeal to Syria for help against Baasha, king of Israel (c. 908-886 B.C.). Baasha, pushing his frontier southward to within five miles of Jerusalem, proceeded to fortify Ramah as a border fortress commanding the capital of Judah (1 Kings 15:17). Asa desperately sent what was left of the Temple and royal treasury, despoiled so recently by the Egyptian pharaoh Shishak, to Ben-hadad as a bribe to entice Syria into an alliance with himself against Israel. This strategy was at least immediately successful, for Ben-hadad invaded northern Israel and forced Baasha to abandon Ramah (15:20-22). But Asa committed a grievous mistake, for in courting the favor of Damascus against Israel, he granted Ben-hadad an unparalleled opportunity for aggrandizement and gave a common enemy of both the Northern and the Southern kingdoms a great advantage.
    Formerly scholars almost universally distinguished between Ben-hadad I, son of Tabrimmon (who was the son of Hezion the contemporary of Asa and Baasha; 15:18), and Ben-hadad the contemporary of Elijah and Elisha. Only occasionally did a biblical scholar such as T. K. Cheyne recognize the possibility that the two might be identical (*Encyclopaedia Biblia,* 1:531-32). Still, the majority maintained that the so-called Ben-hadad I died during the early years of the reign of Omri or Ahab (c. 865 B.C.) and was succeeded by Ben-hadad II. However, evidence furnished by the stela of Ben-hadad argues strongly for the identity of Ben-hadad I and Ben-hadad II (cf. *Bulletin of the American Schools of Oriental Research*: 83:14-22). In addition, careful research on the vexing problems of the chronology of the kings of Israel and Judah of this period has resulted in the reduction of years reigned, notably of Israel's kings, and obviated any serious objection to the equation on the grounds of an impossibly long reign for Ben-hadad I.
    A further argument commonly urged against the identification of Ben-hadad I with Ben-hadad II is the word of the vanquished Syrian monarch to King Ahab of Israel after the latter's notable victory at Aphek (modern Fiq) three miles E of the Sea of Galilee, recorded in 20:34: "The cities which my father took from your father I will restore, and you shall make streets for yourself in Damascus as my father made in Samaria." This allusion can hardly be to Ahab's father Omri (c. 885-874 B.C.), who founded the metropolis of Samaria as the capital of the Northern Kingdom, for

available sources do not lend the least support to the hypothesis that the latter incurred a defeat in a coalition with Syria. The term *father*, especially when used of royalty, must frequently be construed as "predecessor," as is commonly illustrated by the monuments. Doubtless towns taken from Israel by early Syrian kings such as Hezion or Tabrimmon are meant. Ben-hadad's use of the term *Samaria* was evidently formulaic. The city had been so strategically situated and enjoyed such a prosperous growth that soon after its establishment by Omri its name was used of the whole Northern Kingdom of which it was the capital. Ben-hadad I warred against Ahab of Israel (20:1). Ahab's brilliant strategy won not only this battle but also the one during the following year at Aphek (1 Kings 20:26-43).

The next year, however, the appearance on the horizon of a powerful Assyrian army marching toward Syria-Palestine compelled Ahab and his hereditary foe Ben-hadad to align themselves in a general coalition of neighboring kings to block the ambitious Assyrian invasion southward. The Monolith Inscription, now in the British Museum, records the military expeditions of Shalmaneser III (859-824 B.C.) and includes a description of his clash with the Syrian coalition headed by "Hadadezer [Ben-hadad], of Aram (Damascus)" in 853 B.C. The battle took place at Qarqar north of Hamath in the Orontes Valley, a strategic fortress city that guarded the approaches of lower Syria. Ahab "of Israel" is mentioned along with Ben-hadad of Damascus. Ben-hadad furnished twelve hundred chariots as compared to Ahab's two thousand, but Hadadezer (Ben-hadad) furnished twice as many soldiers, twenty thousand against Ahab's ten thousand. Shalmaneser's venture was evidently not successful, despite his extravagant boasts. In 848 B.C. Shalmaneser III made another thrust into Syria. He was again met by a coalition of "twelve kings of the seaboard" headed by Adadidri (Hadadezer of Damascus, i.e., Ben-hadad I). Ben-hadad I's long energetic reign came to an end about 843 B.C., and by 841 B.C. Hazael, an influential official, had succeeded to the throne.

3. Ben-Hadad II, another Aramaean king who ruled at Damascus. He was the son of Hazael. The latter sat on the throne at Damascus from c. 841 to 801 B.C. Ben-hadad II was a weak ruler who failed to protect the far-reaching conquests of his father, and Israel began to regain its fortunes. Although Aramaean power suffered in S Syria, Ben-hadad II displayed remarkable vitality in the N, as shown by the important stela of Zakir, king of Hamath, discovered in 1903 at modern Afis, SW of Aleppo in N Syria. This significant monument, published by its discoverer H. Pognon in 1907, makes reference in lines 4 and 5 to Ben-hadad II under the Aram. form of his name "Bar hadad, son of Hazael, king of Aram." He is presented as heading a coalition of kings against

"Zakir, king of Hamath and Luash." The cause of the attack was the merger of two powerful independent states, Hamath and Luash. This political maneuver so upset the balance of power in Syria and was attended with such a serious threat to the autonomy of Damascus and other Syrian states that they were ready to go to war in order to break it up. Ben-hadad II especially had reason to be made sensitive to any added threat to Syrian power since his losses to Israel in the S had seriously curtailed his sway in that direction. Zakir's victory over the coalition, in the celebration of which he set up his stela, furnished another indication of the essential weakness of Ben-hadad II's might. In fact, his reign made possible Israel's power under Jeroboam II (c. 786-746 B.C.). M.F.U.

BIBLIOGRAPHY: R. deVaux, *Revue Biblique* 43 (1934): 512-18; W. F. Albright, *Bulletin of the American Schools of Oriental Research* 89 (Feb. 1942): 23-29; M. F. Unger, *Israel and the Aramaens of Damascus* (1957); J. Pritchard, ed., *Ancient Near Eastern Texts* (1969), pp. 271-81.

BEN-HA'IL (ben-ha'il; "son of strength," that is, "warrior"). One of the "officials" of the people sent by Jehoshaphat to teach the inhabitants of Judah (2 Chron. 17:7), 875 B.C.

BENHA'NAN (ben-ha'nan; "son of one gracious"). The third named of the four "sons" of Shimon, of the tribe of Judah (1 Chron. 4:20).

BEN-HE'SED (ben-he'sed; the son of Hesed). The name of one of Solomon's deputies in the districts of Arubboth, Socoh, and Hepher (1 Kings 4:10), after 960 B.C.

BEN-HINNOM, VALLEY OF. *See* Hinnom, Valley of.

BEN-HUR' (ben-hur). The name of Solomon's governor of the district of Ephraim (1 Kings 4:8).

BENI'NU (be-nî'nū; "our son"). A Levite who sealed the covenant with Nehemiah (Neh. 10:13), 445 B.C.

BENJAMIN (ben'ja-min; "son of my right hand," or perhaps, "son of the South," Southerner). The name of the youngest son of Jacob (see below) and two other biblical personages.

1. A man of the tribe of Benjamin, second named of the seven sons of Bilhan, and the head of a family of "mighty men of valor" (1 Chron. 7:10).

2. An Israelite, one of the "sons of Harim," who divorced his foreign wife after the Exile (Ezra 10:32), 456 B.C. He seems to be the same person who had assisted in rebuilding (Neh. 3:23) and purifying (Neh. 12:34) the walls of Jerusalem.

BEN'JAMIN (ben'ja-min; "son of my right hand," or perhaps, "son of the South," Southerner). A son of Bilhan and a son of Harim (*see* article above) as well as the youngest of the sons of

Jacob, and the second by Rachel (Gen. 35:18), born about 1900 B.C.

Personal History. Benjamin was probably the only son of Jacob born in Palestine. His birth took place on the road between Bethel and Ephrath (Bethlehem), a short distance from the latter. His mother died immediately and with her last breath named him Ben-oni ("son of my pain"), which name the father changed. We hear nothing more of Benjamin until the time when his brothers went into Egypt to buy food. Jacob kept him at home, for he said, "I am afraid that harm may befall him" (Gen. 42:4). The story of his going to Joseph, the silver cup, etc., is familiar and discloses nothing beyond a strong affection manifested for him by his father and brothers.

The Tribe of Benjamin. In Gen. 46:21 the immediate descendants of Benjamin number ten, whereas in Num. 26:38-40 only seven are enumerated, and some even under different names. This difference is probably owing to the circumstance that some of the direct descendants of Benjamin died at an early period, or, at least, childless.

Numbers. At the first census the tribe numbered 35,400, ranking eleventh, but increased to 45,600 at the second census, ranking seventh.

Position. During the wilderness journey Benjamin's position was on the W side of the Tabernacle with his brother tribes of Ephraim and Manasseh (Num. 2:18-24). We have the names of the leader of the tribe when it set out on its long road (2:22); of the spy (13:9); of the families of which the tribe consisted when it was marshaled at the great halt in the plains of Moab, near Jericho (26:38-41, 63), and of the leader who was chosen to assist at the dividing of the land (34:21).

Territory. The proximity of Benjamin to Ephraim during the march to the Promised Land was maintained in the territories allotted to each. Benjamin lay immediately to the S of Ephraim, and between him and Judah.

Subsequent History. We may mention, among the events of note, that they assisted Deborah (Judg. 5:14); they were invaded by the Ammonites (10:9); that they were almost exterminated by the other tribes because they refused to give up the miscreants of Gibeah (chaps. 19-20); that the remaining six hundred were furnished with wives at Jabesh-gilead and Shiloh (chap. 21). To Benjamin belongs the distinction of giving the first king to the Jews, Saul being a Benjamite (1 Sam. 9:1-2; 10:20-21). After the death of Saul they declared themselves for Ish-bosheth (2 Sam. 2:15; 1 Chron. 12:29). They returned to David (2 Sam. 3:19-20; 19:16-17). David having at last expelled the Jebusites from Zion, making it his own residence, the close alliance between Benjamin and Judah (Judg. 1:8) was cemented by the circumstance that while Jerusalem actually belonged to the district of Benjamin, that of Judah was immediately contiguous to it. After the death of Solomon, Benjamin espoused the cause of Judah, and the two formed a kingdom by themselves. After the Exile, also, these two tribes constituted the flower of the new Jewish colony (cf. Ezra 4:1; 10:9). The prediction of Jacob regarding Benjamin's future lot, or the development of his personal character in his tribe, is brief: "Benjamin is a ravenous wolf;/In the morning he devours the prey,/And in the evening he divides the spoil" (Gen. 49:27). The events of history cast light on that prediction, for the ravening of the wolf is seen in the exploits of Ehud the Benjamite (Judg. 3), in Saul's career, and especially in the whole matter of Gibeah, so carefully recorded in Judg. 20. And again, the fierce wolf is seen in the fight in 2 Sam. 2:15-16, at Gibeon, and in the character of Shimei. Some find much of the wolf of Benjamin in Saul of Tarsus, "ravaging the church."

Archaeology. The famous letters from the eighteenth century B.C. recovered from the site of the Middle-Euphrates city of Mari since 1933 mention the Banu Yamina, "sons of the right," i.e., "sons of the South" (Southerners), who were roving Bedouin in this vicinity at the time. Although some scholars (such as A. Parrot) are tempted to connect these wandering bands with the biblical Benjamites, or Benjaminites, and A. Alt allowed the possibility, yet the biblical tribe was born in Palestine and is never said to have been in Mesopotamia. The name *Benjamin*, meaning "son of the right," "son of the South," or "Southerner," was a name likely to occur in various places, especially so at Mari, where the corresponding term "sons of the left," i.e., "sons of the North" or "Northerners," is found. Directions N and S in the ancient Near East were determined by facing E toward the sunrise—so left was N and right was S.   M.F.U.

BEN'JAMITE (ben'ja-mīt; 1 Sam. 9:21; 22:7; 2 Sam. 16:11). The patronymic title of the descendants of the patriarch *Benjamin* (which see).

BE'NO (be'nō; "his son"). The only son, or the first of the four sons, of Jaaziah the Levite, of the family of Merari, in 1 Chron 24:26-27.

BEN-O'NI (ben-ō'ni; "son of my pain"). The name given by the dying Rachel to her youngest son, but afterward changed (Gen. 35:18) by his father to *Benjamin* (which see).

BEN-ZO'HETH (ben-zō'heth; "son of Zoheth"). A person named (1 Chron. 4:20) as the second son of Ishi, a descendant of Judah, or it may be that he was grandson of Ishi, being the son of Zoheth himself.

BE'ON (bē-on'). Perhaps an early scribal error for "Meon," one of the places fit for pasturage; Num. 32:3-4, "a land for livestock." It is more properly called Beth-baal-meon (Josh. 13:17), more briefly Baal-meon (Num. 32:38), and Beth-meon (Jer. 48:23).

BE'OR (bē'or).

1. The father of Bela, one of the kings of Edom (Gen. 36:32; 1 Chron. 1:43).

2. The father of Balaam, the prophet hired by Balak to curse the children of Israel (Num. 22:5), about 1400 B.C. He is also mentioned in 2 Pet. 2:15.

BE'RA (bē'ra). King of Sodom at the time of the invasion of the five kings under Chedorlaomer, which was repelled by Abraham (Gen. 14:2, 17, 21), twenty-first century B.C.

BER'ACAH (ber'a-ka; a "blessing").

1. One of the thirty Benjamite warriors who joined David at Ziklag (1 Chron. 12:3).

2. A valley between Bethlehem and Hebron, not far from En-gedi; noted as the place where Jehoshaphat overcame the Moabites and Ammonites (2 Chron. 20:26).

BERACHI'AH. See Berechiah.

BERAI'AH (ber-aī-a; "created by Jehovah"). Next to the last named of the sons of Shimei and a chief Benjamite of Jerusalem (1 Chron. 8:21).

BERAKI'AH. See Berechiah.

BERE'A (be-rē'a). A Macedonian city at the foot of Mt. Bermius, once a large and populous city and the residence of many Jews, whose concern for careful criticism in the study of the Scriptures was commended by Paul (Acts 17:10-13). Berea is now known as Verria, a place of more than thirty thousand people.

BIBLIOGRAPHY: Strabo *Geography of Strabo* 7.

View from the walls of ancient Berea

BERECHI'AH (ber-a-kī'a; "blessed by Jehovah").

1. Either one of the sons (according to most authorities) or a brother of Zerubbabel, of the royal line of Judah (1 Chron. 3:20), 536 B.C.

2. The son of Shimea and father of Asaph, the celebrated singer (1 Chron. 6:39, KJV, "Bera-

chiah"; 15:17), 1000 B.C. He was one of the "gatekeepers for the ark" when it was moved from the house of Obed-edom (15:23).

3. The son of Asa, and one of the Levites that dwelt in the villages of the Netophathites after the return from Babylon (1 Chron. 9:16), about 536 B.C.

4. The son of Meshillemoth, and one of the "heads" of Ephraim who enforced the prophet Oded's prohibition of the enslavement of their Judaite captives by the warriors of the Northern Kingdom (2 Chron. 28:12), 741 B.C.

5. The son of Meshezabel and father of Meshullam, who repaired a part of the walls of Jerusalem (Neh. 3:4, 30). His granddaughter was married to Jehohanan, the son of Tobiah (6:18).

6. The son of Iddo and father of Zechariah the prophet (Zech. 1:1, 7), before 520 B.C.

7. The father of the Zechariah mentioned in Matt. 23:35 as having been murdered by the Jews; and perhaps the same as Jehoida the priest (cf. 2 Chron. 24:20-22). See Zechariah.

BE'RED (be'red).

1. A son of Shuthelah and grandson of Ephraim (1 Chron. 7:20), supposed by some to be identical with Becher (Num. 26:35).

2. A town in the S of Palestine (Gen. 16:14), near which lay the well Lahai-roi (Beer-lahai-roi), supposed by some to be at El-Khulasah, twelve miles from Beersheba.

BEREKI'AH. See Berechiah.

BE'RI (be'rî; "well, fountain"). A son of Zophah, and a mighty warrior of the tribe of Asher (1 Chron. 7:36).

BERI'AH (be-ri'a; perhaps "prominent," cf. Arab. *bara'a,* "to excel").

1. The last named of the four sons of Asher, and father of Heber and Malchiel (Gen. 46:17; 1 Chron. 7:30). His descendants were called Beriites (Num. 26:44-45).

2. A son of Ephraim, so named on account of the state of his father's house when he was born. Some of Ephraim's sons had been killed by men of Gath "because they came down to take their livestock" (1 Chron. 7:21).

3. A Benjamite, and apparently son of Elpaal. He and his brother Shemed were ancestors of the inhabitants of Aijalon and expelled the people of Gath (1 Chron. 8:13). His nine sons are enumerated in vv. 14-16.

4. The last named of the four sons of Shimei, a Levite of the family of Gershon (1 Chron. 23:10-11). His posterity was not numerous and was reckoned with that of his brother Jeush.

BERI'ITES (be-rî'īts). Only mentioned in Num. 26:44, these are the descendants of *Beriah* (which see), son of Asher (Gen. 46:17; Num. 26:45).

BE'RITES (be'rīts). A people mentioned only in

2 Sam. 20:14, in the account of Joab's pursuit of Sheba, son of Bichri. Being mentioned in connection with Abel Beth-maacah, they seem to have lived in northern Palestine. Thompson (*The Land and the Book*) places them at Biria, N of Safed. Biria he identifies with Beroth, a city of upper Galilee, not far from Cadesh, where, according to Josephus (*Ant.* 5.1.18), the northern Canaanite confederacy pitched camp against Joshua. The story is told in Josh. 11, where, however, the camp is located at the waters of Merom.

BIBLIOGRAPHY: J. M. Thompson, *The Land and the Book* (1886), 2:74.

BE'RITH. *See* Gods, False: Baal-berith.

BERNI'CE (ber-nî'se). The eldest daughter of Herod Agrippa I by his wife Cypros. *See* Herod: Princesses of the House of.

BERO'DACH-BAL'ADAN (be-rō'dak-bal'a-dan). The king of Babylon who sent friendly letters and a gift to Hezekiah upon hearing of his sickness (2 Kings 20:12). He is also called, in Isa. 39:1, *Merodach-baladan* (which see).

BEROE'A. *See* Berea.

BERO'THAH (be-rō'tha; Ezek. 47:16), or **Bero'thai** (be-rō'thī; "wells," 2 Sam. 8:8). Ezekiel mentions Berothah, in connection with Hamath and Damascus, as forming the northern boundary of the Promised Land as restored in his vision. Now identified with Bereitan in the Beqa about thirty-five miles N of Damascus.

BE'ROTHITE (be'rō-thīt). An epithet of Naharai, Joab's armor bearer (1 Chron. 11:39), probably as a native of *Beeroth* (which see).

BERYL. *See* Mineral Kingdom.

BE'SAI (be'sī). One of the heads of the Temple servants, whose descendants returned from Babylon (Ezra 2:49; Neh. 7:52), 536 B.C.

BESODE'IAH (bes-o-dē'ya; "in the counsel of Jehovah"). The father of Meshullam, who repaired "the Old Gate" of Jerusalem (Neh. 3:6), 445 B.C.

BESOM (bē'som; a "broom"; Isa. 14:23, KJV, "besom of destruction"). To sweep away, as with a broom, is a metaphor still frequent in the East for utter ruin. Jehovah treats Babylon as rubbish and sweeps it away, destruction serving Him as a broom.

BESOR (bē'sor). A brook flowing into the Mediterranean, about five miles S of Gaza South, and the place where two hundred of David's men remained while the other troops pursued the Amalekites (1 Sam. 30:9-10, 21). The present Wadi es Sheriah, according to some; others claim its location in the Wadi Ghazzeh.

BE'TAH (bē'ta; "confidence"). Called Tibhath (1 Chron. 18:8), a city of Syria-Zobah, captured by David (2 Sam. 8:8) and yielding a large spoil of "bronze." Probably a city on the eastern slope of the Anti-Lebanon Mountains; NIV, Tebah.

BE'TEN (be'ten; "belly, hollow"). One of the cities on the border of the tribe of Asher (Josh. 19:25 only). Identified perhaps with *Abṭun* E of Mt. Carmel.

BETH (ב) (bāth; "house"). The name of the second letter of the Heb. alphabet (corresponding to Gk. beta [β], Lat. B), so named because originally the representation of a rude dwelling. As an appellative, Beth is the most general word for "house" (Gen. 24:32; 33:17; Judg. 18:31; 1 Sam. 1:7). From this general use the transition was natural to a house in the sense of a "family." Beth is frequently employed in combination with other words to form the names of places.

BETHAB'ARA (beth-ab'a-ra; "house of the ford"). In the KJV, the place on the E bank of the Jordan where John was baptizing (John 1:28); placed by Conder at the ford 'Abarah, just N of Beisan. The NASB and NIV read "in Bethany beyond the Jordan." Many of the best Gk. manuscripts have "Bethany" instead of "Bethabara." This is not the Bethany near Jerusalem. The sixth-century Madeba map shows Bethabara on the W bank of the Jordan near the traditional site of Jesus' baptism.   H.F.V.

BETH-A'NATH (beth-a'nath; "house of the goddess"). Anath, modern el-Ba'neh, twelve miles E of Acre, a fortified city of Naphtali, named with Beth-shemesh (Josh. 19:38; Judg. 1:33), from neither of which the Canaanites were expelled, although they were made tributaries (1:33).

BETH-A'NOTH (beth-a'nōth; "house of [the goddess] Anath"). A town in the mountains of Judah (Josh. 15:59), possibly located just N of Hebron.

Traditional site of the tomb of Lazarus, Bethany

BETH'ANY (beth'a-ni; "house, place of unripe figs").

1. A place on the E of the Jordan, the name of

which is substituted in the NASB and NIV for *Beth-abara* (which see; *see also* John 1:28).

2. A village situated on the eastern slope of Mt. Olivet, fifteen furlongs (about one and one-half miles) from Jerusalem. It is called also the *house of misery* on account of its lonely situation and the invalids who congregated there. It was the home of Lazarus and was associated with important events in Scripture history (Matt. 21:17; 26:6; Mark 11:11; 14:3; Luke 24:50; John 11:1; 12:1); called now Azariyeh, or Lazariyeh, "the place of Lazarus."

BIBLIOGRAPHY: W. M. Thompson, *The Land and the Book* (1886), 1:347, 367, 406, 408-16; J. Finegan, *Archaeology of the New Testament* (1969), pp. 89-95, 238.

BETH-AR'ABAH (beth-ar'a-ba; "house of the desert"). A town on the N end of the Dead Sea, and one of six cities belonging to Judah on the N border of the tribe (Josh. 15:6, 61); possibly to be located at modern 'Ain el-Gharbah SW of Jericho. It was afterward included in the list of the towns of Benjamin (18:22; "Arabah," 18:18).   H.F.V.

BETH-ARAM. *See* Beth-haram; Beth-haran.

BETH-AR'BEL (beth-ar'bel; "house of Arbel"). In Hos. 10:14 we read of Ephraim, "All your fortresses will be destroyed,/As *Shalman* [which see] destroyed Beth-arbel in the day of battle." "Beth-arbel is hardly the Arbela of Assyria—which became celebrated through the victory of Alexander—since the Israelites could scarcely have become so well acquainted with such a remote city, but in all probability the Arbela in Galiloea Superior, a place in the tribe of Naphtali between Sephoris and Tiberias" (K. & D., *Com.*). If so, it is to be identified with a site NW of Tiberias. Some would locate it E of the Jordan in Gilead. It is present-day Irbid, four miles NW of Tiberias.

BETH-ASH'BEA (beth-'ash'be-a). The place where "the families of the house of the linen workers" resided. The KJV renders just Ashbea and mentions him as the head of this branch of the descendants of Shelah, the son of Judah (1 Chron. 4:21).

BETH-A'VEN (beth-ā'ven; "house of nothingness," i.e., "idolatry"). A place in the mountains of Benjamin (Josh. 7:2; 18:12; 1 Sam. 13:5), E of Bethel (Josh. 7:2), and between it and Michmash (1 Sam. 13:5).

The place mentioned in Hos. 4:15 is not the same, but, as Amos 4:4 and 5:5 clearly show, a name that Hosea adopted from Amos 5:5 for Bethel (the present Beitin) to show that Bethel, the house of God, had become Beth-aven, the house of idols, through the setting up of the golden calf there (1 Kings 12:29).

BETH-AZMA'VETH (beth-az-ma'veth). A village of Benjamin, the inhabitants of which, forty-two in number, returned with Zerubbabel from Bab-

ylon (Neh. 7:28; "Azmaveth," 12:29; Ezra 2:24). Its present site is Hizmeh, between Geba and Anathoth.

BETH-BA'AL-ME'ON (beth-ba'ăl-mē'on; "house of Baal-meon"). One of the places assigned to Reuben in the plains E of the Jordan (Josh. 13:17), known formerly as Baal-meon (Num. 32:38) or Beon (32:3), to which the Beth was possibly a Heb. prefix. It is identified with the present ruins of Ma'in, in N Moab, four miles SW of Medeba. It is mentioned on the Moabite Stone, 9.30, as held by King Mesha.

BETH-BA'RAH (beth-ba'ra). A chief ford of the Jordan. Possibly the place of Jacob's crossing (Gen. 32:22), S of the scene of Gideon's victory (Judg. 7:24), and where Jephtha slew the Ephraimites (12:4). Location uncertain.

BETH-BIR'I (beth-bir'î). A town of Simeon, inhabited by the descendants of Shimei (1 Chron. 4:31); the Beth-lebaoth of Josh. 19:6, or simply Lebaoth (15:32). Not identified with any present locality.

BETH'CAR (beth-kar'; "sheep house"). The place to which the Israelites pursued the Philistines from Mizpah (1 Sam. 7:6-12). From the unusual expression "below Bethcar," it would seem that the place itself was on a height with a road at its foot. Its situation is not known.

BETH-DA'GON (beth-dā'gon; "house of Dagon," the fish god).

1. A city in the low country of Judah, about five miles from Lydda, near Philistia (Josh. 15:41). Present Khirbet Dajûn.

2. A town near the SE border of Asher (Josh. 19:27).

BETH-EDEN (beth-ē'den; Heb. *bêt 'eden,* "house of delight"). In the KJV a place named "House of Eden" occurs in the prophecy of Amos against Damascus (Amos 1:5). Some scholars have thought that the prophecy refers to the Aramaean city-states of Damascus and Bit-adini. The reading of the LXX is "from the men of Haran," since Haran was apparently in Bit-adini. The reference to "the people of Eden" (KJV, "children of Eden") in 2 Kings 9:12 and Isa. 37:12, along with the Eden mentioned in Ezek. 27:23, seem also to refer to Bit-adini.   R.K.H.

BETH-E'KED (beth-e'ked); **of the shepherds** (lit., "house of binding of the shepherds"). The translation in the NASB and NIV of 2 Kings 10:12, 14 of a place on the road between Jezreel and Samaria. When Jehu was on his way to Samaria, he encountered forty-two members of the royal ramily of Judah, whom he slaughtered at the well or pit attached to the place. The KJV renders "shearing house." It is commonly identified with Beit Kad, sixteen miles NE of Samaria.

BETH'EL (beth'el; "house of God").

1. A town about ten miles N of Jerusalem, originally Luz (Gen. 28:19). It was here that Abraham encamped (12:8; 13:3), and the district is still known as suitable for pasturage. It received the name of Bethel, "house of God," because of its nearness to or being the very place where Jacob dreamed (28:10-22). Bethel was assigned to the Benjamites, but they appear to have been either unable to take it or careless about doing so, as we find it taken by the children of Joseph (Judg. 1:22-26). It seems to have been the place to which the Ark was brought (Judg. 20:26-28). It was one of the three places that Samuel selected in which to hold court (1 Sam. 7:16), and Jeroboam chose Bethel as one of the two places in which he set up golden calves (1 Kings 12:28-33). King Josiah removed all traces of idolatry and restored the true worship of Jehovah (2 Kings 23:15-20). Bethel was occupied by people returning from Babylon (cf. Ezra 2:28 with Neh. 11:31).

Bethel is identified with modern Beitin. It stands upon the point of a low rocky ridge, between two shallow wadis, which unite, the water then falling into the Wadi Suweinit toward the SE.

W. F. Albright and J. L. Kelso excavated Beitin in 1934, and Kelso resumed work in 1954 and continued in 1957 and 1960 on behalf of the American Schools of Oriental Research and Pitts-

burgh Theological Seminary. Although there was a village at Beitin as early as 3200 B.C., continuous occupation of the site apparently began just before 2000 B.C. During the sixteenth century the settlement was enlarged and surrounded with an eleven-foot-thick stone wall and possessed some of the best-laid masonry of that period yet discovered in Palestine. About 1235 the city was destroyed in a great fire that left debris five feet thick in places. Evidently this conflagration is to be attributed to the Israelite conquest of Judges 1:22-25. The subsequent Israelite level of occupation has construction strikingly inferior to Canaanite levels, but the period of David and Solomon shows noticeable recovery. No sanctuary dating to the days when Jeroboam I instituted calf worship there has yet been recovered. Although Bethel was only a small village during Nehemiah's day (fifth century B.C.), it became an important place during the Hellenistic period and grew even larger in Roman and Byzantine days. Remains in the area show that the city continued to exist throughout the Byzantine era but apparently disappeared when the Muslims took over Palestine.   M.F.U.; H.F.V.

2. Knobel suggests that this is a corrupt reading for Bethul or Bethuel (Josh. 19:4; 1 Chron. 4:30), in the tribe of Simeon.

BIBLIOGRAPHY: M. Avi-Yonah, ed., *Encyclopedia of Ar-*

Grassed over remains of ancient Bethel

chaeological Excavations in the Holy Land (1975), 1:190-93.

BETH-EL, MOUNT. The KJV rendering for the southern range of mountains belonging to Bethel (Josh. 16:1-2). Bethel is here distinguished from Luz because the reference is not to the town of Bethel but to the mountains, from which the boundary ran out to Luz. The NASB and NIV render "hill country."

BETH'ELITE (beth'e-līt). A name by which Hiel, who rebuilt Jericho (1 Kings 16:34), was called, being a native of *Bethel* (which see) in Benjamin.

BETH-E'MEK (beth-e'mek; "house of the valley"). A city of Asher, in the S of the valley of Iphtahel (Josh. 19:27), not yet discovered; possibly Tell Mimas, near 'Amqa, 6½ miles NE of Acre.

BE'THER (be'ther; "separation"). A range of mountains named in Song of Sol. 2:17, perhaps the same as the "mountains of spices" (8:14). The NIV renders Bether as "rugged hills."

BETHES'DA (beth-ez'da; Gk. from Aram. *Beth hesdā*, "house of grace"). A spring-fed pool with five porches where invalids waited their turn to step into the mysteriously troubled waters that were supposed to possess healing virtue (John 5:2-4). The last part of v. 3 and all of v. 4, which mention a periodic disturbance of the water by an angel, are placed in brackets in the NASB because there is not sufficient attestation by early texts. Here Jesus healed the man who was lame for thirty-eight years (5:5-9). The place is now thought to be the pool found during the repairs in 1888 near St. Anne's Church in the Bezetha quarter of Jerusalem not far from the Sheep's Gate and Tower of Antonia. It is below the crypt of the ruined fourth-century church and has a five-arch portico with faded frescoes of the miracle of Christ's healing.   M.F.U.

BIBLIOGRAPHY: J. M. Thompson, *The Land and the Book* (1886), 3:387; J. Finegan, *Archaeology of the New Testament* (1969), pp. 143-44, 147.

Site of the pool of Bethesda

BETH-E'ZEL (beth-e'zel; "a place near"). A town mentioned in Mic. 1:11 in southern Judah, now identified with Deir el-'Asal about two miles E of Tell Beit Mirsim.

BETH-GA'DER (beth-ga'der; "walled house"). A place in the tribe of Judah, of which Hareph is named as "father" or founder (1 Chron. 2:51). Probably identical with *Gedor* (which see) of Josh. 15:58, or Geder.

BETH-GA'MUL (beth-ga'mul; "house of recompense"). A city of Moab (Jer. 48:23). It is identified with Khirbet Jemeil, six miles E of Dibon, between the Arnon and Ummer Raṣās.

BETH-GIL'GAL (beth-gil'gal; "house of Gilgal," Neh. 12:29). A place from which the sons of the singers gathered together for the celebration of the rebuilding of the walls of Jerusalem; doubtless the same as *Gilgal* (which see).

BETH-HACCHE'REM (Neh. 3:14, NASB; beth-hak-e'rem), **Beth Hakkerem** (Neh. 3:14; Jer. 6:1, NIV; pronunciation the same as above), **Bethhaccerem** (Neh. 3:14; Jer. 6:1, KJV; Jer. 6:1, NASB; beth-hak'se-rim; marg., Jer. 6:1, NASB, "house of the vineyard"). A Judean town of such commanding height as to be a place for signaling upon occasions of invasion. It is now identified with Ramat-rahel in the southern suburbs of Jerusalem. Yohanan Aharoni excavated there five seasons (1954-62) for the Hebrew University and the University of Rome. The history of the site extends from about the ninth century B.C. to the Arab period. In strata V-A (*see* 608-586 B.C.) one of the last kings of Judah built an imposing palace; Aharoni originally supposed the builder was Jehoiakim (609-587 B.C.; *see* Jer. 22:13-19). A stamped jar handle with the inscription "Belonging to Eliakim, steward of Yaukin" (Jehoiachin, son of Jehoiakim), was found in the ruins. Evidently this citadel was destroyed by Nebuchadnezzar.

BETH-HAG'GAN (beth-hag'an; "house of the garden"). A place by way of which King Ahaziah fled from Jehu (2 Kings 9:27, NASB, "garden house"). The "garden house" cannot have been in the royal gardens but must have stood at some distance from the city of Jezreel, as Ahaziah went away by the road leading to it and was not wounded till he reached the height of Gur, near Ibleam.

BETH-HA'RAM (beth-hâ'ram). A town of Gad, opposite Jericho and six miles E of the Jordan (Josh. 13:27). Named Julias, or Livias, by Herod, after the wife of Augustus; the present Tell er Rameh at the mouth of the Wadi Hesban, a source of the celebrated hot springs where King Herod had a palace. Also called *Beth-haran* (which see).

BETH-HA'RAN (beth-ha'ran). A fenced city E of the Jordan, "built," i.e., restored and fortified, by the Gadites (Num. 32:36). The same as *Beth-ha-ram* (which see).

BETH-HOG'LAH (beth-hog'la; "house of a partridge," Josh. 15:6; 18:19). A place on the border of Judah and of Benjamin, and belonging to the latter tribe (18:21). The name and location are to be found at 'Ain Hajlah, four miles SE of Jericho.

BETH-HO'RON (beth-hō'ron; "house or place of the hollow"). The name of two towns, an "upper" and a "lower" (Josh. 16:3, 5; 1 Chron. 7:24; 2 Chron. 8:5), on the road from Gibeon to Azekah (Josh. 10:10-11) and the Philistine plain (1 Sam. 13:18). Beth-horon lay on the boundary line between Benjamin and Ephraim (Josh. 16:3, 5; 18:13-14), was assigned to Ephraim, and was given to the Kohathites (21:22; 1 Chron. 6:68). It is said (7:24) that Sheerah built Beth-horon, both upper and lower, along with Uzzen-sheerah. The building referred to was merely an enlarging and fortifying of these towns. Sheerah was probably an heiress who had received these places as her inheritance and caused them to be enlarged by her family.

"These places still exist and are called by Arabic names meaning 'upper' and 'lower.' They are separated by about half an hour's journey. The upper village is about four miles from Gibeon, the road always on the *ascent*. The *descent* begins from the upper to the lower village, and that road is one of the roughest and steepest in Palestine; it is still used as the road from the coast and is a key to the country; it was afterward fortified by Solomon. Old tanks and massive foundations exist" (Harper, *Bible and Mod. Dis.*, p. 159).

It was along this pass that Joshua drove the allies against whom he went out in defense of the Gibeonites (Josh. 10:10); and by the same route one of three companies of Philistine raiders came against Israel (1 Sam. 13:18).

The importance of the road upon which the two Beth-horons were situated, the main approach to the interior of the country from the hostile districts on both sides of Palestine, at once explains and justifies the frequent fortification of these towns at different periods of their history (1 Kings 9:17; 2 Chron. 8:5; 1 Macc. 9:50; Judg. 4:4-5).

BETH-JESH'IMOTH (beth-jesh'i-mōth; "house or place of deserts"). A town in Moab, not far E of the mouth of the Jordan and just N of the Dead Sea (Num. 33:49; Josh. 12:3; 13:20; Ezek. 25:9). Belonging to Sihon, king of the Amorites (Josh. 12:3). It is to be identified with Tell el 'Azeima).

BETH-JES'IMOTH. Another form of *Beth-jesh-imoth* (which see). In NT times Besimoth (Tell el 'Azeimeh).

BETH-LE-APH'RAH (beth-le-af-ra; "house or place of dust"; so in NASB, Mic. 1:10; "house of Aphrah" in the KJV; Beth Ophrah in the NIV).

Site unknown, but apparently in Philistine territory.

BETH-LEBA'OTH (beth-le-ba'ōth; "house of lionesses"). A town in the lot of Simeon (Josh. 19:6), in the extreme S of Judah (15:32), where it is given as *Lebaoth*. The location of the site is near Sharuhen, but unknown.

BETH'LEHEM (beth'le-hem; "house of bread").

1. A town in Palestine, near which Jacob buried Rachel, then known as Ephrath (Gen. 35:19; 48:7). It is also called Bethlehem Ephrathah (Mic. 5:2), Bethlehem in Judah (1 Sam. 17:12), Bethlehem of Judea (Matt. 2:1), and the city of David (Luke 2:4; cf. John 7:42). The old name, Ephrath, or Ephrathah, lingered long after Israel occupied Palestine (Ruth 1:2; 4:11; 1 Sam. 17:12; Ps. 132:6; Mic. 5:2; etc.). The city overlooks the main highway to Hebron and Egypt. The site of the city on a commanding limestone ridge of the Judean highland has never been disputed.

Bethlehem

After the conquest Bethlehem fell to Judah (Judg. 17:7; 1 Sam. 17:12; Ruth 1:1-2); Ibzan of Bethlehem judged Israel after Jephthah (Judg. 12:8); Elimelech, the husband of Naomi and father-in-law of Ruth, was a Bethlehemite (Ruth 1:1-2), as was Boaz (2:1, 4).

David was born in Bethlehem, and here he was anointed as future king by Samuel (1 Sam. 16:1); here was the well from which David's three heroes brought him water (2 Sam. 23:15-16), thought to be the same three wells still existing in the N side of the village; it was the birthplace of the Messiah (Matt. 2:1), and its male children were slain by order of Herod (2:16, cf. Jer. 31:15; Mic. 5:2). This Bethlehem is about five miles S of Jerusalem, and elevated 2,460 feet above sea level. In Bethlehem stands the Basilica of the Nativity, marking the traditional site of the birth of Christ.

2. A town in the portion of Zebulun, named only in connection with Idala (Josh. 19:15). It is to be located at Beit Lahm, seven miles NE of Nazareth.

BIBLIOGRAPHY: F. M. Abel, *Géographie de la Palestine* (1938), 2:276-77; J. W. Crowfoot, *Early Churches in Palestine* (1941), pp. 22-30, 77-85; C. Kopp, *Holy Places of the Gospels* (1961); S. Perowne, *Holy Places of Christendom* (1976), pp. 15-23; J. Finegan, *Archaeology of the New Testament* (1969), pp. 18-26, 33, 35, 121-22, 169; Y. Aharoni, *The Land of the Bible* (1979), pp. 242, 248, 266.

BETH'LEHEM IN JU'DAH (beth'le-hem in jū'da). A more distinctive title (Judg. 17:7-9; 19:1; etc.; Ruth 1:1-2; 1 Sam. 17:12) of *Bethlehem*, no. 1 (which see). KJV reads "Beth-le-hem-judah."

BETH'LEHEMITE (beth'-le-hem-īt). An inhabitant of *Bethlehem* (which see) in Judah (1 Sam. 16:1, 18; 17:58; 2 Sam. 21:19).

BETH'LEHEM-JUDAH. *See* Bethlehem in Judah.

BETH-MA'ACAH (beth-ma'a-ka; "house of Maakah"). A place to which Joab went in pursuit of Sheba the son of Bichri (2 Sam. 20:14). It was quite close to Abela, so that the names of the places are connected in v. 15 and afterward as Abel-beth-maacah (thus always in the NIV; *see also* 1 Kings 15:20; 2 Kings 15:29; all NASB); also called Abel-maim (2 Chron. 16:4). The modern site is Tell Abil, about 2½ miles WNW of Laish (Dan) and 6 miles WNW of Caesarea Philippi (Paneas) near the sources of the Jordan River.

BETH-MAR'CABOTH (beth-mar'ka-bŏth; "place of chariots"). A town of Simeon, in the extreme S of Judah, in which some of the descendants of Shimei dwelt (Josh. 19:5; 1 Chron. 4:31). Site uncertain.

BETH-ME'ON (beth-mē'on; "house of habitation"). A place in the tribe of Reuben (Jer. 48:23); elsewhere (Josh. 13:17) in the full form *Beth-baal-meon* (which see). *See also* Baal-meon.

BETH-MILLO. The name of the citadel of Shechem (Judg. 9:6, 20; "house of Millo," KJV), the garrison of which joined in proclaiming Abimelech their king. *See* Millo.

BETH-NIM'RAH (beth-nim'ra; "house of the leopard"). One of the towns "built," i.e., fortified, by the tribe of Gad (Num. 32:36); called simply *Nimrah* (which see) in 32:3.

BETH OPHRAH. *See* Beth-le-Aphrah.

BETH-PALET. *See* Beth-pelet.

BETH-PAZ'ZEZ (beth-paz'ez; "house of dispersion"). A city of Issachar (Josh. 19:21). Probably modern Kerm el-Hadetheh.

BETH-PE'LET (beth-pe'let; "house of escape"). A town in the S of Judah (Josh. 15:27), assigned to Simeon and inhabited after the captivity (Neh. 11:26). Location uncertain.

BETH-PE'OR (beth-pē'or; "house, or temple, of Peor"). A place in Moab E of the Jordan, abominable for its idolatry. It belonged to Reuben (Josh. 13:20; Deut. 3:29; 4:46). It was the last halting place of the children of Israel, and in the valley nearby Moses rehearsed the law to Israel and was buried (4:44-46; 34:6).

BETH'PHAGE (beth'fa-ji; Aram. "house of unripe figs"). On the Mount of Olives, and on the way from Jerusalem to Jericho, close to Bethany. A Sabbath day's journey from Jerusalem (Matt. 21:1; Mark 11:1; Luke 19:29). No trace of it now remains. It is not mentioned once in the OT, though frequently in the Talmud. Now called Abu Dīs.

BETH-PHELET. *See* Beth-pelet.

BETH-RA'PHA (beth-ra'fa; "house of Rapha, or giant"). A name occurring in the genealogy of Judah as a son of Eshton (1 Chron. 4:12).

BETH-RE'HOB (beth-re'hob; "roomy [?] house"). A place near which lay the valley of the town of Laish or Dan (Judg. 18:28). This valley is the upper part of the Huleh lowland, through which the central source of the Jordan flows, and by which Laish-Dan, the present Tell el Qadi, stood. The Ammonites secured foot soldiers from Beth-rehob to fight against David (2 Sam. 10:6; Rehob, v. 8).

BETHSA'IDA (beth-sā'i-da; Gk. from Aram. *bēt ṣaydā,* "house or place of fishing").

1. A city in Galilee, on the NE coast of the Sea of Tiberias (John 1:44; 12:21). It was the home of Peter, Andrew, and Philip, and a frequent resort of Jesus. Our Lord upbraided its inhabitants for not receiving His teachings (Luke 10:13). It is probably to be located at Aradj about a mile E of where the Jordan River enters the Sea of Galilee.

2. Bethsaida of Gaulanitis, afterward called Julias. There is every evidence that the city in Gaulanitis, on the E side of the sea, is that "desolate place" where Christ fed the five thousand (Luke 9:10-17) and cured "those who had need of healing." Here He also restored the blind man to sight (Mark 8:22-26), as it would be on the road to Caesarea Philippi, visited next by our Lord (v. 27).

It was originally a small town, but Philip the tetrarch, having raised it to the rank of city, called it Julias, after Julia, the daughter of the Emperor Augustus (Josephus *Ant.* 18.2.1). Philip died and was buried there. It is probably to be identified with et-Tell, a little more than a mile N of the Sea of Galilee. Et-Tell stood on the E bank of the Jordan and seems to have had access to the Sea of Galilee.

BETHSHAN (beth-shan'), or **Beth-shean** (beth-shē'an; Heb. "house of security." But more probably house of the Babylonian god Shahan, Phoenician Sha'an, the Sumerian serpent god). An ancient fortress city strategically commanding the Valley of Esdraelon (Tell el-Husn, "mound of the fortress") also known as NT Scythopolis (modern Beisan). This great fortress site was founded before 3000 B.C. and has a long and interesting occupational history. After Thutmose III's brilliant victory at Megiddo (c. 1482 B.C.), it passed into Egyptian hands and was garrisoned by Egyptian soldiers for almost three hundred years. Two stelae of Seti I and one of Rameses II were uncovered here. At the time of the conquest, around 1400 B.C., the inhabitants of the city and the plain had "chariots of iron" (Josh. 17:16), and the Israelites failed to drive out the Canaanites but developed strongly enough to make them pay tribute (17:12-16). At the battle of Gilboa, around 1000 B.C., the town was either in Philistine hands or in alliance with them, for the Philistines fastened the bodies of Saul and his sons to the wall of the city (1 Sam. 31:10-13; 2 Sam. 21:12-14). The University of Pennsylvania Expedition at Bethshan, 1921-33, unearthed a temple that the excavators identified with the temple of Ashtareth in which Saul's armor was placed (1 Sam. 31:10). First Chron. 10:10 refers to a second temple of Bethshan called the house of Dagon, where Saul's head was hung. The excavations uncovered another temple to the S of the temple of Ashtaroth that Alan Rowe identified with the temple of Dagon. In the reign of Solomon the city gave its name to a district (1 Kings 4:12). No mound in Palestine is more impressive than Bethshan, which yielded a number of Egyptian temples dating to the reigns of Amenhotep III (c. 1413-1377 B.C.), Seti I (1319-1301 B.C.), and Rameses II (1301-1234 B.C.). It has also revealed extensive fortress construction. In the level of City 7, from the reign of Amenhotep III, remains of the commanding officer's residence have been unearthed, showing a spacious kitchen, a lavatory, and an immense silo for storing grain. A Canaanite migdol, or fort tower, designed as a last place of refuge if the walls were breached, was also found.   M.F.U.

BIBLIOGRAPHY: G. M. Fitzgerald, *Archaeology and Old Testament Study*, ed. D. W. Thomas (1967), pp. 185-96.

The impressive mound at Bethshan

BETH-SHE′MESH (beth-she′mesh; "house of the sun").

1. A priestly city (Josh. 21:16; 1 Sam. 6:15; 1 Chron. 6:59) in the tribe of Dan, on the N boundary of Judah (Josh. 15:10), toward Philistia (1 Sam. 6:9, 12). The expressions "went down" (Josh. 15:9-10) and "go up" (1 Sam. 6:20-21) seem to indicate that the town was lower than Kiriath-jearim; and there was a valley of wheat fields attached to the place (6:13). It was a city with "pasture lands" (Josh. 21:16; 1 Chron. 6:59) and contributed to Solomon's expenses (1 Kings 4:9). In an engagement between Jehoash, king of Israel, and Amaziah, king of Judah, the latter was defeated and made prisoner (2 Kings 14:11, 13; 2 Chron. 25:21, 23). In the time of Ahaz the Philistines occupied it (28:18), and to this place the Ark was returned (1 Sam. 6:19). The number killed at Beth-shemesh for irreverently examining the Ark is recorded as 50,070. "In this statement of numbers we are not only struck by the fact that in the Hebrew the seventy stands before the fifty thousand, which is very unusual, but even more by the omission of the copula *waw*, which is altogether unparalleled. ... We can come to no other conclusion than that the number fifty thousand is neither correct nor genuine, but a gloss which has crept into the text through some oversight" (K. & D., *Com.*, ad loc.). The town of Beth-shemesh was small; the usual conclusion is that a copyist's error has crept in here and that only seventy were struck down. The Jewish historian Josephus supports seventy as accurate (*Ant.* 6.1.4). Beth-shemesh was identical with Ir-shemesh (Josh. 19:41) and is preserved in the modern Ain-shems on the NW slopes of the mountains of Judah, a site known today as Tell er-Rumeileh. From 1911 to 1912 Duncan Mackenzie excavated at Beth-shemesh on behalf of the Palestine Exploration Fund, and Elihu Grant directed the Haverford College dig there from 1928 to 1933. The city was founded shortly after 2000 B.C. and fell under Hyksos control from about 1700 to 1550 B.C.; the Hyksos effectively fortified the seven-acre site. The Egyptians destroyed the city by fire about 1500 B.C., but then it prospered during the period 1500-1200 B.C. The Israelites controlled the site between 1200 and 1000, the period of the Judges, but there is evidence of strong Philistine influence at that time. Clearly the period from 1000 to 586 was Israelite, and excavations clearly attest the destruction by Nebuchadnezzar early in the sixth century B.C. The city was never rebuilt.   H.F.V.

2. A city near the southern border of Issachar, between Tabor and the Jordan (Josh. 19:22). Unidentified.

3. One of the "fortified cities" of Naphtali (Josh. 19:35, 38; Judg. 1:33), from which, along with Beth-anath, the Canaanites were not driven out.

4. The name given in the KJV of Jer. 43:13 to On, the Egyptian city usually called *Heliopolis* (so NASB; the NIV reads "temple of the sun"). *See* discussion at On, no. 2; and Sun, Worship of.

BIBLIOGRAPHY: E. Robinson, *Biblical Researches* (1856), 2:224; 3:17-19; M. Avi-Yonah, ed., *Encyclopedia of Archaeological Excavations in the Holy Land* (1975), 1:248-53.

BETH'-SHEMITE (beth-she'mīt). An inhabitant (1 Sam. 6:14, 18) of *Beth-shemesh* (which see) in Judea.

BETH-SHIT'TAH (beth-shi'ta; "house of the acacia"). A town not far from the Jordan to which the Midianites fled from Gideon (Judg. 7:22). It is probably Shattah, N of Bethshan.

BETH-TAP'PUAH (beth-tap'ū-a; "house of apples"). A town about five miles W of Hebron (Josh. 15:53), same as modern Taffuh. Another town in Judah (12:17) was known by the simple name of *Tappuah* (which see).

BETH TOGARMAH (beth-tō-gar'mah). *See* Togarmah.

BETHU'EL (beth-ū'el; perhaps "abode of God").
1. A southern city of Judah, sometimes called Bethul or Bethel (1 Chron. 4:30; Josh. 19:4; 12:16; 1 Sam. 30:27). Named with Eltolad, Hormah, and Ziklag.
2. The son of Nahor by Milcah; the nephew of Abraham and father of Rebekah (Gen. 22:22-23; 24:15, 24, 47). In 25:20 and 28:5 he is called "Bethuel the Aramean" (marg., Syrian). In the narrative of Rebekah's marriage he is mentioned as saying, "The matter comes from the Lord" (24:50); her brother Laban takes the leading part in the transaction.

BE'THUL (beth'ul; contraction for *Bethuel,* which see). A town in the S of Simeon, named with Eltolad and Hormah (Josh. 19:4). Location uncertain.

BETH-ZUR' (beth-zur'; "house of rock"). A strategic elevated fortress about four miles N of Hebron. The site was fortified by Rehoboam (2 Chron. 11:7) and referred to in Nehemiah's time (Neh. 3:16) but was most prominent in Maccabean times. Here Judas Maccabeus defeated the Greeks under Lysias, 165 B.C.

W. F. Albright and O. R. Sellers excavated there in 1931 and Sellers in 1957 for the American Schools of Oriental Research and McCormick Theological Seminary. These digs show that the site was first occupied near the end of the third millennium B.C. and fortified for the first time by the Hyksos in the sixteenth century B.C. The place was abandoned during the fourteenth and thirteenth centuries and then occupied by the Hebrews in the twelfth and eleventh centuries. Hellenistic builders erected strong fortifications there during the second century B.C. The Syrians, Ptolemies, and Maccabeans all apparently sought

to use the site to good advantage during military activities in the third and second centuries B.C.

H.F.V.

BIBLIOGRAPHY: O. R. Sellers, *The Citadel of Beth-Zur* (1933); id., *Bulletin of the American Schools of Oriental Research* 150 (April 1958): 8ff.

BET'ONIM (bet'o-nim; "hollows"). A town in the tribe of Gad (Josh. 13:26), located at Khirbet Batneh on Mt. Gilead.

BETRAY (Gk. *paradidōmi,* "to give into the hands" of another). The term used of the act of Judas in delivering up our Lord to the Jews (Matt. 26:16; Mark 14:10; Luke 22:4, 6).

BETROTHAL. *See* Marriage.

BEU'LAH (bū'la; "married"). A prophetic figurative expression used in the KJV (Isa. 62:4; NASB, "married") describing Palestine restored to God's blessing, not only after the Babylonian Exile but particularly after Israel's present worldwide dispersion and establishment in Palestine in the millennial kingdom. Israel in its relation to Jehovah is as a weak but beloved woman who has Him for her Lord and husband (54:5) and who will yet be cleansed and restored to her Lord.

BEVERAGE. *See* Drink.

BEWITCH. To deceive or delude by satanic and demonic power, as Simon Magus the sorcerer did to the people of Samaria (Acts 8:9, 11, KJV; NASB, "astonish"); to thus charm or fascinate (Gal. 3:1).

BEYOND. The region or country *beyond.* The phrase "beyond the Jordan" frequently occurs in Scripture. To ascertain its meaning we must take into account the situation of the writer. With Moses, writing upon its eastern bank, it usually signified the country W of the river (Gen. 50:10-11; Deut. 3:8, 20), but with Joshua after he crossed the river it meant the reverse (Josh. 5:1; 12:7; 22:7). In Matt. 4:15 "beyond the Jordan" designates, after the two lands already mentioned, a new land after the coming of Jesus, namely, Perea.

BE'ZAI (be'zī). The head of one of the families who returned from Babylon to the number of 324, including himself (Ezra 2:17; Neh. 7:23), 536 B.C. Either he or his family is probably referred to (Neh. 10:18) as sealing the covenant, 445 B.C.

BEZ'ALEL (bez'a-lel; "in the shadow [protection] of God").
1. The craftsman to whom was entrusted the design and construction of the Tabernacle and its furniture in the wilderness. For this work he was specially chosen and inspired by Jehovah. With him was associated Oholiab, though Bezalel appears to have been chief. He was the son of Uri, the son of Hur (Ex. 31:2-11; 35:30; 38:22), c. 1440 B.C.

2. One of the sons of Pahath-moab, who divorced his foreign wife after the captivity (Ezra 10:30), 456 B.C.

BE'ZEK (be'zek; "lightning").

1. The residence of *Adoni-bezek* (which see), and inhabited by Canaanites and Perizzites (Judg. 1:4-5). The location is uncertain but may well be Khirbet Bezqa near Gezer.

2. The gathering place where Saul numbered the forces of Judah and Israel before going to the relief of Jabesh-gilead (1 Sam. 11:8). It is located at modern Khirbet Ibziq, about twelve miles NE of Shechem.

BE'ZER (be'zer).

1. The sixth named of the eleven sons of Zophah, of the descendants of Asher (1 Chron. 7:37).

2. A Reubenite city of refuge E of the Jordan (Deut. 4:43; Josh. 20:8; etc.). It is probably to be located at modern Umm el-Amad, eight miles NE of Madaba. Location uncertain.

BIBLE. The name commonly used to designate the thirty-nine books of the OT and the twenty-seven books of the NT. These sixty-six books constitute a divine library that is nevertheless, in a vital sense, *one* Book.

The Name *Bible*. The development of the expression *the Bible* to designate the "Book of books" is providential. It admirably expresses the unity of the Word of God. The English word *Bible* came originally from the name of the papyrus or byblos reed used extensively in antiquity for making scrolls and books. Byblos (OT Gebal) was so named because, in that Phoenician seaport, trade and manufacture in papyrus writing material was carried on. From about the eleventh century B.C., or even earlier, papyrus rolls grown in the Delta of Egypt were shipped to Gebal. The word *Bible* comes from the Old French through the Lat. *biblia,* from the Gk. Quite naturally the Greeks came to term a book *biblos* or a small book *biblion.* By the second century A.D. Greek Christians called their sacred Scriptures *ta Biblia,* "the Books." When this title was subsequently transferred to the Lat., it was rendered in the singular and through Old French came into English as "Bible."

Other Designations. In the OT and the Apocrypha the sacred writings are called "the books" (LXX, *bibloi,* Dan. 9:2), "the holy books" (1 Macc. 12:9), "the books of the law" (1:56), "book of the covenant" (1:57), etc. In the prologue to Ecclesiasticus the Scriptures are referred to as "the law, the prophets, and the other books (*biblia*) of our fathers." In the NT the common designations for the OT books are "the Scriptures" (writings; Matt. 21:42; Mark 14:49; Luke 24:32; John 5:39; Rom. 15:4), the "holy Scriptures" (Rom. 1:2), "the sacred writings" (2 Tim. 3:15). The Jewish technical division of "the Law," "the Prophets,"

and the "Psalms" or "writings" is recognized in Luke 24:44. Another term for the whole is "the Law and the Prophets" (Acts 13:15; cf. Matt. 5:17; 11:13). The term *Law* is occasionally extended to include the other divisions (John 10:34; 1 Cor. 14:21). Paul also employs the expression "the oracles of God" (Rom. 3:2).

The Terms *Old Testament* and *New Testament*. These terms have come into use since the close of the second century to distinguish the Jewish and the Christian Scriptures. The word *testament* (lit., a will) denotes a covenant. In the RV, accordingly, "testament" is generally corrected to covenant. However, these terms are not altogether accurate for the simple reason that the Mosaic covenant and the legal dispensation were still in operation throughout the lifetime and up to the death of Christ, when "the veil of the temple was torn in two from top to bottom" (Matt. 27:51). This momentous event signified that a "new and living way" (Heb. 10:20) was open for all believers into the very presence of God with no other sacrifice or priesthood necessary save Christ (cf. 9:1-8; 10:19-22). It was only as a result of the death, burial, and resurrection of Christ, the giving of the Holy Spirit at Pentecost (Acts 2), and the preaching of the gospel of grace that actually saw the outworking of the New Covenant.

Languages. The OT is written mostly in Heb.; the NT wholly in Gk. The parts of the OT not in Heb. are Ezra 4:8–6:18; 7:12-26; Jer. 10:11; and Dan. 2:4–7:28. These sections are written in Aram., a related Semitic dialect that, after the exilic period, gradually took the place of Heb. as the common language of the Jews. The ancient Heb. was a Canaanite dialect closely akin to Phoenician and Ugaritic, the latter being a language spoken at Ugarit (modern Ras Shamra) in northern Syria. At Ugarit an important and extensive religious epic literature shedding great light on Canaanite morality and religious practices has been uncovered by Claude Schaeffer and the French expedition (1929-37). NT Gk., so greatly illuminated by important papyri discoveries, particularly from Egypt, has been shown to be not a special sacred dialect, as was formerly thought, but the common Hellenistic speech of the first century A.D. In no phase of its composition does the Bible show itself to be a book for the people more than in its use of the everyday language of the Greek-speaking world of the period.

Division of the Old Testament Books. The thirty-nine books of the OT were anciently divided by the Hebrews into three distinct classes: (1) *The Law* (*Torah*), which consisted of the five books of Moses—Genesis, Exodus, Leviticus, Numbers, and Deuteronomy. These are the oldest of the biblical books, Mosaic in origin but incorporating much earlier material. (2) *The Prophets* (*Nevi'im*), which embraced the four earlier prophets, Joshua, Judges, Samuel, and

Kings and the four later prophets, Isaiah, Jeremiah, Ezekiel, and the Twelve—Hosea, Joel, Amos, Obadiah, Jonah, Micah, Nahum, Habakkuk, Zephaniah, Haggai, Zechariah, and Malachi. These were believed to have been written by those who had the prophetic office as well as the prophetic gift. (3) *The Writings* (*Kethuvim*), which consisted of (a) poetical books—Psalms, Proverbs, Job; (b) the Rolls—Song of Solomon, Ruth, Lamentations, Ecclesiastes, and Esther; and (c) prophetical-historical books—Daniel, Ezra-Nehemiah, and Chronicles. The Heb. books number twenty-four and are identical in content with the thirty-nine of the English order, the difference being made up by the division of Samuel, Kings, and Chronicles into two books respectively instead of one, and by counting the twelve minor prophets individually instead of as one.

Division of the New Testament Books. By the middle of the second century a Christian NT had come into existence. Early distinction had to be made between the generally acknowledged and the disputed books. As enumerated by Eusebius and substantiated by early lists such as the canon of Muratori (about A.D. 170), quotations, versions, and patristic use, the former included the four gospels, Acts, thirteen epistles of Paul, 1 Peter, and 1 John. With these may be placed Hebrews and Revelation. Disputed books included James, Jude, 2 and 3 John, and 2 Peter. However, the complete acceptance of all of the books in our present NT canon may be dated from the councils of Laodicea (about A.D. 363) and Carthage (A.D. 397), which confirmed the catalogs of Cyril of Jerusalem, Jerome, and Augustine.

Origin and Growth. Accepting the internal evidence together with predictive prophecy and divine miracle, the following general conclusions have been arrived at by conservative scholars: (1) The Pentateuch as it stands is historical and dates from the time of Moses. Moses was its author, though it may have been revised and edited later, the additions being just as much inspired as the rest. (Cf. Robert Dick Wilson, *A Scientific Investigation of the O. T.* [1926], p. 11.) In other words, the Pentateuch is one continuous work, the product of a single writer, Moses. This Mosaic unity of the Pentateuch may, however, admit post-Mosaic additions or changes that do not abrogate the authenticity and integrity of the text. It is not inconsistent with Mosaic authorship of the Pentateuch to grant modification of archaic expressions and place names, marginal glosses, or explanatory scribal insertions that evidently crept into the text, and textual errors resulting from inadvertent mistakes of copyists. The latter constitute the legitimate domain of scholarly criticism. An example of an addition is Deut. 34:5-12, which narrates Moses' death and burial. An evident gloss is furnished by Gen. 15:2-3, which is obscure in the Heb. unless one sees that a copyist's explanation eventually got into

the text (cf. KJV and NASB readings); also 14:14 and Deut. 34:1, where Laish is called "Dan," although apparently this place did not receive its later name until after the Mosaic age (Judg. 18:29). "Raamses" (Ex. 1:11) seems clearly a modification of the earlier city Zoan or Avaris. (2) The book of Joshua is a literary unit distinct from the Pentateuch. It dates from the period of Joshua and in all likelihood was written in substance by Joshua himself (cf. 24:26). In any event, it was written early, as numerous internal evidences show. (3) The Song of Deborah (Judg. 5) is unquestionably an authentic monument of the age of the Judges, and the older parts of Judges, at least, are contemporaneous with the events they recount. (4) The age of Samuel, Saul, David, and the monarchy was a period of literary activity and saw the gradual rise of such books as 1 and 2 Samuel, 1 and 2 Kings, and many of the psalms. (5) The Solomonic period saw the development of wisdom literature such as Proverbs, Song of Solomon, and Ecclesiastes. (6) To the period of the Divided Monarchy in the main belongs the extensive prophetic literature of the OT. Obadiah and Joel are probably dated as early as the late ninth century B.C. To the eighth century B.C. belong Amos, Hosea, and Jonah in the Northern Kingdom, and Micah and Isaiah in the Southern Kingdom. Nahum, Zephaniah, Habakkuk, and Jeremiah (including Lamentations) come in the late seventh century B.C. (7) Ezekiel and Daniel are exilic, and (8) Haggai, Zechariah, and Malachi are postexilic, as well as such books as Esther, Ezra, Nehemiah, and Chronicles. Concerning unsound views, it is especially important to note the claim of higher critics that Isa. 40-66 is the work of a "second" or "third" *Isaiah* (which see) living about 540 B.C. or later, and that the book of Daniel is a product of the Maccabean period (c. 167 B.C.) But denials of the unity of Isaiah and the genuineness of *Daniel* (which see) are based upon false assumptions and unsound conclusions, and they are challenged by believing scholars who refuse to abandon the fortress of a high and worthy doctrine of inspiration as set forth in the Word (2 Tim. 3:15; 2 Pet. 1:20-21). Conservative critics also refuse to surrender the historicity of *Jonah* (which see) or the authenticity of *Ezekiel's* (which see) prophecies in the face of critical attack.   M.F.U.

BIBLIOGRAPHY: B. F. Westcott, *The Bible in the Church* (1875); A. S. Peake, *The Bible, Its Origin, Its Significance, and Its Abiding Worth* (1913); R. D. Wilson, *A Scientific Investigation of the Old Testament* (1926); N. B. Stonehouse, ed., *The Infallible Word* (1946); N. Geldenhuis, *Supreme Authority* (1953); R. Preus, *Inspiration of Scripture* (1955); R. L. Harris, *Inspiration and Canonicity of the Bible* (1957); E. J. Young, *Thy Word Is Truth* (1957); F. G. Kenyon, *Our Bible and the Ancient Manuscripts* (1958); J. G. MacGregor, *The Bible in the Making* (1958); J. L. Jensen, *Independent Bible Study* (1963); B. B. Warfield, *Inspiration and Authority of the Bible* (1970); J. R. W. Stott, *Under-*

standing the Bible (1972); L. L. Morris, *I Believe in Revelation* (1976); R. M. Polzin, *Biblical Structuralism* (1977); R. L. Saucy, *The Bible Breathed from God* (1978); N. L. Geisler, *Inerrancy* (1979); J. I. Packer, *God Has Spoken* (1979); E. Radmacher, ed., *Can We Trust the Bible?* (1979); G. B. Caird, *The Language and Imagery of the Bible* (1980); C. J. Barber, *Dynamic Personal Bible Study* (1981); C. C. Ryrie, *What You Should Know About Inerrancy* (1981); R. H. Nash, *The Word of God and the Mind of Man* (1982); J. D. Woodbridge, *Biblical Authority* (1982); D. A. Carson and J. D. Woodbridge, eds., *Scripture and Truth* (1983); S. Kubo and W. F. Specht, *So Many Versions?* (1983); J. F. MacArthur, Jr., *Why I Trust the Bible* (1983); F. F. Bruce, *The Books and the Parchments* (1984); N. L. Geisler and W. E. Nix, *A General Introduction to the Bible,* 2d ed., rev. and enl. (1986).

BIBLIA PAUPERUM (bib'li-a paw'per-um; "Bible of the Poor").

1. The name given to a picture Bible, printed on wood blocks before the invention of movable type. It had forty leaves printed on one side, on which forty scenes from the life of our Lord were depicted, with some OT events, accompanied by an illustrative text or sentence in Lat. It was not intended so much for the poor people as for the indigent friars, who were, doubtless, aided in their preaching by the pictures. The pictures in this book were copied in sculpture, paintings, and altar pieces. The stained-glass windows in Lambeth Chapel were copied from some of them.

2. A work of Bonaventura, in which Bible events are alphabetically arranged and accompanied with notes to aid preachers.

BIBLIOMANCY (Gk. *biblion,* "Bible," and *manteia,* "divination"). A kind of fortune-telling by means of the Bible, consisting of drawing texts of Scripture at random, from which inference was made of duty, future events, etc. It was introduced from paganism, which made a similar use of Homer, Virgil, and other writers. In the twelfth century it was used for the detection of heretics and in the election of bishops. A sort of bibliomancy was in use among the Jews, which consisted in appealing to the very first words heard from anyone reading the Scriptures, and in regarding them as a voice from heaven.

BICH'RI (bik'ri; "firstborn"), or **Bic'ri** (NIV). A Benjamite, whose son Sheba stirred up a rebellion against David after the death of Absalom (2 Sam. 20:1-22), about 967 B.C.

BID'KAR (bid'kar). Jehu's captain and originally fellow officer who cast the body of Jehoram, the son of Ahab, into the field of Naboth after Jehu had killed him (2 Kings 9:25), 842 B.C.

BIER (Heb. *miṭṭâ,* "bed"; but "bier" in 2 Sam. 3:31, KJV, NASB, NIV; Gk. *saros,* open "coffin," funeral "couch," Luke 7:14, rendered "coffin" in the NASB and NIV, but "bier" in the KJV). The original form of the term is "beere," from the Anglo-Saxon *beran,* "to bear." The bier is in fact

a hand-barrow on which to carry a corpse to burial. In Europe it was usually covered by a "hearse," or wagon-shaped framework, for the support of the "pall." A combination of the two placed on wheels makes the modern hearse.

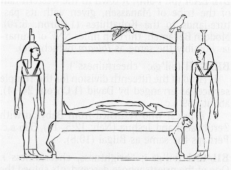

Bier, from an Egyptian bas-relief at Thebes

BIGAMY. *See* Marriage.

BIG'THA (big'tha; from Old Persian *baga + da,* "gift of God"). One of the seven eunuchs or chamberlains who had charge of the harem of Xerxes (Ahasuerus) and were commanded by him to bring in Queen Vashti to the banquet (Esther 1:10), 486-465 B.C.

BIG'THAN, or **Bigtha'na** (big'than or big-tha'na; Old Pers., cf. Bigtha). One of the officials of Xerxes (Ahasuerus) who "guarded the door." He conspired with Teresh against the life of the king and, being exposed by Mordecai, was hanged with his fellow conspirator (Esther 2:21; 6:2), 486-465 B.C.

BIG'VAI (big'va-ī; Old Persian, "happy, fortunate," from *baga,* "good luck").

1. The head of one of the families of Israelites who returned from Babylon with Zerubbabel (Ezra 2:2; Neh. 7:7) with a large number of retainers —2,056, by Ezra's count (Ezra 2:14); 2,067, by Nehemiah's (Neh. 7:19), 536 B.C. At a later period seventy-two males of his family returned with Ezra (Ezra 8:14), about 457 B.C.

2. One of the leaders of the people who subscribed to the covenant with Nehemiah (Neh. 10:16), 445 B.C. Perhaps the same as no. 1.

BIL'DAD (bil'dad). The *Shuhite* (which see), and the second of the three friends of Job who disputed with him as to his affliction and character (Job 2:11). In his first speech (chap. 8) he attributes the death of Job's children to their own transgression. In his second speech (chap. 18) he recapitulates his former assertions of the temporal calamities of the wicked, insinuating Job's wrongdoing. In his third speech (chap. 25), unable to answer Job's arguments, he takes refuge in a declaration of God's glory and man's nothingness. Finally, with Eliphaz and Zophar, he availed himself of the intercession of Job, in obedience to the divine command (42:9).

BIBLIOGRAPHY: J. S. Baxter, *Explore the Book* (1960), 2:9-78.

BIL'EAM (bil'i-am). A town in the western half of the tribe of Manasseh, given with its pasture-lands to the Kohathites (1 Chron. 6:70). Modern Bel'āmeh, thirteen miles NNE of Samaria. Possibly the same as *Ibleam* (which see).

BIL'GAH (bil'ga; "cheerfulness").
1. Head of the fifteenth division for the Temple service, as arranged by David (1 Chron. 24:14), about 989 B.C.
2. A priest who returned from Babylon with Zerubbabel and Jeshua (Neh. 12:5, 18), 536 B.C. Perhaps the same as Bilgai (10:8).

BIL'GAI (bil'ga-ī; "brightness, cheerfulness"). One of the priests whose descendants signed the seal with Nehemiah (Neh. 10:8), 445 B.C. Probably the same as *Bilgah* (which see).

BIL'HAH (bil'ha). The handmaid of Rachel, given to her by Laban (Gen. 29:29). Rachel gave Bilhah to her husband, Jacob, that through her she might have children, about 1938 B.C. Bilhah thus became the mother of Dan and Naphtali (30:3-8; 35:25; 46:25). Her stepson Reuben afterward lay with her (35:22) and thus incurred his father's dying reproof (49:4).

BIL'HAN (bil'han).
1. A Horite chief, son of Ezer, son of Seir, dwelling in Mt. Seir, in the land of Edom (Gen. 36:27; 1 Chron. 1:42).
2. A Benjamite, son of *Jediael* (which see) and father of seven sons (1 Chron. 7:10).

BILL (Heb. *sēper*, "writing"). A word meaning anything that is written, e.g., a "bill of divorcement," KJV; "certificate [or writ] of divorce," NASB (cf. Deut. 24:1, 3; Isa. 50:1; Jer. 3:8; Matt. 19:7, Gk. *biblion*). The words in the KJV of Job 31:35, "that mine adversary had written a book," would be better rendered, "that mine adversary had given me a *bill* of accusation" (i.e., of *indictment*, as in the NIV), a reading reflected in the NASB: "Here is . . . the indictment which my adversary has written." In the KJV of Jer. 32:10-16, 44, "the evidence" (marg., "book") means a *bill* of purchase or sale (NASB and NIV, "deed of purchase"). By "bill" (KJV, NIV, and NASB, from Gk. *gamma*, Luke 16:6-7) a legal instrument is meant, which showed the amount of indebtedness, probably of tenants who paid rent in kind.

BIL'SHAN (bil-shan; possibly from Akkad. *Bēlshun*, "their lord"). The name of one of the leaders of the Jews who returned to Jerusalem with Zerubbabel after the captivity (Ezra 2:2; Neh. 7:7), 536 B.C.

BIM'HAL (bim'hal). A son of Japhlet and the

great-great-grandson of Asher (1 Chron. 7:33).

BIND (*qāshar*). In the command, "You shall bind them as a sign on your hand," etc. (Deut. 6:8), the "words are figurative, and denote an undeviating observance of the divine commands; their literal fulfillment could only be a praiseworthy custom or well-pleasing to God when resorted to as the means of keeping the commands of God constantly before the eye" (K. & D., *Com.*, ad loc.).

BINDING AND LOOSING. In Matt. 16:19 the power of binding and loosing is given to the apostle Peter in connection with "the keys of the kingdom of heaven." A key in Scripture is a symbol of power and authority (Isa. 22:22; Rev. 1:18). Peter was thus given authority to open and close, not with reference to the church but in connection with "the kingdom of heaven." The history of the early church as recorded in the book of Acts makes clear the extent of this trust. It was Peter who opened the door to Christian opportunity on the Day of Pentecost (Acts 2:14; 38-42), to the Samaritans (8:14-17), and to the Gentiles in Cornelius's household at Caesarea (10:34-48). Each of these pivotal passages marked the opening of religious opportunity in a dispensational sense to the Jew, to the racially mixed Samaritans, and to the Gentile. With the gospel of grace reaching out to the Gentiles in chap. 10, the normal course of the age was established. The Holy Spirit, who came at Pentecost to baptize the Jew into the Body of Christ, was now given to Samaritan and Gentile. This marked the extent of Peter's use of the keys of the kingdom of heaven and his power of binding and loosing. There was no other assumption of authority by the apostle (15:7-11). In the Jewish council James, not Peter, presided (15:13; Gal. 2:11-15). The power of binding and loosing was shared by the other disciples (Matt. 18:18). That it merely indicated special apostolic authority and power, and in no sense involved the determination of eternal destiny, is apparent from Rev. 1:18. Christ alone holds the "keys of death and of Hades." To Peter alone was granted the special prerogative of opening gospel opportunity at the beginning of the church age or present period, characterized preeminently by God's grace and extending from the formation of the church at Pentecost by the baptism of the Spirit (cf. Acts 1:5; 11:16 with 1 Cor. 12:13) to the out-taking of this body at the coming of Christ (15:53; 1 Thess. 4:13-17; 2 Thess. 2:1-8).   M.F.U.

BIBLIOGRAPHY: H. J. Cadbury, *Journal of Biblical Literature* 58 (1939): 231-34; J. R. Mantey, *JBL* 58 (1939): 243-49; D. O. Via, Jr., *Review and Expositor* 55 (1958): 22-39.

BIN'EA (bin'i-a). A Benjamite, son of Moza and father of Raphah, of the descendants of King Saul (1 Chron. 8:37; 9:43), about 850 B.C.

BIN'NUI (bin'nū-i; "built").

1. A Levite whose son, Noadiah, was one of those who assisted in weighing the gold and silver designed for the divine service on the restoration from Babylon (Ezra 8:33), about 457 B.C.

2. One of the "sons" of Pahath-moab, who put away his foreign wife on the return from Babylon (Ezra 10:30), 456 B.C.

3. Another Israelite, of the "sons" of Bani, who did the same as above (Ezra 10:38), 456 B.C.

4. A Levite, son of Henadad, who returned with Zerubbabel from Babylon (Neh. 12:8), 536 B.C. He also (if the same) assisted in repairing the walls of Jerusalem (Neh. 3:24), 446 B.C., and joined in the covenant (10:9), 410 B.C.

5. The head of one of the families of Israelites whose followers, to the number of 648, returned from Babylon (Neh. 7:15). In Ezra 2:10 he is called *Bani* (which see), and his retainers are numbered at 642.

BIRD. See Animal Kingdom; Food; Sacrifices.

BIR'SHA (bir'sha). A king of Gomorrah whom Abraham assisted during the invasion of Chedorlaomer (Gen. 14:1-16), about 2050 B.C.

BIRTH. See Child.

BIRTHDAY (Heb. *yôm hūlledet,* Gen. 40:20; Gk. *ta genesia,* Matt. 14:6; Mark 6:21). The custom of observing birthdays is ancient and widely extended. In Persia they were celebrated with peculiar honor and banquets, and in Egypt the king's birthday was observed with great pomp (Gen. 40:20). No reference is made in Scripture to the celebration of birthdays by the Jews themselves although the language of Jeremiah (20:14-15) would seem to indicate that such occasions were joyfully remembered. By most commentators the feasts mentioned in Job 1:13, 18 are thought to have been birthday festivals, but Delitzsch (*Com.,* ad loc.) believes them to have been gatherings held each day in the home of one of the brothers. The feast commemorative of "Herod's birthday" (Matt. 14:6) may have been in honor of his birth or of his accession to the throne (cf. Hos. 7:5). The later Jews regarded the celebration of birthdays as a part of idolatrous worship. In the early church the term *birthdays* was applied to the festivals of martyrs, the days on which they suffered death in this world and were born to the glory and life of heaven.

BIRTHRIGHT (Heb. *bekōrâ;* Gk. *prototokia,* "primogeniture"). The right of the firstborn; that to which one is entitled by virtue of his birth. See Firstborn.

BIRTHSTOOL (Heb. *'obnayim,* a "pair of stones," as a "potter's wheel," and used of a low stool, so called from its resemblance to a potter's wheel). A chair of peculiar form upon which a Hebrew woman sat during childbirth (Ex. 1:16).

BIR'ZAITH (bir'za-ith). A name given in the genealogies of Asher (1 Chron. 7:31) as the son of Malchiel and great-grandson of Asher.

BISH'LAM (bish'lam; "in peace"). Apparently an officer of Artaxerxes in Palestine at the time of the return of Zerubbabel from captivity. He wrote to the king against the Jews who were rebuilding the Temple (Ezra 4:7), 529 B.C.

BISHOP. See Elder; Office; Overseer.

BISHOPRIC (Gk. *episcopē,* "oversight"). A KJV term (Acts 1:20) referring to the ministerial charge of the church; it is replaced in the NASB by the term *office* and in the NIV by the expression *place of leadership.* In liturgical churches the term is used to designate (1) the office and function of a bishop and (2) the district over which he has jurisdiction. *See also* Elder; Office; Overseer.

BITHI'A (bi-thi-a; "daughter of Jehovah") or **Bithiah** (NIV). Daughter of Pharaoh and wife of Mered, a descendant of Judah (1 Chron. 4:17). Her sons are mentioned in the clause beginning "and she conceived and bore." As the pharaohs contracted marriages with royal families alone, Mered was probably a person of some distinction, or Bithia may have been an adopted daughter of Pharaoh. It may be supposed that she became the wife of Mered during captivity.

BITHRON (bith'ron; "cut," "gorge," "ravine"). A term found in the KJV and NIV of 2 Sam. 2:29 but not in the NASB. It refers to a narrow passage in the Arabah (or Jordan Valley) through which Abner and his men went following the death of Asahel.

BITHYN'IA (bi-thin'i-a). The NW province of Asia Minor. It is mountainous, thickly wooded, and fertile. It was conquered by the Romans in 75 B.C. The letters of Pliny to the emperor Trajan show that the presence of so many Christians in the province embarrassed him (1 Pet. 1:1). Paul was not permitted to enter Bithynia (Acts 16:7), being detained by the "Spirit of Jesus."

BIBLIOGRAPHY: E. M. Blaiklock, *The Christian in Pagan Society* (1951); W. M. Ramsay, *Historical Geography of Asia Minor* (1972), pp. 179-96.

BITTER (some form of Heb. *mārar;* Gk. *pikros*). Bitterness in Scripture is symbolic of affliction, misery, servitude (Ex. 1:14; Ruth 1:20; Prov. 5:4), and wickedness (Jer. 4:18). A time of mourning and lamentation is called a "bitter day" (Amos 8:10). The "gall of bitterness" describes a state of extreme wickedness (Acts 8:23), while a "root of bitterness" (Heb. 12:15) expresses a wicked, scandalous person or any dangerous sin leading to apostasy. The waters "made bitter" (Rev. 8:11) is figurative of severe political or providential events. In the KJV of Hab. 1:6 the Chaldeans are called "that bitter and swift nation," i.e., having a *fierce* disposition (so NASB).

BITTER HERBS. Because of the symbolical meaning of bitterness, bitter herbs were commanded to be used in the celebration of the *Passover* (which see) to recall the bondage of Egypt (Ex. 12:8; Num. 9:11). *See* Vegetable Kingdom.

BITTERN. *See* Animal Kingdom: Hedgehog.

BITU'MEN (KJV, "slime"; NASB and NIV, "pitch"). *See* Mineral Kingdom: Pitch.

BIZ'I'OTH'IAH (biz'i'ōthī'a; "contempt of Jehovah"). One of the towns that fell to Judah (Josh. 15:28), probably the same as Baalath-beer (19:8). Site unknown, but apparently located near Beersheba.

BIZJOTH'JAH. *See* Biziothiah.

BIZ'THA (biz'tha; perhaps from Avestan *biz-da,* "double gift"). One of the seven eunuchs of the harem of Xerxes (Ahasuerus) who were ordered to bring Vashti forth for exhibition (Esther 1:10), 486-465 B.C.

BLACK. *See* Colors.

BLACK KITE. *See* Animal Kingdom: Kite.

BLAINS. *See* Diseases: Boils.

BLASPHEMY (Gk. *blasphēmia,* signifies the speaking of evil of God; Heb. *nāqab shēm 'Adōnai,* to "curse the name of the Lord," Isa. 52:5; Rom. 2:24). Sometimes, perhaps, "blasphemy" has been retained by translators when the general meaning "evil-speaking" or "slander" might have been better (Ps. 74:18; Col. 3:8). There are two general forms of blasphemy: (1) Attributing some evil to God, or denying Him some good that we should attribute to Him (Lev. 24:11; Rom. 2:24). (2) Giving the attributes of God to a creature—which form of blasphemy the Jews charged Jesus with (Matt. 26:65; Luke 5:21; John 10:36). The Jews from ancient times have interpreted the command in Lev. 24:16 as prohibiting the utterance of the name Jehovah, reading for it "Adonai" or "Elohim."

Punishment. Blasphemy, when committed in ignorance, i.e., through thoughtlessness and weakness of the flesh, might be atoned for; but if committed "with a high hand," i.e., in impious rebellion against Jehovah, was punished by stoning (Lev. 24:11-16).

New Testament. Blasphemy against the Holy Spirit (Matt. 12:31; Mark 3:29; Luke 12:10), also called the *unpardonable sin,* has caused extended discussion. The sin mentioned in the gospels would appear to have consisted in attributing to the power of Satan those unquestionable miracles that Jesus performed by "the finger of God" and by the power of the Holy Spirit. It is questionable whether it may be extended beyond this one limited and special sin (*see* Sin, The Unpardonable).

Among the early Christians three kinds of blasphemy were recognized: (1) of apostates and *lapsi*

(lapsed), whom the heathen persecutors had compelled not only to deny, but to curse, Christ; (2) of heretics and other profane Christians; (3) blasphemy against the Holy Spirit.

BLASTING. This term, which appears several times in the KJV and once in the NASB, refers to two diseases that attack the grain: one to the withering or burning of the ears, caused by the E wind (Gen. 41:6, 23, 27); the other to the effect produced by a warm wind in Arabia, by which the green ears are turned yellow, so that they bear no grains (K. & D., *Com.*). In the NASB and NIV "blasted" is replaced with "scorched," and "blasting" is replaced with "blight" or "scorching," except in Hag. 2:17, where both the KJV and NASB read "blasting." The NIV, however, retains "blight" in this passage. *See* Mildew.

BLAS'TUS (blas'tus; "sprout, shoot"). The chamberlain of King Herod Agrippa who acted as mediator between the people of Tyre and Sidon and the king (Acts 12:20), A.D. 44.

BLEMISH. A physical or mental defect. As the spiritual nature of a man is reflected in his bodily form, only a faultless condition of the body could correspond to the holiness of a priest. Consequently, all men were excluded from the priesthood, and all animals from being offered as sacrifices, who had any blemish or "defect." These blemishes are described in Lev. 21:17-23; 22:18-25; Deut. 15:21. "A disfigured face" may mean any mutilation, or it could indicate a syphilitic condition. The rule concerning animals extended to imperfections, so that if an animal free from outward blemish was found, after being slain, internally defective it was not offered in sacrifice. *See also* the articles Defect; Diseases: Blemish.

BLESS, BLESSING. Acts of blessing may be considered: (1) When God is said to bless men (Gen. 1:28; 22:17). God's blessing is accompanied with that virtue that renders His blessing effectual and which is expressed by it. Because God is eternal and omnipresent, His omniscience and omnipotence cause His blessings to avail in the present life in respect to all things and also in the life to come. (2) When men bless God (Pss. 103:1-2; 145:1-3; etc.). This is when they ascribe to Him those characteristics that are His, acknowledge His sovereignty, express gratitude for His mercies, etc. (3) Men bless their fellowmen when, as in ancient times under the spirit of prophecy, they predict blessings to come upon them. Thus Jacob blessed his sons (Gen. 49:1-28; Heb. 11:21), and Moses the children of Israel (Deut. 33:1-29). It was the duty and privilege of the priests to bless the people in the name of the Lord (*see* Benediction). Further, men bless their fellowmen when they express good wishes and pray to God in their behalf. (4) At meals. The psalmist says, "I shall lift up the cup of salvation, and call upon the name of the Lord" (Ps. 116:13), an apparent reference to a custom among the Jews. A feast was made of a portion of their thank offerings when, among other rites, the master of the feast took a cup of wine, offering thanks to God for His mercies. The cup was then passed to all the guests, each drinking in his turn. At family feasts, and especially the Passover, both bread and wine were passed and thanks offered to God for His mercies.

BIBLIOGRAPHY: T. H. Gaster, *Journal of Biblical Literature* 66 (1947): 53-62; F. M. Cross and D. N. Freeman, *JBL* 67 (1948): 191-210; L. J. Liebrich, *JBL* 74 (1955): 33-36; E. M. Good, *JBL* 82 (1963): 427-32.

BLESSING, THE CUP OF. A name applied to the wine in the Lord's Supper (1 Cor. 10:16), probably because the same name was given to the cup of wine in the supper of the *Passover* (which see).

BLINDNESS. The Bible speaks of three kinds of blindness: physical, spiritual, and judicial.

Physical Blindness. Instances of physical blindness appear in Scripture (John 9:25). Blindness was sometimes inflicted for political and other purposes in the East (Judg. 16:21; 1 Sam. 11:2). The eyes of captives taken in war were commonly put out. This practice was especially followed by the cruel Assyrians, as well as by the Babylonians and others. Jesus often healed physical blindness during His earthly ministry. In John 9 physical blindness and its cure portray judicial blindness. *See* Diseases.

Spiritual Blindness. Spiritual blindness is that state affecting truth. "And even if our gospel is veiled, it is veiled to those who are perishing, in whose case the god of this world has blinded the minds of the unbelieving, that they might not see the light of the gospel of the glory of Christ, who is the image of God" (2 Cor. 4:3-4). Numerous Scriptures portray the unsaved as blinded and held under the power of Satan (John 8:44; Col. 1:13; Eph. 2:1-2). Salvation involves the taking away of this satanic veil. Spiritual blindness also extends to carnal Christians. Yielding to sin on the part of a believer, or failing to walk by the Spirit, involves diminution of spiritual perception: "And I, brethren, could not speak to you as to spiritual men, but as to men of flesh, as to babes in Christ" (1 Cor. 3:1). The correction of blindness in the carnal believer can only be brought about by a separation from carnality and a yielding to the Holy Spirit (1 Cor. 2:6-16). *See also* Isa. 6:10; 42:18-19; Matt. 15:14.

Judicial Blindness. This phase of blindness or hardness of heart is characteristic of the nation Israel as a result of its rejection of the Messiah. It extends throughout the entire Christian age since the crucifixion of Christ. In Rom. 11:1-5 the apostle describes Israelites as under a double election—the national election and their individual election. He points out that nationally they have been temporarily set aside but that through

individual election of grace, when the present age of the out-calling of the church is completed, Israel will be brought into judgment, refined, and restored to its national election. For this reason Israel's blindness is described by the apostle to be "partial" (Rom. 11:25), thus indicating the remnant of Israel who will be saved in this present age and will become members of the church, the Body of Christ. Judicial blindness of Israel is implied in such great passages of Scripture as Isa. 6:9-10, Jer. 31:35-37, Mark 4:12, Luke 8:10, Acts 28:26-27, John 12:37-41. We are told in 2 Cor. 3:14-16 that a veil is upon the heart of the understanding of Jews "whenever Moses is read." However, when the nation shall turn to the Lord "the veil is taken away." The difficult problem is that although Scripture declares that for their own national sins the Jews are blinded, yet not all of them are blinded, and only partially so for the period of the out-calling of the church. The apostle says, "For I do not want you, brethren, to be uninformed of this mystery, lest you be wise in your own estimation, that a partial hardening has happened to Israel until the fulness of the Gentiles has come in; and thus all Israel will be saved; just as it is written,/'The Deliverer will come from Zion,/He will remove ungodliness from Jacob.'/'And this is My covenant with them,/When I take away their sins'" (Rom. 11:25-27). M.F.U.

BLOOD (Heb. *dām;* Gk. *haima,* "the circulatory life fluid of the body"). A peculiar sacredness was attached to blood because of the idea that prevailed of its unity with the soul. We find this distinctively stated (Gen. 9:4): "Only you shall not eat flesh with its life, that is, its blood." This identification of the blood with the soul, which prevailed in antiquity, appears at first to have no further foundation than that a sudden diminution of the quantity of blood in the body causes death. But this phenomenon itself has the deeper reason that all activity of the body depends on the quantity of the blood. The blood is actually the basis of the physical life; and, so far, the soul, as the principle of bodily life, is preeminently in the blood. We are to understand this only of the sensuous soul, not of the intelligent and thinking soul" (Delitzsch).

Arising from this principle the Scriptures record different directions respecting blood:

As Food. When permission was given Noah to partake of animal food (Gen. 9:4), the use of blood was strictly forbidden. In the Mosaic law this prohibition was repeated with emphasis, though generally in connection with sacrifices (Lev. 3:8; 7:26). "The prohibition of the use of blood has a twofold ground: blood has the soul in itself, and in accordance with the gracious ordinance of God it is the means of expiation for human souls, because of the soul contained in it. The one ground is found in the nature of blood and the other in its destination to a holy purpose, which, even apart from that other reason, withdraws it from a common use" (Delitzsch, *Bib. Psychology*, p. 283). Because of the blood the eating of bloody portions of flesh (Gen. 9:4) or of flesh with blood (Lev. 19:26; 1 Sam. 14:32) is also forbidden. The penalty was that the offender should be "cut off " from the people, which seems to be death, but whether by the sword or by stoning is not known (Lev. 17:14). This prohibition was also made by the apostles and elders in the council at Jerusalem and coupled with things offered to idols (Acts 15:29).

Sacrificial. A well-known rabbinical maxim, recognized by the author of the epistle to the Hebrews (9:22), was "Without shedding of blood there is no forgiveness." The life is in the blood, as is often declared by Moses; the life of the sacrifice was taken, and the blood offered to God, as a representative and substitute for the offerer (Lev. 17:11). *See* Sacrifice; Festivals.

Figurative. "Blood" is often used for *life:* "Whoever sheds man's blood" (Gen. 9:6); "His blood be on us" (Matt. 27:25). "Blood" sometimes is used as a symbol of slaughter (Isa. 34:3; Ezek. 14:19). To "wash his feet in the blood of the wicked" (Ps. 58:10) is to gain a victory with great slaughter. He who "builds a city with bloodshed" (Hab. 2:12) causes the death of the subjugated nations. Wine is called the "blood of grapes" (Gen. 49:11).

BIBLIOGRAPHY: A. M. Stibbs, *The Meaning of the Word "Blood" in Scripture* (1947); L. L. Morris, *Journal of Theological Studies* 3 (1952): 216-27; id., JTS 6 (1955): 77-82; id., *Apostolic Preaching of the Cross* (1955).

BLOOD, AVENGER, or **Revenger of** (Heb. *gô'ēl haddām*, lit., "redeemer of blood"). At the root of the enactments of the Mosaic penal code lies the principle of strict but righteous retribution, the purpose being to eradicate evil and produce reverence for the righteous God. This principle, however, was not first introduced by the law of Moses. It is much older and is found especially in the form of *blood revenge* among many ancient peoples. It appears almost everywhere where the state has not yet been formed or is still in the first stages of development, and consequently satisfaction for personal injury falls to private revenge.

This custom of "blood calling for blood" exists among Arabs of today. If a man is slain there can never be peace between the tribes again unless the man who killed him is slain by the avenger.

By this custom the life, first of all, but after it also the property of the family, as its means of subsistence, was to be protected by the nearest of kin, called a *redeemer.* The following directions were given by Moses: (1) The willful murderer was to be put to death, without permission of compensation, by the nearest of kin. (2) The law of retaliation was not to extend beyond the immediate offender (Deut. 24:16; 2 Kings 14:6;

2 Chron. 25:4; etc.). (3) If a man took the life of another without hatred, or without hostile intent, he was permitted to flee to one of the *cities of refuge* (which see).

It is not known how long blood revenge was observed, although it would appear (2 Sam. 14:7-8) that David had influence in restraining the operation of the law. Jehoshaphat established a court at Jerusalem to decide such cases (2 Chron. 19:10).

BIBLIOGRAPHY: J. Pedersen, *Israel, Its Life and Culture* (1926), 1-2: 420-37.

BLOOD, FLOW, or **Issue, of.** *See* Diseases: Issue.

BLOODY SWEAT. In recording the scene in Gethsemane Luke says that our Lord's sweat "became like drops of blood falling down upon the ground" (22:44). These words are understood by many to express merely a comparison between the size and density of the drops of sweat and those of blood. But *blood* is properly understood here only when compared to the *nature* of the sweat, and we infer that the words imply a *profusion of sweat* mingled with blood. "Phenomena of frequent occurrence demonstrate how immediately the blood, the seat of life, is under the influence of moral impressions. A feeling of shame causes the blood to rise to the face. Cases are known in which the blood, violently agitated by grief, ends by penetrating through the vessels which inclose it, and, driven outward, escapes with the sweat through the transpiratory glands" (Godet, *Com.*, ad loc.). The phenomenon of "bloody sweat" under extreme emotional stress is recognized by medicine and is called *diapedesis*, or the seeping of the blood through the vessels without rupture.

BLOSSOM. Several Heb. terms are translated "blossom" or "blossoms" in the KJV, NIV, and NASB. For the use of the term in the description in the NASB and NIV of the golden lampstand in the Tabernacle, *see* Almond Blossom; for the use of the term in the description in the NASB and NIV of the laver in Solomon's Temple, *see* Lily Blossom.

For the almond tree and the lily plant, *see* Vegetable Kingdom.

BLOSSOM, ALMOND. *See* Almond Blossom; Vegetable Kingdom: Almond.

BLOSSOM, LILY. *See* Lily Blossom; Vegetable Kingdom: Lily.

BLOT. This word is used in the sense of to obliterate; therefore *to blot out* is to destroy or abolish. To blot out sin is to forgive it fully and finally (Isa. 44:22, KJV). To blot men out of God's book is to withdraw His providential favors and to cut them off (Ex. 32:32; cf. Deut. 29:20; Ps. 69:28). When Moses says, in the above passage, "Blot me out from Thy book," we understand the written book as a metaphorical expression, alluding to the custom of making a list of all citizens so that privileges of citizenship might be accorded them. "To blot out of Jehovah's book, therefore, is to cut off from living fellowship with the living God . . . and to deliver over to death. As a true mediator of his people, Moses was ready to stake his own life for the deliverance of the nation if Jehovah would forgive the people their sin. These words were the strongest expression of devoted, self-sacrificing love" (K. & D., *Com.*, ad loc.).

The refusal to blot the name of the saints out of the book of life, etc. (Rev. 3:5), indicates their security and final vindication. A sinful act (Job 31:7) or reproach (Prov. 9:7) is termed a blot (KJV).

BLUE. *See* Colors.

BOANER'GES (bo-a-nur'jēz; Gk. from Aram. "sons of thunder," "noise," *regōshā,* cf. Arab. *rejasa,* "to rumble"—thunder). An epithet used of James and John (Mark 3:17), denoting probably their fiery eloquence (so Jerome) or zeal. It may, however, refer to their quick temper and disposition to violence (Luke 9:52-56). Compare Aram. *riggūshā* (Syr. *regshā,* "tumult"; *rugza,* "anger").   M.F.U.

BOAR. *See* Animal Kingdom: Swine.

BOARDS. *See* Deck of Boxwood.

BOATS. As a farming people inhabiting the central highland region of Palestine, the Israelites, unlike the Phoenicians, were not sea-minded. References to boats inside Palestine are not numerous. There were ferry boats across the Jordan River (2 Sam. 19:18) and small fishing boats that plied the Sea of Galilee (Mark 4:36; John 6:1, 23). David had to depend on the Phoenician navy of Hiram, who helped Solomon build the Hebrew navy. Ezion-geber on the Gulf of Aqaba was the port. Although the Hebrews were a land-loving people, there are a number of references to the boats of other nations (cf. Pss. 107:23; 104:26; Prov. 31:14). Paul used coastal freighters for travel during his missionary journeys. His account of the voyage to Rome in Acts 27 is one of the best-known and most vivid ancient adventures at sea. In OT times Egyptian ships not only traveled along the Nile but the Mediterranean coast. Traffic with Phoenician Byblos (OT Gebal) was especially well known. Those ships, called "Byblos Travelers," transported papyrus for papermaking and brought back various kinds of wood and expensive wines. From early times flat-bottomed boats were capable of hauling heavy stones for Egyptian buildings hundreds of miles on the Nile. Similar flat-bottomed boats, caulked with bitumen, and timber rafts floated on inflated skins, were used on the Tigris and Euphrates rivers. Traffic extended even to India via the Persian Gulf. Perhaps the most famous ships of antiquity were those of the Phoenicians, which plied the Mediterranean and extended Phoenician art and culture as far W as Spain. Those ships were propelled by sails and oars.

M.F.U.

Artist's impression of Roman merchant ship

BO'AZ (bō'az; possibly "fleetness" from Arab. *ba'aza,* "to be nimble").

1. A wealthy Bethlehemite, kinsman to Elimelech, the husband of Naomi. When Naomi and Ruth returned from the country of Moab the latter received permission to glean in the fields of Boaz. He treated her generously, offering her much greater privileges than were usually accorded to gleaners. Finding that the kinsman of Ruth, who was more nearly related to her, would not marry her according to the "levirate law," Boaz voluntarily assumed that law's obligations. He married Ruth, and their union was blessed by the birth of Obed, the grandfather of David (Ruth 1-4), about 1070 B.C.

2. One of the pillars of Solomon's Temple. *See* Jachin.

BO'CHERU (bo'ke-rū; "firstborn"). One of the six sons of Azel, a descendant of King Saul (1 Chron. 8:38).

BO'CHIM (bō'kim; "weepers"). A place near Gilgal that was so named as a reminder of the tears shed by the unfaithful people of Israel upon God's reproving them (Judg. 2:1, 5). It was W of the Jordan, near the Dead Sea, and probably between Bethel and Shiloh.

BODY. The lowest part of man as a triune being, in which his soul and spirit reside (1 Thess. 5:23). In the body of a redeemed man the Holy Spirit dwells (1 Cor. 6:19; 2 Pet. 1:13-14), and his body is said to be peculiarly God's property (1 Cor. 6:20). Its members are to be yielded unto God as instruments of righteousness rather than unto iniquity (Rom. 6:13, 19).

Figurative. The apostle Paul uses the exquisite figure of the human body to portray the spiritual unity of believers in this age, from Pentecost to the out-taking of the church. This mystical body is formed by the baptizing work of the Spirit (1 Cor. 12:13), an operation that not only unites Christians to one another but to Christ (Rom. 6:3-4; Gal. 3:27). "The body" (Gk. *sōma*) is differentiated from the "shadow" (*skia*; Col. 2:17). Thus the ceremonies of the law are figures and shadows realized in Christ. The "body of sin" (Rom. 6:6), called also "the body of this death" (7:24), represents the physical body under the control of the old nature. Unless the Christian walks in the new nature under the power of the Holy Spirit, he will come under the contamination of the old nature, which is not eradicated or destroyed when he becomes a believer. The apostle speaks of a *natural* body in opposition to a spiritual body (1 Cor. 15:44). The spiritual body will be the body after glorification, no longer subject to sin or death. The body that is buried is natural, subject to dissolution. The resurrection body will be spiritual, no longer subject to natural law or to sin.　　　　　　　　M.F.U.

BIBLIOGRAPHY: J. A. T. Robinson, *The Body: A Study in Pauline Theology,* Studies in Biblical Theology, no. 5 (1952); A. L. Oppenheim, *Ancient Mesopotamia* (1964), pp. 198-204; H. W. Wolff, *Anthropology of the Old Testament* (1975); R. H. Gundry, *"Soma" in Biblical Theology* (1976); P. Brand and P. Yancey, *Fearfully and Wonderfully Made* (1980).

BO'HAN (bō'han; a "thumb"). A Reubenite, in whose honor a stone was set up (or named), which afterward served as a boundary mark on the frontier of Judah and Benjamin (Josh. 15:6; 18:17).

BOILS. See Diseases.

BO'KERU. See Bocheru.

BO'KIM. See Bochim.

BOLSTER (Heb. *mᵉra'ashâ,* "at the head"). A KJV term replaced in the NASB by "at his (or its) head." In Gen. 28:18 *mᵉra'ashâ* is rendered *pillow* (which see), but the NASB correctly gives "under his head."

BOLT. See Lock.

BOLT (Heb. *reshep,* a live "coal," an "arrow"). The Heb. term, referring to a bolt of lightning (Ps. 78:48), doubtless has reference to the manner in which lightning strikes the earth.

BOND. The translation of several Heb. and Gk. words; an obligation of any kind (Num. 30:2, 4, 12). It is used to signify oppression, captivity, affliction (Ps. 116:16). We read of the "bond of peace" (Eph. 4:3); and love, because it completes the Christian character, is called the "perfect bond of unity" (Col. 3:14). Bands or chains worn by prisoners were known as *bonds* (Acts 20:23).

BONDAGE. See Service.

BONDMAID, BONDMAN, BONDSERVANT. See Service.

BONE. This word is used figuratively, as "bone of my bones, and flesh of my flesh" (Gen. 2:23), "of his flesh, and of his bones" (Eph. 5:30, KJV; "members of His body," NASB and NIV), to mean the same nature and being united in the nearest relation. Iniquities are said to be in men's *bones* when their bodies are polluted thereby (Job 20:11, KJV); and the state of the national death of Israel scattered among the Gentile nations is represented by the "valley of dry bones" (Ezek. 37:1-14).

BONNET. A KJV term replaced in the NASB and NIV by *caps, headdress,* and *linen turban. See* Dress; Turban.

BOOK (Heb. *sēper;* Gk. *biblos*). The Heb. word is much more comprehensive than our English *book.* It means anything *written,* as a bill of sale or deed of purchase (Jer. 32:12), a bill of accusation or an indictment (Job 31:35), a certificate of divorce (Deut. 24:1, 3), a letter (2 Sam. 11:14), or a volume (Ex. 17:14; Deut. 28:58; etc.). Respecting the material, form, and making of books, *see* Writing.

There are some notable expressions one may paraphrase from Scripture regarding books:

1. "To eat a book" (Ezek. 2:8; 3:2; Rev. 10:9) is a figurative expression meaning to master the contents of the book; to receive into one's innermost being the Word of God.

2. "A sealed book" is one closed up from view (Rev. 5:1-3) or one whose contents were not understood by those reading it (Isa. 29:11). By a book "written inside and on the back" (Rev. 5:1) we understand a roll written on both sides.

3. "Book of the generations" means the genealogical records of a family or nation (Gen. 5:1; cf. Matt. 1:1).

4. "The books" mentioned in Dan. 7:10 perhaps mean books of accounts with servants; or, as among the Persians, records of official services rendered to the king and the rewards given to those who performed them (Esther 6:1-3). The "books" (Rev. 20:12) are referred to in justification of the sentence passed upon the wicked.

5. "The Book of Life" is a figurative expression originating from the ancient custom of keeping genealogical records (Neh. 7:5, 64; 12:22-23) and of registering citizens for numerous purposes (Jer. 22:30; Ezek. 13:9). God is accordingly represented as having a record of all His creation, particularly those under His special care. To be expunged from "the book of life" is to be severed from the divine favor and to incur an untimely death. Moses thus pleads that he might die, rather than that Israel should be destroyed (Ex. 32:32; Ps. 69:28). In the NT "the book of life" refers to the roster of righteous who are to inherit eternal life (Phil. 4:3; Rev. 3:5; 13:8; 17:8; 21:27), from which the saved are not to be blotted out (3:5). In the Apocalypse "the book" (or "books") is presented as the divine record of the works of

the unsaved at the great white throne judgment (20:12, 15), according to which the lost will suffer degrees of eternal punishment.

6. "Book of the Wars of the Lord" represents a memento of a larger literary development in early OT times than is represented in the canonical books. This early literary work, probably poetical, existed in Mosaic times (Num. 21:14). It was likely a collection of odes celebrating God's glorious acts toward Israel and recited over campfires, just as the Bedouin do today. Similarly, "The book of Jashar" (Josh. 10:13; 2 Sam. 1:18) seems to have been an early national chronicle of events in Israel that stretched over several centuries of the early history of the Hebrews.

BOOTH (Heb. *sūkkâ*, "hut," or "lair"; often translated "tabernacle" or "pavilion"). A shelter made of branches of trees and shrubs (Gen. 33:17) and serving as a protection against rain, frost, and heat. Such were also the temporary green shelters in which the Israelites celebrated the feast of Booths (Tabernacles, KJV; Lev. 23:42-43). *See* Cottage; Festivals.

A farmer's makeshift booth

BOOTHS, FEAST OF. The NASB and NIV rendering of the Heb. expression given in the KJV as feast of Tabernacles. *See* Festivals.

BOOTY. *See* Spoil.

BO'OZ. *See* Boaz.

BOR'-ASHAN (bor'a-shan; "smoking furnace"). A place named (1 Sam. 30:30) as the scene of David's hunting exploits; also probably identical with Ashan of Simeon (Josh. 15:42; 19:7).

BORDER (from Heb. *gĕbūl*). Generally a boundary line. Boundary stones were commonly set up to mark off property lines (Deut. 19:14; 27:17; Prov. 22:28; 23:10). Many such markers have been excavated in Babylonia, where demarcation of fields in irrigation areas was especially important. One such "ancient landmark" survives from the reign of Nebuchadnezzar I (c. 1138 B.C.) and

was unearthed at ancient Nippur. *See also* Boundary Mark.

BORN AGAIN. The new birth is a creative life-giving operation of the Holy Spirit upon a lost human soul, whereby in response to faith in Christ crucified (John 3:14-16; Gal. 3:24), the believing one, "dead in ... trespasses and sins" (Eph. 2:1), is quickened into spiritual life and made a partaker of the divine nature and of the life of Christ Himself (Gal. 2:20; Eph. 2:10; Col. 1:27; 1 Pet. 1:23-25; 2 Pet. 1:4). The complete necessity of this spiritual transaction is the result of fallen man's state of spiritual death, his alienation from God, and his consequent utter inability to "see" (John 3:3) or "to enter into" the kingdom of God (3:5). No matter how moral, refined, talented, or religious the natural or unregenerate man may be, he is blind to spiritual truth and unable to save himself (3:6; cf. Ps. 51:5; 1 Cor. 2:14; Rom. 8:7-8). It is clear, therefore, that the new birth is not the reformation of the old nature but the reception of a new nature. *See* Regeneration.   M.F.U.

BORROW, BORROWING. As a matter of law, etc., *see* Loan.

We call attention to the much-debated act of the Israelites in "borrowing" from the Egyptians (Ex. 12:35). This was in response to a divine command (3:22; 11:2); and it suggests a difficulty, seeing that the Israelites did not intend to return to Egypt or to restore the borrowed articles. So considered, the Israelites were guilty of an immoral act. The following are some of the attempts at explanation, briefly stated:

1. The Israelites borrowed, expecting to return in three days; but when Pharaoh refused to allow this, Moses was instructed to demand the *entire* departure of Israel. After the smiting of the firstborn, Israel was thrust out and had no opportunity of returning what she had borrowed.

2. After the borrowing the Egyptians made war upon the Israelites, and this breach of peace justified the latter in retaining the property as "contraband of war."

3. Ewald (*Hist. of Israel,* 2:66) maintains that "since Israel could not return to Egypt, ... and therefore was not bound to return the borrowed goods, the people kept them, and despoiled the Egyptians. It appears a piece of highly retributive justice that those who had been oppressed in Egypt should now be forced to borrow from the Egyptians, and be obliged by Pharaoh's subsequent treachery to retain them, and thus be indemnified for their long oppression."

4. "The only meaning of *shā'al* is to ask or beg; [and the expression] *yash'ilûm* [Ex. 12:36], *lit.,* 'they allowed them to ask'; *i.e.,* the Egyptians ... received their petition with good will, and granted their request. ... From the very first the Israelites asked without intending to restore, and the Egyptians granted their request without any

hope of receiving back, because God had made their hearts favorably disposed to the Israelites" (K. & D., *Com.* on 3:21-22). This view appears to be taken by Josephus (*Ant.* 2.14.6): "They also honored the Hebrews with gifts; some in order to get them to depart quickly and others on account of [neighborly intimacy] with them." It evidently refers to the custom, which is fresh now as always in the unchangeable East, of soliciting a gift on the eve of departure or on the closing of any term of service of any sort whatsoever. That this was the custom in that day, as it is now, is indicated in many Bible references to the giving of gifts (Gen. 12:16; 33:10-11; Judg. 3:15-18; etc.); but more explicitly in the divine command to the Israelites themselves not to "send him away empty-handed" when they released a servant at the beginning of the sabbatical year (Deut. 15:13-15).

BIBLIOGRAPHY: A. Edersheim, *Sketches of Jewish Social Life in the Days of Christ* (1961), pp. 211-12; A. Deissmann, *Light from the Ancient East* (1965), pp. 270, 331.

BOS'CATH. *See* Bozkath.

BO'SOR. *See* Beor.

BOSOM.
1. The bunchy fold of the dress in front of the breast, into which idlers thrust the hand (Ps. 74:11); also used as a pocket or bag in which bread, grain, and other kinds of food were carried (Hag. 2:12; Luke 6:38, KJV; NASB, NIV, "lap"; Gk. *kolpos*). Shepherds thus carried lambs (Isa. 40:11).
2. The front of the body between the arms; hence to "lean on one's bosom" is to so recline at the table that the head covers, as it were, the breast of the one next to him (John 13:23). The expression "carried away . . . to Abraham's bosom" (Luke 16:22) means to obtain the seat next to Abraham, i.e., to be partaker of the same blessedness as Abraham. Christ "is in the bosom of the Father" (John 1:18), i.e., "He who is most intimately connected with the Father, and dearest to Him."

BOTCH. *See* Diseases: Boils.

BOTTLES. Two kinds of containers of liquids were common in ancient times—bottles of skin and earthenware. The latter were easily broken, and recovered pottery and shards constitute one of the most helpful ways the archaeologist has of describing and dating old cultures in both Palestine and Mesopotamia. Beautiful Halafian ware from Tell Halaf in N Mesopotamia goes back to c. 4500 B.C. Obeidan ware from Tell Obeid, near Ur in Babylonia, dates around 3500 B.C.; Warkan ware from Uruk (Erech, Gen. 10:10) 3200 B.C.; Jemdet Nasr ware around 3100 B.C. Jeremiah mentions the potter's earthen vessels (Jer. 19:1, 10; 13:12-14). Bottles, frequently decorated with glass, held tears of mourners (Ps. 56:8) and were placed in tombs. They were popular in Egypt and Palestine. Bottles of skin were manufactured from whole animal hides by slowly drying them. Such leather containers are referred to in Gen. 21:14 and Josh. 9:4. Jesus referred to the wineskin or bottle that bursts when new wine is put into the old skins (Matt. 9:17; Mark 2:22; Luke 5:37). Such skins were also used to churn butter. Skin bottles are found even today in Palestine.

Several Heb. words are given as "bottle" in the KJV. Except for Judg. 4:19; Ps. 56:8, these terms are translated "skin," "wineskin," "jug," or "jar" in the NASB. The NIV translates "skin" in Judg. 4:19 and "scroll" (marg., "wineskin") in Ps. 56:8. When KJV "bottle" is the rendering of Heb. *nēbel,* the NASB and NIV translations are always *jug* or *jar* (both which see).   M.F.U.

Varieties of ancient bottles or pots

BOTTOMLESS PIT (NASB rendering of the Gk. *to phrear tēs 'abussou,* "the pit of the abyss," Rev. 9:1-2; the NIV renders "abyss"). The prisonhouse of the demons. In the end of the age myriads of these imprisoned evil spirits will be set free to indwell, torment, and energize men (9:1-21) to engage in a gigantic attempt to oppose Christ and God's kingdom plans for the Jew in the millennial age to come (16:13-16). At the second coming of Christ, Satan and demons will be remanded to the abyss (20:1-3), a condition that will make possible the Kingdom age on earth (20:3). *See* Abyss; Hell; Lake; Gehenna.   M.F.U.

BOUNDARY MARK (Heb. *gᵉbûl*). This was used to designate the limits of land; it could be a stone, a stake, or other such marker. The removal of such a landmark was prohibited by Mosaic law (Deut. 19:14; 27:17; Prov. 22:28; cf. Job 24:2, "landmarks") on account of the close connection in which a man's possession as the means of his support stood to the life of the man himself. Landmarks were held sacred by other nations; by the Romans, for example, who held them so sacred that removal was punished with death. In Arab fields in Palestine one may sometimes still see stones piled on top of one another for use as a landmark. *See also* Border.

BIBLIOGRAPHY: C. M. Carmichael, *The Laws of Deuteronomy* (1974), pp. 113-14; R. Wardlaw, *Lectures on the*

Book of Proverbs (1982), 3:65-68, 79-82; J. Ridderbos, *Deuteronomy*, Bible Student's Commentary (1984), pp. 211-12, 251-53.

Boundary marker of Marduk, Babylonia

BOW AND ARROW. As a weapon, *see* Armor, Arms.

Figurative. The *bow* signifies *judgments* ready for offenders (Ps. 7:12); sometimes *lying* (Jer. 9:3). "A treacherous bow" (Ps. 78:57; cf. Hos. 7:16) represents *unreliableness*. "The song of the bow" (2 Sam. 1:18) refers to "a song to which the title Kesheth (Heb. word for 'bow') was given, not only because the bow is referred to (v. 22), but because it is a martial ode" (K. & D., *Com.*, ad loc.).

BOW IN THE CLOUDS. *See* Rainbow.

BOWELS. A KJV term translating several Heb. words and the Gk. word *splanchna,* and often indicating the inner parts generally, the inner man, and also the heart. Thus the bowels are made the seat of tenderness and compassion (Gen. 4:30; Ps. 25:6, "tender mercies," KJV, "loving kindnesses," NASB, "great mercy," NIV; Phil. 1:8; Col. 3:12). "My bowels shall sound like an harp" (Isa. 16:11, KJV; "my heart intones like a harp," NASB) is thus explained by Keil and Delitzsch (*Com.*): "Just as the hand or plectrum

touches the strings of the harp, so did the terrible things that he had heard Jehovah say concerning Moab touch the strings of his inward parts, and cause them to resound with notes of pain."

BOWING. An attitude of respect and reverence from the earliest times. Thus Abraham "bowed to the people of the land" (Gen. 23:7); Jacob, when he met Esau, "bowed down to the ground seven times" (33:3); and the brothers of Joseph "bowed down in homage" (43:28). The orientals in the presence of kings and princes often prostrate themselves upon the earth. Such customs prevailed among the Hebrews (Ex. 4:31; 1 Kings 1:53; 2:19; 1 Sam. 24:8).

Bowing is frequently noticed in Scripture as an act of religious homage to idols (Josh. 23:7; Judg. 2:19; 2 Kings 5:18; Isa. 44:15), and also to God (Josh. 5:14; Pss. 22:29; 72:9; Mic. 6:6; etc.).

BOWL. The translation of several Heb. words. We have no means of obtaining accurate information as to the material and precise form of these vessels. In the earliest times they were, doubtless, made of wood and shells of the larger kinds of nuts and were used at meals for liquids, broth, or stew (2 Kings 4:40). Modern Arabs are now content with a few wooden bowls, although those of the rulers are not infrequently made of copper and neatly tinned. Bowls with Heb. inscriptions have been found at Babylon. *See* Dish.

BOWMAN. *See* Armor, Arms.

BOWSHOT. The ordinary distance an archer could shoot an arrow (Gen. 21:16).

BOX OF OIL. *See* Flask.

BOX TREE. *See* Vegetable Kingdom: Box Tree; Cypress.

BOY (Heb. *yeled,* a young "boy" or "child," Joel 3:3; Zech. 8:5; *na'ar,* Gen. 25:27). A term used of those who are from the age of infancy to adolescence.

BO'ZEZ (boz'es). Between the passes through which Jonathan endeavored to cross over to go up to the post of the Philistines there was a sharp rock on one side called Bozez, and one on the other called Seneh (1 Sam. 14:4-5). These rose up like pillars to a great height and were probably the "hills" that Robinson saw to the left of the pass.

BOZ'KATH (boz'kath). A town in the plain of Judah, near Lachish and Eglon (Josh. 15:39); and the birthplace of Adaiah, maternal grandfather of King Josiah (2 Kings 22:1).

BOZ'RAH (boz'ra; "enclosure, fortress").

1. A city of Edom, and residence of Jobab (Gen. 36:33; 1 Chron. 1:44). This is the Bozrah of Isa. 34:6; 63:1; Jer. 49:13, 22; Amos 1:12. It is probably to be identified with present Buseirah SE of the Dead Sea. Bozrah was the metropolis of N

181

Edom (1200-700 B.C.) and was famous for its dyed garments (Isa. 63:1).

2. A place in Moab (Jer. 48:24). Perhaps the same as Bezer.

BRACELET. An article of adornment popular in ancient times, worn on the wrists or arms of both men and women (Ezek. 16:11). Abraham's servant put such a piece of jewelry on Rebekah's wrist (Gen. 24:22). Israelites in the wilderness contributed gold or silver for the vessels of the Tabernacle from such a source (Num. 31:50). Saul wore a bracelet on his arm (2 Sam. 1:10), and archaeology furnishes many examples of royal bracelets, such as those worn by Ashurnasir-pal, Tiglath-pileser, Esarhaddon, and other emperors of Assyria. Bracelets were often gorgeously inlaid with precious stones and pearls and were popular in Egypt and Phoenicia, as well as in Assyria and later in Rome. *See* Dress; Jewel, Jewelry.

M.F.U.

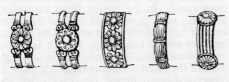

Assyrian bracelets

BRAMBLE. *See* Vegetable Kingdom: Thistles, Thorns.

BRANCH. The rendering of a number of Heb. and Gk. words. In the Scriptures, as well as elsewhere, the family is spoken of as a tree, and its members as branches, twigs, or shoots. From this has arisen a number of *figurative* expressions:

1. A branch or shoot is used as a symbol of *prosperity* (Gen. 49:22; Job 8:16; Prov. 11:28; Ezek. 17:6) and also of *adversity* (Job 15:32; Ps. 80:11, 15).

2. "A rejected branch" (Isa. 14:19) may mean a branch that is withered, or a useless *sucker* starting from the root. The sentence might better be rendered, "But you have been cast out of your tomb like an *offensive* (i.e., useless) branch."

3. "The top of the cedar" and "the topmost of its young twigs" (Ezek. 17:3-4) is used to describe Jehoiachin as king. "They are putting the twig to their nose" (8:17) is obscure as to its meaning. By some the act was thought to be expressive of contempt, similar to "they turn up the nose with scorn." Others understand a reference to the hypocrisy of the Jews who carried branches in honor of Jehovah but held them to the nose in scorn—outward worship but secret contempt. It may be that the branch was of a tree dedicated to Baal and carried by them in his honor. The saying appears to be a proverbial one, but the origin and

meaning have not yet been satisfactorily explained.

4. Christ the *Branch.* A branch is the symbol of kings descended from royal ancestors; and Christ, in respect of His human nature, is called "a shoot *that* will spring from the stem of Jesse, and a branch from his roots" (Isa. 11:1; cf. Jer. 23:5; Zech. 3:8; 6:12). Christians are called branches of Christ, the Vine, with reference to their union with Him (John 15:5-6).

BRAND. In Zech. 3:2 (Heb. *'ûd*) the word means a wooden *poker* with which the fire is stirred, hence any burned wood. The NIV translates it here as "burning stick." A *firebrand* (also Amos 4:11; Isa. 7:4).

BRANDING. "Branding instead of beauty" (Isa. 3:24). In Arabia the application of the *cey* with a red-hot iron plays an important part in the medical treatment of both man and beast. You meet with many men who have been burned not only on their legs and arms but on their faces as well. Branding thus appears to have been used as a symbol for disfigurement, as the contrary of beauty.

BRASS. Replaced in the NASB by "bronze." *See* Metrology; Mineral Kingdom.

BRAY. The loud, harsh cry of a donkey when hungry (Job 6:5). It is used figuratively of the cry of persons when hungry (30:7, marg.). In addition, the KJV of Prov. 27:22 uses *bray* with the sense of *pound* or *crush* as in a mortar. The NASB renders "pound," and the NIV "grind."

BRAZEN SERPENT. *See* Bronze Serpent.

BREAD. The word *bread* in the Bible is used in a wide sense, often occurring as our "food," as in the petition "Give us this day our daily bread." In strictness it denotes baked food, especially loaves. Its earliest reference is found in Gen. 18:5-6.

Material. The best bread was made of wheat, called "flour" or "meal" (Judg. 6:19; 1 Sam. 1:24; 1 Kings 4:22; etc.) and, when sifted, "fine flour" (Gen. 18:6; Lev. 2:1). A coarser bread was made of barley (Judg. 7:13; John 6:9-13). Millet, spelt, beans, and lentils were also used (Ezek. 4:9-12).

Preparation. To make "leavened bread" (Heb. *ḥamēs*, "sour") the flour was mixed with water, kneaded on a small kneading trough, with leaven added. These kneading troughs may have been mere pieces of leather, such as are now used by the Arabs, although the expression "bound up in the clothes" (Ex. 12:34) favors the idea of a wooden bowl. The leavened dough was allowed time to rise (Matt. 13:33; Luke 13:21), sometimes a whole night (Hos. 7:6, "their baker sleepeth all the night," KJV). When the time for making bread was short the leaven was omitted, and *unleavened* cakes were baked, as is customary among the Arabs (Gen. 18:6; 19:3; Ex. 12:39;

1 Sam. 28:24). Such cakes were called in Heb. *maṣṣâ*, "sweetness."

Thin, round cakes made of unleavened dough were baked on heated sand or flat stones (1 Kings 19:6), by hot ashes or coals put on them—"ash-cakes." Such cakes are still the common bread of the Bedouin and poorer orientals. The outside is, of course, black as coal, but tastes good.

Unleavened bread

Old bread is described in Josh. 9:5, 12, as "crumbled" (Heb. *niqqûd*, a "crumb"; KJV and NIV, "mouldy"), a term also applied to a sort of easily crumbled biscuit (KJV, "cracknels").

"From flour there were besides many kinds of confectionery made: (*a*) Oven-baked, sometimes perforated cakes kneaded with oil, sometimes thin, flat cakes only smeared with oil; (*b*) pancakes made of flour and oil, and sometimes baked in the pan, sometimes boiled in the skillet in oil, which were also presented as meat offerings; (*c*) honey cakes (Exod. 16:31), raisin or grape cakes (Hos. 3:1; Cant. 2:5; II Sam. 6:19; I Chron. 16:3), and heart cakes, kneaded from dough, sodden in the pan and turned out soft, a kind of pudding (II Sam. 13:6-9). . . . The various kinds of baked delicacies and cakes had, no doubt, become known to the Israelites in Egypt, where baking was carried to great perfection" (Keil, *Arch.*, 2:126).

Baking. When the dough was ready for baking it was divided into round cakes (literally, "circles of bread," Ex. 29:23; Judg. 8:5; 1 Sam. 10:3; etc.), not unlike flat stones in shape and appearance (Matt. 7:9; cf. 4:3), about a span in diameter and a finger's breadth in thickness. The baking was generally done by the wife (Gen. 18:6), daughter (2 Sam. 13:8), or a female servant (1 Sam. 8:13). As a trade, baking was carried on by men (Hos. 7:4-6), often congregating, according to Eastern custom, in one quarter (Neh. 3:11; 12:38, "Tower of Furnaces"; Jer. 37:21, "bakers' street").

Egyptian Bread-making. The following account of early bread-making is interesting: "She spread some handfuls of grain upon an oblong slab of stone, slightly hollowed on its upper surface, and proceeded to crush them with a smaller stone like a painter's muller, which she moistened from time to time. For an hour and more she labored with her arms, shoulders, loins, in fact, all her body; but an indifferent result followed from such great exertion. The flour, made to undergo several grindings in this rustic mortar, was coarse, uneven, mixed with bran or whole grains, which had escaped the pestle, and contaminated with dust and abraded particles of the stone. She kneaded it with a little water, blended with it, as a sort of yeast, a piece of stale dough of the day before, and made from the mass round cakes, about half an inch thick and some four inches in diameter, which she placed upon a flat flint, covering them with hot ashes. The bread, imperfectly raised, often badly cooked, borrowed, from the organic fuel under which it was buried, a special odor, and a taste to which strangers did not sufficiently accustom themselves. The impurities which it contained were sufficient in the long run to ruin the strongest teeth. Eating it was an action of grinding rather than chewing, and old men were not infrequently met with whose teeth had gradually been worn away to the level of the gums, like those of an aged ass or ox" (Maspero, *Dawn of Civ.*, p. 320).

Figurative. The thin cakes already described were not cut but broken, hence the expression usual in Scripture of "breaking bread" to signify taking a meal (Lam. 4:4; Matt. 14:19; 15:36).

From our Lord's breaking bread at the institution of the Eucharist, the expression *"breaking of"* or *"to break bread,"* in the NT is used for the Lord's Supper (Matt. 26:26) and for the *agape*, or love, feast (Acts 2:46).

"Bread of privation" (lit., "penury") signifies to put one on the low rations of a siege or imprisonment (1 Kings 22:27; Isa. 30:20).

"Bread of painful labors" (Ps. 127:2) means food obtained by toil.

"Bread of tears" (Ps. 80:5) probably signifies a condition of great sorrow.

"Bread of wickedness" (Prov. 4:17) and *"bread obtained by falsehood"* (Prov. 20:17) denote not only living or estate obtained by fraud but that to do evil is as much the portion of the wicked as to eat his bread.

"Cast your bread on the surface of the waters" (Eccles. 11:1) is doubtless an allusion to the custom of sowing seed by casting it from boats into the overflowing waters of the Nile or in any marshy ground. From v. 1 it is evident that charity is implied, and that, while seemingly hopeless, it shall prove at last not to have been thrown away (Isa. 32:20).

"Bread of Life" prefigures Christ as the supplier of true spiritual nourishment (John 6:48-51). He is the bread of heaven, and God's Word, like bread, is the spiritual staff of life (Matt. 4:4).

BIBLIOGRAPHY: W. Foerster, ἐπιούσιος, *Theological Dictionary of the New Testament,* ed. G. Kittel (1964), 2:590-99.

BREAD, SHOW. The KJV term *shewbread* is replaced in the NASB and NIV by *Bread of the*

Presence. See Tabernacle: Typology of the Tabernacle and Furniture.

BREAD OF THE PRESENCE. *See* Tabernacle: Typology of the Tabernacle and Furniture.

BREAKFAST. *See* Meals.

BREASTPIECE, BREASTPLATE. *See* Armor, Arms; High Priest, Dress of.

BREECHES. *See* Priesthood, Hebrew: Symbolical and Typical.

BRETHREN. *See* Brother.

BRIBE, BRIBERY (Heb. *kōper,* "redemption" money).

1. A payment made by a man to redeem himself from capital punishment. The expression "From whose hand have I taken a bribe to blind my eyes with it?" (1 Sam. 12:3) means, "Of whom have I taken anything to exempt from punishment one worthy of death?"

2. (Heb. *shōḥad,* "gift"). A present to avert punishment (2 Kings 16:8; Prov. 6:35), or a bribe taken to "pervert justice" (cf. 1 Sam. 8:3; Ezek. 22:12).

BRICK (Heb. *lᵉbēnâ,* from *lāban,* "to be white," from the whiteness of the clay out of which bricks were made). The earliest mention made of bricks in Scripture is in the account of the building of Babel (Gen. 11:3). In Exodus (chap. 5) we have the vivid description of the grievous hardship imposed upon the Israelites in the making of bricks in Egypt.

Babylonian. The following account taken from Maspero (*Dawn of Civilization,* pp. 622-23) especially applies to Mesopotamia and Egypt: "In the estimation of the Chaldean architects stone was a matter of secondary consideration. As it was necessary to bring it from a great distance and at considerable expense, they used it very sparingly, and then merely for lintels, thresholds, for hinges on which to hang their doors, for dressings in some of their state apartments, in cornices or sculptured friezes on the external walls of their buildings; and even then its employment suggested rather that of a band of embroidery carefully disposed on some garment to relieve the plainness of the material. Crude brick, burnt brick, enameled brick, but always and everywhere brick was the principal element in their construction. The soil of the marshes or of the plains, separated from the pebbles and foreign substances which it contained, mixed with grass or chopped straw, moistened with water, and assiduously trodden under foot, furnished the ancient builders with material of incredible tenacity. This was molded into thin, square brick, eight inches to a foot across and three or four inches thick, but rarely larger. They were stamped on the flat side, by means of an incised wooden block, with the name of the reigning sovereign, and were then dried in the sun. They were sometimes enameled with patterns of various colors." The Babylonian bricks were more commonly burned in kilns than those used at Nineveh, which are chiefly sun-dried like the Egyptian.

Egyptian. Egyptian bricks were not generally baked in kilns but dried in the sun, although a brickkiln is mentioned by Jeremiah (Jer. 43:9; NASB, "brick terrace"; the NIV renders "brick pavement"). Made of clay, they are, even without straw, as firm as when first put up in the reigns of the Thutmoids and others, whose names they bear. When made of the Nile mud they required straw to keep them from falling apart, and when laid up in walls were secured by layers of sticks and reeds. In size they varied from 20 or 17 inches to 14¼ inches long, 8¾ inches to 6½ inches wide, and 7 inches to 4½ inches thick.

A Jewish bride in traditional costume

Brickmaking was regarded as an unhealthy and laborious occupation by the Egyptians and was, therefore, imposed upon slaves. Very naturally, the Hebrews, when enslaved by the pharaohs, were put to this work. The use of brick as building material was, doubtless, quite general, although their fragility often insured early decay. We have illustrations of walls, storehouses, and temples having been built of bricks. The tomb of Rekhmire, grand vizier of Thutmose III (c. 1460 B.C.) depicts Semitic slaves busy with brickmaking. Rameses II (c. 1290 B.C.) rebuilt the older city Zoan-Tanis (Raamses of Ex. 1:11, NASB), and the bricks are stamped with his name.

Jewish. The Jews learned the art of brickmaking in Egypt, using almost the identical method. Even now in Palestine bricks are made from moistened clay mixed with straw and dried in the sun.

Mention is made of the brickkiln in the time of David (2 Sam. 12:31; cf. Nah. 3:14), and Isaiah complains (65:3) that the people built their altars of brick, instead of stone, as the law directed (Ex. 20:25). *See* Handicrafts: Brickmaker.

BIBLIOGRAPHY: G. Maspero, *Dawn of Civilization* (1922), pp. 622-23; H. Frankfort, *Art and Architecture in the*

Ancient Orient (1955); A. Badawy, *Architecture of Egypt and the Ancient Near East* (1966).

BRIDAL GIFT. *See* Marriage.

BRIDE, BRIDEGROOM. *See* Marriage.

Figurative. The church is alluded to (Rev. 21:9) as "the bride, the wife of the Lamb." The meaning is that as the bridegroom rejoices over the bride, so the Lord shall forever rejoice in His people and His people in Him. Christ Himself is also called "the bridegroom" in the same sense (John 3:29).

The figure of marriage is used also in the OT to denote the relationship between Jehovah and the Jewish nation, however with this important contrast. Israel is portrayed as the *wife* of Jehovah (Hos. 2:2, 16, 23), now because of unbelief and apostasy disowned and dishonored, but yet to be restored (2:14-23). The church, on the other hand, is a pure virgin, espoused to Christ (2 Cor. 11:1-2), which could never be true of an adulterous wife, although she is eventually to be restored in grace. In the mystery of the Divine-trinity it can be true that Israel is the adulterous wife of Jehovah (to be forgiven and reinstated), whereas the church is the virgin wife of the Lamb (John 3:29; Rev. 19:6-8). To break down this distinction between Israel, God's elect nation with a unique future when restored (Rom. 11:1-27), and the church, the Body (1 Cor. 12:13-14) and bride of Christ (Eph. 5:25-27), formed by the baptizing work of the Holy Spirit during the period of Israel's national unbelief and setting aside, is to plunge biblical prophecy into confusion.   M.F.U.

BIBLIOGRAPHY: C. Chavasse, *The Bride of Christ* (1939); P. Minear, *Images of the Church in the New Testament* (1960); R. M. Grant, *After the New Testament* (1967).

BRIDECHAMBER. *See* Marriage.

BRIDESMAID, BRIDESMAN. *See* Marriage.

BRIDGE. Bridges were not in use in early biblical times. Rivers were crossed either by ferries or more commonly by fords (Judg. 3:28; 2 Sam. 19:18). Later, however, the Romans constructed masonry bridges, ruins of which survive to our day. A famous ruin of a bridge is the structure built across the Tyropoean Valley at Jerusalem by John Hycranus (134-104 B.C.), called "Robinson's Arch" for its modern discoverer. It was destroyed in 63 B.C. during Pompey's siege. Ruins of a famous Roman bridge are to be found near Beirut in Lebanon, north of the Dog River.   M.F.U.

BRIDLE (Heb. *resen,* "halter," Job 30:11; 41:13, NASB, marg.; Isa. 30:28; *meteg,* strictly the "bit," as rendered in Ps. 32:9, though NIV has "bridle"; *mahsôm,* a "muzzle," only in 39:1; Gk. *chalinos,* "bit," James 3:2; Rev. 14:20). The word *bridle* is used for that portion of the harness by which the driver controls the horse, and consists of the headstall, bit, and reins (Ps. 32:9). The

Assyrians ornamented their bridles to a high degree.

It was customary to fix a muzzle of leather on refractory slaves (see Isa. 37:29). Prisoners of war were similarly treated. One of the Assyrian sculptures represents prisoners with a ring in the lower lip, to which is attached a thin cord held by the king (2 Kings 19:28).

Figurative. The providence of God in leading men and nations away from the completion of their plans is symbolized by the "bridle" and "hook" (2 Kings 19:28; Isa. 30:28; 37:29; Ezek. 29:4). The restraints of law and humanity are called a bridle, and to "cast off the bridle" (Job 30:11) is to act without reference to these.

BRIERS. *See* Vegetable Kingdom: Thistles, Thorns.

BRIMSTONE (Heb. *goprît,* properly "resin"; Gk. *theion,* "flashing"). The Heb. word is connected with *gopher* (Heb. *gōper*) and probably meant the *gum* of that tree. It was thence transferred to all inflammable substances, especially sulfur. The cities of the plain were destroyed by a storm of fire and brimstone (Gen. 19:24, KJV; NIV, "sulfur"). *See also* Mineral Kingdom: Brimstone; Pitch and articles Sodom; Gomorrah.

Figurative. Apparently with reference to Sodom, brimstone is often used in Scripture to denote punishment and destruction (Deut. 29:23; Job 18:15; Ps. 11:6; Isa. 30:33; Ezek. 38:22; Luke 17:29; Rev. 9:17; etc.).

BROKEN HAND, BROKEN FOOT. *See* Diseases.

BRONZE. A unit of money and an alloy. *See* Metrology; Mineral Kingdom.

BRONZE SEA. *See* Laver; Sea, Bronze; Tabernacle of Israel.

BRONZE SERPENT (Heb. *nāhāsh nehoshet,* "serpent of copper"). As the Israelites "set out from Mount Hor by the way of the Red Sea" they rebelled against God and against Moses. Punished by Jehovah with *fiery serpents* (which see), many of them died. At the command of God Moses made the figure of a serpent and set it on a "standard" or pole; whoever of the bitten ones looked at it "lived," i.e., recovered from the serpent's bite (Num. 21:1-9). This bronze serpent afterward became an object of worship, under the name of Nehushtan, and was destroyed by King Hezekiah (2 Kings 18:4).

Figurative. From the words of our Lord (John 3:14) most commentators have rightly inferred that the "bronze serpent" was intended as a type of Christ as the redeemer of the world, as becoming "sin on our behalf" (2 Cor. 5:21) and as bearing our judgment. Cf. the historical fulfillment in Matt. 27:46.

BROOK (Heb. generally *naḥal;* Gk. *cheimarros,* a "torrent").

1. A small stream issuing from a subterranean spring and running through a deep valley, such as the Arnon, Jabbok, Kidron, etc.

2. Winter streams arising from rains, but drying up in the summer (Job 6:15, marg.).

3. The torrent bed, even though it might be without water, so that it is sometimes doubtful whether the bed or stream is meant. The word is sometimes rendered "river," as in the case of the "brook of Egypt," a small torrent in the southern border of Palestine (Num. 34:5; Josh. 15:4, 47).

Figurative. "My brothers have acted deceitfully like a wadi" (or brook, Job 6:15) is an expression of the failure of friends to comfort and help.

BROOM TREE. *See* Vegetable Kingdom.

BROTHER (generally Heb. *'āḥ;* Gk. *adelphos*). Brother is a word extensively and variously used in Scripture. (1) A brother in the natural sense, whether the child of the same father and mother (Gen. 42:4; 44:20; Luke 6:14), of the same father only (Gen. 42:15; 43:3; Judg. 9:21; Matt. 1:2; Luke 3:1, 19), or of the same mother only (Judg. 8:19). (2) A relative, kinsman, in any degree of blood, e.g., a *nephew* (Gen. 14:16; 29:12, 15, marg.), or a *cousin* (Matt. 12:46; John 7:3; Acts 1:14; etc.). (3) One of the same tribe (Num. 8:26; 2 Kings 10:13, marg.; Neh. 3:1). (4) A fellow countryman (Ex. 2:11; 4:18; Matt. 5:47; Acts 3:22; etc.), or one of a kindred nation, e.g., the Edomites and Hebrews (Gen. 9:25; 16:12; Num. 20:14). (5) An *ally, confederate,* spoken of allied nations such as the Hebrews and Tyrians (Amos 1:9) or those of the same religion (Isa. 66:20; Acts 9:30; 1 Cor. 5:11); probably the name by which the early converts were known until they were called "Christians" at Antioch (Acts 11:26). (6) A *friend, associate,* as of Job's friends (6:15; see 19:13; Neh. 5:10), of Solomon, whom Hiram calls his brother (1 Kings 9:13). (7) One of equal rank and dignity (Matt. 23:8). (8) One of the same nature, a *fellowman* (Gen. 13:8; Matt. 5:22; Heb. 2:17). (9) It is applied in the Heb. to inanimate things, as of the cherubim it is said they are "facing one another" (Ex. 25:20; cf. 37:9; lit., *a man his brother*). (10) Disciples, followers (Matt. 25:40; Heb. 2:11-12).

Figurative. As *likeness* of disposition, habits, Jobs says (30:29), "I have become a brother to jackals," i.e., I cry and howl like them. Proverbs 18:9 says, "He also who is slack in his work is brother to him who destroys." The Jewish schools distinguish between a "brother" (i.e., an Israelite by blood) and "neighbor" (a proselyte). The gospel extends both terms to all the world (1 Cor. 5:11; Luke 10:29-37).

BIBLIOGRAPHY: H. F. von Soden, ἀδελφός, *Theological Dictionary of the New Testament,* ed. G. Kittel (1964), 1:144-46.

BROTHERLY KINDNESS (Gk. *philadelphia,* 2 Pet. 1:7). The Gk. term is also rendered "brotherly *love*" (Rom. 12:10); "love of the brethren" (1 Thess. 4:9; Heb. 13:1; 1 Pet. 1:22). It is affection for our brothers, in the broad meaning of which word the Scriptures include as our neighbors all mankind, not excluding our enemies. We are not required to bestow equal love upon all or recognize all as possessing an equal claim to it. It does not make men blind to the qualities of their fellows. While it requires obedience to the golden rule, a special and warmer love for our brothers in Christ is urged. Brotherly love requires the best construction of a neighbor's conduct, effort, and sacrifice for others, and forgiveness of injuries. *See* Charity.

BROTHERLY LOVE. *See* Brotherly Kindness.

BROTHERS OF OUR LORD. In Matt. 13:55 "James and Joseph and Simon and Judas" are named as the brothers of Jesus, whereas sisters are mentioned in v. 56. The sense in which the terms "brothers and sisters" are to be taken has been a matter of great discussion, some contending that they are to be regarded in their literal sense, others in the more general sense of relatives. Several theories in support of the latter view have been advanced:

1. That they were our Lord's first cousins, the sons of Alphaeus (or Cleopas) and Mary the sister of the virgin. Against this view it is argued that there is no mention anywhere of *cousins* or *kinsmen* of Jesus according to the flesh, although the term *cousin* (Gk. *anepsios*) is well known in NT vocabulary (Col. 4:10); also the more exact term "son of Paul's sister" (Acts 23:16); also "relative" occurs several times (Mark 6:4; Luke 1:36, 58; John 18:26; Acts 10:24), as well as "kinsman" (Rom. 9:3). Thus it seems strange that if the *brothers of our Lord* were merely cousins they were never called such.

2. That they were sons of Joseph by a former marriage with a certain Escha, or Salome, of the tribe of Judah. The only ground for its possibility is the apparent difference of age between Joseph and Mary.

3. That they were the offspring of a levirate marriage between Joseph and the wife of his deceased brother, Cleopas. This, however, is a mere hypothesis.

The arguments for their being the full brothers of Jesus are numerous and, taken collectively, are very strong. (1) The words "first-born son" (Luke 2:7) appear to have been used with reference to later-born children. (2) The declaration that Joseph "kept her a virgin until she gave birth to a Son" (Matt. 1:25) does not necessarily establish the perpetual virginity of Mary. We must remember that "the evangelist employed the term 'first-born' as an historian, from the time when his gospel was composed, and consequently could *not* have used it had Jesus been present to his historical consciousness as the *only* son of Mary. But Jesus, according to Matthew (12:46-48; 13:55-56), had also brothers and sisters, among whom he was the *first-born*" (Meyer, *Com.,* on Matt. 1:25). (3) They are constantly spoken of *with* the virgin Mary and with no shadow of a hint that they were not her children. The *mother* is mentioned at the same time (Mark 3:31; Luke 8:19; John 2:12; Acts 1:14), just as in Matt. 13:55-56 the *father* and *sisters* are likewise mentioned along with Him.

BIBLIOGRAPHY: C. Harris, *Dictionary of Christ and the Gospels,* ed. J. Hastings (1906), 1:232-37; J. B. Mayor, *Dictionary of the Bible,* ed. J. Hastings (1919), 1:320-26; H. E. Jacobs, *International Standard Bible Encyclopedia,* ed. J. Orr (1939), 1:518-20; J. B. Lightfoot, *St. Paul's Epistle to the Galatians* (1970), pp. 88-128; J. B. Mayor, *Epistle of James* (1977), pp. 3-65.

BROTHER'S WIFE (Heb. *yᵉbemet,* Deut. 25:7; "sister-in-law," Ruth 1:15). *See* Marriage, Levirate.

BROWN (Heb. *ḥûm,* lit., "scorched"). The term applied in the KJV to the dark-colored sheep removed from Jacob's flocks by Laban (Gen. 30:32-40). The NASB renders "black," and the NIV "dark-colored." *See* Colors.

BUILDERS. *See* Handicrafts.

BRUISED. The rendering of at least eleven Heb. and Gk. words is used in Scripture in a figurative sense. Thus Satan is said to bruise the heel of Christ (Gen. 3:15), i.e., to afflict the humanity of Christ and to bring suffering and persecution on His people. The serpent's poison is in his head, and a wound in that part is fatal. So Christ is said to bruise the head of Satan when He crushes his designs, despoils him of his power, and enables His people to rise superior to temptation (Rom. 16:20). Our Lord was bruised when He had inflicted upon Him the punishment due to our sins (Isa. 53:5, 10). Weak Christians are bruised reeds, which Christ will not break (Isa. 42:3).

BRUISES. *See* Diseases.

BRUTISH (Heb. *ba'ar,* "to be like an animal"). A KJV term applied to one whose mental and moral perceptions are dulled by ignorance (Prov. 12:1), idolatry (Jer. 10:8, 14, 21). "The word must be explained from Ps. 92:6, 'brutish,' foolish, always bearing in mind that the Hebrew associated the idea of godlessness with folly, and that cruelty naturally follows in its train" (Keil, *Com.,* on Ezek. 21:31). The NASB and NIV render "stupid."

BUBAS'TIS (bu-bas'tis). *See* Pi-beseth.

BUCK. *See* Animal Kingdom: Deer; Roebuck.

BUCKET. A skin vessel with which to draw water (Isa. 40:15). In John 4:11 the Gk. word *antlēma* is used.

Figurative. Bucket is used (Num. 24:7) for abundance, as water is the leading source of prosperity in the burning East. The nation is personified as a man carrying two buckets overflowing with water.

BUCKLER. *See* Armor: Defensive Weapons.

BUFFET (Gk. *kolaphizo,* to "strike with the fist"). Rude maltreatment in general, whether in *derision* (Matt. 26:67; Mark 14:65, KJV, "buffet"; NASB, "beat"), *opposition* (2 Cor. 12:7-9, where Paul states that Christ sent "a messenger of Satan to *buffet* me" that "the power of Christ may dwell in me"), or *punishment* (1 Pet. 2:20, KJV, "buffet"; NASB, "harshly treated"; NIV, "receive a beating").

BUILDING. *See* Architecture; House.

Figurative. "To build" is used with reference to children and a numerous progeny (Ruth 4:11; 2 Sam. 7:27); and to the founding of a family. The church is called a building (1 Cor. 3:9; etc.); and the resurrection body of the Christian is called a building in contrast to a tent, symbolic of this mortal body (2 Cor. 5:1).

BIBLIOGRAPHY: G. Conteneau, *Everyday Life in Babylon and Assyria* (1954); National Geographic Society, *Everyday Life in Ancient Times* (1964); A. Badawy, *Architecture in Ancient Egypt and the Near East* (1966).

BUK'KI (buk'i).

1. The son of Jogli and leader of the tribe of Dan, appointed by Moses as one of the commission to divide the inheritance among the tribes (Num. 34:22), c. 1400 B.C.

2. The son of Abishua and father of Uzzi, being great-great-grandson of Aaron (1 Chron. 6:5, 51).

BUKKI'AH (bu-kī'a). A Kohathite Levite, of the sons of Heman, the leader of the sixth band in the Temple music service. The band consisted of himself and eleven of his kindred (1 Chron. 25:4, 13), 1000 B.C.

BUL (būl). The eighth ecclesiastical month of the Jewish year (1 Kings 6:38). *See* Time.

BULBS (Heb. *kaptōr*). Part of the ornamentation of the seven-branched lampstand in the Tabernacle (Ex. 25:31-36; 37:17-22; marg., "calyx"). The term is distinct from KJV "flower," NASB "lily blossom," NIV "buds." In the KJV "bulbs" is rendered "knops."

BULL, BULLOCK. *See* Animal Kingdom: Ox.

Figurative. In this sense *bull* represents powerful, fierce, and insolent enemies (Pss. 22:12; 68:30; Isa. 34:7).

BULRUSH. *See* Vegetable Kingdom: Reeds, Rushes.

BULWARK. Bulwarks in Scripture appear to have been rural towers, answering the purpose of the modern bastion. They were usually erected at certain distances along the walls, generally at the corners, and upon them were placed the military engines. *See* Fortifications.

BU'NAH (bū'na; "discretion"). The second of the sons of Jerahmeel, the grandson of Perez, the son of Judah (1 Chron. 2:25).

BUNCH. The rendering of several Heb. words, such as a bunch of hyssop (Ex. 12:22), a bunch of raisins (2 Sam. 16:1, KJV), the bunch of a camel (Isa. 30:6, KJV).

BUNDLE. Anything bound together, such as a "bundle of myrrh" (Song of Sol. 1:13, KJV; NASB, "pouch"; NIV, "sachet"), of "wheat" (Matt. 13:30), of "sticks" (Acts 28:3). It is also used of money in a purse (Gen. 42:35).

Figurative. The speech of Abigail to David (1 Sam. 25:29) is rendered "The life of my lord shall be bound in the *bundle* of the living," and the words seem to refer to the safer preservation of the righteous on the earth. The metaphor is taken from the custom of binding up valuable things in a bundle to prevent injury.

BUN'NI (bun'i; "built"). One of the Levites who made public prayer and confession (Neh. 9:4) and joined Nehemiah in the covenant after the return from Babylon (10:15), 445 B.C.

BURDEN (Heb. *maśśā'*, a "lifting up"). This word is often used in the familiar meaning of a load. It also frequently has the meaning of an *oracle* from God; sometimes as a denunciation of evil (Isa. 13:1; Nah. 1:1; Mal. 1:1), and also merely as a message, whether joyous or afflictive (Zech. 9:1; 12:1).

BURIAL. Burial customs favored by ancient peoples differed from one culture to another.

Hebrew. Interment in Bible times followed soon after death, as is evident in the narratives of the burial of Sarah (Gen. 23:1-20), Rachel (35:19, 20), and Rebekah's nurse (35:8). The Hebrews did not normally cremate, except in most unusual cases of emergency, as in the case of Saul and his sons (1 Sam. 31:11-13). Neither did they generally use coffins or embalm. Joseph's burial in a coffin (Gen. 50:26) and his being embalmed (as was his father, Jacob, 50:2-3) are to be explained as due to his eminent position in Egypt. Ordinarily a body, after being washed (Acts 9:37) and wrapped in a cloth or closely bound in bands (Matt. 27:59; John 11:44), was carried on a simple bier to the grave or vault (2 Sam. 3:31; Luke 7:14), which was commonly a natural cave artificially cut out of the rock (Gen. 25:9-10; Matt. 27:60). Unguents and perfumes were applied to the body if they could be afforded (John 12:3, 7; 19:39), or fragrant incense was burned (Jer. 34:5). Mourners lamented with loud demonstrations of grief (Mark 5:38) and were often hired (Jer. 9:17).

Egyptian. Egyptians took great pains to prepare their dead for the future life. Under the early dynasties graves with stone superstructures (*mastaba*) built over them were used, and food and other essential commodities for the afterlife were placed near the body. The practice of placing one *mastaba* upon another resulted in a step pyramid, such as the famous one at Saqqara from Dynasty III. From these developed the square-based, perfect pyramids. These colossal structures, the most famous of which are located at Gizeh from Dynasty IV, are architectural wonders that still amaze the world. In the complex interior of these great masses of stone the mummified bodies of royalty were interred. The intricate process of mummification, including embalming, required seventy days during which the internal organs, except the heart, were removed and stored away in special animal-headed jars. The brains of the deceased were also removed and a resinous paste and linen used to stuff the body, while the body itself was carefully wrapped with linen bandages and cords. Jewels and scarabs were used to adorn the corpse, the latter enabling the mummy to be identified and dated. The mummy was set in a case, which was painted with the face of the deceased. The discovery of the lavish intact tomb of Tutankhamen (1922), a pharaoh of the fourteenth century B.C. (late Amarna Period) revealed incredible burial splendor. A whole series of fine metal coffins, including one of solid gold inlaid with lapis lazuli and carnelian, was uncovered, as well as exquisite death masks of the ruler.

Tomb of the Herods, with rolling stone door

Babylonian. Like the Egyptians, the Babylonians took great pains to prepare for the future life. The famous royal tombs from the First Dynasty of Ur, discovered by Sir Leonard Woolley and dating from about 2500 B.C., reveal rooms and vaults of brick and stone. The occupant of one of the tombs, identified by a lapis lazuli cylinder as Queen Puabi, lay upon a wooden bier, a golden cup near her hand. She wore an elaborate headdress, ornate earrings, and a golden comb with golden flowers set with lapis lazuli. Mass burials were discovered in several tombs. Twenty-five persons were interred with the queen. Other graves contained the remains of as many as six men and sixty-eight women. Even chariots filled with treasures were driven into these tombs. Superb gold daggers, bowls, animals, helmets, and other exquisitely wrought objects were interred with the deceased. But the graves of the common people were found to be simple rectangular pits. The body was wrapped in matting or put in a coffin of wood, clay, or wickerwork. Personal belongings as well as food and drink for the afterlife were placed in the grave. Kind provisions for the dead appear in the carefully folded hands in which there was a cup, once doubtless filled with water, for the need of the sleeper. Later Babylonians burned their dead and deposited their ashes in ornate funerary urns, as did Greeks and Romans. Hebrews in later times also practiced cremation, as is indicated by the numerous ossuaries found in NT Palestine.

Philistine. The Philistines around the twelfth century B.C. interred in clay coffins, numbers of which have been found in Palestine.

See also Dead, The.

BIBLIOGRAPHY: K. M. Kenyon, *Digging Up Jericho* (1957), pp. 233-55; G. E. Wright, *Biblical Archaeologist* 22, no. 3 (1959): 54-66; J. B. Payne, *Theology of the Older Testament* (1962), pp. 443-62; J. E. Callaway, *BA* 24 (1963): 74-91; R. de Vaux, *Ancient Israel: Its Life and Institutions* (1961), pp. 56-59.

BURNING. *See* Branding.

BURNING BUSH. *See* articles Bush; Vegetable Kingdom: Burning Bush.

BURNING INSTEAD OF BEAUTY. *See* Branding.

BURNT OFFERING, SACRIFICE. *See* Sacrifices.

BURY, BURYING PLACE. *See* articles Dead, The; Tomb.

BUSH (Heb. *seneh*, "bramble"; Gk. *batos*). The burning bush in which Jehovah manifested Himself to Moses at Horeb (Ex. 3:2; etc.; Deut. 33:16; Mark 12:26; Acts 7:30, 35). This was probably the bramble. *See* Vegetable Kingdom: Burning Bush.

Figurative. The thornbush or "bramble," in contrast with the more noble and lofty trees (Judg. 9:15), represented the Israelites in their humiliation as a people despised by the world. The *burning* bush represents Israel as enduring the fire of affliction, the iron furnace of Egypt (Deut. 4:20), chastened but not consumed. *See* Vegetable Kingdom.

BUSHEL. *See* Metrology: Dry Measures of Capacity.

BUSYBODY (Gk. *periergos,* "working around," 1 Tim. 5:13; to "be overbusy," 2 Thess. 3:11; *allotriepiskopos,* "one who supervises others' affairs," 1 Pet. 4:15, NASB; "troublesome meddler"). A meddlesome person, emphatically condemned in the above passages.

BUTLER (Heb. *mashqeh,* "one who gives drink"). A *cupbearer* (which see), as the Heb. word is rendered in the KJV, NIV, and NASB of 2 Chron. 9:4, and an officer of honor in the royal household of Egypt (Gen. 40:1, 13). It was his duty to fill and bear the drinking vessel to the king. Nehemiah was cupbearer to King Artaxerxes (Neh. 1:11; 2:1). Where the KJV renders "butler," the NASB and NIV render *cupbearer* (which see).

BUTTER (Heb. *hem'â,* "grown thick"). Although always rendered butter in the KJV, critics usually agree that the Heb. word means "curdled milk" or curds. Indeed, it is doubtful whether butter is meant in any passage except Prov. 30:33, "the churning of milk produces butter." The other passages will better apply to curdled milk than to butter. The ancient method of making butter was probably similar to that followed by the modern Bedouin. The milk is put into a skin, the tanned hide of a whole goat; this skin is hung up on a light frame, or between two poles, and pushed steadily from side to side till the butter is ready. "When the butter has come, they take it out, boil or melt it, and then put it into *bottles* made of goats' skins. In winter it resembles candied honey; in summer it is mere oil" (Thompson, *The Land and the Book,* 1:393).

BIBLIOGRAPHY: W. M. Thompson, *The Land and the Book* (1886), 1:393.

BUZ (būz; "contempt").

1. The second son of Nahor and Milcah (Gen. 22:21).

2. The father of Jahdo, of the tribe of Gad (1 Chron. 5:14).

3. One of three tribes of northern Arabia. In Jer. 25:23 the following are mentioned: "Dedan, Tema, Buz, and all who cut the corners of their hair."

BU'ZI (būz'i). A priest, father of Ezekiel the prophet (Ezek. 1:3), before 595 B.C.

BUZ'ITE (būz'īt). A term indicating the ancestry of Elihu, found only in Job 32:2, 6, "Elihu the son of Barachel the Buzite," indicating ancestry from the Arabian tribe of Buz.

BUZZARD. *See* Animal Kingdom.

CAB. The cab (KJV) or kab (NASB, NIV) was a dry measure of capacity. *See* Metrology.

CAB'BON (kab'on). A place in the plain of Judah (Josh. 15:40); possibly the same as Machbena (1 Chron. 2:49; Macbenah, NIV).

CA'BUL (ka'bul; perhaps "sterile, worthless"), i.e., fettered land (Heb. *kebel,* "a fetter").

1. A city on the E border of Asher, at its N side (Josh. 19:27), probably identical with the village of *Kabul,* nine miles SE of Acre.

2. A district of Galilee, containing twenty "cities," which Solomon gave to Hiram, king of Tyre, in return for services rendered in building the Temple. When Hiram saw them he was displeased, and he said, " 'What are these cities which you have given me, my brother?' So they were called the land of *Cabul* to this day" (1 Kings 9:13). These cities were occupied chiefly by a heathen population and were probably in bad condition. Or it may have been that, as the Phoenicians were a seafaring people, Hiram would have preferred to have had coastal cities rather than those inland.

CAESAR (sē'zer). A name taken by—or given to—all the Roman emperors after Julius Caesar. It was a sort of title, like Pharaoh, and as such is usually applied to the emperors in the NT, as the sovereigns of Judea (John 19:15; Acts 17:7). It was to him that the Jews paid tribute (Matt. 22:17; Luke 23:2), and to him that such Jews as were *cives Romani* had the right of appeal (Acts 25:11); in which case, if their cause was a criminal one, they were sent to Rome (25:12, 21). The Caesars mentioned in the NT are Augustus (Luke 2:1), Tiberius (3:1; 20:22), Claudius (Acts 11:28), and Nero (25:8). *See* each name.

CAESARE'A (sē-sa-rē'a; "pertaining to Caesar").

Caesarea Maritima (i.e., "Caesarea by the

sea"). This Caesarea, so called to distinguish it from Caesarea Philippi—or simply **Caesarea**—was situated on the coast of Palestine on the great road from Tyre to Egypt, and about halfway between Joppa and Dora (Josephus *Wars* 1.21.5), or about twenty-seven miles S of Haifa. The distance from Jerusalem is given by Josephus (*Ant.* 13.11.2; *Wars* 1.3.5) as six hundred stadia; the actual distance in a direct line is forty-seven miles. Philip stopped at Caesarea at the close of his preaching tour (Acts 8:40). Paul, to avoid Grecians who wished to kill him, was taken to Caesarea before embarking for Tarsus (9:30). Here dwelt Cornelius the centurion, to whom Peter came and preached (10:1; 11:11), and to this city *Herod* (which see) resorted after the miraculous deliverance of Peter from prison (12:19). Later Paul visited Caesarea several times (18:22; 21:8, 16) and was sent there by the Roman commander at Jerusalem to be heard by Felix (23:23, 33; 25:1-14); and from Caesarea he started on his journey to Rome (27:1).

Although small excavations were conducted at Caesarea in 1945, 1951, and 1956, large-scale archaeological work did not begin there until 1959. In that year A. Frova launched the Italian Archaeological Mission dig at the theater (1959-63), where he found an inscription mentioning Pontius Pilate and the emperor Tiberius. The theater has been restored and is used periodically for musical and dramatic performances.

In 1960 the Edwin A. Link Underwater Archaeological Expedition explored the harbor area and plotted the breakwaters. Since 1980 an international consortium of four universities, headed by the Israel Center for Maritime Studies and directed by Avner Raban, has been working on the harbor of Caesarea. The effort is called the Caesarea Ancient Harbor Excavation Project. The project has been conducting a survey and excavation that has provided important new information on Roman harbor design and construction. Two immense breakwaters were constructed to frame outer and inner basins. Hydraulic concrete was used in a sophisticated way, and sluice gates and subsidiary breakwater provided protection against siltation.

During the years 1960-62, A. Negev excavated on behalf of the National Parks Authority in the Crusader town. The Crusader fortifications of the thirteenth century A.D. and the great moat were uncovered, as were remains of the temple Herod built in honor of Augustus, and part of the Roman pier. A consortium of twenty-two American, Canadian, and Israeli universities, under the direction of Dr. Robert Bull of Drew University, contributed talent and money to uncover the ancient site in an ongoing project that began in 1970. Since that time teams have worked at the site every season, exploring the water system and excavating houses, the gate area, and the aqueducts. Two aqueducts and a Mithras shrine (the first in Palestine) have been uncovered and work has been done on the second-century A.D. hippodrome. Caesarea was a great city, and it is only beginning to emerge from the sand dunes. Population estimates run as high as 250,000, and it is judged to have occupied an area half the size of Manhattan Island.

Remains of the aqueduct at Caesarea

Caesarea Philippi (sē-sa-rē′a fi-lip′i; "Caesarea of Philip"). A town in the northern part of Palestine, about 120 miles from Jerusalem, 50 from Damascus, and 30 from Tyre, near the foot of Mt. Hermon. It was first a Canaanite sanctuary for the worship of Baal; perhaps Baal-hermon (Judg. 3:3; 1 Chron. 5:23). It was called by the Greeks Paneas because of its cavern, which reminded them of similar places dedicated to the worship of the god Pan. In 20 B.C. Herod the Great received the whole district from Augustus and dedicated a temple to the emperor. Herod Philip enlarged it and called it Caesarea Philippi to distinguish it from his father's on the seacoast. It was the northern limit of Christ's travels in the Holy Land (Matt. 16:13; Mark 8:27). The site of

Caesarea is Banias, a paltry village.   H.F.V.

BIBLIOGRAPHY: *Caesarea.* E. M. Blaiklock, *Cities of the New Testament* (1965), pp. 72-76; M. Avi-Yonah, ed., *Encyclopedia of Archaeological Excavations in the Holy Land* (1975), 1:270-85.

Caesarea Philippi. J. H. Kitchen, *Holy Fields* (1955), pp. 45-47.

CAGE (*kᵉlûb*). A "basket" or "cage" for keeping birds (Jer. 5:27) and fruit (Amos 8:1). On the Taylor Prism in the British Museum, Sennacherib says of Hezekiah: "Himself like a caged bird, I shut up in Jerusalem. . . ." A place of confinement for prisoners in transit (Ezek. 19:9).

CA′IAPHAS (ka′ya-fas). A surname, the original name being Joseph (Josephus *Ant.* 18.2.2); but, the surname becoming his ordinary and official designation, it was used for the name itself. Caiaphas was the high priest of the Jews in the reign of Tiberius Caesar, at the beginning of the Lord's public ministry (Luke 3:2) and also at the time of His condemnation and crucifixion (Matt. 26:3, 57; etc.). He was appointed to this dignity through the curator Valerius Gratus (probably A.U.C. 770-88 or 789, Meyer, *Com.,* on Luke) and held it during the whole procuratorship of Pontius Pilate, but was deposed by the proconsul Vitellus, A.D. about 38. Caiaphas was the son-in-law of Annas, with whom he is coupled by Luke (*see* below). His wife was the daughter of Annas, or Ananus, who had formerly been high priest and who still possessed great influence and control in sacerdotal matters.

After the miracle of raising Lazarus from the dead Caiaphas advocated putting Jesus to death. His language on this occasion was prophetic, though not so designed: "You know nothing at all, nor do you take into account that it is expedient for you that one man should die for the people, and that the whole nation should not perish" (John 11:49-50). After Christ was arrested He was taken before Annas, who sent Him to Caiaphas, probably living in the same house. An effort was made to produce false testimony sufficient for His condemnation. This expedient failed; for, though two persons appeared to testify, they did not agree, and at last Caiaphas put our Savior Himself upon oath that He should say whether He was indeed the Christ, the Son of God, or not. The answer was, of course, in the affirmative, and was accompanied with a declaration of His divine power and majesty. The high priest pretended to be greatly grieved at what he considered our Savior's blasphemous pretensions, and appealed to His enraged enemies to say if this was not enough. They answered at once that He deserved to die, but, as Caiaphas had no power to inflict the punishment of death, Christ was taken to Pilate, the Roman governor, that His execution might be duly ordered (Matt. 26:3, 57; John 18:13, 28). The bigoted fury of Caiaphas exhibited itself also against the first efforts of the apostles (Acts 4:6-21). What became of Caiaphas after his deposition is not known.

The expression in Luke 3:2, "In the high priesthood of Annas and Caiaphas," has led some to maintain that Annas and Caiaphas then discharged the functions of the high priesthood by turns; but this is not reconcilable with the statement of Josephus. Others think that Caiaphas is *called* high priest because he then actually exercised the functions of the office, and that Annas is so called because he formerly filled the position. But it does not thus appear why, of those who held the priesthood before Caiaphas, Annas in particular should be named, and not others who had served the office more recently than Annas. Meyer (*Com.*, ad loc.) says: "Annas retained withal very weighty influence (John 18:12, sq.), so that not only did he continue to *be called by the name*, but, moreover, he also partially *discharged the functions* of high priest." Edersheim (*Life and Times of Jesus*, 1:264): "The conjunction of the two names of Annas and Caiaphas probably indicates that, although Annas was deprived of the pontificate, he still continued to preside over the Sanhedrin" (cf. Acts 4:6).

BIBLIOGRAPHY: F. F. Bruce, *Commentary on the Book of Acts,* New International Commentary on the New Testament (1954), pp. 97-98; W. Hendricksen, *Gospel of John,* New Testament Commentary (1954), 2:162-65, 384-98; C. J. Barber, *Searching for Identity* (1975), pp. 108-19; C. K. Barrett, *Gospel According to John* (1978), pp. 404ff., 483-92, 515-51.

CAIN (kān; a "smith, spear"). The firstborn of the human race, and likewise the first murderer and fratricide. His history is narrated in Gen. 4.

Sacrifice. Cain was the eldest son of Adam and Eve, and by occupation a tiller of the ground. He and his brother offered a sacrifice to God, Cain of the fruit of the ground and Abel of the firstlings of his flock. Cain's temper and offering (being bloodless) were not acceptable, while Abel's received the divine approval.

Murder. At this Cain was angered, and, though remonstrated with by the Almighty, he fostered his revenge until it resulted in the murder of his brother. When God inquired of him as to the whereabouts of Abel he declared, "I do not know," and sullenly inquired, "Am I my brother's keeper?" (v. 9). The Lord then told him that his crime was known, and pronounced a curse upon him and the ground that he should cultivate. Cain was to endure, also, the torments of conscience, in that the voice of his brother's blood would cry unto God from the ground. Fearful lest others should slay him for his crime, he pleaded with God, who assured him that vengeance sevenfold would be taken on anyone who should kill him. He also gave him "a sign," probably an assurance that his life should be spared. Cain became a fugitive, and journeyed into the land of Nod, where he built a city that he named after his son Enoch. His descendants are named to the

sixth generation and appear to have reached an advanced stage of civilization, being noted for proficiency in music and the arts.

The NT references to Cain are Heb. 11:4, where it is recorded, "By faith Abel offered to God a better sacrifice than Cain"; 1 John 3:12; Jude 11.

BIBLIOGRAPHY: S. N. Kramer, *History Begins at Sumer* (1981), pp. 14-17.

CAI'NAN (kā'i-nan). The son of Arphaxad and father of Shelah, according to Luke 3:35-36. He is nowhere named in the Heb. text, nor in any of the versions made from it, such as the Samaritan, Aram., Syr., Vulg., etc. It is believed by many that the name was not originally in the text, even of Luke, but is an addition of careless transcribers from the LXX.

See also Kenan for the NASB and NIV rendering of KJV "Cainan" in Gen. 5:9-14; 1 Chron. 1:2.

CAKE, CAKES. *See* Bread.

CA'LAH (ka'la). An ancient city of Assyria built by *Nimrod* (which see) or by people from his country (Gen. 10:11). Shalmaneser I (c. 1280-60 B.C.) made this place famous in his day. By the time of the great conqueror Ashurnasirpal II (883-59 B.C.) the site had fallen into decay. But this eminent warrior chose Calah as his capital. At this site, now represented by the mound of Nimrud, the young Assyriological pioneer Austen Henry Layard began his excavations in 1845. At the very outset of these diggings the splendid palace of Ashurnasirpal II was discovered with colossal winged man-headed lions guarding the palace entrance. In a small temple nearby a statue of Ashurnasirpal II was found in a perfect state of preservation. Numerous inscriptions of the king also came to light. Calah remained the favorite haunt of Assyrian kings for a century and a half. Here Layard recovered the famous Black Obelisk of Shalmaneser III in 1846, which, among other captives, portrays Jehu of Israel (c. 842-15 B.C.) bringing tribute to his Assyrian overlord. M. E. L. Mallowan led a dig at Calah for the British School of Archaeology in Iraq from 1949 to 1961. He completed excavation of Ashurnasirpal's magnificent palace, covering six acres. This is now the best preserved of Assyrian royal dwellings. He also discovered and largely excavated Shalmaneser's great fort, eighteen acres in size, which lay just inside the five-mile circuit of the city wall at its SE edge. This is the most extensive military installation yet discovered in ancient Assyria. Calah was the staging ground from which the Assyrians launched their attack on Samaria, and to Calah Sargon II brought the booty and captives after the fall of Samaria (723/2 B.C.).

Valuable antiquities from Calah are housed in the British Museum in London, the Metropolitan Museum of Art in New York, the University Museum at Philadelphia, and the Museum of Fine Arts in Boston.   M.F.U.; H.F.V.

Winged man-headed beast, a guardian of the palace gate of Ashurnasirpal at Calah

BIBLIOGRAPHY: M. E. L. Mallowan, *Nimrud and Its Remains*, 2 vols. (1966); D. Dates, *Studies in the Ancient History of Northern Iraq* (1968).

CALAMUS. *See* Vegetable Kingdom: Reeds, Rushes.

CAL'COL (kal'kol). One of the four sons of Mahol, who were famous for their wisdom before the time of Solomon (1 Kings 4:31), before 960 B.C. In 1 Chron. 2:6 he and his brothers are given as the sons of Zerah, of the tribe of Judah.

CALDRON. The rendering of several Heb. words, all meaning a vessel for boiling flesh, either for domestic or ceremonial purposes. The term appears only once in the NASB (1 Sam. 2:14) and twice in the NIV (1 Sam. 2:14; Job 41:31), but is frequent in the KJV (1 Sam. 2:14; 2 Chron. 35:13; Job 41:20; Jer. 52:18, 19; Ezek. 11:3, 7). Metallic vessels of this kind have been found in Egypt, Babylonia, and Mesopotamia.

CA'LEB (kā'leb; a "dog").

1. The son of *Jephunneh* (which see), the Kenizzite, and head of one of the families of Judah. The first mention of Caleb was his appointment at the age of forty years (Josh. 14:6-7) as one of the twelve spies sent by Moses to explore Canaan (Num. 13:6, 17-25), c. 1440 B.C.

On their return all the spies agreed respecting the preeminent goodness of the land but differed in their advice to the people. While the ten others announced the inability of Israel to overcome the Canaanites, Caleb and Joshua spoke encouragingly. They admitted the strength and stature of the people and the greatness of the walled cities but were far from despairing. Caleb, stilling the people before Moses, exhorted them earnestly and boldly, "We should by all means go up and take possession of it, for we shall surely overcome it" (Num. 13:30). For this act of faithfulness, repeated the following day, Caleb and Joshua barely escaped being stoned by the people (14:10). Moses announced to the congregation, however, that they alone, of all the people over twenty years of age, should enter into the Promised Land, and in a plague that shortly followed the other spies died (14:26-38). A special promise was given to Caleb that he should enter the land that he had trodden upon, and that his seed should possess it (14:24).

We find no further mention of Caleb until about forty-five years after. The land was being divided, and he claimed the special inheritance promised by Moses as a reward of his fidelity. His claim was admitted, and Joshua added his blessing. Caleb, who at the age of eighty-five was still as strong for war as when he was forty, drove out the Anakim from Hebron (Josh. 14:6-15; 15:14). He then attacked Debir (Kiriath-sepher), to the SW of Hebron. This town must have been strong and hard to conquer, for Caleb offered a prize to the conqueror, promising to give his daughter Achsah for a wife to anyone who should take it. Othniel, his nephew, took the city and secured Achsah and a tract of land (15:13-19). We have no further information respecting Caleb's life or death.

Concerning the taking of Debir, Keil notes: "There is no discrepancy between the accounts of the taking of Debir (Josh. 11:21-22; 15:13-19), for the expulsion of its inhabitants by Joshua did not preclude the possibility of their returning when the Israelitish armies had withdrawn to the north" (*Com.*).

2. The last named of the three sons of Hezron (1 Chron. 2:18), of the descendants of Judah, in 1 Chron. 2:9, where he is called *Chelubai* (which see; still Caleb in the NIV). His sons by his first wife, Azubah, or *Jerioth* (which see), were Jesher, Shobab, and Ardon (v. 18). After her death he married Ephrath, by whom he had Hur (v. 19) and perhaps others (v. 50). He had also several children by his concubines, Ephah and Maacah (vv. 46, 48).

3. In the KJV and NIV of 1 Chron. 2:50, a son of Hur. *See* the NASB for a better reading.

CA'LEB-EPH'RATHAH (kā'leb-ef'ra-tha). Only in 1 Chron. 2:24: "And after the death of Hezron in Caleb-ephrathah," etc. "The town or village in which Caleb dwelt with his wife Ephrath may have been called Caleb of Ephrathah, if Ephrath had brought this place as a dower to Caleb (comp. Josh. 15:18). Ephrathah or Ephrath was the ancient name of Bethlehem, and with it the name Ephrath is connected, probably so called after her birthplace. If this supposition is well founded, then Caleb of Ephrathah would be the little town of Bethlehem" (Keil, *Com.*). Many scholars, however, adopt the LXX reading, "After the death of Hezron Caleb came unto Ephrath, the wife of Hezron, his father."

CALENDAR (Lat. *calendarium,* from *calere,* "to call," because the priests *called* the people to notice that it was new moon). An ecclesiastical almanac indicating the special days and seasons to be observed.

Chaldean. Their years were vague years of 360 days. The twelve equal months of which they were composed bore names that were borrowed, on the one hand, from events in civil life, such as "Simanu," from the making of brick, and "Addaru," from the sowing of seed, and, on the other, from mythological occurrences whose origin is still obscure, such as "Nisanu," and "Elul." The adjustment of this year to astronomical demands was roughly carried out by the addition of a month every six years, which was called a second Adar, Elul, or Nisan, according to the place in which it was intercalated. The neglect of the hours and minutes in their calculations of the length of the year became with them, as with the Egyptians, a source of serious embarrassment, and we are still ignorant as to the means employed to meet the difficulty.

Egyptian. Very early the Egyptians divided the year into twelve months of 30 days each, with a sacred period of 5 feast days intercalated at the end of the year. The year began when Sirius first appeared on the eastern horizon at sunrise (July 19 on our calendar). Since this calendar year was a quarter of a day shorter than the solar year, it gained a full day every 4 years, and a full year in 1,460 years. An astronomical event such as the heliacal rising of Sirius, when computed on the basis of the Egyptian calendar, may therefore be reckoned and dated within four years in terms of our reckoning, i.e., in years b.c. This is the calendar that Julius Caesar introduced into Rome and that was bequeathed to us by the Romans (see below), thus being in operation for over six millennia.

Jewish. The Israelites divided their year according to natural phenomena exclusively, combining the solar and lunar year. The months began with the new moon, but the first month was fixed (after the Exodus and by the necessities of the Passover) by the ripening of the earliest grain, namely, barley. The lunar month averaging 29½ days, a year of twelve months of 30 and 29 days alternately resulted; but this involved a variation of 11 and 22 days alternately in eighteen out of nineteen years. To reconcile this lunar year with the year of the seasons, a thirteenth month was inserted about once in three years. That the Jews had calendars wherein were noted all the feasts, fasts, and days on which they celebrated any great event of their history is evident from Zech. 8:19. Probably the oldest calendar is the *Megillath Taanith* ("volume of affliction"), said to have been drawn up in the time of John Hyrcanus, before 106 b.c. In table 1, "The Jewish Calendar," it is assumed, as usual, that the first month of the Hebrew ecclesiastical year, Abib or Nisan, answers nearly to half March and half April, the earliest possible commencement of the lunar year being on our fifth of March. *See* Chronology.

Roman. The ancient Roman year consisted of twelve lunar months, of 29 and 30 days alternately, making 354 days; but a day was added to make the number odd, which was considered more fortunate, so that the year consisted of 355 days. This was less than the solar year by 10 days and a fraction. Numa is credited with attempting to square this lunar year of 355 days with the solar of 365; but how he did it is not known for certain. The Decemviri, 450 b.c., probably introduced the system of adjustment afterward in use, namely, by inserting biennially an intercalary month of 23 days between February 24 and 25, and in the fourth year a month of 22 days between February 23 and 24. But this gave the year an average of 366¼ days, or one too many; and it was the business of the pontiffs to keep the calendar in order by regular intercalation. Their neglect produced great disorder. The mischief was finally remedied by Julius Caesar, with the assistance of the mathematician Sosigenes. To bring the calendar into correspondence with the seasons, the year 46 b.c. was lengthened so as to consist of fifteen months, or 445 days, and the calendar known as the Julian was introduced January 1, 45 b.c. The use of the lunar year and the intercalary month was abolished, and the civil year was regulated entirely by the sun. Caesar fixed this year to 365¼ days, which is correct within a few minutes. After this the ordinary year consisted of 365 days, divided into twelve months, with the names still in use.

Gregorian. The method adopted by Caesar answered a good purpose for a short time, but after several centuries astronomers began to discover a discrepancy between the solar and the civil year. The addition of the day every fourth year would be correct if the solar year consisted of exactly 365¼ days, whereas it contains only 365 days, 5 hours, 47 minutes, 51½ seconds. This makes the Julian year longer than the true solar year by about 12 minutes. In 1582 the Julian year was found to be about 10 days behind the true time, the vernal equinox falling on March 11 instead of March 21, its date at the Council of Nice, a.d. 325. Pope Gregory issued an edict causing October 5 to be called the 15th, thus suppressing 10 days, and making the year 1582 to consist of only 355 days; thus restoring the concurrence of the solar and civil year, and consequently the vernal equinox to the place it occupied in 325, namely, March 21. In order that this

Table 1
The Jewish Calendar

Names of Months		Festivals	Season	Weather	Crops
Hebrew	English				
A'BIB (Heb. *'ābib,* "green ears"), or NI'SAN. Thirty days; first of *sacred,* seventh of *civil,* year.	March-April	1. New moon (Num. 10:10; 28:11–15). *Fast* for Nadab and Abihu (Lev. 10:1–2). 10. Selection of paschal lamb (Ex. 12:3). *Fast* for Miriam (Num. 20:1) and in memory of the scarcity of water (20:2). 14. Paschal lamb killed in evening (Ex. 12:6). Passover begins (Num. 28:16). Search for leaven. 15. First day of Unleavened Bread (Num. 28:17). After sunset sheaf of barley brought to Temple. 16. "First fruits," sheaf offered (Lev. 23:10–15). Beginning of harvest, fifty days to Pentecost (Lev. 23:15). 21. Close of Passover, end of Unleavened Bread (Lev. 23:6). 15 and 21. Holy convocations (Lev. 23:7). 26. *Fast* for the death of Joshua.	Spring equinox	*Wind* S; sometimes sirocco. Fall of the "late" or spring rains (Deut. 11:14). The melting snows of Lebanon and the rains fill the Jordan channel in places, and the river overflows its lower plain in places (Josh. 3:15; cf. Zech. 10:11).	*Barley* harvest begins in the plain of Jericho and in the Jordan Valley; *wheat* coming into ear; uplands brilliant with shortlived vegetation and flowers.
ZIF (Heb. *ziw,* "brightness"), or I'JAR. Twenty-nine days; second *sacred,* eighth of *civil,* year.	April-May	1. New moon (Num. 1:18). 6. *Fast* of three days for excesses during Passover. 10. *Fast* for death of Eli and capture of Ark (1 Sam. 4:11–17). 15. "Second" or "little" Passover, for those unable to celebrate in Abib; in memory of entering wilderness (Ex. 16:1). 23. *Feast* for taking of Gaza by S. Maccabeus; for taking and purification of the Temple by the Maccabees. 27. *Feast* for the expulsion of the Galileans from Jerusalem. 28. *Fast* for the death of Samuel (1 Sam. 25:1).	Summer	*Wind* S; showers and thunderstorms rare (1 Sam. 12:17–18). Sky generally cloudless till end of summer.	Principal harvest month in lower districts. *Barley* harvest general (Ruth 1:22); *wheat* ripening on the uplands; *apricots* ripen. In Jordan Valley hot winds destroy vegetation.
SI'VAN (Heb. *sîwān*). Thirty days; third of *sacred,* ninth of *civil,* year.	May-June	1. New moon. 2. "*Feast* of Pentecost," or "Feast of Weeks," because it came seven weeks after Passover (Lev. 23:15–21). 15, 16. Celebration of victory over Bethshan (1 Macc. 5:52; 12:40–41). 17. *Feast* for taking Caesarea by Hasmonaeans. 22. *Fast* in memory of Jeroboam's forbidding subjects to carry firstfruits to Jerusalem (1 Kings 12:27). 25. *Fast* in memory of rabbis Simeon, Ishmael, and Chanina; *feast* in honor of judgment of Alexander the Great, in favor of Jews against Ishmaelites, who claimed Canaan. 27. *Fast,* Chanina being burned with books of law.		*Wind* NW, also E; and *khamseen,* or parching wind from southern deserts. Air still and brilliantly clear.	*Wheat* harvest begins on uplands; *almonds* ripen; grapes begin to ripen; *honey* of the Jordan Valley collected May to July.

Names of Months		Festivals	Season	Weather	Crops
Hebrew	English				
TAM'MUZ (Heb. *tammūz*). Twenty-nine days; fourth of *sacred*, tenth of *civil*, year.	June-July	1. New moon. 14. *Feast* for abolition of a book of Sadducees and Bethusians, intended to subvert oral law and traditions. 17. *Fast* in memory of tablets of law broken by Moses (Ex. 32:19); and taking of Jerusalem by Titus.	Hot season	*Wind* usually NW, also E, and *khamseen* from S. Air still and clear; heat intense; heavy dews.	*Wheat* harvest on highest districts; various *fruits* ripe. Springs and vegetation generally dried up. Bedouins leave steppes for mountain pastures. Elsewhere, country parched, dry and hard—"a dreary waste of withered stalks and burned-up grass" ("stubble," KJV).
AB (Heb. *'âb*, "fruitful"). Thirty days; fifth of *sacred*, eleventh of *civil*, year.	July-August	1. New moon; *fast* for death of Aaron, commemorated by children of Jethuel, who furnished wood to Temple after the captivity. 9. *Fast* in memory of God's declaration against murmurers entering Canaan (Num. 14:29–31). 18. *Fast*, because in the time of Ahaz the evening lamp went out. 21. *Feast* when wood was stored in Temple. 24. *Feast* in memory of law providing for sons and daughters alike inheriting estate of parents.		*Wind* E. Air still and clear; heat intense; heavy dews.	Principal *fruit* month—grapes, figs, walnuts, olives, etc.; *grape gathering* begins (Lev. 26:5).
E'LUL (Heb. *'ĕlûl'*, good for "nothing"). Twenty-nine days; sixth of *sacred*, twelfth of *civil*, year.	August-September	1. New moon. 7. *Feast* for the dedication of Jerusalem's walls by Nehemiah. 17. *Fast*, death of spies bringing ill report (Num. 14:36–37). 21. *Feast*, wood offering. 22. *Feast* in memory of wicked Israelites, who were punished with death. (Throughout the month the cornet is sounded to warn of approaching new civil year.)		*Wind* NE. Heat still intense (2 Kings 4:18–20), much lightning, but rain rarely.	*Grape gathering* general; harvest of *dourra* and *maize*; *cotton* and *pomegranates* ripen.
ETH'ANIM (Heb. *'ĕtānîm*, "permanent"), or TIS'RI. Thirty days; seventh of *sacred*, first of *civil*, year.	September-October	1. New moon; *New Year; feast* of Trumpets (Lev. 23:24; Num. 29:1–2). 3. *Fast* for murder of Gedaliah (2 Kings 25:25; Jer. 41:2); high priest set apart for the Day of Atonement. 7. *Fast* on account of worship of golden calf 10. Day of Atonement, *"the fast"* (Acts 27:9), i.e., the only one required by the law; the first day of jubilee years. 15–21. *Feast* of Booths. 22. Holy convocation, palms borne, prayer for rain. 23. *Feast* for law being finished; dedication of Solomon's Temple.	Seed time, grain ripening	*Wind* NE. Dews heavy. Former or "early," i.e., autumnal, rains begin (Joel 2:23) to soften the ground (Deut. 11:14); nights frosty (Gen. 31:40).	Plowing and sowing begin as soon as the ground is softened by the rain—in any weather as the time runs short (Prov. 20:4: Eccles. 11:4); *cotton* harvest.
BUL (Heb. *bûl*), or MARCHESH'-VAN. Twenty-nine days; eighth of *sacred*, second of *civil*, year.	October-November	1. New moon. 6, 7. *Fast* because Nebuchadnezzar blinded Zedekiah (2 Kings 25:7; Jer. 52:10). 17. Prayer for rain. 19. *Fast* for faults committed during feast of Booths. 23. Memorial of stones of altar profaned by Greeks (1 Macc. 4:44). 26. *Feast* in memory of recovery after the captivity of places occupied by the Cuthites.		*Wind* N, NW, NE, S, SW. Rainy month, partly fine; rains from S and SW.	*Wheat* and *barley* are sown; *grape gathering* in northern Palestine; *rice* harvest; *fig* tree laden with fruit; *orange* and *citron* blossom; almost all vegetation has disappeared.

Names of Months		Festivals	Season	Weather	Crops
Hebrew	English				
CHIS'LEV (Heb. *kis-lēw*). Thirty days; ninth of *sacred*, third of *civil*, year.	November-December	1. New moon. 2. *Fast* (three days) if no rain falls. 3. *Feast* in honor of Hasmonaeans' throwing out idols placed in Temple court by Gentiles. 6. *Feast* in memory of roll burned by Jehoiakim (Jer. 36:23). 7. *Feast* in memory of death of Herod the Great. 14. *Fast*, absolute if no rain. 21. *Feast* of Mt. Gerizim; plowing and sowing of Mt. Gerizim with tares, as Samaritans had intended to do with Temple ground. 25. *Feast* of the dedication of the Temple, or of Lights (eight days) in memory of restoration of Temple by Judas Maccabeus.	Winter begins (John10:23)	Snow on mountains and stormy. Greatest amount of rainfall during year in December, January, and February.	Trees bare, but plains and deserts gradually become green pastures.
TE'BETH (Heb. *tē-bēt*). Twenty-nine days; tenth of *sacred*, fourth of *civil*, year.	December-January	1. New moon. 8. *Fast* because the law was translated into Gk. 9. *Fast*, no reason assigned. 10. *Fast* on account of siege of Jerusalem by Nebuchadnezzar (2 Kings 25:1). 28. *Feast* in memory of exclusion of Sadducees from the Sanhedrin.	Mid-winter	*Wind* N, NW, NE. Coldest month; rain, hail, and snow (Josh. 10:11) on higher hills, and occasionally at Jerusalem.	Flocks leave highlands for the Jordan Valley, and its cultivation begins; *oranges* ripening, and lower districts green with grain.
SHE'BAT (Heb. *shᵉ-bāt'*), or SE'BAT. Thirty days; eleventh of *sacred*, fifth of *civil*, year.	January-February	1. New moon. 2. Rejoicing for death of King Alexander Jannaeus, enemy of the Pharisees. 4 or 5. *Fast* in memory of death of elders, successors to Joshua. 15. Beginning of the year of Trees (which see). 22. *Feast* in memory of death of Niscalenus, who ordered images placed in Temple, and who died before execution of his orders. 23. *Fast* for war of the Ten Tribes against Benjamin (Judg. 20); also idol of Micah (18:11–31). 29. Memorial of death of Antiochus Epiphanes, enemy of Jews.	Winter	*Wind* N, NW, NE. Gradually growing warmer. Toward end of month the most pleasant "cool season" begins.	*Almond* and *peach* blossom in warmer and sheltered localities; *oranges* ripe.

Names of Months		Festivals	Season	Weather	Crops
Hebrew	English				
A'DAR (Heb. *'ädär*, "fire"). Twenty-nine days; twelfth of *sacred*, sixth of *civil*, year.	February-March	1. New moon. 7. *Fast* because of Moses' death (Deut. 34:5). 8, 9. Trumpet sounded in thanksgiving for rain, and prayer for future rain. 12. *Feast* in memory of Hollianus and Pipus, two proselytes, who died rather than break the law. 13. *Fast* of Esther (Esther 4:16). *Feast* in memory of Nicanor, enemy of the Jews (1 Macc. 7:44). 14. The first *Purim*, or lesser *Feast* of Lots (Esther 9:21). 15. The great *Feast of Purim* (which see). 17. Deliverance of sages who fled from Alexander Jannaeus. 20. *Feast* for rain obtained in time of drought, in time of Alexander Jannaeus. 23. *Feast* for dedication of Zerubbabel's Temple (Ezra 6:16). 28. *Feast* to commemorate the repeal of decree of Grecian kings forbidding Jews to circumcise their children.	Cold and rainy season, or spring	*Wind* W. Thunder and hail frequent, sometimes snow. The late rains begin, on which plenty or famine, the crops and pasture depend.	In the Jordan Valley cultivation draws to an end, and *barley* ripens.

difference might not recur it was further ordained that every hundredth year (1800, 1900, etc.) should not be counted as a leap year, except every fourth hundredth, beginning with 2000. In this way the difference between the civil and solar years will not amount to a day in five thousand years. The pope was promptly obeyed in Spain, Portugal, and part of Italy. The change took place in France the same year by calling the 10th the 20th day of December. Gradually other countries adopted this style.

Ecclesiastical. Originally the ecclesiastical calendar was only an adaptation of Greek and Roman calendars, although Christian influence is seen in two calendars as early as the middle of the fourth century. This influence is shown in the setting of the Christian week side by side with the pagan, while the other, A.D. 448, contains Christian feast days and holidays, though as yet few, namely, four festivals of Christ and six martyr days. The earliest known *pure Christian* calendar is of Gothic origin, from Thrace, in the fourth century. It is a fragment, merely 38 days, but contains mention of seven saints.

Originally the martyrs were celebrated only where they suffered, and each church had its own calendar, but in the Middle Ages the Roman calendar spread throughout the Western church. From the eighth century combined calendars of saints and martyrs were made and are found in great numbers. They are designed to suit all times and are supplied with means to ascertain the movable feasts, especially Easter.

The present Saints' Calendar of the Roman Catholic church is copious and may be found more or less complete in its almanacs.

The German Lutheran church retained the Roman calendar (with the saints' days of that age) at the Reformation. An Evangelical Calendar for the use of the Evangelical Church of Germany is issued annually.

The calendar of the Church of England may be found in the large edition of the Prayer Book, and consists of nine columns, containing (1) the golden number or cycle of the moon; (2) days of the month in numerical order; (3) dominical or Sunday letter; (4) calends, nones, and ides; (5) holy days of the church, as also some festivals of the Roman church, for convenience rather than reverence; (6-9) portions of Scripture and of the Apocrypha, appointed for the daily lessons.

BIBLIOGRAPHY: P. Nilsson, *Primitive Time Reckoning* (1920); J. Morgenstern, *Hebrew Union College Annual* (1924), 1:13-78; S. Langdon, *Babylonian Menologies and the Semitic Calendars* (1935); J. Lewy and H. Lewy, *HUCA* 17 (1941): 1-152; J. Morgenstern, *HUCA* 20 (1947): 1-36; id., 21 (1948): 365-496; R. Parker, *Calendars of Ancient Egypt* (1950); J. van Goudoever, *Biblical Calendars* (1961); J. Morgenstern, *Journal of Biblical Literature* 83 (1964): 109-18; D. J. A. Clines, *JBL* 93 (1974): 22-40.

CALF. The young of the ox species. The frequent mention in Scripture of calves is due to their common use in sacrifices. The "fattened calf" was considered by the Hebrews as the choicest of animal food. It was stall-fed, frequently with reference to a particular festival or extraordinary sacrifice (1 Sam. 28:24; Amos 6:4; Luke 15:23). The allusion in Jer. 34:18-19 is to an ancient custom of ratifying a *covenant* (which see). *See* Animal Kingdom: Ox.

Figurative. The expressions "calves of our lips" (Hos. 14:2, KJV) and "fruit of our lips" (Heb. 13:15, KJV) signify *prayers* or *thanksgiving,* young oxen being considered as the best animals for thank offerings.

CALF, GOLDEN. The idolatrous image of a young bull set up at Mt. Sinai (Ex. 32:2-4) and later by Jeroboam at Bethel and Dan (1 Kings 12:28). The young bull symbolized vitality and strength, and the Israelites sought to worship Jehovah under this representation. Doubtless the prevalence of bull worship in Egypt suggested this animal. Jeroboam also had likely seen the bull Apis worshiped in Egypt while he was a refugee at the court of Shishak (11:40), but ancient tradition also influenced him, for he quotes Ex. 32:4 in advertising his new cult. Common among western Semites are gods represented as standing on an animal's back or as seated on an animal-borne throne. What Jeroboam likely did was to represent the invisible Jehovah astride a young bull of gold. It is inconceivable that he would resort to the crass idea of actually expecting worship of a golden calf itself.   M.F.U.

CALF, WORSHIP OF. *See* Gods, False.

CALKER. *See* Handicrafts.

CALL, CALLING (Heb. usually *qārā;* Gk. *kaleō,* to "call").

To Call for Help. Hence, to pray. We first meet this expression in Gen. 4:26: "Then men began to call upon the name of the Lord" (see also Pss. 79:6; 105:1; Isa. 64:7; Jer. 10:25; Zeph. 3:9). In this sense of invoking God in prayer, with an acknowledgment of His attributes, confession of sins, etc., "call" is used in the NT (Acts 2:21; 7:59; 9:14; Rom. 10:12; 1 Cor. 1:2).

Divine Call. The word *call* is used in Scripture with the following significations: (1) In the sense of "to name," "to designate" (Gen. 16:11; Deut. 25:10), and in the sense of "to be," e.g., "His name will be called Wonderful" (Isa. 9:6); i.e., He shall be wonderful, and so acknowledged. (2) In the designation of individuals to some special office or work, as the call of Bezalel (Ex. 31:2), of judges, prophets, apostles, etc. (Acts 13:2); of nations to certain functions, privileges, or punishments (Lam. 2:22); particularly of Israel (Deut. 7:6-8; Isa. 41:9; 42:6; Hos. 11:1). (3) A condition of life, "Let each man remain in that condition in which he was called" (1 Cor. 7:20).

Call to Salvation. "To call" signifies to invite to the blessings of the gospel, to offer salvation through Christ. This calling is, we believe, general, extending to all mankind. There is likewise a calling by the Spirit that is not resisted and clearly described as an efficacious calling. The efficacious calling of God is tantamount to His sovereign choice. There are now two elect companies in the world—Israel and the church. Both alike appear in Scripture as called by God. Israel's calling is national, whereas the calling of those who compose the church is individual. It is wholly within the bounds of the efficacious calling that believers are termed *the called ones.* They are thus distinguished from the general mass who though subject to a general call are not efficaciously called. The efficacious call is the work of God in behalf of each elect person under grace. They are referred to as "those who are called according to His purpose" (Rom. 8:28). The apostle goes on to declare that those whom God foreknew, He predestined; those whom He predestined, He called; those whom He called, He justified; and those whom He justified, He glorified (8:29-30). Calling, then, is that choice on the part of God of an individual through an efficacious working in his mind and heart by the Holy Spirit so that the will of the one who is called operates by its own determination in the exercise of saving faith. In this way two great necessities are provided; namely, only those are called whom God has predestined to be justified and glorified and those who are thus called choose from their own hearts and minds to accept Christ as Savior.

M.F.U.

CAL'NEH (kal'ne).

1. An ancient Babylonian city pertaining to Nimrod's kingdom (Gen. 10:10). Its location is uncertain, and because of this some scholars emend the Heb. to *kŭllānâ,* "all of them." Some have identified Calneh with Nippur, an important excavated city in central Babylonia. Others see a connection with Kulunu, an ancient important city near Babylon. Another possibility is that Calneh is Hursagkalama, a twin city of Kish.

2. Calneh mentioned in Amos 6:2 together with Hamath may be Kullani, modern Kullanhu, about six miles distant from Arpad. It was conquered and annexed to Assyria by Tiglath-pileser in 738 B.C.

CAL'NO (kal'nō). A city referred to in Isa. 10:9 as offering futile resistance to the military power of Assyria. Doubtless the same as Calneh (no. 2).

CAL'VARY (Gk. *kranion,* a "skull," but having its English form from the translators' having literally adopted the Lat. word *calvaria,* a bare "skull"; the Gk. is the interpretation of the Heb. *Golgotha,* which see; the word occurs once, in Luke 23:33, KJV.) Calvary refers to the place where Christ was crucified, designated as the place of a skull (Golgotha), either because of the shape of the mound or elevation or because it was a place of execution. Some claim that Moriah and Calvary are identical. The shift of the city wall from time to time renders it difficult to locate the spot.

It would probably have been a prominent place near the public highway, for the Romans selected such places for public executions.

From the fourth century to the present day the sites of Calvary and of the Holy Sepulcher have been shown within the precincts of the church of the Holy Sepulcher, a Crusader construction, standing where Constantine's Basilica was raised. Others identify the spot with "Gordon's Calvary," N of the present N wall.

BIBLIOGRAPHY: G. H. Dalman, *Sacred Sites and Ways* (1935), pp. 341-81; C. Maston, *The Garden Tomb, Jerusalem* (1941); A. Parrot, *Golgotha and the Church of the Holy Sepulcher* (1957); C. C. Dobson, *The Garden Tomb and the Resurrection* (1958); L. E. Cox Evans, *Palestine Exploration Quarterly* 100 (1968):112-36.

Gordon's Calvary

CAMEL. For a description of the camel, *see* Animal Kingdom.

Figurative. "It is easier for a camel to go through the eye of a needle, than for a rich man to enter the kingdom of God" (Matt. 19:24) is a proverbial expression to show how difficult it is for a rich man who has the many temptations of wealth to leave them for the sake of Christ. The objection is made that the metaphor of an animal passing through a needle's eye is a bad one, and that the Gk. *kamēlos* ought to be read *kamilos,* a "cable," "as for a *rope* to pass," etc. There appears, however, to be no such Gk. word as *kamilos,* a "cable." "To render the word by a *narrow gate,* a narrow *mountain pass,* or anything but a *needle* is inadmissible" (Meyer, *Com.,* ad loc.).

"You blind guides, who strain out a gnat and swallow a camel!" (Matt. 23:24) is a proverb applied to those who superstitiously strive to avoid small faults and yet do not scruple to commit great sins. This is a reference to the custom of the Jews in straining their wine in order that there might be no possibility of swallowing with it any unclean animal, however minute (Lev. 11:42).

BIBLIOGRAPHY: *See* Animal Kingdom: Camel.

CAMEL'S HAIR. The long hair of the camel, which is somewhat woolly in texture, becomes toward the close of spring loose and is easily pulled away from the skin. The modern Arabs still weave it into a coarse sort of cloth for tent covers and coats for shepherds and camel drivers. Garments of this material were worn by John the Baptist in the wilderness (Matt. 3:4).

Figurative. It was an outward mark of that deadness to carnal enjoyment and mortification that marked John's mission as God's prophet in the apostasy of Israel. In this he imitated his great predecessor and type, Elijah (2 Kings 1:8), in a time of similar degeneracy (see Zech. 13:4).

CA'MON. *See* Kamon.

CAMP, ENCAMPMENT (Heb. *mahăneh,* "place of pitching a tent," from *hānâ,* "to pitch a tent"). A term applied to any band or company presenting a regular and settled appearance; a nomad party at rest (Gen. 32:21); an army or caravan when on its march (Gen. 32:7-8; Ex. 14:9; Josh. 10:5), and the resting place of an army or company (Ex. 16:13). Sometimes the verb refers to the casual arrangement of a siege (Ps. 27:3) or campaign (1 Sam. 4:1). Among nomadic tribes war never attained the dignity of a science, and their encampments were consequently devoid of all the appliances of more systematic warfare. The art of laying out an encampment appears to have been well understood in Egypt long before the departure of the Israelites from that country, and it was there, doubtless, that Moses became acquainted with that mode of encampment that he introduced among the Israelites.

Camp of Israel.

Arrangement. During the sojourn in the wilderness, when the people had to be kept for a long period in a narrow space, it was necessary for the sake of order and safety to assign the several tribes and families to their respective positions, leaving as little as possible to personal rivalry or individual caprice. With the exception of some scattered hints, our information respecting the camp of Israel is found in Num. 2-3. The Tabernacle occupied the center of the camp, following the common practice in the East of the leader of a tribe having his tent in the center of the others. It should be borne in mind that Jehovah, whose tent was the Tabernacle, was the leader of Israel. The tents nearest to the Tabernacle were those of the Levites, whose business it was to watch it; the family of Gershon pitched to the W, that of Kohath to the S, and that of Merari to the N. The priests occupied a position to the E, opposite the entrance of the Tabernacle (3:38). The priests and Levites were under the immediate supervision of Moses and Aaron (1:53; 3:21-38). The host of Israel was divided into four divisions and encamped in the following order: first, on the E, Judah, having associated with him Issachar and Zebulun; on the S, Reuben, Simeon, and Gad; on the W, Ephraim, Manasseh, and Benjamin; on the N, Dan, Asher, and Naphtali. Each division had its separate *standard* (which see), and each family had a separate standard, around which it was to pitch its tents (1:52). The order of encampment was preserved on the march (2:17), the signal for which was given by a blast of the two silver trumpets (10:5). Sentinels were probably placed at the gates (Ex. 32:26-27) in the four quarters of the camp. This was evidently the case in the camp of the Levites (cf. 1 Chron. 9:18, 24; 2 Chron. 31:2).

ISRAEL CAMPED AROUND THE TABERNACLE

	NAPHTALI 53.400	ASHER 41.500	DAN 62700	
EPHRAIM 40.500				JUDAH 74.500
MANASSEH 32.200		TABERNACLE		ISSACHAR 54.400
BENJAMIN 35.400				ZEBULUN 57.400
	GAD 45.650	SIMEON 59.300	REUBEN 46.500	

Camp of Israel

Sanitary Regulations. The encampment of Israel, being that of the Lord's host, and with the Lord Himself symbolically resident among them, was ordered to be kept in a state of great cleanliness. This was for the twofold purpose of preserving the health of so great a number of people and preserving the purity of the camp as the dwelling place of God (Num. 5:3; Deut. 23:14). The dead were buried outside of the camp (Lev. 10:4-5); lepers were excluded till their leprosy departed (13:46), and likewise all others with loathsome diseases (15:2; Num. 5:2) or personal uncleanness (Deut. 23:10-13); those defiled by contact with the dead, whether slain in battle or not, were excluded from the camp for seven days; captives remained for a while outside (Num. 31:19; Josh. 6:23); the ashes from the sacrifices were carried to an appointed place outside of the camp, where the entrails, skin, horns, and all that was not offered in sacrifice, were burned (Lev. 4:11-12; 6:11; 8:17); the execution of criminals took place outside of the camp (24:23; Num. 15:35-36; Josh. 7:24), as did the burning of the young bull for the sin offering (Lev. 4:12). An important sanitary regulation is mentioned in Deut. 23:12-14. The

encampment of the Israelites in the wilderness left its traces in their subsequent history. The Temple, so late as the time of Hezekiah, was still the camp of Jehovah (2 Chron. 31:2, KJV, "the tents of the Lord"; cf. Ps. 78:28), and the multitudes who flocked to David were "a great army like the army of God" (1 Chron. 12:22, lit., "a great *camp*, like the *camp* of God").

Military. We have no definite information concerning the military encampments of Israel in later times. Formed merely for the occasion, and as circumstances might admit, they could scarcely be brought under precise or stringent regulations. They were pitched in any suitable or convenient situation that presented itself—sometimes on a height (1 Sam. 17:3; 28:4; etc.), or near a spring or well (Judg. 7:1; 1 Sam. 29:1). The camp was surrounded by the rampart (17:20; 26:5-7), which some explain as an earthwork thrown up around the encampment, others as the barrier formed by the baggage wagons. We know that, in the case of a siege, the attacking army, if possible, surrounded the place attacked (1 Macc. 13:43) and drew a line about it (2 Kings 25:1), which was marked by a breastwork of earth (Isa. 62:10; Ezek. 21:22; cf. Job 19:12) for the double purpose of preventing the escape of the besieged and of protecting the besiegers from their sallies. To guard against attacks sentinels were posted (Judg. 7:19; 1 Macc. 12:27) around the camp, and the neglect of this precaution by Zebah and Zalmunna probably led to their capture by Gideon and the ultimate defeat of their army (Judg. 8:21). The valley that separated the hostile camps was generally selected as the fighting ground (1 Sam. 4:2; 14:15; 2 Sam. 18:6) upon which the contest was decided, and hence the valleys of Palestine have played so conspicuous a part in its history (Josh. 8:13; Judg. 6:33; 2 Sam. 5:22; 8:13; etc.). When the fighting men went forth to the place selected for marshaling the forces (1 Sam. 17:20), a detachment was left to protect the camp and baggage (17:22; 30:24). The beasts of burden were probably tethered to the tent pegs (2 Kings 7:10; Zech. 14:15).

CAMPHIRE. *See* Vegetable Kingdom: Henna.

CA′NA (kā′na). "Cana of Galilee," a name found in the gospel of John only, but in such references no clue is given as to its locality; supposed to be near Capernaum. Cana of Galilee is distinguished from Cana of Asher (Josh. 19:28, NASB and NIV, "Kanah"). It was the birthplace of Nathanael (John 21:2) and honored as the scene of Christ's first recorded miracle (2:1, 11; 4:46). North of Nazareth lie the two sites that have at various times been regarded as representing Cana of Galilee. The one is the Christian village of Kefr Kenna, about four miles NE of Nazareth, accepted before the Crusades as the true site; the other site is Khirbet, four or five miles farther N. Though the former is usually pointed out to tourists as the true site, scholars are increasingly leaning to acceptance of the latter.

BIBLIOGRAPHY: M. Pearlman and Y. Yannai, *Historical Sites of Israel* (1960); J. Finegan, *The Archaeology of the New Testament* (1969), p. 66.

Traditional site of Cana of Galilee (Kefr Kenna)

CA'NAAN, CA'NAANITES (kā'nan, kā'na-nīt). In Gen. 10:6, 15-18, Canaan is listed as the fourth son of Ham, the father of "Sidon, his first-born, and Heth and the Jebusite and the Amorite and the Girgashite and the Hivite and the Arkite and the Sinite and the Arvadite and the Zemarite and the Hamathite."

The Name. The Canaanites were the inhabitants of Canaan, the more ancient name of Pales-

CANAAN
after the Israelite
settlement

Sidon
Damascus
Dan
Achzib
Kadesh
Hazor
Acco Ramah
Rehob
Chinnereth
Nahalol
Aphek
Sea of
Ashtaroth
Kitron
Chinnereth
Megiddo
Dor
Jezreel
Taanach
Beth-shan
Ramoth-gilead
Ibleam
Jabesh-gilead
Mount Ebal
Shechem
Succoth
Mount Genzim
Aphek
Shiloh
AMMON
Gezer
Bethel Gilgal
Gibeon
Heshbon
Ashdod Ekron Aijalon
(Jerusalem)
Ashkelon
Gath Bethlehem
Medeba
Gaza
Lachish
Hebron
Dibon
Debir
Aroer
Beersheba
0 25 50 km
0 10 20 30 miles
Zoar
Border of Canaan
Philistine city
Mount Halak
Area controlled
Tamar
by Israelites
Kadesh-barnea
EDOM

GREAT SEA
PHILISTIA
Jordan
Salt Sea
MOAB

tine. The Heb. form of Canaan apparently was taken from Hurrian, signifying "belonging to the land of red-purple." From the fourteenth century B.C. on this designation came to be employed of the country in which the "Canaanite" or Phoenician traders exchanged for their commodities their most important commercial product, red-purple, which was obtained from the murex mollusks of coastal Palestine and used for dyeing. In the Amarna Letters the "land of Canaan" is applied to the Phoenician coast, and the Egyptians called all western Syria by this name. By the time of the conquest the term *Canaan* signified the territory later called Palestine.

Territory. The term "land of Canaan" covers all Palestine W of the Jordan (Num. 34:2-12). This territory was situated between the great ancient empires of the Tigris-Euphrates and Halys rivers on the one hand and the great Egyptian empire of the Nile on the other. It was providential that the nation Israel, with its testimony to the knowledge of the one true God and with its obligation to make known that fact, should inherit a country that formed a geographical bridge between the ancient centers of pagan civilization.

Civilization. The Canaanites were talented and developed the arts and sciences early. Stout walled cities have been excavated, and their construction was much superior to that of later Israelite buildings. They excelled in ceramic arts, music, musical instruments, and architecture. The Solomonic Temple was planned with the help of Phoenician artisans and architects. Craftsmen of Hiram of Tyre executed much of the work (1 Kings 7:13-51). Decorations, architectural motifs, and general styling were heavily indebted to Syro-Phoenician art. From all sections of Palestine, well-executed fortifications, ornate palaces, and temples contrast strongly to the strata containing inferior Hebrew construction. The art treasures in ivory, gold, and alabaster recovered from Canaanite Megiddo demonstrate Canaanite architectural elegance. Many of the treasures from Ras Shamra-Ugarit tell the same story. However, by the time of the Israelite conquest, Canaanite civilization had become decadent and was ripe for destruction. Among Canaanite cities that have been excavated are Jericho, Bethel, Libnah, Debir (Kiriath-sepher), Megiddo, Taanach, Beth-shean, Beth-shemesh, Byblos, Ras Shamra, and Gezer.

Religion. New vistas of knowledge of Canaanite cults and their degrading character and debilitating effect have been opened up by the discovery of the Ras Shamra religious epic literature from Ugarit in N Syria. Thousands of clay tablets stored in what seems to be a library between two great Canaanite temples dating from c. fifteenth-fourteenth century B.C. give a full description of the Canaanite pantheon. Canaanite fertility cults are seen to be more base than elsewhere in the ancient world. The virile monotheistic faith of the Hebrews was continually in peril of contamination from the lewd nature worship with immoral gods, prostitute goddesses, serpents, cultic doves, and bulls. El, the head of the pantheon, was the hero of sordid escapades and crimes. He was a bloody tyrant who dethroned his father, murdered his favorite son, and decapitated his daughter. Despite these enormities, El was styled "father of years" (*abu shanima*), "the father of man" (*abu adami,* "father bull"), i.e., the progenitor of the gods. Baal, the widely revered Canaanite deity, was the son of El and dominated the Canaanite pantheon. He was the god of thunder, whose voice reverberated through the heavens in the storm. He is pictured on a Ras Shamra stela brandishing a mace in his right hand and holding in his left hand a stylized thunderbolt. The three goddesses were Anath, Astarte, and Ashera, who were all three patronesses of sex and war. All were sacred courtesans. Other Canaanite deities were Mot (death); Reshep, the god of pestilence; Shulman, the god of health; Koshar, the god of arts and crafts. These Canaanite cults were utterly immoral, decadent, and corrupt, dangerously contaminating and thoroughly justifying the divine command to destroy their devotees (Deut. 20:17).

Conquest. After their victories in Transjordan over Sihon, king of the Amorites, and Og, king of Bashan, Israel under Joshua's leadership passed over the Jordan and began their conquest. The story is told in Josh. 1-12, and the allocation of the land to the various tribes is recounted in chaps. 13-22. After the destruction of Jericho (around 1400 B.C., according to Garstang and in agreement with underlying OT chronology) and Ai (6:1-8:29), the conquest of southern Canaan (chap. 10) and northern Canaan (11:1-5) is described. In 11:16-12:24 the conquest is summarized. The events recorded in the Bible are evidently highly selective. Summary statements embrace other conquests not specifically described in the book (cf. 21:43-45). Those that were included were considered sufficient to accomplish the author's purpose of proving God's faithfulness in giving them the land for their possession.

Language. Languages of Canaan included Phoenician and Ugaritic. Hebrew seems to have been adapted from a Canaanite dialect. It originated from the old Phoenician alphabet. The origin of this proto-Semitic alphabet is still obscure. Examples of this rude script discovered at Serabit el Khadem in the Sinai Peninsula in 1904-5 push alphabetic writing back to pre-Mosaic times. It is interesting that this early (Sinai Heb.) script was found in the general region where Moses was told to write (Ex. 17:8-14). But it is scarcely credible that the alphabet was invented in the desert wastes of the Sinai Peninsula. Since 1930 several brief inscriptions dated between 1700 and 1550

have been found in Palestine and are more archaic than the letters from Serabit el Khadem. These apparently belong to the same alphabet. Proto-Sinaitic was demonstrably affected by Egyptian characters, in both the form of the letters and in the limitation of the alphabet to consonants. The alphabet itself was in all likelihood invented in Hyksos Egypt, or conceivably in Palestine at this or an earlier period. But old Heb. goes back to the patriarchal age. Did Abraham find the Heb. language in Palestine, or did he bring it with him from Haran? The Hebrew patriarchs presumably spoke an Aram. dialect while in Mesopotamia before their entrance into Palestine, but once in Palestine "they adopted a local Canaanite dialect which was not identical with the standard speech of the sedentary Canaanites, as may be linguistically demonstrated" (Albright, *From the Stone Age to Christianity*). This conclusion seems valid because old Heb. is practically the same as Phoenician. Apparently it appears in the traditional name of Heb., "the language of Canaan" (Isa. 19:18). It is furthermore attested by early Canaanite and Heb. inscriptions. These appear in Ugaritic about 1400 B.C., Canaanite inscriptions from Byblos and inscriptions from Cyprus, Sardinia, Carthage, and other colonies in the western Mediterranean. Inscriptions made in Heb. from Palestine including the Gezer Calendar (c. 925 B.C.), the Moabite Stone (c. 850 B.C.), the Samaritan Ostraca (c. 776 B.C.), the Siloam Inscription (c. 701 B.C.), and the Lachish Letters (589 B.C.) add further epigraphic evidence of the close association of biblical Heb. with Phoenician and other Canaanite dialects.   M.F.U.

BIBLIOGRAPHY: J. Gray, *The Canaanites* (n.d.); W. F. Albright, *Archaeology and the Religion of Israel* (1953); D. J. Wiseman, *The Alalakh Tablets* (1953); K. M. Kenyon, *Archaeology in the Holy Land* (1960); J. Gray, *The Legacy of Canaan* (1965); G. E. Wright, ed., *Bible and the Ancient Near East* (1965), pp. 438-87; K. M. Kenyon, *Amorites and Canaanites* (1966); W. F. Albright, *Yahweh and the Gods of Canaan* (1968); G. R. Driver and J. C. L. Gibson, *Canaanite Myths and Legends* (1978); D. J. Wiseman, ed., *Peoples of Old Testament Times* (1973), pp. 29-52.

CA'NAANAEAN, SI'MON THE (Matt. 10:4; Mark 3:18). *See* Simon, no. 2.

CAN'DACE (kan'dā-se). The title of the queen of the Ethiopians whose high treasurer was converted to Christianity under the preaching of Philip the evangelist (Acts 8:27), A.D. 34. Candace was probably a distinctive appellation borne by successive queens, similar to Pharaoh, Ptolemy, etc., which were titles. The country over which she ruled was that region in Upper Nubia called by the Greeks Meroë, where George Reisner identified pyramid tombs of reigning Candaces of Ethiopia constructed from c. 300 B.C. TO A.D. 300.

CANDLE. This term appears frequently in the

KJV where "lamp" or "light" would be the more literal reading. *See* Lamp.

CANE. *See* Vegetable Kingdom.

CANKER. *See* Diseases: Gangrene.

CANKERED. *See* Diseases.

CANKERWORM. *See* Animal Kingdom: Locust.

CAN'NEH. Mentioned only in Ezek. 27:23, and probably a contracted form of the earlier Calneh (Gen. 10:10).

CANON OF SCRIPTURE, THE NEW TESTAMENT. Although the churches of the West are divided as to the position of the OT Apocrypha, they have joined in ratifying one canon of the NT.

The Apostles. They claimed for their writings a public use (Col. 4:16; 1 Thess. 5:27; 1 Tim. 4:13; Rev. 22:18) and an authoritative power (2 Thess. 2:6; 1 Tim. 4:1-6; Rev. 22:19), and Peter (2 Pet. 3:15-16) places the epistles of Paul in significant connection with "the rest of the Scriptures."

Apostolic Fathers. In the writings of the apostolic Fathers, A.D. 70-120, with the exception of Jude, 2 Peter, and 2 and 3 John, with which no coincidences occur, and 1 and 2 Thessalonians, Colossians, Titus, and Philemon, with which the coincidences are questionable, all the other epistles were clearly known, and used by them; but still they are not quoted with the formulas that preface citations from the OT.

Apologists. The next period, A.D. 120-170, the age of the apologists—carries the history of the formation of the canon one step further. The facts of the life of Christ acquired a fresh importance in controversy with Jew and Gentile. The oral tradition, which still remained in the former age, was dying away, and a variety of written documents claimed to occupy its place. It was then that the canonical gospels were definitely separated from the mass of similar narratives in virtue of their outward claims, which had remained, as it were, in abeyance during the period of tradition.

From A.D. 170 to 305. The testimony of Irenaeus, Clement of Alexandria, and Tertullian extends to the four gospels, Acts, 1 Peter, 1 John, thirteen epistles of Paul, and the Apocalypse; and, with the exception of the Apocalypse, no one of these books was ever afterward rejected or questioned until modern times.

From A.D. 303 to 97. The persecution of Christians by the Roman emperor Diocletian, which began with that emperor's edict against Christians in A.D. 303 and continued until A.D. 313, was directed in a great measure against the Christian writings, and some obtained protection by surrendering the sacred books. The Donatists may be regarded as maintaining in its strictest integrity the popular judgment in Africa on the contents of the canon of Scripture, and Augus-

tine allows that they held in common with the Catholics the same "canonical Scriptures," and were alike "bound by the authority of both Testaments." The canon of the NT, as commonly received at present, was ratified by the third Council of Carthage (A.D. 397) and from that time was accepted throughout the Latin church, though occasional doubts as to Hebrews still remained. Meanwhile the Syrian churches still retained the canon of the Peshito. The churches of Asia Minor seem to have occupied a mean position between the East and West. With the exception of the Apocalypse, they received generally all the books of the NT as contained in the African canon.

The Reformation. At the era of the Reformation the question of the NT canon became again a subject of great though partial interest. The hasty decree of the Council of Trent, which affirmed the authority of all the books commonly received, called out the opposition of controversialists, who quoted and enforced the early doubts. Erasmus denied the apostolic origin of Hebrews, 2 Peter, and the Apocalypse, but left their canonical authority unquestioned. Luther set aside Hebrews, Jude, James, and the Apocalypse at the end of his version, and spoke of them and the remaining Antilegomena with varying degrees of disrespect, though he did not separate 2 Peter and 2 and 3 John from the other epistles.

Calvin. Calvin, although he denied the Pauline authorship of Hebrews, and at least questioned the authenticity of 2 Peter, did not set aside their canonicity, and he noticed the doubts as to James and Jude only to dismiss those doubts. The language of the Articles of the Church of England with regard to the NT is remarkable. In the Articles of 1552 no list of the books of Scripture is given; but in the Elizabethan Articles (1562, 1571) a definition of Holy Scripture is given as "the canonical books of the Old and New Testament, *of whose authority was never any doubt in the Church*" (Art. 6). This definition is followed by an enumeration of the books of the OT and of the Apocrypha; and then it is said summarily, without a detailed catalog, "All the books of the New Testament, as they are commonly received, we do receive and account them canonical." A distinction thus remains between the "canonical" books, and such "canonical books as have never been doubted in the church"; and it seems impossible to avoid the conclusion that the framers of the Articles intended to leave a freedom of judgment on a point on which the greatest of the Continental Reformers, and even of Romish scholars, were divided.

BIBLIOGRAPHY: *Old Testament:* W. H. Green, *General Introduction to the Old Testament: The Canon* (1898); H. B. Swete, *Introduction to the Old Testament in Greek* (1902); H. R. Ryle, *The Canon of the Old Testament* (1909); S. Zeitlin, *An Historical Study of the Canonization of the Hebrew Scriptures* (1933); B. J. Roberts, *Old Testament Texts and Versions* (1951); C.

H. Dodd, *The Bible Today* (1952); R. L. Harris, *Inspiration and Canonicity of the Bible* (1957); C. F. H. Henry, ed., *Revelation and the Bible* (1958), pp. 153-68; R. K. Harrison, *Introduction to the Old Testament* (1969), pp. 260-88. G. L. Archer, Jr., *Survey of Old Testament Introduction* (1974), pp. 66-80.

New Testament: T. Zahn, *Geschichte des Neuen Testament Kanons* (1888-92); B. F. Westcott, *General Survey of the History of the Canon of the New Testament* (1896); E. J. Goodspeed, *Formation of the New Testament* (1926); C. L. Mitton, *The Formation of the Pauline Corpus* (1955); F. V. Filson, *Which Books Belong in the Bible?* (1957); A. Souter, *Text and Canon of the New Testament* (1960); W. Barclay, *Making of the Bible* (1961); K. Aland, *The Problem of the New Testament Canon* (1962); C. F. D. Moule, *Birth of the New Testament* (1981), pp. 235-69.

CANON OF SCRIPTURE, THE OLD TESTAMENT.

If the testimony of Scripture is accepted, that God is the author of the Bible and that the Holy Spirit worked upon men to receive and record His word for future generations, the important question was bound to arise (since many religious books were written during the OT period), *what particular books enjoy divine origin and hence are divinely authoritative?* This and similar problems concerning the origin of the thirty-nine books of the OT and the twenty-seven of the NT constitute a historical inquiry concerning man's response to God's operation in giving the sacred oracles.

The Meaning of the Term. The canon of sacred Scripture is a phrase by which the catalog of the authoritative sacred writings is designated. The word for the expression, of Gk. derivation, *kanōn,* and possibly a loan word from Semitic (Heb. *qāneh;* Akkad. *qānu*), originally signified a reed or measuring rod. Actually it indicated "that which measures"; that is, a standard, norm, or rule; specifically, "that which is measured" by that standard, norm, or rule. Those books that were measured by the standard or test of divine inspiration and authority and were adjudged to be "God-breathed" were included in "the canon." The term thus came to be applied to the catalog or list of sacred books thus designated and honored as normative, sacred, and binding. Athanasius (c. A.D. 350) was the first person known with certainty to apply the term to sacred Scripture. Thereafter the concept became general both in the Greek and Latin churches. The Jewish idea was expressed technically in terms of a ritualistic formula known as "defiling the hands." The most likely explanation of this enigmatic phrase seems to be that of George Robinson Smith; namely, that the hands that had touched the sacred writings, that is, those that were really God-inspired, were rendered "taboo" with respect to handling anything secular. The high priest (Lev. 16:24) washed not only when he put on the sacred garments on the Day of Atonement but when he took them off. This seems to be the thought; when

writings were holy they were said to "defile the hands."

Contents of the Hebrew Canon. The standard or Masoretic text (MT) of the OT contains twenty-four books, beginning with Genesis and concluding with 2 Chronicles. The arrangement is such that there are only twenty-four books instead of thirty-nine as in the Protestant canon, but the subject matter is exactly the same. In other words, the OT canon of Protestantism is identical with that of the ancient Jews. The only difference is in the order and division of the books. In these matters the Protestant canon has been affected by the LXX, the version of the OT in Gk. dated about 250-160 B.C. The Gk. version divides Samuel, Kings, Chronicles, Ezra-Nehemiah each into two books (making eight instead of four). The twelve minor prophets are divided into twelve instead of being counted as one, as in the Heb. This totals fifteen additional books, accounting for the thirty-nine. Modern Heb. Bibles from the sixteenth century on also have the books divided into thirty-nine but retain the ancient threefold division, Genesis opening and 2 Chronicles closing the canon. The twenty-four-book division of the MT into the *law,* the *prophets,* and the *writings* is as follows:

The Law (5 books)
   Genesis, Exodus, Leviticus, Numbers, Deuteronomy
The Prophets (8 books)
   1. The Former Prophets (4 books) Joshua, Judges, Samuel, Kings
   2. The Latter Prophets (4 books)
      (1) Major (3 books) Isaiah, Jeremiah, Ezekiel
      (2) Minor (1 book): The Twelve: Hosea, Joel, Amos, Obadiah, Jonah, Micah, Nahum, Habakkuk, Zephaniah, Haggai, Zechariah, Malachi
The Writings (11 books)
   1. Poetical (3 books) Psalms, Proverbs, Job
   2. Five Rolls (5 books) Song, Ruth, Lamentations, Ecclesiastes, Esther
   3. Historical (3 books) Daniel, Ezra-Nehemiah, Chronicles

The Critical View of the Formation of the Canon of the Old Testament. This hypothesis, which is a naturalistic attempt to account for the threefold division of the Heb. Scriptures, maintains the gradual development of the Heb. OT under three claims.

The First Claim: The Hebrew Canon First Consisted of the Pentateuch and That Alone.

1. This is implied, the critics contend, in the expressed reverence paid to the Mosaic law in the postexilic writings. The compiler of the Chronicles and Ezra-Nehemiah, it is stated, assumes the authority of the law in its finished form throughout the narration of postexilic history. Malachi

4:4 appeals to the law of Moses as a sacred standard of doctrine for all Israel.

Reply. But there is ample reason for an emphatic reference to the law of Moses after the Exile. The catastrophe of the fall of the Northern Kingdom (2 Kings 17:13-41) and the later captivity of Judah are time and again attributed to infraction of the law and the prophets. These are joined together alike as binding upon Judah and Israel (Isa. 5:24; 30:9; Amos 2:4-6). It would be natural after the restoration to give special attention to that to which former disobedience had brought suffering and captivity. The question of whether or not the law of Moses was received as authoritative centuries before the Exile is not in view. The reason Ezra stresses the law of Moses is that the specific evils current in the young restored community—foreign religions, Sabbath desecration, and neglect of adequate Temple worship (Neh. 10:29)—were covered most comprehensively by the requirements of the law. The prophetic injunctions, although rooted in the Mosaic revelation, were not so direct and pointed.

2. It is suggested, it is contended, in the special deference accorded the Pentateuch in later times. In this connection the critical theory stresses the Torah as the mainstay of Judaism and the object of Antiochus Ephiphanes's wrath (168 B.C.; 2 Macc. 5:16). The Pentateuch was not only the first installment of the translation of the OT into Gk., but the only portion carried out with the accuracy demanded by an authoritative edition. Philo attributes to Moses and the law the highest gift of inspiration.

Reply. It is true that the law is exclusively spoken of in 1 Maccabees as adhered to by the faithful and forsaken by the godless (1:52; 2:21, 26-27), but who would be so bold as to assert on that account that there were no other books in the canon at that late date? As far as the evidence from the LXX is concerned, the fact of an inferior translation for the prophets and the writings as compared with the law, even if it could be proved, might rest upon any number of other factors and not on a supposed noncanonization of the prophets and the writings. Philo's finespun theory of inspiration, like later rabbinical speculations, is mere fancy and offers no real weight.

3. It is implied, the critics say, in the employment of the Torah in the synagogue service. From the Torah alone lessons were systematically read in public services of the synagogue. Not until later times (cf. Luke 4:17-21) were lessons added from the prophets and then only to supplement and illustrate the Torah.

Reply. Readings were confined to the law originally, not because it alone was canonical, but because the divine covenant relation with Israel rested upon it and hinged upon its faithful observation. This alone would give sufficient reason that from the first institution of the synagogue the law should have a place in the worship. It would be only natural that soon selections from the prophets would be attempted to illustrate and amplify the law. The writings (Heb. *kethubim*) were more adaptable for reading on special occasions. The psalms were sung in the Temple and the five rolls were read on festal days. Selections from Job, Ezra-Nehemiah, Chronicles, Daniel, and Proverbs were read throughout the entire night preceding the Day of Atonement.

4. It is implied by the subsequent use of "the law," signifying the whole Heb. canon. This expression is assumed by critics to be a reminiscence of a much earlier usage as well as a recognition of the higher esteem in which the law was held (John 10:34-35; 15:25). Jesus refers to the Psalms as the law. In 1 Cor. 14:21 Isaiah is alluded to under the same designation.

Reply. As the foundation of the whole Hebrew religious and liturgical system, it was natural for the name of the Pentateuch to be figuratively applied to the whole, a part denoting the entirety. With perfect propriety all Scripture may be designated "the law" since it constitutes the revelation of God's purpose and will.

5. The Samaritan Pentateuch points at least to the high probability that around 432 B.C. the Torah (the law) alone was canonical. Why did the Samaritans take only the Pentateuch? The critics see in this anomaly "presumptive evidence" that around 432 B.C. (cf. Neh. 13:29) the Torah alone was canonical among Jerusalem Jews.

Reply. The mutilated canon of the Samaritans evidently originated like heretical sects in general. These groups accept what suits their own particular purposes, arbitrarily rejecting the rest. That the Samaritans did this is suggested by their deliberate alteration of Deut. 27:4 to read Mt. Gerizim instead of Mt. Ebal, in order to get divine sanction for the construction of their rival temple there. Since they deliberately did this, it is scarcely possible that they would have hesitated to reject any part of the sacred canon that spoke approvingly of worship at Shiloh or Jerusalem. Recognizing the force of this argument, Ryle (*The Canon of the Old Testament,* pp. 92-93) suggests the inclusion of books such as Joshua or Hosea that would have been inoffensive to the purposes of the Samaritans, had these writings at that time been canonical. But would a few isolated books outside the Pentateuch have offered any advantage? It would have in reality spoiled the unity and completeness that the Pentateuch afforded. The Samaritans were thus, as W. H. Green clearly remarks (*General Introduction to the Old Testament, The Canon* [1898], p. 100), "necessarily limited to the Pentateuch irrespective of the extent of the Jewish canon at the time."

The Second Claim: The Prophets Were Not Added to the Hebrew Canon Until Between 300 B.C. and 200 B.C. The critical view acknowledges that the steps by which the prophets became canonical over a century and a half after the law "are, indeed, in a great measure hidden from our view" and that the evidence is "scanty" (Ryle, op. cit., pp. 95-96). However, they insist upon the claim.

1. It is implied, they claim, by the unpopularity of the prophets during the canonical period. As long as the prophets were not well received, it is maintained that it was unlikely for their utterances and their writings to have been regarded as having canonical authority. Supposedly not until the power and prestige of the prophets were enhanced toward the end of the exilic period were the prophetic writings collected and canonized. This erroneous presupposition fails to see the real nature of Scripture inspiration. The inspired Word of God possesses intrinsic binding authority and did not have to wait for intervals of time to give it this quality. Moreover, this quality is independent of the popularity or unpopularity of the prophet or the reception or rejection of his message. It is unwarrantedly assumed that "the incorporation of recent or almost contemporary work in the same collection with the older prophets would not have been approved" (Ryle, p. 106). But why should it not have been approved if inspired and thus possessing intrinsic authority? Why did many years have to slip away, for example, before Malachi's writings, written about 445 B.C., would be accepted, as Ryle contends?

2. It is suggested by the date of the compilation of the book of Isaiah. Chapters 1-39 are in the main ascribed to Isaiah, whereas chapters 40-66, considered as non-Isaianic and late postexilic, were added when the prophetical writings were being collected. The real author of this section being completely forgotten, they were simply appended to Isaiah's genuine prophecies.

Reply. Only the critical hypothesis demands a long interval of time to attempt to offer some rational explanation for the unaccountable oblivion of the so-called second Isaiah. Not the internal evidence of the book itself, considered as a genuine work of Isaiah, but the assumptions of the critics, create the unanswerable question: How could so prominent a prophet with such unusual literary skill, who wrote near the end of the Exile, be so completely forgotten that he was confused with another who lived at an entirely different time and under different circumstances?

3. It is implied in the date of the composition of the book of Daniel. Wildeboer concisely states the critical position: "At what time the division of the prophets was closed we are not informed. But on account of Dan. 9:2, whose author, living about 165 B.C., seems to know 'the books' as a collection with definite limits, and because the book of Daniel itself was unable to obtain a place in the second section, we fix the *terminus ad*

quem about 200 B.C." (*Origin of the Canon of the Old Testament* [1895], p. 116).

Reply. The critical date of Daniel, about 167 B.C., is largely dictated by rationalistic presuppositions with regard to miracles and prophecies. There is no valid reason for rejecting the Danielic authorship that the book claims for itself. It is not true that the book was unable to obtain a place in the prophetic section of the canon. The rightful place, according to the Jewish criteria for arranging the threefold division, is in the third division. But if the book was not written until about 167 B.C., it may be asked, How did it gain credence in such a short time as to be quoted in 1 Macc. 2:59-60? Or again it may be asked, Why should it have been translated into Gk. with other canonical books when, according to the uniform admission of the critics, this book would not have been in the canon at all if it were not considered to be the genuine work of the prophet Daniel?

The Third Claim. The Writings Were Not Canonized Until After the Prophets, Between 160 B.C. and 105 B.C. The general position is that no steps were taken toward the formation of a third division until the second was closed. Reasons cited to support this presupposition are as follows:

1. Much time had to elapse after Malachi for the general conviction to crystallize that prophecy had ceased and no more prophets were to be expected. Otherwise, it is contended, Ezra-Nehemiah and Chronicles would have been placed with the other historical books, such as Samuel and Kings, and Daniel would have been inserted with other prophecies into the second section, if that division had not been previously closed when they were finally considered canonical.

Reply. The order of the Heb. canon is not the result of the character or contents of the various books. It is due to the official status or position of their authors. There is no need to assume that the second division was closed and could not be opened to admit these books.

2. The general freedom and inaccuracy of the Gk. rendering of the writings are proof against their canonization before 160 B.C. Dillmann, for example, maintains that the additions to Esther and Daniel in the Gk. and the recasting of Chronicles and Ezra in the apocryphal Esdras furnish evidence that these books were not regarded as authoritative as the law and the prophets.

Reply. It would be strange if stories so vivid and remarkable as Esther and Daniel would not arouse popular imagination. Later Targumic legends connected with the law are answer enough that canonicity is no bar to imaginative additions. The evidence from the LXX has been doubtlessly overdone, and it is a subtle fallacy to assume that canonization always insures accurate translation or precludes imaginative fancy.

3. The evidence of the prologue to Ecclesiasticus is opposed to the canonicity of the writings before 160 B.C. The supposed "vagueness" with

which the author of the prologue about 132 B.C. refers to the third division is construed as a testimony to the late canonization of the writings.

Reply. However, this argument is invalid. So far from an imagined "vagueness," the language is remarkably definite. Actually the designation is comprehensive. By referring to the third division as "the rest of the books" or "the other books of the fathers" the designation is just as unambiguous in the light of the miscellaneous contents of these writings as is the term "the law and the prophets." In fact, this statement in the prologue is in full agreement with the history of Josephus, who, flatly denying the critical hypothesis, asserts that the canon was completed and closed in the days of Artaxerxes (465-425 B.C.) and that since that time "not a soul has ventured to add or to remove or to alter a syllable" of the ancient records (*Contra Apionen* 1:8). There is no proof, despite the theorizing of the critics that, in the long interval between Malachi and the translator of Ecclesiasticus, the third division of the canon was still in the process of formation, much less that it was not formed until 160 B.C. or later.

The Correct and Conservative View of the Development of the Hebrew Canon. The OT books were written with the immediate idea of being held sacred and divinely authoritative. Being divinely inspired, they possessed the stamp of canonicity from the first. The prophets were conscious that they were speaking the Word of God by inspiration. Often they prefix their spoken and written messages with an authoritative "the word of the Lord came," or some similar expression (cf. Ex. 4:15-16; 1 Kings 16:1; 2 Kings 7:1; Jer. 13:1; Ezek. 1:3). Early in the history of Israel, God began the formation of the book that was to constitute the revelation of Himself to man. The Decalogue was inscribed on stone (Deut. 10:4-5), Moses' laws were written in a book (31:24-26), and copies of this book were made (17:18). Samuel also wrote in a book (1 Sam. 10:25). The prophets wrote their inspired message (Jer. 36:32); Ezra read the law publicly (Neh. 8:3). However, the precise way in which the entire group of OT books was set apart and divinely inscribed as the Word of God is hidden from our eyes. Jewish tradition attributes these remarkable achievements to Ezra and the men of the Great Assembly, but these facts are also far from being clear. Because the writings of the prophets, as soon as they were issued, had tremendous authority as inspired Scripture, no formal declaration of their canonicity was needed to give them sanction. The divine author who inspired these writings, we may reasonably believe, acted providentially in behalf of their acceptance by the faithful. However, their inspiration and consequent divine authority were inherent and not dependent on human reception or lapse of time to give them prestige or until there were no more living prophets, *or any other factor.* Canonical authority is not derived from the sanction of Jewish priests and leaders or from the Christian church. *That authority is in itself.*

This view of the formation of the canon, however, is not the mere history of the production of the various books. That OT authors were fully conscious of their inspiration is clear from the internal evidence of the books themselves. There is no need, however, to think that they simply deposited their oracles in the Temple, the oracles thereby immediately being considered part of the sacred canon. Inspired Scripture had to face opposition and sometimes destruction, as Jer. 36:1-32 indicates. Canonization of books is not to be confused with their collection. Books were not made canonical by reason of their collection. They were collected because they were canonical, that is, possessed of divine authority by virtue of their inspired character. It is to be feared that modern scholars, in making the collection and arrangement of Bible books a primary element in canonization, have created an artificial idea that has led to serious misunderstanding and unsound views. The Jews had a canon of Scripture long before their holy writings were formally arranged in the threefold division and as a unified whole.

The real basis of the threefold division of the Heb. Scriptures is evidently the official position of the individual authors. Moses was the writer of the books of the law in the first division. The writers in the second division were those who had the prophetic office, that is, the official status and calling of a prophet, as well as the prophetic gift (the enduement of inspiration). The authors in the third category had the prophetic gift but not the prophetic office. They were not *officially* prophets. David and Solomon were kings; Ezra was a scribe; Daniel, a government official; Nehemiah, a civil governor. This view seems to be the simplest and most satisfactory of all.

The Christian Canon of the Old Testament. In proportion as the Fathers were more or less absolutely dependent on the LXX for their knowledge of OT Scriptures, they gradually lost in common practice the sense of the difference between the books of the Heb. canon and the Apocrypha. The history of the Christian canon is to be sought from definite catalogs and not from isolated quotations. But even this evidence is incomplete and unsatisfactory, few of the catalogs being really independent. They evidently fall into two great classes, Hebrew and Latin; the former, again, exhibits three distinct varieties, which are to be traced to the three original sources from which the catalogs were derived. The first may be called the pure Heb. canon, which is that of the Church of England. The second differs from this by the *omission* of the book of Esther. The third differs by the *addition* of Baruch, or "the letter." During the first four centuries this Heb. canon was the only one that was distinctly recognized, and it was supported by the combined authority of those Fathers whose critical judgment was entitled to the greatest weight. The real divergence as to the contents of the OT canon is to be traced to Augustine, whose wavering and uncertain language on the point furnishes abundant materials for controversy. In the famous passage (*De Doct. Christ.* 2.8 [13]) he enumerates the books that are contained in "the whole canon of Scripture," and includes among them the apocryphal books without any clear mark of dysfunction. The Council of Trent pronounced the enlarged canon, including the apocryphal books, to be deserving in all its parts of "equal veneration," and added a list of books to prevent the possibility of doubt. The Reformed churches agreed in confirming the Heb. canon of Jerome and refused to allow any dogmatic authority to the apocryphal books; but the form in which this judgment was confirmed varied considerably in the different confessions. The English church (Art. 6) appeals directly to the opinion of Jerome, and concedes to the apocryphal books, including 4 Esdras and the Prayer of Manasses, a use "for example of life and instruction of manners," but not for the establishment of doctrine.   M.F.U.

CANOPY. *See* Curtains.

CANTICLES. *See* Song of Solomon.

CAP. The headdress of the priests. *See* Dress: Garments.

CAPERBERRY. The rendering in Eccles. 12:5 (NASB) of Heb. *'ăbiyyônâ,* "provocative of desire," to form the reading "the caperberry is ineffective." The KJV reads "desire shall fade"; the NIV, "desire is no longer stirred." *See* Vegetable Kingdom.

CAPER'NAUM (ka-per'nā-um; "town of Nahum"). A city of Galilee, frequently mentioned by the evangelists in connection with the life of our Lord. It was on the western shore of the "Sea of Galilee" (Matt. 4:13; cf. John 6:24), lower than Nazareth and Cana, from which the road to it was one of descent (John 2:12; Luke 4:31). It was of sufficient size to be called a "city" (Matt. 9:1; Mark 1:33), and had its own synagogue, in which our Lord frequently taught (John 6:59; Mark 1:21; Luke 4:31-38)—a synagogue built by the centurion of the detachment of Roman soldiers that appears to have been quartered in the place (7:2; Matt. 8:8). But besides the garrison there was also a customs station, where the dues were gathered both by stationary (9:9; Mark 2:14; Luke 5:27) and by itinerant (Matt. 17:24) officers.

Capernaum was the residence of Jesus and His apostles, and the scene of many miracles and discourses. At Nazareth He was "brought up," but Capernaum was emphatically His "own city"; it was when He returned to it that He is said to have been "at home" (Mark 2:1). Here He chose the evangelist Matthew, or Levi (Matt. 9:9). The brothers Simon Peter and Andrew belonged to Capernaum (Mark 1:29), and it is perhaps allowable to imagine that it was on the sea beach that they had the quiet call that was to make them forsake all and follow Him (1:16-17; cf. v. 28). Here Christ worked the miracle on the centurion's servant (Matt. 8:5; Luke 7:1-2), on Simon's wife's mother (8:14; Mark 1:30; Luke 4:38), the paralytic (Matt. 9:1-2; Mark 2:1-3; Luke 5:18), and the man afflicted with an unclean demon (Mark 1:32; Luke 4:33). At Capernaum the incident of the child occurred (Mark 9:36-37; Matt. 18:1-6); and in the synagogue there was spoken the wonderful discourse of John 6 (see v. 59).

The doom pronounced against Capernaum and the other unbelieving cities (Matt. 11:23) has been remarkably fulfilled. Tell Hum, its generally accepted site, is an uninhabited place two and a half miles SW of where the Jordan enters the Sea of Galilee. The Franciscans acquired the site in 1894, and in 1905 H. Kohl and C. Watzinger, working for the German Oriental Society, uncovered part of the ruins of the synagogue. From 1905 to 1914 the Franciscan W. Hinterkeuser worked in the area of the synagogue and the octagonal church that stood to the S of it. G. Orfali restored part of the synagogue and worked on the octagonal church from 1921 to 1926. And since 1968 V. Corbo and S. Loffreda have been excavating inside and around the synagogue, on the site of the octagonal church, and on adjacent parts of the town. The dominant structure of Tell Hum is the limestone synagogue, which the excavators have now dated about A.D. 400. Under the floor of this synagogue in 1981 were excavated ruins of a first-century synagogue of basalt. The octagonal church, that stands between the synagogue and the seashore, covers a first-century house that the excavators conclude was the house of Peter.   H.F.V.

BIBLIOGRAPHY: C. C. McCown, *Ladder of Progress in Palestine* (1943), pp. 257-60, 267-72; E. F. F. Bishop, *Catholic Biblical Quarterly* 15 (1953), pp. 427-37; C. Kopp, *The Holy Places of the Gospels* (1963), pp. 171-79.

Capernaum

CAPH'TOR (kaf'tor). The place from which the Philistine groups mentioned by Jeremiah (Jer. 47:4) and Amos (Amos 9:7) originally came. It is probably to be identified with *Kap-ta-ra* or Crete, which under second millennium B.C. Minoan rule controlled the Aegean. The Caphtorim originated in Egypt (Gen. 10:14), and evidently migrated in the third millennium (B.C.) to establish the Minoan civilization with others. Caphtor is described as an "island," or a "coastland." R.K.H.

CAPHTORIM (kaf-tor-im'). The inhabitants of Caphtor or Crete (Deut. 2:23). Originally migrants from Egypt (Gen. 10:14), they formed part of the Sea Peoples, settling finally in Canaan. *See* Philistines.

CAPITAL. In modern architecture, the upper, ornamental part of a column. Once (2 Chron. 3:15) the Heb. *ṣepet,* "to encircle," is so rendered; elsewhere (1 Kings 7:16-20; Jer. 52:22) the term is the rendering of the Heb. *kōteret,* and refers to the capitals of the Temple pillars.

CAPPADO'CIA (kap-a-dō'shi-a). A province in the eastern part of Asia Minor whose boundaries were changed several times by the Roman emperors. In NT history it comprised Lesser Armenia. On the Day of Pentecost it was represented at Jerusalem (Acts 2:9), and Peter refers to it (1 Pet. 1:1); hence its interest for the Bible reader.

CAPSTONE. *See* Cornerstone.

CAPTAIN. This word is the rendering of numerous Heb. and several Gk. words, some of which require special consideration. *See* Shipmaster.

1. Prince or Leader (Heb. *śar;* Gk. *chiliarch;* usually "official" or "leader" in the NIV), a military title (1 Sam. 22:2); also rendered "chief" (Gen. 40:2; 41:9; *see* article Chief), "commander" (2 Sam. 23:19; Dan. 1:7), "ruler" (Judg. 9:30), "governor" (1 Kings 22:26). The "captain of the guard" (Acts 28:16, KJV) was the commander of the pretorian troops. The rank or power of an Israelite captain was designated by the number of men under his command as "captain of fifty," or "captain of a thousand"; and the commander of the whole army was called the "captain of the host." *See* Army; Officer.

2. Ruler (Heb. *qāṣîn;* usually "commander" in the NIV), sometimes denotes a military (Josh. 10:24; Judg. 11:6-11; Isa. 22:3), sometimes a civil, command (Isa. 1:10; 3:6); in Isaiah rendered "ruler," or "leader" (NIV).

3. Adjutant (Heb. *shālîsh*), properly a *third* man, or one of three. Some conclude from this that the term was applied to a higher order of soldiers, who fought from chariots and were so called because each chariot contained *three* soldiers, one of whom managed the horses while the others fought (Ex. 14:7; 2 Sam. 23:8; etc.). Others hold to the opinion that the *shālîsh* were third

officers in rank after the king, or commanded a third part of the army.

4. The "officer" or "captain of the temple" (Luke 22:4; Acts 4:1; 5:24) was not a military officer but a priest who had command of the Levitical Temple police, called by Jewish writers "the man of the temple mount" (Edersheim, *The Temple,* p. 119). His duty was to visit the posts during the night and see that the sentries were doing their duty.

Figurative. Christ is called the "captain of our salvation" (Heb. 2:10, KJV; Gk. *archēgos*), because He is the "author" (NASB and NIV) of His people's salvation and their leader. Jehovah announces Himself to Joshua (5:14) as the "captain of the host," i.e., the head and protector of His people (Dan. 8:11, rendered "commander").

CAPTIVE. Persons taken prisoner during war. As ancient inscriptions and reliefs show, they were treated with great indignities and cruelty. Those who surrendered were led out with halters, as if for execution (1 Kings 20:32); the victors set their feet upon the necks of captured kings and nobles (Josh. 10:24); cut off their thumbs, toes, or ears (Judg. 1:7; 2 Sam. 4:12; Ezek. 23:25) and put out their eyes (2 Kings 25:7). Captives were suspended by the hand (Lam. 5:12); made to lie down and be walked or driven over (Isa. 51:23); thrown among thorns, sawn in two, beaten to pieces with threshing machines, or had severe labor imposed upon them (Judg. 8:7; 2 Sam. 12:31; 1 Chron. 20:3). When a city was captured the men were usually put to death, the women and children sold as slaves (2 Chron. 28:8-15; Ps. 44:12; Isa. 47:3; Joel 3:3; Mic. 1:11) or exposed to most cruel treatment (2 Kings 8:12; Esther 3:13; Isa. 13:16, 18; Nah. 3:5-6; Zech. 14:2). Sometimes the people were transported (2 Kings 24:12-16; Jer. 20:5; 39:9-10) or made tributary (2 Sam. 8:6; 2 Kings 14:14).

CAPTIVITY (properly some form of *shābâ,* to "take captive"; often expressed by other Heb. words). This word may be taken in the strict sense of imprisonment, but in relation to the people of Israel it has come to mean expatriation. Captives and captivity are used in Scripture very much in the sense of exile, yet with the notion that this state of exile was compulsory and that the persons thus exiled were in a dependent and oppressed condition. The violent removal of the entire population of a city or district is not an uncommon event in ancient history and was much more humane than the selling of captives into slavery. Such deportation might arise from one of two motives —the desire to rapidly populate new cities, built for pride or policy; or to break up hostile organizations. In addition to the destruction of national existence such exile was made the more bitter from the sanctity attributed to special places and the local attachment to deity. Removal was thought to sever a people from the care and protection of their god; indeed, it implied the defeat of such deity. Tiglath-pileser of Assyria (745-727 B.C.) inaugurated the practice of transporting whole conquered populations to distant parts of his empire (1 Kings 15:29). In this policy he was followed by many of his royal successors including Sargon, Sennacherib, and Esarhaddon, and by Babylonian rulers, notably Nebuchadnezzar II (605-562 B.C.).

The bondage of Israel in Egypt, and their subjugation at different times by the Philistines and other nations, are sometimes spoken of as captivities; the Jews themselves reckon their national captivities as four—the Babylonian, Persian, Grecian, and Roman. The general use of the term, however, is applied to the forcible deportation of the Jews under the Assyrian or Babylonian kings (Matt. 1:17).

Captivity of Israel. The removal of the ten tribes, though often spoken of as a single event, was a complex process. The larger part of the people were carried away, not to Babylon, but to Assyria. The period during which their removal was gradually effected was not less than 150 years. There were two of these captivities: (1) In the reign of Pekah, king of Israel, Tiglath-pileser III carried away in 732 B.C. the trans-Jordanic tribes (1 Chron. 5:26) and the inhabitants of Galilee (2 Kings 15:29; cf. Isa. 9:1) to Assyria. (2) In the reign of Hoshea, king of Israel, Shalmaneser, king of Assyria, twice invaded (2 Kings 17:3, 5) the kingdom that remained, and his successor Sargon II took Samaria in 722 B.C., carrying away 27,290 of the population as he tells in his Khorsabad Annals. Later Assyrian kings, notably Esarhaddon (681-668 B.C.), completed the task.

Captivity of Judah. The carrying away of the people of Judah was not accomplished at once, either. Sennacherib, about 701 B.C., is stated to have carried into Assyria 200,000 captives from the Jewish cities that he took (2 Kings 18:13). Three distinct deportations are mentioned in 24:14 (including 10,000 persons) and 25:11, one in 2 Chron. 36:20, three in Jer. 52:28-30 (including 4,600 persons), and one in Dan. 1:3. The two principal ones were: (1) when Jehoiachin with all his nobles, soldiers, and artificers were carried away; and (2) that which followed the destruction of Jerusalem and the capture of Zedekiah, 586 B.C. (Albright, 587 B.C.). The three mentioned by Jeremiah may have been contributions from the more distinguished portions of the captives, and the captivity of certain selected "children" (Dan. 1:3), 607 B.C., may have occurred when Nebuchadnezzar was a colleague of his father, Nabopolassar.

Condition of Captives. The condition of the captives must have had many an element of bitterness. They were humiliated with the memory of defeat and present bondage; if faithful to Jehovah they were subject to bitter scorn and derision (Ps. 137:3-5); they were required to pay for their existence in heavy services and tributes; those of high-priestly, noble, or royal origin were treated with indignity (Isa. 43:28; 52:5). On the other hand, they were treated not as slaves but as colonists. There was nothing to hinder a Jew from rising to the highest eminence in the state (Dan. 2:48) or holding the most confidential office near the person of the king (Neh. 1:11; Tobit 1:13, 22). The advice of Jeremiah (29:5; etc.) was generally followed. The exiles increased in numbers and in wealth. They observed the Mosaic law (Esther 2:10; Tobit 14:9). They kept up distinctions of rank among themselves (Ezek. 20:1). Their genealogical tables were preserved, and they were at no loss to tell who was the rightful heir to David's throne. They had neither place nor time of national gathering, no temple, and they offered no sacrifice. But the rite of circumcision and their laws respecting food, etc., were observed; their priests were with them (Jer. 29:1); and possibly the practice of erecting synagogues in every city (Acts 15:21) was begun by the Jews in the Babylonian captivity.

Literature. The captivity had also a contemporaneous literature. Tobit presents a picture of the inner life of a family of Naphtali among the captives of Nineveh. Baruch was written by one whose eyes, like those of Ezekiel, were familiar with the gigantic forms of Assyrian sculpture. Several of the psalms appear to express the sentiments of Jews who were either partakers or witnesses of the Assyrian captivity. But it is from the three great prophets, Jeremiah, Ezekiel, and

Sculpture of the captivity

Daniel, that we learn most of the condition of the children of the captivity.

Duration. Jeremiah (25:12; 29:10) predicted that the captivity should last for seventy years, which has aroused much discussion. The best explanation of the chronological problem involved is that there were two, if not more, coordinate modes of computing the period in question, used by the sacred writers, one *civil,* extending from the first invasion by Nebuchadnezzar to the decree of Cyrus, 605-537 B.C.; and the other *ecclesiastical,* from the burning of the Temple to its reconstruction, 586-515 B.C. The Babylonian captivity was brought to a close by the decree (Ezra 1:2) of Cyrus, 537 B.C. and the return of a portion of the nation under Sheshbazzar, or Zerubbabel, 535 B.C., Ezra, 458 B.C., and Nehemiah, 444 B.C. The number who returned upon the decree of 537 B.C. was 42,360, besides servants. Among them about 30,000 are specified (cf. Ezra 2 and Neh. 7) as belonging to the tribes of Judah, Benjamin, and Levi. It has been inferred that the remaining 12,000 belonged to the tribes of Israel (cf. Ezra 6:17). Those who were left in Assyria (Esther 8:9, 11), and kept up their national distinctions, were known as *The Dispersion* (which see; John 7:35; James 1:1; 1 Pet. 1:1).

The Ten Tribes. Of these little is known. (1) Some returned and mixed with the other Jews (Luke 2:36; Phil. 3:5; etc.). (2) Some were left in Samaria, mingled with the Samaritans (Ezra 6:21; John 4:12), and became bitter enemies of the other Jews. (3) Many remained in Assyria and were recognized as an integral part of the Dispersion (see Acts 2:9; 26:7). (4) Most, probably, apostatized in Assyria, adopted the usages and idolatry of the nations among whom they were planted, and became wholly swallowed up in them.

Cause and Effects of Captivity. The captivity in Babylon was the result that justly befell the covenant people from their becoming assimilated to heathen states. By accepting other gods they broke their covenant with Jehovah and placed themselves beyond His protection. "Repentance, and a return to the ancient, the everlasting, and the true God, from the delirium, the charms, and the seductions of the world, had indeed been for centuries the cry of the best prophets, ever growing in intensity" (Ewald, *Hist. of Israel*). They now came to God in penitence and earnest prayer. The clearest proof of repentance is found in the establishment of four fast days, celebrated in four different months (Isa. 58:3-12; Zech. 7:5; 8:19). Thus the Jews who returned from captivity were remarkably free from the old sin of idolatry, and a great spiritual renovation, in accordance with the divine promise (Ezek. 36:24-28), was wrought in them. A new and deep reverence for at least the letter of the law and the institutions of Moses was probably the result of the religious services in the synagogue. The Exile was also a period of change in the vernacular language of the Jews (see Neh. 8:8), and a new impulse of commercial enterprise and activity was developed.

For an excellent discussion of the chronology of this period see David N. Freedman, "The Babylonian Chronicle," *The Biblical Archaeologist* 19, no. 3 (1956): 5-60.

Captivity Under the Romans. The Jews' fate at the hands of the Romans far better deserves the name of captivity; for, after the massacre of many thousands, the captives were reduced to real bondage. Josephus tells us that 1.1 million men fell in the siege of Jerusalem by Titus, and 97,000 were captured in the whole war. Those under seventeen were sold into private bondage; of the rest some were sent to the Egyptian mines, others into the provinces to be destroyed at the theaters by the sword and wild beasts (*Wars* 6.9.3).

An equally dreadful destruction fell upon the remains of the nation, which had once more assembled in Judea under the reign of Hadrian, and by these two wars the Jewish population must have been effectually extirpated from the Holy Land.

Figurative. "People of the exile" denotes those who were in captivity, or their posterity (Ezra 4:1). "The Lord turned the captivity of Job" (Job 42:10, KJV) means that He released him from his sufferings and restored him to prosperity. "He led captive a host of captives" (Eph. 4:8) is a figurative allusion to the victory of Christ over the enemies of Himself and His kingdom.

Prophetic. The OT speaks of a future restoration of Israel to God's favor in Palestine and as head of the nations in the coming age (the Millennium). Isaiah (11:11) calls it a "second" restoration. The Jews have never been restored but "once" and that was from Babylon. The Egyptian deliverance was not a restoration, because Palestine was never in their possession until conquered by Joshua. The "second" and final restoration will be from their present worldwide dispersion (Isa. 43:5-7; Jer. 16:14-15; 24:6) after the completion of "the times of the Gentiles" (Luke 21:24) at the second advent of Christ (Matt. 24:29-30). It will be a restoration in unbelief (Ezek. 36:24-27) to be followed by judgment and chastening in "a great tribulation" (Jer. 30:4-7; Dan. 12:1; Matt. 24:21-31) previous to their conversion (Zech. 12:10; 1 Cor. 15:8). It will be a national restoration (Ezek. 37:1-22; Rom. 11:25) and will usher in the mediatorial, Davidic, messianic kingdom on earth. This millennial age with the Jew in his God-ordained position as a priestly nation at the head of the nations (Zech. 3:1-10) will constitute the last of God's ordered ages in time (Rev. 20:1-10) before the dawn of the eternal state (Rev. 21-22).　　M.F.U.

BIBLIOGRAPHY: C. F. Pfeiffer, *Exile and Return* (1962); P. R. Ackroyd, *Exile and Restoration* (1968).

CARBUNCLE. A KJV term. It is replaced in the NASB and NIV by either *crystal* or *emerald. See* Mineral Kingdom.

CARCAS (car'cas). One of the seven eunuchs of King Ahasuerus (or Xerxes, NIV) of Persia (Esther 1:10).

CARCASS. The dead body of man or beast. According to the Mosaic law: (1) The dead body of a human being rendered unclean the tent (or house) in which the man had died, with any open vessels therein, for seven days. It was no less defiling to touch the dead. (2) Contact with the carcass of any animal rendered the one touching, carrying, or eating it unclean until evening (Lev. 11:39). For fuller particulars, *see* Uncleanness; Dead, The.

CAR'CHEMISH (kar'kem-ish). A Hittite city on the right bank of the Euphrates commanding one of the best fords of that river (Isa. 10:9; Jer. 46:2). Located about sixty miles NE of Aleppo, the site was excavated by Sir Leonard Woolley and T. E. Lawrence for the British Museum. An important Hittite culture was revealed, and the city formed the E capital of the Hittite Empire. It lay just W of Haran and may have been visited by Abraham on his trek to Palestine. Sargon II of Assyria (c. 718 B.C.) took Carchemish. To this place Josiah went to do battle with Pharaoh Neco of Egypt (2 Chron. 35:20-22). And it was here that Nebuchadnezzar II defeated Neco (605 B.C.), the event that inaugurated the splendid neo-Babylonian Empire and presaged the Babylonian captivity of the Southern Kingdom.   M.F.U.

BIBLIOGRAPHY: D. G. Hogarth and C. L. Woolley, *Carchemish*, 3 vols. (1914-52); D. J. Wiseman, *Chronicles of the Chaldaean Kings* (1956); J. Pritchard, ed., *Ancient Near Eastern Texts* (1969), pp. 240-42, 275-79, 283-85.

CARE, CARES (Gk. *merimma*). The Gk. word has the sense of being drawn in different directions, and answers to our *distraction.* It is translated "anxiety" in 1 Pet. 5:7, where it is contrasted with *melō,* to "be of interest" to, and may be read, "Casting all your anxiety upon Him, because He cares for you" (cf. Ps. 55:23; Luke 8:14; 21:34). In Matt. 13:22 and Mark 4:19, the "worries of the world" are anxiety about things pertaining to this earthly life. Paul uses the same word, "concern for all the churches" (2 Cor. 11:28).

CARE'AH. *See* Kareah.

CARITES (car'ītes). Probably the same as the Kerethites or the *Cherithites* (which see).

CAR'MEL (kar'mel; a plant, "field, park, garden").
    1. As a common noun, rendered "fruitful garden" or "fertile field" (Isa. 10:18; 29:17; 32:15-16), "fruitful field" (Isa. 16:10; Jer. 48:33), "fruitful land" (2:7). In 2 Kings 19:23; 2 Chron. 26:10, KJV, it is incorrectly rendered as a proper name,

"Carmel" (NASB, "fertile fields"; NIV, "fertile lands").
    2. A prominent headland of Palestine, bounding on the S the Bay of Acre, and running out almost into the Mediterranean, bearing about S-SE for more than 12 miles, ending suddenly by an eastern bluff. Its average height is 1,500 feet. Carmel fell within the lot of the tribe of Asher (Josh. 19:26), which was extended as far S as Dor, probably to give the Asherites a share of the rich grain-growing plain of Sharon. The king of "Jokneam in Carmel" was one of the Canaanite chiefs who fell before the arms of Joshua. From earliest times the gardenlike loveliness of Carmel was sacred to the Canaanite Baal and other oracles.

View from Mt. Carmel

    That which has made Carmel most familiar is its connection with the history of Elijah and Elisha. Here Elijah brought back Israel to allegiance to Jehovah and killed the prophets of the foreign and false god (1 Kings 18:20-40). Here Elisha received the visit of the bereaved mother whose son he was soon to restore to her arms (2 Kings 4:25). Carmel may have been the location of an incident that took place near the end of Elijah's life: fire coming "down from heaven" and consuming the two "fifties" of the guard Ahaziah had dispatched to take Elijah prisoner, for having stopped the messengers to Baalzebub the god of Ekron (1 Kings 1:9-15).
    Carmel is still clothed with the same excellency of wood that supplied the prophets of Israel and Judah alike with one of their most favorite illustrations (Isa. 33:9; Mic. 7:14, see marg.).

3. A town in the mountainous country of Judah (Josh. 15:55), familiar as the residence of Nabal (1 Sam. 25:2, 5, 7, 40), and the native place of David's favorite wife, "Abigail the Carmelitess" (1 Sam. 27:3; 1 Chron. 3:1). This was doubtless the Carmel at which Saul set up "a monument" after his victory over Amalek (1 Sam. 15:12). It is now called Kermel, about nine miles SE of Hebron.

CAR'MELITE (kar'mel-īt). The designation of Nabal (1 Sam. 30:5; 2 Sam. 2:2; 3:3) and his wife Abigail (1 Sam. 27:3; 1 Chron. 3:1, "Carmelitess"); also of Hezro, one of David's warriors (2 Sam. 23:35), probably from being an inhabitant of *Carmel* (which see) in Judah.

CAR'MI (kar'mi; "vine-dresser").
1. The fourth son of Reuben (Gen. 46:9; Ex. 6:14), about 1870 B.C. His descendants were called Carmites (Num. 26:6).
2. The son of Hezron (Judah's grandson), and father of Hur (1 Chron. 4:1). He is elsewhere called Caleb (2:18), or Chelubai (2:9).
3. The son of Zabdi (of the tribe of Judah), and father of Achan, the traitor (Josh. 7:1; 1 Chron. 2:7), before 1400 B.C.

CAR'MITES (kar'mīts). The patronymic of the descendants of *Carmi* (which see), the Reubenite (Num. 26:6).

CARNAL. *See* Flesh.

CARNELIAN (car-nē'lyan). A precious stone rendered by "sardius" in the NASB. *See* Mineral Kingdom: Sardis.

CAROUSE (Gk. *kōmos*, a "carousel"). In the Gk. writings, this term referred to a nocturnal and riotous procession of half-drunken people who paraded after supper through the streets with torches and music in honor of Bacchus or some other deity, and sang and played before the houses of their friends; hence it was used generally of feasts and drinking parties that were protracted into the night and during which people indulged in revelry (Rom. 13:13; Gal. 5:21; 1 Pet. 4:3).

CARPENTER (Heb. *ḥārāsh*, "artisan," 2 Sam. 5:11; 1 Chron. 14:1; etc.; Gk. *tektōn*, Matt. 13:55; Mark 6:3). A general term, including an artificer in stone and metal, as well as wood. *See* Handicrafts: Builders; Wood, Workers in.

CAR'PUS (kar'pus; "fruit"). A Christian of Troas with whom the apostle Paul states that he left a cloak (2 Tim. 4:13), probably when passing through Asia Minor for the last time before his martyrdom at Rome.

CARRION VULTURE. *See* Animal Kingdom: Vulture.

CARSHE'NA (kar-she'na). The first named of the seven "wise men" or chief rulers of the court of Xerxes (Ahasuerus), with whom he consulted as to what course he should pursue toward Vashti, who had refused to appear at the royal banquet (Esther 1:14). The name is evidently Old Persian, signifying "plowman."

CART (Heb. *'ăgālâ*), something "revolving"; sometimes rendered "chariot," Ps. 46:9; "wagon," Gen. 45:19, 21, 27; 46:5). A two-wheeled vehicle used for transporting persons (Gen. 45:19; Num. 7:8) or freight (1 Sam. 6:7-8). Carts were drawn by cattle (2 Sam. 6:3, 6) and are to be distinguished from the war chariots drawn by horses. The wheels were sometimes made of solid blocks of wood, sometimes with spokes, as represented on the monuments of Egypt and Nineveh.

Ox cart

Figurative. The expression "Woe to those who drag iniquity . . . and sin as if with cart ropes" (Isa. 5:18) is understood by some to refer to the binding of burdens upon carts, and so to the enslaving power of sin. Others use "cart rope" in the sense of a trace and think that the metaphor is used to illustrate the heavy burdens that must be drawn by the sinner.

CARVE, CARVING. *See* Handicrafts.

CASEMENT. *See* articles Lattice; House.

CASIPH'IA (ka-sif'i-a). A "place" of the Persian Empire where Levites settled during the captivity, and where Iddo and others joined Ezra (Ezra 8:17). Its location is unknown.

CAS'LUHIM (kas'lū-him), **Cas'luhites** (NIV). Mizraite people or tribe (Gen. 10:14). The only clue we have as yet to the position of the Casluhim is their place in the list of the sons of Mizraim between the Pathrusim and the Caphtorim, making it probable that they were located in Upper Egypt.

CASSIA. *See* Vegetable Kingdom.

CASTANETS. *See* Music.

CASTAWAY. *See* Disqualified.

CASTLE. In addition to its meaning of fortress or stronghold (1 Chron. 11:7), castles were, probably, towers used by the priests for observation and for making known, through the sounding of trumpets, anything discovered at a distance (1 Chron. 6:54). The "castles" in the KJV of Gen. 25:16 may have been enclosures for flocks or cattle, watchtowers from which shepherds watched their flocks. The NASB and NIV render "camps." The "castle" in the KJV of Acts 21:34 refers to the barracks (so NASB and NIV) of the Roman soldiers in the fortress of Antonia, adjacent to the Temple.

CAST METAL SEA. *See* Laver; Sea, Bronze.

CAS'TOR AND POL'LUX (kas'tor and pol'ux). The Dioscuri, i.e., sons of Jupiter; Castor being a horse-tamer, and Pollux (Gk. *Polydeucēs*) the master of the art of boxing. They were the ideal types of bravery and dexterity in fight and thus became the tutelary gods of warlike youth. They were supposed to lend their aid to the mariner, who, in case of a storm, prayed to them, and vowed to sacrifice a lamb to them as soon as the storm ceased. The ship in which Paul sailed from Malta had Castor and Pollux for its figurehead (Acts 28:11).

CASTOR OIL PLANT. *See* Vegetable Kingdom.

CAT. *See* Animal Kingdom.

CATERPILLAR. *See* Animal Kingdom: Locust.

CATHOLIC EPISTLES. At the end of the epistles stand seven—James, 1 and 2 Peter, 1, 2, 3 John, and Jude—which bear the name of *catholic,* or *general.* This title is inaccurate, for two of them, 2 and 3 John, are addressed to individuals, and two more to a designated circle of readers; James to "the twelve tribes who are dispersed abroad" and 1 Peter to "those who reside as aliens, scattered throughout," etc. The following explanations have been given of the term: (1) these epistles are "general letters of instruction, the name at first applied only to a part, but afterward including even those addressed to private persons"; (2) because the different apostles wrote them; (3) because of the *catholic* doctrine taught in them; (4) 1 Peter and 1 John, having from the beginning been received as authentic, obtained the distinction of being *catholic,* or universally accepted; as the others came to be thus received, they also were called catholic.

BIBLIOGRAPHY: P. J. Gloag, *Introduction to the Catholic Epistles* (1887); C. R. Erdman, *The General Epistles* (1918); J. Calvin, *Commentaries on the Catholic Epistles* (1959); D. E. Hiebert, *An Introduction to the Non-Pauline Epistles* (1962). For individual commentaries see *The Minister's Library* (1985), pp. 216-26.

CATTLE. *See* Animal Kingdom.

CAVALRY. *See* Army; War.

CAU'DA (caw'da). *See* Clauda.

CAUL. A KJV term replaced in the NASB by (1) "lobe of the liver" (Lev. 3:4; lit., "surplus tissue"); "chest" (Hos. 13:8); and "headbands" (Isa. 3:18), and in the NIV by "covering of the liver,"

"rip them open," and "headbands," respectively.

CAUSEWAY (Heb. *mᵉsillâ* from *sālal,* to "throw up"). A KJV term referring to the "ascending highway" (NASB), or "upper road" (NIV), leading from the lower city up to the Temple site (1 Chron. 26:16, 18). In the NASB of 2 Chron. 9:4, 11, it is called a "stairway" and "steps."

CAVE. The chalky limestone of which the rocks of Syria and Palestine chiefly consist presents, as in the case in all limestone formations, a vast number of caverns and natural fissures, many of which have also been artificially enlarged and adapted to various purposes, both of shelter and defense. The most remarkable caves noticed in Scripture are: (1) that in which Lot dwelt after the destruction of Sodom (Gen. 19:30); (2) the cave of Machpelah (23:17); (3) cave of Makkedah (Josh. 10:16); (4) cave of Adullam (1 Sam. 22:1); (5) cave of Engedi (24:3); (6) the cave in which Obadiah concealed the prophets (1 Kings 18:4), which was probably in the northern part of the country, where abundant caves fit for such a purpose might be pointed out; (7) Elijah's cave in Horeb (19:9), the locality of which cannot be determined; (8, 9) the rock sepulchers of Lazarus and of our Lord (John 11:38; Matt. 27:60).

Caves were used as habitations (Num. 24:21; Song of Sol. 2:14; Jer. 49:16; Obad. 3), as places of refuge (Judg. 6:2; 1 Sam. 14:11), and as prisons (Isa. 24:22; Zech. 9:11). *See also* Cottage; Dwelling.

CEDAR. *See* Vegetable Kingdom.

CEDRON. *See* Kidron.

CELLAR. An underground vault for storage of wine and oil (1 Chron. 27:27-28). The NIV, however, renders "wine vats" here. The word is also used to denote the *treasury* of the Temple (1 Kings 7:51) and of the king (14:26). *See* House.

CEN'CHREA (sen'kre-a; "millet"). The eastern harbor of Corinth, the modern name of which is still Kenchreae, although the popular name is Kikries. It is about eight miles from Corinth. Paul once sailed from this port (Acts 18:18). He also makes reference in Rom. 16:1 to the church established there.

CENSER (Heb. *mahtâ,* a "firepan"; *miqteret,* "vessel for burning incense," from *qātar,* "burn incense"). The vessel upon which the incense was burned in the sanctuary, and which was appointed to be set every morning on the altar of incense when the priest went in to trim the lamps and again when he lighted them in the evening (Ex. 30:7-8). Yearly, on the Day of Atonement, the high priest entered the Holy of Holies, bearing the censer, and threw upon the burning coals the incense, holding the censer in his hand while the incense burned (Lev. 16:12-13).

No description is given of the censer, and therefore we are left in doubt as to its form and appearance. The probability is that, inasmuch as all fire upon which incense was burned was taken from the "bronze altar," every censer had a handle by which it could be carried. They are mentioned among the vessels of the Tabernacle, which were to be wrapped up in proper coverings when the order was given to march (Num. 4:14, NASB and NIV, "firepans"); and from Lev. 10:1; Num. 16:6, 17, in which each ministering priest is spoken of as having his censer, it would seem that they existed in considerable numbers.

As to material, the censers were made of "bronze," and from the fact that the censers of the rebels were used as plates to cover the altar (16:38-39) it would seem that they were simply square sheets, folded at the corners like the modern sheet-iron pan. Solomon prepared "firepans of pure gold" for the Temple (1 Kings 7:50; 2 Chron. 4:22). In Rev. 5:8; 8:3, 5, the angel is represented with a golden censer.

The word *thumiastērion,* "place of fumigation," is rendered "censer" in the KJV of Heb. 9:4; more correctly, "altar of incense" in the NASB and NIV.

CENSUS. This term does not occur in the KJV, although found in the original (Matt. 17:25, *kēnsos,* KJV, "tribute"). The act is, however, referred to in the Heb. *mipqād,* or *peqūddâ,* "numbering"; and the Gk. *apographē,* "enrollment."

Old Testament. According to the law of Moses (Ex. 30:12-14) every male Israelite of twenty years old and upward was enrolled in the army and was to pay half a shekel as atonement money. The following instances of a census being taken are given in the OT: (1) Under the express direction of God (Ex. 38:26), in the third or fourth month after the Exodus during the encampment at Sinai, chiefly for the purpose of raising money for the Tabernacle. The numbers then taken amounted to 603,550 men. (2) In the second month of the second year after the Exodus (Num. 1:2-3). This census was taken for a double purpose: (a) To ascertain the number of fighting men from the age of twenty to fifty. (b) To ascertain the amount of the redemption offering due on account of all the firstborn, both of persons and cattle. The Levites, whose numbers amounted to 22,000, were taken in lieu of the firstborn males of the rest of Israel, whose numbers were 22,273, and for the surplus of 273, a money payment of 1,365 shekels, or five shekels each, was made to Aaron and his sons (3:39, 51). (3) Thirty-eight years afterward, previous to the entrance into Canaan, when the total number, excepting the Levites, amounted to 601,730 males, showing a decrease of 1,870 (26:51). (4) In the reign of David the men of Israel above twenty years of age were 800,000, and of Judah 500,000, total 1,300,-000. The book of Chronicles gives the numbers of Israel 1,100,000, and of Judah 470,000, total 1,570,000, but informs us that Levi and Benjamin were not numbered (1 Chron. 21:6; 27:24). The time of this census belongs undoubtedly to the closing years of David's reign. The wrong of this census is thought by some to have consisted in the omission to collect the atonement money (see above), but the following explanation seems the correct one: "The true kernel of David's sin was to be found, no doubt, in self-exaltation, inasmuch as he sought for the strength and glory of his kingdom in the number of the people and their readiness for war" (K. & D., *Com.,* 2 Sam. 24:1-9). (5) The census of David was completed by Solomon by causing the foreigners and remnants of the conquered nations resident within Palestine to be numbered. Their number amounted to 153,600 (1 Kings 5:15; 2 Chron. 2:17-18), and they were employed in forced labor on great architectural works (Josh. 9:27; 1 Kings 9:20-21; 1 Chron. 22:2). The numbers in the armies under the several kings between Solomon and the captivity assist us in estimating the population at the various times referred to. The census taken of those who returned with Zerubbabel was to settle the inheritances in Palestine and to ascertain the family genealogies. The number was 42,360 (Ezra 2:64).

New Testament. Luke, in his account of the "taxing," says a decree went out from Augustus that "a census be taken of all the inhabited earth" and in the Acts alludes to a disturbance raised by Judas of Galilee in the days of the "census" (Luke 2:1-2; Acts 5:37). The Roman census under the Republic consisted, so far as the present purpose is concerned, in an enrollment of persons and property by tribes and households.

The Gk. expression *apographē* (Luke 2:2; Acts 5:37; "taxing," KJV), referred to an enrollment (or registration) in the public records of persons, together with their property and income, as the basis of an *apotimēsis,* "census," or valuation, i.e., that it might appear how much tax should be levied upon each one. Another form of the same Gk. verb (*apographesthai*) is used in Heb. 12:23, "To the general assembly and church of the first-born, who are enrolled." The English word conveys to us more distinctly the notion of a tax or tribute actually levied, but it appears to have been used in the sixteenth century for the simple assessment of a subsidy upon the property of a given county, or the registration of the people for the purpose of a poll tax. The word *apographē* by itself leaves undetermined the question whether the returns made were of population or property. In either case "census" would have seemed the most natural Latin equivalent. Two distinct registrations, or taxings, are mentioned in the NT, both of them by Luke. The first is said to have been the result of an edict of the emperor Augustus, that "a census be taken of all the inhabited earth" (Luke 2:1), and is connected by the evangelist with the name of Cyrenius, or *Quirinius* (which see). The second, and more important (Acts 5:37), is distinctly associated, in point of time, with the revolt of Judas of Galilee. The account of Josephus brings together the two names that Luke keeps distinct, with an interval of several years between them.

BIBLIOGRAPHY: W. M. Ramsay, *Was Christ Born in Bethlehem?* (1898); E. M. Blaiklock, *The Century of the New Testament* (1962); id., *Archaeology of the New Testament* (1970).

CENT. A unit of money. *See* Metrology.

CENTURION. The captains of the sixty *centuries* (companies of one hundred men) in the Roman legion. The centurion carried a staff of vinewood as his badge of office. There were various degrees of rank among the centurions according as they belonged to the three divisions of the *triarii, principes,* and *hastati,* and led the first or second *centuria* of one of the thirty *manipuli.* The first centurion mentioned in Scripture is the one who in our Lord's early ministry sent a request that He would heal his dying servant (Matt. 8:5-10). The other is Cornelius, an early convert to Christianity (Acts 10:1). Others are mentioned (Luke 7:2, 6; also in Acts). *See* Army.

CE'PHAS (sē'fas; Aram. "rock, stone"). A surname that Christ bestowed upon Simon Peter (John 1:42; 1 Cor. 1:12, 3:22; 9:5; 15:5).

CERTIFICATE OF DEBT (Gk. *cheirographon,* "what one has written with his own hand"). Applied figuratively in Col. 2:14 to the Mosaic law, which shows men to be chargeable with offenses for which they must pay the penalty. KJV, "the handwriting of ordinances." The NIV renders "the written code."

CE'SAR. *See* Caesar. **Cesare'a.** *See* Caesarea.

CHAFF. Most generally "chaff" is the rendering of the Heb. *môṣ,* the refuse of winnowed grain, consisting of husks and broken straw. In the East it was the custom to burn chaff, in case, with the changing wind, it might be blown again among the grain (Job 21:18; Pss. 1:4; 35:5; Isa. 17:13; 29:5; 41:15; Hos. 13:3; Zeph. 2:2).

In Isaiah (33:11) the word rendered "chaff" is *ḥāshash* and means "dry grass, hay." It only occurs in the above passage.

Hebrew *teben,* "chaff" in the KJV of Jer. 23:28 (but "straw" in the NASB and NIV), is elsewhere translated "straw" (Ex. 5:7-10; KJV, NASB, NIV). The "stubble" mentioned in Job 21:18 is *cut straw. See also* Vegetable Kingdom.

In Daniel (2:35) the Aram. word *'ûr* occurs.

Figurative. From its being the lighter and, comparatively speaking, worthless portion of the grain, *chaff* is used in Scripture as an emblem of that which is, in doctrine or morals, of a similar nature; of false teaching, evildoers, who must come to naught (Ps. 1:4; Isa. 33:11; Matt. 3:12).

CHAIN. The rendering of several Heb. and Gk. words. From ancient times chains have been used, as at present, both for ornament, bondage, and badges of office.

Badge of Office. Instances of such are the golden chain on Joseph's neck (Gen. 41:42; Heb. *rābîd,* NASB, "necklace," lit., "collar") and the one promised to Daniel (Dan. 5:7; Aram. *hamᵉnûkā',* "necklace"). In Egypt it was one of the insignia of a judge, who wore an image of truth attached to it; it was also worn by the prime minister. In Persia it was considered not only a mark of royal favor, but a token of investiture. In Ezek. 16:11 the chain or necklace is mentioned as the symbol of sovereignty.

Ornamental. Chains for ornamental purposes were worn by men, as well as women, in many countries, both of Europe and Asia, and probably this was the case among the Hebrews (Prov. 1:9; Heb. *'ānāq,* "neck," NASB, "ornaments about your neck"). In addition to necklaces of pearls, corals, etc., other chains were worn (Judith 10:4), hanging down as far as the waist or even lower. Mention is made of "ankle chains" (Isa. 3:20; Heb. *ṣᵉ'ādôt,* "step-chains," rendered "ornaments of the legs"), which were attached to ankle-rings to shorten the step and give it elegance.

Chains. Chains were used to confine prisoners in a manner similar to our handcuffs (Judg. 16:21; 2 Sam. 3:34; Jer. 39:7; Heb. *nᵉḥōshet,* "bronze chains," sometimes rendered "fetters"). The Romans frequently fastened the prisoner with a light chain to the soldier guarding him, as was the case with Paul (Acts 28:20; Eph. 6:20; 2 Tim. 1:16); and when the utmost security was desired two chains were used (Acts 12:6). Isaiah speaks (Isa. 40:19) of silver chains in connection with idols, which may have been for ornament or to fasten them to their shrines.

Figurative. Chains are used as a symbol of oppression or punishment (Ps. 149:8; Lam. 3:7; Ezek. 7:23; etc.).

CHALCE'DONY (kal-sē'do-ni). *See* Mineral Kingdom.

CHAL'COL. *See* Calcol.

CHALDE'A (kal-dē'a; from Accad. *kaldu*). Originally a small territory in southern Babylonia at the head of the Persian Gulf, but later, after the neo-Babylonian Empire of Nebuchadnezzar II (605-562 B.C.), the term came to include practically all of Babylonia extending N of Hit southward to the gulf.   M.F.U.

CHALDEAN (kal-dē'an). A native of Chaldea. *See* Babylonia. The Chaldeans were a warlike, aggressive people from the mountains of Kurdistan. Apparently they were Haldians (or Khaldians), the inhabitants of Urartu, that is, Ararat or Armenia. The ancient Chaldeans are mentioned in the Babylonian inscriptions. They began to appear in Assyrian notices in the reign of Ashurnasirpal II (883-859 B.C.), though their existence as a people goes back well beyond 1000 B.C. When Tiglath-pileser III (745-727 B.C.) became king of Assyria he conquered Babylon. Here the Chaldeans and roving Aramaean tribes were constantly disturbing the native king. In 731 B.C. Ukinzer, who came from one of the Chaldean cities, made himself king of Babylon. However, he was deposed by Tiglath-pileser III in 728 B.C., who ascended the throne of Babylon and ruled under the name of Pul. Pul was followed on the Assyrian throne by Shalmaneser IV (726-722 B.C.). He was in turn succeeded on the throne of Babylon by Merodach-Baladan, a Chaldean. Merodach-Baladan was conquered by Sargon but continued as king until 709 B.C., when the latter became king of Babylon as well as of Assyria. At the time of Hezekiah (702 B.C.), Merodach-Baladan, son of Baladan, ruled in Babylon. It was not until about 625 B.C. that Chaldean power began to assert itself over Assyria. Nabopolasser at that time rebelled against Assyria and established the new Babylonian Empire. He reconstructed the city of Babylon. In the fourteenth year of his reign (612 B.C.) with Cyaxares the Mede and the Scythian king he captured Nineveh and laid it waste (cf. Nah. 3:1-3). In 605 B.C. he was succeeded by his son Nebuchadnezzar II. Under Nebuchadnezzar, Judah and Jerusalem were carried captive to Babylon, and the Chaldean armies overran the Fertile Crescent, with Nebuchadnezzar making the Babylon of his day the most splendid city of antiquity (cf. Dan. 4:30). Nebuchadnezzar was succeeded by his son Evil-Merodach (562-560 B.C.), who was murdered by his brother-in-law Neriglissar (560-558 B.C.). The next king, Labashi-Marduk, reigned only three months and was succeeded by the usurper Nabonidus, whose son Belshazzar (Dan. 5) was coregent until the fall of the Chaldean Empire in 539 B.C.   M.F.U.

BIBLIOGRAPHY: D. J. Wiseman, *Chronicles of the Chaldaean Kings* (1956); H. W. F. Saggs, *The Greatness That Was Babylon* (1962); G. Roux, *Ancient Iraq* (1964).

CHALDEAN ASTROLOGERS. Because of their proficiency in the science of astronomy and their skillful practice of astrology, the Chaldeans became a special caste of *astrologers*. In this sense the word is used in the book of Daniel (2:2, 10; 4:7; etc.; NASB, "conjurers"; NIV, "astrologers"). The explanation of this specialized name is easily understood. From 625 B.C. onward the Chaldeans held complete sway in Babylonia. The city of Babylon was their capital and was the center of intellectual life in all western Asia. This intellectual activity was used especially in the study of the stars, both scientific and as a means of divination. Astronomy and astrology were both sought after in the land. Hence Babylon became famous as the home of all sorts of magicians, sorcerers, diviners, and other occultists. As scientists the

Chaldeans founded the exact science of astronomy. For more than 360 years they kept meticulous astronomical records. One of their astounding contributions was to reckon a year of 365 days, six hours, fifteen minutes and forty-one seconds, a calculation that measures within thirty minutes of what modern instruments have worked out. As the Chaldeans reigned in Babylon, it was perfectly natural that they should give their name to the astrologers as well as astronomers who had made the city famous. *See also* Magic.   M.F.U.

CHAL'DEE (kal'dî). *See* Aramaic.

CHALDEES (kal'dîz). This is a variant form of the term *Chaldeans* used in the expression "Ur of the Chaldees" (Neh. 9:7). The qualifying phrase "of the Chaldees [Chaldeans]" is not an anachronism as many critics hold (cf. Finegan, *Light from the Ancient Past* [1946], p. 57). Instead, as in the case of numerous archaic place names, it is a later scribal gloss to explain to a subsequent age, when Abraham's native city Ur and its location had utterly perished, that the city was located in southern Babylonia, then known as Chaldea. After 1000 B.C. the race of the Chaldeans became dominant, and it was, of course, quite natural for the Hebrew scribe to define the then-incomprehensible foreign name by an appellation customary in his own day. Genesis 14 (vv. 2-3, 7-8, 17) offers a good example of such scribal glosses to explain archaic place names.   M.F.U.

CHALK STONES. *See* Mineral Kingdom.

CHAMBER (Heb. ḥuppâ, "canopy"). A bridal couch with curtains (Ps. 19:5; Joel 2:16). The same word is employed by the Jews today for the canopy under which the marriage ceremony is still performed. Also refers to an apartment of a *house* (which see).

Figurative. The term *chamber* is used metaphorically in Pss. 104:3, 13 for the heavens.

The expression "enter into my chambers," etc. (Isa. 26:20, NASB, "rooms"), is figurative of earnest prayer.

The "chambers of the south" (Job 9:9) are the constellations, or, perhaps, in a more general sense, the regions of the southern sky.

"Chambers of imagery" (Heb. "image storerooms," Ezek. 8:12, NASB, "room of his carved images"; NIV, "shrine of his own idol") is used by the prophet to denote the vision that he had of the idolatrous practices of the Jews in Jerusalem. "Image chambers" is the term applied to the rooms or closets in the houses of the people in which idolatrous images were set up and secretly worshiped.

CHAMBERING (Gk. *koitē*, "beds"). A KJV term occurring in Rom. 13:13, where it signifies lewd and licentious conduct, especially illicit intercourse. The NIV renders "sexual immorality."

CHAMBERLAIN (Heb. *sārîs*, "castrated," sometimes translated *"eunuch,"* which see). An officer confidentially employed about the person of the sovereign, such as Potiphar (Gen. 39:1). This officer was introduced into the court by Solomon (1 Kings 4:6; 16:9; 18:3; "over the household"). His duty seems at first to have been the superintendence of the palace and royal etiquette. Later this post became one of special and increasing influence, including the right of introduction to the king. He thus became the chief minister.

Erastus, the "chamberlain" of the city of Corinth, was one of those whose salutations to the Roman Christians are given (Rom. 16:23, NASB, "city treasurer"; NIV, "director of public works"; Gk. *oikonomos*). The office was apparently that of public treasurer or *arcarius*. The *arcarii* were inferior magistrates having charge of the public chest and were under the authority of the Senate.

Blastus, Herod's chamberlain (Acts 12:20; Gk. *koitōn*), was the chief *valet de chambre* of the king and by reason of his office had great influence with Herod.

CHAMELEON. *See* Animal Kingdom.

CHAMOIS. *See* Animal Kingdom: Mountain Sheep.

CHAMPION (Heb. *gibbôr*, 1 Sam. 17:51; elsewhere "mighty man"). The Heb. phrase, rendered "champion" in 17:4, 23, literally is a "man between the two," a go-between, a challenger. So Goliath went between the armies of the Hebrews and Philistines, as the champion of the latter.

CHANCE. The use of this word in Scripture has the sense of to *meet unexpectedly* (2 Sam. 1:6), an occurrence for which there seems to be no explanation (1 Sam. 6:9), a *coincidence* (Luke 10:31), *opportunity* (Eccles. 9:11).

CHANCELLOR. *See* Commander.

CHANNEL. The bed of the sea, or of a river (Ps. 18:15; Isa. 8:7; Heb. *'āpîq*, "valley"). *See* Conduit.

CHAOS. A term not used in Scripture (though see Isa. 34:11, NIV), but in frequent use to designate the unformed mass of primeval matter mentioned in Gen. 1:2. It comes from the Gk. *chaos* ("immeasurable space") and is used by Hesiod for the unfathomable gulf that was supposed to be the first of existing things. Some cosmogonies, such as the Phoenician, retain the biblical terms descriptive of chaos but changed into personal existences; e.g., the Heb. term *bōhû,* "emptiness," is transformed into *Baau,* the producing principle. According to Greek mythology, from chaos arose the Earth, Tartarus, and Love, also Erebus and Night. Ovid describes chaos as a confused mass, containing the elements of all things that were formed out of it. The great majority of the cosmogonies, however, are atheistic, ascrib-

ing creation to inherent ability in matter or to a blind necessity; whereas the Scriptures make it the act of God.

In Babylonian thought, however, matter and spirit are identified with each other and confused. Apsu (male) and Tiamat (female) are not only conceived as gods (spirit) but as cosmic forces (matter). Apsu is the primeval fresh water ocean and Tiamat, the primordial salt water ocean. Their union produces the gods and the universe. Tiamat (chaos) in her war with Marduk is slain and her corpse made into kosmos. Tiamat and *tehôm,* "the deep" of Gen. 1:2, are etymologically equivalent, but whereas the former is a mythical personality confused with matter, the latter is a common noun, without any mythological connotation whatever and simply describes the entire chaotic mass out of which the waters above the firmament were separated on the second day and out of which the dry land emerged on the third day. *Tiamat* and *tehôm,* although cognate, are independent of each other, and both go back to a common proto-Semitic form.

M.F.U.

CHAPITER. A KJV term referring to the upper, ornamental part of a column. In Ex. 36:38; 38:17, 19, 28 it is the translation of Heb. *rō'sh,* "head." The NASB and NIV render "top." *Chapiter* is also the KJV translation of two other Heb. words; for those, *see* Capital.

CHAR'AN. *See* Haran.

CHAR'ASHIM (kar'a-shim; "craftsmen"). A KJV term appearing in 1 Chron. 4:14. It is rendered "craftsmen" in the NASB. The NIV reads "Ge Harashim," a place name identified in the margin as "valley of craftsmen."

CHARIOT. The rendering of several Heb. words and one Gk. word, the indiscriminate use of which makes it difficult to know which kind of vehicle is meant. The same words are employed in speaking of chariots of war, state chariots, and even of wagons. The earliest mention of chariots in Scripture is where Joseph, as a mark of distinction, rode in Pharaoh's second chariot (Gen. 41:43); and later when he went in his own chariot to meet his father (46:29). Chariots also accompanied the funeral procession of Jacob, as a guard of honor (50:9). We next find them used for a *warlike* purpose (Ex. 14:7), when Pharaoh pursued the Israelites with six hundred chariots. Chariots date back to early Sumerian times in Mesopotamia.

Egyptian. From the Egyptian monuments we are able to form a correct idea of that nation's chariots. They were all similar in form, having but two wheels, furnished on the right side with cases for bows and spears and arrows. The framework, wheels, pole, and yoke were of wood, with the wheels sometimes tipped with iron and the axletrees ending with a scythelike projection. The binding of the framework, as well as the harness, were of rawhide or tanned leather; the floor was often made of rope network, to give a more springy footing to the occupants. The chariot was open behind, and here the charioteer entered. The sumptuous gold-stuccoed chariot of Tutankhamun was recovered from his lavish intact tomb.

Philistine war chariot

From the Egyptian sculptures it would seem that an Egyptian army was composed exclusively of infantry and chariots. Chariots were manned sometimes with three men, the warrior, the shield-bearer, and the charioteer; sometimes with only one person. The assumption is that the horsemen and riders (Ex. 14:9; 15:1) were riders in the chariots; and the "officers" (14:7) were chariot-warriors, literally, "third" men, probably selected for their valor.

Assyrian. From the sculptures we learn that the Assyrian chariot resembled the Egyptian in all material points. An early chariot from Sumerian Ur is pictured with solid wooden wheels clamped around a copper core.

Canaanite. The Canaanites had *iron* chariots (Josh. 17:18), "not *scythe* chariots, for these were introduced by Cyrus, but simply chariots tipped with iron" (K. & D., *Com.,* ad loc.). Of these it is recorded that Jabin, king of Canaan, had 900 (Judg. 4:3). The number of chariots that the Philistines had in the time of Saul, namely, 30,000 (1 Sam. 13:5), appears excessive, the probability is that there was a mistake by the copyist, so that it would be more correct to read 3,000. David took from Hadadezer, king of Zobah, 1,000 chariots (2 Sam. 8:4, KJV; NASB, "1,700 horsemen") and later 700 from the Syrians (10:18), who, in order to recover their ground, collected from various countries 32,000 (1 Chron. 19:6-7).

Hebrew. Hitherto the Israelites had few chariots, partly on account of the mountainous nature of the country, partly owing to the prohibition against their multiplying horses. Solomon raised and maintained a force of 1,400 chariots (1 Kings 10:26) by taxation on certain cities. The chariots and the horses were imported chiefly from Egypt (10:29). "Chariot cities" (2 Chron. 1:14) were the depots and stables erected by Solomon on the frontiers of his kingdom, such as Beth-marcaboth, "the house of chariots" (Josh. 19:5).

New Testament. In the NT the only mention made of a chariot, except in Rev. 9:9, is in the case of the Ethiopian eunuch of Queen Candace (Acts 8:28-39).

Figurative. Chariots are frequently alluded to as symbols of power (Pss. 20:7; 104:3; Jer. 51:21; Zech. 6:1-2), hosts, or armies (2 Kings 6:17; Ps. 68:17). Elijah, by his courage, faith, and power with God, saw "the chariots of Israel and its horsemen" (2 Kings 2:12). "Chariot" is likewise used poetically in Scripture to designate the rapid agencies of God in nature (Pss. 68:17; 104:3; Isa. 66:15; Hab. 3:8). "Gold for the model of the chariot, even the cherubim" (1 Chron. 28:18) probably means the cherubim as the chariot upon which God enters or is throned (*see* Cherubim, no. 3). " A chariot of fire and horses of fire" (2 Kings 2:11) signifies some bright effulgence which, in the eyes of the spectators, resembled those objects. "Chariots of the sun" are mentioned (2 Kings 23:11) as being burned by Josiah. Horses and chariots were dedicated to the sun by its worshipers, under the supposition that that divinity was drawn in a chariot by horses. The rabbis inform us that the king and nobles rode in these chariots when they went forth to greet the morning sun.

BIBLIOGRAPHY: C. J. Gadd, *The Assyrian Sculptures* (1934); O. R. Gurney, *The Hittites* (1952); D. J. Wiseman, *The Alalakh Tablets* (1953); Y. Yadin, *Biblical Archaeologist* 23 (1960):62-68.

CHARITY. *See* Brotherly Kindness; Love.

CHARM, CHARMER, CHARMING. *See* articles Magic; Amulet.

CHASE. *See* Hunting.

CHASM (Gk. *chasma*). An impassable space such as is said to exist between "Abraham's bosom" and the lost rich man in one of Jesus' parables (Luke 16:26).

CHASTISEMENT. *See* Discipline.

CHE'BAR (kĭ'bar), **Kebar** (NIV). A river or canal in the "land of the Chaldeans" (Ezek. 1:3), on the banks of which some of the Jews were located at the time of the captivity, and where Ezekiel saw his earlier visions (1:1; 3:15, 23; etc.).

CHECKER WORK. *See* Network.

CHEDORLAO'MER (kedorlaō'mer), **Kedorlao'mer** (NIV). A king mentioned in Gen. 14 as invading the Jordan Valley at the time of Abraham. He is called "king of Elam," a country E of Babylonia at the head of the Persian Gulf (14:1, 4-5). He was allied with three other Mesopotamian kings who fought against the five kings in the region of the Salt Sea. When the rulers of Sodom, Gomorrah, Admah, Zeboiim, and Zoar threw off his hegemony, he attempted to crush all resistance. Abraham clashed with him and rescued Lot. Although all attempts to identify him have thus far failed, the episode is to be dated around the middle of the twenty-first century B.C. according to chronological notations in the MT of the Heb. Bible. Former identification with Hammurabi (c. 1790 B.C.) is now completely untenable.   M.F.U.

CHEEK (Heb. *leḥî*). Smiting on the cheek was considered a great insult (Job 16:10; Lam. 3:30; Mic. 5:1; Luke 6:29). "Thou hast smitten all my enemies on the cheek" (Ps. 3:7) is figurative of utter destruction of those enemies. The cheekbone (KJV) denotes the bone in which the teeth are placed; to break that is to disarm the animal.

CHEESE. The coagulated curd of milk pressed into a solid mass (Job 10:10; 1 Sam. 17:18; 2 Sam. 17:29). The Tyropoean Valley in Jerusalem is the Gk. equivalent for "The Valley of the Cheese Makers." The making of cheese was an important industry in antiquity, and this dairy product was a vital part of the diet of the Jews.

Among the regulations regarding food in the Mishna was that no cheese made by foreigners should be eaten, for fear that it might be derived from the milk of an animal that had been offered to idols.

CHE'LAL (ke'lal; "completion"), **Ke'lal** (NIV). One of the "sons" of Pahath-moab, who divorced his Gentile wife after the return from Babylon (Ezra 10:30), 456 B.C.

CHEL'LUH. *See* Chelluhi, Keluhi (NIV).

CHEL'LUHI (ke'lū-hi). One of the "sons" of Bani, who divorced his Gentile wife after the return from captivity (Ezra 10:35), 456 B.C.

CHE'LUB (ke'lūb), **Ke'lub** (NIV).
1. The brother of Shuhah and father of Mehir, of the tribe of Judah (1 Chron. 4:11).
2. The father of Ezri, who was David's chief gardener (1 Chron. 27:16), after 1000 B.C.

CHELU'BAI (ke-lū'bi). One of the sons of Hezron (1 Chron. 2:9); elsewhere in the same chapter (vv. 18, 42) called Caleb. *See* Caleb, no. 2.

CHEM'ARIM (ke'mā-rim; "servants"?). A KJV term appearing in Zeph. 1:4 to refer to "idolatrous priests" (so NASB and NIV). The Heb. word is found elsewhere (2 Kings 23:5; Hos. 10:5), with the NASB rendering "idolatrous priests," and the NIV "pagan priests." The term refers to the priests appointed by the kings of Judah for the

worship of the high places and the idolatrous worship of Jehovah.

CHE'MOSH (ke'mosh). The leading deity of the Moabites. *See* Gods, False.

CHENA'ANAH (ke-na'a-na), **Kena'anah** (NIV).
1. The fourth named of the seven "sons" of Bilhan, a Benjamite and mighty warrior, apparently, in the time of David (1 Chron. 7:10), about 1000 B.C.
2. The father of the false prophet Zedekiah, which latter opposed Micaiah and encouraged Ahab (1 Kings 22:11, 24; 2 Chron. 18:10, 23), before 850 B.C.

CHEN'ANI (ken'a-ni; "established"), **Ken'ani** (NIV). One of the Levites who conducted the devotions of the people after Ezra had read to them the book of the law (Neh. 9:4), 445 B.C.

CHENANI'AH (ken-a-nī'a; "established by Jehovah"), **Kenani'ah** (NIV). Chief of the Levites who, as master of song (1 Chron. 15:22), conducted the grand musical services when the Ark was removed from the house of Obed-edom to Jerusalem (15:27). He was of the family of Izharites and was appointed over the inspectors of the building of the Temple (26:29), about 1000 B.C.

CHE'PHAR-AM'MONI (ke'far-am'ō-ni; "village of the Ammonites"), **Ke'phar Am'moni** (NIV). A place mentioned among the towns of Benjamin (Josh. 18:24). Site uncertain.

CHEPHI'RAH (ke-fi'ra; "village, hamlet"), **Kephi'rah** (NIV). One of the Gibeonite towns of Benjamin (Josh. 18:26); now *Kefîreh,* about eight miles from Jerusalem. Joshua made peace with its people (9:17). It was occupied after the captivity by a remnant of Benjamin (Ezra 2:25; Neh. 7:29).

CHE'RAN (ke'ran), **Ke'ran** (NIV). The last named of the four sons of Dishon, the Horite chief descended from Seir (Gen. 36:26; 1 Chron. 1:41).

CHER'ETHITES (ker'e-thīts), **Ker'ethites** (NIV).
1. Those tribes of the Philistines who dwelt in the SW of Canaan (1 Sam. 30:14); treated by Ezekiel (25:16) and Zephaniah (2:5) as synonymous with Philistines. The LXX and Syr. rendered the words in these passages by "Cretans," from which it is now known that the *Philistines* (which see) sprang from Crete (cuneiform, "Kaptara").
2. "The Cherethites and the Pelethites," a collective term for David's personal bodyguard (2 Sam. 8:18; 15:18; 20:7, 23; 1 Kings 1:38, 44; 1 Chron. 18:17). The words are adjectives in form, but with a substantive meaning, and were used to indicate a certain rank, literally, the executioners and runners. At a later date they were called "the captains" and "the guards" (2 Kings

11:4, 19; cf. 1 Kings 14:27). The NIV renders "Carites" in 2 Kings 11:4, 19.

CHE'RITH (ke'rith), **Ke'rith** (NIV). A brook in Transjordan where Elijah fled to hide (1 Kings 17:3, 5). The traditional site is now the Wâdi Qelt, a wild glen that runs into the Jordan Valley; but the Bible indicates that it was E of that river, and therefore in Elijah's own native country of Gilead. Wâdi Yabis, opposite Beth-shean, may be the place.

CHER'ETHIM. *See* Cherethites.

CHE'RUB (ke'rub). An Israelite of doubtful extraction, who accompanied Zerubbabel to Judea (Ezra 2:59; Neh. 7:61).

CHER'UB (cher'ub), **Cherubim** (Heb. *kerûbîm;* Gk. *cheroubim*).

Mention in Scripture. Cherubim are mentioned at the expulsion of our first parents from Eden (Gen. 3:24), when their office was "to guard the way to the tree of life," i.e., to render it impossible for man to return to paradise and eat of the tree of life. In this account there is no mention of their nature or form.

We next read of them in connection with the furnishing of the Tabernacle (Ex. 25:18-20), where directions are given to place two golden cherubim upon the top of the Ark of the Covenant. They were to be of "hammered work," i.e., beaten with the hammer and rounded, and not solid. They were fastened to the Mercy Seat (lid of the Ark) and, facing each other, stretched out their wings so as to form a screen over the Mercy Seat. They were called the "cherubim of glory" (Heb. 9:5). Cherubim were also woven into or embroidered upon the inward curtain of the Tabernacle (Ex. 26:1; 36:8) and the veil (26:31).

The two cherubim placed by Solomon in the Holy of Holies (1 Kings 6:23-28; 8:7; 2 Chron. 3:7-14) were made of olive wood, overlaid with gold. They had bodies ten cubits high, and stood upon their feet, like men. The length of their wings was five cubits. They stood "facing the main room," i.e., the Holy Place, the outward wing of each cherub touching the wall and the tip of the other wings touching each other.

Other references are as follows: "He rode on a cherub and flew" (2 Sam. 22:11; Ps. 18:10); the vision of four cherubim (NASB, "living beings"; NIV, "living creatures") seen by Ezekiel (1:5-14; 10:1-22), and that of the "four living creatures" in Rev. 4:6-9.

Form. From an excavated pair of cherubs supporting the throne of King Hiram of Byblos (c. 1200 B.C.) a creature with a lion's body, human face, and conspicuous wings is indicated. The Assyrians and other Semitic peoples used symbolic winged creatures, notably winged lions and bulls, to guard temples and palaces. Egyptians also had winged creatures in some of their temples. Griffins—winged sphinxes having lions'

bodies and eagles' heads were familiar to the Hittites. The cherubim of Solomon are said to have "stood on their feet" (2 Chron. 3:13). Ezekiel says they "appeared to have the form of a man's hand under their wings" (10:8). The representations of the Bible stress the human likeness but also indicate the animal characteristics. Undoubtedly we are to think of the cherub as at Byblos; that is, as a winged lion with human face. In any case, they are celestial creatures belonging to the spiritual realm and not at all to be confounded with any natural identification.

Winged bull from the palace of the Assyrian king Sargon II

The Cherubim and the Throne. As a winged lion with human head, i.e., a winged sphinx, this hybrid animal appears hundreds of times in the iconography of western Asia between 1800 and 600 B.C. The fact that many representations picture the deity or king seated on a throne supported by two cherubs suggests that in the OT the Deity and His throne—both invisible—were similarly supported by symbolical cherubim (cf. W. F. Albright *O.T. Commentary* [1948], p. 148; Graham and May, *Culture and Conscience* [1936], pp. 195-96, 249-50). Archaeology thus greatly illuminates the meaning of the cherubim both in Solomon's Temple and the earlier Tabernacle and enables 1 Sam. 4:4 (cf. Rev. 4:6) to be rendered thus: "the ark of the covenant of the Lord of hosts who sits above the cherubim."

The Meaning. The cherubim from their position at the gate of Eden, upon the cover of the Ark of the Covenant, and in Rev. 4 are evidently connected with vindicating the holiness of God against the presumptuous pride of fallen man, who despite his sin, would "stretch out his hand, and take also from the tree of life" (Gen. 3:22). Upon the Ark of the Covenant they looked down upon the sprinkled blood that symbolizes the perfect maintenance of God's righteousness by the sacrifice of Christ (Ex. 25:17-20; Rom. 3:24-26). The cherubim seem to be actual beings of the angelic order. They do not seem to be identical with the seraphim (Isa. 6:2). The cherubim apparently have to do with the holiness of God as violated by sin; the seraphim with uncleanness in the people of God.   M.F.U.

BIBLIOGRAPHY: W. F. Albright, *Biblical Archaeologist Reader* 1 (1961): 95-97; R. de Vaux, *Ancient Israel: Its Life and Institutions* (1961), pp. 295-304, 319-20; J. B. Payne, *Theology of the Older Testament* (1962), pp. 289-95.

CHES'ALON (kes'a-lon), **Kes'alon** (NIV). One of the landmarks on the W part of the N boundary of Judah (Josh. 15:10). Eusebius and Jerome differ as to its location but agree that it was a large village near Jerusalem. Kesla, ten miles W of Jerusalem, is its present site.

CHE'SED (ke'sed), **Ke'sed** (NIV). The fourth named of the sons of Nahor (Abraham's brother) by Milcah (Gen. 22:22).

CHE'SIL (ke'sil; "a fool"), **Ke'sil** (NIV). A town in the S of Judah (Josh. 15:30), identical with Bethul and Bethuel (19:4; 1 Chron. 4:30; "Bethel," 1 Sam. 30:27).

CHEST. The rendering of two distinct Heb. terms:

1. *'Ārôn,* invariably used for the Ark of the Covenant, with but two exceptions. These exceptions are (1) the "coffin" in which the bones of Joseph were carried to Palestine (Gen. 50:26) and (2) the "chest" in which Jehoiada the priest collected the offerings for Temple repairs (2 Kings 12:9-10; 2 Chron. 24:8-11).

2. *Genāzîm,* used only in the plural, rendered in KJV "chests" (Ezek. 27:24) and "treasuries" (Esther 3:9; 4:7).

CHESTNUT TREE. *See* Vegetable Kingdom.

CHESUL'LOTH (ke-sul'ōth), **Kesul'loth** (NIV). A town of Issachar (Josh. 19:18), probably identical with Chisloth-tabor (v. 12). Modern Iksal, near Nazareth, marks the ancient site.

CHE'ZIB (ke'zib; "deceitful"), **Ke'zib** (NIV). A town in which Judah was when Shelah, his third son, was born (Gen. 38:5); probably the same as Achzib.

CHICKEN (Gk. *nossion,* 2 Esd. 1:30; cf. Matt. 23:37). *See* Animal Kingdom: Cock.

CHICKS. *See* Animal Kingdom: Cock.

CHI'DON (ki'don; a "spear"), **Ki'don** (NIV). Thought by some to be an Israelite on whose threshing floor the accident to the Ark, and the death of Uzza, took place as the Ark was being carried to Jerusalem (1 Chron. 13:9). It is more probable that it was the name of the *place.*

CHIEF. The rendering of a large number of Heb. and Gk. words, frequently in official terms, as "chief cupbearer," "chief officers" (*see* Army), "chief of the Levites" (*see* Levites), *"chief gatekeeper"* (which see), "chief priests" (*see* Priest), "chief ministers" (*see* Synagogue).

The translation of two Heb. terms: (a) *Chief* (Heb. *'allûp,* "leader of a thousand"), the distinguishing title of the head of Edomite or Horite divisions (Gen. 36:15-43; Ex. 15:15; 1 Chron. 1:51,54). *'Allûp* is used rarely of Jews (Zech. 9:7; 12:5-6; "clan[s]," NASB; "governor[s]," KJV; "leaders," NIV), and once of chiefs in general (Jer. 13:21, "captains," KJV; "companions" or "chieftains," marg., NASB; "allies," NIV). (b) *Prince,* Heb. *nāśî,* "anointed" one), "princes of Sihon" (Josh. 13:21; "dukes of Sihon," KJV, "properly *vassals* of Sidon, princes created by the communication or pouring in of power" (K. & D., *Com.,* ad loc.). The Heb. term is rendered "princes" in Ps. 83:11; "chiefs" in Ezek. 32:30 ("princes," KJV, NIV, NASB marg.); and "leaders of men" (NIV; "principal men," KJV) in Mic. 5:5.

CHIEF OF THREE. The official title of *Adino* (which see), the Ezrite (2 Sam. 23:8, NASB, "chief of the captains"; marg., "chief of the three").

CHIEFS OF ASIA. *See* Asiarch.

CHILD, CHILDREN (Heb. properly *yeled;* Gk. *teknon,* something "born"). This term is often used freely in Scripture; thus the descendants of a man, however remote, are called his sons or children. For other uses, see below.

Desire for. It is of children that the house, the family, is built (Gen. 16:2; 30:3, marg., "from her I too may be built"). The conception and bearing of children was a matter of longing and joy among the Israelites, especially to the women (24:60; 30:1; 1 Sam. 1:11). On the ground of the twofold blessing connected with creation and the covenant promise (Gen. 1:28; 12:2, 7; 13:16) a numerous group of children was considered as a special gift of God's grace (Deut. 28:4; Pss. 113:9; 128:3; 144:12; Prov. 17:6; Eccles. 6:3), and sterility in marriage was thought to be a divine punishment (Gen. 16:2; 30:23; 1 Sam. 1:6-20; Isa. 47:9).

Infants. At childbirth women were helped by nurses and midwives, even in the time of the patriarchs (Gen. 35:17; 38:28; Ex. 1:15), although women in the East often give birth so easily as not to need this help. The newborn child, after having the navel cord cut, was bathed in water, rubbed with salt, and wrapped in swaddling clothes (Ezek. 16:4). As a rule, it was nursed and tended by the mother herself (Gen. 21:7; 1 Sam. 1:23; 1 Kings 3:21; Song of Sol. 8:1), excepting in case of weakness or death or in princely families (2 Kings 11:2; cf. Ex. 2:9). After eight days boys were circumcised (*see* Circumcision), and got their names from some memorable circumstance connected with their birth (Gen. 25:25; 35:18; 38:29) or according to the mother's hopes or wishes (4:25; 29:32; 1 Sam. 1:20), but in later times from some relative (Luke 1:61). Forty days after its birth, in the case of a boy, and eighty in the case of a girl, the mother had to offer a sacrifice of purification in the Temple (Lev. 12:1-8), to present the male firstborn to Jehovah and to redeem it with five shekels of silver (Num. 18:15; cf. with Lev. 27:5). The *weaning* of the child did not occur, in some cases, till it was two or three years of age (2 Macc. 7:27). The event was celebrated with festivities (Gen. 21:8) and on special occasions was accompanied by the offering of a sacrifice (1 Sam. 1:23-25).

Training. Both boys and girls in their earlier years were under the training of their mother (Prov. 31:1; 2 Tim. 1:5; 3:15), the daughters, no doubt, remaining so until their marriage. At the age of five years, probably, the boys were trained by their fathers, or in well-to-do families were placed under the care of special tutors (Num. 11:12, marg.; Isa. 49:23; 2 Kings 10:1, 5; Gal. 3:24). This instruction was not only in reading and writing, but also in the law, its commandments and doctrines, and the deeds and revelations of Jehovah to His people (Ex. 12:26; 13:8, 14; Deut. 4:10; 6:7, 20-23; 11:19; Prov. 6:20). Schools were not set up till a comparatively late time, and only in the larger cities.

Children and the Law. In the Ten Commandments reverence for parents is made a condition of children's prosperity (Ex. 20:12; Lev. 19:3; Deut. 5:16). If a child cursed his parents he was under the divine curse (Deut. 27:16) and was to be put to death equally with him who did violence to them (Ex. 21:15, 17; Lev. 20:9; cf. Prov. 20:20; Matt. 15:4). Drunkenness, gluttony, and the like, persevered in against a father's warning, were punished by the elders of the city with stoning (Deut. 21:18-21).

Thus while the law gave parents full authority over their children, it provided also against the abuse of full parental power. The father was not to deprive his firstborn of his rights of inheritance in favor, for example, of a younger son by a second and more loved wife (21:15-17). He could nullify a vow made by his daughter, but he must do so immediately upon hearing it; otherwise he could not prevent its fulfillment (Num. 30:4-5). He had power to marry his daughters, and even to sell them into concubinage, but not to a foreign people (Ex. 21:7-8).

Children seem to have often been taken as bondsmen by creditors for debts contracted by the fathers (2 Kings 4:1; Neh. 5:5; Isa. 50:1). Children who were slaves by birth are called in Scripture those "born in [the] house" (Gen. 14:14; 15:3; 17:23).

Illegitimate. Such children had no legal inheritance (Gen. 21:10; Gal. 4:30); they did not receive the training of legitimate sons (Heb. 12:8, "discipline"; Gk. *paideia*, "education"), were excluded from the congregation (Deut. 23:2), and were despised by their brethren (Judg. 11:2).

Figurative. In the Scriptures, children, like sons or daughters, are used figuratively (1) to express a state of ignorance and of intellectual darkness (Matt. 11:16; 1 Cor. 13:11; 14:20; Eph. 4:14; Heb. 5:13); (2) of persons who are distinguished, whether for good or evil, by some particular quality or power. Thus the expression "sons of light" (Luke 16:8) is applied to those who have a knowledge of God through Christ; the "obedient children" (1 Pet. 1:14) are those submitting themselves readily to the will of God. On the other hand, we have such expressions as "son of hell" (Matt. 23:15), "sons of the evil one" (Matt. 13:38), "sons of this age" (Luke 16:8).

CHILDBEARING (Gk. *teknogonia*). As a part of the curse coming to our first parent, on account of sin, it was said to her, "In pain you shall bring forth children" (Gen. 3:16). Commenting on this, Delitzsch says: "That the woman should bear the children was the original will of God; but it was a punishment that henceforth she was to bear them in sorrow, i.e., with pains which threatened her own life as well as that of the child." The punishment consisted in an enfeebling of nature, in consequence of sin. The language of the apostle, "But women shall be preserved through the bearing of children if they continue in faith and love," etc. (1 Tim. 2:15), implies that a patient endurance of this penalty shall contribute to woman's spiritual benefit.

CHILDBIRTH. *See* Child: Infants.

CHILDREN OF GOD. Persons in this category are only those who of the fallen race are regenerated as a result of faith in Christ. The believer's relationship to God as a child, accordingly, issues from the new birth (John 1:12-13). But all regenerated people are not only children, (that is, born again) but adult sons as well, children of God receiving a place as sons (Gal. 4:5) by *adoption* (which see). The indwelling Spirit gives to the child of God the realization of his sonship or spiritual adulthood (4:1-6). The popular doctrine of the Fatherhood of God and the brotherhood of man is not taught in Scripture. Since man is fallen, a person becomes a child only by faith in Christ, and only members of the Father's family are brothers in any vital spiritual sense. Liberal theological thinking that seeks to break down this important biblical distinction between the children of God and the children of the devil is contrary to divinely revealed truth. It not only robs Christianity of its distinctive message but provokes great harm, confusion, and empty utopian dreaming.   M.F.U.

BIBLIOGRAPHY: J. Jeremias, *Central Message of the New Testament* (1964), pp. 9-30.

CHILDREN OF ISRAEL. *See* Israel.

CHIL'EAB (kil'e-ab; "restraint" [?]), **Kil'eab** (NIV). The second son of David, by Abigail, the widow of Nabal (2 Sam. 3:3), about 1000 B.C. He is called Daniel in the parallel passage (1 Chron. 3:1).

CHIL'ION (kil'i-un; "pining"), **Kil'ion** (NIV). The younger son of Elimelech and Naomi, and husband of Orpah, Ruth's sister-in-law; he died childless in the land of Moab (Ruth 1:2, 5; 4:9), about 1100 B.C.

CHIL'MAD (kil'mad), **Kil'mad** (NIV). A place or country mentioned in conjunction with Sheba and Asshur (Ezek. 27:23). The only name bearing any similarity to it is Charmande, a town near the Euphrates between the Mascus and the Babylonian frontier; but it is highly improbable that this place was of sufficient importance to rank with Sheba and Asshur.

CHIM'HAM (kim'ham; "pining, longing"), **Kim'ham** (NIV). A follower and, according to Josephus (*Ant.* 7.11.4), a son of Barzillai, the Gileadite. Upon David's restoration after Absalom's rebellion, Chimham returned from beyond the Jordan with him and received marked favors at his hand, which were first offered to Barzillai, but declined on account of old age (2 Sam. 19:37-40), 973 B.C. David probably bestowed upon him a possession at or near Bethlehem, on which, in later times, was an inn called after him (Jer. 41:17).

CHIMNEY (Heb. *'ărūbbâ*, "lattice"). The expression "like smoke from a *chimney*" (Hos. 13:3) should be rendered "smoke out of the window" (thus NIV), i.e., "window lattice," as the houses were without chimneys. The same word is elsewhere translated "*window.*" *See* House.

CHIN'NERETH (kin'e-reth; "harp-shaped"), or **Chin'neroth** (kin'e-rōth), **Kin'nereth** (NIV).

1. A fortified city in the tribe of Naphtali (Josh. 19:35 only), of which no trace is found in later writers, and no remains by travelers. By Jerome,

Ruins of synagogue at Chorazin, near Capernaum

Chinnereth was identified with the later Tiberias. On the temple walls of Karnak, at Thebes, Thutmose III (1475 B.C.) gives a list of Canaanitish towns submitting to him, among which Chinnereth is found.

2. Sea of Chinnereth (Num. 34:11; Josh. 13:27), the inland sea, which is most familiarly known to us as the lake of Gennesaret or the Sea of Galilee. This is evident from the mode in which it is mentioned as being at the end of the Jordan opposite to the "sea of the Arabah," i.e., the Dead Sea; as having the Arabah and Ghor below it, etc. (Deut. 3:17; Josh. 11:2; 12:3). In the two latter of these passages it is in a plural form, *Chinneroth.* It seems likely that Chinnereth was an ancient Canaanite name existing long prior to the Israelite conquest.

CHI'OS (ki'os), **Ki'os** (NIV). An island in the Grecian Archipelago, about five miles from the mainland; now Scio. It was once noted for wine. Paul anchored there on his last missionary journey (Acts 20:15).

CHIS'LEV (kis'lev) in the NASB, **Chis'leu** (kĭs'lū; Heb. *kislēw* from Akkad. *kislimu*) in the KJV, **Kis'lev** in the NIV. The name of the third civil or ninth ecclesiastical month adopted from the Babylonians after the captivity (Neh. 1:1; Zech. 7:1). *See* Calendar; Time.

CHIS'LON (kis'lon; "hopeful"), **Kis'lon** (NIV). The father of Elidad, who, as one of the leaders of Benjamin, was selected on the part of that tribe to divide Canaan (Num. 34:21).

CHIS'LOTH-TA'BOR (kis'lōth-ta'bor; "flanks of Tabor"), **Kis'loth Ta'bor** (NIV). A place near Tabor (Josh. 19:12), and probably the same as Chesulloth (v. 18).

CHIT'LISH (chit'lish), **Kit'lish** (NIV). A town in the valley of Judah (Josh. 15:40; "Kithlish," KJV). It is identified by some with Jelemah; by others it is thought to be found in Tell Chilchis; to the SSE of Beit-jibrin.

CHITTIM, KITTIM. *See* Kittim.

CHI'UN. *See* Kiyyun in the general listing; and also Gods, False: Kiyyun.

CHLO'E (klō'e; "verdure"). A female Christian mentioned in 1 Cor. 1:11, some of whose household had informed the apostle Paul of divisions in the Corinthian church. Whether she was a resident of Corinth or not we do not know.

CHOENIX. A foreign measure of capacity. *See* Metrology.

CHOR'ASHAN. *See* Bor-ashan.

CHORA'ZIN (ko-ra'zin), **Kora'zin** (NIV). This city, in the general vicinity of Bethsaida and Capernaum near the Sea of Galilee, was upbraided by Jesus and committed to destruction for its unbelief in the face of His mighty works (Matt. 11:21; Luke 10:13). It is now identified with Kerazeh, about three miles N of Tell Hum (Capernaum).

H. Kohl and C. Watzinger excavated the synagogue at Kerazeh on behalf of the German Oriental Society from 1905 to 1907. J. Ory for the Palestine Department of Antiquities (1926) and Z. Yeivin for the Israel Department of Antiquities (1962-63) continued work on the synagogue, the latter also excavating nearby houses. Since 1983 restoration work on the synagogue has been conducted. The synagogue, of black basalt, measures seventy by fifty feet and dates to the third or fourth centuries A.D. Its design is similar to that of Capernaum, with three monumental entrances facing toward Jerusalem, a roof supported by pillars, stone benches around the wall for the men, and an outside stairway leading to the women's gallery.   M.F.U.; H.F.V.

CHOSEN (Heb. from *bāhar;* Gk. *eklektos*). This term means singled out from others for some special service or station. "Chosen" warriors were picked out as being most skillful or best adapted to some service (Ex. 15:4; Judg. 20:16; NASB, "choice"; NIV, "best"). The Israelites were a "chosen" people, God having set them apart to receive His word and maintain His worship (Ps. 105:43; Deut. 7:6-7). Jerusalem was "chosen" as the seat of the Temple (1 Kings 11-13). Christ was *chosen* (Isa. 42:1) of God to be the Savior of men. The apostles were "chosen beforehand by God" to be witnesses of the resurrection (Acts 10:41). The declaration, "Many are called, but few are chosen," means that the invitation is extended to many but that only few profit thereby so as to be finally accepted (Matt. 22:14). *See* Election.

CHOZE'BA. *See* Cozeba.

CHRIST (Gk. *Christos;* "anointed"). The official title of our Savior (occurring first in 2 Esd. 7:28-29, and constantly in the NT), as having been consecrated by His baptism and the descent of the Holy Spirit as our Prophet, Priest, and King. *See* Jesus.

CHRIST, ASCENSION OF. *See* Ascension.

CHRIST, CRUCIFIXION OF. *See* Crucifixion.

CHRIST, DEATH OF. *See* Atonement; Crucifixion.

CHRIST, DIVINITY OF. *See* Incarnation.

CHRIST, HUMANITY OF. *See* Incarnation.

CHRIST, LIFE OF. *See* Jesus.

CHRIST, OFFICES OF. *See* Jesus.

CHRIST, PERSON OF. *See* Kenosis.

CHRIST, RESURRECTION OF. *See* Resurrection.

CHRISTIAN. A Christian is a believer in and a follower of Jesus Christ the Messiah. This name is more widely employed than any other designation of those who believe unto salvation. However, it occurs in the Scriptures only three times: "And the disciples were first called Christians in Antioch" (Acts 11:26); "and Agrippa replied to Paul, 'In a short time you will persuade me to become a Christian' " (26:28); "If anyone suffers as a Christian, let him not feel ashamed" (1 Pet. 4:16). The term *Christian* is clearly a Gentile designation for believers because the word *Christ,* upon which the term was constructed, suggests recognition of the Messiah, which no unbelieving Jew was prepared to do. Becoming a Christian, according to the NT, is a definite act with significant results. According to Lewis Sperry Chafer, no fewer than thirty-three simultaneous and instantaneous divine undertakings and transformations, which collectively constitute the salvation of a soul, take place the moment one exercises faith in Christ and is saved. Among these is that a believer in Christ has the guilt of his sins removed. Second, he is taken out of Adam, the sphere of condemnation, and placed in Christ, the sphere of righteousness and justification. Third, he is given a new standing by virtue of his being placed "in Christ" by the Spirit's baptizing work (1 Cor. 12:13; Rom. 6:3-4). A Christian then, as Chafer says, "Is not one who does certain things for God but . . . one for whom God has done certain things; he is not so much one who conforms to a certain manner of life as he is one who has received the gift of eternal life; he is not one who depends upon a hopelessly imperfect state but rather one who has reached a perfect standing before God as being in Christ" (*Systematic Theology,* 7:75).   M.F.U.

BIBLIOGRAPHY: L. S. Chafer, *Systematic Theology* (1945), 4:92-100; 5:146-48; 6:254-55; 7:73-75; P. J. Gloag, *Acts of the Apostles* (1979), 1:402-4.

CHRISTIANITY. The body of doctrine that consists of the teachings and way of life made possible by the death, burial, and resurrection of Christ and the giving of the Holy Spirit. These teachings were committed by Christ to His disciples and particularly by special divine revelation to the apostle Paul, so that what was provided by Christ is given full-fledged doctrinal expression by the apostle. Other NT writers give various aspects of Christian doctrine, but the most developed revelation concerning the Person and work of Christ and of the Holy Spirit for the normal, established course of the age was given to Paul. His doctrinal epistles demonstrate that Christianity, although having its roots in Judaism, is not Judaism or a mixture of Judaism. It is a way of life, of salvation, the full expression of the gospel of the grace of God for this age in which God is visiting the Gentiles and "taking from among [them] a people for His name" (Acts

15:14). After this period Christ will return and "rebuild the Tabernacle of David which has fallen" (15:16), i.e., restore Israel for blessing in the coming millennial age.

To many, Christianity is a general term descriptive of all that is not Jewish. To others it is synonymous with Christendom. In such cases, little attention is given to the distinctive features of Christian truth.   M.F.U.

BIBLIOGRAPHY: Marcus Aurelius Augustinus *The City of God* (numerous trans.); L. S. Chafer, *Systematic Theology* (1948), 7:75-77.

CHRIST'MAS ("Christ's Mass," or "Festival"). The annual festival held by the Christian church in memory of the birth of Christ. It begins with the evening of December 24 (called *Christmas Eve*) and continues until Epiphany (January 6), the whole period being called *Christmastide*. It is more particularly observed on December 25, called *Christmas Day*, or simply *Christmas*.

As to whether our Lord's birth really occurred on December 25 ancient authorities are not agreed. Clement of Alexandria says that some place it on April 20, others on May 20, whereas Epiphanius states that in Egypt Jesus was believed to have been born on January 6. For a long time the Greeks had no special feast corresponding to Christmas Day. Chrysostom, in a Christmas sermon, A.D. 386, said: "It is not ten years since this day was clearly known to us, but it has been known from the beginning to those who dwell in the West." The Western church unanimously agreed upon this date, and the Eastern church adopted it without much contradiction.

As mentioned above, the period from Nativity to Epiphany was consecrated. The four Sundays preceding Christmas were incorporated with the cycle, under the title of the Advent, as a preparation for the festival. On Christmas Day, in the Roman Catholic church, three masses were celebrated, namely, at midnight, dawn, and in the daytime, a custom still observed in collegiate and cathedral churches. "A mystical explanation of the three masses is given, and they are supposed to figure the three births of our Lord: of His Father before all ages, of the Blessed Virgin, and in the hearts of the faithful" (*Cath. Dict.*, s.v.).

Several non-Christian elements have crept into the observance of Christmas. The use of lighted tapers reminds us of the Jewish feast of purification. The giving of presents was a Roman custom, whereas the yule tree and the yule log are remnants of old Teutonic nature worship. Gradually the festival sank into mere revelry. In England an abbot of misrule was chosen in every large household; in Scotland an abbot of unreason, who was master of the house during the festival. The custom was forbidden by Parliament in 1555; and the Reformation brought in a refinement in the celebration of Christmas by emphasizing its Christian elements.

BIBLIOGRAPHY: Clement of Alexander *The Stromata* 1.21; Marcus Aurelius Augustinus *De Trinitate* 4.5; A. Hislop, *The Two Babylons* (1939), pp. 101-2.

CHRISTS, FALSE (Gk. *pseudochristoi*). Those who falsely claim to be the Messiah, and against whom our Lord warned His disciples (Matt. 24:24; Mark 13:22). About twenty-four such persons have had more or less prominence.

See Antichrist.

CHRONICLES, BOOKS OF. In the Heb. these two historical books were originally one work. The twofold LXX division did not become effective in modern Heb. Bibles until the sixteenth century. The term *Chronicle*, from the Heb. *divre hayyamim* ("events or annals of the days," i.e., "times," cf. 1 Chron. 27:24), was suggested by Jerome who said "the name might be better called a Chronicle of the entire divine history." The LXX styled the two books inaccurately *Paralipomena*, i.e., "things passed over or omitted" (from the books of Samuel and Kings), construing Chronicles as a mere supplement to these works. In the Heb. canon the books of Chronicles come at the end of the third and last section.

Purpose. First and Second Chronicles catalog the history of priestly worship from the death of Saul to the conclusion of the Babylonian captivity, when the book of Ezra takes up the account. Samuel and Kings present a prophetic standpoint over against the priestly approach of Chronicles. These books interpret the history of the Jerusalem priesthood in its growth and development from the time of David. Chronicles is not a mere supplement to the parallel books of Samuel and Kings, but emphasizes only those aspects of history that illustrate the observance of the priestly laws of Moses as a way to spiritual prosperity in Israel. Priestly genealogies and faithful Jehovah-worshiping kings are given prominence. The kings of the Northern Kingdom are, accordingly, passed over along with prophetic aspects, which are brought to the fore in Samuel and Kings:

Outline.
  I. Genealogies from Adam to Saul (1 Chron. 1:1–9:44)
     A. From Adam to Jacob (1:1–2:2)
     B. Jacob's posterity (2:3–9:44)
  II. David's history (10:1–29:30)
     A. Saul's death (10:1-14)
     B. Zion's capture and David's warriors (11:1–12:40)
     C. David's kingship (13:1–21:30)
     D. David's contribution to Tabernacle worship (22:1–29:30)
  III. Solomon's history (2 Chron. 1:1–9:31)
     A. His prosperity (1:1-17)
     B. His construction of the Temple (2:1–7:22)
     C. His work and death (8:1–9:31)
  IV. History of the Judahite Kings (10:1–36:23)

A. From Rehoboam to Zedekiah (10:1–36:21)

B. Cyrus's edict (36:22-23)

Author and Date. Ezra is traditionally fixed as the author of Chronicles. W. F. Albright defends this thesis that the chronicler is Ezra and that he wrote between 400 and 350 B.C. Negative critics commonly assign the book considerably later. R. Pfeiffer sees nothing wrong with a date as late as 250 B.C. No conclusive argument can be advanced against authorship by Ezra around 400 B.C. or somewhat earlier. Arguments for a later date derived from the language and spirit of the work are not potent, since the diction of the chronicler is generally confessed to be similar to that of Ezra-Nehemiah and to come from the same period. Arguments based on the genealogies in 1 Chron. 3:17-24 are inconclusive, for the text as it stands does not permit determining whether five or eleven generations are listed after Zerubbabel and, accordingly, whether the last generation belongs to the period around 400 B.C. or around 270 B.C.

Historical Authenticity. Critics have customarily depreciated the historical reliability of the chronicler's work. As W. F. Albright says, "Chronicles contains a considerable amount of original material dealing with the history of Judah which is not found in Kings and . . . the historical value of this original material is being established by archaeological discoveries" (*Bulletin Am. Schools of Oriental Research* 100 [1945]: 18). It is quite evident also that the writer's wide use of sources and his meticulous references to them disprove the critical notion that he was an inaccurate historian. The priestly slant of the book, as W. A. L. Elmslie correctly says, is "invaluable for the light it gives on the post-exilic priestly standpoint toward the past" (*How Came Our Faith* [1949], p. 39) and must be evaluated on this score.

Other "Chronicles." It is known that the books of Chronicles and Ezra, though put into their present form by one hand, contain in fact extracts from the writings of many different writers, which were extant at the time the compilation was made. For the full account of the reign of David the compiler made copious extracts from the books of Samuel the seer, Nathan the prophet, and Gad the seer (1 Chron. 29:29). For the reign of Solomon he copied from "the records of Nathan," from "the prophecy of Ahijah the Shilonite," and from "the visions of Iddo the seer" (2 Chron. 9:29). Another work of Iddo, "the treatise (or interpretation, *Midrash*) of the prophet Iddo," supplied an account of the acts and the ways and sayings of King Abijah (13:22); while yet another book of Iddo concerning genealogies, with the book of the prophet Shemaiah, contained the acts of King Rehoboam (12:15). For later times the "Book of the Kings of Israel and Judah" is repeatedly cited (25:26; 27:7;

32:32; 33:18; etc.), and "the records of the Hozai" (33:19, marg., "seers"); and for the reigns of Uzziah and Hezekiah "the vision of Isaiah the prophet" (26:22; 32:32). Besides the above-named works there was also the public national record mentioned in Neh. 12:23. These chronicles of David are probably the same as those above referred to, written by Samuel, Nathan, and Gad. From this time the affairs of each king's reign were regularly recorded in a book (1 Kings 14:29; 15:7; etc.); and it was doubtless from this common source that the passages in the books of Samuel and Kings identical with the books of Chronicles were derived (Smith, *Bib. Dict.*, s.v.).

M.F.U.

BIBLIOGRAPHY: J. M. Myers, *I Chronicles*, The Anchor Bible (1965); id., *II Chronicles*, The Anchor Bible (1965); G. L. Archer, Jr., *Survey of Old Testament Introduction* (1974), pp. 404ff.; E. R. Thiele, *Mysterious Numbers of the Hebrew Kings* (1983).

CHRONOLOGY, NEW TESTAMENT. When the chronology in mind is the scientific measurement of time according to the revolutions of the heavenly bodies, it is said to be *astronomical;* when the chronology refers to particular events occurring among men on earth, it is called *historical.*

Difficulties of Chronology. The chronology of the NT relates alike to the dates when the several books of which it is composed were written and to the historicity of the facts recorded in their contents. Thus the origin of the Christian era is involved. But the modern chronologist is confronted with considerable difficulty at the very outset to fix the *exact date* of the birth of Jesus Christ, as the founder of Christianity, which synchronizes with the beginning of the Christian era. This is because he is compelled to base his computation on dateless documents written in a remote antiquity. For neither sacred nor secular authors in those times were at all accustomed to record historical facts under distinct dates. All demands were satisfied when known occurrences were referred to definite periods, as within a certain generation, or under a specific dynasty, or within the reign of a given ruler already familiar to the contemporaries addressed; for our modern method of historical notation according to the calendar was something altogether unknown to the ancients. A fine illustration of the ancient method is furnished in the third gospel, wherein a chronological minute is made of the beginning of John the Baptist's ministry, compacting away and synchronizing in a single sentence the names of the ruling Caesar at Rome, the several political rulers of Palestine under that emperor, the territories over which they presided, and even the high priests of the Jewish religion at Jerusalem (Luke 3:1-2). Now it does not follow that because such documents were dateless they were unhistorical, or in any sense to be discredited.

Rather, because that practice was the universal custom of the times with historians, a departure from the method would at once justify a suspicion against an ancient document as unauthentic and incredible.

Basis of Computation. The argument relies upon three facts: (1) the star of the ancient wise men, a scientific conclusion; (2) the death of Herod the Great, with special reference to an eclipse of the moon; and (3) the enrollment of the Jewish population at the birth of Christ, by the Roman Quirinius. Edward Robinson states: "The present Christian era, which was fixed by the abbot Dionysius Exiguus in the 6th century, assumes the year of the Christian era as coincident with the year 754 from the building of Rome. Our era begins in any case more than four years too late; i.e., from four to five years at least after the actual birth of Christ. This era was first used in historical works by the Venerable Bede early in the 8th century and was not long after introduced in public transactions by the French kings Pepin and Charlemagne" (*Greek Harmony of the Gospels*).

Dionysius Exiguus did not give origin to the Christian era, he merely computed it. Considering the *data* then at his command, his work is as remarkable for its difficulty as for its measure of success. However, the *common consensus* of eminent biblicists is that he erred in his conclusion by at least four years: that the beginning of the Christian era should properly have been dated at A.U.C. (*ab urbe condita*, "from the founding of the city" of Rome) 750 instead of 754, which would have been coincident with 4 B.C. of our present chronology. There are several scientific and historical *data* now to be considered as determinative of the time of the birth of Jesus Christ, upon which the Christian era is based.

Star of the Wise Men. Matthew alone notes the passage of the *magi*, who had crossed the deserts of the East, guided by the presence of a strange star, to the feet of the infant Jesus. They ask of Herod, "Where is He who has been born King of the Jews? For we saw His star in the east, and have come to worship Him" (Matt. 2:2). The appearance of a star was the predicted sign of the Messiah's birth as made by Balaam, the Moses of the Midianites. It reads: "A star shall come forth from Jacob, and a scepter shall rise from Israel.... One from Jacob shall have dominion" (Num. 24:17, 19).

In reference to the star of the magi Schaff remarks: "The Savior was not without a witness among the heathen. Wise men from the East —i.e., Persian magi, of the Zend religion, in which the idea of a Zoziosh, or *redeemer*, was clearly known—guided miraculously by a star or meteor created for the purpose, came and sought out the Savior to pay Him homage" (Smith, *Bib. Dict.*, 2:1349, Hackett's ed.).

Jewish Intimations. With reference to Ba-

laam's prediction, the Jewish rabbis wrote in their Talmud: "When the Messiah shall be revealed there shall rise up in the east a star flaming with six colors" (R. Frey, *Messiah*, p. 137). "The star shall shine forth from the east, *and this is the star of the Messiah*. It shall shine forth from the east for fifteen days, and if it be prolonged it will be for the good of Israel" (Edersheim, *Jesus of Nazareth*, 1:212).

Those Jews who are still looking for their Messiah to come confidently expect a star to appear as the *sign of His Advent*. So it was also in the early centuries of Christianity; and this explains why that celebrated messianic imposter succeeded so well in the reign of Hadrian, A.D. 132-35, who assumed the name Bar-Kokheba, i.e., "the son of a star," and issued coins bearing a star in allusion to Balaam's prediction. In his open rebellion against the Romans he found a large following of the Jews, but when made a prisoner he promised that if his captors killed him he would prove his messiahship by rising from the dead. The Romans took him at his word and cut off his head. Because he did not rise as he had promised, the Jews became disgusted and named him Bar-Kozibar, i.e., "the son of a lie!" (see Schaff, *Hist. Christ. Church*, 1:402).

Schaff also mentions the learned rabbi named *Abarbanel*, or *Abrabanel*, as authority for the tradition of the Jews, "There was a conspicuous conjunction of planets . . . three years before the birth of Moses, in the sign Pisces," and that another "would occur before the Messiah's birth." This was fifty years before Kepler published his discovery of the conjunction of the planets Jupiter, Saturn, and Mars, in the sign Pisces, at the birth of Jesus. Kepler's discovery has since been verified by other eminent astronomers, "including Schubert, of Petersburg; Charles Pritchard, of London, honorable secretary of the Royal Astronomical Society; and Ideler and Encke, of Berlin." "Dean Alford accepts this view. . . . The mathematical calculation of Wieseler, placing the date of the appearance of the star at A.U.C. 750 is coincident with 4 B.C., the time of the corrected chronology of the nativity." "It is pronounced by Pritchard to be 'as certain as any celestial phenomenon of ancient date.' " "If we accept the results of these calculations of astronomers, we are brought to within two years of the nativity, viz., between A.U.C. 748 (6 B.C.) (Kepler) and 750 (4 B.C.) (Wieseler). The differences arise, of course, from the uncertainty of the time of the departure and length of the journey of the magi" (*Hist.* 1:115-16, 119).

Chinese Notations. Edersheim mentions the astronomical tables of the Chinese as being honored by Humboldt, which contains an account of this star; and that "Pingre and others have designated it as a comet," whose appearance was coincident with the visit of the magi, which would "seem to go before (them) in the direction of, and stand over, Bethlehem." "And here the subject must, in the present state of information, be left" (*Jesus the Messiah,* 1:213).

Death of Herod the Great. He was sometimes known as Herod I (*see* article Herod). The first gospel relates that "Jesus was born in Bethlehem of Judea in the days of Herod the king" (Matt. 2:1; cf. Luke 1:5). Josephus, the celebrated Jewish priest and historian, born A.D. 37, affirms in both his historical works that Herod died in Jericho, in the valley of the Jordan, A.U.C. 750, or 4 B.C. It is known that his death occurred just before the Jewish Passover, on March 13. This writer further remarks that on "that very night there was an eclipse of the moon" (*Ant.* 7.7.6.4.; *Wars* 1.1.8). The fact of the eclipse is conspicuous for the reason that it is the only one mentioned by this writer and that this circumstance furnishes a certain astronomical *datum* for determining the nativity, since Herod was then alive and sought the child's life.

When the magi inquired of Herod respecting Him "*born King of the Jews,*" it filled him with consternation. "Herod the king . . . was troubled, and all Jerusalem with him." Fearing that the royal infant would be his supplanter, he "sent and slew all the male children . . . from two years old and under." Joseph meanwhile had fled with the holy family into Egypt, "until the death of Herod," when an angel directed him to return to the land of Israel, "for those who sought the Child's life are dead" (Matt. 2:2-20). Now, Josephus relates that Herod, just five days before he died, killed his own son Antipater, which reveals his horrible character. This fact seems to have been confused with the account of the massacre of the infant children at Bethlehem when the report reached the emperor at Rome. Thereupon Macrobius states that Augustus Caesar, recalling Herod's Jewish hatred of swine, said, "It is better to be Herod's hog than to be his son" ("Melius est Herodis porcum esse quam filium," *Saturnalia Convivia* 2.4).

It is obvious that Jesus was born at least several months before the death of Herod; that the murder of the innocents occurred between the birth of our Lord and the death of Herod; and withal, the moon's eclipse on that "very night" of his death renders it scientifically certain and ascertainable by mathematical calculation that Herod departed this life on March 13, A.U.C. 750, which is identical with the year 4 B.C. the year assumed as that of the nativity.

Enrollment of Cyrenius (Quirinius). Schaff gives Franciscus Junius as the authority for the historical statement that "*the agent* through whom Saturninus carried out the census in Judea *was the governor Cyrenius,* according to Luke, ch. 2."

Another chronological *datum* for determining the year of Christ's birth is furnished by the third gospel: "Now it came about in those days that a decree went out from Caesar Augustus, that a census be taken of all the inhabited earth. This was the first census taken while Quirinius was governor of Syria. And all were proceeding to register for the census, everyone to his own city. And Joseph also went up from Galilee, from the city of Nazareth, to Judea, to the city of David, which is called Bethlehem, because he was of the house and family of David, in order to register along with Mary. . . . And she gave birth to her first-born son" (Luke 2:1-7).

Method of Registration. This was a Roman registration conducted by the Jewish method. Every person was required to resort to his own tribal territory in order to be entered in the registry. By this simple but most significant circumstance Joseph and Mary left their residence in Galilee and came to their ancestral Bethlehem, in the territory of Judah, where Jesus was born; and Micah's prediction of the Messiah's birth was circumstantially realized: "But as for you, Bethlehem Ephrathah . . . from you One will go forth for Me to be ruler in Israel" (Mic. 5:2).

A head tax was imposed upon all men and women between the ages of fourteen and sixty-five (Schaff). Edersheim says: "In consequence of the decree of Caesar Augustus, Herod (the Great) directed a general registration to be made after the Jewish rather than the Roman manner. . . . All country people were to be registered in their own city; meaning thereby the town to which the village or place where they were born was attached. In so doing the house or lineage of each was marked. According to the Jewish mode of registration the people would have to be enrolled according to tribes, families, or clans, and the house of their father. . . . In the case of Joseph and Mary, whose descent from David was not only known, but where, for the sake of the unborn Messiah, it was most important that this should be distinctly noted, it is natural that in accordance with Jewish law they should go to Bethlehem" (*Jesus the Messiah,* 1:182-83).

The Two Registrations. There has been in the past an interesting question: How could Cyrenius conduct an enrollment of the Jews at the birth of Christ, 4 B.C. when it is a known fact that he was appointed governor of Syria and made a registry ten years later, namely, in A.D. 6? The answer is that Cyrenius was *twice* appointed to this service. In the first instance it was a census of the *population,* taken with a view of replacing their tribute to the empire in produce by a head tax in money; and in the second it was a registration of their *property.* The census occurred 4 B.C. to A.D. 1. It was begun by Sentius Saturninus, was then continued by Quintilius Varus until 4 B.C. and concluded by Cyrenius from the year 4 B.C. to A.D. 1, the time of the nativity. Luke expressly says, "*This was the first census*" (2:2). The second enrollment by Cyrenius occurred A.D. 10-14, according to the correct chronology.

Now, Luke makes historical notation of *both* enrollments in a way that indicates a perfect understanding of them on the part of his contemporaries. He refers to the first as a principal fact connecting it with the birth of Jesus; he refers to the second enrollment incidentally, in narrating what Gamaliel said in defense of the apostles before the Sanhedrin. In recounting different rebellions against the Romans in that country, Gamaliel said, "After this man Judas of Galilee rose up *in the days of the census*" (cf. Luke 2:1-3; Acts 5:37). It is of this registration that Josephus says: "Under his administration [Cyrenius's as procurator of Judea] it was that a certain Galilean whose name was Judas prevailed with his countrymen to revolt" (*Wars* 2.8.1); "I mean that Judas who caused the people to revolt when Cyrenius came to take an account of the estates of the Jews" (*Ant.* 20.5.2).

The latest word on these enrollments is that of the eminent Augustus W. Zumpt, the classical scholar and archaeologist of Berlin, whose researches have secured us "full historical probability; and whose conclusions of the date of the birth of Christ at the time of the census taken 4 B.C. by Cyrenius is endorsed by the scholarly Mommsen, and accords with the view of Ideler, Bergmann, Browne, Ussher, and Sanclemente" (Schaff).

Patristic References. These have their evidential value, coming from those who were so near in the succession of the apostles and corroborating the historical character in the common understanding of their contemporaries respecting the census taken by Cyrenius at the time of the nativity. Manifold strength is added to these references in that they appeal directly to the registries of the Roman government for the truth of what they say. Justin Martyr (born A.D. 105) says: "Now there is a village in the land of the Jews, thirty-five stadia from Jerusalem, in which Christ was born, as you can ascertain also from the registries of the taxing under Quirinius [Cyrenius] your first procurator in Judea" (*First Apology*, chap. 34). Now, as Justin was defending the Christians from persecutions by the government, nothing could have been more unfortunate and fatal to his claim if the appeal to the public registries was false; but nothing could be stronger in evidence if the appeal was verified by the registration. This remark applies alike to Tertullian of Carthage (born A.D. 160) who was a highly gifted lawyer, and who, writing with a different design from a different country, refers to the same enrollment, and the same *period*, when he says: "There is historical proof that at this very time a census had been taken in Judea by Sentius Saturninus, which might have satisfied their inquiry respecting the family and descent of Christ" (*Marcion* 4.19).

Accounts of Historians. Schaff cites with approval several high authorities as historians on this subject. He says: "Cassiodorus and Suidas expressly assert the fact of a general census, and add several particulars which are not derived from Luke; e.g., Suidas says that Augustus elected twenty commissioners of high character and sent them to all parts of the empire to collect statistics of the population. . . . Hence Huschke, Wieseler, Zumpt, Plumptre, and McClellan accept their testimony as historically correct. . . . Wieseler quotes also John Malala, the historian of Antioch, as saying . . . that 'Augustus in the thirty-ninth year and tenth month of his reign (i.e., 5 or 6 B.C.) issued a decree for a general registration throughout the empire.' Julius Caesar had begun a measurement of the whole empire, and Augustus completed it" (*Hist. Christ. Church*, 1:124-25, n. 4).

Affirmation of an Enemy. It is greatly to our advantage in the investigation of the truth of the gospels to cite the testimony of a conspicuous adversary of Christianity who lived in the early centuries of the era, touching this census taken by Cyrenius at the time of the nativity—Julian, born 331, a Roman emperor, known as "the Apostate," because, having been brought up a Christian, he repudiated this religion when he came to the throne. When in possession of all the archives of the empire he wrote against the Christians as one so conscious of the certainty of his source of information that he adopted a defiant tone, especially in reference to the enrollment of Joseph and Mary at Bethlehem, as mentioned by Luke. There is absolutely no known record of evidence that Jesus was "enrolled as one of Caesar's subjects," unless it was at the time which Julian affirms. He says: "Jesus, whom you celebrate, was one of Caesar's subjects. If you dispute it, I will prove it. . . . For yourselves allow that He was enrolled with His father and mother in the time of Cyrenius." "But Jesus having persuaded a few among you, and those the worst of men, has now been celebrated about three hundred years, having done nothing in His lifetime worthy of remembrance, unless anyone thinks it a mighty matter to heal lame and blind people, and exorcise demoniacs in the villages of Bethsaida and Bethany" (Lardner, *Works*, 7:626-27).

Monumental Inscription. A monument has been unearthed at Rome between the Villa Hadriani and the Via Tiburtina. The name of him to whom the monument was dedicated is obliterated. Bergmann, Mommsen, and Merivale refer it to Cyrenius. Then it reads: "Quirinius as proconsul obtained Asia as his province. As legate of the deified Augustus a second time, he governed Syria and Phoenicia" (*see* Schaff, *Hist. Christ. Church*, 1:122-23).

Christ's Confirmation. There is a direct implication of Christ's loyalty, as "one of Caesar's subjects," to "the powers that be," as on the notable occasion when He met the Jews with the answer *"Render to Caesar the things that are*

Caesar's" (Matt. 22:15-22). This wonderfully wise reply that silenced His adversaries is a record that is exactly accordant with the witness of the emperor, who as the head of the imperial government had in his possession, for reference, all the registrations of the Jews.

These, then, are the three principal arguments respecting the birth of Jesus, and therefore dating properly the Christian era at least four years earlier, namely: (1) that based upon the science of astronomy relating to the star of the magi, as developed by Kepler and improved by other astronomers; (2) the death of Herod the Great, dated by the eclipse of the moon; and (3) the argument based on history due to the researches of Zumpt in regard to the date of Cyrenius's registration of the Jews. Respecting this census, in distinction from a later registration by the same person as indicated by Luke, the patristic appeals made by Justin and Tertullian to the documents in the possession of the government; the assumption of fact in the declaration by the emperor Julian, who directly connects Christ with the census-taking of Cyrenius and His parents' registration; the confirmatory testimony of the secular historians Cassiodorus, Suidas, and John Malala of Antioch to a universal registration throughout the world; the monumental reference at Rome to the same transaction of Cyrenius; and Christ's own conduct in holding Himself to be "a subject of Caesar" by paying the usual imperial tribute to the receivers, are all so many facts corroborating the statement of Luke as historical and fixing the beginning of the Christian era at least four years earlier than our present chronology does.

Books of the New Testament. An approximate chronology of the dates of the NT books can be computed (tables 2, 3), although there is varied opinion among noted scholars concerning those dates. Eminent orthodox Christian writers have generally held to earlier dates for the writing of the gospels and the Acts than have those holding more or less liberal views respecting the Scriptures.

BIBLIOGRAPHY: G. Ogg, *Chronology of the Public Ministry of Jesus* (1940); H. J. Cadbury, *Book of Acts in History* (1955); N. Walker, *Novum Testamentum* 3 (1959): 317-20; A. Jaubert, *New Testament Studies* 7 (1960): 1-30; B. I. Reike, *New Testament Era* (1968); G. Ogg, *Chronology of the Life of Paul* (1968); H. W. Hoehner,

Chronological Aspects of the Life of Christ (1977); J. Smith, *Voyage and Shipwreck of St. Paul* (1978); R. Jewett, *A Chronology of Paul's Life* (1979); S. L. Bowman, *Historical Evidences of the New Testament;* F. F. Bruce, *New Testament History* (1969).

CHRONOLOGY, OLD TESTAMENT. Of great importance is the location of events recorded in the OT in the frame of extrabiblical history. Although many great problems still exist in this correlation, substantial strides in archaeological research have set the OT fairly accurately in the ancient biblical world in general.

Early Chronology of Genesis. The initial chapters of the Bible do not indicate the date of the creation of the world or of man. Genesis 1:1 evidently puts the origin of the universe in the dateless past. According to Genesis, the appearance of man upon the earth is set forth as a result of a direct creative act of God and occurred at least over four millennia B.C. and perhaps as early as 7,000-10,000 years B.C. Byron Nelson, a conservative, argues for even greater antiquity of man (*Before Abraham, Prehistoric Man and Bible Life* [1948], p. 95). This, however, seems scarcely in focus with the indications of the Genesis account. On the other hand, the compressed chronology of Archbishop Ussher, who assumes unbroken succession of father-son relationship in the genealogical lists of Gen. 5 and 11, and who places the creation of man around 4,000 B.C., is untenable in the light of attested archaeological facts. For discussion of the problems involved see B. Ramm, *The Christian View of Science and Scripture* (1955).

Pre-Patriarchal Chronology. The Neolithic, Chalcolithic, and Early Bronze ages.

Neolithic Age (c. 8000-4500 B.C.) The first appearance of pottery (c. 5500 B.C.).

Chalcolithic Age (c. 4000-3000 B.C.). Introduction of copper and of stone implements, advance in pottery, early building activity, simple writing in Babylonia on clay (c. 3400 B.C.), irrigation cultures.

Early Bronze Age (3000-2000 B.C.). The beginning of first great states, Babylonia and Egypt. Babylonia. Three Periods:

1. Early Dynastic Period (c. 2800-2360 B.C.).

2. Old Akkadian Period (c. 2360-2180 B.C.). Mesopotamian Period of the great empire of Sar-

Table 2
Chronology of the Historical Books of the New Testament

Book	Writer	Place	Those Addressed	Date[1]	Key Thought
Synoptic gospels:					
First gospel	Matthew	Judea	Jewish Christians	60-65	Jesus the true Messiah
Second gospel	Mark	Rome	Roman Christians	60-65	Jesus the Son of man
Third gospel	Luke	Caesarea	Greek Christians	58-65	Jesus Redeemer of mankind
Fourth gospel	John	Ephesus	Christian church	90-100	Jesus incarnate Son of God
Acts of the Apostles	Luke	Rome	Gentile world	58-65	Origin of apostolic churches

1. Dates are approximate and may differ slightly from those given in the articles on the respective books.

gon I followed by Rimush, Manishtusu, Naram-Sin, and Shargalisharri.

3. The Gutian Period (c. 2180-2070 B.C.) and Sumerian renaissance under the Third Dynasty of Ur (c. 2070-1960 B.C.).

Egypt. Four Periods:

1. Predynastic Period (c. 5000-2900 B.C.).

2. Protodynastic Period (Dynasties I-II, c. 2900-2700 B.C.).

3. The Old Kingdom (Dynasties III-IV, c. 2700-2200 B.C.), the great pyramids, vast imperial power.

4. First Intermediate Period (Dynasties VII-XI, c. 2200-2000 B.C.).

Patriarchal to Davidic Era (c. 2000-1000 B.C.). The Middle Bronze Age and the Late Bronze Age.

Middle Bronze Age (c. 2000-1500 B.C.). Developments in Mesopotamia, Egypt, and Palestine:

Mesopotamia. Abraham's birth at Ur (c. 2160 B.C., according to the OT chronology preserved in the MT); Abraham's entrance into Canaan (c. 2086 B.C.); Amorite invasion; establishment of Amorite dynasty from Mediterranean to Babylonia (c. 2000-1700 B.C.), the Mari Age, revealed by excavations at the Middle Euphrates city (c. eighteenth century B.C.); First Dynasty of Babylon (c. 1850-1550 B.C.), the great Hammurabi (c. 1700 B.C.), Indo-Iranian-Hurrian invasion (eighteenth and seventeenth centuries B.C.), destruction of Babylon (c. 1550 B.C.) by Hittites.

Egypt. The Great Middle Kingdom, Dynasty XII (c. 1990-1775 B.C.), Egyptian control of Palestine-Syria, Egyptian sojourn of Israel (c. 1870-1440 B.C., chronology of MT), Joseph becomes prime minister, and Jacob stands before one of the powerful pharaohs of this dynasty (Amenemes I-IV or Senwosret I-III); Israel continues in Egypt during the Hyksos period of foreign domination (c. 1775-1546 B.C.), is oppressed by the great Thutmose III (c. 1482-1450 B.C.) of the

Table 3
Chronology of the New Testament Epistles and the Apocalypse

Writing	Place	Those Addressed	Date[1]	Key Thought
THE PAULINE EPISTLES				
Earliest Epistles				
1 Thessalonians	Corinth	Thessalonian Christians	52	Second advent of Jesus Christ
2 Thessalonians	Corinth	Thessalonian Christians	53	Misunderstanding concerning advent corrected
Mid-Ministry Epistles				
Galatians	Corinth or Ephesus	The church in Galatia	58	Salvation by faith
1 Corinthians	Macedonia	The church in Corinth	55	Resurrection of Jesus Christ
2 Corinthians	Macedonia	The church in Corinth	56	Defense of his apostleship
Romans	Corinth	The Christians at Rome	57	Power of sin and grace
Prison Epistles				
Philemon	Rome	Onesimus's master	61–62	Onesimus's slavery or freedom
Philippians	Caesarea or Rome	The church at Philippi	62	Spiritual encouragements given
Ephesians	Rome	The church at Ephesus	61–62	Unity of Christians
Colossians	Rome	The church at Colosse	61–62	Correction of heretical views
Pastoral Epistles				
1 Timothy	Macedonia	Timothy	64–66	Church officers and their duties
2 Timothy	Rome	Timothy	64 or 67	Paul's coming death near
Titus	Macedonia or Greece	Titus of Crete	64–66	Persons for church offices
THE CATHOLIC (OR GENERAL) EPISTLES				
Hebrews	Palestine	Jewish Christians	63–64	High priesthood of Jesus Christ
James	Jerusalem	Jerusalem	48–49	Duties: prayer, faith, works
1 Peter	Babylon	The dispersed Jews	64	Encouragement in Christian duties
2 Peter	Unknown	The church at large	66–67	New heavens and new earth
1 John	Judea	The general church	85–90	Love of Jesus and the brethren
2 John	Ephesus	Elect lady and children	85–90	Loyal obedience to Jesus Christ
3 John	Ephesus	Beloved Gaius	85–90	The state of the church
Jude	Unknown	Believers in general	66–67	Defense of the faith
BOOK OF THE APOCALYPSE				
Revelation	Patmos[2] or Ephesus	Seven churches of Asia	68–69[2] or 96–98	The consummation of all things

Revised R.K.H.; H.F.V.

1. Dates are approximate and may differ slighty from those given in the articles on the respective books.
2. If the apostle John was banished to Patmos under the reign of Nero, *as the internal evidence indicates*, he wrote the Apocalypse about A.D. 68 or 69, which was after the death of that emperor; but the gospel and epistles some years later. This view is advocated or accepted by Neander, Lücke, Bleek, Ewald, DeWette, Baur, Higenfeld, Reuss, Düsterdieck, Weiss, Renan, Aubé, Stuart, Davidson, Cowles, Bishop Lightfoot, Westcott, and Schaff. The great majority of older commentators, and among the later ones Elliott, Alford, Hengstenberg, Ebrard, Lange, Godet, Lee, and others, favor the traditional date, *as the external evidence indicates*, which is after Domitian's death in A.D. 96. John is said to have died a natural death in the reign of Trajan, about A.D. 98 (see Schaff, *Hist. Christ. Church,* 1:429, 834). S.L.B.

New Kingdom (Dynasty XVIII), and quits the country under Amenhotep II (c. 1450-1425 B.C.).

Palestine. Abraham enters Canaan (c. 2086 B.C.), Patriarchal Period (2086-1871 B.C., chronology of the MT).

Late Bronze Age (c. 1500-1200 B.C.). Developments in Egypt, Mesopotamia, Asia Minor, Palestine, and Greece:

Egypt—New Kingdom. Two Dynasties:

1. Dynasty XVIII (c. 1570-1319 B.C.), Thutmose III (c. 1482-1450 B.C.), Amenhotep II (c. 1450-1425 B.C.), Israel quits Egypt (c. 1440), enters Canaan (c. 1400 B.C.). Important pharaohs of Amarna Period, Amenophis III (c. 1413-1377), Amenophis IV (Akhnaton; c. 1377-1360 B.C.); solar monotheism.

2. Dynasty XIX (c. 1319-1200 B.C.), principal pharaohs Seti I (c. 1319-1301 B.C.), Rameses II the Great (c. 1301-1234 B.C.), wars with the Hittites at Kadesh (c. 1298), treaty with them (c. 1280), reign of Merenptah (c. 1235-1227), first mention of Israel in his stela (c. 1230).

Mesopotamia. Kassites in Babylonia (c. 1500-1150 B.C.), Mitannian state in northern Mesopotamia (c. 1500-1370), war between Egypt and Mitanni, conquests of Hittites (c. 1375).

Asia Minor. Hittite Empire (c. 1600-1200 B.C.), clash with Egypt at Kadesh (c. 1298 B.C.), treaty with the Egyptians (c. 1280).

Palestine. Two Major Periods:

1. Amarna Period (c. 1400-1360), destruction of Jericho (c. 1400), entrance of Hebrews into Palestine (c. 1400), conquest of Palestine (c. 1400-1360, Masoretic chronology).

2. Early Period of the Judges (c. 1360-1200 B.C.), oppression of Cushan-Rishathaim (c. 1361-1353 B.C.), deliverance by Othniel, period of peace (c. 1353-1313 B.C.; Judg. 3:11), oppression by Eglon of Moab (c. 1319-1295 B.C.), period of peace after Ehud (c. 1295-1215; Judg. 3:12-30), oppression by Jabin (c. 1215-1195 B.C.; Judg. 4:1-24).

The Greek World. Height of Minoan Civilization (fifteenth century), downfall of Crete (c. 1400), Mycenaean Civilization in Greece, trade with Asia (c. 1400-1300 B.C.).

Early Iron Age (c. 1200-1000 B.C.). Developments in Egypt, Mesopotamia, and Palestine:

Egypt. Dynasty XX (c. 1200-1085 B.C.), Rameses III (c. 1198-1167 B.C.) stems invasion of sea peoples (c. 1191 B.C.), Philistines settle in large numbers in southwestern Palestine, Egypt loses hold on Palestine (after c. 1150 B.C.).

Mesopotamia. General weakness of rulers with the oppression of the great Tiglath-pileser I, who held northern Syria from c. 1105 to 1100 B.C.

Palestine. Middle part of the period of the Judges, deliverance by Deborah (Judg. 4-5), an era of peace for forty years (c. 1195-1155 B.C.), Midianite oppression for seven years (c. 1155-1148 B.C.), era of peace under Gideon (c. 1148-1108), Abimelech king at Shechem (c. 1108-1105 B.C.), Philistine ascendancy (c. 1089-1059 B.C.),

Samson (c. 1085-1065 B.C.), judgeship of Eli (c. 1065-1050 B.C.), Saul and beginning of the monarchy (c. 1020-1004 B.C.), David king (c. 1004).

Table 4
Kings of Judah and Israel[1]

Judah		Israel	
Rehoboam	931–913 B.C.	Jeroboam I	926–909 B.C.
Abijam		Nadab	909–908 B.C.
(or Abijah)	913–910 B.C.	Baasha	908–886 B.C.
Asa	910–869 B.C.	Elah	886–885 B.C.
Jehoshaphat	873–848 B.C.	Zimri	885 B.C.
Jehoram		Tibni	885–880 B.C.
(or Joram)	853–841 B.C.	Omri	885–874 B.C.
Ahaziah	841 B.C.	Ahab	874–853 B.C.
Athaliah	841–835 B.C.	Ahaziah	853–852 B.C.
Joash (or		Jehoram	852–841 B.C.
Jehoash)	835–796 B.C.	Jehu	841–814 B.C.
Amaziah	796–767 B.C.	Jehoahaz	814–798 B.C.
Uzziah (or		Joash (or	
Azariah)	792–740 B.C.	Jehoash)	798–782 B.C.
Jotham	750–732 B.C.	Jeroboam II	793–753 B.C.
Ahaz	735–715 B.C.	Zechariah	753–752 B.C.
Hezekiah	715–686 B.C.	Shallum	752 B.C.
Manasseh	696–642 B.C.	Menahem	752–742 B.C.
Amon	642–640 B.C.	Pekahiah	742–740 B.C.
Josiah	640–609 B.C.	Pekah	752–732 B.C.
Jehoahaz	609 B.C.	Hoshea	732–723 B.C.
Jenoiakim	609–597 B.C.	Fall of Samaria	723/722 B.C.
Jehoiachin	597 B.C.		
Zedekiah	597–586 B.C.		
Fall of			
Jerusalem	586 B.C.		

1. Dates are adapted from the chronology of E.R. Thiele and include coregencies.

The Era of the Hebrew Kings (c. 1000-586 B.C.). Developments in Palestine, Egypt, and Mesopotamia.

Palestine. (1) The United Monarchy: David (c. 1004-965 B.C.), Solomon (c. 965-926 B.C., according to J. Begrich); and (2) the Dual Monarchy (c. 926-586 B.C.; see table 4, "Kings of Judah and Israel").

Egypt. Libyan, Ethiopian, and Saite Dynasties: Libyan Dynasties XXII-XXIV (c. 935-712 B.C.), Pharaoh Shishak, who invaded Palestine.

Ethiopian Dynasty XXV (c. 712-663 B.C.), Assyria conquered Egypt (c. 760 B.C.).

Saite Dynasty XXVI (c. 663-525 B.C.), Pharaoh Neco (c. 609-597 B.C.), Hophra (c. 588-569 B.C.); Neco defeated by Chaldeans at Haran (c. 609 B.C.) and at Carchemish (c. 605 B.C.).

Mesopotamia. Assyrian Empire and Chaldean Period.

Assyrian Empire in a weakened form (c. 1000-880 B.C.), great conqueror Ashurnasirpal II (883-859 B.C.), Shalmaneser III (858-824 B.C.), Battle of Qarqar (853 B.C.), Assyrian push stopped by Ahab and Assyrian coalition. Tiglath-pileser III (747-727 B.C.) conquered coastal plain of Galilee, Gilead, and Damascus (733-732 B.C.); Samaria besieged by Shalmaneser V (727-722 B.C.), captured by Sargon II (721 B.C.), 27,290 leading citizens being carried into exile; Sennacherib (705-681 B.C.) invaded Judea at the time of Hezekiah (c. 701 B.C.), Assyrian world power, Esarhaddon (681-669 B.C.) conquered Egypt, Ashurbanipal

(669-626 B.C.), decline of Assyria, fall of Asshur to the Medes (614 B.C.), Nineveh destroyed by the Medes and Babylonians (612 B.C.).

The Chaldean Period (c. 612-539), defeat of Assyria and Egypt under Neco at Haran (c. 609 B.C.), Nebuchadnezzar II (c. 605-562 B.C.), captivity of Judah, destruction of Jerusalem (c. 586 B.C.).

The Era of the Exile and Return (587-400 B.C.). Developments in Palestine, the Persian Empire, and Greece.

Palestine. Deportation of the leading citizens of Judah including Daniel (605 B.C.) and Ezekiel (597 B.C.), destruction of Jerusalem (587 B.C.), Cyrus's proclamation (538 B.C.), return under Zerubbabel (536 B.C.), Temple rebuilt (520-515 B.C.), Ezra's return (458 B.C.), Nehemiah's return (444 B.C.), Malachi (435 B.C.).

Persian Empire. Persia conquers Babylon (539 B.C.), death of Cyrus (530 B.C.), Cambyses (530-522 B.C.), conquers Egypt (525 B.C.), Darius I the Great (522-486 B.C.), Behistun Inscription; defeat at Marathon (490 B.C.), Ahasuerus (486-465 B.C.), campaign against Greece, defeat at Salamis (480 B.C.), Artaxerxes I (465-424 B.C.), Xerxes II (424-423 B.C.), Darius I (423-404 B.C.), Artaxerxes II (404-358 B.C.), Artaxerxes III (358-338 B.C.), Arses (338-336 B.C.), Darius III (336-331 B.C.).

Greece. The Greeks defeat the Persians at Marathon (490 B.C.), Salamis (480 B.C.), golden age at Athens, Pericles (460-429 B.C.), Herodotus (485-425 B.C.), Socrates (469-400 B.C.), Plato (430-350 B.C.), Aristotle (384-322 B.C.).

The Greek Era (333-63 B.C.). Developments in the Macedonian Empire and in the kingdoms that emerged from that empire by 275 B.C., following the death of Alexander the Great in 323, B.C.

Macedonian Empire. The reigns of Philip II of Macedonia (359-336 B.C.) and his son Alexander the Great (336-323 B.C.); Alexander the Great's conquest of Persia, arrival in India (327 B.C.), death in Babylon (323 B.C.),

Macedonian Kingdom. Rule of Macedonia by a line of kings followed by the establishment of the country as a Roman province in 146 B.C.

Egypt. Rule of Egypt by a dynasty begun by Ptolemy I (Soter), a general of Alexander the Great. Maintenance of the kingdom in relative strength through Ptolemies I-V, but a decline afterward; establishment of Egypt as a Roman province in 30 B.C. The Ptolemies from 323 B.C. to 180 B.C.:

Ptolemy I	323-285 B.C.
Ptolemy II	285-246 B.C.
Ptolemy III	246-221 B.C.
Ptolemy IV	221-203 B.C.
Ptolemy V	203-180 B.C.

Syria. Following the death of Alexander the Great, the rule of Syria by a dynasty founded by Seleucus I Nicator, an officer in Alexander's army; the conquest of Babylon by Seleucus in 312 B.C. and the beginning of the formal counting of the Seleucid Dynasty; maintenance of the kingdom in relative strength through Antiochus VII; following that ruler, continuation of the kingdom in a weak form until Pompey's conquest; the establishment of Syria as a Roman province in 64 B.C. The Seleucid rulers from 312 B.C. to 129 B.C.:

Seleucus I	312-280 B.C.
Antiochus I	280-261 B.C.
Antiochus II	261-247 B.C.
Seleucus II	247-226 B.C.
Seleucus III	226-223 B.C.
Antiochus III (The Great)	223-187 B.C.
Seleucus IV	187-175 B.C.
Antiochus-Epiphanes IV	175-163 B.C.
Antiochus-Epiphanes V	163-162 B.C.
Demetrius I	162-150 B.C.
Alexander Balas	150-145 B.C.
Antiochus VI	145-141 B.C.
Demetrius II	145-138 B.C.
Antiochus VII	139-129 B.C.

Pergamum. Under the Attalids until Attalus III (139-133 B.C.), who bequeathed his kingdom to Rome.

Bithynia. Under kings until Nicomedes III (94-74 B.C.) bequeathed his kingdom to Rome.

Pontus. Under Mithridates I (337-301) and his successors until conquered by Rome (50 B.C.).

Galatia. Came under Roman rule on the death of Amyntas (37-25 B.C.).

Parthian Kingdom (248 B.C.). Extended sway to India. Defeated Crassus and threatened Syria and Asia Minor; repulsed by the Romans (39 B.C.), the kingdom continued, but with declining power until A.D. 224.

Greek Cities. Allied with Rome against Macedonia, but Rome gradually absorbed Greece; destruction of Corinth (146 B.C.) ended resistance, Greece organized as separate Roman province (27 B.C.).

Palestine. Under strong Egyptian power until 198 B.C., when Syria gained ascendancy. Maccabean revolt against Greek paganizing civilization 167 B.C. The Maccabean rulers from 166 to 63 B.C.:

Judas Maccabaeus	166-160 B.C.
Jonathan	160-142 B.C.
Simon	142-134 B.C.
John Hyrcanus	134-104 B.C.
Aristobulus	104-103 B.C.
Alexander Jannaeus	103-76 B.C.
Alexandra	76-67 B.C.
Aristobulus II	66-63 B.C.

Rome under Pompey assumed control over Palestine 63 B.C.

Nabataean Kingdom. By 300 B.C. the Nabataeans were in possession of ancient Edom. From Petra, their capital, their power extended in all directions. Their control was limited by the Romans from 63 B.C. on, but they did not become a Roman province until A.D. 106.   M.F.U.

BIBLIOGRAPHY: J. B. Payne, *Outline of Hebrew History* (1954); W. C. Hayes, M. B. Rowton, and F. H. Stubbins, *The Cambridge Ancient History: Chronology* (1962); R. W. Ehrich, *Chronologies in Old World Archaeology* (1966); K. A. Kitchen, *Ancient Orient and the Old Testament* (1966), pp. 33-78; R. K. Harrison, *Introduction to the Old Testament* (1969), pp. 147-98; E. R. Thiele, *A Chronology of the Hebrew Kings* (1977); id., *The Mysterious Numbers of the Hebrew Kings* (1983).

CHRYSOLITE, CHRYSOPRASE. *See* Mineral Kingdom.

CHUB (kûb; only Ezek. 30:5, KJV). A nation in alliance with Egypt, and probably near it. Some read *Lub* (or, NIV, "Libya"), a singular form of *Lubîm* (Libyans), which elsewhere occurs only in the plural. Some propose *Nûb* (Nubia), as the Arab. version has Noobeh. But these emendations are only conjectures.

CHUN *See* Cun.

CHURCH (Gk. *ekklēsia,* "called out," *ek* "out," *kaleo* "to call").

The Term, General Use. The word *church* is employed to express various ideas, some of which are scriptural, others not. It may be used to signify: (1) The entire body of those who are saved by their relation to Christ. (2) A particular Christian denomination. (3) The aggregate of all the ecclesiastical communions professing faith in Christ. (4) A single organized Christian group. (5) A building designated for Christian worship.

Simple New Testament Usage. In the NT the church comprehends the whole number of regenerated persons specifically from Pentecost to the first resurrection (1 Cor. 15:52; 1 Thess. 4:13-17) united organically to one another and to Christ by the baptizing work of the Holy Spirit (Rom. 6:3-4; 1 Cor. 12:12-13; Gal. 3:27; Eph. 4:5; Col. 2:10-12). According to the NT definition the church is the mystical Body of Christ of which He is the head (Eph. 1:22-23), being a holy temple for the habitation of God through the Spirit (2:21-22), "one flesh" with Christ (5:30-31), and espoused to Him as a pure virgin to one husband (2 Cor. 11:2-4). The word *ekklēsia,* however, is employed of any assembly, and the word in the Gk. language imples no more; for example, the town meeting or "assembly" (*ekklēsia*) at Ephesus (Acts 19:39), and Israel called out of Egypt and spoken of as a "congregation," *ekklēsia,* in the wilderness (Acts 7:38), but in no sense was it a NT church except as a type of that which was to come. In addition to the church as the Body of Christ, we find other meanings attached to the word in the NT. It refers sometimes to the company of believers in a single province or city (cf. Rev. 2-3), or those meeting in a particular place of worship. It is applied even to bodies of professed believers who have largely departed from the true faith and practice, though in such cases the title is no longer appropriate except as a reminder of what they once were or professed to be, or only as a convenient designation, the significance of which in such cases is wholly lost.

The Beginning of the Church. That the true church as the Body of Christ began on the Day of Pentecost may be demonstrated in various ways. (1) Christ Himself declared it to be yet future. (2) It was founded upon the death, resurrection, and ascension of Christ, and such an accomplished fact was not possible until Pentecost (Gal. 3:23-25). (3) There could be no church until it was purchased with Christ's precious blood (Eph. 5:25-27), until He arose to give it resurrected life (Col. 3:1-3), until He ascended to be head over all things to the church (Eph. 1:20-23), and until the Spirit came on Pentecost, through whom the church would be formed into one body by the baptism of the Spirit. (4) The baptism of the Spirit prophesied by John (Matt. 3:11; Mark 1:8; Luke 3:16-17; John 1:33) was still future at Acts 1:5. That it occurred between 1:5 and 11:16 is evident by a comparison of these two verses. It is obvious that the Holy Spirit, who came at Pentecost, arrived to perform among His various ministries of regenerating, sealing, indwelling, and filling, His distinctive ministry for this age of baptizing into Christ, that is, into His Body, the church (1 Cor. 12:13). It was just as impossible, considering the baptizing work of the Holy Spirit, that the church would have been formed before Pentecost as it was impossible that it should not have been formed after that date. Other views as to the time of the founding of the church include the period of Christ's earthly ministry, the days of Abraham, and the lifetime of Adam.

Purpose and Completion of the Church. There is abundant Scripture that points to God's principal purpose in this particular age as the outcalling of the church, the Body of Christ, from both Gentiles and Jews (Acts 15:14-18). This pivotal passage from Acts indicates God's divine purpose for this age in taking out from among the Gentiles a people for His name. The gospel has never anywhere saved all but in every place it has called out some. The church is thus still in the process of formation, principally from among Gentiles with comparatively few Jews, who constitute the remnant according to the election of grace (Rom. 11:5). When the Body of Christ is complete, it will be removed, or translated, from the earthly scene (1 Cor. 15:51-53; 1 Thess. 4:15-17; 2 Thess. 2:1; Rev. 3:10). After the out-taking of the church, the end-time apocalyptic judgments will fall upon Gentiles and unbelieving Jews. However, a remnant will be saved out of this "time of Jacob's distress" (Jer. 30:7), and the advent of Christ in glory will mark the setting up of the millennial kingdom with the nation Israel reinstated in priestly communion and blessing (Zech. 3:1-10) as the light of the world (4:1-14). Three views are held among premillennialists as to the time of

Christ's return: before, in the middle of, and at the end of the Tribulation.

Relation Between Christ and the Church. Seven NT figures set forth this relation: (1) the Shepherd and the Sheep (John 10); (2) the Vine and the Branches (John 15); (3) the Cornerstone and the Stones of the Building (1 Cor. 3:9; Eph. 2:19-22; 1 Pet. 2:5); (4) High Priest and the Kingdom of Priests (Heb. 5:1-10; 6:13–8:6; 1 Pet. 2:5-9; Rev. 1:6); (5) the Head and the Many-Membered Body (1 Cor. 12:12-13, 27; Eph. 4:4); (6) the Last Adam and the New Creation (1 Cor. 15:22, 45; 2 Cor. 5:17); (7) the Bridegroom and the Bride (John 3:29; 2 Cor. 11:2; Eph. 5:25-33; Rev. 19:7-8).

The Unity of the Church. Our Lord's remarkable intercession for Christian unity in John 17:11, 20-23 was answered in the outpouring of the Holy Spirit at Pentecost and the Spirit's advent to baptize all who believe in Christ into one Body. Christian unity is thus a reality—a position as a result of being "in Christ." It is not organizational unity but the unity of a living organism. The task of Christians is to realize this positional unity as an actuality by Christlike conduct (Eph. 4:1-3) based on sound doctrine (4:4-6). Only then can positional unity become experiential.

Roman Catholic and Protestant Statements. The authoritative utterances of Catholics and of Protestants illustrate this difference of view. For example, the *Catechism of Trent* (Roman Catholic) says: "The church is one, because, as the apostle says, there is 'one Lord, one faith, one baptism;' but more especially because it has one invisible ruler, Christ, and one visible, viz., the occupant for the time being of the chair of St. Peter at Rome." Luther's *Larger Catechism* says: "I believe that there is upon earth a certain community of saints composed solely of holy persons, under one Head, collected together by the Spirit; of one faith and one mind, endowed with manifold gifts, but united in love and without sects and divisions." The Church of England (Art. 19) says: "A congregation of faithful men, in which the pure word of God is preached, and the sacraments duly administered according to Christ's ordinance, in all those things that of necessity are requisite to the same." This is also the definition given by the Methodist church. These quotations might be greatly multiplied; but enough is given to show the main line of divergence and the position and trend of Protestant doctrine upon this subject.

The Ethics of the Church. As visible institutions churches must exercise government over their members. What rules of conduct they may properly impose and enforce is, however, a question of great importance. If the church is, as Roman Catholics hold, infallible, because divinely inspired, then all that the church may require is of divine obligation. If the churches, as some seem to hold, are merely voluntary human societies formed for Christian purposes, then such rules as from a human standpoint may seem appropriate are binding upon those who enter and remain in their communion; though at the same time the obligation of entering or remaining becomes, to say the least, greatly reduced. But if, according to the Protestant view, the churches are divine-human institutions, and not infallible, the rules of conduct must accord with the teachings of the infallible Word. The ethical standard of the visible church must be simply that of the Holy Scriptures, otherwise the true idea of the church is lost sight of and the church assumes either too much or too little. Only by adhering to the Word of God as the "rule of faith and practice" can the churches save themselves from the two extremes: on the one hand, that of unduly magnifying the authority of the visible church, or, on the other, that of laying aside its highest claim to recognition and obedience.

M.F.U.

BIBLIOGRAPHY: S. Cox, *The Expositor* (1896), 3:223-336; F. J. A. Hoyt, *The Christian Ecclesia* (1897); T. M. Lindsay, *The Church and the Ministry in the Early Centuries* (1907); R. N. Flew, *Jesus and His Church* (1943); A. von Schlatter, *The Church in the New Testament Period* (1955); G. W. Bromiley, *Unity and Disunity of the Church* (1958); R. A. Cole, *The Body of Christ* (1964); R. P. Martin, *Worship in the Early Church* (1964); R. L. Saucy, *The Church in God's Program* (1972).

CHURL (Heb. *kîlay*, "withholding," Isa. 32:5, 7). A fraudulent person, a deceiver. The NIV renders "scoundrel."

CHURLISH (Heb. *qāsheh*, "severe"). A KJV word descriptive of a coarse, ill-natured fellow (1 Sam. 25:3). The NASB renders "harsh," the NIV "surly."

CHU'SHAN-RISHATHA'IM. *See* Cushan-rishathaim.

CHU'ZA (koo'za; Aram. *chuza'*, "jug"), **Ku'za** (NIV). The "steward" of Herod (Antipas), whose wife, *Joanna* (which see), having been cured by our Lord either of possession by an evil spirit or of a disease, became attached to that body of women who accompanied Him on his journeyings (Luke 8:3).

CILIC'IA (si-lish-a). The southeasterly province of Asia Minor along the Mediterranean Sea, with Tarsus, the birthplace of Paul, its capital. A Roman province, 67 B.C. The Jews of Cilicia had a synagogue at Jerusalem (Acts 6:9). Paul learned his trade of tent making here, and visited it soon after his conversion (Gal. 1:21; Acts 9:30). It was famous for its goats' hair. Cicero was once consul of it. Its climate was pleasant and attracted Greek residents (15:41; 21:39).

CINNAMON. *See* Vegetable Kingdom.

CIN'NERETH. *See* Chinnereth.

237

A Jewish baby boy is circumcised

CIRCLE. *See* Vault.

CIRCUIT. (1) In 1 Sam. 7:16 (Heb. *sābab*, to "revolve"), a regular tour of inspection by Samuel when he "judged" Israel. (2) In Job. 22:14 (KJV; NASB marg.) the Heb. word *ĥûg*, "circle," appears in reference to the heavens. *See* Vault. (3) The act of going around (Heb. *tᵉqûfāh*, "revolution"), the *apparent* diurnal revolution of the sun around the earth (Ps. 19:6). The word in Ex. 34:22 and 2 Chron. 24:23 is rendered "turn of the year"; in 1 Sam. 1:20 it refers to the term of pregnancy (NASB marg., "the *circuit* of the days"; NIV, "the course of time").

CIRCUMCISION (Heb. *mûlâ;* Gk. *peritomē,* a "cutting around"). The ceremony of circumcision consisted in cutting away the foreskin, i.e., the hood or fold of skin covering the head of the male organ. This is generally done by means of a sharp knife, but in more primitive times sharp stones were used (Ex. 4:25; Josh. 5:2, "flint knives"). As a rule this act was performed by the father (Gen. 17:23), although it might be done by any Israelite, and, if necessary, women as well (Ex. 4:25), but never by a Gentile. In later times the operation was, in the case of adults, performed by a doctor. The Jews of the present day entrust it to a person called a *mohel* appointed especially for the purpose. In later times the naming of the child accompanied the act of circumcision (Luke 1:59).

History. After God had made a covenant with Abraham (Gen. 15) He commanded that, as a token of the covenant, every male should be circumcised; not merely the children and bodily descendants of Abraham, but also those born in his house and purchased slaves, and that in the case of children it occur on the eighth day after birth. Every one not so circumcised was to be "cut off from his people" as having "broken My covenant" (17:14).

Circumcision was formally enacted as a legal institute by Moses (Lev. 12:3; John 7:22-23) and was made to apply not only to one's own children, but to slaves, home-born or purchased, and to foreigners before they could partake of the Passover or become Jewish citizens (Ex. 12:48).

During the wilderness journey circumcision fell into disuse. This neglect is most satisfactorily explained as follows: the nation, while bearing the punishment of disobedience in its wanderings, was regarded as under temporary rejection by God and was therefore prohibited from using the sign of the covenant.

As the Lord had only promised His assistance on condition that the law given by Moses was faithfully observed, it became the duty of Joshua, upon entering Canaan, to perform the rite of circumcision upon the generation that had been born in the wilderness. This was done immediately upon crossing the Jordan, at or near Gilgal (Josh. 5:2-8).

From this time circumcision became the pride of Israel, they looking with contempt upon all those people not observing it (Judg. 14:3; 15:18; 1 Sam. 14:6; Isa. 52:1; etc.). It became a rite so distinctive of them that their oppressors tried to prevent their observing it, an attempt to which they refused to submit (1 Macc. 1:48, 50, 60, 62).

The process of restoring a circumcised person to his natural condition by a surgical operation was sometimes undergone from a desire to assimilate themselves to the heathen around them, or that they might not be known as Jews when they appeared naked in the games. Paul cautions the Corinthians against taking recourse to this practice from an excessive anti-Judaistic tendency (1 Cor. 7:18-19). The attitude that Christianity, at its introduction, assumed toward circumcision was one of absolute hostility so far as the necessity of the rite to salvation or its possession of any religious or moral worth were concerned (Acts 15:5; Gal. 5:2).

Pagan. Circumcision was practiced by the Edomites, Moabites, Ammonites, and Egyptians, but among the last only by the priests and those who wanted to be initiated into the sacred mysteries. The practice has also been found to exist among the Ethiopians, Colchians, Congo blacks, and many savage tribes in the heart of Africa; also among American Indian tribes, e.g., the Salivas, the Guamos, the Octamotos on the Orinoco, among the inhabitants of Yucatan and of Mexico, and further, among the Fiji Islanders.

Significance. With respect to the symbolical significance of circumcision, it is said to have originated in phallus worship, but if so this would have no bearing on the Israelite view of the rite. It was practiced, according to some, because of its medical advantages, such as the warding off of disease through ease in cleanliness, or that it served to increase the generative powers, but these can hardly be received as proper explanations, for whole nations not practicing circumcision appear as healthy and fruitful. Nor can the rite be brought into connection with the idea of sacrifice, "the consecration of a part of the body for the whole," or even "as an act of emasculation in honor of the Deity, that has gradually dwindled down to the mere cutting away of the foreskin."

We must rather look for the significance of this rite in the fact that the corruption of sin usually manifests itself with peculiar energy in the sexual life, and that the sanctification of the life was symbolized by the purifying of the organ by which life is reproduced. But, as spiritual purity was demanded of the chosen people of God, circumcision became the external token of the covenant between God and His people. It secured to the one subjected to it all the rights of the covenant, participation in all its material and spiritual benefits; while, on the other hand, he was bound to fulfill all the covenant obligations. It had not, however, of a sacramental nature; it was not a vehicle through which to convey the sanctifying influences of God to His people, but was simply a token of the recognition of the covenant relation existing between Israel and God.

The circumcision of the child on the eighth day seems to have been founded on the significance attached to the number seven, so far as that number denotes a period of time. On the eighth day, when a new cycle of life began, the child entered into covenant with God. Again, it was not until the eighth day that the child was supposed to possess an independent existence.

Figurative. Circumcision was used as a symbol of purity of heart (Deut. 10:16; 30:6; cf. Lev. 26:41; Jer. 4:4; 9:25; Ezek. 44:7). "Who am of uncircumcised lips" (Ex. 6:12, KJV; NASB, see marg.; NIV, "faltering lips"). Here Moses would seem to imply that he was unskilled in public address, as the Jews considered circumcision a perfecting of one's powers. Circumcision is also figurative of a readiness to hear and obey (Jer. 6:10, NASB, see marg.).

Christian Circumcision. Christians are said to be circumcised in Christ (Col. 2:11). This circumcision is asserted to be "circumcision made without hands," that is, a spiritual reality and not a physical rite, the antitype and not the type. Physical circumcision was a putting off of a part of the flesh as a symbol of covenant relationship of God's people with a holy God. Christian circumcision is "removal of" not a part, but the entire "body of the flesh." "The body of the flesh" is the physical body controlled by the old fallen nature that all possess, saved as well as unsaved. The "removal of" is positional truth, that is, truth that arises as a result of the believer's being placed in Christ by the Spirit's baptizing work. Because the sin nature was judged by Christ in His death, so the believer by virtue of his organic union and identification with his Lord shares that "removal" that Christ accomplished, just as he shares Christ's fullness and is declared to be "complete" in Him. (2:10). The believer's circumcision is not only a spiritual reality consisting in the putting off of the body of the flesh; it

is more precisely Christ's circumcision, effected by Him and imputed to the believer: "In Him you were also circumcised . . . by the circumcision of Christ" (2:11). Our Lord's circumcision mentioned in this passage has no reference to His physical circumcision when He was eight days old, but is a meaningful term the apostle applies to Christ's death to the sin nature. It is the truth enunciated in Rom. 6:10, "For the death that He died, He died to sin, once for all," and 8:3, "For what the Law could not do, weak as it was through the flesh, God did: sending His own Son in the likeness of sinful flesh and as an offering for sin, He condemned sin in the flesh." It is thus apparent that the baptizing work of the Holy Spirit (Rom. 6:3-4; 1 Cor. 12:13; Col. 2:12) effects spiritual circumcision.

BIBLIOGRAPHY: R. deVaux, *Ancient Israel: Its Life and Institutions* (1961), pp. 461ff.; M. F. Unger, *Baptism and Gifts of the Holy Spirit* (1974), pp. 91-92.

CIS. See Kish.

CISTERN (Heb. *b'ōr*, or *bôr*, "a dug place"). A receptacle for holding water (Prov. 5:15; Eccles. 12:6; Isa. 36:16; Jer. 2:13). Sometimes these were dug around a spring to retain the water coming from it. Those that generally bore the name of cisterns were covered reservoirs dug out of the earth or rock, into which, in the rainy seasons, the rain or a flowing stream was conducted for storage. The absence of rain during the summer months (May to September) makes it necessary to collect and preserve the water, which falls in abundance during the remainder of the year. These cisterns were usually large pits, but sometimes were extensive vaults open only by a small mouth. The mouth was closed with a large flat stone, over which sand was spread to prevent easy discovery (Song of Sol. 4:12, "rock garden"). Mud would naturally accumulate at the bottom of these cisterns, so that anyone falling would be likely to perish (Jer. 38:6; Ps. 40:2).

In cities, the chief dependence for water being upon cisterns, they were carefully made, either hewn out of the rock or constructed of masonry.

Empty cisterns were sometimes used as prisons; thus Joseph was cast into a pit (Gen. 37:22); and Jeremiah was also thrown into one (Jer. 38:6).

Figurative. (1) The crushing of the wheel at the cistern, used to draw up the bucket, is used (Eccles. 12:6) as an image of the dissolution of the bodily powers. (2) To "drink water from your own cistern" (Prov. 5:15) means to confine one's self to pleasures legitimately his own. (3) "Broken cisterns" (Jer. 2:13), tanks not only without feeding springs, but unable even to retain the water flowing into them, are symbols of all earthly, as compared with heavenly, means of satisfying man's highest needs.

BIBLIOGRAPHY: J. B. Pritchard, *Biblical Archaeologist* 19 (1956): 66-74; N. Glueck, *Rivers in the Desert* (1959), pp. 94-97; R. de Vaux, *Ancient Israel: Its Life and Institutions* (1961), pp. 238-40; R. Forbes, *Studies in Ancient Technology* (1964), 1:152.

CITADEL (Heb. *bî'rāh).* A specially fortified defensive structure usually located within a city (2 Sam. 12:26; 1 Kings 16:18; 2 Kings 15:25; Esther 1:2, 5; 2:3, 5, 8). *See* Fortified City.

CITIES. *See* City.

CITIES, UNDERGROUND. *See* Edrei.

CITIES OF REFUGE. When the Israelites had come into the land of Canaan they were to choose towns conveniently situated as "cities of refuge," to which the manslayer who had killed a person by accident might flee. Three of these cities were located on each side of the Jordan (six in all). Those on the W of the Jordan were Kedesh in Galilee (1 Chron. 6:76), Shechem in Ephraim (Josh. 21:21; 1 Chron. 6:67), Hebron in Judah (Josh. 21:11; 2 Sam. 5:5; 1 Chron. 6:55); on the E of the Jordan were Bezer, in the plain of Moab (Deut. 4:43; Josh. 20:8); Ramoth in Gilead, in the tribe of Gad (Deut. 4:43; Josh. 21:38; 1 Kings 22:3); and Golan, in Bashan, in the half tribe of Manasseh (Deut. 4:43; Josh. 21:27; 1 Chron. 6:71). They were also Levitical cities. *See* Levite.

CITIES OF REFUGE

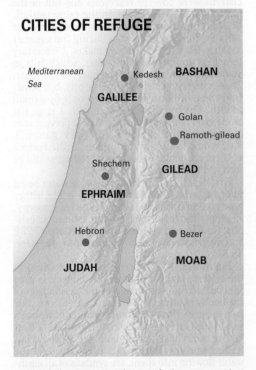

The following were the regulations respecting the asylum offered by the cities of refuge. The *Avenger of Blood* (which see, under Blood, Avenger of) was allowed to kill the manslayer if

he overtook him before reaching the city (Num. 35:19). Before he could avail himself of the shelter the fugitive had to undergo a trial and prove to the congregation that the killing was accidental (35:12, 24); if acquitted of intentional killing he had to remain within the city or its suburbs until the death of the high priest, and if found outside its limits he might be put to death by the blood avenger (35:25-28).

According to the rabbis, in order to aid the fugitive it was the business of the Sanhedrin to keep the roads leading to the cities of refuge in the best possible repair. No hills were left, every river was bridged, and the road itself was to be at least thirty-two cubits broad. At every turn were guideposts bearing the word "Refuge," and two students of the law were appointed to accompany the fleeing man and to pacify, if possible, the avenger, should he overtake the fugitive.

CITIES OF THE VALLEY. These cities were five in number: Sodom, Gomorrah, Admah, Zeboiim, and Bela or Zoar (Gen. 13:12; 19:29). The biblical notices that the district of the Jordan where these cities were situated was extremely fertile and well peopled (c. 2065 B.C. according to the preserved chronology of the MT), but that not long afterward was abandoned, are in agreement with archaeological facts (*see* W. F. Albright, *The Archaeology of Palestine and the Bible,* pp. 133ff.). It is now fairly certain that these cities were located in the valley of Siddim (14:3) and that this was the region in the southern portion of the Dead Sea now covered with water. The ruins of Bab ed-Dra' E of the Dead Sea probably belong to the age of Sodom and Gomorrah. The town probably came to an end in the twenty-third century B.C., but tombs in the area continued to be used down into the twenty-first century. The valley of Siddim with its towns was overtaken by a great catastrophe around the middle of the twenty-first century B.C (19:23-28). It was "full of tar pits" (14:10); petroleum deposits are still found in the area. Being on a great fault that forms the Jordan Valley and the Dead Sea of the Arabah, this region has been noted throughout history for its earthquakes. The cataclysm, although Scripture records only the miraculous elements, was doubtless due to violent earthquakes in which the salt and free sulphur of this area were mingled, which resulted in a gigantic explosion, hurling into the sky red-hot salt and sulphur, literally raining fire and brimstone over the whole plain (19:24-28). The instance of Lot's wife being turned into a pillar of salt is reminiscent of the great salt mass in the valley, the Mount of Sodom, called by the Arabs "Jebel Usdum." It is a spur some five miles long extending N and S at the SW end of the Dead Sea. Somewhere, inundated by the slowly rising water of the southern part of the salt lake, the cities of the valley are evidently to be found. In NT times their ruins were still visible, not yet being covered with water (Tacitus *History* 5.7; Josephus *Wars* 4.4).

BIBLIOGRAPHY: Tacitus *Annals* 5.7; F. Josephus *Wars* 4.4; W. F. Albright, *Bulletin of the American Schools of Oriental Research* 13 (Feb. 1924): 5ff.; id., *BASOR* 14 (April 1924): 2-12; G. E. Wright, *BASOR* 71 (Oct. 1938): 27ff.; J. P. Harland, *Biblical Archaeologist* 5 (1942): 17ff; id., *BA* 6 (1943): 41ff.   M.F.U.

CITIZENSHIP (Gk. *politeia*). The rights and privileges of a native or adopted citizen as distinguished from a foreigner.

Hebrew. As the covenant people, and according to the Mosaic constitution (which was framed on a basis of religious rather than of political privileges and distinctions), the idea of the commonwealth (Eph. 2:12) was merged into that of the *congregation* (which see).

Roman (Lat. *civitas*). In the fullest sense citizenship included the right of voting, of being elected to a magistracy, of appeal to the people, of contracting a legal marriage, and of holding property in the Roman community. "As a rule, the Jewish communities in Roman cities are to be regarded in the light of *private associations of settlers,* which were recognized by the state and on which certain rights were conferred, but the members of which did not enjoy the rights of citizenship" (Schürer, *History of the Jewish People,* 2:270). Still there were quite a large number of towns in which the Jews enjoyed the *rights of citizenship,* as enumerated above. Individual Jews also had the rights of citizenship conferred upon them, such as Paul (Acts 21:39; 22:28).

BIBLIOGRAPHY: A. N. Sherwin-White, *The Roman Citizenship* (1939); R. M. Grant, *Early Christianity and Society* (1978), pp. 1-95.

CITRON WOOD. A prized ornamental fragrant wood of the cypress family enumerated as a luxury product of Babylon (Rev. 18:12, NASB; "thyine wood," KJV). *See* Vegetable Kingdom.

CITY (Heb. *'îr,* poetical *qiryâ*). In the most ancient times the only distinction between village and city was that an assemblage of houses and buildings surrounded by a wall was reckoned a city and one without such surroundings was a village (Lev. 25:29-31; 1 Sam. 6:18; Ezek. 38:11).

Later, cities became distinguished by a large number of houses, as well as by the size, solidity, and magnificence of the buildings. "Cities and their villages" are commonly mentioned in the apportionment of the land to the tribes of Israel (Josh. 13:23, 28; 15:32, 36, 41; etc.), from which we infer that some villages belonged to and were dependent upon the cities. Naturally, with increased population and extension, villages and towns developed into cities, e.g., Hazaraddar (Num. 34:4), which was perhaps Hezron and Addar (Josh. 15:3); the two places being, probably, near together and growing into one. This may account for the fact that many places are designated now cities, not villages, as Bethlehem (John 7:42, "village"; Luke 2:4, "city").

The earliest notice in Scripture of city-building is the reference in Genesis to the city built by Cain and named after his son, Enoch (Gen. 4:17). After the confusion of tongues the descendants of Nimrod founded Babel, Erech, etc., in the land of Shinar; as well as Nineveh, Rehoboth-Ir, etc. (10:10-12, 19). Such cities as Ur, Nippur, Kish, Eridu, Lagash, Nineveh, Asshur, etc., have been excavated and go back to 3,000 B.C. or earlier. The earliest biblical description of a city is that of Sodom (19:1-22), but cities existed in early times on the sites of Jerusalem, Hebron, and Damascus; and it is plain that the Canaanite, who was "in the land" before the coming of Abraham, had already built cities. We read that the Israelites during their sojourn in Egypt were employed in building or fortifying the "storage cities" of Pithom and Rameses (Ex. 1:11).

Hebrew Cities. The cities of Palestine were, judging from the large number mentioned in Joshua, relatively small, like most cities of ancient times. They were like oriental cities of today, built with narrow, crooked streets (Eccles. 12:4; Song of Sol. 3:2) with many squares near the gates, where markets and courts were held (Gen. 23:10; Ruth 4:1; Matt. 6:5; etc.). Few of the streets were paved, although, according to Josephus (*Ant.* 8.7), Solomon had the roads leading to Jerusalem laid with black stone. More certain are the statements that Herod the Great paved the main street in Antioch, and Herod Agrippa III paved Jerusalem with white stones. Many cities were surrounded with high walls, having strong gates and bronze or iron bars (Deut. 3:5; 1 Kings 4:13), and provided with watchtowers (2 Sam. 18:24; 2 Kings 9:17).

Later, especially under the kings, many places, particularly frontier towns and chief cities, and above all, Jerusalem, were strengthened by the erection of thick walls with battlements (2 Chron. 26:6; Zeph. 1:16) and high towers raised partly over the gates (2 Sam. 18:24; 2 Kings 9:17), partly at the corners of the walls (2 Chron. 14:7; 32:5). Ditch and rampart were provided for the outside of the walls (2 Sam. 20:15; Isa. 26:1). Jerusalem's walls have been uncovered dating back to Jebusite times before 1000 B.C.

Government. The government of Jewish cities was vested in a council of officers with judges (Deut. 16:18), who were required to be priests. Under the kings we find mention of a "governor" (1 Kings 22:26; 2 Chron. 18:25). After the captivity Ezra made similar arrangements for the appointment of judges (Ezra 7:25). *See* Citizenship.

BIBLIOGRAPHY: A. H. M. Jones, *Cities of the Ancient Roman Provinces* (1937); W. M. Ramsay, *The Cities of St. Paul* (1960); R. J. Braidwood and G. R. Willey, eds., *Courses Toward Urban Life* (1962); E. Anati, *Palestine Before the Hebrews* (1963); A. N. Sherwin-White, *Roman So-*

ciety and Roman Law in the New Testament (1963); A. L. Oppenheim, *Ancient Mesopotamia* (1964), pp. 109-42; L. Lampl, *Cities and Planning in the Ancient Near East* (1968); M. Hammond, *The City in the Ancient World* (1972).

CITY, FENCED. *See* Fortified City.

CITY, HOLY. Another name of Jerusalem (Neh. 11:1; Dan. 9:24), probably from the feeling that the sacredness of the Temple extended in some measure over the city. It is so distinguished in the East to the present day.

CITY, LEVITICAL. *See* Levitical Cities.

CITY, SACERDOTAL. *See* Priest.

CITY, STORAGE. Two such cities, *Pithom* and *Raamses* (*see* Rameses), were built by the Israelites while in Egypt (Ex. 1:11), in which the produce of the land was housed. The Jewish kings had similar places of public deposit (1 Kings 9:19; 2 Chron. 8:4, 6; 16:4).

CITY, TREASURE. *See* City, Storage.

CITY OF DAVID. A portion of the SE hill of Jerusalem, including Mt. Zion, where the fortress of the Jebusites stood. This fortress was reduced by David, who built a new palace and city, named after him (1 Chron. 11:5).

Bethlehem, the native town of David, is also called, from that circumstance, the city of David (Luke 2:11).

CITY OF DESTRUCTION; (*'ir haheres;* "city of destruction"; "Ir-hahares," KJV). This place is mentioned only in Isa. 19:18. Various explanations are given as to the meaning of the word the NASB and NIV render "City of Destruction":

1. "The city of the sun," a translation of the Egyptian sacred name of Heliopolis. This is the reading in a number of ancient manuscripts and is the marginal reading for the verse in the NASB and NIV.
2. "The city of Heres," a transcription in the second word of the Egyptian sacred name of Heliopolis, Ha-ra, "the abode [lit., "house"] of the sun."
3. "A city destroyed," meaning that one of the five cities mentioned would be destroyed, according to Isaiah's idiom.
4. "A city preserved," meaning that one of the five cities mentioned would be preserved. A careful examination of the nineteenth chapter of Isaiah, and the eighteenth and twentieth, which are connected with it, makes the third explanation and the NASB and NIV rendering most likely.

CITY OF GOD. A name given to Jerusalem (Ps. 46:4; cf. 48:1, 8), the appropriateness of which is evident from Deut. 12:5: "The place which the Lord your God shall choose from all your tribes, to establish His name there for His dwelling, and there you shall come."

CLAU'DA (klaw'da). A small island twenty-two miles S of the W end of Crete. Pliny calls it Gaudos. Ptolemy calls it Klaudos; it is now called Gavdos. Paul passed this island on his voyage to Rome (Acts 27:16).

CLAU'DIA (klaw'di-a; feminine of "Claudius"). A Christian woman mentioned in 2 Tim. 4:21. By some she is thought to have been the daughter of the British king Cogidunus, and the wife of Pudens (mentioned in the same verse), having been sent to Rome to be educated; that there she was the *protégée* of Pomponia (wife of the late commander in Britain, Aulus Plautius) and became a convert to Christianity. On the other hand, it may be said that this attempt at identification rests on no other foundation than the identity of the names of the parties, which, in the case of names so common as Pudens and Claudia, may be nothing more than a mere accidental coincidence (Conybeare and Howson, *The Life and Epistles of St. Paul*, 2:484, n.).

BIBLIOGRAPHY: W. J. Conybeare and J. S. Howson, *The Life and Epistles of Paul* (1953), p. 704.

CLAU'DIUS (klaw'di-us; Gk. perhaps from *claudus,* "lame").

1. The fourth Roman emperor (excluding Julius Caesar), who succeeded Caligula, January 25, A.D. 41. He was the son of Drusus and Antonia, and was born August 1, 10 B.C. at Lyons, in Gaul. Losing his father in infancy, he was left to the care and society of domestics, and despised by his imperial relatives. Notwithstanding the weakness of intellect resulting from this neglect, he devoted himself to literary pursuits and was the author of several treatises. On the murder of Caligula he hid himself through fear of a similar fate but was found by a soldier, who saluted him as emperor.

He was taken, almost by force, to the Senate, and constituted emperor chiefly by the pretorian guards, under the promise of a largess to each soldier. According to Josephus, the throne was, in a great measure, finally secured to him through the address and solicitation of Herod Agrippa. This obligation he returned by great favors to Agrippa, enlarging his territory, and appointing his brother to the kingdom of Chalcis (Josephus *Ant.* 19.5.1), giving to this latter also, after Agrippa's death, the presidency over the Temple at Jerusalem (*Ant.* 20.1.3). The Jews were generally treated by him with indulgence, especially those in Asia and Egypt (*Ant.* 19.5.2.3; 20.1.2), although those in Palestine seem to have, at times, suffered much oppression at the hands of his governors. About the middle of his reign all Jews who lived at Rome were banished (Acts 18:2), probably A.D. 49. The conduct of Claudius during his reign insofar as it was not under the influence of his wives and freedmen, was mild and popular, and he made several beneficial enactments. Having married his niece, Agrippina, she prevailed upon him to bypass his own son, Britannicus, in favor of her son, Nero, by a former marriage; but discovering that he regretted this step she poisoned him, A.D. 54.

2. Claudius Lysias (Acts 23:26) *See* Lysias.

BIBLIOGRAPHY: R. Graves, *I, Claudius* (1934); V. M. Scramuzza, *The Emperor Claudius* (1940).

CLAW. The sharp hooked end of the foot of a bird (Dan. 4:33). The KJV uses "claw" where the NASB and NIV render "hoofs" (Zech. 11:16) or are silent (KJV, "cleft into two claws," versus NASB, "hoof split in two"; both Deut. 14:6). *See* Hoof; Nail, no. 4.

Figurative. The expression "tear their claws in pieces" (Zech. 11:16; NASB and NIV, "tear off their hoofs") means to seize upon and eat the last morsel of flesh or fat.

CLAY. *See* Mineral Kingdom.

CLEAN, CLEANNESS. The rendering of several Heb. and Gk. words, having the primary meaning of freedom from dirt or filth, and then of moral purity. Generally, however, they signify freedom from ceremonial defilement. *See* Purification; Purity; Uncleanness.

CLEFT. The rendering of several Heb. words.

1. A space or opening made by cleavage, as a fissure in a building (Isa. 22:9, "breaches"; Amos 6:11, KJV); crevice in a rock (Song of Sol. 2:14; Isa. 2:21; Jer. 49:16).

2. The split in the hoof of an animal (Deut. 14:6, KJV; NASB and NIV, "split").

CLEM'ENT (klem-ent; "merciful"). A person (apparently a Christian of Philippi) mentioned by Paul (Phil. 4:3) as one whose name was in the Book of Life. This Clement was, by the ancient church, identified with the bishop of Rome of the same name.

CLE'OPAS (klē'ō-pas; contraction of Gk. *kleopatros,* "of a renowned father"). One of the two disciples who were going to Emmaus on the day of the resurrection, when Jesus drew near and conversed with them (Luke 24:18). He questioned them as to the subject of their conversation, chided them for their ignorance and unbelief, and expounded to them the Scriptures that foretold His sufferings and glory. Arriving at Emmaus, they secured His presence at the evening meal, during which He was made known to them. They hastened back to Jerusalem and acquainted the disciples with what they had seen and heard. Cleopas must not be confounded with *Clopas* of John 19:25.

CLE'OPHAS. *See* Clopas.

CLERK (Acts 19:35). *See* Town Clerk.

CLOAK. An article of *dress* (which see). KJV and NIV "cloak" is sometimes rendered "coat" (Matt. 5:40; Luke 6:29) or "garment" (Isa. 59:17) in the NASB. Conversely, KJV "raiment" (Ex. 22:26, 27; Deut. 24:13; Judg. 3:16), "veil" (Ruth 3:15), and "garment" (Matt. 9:20; 14:36; Mark 5:27, 6:56;

Luke 8:44; Acts 12:8) are often given in the NASB and NIV as "cloak." The Gk. word for *cloak* in 2 Tim. 4:13 is a different word for *cloak* than in other NT passages (NASB).

Figurative. In the KJV "cloak" appears for that which conceals, or for a pretext or excuse (cf. NASB Isa. 59:17; John 15:22; 1 Thess. 2:5; 2 Tim. 4:13; 1 Pet. 2:16).

CLO'PAS (Gk. klō'pas). The husband of *Mary* (which see), the sister of Christ's mother (John 19:25); probably a Grecized form of *Alphaeus* (which see). He is the father of James the Less and his brother Joseph, or Joses (Matt. 10:3; Mark 3:18; Luke 6:15; Acts 1:13; cf. Mark 15:4).

CLOSET (Heb. *ḥuppâ,* "canopy"; Gk. *tameion*). A KJV term rendered in the NASB by "bridal chamber" (Joel 2:16; Ps. 19:5) and "inner room" (Matt. 6:6; Luke 12:3). The NIV renders Joel 2:16 by "chamber"; Ps. 19:5 by "pavilion"; Matt. 6:6 by "room"; and Luke 12:3 by "inner rooms."

CLOTH, CLOTHES, CLOTHING. *See* Dress.

CLOTHES, RENDING OF. *See* Rend.

CLOUD. The allusions to clouds in Scripture, as well as their use in symbolical language, can only be understood when we remember the nature of the climate, where there is hardly a trace of cloud from the beginning of May to the close of September. During this season clouds so seldom appear and rains so seldom fall as to seem phenomenal, as was the case with the harvest rain invoked by Samuel (1 Sam. 12:17-18) and the little cloud, not larger than a man's hand, which Elijah declared to be a sure promise of rain (1 Kings 18:44).

Clouds are referred to as showing the power and wisdom of God in their formation (Pss. 135:6-7, NASB, "vapors," 147:8), and causing them to hold and dispense rain (Job 37:10-12; Prov. 3:20). They are called the "clouds of heaven" (Dan. 7:13), "clouds of the sky" (Matt. 24:30), "floodgates of the sky" (Gen. 7:11), "windows above" (Isa. 24:18), "water jars of the heavens" (Job 38:37), God's "upper chambers" (Ps. 104:3, 13), "dust beneath His feet" (Nah. 1:3).

Man's ignorance is illustrated by his inability to number the clouds (Job 38:37), to account for their spreading (36:29), to understand how God "establishes" and "layers" them (37:15-16), to cause them to rain (38:34), or stay them (38:37).

Figurative. Living much in the open air and being of a poetical nature, the people of the East would naturally make clouds figurative of many things. Thus clouds are the symbol of armies and multitudes of people (Isa. 60:8; Jer. 4:13; Heb. 12:1). The sudden disappearance of threatening clouds from the sky is a figure for the wiping out of transgressions (Isa. 44:22). A day of clouds is taken for a season of calamity and of God's judgment (Ezek. 30:3; 34:12; Joel 2:2). Naturally the cloud is a symbol of transitoriness (Job 30:15; Hos. 6:4). The cloud without rain is the proverb for the man of promise without performance (Prov. 25:14; Isa. 25:5; Jude 12). A wise ruler is said to be as the "light of . . . a morning without clouds" (2 Sam. 23:4), while the favor of a king is compared to "a cloud with the spring rain" (Prov. 16:15). "Clouds that return after the rain" is figurative of the infirmities of old age; i.e., as after a rain one expects sunshine, so after pains one longs for comfort. As clouds in hot countries veil the oppressive glories of the sun, they are used to symbolize the divine presence, which they entirely or in part conceal (Ex. 16:10; 33:9; Num. 11:25; Job 22:14; Ps. 18:11-12; Isa. 19:1). *See* Pillar of Cloud, Shekinah.

CLOUD, PILLAR OF. *See* Pillar.

CNI'DUS (nî'dŭs). A town at the extreme SW of Asia Minor, upon land jutting out between the islands of Rhodes and Cos (Acts 21:1). Venus was worshiped there; Paul sailed by this place (27:7).

COAL. Two Heb. words are rendered "coal" or "coals":

1. One (*pehām*) would seem to be applied to coals not yet lighted. It occurs three times— twice when the smith working with the coals is mentioned (Isa. 44:12; 54:16), and in Proverbs (26:21, "as coals are to burning coals," KJV; NASB and NIV render "charcoal"), where unlighted coals must be meant.

It has been disputed whether the Hebrews had mineral coal or merely charcoal. There is strong reason, however, to believe that the former was used in ancient times. The mountains of Lebanon contain seams of coal that have been worked in recent times and were probably known to the Phoenicians. Charcoal was the "coal" in common use; thus coals of juniper or broom are mentioned (Ps. 120:4).

2. The other word (*gahelet*, "kindling") signifies an ignited or *live* coal, and is mentioned frequently (2 Sam. 14:7; Job 41:21; Ps. 18:8; Isa. 44:19; Ezek. 24:11; etc.); often with the addition of "burning" or of "fire" (Lev. 16:12; 2 Sam. 22:13; Isa. 6:6; etc.).

The term "live coal" (Heb. *rişpâ*, Isa. 6:6, KJV) appears to have been a hot stone used for baking upon (*see* 1 Kings 19:6, "a bread cake baked on hot stones," Heb. *reşep*).

In the NT "charcoal fire" (John 18:18) was probably made on a chafing dish, used in the East for the sake of warmth. *See* Fuel.

Figurative. The expression "They will extinguish my coal which is left" (2 Sam. 14:7) refers to the burning coal with which one kindles a fire and is obviously a metaphor for extinguishing one's family.

"Coals of fire" (2 Sam. 22:13; Ps. 18:12; etc.) is by some thought to be a figure for lightning proceeding from God. The flame of red-hot coals

pours out of Him as out of a glowing furnace. This description is based entirely upon Ex. 19:18, where the Lord comes down upon Sinai in smoke and fire.

"You will heap burning coals on his head" (Prov. 25:22; Rom. 12:20) represents the shame and confusion which men feel when their evil is requited by good.

COAST. An inaccurate rendering of several terms, meaning *border,* except in the expression "sea coast." *See* Seacoast, Seashore.

COASTLAND (Heb. *î*). Any maritime district; whether belonging to a continent or to an island; thus it is used of the shore of the Mediterranean (Isa. 20:6; 23:2, 6) and of the coasts of Elishah (Ezek. 27:7), i.e., of Greece and Asia Minor. Occasionally coastlands is specifically used of an island, as in Caphtos of Crete (Jer. 47:4); but more generally it is applied to any region separated from Palestine by water, as described in 25:22. The "many coastlands" (Ezek. 27:3) may have been the islands and coasts of Arabia, on the Persian Gulf and Erythraen Sea. The KJV renders this word "island" or "isle."

COAT. *See* Dress.

COAT OF MAIL. *See* Armor; Arms.

CO'BRA. *See* Animal Kingdom: Serpent.

COCK, THE. On tombs this is a Christian symbol of the resurrection, the herald of life after the night of death. It is also a symbol of vigilance. For the bird, *see* Animal Kingdom.

COCKATRICE. *See* Animal Kingdom: Serpent.

COCKCROWING. The habit of the cock in the East of crowing during the night at regular times gave rise to the expression "cockcrowing" to indicate a definite portion of time (Mark 13:35). The Romans called the last watch of the night, the break of day at about three o'clock, *gallicinium;* and the Hebrews designated the cockcrowing period by words signifying "the singing of the cock." Among the Hebrews we find no mention of the flight of the hours of the night except the crowing of the cock. *See* Time.

COCKLE. *See* Vegetable Kingdom. Stinkweed.

COCKOW, CUCKOO. *See* Sea Gull.

CODE OF HAMMURABI. *See* Hammurabi.

COFFER. A KJV term referring to the small box the Philistines placed upon the cart with the Ark (1 Sam. 6:8, 11, 15), and in which they placed the golden mice and tumors that formed their trespass offering.

COFFIN (Heb. *'ārôn*, Gen. 50:26, "and he was . . . placed in a coffin in Egypt"). Undoubtedly a mummy chest made of sycamore wood that was deposited in a room, according to Egyptian custom, and carried away with Israel at the Exodus. *See* Burial; Dead, The.

The same Heb. word is rendered "chest" (2 Kings 12:10) and frequently *"ark"* (which see).

COIN. *See* Metrology: Measures of Value, or Money.

COL-HO′ZEH (kol-hō′zeh; "all-seeing"). A descendant of Judah, being the son of Hazaiah, and father of one Baruch (Neh 11:5), before 445 B.C. He also had a son named Shallum, who repaired part of the wall of Jerusalem after the captivity (Neh. 3:15).

COLLAR. Any aperture as in Job 30:18 the opening by means of which the shirt was put on. Job, whom the Lord "smote . . . with sore boils from the sole of his foot to the crown of his head," would have found any garment painfully binding.

The term *collars* (from Heb. *neṭîpâ*) appears in the KJV of Judg. 8:26 but is replaced by "pendants" in the NASB and NIV. In Isa. 3:19 the same Heb. term is given as "chains" in the KJV, "dangling earrings" in the NASB, and "earrings" in the NIV.

COLLECTION.

1. Joash ordered a collection for the repairing of the Temple (2 Chron. 24:6, 9; NASB, "levy"; NIV, "tax"). A chest was placed by the high priest at the entrance of the Temple to receive the same. By making a distinction between this money and that given for the use of the priests a special appeal was made to the liberality of the people.

2. In the early age of the Christian church the Christians of Palestine suffered greatly from poverty, probably due to ostracism. Paul made appeals to the Gentile Christians for aid (Acts 24:17; Rom. 15:25-26; 2 Cor. 8-9; Gal. 2:10), recommending collections to be taken for this purpose on the "first day of every week" (1 Cor. 16:1-3).

COLLEGE. *See* Second Quarter.

COLONY. The city of Philippi was gifted by Caesar Augustus with the privileges of a colony (*colonia*). Antioch in Pisidia and Alexandria in Troas both possessed the same character, but Philippi is the first case to which Scripture (Acts 16:12) calls our attention to this distinction. When the Romans conquered a town they planted a body of their own citizens within it as a kind of garrison, usually to the number of three hundred. These constituted a "colony of Roman citizens" (Lat. *colonia cibium Romanorum*), a sort of little Rome. Such a colony was free from taxes and military duty, its position as an outpost being regarded as an equivalent. It had its own constitution (a copy of the Roman) and elected its own senate and other offices of state. To this constitution the original inhabitants had to submit (Seifert, *Dict. Class. Ant.,* s.v.).

BIBLIOGRAPHY: A. N. Sherwin-White, *The Roman Citizenship* (1939); E. M. Blaiklock, *Cities of the New Testament* (1965).

COLORS. The color sense, i.e., the distinction of color impressions in sensation, perception, and nomenclature, follows the same law as all human development—the law of progress from coarse to fine. The Jews had not reached such an advanced state of art that we should expect a wide acquaintance with colors. There are not, therefore, many colors mentioned in Scripture, and these may be arranged in two classes—those applied to natural objects, and artificial mixtures employed in *dyeing* (which see) or *painting* (which see).

Natural These were five: white, black, red, yellow, and green.

White. This term embraces the relatively as well as the absolutely white. In the full sense of the word the rays of the sun and those proceeding from a body raised to white heat are white, because all the colors of the spectrum are united in them. But even the daylight is not absolutely colorless, and the direct light of the sun seems yellowish or, to speak poetically, golden. We are, therefore, prepared for a varied use of the term "white." Thus Matthew (17:2) writes, "His garments became as white as light"; and our Lord said, "Look on the fields, that they are white (NIV, "ripe") for harvest" (John 4:35); the ripening ears are white as distinguished from the green blade. The most common term is Heb. *lābān,* which is applied to such objects as milk (Gen. 49:12), manna (Ex. 16:31), snow (Isa. 1:18), horses (Zech. 1:8), and clothing (Eccles. 9:8). Hebrew *ṣaḥ,* "sunny," dazzling white, is applied to the complexion (Song of Sol. 5:10; NIV, "radiant"); *ḥiwwār,* a term of a later age, to snow (Dan. 7:9 only) and to the paleness of shame (Isa. 29:22); *'sîb,* to the hair alone. Another class of terms arises from the textures of a naturally white color. These were, without doubt, primarily applied to the material; but the idea of color is also prominent, particularly in the description of the curtains of the Tabernacle (Ex. 26:1) and the priests' vestments (28:6).

Black. Black and white are the extremest contrasts in Scripture, the former being where light and its colors have vanished. But the term is used relatively and includes the dark hues that approach black. The shades of this color are expressed in the terms *sheḥôr,* "dusky," applied to the hair (Lev. 13:31; Song of Sol. 5:11); the complexion (1:5; NIV, "dark"), particularly when affected with disease (Job 30:30); horses (Zech. 6:2, 6); *ḥûm,* lit., "scorched," is applied to sheep (Gen. 30:32) and expresses the color produced by influence of the sun's rays; *qādar,* lit., "to be dirty," is applied to a complexion blackened by sorrow or disease (Job 30:30), a clouded sky (1 Kings 18:45), night (Mic. 3:6; Jer. 4:28; Joel 2:10; 3:15), a turbid brook (whence possibly *Kidron*), particularly when rendered so by melted snow (Job 6:16). In many of these passages the NIV renders "dark" or "darkened" for "black."

Red (Heb. *ādōm*) is applied to blood (2 Kings 3:22), a garment sprinkled with blood (Isa. 63:2), a heifer (Num. 19:2), stew made of lentils (Gen. 25:30), a horse (Zech. 1:8; 6:2), wine (Prov. 23:31), the complexion (Gen. 25:25; Song of Sol. 5:10; Lam. 4:7, NASB and NIV, "ruddy"). *Reddish* is applied to a leprous spot (Lev. 13:19; 14:37). *Śārōq,* lit., "fox-colored," "bay," is applied to a horse (KJV, "speckled"; NIV, "red," Zech. 1:8) and to a species of vine bearing a purple grape (Isa. 5:2, NASB, see marg.). This color was symbolical of bloodshed (Zech. 6:2; Rev. 6:4; 12:3).

Yellow. This seems to have been regarded as a shade of green, for the same term *greenish* is applied to gold (Heb. *yᵉraqraq,* Ps. 68:13; NIV, "shining gold"), and to the leprous spot (Lev. 13:49).

Green, though frequently used, seldom refers to color. The Heb. terms are *ra'ănān,* applied to what is "vigorous" and "flourishing" (Job 15:32; Ps. 52:8); also used of that which is "fresh," as oil (Ps. 92:10); and *yereq,* having the radical signification of "putting forth," "sprouting," and is used indiscriminately for all food products of the earth (Gen. 1:30; 9:3; Ex. 10:15; Isa. 15:6). Sometimes it is used for the sickly yellowish hue of mildewed grain (*see* Mildew), and also for the entire absence of color produced by fear (Jer. 30:6, "pale"). "Green" is used incorrectly in the KJV for *white* (Gen. 30:37; Esther 1:6), *young* or *new* (Lev. 2:14; 23:14), *moist* or *fresh* (Judg. 16:7-8), *sappy* or *well watered* (Job 8:16), and *unripe* or *early* (Song of Sol. 2:13).

Artificial. These were four: purple, blue, red (or crimson), and vermilion. Dyeing, although known at an early period (Gen. 38:28; Ex. 26:1), is not noticed as a profession in the Bible; and the Jews were probably indebted to the Egyptians and Phoenicians for their dyes and the method of applying them. These dyes were purple (light and dark, the latter being the "blue" of the NASB and KJV) and crimson; vermilion was introduced later.

Purple (Heb. *'argāmān*). A brilliant red-blue color prized by the ancients for dyeing garments (Prov. 31:22; Jer. 10:9). The chief source of the famous Tyrian purple was the tiny mollusk (*Murex trunculus*) found along the coast of Phoenicia and adjacent lands. It was exported far and wide as a staple commodity of Phoenician commerce (Ezek. 27:7, 16). Murex shells were found at the seaport of ancient Ugarit (modern Ras Shamra) demonstrating that purple was manufactured there about 1400 B.C. Great labor was required to extract the purple dye and hence only royalty and the wealthy could afford the resulting richly colored garments (Esther 8:15; Dan. 5:7; 1 Macc. 10:20, 62, 64; 2 Macc. 4:38; Luke 16:19; Rev. 17:4). Such a robe was placed on Jesus as a jest, making mockery of His claims to kingship.

Purple prefiguring Christ's kingship was largely used in the Mosaic Tabernacle (Ex. 25:4; 26:1, 31, 36) and in the high priest's dress (28:5-6, 15; 39:29).

"The dye taken from these shellfish is not their blood, but the slimy secretion of a gland which they have in common with all snails. This secretion is not at first red or violet, but whitish. When exposed to the sunlight, however, it begins to color like a photographic surface, and, passing through shades of yellow and green, settles into the purple color, which is a combination of red and violet light; this mixed color, having sometimes more of a blue, sometimes more of a red hue, is ineffaceable. Purple was a monopoly of the Phoenicians. They, not only on their own but on other coasts, discovered shellfish yielding purple; but the oldest site of the purple trade was Tyre itself. At the present day, in the neighborhood of the miserable ruined village that bears the name of Tyre, there are found traces of these purple dyeworks that were celebrated far into the Christian era. Purple was still costly in the time of the Roman supremacy. A mantle of the best purple of Tyre, such as the luxurious habits of the empire required, cost ten thousand sesterces, i.e., over five hundred dollars" (Delitzsch, *Iris*, p. 65). Robes of a purple color were worn by kings (Judg. 8:26) and by the highest officers, civil and religious. They were also worn by the wealthy (Jer. 10:9; Ezek. 27:7; Luke 16:19; Rev. 17:4; 18:16).

Blue (Heb. *tᵉkēlet*). This dye came from a species of shellfish found on the coast of Phoenicia and called by modern naturalists *Helix Ianthina*. The tint is best explained by the statements of Josephus (*Ant.* 3.7.7) and Philo that it was emblematic of the sky, in which case it represents, not the light blue of our northern climate, but the deep dark hue of the eastern sky. The KJV has rightly described the tint in Esther 1:6 (marg.) as *violet*. This color was used in the same way as purple. Princes and nobles (Ezek. 23:6; Ecclus. 40:4) and the idols of Babylon (Jer. 10:9) were clothed in robes of this color; the tassles of the Hebrew dress were to be of this color (Num. 15:38).

Red or Crimson (Isa. 1:18; Jer. 4:30; etc.). This color is expressed in Heb. by several different terms: *Shānî* (Gen. 38:28-30), *tôla'at-shānî* (Ex. 25:4), or simply *tôla'at* (Isa. 1:18); *karmîl* (NASB and NIV, "crimson," 2 Chron. 2:7, 14; 3:14) was introduced at a late period, probably from Armenia, to express the same color. The first term expresses the brilliancy of the color, the second the worm or grub from which the dye was procured. This is a small insect the size of a pea, which draws its nourishment from the oak and other plants by piercing them, the tint produced being *crimson* rather than scarlet. The only natural object to which it is applied in Scripture is the lips, which are compared to a "scarlet thread" (Song of Sol. 4:3). Robes of this color were worn by the wealthy (2 Sam. 1:24; Prov. 31:21; Jer. 4:30; Lam. 4:5, NASB, see marg.; Rev. 17:4). This color was among the Greeks and Romans the proper color for the military cloak; and so it is a scarlet cloak which, according to Matthew, is put on Jesus by the soldiers in Pilate's judgment hall. Mark and John say "purple," for the language of the people did not distinguish the two kinds of red. *See* article Scarlet.

Vermilion (Heb. *shāshēr*). This was a pigment used in fresco paintings, either for drawing figures of idols on the walls of temples (Ezek. 23:14; NIV, "red"), for coloring the idols themselves (Wisd. of Sol. 13:14), or for decorating the walls and beams of houses (Jer. 22:14, NASB and NIV, "red"). Vermilion was a favorite color among the Assyrians, as is still attested to by the sculptures of Nimroud and Khorsabad.

Sacred, or **Sacerdotal.** Purple, blue, scarlet, and white were the four colors prescribed by Moses. Of *four* colors were the ten curtains of the Tabernacle, the veil, the curtain that hung at the entrance of the Holy Place, and the entrance into the court; the ephod, the girdle, and the breastplate of the high priest. Of *three* colors, namely, blue, purple, and scarlet, were the pomegranates that adorned the robe of the ephod. Of *one* color, white, were his under robe and miter, or turban; of *blue* were the fifty loops of the curtain, the cord by which the breastplate was fastened to the ephod, and that by which the diadem was attached to the miter. Of *one* color also, sometimes blue, sometimes purple, were the coverings of the sacred furniture of the Tabernacle when it was carried from place to place; and of *one* color, white, were the clothes of the ordinary priests, with, probably, the exception of the varicolored girdle or sash.

Figurative. *White* has a direct significance because light is white. White denotes purity or, what is nearly the same, holiness. The priests wore white as servants of the Holy One and as examples in holiness. White was also the ground color of the veil that divided the sanctuary, of the curtains, and of the attire of the high priest. Garments of salvation are certainly garments of light (Ps. 27:1, "The Lord is my light and my salvation"; cf. Rev. 19:8). White was also the sign of *festivity* (Eccles. 9:8) and *triumph* (Zech. 6:3; Rev. 6:2). As the color of light (cf. Matt. 17:2), white was the symbol of *glory* and *majesty* (Dan. 7:9; Ezek. 9:3; Matt. 28:3; John 20:12).

Black, as the opposite of white or light, denotes *mourning, affliction, calamity,* and *death* (KJV, Jer. 14:2; Lam. 4:8; 5:10). It was also the sign of *humiliation* (Mal. 3:14, lit., "in black") and the omen of *evil* (Zech. 6:2; Rev. 6:5).

Red is the color of fire, and therefore of life; the blood is red because life is a fiery process. But *red,* as contrasted with white, is the color of selfish, covetous, passionate life. Sin is called red inasmuch as it is a burning heat that consumes man (Isa. 1:18). Red (crimson), as representing blood, designates the life principle of man and beast (Gen. 9:4-6) and the essential element of atonement (Isa. 63:2; Heb. 9:22).

Green was the emblem of *freshness, vigor,* and *prosperity* (Pss. 52:8; 92:14).

Blue. The purple blue, or hyacinth, points to heaven, and was the symbol of revelation. Among the Hebrews it was the Jehovah color, the symbol of the revealed God (cf. Ex. 24:10; Ezek. 1:26). Delitzsch says: "Blue denotes the softened divine majesty condescending to man in grace" (*Iris,* p. 48). It also represented reward.

Purple, the dress of kings, was associated with *royalty* and *majesty* (Judg. 8:26; Esther 8:15; Song of Sol. 3:10; 7:5; Dan. 5:7, 16, 29). M.F.U.

COLOS'SAE, or **Colos'se** (ko-lo-se). A city of mercantile importance on the Lycus, in Phrygia, about twelve miles above Laodicea. The most competent commentators think that the Christian church there was founded by Epaphras (Col. 1:2, 7; 4:12) and believe 2:1 proves that Paul had not been there previous to writing the epistle. The city was destroyed by an earthquake in the ninth year of Nero and was then rebuilt. The modern town Chonas is near the ruins. *See* Sherman E. Johnson, "Laodicea and Its Neighbors," *Biblical Archaeologist* 13, no. 1 (1950): 5-7.

Site of ancient Colossae

COLOS'SIANS, BOOK OF. An epistle of Paul written apparently from his Roman imprisonment (Acts 28:30-31; Col. 4:3, 10, 18). Belonging also to this third group of Pauline epistles are Philemon, Ephesians, and Philippians.

Occasion and Date. The epistle is a strong polemic against a Judaic-Gnostic heresy with its ceremonialism and doctrine of emanations. This unsound teaching sought to reduce Christianity to a legal system and Christ to the position of a lesser god. Paul directed the impact of revealed truth against the Jewish element (circumcision, meats, drinks, fast days, new moons, and Sabbaths; 2:11-16), an ascetic element (2:20-23), and a false philosophical and speculative element (2:8), with the worship of intermediary beings

(2:18-19). Apparently, Epaphras and his colleagues were unable to handle this situation and went to Rome to consult Paul about it (1:7-8). The letter of reply was sent by Tychicus and Onesimus (4:7-9) toward the middle of Paul's two-year imprisonment at Rome, about A.D. 60.

Plan. Paul attacks the errors at Colossae by the clear presentation of counter truths. After first giving thanks for the Colossians' achievements and interceding for their progress (1:1-12), he expounds the supremacy of Christ over all principalities and powers (1:13-19), the fullness of His redemption (1:20-23), and his own hardship in making known the gospel message (1:24–2:3). He warns the Colossian church against philosophic errors that set aside the provision of full deliverance from sin and freedom from legalism (2:4-15). He warns them accordingly to reject ritual prescriptions and the worship of inferior beings (2:16-19), emphasizing their complete position in Christ (2:20–3:4). He urges them to appropriate Christ's death and resurrection in practical Christian living (3:5-17) and in discharging the various special relations of life (3:18–4:6). He explains the mission of Tychicus and Onesimus (4:7-9) and sends salutations (4:10-17), ending with a benediction (4:18).

Outline.

I. Introduction (1:1-12)
II. Doctrinal exposition (1:13–2:3)
  A. Redemption (1:13-14)
  B. Person of Christ (1:15-19)
  C. The work of Christ (1:20-23)
  D. The apostle's participation in Christ's program (1:24–2:3)
III. Doctrinal polemicism (2:4–3:4)
  A. Against false philosophy (2:4-8)
  B. In behalf of the Person and work of Christ (2:9-15)
  C. Resulting obligations (2:16–3:4)
IV. Doctrinal practice (3:5–4:6)
  A. Practical appropriation of the death and resurrection of Christ (3:5-17)
  B. Appropriation of Christ's death and resurrection in domestic life (3:18–4:1)
  C. Appropriation of the death and resurrection in relation to the world (4:2-6)
V. Personal matters (4:7-17)
  A. The mission of Tychicus and Onesimus (4:7-9)
  B. Salutations from Paul's associates (4:10-14)
  C. Paul's own greetings (4:15)
  D. The Laodicean message (4:16-17)
VI. Conclusion (4:18)   M.F.U.

BIBLIOGRAPHY: H. C. G. Moule, *Colossian and Philemon Studies: Lessons in Faith and Holiness* (n.d.); W. R. Nicholson, *Popular Studies in Colossians* (n.d.); J. Eadie, *Commentary on the Epistle of Paul to the Colossians* (1957); C. F. D. Moule, *The Epistles of Paul the Apostle to the Colossians and to Philemon* (1958); J. B. Lightfoot, *St. Paul's Epistles to the Colossians and to Philemon* (1959); W. Hendricksen, *Exposition of Colossians and Philemon* (1964); E. Lohse, *Colossians and Philemon* (1971); R. P. Martin, *Colossians: The Church's Lord and the Christian's Liberty* (1971); H. C. G. Moule, *Studies in Colossians and Philemon* (1977); W. G. Scroggie, *Studies in Philemon* (1977); F. B. Westcott, *Colossians: A Letter to Asia* (1981).

COLT. *See* Animal Kingdom: Donkey; Horse.

COLUMNS OF A BOOK (Heb. *delet*). In Jer. 36:23 it is said that "when Jehudi had read three or four columns, the king cut it [the roll] with a scribe's knife." The columns were the four-cornered squares into which the rolls were divided.

COMB. A honeycomb. *See* Honey; Animal Kingdom: Bees.

COMFORT (Heb. *nāham,* "to comfort," "give forth sighs"; Gk. *parakaleō,* to "call alongside," "help"). Our English word is from Lat. *confortare (con fortis),* "to strengthen much," and means to ease, encourage, inspirit, enliven.

As pertaining to the life of the believer it is the consolation and support that results from the gracious work of the indwelling Comforter, making clear to him his part in the great redemption, assuring him of the Savior's love, and imparting peace and joy. The Gk. noun is often translated *Helper* (which see) in the NT. *See also* Holy Ghost.

COMFORTER, THE *See* Holy Spirit.

COMING OF CHRIST, THE. This great event, so prominent in both the OT and the NT, is a subject of much controversy, hostility, and ignorance. It has been commonly set forth as one great cataclysmic event ending time and ushering in eternity with a concomitant so-called general resurrection and general judgment. This view, however, involves insuperable difficulties when the aggregate teaching of the Word is approached inductively. The various scriptural statements can only be reconciled under the view that the coming of the Christ will consist of two phases—a coming *for* His church, the Body of Christ (1 Thess. 4:13-18; 1 Cor. 15:53; 2 Thess. 2:1; Rev. 3:10), and a coming *with* His church (Rev. 19:11-16). His coming for His church will result in its removal from the earthly scene to heaven. This climactic event will usher in a period of trouble at the end of the age, known as Daniel's seventieth week. At the conclusion of this period (at least seven years in length) in which human wickedness and rebellion will reach their height, Christ will return with His glorified saints to conquer His enemies (Ps. 2; Zech. 14; Isa. 11) and to set up His millennial kingdom. This mediatorial Davidic kingdom will be the last of God's ordered ages in time. Only after it has run its course and Satan is loosed and all sinners judged (Rev. 20:11-15) will the eternal state be brought in.   M.F.U.

BIBLIOGRAPHY: S. P. Tregelles, *The Hope of Christ's Sec-*

ond Coming (n.d.); J. F. Walvoord, *The Return of the Lord* (1955); W. K. Harrison, *Hope Triumphant* (1966); G. C. Berkouwer, *The Return of Christ* (1972); H. A. Ironside and F. C. Ottman, *Studies in Biblical Eschatology* (1983).

COMMANDER (Aram. *beʿel-teʿēm*, "lord of judgment"). The title of the Persian governor of Samaria (Ezra 4:8-9, 17; "chancellor," KJV; "commanding officer," NIV).

COMMANDMENTS, THE TEN. *See* Decalogue.

COMMERCE. The exchange of products among men must have begun with the earliest history of mankind. The descendants of Cain in Gen. 4 initiated urban living, articles of art and craftsmanship (4:21-22), and engaged in commerce. The construction of the Noahic ark implied interchange of goods.

Babylonia. Among the early pre-Semitic Sumerians artistic craftsmanship and trade flourished as revealed by the exquisite jewelry and art objects recovered from the royal tombs at Ur dating no later than 2500 B.C. From the earliest levels of Mesopotamian cities evidences of extended commerce are recovered. Babylonia was from most ancient times a great merchant nation dispensing wares by canal and riverboat and by desert caravan. The city of Ur was a center of all kinds of manufacture, especially woolen goods. Babylonian merchants scattered widely, not only trafficking in their goods but peddling their arts and cuneiform system of writing. The Assyrian merchants invented the idea of checks—clay tablets denominating equivalent worth in silver. Ancient Sumerian and Akkadian kings imported cedarwood from Lebanon. The Fertile Crescent was a veritable beehive of camel caravans and river-going ships. Early syndicates of merchants controlled these trade routes stretching between Ur on the Lower Euphrates, Mari on the Middle Euphrates, and Palmyra and Damascus westward, linking the lucrative trade marts of Egypt via Palestine-Syria.

Phoenicia. It was one of the greatest merchant nations of antiquity. Probably before 2400 B.C. they sailed boats between the coastal emporiums and Egypt; through the centuries there was a continuous flow of commerce between Tyre, Sidon, Gebal (Byblos), and Egypt. The latter city was especially known for the papyrus trade, lucrative commerce in Tyrian dyes and other commodities, as well as images of the goddess Astarte and the "Lady of Byblos." Tyre and Sidon as great commercial markets appear prominently in the OT (Isa. 23:8; Ezek. 27).

Egypt. Egyptians engaged early in land and sea traffic. They imported cedarwood from Lebanon, pine from Cilicia, amber from the shores of the Baltic, and tin to alloy copper for making bronze. Tiny Palestine was the bridge over which the ceaseless camel-caravan traffic flowed. Such a caravan laden with spices and perhaps nuts,

balm, and other commodities carried Joseph into Egypt (Gen. 39:1). Egyptian sailors plied the Red Sea. Caravan routes extended S carrying Egyptian grain in exchange for many exotic products.

Men carrying saplings in baskets from the shore to the ships

Israel. Until Solomon's time the Hebrews were a simple agricultural and pastoral people. Solomon's diplomacy, foreign marriages, his control of the trade routes, his traffic in horses and chariots (1 Kings 10:28-29) between Kue (Cilicia) and Egypt, his construction of chariot cities, and his voyages with Hiram of Tyre to Ophir (9:26-28; 10:22) yielded the king an immense revenue and greatly extended Hebrew commerce. It is now known that Solomon's smelteries had their counterparts in Phoenician metal refineries of Sardinia and Spain. Solomon's fleets putting out from Ezion-Geber laden with smelted ore brought back valuable goods obtainable in Arabian ports or from the adjacent coasts of Africa. Solomon's affluence was perhaps never equaled by his successors, but thereafter trade not only flourished through Palestine but the Jews enjoyed in their markets, or *suks,* exotic wares from Babylonia, Assyria, the Land of the Hittites, Egypt, Arabia, and far-off Ophir. After the Babylonian captivity the commercial bent of the people was even more permanently fixed, and they never regained the simple pastoral nature or their economy of the earlier period.

Greece (c. 700 B.C.). The Greeks became noted as great seagoing merchants in the Mediterranean world. As early as 650 B.C. they had trading posts in Egypt. Oil, wine, honey, and exquisite Greek pottery were transported wherever ships could sail in the ancient civilized world. In this commercial activity they were preceded in the Aegean area by the highly developed culture and commerce of the Minoans and Mycenaeans—roughly contemporary with Moses and the period of the Judges.

Aramaeans. From the sixth century on Aramaean merchants became prominent all over the Fertile Crescent, and they extended their commodities, culture, and language so that the cumbersome cuneiform language was pushed out, and later even Heb. became a virtually dead language. As a result, by the first century A.D. Aram. was the *lingua franca* of all SW Asia; it was therefore the native language of Jesus and His disciples.

COMMISSIONER (Aram. *sārak,* for the Heb. *shōṭēr,* and used only in Dan. 6; the KJV reads "presidents," and the NIV, "administrators"). According to Dan, 6:2 Darius not only appointed 120 satraps for all the provinces and districts of his kingdom, but he also placed the whole body of satraps under a government council consisting of three commissioners who were to deal with the individual satraps. This triumvirate, or higher authority of three, was not newly instituted by Darius, but already existed in the Chaldean kingdom under Belshazzar (5:7) and was only continued by Darius. Daniel was one of the commissioners.

BIBLIOGRAPHY: F. C. Grant, *Economic Background of the Gospels* (1972); M. I. Finley, *Ancient Economy* (1973).

COMMUNION. *See* Lord's Supper.

COMMUNITY OF GOODS, CHRISTIANITY versus **Communism.** The infant church in Acts presents us with a type of Christian community of goods that was the result of spiritual revival. "And all those who had believed were together, and had all things in common," etc. (Acts 2:44). "And the congregation of those who believed were of one heart and soul; and not one of them claimed that anything belonging to him was his own; but all things were common property to them," etc. (4:32). Some have construed this as a picture of Christian communism. In view of the widespread advance of Marxist communism in the twentieth century it is necessary to see the unique features of this early Christian community of goods in the book of Acts.

First, it took place only in Jerusalem and was probably the result of the abysmal poverty of the church in that city on one hand and spiritual revival on the other. There is no trace of it in any other church. On the contrary, the rich and poor continued to live side by side in what was evidently a free capitalistic society (1 Cor. 16:2; 2 Cor. 9:5–7; 1 Tim. 6:17; James 5:1).

This community of goods was not ordained as a legal necessity in contrast to the contemporary Essenes (which see). It was purely voluntary as it developed from the free working of the Holy Spirit in revival power (Acts 5:3-4).

Ananias's sin was in his pretending to give more than he really had, an exhibition of base hypocrisy in the midst of heaven-sent revival. The community of property practiced by the infant church was a reflection of that community of goods that existed in the case of Jesus Himself and His disciples, the want of all being paid for from a common treasury. Twentieth-century communism was an attempt to achieve a classless society where all exploitation of man by man would disappear, each one contributing according to his ability and receiving according to his need in an environment of plenty for all, in the process of

the development of which the state, essentially a coercive agency in the hands of an oligarchy, will pass away.

The tragic blunder of Marxist communism was its anti-God, anti-Christ program, which lacked respect for individual personality, and was bereft of the fine ethical and spiritual qualities that only the Jewish-Christian spiritual heritage contained in the OT and NT can supply. A definition of communism specifies a type of highly socialized civilization that has never yet been attained, but toward which the communist party of the Union of Soviet Socialist Republics strove. To understand Marxist communism fully, one must scrutinize the type of society that is the communist dream and the underlying philosophy motivating communists to seek the realization of that society.

Karl Marx (1818-83) and Friedrich Engels (1820-95) created a theory of communism, borrowing various philosophical ideas from Hegel, David Smith, Claude St. Simon, and François Fourier. Lenin and Stalin, somewhat revising the Marx-Engels definition of the state to come, gave a description that was cited by communist parties of the USSR and other countries. This system would include the public and collective ownership of productive means in contrast to private ownership, a highly planned industrial and agricultural economy, replacement of class distinctions and state power by free association of city and farm workers, abandonment of socialism "from each according to his ability, from each according to his work" for communism "from each according to his ability to each according to his needs," a free realization of personality for the individual because of elimination of personal economic concern, and encouragement of art and science.

The blunders of Marxist (rather, Soviet) communism were these: (1) a realization of the blessings of God without God; (2) a realization of material blessings without spiritual values; (3) a realization of freedom through slavery; (4) the dream that artistic, scientific advancement and economic security can solve all human difficulties; (5) asserting the highest collective good by denying the worth of the individual human personality.

To the purely natural, materialistic-minded person communism is attractive. However, it strikes violently at Jesus' teaching: "For what will a man be profited, if he gains the whole world and forfeits his soul? Or what will a man give in exchange for his soul?" (Matt. 16:26). In its advocacy of the violent, bloody overthrow of capitalistic society, communist theory acknowledged and its practices showed a complete disregard of ethical and moral restraint in its subversive activities, its home administration, its international diplomacy, or any phase of its dealings. Murder, hatred, dishonesty, deceit, and treachery–anything that actually achieved their goals was acceptable to them. Their materialism completely disregarded spirituality. Soviet communism was for decades a source of persecution of the Christian church in many countries.

Reform from communist rule in central eastern Europe began in earnest in Poland with the Solidarity movement and spread to Hungary, Bulgaria, the Baltic Republics, Czechoslovakia, East Germany, Albania, Romania. In 1985, Mikhail Gorbachev became the leader of the Soviet Union and discontinued his predecessor's policy of intervening in Soviet satellite countries with military force to preserve communist rule. He instead urged communist leaders to seek ways to gain popular support for their rule, but when elections were held in many countries, communist leaders were ousted. The 1989 collapse of the Berlin Wall, perhaps the most visible symbol of the division between the communist and free worlds, was the culmination of the revolutionary changes sweeping through eastern Europe in the 1980s. The collapse of communism in east central Europe spread to the Soviet Union itself, leading to its dissolution, and soon the cold war ended. The Christian church in former Soviet countries has enjoyed a new freedom while experiencing new challenges that a free society brings, such as materialism. The communist system still prevails in nations such as China, Cuba, and North Korea, where the Christian church continues to be oppressed.

BIBLIOGRAPHY: F. F. Bruce, *The Acts of the Apostles,* New International Commentary on the New Testament (1965), pp. 101, 130-33; P. J. Gloag, *Acts of the Apostles* (1979), 1:155-68.

COMPASS (Heb. *mĕḥûgâ*). An architect's tool which, as the Heb. word suggests ("circle"), was used to define round or circular measurement (Isa. 44:13).

COMPASSION. In many instances *compassion* is the rendering of Heb. words elsewhere translated *mercy* (which see). It is also the rendering of the Heb. *ḥāmal* (to "be gentle, clement"; "concern" in the NIV), as in 1 Sam. 23:21. In Ex. 2:6 the rendering is "pity" and in 1 Sam. 15:3, 15; 2 Sam. 21:7 it is rendered "spared," as in 2 Chron. 36:15, 17 where we read that God "had compassion on His people and on His dwelling place," i.e., He *spared* them. It is written that "the Lord is full of compassion" (James 5:11), and that "just as a father has compassion on his children, so the Lord has compassion on those who fear Him" (Ps. 103:13).

CONANI'AH (cō-na-nī'ah). The Levitical brother of Shemei who was charged with preparing storage space in the Temple and caring for the contributions placed therein according to the command of King Hezekiah (2 Chron. 31:12, 13; 35:9).

CONCISION (Gk. *katatomē,* "cutting down, mutilation"). A contemptuous term used by Paul (Phil. 3:2, KJV) to denote the zealous advocates of circumcision, as though he would say, "Keep your eye on that boasted circumcision, or, to call it by its true name, 'concision,' or 'mutilation.' " The NASB renders "false circumcision," marg., lit., "mutilation."

In Gal. 5:12 Paul speaks more pointedly; "Would that those who are troubling you would even mutilate themselves," marg., "cut themselves off."

CONCUBINE (Heb. *pîlegesh,* derivation uncertain). A secondary or inferior wife.

Roman and Greek. Among the Romans it was only at a comparatively late period that concubinage acquired any kind of legal sanction, and the *concubine* came to be substituted for the *mistress.* Among the Greeks, however, the distinction between wife and concubine was established early, the former being for the begetting of legitimate children and taking charge of the affairs of the house, the other for performing daily ministrations about the person.

Hebrew. Concubinage came early into general practice, for we read (Gen. 22:24) of Bethuel, the father of Rebekah, having not only his wife Milcah, but also a concubine, Reumah, who bore him four children. Indeed, concubinage substantially appeared when Abraham took Hagar as a sort of wife, by whom Sarah hoped he would have children —to be reckoned, in some sense, as her own, and to take rank as proper members of the family (16:1-3). In the next generation of the chosen family we find no mention of a state of concubinage; Isaac seems to have had no partner to his bed but Rebekah and no children but Esau and Jacob. But the evil reappears in the next generation in an aggravated form: Esau multiplying wives at pleasure, and Jacob taking first two wives and then two concubines.

Nor was the practice ever wholly discontinued among the Israelites, for we see that the following men had concubines, namely, Eliphaz (Gen. 36:12), Gideon (Judg. 8:30-31), Saul (2 Sam. 3:7), David (5:13), Solomon (1 Kings 11:3), Rehoboam (2 Chron. 11:21), Abijah (13:21). Indeed, in process of time concubinage appears to have degenerated into a regular custom among the Jews, and the institutions of Moses were directed to prevent excess and abuse by wholesome laws and regulations (Ex. 21:7-9; Deut. 21:10-14). The unfaithfulness of a concubine was considered criminal (2 Sam. 3:7-8) and was punished with scourging (Lev. 19:20). In Judg. 19 the possessor of a concubine was called her "husband," her father is called the "father-in-law," and he the "son-in-law," showing how nearly the concubine approached to the wife.

Sometimes, to avoid debauchery, a female slave would be given to the son, was then considered as one of the children of the house, and retained her rights as concubine even after the marriage of the son (Ex. 21:9-10).

Christianity restores the sacred institution of marriage to its original character, and concubinage is ranked with fornication and adultery (Matt. 19:5; 1 Cor. 7:2). Still the practice of concubinage yielded only in the slowest and most gradual manner even to our Lord's explicit teachings.

BIBLIOGRAPHY: E. Westermarck, *The History of Human Marriage* (1925), 3:35ff.; L. M. Epstein, *Marriage Laws in the Bible and the Talmud* (1942), pp. 37-44, 61-63, 71-76; E. Neufeld, *Ancient Hebrew Marriage Laws* (1944), pp. 118-34; L. M. Epstein, *Sex Laws and Customs in Judaism* (1967), p. 69.

CONCUPISCENCE (Gk. *'epithumia,* a "longing," Rom. 7:8; Col. 3:5; 1 Thess 4:5). A KJV term referring to evil desire, generally in the sense of indwelling sin. The NASB renders "coveting," "evil desire," and "lustful passion." The NIV translates "covetous desire," "evil desires," and "passionate lust."

CONDEMNATION. The Gk. word *krima* is translated "judgment" and (often wrongly) "damnation." Condemnation signifies the declaring of an evildoer to be guilty; the punishment inflicted (1 Cor. 11:32, 34); testimony by good example against malefactors (Matt. 12:41-42). We use the word with the lighter meaning of censure, disapproval, blame, etc. As far as the justified believer is concerned, he faces no condemnation or judgment (Rom. 8:1). The guilt of his sin has been removed (Rom. 3:7), and he stands positionally "in Christ" and hence accepted "in the Beloved" (Eph. 1:6).

CONDUIT (Heb. *te'ālâ,* a "channel," Job 38:25; "trench," 1 Kings 18:32-38). The aqueduct made by Hezekiah to convey the water from the upper spring of Gihon into the western part of Jerusalem (2 Kings 18:17; 20:20; Isa. 7:3; 36:2). It was a tunnel (discovered in 1880) cut through solid rock from both ends for a total of about seventeen hundred feet. Evidently it was constructed just before the attack of Sennacherib of Assyria in 701 B.C. It seems to have been at first an open trench, but closed with masonry at the approach of the Assyrians. The aqueduct, though much injured and not serviceable for water beyond Bethlehem, still exists; the water is conveyed from about two miles S of Bethlehem, crossing the valley of Hinnom on a bridge of nine arches.

CONEY. *See* Animal Kingdom: Rock Badger.

CONFECTION. A KJV term for *perfume* (so NASB, Ex. 30:55) made for use in the Temple. In the NIV (Ezek. 27:17), a word that may refer to a kind of cake (cf. NASB marg.).

CONFECTIONER. *See* Handicrafts: Perfumer; Oils and Ointment; Perfume.

CONFESSION (Heb. from *yādâ,* lit., to "use,"

i.e., extend the hand). Used in the OT in the sense of acknowledging one's sin (Lev. 5:5; Job 40:14; Ps. 32:5). In the prayer of Solomon at the dedication of the Temple he uses the expression "confess Thy name" (1 Kings 8:33, 35; 2 Chron. 6:24, 26), doubtless meaning the acknowledgment of Jehovah as the one against whom the Israelites might sin, and the justice of punishment meted out by Him.

The Gk. word rendered "confession" is *homologeō,* lit., to "say the same thing," i.e., not to deny and so to admit or declare one's self guilty of what he is accused. It is also used in the sense of a *profession,* implying the yielding or change of one's conviction (John 12:42; Rom. 10:9-10; 1 Tim. 6:13; etc.).

CONFUSION OF TONGUES. *See* Babel; Tongues, Speaking in.

CONGREGATION (Heb. *'ēdâ,* "assembly," *mô'ēd,* "festive gathering").

The Hebrew People. The term referred to the Hebrew people in a collective capacity under their peculiar aspect as a holy community, held together by religious rather than political bonds. Sometimes it is used in a broad sense as inclusive of foreign settlers (Ex. 12:19); but more properly as exclusively appropriate to the Hebrew element of the population (Num. 15:15, NASB, "assembly"; NIV, "community"). Every circumcised Hebrew was a member of the congregation and took part in its proceedings, probably from the time that he bore arms. It is important, however, to observe that he acquired no political rights in his individual capacity, but only as a member of a *house;* for the basis of the Hebrew polity was the house, from which was formed in an ascending scale the *family* or collection of houses, the *tribe* or collection of families, and the *congregation* or collection of tribes.

The Comitia, or Legislative Assemblies. The persons composing the Comitia were judges, heads of families, genealogists (Heb. *shōṭerîm*), elders, and the princes of the tribes. These representatives formed the *congregation.* Cf. Ex. 12:3, "the congregation of Israel"; v. 21, "the elders of Israel"; further, Deut. 31:28, where we read, "the elders of your tribes and your officers"; and in v. 30, "all the assembly of Israel" (KJV, "all the congregation of Israel"). Thus both expressions are in every case identical, and *congregation* or *assembly* of Israel means the people of Israel present in their representatives.

Meetings. The Comitia was convened by the judge or ruler for the time being, or, in case of his absence, by the high priest (Josh. 23:1-2; Num. 10:2-4). The place of assembling appears to have been at the door of the Tabernacle (Num. 10:3; 1 Sam. 10:17); although some other place, commonly of some celebrity, might be selected (Josh. 24:1; 1 Sam. 11:14-15; 1 Kings 12:1). While in the wilderness the summons was given by blowing the holy trumpets; the blowing of *one* trumpet being the signal for a select convention, composed merely of the heads of the clans or associated families, and of the princes of the tribes; the blowing of two trumpets, the signal for convening the great assembly, composed not only of the above, but also of the elders, judges, genealogists, and, in some instances, of the whole body of the people (Num. 10:2-4). When Israel was settled in Palestine, notification of the assembly was sent by messengers.

Powers. In the congregation the rights of sovereignty were exercised, such as declaring war (Judg. 20:1, 11-14), making peace (21:13-20), and concluding treaties (Josh. 9:15-21). Civil rulers and generals, and eventually kings, were chosen (1 Sam. 10:17-24; 2 Sam. 5:1-3; 1 Kings 12:20). The congregation acted without instructions from the people, on its own authority, and according to its own views; still it was in the habit of proposing to the people its decisions for ratification (1 Sam. 11:14-15; cf. Josh. 8:33).

In the later periods of Jewish history the congregation was represented by the *Sanhedrin* (which see), and the term *Synagogue* (which see), applied in the LXX exclusively to the congregation, was transferred to the place of meeting. In Acts 13:43, however, it is used in a modern sense of an assemblage.

BIBLIOGRAPHY: B. F. Streeter, *The Primitive Church* (1929); W. F. Albright, *Recent Discourses in Bible Lands* (1955), pp. 134ff.; J. Y. Church, *Journal of Theological Studies* 49 (1948): 130-42; E. Schweitzer, *Theology Today* 13 (1957): 471-83; J. A. Thompson, *Journal of Semitic Studies* 10 (1965): 222-40.

CONGREGATION, MOUNT OF. *See* Assembly, Mount of.

CONGREGATION, TABERNACLE OF. *See* Tabernacle.

CONI'AH (cō-nī'a). Another form of *Jehoiachin* (which see).

CONSCIENCE (Lat. *conscientia,* "consciousness"; Gk. *suneidēsis*). The awareness that a proposed act is or is not conformable to one's ideal of right and manifesting itself in the feeling of *obligation* or *duty.* The OT usually expresses the idea as "having [something] on the heart" (so the NIV in Gen. 20:5, 6; 1 Sam. 25:31; Job 27:6). Conscience is not so much a distinct faculty of the mind, like perception, memory, etc., as an exercise of the judgment and the power of feeling, as employed with reference to moral truth. It implies the moral sense "to discern good and evil" (Heb. 5:14) and a feeling, more or less strong, of responsibility. Thus it will appear to be wrong to name conscience "the voice of God," although it is true that the testimony of conscience certainly rests on the foundation of a divine law in man, the existence of which, its

claims and judgments, are removed from his subjective control.

If a man knows his doing to be in harmony with this law his conscience is *good* (Acts 23:1; 1 Tim. 1:5, 19; Heb. 13:18; 1 Pet. 3:16, 21), *pure* (1 Tim. 3:9; 2 Tim. 1:3), and *void of offense.* If what he does is *evil,* so also is his conscience, inasmuch as it is conscious of such evil (Heb. 10:22); it is *defiled* (Titus 1:15; 1 Cor. 8:7) when it is stained by evil deeds; or *seared with a branding iron* (1 Tim. 4:2) when it is branded with its evil deeds, or cauterized, i.e., made insensible to all feeling.

Paul lays down the law that a man should follow his own conscience, even though it be weak; otherwise moral personality would be destroyed (1 Cor. 8:10-13; 10:29).

BIBLIOGRAPHY: C. A. Pierce, *Conscience in the New Testament,* Studies in Biblical Theology 15 (1955); W. Lillie, *Studies in New Testament Ethics* (1961); J. G. McKenzie, *Guilt: Its Meaning and Significance* (1962), pp. 21-54, 138-58; R. H. Niebuhr, *The Responsible Self* (1963); H. Thielicke, *Theological Ethics: Foundations* (1966), pp. 298-358.

CONSECRATION. The rendering of several Heb. and Gk. words. It is the act of setting apart any person or thing to the worship or service of God.

The Law of Moses. This law ordained that the firstborn, both of man and beast, should be consecrated to Jehovah; also that all the race of Abraham was in a peculiar manner consecrated to His worship, whereas the tribe of Levi and family of Aaron were more immediately consecrated to His service (Ex. 13:2; Num. 3:12; 1 Pet. 2:9). There were also consecrations, voluntary and of temporary or abiding nature (*see* Vow). Thus Hannah devoted her son Samuel to a lifetime of service in the Tabernacle (1 Sam. 1:11); and David and Solomon appointed the Nethinim or Temple servants to a similar service in the Temple (Ezra 8:20). The Hebrews sometimes devoted to the Lord their fields and cattle, spoils taken in war (Lev. 27:28-29), vessels (Josh. 6:19), profits (Mic. 4:13), individuals (Num. 6:2-13; 1 Sam. 1:11; Luke 1:15), and nations (Ex. 19:6).

In the NT all Christians are consecrated persons. They are not only "a holy nation" but also "a royal priesthood" (1 Pet. 2:9). The NT also recognizes special consecrations, as to the work of the Christian ministry or to some particular service connected with it (Acts 13:2-3; 1 Cor. 12:28). *See* Ordination.

CONSOLATION. *See* Comfort; Holy Ghost.

CONSTELLATIONS. *See* Astronomy; Star.

CONSUMPTION. The translation in the KJV of two Heb. words, one referring to a wasting disease (cf. KJV, NIV, and NASB of Lev. 26:16; Deut. 28:23) and the other to an end or consummation of things (Isa. 10:22-23; 28:22; NIV, "destruction").

CONTAMINATION (Heb. *nega'*; Gk. *alisgēma*), a Hellenistic word (Acts 15:20). The contamination referred to here alludes to meat sacrificed to idols. After the sacrifice was concluded, a portion of the victim was given to the priests, the rest being eaten in honor of the gods, either in the temples or a private house. Some salted the flesh and laid it up for future use, while others sold it in the market (1 Cor 10:25; cf. 8:1, 7, 10). Of course this flesh, having been offered to idols, was an abomination to the Jews; any use of it was thought to infect the user with idolatry. The Council of Jerusalem directed that converts decline invitations to such feasts and refrain from the use of such meat, that no offense might be given (Acts 15:28-29). The OT use (so translated only in the NIV) refers to objects that have become impure ceremonially by mildew or other means (Lev. 13:47, 49, 52, 54). The NASB renders the Heb. *nega'* "mark."

CONTENTMENT (Gk. *autarkeia*). The word means "sufficiency" and is so rendered in 2 Cor. 9:8. It is that disposition of mind in which one is, through grace, independent of outward circumstances (Phil. 4:11; 1 Tim. 6:6, 8), so as not to be moved by envy (James 3:16), anxiety (Matt. 6:24, 34), and discontent (1 Cor. 10:10).

CONTRACT. *See* Covenant.

CONVERSION (Gk. *epistrophē*, Acts 15:3, rendered "conversion," lit., "turning toward"). A term denoting, in its theological use, the "turning " of a soul from sin to God. The verb (*epistrephō*) is sometimes rendered in the NT "to convert," sometimes simply "to turn." In its *active* sense it represents the action of one who is instrumental in "turning" or "converting" others (Luke 1:16; Acts 26:18; James 5:19-20); *intransitively*, the action of men in their own conversion, i.e., the action of men empowered by divine grace to "turn" from sin "toward" God (Acts 3:19).

The Heb. terms of the OT have a similar significance and use (Pss. 19:7; 51:13; Jer. 31:18; Ezek. 33:11). There is a measure of freedom in Scripture in the use of these terms that should put us on our guard against attempts at too rigid a definition. But in a general way it may be said that conversion in the Scriptures has a more exact and *restricted* meaning than is ascribed to it in common religious phraseology. Conversion is not justification, or regeneration, or assurance of reconciliation, however closely these blessings may be connected with true conversion. Like repentance and faith, both involved in conversion, conversion is an act of man which he is enabled to perform by divine grace.

Justification and regeneration are acts of God, which He invariably accomplishes for those who are converted, i.e., for those who, with repentance and faith, "turn" away from sin "toward"

Him (Acts 3:19). For a full and discriminating statement of the doctrine of conversion, *see* Pope, *Comp. Christian Doc.*, 3:367-71. *See* Repentance.

BIBLIOGRAPHY: W. James, *Varieties of Religious Experience* (1902); E. Routley, *The Gift of Conversion* (1957); id., *Conversion* (1959); R. O. Ferm, *The Psychology of Christian Conversion* (1959); W. Barclay, *Turning to God* (1963); L. L. Morris, *The Abolition of Religion* (1964); J. K. Grider, *Repentance unto Life* (1965).

CONVICTION (Gk. *elegchō*, to "convict," "reprove," John 8:46, KJV, "convinceth"; NIV, "prove"; in 1 Cor. 14:24, KJV and NIV, "convinced" is in RV "reproved"; etc.). The meaning of conviction as a law term is *being found guilty*. In common language it means *being persuaded* or *convinced*. In *theology* it means *being condemned* at the bar of one's own conscience as a sinner in view of the law of God. It is the antecedent to repentance and is often accompanied by a painful sense of exposure to God's wrath. It is the work of the Holy Spirit, showing the heinousness of sin and the soul's exposure to divine wrath. The means of conviction are various: gospel truth, the law read or heard, reflection, affliction, calamity, etc. It often comes suddenly, and may be stifled, as it surely is if not heeded.

CONVOCATION (Heb. *miqrā'*, a "holy assembly"). A meeting of the people for the worship of Jehovah (Ex. 12:16; etc.). The following occasions were to be held as convocations: the *Sabbaths* (Lev. 23:2-3); the *Passover,* the first and the last day (Ex. 12:16; Lev. 23:7-8; Num. 28:18, 25); *Pentecost,* the *feast of Weeks* (Lev. 23:21; Num. 28:26); the *feast of Trumpets* (Lev. 23:24; Num. 29:1); the *feast of Tabernacles,* first and last day (Lev. 23:35-36; Num. 29:12); the one great *fast,* the annual *Day of Atonement* (Lev. 23:27; Num. 29:7).

One great feature of the convocation was that no work was to be done on these days, except what was necessary for the preparation of food; on the Sabbath even this was prohibited (Ex. 35:2-3).

See also Festivals.

COOK, COOKING. *See* Food.

COOS. *See* Cos.

COPPER. *See* Mineral Kingdom.

COPPERSMITH. A worker in any kind of metals; probably Alexander was so called (2 Tim. 4:14) because copper was in such common use. *See* Handicrafts.

COR. *See* Kor.

CORAL. *See* Animal Kingdom; Mineral Kingdom.

CORBAN (kor'ban; Gk. *korban,* an "offering"). A name common to any sacred gift; the term in general use to denote sacrifice, its equivalent (Ex.

28:38) being "holy gifts." All things or persons consecrated (or vowed) for religious purposes became *corban* and fell to the sanctuary. The Pharisees taught that "if a man says to his father or his mother, anything of mine you might have been helped by is *Corban* [i.e., devoted]" (Mark 7:11), he thereby consecrated all to God and was relieved from using it for his parents. This Jesus declared to be contradictory of the command that taught children to honor their parents. *See* Vows.

CORD. The rendering of several Heb. words, the most comprehensive of which is *ḥibbēl*, from the root meaning to "twist," hence the English "cable." The term *cord* includes in its meaning rope, twine, thread, thongs, etc.

Material. The material of which cord was made varied according to the strength required. Flax was used for making ropes, string, and various kinds of twine; date tree fibers for large ropes; and strips of camel hide for strongest rope.

Uses. The following uses of cord are mentioned: (1) For fastening a tent (Ex. 35:18; 39:40; Isa. 54:2). (2) For leading or binding animals, as a halter or rein (Ps. 118:27; Hos. 11:4). (3) For yoking them either to a cart (Isa. 5:18) or a plow (Job 39:10). (4) For binding prisoners (Judg. 15:9, 11-12; Pss. 2:3; 129:4; Ezek. 3:25). (5) For bowstrings (Ps. 11:2) made of catgut; such are spoken of in Judg. 16:7 ("fresh cords [NIV, "thongs"] that have not been dried"). (6) For the ropes or "tackle" of a vessel (Isa. 33:23). (7) For measuring ground (2 Sam. 8:2; Ps. 78:55; Amos 7:17; Zech. 2:1); hence *cord* or *line* became an expression for an inheritance (Josh. 17:14; 19:9; Ps. 16:6; Ezek. 47:13) and even for any defined district (Deut. 3:4). (8) For fishing and snaring. (9) For attaching articles of dress, as the chains of "twisted cordage work" and the "blue cord" worn by the high priests (Ex. 28:14, 22, 24, 28, 37; 39:15, 17, 21, 31; Num. 15:38). (10) For fastening awnings (Esther 1:6). (11) For attaching to a plummet. (12) For drawing water out of a well or raising heavy weights (Josh. 2:15; Jer. 38:6, 13).

CORE. *See* Korah.

CORIANDER. *See* Vegetable Kingdom.

CORINTH (kor'inth). A prominent Gk. city evangelized by Paul.

Physical Description. As Greece's most splendid commercial city, Corinth was located just S of the narrow isthmus connecting central Greece with the Peloponnesus. Its strategic situation made it the mecca of trade between the East and West. Its eastern port was Cenchrae (cf. Rom. 16:1) and its western emporium Lechaeum. The city derived rich income from the transport of cargoes across the narrow isthmus (a distance less than five miles). Not until A.D. 1881-93 was the present canal dug, saving a perilous two-hundred-mile trip around the stormy Cape Malea.

Alexander the Great, Julius Caesar, and Nero (who turned the first spade of dirt with a golden shovel) realized the practicality of such a waterway. But all ancient attempts came to nought and were abandoned. The modern engineering feat is four miles in length, spanned by the 170-foot-high bridge.

History. The occupation of the site goes back to Neolithic times (cf. John G. O'Neill, *Ancient Corinth*, part I: *From the Earliest Times to 404 B.C.* [1930]). The cult of Aphrodite was cultivated there early. Corinth was an aggressive colonizing city in the eighth and seventh centuries B.C.; Corinthian bronze and pottery became proverbial. The Romans completely destroyed it in 146 B.C. Julius Caesar restored it (46 B.C.), and it grew so rapidly that it was made Achaia's capital and the seat of the proconsulship by Augustus (cf. Acts 18:12). Its prosperity continued until the city was taken by the Turks in 1458. A terrific earthquake destroyed the old city in 1858, and a new city was constructed about three and one-half miles from the old city.

Archaeology. The American School of Classical Studies has been excavating at Corinth since 1896, except for war years. Much of their attention has centered on the agora, which was seven hundred feet from E to W and three hundred feet from N to S. Following the natural configuration of the land, the southern section was about thirteen feet higher than the northern part. At the dividing line of the two levels stood the bema where public officials could address crowds and render judgment; no doubt Paul stood before Gallio there (Acts 18:12-13). The bema was flanked by a row of central shops. Along the S side of the agora lay an immense stoa filled with shops of meat and wine merchants, probably the "shambles" (1 Cor. 10:25) where Paul told the Corinthians they could buy meat with a clear conscience. At the E end of the agora and S of the stoa stood two similar basilicas used as law courts. Built in the first century A.D., they may well have been the places where the litigious Corinthian Christians went to court against their brethren (1 Cor. 6).

On a rocky terrace overlooking the western side of the agora stood a temple of Apollo. Built during the sixth century B.C., it measured 174 feet long by 69 feet wide, and the 38 columns of its peristyle stood almost 24 feet in height. These were especially impressive because they consisted of single shafts of stone instead of being built up with drums, as was the usual practice. In the 1980s work has been going on at the theater, just to the NW of the agora.

The American School has also been working at the site of the Isthmia (about six miles from ancient Corinth), where the Isthmian Games were held in honor of Poseidon (cf. 1 Cor. 9:24-27). The excavators have uncovered the temple of Poseidon, the 650-foot stadium, the

Bema or judgment seat at Corinth on which Gallio stood when hearing Paul's case

theater, an impressive propylaea to the sanctuary, and Roman baths of a period later than the NT.   H.F.V.

BIBLIOGRAPHY: J. G. O'Neill, *Ancient Corinth* (1930); O. Broneer, *Biblical Archaeologist* 14 (1951): 78-96; American School of Classical Studies, *Ancient Corinth* (1954); H. J. Cadbury, *The Book of Acts in History* (1955); G. E. Wright, *BA* 25 (1957): 261.

CORINTHIANS, FIRST EPISTLE.

Authorship. The Pauline authorship of 1 Corinthians is abundantly attested to from the first century onward. Clement of Rome, the Didache, Ignatius, Polycarp, Hermas, Justin Martyr, and Athenagoros all lend their voice in support of the genuineness of the epistle. Irenaeus contains more than 60 quotations from 1 Corinthians; Clement of Alexandria quotes it more than 130 times; Tertullian quotes some 400 times. First Corinthians stands at the head of the Pauline epistles in the Muratorian canon. Internal evidence is also abundant (cf. 1:1; 3:4; 9:1; 16:21). The way the book dovetails with the history in Acts also confirms it.

Occasion and Date. The occasion of the epistle was a letter of inquiry from Corinth concerning marriage and the eating of meats offered to idols (1 Cor. 7:1; 8:1-13). This led the apostle to write concerning the deepening divisions, increasing contentions, and unjudged sin in the church (1:10-12; 5:1). The factions were due not to open heresies, but to the carnality of the Corinthians and to their being carried away by admiration for Gk. wisdom and eloquence. The moral pollution of their city, which was notorious, was a continual temptation to them. Minor disorders took the form of abuse of spiritual gifts, particularly tongues and the sign gifts (14:1-28). False ideas concerning the resurrection were also corrected (chap. 15). The date of the epistle varies with critical opinion. We know it was written from Ephesus (16:8). It was seemingly written in the latter half of Paul's three-year ministry in that city (Acts 20:31; cf. 19:8-22). The spring of A.D. 54

or 55 is perhaps correct, although some would date it as late as A.D. 59.

Outline. In correcting the current evils in the church, the apostle presents the contents in the following plan:

I. Introduction (1:1-9)
II. Rebuke of their divisions (1:10–4:21)
III. The problem of their sensual immorality (5-7)
   A. Judgment of incest (5:1-13)
   B. Parenthetical—the lawsuits in heathen courts (6:1-11)
   C. Fornication and the sacredness of the body (6:12-20)
   D. Marriage and divorce (7)
IV. The problem of food offered to idols (8:1–11:1)
   A. General tenets (8)
   B. The precept of forbearance (9)
   C. Illustration from ancient Israel (10:1-13)
   D. Rebuke of idolatry (10:14-22)
   E. Christian liberty (10:23–11:1)
V. Problem of public worship (11:2–14:40)
   A. Dress of women in public worship (11:2-16)
   B. Regulations of the Lord's Supper (11:17-34)
   C. Regulations concerning spiritual gifts (12-14)
VI. Doctrine of the resurrection (15)
VII. Practical concerns of Paul (16:1-8)
VIII. Conclusion (16:19-24)

BIBLIOGRAPHY: A. Robertson and A. Plummer, *A Critical and Exegetical Commentary on the First Epistle of St. Paul to the Corinthians*, International Critical Commentary (1914); J. Moffat, *Commentary on I Corinthians* (1938); C. Hodge, *An Exposition of the First Epistle to the Corinthians* (1965); C. K. Barrett, *A Commentary on the First Epistle to the Corinthians* (1968); H. Conzelman, *I Corinthians*, Hermenia (1975); F. L. Godet, *Commentary on First Corinthians* (1977); F. F. Bruce, *1 and 2 Corinthians* (1980); T. C. Edwards, *A Commentary on the First Epistle to the Corinthians* (1980); J. F. MacArthur, Jr., *First Corinthians*, The MacArthur New Testament Commentary (1984); H. Olshausen, *A Commentary on Paul's First and Second Epistles to the Corinthians* (1984).

CORINTHIANS, SECOND EPISTLE.
This great epistle presents the vindication of Paul's apostleship and sets forth in a remarkable way the glory of the Christian ministry. The epistle discloses the heart of Paul and his conduct under physical weakness and persecution from the legalizers.

Authenticity. The internal evidence of 2 Corinthians vividly attests its genuineness. The distinctive elements of Pauline theology and eschatology are clearly seen throughout. However, the letter is not doctrinal or didactic, but intensely personal. Its absorbing interest is a recital of the events with which the apostle and the Corinthians were struggling at the time. A great deal is lacking concerning the circumstances calling forth the epistle, but the references to these events that do exist are so manifestly made in good faith that it is difficult to reject Pauline authorship. External evidence, while not so clear as in the case of 1 Corinthians, yet is unambiguous in establishing the existence and the use of the letter, especially in the second century. Although Clement of Rome is silent, the epistle is quoted by Polycarp. It is referred to in the epistle of Diognetus 5:12. It is sufficiently corroborated by Irenaeus, Theophilus, Athenagoras, Tertullian, and Clement of Alexandria.

Date and Connection with First Corinthians. It was written from Macedonia, likely from Philippi, in the fall of A.D. 54 or 55, the same year in which 1 Corinthians was written or in the autumn of the succeeding year. After Paul sent 1 Corinthians, it seems evident that news reached the apostle of growing opposition led by the Judaizing party. Paul was constrained to pay an immediate visit and found the reports only too true. Perhaps he was openly flouted before the congregation at Corinth. Returning to Ephesus he wrote a severe epistle that he sent on through the hand of Titus. Before Titus could return, events took a disastrous turn at Ephesus, and Paul had to flee at the peril of his life. He went to Troas but, unable to await patiently there for tidings of the Corinthian issue, he crossed into Macedonia and met Titus there, possibly in Philippi. The news, happily, was reassuring. He then wrote a second epistle and sent it on by Titus and others.

Value. The letter is chiefly of value in showing us the concern of the apostle for his converts. In the circumstances of the epistle we find the intensity of his emotions and his great love for them. Second Corinthians is also extremely valuable in setting forth the lofty character and the challenge of the Christian ministry. Paul sets forth his high calling as the most glorious work in which a man can engage. The apostle himself received the ministry as divine, and he accepted it with supreme devotion. Through all the sufferings, testings, and buffetings that he suffered, we yet discern his triumphing in Christ.

Outline. The epistle may be divided into three parts:

I. Paul's guiding principle of conduct (1:1–7:16)
II. The collection for the poor saints at Jerusalem (8:1–9:15)
III. Paul's defense of his apostolic ministry (10:1–13:14)

BIBLIOGRAPHY: A. Plummer, *A Critical and Exegetical Commentary on the Second Epistle of St. Paul to the Corinthians,* International Critical Commentary (1956); P. E. Hughes, *Paul's Second Epistle to the Corinthians* (1962); C. Hodge, *An Exposition of the Second Epistle to the Corinthians* (1965); C. K. Barrett, *A Commentary on the Second Epistle to the Corinthi-*

ans (1973); A. P. Stanley, *Epistles of St. Paul to the Corinthians* (1981).

CORMORANT. *See* Animal Kingdom.

CORN. *See* Vegetable Kingdom.

CORNELIUS (kor-nē'li-us). A devout Roman proselyte, the first representative Gentile introduced to the gospel of grace.

Personal History. He was probably of the *Cornelii,* a noble and distinguished family at Rome (Acts 10:1-2).

His Spiritual Status. Was Cornelius saved before Peter's visit? A careful answer to this must be that he was *not* saved (Acts 11:14), his devotion, alms, prayers, and visions (10:2-3) merely signifying that he was a Jewish proselyte. If he were regenerated, he most certainly was not baptized, indwelt, and sealed by the Holy Spirit as is every believer in this age.

Dispensational Importance. The case of Cornelius marked the giving of the Holy Spirit to the Gentiles to undertake for them every ministry committed to Him in this present age, namely, the ministry of regeneration, baptism, indwelling, sealing, and filling. The scene at Caesarea pictures the first representative Gentiles being baptized into the mystical Body of Christ and becoming "fellow heirs" with the Jews and partakers of His promise in Christ by the gospel (Eph. 3:6). In the book of Acts the gospel had now gone to the Jew (chap. 2), to the racially mixed Samaritan (chap. 8), and now to the Gentile (chap. 10). With the introduction to the latter the normal order of the age is established, when *every* believer, upon no other condition than simple faith in the finished redemptive work of Christ, is regenerated, baptized into the Body of Christ, indwelt perpetually, and sealed eternally, with the added privilege and duty of being filled continually as conditions for filling are complied with. Moreover, Cornelius's case marked the introduction of the gospel to the Gentiles. For the last time Peter used the "keys of the kingdom of heaven" (cf. 2:14; 8:14-15). He is the one who was sent to Cornelius, preached the sermon, and unlocked the message of grace (10:34-35). When this simple dispensational distinction in the case of Cornelius as well as in the case of the pivotal passages, Acts 2 and Acts 8, has not been made, the doctrine of the Holy Spirit in the Acts has become a grand jumble in modern cultism.

M.F.U.

BIBLIOGRAPHY: M. F. Unger, *The Baptism and Gifts of the Holy Spirit* (1974), pp. 69-72.

CORNER GATE. This gate was at the NW corner of Jerusalem (2 Kings 14:13; 2 Chron. 25:23). *See* Jerusalem.

CORNERSTONE (Job 38:6; Isa. 28:16). The stone at the corner of two walls that unites them; specifically, the stone built into one corner of the foundation of an edifice as the actual or nominal starting point of a building. From a comparison of passages we find mention of "a costly cornerstone for the foundation" (Isa. 28:16), "a stone for a corner" (Jer. 51:26, from which it would appear that cornerstones were placed in different positions as regards elevation). The expressions "the chief corner stone" (Ps. 118:22; "capstone" in NIV) and the "top stone" (Zech. 4:7; "capstone" in NIV) seem to warrant the conclusion that the "cornerstone" is a term equally applicable to the chief stone at the top and that in the foundation.

Figurative. The term "cornerstone" is sometimes used to denote any principal person, such as the princes of Egypt (Isa. 19:13). Christ is called the "corner stone" in reference to His being the foundation of the Christian faith (Eph. 2:20) and the importance and conspicuousness of the place He occupies (Matt. 21:42; 1 Pet. 2:6).

CORNET. See Music.

COROS. A foreign measure of capacity. See Metrology.

CORRECTION (Heb. *yāsar,* to "instruct," "chastise"; *yākah,* to "manifest," "reason with," "reprove"). In "He that *chastiseth* the heathen, shall not he *correct?*" (Ps. 94:10, KJV; italics added; NASB, "He who chastens the nations, will He not *rebuke?*" italics added) both Heb. words are used in the above order. The man is considered happy whom God thus *correcteth* (Job 5:17, KJV; NASB, "reproves"). The Scriptures are for *correction* (2 Tim. 3:16). In the Bible the word has the same double meaning as in other English literature, namely, *to reform, rectify,* free from errors, and to chastise or punish; the act of *correcting. See* Discipline.

CORRUPTION. The rendering of several Heb. and Gk. words, signifying (1) the decay of the body (Job 17:14; Ps. 16:10, KJV; NASB renders "the pit," NIV "decay"); (2) the blemishes that rendered an animal unfit for sacrifice (Lev. 22:25); (3) the demoralization of heart and life through sin (Gen. 6:12; Deut. 9:12), resulting in those sinful habits and practices that defile and ruin men (Rom. 8:21; 2 Pet. 2:19); (4) everlasting ruin (Gal. 6:8; NIV, "destruction").

CORRUPTION, MOUNT OF. See Destruction, Mount of.

COS (kōs), **Co'os.** A small island (111 sq. miles) in the Aegean Sea; the birthplace of Hippocrates; celebrated for wines and beautiful fabrics. It is now called Kos and has a population of more than twenty thousand. Paul spent the night on the island while on his voyage to Judea from Miletus (Acts 21:1).

CO'SAM (kō'sam). The son of Elmadam and father of Addi, in the line of Joseph the husband of Mary (Luke 3:28).

COTTAGE. A KJV term for a shelter, replaced in the NASB and NIV by "shelter" (Isa. 1:8; Heb. *sūkkâ*), "shack," or "hut" (Isa. 24:20; Heb. *mᵉlûnâ*), and "caves" (Zeph. 2:6; Heb. *kᵉrôt*). The *sūkkâ,* frequently rendered "booth," was a hut made of boughs for the purpose of temporary shelter. Being of slight structure, when the fruits were gathered the shelters were either taken down or blown down by the winds of winter (Job 27:18, "booth," KJV; "hut," NASB and NIV).

The *mᵉlûnâ* was a night lodge, or impermanent place of dwelling (from *lûn,* "to spend the night"). Usually it was merely the rough hut in which the vintager was sheltered (Isa. 1:8, "lodge," KJV; "hut," NASB and NIV). In Isa. 24:20 it is a hanging bed.

The *kᵉrôt,* lit., "diggings," were probably excavations made by the shepherds as a protection against the sun (Zeph. 2:6). The NIV takes it as a reference to the Kerethites (*see* Cherithites).

COTTON. See Vegetable Kingdom.

COUCH. See Bed.

COULTER (Heb. *'ēt,* 1 Sam 13:20-21, KJV). The term *coulter* is replaced in the NASB and NIV by *mattock,* but the Heb. word behind it is elsewhere rendered "plowshare" in the KJV, NIV and NASB (Isa. 2:4; Mic. 4:3; Joel 3:10), as it is in the majority of the ancient versions. See Mattock; Plowshare.

COUNCIL. In the OT *council* is the rendering of the Heb. *rigmâ,* lit., a "heap" (Ps. 68:27, KJV; NASB, NIV, "throng"), a group or company of persons. Two Gk. words are thus rendered in the NT:

1. A consultation of persons (Matt. 12:14, *sumboulion*). In Acts 25:12 reference is made to a board of assessors or advisers, with whom the governors of the provinces took counsel before rendering judgment.

2. Any assembly for the purpose of deliberating or judging (*sunedrion,* a "sitting together"). Among the Jews these councils were: (1) The Sanhedrin. (2) The lesser courts (Matt. 10:17; Mark 13:9, see marg.), of which there were two at Jerusalem and one in each town of Palestine. *See* Law, Administration of.

COUNSELOR. In general, an adviser upon any matter (Prov. 11:14; 15:22; 2 Chron. 25:16; etc.), especially the king's state adviser (2 Sam. 15:12; Ezra 7:28; 1 Chron. 27:33; etc.), and one of the chief men of the government (Job 3:14; 12:17; Isa. 1:26; 3:3; etc.). In Mark 15:43 and Luke 23:50 the word probably designates a member of the Sanhedrin.

COUPLING (Heb. *ḥābar,* "to join"). The wooden beams for fastening a building (2 Chron. 34:11). The NIV renders "joists."

COURIER (Heb. *rûṣ,* a "runner"). Complete establishments of couriers formed a part of royal establishments (2 Chron. 30:6, 10; "posts," KJV), their purpose being to carry by foot messages as swiftly as possible. Jeremiah shows that a regular postal service of this sort existed in his time (Jer. 51:31, "One courier runs to meet another"), clearly implying that couriers were wont to be maintained by relays of special messengers regularly organized for their work. The same sort of postal communication is referred to in Esther 3:15; 8:13-14.

COURSE. This word is used in Scripture in the sense of *advance, progress* (2 Thess. 3:1, KJV; NASB and NIV, "spread rapidly"), *race*, a *career* (2 Tim. 4:7), *path, direction* (Jer. 23:10), *running*, as of a horse (Jer. 8:6).

COURSE OF PRIESTS AND LEVITES. *See* Division of the Priests and Levites.

COURT (Heb. usually *ḥāṣēr*). An open enclosure; applied in Scripture mostly to the enclosures of the *Tabernacle* and *Temple* (both which see). It also means a yard of a prison (Neh. 3:25; Jer. 32:2), a private house (2 Sam. 17:18), or a palace (2 Kings 20:4; Esther 1:5; etc.).

"Court for owls" (Isa. 34:13, KJV) is rendered by Delitzsch (*Com.*, ad loc.) "pasture for ostriches" (cf. NASB). He says that the Heb. word corresponds to the Arab. for green, a green field, and takes it in the sense of a grassy place such as is frequented by ostriches. In Amos 7:13 the Heb. word for "house" is rendered "court" in the KJV, "residence," in the NASB (marg., lit. "house"), and "sanctuary" in the NIV. *See* House.

In the NT the Gk. *aulē* designates an open court (Rev. 11:2), whereas "kings' courts" is the rendering of the Gk. word *basileion*, a "palace."

COURTS, JUDICIAL. *See* Law, Administration of.

COUSIN. The rendering of the Gk. *sungenēs*, a blood relative or "kinsman," as translated elsewhere.

COVENANT (Heb. *berît*, "cutting"). The term applied to various transactions between God and man, and man and his fellowman. In Obadiah (v. 7) it is rendered "allied." In the NT the word *diathēkē*, "disposition" or "will" respecting a person or thing, is used; sometimes it is translated *"Testament"* (which see), at other times "covenant."

Application of the Term. Properly used of a compact between man and man; either between tribes or nations (1 Sam. 11:1; Josh. 9:6, 15), or between individuals (Gen. 21:27), in which each party bound himself to fulfill certain conditions and was promised certain advantages. In making covenants God was solemnly invoked as a witness (31:53), whence the expression "a covenant of the Lord" (1 Sam. 20:8; cf. Jer. 34:18-19; Ezek. 17:19), and an oath was sworn (Gen. 21:31). Ac-

cordingly, a breach of covenant was regarded as a heinous sin (Ezek. 17:12-20). The marriage contract is called "the covenant of . . . God" (Prov. 2:17). As a witness to the covenant a gift was presented (Gen. 21:30) or a heap of stones set up (31:52).

It is also improperly used of a covenant between God and man. As man is not in the position of an independent covenanting party, such a covenant is not strictly a mutual compact but a promise on the part of God to arrange His providences for the welfare of those who should render Him obedience.

Covenants Mentioned. The following covenants are mentioned in Scripture:

The Covenant with Noah. In this covenant God assured Noah that judgment would not again come to men in the form of a flood; and that the recurrence of the seasons and of day and night should not cease (Gen. 9; Jer. 33:20).

The Covenant with Abraham. The condition of this covenant was that Abraham was to leave his country, kindred, and father's house, and follow the Lord into the land that He would show him. The promise was a fourfold blessing: (1) increase into a numerous people; (2) material and spiritual prosperity—"I will bless you"; (3) the exaltation of Abraham's name—"make your name great"; (4) Abraham was not only to be blessed by God, but to be a blessing to others, implicitly by the coming of the Messiah through his descendants (Gen. 12:1-3). Later this covenant was renewed, and Abraham was promised a son and numerous posterity (chap. 15). About fourteen years after the making of the covenant it was renewed, with a change of his name and the establishment of circumcision, which was to be the sign of accepting and ratifying the covenant (chap. 17).

The Covenant with Israel. This took place at Sinai, when the people had intimated their acceptance of the words of the covenant as found in the Ten Commandments (Ex. 34:28; 24:3) and promised to keep the same. Their obedience to the commands of the law was to be rewarded by God's constant care of Israel, temporal prosperity, victory over enemies, and the pouring out of His Spirit (Ex. 23:20-33). The seal of this covenant was to be circumcision and was called "His covenant" (Deut. 4:13). It was renewed at different periods of Jewish history (chap. 29; Josh. 24; 2 Chron. 15, 23, 29, 34; Ezra 10; Neh. 9-10).

The Covenant with David. This was in reality but another and more specific form of the covenant with Abraham; its main object was to mark with greater exactness the line through which the blessing promised in the Abrahamic covenant was to find accomplishment. The royal seed was from then on to be in the house of David (2 Sam. 7:12; 22:51), and, especially in connection with the One who was to be preeminently the child of promise in that house, all good, first to Israel and then to all nations, should be realized (Pss. 2; 22; Isa. 9:6-7; etc.).

In adaptation to human thought such covenants were said to be confirmed by an oath (Deut. 4:31; Ps. 89:3).

Ceremonies. Covenants were not only concluded with an oath (Gen. 26:28; 31:53; Josh. 9:15; 2 Kings 11:4), but, after an ancient custom, confirmed by slaughtering and cutting a victim into two halves between which the parties passed, to intimate that if either of them broke the covenant it would fare with him as with the slain and divided beast (Gen. 15:9-10, 17-18; Jer. 34:18-20). Moreover, the covenanting parties often partook of a common meal (Gen. 26:30; 31:54; cf. 2 Sam. 3:20 with v. 12), or at least of some grains of salt. *See* Covenant of Salt.

According to the Mosaic ritual, the blood of the victim was divided into halves; one-half was sprinkled upon the altar and the other upon the people (Ex. 24:6-8). The meaning of this seems to be that, in the sprinkling of the blood upon the altar, the people were introduced into gracious fellowship with God and atonement made for their sin. Through the sprinkling of the blood upon the people Israel was formally consecrated to the position of God's covenant people.

BIBLIOGRAPHY: G. E. Mendenhall, *Biblical Archaeologist* 17 (March 1954): 50-76; id., *Law and Covenant in Israel and the Ancient Near East* (1955); J. D. Pentecost, *Things to Come* (1958), pp. 65-128; M. G. Kline, *Treaty of the Great King* (1963); D. J. McCarthy, *Treaty and Covenant*, Analecta Biblica 21 (1963); id., *Catholic Biblical Quarterly* 27 (1965): 217-40; C. C. Ryrie, *Dispensationalism Today* (1965); G. M. Tucker, *Vetus Testamentum* 15 (1965): 487-503; K. A. Kitchen, *Ancient Orient and Old Testament* (1967), pp. 90-102; D. R. Hillers, *Covenant: The History of a Biblical Idea* (1969).

COVENANT OF SALT (Heb. *beˆrît melaḥ*). Covenanting parties were accustomed to partake of salt, thus making a *covenant of salt* (Num. 18:19; 2 Chron. 13:5), i.e., one that was inviolably sure. The meaning appears to have been that the salt, with its power to strengthen food and keep it from decay, symbolized the unbending truthfulness of that self-surrender to the Lord embodied in the sacrifice, by which all impurity and hypocrisy were repelled.

BIBLIOGRAPHY: H. C. Trumbull, *The Covenant of Salt* (1899); J. E. Latham, *The Religious Symbolism of Salt* (1982).

COVENANT, THE NEW. In the NT we read of only two covenants—the *New* and the *Old,* the former brought in and established by Christ, and the latter in consequence ceasing to exist. The *Old,* i.e., the covenant of law, with all its outward institutions and ritualistic services, is regarded as the *Old* because its full and formal ratification took place before the other. In *germ* the *New* Covenant (or that of *grace*) existed from the first; and partial exhibitions of it have been given all

through the world's history. It was involved in the promise of recovery at the Fall.

BIBLIOGRAPHY: J. D. Pentecost, *Things to Come* (1958), pp. 116-28.

COVERED WAY FOR THE SABBATH. *See* Sabbath, Covered Way for.

COVERING THE HEAD IN PRAYER (1 Cor. 11:4-6). "The Jewish men prayed with the head covered, nay, even with a veil before the face. Greek usage required that the head should be bare on sacred occasions; and this commended itself to Paul as so entirely in accordance with the divinely appointed position of man (v. 3) that for the man to cover his head seemed to him to cast dishonor on that position. His head ought to show to all (and its being uncovered is the sign of this) that no man, but, on the contrary, Christ, and through Him God Himself, is Head (Lord) of the man. . . . A woman, when praying, was to honor her head by having a sign upon it of the authority of her husband, which was done by having it covered; otherwise she dishonored her head by dressing, not like a married wife, from whose headdress one can see that her husband is her head, but like a loose woman, with whose *shorn* head the uncovered one is on a par" (Meyer, *Com.,* ad loc.). The above command does not refer to private or family prayer.

COVETOUSNESS (Heb. *ḥāmad,* to "desire"; *beṣa',* "dishonest gain"; Gk. *pleoneksia,* "the wish to have more"). An inordinate desire for what one has not; in NASB this word is translated "greed"; its basis lies in discontentment with what one has. It has an element of lawlessness and is sinful because it is contrary to the command "Being content with what you have" (Heb. 13:5), because it leads to trust in "the uncertainty of riches," to love of the world, to forgetfulness of God, and is idolatry (Col. 3:5), setting up wealth instead of God. It ranks with the worst sins (Mark 7:22; Rom. 1:29). Our Lord especially warns against it (Luke 12:15), as does Paul (Eph. 5:3; etc.). A man may be *covetous,* eager to obtain money, and not *avaricious* or *penurious,* i.e., unwilling to part with money, or *sordid* and *niggardly,* i.e., mean in his dealings. He may or may not be miserly.

The verb is also used in a good sense (1 Cor. 12:31, KJV, NIV; NASB, "but earnestly *desire* the greater gifts").

COW, COWS. *See* Animal Kingdom: Ox.

Figurative. Cows are used figuratively of proud and wealthy rulers (Amos 4:1); and of years of plenty ("fat," Gen. 41:2; 26:29) and years of scarcity ("lean").

COZ. *See* Koz.

COZ'BI (kos'bi; "false"). The daughter of Zur, a Midianite leader. While in the act of committing lewdness with Zimri, an Israelite leader, she was slain by Phinehas, who thrust a spear through them both (Num. 25:6-8, 15, 18), about 1401 B.C.

COZE'BA (ko-zē'ba; "deceitful"). A city in the lowlands of Judah, "the men" of which are named among the descendants of Shelah (1 Chron. 4:22). The same as Chezib (Kezib) and Achzib (Akzib; Gen. 38:5; Josh. 15:44).

CRACKLING (Heb. *qôl*, "voice," i.e., noise). "The crackling of thorn bushes under a pot" (Eccles. 7:6) is a proverbial expression for a roaring but quickly extinguished fire.

CRACKNEL. *See* Bread.

CRAFT, CRAFTSMAN. *See* Handicrafts.

CRAFTINESS, CRAFTY (Heb. *'āram*, to "be bare," "cunning," "subtlety"; Gk. *panourgia*, "adroitness," "unscrupulousness"). The terms used in the Bible as applied to the sly, subtle, wily, deceitful, and fraudulent. The NASB also renders "shrewd," "crafty," etc. (Job 5:12-13; Ps. 83:3; Luke 20:23; 1 Cor. 3:19; 2 Cor. 4:2; 12:16; etc.).

CRANE. *See* Animal Kingdom.

CREATION. The work of God in bringing into existence the universe, including both the material and the spiritual worlds; in a more restricted sense, the bringing into existence and into its present condition the earth and the system to which it belongs.

Christian View. According to Christian doctrine, God alone is eternal. The system or systems of the material universe, as well as matter itself, also spiritual beings, except God, had a beginning. They were absolutely created, made "out of nothing," by the power of the almighty will. The first sentence of the Apostles' Creed is to be taken in its broadest and deepest sense, "I believe in God the Father Almighty, Maker of heaven and earth."

The record of the creation in Genesis relates principally in its details to the creation of the earth, or the system to which the earth belongs, and to the creation of man. The first words of the record, however, suggest a still broader conception. Taking the account as a whole, we have revealed a succession of creative acts, constituting together one great process of creation. And whatever interpretations have been given as to the various stages of this process, or the "days" of creation, or of other particulars, the fact of chief import remains unclouded—that to God is ascribed the work of bringing into existence, by the free exercise of His creative power, the world and all orders of beings that live within it. This is the uniform teaching of the OT Scriptures (Ps. 33:6; Isa. 45:18; Jer. 10:12; etc.). The doctrine of the NT upon this subject is not merely a repetition but in some respects a development, or further unfolding, of that contained in the OT. Thus,

with greater explicitness the existence of superhuman intelligence is attributed in the NT Scriptures to divine creative power. As the heavenly and spiritual world comes more clearly into view in the NT, along with this comes the declaration that all spiritual beings outside of God owe their origin to Him. Also, that creative "Word of the Lord," upon which such stress is laid in the OT, is identified in the NT with Christ. The second Person of the Trinity is revealed as the One most directly connected with the work of creation. In Him creation has its explanation and its end (see John 1:3; 1 Cor. 8:6; Eph. 3:9-11; Col. 1:16; Heb. 1:2; 2:10).

Babylonian View. This polytheistic version of creation is contained in the seven-tablet *Enuma elish*, recovered mainly from the library of Ashurbanipal (668-626 B.C.) at Nineveh. It hopelessly confuses divine spirit and cosmic matter by an irrational mythological identification of the two. Apsu and Tiamat, the parents of the gods, are personifications of cosmic matter (the primordial sweet and salt water oceans respectively). Their offspring personify cosmic spaces and natural forces. Spirit and cosmic matter are made coexistent and coeternal in an account spiritually, morally, and philosophically confusing and incomparably inferior to the Genesis account of beginnings.

Importance of Doctrine. True doctrine upon this subject is both theoretically and practically of fundamental importance. (1) In relation to God, whose eternal greatness and majesty can be felt by us only when we conceive of Him as "before all worlds" and the Creator of all. (2) Here, first of all, true religion establishes its claim upon us; for He who has created us and all things may rightfully require our worship and service. (3) In the creation we find also a true revelation, and he who recognizes this must admit the possibility and even the probability of more particular revelations. The objection to miracles in connection with revelation vanishes when one begins by accepting the miracle of creation. (4) This doctrine underlies all true repose of faith; for only when we apprehend the broad and wholesome teaching of the Scriptures upon this subject can we fully commit ourselves unto God as unto "a faithful Creator."

Concordant Views and Modern Science. Acute present-day problems hinge on the interpretation of the creative six days of Gen. 1 in the light of modern scientific findings, especially in the field of geology (cf. Bernard Ramm, *The Christian View of Science and Scripture* [1955], pp. 173-299). (1) *The Twenty-Four-Hour-Day View* holds that creation was effected in six days. (2) *The Purely Religious View* divorces the theological account in Genesis from scientific relevance or reconciliation. In making apparent peace with geology this view tends to make theology irrelevant and thus unnecessary and inconsequential.

(3) *The New Diluvial View* of George McCready Price (*The New Geology* [1923]), attempts to explain geological phenomena by the Noahic Flood (cf. also Byron Nelson, *The Deluge Story in Stone* [1931]; A. M. Rehwinkel, *The Flood* [1951]); and H. W. Clark, *The New Diluvialism* [1946]). This so-called New Catastrophism clashes with present-day uniformitarian geology (but cf. 2 Pet. 3:1-10) and is a modern modification of the older views of successive catastrophes of Cuvier and Agassiz. (4) *The Local Creation View* of John Pye Smith limits Gen. 1 to the re-creation of the general Middle Eastern World (*On the Relation Between the Holy Scriptures and Certain Parts of Geological Science* [1840]). Smith, however, in trying to reconcile Scripture with geology in this way cheapens the Genesis account. (5) *The Gap Theory* postulates creation in Gen. 1:1, followed by catastrophe (1:2), succeeded by re-creation (1:3-31). This view, popularized by G. H. Pember (*Earth's Earliest Ages* [1876]), Harry Rimmer (*Modern Science and the Genesis Record* [1937]), and the *Scofield Reference Bible*, goes back at least to Thomas Chalmers (*Works*, 1:228; 12:369), J. H. Kurtz (*Bible and Astronomy*, 3d ed. [1857]), and J. G. Rosenmuller (*Antiquissima Telluris Historia a Mose* [1736-1815]). It provides *time* but fails to account for geological *sequence*, besides being exegetically weak. (6) *The Age-Day View* considers the Genesis days to be geologic eras and has been defended by the geologist J. W. Dawson and more recently by E. K. Gedney (*Modern Science and the Christian Faith*, 2d ed. [1950]). Gedney affirms that the theory of progressive creationism with the age-long interpretation of the term *day* can account for the facts of geology. (7) *Pictorial Day* and *Moderate Concordism* coupled with progressive creationism. This is Bernard Ramm's view (op. cit., pp. 218-29). (8) *Re-creation-Revelation View* holds that Gen. 1:1-2 does not describe primeval creation *ex nihilo* celebrated by the angels (Job 38:7; Isa. 45:18) but a much later refashioning of a judgment-ridden earth in preparation for a new order of creation —man. The six days that follow are *re-creation*, revealed to man in six literal days (cf. Merrill F. Unger, "Rethinking the Genesis Account of Creation," *Bibliotheca Sacra* 115 [Jan. 1958]: 27-35).

P. J. Wiseman (*Creation Revealed in Six Days* [1948]) espouses the view of revelation of creation (not re-creation) in six twenty-four-hour days.

BIBLIOGRAPHY: B. L. Ramm, *Christian View of Science and Scripture* (1954); P. A. Zimmerman, ed., *Darwin, Evolution, and Creation* (1959); R. E. D. Clark, *The Universe: Plan or Accident* (1961); H. M. Morris, *The Twilight of Evolution* (1964); J. C. Whitcomb, Jr., *The Origin of the Solar System* (1964); B. C. Nelson, *After Its Kind* (1965); E. Shute, *Flaws in the Theory of Evolution* (1966); R. E. D. Clark, *The Christian Stake in Science* (1967); W. Frair and P. W. Davis, *Case for Creation* (1967); A. E. Wilder Smith, *Man's Origin, Man's Destiny* (1968); B. Davidheiser, *Evolution and Christian Faith* (1969); E. O. James, *Creation and Cosmology* (1969); A. E. Wilder Smith, *Creation of Life* (1970); P. A. Zimmerman, ed., *Rock Strata and the Bible Record* (1970); W. E. Lammerts, ed., *Scientific Studies in Special Creation* (1971); H. M. Morris, *Scientific Creationism* (1974); id., *The Troubled Waters* (1974); A. M. Rehwinkel, *The Wonder of Creation* (1974); A. C. Custance, *The Doorway Papers* (1975); H. M. Morris, *The Scientific Case for Creation* (1977); D. A. Young, *Creation and the Flood* (1977).

CREATURE (Heb. *nepesh*, a "breathing" creature; Gk. *ktisis*, a "making," "thing made"; *ktisma*, "formation").

1. In the OT "creature" is a general term for any animal (Gen. 1:21, 24, etc.).

2. In the NT, the NASB renders "creation"; it is used as: (1) A term for the whole creation or for any created object, e.g., "Everything created by God is good; NIV, "Everything God created is good");" (1 Tim. 4:4, NASB; KJV, "Every creature of God is good"; NIV, "Everything God created is good"); "Nor height, nor depth, nor any other created thing" (Rom. 8:39; etc.). (2) Humanity individually or collectively. "Preach the gospel to all creation" (Mark 16:15); "The creation was subjected," etc. (Rom. 8:20).

CREATURES, LIVING. A term appearing frequently in the KJV (cf. Ezek. 1:5, 13-15, 17, 19-20; where the NASB renders "living creature" or "living creatures") and the NASB and NIV (cf. Rev. 4:8, 14-15, 19; where the KJV renders "beasts"). See Cherub, Cherubim.

CREDITOR. See Debt; Loan.

CREEPING LOCUST. See Animal Kingdom: Locust.

CREEPING THINGS (Heb. *sheres*, an active mass of minute animals; or, Heb. *remeś*, "creeping"), a term used in Scripture (Gen. 1:24; 6:7; etc.) to designate reptiles, insects, aquatic creatures, and the smaller mammals.

CRES'CENS (kres'enz; "growing"). An assistant of the apostle Paul, who left Rome for Galatia (2 Tim. 4:10). Nothing further of him is known for certain (Ellicott, *Com.*, ad loc.).

CRESCENT ORNAMENTS. See Dress.

CRE'TANS (krē'táns). See Crete.

CRETE. A large island in the Mediterranean, about 150 miles in length and from 6 to 35 miles wide. It lies 60 miles S of Cape Malea in the Peloponnesus. Anciently it was the home of the great Minoan civilization. It is mountainous, and its famous peak is Mt. Ida. The vessel carrying Paul on his way to Rome sailed along the southern coast of the island, where it was overtaken by a storm (Acts 27:7-21). Cretans were among those specially mentioned as attending the great feast of Pentecost (2:11). The Cretans had a name in ancient times for being good sailors, skilled archers, and experts in ambush.

Coastal view of the island of Crete

The ancient notices of their character fully agree with the quotation that Paul produces from "a prophet of their own" (Titus 1:12): "Cretans are always liars, evil beasts, lazy gluttons." The classics abound with allusions to the untruthfulness of the Cretans; and it was so frequently applied to them that *krētizein,* "to act the Cretan," was a synonym for to *play the liar.* Paul sent Titus to organize the church there.

Though archaeological work on Crete is extensive, it concerns the Minoan civilization and is not germane to biblical studies. *Caphtor* (which see), home of the Philistines, is usually identified with Crete.

CRIB. A KJV term replaced by *manger* (which see).

CRICKET. *See* Animal Kingdom.

CRIMSON. *See* Colors.

CRIPPLE, CRIPPLED. *See* Diseases: Lame, Lameness; Maimed.

CRISPING PIN. *See* Purse.

CRIS'PUS (kris'pus; "curled"). Chief of the Jewish synagogue at Corinth (Acts 18:8), converted and baptized by the apostle Paul (1 Cor. 1:14). According to tradition, he afterward became bishop of Aegina.

CROCODILE. *See* Animal Kingdom.

CROCUS. *See* Vegetable Kingdom.

CROOKBACKED (Heb. *gibbēn,* to be "arched," or "contracted"). A humpback (Lev. 21:20, 21) was one of the blemishes that unfitted a priest for the sacred service of the sanctuary. *See also* Diseases: Hunchback.

CROP. That part of the bird that held the food and that, with its feathers, was cast among the ashes at the side of the altar and not burned with the rest of the fowl (Lev. 1:16). *See* Sacrifice.

CROSS (Gk. *stauros,* a "stake"; Lat. *crux*). The cross that was used as an instrument of death (*see* Crucifixion) was either a plain vertical stake to which the victim was fastened, with the hands tied or nailed above the head, or such a stake provided with a crossbar, to which the victim was fastened with the arms outstretched. Of this latter kind three varieties were known, so that there were four forms of the cross: (1) simple (Lat. *simplex*), | ; (2) St. Andrew's (*decussata*), × (3) St. Anthony's (*commissa*), ⊤ ; (4) the Latin (*immissa*), + .

Other forms have been invented and used as emblems, e.g., the Greek cross, consisting of four equally long arms, + ; double cross, ‡ whose upper bar refers to the inscription by Pilate on the cross of Jesus; and the triple, ‡ , ‡ , of which the first is used by the pope, the second by the Raskolniks.

In addition to the transverse bar there was sometimes a peg or other projection, upon which the body of the sufferer rested, to prevent his weight from tearing away the hands.

Emblem. That the cross was widely known as an emblem in pre-Christian times has been clearly shown by independent investigators. Indeed, it was a well-known heathen sign. The vestments of the priests of Horus, the Egyptian god of light, are marked + . At Thebes, in the tombs of the kings, royal cows are represented plowing, a calf playing in front. Each animal has a + marked in several places on it. Rassam found buildings at Nineveh marked with the Maltese cross. Osiris, as well as Jupiter Ammon, had for a monogram a + . The cross is found marked on Phoenician monuments at an early date.

In Christian times the cross, from being in itself the most vile and repulsive of objects, became in the minds of believers the symbol of all that is holy and precious. As Christ is "the power of God and the wisdom of God" unto salvation, it is but natural that those who experience the power of this salvation should glory in the cross. The exact time of its adoption as a Christian emblem is unknown. In the pre-Constantine period the sign of the cross seems to have been quite generally recognized by primitive Christians. They appear to have contemplated it only as a symbol, without any miraculous energy, and associated it with that which was hopeful and joyous. On the tombstones of the early Christians the cross was the emblem of victory and hope. It was only after superstition took the place of true spiritual devotion that the figure of the cross was used or borne about as a sacred charm.

In the latter part of the third century people signed the cross in token of safety and laid stress on figures of it as a preservative against both spiritual and natural evil. This superstitious feeling was stimulated by the discovery of what was held to be the real cross upon which our Lord suffered. The empress Helena, mother of Constantine, about A.D. 326 visited Palestine and was shown three crosses by a Jew. In order to know which was the genuine one, Macarius, bishop of Jerusalem, suggested that they be tested by their power of working miracles. Only one being reported as possessing this quality, it was declared to be the real cross.

As Signature. As early as the sixth century it had become the custom to place three crosses (+ + +) near the signature of important documents, these having the value of an oath on the part of the signer. Priests added it to their signatures, and bishops, as a sign of the dignity of their office, placed it before their signatures. Crosses were used in diplomatic documents as early as the fifth century. By tradition the cross is now used as a signature by those unable to write.

Figurative. The *cross* is used in Scripture, in a general way, for what is painful and mortifying to the flesh (Matt. 16:24). After the resurrection of our Lord the cross is spoken of as the representative of His whole sufferings from His birth to His death (Eph. 2:16; Heb. 12:2) and for the whole doctrines of the gospel (1 Cor. 1:18; Gal. 6:14); whereas the opposers of the gospel were spoken of as enemies of the cross (Phil. 3:18). "The cross of Christ" (1 Cor. 1:17) represents that Christ was crucified for man and thereby procured His salvation.

BIBLIOGRAPHY: L. L. Morris, *Apostolic Preaching of the Cross* (1955); Y. Yadin, *Israel Exploration Journal* 21 (1971): 1-12; id., *IEJ* 23 (1973): 18-22; M. Wilcox, *Journal of Biblical Literature* 96 (1977): 85-99.

CROWN. This ornament, which is both ancient and universal, probably originated from the headbands used to prevent the hair from being disheveled by the wind. Such headbands are still common, and they may be seen on the sculpture of Persepolis, Nineveh, and Egypt; they gradually developed into turbans, which by the addition of ornamental or precious materials assumed the dignity of miters or crowns. The use of them as ornaments probably was suggested by the natural custom of encircling the head with flowers in token of joy and triumph (Wisd. of Sol. 2:8; Judith 15:13).

Several words in Scripture are rendered "crown":

Nēzer (lit, something "set apart," "consecration"; hence *consecrated* hair, as of a Nazirite) is supposed to mean a "diadem." It was applied to the plate of gold in front of the high priest's miter (Ex. 29:6; 39:30); also to the diadem that Saul wore in battle and which was brought to David (2 Sam. 1:10), and that which was used at the coronation of Joash (2 Kings 11:12). The crown was in universal use by priests and in religious services. Egyptian crowns such as that worn by Tutankhamen were elaborate and richly adorned with royal emblems. The crown worn by the kings of Assyria was a high turban frequently adorned with flowers, etc., and arranged in bands of linen or silk. Originally there was only one band, but later there were two, and the ornaments were richer.

Shalmaneser of Assyria wearing crown

'Aṭārâ, "circlet"; (Gk. *stephanos*). A more general word for crown and used for crowns and head ornaments of various sorts. When applied to the crowns of kings it appears to denote the state crown as distinguished from the diadem, as, probably, the crown taken by David from the king of Ammon at Rabbah and used as the state crown of Judah (2 Sam. 12:30). As to the shape of this Hebrew crown we can form an idea only by reference to ancient crowns. The diadem of two or three headbands may have signified dominion over two or three countries. In Rev. 12:3; 13:1; 19:12, allusion is made to *many* "crowns" (KJV; NASB, "diadems") worn in token of extended dominion.

Kether, "diadem," refers to the ancient Persian crown (Esther 1:11; 2:17; 6:8), which was, doubtless, the high cap or tiara so often mentioned by Greek historians.

Other Heb. terms rendered "crown" are *zēr,* a wreath or border of gold around the edge of the Ark of the Covenant (Ex. 25:11, KJV, etc.; NIV, "molding"); and *qodqōd,* the crown of the human head (Gen. 49:26; etc.). The Gk. word *stemma* is used only once in the NT (Acts 14:13) for the "garlands" (NIV, "wreaths") used with victims.

Figurative. The crown was a symbol of victory

and reward, victors being crowned in the Grecian games. These crowns were usually made of leaves that soon began to wither. In opposition to these is the incorruptible crown (1 Cor. 9:25, NASB, "wreath," cf. 2 Tim. 2:5), a crown of life or of glory (James 1:12; 1 Pet. 5:4; Rev. 2:10). The meaning of the crown of thorns placed on the head of Jesus (Matt. 27:29) was to insult Him under the character of the king of the Jews. The crown is also used as an emblem of an exalted state (Prov. 12:4; 17:6; Isa. 28:5; Phil. 4:1; etc.).

CROWN OF THORNS. The Roman soldiers made a crown out of some thorny plant and crowned our Lord in mockery (Matt. 27:29). "The object was not to cause suffering, but to excite ridicule; so that while we cannot altogether dissociate the idea of something painful from this crown of thorns we must not conceive of it as covered with prickles, which were intentionally thrust into the flesh. It is impossible to determine what *species* of thorn it was" (Meyer, *Com.,* ad loc.). *See also* Vegetable Kingdom: Thistle, Thorns.

CRUCIFIXION. This form of punishment was in use among the Egyptians (Gen. 40:19), the Carthaginians, the Persians (Esther 7:10), the Assyrians, Scythians, Indians, Germans, and from earliest times among the Greeks and Romans. After the conquest of Tyre, Alexander the Great ordered two thousand Tyrians to be crucified as punishment for the resistance which that city made. Crucifixion was abolished by Constantine, probably toward the end of his reign, owing, doubtless, to his increasing reverence for the cross. Punishment by the cross was confined to slaves or to malefactors of the worst class. Exemption from it was the privilege of Roman citizenship.

Among the Jews. Whether this mode of execution was known to the ancient Jews is a matter of dispute. The Heb. words apparently alluding to crucifixion are *tālâ* and *yāqaʿ,* generally rendered in the KJV "to hang" (Num. 25:4, NASB, "execute," NIV, "kill"; Deut. 21:22; 2 Sam. 18:10). The Jewish account of the matter is that the exposure of the body tied to a stake by the hands took place after death. The placing of the head on an upright pole has been called crucifixion. Crucifixion *after* death was not rare, the victim being first killed in mercy. The Jews probably borrowed this punishment from the Romans.

Among the Jews, as well as among the Romans, crucifixion was considered the most horrible form of death; to a Jew it would seem the more horrible from the curse "He who is hanged is accursed of God" (Deut. 21:23). Our Lord was condemned to it by the popular cry of the Jews (Matt. 27:23) on the charge of sedition against Caesar (Luke 23:21-23).

Process. Crucifixion was preceded by scourging with thongs, to which were sometimes added nails, pieces of bone, etc., to heighten the pain, often so intense as to cause death. In our Lord's case, however, this infliction seems neither to have been the legal scourging after sentence nor examination by torture (Acts 22:24) but rather a scourging *before* the sentence to excite pity and procure immunity from further punishment (Luke 23:22; John 19:1). The criminal carried his own cross, or a part of it, in which case another person was compelled to share the burden (Luke 23:26). The place of execution was outside the city (1 Kings 21:13; Acts 7:58; Heb. 13:12); arriving there, the condemned was stripped of his clothes, which became the property of the soldiers (Matt. 27:35); and the cross having been previously erected, he was drawn up and made fast to it with cords or nails, although sometimes he was first fastened to the cross and then raised. The limbs of the victim were generally three or four feet from the earth. Before the nailing or binding took place a medicated cup was given out of kindness to confuse the senses and deaden the pangs of the sufferer (Prov. 31:6), usually of "wine mixed with myrrh," because myrrh was soporific. The Lord refused it that His senses might be clear (Matt. 27:34; Mark 15:23).

If the nailing was the most painful mode in the first instance, the other was more so in the end, for the sufferer was left to die of sheer exhaustion, and when simply bound with thongs, it might take days to accomplish the process. Instances are on record of persons surviving for nine days. Owing to the lingering character of this death our Lord was watched, according to custom, by a party of four soldiers (John 19:23), with their centurion (Matt. 27:54), to prevent His being taken down and resuscitated. Fracture of the legs was resorted to by the Jews to hasten death (John 19:31). This was done to the two thieves crucified with Jesus but not to Him, for the soldiers found that He was dead already (19:32-34). The unusual rapidity of the Lord's death was due to the depth of His previous agonies or may be sufficiently accounted for simply from peculiarities of constitution. Pilate expressly satisfied himself as to the actual death by questioning the centurion (Mark 15:44). In most cases the body was allowed to rot on the cross by the action of the sun and rain or to be devoured by birds and beasts. Interment was generally, therefore, forbidden, but in consequence of Deut. 21:22-23 an exception was made in favor of the Jews (Matt. 27:58).

BIBLIOGRAPHY: J. Finegan, *Light from the Ancient Past* (1946), pp. 252, 292, 431; M. Hengel, *Crucifixion in the Ancient World* (1977).

CRUSE. The rendering in the KJV of three Heb. words:

1. *Ṣappaḥat,* lit., "spread out," usually thought to be a *flask,* but more likely a shallow *cup* for holding water (1 Sam. 26:11, 12, 16; 1 Kings 19:6) or oil (1 Kings 17:12, 14, 16), al-

though the NASB and NIV consistently render the term as "jar" or "jug." "In a similar case in the present day this would be a globular vessel of blue porous clay, about nine inches diameter, with a neck of about three inches long, a small handle below the neck, and opposite the handle a straight spout, with an orifice about the size of a straw, through which the water is drunk or sucked" (Smith, *Bib. Dict.,* s.v.).

2. *Baqbuq,* so called from the *gurgling* sound in emptying (1 Kings 14:3; NASB, NIV, "jar"), an "earthenware jar" (Jer. 19:1, 10, NASB).

3. *Ṣelōḥit,* perhaps from the root *ṣlḥ,* occurs in the Bible only in 2 Kings 2:20. It probably described a shallow dish or a flat cooking pan. The NIV renders it "bowl."

CRYSTAL *See* Mineral Kingdom.

CUBIT. A linear measure. *See* Metrology.

CUCKOO. *See* Animal Kingdom: Sea Gull.

CUCUMBER. *See* Vegetable Kingdom.

CUMI. *See* Kum.

CUMIN. *See* Vegetable Kingdom: Cummin.

CUN (kūn; 1 Chron. 18:8). A city of Hadadezer, king of Syria, in Zobah, on the way to the Euphrates, and plundered by David for bronze with which to build the Temple. It was called Berothai (2 Sam. 8:8); probably the same as *Berothah* (Ezek. 47:16; which see).

CUNEIFORM. *See* Assyria.

CUP. The rendering, mostly in the OT, of the Heb. *kōs;* in the NT, of the Gk. *protērion.* Note that other Heb. terms are so translated as well.

Egyptian. These were varied in form, the paintings upon the tombs representing many of

Passover cup

elegant design, while others are deficient in both form and proportion. Many were of gold and silver (Gen. 44:2; cf. Num. 7:84), some being richly studded with precious stones, inlaid with vitrified substances in brilliant colors, and even enameled. They were also made of hard stones, pottery, glass, and porcelain.

Assyrian. Cups and vases among the Assyrians were even more varied in form and design than those of the Egyptians. The materials employed were about the same—precious metals, copper, bronze, glass, and pottery, both glazed and unglazed. Some of their drinking cups terminate in the head of a lion, with a handle. Other festal cups are more like bowls in form and are fluted.

Hebrew. The cups of the Jews, whether of metal or earthenware, were probably borrowed from Egypt or from the Phoenicians, who were celebrated in that branch of workmanship. In Solomon's time all his drinking vessels were of gold (1 Kings 10:21). The cups mentioned in the NT were often, no doubt, made after Greek and Roman models. In Isa. 22:24 the Heb. word translated "cups" (*'aggān*) in the KJV is given as "bowls" in the NASB and NIV; elsewhere it is rendered as "basins" (Ex. 24:6) and "goblet" (Song of Sol. 7:2). The cups in 1 Chron. 28:17 were bowls for libation ("pitchers," NASB and NIV; Heb. *qaśwâ*); the same Heb. term is incorrectly rendered "covers" in the KJV of Ex. 25:29; 37:16; Num. 4:7. The NASB more correctly translates "jars," whereas the NIV translates "pitchers" except in Num. 4:7, where it has "jars."

Cup of Divination. The use of such cups was a practice common to Syria and Egypt as early as the time of the patriarch Jacob. Otherwise the question, "Is not this the one from which my lord drinks, and which he indeed uses for divination?" (Gen. 44:5) would have lost half its force with the brothers of Joseph. Among the Egyptians this sort of divination consisted of pouring clean water into a goblet and then looking into the water for representations of future events, or in pouring water into a goblet or dish, dropping in pieces of gold or silver or precious stones, and observing and interpreting the appearance of the water. Melted wax was also poured into the water and the will of the gods interpreted by the variously shaped figures formed in this way. But we cannot infer from this that Joseph adopted this superstitious practice. The intention of the statement was simply to represent the goblet as a sacred vessel and Joseph as acquainted with the most sacred things.

Figurative. "Cup" is employed in both Testaments in some curious metaphorical phrases: "The portion of their cup" is a general expression for the condition of life, prosperous or miserable (Pss. 11:6; 16:5; 23:5).

A "cup" is also the natural type of sensual allurement (Prov. 23:31; Jer. 51:7; Rev. 17:4;

18:6). Babylon is termed a "golden cup" to express its splendor and opulence.

"Cup of consolation" (Jer. 16:7). It was the oriental custom for friends to send dishes of food and wine (the cup of consolation) to console relatives in mourning (cf. 2 Sam. 3:35; Prov. 31:6).

"Cup of salvation" (Ps. 116:13) is probably the drink offering lifted in thanksgiving to God (Num. 15:5; 28:7).

"Cup of blessing" (1 Cor. 10:16; called the "cup of the Lord," v. 21), i.e., the cup over which the blessing is spoken, when the wine contained in it is expressly consecrated by prayer to the sacred use of the Lord's Supper. It is called in Jewish writings, just as by Paul, "the cup of blessing," and is supposed to refer to the third cup of wine drunk at the Passover feast, over which a special blessing was spoken. In 10:21 it is contrasted with the "cup of demons," i.e., the cup drunk at heathen feasts.

The "cup of His anger" (Isa. 51:17; Rev. 14:10), "cup of reeling" (51:22; Zech. 12:2), and "cup of horror and desolation" (Ezek. 23:33) are figures representing the effects of Jehovah's wrath upon the wicked. God is represented as the master of a banquet, dealing madness and stupor of vengeance to guilty guests. There is in the prophets no more frequent or terrifying image, and it is repeated with pathetic force in the language of our Lord's agony (Matt. 26:39, 42; John 18:11).

CUPBEARER (Heb. *mashqeh,* "one who gives drink to"). That officer of the household who tasted the wine and passed it to those at the table. He was often chosen for his personal beauty and attractions and in ancient oriental courts was always a person of rank and importance. From the confidential nature of his duties and his frequent access to the royal presence, he possessed great influence. The chief cupbearer, or butler, to the king of Egypt was the means of raising Joseph to his high position (Gen. 41:9). Rabshakeh appears from his name to have filled a like office in the Assyrian court (2 Kings 18:17). Nehemiah was cupbearer to Artaxerxes Longimanus, king of Persia (Neh. 1:11; 2:1). Cupbearers are mentioned among the attendants of Solomon (1 Kings 10:5; 2 Chron. 9:4).

CURE. *See* Diseases, Treatment of.

CURIOUS ARTS (Gk. *ta perierga,* "devious works"). A KJV term referring to magic (so NASB, Acts 19:19; "sorcery," NIV), spoken of the black art as practiced by the Ephesian conjurers. The allusion is doubtless to the *Ephesian spells,* i.e., charms, consisting of letters or monograms, written on parchment and worn like amulets. *See* Magic; Sorcery.

CURSE. The rendering of several Heb. and Gk. words. Many instances of cursing are recorded in Scripture. Thus God cursed the serpent that had seduced Eve (Gen. 3:14); Cain, who slew his brother (4:11). He promised Abraham that He would curse those who should curse him. These divine maledictions are not merely imprecations or the expressions of impotent wishes, but they carry their effects with them and are attended with all the miseries they denounce or foretell. Curses delivered against individuals by holy men (9:25; 49:7; Deut. 27:15; Josh. 6:26) are not the expressions of revenge, passion, or impatience; they are *predictions,* and, therefore, not such as God condemns.

The Mosaic law forbade the cursing of father or mother (Ex. 21:17) on pain of death, of the ruler of his people (22:28), of one that is deaf (Lev. 19:14) or perhaps absent so that he could not hear. Blasphemy, or cursing God, was a capital crime (24:11, 14-15). *See* Anathema.

CURTAINS. The rendering of three Heb. terms.

1. *Yerî'â,* the ten "curtains" of fine linen, and also the eleven of goats' hair that covered the Tabernacle (Ex. 26:1-13; 36:8-17). The charge of these curtains and of the other textile fabrics of the Tabernacle was laid on the Gershonites (Num. 4:4-25). Having this definite meaning, the word became a synonym for the Tabernacle (2 Sam. 7:2). Sometimes it means the sides of a tent (Isa. 54:2; Jer. 4:20; 10:20).

2. *Māsāk,* the "screen" for the doorway of the Tabernacle (Ex. 26:36; etc.), and also for the gate of the court around the Tabernacle (Ex. 27:16; etc.). *See* Tabernacle.

3. *Daq,* "fineness," occurs in the expression "stretches out the heavens like a curtain" (Isa. 40:22; NIV, "canopy") and appears to have been a fabric such as is used by rich orientals for a screen over their courts in summer.

CUSH (Heb. *kûsh*).

1. A son (probably the eldest) of Ham. In the genealogy of Noah's children it is said, "Cush became the father of Nimrod" (Gen. 10:8; 1 Chron. 1:10). A number of his descendants are also mentioned.

2. A Benjamite, mentioned in the title of Ps. 7, of whom nothing more is known than that the psalm is there said to have been composed "concerning" him, 1000 B.C. He appears to have been an enemy of David and in search of an opportunity of injuring him but to have been unsuccessful (v. 15).

3. **Land of.** The ancient designation of Ethiopia, that section of Africa contiguous to Egypt and the Red Sea, now again known as Ethiopia (2 Kings 19:9; Esther 1:1, see marg.; Ezek. 29:10, marg.). In Gen. 2:13 and 10:8, the reference is to an earlier Asiatic (Mesopotamian) Cush, probably the Kassites (Cossaeans).

CU'SHAN (ku'shan). Another form of Cush or perhaps an Arabian country occupied by Cushites (Hab. 3:7).

CU'SHAN-RISHATHA'IM (ku'shan-rish-a-tha'-

im). Evidently an obscure Hittite conqueror who, having annexed Mesopotamia (Mitanni), overran Palestine (Judg. 3:7-10). He left traces of his conquests at Bethshan, the stout Esdraelon fortress, and in other places (John Garstang, *Joshua-Judges*, pp. 62, 364). The event is likely to be placed c. 1361-1353 b.c., in the latter part of the reign of Tutankhamen (c. 1366-1357 b.c.) and the first years of the regime of his general Haremhab, when Egyptian influence in Syria-Palestine had waned.   m.f.u.

BIBLIOGRAPHY: R. T. O'Callaghan, *Aram Naharaim* (1948), pp. 122-23, 139ff.; A. Malamat, *Journal of Near Eastern Studies* 13 (1954): 231ff.

CU'SHI (ku'shi; "Cushite," or "Ethiopian").

1. The messenger sent by Joab to announce to David the success of the battle against Absalom and the death of the young prince (2 Sam. 18:21-23, 31-32), about 970 b.c.

2. The father of Shelemiah, and great-grandfather of Jehudi, which latter was sent by the Jewish magnates to invite Baruch to read his roll to them (Jer. 36:14), before 604 b.c.

3. The son of Gedaliah and father of the prophet Zephaniah (Zeph. 1:1), before 620 b.c.

CUSHITE. See Cush.

CUSHITE WOMAN. Zipporah, the wife of Moses, is so described (Num. 12:1); elsewhere she is called the daughter of a Midianite (Ex. 2:21; cf. v. 16). Reference is probably made here to the Arabian Ethiopia or Cush. Ewald and Keil and Delitzsch think that allusion is made to another wife whom Moses married after the death of *Zipporah* (which see).

CUSHION. See articles Bed; Pillow.

CUSTOM (Heb. *hǎlak*, "way tax," Ezra 4:13, 20; Gk. *telos*, "tax," 1 Macc. 11:35; Matt. 17:25; Rom. 13:7). See Tax.

CUSTOM, RECEIPT OF (Gk. *telōnion*). A KJV term signifying "tollhouse" (Matt. 9:9; Mark 2:14; Luke 5:27).

CU'THAH, or **Cuthah** (ku'tha). The name of a city of Babylonia mentioned only twice in the OT. In one passage (2 Kings 17:30) it is connected with the worship of the god Nergal; in the other (17:24) it is mentioned along with Babylon and other cities as furnishing the people who were deported and settled in Samaria. The city of Cuthah was located a short distance E of Babylon, where the village of Tell-Ibrahim now marks its former site. It was one of the most important cities of ancient Babylonia. In the opinion of some it was the capital city of an ancient kingdom that existed before the city of Babylon had risen to power in the country. However that may be, the city continued to be a center of power through the Assyrian period, and many Assyrian kings halted there to pay tribute of worship at the shrine of its great god Nergal, whose temple,

known by the name of E-shid-Lam, has been found in the ruins at Tell-Ibrahim. After the taking of Samaria by the Assyrians, Sargon king of Assyria transported inhabitants from Avva, Babylon, Hamath, and Sepharvaim to Samaria to take the place of those who had been removed into captivity. These people became known as Samaritans in later times, and a long enmity existed between them and the Jews. Among them the people of Cuthah must have been prominent either because of numbers or of ability, for the new settlers were long called Cutheans. The history of Cuthah shows periods of power and of decay. Sennacherib, king of Assyria who destroyed Babylon, claims to have conquered Cuthah in one of his great campaigns; and Nebuchadnezzar in a later day rebuilt and otherwise restored and beautified its temple. Cuthah had two rivers or canals and therefore probably possessed some commercial importance.   r.w.r.

CUTS (in the flesh, Lev. 19:28; 21:5; Jer. 48:37). Unnatural disfigurement of the body was prohibited by Moses and seems to refer to the scratching of the arms, head, and face, common in times of mourning among the people of the East. The law gave the further prohibition, "Nor make any tattoo marks on yourselves" (Lev. 19:28), a custom common among the savage tribes, and still seen in Arabia. This prohibition had reference to idolatrous usages but was intended to inculcate upon the Israelites a proper reverence for God's creation.

The priests of Baal cut themselves with knives to propitiate the god "according to their custom" (1 Kings 18:28). Herodotus says the Carians, who resided in Europe, cut their foreheads with knives at festivals of Isis, in this respect exceeding the Egyptians, who beat themselves on these occasions (Herodotus 2.61). Lucian, speaking of the Syrian priestly attendants of this mock deity, says that, using violent gestures, they cut their arms and tongues with swords. Tattooing indicated allegiance to a deity, in the same manner as soldiers and slaves bore tattooed marks to indicate allegiance or adscription. This is evidently alluded to in the book of Revelation (13:16; 17:5; 19:20) and, though in a contrary direction, by Ezekiel (9:4), by Paul (Gal. 6:17), and perhaps by Isaiah (44:5) and Zechariah (13:6) (Smith, *Bib. Dict.*, s.v.). See Mark.

CUTTING OFF from the people. See Excommunication.

CUZA See Chuza.

CYMBAL. See Music.

CYPRESS. See Vegetable Kingdom.

CYPRUS (sī'prus). A large island in the Mediterranean sixty miles off the coast of Syria. Its length is about 138 miles and its greatest width 60 miles. It was once inhabited by the Phoenicians. In 447

B.C. the Greeks controlled it; in 58 B.C. it fell to the Romans. At the death of Alexander the Great it had been incorporated with Egypt, and it was an imperial province in 27 B.C. The first NT notice of Cyprus is in Acts 4:36, where it is mentioned as the native place of Barnabas. It appears prominently in connection with the early spread of Christianity (11:19-20). Paul and Barnabas visited it A.D. 44, and it was Paul's first missionary field (13:4-13). The Kittim of Gen. 10:4 and the Chittim of Isa. 23:1 (rendered "Cyprus" in the NIV) referred initially to the inhabitants of Citium and later to the inhabitants of the whole island. Cyprus was known as Elishah in Ezek. 27:7. Among the more important excavations on the island are those at *Paphos* (which see) and *Salamis* (which see).

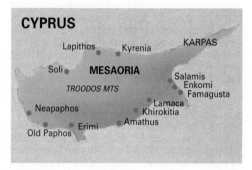

CYRE'NE (sī'rē'nē). A city founded by the Greeks upon a beautiful tableland eighteen hundred feet above sea level. It was the capital of the district of Cyrenaica in Africa. It was a Greek city but contained many Jews. Cyrene was represented in Jerusalem at Pentecost (Acts 2:10). Simon, one of its people, helped Jesus bear His cross (Matt. 27:32). Cyrenian Jews had a synagogue at Jerusalem (Acts 6:9).

Cyrene was a great city in antiquity. The central part of the city was surrounded by a wall four miles in circumference, but large temples and other isolated structures stood far outside the walls. At its height it was said to have had a population of more than 100,000. It was noted among the ancients for its intellectual life, and its medical school was famous. The city was dealt an irreparable blow by the Jewish revolt of A.D. 115-16 and the measures taken by the Roman government to quell it. It was descibed as deserted in the fourth century. Several fine buildings and some excellent sculpture were excavated there early in this century.   H.F.V.

CYRE'NIAN (sī'rē'ni-an; "of Cyrene," Matt. 27:32). A native of Cyrene, or Cyrenaica, in Africa (cf. Mark 15:21; Acts 11:20; etc.).

CYRE'NIUS (sī-rē'ni-us; whose full name was "Publius Silpicius Quirinus"). The second person bearing that name to be mentioned in Roman history, he was consul with M. Valerius Messala. Some years after (A.D. 6) he was made governor of Syria; he decreed that a census, or enrollment, take place there and in Judea. He was a favorite with Tiberius, and on his death (A.D. 21) he was buried with public honors by the Senate at the request of the emperor. The census mentioned above seems, in Luke 2:2, to be identified with one that took place at the time of the birth of Christ, when Sentius Saturnius was governor of Syria. From this has arisen considerable difficulty, which has been variously solved, either by supposing some corruption in the text of Luke or by giving some unusual sense to his words. But A. W. Zumpt, of Berlin, has shown it to be probable that Quirinus (as rendered in the NIV) was *twice* governor of Syria and, by striking and satisfactory arguments, fixes the time of his governorship from 4 B.C. to A.D. 1; the second A.D. 6-10. *See* Chronology, NT.

CY'RUS (sī'rus) II, the Great. The conqueror of Babylon and ruler of that city from 539 B.C. until his death in 530 B.C. and founder of the vast Persian Empire. This great humane ruler holds an important position both in biblical prophecy (Isa. 41:25; 44:28; 45:1-13) and history (Ezra 1:1-8; 4:3-5; 2 Chron. 36:22-23; Dan. 1:21; 10:1).

Early History. Cyrus II came to the throne of Anshan, an Elamite region, around 559 B.C. He clashed with a Median king, Astyages. When the Median army rebelled, Cyrus victoriously took Ecbatana, and the Persians became ascendant.

Conquests. Cyrus II extended his conquests with lightninglike rapidity, defeating Croesus, king of Lydia c. 546 B.C. Babylon fell to him in 539 B.C. Thus he laid the foundations for the vast Persian Empire under whose dominion Judea was to remain a province for the next two centuries. Cyrus established his capital at Pasargadae in the land of Parsa. On a ruined palace there the repeated inscription can still be read, "I, Cyrus, the king, the Achaemenid." From this palace comes the earliest extant Persian relief, a four-winged genius, perhaps representing the deified Cyrus.

Decree. This edict recorded in 2 Chron. 36:22-23 and Ezra 1:2-3 gave permission to the Hebrew captives to go back to Palestine to rebuild their Temple. "Thus says Cyrus king of Persia, 'The Lord, the God of heaven, has given me all the kingdoms of the earth, and He has appointed me to build Him a house in Jerusalem, which is in Judah. Whosoever there is among you of all His people, may his God be with him! Let him go up to Jerusalem . . . and rebuild the house of the Lord.' "

Inscriptions. The famous cylinder of Cyrus found by Hormuzd Rassam in the nineteenth century is in remarkable agreement with the royal edict as set forth in the Bible. "From . . . Ashur and Susa, Agade, Ashnunnak, Zamban, Meturnu,

Cylinder referring to the taking of Babylon by Cyrus

himself as a man of destiny and gives background to the prophetic message of the Hebrew seer. "Marduk . . . sought a righteous prince, after his own heart, whom he took by the hand, Cyrus, king of Anshan, he called by name, to lordship over the whole world he appointed him . . . to his city Babylon he caused him to go . . . his numerous troops in number unknown, like the water of a river, marched armed at his side. Without battle and conflict he permitted him to enter Babylon. He spared his city Babylon a calamity. Nabunaid, the king, who did not fear him, he delivered into his hand" (Rogers, op. cit., p. 381).

His Capital. Cyrus established his main capital at Pasargadae, about forty-five miles NE of the later city of Persepolis. The royal complex seems to have consisted of several pavilions set among gardens and surrounded by a masonry wall about thirteen feet thick. Though archaeological soundings were made at the site earlier, the main work was done by Ali Sami, then director of the Archaeological Institute at Persepolis (1949-54) and David Stronach, director of the British Institute of Persian Studies in Tehran (1961-63). At the SW edge of Pasargadae stands the tomb of Cyrus. Its stepped base measures about 45 by 38 feet, and the tomb chamber itself about 17 by 17 feet and 19 feet high. Its gabled roof stands to a height of about 35 feet from the ground. About a half mile to the NE of the tomb stood a complex of palaces: an audience hall, a garden pavilion, a gatehouse, and a residential palace. About another half mile to the NE lay a citadel area, and approximately a half mile NE of that was a sacred area with two freestanding limestone plinths, which may have been fire altars, and a terraced mound that may have been a stage for sacrificial rites.

End. Cyrus was slain in battle 530 B.C. and buried in a still extant tomb at Pasargadae. In the small burial chamber a golden sarcophagus received Cyrus's body. Plutarch (A.D. 90) says the tomb bore this inscription: "O man, whosoever thou art and whencesoever thou comest, for I know that thou wilt come, I am Cyrus and I won for the Persians their empire. Do not, therefore, begrudge me this little earth which covers my body."   M.F.U.; H.F.V.

BIBLIOGRAPHY: A. T. Olmstead, *The History of the Persian Empire* (1948); R. N. Frye, *Heritage of Persia* (1963); J. C. Whitcomb, Jr., *Darius the Mede* (1963); D. J. Wiseman, et al., *Notes on Some Problems in the Book of Daniel* (1965), pp. 9-16; R. Drews, *Journal of Near Eastern Studies* 33 (1974): 387-93.

Deri, with the territory of the land of Gutium, the cities on the other side of the Tigris, whose sites were of ancient found—the gods, who dwell in them, I brought back to their places and caused them to dwell in a habitation for all time. All their inhabitants I collected and restored them to their dwelling places . . . may all the gods whom I brought into their cities pray daily before Bel and Nabu for long life for me" (R. W. Rogers, *Cuneiform Parallels to the Old Testament* [1912], p. 383). This royal edict shows that Cyrus reversed the inhumane policy of displacing whole populations, as practiced by Assyrian and Babylonian conquerors. Thus his clemency and religious toleration with regard to the Jewish captives are readily understood. Further, it is clear how the Hebrew prophet sang of Cyrus as the deliverer whom Jehovah would raise up (Isa. 45:1-4). Although the Hebrew prophet spoke of the great conqueror as anointed by the Lord for the particular task of restoring the Jewish captives, Cyrus claimed to be commissioned by the god Marduk. The famous inscription of the victor, preserved on a clay cylinder, contains the amazing story of triumphs of one who plainly saw

DAB'AREH. This name is incorrectly spelled in the KJV and should be *Daberath* (which see).

DAB'BESHETH (dab'e-sheth; "hump"). A town on the border of Zebulun (Josh. 19:11). Its location has not been positively identified.

DAB'ERATH (dab'e-rath; "pasture"). A Levitical town of Issachar (Josh. 19:12; 21:28; 1 Chron. 6:72). It lay at the western foot of Mt. Tabor. It is the present insignificant village of Deburieh.

DAGGER. Any sharp instrument, especially a weapon of war (Judg. 3:16, 21-22). *See* Armor.

DAGON. *See* Gods, False.

DAILY. Occurs in the KJV as the rendering of the Gk. *'epiousios*, "necessary" (Matt. 6:11; Luke 11:3), so that the phrase really means "the bread of our necessity," i.e., necessary for us.

DAILY OFFERING, or **Sacrifice.** *See* Sacrifice.

DALAI'AH. *See* Delaiah.

DALE, THE KINGS. *See* Shaveh, Valley of.

DA'LETH (ד) (da'leth). The fourth letter of the Heb. alphabet. From Semitic "daleth" came Gk. *delta* δ, whence Lat. and English "d." See Ps. 119, section 4, where this letter begins each verse in the Heb.

DALMANU'THA (dal-ma-nū'tha). A place on the W coast of the Sea of Galilee, into parts of which Christ was said to have gone ("Magadan," Matt. 15:39). Dalmanutha itself is mentioned only in Mark 8:10. The place is identified with a village called Ain-el-Barideh—the "cold fountain." The village proper is called el-Mejdel, possibly the "Migdal-el" of Josh. 19:38.

BIBLIOGRAPHY: D. Baly, *Geographical Companion to the Bible* (1963), p. 120; G. H. Dalman, *The Words of Christ* (1981), pp. 66ff.

DALMA'TIA (dal-mā'shi-a). A district E of the Adriatic, being a Roman province; a place visited by Titus (2 Tim. 4:10). According to Rom. 15:19 Paul himself had once preached there, the place being referred to as Illyricum.

DAL'PHON (dal'fon). The second of the ten sons of Haman, killed by the Jews on the thirteenth of Adar (Esther 9:7).

DAM (Heb. *'ēm,* "mother"). A KJV term; *see* Mother.

DAMAGES. Remuneration or restitution prescribed in case of offense against the person, property, or name of another. *See* Law.

DAM'ARIS (dam'a-ris; "gentle"). An Athenian woman converted to Christianity by Paul's preaching (Acts 17:34). Chrysostom and others believed her to have been the wife of Dionysius the Areopagite but apparently for no other reason than that she is mentioned with him in this passage.

DAM'ASCENES (dam'a-sēns). Inhabitants of Damascus (2 Cor. 11:32).

DAMAS'CUS (da-mas'kus). Said to be the oldest city in the East.

Situation. Damascus lies about seventy miles from the seaboard, just E of the Anti-Lebanon Mountains, in the valley of the Abana, a great plain about 2,300 feet above the sea and thirty miles by ten in extent. This plain is called the Ghutah and is generously watered by the Abana (modern Barada) and Pharpar (Awaj) rivers. It is fertile, abounding in gardens, orchards, and meadows. It is to Abana that Damascus chiefly owes her importance and stability. Another important factor is that the city lies on the border of the desert and that she is situated on the natural highway from the E to the W. Three great roads lead out of the city to the W, S, and E. The western, or southwestern, road travels by Galilee to the Levant and the Nile. The southern, which leaves the city by the "Gates of God," takes the pilgrims to Mecca. The eastern is the road to Baghdad.

History. Josephus (*Ant.* 1.6.4) says that Damascus was founded by Uz, son of Aram. It is first mentioned in Scripture in connection with Abraham (Gen. 14:15), whose steward was a native of the place (15:2). We may gather from the name of this person, as well as from the statement of Josephus, which connects the city with the Aramaeans, that it was a Semitic settlement.

In the time of David the Syrians of Damascus supported Hadadezer king of Zobah, with whom David was at war (2 Sam. 8:5; 1 Chron. 18:5). But the Syrians were defeated, and David became master of the whole territory, garrisoning it with Israelites (2 Sam. 8:6). In the reign of Solomon, *Rezon* (which see) became master of Damascus (1 Kings 11:23-25). The family of Hadad appears to have recovered the throne, as we find Ben-hadad in league with Baasha of Israel against Asa (1 Kings 15:18-19; 2 Chron. 16:2-3), and later in league with Asa against Baasha (1 Kings 15:20). The defeat and death of Ahab at Ramoth-gilead (1 Kings 22:15-37) enabled the Syrians of Damascus to resume the offensive. Their bands ravaged

Restored gateway to the city of Dan

Israel during Jehoram's reign and laid siege to Samaria.

Hazael, the servant of Ben-hadad, murdered the king (2 Kings 8:15) and was soon after defeated by the Assyrians. He and his son waged successful war against Israel and Judah, but Joash defeated the Syrians three times and recovered the cities of Israel (2 Kings 13:3, 22-25). Jeroboam II (about 783 B.C.) is said to have recovered Damascus (2 Kings 14:28). Later (about 735 B.C.) Rezin, king of Damascus, and Pekah, king of Israel, laid unsuccessful siege to Jerusalem (2 Kings 16:5), but Elath—built by Azariah in Syrian territory—having been taken by Rezin, Ahaz sought the aid of Tiglath-pileser (2 Kings 16:7-8). Rezin was slain, the kingdom of Damascus brought to an end, the city destroyed, and its inhabitants carried captive into Assyria (v. 9; cf. Amos 1:5). It was long before Damascus recovered from this serious blow. We do not know at what time Damascus was rebuilt, but Strabo says that it was the most famous place in Syria during the Persian period. At the time of the gospel history and of the apostle Paul it formed a part of the kingdom of Aretas (2 Cor. 11:32), an Arabian prince, who held his kingdom at the pleasure of the Romans.

The mention of Damascus in the NT is in connection with the conversion and ministry of *Paul* (which see).

BIBLIOGRAPHY: M. F. Unger, *Israel and the Aramaeans of Damascus* (1957); C. Thubron, *Mirror to Damascus* (1967).

DAM'MIM (dam'im). *See* Ephes-dammim, Pasdammim.

DAMNATION (rendering of several Gk. terms, denoting judgment, destruction, etc.). A word used to denote the final loss of the soul, but not to be always so understood. Thus, in place of the KJV expression "damnation," the NASB renders "destruction" (2 Pet. 2:1); "condemnation" (Rom. 13:2; 14:23); and "judgment" (1 Cor. 11:29). Just what it is to which the offender may be condemned lies with God. Some suppose temporal judgments from God and the censure of wise and good men. *See* Punishment.

DAMSEL. *See* Girl.

DAN ('judge"). The fifth son of Jacob and the first of Bilhah, Rachel's maid (Gen. 30:6).

Personal History. Of the patriarch himself no incident is preserved. By the blessing of Jacob on his deathbed it was settled that Dan and his other sons by handmaids should be legally entitled to a portion of the family inheritance.

Tribe of Dan. Only one son is attributed to Dan (Gen. 46:23), but it may be observed that "Hushim" is a plural form, as if the name not of an individual but of a family. At the Exodus the tribe of Dan numbered 62,700 warriors (Num. 1:39) and at the second census 64,400, holding their rank as second.

Position in Camp. Dan's position in the journey was on the N of the Tabernacle, with Asher and Naphtali. The standard of the tribe was of white and red and the crest upon it an eagle, the great foe to serpents. Jacob had compared Dan to a serpent. Ahiezer substituted the eagle, the destroyer of serpents, as he shrank from carrying an adder upon his flag.

Prominent Persons. One who played a prominent part in the wandering was "Oholiab, the son of Ahisamach, of the tribe of Dan" (Ex. 31:6). Samson was also a Danite (Judg. 13:2).

Territory. Dan was the last of the tribes to receive its portion, which was the smallest of the twelve. It had, however, great natural advantages, was fertile, and had also a line of seacoast, which seems to have led the tribe to engage in fishing and commerce, for in the war of Sisera and Barak, Dan remained in ships (Judg. 5:17). It included the cities of Joppa, Lydda, and Ekron.

Capture of Laish. Crowded by the Amorites from the rich lowlands up into the mountains, the Danites turned their attention to territory in the N of Palestine. A force of 600 men was sent, who captured and burned Laish, afterward rebuilding it and naming it Dan (Judg. 18:14-29). This city, with others, was laid waste by Ben-hadad (1 Kings 15:20; 2 Chron. 16:4), and this is the last mention of the place. It is now called Tell el Kâdy ("mound of the judge").

DAN, CAMP OF (Judg. 13:25; 18:12, "Mahanehdan"). The name given to the district in which the Danites pitched before emigrating northward; or perhaps the location of some Danite families that remained.

Restored shrine at Dan

DAN, CITY OF.

1. Formerly Laish, but taken by the Danites and called Dan. Dan stood at the northern border of Canaan (Judg. 20:1) and the northern border of the Northern Kingdom during the period of the Divided Kingdom. Here Jeroboam instituted calf worship after he led the ten tribes out of the Hebrew monarchy (1 Kings 12:29-33). The sixty-five-foot-high mound covers about fifty acres. Avraham Biran began an Israel Department of Antiquities dig there in 1966, and work has gone on to the present. Excavations have demonstrated that the city was founded about 2500 B.C. Of special interest was the discovery of a high place dating to the Israelite period and evidently passing through two stages of construction. The lower, apparently constructed by Jeroboam I in the tenth century B.C., was about twenty by sixty-one feet in size. The upper, of Ahab's day, measured sixty by sixty-two feet and was approached by a monumental flight of steps twenty-seven feet wide. A great double gateway was uncovered on the E side of the Israelite city. It was probably built by Jeroboam I.

2. There is a reference in Ezek. 27:19 in the KJV to "Dan also" (Heb. *wedan*), but the NASB has it correctly "Vedan," which has been believed to be Aden in Arabia, once the chief trading port of Arabia before the rise of Mochar. The NIV, however, renders "Danites." H.F.V.

"DAN TO BE'ER-SHEBA." Dan being the northern boundary of Canaan and Beer-sheba its most southerly town, this proverbial saying expressed the extreme length of the land (Judg. 20:1; 1 Sam. 3:20).

DANCE.

Egyptian. Among the Egyptians the dance consisted mostly of a succession of figures in which the performers endeavored to exhibit a great variety of gesture. Men and women danced at the same time or in separate parties, but women were generally preferred for their superior grace and elegance. Some danced to slow airs, adapted to the style of their movement—the attitudes they assumed frequently partook of a grace not unworthy of the Greeks—and others preferred a lively step, regulated by an appropriate tune. Graceful attitudes and expressive gestures were the general style of their dance, but, as in other countries, the taste of the performance varied according to the rank of the person by whom they were employed, or their own skill. The dance at the house of a priest differed from that among the uncouth peasantry or the lower classes of townsmen.

It was not customary for the upper orders of Egyptians to indulge in this amusement, either in public or private assemblies, and none appears to have practiced it but the lower ranks of society and those who gained their livelihood by attending festive meetings.

The dresses of the female dancers were light and of the finest texture, showing by their transparent quality the form and movement of the limbs. They generally consisted of a loose-flowing robe, reaching to the ankles, occasionally fastened tight at the waist. Round the hips was a small narrow girdle, adorned with beads or ornaments of various colors. Slaves were taught dancing as well as music, and in the houses of the rich, besides their other occupations, that of dancing to entertain the family or a party of friends was required of them. Free Egyptians also gained a livelihood by performing. The dances of the lower orders generally had a tendency toward a species of pantomime; the peasantry were more delighted with ludicrous and extravagant dexterity than with gestures that displayed elegance and grace. The Egyptians also danced at the temples in honor of the gods, and in some processions, as they approached the precincts of the sacred courts.

Greek. Though the Greeks employed women who practiced music and dancing to entertain the guests, they looked upon the dance as a recreation in which all classes might indulge and an accomplishment becoming a gentleman. But if the dances became occasions for excess or effeminacy, the Greeks regarded them as indecent for men of wisdom and character.

Roman. The Romans, on the contrary, were far from considering dance worthy of a man of rank or of a sensible person. Cicero says: "No man who is sober dances, unless he is out of his mind, either when alone or in any decent society, for dancing is the companion of wanton conviviality, dissoluteness, and luxury."

Hebrew. Among the Jews, dancing was always a favorite social pastime among girls and women (Jer. 31:4), imitated by children playing on the street (Job 21:11; Matt. 11:17; Luke 7:32), and was engaged in by female companies in honor of national joys, especially victories (1 Sam. 18:6) and religious festivities (Ex. 15:20; Judg. 21:21). On such occasions, at least in more ancient times, men also testified to the joy of their hearts by dancing (2 Sam. 6:5, 14). A religious meaning belonged also to the torch dance, which was performed later by men in the Temple on the first evening of the feast of Booths. The dances probably consisted only of circular movements with artless rhythmical steps and lively gesticulations and were accompanied by women beating tambourines (Judg. 11:34). At national festivities, other instruments were played (Pss. 68:25; 150:3-5). Of public female dancers, as are frequently found in the modern East, there is not a trace to be found in OT times. Such dancing as that of Herodias's daughter before men at a voluptuous banquet (Matt. 14:6; Mark 6:22) was first introduced among the Jews through the influence of corrupt Greek customs. It was also a Jewish custom for young ladies to dance at private entertainments.

The Jewish dance was performed by the sexes separately. There is no evidence from sacred history that the diversion was promiscuously enjoyed, except perhaps when the deified calf had been erected in imitation of the Egyptian festival of Apis, and all classes of Hebrews intermingled in the frantic revelry. In the sacred dances, although both sexes seem to have frequently borne a part in the procession or chorus, they remained in distinct and separate companies (Ps. 68:25; Jer. 31:13). The dances of the virgins at Shiloh were certainly part of a religious festivity (Judg. 21:19-23).

A form of religious dancing was sometimes made part of the public worship of the early Christians. The custom was borrowed from the Jews, in whose solemn processions choirs of young men and maidens, moving in time with solemn music, always bore a part. It must not be supposed that the "religious dances" had any similarity to modern dance. They were rather processions, in which all who took part marched in time with the hymns that were sung. The custom was early laid aside, probably because it might have led to the adoption of such objectionable dances as were employed in honor of the pagan deities. Prohibitions of dancing as an amusement abound in the church Fathers and in the decrees of the councils.

Figurative. Dancing in the Scriptures is symbolic of joy in contrast with mourning (Ps. 30:11; etc.).

BIBLIOGRAPHY: W. E. O. Oesterley, *The Sacred Dance* (1923); C. Sachs, *World History of the Dance* (1937); J. Pedersen, *Israel, Its Life and Culture* (1940), 3-4:759; E. L. Backman, *Religious Dances in the Christian Church and in Popular Medicine* (1952); A. Sendry, *Music in Ancient Israel* (1969), pp. 441ff.

DANIEL (dan'yel; "God is my judge"). The name of the prophet (which see) who ministered in Babylon, and of two other persons in the Bible.

1. The son of David, the second by the Carmelitess *Abigail* (which see; 1 Chron. 3:1). In the parallel passage (2 Sam. 3:3), this child is called Chileab.

2. A priest of the family of Ithamar who returned from the Exile with Ezra (Ezra 8:2), about 457 B.C. He is probably the same as the priest Daniel who joined in the covenant drawn up by Nehemiah (Neh. 10:6) in 445 B.C.

DAN'IEL (dan'yel; "God is my judge"). One of three persons in Scripture with this name (for the other two, see immediately above). The life and prophecies of this celebrated prophet and minister at the court of Babylon are contained in the book bearing his name. Nothing is known of his parentage or family, but he appears to have been of royal or noble descent (Dan. 1:3) and to have possessed considerable personal endowments (1:4).

Early Life. He was taken to Babylon while yet a boy, together with three other Hebrew youths of rank—Hananiah, Mishael, and Azariah—at the first deportation of the people of Judah in the fourth year of Jehoiakim (604 B.C.).

Enters the King's Service. He and his companions were obliged to enter the service of the royal court of Babylon, on which occasion he received the Chaldean name *Belteshazzar,* according to the Eastern custom of taking a new name when a change takes place in one's condition of life, and more especially if his personal liberty is thereby affected (cf. 2 Kings 23:34; 24:17). Daniel, like Joseph, gained the favor of his guardian and was allowed by him to carry out his wise intention of abstaining from unclean food and idolatrous ceremonies (1:8-16). His prudent conduct and absolute refusal to comply with such customs were crowned with the divine blessing and had important results.

Interprets Dreams. After three years of discipline Daniel was presented to the king, and shortly afterward he had an opportunity to exercise his peculiar gift (2 Kings 1:17) of interpreting dreams—not only recalling the forgotten vision of the king but also revealing its meaning (2:14-45). As a reward he was made "ruler over the whole province of Babylon" and "chief prefect over all the wise men of Babylon" (2:48). Later he interpreted another of Nebuchadnezzar's dreams to the effect that he was to lose for a time his throne but was to be restored to it after his humiliation had been completed (chap. 4).

In Retirement. Under the unworthy successors of Nebuchadnezzar Daniel appears to have occupied an inferior position (Dan. 8:27) and no longer to have been "chief of the magicians" (4:8-9), probably living at Susa (8:2). In the first year of King Belshazzar (7:1), about 555 B.C., he was both alarmed and comforted by a remarkable vision (chap. 7), followed by another two years later (chap. 8), which disclosed to him the future course of events and the ultimate fate of the most powerful empires of the world, in particular their relations to the kingdom of God and its development to the great consummation.

Restored to Office. He interpreted the handwriting on the wall that disturbed the feast of Belshazzar (Dan. 5:10-28), and, notwithstanding his bold denunciation of the king, the latter appointed him the "third ruler in the kingdom" (5:29). After the fall of Babylon Darius ascended the throne and made Daniel the first of the "three commissioners" of the empire (6:2). In deep humiliation and prostration of spirit he then prayed to the Almighty in the name of his people for forgiveness of their sins and for the divine mercy in their behalf; and the answering promises that he received far exceeded the tenor of his prayer, for the visions of the seer were extended to the end of Judaism (chap. 9).

Persecution. His elevation to the highest post of honor and the scrupulous discharge of his official duty aroused the envy and jealousy of his colleagues, who conspired against him. They persuaded the monarch to pass a decree forbidding anyone for thirty days to offer prayer to any person save the king. For disobeying that order the prophet was thrown into a den of lions but was miraculously saved and again raised to the highest post of honor (chap. 6).

Patriotism. He lived to enjoy the happiness of seeing his people restored to their own land, and although his advanced age would not allow him to be among those who returned to Palestine, he never ceased to occupy his mind and heart with his people and their concerns (Dan. 10:12). At the accession of Cyrus he still retained his prosperity (1:21; 6:28).

Visions. In the third year of Cyrus he had a series of visions in which he was informed of the minutest details respecting the future and sufferings of his nation to a period of their true redemption through Christ, as also a consolatory notice to himself to proceed calmly and peaceably to the end of his days and then await patiently the resurrection of the dead (chaps. 10-12). It is not worthwhile to mention here the various fables respecting the later life and death of Daniel, as all accounts are vague and confused.

Character. In the prophecies of Ezekiel, mention is made of Daniel as a pattern of righteousness (Ezek. 14:14, 20) and wisdom (28:3), and, since Daniel was still young at that time (594-588 B.C.), some have believed that another prophet or the legendary Danel of the Ugaritic epic literature of the fourteenth century B.C. discovered at Ras Shamra, Syria, in 1929-37, must be referred to. But Daniel was conspicuous for purity and knowledge at an early age (Dan. 1:4, 17, 20), and he was probably more than thirty years of age at the time of Ezekiel's prophecy. *See* Daniel, Book of.

BIBLIOGRAPHY: T. Kirk, *Daniel the Prophet* (1906); C. E. Macartney, *The Greatest Men of the Bible* (1941), pp. 186-97; W. S. LaSor, *Great Personalities of the Old Testament* (1965), pp. 164-73.

DANIEL, BOOK OF. One of the most important prophetic books of the OT, indispensable as an introduction to NT prophecy dealing with the "times of the Gentiles" (Luke 21:24), the manifestation of the man of sin, the Great Tribulation, the second coming of Christ, the resurrection, and the judgments. Daniel's visions encompass the whole period of Gentile world rule to its destruction and the setting up of the messianic kingdom.

Contents.

I. Daniel's visions under Nebuchadnezzar; personal history to the reign of Cyrus (1:1–6:28)
  A. Reasons for Daniel's fame and prosperity (1:1-21)
  B. Vision of Gentile world empire; Christ and His second advent (2:1-49)
  C. Deliverance from the fiery furnace (3:1-30)
  D. Nebuchadnezzar's tree vision (4:1-37)

E. Belshazzar's feast and the fall of Babylon (5:1-31)

F. Deliverance from the lion's den (6:1-28)

II. Daniel's great prophetic visions (7:1–12:13)

A. The four beasts and the second coming of Christ (7:1-28)

B. Vision of the ram and the male goat (8:1-27)

C. Vision of the seventy weeks (9:1-27)

1. The first advent (9:20-26)

2. Israel's final tribulation and the second advent (9:27)

D. The vision of God's glory (10:1-21)

E. Rule of the Ptolemies and Seleucidae; end-time events (11:1-45)

F. The Great Tribulation (12:1)

G. The resurrections (12:2-3)

H. Daniel's concluding message (12:4-13)

The Danielic Authorship. A Maccabean date (c. 167 B.C.) and the rejection of the traditional Danielic authorship are alleged assured achievements of modern criticism. Those views, however, are built upon a number of highly plausible fallacies.

1. It is argued that Daniel's prophecy was placed among writings in the third section of the Heb. canon and not among the prophets in the second division because it was not in existence when the canon of the prophets was closed, allegedly between 300 and 200 B.C. That conclusion is based upon the unsound critical theory of canonization and also fails to take into account the official status of the prophet as a determining factor in the formation of the Heb. canon. Although possessing the prophetic gift (Matt. 24:15), Daniel everywhere appears as a statesman and not as a prophet.

2. It is assumed that because Daniel is not mentioned in the list of writers in the book of Ecclesiasticus (c. 180 B.C.) that the book, therefore, did not exist at that time. Such an argument from silence is dubious, as neither Asa, Jehoshaphat, or Ezra is mentioned. Discovery of fragments of Daniel among the Dead Sea Scrolls dating to 150 B.C. or earlier has helped to question some of the liberal conclusions about authorship and date.

3. It is maintained that the author of Daniel makes erroneous statements about history of the sixth century B.C., which would be incredible on the part of one who really lived during that period. The campaign of Nebuchadnezzar referred to in 1:1 is given as an example. But that again is an argument from silence, for no extant source has proved that reference erroneous. Numbers of alleged discrepancies in chap. 5 have been obviated or cleared up by archaeological light, such as the existence of Belshazzar as king, who is called the son of (meaning nothing more than the royal successor of) Nebuchadnezzar.

4. Alleged literary features of Daniel are ad-

duced to prove its late date. There is no reason at all to conclude, for instance, that the three Gk. words, names of musical instruments (Dan. 3:10), "demand a date" after the conquest of Palestine by Alexander the Great (332 B.C.), as S. R. Driver (*Introduction to the Literature of the O.T.*, p. 508) contends. It is becoming increasingly evident that Greek culture penetrated the Near East at a much earlier date than had formerly been supposed. Nebuchadnezzar's court was evidently highly cosmopolitan. If Jewish captives were required to furnish music (Ps. 137:3), why is it so incredible to believe that Greeks from Ionia, Lydia, Cilicia, and Cyprus were required to do the same? A slight Persian influence is certainly not astonishing since Daniel lived on into the Persian period. Neither is there anything decisive against Danielic authorship in the considerable Aram. portions of the book.

5. The critical claim that the reference to Daniel in Ezekiel (14:14, 20; 28:3) is to the ancient Semitic legendary figure of Danel, who renders justice in the Ras Shamra poems of the fourteenth century B.C., is highly plausible but certainly unsound. Why should Ezekiel classify a pagan figure with holy men such as Job and Noah? The fact is that the Ezekiel references furnish comparative historical evidence of the historicity of Daniel.

Interpretation. Considerable difference in interpretation of the great visions of Daniel is set forth by amillennial and premillennial commentators. Premillennialists contend that there will yet be established a future kingdom of Israel. Amillennialists generally view the first coming of Christ as an event initiating a spiritual messianic kingdom. Premillennialists, on the other hand, see this as a vision of the destruction of the Gentile world system, and consider the stone that "became a great mountain and filled the whole earth" of the monarchy vision (2:31-45) as being the establishment of the kingdom over Israel. Such a destruction of Gentile world governments did not occur at the first advent of Christ. The Roman Empire was then at its height. Since the crucifixion, the Roman Empire has followed out the history marked in Daniel's great monarchy vision. Gentile world power still continues, and it will end only by catastrophic judgment at Armageddon (Rev. 16:14; 19:21). Likewise, in the great visions of chaps. 7 and 8, a difference of interpretation prevails. Premillennialists see the great beasts portrayed in chap. 7 as picturing the outward voracious nature of the same world empires and Gentile world rule as exhibited in the monarchy vision of chap. 2. The "lion" of Dan. 7:4 is Babylon; the "bear" (7:5) is Media-Persia; the "leopard" (7:6) is Greece under Alexander; the nondescript beast of 7:7 is the Roman Empire; 7:8 gives a vision of the end of Gentile world dominion. Gentile world dominion in the end time will have "ten horns" (that is, ten kings,

Rev. 17:12), corresponding to the ten toes in the monarchy vision. The "little" horn of Dan. 7:8 prefigures Antiochus Epiphanes and through him the final beast (2 Thess. 2:4-8; Rev. 13:4-10). The second coming of Christ in glory to set up His earthly kingdom is described in Dan. 7:9-12. In Dan. 8 the vision of the "ram" with the two horns and the "male goat" with the one conspicuous horn symbolizes the transfer of world power from Media-Persia in the East to Greece under Alexander in the West. The little horn prefigures Antiochus Epiphanes and through him the final Antichrist. The vision of the seventy weeks of chap. 9 constitutes one of the pivotal prophecies of the Bible, whether the amillennial interpretation of it as historical or the premillennial view as prophetic is adopted. Many prophetic Bible teachers hold that the *seventieth week* (which see) is yet future and corresponds to the Great Tribulation discoursed upon by our Lord in Matt. 24:21. Premillennialists, accordingly, see a gap between 9:26 and 9:27 in which they place the church period between the first and second advents. Amillennialists deny the "gap theory" and interpret the seventy weeks as fulfilled in connection with the first advent and the death of Christ and events closely connected with it. Daniel 11:1–12:13 gives a prophetic panorama from Darius to the man of lawlessness (2 Thess. 2:3-4). The spirit of prophecy returns to Daniel's day. Daniel traces the remaining history of the Persian Empire to Alexander, the "mighty king" of Greece (Dan. 11:3). The division of Alexander's empire into four parts (11:4), as already predicted in 8:22, is here again foretold. Daniel 11:4-20, in a most amazing fashion, minutely traces the wars between the Ptolemies and the Seleucids of Syria. Antiochus Epiphanes occupies the vision down to v. 36. From 11:36 the interpretation broadens out to the final little "horn." His prosperity continues until "the indignation" is accomplished (v. 36). "The indignation" is the Great Tribulation (12:1; Matt. 24:21). Daniel 11:38-45 portrays the little horn's career as an irresistible conqueror (vv. 40-44). He establishes the headquarters of his authority in Jerusalem. From this period begins the Great Tribulation, which lasts for 3½ years (7:25; 12:7, 11; Rev. 13:5). Thus the book of Daniel, according to premillennialists, portrays the destruction of Gentile world power under the beast or little horn. That is effected by the second coming of Christ and the establishment of the kingdom over Israel.   M.F.U.

BIBLIOGRAPHY: E. W. Hengstenberg, *Authenticity of Daniel and the Integrity of Zechariah* (1848); R. Anderson, *Daniel in the Critic's Den* (1902); J. A. Montgomery, *A Critical and Exegetical Commentary on the Book of Daniel* (1927); E. J. Young, *The Prophecy of Daniel* (1949); R. D. Culver, *Daniel and the Latter Days* (1954); R. Anderson, *The Coming Prince* (1957); E. J. Young, *Daniel's Vision of the Son of Man* (1958); J. C. Whitcomb, Jr., *Darius the Mede* (1959); H. C. Leupold, *Exposition of Daniel* (1961); N. W. Porteous, *Daniel; a Commentary* (1965); S. P. Tregelles, *Remarks on the Prophetic Visions of the Book of Daniel* (1965); J. F. Walvoord, *Daniel: The Key to Prophetic Revelation* (1971); L. J. Wood, *A Commentary on Daniel* (1973); G. H. Lang, *The Histories and Prophecies of Daniel* (1974); C. Boutflower, *In and Around the Book of Daniel* (1977); D. Ford, *Daniel* (1978); E. B. Pusey, *Daniel the Prophet* (1978); J. G. Baldwin, *Daniel; an Introduction and Commentary* (1979); R. D. Wilson, *Studies in the Book of Daniel*, 2 vols. in 1 (1979); R. D. Culver, *The Histories and Prophecies of Daniel* (1980); F. A. Tatford, *Daniel and His Prophecy* (1980); C. L. Feinberg, *Daniel: The Man and His Visions* (1981); A. B. Michelson, *Daniel and Revelation: Riddles or Realities?* (1984); W. S. Towner, *Daniel* (1984). For different viewpoints see *The Minister's Library* (1985).

DAN'ITE (Judg. 13:2; 18:1, 11; 1 Chron. 12:35). One of the tribe of *Dan* (which see).

DAN-JA'AN (dan-jā'an; 2 Sam. 24:6). The LXX and the Vulg. read "Dan in the woods." Opinions differ as to whether this is identical with Dan or Laish, or the ancient site called Danian in the mountains above Khan en-Nakura, S of Tyre, or a place near Gilead.

DAN'NAH (dan'na; "murmuring"). A city in the mountains of Judah, about eight miles from Hebron (Josh. 15:49).

DA'RA (da'ra). A contracted or corrupt form (1 Chron. 2:6) of the name *Darda* (which see).

DAR'DA (dar'da). A son of Mahol, one of the four men of great fame for their wisdom but surpassed by Solomon (1 Kings 4:31), before 960 B.C. In 1 Chron. 2:6, however, the same four names occur again as "sons of Zerah," of the tribe of Judah, with the slight difference that Darda appears as Dara. Although the identity of these persons with those in 1 Kings 4 has been much debated, they are doubtless the same.

DARIC, or **Drachma.** A weight and a unit of money. *See* Metrology.

DARI'US, THE KING OF PERSIA (da-rī'us; Darius Hystaspes in KJV; 521-486 B.C.; Ezra 4:5, 24; 5:5-7; 6:1, 12, 15; Hag. 1:1; 2:10; Zech. 1:1, 7; 7:1). The restorer of the Persian Empire founded by Cyrus the Great (*see* Cyrus). Cyrus was succeeded in 529 B.C. by his son Cambyses, who added first Phoenicia and Cyprus, and afterward Egypt, to the new empire. In part because Cambyses had been away too long on his campaigns and had lost touch with the people, Smerdis, the younger son of Cyrus, led a revolt in Persia. On hearing of this, Cambyses jumped on his horse to return and deal with the situation and apparently wounded himself with his own dagger. When he died from the wound, Darius, the son of Hystaspes, headed an insurrection of the nobles against Smerdis, which succeeded in dethroning Smerdis. Darius was descended, collaterally with Cyrus, from the ancient royal line of Persia. The reign of Darius belongs more to general than to Bible history, but, as he had great influence on the history of the world as well as upon the fortunes of the Jews, we must notice the leading stages of his career. For our information we are indebted not only to the Greek historians but to his own inscriptions, written in the old Persian cuneiform alphabet, whose decipherment also gave the key to the more ancient and complex Assyrian and Babylonian system of ideograms and syllable signs.

Period of Revolt. The genius for universal rule possessed by Cyrus, his power of conciliation, and his generosity and tolerance had kept his heterogeneous empire in peace and contentment for seventeen years after the submission of the Lydians and Greeks of Asia Minor and nine years after the capture of Babylon. But during the reign of Cambyses discontent and misrule prepared the way for open revolt, which at the accession of Darius spread to all parts of his dominions. But the energy and military skill of Darius everywhere prevailed, and the whole formidable uprising was quelled after six years' work of stern repression, so that by 515 B.C. the sole authority of Persia was recognized in all the lands that had been subdued by Cyrus and Cambyses.

Period of Reorganization. Cyrus had made it his policy to interfere as little as possible with the modes of government followed by his several subject states. For example, in many countries the native kings were confirmed and encouraged in their autonomous administration upon the payment of a reasonable tribute, and in the smaller states native governors looked after the royal revenues and at the same time ruled their people in accordance with traditional methods. That system was changed by Darius, who abolished the local kingdoms and principalities and divided the empire into "satrapies," each satrap being a Persian official with supreme authority in civil affairs and a division of the imperial army to support him and maintain the government against all outside attacks. Judges were also appointed with fixed circuits. A system of posts was established, with royal roads extending everywhere for the transmission of dispatches and rescripts to and from the capital cities of Susa or Ecbatana or Pasargadae. This governmental system was an advance over the old Assyrian despotism, in that the sovereign ruled by delegated power. What is of particular importance to Bible readers is the application of the system to Palestine. There the returning exiles expected to found an autonomous princedom, but under Darius there was erected instead the Persian province of Judah, with imperial supervision over matters civil and religious.

Period of Foreign Conquests. Not content with the empire that fell to him by succession, Darius planned and carried out vast schemes of foreign conquest. The most important of those were the acquisition, about 512 B.C., of northwestern India and the subjection, about 508 B.C., of the coastland between the Bosporus and the Grecian state of Thessaly. Once northwestern India was acquired, the navigation of the lower Indus was controlled and the trade of India opened up by way of the Persian Gulf, with an enormous increase of imperial revenue. The expedition that acquired the coastland crossed the Bosporus and conquered maritime Thrace and Macedonia. Thus the Persian dominions extended from the Caucasus to the borders of northern Greece and "from India to Ethiopia" (Esther 1:1).

Period of the Grecian Wars. These, as is well known, were precipitated by disturbances among the Greeks of the Asiatic coast. The revolt of the subject cities, in 501 B.C., was supported for a time by the European states of Athens and Eretria. It lasted till 494 B.C., and after its complete suppression steps were immediately taken by Darius for vengeance upon the foreigners. The first great expedition by land and sea in 493 did not quite reach its destination, and the second by sea in 490 was frustrated by the world-famous defeat at Marathon. These expeditions were led by generals of Darius, and he made plans for a third that he was to command in person. A revolt in Egypt in 487 and his own death in 486 put an end to the designs. He was succeeded by his son Xerxes, the Ahasuerus of the book of Esther, whose mother was a daughter of Cyrus the Great.

Relief of Darius

Darius and the Jews. The exiles who returned under the protection of Cyrus (537 B.C.), having begun their political and religious life at Jerusalem, were thwarted in their efforts to rebuild the Temple by the Samaritans and other adversaries, who accused them of intrigue and sedition against the Persian government. Cyrus, being occupied with his eastern wards, did not take upon himself to interfere for the prosecution of the work. His successor, Cambyses, had little sympathy with his struggling subjects. Thus the restoration of the sanctuary, so essential in all ways to the progress of the little nation, was delayed for seventeen years (Ezra 4:24). The accession of Darius gave new hope to the leaders of the Jews. In 520 B.C. the prophets Haggai and Zechariah stirred up the people to renewed efforts, and under their inspiration Zerubbabel, the civil leader of the colony, set earnestly to work (5:1-2). An appeal to Darius by Tattenai, the satrap of Syria (5:3-17), embodying a memorial from the leaders of the Jews, resulted in the confirmation of their contention that their proceedings were not only lawful but were actually carried on under royal authority. Darius gave orders that search should be made, with the result that in Ecbatana the edict of Cyrus was found containing all that the Jews had claimed (6:1-5). Darius therefore made a new proclamation insisting that no obstacle should be put in the way of the people of Jerusalem, that the Temple should be rebuilt, that interference with the work should be a capital offense, and that contributions should be made in money and goods from the king's local revenues toward the expenses of the restoration (6:6-12). Accordingly the satrap and his officers "with all diligence" carried out the orders of Darius (6:13-15), with the result that the Temple was finished and dedicated in the sixth year of Darius (515 B.C.).   H.F.V.

BIBLIOGRAPHY: A. T. Olmstead, *History of the Persian Empire* (1948); J. B. Pritchard, ed., *Ancient Near Eastern Texts* (1969), pp. 221, 316; G. C. Cameron, *National Geographic Magazine* 98 (Dec. 1950): 825-44; C. F. Pfeiffer and H. F. Vos, *Wycliffe Historical Geography of Bible Lands* (1967), pp. 188, 210, 238, 263, 268, 271-73, 277, 281, 331-32, 435-36.

DARIUS THE MEDE (Dan. 5:31; 6:1, 6, 9, 25, 28; 9:1; 11:1). This person is to be identified with Gobryas (Gubaru), the governor of Babylon under Cyrus. Darius is most certainly another name for Gubaru. That he was styled "king" is to be regarded as not inaccurate in describing a man of Gubaru's authority since he was *amēl pīḫāte* of the city or province of Babylon, neither does this title usurp the absolute sovereignty of *Cyrus* (which see). Moreover, it is not necessary to discover cuneiform tablets dated according to the years of Darius's reign in order to substantiate the biblical datings. These biblical datings of Darius's reign (9:1; 11:1) are exactly paralleled by the datings of Belshazzar's reign (7:1; 8:1). This conclusion is warranted since it is now known that the author of Daniel took into consideration Belshazzar's secondary position in the Babylonian Empire (cf. 5:7, 16, 29). Neither does the author of Daniel, while attributing far-reaching administrative powers to Darius, detract from his subordination to Cyrus. Darius is said to have "received the kingdom" (5:31) and to have been "made king over the kingdom of the Chaldeans" (9:1). Behind these statements is the implication that Darius was not the supreme ruler of the

Persian Empire. Daniel 6:28 portrays Daniel as prospering not in the consecutive reigns of two independent sovereigns but during the reigns of two contemporary rulers, one being subordinate to the other. "So this Daniel enjoyed success in the reign of Darius *and* in the reign of Cyrus the Persian." Gubaru (Gobryas), it is now known, appointed governors in Babylon after the fall of the city, and Cyrus departed for Ecbatana before the end of the year. The only possible ruler of Babylon was Darius, since Cambyses did not reign as sub-king until the following year, being removed from that honorary position after a few months, while Gubaru continued as governor of Babylon and of a region called the "District Beyond the River" for some years. Since the territory ruled by Gubaru was coextensive with the Fertile Crescent and included many different peoples and races, the description in 6:25-28 of Darius's decree is explainable. Neither does the decree of Darius in 6:7, 12 exclude the possibility of his being a subordinate ruler. Darius's second decree (6:26), which was published to annul the first, was addressed to "all the dominion of *my kingdom,*" not the entire Persian Empire. "To all the peoples, nations, and men of every language who were living in all the land" (6:25) does not claim universal sovereignty for Darius. Moreover, Gubaru was doubtless "the son of Ahasuerus" (9:1) and also a Mede. In the light of these various facts, it is maintained that Darius the Mede is to be identified with Gubaru the governor of Babylon and that the book of Daniel is accurate in this historical reference. (The writer is indebted for this material to John C. Whitcomb, Jr., who wrote his master of divinity thesis on *The Historicity of Darius the Mede in the Book of Daniel,* now published as *Darius the Mede.*)   M.F.U.

BIBLIOGRAPHY: J. C. Whitcomb, Jr., *Darius the Mede* (1963).

DARIUS THE PERSIAN (Neh. 12:22). This Darius was almost certainly Darius II (423-404 B.C.), who ruled after the Artaxerxes during whose reign Nehemiah was so active (for discussion, see *Wycliffe Bible Commentary,* p. 443).   H.F.V.

DARKNESS (Heb. *hōshek,* "the dark"; Gk. *skotos*). In the physical sense, darkness is specially noticed, on three occasions, in the Scriptures:

1. At the period of creation, when darkness, it is said, "was over the surface of the deep," the dispelling of which by the introduction of light was the commencement of that generative process by which order and life were brought out of primeval chaos (Gen. 1:2-4).

2. The plague of darkness in Egypt (Ex. 10:21), "darkness which may be felt." *See* Plagues of Egypt.

3. The awful moment of our Lord's crucifixion, when "from the sixth hour darkness fell upon all the land until the ninth hour" (Matt. 27:45). Some, chiefly ancient writers, have insisted upon

rendering "upon all the *earth*," and account for it by an eclipse of the sun. But an eclipse of the sun could not be visible to the whole world, and, moreover, there could not have been an eclipse, for it was the time of full moon, when the moon could not come between the sun and the earth. The darkness would, therefore, seem to have been confined to Palestine and may have been caused by an extraordinary and preternatural obstruction of the light of the sun by the sulphurous vapors accompanying the earthquake that then occurred.

The "thick darkness where God was" (Ex. 20:21, KJV and NIV) was doubtless the "thick darkness" in which "the Lord said that he would dwell" (1 Kings 8:12, KJV; NIV has "dark cloud"), and has reference to the cloud upon the Mercy Seat. "Clouds and thick darkness surround Him" (Ps. 97:2) refers to the inscrutability of the divine nature and working. The darkness connected with the coming of the Lord (Isa. 13:9-10; Joel 2:31; Matt. 24:29; etc.) has reference to the judgments attendant on His advent.

Figurative. Darkness is used as a symbol of ignorance and spiritual blindness (Isa. 9:2; John 1:5; 1 John 2:8; etc.). With respect to the gloom associated with darkness it becomes significant of sorrow and distress; hence, "a day of darkness" is the time of calamity and trouble (Joel 2:2). Isaiah 8:22; 9:2; 13:10; etc., refer to the unlighted streets of Eastern countries and indicate the despair and wretchedness of the lost. Darkness affording a covering for the performance of evil, "the unfruitful deeds of darkness" (Eph. 5:11) is employed to designate the more flagrant exhibitions of unrighteousness. Darkness is used to represent the state of the dead (Job 10:21; 18:18).

BIBLIOGRAPHY: D. W. Thomas, *Journal of Semitic Studies* 7 (1962): 191-200.

DAR'KON (dar'kon). One whose children, or descendants, were among the servants of Solomon who returned from Babylon with Zerubbabel (Ezra 2:56; Neh. 7:58), about 458 B.C.

DARLING. In the KJV "darling" appears as the translation of the Heb. *yāḥîd* in Pss. 22:20; 35:17. The Heb. term has the meaning of "united," "only," hence "beloved"; the NASB renders "my only life," the NIV, "my precious life."

In the NASB and NIV "darling" appears in the Song of Solomon as the translation of Heb. *ra'yâ,* "attendant maidens." The KJV and RV render "O my love."

DART. The KJV rendering of several Heb. and Gk. words, referring to an arrow or light spear. The Hebrews are supposed to have discharged the arrow while on fire, to which allusion may be made in Deut. 32:23, 42; Ps. 7:13; 120:4; Zech. 9:14; Eph. 6:16. *See* Armor.

DA'THAN (dā'than; "of a spring," or "well"). A Reubenite chieftain, son of Eliab, who joined the conspiracy of Korah the Levite, and, with his accomplices, was swallowed up by an earthquake (Num. 16:1-35; 26:9; Deut. 11:6; Ps. 106:17), about 1435 B.C.

DAUGHTER (Heb. *bat,* feminine of *bēn,* "son"; Gk. *thugatēr*). This word is used in Scripture, like son, with some latitude. In addition to its usual and proper sense of daughter, born or adopted, it is used to designate *a step-sister,* niece, or *any* female descendant (Gen. 20:12; 24:48; Deut. 23:17). More generally still it is used of the female branch of a family, or female portion of community, as "the daughters of Moab," of "the Philistines," "of Aaron" (Num. 25:1; 2 Sam. 1:20; Luke 1:5). Small towns were called daughters of neighboring large mother cities, as "Heshbon, and in all her daughters" (Num. 21:25, NASB marg.); so Tyre is called the daughter of Sidon (Isa. 23:12).

Cities were commonly personified as women and so, naturally, had the designation given to them of *daughters* of the country to which they belonged, as "daughter of Zion," "daughter of Jerusalem" (Isa. 37:22; etc.). The condition of daughters, that is, of young women, in the East, their employments, duties, etc., may be gathered from various parts of the Scriptures. Rebekah drew and fetched water; Rachel kept sheep, as did the daughters of Jethro, though he was a priest, or a prince, of Midian. They superintended and performed domestic services for the family. Tamar, though a king's daughter, baked bread.

DAUGHTER-IN-LAW (Heb. *kallâ;* Gk. *numphē*). The word literally means a "bride" and is applied to a son's wife.

DA'VID.

David's name in Heb. means "beloved" or possibly "chieftain," as evidence from the Mari Letters indicates. Reference in these tablets to the plundering "Benjamites" is indicated by the word *dawîdum* ("leader"), but the connection between that term and Israel's most famous king is conjectural. He was born in Bethlehem, the youngest son of a sheikh of that town named Jesse (1 Sam. 16:1). Apparently David had seven older brothers (1 Sam. 16:10). These are listed in table 5, "David's Family Register," along with other members of his immediate family.

Early History. His boyhood was spent as a shepherd. He was eminently gifted, being skilled in playing the lyre (1 Sam. 16:16-18). David was conspicuous for valor, slaying a lion and a bear in defense of his father's flocks (17:34-36). As a humble shepherd boy he was anointed as Saul's successor by Samuel (16:1-13).

His Relations with Saul. As a result of Saul's disobedience to the divine command, he was rejected from the kingship and afflicted with melancholy, jealousy, and hatred. David was summoned when an evil spirit, or demon, by God's permission came upon Saul. David played so well that Saul was refreshed and the evil spirit departed from him (1 Sam. 16:14-23). When Saul's condition presumably improved, David returned to his pastoral pursuits at Bethlehem. On a visit to his brethren, who were fighting in Saul's army against the Philistines, the young shepherd, whose valiant spirit was nurtured by communion with God, was outraged by the cowardice of Saul's army before the Philistine giant-champion, Goliath. David's notable victory over the giant with a simple shepherd's sling and pebbles from the brook gained him national reputation. It was then that Saul made adequate inquiry concerning David's family connections. The result was that David was adopted into the court (17:55–18:2). As a warrior-courtier the young man won the loyal friendship of Saul's son Jonathan (18:1-4). Further clashes with the Philistines greatly enhanced David's reputation. Saul's insane jealousy and hatred against David were aroused when the women of Israel greeted the returning heroes with the song: "Saul has slain his thousands, and David his ten thousands" (18:5-9). From that point on, David's life was in constant jeopardy. But he behaved himself so wisely that he attracted universal respect and love. Saul attempted to get rid of him by demanding that he slay one hundred Philistines and provide proof of the fact. David performed the feat and received Michal, Saul's daughter as wife. As

a consequence he was saved from death only by the loyalty of Jonathan and Michal.

A Fugitive and an Outlaw. The next several years of David's life were spent fleeing from Saul's rage. Michal was given in marriage to another and was not restored to David until after Saul's death. David saw Jonathan only in secret. He fled to Samuel at Ramah, then fled to Nob where, on the pretext of a secret mission from Saul, he gained an answer from the oracle, food, and the sword of Goliath. He then fled to Achish, king of Gath, where, as the slayer of Goliath, he feigned madness in order to avoid death at the hands of the Philistines (21:10-15). As an outlaw, David at the head of a band of supporters made the Cave of Adullam his headquarters (22:1-2). In that wild and mountainous region he was hunted like an animal. On several occasions Saul was at David's mercy, but David spared his life.

Service Under Achish. Wearied with his wandering life, he at length crossed the Philistine frontier, not as before, in the capacity of a fugitive, but at the head of a sizable force of six hundred men (27:1-2). Achish, king of Gath, gave him, after the manner of Eastern kings, the city of *Ziklag* (which see) on the Philistine frontier (27:6). From the Philistines David learned much military knowledge. While he was away from Ziklag the Amalekites burned the city and carried off the women and children. David was able to overtake the raiders and recover a vast amount of spoil. Two days after that victory an Amalekite

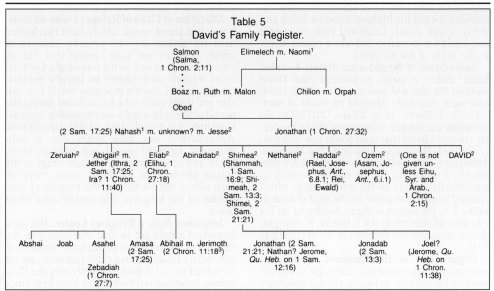

Table 5
David's Family Register.

				Salmon (Salma, 1 Chron. 2:11)		Elimelech m. Naomi[1]				
				Boaz m. Ruth m. Malon			Chilion m. Orpah			
				Obed						
		(2 Sam. 17:25) Nahash[1] m. unknown? m. Jesse[2]					Jonathan (1 Chron. 27:32)			
Zeruiah[2]	Abigail[2] m. Jether (Ithra, 2 Sam. 17:25; Ira? 1 Chron. 11:40)	Eliab[2] (Elihu, 1 Chron. 27:18)	Abinadab[2]	Shimea[2] (Shammah, 1 Sam. 16:9; Shimeah, 2 Sam. 13:3; Shimei, 2 Sam. 21:21)	Nethanel[2]	Raddai[2] (Rael, Josephus, Ant., 6.8.1; Rei, Ewald)	Ozem[2] (Asam, Josephus, Ant., 6.1.1)	(One is not given unless Eihu, Syr. and Arab., 1 Chron. 2:15)	DAVID[2]
Abshai Joab Asahel Zebadiah (1 Chron. 27:7)	Amasa (2 Sam. 17:25)	Abihail m. Jerimoth (2 Chron. 11:18[3])		Jonathan (2 Sam. 21:21; Nathan? Jerome, *Qu. Heb.* on 1 Sam. 12:16)			Jonadab (2 Sam. 13:3)	Joel? (Jerome, *Qu. Heb.* on 1 Chron. 11:38)	

1. The line through David is given in Ruth 1:1–5; 4:10–22; 1 Chron. 2:11–15. For a discussion of the identity of Nahash, *see* the article Nahash, no. 2.
2. Jesse's children and some of his grandchildren are listed in 1 Chron. 2:13–17. Additions and alternate readings are given in parentheses.
3. The KJV of 2 Chron. 11:18 can be read as listing Rehoboam as Abihail's husband, but the NASB and NIV readings clearly give his name as Jerimoth.

arrived with the news of Saul's death at Mt. Gilboa.

Early Activity as King. Saul's death resulted in a crisis in the political history of Israel, and a period of civil war followed. David took up his residence at Hebron in the hill country of Judah, some nineteen miles SW of Jerusalem. There he was anointed king over the house of Judah and reigned 7½ years over that tribe (2 Sam. 2:1-11). Meanwhile the long civil war between the house of Saul and the house of David eventuated in extermination of the house of Saul and David's being anointed king over all Israel (2:8–5:5). The most important event of his early reign was capturing *Jebusite* (which see) *Jerusalem* (which see) and making that the capital of his realm. Despite the apparent impregnable defense of the place, David took the stronghold, evidently by ascending the stout walls with a grappling hook. Although David's men probably scaled the walls of Jerusalem and did not gain entrance to the Jebusite fortress as previously believed, through the city's underground water system, archaeology has proved conclusively that the "stronghold of Zion" and subsequently "the city of David" (5:7), which the king constructed, were situated on the Eastern hill above the Gihon fountain and not on the so-called Western hill of Zion. Having conquered the city, David made it his capital, displaying great wisdom in that decision. The city stood on the border of Judah and Israel, and its neutral location tended to allay the jealousy between the northern and southern portions of his kingdom. Its liberation from the Canaanites opened the highway between Judah and the N, which greatly facilitated both commerce and foreign intercourse and was a potent factor in the unity of the kingdom.

Subjugation of Neighboring States. A united Israel under a virile personality like David aroused the fear and jealousy of the Philistines, who were decisively defeated by David (2 Sam. 5:17-25; 1 Chron. 18:1; 2 Sam. 21:15-22). So complete was David's subjugation of the inveterate enemy of Israel that their power was effectively nullified. David also conquered the Moabites, Aramaeans, Ammonites, Edomites, and Amalekites (8:10; 12:26-31). He was enabled to build up a substantial empire for his son Solomon, which reached from Ezion-geber on the Gulf of Aqabah in the S to the region of Hums bordering on the city-state of Hamath in the N (see W. F. Albright, *Archaeology and the Religion of Israel* [1931], p. 131).

Organization of the Kingdom. David's administrative achievements, although overshadowed by his colorful, personal, skillful diplomacy and brilliant military strategy, were outstanding. That is clearly reflected in the extensive kingdom he left behind him and the preservation of accounts of efficient organization (cf. 1 Chron. 22:17–27:34). His kingdom was organized, in part at least, on Egyptian models (cf. Albright, *Archaeology and the Religion of Israel,* p. 120). Among official Egyptian institutions, which he copied, probably through Phoenician or other channels, was the division of the functions between the "recorder" *mazkir,* the "secretary" *sopher* (18:15-16), and the "charge of thirty" (cf. 27:6). He also efficiently organized his army (2 Sam. 8:16), which included a special personal bodyguard of mercenaries, presumably of Philistine extraction, called Cherethites and Pelethites (8:18).

Establishment of Levitical Cities. Although these cities included the cities of refuge (Num. 35), which were provided for by Moses before entrance into the land and established by Joshua after the conquest (Josh. 21:2), it was unlikely that before the time of Saul or David many of these places, such as Gezer, Ibleam, Taanach, Rehob Jokneam, and Nahalo (cf. chap. 21) were actually apportioned to the Levitical priests, since these places were not in Israelite hands before that time. Towns such as Eltekeh and Gibbethon were under Philistine domination previous to the Davidic era. And such small places as Allemeth and Anathoth in the tribe of Benjamin could scarcely have been established as Levitical towns previous to the removal of the Tabernacle to Nob in the time of Saul. It seems likely that they were apportioned to the Levites after David's conquest of Jebusite Jerusalem, making it his capital, since there is no doubt that he planned some kind of administrative reorganization of the Israelite confederation.

Allocation of Cities of Refuge. A wise administrator like David would hardly have overlooked need for asylum for one unjustly accused of crime. Scholars are quite certain that the six cities of refuge as well as the forty-eight Levitical cities figured prominently in David's political reorganization. Such a provision would rule out clan and tribal feuds, which flourished during the period of the judges and were commonly destructive (Judg. 8:1-4; Josh. 19:1–21:25). David's wise statesmanship was fully aware that a well-grounded kingdom would not tolerate blood feuds, and he was quick to take advantage of the Mosaic provision of six refuge cities, three on each side of the Jordan, for the purpose of consolidating the kingdom and contributing to its peace.

Jerusalem Made a Religious Center. His most important single act in that direction was the removal of the Ark to Jerusalem from Kiriath-jearim, where Israel's sacred chest had been, except for a brief period at Beth-shemesh after the Philistines, in whose territory it had been kept since the battle of Ebenezer (c. 1050 B.C.), had brought it back to Israel. The first attempt to bring up the Ark proved abortive (cf. 2 Sam. 6:11-15; 1 Chron. 15:13), because it was not carried according to prescribed Mosaic regulations (Num. 4:5, 15, 19), and David's resort to the Philistine expedient of a new cart drawn by cows (cf. 1 Sam. 6:7-8) led to the death of Uzzah. Finally after four months and with great religious celebration the Ark was brought up to the city of David (2 Sam. 6:12-15) when David was "dancing before the Lord . . . wearing a linen ephod" (6:14). The ephod, now illustrated from the Assyrian and Ugaritic texts, was formerly an ordinary garment worn apparently especially by women. Not until later centuries did the ephod become restricted to religious and, subsequently, to priestly use. In Israel, however, it early became a distinctive part of the dress of the Levitical priesthood. Its use by David on this occasion was evidently in his capacity as Yahweh's anointed king and as His special representative. The Davidic tent was certainly copied after the specifications of the Mosaic prototype, like the one that had existed at Nob (1 Sam. 21:1, 9).

Organization of Sacred Music. Despite modern criticism's denial that David organized Hebrew sacred music, archaeological findings tend to show there is nothing incongruous in the light of conditions existing in the ancient Near Eastern world around 1,000 B.C. with the biblical representation of David as a patron saint of Jewish hymnology and the organizer of Temple music. Palestinian musicians were well known in antiquity, as shown by the Egyptian and Mesopotamian monuments in the early nineteenth century B.C. Semitic craftsmen carried musical instruments with them when they went down into Egypt, as is shown by the famous relief from Beni-Hasan, 169 miles above Cairo. The epic religious literature discovered at Ras Shamra portrays the singers (*sharim*) as forming a special class of personnel at Ugarit as early as 1400 B.C. The OT narratives themselves give considerable prominence to David's musical and poetical gifts. Musical guilds have been shown by archaeological and linguistic evidence to have been prominent among the Canaanites.

Resolve to Build a Temple. After this event the king, contrasting his cedar palace with the curtains of the Tabernacle, was desirous of building a temple for the Ark. He communicated his desire to the prophet Nathan, who, without waiting to consult God, replied: "Go, do all that is in your mind, for the Lord is with you." But the word of God came to Nathan that same night telling him that David was not to build a house for God to dwell in, that he had been a man of war, that God would first establish his house, and that his son should build the Temple (2 Sam. 7; 1 Chron. 17). Encouraged by the divine sanction and by the promises given him, David henceforth made it one of the great objects of his reign to gather means and material for this important undertaking.

Mephibosheth. When David had taken up his abode in Jerusalem, he inquired whether there yet survived any of Saul's descendants to whom he might show kindness. Through Ziba, an old servant of Saul, he learned of Mephibosheth, a son of Jonathan. He sent for Mephibosheth, returned him Saul's family possessions, and gave him a place at the king's table (2 Sam. 9:13).

Three Years' Famine. About this time a three years' famine terrified Israel, which induced David to inquire of the Lord the cause of the judgment. The Lord replied, "It is for Saul and his bloody house, because he put the Gibeonites to death." Nothing further is known about the fact itself. The Gibeonites were sent for, and upon their requisition David gave up to them two sons of Rizpah, a concubine of Saul, and five sons of Merab, whom she had borne to Adriel. These were slain, and their bodies, left uncared for, were watched over by Rizpah. Word was brought to David, who had the bones of the crucified men, together with those of Saul and Jonathan, which were brought from Jabesh-gilead, honorably deposited in the family tomb at Zela, in the tribe of Benjamin. It is probable that this was the time when David spared Mephibosheth, in order to fulfill his covenant with Jonathan (21:1-14).

David's Adultery. The notion of the East, in ancient and modern times, has been that a well-filled harem is essential to the splendor of a princely court. That opened a dangerous precipice in David's way and led to a most grievous fall. Walking upon the roof of his house, he saw a woman washing herself. The beauty of the woman excited David's lust, and he inquired of his servants who she was. "Bathsheba, the daughter of Eliam, the wife of Uriah the Hittite," was the reply. Despite the fact that she was the wife of another, David sent for her, and she appears voluntarily to have acceded to his sinful purpose. In order to cover up his sin and secure Bathsheba for his wife, David sent Uriah into battle under circumstances that caused his death and thus added murder to his other crime. The clouds from this time gathered over David's fortunes, and the Lord told him, "The sword shall never depart from your house" (12:10). There followed the outrage of his daughter Tamar by his eldest son, Amnon, and the murder of the latter by the servants of Absalom (11:1–13:29).

Absalom's Rebellion. Absalom fled and went to Talmai, the son of Ammihud, king of Geshur, where he remained three years. After this he was recalled to Jerusalem but lived "two full years in Jerusalem, and did not see the king's face." He then sent for Joab and through his mediation was admitted into his father's presence (chap. 14). Absalom soon began to aspire to the throne, and, under pretense of wanting to fulfill a vow, he gained permission to go to Hebron, where he strengthened his conspiracy. Hearing of Absalom's conduct, David fled from Jerusalem (15:14) and passed over Jordan, about 974 B.C. Mahanaim was the capital of David's exile, as it had been of the exiled house of Saul (17:24; cf. 2:8, 12). His forces were arranged under the three great military officers who remained faithful to his fortunes—Joab, captain of the host; Abishai, captain of "the mighty men"; and Ittai, who seems to have taken the place of Benaiah as captain of the guard (18:2). On Absalom's side was David's nephew, Amasa (17:25). The final battle was fought in the "forest of Ephraim" and terminated in the accident leading to the death of Absalom (18:1-33). The return was marked at every stage by rejoicing and amnesty (19:16-40; 1 Kings 2:7), and Judah was first reconciled. The embers of the insurrection still smoldered (2 Sam. 19:41-43), and David's hereditary enemies of the tribe of Benjamin were trampled out by the mixture of boldness and sagacity in Joab, now, after the murder of Amasa, once more in his old position (chap. 20). David again reigned in peace at Jerusalem.

Three Days' Pestilence. This calamity visited Jerusalem at the warning of the prophet Gad. The occasion that led to this warning was the census of the people taken by Joab at the king's orders (2 Sam. 24:1-9; 1 Chron. 21:1-7; 27:23-24). Joab's repugnance to the measure was such that he refused to number Levi and Benjamin (21:6). The king also hesitated to number those who were under twenty years of age (27:23), and the final result was never recorded in the "chronicles of King David" (27:24). Outside the walls of Jerusalem, Araunah, or Ornan, a wealthy Jebusite, perhaps even the ancient king of Jebus (2 Sam. 24:23), possessed a threshing floor (1 Chron. 21:20). At that spot an awful vision appeared, such as is described in the later days of Jerusalem, of the angel of the Lord stretching out a drawn sword between earth and sky over the city. The scene of such a phenomenon at such a moment was at once marked out for a sanctuary. David demanded and Araunah willingly granted the site; the altar was erected on the rock of the threshing floor; the place was called by the name "Mount Moriah" (2 Chron. 3:1); and for the first time a holy place, sanctified by the vision of the divine Presence, was recognized in Jerusalem. It was this spot that afterward became the altar of the Temple and therefore the center of the national worship.

Adonijah's Conspiracy. Adonijah, one of David's elder sons, feared that the influence of Bathsheba might gain the kingdom for her own son Solomon and declared himself to be the successor to his father (1 Kings 1).

Solomon Made King. The plot was stifled, and Solomon's inauguration took place under his father's auspices (1 Kings 1:1-53). By this time David's infirmities had grown upon him. An attempt was made to restore the warmth of his exhausted frame by the introduction of the young Shunammite Abishag (1:1; 2:17). His last song is preserved—a striking union of the ideal of the just

rule he had pursued and of the difficulties he had felt in realizing it (2 Sam. 23:1-7). His last recorded words to his successor are general exhortations to duty, combined with warnings against Joab and Shimei and charges to remember the children of Barzillai (1 Kings 2:1-9).

Death. He died at the age of seventy (2 Sam. 5:4) and "was buried in the city of David" (1 Kings 2:10-11), about 960 B.C. After the return from the captivity "the tombs of David" were still pointed out between "the artificial pool and the house of the mighty men" (Neh. 3:16). His tomb, which became the general sepulcher of the kings of Judah, was pointed out in the latest times of the Jewish people. The edifice, shown as such from the Crusades to the present day, is on the western hill of modern Jerusalem, commonly called Mt. Zion, under the so-called "Coenaculum," but it cannot be identified with the tomb of David, which was within the walls of the "city of David" on the southeastern hill.

Perhaps the best way to understand the family of David will be to study table 6, "David's Family," in which are given his wives, children, and grandchildren, so far as known. The royal line was carried on through a union of the children of Solomon and Absalom.

Character. "If we proceed to put together, in its most general features, the whole picture of David which results from all these historical testimonies, we find the very foundations of his character to be laid in a peculiarly firm and unshaken trust in Jehovah, and the brightest and most spiritual views of the creation and government of the world, together with a constant, tender, and sensitive awe of the Holy One in Israel, a simple, pure striving never to be untrue to him, and the strongest efforts to return to him all the more loyally after errors and transgressions. . . . His mouth continually overflows with heartfelt praise of Jehovah, and his actions are ever redolent of the nobility inspired by a real and living fear of him (for the errors by which he is carried away stand out prominently just because of their rarity). . . . In the clear daylight of Israel's ancient history David furnishes the most brilliant example of the noble elevation of character produced by the old religion" (Ewald, *Hist. of Israel,* 3:57-58).

Critics sometimes focus upon seeming contradictions in David's life, yet an examination of those so-called discrepancies reveals not contradiction but the uncompromising honesty of the scriptural text.

First Samuel 13:14. "How," ask some, "could a man after God's own heart have murdered Uriah, seduced Bathsheba, and tortured the Ammonites?" An extract from one who is not a too-indulgent critic of sacred characters expresses at once the common sense and the religious lesson of the whole matter. "David, the Hebrew king, had fallen into sins enough—

blackest crimes—there was no want of sin. And, thereupon, the unbelievers sneer, and ask, 'Is this your man according to God's heart?' The sneer, I must say, seems to me but a shallow one. What are faults, what are the outward details of a life, if the inner secret of it, the remorse, the temptations, the often-baffled, never-ended struggle of it, be forgotten? All earnest souls will ever discern in [David's life] the faithful struggle of an earnest human soul toward what is good and best. Struggle often baffled—sore baffled —driven as into entire wreck, yet a struggle nev-

er ended, ever with tears, repentance, true unconquerable purpose, begun anew" (Carlyle, *Heroes and Hero-worship*, 1:277).

First Samuel 16:18; 17:42, 56. There seems a contradiction between these two passages, the one representing David as a "mighty man of valor, a warrior," the others as "but a youth." The first description of David "does not presuppose he had already fought bravely in war, but may be perfectly explained from what David himself afterward affirmed respecting his conflicts with lions and bears (17:34-35). The courage and

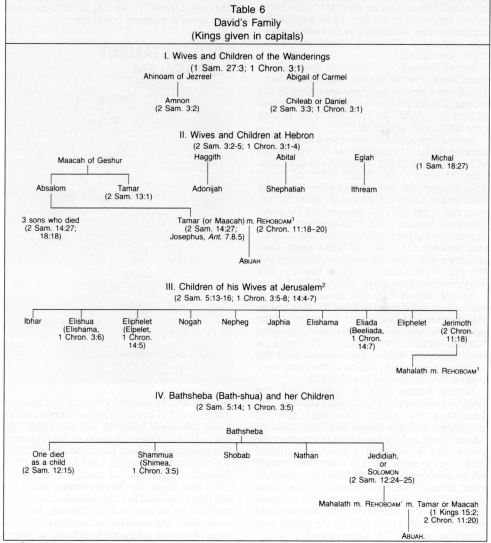

Table 6
David's Family
(Kings given in capitals)

I. Wives and Children of the Wanderings
(1 Sam. 27:3; 1 Chron. 3:1)

Ahinoam of Jezreel — Amnon (2 Sam. 3:2)

Abigail of Carmel — Chileab or Daniel (2 Sam. 3:3; 1 Chron. 3:1)

II. Wives and Children at Hebron
(2 Sam. 3:2-5; 1 Chron. 3:1-4)

Maacah of Geshur — Absalom; Tamar (2 Sam. 13:1)
 Absalom — 3 sons who died (2 Sam. 14:27; 18:18)

Haggith — Adonijah
Abital — Shephatiah
Eglah — Ithream
Michal (1 Sam. 18:27)

Tamar (or Maacah) m. Rehoboam[1] (2 Sam. 14:27; Josephus, *Ant.* 7.8.5) (2 Chron. 11:18–20)
 Abijah

III. Children of his Wives at Jerusalem[2]
(2 Sam. 5:13-16; 1 Chron. 3:5-8; 14:4-7)

Ibhar; Elishua (Elishama, 1 Chron. 3:6); Eliphelet (Elpelet, 1 Chron. 14:5); Nogah; Nepheg; Japhia; Elishama; Eliada (Beeliada, 1 Chron. 14:7); Eliphelet; Jerimoth (2 Chron. 11:18)
 Mahalath m. Rehoboam[1]

IV. Bathsheba (Bath-shua) and her Children
(2 Sam. 5:14; 1 Chron. 3:5)

Bathsheba

One died as a child (2 Sam. 12:15); Shammua (Shimea, 1 Chron. 3:5); Shobab; Nathan; Jedidiah, or Solomon (2 Sam. 12:24–25)
 Mahalath m. Rehoboam[1] m. Tamar or Maacah (1 Kings 15:2; 2 Chron. 11:20)
 Abijah.

1. Rehoboam was the son of Solomon.
2. Bathsheba (Bath-shua) and her children are listed separately below. In addition, there were ten concubines (2 Sam. 5:13; 15:16), whose children (1 Chron. 3:9) are not named.

strength which he then displayed furnished sufficient proofs of heroism for anyone to discern in him the future warrior" (Keil, *Com.*).

First Samuel 17:55-58. How can we reconcile Saul's and Abner's ignorance of David, who had been musician and armor bearer to Saul (16:14-23)? Keil and Delitzsch (*Com.*) explain as follows: "The question put by Saul does not presuppose an actual want of acquaintance with the person of David and the name of his father, but only ignorance of the social condition of David's family, with which both Abner and Saul may hitherto have failed to make themselves more fully acquainted." Some explain by saying that after David played before Saul he returned to his home (which appears to be the fact, 18:2), and that his appearance had so changed as to make recognition impossible (Thomson, *Land and Book*, 2:366, American ed.).

Second Samuel 5:3. The three anointings of David need give no trouble. The first (1 Sam. 16:13) was a private, prophetic anointing; by the second (2 Sam. 2:4) he was publicly recognized as king over Judah; by the third (5:3), as king over both Judah and Israel.

Second Samuel 5:6-9. Some see a discrepancy between the fact of the capture of "the stronghold of Zion" and the taking of Goliath's head to Jerusalem (1 Sam. 17:54). Ewald (*Hist. of Israel*, 3:72) answers that clearly David did not carry the head to Jerusalem till afterward, when he was king. Keil (*Com.* of 17:54) explains that the assertion made by some, that Jerusalem was not yet in possession of the Israelites, rests upon a confusion between the citadel of Jebus upon Zion, which was still in the hands of the Jebusites, and the city of Jerusalem, in which Israelites had dwelled a long time (Josh. 15:63; Judg. 1:8).

Second Samuel 6:20. The proud daughter of Saul was offended at the fact that the king had on this occasion let himself down to the level of the people. She taunted him with having stripped himself, because while dancing and playing he wore somewhat lighter garments (such as the ordinary priestly garb) instead of the heavy royal mantle (Ewald, *Hist. of Israel*, 3:127).

Second Samuel 24:1. In 2 Sam. 24:1, the Scripture observes that God moved David against Israel to say, "Go, number Israel and Judah," yet in 1 Chron. 21:1 it is alleged that Satan stood up against Israel and provoked David to number the people. But the meaning is that God permitted Satan thus to move David in order that through his act an opportunity might arise for the punishment of Israel's sin. The command of David was not sinful in itself but became so from the spirit of pride and vanity out of which it originated and which was shared with him by the people over whom he ruled (W. M. Taylor, *David*, p. 371).

M.F.U.

BIBLIOGRAPHY: F. W. Albright, *Archaeology and the Religion of Israel* (1931), p. 131; F. B. Meyer, *David: Shepherd, Psalmist, King* (1953); A. W. Pink, *The Life of David*, 2 vols. (1958); D. W. Thomas, *Documents Illustrative of Old Testament Times* (1958), pp. 195-201; W. M. Taylor, *David: King of Israel* (1961); R. A. Carlson, *David: The Chosen King* (1964); J. Bosch, *David—The Biography of a King* (1966); K. M. Kenyon, *Jerusalem: Excavating 3000 Years of History* (1967); W. D. Davies, *The Gospel and the Land* (1974); K. M. Kenyon, *Digging Up Jerusalem* (1974); W. G. Blaikie, *The First Book of Samuel* (1978); id., *The Second Book of Samuel* (1978); L. J. Wood, *Israel's United Monarchy* (1979); W. G. Blaikie, *David, King of Israel* (1981); F. W. Krummacher, *David, The King of Israel* (1983).

DAVID, CITY OF.

1. Bethlehem of Judah was occasionally called "the city of David" (Luke 2:4, 11) because David grew up as a shepherd boy there.

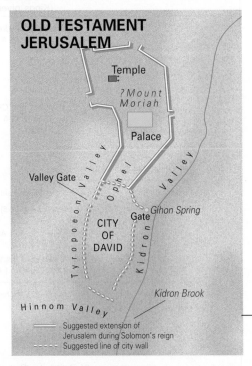

OLD TESTAMENT JERUSALEM

Temple

?Mount Moriah

Palace

Valley Gate

Ophel

Tyropoeon Valley

Kidron Valley

Gihon Spring

Gate

CITY OF DAVID

Kidron Brook

Hinnom Valley

——— Suggested extension of Jerusalem during Solomon's reign

- - - - Suggested line of city wall

2. The ancient portion of the city of Jerusalem, that eastern hill inhabited by the Jebusites before it was conquered by David, was also called "the city of David." David's account of the capture of "the stronghold of Zion, that is the city of David," is recounted in 2 Sam. 5:6-8 and 1 Chron. 11:4-8. Situated on a plateau of commanding height, 2,500 feet above the Mediterranean and 3,800 feet above the Dead Sea, the Jebusite fortress was enclosed by natural rock for defense. Its stout walls, gates, and towers were considered impregnable. So secure did the native Jebusite defenders consider themselves that they taunted David and the Israelite besiegers with the words: " 'You shall not come in here, but the blind and lame

shall turn you away'; thinking, 'David cannot enter here' " (2 Sam. 5:6). Despite its supposed impregnability, David captured the fortress, most likely by ascending the stout walls with a grappling hook, and when the citadel was stormed he said, "Whoever would strike the Jebusites, let him reach the lame and the blind, who are hated by David's soul" (5:8).

The ancient water system of Jerusalem is now well known. The fifty-foot-high watercourse ("Warren's Shaft") has been uncovered as the result of the excavations of the Palestine Exploration Fund, revealing that the inhabitants of the city (c. 2000 B.C.) had made a rock-cut passage, similar to that at Gezer and at Megiddo, to enable them to secure water from the Gihon spring without having to go outside the city walls. From the cave into which the Gihon spring entered, a horizontal tunnel had been driven back into the hill some thirty-six feet W and twenty-five feet N. This conduit conducted the water into an old cave that served as a reservoir. Running up from that was a vertical tunnel at the upper end of which the women could stand to lower their jugs to get water. The Jebusite bastion with its twenty-foot-thick wall has been verified by British archaeologists. Thus the city of David overlooks the Kidron and Hinnom valleys. David apparently did little to beautify the Jebusite city. Solomon, however, adorned it with magnificent buildings and made a worthy site of the Hebrew capital.

M.F.U.

BIBLIOGRAPHY: J. Simons, *Jerusalem in the Old Testament* (1952); M. Avi-Yonah, *Jerusalem* (1960); J. Jeremias, *Jerusalem in the Time of Jesus* (1967); N. Avigad, *Discovering Jerusalem* (1983), pp. 24-29, 54-55, 77.

DAWN (Heb. *bōqer*).
  Figurative. Dawn is illustrative of the glory of the church (Song of Sol. 6:10); the love of God is compared to the breaking of the day; the dawn (Isa. 58:8); the wings of the dawn is figurative of rapid movement (Ps. 139:9). In the expression "as the dawn is spread over the mountains" (Joel 2:2), the prophet refers to the bright glimmer or splendor that is seen in the sky as a swarm of locusts approaches; from the reflection of the sun's rays on their wings (K. & D.; *Com.*, ad loc.). *See also* Morning; Time.

DAY. *See* Time.

DAY OF ATONEMENT. *See* Festivals.

DAY OF CHRIST. This is the period connected with reward and blessing of saints at the coming of Christ for His own. The expression occurs in 1 Cor. 1:8; 5:5; 2 Cor. 1:14; Phil. 1:6, 10; 2:16. In 2 Thess. 2:2 the KJV has the day of Christ incorrectly for the Day of the Lord. The day of Christ is not the Day of the Lord. The latter is connected with earth judgments (Rev. 4:1–19:16), which will come after the out-taking of the church, the Body of Christ, and its glorification and judg-

ment for works at the judgment seat of Christ. The Day of the Lord (Isa. 2:12; Rev. 19:11-21) cannot occur until after the church is completed (2 Thess. 2:2-12).   M.F.U.

DAY OF JUDGMENT. *See* Judgment.

DAY OF THE LORD. This is the protracted period commencing with the second advent of Christ in glory and ending with the cleansing of the heavens and the earth by fire preparatory to the new heavens and the new earth of the eternal state (Isa. 65:17-19; 66:22; 2 Thess. 2:2; 2 Pet. 3:13; Rev. 21:1). The Day of the Lord as a visible manifestation of Christ upon the earth is to be distinguished from the day of Christ. The latter is connected with the glorification of the saints and their reward in heaven prior to their return with Christ to inaugurate the Day of the Lord. The Day of the Lord thus comprehends specifically the closing phase of the Tribulation and extends through the millennial kingdom. Apocalyptic judgments (Rev. 4:1–19:6) precede and introduce the Day of the Lord.   M.F.U.

DAY'S JOURNEY. *See* Metrology: Linear Measurements.

DAYSMAN (Heb. *yākaḥ*, to "set right"). An umpire or arbitrator (Job 9:33); an old English word derived from *day*, in the specific sense of a day fixed for a trial. The meaning seems to be that of someone to compose our differences, the laying on of whose hand expresses power to judge between the two persons. The NIV thus renders, "someone to arbitrate." There might be one on a level with Job, the one party, but Job knew of none on a level with the Almighty, the other party (1 Sam. 2:25). Such a mediator we have in Jesus Christ (1 Tim. 2:5).

DAYSPRING (Heb. *shahar*, Job 38:12, KJV; Gk. *anatolē*, Luke 1:78, KJV). The NIV translates "dawn" and "rising sun" respectively. The first streak of daylight, the dawn; and so the early revelation of God in Christ to the soul.

DAYSTAR (Gk. *phōsphoros*, "light-bearing"; Lat. *Lucifer*). The KJV rendering of "morning star," the planet Venus (2 Pet. 1:19). The meaning of the passage is that the prophets were like a *lamp*, but Christ Himself is the light of dawn, heralded by the "morning star" (Rev. 2:28; 22:16).

DEACON (Gk. *diakonos*, of uncertain origin). One who executes the commands of another, a servant.
  In a General Sense. The term is applied to the "servant" of a king (Matt. 22:13); ministers (Rom. 13:4; lit., "deacons of God," i.e., those through whom God carries out His administration on earth); Paul and other apostles (1 Cor. 3:5; 2 Cor. 6:4; 1 Thess. 3:2). As teachers of the Christian religion are called "servants of Christ"

in 2 Cor. 11:23; Col. 1:7; 1 Tim. 4:6, Christ is called the "servant [lit., "deacon," Rom. 15:8] to the circumcision," as devoting Himself to the salvation of the Jews. In addition to this general use of the word it was given a more specific meaning:

Officer of the Church. In the NT, deacons, or helpers, appear first in the church at Jerusalem. The Hellenistic Christians complained that their widows were neglected in favor of the Hebrew Christians "in the daily serving of food" (Acts 6:1). This was a natural consequence of the rapid growth of the society and of the apostles' having more than they could properly attend to. Upon the recommendation of the apostles "seven men of good reputation, full of the Spirit and of wisdom" were selected and set apart by prayer and laying on of hands. Deacons primarily were assigned the duty of ministering to the poor and the oversight of temporal affairs of the Christian societies, yet retaining, as in the case of Stephen and Philip, the right to teach and baptize. The qualifications for this office, as enumerated by Paul (1 Tim. 3:8-13), were of a nature to fit them for mingling with the church in most familiar relations, to ascertain and relieve the wants of the poorer members with delicacy, and freedom from temptation to avaricious greed. On offering themselves for their work, deacons were to be subject to a strict scrutiny (3:10).

In the Early Church. A difference of opinion respecting the function of deacons prevailed in the early church. Some contended that *no* spiritual function had been assigned them (Council of Constantinople, Can. 18), whereas Ignatius styles them "ministers of the mysteries of Christ." Tertullian classes them with bishops and presbyters as guides and leaders to the laity. They evidently occupied the position of assistants to the higher clergy, exercising the spiritual functions or not, according to the sentiment of the age or wish of those whom they assisted. The deacons, also called "Levites," received a different ordination from the presbyters, both as to form and the power it conferred; for in the ordination of a presbyter the presbyters who were present were required to join in the imposition of hands with the bishop, but the ordination of a deacon might be performed by the bishop alone.

The Duties of the Deacon. The duties of the deacon included: (1) To assist the bishop and presbyter in the service of the sanctuary, especially to care for utensils, etc., of the holy table. (2) In the administration of the Eucharist, to hand the elements to the people but not to consecrate the elements. (3) To administer baptism. (4) To receive the offerings of the people. (5) Sometimes, as the bishop's special delegates, to give to the penitents the solemn imposition of hands, the sign of reconciliation. (6) To teach and catechize the catechumens. (7) In the absence of bishop and presbyter to suspend the inferior

clergy. In addition there were many minor duties. Deacons often stood in close relations with the bishop and not infrequently looked upon ordination to the presbyterates as a degradation. The number of deacons varied with the wants of the individual church. The qualifications of a deacon were the same as those required for bishops and presbyters (3:1-13).

In the Modern Church. Today deacons are found as a distinct order of the clergy in the Roman Catholic, Church of England, Episcopal, Methodist Episcopal, and German Protestant churches. For the most part, their duties are the same and consist of helping the clergy in higher orders. In the Presbyterian and Congregational churches they are laymen who care for the poor, attend to the temporal affairs of the church, and act as spiritual helpers to the minister (see Schaff, *Hist. Christ. Ch.,* 1:135; Hurst, *Hist. Christ. Ch.,* p. 25; McClintock and Strong, *Cyclopedia*).

BIBLIOGRAPHY: J. McCord and T. H. L. Parker, *Service in Christ* (1966).

DEACONESSES. Female helpers who had the care of the poor and the sick among the women of the church. This office was needed because of the rigid separation of the sexes in that day. Paul mentions Phoebe as a deaconess of the church of Cenchrea, and it seems probable that Tryphaena, Tryphosa, and Persis, whom he commends for labor in the Lord, were deaconesses (Rom. 16:1, 12).

In the Early Church. In the early church the apostolic constitution distinguished "deaconesses" from "widows" and "virgins" and prescribed their duties. The office of deaconess in the Eastern church continued down to the twelfth century. It was frequently occupied by the widows of clergymen or the wives of bishops, who were obliged to forgo the married state to enter upon their sacred office.

Qualifications. Piety, discretion, and experience were in any case the indispensable prerequisites in candidates. During the first two centuries the church more carefully heeded the advice of Paul that the deaconess should have been the wife of one husband and that the church should admit to the office only those who had been thoroughly tested by previous trusts, having provided hospitality to strangers, washed the saints' feet, relieved the afflicted, diligently followed every good work, etc. (1 Tim. 5:10). But at a later period there was more laxity, and younger and more inexperienced women were admitted.

Ordination. The question of their ordination has been much debated. They were inducted into office by the imposition of hands; of that there is abundant proof. Such a practice, however, would not necessarily imply their right to fulfill the sacred functions of the ministry.

Duties. The need of such helpers arose from

the customs and usages of the ancient world, which forbade the intimate association of the sexes in public assemblies. They were to instruct the female catechumens, to assist in the baptism of women, to anoint with holy oil, to minister to believers who were languishing in prison, to care for the women who were in sickness or distress, and sometimes to act as doorkeepers in the churches. It is plain that the deaconesses had other duties than those of keepers of the entrances of the church appointed for women, or even as assistants in baptism or instructors of candidates; they were employed in those works of charity and relief where heathen public opinion would not permit the presence of the deacons.

BIBLIOGRAPHY: C. C. Ryrie, *The Role of Women in the Church* (1972); S. Stephens, *A New Testament View of Women* (1980).

DEAD, BAPTISM FOR THE. *See* Baptism.

DEAD, THE.

Egyptian. The great care of the Egyptians was directed to their condition after death. They expected to be received into the company of that being who represented divine goodness, if pronounced worthy at the great judgment day, and to be called by his name was the fulfillment of all their wishes. The dead were all equal in rank —king and peasant, the humblest and the hero. Virtue was the basis of admission into the land of the blessed, and it brought reunion with the deity. The body was bound up so as to resemble the mysterious ruler of Amenti (Hades); it bore some of the emblems peculiar to him. And bread, in a form that belonged exclusively to the gods, was given to the deceased in token of his having assumed the character of that deity.

Burial services were performed by the priests (of the grade who wore the leopard skin) at the expense of the family. If the sons or relations were of the priestly order they could officiate, and the members of the family had permission to be present. The ceremonies consisted of a sacrifice (incense and libation being also presented) and a prayer. These continued at intervals as long as the family paid for them. The body after *embalming* (which see) was frequently kept in the house, sometimes for months, in order to gratify the desire to have those who were beloved in life as near as possible after death. The mummy was kept in a movable wooden closet, drawn on a sledge to and from the altar, before which frequent ceremonies were observed. It was during this interval that the feasts were held in honor of the dead. Sometimes the mummy was kept in the house because the family did not own a burial plot or was denied the rites of burial on account of accusations brought against or debt contracted by the dead or his sons. That was considered a great disgrace, only to be removed by the payment of the debt, liberal donations in the service of religion, or the influential prayers of the

priests. The form of the ritual read by the priest in pronouncing the acquittal of the dead was preserved in the tombs, usually at the entrance passage. In this ritual the deceased was made to enumerate all the sins forbidden by the Egyptian law and to assert his innocence of each, persons of every rank being subjected to the ordeal. Every large city, as Thebes, Memphis, and some others, had its lake where the ceremonies were practiced. The Egyptians did not permit the extremes of degradation to be offered to the dead that the Jews sometimes allowed, and the body of a malefactor, though excluded from the precincts of the necropolis, was not refused to his friends for burial.

Hebrew. Immediately when life departed it was the duty of a friend or son to close the eyes of the dead (Gen. 46:4) and to kiss the face (50:1). The body was washed, wrapped in a linen cloth (Matt. 27:59; etc.), or the limbs separately wound with strips of linen (John 11:44), placed in a coffin (Luke 7:14), and, if not buried immediately, laid out in an upper room (2 Kings 4:21; Acts 9:37).

The Embalming. The embalming of the dead took place after the Egyptian fashion in the case of Jacob and Joseph (Gen. 50:2, 26) but only imitated the rich or distinguished by anointing the dead with costly oil (John 12:7) and wrapping them in linen with spices, especially myrrh and aloes (John 19:39-40).

The Burning of Bodies. The burning of bodies occurred to secure them from mutilation (1 Sam. 31:12), in which case the bones were afterward buried (v. 13); in times of war, where the multitude of deaths made burial impossible (Amos 6:10); or as a punishment inflicted on great criminals (Lev. 20:14; 21:9). The making of "a very great fire," usual when kings were buried (2 Chron. 16:14; 21:19; Jer. 34:5), was a consuming of sweet-scented substances in honor of the dead. On high state occasions the vessels, bed, and furniture used by the deceased were burned also. Such was probably the "very great fire" made for Asa. If a king was unpopular or died disgraced (2 Chron. 21:19) the practice was not observed.

Funeral and Burial. To remain unburied was considered the greatest indignity that could befall the dead (1 Kings 13:22; 16:4; Jer. 7:33; etc.) because the corpse soon became the prey of wild beasts (2 Kings 9:35). The law ordered that criminals should be buried on the day of execution (Deut. 21:23; Josh. 8:29).

The speedy burial of the dead did not prevail in ancient times (Gen. 23:2) but arose when the law made dead bodies a cause of uncleanness (Num. 19:11-19; cf. Acts 5:6, 10).

To bury the dead was a special work of affection (Tobit 1:21; 2:8), an imperative duty of sons toward their parents (Gen. 25:9; 35:29; Matt. 8:21), and next devolved upon relatives and friends (Tobit 14:13). The body was carried to the grave in a coffin, often uncovered, on a bier borne by men, with a retinue of relatives and friends (2 Sam. 3:31; Luke 7:12-14; Acts 5:6, 10). Those prominent because of position, virtue, or good deeds were followed by a vast multitude (Gen. 50:7, 14; 1 Sam. 25:1; 2 Chron. 32:33).

The custom seems to have prevailed, as early as our Lord's life on earth, of having funeral orations at the grave. Even at the funeral of a pauper, women chanted the lament, "Alas, the lion; alas, the hero!" or similar words, whereas great rabbis were wont to bespeak for themselves a warm funeral oration. After the funeral a meal was served (2 Sam. 3:35; Hos. 9:4; Ezek. 24:17), which later became scenes of luxurious display (Josephus *Wars* 2.11). *See* Embalming; Mourning; Tomb.

The word rendered "departed spirit" or "dead" (Job 26:5; Ps. 88:10; Prov. 2:18; 9:18; 21:16; Isa. 14:9; 26:14, 19) is Heb. *rāphā'*, the "relaxed," i.e., those who are bodiless in the state after death.

DEAD SEA, THE. In Scripture it is called the *Salt Sea* (Gen. 14:3; Num. 34:12; etc.), the *Sea of the Arabah* (Deut. 3:17; 4:49; etc.; KJV also renders it *Sea of the Plain*), *Eastern Sea* (Ezek. 47:18; Joel 2:20; Zech. 14:8, KJV, "former"). The name *Dead Sea* has been applied to it since the second century, and it was also called the *Asphalt Sea* by early writers.

The Dead Sea lies in the southern end of the Jordan Valley, occupying the fifty-three deepest miles, with an average breadth of nine to ten miles. The surface is 1,290 feet below the level of the Mediterranean, but the bottom is as deep again; soundings having been taken of 1,300 feet in the NE corner, under the hills of Moab. From there the bed shelves rapidly, till the whole southern end of the sea is only from eight to fourteen feet in depth. These figures vary from year to year. After a rainy season the sea will be as much as fifteen feet deeper and at the southern end more than a mile longer. It is fed by the Jordan and four or five smaller streams, which pour into it millions of tons of water a day. It has no outlet but is relieved by evaporation, often so great as to form a very heavy vapor. This evaporation causes the bitterness of the sea. The streams that feed it are unusually saline, flowing through nitrous soil and fed by sulfurous springs. Chemicals, too, have been found in the waters of the sea, probably introduced by hot springs in the sea bottom. Along the shores are deposits of sulfur and petroleum springs, whereas the surrounding strata are rich in bituminous matter. At the SE end a ridge of rock salt three hundred feet high runs for five miles, and the bed of the sea appears to be covered with salt crystals. "To all these solid ingredients, precipitated and concentrated by the constant evaporation, the Dead Sea owes its extreme bitterness and buoyancy. While the water of the ocean contains from 4 to 6 percent of solids

in solution, the Dead Sea holds from 30 to 33 percent. The water is nauseating to the taste and oily to the touch, leaving upon the skin, when it dries, a thick crust of salt. But it is very brilliant. Its buoyance is so great that it is difficult to sink the limbs deep enough for swimming.

"Its shore is a low beach of gravel, varied by marl or salt marsh. Twice on the west side the mountain cliffs come down to the water's edge, and on the east coast there is a curious peninsula, El-Lisan (or the Tongue), though the shape is more that of a spurred boot. Ancient beaches of the sea are visible all round it, steep banks from five to fifty feet of stained and greasy marl, very friable, with heaps of rubbish at their feet, and crowned with nothing but their own bare, crumbling brows. Behind these terraces of marl the mountains rise precipitous and barren on either coast. To the east the long range of Moab, at a height of two thousand five hundred to three thousand feet above the shore, is broken only by the great valley of the Arnon. . . . On the west coast the hills touch the water at two points, but elsewhere leave between themselves and the sea the shore already described, sometimes one hundred yards in breadth, sometimes one and a half miles. From behind the highest terrace of marl the hills rise precipitously from two thousand to two thousand five hundred feet."

The prophet Ezekiel (Ezek. 47:1-12) gives a wonderful vision of a stream of water issuing from the Temple and with increasing volume sweeping down to the Dead Sea and healing its bitter waters, "teaching that there is nothing too sunken, too useless, too doomed, but by the grace of God it may be redeemed, lifted, and made rich with life" (Smith, *Hist. Geog.,* pp. 499-512).

BIBLIOGRAPHY: G. A. Smith, *Historical Geography of the Holy Land* (1894), pp. 320-34; D. Baly, *Geography of the Bible* (1957), pp. 202-6; id., *Geographical Companion to the Bible* (1963), pp. 13, 21, 47-57; G. A. Turner, *Historical Geography of the Holy Land* (1973), pp. 271-96.

DEAD SEA SCROLLS, THE. Since 1947, when a Bedouin shepherd stumbled upon a cave (about seven miles S of Jericho and a mile from the Dead Sea) containing many scrolls of leather covered with Heb. and Aram. writing, biblical studies have been considerably altered by what have come to be known as the Dead Sea Scrolls.

The Discoveries. When all of the great manuscripts from this cave (known as Cave 1) were assembled in the possession of the state of Israel, they included a complete Isaiah, a partial Isaiah, a Habakkuk commentary (including two chapters of Habakkuk), The Manual of Discipline (rules for members of the religious community living nearby), Thanksgiving Hymns, a Genesis Apocryphon (apocryphal accounts of some of the patriarchs) and Wars of the Sons of Light Against the Sons of Darkness (an account of a real or

The caves at Qumran

spiritual war between some of the Hebrew tribes and tribes E of the Jordan).

This cache of documents stimulated exploration of some 270 caves in the vicinity of Cave 1, with the result that a total of 11 caves were found to contain manuscripts like those discovered in Cave 1. In Cave 2 there were about one hundred fragments of Exodus, Leviticus, Numbers, Deuteronomy, Jeremiah, Job, Psalms, and Ruth. Cave 3 contained the famous copper scrolls, with directions to sites where treasure was located. To date none of this treasure has been found. Cave 4 contained fragments of about one hundred bib-

lical scrolls representing all the OT books except Esther. A fragment of Samuel, dating to the third century B.C. and believed to be the oldest known piece of biblical Heb., came from this cave. Caves 5-10 had a variety of scroll fragments too diverse to list here. Prize pieces from Cave 11 included very fine portions of Psalms and Leviticus. The former included forty-eight psalms, forty-one biblical and seven nonbiblical. It should be noted that biblical manuscripts accounted for only a fraction of the scroll fragments; e.g., some forty thousand fragments of an unknown number of manuscripts turned up in Cave 4.

As all this material came to light, interest centered on the ruin Khirbet Qumran, located on a plateau between Cave 4 and the Dead Sea. G. Lankester Harding, director of the Department of Antiquities for the state of Jordan, and Father R. de Vaux of the Ecole Biblique in Jerusalem dug there in 1951 and 1953 to 1956. Evidently this was the center of the religious community (largely celibate) responsible for copying and assembling the library found in the eleven caves. Many scholars have classified them as Essenes, but not all are convinced of that identification.

The general date of the scrolls is bound up with the date of the community and is established on the basis of at least five lines of evidence: (1) carbon 14 tests on linen wrappings of the scrolls (range of c. 327 B.C.-A.D. 73); (2) coins found in

View from remains of Qumran settlement toward the Dead Sea

the community, dating from 325 B.C. to A.D. 68; (3) pottery chronology for the jars in which the scrolls were found, as well as other pottery found in the community center and the scroll caves; (4) comparative paleography (science of handwriting); (5) linguistic analysis of Aram. documents found in the caves.

One of the Dead Sea Scroll jars

Discoveries in the Qumran area sparked interest in other cave investigation. From caves in the Wadi Murabba'at (twelve miles S of Qumran) in 1952 came fragments in Heb. of five leather scrolls: two of Exodus and one each of Genesis, Deuteronomy, and Isaiah. Bedouin later found in this area an incomplete scroll of the minor prophets and fragments of Genesis, Numbers, and Psalms. At Khirbet Mird in the Wadi en-Nar, six miles SW of Qumran, a Belgian expedition found biblical materials (dating to the fifth through eighth centuries) consisting of portions of Mark, John, and Acts in Gk. and Joshua, Luke, John, Acts, and Colossians in Syr. In 1960 an Israeli team found Heb. fragments of Pss. 15 and 16, Ex. 13, and Num. 20 in caves in the Nahal Hever gorge, about three miles S of En-gedi. They also found a considerable collection of Bar Kochba materials there. Then at Masada, Yigael Yadin found the following first-century A.D. materials: Pss. 81-85 and 150, fragments of Genesis, Lev. 8-12, Deuteronomy, and Ezekiel.

The Significance of the Dead Sea Scrolls. The big question yet to be answered is what all the magnificent discoveries near the Dead Sea have done for biblical studies. In the first place, they pushed the history of the Heb. text back a thousand years. Before the discovery of these texts, the oldest Heb. manuscript of any length dated to the ninth century A.D. The Isaiah manuscript and other materials from Qumran dated to the second century B.C. or earlier. Second, the Dead Sea Scrolls have thrown much light on the meanings of individual words often not clearly understood from their OT usage. Third, some higher critical views have been brought into question by the scroll discoveries. For example, the supposed second-century date for the composition of Daniel is difficult to support when a Dead Sea manuscript of Daniel dates to about 120 B.C. Likewise, a second- or first-century B.C. date for the composition of Ecclesiastes can hardly be maintained when part of Ecclesiastes, dating about 175 to 150 B.C., is produced from Cave 4. Moreover, the Dead Sea Scrolls do not support the existence of a deutero- or trito-Isaiah, at least during the second century B.C. The two Isaiah manuscripts from Cave 1 treat the book as a unit. Fourth, the Dead Sea Scrolls confirm the accuracy of the OT text. The new information shows that there were three or four families of texts, of which the Masoretic, or traditional Heb., text was one. But even though the Masoretic family of texts had to compete with the other textual traditions, it did not greatly diverge from them in most OT books, and the differences have a bearing only on minor points. Probably it is reasonably correct to say that there is at least 95 percent agreement between the various biblical texts found near the Dead Sea and the OT we have had all along. Most of the variations are minor, and none of the doctrines has been put in jeopardy. The Dead Sea Scrolls reveal a miracle of preservation of the text in transmission. In fact, when the *Revised Standard Version* translation committee was preparing that new version, they finally decided to adopt only thirteen improvements on the MT of Isaiah based on the complete Isaiah manuscript from Cave 1. Later Millar Burrows, a member of the committee, concluded that only eight of the changes were warranted. Last, the Dead Sea Scrolls demonstrate that the contents of John's gospel reflect the authentic Jewish background of John the Baptist and Jesus and the writer, rather than an alleged Hellenistic or later Gnostic orientation.   H.F.V.

BIBLIOGRAPHY: C. Rabin, *The Zadokite Documents* (1952); H. H. Rowley, *The Zadokite Fragments and the Dead Sea Scrolls;* M. Burrows, *The Dead Sea Scrolls* (1955); G. Vermes, *Discoveries in the Judean Desert* (1956); T. H. Gaster, *The Scriptures of the Dead Sea Sect* (1957); A. Y. Samuel, *The Treasures of Qumran* (1957); M. Burrows, *More Light on the Dead Sea Scrolls* (1958); F. M. Cross, *Ancient Library of Qumran* (1958);

W. S. LaSor, *Bibliography of the Dead Sea Scrolls, 1948-1957* (1958); J. T. Milik, *Ten Years of Discovery in the Wilderness of Judaea* (1959); J. M. Allegro, *The Treasure of the Copper Scroll* (1960); R. K. Harrison, *The Dead Sea Scrolls* (1961); A. Dupont-Sommer, *The Essene Writings from Qumram* (1962); G. Vermes, *The Dead Sea Scrolls in English* (1962); G. R. Driver, *The Judaean Scrolls* (1965); J. de Waard, ed., *A Comparative Study of the Old Testament Text in the Dead Sea Scrolls and in the New Testament* (1966); M. Black, *The Scrolls and Christian Origins* (1969); J. R. Rosenbloom, *The Dead Sea Isaiah Scroll* (1970); B. Jongeling, *Classified Bibliography of the Finds of the Desert of Judah, 1958-1969* (1971); R. de Vaux, *Archaeology and the Dead Sea Scrolls* (1973); J. A. Fitzmeyer, *The Dead Sea Scrolls: Major Publications and Tools for Study* (1975); G. Vermes, *The Dead Sea Scrolls: Qumran in Perspective* (1977); J. C. Trever, *The Dead Sea Scrolls: A Personal Account* (1978).

DEAF (Heb. *ḥērēsh;* Gk. *kōphos,* "blunted"). Moses protected the deaf by a special statute. "You shall not curse a deaf man" (Lev. 19:14). This was because the deaf could not hear and were therefore unable to defend themselves.

Figurative. Deafness is symbolic of inattentiveness or inability (Isa. 29:18; 35:5; Matt. 11:5; etc.).

DEAL. *See* Metrology.

DEARTH (Heb. *rā'āb,* "hunger"; Gk. *limos,* "scarcity"). KJV rendering of "famine" (Ruth 1:1; etc.). *See* Famine.

DEATH. A term that, in its application to the lower orders of living things, as animals and plants, denotes the extinction of vital functions, so that their renewal is impossible. With reference to human beings the term is variously defined according to the view held of human nature and life. The answer to the question, What is death? depends upon the answer given in the first place to the question, What is man? *See* Immortality.

Scripture Doctrine. The general teaching of the Scriptures is that man is not only a physical but also a spiritual being; accordingly, death is not the end of human existence, but a change of place or conditions in which conscious existence continues. (1) The doctrine of the future life is less emphatically taught in the OT than in the NT. The OT Scriptures, however, frequently refer to death in terms harmonious with that doctrine (Eccles. 12:7; 2 Sam. 12:23; Ps. 73:24; Job 14:14; Isa. 28:12). (2) In the NT this dark subject receives special illumination. In many cases essentially the same forms of representation are employed. Death is "a departure," a "being absent from the body," an "unclothing," a "sleep," but with all is the clear and strong announcement that Christ "brought life and immortality to light through the gospel" (2 Cor. 5:1-4; John 11:13; 2 Tim. 1:10; 4:6-7; etc.). (3) Death as a human experience, according to the Scriptures, is the result and punishment of sin. "The wages of sin is death." And though the word is often used in a spiritual sense to denote the ruin wrought in man's spiritual nature by sin, yet in the ordinary physical sense of the word, death is declared to have come upon the human race in consequence of sin. No such declaration is made as to the death of lower creatures (Gen. 2:17; 3:19; Rom. 5:12; 6:23; James 1:15). (4) A principal part of Christ's redemptive work is the abolishment of death. This is seen in part in man's present state, in the salvation that Christ effects from sin, which is "the sting of death," and in the taking away of the fear of death from true believers. The complete work of Christ in this respect will appear in the resurrection (2 Tim. 1:10; 1 Cor. 15:22, 56-57; Heb. 2:14-15).

Man and Lower Creatures. The Scriptures make a deep distinction between the death of human beings and that of irrational creatures. For the latter it is the natural end of the existence; for the former it is an unnatural experience to which they are reduced because of sin, which is also unnatural. Man was not created to die.

The Scriptures nowhere affirm that death did not prevail over the lower creatures before the Fall of man. Thus upon this point there is no conflict between the Scriptures and geology.

It does not follow, because man was created immortal, that his permanent abiding place was to be this world. The OT Scriptures give two examples of men, Enoch and Elijah, who passed into the other world but "did not see death." (See Martensen's *Christ. Dogm.,* Watson's *Institutes,* Pope's *Compend. Christ. Theol.,* Laidlaw's *Bible Doctrine Concerning Man.*)   E.MCC.

BIBLIOGRAPHY: L. A. Muirhead, *The Terms Life and Death in the Old and New Testament* (1908); R. A. S. Macalister, *The Philistines: Their History and Civilization* (1914); W. M. F. Petrie, *Social Life in Ancient Egypt* (1932); L. L. Morris, *The Wages of Sin* (1955); G. Murray, *Five Stages of Greek Religion* (1955); L. Boettner, *Immortality* (1958); T. C. Vriezen, *Outline of Old Testament Theology* (1958); R. Summers, *The Life Beyond* (1959); R. Martin-Achard, *From Death to Life: A Study of the Development of the Doctrine of the Resurrection in the Old Testament* (1960); L. L. Morris, *The Biblical Doctrine of Judgement* (1960); A. H. Gardiner, *Egypt of the Pharaohs* (1961); S. N. Kramer, *The Sumerians: Their History, Culture and Character* (1963); R. H. Barrow, *The Romans* (1964); R. H. Charles, *Eschatology: Hebrew, Jewish, and Christian* (1964); H. D. F. Kitto, *The Greeks* (1964); G. L. Dickinson, *The Greek View of Life* (1966); J. Carcopino, *Daily Life in Ancient Rome* (1966); J. A. Motyer, *After Death: A Sure and Certain Hope?* (1966); H. Thielicke, *Death and Life* (1970).

DEBATE. In the KJV, in addition to the usual meaning of friendly discussion, debate means quarrel, strife; thus, "Ye fast for strife and *debate*" (Isa. 58:4, RV, "contention," Heb. *maṣṣâ*). Among evils of the Gentiles given in the epistle to the Romans (1:29) Paul includes debate; the rendering of Gk. *eris,* "wrangling," "strife" (KJV and NIV).

DE'BIR (de'bîr), or **Kiriath-sepher**.

1. A king of Eglon, one of the five Amorite kings whom Joshua defeated and hanged (Josh. 10:3, 5, 16, 26).

2. A highland city of Judah about a dozen miles SW of Hebron, or about the same distance SE of Lachish. It was conquered by Joshua (Josh. 10:38-40). Later reoccupied, it was retaken by Othniel (15:7, 15, 17). The Canaanites called it Kiriath-sepher ("book town") or Kiriath-sanna (15:15, 49). W. F. Albright and Melvin Grove Kyle identified it as Tell Beit Mirsim and excavated there in 1926, 1928, 1930, and 1932. The site was found to have been occupied about 2200 B.C. and later to have become a Hyksos city with considerable prosperity. Destroyed about 1550, it was rebuilt as a Canaanite city. This in turn was leveled by fire late in the thirteenth century, a destruction believed to have been perpetrated by the Israelites. Several more rebuildings and destructions occurred before the final destruction by Nebuchadnezzar in 586, after which Debir was never rebuilt. Albright's work at the site contributed considerably to the development of pottery chronology. Not all have been convinced that Tell Beit Mirsim was the site of Debir. Some scholars have located it at Khirbet Terrameh, five miles SW of Hebron, and others at Khirbet Rabud, nine miles SW of Hebron.

Scythopolis, one of the towns of Decapolis

3. There was another Debir in Gad (Josh. 13:26) not far from Mahanaim, possibly the same as Lo-debar (2 Sam. 17:27).   M.F.U.; H.F.V.

BIBLIOGRAPHY: W. F. Albright, *Archaeology and Old Testament Study,* ed. D. W. Thomas (1967), pp. 207-20; id., *Encyclopedia of Archaeological Excavations in the Holy Land,* ed. M. Avi-Yonah (1970), 2:567-73.

DEB'ORAH (deb'ō-ra; a "bee").

1. The nurse of Rebekah (Gen. 35:8), whom she accompanied from the house of Bethuel (24:59). She is mentioned by name only on the occasion of her burial under the oak tree of Bethel, named in her honor Alon-bacuth (lit., "oak of weeping," 35:8).

2. A prophetess, "the wife of Lappidoth," who judged Israel (Judg. 4:4) in connection with Barak, about 1120 B.C. After the death of Ehud the children of Israel fell away from the Lord and were given into the hands of "Jabin, king of Canaan, who reigned in Hazor." He oppressed them severely for twenty years.

At this time Deborah, "the prophetess," dwelt under a palm tree (which bore her name) between Ramah and Bethel in the hill country of Ephraim, and there the people came to her for judgment. She sent an inspired message to *Barak* (which see), bidding him assemble ten thousand men of Naphtali and Zebulun at Mt. Tabor, for Jehovah would draw Sisera (Jabin's general) and his host to meet him at the river Kishon and would deliver them into his hand. Barak agreed, but only on the condition that Deborah would accompany him. Deborah consented but assured him that the prize of victory, the defeat of the hostile general, should be taken out of his hand, for Jehovah would sell Sisera into the hand of a woman (Jael). "And the Lord routed Sisera and all his chariots and all his army, with the edge of the sword before Barak." Sisera, taking refuge in the tent of Heber the Kenite, was slain by Heber's wife, Jael. This success was followed up until Jabin was overthrown, and the land had rest for forty years.

This remarkable ode contained in Judg. 5 is a poetic version of the same material contained in prose in chap. 4. It is universally acclaimed an early masterpiece of Heb. poetry. Critics laud it as one of the first songs in Heb. literature. Deborah has been widely acclaimed as its author. It is remarkable for its vividness of imagery, preserved archaisms, and insight into the rude, barbaric life of the twelfth century B.C.

DEBT.

1. The rendering of several Heb. and Gk. words, with the general meaning of something *due.* In the Mosaic law the duty of aiding the poor was strongly emphasized (Deut. 15:7-15; cf. Ps. 37:26 and Matt. 5:42). All loans to fellow Israelites were to be forgiven every seven years (Deut. 15:2), and usury was looked upon with deepest contempt (Prov. 28:8; Ezek. 18:8, 13, 17; etc.). In any case of debt the creditor was expected to manifest the utmost consideration for the debtor, as a brother Israelite. Written notes of obligation were, at least after the period of exile, regularly in vogue (Josephus *Ant.* 16.10.8; *Wars* 2.17.6). The "bonds" mentioned in the parable (Luke 16:6) may have been written on wax-covered tablets, or parchment, from which the numbers might easily be effaced. Of these "bonds" there were two kinds. The most formal, *shetar,* was not signed by the debtor but only by the witnesses, who wrote their names (or marks) immediately

below the lines of the document to prevent fraud. Generally it was further attested by the Sanhedrin of three, and contained the names of creditor and debtor, the amount owed, and the date, together with a clause attaching the property of the debtor. In fact, it was a kind of mortgage. When the debt was paid, the legal obligation was simply returned to the debtor; if paid in part, either a new bond was written or a receipt given. The bond mentioned in the parable was different, being merely an acknowledgment of debt for purchases made and signed only by the debtor, witnesses being dispensed with.

2. The Scripture spelled out regulations respecting debtors. The creditor might secure what was due him by means of a mortgage, pledge, or bondsman. (1) If a pledge was to be taken for a debt the creditor was not allowed to enter the debtor's house and take what he pleased, but was to wait without (Deut. 24:10-11; cf. Job 22:6; 24:7-9). (2) A mill or millstone, or an upper garment, received as a pledge was not to be kept overnight. These appear to be only examples of those things that the debtor could not, without great inconvenience, dispense with (Ex. 22:26-27; Deut. 24:6, 12). (3) A debt could not be exacted during the sabbatic year (Deut. 15:1-15), but at other times the creditor might seize, first, the hereditary land, to be held until the year of jubilee; or, second, the debtor's house, which could be sold in perpetuity unless redeemed within a year (Lev. 25:25-33). Third, the debtor might be sold, with wife and children, as hired servants (not slaves) until the jubilee (25:39-41). (4) A person becoming bondsman or surety was liable in the same way as the original debtor (Prov. 11:15; 17:18).

BIBLIOGRAPHY: R. deVaux, *Ancient Israel: Its Life and Institutions* (1961), pp. 172-73; S. Baron, *A Social and Religious History of the Jews* (1962), 1:161, 195, 261.

DEBTOR. See Debt.

DECALOGUE (Gk. *deka*, "ten"; *logos*, "word"). *See* Ten Commandments.

DECAP'OLIS (Gk. de-kap'o-lis; "ten cities"). A district containing ten cities in the NE part of Galilee, near the Sea of Galilee (Matt. 4:25; Mark 5:20; 7:31).

The cities were Scythopolis, Hippos, Gadara, Pella, Philadelphia, Gerasa, Dion, Canatha, Raphana, and Damascus. Damascus is the only one now entitled to the name of city. They were built originally by the followers of Alexander the Great and rebuilt by the Romans in 65 B.C., by whom they had certain privileges conferred upon them. These were typical Greco-Roman cities with their forums, pagan temples, baths, theaters, hippodromes, and other accoutrements. They were a thorn in the side of the Jews because they introduced nonsupernaturalistic ideas and elements of non-Jewish life-style and architecture into

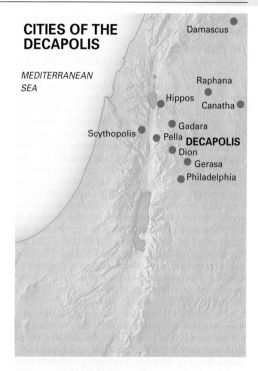

CITIES OF THE DECAPOLIS

MEDITERRANEAN SEA

Damascus

Raphana

Hippos
Canatha

Gadara

Scythopolis   Pella **DECAPOLIS**
Dion

Gerasa

Philadelphia

Palestine during the Roman period. The excavations at Jerash (*Gergesa*, which see) especially illustrate the nature of these cities.   H.F.V.

DECISION, VALLEY OF. A figurative name (Joel 3:14) for the valley of *Jehoshaphat* (which see). The prophet gives in this passage a description of the nations streaming into the valley of judgment, following it with that of the appearance of Jehovah upon Zion in terrible glory as the judge of the nations and as a refuge of His people Israel.

DECK OF BOXWOOD (Heb. *qeresh*, a "plank," usually rendered "board"). Deck of a ship (Ezek. 27:6) made of the tough, heavy wood of the box tree and said to be inlaid with ivory. The KJV renders "bench." The same Heb. term is used (Ex. 26:15-29) for the boards of the *Tabernacle* (which see).

DECREE. The rendering of a number of Heb. and Gk. words, sometimes translated "law," "edict." The enactments of kings in the East were proclaimed publicly by criers (Jer. 34:8-9; Jonah 3:5-7) who are designated in Dan. 3:4; 5:29 by the term, *kārôzā'*, "herald." Messengers, sent for that purpose, carried them to distant provinces, towns, and cities (1 Sam. 11:7; Ezra 1:1; Amos 4:5), and they were publicly announced at the gate of the city or other public place. In Jerusalem they were announced in the Temple, where large numbers of people assembled, for which reason the prophets often uttered their prophecies there.

DE'DAN (dē'dan).

1. A son of Raamah, son of Cush (Gen. 10:7; 1 Chron. 1:9).

2. A son of Jokshan, son of Abraham and Keturah (Gen. 25:3; 1 Chron. 1:32). The usual opinion respecting these founders of tribes is that they first settled among the sons of Cush, wherever these latter may be placed; the second, on the Syrian borders, about the territory of Edom. But Gesenius and Winer have suggested that the name may apply to one tribe; and this may be adopted as probable on the supposition that the descendants of the Keturahite Dedan intermarried with those of the Cushite Dedan, whom the writer places, presumptively, on the borders of the Persian Gulf. The theory of this mixed descent gains weight from the fact that in each case the brother of Dedan is named Sheba. The passages in the Bible in which Dedan is mentioned (besides the genealogies above referred to) are contained in the prophecies of Isaiah (21:13), Jeremiah (25:23; 49:8), and Ezekiel (25:13; 27:15, 20; 38:13) and are in every case obscure. The probable inferences from these mentions of Dedan are (1) that Dedan, son of Raamah, settled on the shores of the Persian Gulf, and his descendants became caravan merchants between that coast and Palestine; (2) and that Jokshan, or a son of Jokshan, by intermarriage with the Cushite Dedan formed a tribe of the same name, which appears to have had its chief settlement in the borders of Edom, and perhaps to have led a pastoral life. A native indication of the name is presumed to exist in the island of *Dadan,* on the borders of the gulf (Smith).

BIBLIOGRAPHY: J. Simons, *The Geographical and Topographical Text of the Old Testament* (1959), p. 21; J. Thompson, *The Bible and Archaeology* (1982), p. 225.

DEDANIM. *See* Dedan.

DEDICATE (Heb. *ḥānak,* to "initiate"; Gk. *qādash,* to "pronounce clean"). A religious service whereby anything is dedicated or consecrated to the service of God; as the dedication of the Tabernacle by Moses (Ex. 40; Num. 7); the altar (Num. 7:84, 88); the Temple, by Solomon (1 Kings 8); the Temple, by the returned exiles (Ezra 6:16-17); the Temple built by Herod (Josephus *Ant.* 15.11.6; *see* Temple). Dedicatory solemnities were observed with respect to cities, walls, gates, and private houses (Deut. 20:5; Ps. 30, title; Neh. 12:27). The custom still lingers in the dedication of churches, "opening" of roads, bridges, etc.

DEDICATION, FEAST OF. *See* Festivals.

DEED. *See* Land.

DEEP. The rendering of several Heb. and Gk. words used to denote (1) the grave or abyss (Rom.

10:7; Luke 8:31, KJV); (2) the deepest part of the sea (Pss. 69:15; 107:24, 26); (3) the waters at creation (Gen. 1:2); (4) hell, the place of punishment (Luke 8:31; Rev. 9:1; 11:7, KJV). *See also* Depths.

DEER. *See* Animal Kingdom.

DEFECT. A "blemish" (Heb. *mûm*), and usually so rendered, either *physical* (Lev. 21:17-23; 22:20-21; 2 Sam. 14:25) or *moral* (Deut. 32:5; Job 11:15). The NIV renders the last two passages "to their shame" and "without shame," respectively. *See also* Diseases: Blemish; Disfigured Face.

DEFILE. The rendering of several Heb. and Gk. words, generally meaning uncleanness in a figurative or ceremonial sense. Many blemishes of person and conduct were, under the Mosaic law, considered defilements. Under the gospel moral defilement is specially emphasized (Matt. 15:18; etc.). *See* Uncleanness.

DEGREE (Heb. *ma'ălâ,* a "step"). This term is used of a group of Levites "of the second degree" (1 Chron. 15:18, KJV; NASB and NIV, "rank") in the sense of rank or order of enumeration. David, in the expression "Thou ... hast regarded me according to the standard of a man of high degree" (17:17), seems to mean, "Thou hast visited me in reference to my elevation." In Ps. 62:9 "degree" is evidently used in the sense of condition or rank (cf. NIV, "highborn"), as also in Luke 1:52 and James 1:9 (Gk. *tapeinos,* "depressed, humiliated," *see* KJV). In 1 Tim. 3:13 (Gk. *bathmos*) the meaning is "position" (or "standing," NASB and NIV). In reference to degree as applied to measurement, *see* Dial.

DEGREES, SONG OF. *See* Ascents, Song of.

DEHA'VITES (dē-ha'vīts). Ezra 4:9 only, KJV; RV, "Dehaites;" NIV, "of" (as a relative pronoun construction in "Elamites *of* Susa"). One of the tribes transported by the king of Assyria to "the cities of Samaria" at the time of the captivity of Israel, 721 B.C. As they are named in connection with the Susanchites, or Susianans, and the Elamites, they may be the widely diffused Aryan Daï, or Dahi, mentioned by Herodotus (1.125) among the nomadic tribes of Persia (Smith, *Bib. Dict.,* s.v.).

If Daï were transported by the Assyrians to Samaria it must have been a small detached section of the tribe analogous to the Hittites of S Palestine. The Daoi of Herodotus, the Dahae of Pliny and Virgil, were a warlike and "numerous nomad tribe who wandered over the steppes to the east of the Caspian. Strabo has grouped them with the Sacae and Massagetae as the great Scythian tribes of inner Asia to the north of Bactriana." In the time of Alexander and later they were found around the rivers Oxus and Jaxartes. The name also appears in the vicinity of the Sea of Azof and of the river Danube. But all these places are far beyond the horizon of Assyria, and the Assyrians never mention such a race. On the whole, we are inclined to regard the identification as an interesting suggestion rather than an established fact.   w.h.

DEKAR. See Ben-Dekar.

DELAI'AH (de-lī'a; "freed by Jehovah").

1. One of the sons of Elioenai, a descendant of the royal line from Zerubbabel (1 Chron. 3:24). He probably belongs to the tenth generation before Christ (see Strong's *Harmony of the Gospels,* p. 17), about 300 B.C.

2. The head of the twenty-third division of the priestly order in the arrangement by David (1 Chron. 24:18), about 980 B.C.

3. The "sons of Delaiah" were among those that returned to Zerubbabel from certain parts of the Assyrian dominions but who had lost their genealogical records (Ezra 2:60; Neh. 7:62), 536 B.C.

4. The son of Mehetabel and father of the Shemaiah who advised Nehemiah to escape into the Temple from the threats of Sanballat (Neh. 6:10), 445 B.C.

5. A son of Shemaiah and one of the officials to whom Jeremiah's first roll of prophecy was read (Jer. 36:12). He afterward vainly entreated the king (Jehoiakim) to spare the roll from the flames (v. 25), 606 B.C.

DELI'LAH (de-lī'la; "coquette"). A courtesan who dwelt in the valley of Sorek and was loved by Samson (Judg. 16:4-18), about 1060 B.C. Samson was tricked by her into revealing the secret of his strength and the means by which he might be overcome; she was bribed by the lords of the Philistines, who gave her the large sum of 1,100 pieces of silver for her services, into doing this. She was probably a Philistine and one who used her personal charms for political ends.

BIBLIOGRAPHY: C. E. Macartney, *The Way of a Man with a Maid* (1974); G. Bush, *Notes on Judges* (1981), pp. 205-31; J. M. Lang and T. Kirk, *Studies in the Book of Judges,* 2 vols. in 1 (1983), 2:152-228.

DELUGE. See Flood.

DE'MAS (dē'mas). A companion of the apostle Paul (called by him his fellow worker in Philem. 24; see also Col. 4:14) during his first imprisonment at Rome. At a later period (2 Tim. 4:10) we find him mentioned as having deserted the apostle because he "loved this present world," A.D. 66.

DEME'TRIUS (de-mē'tri-us).

1. A silversmith of Ephesus who made "silver shrines of Artemis" (Acts 19:24), i.e., probably, silver models of the temple or of its chapel, in which, perhaps, a little image of the goddess was placed. These, it seems, were purchased by foreigners who either could not perform their devotions at the temple itself or who, after having

done so, carried them away as memorials or for purposes of worship. Demetrius, becoming alarmed at the progress of the gospel under the preaching of Paul, assembled his fellow-craftsmen and incited a tumult by haranguing them on the danger that threatened the worship of Artemis and, consequently, the profits of their craft. The tumult was quieted by the tact and boldness of the town-clerk, and Paul departed for Macedonia, A.D. (perhaps autumn) 55.

2. A Christian mentioned with commendation in 3 John 12, A.D. about 90. Further than this nothing is known of him.

DEMON (Gk. *daimōn,* and its derivative *daimonion*). Used once in the NT (Acts 17:18, NIV, "foreign gods"; NASB, "deities," *see* marg.) for deity, but usually referring to the ministers of the devil (Luke 4:35; 9:1, 42; John 10:21; etc.); inferior spirit beings, Satan's angels who "did not keep their own domain" (Jude 6; Matt. 25:41; Rev. 12:7, 9). Satan is called the "ruler of the demons" (Matt. 9:34; 12:24; Mark 3:22; Luke 11:15; Gk. *archonti tōn daimoniōn*). Demons are said to enter into the body of a person to vex him with diseases (Matt. 9:33; 17:18; Luke 4:35, 41; 8:30, 32-33; etc.), and a person was believed to be possessed by a demon when he suffered from some exceptionally severe disease (4:33; 8:27) or acted and spoke as though mad (Matt. 11:18; Luke 7:33; John 7:20; etc.). According to a Jewish opinion that passed over to the Christians, demons are the gods of the Gentiles and the authors of idolatry. Paul, teaching that the gods of the Gentiles are a fiction (1 Cor. 8:10-13), makes the beings answering to the heathen conceptions of the gods to be *demons,* to whom he says they really sacrifice (10:20); in 1 Tim. 4:1 deceitful lies are attributed to demons. They are represented as "kept in eternal bonds under darkness for the judgment of the great day" (Jude 6; cf. 2 Pet. 2:4).

BIBLIOGRAPHY: R. C. Thompson, *The Devils and Evil Spirits of Babylonia* (1903); id., *Semitic Magic* (1908); C. H. Kraeling, *Journal of Biblical Literature* 59 (1940): 147-57; E. Langton, *Essentials of Demonology* (1949); M. F. Unger, *Biblical Demonology* (1957); R. Gilpin, *Demonologia Sacra* (1982).

DEMONIAC (Gk. *daimonizomai,* "to be under the power of a demon," rendered "demon possessed" or "demoniac"). A term frequently used in the NT of one under the influence of a demon. The verb "to be demonized" occurs, in one form or another, seven times in Matthew, four times in Mark, once in Luke, and once in John.

Nature. By some, demoniacs are believed to have been "persons afflicted with especially severe diseases, either bodily or mental (such as paralysis, blindness, deafness, loss of speech, epilepsy, melancholy, insanity, etc.), whose bodies, in the opinion of the Jews, demons had entered." But the evidence points to actual possession by spirits. "The demonized were incapable of separating their own consciousness and ideas from the influence of the demon, their own identity being merged, and to that extent lost, in that of their tormentors. In this respect the demonized state was also kindred to madness" (Edersheim, *Life of Jesus*, 1:608).

The evangelists constantly distinguish between demonic possession and all forms of mere disease, although sometimes they occurred together. Thus, Christ "cast out the spirits . . . and healed all who were ill" (Matt. 8:16); they "brought to Him all who were ill . . . demoniacs, epileptics, paralytics" (4:24); "they began bringing to Him all who were ill and those who were demon-possessed" (Mark 1:32; cf. v. 34). Matthew (9:32-33) keeps the possession distinct from the dumbness when he writes, "A dumb man, demon-possessed." Jesus called His disciples "together, and gave them power and authority over all the demons, and to heal diseases" (Luke 9:1; cf. Matt. 10:1). In Mark 6:13 they "were casting out many demons and were anointing with oil many sick people and healing them" (cf. 3:15; Luke 6:17-18).

The evangelists constantly assert that the actions and utterances in demonic possessions were those of the evil spirits. The demons are the actual *agents* in the cases. There are many statements indicating this: "The unclean spirits . . . would fall down before Him and cry out, saying," etc. (Mark 3:11); "the demons began to entreat Him" (Matt. 8:31); "and throwing him into convulsions, the unclean spirit cried out with a loud voice, and came out of him" (Mark 1:26; Luke 4:35). Of a similar tenor are Mark 9:20-26; Luke 8:2; 9:42; Acts 5:16.

Some of the facts recorded are not compatible with any theory of mere disease, bodily or mental. One of these facts is found in the case recorded by three evangelists (Matt. 8; Mark 5; Luke 8), where the demons asked and received from Christ permission to pass from the demoniac into the herd of swine. Again, there is the habitual assertion of Christ's divinity by these spirits and our Lord's recognition of the fact, while as yet not only the people but also the disciples did not know who He was, e.g., "I know who You are —the Holy One of God!" (Mark 1:24; Luke 4:34); "What have we to do with You, Son of God?" (Matt. 8:29; cf. Mark 3:11; Luke 4:41). That this was a genuine recognition, and was so understood by our Savior, appears in several places in Scripture, for Mark said (1:34), "He was not permitting the demons to speak, because they knew who He was," and again (3:12), "He earnestly warned them not to make Him known," and in Luke (4:41) we read, "And rebuking them, He would not allow them to speak, because they knew Him to be the Christ." Epilepsy, lunacy, and insanity do not meet these several facts. Alford calls attention to a sort of double consciousness indicated in some of these cases, the utterance seeming to come at times from the man and not from the evil spirit. In Acts 19:13-17 we find a distinction between "the evil spirit" and "the man, in whom was the evil spirit," who leaped on the sons of Sceva and overcame them.

Jesus treated cases of demonic possession as realities. He is not only described as "rebuking," "commanding," and "casting out" the unclean spirits, but His direct addresses to them are recorded. Thus in Mark 5:8-12 and Matt. 8:28-32 Jesus addresses the demons who are called "Legion," commanding them to leave and finally granting them permission to enter a nearby herd of swine. Again (Mark 1:25; Luke 4:35), He directly addressed the unclean spirit: "Be quiet, and come out of him!" Was this all a show and a pretense on His part? He went further yet, for He deliberately argued with the Jews on the assumption of the reality of demonic possession, affirming that His casting out demons by the Spirit of God proved that the kingdom of God had come to them (Matt. 12:23-28; Luke 11:14-26). Questioning their inability to cast out an evil spirit, Jesus told the disciples, "This kind cannot come out by anything but prayer" (Mark 9:29). When the seventy returned with joy and said to him, "Lord, even the demons are subject to us in Your name," His answer was to the same effect: "I was watching Satan fall from heaven like lightning" (Luke 10:17-18). We are further informed (Mark 3:14-15) that in the solemn act of calling and appointing the apostles "He appointed twelve, that they might be with Him, and that He might send them out to preach, and to have authority to cast out the demons." Clearly demonism was regarded by our Lord as a stern reality.

Cure. "The New Testament furnishes the fullest details as to the manner in which demoniacs were set free. This was always the same. It consisted neither in magical means nor formulas of exorcism, but always in the word of power which Jesus spake or intrusted to His disciples, and which the demons always obeyed. In one respect those who were demonized exhibited the same phenomenon: they all owned the power of Jesus" (Edersheim, *Life and Times of Jesus*, 1:480).

BIBLIOGRAPHY: A. Edersheim, *Life and Times of Jesus the Messiah* (1956), 1:608.

DEN. The rendering of one Gk. and several Heb. words, meaning a *lair* of wild beasts (Job 37:8; Pss. 104:22; 10:9; where it is rendered "lair" or "cover" [NIV]); a *hole* of a venomous reptile (Isa. 11:8); a *fissure* in the rocks, caves used for hiding (Judg. 6:2; "holes in the ground," Heb. 11:38, NASB; cf. Heb. 11:38; Rev. 6:15, NASB, KJV, NIV), or resort for thieves (Matt. 21:13; Mark 11:17; Luke 19:46). For "Den of Lions" *see* Daniel.

DENARIUS. *See* Metrology: Measures of Value, or Money.

DENIAL.

1. Heb. *kāḥash,* to be "untrue, disown" (Josh. 24:27; Prov. 30:9).

2. Gk. *aparneomai,* to "affirm that one has no acquaintance or connection with another"; of Peter's denying Christ (Matt. 26:34, 69-75); Mark 14:30, 66-72; Luke 22:34, 61); to deny one's self, to lose sight of one's self and one's own interests (Matt. 16:24; Mark 8:34; Luke 9:23).

3. Gk. *arneomai,* to "deny" an assertion (Mark 14:70) or event (Acts 4:16). Used of followers of Jesus who, for fear of death or persecution, deny that Jesus is their master and desert His cause (Matt. 10:33; Luke 12:9; 2 Tim. 2:12); and, on the other hand, of Jesus denying that one as His follower (Matt. 10:33; 2 Tim. 2:12). "Denying" God and Christ is used of those who, by teaching false doctrines and introducing "destructive heresies" apostatized from God and Christ (2 Pet. 2:1; 1 John 2:22-23; Jude 4). Denying "ungodliness and worldly desires" (Titus 2:12) is to abjure, renounce.

4. Self-denial, in the scriptural sense, is the renouncing of all those pleasures, profits, views, connections, or practices that interfere with the true interests of the soul. One's understanding must be denied in preference of divine instruction (Prov. 3:5-6); the will must be denied so far as it opposes the will of God (Eph. 5:17); the affections when they become inordinate (Col. 3:5); the physical nature when opposed to righteousness (Rom. 6:12-13); position (Heb. 11:24-26), monetary gain (Matt. 4:20-22), and friends and relatives (Gen. 12:1) must be renounced if they stand in the way of religion and usefulness. One's own righteousness must be relinquished, so as not to depend upon it (Phil. 3:8-9); even life itself must be laid down if called for in the cause of Christ (Matt. 16:24-25).

DENIAL OF CHRIST. *See* Peter.

DEPRAVITY.
In theology the term *depravity* denotes the sinfulness of man's nature. *See* Sin, Original.

DEPTH. *See* Deep.

DEPTHS.
The expression "the depths of the earth" (Ps. 63:9), also rendered "the lower parts of the earth" (Ezek. 26:20), properly means *valleys;* hence, by extension, *sheol* (which see), or the underworld as the place of the dead. The "lower parts of the earth" ("earth beneath," NIV) in Isa. 44:23 is not hades but the interior of the earth with its caves, pits, and deep abysses. The "depths of the earth" (Ps. 139:15) is also used figuratively for any hidden place, such as the womb. *See also* Deep.

DEPUTY.
The rendering of several words:

1. *Nīṣṣāb* ("appointed"), a *prefect;* one set over others (1 Kings 4:5; etc.; "officer," KJV).

2. *Peḥâ,* Esther 8:9; 9:3; NASB and NIV, "gov-

ernor," the Persian prefect W of the Euphrates; modern form, *pasha.*

3. *Anthupatos,* "in lieu of anyone," a *proconsul.* The emperor Augustus divided the Roman provinces into senatorial and imperial. The former were presided over by the proconsuls appointed by the Senate; the latter were administered by legates of the emperor, sometimes called propraetor (Acts 13:7-8, 12; 18:12).

DER′BE (der′bi).
A small town at the foot of Mt. Taurus, about sixteen miles E of Lystra. Paul and Barnabas gained many converts here, among them possibly Gaius (Acts 14:6, 20; 20:4). Paul passed through the place on his second missionary journey (16:1). Inscriptions found at Kerti Hüyük now fix that mound as the site of ancient Derbe. It is located some fifteen miles NW of Karaman (sixty-six miles by road SE of Konya).

H.F.V.

BIBLIOGRAPHY: M. Ballance, *Anatolian Studies* 7 (1957), pp. 147ff.; W. M. Ramsay, *Cities of St. Paul* (1960), pp. 385ff.

Derbe lay at the foot of Mt. Taurus

DERISION
(Heb. *la‘ag,* to "stammer, imitate" in derision). "Derision" (Job 34:7, NASB; "scorning," KJV and NIV) is blasphemy, and one who "drinks up derision like water" gives himself up to mockery in order to find satisfaction in it (cf. 15:16). It is used of the treatment accorded the godly by their enemies (Pss. 44:13; 79:4; Heb. *qeles,* a "laughingstock").

DESERT.
A term scarcely distinguished in ordinary language from *wilderness,* and in the English Bible the terms are used indiscriminately. In one place we find a Heb. term treated as a proper name and in another translated as a common name.

1. *Midbār,* "pasture"; Ex. 3:1; 5:1; etc. (KJV), usually rendered "wilderness" (Gen. 14:6; etc.), and applied to the country between Palestine and Egypt, including Sinai (Num. 9:5). When used with the article *midbār* denotes the wilderness of Arabia (1 Kings 9:18). Such pastureland in the

East is often an extensive plain or steppe, which during the drought and heat of summer becomes utterly parched and bare, so that the transition from pastureland to desert was quite easy and natural. That the word comprehends both meanings is evident from Ps. 65:12 and Joel 2:22. But in the greater number of passages, the idea of sterility is the prominent one (Gen. 14:6; 16:7; Deut. 11:24; etc.). In the poetical books "desert" is found as the translation of *midbār* (Deut. 32:10; Job 24:5; Jer. 25:24).

2. *'Ārābâ* ("sterility"; rendered either "Arabah" or "desert" in Isaiah, Jeremiah, and Ezekiel; elsewhere usually "plain"). Although this term primarily meant *plain*, it was not in the sense of pasture but rather that of hollow or level ground, and especially the level of the Jordan Valley, extending to the Red Sea (Deut. 1:1; 2:8; Josh. 12:1; hence also "sea of the *Arabah*" or "desert," Deut. 4:49; namely, the Dead Sea). In the East, wide, extended plains are liable to drought and consequent barrenness; hence the Heb. language describes a *plain*, a *desert*, and an *unfruitful waste* by the same word.

3. *Yeshîmôn* ("desolation"; rendered "wilderness," Deut. 32:10; Ps. 68:7; "desert," Ps. 107:4) is used with the definite article apparently to denote the waste tract on both sides of the Dead Sea. In such cases it is treated as a proper name in some translations; thus "the top of Pisgah, which looketh toward *Jeshimon*" (Num. 21:20, KJV; NASB, *see* marg.; the NIV has "wasteland"). This term expresses a greater extent of uncultivated country than do the others (1 Sam. 23:19, 24; Isa. 43:19-20).

4. *Ḥorbâ* ("desolation") is generally applied to what has been made desolate by man or neglect, rendered "ruin" in NASB and NIV (Ezra 9:9; Ps. 109:10). The only passage in which it expresses a natural waste or "desert" is Isa. 48:21, where it refers to Sinai. It is rendered "waste places" (Ps. 102:6; NIV, "ruins"), "deserts" (Isa. 48:21), and "ruins" (Ezek. 13:4). The Gk. word in the NT (*erēmos*) has the general meaning of "solitary," "uninhabited," and is sometimes rendered "wilderness."

Figurative. "Desert" or wilderness is used in Scripture as the symbol of temptation, solitude, and persecution (Isa. 27:10; 33:9); of nations ignorant or neglectful of God (32:15; 35:1); of Israel when she had forsaken God (40:3). The desert was supposed to be inhabited by evil spirits or at least occasionally visited by them ("waterless places," Matt. 12:43; Luke 11:24).

For figurative and nonfigurative use, *see also* Wilderness.

BIBLIOGRAPHY: D. Baly, *The Geography of the Bible* (1957), pp. 63-66, 95-96, 103-5, 252-66; Y. Aharoni, *The Land of the Bible* (1979), p. 35.

DESERT OWL. *See* Animal Kingdom: Owl; Peacocks.

DESIRE OF ALL NATIONS (lit., the "delight" or "costly" of all the nations). An expression (Hag. 2:7) understood by most of the earlier commentators as a title of the Messiah. Heb. *ḥemdâ* ("desire") is the valuable possessions of the heathen, their gold and silver (v. 8). The thought is that the shaking will be followed by this result, or produce this effect, that all that is valuable will come to fill the Temple with glory. The NASB renders "wealth of all nations," and the NIV, "desired of all nations."

DESOLATION, ABOMINATION OF. *See* Abomination.

DESTROYER (Heb. *mashḥît*, an "exterminator," Ex. 12:23). The agent employed in the slaying of the firstborn (Heb. 11:28; Gk. *hō holothrenōn*), the angel or messenger of God (2 Sam. 24:15-16; 2 Kings 19:35; Ps. 78:49; Acts 12:23).

DESTRUCTION (Heb. *'abaddôn*, a "perishing"). A "place of destruction" (Ps. 88:11), or abyss, and nearly equivalent to *Sheol* (which see). In several places (Job 26:6; 31:12; Prov. 15:11) NASB renders simply "Abaddon." *See* Abaddon.

DESTRUCTION, MOUNT OF. A hill near Jerusalem where Solomon established high places for the worship of Ashtoreth, Chemosh, and Milcom, afterward overthrown by Josiah (2 Kings 23:13-14). The NIV describes it as the "Hill of Corruption." Tradition locates it at the rise immediately S of the Mount of Olives.

DETESTABLE. *See* Abomination.

DEU'EL (dū'el; "known of God"). Father of Eliasaph, head of the tribe of Gad at the time of the numbering of the people at Sinai (Num. 1:14; 7:42, 47; 10:20), about 1438 B.C. He is mentioned again (2:14), although the KJV reading of the verse gives Reuel in place of Deuel, reflecting the text of a number of ancient MSS and having to do with the similarity of the Heb. letters *D* and *R*.

DEUTERONOMY, BOOK OF. The last book of the Pentateuch, completing the five books of Moses. The Jews called it "five-fifths of the law." It follows logically after Numbers; Numbers carries the history of the nation Israel to the events in the Plains of Moab to the E of Jericho, and Deuteronomy winds up the Mosaic age with three discourses from Moses just before his death and the entrance of the people into the land of Canaan.

Name. The name comes from the LXX through an inaccurate translation of Deut. 17:18, which is correctly rendered, "This is the copy (or repetition) of the law" (cf. NASB, KJV, NIV). It is apparent that the book is not a "second law" distinct from the law given at Sinai, as the name of the work might suggest. It is simply a partial restatement and exposition of former laws to the new generation that had been reared in the wilderness. The Jewish name of the book is *'Elleh haddevarim,* "These are the words" or simply *Devarim,* "Words." In Jewish tradition it is called *Mishneh Torah,* meaning "repetition" or "copy of the law" (17:18).

Author. In the most explicit terms the book itself asserts its authorship by Moses. "So Moses wrote this law and gave it to the priests, the sons of Levi who carried the ark of the covenant of the Lord, and to all the elders of Israel" (Deut. 31:9). "And it came about, when Moses finished writing the words of this law in a book until they were complete, that Moses commanded the Levites who carried the ark of the covenant of the Lord, saying, 'Take this book of the law and place it beside the ark of the covenant of the Lord your God, that it may remain there as a witness against you' " (31:24-26). No other book of the Pentateuch bears so emphatic a testimony of its Mosaic authorship. It is of unusual interest that critics most dogmatically reject the Mosaic authorship of this book in the face of these clear assertions. Over against these critical claims conservative scholars see ample evidence to maintain the Mosaic authenticity of this book. The general character of the writing, its code of conquest, its exhortatory nature, its plan as a military lawbook of a pilgrim people about to enter Canaan, together with the scope and spirit of the writing are peculiarly suited for the Mosaic era and completely unsuitable for a later age. Moses is mentioned more than forty times in the book, mostly as the authoritative author of the subject matter. The first person predominates. The language purports to come directly from Moses. If Moses is not the actual author, the book can hardly be excused from being a literary forgery, scarcely worthy of canonical Scripture.

Treaty Form. Second millennium B.C. Near Eastern treaties imposed upon a vassal by an overlord or a great king such as a Hittite ruler had a remarkably consistent form: (1) a preamble, identifying the author of the covenant; (2) historical prologue stating previous relations between the two parties (if any), and past benefactions by the overlord; (3) basic and detailed stipulations stating the obligations imposed by the sovereign ruler upon the vassal; (4) deposit of a copy of the covenant in the vassal's most sacred repository; (5) periodic public reading of the covenant by the vassal; (6) witnesses, generally the gods of the countries involved; (7) curses for breaking the covenant; (8) blessings for keeping it; (9) a formal oath of obedience; (10) a solemn ratification ceremony; (11) a formal procedure for acting against rebellious vassals. Covenants coming from first millennium B.C. sources are the same except that they do not have the historical prologue.

The covenant form was Hittite in origin. Not every element has survived in Scripture, but when Exodus, Leviticus, Numbers, and Deuteronomy are put together, one can get an excellent idea of how the treaties worked. As far as Deuteronomy is concerned, it can be analyzed on the basis of the covenant form common in the second millennium B.C.: (1) preamble: Deut. 1:1-5; (2) historical prologue: Deut. 1:6–3:29; (3) stipulations: Deut. 4:5-11 (basic) and 12-26 (detailed); (4) provisions for depositing a copy in a sacred repository: Deut. 31:9, 24-26; (5) provision for periodic public reading: Deut. 31:10-13; (6) identification of the witness: Deut. 31:26 (the law book itself as witness); (7) curses: Deut. 28:15-68; (8) blessings: Deut. 28:1-14; (9) oath of obedience: not specific in Deut., but *see* Ex. 24:7; (10) provision for a ratification ceremony, specified in this case as a covenant-renewal ceremony: Deut. 27:5-7; (11) provision for dealing with rebellious vassals: foreshadowed in Deut. 30:17-19; this is the so-called "controversy" (Heb. *rîb*) procedure; *see* Hos. 4:1; 12:2, and elsewhere.

Critical View of Authorship. Deuteronomy has a central place in higher criticism of the Pentateuch. Rationalists maintain that it was written by an anonymous prophetic writer in the spirit of Moses between 715 and 640 B.C. It is claimed that it was first published in the eighteenth year of King Josiah, to bring about his great religious reformation (2 Kings 22-23). The principal reason assigned for the Josianic date is that the OT books do not give explicit witness to Deuteronomy, especially in the matter of the law of the central sanctuary (Deut. 12:1-7). It is, accordingly, assumed not to have had an existence previously to Josiah's time. But an unbiased view of the Pentateuch reveals that the laws of Deuteronomy were both known and observed, existing in the form of written codified statutes, and made a marked impression on the Israelites from the period of their actual entrance into the land of Canaan. Examples are abundant. The ban concerning Jericho (Josh. 6:17-18) follows Deut. 13:15-17. When Ai was captured, Israel took only "the cattle and the spoil" (Josh. 8:27) in keeping with Deut. 20:14. The body of the king of Ai was taken down from the gibbet before nightfall (Josh. 8:29, cf. Deut. 21:23). The altar on Mt. Ebal (Josh. 8:30-31) recalls Deut. 27:4-6. Many other evidences occur. The law of the central sanctuary, i.e., of worshiping only "at the place which the Lord your God shall choose," was also known in early Israel, as is proved by the fact that the E Jordanic tribes disavowed their memorial when accused by their fellow tribesmen of building an altar of their own (Josh. 22:29, 31; cf. Deut. 12:5). Elkanah went up annually to Shiloh, Israel's early sanctuary (1 Sam. 1:3, 7). After the destruction of the central sanctuary, Samuel sacrificed at Mizpah, Ramah, and Bethlehem, evidently taking advantage of the law of Deut. 12:10-11 because of the time of war. Hezekiah's revival (2 Kings 18:4, 22) is inconceivable without a knowledge of Deuteronomy and its unique law of the central sanctuary. Eighth-century prophets knew the law also. By their unsound views of Deuteronomy the partitionists have been led to discard Mosaic authenticity of the entire Pentateuch and have landed in a quagmire of doubt and uncertainty.

Contents.

I. First Mosaic discourse (1:1–4:43)
II. Second Mosaic discourse (4:44–26:19)
III. Third Mosaic discourse (27:1–30:20)
IV. Historical appendixes (31:1–34:12)
    A. Moses' last words and Joshua's appointment (31:1-30)
    B. Moses' song and exhortation (32:1-47)
    C. Moses' sight of the Promised Land (32:48-52)
    D. Moses' parting blessing (33:1-29)
    E. Death and burial of Moses (34:1-12)

M.F.U.; R.K.H.

BIBLIOGRAPHY: G. T. Manley, *The Book of the Law* (1957); J. Muilenburg, *Vetus Testamentum* 9 (1959); 347ff.; M. G. Kline, *Treaty of the Great King* (1963); D. J. McCarthy, *Treaty and Covenant* (1963); D. R. Hillers, *Treaty-Curses and the Old Testament Prophets* (1964); J. A. Thompson, *Ancient Near Eastern Treaties and the Old Testament* (1964); S. R. Driver, *A Critical and Exegetical Commentary on Deuteronomy,* International Critical Commentary (1965); E. W. Nicholson, *Deuteronomy and Tradition* (1967); R. K. Harrison, *Introduction to the Old Testament* (1969), pp. 635-62; S. J. Schultz, *Deuteronomy: The Gospel of Love* (1971); G. L. Archer, Jr., *Survey of Old Testament Introduction* (1974), pp. 251-62.

DEVIL (Gk. *diabolos,* "accuser").

1. One who slanders another for the purpose of injury, a maligner, e.g., a "malicious gossip" (1 Tim. 3:11; 2 Tim. 3:3; Titus 2:3).

2. "Goat demon" (or "goat idol," NIV) is the rendering of the Heb. *śā'îr,* "hairy" (Lev. 17:7; Isa. 13:21; 34:14, marg.). These were demon spirits that inhabited the desert and whose evil influence was sought to be averted by sacrifice. The Israelites brought this superstition and the idolatry to which it gave rise from Egypt, where goats were worshiped as gods; these were the gods whom the Israelites worshiped in Egypt (Josh. 24:24; Ezek. 20:7; 23:3, 8-9; etc.).

3. In Deut. 32:17 and Ps. 106:37 the term rendered "demon" is "shade" (Heb. *shēd,* "demon") and means an idol, since the Jews regarded idols as demons that caused themselves to be worshiped by men.

4. The greatest of all fallen spirits (Matt. 4:8-11; Rev. 12:9; etc.). This epithet refers to him as the "accuser of the brethren" (12:10). In this role he is granted a certain power of "sifting" carnal believers (Luke 22:31-32; cf. Job 1:6-11; 1 Cor. 5:5; 1 Tim. 1:20). Although this may even involve physical death, Satan's power over the believer is strictly permissive and limited, and believers are kept in faith through the advocacy of Christ

(1 John 2:1). At the commencement of the Great Tribulation, Satan's privilege of access to God as accuser will be terminated (Rev. 12:7-11). At Christ's glorious second advent Satan will be chained for the Millennium (20:2). Finally, he will be loosed for a short time (20:3; 7-8) and will head a final attempt to overthrow God's kingdom. Defeated in this, he will be hurled to his eternal doom in the lake of fire. *See* Satan.

BIBLIOGRAPHY: E. Langton, *Essentials of Demonology* (1949); E. M. Bounds, *Satan: His Personality, Power and Overthrow* (1963); L. S. Chafer, *Satan: His Motives and Methods* (1964); J. D. Pentecost, *Your Adversary the Devil* (1969); E. M. B. Green, *I Believe in Satan's Downfall* (1981); R. Gilpin, *Demonologia Sacra* (1982).

DEVOTED THING. *See* Anathema.

DEW (Heb. *ṭal*). "The dews of Syrian nights are excessive; on many mornings it looks as if there had been heavy rains, and this is the sole slackening of the drought which the land feels from May till October" (Smith, *Hist. Geog.,* p. 65; Judg. 6:38; Song of Sol. 5:2; Dan. 4:15). This partial refreshment of the ground is of great value and would alone explain all the oriental references to the effect of dew. Thus it is coupled as a blessing with rain, or mentioned as a source of fertility (Gen. 27:28; Deut. 33:13; Zech. 8:12), and its withdrawal is considered a curse (2 Sam. 1:21; 1 Kings 17:1; Hag. 1:10).

Figurative. Dew in the Scriptures is a symbol of the beneficent power of God, which quickens, revives, and invigorates the objects of nature when they have been parched by the burning heat of the sun (Prov. 19:12; Hos. 14:5). The silent, irresistible, and rapid descent of dew is used to symbolize the sudden onset of an enemy (2 Sam. 17:12). "Thy youth are to Thee as the dew" (Ps. 110:3) is believed to be a figure of abiding youthful vigor. Dew is a token of exposure in the night (Song of Sol. 5:2; Dan. 4:15; etc.); the symbol of something transient (Hos. 6:4; 13:3); and, from its noiseless descent and refreshing influence, the emblem of brotherly love and harmony (Ps. 133:3).

DIADEM. The rendering of several Heb. words and, in the NASB, one Gk. word.

1. *Ṣānîp,* something wound about the head (Isa. 62:3, lit., "turban"); spoken of as the "turban" of men (Job 29:14), of women (Isa. 3:23), of the high priest (Zech. 3:5), as well as the tiara of a king (Isa. 62:3).

2. *Ṣepîrâ,* circlet (Isa. 28:5), a royal tiara or, "wreath" (NIV).

3. *Miṣnepet* (Ezek. 21:26, KJV), the royal diadem, like *ṣānîp,* but the *turban* (so NASB and NIV) of the high priest, as it is used in every instance in the Pentateuch, from which Ezekiel has taken the word.

4. *Diadēma.* This Gk. word is rendered "crowns" in three passages of the KJV and NIV (Rev. 12:3; 13:1; 19:12), but the NASB correctly

gives "diadem." A *diadem* (*diadēma*) and *crown* (*stephanos*) are distinct from one another. The latter is a crown in the sense of a chaplet, wreath, or garland; the "badge of victory in the games, of civic worth, of military valor, of nuptial joy, of festal gladness." *Diadem* is a crown as the badge of royalty.

What the "diadem" of the Jews was we do not know. That of other nations of antiquity was a band of silk, two inches broad, bound around the head and tied behind, the invention of which is attributed to Liber. Its color was generally white; sometimes, however, it was blue, like that of Darius, and it was sown with pearls or other gems. *See also* Priest, High; Turban.

High Priest's turban or "diadem"

DIAL (Heb. *ma'ălâ,* "step"). Used for the measurement of time, erected by Ahaz (2 Kings 20:9-11; Isa. 38:8) and called the "steps of Ahaz" (KJV; NASB and NIV, "stairway"). As *ma'ălâ* may signify either one of a flight of steps or degree, we might suppose the reference to be a dial plate with a gnomon indicator; but, in the first place, the expression points to an actual succession of steps, that is to say, to an obelisk upon a square or circular elevation ascended by steps, which threw the shadow of its highest point at noon upon the highest steps, and in the morning and evening upon the lowest, either on the one side or the other, so that the obelisk itself served as a gnomon. The step dial of Ahaz may have consisted of twenty steps or more, which measured the time of day by half hours, or even quarters. If the sign was given an hour before sunset, the shadow, by going back ten steps of half an hour each, would return to the point at which it stood at twelve o'clock. When it is stated that "the sun returned" (KJV), this does not mean the sun in the heaven but the sun upon the sundial, upon which the illumined surface moved upward as the shadow retreated, for when the shadow moved back the sun moved back as well. The event is intended to be represented as a miracle,

Ancient Dibon, Jordan

and a miracle it really was (Delitzsch, *Com.,* on Isa. 38:7-8).

DIAMOND, or **ADAMANT.** *See* Mineral Kingdom.

DIANA. *See* Gods, False: Artemis.

DIB'LAH (dib'la). A place mentioned only in Ezek. 6:14, as if situated at one of the extremities of the land of Israel. It is natural to infer that Diblah was in the N. The only name in the N at all like it is Riblah, and the letters *D* and *R* are so much alike in Heb. and so frequently interchanged, owing to the carelessness of copyists, that there is a strong possibility that Riblah is the correct reading.

DIB'LAIM (dib'lā-im; "cakes" [of dried figs?]). The name of the father of Gomer, the wife of Hosea (Hos. 1:3), about 750 B.C.

DIB'LATH. *See* Diblah.

DI'BON (di'bon; "pining").

1. A town on the E side of Jordan, in the rich pastoral country that was taken possession of and rebuilt by the children of Gad (Num. 32:3, 34). From this circumstance it possibly received the name of Dibon-gad. Its first mention is in the ancient fragment of poetry (21:30), and from this it appears to have belonged originally to the Moabites. We find Dibon counted to Reuben in the lists of Joshua (13:9, 17). In the time of Isaiah and Jeremiah, however, it was again in possession of Moab (Isa. 15:2; Jer. 48:18, 22; cf. v. 24). In the same denunciations of Isaiah it appears, probably, under the name of Dimon.

Dibon, capital of the Moabite kingdom, is located about forty miles S of Amman and thirteen miles E of the Dead Sea. Here the famous Moabite Stone was found in 1868. The American Schools of Oriental Research excavated there from 1950 to 1953 and in 1955 and 1956 under the leadership of F. V. Winnett, W. L. Reed, A. D. Tushingham, and W. M. Morton. Excavation has shown that the site was occupied as early as about 3000 B.C. and intermittently until Byzantine and Arab times. During the first three seasons of excavation, attention concentrated on the defenses of the eastern and southeastern edges of the mound. The beautifully built wall stood there from the middle of the ninth century to Nebuchadnezzar's destruction in 582. During the last season of excavation interest centered on the northern gate area, dating to the tenth-eighth centuries. On the summit of the mound stood an official building that may have been a temple or a palace with a royal chapel.

2. One of the towns reinhabited by the men of Judah after the return from captivity (Neh. 11:25). From its mention with Jekabzeel, Moladah, and other towns of the S there can be no doubt that it is identical with *Dimonah* (which see).   H.F.V.

BIBLIOGRAPHY: F. V. Winnett, *Bulletin of the American Schools of Oriental Research* 125 (1952): 7-20; A. D. Tushingham, *BASOR* 133 (1954): 6-26; W. H. Morton, *BASOR* 140 (1955): 4-7; A. H. van Zyl, *The Moabites* (1960); F. V. Winnett and W. L. Reed, *Annual of the American Schools of Oriental Research* 26-27 (1964).

DI'BON-GAD (di'bon-gad). One of the halting places of the Israelites (Num. 33:45-46). It was, no doubt, the same place that is generally called Dibon, no. 1.

DIB'RI (dib'ri; perhaps "eloquent"). A Danite, father of Shelomith, a woman whose son was stoned to death at Moses' command for blaspheming the name of the Lord (Lev. 24:11), 1420 B.C.

DIDRACHM. *See* Metrology: Measures of Value, or Money; and also the article Tribute Money.

DID'YMUS (did'i-mus; "twin"). A surname (John 11:16) of the apostle Thomas.

DIET (Heb. *'ārūḥâ*). The daily "allowance" (so NASB and NIV) of food apportioned by Evil-merodach, king of Babylon, to his royal captive Jehoiachin, king of Judah (Jer. 52:34). *See also* Food.

DIGIT. The digit or finger was a linear measure. *See* Metrology.

DIGNITIES (Gk. plural of *doxa,* "glory"). A KJV term for persons higher in honor (2 Pet. 2:10; Jude 8), probably angels as spiritual beings of preeminent dignity. The NASB translates the Gk. term with the expression "angelic majesties" and gives marginal readings of "glories" and "angelic glories." The NIV renders "celestial beings" in both passages.

DIK'LAH (dik'la). The name of a son of Joktan (Gen. 10:27; 1 Chron. 1:21). His descendants probably settled in Yemen and occupied a portion of it a little to the E of the Hejaz.

DIL'EAN (dil'i-an). A town in the low country of Judah (Josh. 15:38). Probably Tell en Negileh.

DILL. *See* Vegetable Kingdom.

DIM'NAH (dim'na; "dunghill"). A Levitical city in Zebulun (Josh. 21:35). In 1 Chron. 6:77 Rimmono is substituted for it.

DI'MON, THE WATERS OF (di'mon). A stream on the E of the Dead Sea, in the land of Moab, against which Isaiah utters denunciations (Isa. 15:9). Gesenius conjectures that the two names Dimon and Dibon are the same.

DIMO'NAH (di-mō'na). A city in the S of Judah (Josh. 15:22), perhaps the same as Dibon in Neh. 11:25.

DI'NAH (dī'na; "justice"). The daughter of Jacob by Leah (Gen. 30:21) and full sister of Simeon and Levi. While Jacob dwelt in Shechem, Dinah was seduced by Shechem, the son of Hamor, prince of the country (chap. 34). She was probably thirteen to fifteen years of age, the ordinary period of marriage in the East. Shechem proposed to make the usual reparation by paying a sum to the father and marrying her (Deut. 22:28-29), but Jacob declined to negotiate until he had made known the facts to his sons and conferred with them. Hamor proposed a fusion of the two peoples by the establishment of intermarriage and commerce. The sons, bent upon revenge, demanded, as a condition of the proposed union, the circumcision of the Shechemites. They assented, and on the third day, when the men were disabled, Simeon and Levi slew them all and took away their sister. Dinah probably continued unmarried and went with her father into Egypt (Gen. 46:15), about 1950 B.C.

DI'NAITE (dī'na-īt). A name given to a part of the colonists placed in Samaria after it was taken by the Assyrians (Ezra 4:9, KJV; the NIV has "judges"). "They remained under the dominion of Persia, and took part with their fellow-colonists in opposition to the Jews under Artaxerxes, but nothing more is known of them" (Smith, *Bib. Dict.,* s.v.). They may have been the Armenian peoples known as Dayani to the Assyrians.

DINE, DINNER. *See* Eating; Food.

DIN'HABAH (din'haba). A city of Bela, king of Edom (Gen. 36:32; 1 Chron. 1:43). Location uncertain.

DIONY'SIUS THE AREOPAGITE (di-o-nish'i-us the a-rē-o'pa-gīt, Acts 17:19-34). An eminent Athenian converted to Christianity by the preaching of Paul on Mars' Hill. Nothing further is related of him in the NT, but Suidas recounts that he was an Athenian by birth and eminent for his literary attainments, that he studied first at Athens and afterward at Heliopolis, in Egypt. The name of Dionysius has become important in church history from certain writings formerly believed to be his but now known to be spurious and designated as the Pseudo-Dionysian writings.

DIOT'REPHES (dī-ot're-fez; "brought up or nourished by Jove"). A person condemned by the apostle John in his third epistle. Desiring preeminence, he refused to see the letter sent by John, thereby declining to submit to his direction or acknowledge his authority. He circulated malicious slanders against the apostle and exercised an arbitrary and pernicious influence in the church (3 John 9-10).

DISCERNING OF SPIRITS (NASB and NIV, "distinguishing the spirits"). A spiritual gift enjoyed by certain Christians in the apostolic age and enabling them to judge from what spirits the utterances they heard proceeded, whether from the Holy Spirit, human, or demonic spirits, thus preserving the church from misleading influences (1 Cor. 12:10; cf. 1 Cor. 14:29; 1 John 4:1).

DISCHARGE. See Diseases: Issue.

DISCIPLE. This term occurs in the OT as the rendering of Heb. *limmūd,* one "instructed," Isa. 8:16; 50:4; rendered "taught" in 54:13.

In the NT it is the rendering of the Gk. *mathētēs,* "learner," and occurs frequently. The meaning applies to one who professes to have learned certain principles from another and maintains them on that other's authority. It is applied principally to the followers of Jesus (Matt. 5:1; 8:21; etc.); sometimes to those of John the Baptist (9:14) and of the Pharisees (22:16). It is used in a special manner to indicate the twelve (10:1; 11:1; 20:17).

DISCIPLINE. From the Gk. *paideuō,* "to instruct, train, correct." The action of the heavenly Father toward His disobedient child that he should "not be condemned along with the world" (1 Cor. 11:31-32). This correction of the Father of His own offspring (Heb. 12:6) must in no way be connected with condemnation: "There is therefore now no condemnation for those who are in Christ Jesus" (Rom. 8:1); "He who believes in Him is not judged" (John 3:18). A regenerated child of God has the position of a son, stands in the imputed merits of Christ, and cannot come into condemnation. Discipline, therefore, is confined to members of the family, and it may be (1) preventive, as in the case of the apostle Paul, who was given a thorn in the flesh to keep him humble (2 Cor. 12:7-9); (2) corrective, which is the disciplinary moving of the Father against His wayward child for the good of the child; (3) enlarging, the object being to "share His holiness," to bring forth the "fruit of righteousness" (Heb. 12:11; John 15:2); (4) vindicatory, as in the case of Job who vindicated God against the challenge and accusations of Satan that the patriarch did not really love God apart from his family, his possessions, and himself. There is a difference

between disciplining and scourging. The latter represents the divine conquering of the human will that the redeemed life may be completely yielded to God (Rom. 12:1-2; cf. Heb. 12:6).

M.F.U.

BIBLIOGRAPHY: E. Schweitzer, *Leadership and Discipleship* (1960); K. H. Rengstorf, μαθητης, *Theological Dictionary of the New Testament,* ed. G. Kittel (1967), 4:425-61.

DISDAIN (Heb. *bāzâ,* "to tread under foot, to despise"; KJV, "to scorn"). Rendered in Esther 3:6 "[Haman] disdained [NIV, "scorned"] to lay hands on Mordecai alone," and elsewhere "joke" (Job 12:4), "contempt" (Esther 1:17), "careless" (Prov. 19:16), "despise" (Ps. 73:20; Isa. 53:3; Heb. *qālas,* "to despise, refuse"; KJV and NIV, "to scorn"), spoken of Jerusalem's refusing payment for her adulteries, unlike what an ordinary prostitute would do (Ezek. 16:31).

DISEASES. In treating this subject we call attention to the several diseases mentioned in Scripture. Discussion of the treatment of disease is given in a separate article below. Under the latter we introduce medicine, physician, remedies, and so forth.

Ague. See Fever.

Blains. See Boils.

Blemish (Ex. 12:5; 29:1; etc.; Lev. 21:18-21, NASB and NIV, "defect." The rendering of several Heb. words). Any deformity or spot. Such a disfigurement disqualified its possessor from becoming a priest.

Blindness (Heb. *'iwwārôn,* Deut. 28:28). Eye infections are among the most common of all the diseases of Bible lands. Ophthalmia and other destructive diseases prevail to a frightful extent in Egypt. Among the lower classes it has been the exception to see both eyes perfect. A large proportion of the population has lost one eye, and the number of totally blind is excessive. Although the ravages of eye disease are not so frightful in Palestine and Syria, they are sufficiently so to illustrate the frequent (more than sixty) references to blindness in the Bible. The causes are the heat, sunlight, dust, and, most of all, unclean habits, all of which favor the spread of diseases, which often in a single day destroy the eye.

Blood, Flow of. See Issue.

Boils (Heb. *sheḥîn,* Ex. 9:9-10). These are of several kinds: (1) Simple boils, which may be single or come out in large numbers and successive crops (Job 2:7; NIV, "sores"), causing much suffering and some danger to the patient. They consist of a core, which is a gangrenous bit of skin and subcutaneous tissue, surrounded by an angry, inflamed and suppurating nodule, which finally bursts and lets out the core, after which the seat of the boil heals, leaving a permanent scar. (2) Carbuncles. These are large boils, with a number of openings, leading to a considerable mass of dead cellular tissue and giving exit to the discharge of the same. Such was probably Hezekiah's boil (2 Kings 20:7; Isa. 38:21). (3) Malignant pustules. These are due to infections from animals having splenic fever. The virus is carried by insects or in wool or hides or otherwise, and produces a black spot where it enters, surrounded by a dark livid purplish or dusky red zone, with vesicles and a hard area of skin infiltrated with anthrax bacilli. If the focus of the disease is not destroyed the blood is rapidly poisoned, and the patient dies. (4) Probably all skin diseases in which there is suppuration in and beneath the skin would have been included in the generic designation of boils.

Broken Hand, Broken Foot (Lev. 21:19). A disqualification for the priesthood. Clubfoot and clubhand would also disqualify.

Bruises (Isa. 1:6; Jer. 30:12; Nah. 3:19, KJV; NASB often renders "crush"; several Heb. words). Familiar accidents, often far more serious than would be supposed from their external marks.

Canker. See Gangrene.

Cankered. A KJV term rendered "rusted" in the NASB.

Cripple, Crippled. See Lame, Lameness; Maimed.

Crookbacked. See Hunchback.

Discharge (Lev. 15:2). Renders a person unclean. See Issue.

Disfigured Face (Heb. *ḥāram*, to be "blunt," Lev. 21:18). A disqualification for the priesthood.

Dropsy (Gk. *hudrōpikos,* "watery," Luke 14:2). This is a symptom of a number of diseases, mostly of the heart, liver, kidneys, and brain, causing collections of water in the cavities of the body, or on its surface, or in the limbs. It is curable only if the disease causing it is amenable to treatment.

Dwarf. Dwarfs were not allowed in the priesthood (Lev. 21:20).

Dysentery (Gk. *dusenteria,* Acts 28:8). This disease is common in the East and often fatal, not merely by its own violence but by the abscess of the liver that it frequently causes. It is supposed to be the disease of the bowels (2 Chron. 21:15, 19) that afflicted Jehoram.

Eczema. See Scab.

Emerods. See Hemorrhoids.

Fever (Heb. *qaddaḥat,* Lev. 26:16, KJV, "ague"). This doubtless covered all the fevers of the land. They were intermittent, remittent, typhoid, typhus, besides the febrile states accompanying the various inflammations and eruptive diseases such as measles. Malarial fevers were the most characteristic. They prevailed especially in late summer and early autumn. In the former swamps of the Hûleh and the irrigated gardens about the cities malignant types of these fevers attacked those who slept in the area of infection and those who worked in the poisonous atmosphere. Not infrequently patients died in the second or third paroxysm of such fevers. When they did not die from the violence of the poison they often dragged on through weary months of constantly recurring attacks and suffered from congestion or abscess of the liver or spleen and other internal disorders.

Flat Nose. See Disfigured Face.

Flow of Blood. See Issue.

Flux. See Dysentery.

Gangrene (2 Tim. 2:17, KJV, "canker"). Mortification of any part of the body. The reference is probably to the variety known as senile gangrene. This disease begins at the end of a toe or finger as a blackish spot that gradually spreads over the rest of the toe, then to the other toes, the foot, and leg, until at last the patient dies of blood poisoning. Even early and free amputation generally fails to save the life, as the disease is in the constitution and reappears in the stump. This course of the destructive process corresponds well with that of "worldly and empty chatter," which "leads to further ungodliness."

Halt, Halteth. See Lame, Lameness.

Hemorrhage. See Issue.

Hemorrhoids (Heb. *'ophĕl,* "tumor," Deut. 28:27; etc.). A painful disease promoted especially by the sedentary habits of the East and thus quite common there. Although amenable to the skills of the West, the popular medicine of the East had no cure for it; it was, therefore, a terrible disease to be visited with (1 Sam. 5:6, 9, 12; 6:4-5, 11).

Hunchback (Heb. *gĭbbēn,* "arched," Lev. 21:20). In the East it is quite common to see young girls carrying children on their shoulders or perched on their hips. Many of these fall and experience irreparable injuries to their spines. Scrofulous disease of the spine is also common and often results in angular curvature. The specimens of deformity of this class that are to be seen in Syria and Palestine are lamentable. Those afflicted with such deformities were not allowed in the Temple service.

Infirmity. A word used in the KJV in three senses: (1) *impurity* (Lev. 12:2, NASB, "menstruation"); (2) *deformity* (Luke 13:12); (3) a general term for *disability* (John 5:5; 1 Tim. 5:23). Besides these senses it is used figuratively for mental and spiritual weaknesses (Rom. 8:26; etc.).

Inflammation or **Swelling.** A general and well-understood term (Lev. 13:28; Deut. 28:22).

Itch (Heb. *ḥeres,* Deut. 28:27). It is probable that the word translated "itch" in this passage refers to some other tormenting skin disease, such as eczema or prurigo, whereas that translated "scab," RV, "scurvy" (Heb. *gārāb;* Arab. *jarab*), is the true itch. *Jarab* is the classical name of this disease and is used for it in common speech to this day (*see* Scurvy). Itch is a skin disease produced by the entrance of a parasitic insect into the substance of the skin. It causes intolerable itching, and the scratching produces deep furrows and excoriations. If left to itself it is interminable. Although curable by proper medical treatment, this was probably unknown to the Hebrews. *See also* Scab.

Lame, Lameness. The translation of one Gk. and several Heb. words referring to impairment or loss of power in walking, whether from rigidity, amputation, or deformity. Lameness was a barrier to the priestly office.

In the NASB and NIV "crippled" appears in place of KJV "lame" as the translation of Heb. *nākeh,* and in place of KJV "maimed" as the translation of Gk. *kullos.* Heb. *pāsaḥ* is translated "maimed" in both the KJV and NASB, but "lame" in the NIV.

Gk. *chōlos,* "limping," is translated "halt" or "lame" in the KJV and "lame" in the NASB and NIV (Luke 7:22; 14:21; John 5:3).

Leprosy (Heb. *ṣāra'at*). The term is of uncertain origin and meaning but is clearly a comprehensive designation of a disease marked by a variety of skin afflictions, only one form of which was malignant. There was also a *ṣāra'at* of materials, which may have corresponded to mildew (Lev. 13:47-59), and another of buildings (Lev. 14:34-53), possibly indicating dry rot of timbers or mineral efflorescence of stone walls.

The priests had to be consulted in all cases of suspected *ṣāra'at,* and Lev. 13 supplied them with detailed diagnostic directions that contained obscure medical terminology. The affliction could be marked by swellings under the skin, pink spots or reddish areas of skin, or could have arisen on the site of an earlier boil or burn. Although it may have come into being suddenly, most cases would be well developed when the priests examined them, because the fear of *ṣāra'at* was so great in antiquity that its victims would go to the priests only as a last resort.

Benign Infections. If the sufferer exhibited a variety of eruptions (*mishpaḥat*), or patches of whitish skin on the body (vitiligo), or reddish patches covered with white scales occurring on the scalp, back, elbows, or knees (psoriasis), he or she was quarantined for two weeks. If during that time the condition did not deteriorate, the sufferer was released as "clean" even though his or her body might be covered with the eruption.

Malignant Infections. If the priest discovered white hairs on the lesion and evidence that it had penetrated the skin, the person was quarantined for two weeks as a suspected leper. After that time, if the lesion exhibited "raw flesh" (*bāśār ḥay*) such as skin ulcers or was marked by bright pink patches of skin and was obviously spreading, the sufferer was diagnosed as a leper and prohibited from living in the community as an "unclean" person. If he was healed subsequently, the priest employed cleansing rituals to restore the person to community life (Lev. 14:1-32). *See* the article Leprosy and the Mosaic Law.

Cause. The cause of leprosy is now known to be a bacillus similar to the one that produces tuberculosis, and modern medicine has classified the disease in terms of two main types, lepromatous and non-lepromatous, with some borderline cases. The lepromatous form is the most severe and is marked initially by lack of pigment and numbness in certain areas of the skin. Nodules (knoblike swellings) occur in various areas of the body and generally ulcerate. Other ulcers form on the feet and affect the bones, and as the disease progresses the hands and feet become distorted and the limbs swollen. Many peripheral nerves are affected, as are internal organs, and the condition of the patient is frequently complicated by gangrene. Tubercular lesions often arise on the face, and the skin of the forehead and cheeks puckers to produce a characteristic lionlike look. In severe cases most of the skin may thicken and become red.

Non-lepromatous Leprosy. Non-lepromatous leprosy is less severe in character. One variety is marked by patches of skin that have lost sensation and color but has few lesions and is usually noninfective. Another has rough-looking lesions that may either be pale or reddish; a third involves some nerves that become thick and sometimes ulcerate when nodules develop.

Ṣāra'at and Clinical Leprosy. Although some modern doctors have attempted to deny the identification between *ṣāra'at* and clinical leprosy (Hansen's disease), the correspondence of the Levitical narrative with the signs and symptoms of lepromatous leprosy is so striking as to demand careful consideration. Those who repudiate the identification have been unable to suggest an alternative disease that would have so terrified the peoples of antiquity.

Leprosy in Biblical Persons. The leprosy that afflicted Moses (Ex. 4:6) was not of the malignant variety and may have been the same as Miriam's (Num. 12:9-16), perhaps leucoderma. Naaman's affliction was also of a nonmalignant kind (2 Kings 5), possibly also leucoderma, in which pale patches of skin develop on the body. Whatever the affliction, it was transmitted subsequently to Gehazi (2 Kings 5:19-27). What was probably a small colony of men with malignant leprosy was mentioned in 2 Kings 7:3-10, and it was probably this same condition that afflicted Uzziah (2 Chron. 26:19-21). There is little doubt that most NT persons described as lepers did in fact have Hansen's disease (Luke 5:12-15; 17:11-19). By contrast, Simon the leper probably had a nonmalignant *ṣāra'at* such as vitiligo (Matt. 26:6; Mark 14:3).

Leprosy Today. Just as in biblical times, lepers can be encountered occasionally in public in the Near East today. Despite its abhorrent character, the disease is not contracted easily by persons in normal health.

Lunacy, Lunatick. *See* Madness.

Madness (Heb. *shiggā'ôn,* "raving," Deut.

28:28). Madmen are mentioned twice (1 Sam. 21:15; Prov. 26:18). Insanity is much more rare in the East than in the West, and little or no treatment is used. It is considered of merit to feed and clothe the insane if needy.

Maimed. A general term for severely injured. Although the term appears in the KJV, NIV, and NASB of Lev. 22:22, elsewhere the NASB and NIV render "crippled" in place of "maimed" (Matt. 15:30-31; Luke 14:13, 21). The only instance in the KJV of the term *cripple* is in Acts 14:8 ("lame," NASB), although the word appears numerous times in the NASB and NIV.

Murrain (Heb. *deber,* "pestilence"). A KJV term appearing once in the Bible (Ex. 9:3) in connection with the plagues of Egypt. The Heb. term is rendered "pestilence" in the NASB and "plague" in the NIV. We have no means of knowing what the epidemic was that constituted the fifth plague (Ex. 9:1-6). It may have been splenetic fever, which sometimes prevails extensively.

Palsy. See Paralysis.

Paralysis (Gk. *paralutikos,* "loosened," Matt. 4:24; 9:2; etc.). Paralysis comes from several causes: (1) Inflammation of the brain or spinal cord. In the East this is specially common in infancy, and in many cases leads to partial paralysis, as of the shoulder, arm, one or both legs, and sometimes the nerve of speech or hearing, or both. (2) Injuries of the spinal column. These are more apt to occur in adult life. (3) Pressure from curvature of the spine, or from tumors or other cause. (4) Apoplexy. The paralysis from the latter cause is sometimes cured. That from the others is incurable. The cases brought to our Savior were undoubtedly of the incurable sort and probably involved at least the lower limbs.

Pestilence (Heb. *deber;* Gk. *loimos,* "plague"). A general term for diseases that attack large numbers of persons at the same time. They are not known to be due to germs. We have no means of knowing what particular pestilences from time to time scourged the Israelites.

Running Sore. See Wen.

Scab (Heb. *sappaḥat,* Lev. 13:2, 6-7; 14:56). A similar root appears in the form of a verb (Isa. 3:17), *sāpaḥ,* to "affict with a scab." Both refer to the crust that forms on skin eruptions. The NIV usually renders "rash" or "sore." Such are common in many skin diseases and do not indicate any particular kind. Many diseases of the scalp produce them and cause the hair to fall out; this is regarded as a special calamity for women (3:17). The term *yallepet* (Lev. 21:20; 22:22) refers to some crustaceous disease of the skin of animals (NIV, "running sores"). The disease of horses, in which there is a scabby, eczematous state of the pastern, known in English as "scratches," is called *jarab* (itch) in Arab.

The Heb. term *garab* is translated "scab" in the KJV and NASB of Deut. 28:27 ("festering sore" in the NIV) but as "scurvy" (KJV), "eczema"

(NASB), or "festering sore" (NIV) in Lev. 21:20; 22:22.

Scale (Lev. 13:30, 35; 14:54). A somewhat general term for *eruptions.*

Scall. See Scale.

Scurvy (RV, Deut. 28:27, for NASB "scab" and NIV "itch"). We have given our reasons under *Itch* for preferring the rendering "itch" for the Heb. *garab* here, instead of for *ḥeres,* as in KJV, RV, and NIV. We do not see any reason to render it RV "scurvy." Neither do we believe the rendering of the same word (Lev. 21:20; 22:22), KJV, RV, "scurvy," any better; "itch" is its proper rendering (cf. the NASB reading of the same text, which renders "eczema" for Heb. *garab*). This would remove *scurvy* from the list of diseases mentioned in Scripture.

Sores (Lev. 22:22; Luke 16:20; Rev. 16:11). A general term for ulcers. *See also* Wen.

Tumors. See Hemorrhoids.

Wen (Heb. *yabbelet*). A KJV term appearing once in the Bible (Lev. 22:22) and rendered "running sore" in the NASB and "warts" in the NIV. A "wen" was a cyst containing sebaceous and other substances, spoken of only in connection with animals intended for sacrifice (22:22) but also common in men.

Withered (Heb. *yābēsh*). The Nazirite's skin is spoken of as withered (Lam. 4:8), i.e., wrinkled and dry ("shriveled" in the NIV). A "withered hand" (Matt. 12:10; cf. 1 Kings 13:4-6) is one in which the muscles, and often the bones themselves, are shrunken owing to loss of nerve power or stiffening of joints. Not infrequently the limb is much shorter, as well as more slender, than natural. When resulting from anything but recent disuse it is incurable.

Worms. The worms that ate Herod (Acts 12:23) may have been maggots bred in some gangrenous sore.

Wounds. Wounds are frequently alluded to. The binding up and pouring in oil and wine (Luke 10:34) was as good an antiseptic treatment as was then known.

BIBLIOGRAPHY: R. L. Moody, *Antiquity of Disease* (1923); A. R. Short, *The Bible and Modern Medicine* (1953); S. I. MacMillan, *None of These Diseases* (1984); R. K. Harrison, *The International Standard Bible Encyclopedia,* vol. 3, s.v. "Leper."

DISEASES, TREATMENT OF. The Hebrews were greatly inferior in scientific culture to their powerful neighbors Egypt, Assyria, and Greece. We have no allusion in the OT to scientific schools, and it is improbable that such existed. There were schools for the education of religious teachers, but we have no reason to believe that anything was taught in them except the Heb. language itself and the various branches of canon law and interpretation. While their neighbors were cultivating mathematics, astronomy, history, logic, metaphysics, law, and medicine, and their learned men were committing all that they knew to inscribed bricks, stone, papyrus rolls, and books full of treatises, the ancient Hebrews left us very little in the way of literature or science except the canonical Scriptures and the Apocrypha. Only by the most laborious search can we find in these Scriptures hints as to the scientific belief and practice that the Hebrews may have derived from their residence in Egypt and interaction with their more enlightened and progressive rivals. The Talmud, the function of which was to gather up all that tradition had transmitted and expound it by all that the ingenuity of its astute authors could furnish, does nothing to change our judgment that the Hebrews had little or no notion of the movement of the human mind that was taking place in other lands.

We have no reason to suppose that medicine affords any exception to the general state of the sciences among the Hebrews. It is exceedingly difficult to establish from the Bible the existence of such a science or of a proper order of medical practitioners in the earlier stages of Hebrew history. The allusions to the offices of the midwives (Gen. 35:17; 38:28; Ex. 1:15) give us no reason to suppose that they were an educated class, or had any knowledge of their art greater than is possessed by their successors in Syria at the present day. The simple operation of circumcision was probably performed by heads of families or their dependents (17:10-14; 34:24), or at times women (Ex. 4:25). The law provided that one who injured another should "pay for his loss of time and shall take care of him until he is completely healed" (Ex. 21:19). But this healing does not state or necessarily imply a physician. Physicians embalmed Jacob (Gen. 50:2), but they were Egyptians, not Hebrews. Job mentions physicians (13:4). Even as late as the time of Joram (850 B.C.), although he returned to Jezreel to be healed of wounds and sickness (2 Kings 8:29), no mention is made of doctors. It is uncertain whether Asa's physicians (2 Chron. 16:12, 915 B.C.) were natives or foreigners. The poetical allusion (Jer. 8:22, 626 B.C.) is in the form of a question, "Is there no balm in Gilead? Is there no physician there?" Although it is implied that physicians were then recognized as a guild, that does not make certain that they were more than users of balsams and ointments for wounds. A few passages in Proverbs and one in Ecclesiastes have been quoted to prove that Solomon was versed in medicine (Prov. 3:8; 12:18; 17:22; 20:30; 29:1; Eccles. 3:3); but such an interpretation is quite fanciful. The allusions to diseases and remedies also tend to show that the conceptions of medicine were crude and popular. Of the diseases and deformities mentioned in the Pentateuch and Joshua, we know about boils, blindness, bruises, dwarfs, hemorrhoids, dysentery, infirmity, inflammation, itch, lameness, madness, paralysis,

and wounds. Yet the most cursory glance at these terms shows that they are popular, not scientific. Of the treatment of these, except ceremonial and sacerdotal, we have not the faintest hint. The few remedies mentioned are evidently popular ones, such as mandrakes, balm; or ingredients in unguents used for sacred purposes, not for healing, such as calamus, cassia, cinnamon, myrrh, galbanum, onycha, stacte, frankincense; or condiments, such as coriander.

Thus for the period of Hebrew history to the end of the OT the Scripture reveals hardly a trace of medical science or art. This seems remarkable considering the long residence of Israel in Egypt where medicine was well established and cultivated to a high degree of excellence for those days. The Egyptians, owing to the practice of embalming, were well acquainted with human anatomy, as well as with that of the domestic animals. They also had a system of pathology and a considerable materia medica. They cultivated medicine to the point of dividing it into specialties as in modern times. But the Israelites in Egypt were apparently separated, and there is no reason to believe that any of them except Moses carried away any of the learning of Egypt. Although a considerable number of hygienic precepts exist in the Mosaic law, such as circumcision, burying of excrements, etc. (Deut. 23:13), it is a strained interpretation to refer them to the medical knowledge or skill of the lawgiver. There was a tendency in all serious sickness to fall back on religious ritual and ultimately on divine providence (Ex. 15:26; Pss. 103:3; 147:3; Isa. 30:26; Jer. 17:14; 30:17). When Asa "did not seek the Lord, but the physicians" (2 Chron. 16:12), the record speaks reproachfully. It is impossible to tell whether his diseased and swollen feet were dropsical or elephantiasical. The term *feet* was sometimes used euphemistically of the sexual organs (cf. Ruth 3:4-8), and if this is intended here the reference could be to some form of venereal disease.

In the time of Christ the Jews had become enlightened by contact with Egypt, Babylon, Greece, and Rome. They certainly cultivated philosophy, law, and medicine. In the NT are mentioned dropsy, gangrene, dysentery, paralysis, and epilepsy. Physicians were a regular profession (Matt. 9:12; Mark 2:17; Luke 4:23; 5:31). Luke was the "beloved physician" (Col. 4:14). Physicians were numerous (Mark 5:26; Luke 8:43). They doubtless practiced according to the system then in vogue in the Greek and Roman world. But the vast number of the unrelieved stands out on every page of the gospels and gives to the ministry of Christ its peculiar hold on the people.

The following animal and vegetable substances used in medicine are alluded to under their several headings in the articles Animal Kingdom and Vegetable Kingdom: anise, balm, calamus, cassia, cinnamon, cummin, dill, galbanum, gall, hyssop, leech, mandrake, mint, myrrh, stacte, wine.   G.E. POST

BIBLIOGRAPHY: R. K. Harrison, *Healing Herbs of the Bible* (1966).

DISFIGURED FACE. See Diseases.

DISGUISE. In 2 Cor. 11:13, Paul, characterizing false prophets, says of them that they are "deceitful workers, disguising themselves as apostles of Christ. And no wonder, for even Satan disguises himself as an angel of light" (vv. 14-15). The Gk. is *metaschēmatizō* and means "to assume the appearance of another." It is translated "transformed" in the KJV and "masquerades" in the NIV. The persons of whom Paul speaks were servants of Satan, but in working against the apostle in doctrine and act they hypocritically assumed the mask of an apostle, though they were opposite of a true apostle.

DISH. The rendering of several Heb. and Gk. terms:

1. *Sēpel,* "low." Probably a shallow pan (a "dish" [NASB and NIV, "bowl"] of "curds," curdled milk, Judg. 5:25; "bowl" of water, 6:38).

2. *Sēlāhâ,* something to "pour" into, probably a platter (2 Kings 21:13, NASB, KJV, NIV, "dish."

3. *Qeʻārâ,* something "deep," the gold "dishes" of the Tabernacle (Ex. 25:29; 37:16; Num. 4:7; 7:13).

4. *Trublion* (Matt. 26:23; Mark 14:20, NASB and NIV, "bowl"), probably the same as no. 3.

In ancient Egypt and Judea each person broke off a small piece of bread, dipped it into the dish, and brought it to the mouth with a small portion of the contents of the dish. To partake of the same dish or bowl was to show special friendliness and intimacy.

DIʻSHAN (dīʼshan; another form of *Dishon,* "antelope"). The name of the youngest son of Seir the Horite, father of Uz and Aran, and head of one of the original tribes of Edom (Gen. 36:21, 28, 30; 1 Chron. 1:38, 42).

DIʻSHON (dīʼshon; "antelope"). The name of two descendants of Seir the Horite.

1. Seir's fifth son, and head of one of the original Edom tribes (Gen. 36:21, 30; 1 Chron. 1:38).

2. Seir's grandson, the only son of Anah, and brother of Oholibamah, Esau's second wife (Gen. 36:25; 1 Chron. 1:41).

DISPENSATIONS (Gk. *oikonomia,* "management of a household," hence English "economy").

A dispensation is an era of time during which man is tested in respect to obedience to some definite revelation of God's will. Seven such dispensations are recognized by many premillennialists. Other premillennialists speak of only three or four. Still others prefer not to be classed as

dispensationalists at all. Those who hold to seven list them as follows:

Innocence. Man was created innocent, set in an ideal environment, placed under a simple test and warned of the result of disobedience. The woman fell through pride; the man, deliberately (1 Tim. 2:14). Although God restored the sinning creatures, the dispensation came to an end at the judgment of the expulsion (Gen. 3:24).

Conscience. By an act of disobedience man came to an experiential knowledge of good and evil. Driven out of Eden and placed under the Adamic covenant, man was accountable to do all known good and to abstain from all known evil and to come before God by sacrifice. The result of this testing was complete degeneration ending in the judgment of the Flood (Gen. 6-9).

Human Government. The declaration of the Noahic covenant after the Flood (Gen. 8:20–9:27) put man under a new test, featured by the inauguration of human government, the highest function of which was the judicial taking of life. Man is responsible to govern the world for God. That responsibility rests upon the whole race, Jew and Gentile. With the failure of Israel under the Palestinian covenant (Deut. 28:64) and the consequent judgment of the captivities, "the times of the Gentiles" began (Luke 21:24). The world is still Gentile-governed, and hence this dispensation overlaps other dispensations and will not strictly come to an end until the second coming of Christ.

Promise. This era went from the call of Abraham (Gen. 12:1) to the giving of the Mosaic law (Ex. 19:8). The dispensation was under the Abrahamic covenant and was exclusively Israelite.

Law. This era reaches from Sinai to Calvary. The period was a time of teaching used to bring Israel to Christ and was governed by the Mosaic covenant (Ex. 20:1–31:18).

Grace. This period began with the death and resurrection of Christ (Rom. 3:24-26; 4:24-25). The point of testing is no longer legal obedience to the law as a condition of salvation but acceptance or rejection of Christ with good works as the fruit of salvation (John 1:12-13; 3:36; 1 John 5:10-12). The predicted end of the testing of man under grace is the apostasy of the professing church (2 Tim. 3:1-8) and the subsequent apocalyptic judgments.

The Kingdom. This is the last of the ordered ages regulating human life on the earth, previous to the eternal state. It involves the establishment of the kingdom covenanted to David (2 Sam. 7:8-17; Zech. 12:8; Luke 1:31-33). This will include Israel's restoration and conversion (Rom. 11:25-27) and her rehabilitation as a high-priestly nation in fellowship with God and as head over the millennial nations (Zech. 3:1-10; 6:9-15).

BIBLIOGRAPHY: W. G. Scroggie, *Ruling Lines of Progressive Revelation* (n.d.); L. S. Chafer, *Dispensationalism*

(1936); L. T. Talbot, *God's Plan of the Ages* (1936); G. E. Ladd, *Crucial Questions About the Kingdom of God* (1952); E. Sauer, *From Eternity to Eternity* (1954); C. B. Bass, *Backgrounds to Dispensationalism* (1960); C. C. Ryrie, *Dispensationalism Today* (1965).

DISPERSION OF ISRAEL (Gk. *diaspora;* John 7:35; rendered "dispersed," James 1:1; "scattered," 1 Pet. 1:1). Jewish communities settled in almost all the countries of the civilized world, remaining on the one hand in constant communication with the mother country and, on the other, in active interaction with the non-Jewish world.

Causes. These were of different kinds: the deportation by the Assyrian and Babylonian conquerors of large masses of the nation into their eastern provinces; the carrying of hundreds of Jewish captives to Rome by Pompey. Of greater importance, however, were the voluntary emigrations of Jewish settlers during the Greco-Roman period to the countries bordering on Palestine, and to all the chief towns of the civilized world, for the sake chiefly of trade. The Diadochoi (successors of Alexander the Great), in order to build up their many kingdoms, offered citizenship and many other privileges to immigrants. Attracted by these circumstances and perhaps influenced by adverse events at home, large numbers of Jews were induced to settle in Syria, Egypt, and Asia Minor, as well as in all the more important ports and commercial cities of the Mediterranean Sea.

Extent. We have strong and varied evidence that the dispersion became quite widespread. The Roman Senate dispatched a circular (139-138 B.C.) in favor of the Jews to the kings of Egypt, Syria, Pergamos, Cappadocia, and Parthia, and to a great number of provinces, towns, and islands of the Mediterranean Sea (1 Macc. 15:16-24). It may therefore be safely inferred that there was already a number of Jews in all these lands. *See also* the list of countries from which Jews had come to Jerusalem (Acts 2:9-11).

In Mesopotamia, Media, and Babylonia lived the descendants of the members of the ten tribes and of the kingdom of Judah carried there by the Assyrians and Chaldeans. The "ten tribes" never returned at all from captivity, neither must the return of the tribes of Judah and Benjamin be conceived of as complete. These eastern Jewish settlements may also have been increased by voluntary additions, and the Jews in the provinces were "an immense multitude" (Josephus *Ant.* 11.5.2).

Josephus names Syria as the country in which was the largest percentage of Jewish inhabitants, and its capital, Antioch, was specially distinguished in this respect. In Damascus, according to Josephus, ten thousand (or according to another passage, eighteen thousand) Jews were said to have been assassinated during the war. Agrippa is the authority for the statement that Jews

had settled in Bithynia and in the uttermost corners of Pontus, which is confirmed by Jewish inscriptions in the Gk. language found in the Crimea. The entire history of the apostle Paul shows how widely the Jews had settled all over Asia Minor.

Most important with regard to the history of civilization was the Jewish colony in Egypt, especially in Alexandria. Long before the time of Alexander the Great, Jewish immigrants were found there. In the time of Jeremiah many Jews went to Egypt out of fear of the Chaldeans (Jer. 41:17-18), in opposition to the warning of the prophet (chaps. 42-43), and settled in various parts of the country (44:1). Nebuchadnezzar appears, during his invasion of Egypt, to have carried to Babylon a considerable number of Jews from Alexandria.

The Jewish dispersion penetrated westward from Egypt and was numerously represented in Cyrenaica. That it reached Greece is evident from the fact that Paul found synagogues in Thessalonica, Berea, Athens, and Corinth (Acts 17:1, 10, 17; 18:4, 7). Jews were also found in almost all the islands of the Grecian Archipelago and the Mediterranean Sea, in some of these in large numbers.

In Rome there was a Jewish community numbering thousands, first appearing in that city during the time of the Maccabees. Judas Maccabeus sent an embassy to obtain assurances of its friendship and assistance (1 Macc. 8:17-32); another was sent by Jonathan (12:1-4), and a third by Simon (140-139 B.C.), which effected an actual offensive and defensive alliance with the Romans (14:24; 15:15-24).

But the settlement of Jews at Rome dates only from the time of Pompey, who after his conquest of Jerusalem (63 B.C.) took numerous Jewish prisoners of war with him to Rome. Sold as slaves, many of them were afterward given their liberty and, granted Roman citizenship, formed a colony beyond the Tiber. They were expelled from Rome under Tiberius and again by Claudius. But the Jews soon returned and, although looked down upon by the Romans, increased in wealth and numbers.

Jewish Communities in the Dispersion. Of course there was only one way in which the scattered Israelites could maintain their native religion and usages—by organizing themselves into independent communities. That as a rule they were in the habit of doing, the nature of the organization varying according to time and place. Information respecting this feature of the Dispersion in the East, Asia Minor, and Syria is meager. In Alexandria and Cyrene they formed an independent municipal community within or coordinate with the rest of the city. An important light is thrown upon the constitution of communities of the Dispersion by a Jewish inscription found in Berenice, in Cyrenaica (probably 13 B.C.), from which we find that the Jews of Berenice formed a distinct community, with *nine archons* at its head. With regard to the constitution of the Jewish communities of Rome and of Italy, generally we are most thoroughly informed through the large number of Jewish epitaphs found in the cemeteries of Rome and Venosa. From these inscriptions we gather that the Jews living in Rome were divided into a large number of separate and independently organized communities, each having its own synagogue, *gerousia* (assembly of elders), and public officials. Two important privileges were allowed them: *the right of administering their own funds* and *jurisdiction over their own members*. Rome also granted them *exemption from military service*. In the older cities of Asia Minor, Syria, and Phoenicia there were instances in which individual Jews had the rights of citizenship conferred upon them, e.g., Paul (Acts 21:39). But as a rule the Jewish communities are to be considered as *private associations of settlers*. These had the right to claim the protection of the laws and enjoy the comforts and amenities of life.

Religious Life. Constant contact could not fail to have its effect upon the Jews in their development. The cultured Jews were not only Jews, but Greeks also, in respect to language, education, and habits; yet they were Jews and felt themselves in all essentials to be in unison with their brethren in Palestine. One of the principal means employed for preserving and upholding the faith of their fathers was the *synagogue* (which see).

There was also a *temple* at Leontopolis, with a regular Jewish temple service (160 B.C.-A.D. 73). *See* Temple. Collections were regularly received in every town and at particular seasons were forwarded to Jerusalem. The language employed in the religious services appears to have been usually Gk.

BIBLIOGRAPHY: N. H. Snaith, *The Jews from Cyrus to Herod* (n.d.); S. Baron, *A Social and Religious History of the Jews* (1952).

DISPERSION OF MANKIND. This dispersion was the result of the confusion of tongues at Babel (Gen. 11:6-9). In 10:5, 20, 31, we are told that the posterity of Noah were divided in their lands, all of them according to their own language, family, and nation, so that their distribution was undoubtedly conducted under the ordinary laws of colonization. The tenth chapter of Genesis presents an account of the principal descendants of Noah, followed by the description of that event that led to the division of the race into many nations with different languages. Table 7, "Tribes Descended from Noah's Sons" (p. 313), shows the principal tribes that have been identified. For archaeological illumination of the Table of Nations (chap. 10) *see* Merrill F. Unger, *Archaeology and the Old Testament* (1954), pp. 73-104.

DISQUALIFIED (Gk. *'adokimos,* "not ap-

proved," "disqualified"). A term borrowed from the athletic games in which the contestant, being examined, is found to be rejected from receiving the prize because of the infraction of some rule of the game. In 1 Cor. 9:27 the apostle is giving instruction concerning *rewards* and not *salvation.* These two lines of truth, though saliently differentiated in Scripture, are commonly confused in theological thinking. Salvation, which is by "grace through faith" totally apart from "works" (Eph. 2:8-10) is not subject to loss or forfeiture, inasmuch as it is a divine gift and rests on the sure foundation of God's faithfulness (John 3:16; 4:10; Rom. 6:23). Rewards, on the other hand, are gained by works performed after one is saved (Matt. 10:42; Luke 19:17; 2 Tim. 4:7-8; Rev. 2:10; 22:12). Furthermore, salvation is a present possession of the believer (John 3:36; 5:24; 6:47), whereas rewards are a future realization to be dispensed at the Lord's coming (Matt. 16:27; 1 Cor. 3:11-23; 2 Tim. 4:8).   M.F.U.

DISSIPATION (Gk. *asōtia*). The characteristic of an abandoned man, denoting a dissolute life, profligacy (Eph. 5:18; Titus 1:6; 1 Pet. 4:4; the KJV frequently renders "riot"). A similar definition of the word is given in the parable of the prodigal: "He squandered his estate with *loose living*" (Luke 15:13; "riotous," KJV; "wild," NIV). *See* Carouse.

DIVERS, DIVERSE (Heb. *kil'ayim,* "of two sorts"). The Jews were forbidden to bring together different kinds of materials, animals, or products, such as (1) weaving garments of two kinds of stuff, particularly of wool and linen; (2) sowing a field with mixed seed; (3) yoking an ox and an ass together; or (4) breeding together animals of different species, e.g., to procure mules (Lev. 19:19; Deut. 22:9-11). The enactment concerning cloth would probably be better understood if we knew the exact meaning of Heb. *sha'atnēz,* rendered "linen and woollen" (Lev. 19:19, KJV; NASB and NIV, "two kinds of material mixed together") and "garment of divers sorts" (Deut. 22:11, KJV; NIV, "wool and linen woven together"). Perhaps the best explanation is "stuff of large meshes" (Koehler).

DIVIDING WALL, BARRIER OF. The expression used by Paul to designate the Mosaic law as the dividing line between the Jews and Gentiles (Eph. 2:14). The argument of the verse is as follows: Christ has procured peace. Then follows a statement of how Christ became our peace, having "made both groups into one," not so that one part assumed the nature of the other, but so that the separation of the two was done away with, and both were raised to a *new* unity. Then we have the statement in further explanation, "And broke down the barrier of the dividing wall," thus removing the enmity that existed between Jews and Gentiles. As to any special wall or fence being alluded to, commentators are divided, some believing it to refer to the stone screen in the Temple marking off the court of the Gentiles, whereas others believe it meant the wall in large towns marking off the Jewish districts.

DIVINATION (div-i-nā'shun). Divination, the art of obtaining secret knowledge, especially of the future, is a pagan counterpart of prophecy. Careful comparison of Scripture will reveal that inspirational divination is by demonic power, whereas genuine prophecy is by the Spirit of God. The biblical attitude toward divination is distinctly hostile (Deut. 18:10-12). The prophet of Jehovah is contrasted with diviners of all sorts and is set forth as the only authorized medium of supernatural revelation. Baalam (Num. 22-24) was a pagan diviner but rose to the status of a bona-fide prophet of the Lord, although he reverted to paganism. In Isa. 3:2; Jer. 29:8; Ezek. 22:28 the diviner is classified with the prophet, but this does not mean condonement of divination. It points rather to the apostasy and pagan contamination of the era. The worship of the true God is basically at variance with divination of every sort. Seeking knowledge of the future from any source other than the God of Israel was an insult to His

holy Being and the revelation of Himself and His purpose for men. *See also* Magic.

BIBLIOGRAPHY: T. W. Davies, *Magic, Divination and Demonology Among the Hebrews and Their Neighbors* (1898); M. Summers, *The Geography of Witchcraft* (1927); A. Guillaume, *Prophecy and Divination Among the Hebrews and Other Semites* (1938); K. Seligman, *The History of Magic* (1948); M. F. Unger, *Archaeology and the Old Testament* (1954), pp. 73-104; A. L. Oppenheim, *Interpretation of Dreams in the Ancient Near East* (1956); id., *Ancient Mesopotamia* (1964), pp. 206-27.

DIVISION OF THE PRIESTS AND LEVITES. The number of the priests and Levites had so increased that David divided them into twenty-four divisions ("courses," KJV), with a president at the head of each. The order in which each of these divisions took its turn was determined by lot, a new division being appointed every week. The duties began with one Sabbath and ended on the next (2 Kings 22:9; 2 Chron. 23:8; *see also* 1 Chron. 24:1-19, where the twenty-four divisions are enumerated; and 27:1). Further information on the priests can be found in the articles Levites; Priests.

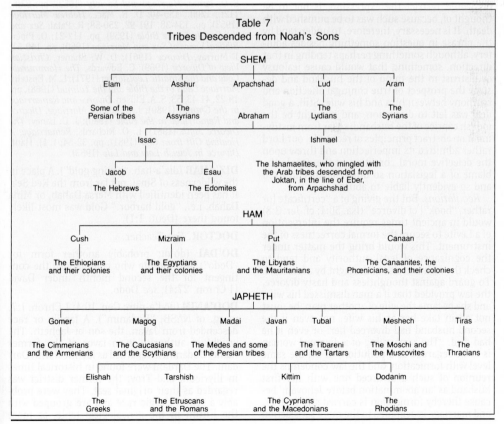

Table 7
Tribes Descended from Noah's Sons

SHEM

Elam	Asshur	Arpachshad	Lud	Aram
Some of the Persian tribes	The Assyrians	Abraham	The Lydians	The Syrians

Issac		Ishmael

Jacob	Esau	The Ishamaelites, who mingled with the Arab tribes descended from Joktan, in the line of Eber, from Arpachshad
The Hebrews	The Edomites	

HAM

Cush	Mizraim	Put	Canaan
The Ethiopians and their colonies	The Egyptians and their colonies	The Libyans and the Mauritanians	The Canaanites, the Phœnicians, and their colonies

JAPHETH

Gomer	Magog	Madai	Javan	Tubal	Meshech	Tiras
The Cimmerians and the Armenians	The Caucasians and the Scythians	The Medes and some of the Persian tribes		The Tibareni and the Tartars	The Moschi and the Muscovites	The Thracians

Elishah	Tarshish	Kittim	Dodanim
The Greeks	The Etruscans and the Romans	The Cyprians and the Macedonians	The Rhodians

DIVORCE (Heb. *kerîtût;* Gk. *apostasion,* "cutting," "separating").

Jewish Law. A legal separation between man and wife by means of a formal process of some sort. As the ordinances respecting marriage have in view the hallowing of that relationship, so also was the Mosaic regulation in respect of divorce (Deut. 24:1-4). From this we learn that a man, finding in his wife something shameful or offensive, dismissed her from his house with a certificate of divorce.

Temporary Expedient. Divorce, giving a certificate, and causes of divorce seem to have been accepted by Moses by hereditary usage and allowed because of the people's hardness of heart (Matt. 19:7-8). The question of divorce was entirely at the will of the husband; the wife, not possessing equal privileges with the husband, had no right of divorce. The action of Salome and others was done in defiance of the law and in imitation of Roman licentiousness.

Ground of Divorce. There have been many interpretations of the expression "anything indecent" given as the ground of divorce. It occurs also in Deut. 23:14 of things that profane the camp of Israel, and denotes something shameful or offensive. Adultery, to which some of the rabbis would restrict the expression, is not to be thought of, because such was to be punished with death. It is necessary, therefore, to understand by the phrase in question something besides adultery, although something perhaps tending in that direction, something that would cause jealousy or distrust in the mind of the husband and destroy the prospect of true conjugal affection and harmony between him and his wife. Still, a good deal was left to discretion, and it might be the foolish caprice of the husband; so far from justifying it on abstract principles of rectitude, our Lord rather admitted its imperfection and threw upon the defective moral condition of the people the blame of a legislation so unsatisfactory in itself and so evidently liable to abuse.

Regulations. But the giving of a "certificate [or rather, "book"] of divorce" (Isa. 50:1; cf. Jer. 3:8) would in ancient times require the intervention of a Levite to secure the formal correctness of the instrument. This would bring the matter under the cognizance of legal authority and tend to check the rash exercise of the right by a husband. To guard against thoughtless and hasty divorce, the law provided that if a man dismissed his wife, and she became the wife of another man, he must not again take her as his wife, not even if the second husband had divorced her, or even if he had died. "The remarrying of a divorced woman is to be regarded as a pollution, or on the same level with fornication, and the law condemns the reunion of such a divorced one with her first husband as 'an abomination before Jehovah,' because thereby fornication is carried still further, and marriage is degraded to the mere satisfaction

of sexual passion" (Keil, *Bibl. Arch.,* 2:173-75).

Christian Law. The teachings of Jesus on the subject of divorce are found in Matt. 5:31-32; 19:3-10; Mark 10:2-12; and Luke 16:18. Briefly they are these: (1) The liberty given to a man by the Mosaic law to put away his wife (Deut. 24:1-4) was because of the hardness of the Jewish heart. (2) He who divorces his wife, except for fornication, and marries another commits adultery (Matt. 19:9) and leads her to commit the same crime (Matt. 5:32). (3) He who marries a divorced woman commits adultery, and the woman who puts away her husband and marries another man (Mark 10:12) incurs the same kind of guilt. This last refers to the custom among the Greeks and Romans, namely, that the wife might also be the divorcing party. In Matt. 19:9 the one exception in favor of divorce is given, namely, *fornication,* perhaps some form of sexual immorality, although the meaning of the term is uncertain. It was evidently not adultery, which is described by a different word.

BIBLIOGRAPHY: W. Smith, ed., *Dictionary of Christian Antiquities* (1917), 2:1110-14; R. H. Charles, *Teaching of the New Testament on Divorce* (1921); E. Neufeld, *Ancient Hebrew Marriage Laws* (1944), pp. 176-88; K. E. Kirk, *Marriage and Divorce* (1948), pp. 33-56; E. O. James, *Marriage and Society* (1952), pp. 93ff., 112f., 120ff., 135-40; D. R. Mace, *Hebrew Marriage* (1953), pp. 134-38, 191-92, 250-58; R. Patai, *Sex and the Family in the Bible* (1959), pp. 112-21; O. Piper, *Biblical Views of Sex and Marriage* (1960), pp. 140-51; J. Murray, *Divorce* (1961); D. W. Shaner, *Christian View of Divorce* (1969); C. Edwards, *The Hammurabi Code and the Sinaitic Legislation* (1971); L. M. Epstein, *Marriage Laws in the Bible and the Talmud* (1968), pp. 19-22, 41-43, 53; S. A. Ellison, *Divorce and Remarriage in the Church* (1980); J. E. Adams, *Marriage, Divorce and Remarriage in the Bible* (1980); J. C. Laney, *The Divorce Myth* (1981); L. O. Richards, *Remarriage: A Healing Gift from God* (1981), pp. 32-54; I. H. Haut, *Divorce in Jewish Law and Life* (1983).

DIZ'AHAB (diz'a-hab, "having gold"). A place in the wilderness of Sinai, not far from the Red Sea. It has been identified with Mersa Dahab, or Mina Dahab, i.e., "gold harbor." Gold was most likely found there (Deut. 1:1).

DOCTOR. *See* Teacher.

DO'DAI (dō'dī; probably another form for "Dodo"). An Ahohite who commanded the contingent for the second month under David (1 Chron. 27:4); *see* Dodo.

DOD'ANIM (dōd'a-nim; Gen. 10:4; 1 Chron. 1:7, marg. of NASB, "Rodanim"). A family or race descended from Javan, the son of Japheth. The weight of authority is in favor of the former name. Dodanim is regarded as identical with Dardani. The Dardani were found in historical times in Illyricum and Troy; the former district was regarded as their original seat. They were probably a semi-Pelasgic race and are grouped with the Kittim in the genealogical table, as more closely related to them than to the other branches of the Pelasgic race.

DOD'AVAHU (dod'a-va-hū; "beloved of Jehovah"). A man of Mareshah, in Judah, and father of the Eliezer who predicted to Ahaziah the wreck of Jehoshaphat's fleet (2 Chron. 20:37), 874 B.C.

DO'DO (dō'dō). Perhaps a shortening of Dodavahu.

1. A descendant of Issachar, father of Puah, and grandfather of the judge Tola (Judg. 10:1), after 1300 B.C.

2. An Ahohite, father of Eleazar, one of David's three mighty men (2 Sam. 23:9; 1 Chron. 11:12), before 1000 B.C. He seems to be the same as the *Dodai* (which see) mentioned in 1 Chron. 27:4 as commander of the second division of the royal troops under David.

3. A Bethlehemite, and father of Elhanan, one of David's thirty heroes (2 Sam. 23:24; 1 Chron. 11:26), before 1000 B.C.

DOE. *See* Animal Kingdom.

DO'EG (dō'eg). An Edomite, and chief of Saul's herdsmen ("keeper of the king's mules," Josephus *Ant.* 6.12.1). He was at Nob when Ahimelech gave David assistance by furnishing him with consecrated bread and the sword of Goliath (1 Sam. 21:7). Doeg informed the king of this, and, when others refused to obey his command, slew Ahimelech and his priests to the number of eighty-five persons (1 Sam. 22:9-19), about 1000 B.C. This "act called forth one of David's most severe imprecative prayers (Ps. 52), of which divine and human justice seem alike to have required the fulfillment."

BIBLIOGRAPHY: C. E. Macartney, *Chariots of Fire* (1951), pp. 104-13.

DOG. *See* Animal Kingdom.
Figurative.

1. In Bible times, as now, troops of hungry and half-wild dogs roamed the fields and the streets feeding upon dead bodies and other refuse (1 Kings 14:11; 16:4; 21:19, 23; 2 Kings 9:10, 36; Jer. 15:3; etc.) and thus became objects of dislike. Fierce and cruel enemies were called *dogs* (Ps. 22:16, 20; Jer. 15:3).

2. The dog being an *unclean* animal, the terms "dog," "dead dog," "dog's head" were used as terms of reproach, or of humiliation if speaking of one's self (1 Sam. 24:14; 2 Sam. 3:8; 9:8; 2 Kings 8:13).

3. In the East "dog" is used for impure and profane persons and was used by the Jews respecting the Gentiles (Matt. 15:26).

4. False apostles are called "dogs" on account of impurity and love of gain (Phil. 3:2).

5. Those who are shut out of the kingdom of heaven are also called "dogs" (Rev. 22:15) on account of their vileness, probably a reference to homosexuality.

DOLEFUL CREATURES. *See* Animal Kingdom: Owl.

DONKEY. *See* Animal Kingdom.

DOOR. As the opening for entering and leaving, it is an essential part of a tent or house.

Figurative. "I will give . . . the valley of Achor as a door of hope" (Hos. 2:15) refers, doubtless, to the defeat of Israel through the sin of *Achan* (which see), the encouragement given by Jehovah, and Joshua's uninterrupted success (Josh. 7).

A "wide" or "open" door is used by Paul (1 Cor. 16:9; 2 Cor. 2:12; Col. 4:3) as a symbol of the favorable opportunity for apostolic work. Our Lord speaks of Himself as "the door" (John 10:9), and John of "a door standing open in heaven" (Rev. 4:1).

DOORKEEPER (Heb. *shô'ēr;* Gk. *thurōros*). "Doorkeepers for the ark are named (1 Chron. 15:23-24 [NASB, "gatekeeper"]), whose duty was thought to be to guard the door of the Tabernacle, so as to prevent anyone from coming carelessly to the ark." Persons were appointed to keep the street door of houses, and these were sometimes women (John 18:16-17; Acts 12:13).

"Doorkeeper" in the KJV and NIV of Ps. 84:10 does not convey the right meaning of the original. It means one "at the threshold" (so NASB), either a beggar asking alms or a passerby merely looking in.

DOORPOST. Moses exhorted the Israelites to write the divine commands "on the doorposts of your house and on your gates" (Deut. 6:9; Heb. *mezūzâ*). These words were figurative and are expected to be understood spiritually. Placing inscriptions about the door of the house was an ancient Egyptian custom and was evidently followed by the Israelites in early times. Portions of the law were either carved or inscribed upon the doorposts — or else written upon parchment and enclosed in a cylinder or reed and fixed on the right-hand doorpost of every room in the house. *See also* Threshold.

DOPH'KAH (dof'ka). One of the encampments of Israel in the desert, their eighth station (Num. 33:12-13). It was located between Rephidim and the Red Sea; there has been no satisfactory identification.

DOR (dōr; "dwelling"). An ancient city of the Canaanites, referred to as "the heights of Dor" (Josh. 11:2; 12:23). Its people were tributary to King Solomon (Judg. 1:27; 1 Kings 4:11). It was a Phoenician settlement on the coast of Syria and is identified with Khirbet el-Buri, about eight miles N of Caesarea. The site was excavated by John Garstang for the British School of Archaeology in 1923 and 1924 and J. Leibovitch for the Israel Department of Antiquities in 1950 and 1952. Excavations have shown the place to have

Seashore at Dor

Dove

been occupied first by the Egyptians in the fifteenth or fourteenth centuries B.C. It developed an important harbor and had close relations with Cyprus and the Aegean world. The most important remains dated to the Hellenistic-Roman period and included temples to Zeus and Astarte, and a theater, probably dating to the second or third century A.D.　　　　　　　　　　H.F.V.

DOR'CAS (dor'kas; "gazelle"). A charitable and pious Christian woman of Joppa whom Peter restored to life (Acts 9:36-41). The sacred writer mentions her as "a certain disciple named Tabitha (which translated in Greek is called Dorcas)," probably because she was a Hellenistic Jewess and was called Dorcas by the Greeks, whereas to the Jews she was known by the name *Tabitha* (which see).

DO'THAN (dō'than; probably, "two wells"). An upland plain on the caravan route from Syria to Egypt, about eleven miles N of Samaria and noted for its excellent pasturage; the scene of Joseph's forced slavery and also of Elisha's vision of the mountain full of horses and chariots (Gen. 37:17; 2 Kings 6:13). One of the two wells found there now has the name "the pit of Joseph" (Jubb Yusuf). It was the usual sort of pit or pond dug even now by Arabs and shepherds to get rain water, with sloping sides, perhaps ten feet deep. The excavation at the mound of Dothan, sixty miles by road N of Jerusalem, was conducted by Joseph P. Free of Wheaton College (Ill.) for nine seasons from 1953 to 1964. Twenty levels of occupation were identified, extending from about 3000 B.C. to A.D. 1200 to 1400. Part of a thriving Iron Age city, contemporary with Elisha, was uncovered. A larger two-story administrative building constructed during Solomon's reign and rebuilt at about 800 B.C. came to light during the 1958 season. The Assyrian conquest of 725-722 B.C. was abundantly evident in destruction at the site. The great find of the 1959 season was the richest tomb yet found in Palestine. Used from 1400 to 1100 B.C., it contained more than 3,200 pottery vessels.　　　　　　　　　H.F.V.

BIBLIOGRAPHY: M. Avi-Yonah, ed., *Encyclopedia of Archaeological Excavations in the Holy Land* (1975), 1:337-39.

DOUBLE. The rendering of several Heb. and Gk. words has many meanings. Thus the *breastplate* (which see) was to be folded double (Ex. 39:9). "Double the money" had the same value as before, with an equal value added to it (Gen. 43:12, 15). "She has received of the Lord's hand *double* for all her sins" (Isa. 40:2, italics added) does not mean twice as much as she *deserved* but *ample* punishment through her twofold captivity, the Assyrian and Babylonian. "Instead of your shame you will have a double portion" (Isa. 61:7) refers to the double possession of land, not only that which they had inherited but extending far beyond their former borders. *See* Inheritance.

Double heart, *double* tongue, *double* mind are opposed to one that is simple, unequivocal, sincere (James 1:8; 4:8).

DOUBT. That state of mind that hesitates between two contradictory conclusions. It may have some degree of belief, checked by a consciousness of ignorance. In this case it is provisional, waiting for more light. The NT gives several instances of this as worthy to be reasoned with.

Absolute disbelief is the belief of the opposite of that which faith holds.

DOUGH (Heb. *bāṣēq*, "swelling" from fermentation, Ex. 12:34, 39; Jer. 7:18; etc.; *'arîsâ*, "meal"). Mention is made of Israel's carrying their dough with them, before it was leavened, when they left Egypt (Ex. 12:34). Dough was sometimes baked with or without leaven. *See* Bread.

DOVE. *See also* Animal Kingdom.

Turtledoves and pigeons were the only birds that could be offered in sacrifice, being usually selected by the poor (Gen. 15:9; Lev. 5:7; 12:6; Luke 2:24); and to supply the demand for them dealers in these birds sat about the precincts of the Temple (Matt. 21:12; etc.). *See* Animal Kingdom.

Figurative. The dove was the symbol of reconciliation with God (Gen. 8:8, 10) and has since been the emblem of peace. It is also a noted symbol of tender and devoted affection (Song of Sol. 1:15; 2:14; etc.) and likewise of mourning (Isa. 38:14; 59:11, NASB and NIV, "moan").

The dove symbolizes the Holy Spirit that descended upon our Savior at His baptism with that peculiar hovering motion that distinguishes the descent of a dove (Matt. 3:16; Mark 1:10; Luke 3:22; John 1:32).

DOVE COTE. "When traveling in the north of Syria many years ago I noticed in certain villages tall square buildings without roofs, whose walls were pierced inside by numberless pigeon-holes. In these nestled and bred thousands of these birds. Their foraging excursions extended many miles in every direction, and it is curious to notice them returning to their 'windows' like bees to their hives or like clouds pouring over a sharp ridge into the deep valley below (*see* Isa. 60:8). I have never seen them in Palestine" (Thomson, *Land and Book*).

DOVE'S DUNG. See Animal Kingdom.

DOWRY (Heb. *mōhar*, "price" paid for a wife; Gen. 34:12; Ex. 22:17; 1 Sam. 18:25). In arranging for marriage, as soon as paternal consent was obtained, the suitor gave the bride a betrothal or bridal gift, as well as presents to her parents and brothers. In more ancient times the bride received a portion only in exceptional cases (Josh. 15:18-19; 1 Kings 9:16). The opinion that the Israelites were required to buy their wives from the parents or relatives seems to be unfounded. The *mōhăr* in the OT was not "purchase money" but the bridal gift that the bridegroom, after receiving the bride's assent, gave to *her,* not to the parents or relatives. *See* Marriage.

BIBLIOGRAPHY: E. Neufeld, *Ancient Hebrew Marriage Laws* (1944), pp. 94-110; R. de Vaux, *Ancient Israel: Its Life and Institutions* (1961), p. 28.

DOXOLOGIES (Gk. *doxologia,* "giving glory"). Ascriptions of glory or praise to God.

Scriptural. These abound in the Psalms (e.g., 96:6; 112:1; 113:1) and were used in the synagogue. The apostles naturally used them (Rom. 11:36; Eph. 3:21; 1 Tim. 1:17). We have also examples of celestial doxologies (Rev. 5:13; 19:1). The song of the angels in Luke 2:13-14 is a doxology. As to the doxology in Matt. 6:13, *see* Lord's Prayer.

Liturgical. Three doxologies of special note have been used in church worship from an early time: (1) The *Lesser Doxology,* or *Gloria Patri,* originally in the form "Glory be to the Father, and to the Son, and to the Holy Ghost," to which was added later, "world without end," and still later brought to its present form: "Glory be to the Father, and to the Son, and to the Holy Ghost, as it was in the beginning, is now, and ever shall

be, world without end. Amen." (2) The *Greater Doxology,* or *Gloria in Excelsis,* called also the *Angelic Hymn.* (3) The *Trisagion,* as old as the second century, beginning, "Therefore, with angels and archangels, and with all the company of heaven, we laud and magnify Thy glorious name."

BIBLIOGRAPHY: L. G. Champion, *Benedictions and Doxologies in the Epistles of Paul* (1934).

DRACHMA. The drachma or daric was a weight and a coin. *See* Metrology.

DRAG, or **Dragnet** (Heb. *mikmeret*). The drag is mentioned in the KJV as being the object of worship by fishermen (Hab. 1:15-16). It was a large fishing net, the lower part of which, when sunk, touched the bottom, while the upper part floated on the top of the water. The NASB renders "net" (which see).

DRAGON. See Animal Kingdom.

Figurative. In the NT "dragon" (Gk. *drakōn*) is found only in Rev. 12:3-4, 7-9, 13-17; 13:2, 4, 11; 16:13; 20:2 and is used figuratively of Satan. The reason for this scriptural symbol is to be sought not only in the union of gigantic power with craft and malignity, of which the serpent is the natural emblem, but also in the record of the serpent's participation in the temptation (Gen. 3).

In Christian art the dragon is the emblem of sin in general and idolatry in particular, having usually the form of a gigantic winged crocodile.

DRAGON'S WELL. Probably the fountain of Gihon, on the W side of Jerusalem (Neh. 2:13).

DRAM. Better, a daric or a drachma. This was a weight and a unit of money. *See* Metrology.

DRAUGHT (Gk. *'aphedrōn*). A privy or sink; the word is found only in the KJV, Matt. 15:17; Mark 7:19. *See* Refuse.

DRAUGHT HOUSE (Heb. *mahărā'â,* lit., "easing one's self"). A privy or sink. Jehu, in contempt of Baal, ordered his temple to be destroyed and the place turned into a receptacle for rubbish or excrement (2 Kings 10:27, KJV only). The NASB and NIV render "latrine."

DRAWER OF WATER (Heb. *sho'eb mayim,* "drawer of water"). In the East water is often carried from the rivers or wells by persons who make it their trade, carrying the water in goatskins slung on their backs, with the neck brought around under the arm to serve as a mouth. It was a hard and servile employment (Deut. 29:11), to which the Gibeonites were condemned (Josh. 9:21, 23).

DRAWERS. *See* Dress.

DREAM (Heb. *hălôm;* Gk. *onar*). "The dream is a domain of experience, having an intellectual, ethical, and spiritual significance. Living in an earthly body, we have, as the background of our

A Jewish bride in traditional dress

being, a dim region, out of which our thinking labors forth to the daylight, and in which much goes forward, especially in the condition of sleep, of which we can only come to a knowledge by looking back afterward. Not only many poetical and musical inventions, but, moreover, many scientific solutions and spiritual perceptions, have been conceived and born from the life of genius awakened in sleep.

"Another significant aspect of dreaming is the ethical. In the dream one's true nature manifests itself, breaking through the pressure of external relations and the stimulation of the waking life. From the selfishness of the soul, its selfish impulses, its restlessness stimulated by selfishness, are formed in the heart all kinds of sinful images, of which the man is ashamed when he awakens, and on account of which remorse sometimes disturbs the dreamer. The Scriptures appear to hold the man responsible, if not for dreaming, at least for the character of the dream (Lev. 15:16; Deut. 23:10).

"A third significant aspect of dreams is the spiritual: they may become the means of a direct and special intercourse of God with man. The witness of conscience may make itself objective and expand within the dreamlife into perceptible transactions between God and man. Thus God warned Abimelech (Gen. 20) and Laban (31:24) in a dream, and the wife of Pilate warned her husband against being concerned in the death of the Just One." The conviction of the sinfulness and nothingness of man is related by Eliphaz as realized in a dream (Job 4:12-21).

The special will of God was often revealed to men through dreams. Such are the dreams of Jacob in Bethel (Gen. 28:12) and in Haran (31:10-13), the dream of Solomon in Gibeon (1 Kings 3:5), the dreams of Joseph the husband of Mary (Matt. 1:20), the night visions of Paul (Acts 16:9; 18:9; 23:11; 27:23). From 1 Sam. 28:6 we infer that God did at times answer sincere inquirers. Concerning the future the dreams of Nebuchadnezzar and Daniel are examples.

"Waking visions probably are to be distin-

guished from these prophetic dream visions, which the seer, whether by day (Ezek. 8:1; Dan. 10:7; Acts 7:55; 10:9-16) or by night (cf. Acts 16:9; 18:9), receives in a waking state."

The dreams of Joseph in his father's house (Gen. 37:5-11), which figuratively predicted to him his future eminence over the house of Jacob, the dreams of the chief butler and the chief baker of Pharaoh (chap. 40), and the dream of the soldier in the Midianitish camp in the time of Gideon (Judg. 7:13) are illustrations of dreams of presentiment.

According to Num. 12:6, dreams and *visions* (which see) are the two forms of the prophetic revelations of God. Too much reliance is not to be placed upon dreams (Eccles. 5:7).

"A good dream" was one of the three things —namely, a good king, a fruitful year, and a good dream—popularly regarded as marks of divine favor; and so general was the belief in its significance that it passed into this popular saying: "If anyone sleeps seven days without dreaming call him wicked" (as being unremembered by God) (*see* Delitzsch, *Biblical Psychology,* pp. 324ff.).

Because the dream was looked upon as a communication from the gods there arose those who professed the ability to interpret them (*see* Magic). They were not to be listened to if they taught anything contrary to the law (Deut. 13:1-3; Jer. 27:9; etc.). Instances are given of God's aiding men to understand dreams and the divine lessons taught thereby, e.g., Joseph (Gen. 40:5-23; 41:1-32), Daniel (Dan. 2:19-30; 4:8).

BIBLIOGRAPHY: A. L. Oppenheim, *The Interpretation of Dreams in the Ancient Near East* (1956); F. J. Delitzsch, *A System of Biblical Psychology* (1966), pp. 324ff.

DREAMS, DIVINATION BY. *See* Magic: Various Forms.

DREGS.

1. The rendering of the Heb. *shemer,* Ps. 75:8, elsewhere "aged" or "lees" of wine. As the wine was strained when about to be used, so the psalmist uses the figure of the strained wine being a portion of the righteous, whereas the wicked shall drink the dregs.

2. Heb. *qŭbba'at,* "goblet," Isa. 51:17, 22. Rendered "the chalice of reeling you have drained to the dregs," but better, "the chalice of My anger."

DRESS. In treating this subject we call attention to (1) materials, color, and ornamentation; (2) garments, forms, names, etc.; (3) usages relating to it. A discussion of the term *dress* in the sense of tilling the soil appears in the article following.

Materials. The first mention of clothing that occurs in Scripture is of the simple garments made by Adam and Eve from fig leaves (Gen. 3:7), which were followed by those made of the skin of animals (3:21). Skins were not wholly disused at later periods; the "mantle" worn by Elijah appears to have been the skin of a sheep or some other animal with the wool left on. It was characteristic of a prophet's office from its mean appearance (Zech. 13:4; cf. Matt. 7:15). Cloaks of sheepskin still form an ordinary article of dress in the East. The art of weaving hair was known to the Hebrews at an early period (Ex. 26:7; 35:6); the sackcloth used by mourners was of this material. John the Baptist's robe was of camel's hair (Matt. 3:4). Wool, we may presume, was introduced at an early period, the flocks of the pastoral families being kept partly for their wool (Gen. 38:12); it was at all times largely employed, particularly for the outer garments (Lev. 13:47; Deut. 22:11; etc.). Flax was no doubt used in the earliest times to make linen garments. Of silk there is no mention at an early period, unless it is in Ezekiel (16:10, 13).

White was considered the most appropriate color for cotton cloth, and purple for others. Ornamentation was secured by (1) weaving with previously dyed threads (Ex. 35:25); (2) gold thread; (3) introduction of figures, either woven into the cloth or applied by needlework. Robes decorated with gold (Ps. 45:13), and at a later period with silver thread (cf. Acts 12:21), were worn by royal personages; other kinds of embroidered robes were worn by the wealthy both of Tyre (Ezek. 16:13) and Palestine (Judg. 5:30; Ps. 45:14). From the period of Moses the art was maintained among the Hebrews; the Babylonians and other Eastern nations (Josh. 7:21; Ezek. 27:24), as well as the Egyptians (v. 7), excelled in it. Although the art of dyeing seems to have been flourishing in Palestine, dyed robes were imported from foreign countries (Zeph. 1:8), particularly from Phoenicia, and were not much used on account of their expensiveness; purple (Prov. 31:22; Luke 16:19) and scarlet (2 Sam. 1:24) were occasionally worn by the wealthy. The surrounding nations were more lavish in their use of them; the wealthy Tyrians (Ezek. 27:7), the Midianitish kings (Judg. 8:26), the Assyrian nobles (Ezek. 23:6), and Persian officers (Esther 8:15) are all represented in purple.

Garments. From the simple loincloth, or apron, dress gradually developed in amount and character according to climate and condition and taste of the wearer. Regarding the clothing of the patriarchs and ancient Israelites, the Beni Hasan tableau (c. 1900 B.C.) from Egypt provides a good illumination of the appearance of Abraham and his contemporaries. It was not limited to what was indispensable to cover nakedness, for we read of various forms of clothing (Gen. 24:53; 37:3) and costly garments of fine linen (41:42; 45:22).

The making of clothes among the Israelites was always the business of the housewives, in which women of rank equally took part (1 Sam. 2:19; Prov. 31:22-24; Acts 9:39).

Although the costume of men and women was similar, there was an easily recognizable distinc-

tion between the male and female attire of the Israelites. Accordingly the Mosaic law forbids men to wear women's clothes and vice versa (Deut. 22:5).

The Dress of Men. Among the Israelites these were a *tunic* or *coat* (Heb. *kuttōnet,* Ex. 28:4, 39; 29:5; 2 Sam. 15:32; Gk. *chitōn,* Matt. 5:40; Mark 6:9; Luke 3:11; 6:29; etc.). This was the simplest of all the garments worn, corresponding to an ordinary shirt or nightgown. It was probably made of two pieces sewn together at the sides, or else formed of one piece, with a place cut for the head to pass through. It afforded so slight a covering that persons who had on nothing else were called naked (1 Sam. 19:24, marg.; 2 Sam. 6:20; John 21:7). Another kind reached to the wrists and ankles. It was in either case fastened around the loins with a *girdle* (*see* below), and the fold formed by the overlapping of the robe served as an inner pocket. Such a garment was worn by the priests and probably by Joseph (Gen. 37:3, 23) and Tamar (2 Sam. 13:18).

Outer Tunic (Heb. *me'il*). This was a looser and a longer sort of a tunic reaching to near the ankles; open at the top also as to be drawn over the head, and having holes for the insertion of the arms. As an article of ordinary dress it was worn by kings (1 Sam. 24:4), prophets (28:14), nobles (Job 1:20), and youths (1 Sam. 2:19). It may, however, be doubted whether the term is used in its specific sense in these passages and not rather for any robe that chanced to be worn over the *kuttōnet* (*see* above). Where two tunics are mentioned (Luke 3:11) as being worn at the same time, the second would be a *me'il;* travelers generally wore two, but the practice was forbidden to the disciples (Matt. 10:10; Luke 9:3).

Mantle, or Cloak (Heb. *śimlâ,* and other terms). A piece of cloth nearly square, a sort of blanket or plaid. In pleasant weather it was more conveniently worn over the shoulders than being wrapped around the body. Although it answered the purpose of a cloak, it was so large that burdens, if necessary, might be carried in it (Ex. 12:34; 2 Kings 4:39). The poor wrapped themselves up wholly in this garment at night, spread the leather girdle upon a rock and rested the head upon it, as is customary to this day in Asia. Moses, therefore, enacted as a law what had been a custom, that the upper garment, when given as a pledge, should not be retained overnight (Ex. 22:25-26; Deut. 24:13; Job 22:6; 24:7). In the time of Christ creditors did not take the upper garment or cloak, which it was not lawful for them to retain, but the coat or tunic, which agrees with the representation of Jesus (Matt. 5:40). There having occurred an instance of the violation of the Sabbath (Num. 15:32-41), Moses commanded that there should be a fringe upon the four corners of this garment, together with a blue cord or "riband," to remind the people of the heavenly origin of His statutes (Matt. 9:20;

Luke 8:44). *See* Hem in the general listing. The prophet's mantle was, probably, as a rule a simple sheepskin with the wool turned outward.

Breeches or Drawers (Heb. *miknās*, "hiding"). A garment worn under the tunic for the fuller covering of the person. These trousers were worn by the priests but do not appear to have been in general use among the Hebrews. *See* Priest, Dress of.

Girdle (the rendering of one Gk. and several Heb. words). The tunic when it was not girded impeded the person who wore it in walking. Those, consequently, who perhaps at home went ungirded, went out girded (2 Kings 4:29; 9:1; Isa. 5:27; Jer. 1:17; John 21:7; Acts 12:8). There were formerly, and are to this day, two sorts of girdles in Asia: a common one of leather six inches broad and furnished with clasps, with which it is fastened around the body (2 Kings 1:8; Matt. 3:4; Mark 1:6); the other a valuable one of flax or cotton, sometimes of silk or of some embroidered fabric, a handbreadth broad, and supplied with clasps by which it was fastened over the forepart of the body (Jer. 13:1). The girdle was bound around the loins, whence the expression, "gird up your loins" (Jer. 1:17; 1 Kings 18:46; Isa. 11:5). The Arabs carry a knife or a dagger in the girdle. This was the custom among the Hebrews (1 Sam. 25:13; 2 Sam. 20:8-10), a fact that is confirmed from the ruins of Persepolis. The girdle also answers the purpose of a pouch, to carry money and other necessary things (2 Sam. 18:11; Matt. 10:9; Mark 6:8).

Cap, or Turban. The words for headdress in the OT (Heb. *miṣnepet*, the high priest's "turban," NASB ["mitre," KJV], Ex. 28:4; *migbā'â*, the "cap," NASB ["bonnet," KJV, "headband," NIV], worn by the priests, Ex. 28:40; *ṣanîp*, a "turban," Zech. 3:5, or "diadem," Isa. 62:3; *pe'er*, a decoration, garland, headdress, or turban, cf. Ezek. 24:17; *ṭebûlîm*, a "turban," Ezek. 23:15 all belong to men of rank. Israelites, as a rule, seem not to have worn any cap but to have confined their hair with a band or wrapped a cloth—generally known by us as a turban—around the head, as is still done in Arabia. *See also* the following in the general listing: Crown; Diadem; Turban.

Robe, or Ephod. The *ephod* (*see* article in the general listing) and the *me'îl*, according to the Mosaic law, were appropriately garments of the *high priest* (which see) but were sometimes worn by other illustrious men (Ex. 28:4, 6, 12; 1 Sam. 18:4; 2 Sam. 6:14; Job 29:14; Ezek. 26:16).

Sandals, Shoes. The covering for the feet were *sandals* (Heb. *na'al;* Gk. *hupodēma*, "bound under" the feet), of leather and fastened with thongs. They were taken off upon entering a room or a holy place (Ex. 3:5; Josh. 5:15), whereas the poor and mourners went barefoot (2 Sam. 15:30; Isa. 20:2; Ezek. 24:17, 23). Men of rank had these sandals put on, taken off, and carried after them by slaves (Matt. 3:11; Mark 1:7; John 1:27).

The Dress of Women. The difference between the dress of men and women was small, consisting chiefly in the fineness of the materials and the length of the garment. The dress of the hair in the two sexes was different, and another mark of distinction was that women wore veils.

Tunic. Women wore the tunic as an *under dress* (Song of Sol. 5:3), but it was probably wider, longer, and of finer material; the well-to-do wore also *shirts* (Heb. *sādîn*, "wrapper," Isa. 3:23, "undergarments"; NIV, "linen garments"), and a kind of second tunic, provided with sleeves and reaching to the ankles.

Girdle, or Belt. This was frequently of fine woven stuff (Prov. 31:24), studded with precious stones and worn lower down on the loins and more loosely than by men.

Headdress. This could be of several types: (1) *Veil.* That of the lower class of Israelite women is unknown, but the *veil* was regarded from ancient times by women of character as indispensable. Various kinds are mentioned: "The oldest kind seems to be (Heb. *sa'îp*, to "wrap," Gen. 24:65; 38:14, 19), a cloak-like veil, a kind of mantilla which at a later time . . . was called *rādîd*, ("spreading," Song of Sol. 5:7; Isa. 3:23)." The *re'ālâ* ("fluttering," Isa. 3:19) are veils flowing down from the head over the temples, hence waving with the action of walking, which were so adjusted to the eyes as to be seen through. Many understand *ṣammâ* (to "fasten" on; Song of Sol. 4:1, 3; 6:7; Isa. 47:2) to be a veil covering breast, throat, and chin, such as is still worn in Syria and Egypt. (2) The *mitpaḥat*, "cloak" (Ruth 3:15; Isa. 3:22; both NASB ["shawl," NIV]; but "veil" and "wimple," respectively, in the KJV), a sort of shawl or broad garment, probably similar to the mantle (or cloak) worn by men. "As the cloaks worn by the ancients were so full that one part was thrown upon the shoulder and another gathered up under the arm, Ruth, by holding a certain part, could receive into her bosom the corn which Boaz gave her" (Edersheim, *Sketches of Jewish Life*). (3) The *kerchief* (NASB and NIV, "veil," Heb. *mispāḥâ*, "spread" out, Ezek. 13:18, 21) is understood by some as a close-fitting cap; but others believe it to have been a long veil or headdress. "The Eastern women bind on their other ornaments with a rich embroidered handkerchief, which is described by some travelers as completing the headdress and falling without order upon the hair behind." In patriarchal times wives (Gen. 12:14) and young women (24:15) went about, especially when engaged in their household duties, without veils; and yet in early times the betrothed veiled herself in the presence of the bridegroom (24:65), and lewd women veiled themselves (38:15).

Sandal. Sandals consisted merely of soles strapped to the feet, but ladies also wore costly slippers, often made of sealskin (Ezek. 16:10, NASB, "porpoise skin"; NIV, "leather"), probably also of colored leather. Ladies of rank appear to have paid great attention to the beauty of their sandals (Song of Sol. 7:1). They were embroidered or adorned with gems and so arranged that the pressure of the foot emitted a delicate perfume. (5) *Stomacher* (KJV, Heb. *pᵉtîgîl*), a term of doubtful origin, but probably a holiday dress (Isa. 3:24; NIV, "fine clothing"). The garments of females were terminated by an ample border of fringe, which concealed the feet (47:2; Jer. 13:22).

Luxurious Articles of Dress. In addition to the essential and common articles of dress already mentioned, a great many more of an ornamental kind were in use, especially among women of luxurious habits. In rebuking the women of Jerusalem, Isaiah (3:16-24) mentions a number of these articles of luxurious dress. There is doubt as to the precise meaning of some of the words employed in the description, and little comparatively can now be known of the exact shape and form of several of the articles mentioned.

Tinkling Ornaments. Rings of gold, silver, or ivory, worn around the ankles, which made a tinkling sound as the wearer walked. *See* Anklet in the general listing.

Headbands or Frontlets. Plaited bands of gold or silver thread worn below the hairnet and reaching from ear to ear ("cauls," Isa. 3:18, KJV, is one name for such an item of dress; NIV has "headbands").

Crescent ornaments (Heb. *saḥărōn,* a round "pendant"; "round tires," KJV; NIV, "crescent necklaces"). The new moon was a symbol of increasing good fortune and as such was the most approved charm against the evil eye; the ornament fastened around the neck and hung down upon the breast (Judg. 8:21).

"Necklaces" and "Earrings" (KJV, "chains").

Bracelets (*see* article in the general listing). According to the Targum, these were chains worn upon the arm, or spangles upon the wrist, answering to the spangles upon the ankles.

Caps (Heb. *pᵉ'ēr,* "embellishment"; "bonnets," KJV). These are only mentioned in other parts of Scripture as worn by men.

Ankle Chains ("ornaments of the leg," KJV). A chain worn to shorten and give elegance to the step. *See* Anklet in the general listing.

Sashes (Heb. *qishshūr*).

Perfume Boxes (Heb. *nepesh,* "breath"; "tablets," KJV). Smelling bottles.

Amulet (Heb. *lāḥash,* "whisper"). Gems or metal plates with an inscription upon them, worn as protection as well as ornament. *See* Amulet; Earring, both in the general listing.

Rings (both ear and nose). *See* article in the general listing.

Festal Robes (Heb. *mahălāsâ;* "changeable

suits," KJV). Gala dresses, not usually worn, but taken off when at home.

Money Purses (Heb. *harît,* "cut" out; "crisping pins," KJV; "satchel," RV). Pockets for holding money (2 Kings 5:23, NIV, "bags"), generally carried by men in the girdle or in a purse.

Hand Mirrors ("glasses," KJV).

Fine Linen (Heb. *sādîn,* to "envelope"). Veils or coverings of the finest linen, Sindu cloth.

Headdress ("hoods," KJV).

Veils (*see* above). Probably delicate veillike mantles thrown over the rest of the clothes.

Of course, garments varied greatly in material and ornamentation according to ability and taste. Kings and men of rank always had a large wardrobe, partly for their own use (Prov. 31:21; Job 27:16; Luke 15:22), partly to give away as presents (Gen. 45:22; 1 Sam. 18:4; 2 Kings 5:5; 10:22; Esther 4:4; 6:8, 11).

Dress of Foreign Nations Mentioned in the Bible. That of the Persians is described in Dan. 3:21 in terms that have been variously understood, but which may be identified in the following manner: (1) the *sarbāl* ("trousers," NASB and NIV; "coat," KJV), *underclothing,* worn next the person; (2) *paṭîsh* ("coat," NASB; "hosen," KJV; "robes," NIV), probably the outer tunic; (3) *karbᵉlâ* ("caps," NASB; "hats," KJV; "turbans," NIV); whereas (4) the "other clothes," *lᵉbûsh,* may mean coverings for the head and feet. In addition to these terms we have notice of "a garment of fine linen" (Heb. *takrîk*), so called from its ample dimensions (Esther 8:15). References to Roman or Greek dress are few.

Customs Relating to Dress. "The length of the dress rendered it inconvenient for active exercise; hence the outer garments were either left in the house by a person working close by (Matt. 24:18) or were thrown off when occasion arose (Mark 10:50; John 13:4; Acts 7:58), or, if this was not possible, as in the case of a person traveling, they were girded up (1 Kings 18:46; 2 Kings 4:29; 9:1; cf. 1 Pet. 1:13). On entering a house the upper garment was probably laid aside and resumed on going out (Acts 12:8). The number of suits possessed by the Hebrews was considerable; a single suit consisted of an under and upper garment. The presentation of a robe in many instances amounted to installation or investiture (Gen. 41:42; Esther 8:15; Isa. 22:21); on the other hand, taking it away amounted to dismissal from office (2 Macc. 4:38). The production of the best robe was a mark of special honor in a household (Luke 15:22). The number of robes thus received or kept in store for presents was very large and formed one of the main elements of wealth in the East (Job 27:16; Matt. 6:19; James 5:2); so that to have clothing was equal to being wealthy and powerful (Isa. 3:6-7)" (Smith, *Bib. Dict.,* s.v.; Jahn; Keil).

BIBLIOGRAPHY: A. Erman, *Life in Ancient Egypt* (1894), pp. 200-233; H. F. Lutz, *Textiles and Customs Among the*

WOMEN'S DRESS IN BIBLE TIMES

MEN'S DRESS IN BIBLE TIMES

People of the Ancient Near East (1923); A. C. Bouquet, Everyday Life in New Testament Times (1954); M. G. Houston, Ancient Egyptian and Persian Costume and Decoration (1954); J. B. Pritchard, ed., The Ancient Near East in Pictures (1954), figs. 1-66; A. Edersheim, Sketches of Jewish Social Life in the Days of Christ (1961), pp. 155, 216-25; E. E. Platt, Andrews University Seminary Studies 17 (1979): 71-84, 189-201.

DRESS. A term used in the KJV in the following senses: (1) to till the soil (Heb. 'ābad, to "serve," Gen. 2:15; Deut. 28:39; Gk. geōrgeō, Heb. 6:7), (2) to prepare food (Heb. 'āśâ, to "make," Gen. 18:7-8; 1 Sam. 25:18; 2 Sam. 12:4; 13:5, 7; etc.), (3) to trim lamps (Heb. yāṭab, "make right," Ex. 30:7).

DRINK. As a drink, water took first place, although milk was also used extensively but was considered food (which see). For the better quenching of thirst the common people used a sour drink (Ruth 2:14), a sort of vinegar mixed with oil, perhaps also sour wine. The well-to-do drank wine, probably mixed with water, and often also spiced; also a stronger intoxicating drink, either date wine or Egyptian barley wine. See Wine.

Figurative. To "drink water from your own cistern" (Prov. 5:15) is to enjoy the lawful pleasures of marriage. To "drink the blood" (Ezek. 39:18) is to be satiated with slaughter. To drink water "by measure" (4:11) denotes scarcity and desolation.

DRINK, STRONG (Heb. shēkār, "intoxicant"; Gk. sikera). Any intoxicating beverage. The Hebrews seem to have made wine (which see) of pomegranates (Song of Sol. 8:2) and other fruits. In Num. 28:7 strong drink is clearly used as an equivalent to wine. "The following beverages were known to the Jews: (1) Beer, which was largely consumed in Egypt under the name of zythus, and was thence introduced into Palestine. It was made of barley; certain herbs, such as lupin and skirrett were used as substitutes for hops. (2) Cider, which is noticed in the Mishna as apple wine. (3) Honey wine, of which there were two sorts—one consisting of a mixture of wine, honey, and pepper; the other a decoction of the juice of the grape, termed debash (honey) by the Hebrews, and dibs by the modern Syrians. (4) Date wine, which was also manufactured in Egypt. It was made by mashing the fruit in water in certain proportions. (5) Various other fruits and vegetables are enumerated by Pliny as supplying materials for factitious or homemade wine, such as figs, millet, the carob fruit, etc. It is not improbable that the Hebrews applied raisins to this purpose in the simple manner followed by the Arabians, viz., by putting them in jars of water and burying them in the ground until fermentation takes place" (Smith, Bib. Dict., s.v.).

DRINK OFFERING. See Sacrificial Offering.

DROMEDARY. See Animal Kingdom.

DROPSY. See Diseases.

DROSS (Heb. sîg, "refuse"). The impurities separated from silver, etc., by the process of melting (Prov. 25:4; 26:23); also the base metal itself prior to smelting (Isa. 1:22, 25; Ezek. 22:18-19).

Figurative. Dross is used to represent the wicked (Ps. 119:119; Prov. 26:23), sin (Isa. 1:25), and Israel (Ezek. 22:18-29).

DROUGHT. The rendering of a number of Heb. words. In Palestine there is little if any rain from May till October, and consequently this is the season of drought. The copious dews nourish only the more robust plants, and as the season advances the grass withers, unless watered by rivulets or the labor of man. In the drought of summer (Gen. 31:40; Ps. 32:4, see marg.), the parched ground cracks, the heaven seems like bronze and the earth as iron (Deut. 28:23), prairie and forest fires are not uncommon (Isa. 5:24; 9:18; etc.).

DROWN (Gk. katapontizō). Drowning was not a Jewish method of capital punishment, neither was it a practice in Galilee, but belonged to the Greeks, Romans, Syrians, and Phoenicians (Matt. 18:6).

DRUM. See Music.

DRUNK, DRUNKARD (Heb. some form of shākār, to be "tipsy"; Gk. metheuō). Noah, who was probably ignorant of the fiery nature of wine, affords us the first instance of intoxication (Gen. 9:21). That the excessive use of strong drink was not uncommon among the Jews may be inferred from the striking figures furnished by its use and effect and also from the various prohibitions and penalties (Ps. 107:27; Isa. 5:11; 24:20; 49:26; 51:17, 21-22; Hab. 2:15-16). The sin of drunkenness is strongly condemned in the Scriptures (Rom 13:13; 1 Cor. 5:11; 6:10; Eph. 5:18; 1 Thess. 5:7-8).

Figurative. Men are represented as drunk with sorrow, afflictions, and God's wrath (Isa. 63:6; Jer. 51:57; Ezek. 23:33); also those under the power of superstition, idolatry, and delusion, because they do not use their reason (Jer. 51:7; Rev. 17:2). Drunkenness sometimes denotes abundance, satiety (Deut. 32:42; Isa. 49:26). "To add drunkenness to thirst" (Deut. 29:19, KJV; NASB and NIV, "to destroy the watered land with the dry") is a proverbial expression meaning the destruction of one and all.

DRUSIL'LA (drū-sil'a). Youngest daughter of Herod Agrippa I, by his wife Cypros, and sister of Herod II, was only six years old when her father died in A.D. 44 (Josephus Ant. 19.9.1; 20.7.1-2). She was promised early in marriage to Epiphanes, son of Antiochus, but the match was broken off in consequence of his refusing to perform his promise of conforming to the Jewish religion. She was married to Azizus, king of Edessa, but afterward was induced by Felix, procurator of Judea, to leave Azizus and become his wife. In Acts 24:24 she is mentioned in such a manner that she may be naturally supposed to have been present when Paul preached before Felix in A.D. 57. *See also* Herod: Princesses of the House of the Herods.

DUKE (Lat. *dux,* a "leader"). Used in the KJV but not in the NASB and NIV. *See* Chiefs; Governors.

DULCIMER. *See* Music.

DU'MAH (dū'ma; "silence").
1. A son of Ishmael, most probably the founder of an Ishmaelite tribe of Arabia, and so giving a name to the principal place or district inhabited by that tribe (Gen. 25:14; 1 Chron. 1:30; Isa. 21:11, marg.).
2. A town in Judah (Josh. 15:52), the same as Daumeh, about ten miles SW of Hebron.
3. The region occupied by the Ishmaelites in Arabia (Gen. 25:14; 1 Chron. 1:30), retained in the modern Dumat el Jeudel.
Figurative. As used in Isa. 21:11, marg., Dumah seems to be symbolical, meaning deep, utter "silence," and therefore the land of the dead (Pss. 94:17; 115:17).

DUMB (Heb. *'illēm,* "speechless"; Gk. *kōphos,* "blunted," as to tongue, i.e., unable to speak, or as to ear, i.e., deaf). Dumbness has the following meanings: (1) inability to speak by reason of natural infirmity (Ex. 4:11; Matt. 15:30; Luke 1:20; etc.); (2) by reason of want of knowing what to say or how to say it (Prov. 31:8); unwillingness to speak (Ps. 39:2, 9).

DUNG. *See* Refuse.

DUNG GATE. *See* Refuse Gate.

DUNGEON. *See* Prison.

DUNGHILL. The rendering in KJV of three Heb. words and one Gk., and meaning: (1) a heap of manure (Isa. 25:10; Luke 14:35; NASB and NIV, "manure pile"); (2) privy (2 Kings 10:27, "draughthouse," NASB, "latrine," Dan. 2:5, NASB and NIV, "rubbish heap"; NIV, "piles of rubble").
Figurative. To sit upon a dung heap denoted the deepest degradation and ignominy (1 Sam. 2:8; Ps. 113:7; Lam. 4:5).

DU'RA (dū'ra; Akkad. *dūru,* "circuit," "wall"). A plain in the province of Babylon in which Nebuchadnezzar set up a golden image (Dan. 3:1). It is supposed that the site of the image is identified in one of the mounds discovered in the territory. Several localities in Babylon were called Duru. There is a river by this name, with Tulūl Dūra near by.

DUST. In the countries suffering from severe droughts the soil is often converted into dust, which, agitated by violent winds, brings terrific and desolating storms. Among the punishments against the Hebrews, in the event of forsaking Jehovah, was that, instead of rain, dust and ashes ("powder") should fall from heaven (Deut. 28:24).
Figurative. To put dust on the head was the sign of the deepest grief (Josh. 7:6); sitting in the dust denotes degradation (Isa. 47:1); the "mouth in the dust" (Lam. 3:29) symbolizes suppliant and humble submission. Dust may mean the *grave* (Job 7:21), *death* itself (Gen. 3:19; Ps. 22:15), a *numerous people* (Num. 23:10) or *low condition* (1 Sam. 2:8). The *shaking off the dust* is a sign of merited *contempt* with which the people rejecting the truth are reduced to the level of the Gentiles (Matt. 10:14; Acts 13:51). To "lick the dust" signifies the most abject submission (Ps. 72:9). To "throw dust" at anyone (2 Sam. 16:13) may signify contempt or, as some believe, to demand justice (Acts 22:23). *See* Mourning.

DUTY (Heb. *dābār,* a "matter," 2 Chron. 8:14; Ezra 3:4, KJV). The task of each day. NASB renders "according to the daily rule" or "as each day required." The other use of the word is that which a man owes to his wife or his deceased brother's widow (Deut. 25:5; 7; Heb. *'ônâ,* "cohabitation"). In the NT the word is the rendering of the Gk. *opheideō,* to "be under obligation" (Luke 17:10; Rom. 15:27, KJV), and signifies that which ought to be done.
Duty implies *obligation.* Such is the constitution of the human mind that no sooner do we perceive a given course to be *right* than we recognize also a certain *obligation* resting on us to pursue that course. Duties vary according to one's relations. Thus a person has duties to one's self, the family, the state, and God. As his most supreme relation is to God, and as God's commands are always right, therefore one's chief obligation is to God (1 Cor. 10:31).

DWARF (Heb. *daq,* "beaten" small, as in Lev. 16:12, NASB, "finely ground"). An incorrect rendering for a *lean* or emaciated person (Lev. 21:20). Such a person was included among those who could not serve in the sanctuary. *See* Blemish.

DWELL. *See* House, Tent.
Figurative. God "dwelling in light" is said in respect to His independent possession of His own glorious attributes (1 Tim. 6:16; 1 John 1:7); He *dwells in heaven* in respect to His more immediate presence there (Ps. 123:1, "who art enthroned in the heavens"); Christ *dwelt* (tabernacled) upon earth during His incarnation. To dwell has the sense of *permanent* residence. "May God enlarge Japheth, and let him *dwell* in the tents of Shem" (Gen. 9:27, italics added).
"To dwell under one's vine and fig tree"

(1 Kings 4:25, KJV) is to enjoy the possession of a home in his own right. God dwells in the church (Eph. 3:17-19) through the Holy Spirit (1 Cor. 3:16; 2 Tim. 1:14); and believers are exhorted to "let the word of Christ richly dwell within you" (Col. 3:16; Ps. 119:11).

To "dwell in the depths," literally, "make deep for dwelling" (Jer. 49:8), seems to refer to a custom still common in Eastern countries of seeking refuge from danger in the recesses of rocks and caverns, etc.

DWELLING. The rendering of a number of Heb. and Gk. words. Human dwellings have varied from the earliest day to the present—caves, booths, tents, houses, and palaces—according to the character of the country, mode of living, and occupation, as well as the degree of culture.

DYERS. See Handicrafts.

DYSENTERY. See Diseases.

EAGLE. *See* Animal Kingdom.

Figurative. Of great and powerful kings (Ezek. 17:3; Hos. 8:1); of the renovating and quickening influences of the Spirit in the godly, referring to the eagle's increase of vigor after moulting (Ps. 103:5; Isa. 40:31); of God's strong and loving care of His people (Ex. 19:4; Deut. 32:11); the melting away of riches is symbolized by the swiftness of the eagle's flight (Prov. 23:5), also the rapidity of the movement of armies (Deut. 28:49; Jer. 4:13; 48:40) and the swiftness of man's days (Job 9:26); the height and security of its dwelling symbolizes the fancied but fatal security of the wicked (Jer. 49:16; Obad. 4). "Extend your baldness like the eagle" (Mic. 1:16) is "a reference to the bearded vulture, or more probably the carrion vulture, which has the front of the head completely bald and only a few hairs at the back of the head. The words cannot possibly be understood as referring to the yearly moulting of the eagle itself" (K. & D., *Com.*, ad loc.).

EAGLE OWL. *See* Animal Kingdom: Owl.

EAR. The organ of hearing. We learn from Scripture that blood was put upon the right ear of the priests at their consecration (Ex. 29:20; Lev. 8:23) and of the healed leper in his cleansing (14:14). They were often adorned with rings (*see* Earring), and servants who refused to leave their masters had to stand against a door as an awl was bored through the ear as a mark of perpetual servitude (Ex. 21:6; Deut. 15:17).

Figurative. "Uncover my ear" (1 Sam. 20:2, marg.) is to reveal; to have the "ears dull" (Isa. 6:10) or "closed" (Jer. 6:10, marg., "uncircumcised") is to be inattentive and disobedient; the regard of Jehovah to the prayer of His people is expressed thus: "His ears are open to their cry" (Ps. 34:15).

EARRING.

Egyptian. The earrings usually worn by Egyptian women were large, round, single hoops of gold, from 1½ to 2 1/3 inches in diameter, and frequently of a still greater size or made of six rings soldered together. Sometimes a snake, whose body was of gold set with precious stones, was worn by persons of rank as a fashionable caprice, but it is probable that this emblem of majesty was usually confined to members of the royal family. Earrings of other forms have been found at Thebes, but their date is uncertain, and it is difficult to say if they are of an ancient Egyptian age or of Greek introduction. Of these the most remarkable were a dragon and another elegant, fancy shape. A few were of silver, and plain hoops, like those made of gold already noted, but less massive, being of the thickness of an ordinary ring. At one end was a small opening, into which the curved extremity of the other caught after it had been passed through the ear. Others were in the form of simple studs. The ancient Assyrians, both men and women, wore earrings of exquisite shape and finish; those on the later monuments are generally in the form of a cross.

Hebrew. Rings and amulets were worn.

Ring (Heb. *nezem*). Used both as a *nosering* and an *earring*, and differing little if any in form. It certainly means an earring in Gen. 35:4 but a nose jewel in 24:47; Prov. 11:22; Isa. 3:21; its meaning is doubtful in Judg. 8:24-25 (though the NIV has "earring"); Job 41:22.

Amulet (Heb. *laḥash*, "whispering"). This word, rendered in the KJV "earrings" (Isa. 3:20), is "amulets" in the NASB and "charms" in the NIV. These latter more correctly represent the Heb. word (meaning "incantations"). Amulets were gems or metal charms with an inscription upon them, worn for protection as well as ornament. On this account they were surrendered along with the idols by Jacob's household (Gen. 35:4). Chardin describes earrings, with talisman-

Gold earrings of Bible times discovered in the Jericho hills

ic figures and characters on them, as still existing in the East. Jewels were sometimes attached to the rings. The size of the earrings still worn in Eastern countries far exceeds what is usual in the West; hence they formed a handsome present (Job 42:11) or offering to the service of God (Num. 31:50). Earrings were worn by both sexes (Ex. 32:2). *See also* Dress.

EARTH. The rendering of several Heb. and Gk. words. (*See* Mineral Kingdom.)

Soil (Heb. *'ădāmâ*), or ground, as in Gen. 9:20, where the word used for farming is literally "man of the ground." The *earth* supplied the elementary substance of which man's body was formed (2:7). According to the law, earth or rough stones were the material out of which altars were to be raised (Ex. 20:24); thought by some to symbolize the elevation of man to God. Others think it teaches that the earth, which has been involved in the curse of sin, is to be renewed and glorified by the gracious hand of God. Naaman's request for "two mules' load of earth" (2 Kings 5:17) was based on the belief that Jehovah, like heathen deities, was a local god and could be worshiped acceptably only on His own soil.

Land (Heb. *'ĕrĕṣ*). K. & D. (*Com.*, on Gen. 2:5) thus distinguish between "field" (Heb. *śādeh*) and "earth." "*Śādeh* is not the widespread plain of the earth, the broad expanse of land, but a field of arable land, which forms only a part of the earth or ground." The term is applied in a more or less extended sense: (1) to the whole world (Gen. 1:1); (2) to land as opposed to sea (1:10); (3) to a country (21:32); (4) to a plot of ground (23:15); (5) to the ground on which a man stands (33:3); (6) to the inhabitants of the earth (6:11; 11:1); (7) to heathen countries, as distinguished

from Israel, especially during the theocracy (2 Kings 18:25; 2 Chron. 13:9; etc.); (8) in a spiritual sense it is employed in contrast with heaven, to denote things carnal (John 3:31; Col. 3:2, 5).

EARTHEN VESSEL or **Earthenware.** *See* Pot, Potter.

EARTHQUAKE (Heb. *ra'ash,* "vibration"; Gk. *seismos*). A tremulous motion or shaking of the earth caused by the violent action of subterraneous heat and vapors. There can be no doubt that Palestine has been subject both to volcanic agency and to occasional earthquakes. The recorded instances, however, are few; the most remarkable occurred in the reign of Uzziah (Amos 1:1), which Josephus connected with the sacrilege and consequent punishment of that monarch (cf. 2 Chron. 26:16-23). Of the extent of that earthquake, of the precise localities affected by it, or of the desolations it may have produced—of anything, in short, but the general alarm and consternation occasioned by it—we know absolutely nothing. Earthquakes are mentioned in connection with the crucifixion (Matt. 27:51-54), the resurrection (28:2), and the imprisonment of Paul and Silas (Acts 16:26). These, like those recorded in connection with the death of Korah (Num. 16:32) and Elijah's visit to Mt. Horeb (1 Kings 19:11), would seem to have been miraculous rather than natural phenomena. Josephus (*Ant.* 14. 52) gives an account of an earthquake that devastated Judea (31 B.C.). The second advent of Christ will be preceded and attended by gigantic earthquakes (Rev. 16:18-19; Zech. 14:4-5).

Figurative. Earthquakes are symbolic of the judgments of God (Isa. 24:20; 29:6; Jer. 4:24; Rev. 8:5) and of the overthrow of nations (Hag. 2:6, 22; Rev. 6:12-13; 16:18-19).

BIBLIOGRAPHY: E. J. Arieh, *Geological Survey of Israel* 43 (1967): 1-14.

EAST. The direction toward the rising of the sun, denoted by the Heb. word *mizrāḥ,* "rising" (Josh. 11:3; Ps. 103:12; Zech. 8:7), used when the E is distinguished from the W or from some other quarter of the compass (Dan. 8:9; 11:44). Since the Hebrews faced the rising of the sun in telling direction, the E was "the front" (Heb. *qedem,* "what is the front"; Gen. 13:14; 28:14; Ezek. 47:18). This Heb. word is also used in a geographical sense to describe a spot or country immediately *before* another in an easterly direction (Gen. 2:8; 3:24; 13:11). In Matt. 2:2, 9 the Gk. expression for E means "rising," *anatolē,* "for we saw His star in the east," that is, in its rising.

EAST, CHILDREN OF THE. *See* East, Sons of the.

EAST, SONS OF THE. Hebrew idiom for "Easterners" applied to peoples living E of Palestine (Judg. 6:3, 33; 7:12; 8:10; 1 Kings 4:30; etc.).

EAST GATE. *See* Potsherd Gate.

EAST WIND (Heb. *qādîm,* "east"). *See* Winds.

EASTER (Gk. *pascha,* from Heb. *pesaḥ*). The *Passover* (which see), and so translated in every passage except in the KJV: "intending after Easter to bring him forth to the people" (Acts 12:4). In the earlier English versions Easter had been frequently used as the translation of *pascha.* At the last revision Passover was substituted in all passages but this. *See* Passover.

The word *Easter* is of Saxon origin, Eastra, the goddess of spring, in whose honor sacrifices were offered about Passover time each year. By the eighth century Anglo-Saxons had adopted the name to designate the celebration of Christ's resurrection.

BIBLIOGRAPHY: N. M. Denis-Boulet, *Christian Calendar* (1960).

EASTERN SEA. The Dead Sea was called the East (KJV) or Eastern Sea (Joel 2:20; Ezek. 47:18), whereas the Mediterranean Sea was called the West (KJV) or Great Sea (Num. 34:6). *See* Dead Sea.

EATING. *See* Food, Hospitality.

Figurative. "To eat" is spoken metaphorically of meditating upon and assimilating the Word of God (Jer. 15:16; Ezek. 3:1-3; Rev. 10:9-10) and familiar intercourse (Luke 13:26; cf. Titus 1:16). To eat the "spoil of your enemies" (Deut. 20:14, marg.) is to make use of it for one's own maintenance. Eating and drinking signifies enjoying one's self (Eccles. 5:18) or to live in the ordinary way as distinguished from asceticism (Matt. 11:18; cf. Acts 10:41).

E'BAL (ē'bal; to be "bare," a "stone").

1. A variant reading (1 Chron. 1:22) for *Obal* (which see).

2. One of the sons of Shobal, son of Seir the Horite, of Edom (Gen. 36:23; 1 Chron. 1:40).

3. A mountain opposite Gerizim (Deut. 11:29; Josh. 8:30, 33). In Deut. 27:4 the Samaritan Pentateuch has Gerizim instead of Ebal. The modern name is Jebel Eslamiyeh (2,950 feet) N of Shechem (see L. H. Grollenberg, *Atlas of the Bible*

Mt. Ebal and Mt. Gerizim

[1956], p. 148). From Ebal the law of Moses was recorded and read by Joshua with the blessings and the cursings (Josh. 8:30-35), the blessing set upon Mt. Gerizim and the curse upon Mt. Ebal (Deut. 11:29), which is known as the Mount of Cursing.   M.F.U.

E'BED (e'bed; "servant").

1. The father of *Gaal* (which see), who headed the insurrection at Shechem against Abimelech (Judg. 9:26-35), about 1100 B.C.

2. Son of Jonathan and head of the descendants of Adin, who returned (to the number of fifty males) from the captivity (Ezra 8:6), about 457 B.C.

E'BED-ME'LECH (e'bed-me'lek; "servant of a king"). Probably an official title equal to *king's slave,* i.e., *minister;* an Ethiopian at the court of Zedekiah, king of Judah, who was instrumental in saving the prophet Jeremiah from the dungeon and famine (Jer. 38:7-13). For the kindness he was promised deliverance when the city should fall into the enemy's hands (39:15-18), 589 B.C. He is designated a eunuch, and he probably had charge of the king's harem, an office that would give him free private access to the king.

EB'EN-E'ZER (eb'en-ē'zer; "stone of the help"). A stone set up by Samuel after a defeat of the Philistines as a memorial of the "help" received on the occasion from Jehovah (1 Sam. 7:12). Its position is carefully defined as between Mizpah and Shen. The site is currently identified with Izbet Sartah, about two miles E of *Aphek* (which see). Moshe Kochavi of Tel Aviv University directed a dig there for four seasons in the years 1976 to 1978. He found three occupational layers covering the period c. 1200-1000 B.C. From the lowest level came an ostracon bearing the earliest proto-Canaanite alphabet that has yet come to light. Level II evidently was abandoned c. 1050, about the time of the battle that resulted in the Israelite loss of the Ark of the Covenant. About 1000 B.C. the site was reoccupied briefly and then abandoned to the present.   H.F.V.

E'BER (ē'ber).

1. The son of Shelah and father of Peleg, being the third postdiluvian patriarch after Shem (Gen. 10:24; 11:14; 1 Chron. 1:18, 25). He is claimed as founder of the Hebrew race (Gen. 10:21; Num. 24:24). In Luke 3:35 his name is anglicized Heber.

2. The last named of the seven chiefs of the Gadites in Bashan (1 Chron. 5:13; "Heber," KJV).

3. The oldest of the three sons of Elpaal the Benjamite; and one of those who rebuilt Ono and Lod and their towns (1 Chron. 8:12), 535 B.C.

4. A Benjamite and son of Shashak (1 Chron. 8:22; "Heber," KJV), before 598 B.C.

5. The head of the priestly family of Amok in

the time of the return from the Exile under Zerubbabel (Neh. 12:20), 535 B.C.

E'BEZ (ē'bez). A city allotted to the tribe of Issachar following the conquest of Canaan under Joshua.   E.H.M.

EBI'ASAPH (e-bi'a-saf; "gatherer"). The son of Elkanah and father of Assir, in the genealogy of the Kohathite Levites (1 Chron. 6:23). In v. 37 he is called a son of Korah. From a comparison of that circumstance with Ex. 6:24 most interpreters have identified him with *Abiasaph* (which see) of the latter passage; but (unless we understand not three sons of Korah to be meant but only three in regular descent) the pedigrees of the two cannot be made to tally. From 1 Chron. 9:19 it appears he had a son named Kore. In 26:1 his name is abbreviated to Asaph.

EBLA (eb'la; Tell Mardikh). This city, unmentioned in Scripture but known from ancient cuneiform texts, was located about thirty miles S of Aleppo in Syria. Italian archaeologists under Paolo Matthiae of the Italian Archaeological Mission to Syria began excavating the 140-acre mound in 1964, but the site was only identified by its ancient name in 1968, when a broken inscribed statue was discovered. In 1974 a collection of forty-two large clay tablets dating to about 2300 B.C. was uncovered, and in the following year a large hoard of fifteen thousand tablets came to light. They were written in Eblaite, an early NW Semitic dialect close to the Heb. and Canaanite, but including many Sumerian loanwords. The language is sophisticated and obscure, making decipherment extremely difficult and uncertain.

Excavations showed that the ancient city could be entered through four gates set in the reinforced walls. The upper or acropolis area included the royal residences and administrative buildings, whereas the lower part of the mound was subdivided into four sections that included the homes of the workers. From the tablets, insofar as they have been deciphered correctly, Ebla appears to have been a prominent commercial center in the ancient Near East, reaching its greatest degree of influence between 2400 and 2000 B.C. (level IIB). The Eblaites traded with surrounding nations in timber, textiles, grain, metals, and marble. When Eblaite influence was at its height the city-state may well have threatened commercial interests as far away as Mesopotamia and Egypt.

The city evidently began as a prehistoric settlement about 3500 B.C. (levels I-IIA), and at its most prosperous point boasted a population of about 260,000. After its destruction about 2000 B.C. by Naram-Sin, the city was rebuilt but on a smaller scale. The rise of the Amarna Age (fifteenth and fourteenth centuries B.C.), when Egypt dominated the Near East, brought a decline in Ebla's

commercial importance, and the site ultimately became a burial ground in Roman times.

Names similar to those of some OT personages have allegedly been recognized in the Ebla tablets, including Abraham, Saul, Israel, and David. One of the cosmological texts recorded some elements of creation in the same order as that found in Genesis, while another referred to a devastating flood sent by the gods. One of the chief Eblaite deities was Dagan, who was represented in the tablets as having male hands but a fish's body. Chemosh and Ishtar are mentioned in the tablets, and reference to them is also made in OT narratives.

Early reports from Tell Mardikh suggested that the Ebla materials would have great importance for the early history of the Hebrews. But the difficulties encountered in translating the language have led to considerable uncertainty about the names of persons and places; and until these matters are resolved, it is difficult to obtain a satisfactory correlation. What is evident, however, is that a flourishing culture was able to communicate in a highly sophisticated written form some 2,500 years before Christ was born. There is thus no reason for questioning the authenticity of written communications in a comparable period of OT history. But much more investigation and study will need to be undertaken before assured comparisons between Ebla and OT personages can be made.   R.K.H.

EBONY. See Vegetable Kingdom.

EBRONAH. See Abronah.

ECBA'TANA (ek-ba'ta-na). A capital city of Cyrus the Great, about 300 miles north of Susa. It was originally the chief city of Media before Cyrus brought Media under Persian control. The city is now known as Hamadan.   E.H.M.

ECCLESIAS'TES, BOOK OF (e-klē'zi-as'tēz). The superscription in 1:1 designates the book as "the words of the Preacher, the son of David, king in Jerusalem." "The Preacher," Heb. *qōheleth,* apparently describes one who holds or addresses an assembly, Heb. *qāhal.* This is the meaning evident in the Gk. *ekklēsiastēs,* the Vulg. *concionator,* and the English "preacher." Ecclesiastes was a roll that was read at the feast of Booths. The theme of the book is the vanity of mere earthly things contrasted to the knowledge and service of God.

Contents.
I. The subject discussed: vanity of everything (1:1-3)
II. The subject proved (1:4–3:22)
   A. By the transitoriness of things (1:4-11)
   B. By the existence of evil (1:12-18)
   C. By the emptiness of pleasure, riches, and work (2:1-26)
   D. By the certainty of death (3:1-22)
III. The subject developed (4:1–12:8)

A. In consideration of injustices (4:1-16)
B. In consideration of riches (5:1-20)
C. In consideration of man's end (6:1-12)
D. In consideration of man's sinfulness (7:1-29)
E. In consideration of inscrutable divine providence (8:1–9:18)
F. In consideration of disorders (10:1-20)
G. In consideration of the vanity of youth and age (11:1–12:8)
IV. The conclusion: revere God and observe His commandments (12:9-14)

Authorship. Luther denied the Solomonic authorship, and it is at present common to attribute the book to a much later writer or writers. Few today, even among conservative scholars, defend the Solomonic authorship. However, certain evidences point to the fact that Solomon wrote the book (cf. 1:1). Definite texts in the book refer to Solomon's wisdom (1:16), his pleasures (2:3), his building exploits (2:4-6), his servants (2:7), and his wealth (2:8). If Solomon is not the writer, one must be prepared to defend the position that the author impersonates Solomon, as in the apocryphal Book of Wisdom (cf. Wisd. of Sol. 6-9). Solomonic authorship, it may be said, need not be abandoned as incapable of scholarly defense despite critical unanimity. Roman Catholic scholars Gietmann, Vigouroux, and Cornely-Hagen, as well as some Protestant scholars, have defended the Solomonic authorship.

Unity. Numerous critics such as Winckler, Haupt, Kautzch, and Barton deny unity of authorship and regard the book as composed of many later annotations to the original skeptical treatise in order to give the book an orthodox tone, but the language, style, and theme of the entire book are against this view. Ernst Sellin and Otto Eissfeldt correctly defend the unity of the book, as do many church Fathers such as Jerome and Gregory the Great, and medieval scholastics such as Thomas Aquinas.

BIBLIOGRAPHY: E. W. Hengstenberg, *Commentary on Ecclesiastes* (1860); G. A. Barton, *A Critical and Exegetical Commentary on the Book of Ecclesiastes* (1908); S. Cox, *The Book of Ecclesiastes* (1908); H. L. Ginsberg, *Studies in Koheleth* (1950); R. K. Harrison, *Introduction to the Old Testament* (1969), pp. 1072-84; H. C. Leupold, *Exposition of Ecclesiastes* (1966); C. D. Ginsburg, *Coheleth and Song of Songs* (1968); D. Kidner, *A Time to Mourn, a Time to Dance* (1976); W. C. Kaiser, Jr., *Ecclesiastes: Total Life* (1979); J. M. MacDonald, *The Book of Ecclesiastes Explained* (1982); R. Wardlaw, *Exposition of Ecclesiastes* (1982); R. C. Stedman, *Solomon's Secret* (1985); C. R. Swindoll, *Living on the Ragged Edge* (1985).

ECLIPSE OF THE SUN. No historical notice of an eclipse occurs in the Bible, but there are passages in the prophets that contain manifest allusions to this phenomenon (Joel 2:10, 31; 3:15; Amos 8:9; Mic. 3:6; Zech. 14:6). Some of these notices probably refer to eclipses that occurred about the time of the respective compositions; thus the date of Amos coincides with a total eclipse, which occurred February 9, 784 B.C., and was visible at Jerusalem shortly after noon; that of Micah with the eclipse of June 5, 716 B.C. A passing notice in Jer. 15:9 coincides in date with the eclipse of September 30, 610 B.C., so well known from Herodotus's account (1.74.103). The darkness that overspread the world at the crucifixion cannot with reason be attributed to an eclipse, as the moon was full at the time of the Passover.

ECZEMA. *See* Diseases: Scab.

ED (Heb. *'ēd,* a "witness"). A word inserted in the KJV of Josh. 22:34, apparently on the authority of a few manuscripts and also of the Syr. and Arab. versions, but not existing in the generally received Heb. text. In the NASB and NIV the word used is "witness."

EDAR. *See* Eder.

E'DEN (ē'den; "delight," "pleasantness").
1. Garden of. Biblical notices locate the spot where the temptation and the Fall occurred somewhere in the Tigris-Euphrates valley, evidently in the easternmost third of the Fertile Crescent. "Now a river flowed out of Eden to water the garden; and from there it divided and became four rivers. The name of the first is Pishon.... And the name of the second river is Gihon.... And the name of the third river is Tigris.... And the fourth river is the Euphrates" (Gen. 2:10-14). Pishon and Gihon are presumably canals, called rivers in Babylonia, which connected the Tigris and Euphrates as ancient riverbeds. The KJV Hiddekel (Babylonian *Idigla, Diglat*) is the ancient name of the Tigris. Friedrich Delitzsch located the site of Eden just N of Babylon where the Euphrates and Tigris closely approach each other. A. H. Sayce and others located it near Eridu, anciently on the Persian Gulf, but such identifications are now impossible. Both the Tigris and the Euphrates have shifted their riverbeds in the course of millennia and enormous deposits of silt have drastically changed the entire configuration of lower Babylonia. The important thing is that the book of Genesis locates the beginning of human life in the very region that scientific archaeology has demonstrated to be the cradle of civilization.

2. One of the markets that supplied Tyre with richly embroidered goods (Isa. 37:12; Ezek. 27:23). This city is the "Bit Adini" of the Assyrian monuments, a small kingdom situated on both sides of the Euphrates N of the Balikh River.

3. Son of Joah, and one of the Gershonite Levites who assisted in the reformation of public worship under Hezekiah (2 Chron. 29:12), after c. 719 B.C. He is possibly the same Levite appointed by Hezekiah as one of those who were to

superintend the distribution of the freewill offerings (31:15).

BIBLIOGRAPHY: W. F. Albright, *American Journal of Semitic Languages and Literatures* 39 (1922-23): 15-31; id., *From the Stone Age to Christianity* (1940), p. 6; M. G. Kline, *Westminster Theological Journal* 20 (1957-58): 146-49.

E'DER (ē'der; "a flock," "helper").

1. A city of southern Judah, on the Edomite border (Josh. 15:21), perhaps also the place where Jacob first halted after the burial of Rachel.

2. A chief Benjamite, son of Beriah, resident at Jerusalem (1 Chron. 8:15).

3. The second of the three "sons" (descendants) of Mushi appointed to Levitical offices in the time of David (1 Chron. 23:23; 24:30), after 1000 B.C.

EDIFICATION (Gk. *oikodomē*, "building"). Means building up. A building is therefore called an edifice. Accordingly, the work of confirming believers in the faith of the gospel and adding to their knowledge and grace is appropriately expressed by this term. Christians are said in the NT to be *edified* by understanding spiritual truth (1 Cor. 14:3-5), by the work of apostles, prophets, evangelists, pastors, and teachers (Eph. 4:11-12, "building up"), and by good speech (4:29).

The means to be used for one's upbuilding are the study and hearing of God's Word, prayer, use of the sacraments, meditation, self-examination, and Christian work of every kind. It is our duty to edify or "build up one another" (1 Thess. 5:11) by the exhibition of every grace of life and conversation.

The term is also applied to believers as "living stones" builded up into a habitation for the Lord, constituting the great spiritual temple of God (Eph. 2:20-22; 1 Pet. 2:5).

E'DOM (ē'dom; "red").

1. The name given to *Esau* (which see) after he bartered his birthright for a mess of *red* stew (Gen. 25:30).

2. The name of the country settled by the descendants of Edom. *See* Edomites.

E'DOMITES (ē'do-mīts). The descendants of Esau, who settled in the S of Palestine and at a later period came into conflict with the Israelites (Deut. 23:7); frequently called merely Edom (Num. 20:14-21; 24:18; Josh. 15:1; 2 Sam. 8:14; etc.).

Country. Edom ("Idumaea," KJV) was situated at the SE border of Palestine (Judg. 11:17; Num. 34:3) and was properly called the land or mountain of Seir (Gen. 36:8; 32:3; Josh. 24:4; Ezek. 35:3, 7, 15). The country lay along the route pursued by the Israelites from Sinai to Kadesh-barnea and thence back again to Elath (Deut. 1:2; 2:1-8), i.e., along the E side of the great valley of Arabah. On the N of Edom lay the

territory of Moab, the boundary appearing to have been the "brook Zered" (2:13-14, 18).

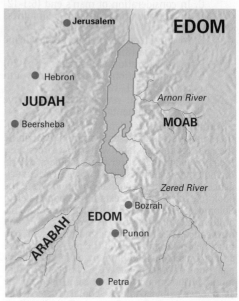

The physical geography of Edom is somewhat peculiar. Along the western base of the mountain range are low calcareous hills. These are succeeded by lofty masses of igneous rock, chiefly porphyry, over which lies red and variegated sandstone in irregular ridges and abrupt cliffs with deep ravines between. The latter strata give the mountains their most striking features and remarkable colors. The average elevation of the summit is about two thousand feet above the sea. Along the eastern side runs an almost unbroken limestone ridge, a thousand feet or more higher than the other. This ridge sinks down with an easy slope into the plateau of the Arabian Desert. Although Edom is thus wild, rugged, and almost inaccessible, the deep glens and flat terraces along the mountainsides are covered with rich soil, from which trees, shrubs, and flowers now spring up luxuriantly.

People. The Edomites were descendants of Esau, or Edom, who expelled the original inhabitants, the Horites (Deut. 2:12). A statement made in Gen. 36:31 serves to fix the period of the dynasty of the eight kings. They "reigned in the land of Edom before any king reigned over the sons of Israel"; i.e., before the time of Moses, who may be regarded as the first virtual king of Israel (cf. Deut. 33:4-5; Ex. 18:16-19). It would also appear that these kings were elected. The chiefs ("dukes," KJV) of the Edomites are named in Gen. 36:40-43 and were probably petty chiefs or sheikhs of their several clans.

History. Esau's bitter hatred toward his brother, Jacob, for fraudulently obtaining his blessing appears to have been inherited by his posterity. The Edomites peremptorily refused to permit the Israelites to pass through their land (Num. 20:18-21). For a period of 400 years we hear no more of the Edomites. They were then attacked and defeated by Saul (1 Sam. 14:47). Some forty years later David overthrew their army in the "Valley of Salt," and his general, Joab, following up the victory, destroyed nearly the whole male population (1 Kings 11:15-16) and placed Jewish garrisons in all the strongholds of Edom (2 Sam. 8:13-14). Hadad, a member of the royal family of Edom, made his escape with a few followers to Egypt, where he was kindly received by Pharaoh. After the death of David he returned and tried to excite his countrymen to rebellion against Israel, but failing in the attempt he went on to Syria, where he became one of Solomon's greatest enemies (1 Kings 11:14-22). In the reign of Jehoshaphat (875 B.C.) the Edomites attempted to invade Israel in conjunction with Ammon and Moab but were miraculously destroyed in the valley of Beracah (2 Chron. 20:22, 26). A few years later they revolted against Jehoram, elected a king, and for half a century retained their independence (21:8). They were then attacked by Amaziah, and Sela, their great stronghold, was captured (2 Kings 4:7; 2 Chron. 25:11-12). Yet the Israelites were never again able to completely subdue them (28:17). When Nebuchadnezzar besieged Jerusalem the Edomites joined him and took an active part in the plunder of the city and slaughter of the Jews. Their cruelty at that time seems to be specially referred to in Ps. 137. It was on account of these acts of cruelty committed against the Jews in the day of their calamity that the Edomites were so fearfully denounced by the later prophets (Isa. 34:5-8; 63:1-4; Jer. 49:17; Lam. 4:21; Ezek. 25:13-14; Amos 1:11-12; Obad. 8-10, 15). On the conquest of Judah, the Edomites, probably in reward for their services during the war, were permitted to settle in southern Palestine and the whole plateau between it and Egypt; but at about the same time they were driven out of Edom proper by the Nabataeans. For more than four centuries they continued to prosper. But during the warlike rule of the Maccabees they were again completely subdued and even forced to conform to Jewish laws and rites and submit to the government of Jewish prefects. The Edomites were then incorporated into the Jewish nation, and the whole province was often termed by Greek and Roman writers "Idumaea." Immediately before the siege of Jerusalem by Titus, twenty thousand Idumaeans were admitted to the Holy City, which they filled with robbery and bloodshed. From this time the Edomites, as a separate people, disappear from the pages of history. Scriptural indications that they were idolaters (2 Chron. 25:14-15, 20) are amply confirmed and illuminated by discoveries at Petra. For a discussion of the degrading practices of Edomite religion, see George L. Robinson, *The Sarcophagus of an Ancient Civilization.*

BIBLIOGRAPHY: D. N. Freedman and E. F. Campbell, eds., *Biblical Archaeologist Reader* 2 (1964): 51-58; T. C. Vriezen, *Oudtestament Studien* 14 (1965): 330-53; N. Glueck, *The Other Side of Jordan* (1970); D. J. Wiseman, ed., *Peoples of Old Testament Times* (1973), pp. 229-58.

ED'REI (ed're-i; "mighty").

1. A fortified town of northern Palestine, situated near Kedesh and Hazor (Josh. 19:37), site not known.

2. One of the metropolitan towns of Bashan beyond the Jordan (Josh. 12:4; 13:12; Deut. 3:10), and the place where King Og was defeated by the Israelites (Num. 21:33-35; Deut. 1:4; 3:1-3). It afterward fell to eastern Manasseh (Josh. 13:31; Num. 32:33).

"Its present name, *Ed-Dera'-ah* [Deraa]; first discovered by Consul Wetzstein in 1860, explored and mapped since by Schumacher in 1886. Accounts of this wonderful city have been given by others. It is a *subterranean* city. There is a small court, twenty-six feet long, eight feet three inches wide, with steps leading down into it, which has been built as an approach to the actual entrance of the caves. Then come large basaltic slabs, then a passage twenty feet long, four feet wide, which slopes down to a large room, which is shut off by a stone door so this underground city could be guarded.

"Columns ten feet high support the roof of the chambers into which you now enter. These columns are of a later period, but there are other supports built out of the basaltic rock. Then come dark and winding passages—a broad street, which had dwellings on both sides of it, whose height and width left nothing to be desired. The temperature was mild, no difficulty in breathing; several cross streets, with holes in the ceiling for air; a marketplace, a broad street with numerous shops in the walls; then into a side street, and a great hall, with a ceiling of a single slab of jasper, perfectly smooth and of immense size. Airholes are frequent, going up to the surface of the ground about sixty feet. Cisterns are frequent in the floors. Tunnels partly blocked, too small for anyone now to creep through, are found. The two travelers from whom I have quoted believe that a far greater city exists than the portion they explored.

"This remarkable subterranean city was presumably hollowed out to receive the population of the upper town in times of danger, and the people were thus prepared to stand a siege on the part of the enemy for as long as their magazines were filled with food, their stables with cattle, and the cisterns with water.

"If, however, the enemy had found out how to cut off their supply of air by covering up the airholes the besieged would have had to surrender or perish. The average depth of the city from the surface of the ground is about seventy feet" (Harper, *Bib. and Mod. Dis.*, pp. 127-29).

This important Amorite town was located about ten miles N of Ramoth-gilead on one of the eastern tributaries of the Yarmuk River. Today Deraa has a population of some ten thousand.

EDUCATION. Although nothing is more carefully inculcated in the law than the duty of parents to teach their children its precepts and principles (Ex. 12:26; 31:8, 14; Deut. 4:5, 9-10; 6:2, 7, 20; etc.), there is little trace among the Hebrews in earlier times of education in any other subject. Exception to this statement may perhaps be found in the instances of Moses himself, who was brought up in all Egyptian learning (Acts 7:22); of the writer of the book of Job, who was evidently well versed in natural history and in the astronomy of the day (Job 38:31; 39-41); of Daniel and his companions in captivity (Dan. 1:4, 17); and, above all, in the intellectual gifts and acquirements of Solomon, which were even more renowned than his political greatness (1 Kings 4:29, 34; 10:1-9; 2 Chron. 9:1-8). In later times the prophecies and comments on them, as well as on the earlier Scriptures, together with other subjects, were studied. Parents were required to teach their children some trade. *See* Children; Father; Schools.

BIBLIOGRAPHY: W. M. Ramsay, *The Education of Christ* (1909); F. H. Swift, *Education in Ancient Israel* (1919); H. T. Kuist, *The Pedagogy of St. Paul* (1925); A. Erman, *Literature of the Ancient Egyptians* (1927); W. F. Albright, *Bulletin of the American Schools of Oriental Research* 86 (April 1942): 28-31; id., *BASOR* 92 (Dec. 1943): 16-26; L. J. Sherill, *The Rise of Christian Education* (1944); G. R. Driver, *Hebrew Writing—From Pictograph to Alphabet* (1948); S. N. Kramer, *Journal of the American Oriental Society* 59 (1949): 199-215; G. E. Mendenhall, *Biblical Archaeologist* 11 (1949): 1-19; S. N. Kramer, *From the Tablets of Sumer* (1956); E. W. Heaton, *Everyday Life in Old Testament Times* (1957); W. Barclay, *Educational Ideals of the Ancient World* (1959); S. N. Kramer, *The Sumerians: Their History, Culture, and Character* (1963); H. H. Horne, *Jesus the Master Teacher* (1964); I. A. Muirhead, *Education in the New Testament* (1965); G. H. Blackburn, *Aims of Education in Ancient Israel* (1966); W. D. Davies, *The Setting of the Sermon on the Mount* (1966), pp. 415-35; D. Daube, *New Testament Studies* 19 (1972): 1-15; S. Safrai and M. Sterns, eds., *Jewish People of the First Century* (1976), 2:945-70; J. Harris, *The Teaching Methods of Christ* (1984).

EFFECTIVE CALLING. *See* Call.

EFFECTIVE PRAYER. In James 5:16 we read, "The effective [Gk. *energoumenē*] prayer of a righteous man can accomplish much." The participle here has not the force of an adjective but gives the reason that the prayer of a righteous man has outward success. The RV renders appropriately, "The supplication of a righteous man availeth much in its working."

EGG. Deuteronomy 22:6 prohibits the taking of a sitting bird from its eggs or young. Eggs are mentioned as abandoned (Isa. 10:14); also of the adder (59:5). The egg is contrasted with a *scorpion* (which see, Animal Kingdom), as an article of food (Luke 11:12). Eggs were extensively used as *food* (which see). *See also* Animal Kingdom: Bird.

Figurative. "The white of an egg" is used (Job 6:6, "the juice of purslain," RV marg.) as a symbol of something *insipid*.

EG'LAH (eg'la; "heifer"). One of David's wives during his reign in Hebron and the mother of his son Ithream (2 Sam. 3:5; 1 Chron. 3:3), about 1000 B.C. The clause appended to Eglah's name, namely, "David's wife," is not added to show that Eglah was David's principal wife, which would necessitate the conclusion drawn by the rabbis that Michal was the wife intended (Keil, *Com.*).

EG'LAIM (eg'la-im; Isa. 15:8). *See* Eneglaim.

EG'LATH SHELISHI'YAH (eg'lath shel-i-shi'-yah). A Moabite city whose location is uncertain but probably in the S of that country (Isa. 15:5; Jer. 48:34).   E.H.M.

EG'LON (eg'lon; "calflike").

1. A Moabite king. When Israel once again forsook the Lord, the Lord strengthened Eglon against them. The king allied himself with the Ammonites and the Amalekites, invaded the land, and took "the city of the palm trees" (Judg. 3:13), i.e., Jericho (c. 1300 B.C.). Sixty years had passed since Jericho had been destroyed by Joshua. During that time the Israelites had rebuilt the ruined city, but they had not fortified it on account of the curse pronounced by Joshua upon anyone who should restore it as a fortress. Thus the Moabites could easily conquer it and, using it as a base, reduce the Israelites to servitude. Here Eglon built a palace (Josephus *Ant.* 5.4.1.), which he occupied at least in the summer months (3:20).

After the Israelites had served him eighteen years the Lord raised up a deliverer in the person of *Ehud* (which see), a Benjamite. He was sent to carry a tribute to the king, and after he had done so retired with his attendants. Returning to the king, whom he found in his summer parlor, he informed him that he had a secret message from God. Eglon dismissed his attendants and rose to receive the divine message with reverence. Then Ehud plunged a dagger into the body of the king, whose obesity was such that the weapon was buried to the handle and Ehud could not draw it out again. Ehud locked the door of the room, went out through the porch, and escaped to Seirah, in Mt. Ephraim. Through delicacy the servants waited for a long time before they opened the door, when they found Eglon dead on the floor (3:12-26).

2. An Amorite city in the western lowlands that

was conquered by Joshua (Josh. 10:3, 23; 12:12; 15:39).

E'GYPT (ē'jipt). The ancient Egyptians knew their native country by the term *Kemet* (the "black land"), from its dark-colored Nile mud in contrast with the golden sands of the desert. The most common designation was Touï, the two countries, meaning Upper and Lower Egypt. The Canaanites called the land "Miṣri." The Heb. name employed in the OT, "Miṣrayim," is probably a dual, suggesting also the twofold ancient division of the country. Modern Arabs call it "Miṣr." The Greeks called it "Aigyptos" as early as the Homeric period.

Territory and Divisions. In ancient times Egypt consisted mainly of (1) the narrow strip of land watered by the Nile, extending from Memphis or Cairo as far as the First Cataract and (2) the so-called Delta (from its resemblance to that letter of the Gk. alphabet), the pie-shaped area between the Mediterranean Sea and Cairo (measuring c. 125 miles N and S and 115 E and W). This geographic configuration of the country gave rise to the term Upper Egypt, denoting the long, narrow fertile valley, and Lower Egypt, constituting the Delta. Egypt was accordingly about 725 miles long from the Mediterranean to the First Cataract and its breadth never more than 30 miles, while its cultivated area did not exceed 10 miles. It was thus a long and narrow country, its extremely fertile land comprising less than 13,000 square miles. Egypt in a definite sense is the "gift of the Nile," as the ancient Greeks said. It depended upon the exceedingly rich alluvial mud deposited by the annual inundation of the river from June to October. Irrigation was indispensable, and agriculture was the foundation of its economy.

MEDITERRANEAN SEA

Alexandria

LAND OF GOSHEN — Tanis (Raamses) — Bubastis — JUDAH

Heliopolis (On)

Cairo

Memphis — Lake Moeris — SINAI

Heracleopolis

River Nile — ▲ Mt Sinai

Oxyrhynchus

EGYPT — RED SEA

Hermopolis — 0 — 200 km

0 — 80 miles

Thebes — Karnak — Luxor

Bounded on either side by untraversable deserts and mountains, the sea on the N, an exceedingly narrow valley, and the river obstructed by cataracts on the S, Egypt was an isolated land. This geographic isolation was a prominent factor in its long and splendid history and brilliant civilization.

Inhabitants. The ancient Egyptians were Hamitic peoples (Gen. 10:6). Later on an invasion from Babylonia, predominantly Semitic, came into the country and left its imprint upon the language and culture. Other elements such as the Nubian entered into the Egyptian mixture. At a late date the country was divided into forty-two nomes, or provinces, twenty in Lower and twenty-two in Upper Egypt.

Egyptian is Hamitic, but may properly be called Hamito-Semitic. The following linguistic areas may be noted: (1) Old Egyptian, Dynasties I-VIII, included the language of the Pyramid Texts. (2) Middle Egyptian, the literary tongue of Dynasties IX-XVIII, and the vernacular language of the early part of the period, which became the classical norm imitated in later eras. (3) Late Egyptian, Dynasties XIX-XXIV, which exists on business documents and to some extent in literary works. (4) Demotic, denoting the language in a popular script from Dynasties XXV to late Roman times, 700 B.C. until after A.D. 450. (5) Coptic, third century A.D. onward, the language of the Copts, the Christian descendants of the ancient Egyptians.

The earliest writing was hieroglyphic, or picture language, including representations of common objects and geometric symbols. As early as the Old Kingdom scribes began to do away with cumbersome pictures in order to facilitate rapid writing. By the eighth century B.C. a demotic or popular writing came into vogue and was cursive in form. In 1799 Napoleon's expedition discovered the Rosetta Stone, a piece of black basalt bearing an inscription in hieroglyphics, demotic and Gk. This discovery, now in the British Museum, furnished the key to the decipherment of the Egyptian language. This feat was accomplished by the Frenchman François Champollion in 1822.

History. Manetho, a priest of Sybennytos, c. 290 B.C., wrote a history of Egypt in Gk. He divided the history of united Egypt into thirty royal dynasties. The new minimal chronology begins the first of his dynasties around 2900 B.C. Our knowledge of the early and pre-dynastic periods comes from more recent archaeological discovery.

Early and Pre-Dynastic Periods (c. 5000-2900 B.C.). Neolithic cultures appear from discoveries at Deir Tasa in Middle Egypt, in the Fayum and at Merimdeh Beni-Salameh. Chalcolithic remains appear at Badari. Copper and fine pottery were used as well as green malachite for eye paint. Akin to the Badarians were the succeeding Amratians. The civilization of these people is to be dated around the middle of the fifth millennium B.C. and marks the beginning of the pre-dynastic period. Cemeteries and village sites of Amratian culture exist from Badari to lower Nubia. They used copper and plied the Nile in boats made of bundles of papyrus. Their graves are distinctive, consisting of shallow oval pits accompanied by food, ornaments, and weapons. The Amratian period was succeeded by the Gerzean. Pear-shaped maces, wavy-handled jars of clay, stone vessels of animal shapes, and amulets representing the falcon, the cow, the bull, the toad, and the fly were uncovered. In this period emerged the independent districts, each denoted by an ensign representing a plant or animal. Later the Greeks called them "nomes."

Eventually two powerful states came into existence, one in Upper Egypt and the other in the Delta. Ombos, near the modern town of Naqada, became the capital of Upper Egypt. The symbol of this kingdom was the so-called lotus. Behdet, near Alexandria, became the capital of Lower Egypt. The symbol of this kingdom was the papyrus that grows so luxuriously in the marshes of the Delta. Even after Egypt became a united country the two-kingdom tradition persisted. The rulers of all Egypt bore the title "king of Upper and Lower Egypt," and the symbol became a device in which the lotus and papyrus were combined. The OT Heb. name for Egypt remained literally "the two Egypts."

The Proto-Dynastic Period (Dynasties I and II, c. 2900-2700 B.C.). According to Manetho, Menes was the first king and reigned at This, not far from the great bend of the Nile below Thebes, near present-day Girga. The First and Second Dynasties are often called Thinite. The cemetery of the Thinite kings was in the desert near This, close to present-day Abydos. Sir W. M. Flinders Petrie excavated most of the tombs of this dynasty. Like so many of the burial places of ancient Egyptians, the royal tombs at Abydos had already been plundered. Enough of the contents remained, however, to yield a profusion of jewelry, stone vases, copper vessels, and other objects. Names of a number of the kings were found, including Narmer, Aha, and Zer. The slate palette of Narmer found at Hieronkonpolis has on the reverse the conspicuous figure of the king raising a mace to crush the skull of his enemy, whom he holds by the hair. On the king's head is a helmet-like crown of Upper Egypt. Behind the king is his servant bearing the king's sandals and a water vessel. Heads of Hathor the cow-goddess are around the king's belt and at the top of the palette. The falcon, as a royal symbol, holds a rope attached to a human head. Six papyrus stalks, symbolizing the marshes of Lower Egypt, are depicted beneath the falcon. Below is a single barbed harpoon head and a rectangle representing a lake. The entire representation means that the falcon king has taken captive the people of the region of the Harpoon Lake in Lower Egypt.

The Old Kingdom, Dynasties III-IV (c. 2700-2200 B.C.). With his capital at Memphis, King Zoser of the Third Dynasty built the famous Step Pyramid at Saqqara, the earliest large stone structure known in history, 190 feet high. Khufu, founder of the Fourth Dynasty, built the greatest of the pyramids at Gizeh. It was originally 481 feet high, 755 feet square at the base, covering almost thirteen acres; 2,300,000 blocks of limestone, each weighing about 2½ tons, were required in its construction. Khafre, the successor of Khufu, constructed the second pyramid at Gizeh. Its present height is 447½ feet and it is not considerably smaller than the Great Pyramid. The head of the great Sphinx, which stands to the E of the second pyramid, probably represents Khafre. Kings of the Fifth and Sixth Dynasties had inscriptions carved on the walls and inner passages of the pyramids. These are now known as the Pyramid Texts and deal with the glorious future life of the deceased kings in the presence of the sun-god. The Pyramid Texts frequently have the form of couplets with parallel thought arrangement, an early form of poetry that was to be used by the Hebrews two millennia later.

Great Pyramid at Gizeh

First Intermediate Period (Dynasties VII-XI, c. 2200-1900 B.C.). The pharaohs of this period were comparatively weak and ruled at Memphis and at Herakleopolis, some seventy-seven miles S of Cairo. In the Eleventh Dynasty the Intefs and the Mentuhoteps ruled at Thebes, which was later destined to become Egypt's greatest capital.

Egypt's Strong Middle Kingdom (Dynasty XII, c. 1900-1775 B.C.). These kings were native Thebans, but they ruled at Memphis and in the Fayum. This period was contemporary with the patriarchal period in Palestine. Joseph became prime minister of and Jacob stood before one of the powerful pharaohs of this dynasty (Amenemes I-IV or Senwosret I-III). This period marked the classical efflorescence of Egyptian literature. Amenemes I composed a series of proverbs for his son. The Tale of Sinuhe portrays conditions in Syria and Palestine under the power of Egypt at this time. Senwosret III pushed the Egyptian Empire to the Second Cataract and extended his power into Syria. There was great commercial activity. A canal was constructed connecting the Red Sea to the nearest branch of the Nile in the eastern Delta. The mining industry in Sinai was developed into a permanent industry. Jewelry and art work from this period show remarkable design and accuracy of construction. The famous tomb of Khnumhotep II, a powerful noble under Senwosret II who lived at Beni Hasan 169 miles above Cairo, depicts the visit of thirty-seven Asiatics to Egypt about 1900 B.C. These Semites bringing gifts remind us of Abraham's going down into Egypt. The picture gives an inscription reading: "The arrival, bringing eye paint, which 37 Asiatics bring to him." Their leader has the good Heb. name "Sheikh of the highlands Ibshe."

Second Intermediate Period (Dynasties XII-XVII, c. 1775-1570 B.C.). The strong Middle Kingdom was succeeded by Dynasties XIII and XIV, characterized by weakness and futile struggles. This period of turmoil was followed by the invasion of the Hyksos, literally, "rulers of the foreign lands," commonly called the "Shepherd Kings." These foreign princes reigned almost a century and a half, comprising Dynasties XV-XVI. The Hyksos seem to have been mainly Semitic with probable intermixture of Hittites and Hurrians. Avaris in the Delta was their capital. As the Hyksos period ran its course, Dynasty XVII came into power at Thebes. The last king of this dynasty, named Ahmose, completely expelled the Hyksos. The Hyksos introduced the horse and the chariot into the Nile Valley and contributed to their empire-building activities.

The New Empire, (Dynasties XVIII-XX, c. 1570-1150 B.C.). This was the heyday of Egyptian splendor and building activity, as evidenced by the vast temple at Karnak. Great pharaohs of this era include Amenhotep I, c. 1546-1525, Thutmose I, c. 1525-1508, Thutmose II, c. 1508-1504, Queen Hatshepsut, c. 1520-1482. She was succeeded by Thutmose III, the great conqueror and builder, c. 1482-1450. This warrior conducted seventeen campaigns and extended the empire to its widest limits in Palestine, Syria, and the regions of the upper Euphrates and on the Nile up to the Fourth Cataract. At the battle of Megiddo, c. 1482 B.C., he defeated the Hittites. According to the chronology preserved in the MT, he was probably the pharaoh of the oppression. Amenhotep II, c. 1450-1425, was apparently the pharaoh under whom the children of Israel left the country. The great empire began to decline after Thutmose III. Amenhotep III reigned from c. 1412 to 1375 (the Amarna period) and was followed by his son Amenhotep IV, c. 1375-1366. This religious zealot is better known by the name of Akhnaton and is famous for his solar monotheism. This cult was a reaction against the well-entrenched religion of Amon, the sun-god of Thebes. Akhnaton established a new capital at Akhetaton (modern el-Amarna, where the famous Amarna Letters were discovered in 1887), nearly three hundred miles below Thebes. Frantic calls for help against encroaching Habiru fill the Amarna correspondence. Under Tutankhamen (c. 1358-1352) the capital was reestablished at Thebes. The lavish, intact tomb of this pharaoh was discovered in 1922 by Howard Carter. Dynasty XIX was initiated by a general named Harmhab, c. 1353-1319, who restored traditional religion and organization. Rameses I reigned for only a year, c. 1319, and was succeeded by Sethi I, c. 1318-1299. He showed imperial tendencies and began the reconquest of Palestine-Syria, which his great son Rameses II, c. 1299-1232, carried forward. This great pharaoh, comparable to Thutmose III, clashed with the Hittites around 1293 at Kadesh on the Orontes. About a decade later he made a treaty with the Hittites. Merenptah (Merneptah), c. 1232-1222, succeeded the great conqueror. In his famous stela, Israel is mentioned for the first time, and Merneptah claims to have destroyed them. Dynasty XX (c. 1200-1085) had about ten rulers by the name of Rameses. Rameses III (c. 1198-1167) was the greatest. He repulsed the invading Sea Peoples, including the Philistines. After him decline set in rapidly.

Model boat from Egyptian tomb

The Decline (Dynasties XXI-XXX, c. 1085-332 B.C.). During Dynasty XXI (c. 1085-945 B.C.), the high priests of Amon at Thebes, Herihor and his successors, and nobles of Tanis, Smendes and his successors, strove for supremacy. Meanwhile there was a Libyan penetration of the country and Sheshonk I (biblical Shishak), a Libyan, seized the throne, inaugurating Dynasty XXII (c. 945-745). Bubastis in the E Delta was now the capital. Dynasties XXIII-XXIV (c. 745-712) were likewise Libyan. Dynasty XXV (c. 712-663) was Nubian. By the middle of the eighth century B.C. a strong Nubian kingdom came into existence with a capital at Napata, just below the Fourth Cataract. By around 721 B.C. Piankhi, a Nubian king, advanced up the Nile and eventually captured Memphis. Shabaka, a brother of Piankhi, established the Nubian and Ethiopian Dynasty XXV (c. 712-663). Taharka, a son of Piankhi, was the last ruler. Around 680 B.C. Egypt became imperiled by the Assyrians. Esarhaddon conquered the Delta, and Taharka surrendered Lower Egypt. When the Assyrian army was withdrawn, Taharka once more became ruler of the whole country. Under Ashurbanipal the Assyrians made a new invasion (c. 667 B.C.). Ashurbanipal's second campaign eventuated in the sacking of Thebes (c. 663, Nah. 3:8-10). Dynasty XXVI (c. 663-525) was founded by Psamtik (Psammetichus). It is sometimes called the Saite Dynasty, since the capital was at Sais in the Delta. He was a practical vassal of the Assyrians until about 650, when the Assyrians had to withdraw their occupational forces because of a Babylonian revolt. Egyptian glory momentarily returned. Psamtik was succeeded by his son Necho II (c. 609-593). It was he who slew Josiah at Megiddo (c. 608) when the latter opposed his march toward Assyria. He was utterly routed by Nebuchadnezzar II and lost all of Egypt's Asiatic possessions (2 Kings 24:7). Henceforth Necho confined his energies chiefly to Egypt, as did his son Psamtik II. The latter's son Apries (Hophra) unsuccessfully challenged Nebuchadnezzar's invasion of Palestine when Jerusalem fell (587 B.C.). Hophra lost his life in a civil war with Amasis II (c. 569-525), who succeeded him. In the days of Amasis, Nebuchadnezzar attempted to invade Egypt. At the end of his reign Amasis witnessed the rise of Cyrus the Great and the Persian Empire. His son Psamtik III reigned only a few months when he fell at Pelusium (525 B.C.) before the invading forces of Cyrus's son and successor, Cambyses II. During Dynasties XXVII-XXX Egypt was under Persian rule. In 332 B.C. the country was conquered by Alexander the Great. After his death in 323 B.C., the land came under the rule of the Ptolemies until the death of Cleopatra, 30 B.C., when it became a province of Rome.

Religion. The Egyptian religion was an utterly bewildering polytheistic conglomeration in which many deities of the earliest periods, when each town had its own deity, were retained. Re, the sun-god, was worshiped at Heliopolis (On). Osiris, god of the Nile, became the god of fertility. With the ascendancy of Thebes, the local god Amon was elevated and finally identified with Re under the compound Amon-Re. The moon also was worshiped as a god. Ptah, a god of Memphis, was known as the "great chief of artificers." It would be practically impossible to list all the gods sacred to Egyptians. Every object beheld, every phenomenon of nature, was thought to possess a spirit that could choose its own form, occupying the body of a crocodile, a fish, a cow, a cat, etc. Hence the Egyptians had numerous holy animals, principally the bull, the cow, the cat, the baboon, the jackal, and the crocodile. Some of the deities were composite, with human bodies and animal heads. Thoth, the scribe of the gods, had the head of an ibis; Horus, the sun-god, that of a hawk. The idea of a universal god found expression under Akhnaton, and for a brief period Aton was distinguished from the material sun. Despite crude nature worship among the Egyptians, there was a remarkable understanding of ethical conduct and, notably, mortality. Great pains were taken to insure the welfare of the deceased in the hereafter.

Relations with Israel. According to biblical chronology preserved in the MT of the Heb. Bible, Jacob and his family went down into Egypt somewhere in the neighborhood of 1871 B.C., under the Twelfth Egyptian Dynasty of the Middle Kingdom. Abraham, early in the history of this powerful government, had gone down into Egypt in time of famine (Gen. 12:10-20) as the aged Jacob and his sons did in this later period under like circumstances (46:6). Archaeology has yielded a number of evidences of Israel's sojourn in Egypt, among which are Egyptian personal names of Levites such as Moses, Assir, Pashhur, Hophni, Phinehas, Merari, and Putiel. These are all incontestably Egyptian. Another indication is the Canaanite place names in the Delta before the New Empire, such as Succoth (Ex. 12:37), Baal-zephon (14:2), Migdol (14:2), Zilu, and very likely Goshen itself (8:22; 9:26; W. F. Albright, *From the Stone Age to Christianity* [1940], p. 184). The Egyptian plagues abound in authentic local coloring. About 1441 B.C. (Masoretic chronology), the Hebrews left Egypt after a 430-year sojourn (12:40-41). This date is supported by the data in 1 Kings 6:1, which places the Exodus as 480 years before the fourth year of Solomon's reign (c. 961 B.C.). Adding 480 to 961 gives 1441 B.C. Scholars such as Albright argue for a c. 1290 B.C. date. H. H. Rowley places it around 1225 B.C. Besides telescoping the period of the Judges, these later dates virtually rule out the possibility of fitting the biblical chronology into the frame of contemporary history. John Garstang's excavations at Jericho favor the date c. 1441, and general conditions in Palestine, reflected in the Amarna Letters, do not make the equation impossible. Moreover, contemporary Egyptian history under the Eighteenth Dynasty permits the 1441 B.C. date. (For the early date and its arguments, see Merrill F. Unger's *Archeology and the Old Testament* [1954], pp. 140-48 and objections to the early date, pp. 149-52.)

The son and successor of Rameses II, Merenptah, set up a victory stela. This important monument found in the pharaoh's mortuary temple at Thebes, in twenty-eight closely packed lines of inscription, celebrates his triumph over his enemies. The first extrabiblical mention of Israel occurs on this inscription. The concluding portion of the stela reads as follows:

Askelon is carried captive; Gezer is conquered.

Nile River at Cairo

Yanoam is made as though it did not exist.
The people of Israel is desolate; it has no
  offspring;
Palestine has become a widow for Egypt.
All lands are united; they are pacified.
Everyone that is turbulent is bound by King
  Merenptah, giving life like Re every day.

Other notable contacts with Egypt occurred in
the days of Solomon, who married an Egyptian
princess, and in the days of Rehoboam, when
Judah and also Israel, as archaeology has shown,
were overrun and plundered by Shishak. In the
days of Jeremiah, on the eve of the fall of Jerusalem, the prophet denounced the people for leaning upon Egypt. After the fall of the city and the
murder of Gedaliah, Jeremiah and a number of
those left in the land migrated to Egypt. In later
periods, after Alexander's conquests and death,
numerous Jews settled in Egypt, notably in Alexandria, under the favorable treatment of the
Ptolemies.   M.F.U.

BIBLIOGRAPHY: G. Rawlinson, *History of Ancient Egypt*, 2
vols. (1881); J. H. Breasted, *Ancient Records of Egypt*,
5 vols. (1906-7); W. M. F. Petrie, *Egypt and Israel*
(1911); J. H. Breasted, *History of Egypt* (1919); A.
Erman, *Literature of the Ancient Egyptians* (1927);
W. M. F. Petrie, *Social Life in Ancient Egypt* (1932); H.
Frankfort, *The Intellectual Adventure of Ancient Man*
(1946); J. M. A. Janssen, *Annual Egyptological Bibliography* (1948-   ); R. A. Parker, *Calendars of Ancient
Egypt* (1950); id., *Journal of Near Eastern Studies* 16
(1957): 39-43; J. Cerny, *Ancient Egyptian Religion*
(1952); W. C. Hayes, *The Scepter of Egypt*, 2 vols.
(1953-59); M. F. Unger, *Archaeology of the Old Testa-
ment* (1954), pp. 140-48; H. E. Winlock, *Models of
Daily Life in Ancient Egypt* (1955); G. Steindorff and
K. C. Steele, *When Egypt Ruled the East* (1957);
P. Montet, *Everyday Life in Egypt in the Days of
Ramses the Great* (1958); A. H. Gardiner, *Egypt of the
Pharaohs* (1961); H. Kees, *Ancient Egypt, A Cultural
Topography* (1961); K. A. Kitchen, *The Joseph Narra-
tive and Its Egyptian Background* (1962); J. A. Wilson,
Signs and Wonders upon Pharaoh (1964); id., *The Bur-
den of Egypt* (1965); W. C. Hayes, *Most Ancient Egypt*
(1965); J. van Seters, *The Hyksos* (1966); D. B. Redford,

Egyptian wall painting

Orientalia 39 (1970): 1-51; W. M. F. Petrie, *A History of Egypt from the 19th to 30th Dynasties* (1972).

EGYPT, BROOK OF. Present-day Wadi el-Arish is a wide, shallow stream bed forming the southern boundary of Judah. It drains surplus water of the wet season from the wilderness of Paran into the Mediterranean. It forms a line of demarcation between Sinai and Palestine (Num. 34:5). It is some ninety-six miles NE of Kantara, the point of crossing the Suez Canal into Egypt proper.

E'HI (ē'hī; "brotherly"). One of the "sons" of Benjamin (Gen. 46:21). He is probably the grandson called *Ahiram* (which see) in Num. 26:38. In the parallel passage (1 Chron. 8:6) he seems to be called *Ehud* (which see).

E'HUD (ē'hud).

1. A descendant of Benjamin, progenitor of one of the clans of Geba that moved to Manahath (1 Chron. 8:6). He seems to be the same as Ahiram (Num. 26:38), and if so, Ahiram is probably the right name, as the family is called Ahiramites. In 1 Chron. 8:1 the same person seems to be called Aharah, and perhaps also Ahoah in v. 4; Ahijah, v. 7; and Aher, 7:12.

2. The third named of the seven sons of Bilhan, the son of Jediael and grandson of the patriarch Jacob (1 Chron. 7:10).

3. A judge of Israel, the son (descendant) of Gera, a Benjamite (Judg. 3:15). The name Gera was hereditary among the Benjamites (see Gen. 46:21; 2 Sam. 16:5; 1 Chron. 8:3, 5).

This Ehud was the second judge of Israel, or rather of that part of Israel that he delivered from the Moabites. Israel having lapsed into idolatry, the Lord strengthened Eglon, the king of Moab, against them. With the assistance of the Ammonites and the Amalekites he invaded the land, took Jericho (Judg. 3:12-13), and held Israel under tribute eighteen years (c. 1314-1295 B.C.).

Sent by the children of Israel, Ehud brought a tribute to Eglon. He departed with those who bore the gift, but, turning "back from the idols which were at Gilgal," he presented himself before the king in his "cool roof chamber." He secured the dismissal of the attendants by declaring that he had a "secret message" for Eglon; when they were alone, Ehud said, "I have a message from God for you," and the king rose to receive it with reverence. Immediately Ehud, who was left-handed, drew a dagger from his right thigh and plunged it so deeply into Eglon's abdomen that the fat closed upon the hilt and Ehud could not withdraw it. Leaving the room, he locked the door and fled past the idols into Seirah.

Ehud now summoned the Israelites to Seirah, in the mountains of Ephraim. First taking the fords of Jordan, he fell upon the Moabites, defeating them with a loss of 10,000 of their best men.

And so the land had rest for eighty years (Judg. 3:15-30).

"The conduct of Ehud must be judged according to the spirit of those times, when it was thought allowable to adopt any means of destroying the enemy of one's nation. The treacherous assassination of the hostile king is not to be regarded as an act of the Spirit of God, and therefore is not set before us as an example." Beyond his commission as deliverer of Israel we do not suppose that God gave Ehud any special commands but left him to the choice of such measures and plans of conquest as his own judgment and skill might devise.

BIBLIOGRAPHY: L. J. Wood, *Distressing Days of the Judges* (1975), pp. 171-75; A. R. Fausset, *A Critical and Expository Commentary on the Book of Judges* (1977), pp. 61-75; G. Bush, *Notes on Judges* (1981), pp. 42-56; J. M. Lang and T. Kirk, *Studies in the Book of Judges*, 2 vols. in 1 (1983), 1:34-37.

E'KER (e'ker). The youngest of the three sons of Ram, the grandson of Hezron (1 Chron. 2:27).

EK'RON (ek'ron; "extermination"). A city of the Philistines, about eleven miles from Gath. It belonged successively to Judah (Josh. 13:3) and Dan (19:43) and to the Philistines (1 Sam. 5:10). Here the Ark was carried (5:10; 6:1-8). Baal-zebub was worshiped here (2 Kings 1:2). Ekron is now located at Tel Miqne, near Revadim, about twenty-five miles W of Jerusalem. Excavations at the site are being led by Trude Dothan of the Hebrew University in Jerusalem and Seymour Gitin of the Albright Institute in Jerusalem. Finds demonstrate that Miqne was occupied during the Early, Middle, and Late Bronze ages (c. 3000-1200 B.C.); and around 1200 B.C. the Philistines founded the first urban settlement there. The last fortified city was probably destroyed by Sennacherib of Assyria during his 701 B.C. campaign in Judah.　　　　　　　　　　H.F.V.

BIBLIOGRAPHY: R. A. S. Macalister, *The Philistines, Their History and Civilization* (1911), pp. 64-65, 74-76.

EK'RONITE (ek'ron-īt; Josh. 13:3; 1 Sam. 5:10). An inhabitant of the Philistine city of *Ekron* (which see).

EL (el). This is a name by which God is called in the OT—El, the God Elohim of Israel (Gen. 33:20). In prose it occurs more frequently with the modifier—El Elyon ("God, Most High," 14:18), El Shaddai ("God Almighty," 17:1), El Hai ("the living God," Josh. 3:10), commonly the plural of majesty Elohim. In poetry *el* is common. The word often stands alone without any adjunct (Pss. 18:31; 68:21; Job 8:3). *El* is a generic name for God in NW Semitic (Heb. and Ugaritic), and as such it is also employed in the OT for heathen deities (Ex. 34:14; Isa. 44:10). The original generic term was *'ilum*, which, dropping the mimation and the nominative case ending *u*, became *el* in Heb. The word is derived from the root *'wl,* "to be strong, powerful," meaning "the strong one." In Canaanite paganism as reflected in the Phoenician historian Philo of Byblos, A.D. 100, and particularly in the epic religious literature unearthed at Ras Shamra, ancient Ugarit in N Syria, 1929-37, El was the head of the Canaanite pantheon. According to Philo, El had three wives, who were also his sisters. This fluidity of relationship is in accordance with the general irrationality and moral grossness of Canaanite cults. According to Philo, El was a bloody tyrant who dethroned his own father, Uranus, murdered his favorite son, and decapitated his daughter. The Ugaritic poems present him also as a lustful, morbid character. Despite these crimes, El was considered the exalted "father of years" (*abu shanima*), the "father of man" (*abu adami*), and "father bull," that is, the progenitor of the gods. Like Homer's Zeus, El was the father of men and gods. The utter moral abandon of El, as well as that of his son, Baal, and his three sister-wives, who were patronesses of sex and war, point to the degrading effects of Canaanite religion and offer adequate moral explanation for the inflexibly stern attitude of the OT toward the religion of the Canaanites and to the Canaanites themselves. The Ras Shamra literature speaks of Canaan as the "land of El," where this deity was absolute in authority over lesser gods. El rapidly declined, however, and was largely supplanted by the worship of Baal, who was equally demoralizing. The Heb. name of God, El, has, of course, no connection with paganism, but is a simple generic term.

M.F.U.

BIBLIOGRAPHY: M. H. Pope, *El in the Ugaritic Texts* (1955); F. M. Cross, *Theological Dictionary of the Old Testament,* ed. G. J. Botterweck and H. Ringgren (1977), 1:242-60.

E'LA (ē'la). The father of Shimei, one of Solomon's deputies (1 Kings 4:18; "Elah," KJV), after 960 B.C.

EL'ADAH. *See* Eleadah.

E'LAH (ē'la; "oak," any large "evergreen").

1. One of the Edomite chiefs in Mt. Seir (Gen. 36:41; 1 Chron. 1:52).

2. In the KJV, the father of Shimei. *See* Ela.

3. The son and successor of Baasha, king of Israel (1 Kings 16:8-10). He reigned for only part of two years (c. 886-885 B.C.) and was then killed while drunk by Zimri, in the house of his steward Arza (in Tirzah), who was probably a confederate in the plot. He was the last king of Baasha's line, and by this catastrophe the predictions of the prophet Jehu (16:1-4) were accomplished.

4. The father of Hoshea, last king of Israel (2 Kings 15:30; 17:1), c. 732-724 B.C.

5. One of the three sons of Caleb, the son of Jephunneh (1 Chron. 4:15), c. 1380 B.C. In KJV (NASB marg.) this passage ends with the words "even (or *and*) Kenaz," showing that a name had been dropped out before it (Keil, *Com.*). The NIV, however, reads, "The son of Elah: Kenaz."

6. The son of Uzzi, and one of the Benjamite heads of families who were taken into captivity (1 Chron. 9:8), or rather, perhaps, returned from it and dwelt in Jerusalem, 536 B.C.

7. The Valley of Elah located eleven miles SW from Jerusalem, the scene of Goliath's death at the hands of David (1 Sam. 17:2; 21:9). It is the modern Wadi es-Sunt, or valley of the acacia tree. Its entrance from the Philistine plain is commanded by the famous Tell-es-Sâfiyeh.

Valley of Elah, where David fought Goliath

E'LAM (ē'lam; "hidden"). The name of an ancient land (*see* article below) and of several persons in the Bible.

1. The first named of the sons of Shem (Gen. 10:22; 1 Chron. 1:17). His descendants probably settled in that part of Persia that was afterward frequently called by this name.

2. A head man of the tribe of Benjamin, one of the sons of Shashak, resident at Jerusalem at the captivity or on the return (1 Chron. 8:24), 536 B.C.

3. A Korahite Levite, fifth son of Meshelemiah, who was one of the gatekeepers of the Tabernacle in the time of David (1 Chron. 26:3), 1000 B.C.

4. The progenitor of a family who returned with Zerubbabel (536 B.C.) to the number of 1,254 (Ezra 2:7; Neh. 7:12). A further detachment of 71 men came with Ezra (8:7). It was, probably, one

of this family, Shecaniah son of Jehiel, who encouraged Ezra in his efforts against the indiscriminate marriages of the people (10:2), and six of the "sons of Elam" accordingly put away their foreign wives (10:26).

5. In the same set of lists is a second Elam, whose sons, to the same number as in the former case, returned with Zerubbabel (Ezra 2:31; Neh. 7:34), and which, for the sake of distinction, is called "the other Elam." "The coincidence of numbers is curious, and also suspicious, as arguing an accidental repetition of the foregoing name" (Smith, *Dict.*, s.v.).

6. One of the leaders of the people who signed the covenant with Nehemiah (Neh. 10:14), 445 B.C.

7. One of the priests who accompanied Nehemiah and took part in the dedication of the new wall of Jerusalem (Neh. 12:42), 445 B.C.

E'LAM (ē'lam; Heb. *'ēlām;* Akkad. *elamtu,* "highland"). The land beyond the Tigris and E of Babylonia, bounded on the N by Assyria and Media and on the S by the Persian Gulf. Its capital was the ancient city of Susa, OT Shushan (KJV). Elam was the center of an ancient political power. Eannatum of Lagash was the first known person to mention Elam. He claims to have conquered it, but not much later, under one of his successors, the Elamites plundered Lagash. The great Sargon of Agade called himself "conqueror of Elam." His successor, Naram-Sin, mastered the entire land of Elam. As the result of the victories of this great Semitic dynasty of Agade (c. 2400-2200 B.C.), the Elamites were kept in subjection for more than three hundred years. After the destruction of the Third Dynasty of Ur, c. 1960 B.C., Kudur Mabuk became master of Larsa and was succeeded by his sons, Warad-Sin and Rim-Sin. The great Hammurabi defeated Rim-Sin. Later on an Elamite conqueror carried the Code of Hammurabi to Susa, where it was recovered in A.D. 1901-2. In the Abrahamic era, Chedorlaomer, king of Elam, was powerful in Lower Babylonia and conquered even the country on the Jordan (Gen. 14:1-11). In the eighth and seventh centuries B.C. the mighty Assyrian Empire intermittently had to struggle with the troublesome Elamites. About 645 B.C. Susa was taken. The Chaldeans conquered the Elamites (cf. Ezek. 32:24), and Susa became a capital of the Persian Empire. Some Elamites were forcibly settled in Samaria and joined in harassing the Jews in their attempts to rebuild the Temple (Ezra 4:9). Elamites were prominently present on the Day of Pentecost, when the Holy Spirit came (Acts 2:9).

M.F.U.

BIBLIOGRAPHY: E. Herzfeld, *Iran in the Ancient Near East* (1941); J. Gray, *Archaeology and the Old Testament World* (1965); J. A. Thompson, *The Bible and Archaeology* (1982), p. 154.

EL-AMARNA. *See* Amarna, el-.

E'LAMITES (ē'la-mīts; Ezra 4:9; Acts 2:9). The original inhabitants of the country called Elam; they were descendants of Shem and perhaps received their name from an actual man, Elam (Gen. 10:22).

EL'ASAH (el'a-sa; "God has made").

1. One of the sons of Pashhur, a priest, who renounced his Gentile wife, whom he had married during the captivity or after (Ezra 10:22), 457 B.C.

2. The son of Shaphan, one of the two men sent on a mission by King Zedekiah to Nebuchadnezzar at Babylon. At the same time they took charge of the letter of Jeremiah the prophet to the captives in Babylon (Jer. 29:3), about 593 B.C.

E'LATH (e'lath, e'loth; "great trees"). A site located on the NE end of the Gulf of Aqaba. On their northward trek from Sinai the Israelites passed Elath (Deut. 2:8), which was then a tiny village E of the later Eloth and that was beside Ezion-geber. Ezion-geber, modern Tell el Keleifeh, excavated by Nelson Glueck, lay E of Elath, but from the tenth to the fifth century B.C. the place was known as Ezion-geber, later as Elath. Because of its strategic location Ezion-geber passed back and forth between Edomites and Jews in the two centuries between David and Uzziah (2 Kings 14:22; 16:6). It was also a strategic stopping place for caravans coming from Arabia.

EL-BE'RITH (el-be'rīth). The god (Judg. 9:46). *See* Gods, False: Baal-berith.

EL-BETH'EL (the "God of Bethel"). The name given by Jacob to the altar that he erected at Bethel on his return from Laban (Gen. 35:7). It was built in memory of God's appearance to him in the vision of the "ladder" (cf. 28:12-22).

EL'DAAH (el'da; "God of knowledge"). The last named of the five sons of Midian, Abraham's son by Keturah (Gen. 25:4; 1 Chron. 1:33), after 2,000 B.C.

EL'DAD (el'dad; "God has loved"). One of the seventy elders appointed to assist Moses in the administration of justice, c. 1440 B.C. These elders were assembled before the door of the Tabernacle and received the spirit of prophecy from God (Num. 11:24-25). Eldad is mentioned along with Medad, another elder, as having received the same gift, although for some reason they were not with the other elders but remained in the camp. A young man brought word to Moses that these two persons were prophesying in the camp, and Joshua entreated Moses to forbid them. But Moses replied: "Are you jealous for my sake? Would that all the Lord's people were prophets, that the Lord would put His Spirit upon them!" (11:26-29). The mode of prophesying, in the case of Eldad and Medad, was probably the spontaneous production of hymns chanted forth to the people. Compare the case of Saul (1 Sam. 10:11).

ELDER (Heb. *zāqēn,* "old"; Gk. *presbuteros,* "older"; English "presbyter"). In early times books were scarce, and the aged of the tribes were the depositories of the traditions of bygone generations. The old men, moreover, had the most experience and were the heads of large families, over whom they exercised supreme authority. Great reverence was paid to the aged among the Hebrews and other nations (Deut. 32:7; Job 12:12; Prov. 16:31). Because old age was identified with matured wisdom, knowledge, and experience, and a reward for a virtuous and godly life, the aged were from time immemorial chosen to fill the official positions in the community. The name *elder* came to be used as the designation for the office itself.

In the Old Testament. The term *elder* is applied to various offices: to Abraham's "oldest" servant (RV, "elder," i.e., *major-domo;* NIV, "chief servant," Gen. 24:2); the officers of Pharaoh's household (50:7); and David's head servants (2 Sam. 12:17). "The elders of Gebal" (Ezek. 27:9) are understood to be the *master workmen.* The elders of Egypt (Gen. 50:7) were probably the state officers, and the term denoting a political office applied not only to the Hebrews and Egyptians but also to the Moabites and Midianites (Num. 22:7). "According to patriarchal custom the fathers, standing by the right of birth (primogeniture) at the head of the several tribes and divisions of tribes, regulated the relations of the tribes and clans, punished offenses and crimes, and administered law and equity. Thus from the heads of tribes, clans and families proceeded the *elders,* who, even before the time of Moses, formed the superiors of the people. For Moses and Aaron, on their arrival in Egypt, gathered the elders of Israel to announce to the people their divine commission to lead them out of the bondage of Egypt (Ex. 3:16, 18; 4:29)." They accompanied Moses in his first interview with Pharaoh (3:18); through them Moses gave his communications and commands to the people (19:7; Deut. 31:9). They were his immediate attendants in all the great transactions in the wilderness (Ex. 17:5), and seventy of them accompanied Moses to Sinai (24:1). Seventy of them were also appointed to bear the burden of government with Moses (Num. 11:16-17). As in the legislation of Moses certain things were committed to the charge of the elders of each particular city (Deut. 19:12; 21:3; etc.), it was clearly implied that the people, on their settlement in Canaan, were expected to appoint persons ("elders") who would see that divine regulations were executed in the several districts (see Josh. 20:4; Judg. 8:16; Ruth 4:2; etc.). In the Psalms and the Prophets, elders are spoken of as a distinct class with an official character and occupying a somewhat separate position (Ps. 107:32; Lam. 2:10; Ezek. 14:1; etc.). After the return from the Exile, the office rose into higher significance and fuller organization.

With every *synagogue* (which see) there was connected a government of elders, varying in number according to the population attached to it. The rulers of the synagogue and the elders of the people were substantially one, and a certain number of those elders belonged to the *Sanhedrin* (which see).

In the New Testament. They were associated sometimes with the chief priests (Matt. 21:23), sometimes with the chief priests and scribes (16:21), or the council (26:59), always taking an active part in the management of public affairs. Luke speaks of the whole order by the collective term of eldership (Gk. *presbuterion;* Luke 22:66; Acts 22:5). There is no specific account of the origin of the eldership in the apostolic church. We find officers called interchangeably *elders* or *presbyters* and *bishops* (Gk. *episkopos,* "superintendent"). This office pertained to local congregations, was extended as the churches multiplied, and was distinguished from that of deacon. Elders first came into prominence on the scattering abroad of the disciples and the withdrawing of the apostles from Jerusalem, following the death of Stephen. They were associated with James to give direction to the affairs of the church, appear to have been a well-known and established class of officials (11:30), and came into greater prominence in association with the apostles (15:2). With the "brethren" they constituted the council at Jerusalem to which was referred the question of circumcision, and they united with the apostles and the church in sending to Antioch and other churches delegates who should convey the decision of the council (15:22-23). When Paul visited Jerusalem for the last time he went in to James, the president, where he found all the elders assembled (21:18-25). The "elders" of the NT church were the "pastors" (Eph. 4:11), "overseers" (Acts 20:28; etc.), the leaders who "have charge" (Heb. 13:7; 1 Thess. 5:12; etc.) of the flock. They were also the regular teachers of the congregation, whose duty it was to expound the Scriptures and administer the sacraments (1 Tim. 3:2; Titus 1:9). The Jewish Christians, following the pattern of the synagogue as well as of political administration of cities, which was vested in a senate or college, readily adopted the *presbytery.* Consequently we meet it everywhere in the plural, as a corporation at Jerusalem (Acts 11:30; 15:4, 6, 23; 21:18), at Ephesus (20:17, 28), at Philippi (Phil. 1:1), at the ordination of Timothy (1 Tim. 4:14; etc.).

"The essential identity of presbyters and bishops in the apostolic age is a matter of well nigh absolute historic demonstration. The same officers of the church of Ephesus are alternately called presbyters and bishops. Paul sends greetings to the bishops and deacons of Philippi, but omits the presbyters because they were included in the first term, as also the plural indicates. In the pastoral epistles, when Paul intends to give the qualifications for all church officers he again mentions two, bishops and deacons, but the term presbyters afterward for bishops. Peter urges the presbyters to 'tend the flock of God, and to fulfill the office of bishops,' with disinterested devotion and without lording it over the charge allotted them. The interchange of terms continued in use to the close of the 1st century, as is evident from the epistle of Clement of Rome (about 95 A.D.), and still lingered toward the close of the second" (Schaff, *Hist. Christ. Church*). The reason for the use of two terms for persons having the same essential functions has given rise to much discussion.

Two general suggestions have been made: (1) The term presbyter has been claimed to be of Jewish derivation and to have been used at first only by Jewish-Christian congregations. In communities where a Christian church had sprung from the bosom of a local synagogue, and was therefore chiefly under the control of Jewish tradition and thought, the term *presbyter,* which was the name of the governing body of the synagogue, would be naturally transferred to officers of similar function in the Christian societies. It is likewise true that the term *bishop* is used to designate one of like official duty in the churches of almost exclusively Gentile origin. (2) A second theory is that the bishop of the Christian church was analogous in office and function to that of the president of the pagan fraternities or clubs. To administer the funds of these organizations became a matter of primary importance, and the officer charged with this duty was termed an *episcopos.*

The peculiar environment of the first Christian believers compelled like provision for the exercise of systematic charities. Most of the early disciples were of the poorer class, and many more, upon profession of the Christian faith, became outcasts from their families and homes.

In the Modern Church. (1) In the Roman Catholic church, the Church of England, and the Protestant Episcopal church, "priest" is generally used instead of "presbyter" or "elder," to designate the second order in the ministry (the three orders being bishops, priests, and deacons). (2) In the Methodist church only two orders of ministers are recognized, elders and deacons, the bishops being chosen (*primus inter pares*) as superintendents. (3) Among Congregationalist and all churches having the presbyterian form of government the two orders of elders and deacons are recognized. Among Presbyterians there are two classes of elders: teaching elders (pastors) and ruling elders (laymen).

BIBLIOGRAPHY: L. Koehler, *Hebrew Man* (1956); R. de Vaux, *Ancient Israel: Its Life and Institutions* (1961); G. Bornkamm, πρεσβυτερος, *Theological Dictionary of the New Testament,* ed. G. Friedrich (1968), 6:651-81.

EL'EAD (el'e-ad; "God has testified"). A descendant of Ephraim (1 Chron. 7:20-21), but whether through *Shuthelah* (which see) or a son of the patriarch (the second Shuthelah being taken as a repetition of the first, and Ezer and Elead as his brothers) is not determined.

EL'EADAH (el'e-a-da; "God has decked"). One of the sons (rather than later descendants, as the text seems to state) of Ephraim (1 Chron. 7:20; perhaps the same as *Elead* (which see) of v. 21, since several of the names (*see* Tahath) in the list appear to be repeated.

ELEA'LEH (e-le-a'le; "God has ascended"). A town of the Amorites, in the country E of the Jordan, in the tribe of Reuben (Num. 32:3-37). Prophetic threats were uttered against it (Isa. 15:4; Jer. 48:34). The present El-Al, about a mile N from Heshbon, marks the site.

ELE'ASAH (el-e'a-sa). More properly *Elasah* (which see).

1. The son of Helez, one of the descendants of Judah, of the family of Hezron (1 Chron. 2:39).

2. Son of Rapha, or Rephaiah, a descendant of Saul through Jonathan and Merib-baal, or Mephibosheth (1 Chron. 8:37; 9:43), after 1030 B.C.

ELEA'ZAR (el-e-a'zar; "God is helper"). A common name among the Hebrews.

1. The high priest. The third son of Aaron by Elisheba, daughter of Amminadab (Ex. 6:23; 28:1). He married a daughter of Putiel, who bore him Phinehas (6:25), c. 1440 B.C.

After the death of Nadab and Abihu, who had no children (Lev. 10:12; Num. 3:4), Eleazar was appointed chief over the principal Levites, to have the oversight of those who had charge of the sanctuary (3:32). After the destruction of Korah and his company, Eleazar gathered up their censers out of the fire to make plates for a covering of the altar of burnt offering (16:37-39). With his brother Ithamar he ministered as a priest during their father's lifetime.

Immediately before the death of Aaron, Moses went with them both to Mt. Hor, where he invested Eleazar with the sacred garments, as the successor of Aaron in the office of high priest (Num. 20:25-29), about 1402 B.C. One of his first duties was, in conjunction with Moses, to superintend the census of the people (26:1-4). He also assisted at the inauguration of Joshua (27:18-23) and at the division of the spoil taken from the Midianites (31:21). After the conquest of Canaan he took part in the division of the land (Josh. 14:1). The time of his death is not mentioned in Scripture. Josephus says that it took place about the same time as Joshua's, twenty-five years after the death of Moses. The high priesthood is said to have remained in the family of Eleazar until the time of Eli, into whose family, for some reason unknown, it passed until it was restored to the family of Eleazar in the person of Zadok

(2 Sam. 8:17; 1 Chron. 6:8; 24:3; 1 Kings 2:27) (Smith, s.v.).

2. An inhabitant of Kiriath-jearim, who was set apart by his fellow townsmen to attend upon the Ark while it remained in the house of his father, Abinadab, after it had been returned to the Hebrews by the Philistines (1 Sam. 7:1-2), before 1030 B.C. It is not stated that Eleazar was a Levite, but that is very probable, because otherwise they would hardly have consecrated him to be the keeper of the Ark, but would have chosen a Levite for the purpose.

3. The son of Dodo the Ahohite, that is, possibly a descendant of Ahoah, of the tribe of Benjamin (2 Sam. 23:9; 1 Chron. 8:4), one of the three most eminent of David's thirty-seven heroes, who fought "until his hand was weary" in maintaining with David and the other two a daring stand after "the men of Israel had withdrawn." He was also one of the same three when they broke through the Philistine host to gratify David's longing for a drink of water from the well of his native Bethlehem (2 Sam. 23:9-17; 1 Chron. 11:12), about 998 B.C.

4. A Levite, son of Mahli and grandson of Merari (after 1400 B.C.). He is mentioned as having had only daughters, who were married by their "brothers," i.e., cousins (1 Chron. 23:21-22; 24:28).

5. The son of Phinehas, and associated with the priests and Levites in taking charge of the sacred treasure and vessels restored to Jerusalem after the Exile (Ezra 8:33), about 457 B.C. It is not definitely stated, however, whether he was a priest or even a Levite.

6. One of the descendants of Parosh, an Israelite (i.e., layman) who, on returning from Babylon, renounced the Gentile wife whom he had married (Ezra 10:25), 456 B.C.

7. One of those who encompassed the walls of Jerusalem when they were completed (Neh. 12:42), 445 B.C. He is probably the same as no. 5.

8. The son of Eliud, in the genealogy of Jesus Christ (Matt. 1:15).

ELECT (Heb. *bāḥir,* "chosen"; so rendered in 2 Sam. 21:6). Used to denote those selected by God for special office, work, honor, etc. (Isa. 42:1; 45:4; 65:9, 22, all KJV; NASB, NIV, "chosen"). The term was sometimes applied in the early church (1) to the whole body of baptized Christians; (2) to the highest class of catechumens *elected* to baptism; and (3) to the newly baptized, as especially admitted to the full privileges of the profession.

ELECTION (Gk. *eklogē,* "choice," a "picking out").

Bible Meaning. This word in the Scriptures has three distinct applications. (1) To the divine choice of nations or communities for the possession of special privileges with reference to the performance of special services. Thus the Jews were "a chosen nation," "the elect." Thus also in the NT, bodies of Christian people, or churches, are called "the elect." (2) To the divine choice of individuals to a particular office or work. Thus Cyrus was elected of God to bring about the rebuilding of the Temple, and thus the twelve were chosen to be apostles and Paul to be the apostle to the Gentiles. (3) To the divine choice of individuals to be the children of God, and therefore heirs of heaven.

It is with regard to election in this third sense that theological controversies have been frequent and at times most fierce. Calvinists hold that the election of individuals to salvation is absolute, unconditional, by virtue of an eternal divine decree. Arminians regard election as conditional upon repentance and faith; the decree of God is that all who truly repent of their sins and believe on the Lord Jesus Christ shall be saved. But every responsible person determines for himself whether or not he will repent and believe. Sufficient grace is bestowed upon everyone to enable him to make the right decision.

The Calvinistic View. The Westminster Confession, the standard of the Church of Scotland and of the various Presbyterian churches of Europe and America, contains the following statement: "God from all eternity did by the most wise and holy counsel of His own free will freely and unchangeably ordain whatsoever comes to pass; yet so as thereby neither is God the author of sin, nor is violence offered to the will of the creatures, nor is the liberty or contingency of second causes taken away, but rather established. Although God knows whatsoever may or can come to pass upon all supposed conditions, yet hath He not decreed anything because He foresaw its future, or as that which would come to pass upon such conditions. By the decree of God, for the manifestation of His glory some men and angels are predestinated unto everlasting life and others foreordained to everlasting death. These angels and men, thus predestinated and foreordained are particularly and unchangeably designed, and their number is so certain and definite that it cannot be either increased or diminished. Those of mankind that are predestinated unto life, God, before the foundation of the world was laid, according to His eternal and immutable purpose, and the secret counsel and good pleasure of His will, hath chosen in Christ unto everlasting glory, out of His mere free grace and love, without any foresight of faith, or good works, or perseverance in either of them, or any other thing in the creature, as conditions or causes moving Him thereto; and all to the praise of His glorious grace. As God hath appointed the elect unto glory, so hath He, by the eternal and most free purpose of His will, foreordained all the means thereunto. Therefore, they who are elected, being fallen in Adam, are redeemed by Christ, are effectually called unto faith in Christ, by His Spirit working in due season; are justified, adopted, sanctified, and kept by His power through faith unto salvation. Neither are any other redeemed by Christ, effectually called, justified, adopted, sanctified, and saved, but the elect only. The rest of mankind God was pleased, according to the unsearchable counsel of His own will, whereby He extendeth or withholdeth mercy, as He pleaseth, for the glory of His sovereign power over His creatures, to pass by, and to ordain them to dishonor and wrath for their sin, to the praise of His glorious justice."

In support of this doctrine several arguments are made by Calvinistic theologians: (1) According to the Scriptures election is not of works but of grace; and that it is not of works means that it is not what man does that determines whether he is to be one of the elect or not. For the descendants of Adam this life is not a probation. They stood their probation in Adam and do not stand each one for himself. (2) The sovereignty of God in electing men to salvation is shown by the fact that repentance and faith are gifts from God. These fruits of His Spirit are the consequences and signs of election and not its conditions. (3) The salvation that is of grace must be of grace throughout. The element of works or human merit must not be introduced at any point in the plan. And that would be the case if repentance and faith were the conditions of election. (4) The system of doctrine called Calvinistic, Augustinian, Pauline, should not be thus designated. That though taught clearly by Paul, particularly in Rom. 8:9, it was taught also by others of the writers of sacred Scripture, and by Christ Himself. Reference is made to Matt. 11:25-26; Luke 4:25-27; 8:10; John 6:37, 39; etc. (5) That the sovereignty of God is evidenced in dispensing saving grace is illustrated also in His establishing the temporal conditions of mankind. Some are born and reared in the surroundings of civilization, others of barbarism. And precisely so some are blessed with the light of the gospel, while others, dwelling in pagan lands, are deprived of that light and consequently are not saved.

This system of strict Calvinism above outlined has received various modifications by theologians of the Calvinistic school. The General Assembly of the Presbyterian Church in the United States of America, May 1903, adopted the following: "We believe that all who die in infancy, and all others given by the Father to the Son who are beyond the reach of the outward means of grace, are regenerated and saved by Christ through the Spirit, who works when and where and how He pleases."

The Arminian View. The Arminian view of election has been in recent years more generally accepted than formerly, even among denominations whose teaching has been Calvinistic or indefinite upon this point. This view grounds itself, in opposition to Calvinism, upon the universality

of the atonement and the graciously restored freedom of the human will. Election, accordingly, is not absolute but conditional, contingent upon the proper acceptance of such gifts of grace as God by His Spirit and providence puts within the reach of men. Inasmuch as this subject involves the character and method of the divine government and the destiny of the entire race, the following should be said: (1) According to the Arminian doctrine the purpose of God to redeem mankind was bound up with His purpose to create. The Lamb of God was "slain from the foundation of the world" (Rev. 13:8, KJV, NIV). God would not have permitted a race of sinners to come into existence without provision to save them. Such provision must not be for only a part but for the whole of the fallen race. To suppose the contrary is opposed to the divine perfections. To doom to eternal death any number of mankind who were born in sin and without sufficient remedy would be injustice. (2) The benefits of the atonement are universal and in part unconditional. They are unconditional with respect to those who, through no fault of their own, are in such a mental or moral condition as to make it impossible for them either to accept or reject Christ. A leading denomination emphasizes the doctrine that "all children, by virtue of the unconditional benefits of the atonement, are members of the kingdom of God." This principle extends to others besides children, both in heathen and Christian lands. God alone is competent to judge the extent to which, in varying degrees, human beings are responsible, and therefore the extent to which the unconditional benefits of the atonement may be applied. (3) The purpose or decree of God is to save all who do not, actually or implicitly, willfully reject the saving offices of the Lord Jesus Christ. Among those who have not heard the gospel may exist "the spirit of faith and the purpose of righteousness." Thus even those who have no knowledge of the historic Christ virtually determine whether or not they will be saved through Christ. They to whom the gospel is preached have higher advantages and more definite responsibilities. To them, repentance toward God and faith in the Lord Jesus Christ are the conditions of salvation. (4) Upon all men God bestows some measure of His grace, restoring to the depraved will sufficient freedom to enable them to accept Christ and be saved. Thus, in opposition to Calvinists, Arminians assert that not only Adam, but also his depraved descendants are in a stage of probation.

In behalf of this doctrine the following is argued: (1) That the whole trend of the Scriptures is to declare the responsibility of men and their actual power to choose between life and death. (2) That the Scriptures explicitly teach that it is the will of God that all men should be saved. Only those perish who wickedly resist His will (1 Tim. 2:4; 4:10; John 5:40; Acts 7:51; etc.). (3) That the

Scriptures declare the universality of Christ's atonement, and in some degree the universality of its benefits (Heb. 2:9; John 1:29; 3:16-17; 1 Cor. 15:22; Rom. 5:18-19; and many other passages). (4) That the doctrine of unconditional election necessarily implies that of unconditional reprobation; and that is to charge God with cruelty. (5) That unconditional election also necessarily implies the determinate number of the elect, a point that Calvinists hold, though they admit that they have for it no explicit teaching of Scripture. To the contrary, the Scriptures not only generally but particularly teach that the number of the elect can be increased or diminished. This is the purport of all those passages in which sinners are exhorted to repent, or believers warned against becoming apostate, or to "make certain about His calling and choosing you" (Matt. 24:4, 13; 2 Pet. 1:10; etc.). (6) That the Scriptures never speak of impenitent and unbelieving men as elect, as in some cases it would be proper to do if election were antecedent to repentance and faith and not conditioned thereby. (7) That the whole theory of unconditional election is of the same tendency with fatalism. (8) That the logic of unconditional election is opposed to true evangelism. (9) That the essential features of the Arminian doctrine of election belong to the primitive and truly historic doctrine of the church. Augustine was the first prominent teacher of unconditional election, and he, regardless of the logical inconsistency, granted that reprobation is not unconditional. This doctrine of Augustine was first formally accepted by the church in A.D. 529, in the Canons of the Council of Orange, approved by Pope Boniface II. The prominence of unconditional election in the theory of Protestantism is due largely to the influence and work of John Calvin, who, at the age of twenty-five, wrote his *Institutes,* in which he not only set forth the Augustinian doctrine of unconditional election, but also taught unconditional reprobation. John Wesley and his followers were responsible in a large degree for reviving and developing the doctrine of Arminius.

The limits of this article do not permit an examination of the contested passages of Scripture. For that, the reader should refer to works of systematic theology and to the commentaries.

E.MCC.

BIBLIOGRAPHY: R. Watson, *Theological Institutes,* 2 vols. (1843), 2:311-35, 370; J. Miley, *Systematic Theology,* 2 vols. (1892), 2:260-63; W. R. Cannon, *The Theology of John Wesley* (1946), pp. 90-106; H. H. Rowley, *The Biblical Doctrine of Election* (1950); J. Calvin, *Institutes of the Christian Religion,* Library of Christian Classics (1960), 3:21-24; B. B. Warfield, *Biblical and Theological Studies* (1952), pp. 270-333; G. C. Berkouwer, *Divine Election* (1960).

ELECTRUM. *See* Glowing Metal.

EL-'ELO'HE-IS'RAEL (el'e-lo'hē-iz'ra-el; the "mighty God of Israel"). Jacob called by this name an altar pitched before Shechem (Gen. 33:20) in accordance with his vow (28:20-22) to give glory to the "God of Israel."

ELEMENTS (Gk. *stoicheion,* "orderly"). The component parts of the physical universe. "The elements will melt with intense heat" (2 Pet. 3:10, 12), i.e., be reduced to as confused a chaos as that from which it was first created.

Figurative. The term is used figuratively of the elementary parts of religion (Heb. 5:12), the elements of religious training, or the ceremonial precepts common alike to the worship of the Jews and Gentiles (Gal. 4:3, 9); the ceremonial requirements, especially of Jewish tradition (Col. 2:8, 20). These types, "weak" and "beggarly" (KJV; the NIV renders, "basic principles of this world"), were suited to a condition of comparative childhood, in which appeals must be made to the senses.

E'LEPH. *See* Haeleph.

ELEPHANT. *See* Animal Kingdom.

ELHA'NAN (el-ha'nan; "God is gracious").

1. A distinguished warrior in the time of King David, who performed a memorable exploit against the Philistines, though in what that exploit exactly consisted and who the hero himself was it is not easy to determine (about 989 B.C.). Second Sam. 21:19 says that he was the "son of Jaare-oregim the Bethlehemite" and that he "killed Goliath the Gittite, the shaft of whose spear was like a weaver's beam." In the KJV the words "the brother of " are inserted to bring the passage into agreement with 1 Chron. 20:5, which states that "Elhanan the son of Jair killed Lahmi the brother of Goliath the Gittite, the shaft of whose spear," etc. Of these two statements the latter is correct, the former containing a textual corruption. See E. Young, *Introduction to the O. T.* (1949), p. 182.

2. The name Elhanan also occurs as that of "the son of Dodo" (2 Sam. 23:24; 1 Chron. 11:26). He is given as one of "the thirty" of David's guard. Perhaps his father had both names. "This Elhanan is not the same as the one mentioned above" (Keil, *Com.*).

E'LI (ē'lī; "high," i.e., "God is high"). The name of a high priest mentioned in 1 Sam. (see below) and that of the father-in-law of Joseph, the maternal grandfather of Jesus (Luke 3:23; "Heli," KJV).

E'LI (ē'lī; "high," i.e., "God is high"). This Eli (for the other, *see* article above), a high priest, was descended from Aaron through Ithamar (Lev. 10:1-2, 12), as appears from the fact that Abiathar, who was certainly a lineal descendant of Eli (1 Kings 2:27), had a son, Ahimelech, who is expressly stated to have been "of the sons of Ithamar" (1 Chron. 24:3; cf. 2 Sam. 8:17).

High Priest. Eli is generally supposed to have been the first of the line of Ithamar who held the office of high priest (Josephus *Ant.* 5.11.5). How the office ever came into the younger branch of the house of Aaron we are not informed, but it is very evident that it was no unauthorized usurpation on the part of Eli (1 Sam. 2:27-30).

Judge. Eli also acted as judge of Israel, being the immediate predecessor of Samuel (7:6, 15-17), the last of the judges. He was also the first judge who was of priestly descent and is said to have judged Israel forty years (4:18).

Sons. His sons, Hophni and Phinehas, conducted themselves so outrageously that they excited deep disgust among the people and rendered the services of the Temple odious in their eyes (2:12-17, 22). Of this misconduct Eli was aware but contented himself with mild and ineffectual remonstrances (2:23-25) where his station required severe and vigorous action (3:13).

Prophetic Warnings. A prophet was sent to announce the destruction of the house of Eli, as a sign of which both his sons should be slain in one day, a faithful priest should be raised up in his place, and those who remained of Eli's house should come crouching to him with the prayer to be put into one of the priests' offices to earn a morsel of bread (2:27-36). Another warning was sent to Eli by the mouth of the youthful Samuel (3:11-18).

Death. At last the Israelites rose against the Philistines but were defeated near Ebenezer. They then took the Ark of the Covenant into the camp, hoping thereby to secure the help of God; but in a succeeding engagement they suffered a still greater defeat, in which Eli's sons were slain. When tidings were brought to Eli that Israel was defeated—that his sons were slain and the Ark of God was taken—he "fell off the seat backward beside the gate, and his neck was broken and he died, for he was old and heavy" (1 Sam. 4:18), about 1050 B.C. The final judgment upon Eli's house was accomplished when Solomon removed Abiathar from his office and restored the line of Eleazar in the person of Zadok (1 Kings 2:27).

Character. The recorded history of Eli presents to us the character of Eli in three different aspects: (1) The devoted high priest. He takes particular interest in Hannah when he understands her sorrows and bestows upon her his priestly benediction (1:17; 2:20). He recognizes the divine message and bows in humble submission to the prophecy of his downfall (3:8, 18) and shows his profound devotion to God by his anxiety for the Ark and his sudden fall and death at the tidings of its capture. We can find in him no indication of hypocrisy or lack of faith in God. (2) As judge. The fact that he judged Israel seems to prove that his administration was, on the whole, careful and just. But his partiality appears when his own sons are the offenders. (3) As father. Eli let his paternal love run away with his judgment;

his fondness for his sons restrained him from the exercise of proper parental authority.

BIBLIOGRAPHY: W. R. Arnold, *Ephod and Ark* (1917), pp. 14-15; W. F. Albright, *Archaeology and the Religion of Israel* (1956), pp. 201-2.

ELI'AB (e-lī'ab; "God is father").

1. A son of Helon and the leader of the tribe of Zebulun, who assisted Moses in numbering the people (Num. 1:9; 2:7; 10:16), about 1440 B.C. He is mentioned (7:24-29) as presenting the offering of his tribe at the dedication of the Tabernacle.

2. A Reubenite, son of Pallu (or Phallu), whose family was principal in the tribe, and father or progenitor of Dathan and Abiram, the leaders in the revolt against Moses (Num. 16:1, 12; 26:8-9; Deut. 11:6), c. 1425 B.C. Eliab had another son, Nemuel (Num. 26:9).

3. The eldest brother of David (1 Chron. 2:13) and first of the sons of Jesse, who was presented to Samuel when he came to Bethlehem to anoint a king (1 Sam. 16:6), about 1013 B.C. Eliab, with his next two younger brothers, was in the army of Saul when threatened by Goliath; it was he who made the contemptuous inquiry, with which he sought to screen his own cowardice, when David proposed to fight the Philistine, "With whom have you left those few sheep in the wilderness?" (17:28). His daughter Abihail married her second cousin, Rehoboam, and bore him three children (2 Chron. 11:18-19). Eliab is supposed to be the same as Elihu, "one of David's brothers" (1 Chron. 27:18).

4. An ancestor of Samuel the prophet, being a Kohathite Levite, son of Nahath and father of Jeroham (1 Chron 6:27). In the other statements of the genealogy this name appears to be given as Elihu (1 Sam. 1:1) and Eliel (1 Chron. 6:34).

5. A valiant man, one of the Gadites who joined David in the stronghold in the wilderness (1 Chron. 12:9).

6. A Levite, who was one of the second rank of those appointed to conduct the music of the sanctuary in the time of David and whose part was to play "with harps tuned to alamoth." He also served as gatekeeper (1 Chron. 15:18, 20; 16:5), about 986 B.C.

ELI'ADA (e-lī'a-da; "God is knowing").

1. One of the youngest sons of David, born at Jerusalem, the child (as it would seem) of one of his wives and not of a concubine (2 Sam. 5:16; 1 Chron. 3:8-9), after 1000 B.C. In 14:7 the name appears in the form Beeliada (whom the "master has known"). As to the difficulty of David's using a name that contained Baal for one of its elements, it is doubtful whether that word, which literally means "master," or "husband," had in David's time acquired the bad sense that Baal worship in Israel afterward imparted to it (Kitto, s.v.).

2. The father of Rezon, who fled from the service of Hadadezer, king of Zobah, and became a

captain of Syrian marauders who annoyed Solomon during his reign (1 Kings 11:23-24), after 960 B.C.

3. A Benjamite and mighty man of war, who led 200,000 archers of his tribe to the army of Jehoshaphat (2 Chron. 17:17), 875 B.C.

ELI'AHBA (e-lī'a-ba; "God will hide"). A Shaalbonite, one of David's thirty chief warriors (2 Sam. 23:32; 1 Chron. 11:33), about 1000 B.C.

ELI'AKIM (e-lī'a-kim; "God will establish").

1. Son of Hilkiah and "over the household" of King Hezekiah (2 Kings 18:18; 19:2). He succeeded Shebna in this office after the latter had been removed from it as a punishment for his pride (Isa. 22:15-20), after 719 B.C. He was one of the three persons sent by Hezekiah to receive the message of the invading Assyrians (2 Kings 18:18; Isa. 36:3, 11, 22) and afterward to report it to Isaiah. Eliakim was a good man, as appears by the title emphatically applied to him by God, "My servant Eliakim" (22:20), and as was shown by his conduct on the occasion of Sennacherib's invasion (2 Kings 18:18, 26, 37; 19:1-5) and also in the discharge of the duties of his high station (Isa. 22:20-21).

The office that Eliakim held has long been a subject of perplexity to commentators. The ancients, including the LXX and Jerome, understood it of the priestly office. But it is certain, from the description of the office in Isa. 22, and especially from the expression in v. 22, "I will set the key of the house of David on his shoulder," that it was the king's house, and not the house of God, of which Eliakim was made prefect (Smith, *Dict.,* s.v.; Delitzsch, *Com.*). Most commentators agree that Isa. 22:25 does not apply to him, but to Shebna. Delitzsch, however, says: "Eliakim himself is also brought down at last by the greatness of his power on account of the nepotism to which he has given way."

2. The original name of *Jehoiakim* (which see), king of Judah (2 Kings 23:34; 2 Chron. 36:4).

3. A priest in the days of Nehemiah who assisted at the dedication of the new wall of Jerusalem (Neh. 12:41), 445 B.C.

4. Son of Abiud and father of Azor, of the posterity of Zerubbabel (Matt. 1:13). He is probably identical with Shecaniah (1 Chron. 3:21).

5. The son of Melea and father of Jonam, in the genealogy of Christ (Luke 3:30), probably the grandson of Nathan, of the private line of David's descent, considerably after 1000 B.C.

E'LIAM (e'li-am; "God of the people").

1. The father of Bathsheba, the wife of Uriah and afterward of David (2 Sam. 11:3). In the list of 1 Chron. 3:5 the names of both father and daughter are altered, the former to Ammiel and the latter to Bath-shua.

2. Son of Ahithophel, the Gilonite, one of David's "thirty" warriors (2 Sam. 23:34), about

1000 B.C. The name is omitted in the list of 1 Chron. 11, but is now probably discernible as "Ahijah the Pelonite." The ancient Jewish tradition, preserved by Jerome, is that the two Eliams are one and the same person (Smith, *Dict.*).

ELI'AS (e-lī'as), the Grecized form in which the name of Elijah is given in the KJV of the Apocrypha and NT.

ELI'ASAPH (e-lī'a-saf; "God has added").

1. The son of Deuel (or Reuel), head of the tribe of Gad at the time of the census in the wilderness of Sinai (Num. 1:14; 2:14; 7:42, 47; 10:20), about 1438 B.C.

2. The son of Lael and leader of the family of Gershonite Levites (Num. 3:24).

ELI'ASHIB (e-lī'a-shib; "God will restore"). A common name among the Israelites, especially in the latter period of OT history.

1. A son of Elioenai, one of the last descendants of the royal family of Judah (1 Chron. 3:24).

2. A priest in the time of King David, head of the eleventh "lot" in the order of the "officers" of the sanctuary (1 Chron. 24:12), about 989 B.C.

3. A Levitical singer who divorced his Gentile wife after the Exile (Ezra 10:24), 556 B.C.

4. An Israelite of the lineage of Zattu, who did the same (Ezra 10:27), 456 B.C.

5. An Israelite of the lineage of Bani, who did the same (Ezra 10:36), 456 B.C.

6. The high priest of the Jews in the time of Nehemiah (445 B.C.). With the assistance of his fellow priests he rebuilt the eastern city wall adjoining the Temple (Neh. 3:1). His own mansion was, doubtless, situated in the same vicinity (3:20-21). Eliashib was related in some way to Tobiah the Ammonite, for whom he prepared an anteroom in the Temple, a desecration that excited the pious indignation of Nehemiah (13:4, 7). One of the grandsons of Eliashib had also married the daughter of Sanballat the Horonite (13:28). There seems to be no reason to doubt that the same Eliashib is referred to, in Ezra 10:6, as the father of Jehohanan with whom Ezra consulted concerning the transgression of the people in taking Gentile wives. He is evidently the same as the son of Joiakim mentioned in the succession of high priests (Neh. 12:10, 22).

ELI'ATHAH (e-lī'a-tha; "God has come"). The eighth named of the fourteen sons of the Levite Heman, and a musician in the time of David (1 Chron. 25:4). With twelve of his sons and brothers he had the twentieth division of the Temple service (25:27), about 970 B.C.

ELI'DAD (e-lī'dad; "God of his love"). Son of Chislon (NIV, Kislon), and a leader of the tribe of Benjamin who represented his tribe among the commissioners appointed to divide the Promised Land (Num. 34:21), c. 1390 B.C.

ELIEHOE'NAI (el-i-hō'-e'nī; "toward Jehovah" are "my eyes").

1. The seventh son of Meshelemia, one of the Korhite gatekeepers of the Temple (1 Chron. 26:3; "Elioenai," KJV), about 960 B.C.

2. A son of Zerahiah, of the "sons of Pahath-moab," who returned with 200 males from the Exile (Ezra 8:4), 457 B.C.

E'LIEL (e'lī-el; "God is God").

1. One of the leaders of the tribe of Manasseh, on the E of the Jordan, a mighty man (1 Chron. 5:24).

2. The son of Toah and father of Jeroham, ancestors of Heman the singer and Levite (1 Chron. 6:34); probably identical with the Eliab of v. 27 and of the Elihu of 1 Sam. 1:1.

3. One of the descendants of Shimei, and leader of a Benjamite family in Jerusalem (1 Chron. 8:20).

4. One of the descendants of Shashak, and also leader of a Benjamite family in Jerusalem (1 Chron. 8:22).

5. "The Mahavite," one of David's distinguished warriors (1 Chron. 11:46), 991 B.C.

6. Another of the same guard, but without any express designation (1 Chron. 11:47).

7. One of the Gadite heroes who came across the Jordan and joined David in his stronghold in the wilderness (1 Chron. 12:11); possibly the same as no. 5 or 6, about 1000 B.C.

8. One of the eighty Hebronite Levites who assisted David in the removal of the Ark to Jerusalem (1 Chron. 15:9, 11), about 982 B.C.

9. One of the Levites appointed by Hezekiah to have charge of the offerings and tithes dedicated in the Temple (2 Chron. 31:13), about 719 B.C.

ELIE'NAI (el-i-ē'ni; "toward God are my eyes"). A descendant of Shimei, and a leader of one of the Benjamite families resident at Jerusalem (1 Chron. 8:20).

ELIE'ZER (el-i-ē'zer; "God of help").

1. "Eliezer of Damascus," mentioned in Gen. 15:2-3, apparently a house-born domestic and steward of Abraham and hence likely, in the absence of direct issue, to become the patriarch's heir, about 2070 B.C. The common notion is that Eliezer was Abraham's house-born slave, adopted as his heir, and meanwhile his chief servant, the same who afterward was sent into Mesopotamia to seek a wife for Isaac. "This last point we may dismiss with the remark that there is not the least evidence that 'the elder servant of his house' (Gen. 24:2 KJV) was the same with Eliezer" (Kitto).

Much difficulty has arisen from the seeming contradiction in the two expressions "Eliezer of Damascus" and "one born in my house" (Gen. 15:2-3). The question arises as to how Eliezer could have been a house-born slave, seeing that Abraham's household was never in Damascus.

The answer is that the expression "the heir of my house" literally translated is "the son of possession of my house" and is exactly the same as the phrase in v. 3, "the son of my house ["one born in my house," NASB; NIV, however, "a servant in my house"] is my heir." This removes every objection to Eliezer's being of Damascus and leaves it more probable that he was not a servant at all but a near relative, perhaps nearer than Lot. Some, indeed, identify Eliezer with Lot, which would afford an excellent explanation if Scripture afforded sufficient grounds for it (Keil, *Com.*; Kitto).

2. The second of the two sons of Moses and Zipporah, born during the exile in Midian, to whom his father gave this name, "for he said, 'the God of my father was my help, and delivered me from the sword of Pharaoh' " (Ex. 18:4; 1 Chron. 23:15), before 1440 B.C. He remained with his mother and brother, Gershom, in the care of Jethro, his grandfather, when Moses returned to Egypt (Ex. 18:2-4). Jethro brought Zipporah and her two sons back to Moses in the wilderness after the Exodus from Egypt (18:5). Eliezer had one son, Rehabiah, from whom sprang a numerous posterity (1 Chron. 23:17; 26:25-26). Shelomoth, in the reigns of Saul and David (v. 28), had the care of all the treasures of things dedicated to God and was descended from Eliezer in the sixth generation, if the genealogy in 26:25 is complete.

3. A son of Becher and grandson of Benjamin (1 Chron. 7:8).

4. One of the priests who blew the trumpets before the Ark when it was brought to Jerusalem (1 Chron. 15:24), about 982 B.C.

5. Son of Zichri, and "chief officer" of the Reubenites in the reign of David (1 Chron. 27:16).

6. A prophet (son of Dodavahu, of Mareshah) who foretold to *Jehoshaphat* (which see) that the fleet he had fitted out in partnership with Ahaziah would be wrecked (2 Chron. 20:37), after 875 B.C.

7. A leader of the Jews during the Exile, sent by Ezra with others from Ahava to Casiphia to induce some Levites and Temple servants to join the party returning to Jerusalem (Ezra 8:16), 457 B.C.

8, 9, 10. A priest (descendant of Jeshua), a Levite, and an Israelite (of the lineage of Harim), who divorced their Gentile wives after the Exile (Ezra 10:18, 23, 31), 456 B.C.

11. Son of Jorim and father of Joshua, of the private lineage of David prior to Shealtiel (Luke 3:29), before 588 B.C.

ELIHOE'NAI. See Eliehoenai.

ELIHO'REPH (el-i-hō'ref; "God of autumn"). Son of Shisha, and appointed, with his brother Ahijah, secretary by Solomon (1 Kings 4:3), 959 B.C.

ELI'HU (e-lī'hū; "my God is he").

1. The son of Tohu and grandfather of Elkanah, Samuel's father (1 Sam. 1:1). In the statements of the genealogy of Samuel in 1 Chronicles, the name *Eliel* (which see) occurs in the same position—son of Toah and father of Jeroham (6:34); and also *Eliab* (which see; 6:27), father of Jeroham and grandson of Zophai. The general opinion is that Elihu is the original name, and the two latter forms are copyists' variations of it.

2. One of the captains of Manasseh (1 Chron. 12:20) who followed David to Ziklag on the eve of the battle of Gilboa and who assisted him against the Amalekites (1 Sam. 30), about 1001 B.C.

3. One of the very able-bodied members of the family of Obed-edom (a grandson by Shemaiah) who were appointed gatekeepers of the Temple under David (1 Chron. 26:7), after 1000 B.C. Terms applied to all these gatekeepers appear to indicate that they were not only "strong men," as in the KJV, but also fighting men (*see* vv. 6-8, 12, in which the Heb. words for army and warriors, or heroes, occur).

4. A "chief officer" of the tribe of Judah, said to be "one of David's brothers" (1 Chron. 27:18) and hence supposed by some to have been his eldest brother, Eliab (1 Sam. 16:6), 1000 B.C.

5. One of Job's friends. He is described as "the son of Barachel the Buzite, of the family of Ram" (Job 32:2). This is usually understood to imply that he was descended from Buz, the son of Abraham's brother Nahor. For his part in the remarkable discussion, *see* Job.

ELIJAH (e-lī'ja; "my God is Jehovah"). The name of the great prophet (which see) and three other biblical characters.

1. One of the "sons of Jeroham," and head of a Benjamite family resident at Jerusalem (1 Chron. 8:27).

2. A priest of the "sons of Harim," who divorced his Gentile wife on returning from the Exile (Ezra 10:21), 456 B.C.

3. One of the "sons of Elam," who divorced his Gentile wife on returning from the Exile (Ezra 10:26), 456 B.C.

ELI'JAH (e-lī'ja; "my God is Jehovah"). The prophet Elijah came from Tishbeh in Gilead, a district that shared deeply in the miseries of the kingdom of the ten tribes. Nothing is known concerning his family or birth.

The better to understand his history, let us briefly consider the condition of affairs when Elijah made his appearance. Ahab had taken Jezebel, a Canaanite woman and daughter of Ethbaal, for his wife. Of a weak and yielding character, he allowed Jezebel to establish the Phoenician worship on a grand scale—priests and prophets of Baal were appointed in crowds—the prophets of Jehovah were persecuted and slain or only escaped by being hid in caves. It seemed the last remnants of true religion were about to perish. Jezebel had also induced Ahab to issue orders for the violent death of all the prophets of Jehovah who, since the expulsion of the Levites, had been the only firm support of the ancient religion (*see* 1 Kings 18:4, 13, 22; 19:10, 14; 2 Kings 9:7).

Appears Before Ahab. Elijah suddenly appeared before Ahab and proclaimed the vengeance of Jehovah for the apostasy of the king. "As the Lord, the God of Israel lives, before whom I stand, surely there shall be neither dew nor rain these years, except by my word" (1 Kings 17:1). This was probably the conclusion of a warning given the king of the consequences of his iniquitous course (about 870 B.C.). Warned by God, Elijah went and hid by Cherith, perhaps the present Wadi Kelt. There he remained, supported by ravens, until the brook dried up. Then another refuge was provided for him at *Zarephath* (which see). "Then the word of the Lord came to him, saying, 'Arise, go to Zarephath . . . and stay there.' " At the gate of the city he met the woman who was to sustain him, herself on the verge of starvation. Obedient to his request to prepare him food, she was rewarded by the miracle of the prolonging of the meal and oil and the restoration of her son to life after his sudden death (17:8-10, 16, 21-22).

Second Appearance Before Ahab. For three years and six months there had been no rain (James 5:17). At last the full horrors of famine, caused by the failure of the crops, descended on Samaria. Elijah, returning to Israel, found Ahab still alive and unreformed, Jezebel still worshiping her idols, and the prophets of Baal still deceiving the people. Elijah first presented himself (1 Kings 18) to Obadiah, the principal servant of Ahab and a true servant of God. He requested him to announce his return to Ahab, and Obadiah, his fears having been removed by the prophet, consented. The conversation between Ahab and Elijah, when they met soon after, began with the question of the king, "Is this you, you troubler of Israel?" Elijah answered unhesitatingly, "I have not troubled Israel, but you and your father's house have, because you have forsaken the commandments of the Lord, and you have followed the Baals" (vv. 17-18). He then challenged Ahab to exercise his authority in summoning an assembly to Mt. Carmel that the controversy between them might be decided.

On Carmel. Whatever his secret purposes were, Ahab accepted this proposal, and the people also consented. Fire was the element over which Baal was supposed to preside so Elijah proposed (wishing to give them every advantage) that two oxen be slain and each laid upon a separate altar, the one for Baal, the other for Jehovah; whichever should be consumed by fire would proclaim whose the children of Israel were and whom it was their duty to serve (vv. 23-24). There are few more sublime stories in history than this. On the one hand the servant of Jehovah, attended by his one servant, with his wild, shaggy hair, his scanty garb, and sheepskin cloak, but with calm dignity of demeanor and the minutest regularity of procedure. On the other hand the prophets of Baal and Ashtaroth—doubtless in all the splendor of their vestments (2 Kings 10:22), with the wild din of their vain repetitions and the maddened fury of their disappointed hopes —and the silent people surrounding all; these form a picture that brightens into fresh distinctness every time we consider it. The Baalites were allowed to make trial first. All day long these false prophets cried to Baal; they leaped upon the altar, and mingled their blood with that of the sacrifice—but all was in vain, for at the time of the evening sacrifice the altar was still cold and the ox unconsumed— "there was no voice, no one answered, and no one paid attention" (1 Kings 18:29). Then Elijah repaired the broken altar of Jehovah, and, having laid his ox on it and drenched both altar and sacrifice with water until the trench about them was filled, he prayed, "O Lord, the God of Abraham, Isaac and Israel, today let it be known that Thou art God in Israel, and that I am Thy servant, and that I have done all these things at Thy word." The answer was all that could be desired, for the "fire of the Lord fell, and consumed the burnt offering and the wood and the stones and the dust, and licked up the water that was in the trench." The people acknowledged the presence of God, exclaiming with one voice, "The Lord, He is God; the Lord, He is God." By Elijah's direction the priests were slain and Ahab informed that he might take refreshment, for God would send the desired rain (vv. 31-44).

Prays for Rain. Elijah prayed, God heard and answered; a little cloud arose, and, diffusing itself gradually over the entire face of the heavens, emptied its refreshing waters upon the whole land of Israel. Ahab rode to Jezreel, a distance of at least sixteen miles; the prophet also "girded up his loins and outran Ahab to Jezreel" (v. 46).

Flees from Jezebel. The prophets of Baal were destroyed and Ahab was cowed, but Jezebel remained undaunted. She made a vow against the life of the prophet, who, attended by his servant—according to Jewish tradition, the boy of Zarephath—took refuge in flight. The first stage in his journey was "Beersheba, which belongs to Judah." Leaving his servant in the town he set out alone into the wilderness (19:1-4).

Under the Juniper Tree. The labors, anxieties, and excitement of the last few days had proved too much even for that iron frame and stern resolution. His spirit was broken, and, sitting beneath a juniper tree, Elijah wished for death. "It is enough; now, O Lord, take my life, for I am not better than my fathers." But sleep and food, miraculously furnished, refreshed the weary

Mt. Carmel, near Elijah's altar

This figure of Elijah marks the traditional site of the prophet's confrontation with the prophets of Baal.

prophet, and he went forward in the strength of that food to Mt. Horeb, a journey of forty days (vv. 4-8).

At Horeb. After he rested in a cave one night the voice of the Lord came to him in the morning, asking, "What are you doing here, Elijah?" And then he again unburdened his soul and told his grief: "I have been very zealous for the Lord, the God of hosts, for the sons of Israel have forsaken Thy covenant . . . I alone am left; and they seek my life, to take it away" (vv. 9-10). He was directed to stand outside the cave, and "the Lord was passing by" (v. 11) in all the terror of His most appalling manifestations. The fierce wind tore the solid mountains and shivered the granite cliffs of Sinai; the earthquake crash reverberated through the defiles of those naked valleys; the fire burned in the incessant blaze of Eastern lightning. Elijah's own mode of procedure had been like these in their degree, but the conviction was now forced upon him that in none of these was Jehovah to be known. Then came the whisper of the "still small voice" (v. 12, KJV; NIV, "a gentle whisper"). Elijah knew the call and, stepping forward, hid his face in his mantle and waited for the divine communication. Three commands were laid upon him—to anoint Hazael king over Syria; Jehu the son of Nimshi, king

over Israel; and Elisha the son of Shaphat to be his own successor. Of these three commands the first two were reserved for Elisha to accomplish; the last one was executed by Elijah himself (vv. 15-18).

Finds Elisha. The prophet soon found Elisha at his native place, Abel-meholah. Elisha was plowing at the time, and Elijah, without uttering a word, cast his mantle, the well-known sheepskin cloak, upon him, as if by that familiar action (which was also a symbol of official investiture) claiming him for his son. The call was accepted, and then began the long relationship that continued until Elijah's removal (vv. 19-21).

Reproves Ahab and Jezebel. For about six years we find no notice of Elijah, until God sent him once again to pronounce judgment upon Ahab and Jezebel for the murder of the unoffending *Naboth* (which see). Just as Ahab was about to take possession of the vineyard he was met by Elijah, who uttered the terrible curse (21:19-24), 860 B.C. Ahab, assuming penitence and afterward proving his sincerity, was rewarded by a temporary arrest of judgment; but it took effect upon his wicked consort and children to the very letter.

Elijah and King Ahaziah. Ahaziah had succeeded Ahab, his father, upon his death and in the second year of his reign met with a serious accident. Fearing a fatal result, he sent to Ekron to learn at the shrine of Baal of the issue to his illness, but the angel of the Lord told Elijah to go forth and meet the messengers of the king. Questioned by Ahaziah as to the reason for their early return the messengers told him of their meeting the prophet and his prediction. From their description of him Ahaziah recognized Elijah, the man of God. Enraged he sent a captain with fifty men to take Elijah. The officer addressed the prophet by the title most frequently applied to him, " 'O man of God, the king says, "Come down." ' And Elijah answered and said to the captain of fifty, 'If I am a man of God, let fire come down from heaven and consume you and your fifty.' Then fire came down from heaven and consumed him and his fifty" (2 Kings 1:9-10). A second company shared the same fate. The altered tone of the leader of the third party, and the assurance of God that His servant need not fear, brought Elijah down. But the king gained nothing. The message delivered before was repeated to his face, and the king died shortly after (vv. 11-17). This was Elijah's last interview with the house of Ahab, and his last recorded appearance in person against the Baal worshipers, c. 852 B.C.

Warns Jehoram. Jehoram, king of Judah, had married the daughter of Ahab and walked "in the way of the kings of Israel," as did the house of Ahab. Elijah sent him a letter denouncing his evil doings and predicting his death (2 Chron. 21:12-15). That is Elijah's only communication with the Southern Kingdom of which any record remains.

Closing Scenes. The faithful prophet's warfare was now accomplished, and God would translate him in a special manner to heaven. Conscious of that, he determined to spend his last moments in imparting divine instruction to, and pronouncing his last benediction upon "the sons of the prophets" who were at Bethel and Jericho. It was at Gilgal—probably not the ancient place of Joshua and Samuel but another of the same name still surviving on the western edge of the hills of Ephraim—that the prophet received the divine intimation that his departure was at hand. Here he requested Elisha, his constant companion, to remain while he went on an errand of Jehovah. Perhaps the request was made because of the return of his old love for solitude, perhaps he desired to spare his friend the pain of too sudden a parting, or, it may be, he desired to test the affection of the latter. But Elisha would not give up his master, and they went together to Bethel (2 Kings 2:1-4). The sons of the prophets, apparently acquainted with what was about to happen, inquired of Elisha if he knew of his impending loss. His answer shows how fully he was aware of it. "Yes, I know; be still" (vv. 3, 5). Again Elijah attempted to escape to Jericho, and again Elisha protested that he would not be separated from him. Under the plea of going to Jordan, Elijah again requested Elisha to tarry, still with no success, and the two set off together toward the river. Fifty men of the sons of the prophets ascended the heights behind the town to watch what would happen. Reaching the river, Elijah rolled up his mantle as a staff, struck the waters, which divided, and the two went over on dry ground. What followed is best told in the simple words of the narrative: "Now it came about when they had crossed over, that Elijah said to Elisha, 'Ask what I shall do for you before I am taken from you.' And Elisha said, 'Please, let a double portion of your spirit be upon me.' And he said, 'You have asked a hard thing. Nevertheless, if you see me when I am taken from you, it shall be so for you; but if not, it shall not be so.' Then it came about as they were going along and talking, that behold, there appeared a chariot of fire and horses of fire which separated the two of them. And Elijah went up by a whirlwind to heaven." Elisha, at the wonderful sight, cried out, like a bereaved child, "My father, my father, the chariots of Israel and its horsemen!" The mantle of his master had, however, fallen upon Elisha as a pledge that the office and spirit of the former were now his own (vv. 6-13).

Character. Elijah's character is one of moral sublimity. His faith in God seemed to know no limit or questioning. His zeal for Jehovah was an all-absorbing motive of his life, so that he justly said, "I have been very zealous for the Lord, the God of hosts." No danger or duty was too severe to shake his confidence—no labor too great for his Lord. His courage was undaunted, even in the presence of royalty or famine. His obedience was as simple and unquestioning as a child's. Tender of soul, he could sympathize with the widow when she lost her child or weep over the sad condition of his deluded countrymen. Stern in principle, he was; in his opposition to sin, as fierce as the fire that more than once answered his command. He was by nature a recluse, only appearing before men to deliver his message from God and to enforce it by a miracle, and then disappearing from sight again.

The Ravens. Much ingenuity has been devoted to explaining away the obvious meaning of Elijah's ravens (1 Kings 17:4, 6). Some suppose that the brook Cherith was a place where ravens congregated and that Elijah took from their nests morning and evening the food they brought to their young. Others have explained '*ōrᵉbîm* to mean "Arabians"; others, the inhabitants of Orbo, or Oreb; and some have thought that the word might mean "merchants," from '*ārab*, "to traffic." The text, however, plainly records a miracle (Whedon, *Com.,* ad loc.).

Elijah's Mocking. Some have objected that Elijah's mockery of Baal's prophets was not in accordance with the spirit of Scripture—"not returning evil for evil, or insult for insult, but giving a blessing instead" (1 Pet. 3:9). "In the case of Elijah ridicule was a fit weapon for exposing the folly and absurdity of idol worship. The prophet employed it with terrible effect" (Haley, *Dis.*).

Letter to Jehoram. This letter has been considered a great difficulty, on the ground that Elijah's removal must have taken place before the death of Jehoshaphat and, therefore, before the accession of Jehoram to the throne of Judah. That Jehoram began to reign during the lifetime of his father, Jehoshaphat, is stated in 2 Kings 8:16. He probably ascended the throne as viceroy or associate some years before the death of his father.

BIBLIOGRAPHY: F. W. Krummacher, *Elijah the Tishbite* (n.d.); J. R. MacDuff, *Elijah, the Prophet of Fire* (1956); R. S. Wallace, *Elijah and Elisha* (1957); H. H. Rowley, *Man of God* (1963), pp. 37-65.

ELI'KA (e-lī'ka; perhaps "God has spewed out," "rejected"). A Harodite, and one of David's thirty-seven distinguished warriors (2 Sam. 23:25), about 1000 B.C.

E'LIM (ē'lim; "trees"). Second station of Israel in the desert (Ex. 15:27; Num. 33:9), where they encamped for a month (Ex. 16:1). Here were "twelve springs of water and seventy date palms." The present Wadi Gharandel.

ELIM'ELECH (e-lim'e-lek; "God is king"). A man of the tribe of Judah who dwelt in Bethlehem in Judah in the days of the judges, probably before 1070 B.C. In consequence of a great famine in the land, he went with his wife, Naomi, and his two sons, Mahlon and Chilion, to dwell in Moab, where he and his two sons died (Ruth 1:2-3; 2:1, 3; 4:3, 9).

ELIOE'NAI (e-li-o-ē'ni; a contracted form of the name Elihoenai).

1. The eldest son of Neariah, son of Shemaiah, of the descendants of Zerubbabel (1 Chron. 3:23-24).

2. A leader of the Simeonites (1 Chron. 4:36).

3. The fourth son of Becher, son of Benjamin (1 Chron. 7:8).

4. Seventh son of Meshelemiah (1 Chron. 26:3, KJV). *See* Eliehoenai, no. 1.

5. A priest of the sons of Pashhur, who, at the instigation of Ezra, put away his Gentile wife and offered a ram for a trespass offering (Ezra 10:22), 456 B.C. He is, perhaps, the same mentioned in Neh. 12:41 as one of the priests who accompanied Nehemiah with trumpets at the dedication of the wall of Jerusalem, 445 B.C.

6. An Israelite (*singer*) of the sons of Zattu, who likewise divorced his Gentile wife after the Exile (Ezra 10:27), 456 B.C.

ELI'PHAL (e-lī'fal; "God his judge"). Son of Ur, and one of David's mighty men (1 Chron. 11:35), about 1000 B.C. *See* Eiphelet, no. 3.

ELIPH'ALET. *See* Eliphelet, no. 2.

ELI'PHAZ (el'ī'faz; "God of gold," or "God is fine gold").

1. A son of Esau by Adah, his first wife, and father of several Edomite tribes (Gen. 36:4, 10-11, 16; 1 Chron. 1:35-36).

2. One of the three friends who came to console Job in his affliction. They had agreed to meet together for this purpose, but, overcome with feeling at the condition of their friend, they sat down in silence for seven days (Job 2:11). Eliphaz is called "the Temanite" and was probably of Teman in Edom. As Eliphaz the son of Esau had a son named Teman, from whom the place took its name, there is reason to conclude that this Eliphaz was a descendant of the former Eliphaz (Kitto). He is the first speaker among the friends and probably the eldest among them. He begins his orations with delicacy and conducts his part of the controversy with considerable address (chaps. 4-5, 15, 22). On him falls the main burden of the argument that God's retribution in this world is perfect and certain and that, consequently, suffering must be a proof of previous sin. The great truth brought out by him is the unapproachable majesty and purity of God (4:12-21; 15:12-16). But still, with the other two friends, he is condemned because they "have not spoken of Me what is right" (42:7). "In order that they may only maintain the justice of God they have condemned Job against their better knowledge and conscience" (Delitzsch). Through sacrifice and intercession of Job all three are pardoned.

BIBLIOGRAPHY: J. S. Baxter, *Explore the Book* (1962), 3:23-80.

ELIPH'ELE'HU (e-lif'e-lē'hu; "whom God makes distinguished"). A Merarite Levite, one of the gatekeepers appointed by David to "lead with lyres tuned to the sheminith" on the occasion of bringing up the Ark to the city of David (1 Chron. 15:18, 21), about 982 B.C.

ELIPH'ELET (e-lif'e-let; "God of deliverance").

1. The third of the nine sons of David, born at Jerusalem, by Bathsheba (1 Chron. 3:6; 14:5). In the latter passage the name is given in a contracted form, *Elpelet* (*Elpalet*, KJV), about 989 B.C.

2. The ninth of the same (1 Chron. 3:8; 14:7; 2 Sam. 5:16). It is believed that there were not two sons of this name but that one is merely a transcriber's repetition. The two are certainly omitted in Samuel, but, on the other hand, they are inserted in two separate lists in Chronicles, and in both cases the number of the sons is summed up at the close of the list.

3. One of David's distinguished warriors, called "the son of Ahasbai, the son of the Maacathite" (2 Sam. 23:34) but, by some error and abbreviation, *Eliphal* (which see) son of Ur, in 1 Chron. 11:35.

4. The third of the three sons of Eshek, of the posterity of Benjamin, and a descendant of King Saul through Jonathan (1 Chron. 8:39).

5. One of the three sons of Adonikam, who returned from Babylon with his brothers and sixty males (Ezra 8:13), 457 B.C.

6. A descendant of Hashum, who divorced his Gentile wife after the Exile (Ezra 10:33), 456 B.C.

ELIS'ABETH. *See* Elizabeth.

ELISE'US. *See* Elisha.

ELI'SHA (e-lī'sha; Heb. *ʾelîshaʿ*, "God his salvation"). The son of Shaphat, of Abel-meholah (in or near the Jordan Valley).

Call. Elisha, a husbandman, was plowing with a number of companions, himself with the twelfth plow. Elijah, on his way from Horeb to Damascus, found Elisha and threw upon his shoulders his mantle—a token of investiture with the prophet's office and adoption as a son. Elisha accepted the call. Delaying only long enough to kiss his father and mother and give a farewell feast to his people, he "arose and followed Elijah and ministered to him" (1 Kings 19:19-21), about 856 B.C.

Elijah's Ascension. We hear no more of Elisha until he accompanied his master to the other side of the Jordan, witnessed his ascension there, with his fallen mantle parted the waters, and was welcomed by the sons of the prophets as the successor of Elijah (2 Kings 2:1-15), 846 B.C.

At Jericho. After that he dwelt at Jericho (2:18). The town had lately been rebuilt by Hiel (1 Kings 16:34) and was the residence of a body of the "sons of the prophets" (2 Kings 2:5). While he was there the citizens of the place complained to him of the foulness of its waters. He remedied the evil by casting salt into the water at its source in the name of Jehovah (2:19-22).

The oasis of Jericho

Mocked. Leaving Jericho he went to Bethel and upon nearing the town was met by a number of children who mockingly cried, "Go up, you baldhead." This dishonor to God through His prophet was sternly rebuked by Elisha, and "two female bears came out of the woods and tore up forty-two lads of their number. And he went from there to Mount Carmel, and from there he returned to Samaria" (2:23-25). Objection has been made to the severity of the punishment visited upon the mocking children. "It is not said that they were actually slain (the expression is *bāqa'*, 'to rend,' which is peculiarly applicable to the claws of the bear). It is by no means certain that all of them were killed" (McClintock and Strong, s.v.). Kitto thinks that these children had been instigated by their idolatrous parents to mock Elisha, and that by this judgment the people of Bethel were to know that to dishonor God's prophets was to dishonor Him.

Assists Jehoram. Jehoram, king of Israel, and the kings of Judah and Edom were united in a campaign against Moab, endeavoring to suppress a revolt that occurred shortly after the death of Ahab. A difficulty arose from the lack of water. Elisha, being appealed to, requested a minstrel to be brought, and at the sound of the music the

hand of Jehovah came upon him. He ordered pits to be dug to hold the abundant supply of water that he prophesied would be given them. The water that preserved their lives became the source of destruction to their enemies, for the next morning "the sun shone on the water, and the Moabites saw the water opposite them as red as blood. Then they said, 'This is blood; the kings have surely fought together, and they have slain one another. Now therefore, Moab, to the spoil!' But when they came to the camp of Israel, the Israelites arose and struck the Moabites, so that they fled before them; and they went forward into the land, slaughtering the Moabites" (3:4-24).

Widow's Oil. A widow of one of the sons of the prophets was in debt and her two sons about to be taken from her and sold by her creditors, as by law they had power to do (Lev. 25:39). In her extremity she implored the prophet's assistance. Inquiring into her circumstances he learned that she had nothing in the house but a jar of oil. This Elisha caused (in his absence, 4:5) to multiply until the widow had filled with it all the vessels she could borrow, and thus she procured the means of payment (4:7). No place or date of the miracle is mentioned.

The Shunammite. On his way between Carmel and the Jordan Valley Elisha called at Shunem. Here he was hospitably entertained by a rich and godly woman. Desiring to have him as a guest on his frequent visits, she prepared a chamber for his use. This room, called *'aliyyâ* (the upper chamber), is the most desirable of the house, being secluded and well fitted. Elisha, grateful for the kindness shown him, asked the woman if she would have him seek a favor for her of the king or captain of the army. She declined the prophet's offer, saying, "I live among my own people." Gehazi, Elisha's servant, reminded him of the Shunammite's childless condition, and a son was promised her, which in due time was born (4:8-17). When the child was large enough he went out to his father in the field. While there he was (probably) sunstruck, and soon died. The mother laid the dead child upon the prophet's bed, and hastening to the prophet in Carmel she made him acquainted with her loss. Gehazi was sent before to lay Elisha's staff upon the face of the child. The child's life did not return, and Elisha shut himself up with the dead boy. Praying to God, he "stretched himself on him; and the flesh of the child became warm" (4:18-37).

At Gilgal. It was a time of famine, and the food of the prophets was limited to any herbs that could be found. A large pot was put on at the command of Elisha, and one of the company brought in his blanket full of such wild vegetables as he had collected and emptied it into the stew. But no sooner had they begun their meal than the taste betrayed the presence of some obnoxious herb, and they cried out, "O man of God, there is death in the pot." In this case the cure was effected by meal that Elisha cast into the caldron (4:38-41). The next miracle probably occurred at the same time and place. A man from Baal-shalishah brought a present to Elisha of the firstfruits, which, under the law (Num. 18:8, 12; Deut. 18:3-4), were the perquisites of the ministers of the sanctuary—twenty loaves of new barley and full ears of corn in the husk (perhaps new garden grain). This, by the word of Jehovah, was rendered more than sufficient for a hundred men (4:42-44).

Naaman Cured. Naaman, captain of the army of Syria, was afflicted with leprosy, and that in its most striking form, the white variety (5:1, 27). Hearing of Elisha, he informed the king, who sent him with a letter to the king of Israel. "And now," so ran Benhadad's letter, "as this letter comes to you, behold, I have sent Naaman my servant to you, that you may cure him of his leprosy." Accompanying the letter were rich presents of gold, silver, and "ten changes of clothes." The king of Israel saw only one thing in the transaction—a desire on the part of Benhadad to pick a quarrel with him. The prophet, hearing of the matter, sent word to the king, "Now let him come to me, and he shall know that there is a prophet in Israel." So Naaman stood with his retinue before Elisha's house. Elisha sent a messenger to the general with the simple instruction to bathe seven times in the Jordan. Naaman was enraged at the independent behavior of the prophet and the simplicity of the prescription but, persuaded by his servants, obeyed Elisha and was healed. Returning to the prophet, he acknowledged the power of God and entreated Elisha to accept the present he had brought from Damascus. This Elisha firmly refused and dismissed him in peace (5:1-27).

Ax Raised. When the home of the prophets became too small, it was resolved to build nearer the Jordan. While one of them was felling a tree the axe head flew off and fell into the water. Appeal was made to Elisha, who "cut off a stick, and threw it in there, and made the iron float" (6:1-7).

Syrians Thwarted. The Syrians warred against Israel, but their plans, however secret, were known to Elisha, who disclosed them to the king of Israel, and by his warnings saved the king "more than once or twice." The king of Syria, learning that Elisha the prophet told of his plans, sent a detachment of men to take him. They came by night and surrounded Dothan, where Elisha resided. His servant was the first to discover the danger and made it known to his master. At Elisha's request the eyes of the young man were opened to behold the spiritual guards who protected them. In answer to Elisha's prayer, the Syrians were blinded, and Elisha offered to lead them to the place and person they sought. He conducted them to Samaria, where their blindness was removed and they found themselves in the presence of the king and his troops. The king, eager to destroy them, asked, "My father, shall I kill them? Shall I kill them?" Elisha's object was gained when he showed the Syrians the futility of their attempts against him. He, therefore, refused the king permission to slay them and, having fed them, sent them away to their master (6:8-23). "Was the deception (6:19) practiced toward the Syrians justifiable? Various answers have been given. Keil and Rawlinson apparently regard Elisha's statement simply in the light of a 'stratagem of war.' Thenius says: 'There is no untruth in the words of Elisha; for his home was not in Dothan, where he was only residing temporarily, but in Samaria; and the words "to the man" may well mean to his house.' Some regard the prophet's language as mere irony" (Haley, *Alleged Dis.*).

Famine in Syria. Ben-hadad, the king of Syria, now laid siege on Samaria, and its inhabitants were driven to great straits by reason of famine. Roused by an encounter with a ghastly incident, Jehoram, the king (Josephus *Ant.* 9.4.4), vented for some reason his wrath upon Elisha, and with an oath he said, "May God do so to me and more also, if the head of Elisha the son of Shaphat remains on him today" (6:31). An emissary started to execute the sentence, but Elisha, warned of the danger, told those present not to admit him, assuring them that the king himself was coming in haste to stay the result of his rash exclamation (so interprets Josephus, *Ant.* 9.4.4). To the king Elisha promised that within twenty-four hours food should be plentiful. The next day the Syrian camp was found deserted; the night before, God had caused the Syrians to hear the noise of horses and chariots and, believing that Jehoram had hired against them the kings of the Hittites and the king of Egypt, had fled in panic and confusion. Thus God, according to the words of Elisha, delivered Samaria. Another prediction was also accomplished, for the distrustful lord who doubted the word of Elisha was trampled to death by the famished people rushing through the city gates to the forsaken tents of the Syrians (6:24–7:20).

Shunammite's Property Restored. Elisha, aware of the famine God was about to bring upon the land, had advised his friend the Shunammite of it that she might provide for her safety. She left Shunem for the land of the Philistines and remained there during the dearth. At the end of the seven years she returned and found her house and land appropriated by some other person. When she came to the king to ask redress he was listening to a recital by Gehazi of the great things that Elisha had done, the crowning feat being that which he was then actually relating—the restoration to life of the boy of Shunem. The woman was instantly recognized by Gehazi. "My lord, O king, this is the woman and this is her son, whom Elisha restored to life." The king immediately ordered her land to be restored, with the value of its produce during her absence (8:1-6).

Elisha at Damascus. We next find Elisha at Damascus, where he went to anoint Hazael to be king over Syria. Ben-hadad was prostrate with his last illness and sent Hazael with a princely present to inquire of Elisha, "Will I recover from this sickness?" The answer of Elisha, though ambiguous, contained the unmistakable conclusion, "The Lord has shown me that he will certainly die." The prophet fixed his earnest gaze upon Hazael and burst into tears. Inquired of as to the cause of his grief, Elisha told him that he would be king and bring great evil upon the children of Israel. Hazael returned and told the king that the prophet had predicted his recovery. That was the last day of Ben-hadad's life, for on the morrow he was smothered, and Hazael reigned in his stead (8:7-15).

Jehu Anointed. While Hazael was warring against the combined force of the kings of Israel and Judah (8:28) Elisha sent one of the sons of the prophets to anoint Jehu the son of Jehoshaphat king over Israel and to prophesy concerning the fearful overthrow of the house of Ahab (9:1-10).

Death. We next find Elisha upon his deathbed. Here he was visited by Joash, the grandson of Jehu, who came to weep over the departure of the great and good prophet. The king was given a test and told that he would strike Syria but three times, whereas if he had shown more energy in striking the ground with the arrows he should have completely destroyed his foe (13:14-19).

In His Tomb. The power of the prophet did not end with his death, for even in his tomb he restored the dead to life. A funeral was going on in the cemetery that contained the sepulcher of Elisha. Seeing a band of Moabites near by, the friends of the dead man hastily put him into the tomb of the prophet. The mere touch of his remains had power, for the man "revived and stood up on his feet" (13:20-21).

Character. Elisha presents a striking contrast to his master, Elijah, who was a true Bedouin child of the desert. Elisha, on the other hand, was a civilized man, preferring companionship, dwelling in cities, and often in close connection with kings. Elijah was a man whose mission was to accuse of sin or bring judgment upon men because of it; Elisha, while defending the ancient religion, came as a healer, and his miracles were those of restoring to life, increasing the widow's oil, making pure the bitter waters. There were tender sympathy for friends, tears for his country's prospective woes. And yet there was firmness in maintaining that which was right, sternness of judgment, and seeming forgetfulness of self. "In spite of all the seductions to which he was abundantly exposed through the great consideration in which he was held he retained at every period of his life the true prophetic simplicity and purity and contempt for worldly wealth and advantages" (Ewald, *History of Israel,* 4:83).

BIBLIOGRAPHY: L. Bronner, *The Stories of Elijah and Elisha* (1968); F. W. Krummacher, *Elisha: A Prophet for Our Times* (1976).

ELI'SHAH (e-lī′sha). The oldest of the four sons of Javan (Gen. 10:4; 1 Chron. 1:7). He seems to have given his name to "the coastlands of Elishah," which are described as exporting fabrics of purple and scarlet to the markets of Tyre (Ezek. 27:7). Elishah is Kittim or Cyprus (G. E. Wright and F. Filson, *Westminster Historical Atlas to the Bible* [1945], p. 109). It is the Alashia of the Amarna Letters. Cyprus with the Peloponnesus and the islands and coasts of the Aegean were rich in purple shells.

ELISH'AMA (e-lish′a-ma; "God of hearing").

1. The son of Ammihud, and head of the tribe of Ephraim at the Exodus (Num. 1:10; 2:18; 7:48, 53; 10:22), c. 1440 B.C. From the genealogy in 1 Chron. 7:26 we find that he was the grandfather of Joshua.

2. The second of the nine sons of David, born at Jerusalem, by Bathsheba (1 Chron. 3:6), called in the parallel passages (2 Sam. 5:15; 1 Chron. 14:5) by apparently the more proper name *Elishua* (which see).

3. The seventh of the same series of sons (1 Chron. 3:8; 14:7). According to Samuel (2 Sam. 5:14-16) there were only eleven sons born to David after his establishment in Jerusalem, and Elishama is eleventh of the series, after 1000 B.C.

4. An Israelite of the family of David, father of Nethaniah, and grandfather of Ishmael, who slew Gedaliah, the ruler appointed by Nebuchadnezzar over the people that were left in Judea (2 Kings 25:25; Jer. 41:1), before 588 B.C.

5. An Israelite of the tribe of Judah and son of Jekamiah. In the Jewish tradition preserved by Jerome (*Quaestiones hebraicae* on 1 Chron. 2:41) he appears to be identified with no. 4.

6. One of the two priests sent with the Levites by Jehoshaphat to teach the law through the cities of Judah (2 Chron. 17:8), after 875 B.C.

7. A royal scribe, in whose chamber the roll of Jeremiah was read to him and other magnates. Afterward it was deposited for a time (Jer. 36:12, 20, 21), about 604 B.C.

ELISH'APHAT (e-lish′a-fat; "God of judgment"). Son of Zichri. One of the captains of hundreds by whose aid Jehoiada the priest placed Joash on the throne of Judah and overthrew Athaliah, the usurper (2 Chron. 23:1ff.), about 836 B.C.

ELISH'EBA (e-lish′e-ba; "God of the oath," i.e., worshiper of God). Daughter of Amminadab and sister of Nahshon, the captain of the Hebrew host

(Num. 2:3). She became the wife of Aaron and hence the mother of the priestly family (Ex. 6:23), about 1440 B.C.

ELISH'UA (e-lish'ū-a; "God of supplication"). One of the sons of David born at Jerusalem (2 Sam. 5:15; 1 Chron. 14:5), called *Elishama* (which see) in the parallel passage (1 Chron. 3:6), after 1000 B.C.

ELI'UD (e-līud; "God of majesty"). Son of Achim and father of Eleazar; the fifth in ascent in Christ's paternal genealogy (Matt. 1:14-15), about 200 B.C. (McClintock and Strong, *Cyclopedia*).

ELIZ'ABETH (e-liz'a-beth; Gk. *Elisabeth*, from Heb. *'Elîshēbâ'*, "God her oath"). The wife of Zacharias and mother of John the Baptist. She was a descendant of Aaron, and of her and her husband this exalted character is given by the evangelist: "They were both righteous in the sight of God, walking blamelessly in all the commandments and requirements of the Lord" (Luke 1:5-6). They remained childless until well advanced in years, when an angel foretold to Zacharias the birth of John while he was "performing his priestly service before God" in the Temple. Upon asking for a sign that this miracle would indeed occur, Zacharias lost his speech. After Zacharias returned home, Elizabeth conceived (1:7-24). For five months she concealed the favor God had granted her, but the angel Gabriel revealed to the virgin Mary this miraculous conception as an assurance of the birth of the Messiah by herself (1:24-38). Mary visited her cousin Elizabeth, and they exchanged congratulations and praised God together; Mary abode with her for three months (1:39-56). When the child was circumcised Elizabeth named him John. Her friends objected that none of her kindred had that name, and an appeal was made to Zacharias; he wrote upon a tablet, "His name is John," and immediately speech was restored to him (1:58-64), 6 B.C.

ELIZ'APHAN (e-liz'a-fan; "God has concealed").
1. The second son of Uzziel, and chief of the Kohathite Levites at the Exodus (Num. 3:30; Ex. 6:22), 1441 B.C. He, with his elder brother, Mishael, was directed by Moses to carry away the corpses of their sacrilegious cousins, Nadab and Abihu (Lev. 10:4). In Exodus and Leviticus the name is contracted into Elzaphan. His family took part in the ceremony of bringing the Ark to Jerusalem in the time of David (1 Chron. 15:8) and were represented in the revival under Hezekiah (2 Chron. 29:13).
2. Son of Parnach and leader of the tribe of Zebulun, appointed to assist Moses in the division of the land of Canaan (Num 34:25).

ELI'ZUR (e-lī'zur; "God his rock"). Son of Shedeur and head of the tribe of Reuben at the Exodus (Num. 1:5; 2:10; 7:30, 35; 10:18), 1440 B.C.

ELKA'NAH (ĕl-kā'nà; "whom God has acquired"). The name of several men, all apparently Levites. There is much difficulty and uncertainty in discriminating among the various individuals who bear this name.
1. The second son of Korah, according to Ex. 6:24, where his brothers are represented as being Assir and Abiasaph. But in 1 Chron. 6:22-23, Assir, Elkanah, and Ebiasaph are mentioned in the same order, not as the three sons of Korah, but as son, grandson, and great-grandson, respectively, and that seems to be correct.
2. Son of Shaul, or Joel, and father of Amasai, and ninth in descent from Kohath the son of Levi (1 Chron. 6:25, 36).
3. Son of Ahimoth, or Mahath, being father of Zuph, or Zophai, and great-grandson of the one immediately preceding (1 Chron. 6:26, 35).
4. Another Kohathite Levite, in the line of Heman the singer. He was the son of Jeroham and father of Samuel (1 Chron. 6:27-28, 33-34), about 1106 B.C. He is described (1 Sam. 1:1-2) as living at Ramathaim-zophim, in Mt. Ephraim, otherwise called Ramah, and as having two wives, Hannah and Peninnah, with no children by the former till the birth of Samuel in answer to the prayer of Hannah. We learn also that he lived in the time of Eli the high priest, and that he was a pious man, going up yearly to Shiloh to worship and offer sacrifice (1:3). After the birth of Samuel, Elkanah and Hannah continued to live at Ramah and had three sons and two daughters (2:21). Elkanah the Levite is called an Ephraimite because, so far as his civil standing was concerned, he belonged to the tribe of Ephraim, the Levites being reckoned as belonging to those tribes in the midst of which they lived.
5. The father of Asa, and head of a Levitical family resident in the "villages of the Netophathites" (1 Chron. 9:16), long before 536 B.C.
6. A man of the family of Korahites, who joined David while he was at Ziklag (1 Chron. 12:6), about 1002 B.C. He probably resided in the tribe of Benjamin, which included four Levitical cities. Perhaps he was the same person who was one of the two gatekeepers for the Ark when it was brought to Jerusalem (15:23), about 982 B.C.
7. The chief officer in the household of Ahaz, king of Judah, slain by Zichri the Ephraimite when Pekah invaded Judah (2 Chron. 28:7), about 735 B.C.

BIBLIOGRAPHY: F. Josephus *Ant.* 5.10.2-4; J. Kitto, *Daily Bible Illustrations* (1982), 1:597-602; C. J. and A. A. Barber, *You Can Have a Happy Marriage* (1984), pp. 55-66.

EL'KOSH (el'kosh; uncertain derivation). The birthplace of the prophet Nahum, from which he is called "the Elkoshite" (Nah. 1:1). Two Jewish traditions assign widely different localities to Elkosh. In the time of Jerome it was believed to be a small village of Galilee, called to the present day

Helcesaei (or Helcesei, Elcesi), which belief is more credible than the one that identifies Elkosh with a village on the eastern side of the Tigris, NW of Khorsabad. This place, Alkush, is a Christian village, where the tomb of the prophet is shown in the form of a simple plaster box of modern style. Others place Elkosh in Judah. It is impossible to be definite about its location at the present time.

EL'KOSHITE (el'ko-shīt). *See* Elkosh.

ELLAS'AR (el-la'sar). A city of Babylonia, mentioned twice in Genesis (14:1, 9). Ellasar was located in southern Babylonia, between Ur and Erech, on the left bank of the great canal Shatt-en-Nil. The site of the city is now marked by the little mound called by the natives Senkereh. In an early period, Ellasar played an important role in Babylonia. In southern Babylonia, it was the center of the sun worship (called in Babylonian *Shamash*), as Sippar in northern Babylonia was the chief place of the same worship. The Babylonian form of the city's name was Larsa, and in later times it was known to the Greeks as Larissa. Its origin is entirely unknown to us, but its holy character and its religious leadership point to high antiquity. About 2400 B.C. Ellasar was filling an influential place in Babylonia. It had then the leadership in southern Babylonia, and the kings of Larsa were at the same time kings of Sumer and Akkad. Of the dynasty that then ruled in Ellasar we know the names of only two kings, Nur-Ramman and Sin-iddina, the latter of whom built an important canal that connected the Shatt-en-Nil with the Tigris River. Shortly after this time Ellasar was conquered by an invasion from Elam, and the Elamite king Kudur-Mabug, at that time a great conqueror even in the West, possessed the city. He did not, however, reside in the conquered city but was represented there by his son, Eri-Aku, who is also known in the Babylonian inscriptions by the name of Rim-Sin. He was later conquered by Hammurabi, king of Babylon, who annexed the whole territory to the newly founded Babylonian empire.

W. K. Loftus excavated there in 1854 and extracted numerous tablets and worked around the ziggurat and temple of the city, but he established no clear chronology of the site. André Parrot of the Louvre excavated at Larsa in 1932 and 1933 and worked out the history of this important city-state from the Ur III period (about 2000 B.C.) to the Neo-Babylonian period (c. 600 B.C.) and uncovered the temple of the sun-god Shamash and the royal palace. The French reopened the dig in 1967 and have since recovered materials useful for the study of ancient Mesopotamian civilization.

ELM. *See* Vegetable Kingdom: Oak.

ELMA'DAM (el-ma'dam). Son of Er and father of Cosam, one of the ancestors of Christ in the private line of David (Luke 3:28). He is not mentioned in the OT.

ELNA'AM (el-na'am; "God his delight"). Father of Jeribai and Joshaviah, two of David's distinguished warriors (1 Chron. 11:46), about 1000 B.C. "In the Septuagint the second warrior is said to be the son of the first, and Elnaam is given himself as a member of the guard."

ELNA'THAN (el-na'than; "God the giver").
1. An inhabitant of Jerusalem, whose daughter Nehushta was the mother of Jehoiachin, king of Judah (2 Kings 24:8), before 597 B.C. He was, perhaps, the same as the son of Achbor sent by Jehoiakim to bring the prophet Uriah from Egypt (Jer. 26:22) and in whose presence the roll of Jeremiah was read, for the preservation of which he interceded with the king (36:12, 25).
2, 3, 4. Three of the Israelites of position and understanding sent by Ezra to invite the priests and Levites to accompany him to Jerusalem (Ezra 8:16), 457 B.C.

ELO'HIM (e-lō'hîm; Heb. plural *'ĕlōhîm;* singular *'ĕlôah,* "mighty"). A term sometimes used in the ordinary sense of *gods,* whether true or false (Ex. 12:12, 32:4; etc.), including Jehovah (Ps. 76:7; Ex. 18:11; etc.). W. Henry Green (*Hom. Mag.* [Sept. 1898]: 257ff.) thus summarizes the principles regulating the use of Elohim and Jehovah in the OT: "1. Jehovah represents God in His special relation to the chosen people, as revealing Himself to them, their guardian and object of their worship; Elohim represents God in His relation to the world at large, as Creator, providential ruler in the affairs of men, and controlling the operations of nature. 2. Elohim is used when Gentiles speak or are spoken to or spoken about, unless there is a specific reference to Jehovah, the God of the chosen people. 3. Elohim is used when God is contrasted with men or things, or when the sense requires a common rather than a proper noun."

BIBLIOGRAPHY: W. Eichrodt, *Theology of the Old Testament* (1967), pp. 15-92; C. Brown, ed., *New International Dictionary of New Testament Theology* (1971), 2:66-82; R. E. Clements, *Old Testament Theology* (1978), pp. 53-78; W. Dyrness, *Themes in Old Testament Theology* (1979), pp. 44-46.

ELO'I (e-lō'i; Aram. "My God"). An exclamation from Ps. 22:1 quoted by our Savior (Mark 15:34) while on the cross.

E'LON (e-lon; "oak").
1. A Hittite, father of Basemath (Gen. 26:34), or Adah (36:2), wife of Esau.
2. The second of the three sons of Zebulun (Gen. 46:14) and head of the family of Elonites (Num. 26:26).
3. An Israelite of the tribe of Zebulun and judge for ten years (Judg. 12:11-12).
4. One of the towns in the border of the tribe

of Dan (Josh. 19:43), doubtless the same as Elonbeth-hanan (1 Kings 4:9). Its site has not been identified.

E'LONBETH-HA'NAN (e'lon-beth-ha'nan). The same as *Elon,* no. 4.

E'LONITE (ē'lon-īt). The patronymic applied to the descendants of *Elon* (which see), the son of Zebulun (Num. 26:26).

E'LOTH (ē'loth). Another form (1 Kings 9:26; etc.) of the city of *Elath* (which see).

ELPA'AL (el-pa'al; "God's doings"). The second of the two sons of Shaharaim by his wife Hushim, and progenitor of a numerous progeny. He was a Benjamite (1 Chron. 8:11-12, 18).

ELPA'LET. A contracted form in the KJV (1 Chron. 14:5) of the name *Eliphalet;* the NASB gives *Eliphelet* (which see, no. 1); the NIV reads "Elpelet."

EL-PA'RAN (el-pā'ran; "oak of Paran"). "The one oasis which is in mid-desert, on the great highway across the wilderness of Paran, known in later times as 'Qala' at Nukhl, . . . more commonly 'Castle Nakhl,' 'Castle of the Palm' " (Trumbull, *Kadesh-barnea,* p. 37). It was at "El-paran, which is by the wilderness," that Chedorlaomer halted before starting northward into Canaan (Gen. 14:5-6). Ishmael dwelt in the wilderness of Paran, after he and his mother were expelled through the influence of Sarah (21:21).

ELPE'LET (el-pe'let). A contracted form in the NASB and NIV (1 Chron. 14:5) of the name *Eliphelet* (which see, no. 1).

EL'TEKEH (el'te-keh), **Elteke** (el-te-ke). A Danite town assigned to the Levites (Josh. 19:44; 21:23). The site was destroyed by Sennacherib, c. 701 B.C., and in its vicinity a decisive battle was fought by the Assyrians and the Egyptians. Its site is uncertain.   M.F.U.

EL'TEKON (el'te-kon; "God is straight"). One of the towns of the tribe of Judah, in the mountain district (Josh. 15:59); not identified.

ELTO'LAD (el-to'lad; perhaps "God is generator"). One of the cities in the S of Judah (Josh. 15:30) allotted to Simeon (19:4) and in possession of that tribe until the time of David (1 Chron. 4:29), when it is called simply Tolad; not identified.

E'LUL (e'lūl; Heb. *'elûl* from Akkad. *ulūlu*). The sixth month of the ecclesiastical, and twelfth of the civil, year of the Jews. *See* articles Calendar; Time.

ELU'ZAI (e-lu'za-i; "God is my strength"). One of the Benjamite warriors who joined David at Ziklag (1 Chron. 12:5), a little before 1000 B.C.

EL'YMAS (el'i-mas; probably from the Arab. *aliman,* "a wise man"). A Jew named Bar-jesus, who

had attached himself to the proconsul of Cyprus, Sergius Paulus, when Paul visited the island (Acts 13:6-12). Upon his endeavoring to dissuade the proconsul from embracing the Christian faith he was miraculously struck blind by the apostle (A.D. 44).

EL'ZABAD (el'za-bad; "God has given").

1. The ninth of the eleven Gadite heroes who joined David in the wilderness of Judah (1 Chron. 12:12), before 1000 B.C.

2. One of the sons of Shemaiah, the son of Obed-edom, the Levite. He served as a gatekeeper to the house of the Lord under David (1 Chron. 26:7), after 1000 B.C.

EL'ZAPHAN (el'za-fan); a contracted form (Ex. 6:22; Lev. 10:4) of the name *Elizaphan* (which see).

EMBALM (Heb. *ḥānaṭ,* "to spice"). The process of preserving a corpse by means of spices (Gen. 50:2-3, 26). *See* Handicrafts: Embalming.

EMBROIDERER. *See* Handicrafts.

E'MEK-KE'ZIZ (e'mek-ke'ziz). A city of Benjamin (Josh. 18:21), the name of which is still preserved in the Wadi el Kaziz, on the road from Jerusalem to Jericho, SE of the Apostles' well. The KJV renders it "valley of Keziz."

EMERALD. *See* Mineral Kingdom.

EMERODS. *See* Diseases: Hemorrhoids.

E'MIM (ē'mim). The giant aborigines dispossessed by Moab. In Gen. 14:5-7 (cf. Deut. 2:10-12, 20-23) we find all the region E of the Jordan once occupied by a series of races mostly described as giants—the Rephaim in Bashan, the Zamzummin dispossessed by the Ammonites (2:20-21); possibly the same as the Zuzim of Gen. 14:5, the Emim by the Moabites, and the Horim by the Edomites. The "Emims" of the KJV is an incorrect double plural. *See also* Giant.

E'MITES. *See* Emim.

EMMAN'UEL. *See* Immanuel.

EMMA'US (e-mā'us; "hot baths"). A town seven and a half miles from Jerusalem (sixty furlongs), the scene of Christ's revelation of Himself after His resurrection (Luke 24:13). Its real site is disputed, however. A number of places are held, by tradition and otherwise, to be the original site of Emmaus. Among them are Amwas (about twenty miles from Jerusalem and, apparently, too far away); Kolonieh (only about thirty-four stades or furlongs from Jerusalem, a little over three miles, and thus too close); and El-Qubeibeh, on the road to Joppa, about the right distance from Jerusalem (about seven and one-half miles). Materials recovered there date to the NT period.
                                                         H.F.V.

BIBLIOGRAPHY: J. Finegan, *Archaeology of the New Testament* (1969), pp. 177-80; M. Avi-Yonah, ed., *Encyclope-*

dia of *Archaeological Excavations in the Holy Land* (1976), 2:362-64.

Fields near En-Dor

EM'MOR. *See* Hamor.

EN- (Heb. *'ēn,* "fountain"). A prefix given to many names of places in Heb. because there was a living spring in the vicinity.

ENA'IM. *See* Enam.

E'NAM (ē'nam). One of the cities of Judah in the lowland (Josh. 15:34). From its mention with towns that are known to have been near Timnath this is probably the place in the gateway (KJV, "an open place") in which Tamar sat before her interview with her father-in-law (Gen. 38:14). The NIV reads "Enaim" in the latter passage.

E'NAN (ē'nan; "fountain"). The father of Ahira, who was leader of the tribe of Naphtali at the time of the numbering of Israel in the desert of Sinai (Num. 1:15; 2:29; 7:78, 83; 10:27), c. 1440 B.C.

ENCAMPMENT. *See* Camp.

ENCHANTER, ENCHANTMENT. The practice of magic or the speaking of certain words whereby evil forces are invoked in order to achieve supernatural effects over human beings, animals, or natural phenomena was known in Bible times. This category includes magic (Ex. 7:11), conjuration, exorcism (Acts 19:13-17), sorcery (8:9, 11; 13:8, 10). This traffic in quackery or bona fide spiritism was forbidden by the law of Moses (Deut. 18:10). Sometimes magic is not easily distinguished from divination in the English versions (cf. Num. 23:23; 24:1; 2 Kings 17:17; Jer. 27:9).

See also Magic: Various Forms.

BIBLIOGRAPHY: T. W. Davies, *Magic, Divination and Demonology Among the Hebrews and Their Neighbors* (1898); M. F. Unger, *Biblical Demonology* (1952), pp. 107-18.

END OF THE WORLD. *See* Eschatology.

EN'-DOR (en'dor; "fountain of Dor"). A town about four miles from the S foot of Mt. Tabor. It

is probably located at Khirbet Safsafa, about a mile NE of the village of Indur. The numerous caves in the hillsides suggest a fit dwelling place for such persons as the spiritistic medium to whom *Saul* (which see) resorted (1 Sam. 28:7). *See* also Josh. 17:11 and Ps. 83:10.

ENE'AS (ē-nē'as). *See* Aeneas.

ENEG'LAIM (en-eg'la-im; "fountain of two calves"), **En Eglaim** (NIV). A place mentioned by Ezekiel (47:10; "En-eglaim," KJV) in the vision of holy waters. Identified with Ain Hajlah, N of the Dead Sea, W of the Jordan.

EN-GAN'NIM (en-gan'im; "fountain of gardens").

1. A city of Issachar (Josh. 19:21; "Anem," 1 Chron. 6:73) allotted to the Levites (Josh. 21:29). It is located fifteen miles S of Mt. Tabor and is the scene of Ahaziah's escape from Jehu (2 Kings 9:27, "garden house"). It is identified with modern Jenin, a prosperous town at the southern edge of the plain of Esdraelon.

2. A town in Judah (Josh. 15:34) whose location is unknown.

ENGE'DI (en-ge'di; "fountain of the wild goat"). A town, also called the city of palm trees (i.e., Hazazon-tamar, Gen. 14:7; 2 Chron. 20:2), and wilderness situated about thirty miles SE of Jerusalem, on the W shore of the Dead Sea. It is full of rocks and caves (1 Sam. 23:29; Ezek. 47:10). The source of the spring from which it derives its name is on the side of the mountain about six hundred feet above the sea.

It is a fertile place and most suitable for refuge. The strongholds of David (23:29; 24:22) must have been situated by the water, and the cave is described as being below them.

It was immediately after an assault upon the "Amorites, who lived in Hazazon-tamar," that the five Mesopotamian kings were attacked by the rulers of the plain of Sodom (Gen. 14:7; cf. 2 Chron. 20:2). Saul was told that David was in the "wilderness of Engedi," and he took "three thousand chosen men from all Israel, and went to seek David and his men in front of the Rocks of the Wild Goats" (1 Sam. 24:1-4). At a later period Engedi was the gathering place of the Moabites and Ammonites who went up against Jerusalem and fell in the valley of Beracah (2 Chron. 20:2, 26). The vineyards of Engedi were celebrated by Solomon (Song of Sol. 1:14), its balsam by Josephus, and its palms by Pliny.

At Tell el-Jurn, just S of the springs of Engedi, Benjamin Mazar led a Hebrew University and Israel Exploration Society dig from 1961 to 1965. He found no evidence of occupation in the time of David, but that is not surprising because the area probably was quite wild when David and his band hid there. Five periods of occupation were uncovered on the tell, dating from the last days of the Judean kingdom to the Roman-Byzantine period. A large fort stood in the middle of the city during the Hasmonean (Maccabean) period (Stratum III) and again in Herodian-Roman days (Stratum II). This latter city and fort were burned about the time of the destruction of Jerusalem in A.D. 70. The place was again occupied during the Roman-Byzantine period. Mazar also excavated a Chalcolithic worship center (c. 3500 B.C.) just N of the spring of Engedi.   H.F.V.

BIBLIOGRAPHY: W. F. Albright, *Bulletin of the American Schools of Oriental Research* 18 (April 1925): 11-15; B. Mazar, *Archaeology* 16 (1963): 99-107; B. Mazar and J. Dunayevsky, *Israel Exploration Journal* 14 (1964): 121-30; M. Avi-Yonah, ed., *Encyclopedia of Archaeological Excavations in the Holy Land* (1976), 2:370-80.

ENGINE. A term applied in Scripture exclusively to military affairs. *See* Armor.

ENGRAVER. *See* Handicrafts: Carver.

EN-HAD'DAH (en-had'a). A city on the border of Issachar (Josh. 19:21); according to Knobel either the place by Gilboa called Judeideh, or else el-Hadethah, six miles E of Mt. Tabor.

EN-HAK'KORE (en-hak'o-re; "fountain of the crier"). A spring that burst forth at the cry of Samson (Judg. 15:19). It has been identified with Ayun Kara, near Zoreah.

EN-HA'ZOR (en-ha'zor; "fountain of the village"). One of the fortified cities in the inheritance of Naphtali, distinct from Hazor (Josh. 19:37). Probably Khirbet Hasireh near Hazzur.

ENLIGHTENED (from Gk. *photizō*, to "give light"). A term meaning imbued with a saving knowledge of the gospel, and so applied to Christians (Heb. 6:4; 10:32). In the early Christian church it was used to denote the baptized.

EN-MISH'PAT (en-mish'pat; "fountain of judgment"). The earlier name (Gen. 14:7) for *Kadesh* (which see).

ENMITY (Heb. *'êbâ*; Gk. *echthra*). Deep-rooted hatred or irreconcilable hostility. God established perpetual enmity, not only between the serpent and the woman, but also between the human and the serpent race (Gen. 3:15). Friendship with the world (i.e., the corrupt part of it) is declared to be "enmity with God" (James 4:4, KJV; NASB, "hostility toward God"; NIV, "hatred toward God"), or being at variance with His plans for the promotion of righteousness (cf. 1 John 2:15-16). So also the carnal mind is "hostile toward God" (Rom. 8:7-8), or opposed to His nature and will. The ceremonial law is called "enmity" (Eph. 2:15-16), referring to the hostility between Jew and Gentile, and due to Judaical limitations and antagonisms and especially the alienation of both Jew and Gentile from God.

E'NOCH (ē'nok; "dedicated," "initiated"). The

Waterfall at Engedi

name of two men, two others having their name given as *Hanoch* (which see), and the name of a city.

1. The eldest son of Cain, who gave his own name to the city he built (Gen. 4:17-18).

2. The son of Jared (Gen. 5:18) and father of Methuselah (5:21; Luke 3:37). After the birth of Methuselah, in his sixty-fifth year, he lived 300 years. Following his son's birth it is said (Gen. 5:22-24) that Enoch "walked with God three hundred years . . . and he was not, for God took him." As a reward of his sanctity he was transported into heaven without dying, and thus the doctrine of immortality was plainly taught under the old dispensation. In the epistle to the Hebrews (11:5) the issue of Enoch's life is clearly marked. Jude (vv. 14-15) quotes from a prophecy of Enoch, but whether he derived his quotation from tradition or from writing is uncertain. The voice of early ecclesiastical tradition is almost unanimous in regarding Enoch and Elijah as the "two witnesses" (Rev. 11:3).

3. The first city mentioned in Scripture (Gen. 4:17), which was built by Cain; it lies E of Eden and in the land of Nod.

BIBLIOGRAPHY: E. K. Cox, *Lives That Oft Remind Us* (1940), pp. 18-25; C. J. and A. A. Barber, *Your Marriage Has Real Possibilities* (1984), pp. 49-57.

E'NOS. The Gk. (and less correct) way of rendering OT *Enosh* (which see).

E'NOSH (ē'nosh; "a man"). The son of Seth and grandson of Adam (Gen. 5:6-11; Luke 3:38) who lived 905 years. He was remarkable on account of a singular expression used respecting him in Gen. 4:26, "Then men began to call upon the name of the Lord." Two explanations are given of this passage: (1) "Then began men to call themselves *by the name* of the Lord," in order, it would seem, to distinguish themselves from those who were already idolaters and were termed children of men; and, (2) "Then men *profanely* called on the name of the Lord," intimating that at that period idolatry began to be practiced among men.

"ENQUIRE OF THE LORD." *See* "Inquire of the Lord."

EN-RIM'MON (en'rim'on; "fountain of a pomegranate"). A place occupied by the descendants of Judah after the Exile (Neh. 11:29), apparently the same as "Ain and Rimmon" (Josh. 15:32). It seems probable that they were so close together that in the course of time they grew into one. It is identified with Umm er-Rummāmin, nine miles N of Beersheba.

EN-RO'GEL (en-rō'gel; "fountain of the treaders"). The "foot fountain," also called the "fullers' fountain." Here the fullers cleansed their garments by treading them in the water of the spring (Josh. 15:7; 18:16; 2 Sam. 17:17; 1 Kings

1:9). This is the well of Job, "Bir Eyub," or the well of Jeremiah, located just below the junction of the valley of Hinnom and that of the Kidron, SE of the hill Op'hel. Gihon Spring, with which En-Rogel is sometimes confused, is farther N. Here Adonijah declared himself king (1 Kings 1:5-10).

BIBLIOGRAPHY: J. Simons, *Jerusalem in the Old Testament* (1952), pp. 48-50.

EN-SHE'MESH (en-she'mesh; "fountain of the sun"). A landmark between Judah and Benjamin (Josh. 15:7; 18:17), E of the Mount of Olives and said to be the only spring on the way to Jericho, now called Ain-Haud, or "well of the apostles."

ENSIGN. *See* Banner; Standard.

EN-TAP'PUAH (en-tap'u-a; "fountain of Tappuah"). A spring near the city of *Tappuah* (which see), used for that place in Josh. 17:7 (cf. v. 8).

ENVY (Heb. *qin'â;* Gk. *phthonos*). (1) That discontented feeling that arises in the selfish heart in view of the superiority of another, nearly tantamount to jealousy (Ps. 37:1; 73:3; Prov. 24:1, 19; Phil. 1:15; etc.). (2) That malignant passion that sees in another qualities that it covets, often resulting in hate for their possessor (Matt. 27:18; Rom. 1:29; etc.).

Envying is ill will, malice, spite (James 3:14, NASB, "jealousy"). It is accompanied by every "evil thing" (v. 16). It always desires and often strives to degrade others, not so much because it aspires after elevation as because it delights in obscuring those who are more deserving. It is one of the most odious and detestable of vices.

EPAE'NETUS (e-pe'nē-tus; "praised"). A Christian at Rome, greeted by the apostle Paul in Rom. 16:5 and designated as his beloved and the "first convert to Christ from Asia."

EP'APHRAS (ep'a-fras; probably a contraction of Epaphroditus). An eminent teacher in the church of Colossae, called by Paul his "beloved fellow bond-servant" and "a bondslave of Jesus Christ" (Col. 1:7; 4:12), A.D. 62. It has been inferred from 1:7 ("as you learned it from Epaphras") that he was the founder of the Colossian church. Lardner thinks that the expression respecting Epaphras in 4:12, *ho ex humōn* ("one of your number"), is quite inconsistent with the supposition of his being the founder of the church, since the same phrase is applied to Onesimus, a recent convert. The words are probably intended to identify these individuals as fellow townsmen of the Colossians. He was at this time with Paul in Rome and is afterward mentioned in the epistle to Philemon (v. 23), where Paul calls him "my fellow prisoner." The martyrologies make Epaphras to have been the first bishop of Colosse and to have suffered martyrdom there.

BIBLIOGRAPHY: H. S. Seekings, *Men of the Pauline Circle* (1914), pp. 147-53; H. C. Lees, *St. Paul's Friends*

(1918), pp. 146-59; D. E. Hiebert, *Personalities Around Paul* (1973), pp. 145-52.

EPAPHRODI′TUS (e-paf-ro-dī′tus; belonging "to Aphrodite," or Venus). A messenger of the church of Philippi to the apostle Paul during his imprisonment at Rome and entrusted with their contributions for his support (Phil. 2:25; 4:18). Paul seems to have held him in high appreciation, calling him his "brother," "fellow worker," and "fellow soldier." While in Rome he contracted a dangerous illness brought on by his ministering to the apostle (2:27-30). On his return to Philippi he was the bearer of the epistle to the church there. Grotius and some other critics conjecture that Epaphroditus was the same as Epaphras mentioned in the epistle to the Colossians. But though the latter name may be a contraction of the former, the fact that Epaphras was most probably in prison at the time sufficiently marks the distinction of the two persons.

BIBLIOGRAPHY: H. S. Seekings, *Men of the Pauline Circle* (1914), pp. 157-64; H. C. Lees, *St. Paul's Friends* (1918), pp. 192-209; D. E. Hiebert, *Personalities Around Paul* (1973), pp. 153-60.

EPE′NETUS. *See* Epaenetus.

E′PHAH (ē′fà; "gloom").

1. The first named of the five sons of Midian (Gen. 25:4; 1 Chron. 1:33). His descendants formed one of the tribes of the desert connected with the Midianites, Shebaites, and Ishmaelites (Isa. 60:6-7) and had its seat on the E coast of the Elanitic Gulf.

2. A concubine of Caleb, the son of Hezron, of the tribe of Judah (1 Chron. 2:46).

3. One of the sons of Jahdai, probably a descendant of one of the sons of the foregoing (1 Chron. 2:47).

EPHAH (ē′fà). A measure for grain. *See* Metrology: Dry Measures of Capacity.

E′PHAI (e′fī; "birdlike"). A Netophathite whose sons were among the "commanders of the forces" left in Judah after the deportation to Babylon and who submitted themselves to Gedaliah, the Babylonian governor (Jer. 40:7-8). They warned Gedaliah of the plots against him, but he did not believe them (vv. 13-16), and they were probably massacred with him by Ishmael (41:2-3), 588 B.C.

E′PHER (e′fer; "gazelle").

1. The second named of the sons of Midian (Gen. 25:4; 1 Chron. 1:33) and Abraham's son by Keturah.

2. An Israelite of the tribe of Judah, apparently of the family of Caleb, who was the son of Jephunneh (1 Chron. 4:17).

3. The head of one of the families of Manasseh, who were carried away by Tilgath-pileser (1 Chron. 5:21-26), before 727 B.C.

E′PHES-DAM′MIM (e′fes-dam′im; "boundary

of blood," 1 Sam. 17:1). Called Pasdammim (1 Chron. 11:13). The bloody contests between Israel and the Philistines gave it its name. It is modern Beit Fased ("house of bleeding").

EPHESIANS. *See* Ephesus.

EPHESIANS, EPISTLE TO. Perhaps the most sublime of all the Pauline epistles. No part of NT revelation sets forth more clearly or more profoundly the believer's position "in Christ" and the results that should be obtained in his practical experience. In contrast to Colossians and Galatians it is remarkably free of controversial elements. As Salmon notes, there have been students "who with an incredible lack of insight have construed it as an insipid production or a tedious and unskillful compilation" (*Exp. Gk. Testament,* 3:208).

Authorship and Authenticity. Ephesians has a strong claim to Pauline authenticity, both externally and internally. Clement of Rome, Ignatius, Polycarp, Hermas, Clement of Alexandria, Tertullian, Irenaeus, and Hippolytus give evidence of early and continued use of the epistle. Internal evidence is likewise decisive. The writer twice mentions his name (1:1 and 3:1). The organization of material is Pauline, beginning with doctrine (chaps. 1-3) and ending with experience based upon the doctrine (chaps. 4-6). The language is definitely Pauline. According to Lewis, "out of 155 verses in Ephesians, seventy-eight are found in Colossians in varying degrees of identity" ("The Epistle to the Ephesians," *Int. Stand. Bible Ency.,* p. 956). First Peter, Hebrews, and the Apocalypse apparently show acquaintance with Ephesians, indicating that Ephesians is earlier than any of the three. Ephesians was written from Rome in A.D. 64 (Acts 20-27). Tychicus was the bearer, together with the epistles of Colossians and Philemon. Since Ephesians is the most impersonal of Paul's letters and the words "to the Ephesians" are not in the best manuscripts, it seems that the letter was intended to be circularized, being sent to several churches, and may be referred to in Col. 4:16 as the "letter that is coming from Laodicea." The letter would then be addressed "to the saints who are faithful in Christ Jesus anywhere." The theme of the epistle confirms this view.

Although the genuineness of the epistle has been denied by Schleiermacher, de Wette, and others, there are strong arguments in its favor. Coleridge called it "the divinest composition of man."

Position. The apostle's real object in writing this epistle is to set forth the believer's union with Christ (1:3-14; 2:1-10), relating this to the union of Jew and Gentile in Christ (2:11-22). With the distinctive revelation of this truth to Paul (3:10-13), these sections give the believer's standing in Christ and are doctrinal. Chapters 4-6 are practical and give our state. In the doctrinal section Paul offers two remarkable prayers that the power of the believer's position "in Christ" be understood and by faith be made an experience (1:15-23; 3:14-21). The practical exhortation based on the believer's position in Christ (4:1–6:9) pertains to his walk, which should be consonant with his position. Presented in 6:10-20 is the spiritual warfare of the Spirit-filled believer who through knowledge and faith translates his position into an everyday experience.

Outline.

    I. Salutation (1:1-2)
   II. The believer's position in Christ (1:3–3:21)
      A. The elements of his position (1:1-14)
      B. Prayer for knowledge and faith to appropriate the power of the position (1:15-21)
      C. Christ the Head of the church (1:22-23)
      D. Method of Gentile salvation (2:1-10)
      E. Union of Jew and Gentile in Christ (2:11-18)
      F. The church as a temple inhabited by the Spirit (2:19-22)
  III. The church as a special divine revelation (3:1-12)
      A. Hidden in past ages (3:1-6)
      B. Revealed especially to the apostle Paul (3:7-12)
      C. Second prayer for knowledge and faith to appropriate the power of the position (3:13-21)
  IV. The walk of the believer in Christ (4:1–6:9)
      A. The walk worthy (4:1-3)
      B. The walk as an expression of doctrinal unity (2:4-6)
      C. The walk as a ministry of gifts (3:7-16)
      D. The walk as a regenerated man (4:17-29)
      E. The walk of the believer indwelt by the Spirit (4:30-32)
      F. The walk as a child in God's family (5:1-33)
      G. The walk of children and servants (6:1-9)
   V. The warfare of the Spirit-filled believer in Christ (6:10-22)
      A. His power (6:10)
      B. His armor (6:11)
      C. His foes (6:12-17)
      D. His resources (6:18-22)
  VI. Benediction (6:23-24)   M.F.U.

BIBLIOGRAPHY: T. K. Abbott, *A Critical and Exegetical Commentary on the Epistles to the Ephesians and Colossians,* International Critical Commentary (1897); H. C. G. Moule, *Ephesian Studies: Lessons in Faith and Walk* (1900); B. F. Westcott, *St. Paul's Epistle to the Ephesians* (1958); F. Foulkes, *The Epistle of Paul to the Ephesians* (1963); C. Hodge, *A Commentary on the Epistle to the Ephesians* (1966); W. Hendriksen, *Exposition of Ephesians,* New Testament Commentary (1967); H. A. Kent, Jr., *Ephesians: The Glory of the Church* (1971); R. C. Stedman, *Riches in Christ* (1976);

H. C. G. Moule, *Studies in Ephesians* (1977); C. L. Mitton, *Ephesians,* New Century Bible (1978); J. A. Robinson, *Commentary on Ephesians* (1979); J. R. W. Stott, *God's New Society* (1979); E. M. Blaiklock, *New International Dictionary of Biblical Archaeology* (1983), p. 181; R. E. Pattison and H. C. G. Moule, *Exposition of Ephesians: Lessons in Grace and Godliness* (1983); F. F. Bruce, *The Epistles to the Colossians, to Philemon, and to the Ephesians,* New International Commentary on the New Testament (1984).

EPH'ESUS (ef'e-sus). The capital of proconsular Asia; an opulent city on the W coast of Asia Minor, located on the banks of the Cayster and about forty miles SE of Smyrna. Its harbor was ample.

Ruins of the Temple of Artemis, Ephesus

History. Ephesus was an ancient city when Paul arrived. By the middle of the second millennium B.C., settlers of Asiatic origin inhabited the site. During the eleventh century B.C., Athenians arrived and gradually assimilated the older population. After varying periods of independence and absorption into neighboring empires, Ephesus came into the Roman Empire in 133 B.C. as part of the province of Asia. Though suffering terribly during the civil wars of the first century B.C., Ephesus enjoyed great prosperity under Rome during the first and second centuries A.D., when the city must have had a population of about a half million. Here the Roman governor resided, and here Paul conducted the longest of his city ministries (two years and nine months, Acts 19:8, 10). The city's importance lay in its political prominence, its economic clout derived from its position on major trade routes, and its religious leadership as a center for the worship of Diana, or Artemis. By the middle of the third century signs of decay appeared in the city, and in 263 Goths raided Ephesus and dealt it a blow from which it never recovered. By the tenth century the prosperous city of Roman times was completely deserted and invaded by marshes.

Religion. The Ephesians worshiped the Asiatic goddess Artemis, or Diana (*see* Gods, False), whose temple, one of the seven wonders of the world, made the city famous. After the temple was destroyed by fire (356 B.C.), it was immediately rebuilt. It is said that some of the magnificent columns are incorporated into the Church of St. Sophia.

There were many Jews in the city who were more or less influenced by Christianity (Acts 2:9; 6:9). Timothy was the bishop of the church founded by Paul. To this church Paul addressed one of his epistles. According to Eusebius John spent his last years in Ephesus. John opposed the doctrines of Nestorius, and Paul opposed the idolatry of those who made or worshiped shrines or practiced magic (19:13). His opposition resulted in a serious riot.

Several important councils were held in Ephesus, among which was the third ecumenical council (June 22–August 31, A.D. 431). A small Turkish town today represents the once noted city, which is called Ayasaluk.

Archaeology. The archaeological history of Ephesus began on May 2, 1863, when the British architect John T. Wood started his search for the temple of Artemis, or Diana. He did not actually discover the ruins of the temple itself (outside the city) until December 31, 1869; after that he worked for five years at the temple site. In 1904-5 D. G. Hogarth did further work on the temple. The temple platform was 239 feet wide and 418 feet long. A flight of ten steps led up to the pavement of the platform. The temple itself was 180 feet wide and 377 feet long, and the roof was supported by 117 60-foot columns. These were 6 feet in diameter and 36 of them were sculptured at the base with life-sized figures.

Theater at Ephesus

The Austrian Archaeological Institute began to excavate the city of Ephesus in 1897 and continued there for sixteen years under the leadership of Otto Bendorf and Rudolf Heberdey. In part subsidized by Rockefeller money, the Austrians worked there again from 1926 to 1935, and they have been working annually at the site since 1954. To date they have uncovered about 25 percent of the city. Today one can walk down the ancient streets past the odeion (covered concert hall), the Roman agora, the town hall, the temple of Hadrian, the magnificent library of Celsus (now restored), the Hellenistic agora, the great theater (where the mob scene of Acts 19 occurred), and much more. The Austrians have also done some work at the site of the temple of Artemis, or Diana, and on the Church of St. John, on the hill overlooking the temple. The traditional burial place of the apostle John was located there and was enclosed by a church in the fourth century and covered by a great domed church in the days of Justinian (527-565).   H.F.V.

BIBLIOGRAPHY: E. M. Blaiklock, *The Christian in Pagan Society* (1951); id., *The Cities of the New Testament* (1965). W. M. Ramsay, *The Letters to the Seven Churches* (1963);

EPH'LAL (eph'lal). The son of Zabad (1 Chron. 2:37), a descendant of Judah through Hezron, Jerahmeel, and *Sheshan* (which see).   E.H.M.

E'PHOD (ē-fod; "a covering").

The Ephod and the Jewish Priesthood. A sacred garment of gold, blue, purple, scarlet, and fine twined linen worn by the Jewish high priest (Ex. 28:4-9). The ephod fit closely around the shoulders and was held on by two straps. A hole in the top admitted the head. On top of each of the shoulder straps an onyx stone was encased in a filigree setting of gold and engraved with the names of six tribes of Israel (28:9; 39:6-7). The robe of the ephod was a garment different from the ephod. It was blue, sleeveless, and fringed at the bottom with bells of gold and pomegranates of blue, gold, purple, and scarlet (28:31-35; 39:22-26). Ordinary priests wore a simpler linen ephod (1 Sam. 22:18); Samuel also wore such an ephod as a child (2:18), as did David when officiating before the Ark as king (2 Sam. 6:14). *See also* Priest, High.

The Ephod and Archaeology. Old Assyrian cuneiform tablets of the nineteenth century B.C. and the Ugaritic texts of the fifteenth show that an ephod (*epadu*), such as is mentioned in the OT as an important part of the holy attire of the Levitical priesthood, was formerly an ordinary garment, worn especially, it would seem, by women. Only after many centuries did the *epadu* come to be restricted to religious and subsequently to priestly use. In Israel, however, it came early to be a distinctive part of the sacred dress of the Levitical priesthood. It was as Israel's anointed king and accordingly as a special representative of Jehovah that David wore a linen ephod on the occasion of the transfer of the Ark of God to his capital city, Jerusalem.   M.F.U.

BIBLIOGRAPHY: F. Josephus *Ant.* 3.7.3; J. Morgenstern, *The Ark, the Ephod and the Tent of Meeting* (1945); R. de Vaux, *Ancient Israel: Its Life and Institutions* (1961), pp. 349-52.

E'PHRAIM (ē'fra-im; "fruitful"). The second son of Joseph by Asenath, the daughter of Potiphera (Gen. 46:20), born during the seven years of plenty, about 1880 B.C.

Personal History. The first incident in Ephraim's history is the blessing of his grandfather, Jacob. Contrary to the intention of Joseph, Ephraim was preferred to Manasseh by Jacob, and upon him was conferred the birthright blessing (Gen. 48:17-19). Before Joseph's death Ephraim's family had reached the third generation (50:23), and it may have been about this time that the conflict mentioned in 1 Chron. 7:21 occurred, when some of his sons were killed and when Ephraim named one of his sons Beriah to perpetuate the memory of the disaster that had fallen on his house.

The Tribe of Ephraim. At the census in the wilderness of Sinai (Num. 1:32-33; 2:19) its numbers were 40,500, ranking tenth, and at the second census, had decreased to 32,500, ranking eleventh.

Position. During the march through the wilderness the position of the sons of Joseph and Benjamin was on the W of the Tabernacle (2:18-24), and the head of Ephraim was Elishama, the son of Ammihud (1:10). According to rabbinical authority the standard of Ephraim was a golden flag on which the head of a calf was depicted. The representative of Ephraim among the spies was the great hero "Hoshea, the son of Nun," whose name was changed by Moses to the more distinguished form (Joshua), in which it is familiar to us.

Territory. The boundaries of Ephraim are given in Josh. 16 (cf. 1 Chron. 7:28-29). We are not able to trace this boundary line exactly, but Ephraim occupied the center of Palestine, embracing an area about forty miles in length from E to W and from six to twenty-five in breadth from N to S. It extended from the Mediterranean to the Jordan, having on the N the half tribe of Manasseh and on the S Benjamin and Dan (Josh. 16:5-8; 18:7; 1 Chron. 7:28-29). The tribes of Ephraim and Manasseh at first were not contented with the size of their allotted portions and were told by Joshua to go boldly and expel the inhabitants of the adjacent mountain and woodland country and occupy it (Josh. 17:14-18).

Subsequent History. The "tent of meeting" was set up in Ephraim at Shiloh (Josh. 18:1). By this circumstance the influence of the tribe was increased, and we find it bearing itself haughtily. We have an example of this in the Ephraimites' remonstrance to Gideon after his first victory, which that leader deemed prudent to pacify by a flattering answer (Judg. 7:24-25; 8:1-3). With Jephthah they were still more incensed because, as they said, he had not solicited their aid. Jephthah boldly attacked and defeated them (12:1-6). At first the Ephraimites did not submit to the authority of David (2 Sam. 2:8-9). Although after the death of Ish-bosheth a large body of them went to Hebron to join David and that monarch could speak of Ephraim as the strength ("helmet") of his head, the jealousy against Judah sometimes broke out (2 Sam. 19:40-43; 1 Chron. 12:30; Ps. 60:7). David had his ruler in Ephraim (1 Chron. 27:20), and Solomon one of his twelve deputies (1 Kings 4:8). Still the spirit and weight of the tribe were so great that Rehoboam found it necessary to go to Shechem, a city within its borders, for his inauguration (1 Kings 12:1). And then, on his foolish refusal of their demands, the ten tribes revolted and established a different mode of worship (chap. 12). After this Ephraim was the main support of the Northern Kingdom, which came to be designated by its name, and its reunion with Judah became the hope of the prophets as the fulfillment of Israel's glory (Isa. 7:2; 11:13; Ezek. 37:15-22). After the captivity "sons of Ephraim" dwelt in Jerusalem (1 Chron. 9:3).

BIBLIOGRAPHY: D. Baly, *The Geography of the Bible* (1957), pp. 170-76.

E'PHRAIM, CITY OF. This town was mentioned as being in the wilderness (John 11:54). It lay NE of Jerusalem. Christ found refuge there when threatened with violence by the priests in consequence of raising Lazarus from the dead. Identified as et Taiyibeh, about five miles NE of Bethel and fifteen miles N of Jerusalem.

E'PHRAIM, FOREST OF. When David's army had advanced into the field against Israel (those who followed Absalom) a battle was fought "in the forest of Ephraim" (2 Sam. 18:6). All the circumstances connected with the battle indicate that it took place E of the Jordan. Absalom had encamped in Gilead, and it is not stated that he had recrossed the Jordan; v. 3 ("be ready to help us from the city") presupposes that the battle took place near Mahanaim, and that after the victory David and his army returned there.

E'PHRAIM, GATE OF. This was one of the gates of Jerusalem on the N side of the city (2 Kings 14:13; 2 Chron. 25:23).

The hill country of Ephraim, near Samaria

E'PHRAIM, MOUNT OF. Also called by other names, such as the "hill country of Israel" (Josh. 11:21) and the "hills" or "mountains of Samaria" (Jer. 31:5-6; Amos 3:9). In the NASB it is called the "hill country of Ephraim"; NIV, "hills of Ephraim." Joshua's burial place was among these mountains, at Timnath-heres, on the N side of Mt. Gaash (Judg. 2:9). The earliest name given to the central range of mountains in Samaria was Mt. Ephraim, just as the whole tableland of Judah was called Mt. Judah.

E'PHRAIM, WOOD OF. See Ephraim, Forest of.

E'PHRAIMITE (ē'frā-mīt). A descendant of the patriarch Ephraim (Judg. 12:5; 1 Sam. 1:1; 1 Kings 11:26); also rendered *Ephrathite* (which see). The narrative in Judges seems to indicate that the Ephraimites had a peculiar accent, or patois, similar to that which in later times caused the speech of the Galileans to betray them at Jerusalem (Matt. 26:73).

E'PHRAIN. See Ephron, no. 3.

EPH'RATAH. Another spelling of *Ephrathah*, no. 2 (which see).

EPH'RATHAH (ef'ra-tha), or **Eph'rath** (ef'rath; "fruitfulness, fruitful").

1. The second wife of Caleb the son of Hezron. She was the mother of Hur (1 Chron. 2:19) and grandmother of Caleb the spy (v. 50; 4:4), probably 1440 B.C.

2. The ancient name of Bethlehem in Judah (Gen. 35:16, 19; 48:7), both of which passages distinctly prove that it was called Ephrath or Ephrathah in Jacob's time. The meaning of the passage "Behold, we heard of it in Ephrathah" (Ps. 132:6) is much disputed. The most obvious reference is to *Bethlehem* (which see), which is known in other places by that name.

EPH'RATHITE (ef'ra-thīt).

1. An inhabitant of Bethlehem (Ruth 1:2).

2. An Ephraimite (1 Sam. 1:1; 1 Kings 11:26).

E'PHRON (e'fron; perhaps "fawnlike").

1. The son of Zohar, a Hittite; the owner of a field that lay facing Mamre, or Hebron, and contained a cave that Abraham bought from him for 400 shekels of silver (Gen. 23:8-18; 25:9; 49:29-30; 50:13), perhaps about 1950 B.C.

2. A mountain of the "cities" that formed one of the landmarks on the N boundary of the tribe of Judah (Josh. 15:9). It was probably the steep mountain ridge on the W side of the Terebinth valley (Wadi Beit Hanina).

3. A city of Israel that, with its dependent hamlets, Abijah and the army of Judah captured from Jeroboam (2 Chron. 13:19). C. V. Raumer and others identify Ephron (KJV, "Ephrain") both with Ophrah of Benjamin that, it is conjectured, was situated near or in Taiyibeh to the E of Beth-

el, and with the city of Ephraim (Keil, *Com.*, ad loc.).

EPICURE'ANS, THE (ep-i-ku-rē'anz). The name derives from Epicurus (342-271 B.C.), a philosopher of Attic descent whose "Garden" at Athens rivaled the "Porch" and the "Academy" in popularity. The doctrines of Epicurus found wide acceptance in Asia Minor and Alexandria, and they gained a brilliant advocate at Rome in Lucretius (95-50 B.C.). The object of Epicurus was to find in philosophy a practical guide to happiness. True pleasure and not absolute truth was the end at which he aimed; experience and not reason the test on which he relied. It is obvious that a system thus framed would degenerate by a natural descent into mere materialism, and in this form Epicurism was the popular philosophy at the beginning of the Christian era (cf. Diog. 50.10.5.9). When Paul addressed "the Epicurean and Stoic philosophers" (Acts 17:18) at Athens the philosophy of life was practically reduced to the teaching of those two antagonistic schools (Smith).

BIBLIOGRAPHY: N. W. DeWitt, *Epicurus and His Philosophy* (1954); id., *Paul and Epicurus* (1954); E. Brehier, *Hellenistic and Roman Age* (1965); B. Farrington, *The Faith of Epicurus* (1967).

EPISTLE (Gk. *epistolē*, a "written message"). The term employed to designate twenty-one out of twenty-seven of the writings of the NT, whereas Luke and the Acts are both prefaced by an epistle to Theophilus, a friend of the evangelist. They are known as *Paul's Epistles* and the *Catholic* or *General Epistles.*

Paul's Epistles. Paul's epistles number fourteen (if we include Hebrews) and are arranged in the NT not in the order of time as to their composition but rather according to the rank of the places to which they were sent. It is not known by whom they were thus arranged. Paul's letters were, as a rule, written by an amanuensis under his dictation, after which he added a few words in his own hand at the close. The epistles to Timothy and Titus are called pastoral epistles, because they contain pastoral instructions from a pastor to a pastor.

Ephesians, Philippians, Colossians, and Philemon are known as prison epistles because they were written during Paul's Roman imprisonment.

The Catholic or General Epistles. The Catholic epistles are so called because they were not addressed to any particular church or individual but to Christians in general. Of these, three were written by John, two by Peter, and one each by James and Jude. This division is strictly accurate, for 1 Peter and 2 and 3 John, although addressed to particular persons, have little in them that is properly local and personal.

EPISTLES, SPURIOUS. Many of these are lost,

but several are extant, of which the following are the principal:

1. The *Epistle of Paul to the Laodiceans.* Marcion received as genuine an "Epistle of Paul to the Laodiceans," early in the second century, but it is doubtful whether it is the Lat. one now extant. The original epistle was probably a forgery founded on Col. 4:16, "And when this letter is read among you, have it also read in the church of the Laodiceans, and *you, for your part read my letter that is coming from Laodicea.*" Some have endeavored to identify it with a genuine epistle; Grotius thought it to be the epistle to the Ephesians; Theophylact believed it to be 1 Timothy, whereas others hold it to be 1 John, Philemon, etc.

2. *Third Epistle of Paul to the Corinthians.* John Calvin, Louis Cappell, and others think that Paul wrote many other epistles besides those now known, basing their opinion on 1 Cor. 5:9. There is still extant, in the Armenian language, an epistle from the Corinthians to Paul, together with the apostle's reply. This epistle is quoted as Paul's by St. Gregory the Illuminator in the third century.

3. The *Epistle of Peter to James* is an ancient forgery. Origen says that it was not to be reckoned among the ecclesiastical books, and that it was not written by Peter or any other inspired person. It is thought to be a forgery of some Ebionite in the beginning of the second century.

4. The *Epistles of Paul and Seneca* consist of eight long letters from the philosopher Seneca to the apostle Paul, with six from Paul to Seneca. Their antiquity is doubted. They are mentioned by Jerome and Augustine and are generally rejected as spurious.

5. The *Epistle of Lentulus* to the Roman Senate, giving a description of the Person of Christ, and some pretended epistles of the virgin Mary, are generally rejected. *See* Bible.

BIBLIOGRAPHY: J. Moffat, *An Introduction to the Literature of the New Testament* (1923), pp. 44-58; C. K. Barrett, *The New Testament Background* (1961), pp. 27-29; A. Deissmann, *Light from the Ancient East* (1965), pp. 217-38; A. L. Oppenheim, *Letters from Mesopotamia* (1967); W. A. Beardsley, *Literary Criticism of the New Testament* (1970); J. A. Fitzmyer, *Journal of Biblical Literature* 93 (1974): 201-25.

EPOCH. A point of time distinguished by some remarkable event, and from which succeeding years are numbered. *See* Era; Dispensation.

ER (ūr; "watchful").

1. The eldest son of the patriarch Judah by Shuah, a Canaanitess (Gen. 38:2-3). "Er . . . was evil in the sight of the Lord, so the Lord took his life" (v. 7; Num. 26:19). What the nature of his sin was is not apparent, but, from his Canaanitish birth on his mother's side, it was probably connected with the abominable idolatries of Canaan (Smith).

2. The son of Shelah and grandson of Judah (1 Chron. 4:21).

3. The son of Joshua and father of Elmadam, in the ancestry of Joseph, the husband of Mary (Luke 3:28).

ERA. A period during which years are numbered and dates are reckoned from some historical event.

Jewish. The ancient Jews used several eras in their computations: (1) from Gen. 7:11 and 8:13 it appears that they reckoned from the lives of the patriarchs or other illustrious persons; (2) from the Exodus from Egypt (Ex. 19:1; Num. 1:1; 33:38); (3) from the building of the Temple (1 Kings 9:10; 2 Chron. 8:1) and the reigns of the kings of Judah and Israel; (4) from the Babylonian captivity (Ezek. 1:1; 33:21; 40:1) and the dedication of the second Temple; (5) from the era of the Seleucidae, dating from the occupation of Babylon by Seleucus Nicator (312 B.C.); (6) from the time when their princes began to reign (1 Kings 15:1; Isa. 36:1; Jer. 1:2-3; also Matt. 2:1; Luke 1:5; 3:1); (7) since the compilation of the Talmud the Jews have reckoned their years from the creation of (year of) the world, which they fix at 3761 B.C.

Ancient Heathen. (1) The first olympiad was placed in the year of the world 3228, and 776 B.C.; (2) the taking of Troy by the Greeks, year of the world 2820 and 1184 B.C.; (3) the voyage undertaken for the possession of the golden fleece, year of the world 2760; (4) the foundation of Rome, 753 B.C.; (5) the Era of Nabonassar, 747 B.C.; (6) the Era of Alexander the Great, or his last victory over Darius, 330 B.C.; (7) the Julian Era, dating from the reform of the calendar by Julius Caesar, 45 B.C., Jan. 1; (8) the Era of Diocletian, being the beginning of the first Egyptian year after the accession of that emperor, A.D. 284, August 29; (9) among the Muslims, the Hegira, A.D. 622; and (10) among the modern Persians, the Era of Yezdegird III, A.D. 632, June 16.

Christian. For a long time the Christians had no era of their own but followed those in common use in the different countries. In the western part of the Roman Empire the *Consular* Era was used until the sixth century after Christ. The *Era of Diocletian,* called by the Christians the "Era of Martyrs" (*Aera Martyrum*) because of persecutions in his reign, is still used by the Ethiopians and Copts. The *Era of the Armenians* was adopted when the Armenians, at the Council of Tiben, separated from the main body of the Eastern church by rejecting the Council of Chalcedon, A.D. 552. The idea of counting from Christ's birth was introduced in the sixth century by Dionysiuus Exiguus, who supposed that Christ was born December 25, 1 B.C. (a date now universally considered to be at least three years too late), and was in the eleventh century adopted by the popes. It has since been in universal use in the Western church.

The present reckoning of the New Year, January 1, was established only over a long period. The date observed by Dionysius, December 25, was used for some time, as was March 25, the date of the annunciation. When the Gregorian calendar was published in 1582 by Pope Gregory XIII, it established January 1 as the beginning of the New Year, and countries that were predominantly Roman Catholic quickly adopted the new method. The Eastern church and the Protestants did not recognize the new calendar until much later. Britain, for example, observed December 25 as the New Year until the fourteenth century, when it began to observe March 25 as the date; it did not shift from the Julian to the Gregorian calendar until 1752. Greece did not adopt the Gregorian calendar until 1923, and Turkey not until 1928. *See also* Chronology.

E'RAN (e'ran; "watchful"). Son of Shuthelah (eldest son of Ephraim) and head of the family of the Eranites (Num. 26:36).

E'RANITES (e'ran-īts). Descendants of Eran (Num. 26:36).

ERAS'TUS (e-ras'tus; "beloved"). A Corinthian and one of Paul's disciples whose salutations he sends from Corinth to the church at Rome as those of "the city treasurer" (Rom. 16:23). The word so rendered is *oikonomos* (Vulg., *arcarius*) and denotes an officer or steward of great dignity in ancient times (Josephus *Ant.* 7.8.2); the conversion of such a man to the faith of the gospel was proof of the wonderful success of the apostle's labors in that city. We find Erastus with Paul at Ephesus as one of his attendants or deacons, and he was sent along with Timothy into Macedonia while the apostle himself remained in Asia (Acts 19:22). They were both with the apostle at Corinth when he wrote, as above, from that city to the Romans; at a subsequent period Erastus was still at Corinth (2 Tim. 4:20), which would seem to have been his usual place of abode.

BIBLIOGRAPHY: G. S. Duncan, *St. Paul's Ephesian Ministry* (1929); D. E. Hiebert, *Personalities Around Paul* (1973), pp. 161-63.

E'RECH (ē'rek; Akkad. *Uruk*). This city of Nimrod (Gen. 10:10), lying on the left bank of the Euphrates, is represented by modern Warka, situated about a hundred miles SE of Babylon in a marshy region of the Euphrates. Excavations at Erech have been an effort of the German Oriental Society. Julius Jordan worked there in 1912 and 1913; Jordan and later A. Nöldeke excavated at the site from 1928 to 1939. Heinrich Lenzen launched a new series of excavations in 1954. The earliest ziggurat or stage tower, the earliest cylinder seals, and the earliest known writing in the world (c. 3400-3300 B.C.) appeared at the site. Several mounds encase the ruins of ancient Uruk; four of these cover the remains of temples, the largest of which was dedicated to Inanna, Lady of the Heavens. Another mound contains the palace of a Babylonian king. Occupation of the site goes back to the fifth or fourth millennium B.C. The whole area of the city, surrounded by a wall, is 5½ square miles in extent.   H.F.V.

BIBLIOGRAPHY: H. W. Eliot, *Excavations in Mesopotamia and Western Iran* (1950); C. F. Pfeiffer and H. F. Vos, *Wycliffe Historical Geography of Bible Lands* (1967) pp. 11ff.

Ledger tablet from Uruk (Erech) inscribed in Sumerian cuneiform

E'RI (e'ri; "watching"). The fifth son of the patriarch Gad (Gen. 46:16) and ancestor of the Erites (Num. 26:16).

E'RITES (e'rīts). Descendants of the Gadite Eri (Num. 26:16).

ESA'IAS. *See* Isaiah.

ESARHAD'DON (e-sar-had'on; "Ashur" has given a brother). An eminent and powerful Assyrian emperor, successor of Sennacherib. He reigned 680-669 B.C.

Accession. Sennacherib was assassinated in 681 B.C. by his two sons Adrammelech and Sharezer as a result of their jealousy of Esarhaddon, the emperor's favorite (cf. 2 Kings 19:37; Isa. 37:38). Esarhaddon was away conducting a campaign, and he immediately returned to Nineveh. The murderers escaped to Armenia.

Accomplishments. The most important achievement of Esarhaddon was the restoration of the city of Babylon, destroyed by his father, Sennacherib. ". . . At the beginning of my rule, in the first year of my reign, when I took my seat upon the royal throne in might, there appeared favorable signs in the heavens and upon earth . . . through the soothsayers' rites encouraging oracles were disclosed, for the rebuilding of Babylon and the restoration of Esagila (temple of the gods). They caused the command (oracle) to be written down" (D. D. Luckenbill, *Ancient Records of Assyria and Babylonia II*, sec. 646). Esarhaddon continues his description of the rebuilding of Babylon. "I summoned all my artisans and the people of Babylon in their totality

... Babylon I built anew, I enlarged, I raised aloft, I made magnificent" (ibid., sec. 647). Esarhaddon also defeated Taharka, the pharaoh of Egypt. The triumph over Taharka was commemorated by the victory stela set up at Senjirli in N Syria, recovered in 1888 by the Germans. The king is depicted with a mace in his left hand, and with his right he pours out a libation to the gods, symbolized at the top of the stela. Ropes extending to the lips of two figures at his feet are shown in his left hand. Taharka is evidently one of the figures. The other seems to be Ba'alu of Tyre. Esarhaddon thus boasts of himself, "I am powerful, I am all powerful. I am a hero, I am gigantic, I am colossal," and for the first time an Assyrian monarch assumed the new title, "king of the kings of Egypt," boasting concerning Taharka, king of Egypt and Ethiopia: "daily without cessation I slew multitudes of his men and him I smote five times with the point of my javelin with wounds from which there was no recovery. Memphis, his royal city, in half a day, with mines, tunnels, assaults, I besieged, I captured, I destroyed, I defeated, I burned with fire" (ibid., secs. 577-83).   M.F.U.

BIBLIOGRAPHY: D. J. Wiseman, *The Vassal Treaties of Esarhaddon* (1958); J. B. Pritchard, ed., *Ancient Near Eastern Texts* (1969), pp. 289-94.

Reproduction of the stone prism

E'SAU (ē'saw; "hairy," Gen. 25:25). His surname, Edom, was given him from the *red* stew he ate (Gen. 25:30). He is the eldest son of Isaac by Rebekah, and twin brother of Jacob.

We have no account of the early life of Esau beyond an incident or two connected with his birth (Gen. 25:22-26), about 2001 B.C. As he grew up Esau became "a skillful hunter, a man of the field." He was, in fact, a thorough "son of the desert," who delighted to roam free as the wind of heaven, and who was impatient at the restraints of civilized or settled life. Still his father loved him, and none the less for the savory venison the son brought to him (25:28).

Sells His Birthright. Coming in one day from the chase hungry and longing for food he saw Jacob enjoying a dish of stew and asked him to share his meal with him. Jacob set a price upon the food: the birthright of his brother. This was, indeed, a large demand, for the birthright secured to its possessor immunities and privileges of high value—the headship of the tribe, both spiritual and temporal, and the possession of the great bulk of the family property, and carried with it the covenant blessing (Gen. 27:28-29, 36; Heb. 12:16-17). Urged by hunger, however, Esau acceded to Jacob's demands, secured the food, and "despised his birthright" (Gen. 25:29-34).

Marries. At the age of forty Esau married two wives in close succession. They were both Canaanites and, on account of their origin, were not acceptable to Isaac and Rebekah. The latter was especially grieved. "I am tired of living," she said (Gen. 27:46), "because of the daughters of Heth." (1) His first wife was Adah, the daughter of Elon the Hittite (36:2), called Basemath in 26:34. (2) His second wife was Oholibamah, the daughter of Anah (36:2), as all the accounts agree, except that in 26:34, where by some error or variation of names she is called Judith, the daughter of Beeri the Hittite. (3) Esau's third wife, taken from his own kindred, was Basemath (otherwise called Mahalath, 28:9), sister of Nebaioth and daughter of Ishmael (36:3).

Loses His Father's Blessing. When Isaac had grown old and feeble he wished in the consciousness of approaching death to give his blessing to his elder son. Without regard to the words that were spoken by God with reference to the children before their birth, and without taking any notice of Esau's frivolous barter of his birthright and his ungodly connection with the Canaanites, Isaac maintained his preference for Esau. He commanded him to hunt game and prepare him a savory dish that he might eat and bless him. Rebekah sought to frustrate this plan, desiring to secure the inheritance for Jacob. Jacob successfully simulated Esau and secured the desired blessing but had scarcely done so when Esau returned. When told that his brother had secured the prize he cried out, "Bless me, even me also, O my father!" Entreated again and again, even with tears, Isaac at length said to him: "Behold, away from the fertility of the earth shall be your dwelling, and away from the dew of heaven from above. And by your sword you shall live, and your brother you shall serve; but it shall come about when you become restless, that you shall break his yoke from your neck" (Gen. 27:1-40). Thus deprived forever of his birthright by virtue of the irrevocable blessing, Esau hated his brother and vowed vengeance. But he said to himself, "The days of mourning for my father are near; then I will kill my brother Jacob." When Esau heard that his father had commanded Jacob to take a wife of the daughters of his kinsman Laban, he also resolved to see if by a new alliance he could win his parents' acceptance. He accordingly married his cousin Mahalath, the daughter of Ishmael (28:6-9).

Removes to Mt. Seir. Esau probably moved soon after this to Mt. Seir, still retaining, however, some interest in his father's property in southern Palestine. It is probable that his own habits and the idolatrous practices of his wives and growing family continued to excite and even increase the anger of his parents, and that he, consequently, considered it more prudent to remove his household to a distance (Gen. 32:3).

Reconciled to Jacob. Esau was residing at Mt. Seir when Jacob returned from Paddan-aram, and Jacob, fearing lest Esau should desire to take revenge for former injuries, sent messengers in order, if possible, to appease his wrath. In reply to his conciliatory message Esau came to meet him with 400 armed men. Jacob was greatly afraid and distressed; what must have been his surprise, when they neared each other, to see Esau running with extended arms to greet and embrace him! Esau "fell on his neck and kissed him, and they wept." Jacob had prepared a present for Esau, which he at first refused to take, but afterward accepted. Esau's offer to march with Jacob as a guard was declined, and Esau returned to Mt. Seir (Gen. 32:3–33:16).

Later History. It does not appear that the two brothers met again until the death of their father. Mutual interest and fear constrained them to act honestly, and even generously, toward each other at this solemn interview. They united in laying the body of Isaac in the cave of Machpelah (Gen. 35:29). Then "Esau took . . . all his cattle and all his goods which he had acquired in the land of Canaan"—such, doubtless, as his father, with Jacob's consent, had assigned to him —"and went to another land away from his brother Jacob" (36:6). Esau is once more presented to us (36:43) in a genealogical table, in which a long line of illustrious descendants is referred to "Esau, the father of the Edomites."

Spiritual Message. Esau serves as a good illustration of the natural man of the earth (Heb. 12:16-17). In many respects a more honest man than Jacob, he was nevertheless destitute of faith. This was manifest in his despising the birthright because it was a spiritual thing, of value only as faith could see that value. The birthright involved the exercise of the priestly rights vested in the family head until the establishment of the Aaronic priesthood. The Edenic promise of one who would "bruise" Satan was fixed in the family of Abraham (Gen. 3:15); the order of promise was Abel, Seth, Shem, Abraham, Isaac, *Esau*. As the

firstborn Esau was in the distinct line of the promise to Abraham: "and in you all the families of the earth shall be blessed" (12:3). For all that was revealed, these great messianic promises might have been realized in Esau. For a fleeting, fleshly gratification Esau sold this birthright. Although Jacob's understanding of the birthright at the time was undoubtedly carnal and faulty, his desire for it, nevertheless, evidenced true faith. "For he who comes to God must believe that He is, and that He is a rewarder of those who seek Him" (Heb. 11:6).

BIBLIOGRAPHY: A. Whyte, *Bible Characters: Old Testament* (n.d.), pp. 99-105.

ESCHATOLOGY (from Gk. *eschatos,* "last," and *logos,* "study"). A theological term employed to designate the doctrine of last things, particularly those dealing with the second coming of Christ and the events preceding and following this great event.

Common Concept. It is quite customary in treatises on systematic theology to find an abbreviated eschatology and to discover a prevailing agnostic attitude that much cannot be known. This curtailment of such an important phase of biblical theology is a severe hindrance to the edification of the present-day church. Creedal systems and traditionalism have held the field in this realm of theological thinking as in no other. When one considers that approximately 25 percent of divine revelation was prophetic when written, it is a tragedy to reduce this realm of theology to the events immediately clustering around the second advent of Christ.

Correct Concept. Properly understood, eschatology includes more than just Christ's second coming. As Lewis Sperry Chafer says, "This, the last major division of systematic theology, is concerned with things to come and should not be limited to things which are future at some particular time in human history but should contemplate all that was future in character at the time its revelation was given. . . . A worthy eschatology must employ all prediction whether fulfilled or unfulfilled at a given time. In other words, a true eschatology attempts to account for all the prophecy set forth in the Bible" (Lewis Sperry Chafer, *Systematic Theology,* 4:255).

General Scope. Eschatology is of broad significance.

1. Properly understood, it embraces the far-reaching prophecy concerning the Lord Jesus Christ as Prophet, Priest, and King, as the promised seed, and with regard to the two advents.

2. It embraces prophecy concerning Israel's covenants, the four major covenants being that made with Abraham, that given through Moses, that made with David, and the New Covenant yet to be made in the messianic kingdom.

3. It embraces prophecy concerning the Gen-

tiles—their "times" (Luke 21:24) and their judgment.

4. It embraces prophecies concerning Satan, evil, the "man of sin," etc.

5. It embraces prophecy concerning the end of apostate Christendom.

6. It embraces prophecy concerning the church, involving the translation of the living saints, the judgment seat of Christ, the marriage of the Lamb, and the return of the glorified church to reign with Christ. A full-scale study of these great prophetic themes will include the judgments, the resurrections, the mediatorial messianic kingdom, and the eternal state.

M.F.U.

BIBLIOGRAPHY: H. A. A. Kennedy, *St. Paul's Conception of the Last Things* (1908); R. H. Charles, *Critical History of the Doctrine of a Future Life in Israel, in Judaism, and in Christianity* (1913); L. S. Chafer, *The Kingdom in History and Prophecy* (1915); G. Vos, *Pauline Eschatology* (1930); W. C. Robinson, *Christ the Hope of Glory* (1945); G. E. Ladd, *Crucial Questions About the Kingdom of God* (1952); W. D. Davies and D. Daube, eds., *Background of the New Testament and Its Eschatology* (1956); J. D. Pentecost, *Things to Come* (1958); A. J. McClain, *The Greatness of the Kingdom* (1959); H. A. Ironside and F. C. Ottman, *Biblical Eschatology* (1983).

ESDRAE'LON, PLAIN OF (es-dra-ē'lon). This name is the Gk. modification of Jezreel ("God sows"). It is a large plain about twenty miles long and fourteen miles wide, famous for its fertility due to soil washed down from the neighboring mountains of Galilee and the highlands of Samaria. Esdraelon drains into the Mediterranean by the Wadi Kishon where Deborah's ancient battle was fought (Judg. 4:7; 5:21) and Elijah conducted his contest with the priests of Baal (1 Kings 18:40). Important towns in ancient times, such as Taanach, Megiddo, and Bethshan, were built around the edge of the plain by Canaanite chariot kings. The valley has been a famous battleground through the centuries. Here the great Egyptian Thutmose III fought the confederate princes of Syria and Palestine. Here King Saul was slain by the Philistines (1 Sam. 31:1-3), and here the conquering Israelites faced the Canaanite kings (Josh. 17:16). In the prophetic Scriptures the last great battle of the age will be fought at Armageddon, the ancient hill of the valley of Megiddo W of Jordan in the plain of Jezreel (Rev. 16:14-16). This great conflict will be that in which Christ and His coming glory will deliver the Jewish remnant besieged by the Gentile world powers under the Beast and the False Prophet (16:13-16; Zech. 12:1-9). Apparently the besieging hosts, alarmed by the signs preceding the Lord's advent (Matt. 24:29-30), fall back to Megiddo after the events of Zech. 14:2, where their destruction begins, with the decimation completed in Moab and the plains of Edom (Isa. 63:1-6).

M.F.U.

BIBLIOGRAPHY: D. Baly, *Geography of the Bible* (1957), pp. 148-54; id., *Geographical Companion to the Bible* (1963), pp. 70, 74-76, 84-86.

Plain of Esdraelon from Megiddo

E'SEK (ē'sek; "contention"). One of the three wells dug by Isaac's herdsmen in the valley of Gerar and so named because the herdsmen of Gerar disputed concerning its possession (Gen. 26:20).

ESH'AN (esh'an; "support"). The third named of a group of nine towns in the country around Hebron in Judah (Josh. 15:52). As the LXX reading is "Somah," Knobel conjectures that Eshan is a corrupt reading for "Shema" (1 Chron. 2:43) and connects it with the ruins of Simia, S of Daumeh (K. & D., *Com.*).

ESH'BAAL (esh'ba-al; "man of Baal"). The fourth son of King Saul (1 Chron. 8:33; 9:39). He is doubtless the same person as Ish-bosheth (1 Sam. 31:2, cf. 2 Sam. 2:8), since it was the practice to change the obnoxious name of Baal into Bosheth or Besheth, as in the case of Jerub-besheth for Jerubbaal and (in this genealogy) Mephibosheth for Merib-baal. The Heb. term *bōshĕth*, meaning "shame," expressed the horror pious Jehovistic worshipers felt toward the degenerate cults of Canaan.

ESH'BAN (esh'ban). The second named of the

Model of the stronghold at Megiddo

four sons of Dishon, the Horite (Gen. 36:26; 1 Chron. 1:41).

ESH'COL (esh'kol; "a bunch, cluster").

1. A young Amorite chief who, with his brothers Aner and Mamre, being in alliance with Abraham, joined him in recovering Lot from the hands of Chedorlaomer and his confederates (Gen. 14:13, 24), about 1955 B.C.

2. A valley in the neighborhood of Hebron, the one in which the spies found large grapes (Num. 13:23-24). The valley probably took its name from the distinguished Amorite mentioned above.

ESH'EAN. See Eshan.

E'SHEK (e'shek; "oppression"). A brother of Azel, a Benjamite, one of the late descendants of King Saul; the father of Ulam, the founder of a large and noted family of archers (1 Chron. 8:39).

ESH'KALONITE. See Ashkelonite.

ESH'TAOL (esh'ta-ol). A town in the northern part of the hilly region, at first assigned to Judah (Josh. 15:33), but afterward to Dan (19:41). Samson was born at or near Eshtaol (Judg. 13:24-25; 16:31). From Eshtaol and the neighboring Zorah the Danites started on their expedition to secure more territory at Laish (18:2). Its location has been fixed at Eshwa' near Zorah, and thirteen miles NW of Jerusalem.

ESH'TAO'LITE (esh'ta-o'līt). An inhabitant of Eshtaol (1 Chron. 2:53).

ESHTA'RAH (esh-ta'ra). Otherwise known as Be Eshtarah (or Be-eshterah, NASB), this was a city allocated to the Gershonites as one of the Levitical cities E of the Jordan and in the territory of East Manasseh (Josh. 21:27).   E.H.M.

ESHTEMO'A (esh'te-mō'a), or **Esh'temoh** (esh'-te-mō; "obedience," Josh. 15:50). A mountain town of Judah, and afterward ceded to the priests (Josh. 21:14; 1 Chron. 4:17, 19). David, when at Ziklag, sent some of his spoil to the elders of Eshtemoa (1 Sam. 30:28), and Ishbah is mentioned (1 Chron. 4:17) as its "father," i.e., lord. It is the present Semua, a village S of Hebron, with considerable ruins dating from ancient times.

ESH'TON (esh'ton; "restful"). A man of Mehir and grandson of Chelub, of the tribe of Judah (1 Chron. 4:11-12).

ES'LI. See Hesli.

ESPOUSAL. The mutual agreement between parties to marry. See Marriage.

Figurative. This social institution is alluded to figuratively in the relationship of the church as the bride of Christ (John 3:29; 2 Cor. 11:2; Eph. 5:25-32; Rev. 19:6-8). It is important to distinguish between Israel and the church. Israel is the wife of Jehovah (Hos. 2:2, 16-23) now disowned but some day to be restored. This relationship is not to be confused with that of the church of Christ. The church is a virgin espoused to one husband, which could never be said of an adulterous wife to be restored in grace. Israel is, accordingly, to be the forgiven and restored wife of Jehovah. Such relationships in dealing with deity, being figurative and expressing spiritual relationship, are not inconsonant or contradictory. First Cor. 10:32 clearly names three classes in this present age—Jews, Gentiles, and the church of God. All the unsaved are either Jews or Gentiles in this age. All saved people, whether Jews or Gentiles, are members of the church, the Body of Christ, a distinct entity formed at Pentecost by the advent of the Spirit performing His baptizing work (Acts 1:5; 11:16) and to be completed at the coming of the Lord (1 Cor. 15:53; 1 Thess. 4:13-17; 2 Thess. 2:1).   M.F.U.

ES'ROM. A KJV term (Matt. 1:3; Luke 3:3). See Hezron.

ESSENCE, THE DIVINE. Essence (from the Lat. verb *esse*, "to be") signifies that which a person or thing is in himself or itself, apart from all that is accidental. Substance is a term of equivalent meaning. These terms are held by some to be more appropriate in philosophy than in theology. The Scriptures, it is true, contain no such abstract terms as essence and substance. At the same time it must be admitted that some of the names under which God has revealed Himself, such as Elohim and Jehovah, refer directly to the eternal, divine essence. Therefore, theology has often made large use of these terms in its attempts to arrive at the proper and scriptural conception of God. The principal points in dispute have been, first, as to what extent, if any, the divine essence can be known to us; and, second, as to the relation existing between the attributes of God and His essence. The view best substantiated is that the attributes of God are not merely subjective conceptions, based upon certain only relatively true Scripture revelations, but that the attributes made known to us through the Scriptures are manifestations of what God is in Himself. They are the living realization of His essence. Accordingly, although the divine essence is incomprehensible, we have nevertheless some measure of true knowledge of God, knowledge that relates to His very essence. (See God, Attributes of.) For full and discriminating discussion see Dorner, *System of Christian Doctrine,* 1:187-206; Pope, *Compendium of Christian Doctrine,* 1:246-52; Van Oosterzee, *Christian Dogmatics,* 1:234-38; Hodge, *Systematic Theology,* 1:366-70.   E.MCC.

ESSENES' (es-sēnz'). A Jewish religious community, though differing in many respects from traditional Judaism.

Identity. An ascetic community of men in Palestine and Syria forming the first cells of organized monasticism in the Mediterranean world. Their main colonies were near the northern end of the Dead Sea and around En-gedi. The phenomenal discovery of nonbiblical literature among the famous Dead Sea Scrolls, including "The Manual of Discipline" and "The Commentary on Habakkuk," has shed a great deal of light on pre-Christian sects. The sect that owned and produced the Dead Sea Scrolls had striking affinities with the Covenanters of Damascus, the Essenes, the Therapeutae of Egypt, and the John the Baptist movement. Millar Burrows has shown that the Judean Covenanters (his term for the Essenes) are the same Jewish sect as the Covenanters of Damascus. This material corroborates Philo and Josephus, heretofore the primary sources for an understanding of the Essenes. For a comparison of this archaeological material with the older sources see W. H. Brownlee, "A Comparison of the Covenanters of the Dead Sea Scrolls with Pre-Christian Jewish Sects," *The Biblical Archaeologist* 13 (Sept. 1950): 50-72, dealing specifically with the Essenes.

Origin. The origin of the Essenes is as obscure as their name. Josephus first mentions them (*Ant.* 13.5.9) in the time of Jonathan the Maccabee (about 150 B.C.) and speaks expressly of Judas, an Essene (105-104 B.C.). This would place the origin of the order in the second century before Christ. It is questionable whether they proceeded simply from Judaism or whether foreign and especially Hellenistic elements did not also have an influence in their origin.

Organization. Their whole community was strictly organized as a single body, at the head of which were presidents (Gk. *epimelētai*) to whom the members were bound in unconditional obedience. One wishing to enter the order received three badges—a pickaxe, an apron, and a white garment. After a year's probation he was admitted to the purification ceremonies. Another probation of two years followed, after which he was allowed to participate in the common meals and to become a full member. At that time the new member took a fearful oath in which he bound himself to absolute openness to his brethren and secrecy concerning the doctrines of the order to nonmembers. Only adults were admitted as members, but children were received for instruction in the principles of Essenism. Josephus says that the Essenes were divided into four classes according to the time of their entrance, the children being the first class, those in the two stages of the novitiate the second and third class, and the members proper the fourth class.

Discipline. Transgressions of members were tried by a court, and sentence was never pronounced by a vote of less than one hundred. What was once decided by that number was unalterable.

Excommunication was equivalent to a slow death since an Essene could not take food prepared by strangers for fear of pollution. The strongest tie by which the members were united was the absolute community of goods. It was a law among the Essenes that those who came to them must let what they had be common to the whole order. They also had stewards appointed to take care of their common affairs. They chose fitting persons as receivers of revenues and of the produce of the earth, and priests for the preparation of the bread and food. There was one purse for all, and common expenses, common clothes, and common food at common meals. The needy of the order, such as the sick and the aged, were cared for at common expense, and special officers were appointed in every town to care for the wants of the traveling brethren. The daily labor of the members was strictly regulated. After prayer they were dismissed to their work by the presidents. They reassembled for purifying ceremonies and the common meal, after which they went to work again, to reassemble for the evening meal. Although their chief employment was agriculture, they carried on crafts of every kind, but trading (thought to lead to covetousness) and the making of weapons or any utensils that might injure men was forbidden.

Ethics, Manners, and Customs. Philo competes with Josephus in sounding the praises of the Essenes. According to these authorities their life was moderate, simple, and unpretentious. They condemned sensual desires as sinful and abstained from wedlock but chose other people's children while they were pliable and fit for learning. They took food and drink only till they had had enough, contenting themselves with the same dish day by day and rejecting great expense as harmful to mind and body. They did not cast away clothes and shoes until they were utterly useless and sought to acquire only what was needed for the wants of life.

In addition to the general features of simplicity and moderation mentioned above we call attention to the following special points: (1) There was no *slave* among them, but all were *free*, mutually working for each other. (2) *Swearing* was forbidden as worse than perjury: "For that which does not deserve belief without an appeal to God is already condemned." (3) They *forbade anointing with oil*, regarding a rough exterior as praiseworthy. (4) *Bathing in cold water* was compulsory before each meal, after performing the functions of nature, or coming in contact with a member of a lower class of the order. (5) They considered *white* raiment as seemly for all occasions. (6) *Great modesty* was inculcated. In performing natural functions they dug with the pickaxe—which each member received—a hole one foot deep, covered themselves with a mantle (not to offend the brightness of God), relieved themselves, and filled the hole again. In *bathing* they bound an apron about their loins; they avoided *spitting* forward or to the right hand. (7) They sent gifts of incense to the Temple but *offered no animal sacrifices* because they esteemed their own sacrifices more valuable. (8) The chief peculiarity of the Essenes was their common meals, which bore the character of *sacrificial feasts.* The food was prepared by priests, with the observance, probably, of certain rites of purification; an Essene was not permitted to partake of any other food than this. The opinion that the Essenes abstained from *flesh* and *wine* is not supported by the older authorities.

Theology. The Essenes held fundamentally the Jewish view of the world, entertaining an absolute belief in providence, which they held in common with the Pharisees. Next to God the name of Moses the lawgiver was an object of the greatest reverence with them, and whoever blasphemed it was punished with death. In their worship the Holy Scriptures were read and explained. The Sabbath was so strictly observed that on that day they did not remove a vessel or even perform the functions of nature, and they seem to have kept to the priesthood of the house of Aaron.

They must have held their angelology in high esteem as their novices had to swear carefully to preserve the names of the angels. Concerning their doctrine of the *soul* and of its *immortality* Josephus writes: "They taught that bodies are perishable, but souls immortal, and that the latter dwelt originally in the subtlest ether, but being debased by sensual pleasures united themselves with bodies as with prisons; but when they are freed from the fetters of sense they will joyfully soar on high as if delivered from long bondage. To the good (souls) is appointed a life beyond the ocean, where they are troubled by neither rain nor snow nor heat, but where the gentle zephyr is ever blowing. . . . But to the bad (souls) is appointed a dark, cold region full of unceasing torment."

A strange phenomenon presented on Jewish soil is the peculiar conduct of the Essenes with respect to the sun. To this they turned while praying, in opposition to the Jewish custom of looking toward the Temple. From this and other customs it would appear that they were in earnest in their religious estimation of the sun.

In conclusion we may observe that "Essenism is merely Pharisaism in the superlative degree." It was, however, influenced by foreign systems of theology and philosophy, of which four have been proposed, namely, Buddhism, Parseeism, Syrian heathenism, and Pythagoreanism.

The Essenes disappeared from history after the destruction of Jerusalem. Though not directly mentioned in Scripture they may be referred to in Matt. 19:11-12; Col. 2:8, 18, 23.

BIBLIOGRAPHY: W. H. Brownlee, *Dead Sea Manual of Discipline* (1951); F. M. Cross, *Ancient Library of Qumran* (1958); M. Black, *The Scrolls and Christian Origins* (1961); A. Dupont-Sommer, *Essene Writings from Qumran* (1961); R. K. Harrison, *The Dead Sea Scrolls* (1971); G. W. Buchanan, *International Standard Bible Encyclopedia* (1982), 2:147-55.

ES'THER (es'ter). The Jewish maiden chosen by Ahasuerus to be queen. Esther was the new, and probably Persian, name given on her introduction to the royal harem. Her proper Heb. name was *Hadassah,* "Myrtle" (which see). As to the signification of Esther, it is "Ishtar," the name of the great Babylonian goddess. Gesenius quotes from the second Targum on Esther: "She was called Esther from the name of the star Venus, which in Greek is Aster (i.e., *astēr,* English, 'star')." Esther was the daughter of Abihail, a Benjamite and uncle of Mordecai (Esther 2:15). Her ancestor Kish had been among the captives led away from Jerusalem by Nebuchadnezzar. Left an orphan, Esther was brought up by her cousin Mordecai, who held an office in the palace at Susa (Esther 2:5-7).

Chosen Queen. Ahasuerus, Xerxes I (486-465 B.C.), having divorced his wife because she refused to comply with his drunken commands, ordered that a search be made for the most beautiful maiden to be her successor. Those selected were placed in the custody of "Hegai, who was in charge of the women." The final choice among them remained with the king himself. That choice fell upon Esther, for "the king loved Esther more than all the women, and she found favor and kindness with him more than all the virgins, so that he set the royal crown on her head and made her queen instead of Vashti" (2:8-17), about 478 B.C.

Saves Her People. Esther, in obedience to Mordecai, had not made known her parentage and race (Esther 2:10). But Haman, the Agagite, angry with Mordecai because he "neither bowed down nor paid homage to him," represented to the king that the Jews scattered through his empire were a pernicious nation. The king gave Haman full power to kill them all and seize their property (chap. 3). Upon being informed of this by Mordecai, Esther, who seemed herself to be included in the doom of extermination, resolved to plead for her people. She decided to present herself unbidden to the king, which was not according to law (4:16). She did so and, obtaining favor in his sight, made known her request: that the king and Haman would attend a banquet that she had prepared that day. At the banquet the king renewed his willingness to grant Esther any request she might make. She extended another invitation to both of them for the next day and promised to reveal her wishes then (chap. 5). The next day Esther pleaded for her people and denounced Haman. The laws of the empire would not allow the king to recall a decree once uttered, but the Jews were authorized to stand upon their defense and this, with the change in the intentions of the court known, averted the worst con-

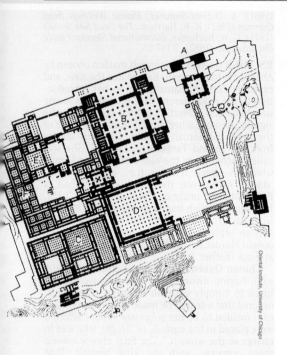

Plan of Persepolis

sequences of the decree. The Jews established a yearly feast in memory of their deliverance called *Purim,* which is observed to this day (9:20-32).

Character. "The character of Esther, as she appears in the Bible, is that of a woman of deep piety, faith, courage, patriotism, and caution, combined with resolution; a dutiful daughter to her adopted father, docile and obedient to his counsels, and anxious to share the king's favor with him for the good of the Jewish people. That she was a virtuous woman, and, as far as her situation made it possible, a good wife to the king, her continued influence over him for so long a time warrants us to infer. There must have been a singular charm in her aspect and manners since she obtained favor in the sight of all that looked upon her (Esther 2:15)" (McClintock and Strong, *Cyclopedia*).

BIBLIOGRAPHY: W. M. Taylor, *Ruth the Gleaner and Esther the Queen* (1961); C. J. and A. A. Barber, *You Can Have a Happy Marriage* (1984), pp. 107-18.

ESTHER, BOOK OF. The book is named from its principal character whose Heb. name *Hadassah* (myrtle) was changed to the Persian name *Esther* (which see). The Jews call it Megilloth Esther, that is, the Esther Roll, and it is in the third section of the Heb. Scriptures with the four other rolls, including the Song of Solomon, Ruth, Lamentations, and Ecclesiastes. These rolls were short and read on special feast days.

The Esther Roll was read at the feast of Purim.

Design. The purpose of the book is to demonstrate God's providential care of His people in their trials and persecutions and to furnish an explanation of the origin of the important feast of Purim, first mentioned in 2 Macc. 15:36.

Authenticity. It is common in critical circles to deny the historicity of the story except as history may be fictionalized. A. Bentzen, accordingly, describes the book as an "historical novel" but is forced to confess "that the story teller knows something of the administration of the Persian kingdom and especially the construction of the palace at Shushan" (*Introduction to the O.T.* [1948] 2:192). The author's undeniable knowledge of Persian life and customs and his manifestly historical intent (cf. 10:2) militate against the critics' contention of a fictional narrative. For example, it is alleged that Mordecai would have to be well over a hundred years old to have gone in the first deportation in 597 B.C. The relative pronoun of this verse evidently refers to Kish, Mordecai's great-grandfather; hence, this difficulty is obviated. It is also contended that Vashti, Esther, and Mordecai are unknown to secular history in the reign of Xerxes I (c. 485-465 B.C.). But Esther evidently did not become queen until the seventh year of Xerxes's reign, c. 478 B.C., after his return from his defeat in Greece, c. 480 B.C., when Herodotus specifically says he paid attention to his harem. It is true that the queen is said to have been Amestris, but certainly Xerxes, from what we know of him personally and of his splendor and power, may well have had many other wives, if Solomon, king over tiny Syria-Palestine, had "seven hundred wives, princesses, and three hundred concubines" (1 Kings 11:3). The contention that Esther (Ishtar), Mordecai (Marduk), and Vashti (the name of a Persian deity) were merely fictional names is pure supposition carrying no weight with the devout student.

The arguments against the genuineness of the story of Esther are these: (1) The narrative implies that Vashti and Esther were the legitimate wives of "the great king" (Esther 1:19; 2:4). The only wife of Xerxes known to history, however, was Amestris, married to him before the third year of his reign and who continued to be queen after his death. To this it is replied that the disgrace of Vashti may have been only temporary, and she may afterward have been restored to her queenship; or that Vashti and Esther were secondary wives, the latter certainly being selected from the king's harem. The title "queen" may have been used as a special honor in indicating the favor Esther had obtained with the king. (2) The king could not legally, and therefore it is supposed would not, marry a wife not belonging to one of the seven great Persian families. "The marriage of Ahasuerus with a Jewess, even if we regard it as a marriage in the fullest sense, would not be more illegal or more abhorrent to Persian notions than Cambyses's marriage with his full sister. It is, therefore, just as likely to have taken place. If, on the other hand, it was a marriage of the secondary kind, the law with respect to the king's wives being taken from the seven great families would not apply to it" (Rawlinson, *Historical Illustrations of the Old Testament*).

Authenticity and Date. The book is anonymous. It is to be placed sometime during or near the reign of Artaxerxes Longimanus (c. 464-425 B.C.). This also accounts for its literary phenomena, since its diction is reminiscent of such late books as Ezra, Nehemiah, and Chronicles. Critics who doubt the historicity of the book put it later in the Gk. (third century B.C.) or Maccabean period (second century B.C.).

Contents.
I. The Jews in danger (1:1–3:15)
 A. Esther made queen (1:1–2:23)
 B. Haman's plot against the Jews (3:1-15)
II. The Jews delivered (4:1–10:3)
 A. Esther's courage brings deliverance (4:1–7:10)
 B. Vengeance over the Jews' enemies (8:1–9:19)
 C. The feast of Purim (9:20-32)
 D. Mordecai's elevation at court (10:1-3)

BIBLIOGRAPHY: J. V. McGee, *An Exposition of the Book of Esther* (1951); L. B. Paton, *A Critical and Exegetical Commentary on the Book of Esther,* International Critical Commentary (1951); R. K. Harrison, *Introduction to the Old Testament* (1969), pp. 1085-1102; J. C. Whitcomb, Jr., *Esther: The Triumph of God's Sovereignty* (1979); A. Raleigh, *The Book of Esther* (1980).

ESTHER, FAST OF. *See* Festivals: Postexilic.

E'TAM (ē'tam; "hawk ground").
1. The "rock of Etam" was the place to which Samson retired after his slaughter of the Philistines (Judg. 15:8, 11). It is probably to be located near Zorah at 'Arak Isma'in.
2. A city of Judah fortified by Rehoboam (2 Chron. 11:6), probably, from its position in the list, near Bethlehem and Tekoa. The Talmudists locate the sources of the water from which Solomon's gardens and pleasure grounds were fed there, from which it has been inferred that the site was identical with that of Solomon's Pools at el-Eurak, near Bethlehem. Probably it is the same Etam mentioned in 1 Chron. 4:3.

ETERNAL LIFE. This is a priceless treasure, the gift of God. It is not to be confused with mere endless existence, which all possess, saved as well as unsaved. Christ said, "I came that they might have life, and might have it abundantly" (John 10:10). This life is nothing less than "Christ in you, the hope of glory" (Col. 1:27). It is likened to a birth from above (John 3:3; 1:13) and is dependent upon receiving Christ as Savior. "He who has the Son has the life; he who does not have the Son of God does not have the life" (1 John 5:12). Eternal life must not be confused

with natural life. This form of life is subject to death and is derived by human generation. Spiritual life has a beginning but no end. The difference is that one possessing mere natural life will be separated eternally from God in the lake of fire, whereas the one possessing eternal life will be united and in fellowship with God for all eternity. Thus, separation from God is eternal death; union with God is eternal life. M.F.U.

BIBLIOGRAPHY: J. Barr, *Biblical Words for Time* (1960).

ETERNITY. This is an essential attribute of God. It is the infinitude of God in relation to duration, as His omnipresence is His infinitude in relation to space. His existence is without beginning and will never end. The thought of this divine attribute is necessarily included in that of God's absolutely independent existence. The eternity of God is declared in many places in the Scriptures. See Pss. 90:2; 102:26-28; Isa. 44:6; 47:15; 1 Tim. 6:16; 2 Pet. 3:8; Rev. 1:4.

BIBLIOGRAPHY: H. Sasse, αἰών, *Theological Dictionary of the New Testament,* ed. G. Kittel (1964), 1:197-209.

E'THAM (ē'tham). A place to the E of the present Suez Canal, on the border of the desert, where Israel made its second station after leaving Egypt (Ex. 13:20; Num. 33:6). At this point the Israelites were ordered to change their route (Ex. 14:2).

E'THAN (ē'than; "perennial, permanent").
1. One of the four persons ("Ethan the Ezrahite, Heman, Calcol and Darda") who were so renowned for their perception that it is mentioned to the honor of Solomon that his wisdom excelled theirs (1 Kings 4:30-31). Ethan is distinguished as "the Ezrahite" from the others who are called "sons of Mahol," unless the word *Mahol* is taken for "sons of music, dancing," etc., in which case it would apply to Ethan as well as to the others. In 1 Chron. 2:6 they are all given as "sons of Zerah." In the title to Ps. 89 an "Ethan the Ezrahite" is named as the author.
2. Son of Zimmah and father of Adaiah, in the ancestry of the Levite Asaph (1 Chron. 6:42). In v. 21 he seems to be called Joah, the father of Iddo.
3. Son of Kishi, or Kushaiah, a Levite of the family of Merari. He was appointed one of the leaders of the Temple music by David (as singer, 1 Chron. 6:44, or player on cymbals, 15:17, 19), about 960 B.C. In the latter passages he is associated with Heman and Asaph, the heads of two other families of Levites; and, inasmuch as in other passages of these books (25:1, 6) the names are given as Asaph, Heman, and Jeduthun, it has been conjectured that this last and Ethan were identical. There is at least great probability that Ethan the singer was the same person as Ethan the Ezrahite (*see* no. 1), whose name stands at the head of Ps. 89. It is an unlikely coincidence that there should be two persons named Heman

and Ethan so closely connected in two different tribes and walks of life.

ETH'ANIM (eth'a-nim). Another name for the month *Tisri. See* Time.

ETH'BAAL (eth'bā-al; "with Baal"). A king of Sidon, father of Jezebel, the wife of Ahab (1 Kings 16:31), before 875 B.C. According to Josephus (*Against Apion* 1.18; cf. *Ant.* 8.13.1-2), Ethbaal is called Ithobalus by Menander, who also says that he was a priest of Astarte, and, having put the king, Pheles, to death, assumed the scepter of Tyre and Sidon, lived sixty-eight years, and reigned thirty-two. We see here the reason Jezebel, the daughter of a priest of Astarte, was so zealous a promoter of idolatry.

E'THER (e'ther; "abundance"). One of a group of nine cities in the plain of Judah (Josh. 15:42), but eventually assigned to Simeon (19:7). Now identified with Khirbet el-'Ater, one mile NW of Beit Jibrin.

ETHIO'PIA (ē-thi-ō'pi-a; Heb. *kûsh*). Lying S of Egypt, corresponding to what is now called the Sudan, i.e., the country of the blacks. It was known to the Hebrews (Isa. 18:1; 45:14; Zeph. 3:10). The name *Cush* (KJV, "Ethiopia") is found in the Egyptian Keesh, evidently applied to the same territory. In the description of the Garden of Eden, an Asiatic Cush is mentioned (Gen. 2:13). In all other passages the words *Ethiopia* and *the Ethiopians*—with one possible exception, "the Arabs who bordered the Ethiopians" (2 Chron. 21:16), which may refer to Arabians opposite Ethiopia—may be safely considered to mean an African country and people or peoples (Kitto). The languages of Ethiopia are as various as the tribes. In Ps. 68:31, Isa. 45:14, and probably Zeph. 3:10, the calling of Ethiopia to the service of the true God is foretold. The case of the Ethiopian eunuch (Acts 8:27-39) indicates the spread of the old dispensation influence in that country and the introduction of the new. The NIV regularly uses the transliteration "Cush" except in Jer. 13:23 and Acts 8:27, where it is "Ethiopian."

BIBLIOGRAPHY: E. A. T. W. Budge, *The Egyptian Sudan* (1907); id., *A History of Ethiopia, Nubia, and Abyssinia* (1928); D. Dunham, *The Royal Tombs of Kush,* 4 vols. (1950-57); G. Steindorff and K. C. Steele, *When Egypt Ruled the East* (1957); E. Ullendorff, *The Ethiopians* (1960); id., *Ethiopia and the Bible* (1968).

ETHIO'PIAN (ē-thi-ō'pi-an; *see* 2 Chron. 14:9; Jer. 13:23; 38:7, 10, 12). An inhabitant of *Ethiopia* (which see) or Cush; used of Zerah and Ebed-melech.

ETHIO'PIAN EUNUCH. Chief officer of Candace, the Ethiopian queen, who was converted to Christianity through the instrumentality of Philip, the evangelist (Acts 8:27). He is described as being "in charge of all her treasure." In the East

eunuchs were taken not only to be overseers of the harem but also generally to fill the most important posts of the court. Tradition calls the Ethiopian by the names *Indich* and *Fudich* and makes him without historical proof, but not improbably, the first preacher of the gospel among his countrymen. *See* Candace; Eunuch.

ETHIOPIAN WOMAN. *See* Cushite Woman.

ETH-KA'ZIN (eth-ka'zin; "time of a judge"). A city near the eastern boundary of Zebulun (Josh. 19:13), not identified.

ETH'NAN (eth'nan; "a gift"). A descendant of Judah, one of the sons of Helah, the wife of Ashhur (1 Chron. 4:7).

ETH'NI (eth'ni; "munificent"). The son of Zerah and father of Malchijah, a Levite of the family of Gershom (1 Chron. 6:41).

EUBU'LUS (ū-bu'lus, "good in counsel"). A Christian at Rome whose greeting Paul sent to Timothy during his last imprisonment (2 Tim. 4:21), A.D. 66.

EUCHARIST (ū'kar-ist; Gk. *eucharistia*, "giving of thanks"). One of the names of the *Lord's Supper* (which see). *See also* Agape.

EUNI'CE (ū'nis; "good victory"). The mother of Timothy and the wife of a Greek (Acts 16:1; 2 Tim. 1:5), A.D. before 66. In both passages reference is made to her faith.

EUNUCH (Gk. *eunouchos;* Heb. *sārîs*). The Gk. word means literally "bed keeper," i.e., one who has charge of beds and bedchambers. The original Heb. word clearly implies the incapacity that mutilation involves. Castration, according to Josephus (*Ant.* 4.8.40), was not practiced by the Jews upon either man or animals; and the law (Deut. 23:1; cf. Lev. 22:24) dealt severely with this kind of treatment of any Israelite. It was a barbarous custom of the East to treat captives thus (Herodotus *History* 3. 49; 6. 32), not only those of tender age, but, it should seem, when past puberty. The "officer" Potiphar (Gen. 37:36; 39:1, KJV marg., "eunuch") was an Egyptian, married, and the "captain of the bodyguard." In the Assyrian monuments a eunuch often appears, sometimes armed and in a warlike capacity or as a scribe noting the number of heads and amounts of spoil, as receiving the prisoners, and even as officiating in religious ceremonies. The origination of the practice is ascribed to Semiramis and is no doubt as early, or nearly so, as Eastern despotism itself. The complete assimilation of the kingdom of Israel, and latterly of Judah, to the neighboring models of despotism, is traceable in the rank and prominence of eunuchs (2 Kings 8:6; 9:32; 23:11; 25:19; Isa. 56:3-4; Jer. 29:2; 34:19; 38:7; 41:16; 52:25). They mostly appear in one of two relations, either in the military as those set over "the men of war," greater trustworthiness possibly counterbalancing inferior courage and military vigor, or associated, as we mostly recognize them, with women and children. We find the Assyrian Rab-saris, or chief eunuch (2 Kings 18:17) employed together with other high officials as ambassador. Some think that Daniel and his companions were in this manner treated (2 Kings 20:17-18; Isa. 39:7; cf. Dan. 1:3, 7). The court of Herod had its eunuchs (Josephus *Ant.* 15.7.4; 16.8.1), as did that of Queen Candace (Acts 8:27). We must remember that both the Heb. and Gk. terms were sometimes applied to those filling important posts, without regard to bodily mutilation.

Figurative. The term is employed figuratively by our Lord (Matt. 19:12) with reference to the power, whether possessed as a natural disposition or acquired as a property of grace, of maintaining an attitude of indifference toward fleshly desires and temptations.

BIBLIOGRAPHY: R. de Vaux, *Ancient Israel: Its Life and Institutions* (1961), pp. 121, 225; K. A. Kitchen, *Journal of Egyptian Archaeology* (1961), 47:158-64; id., *Ancient Orient and Old Testament* (1966), pp. 165-66; G. Kalish, *Studies in Honor of John A. Wilson* (1970), pp. 55-62.

EUO'DIA (ū-ō'di-a; "a good journey"). A female member of the church at Philippi who seems to have been at variance with another female member named Syntyche (A.D. 58-60). Paul describes them as women who had "shared my struggle in the cause of the gospel," and implores them to "live in harmony" (Phil. 4:2-3).

BIBLIOGRAPHY: D. E. Hiebert, *Personalities Around Paul* (1973), pp. 164-66.

EUPHRA'TES (ū-frā'tēz; Heb. *perāt*, to "break" forth; Gk. *Euphratēs*). This river rises in the mountains of Armenia Major and flows through Assyria, Syria, Mesopotamia, and the city of Babylon, from 1,700 to 1,800 miles into the Persian Gulf. It is navigable for small vessels for 1,200 miles from its mouth. It floods like the Nile, becoming swollen in the months of March, April, and May by the melting of the snows. It was the natural boundary of the empire, so that to cross the Euphrates was to cross the Rubicon. It was the western boundary of Mesopotamia, dividing it from the "Land of Hatti," which included all land between the Euphrates and the Mediterranean; Babylon lay upon this, as Nineveh did upon the Tigris River. It flowed by other ancient cities, such as Carchemish (2 Chron. 35:20) and Sippar, Agade, Borsippa, and Ur. It served, like the Nile, to irrigate the country by means of artificial canals, making the desert, according to Xenophon, to become a garden of fertility. It is referred to under various names in Scripture (Gen. 2:14; 15:18; Deut. 1:7; 11:24; Josh. 1:4; 2 Sam. 8:3; 2 Kings 23:29; 24:7; 1 Chron. 5:9; 18:3; 2 Chron. 35:20; Jer. 13:4; 51:63). It is sometimes called the "flood."

BIBLIOGRAPHY: S. A. Pallis, *The Antiquity of Iraq* (1956), pp. 4-7; J. J. Finkelstein, *Journal of Near Eastern Studies* 21 (1962):73-92; T. Jacobsen, *Toward the Image of Tammuz* (1970), pp. 231-43.

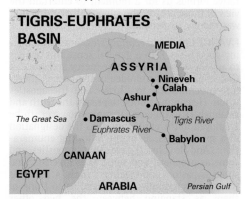

TIGRIS-EUPHRATES BASIN

EURA'QUILO (ū-ra'kwilō; KJV *Euroclydon;* Gk. *Euroklydōn;* "east" and "wave," an "east waver"). The gale of wind in the Adriatic Gulf that off the S coast of Crete seized the ship in which Paul was finally wrecked on the coast of Malta (Acts 27:14). This gale in particular is described, and its circumstances are verified by abundant illustrations from experiences of modern seamen in the Levant. As to the direction of the wind we quote: "The wind came *down from* the *island* and drove the vessel *off the island;* whence it is evident that it could not have been southerly. If we consider further that the wind struck the vessel when she was *not far* from Cape Matala (Acts 27:14), that it drove her *toward Claudia* (v. 16; ["Clauda," NASB]), which is an island twenty miles to the S.W. of that point, and that the sailors feared lest it should drive them into the Syrtis, on the African coast (v. 17), an inspection of the chart will suffice to show us that the point from which the storm came must have been N.E., or rather to the E. of N.E., and thus we may safely speak of it as coming [from] the E.N.E." (Conybeare and Howson, *Life and Epistles of St. Paul,* 2:326). The NIV, therefore, refers to it as the "northeaster."

BIBLIOGRAPHY: E. D. S. Bradford, *Paul the Traveller* (1974), pp. 223-24, 226-27; J. Smith, *The Voyage and Shipwreck of Paul* (1979), pp. 119-21, 287-89.

EU'TYCHUS (ū'ti-kus; "good fortune"). A young man of Troas who attended the preaching of Paul. The services were held in the third story of a house, the sermon long, lasting until midnight, and the air heated by the large company and the many lamps. Under those circumstances Eutychus was overcome with sleep and fell from the window in which he was sitting into the court below "and was picked up dead." Paul went down and, extending himself upon the body, embraced it, like the prophets of old (1 Kings 17:21; 2 Kings 4:34). He then comforted his friends, "Do not be troubled, for his life is in him." Before

Paul departed in the morning they brought the young man to him alive and well (Acts 20:5-12). Bloomfield (*New Testament*) proves that the narrative forbids us for a moment to entertain the view of those critics who suppose that animation was merely suspended.

EVANGELIST (Gk. *evangelistēs,* one "announcing good news"). In a general sense this applies to anyone who proclaims the mercy and grace of God, especially as unfolded in the gospel; therefore preeminently to Christ, and the apostles whom He commissioned to preach the truth and establish His kingdom. It came, however, to be employed in the early church as the designation of a special class, as in the following enumeration: "And He [Christ] gave some as apostles, and some as prophets, and some as evangelists, and some as pastors and teachers" (Eph. 4:11). This passage, accordingly, would lead us to think of them as standing between the two other groups—sent forth as missionary preachers of the gospel by the first, and as such preparing the way for the labors of the second. The same inference would seem to follow the occurrence of the word as applied to Philip (Acts 21:8). It follows from what has been said that the calling of the evangelist is the proclamation of the glad tidings to those who have not known them, rather than the instruction and pastoral care of those who have believed and been baptized. It follows also that the name denotes a *work* rather than an *order.* The evangelist might or might not be a bishop-elder or a deacon. The apostles, so far as they evangelized (8:25; 14:7; 1 Cor. 1:17), might claim the title, though there were many evangelists who were not apostles (Smith, *Bib. Dict.,* s.v.). In later liturgical language the term applied to the reader of the gospel for the day.

BIBLIOGRAPHY: E. M. B. Green, *Evangelism in the Early Church* (1970).

EVE (ēv; Heb. *ḥawwâ,* "life giver"). The name given by Adam to the first woman, his wife (Gen. 3:20). It is supposed that she was created on the sixth day, after Adam had reviewed the animals. The naming of the animals led to this result, because "there was not found a helper suitable for him." Then God caused a deep sleep to fall upon the man, and took one of his ribs and fashioned it into a woman, and brought her to Adam (2:18-22). Through the subtlety of the serpent, Eve was beguiled into a violation of the one commandment imposed upon her and Adam: she took of the fruit of the forbidden tree and gave some to her husband. Her punishment was an increase of sorrow and pain in childbirth (3:16). "That the woman should bear children was the original will of God; but it was a punishment that henceforth she was to bear them in sorrow, i.e., with pains which threatened her own life as well as that of the child" (Delitzsch). Three sons of Eve are named—Cain (4:1), Abel (v. 2), and Seth

(5:3)—though the fact that there were other children is recorded (5:4).

BIBLIOGRAPHY: J. J. Davis, *Paradise to Prison* (1975), pp. 59-95; C. J. and A. A. Barber, *Your Marriage Has Real Possibilities* (1984), pp. 17-28.

EVEN, EVENING, EVENTIDE. *See* Time.

EVENING SACRIFICES. *See* Sacrifice.

EVERLASTING. *See* Eternity.

E'VI (ē'vi; "desirous"). One of the five kings of the Midianites slain by the Israelites in the war arising out of the idolatry of Baal-peor, induced by the suggestion of Balaam (Num. 31:8), and whose lands were afterward allotted to Reuben (Josh. 13:21), 1441 B.C.

EVIDENCE. The rendering in the KJV (Jer. 32:10-16) of Heb. *sēper,* "book," as it is usually rendered in the KJV, or "writing," hence a document of title, i.e., a *deed* (so NASB and NIV); and of Gk. *elegchos,* "proof," cf. Heb. 11:1, "evidence," KJV; "conviction," marg., "evidence," NASB.

EVIL. The comprehensive term under which all disturbances of the divinely appointed harmony of the universe are included. Christian doctrine, in accordance with the Scriptures, carefully distinguishes between physical and moral evil.

Physical Evil. It is often called natural evil and is disorder in the physical world. Such physical causes as militate against physical well-being are therefore called evils. That such evils are, to some extent at least, the effect or penalty of sin is a clear teaching of Scripture (Gen. 3:10-12; 6:13). To what extent physical sufferings are the necessary means to greater good is, however, a great question.

Moral Evil. This is sin, disorder in the moral world. It is the failure of rational and free beings to conform in character and conduct to the will of God. This is the greatest evil (*see* Rom. 1:18-32). How the existence of evil is compatible with the goodness of God is the question of *theodicy.* For discussion of moral evil *see* Sin.

BIBLIOGRAPHY: C. S. Lewis, *The Problem of Pain* (1965); W. Fitch, *God and Evil* (1969); A. E. Wilder-Smith, *The Paradox of Pain* (1971); J. W. Wenham, *The Goodness of God* (1974).

EVILDOER. One who is bad; from the Heb. *rā'â,* to "break," and so to render worthless (Pss. 37:1; 119:115; Isa. 1:4; etc.). The Gk. word (*kakopoios*) is identical with the English (1 Pet. 2:12, 14; 4:15).

EVIL-FAVOREDNESS. In the KJV (Deut. 17:1; NASB and NIV, "defect") a term for a blemish, scurvy, wound, etc., that made an animal unfit for sacrifice (cf. Lev. 22:22-24).

E'VIL-MERO'DACH (ē'vil-me-rō'dak). The name of a king of Babylon mentioned twice in the OT (2 Kings 25:27 and Jer. 52:31). The name, in the Babylonian language, is written *Amel-Marduk;* i.e., man (or servant) of the god Marduk, or Merodach. Evil-merodach was the son and successor of Nebuchadnezzar and reigned 562-560 B.C. Of his reign we have but meager details. According to Berosus and the canon of Ptolemy he was slain by his sister's husband, Neriglissar, who then made himself king in his stead. Josephus, probably following Berosus in this, makes him odious because of debauchery and cruelty. The OT narrates a kind and high-spirited act of his doing. In the first year of his reign he released from prison Jehoiachin, king of Judah, who had been in confinement thirty-seven years; "he spoke kindly to him" (2 Kings 25:28) and gave him a portion at his table for the rest of his life, honoring him above the other vassal kings who were at Babylon.

EWES. The rendering in the KJV of several Heb. words for the female sheep. *See* Animal Kingdom: Sheep.

EXACTOR (Heb. *nāgaś,* to "drive, tax, tyrannize," Isa. 60:17). A word used to signify a driver (taskmaster, Ex. 3:7; Job 3:18; Isa. 9:3), or simply a driver of animals (Job 39:7); hence, exactor of debt (or tribute, Dan. 11:20; Zech. 9:8); hence, with oriental ideas of tyranny, a ruler (Isa. 3:12; 14:2; Zech. 10:4). In the passage, Isa. 60:17, it seems to mean magistracy, and we may read "righteousness shall be a substitute for the police force in every form" (Delitzsch, *Com.*).

EXCHANGER (Matt. 25:27, KJV). A *broker* or *banker,* i.e., one who exchanges money for a fee and loans out to others for a rate of interest. The NASB replaces the KJV expression with "in the bank," giving a marginal reading of "to the bankers" (thus also the NIV). *See* Bank.

EXCOMMUNICATION. "A cutting off, deprivation of communion, or the privileges of intercourse; specifically, the formal exclusion of a person from religious communion and privileges" (*Cent. Dict.,* s.v.).

Jewish. The distinction between two kinds has been handed down: The *temporary* exclusion and the *permanent* ban, *ḥērem,* "The Anathema" (which see). The former of these, the *ban of the synagogue,* was among the later Jews the excommunication or exclusion of a Jew, usually for heresy or alleged blasphemy, from the synagogue and the congregation or from familiar intercourse with the Jews. This was a modification of the *anathema,* and owes its origin to Ezra 10:8, where we find that the *ḥērem* (anathema) excluded the man from the congregation and anathematized his goods and possessions but did not consist in putting him to death. This ecclesiastical ban was pronounced for twenty-four different offenses, all of which Maimonides picked out from the Talmud. In the event of the offender's showing signs of penitence it might be revoked.

The excommunicated person was prohibited the use of bath, razor, and the convivial table, and no one was allowed to approach him within four cubits' distance. The term of punishment was thirty days, and it was extended to a second and third thirty days, if necessary. If still rebellious the offender was subjected to the second and severer excommunication, the *ḥērem.*

In the NT, Jewish excommunication is brought before us in the case of the blind man (John 9:22). It was exclusion from the synagogue, i.e., the *nidûî.* Some think that our Lord in Luke 6:22 referred specifically to three forms of Jewish excommunication.

Christian. Excommunication in the Christian church is not merely founded on the natural rights possessed by all societies or in imitation of the Jews. It was instituted by our Lord (Matt. 18:15-17) and consists in the breaking off of all further Christian, brotherly fellowship with one who is hopelessly obdurate. We find the apostle Paul claiming the right to exercise discipline over his converts (2 Cor. 1:23; 13:10) and that formal excommunication on the part of the church was practiced and commanded by him (1 Cor. 5:11; 1 Tim. 1:20; Titus 3:10). The formula of *delivering* or *handing over to Satan* (1 Cor. 5:5; 1 Tim. 1:20) has been open to a difference of interpretation. Some interpret it as being merely a symbol for excommunication, which involves "exclusion from all Christian fellowship, and consequently banishment to the society of those among whom Satan dwelt, and from which the offender had publicly severed himself" (David Brown, in Schaff's *Popular Com.,* 3:180). Alfred Plummer (*Pastoral Epistles,* pp. 75ff.) says that "this handing over to Satan was an apostolic act—a supernatural infliction of bodily infirmity, or disease, or death, as a penalty for grievous sin. It is scarcely doubtful that St. Paul delivered Hymenaeus and Alexander to Satan, in order that Satan might have power to afflict their bodies, with a view to their spiritual amelioration."

Nature of Excommunication. We thus find that excommunication consisted in (1) separation from the communion of the church; (2) having as its *object* the good of the sufferer (1 Cor. 5:5) and protection of sound members (2 Tim. 3:17); (3) that it was wielded by the highest ecclesiastical officer (1 Cor. 5:3; Titus 3:10), promulgated by the congregation to which the offender belonged (1 Cor. 5:4), and in spite of any opposition on the part of a minority (2 Cor. 2:6); (4) that it was for an indefinite duration or for a period; (5) that its duration might be abridged at the discretion and by the indulgence of the person imposing the penalty (v. 8); (6) that penitence was the condition of restoration (v. 7); and (7) that the sentence was publicly revered (v. 10) as it was publicly declared (v. 10).

BIBLIOGRAPHY: J. Bannerman, *The Church of Christ*

(1960), 2:186-200; G. W. Buchanan, *Consequences of the Covenant* (1970), pp. 305-13.

EXECUTION. *See* Punishments.

EXECUTIONER. The Heb. word describes, in the first instance, the office of executioner, and, secondarily, the general duties of the bodyguard of a monarch. Thus Potiphar was "captain of the executioners" (Gen. 37:36, KJV marg.; NIV, "captain of the guard"). That the "captain of the guard" occasionally performed the duty of an executioner himself appears in 1 Kings 2:25, 34. Nevertheless the post was one of high dignity. The Gk. *spekoulatōr* (Mark 6:27) is borrowed from the Lat. *speculator;* originally a military spy or scout, but under the emperors transferred to the bodyguard.

EXERCISE, BODILY. Exercise or training of the body, i.e., gymnastics (1 Tim. 4:8). The apostle appears to disparage not the athletic discipline, but rather that ascetic mortification of the fleshly appetites and even innocent affections (cf. 1 Tim. 4:3; Col. 2:23) characteristic of some Jewish fanatics, especially the *Essenes* (which see).

EXHORTATION (Gk. *paraklēsis,* lit., a "calling near," "invitation"). It appears to have been recognized in the apostolic church as a special supernatural or prophetic function (Rom. 12:8), probably a subordinate exercise of the general faculty of teaching (1 Cor. 14:3). It has been defined as "the act of presenting such motives before a person as may excite him to the performance of duty." The NIV usually renders the idea as "encourage." The Scriptures enjoin ministers to exhort men, i.e., to rouse them to duty by proposing suitable motives (Isa. 58:1; Rom. 12:8), and it was also the constant practice of prophets (Isa. 1:17; Jer. 4:14; Ezek. 37), apostles (Acts 11:23), and of Christ Himself (Luke 3:18) (McClintock and Strong, *Cyclopedia,* s.v.).

EXODUS, THE. The great deliverance extended to the Israelites when "the Lord brought the sons of Israel out of the land of Egypt" (Ex. 12:51), "with a mighty hand and an outstretched arm" (Deut. 26:8), that is, "with full manifestation of divine power."

Preparatory History. The quiet life of the patriarchs terminated in the circumstances subsequent to the selling of Joseph to the Ishmaelites and his later exaltation as viceroy in Egypt. According to the biblical chronology preserved in the MT of the Heb. Bible, the Israelites emigrated to Egypt around 1871 B.C. under the Twelfth Egyptian Dynasty of the Middle Kingdom c. 2000-1780 B.C. Multiplying rapidly in Egypt in the land of Goshen (Gen. 46:26-34) and identified with the area around the Wadi Tumilat in the eastern part of the Nile Delta, the children of Israel soon became an important factor in Egyptian life. The land of Goshen was one of the richest parts of Egypt, "the best of the land"

(47:11). Divine favor plus their happy location were factors in their increasing strength. Many scholars place Joseph's rise to power much later, during the Hyksos Period, c. 1700 B.C., under the unnecessary supposition that it would be "a historical misrepresentation" to imagine that a young Semitic foreigner would have been elevated to such power under a native Egyptian dynasty like the Twelfth or the Eighteenth, but that such an event would be likely under the Semitic conquerors of Egypt, called the Hyksos. Unfortunately, the period 1780-1546 B.C. is one of great obscurity in Egypt, and the Hyksos conquest is as yet imperfectly understood. Although the history of Joseph cannot yet be placed in the frame of known Egyptian history, Israel was in Egypt during this period of confusion and turmoil, and the notice of the accession of an oppressive pharaoh called "a new king . . . who did not know Joseph" (Ex. 1:8) has reference to one of the pharaohs of the New Empire, after the expulsion of the despised Asiatics from Egypt. Consistent with this is the fact that the Israelites were settled about the Hyksos capital of Egypt in the "plain of Tanis" called "the field of Zoan" (Ps. 78:12).

Deliverance. The ten plagues, like the story of Joseph, are replete with authentic local coloring. The plagues were supernatural and consisted of events and phenomena that were natural to Egypt, but with greater intensity and in unusual sequence. Israel's exit from Egypt, as outlined in the Bible narrative (Ex. 12:37; 13:17-18, 20; 14:1-2), has incited a vast amount of skepticism and debate among scholars. However, with increased archaeological knowledge, the biblical itinerary is more and more credible.

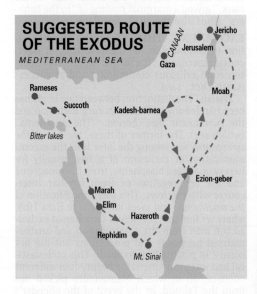

SUGGESTED ROUTE OF THE EXODUS

MEDITERRANEAN SEA

CANAAN

Jericho
Jerusalem
Gaza
Rameses
Moab
Succoth
Kadesh-barnea
Bitter lakes
Ezion-geber
Marah
Elim
Hazeroth
Rephidim
Mt. Sinai

Route of the Exodus. In tracing this itinerary,

it is important to observe that the translation of the Heb. *Yam Sup* ("Red Sea") is plainly incorrect. The proper rendering is "Reed" or "Marsh" Sea. That this can scarcely denote the Red Sea or even its northeastern arm, the Gulf of Suez, is attested by the fact that no reeds exist in the Red Sea, and that the body of water the Israelites actually passed through formed a natural barrier between Egypt and the Sinai wilderness. On the other hand, to reach the Red Sea or its arm, the Gulf of Suez, they would have had to traverse a vast expanse of desert. The account most certainly implies the proximity of the Reed Sea to Succoth, modern Tell el-Mashkutah, some thirty-two miles southeastward of their starting places from Rameses (Avaris, Ex. 12:37). The Reed or Papyrus Sea, which the Israelites miraculously went through, "may reasonably be supposed to be the Papyrus Lake or Papyrus Marsh known from an Egyptian document of the thirteenth century to be located near Tanis" (W. F. Albright, "The Old Testament Archaeology," *O. T. Commentary* [1948], p. 142). The crossing of the Reed Sea was doubtless in the area around Lake Timsah and just S of it. The topography of this region has been changed to some extent since the digging of the Suez Canal. At least one body of water, Lake Ballah, has disappeared. The vicinity of Lake Timsah between Lake Ballah and the Bitter Lakes may well have been more marshy than it is at present. The starting point for the tracing of the biblical route of the Exodus was the identification of Rameses (Avaris). This city was the Hyksos capital, built c. 1720 B.C. It is located in the NE part of the Delta. Leaving Rameses (Avaris), the fleeing Israelite captives began their journey toward Canaan. The direct military route lay immediately parallel to the Mediterranean coast, past the Egyptian frontier fortress of Zilu (Thiel) and thence by "the way of the land of the Philistines" (13:17). This well-guarded and carefully traveled highway giving access to the Egyptian empire in Palestine and lower Syria would have brought the Israelites into immediate open conflict. Their morale and military organization were not equal to this. Quitting Succoth, located some ten miles E from Pithom (1:11) and now identified with Tell Retabeh, the Israelites set camp on the frontier of "the wilderness to the Red (Reed) Sea" (13:18-20), that is, the region of Lake Timsah. Pi-hahiroth, said to be "between Migdol and the sea" and "in front of Baal-zephon" (14:2), was most evidently Egyptian Pi-hathor in the general vicinity of Tanis. Migdol and Baal-zephon are Semitic names perfectly normal for this part of Egypt and attested to by the inscriptions. However, their exact positions have not yet been determined, hence the Israelites in their circuitous journey (13:18) may have gone farther northward than is commonly thought and crossed the water in the region of Lake Ballah. At any rate, the route outlined in the Bible bears every evidence of reliability.

EXODUS, THE DATE OF. The date of Israel's departure from Egypt involves difficult problems, and the subject is filled with confusion. Setting aside extreme views like those of Gardner, Hall, Wreszinski, and others, who regard the story of the Exodus as a garbled version of the Egyptian saga of Hyksos expulsion, or like those of Petrie, Eerdmans, Rowley, and others, who give it a very late date under Merneptah or even somewhat later, only two principal views exist. The first places the event around 1441 B.C. in the reign of Amenhotep II of the Eighteenth Dynasty; the second places it around 1290 B.C. in the reign of Rameses II in the Nineteenth Dynasty.

The Biblical Date. Although any view of the Exodus date is so plagued with problems that many scholars contend that "the complete harmonization" of the biblical account "and our extra-Biblical material is quite impossible," it is, nevertheless, true on the basis of many considerations that the early date view (1441 B.C.) is the biblical one. This is denied by many on the basis of Ex. 1:11 and other evidence. But if one carefully surveys all the scriptural evidence, taking into consideration the whole time scheme underlying the Pentateuch and the early history of Israel to the time of Solomon, it is clear that the OT places this great redemptive event around the middle of the fifteenth century B.C., rather than a full century and a half later. Evidence both within and without the Bible in support of this is not easily set aside.

Explicit Scriptural Statement Places the Exodus about 1441 B.C. In 1 Kings 6:1 it is explicitly stated that Solomon "began to build the house of the Lord" "in the four hundred and eightieth year after the sons of Israel came out of the land of Egypt." The fourth year of Solomon's reign, when he is said to have begun to build the Temple, would be about 961 B.C. Since Solomon ruled forty years (11:42), the fourth year of his reign would be variously computed by modern chronologists: 958 B.C. (Albright), 967 B.C. (Thiele), 962 B.C. (Begrich). Taking the year 961 B.C., which cannot be far wrong, the date 1441 B.C. as the date of the Exodus is computed, and 1871 B.C. as the time of the entrance of Israel into Egypt, since the sojourn there extended to 430 years (Ex. 12:40-41). Albright's date of the Exodus (1290 B.C.) and H. H. Rowley's (1225 B.C.) must reject 1 Kings 6:1 as late and completely unreliable, despite the fact that the chronological notice it gives has every evidence of authenticity and obviously fits into the whole time scheme underlying the Pentateuch and the books of Joshua and Judges (cf. J. W. Jack, *The Date of the Exodus* [1925], pp. 200-16). Scholars who thus drastically curtail the period of the Judges by a century and a half or two centuries, which the biblical figures place about 1400 to 1050 B.C., practically reject the possibility of fitting the biblical chronology into the framework of contemporary history.

Contemporary Egyptian History Allows the 1441 B.C. Date of the Exodus. This date falls very likely toward the opening years of the reign of Amenhotep II (c. 1450-1425 B.C.), son of the famous conqueror and empire-builder Thutmose III (c. 1482-1450 B.C.). The commanding person of Thutmose III, one of the greatest of the pharaohs, furnishes an ideal figure for the events of the Exodus. In the contemporary records of Amenhotep II, who would be the pharaoh who hardened his heart and would not let the children of Israel go, of course no references occur to such national disasters as the ten plagues and the loss of the Egyptian army in the Red (Reed) Sea, much less to the escape of the Hebrews. But this circumstance is to be expected. The Egyptians were the last people to record their misfortunes. Nor is there any sign upon the mummy of Amenhotep II, discovered in 1898, to show that he was drowned at sea. Nor does the Bible state that he was or that he personally accompanied his army into the water (Ex. 14:23-31). If Amenhotep II was the reigning pharaoh of the Exodus, his eldest son was slain in the tenth plague (12:29). It seems clear from the monuments that Thutmose IV (c. 1425-1412) was not the eldest son of Amenhotep II. The so-called Dream Inscription of Thutmose IV, recorded on an immense slab of red granite between the paws of the Sphinx at Gizeh, recounts the prophecy that the young Thutmose would one day be pharaoh. Such a prophecy would have been pointless had the young man been the firstborn son of Amenhotep, since the law of primogeniture was in force in Egypt at that time. Thutmose III was a great builder and employed Semitic captives in his wide-scale construction projects. His vizier, named Rekhmire, left a tomb on which scenes of brick-making are depicted, recalling Ex. 5:6-19. Semitic foreigners are significantly found among the bricklayers on this tomb. The bricklayers are quoted as saying "He supplies us with bread, beer and every good thing," while the taskmasters warn the laborers: "The rod is in my hand; be not idle." Finally Joseph died and "a new king arose over Egypt, who did not know Joseph" (1:8). This ruler seems to have been the founder or an early king of the powerful Eighteenth Dynasty (1546-1319 B.C.). Because the Hyksos invasion of Egypt was led by Semites and not by Hurrians or Indo-Aryans, as recent studies have shown (W. F. Albright, *The O. T. and Modern Study* [1951], p. 44), it appears that the expulsion of the Hyksos around the middle of the sixteenth century B.C. was the important event that resulted in the oppression of the Israelites. Not until about 1570 B.C. were the Hyksos invaders driven out and the powerful Eighteenth Dynasty founded. Very likely under the

kings of the Eighteenth Dynasty who preceded Thutmose III—Amenhotep I (1546-1525 B.C.), Thutmose I (1525-1508 B.C.), and Thutmose II (1508-1504 B.C.)—and under Queen Hatshepsut (1504-1482 B.C.), the Hebrew bondage became increasingly severe. About 1520 B.C. Moses was born, probably during the reign of Thutmose I, whose daughter, the well-known Hatshepsut, seems to have been the princess who found the baby Moses among the reeds by the riverside (2:5-10). After a struggle with Queen Hatshepsut, Thutmose III came into power about 1486 B.C. This event doubtless inaugurated the last and most severe phase of Israelite oppression.

Egyptian priest with offering-table, c. 1450 B.C.

Contemporary Events in Palestine Substantiate the 1441 B.C. Date of the Exodus. If the Exodus took place around 1441 B.C. the Israelites entered Canaan around 1401 B.C. Is there any evidence of such an invasion in extrabiblical monuments? The Amarna Letters, which concern this very period (c. 1400-1366 B.C.), refer to such an invasion, as has been known virtually from their discovery in 1886. These invaders, called Habiru, are sometimes equated etymologically with the Hebrews. There are many serious problems involved, and the best scholars are divided on the matter, but the statement of J. W. Jack is still pertinent, especially in the light of plain statement and clear intimations of the OT concerning the date of the Exodus. "Who are these invaders of south and central Palestine. . . . Who else could they be but the Hebrews of the Exodus, and have we not here the native version of their entry into the land?" (*The Date of the Exodus*, p. 128). For a full discussion see Jack, pp. 119-41.

In the Amarna Letters the correspondence of Abi-Hiba, governor of Jerusalem, with Pharaoh Akhnaton (c. 1370 B.C.), Egyptian military aid is requested against the Habiru (but *see* article Amarna, el-). The fall of Jericho favors the 1441 B.C. date of the Exodus as a result of the excavations of Ernest Sellin (1907-9) and especially those of John Garstang (1930-36). City D, which was taken by Joshua and the invading Israelites, was constructed about 1500 B.C., and fell around 1400 B.C. Moreover, the Egyptian empire was falling through the fingers of Pharaohs Amenhotep III and IV about 1400-1360, precisely when the Hebrews would have been conquering Canaan, according to the early date of the Exodus.

Objections to the Biblical Date. Many scholars who set aside OT chronological notices as frequently of little historical value would strenuously object to calling the 1441 B.C. date of the Exodus the biblical one. They would place it around 1290 B.C., urging the following objections:

1. It would be very improbable that Israel would have entered Egypt before the Hyksos period. Abraham went to Egypt and moved freely in high circles under the Middle Kingdom (Gen. 13:10-12), and there is no reason Joseph may not have done so at a later pre-Hyksos period, especially when his exaltation is presented in the OT narratives as entirely providential. Moreover, the details of the story have a strong Egyptian and not a Hyksos (Semitic) coloring. Had the reigning king been Hyksos, the Hebrew shepherds would not have been segregated in Goshen and

Rameses II

a point made of the fact that "every shepherd is loathsome to the Egyptians" (46:34).

2. Exodus 1:11 is supposed to place the Exodus definitely later. But 1 Kings 6:1 is just as explicit for the earlier date. The question is, Are these two notices at variance with one another? The explanation is that Rameses (Avaris) is a modernization of its older name, and the fact that this site was called Rameses only from about 1300 to 1100 B.C. is not a decisive argument against the early date. The reference in Ex. 1:11 must be to the older city Avaris where the oppressed Israelites labored centuries earlier. Since Avaris was once a flourishing city before the Hyksos were driven out (c. 1570 B.C.), there was plenty of time for the Israelites in bondage to have constructed the earlier city as they went down into Egypt about 1870 B.C. Moreover, it is hardly conceivable that such renowned conquerors and builders as Thutmose III and Amenhotep II would have abandoned all interest in the Delta area, because this rich and vital territory was necessary to the security of their Asiatic domain.

3. Archaeological evidence from Transjordan, Lachish, and Debir allegedly disproves the early date of the Exodus. Nelson Glueck's surface explorations in Transjordan and in the Arabah are supposed to demonstrate that there was a gap in the sedentary population of this region from about 1900 to about 1300 B.C., so that had Israel come up out of Egypt about 1400 there would supposedly have been no Edomite, Ammonite, and Moabite kingdoms to resist their progress. Only scattered nomads would have met them (cf. Num. 20:14, 17-18). But there is nothing in the narrative to demand anything more than a simple agricultural economy that would have left little or no material remains. Also archaeological evidence at Lachish and Debir is not sufficiently evident to set aside the whole testimony supporting the earlier date. The destruction of Bethel, Lachish, and Debir is claimed to have occurred about 1230 B.C., and therefore to support a late date for the Exodus. Those cities fell about the same time and near the beginning of the Conquest, according to the Joshua narrative. But it is important to note that although Joshua captured Bethel, Lachish, and Debir, nothing is said about destroying them; he burned only Ai, Jericho, and Hazor (Josh. 6:24; 8:19; 11:13). Some of Joshua's conquests were not permanent. We know that Debir had to be recaptured later (Josh. 15:13-17), and possibly the others did also. If dates of destruction at Bethel, Lachish, and Debir are correct, they may well refer to attacks during the days of the Judges instead of to Joshua's conquests.   M.F.U.; H.F.V.

EX'ODUS, BOOK OF (ek'so-dus; from the Gk. *ex,* "out," and *hodos,* "way," "a going out"). Whereas Genesis is the book of origins, Exodus is the book of redemption. Delivered out of Egyptian bondage, the newly constituted nation is endowed with the law, priesthood, and sacrificial system, providing for the worship and regulation of a redeemed people.

Name. The book is named from the Lat. "exodus," through the LXX *exodus,* signifying "out-going" or "departure" (cf. 19:1; Heb. 11:22). The ancient Hebrews, in accordance with their practice of designating the holy books from one or more of the opening words, called it *we ʾelleh sheMōt* ("and these are the names"), or simply *sheMōt,* ("names").

Aim. The book of Exodus deals with the great event of the redemption from Egypt. It typifies our redemption and traces the constitution of Jacob's descendants as a theocratic nation at Mt. Sinai. God, who until this time had been related to the Israelites only through the Abrahamic covenant, now brings Himself in relationship to them nationally through redemption. As a people selected to bring forth the promised Redeemer, they are put under the Mosaic covenant. The divine Presence resides among them under the cloud of glory. The constitution, Tabernacle, priesthood, and sacrificial system are minutely typical of the Person and work of Christ (note the message of the book of Hebrews). Exodus is preeminently the book of redemption.

Outline.

I. The Hebrews in Egypt (1:1–12:36)
II. The Hebrews in the wilderness (12:37–18:37)
III. The Hebrews at Sinai (19:1–40:38)

Critical View. As in the case with Genesis and the rest of the Pentateuch, higher critics deny the Mosaic authorship and authenticity of Exodus, claiming that the book is a compilation of J, E, and P sources. This partitionist theory, however, is constructed upon shaky presuppositions involving false literary criteria and philosophic hypotheses, notably the erroneous notion that the development of Israel and Israel's institutions were in no way different from the progressive, evolutionary development of other peoples. Sound views of inspiration must reject the essential claims of this so-called Graf-Keunen-Wellhausen theory of pentateuchal criticism as being incompatible with the claims of the Pentateuch itself and its foundational place in the whole scheme of divine revelation and redemptive history.

Conservative View. The book of Exodus is historical and from the time of Moses, who is its author. As with the other books of the Pentateuch, the great lawgiver may have used ancient sources, oral or written, but the Pentateuch bears the unmistakable hand of a one-author unity and bears the impress everywhere—in miracle, prophecy, type, and symbol—of divine inspiration, historicity, and authenticity.

BIBLIOGRAPHY: S. R. Driver, *The Book of Exodus* (1953); G. E. Mendenhall, *Law and Covenant in Israel and the* *Ancient Near East* (1955); C. de Wit, *The Date and Route of the Exodus* (1960); K. A. Kitchen, *Ancient Orient and Old Testament* (1966), pp. 57-75; U. Cassuto, *A Commentary on the Book of Exodus* (1967); R. K. Harrison, *Introduction to the Old Testament* (1969), pp. 556-58; J. J. Davis, *Moses and the Gods of Egypt: Studies in Exodus* (1971); R. A. Cole, *Exodus, an Introduction and Commentary,* Tyndale Old Testament Commentaries (1973); B. S. Childs, *The Book of Exodus* (1974); G. Bush, *Notes on Exodus,* 2 vols. (1976); J. J. Bimson, *Redating the Exodus and Conquest* (1981); C. R. Erdman, *The Book of Exodus* (1982); G. Wagner, *Practical Truths from Israel's Wanderings* (1982).

EX'ORCISM (ek'sor-sizm). The practice of using magical words and ceremonies to expel evil spirits or demons. The phenomenon was characteristic of heathenism. The Jews at Ephesus encountered by Paul (Acts 19:13-19) illustrate an attempt to mix pagan traffic in demonology with expulsion of evil spirits by the power of God. *See also* Magic: Various Forms.   M.F.U.

EXPEDIENCY, EXPEDIENT (Gk. *sumpherō,* to "advantage"). "The principle of doing what is deemed most practicable or serviceable under the circumstances." A familiar rule of expediency is that laid down by the apostle Paul: "Therefore, if food causes my brother to stumble, I will never eat meat again, that I might not cause my brother to stumble" (1 Cor. 8:13). The occasion of this declaration was his writing to the Corinthians respecting the Christian's attitude toward *flesh offered up to idols* (which see). This would give offense to those with scrupulous consciences, while others, like Paul, might make light of the matter, so far as personal feeling was concerned. "It is impossible to state more strongly than does the apostle the obligation to refrain from indulging in things indifferent when the use of them is an occasion of sin to others. Yet it is never to be forgotten that this, by its very nature, is a principle the application of which must be left to every man's conscience in the sight of God. No rule of conduct founded on expediency can be enforced by church discipline. It was right in Paul to refuse to eat flesh for fear of causing others to offend, but he could not justly be subjected to censure had he seen fit to eat. The same principle is illustrated in reference to circumcision. The apostle utterly refused to circumcise Titus, and yet he circumcised Timothy, in both cases acting wisely and conscientiously. Whenever a thing is right or wrong, according to circumstances, every man must have the right to judge of those circumstances. Otherwise he is judge of another man's conscience, a new rule of duty is introduced, and the catalogue of *adiaphora* (i.e., things indifferent or nonessential), which has existed in every system of ethics from the beginning, is simply abolished" (T. W. Chambers in Meyer, *Com.* on 1 Cor. 8).

EXPERIENCE. We speak of our knowledge of

sins forgiven and enjoyment of the favor of God as our Christian *experience*. It means the practical acquaintance with the work of God in man that results in the consciousness of salvation. Thus experience is the personal trial of all things and the consequent knowledge of it.

EXPIATION. In the theological sense, this term denotes the end accomplished by certain divinely appointed sacrifices in respect to freeing the sinner from the punishment of his sins. The sacrifices recognized as expiatory are the sin offerings of the OT dispensation (*see* Offering; Sacrifice), and, preeminently, the offerings that Christ made of Himself for the sins of the world (*see* Atonement).

The above definition is made somewhat general for the purpose of including both of the theories that accept expiation in any real sense.

Calvinistic View. The Calvinistic or Satisfaction view teaches that the sacrifice of Christ was expiatory in the sense that Christ suffered vicariously the punishment of the sins of the elect. The expiation thus is absolute in behalf of the limited number for whom it is made. For the nonelect, or reprobate, there is no expiation. *See* Election.

Arminian View. The Arminian theory of expiation holds that the sacrificial sufferings of Christ were not of the nature of punishment, but were a divinely appointed, though conditional, substitute for the punishment of the sins of all mankind. The sacrifice of Christ is expiatory in the sense that all who truly repent of their sins and believe on Christ have, on account of that sacrifice, their guilt canceled, the punishment of their sins remitted.

The two theories are alike in regarding Christ's sacrifice as the objective ground of forgiveness.

Moral Influence View. The third prominent theory of the atonement, the moral influence theory, admits of no necessity for sacrificial expiation and denies the expiatory character of sacrifices. According to this theory, Christ died to provide an example of devotion to truth and duty—the kind of devotion that might lead to a martyr's death.

As to the fact of expiation by sacrifice, the following should be noted:

1. The idea of expiation, or of seeking reconciliation with Deity through sacrifices, is a common feature of most if not all forms of religion. It is a fair supposition that, despite all the false conceptions held in connection with the idea, some measure of important truth lies at the bottom.

2. Among the sacrifices appointed by God under the OT dispensation, there were sacrifices for which the purpose was clearly expiatory. Not only the simple and most natural understanding of such sacrifices, but also the divine teaching concerning them, was that they stood in important relation to the forgiveness of sins (*see* Lev. 17:11). Preeminent among these were the sacrifices on the great annual Day of Atonement. *See* Sacrifices; Offerings; Atonement, Day of. It is not, however, to be understood that the blood of beasts of itself had expiatory value and effect, or that the offerings in a mechanical or commercial way brought about reconciliation (*see* Ps. 50; Isa. 1; Amos 5:22). It was only because of divine grace that these sacrifices availed for reconciliation. The sacrifices were not only appointed by God, but were also provided by Him (Lev. 17:11; Ps. 50:10).

3. In the NT dispensation, of which the OT was predictive and for which it was preparatory, the sacrifice that Christ offered of Himself is conspicuously set before us as the ground of the forgiveness of sins. Christ is "the Lamb of God who takes away the sin of the world." He is the "Lamb . . . slain" "from the foundation of the world." It was Christ's own declaration that His blood was shed "for forgiveness of sins" (see John 1:29; Rev. 13:8; Matt. 26:28; *see also* John 3:14; Col. 1:14, 20; Heb. 9:13-14; 10:1-12; etc.).

As to the necessity of expiation, from which it arises, *see* Atonement.   E.MCC.

BIBLIOGRAPHY: C. H. Dodd, *The Bible and the Greeks* (1954), pp. 82-95; L. L. Morris, *Apostolic Preaching of the Cross* (1965), pp. 144-213.

EYE. Used as the symbol of a large number of objects and ideas, as in the following: (1) frequently a *fountain;* (2) *color* (Num. 11:7, in the Heb.; *see* marg., KJV); (3) the *face* or *surface* (Ex. 10:5, 15; Num. 22:5, 11, as "the surface, i.e., eye of the land"); the expression "between the eyes" means the *forehead* (Ex. 13:9, 16, see marg.); (4) in Song of Sol. 4:9, KJV, "eye" is better rendered "glance" in the NASB and NIV; (5) "eye" (marg., KJV, Prov. 23:31, for "colour") is applied to the beads or bubbles of wine when it is poured out (NASB, NIV, "sparkles"; NASB marg., "gives its eye"); (6) "before the eyes" (KJV, Gen. 23:11, 18; Ex. 4:30) is better translated in the NASB as "in the presence of," "in the sight of"; "in the eyes" (KJV, Gen. 19:8) of anyone means according to his judgment or opinion ("whatever you like," NASB and NIV); (7) to "set the eyes" (Gen. 44:21; Job 24:23; Jer. 39:12, marg.) upon anyone is to regard with favor, but may also be used in a negative sense (Amos 9:8); (8) many of the passions, such as envy, pride, pity, etc., being expressed by the eye, such phrases as the following occur: "evil eye" (Matt. 20:15, marg., i.e., "envious," thus also NIV); "bountiful eye" (Prov. 22:9, KJV; NIV, "generous"); "seductive eyes" (Isa. 3:16); "eyes full of adultery" (2 Pet. 2:14); "the lust of the eyes" (1 John 2:16); "the desire of your eyes" (Ezek. 24:16) denotes whatever is a great delight; (9) to guard as the "apple [pupil] of the eye" (Deut. 32:10; Zech. 2:8) is to preserve with special care; "as the eyes of servants look to the hand of their master" (Ps. 123:2) is an expression that seems to indicate that masters, especially in the presence of strangers, communicated with their servants by certain motions of their hands.

EYES, BLINDING OF. *See* Punishments.

EYES, COVERING OF THE (Gen. 20:16, KJV; NASB, *see* marg.). A phrase of much disputed significance, understood by some to mean that Abimelech advised Sarah and her women, while in or near towns, to conform to the general custom of wearing *veils* (*see* Dress). Another view is the following: "By the 'covering of the eyes' we are not to understand a veil, which Sarah was to procure for a thousand shekels, but it is a figurative expression for an atoning gift, . . . so that he may forget a wrong done, and explained by the analogy of the phrase he covereth the faces of the judges, i.e., he bribes them (Job 9:24)" (K. & D., *Com.*, ad loc.). The NIV renders "cover the offense."

EYES, PAINTING THE. Refers rather to the eyelids. An ancient practice known to the Hebrews and to the Egyptians millennia before them. About 4000 B.C. the Badarians of Egypt were accustomed to grind green malachite on slate palettes to use for eye paint. This was not only a beauty aid but an excellent germicide. It is still used by Africans and is particularly effective when spread around the eyes as protection against flies. One of the finest monuments of Narmer, one of the kings of the First Dynasty of Egypt, c. 2900 B.C., is a palette found at Hierakonpolis. The palette, similar to those on which the Egyptians had long ground eye paint, is of a very large size befitting a great king. The painting of the eyelids was doubtless copied by the Hebrews from their Egyptian, Phoenician, and Mesopotamian neighbors. Jezebel is spoken of as having "painted her eyes" (2 Kings 9:30). This practice was also very common in Phoenicia. Painting of the eyes is mentioned among other methods that women used to win admiration. Compare Jer. 4:30: "enlarge your eyes with paint" and Ezek. 23:40: "for whom you bathed, painted your eyes, and decorated yourselves with ornaments." Eye paint was also prepared from antimony ore, which when pulverized produced a black powder with metallic brilliancy. It was generally made into an ointment and applied to the eyebrows and eyelashes with an eye pencil.   M.F.U.

EYE SALVE (Gk. *kollourion,* diminutive of *kollura,* coarse bread of cylindrical shape). A preparation shaped like a *kollura,* composed of various materials and used as a remedy for tender eyelids (Rev. 3:18).

E'ZAR. *See* Ezer.

EZ'BAI (ez'bye). The father of Naarai, one of David's mighty men (1 Chron. 11:37), after 1000 B.C.

EZ'BON (ez'bon).

1. The fourth son of the patriarch Gad (Gen. 46:16), also called (Num. 26:16) Ozni.

2. The first named of the sons of Bela, the son of Benjamin (1 Chron. 7:7).

EZEKI'AS. A Gk. form (Matt. 1:9-10, KJV) of the name of King *Hezekiah* (which see).

EZE'KIEL (e-zēk'yel; Heb. *yᵉhezqē'l,* "God will strengthen"). The son of a priest named Buzi, and one of the four greater prophets.

Ezekiel was taken captive in the captivity of Jehoiachin, eleven years before the destruction of Jerusalem (2 Kings 24:12-15). He was a member of a community of Jewish exiles who settled on the banks of the Chebar, a "river" or canal of Babylonia. It was by this river, "in the land of the Chaldeans," that God's message first reached him (Ezek. 1:3). His call took place "in the fifth year of King Jehoiachin's exile" (1:2; 592 B.C.). It now seems generally agreed that it was the thirtieth year from the new era of Nabopolassar, father of *Nebuchadnezzar* (which see). We learn from an incidental allusion (24:18)—the only reference that he makes to his personal history—that he was married and had a house (8:1) in his place of exile and lost his wife by a sudden and unforeseen stroke. He lived in the highest consideration among his companions in exile, and their elders consulted him on all occasions (8:1; 11:25; 14:1; 20:1; etc.). The last date he mentions is the twenty-seventh year of the captivity (29:17), so that his mission extended over twenty-two years.

He is distinguished by his firm and inflexible energy of will and character, and we also observe a devoted adherence to the rites and ceremonies of his national religion. Ezekiel is no cosmopolite, but displays everywhere the peculiar tendencies of a Hebrew educated under Levitical training. We may also note in Ezekiel the absorbed recognition of his high calling, which enabled him cheerfully to endure any privation or misery, if thereby he could give any warning or lesson to his people (chap. 4; 24:15-16; etc.), whom he so ardently loved (9:8; 11:13).

EZEKIEL, BOOK OF. This major prophecy takes the name of the prophet whose writing it records. Ezekiel was the son of a priest named Buzi and without doubt a priest himself (1:3). Together with King Jehoiachin he was taken captive to Babylon in 597 B.C. He settled in Babylonia in a place called Tel-abib (1:1; 3:15) by the River Chebar, a great canal SE of Babylon. He began his ministry in the fifth year of the captivity of Jehoiachin when he was about thirty years old (cf. 1:1). His ministry lasted about twenty-two years, until 571 B.C. (29:17), his last dated prophecy. It is not certain whether he survived to see King Jehoiachin liberated by Evil-Merodach in 560 B.C.

Authorship and Date. The unity and authenticity of the book of Ezekiel were not seriously attacked until comparatively recent times. As late as 1924 Gustav Hoelscher observed that the critical knife had been laid on practically all the OT prophetic books except Ezekiel's prophecy. Accordingly, following the methods of Duhm, he dissected the book, leaving not much more than one-tenth of it as authentic—the comparatively few rhythmical sections. The rest, the prosaic parts, he assumed were written by fifth-century authors.

V. Herntrich, *Ezekielprobleme* (1932), although largely rejecting Hoelscher's theses, approached the book in essentially the same way. W. A. Irwin rejects chaps. 40-48 entirely and accepts only 250 verses of the rest. (*The Problem of Ezekiel* [1943]). In 1930 C. C. Torrey rejected the book as a pseudoepigraph of Palestinian origin and dated it c. 230 B.C. (*Pseudo-Ezekiel and the Original Prophecy* [1930], p. 150). N. Messel (1945), and A. Bentzen (1949), advocate similar if not such drastic views. Criticism of Ezekiel illustrates the wearisome story of negative criticism. It is conceived in doubt and born in complete confusion and uncertainty. The critics' subtle attempts to solve the so-called problem of Ezekiel need not trouble the Christian student who firmly believes in and has a vital knowledge of the supernatural in his own experience. Negative critical views are largely dictated by disbelief in the supernatural. Because it contains so many supernatural visions and so much apocalyptic imagery, which, as with the book of Daniel, is reflected in the book of Revelation, it was inevitable that negative criticism would dismember the book of Ezekiel despite manifold evidences of its genuineness, which the older critics like Cornill freely admitted (*Einleitung*, p. 76). The arrangement and plan, the accurate dating, the use of the first person, and the clear-cut prophetic purpose all point to genuine authorship by Ezekiel.

Purpose. Ezekiel's mission was one of comfort to the captives in Babylon, constituting "the whole house of Israel" (cf. 37:11, 15-24). He directed his prophecies toward demonstrating that Jehovah was justified in permitting the captivity of His people; this is the dominant theme in chaps. 8-33. Proof is presented that instead of wiping them out, as God had done with other nations who had committed similar abominations, His dealing with His own covenant people was preventive and corrective. The purpose was to instruct them to know that He was God, that the neighboring nations exulting over their fall would be judged (25:1–32:32), and that the nation would finally be restored in the mediatorial Davidic kingdom (33:1; 48:35). The phrase "you [or "they"] will know that I am the Lord" occurs more than thirty times in 6:7–39:28.

Contents.

I. Introduction: Ezekiel's call and commission (1:1–3:27)

II. Prophecies against Judah and Jerusalem (4:1–24:27)

III. Prophecies against surrounding nations (25:1–32:32)
   A. Against Ammon (25:1-7)
   B. Against Moab (25:8-11)
   C. Against Edom (25:12-14)
   D. Against Philistia (25:15-17)
   E. Against Tyre (26:1–28:19)
   F. Against Sidon (28:20-26)
   G. Against Egypt (29:1–32:32)

IV. Prophecies of Israel's final restoration (33:1–48:35)
   A. Events preceding the restoration (33:1–39:29)
      1. Wicked purged out (33:1-33)
      2. False shepherds give way to true Shepherd (34:1-31)
      3. Restoration of the land (35:1-15)
      4. Restoration of the people (36: 15–37:28)
      5. Judgment of enemies (38:1–39:24)
      6. Vision of the restored nation (39: 25-29)
   B. Worship in the Kingdom (40:1–48:35)
      1. Millennial temple (40:1–43:27)
      2. Millennial worship (44:1–46:24)
      3. Millennial land (47:1–48:35)

BIBLIOGRAPHY: C. L. Feinberg, *The Prophecy of Ezekiel* (1969); R. K. Harrison, *Introduction to the Old Testament* (1969), pp. 822-55; J. B. Taylor, *Ezekiel*, Tyndale Old Testament Commentaries (1969); R. Alexander, *Ezekiel* (1976); E. W. Hengstenberg, *The Prophecies of the Prophet Ezekiel* (1976); F. A. Tatford, *Dead Bones Live* (1977); P. Fairbairn, *An Exposition of Ezekiel* (1979).

E'ZEL (ē'zel; "separation"). The memorial stone, place of the meeting and parting of David and Jonathan (1 Sam. 20:19). The marg. of the KJV has "that showeth the way"; the marg. of the RV has "this mound."

E'ZEM (ē'zĕm; a "bone"). A city in the tribe of Simeon, originally included within the southern territory of Judah, near Baalah (or Balah or Bilhah) and Eltolad (Josh. 15:29; 19:3; 1 Chron. 4:29). Probably Ummel 'Azam, eleven miles SE of Beersheba.

E'ZER (ē'zer; "help").

1. The father of Hushah, one of the posterity of Hur, of the tribe of Judah (1 Chron. 4:4).

2. A son (or descendant) of Ephraim who, with Elead, was slain by the aboriginal inhabitants of Gath "because they came down to take their livestock" (1 Chron. 7:21).

3. The first named of the Gadite champions who went to David at Ziklag (1 Chron. 12:9), after 1000 B.C.

4. The son of Jeshua, the "official of Mizpah" who repaired part of the city walls near the armory (Neh. 3:19), 445 B.C.

5. One of the priests who assisted in the dedica-

tion of the walls of Jerusalem under Nehemiah (Neh. 12:42), 445 B.C.

6. One of the sons of Seir, a chief "descended from the Horites" (Gen. 36:21, 27, 30; 1 Chron. 1:38, 42).

EZION-GEBER (e′zi-on-gē′ber). Solomon's naval base at the head of the Gulf of Aqaba (1 Kings 9:26) has been identified with Tell el-Kheleifeh, about 500 yards from the shore of the gulf. Nelson Glueck led a Smithsonian-American Schools of Oriental Research dig there during the spring seasons of 1938 to 1940. What he found was a heavily fortified site an acre and a half in extent and having five periods of occupation, from Solomon's day to the fourth century B.C. In the NW corner of the site he found an installation that he identified as a copper smelting and refining plant. Subsequently he decided the structure was not a smeltery but a citadel also used as a storehouse or granary, and he concluded that Tell el-Kheleifeh may have been only a satellite of Ezion-geber instead of the port itself. The tell is not on the seacoast. Archaeological work in the southern Arabah has shown that the copper industry in the area did not date to Solomon's day, and various scholars have suggested that Ezion-geber may have been on the island of Jezira Fara'un, about 300 yards from the shore at Eilat. *See* J. J. Davis, *The New International Dictionary of Biblical Archaeology* (1983), pp. 189-91.

H.F.V.

The shoreline of Eilat, near ancient Ezion-geber

EZ′NITE (ez′nīt). Apparently the patronymic of *Adino* (which see) given (2 Sam. 23:8) as chief among David's captains. Concerning this doubtful rendering, Luther expresses the following opinion: "We believe the text to have been corrupted by a writer, probably from some book in an unknown character and bad writing, so that *orer* should be substituted for *adino,* and *ha-ez-nib* for *eth hanitho*"; that is to say, the reading in the Chronicles (1 Chron. 11:11), "he lifted up

his spear," should be adopted (K. & D., *Com.*). This is done in the NIV.

EZ′RA (ez′ra; "help"). The name of two persons connected with the return of the Jews from Babylon.

1. The priest who led the second expedition of Jews back from Babylonian exile into Palestine, and the author of the book bearing his name (*see* the last four chapters, in which he speaks in the first person). Ezra was a lineal descendant of Phinehas, the grandson of Aaron (Ezra 7:1-5), being a son of Seraiah, who was the grandson of Hilkiah, high priest in the reign of Josiah. He is described as a "scribe skilled in the law of Moses" (v. 6); "a scribe, learned in the words of the commandments of the Lord and His statutes to Israel" (v. 11); "Ezra the priest, the scribe of the law of the God of heaven" (v. 12).

Ezra's priestly extraction acted as a powerful lever for directing his vigorous efforts specifically to the promotion of religion and learning among his people. It is recorded (7:10) that he "had set his heart to study the law of the Lord, and to practice it, and to teach His statutes and ordinances in Israel." Living in Babylon he gained the favor of King Artaxerxes, and obtained from him a commission to go up to Jerusalem (about 459 B.C.). The king's commission invited all the Israelites, priests, and Levites in the whole empire, who so wished, to accompany Ezra. Of these a list amounting to 1,754 is given (chap. 8); and these, doubtless, form part of the full list of the returned captives contained in Nehemiah (chap. 7), and in duplicate (Ezra 2). Ezra was allowed to take with him a large freewill offering of gold and silver, and silver vessels contributed by the Jews, by the king himself, and by his counselors. He was also empowered to draw upon the king's treasures beyond the river for any further supplies required, and all priests, Levites, and other ministers of the Temple were exempted from taxation. Ezra received authority to appoint magistrates and judges in Judea, with power of life and death over all offenders (7:11-28). His credentials were endorsed by the seven principal members of the royal council (v. 14).

Ezra assembled the Jews who accompanied him on the banks of the Ahava River, where they camped for three days. As mentioned above, the number was about 1,500 and included several of high-priestly and Davidic descent. Upon inspection he found that they did not have a single Levite among them. He sent a deputation to Casiphia, where many of them lived, and succeeded in adding 38 Levites and 220 Temple servants to the expedition (8:15-20). The valuable offerings to the Temple he placed in the custody of 12 of the most distinguished priests and Levites, but such was his trust in God and his lofty courage, that he refrained from asking the king for protection (v. 22). After fasting "that we might humble ourselves before our God" (vv. 21-23), the company started on its journey on the twelfth day of the first month (in the spring) of the seventh year of Artaxerxes I.

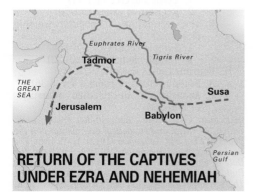

RETURN OF THE CAPTIVES UNDER EZRA AND NEHEMIAH

It reached Jerusalem without incident at the beginning of the fifth month (7:8). Three days after the company's arrival the treasures were weighed and delivered to the proper custodians, burnt sacrifices were offered by the returned exiles, and the king's commissions were delivered to viceroys and governors (8:32-36). In accordance with the royal decree, Ezra was now to be firmly established in Jerusalem as chief judge, empowered to settle everything relating to the religion of the Jews and the life that was regulated by it. Ezra soon found, to his great distress, that the people of Jerusalem had paid no regard to the law forbidding the marriage of Israelites with heathen. Overwhelmed by his emotion, he tore his robe, pulled his hair, and "sat down appalled." Men of tender conscience gathered around him, and all remained in mourning until the hour of the evening sacrifice, when Ezra poured out his soul in prayer (9:1-15). By this time a great congregation had gathered about Ezra, and "wept bitterly." At length Shecaniah declared the guilt of the people and their wish to comply fully with the law. A general assembly was called to meet in Jerusalem within three days to decide what course should be pursued. The people assembled on the twentieth day of the ninth month amid a great storm of rain, and having confessed their sin, they proceeded to remedy the situation with order and deliberation. All the heathen wives were put away, including those who had borne children, by the beginning of the new year (chap. 10).

Whether Ezra remained after the events recorded above, occupying about eight months, or returned to Babylon, is not known. It is conjectured by some that Ezra remained governor until superseded by Nehemiah; others think that he continued his labors in conjunction with Nehemiah. Our next mention of him is in connection with Nehemiah after the completion of the walls

of Jerusalem. The functions he executed under Nehemiah's government were purely of a priestly and ecclesiastical character, such as reading and interpreting the law of Moses to the people, praying for the congregation, assisting in the dedication of the walls, and proclaiming the religious reformation effected by Nehemiah (Neh. 8:9; 12:26). In the sealing of the covenant (10:1-27), Ezra perhaps was listed under the patronymic Seraiah or Azariah (v. 2). As Ezra is not mentioned after Nehemiah's departure for Babylon, and as everything fell into confusion in Nehemiah's absence, it is not unlikely that Ezra had again returned to Babylon before Nehemiah.

Ezra had a profound love for the Word of God, and "set his heart to study the law of the Lord" (Ezra 7:10); he was a man of excellent judgment (7:25), of a conscience (9:3) that led him to deplore sin deeply and strenuously oppose it. So great was his sense of dependence upon God that every step he took was marked by some devout acknowledgment of the divine help, "according to the hand of the Lord my God" (7:6, 9, 27-28; 8:22, 31).

2. The head of one of the twenty-two divisions of priests that returned from captivity with Zerubbabel and Jeshua (Neh. 12:1), 536 B.C. The same name appears in v. 13, where it is stated that his son, Meshullam, was head of his family in the time of the high priest Joiakim (*see* v. 12); also in v. 33, as one of the chief Israelites who formed the first division that made the circuit of the walls of Jerusalem when rebuilt, 445 B.C.

3. A descendant of Judah (1 Chron. 4:17, KJV). *See* Ezrah.

BIBLIOGRAPHY: G. Rawlinson, *Ezra and Nehemiah: Their Lives and Times* (1890).

EZRA, BOOK OF. In the ancient Heb. Scriptures Ezra and Nehemiah were classified as one book called "the Book of Ezra." Since 1448, Heb. Bibles have contained the twofold arrangement of Ezra and Nehemiah, as in our English renderings. In the LXX Ezra and Nehemiah follow Chronicles. That seems a more logical idea since Ezra and Nehemiah carry on the history at the point where Chronicles leaves off, and since the Masoretic notes on the Writings stand as the conclusion of Nehemiah and not Chronicles. Critics commonly consider Chronicles, Ezra, and Nehemiah as originally a single work, but the reasons given for that are not completely satisfying.

Authorship and Date. There is no solid reason to give up the supposition that Ezra is the author, despite the theorizing of modern critics. It is possible that a later inspired compiler consulted Ezra's memoirs written in the first person (7:27–9:15). However, it is very likely that Ezra himself compiled that material as a framework for the book and filled out the remaining parts written in the third person from other sources to make it a unified whole. Assuming that Ezra is also the author of Chronicles, according to tradition, then the book of Ezra must have followed Chronicles somewhere during the period of 430-400 B.C. or a little later. Ezra's activity is evidently to be placed during the reign of Artaxerxes I (465-414 B.C.), but Chronicles and the book of Ezra may have been written considerably later. Modern negative criticism construes the book as a compilation dating at least a century or more subsequent to Ezra's time. It is therefore accorded little historical authenticity. Such invalid criticism as the claim of the nonhistoricity of the title "king of Persia" (1:1-2; etc.) is often made. The term, as common sense would suggest, is used interchangeably with related terms and occurs in the same passages (1:1-2, 7-8; 7:1, 7), as one would now refer to "the president" or "the president of the United States" without implying by the latter term that a new nation had superseded the United States. A heathen king, moreover, although a "king of kings" might naturally be called simply "king of Persia," even if such usage is rare on the monuments. Critics make the charge of chronological confusion in 4:6-23. Events in the reign of Xerxes (485-465 B.C.) and Artaxerxes (465-424 B.C.) come before events in the reign of Darius (521-485 B.C.) in chap. 5, but Ezra simply finishes one subject before proceeding to the next, even at the expense of chronological sequence, which any other writer would be inclined to do. The decree of Cyrus recorded in Heb. (1:1-4) and Aram. (6:3-5) is supposed to involve contradiction, but the one in Heb. was evidently made by Cyrus when he first conquered Babylon and naturally has a Jewish coloring. The second, in Aram., was evidently a formal record drawn up for the official archives at Ecbatana and consequently has a Babylonian coloring. There is no reason to suppose that both are not historical and authentic.

Outline.

I. Return under Zerubbabel (1:1–6:22)
  A. First return of the captives (1:1–2:70)
    1. Cyrus's decree (1:1-11)
    2. Register of exiles (2:1-70)
  B. The restoration of popular worship (3:1–6:22)
    1. Temple rebuilt (3:1–6:15)
    2. Temple dedicated (6:16-22)
II. Reforms under Ezra (7:1–10:44)
  A. Second return of exiles (7:1–8:36)
  B. Abolishment of heathen marriages (9:1–10:44)

BIBLIOGRAPHY: C. C. Torrey, *Ezra Studies* (1910); L. W. Batten, *A Critical and Exegetical Commentary on the Books of Ezra and Nehemiah* (1913); H. E. Ryle, *The Books of Ezra and Nehemiah* (1917); J. S. Wright, *The Date of Ezra's Coming to Jerusalem* (1947); id., *The Building of the Second Temple* (1958); H. H. Rowley, *The Servant of the Lord and Other Essays* (1965); R. K. Harrison, *Introduction to the Old Testament* (1969), pp. 1135-45; R. W. Klein, *Magnalia Dei: The Mighty Acts of God*, ed. F. M. Cross (1976), pp. 361-76; D. K. Kidner, *Ezra and Nehemiah: An Introduction and Commentary*, Tyndale Old Testament Commentaries (1979); W. F. Adeney, *Ezra and Nehemiah* (1980).

EZ'RAH (ez'ra). A descendant of Judah, the father of several sons. His own parentage is not given (1 Chron. 4:17).

EZ'RAHITE (ez'ra-hīt). The patronymic of the Levites Heman and Ethan (1 Kings 4:31; titles of Pss. 88, 89). Their Levitical descent is not at variance with the epithet Ezrahite (or Ezrachite), for they were incorporated into the Judean family of Zerach. Thus the Levite (Judg. 17:7) is spoken of as belonging to the family of Judah because he dwelt in Bethlehem in Judah.

EZ'RI (ez'ri; "helpful"). Son of Chelub, he "had charge of the agricultural workers who tilled the soil" during King David's reign (1 Chron. 27:26), after 1000 B.C.

EZ'RITE. *See* Abi-ezrite.

FABLE (Gk. *muthos,* "myth"). A fictitious story employed for the purpose of enforcing some truth or precept. Neander, *Life of Christ,* thus distinguishes between the parable and fable: "The parable is distinguished from the fable by this, that, in the latter qualities or acts of a higher class of beings may be attributed to a lower, e.g., those of men to brutes; while in the former the lower sphere is kept perfectly distinct from that which it seems to illustrate. The beings and powers thus introduced always follow the law of their nature, but their acts, according to this law, are used to figure those of a higher race." Of the fable, as thus distinguished from the parable, we have but two examples in the Bible: (1) that of the trees choosing their king, addressed by Jotham to the men of Shechem (Judg. 9:8-15); (2) that of the cedar of Lebanon and the thistle, as the answer of Jehoash to the challenge of Amaziah (2 Kings 14:9).

In the NT fable is used for *invention, falsehood,* "cleverly devised tales," or (NIV) "cleverly invented stories" (2 Pet. 1:16). "The fictions of the Jewish theosophists and Gnostics, especially concerning the emanations and orders of the eons, i.e., spirits of the air, are called myths" (1 Tim. 1:4; 4:7, "fables," KJV; 2 Tim. 4:4; Titus 1:14).

FACE. There is nothing peculiar in the use of this word in Scripture, except with reference to God. Applied to God, it denotes His *presence.* In such phrases as seeing the Lord "face to face," "the face of the Lord is against evildoers," it is evidently all one with God's manifested presence. The declaration made by Jehovah to Moses, "No man can see Me and live" (Ex. 33:20), seems to contradict the joyful assertion of Jacob, "I have seen God face to face, yet my life has been preserved" (Gen. 32:30). The apparent discrepancy is to be explained by the different respects in which the expression is used in the two cases. The face

of God, as involving the full blaze of His manifested glory, no mortal can see and survive; but when veiled and appearing with the softened radiance of the human countenance, revived and quickened life is the natural result. The word is also used in the sense of favor (Ps. 67:1; Dan. 9:17) and signifies also *anger,* justice, severity (Gen. 16:6, 8; Ex. 2:15; Rev. 6:16, KJV; NASB, "presence"), it being natural to express these feelings in one's countenance. "To set one's face" denotes to determine fully and resolve, and "to fall on the face" is an attitude of *fear* and *reverence.* To see one "face to face" is to enjoy a direct, clear sight of him and not a reflection in a mirror.

FACES, BREAD OF. The *bread of the Presence* (which see, in the article Tabernacle), which was always set before God.

FAINTHEARTED (Gk. *oligopsuchos,* "little spirited"). Often occurs in the LXX and signifies one who is laboring under such trouble that his heart sinks within him; it may also mean one's despairing of working out his salvation (1 Thess. 5:14).

FAIR. The rendering in the KJV of several Heb. and Gk. words. In the East exposure to the sun makes a great difference in the complexion of women. Those of high condition carefully avoid such exposure and retain their fairness, which becomes a distinguishing mark of quality as well as an enhancement of beauty (so NASB and NIV; Gen. 12:11-13; Song of Sol. 1:15-16).

FAIR HA′VENS (Gk. *kaloi limenes,* "good harbors"). A harbor in the island of Crete (Acts 27:8) near the city of Lasea, two leagues E of Cape Matala and due S of the ancient Minoan center of Phaestos. It still bears the same name in the modern Gk. dialect, Kali Limenes.

FAIRS. *See* Wares.

Fair Havens, Crete

FAITH (Gk. *pistis*). Belief or trust—especially in a higher power. The fundamental idea in Scripture is steadfastness and faithfulness.

Scripture's Use of the Word. The word is used in Scripture (1) most frequently in a subjective sense, denoting a moral and spiritual quality of individuals, by virtue of which men are held in relations of confidence in God and fidelity to Him; and (2) in an objective sense, meaning the body of truth, moral and religious, which God has revealed—that which men believe. Examples of this use of the word are not numerous, though they occur occasionally, as in Phil. 1:27; 1 Tim. 1:19; 6:20-21; Jude 3, 20.

The word occurs only twice in our English version of the OT, the idea being expressed by other terms, such as "trust," etc.

This article is confined in the further discussion to faith in the sense first named. The following points are of chief importance:

Philosophical. Faith, viewed philosophically, must be regarded as lying at the basis of all knowledge. Anselm's famous utterance *"Crede ut intelligas,"* "Believe that you may know," expresses the truth in contrast with the words of Abelard, *"Intellige ut credas,"* "Know that you may believe." Truths perceived intuitively imply faith in the intuitions. Truths or facts arrived at by logical processes, or processes of reasoning, are held to be known because, first of all, we have confidence in the laws of the human mind. Our knowledge obtained through the senses has underneath it faith in the senses. To this extent Goethe spoke wisely when he said, "I believe in the five senses." A large part of knowledge rests upon human testimony, and of course this involves faith in the testimony.

The distinction between matters of faith and matters of knowledge must not be drawn too rigidly, inasmuch as all matters of knowledge are in some measure matters also of faith. The distinction, when properly made, chiefly recognizes the different objects to which our convictions relate, and the different methods by which we arrive at these convictions. The convictions themselves may be as strong in the one case as in the other.

Theological. Faith in the theological sense contains two elements recognized in the Scriptures: there is an element that is intellectual and also an element, of even deeper importance, that is moral. Faith is not simply the assent of the intellect to revealed truth; it is the practical submission of the entire man to the guidance and control of such truth. "The demons also believe, and shudder."

Indispensable as is the assent of the intellect, that alone does not constitute the faith upon which the Scriptures lay such emphasis. The essential idea is rather that of fidelity, faithfulness, steadfastness. Or, as has been well said, "Faith, in its essential temper, is that elevation of soul by which it aspires to the good, the true, and the divine." In illustration may be cited particularly John 3:18-21; Rom. 2:7; 4:5; Heb. 11; James 2:14-26.

Intellectual. Viewed more particularly with reference to its intellectual aspect, faith is properly defined as the conviction of the reality of the truths and facts that God has revealed, such conviction resting solely upon the testimony of God.

These truths and facts are to a large extent beyond the reach of the ordinary human processes of acquiring knowledge. Still, they are of the utmost importance in relation to human life and salvation. God has therefore revealed them. And they who accept them must do so upon the trustworthiness of the divine testimony. This testimony is contained in the Holy Scriptures. It is impressed moreover by the special sanction of the Holy Spirit. (*See* John 3:11, 31-33; 16:8-11; 1 John 5:10-11, and many other places.)

Results of Faith. They who receive the divine testimony and yield to it become partakers of heavenly knowledge. Their knowledge comes by faith, yet nonetheless it is knowledge. The Scriptures, it is true, recognize the difference between walking by faith and walking by sight, and thus the difference between the objects and methods of sense-perception and those of faith. Also the difference is noted between the acquisition of human learning and philosophy and the contents of the divine revelation. But still the Scriptures represent true believers as persons who "know the things freely given to us by God." Christ said to His disciples, "To you it has been granted to know the mysteries of the kingdom of God" (Luke 8:10; *see* also John 8:31-32; 1 Cor. 1:5-6, 21-30; 2:9-16; Eph. 1:17; 1 Tim. 2:4).

Reason and Faith. The relation of reason to faith is that of subordination, and yet not that of opposition. The truths of revelation are in many cases above reason, though not against it. Such truths were revealed because reason could not discover them. They are therefore to be accepted, though the reason cannot demonstrate them. But this inability of reason to discover or to demonstrate is one thing; irrationality, as involving absurdity, or contradiction of the intuitions of the intellect or conscience, or contradiction of well-established truth, is another.

Reason has its justly recognized and appropriate function in examining and weighing the evidences of revelation, as well as in interpreting or determining the force of the terms in which the revelation is given. But when the reality and meaning of revelation are thus reached, reason has done its work, and it remains for faith to accept the contents of the revelation, whatever they may be.

It should be said, however, that the evidence of the saving truth of revelation, most convincing for many, is not that which appeals directly to reason. Many lack ability or opportunity to investigate the rational evidences of Christianity. But to them with all others the announcement of the truth comes attended by the ministration or direct testimony of the Holy Spirit. They are thus made to feel that they ought to repent and believe the gospel. If they yield to this conviction they obtain forgiveness of their sins and become new creatures in Christ Jesus. The Spirit bears witness to their acceptance with God. And thus in the experience of salvation they have unquestionable proof of the reality of revelation. In all this reason is subordinate to faith but by no means opposed to it (1 Cor. 1:21-31; John 16:8-11; Rom. 8:14-17; 1 John 5:9-11).

Condition of Salvation. As has been assumed in the foregoing, faith is the condition of salvation. It is not the procuring cause but the condition, or instrumental cause. It is frequently associated in the Scriptures with repentance; thus the conditions of salvation, as commonly stated in Protestant doctrine, are repentance and faith. But in reality true faith and true repentance are not separate or to be distinguished too rigidly from each other. Faith is fundamental. Repentance implies faith. Faith is not saving faith unless it includes repentance. (*See* Repentance.) Saving faith may therefore be properly defined for those who have the light of the gospel as such belief in the Lord Jesus Christ as leads one to submit completely to the authority of Christ and to put complete and exclusive trust in Him for salvation. (*See* John 3:14-16.)

Faith, which is the condition of salvation, is also, in an important measure, one of the results of salvation. In the justified and regenerated soul, faith is deepened and developed by the influence of the Holy Spirit. In its essential quality faith is unchanged, but it acquires greater steadiness, and as the Word of God is studied and its contents spiritually apprehended faith becomes broader and richer in the truths and facts that it grasps.

Thus in its beginning and completion faith is one of the fruits of the Spirit (Gal. 5:22). E.MC.

BIBLIOGRAPHY: W. H. P. Hatch, *The Pauline Idea of Faith* (1917); C. H. Dodd, *The Bible and the Greeks* (1935); J. Barr, *Semantics of Biblical Language* (1961); J. G. Machen, *What Is Faith?* (1962); B. B. Warfield, *Biblical and Theological Studies* (1962); N. Turner, *Christian Words* (1980), pp. 153-58.

FAITH, RULE OF. In the early church, the summary of doctrines taught to catechumens and to which they were obliged to subscribe before baptism. It was afterward applied to the Apostles' Creed. In modern theology it denotes the true source of our knowledge of Christian truth.

Protestant Doctrine. One of the chief doctrinal elements of the Reformation was the sufficiency of the Scriptures for faith and salvation. Thus the Methodist church teaches: "The Holy Scriptures contain all things necessary to salvation; so that whatsoever is not read therein, nor may be proved thereby, is not to be required of any man that it should be believed as an article of faith, or be thought requisite or necessary to salvation" (*Meth. Dis.* 5.5).

Roman Catholic Teaching. It emphasizes the role of the church: "The Church is the ordinary and the infallible means by which we know what the truths are which God has revealed. The testimony of the Church is the *rule* by which we can distinguish between true and false doctrine. . . . A person must believe that the Church cannot err, and that whatever it teaches is infallibly true" (*Cath. Dict.*, s.v.).

FAITH, THE CHRISTIAN. "To those who receive the light, in the sense of not refusing it, revelation is one whole, and all its glorious system of truth is received and surely believed. To them it is both objectively and subjectively *the Faith;* and, inasmuch as Christianity has brought it in all fullness into the world, it is to them the *Christian Faith.* This phrase has therefore a larger meaning. It signifies that it is not their philosophy simply, the glory of their reason, the tradition they have derived from their fathers, but the rich inheritance which the Holy Spirit has given to that one supreme faculty of their souls, the faith which is the *evidence of things not seen.* It is a body of truth which, as reason did not give it, so reason cannot take it away. It is a region in which they walk by faith, which their faith habitually visits, in which their faith lives, and moves, and has its being" (Pope, *Compendium of Christian Theology,* p. 45).

FAITHFULNESS (Heb. *ʾĕmûnâ,* "faithfulness, stability"). An attribute ascribed to God in many places, especially in the Psalms (36:5; 89:2, 5, 8; Isa. 11:5; etc.), which exhibits His character as worthy of the love and confidence of man and assures us that He will certainly fulfill His promises as well as execute His threats against sin. It covers "temporal blessings (1 Tim. 4:8; Ps. 84:11; Isa. 33:16); spiritual blessings (1 Cor. 1:9); support in temptation (10:13) and persecution

(1 Pet. 4:12-13; Isa. 41:10); sanctifying afflictions (Heb. 12:4-12); directing in difficulties (2 Chron. 32:22; Ps. 32:8); enabling to persevere (Jer. 32:40), and bringing to glory (1 John 2:25)."

Faithfulness is also predicated of men: "he was a *faithful* man" (Heb. "trustworthy," Neh. 7:2); "who then is the faithful and sensible steward ...?" (Luke 12:42; etc.). *The faithful* was the general and favorite name in the early church to denote baptized persons.

FALCON. *See* Animal Kingdom: Falcon; Vulture.

FALL OF MAN. A term of theology that is not found in Scripture, though the essential fact is a matter of Scripture record and of clear though not frequent reference. The particular account is in Gen. 3. The most explicit NT references are Rom. 5:12-21; 1 Cor. 15:21-22, 45-47; 2 Cor. 11:3.

The character of the primitive record in Genesis has been the subject of much discussion. Some have contended that the account is purely literal; others, that it is figurative, poetic, or allegorical; still others, rationalistic or semirationalistic, relegate the whole matter to the realm of the mythical. This last view, of course, cannot be consistently held by anyone who accepts the Scriptures as of divine authority.

It must be admitted that the account leaves room for many questions both as to its form and its meaning in relation to incidental details. But still, the great underlying, essential facts are sufficiently clear, especially when the account is taken in connection with other Scriptures. They are as follows:

Bible Doctrine. The Fall of our first ancestors was an epoch or turning point in the moral history of the race. It was in itself an epoch of great and sad significance and of far-reaching results.

Man at his creation was in a state of moral purity. In connection with his freedom there was of necessity the possibility of sin. But still there was no evil tendency in his nature. God pronounced him, with other objects of His creation, "good." He was made in the image and likeness of God.

As a moral being man was placed by God in a state of probation. His freedom was to be exercised and tested by his being under divine law. Of every tree in the garden he might freely eat, except the tree of knowledge of good and evil. At one point there must be restraint, self-denial for the sake of obedience. "For what will a man be profited, if he gains the whole world, and forfeits his soul?" (Matt. 16:26).

The temptation to disobedience came from an evil source outside himself. In Genesis only the serpent is mentioned. In the NT the tempter is identified as Satan, who employed the serpent as his instrument (1 Cor. 11:3, 14; Rom. 16:20; Rev. 12:9).

The temptation came in the form of an appeal to man's intellect and to the senses. The forbidden fruit was presented as "good for food" and "desirable to make one wise." Thus the allurement was in the direction of sensual gratification and intellectual pride.

At the beginning of the sin lay unbelief. The tempted ones doubted or disbelieved God and believed the tempter. And thus, under the strong desire awakened by the temptation, they disobeyed the divine command.

By this act of disobedience "sin entered into the world, and death through sin." Shame and alienation from God were the first visible consequences. The image of God, which contained among its features "righteousness and holiness of the truth," was marred and broken, though not completely lost. (*See* Image of God.) Expulsion from Eden followed. The ground was cursed on account of sin. Sorrow and toil and struggle with the evil in human nature became the lot of mankind.

Theological Views. The theological treatment of this topic should be particularly noted:

A favorite view of rationalistic or evolutionist theologians is that the Fall was a necessary incident in man's moral development. The Fall is sometimes, therefore, spoken of as "a fall upward." It was a step forward from the savage or animal state to the practical knowledge of good and evil and thus, through the experience of sin, toward the goal of developed moral purity. But this view ignores the essential evil of sin. It makes sin only an imperfect or disguised good and is, for that reason and others, opposed to the plain teaching of Scripture.

The Calvinistic types of theology regard the Fall in two ways: (1) the supralapsarian, or most rigid view, includes the Fall under the divine decree; (2) the sublapsarian, the less rigid but less logically consistent view, represents the divine decree as relating to the condition produced by the Fall. Out from the race fallen in Adam God elected a certain number to salvation.

The Arminian theology regards the Fall not as predetermined by a divine decree but as foreseen and provided against by divine grace. It asserts that, but for the redemptive purpose of God in Christ, the race of fallen descendants of Adam would not have been permitted to come into existence. When man fell he did not "fall upward," but he fell into the arms of redeeming mercy. Probation is still the condition of mankind. For though man is fallen and therefore under the bondage of sin, through Christ (the second Adam) man has his moral freedom restored to such an extent that he can avail himself of the provisions God has made for his salvation.

The Fall and Archaeology. The so-called Myth of Adapa has often been adduced as offering a parallel to the Bible account of the Fall of man. This claim, however, is ill-founded. There is not the slightest reason to look for the Fall in the literature of the Babylonians, as such a concept is contrary to their whole system of polytheistic speculation. In Genesis man is created in the image of a holy God. But the Babylonians, like other ancient pagan peoples (notably the Greeks and the Romans), fashioned their gods, good and bad, in the image of man. Such deities schemed, hated, fought, and killed one another. They were of such dubious moral character, it was impossible that they be thought of as creating anything morally perfect. Neither could man formed out of the blood of such deities (the Babylonian notion) possess anything but an evil nature. No fall was possible because man was created evil and in heathenistic thought had no state of innocence from which to fall. Nevertheless, further features of the legend of Adapa are interesting by way of similarity or contrast. The "food of life" corresponds to "fruit" of the "tree of life" (Gen. 3:3, 22). The two accounts are in agreement that eternal life could be obtained by eating a certain kind of food. Adam, however, forfeited immortality for himself because of the sinful desire to be "like God" (3:5). Consequently, he was exiled from the garden lest he should "take also from the tree of life, and eat, and live forever" (3:22). Adapa was already endued with wisdom by the gods. He failed to become immortal not because of disobedience or presumption, like Adam, but because he was obedient to his creator, Ea, who deceived him. The Babylonian tale, like the biblical narrative, deals with the perplexing question of why man must suffer and die. In contrast, the answer is not that man fell from his moral integrity and that sin into which he fell involved death, but that man forfeited his opportunity to gain eternal life in consequence of being deceived by one of the gods. The origin of human sin is not at all in view in the Adapa story. This is basic in the theologically pivotal third chapter of Genesis. The two narratives, the biblical and the Babylonian, are poles apart despite superficial resemblances.   E.MCC.; M.F.U.

BIBLIOGRAPHY: J. Murray, *The Imputation of Adam's Sin* (1959); E. E. Sauer, *The King of the Earth* (1962); J. G. Machen, *The Christian View of Man* (1965); J. Daane, *International Standard Bible Encyclopedia* (1982), 2:247-79; D. MacDonald, *The Biblical Doctrine of Creation and the Fall* (1984).

FALLOW DEER. *See* Animal Kingdom: Roebuck.

FALLOW GROUND. A field plowed up and left for seeding and summer fallow, properly conducted is a sure method of destroying weeds (Jer. 4:3; Hos. 10:12).

FALLOW YEAR. *See* Sabbath.

FALSE CHRISTS. Those who falsely claim to be the Messiah, as foretold by Jesus (Matt. 24:24; Mark 13:22). Nothing is known of the historical

fulfillment of this prophecy, but Josephus (*Wars* 7.11.1) mentions Jonathan as a pretender.

FALSE PROPHET, THE. The second beast of Rev. 13:11-18 (cf. 16:13; 19:20; 20:10). Twice he is associated with the first Beast (Antichrist) and once with the Dragon (Satan). As the Dragon and the first Beast are persons, so must he be a person. Jesus had a prophetic foreview of him when He said, "For false Christs and false prophets will arise and will show great signs and wonders, so as to mislead, if possible, even the elect" (Matt. 24:24). Here our Lord distinguishes between false christs and false prophets. It seems clear, therefore, that the Antichrist and the false prophet cannot be the same. The false prophet will be a miracle worker. By evil, supernatural power he will bring down fire from heaven and will command the people of the Tribulation period to make an "image to the Beast" in order to worship it, having power to give life to the image to cause it to speak and to demand that all who will not worship it be put to death (Rev 13:14-15). "And he causes all, the small and the great, and the rich and the poor, and the free men and the slaves, to be given a mark on their right hand, or on their forehead, and he provides that no one should be able to buy or to sell, except the one who has the mark, either the name of the beast or the number of his name" (13:16-17). He will thus be a consummation of deception and wickedness, this being signified by his mystical number, 666. As an aide to the Antichrist, he is one of the principal characters revolting against God at the end time, immediately prior to Christ's second advent.   M.F.U.

FAMILIAR SPIRIT (Heb. *'ōb*). A divining demon present in the physical body of the conjurer. "A man or a woman who is a medium or a spiritist" [lit., "a familiar spirit within them"] shall surely be put to death. They shall be stoned with stones, their bloodguiltiness is upon them" (Lev. 20:27, *see* marg.). The term *familiar* is used to describe the demon because it was regarded by the English translators as a servant ("famulus"), belonging to the family ("familiaris"), who was on intimate terms with and might be readily summoned by the one possessing it. Thus a familiar spirit is a divining demon, and the ancient world, as well as the modern, had traffic in spiritism, not as mere trickery but as a spiritual reality of evil nature. The significance of the Heb. term *'ob* is disputed. It may be related to the Arab. root *'awaba* ("to return"), with reference to the divining spirit who periodically returns to the medium. The most common view, however, associates the fundamental etymological significance with "something hollow," such as "wineskins" (Job 32:19). Assuming the fundamental notion of "hollowness," various explanations are suggested as accounting for it, such as calling the divining spirit an *'ōb* because of the hollow tone of its voice as if issuing from a cave or opening in the ground. Greek and Roman oracles, which were considered to communicate with the spirit world, were commonly situated among the deep caverns. This was notably true of Apollo's famous oracle at Delphi. (*See* T. K. Oesterreich, *Possession, Demoniacal and Other*, pp. 312ff.; E. Langton, *Essentials of Demonology*, pp. 96-98.) Gesenius has the idea that the connection between "bottle" and "necromancer" probably arose "from regarding the conjurer, while possessed by the demon, as a bottle, i.e., vessel, case, in which the demon was contained" (*Hebrew and English Lexicon*, ad loc.). *See* Necromancer; Spiritist; Demons; Divination; and Magic: Various Forms.   M.F.U.

BIBLIOGRAPHY: *See* under Demons; Divination.

FAMILY. The family relation is the institution of God lying at the foundation of all human society. Christian ethics leave nothing wanting of the main elements of that institution. It confirms monogamy: "Have you not read, that He who created them from the beginning made them male and female, and said, 'For this cause a man shall leave his father and mother, and shall cleave to his wife' " (Matt. 19:5; Mark 10:6-7). So Christian legislation is clear and positive respecting the relation of marriage, of parents and children, of masters and servants, and the regulation of all the household. Parental obligations include the maintenance of children (1 Tim. 5:8) and their education in its fullest sense (Ex. 12:26-27; Deut. 6:6-7; Eph. 6:4).

The filial obligations are obedience (Luke 2:51; Eph. 6:1; Col. 3:20), reverence (Ex. 20:12; cf. Eph. 6:1-2), and grateful requital (1 Tim. 5:4; cf. John 19:26). The moral teaching of Christianity has a marked bearing on the relation between master and servants. Although the mutual rights, duties, and responsibilities are not in their widest range a matter of direct statute in the Scriptures, the principles laid down by Paul are of permanent application. On the employer's side there is the obligation of justice (Col. 4:1); on the side of the servants there is enjoined the duty of obedience, fidelity, and honesty (Titus 2:9-10; Col. 3:22-23; Eph. 6:5-6). Thus the family occupies a prominent place throughout Scripture, is the first form of society, and has continued to be the germ and representative of every fellowship.

BIBLIOGRAPHY: D. Jacobsen, *The Social Background of the Old Testament* (1942); E. Neufeld, *Ancient Hebrew Marriage Laws* (1944); D. R. Mace, *Hebrew Marriage* (1953); E. A. Judge, *Social Pattern of the Christian Groups of the First Century* (1960); R. de Vaux, *Ancient Israel: Its Life and Institutions* (1961), pp. 19-64; A. N. Sherwin-White, *Roman Society and Roman Law in the New Testament* (1963).

FAMILY, or **Father's Household.** One of the divisions of the people of Israel. *See* Israel, Classification of.

FAMINE. Occupies a conspicuous place in Scripture among the troubles with which God's people had to contend. It is mentioned as one of the scourges that God sent to chastise men for their wickedness (Lev. 26:21, 26; Ps. 105:16; Lam. 4:4-6; Ezek. 14:21).

Causes. Several causes of famine are given: (1) God's blessing withheld (Hos. 2:8-9; Hag. 1:6). (2) Want of seasonable rain (1 Kings 17:1; Jer. 14:1-4; Amos 4:7-8). "In Egypt a deficiency in the rise of the Nile, with drying winds, produces the same results. The famines recorded in the Bible are traceable to both these phenomena; and we generally find that Egypt was resorted to when scarcity afflicted Palestine. In the whole of Syria and Arabia the fruits of the earth must ever be dependent on rain, the watersheds having few large springs and the small rivers not being sufficient for the irrigation of even the level lands. If, therefore, the heavy rains of November and December fail, the sustenance of the people is cut off in the parching drought of harvest time, when the country is almost devoid of moisture" (Smith, *Dict.*, s.v.). (3) Rotting of seed in the ground (Joel 1:17). (4) Scorching wind and mildew (Amos 4:9; Hag. 2:17). (5) Devastation by enemies (Deut. 28:33, 51). In addition to the above causes may be given the imperfect knowledge of agriculture that prevailed, in consequence of which men had few resources to stimulate or, in unfavorable seasons and localities, to aid the productive powers of nature. Means of transit were defective, rendering it often impossible to relieve the wants of one region even when there was plenty in another. Despotic governments and frequent wars and desolation greatly interrupted agricultural industry.

Characteristics. These famines were often long (Gen. 41:27) and of great severity (12:10; 2 Kings 8:1; Jer. 52:6), accompanied with wars (14:15; 29:18) and followed by pestilence (42:17; Ezek. 7:15; Matt. 24:7). During the time of famine people fed upon wild herbs (2 Kings 4:39-40), donkey's flesh, dung (6:25; Lam. 4:5), and human flesh (Lev. 26:29; 2 Kings 6:28-29), while provisions were sold by weight and water by measure (Ezek. 4:16).

Instances. Famines are mentioned as occurring in the days of Abraham (Gen. 12:10), of Isaac (26:1), of Joseph (41:53-56), of the Judges (Ruth 1:1), of David (2 Sam. 21:1), of Ahab (1 Kings 17:1; 18:2), of Elisha (2 Kings 4:38), during the siege of Samaria (6:25), in the time of Jeremiah (Jer. 14:1-6), during the siege of Jerusalem (2 Kings 25:3), after the captivity (Neh. 5:3), in the reign of Claudius Caesar (Acts 11:28), before the destruction of Jerusalem (Matt. 24:7).

Figurative. Famine is symbolic of the withdrawal of God's word (Amos 8:11-12) and the destruction of idols (Zeph. 2:11).

FAN. *See* Winnow; Winnowing Fork.

Figurative. Used in the KJV to mean *scatter,* as enemies (Isa. 41:16); to cause defeat and dispersion on the border of the land (Jer. 15:7).

FANNERS. The rendering in the KJV of Jer. 51:2; the NASB and NIV give "foreigners"; NASB marg., "winnowers." *See* Winnow.

FARM. *See* Agriculture.

FARMER, FARMERS, FARMING. One Gk. and several Heb. terms are behind these English ones. *Farming* (Gen. 9:20) is from Heb. *'īsh 'ǎdāmâ,* lit., "man of the soil"; the term is given as "husbandman" in the KJV. *Farmer* and *farmers* are from Heb. *hārash* (Isa. 28:24); Heb. *'ikkār* (Isa. 61:5; Jer. 14:4; 31:24; 51:23; Amos 5:16; 9:13; Joel 1:11); and Gk. *geōrgos,* "land worker" (cf. 2 Tim. 2:6; James 5:7). The terms *husbandman, plowman,* and *vinedressers* are sometimes the rendering for the Heb. and Gk. terms, but *husbandman* does not appear in the NASB and NIV. Farming is among the most ancient and honorable occupations (*see* above; and also Gen. 26:12, 14; 37:7; Job. 1:3). The various operations of farming (*see* Agriculture), such as the sowing of seed, harvesting, etc., furnish many apt illustrations in Scripture.

FARTHING. The farthing (KJV), cent (NASB), or penny (NIV) was a unit of money. *See* Metrology.

FAST, FASTING (Heb. *ṣûm,* to "cover" the mouth; Gk. *nēsteuō,* to "abstain"). In the early ages men subsisted largely upon the spontaneous productions of the earth and the spoils of the chase; owing to the uncertainty of obtaining food, fasting was often compulsory. Superstitious ignorance could easily interpret this compulsion into an expression of divine will, and so consider fasting as a religious duty. It was believed that the gods were jealous of the pleasures of men and that abstinence would propitiate their favor. As a result we find that fasting as a religious duty is almost universal.

Jewish. The word *fasting* (Heb. *ṣûm*) is not found in the Pentateuch but often occurs in the historical books (2 Sam. 12:16; 1 Kings 21:9-12; Ezra 8:21) and the prophets (Isa. 58:3-5; Joel 11:14; 2:15; Zech. 8:19; etc.). The expression used in the law is "humble your souls" (Lev. 16:29-31; 23:27; Num. 30:13), implying the sacrifice of the personal will, which gives to fasting all its value.

The Jewish fasts were observed with various degrees of strictness. When the fast lasted only a single day it was the practice to abstain from food of every kind from evening to evening, whereas in the case of private fasts of a more prolonged character it was merely the ordinary food that was abstained from. To manifest a still profounder humbling of the soul before God is repentance and mortification on account of one's sin and the punishment with which it had been visited. It was

not unusual to put on sackcloth, rend the garments, and scatter ashes over the head (2 Sam. 13:19; 1 Kings 21:27; 1 Macc. 3:47; Lam. 2:10; Jonah 3:5-8). In 1 Sam. 7:6 it is said that Israel "drew water and poured it out before the Lord, and fasted on that day." To "pour out your heart like water" (Lam. 2:19) seems to denote inward dissolution through pain and misery. In connection with the fast it would be a practical confession of misery and an act of deepest humiliation before the Lord.

The Mosaic law prescribed only one public occasion of strict fasting, namely, once a year on the great *Day of Atonement* (*see* Festivals). This observance seems always to have retained some prominence as "the fast" (Acts 27:9). But as to the nature of the observance we are nowhere expressly informed, excepting that "it shall be a holy convocation for you" (Lev. 23:27-29). The Hebrews, in the earlier period of their history, were in the habit of fasting whenever they were in hard and trying circumstances (1 Sam. 1:7), misfortune, and bereavement (20:34; 31:13; 2 Sam. 1:12), in the prospect of threatened judgments of God (12:16; 1 Kings 21:27), on occasions of falling into grievous sin (Ezra 10:6), or to avert heavy calamity (Esther 4:1, 3, 16). Extraordinary fasts were appointed by the theocratic authorities on occasions of great national calamity in order that the people might humble themselves before the Lord on account of their sins, thus averting His wrath and getting Him to look upon them again with favor (Judg. 20:26; 1 Sam. 7:6; 2 Chron. 20:3; Joel 1:14; 2:12; Jer. 36:9; Ezra 8:21; Neh. 1:4; 2 Macc. 13:12).

Postexilic. There is no mention of any other periodic fast than that on the Day of Atonement in the OT, except in Zech. 7:1-7; 8:19. These anniversary fast days were observed from about the time of the captivity and were as follows: (1) The seventeenth day of the fourth month, namely, Tammuz, or July. This fast was instituted in memory of the capture of Jerusalem (Jer. 52:6-7; Zech. 8:19). (2) The ninth day of the fifth month, Ab, or August, in memory of the burning of the Temple (2 Kings 25:8-9; Zech. 7:3; 8:19). (3) The third of the seventh month, Tishri, or October, in memory of the death of Gedaliah (Jer. 41:4; Zech. 7:5; 8:19). (4) The tenth day of the tenth month, Tebeth, or January, in memory of the commencement of the attack on Jerusalem (2 Kings 25:1; Jer. 52:4; Zech. 8:19). (5) The fast of *Esther* (which see), kept on the thirteenth of Adar (Esther 4:16). "Subsequent to the captivity, and with the growth of the Pharisaic spirit, the fasts became much more frequent generally, till ere long they assumed the form of ordinary pious exercises, so that the Pharisees fasted regularly on the second and fifth day of every week (Matt. 9:14; Luke 18:12), while other Jewish sects, such as the Essenes and Therapeutae, made their whole worship to consist principally of fasting."

For new archaeological light on the practices of these pre-Christian Jewish sects *see* W. H. Brownlee, "A Comparison of the Covenanters of the Dead Sea Scrolls with Pre-Christian Jewish Sects," *Biblical Archaeologist* 13 (Sept. 1950): 50-72. There was, however, no fasting on the Sabbath, on festival and celebration days in Israel, and on the day immediately preceding the Sabbath or a festival (Judith 8:6). That in the lapse of time the practice of fasting was lamentably abused is shown by the testimony of the prophets (Isa. 58:3-6; Jer. 14:12; Zech. 7:5).

New Testament. In the NT the only references to the Jewish fasts are the mention of "the fasts" in Acts 27:9 (generally understood to denote the Day of Atonement) and the allusions to the weekly fasts (Matt. 9:14; Mark 2:18; Luke 5:33; 18:12). These fasts originated some time after the captivity. They were observed on the second and fifth days of the week, which, being appointed as the days for public fasts (because Moses was supposed to have ascended the mount for the second tables of the law on a Thursday and to have returned on a Monday), seem to have been selected for these private voluntary fasts.

Our Lord sternly rebuked the Pharisees for their hypocritical pretenses in the fasts that they observed (Matt. 6:16-18). He abstained from appointing any fast as part of His own religion (9:14-15; 11:18-19). Prayer and fasting are mentioned (17:21; Mark 9:29, *see* marg.) as means for promoting faith and as good works. Mention is made of fasting in the apostolic church (Acts 13:3; 14:23; 2 Cor. 6:5). In the last passage the apostle probably refers to *voluntary fasting,* as in 2 Cor. 11:27 he makes a distinction between fasting and "hunger and thirst" (KJV).

Christian Church. After the Jewish custom, fasting was frequently joined with prayer that the mind, unencumbered with earthly matter, might devote itself with less distraction to the contemplation of divine things. As the Pharisees were accustomed to fast on Monday and Thursday, the Christians appointed Wednesday and especially Friday as days of half-fasting or abstinence from flesh in commemoration of the passion and crucifixion of Jesus. They did this with reference to the Lord's words "But the days will come when the bridegroom is taken away from them, and then they will fast" (Matt. 9:15).

In the second century arose also the custom of fasts before Easter, which, however, differed in length in different countries, being sometimes reduced to forty hours, sometimes extended to forty days or at least to several weeks. Perhaps equally ancient are the nocturnal fasts or vigils before the high festivals, suggested by the example of the Lord and the apostles. On special occasions the bishops appointed extraordinary fasts and applied the money saved to charitable purposes, a usage that often became a blessing to the poor.

By the sixth century fasting was made obligatory by the Second Council of Orleans (A.D. 541), which decreed that anyone neglecting to observe the stated time of abstinence should be treated as an offender. In the eighth century it was regarded as praiseworthy, and failure to observe subjected the offender to excommunication. In the Roman Catholic and Greek churches fasting remains obligatory, whereas in most Protestant churches it is merely recommended.

BIBLIOGRAPHY: J. Pedersen, *Israel, Its Life and Culture* (1940), 3-4:11-12, 456-58; I. Abrahams, *Studies in Pharisaism and the Gospels,* 2 vols. in 1 (1967), 1:121-28.

FAT (Heb. *ḥēleb*). "The Hebrews distinguished between the suet or pure fat of an animal and the fat which was intermixed with the lean (Neh. 8:10). Certain restrictions were imposed upon them in reference to the former: some parts of the suet, viz., about the stomach, the entrails, the kidneys, and the tail of a sheep, which grows to an excessive size in many Eastern countries and produces a large quantity of rich fat, were forbidden to be eaten in the case of animals offered to Jehovah in sacrifice (Lev. 3:3, 9, 17; 7:3, 23). The ground of the prohibition was that the fat was the richest part of the animal, and therefore belonged to God (3:16). The presentation of the fat as the richest part of the animal was agreeable to the dictates of natural feeling, and was the ordinary practice even of heathen nations. The burning of the fat of sacrifices was particularly specified in each kind of offering" (Smith, *Dict.,* s.v.). *See* Fat Tail.

Figurative. Next to blood, the bearer of life (Lev. 17:14), the fat stood as the sign of healthfulness and vigor. "The fat of the land," "the fat of lambs, and rams, . . . and goats," even "the fat of the mighty," though to our view somewhat peculiar expressions, were familiar to the Hebrews as indicating the choicest specimens or examples of the several objects in question (Gen. 45:18; Deut. 32:14; Num. 18:12, marg., "fat"; 2 Sam. 1:22).

FATHER (Heb. *'āb;* Gk. *patēr,* lit., "nourisher," "protector").

Meanings. This word, besides its natural sense of progenitor (Gen. 19:31; 44:19; etc.), has a number of other meanings: (1) Any ancestor, near or remote (1 Kings 15:11; 2 Kings 14:3), e.g., a *grandfather* (Gen. 28:13; 31:42; 32:9; etc.), a *great*-grandfather (Num. 18:1-2; 1 Kings 15:11, 24; etc.); frequently in the plural *fathers,* i.e., *forefathers* (Gen. 15:15; Ps. 45:16). (2) Founder, i.e., the first ancestor of a tribe or nation (Gen. 10:21; 17:4-5; 19:37; etc.) Here we may refer to Gen. 4:21, "the father of all those who play the lyre and pipe," i.e., the founder of a family of musicians, the inventor of the art of music. Jubal was "the father of those who dwell in tents" (4:20). The term also refers to the author of a family or society of persons animated by the same spirit as himself; thus Abraham was "the father of all who believe" (Rom 4:11); also the *author* or maker of anything, especially a *creator* ("has the rain a *father?*" Job 38:28). In this sense God is called the "father" of men and angels (Isa. 63:16; 64:8; Eph. 3:14-15; etc.). He is also called the "Father of lights," i.e., stars (James 1:17). The above topical senses come from the notion of *source, origin;* others are drawn from the idea of paternal love and care, the honor due a father, etc. (3) Benefactor, as doing good and providing for others as a father (Job 29:16, "I was a father to the needy"). Eliakim, the prefect of the palace, was called "a father to the inhabitants of Jerusalem" (Isa. 22:21). The Messiah is the "Eternal Father" (9:6); God, the *father* of the righteous and of kings (2 Sam. 7:14; 1 Chron. 17:13; Ps. 89:26). (4) Teacher, from the idea of paternal instruction (1 Sam. 10:12); priests and prophets as teachers were called *father* (2 Kings 2:12; 5:13; etc.). In a similar sense the prime minister, as chief adviser, is called the king's father (Gen. 45:8). (5) Intimate relationship, as,"If I call to the pit, 'You are my father' " (Job 17:14).

Place and Authority. The position and authority of the father as the head of the family is expressly assumed and sanctioned in Scripture as a likeness to that of the Almighty over His creatures. It lies, of course, at the root of that so-called patriarchal government (Gen. 3:16; 1 Cor. 11:3) that was introductory to the more definite system that followed but did not wholly supersede it. "While the father lived he continued to represent the whole family, the property was held in his name, and all was under his superintendence and control. His power, however, was by no means unlimited or arbitrary, and if any occasion arose for severe discipline or capital punishment in his family he was not himself to inflict it, but to bring the matter before the constituted authorities" (Deut. 21:18-21). The children, and even the grandchildren, continued under the roof of the father and grandfather; they labored on his account and were the most submissive of his servants. The property of the soil, the power of judgment, the civil rights belonged to him only, and his sons were merely his instruments and assistants. The father's blessing was regarded as conferring special benefit and his malediction special injury to those on whom it fell (Gen. 9:25, 27; 27:27-40; 48:15-16, 20; chap. 49); and so also the sin of a parent was held to affect, in certain cases, the welfare of his descendants (2 Kings 5:27). The father, as the head of the household, had the obligation imposed upon him of bringing up his children in the fear of God, making them well acquainted with the precepts of the law, and generally acting as their instructor and guide (Ex. 12:26; Deut. 6:20; etc.). Filial duty and obedience to both parents were strictly enforced by Moses (Ex. 20:12); and any outrage against either

parent, such as a blow (21:15), a curse (v. 17; Lev. 20:9), or incorrigible rebellion against their authority (Deut. 21:18-21) was made a capital offense.

BIBLIOGRAPHY: D. R. Mace, *Hebrew Marriage* (1953), pp. 184-220; P. A. H. de Boer, *Fatherhood and Motherhood in Israelite and Judean Piety* (1974); K. Kerenyi, *Zeus and Hera: Archetypal Image of Father, Husband and Wife* (1975); T. A. Smail, *The Forgotten Father* (1980); D. B. Lockerbie, *Fatherlove* (1981).

FATHER, GOD THE. A term that represents several scriptural conceptions.

1. The term designates the first Person of the Trinity. God has revealed Himself as Father, Son, and Holy Spirit. To the Eternal Son the Father stands related as to no other being and finds in the Son the perfect and infinite object of His love. With this highest meaning in view the apostles speak of God as the "Father of our Lord Jesus Christ" (1 Pet. 1:3; *see* 1 Cor. 8:6; Eph. 1:17). Thus also, although Christ taught His disciples to address God in prayer as "our Father," He did not use that form Himself. He spoke of God as "My Father" and "your Father," but at the same time He made plain that He distinguished between the relation in which they stood to God and that in which He Himself stood. The first words of the Apostles' Creed, "I believe in God the Father Almighty," are first of all a recognition of this deep truth of Holy Scriptures. *See* Trinity.

2. In the OT God is in quite a number of conspicuous instances called the Father of the Jewish nation. The chosen nation owed its origin and continued existence to His miraculous power and special care. As their Father He loved, pitied, rebuked, and required the obedience of His people (*see* Deut. 32:6; Hos. 11:1; Pss. 103:13; 68:5; Mal. 1:6).

3. In the NT, which brings the fact of the Fatherhood of God into greater prominence and distinctness, God is represented as the Father of various objects and orders of beings that He has created. The term thus used refers to the natural relationship between God and His creatures and has a significance more or less profound according to the different natures and capacities of these objects or orders of beings. Thus God is "the Father of lights," the heavenly bodies (James 1:17). He is also "the Father of spirits" (Heb. 12:9). He is particularly the Father of man, created after His image (Acts 17:26; Luke 3:8).

4. God is in a special sense the Father of His redeemed and saved people. Although the hope of the gospel rests upon the fact of the fatherly love of God for mankind even in its sinfulness (*see* John 3:16; Luke 15:11-32), still, only they who are actually saved through Jesus Christ are admitted to the privileges of children in the divine household. Christ taught only His disciples to pray "our Father." He said to the unbelieving Jews, "You are of your father the devil" (John 8:44). The spiritual and moral relationship de-

stroyed by sin must be restored by gracious, divine renewal (1:12; Rom. 8:14-16; etc.). *See* Adoption.   E.MCC.

BIBLIOGRAPHY: J. Baillie, *Our Knowledge of God* (1930); G. Vos, *Biblical Theology* (1948), pp. 381-97; A. W. Tozer, *Knowledge of the Holy* (1961); L. Strauss, *The First Person* (1967); C. C. Ryrie, *A Survey of Bible Doctrine* (1972), pp. 11-35.

FATHER-IN-LAW. One giving a daughter in marriage (Ex. 3:1; 4:18); one related by affinity (Gen. 38:25; 1 Sam. 4:19, 21). A wife's father (John 18:13).

FATHER'S BROTHER (Heb. *dôd*). Strictly *one beloved* (Isa. 5:1); an *uncle* (Num. 36:11; 2 Kings 24:17); in Ex. 6:20 used in the feminine, *father's sister,* an aunt.

FATHER'S HOUSEHOLD. The name given to *families* among the Israelites (Josh. 22:14; cf. 7:14, 16-18). *See* Israel, Classification of.

FATLING. An animal put up to be fattened for slaughter (Heb. *merî',* 2 Sam. 6:13; Isa. 11:6; Ezek. 39:18; *see* 1 Kings 4:23; Matt. 22:4). In the KJV *fatling* is the term used for a choice *sheep* (which see), especially of the fat-tailed variety (Heb. *mēaḥ;* Ps. 66:15).

FAT TAIL (Heb. *'alyâ*). Moses prescribed that in certain sacrifices the tail of the animal should be burned upon the altar, namely, the ram of consecration (Ex. 29:22), the lamb of the peace offering (Lev. 3:9), and the lamb of the trespass offering (7:3). The fat tail was esteemed the most delicate portion of the animal. The fat is contained in the broad part of the tail, from which the true tail hangs. *See* Fat.

FATTENED FOWL (Heb. *barbūrîm 'ăbûsîm*). Mentioned among the daily provisions for Solomon's table (1 Kings 4:23; NIV, "choice fowl"). Evidently the "lark-heeled cuckoo" is meant. The cuckoo is a delicacy in Greece and Italy, even today (L. Koehler, *Lexicon,* ad loc.). *See* Animal Kingdom.

FEAR (Heb. *yir'â,* "reverence," and other Heb. words meaning "terror," Ex. 15:16; etc.; "carefulness," Josh. 22:24, NASB; "concern," Prov. 29:25; "fright," Job 41:33; Gk. *phobos,* "dread, terror," Matt. 14:26; etc.). Fear is that affection of the mind that arises with the awareness of approaching danger. The fear of God is of several kinds: superstitious, which is the fruit of ignorance; servile, which leads to abstinence from many sins through apprehension of punishment; and filial, which has its spring in love and prompts to care not to offend God and to endeavor in all things to please Him. It is another term for practical piety and comprehends the virtues of the godly character (Ps. 111:10; Prov. 14:2), whereas its absence is characteristic of a wicked and depraved person (Rom. 3:18). It is produced in the soul by the Holy Spirit, and great blessing is pronounced upon those who possess this trait: His angels protect them (Ps. 34:7); they "abide in the shadow of the Almighty" (91:1). This fear would subsist in a pious soul were there no punishment of sin. It dreads God's displeasure, desires His favor, reveres His holiness, submits cheerfully to His will, is grateful for His benefits, sincerely worships Him, and conscientiously obeys His commandments. Fear and love must coexist in us in order that either passion may be healthy and that we may please and rightly serve God. "The fear of the Lord" is used for the worship of God, e.g., "I will teach you the fear of the Lord" (34:11) and for the law of God (19:8-9). The "fear of Isaac" (Gen. 31:42, 53) is God, whom Isaac worshiped with reverent awe. The "fear of man" is that dread of the opinions of our neighbors that makes us cowards in the performance of those duties that we fancy they do not practice (Prov. 29:25).

BIBLIOGRAPHY: W. Barclay, *A New Testament Wordbook* (n.d.), pp. 92-96; J. Murray, *Principles of Conduct* (1957), pp. 229ff.; R. Morosco, *Journal of Psychology and Theology* 1, no. 2 (1973): 43-50.

FEAST. *See* Banquet; Festivals.

FEAST OF CHARITY. *See* Agape.

FEEBLE KNEES. A term used to express the results of overexertion, as in an athletic contest, and, figuratively, of *weariness of mind, low spirits* (Heb. 12:12).

FEEBLEMINDED. *See* Fainthearted.

FEELING. In Eph. 4:19 we find this: "and they, having become callous, have given themselves over to sensuality," etc. The Gk. word *apalegeō* means "to become insensible to pain, callous, and so indifferent to truth, honor, or shame," i.e., without *feeling.* The writer of the epistle to the Hebrews (4:15) tells us that "we do not have a high priest who cannot sympathize with our weaknesses." Here we have the Gk. *sumpatheō,* "to feel for, to have compassion on." Dorner thus speaks of feeling as an element of man's nature: "In *feeling* he has existence within himself, in *will* he exists in a state of movement from self outward, in *knowledge* in movement from without inward. . . . Like the other spiritual faculties, so called, *feeling* is receptive of infinite as of finite truth. Feeling is a third element alongside of knowledge and will. The strength of feeling depending very much on individual mental temperament, this forms no security for the purity or healthiness of religious feeling. With respect to the contents of feeling, in religious feeling the reference to a definite idea of God will likewise exert an influence, and upon its accurate or confused character—in short, upon its completeness—will the nature of religion depend. A religion, for example, acquainted merely with God's physical attributes will stand lower than one that has heard of His holiness, or, still more, of His love. Feeling alone, occupied merely with self and brooding upon self, may easily become one-sided and selfish. Knowledge, as the product of revelation, we call *illumination.* Revelation must possess power by its contents to inspire and intensify the *will,* and under this aspect it is *quickening,* while the *feeling* (the spiritual consciousness of self or life) is enhanced in freedom and blessedness" (Dorner, *Christian Doctrine,* 2:109, 119).

FEET. *See* Foot.

FE'LIX (fē'lix; "happy"). The Roman procurator before whom Paul was arraigned (Acts 24).

Elevation and Crimes. He was originally a slave and for some unknown service was freed by Claudius Caesar. He was appointed by this emperor procurator of Judea with the banishment of Ventidius Cumanus, probably A.D. 53. Suetonius speaks of the military honors that the emperor conferred upon him and specifies his appointment as governor of the province of Judea, adding an innuendo that loses nothing by its brevity, namely, that he was the husband of three queens or royal ladies (*"trium reginarum maritum"*). Tacitus in his *History* declares that during his governorship in Judea he indulged in all kinds of cruelty and lust, exercising regal power with the disposition of a slave; and in his *Annals* (11.54) he represents Felix as considering himself licensed to commit any crime, relying on the influence that he possessed at court. Having a grudge against Jonathan, the high priest who had expostulated with him on his misrule, he made use of Doras, an intimate friend of Jonathan, in order to get him assassinated by a gang of villains, who joined the crowds that were going up to the Temple worship. The crime led subsequently to countless evils by the encouragement that it gave to the Sicarii, or leagued assassins of the day, to whose excesses Josephus ascribes, under Providence, the overthrow of the Jewish state. While in office he became enamored of Drusilla, a daughter of King Herod Agrippa, who was married to Azizus, king of Emesa, and through the influence of Simon, a magician, prevailed upon her to consent to a union with him. With this adulteress Felix was seated when Paul reasoned before him (Acts 24:25). Another Drusilla is mentioned by Tacitus as being the (first) wife of Felix.

Hears Paul. Paul, having been arrested at Jerusalem, was sent by Claudius Lysias to Felix at Caesarea (Acts 23:23-33), where he was confined in Herod's judgment hall until his accusers came. They arrived after five days, headed by Ananias, the high priest. Their case was managed by Tertullus, who, to conciliate Felix, expressed gratitude on the part of the Jews, "Since we have through you attained much peace, and since by your providence reforms are being carried out for this nation, we acknowledge this in every way and everywhere, most excellent Felix" (24:2-3). He then proceeded to accuse Paul, charging him, first, with sedition; second, with being "a ringleader of the sect of the Nazarenes"; and, third, with an attempt to profane the Temple at Jerusalem (vv. 5-6). The evident purpose was to persuade Felix to give up the apostle to the Jewish courts, in which case his assassination would have been easily accomplished. Felix now gave the prisoner permission to speak, and the apostle, after briefly expressing his satisfaction that he had to plead his cause before one so well acquainted with Jewish customs, refuted Tertullus step by step. Felix deferred inquiry into the case for the present. "When Lysias the commander comes down," he said, "I will decide your case." Meanwhile, he placed Paul under the charge of the centurion who had brought him to Caesarea (24:10-23). Some days after, Felix came into the audience chamber with his wife, Drusilla, and the prisoner was brought before them. As a faithful preacher Paul spoke to the Roman libertine and the profligate Jewish princess. As he spoke of righteousness, self-control, and judgment to come, Felix "became frightened." But still nothing was decided. Felix said, "Go away for the present, and when I find time, I will summon you." We are told why the governor shut his ears to conviction, even neglected his official duty, and kept his prisoner in cruel suspense: "He was hoping that money would be given him by Paul" (vv. 24-26). Hence he frequently sent for Paul and had many conversations with him. But his hopes were unfulfilled, and he kept the apostle a prisoner for two years (v. 27).

Summoned to Rome. Meanwhile, the political state of Judea grew more embarrassing. It was during the two years of Paul's imprisonment that disturbances took place in the streets of Caesarea. In the end Felix was summoned to Rome, and the Jews followed him with their accusations. Thus it was that he was anxious "to do the Jews a favor" and "left Paul imprisoned" (Acts 24:27). At Rome he was saved from suffering the penalty due his atrocities by the influence of his brother Pallas.

BIBLIOGRAPHY: H. J. Cadbury, *The Book of Acts in History* (1955), pp. 9ff.

FELLOES. *See* Spoke.

FELLOW. A term occurring in both the KJV and NASB, though not always as the rendering of the same Heb. or Gk. word. Some special KJV uses follow.

1. A contemptuous use of Heb. *'îsh* (1 Sam. 29:4); Gk. *anēr,* words for *man* (so NASB).

2. The rendering of Heb. *rēa'* (Ex. 2:13; Judg. 7:13; NASB, "companion," "friend") or *ḥabbār* (Eccles. 4:10; NASB, "companion"; NIV, "friend").

3. The rendering of Heb. *'āmît,* "neighbor," given as "Associate" in Zech. 13:7. The NIV renders, "the man close to me." *See* Associate; Belial.

FELLOWSHIP. *Fellowship* means companionship, a relation in which parties hold something in common, familiar interaction. Christians have *fellowship* with the Father and the Son (1 John 1:3) and the Holy Spirit (2 Cor. 13:14), and with one another (1 John 1:7). As is the case between men, no one can "know God," i.e., be in fellowship with Him, unless he possess like purposes and feelings (2:3-6), with love (Rom. 8:38-39). The *fellowship* of believers embraces confession of sins one to another with prayer (James 5:16); assembly, with exhortation and stimulation to love and good works (Heb. 10:24-25); partaking of the Lord's Supper (1 Cor. 11:24-25); "contributing to the needs of the saints" (Rom. 12:13; 15:25; Acts 11:29; 1 Cor. 16:1-2; 2 Cor. 8:4; Heb. 13:16); bearing the infirmities of the weak; and pleasing one's neighbor (Rom. 15:1-2). Love for and fellowship with one another are necessary to, and an evidence of, fellowship with God (1 John 4:12). Christ prayed that His people might have fellowship with each other (John 17:21). Fellowship with God is essential to fruitfulness (15:4-5).

FENCE (Heb. *gāḏēr,* an "enclosure"; Pss. 62:3; 80:12, *see* marg.). Fences were built of unmortared stones to protect cultivated lands, sheepfolds, etc. In the crevices of such fences, serpents delighted to hide (cf. Eccles. 10:8; Amos 5:19).

Figurative. In Ps. 62:3 the wicked are compared to a tottering *fence* and leaning wall, i.e., their destruction comes suddenly. *See* Hedge.

A stone fence

FENCED CITY. *See* Fortified City.

FERRET. *See* Animal Kingdom: Gecko.

FERRYBOAT (Heb. *'ăḇārâ,* "crossing"). A vessel for crossing a stream (2 Sam. 19:18, KJV; NIV has "ford"). Floats or rafts for this purpose were used from remote times (1 Kings 5:9, and paintings on Egyptian monuments). A ferryboat still crosses the Jordan ford near Jericho.

FESTAL ROBES. *See* Dress.

FESTIVALS. Besides the daily worship, the law prescribed special festivals to be observed from time to time by the congregation. One Heb. name for festival was *ḥāg* (from the verb signifying to "dance"), which, when applied to religious services, indicated that they were occasions of joy and gladness. The term most fitly designating, and which alone actually comprehended all the feasts, was *mô'ēd,* (a "set time" or "assembly, place of assembly"). This name refers to the stated assemblies of the people—the occasions fixed by divine appointment for meeting together in holy fellowship, i.e., for acts and purposes of worship. There is also the Gk. *heortē* ("festival, holy day"). The date of every Mosaic festival without distinction, no matter what its special object may have been, gave evidence of being connected in some way or other with the number *seven.* So every seventh day, every seventh month, every seventh year, and last, the year that came after the lapse of seven times seven years, was marked by a festival. Again, the Passover and the feast of Booths (Tabernacles, KJV) extended over seven days; the number of special *convocations* (which see) during the year was seven—two at the Passover, one at Pentecost, one at the feast of Trumpets (or New Moon), one on the Day of Atonement, and two at the feast of Booths. All the festivals instituted by the law of Moses may be arranged in two series, septenary and yearly. In addition are the postexilic and doubtful festivals. *See* table 8, "Festivals of Israel."

The Weekly Sabbath. In addition to entire cessation from all work the Sabbath was observed by a holy assembly, the doubling of the morning and evening sacrifices (Num. 28:9-10), and the presentation of new bread in the Holy Place (Lev. 24:8). *See* Sabbath.

The Seventh New Moon, or Feast of Trumpets (Heb. *yôm ṭerû'â,* "day of blowing," Num. 29:1). The feast of the New Moon, which fell on the seventh month, or Tishri. This differed from the ordinary festivals of the new moon because of the symbolic meaning of the seventh or sabbatical month and partly, perhaps, because it marked the beginning of the civil year. This month was distinguished above all the other months of the year by the multitude of ordinances connected with it, the first day being consecrated to sacred rest and spiritual employment, the tenth being the Day of Atonement, whereas the fifteenth began the feast of Booths (Tabernacles, KJV).

Sacrifices. (1) The usual morning and evening sacrifices, with their grain and drink offerings. (2) The ordinary sacrifice for the New Moon, except the sin offering, namely, two young bulls, one ram, seven yearling lambs, with their grain and drink offerings (Num. 28:11-14). (3) Another festive offering of one young bull, one ram, seven lambs, with their grain and drink offerings, together with "one male goat for a sin offering, to make atonement for you" (Num. 29:1-6).

Observance. This day was observed as a feast day, in the strict sense, by resting from all work,

Blowing the "shofar" trumpet at the Western Wall in Jerusalem on the eve of the Feast of Trumpets

and as a holy convocation, by the blowing of horns. In later times, while the drink offering of the sacrifice was being poured out, the priests and Levites chanted Ps. 81, whereas in the evening sacrifice they sang Ps. 29. Throughout the day trumpets were blown at Jerusalem from morning to evening. In the Temple it was done even on a Sabbath, but not outside its walls. "The Day of Atonement, which falls on this month, provides full expiation of all sins and the removal

of all uncleanness; and the Feast of Tabernacles, beginning five days thereafter, provides a foretaste of the blessedness of life in fellowship with the Lord. This significance of the seventh month is indicated by the sounding of trumpets, whereby the congregation present a memorial of themselves loudly and strongly before Jehovah, calling on him to vouchsafe the promised blessings of grace in fulfillment of his covenant" (Keil, *Arch.*, 2:10). The fact that Tishri was the great month for sowing might easily have suggested the thought of commemorating on this day the finished work of creation, and thus the feast of Trumpets came to be regarded as the anniversary of the beginning of the world. The rabbis believed that on this day God judges all men, and that they pass before Him as a flock of sheep passes before a shepherd.

Sabbatic Year. The septennial rest for the land from all tillage and cultivation as enjoined by Moses (Ex. 23:10-11; Lev. 25:2-7; Deut. 15:1-10; 31:10-13).

Names. The Mosaic titles express features of their observance. These are (1) "Rest of Entire Rest" (Heb. *shabbat shabbātôn,* "Sabbath of Sabbatism," Lev. 25:4; NASB and NIV, "a sabbath rest"), because the land was to have a complete rest from cultivation; (2) "Year of Rest" (Heb. *sh*e*nat shabbātôn,* "Year of Sabbatism," Lev. 25:5; NASB, "sabbatical year"; NIV, "year of rest"), because the rest was to extend through the year; (3) "Release" (Heb. *sh*e*miṭṭâ,* Deut. 15:1-2, KJV), or more fully, the "Year of Release" (Heb. *sh*e*nat hashsh*e*miṭṭâ,* 15:9; NASB, "year of remission"; NIV, "year for canceling debts"), because in it all debts were remitted; (4) "The Seventh Year" (Heb. *sh*e*nat hashsheba',* Deut. 15:9), because it was to be celebrated every seventh year.

Design. The spirit of the sabbatic year is that

Cycle or Historic Period	Name of Observance	Reference in the Scripture or Apocrypha
Septenary (or cycles of Sabbaths)	Weekly Sabbath	Ex. 20:8–11; 31:12–17; Lev. 23:12
	Seventh New Moon, or Feast of Trumpets	Num. 28:11–15; 29:1–6
	Sabbatic Year, i.e., every seventh year	Ex. 23:10–11; Lev. 25:2–7
	Year of Jubilee	Lev. 25:8–16; 27:16–25
	New Moon	Num. 10:10; 28:11–15
Yearly	Feast of Passover and Unleavened Bread	Ex. 12:1–28; 23:15; Lev. 23:4–8; Num. 28:16–25; Deut. 16:16; 18:1–8
	Pentecost, or Feast of Weeks	Ex. 34:22; Lev. 23:15–16; Num. 28:26; Deut. 16:10, 16
	Day of Atonement	Ex. 30:10–30; Lev. 16:1–34; Num. 29:7–11
	Feast of Booths (Tabernacles)	Lev. 23:34–42; Num. 29:12–38; Deut. 10:13–16; Neh. 8:13–18; John 7:2, 37
Postexilic	Feast of Purim	Esther 9:24–32
	Feast of Dedication	1 Macc. 4:52–59; 2 Macc. 10:5–8; John 10:22

Table 8
Festivals of Israel

of the weekly Sabbath. The rest that the land was to keep in the seventh year was not to increase its fruitfulness by lying fallow or merely to be a time of recreation for laboring men and beasts, needful and useful as that may be. It was rather to afford true spiritual rest and quickening, with their attendant life and blessing. "Thus Israel, as the people of God, was to learn two things: First, that the earth, though created for man, was not merely that he might turn its powers to his own profit, but that he might be holy to the Lord and participate also in his blessed rest; next, that the goal of life for the congregation of the Lord did not lie in that incessant laboring of the earth which is associated with sore toil in the sweat of the brow (Gen. 3:17, 19), but in the enjoyment of the fruits of the earth, free from care, which the Lord their God gave and ever would give them if they strove to keep his covenant and to take quickening from his law" (Keil, *Arch.,* 2:12). Such an institution as the sabbatic year might seem, at first sight, to be impracticable. But we are to remember that in no year was the owner of land allowed to reap the whole harvest (Lev. 19:9; 23:22). Unless the remainder was entirely gleaned there might easily have been enough to insure quite a spontaneous crop the ensuing year, while the vines and olives would yield fruit of themselves. Then, too, the unavoidable inference from 25:20-22 is that the owners of land were to lay by grain in previous years for their own and their families' need.

Time, Observance. The sabbatic year, like the year of Jubilee, began on the first day of the civil year, namely, the first of the month Tishri. Although this was the time fixed for the celebration of the sabbatic year during the time of the second Temple, the tillage and cultivation of certain fields and gardens had already begun to be left off in the sixth year. Thus it was ordained that fields upon which trees were planted were not to be cultivated after the feast of Pentecost of the sixth year, whereas the cultivation of grainfields was to cease from the feast of the Passover (Mishna, *Shebith* 1.1-8). The keeping of the sabbatic year is distinctly attested to by 1 Macc. 6:49, 53, and Josephus (*Ant.* 13.8.1; 14.10.6; 15.1.2; etc.), and it was observed also by the Samaritans (Josephus *Ant.* 11.8.6).

Laws. The laws respecting this year were four in number: (1) The soil, the vineyards, and the olive groves were to have perfect rest (Ex. 23:10-11; Lev. 25:2-5). Rabbinical regulations carried the law to such an extent that anything planted wittingly or unwittingly had to be plucked up by its roots (Mishna, *Terum* 2.3). (2) The spontaneous growth of the fields or of trees (cf. Isa. 37:30) was for the free use of the poor, the hireling, the stranger, servants, and cattle (Ex. 23:10-11; Lev. 25:2-7). An especially fruitful harvest was promised for the sixth year (25:20-21). (3) Debts, with the exception of ones owed by foreigners, were to

be canceled (Deut. 15:1-4). This does not seem to denote the entire renunciation of what was owed but entailed not pursuing it during the sabbatic year. This enactment did not forbid the voluntary payment of debts but their enforced liquidation, and also that no poor man should be oppressed by his brother. (4) Finally, at the feast of Booths in this year, the law was to be read to the people—men, women, children, and strangers—in solemn assembly before the sanctuary (Deut. 31:10-13).

The sabbatic year seems to have been systematically neglected. Hence Jewish tradition explains (*see* 2 Chron. 36:21) that the seventy years' captivity was intended to make up for the neglect of sabbatical years. After the return from captivity this year was most strictly observed.

Jubilee (Heb. *yôbēl,* a "blast" of a trumpet). Usually in connection with the year of Jubilee (Lev. 25:28); also called the "year of liberty" (Ezek. 46:17; NIV, "year of freedom"). Its relation to the sabbatic year and the general direction for its observance are found in Lev. 25:8-16, 23-55. Its bearing on lands dedicated to Jehovah is given in 27:16-25. It is not mentioned in Deuteronomy, and the only other reference to it in the Pentateuch is in Num. 36:4.

Worshiper holding the four species used to mark the Feast of Tabernacles

Time. After the lapse of seven Sabbaths of years, or seven times seven years, i.e., forty-nine years, the trumpet was to sound throughout the whole land, and the fiftieth year was to be announced and hallowed as the Jubilee year. This was not the forty-ninth year, as held by some chronologists. Decisive against this view is the fact "that in Lev. 25:10[-13] not only is the fiftieth year expressly named as the year of Jubilee, but the forty-nine years which make seven Sabbatic years are expressly distinguished from it" (Winer, "Jubeljahr," in *R. W. Buch*).

Observance. It should be noticed that the observance of Jubilee was to become obligatory upon the Israelites after they had taken possession of the Promised Land and had cultivated the soil for forty-nine years. The ancient Talmudic tradition, which appears to be correct, is that the first sabbatic year was the twenty-first, and the first Jubliee the sixty-fourth after the Jews came into Canaan, for it took them seven years to conquer it and seven more to distribute it. The only enactment as to the *manner* of its observance is that there should be announced with the blowing of trumpets the Jubilee that proclaimed to the covenant nation the gracious presence of its God. Because the Scriptures do not record any particular instance of the public celebration, some have denied or questioned whether the law of Jubilee ever came into actual operation. In favor of its actual observance are (1) the probability arising from the observance of all the other festivals; (2) the law of the inalienability of landed property that really did exist among the Hebrews (Num. 36:4, 6-7; Ezek. 46:17); (3) the unanimous voice of Hebrew tradition.

Laws. The law stated three respects in which the Jubilee was to be hallowed, i.e., separated from other years: rest for the soil, reversion of landed property, and manumission of Israelites.

Rest for the Soil. No sowing, reaping, or gathering from the unpruned vine (Lev. 25:11). Thus the soil enjoyed a holy rest, man was freed from the sore labor of sowing and reaping, and in blessed rest was to live and enjoy the bounty provided by Jehovah in the sixth year (v. 21).

Reversion of Landed Property (Lev. 25:10-34; 27:16-24). The law of Moses provided that all the Promised Land was to be divided by lot among the Israelites, and then it was to remain absolutely inalienable. Therefore, at Jubilee all property in fields and houses situated in villages or unwalled towns, which the owner had been obliged to sell through poverty and that had not been redeemed (*see* Redemption), was to revert without payment to its original owner or his lawful heirs. The only exceptions were houses in walled cities, which remained with the buyer unless redeemed within one year (25:29-30), and those fields which, unless redeemed by the owner, had been sold and thereby rendered unredeemable (27:17-21), in which case they reverted to the priests.

Manumission of Israelites. Every Israelite who through poverty had sold himself to one of his countrymen or to a foreigner settled in the land, if he had been unable to redeem himself or had not been redeemed by a kinsman, was to go out free with his children (Lev. 25:35-43, 47-54).

Thus ownership of a person was changed into a matter of hire (vv. 40, 53). It would seem that there must have been a perfect remission of all debts in the year of Jubilee from the fact that all persons in bondage for debt were released, and all landed property of debtors was freely returned. Thus the Jubilee year became one of freedom and grace for all suffering, bringing not only redemption to the captive and deliverance from want to the poor, but also release to the whole congregation of the Lord from the sore labor of the earth, representing the time of refreshing (Acts 3:19) that the Lord provides for His people. For in this year every kind of oppression was to cease and every member of the covenant people to find his redeemer in the Lord, who brought him back to his possession and family.

New Moon (Heb. *r'ōsh ḥōdesh*, "beginning of a month," Num. 10:10; 28:11). The ordinary new moons, i.e., all except the seventh, were raised out of the rank of ordinary days, but not to that of festivals. They may be called demi-feast days and will therefore be inserted here.

Origin. Many nations of antiquity celebrated the returning light of the moon with festivals, sacrifices, and prayers. Some believe that the object of Moses in providing for this occasion was to suppress heathen celebrations of the day. There was, however, a deeper meaning in this observance. The new moon stood as the representative of the month. For an individual day, a burnt offering that emphasized consecration to the Lord rather than atonement was sufficient. But for the month, because of sins committed and remaining unexpiated during the course of the month, a special sin offering for atonement was required. Thus, on the ground of the forgiveness and reconciliation with God thereby obtained, the people might be able in the burnt offering to consecrate their lives anew to the Lord.

Mode of Ascertaining the New Moon. As the festivals, according to the Mosaic law, were always to be celebrated on the same day of the month, it was necessary to fix the commencement of the month. This was determined by the appearance of the new moon; for the new moon was reckoned not by astronomical calculation, but by actual personal observation. On the thirtieth day of the month watchmen were placed on commanding heights around Jerusalem to watch the sky. As soon as each of them detected the moon he hastened to a house in the city kept for this purpose and was there examined by the president of the Sanhedrin. When the evidence of the appearance was deemed satisfactory, the president stood up and formally announced it, uttering the words, "It is consecrated." The information was immediately sent throughout the land from the Mount of Olives by beacon fires on the tops of the hills. The religious observance of the day of the new moon may plainly be regarded as the consecration of a natural division of time.

Sacrifices. These were of two types: (1) the usual morning and evening sacrifices, with their grain and drink offerings, and (2) special sacrifices, consisting of two young bulls, one ram, and seven lambs of the first year, as a burnt offering, with their grain and drink offerings. A goat was also presented as a sin offering, at which time the priests blew the silver trumpets (Num. 10:10; 28:11-15). It is evident from the writings of the prophets and from postexilic documents that the New Moon was an important national festival. It was often called a feast along with the Sabbath (Ps. 81:3; Isa. 1:13; Ezek. 46:1; Hos. 2:11), on which all business ceased (Amos 8:5), the pious Israelites waited on the prophets for edification (2 Kings 4:23), many families and clans presented their annual thank offerings (1 Sam. 20:6, 29), social gatherings and feasting were indulged in (vv. 5, 24), and the most devout persons omitted fasting (Judith 8:6).

The Passover and Feast of Unleavened Bread. Passover and the feast of Unleavened Bread as a unit constituted the most important of the three great annual festivals of Israel.

Name and Significance. It was indifferently called the feast of the Passover and the feast of Unleavened Bread, but where the object was to mark the distinction between the Passover as a sacrifice and as a feast following the sacrifice, the latter was designated the feast of Unleavened Bread (Lev. 23:5-6). The Heb. word *pesaḥ* (from *pāsaḥ*, to "leap over," figuratively, to "spare, show mercy") denotes (1) an overstepping and (2) the paschal sacrifice by virtue of which the passing over was effected (Ex. 12:21, 27, 48; 2 Chron. 30:15). The paschal meal was on the evening of the 14th Nisan, and the seven days following are called the feast of Unleavened Bread (Lev. 23:5-6), hence the expression "the morrow of the Passover" for the 15th Nisan (Num. 33:3; Josh. 5:11, *see* marg.). The whole feast, including the paschal eve, is called the festival of Unleavened Bread (Ex. 23:15; Lev. 23:6; Ezra 6:22; Luke 22:1, 7; Acts 12:3; 20:6); but the simple name "Passover" (Heb. *pesaḥ*) is the one commonly used by the Jews to the present day for the festival of Unleavened Bread (2 Chron. 30:15; 35:1, 11; Mark 14:1; Gk. *pascha*).

Institution. The Passover was instituted in memory of Israel's preservation from the last plague visited upon Egypt (the death of the firstborn) and their deliverance from bondage (Ex. 12:1-28). "The deliverance of Israel from Egypt was accompanied by their adoption as the nation of Jehovah. For this a divine consecration was necessary that their outward severance from Egypt might be accompanied by an inward severance from everything of an Egyptian or heathen nature. This consecration was imparted by the Passover, a festival which was to lay the foundation of Israel's birth (Hos. 2:15; Ex. 6:6-7) into

the new life of grace and fellowship with God and to perpetuate it in time to come" (K. & D., *Com.*, on Ex. 12).

Observance. Observances connected with the Passover are in two categories, those established at the keeping of the first Passover and those enacted after the Exodus.

Before the Exodus. At its first institution, just before the Exodus, the keeping of the Passover was as follows: Every head of a family chose a male of the first year without blemish from the small cattle, i.e., from the sheep or goats, on the 10th Nisan (Ex. 12:3). Later it became the fixed practice to take a lamb. On the 14th Nisan the animal was slain "at twilight" (12:6); according to the Karaite Jews between actual sunset and complete darkness but understood by the Pharisees and rabbis as the time when the sun begins to descend to its real setting (from 3:00 to 6:00 P.M.). A bunch of hyssop was dipped in the blood of the animal and applied to the two posts and the lintel of the house where the meal was to be eaten. Then the whole animal, without a broken bone, was roasted and eaten by each family, including slaves and strangers, if circumcised. If the number of the family was too small, the neighboring family might join in the eating. It was eaten that same night with unleavened bread and bitter herbs, probably endives, wild lettuce, which are eaten by Jews of the present day in Egypt and Arabia with the paschal lamb. The meal was eaten the same evening, all who partook having their loins girded, shoes on their feet, and a staff in hand, ready to march out of Egypt. What of the lamb could not be eaten was to be burned the next morning, and nothing of it was to be carried out of the house (12:1-13, 21-23, 43-51). According to Jewish authorities this was called the "Egyptian" Passover in distinction from the "Permanent" Passover. The paschal lamb was a sacrifice, combining in itself the significance of the sin offerings and holy offerings, i.e., it shadowed reconciliation as well as glad fellowship with God; the lamb suffered instead of the partakers. There being no fixed sanctuary, the houses were converted into such places of grace or altars, and the blood put on the posts and lintel of the door was the sign that the house was to be spared. This sparing and reconciliation accomplished through forgiveness of sins was immediately associated with the meal, and thus the *sacrificium* became the *sacramentum*, the sacrificial flesh a means of grace. The unleavened bread symbolized the spiritual purity after which Israel in covenant with the Lord is to strive, and the bitter herbs were intended to call to mind the bitter experiences that the Israelites had suffered in Egypt.

After the Exodus. The following supplementary enactments were introduced after the Exodus: all male members of the congregation were to appear before the Lord with "the choice first fruits" (Ex. 23:14-19), the first sheaf of the harvest to be offered on "the day after the sabbath" (Lev. 23:10-14; *see also* the article First Fruits); those prevented from keeping the Passover on the 14th Nisan were to observe it on the fourteenth of the following month (Num. 9:6-14); special sacrifices were to be offered each day of the festival (28:16-25); the paschal animals were to be slain in the national sanctuary and the blood sprinkled on the altar instead of the doorposts and lintels of the homes (Deut. 16:1-8).

Feast of Unleavened Bread. The feast of Unleavened Bread immediately followed the Passover and lasted seven days, from the 15th to the 21st Nisan (or Abib). On each of those days, after the morning sacrifice, a sacrifice in connection with the feast was presented; unleavened bread alone was eaten (Ex. 12:15-20; 13:6-7; Deut. 16:3-8.

Sacrifices. (1) The usual morning and evening sacrifices, with their grain and drink offerings. (2) Two young bulls, one ram, seven lambs of the first year, with their grain and drink offerings. These were presented after the morning sacrifice (Num. 28:19-24).

Convocations. The first and seventh days of the feast were celebrated by a holy convocation and resting from work, with the exception of preparing food. On the intervening days work might be carried on unless the weekly Sabbath fell on one of them, in which case the full strictness of Sabbath-keeping was observed, and the special feast sacrifice was not presented until after the Sabbath offering.

Barley Sheaf. On the second feast day (16th Nisan) the first sheaf of the new harvest (barley) was symbolically offered to the Lord by waving —not burning on the altar—accompanied with a lamb of the first year for a burnt offering, with its grain and drink offerings. Previous to this offering neither bread nor roasted grain of the new harvest was allowed to be eaten (Lev. 23:9-14). Those attending presented freewill, burnt, and holy offerings of sheep and oxen (Ex. 23:15, 19; Deut. 16:2), and sacrificial meals were eaten. The feast closed on the 21st, with rest from work and a holy convocation.

History. Scripture records that the Passover was kept on the evening before the Israelites left Egypt (Ex. 12:28), the second year after the Exodus (Num. 9:1-5), and then not again until they entered Canaan (Ex. 13:5; Josh. 5:10). Only three instances are recorded in which the Passover was celebrated between the entrance into the Promised Land and the Babylonian captivity, namely, under Solomon (2 Chron 8:13), under Hezekiah when he restored the national worship (30:15), and under Josiah (2 Kings 23:21; 2 Chron. 35:1-19). But the inference that the Passover was celebrated only on those occasions seems the less warranted, that in later times it was so punctually and universally observed.

Postexilic Observance. After the return of the Jews from captivity the celebration of the Passover, like that of other institutions, became more regular and systematic; and its laws, rites, manners, and customs have been faithfully transmitted to us. These were the same as those in the time of Christ and His apostles and are, therefore, of the utmost importance and interest to us in understanding the NT. We give the various practices in connection with the days of the festival on which they were respectively observed.

1. The Great Sabbath (10th Nisan). The Sabbath immediately preceding the Passover, it is so called because, according to tradition, the 10th of Nisan, when the paschal lamb was to be selected, originally fell on the Sabbath. In later legislation the animal was not required to be set aside four days beforehand, yet the Sabbath was used for the instruction of the people in the duties of this great festival. In addition to the regular ritual, special prayers bearing on the redemption from Egypt, the love of God to Israel, and Israel's obligation to keep the Passover, were prescribed for that Sabbath. Malachi 3:1–4:6 was read as the lesson of the day, and discourses were delivered explaining the laws and domestic duties connected with the festival. This is likely the Sabbath referred to in John 19:31.

2. The 13th Nisan. On the evening of the 13th Nisan, which, until that of the 14th, was called the "preparation for the Passover" (John 19:14), every head of a family searched for and collected by the light of a candle all the leaven. Before beginning the search, he pronounced the following benediction: "Blessed art thou, O Lord our God, King of the universe, who has sanctified us with thy commandments, and hast enjoined us to remove the leaven." After the search he said, "Whatever leaven remains in my possession which I cannot see, behold, it is null, and accounted as the dust of the earth."

3. The 14th Nisan. This day, called until the evening *the preparation for the Passover,* was also known as the "first day" of Passover (Lev. 23:5-7). Handicraftsmen, with the exception of tailors, barbers, and laundresses, were obliged to cease from work, either from morning or from noon, according to the custom of the different places in Palestine. No leaven was allowed to be eaten after noon, when all that had been found either on this day or the preceding one was to be burned. On the 14th Nisan every Israelite who was physically able, not in a state of Levitical uncleanness, or further distant from Jerusalem than fifteen miles, was to appear before the Lord with an offering proportionate to his means (Ex. 23:15; Deut. 16:16-17). Women, though not legally bound to appear in the sanctuary, were not excluded (1 Sam. 1:7; Luke 2:41-42).

4. Offering of the Paschal Lamb. The lamb was to be free from all blemish and neither less than eight days nor more than exactly one year old.

Each paschal lamb was to serve a "company" of not less than ten nor more than twenty, the representatives of each company going to the Temple. The daily evening sacrifice (Ex. 29:38-39), usually killed at the eighth and a half hour (i.e., 2:30 P.M.), and offered up at the ninth and a half hour (i.e., 3:30 P.M.), was on this day killed at 1:30 and offered at 2:30 P.M., an hour earlier. And if the 14th of Nisan happened on a Friday, it was killed at 12:30 and offered at 1:30 P.M., two hours earlier than usual, so as to avoid any needless breach of the Sabbath.

Before the incense was burned or the lamps were trimmed, the paschal sacrifice had to be offered. It was done in this way: The first of the three festive divisions, with their paschal lambs, was admitted within the court of the priests. Each division was to consist of not less than thirty persons. Immediately, the massive gates were closed behind them, and the priests blew a threefold blast from their silver trumpets when the Passover was slain; altogether, the scene was most impressive. All along the court up to the altar of burnt offering priests stood in two rows, the one holding golden, the other silver, bowls. In these the blood of the paschal lambs, which each Israelite slew for himself (as representative of his company at the paschal supper), was caught up by a priest, who handed it to his colleague, receiving back an empty bowl, and so the bowls with the blood were passed up to the priest at the altar, who jerked it in one jet at the base of the altar. While this was going on, a most solemn "hymn" of praise was raised, the Levites leading in the song and the officers either repeating after them or merely responding. "The *Hallel* [which see] was recited the whole time, and if it was finished before all the paschal animals were slain it might be repeated a second and even a third time. Next the sacrifices were hung up on hooks along the court, or laid on staves which rested on the shoulders of two men (on Sabbaths they were not laid on staves), then flayed, the entrails taken out and cleansed, and the inside fat separated, put in a dish, salted, and placed on the fire of the altar of burnt offering. This completed the sacrifice.

"The first division of officers being dismissed, the second entered, and finally the third, the service in each case being conducted in precisely the same manner. Then the whole service concluded by burning the incense and trimming the lamps for the night." If it was the Sabbath, the first division waited in the court of the Gentiles, the second between the ramparts, i.e., the open space between the walls of the court of the women and the trellis work in the Temple, whereas the third remained in its place. At dark all went out to roast their paschal sacrifices. According to Jewish ordinance, the paschal lamb was roasted on a spit of pomegranate wood, the spit passing through from mouth to vent. If it touched the oven, the part so touched was to be cut away, thus carrying out the idea that the lamb must not be defiled by any contact with foreign matter. It was not to be "sodden," because the flesh must remain pure, without the addition even of water, and no bone of it was to be broken.

5. The Paschal Supper. As the guests gathered around the paschal table they were arrayed in their best festive garments, joyous and at rest, as became the children of a king. To express this idea the rabbis insisted that at least a part of the feast should be partaken in a recumbent position. The left elbow was placed on the table, the head resting on the hand, with sufficient room between each guest for the free movement of the right hand. This explains in what sense John "was reclining on Jesus' breast," and afterward "leaning back thus on Jesus' breast," when he leaned back to speak to Him (John 13:23, 25; Luke 22:14). The father, or other person presiding, took the place of honor at the table, probably somewhat raised above the rest.

The paschal supper commenced by the head of the "company" pronouncing a benediction over the first cup of wine, which had been filled for each person. It was then drunk, and a basin of water and a towel were handed around or the guests got up to wash their hands (John 13:4-5, 12), after which the appropriate blessing was pronounced.

These preliminaries ended, a table was brought in, upon which was the paschal meal. The president of the feast first took some of the herbs, dipped them in the sauce (Heb. *charoseth*), ate some, and gave to the others (Matt. 26:23; John 13:26). Immediately after this all the dishes were removed from the table (to excite curiosity), and the second cup of wine was filled. Then the son asked his father as follows: "Wherefore is this night distinguished from all other nights? For on all other nights we eat leavened or unleavened bread, but on this night only unleavened bread? On all other nights we eat any kind of herbs, but on this night only bitter herbs? On all other nights we eat meat roasted, stewed, or boiled but on this night only roasted? On all other nights we dip [the herbs] only once, but on this night twice?" In reply the head of the house related the whole national history, commencing with Terah, Abraham's father, Israel's deliverance from Egypt, and the giving of the law.

The paschal dishes were now placed back upon the table. The president took up in succession the dish with the Passover lamb, that with the bitter herbs, and that with the unleavened bread, briefly explaining the importance of each; the first part of the Hallel was sung (Pss. 113 and 114), with this brief thanksgiving at the close: "Blessed art thou, Jehovah our God, King of the universe, who hast redeemed us and redeemed our fathers from Egypt." The second cup of wine was then drunk, and hands were washed a second time, with the same prayer as before, and one of the two unleavened cakes broken and "thanks given."

Pieces of the broken cake, with "bitter herbs" between them and "dipped" in the *charoseth,* were next handed to each of the company. This, in all probability, was the "dipped morsel" which, in answer to John's inquiry about the betrayer, the Lord "gave" to Judas (John 13:25-30; cf. Mark 14:22; Luke 22:21).

The paschal supper itself consisted of the unleavened bread, with bitter herbs, of the so-called *Chagigah* (i.e., a voluntary peace offering made by private individuals), and the paschal lamb itself. After that nothing more was to be eaten, so that the flesh of the paschal sacrifice might be the last meat partaken of. But since the cessation of the paschal sacrifice, the Jews conclude the supper with a piece of unleavened cake called the *Aphikomen,* or after dish. Hands were again washed, the third cup was filled, and grace after meat said. The service concluded with the fourth cups over which the second portion of the Hallel was sung (Pss. 115-18), the whole ending with the so-called "blessing of the song."

6. The 15th Nisan, Unleavened Bread. On this day there was a holy convocation, and it was one of the six days on which, as on the Sabbath, no manner of work was allowed, with this exception: whereas on the Sabbath the preparation of necessary food was not allowed (Ex. 16:5, 23, 29; 35:2-3), on holy convocation it was permitted (12:16; Lev. 23:7; Num. 28:18). The other five days on which the Bible prohibits servile work are the seventh of this festival, the day of Pentecost, New Year's Day, and the first and last of the feast of Booths (Tabernacles, KJV).

In addition to the ordinary sacrifices there were offered on this and the following six days two bulls, a ram, and seven lambs of the first year (with grain offerings) for a burnt offering, and a goat for a sin offering (28:19-23). Besides these public sacrifices voluntary offerings were made by each individual appearing before the Lord in Jerusalem (Ex. 23:15; Deut. 16:16). The Jewish canon prescribed that this freewill offering should be a burnt offering, worth not less than sixteen grains of corn; a festive offering of not less value than thirty-two grains; and a peace, or joyful offering (27:7), the value to be determined by the offerer (16:16-17).

7. The 16th Nisan, Cutting the Barley Sheaf. This day was also called "the day after the Sabbath"; and on it the omer of the first produce of the harvest (i.e., barley) was waved before the Lord (Lev. 23:10-14). Though for obvious reasons it was customary to choose barley grown in the sheltered Ashes valley across the Kedron, there were no restrictions, save that the barley was to be grown in Palestine and without being forced by manuring and artificial watering. On the 14th Nisan, delegates from the Sanhedrin had marked out the spot where the first sheaf was to be cut by tying together in bundles, while still standing, the barley to be reaped. When the time came for cutting the sheaf (i.e., the evening of the 15th Nisan, even though it was a Sabbath), just as the sun went down, three men, each with a sickle and basket, set formally to work. In order to bring out all that was distinctive in the ceremony, they first asked the bystanders the following questions three times each: "Has the sun gone down?" "With this sickle?" "Into this basket?" "On this Sabbath?" and, last, "Shall I cut?" Having each time been answered in the affirmative, they cut down the barley to the amount of one ephah (nearly three and a half pecks). The ears were brought into the court of the Temple and threshed out with canes or stalks, so that the grains might not be crushed. The grain was then "parched" on a perforated pan, so that each grain might be touched by the fire, and finally exposed to the wind. It was then ground and sifted to the required fineness, which was ascertained by one of the "Gizbarim" (treasurers) plunging his hand into it. The sifting process was continued as long as any of the flour adhered to the hand. In this manner the prescribed omer of flour was secured and offered in the Temple on the 16th Nisan. Whatever was in excess of an omer was redeemed and could be used for any purpose. The omer of flour was mixed with a "log" of oil, and a handful of frankincense put upon it. It was then waved before the Lord, and a handful taken out and burned on the altar (2:15-16). This was what is popularly, though not correctly, called "the presentation of the first, or wave sheaf."

8. The 17th to the 20th Nisan. These days constituted a half holy day and were "the lesser festival." As regards work during this period, all that was necessary for the public interest or to prevent private loss was allowed, but no new work of any kind for public or private purposes might be begun. The following work was allowed: irrigating dry land; digging watercourses; repairing conduits, reservoirs, roads, marketplaces, and baths; and whitewashing tombs, etc. Dealers in fruit, garments, or utensils were allowed to sell privately what was required for immediate use. In the Temple the additional sacrifices appointed for the festival were offered up, and the lesser Hallel was sung instead of the greater.

9. The 21st Nisan, or the Last Day of the Passover. The last day of the Passover was observed by a holy convocation and was celebrated in all respects like the first day, except that it did not commence with the paschal meal.

10. The second, or Little Passover. Anyone prevented by Levitical defilement, disability, or distance from keeping the regular Passover might observe the "second," or the "little Passover," exactly a month later (Num. 9:9-12). In this "second" Passover both leavened and unleavened bread might be kept in the house; the Hallel was

not to be sung at the paschal supper; no *Chagigah* was offered. The supper could not be eaten by any defiled person.

11. Release of Prisoners. It is not certain whether the release of a prisoner at the Passover (Matt. 27:15; Mark 15:6; Luke 23:17; John 18:39) was a custom of Roman origin, or whether it was an old Jewish custom that Pilate allowed them to retain.

12. Preparations for the Passover. A month previous (the 15th Adar) bridges and roads had been repaired for the use of pilgrims. This was also the time for administering the testing draught to women suspected of *adultery* (which see), for burning the red heifer (Num. 19:1-5), and for boring the ears of those wishing to remain in bondage. One of these preliminary arrangements is especially interesting when recalling the words of the Savior. Any dead body found in the field was buried where found, and, as the pilgrims coming to the feast might have contracted "uncleanness" by unwittingly touching such graves, it was ordered that all tombs should be whitened a month before the Passover. Evidently it was in reference to what our Lord saw going on around Him at the time He spoke that He compared the Pharisees to "whitewashed tombs which on the outside appear beautiful, but inside they are full of dead men's bones and all uncleanness" (Matt. 23:27). Two weeks before the Passover, and at the corresponding time before the other two great festivals, the flocks and herds were to be tithed and the treasure chests publicly were opened and emptied. Last, "many went up to Jerusalem out of the country before the Passover, to purify themselves" (John 11:55; cf. 1 Cor. 11:27-28).

Modern Jewish Passover

Present Observance. The Jews of today continue to celebrate the Passover largely as in the days of the second Temple. Several days before the festival all utensils are cleansed; on the eve of the 13th Nisan the master of the house with a candle or lamp searches most diligently into every hole and crevice of the house to discover any leaven that may remain about the premises. Before doing so he pronounces the benediction, following with the formal renunciation of all leaven. On the 14th Nisan (the Preparation Day) all the firstborn males above thirteen years of age fast in commemoration of the sparing of the Jewish firstborn in Egypt. On this evening the Jews, arrayed in festive garments, offer up the appointed prayers in the synagogue. Returning to their homes, they find them illuminated and the tables spread with the following food: three unleavened cakes on a plate; the shank bone of a shoulder of lamb, having a small bit of meat on it, and an egg roasted hard in hot ashes in another dish; bitter herbs in a third dish; and the sauce (Heb. *charoseth*) and salt water, or vinegar, in two cups. The whole family, including the servants, are gathered around the table. With blessings and benedictions, they partake of the food, together with four cups of wine. The same service is repeated the following evening, for the Jews have doubled the days of holy convocation.

Pentecost (Gk. *Pentēkostē,* "fiftieth," i.e., "day"). The second of the three great annual festivals, the others being the Passover and Tabernacles. The most important Bible passages relating to it are Ex. 23:16; Lev. 23:15-22; Num. 28:26-31; Deut. 16:9-12.

Names and Significance. This festival is called (1) the feast of Weeks (Ex. 34:22; Deut. 16:10, 16; 2 Chron. 8:13), because it was celebrated seven complete weeks, or fifty days, after the Passover (Lev. 23:15-16); (2) the feast of the Harvest (Ex. 23:16), because it concluded the harvest of the later grains; and (3) the day of the first fruits (Num. 28:26), because the first loaves made from the new grain were then offered on the altar (Lev. 23:17; *see also* the article First Fruits).

Origin and Import. The Scriptures do not clearly attach any historical significance to this festival but seem to teach that Pentecost owes its origin to the harvest that terminated at this time. It is to be expected that, in common with other nations of antiquity who celebrated the ingathering of grain by offering to a deity among other firstling offerings the fine flour of wheat, the Jews would recognize Jehovah's bounty with the first fruits of their harvest. The Jews, at least as early as the days of Christ, connected with the Passover and commemorated on the 6th Sivan the giving of the Ten Commandments. It was made out from Ex. 19 that the law was delivered on the fiftieth day after the Exodus. It has been conjectured that a connection between the event and the festival may possibly be hinted at in the reference to the observance of the law in Deut. 16:12. Pentecost was essentially linked to the Passover—the festival that above all others expressed the fact of a race chosen and separated from other nations—and was the solemn termination of the consecrated period.

The Time of the Festival. The time fixed for celebrating Pentecost is the fiftieth day from "the day after the Sabbath" of the Passover (Lev. 23:11, 15-16); or, as given in Deut. 16:9, seven full weeks after the sickle was put to the corn. The precise meaning of the word *Sabbath* in this connection, which determines the date for celebrating this festival, has been from time immemorial a matter of dispute. The Boethusians and the Sadducees in the time of the second Temple, and the Karaites since the eighth century of the Christian era, have taken "Sabbath" in the sense of the "seventh day of the week" and have maintained that the omer was offered on the day following that weekly Sabbath that might happen to fall within the seven days of the Passover. This would make Pentecost always come on the first day of the week. Many arguments are presented against this, showing that such an opinion involves many arbitrary and improbable arrangements. Commenting on Lev. 23:15-22, Keil and Delitzsch (*Com.,* ad loc.) say that "*Sabbaths* (v. 15) signifies weeks. Consequently, 'the morrow after the seventh Sabbath' (v. 16) is the day after the seventh week, not after the seventh Sabbath." It is therefore evident that the Jews, who during the second Temple kept Pentecost fifty days after the 16th Nisan, rightly interpreted the injunction in 23:15-22. The fiftieth day, according to the Jewish canons, may fall on 5th, 6th, or 7th Sivan.

Observance, Pentateuchal. The Mosaic ordinances provided that on the Day of Pentecost there was to be a holy convocation, on which no manner of work was to be done; all the able-bodied men of the congregation were to be present (unless legally precluded) at the sanctuary; and a special sacrifice was to be offered (Lev. 23:15-22; Num. 28:26-31). The sacrifices offered were (1) the morning and evening sacrifices, with their grain and drink offerings; (2) a burnt offering, consisting of seven lambs, one young bull, two rams, with their grain and drink offering (Lev. 23:18; Num. 28:26-31); (3) the two wave loaves, the new grain offering, of two-tenths of an ephah of new flour (Lev. 23:17); and (4) with the loaves, a kid of the goats for a sin offering and two lambs for a peace offering. The firstling loaves, with the two lambs (peace offering), were devoted to the Lord by waving, as a thank offering for the harvest that had been gathered in during the seven previous weeks. The words "You shall bring in from your dwelling places two loaves of bread for a wave offering" (Lev. 23:17) are not to be understood as if every head of a house was to bring two such loaves, but that the two loaves were presented for the whole people. "From your dwelling places" appears to mean that they were to be loaves prepared for the daily nourishment of the house and not specially for a holy purpose or paid for out of the treasury. They were freewill offerings, presented by each person in proportion to

the blessings received from God. These might be burnt, grain, drink, or thank offerings (Deut. 16:10). This festival was to be a season of rejoicing, in which were to share the children, men and women servants, the Levites, the stranger, the orphan, and the widow (16:11). Israel was also to recall her bondage in Egypt and was admonished to keep the divine law (16:12).

Observance, Postexilic. From Acts (2:9-11) we infer that, perhaps more than to any other great festival, the Jews came from distant countries to Jerusalem. On the day before Pentecost the pilgrims entered Jerusalem, and the approach of the holy convocation was proclaimed in the evening by blasts of the trumpets. The great altar was cleansed in the first watch, and immediately after midnight the Temple gates were thrown open. Before the morning sacrifice all burnt and peace offerings brought by the people were examined by the priests. The following order was observed for the various sacrifices: (1) The regular morning sacrifice. (2) The festive offerings, as prescribed (Num. 28:26-31); the Levites chanting the Hallel, in which the people joined. (3) The firstling loaves, with their accompanying offerings. These loaves were prepared as follows: "Three *seahs* of new wheat were brought to the temple, threshed like other [grain] offerings, ground and passed through twelve sieves, and the remainder was redeemed and eaten by anyone. Care was taken that the flour for each loaf should be taken separately from one and a half *seah;* that it should be separately kneaded with luke-warm water (like all thank offerings), and separately baked in the temple itself. The loaves were made the evening preceding the festival; or, if that fell on the Sabbath, two evenings before. These loaves, with the two lambs, formed part of the same wave offering." (4) The freewill offerings of the people, which formed the cheerful and hospitable meal of the family and to which the Levite, the widow, the orphan, the poor, and the stranger were invited.

Present-Day Observance. This festival is annually and sacredly kept by Jews on the 6th and 7th Sivan—i.e., between the second half of May and the first half of June, thus prolonging it to two days. In accordance with the injunction in Lev. 23:15-16, the Jews regularly count every evening the fifty days from the second day of Passover until Pentecost and recite a prayer over it. The three days preceding the festival, on which the Jews commemorate the giving of the law, are called "the three days of separation and sanctification," because the Lord commanded Moses to set bounds about the mount and that the people should sanctify themselves three days prior to the giving of the law (Ex. 19:12, 14, 23).

On the preparation day the synagogues and private houses are adorned with flowers and fragrant herbs; the males purify themselves by immersion and confession of sins, put on festive garments, and go to the synagogue, where, after evening prayer, the hallowed nature of the festival is proclaimed by the cantor in the blessing pronounced over a cup of wine. The same is also done by every head of a family before the evening meal. After supper, either in the synagogue or in private houses, the reading of Scripture continues all night, the reason given being that, when God was about to reveal His law to Israel, He had to awaken them from sleep; to remove that sin they now keep awake during the night.

In the general festival service of the morning special prayers are inserted for the day, which set forth the glory of the Lawgiver and of Israel; the Great Hallel is recited; the lesson from the law (Ex. 19:1, 20, 25), the *Maphtir* (Num. 18:26-31), and the lesson from the prophets (Ezek. 1:1-28; 3:12) are read, the evening prayer (*Musaph*) is offered, and the benediction is received by the congregation, their heads covered by the fringed wrapper. On the second evening they again go to the synagogue, using there the ritual for the festivals, in which are again inserted special prayers for the occasion, chiefly those on the greatness of God and on the giving of the law and the Ten Commandments. The sanctification of the festival is again pronounced, both by the prelector in the synagogue and by the heads of the families at home. Prayers different from those of the first day, also celebrating the giving of the law, are mingled with the ordinary prayers; the Hallel is recited, as well as the book of Ruth; the lesson read from the law is Deut. 15:19–16:17, and the lesson from the prophets is Hab. 2:20–3:19, or 3:1-19; prayer is offered for departed relatives; the *Musaph Ritual* is recited; the priests pronounce the benediction; and the festival concludes after the afternoon service, as soon as the stars appear or darkness sets in.

Atonement, Day of (Heb. *yôm hakkippūrîm*). The day appointed for a yearly, general, and perfect expiation for all the sins and uncleanness that might remain, despite the regular sacrifices.

Significance. The Levitical ritual was a constant reminder that "the Law . . . can never by the same sacrifices year by year, which they offer continually, make perfect those who draw near" (Heb. 10:1). Even with the most scrupulous observance of the prescribed ordinances many sins and defilements would still remain unacknowledged and therefore without expiation. This want was met by the appointment of a yearly, general, and perfect expiation of all the sins and uncleanness that had remained unatoned for and uncleansed in the course of the year (Lev. 16:33). Thus on the Day of Atonement Israel was reconciled unto Jehovah, which was necessary before the feast of Booths, the feast that prefigured the ingathering of all nations. In connection with this point it may also be well to remember that the Jubilee year was always proclaimed on the Day of Atonement (25:9).

Time. The tenth day of the seventh month, or Tishri (October), and the fifth of Atonement (Lev. 16:1-34; Num. 29:7-11). The day was a high Sabbath, on which no work was done. All the people were to afflict their souls, i.e., to fast (from the evening of the ninth to the evening of the tenth), under penalty of being cut off from Israel (Lev. 23:27-32). The chronological link connecting the Day of Atonement with the death of Aaron's sons (10:1-5) was intended to point out that event as leading to it and also to show the importance and holiness attached to an entrance into the inmost sanctuary of God (16:1-2).

Sacrifices. From Lev. 16:5-28 and Num. 29:7-11, it would appear that the sacrifices for the day were as follows: (1) The ordinary morning sacrifice. (2) The expiatory sacrifices for the priesthood, namely, a young bull. (3) The sin offering for the people, a kid from the goats for Jehovah and another for Azazel. (4) The festive burnt offerings of the priests and people and, with them, another sin offering. (5) The ordinary evening sacrifice. If the Day of Atonement fell on a Sabbath, the ordinary Sabbath sacrifices were offered besides all these.

Ceremonies. Ceremonies on the Day of Atonement were connected with the preparations for the high priests, the expiatory rites, and the festive offerings.

Preparation. The center point of this feast was the expiation offered by the high priest after the morning sacrifice. In later times, at least, the high priest underwent a special preparation for this service. Seven days before, he had left his own home and taken up his residence in the Temple chambers. A substitute was provided, lest the high priest should die or become Levitically unclean. During this week he practiced the various priestly duties, such as sprinkling the blood, burning incense, lighting the lamps, offering the daily sacrifices, etc.; for every part of the service on Atonement Day depended upon the high priest, and he could make no mistake. Further, he was to abstain from all that could render him unclean or disturb his devotions. On the morning of the Day of Atonement the high priest bathed his entire person, not in the place ordinarily used by the priests but one specially set apart for him. He then put on the holy garments—the coat, drawers, girdle, and headdress of white cloth—thus signifying that he was entirely cleansed from the defilement of sin and was arrayed in holiness.

Expiatory Rites. After everything was ready, the high priest slew the bull (the sin offering for himself and his house), then filled a censer with burning coals from the altar of burnt offering, and, putting two handfuls of incense into a vase, bore them into the Holy of Holies. He poured the incense upon the coals, "that the cloud of incense may cover the mercy seat." As the burning incense was a symbol of prayer, this covering of the

Mercy Seat with the cloud of incense was a symbolic covering of the glory of the Holy One with prayer to God, and thus served as to protect the worshiper. The high priest now returned to the altar of burnt offering to fetch some of the blood of the bull, which he sprinkled upon the Mercy Seat ("on the east side," Lev. 16:14) and seven times upon the ground before it. After this he slew the goat selected for a sin offering and did the same as with the blood of the bull, namely, sprinkled it upon and before the Mercy Seat. He thus made atonement for the Holy of Holies because of the uncleanness of both priests and people (v. 16). He was now required to atone for the "tent of meeting," which he did by sprinkling the blood of both the bull and the goat, first on the horns of the golden altar once, and then seven times toward the altar, on the ground (*see* Ex. 30:10). Atonement having been made for the building, the high priest was to expiate the altar of burnt offering, which he did by first putting some of the blood of the bull and the goat upon the horns of the altar and sprinkling it seven times. Thus the dwelling, the court, and all the holy things were expiated and cleansed. The question as to how often the high priest went into the Holy of Holies on this day is not of great importance. The biblical account seems to indicate that he entered four times: (1) with the incense, while a priest continued to agitate the blood of the bull lest it should coagulate; (2) with the blood of the bull; (3) with the blood of the goat; and (4) to bring the censer, which, according to the Talmud, was done after the evening sacrifice. The high priest then, going out into the court of the Tabernacle, laid his hands on the head of the scapegoat, confessing over it all the sins and transgressions of the people. It was led away into the wilderness by a man standing ready and there let go free to signify the carrying away of Israel's sins that God had forgiven. *See* Azazel.

Festive Offerings. The high priest then went into the Tabernacle, took off his white garments, laid them down there (because they were to be worn only in the expiatory ritual of this day), washed himself in the Holy Place (in the laver of the court), put on his usual official robes, and completed his own and the people's burnt offering in the court, at the same time burning the fat of the sin offerings on the altar. But both of the sin offerings were carried outside of the camp and burned with skin, flesh, and dung. The persons who had taken the live goat into the wilderness and burned the sin offerings outside the camp were, before they returned into it, to wash their clothes and bathe their bodies (Lev. 16:2-29). "This act of expiation for the people and the holy places being finished, there was presented immediately before the evening sacrifice, according to Jewish tradition, the offering prescribed for the feast of the day, a goat as sin offering, a bullock, a ram, and several lambs as burnt offerings, with

the corresponding meat and drink offerings (Num. 29:7-11), and therewith the feast of the day was closed." According to the rabbis, the high priest on this day performed all the duties of the regular daily service; sprinkled the blood eight times, once toward the ceiling and seven times on the floor; and after returning the third time from the Holy of Holies to the Holy Place sprinkled the blood of bull and goat toward the veil, mixed the blood of the two animals together, and sprinkled the altar of incense with the mixture, pouring out what remained at the foot of the altar of burnt offerings. The two goats were similar in appearance (size and value); the lots with which they were chosen were originally of boxwood, later of gold. The high priest, as soon as he received the signal that the goat had reached the wilderness, read some lessons from the law and offered prayer. Very strict rules are given by the Mishna for the fasting of the people.

Modern Observance. The strict Jews, on the day previous to the Day of Atonement, provide a cock slain by a lower-ranking rabbi; the person whose property it is then takes the fowl by the legs, swings it over the heads of himself and company, and at the same time prays to God that the sins committed by them during the year may enter the fowl. This fowl seems to be a substitute for the scapegoat of old. In the evening, after a sumptuous meal, they go to the synagogue dressed in their best. After a blessing by the clerk, each contributes toward the free gift offering, after which begins the evening prayer. The reader, the chief rabbi, and many of the congregation are clad with the shrouds in which they are to be buried, continuing in prayer and supplication for upward of three hours. Some remain all night, and those who go to their homes come again in the morning at five o'clock and remain until dark. The following is the order for the day: morning prayers; the usual prayers and supplications peculiar to the day; reading the portion from Lev. 16, the *maphter* (Num. 19:7-11), the portion from the prophets (Isa. 57:14–58:14); the prayer of the *musaph,* i.e., "addition," which makes mention of the additional sacrifices (Num. 29:7) and supplicates Jehovah to be favorable; the offering of the day from 29:7-28. They abstain from food altogether during the day. *See* Expiation.

Booths (or Tabernacles), Feast of. The third of the great annual feasts, the other two being the Passover and Pentecost.

Names. (1) The festival of Tents (Heb. *ḥag hassūkkôt,* "Feast of Booths," 2 Chron. 8:13; Ezra 3:4; Zech. 14:16, 18-19; Gk. *skēnopēgia,* John 7:2, "Feast of Booths") was so called because the Israelites were commanded to live in booths during its continuance (cf. Lev. 23:43). (2) The feast of Ingathering (Heb. *ḥag hā'āsip,* Ex. 23:16, "Feast of the Harvest"; 34:22), because it was held after the ingathering of the harvest

Booth or "succa" used on the feast of Booths

and fruits. (3) The festival of Jehovah (Heb. *ḥag YHWH*, Lev. 23:39, "feast of the Lord"), or simply *the festival* (1 Kings 8:2; 2 Chron. 5:3, "the feast"), because it was the most important or well known. The principal passages referring to this feast are Ex. 23:16; Lev. 23:34-36; 39:43; Deut. 16:13-15; 31:10-13; Neh. 8.

Origin and Import. The origin of this feast is connected by some with Succoth, the first halting place of the Israelites on their march out of Egypt, and the booths are taken to commemorate those in which they lodged for the last time before they entered the desert. It was ordered by Moses in the regulations he gave to the Israelites respecting their festivals, and it unites two elements: the ingathering of the labor of the field (Ex. 23:16), the fruit of the earth (Lev. 23:39)—or the ingathering of the threshing floor and the wine press (Deut. 16:13)—and the dwelling in booths, which were to be matters of joy to Israel (Lev. 23:41-43; Deut. 16:14). The dwelling in booths was to be a reminder to them of the fatherly care and protection of Jehovah while Israel was journeying from Egypt to Canaan (Deut. 8:7-18). "In comparison with the 'house of bondage' the dwelling in booths on the march through the wilderness was in itself an image of freedom and happiness" (K. & D., *Com.,* ad loc.). Such a reminder of God's loving care and Israel's

dependence would, naturally, keep the Israelites from pride and conceit.

Time of the Festival. It began on the 15th of Tishri (the seventh month), five days before the Day of Atonement, and although, strictly speaking, it lasted only seven days (Deut. 16:13; Lev. 23:36; Ezek. 45:25), another day was added (Neh. 8:18). This day was observed with a sabbatic rest.

Observance. To distinguish between the pentateuchal enactments and the rites, ceremonies, etc., that gradually developed, we divide the description of its observance into three sections: Mosaic, postexilic, and post-Dispersion.

Mosaic. On the first day of the feast, booths were constructed of fresh branches of fruit and palm trees, "boughs of leafy trees and willows." These were located in courts, streets, public squares, and on house roofs. In these all home-born Israelites were to dwell during the festival, in memory of their fathers' dwelling in booths after their exodus from Egypt (Lev. 23:40; Neh. 8:15). The day was also to be observed as a Sabbath and a holy convocation, in which no secular work was to be done, and all abled-bodied male members of the congregation not legally precluded were to appear before the Lord. The booth in Scripture is not an image of privation and misery but of protection, preservation, and shelter from heat, storm, and tempest (Pss. 27:5; 31:20; Isa. 4:6). Table 9 lists the sacrifices offered during this festival.

Table 9
Sacrifices During the Feast of Booths

Day	Bulls	Rams	Lambs	Goats[1]
First	13	2	14	1
Second	12	2	14	1
Third	11	2	14	1
Fourth	10	2	14	1
Fifth	9	2	14	1
Sixth	8	2	14	1
Seventh	7	2	14	1
Total for the seven days	70	14	98	7
Eighth	1	1	7	1

1. The sin offering.

Each bull, ram, and lamb was accompanied with its prescribed grain and drink offering. The above sacrifices were offered after the regular morning sacrifice (Num. 29:12-34). Every sabbatical year the law was to be read publicly in the sanctuary on the first day of the festival (Deut. 31:10-13). The six following days were half festivals, probably devoted to social enjoyments and friendly gatherings, when every family head was to extend hospitality, especially to the poor and the stranger (16:14). To these seven days there was added an eighth, the twenty-second of the month, as the close of the feast. This day was observed with a sabbatic rest and holy convocation but had only a simple sacrifice, similar to the first and tenth days of the seventh month (Num. 29:35-38; *see* table 9). There is only one instance recorded of this festival's being celebrated between the entrance into the Promised Land and the Babylonian captivity (1 Kings 8:2; 2 Chron. 7:8-10; Neh. 8:17).

Postexilic. After the Babylonian captivity the feast of Booths began to be strictly and generally kept, and more minute definitions and more expanded applications of the concise pentateuchal injunction were imperatively demanded, in order to secure uniformity of practice, as well as to infuse devotion and joy into the celebration.

It was ordained that the booth must be a detached and temporary habitation, constructed for the festival and not for permanent residence; the interior must neither be higher than twenty cubits nor lower than ten palms; it must have not less than three walls and must be so thatched as to admit the view of the sky and the stars. The part open to the rays of the sun was not to exceed the part shaded by the cover; it must not be under a tree, or covered with a cloth or with anything that contracts defilement or does not derive its growth from the ground. The furniture of the booths must be of the plainest, and only such as was fairly necessary. Every Israelite was to dwell in the booth during the whole of the seven days of the festival, while his house was to be only his occasional abode; and he was only to quit the booth when it rained heavily. Even a child, as soon as it ceased to be dependent upon its mother, must dwell in the booth. The only persons exempt were those deputed on pious missions, invalids, nurses, women, and infants.

There was a controversy between the Pharisees and Sadducees respecting the use of the branches of trees mentioned in Lev. 23:40; the latter, from Neh. 8:15-16, understanding them to be for the erection of the booths, whereas the Pharisees applied them to what the worshipers were to carry in their hands. The rabbis ruled that the *aethrog,* or citron, was the fruit of the "beautiful trees," and "the boughs of leafy trees" meant the myrtle, provided it did not have more berries than leaves. Every worshiper carried the *aethrog* in his left hand, and in his right the *lulab,* or palm, with myrtle and willow branch on either side of it tied together on the outside with its own kind, though on the inside it might be fastened with a gold thread. The *lulab* was used in the Temple on each of the seven festive days; even children, if able to shake it, were required to carry one.

1. The day before the feast, 14th Tishri, was the *Preparation Day.* On this day the pilgrims came to Jerusalem and prepared all that was necessary for the solemn observance of the festival. When evening set in, the blasts of the priests' trumpets on the Temple mount announced the advent of the feast. As at the Passover and at Pentecost, the altar of burnt offering was cleansed during the

first night watch, and the Temple gates were thrown open immediately after midnight. The time until the beginning of the ordinary morning sacrifice was occupied in examining the various sacrifices and offerings that were to be brought during the day. If this day was the Sabbath all *lulabs* had to be deposited somewhere in the Temple, as it was contrary to law to carry the palms from the booths of the pilgrims to the Temple on the Sabbath.

2. On the first day of the feast, 15th Tishri, while the morning sacrifice was being prepared, a priest, accompanied by a joyous procession and with music, went down to the Pool of Siloam, where he drew water into a golden pitcher capable of holding three *logs.* On the Sabbaths the water was brought from a golden vessel in the Temple itself, to which it had been carried from Siloam the preceding day. At the same time that the procession started for Siloam, another went to a place in the Kidron Valley (i.e., Motza), to which they brought willow branches. These they stuck on either side of the great altar, bending them over so as to form a canopy. The priest who had gone to Siloam timed his return so as to join his brother priests as they carried the sacrifice to the altar. On reaching the water gate he was welcomed by three blasts of the trumpet. He ascended the steps of the altar with another priest, who carried a pitcher of wine for a drink offering. They turned to the left, where there were two silver basins with holes in the bottom; the basin for the water at the W with a narrower hole, that for the wine at the E with wider hole, so that both might empty at the same time. Into these respective basins the water and wine were poured; the people shouting to the priest, "Raise thy hand," to show that he really poured the water into the basin. The reason for this was that Alexander Jannaeus, a Sadducee (about 95 B.C.), had shown his contempt for the Pharisees by pouring the water upon the ground. He was pelted by the people with their *aethrogs,* and the soldiers, being called in, killed nearly six thousand Jews in the Temple.

As soon as the altar was decorated with the willow branches the morning sacrifice was offered, followed by the special festive sacrifices. While these sacrifices were being offered, the Levites chanted the Great Hallel, as at the Passover and Pentecost. When the choir came to the words "Give thanks to the Lord" (Ps. 118:1), again when they sang, "O Lord, do save, we beseech Thee" (118:25), and once more at the close, "Give thanks to the Lord" (118:29), all the worshipers shook their *lulabs* toward the altar. The chant finished, the priests marched around the altar, exclaiming, "Hosanna, O Jehovah; give us help, O Jehovah, give prosperity" (cf. 118:25). The benediction was then pronounced, and the people dispersed, amid the repeated exclamation "How beautiful art thou, O altar!" or "To Jehovah and thee, O altar, we give thanks!" This prayer for succor was applied to Christ when the multitude greeted Jesus on His entry into Jerusalem (Matt. 21:8-9; John 12:12-13).

Each pilgrim went to his booth, there to enjoy his social repast with the Levite, the stranger, etc. On the first day of the festival every Israelite carried about his *lulab*, or palm, all day—to the synagogue, on his visits to the sick and mourners.

3. The second through sixth days of the feast, 16th-20th Tishri, were called also *the middle days of the feast* (John 7:14), or *the lesser festival*. These days were half holy days, on which necessary food or raiment might be privately purchased, and work required for the observance of the festival might be performed. During these days the sacrifices were offered, the palm and the citron were used, and the priests marched around the altar as on the first day of the festival, with the exception that the number of animals offered diminished daily.

4. The seventh or *the last day of the feast,* fell on the 21st Tishri (but according to some authorities this title was given to the 22nd Tishri). This seventh day of the festival was distinguished from the other days as follows: after the *Musaph,* or special festival sacrifices of the day, the priests marched seven times around the altar instead of once, as on other days; the willows that surrounded the altar were then so thoroughly shaken by the people that the leaves lay thickly on the ground; the people also brought palm branches and beat them to pieces at the side of the altar, from which the day was called *the day of willows* and *the branch-threshing day.* This over, the children who were present threw away their palms and ate their *aethrogs,* or citrons; on the afternoon of this day the pilgrims began to move the furniture from the booths, the obligation to dwell in them ceasing at that time. This, the great Hosanna day, was regarded as one of the four days whereon God judges the world. It seems altogether probable that it was on this day that Jesus uttered those memorable words, "If any man is thirsty, let him come to Me and drink" (John 7:37).

5. The eighth day of the feast, 22nd Tishri, was added as the close of the festival and was observed with sabbatic rest and holy convocation. It had only a simple sacrifice (similar to the first and tenth day of the seventh month; *see* table 9, "Sacrifices Offered During the Feast of Booths"). The people no longer dwelt in booths, the joyful procession for the drawing of water was discontinued, the illumination of the court of the women ceased, and the palms and willows were not used.

The ceremony of drawing the water was repeated every morning during the seven days of the festival but was discontinued on the eighth.

When the feast of Booths fell on a sabbatic

year, the reading of portions of the law (Deut. 31:10-13) was afterward confined to one book of the Pentateuch, the number of synagogues in which the law was read every week rendering it less needful to read extensive portions in the Temple. A peculiarity of this festival was that on the first seven days all twenty-four divisions of the priests officiated, whereas at all the other festivals only those upon whom the lot fell served (cf. 1 Chron. 24:7-19). On the eighth day the twenty-four divisions were not all present; only those upon whom the lot fell. As the close of the first day of the feast was celebrated, the "joy of the pouring out of the water," the worshipers descended to the court of the women, where great preparations had been made. Four golden candelabra were there, each with four golden bowls, a ladder resting against each candelabra and upon them standing four sons of the priests holding pitchers of oil with which they fed the lamps, while the cast-off breeches and girdles of the priests served for wicks. The light from these lamps illuminated the whole city, and around them danced men with lighted torches in their hands, singing hymns and songs of praise. The Levites, stationed on the fifteen steps that led into the court, corresponding to the fifteen psalms of degrees, i.e., *steps* (Pss. 120-134, "ascents"), accompanied the songs with harps, lyres, cymbals, and other musical instruments. The dancing, as well as the music, continued until daybreak. It is probable that Jesus referred to this custom when He spoke those well-known words "I am the light of the world" (John 8:12).

Since the Dispersion. Except for the adaptation of the rites to the altered condition of the nation, the Jews of the present day continue to celebrate the feast of Booths as in the days of the second Temple.

As soon as the Day of Atonement is over, every orthodox Jew begins to erect the booth in which he and his family are to take up their abode during the festival, and he also provides himself with a *lulab* (palm) and *aethrog* (citron). The festival commences on the eve of 14th Tishri (Preparation Day). All the Jews, attired in festive garments, resort to the synagogues, where, after the evening prayer, the hallowed nature of the festival is proclaimed by the cantor in the blessing pronounced over the wine. After the evening service every family goes to its booth, which is illuminated and adorned with leaves and fruit and in which the first festive meal is taken. Before this is eaten, the head of the family pronounces the sanctity of the festival over a cup of wine. Each member of the family washes his hands, pronouncing the prescribed benediction while drying them, and all begin to eat. Orthodox Jews sleep in the booths all night.

The following morning, the first day of the feast, they go to the synagogue, holding the palms and citrons in their hands, laying them down during the former part of the prayer, but taking them up after the eighteen benedictions, when about to recite the Hallel. Holding the palm in the right hand and the citron in the left, they recite the following prayer: "Blessed art Thou, O Lord our God, King of the universe, who hast sanctified us with Thy commandments, and hast enjoined us to take the palm branch." Then each turns his citron upside down and waves his palm branch three times toward each point of the compass, and the legate of the congregation pronounces the benediction; the Hallel is chanted; the lessons are read from the law (Lev. 22:26; 23:44; Num. 29:12-16) and from the prophets (Zech. 14:1-21). After this the *Musaph* prayer is recited; when the reader comes to the passage where the word *priests* occurs, the Aaronites and the Levites rise, and, after the latter have washed the hands of the former, the priests, with uplifted hands, pronounce the priestly benediction (Num. 6:24-27) upon the congregation, whose faces are veiled with the *Talith.* The elders then march around the ark, in the center of the synagogue, the legate carrying the scroll and the rest of the palm branches, repeating the *Hosanna* and waving the palms in memory of the procession around the altar. The morning service concluded, the people again go to their booths to partake of the festive meal with the poor and the stranger. About five or six o'clock they recite, in the synagogue, the *Minchah* prayer, answering to the daily evening sacrifice in the Temple.

The ritual and rites of the second evening and morning are similar to those of the first; the lesson from the prophets, however, is from 1 Kings 8:2-21. After the afternoon service of this day the middle days of the festival begin, which last four days, when the ritual is like that of ordinary days, a few prayers being inserted in the regular formula; lessons are read on each day, and the procession goes around the ark.

The seventh day, i.e., *the Great Hosanna,* is celebrated with peculiar solemnity, inasmuch as it is believed that on this day God decrees the rain for the future harvest. On the evening previous every Israelite supplies himself with a small bunch of willows tied with palm bark. Some pious Jews read all night from Deuteronomy, the Psalms, the Mishna, etc., and are immersed before the morning prayer. Candles are lighted at the time of morning service, and after the morning prayer (similar to those of the preceding days) seven scrolls are taken from the ark, from one of which the lesson is read. After prayer the procession, headed by the rabbi and the legate, with those carrying the scrolls, goes seven times around the ark or the reading desk, reciting the Hosannas and waving their palms. The palms are then laid down and the willows beaten.

On the evening of the seventh day the festival commences, which concludes the whole cycle of the feast. Being a day of holy convocation, the

Kiddush (i.e., proclamation) of its sanctity is offered. On the following morning, in the synagogue, the prayers of the first two days are offered; the special lesson of the day is read; the *Musaph,* or additional prayer, is offered, and the priests pronounce the benediction. The people no longer take their meals in the booths on this day. On the evening of this day begins the festival called *the Rejoicing of the Law.* The eighteen benedictions are recited. All the scrolls are taken from the ark, into which a lighted candle is placed. A procession of distinguished members is headed by the legate; they hold the scrolls in their hands and go around the reading desk; the scrolls are then put back into the ark, except the one placed upon the desk, from which is read the last chapter of Deuteronomy. All persons in the synagogue are called to the reading, including children. The evening service over, the children leave the synagogue in procession, carrying banners with sundry Heb. inscriptions.

On the following morning the Jews resort again to the synagogue, recite the *Hallel* after the eighteen benedictions, empty the ark of all its scrolls, put a lighted candle into it, and with the scrolls go around the reading desk amid jubilant songs. The scrolls are returned to the ark, with the exception of two, from one of which is read Deut. 33. Four persons are at first called, then all the little children, and then again several adults. The first of these is known as *the Bridegroom of the Law,* and after the cantor has addressed him in a lengthy Heb. formula the last verses of the Pentateuch are read. Following the reading, all the people exclaim, "Be strong!" Genesis 1:1–2:3 is read, to which another is called who is known as *the Bridegroom of Genesis,* to whom is delivered a Heb. formula; the *Maphtir* (i.e., Num. 29:35–30:1) is read from another scroll; the *Mustaph,* or additional special prayer for the festival, is said; and the service is concluded. The rest of the day is spent in rejoicing and feasting.

The design of this festival is to celebrate the annual completion of the perusal of the Pentateuch, inasmuch as on this day the last section of the law is read. Hence the name of the festival, *The Rejoicing of Finishing the Law.*

Postexilic Festivals. To the yearly festivals instituted by the Mosiac law several were added after the Exile, of which two, Purim and the feast of Dedication, were as regularly kept as the Mosaic yearly feasts.

Purim (Heb. *pûrîm,* "lots," Esther 9:26, 31). This feast was instituted by Mordecai, at the suggestion of Esther, in memory of the extraordinary deliverance of the Jews of Persia from the murderous plot of Haman. It was generally adopted, though not at first without opposition.

Name and Significance. The name *Purim,* "lots," was given to this festival because of the casting of lots by Haman to decide when he should carry into effect the decree issued by the

Purim rattle, shaken by children when Haman is named

king for the extermination of the Jews (Esther 9:24). The name was probably given to the festival in irony.

Observance. The only directions given respecting the observance of the festival is that Mordecai ordered the 14th and 15th of Adar to be kept annually by the Jews; that these two days should be days of feasting and joy, of the interchange of presents, and of sending gifts to the poor; and that the Jews agreed to continue the observance of the festival as it was begun (Esther 9:17-24). No mention is made of any special sacrifice. At the present day the festival is kept as follows: the day preceding (13th Adar) is kept as a fast day (called "the Fast of Esther"), in accordance with the command of the queen (4:15-16). Sundry prayers, expressive of repentance, etc., are introduced into the ritual for the day. As on all fast days, Ex. 32:11-14 and 34:1-11 are read as the lesson from the law, and Isa. 55:6–56:8 as the Haphtarah. If 13th Adar falls on a Sabbath, the fast is kept on the previous Thursday. As soon as the stars appear the festival commences, candles are lighted, and all the Jews go to the synagogue, where, after the evening service, the benediction is pronounced, and the book of Esther is read by the prelector. As often as the name of Haman is mentioned in the reading, the congregation stamps on the floor, saying, "Let his name be blotted out. The name of the wicked shall rot!" while the children shake rattles. After the reading the congregation exclaims, "Cursed be Haman; blessed be Mordecai!" etc.; the benediction is said, and all go home and partake of milk and eggs. On the 14th, in the morning, the people go to the synagogue; several prayers are inserted into the regular ritual; Ex. 17:8-16 is read as the lesson from the law, and Esther, as on the previous evening. The rest of the festival is given up to rejoicing, exchanging of presents, games, etc. Rejoicing continues on the 15th, and the festival terminates on the evening of this day.

Dedication, Feast of (Heb. *ḥanûkkâ*). In 1 Macc. 4:52-59 it is called "the dedication of the altar," and by Josephus (*Ant.* 12.7.7) "the feast of lights." It was a popular and joyous festival commemorating the purifying of the Temple, the removal of the old polluted altar, and the restoration of the worship of Jehovah by Judas Maccabeus, 164 B.C.

This feast began on the 25th Chisleu (December) and lasted eight days but did not require attendance at Jerusalem. Assembled in the Temple or in the synagogues of the places where they resided, the Jews sang "Hallel," carrying palm and other branches; and there was a grand illumination of the Temple and private houses. The origin of the illumination of the Temple is unknown, although tradition says that when the sacred "lampstands" of the restored Temple were to be lighted only one flagon of oil, sealed with the signet of the high priest, was found to feed the lamps. This was *pure* oil, but only sufficient for one day—when by a miracle the oil increased, and the flagon remained filled for eight days, in memory of which the Temple and private houses were ordered to be illuminated for the same period. No public mourning or fast was allowed on account of calamity or bereavement. The festival did not require anyone to abstain partially or completely from his ordinary occupation, and unlike some other celebrations it was not marked by a holy assembly at the beginning and the end. The celebration was always of a joyous, exuberant character which commemorated the restoration of the worship of the Temple (1 Macc. 4:41-49). The similarity between this festival and the "feast of Booths" would seem to indicate some intended connection between the two. Without doubt, our Lord attended this festival at Jerusalem (John 10:22). It is still observed by the Jews.

Festivals as Types. According to many Bible teachers, the seven feasts of the Lord (Lev. 23) constitute a prophecy and foreshadowing of future events, part of which have been fulfilled and part are yet to be fulfilled. They are "a mere shadow of what is to come," of which Christ is the body or substance (Col. 2:16-17). The seven annual feasts may be divided into two sections of four and three. The first section includes the Passover, the feast of Unleavened Bread, the feast of First Fruits, and Pentecost. The second group, separated by a four-month period, includes the feast of Trumpets, the Day of Atonement, and the feast of Booths. The three great festivals were the Passover, Pentecost, and Booths. The first four feasts foreshadow truths concerning this present gospel age. The last three foreshadow blessings in store for Israel. The first four are historic; the last three, prophetic. Those who hold the typical view of the Hebrew feasts teach the significance of each as follows:

Passover. The Passover (Lev. 23:4-5) speaks of Calvary and of redemption by blood from Egypt, a type of the world; from Pharaoh, a type of

Satan; and from Egyptian servitude, a type of sin. The festival speaks of our redemption from sin by the Lamb of God (1 Pet. 1:19), Christ being our Passover (1 Cor. 5:7).

Unleavened Bread. Unleavened Bread (Lev. 23:6-8) typifies the holy walk of a believer after redemption (1 Cor. 5:8; 11:23-33; 2 Cor. 7:1; Gal. 5:7-9). The divine order is eloquent. First, redemption, followed by a holy walk. The eating of unleavened bread and the putting away of all leaven from the household portrays holiness, as leaven is a figure of "malice and wickedness" (1 Cor. 5:8) and is not befitting a believer's walk.

First Fruits. First Fruits (Lev. 23:9-14) is typical of resurrection, first of Christ's, then of "those who are Christ's at His coming" (1 Cor. 15:23; 1 Thess. 4:13-18). When the priest on the day of Christ's resurrection waved the sheaf of first fruits in the Temple, it was before a torn veil and was but an antiquated form, for the substance had come and the shadow had passed away. Joseph's empty tomb proclaimed that the great first fruit sheaf had been reaped and waved in the heavenly Temple. This feast has been completely fulfilled in Christ. (*See also* the article First Fruits.)

Pentecost (Lev. 23:15-22). The type of the feast of Pentecost is the coming of the Holy Spirit at Pentecost to form the church, the Body of Christ. Because the church is not yet glorified and contains evil, leaven is present (Matt. 13:33). The two loaves are not a sheaf of separate stalks loosely tied together but a union of particles making loaves or a homogeneous body. At the Pentecost following Christ's resurrection, the Holy Spirit, by His baptizing work, formed the separate disciples into one organism, the Body of Christ (cf. Acts 1:5 with 11:16 and 1 Cor. 12:13). The church had to begin on Pentecost because it was the first historical instance of the Spirit's baptizing work (cf. Merrill F. Unger, *The Baptizing Work of the Holy Spirit* [1953], pp. 53-65). Although leaven was in the two loaves offered at Pentecost, typifying Jew and Gentile made one in Christ (cf. Eph. 3:1-10), yet the leaven was baked, that is, sin in those who are redeemed has been judged in Christ. The four-month period between Pentecost and Trumpets was occupied in gathering in the harvest, typical of the present church period before Christ restores Israel.

Trumpets. Trumpets (Lev. 23:23-25) speaks of the regathering of Israel to its homeland after the out-gathering of the church. Matthew 24:31 speaks of the Son of Man at His second advent sending His angels with a great sound of a trumpet to gather together His elect (of Israel) from the four winds, from one end of heaven to the other.

Day of Atonement. The Day of Atonement (Lev. 23:26-32) envisions Israels' national cleansing from sin (Rom. 11:25) and refers to the time when a "fountain will be opened for the house of David and for the inhabitants of Jerusalem, for sin and for impurity" (Zech. 13:1). It portrays their future conversion as a nation at the second advent of Christ (12:9-14).

Booths. The antitype of Booths (or Tabernacles; Lev. 23:33-43) has not yet appeared. Peter anticipated it, however, on the mount of transfiguration when he said, "Lord, it is good for us to be here; if You wish, I will make three tabernacles here, one for You, and one for Moses, and one for Elijah" (Matt. 17:4). What Peter desired, the dwelling of heavenly and earthly people on the earth, was not possible in that age but will be possible in the conditions of the mediatorial Davidic kingdom. Then the kingdom of the heavens will bring heaven and earth in closer union. The feast of Booths is thus prophetic of Israel's millennial rest. The feast of Booths is a memorial to Israel, going back to Egypt and forward to millennial rest, as the Lord's Supper now points back to a finished redemption until Christ appears. The eighth day following the Sabbath (Lev. 23:39) points to the new heaven and the new earth following the Millennium and to the dispensation of the fullness of time before the eternal state.   M.F.U.

BIBLIOGRAPHY: *Pentecost:* H. Darby, trans., *Mishnah*, Menahot, 10:3; *Talmud*, Manahot, 65a; H. Schauss, *The Jewish Festivals* (1938), pp. 86ff.; L. Finkelstein, *The Pharisees* (1946), pp. 115ff.

Purim: J. H. Greenstone, *Jewish Feasts and Fasts* (1946).

See also G. F. Moore, *Judaism in the First Three Centuries of the Christian Era* (1927), 2:40-54; H. Schauss, *Jewish Festivals* (1958), pp. 284-88; J. Pedersen, *Israel, Its Life and Culture* (1940), 3-4:377-78; R. de Vaux, *Ancient Israel: Its Life and Institutions* (1961), pp. 468-517.

FES'TUS, POR'CIUS (fes'tus, pōr'shus). The successor of Felix as the Roman governor of Judea, appointed by the emperor Nero probably in the autumn of A.D. 60 (Conybeare and Howson, *Life and Epistles of St. Paul*). Three days after his arrival at Caesarea (the political metropolis) he went up to Jerusalem. Here he was met by the "chief priests and the leading men of the Jews," who "brought charges against Paul." They requested, as a favor, that he would allow Paul to be brought up to Jerusalem; the plea, doubtless, was that he should be tried before the Sanhedrin. The real purpose, however, was to kill him while on the way. Festus refused to comply and told them that they must meet the accused face to face at Caesarea. After eight or ten days Paul was summoned before Festus and asked whether he was willing to go to Jerusalem; but the apostle, knowing full well the danger that lurked in this proposal and conscious of the rights he possessed as a Roman citizen, refused to accede and replied boldly to Festus, concluding with, "I appeal to Caesar." About this time Herod Agrippa, with his sister Bernice, came on a complimentary visit to

Festus and was consulted by the governor. The result was an interview between the three and Paul, in which the latter delivered a famous discourse and was pronounced innocent. But because he had appealed to Caesar, Festus sent him to Rome (Acts 25-26). A few other facts are mentioned concerning Festus. Judea was in the same disturbed state that it had been in under the procuratorship of Felix. He took part with Agrippa against the priests, who built a wall to obstruct Agrippa's view of the Temple but allowed an appeal to Nero, who decided in favor of the Jews. He probably died in the summer of A.D. 62. *See* Paul.

BIBLIOGRAPHY: E. M. Blaiklock, *The Century of the New Testament* (1962), pp. 84, 87, 97, 99, 103; F. F. Bruce, *Paul: Apostle of the Heart Set Free* (1977), pp. 254, 359, 362f., 377.

FETTERS. An archaic term for shackles or chains used for binding prisoners either by the wrists or ankles (Judg. 16:21; 2 Kings 25:7; 2 Chron. 33:11; Mark 5:4). In the original several words are used; the NASB and NIV usually render "chains," but sometimes the NASB has "fetters" (so 2 Kings 25:7).

The Egyptians enclosed the hands of their prisoners in an elongated shackle of wood, made of two opposite segments nailed together at each end.

FEVER. *See* Diseases.

FIDELITY (Gk. *pistis*). "That grace in the servant which shows him to be worthy of his Master's trust. Thus our Lord says, 'Who then is that faithful and wise steward,' etc. (Luke 12:42, KJV). Paul gives the description of the faithful servant as 'showing all good fidelity' (Titus 2:10, KJV). The same word which expresses our trust in God's fidelity expresses his trust in ours. It is a grace which stands alone as having the epithet *good,* and it must pervade the whole of life. Here then are all the elements of our ethics: the Master commits a trust, and the trustworthy servant shows fidelity in all things. It may be that the very faith which trusts God is the strength of the faithfulness which God may trust. Fidelity extends to the whole of life, with special reference to our individual vocation. Nothing is excluded from the sphere of this duty. Fidelity, as the test applied to service, is guarded by threatenings and stimulated by the hope of reward" (Matt. 25:23, 26, 30; Pope, *Compendium of Christian Theology,* 3:220-23).

FIELD (Heb. *śādeh,* "smoothness"). This word does not exactly correspond to our "field." The two words agree in describing *cultivated* land but differ in point of extent, the *śādeh* being specifically applied to what is unenclosed, whereas *field* conveys the notion of enclosure. On the one hand *śādeh* is applied to any cultivated ground, whether *pasture* (Gen. 29:2; 31:4; 34:7; Ex. 9:3), *tillage* (Gen. 37:7; 47:24; Ruth 2:2-3; Job 24:6; Jer.

26:18; Mic. 3:12), *forest* (2 Sam. 14:25; Ps. 132:6, *see* marg.), or *mountaintop* (Judg. 9:32, 36; 1 Sam. 1:21). In some instances it is in marked opposition to the neighboring wilderness, as the field or land of Shechem (Gen. 33:19; NIV, "plot"), of Moab (36:35 [NIV, "country"]; Num. 21:20 [NIV, "valley"]; Ruth 1:1 [NIV, "country"]), and the valley of Siddim (Gen. 14:3, 8).

Man and donkey in a field near Eglon

On the other hand, the *śādeh* is contrasted with what is enclosed, whether a *vineyard* (Ex. 22:5; Lev. 25:3-4), a *city* (Deut. 28:3, 16, *see* marg.), or *unwalled villages* ranking in the eyes of the law as fields (Lev. 25:31; NIV, "open country"). The term often implies a place remote from a house (Gen. 4:8; 24:63), a sense more fully expressed by "the open field" (Lev. 14:7, 53; 17:5; Num. 19:16) and naturally coupled with the idea of exposure and desertion (Jer. 9:22; Ezek. 16:5; 32:4; 33:27; 39:5).

Fields were marked off by stones, which could be easily removed (Deut. 19:14; 27:17; cf. Job 24:2; Prov. 22:28; 23:10). Being unfenced, fields were liable to damage from straying cattle (Ex. 22:5), hence the necessity of constantly watching flocks and herds. From the absence of enclosures cultivated land of any size might be termed a *field,* whether of limited area (Gen. 23:13, 17; Isa. 5:8), one's entire inheritance (Lev. 27:16-24; Ruth 4:5 [NIV, "land"]; Jer. 32:9), or public land about a town (Gen. 41:48; Neh. 12:29; not applied, however, to the "suburbs" of Levitical cities immediately adjacent to the walls and considered part of the town; Josh. 21:11-12), and lastly the territory of a people (Gen. 14:7; Num. 21:20, NASB, "country," "land," etc.; NIV, "valley").

Fields were occasionally named after remarkable events, such as *Helkath-hazzurim,* "the field of strong men" (2 Sam. 2:16), or the use to which they may have been put, such as "the fuller's field" (2 Kings 18:17; NIV, "Washerman's Field") or "the Potter's Field" (Matt. 27:7).

The expression "fruitful garden" (Isa. 10:18),

"fruitful field" (16:10), and "fertile field" (Isa. 29:17; 32:15-16) are not connected with *ṡādeh* but with *karmel* (a "park" or well-kept wood), as distinct from a wilderness or forest (2 Kings 19:23; Isa. 37:24).

FIFTIES. *See* Israel, Classification of.

FIG. *See* Vegetable Kingdom.

FIG LEAVES. *See* Dress.

FIGHT. *See* Warfare.

FILLET. An erroneous rendering in the KJV of *ḥūshshāqîm* ("joinings," Ex. 27:17; 38:17, 28), the *bands* (so NASB and NIV) that joined together the tops of the pillars around the court of the *Tabernacle* (which see) and from which the curtain was suspended (Ex. 27:10-11; etc.); *ḥûṭ*, "thread" (as elsewhere rendered), i.e., a *measuring line* (so NASB, marg., Jer. 52:21).

FILTH, FILTHY. The rendering of several Heb. and Gk. words meaning "foul matter" or "anything that soils or defiles." In 2 Chron. 29:5 and Ezra 6:21 the filth or "uncleanness" and "impurity" from which the Jews were to cleanse the Temple and themselves was the abomination of idolatry. Filth is used as the equivalent of *moral impurity* (Ezek. 36:25; James 1:21; cf. 2 Cor. 7:1). In 1 Cor. 4:13 it is used to denote *outsweepings*, that which is worthless, i.e., "the scum of the world." The expression "and its filthiness may be melted in it" (Ezek. 24:11; NIV, "impurities") seems to mean that the pot was to be placed empty upon the fire that the rust might be burned away by the heat. The *filthiness* of the pot was the rust on it.

FINE, FINES. (Heb. *middâ*). A term referring to something measured out (2 Kings 23:33; Ezra 4:20). The KJV renders the term "tribute." The NIV has "levy" and "taxes" respectively. *See* Punishments.

FINE LINEN. *See* Dress; Linen; Vegetable Kingdom: Flax; Sheet.

FINERING. Refining. *See* Handicrafts: Metalworker.

FINGER.

Figurative. Denotes the special and immediate agency of anyone. The Egyptian magicians said of the plagues, "This is the finger of God," i.e., done by God Himself (Ex. 8:19). The tablets of stone were said to have been "written by the finger of God" (31:18) under His personal direction. The heavens are said to be the work of God's fingers, i.e., His power (Ps. 8:3); and Christ said, "If I cast out demons by the finger of God" (Luke 11:20).

"The pointing of the finger" (Isa. 58:9) signifies a scornful pointing with the fingers at humbler men and especially at such as are godly. "Four fingers" is the measure of thickness used by Jeremiah (52:21).

FINGER or **Digit.** A linear measure. *See* Metrology.

FINING POT. A crucible or refining pot (so NASB). *See* Handicrafts: Metalworker.

FINISHER (Gk. *teleiōtēs*, "completer"). Spoken of Jesus (Heb. 12:2, KJV) as one who in His own person raised faith to its perfection and so set before us the highest example of faith. The NASB and NIV give "perfecter."

FINS. A distinctive mark of such fish as might be eaten under the Mosaic law (Lev. 11:9-10, 12; Deut. 14:9-10). *See* Food.

FIR. *See* Vegetable Kingdom: Cypress; Fir; Juniper.

FIRE. The discovery of fire antedates history and seems to be assumed in the first sacrifice of Cain and Abel (Gen. 4:3-4). No nation has yet been discovered that did not know the use of fire, but the way in which it was first procured is unknown. Entering so largely into the life of men it has naturally been the subject of many legends. The ancient Chaldeans looked upon Gibir (or Gibil), the lord of fire, as their most powerful auxiliary against the Annunaki, an order of inferior but malicious beings. Gibir is addressed as the one who lightens up the darkness, who melts the copper and tin, the gold and silver. According to Greek mythology Prometheus, when Zeus denied fire to mortals, stole it from Olympus and brought it to men in a hollow reed. For this he was punished by being chained on a rock in the wilds of Scythia.

The various uses of fire are given in the following sections:

Domestic. The preparation of food presupposes the use of fire, which the Israelites seem, at least in later times, to have produced by striking steel against flint (2 Macc. 10:3), although the oldest method known was that of rubbing two pieces of wood together. Besides for cooking purposes fire is often needed in Palestine for warmth (Jer. 36:22; Mark 14:54; John 18:18). Sometimes a hearth with a chimney was constructed, on which lighted wood or a pan of charcoal was placed. In Persia a hole made in the floor is sometimes filled with charcoal, on which a sort of table is set covered with a carpet. The company draws the carpet over their feet. Rooms are warmed in Egypt with pans of charcoal. The use of charcoal in reducing and fashioning metals was well known among the Hebrews. *See* Handicrafts: Metalworker.

Laws Regulating Fire. The law forbade any fire to be kindled on the Sabbath, even for culinary purposes (Ex. 35:3; Num. 15:32-36). This did not, probably, forbid the use of fire for warmth. The dryness of the land in the hot season made fires more likely to occur (Judg. 9:15), and the law ordered that anyone kindling a fire that caused damage to grain should make restitution (Ex. 22:6; cf. Judg. 15:4-5; 2 Sam. 14:30).

Religious. Fire was used to consume the burnt offerings and the incense offering, beginning with the sacrifice of Noah (Gen. 8:20) and continuing in the ever-burning fire on the altar. "In the sacrificial flame the essence of the animal was resolved into vapor; so that when a man presented a sacrifice in his own stead, his inmost being, his spirit, and his heart ascended to God in the vapor, and the sacrifice brought the feeling of his heart before God" (K. & D., *Com.*). This altar fire was miraculously sent from God (Lev. 6:9, 13; 9:24), like the fire of Jehovah that consumed the sacrifices of David and Solomon (1 Chron. 21:26; 2 Chron. 7:1). Keil and Delitzsch (*Com., Lev.* 9:24) say: "The miracle recorded in this verse did not consist in the fact that the sacrificial offerings placed upon the altar were burned by fire which proceeded from Jehovah, but in the fact that the sacrifices, which were already on fire, were suddenly consumed by it." Fire was to be constantly burning upon the altar without going out, in order "that the burnt offering might never go out, because this was the divinely appointed symbol and visible sign of the uninterrupted worship of Jehovah, which the covenant nation could never suspend either day or night without being unfaithful to its calling" (K. & D., *Com.,* Lev. 6:12). If by any calamity the sacred fire was extinguished, according to the Talmud it was only to be rekindled by friction. Fire for sacred purposes obtained elsewhere than from the altar was called "strange fire," for the use of which Nadab and Abihu were punished with death by fire from God (Lev. 10:1-2; Num. 3:4; 26:61). When the Israelites returned with booty taken from the Midianites, Eleazer, whose duty it was to see that the laws of purification were properly observed, told them that "the statute of the law" was that all articles that could bear it were to be drawn through the fire and then sprinkled with the water of purification (31:21-23). The animals slain for sin offerings were afterward consumed by fire outside of the camp (Lev. 4:12, 21; 6:30; 16:27; Heb. 13:11). The Nazirite, on the day when the time of his consecration expired, shaved his head and put the hair into the altar fire under the peace offering that was burning, thus handing over and sacrificing to the Lord the hair that had been worn in honor of Him (Num. 6:18).

Penal. Capital punishment was sometimes aggravated by burning the body of the criminal after death (Lev. 20:14; 21:9; Josh. 7:25; 2 Kings 23:16). *See* Punishments; Warfare.

Figurative. Fire was a symbol of the Lord's presence and the instrument of His power, either in the way of approval or of destruction (Ex. 14:19, 24; Num. 11:1, 3; etc.). Thus Jehovah appeared in the burning bush and on Mt. Sinai (Ex. 3:2; 19:18). In the midst of fire He showed Himself to Isaiah, Ezekiel, and John (Isa. 6:4-5;

Ezek. 1:4-5; Rev. 1:12-14) and will so appear at His second coming (2 Thess. 1:7). Jehovah guided the Israelites through the wilderness with the pillar of fire (Ex. 13:21). God is compared to fire, not only because of His glorious brightness but on account of His anger against sin, which consumes sinners as fire does stubble (Deut. 32:22; Isa. 10:17; Ezek. 21:31-32; Heb. 12:29). Fire is illustrative of the church's overcoming her enemies (Obad. 18); the Word of God (Jer. 5:14; 23:29); the Holy Spirit (Isa. 4:4; Acts 2:3-4); the zeal of saints (Pss. 39:3; 119:139) and of angels (104:4; Heb. 1:7); of lust (Prov. 6:27-29) and of wickedness (Isa. 9:18); of the tongue (Prov. 16:27; James 3:6); the hope of hypocrites (Isa. 50:11); persecution (Luke 12:49-53); and of judgment (Jer. 48:45; Lam. 1:13; Ezek. 39:6). Fire, in its symbolic use, is also spoken of as purifying —the emblem of a healing process effected upon the spiritual natures of persons in covenant with God (Isa. 4:5-6; Mal. 3:2-3).

BIBLIOGRAPHY: R. de Vaux, *Ancient Israel: Its Life and Institutions* (1961), pp. 406-56; J. Morgenstern, *Fire upon the Altar* (1963).

FIRE, STRANGE. *See* Fire: Religious.

FIRE BAPTISM. *See* Molech, Worship of; Baptism.

FIREBRAND.

1. A "torch" used by Samson (Judg. 15:4), probably made of resinous wood or other material. His tying the foxes tail to tail was to prevent their running into their holes and to impede their progress for a more effectual execution. Similar conflagrations produced by animals, particularly foxes, were well known to Greeks and Romans.

2. The ends of wooden pokers (lit., "fire stirrers"), that would not blaze anymore but only continued smoking (Isa. 7:4; Amos 4:11). The NIV translates "smoldering stubs" and "burning stick" respectively.

FIREPAN. An ashpan or vessel used for taking away the coals from the fire on the altar (Ex. 27:3; Lev. 16:12; etc.). *See also* Snuffers.

FIRES (Heb. *'ûr*). In Isa. 24:15 (KJV) we read, "Glorify ye the Lord in the fires," but which is better rendered "east," as in the NASB and NIV. The lands of the Asiatic East were called *'ûrîm*, "the lands of light," i.e., the sunrising, as opposed to the "west" (NASB and NIV; the KJV reads, "from the sea").

FIRE WORSHIP, or Pyrolatry. As a symbol of purity, or of the divine presence and power, or as one of the constituent elements, or as typifying the destructive element in nature, fire has been from early times the object of worship by many peoples, e.g., the ancient Persians and Medes. The faith of the magi made the elements of nature the direct objects of worship. These were fire, water, earth, and air, of which the first was considered the most energetic and sublime. So the priest built an altar, and the sacred fire caught from heaven was kindled and always kept burning. The priest was the holy magus. No other might attend the altars or conduct the mystic rites. No breath of mortal might be blown upon the sacred flame without pollution; the burning of dead bodies was a horrid profanation, and of the sacrificial offerings only a fragment of fat was given to the flame. This worship among the Canaanites is frequently referred to in the Scriptures, and the people were warned against joining in its abominations (Lev. 18:21; Deut. 12:31; 1 Kings 11:7; 2 Chron. 28:3; Ezek. 16:20-21; etc.). In spite of these warnings, however, the people caused their children to pass through the fire to Molech. *See* Gods, False.

Fire worship was also practiced among the Carthaginians, Scythians, the ancient Germans, and the ancient inhabitants of Great Britain. Traces of it are also found in Mexican and Peruvian worship. The Mexican god of fire, Xiuhtecutli (the Lord of Fire), was an ancient deity. He is represented naked, with his chin blackened and with a headdress of green feathers, carrying on his back a kind of serpent with yellow feathers, thus combining the fire colors. Sacrifices were offered to him daily. In every house the first libation and the first morsel of bread were consecrated to him. And as an instance of the astounding resemblance between the religious development of the Old World and that of the New, the fire in Mexico, as in ancient Iran and other countries of Asia and Europe, must in every house be extinguished on a certain day every year. The priest of Xiuhtecutli kindled fire anew by friction before the statue of the god. "At set of sun" of this day "all who had prisoners of war or slaves to offer to the deity brought forward their victims, painted with the colors of the god, danced along by their side, and shut them up in a building attached to the teocalli of fire. At midnight each owner severed a lock of the hair of his slave or slaves, to be carefully preserved as a talisman. At daybreak they brought out the victims, the priests took them upon their shoulders and flung their human burden upon the fire" (Reville, *Religions of Mexico and Peru,* pp. 62ff., 83). Among the Peruvians, "fire, considered as derived from the sun, was the object of profound veneration. Strange as it may seem at first sight, the symbol of fire was stones. But . . . stones were thought to be animated by the fire that was supposed to be shut up within them, since it could be made to issue forth by a sharp blow. A perpetual fire burned in the Temple of the Sun and in the abode of the Virgins of the Sun. It was supposed that fire became polluted and lost its divine nature by too long contact with men. The fire must be renewed from time to time, and this act was performed yearly by the chief priest of Peru, who kindled

wood by means of a concave golden mirror" (ibid., pp. 162-63).

FIRMAMENT (Heb. *rāqîa',* "expanse," Gen. 1:6, 14-15, 17, KJV; NASB and NIV render "expanse"). The pure and transparent expanse that envelops the globe. This was made by God on the second day of creation for the purpose of separating the sea from the clouds. As used in the record of creation, firmament includes not merely the lower heavens, or atmospheric sky, with its clouds and vapors, but the whole visible expanse up to the region of the stars; for it is said that on the fourth day God made in the firmament sun, moon, and stars. A controversy has arisen respecting the sense attached by the Hebrew writers to "firmament," chiefly on account of the ancient translations given of it, and the poetic representations found of the upper regions of the visible heavens in some parts of Scripture. The LXX renders *stereōma,* meaning generally "some compact mass," while the Vulg. has *firmamentum,* a "prop" or "support." Hence it has been argued that the Hebrews understood by the word something solid, capable of bearing up the waters that accumulate in masses above, and even of having the heavenly bodies affixed to it as to a crystalline pavement. As proof of this view such passages are quoted as speak of the foundations of heaven shaking (2 Sam. 22:8), of its pillars trembling (Job 26:11), of the windows or doors of heaven (Ps. 78:23; Mal. 3:10), of the gates of the sky (Gen. 7:11), or of the sky's being "strong as a molten mirror" (Job 37:18). But these expressions are manifestly of a figurative nature.

FIRST-BEGOTTEN. *See* Firstborn.

FIRSTBORN (several Heb. words from *bākar,* "to burst forth"; Gk. *prōtotokos*). Applied equally to animals and human beings. By the firstborn, in a religious point of view, we are to understand the first of a mother's offspring (Ex. 12:12). *See* Inheritance.

Figurative. The expression "firstborn" stands for that which is most excellent. Thus Jesus Christ is head of the "church of the first-born" (Heb. 12:23). "The firstborn of the poor" (Isa. 14:30, KJV) means the *poorest of the poor.* "The first-born of death" (Job 18:13) is the disease that Bildad has in his mind as the one more terrible and dangerous than all others. Diseases are conceived of as the children of death.

BIBLIOGRAPHY: R. de Vaux, *Ancient Israel: Its Life and Institutions* (1961), pp. 41-42; J. B. Lightfoot, *St. Paul's Epistles to the Colossians and Philemon* (1966), pp. 152f.; N. Turner, *Christian Words* (1982), pp. 175-76.

FIRSTBORN, DESTRUCTION OF. *See* Plagues of Egypt.

FIRSTBORN IN ISRAEL. In memory of the death of Egypt's firstborn and the preservation of the firstborn of Israel, all the firstborn of Israel, both of man and beast, belonged to Jehovah (Ex. 13:2, 15; cf. 12:11-13).

Sanctification of the Firstborn of Man. This was closely connected with Israel's deliverance from Egypt, and the object of that deliverance was their sanctification. Because Jehovah had delivered the firstborn of Israel, they were to be sanctified to Him. The fundamental element upon which this sanctification rests is evidently the representative character of the firstborn, standing for the entire offspring. Moreover, the firstborn of newly married people were believed to represent the prime of human vigor (Gen. 49:3; Ps. 78:51). Then, too, all Israel were in outward standing and covenant relationship the Lord's firstborn, being the national representatives of a redeemed church, to be brought out of every kindred, tongue, and people, and as such they were a nation of priests (Ex. 4:22-23; 19:6).

Redemption. The firstborn was the priest of the whole family. The honor of exercising the priesthood was transferred, by the command of God through Moses, from the tribe of Reuben, to whom it belonged by right of primogeniture, to that of Levi (Num. 3:12-16; 8:18-19). In consequence of the fact that God had taken the Levites to serve Him as priests, the firstborn of the other tribes were redeemed. They were presented to the Lord when a month old and, according to the priest's estimation, were redeemed by a sum not exceeding five shekels (18:16). When the Levites were set apart Moses numbered the firstborn of Israel to exchange them for the Levites. The number of the firstborn of the twelve tribes amounted to 22,273 of a month old and upward. Of this number 22,000 were exchanged for the 22,000 Levites. This left 273 to be redeemed, whose redemption money (1,365 shekels) was to be paid to Aaron and his sons as compensation for the persons who properly belonged to Jehovah (Num. 3:40-51). The Jewish doctors held that if the child died before the expiration of thirty days the father was excused from payment; if the child was sickly, or appeared otherwise to be inferior to children generally, the priest could estimate it at less than five shekels; or, if he found the parents were poor, he might return the money after the ceremony. When the mother's days of purification were accomplished and she could appear in the Temple, she brought the child to the priest to be publicly presented to the Lord (Luke 2:22). The Jews still observe this law of redemption when the firstborn male is thirty days old, inviting to their house friends and a priest to a meal on the following day. The priest, having invoked the divine blessing upon the meal and offered some introductory prayers, etc., looks at the child and the redemption money placed before him and asks the father to choose between the money and the child. Upon the father's reply that he would rather pay the redemption money, the priest takes it, swings it around the head of the child, in token of his vicarious authority, saying, "This is for the firstborn; this is in lieu of it; this redeems it," etc. When the firstborn is thirteen years old he fasts the day before the feast of Passover, in commemoration of the sparing of the firstborn in Egypt.

Redemption of the Firstborn of Animals.

Of Clean Animals. The firstborn male animal was devoted to the Lord and, if a clean animal, was sacrificed to Him. It was to be brought to the sanctuary within a year, dating from the eighth day after birth, and there offered in sacrifice; the blood sprinkled upon the altar, the fat burned upon it, while all the remaining flesh (such as the breast and the right shoulder in the case of peace offerings) belonged to the priest (Num. 18:17-18; cf. Ex. 13:13; 22:30; 34:20; Neh. 10:36). If the animal had some severe blemish—happened to be blind or lame—it was eaten at home by the owner. Before the sacrifice the animal was not to be used for any work, as it belonged to the Lord (Deut. 15:19-21).

Of Unclean Animals. The firstborn of unclean animals were to be redeemed according to the valuation of the priest, with the addition of a fifth; and if this was not done it was to be sold at the estimated value. By this regulation the earlier law, which commanded that a donkey should either be redeemed with a lamb or put to death (Ex. 13:13; 34:20), was modified in favor of the revenues of the sanctuary and its servants. Nothing, however, that a man had devoted (banned) to the Lord of his property (man, beast, or field) was to be sold or redeemed, because it was most holy (Lev. 27:28-29). The same was true with regard to the produce of the soil—i.e., the products of agriculture—the first of which (i.e., the best of the *firstlings*) were sacred to the Lord (Ex. 23:19; Deut. 18:4). *See* First Fruit.

Birthright (Heb. *beḳōrâ*). The term applied to the peculiar advantages, privileges, and responsibilities of the firstborn among the Israelites. The firstborn was the object of special affection to his parents and inherited peculiar rights and privileges. Before these are given it will be proper to call attention to the fact that, in case a man married a widow with children by a former husband, the firstborn, as respected the second husband, was the eldest child by the second marriage. Attention is also called to the additional fact that, before the time of Moses, the father might transfer the right of primogeniture to a younger child; but the practice occasioned much contention (Gen. 25:31-32), and a law was enacted overruling it (Deut. 21:15-17). The rights and privileges of the firstborn were as follows:

1. The firstborn received a double portion of the estate, the other sons single and equal portions. For example, if there were five sons the property would be divided into six portions, of which the eldest son received two-sixths, each of the others one-sixth. Where there were two

wives, one loved, the other hated, the father was not to prefer the later-born son of the favorite wife to the older firstborn of the hated one, but was to give the right of primogeniture (with two portions of the estate) to the beginning of his strength (Deut. 21:15-17). Jacob took away the right of primogeniture from Reuben because of Reuben's incestuous conduct (Gen. 49:3-4; cf. 35:22) and transferred it to Joseph by adopting his two sons (48:20-22; 1 Chron. 5:1).

2. The firstborn was the head of the whole family. Originally the priesthood belonged to the tribe of Reuben, as the firstborn, but was transferred to the tribe of Levi (Num. 3:12-16; 8:18). The firstborn enjoyed an authority over those who were younger similar to that possessed by a father (Gen. 35:23; 2 Chron. 21:3). As head of the family he had also, according to patriarchal custom, to provide food, clothing, and other necessities in his house for his mother till death, and his unmarried sisters till their marriages.

BIBLIOGRAPHY: *See* under Firstborn.

FIRST DAY OF THE WEEK. *See* Lord's Day, Sunday.

FIRST FRUIT (Heb. *rē'shît,* "first"; *bikkûr,* "first ripe"; Gk. *aparchē,* "beginning"). Like the firstborn of man and beast, the first fruits were sacred to Jehovah, as Lord of the soil (Ex. 23:19; Deut. 18:4; etc.).

Character of. In general, *first fruits* included those in the raw state (grain and fruit); those prepared for use as food (wine, oil, flour, and dough), including wool (Ex. 22:29; 23:19; 34:26; Deut. 18:4; etc.). The firstling sheaf at the *Passover* (*see* Festivals) was presented by the congregation before the commencement of the grain harvest (Lev. 23:10-11). Josephus says that the sheaf was of barley and that until this ceremony had been performed, no harvest work was to be done (*Ant.* 3.10.5). The firstling loaf at *Pentecost* (*see* Festivals) was presented when the harvest was completed. Two of these loaves, made of the new flour (wheat) and leavened, like the sheaf above mentioned, were waved before the Lord (Lev. 23:17; Ex. 34:22; Num. 28:26).

Offering of First Fruits. Regarding the *firstling see* the discussion of Passover and Pentecost in the article Festivals. No private offerings of first fruits were allowed before the public oblation of the two loaves (Lev. 23:15, 20). The law nowhere specifies the amount that was to be given in the shape of offerings of this kind but leaves it to each individual's discretion; it only provided that the choicest portions were always to be offered (Num. 18:12). Neither is it stated in the law what were to be the different products of the soil from which firstlings were to be offered, but that the whole produce of husbandry was meant is implied in the spirit of the law itself. Accordingly, in the time of Hezekiah, firstlings of grain, wine, oil, honey, and of the whole produce of the soil were offered (2 Chron. 31:5). This may further be inferred from the regulation to the effect that, of every tree bearing edible fruit that any Israelite might plant, the fruits of the fourth year, the earliest period at which they could be eaten, were to be sacred to the Lord; and, consequently, they must have been presented to Him as an offering (Lev. 19:23-25).

Manner of Offering. The first fruits were brought in a basket to the sanctuary and presented to the priest, who was to set the basket down before the altar. Then, the offerer recited the story of Jacob's going to Egypt and the deliverance of his posterity from there. He then acknowledged the blessings with which God had visited him (Deut. 26:2-11). It being found almost impracticable for every Israelite to go on this mission to Jerusalem, the following custom arose. The inhabitants of a district prepared a basket with seven kinds of ripe fruit arranged in the following order: barley in the bottom, then wheat, olives, dates, pomegranates, figs, and grapes. This basket was watched all night by a company of at least twenty-four persons, who stayed in the open marketplace, being afraid to go into a house lest the death of a resident should cause pollution. In the morning the company set out for Jerusalem. An ox (to be the peace offering) went before them with gilded horns and an olive crown upon its head, as the people sang, "I was glad when they said to me, 'Let us go to the house of the Lord' " (Ps. 122:1). Upon their approaching Jerusalem a messenger was sent to announce their arrival, and the first fruits tastefully arranged. The officiating priest, the Levites, and the treasurers went out to meet them (the number of officials depending upon the size of the party) and accompanied them into the city, singing as they entered, "Our feet are standing within your gates, O Jerusalem" (122:2). The piper, who led the music of the party, continued to play until the procession came to the mount of the Temple. Here everyone, even the king, took his own basket upon his shoulders and went forward till they came to the court of the Temple, singing, "Praise the Lord! Praise God in His sanctuary," etc. (150:1). The Levites responded with "I will extol Thee, O Lord!" etc. Then pigeons, which were hung about the baskets, were taken for burnt offerings. With the baskets still upon their shoulders, everyone began the story of Jacob until he came to the words "My father was a wandering Aramaean" (*see* Deut. 26:3-5), when he let down his basket, holding it by the brim. The priest then put his hands under it and waved it, the offerer continuing to recite the story. When he reached 26:10, "And now behold, I have brought the first of the produce," he put the basket beside the altar and, having prostrated himself, departed. After passing the night in Jerusalem the pilgrims returned the following day to their homes.

Exemptions. Exemptions were made in the

case of those who simply possessed the trees, without owning the land, for they could not say, "The ground which Thou, O Lord, hast *given me.*" Those living beyond the Jordan could not bring first fruits in the proper sense of the libation, not being able to say the words of the service, from "a land flowing with milk and honey" (Deut. 26:10-15). A proselyte, though bringing the offering, was not to recite the service, being unable to say, "I have entered the land which the Lord swore to *our fathers to give us*" (26:3, italics added). Stewards, servants, slaves, women, sexless persons, and hermaphrodites were not allowed to recite the service, because they could not use the words "I have brought the first of the produce of the ground which Thou, *O Lord hast given me*" (26:10, italics added), they having originally no share in the land.

Historical. After the time of Solomon the corruption of the nation led to neglect of these as well as of other legal enactments, and their restoration was among the reforms brought about by Hezekiah (2 Chron. 31:5, 11). Nehemiah also, after the captivity, reorganized the offerings of first fruits of both kinds and appointed places to receive them (Neh. 10:35, 37; 12:44). An offering of first fruits, brought to Elisha, was miraculously increased so as to feed one hundred persons (2 Kings 4:42-44). First fruits were sent to Jerusalem by Jews living in foreign countries (Josephus *Ant.* 16.6.7).

Figurative. Of the Jewish nation it was said, "Israel was holiness unto the Lord, and the *firstfruits* of his increase" (Jer. 2:3, KJV, italics added). In the NT first fruits are emblematic of abundance and excellence and a sample of full harvest. Paul says that Christians have "the first fruits of the Spirit" (Rom. 8:23), i.e., the first manifestations of the Spirit in the gospel dispensation. Christ was "the first fruits of those who are asleep," i.e., the first who rose from the dead (1 Cor. 15:20, 23; 16:15; cf. Rom. 11:16). Converts are called "firstfruits," such as Epaenetus (16:5, KJV).

FISH. *See also* Animal Kingdom.

Figurative. This term is used to signify the inhabitants of Egypt (Ezek. 29:4-5), the visible church (Matt. 13:48), and defenseless people taken by the Chaldeans (Hab. 1:14). In Christian symbolism the fish is of great significance. "It is among the earliest art forms, and pertains to a period of Church history which causes it to be among the most interesting and important objects in the whole range of Christian symbolism. It is generally thought to be the symbol of Christ. The word in Greek was made up of the initial letters of the words in the article of faith so dear to the early Church: I, Ἰησοῦς, Jesus; X, Χριστός, Christ; Θ, Θεοῦ, of God; Y, Υἱός, Son; Σ, Σωτήρ, Savior—Jesus Christ, Son of God, Savior. The fish is also used to represent Christ's

disciples. Probably, as suggested by Tertullian, the water and the rite of baptism were prominently in their thought, while secondary reference may have been had to the parable of the net or to the command of Christ to Peter and Andrew, 'Follow me, and I will make you fishers of men'" (Matt. 4:18-19).

BIBLIOGRAPHY: G. S. Cansdale, *Animals of Bible Lands* (1970), pp. 212-23; J. D. M. Derrett, *Law in the New Testament* (1970), pp. 247-65.

FISHER. In addition to the usual meaning, the Lord called His disciples "fishers of men" (Matt. 4:19; Mark 1:17). *See* Fishing.

FISH GATE (Heb. *sha'ar haddāgîm*, "gate of the fishes"). The name (2 Chron. 33:14; Neh. 3:3; 12:39) of one of the gates of *Jerusalem* (which see). It probably took its name from the fact of fish being brought through it on the way to the city, or from the fish market being located near it. *See also* Gate.

FISHHOOK.

1. The prophet Amos (4:2), in denouncing the voluptuous grandees of Samaria, predicted that God "will take you away with meat hooks, and the last of you with fish hooks." The reference is undoubtedly to the practice of Egyptians, Assyrians, and other ancient conquerors of putting fishhooks in the lips of captives (*see* 2 Chron. 33:11, RV marg.).

2. A ring placed in the mouth of fish and attached to a cord to keep them alive in the water (Job 41:1-2). *See* Fishing.

FISHING. This trade has always been an industry pursued by a large number of people in Palestine. They are exceedingly fond of fish and pay double to triple the price for it that they do for meat. Several methods of taking fish are mentioned in the Bible: (1) *Angling* with a hook, also called *casting a line* (Isa. 19:8; Hab. 1:15; Job 41:1; Amos 4:2). (2) *Spearing* (Job 41:7). In this passage the reference is to the crocodile, but it is included under the generic idea of fish as conceived by the Hebrew mind, i.e., a creature living more or less in the water. (3) *Netting.* They used the *cast net* (Ezek. 26:5, 14; 32:3; 47:10; Hab. 1:15, 17; Mic. 7:2; Eccles. 7:26; Matt. 4:18-21; Mark 1:16-19; etc.). This consists of a net with fine mesh and of a circular form, about fifteen feet in diameter. The margin is loaded with leaden sinkers. To the center of the net is attached a long piece of fishline. This is held in the left hand, while the net, which has been previously gathered up in the right, is cast by a broad sweep of the arm over an area of the shallow water close to the shore, where the fisherman has previously observed a school of fish. The center of the net is now drawn up by means of the cord, and the fisherman wades into the water and secures the catch. The *seine* is also used. Half of it is loaded into one boat and the other half in another, and the boats then separate, playing out the net as they go and enclosing a vast area of the water. When all the net has been played out the boats draw it toward the shore and land the ends of the net. The two crews then commence to draw in their respective ends, thus enclosing the fish and gradually landing them (Matt. 13:48). At other times the two boats enclose a circle in the water and draw the fish into the boats (Luke 5:4-9). The seine is also mentioned in the OT (Isa. 19:8; Hab. 1:15). Four of Christ's twelve disciples were fishermen. Christ promised them that they should become fishers of men (Mark 1:17; etc.). G.E.P.

Fisherman casting a net

FITCHES. A KJV term, replaced in the NASB and NIV by *cummin* (Heb. *qeṣah,* "black cummin"; Isa. 28:25, 27) and *spelt* (Heb. *kŭssemet;* Ezek. 4:9). *See* Vegetable Kingdom: Cummin; Spelt.

FLAG. *See* Standard.

FLAG. *See* Vegetable Kingdom: Reeds and Rushes.

FLAGONS. A KJV term rendered "jars" (Heb. *nēbel;* Isa. 22:24) or "raisin cakes" (Heb. *'ăshîshâ;* 2 Sam. 6:19; Song of Sol. 2:5; Hos. 3:1) in the NASB and NIV.

FLAKE. *See* Folds.

FLAME. In Job 18:5 it is predicted that "the light of the wicked goes out, and the flame [Heb. *shābîb,* "flame"] of his fire gives no light." *Flame* here probably refers to the lamp hanging in the tent (cf. 21:17; 29:3). *See also* Fire.

FLANK. The translation of two Heb. terms, *yarᵉkâ* (Gen. 49:13; "border" in NIV) and *kātēp* (Ezek. 25:9), referring to the far or side border or boundary of a territory. Rarely, in the KJV, it is the term for the internal muscles of the loins near the kidneys (*see* Loins).

FLASK (Heb. *pak,* 2 Kings 9:1, 3; Gk. *alabastron,* Mark 14:3). Used for holding oil or perfumery. The KJV uses "box of oil" or "box of ointment," whereas the NASB rendering is "flask of oil" or "vial of . . . ointment," and the NIV, "ala-

baster jar" (*see* Mark 14:3). First Sam. 10:1, KJV, uses "vial."

FLAT NOSE. *See* Diseases: Disfigured Face.

FLAX. *See* articles Dress; Linen; Vegetable Kingdom: Flax.

FLEA. *See* Animal Kingdom.

FLEECE (Heb. *gēz,* "sheared," Job. 31:20; cf. Deut. 18:4). The wool of a sheep, whether on the living animal, shorn off, or attached to the flayed skin. The miracle of Gideon's fleece (Judg. 6:37-40) consisted of the dew having fallen one time upon the fleece, without any on the floor, whereas at another time the fleece remained dry while the ground was wet with dew.

FLEET (Heb. *'ŏnî,* "conveyance"; 1 Kings 9:26-27; etc.). Solomon built the Hebrew navy (merchant marine) with the help of Hiram king of Tyre. *See* Ezion-geber; Ship.   H.F.V.

FLESH. This word has various meanings, as follows: (1) In a general sense of the whole animal creation, man or beast (Gen. 6:13, 17, 19; 7:15-16, 21; 8:17; Matt. 24:22, marg.; 1 Pet. 1:24). (2) Of the flesh of the living body, both of men and beasts (Gen. 41:2, 19, marg.; Job 33:21; 1 Cor. 15:39); and as distinguished from other parts of the body, e.g., from bones (Luke 24:39). (3) In the sense of our word *meat,* i.e., the flesh of cattle used for food (Lev. 7:19; cf. Ex. 16:12; Num. 11:4, 13, marg.; *see* Food). (4) The body as distinguished from the *spirit* (Job 14:22, marg.; 19:26; John 6:52; 1 Cor. 5:5; 2 Cor. 4:11; 7:1; 1 Pet. 4:6); so also "flesh and blood" was used as a longer phrase for the whole animal nature or mankind (Heb. 2:14). (5) Human nature, mankind (Gen. 2:23; Matt. 19:5-6; 1 Cor. 6:16; Eph. 5:28-31); also of the incarnation of Christ (John 1:14; 6:51; Rom. 1:3; Eph. 2:15; Col. 1:22; Heb. 5:7; 10:20; etc.). (6) Natural or physical origin, generation, relationship (Gen. 29:14; 37:27; Judg. 9:2; 2 Sam. 5:1; 19:13; John 1:13; Rom. 9:8; Heb. 2:11-14; 12:9, marg.); of one's countryman (Rom. 9:3; 11:14, marg.; Gal. 4:23); a fellowmortal (Isa. 58:7). (7) The sensuous nature of man, "the animal nature," without any suggestion of depravity, sexual desire (John 1:13; NIV, "human decision"); with cravings that excite to sin (Matt. 26:41; Mark 14:38; NIV, "body"). (8) Mere human nature, the earthly nature of man apart from divine influence and therefore prone to sin and opposed to God; accordingly it includes in the soul whatever is weak, low, debased, tending to ungodliness and vice (*see* Rom. 8:3, 5-9; 2 Cor. 7:5; Gal. 5:16; Eph. 2:3). The NIV usually renders "the sinful nature" in such uses. (9) As a modest, general term for the secret parts (Gen. 17:11; Ex. 28:42; Lev. 15:2-3, 7, 16, 19, marg.; 2 Pet. 2:10; Jude 7). *See* Food.

BIBLIOGRAPHY: J. A. T. Robinson, *The Body* (1952), pp. 11-16; C. Tresmontant, *A Study of Hebrew Thought*

(1960), pp. 83-124; D. E. H. Whiteley, *The Theology of St. Paul* (1964); H. W. Wolff, *Anthropology of the Old Testament* (1974), pp. 26-31; N. Turner, *Christian Words* (1982), pp. 176-78.

FLESH AND BLOOD. An expression denoting man as fallible, liable to err (Matt. 16:17; Gal. 1:16; Eph. 6:12).

FLESHHOOK (Heb. *mizlāgâ;* Ex. 27:3; 38:3; Num. 4:14; 1 Chron. 28:17; 2 Chron. 4:16). An instrument used in sacrificial services; probably a *fork* (which see; so NASB and NIV), with its tines bent back to draw away the flesh. The implement in 1 Sam. 2:13-14 (Heb. *mazlēg*) is stated to be three-pronged and was apparently a fork used for sacrificial purposes.

BIBLIOGRAPHY: C. R. Erdman, *The First Epistle of Paul to the Corinthians* (1928), pp. 73-96.

Flock of sheep near Bethlehem

"FLESH OFFERED TO IDOLS." *See* Things Sacrificed to Idols.

FLESH POT. *See* Pots of Meat.

FLIES. *See* Animal Kingdom.

FLINT. *See* Mineral Kingdom.

FLOAT. *See* Raft.

FLOCK.
   Figurative. In addition to the usual sense of sheep (*see* Animal Kingdom), taken collectively the term is applied both to Israel as a nation in covenant relation to Jehovah as well as to the NT church (Isa. 40:11; Matt. 26:31; Luke 12:32; 1 Pet. 5:2-3). "Flock doomed to slaughter" (Zech. 11:4) is an expression that may be applied either to a flock that is being slaughtered or to one that is destined to be slaughtered in the future. From v. 11 Israel is the flock referred to, not the human race. "Israel was given up by Jehovah into the hands of the nations or imperial powers to punish it for its sin. But as these nations abused the power intrusted to them and sought utterly to destroy the nation of God, which they ought only to have chastised, the Lord takes charge of his people as their shepherd" (K. & D., *Com.,* ad loc.).

FLOOD, or **Deluge.** The account of this phenomenal world-engulfing event is recounted in Gen. 6-9. It comprehends the bulk of space given by divine revelation to the events in the early redemptive history of man, eclipsing even the space given to the creation and the Fall.

   The Bible Account. The historical recital in Genesis pointedly sets forth the wickedness of man as the cause of the Flood (6:5-7, 11-13); Noah's building of an ark in which he and his family were to be saved during the coming flood; the entrance of Noah, his family, and the animals into the ark; and God's deliverance from the catastrophe because of Noah's righteousness. Isaiah 54:9 refers to the Flood as "the waters of Noah." Jesus put His sanction upon the historicity of the event (Matt. 24:37-39; Luke 17:26-27). Peter spoke of "the patience of God kept waiting in the days of Noah, during the construction of the ark, in which a few, that is, eight persons, were brought safely through the water" (1 Pet. 3:20) and cites it as an example of God's righteous judgment (2 Pet. 2:5). The Flood events are outlined in table 10, "The Biblical Account of the Flood."

Table 10 The Biblical Account of the Flood	
Event	Genesis
Noah, in his six hundredth year, enters the ark with his family and the animals	7:1-9
The rain begins on seventeenth of second month and lasts forty days	7:10-17
The rain ceases; the waters prevail	7:18-24
The ark rests on Ararat, seventeenth day of seventh month	8:1-4
Tops of mountains visible, first day of tenth month	8:5
Raven and dove sent out	8:6-9
Dove sent out again seven days after and returns with olive branch	8:10-11
Dove sent out the third time, after seven days, and does not return	8:12
Ground becomes dry, six hundred and first year, first month and first day; covering of the ark removed	8:13
Noah leaves the ark, second month, twenty-seventh day	8:14-19

   Primitive Tradition of a Flood. The tradition of the Flood was persistent among ancient oriental peoples. In lower Mesopotamia, the ancestral home of Abraham, the Flood was well remembered as a great catastrophe in human history and was preserved through oral tradition and upon cuneiform tablets. The Sumerian King List (see Thorkild Jacobsen, *The Sumerian King List, Assyriological Studies,* vol. 11 [1939]), after recording eight antediluvian kings, interrupts the sequence with the following significant statement before proceeding to the postdiluvian rulers: "[Then] the Flood swept over [the earth]. After the flood had swept over [the earth] and when kingship was lowered [again] from heaven kingship was [first] in Kish." (See A. Leo Oppenheim, in *Ancient Near Eastern Texts* [1950], p. 265.) In ancient times the Tigris-Euphrates valley was subject to frequent floods when these great rivers overflowed their banks. Evidence of a flood at Ur and at Kish has been construed as pointing to the biblical Deluge. But the flood at Ur dates to early in the fourth millennium B.C., the one at Kish about 2800 B.C. Moreover, a flood at Fara (halfway between Ur and Babylon) dated well before 3000 B.C.; and no evidence of a flood turned up at Obeid, four miles from Ur. According to the scriptural representations the Flood was a worldwide catastrophe.

The Sumerian Account of the Flood. The oldest version of the Flood is the Sumerian record on a cuneiform tablet from ancient Nippur in north central Babylonia dating before the second millennium B.C. The third column on the tablet introduces the Flood. The Flood hero is named Ziusudra, a king-priest. The next column portrays Ziusudra receiving a communication from the gods. In column five the deluge has broken upon the world, and the hero is riding in a huge boat:

> When for seven days and seven nights
> The flood had raged over the land
> And the huge boat had been tossed on the great
>   waters by the storms,
> The sun god arose shedding light in heaven
>   and on earth.
> Ziusudra made an opening in the side of the
>   great ship.
> Before the sun god he bowed his face to the
>   ground.
> The king slaughtered an ox, sheep he sacrificed
>   in great numbers.

(J. Finegan, *Light from the Ancient Past* [1946], p. 27.) In the last column Ziusudra is immortalized and conducted to a paradise called "the Mountain of Dilmun."

The Babylonian Account of the Flood. This account constitutes the eleventh book of the Assyro-Babylonian epic of Gilgamesh. These tablets were unearthed at ancient Nineveh in 1853 by H. Rassam. Not until 1872 were they deciphered and recognized as a startling extrabiblical account of the Flood. The Flood account as contained in the Gilgamesh epic offers the most striking and detailed similarity to Gen. 6-8. Ziusudra, the Sumerian Noah, appears as Utnapishtim, "day of life." Gilgamesh, a demi-god and king of Uruk (biblical Erech, 10:10), in search of the secret of immortality, finds the immortalized Flood hero Utnapishtim. In explaining the secret of his immortality, he recounts the cause of it as his passing through the experience of the Flood and being given eternal life as a result. In Utnapishtim's account the gods determine to destroy the earth by a deluge. According to divine directions the Babylonian hero constructs an enormous boat in the form of a cube, pitching it with bitumen

inside and out, and taking aboard gold, silver, his family, craftsmen, beasts of the field, and a boatman. The fierce storm is pictured as "gathering with the first glow of dawn." Adad, the god of tempest and rain, roared. The Annunaki gods lifted up their torches, emblazoning the land with lightning flashes:

> The gods were frightened by the deluge,
> And shrinking back they ascended to the
>   heavens of Anu.
> The gods crouched like dogs.
>   (11, lines 113-15)

At the terrible decimation of human life the gods wept. Six days and six nights the storm raged; on the seventh day the Flood ceased. The Babylonian hero looked out from the boat and surveyed the catastrophic scene:

> I looked at the weather: stillness had set in,
> And all mankind had turned to clay.
> The landscape was as level as a flat roof.
> I opened a hatch, and light fell upon my face.
> Bowing low, I sat and wept,
> Tears running down on my face.
>   (lines 132-37)

The poem tells how the ship landed on Mt. Nisir, commonly identified with Pir Omar Gudrun in the mountain country E of ancient Assyria, a peak of about nine thousand feet. As Mt. Nisir held the ship captive, the Babylonian hero sent out birds:

> When the seventh day arrived,
> I sent forth and set free a dove
> The dove went forth, but came back;
> There was no resting place and she turned
>   round.
> Then I sent forth and set free a swallow,
> The swallow went forth, but came back;
> There was no resting place for it and she
>   turned round.
> Then I sent forth and set free a raven.
> The raven went forth and, seeing that the
>   waters had diminished,
> He eats, circles, caws, and turns not round.
> Then I let out [all] to the four winds and
>   offered a sacrifice.   (lines 145-55)

When sacrifices were offered to the gods,

> The gods smelled the savor,
> The gods smelled the sweet savor,
> The gods crowded like flies about the
>   sacrificer.   (lines 156-61)

The account ends with the gods engaged in altercation concerning the responsibility of the Flood and with Utnapishtim and his wife being immortalized.

> Hitherto Utnapishtim has been but human.
> Henceforth Utnapishtim and his wife shall be
>   like unto us gods.

Utnapishtim shall reside far away, at the mouth of the rivers!

A Comparison of Biblical and Babylonian Accounts.

Scholars have given much attention to the similarities and differences in the biblical and the Babylonian accounts of the Flood.

The Resemblances. The two accounts are similar on a number of points. (1) Both accounts represent the Flood as definitely planned: by the one true God in Genesis; by numerous quarreling deities in the Babylonian version, who childishly disclaim responsibility when they see the terrific havoc being wrought. (2) In each case the judgment is revealed to the Flood hero. (3) Both accounts set forth defection in the human race as the cause. In the Genesis account it is the outrageous sin of the antediluvians and has no blurred moral element. In the Babylonian account the moral element is blurred as a consequence of a complete lack of sin or distinction between the righteous and unrighteous. (4) In each case the hero is delivered with his family and with animals, although the number surviving in the Babylonian account is larger than in the biblical account. (5) A huge boat appears in both cases, the Babylonian vessel having a displacement about five times that of Noah's ark. Both are pitched to make them watertight. (6) Both stories indicate physical causes of the catastrophe. Violent winds, rain, and electrical storms constitute the causes in the pagan account. In the Genesis account nothing short of a globe-encircling catastrophe is indicated. "All the fountains of the great deep burst open, and the floodgates of the sky were opened" (Gen. 7:11). This can only mean lowering the mountainous regions and raising of ocean beds in violent shiftings of the earth's crust. The openings of the "floodgates of the sky" seem to indicate a complete atmospheric change, signified by the rainbow (9:13). Prior to the Flood atmospheric rain is not recorded (cf. 2:5-6). The huge sources of water seemingly came from large subterranean springs and from the condensation of a huge vapor mist that covered the earth instead of clouds. Second Pet. 3:6 disputes any contention that the Bible presents the Flood as merely local, no matter what geological, astronomical, or other difficulties such a representation may offer. (7) The account of the duration of the Flood is given in both stories—a total of 371 days in the biblical account; only 6 days in the Babylonian. Both give similar striking details that are almost sensational. The sending out of the birds and the landing of the ship on a mountain are examples. The Bible account specifies "the mountains of Ararat" (Gen. 8:4). The name is identical with the Assyrian name *Urartu,* denoting the general mountainous territory of Armenia, N of Assyria (cf. 2 Kings 19:37; Isa. 37:38; Jer. 51:27). The landing of the Babylonian boat was on Mt. Nisir, E of Assyria. The biblical account of sending out of birds, with a raven sent out first and a dove released on three occasions, is much more reasonable than the sending out of a dove first, a swallow second, and finally a raven. The raven normally would be sent out first since it is a flesh-eating bird and can withstand inclement weather. (8) In both cases the hero worships after his deliverance. Utnapishtim offers sacrifice and pours out a libation, burning "sweet cane, cedar and myrtle." Noah similarly offers burnt offerings. In both cases the deity "smelled" the soothing fragrance (Gen. 8:21). (9) Both heroes are recipients of special blessings after the catastrophe. Divinity and immortality are granted Utnapishtim and his wife. Noah is blessed with the power of multiplying and replenishing the earth and to exercise dominion over the animals, originally given at creation. He is given reassurance that there will never again be a flood of such proportions.

The Differences. Despite the startling similarity between the biblical and Babylonian accounts of the Flood, the underlying differences are much more significant and fundamental. (1) The two accounts are completely different in their theological concepts. The chaste monotheism of Genesis elevates every aspect of the Flood story. In contrast, the crass polytheism of the cuneiform accounts discredits the Babylonian story at every turn. Whereas the Genesis account attributes the Flood to the one infinitely powerful and holy God, the Babylonian tradition comprehends a crowd of quarreling, disagreeing, self-accusing deities who either crouch in fear "like dogs" or "swarm like flies" around the sacrifice offered by the Flood hero. (2) The two accounts are poles apart in their moral concepts. The ethical element in the cuneiform story is completely blurred with hazy views of sin. The cause of the Flood is entirely confused, and the justice of it compromised. The whole episode is more the result of the caprice of the gods than a necessary punishment for sin. As a result, the ethical and didactic value of these stories is greatly depreciated. In contrast, the solid morality of the biblical account gives the Genesis story the highest didactic and spiritual value. (3) The two accounts differ in their philosophic concepts. The Babylonian account hopelessly confuses spirit and matter and makes both eternal. The causation is attributed to a multitude of deities. Thunder is Adad, the god of storm and rain, in action. It is Ninurta, the god of winds and irrigation, that causes the dikes to give way. Lightning is the activity of the Annunaki, judges of the underworld, who "raise their torches," illuminating the land. The picture of the one supreme God as Creator and Sustainer of all, who controls all the phenomena of His creation, is in striking contrast.

Explanation of the Similarities. The most

widely accepted explanation is that the Hebrew borrowed from the Babylonian account. To the conservative student, this is incredible. The unsurpassed loftiness of the monotheistic account in the light of the utter crudity of the Babylonian tradition renders this view not only extremely unlikely but practically impossible, especially as the theory cannot be proved. It is also extremely unlikely that the Babylonians borrowed from the Hebrew, inasmuch as the earliest known tablets are considerably older than the book of Genesis, upon any consideration of the date of the latter. It is possible, however, that the Hebrew account may have been current in some form or other centuries before it assumed its present form. The likely explanation is that both the Hebrew and Babylonian accounts go back to a common source of fact, which originated in an actual occurrence. The Flood occurred sometime long before 4000 B.C. The memory of this great event persisted in tradition. The Babylonians received it in a completely corrupted and distorted form. Genesis portrays it as it actually occurred, and as the Spirit of God gave it to meet special needs in the history of redemption.   M.F.U.; H.F.V.

BIBLIOGRAPHY: B. C. Nelson, *The Deluge Story in Stone* (1931); A. Heidel, *The Gilgamesh Epic and Old Testament Parallels* (1949); A. M. Rehwinkel, *The Flood* (1951); B. L. Ramm, *A Christian View of Science and Scripture* (1954); A. Parrot, *The Flood and Noah's Ark* (1955); J. C. Whitcomb, Jr., and H. M. Morris, *The Genesis Flood* (1961); D. W. Patten, *The Biblical Flood and the Ice Epoch* (1966); W. G. Lambert and A. R. Millard, *Atrahasis: The Babylonian Story of the Flood* (1969); J. B. Pritchard, ed., *Ancient Near Eastern Texts* (1969), pp. 72-99, 104-6; F. A. Filby, *The Flood Reconsidered* (1970); D. A. Young, *Creation and the Flood* (1977). For the various viewpoints espoused by these writers, see *The Minister's Library* (1985), 1:134-36.

FLOOR. A level, or open area, such as the place or square near the gates of oriental cities (1 Kings 22:10; 2 Chron. 18:9; KJV, "void place" in both passages). *See* House; Threshing Floor.

FLOUR. Ground grain used for making bread, the support of life in the ancient world. At first barley alone was ground, but afterward wheat, as only the poor used barley. As to the method of making flour, both mortars and mills were employed. *See* Bread; Mills. Fine flour was presented in connection with sacrifices in general, and by the poor as a sin offering (Lev. 5:11-13).

FLOWER, FLOWERS. Several Heb. terms are translated "flower" or "flowers" in the KJV, NIV, and NASB. The Heb. term applied to the floral ornaments on the golden lampstand (Ex. 25:31-36; 37:17-22) and to the artificial lily ornaments around the edge of the laver ("molten sea," KJV) in Solomon's Temple (1 Kings 7:26; 2 Chron. 4:5) is Heb. *peraḥ* (lit., "blossom"). In the KJV of the passages mentioned, the Heb. term is rendered by "flowers" and "flowers of lilies." In the NASB the rendering is "flowers" and "blossom,"

as in "lily blossom." In the NIV it is "lily blossom" in both places. The term is distinct from KJV "knop," NASB, "bulb." *See* Laver; Sea, Bronze; Tabernacle of Israel.

For the flower as a plant, *see* Vegetable Kingdom.

Figurative. Flowers, from their speedy decay, are representative of the shortness of human life (Job 14:2; Ps. 103:15; 1 Pet. 1:24); the speedy downfall of the kingdom of Israel (Isa. 28:1); and the sudden departure of the rich (James 1:10-11).

FLOW OF BLOOD. *See* Diseases: Issue.

FLUTE. *See* Music.

FLUX. *See* Diseases: Dysentery.

FLY. *See* Animal Kingdom.

FOAL. A donkey's colt (Gen. 49:11; Zech. 9:9; Matt. 21:5). *See* Animal Kingdom: Donkey; Horse.

FOAM. *See* Stick.

FODDER (Heb. *mispô,* "collected"; Gen. 42:27; 43:24; Judg. 19:19, 21; Isa. 30:24; "provender," KJV). In the account of King Solomon's stables (1 Kings 4:28) we read, "They also brought barley and straw for the horses and swift steeds," etc. Barley seems to have been the ordinary food of cattle in Palestine and the southern lands, where oats are not cultivated. As they make little hay in these countries, they are careful with their straw, which they cut up fine and mix with barley and beans. Balls made of bean and barley meal, or of pounded kernels of dates, are fed. The "salted fodder" ("provender," KJV) mentioned in Isa. 30:24 was a mash (composed of barley and vetches, or things of that kind) made more savory with salt and sour vegetables. According to Wetzstein, it is ripe barley mixed with salt or salt vegetables.

The original word properly signifies a mixture (Job 24:5; Isa. 30:24).

FOLDS. The dewlaps or flabby parts in the belly of the crocodile or "Leviathan" (Job 41:23), which are firmly attached to the body and do not hang loosely as on the ox. KJV renders "flake."

FOLLOWER. *See* Imitator.

FOLLY. *Silliness* (*see* Prov. 5:23; etc.); *emptiness* (*see* Gen. 34:7, KJV; "disgraceful thing," NIV); and many others (Job 24:12; Ps. 85:8; Eccles. 2:3; 2 Tim. 3:9). In Jer. 23:13, an "offensive thing" (NASB; "folly," KJV; "repulsive thing," NIV). As a word in common use, *folly* is a weak or absurd act, and *foolishness* is a want of wisdom or judgment.

FOOD. Represented in the original by several Heb. and Gk. words.

In Early Times. The articles of food used by men are determined largely by the products of the country that they inhabit and change with the growth of culture. At first men lived upon roots, vegetables, and the fruit of trees, all of which articles were known by the general name of *food* (Heb. *leḥem,* Gen. 1:29; 2:16). It was not until after the Flood that God allowed man the use of the flesh of animals (9:3), but it is probable that the Cainite Jabal, "the father of those who dwell in tents and have livestock" (4:20), used not only the milk and wool obtained from the herd but also ate of the flesh of the cattle. That before the Flood the flesh of animals was converted into food may be inferred from the division of animals into clean and unclean (7:8), and after the Flood it is expressly mentioned that animals were slain for food (9:3-4).

In the Patriarchal Age. The flesh of animals, both tame and wild, was eaten. Leguminous food (i.e., beans, peas, etc.) was used, and a preparation of *lentils* (which see) seems to have been a common and favorite dish (Gen. 25:34). Use was also made of honey, spices, and nuts (43:11). As early as the time of Abraham the art of preparing bread was carried to some degree of perfection.

Among the Egyptians. The Egyptians had a great variety of foods, and their wall paintings reveal much concerning the manner of eating. Genesis 40 tells of an occasion when the king elevated his chief butler and baker. The plentiful foods served at a typical palace banquet included fowl, fish of all sorts, barley beer, and elaborate condiments. Huge jars of wine were brought in, and guests were given bent glass tubes that they dipped directly into the jars. Both men and women attended feasts. Male guests were clean shaven; they wore white banquet garments, and elaborate jewels around their necks. The women wore long white gowns of transparent fineness with exquisite jewelry. Paintings of the city of Akhetaton, built c. 1387-1366 B.C., show us the king and his wife Nofretete and his three young daughters feasting in their wide banqueting hall. Fragrant garlands hanging from pillars added to the festal scene. Slaves waved ivory-handled ostrich fans to cool the heated atmosphere of the Egyptian evening. The banqueting table was attractively arranged with bright cushioned chairs.

Among the Mesopotamians. The lower Mesopotamian region offered many species of legumes to choose from. Beans, lentils, peas, kidney beans, onions, cucumbers, eggplants, pumpkins, and wheat and barley were considered indigenous. The date palm and other fruit trees abounded. An early Baylonian domestic scene portrays a mother from Ur feeding a bunch of the famous Euphrates dates to her baby on her knee. One of the earliest banquet scenes that exists is recorded on a tiny lapis lazuli cylinder seal in the museum of the University of Pennsylvania. This interesting art object, executed c. 3000 B.C., depicts a banquet of the now-famous Queen Puabi. Fleece-skirted domestics dispense goblets of wine to guests seated on small stools. Other palace servants wave fans. A musician stands on one side performing on a harp (M. S. and J. Lane Miller, *Encyclopedia of Bible Life* [1944], pp. 229-319).

A family meal

Among the Israelites. While in Egypt the Israelites shared in the abundance of that land, where they "sat by the pots of meat" and "ate bread to the full" (Ex. 16:3); and they recalled in the wilderness with regret and murmuring the fish, the cucumbers, the melons, the leeks, the onions, and the garlic (Num. 11:5).

Articles Prohibited. Animals as food was limited by the Mosaic law: (1) By the primeval distinction between clean and unclean, the following were forbidden to be used as food: quadrupeds that do not chew the cud or have cloven feet (Lev. 11:4-8; Deut. 14:7-8); fish without scales and fins, e.g., eels and all shellfish (Lev. 11:9-12); birds of prey and such as feed upon worms and rotting flesh (11:13-19); serpents and creeping insects; insects that sometimes fly and sometimes go upon their feet, with the exception of some of the locust kind (11:20-24, 42). (2) By the sacrificial ordinances was forbidden the eating of all blood of cattle and birds and bloody flesh (Lev. 3:17; 7:26; 17:10-14; Deut. 12:16, 23; cf. Gen. 9:4; 1 Sam. 14:32-34); the fatty portions that, in the sacrifice of oxen, sheep, and goats, were burned upon the altar (Lev. 3:17; 7:23, 25); also everything consecrated to idols (Ex. 34:15). (3) For sanitary reasons, doubtless, the following was forbidden as food: the flesh of cattle that had fallen down dead or had been torn by wild beasts (Ex. 22:31; Lev. 11:39-40; Deut. 14:21) as well as food prepared with water on which the dead body of an unclean insect had fallen (Lev. 11:31, 33-34); also all food and liquids remaining in an uncovered vessel in the tent or chamber of a dying or dead man (Num. 19:14-15). In addition, it was forbidden to "boil a kid in the milk of its mother" (Ex. 23:19; 34:26; Deut. 14:21). The reason for this is that the Canaanites may have employed such a practice in one of their sacred rituals. Besides these, according to ancient tradition, the Israelites, perhaps from a feeling of reverence, denied themselves the use of the sinew of the hip (Gen. 32:32).

Articles Allowed. These were partly vegetable and partly animal, with salt for seasoning. Grain formed the chief nourishment, especially wheat kernels roasted in the fire—still a favorite food in Palestine, Syria, and Egypt. It was also frequently baked into bread. Milk was an article of daily food—not only the milk of cows but also of sheep and goats (Deut. 32:14; Prov. 27:27), sometimes sweet, sometimes sour, thick, or curdled. The latter still forms, after bread, the chief food of the poorer classes in Arabia and Syria, and it appears on the tables of well-to-do persons. The Israelites, no doubt, prepared *cheese* of different kinds, and likely *butter* (30:33). Also used was the honey of bees; perhaps also grape honey (sweet grapes boiled to a syrup) and wood honey of wild bees (1 Sam. 14:25; Matt. 3:4), in which Palestine was rich; also raisins, dried figs (25:18), date cakes (2 Sam. 16:1), and various fresh fruits. Of *vegetables* those chiefly used were pulse, lentils, and beans, with onions, garlic, and cucumbers; also green herbs—sometimes raised in gardens (1 Kings 21:2), sometimes growing in the fields (Prov. 15:17). *Animal food*—the flesh of oxen, sheep, and goats—ranks first, although the flesh of calves, lambs, and kids was greatly prized; perhaps, also, that of pigeons and turtledoves. The rich had upon their tables deer, gazelle, roebuck, and various kinds of winged game (1 Kings 4:23; Neh. 5:18). *Fish* were supplied in great abundance from the lake of Gennesaret (John 21:11; cf. Matt. 14:17; 15:34), whereas in earlier times the Phoenicians brought fish to Jerusalem from the sea (Neh. 13:16). *Locusts* were eaten by the poorer people (Lev. 11:22; Matt. 3:4; Mark 1:6); sometimes salted and roasted (or fried), sometimes boiled in water and buttered.

Preparation of Food. Grain was eaten at first without any preparation, and the custom of eating it thus had not entirely disappeared in the time of Christ (Matt. 12:1). After the uses of fire were known, grain was parched. Later the introduction of the mortar and mill furnished flour, which was made into *bread* (which see). As to the preparation of vegetables and flesh, we learn that as early as the time of Isaac it was customary to prepare soup of lentils (Gen. 25:29, 34) and flesh (27:9, 14). Vegetables, pulse, and herbs were cooked in pots (2 Kings 4:38-39; cf. Num. 11:8; Judg. 6:19; 1 Sam. 2:14) and seasoned with oil. Roasting on a spit was perhaps the oldest way of cooking flesh but less common among the Israelites than boiling. Roast flesh was used only by the rich and better classes (2:15), as is still the case in the East. When cooked in pots (2:14; 2 Chron. 35:13), it was lifted out with a three-pronged fork and brought to the table with the broth (Judg. 6:19). All the flesh of the slain animal, owing to the difficulty of keeping it in warm climates, was cooked at once. The Israelites seem to have boiled the flesh of young animals in milk. Locusts were frequently roasted, as they still are in the East.

"Their wings and feet are taken off and their intestines extracted; they are salted, fixed upon a sharp piece of wood, placed over the fire, and at length eaten. They are likewise prepared by boiling them. Sometimes they are salted and preserved in bottles and, as occasion requires, are cut in pieces and eaten" (Lev. 11:22; Matt. 3:4). *Salt* (which see) was anciently used (Num. 18:19; 2 Chron. 13:5). In most ancient times the animal was killed by the master of the house, and the cooking was done by his wife (Gen. 18:2-6) with the help of female slaves. In the houses of the upper classes there were also special cooks (1 Sam. 9:23-24) and in the larger cities bakers (Hos. 7:4).

Women grinding grain

Meals. Besides a simple breakfast the Israelites had two daily meals; at midday (Gen. 18:1-8; 43:16, 25; Ruth 2:14; 1 Kings 20:16) and their principal meal at about six or seven in the evening (Gen. 19:1-3; Ruth 3:7). They were accustomed to wash their hands both before and after eating (Matt. 15:2; Mark 7:2-3; Luke 11:38), because food was lifted to the mouth with the fingers (*see* Washing). Prayers were also offered (1 Sam. 9:13). In the older times it was the custom to sit at the table (Gen. 27:19; Judg. 19:6; 1 Sam. 20:5, 24; 1 Kings 13:19-20), but later it was usual to recline upon cushions or divans. The food was taken to the mouth with the right hand, a custom still prevalent in the East (Ruth 2:14; Prov. 26:15; John 13:26). *See* Banquet; Drink.

BIBLIOGRAPHY: H. N. and A. L. Moldenke, *Plants of the Bible* (1952); A. C. Bouquet, *Everyday Life in New Testament Times* (1954), pp. 69-79; R. J. Forbes, *Studies in Ancient Technology* 3 (1955): 50-105; 5 (1957): 78-88.

FOOL. Represented by a large number of Heb. and Gk. words. The word is used in Scripture with respect to *moral* more than to intellectual deficiencies. The "fool" is not so much one lacking in mental powers, as one who misuses them; not one who does not reason, but reasons wrongly. In Scripture the "fool" primarily is the person who casts off the fear of God and thinks and acts as if he could safely disregard the eternal principles of God's righteousness (Ps. 14:1; Prov. 14:9; Jer. 17:11; etc.). Yet in many passages, especially in Proverbs, the term has its ordinary use and denotes one who is rash, senseless, or unreasonable. The expression "you fool" (Matt. 5:22) is used in the *moral* sense, means "wicked," and seems to be equivalent to judging one as worthy of everlasting punishment. *See* Folly.

FOOLISHNESS. *See* Folly; Fool.

FOOT. The word *feet* is sometimes used in Scripture for the sake of delicacy, to express the parts and the acts that it was not allowed to name. Hence, "the hair of the feet," "to open the feet," etc. In the KJV "to cover the feet" (1 Sam 24:3; Judg. 3:24, *see* marg.) is a euphemism for performing the necessities of nature, as it is the custom in the East to cover the feet. The Jews neglected the feet and bared them in affliction (2 Sam. 15:30; 19:24; Ezek. 24:17); stamped them on the ground in extreme joy or grief (6:11; 25:6); showed respect by falling at the feet (1 Sam. 25:24; 2 Kings 4:37; Esther 8:3; Mark 5:22), showed reverence by kissing another's feet (Luke 7:38), showed subjection by licking the dust from the foot (Isa. 49:23); whereas the subjugation of enemies was expressed by placing the foot on their necks (Josh. 10:24; Ps. 110:1). The feet of enemies were sometimes cut off or maimed (Judg. 1:6-7; 2 Sam. 4:12). Uncovering the feet was a mark of adoration (Ex. 3:5).

Figurative. "To be at any one's feet" is used for being at the service of another, following him, or receiving his instruction (Judg. 4:10; Acts 22:3, *see* marg.). The last passage, in which Paul is described as being brought up "at the feet of Gamaliel" (KJV; NIV, "under Gamaliel") will appear still clearer if we understand that, as the Jewish writers allege, pupils actually did sit on the floor before, and, therefore, at the feet of, the doctors of the law, who themselves occupied an elevated seat. "He set my feet upon a rock" (Ps. 40:2) expresses the idea of stability. "Thou has set my feet in a large place" (31:8) denotes liberty. "Slipping" of the feet is figurative for yielding to temptation (Job 12:5; Pss. 17:5; 38:16; 94:18). "Trampling" under foot (Isa. 26:6; Lam. 1:15) implies complete destruction. To "dip" or "bathe" one's feet in oil or butter (Deut. 33:24; Job 29:6) is to possess abundance; to "shatter them in blood" (Ps. 68:23), of victory. To keep "the feet of His godly ones" (1 Sam. 2:9) is to preserve them from stumbling. To "set" one's foot in a place signifies to take possession (Deut. 1:36; 11:24). "Water it with your foot" (11:10) refers to irrigation, which was effected by foot pumps and by turning the small streams of the

garden with the foot. A striking phrase, borrowed from the feet, is used by Paul (Gal. 2:14): "When I saw that they were not straightforward"; literally, walking "with a straight foot."

FOOTMAN. Employed in the KJV in two senses: (1) as a military term for the infantry in the *army* (which see), and (2) in the special sense of a *runner* (which see).

FOOTSTEPS. Footprints are held to be indicative of one's character, their direction a proof of his tendencies. Therefore to watch one's footsteps is to seek a cause for accusation (Ps. 17:5, 11, KJV).

FOOTSTOOL (Heb. *kebesh,* sometimes "trodden" upon). An article of furniture used to support the feet when sitting in state, as upon a throne (2 Chron. 9:18). The divine glory that resided symbolically between the cherubim above the Ark of the Covenant is supposed to use the Ark as a footstool (1 Chron. 28:2; Pss. 99:5; 132:7). The earth is called God's footstool by the same expressive figure that represents heaven as His throne (110:1; Isa 66:1; Matt. 5:35).

FOOT WASHING. *See* Ablution.

FORBEARANCE (Gk. *anochē,* a "holding back, delaying," Rom. 2:4; 3:25). "The forbearance of God and his long suffering—the two terms exhausting the one idea—denote the disposition of God, in accordance with which he indulgently tolerates sins and delays their punishment" (Meyer, *Com.,* ad loc.). Philippians 4:5 mentions a "forbearing spirit" (Gk. *epieikēs*), elsewhere rendered "gentle."

FORCED LABOR (Heb. *mâs,* a "consuming"). Spoken mostly of tribute to be paid in service (1 Kings 9:21), a condition of serfdom (Josh. 16:10; 17:13; Judg. 1:28). Thus we see that Adoram was appointed overseer over the tributary service in the time of Solomon (2 Sam. 20:24; 1 Kings 4:6). The KJV renders this concept as "tribute."

FORCES (Heb., specially *ḥayil,* "strength"). In a military point of view it is applied to army, fortifications, etc. In Isa. 60:5, 11, KJV, the phrase "forces of the Gentiles" seems to be used in its widest sense to denote not only the subjugation of the heathen but also the consecration of their *wealth* (the NASB renders "wealth of the nations," and the NIV, "riches of the nations").

FORD. A shallow place in a river or other body of water that may be crossed on foot or by wading (Gen. 32:22; Josh. 2:7; Judg. 3:28; 12:5-6; Isa. 16:2). The fords of the Jordan are frequently mentioned. A little above the Dead Sea two fords cross the Jordan near Jericho, passable most of the year, connecting roads from the Judean hills with highways from Gilead and Moab. The passage from Samaria into Gilead was made easy by an extraordinary number of fords through the Jordan. The depth of the Jordan fords varies from three feet to as much as ten or twelve. Mention is also made of the ford of the Jabbok (Gen. 32:22) and of the Arnon (Isa. 16:2). The "fords" (Jer. 51:32) of the Euphrates "are not merely those over the main river, but also those over the canals cut from it to add strength, whether fords, ferries, or light wooden bridges, which must have existed alongside the one stone bridge over the river for purposes of intercourse" (Orelli, *Com.*, ad loc.).

Jordan River

FOREHEAD (Heb. *mēṣaḥ,* to "shine"). The practice of veiling the face in public for women of the higher classes—especially married women—in the East, sufficiently stigmatizes with reproach the unveiled faces of women of bad character (Gen. 24:65; Jer. 3:3). Reference is made to this when Israel is called "stubborn" (lit., "of a hard forehead," *see* marg.), whereas courage is promised to the prophet when Jehovah says, "I have made your face as hard as their faces" (Ezek. 3:7-8). The custom among many oriental nations both of coloring the face and of impressing on the body marks indicative of devotion to some special deity or religious sect is mentioned by various writers. In Ezekiel (9:4-6) we read that the Heb. letter ת (in early times made in the form of a cross) should be placed upon the forehead of those who mourned the abominations of Israel, that they might be spared (*see* Rev. 7:3; 9:4; 14:1; 22:4); in the opposite sense as servants of Satan (13:16-17; 14:9; etc.). The "jewels for the forehead," mentioned in KJV (Gen. 24:22, marg.; Ezek. 16:12), were in all probability nose rings (Isa. 3:21) as the NIV translates.

FOREIGNER (Heb. *nokrî* "stranger," Deut. 15:3; Obad. 11; *tôshāb,* cf. Ex. 12:45, "dweller," as distinguished from a native, rendered "sojourner"; also Gk. *paroikos,* "dwelling near," Eph. 2:19, rendered "aliens," or [NIV] "foreigners"). One living in a country of which he is not a native, i.e., in the Jewish sense, a Gentile. The kingdom of God, temporarily limited to the peo-

ple of Israel, still bore within it the germ of universality, of diffusion among all people. The covenant made with Abraham was from the beginning not exclusively confined to the natural posterity of Israel's twelve sons. As a practical proof that the redemption that was to be prepared through him and his seed was intended to all races of the earth, Abraham was commanded to circumcise every male belonging to his house. Hereby his servants, who amounted to hundreds, were included in his house, made partakers of the covenant promises, and incorporated with the promised seed.

Privileges. When the Israelites went up out of Egypt a large, mixed multitude of foreigners accompanied them (Ex. 12:38; Num. 11:4; Josh. 8:35) and were not rejected by them. Among the Israelites there were at all times individuals of other (pagan) peoples. To such were granted toleration and several privileges, in return for which compliance with the following regulations was insisted upon. They were required, for example, not to blaspheme the name of Jehovah (Lev. 24:16); not to indulge in idolatrous worship (20:2); not to commit acts of indecency (18:26); not to do any work on the Sabbath (Ex. 20:10); not to eat leavened bread during the Passover (12:19); not to eat any manner of blood or flesh of animals that had died a natural death or had been torn by wild beasts (Lev. 17:10, 15). Under such circumstances the law accorded to foreigners not only protection and toleration but equal civil rights with the Israelites. They could even acquire fixed property, lands (25:47) and offer sacrifices to the Lord (Num. 15:15, 26, 29).

Citizenship. Should he desire to enjoy the full rights of citizenship a stranger submitted to circumcision, thus binding himself to observe the whole law, in return for which he was permitted to enjoy to the full the privileges and blessings of the people of the covenant (Rom. 9:4), with whom, in virtue of this right, he was now incorporated (Ex. 12:48). The parties excluded from this fellowship were the Edomites and Egyptians resident in Israel— only, however, till the third generation (Deut. 23:7-8); the seven Canaanitish nations doomed to destruction and excluded forever (Ex. 34:15-16; Deut. 7:1-4); the Ammonites and Moabites, "even to the tenth generation" —i.e., forever—because of their opposition to the Israelites entering Canaan (23:3).

Figurative. "Foreigners" in Eph. 2:19 (KJV and NIV) denotes those who, in their natural condition of sin, are without citizenship in God's kingdom, as opposed to "fellow citizens." In 1 Pet. 2:11 "aliens" are those who live as strangers on the earth, i.e., with their citizenship in heaven (cf. Phil. 3:20).

BIBLIOGRAPHY: J. Pedersen, *Israel, Its Life and Culture* (1940), 3-4:272ff., 585.

FOREIGN WOMEN. *See* article Harlot, Whore.

FOREKNOWLEDGE. *See* God, Attributes of.

FOREORDINATION. *See* Election.

FORERUNNER (Gk. *prodromos*). One who is sent before to take observations or act as a spy, a scout, a light-armed soldier. In Heb. 6:20 (KJV) it is used in the sense of one who comes in advance to a place where the rest are to follow, namely, Jesus Christ (cf. John 14:2).

FORESHIP. A KJV term appearing in Acts 27:30, 41. It refers to the *bow* of a ship (so NASB and NIV).

FORESKIN. The loose fold of skin on the distinctive member of the male sex, which was removed in *circumcision* (which see), leaving the *glans penis* artificially uncovered. Circumcision being a symbol of purification, the foreskin was a type of corruption; hence the phrase "foreskin of the heart" (KJV of Deut. 10:16, marg.; Jer. 4:4) to designate a carnal or heathenish state (Rom. 2:29). It was sometimes brought as a trophy of slain Gentiles (1 Sam. 18:25; 2 Sam. 3:14).

FORESKINS, HILL OF. *See* Gibeath-haaraloth.

FOREST. *See* Vegetable Kingdom.

Figurative. Forest is used symbolically to denote a city, kingdom, and the like (Ezek. 20:46-47, where "the south" denotes the kingdom of Judah). Kingdoms that God has threatened to destroy are represented under the figure of a forest destined to be burned (Isa. 10:17-19, 34, where the briars and thorns denote the common people, whereas "the glory of his forest" are the nobles and others of high rank. *See also* 32:19; 37:24; Jer. 21:14; 22:7; etc.). The forest is the image of unfruitfulness as contrasted with a cultivated field or vineyard (Isa. 29:17; 32:15; Jer. 26:18; Hos. 2:12).

FORGIVENESS. One of the most widely misunderstood doctrines of Scripture. It is not to be confused with human forgiveness that merely remits a penalty or charge. Divine forgiveness is one of the most complicated and costly undertakings, demanding complete satisfaction to meet the demands of God's outraged holiness.

In the Old Testament. "The priest shall make atonement for them, and they shall be forgiven" (Lev. 4:20). However, OT sacrifices had only a typical significance and served as a covering (Heb. *kāpar*, "to cover, to aid," Deut. 21:8; Gen. 50:17; etc.) from sin until the appointed time when God should deal finally with sin through the death of Christ. It is thus obvious that the transaction was to some extent incomplete on the divine side. Of necessity sin was let pass. However, the offender received full forgiveness (cf. Rom. 3:25; Acts 17:30).

For the Unsaved. Forgiveness under this consideration is never an isolated operation but is always connected as an integral part of the whole divine undertaking for man called "salvation." Forgiveness is only one of the many transformations wrought by God in the unsaved in response to simple faith in Christ. Thus forgiveness of sin is not equivalent to salvation. It is merely negative. All else in the comprehensive term *salvation* is gloriously added (John 10:28; Rom. 5:17).

For the Believer Who Sins. The great foundational truth respecting the believer in relationship to his sins is the fact that his salvation comprehends the forgiveness of all his trespasses past, present, and future so far as condemnation is concerned (Rom. 8:1; Col. 2:13; John 3:18; 5:24). Since Christ has vicariously borne all sin and since the believer's standing in Christ is complete, he is perfected forever in Christ. When a believer sins, he is subject to chastisement from the Father but never to condemnation with the world (1 Cor. 11:31-32). By confession the Christian is forgiven and restored to fellowship (1 John 1:9). It needs to be remembered that were it not for Christ's finished work on the cross and His present intercession in heaven, the least sin would result in the sinner's banishment from God's presence and eternal ruin.

Sin unto Death. Persistent or scandalous sin in the believer in face of divine grace and his perfect standing in Christ may eventuate in a sin resulting in physical death. "If anyone sees his brother committing a sin not leading to death, he shall ask and God will for him give life to those who commit sin not leading to death. There is a sin leading to death; I do not say that he should make request for this" (1 John 5:16; cf. 1 Cor. 5:1-5). Both John 15:2 and 1 Cor. 11:30 point out that God reserves the right to cut off the physical life of a believer who has ceased to be a worthy witness in the world. Such a cutting off does not mean that the one who has died is lost. It merely signifies more drastic chastisement to the end that a believer might not be condemned with the world (11:31-32).

The Unpardonable Sin. This was a specific sin possible only during the earthly life of our Lord, when He was ministering in the power of the Holy Spirit. Under those unique conditions a person who attributed to Satan the power of the Holy Spirit, so visibly and openly manifested, was guilty of this peculiar sin. For this reason there could be no forgiveness in the age then present or in the age immediately following (Matt. 12:22-32; Mark 3:22-30). Since no such conditions exist in this age, the unpardonable sin is now impossible. An unpardonable sin and the gospel of "whosoever will" cannot coexist. Were such a sin possible today, every gospel invitation would specifically shut out those who had committed such a trespass.

As an Obligation Among Men. The believer who belongs to this age is exhorted to be kind to believers and unbelievers, tenderhearted and forgiving to one another "as God in Christ also has forgiven you" (Eph 4:32). The basis of the plea for such forgiveness is that one has been himself so graciously forgiven.

BIBLIOGRAPHY: F. H. Wales, *Forgiveness of Sins* (1940); V. Taylor, *Forgiveness and Reconciliation* (1941); H. R. Macintosh, *Christian Experience of Forgiveness* (1947); J. G. Emerson, Jr., *The Dynamics of Forgiveness* (1964).

FORK. The translation of one Gk. and several Heb. terms.

1. Gk. *ptuon* (Matt. 3:12; Luke 3:17) and Heb. *mizreh* (Isa. 30:24; Jer. 15:7), a *winnowing fork* (which see), given in the KJV as a "winnowing fan."

2. Heb. *mazlēg* (1 Sam. 2:13-14), a *fleshhook* (so KJV; which see) for taking joints of meat out of the boiling pot.

3. Heb. *mizlāgâ*, other forks connected with the altar (Ex. 27:3; 38:3; Num. 4:14) and Temple (1 Chron. 28:17; 2 Chron. 4:16); the Heb. term is rendered *fleshhook* (which see) in the KJV.

4. Heb. *shelōsh qillshôn*, "three of prongs" (1 Sam. 13:21), a three-pronged fork, i.e., pitchfork, with which to handle hay, straw, etc.

FORM, LIKENESS. Terms used in several ways in the Bible.

1. An "appearance, shape, likeness" (Heb. *temûnâ*). Jehovah, upon the sedition of Aaron and Miriam, made this distinction between a prophet, as usually known, and Moses: "If there is a prophet among you, I, the Lord, shall make Myself known to him in a vision. . . . Not so, with My servant Moses, he is faithful in all My household; with him I speak mouth to mouth, even openly, and not in dark sayings, and he beholds the *form* ["similitude," KJV] of the Lord" (Num. 12:6-8, italics added; cf. Deut. 4:12, 15-16). The *form* of Jehovah was not the essential nature of God, His unveiled glory—for this no mortal man can see (Ex. 33:18-23)—but a form that manifested the invisible God in a clearly discernible mode, differing from the vision of God in the form of a man (Ezek. 1:26; Dan. 7:9, 13), or of the angel of Jehovah. "God talked with Moses without figure, in the clear distinctness of a spiritual communication, whereas to the prophets he only revealed himself through the medium of ecstasy or dream" (K. & D., *Com.* on Num. 12:6-8).

2. A "model," a "pattern" (as in 2 Kings 16:10) of an altar; an *image*, something cast, as of oxen (2 Chron. 4:3; "similitude," KJV; "figures," NIV), a *likeness* (Gen. 1:26), "appearance" (Ezek. 1:16), Heb. *demût*. The verb *dāmâ* (to "liken" or "compare" is used in Hos. 12:10 ("similitude," KJV) in the sense of employing parables. The Heb. *tabnît* is used in Ps. 106:20; 144:12 in the sense of likeness, though the term is translated "image" ("similitude," KJV).

3. In the NT the Gk. is *homoios* ("similar") and means that which is like, or similar (Rom. 5:14;

Heb. 7:15; "similitude," KJV), a *likeness* as of man to God (James 3:9; "similitude," KJV; *see demût*, above).

FORNICATION (Gk. *porneia*). Used of illicit sexual intercourse in general (Acts 15:20, 29; 21:25; cf. 1 Cor. 5:1; 6:13, 18; 7:2; etc.). It is distinguished from "adultery" (Gk. *moicheia*, in Matt. 15:19; Mark 7:21). The NIV usually translates *porneia* as "sexual immorality" and *moicheia* as "adultery." Jahn (*Biblical Archaeology*, sec. 158) thus distinguishes between adultery and fornication among nations where polygamy exists: "If a married man has criminal intercourse with a married woman, or with one promised in marriage, or with a widow expecting to be married with a brother-in-law, it is accounted *adultery*. If he is guilty of such intercourse with a woman who is unmarried it is considered *fornication*." At the present time adultery is the term used of such an act when the person is married, fornication when unmarried; and *fornication* may be defined as lewdness of an unmarried person of either sex. Its prohibition rests on the ground that it discourages marriage, leaves the education and care of children insecure, depraves and defiles the mind more than any other vice, and thus makes one unfit for the kingdom of God (1 Cor. 6:9; etc.). Our Lord forbids the thoughts that lead to it (cf. Matt. 5:28).

Figurative. The close relationship between Jehovah and Israel is spoken of under the figure of marriage, Israel being the unfaithful wife of the Lord, now rejected but yet to be restored. The church of the NT is a pure virgin espoused to Christ (2 Cor. 11:2) and thus differentiated from the nation Israel (1 Cor. 10:32). The worship of idols is naturally mentioned as *fornication* (Rev. 14:8; 17:2, 4; 18:3; 19:2, KJV; NASB, "immorality"; NIV, "adulteries"); as also the defilement of idolatry, as incurred by eating the sacrifices offered to idols (Rev. 2:21, KJV; NASB, and NIV, "immorality"). *See* Idolatry.

BIBLIOGRAPHY: D. R. Mace, *Hebrew Marriage* (1953), pp. 221-67; W. G. Cole, *Sex and Love in the Bible* (1959), pp. 230-67; J. Jensen, *Novum Testamentum* 20 (1978): 161-84.

FORT, FORTIFICATION, FORTRESS. The Hebrew people, never well equipped with arms or possessing military knowledge and surrounded by powerful neighbors, learned early that it was "better to take refuge in the Lord than to trust in princes" (Ps. 118:9). In the theocracy the divine ideal was that protection was in faith in the God of Israel. Such burning faith in God's power protected Moses, Joshua, Deborah, Samson, Jonathan, David, and other national heros; yet early in her history Israel had to fight to survive.

Pre-Israelite Fortification. When Joshua and Israel invaded Palestine, they faced formidable Canaanite defenses. Stoutly walled cities erected on mounds that seemed to reach to heaven dot-

Ruins at the fortified city of Bethshan

ted the "land flowing with milk and honey." Canaanites were famous for their masonry and by 2000 B.C. had erected massive defenses. Such excavated sites as Jericho, Shechem, Taanach, Lachish, Gezer, and Bethshan have yielded plentiful information concerning the formidableness of Canaanite fortifications. The reports of the Mosaic spies were literally true. They did find great fortified strongholds. Even before the Phoenicians, their Amorite predecessors from c. 2500 B.C. had massive fortifications. Megiddo, the old Amorite fort overlooking Esdraelon, had an area of twenty acres. The recital of the Israelite struggle to control the strongholds of the Amorites, Hittites, Perizzites, and Jebusites is true to archaeological excavations. The impregnable walls of Jebusite Jerusalem, which David finally took, have been fully verified. At Ugarit in North Syria a cuneiform tablet was found that listed the military equipment kept in the royal Ugaritic arsenal. At Ras Shamra there was a lively trade in horses. Jericho's famous walls are featured in the biblical narrative as well as in their archaeological excavations. The taking of Jericho has been to a large extent verified by the archaeologist's spade. At Jericho, John Garstang located a series of walled cities, one above another: City A was dated at 3000 B.C., and City B was dated c. 2500 B.C. City C was larger than its predecessors and was surrounded by stout walls with a stone glacis and an outer moat. This city belonged to the Hyksos era and suffered destruction c. 1500 B.C. City D, taken by Joshua, was constructed c. 1500 B.C. The wall originally reached perhaps thirty feet. Like Jericho, Bethel was occupied almost constantly from 2000 B.C. or earlier and had well-constructed city walls. The stout fortifications of Bethel were consumed by a terrific fire.

Fortifications Under Monarchy. A good example of an early citadel of Israel is Saul's fortress in Gibeah (present Tell el-Ful), located in the hill country about four miles N of Jerusalem. It was excavated in 1922-23 by W. F. Albright. At the bottom of the mound, the first fortress showed traces of destruction by fire and is probably the

one mentioned in Judg. 20:40 (cf. W. F. Albright, in *Young's Analytical Concordance*, 20th ed. [1946], p. 32). The second fortress, just above the first, is identified with Saul's stronghold. The structure is 170 feet by 155 feet and had casemated walls and separately bonded corner towers. The outer wall was about six feet thick and was defended by a sloping base. The castle comprised two stories and contained a massive stone staircase. Above Saul's structure is a third fortress characterized by a series of stone piers. This citadel suffered destruction by fire, perhaps in the Syro-Ephraimite wars. Egyptian art records two of the towers of the military architects at Gibeah. Together these "fenced" cities constituted a strong system of defense. The most notable link in the chain was Bethshan, guarding the eastern approaches to the famous battlefield of Esdraelon. In fact, Tell el-Husn, modern name of Bethshan, means "Mount of the Fortress." Clarence Fisher, Alan Rowe, and other excavators have unearthed fortress constructions at this important site. Megiddo was another fortified location (Josh. 12:21; Judg. 5:19; 2 Kings 23:29). It not only had a strong wall, gates, and towers but, during Solomon's era, was probably one of his chariot cities. Lachish in southeastern Palestine was another famous fort, excavated by J. L. Starkey and others.

Remains of the northern palace at the fortified city of Megiddo

Other Fortresses of Bible Times. Samaria, founded by Omri and made glorious by the Omri dynasty of the ninth century B.C., had a great bastion. Jeroboam II of the eighth century made it almost impregnable with high walls and formidable fortifications. Damascus was another ancient city whose NT walls are familiar from the experiences of Paul. From a house built on the city wall he escaped in a basket (Acts 9:25). The Greek city of Athens was also fortified, and the city walls connected the capital with her harbor at Piraeus. Corinth was another famous fortified site. Syracuse on the island of Sicily also had mighty fortifications in Bible times. This famous fortress stemmed the invasion of the Carthaginians for thirty-eight years, thus defending Hellenic culture in the mid-Mediterranean. Ancient Babylon, Nineveh and Ashur, Ur and other Mesopotamian cities were mighty fortresses from ancient times. The Babylon of Nebuchadnezzar II, as revealed by the records of Herodotus and the accounts of Robert Koldewey, possessed mammoth walls that stretched across the Tigris-Euphrates plain about the city. The incredible splendors of the city, including its "hanging gardens," its famous Ishtar Gate, ziggurat, and temples, were thus defended by a vast system of fortifications. The Ishtar Gate bore reliefs of bulls and dragons, symbolic of Chaldean prowess. This ornate, square-towered portal guarded the city's entrance to the north wall. Assyrian kings such as Sargon II adorned and defended their palaces with massive gates. The Roman walls of Paul's time, which had already existed for centuries, were formidable but never as famous as those at Jerusalem. The remains of many ancient gates are to be found at Rome.

Figurative. As illustrative of divine protection to those who trust Him, the Lord is compared to a fortress (2 Sam. 22:2; Pss. 18:2; 31:3; 71:3; etc.). "The fortified city will disappear from Ephraim" (Isa. 17:3) is an expression signifying that she loses her fortified cities, or fortresses, that were once her defense. To overthrow one's fortress or fortification is to rob it of defense, i.e., to humiliate (25:12). Of the righteous man it is said, "His refuge will be the impregnable rock" (33:16), i.e., God's protection shall be to him as the impregnable walls of a fortress upon a rock. "I have set thee for a tower and a *fortress* among my people" (Jer. 6:27, KJV), is rendered by Orelli, *Com.,* ad loc., "an assayer to my people, a piece of ore" (Heb. from *beṣer,* "broken off"), "that thou mayest test their walk." The NIV translates, "I have made you a tester of metals and my people the ore, that you may observe and test their ways."

BIBLIOGRAPHY: Y. Yadin, *Art of Warfare in Bible Lands,* 2 vols. (1963); C. Herzog and M. Gichon, *Battles of the Bible* (1978).

FORTIFIED CITY. The rendering of several Heb. words; sometimes translated "fortresses" (2 Chron. 11:11), "battle towers" (Isa. 29:3). The broad distinction between a city and a village in biblical language consisted in the possession of walls. The city had walls, the village was unwalled or had only a watchman's tower, to which the villagers resorted in times of danger. A threefold distinction is thus obtained: (1) cities, (2) unwalled villages, and (3) villages with castles or towers (1 Chron. 27:25). The district E of the Jordan, forming the kingdoms of Moab and Bashan, is said to have abounded from early times in castles and fortresses, besides unwalled towns, such as were built by Uzziah to protect the cattle

and to repel the inroads of neighboring tribes (Deut. 3:5; 2 Chron. 26:10). When the Israelites entered Canaan they found many fortified cities (Num. 13:28; 32:17; Josh. 11:12-13; Judg. 1:27-33), some of which held out for a long period, e.g., Jerusalem was held by the Jebusites till the time of David (2 Sam. 5:6-7; 1 Chron. 11:5). *See* Cities.

FORTUNA'TUS (for-tū-nā'tus; "fortunate"). A disciple of Corinth, of Roman birth or origin, as his name indicates, who visited Paul at Ephesus and returned, along with Stephanas and Achaicus, in charge of that apostle's first epistle to the Corinthian church (1 Cor. 16:17). "The household of Stephanas" is mentioned in 1:16 as having been baptized by Paul himself; perhaps Fortunatus and Achaicus were members of that household. There is a Fortunatus mentioned at the end of Clement's first epistle to the Corinthians who was possibly the same person.

FORUM APPII. *See* Appii Forum.

FOUNDATION. The lowest part of a building, and on which it rests.

Figurative. By foundation is sometimes understood the *origin* (Job 4:19), where men are represented as dwelling in clay houses, whose foundation, i.e., *origin,* was in the dust (cf. Gen. 2:7; 3:19). It is also used in the sense of *beginning,* as "the foundation of the world" (Matt. 13:35; 25:34; etc.). The expression is illustrative of Christ: "Behold, I am laying in Zion a stone, a tested stone," etc. (Isa. 28:16; 1 Cor. 3:11); of the doctrines of the apostles (Eph. 2:20); the first principles of the gospel (Heb. 6:1-2); the Christian religion (2 Tim. 2:19); of the righteous (Prov. 10:25). The wise man is one who lays his foundation upon a rock (Luke 6:48); the good minister, who builds on the true foundation—Jesus Christ (1 Cor. 3:10-11).

FOUNDER. *See* Handicrafts: Metalworker.

FOUNTAIN. A natural source of living water. The same word as "eye" in Heb., *'ayin* (Deut. 8:7; 33:28), sometimes rendered "spring" (as in the NIV). It is also spoken of an inflow of the sea (Gen. 7:11; 8:2; NIV, "springs"). An artificial source of flowing water, such as a cistern or a reservoir, may be denoted by the Heb. word *māqôr* (Pss. 36:9; 68:26; Prov. 5:18; 13:14; 14:27; Jer. 2:13). The Gk. *pēgē* is rendered "fountain" in James 3:11 ("spring" in the NIV). In Gen. 16:7; Lev. 11:36; 1 Sam. 29:1; Prov. 8:28; Rev. 7:17; 14:7; 8:10; 21:6, KJV "fountain" is replaced in the NASB and NIV by *spring* (which see).   M.F.U.

Figurative. Of God (Ps. 36:9; Jer. 17:13); of Christ (Zech. 13:1); of Israel, as the father of a numerous posterity (Deut. 33:28); of a good wife (Prov. 5:18); of spiritual wisdom (16:22; 18:4; both "well-spring" in the KJV). In Ps. 87:7; Song of Sol. 4:12; Isa. 41:18; Joel 3:18, KJV "fountain" is replaced in the NASB and sometimes in the NIV by *spring* (which see). *See* Spring; Well; Eye.

FOURTH OF A SHEKEL. A unit of money. *See* Metrology.

FOWL. *See* the articles Food; Sacrifices; and Animal Kingdom: Bird.

FOWLER. *See* Trapper.

FOX. *See also* Animal Kingdom.

Figurative. The proverbially cunning character of the fox is alluded to in Scripture, as in Ezek. 13:4, where the prophets of Israel are said to be like foxes (NIV, "jackals") among ruins; and in Luke 13:32, where our Lord calls Herod "that fox." The fox's fondness for grapes is alluded to in Song of Sol. 2:15.

FRANKINCENSE. *See* Incense; Vegetable Kingdom: Galbanum.

FRAUD. *See* Law.

FRAY (Heb. *ḥārad,* to "frighten"; Deut. 28:26; Jer. 7:33; Zech. 1:21; all KJV only). The English term appearing in the KJV of the passages listed immediately above is not the modern *fray* but rather is an old word signifying to frighten or scare away. The NASB replaces KJV "fray" with "frighten" or "terrify," and the Heb. term is given a variety of renderings throughout the NASB. The NIV uses "fray" in Job 39:21 as a translation of Heb. *nesheq,* rendered by the NASB as "weapons."

FREEDMAN (Gk. *apeleutheros,* one "set free"). A person who has been freed (1 Cor. 7:22). In Gal. 4:22-23, 30, a strong distinction is drawn between the free woman and the bondwoman. *See* Freedom.

FREEDMEN, SYNAGOGUE OF THE (Lat., "freedmen"). This occurs only once in the NT: "But some men from what is called the Synagogue of the Freedmen" (Acts 6:9). The interpretation of this word has been various. Some believe these men ("Libertines," as is rendered in the KJV) were released Roman slaves, who having embraced Judaism had their synagogue at Jerusalem. Others, owing to the geographical names given to other synagogues in the same verse, infer that this must have the same meaning and suppose that Jews dwelling in Liberatum (KJV, "Libertines"), a city or region in proconsular Africa, are meant. Others, with far greater probability, appeal to Philo and understand the word as denoting Jews who had been made captive by the Romans under Pompey but were afterward set free, and who, although they had fixed their abode at Rome, had built at their own expense a synagogue at Jerusalem, which they frequented when in that city.

FREEDOM (Heb. *ḥūpshâ,* "liberty"; Gk. *politeia,* "citizenship," Acts 22:28).

Hebrew. Every Israelite (man or woman) who had become a slave might not only be redeemed at any time by his relatives but, if this did not take place, was bound to receive his freedom without payment in the seventh year, with a present of cattle and fruits (Ex. 21:2; Deut. 15:12-15). Indeed all slaves of Hebrew descent, with their children, obtained freedom without ransom in the Jubilee year (Lev. 25:39-41). If the man was single when he went into slavery, he was liberated alone; whereas the wife brought into slavery with her husband received her freedom at the same time with him (Ex. 21:2-4; Jer. 34:8-9). The emancipation of slaves among Greeks and Romans was tolerably common. The Greeks had no special legal form for the process and consequently no legal differences in the legal *status* of freedom. At Athens they took the position of resident aliens and were under certain obligations to their liberators as patrons.

Roman. Among the Romans emancipation was either formal or informal. Of formal emancipation there were three kinds: (1) The *manumissio vindictā,* in which the owner appeared before the magistrate with the slave. A Roman citizen laid a staff upon the slave's head and declared him free, whereupon the master, who was holding the slave with his hand, let him go as a symbol of liberation. (2) The *manumissio censu,* in which the master enrolled the slave's name in the list of citizens. (3) The *manumissio testāmentō,* or manumission by will, in which the master declared his slave free or bound his heir to emancipate him. Informal emancipation took place in virtue of an oral declaration on the part of the master in the presence of friends, or by letter, or by inviting the slave to the master's table. After formal emancipation they at once became Roman citizens but, not being freeborn, were not eligible to office and were excluded from military service. Informal emancipation conferred only practical freedom without civil rights (Seyffert, *Dictionary of Classical Antiquity*, s.v. *manumissio testāmentō*). Freedom is used (Acts 22:28; cf. 21:39) for *citizenship* (which see).

An Attribute of God. This is declared by the apostle Paul, in harmony with the unanimous testimony of the Scriptures, in the words "Who works all things after the counsel of His will" (Eph. 1:11). By this term theology expresses the fact that God is a self-determining agent, a free personal Being acting purely in accordance with His own perfections. The reason of the divine purpose and act is to be found only in God Himself. Inasmuch as God is eternally and unchangeably what He is, we must recognize in God, in a proper sense, an absolute necessity. But it is a necessity that not only does not conflict but is identical with His perfect freedom. The creation—the existence of all things that are not God—must be referred to the divine freedom. God could be under no necessity to create. But if He creates, His creation, the order and the laws He establishes among them, must reflect His wisdom and goodness and holiness—in a word, Himself. At this point the doctrine of the divine freedom reveals sharply its opposition to Pantheism, which asserts that all things, even sin (the sinfulness of which it denies), are but necessary manifestations or unfoldings of the Divine Being.

The freedom of God is exercised and illustrated in His government of His moral creatures. It has pleased God to create intelligences possessed of moral freedom and to make their ultimate destiny contingent upon the right use of their freedom. This is a necessary feature of the government that God has established over the world of moral beings He has seen fit to create. God has manifested His perfect freedom in creating such a world and adapting His methods to the demanding situations that arise in its history. This view of the divine freedom is to be maintained in opposition to the exaggerated and unscriptural view of the divine sovereignty that, despite all merely verbal qualifications, actually reduces the freedom of moral creatures to nothing and regards their destinies as unalterably fixed by an eternal, divine decree. See Sovereignty of God.

Human. In what has been said above, the freedom of man, as that of other moral intelligences, has been assumed. The doctrine of human freedom, or of free will, the subject of so much controversy, requires particular discussion.

Definition. By freedom of the will, in the proper sense, is meant the power of contrary choice, i.e., the power of the mind to choose in some other direction than that in which the choice is actually made. Theologically freedom refers especially to the power to choose between good and evil, righteousness and unrighteousness. On the one hand, by those who uphold this doctrine, it is asserted that man freely determines his own volitions; on the other, by necessitarians, it is held that these volitions are determined by conditions, influences, and circumstances with which they are connected as rigidly and powerfully as effects are connected with causes in the material world.

Parties to Controversy. Prominent among those who deny human freedom are materialists. This position is also the natural result of Dualism and Pantheism. That form of Theism that fails to recognize the divine freedom finds no freedom in man. The attitude of Calvinistic theology upon this subject has been the occasion of much dispute and probably of some misunderstanding. The extreme doctrines of foreordination, of unconditional election, and of reprobation, held by Calvinists, as well as some of the terms by which they describe man's actual condition, have been claimed by Arminians to be logically equivalent to a denial of man's freedom. And yet it may truly be said that Calvinism, generally speaking, has steadfastly proclaimed the responsibility of man

as a free moral agent. On the whole, belief in the freedom of the will, properly interpreted, may be regarded as the unanimous, if not always coherently spoken, belief of the Christian church.

Theological Interpretation. The doctrine of human freedom relates not only to man's original condition before the Fall but also to his present fallen condition, as that of bondage to sin; and still further to the condition to which he is brought through redemption by Christ. (1) Man was created in the image of God and accordingly was endowed with perfect moral freedom. Sin resulted from the abuse of freedom (see Fall of Man; Sin). (2) In consequence of the sin of the first human pair mankind has inherited a depraved nature, so that while the natural freedom of man is not lost in respect to many things, yet with respect to meeting the requirements of the divine law, man is of himself in a state of complete moral inability (see Rom. 7:19-24). This is to be held in opposition to Pelagianism. (3) The actual condition of mankind as morally fallen is, however, greatly modified by the grace of God that has come to the race through redemption. Through regeneration and sanctification the bondage of sin is completely destroyed, and thus believers become "free indeed."

Arguments for Freedom. There are several arguments for freedom. (1) Appeal is made to universal consciousness. The common experience of men is that while choosing one way they feel that they might choose another. (2) Freedom is essential to all moral responsibility. And moral responsibility is one of the intuitions of the human mind. (3) The denial of freedom must logically lead to the denial of moral distinctions in human affairs. (4) In addition to the above, which are purely rational arguments, is the general force of Scripture teaching, which uniformly represents man as invested with the power of choosing between right and wrong and between sin and salvation.

BIBLIOGRAPHY: J. E. Frame, *Journal of Biblical Literature* (1930), pp. 1-12.

FREEDOM, YEAR OF, or **Jubilee.** *See* Festivals.

FREEMAN. *See* Freedman.

FREEWILL OFFERING. *See* Sacrificial Offering.

FRIEND. A person with whom one has friendly communications (Gen. 38:12, 20; 2 Sam. 13:3; Job 2:11; 19:21; etc.); also a *lover, one beloved* of a woman (Song of Sol. 5:16; Jer. 3:1, 20, NASB, KJV, and NIV, "lovers"); and in Judg. 14:20 it is used in the sense of "the friend of the bridegroom" (John 3:29), who asked the hand of the bride and rendered service at the *marriage* (which see).

The Gk. word *hetairos* (Matt. 11:16, KJV, "fellow"; NIV, "others") is used in kindly address (Matt. 20:13; 22:12; 26:50); one attached by affection (Gk. *philos*) is also frequently used in the NT, as in James 2:23 and 4:4.

BIBLIOGRAPHY: S. Dodds, *Friendship's Meaning and the Heart of God in Nature* (1919), pp. 7-43; A. van Selms, *Journal of Near Eastern Studies* 9 (1950): 65-75.

FRINGE. *See* Tassel.

FROG. *See* Animal Kingdom.

FRONTAL (Heb. *ṭōṭāpâ*, to "bind," only in Deut. 6:8; 11:18; rendered "phylacteries," Ex. 13:16; KJV renders "frontlets," NIV, "symbol"). "The expression in Deut. 6:8, 'Thou shalt bind them for a sign upon thine hand, and they shall be as frontlets between thine eyes,' does not point at all to the symbolizing of the divine commands by an outward sign to be worn upon the hand, or to bands with passages of the law inscribed upon them, to be worn on the forehead between the eyes. . . . The line of thought referred to merely expresses the idea that the Israelites were not only to retain the commands of God in their hearts, and to confess them with the mouth, but to fulfill them with the hand, or in act and deed" (K. & D., *Com.*, ad loc.). But the Jews, after their return from captivity, construed the injunction literally and had portions of the law written out and worn as badges upon their persons. They are still worn by modern Jews and consist of strips of parchment on which are written four passages of Scripture (Ex. 13:2-10, 11-17; Deut. 6:4-9; 13:22). These are rolled up in a case of black calfskin, attached to a stiffer piece of leather having a thong one finger broad and one and a half cubits long. *See* Phylactery.

Frontals (Phylactery) on Orthodox Jew

FRONTLETS. A KJV term; *see* Frontal.

FROST (Heb. *kᵉpôr,* so called from "covering" the ground, Job 38:29; "hoarfrost," Ex. 16:14; Ps. 147:16; also *qāraḥ,* "smooth," as ice, rendered in Job 6:16; 38:29). Frozen dew. It appears in a still night, when there is no storm or tempest, and descends upon the earth as silently as if it were produced by mere breathing (Job 37:10, KJV).

FROWARDNESS. A KJV term referring to perverseness, deceit, or falsehood. The NASB and NIV replace the term with "perversity," "perverseness" (Prov. 2:14; 6:14), or "perverted"

(10:32). *Froward* and *frowardly* likewise have the meaning of perverted, crooked, or deceitful (cf. Prov. 4:24; 10:31; 17:20); a "turning away" from that which is right (Isa. 57:17).

FRUIT. *See* Garden; Vegetable Kingdom.

Figurative. The word *fruit* is often used figuratively in Scripture of offspring, children (Ps. 21:10, marg.; Hos. 9:16); also in such phrases as "fruit of the womb" (Gen. 30:2; Deut. 7:13; etc.); "fruit of his loins" (Acts 2:30, marg.); "fruit of your body" (Ps. 132:11; Mic. 6:7). Also in a variety of forms, such as, "They shall eat of the fruit of their own way," i.e., experience the consequences (Prov. 1:31; Isa. 3:10; Jer. 6:19; 17:10, marg.); boasting is the "fruit of the arrogant heart" (Isa. 10:12); a man's words are called the "fruit of his words," or of his "mouth" or "lips" (Prov. 12:14; 18:20; Heb. 13:15); "fruit of lies" (Hos. 10:13); "the fruit of the righteous" (Prov. 11:30) is his counsel, example, etc.; the "fruit of the spirit" enumerated in Gal. 5:22-23 are those gracious habits that the Holy Spirit produces in the Christian, given more briefly as "goodness and righteousness and truth" (Eph. 5:9); the "fruit of righteousness" (Phil. 1:11) is such good work as springs from a gracious frame of heart. Fruit is also the name given to a charitable contribution (Rom. 15:28).

FRYING PAN. *See* Pan.

FUEL. In most Eastern countries there is a scarcity of wood and other materials for fuel. Consequently almost every kind of combustible matter is eagerly sought for, such as the withered stalks of herbs and flowers (Matt. 6:30), thorns (Ps. 58:9; Eccles. 7:6), and animal excrement (Ezek. 4:12-15). At the present time wood, charcoal, and electricity are employed in the towns of Syria and Egypt, although the people of Palestine use anthracite coal to some extent. *See* Coal.

FUGITIVE. The rendering of several Heb. words, meaning to "wander," a "refugee," "deserter," etc. (Judg. 12:4; Isa. 15:5).

FULLER. *See* Handicrafts: Launderer.

FULLER'S FIELD. A spot near Jerusalem (2 Kings 18:17; Isa. 7:3; 36:2), so near the walls that one speaking there could be heard on them (2 Kings 18:17, 26). The NIV refers to it as the "Washerman's Field." The pool mentioned is probably the one now known as Birket-el-Mamilla, at the head of the Valley of Hinnom, a little W of the Yafa gate. The position of the fuller's field is thus indicated.

FULLER'S SOAP.

Figurative. The powerful cleansing properties of *bōrît,* or soap, are employed by the prophet Malachi (3:2; NIV, "launderer's soap") to represent the prospective results of the Messiah's coming (cf. Mark 9:3). *See* Handicrafts: Launderer.

FULNESS.

1. That portion of the corn and wine that was to be offered to Jehovah as a tithe or first fruits (Ex. 22:29; cf. Num. 18:27).

2. (Gk. *plērōma*, "that which has been filled"). This term has been variously used in Scripture. (a) The "fulness of time" is the time when Christ appeared —"When the fulness of the time came, God sent forth His Son" (Gal. 4:4). (b) The fulness of Christ is the superabundance with which He is filled (John 1:16; Col. 1:19; 2:9). In the last passage, "In Him all the fulness of Deity dwells in bodily form" means that the whole nature and attributes of God are in Christ. (c) The church, i.e., the body of believers, is called the fullness of Christ (Eph. 1:23), as it is the church that makes Him a complete and perfect head.

FULLNESS. *See* Fulness.

FUNERAL.

Egyptian. The body was buried either in the hills, there to be preserved by the sand, or, having been embalmed, it was placed in a sarcophagus of stone whose lid and trough, hermetically fastened with cement, prevented the penetration of any moisture. The soul was supposed to follow the body to the tomb and there to dwell, as in its eternal house, upon the confines of the visible and invisible world. Funeral sacrifices and the regular cultus of the dead originated in the practice of making provision for the sustenance of the "manes" after having secured their lasting existence by the mummification of their bodies. Unless supplied with food the soul (or double) was supposed to wander abroad at night in search of it. Therefore food and vessels of wine and beer were brought to the tomb, that they might enjoy that which was believed to be necessary for the maintenance of their bodies.

Among the Ancient Israelites. What form or ceremonies of obsequies were observed is to us almost unknown, except that the act of interment was performed by the relations (sons, brothers) with their own hands (Gen. 25:9; 35:29; Judg. 16:31; cf. Matt. 8:21-22). In later times the Jews left this office to others, and in Amos 5:16 wailers and professional mourners are mentioned. As soon as possible after death the body was washed (Acts 9:37), then wrapped in a large cloth (Matt. 27:59; Mark 15:46; Luke 23:53), or all its limbs wound with bands (John 11:44), between the folds of which, in cases of persons of distinction, aromatics were laid or sprinkled (19:39-40). At public funerals of princes elaborate shrouds were used, and there was a prodigious expense of perfumes and spices. The body was moved to the grave in a coffin (probably open) or on a bier (2 Sam. 3:31), borne by men (Luke 7:14; Acts 5:6, 10), with a retinue of relatives and friends (2 Sam. 3:31; Luke 7:12). The Talmud speaks of funeral processions with horns, in a long train (Job 21:33), with loud weeping and wailing (2 Sam. 3:32). Female mourners, hired for the purpose, prolonged the lamentation several days. The burial was followed by the funeral meal (2 Sam. 3:35; Jer. 16:5, 7; Ezek. 24:17, 22; Hos. 9:4).

BIBLIOGRAPHY: J. Carcopino, *Daily Life in Ancient Rome* (1940), pp. 49-50; G. L. Dickinson, *A Greek View of Life* (1958), pp. 13-15, 21-23, 33-40; E. A. T. W. Budge, ed., *The Book of the Dead* (1960), pp. 207-16; R. de Vaux, *Ancient Israel: Its Life and Institutions* (1961), pp. 56-61; S. N. Kramer, *The Sumerians: Their History, Culture, and Character* (1963), pp. 89, 129-30; A. L. Oppenheim, *Ancient Mesopotamia* (1964), pp. 79, 103, 234, 300, 333.

FURLONG. *See* Mile in Metrology: Linear Measures.

FURNACE.

1. A smelting oven of limestone; kiln or oven for making bricks (Gen. 19:28; Ex. 19:18; cf. 9:8, 10; Amos 2:1).

2. A large crucible, apparently with an opening at the top for casting in materials (Dan. 3:22-23) and a door at the ground from which to take the metal (v. 26). The Persians used this device for inflicting capital punishment (cf. Jer. 29:22; Hos. 7:7; 2 Macc. 7:5).

3. A cylindrical fire pot such as is commonly used in dwelling houses in the East (Gen. 15:17, KJV; NASB, "oven"; NIV, "fire pot"). They are still in use among the Arabs. NT references to a furnace are found in Matt. 13:42, 50; Rev. 1:15; 9:2.

Figurative. A refining furnace is used figuratively to describe a state of trial (Deut. 4:20; Isa. 48:10).   M.F.U.

FURNACES, THE TOWER OF (Neh. 3:11; 12:38). This was one of the towers of the middle or second wall of Jerusalem, at its NW angle, adjoining the "corner gate" and near the intersection of the present line of the Via Dolorosa with the street of St. Stephen. The NIV refers to it as the "Tower of the Ovens." It may be the same as the "bakers' street" (Jer. 37:21).

FURNITURE. A term used in several ways in the Bible.

1. The rendering in the KJV of the Heb. *kar,* "pad," a camel's litter or canopied saddle (so the NIV), in which females are accustomed to travel in the East at the present day (Gen. 31:34).

2. The name given to the sacred furnishings and their utensils used in the Tabernacle (Ex. 31:7-9; 35:14, "utensils," NASB; "accessories," NIV; 39:33, "furnishings," NASB and NIV; NASB marg., "utensils"; all from Heb. *kelî*, something "prepared"). In Nah. 2:9 the same Heb. word is used for ornamental vessels ("all the pleasant furniture," KJV; "every kind of desirable object," NASB; "the wealth from all its treasures," NIV).

3. For domestic furniture, *see* House: Interior.

FURROW. A trench in the earth made by a plow

(Ps. 65:10). In Hos. 10:10, KJV "two furrows" is replaced in the NASB by "double guilt," and in the NIV by "double sin."

FURY (Heb. *ḥēmâ*, "heat"; or *ḥārôn*, "burning"). In KJV refers to intense anger attributed to God metaphorically or speaking after the manner of men (Lev. 26:28; Job 20:23; Isa. 63:3; etc.). The NASB and NIV render "anger," "wrath." It is the spontaneous reaction of the divine holiness against sin treasured-up and ripe for judgment. *See* Anger.

FUTURE LIFE. *See* Life; Immortality.

G

GA'AL (gā'al; "loathing"). The son of Ebed (Judg. 9:26-49). He was probably a marauder and was welcomed to Shechem because the Shechemites hoped that he would be able to render them good service in their revolt from Abimelech. At the festival at which the Shechemites offered the first fruits of their vintage in the temple of Baal, Gaal strove to kindle their wrath against the absent Abimelech. His rebellious speech was reported to Abimelech by the town prefect, Zebul. On receiving this news, Abimelech rose up during the night with the people that were with him and placed four companies in ambush against Shechem. When Gaal went out in the morning upon some enterprise and stood before the city gate, Abimelech rose up with his army out of the ambush. Gaal fled into the city but was thrust out by Zebul, and we hear of him no more, c. 1108-1105 B.C.

GA'ASH (gā'ash; "quaking"). A mountain in the district of Mt. Ephraim. On the N side of the hill was Timnath-serah, the city given to Joshua (Josh. 24:30). Here Joshua was buried. The "brooks" or *valleys* of Gaash are mentioned in 2 Sam. 23:30 and 1 Chron. 11:32.

GAB'BAI (gab'a-ī; "tax gatherer"). A chief of the tribe of Benjamin who settled in Jerusalem after the captivity (Neh. 11:8), before 445 B.C.

GAB'BATHA (gab'a-tha; Aram. *gabbᵉtā*, "ridge, knoll, hill"). The place mentioned in John 19:13, where it is stated that Pilate, alarmed by the insinuation of the Jews ("If you release this Man, you are no friend of Caesar"), went into the praetorium again and brought Jesus out to them. He then pronounced formal sentence against Jesus, having taken his seat upon the tribunal in a place called "The Pavement" (Gk. *lithostrōton*, "stone strewn"), but in Heb., "Gabbatha." It is probable that the Gk. name was given to the spot from the nature of its pavement, and the Heb. from its

shape. For a long time the pavement in the basement of the Convent of the Sisters of Zion on the Via Dolorosa has been thought to have constituted the courtyard of the fortress Antonia, a garrison Herod the Great constructed on the NW corner of the Temple mount. Thus it was accepted as the place where Herod judged Jesus. In 1966 excavations it was shown, however, that the pavement was laid when the adjacent Hadrianic arch was built in the second century. Thus this pavement could have had nothing to do with Jesus' passion.   H.F.V.

GA'BRIEL (gā'bri-el; "man" or "hero of God"). The word used to designate the heavenly messenger sent to explain to Daniel the visions that he saw (Dan. 8:16; 9:21), who announced the birth of John the Baptist to his father, Zacharias (Luke 1:11-20), and who spoke of the Messiah to the virgin Mary (1:26-38). As to his relation to other angels and archangels, the Scriptures give no information; but in the book of Enoch "the four great archangels, Michael, Raphael, Gabriel, and Uriel," are described as reporting the corrupt state of mankind to the Creator and receiving their several commissions. In the rabbinical writings Gabriel is represented as standing in front of the divine throne, near the standard of Judah. The Muslims regard Gabriel with profound reverence, affirming that to him was committed a complete copy of the Koran, which he imparted in successive portions to Muhammad. He is called in the Koran the Spirit of Truth and the Holy Spirit, and it is alleged that he will hold the scales in which the actions of men will be weighed in the last day.

BIBLIOGRAPHY: A. C. Gaebelein, *Gabriel and Michael, the Archangels, Their Prominence in Bible Prophecy* (1945).

GAD (gad; "fortune"). The name of David's "seer" (see below); and of Jacob's seventh son, the firstborn of Zilpah, Leah's maid, and whole brother to Asher (Gen. 30:9-11; 46:16, 18), perhaps about 1850 B.C.

Personal History. Of the life of the individual Gad son of Jacob, nothing is preserved.

The Tribe of Gad. At the time of the descent into Egypt seven sons are ascribed to him (Gen. 46:16), remarkable from the fact that a majority of their names have plural terminations, as if those of families rather than persons (Smith). At the first census Gad had 45,650 adult males, ranking *eighth;* and at the second census 40,500, ranking *tenth.*

They were attached to the second division of the Israelite host, following the standard of Reuben and camping on the S of the Tabernacle, their chief being Eliasaph the son of Deuel, or Reuel (Num. 1:14; 2:10-16).

In common with Reuben, Gad requested Moses to give them their portion on the E of the Jordan, because they had "an exceedingly large number of livestock." Upon being assured that they would assist their brethren in the conquest of Canaan, Moses granted them their request. The country allotted to Gad appears, speaking roughly, to have lain chiefly about the center of the land E of the Jordan. To Reuben and Gad was given the territory of Sihon, between the Arnon and the Jabbok and as far E as Jazer, the border of the Ammonites, but the division is hard to define (*see* Num. 32:33; Josh. 13:15-21). "The land is high, well suitable for flocks. . . . There is water in abundance, and therefore the vegetation is rich" (Harper, *Bible and Mod. Dis.,* p. 262).

The Gadites were a warlike tribe, and they bravely aided their brethren in the conquest of Canaan (Josh. 4:12; 22:1-4). Surrounded by the Ammonites, Midianites, and many other hostile tribes, they nobly defended their country. One of their greatest victories was that gained over the descendants of Ishmael, the tribes of Jetur, Naphish, and Nodab, from whom they took enormous booty (1 Chron. 5:18-22). The seat of Ish-bosheth's sovereignty was established in this territory, for Abner brought him to Mahanaim, where he reigned (2 Sam. 2:8) and was assassinated. Many, however, of the Gadite chiefs had joined David while in the stronghold (1 Chron. 12:8); and when, years later, he was obliged to flee across the Jordan, he found welcome and help (2 Sam. 17:24, 27-29). In the division of the kingdom, Gad fell to the northern state, and many of the wars between Syria and Israel must have ravaged its territory (2 Kings 10:33). At last, Tiglath-pileser carried the Gadites and the neighboring tribes away as captives into Assyria (15:29; 1 Chron. 5:26).

BIBLIOGRAPHY: D. Baly, *The Geography of the Bible* (1957), pp. 217-31.

GAD (gad; "good fortune"). The "Seer," or "David's seer" (2 Sam. 24:11; 1 Chron. 21:9; 29:29;

2 Chron. 29:25), was a prophet who appears to have joined David when in "the stronghold" and who advised David to leave it for the forest of Hereth (1 Sam. 22:5), before 1000 B.C. We do not hear of him again until he reappears in connection with the punishment inflicted for the numbering of the people (2 Sam. 24:11-19; 1 Chron. 21:9-19). But he was evidently attached to the royal establishment at Jerusalem, for he wrote a book of the acts of David (29:29) and also assisted in settling the arrangements for the musical service of the "house of the Lord" (2 Chron. 29:25).

GAD (gad; "good fortune"). A Canaanite god of fortune, often appearing in Heb. compounds as "Baal-gad" (Josh. 11:17; "Migdal-gad," Josh. 15:37). *See* Gods, False.

GAD'ARA (gad'a-ra). The capital of the Roman province of Peraea, E of the Jordan, about six miles from the Sea of Galilee and opposite Tiberias. Jesus healed the demoniac in Gadara. The modern village Um-Keis is in the midst of ruins intimating the grandeur of the ancient Gadara. *See* Gadarenes.

BIBLIOGRAPHY: M. F. Unger, *Archaeology of the New Testament* (1962), pp. 139-41; E. E. Ellis and M. Wilcox, *Neotestamentica et Semitica* (1969), pp. 181-97.

GADARENES (gad-a-rēnz'). The inhabitants of *Gadara* (which see), mentioned in the account of the healing of the demoniacs (Matt. 8:28, NASB and NIV; but "Gergesenes," KJV; Mark 5:1; Luke 8:26, 37; "Gerasenes" in the NASB and NIV but "Gadarenes" in the KJV).

GAD'DI (gad'i; "fortunate"). A son of Susi, of the tribe of Manasseh, sent by Moses to represent that tribe among the twelve "spies" on their exploring tour through Canaan (Num. 13:11), c. 1441 B.C.

GAD'DIEL (gad-i-el; "fortune of Gad"). A son of Sodi, of the tribe of Zebulun. One of the twelve "spies" sent by Moses to explore Canaan (Num. 13:10), c. 1441 B.C.

GA'DI (ga'di; a "Gadite"). The father of the usurper Menahem, who "went up from Tirzah and came to Samaria, and struck Shallum," king of Israel (2 Kings 15:14), and reigned ten years over Israel (v. 17), about 741 B.C.

GAD'ITES (gad'īts). The descendants of *Gad* (which see), the son of Jacob (Deut. 3:12, 16; 4:43; 29:8; etc.).

GA'HAM (ga'ham; "to burn"). One of the sons of Nahor (Abraham's brother) by his concubine Reumah (Gen. 22:24), about 2100 B.C.

GA'HAR (ga'har). One of the chiefs of the Temple servants whose descendants returned with Zerubbabel from the captivity to Jerusalem (Ezra 2:47; Neh. 7:49), before 536 B.C.

GA'IUS (ga'yus; Lat. Caius).

1. A Macedonian who accompanied Paul on some of his journeys and was seized by the populace at Ephesus (Acts 19:29), A.D. about 54.

2. A man of Derbe who accompanied Paul on his return from Macedonia into Asia, probably to Jerusalem (Acts 20:4).

3. An inhabitant of Corinth, the host of Paul, and in whose house the Christians were accustomed to assemble (Rom. 16:23). He was baptized by Paul (1 Cor. 1:14).

4. The person to whom John's third epistle is addressed (3 John 4). "He was probably a convert of St. John (v. 4), and a layman of wealth and distinction in some city near Ephesus, A.D. after 90. The epistle was written for the purpose of commending to the kindness and hospitality of Gaius some Christians who were strangers in the place where he lived."

GA'LAL (gā'lal; "rolling"). The name of two Levites after the Exile.

1. One of those who dwelt in the villages of the Netophathites and served at Jerusalem (1 Chron. 9:15), about 536 B.C.

2. A descendant of Jeduthun, and father of Shemaiah, or Shammua (1 Chron. 9:16; Neh. 11:17), before 445 B.C.

GALA'TIA (ga-lā'sha). The Roman Galatia was the central region of the peninsula of Asia Minor, with the provinces of Asia on the W, Cappadocia on the E, Pamphylia and Cilicia on the S, and Bithynia and Pontus on the N (Acts 16:6; 18:23; 1 Cor. 16:1; Gal. 1:2; etc.). It would be difficult to define the exact limits; in fact they were freqently changing. At one time there is no doubt that this province contained Pisidia and Lycaonia, and therefore those towns of Antioch, Iconium, Lystra, and Derbe, which are conspicuous in the narrative of Paul's travels.

BIBLIOGRAPHY: W. M. Ramsay, *St. Paul the Traveller and Roman Citizen* (1962), pp. 111-15, 130-36, 140-45, 160-64, 181-90, 196-200, 210-13; E. M. Blaiklock, *Cities of the New Testament* (1966), pp. 22-34; W. M.

Pisidian Antioch, in the region of Galatia

Ramsay, *The Geography of Asia Minor* (1972), pp. 221-54; id., *A Historical Commentary on St. Paul's Epistle to the Galatians* (1978).

GALA'TIANS (gal-ā'shuns). They were called by the Romans *Galli* and were a stream from that torrent of barbarians that poured into Greece in the third century B.C., and that recoiled in confusion from the cliffs of Delphi. Crossing over into Asia Minor they lost no time in spreading over the peninsula with their arms and devastation, dividing nearly the whole of it among their three tribes. They levied tribute on cities and kings and hired themselves out as mercenary soldiers. It became a Roman province under Augustus, reaching from the borders of Asia and Bithynia to the neighborhood of Iconium, Lystra, and Derbe, "cities of Lycaonia." Henceforth this territory was a part of the Roman Empire.

The Galatians had little religion of their own and easily adopted the superstitions and mythology of the Greeks. Paul introduced the gospel among them (Acts 16:6; 18:23; Gal. 1:6-12), visiting them in person. When detained by sickness he sent Crescens to them (2 Tim. 4:10). Soon after Paul left Galatia, missionaries of the Judaizing party came and taught the necessity of circumcision for the higher grade of Christian services, declaring that the apostle did, in effect, preach circumcision (Gal. 5:11), thus casting doubt upon Paul's sincerity. Such teaching caused defection among the converts to Christianity, and he wrote his epistle vindicating himself against the charges of the Judaizing party.

GALATIANS, EPISTLE TO. The letter of the apostle Paul containing his great defense of the gospel of grace against legalistic perversion or contamination.

Early Testimony. The early church gives unambiguous testimony to this document. Marcion put it at the head of his *Apostolikon* (A.D. 140). Athenagoras, Justin Martyr, and Melito quote it. Evidences of it appear in Ignatius and Polycarp. With the other Pauline epistles it appears in the oldest Lat., Syr., and Egyptian translations and in the Muratorian Canon of the second century. No trace of doubt as to the authority, integrity, or apostolic genuineness of the epistle comes from ancient times.

Destination and Date. Although the Pauline authorship of Galatians is well established, its destination, occasion, and date are surrounded by critical difficulties. It was addressed to "the churches of Galatia" (1:2). The Roman province of Galatia included not only Galatia proper, peopled largely by Celts from Gaul, but also portions of Lycaonia, Pisidia, and Phrygia, all situated on the S. The fact that Paul addressed the churches in the S part of Galatia is supported by the following. (1) He and Barnabas had visited the cities of Iconium, Lystra, Derbe, and Pisidian Antioch, all in S Galatia, and had established churches in the vicinity during the first missionary journey (Acts 13:4; 14:19-21). (2) Familiar reference to Barnabas (Gal. 2:1, 9, 13) would be unexplainable in a letter sent to northern Galatia, where Barnabas seems to have been unknown. (3) In the S Galatian cities there were Jews who might have caused the events mentioned in the letter (Acts 13:14-51; 14:1; 16:1-3). If the "South Galatian theory" is subscribed to, Galatians may have been written either at Antioch in Syria at the consummation of the first missionary journey (14:26-28) or at Ephesus in the course of the third missionary journey (19:10). The apostle's visit to Jerusalem (Gal. 2:1-10) is thought to be identical to that alluded to in Acts 11:30. If this is so, Galatians may have been sent from Antioch around A.D. 48, prior to Paul's third visit to Jerusalem to attend the apostolic gathering of chap. 15. According to this theory, Galatians would be the earliest of the apostle's letters. There are strong reasons, however, to support the hypothesis that Galatians was written at Ephesus (52 A.D.) during the same time as the other epistles.

The Occasion. Galatians has been called the "Magna Charta of Christian liberty" and the "Christian's Declaration of Independence." The difficulty that produced this important epistle was caused by Jewish believers who proclaimed a mixture of Judaism and Christianity. Paul had proclaimed the free grace of God for all men through the death of Christ. The legalizers contended that Christianity could only work within the sphere of the Mosaic law. Faith in Christ, involving the free gifts of the Holy Spirit, was not sufficient. Obedience to the Mosaic law (Gal. 2:16, 21; 3:2; 5:4; etc.), which requires observance of festal days and the Sabbath (4:10), was stressed. Had the Judaizers won, Christianity would merely have been a sect within Judaism. The situation called for all the skill and wisdom the great apostle could muster. With invincible logic he vindicated Christianity on the sole basis of man's acceptance of Christ. Men are justified by the finished work of the Redeemer and in no manner by forms and ceremonies. Galatians is an echo of the great truth of justification so masterfully set forth in Romans.

Outline.

I. Introduction (1:1-5)
II. The apostolic vindication (1:6–2:21)
    A. The occasion (1:6-7)
    B. The authenticity of his gospel (1:8-10)
    C. The divine origin (1:11-24)
    D. The official endorsement (2:1-10)
    E. The explanation of his conduct (2:11-21)
III. Doctrinal justification (3-4)
    A. The faulty conduct of the Galatians (3:1-5)
    B. Abraham's example (3:6-9)
    C. Legal deliverance by Christ (3:10-14)
    D. The purpose of the law (3:15-18)
    E. Law related to the promise (3:19-22)
    F. Superiority of the condition under faith compared with that under law (3:23–4:11)
    G. Paul and the Galatians (4:12-20)
    H. The two covenants (4:21-31)
IV. The practical application (5:1–6:10)
    A. Warning of the right use of freedom (5:1-15)
    B. The way to spiritual growth (5:16-26)
    C. Exhortation to patience and brotherly love (6:1-5)
    D. Exhortation to liberality (6:6-10)
    E. Warning against Judaizers (6:11-16)
V. Conclusion (6:17-18)   M.F.U.

BIBLIOGRAPHY: M. C. Tenney, *Galatians: The Charter of Christian Liberty* (1954); E. D. Burton, *A Critical and Exegetical Commentary on the Epistle to the Galatians* (1962); M. Luther, *Lectures on Galatians,* vols. 26-27, *Luther's Works,* trans. J. Pelikan (1963-64); R. A. Cole, *The Epistle of Paul to the Galatians,* Tyndale New Testament Commentaries (1965); J. B. Lightfoot, *The Epistle of St. Paul to the Galatians* (1966); W. Hendricksen, *Exposition of Galatians,* New Testament Commentary (1968); J. R. W. Stott, *The Message of Galatians* (1968); D. Guthrie, *Galatians,* The Century Bible (1974); H. A. Kent, Jr., *The Freedom of God's Sons* (1976); J. Eadie, *Commentary on the Epistle of Paul to the Galatians* (1977); W. M. Ramsay, *A Historical Commentary on St. Paul's Epistle to the Galatians* (1978); M. Luther, *Commentary on Galatians,* trans. E. Middleton (1979); R. G. Gromacki, *Stand Fast in Liberty* (1979); J. Brown, *An Exposition of the Epistle of Paul the Apostle to the Galatians* (1981).

GALBANUM. *See* Vegetable Kingdom.

GAL'EED (gal'ē-ed; "heap of witness"). The name given by Jacob to a pile of stones erected by Jacob and Laban as a memorial of their covenant (Gen. 31:47-48). It is Heb., but the name given by Laban, Jegar-sahadutha, is Aram., known probably to Nahor's family, whereas Abraham and his descendants had learned the kindred Heb. dialect.

GALILE'AN (gal-i-lē'an). A native or inhabitant of Galilee (Matt. 26:69; John 4:45). The Galileans were generous and impulsive, of simple manners, earnest piety, and intense nationalism. They were also excitable, passionate, and violent. The Talmud accuses them of being quarrelsome but admits that they cared more for honor than for money. Their religious observances were simple, differing in several points from those of Judea. The people of Galilee were specially blamed for neglecting the study of their language, charged with errors in grammar, and especially with absurd mispronunciation, sometimes leading to ridiculous mistakes. Thus there was a general contempt in rabbinic circles for all that was Galilean. The Galileans were easily recognized by their dialect and tone, as is seen by the detection of Peter as one of Christ's disciples (Mark 14:70).

The name was applied by way of reproach to the early Christians. Julian generally used this term when speaking of Christ or Christians and called Christ "the Galilean God." He also made a law requiring that Christians be called by no other name, hoping thereby to abolish the name *Christian*. It is said that he died fighting against the Christians and, as he caught the blood from a wound in his side, threw it toward heaven, saying, "Thou hast conquered, O Galilean!"

GAL'ILEE (gal'i-lē; Heb. *gālil*, "circle or circuit"). *Palestine* (which see) was divided into three provinces—Judea, Samaria, and Galilee. Galilee occupied the upper part of the land, being the NW province. In the time of Christ it included more than one-third of western Palestine, extending from the base of Mt. Hermon on the N, to the ridges of Carmel and Gilboa on the S, and from the Jordan to the Mediterranean Sea, about fifty by twenty-five miles in extent. Solomon once offered the tract to Hiram, who declined it, after which Solomon colonized it. It embraced a large northern portion of the tribe of Naphtali and was called Galilee of the Gentiles. There are many Scripture references to it. The first three gospels are occupied largely with Christ's ministry in Galilee. Of His thirty-two parables, nineteen were spoken in Galilee, and twenty-five of His thirty-three great miracles were performed in Galilee. In this province the Sermon on the Mount was spoken. Here the Lord was transfigured.

BIBLIOGRAPHY: D. Baly, *The Geography of the Bible* (1957), pp. 38-39, 184-92; E. Hoade. *Guide to the Holy Land* (1973), pp. 823-954; Y. Aharoni, *The Land of the Bible* (1979), pp. 60-61, 156-58, 220-29, 240-41, 314-16.

GAL'ILEE, SEA OF. This is called by four different names in Scripture: the "Sea of Chinnereth," or "Chinneroth" (Heb. *kinneret*, "harp-shaped"; NIV is "Kinnereth"), the shape of the sea (Num. 34:11; Josh. 12:3; 13:27); the "lake of Gennesaret" (Luke 5:1), the name of the extended plain adjoining the lake; the "Sea of Tiberias" (John 6:1; 21:1), the name used by the natives at this time—Bahr Tarbariyeh; and "Galilee" (Matt. 4:18; 15:29). The lake is about sixty miles from Jerusalem and at one time was thirteen miles long and eight miles wide at its greatest extent, although land reclamation programs have since reduced its length. Its surface is about 700 feet below sea level, and it is about 150 feet deep at its lowest point. The Jordan River flows through it, providing much of its water supply, but that is augmented by springs in the lake floor. The fresh waters of the lake are clean, and they have always been well stocked with a variety of fish. Several towns dotted its shores in NT times, but almost all of them (Bethsaida, Capernaum, Tiberias, etc.) stood on its northern and western shores because the eastern slopes rise more

Sunset over the Sea of Galilee

precipitously from the water. The sea was the highway for considerable traffic between Damascus and the Mediterranean, and the customhouse duties from which Christ took Matthew were of no little import. Hot springs along the western shore, especially at Tiberias, brought multitudes to be cured. The high hills surrounding the below sea-level water combined with abrupt temperature changes contributed to sudden and violent storms on the lake, as various NT passages indicate (*see*, e.g., Mark 4:35-41; 6:45-52; John 6:16-21). It was on and about this lake that Jesus did many of His wonderful miracles. Eighteen of the thirty-three recorded miracles of Christ were probably done in the immediate neighborhood of the Sea of Galilee. In the city of Capernaum alone He performed ten of these.   R.K.H.

BIBLIOGRAPHY: D. Baly, *The Geography of the Bible* (1957), pp. 197-98; Y. Aharoni, *The Land of the Bible* (1979), pp. 111-15, 188-90, 197-98.

GALL.

1. Bitter substance (Heb. *merērâ*). The Heb. term denotes etymologically "that which is bitter"; see Job 13:26, "Thou dost write bitter things against me." Hence the term is applied to the "bile" or "gall" from its intense bitterness (16:13; 20:25); it is also used of the "venom" of serpents (20:14), which the ancients erroneously believed was their gall.

2. Poisonous herb (Heb. *rō'sh*), generally translated "gall" by the KJV, is in Hos. 10:4 rendered "hemlock" ("poisonous weeds," NASB and NIV); in Deut. 32:33 and Job 20:16 *rō'sh* denotes the "poison" or "venom" of serpents. From Deut. 29:8 and Lam. 3:19 (cf. Hos. 10:4), it is evident that the Heb. term denotes some bitter and perhaps poisonous plant. Other writers have supposed, and with some reason (from Deut. 32:32), that some berry-bearing plant must be intended. Gesenius understands this to be "poppies." The capsules of the *Papaveraceae* may well give the name of *rō'sh* ("head") to the plant in question, just as we speak of poppy *heads*. The various species of this family spring up quickly in cornfields, and the juice is extremely bitter. A steeped solution of poppy heads may be "the water of gall" of Jer. 8:14 ("poisoned water," NASB and NIV).

3. Bitter secretion (Gk. *cholē*, "greenish"[?]). It is recorded that just before His crucifixion the Roman soldiers offered the Lord "wine to drink mingled with gall" (Matt. 27:34) and "wine mixed with myrrh" (Mark 15:23). The Jews were in the habit of giving the criminal a stupefying drink before he was nailed to the cross, probably with the purpose of deadening pain. Much discussion has arisen both as to the nature of the drink presented to Jesus and its purpose. Perhaps the following is correct: "gall" is to be understood as expressing the bitter nature of the draught, and its purpose was to reduce the Lord's pain during

the trial of suffering before Him. *See* Vegetable Kingdom.

GALLERY. A term in architecture signifying *projection* of a story or portico, an *offset, terrace* (Ezek. 41:15, marg., "passageway"; 42:3, 5). Their exact form is a matter of conjecture.

GALLEY. *See* Ship.

GAL'LIM (gal'im; "heaps"). A city of Benjamin, N of Jerusalem. It was the native place of Palti, to whom David's wife Michal had been given (1 Sam. 25:44; Isa. 10:30). Site uncertain.

GAL'LIO (gal'i-ō). Proconsul of Achaia (Acts 18:12; etc.). *See* Paul.

GALLON. *See* Metrology: Liquid Measures.

GALLOWS. *See* Punishments.

GAMA'LIEL (ga-mā'li-el; "reward of God").

1. Son of Pedahzur, and the captain of the tribe of Manasseh (Num. 7:54; 10:23), who was appointed to assist Moses in numbering the people at Sinai (1:10; 2:20). He made an offering, as tribal leader, at the dedication of the altar (7:54) and was chief of his tribe when starting on the march through the wilderness (10:23), c. 1440 B.C.

2. The grandson of the great Hillel, and himself a Pharisee and celebrated doctor of the law. His learning was so eminent and his character so revered that he is one of the seven who, among Jewish doctors only, have been honored with the title of *Rabban*. He was called the "Beauty of the Law," and it is a saying of the Talmud that "since Rabban Gamaliel died the glory of the law has ceased." He was a Pharisee, but anecdotes told of him show that he was not confined by the narrow bigotry of the sect. He rose above the prejudices of his party. Candor and wisdom seem to have been the features of his character. That agrees with what we read of him in Acts, where he was "respected by all the people" (W. J. Coneybeare and J. S. Howson, *Life and Epistles of Paul*). When the apostles were brought before the Sanhedrin and enraged the council by their courage and steadfastness, the latter sought to slay them. But this rash proposal was checked by Gamaliel, who, having directed the apostles to withdraw, thus addressed the council: "Men of Israel, take care what you propose to do with these men . . . stay away from these men and let them alone, for if this plan or action should be of men, it will be overthrown; but if it is of God, you will not be able to overthrow them" (Acts 5:34-39). His counsel prevailed, and the apostles were dismissed with a beating. We learn from 22:3 that he was the teacher of the apostle Paul. Ecclesiastical tradition makes him converted and baptized by Peter and Paul, together with his son Gamaliel and with Nicodemus. The Clementine Recognitions (1:65) state that he was secretly a Christian

at this time. But these notices are altogether irreconcilable with the esteem and respect in which he was held even in after times by the Jewish rabbis. The interference of Gamaliel on behalf of the apostles does not prove that he secretly approved of their doctrine. He was a dispassionate judge and reasoned in that affair with the tact of worldly wisdom and experience, urging that religious opinions usually gain strength by opposition and persecution (5:35-37). If not noticed, they are sure not to leave any lasting impression on the minds of the people if devoid of truth (v. 38), and it is vain to contend against them if true (v. 39).

BIBLIOGRAPHY: E. E. Ellis and M. Wilcox, eds., *Neotestamentica et Semitica* (1969), pp. 88-94; E. F. Harrison, *New Dimensions in New Testament Study*, ed., E. N. Longenecker and M. C. Tenney (1974), pp. 251-60.

GAME (Heb. *ṣayid*, the "chase"; *ṣûda*, Gen. 27:3; "venison," KJV). Meat taken in hunting (25:28; 27:5-33).

GAMES. This word occurs but once in Scripture (1 Cor. 9:25, NIV), though frequent reference is made to the things signified by it.

In Bible Lands. A taste for social games in oriental lands goes back to ancient times. Sir Leonard Woolley recovered a fine Sumerian game board from Ur in lower Mesopotamia dating from before 2500 B.C. Dice from nearly every locality of the ancient East have been recovered in ivory, pottery, and numerous other substances. Gaming boards from the Eighteenth Egyptian Dynasty from c. 1560-1350 B.C. have been recovered in large numbers. A gaming board with men of clay going back to almost 5000 B.C. has been discovered in Egypt. In the University Museum at Philadelphia there is a pink alabaster game board from Abydos dated c. 2900 B.C. Ivory strips with one side painted black were used in the place of dice. Marbles go back to early times and were popular in Eighteenth Dynasty Egypt. At Tell Beit Mirsim (Kirjath-sepher) in Palestine a complete set of gaming pieces has been recovered from a royal palace. The Hyksos horsemen who invaded Egypt played at draughts for diversion. They had a square ivory board and used pyramidlike dice. On the pavement in the basement of the Convent of the Sisters of Zion in Jerusalem a second-century gaming board has been discovered. Similar games may be seen cut into the stone of the Egnatian Way in Philippi where it passes through the agora and in the Basilica Julia in the Roman Forum. A gaming board from Crete from a royal recreation room is indescribably magnificent in silver, gold, ivory, and crystal. The board is more than one yard long; its ivory framework is set with gold plate trimmed with mosaic of rock crystal and blue enamel. Around its rim are clustered marguerites with crystal centers set in blue enamel. The top

of the board is incised with nautilus shells, descriptive of the Minoan islanders. Toys abound from ancient Bible times. Miniature houses, animals, and everyday scenes are depicted. Children of the well-to-do were well supplied with diversion. There are dolls with movable joints and lifelike hair. Toys from Tell Beit Mirsim include whistles, rattles, and dolls. In Egypt, elite social groups had hunting parties in the marshes. Carved sticks and wooden boomerangs were used. Harpoons, fishing spears, and bronze fishhooks have been found.

A second-century gaming board from a pavement in the basement of the Convent of the Sisters of Zion, Jerusalem.

Hebrew. With regard to juvenile games, the notices are few. The only recorded sports are keeping tame birds (Job 41:5) and imitating the proceedings of marriages or funerals (Matt. 11:16-17). Physically demanding games were not much followed by the Hebrews; the natural earnestness of their character and the influence of the climate alike indisposed them to exertion. The chief amusement of the men appears to have consisted in conversation and joking (Jer. 15:17; Prov. 26:19). Some type of sport involving young men is alluded to in 2 Sam. 2:14 (*see* marg.). The public games of the Hebrews seem to have been exclusively connected with military sports and exercises; and it is probable that in this way the Jewish youth were instructed in the use of the bow and sling (1 Sam. 20:20; 35:40; Judg. 20:16; 1 Chron. 12:2). In Jerome's day the usual sport consisted in lifting weights as a trial of strength, as was also practiced in Egypt. Dice are mentioned by the Talmudists, probably introduced from Egypt. Public games were altogether foreign to the spirit of Hebrew institutions; the great religious festivals supplied the pleasurable excitement and the feelings of national union that rendered the games of Greece so popular, and at the same time inspired the persuasion that such gatherings should be exclusively connected with religious duties. Accordingly the erection of a *gymnasium* by Jason was looked upon as a heathenish proceeding (1 Macc. 1:14; 2 Macc. 4:12-14). The entire absence of verbal or historical reference to this subject in the gospels shows how little it entered into Jewish life.

Grecian. The more celebrated of the Grecian games were four in number: the Isthmian, which took place on the Isthmus of Corinth in a grove sacred to Poseidon, from 589 B.C., and was held in the first month of spring, in the second and fourth years of each Olympiad (the games to which Paul referred in 1 Cor. 9:24-27); the Nemean, celebrated in the valley of Nemea in honor of Zeus; the Olympian, celebrated in honor of Zeus at Olympia; and the Pythian, held from 586 B.C. on the Crissaean plain, below Delphi, once in four years, in the third year of each Olympiad. The Olympic games were by far the most celebrated, and in describing these we describe the others, with certain differences. They were celebrated once every four years, from 776 B.C., and hence a period of four years was termed an Olympiad, by which period the Greeks reckoned their time. Seyffert reports: "The festival consisted of two parts: *1.* **The presentation of offerings,** chiefly to Zeus, but also to the other gods and heroes, on the part of the Eleans, the sacred embassies, and other visitors to the feast; and *2.* **The contests.** These consisted at first of a simple match in the *stadium* (1 Cor. 9:24-27), the race being run in heats of four, the winners in each heat competing together, the first in the final heat being proclaimed victor; later the runners had to make a circuit of the goal and return to the starting point; then came the long race, where the distance of the *stadium* had to be covered six, seven, eight, twelve, twenty, or twenty-nine times; the fivefold contest, consisting of leaping, running, quoit, spear throwing [discus and javelin throwing today] and wrestling; boxing; chariot racing in the hippodrome; *pancration* (a combination of wrestling and boxing); racing in armor, and competitions between heralds and trumpeters. Originally only men took part in the contests, but after 632 B.C. boys also shared in them. At first the contests were only open to freemen of pure Hellenic descent, but they were afterward opened to Romans. Permission to view the games was given to barbarians and slaves, while it was refused to women. All competitors were obliged to take an oath that they had spent at least ten months in preparation for the games and that they would not resort to any unfair tricks in the contests. Judges, varying in number from one to twelve, but after 348 B.C. always ten, kept guard over the strict observance of all regulations and maintained order. Transgressions of the laws of the games and unfairness on the part of competitors were punished by forfeiture of the prize or by fines of money, which went to the revenue of the temple. The name of the victor, as well as his home, were proclaimed

aloud by the herald and a palm branch presented him by the judges. The actual prize he only received on the last day of the festival. This was originally some article of value, but at the command of the Delphic oracle this custom was dropped, and the victors were graced by a wreath of the leaves of the sacred wild olive, said to have been originally planted by Neracles. Brilliant distinctions awaited the victor on his return home, for his victory was deemed to have reflected honor on his native land at large. He was accorded a triumph, and at Athens received 500 *drachmae,* the right to a place of honor at all public games, and board in the *prytaneum* for the rest of his life" (*Dict. Class. Antiq.*). These games were often held in the Hellenic towns of Palestine, being introduced by Herod into Caesarea and Jerusalem. In the former town he built a stone theater and a large amphitheater. Paul's epistles abound with allusions to the Greek contests (*see* 1 Cor. 4:9; 9:24-27; 15:32; Phil. 3:14; Col. 2:18; 2 Tim. 2:5; 4:7-8; Heb. 10:33; 12:1). A direct reference to the Roman beast-fights (Gk. *ethēriomachēsa*) is made by Paul when he says, "If from human motives I fought with wild beasts at Ephesus" (1 Cor. 15:32). Paul takes for granted that his readers were acquainted with what he describes in such strong language, and that they would take it figuratively, since they knew that his citizenship would exclude him from condemnation to such punishment. It is here a significant *figurative* description of the fight with strong and exasperated enemies.

BIBLIOGRAPHY: W. H. Norton, *Biblical Archaeologist* 19 (1956): 33-35; P. Montet, *Everyday Life in Ancient Egypt* (1958), pp. 99-102; O. Broneer, *Harvard Theological Review* 64 (1971): 169-87; D. L. Miller, *Journal of Biblical Literature* 90 (1971): 309-13.

GAMMAD. *See* Gammadim.

GAM'MADIM (gam'a-dim). Mentioned as defenders of the towers of Tyre (Ezek. 27:11). Various explanations have been given of the meaning of the term, but the most probable is "warriors," "brave men," used as an epithet applied to the native troops of Tyre (marg., "valorous ones"). The RV and NIV render "Men of Gamad." Perhaps Kumidi in northern Syria is meant, mentioned in the Amarna Letters.

GA'MUL (ga'mul; "rewarded"). The chief of the twenty-second division of priests, among whom the services of the sanctuary were distributed by lot in the time of David (1 Chron. 24:17), after 1000 B.C.

GANGRENE. *See* Diseases.

GAP (Heb. *pereṣ,* "breach"). An opening in a wall, "breaches" (Ezek. 13:5; Amos 4:3). Such a break was dangerous in the time of siege.

Figurative. The corruption was so great in Israel that Ezekiel (22:30) declares that not a man could be found who should enter into the gap as a righteous man or avert the judgment of destruction by his intercession.

GARDEN. An enclosed plot of ground carefully cultivated. The term (Heb. *gan;* Gk. *kēpos*) applies to flower gardens (Song of Sol. 6:2), spice plantations (4:16), orchards (6:11), vegetable gardens (Deut. 11:10), and probably parks (2 Kings 9:27; 21:18, 26). Bible lands have been for the most part denuded of their forests. Even groves of non-fruit-bearing trees are rare, except in the neighborhoods of cities and villages. The mountaintops are generally bare. The same is true of the tablelands of the interior. The grainfields and pastures are usually at a distance from the villages, not surrounded by fences or hedges but extending unbroken for miles in every direction, often without a single tree to diversify their surface. On the other hand the vegetable gardens, fruit orchards, mulberry groves, and trees that are cultivated for timber, such as the poplar, are grouped in and around the villages and towns, where they are accessible to the people, can be easily guarded from poachers, and above all where they can be irrigated from the water supply that is the life of the place.

The western landscape exhibits fields and pastures, divided by fences, walls, and hedgerows, interspersed with groves or scattered trees, and dotted with picturesque cottages, with here and there a village or town. The outskirts of the towns are usually more or less waste or barren. On the other hand the eastern landscape consists usually of broad areas sown with uniform crops of cotton or cereals, or terraced hillsides planted with vines, mulberries, or figs, or bleak mountaintops, often with scarcely a shrub to clothe the gray rocks. Not infrequently one may take in at a glance these varied features of the scenery without seeing a single human habitation. Suddenly, on rising above a knoll in the plains or turning an angle in the valleys, one comes upon a scene of ravishing beauty. A village, perched on the top of a rounded hill or clinging to the mountainside, or a city in a broad plain, surrounded and interspersed with luxuriant gardens, orchards, and groves of shade and timber trees, among which wind silvery streams, and over which is a haze that transforms all into a dream. As one enters this paradise the voice of the nightingale, the goldfinch, and the thrush, and the odors and bright colors of innumerable flowers and fruits please the senses. Such a scene greeted Muhammad as he looked from the barren chalk hills of Anti-Lebanon over the oasis of Damascus, and he feared to enter lest he should no longer care for paradise.

An Eastern garden is wholly unlike a Western. It is generally surrounded by a high wall of mud or stone (Prov. 24:31) or hedges or fences (Isa. 5:5), usually composed of a tangle of brambles, thorns, or canes to prevent intrusion. The door has a wooden bolt lock, by the side of which is a hole for the hand to be put through from the outside to reach the lock, which is fastened on the inner face (Song of Sol. 5:4-5). Over the gate or inside the garden is a booth or hut of boughs (Isa. 1:8), or a room, often in the shape of a tower (Mark 12:1), for the watchman. On the trees are scarecrows (Gk. *probaskanion*). These consist of the figure of a man perched on a limb, or of rags tied to the branches, or of the body of a bird. These gardens are not laid out with the precision of the West, with paths and beds. The vegetables, however, are planted in rows by the shallow ditches or furrows through which the water is conveyed to them (Ps. 1:3; Eccles. 2:6). This water is turned from one furrow to another either by a hoe or by moving the earthen bank that separates them by a shove of the foot (Deut. 11:10). Sometimes the vegetables are planted in a sunken parallelogram surrounded by a low, earthen wall, in which an opening is made by the foot until the space is filled with water, and then the earth is shoved back in the same way and retains the water. This process is repeated over the whole plantation. Many gardens have fountains or wells (Song of Sol. 4:15). To this allusion is made in the name *En-gannim,* "Fountain of Gardens," the modern Jennîn. In the orchards and gardens were planted vines, olives (Ex. 23:11), figs, pomegranates, walnuts (Song of Sol. 6:11), flowers (6:2), henna, spikenard, saffron, calamus, cinnamon, frankincense, myrrh, aloes, and various spices (4:13-14), and a great variety of vegetables and fruits. The gardens and parks of Solomon (Eccles. 2:5-6) are supposed to have been in Wadi 'Urtâs, and the "ponds" (v. 6) are still in good preservation. The "king's garden" (2 Kings 25:4; etc.) was near the pool of Siloam,

Terraces with watchtower near Beth-horon

at Bîr Ayyûb, which is probably En-rogel. G.E.P.

Figurative. A "watered garden" (Isa. 58:11; Jer. 31:12) was an emblem of fertility. A "tree planted by the water" (Jer. 17:8; cf. Ps. 1:3) was the emblem of the righteous. A waterless garden (Isa. 1:30) was a desert.

GARDEN HOUSE. The rendering in the NASB and KJV (2 Kings 9:27) of Heb. *bêt haggān*, in the reference to Ahaziah's fleeing "by the way of the garden house," although the NIV retains "Beth Haggan." "The 'garden house' cannot have formed a portion of the royal gardens, but must have stood at some distance from the city of Jezreel, as Ahaziah went by the road thither, and was not wounded till he reached the height of *Gur*, near Jibleam" (Keil, *Com.*). Some think that a place is designated. In Song of Sol. 1:16-17 the bride looks with delight upon the summer house shaded with verdure and containing a couch, inviting luxurious rest.

GARDENER. A class of workmen alluded to in Job 27:18 and mentioned in John 20:15. *See* Agriculture; Garden; Handicrafts: Gardener.

GA'REB (gā'reb; "scabby").

1. An Ithrite, i.e., a descendant of Jethro, or Jether, and one of David's mighty men (2 Sam. 23:38; 1 Chron. 11:40), about 1000 B.C.

2. A hill near Jerusalem, apparently NW (Jer. 31:39).

GARLAND (Gk. *stemma*). In heathen sacrifices it was customary to adorn the animals with fillets and garlands and also to put garlands on the head of the idol before sacrifice. These garlands were generally composed of such trees or plants as were esteemed most agreeable to the god who was to be worshiped. It is recorded (Acts 14:13) that the priest at Lystra came out to meet Paul and Barnabas with "oxen and garlands," but whether to adorn the oxen or the apostles is uncertain.

GARLIC, GARLICK. *See* Vegetable Kingdom.

GARMENTS. When the people proclaimed Jehu king they took their garments and put them under him on the stairs (2 Kings 9:13, KJV; NASB, "garment"; NIV "cloaks"), probably thus making an improvised throne for him. The spreading of garments in the streets before persons to whom it was intended to show particular honor was an ancient and general custom. Thus the people spread their garments in the way before Jesus (Matt. 21:8), while some strewed branches. The simple and uniform shape of garments encouraged the practice of gathering a large number together (Job 27:16; James 5:1-2; cf. Matt. 22:11-12) and of keeping them on hand to present to those whom it was desired to honor (Gen. 35:2; 2 Kings 5:5, "clothes"; 2 Chron. 9:24). *See* Dress.

BIBLIOGRAPHY: M. Radin, *Life of the People in Biblical*

Times (1948), pp. 125-41; A. C. Bouquet, *Everyday Life in New Testament Times* (1954), pp. 56-66.

GAR'MITE (gar'mīt). An epithet of *Keilah* (which see) in the obscure genealogy (1 Chron. 4:19) of *Mered* (which see).

GARNER. A place for storing away anything, especially a granary (Ps. 144:13). *See also* Storehouse.

GARRISON (from Heb. *nāṣab*, to "stand" firm). A military or fortified post (1 Sam. 13:23; 14:1, 6; etc.; 2 Sam. 23:14). In Ezek. 26:11, the KJV rendering, "garrisons," from Heb. *maṣṣēbôt*, is translated "pillars" in the NASB and NIV; the reference is to pillars dedicated to Baal, two of which are mentioned by Herodotus (2.44) as standing in the temple of Hercules at Tyre, one of gold, the other of emerald.

GASH'MU (gash'mū). A prolonged form (Neh. 6:6) of the name *Geshem* (which see).

GA'TAM (gā'tam; "puny"). The fourth named of the sons of Eliphaz the son of Esau, and founder of an Edomite tribe (Gen. 36:11, 16; 1 Chron. 1:36), about 1800 B.C.

GATE (generally the rendering of Heb. *sha'ar*, "opening," and Gk. *pulē*, from *pelō*, "to turn"). The entrance to enclosed grounds, buildings, cities, etc.

Various Names. In the Scriptures we find mentioned: (1) gates of cities, as the "Water Gate," "Gate of Benjamin," etc. (Neh. 1:3; 8:3; Jer. 37:13); the gate of Sodom (Gen. 19:1), of Gaza (Judg. 16:13); (2) gates of fortresses (Neh. 2:8); (3) gates of the *Temple* (which see); (4) gates of tombs (Matt. 27:60, NASB, "entrance"); (5) gates of prisons (Acts 12:10); (6) gates of camps (Ex. 32:26-27; *see* Heb. 13:11-12).

Material. We are not informed as to what materials the Israelites used for the enclosures and gates of their temporary camps. In Egyptian monuments such enclosures are indicated by lines of upright shields, with gates apparently of wicker, defended by a strong guard. Gates of bronze (Ps. 107:16; cf. Isa. 45:2) and of iron (Acts 12:10) were probably only sheeted with plates of these metals. Gates of crystal and of pearls are mentioned in Isa. 54:12; Rev. 21:21 and are supposed to refer to such doors, cut out of a single slab, as are occasionally found in ancient countries. Gates of wood were probably used in Gaza (Judg. 16:3). The doors themselves of the larger gates mentioned in Scripture were two-leaved, plated with metal, closed with locks, and fastened with metal bars (Deut. 3:5; Ps. 107:16; Isa. 45:1-2). Gates not defended by iron were of course liable to be set on fire by an enemy (Judg. 9:52). The gateways of royal palaces and even of private houses were often richly ornamented. Sentences from the law were inscribed on and above the gates (Deut. 6:9). In later Egyptian times the gates of the temples seem to have been intended as places of defense, if not the principal fortifications. The gateways of Assyrian cities were arched or square-headed, sometimes flanked by towers. The entrance to their own royal mansions was a simple passage between two colossal human-headed bulls or lions.

Purposes. The gate was the place for great assemblies of the people (Prov. 1:21), as they passed into and out of the city. This naturally led to the custom of using gates as places for public deliberation; reading the law and proclamations (2 Chron. 32:6; Neh. 8:1, 3); holding court (2 Sam. 15:2; cf. Deut. 16:18; 17:8; Ruth 4:11, marg.; etc.); gathering news (Gen. 19:1) and gossip (Ps. 69:12); attracting the attention of the sovereign or dignitary at his going out or coming in (Esther 2:19, 21; 3:2). The priests and prophets seem to have delivered their discourses, admonitions, and prophecies at the gates (Isa. 29:21; Amos 5:10; Jer. 17:19-20; 26:10). Criminals were punished outside the gates (1 Kings 21:10, 13; Acts 7:58; Heb. 13:12); Pashhur smote Jeremiah and put him in the stocks at the high gate of Benjamin (Jer. 20:2). In heathen cities the open spaces near the gates appear to have been sometimes used as places for sacrifice (Acts 14:13; cf. 2 Kings 23:8). Being positions of great importance, the gates of cities were carefully guarded and closed at nightfall (Deut. 3:5; Josh. 2:5, 7; Judg. 9:40, 44).

Figurative. Gates are thus sometimes taken as representing the city itself (Gen. 22:17; 24:60; Deut. 12:12; Judg. 5:8; Ruth 4:10, marg.; Pss. 87:2; 122:2). "The gates of righteousness" (118:19) are thought to mean the Temple gates. "The gates of death" (Job 38:17; Ps. 9:13) occur as symbols of power and empire. In Matt. 16:18 by the "gates of Hades" must be understood as all aggressions by the empire upon the Christian church.

BIBLIOGRAPHY: R. deVaux, *Ancient Israel: Its Life and Institutions* (1961), pp. 152-53, 166-67, 233-34.

GATEKEEPER (Heb. *shô'ēr*, from *sha'ar*, a "gate"; Gk. *thurōros;* "porter," KJV). As used in the KJV, *porter* has always the sense of doorkeeper, or *gatekeeper*, the term used in the NASB and NIV. In the later books of the OT, written after the building of the Temple, the term is applied to the Levites who had charge of the various entrances (1 Chron. 9:17; 15:18; 2 Chron. 23:19). In 1 Chron. 15:23-24, the KJV and NIV render "doorkeeper" ("gatekeeper," NASB) and in John 18:17 there is reference to the "slave girl . . . who kept the door." In 2 Sam. 18:26; 2 Kings 7:10-11, we meet the keeper of the city gates (cf. Acts 17:13); and a gatekeeper seems to have been usually stationed at the doors of sheepfolds. The gatekeepers of the Temple, who were *guards* as well, numbered 4,000 in David's time (1 Chron. 23:5), were divided into divisions (26:1-19), and

had their posts assigned them by lot (v. 13). They entered upon their service on the Sabbath day and remained a week (2 Kings 11:5-7; those mentioned in vv. 4, 10-11 are probably the king's bodyguard). *See also* Watch.

GATEWAY. *See* Gate.

GATH (gath; "winepress"). One of the cities of the Philistine pentapolis. The site is uncertain, for the city disappeared mysteriously by some unexplained disaster hinted at in Amos 6:2. Tell es-Safi, ten miles E of Ashdod and ten miles SE of Ekron, is favored as its site. This was a famous Crusader location, from which Richard the Lionhearted made his raids on caravans near Beersheba. Araq-'el-Menshiyeh, six miles W of Beit Jibrin, has also been defended as the location of Gath. Wherever the ancient city was, it was the nearest of the large Philistine towns to Hebrew territory. It had a reputation for huge men such as Goliath (1 Sam. 17:4). Achish was king at the time of David and befriended him during Saul's persecution, giving him the town of Ziklag. Subsequently David captured Gath (1 Chron. 18:1). Rehoboam, Solomon's son and successor, fortified it (2 Chron. 11:8). The Aramaean king, Hazael of Damascus, captured Gath in his advance on Jerusalem (2 Kings 12:17).   M.F.U.

BIBLIOGRAPHY: G. E. Wright, *Biblical Archaeologist* 29 (1966): 78-86; Y. Aharoni, *The Land of the Bible* (1979), pp. 287-97, 342, 345, 391-92.

GATH'-HE'PHER (gath-he'fer; "winepress of digging"; Josh. 19:13). A town of Zebulun, in lower Galilee, three miles from Nazareth. It was Jonah's birthplace (2 Kings 14:25), whose reputed tomb is shown at the village of Meshed, at the top of the hill, as Neby-Yûnas. Meshed dates only to Roman times, but Gath-hepher is thought to have stood nearby.

GATH-RIM'MON (gath-ri'mon; "winepress of Rimmon or pomegranate").

1. A Levitical city in the tribe of Dan. It was situated near Joppa, in the plain of Philistia (Josh. 19:45; 21:24; 1 Chron. 6:69). The Gath-rimmon of Josh. 21:25 is evidently a copyist's error, occasioned by the wandering of the eye to the previous verse.

2. Also a city of the same name in the half tribe of Manasseh, called in 1 Chron. 6:70 Bileam.

GAULANI'TIS (gō-la-nī'tis). A province ruled by Herod Antipas, E of the Lake of Galilee. The name is derived from "Golan," one of the cities of refuge in the territory of Manasseh (Josh. 20:8; 21:27; Deut. 4:43). *See* Golan.

GAY. The term in the KJV simply means "magnificent" or "sumptuous."

GA'ZA (ga'za; "stronghold"). Like Damascus, one of the most ancient cities of the world, being a border Canaanite city before Abraham. Its Heb. name is Azzah (KJV, Deut. 2:23; 1 Kings 4:24;

Jer. 25:20). It was the capital of the Philistines. Its earliest inhabitants were the Avvim, who were conquered by a Philistine tribe called the Caphtorim (cf. Josh. 13:2-3). It was the scene of Samson's prowess and humiliation (Judg. 16:1-3); also of Philip's Christian service (Acts 8:26). Modern Gaza (Ghuzzeh) serves as the administrative center of the Gaza Strip, which is crowded with Arab refugees. Ancient Gaza was for long identified with Tell El-Ajjul, four miles SW of modern Gaza; but that mound is now tentatively identified with Beth-Eglaim, and ancient Gaza is thought by some to have stood within the confines of the modern city.   H.F.V.

BIBLIOGRAPHY: T. G. Dowling, *Gaza, A City of Many Battles* (1913); M. Avi-Yonah, ed., *Encyclopedia of Archaeological Excavations in the Holy Land* (1976), 2: 408-17.

Synagogue in shape of star of David at Gaza

GA'ZATHITES. *See* Gazites.

GAZELLE. *See* Animal Kingdom.

GA'ZER. *See* Gezer.

GA'ZEZ (ga'zez; "shearer").
1. A "son" of Caleb (son of Hezron, son of Judah) by his concubine Ephah (1 Chron. 2:46).
2. A grandson of the same Caleb, through his son Haran (1 Chron. 2:46).

GA'ZITES (ga'zīts). The designation of the inhabitants of Gaza (Josh. 13:3; Judg. 16:2).

GAZ'ZAM (gaz'am). The progenitor of one of the families of the Temple servants that returned from the captivity with Zerubbabel (Ezra 2:48; Neh. 7:51), before 536 B.C.

GE'BA (gē'ba; "hill"). A Levitical city of Benjamin (Josh. 21:17; cf. 1 Kings 15:22; 1 Sam. 13:3, 16), situated N of Jerusalem. The Philistines were struck down from "Geba as far as Gezer" by David (2 Sam. 5:25), and Gaza was rebuilt by Asa (1 Kings 15:22; 2 Chron. 16:6). "From Geba to Beersheba" expressed the whole extent of the kingdom of Judah (2 Kings 23:8). It is identified with Jeba, near Michmash.

GEBAL (gē'bal).
1. An ancient Phoenician trading city on the Mediterranean, present-day Gebeil, twenty-five miles N of Beirut (Josh. 13:5, "the land of the Gebalite"; Ezek. 27:9). The Greeks called the city Byblos, meaning "book," because here "paper" was made from imported Egyptian papyrus reeds. On this ancient writing material expense accounts, state correspondence, religious texts, and important documents were inscribed. The Phoenicians of Gebal were expert masons, especially in stonecutting (1 Kings 5:18). Gebalites were also famous for their shipbuilding and caulking (Ezek. 27:9). These famous ships of antiquity were known as "Byblos travelers" and ran between Phoenicia and Egypt. Their cargo consisted of cedar for mummy cases, oils for mummification, fancy woods, etc., returning with gold, metalwares, perfumes, and papyrus reeds. Ships of Byblos sailed the Mediterranean, as did those of Tyre and Sidon. One of the features of the Amarna Letters is the correspondence of Rib-addi with the Egyptian pharaoh; Wenamon tells of his visit to Byblos around 1100 B.C. Near Byblos the voluptuous Adonis rites in honor of Astarte were notorious. Excavations at Gebal were undertaken by Pierre Montet from 1921 to 1924 and continued by Maurice Dunand from 1925 almost until the Lebanese troubles began in 1975. A cross section of Phoenician development from about 5000 B.C. to the Roman period was obtained from the excavation of this single site. The city had an important period of development during the third millennium B.C., when it was surrounded by a massive wall encompassing an area of about twelve acres. Important temples that have come to light are one to Baalat Gebal (lady of Gebal, dating about 2800 B.C.), the "L-shaped temple" (dating a century or more later), and the "obelisk temple" (dating c. 1800 B.C.). Another significant discovery was the royal necropolis, with nine tombs of kings of Byblos. Most ornate was the sarcophagus of Ahiram with its early alphabetic inscription dating about 1000 B.C.

Ruins at Gebal (Byblos)

2. NE Edom, known also as Teman (Ps. 83:7), allied itself with Moabites and Arabians against Israel. H.F.V.

GE'BER (gē'ber; "warrior"). The son of Uri and one of Solomon's deputies, having jurisdiction over Gilead (1 Kings 4:19). His son (probably) had charge of Ramoth-gilead (v. 13), after 1000 B.C.

GE'BIM (ge'bim; "cisterns," Jer. 14:3; in Isa. 33:4, "locusts"). A city of Benjamin, between Anathoth and Nob, mentioned only in Isa. 10:31 and identified by various scholars with Khirbet ed-Duweir. Others suggest Bath el-Battash.

GECK'O. *See* Animal Kingdom.

GEDALI'AH (ged-a-lī'a; "made great by Jehovah").
1. The son of Jeduthun and his second assistant in the Levitical choir selected by David for the Temple service (1 Chron. 25:3, 9), before 960 B.C.
2. A descendant of Jeshua, and one of the priests who divorced their Gentile wives after the Babylonian captivity (Ezra 10:18), 456 B.C.
3. The son of Pashhur, and one of the Jewish officials who, hearing a prophecy of Jeremiah, conspired to accuse and imprison the prophet (Jer. 38:1, 4), 589 B.C.
4. The son of Ahikam (Jeremiah's protector, Jer. 26:24) and grandson of Shaphan. After the destruction of the Temple (587 B.C.), Nebuchadnezzar departed from Judea, leaving Gedaliah as governor. He was stationed, with a Chaldean guard, at Mizpah. Gedaliah had inherited his father's respect for Jeremiah (Jer. 40:5) and was, moreover, enjoined by Nebuzaradan to look after his safety and welfare (39:11-14). Having established his government at Mizpah, the inhabitants, who had fled at the advance of the Chaldean armies when the troops of Zedekiah were dispersed in the plains of Jericho, quitting their retreats, began to gather around him. Gedaliah advised submission and quietness, promising them, on this condition, the undisturbed enjoyment of their possessions. The labors of the field were resumed, and they "gathered in wine and summer fruit in great abundance" (40:12). Jeremiah joined Gedaliah, and Mizpah became the resort of Jews from various quarters (40:6, 12), many of whom, as might be expected at the end of a long war, were in a demoralized state, unrestrained by religion, patriotism, or prudence. The wise, gentle, and prosperous reign of Gedaliah did not secure him from the foreign jealousy of Baalis, king of Ammon, and the domestic ambition of Ishmael, a member of the royal family of Judah (Josephus *Ant.* 10.9.3). The latter came to Mizpah with a secret purpose of destroying Gedaliah. Gedaliah, generously refusing to believe a friendly warning that he received of the intended treachery, was murdered with his Jewish and Chaldean followers, two months after his appointment. After his death the Jews, anticipating the resentment of the king of Babylon, gave way to despair. Many, forcing Jeremiah to accompany them, fled to Egypt under Johanan (2 Kings 25:22-26; Jer. 40:13; 41:18).

GE'DER (ge'der; "walled"). A city of the Canaanites taken by Joshua (Josh. 12:13); identical probably with *Gedor* (which see).

GEDE'RAH (ge-de'ra; "sheepcote"). A city of Judah with a Phoenician title. It is the feminine form of Geder (Josh. 12:13), and its plural is Gederoth (15:41). Identified with Jedireh about twelve miles SW of Lod.

GED'ERATHITE (ged'e-ra-thīt). An epithet of Jozabad, one of David's famous warriors at Ziklag (1 Chron. 12:4), so called from being a native of Gedor or Gederah.

GED'ERITE (ged'e-rīt). An epithet of Baal-hanan, David's overseer of olive and sycamore groves in the low plains of Judah (1 Chron. 27:28), probably so called from being a native of Geder or Gederah.

GED'EROTH (ged'e-rōth; "fortresses"). A town in the "valley" of Judah (Josh. 15:41) captured by the Philistines from Ahaz (2 Chron. 28:18). Possibly modern Qatra, about eleven miles SW of Lod.

GEDEROTHA'IM (ged'e-rō-tha'im; "double wall"). Named (Josh. 15:36) among the valley towns of Judah.

GE'DOR (ge'dor; "a wall").
1. A leader of the Benjamites resident at Jerusalem (1 Chron. 8:31; 9:37), before 536 B.C.
2. An ancient city in the mountains of Judah (Josh. 15:58), some of whose inhabitants joined David at Ziklag (1 Chron. 12:7). It was probably to this town that Jozabad the Gederathite belonged (12:4). Some identify it with Geder. The village is now called Jedûr and is located about seven miles N of Hebron.
3. It is said in 1 Chron. 4:39, "They went to the entrance of Gedor, even to the east side of the valley," etc. It is impossible to determine exactly the location of this Gedor, but it is not to be identified with no. 2.

GE HARASHIM, GE-HAR'ASHIM, (gē-har'-ashim; "craftsmen"). The NASB and NIV render "Joab the father of Ge-harashim" (1 Chron. 4:14). The term refers to the "valley of craftsmen" (cf. 4:14, marg.; Neh. 11:35), not far from Jerusalem. The KJV renders "Charashim."

GEHA'ZI (ge-hā'zī). The servant of Elisha. The first mention of him is his reminding his master of the best mode of rewarding the kindness of the Shunammite woman (2 Kings 4:12-17). He was

461

present when she told the prophet of her son's death and was sent by Elisha to lay his staff upon the face of the child, which he did without effect (4:25-36). The most remarkable incident in his career is that which caused his ruin. When Elisha declined the rich gifts of Naaman, Gehazi coveted at least a portion of them. He therefore ran after the retiring chariots and requested, in his master's name, a portion of the gifts, on the pretense that visitors had arrived for whom he was unable to provide. He asked for a talent of silver and two garments, and the grateful Syrian made him take two talents instead of one. Having hid the spoil, he appeared before Elisha, who asked him where he had been. Upon his answering, "Your servant went nowhere," the prophet denounced his crime and told him that the leprosy of Naaman should cleave to him and to his seed forever. "So he went out from his presence a leper as white as snow" (5:20-27). We afterward find Gehazi recounting to King Joram the great deeds of Elisha, and, in the providence of God, it happened that while he was speaking of the restoration of the child of the Shunammite woman, she appeared with her son before the king to claim her house and lands, of which she had been despoiled during the recent famine. Struck by the coincidence, the king immediately granted her request (8:1-6).

GEHEN'NA (ge-hen'a; Gk. *geenna,* for the Heb. *hinnōm,* the "Valley of Hinnom"). A deep, narrow glen to the S of Jerusalem where the Jews offered their children to Molech. The OT renders "valley of the son of Hinnom," or "Ben Hinnom" (2 Kings 23:10; Jer. 7:31; 19:2-6). In later times it served as a receptacle of all sorts of putrefying matter and all that defiled the holy city, and so became the representative or image of the place of everlasting punishment, especially on account of its ever-burning fires; and to this fact the words of Christ refer when He mentions "the unquenchable fire." "The passages of the New Testament show plainly that the word 'gehenna' was a popular expression for 'hell' of which Jesus and his apostles made use, but it would be erroneous to infer that Jesus and his apostles merely accommodated themselves to the popular expression, without believing in the actual state of the lost." In the NT the word *gehenna* ("hell") falls many times from the lips of Christ in most awesome warning of the consequences of sin (Matt. 5:22, 29-30; 10:28; 18:9; 23:15, 33; Mark 9:43, 45, 47; Luke 12:5). He describes it as a place where their "worm" never dies and their "fire" is never to be quenched. Gehenna is identical in meaning with the "lake of fire" (Rev. 19:20; 20:10, 14-15). Moreover, the "second death" and "the lake of fire" are identical terms (20:14). These latter scriptural expressions describe the eternal state of the wicked as forever separated from God and consigned to the special abode of

unrepentant angels and people in the eternal state. The term *second* is employed relating to the preceding physical death of the wicked in unbelief and rejection of God (John 8:21-24). That the "second death" ("lake of fire" or gehenna) is not annihilation is shown clearly by Rev. 19:20 and 20:10. After 1,000 years in the lake of fire the Beast and false prophet still exist there undestroyed. The phrase "forever and ever" ("to the ages of the ages"), describing the destiny of the lost in Heb. 1:8, also applies to the duration of the throne of God as eternal in the sense of being unending. Thus is represented the punishment of the wicked. Gehenna, moreover, is not to be confused with *Hades* or *Sheol* (which see), which describe the intermediate state of the wicked previous to the judgment and the eternal state. *See* Hades; Lake of Fire; Hell; Hinnom.

M.F.U.

GEL'ILOTH (gel'i-lōth; "circles"). A place on the boundary of Judah and Benjamin (Josh. 18:17) and probably another form of Gilgal (15:7).

GEM. *See* Jewel, Jewelry.

GEMAL'LI (ge-mal'i; "camel driver"). The father of Ammiel, the Danite representative among those who explored the land of Canaan (Num. 13:12), c. 1440 B.C.

GEMARI'AH (gem-a-rī'a; "Jehovah has perfected").

1. The son of Hilkiah who, with Elasah son of Shaphan, was sent to Babylon as ambassador by King Zedekiah. They also took charge of a letter from Jeremiah to the Jewish captives at Babylon, advising them to settle peaceably in the land of captivity, promising deliverance after seventy years and warning them against false prophets (Jer. 29:3), about 597 B.C.

2. The son of Shaphan, one of the nobles of Judah, and a scribe of the Temple in the time of Jehoiakim. Baruch read aloud the prophecies of Jeremiah to the people at the official chamber of Gemariah (or from a window in it), which was attached to the new gate of the Temple built by King Jotham (Jer. 36:10; cf. 2 Kings 15:35). Gemariah's son Micaiah having reported this to his father, Baruch was invited to repeat the reading at the scribe's chamber in the palace before Gemariah and others, who gave an account of the matter to the king (Jer. 36:11-20). He, with the others, heard the divine message with fear. Gemariah and two others entreated the king not to destroy the roll (36:21-25), about 608 B.C.

GENEALOGY (Gk. *genealogia;* Heb. *sēper tôleḏôt,* "the book of the generations"). Accounts or family registers tracing the descent and ancestral relationships of tribes and families. The older histories being usually drawn up on a genealogical basis, "genealogy" is often extended to the whole history, as "the book of the genealogy of

Jesus Christ" includes the whole history contained in that gospel (Matt. 1:1; cf. Gen. 2:4; etc.). This genealogical form of history was not peculiar to the Hebrew or the Semitic races, for the earliest Greek histories were also genealogies.

The Redemptive Purpose of God. God's redemptive purpose took from the first a specific family direction, and it was important that at least the more prominent links in the successive generations of those more closely connected with the development of that purpose should be preserved to future times. It is the genealogy of mankind in its bearing on redemption—reaching through the line of Seth to Noah, then from Noah through the line of Shem to Abraham, then again through the lines of Isaac, Jacob, Judah, and David to Christ— over which the providence of God most carefully watched and which has been most fully exhibited in the historical records of Scripture. The promise of the land of Canaan to the seed of Abraham, Isaac, and Jacob successively, and the separation of the Israelites from the Gentile world; the expectation of the Messiah to spring from the tribe of Judah; the exclusively hereditary priesthood of Aaron with its dignity and emoluments; the long succession of kings in the line of David; and the whole division and occupation of the land upon genealogical principles by the tribes, families, and houses of fathers, gave a deeper importance to the science of genealogy among the Jews than perhaps any other nation.

Different Genealogies. "In Gen. 35:22-26 we have a formal account of the sons of Jacob, the patriarchs of the nation, repeated in Ex. 1:1-5. In Gen. 46 we have an exact genealogical census of the house of Israel at the time of Jacob's going down to Egypt. When the Israelites were in the wilderness of Sinai their number was taken by divine command 'after their families, by the house of their fathers.' According to these genealogical divisions they pitched their tents, and marched, and offered their gifts and offerings, chose the spies, and the whole land of Canaan was parceled out among them."

David, in establishing the Temple services, divided the priests and Levites into divisions and companies, each under the family leader. When Hezekiah reopened the Temple and restored the Temple services, he reckoned the whole nation by genealogies. Zerubbabel's first care seems to have been to take a census of those who had returned from Babylon and to settle them according to their genealogies (see 1 Chron. 9:1-3). In like manner Nehemiah gathered together "the nobles, the officials, and the people to be enrolled by genealogies" (Neh. 7:5). That this system was continued in later times, at least as far as the priests and Levites were concerned, we learn from 12:22; and we have incidental evidence from the apocryphal books (1 Macc. 2:1-5; 8:17; 14:29) of the continued care of the Jews later still

to preserve their genealogies. Another proof is the existence of our Lord's genealogy in two forms, as given by Matthew and Luke. The mention of Zacharias as "of the division of Abija," of Elizabeth as "from the daughters of Aaron," and of Anna the daughter of Phanuel as "of the tribe of Asher" are further indications of the same thing (Luke 1:5; 2:36). From all this it is abundantly manifest that the Jewish genealogical records continued to be kept till near the destruction of Jerusalem; there can be little doubt that the registers of the Jewish tribes and families perished at the destruction of Jerusalem, and not before.

"The Jewish genealogies have two forms, one giving the generations in a descending, the other in an ascending scale. Examples of the descending form may be seen in Ruth 4:18-22, or 1 Chron. 3; of the ascending 1 Chron. 6:33-43, KJV; Ezra 7:1-5. Females are named in genealogies when there is anything remarkable about them, or when any right or property is transmitted through them (see Gen. 11:29; 22:23; 25:1-4; 35:22-26; Ex. 6:23; Num. 26:33; 1 Chron. 2:4, 19, 35, 50, etc.)" (Smith, *Bib. Dict.*, s. v.).

Abbreviated Genealogies. B. B. Warfield showed more than a half-century ago that the Bible genealogies contained gaps ("The Antiquity and Unity of the Human Race," *Studies in Theology* [1932], pp. 235-58). The genealogies in Ex. 6:16-24, Ezra 7:1-5, and Matt. 1:1-17 contain omissions. This is most certainly the case also in the genealogies of Gen. 5 and 11. To use these genealogical lists in Genesis to calculate the creation of man (c. 4004 B.C.), as Archbishop Ussher has done, is not only unwarranted from a comparative study of scriptural genealogies, but incontestably disproved by the well-attested facts of modern archaeology. The total length of the period from the creation of man to the Flood and from the Flood to Abraham is not specified in Scripture. That the genealogies of Gen. 5 and 11 are most assuredly drastically abbreviated and have names that are highly selective is suggested by the fact that each list contains only ten names, ten from Adam to Noah and ten from Shem to Abraham. It is quite evident that symmetry was the goal in constructing these genealogical lists rather than a setting forth of unbroken descent from father to son, in contrast to modern registers of pedigree. Such symmetry with the omission of certain names is obvious from the genealogy of Matt. 1:1-17. This fact is further corroborated by the evident latitude used in ancient Semitic languages in the expressions "begat," "bare," "father," and "son." This usage is completely contrary to English idiom. Thus to "beget" a "son" may mean to beget an actual child or a grandchild or a great-grandchild, or even distant descendants. Usage extends to tribes or countries (Gen. 10:2-22) and even to nonblood relationship. Jehu, the usurper and founder of a new dynasty in Israel and with no blood connection whatever to the house of Omri, is nevertheless called "son of Omri" by Shalmaneser III of Assyria (Daniel David Luckenbill, *Ancient Records of Assyria and Babylonia,* vol. 1, sec. 590). Nebuchadnezzar is called the "father" of Belshazzar, who was actually the son of Nabonidus, a usurper (Dan. 5:2). Accordingly, as J. H. Raven says in the regular recurring formula "A lived . . . years and begat B, and A lived after he begat B . . . years and begat sons and daughters, and B lived . . . years and begat C," B may not be the literal son of A but a distant descendant. If so, the age of A is his age at the birth of the child from whom B is descended. Between A and B, accordingly, many centuries may intervene. The Genesis genealogical lists are not intended to divulge the antiquity of man upon the earth but to set forth in outstanding representative names the line of the promised Redeemer (Gen. 3:15) from Adam to Abraham and to show the effects of sin and the altered conditions brought about by the Flood upon human vitality and longevity. Added evidence that the genealogies of chaps. 5 and 11 contain extensive breaks is demonstrated by the fact that they allow only about 4,000 years from the creation of Adam to Christ. On the other hand, modern archaeology clearly traces sedentary pottery cultures such as that from Tell Halaf well before 4000 B.C.

BIBLIOGRAPHY: W. H. Green, *Bibliotheca Sacra* (1890): 285-304; B. B. Warfield, *Princeton Theological Review* 9 (1911): 1-17; A. Malamat, *Journal of the American Oriental Society* 88 (1968): 163-73; M. D. Johnson, *The Purpose of Biblical Genealogies* (1969); R. R. Wilson, *Genealogy and History in the Biblical World* (1977).

GENEALOGY OF JESUS CHRIST. *See* Chronology, New Testament; Jesus.

GENERATION. The word *generation* in the Scriptures is used in at least three shades of meaning that are closely related and grow out of each other. (1) The basic meaning is that of the production of offspring, in which sense it is applied to the offspring of an individual or successions of offspring noted in a genealogical table and called a "book of the generations," or (NIV) "written account" (Gen. 5:1; 37:2; Matt. 1:17), i.e., lists of successive lines of descent from father to son. (2) A period of time. Differing as the intervals do in this respect, *generation* could never be intended to mark a definite period and must be understood with considerable latitude. The term is used in the sense of time or successive divisions of time. For *generation* in the sense of a *definite* period of time, see Gen. 15:16 and Deut. 23:2-3, 8. As an indefinite period of time: for time *past,* see 32:7; Isa. 58:12, KJV; for time *future,* see Pss. 45:17; 72:5. (3) The word is also taken to denote the persons actually constituting a specific generation, as exponents of its state or character, as in "this generation" (Matt. 11:16),

"an evil and adulterous generation" (12:39), "unbelieving and perverted generation" (17:17), "crooked and perverse generation" (Phil. 2:15). Delitzsch (*Com.,* on Isa. 53:8) thus defines generation: "We must adhere to the ordinary usage, according to which *dôr* signifies an age, or the men living in a particular age; also, in an ethical sense, the entire body of those who are connected together by similarity of disposition (Ps. 14:5)."

BIBLIOGRAPHY: R. R. Wilson, *Genealogy and History in the Biblical World* (1977), pp. 158-59; P. J. Wiseman, *Clues to Creation in Genesis* (1977), pp. 34-45.

GEN'ESIS (jen'e-sis; the book of origins; Gk. *genesis,* "origin"). Traditionally the introductory book of the entire body of Hebrew sacred literature and of revealed truth in general.

Name. The book takes its name from the title given to it in the LXX version, which is derived from the heading of its ten parts *hē biblos geneseōs* (2:4; 5:1; 6:9; 10:1; 11:10; 11:27; 25:12; 25:19; 36:1; 37:2). The Hebrews call the book *berē'shît,* meaning "in the beginning." The recurring phrase "these are the *tôledôt* of" completes the various sections and points to immediately preceding material. It does not serve as a section heading and is comparable to the colophon that ended ancient Babylonian tablets.

Design. As the book of beginnings Genesis recounts the beginning of the physical creation of all plant, animal, and human life, as well as human institutions and social relationships. The book illustrates (as does the entire Bible) the principle of selection. Those events necessary to introduce the drama of human redemption are narrated: the creation, the Fall, the Flood, the call of Abraham, and mention of the promised Redeemer (3:15-16; 12:1-3; 49:10).

Outline.

I. The primeval history of mankind (1:1–11:26)
   A. The creation (1:1–2:25)
   B. From the Fall to the Flood (3:1–5:32)
   C. The Flood (6:1–9:29)
   D. From the Flood to Abraham (10:1–11:26)
II. The patriarchal history of Israel (11:27–50:26)
   A. Abraham (11:27–25:10)
   B. Isaac (25:11–28:9)
   C. Jacob (28:10–36:43)
   D. Jacob's sons, particularly Joseph (37:1–50:26)

Literary Scheme. The narrative of Genesis is hung upon a genealogical skeleton marked by the phrase that occurs ten times: "These are the generations [*tôledôt,* "histories," "family histories," "narratives"] of."

Critical View. Critics partition the book of Genesis and view it as composed of composite sources pieced together by a late exilic or postexilic editor. J, the Jehovist, possibly wrote about 850 B.C., in the S (Judah), employing the name Jehovah. E, the Elohist, is said to have used the name *Elohim*, writing about 750 B.C., in the N (Ephraim). The narrative sections J and E were allegedly fitted into the scriptural history of the origin of the Jewish nation, called the Priestly Code (P), about 500 B.C. This documentary theory, which was subtly developed, highly plausible, and universally popular, is a highly traditional product of modern rationalistic skepticism and is based on false literary criteria, unsound philosophic presuppositions, and a manifest enmity against the miraculous and the prophetic elements that constitute the foundation of the Pentateuch. (*See* R. K. Harrison, *Introduction to the Old Testament* [1969], pp. 542-65.)

Chronology. Genesis leaves both the date of the creation of the world and of man an unsettled question. According to Gen. 1:1 the earth was created in the dateless past. The appearance of man upon the earth is described as accomplished by a direct act of God that occurred at least more than 4,000 years B.C. and perhaps as early as 7,000-10,000 B.C. However, any considerably earlier date for the creation of man such as the evolutionists' greatly expanded ages is out of focus with the Genesis narratives. For detailed discussion of chronology as it relates to the book of Genesis, *see* Abbreviated Genealogies, under Genealogy.

BIBLIOGRAPHY: H. C. Leupold, *Exposition of Genesis*, 2

vols. (1942); S. R. Driver, *The Book of Genesis*, Westminster Commentary (1943); W. H. G. Thomas, *Genesis: A Devotional Commentary* (1946); G. von Rad, *Genesis: A Commentary* (1961); E. A. Speiser, *Genesis*, Anchor Bible (1964); J. J. Davis, *Paradise to Prison: Studies in Genesis* (1975); H. Alford, *The Book of Genesis* . . . (1979); G. Bush, *Notes on Genesis*, 2 vols. (1979); R. S. Candlish, *Studies in Genesis* (1979); W. H. Green, *Unity of the Book of Genesis* (1979); F. J. Delitzsch, *A New Commentary on Genesis*, 2 vols. (1979); G. Ch. Aalders, *Genesis*, Bible Student's Commentary (1981); W. Brueggemann, *Genesis*, Interpretation (1982); J. Strahan, *Hebrew Ideals in Genesis* (1982).

GENITALS. *See* Flesh.

GENNES'ARET (ge-nes'a-ret; "garden of riches"). The earliest use of the name in 1 Macc. 11:67, Genesar. The Targums identify the name with Chinnereth (Deut. 3:17; Josh. 19:35), which is applied both to the lake and the town.

1. The town stood on the W shore of the lake, called in the OT *Chinnereth* (which see), or Kinnereth.

2. The district was a small region of Galilee, on the W shore of the lake, visited by Jesus on His way S to Capernaum (Matt. 14:34).

3. The lake was called in Luke 5:1 the *Sea of Galilee* (which see).

GENTILE.

Old Testament. The Heb. *gôyim* signified the nations, the surrounding nations, *foreigners* as opposed to Israel (Neh. 5:8).

New Testament. (1) The Gk. *ethnos* in the

Gennesaret and the Sea of Galilee

465

singular means a people or nation (Matt. 24:7; Acts 2:5; etc.), and even the Jewish people (Luke 7:5; 23:2; etc.). It is only in the plural that it is used for heathen (Gentiles). (2) *Hellē,* lit., Greek (John 7:35; Rom. 3:9). The KJV is not consistent in its treatment of this word, sometimes rendering it "Greek" (Acts 14:1; 17:4; Rom. 1:16; 10:12), sometimes "Gentile" (2:9-10; 3:9; 1 Cor. 10:32). The latter use of the word seems to have arisen from the almost universal adoption of the Gk. language.

Relation to Israel. What rendered the Jews a distinct and honored class was simply their election by God to the place of His peculiar people, by which they became the recognized depositories of His truth and the consecrated channels of His working among men. The distinction between Israel and other nations, as was shown in the covenant with Abraham, was to be only for a time; and believing Gentiles in no age were excluded from sharing in the benefits conferred upon the Jews when they showed themselves willing to enter into the bond of the covenant.

Hedged in by a multitude of special institutions and taught to consider nonobservance of these customs as uncleanness, as well as blinded by an intense national pride, the Jews seemed often to regard the heathen as only existing for the purpose of punishing the apostasy of Israel (Deut. 28:49-50; 1 Kings 8:33; etc.) or of undergoing vengeance for their enmity toward her (Isa. 63:6).

"Considering the wall of strict separation which, as regards matters of religion the Jews had erected between themselves and the Gentiles, it would not readily occur to one that these latter were also permitted to take part in the worship at Jerusalem. It may be accounted for, however, by reflecting how formal and superficial the connection often is between *faith* and *worship.* To present a sacrifice in some famous sanctuary was often no more than an expression, on the part of the offerer, of a cosmopolitan piety, and not intended to be an expression of the man's creed. This might take place at Jerusalem, for there was no reason why the Jewish people and their priests should discountenance an act intended to do honor to their God, even though it were purely an act of politeness. Accordingly we find the Old Testament itself proceeding on the assumption that a sacrifice might be legitimately offered even by a Gentile" (Lev. 22:25; Schürer, *History of the Jewish People in the Time of Christ,* div. 2, 1:299ff.; also 2:311).

The form that the adhesion of Gentiles to Judaism assumed, and the extent to which they observed the ceremonial laws of the Jews, were of a varied character. Tertullian speaks of Gentiles who, while observing several Jewish ordinances, continued notwithstanding to worship their own deities. On the other hand, those who submitted to circumcision thereby bound themselves to observe the whole law to its fullest extent. Between these two extremes there would be a manifold series of gradations. The "God-fearing" Gentiles mentioned (Acts 10:2, 22; 13:16, 26, 43; 17:17) were probably those who adopted the Jewish mode of worship and attended the synagogues but restricted themselves to certain leading points of the ceremonial law, and so were regarded as outside the fellowship of Jewish communities (Schürer, 2:311ff.). *See* Heathen.

In Prophecy. In the prophetic Word there is a clear distinction between "Jews . . . Greeks or . . . the church of God" (1 Cor. 10:32). In this present age all the saved are members of "the church of God." Unsaved people are either Jews, who are nationally set aside in the present age, or Gentiles. The Word of God clearly outlines the future of the Gentiles. Having their origin in Adam they consequently also have their natural headship in him as do unsaved Jews. Having partaken of the Fall, they are nevertheless the subjects of prophecy that foretells that some of them will yet share as a subordinate people with Israel in her coming kingdom glory (Isa. 2:4; 60:3, 5, 12; 62:2; Acts 15:17). Their condition from Adam to Christ rests upon a fivefold indictment: "separate from Christ, excluded from the commonwealth of Israel, and strangers to the covenants of promise, having no hope and without God in the world" (Eph. 2:12). Consequent upon the death, resurrection, and ascension of Christ, and the advent of the Spirit, admission to gospel privilege was accorded to Gentiles (Acts 10:45; 11:17-18). In the present age from Pentecost to the out-taking of the Body of Christ, God is calling out an elect company from among the Gentiles (15:14) to form the church. The salvation of this age is not a question of sharing Israel's earthly covenants, which even Israel is not now enjoying, but rather the grace brought by Jesus Christ in being privileged to partake of a heavenly citizenship. Prophecy reveals, too, that the mass of Gentiles will not in the present age enter by faith into those blessings. Consequently, Gentiles move on as "the nations" to the end of their stewardship as earth rulers. The termination of this period will be the end of the "times of the Gentiles" (Luke 21:24; cf. Dan. 2:36-44). The nations will thus pass through the Tribulation judgments and will be judged as nations at the second coming of Christ (Matt. 25:31-46). The basis of the judgment will be the treatment of the Jew—"these brothers of Mine." The sheep will enter into the millennial kingdom; the goats, into everlasting fire prepared for the devil and his angels (25:41). "And these will go away into eternal punishment, but the righteous into eternal life" (25:46). The Gentile is also distinctly revealed in the eternal state. After the creation of the new heavens and the new earth, when the New Jerusalem comes down from God out of heaven (Rev. 3:12; 21:2, 10), "the nations shall walk by its light, and the kings of the earth shall bring their glory into it ... and they shall bring the glory and the honor of the nations into it" (21:24-26). Gentiles thus always remain distinct from the nation Israel; therefore, there is no defensible reason for misapplying this great body of Scripture bearing on the Gentiles either to the Jew or to the church of God. *See* Jews; Heathen.

BIBLIOGRAPHY: J. Jeremias, *Jesus' Promise to the Nations* (1958); J. F. Walvoord, *The Nations in Prophecy* (1967).

GENTILES, COURT OF THE. *See* Temple.

GENTLENESS (Heb. *'ānāwâ*, "condescension," Ps. 18:35; Gk. *epieikeia*, "clemency," 2 Cor. 10:1). "All God's going back from the strictness of his rights as against men, all his allowing of their imperfect righteousness and giving a value to that which, rigidly estimated, would have none; all his refusal to exact extreme penalties; all his remembering whereof we are made and measuring his dealings with us thereby" (Trench, *Synonyms of the N.T.*); giving all this, God demands the same spirit of gentleness from us toward others (Matt. 18:23-35). It is the helping grace of God, that practical hearkening on the part of God when called upon for help, and which was manifested in the bettered condition of the psalmist (2 Sam. 22:36; Ps. 18:35). The Gk. words rendered "gentle" or "gentleness," carrying the underlying meaning of affable, kindly, and humble (Gal 6:1; 2 Tim. 2:25; Titus 3:2).

GENU'BATH (ge-nu'bath; "theft"). The son of Hadad, of the royal Edomite family, by the sister of Tahpenes, the queen of Egypt, and reared in Pharaoh's household (1 Kings 11:20). He was born in the palace of Pharaoh, was weaned by the queen herself, and was on the same footing as the sons of the king.

GE'RA (ge'ra). The name of at least three Benjamites, perhaps from *gēr* (Heb. "sojourner").

1. The son of Bela and grandson of Benjamin (1 Chron. 8:3); probably the same as the one mentioned (with some confusion) in vv. 5, 7, unless one of these is identical with no. 2. In Gen. 46:21 he is given as the son of Benjamin and appears there among the descendants of Jacob at the time of his removal to Egypt, about 1871 B.C. In 1 Chron. 7:7, Uzzi occupies the same position as Gera does elsewhere in the genealogy.

2. The father (or ancestor) of Ehud the judge (Judg. 3:15), before 1295 B.C.

3. The father of Shimei, who cursed David when he fled from Absalom (2 Sam. 16:5; 19:16, 18-23; 1 Kings 2:8), before 966 B.C.

GERAH. The smallest weight and coin among the Hebrews. *See* Metrology.

GE'RAR (ge'rar). A Philistine city figuring prominently in the patriarchal narratives of Abraham (Gen. 20:1-2) and of Isaac (chap. 26). Both

of these patriarchs had somewhat similar experiences with their wives and Abimelech (of Gerar). Tell el-Jemmeh (eight miles S of Gaza), partly excavated by the great Egyptian archaeologist Sir Flinders Petrie, used to be identified with Gerar. There is a tendency now to accept Abu Hureira, eleven miles SE of Gaza, as the site of Gerar. D. Alon excavated there in 1956 and found that it was inhabited continually through every period from Chalcolithic times to the Iron Age and was prosperous during the Middle Bronze Age (the patriarchal period).   H.F.V.

BIBLIOGRAPHY: W. M. F. Petrie, *Gerar* (1928); Y. Aharoni, *The Land of the Bible* (1979), pp. 26-27, 191, 201, 218.

Site of Kersa (Kursi) ancient Gergesa

GER'ASA (ger'a-sa). There is a diversity of opinion concerning the location of the place where Jesus healed the demoniac. Kersa, apparently formerly Gergesa, on the eastern shore of the Galilean Sea across from Magdala seems to be the most likely location. It has a topography fitting the details of the narrative (Luke 8:33). There was a Gadara (Muqeis) some half-dozen miles SE of the S end of the Sea of Galilee, but this does not suit Mark 5:13. Thus Christ's miracle of healing is sometimes still identified with Gerasa, the splendid Nabataean city of Jerash, some forty miles SE of the Sea of Galilee in Transjordan, but this seems extremely unlikely in view of the great distance from the scene of Christ's Perean ministry. However, our Lord may have been in this magnificent city. Certainly some to whom He ministered lived in this city, and the result of His ministry certainly extended there (Mark 5:20). Jerash was called the "Pompeii of the East." It is the best-preserved Palestinian city from the Roman era. The British School of Archaeology in Jerusalem, The American Schools of Oriental Research and Yale University have cooperated in the excavations at Jerash during the years 1925 to 1940. In the 1970s restorations were carried out at the south theater. As one approaches the city from the S, he first sees the great triumphal arch of the emperor Hadrian, who visited the city in 129. To the left of the arch sprawls the hippodrome. Beyond that the south gate leads directly into the circular forum, unique in the Greco-Roman world. From the forum, on the left, a great flight of steps led up to the temple of Zeus, begun in A.D. 22. Next to it stood the first-century south theater with seating for some 5,000 people. From the forum northward led the main street of the city, just over a mile long. It was flanked by 260 Ionic and Corinthian columns on each side. All the principal buildings and the best shops had their entrances from this street. To the left on the highest point in town rose the second-century temple of Artemis, patron goddess of the municipality, with its forty-five-foot Corinthian columns. What is especially interesting to the Bible student is that at Jerash the decline of paganism can be traced in masonry, as the form and fabric of pagan temples were incorporated in Christian churches, such as St. Theodore's and the Cathedral. Jerash was rivaled in size by Palmyra and in cultic importance by Syrian Baalbek. *See* Gadara.

H.F.V.

BIBLIOGRAPHY: C. H. Kraeling, ed., *Gerasa, City of the Decapolis* (1938); D. Kirkbride, *Bulletin of the Archaeological Institute, London* 1 (1958): 9-20; M. Avi-Yonah, ed., *Encyclopedia of Archaeological Excavations in the Holy Land* (1976), 2:417-28.

GER'ASENE (Mark 5:1; Luke 8:26). An inhabitant of *Gerasa* (which see). Several manuscripts read *Gerasēnōn,* instead of *Gergesēnōn,* in Matt. 8:28 ("Gadarenes").

GER'GESA (gur'ge-sa). *See* Gerasa.

GERGESENE' (gur'ge-sēnz). The reading in the KJV in the account of the expulsion of the swine from the demoniac by Jesus (Matt. 8:28), instead of Gerasene (Mark 5:1; Luke 8:26).

GER'IZIM (ger'i-zim). The mountain of the Gerizzites, situated opposite Mt. Ebal and over the valley of Shechem, which was about three miles in length and not wider than will allow the hearing of a voice across. Gerizim is 2,849 feet above the Mediterranean and today is called Jebel el-Tor. From its summit much of Palestine can be seen. It was the scene of the parable of the trees and brambles (Judg. 9:7-15). Tradition attempts to locate here Abraham's altar built for the sacrifice of Isaac and also his interview with Melchizedek. After the captivity Manasseh, by permission of Alexander the Great, built a temple on Gerizim, and the Samaritans joined together the worship of idols and the true God (2 Kings 17:33). This temple was destroyed by John Hyrcanus c. 128 B.C. To this day the sect offers annual Paschal sacrifice on the top of the mount according to the prescriptions of Ex. 12. Moses commanded (Deut. 11:29; 27:12-13) that from Mt. Gerizim

the blessings of the law should be proclaimed, while its curses should proceed from Mt. Ebal (cf. Josh. 8:33).

Robert J. Bull of Drew University excavated at Tell er-Ras, a spur on the N slope of Mt. Gerizim, in 1964. There he found remains of a temple of Zeus built in the days of the Roman emperor Hadrian during the second century A.D. Under that were remains of a Hellenistic structure sixty-eight by sixty-five feet, which may have been the Samaritan temple destroyed by Hyrcanus.

H.F.V.

BIBLIOGRAPHY: E. Robinson, *Biblical Researches in Palestine* (1856), 2:275-80; 3:131-32.

GER'SHOM (gur-shom; "sojourner," Ex. 2:22; cf. Arab. *jarash,* "bell").

1. The elder of the two sons of Moses, born to him in the land of Midian by Zipporah (Ex. 2:22; 18:3), before 1441 B.C. He, with his brother, Eliezer, held no other rank than that of simple Levites, while the sons of their uncle Aaron enjoyed all the privileges of the priesthood (1 Chron. 23:15-16), a proof of the rare disinterestedness of Moses. Shebuel, one of his descendants, was appointed ruler of the treasury under David (1 Chron. 26:24).

2. The oldest son of Levi (1 Chron. 6:16-17, 20, 43, 62, 71; 15:7), elsewhere written *Gershon* (which see), as in the NIV.

3. The son of one Manasseh (according to the text), and father of Jonathan, who acted as priest to the Danites who captured Laish (Judg. 18:30); but, according to a more correct reading, he is not different from the son of Moses. The Talmud explains the substitution of "Manasseh" for "Moses" in the text by asserting that Jonathan did the works of Manasseh and was therefore reckoned in his family.

4. A descendant of Phinehas, who went up with Ezra from Babylon (Ezra 8:2), 457 B.C.

GER'SHON (gur-shon; "expulsion"). The eldest of the three sons of Levi, apparently born before the migration of Jacob's family into Egypt (Gen. 46:11; Ex. 6:16), c. 1871 B.C. But though the eldest born, the families of Gershon were outstripped in fame by the descendants of Kohath, from whom sprang Moses and the priestly line of Aaron (1 Chron. 6:2-15). At the census in the wilderness the Gershonites numbered 7,500 males (Num. 3:22), the number of efficient men being 2,630 (4:40). The sons of Gershon had charge of the fabrics of the Tabernacle—the coverings, screen, hangings, and cords (3:25-26; 4:25-26). In the encampment their station was behind the Tabernacle, on the W side (3:23). When on the march, they went with the Merarites, in the rear of the first body of three tribes—Judah, Issachar, Zebulun—with Reuben behind them. In the apportionment of the Levitical cities thirteen fell to the lot of the Gershonites—two in Manasseh beyond the Jordan, four in

Issachar, four in Asher, and three in Naphtali. In the time of David the family was represented by Asaph "the seer" (1 Chron. 6:39-43). It is not easy to see what special duties fell to the lot of the Gershonites in the service of the Tabernacle after its erection at Jerusalem, or in the Temple. They were appointed to "prophesy"—i.e., probably, to utter or sing inspired words, perhaps after the special prompting of David himself (24:1-2). Others of the Gershonites, sons of Ladan, had charge of the "treasures of the house of God, and of the treasures of the dedicated gifts" (26:20-22), among which precious stones are specially named (29:8). In Chronicles the name is, with two exceptions (6:1; 23:6), given in the slightly different form of "Gershom."

GER'SHONITES (gur'shon-īts). The descendants of Gershon, one of the sons of Levi (Num. 3:21; 4:24, 27; Josh. 21:33; etc.). As to the office and duties of the Gershonites, *see* Levites.

GERUTH KIMHAM (ge-rūth' kim'ham). A lodging place near Bethlehem where Johanan and his companions stayed en route to Egypt, where they were fleeing lest they be implicated in and punished for the murder of Gedeliah (Jer. 41:17). *See* Gedeliah.

GE'SHAN (ge'shan). The third son of Jahdai, among the descendants of Caleb (1 Chron. 2:47; "Gesham," KJV), after 1440 B.C.

GE'SHEM (ge'shem; "shower"). An Arab (Neh. 2:19; 6:1), and one of the enemies of the Jews on the return from the Exile, especially in the plots against the life of Nehemiah (6:2), 445 B.C. Geshem, we may conclude, was an inhabitant of Arabia Petraea, or of the Arabian Desert, and probably the chief of a tribe that, like most of the tribes on the eastern frontier of Palestine, was, in the time of the captivity and the subsequent period, allied with the Persians, or with any peoples threatening the Jewish nation; for the wandering inhabitants of the frontier, doubtless, availed themselves largely, in their predatory excursions, of the distracted state of Palestine, and dreaded the reestablishment of the kingdom. The Arabians, Ammonites, and Ashdodites are recorded as having "conspired together to come and fight against Jerusalem" and to hinder its repairing (Neh. 4:8). The name is identical with *Gashmu* (which see), being the Hebraized form with the dropping of the nominative ending "u" and *gashm* resolving into *geshem.*

BIBLIOGRAPHY: A. T. Olmstead, *History of the Persian Empire* (1948), p. 295.

GE'SHUR (ge'shur; "bridge"). A principality in Syria on the E of Jordan, adjoining the N border of the Hebrew territory and lying between Mt. Hermon, Maachah, and Bashan (Deut. 3:13-14; Josh. 12:5). This Aramaean principality was ruled over by Talmai, whose daughter David married

(2 Sam. 3:3). It was the possession of Manasseh, although its original inhabitants were not expelled (Josh. 13:13). It was there Absalom fled after killing Amnon (2 Sam. 13:37-38), and from which Joab returned him to Jerusalem (14:23). It is stated (1 Chron. 2:23) that "Geshur and Aram took the towns of Jair . . . even sixty cities."

GESH'URITES (gesh'u-rīts; Deut. 3:14; Josh. 12:5; 13:2, 11, 13; 1 Sam. 27:8). The inhabitants of *Geshur* (which see), bordering on Aram, to the E of the Jordan.

GE'THER (ge'ther; derivation uncertain). The name of the third son of Aram (Gen. 10:23). He is mentioned in 1 Chron. 1:17 as one of the sons of Shem, probably meaning "grandson of." It is uncertain where his posterity settled.

GETHSEM'ANE (geth-sem'a-ni; Gk. from Aram. "oil press"). The olive grove at the foot of the Mount of Olives, to which Jesus was accustomed to retire (Luke 22:39) with His disciples and which was the scene of His agony (Mark 14:32; Luke 22:39-40; John 18:1). There are two traditional places called Gethsemane. One is the possession of the Latin church, and it consists of a triangular spot, some seventy paces in circumference. It is enclosed by a fence and contains some large and old olive trees, in addition to a flower garden. Adjacent to it stands the Church of All Nations, which encloses a "rock of agony." The Greeks have set up another traditional Gethsemane, located farther up Mount Olivet. Thomson (*Land and Book,* 2:483) says that he inclines to think both are wrong, and he would place the garden in a secluded spot several hundred yards NE of the other traditional sites.

BIBLIOGRAPHY: W. M. Thomson, *The Land and the Book* (1886), 1: 634; G. H. Dalman, *Sacred Sites and Ways* (1935), pp. 321ff.

Gethsemane with the Temple area beyond.

GEU'EL (ge-ū'el; "majesty of God"). The son of Machi, of the tribe of Gad, and one of the men sent by Moses to search the land of Canaan (Num. 13:15), 1440 B.C.

GEZ'ER (gez'er; 2 Sam. 5:25; 1 Chron. 14:16; etc.). An ancient city on the Shephelah above the Maritime Plain, eighteen miles NW of Jerusalem and seventeen miles SE of Jaffa (2 Sam. 5:25; 1 Chron. 14:16, KJV). The site was strategic since it guarded one of the few roads of access from Jaffa to Jerusalem. Tell Jezer is the name of the thirty-three acre mound. Joshua could not conquer the city at the time of the Hebrew conquest, and it remained relatively independent until a pharaoh in Solomon's time gave it to Solomon as dowry when he married the pharaoh's daughter (1 Kings 9:15-17). It then became one of Solomon's chariot cities.

Excavations at Gezer began with the work of R. A. S. Macalister under the sponsorship of the Palestine Exploration Fund, from 1902 to 1909. A. Rowe excavated there for the fund in 1934. Then in 1964 a ten-year project was conducted at Gezer by the Hebrew Union College's Jerusalem School and Harvard. G. Ernest Wright and William C. Dever directed the work. Excavations have shown that Gezer was first occupied in the thirty-third century B.C. and continued with intermissions to be inhabited until the late first century B.C.

The city had a high point of development be-

Pillars used for worship by Canaanites at Tell Gezer

tween 1600 and 1460 B.C. Prosperity and massive building projects were characteristic of this period. A stone wall ten feet thick and reinforced with square towers surrounded the city. The great high place with its row of ten huge sacred pillars came into being early in this period. The water system used to be thought to date near the end of this period, but Dever suggests the possibility that it dated to the Early Iron II period and was contemporary with the great water systems at Megiddo, Hazor, and Gibeon. This water system consisted of a vertical shaft 27 feet deep, which could be entered from just inside the city's S gate. At the bottom of the shaft was a tunnel that extended 132 feet to a 28- by 80-foot cave of unknown depth.

Thutmose III of Egypt destroyed Gezer about 1468, and it lay in ruins for decades thereafter. Then it revived but was destroyed again late in the thirteenth century by the Egyptian pharaoh Merneptah. Abandoned for a time again, it was occupied peacefully by the Philistines during the twelfth and eleventh centuries. Then about 950 an Egyptian pharaoh captured it and presented it to Solomon, after which the city entered another period of prosperity. A casemated wall and a Solomonic gate like that of Megiddo were found at Gezer.

The excavators found traces of the destruction by Pharaoh Shishak in 926 B.C., the Assyrians in the eighth century, and Nebuchadnezzar in the sixth century. The city became important again during the Hellenistic period, and it was a major base of operations against the Maccabean revolt. The town virtually ceased to exist by NT times.

The Gezer calendar, a tenth-century B.C. Heb. inscription citing the annual cycle of agricultural activities, was found there. Albright translated it as follows.

His (or, a man's) two months are (olive) harvest;
His two months are grain planting;
His two months are planting;
His month is hoeing up of flax;
His month is barley harvest;
His month is harvest and festival;
His two months are vine tending;
His month is summer fruit.

BIBLIOGRAPHY: M. Avi-Yonah, ed., *Encyclopedia of Archaeological Excavations in the Holy Land* (1976), 2:428-43; A. F. Rainey, *International Standard Bible Encyclopedia* (1982), 2:458-60.

GEZ'RITES. *See* Girzites.

GHOST. The archaic English form of the German *Geist*, "spirit," and the translation in the KJV of several Heb. and Gk. words signifying "breath, life, spirit"; Job 11:20; Jer. 15:9; Matt. 27:50; John 19:30). In the NT it frequently occurs as the designation of the third Person in the Trinity—the *Holy Ghost* or *Holy Spirit* (which see). The KJV expression "gave up the ghost"

(Gen. 25:17; Lam. 1:19; and elsewhere) simply means "to die" (cf. NASB and NIV readings). *See* Holy Spirit; Spirit.

GIAH (gī′ah). A place near the hill of Ammah, close to Gibeon, where Joab and Abishai overtook Abner as he fled from the contest at the pool of Gibeon (2 Sam. 2:24).

GIANT. An abnormally tall and powerful human being of ancient Bible lands; the rendering of several Heb. words.

Nephilim (nef′i-lim; Heb. *nᵉpîlîm;* Num. 13:13). The form of the Heb. word denotes a plural verbal adjective or noun of passive signification, certainly from *nāpal,* "to fall," so that the connotation is "the fallen ones," clearly meaning the unnatural offspring that were on the earth in the years before the Flood, "and also afterward, when the sons of God came in to the daughters of men, and they bore children to them" (Gen. 6:4). The mention of the great stature of the Nephilim, the sons of Anak, in the evil report that the ten spies brought of the land of Canaan (Num. 13:33) together with the LXX rendering, *gigantes,* suggested the translation *giants.* They were exceedingly wicked and violent so that "every intent" of the thoughts of men's hearts "was only evil continually" (Gen. 6:5). *See* Merrill F. Unger, *Biblical Demonology,* pp. 45-52.

Rephaim (ref′a-im; Heb. *rᵉpā′îm,* "shades, ghosts"). The aboriginal giants who inhabited Canaan, Edom, Moab, and Ammon. In Abraham's time, c. 1950 B.C., Chedorlaomer defeated them. At the period of the conquest, c. 1440 B.C., Og, king of Bashan, is said to have alone remained of this race (Deut. 3:11; Josh. 12:4; 13:12). His huge bedstead of iron is mentioned in particular.

Anakim (an′a-kim; Heb. *′ănāqîm,* "sons of Anak"). In Num. 13:33 the Anakim are classified with the Nephilim on account of their gigantic size.

Emim (em′im), a race that inhabited the country of the Moabites (Gen. 14:5) and that is pictured as "great, numerous, and tall as the Anakim" (Deut. 2:10).

Zamzummmim (zam′zum-im), a giant race inhabiting the land of Ammon (Deut. 2:20).

Other References. From a remnant of the Anakim in Philistine Gath came the famous Goliath (1 Sam. 17:4). Two of the Philistine giants are mentioned in 2 Sam. 21:16-22. The tradition of a giant race persisted in the ancient Near East and goes back in the Genesis account to intercourse between fallen angels and mortal women. Although this so-called angel hypothesis of Gen. 6:1-4 is disclaimed by many Bible students, it is a clear implication of the original. Says W. F. Albright, "Yahweh was believed to have created astral as well as terrestrial beings and the former were popularly called, 'the host of heaven' or 'the sons of God'. In Gen. 6:1ff., for example, . . . the (astral) gods had intercourse with mortal women

who gave birth to heroes (literally, meteors, *nephilim*), an idea that may often be illustrated from Babylonian and Greek mythology. But the Israelite who had this section recited, unquestionably thought of intercourse between angels and women (like later Jews and Christians)" (*From the Stone Age to Christianity* [1940], p. 226).

GIB′BAR (gib′ar; "mighty man," a "hero"). An Israelite whose descendants, to the number of ninety-five, returned with Zerubbabel from Babylon (Ezra 2:20), before 536 B.C. This is probably an error for the remnants of the natives of Gibeon (Neh. 7:25).

GIB′BETHON (gib′e-thon; "mound," a "height"). A Philistine city (Josh. 19:44; 21:23), within the bounds of the tribe of Dan, assigned to the Kohathites (21:23). Nadab, king of Israel, was slain under its walls (1 Kings 15:27; 16:15-16). Possibly to be located at Tell el-Melat, about three miles E of Gezer.

GIB′EA (gib′ē-a; "hill"). One of the sons of Sheva, who was also the father of Machbena (1 Chron. 2:49). The KJV rendering indicates that Gibea was not a person but a place built or occupied in connection with Machbena.

GIB′EAH (gib′ē-a; Heb. *gibᵉ′â*). A "hill," as the word is sometimes rendered.

1. Gibeah of Judah, situated in the mountains of that tribe (Josh. 15:57), where the prophet Habakkuk is said to have been buried. It lay seven miles SW of Bethlehem and is identified with Jeba.

2. Gibeah of Benjamin (Judg. 19:14; 1 Sam. 13:15; 2 Sam. 23:29), known also as "Gibeah of Saul" (1 Sam. 11:4; Isa. 10:29), the scene of the inhumane crime recorded in Judg. 19:12-30, for which the Benjamites were nearly exterminated. It was Saul's birthplace and continued to be his residence after he became king (1 Sam. 10:26; 11:4; etc.), and here the Gibeonites hanged his descendants (2 Sam. 21:6). Saul's Gibeah has been excavated by W. F. Albright. The modern site is Tell el-Fûl, meaning "hill of beans." The site revealed twelve levels of history. An Israelite town, apparently referred to in Judg. 19 and 20, was destroyed by fire. Saul's rustic stronghold with its sturdy polygonal masonry was erected c. 1015 B.C. The outer citadel walls, 170 by 155 feet, were 8 to 10 feet thick. The citadel is composed of two stories with a stone staircase. The casemented walls and separately bonded towers are peculiar to this period. In the audience chamber David played his harp to soothe the demon-possessed Saul (1 Sam. 16:23). Among the interesting objects found were grinding stones, spinning whorls, cooking pots, burnished ware, and a gaming board. Storage bins for oil, wine, and grain, still holding their contents when excavated, were also found in the royal palace.   M.F.U.

3. Gibeah of Phinehas (Josh. 24:33), in the hill country of Ephraim, where Eleazar was buried. It has been identified with Khirbet Jibia, five miles N of Guphria, toward Shechem.

4. Gibeah is rendered "hill" in the following passages: "hill of Moreh" (Judg. 7:1); "hill of God" (1 Sam. 10:5; NIV, "Gibeah of God"); "hill of Hachilah" (23:19; 26:1); "hill of Ammah" (2 Sam. 2:24); "hill Gareb" (Jer. 31:39). It has also been translated "hill" in 2 Sam. 6:3-4 and is the place at Kiriath-jearim where the Ark remained from the time the Philistines returned it until it was taken to Jerusalem (cf. 1 Sam. 7:1-2).

BIBLIOGRAPHY: M. Avi-Yonah, ed., *Encyclopedia of Archaeological Excavations in the Holy Land* (1976), 2:444-46.

GIB'EATH-HAAR'ALOTH ("the hill of foreskins," Josh. 5:3, see marg.). So rendered because the foreskins of the Israelites were buried there when the nation was circumcised.

GIB'EATHITE (gib'ē-a-thīt). A native of Gibeah (1 Chron. 12:3), Shemaah by name, who was the father of two Benjamites who joined David.

GIB'EON (gib'ē-on; "hill city"). One of the Hivite cities that, through deception, effected a league with Joshua (Josh. 9:3-17), thus escaping the fate of Ai and Jericho. It was afterward allotted to Benjamin and was made a Levitical town (18:25; 21:17). After the destruction of Nob by Saul, the Tabernacle was set up here and remained until the building of the Temple (1 Kings 3:4-5; 1 Chron. 16:39; 2 Chron. 1:3, 13). When the Amorite kings besieged Gibeon, Joshua hastened to its relief, and a great battle followed (*see* Joshua). From Jer. 41:16 it would seem that after the destruction of Jerusalem by Nebuchadnezzar, Gibeon again became the seat of government. It produced prophets in the days of Jeremiah (28:1). "The sons of Gibeon" returned with Zerubbabel (Neh. 7:25). Gibeon is located about eight miles NW of Jerusalem on the route to Joppa. Other events in the history of Gibeon include the battle between Ish-bosheth and David (2 Sam. 2:8-17; 3:30) and the execution of the seven sons of Saul (21:1-9). Gibeon was an important place of worship in Solomon's time (1 Kings 3:4; 2 Sam. 20:8). There he had his famous dream. On the Karnak Relief of Pharaoh Shishak, Gibeon is mentioned as one of the trophies of his invasion of Palestine (1 Kings 14:25, "in the fifth year of King Rehoboam"). Shishak's carved reliefs also show captives taken in his Palestinian invasion. (*See* Leon Legrain, *Les Temples de Karnak*.) Gibeon is identified with el-Jib, about six miles NW of Jerusalem. James B. Pritchard excavated there on behalf of the University of Pennsylvania Museum from 1956 to 1962. The most dramatic find there was the "pool" of Gibeon. Measuring thirty-seven feet in diameter and thirty-five feet in depth, this cylindrical cutting had a circular

staircase that led to a stepped tunnel that continued downward another forty-five feet below the pool's floor to a water chamber. Excavations demonstrated that the city was founded about 3000 B.C. Magnificent tomb discoveries documented the Middle Bronze and Late Bronze periods (2000-1200 B.C.). Iron Age I (1200-900 B.C.) apparently was the city's golden age. Near the beginning of the period, a wall about five feet thick and more than a half mile in circumference enclosed the sixteen-acre town.   H.F.V.

BIBLIOGRAPHY: J. B. Pritchard, *Gibeon, Where the Sun Stood Still* (1962); M. Avi-Yonah, ed., *Encyclopedia of Archaeological Excavations in the Holy Land* (1976), 2:446-50; K. N. Schoville, *International Standard Bible Encyclopedia* (1982), 2:462-63.

Fields near El Jib, ancient Gibeon

GIB'EONITES (gib'ē-on-īts). The people of Gibeon and perhaps also of the three cities associated with Gibeon (Josh. 9:17). Upon the victorious advance of the Israelites, the inhabitants of Gibeon attempted to anticipate the danger that threatened them by means of a clever scheme, and to enter into a friendly alliance with Israel. A delegation waited upon Joshua at Gilgal, representing themselves as ambassadors from a far country, desirous of making a league with him. They made this appear probable by taking "worn-out sacks on their donkeys, and wineskins, worn-out and torn and mended, and worn-out and patched sandals on their feet, and worn-out clothes on themselves; and all the bread of their provision was dry and had become crumbled" (9:4-5). They declared that all these tokens of age and wear had come to them upon their journey. Because of these representations they were received as friends and an alliance was made with them. Upon the discovery of the scheme by which they had obtained the protection of the Israelites, they were condemned to be perpetual bondmen, "hewers of wood and drawers of water" for the congregation, and for the house of God and altar of Jehovah (9:23, 27). Saul appears to have broken this covenant and in a fit of enthusiasm or patriotism to have killed some and devised a general massacre of the rest (2 Sam. 21:1-2, 5). This was expiated many years after by giving up seven men of Saul's descendants to the Gibeonites, who hanged them "before the Lord"—as a kind of sacrifice—in Gibeah, Saul's own town (vv. 4, 6, 8-9). From this time there is no mention of the Gibeonites as a distinct people, but many writers include them among the Temple servants, who were appointed for the service of the Temple (1 Chron. 9:2).

GIDDAL'TI (gi-dal'ti; "I have made great"). The ninth son of Heman, and head of the twenty-second division of Levitical musicians in the Tabernacle under David (1 Chron. 25:4, 29), after 1000 B.C. The office of these brothers was to sound the horn in the Levitical orchestra (v. 5, marg.).

GID'DEL (gid'el).
The name of two men whose descendants returned from the captivity with Zerubbabel.

1. One of the Temple servants (Ezra 2:47; Neh. 7:49), before 536 B.C.

2. One of "Solomon's servants," i.e., perhaps of the Canaanite tribes enslaved by Solomon (Ezra 2:56; Neh. 7:58; cf. 1 Kings 9:21), before 536 B.C.

GID'EON (Heb. *gid'ôn,* "tree feller," i.e., "warrior"). The son of Joash the Abi-ezrite, of the tribe of Manasseh; resided at Ophrah in Gilead, beyond the Jordan.

Condition of Israel. Another relapse into evil brought Israel under the oppression of the Midianites for seven years. With Midian were allied Amalek and "the sons of the east" (of Jordan). Their power pressed so severely upon the Israelites that they "made for themselves the dens which were in the mountains and the caves and the strongholds." The allies encamped in their territory, destroyed the crops "as far as Gaza," and left "no sustenance in Israel as well as no sheep, ox, or donkey," so that Israel was greatly impoverished (Judg. 6:1-6). But before helping them the Lord sent an unnamed prophet to reprove them for their disobedience and bring them to repentance.

Call of Gideon. In such a time of distress Gideon was threshing wheat in the winepress to conceal it from the Midianites. While thus engaged the angel of the Lord appeared to him and addressed him in these words: "The Lord is with you, O valiant warrior." To this Gideon made the despondent reply, "If the Lord is with us, why then has all this happened to us?" Then Jehovah (revealing Himself) said, "Go in this your strength and deliver Israel from the hand of Midian. Have I not sent you?" Doubtful of the means by which he might accomplish so great a work, he requested a sign from heaven. This was granted to him; for when he presented his offering of a kid and unleavened cakes, the angel touched it, and it was consumed by fire. Recognizing Jehovah, he was filled with fear; but being comforted he built an altar and called it "The Lord is Peace" (Judg. 6:11-24).

Destroys an Altar of Baal. The first thing for Gideon to do was to purify his father's house from idolatry and sanctify himself by sacrificing a burnt offering. That night God commanded him to tear down the altar of Baal belonging to his father and cut down the grove near it. Then he was to build an altar to the Lord and offer on it a seven-year-old bull of his father's. Assisted by ten servants, Gideon obeyed the vision probably during the following night, through fear of those around. Gideon, being identified as the perpetrator of the act, was in danger of being stoned; but his father took the part of his son and told the people to allow Baal to plead for himself. From this circumstance Gideon received the name of Jerubbaal, i.e., "let Baal contend" (Judg. 6:25-32). *See* Baal.

The Sign of the Fleece. When the Midianites and their allies once more invaded the land of Israel, the Spirit of the Lord came upon Gideon, and he gathered together an army from the tribes of Manasseh, Asher, Zebulun, and Naphtali. Before going into battle he asked for a sign from God of the success of his undertaking. He asked that the dew should fall on a fleece spread upon the threshing floor, while the ground all around should be dry. In the morning the fleece was so wet that Gideon wrung out of it a bowl of water. The next night the wonder was reversed, the soil being wet and the fleece perfectly dry (Judg. 6:36-40). "The sign itself was to manifest the strength of divine assistance to his weakness of faith. Dew, in the Scriptures, is a symbol of the beneficent power of God, which quickens, revives, and invigorates the objects of nature when they have been parched by the burning heat of the sun's rays" (K. & D., *Com.*).

Midianites Defeated. Assured by this double sign, Gideon advanced against the enemy and encamped near the brook Harod, in the valley of Jezreel. (*See* Esdraelon, Plain of.) The army of the Midianites and their allies numbered about 135,000 (Judg. 8:10), whereas the Israelites mustered only 32,000. Nevertheless, "The Lord said to Gideon, 'The people who are with you are too many for Me to give Midian into their hands, lest Israel become boastful, saying, "My own power has delivered me" ' " (7:2). Gideon, therefore, made the usual proclamation (Deut. 20:8), that all the fainthearted might withdraw; and 22,000 availed themselves of this opportunity. Even this number the Lord regarded as too great, and Gideon was commanded to test them in the matter of drinking. Those who knelt to drink were rejected, and only those were chosen who lapped the water with the tongue, "as a dog laps," i.e., to take the water from the brook with the hollow of their hand and lap it into the mouth with their tongues as a dog does. This test reduced the number to 300 men. These took the provision from the people, and the war trumpets, so that every one of the 300 had a trumpet and (as the provisions were probably kept in vessels) a pitcher as well. That night Gideon overheard a man telling of a dream he had had, which was of a cake of barley bread overthrowing a tent. Regarding this dream as indicating divine cooperation, Gideon began the attack without delay. He divided his 300 men into three companies and gave them all trumpets and empty pitchers, with torches in their hands. The pitchers were to hide the burning torches during the advance and to increase the noise at the time of the attack by dashing them to pieces. The noise and sudden lighting up of the burning torches would naturally deceive the enemy as to the numbers of Gideon's army. His clever strategy was eminently successful, and the enemy, thrown into complete confusion, "fled as far as Beth-shittah toward Zererah, as far as the edge of Abel-meholah, by Tabbath" (Judg. 7:1-23).

The Ephraimites. In order to cut off the enemy's retreat at the Jordan, Gideon sent notice to the Ephraimites to "take the waters before them, as far as Beth-barah and the Jordan." The Ephraimites responded, took possession of the waters mentioned, captured the two princes, Oreb and Zeeb, put them to death, and brought their heads to Gideon. This latter act amounted to an acknowledgment of Gideon's leadership, but they were greatly annoyed because he had made war upon and defeated the enemy without first summoning them to the field. Serious consequences were avoided by the tact of Gideon in speaking in a lowly spirit of his doings in comparison with theirs (Judg. 7:24–8-3). The "gleaning of the grapes of Ephraim" is the victory over the Midianites and the capture of the two princes—the "vintage of Abiezer," Gideon's victory with his 300 men.

Destroys Succoth. Passing over the Jordan in pursuit of the Midianites, he was refused assistance by the people of Succoth and Penuel. Upon his return he destroyed both places (Judg. 8:4-17).

Avenges His Brethren. Gideon inquired of the two captive kings of Midian (Zebah and Zalmunna), "What kind of men were they whom you

killed at Tabor?" And they answered, "They were like you, each one resembling the son of a king." He then told them that these persons were his brothers and commanded Jether, his firstborn, to slay them. But because Jether feared to do so, Gideon killed them "and took the crescent ornaments which were on their camels' necks" (Judg. 8:18-21).

Refuses the Crown. Gideon, having so gloriously delivered Israel from the severe and long oppression of the Midianites, was offered by the Israelites a hereditary crown. "The men of Israel" were probably only the northern tribes already mentioned in 6:35, who had suffered most severely from the Midianite oppression and had rallied about Gideon. The temptation to accept the government of Israel was resisted by Gideon, probably because he thought the government of Jehovah in Israel amply sufficient and did not consider himself or his sons called to found an earthly monarchy (Judg. 8:22-23).

Remaining Acts and Death. Gideon made the request that the people should give him the golden earrings taken with the spoil, which they willingly consented to do. They brought him earrings weighing 1,700 shekels (about 50 pounds). With it he made a golden ephod and put it in his own city, Ophrah. This was probably not an image but a magnificent coat made of the gold and purple (*see* Ephod). It proved a snare to Israel, to himself, and to his house: to Israel, because they made it an object of worship; to Gideon and his house, because he invaded the prerogative of the Aaronic priesthood and gave an impetus to the worship of Baal after his death. The evil consequences of this false step in religion was realized in the miserable sequel of Gideon's family. The history of Gideon is concluded in Judg. 8:28-32. The Midianites had been so humiliated that "they did not lift up their heads anymore. And the land was undisturbed for forty years in the days of Gideon." A few other notices are given respecting his family to prepare the way for the history of his sons after his death. "Then Jerubbaal the son of Joash went and lived in his own house," retiring into private life. In addition to the seventy sons born of his many wives, he had a son by his concubine who lived in Shechem, and to this son he gave the name of Abimelech. Gideon died at a "ripe old age" and was buried in his father's tomb at Ophrah, about 1215-1190 B.C.

BIBLIOGRAPHY: A. Malamat, *Palestine Exploration Quarterly* 85 (1953): 61-65; Y. Yadin, *The Art of Warfare in Bible Lands* (1963), pp. 256-60; J. M. Lang and T. Kirk, *Studies in the Book of Judges*, 2 vols. in 1 (1983), 1:81-201.

GIDEO'NI (gid-ē-ō'ni; "warlike"). A Benjamite whose son, Abidan, was a prominent man of his tribe and was employed in numbering the people (Num. 1:11; 2:22; 7:60, 65; 10:24), about 1400 B.C.

GI'DOM (gid-om; "cutting," i.e., "desolation"). A place E of Gibeah, toward the wilderness (of Bethel), where the fleeing Benjamites turned to escape to the rock Rimmon (Judg. 20:45).

GIER EAGLE. *See* Animal Kingdom.

GIFT. The giving and receiving of presents has in all ages been not only a more frequent, but also a more formal and significant proceeding in the East than among ourselves. We cannot offer a more remarkable proof of the important part that presents play in the social life of the East than the fact that the Heb. language possesses no less than fifteen different expressions for the one idea. Several of these have a distinct and specific meaning, indicative of the relation of giver and receiver or of the motive and object of the presentation.

1. From the Heb. root *nātan,* "to give," we have several words meaning a *gratuity* (Prov. 19:6); to secure favor (18:16; 21:14), in religious thankfulness (Num. 18:11), or in dowry (Gen. 34:12), in inheritance (25:6; 2 Chron. 21:3; Ezek. 46:16-17), or as a bribe (KJV, Prov. 15:27; Eccles. 7:7; etc.; NASB and NIV render "bribe").

2. From the Heb. *nāśā',* to "raise," we have words signifying *pecuniary assistance* (Esther 2:18) and a *present* in token of respect (2 Sam. 19:42, KJV). Perhaps the inherent idea of these terms is that of *oblation* to a superior, a *dish of honor* for special guests (2 Sam. 11:8, "present"), the collection or "levy" for the sanctuary (2 Chron. 24:6, 9).

3. More distinctly in the sense of a votive offering is Heb. *minḥâ,* an *oblation* or propitiatory gift (2 Sam. 8:2, 6; 1 Chron. 18:2, 6; etc.), and in several other passages where the word has the idea of *tribute.*

4. Other words are mercenary in character. Thus Heb. *shōḥad* is a gift for the purpose of escaping punishment, presented either as a *bribe* to a judge (Ex. 23:8; Deut. 10:17) or a *present* to a conqueror (2 Kings 16:8).

5. In Gk. the usual terms are generally derived from *didōmi,* to "give," and have a wide meaning, as did the Heb.

"It is clear that the term 'gift' is frequently used where we should substitute 'tribute' or 'fee.' The tribute of subject states was paid not in a fixed sum of money, but in kind, each nation presenting its particular product; and hence the expression 'to bring presents'—to own submission (Pss. 68:29; 76:11; Isa. 18:7). Friends brought presents to friends on any joyful occasion (Esther 9:19, 22), those who asked for information or advice to those who gave it (2 Kings 8:8), the needy to the wealthy from whom any assistance was expected (Gen. 43:11; 2 Kings 15:19; 16:8); on the occasion of a marriage, the bridegroom not only paid the parents for his bride (KJV, 'dowry') but also gave the bride certain presents (Gen. 34:12; cf. 24:22). The nature of the presents was as various as were the occa-

sions. The mode of presentation was with as much parade as possible. The refusal of a present was regarded as a high indignity. No less an insult was it not to bring a present when the position of the parties demanded it (1 Sam. 10:27)" (Smith, *Bib. Dict.,* s.v.).

GIFT OF TONGUES. *See* Tongues, Speaking in.

GIFTS, SPIRITUAL (Gk. *charismata,* "gifts of grace"). Outside of the Pauline epistles this term is used only once in the NT, namely, 1 Pet. 4:10, where it is rendered "special gift," i.e., a *gift of divine grace.* The expression "Each man has his own gift" (1 Cor. 7:7) seems to imply continence or some other gracious endowment in its place. In 2 Cor. 1:11 the "favor" or *gift* was deliverance from great peril to life. Paul calls that which he intends to communicate to the Romans through his personal presence among them a "spiritual gift" (Rom. 1:11), "because in his apprehension all such instruction, comfort, joy, strengthening, etc., as are produced by his labors, are regarded not as procured by his own human individuality, but as a result which the Holy Spirit works by means of him—the gracious working of the Spirit, whose organ he is" (Meyer, *Com.,* ad loc.).

The "free gift," or "gift by the grace" (5:15-16), is the economy of divine grace, by which the pardon of sin and eternal salvation are appointed to sinners in consideration of the merits of Christ laid hold of by faith (cf. 6:23); plural of the several blessings of the Christian salvation (11:29).

In the technical Pauline sense "gifts" denote *extraordinary powers* distinguishing certain Christians and enabling them to serve the church of Christ, the reception of which is due to the power of divine grace operating in their souls by the Holy Spirit (12:6; 1 Cor. 1:7; 12:4, 31; 1 Pet. 4:10); specially the sum of those powers requisite for the discharge of the office of an evangelist (1 Tim. 4:14; 2 Tim 1:6). The fullest list of these charismata, or spiritual gifts, is given in 1 Cor. 12.

Concerning spiritual gifts Cremer says: "Their number is as various as the needs of the Church, and neither the enumeration of 1 Cor. 12, nor of Eph. 4, nor Rom. 12 can be regarded as exhaustive. But those are permanent which are necessary for the government of the Church, and those temporary which had a miraculous element, as the miraculous gifts of the apostles. But among the latter is not to be included the 'gift of proclaiming the Gospel so as to produce faith' (Weiss). The apostolic charismata bear the same relation to those of the ministry that the apostolic office does to the pastoral office, and consist in the power to lay the foundations of the Church. They are therefore not repeated, as the Irvingites hold, for there are no circumstances calling for their repetition" (art. in Schaff-Herzog).

GI'HON (gi'hon; "a gushing fountain").

1. One of the four rivers of Eden (Gen. 2:13). The Gihon and also the Pishon are presumably canals (called rivers in Babylonia) that connected the Tigris and Euphrates as ancient riverbeds. Biblical notices place the Garden of Eden somewhere in the Tigris-Euphrates valley, evidently at the easternmost third of the Fertile Crescent. Shifting riverbeds and the accumulation of enormous deposits of river silt make the task of locating the site of the Pishon or the Gihon virtually impossible, but the other two rivers, Euphrates and Tigris, are well known.

2. The intermittent spring that constituted Jerusalem's most ancient water supply, situated in the Kidron Valley just below the eastern hill (Ophel). This abundant source of water was entirely covered over and concealed from outside the walls and was conducted by a specially built conduit to a pool within the walls where a besieged city could get all the water it needed. "Why should the kings of Assyria come and find abundant water?" the people queried in the time of Hezekiah (2 Chron. 32:2-4). Hezekiah's Tunnel, 1,777 feet long, hewn out of the solid rock and comparable to the tunnels at Megiddo and Gezer, conducted the water to a reservoir within the city. From the top of Ophel the ancient Jebusites (c. 2000 B.C.) had cut a passage through the rock where waterpots could be let down a 40-foot shaft to receive the water in the pool 50 feet back from the Gihon. Early excavations at Jerusalem by the Palestine Exploration Fund under the direction of Sir Charles Warren (1867) resulted in finding the 40-foot rock-cut shaft. It is now known as Warren's Shaft. Conrad Shick in 1891 discovered an ancient surface canal that conveyed water from the Gihon Spring to the old pool of Siloam, located just within the SE extremity of the an-

cient city. Isaiah seems to have alluded to the softly flowing waters of this gentle brook when he spoke poetically of "the gently flowing waters of Shiloah" (Isa. 8:6).   M.F.U.

BIBLIOGRAPHY: K. M. Kenyon, *Jerusalem: Excavation 3000 Years of History* (1967), pp. 15-16, 69-77.

GIL'ALAI (gil'a-li; perhaps "[The Lord] has rolled away"). One of the priests appointed by Nehemiah to aid Zechariah in the musical services under Ezra at the dedication of the walls of Jerusalem (Neh. 12:36), 445 B.C.

Mt. Gilboa

GILBO'A (gil-bō'a). Its name was probably suggested by the spring or fountain about half a mile E of the city of Jezreel, which stood on the western extremity of the mount. Parallel and six miles N of this range is another, called the "hill of Moreh," but called by travelers "Little Hermon." The beautiful valley of Jezreel lies between the two. It was at Gilboa that Saul and his three sons were slain in the battle with the Philistines (1 Sam. 28:4; 31:1, 8; 1 Chron. 10:1). When David heard of the disaster he incorporated in his beautiful ode all the conditions—geographical, military, and social (2 Sam. 1:19-27).

GIL'EAD (gil'i-ad; cf. Arab. *jala'ad,* "to be rough").

1. The mountain region E of the Jordan, called "the hill country of Gilead" (Gen. 31:25), extending from the Sea of Galilee to the upper end of the Dead Sea, about sixty miles long and twenty wide, bounded on the N by Bashan and on the S by Moab and Ammon (13:21; Deut. 3:12-17), now called Jebel Jelâd or Jelûd. Upon it is the site of the ancient city of Ramoth-gilead, now identified by Nelson Glueck with Tell Ramith in the northern part of the country. Its scenery is beautiful; the hills are fertile and crowned with forests. Scripture names oak trees and herds of cattle as being found there (Gen. 37:25; Num. 32:1). Reuben and Gad desired to possess this territory because of their need of pasture for their herds (Deut. 3:12-17). The name *Gilead* is seldom used in the Bible beyond OT history.

Steps leading to Gihon Spring, Jerusalem

2. A city "of wrongdoers," etc. (Hos. 6:8). "Hosea calls Gilead (district) a city of evil-doers, as being a rendezvous for wicked men, to express the thought that the whole land was as full of evil-doers as a city is of men" (K. & D., *Com.*).

3. The son of Machir and grandson of Manasseh; his descendants bore his name as a patronymic (Num. 26:29-30).

4. Father of Jephthah the judge, and descendant of the above (Judg. 11:1-2).

5. Son of Michael and father of Jaroah, of the tribe of Gad (1 Chron. 5:14).

BIBLIOGRAPHY: M. Ottosen, *Gilead: Tradition and History* (1969).

GIL'EADITES, THE (Num. 26:29; Judg. 12:4-5). A branch of the tribe of Manasseh, descended from Gilead. There appears to have been a long-standing feud between them and the Ephraimites, who taunted them with being deserters. See Judg. 12:4, "And the men of Gilead defeated Ephraim, because they said, 'You are fugitives of Ephraim, O Gileadites, in the midst of Ephraim and in the midst of Manasseh.'" "The meaning of these obscure words is probably the following: 'Ye are an obscure set of men, men of no name, dwelling in the midst of two most noble and illustrious tribes.'"

GIL'GAL (gil'gal; "rolling").

1. A place in the Jordan Valley not far from Jericho, called Geliloth (Josh. 18:17). Here the Israelites first encamped after they crossed the Jordan, and here the twelve stones were set up as a memorial (4:19-20). Samuel judged here (1 Sam. 7:16); Agag was slain here (15:33).

2. Gilgal of Elijah and Elisha (2 Kings 2:1; 4:38), a locality probably four miles distant from Bethel and Shiloh.

3. In Josh. 12:23 reference is made to "the king of Goiim in Gilgal." Parker says the word *Goiim* probably means the nomad people who had been driven away by Joshua.

BIBLIOGRAPHY: E. W. Nicholson, *Exodus and Sinai in History and Tradition* (1973), pp. 1-11.

GI'LOH (gī'lō). In the mountains of Judah (Josh. 15:51), the birthplace and the scene of the suicide of the traitor Ahithophel (2 Sam. 15:12; 17:23). Probably the present Khirbet Jala, five miles NNW of Hebron. Giloh stands probably for the original Gilon (cf. 2 Sam. 15:12; 23:34). *See* Gilonite.

GI'LONITE (gī'lon-īt). An epithet of the traitor *Ahithophel* (which see), doubtless from his city, Giloh (2 Sam. 15:12; 23:34).

GIM'EL (ג) (gim'el; "camel"). Gimel is the third letter of the Heb. alphabet, pronounced like English "g" and corresponding to Gk. *gamma*. It stands at the head of the third section of Ps. 119, in which each verse commences with this letter in the Heb.

GIM'ZO (gim'zō; a "place abounding in sycamores"). A town in the low country of Judah (2 Chron. 28:18). Now Jimzu, three miles SE of Lod.

GIN. *See* Snare.

GI'NATH (gi'nath). The father of *Tibni* (which see), king of the northern tribes of Israel (1 Kings 16:21-22).

GIN'NETHOI (gin'e-thō). A corrupt reading (Neh. 12:4) for the name *Ginnethon* (which see).

GIN'NETHON (gin'e-thon; "gardener"). One of the "heads" of the priests who returned from the captivity with Zerubbabel (Neh. 12:4, where the reading is "Ginnethoi") and subscribed to the covenant with Nehemiah (10:6). His son, Meshullam, is mentioned as a contemporary with the high priest Joiakim (12:16), 536-410 B.C.

GIRDLE. As an article of clothing, *see* Dress; Priests, Clothing of.

Figurative. To "gird [or girdle] up the loins" is a common expression in the KJV for putting one's self in readiness for any service that might be required (Luke 12:35); also to "gird your minds for action" (1 Pet. 1:13). The girdle was a symbol of strength, activity, and power (Job 12:18; Isa 23:10, marg.; 45:5; 1 Kings 20:11). Righteousness and faithfulness are called the "girdle" of the Messiah (Isa. 11:5, KJV; NASB and NIV, "belt"), and the perfect adherence of the people of God to His service is spoken of as the "cleaving of the girdle to a man's loins" (Jer. 13:11, KJV). *See* Armor, Arms.

GIR'GASHITES (ger'ga-shīts). One of the seven Canaanite nations whose land was given to Israel. Joshua 24:11 seems to place them W of the Jordan. In Gen. 10:16 and 1 Chron. 1:14 the Girgashite is descended from Canaan. The Girgashites are enumerated among the Canaanite nations only in Gen. 15:21; Deut. 7:1; Josh. 3:10; 24:11; Neh. 9:8.

GIRL (Heb. *yaldâ*, "one born female"). The female counterpart of "boy" (*yeled*). *Yaldâ* is often used of female children (Joel 3:3; Zech. 8:5) but occasionally of a girl of marriageable age, i.e., in her early teens (Gen. 34:4). In Lev. 12:5 a female child was described technically as *neqēbâ*, and this is similar in meaning to *na'ărâ* (2 Kings 5:2, 4; etc.).

GIR'ZITES (Ger'zītes). The name given in 1 Sam. 27:8 to a tribe associated with the Amalekites and Geshurites, "for they were the inhabitants of the land from ancient times, as you come to Shur even as far as the land of Egypt." The three were attacked, plundered, and exterminated by David during his stay in the land of the Philistines. This is all that is known of the tribe, and even the name is in doubt. Girzite (Heb. *haggizrî*) is the rendering of the *qere* of 1 Sam.

27:8, which may be Girzite, Gerizite, or Gerazzite. The Alexandrian manuscript of the LXX has *ton Gezraion;* Vulg. Gerzi and Gezri. The KJV renders Gezrites, which would naturally mean inhabitants of Gezer, but Gezer lies fifty miles distant in the territory of Ephraim and seems too far to have been reached by David on this raid.

W.H.

GISH'PA (gĭsh'pa). One of the two overseers of the Temple servants in Ophel, at Jerusalem, after the captivity (Neh. 11:21); but whether he was himself also of that class is not stated, although this is probable from the fact that his associate, Ziha, was (Ezra 2:43), 445 B.C.

GIT'TAH-HE'PHER. *See* Gath-hepher.

GIT'TAIM (git'a-im; "two winepresses"). The place to which the Beerothites fled (2 Sam. 4:3), perhaps through fear of vengeance for the murder of Ish-bosheth. It is mentioned (Neh. 11:33) in the list of cities inhabited by the Benjamites after the captivity, identified with Gamteti of the Amarna Letters, and located at or near Ramleh.

GIT'TITE (gĭt'īt). An inhabitant, or properly native, of the Philistine city of Gath (Josh. 13:3), 600 of whom attached themselves to David and became part of his bodyguard (2 Sam. 15:18-19). *Obed-edom* (which see), in whose house the Ark was placed for a time (6:10), is called a Gittite, probably from his birthplace, the Levitical city of Gath-rimmon in the tribe of Dan (Josh. 19:45; 21:24).

GIT'TITH (git'ith). A musical term in the titles of Pss. 8, 81, and 84. It may refer to a musical instrument characteristic of Gath.

GI'ZONITE (gī'zo-nīt). An inhabitant of Gizoh, Hashem by name, who was the ancestor of two of David's warriors (1 Chron. 11:34). Gizonite seems to be a corruption of Gunite (*see* Rahlf's LXX); cf. Num. 26:48.

GLASS.

Egyptian. The discovery of glass was made early by the Egyptians and the Phoenicians. The opaque variety was known by the Nile-dwellers as far back as the end of the third millennium B.C. Perfume bottles, bracelets, tear bottles, and beads were manufactured of Egyptian glass from the time of the New Empire on (c. 1500 B.C.). Exquisite shades of blue, yellow, and red, seen today in tomb jewelry, were common among the wealthy. Animals, as well as strings of beads, were made of glass at the time of Thutmose III (c. 1450 B.C.). King Tutankhamen's tomb (fourteenth century B.C.) yielded colorful glass vases and cups.

Phoenician. Phoenicians at an early period produced glass and exquisite jewelry. Pliny recounts how one day a vessel put into the Byblos harbor near the Belus River and landed with blocks of niter; the sailors used this substance to

Glass bottle from Roman period

support cooking utensils on the sandy shore. They were amazed, so the account goes, to find the fires melted salt and sand in a flow of glass. However true this story is, the sand of the Belus River was long famous as an ingredient of fine glass, and some would give Phoenician craftsmen in glass priority over the Egyptian. Sidon was famous for glassware at an early age. In the Byblos district of Lebanon, a new find of Phoenician glassware was made in 1942 in the course of the construction of the Haifa to Tripoli railroad.

Roman. Transparent glass came later as a luxury in the Roman Age. It was a distinct artistic improvement over the opaque variety of ancient Egyptians and Phoenicians. In the NT period after the discovery of transparent Roman glass, Alexandria in Egypt became world-famous as a center of the production of beautiful glassware. This reputation was maintained for a long period. Fine beakers, bowls, flasks and goblets, and bottles both for perfume and wine were costly wares exported throughout the entire Mediterranean world and even as far as Britain. Corinth, after the Pauline period, also developed a reputation for the production of fine Roman glass of varied colors.

Biblical. In the light of transparent Roman glass, the Patmos seer's references become much more comprehensible when he speaks of "a sea of glass mixed with fire" (Rev. 15:2) and when he refers to the New Jerusalem with its street of "pure gold, like transparent glass" (21:21). We also find in the Apocalypse the expression "like clear glass" (21:18). In both passages "glass" is the rendering of the Gk. *hualos.* In the reference of 4:6 and 15:2 the adjectival form of this Gk. word is used, meaning "of glass, transparent." Caution must be exercised, however, in translation references to glass. The familiar KJV passages, "And now we see through a glass, darkly" (1 Cor. 13:12; NIV renders "poor reflection"), and, "Like unto a man beholding his natural face in a glass" (James 1:23), allude to a "mirror" (Gk. *esoptron*), as is rendered in NASB. Probably one of the highly polished metal mirrors such as were in vogue in Egypt, Pompeii, and throughout the Roman world is meant. Among the numerous articles used by fashionable Jewish women in Isaiah's time were "hand mirrors" used for "well-set hair" (Isa. 3:23-24). Evidently these worldly daughters of Zion carried vanity cases as women do today, and a polished bronze mirror is apparently implied (Heb., *gilyōnîn,* "polished metal plates"). When Job said, "Can you, with Him, spread out the skies, strong as a molten mirror?" (Job. 37:18), he had in mind the metal type of "looking glass."   M.F.U.

BIBLIOGRAPHY: A. L. Oppenheim, et al., *Glass and Glass-making in Ancient Mesopotamia* (1970).

Glass bottles from Roman times discovered at Masada

GLASSES. A KJV expression replaced in the NASB by "hand mirrors."

GLASS WORKER. *See* Glass.

GLAZE. The NIV translation of the Heb. phrase otherwise rendered "of silver dross" (Prov. 26:23 and marg.). Glaze was a hard, shiny patina spread over a clay vessel. *See* Glass.

GLEAN. Moses provided a liberal treatment of the poor at the harvest season. In reaping the field the owner was not to "reap to the very corners," etc. (Lev. 19:9-10); i.e., he was not to reap the field to the extreme edge, or gather together the ears left upon the field in the reaping. In the vineyard and olive plantation the fallen fruit was to be left for the distressed and the foreigner (cf. Deut. 24:20-22), hence the proverb of Gideon (Judg. 8:2). *See* Agriculture.

GLEDE. *See* Animal Kingdom.

GLOOM.
1. (Heb. *'apēl,* "dusk"). In Isa. 29:18 this word is rendered "gloom and darkness," as out of which the blind shall see. The KJV renders "obscurity."
2. (Heb. *ḥōshek,* "darkness, destruction, ignorance"). In Isa. 58:10, 59:9, "gloom" ("obscurity," KJV; "darkness," NIV) is again used in connection with darkness and lack of sight.

GLORIFY.
1. To make glorious or honorable, or to cause to appear so (John 12:28; 13:31-32; Acts 3:13; etc.); especially of the resurrection of Christ and His ascension (John 7:39; 12:16).
2. The bringing of Christians to a heavenly condition and dignity (Rom. 8:30).
3. To *glorify* God (1 Cor. 6:20) is to declare His praise by obedience to His law. Thus the "heavens are telling of the glory of God" (Ps. 19:1) in obedience to the law of creation, and much more do men glorify Him by willing obedience to the moral law (1 Cor. 10:31; John 17:5).

GLORY. Usually represents the Heb. *kābōd,* "weight," and Gk. *doxa,* although a number of other words in the original are thus rendered.

In the applications of the word *glory* in Scripture it is easy to trace the fundamental idea involved in it. Properly, it is the exercise and display of what constitutes the distinctive excellence of the subject to which it is spoken; thus, in *respect to God,* His glory is the manifestation of His divine attributes and perfections, or such a visible splendor as indicates the possession and presence of these (Ex. 33:18-22; 16:7, 10; John 1:14; 2:11; 2 Pet. 1:17; etc.). God's "glory is the correlative of his holiness . . . is that in which holiness comes to expression. Glory is the expression of holiness, as beauty is the expression of health." In *respect to man,* His glory is found in the things that reveal His honorable state and character, such as wisdom, righteousness, superiority to passion, or that outward magnificence that is expressive of what, in the lower sphere, bespeaks the high position of its possessor.

"By a very natural extension, the term *glory* is used for the property or possession itself, which tends to throw around its subject a halo of glory, or in some respect to crown it with honor; as when the glory of man is identified with his soul; the glory of Lebanon with its trees (Isa. 60:13); the glory of herbs with the beauty of their flower (40:6); the glory of God with his infinite perfections, and especially with his pure and unchanging righteousness (3:8; 42:8). In this last sense God is the glory of his people (Jer. 2:11; Zech. 2:5), because he is the living root and spring of all that distinguishes them for good; and they are his glory in the outer sense (Jer. 13:11; 33:9), inasmuch as it is through their holy and blessed state, through the wonderful things done for them and by them, that his own glorious perfections are manifested before the eyes of men. There are no applications of the word in Scripture but what may without difficulty be reduced to the one or the other of those now indicated" (*Imp. Dict.,* s.v.).

BIBLIOGRAPHY: A. M. Ramsey, *The Glory of God in the Transfiguration of Christ* (1949); I. Abrahams, *The Glory of God* (1973); J. D. Pentecost, *The Glory of God* (1978).

GLOWING METAL (Heb. *ḥashmal;* LXX *ēlektron,* only in Ezek. 1:4, 27; 8:2, marg., "electrum"). In all these cases it is used, in the attempted description of the visions of the divine glory, in close connection with "brightness" and "the appearance of fire." The Gk. word had a twofold sense—the fossil resin known to us as amber (and so rendered in KJV), and an alloy of gold and silver, now called electrum by mineralogists. It is uncertain whether amber proper was known to the Hebrews; but the idea meant to be conveyed in these passages is plainly that of a brilliant glowing yellow, like amber, or like some highly polished metallic alloy, like brass or electrum. The same idea is clearly brought out in Rev. 1:15 and suggested in Ezra 8:27: "fine shiny bronze, precious as gold."

GLUTTON (Heb. from *zālal,* to "shake," hence to "be loose" morally). A debauchee (Deut. 21:20; Prov. 23:21); "gluttonous" (23:20; 28:7), meaning a free liver, one who is unrestrained (Matt. 11:19; Luke 7:34).

GNASH (Heb. *ḥāraq*). To *grate* the teeth; "He has gnashed at me with His teeth," and "gnash their teeth." Expressions denoting rage or sorrow (Job 16:9; Lam. 2:16).

GNAT. See Animal Kingdom.

GNAWING LOCUST. See Animal Kingdom: Locust.

GNOSTICISM. See Incarnation.

GOAD. An instrument for guiding oxen, the long handle of which might be used as a formidable weapon (Judg. 3:31, "oxgoad," NASB and NIV). The instrument, still used in southern Europe and western Asia, consists of a rod about eight feet long, brought to a sharp point and some-

Goad being used to guide oxen

times cased with iron at the bigger end, to clear the plow of clay.

Figurative. "To kick against the pricks" (Acts 9:5, KJV; not in the NASB; NIV, "goads") or goads was a proverbial expression for unavailing resistance to superior power.

GO'AH (gō'ah). A place near Jerusalem, mentioned by Jeremiah (Jer. 31:39) in his prophecy of the city's restoration. The site is unknown, but probably W of the city.

GOAT. See Animal Kingdom: Goat; Wild Goat; Food; Gods, False: Shaggy Goat; Scapegoat.

GOAT, WILD. See Animal Kingdom: Wild Goat.

GO'ATH. See Goah.

GOAT'S HAIR; SKIN. See Dress; Tabernacle.

GOB (gōb; "a pit," 2 Sam. 21:18-19; called "Gezer," 1 Chron. 20:4). The place where the brother of Goliath of Gath defied Israel but was slain by Jonathan the son of Shimea. In the Syri. version Gob is "Gath," and the Heb. text is uncertain.

GOBLET (Heb. *'aggān*). A trough for washing garments; thus any laver, basin, bowls (Song of Sol. 7:2; cf. Ex. 24:6, "basins"; Isa. 22:24, "bowls"). In form and material the goblet was probably like those found in Egyptian ruins, of silver, gold, bronze, porcelain, and even of wood. See Cup.

GOD.

Names of God. The two essential and personal names of God in the Heb. Scriptures are Elohim and Jehovah (more correctly Yahweh); the former calling attention to the fullness of divine power, the latter meaning "He who is" and thus declaring the divine self-existence. These terms are varied or combined with others to bring out or emphasize certain attributes of the Godhead, such variations or combinations being rendered in our English version "God Almighty," "the Living God," "the Most High," "the Lord," or "the God of Hosts." The English word *God* is identical with the Anglo-Saxon word for "good," and therefore it is believed that the name *God* refers to the divine goodness. (*See* Oehler's *Theol. of Old Test.;* Strong's and Young's concordances.)

Doctrine Defined. The scriptural or Christian doctrine of God must be distinguished not only from antitheistic theories but also from other theories more or less approximating that doctrine. God as revealed through the Scriptures is the one infinite and eternal Being. He is purely spiritual, the supreme personal Intelligence, the Creator and Preserver of all things, the perfect Moral Ruler of the universe; He is the only proper object of worship; He is tri-personal—the Father, Son, and Holy Spirit constituting one Godhead (Gen. 1:1; Ex. 34:14; Pss. 90:1-2; 139:7-12; Job 26; Jer. 23:2-4; Matt. 3:16-17; 28:19; John 4:24;

1 John 4:16; etc.). The above does not present fully, as we shall see later, the contents of revelation concerning God. But it is sufficient for the purpose of making the distinctions named.

Theism. Theism, as the term is most commonly used, is equivalent to monotheism, particularly in the sense of recognizing the one God as distinct from the world, the personal Creator and Governor of all things. Accordingly, the following are specified as: (*a*) *atheism,* avowed opposition to a belief in one supreme God; (*b*) *polytheism,* holding a multiplicity of gods; (*c*) *pantheism,* identifying God with the universe; (*d*) *materialism,* recognizing no existence save that of matter; (*e*) *agnosticism,* denying all knowledge of God and all possibility of knowing Him, thus being in practical effect equivalent to atheism.

Deism. Deism and theism are etymologically equivalent terms, yet a distinction is found in their application. Deism has appeared in various forms, but in general it has been distinct from theism in that, though holding to the existence of a personal God who has created the world, it has regarded God as holding Himself aloof from the world and leaving it to the government of natural laws.

Theism and Christian doctrine. Theism lies at the basis of all Christian doctrine, and yet is not to be regarded as comprehending that doctrine in all its fullness. This must appear most plainly in the consideration of the attributes of God and the mode of the divine Existence.

The Knowledge of God. As to man's knowledge of God two questions have been the subjects of much controversy: the first relating to the possibility of true knowledge of the divine Being, the second the source or method of such knowledge.

First. Can God be known? The Scriptures declare that God is incomprehensible (see Job 11:7; 21:14; 36:26; Ps. 77:19; Rom. 11:33). Perfect or complete knowledge of God is not attainable by man upon the earth. But equally true is that the Scriptures represent God as revealing Himself to man and that a sufficient though limited measure of true knowledge of God is put within the reach of human beings. The important distinction to be maintained at this point is that between partial and perfect knowledge. We cannot comprehend God, and yet we can truly know Him. Our blessedness, our eternal life even, is in such knowledge (see Matt. 11:27; John 17:3; Rom. 1:19-20; Eph. 1:17; Col. 1:10; 1 John 5:20).

The prevailing faith of the Christian church in all ages has been in accord with these teachings of Scripture. Both theological and philosophical speculation, however, have often diverged from this view, and in both directions. For example, defenders of the Arian heresy in the fourth century held that God could be fully known. They thus sought to meet the appeals of their opponents to the unsearchableness of God. The mystics of the Middle Ages also claimed the possibil-

ity of perfect knowledge of God. Through the life of love in God, they held that the soul could contemplate Him immediately and clearly and thus arrive at complete knowledge. In modern times the tendency is to err in the opposite direction. The incomprehensibility of God and His unknowableness are conceived in such a one-sided or exaggerated form as to shut out the possibility of any measure of real knowledge. Agnosticism is an extreme illustration. The doctrine of Mansel in his *Limits of Religious Thought* betrays the same tendency.

Second. As to the source or method of the knowledge of God, it is held by many theologians that the idea, and consequently some knowledge of God, is innate. By this is meant, however, only that all men have naturally a conviction that there is a Being upon whom they are dependent and to whom they are responsible. The arguments for and against this view are too minute and extended to be presented here. Van Oosterzee's statement is weighty: "Belief in God is by no means the necessary product of abstract reasoning, but has its firm basis in the whole nature and being of man." It is also said with much force that the Scriptures do not seek to prove the existence of God but simply assume or assert the fact as one that men ought to be prepared to recognize. The rational proofs of the existence of the divine Being are not, however, to be regarded otherwise than of great value. They are mainly drawn from nature, from history, and from humanity. It is sometimes rashly asserted that arguments built upon these foundations are antiquated or useless. Nevertheless, they remain in all essential respects, whatever may be their changes of form, valid and of great use in confirming and explaining the belief in God that is in some sense natural to every person. It is also to be observed that nature, man, and history bring to us a general revelation from God—a fact recognized throughout Scripture (see Ps. 19:1-3; Acts 14:17; 17:26-27; Rom. 1:19-20; 2:15).

Accordingly, study in these directions yields not only evidences of the existence of the divine Being but also some knowledge of His character.

Special revelation, for which the Holy Scriptures are the appointed vehicle, affords us the necessary and sufficient knowledge of God. The Scriptures throughout are harmonious in their teachings. The God of the OT is also the God of the NT. And yet the Scriptures exhibit a progress in the revelation.

The NT doctrine of God is distinguished from that of the OT, first, in that it presents with peculiar distinctness and fullness the divine fatherhood. Second, it declares likewise the divine sonship of Jesus Christ, God "revealed in the flesh." The God-man is the fullest disclosure of the divine nature and is the Redeemer and Savior of mankind. Third, the distinct divine personality and peculiar office of the Holy Spirit are brought most clearly into view. And thus comes what at most was but intimated in the OT, the doctrine of the Trinity. *See* Trinity.

The Attributes of God. From the Scriptures is derived in the largest measure our knowledge of the attributes of God. By the word *attributes* in this connection is meant the properties or qualities of the divine Being, and particularly those that are made known to us through the revelation that He has given of Himself. They are not to be regarded as mere human conceptions but as true representations of the divine nature. Nor are they to be thought of as otherwise than absolutely inseparable from that nature. They blend harmoniously with each other in the unity of the one Being, God.

Theologians differ to some extent in their statements of the essential truth of Scripture at this point, varying in their use of terms as well as in classification and arrangement. But they generally agree in recognizing the following as the revealed attributes of God, namely: spirituality, infinity, eternity, immutability, self-sufficiency, perfection, freedom, omnipotence, omnipresence, omniscience, justice, truth, love, mercy, and grace.

For discussion of attributes see separate heads.

BIBLIOGRAPHY: C. Hodge, *Systematic Theology* (1946), 1:366-534; L. S. Chafer, *Systematic Theology* (1948), 1:138-282; E. Brunner, *The Christian Doctrine of God* (1949); H. Bavinck, *The Doctrine of God* (1951); K. Barth, *Church Dogmatics* (1957), 1:1:339-560; W. G. T. Shedd, *Dogmatic Theology* (1969), 1:151-546.

GOD, UNKNOWN. Paul, in his address on Mars' Hill, said that he had seen in Athens "an altar with this inscription, 'To an unknown God' " (Acts 17:22-23). That there actually stood at Athens such an altar appears historically certain since Paul appeals to his own observation and does so in the presence of the Athenians themselves. But there are corroborating external proofs, since Lucian, Pausanias, and Philostratus mention altars at Athens consecrated "to the unknown gods." The question naturally arises, What definite god is meant? Different answers have been given, but the following is probably correct. On important occasions, when the reference to a god known by name was wanting, as in public calamities to which no definite god could be assigned as the author, in order to honor or pacify the god concerned by sacrifice and without lighting upon the wrong one, altars were erected that were destined and designated *agnōstō theō* (to the unknown god).

GODDESS. *See* Gods, False.

GODHEAD. As used in theology the term means: (1) The divine notice; deity; (2) the supreme Being, especially as comprehending all His attributes; (3) divinity; a heathen god or goddess. The scriptural term *Godhead* (KJV) is rendered "divine nature" or "deity" in NASB and NIV. "For

since the creation of the world His invisible attributes, His eternal power and divine nature, have been clearly seen, being understood through what has been made" (Rom. 1:20; Gk. *theiotēs*); "For in Him all the fulness of Deity dwells in bodily form" (Col. 2:9; Gk. *theotēs*). In Acts 17:29 the Gk. *theion* is used: "Being then the offspring of God, we ought not to think that the Divine Nature is like gold or silver or stone, an image formed by the art and thought of man."

GODLINESS. The rendering of Gk. *eusebeia,* "reverence," in Scripture meaning *piety toward God* (Acts 3:12, "piety"; 1 Tim. 2:2; 4:7-8; 6:3, 5-6, 11). It is the sum of religious virtues and duties, bringing to its possessor blessedness "for the present life and also for the life to come" (4:8). "The mystery of godliness" (3:16) is the mystery that is held by godliness and nourishes it. Once (1 Tim 2:10) godliness is the rendering of *theosebeia,* "reverence toward God," or (NIV) "profess to worship God."

GODLY ONES (Heb. *ḥasîd,* "pious, just"; "saints," KJV and NIV). Used of pious Israelites, and so of the godly in general (1 Sam. 2:9; 2 Chron. 6:41; Pss. 30:4; 31:23; 37:28; 50:5; 52:9; 79:2; 85:8; 97:10; 116:15; 132:9, 16; 145:10; 148:14; 149:1, 5, 9).

GODS (Heb. *'elōhîm*). This term for deity is used in a threefold connotation in the OT: (1) In a singular sense of the one true God in a plural of majesty or excellence. It is construed with a singular verb or adjective (Gen. 1:1; 2 Kings 19:4, 16; Pss. 7:10; 57:3; 78:56) but with a plural verb only in certain phrases. (2) All gods or deities in general, "the gods of Egypt" (Ex. 12:12); "foreign gods" (Gen. 35:2, 4; cf. Deut. 29:18); "new gods" (32:17). (3) Of judges or prophets as "to whom the word of God came" (John 10:35; Ps. 82:6), and whom God consequently dignified with authority to bear His own name (Ex. 21:6, see marg.; 22:8, "judges"). The medium of Endor said to Saul concerning the spirit she brought up at the seance, "I see a divine being [*'elōhîm*] coming up out of the earth" (1 Sam. 28:13; the NIV has "spirit"). The expression is difficult and unusual in that it is the same word for "God" or "gods," but that this particular reference is not to Jehovah or to heathen deities or demons is evident from Saul's immediate query, "What is his form?" (v. 14); "What form is he of?" KJV. It is apparent that this is another case where *'elōhîm* is employed of a judge or prophet. The designation was plainly apropos of Samuel, the last and greatest of the judges and the first of the prophets. This usage of *'elōhîm* as referring to God's earthly representatives is denied by some critics, and the RSV renders "God" in Ex. 21:6; 22:8; such a rendering is manifestly unsustained by the context and by a general comparison of Scripture.

GODS, FALSE. Under the heading of *idolatry* (which see) will be discussed the general subject of the evil that proved to be so attractive and fatal to the Israelites, namely, the worship of false gods. In this article we only present the gods named in Scripture, whether worshiped by Israel or other nations. They are given in alphabetical order.

Adram′melech (a-dram′e-lek; "Adar is king"). This deity was worshiped in NW Mesopotamia under the name of Adad-Milki, which is a form of the Syrian god Hadad. In honor of Adrammelech the colonists of Samaria, who had been brought from Sepharvaim, burned their children (2 Kings 17:31). The deity is associated with Anammelech. Some have identified the two as being a double god, but this is hypothetical.   M.F.U.

Amon ("the hidden one"). Originally he was merely a local god of Thebes (biblical No-amon, the capital of Upper Egypt; Nah. 3:8; Jer. 46:25, RV). With the rapid ascendancy of this city during the strong New Middle Kingdom under the Eighteenth Egyptian Dynasty (c. 1580-1085 B.C.), the god Amon (Amun) assumed national prominence and was often designated Amon-Re, the sun-god.

Amon-Re, the sun god

A great temple was erected in his honor at Karnak, and it was against the influential priesthood of this deity that the youthful reformer Akhenaton (Akhnaton) revolted when he built a new capital at *Amarna* (which see) where the famous Amarna Tablets were recovered in 1887.

Anam′melech (a-nam′e-lek; "Anu is king"). Anu was the Babylonian god of the sky and one of the gods revered by the people of the Babylonian city Sepharvaim (2 Kings 17:31). When these Sepharvites were transported to Samaria they honored this repugnant deity by burning their children, worshiping him in the fashion of Molech, the god worshiped particularly by the sons of Ammon (1 Kings 11:7). *See* Adrammelech.

'Anat (Anath; a-nat). 'Anat was the patroness of sex and war, the paramour of Aliyan Baal. She is to be identified with the "queen of heaven" to whom Jews offered incense in Jeremiah's day (Jer. 44:19). Lewd figurines of the nude goddess have been dug from Palestinian sites at levels dating from the second and first millennia B.C. It was against the degrading religion of the Canaanites that Moses and Joshua issued such stern warnings to Israel, realizing the utterly debilitating effect of Canaanite cults upon the chaste morality and high spirituality demanded by the worship of Jehovah. *See also* Ashera; Ashtoreth.   M.F.U.

Ar′temis (ar′te-mis). A goddess known among the Greeks as Artemis and among the Romans as Diana. Like Apollo she was armed with bow and arrow, which she used against monsters and giants, but she was also a beneficent and helpful deity. As Apollo was the luminous god of day, she with her torch was a goddess of light by night, and in time became identified with all possible goddesses of moon and night. Her proper domain is that of nature, being a mighty huntress, sometimes chasing wild animals, sometimes dancing, playing, or bathing with her companions. To her all beasts of the field were sacred, but her favorite animal in all Greece was held to be the hind. As goddess of the chase she also had influence in war, and the Spartans sought her favor by the gift of a goat before going into battle.

Artemis (Diana) was also a protectress of youth, especially those of her own sex. Young girls revered the virgin goddess as the guardian of their maiden years and before marriage offered her a lock of their hair, their girdle, and their maiden garment. She was supposed to assist at childbirth. In early times human sacrifices had been offered to Artemis. A relic of this was the yearly custom, observed at Sparta, of flogging the boys till they bled at the altar of a deity known as *Artemis Orthia*.

"Artemis of the Ephesians" was not a Greek divinity, but Asiatic. This is shown by the fact that eunuchs were employed in her worship—a practice quite foreign to Greek ideas. She was not

Artemis (Diana) of Ephesus

Canaanites of the south. However, most biblical references to the name point clearly to some cult object of wood, which might be worshiped or cut down and burned and which was certainly the goddess' image (1 Kings 15:13; 2 Kings 21:7). Her prophets are mentioned (1 Kings 18:19) and the vessels used in her service are referred to (2 Kings 23:4). Her cult object, whatever it was, was utterly detestable to faithful worshipers of Yahweh (1 Kings 15:13) and was set up on the high places beside the "altars of incense" (*ḥammānîm*) and the "stone pillars" (*maṣṣēbôt*). Indeed, the "stone pillars" seem to have represented the male god Baal (cf. Judg. 6:28), while the cult object of Asherah, probably a tree or pole, constituted a symbol of this goddess (see W. L. Reed, *The Asherah in the Old Testament*). But Asherah was only one manifestation of a chief goddess of western Asia, regarded now as the wife, then as the sister, of the principal Canaanite god El. Other names of this deity were Ashtoreth (Astarte) and Anath. Frequently represented as a nude woman bestride a lion, with a lily in one hand and a serpent in the other, and called Qudshu "the Holiness," that is, "the Holy One" in a perverted moral sense, she was a divine courtesan. In the same sense the male prostitutes consecrated to the cult of the Qudshu and prostituting themselves to her honor were called *qᵉdēšîm*, "sodomites" (Deut. 23:18, marg.; 1 Kings 14:24; 15:12; 22:46). Characteristically Canaanite, the lily symbolizes grace and sex appeal and the serpent fertility (W. F. Albright, *Archaeology and the Religion of Israel* [1942], pp. 68-94). At Byblos (biblical Gebal) on the Mediterranean, N of Sidon, a center dedicated to this goddess has been excavated. She and her colleagues specialized in sex and war, and her shrines were temples of legalized vice. Her degraded cult offered a perpetual danger of pollution to Israel and must have sunk to sordid depths as lust and murder were glamorized in Canaanite religion. On a fragment of the Baal Epic, Anath ('Anat) appears in an incredibly bloody orgy of destruction. For some unknown reason she fiendishly butchers mankind, young as well as old, in a most horrible and wholesale fashion, wading ecstatically in human gore up to her knees—even up to her throat—all the while exulting sadistically. In Canaan there was a tendency to employ the plural forms of deities Ashtoreth (Ashtoroth), Asherah (Asherim), and Anath (Anathoth) to summarize all the various manifestations of this deity. In like fashion the Canaanite plural Elohim ("gods") was adopted by the Hebrews to express the excellencies and attributes of the one true God. *See also* Ashtoreth. M.F.U.

regarded as a virgin but as mother and foster-mother, as is clearly shown by the multitude of breasts in the rude effigy. She was undoubtedly a representative of the same power presiding over conception and birth that was adored in Palestine under the name *Ashtoreth*. Her worship, frantic and fanatical after the manner of Asia, was traced back to the Amazons. Her temple at Ephesus was one of the wonders of the world, but its great glory was the "image which fell down from heaven" (Acts 19:35). Images claiming so lofty an origin were to be found in cities other than Ephesus. Once in the year there was a public festival in honor of the goddess at Ephesus, to which all the Ionians who could do so came with their wives and children, bringing costly offerings to Artemis and rich presents for the priests. Great gain came to the silversmiths in making and selling small images of the goddess (cf. 19:23-40).

Ashe′rah (a-she′ra). Plural, Asherim, a pagan goddess who is found in the Ras Shamra epic religious texts discovered at Ugarit in N Syria (1929-37) as Asherat, "Lady of the Sea," and consort of El. She was the chief goddess of Tyre in the fifteenth century B.C. with the appellation Qudshu, "holiness." In the OT Asherah appears as a goddess by the side of Baal, whose consort she evidently came to be, at least among the

Ash′ima (ash′ima). The god of Hamath, introduced by the colonists settled in Samaria by Shalmaneser (2 Kings 17:30).

Ash′toreth (ash′tō-reth). Astarte, a Canaanite goddess. In S Arabia the name is found as 'Athtar

Three Phoenician coins showing Astarte: lower left, Astarte at Tyre; lower right, Astarte in a vehicle.

(apparently from *'athara*, "to be fertile, to irrigate"), a god identified with the planet Venus. The name is cognate with Babylonian Ishtar, the goddess of sensual love, maternity, and fertility. Licentious worship was conducted in honor of her. As Asherah and Anat of Ras Shamra, she was the patroness of war as well as sex and is sometimes identified with these goddesses. The Amarna Letters present Ashtoreth as Ashtartu. In the Ras Shamra Tablets are found both the masculine form 'Athtar and the feminine 'Athtart. Ashtoreth worship was entrenched early at Sidon (1 Kings 11:5, 33; 2 Kings 23:13). Her cult even presented a danger of pollution to early Israel (Judg. 2:13; 10:6); Solomon succumbed to her voluptuous worship (1 Kings 11:5; 2 Kings 23:13). The peculiar vocalization Ashtoreth, instead of the more primitive Ashtaroth, is evidently a deliberate alteration by the Hebrews to express their abhorrence for her cult by giving her the vowels of their word for "shame" (*bōshet*). *See also* Anat; Ashera; Diana.   M.F.U.

Astaroth. *See* Asherah; Ashtoreth.

Astar'te. The Greek name for *Ashtoreth* (which see).

Atar'gatis (a-tar′ga-tis; from Gk. *atargatis* from the Aram. *'Atar* or *'Attar* (Astarte) plus *'Atah*. Probably the same form of the Phrygian *Atis*, a god of vegetation). A Syrian divinity, the great goddess of fertility among the Aramaeans. The worship of this goddess is not alluded to in the OT, but 2 Macc. 12:26 mentions her temple at Carnion in Gilead. She was also worhsiped at Ashkelon, and the concomitants of her cult were those of the mother goddess of the Semites.
                                                                           M.F.U.

Ba'al (bā′al). The common Canaanite word for "master lord." Baal was one of the chief male deities of the Canaanite pantheon, now well known from the religious epic literature discovered at Ras Shamra (ancient Ugarit of the Amarna

Letters) from 1929 to 1937. Baal was the son of El, the father of the gods and the head of the Canaanite pantheon, according to the tablets from Ugarit. He is also designated as "the son of Dagon" (Heb. *dāgān*, "grain"), an ancient Canaanite and Mesopotamian deity associated with agriculture. Baal was thus the farm god who gave increase to family and field, flocks and herds. He was likewise identified with the storm god Hadad, whose voice could be heard in the reverberating thunder that accompanied rain, so necessary for the success of the crops.

Canaanite Worship. The inhabitants of Canaan were addicted to Baal worship, which was conducted by priests in temples and in good weather outdoors in fields and particularly on hilltops called "high places." The cult included animal sacrifice, ritualistic meals, and licentious dances. Near the rock altar was a sacred pillar, or *maṣṣēbâ*, and close by was the symbol of the *'ăshērâ*, both of which apparently symbolized human fertility. High places had chambers for sacred prostitution by male prostitutes (*q*ᵉ*dēshîm*) and sacred harlots (*q*ᵉ*dēshôt*) (1 Kings 14:23-24; 2 Kings 23:7). The gaiety and licentious character of Baal worship always had a subtle attraction for the austere Hebrews bound to serve a holy God under a rigorous moral code.

Baal Names. In times of lapse Hebrews compounded the names of their children with Baal —for example, Jerubbaal (Judg. 7:1); Eshbaal (1 Chron. 8:33; 9:39). Merib-baal (8:34; 9:40), which in times of revival and return to Jehovistic worship were altered, the *baal* element being replaced by "bosheth," meaning "shame." Thus pious Israelites expressed their horror of Baal worship; examples are Jerubbesheth (for Jerubbaal, 2 Sam. 11:21), Ish-bosheth (for Ishbaal, 2:8), Mephibosheth (for Merib-baal; 4:4; 9:6, 10). Numerous place names also occur, such as Baal-gad ("lord of good fortune," Josh. 11:17), Baal-hamon ("lord of wealth," Song of Sol. 8:11), Baal-hazor ("Baal's village," 2 Sam. 13:23), Baal-meon ("lord of the dwelling," Num. 32:38), Baal-peor ("lord of the opening," Deut. 4:3), Baal-tamar ("lord of the palm tree," Judg. 20:33), and others.

Ba'al-berith' (bā′al-be-rîth; "lord of the covenant"). Under this title the great NW Semitic weather god Baal was worshiped at Shechem after the death of Gideon (Judg. 8:33; 9:4). Occasionally he was spoken of as El-berith, "the god of covenant" (9:46). The Canaanites were brought into the Israelite fold by treaty, conquest, or gradual absorption. The Bene Hamor ("sons of the ass") of Shechem were incorporated in such a way. This is indicated from various early references to them and to their god Baal-berith. The sacrifice of an ass was an essential feature of a treaty among the Amorites of the Mari Period (c. 1700 B.C.). (Cf. W. F. Albright, *From the Stone Age to Christianity* [1940], p. 231.)   M.F.U.

Representation of Baal

Ba'alim (bā'al-im; Heb. plural of *Ba'al*). This is a general term including not images of Baal but various concepts of the god. There were numerous Baalim, such as Baal-shamem (lord of heaven) of the Phoenicians and Palmyraeans, Baal-Melkart of the Tyrians, and Baal-Saphon of the Canaanites of Ugarit. There is a distinction, too, between the Baalim, such as Baal-berith, Baal-peor, and Baal-zebub.   M.F.U.

Ba'al-pe'or (bā'al-pē'or; "Baal of Peor"). A Moabite deity worshiped on the summit of Mt. Peor with immoral rites. The name is probably another form of *Chemosh* (which see). The Israelites were seduced into the immorality of this licentious worship in the plains of Moab (Num. 25:1-9; Ps. 106:28; Hos. 9:10).   M.F.U.

Ba'al-ze'bub (bā'al-ze'bub). The form of the name of Baal as worshiped at the Philistine city of Ekron. Baal, under this aspect of worship, was viewed as the producer of flies and hence able to control this pest so common in the East. He was consulted by Ahaziah of Israel, c. 849 B.C. (2 Kings 1:2-16). A NT rendering of the name is Beelzebul, (Beelzebub, KJV) meaning "lord of the (heavenly) habitation." Pharisees called Beelzebub (Beelzebul) the "ruler of the demons" (Matt. 12:24). Our Lord denied that He expelled demons by the power of Beelzebul (Luke 11:19-23). It is

a matter of divine revelation that demonism is the dynamic of idolatry. (1 Cor. 10:20, "No, but I say that the things which the Gentiles sacrifice, they sacrifice to demons, and not to God; and I do not want you to become sharers in demons"). Many of the Jews from the period of the restoration and down through NT times believed that heathen deities were demons. The heathen deities were, of course, nothing, but behind them were evil spirits or demons energizing their worship (cf. Merrill F. Unger, *Biblical Demonology*, pp. 58-61).

Bel (bāl; Akkad. *Bēlû*, cognate of Heb. *ba'al*, "lord"). The patron god of Babylon (Jer. 51:44) identified with Marduk, head of the Babylonian pantheon. The Hebrews called him Merodach. As a sun-god his festival was celebrated in the spring at the beginning of the year, since the sun's rays were then most potent in reviving nature. The Babylonians paid him supreme tribute and exalted him to the headship of their pantheon shortly after 2000 B.C. According to *Enuma elish*, the Babylonian account of creation, Marduk was elevated to this superior position because of his slaying Tiamat, the goddess of chaos. He was worshiped in Esagila, the great temple at Babylon.   M.F.U.

Be'rith. *See* Baal-berith.

Calf Worship.

1. An image was made of gold earrings and other ornaments by the Hebrews and worshiped under the direction of Aaron (Ex. 32:1-6; Deut. 9:16). This was evidently a representation of Jehovah as the God of their deliverance from Egypt. It seems scarcely possible that this incident represents bull worship as witnessed in Egypt, for there the bull was a living animal (Apis). Among many Eastern nations there is evidence of the worship of the bull as the emblem of strength and the symbol of generative power. The winged bull was common among the Assyrians. In Egypt the term *bull* was a favorite title applied to a king or a god.

2. Jeroboam I, after the division of the monarchy, set up two golden calves at Bethel in the south of his country and Dan in the north, to offset interest in the Temple at Jerusalem (1 Kings 12:28-29). This was evidently an accommodation to Canaanite bull cults and certainly cannot mean that the people worshiped the image itself but rather they thought of Jehovah enthroned invisibly above the calf. Among Israel's immediate neighbors—Canaanites, Arameans, and Hittites—"deities were nearly always represented as standing on the back of an animal or as on a throne borne by animals, but never as themselves in animal form" (W. F. Albright, *From the Stone Age to Christianity* [1940], p. 229). The storm god of Mesopotamia, for example, is depicted on second millennium B.C. seal cylinders in the form of a lightning bolt set upright on a bull's back (ibid.). Although concep-

Apis bull figure of Egypt

tionally there is little difference between representing the invisible Deity as enthroned above the cherubim (1 Sam. 4:4; 2 Kings 19:15), or as standing on a bull, except that the former represent beings of the realm of the supernatural that defend the holiness (Gen. 3:24) and throne of God (Isa. 37:16; Rev. 4:6-9), nevertheless Jeroboam's innovation was extremely dangerous. The bull affiliations of Baal, "lord of heaven," were too closely connected with the more degrading aspects of pagan cults to be safe. The Northern Kingdom, consequently, fell to the peril of idolatrous pollution as a result. M.F.U.

Cas'tor (kas'tor) and **Pol'lux** (pol'ux; Gk. *dioskouroi*, "sons of Jupiter"). Castor was a horse tamer and Pollux master of the art of boxing. Castor became mortal, having fallen in a contest with Idas and Lynceus, sons of their paternal uncle Aphareus. Pollux, the immortal son of Zeus, prayed to his father to let him die, too. Zeus permitted him to spend one day among the gods, his peers, the other in the lower world with his beloved brother. According to another story, Zeus, in reward for their brotherly love, set them in the sky as the constellation of the Twins, or the morning and evening star. They are the ideal types of bravery and dexterity in fight.

The ancient symbol of the twin gods at Lacedaemon was two parallel beams, joined by crosspieces, which the Spartans took with them into war. They were worshiped at Sparta and Olympia with Hercules and other heroes. As gods of the sea they were worshiped especially in Ostia, the harbor town of Rome. The only mention of them in Scripture is that the ship in which Paul sailed from Malta bore the sign of "Castor and Pollux" (Acts 28:11, KJV; "Twin Brothers," NASB, see marg.).

Che'mosh (ke-mosh). The national deity of the Moabites, honored with horribly cruel rites like those of Molech, to whom children were sacrificed in the fire. It is interesting archaeologically to note that the anger of Chemosh is said in the famous Moabite Stone to be the reason for Israel's subjugation of Moab (cf. Judg. 11:24). Solomon made a fatal mistake, whatever his reason might have been, of rearing an altar to Chemosh in Jerusalem (1 Kings 11:7). This abomination was not destroyed until Josiah's purge almost three centuries later (2 Kings 23:13). So infatuated were the Moabites with Chemosh that they were known as the "people of Chemosh" (Num. 21:29). M.F.U.

Chi'un. See Kiyyun, below; and also article Kiyyun in the general listing.

Da'gon (dā'gon; Heb. *dāgān*, "corn," evidently a diminutive of *dag*, "fish"). An ancient Mesopotamian deity, transported early to the west. Dagon is generally represented as having the body or trunk of a fish, with a human head and hands, and as being the symbol of water and all the vivifying natural powers that take effect in warm countries through water. The Babylonian-Assyrian, and later Canaanite, Dagon is described by Philo of Byblos as the god of grain. This has been abundantly verified by the N Syrian religious texts from Ras Shamra. There Dagon is associated with agriculture and is described as the father of the great god Baal. Dagon was revered among the early Phoenicians. He had importance as the national god of the Philistines, who set up temples in his honor at Ashdod, Gaza, and elsewhere. Numerous towns were named after him, such as Beth-dagon (Josh. 15:41). His temple has been found at Ugarit near that of Baal, with features

Diana (Artemis)

found in later Hebrew architecture. Instances connected with the temple of Dagon are the scene of Samson's death (Judg. 16:23-30), the experiences connected with the Hebrew Ark at Ashdod (1 Sam. 5:1-7), and the fastening of Saul's head in the temple of Dagon at Bethshan, which has been excavated at this famous fortress site guarding the eastern approaches of Jezreel.
M.F.U.

Diana. *See* Artemis.

Gad. A Canaanite deity rendered "Fortune" (Isa. 65:11, see marg.); the god of good fortune, supposed to be the glorified planet Jupiter. This star is called by the Arabs "the greater luck" as the star of good fortune.

Her'mes (her'mîz). The Greek god who served as messenger for the other gods, identical with Mercury, the Roman god of commerce and protector of the grain trade. Hermes was the son of Zeus and the Naiad, daughter of Atlas. He wore winged sandals and wings on his hat as well. He was inventor of the lyre, herald of the gods, and guide of the dead into the underworld. He was also the god of mining, of crops, and of roads, as well as the patron of trade, and even of theft. He is mentioned in Acts 14:12, where it is stated that the people of Lystra took Paul to be "Hermes, because he was the chief speaker."

Jupiter. *See* Zeus.

Kiyyun (ki'un). The name of this deity should in all likelihood be vocalized Kaiwan or Kewan as representing Akkad. *Kaiwānu,* the name of Ninib or Saturn. The unusual spelling in the MT is evidently the result of the intentional pointing for the vowels of *shiqqûs,* meaning "a detestable thing." Accordingly, the NIV renders it "shrine." The word occurs only once in the Heb. Bible in Amos 5:26, "Kiyyun, your images, the star of your gods." The KJV renders "Chiun."

Mal'cham, or **Malcam** (mal'kam). The national god of the Ammonites equated sometimes with *Molech* or *Moloch* (which see); rendered "Milcom."

Mercury. See Hermes. *See* Milcom.

Me'ni (me'ni; Heb. *mᵉnî,* "destiny" or "fate"). Name of the god of destiny or fortune worshiped by the ancient Hebrews in time of apostasy: "But you who forsake the Lord, who forget My holy mountain, who set a table for Fortune, and who fill cups with mixed wine for Destiny" (Isa. 65:11; see marg.).

Mero'dach (me-rō'dak; the Heb. name for the Akkad. *Marduk*). *See* Bel; Baal. Merodach (Marduk) was the head god of the Babylonian pantheon and the patron god of the city. Merodach's exaltation as head of the Babylonian pantheon is featured in the Babylonian story of creation, *Enuma elish.* He was worshiped by Nebuchadnezzar, the Assyrians, and notably by Cyrus the Great. Cyrus lauds Merodach as a "righteous

prince." Jeremiah 51:44 and Isa. 46:1 mention this deity (rendered "Bel"); also Jer. 50:2, where it is rendered "Marduk" (see marg.). Merodach's name appears compounded with many prominent personages both in and outside of Scripture, and in Bible history in such names as Merodach-baladan and Evil-merodach.   M.F.U.

Mil'com (mil'cum; "their king"). Another form of *Malcham* (which see), the national god of the Ammonites, called (1 Kings 11:5; 2 Kings 23:13) "the abomination of the sons of Ammon." He was worshiped by Solomon and extirpated by Josiah.

Mo'lech (mō'lek; Heb. *melek,* "king"). A Semitic deity honored by the sacrifice of children, in which they were caused to pass through or into the fire. Palestinian excavations have uncovered evidences of infant skeletons in burial places around heathen shrines. Ammonites revered Molech as a protecting father. Worship of Molech was stringently prohibited by Hebrew law (Lev. 18:21; 20:1-5). Solomon built an altar to Molech at Topheth in the valley of Hinnom. Manasseh (c. 696-642 B.C.), in his idolatrous orgy, also honored this deity. Josiah desecrated the Hinnom valley altar, but Jehoiakim revived the cult. The prophets sternly denounced this form of heathen worship (Jer. 7:29-34; Ezek. 16:20-22; 23:37-39; Amos 5:26, marg.). No form of ancient Semitic idolatry was more abhorrent than Molech worship.   M.F.U.

Mo'loch (mō'lok). Another English form (Amos 5:26, marg.; Acts 7:43) of *Molech* (which see).

Ne'bo (ne'bo; Akkad. *Nābû*). A Babylonian deity (Isa. 46:1), the god of wisdom and literature. Borsippa near Babylon was the special center of his worship. The last great Assyrian emperor, Ashurbanipal (669-633 B.C.), the *Osnappar* (which see) of the OT (Ezra 4:10), acted in the interests of Nebo and was a patron of learning and education. An inscription of Ashurbanipal reads thus: "I, Ashurbanipal, learn the wisdom of Nabu, the entire art of writing on clay tablets." In the Nabunaid Chronicle, at the time of the rule of Nabunaid's son Belshazzar, Nabu, together with Bel, was prominent. Speaking of Nabonidus (Akkad. Nabunaid), the Chronicle says: "The king for the month Nisan did not come to Babylon; Nabu did not come to Babylon; Bel did not go forth (from Esagila); the New Year's festival was not celebrated" (Jack Finegan, *Light from the Ancient Past* [1946], p. 190).   M.F.U.

Nehush'tan (ne-hush'tan; a "brazen" or copper "thing"). A contemptuous epithet applied to the *bronze serpent* (which see), which the Israelites had turned into an object of worship (2 Kings 18:4). Among the first acts of Hezekiah was the destruction of all traces of the idolatrous rites that had gained a hold upon the people. Among other objects of superstitious reverence and worship was this serpent, which, in the course of a thousand years, had become invested with a mysterious sanctity that easily degenerated into idolatry.

Ner'gal (ner'gal). The Babylonian sun-god (2 Kings 17:30). The center of his cult was Cuthah, from which Babylonian city, among others, colonists were brought to Samaria after the deportation of the ten tribes (17:24-30). Its site is at Tell Ibrahim, NE of Babylon. Nergal was also the god of pestilence and war and had charge of the netherworld. The name occurs as a formative element in the name of one of Nebuchadnezzar's princes, Nergal-sar-ezer, who held the office of Rab-mag (Jer. 39:3, 13).   M.F.U.

Nib'haz (nib'haz). An idol worshiped by the Avvites, displaced persons from the Assyrian Empire brought to colonize Samaria after the captivity of the Northern Kingdom (2 Kings 17:31). This deity is identified by Hommel with Ibnahaza, an Elamite god.   M.F.U.

Nis'roch (nis'rok). A god with a temple at Nineveh and worshiped by Sennacherib (705-681 B.C.). It was while at worship in the house of this god that Sennacherib was assassinated (2 Kings 19:36-37). This divinity has not as yet been clearly identified. Some construe it as an intentional perversion of the name of Marduk or as a composite containing Ashur; others equate him with Assyrian Nusku.   M.F.U.

Re'phan. *See* Rompha.

Rim'mon (rim'un; "pomegranate"). A Syrian deity worshiped at Damascus, where there was a temple or "house of Rimmon" (2 Kings 5:18). It is probably a contracted form for Hadad-Rimmon, since Hadad was the supreme deity or sun-god of the Syrians. Hadad, with the modification expressed by Rimmon, would be the sun-god of the late summer, who ripens the pomegranate and other fruits. In this sense he has been thought to be the personification of the power of generation, since the pomegranate, with its abundance of seeds, is used in the symbolism of both oriental and Greek mythology, along with the phallus, as a symbol of the generative power, and is also found upon Assyrian monuments.

Rom'pha (rom'fa). A deity said to have been worshiped by the Israelites in the desert (Acts 7:43, "the star of the god Rompha"). The quotation in Acts is from a corrupted translation of Kaiwan (Akkad. *Kaimanu*), the name of Saturn, and was understood to be the god Kiyyun (Amos 5:26). The KJV renders "Remphan," and the NIV, "Rephan." *See* Kiyyun; Sikkuth.

Sat'yr. *See* Shaggy Goat.

Shaggy Goat (Heb. *sā'îr*, "shaggy, hairy"). The reference is clearly to demonic creatures that would dance among the ruins of Babylon (Isa. 13:21, see marg.) and among the remains of Edomite cities (Isa. 34:14). "He goat" or "hairy goat" is what the name commonly refers to, but in Lev. 17:7 ("goat demons") and 2 Chron. 11:15

("satyrs") the reference is clearly to some object of idolatrous reverence. It either refers to idols (thus NIV "goat idols") having the appearance of goats or, more likely, to the demon agencies energizing the idol in question. The demonic reference is clearly indicated by Rev. 18:2 where the language is quoted from the LXX and the word *demons* is used. Thus the prophet has in mind evil spirits. In Greek and Roman mythology a satyr was a sylvan god, Bacchus's companion. As a goatlike creature he had a brutal and lustful nature. The connection between Greek gods and the Hebrew representations is that of the idol and the demon power behind it.

Sic'cuth. *See* Sikkuth.

Sik'kuth (si'kuth). Apparently the proper name of a star deity (Amos 5:26), rendered by ERV, RSV "Sakkuth," but in the KJV and ASV translated "tabernacle" and in the NIV "shrine"; that is, Heb. "Succoth." Interpreted as a proper name, it corresponds to Sakkut, the Babylonian designation of the planet Saturn. The Babylonians also called the planet Saturn *Kaimanu,* in modernized form *Kaiwanu* or *Kiyyun* (which see; 5:26). As in the case of Heb. *Kiyyun,* the vocalization of the Heb. word for "a detestable thing" (*shiggûs*) was given to it, resulting in Sikkuth. *See* Rempha.

Suc'coth-be'noth (suc'oth-be'noth). An idol set up in Samaria (2 Kings 17:30) by displaced Babylonians. This deity has been identified with Zarpanitum, the consort of Marduk, the patron god of Babylon (Rawlinson and Schrader). Others have connected him with the Akkad. expression *sakkut binuti,* the supreme judge of the world. This is construed as a title of Marduk and the form Succoth-benoth represents a Hebraization of it (Delitzsch).   M.F.U.

Tam'muz (tam-uz). Ezekiel refers to the worship of this Babylonian deity in a vision of his apostate brethren who were enamored of this cult. The prophet saw the women weeping for this god at the North Gate of the Jerusalem Temple (Ezek. 8:14). Tammuz was known by the Babylonians as Dumuzi, god of pasture and flocks, of subterranean water, and of vegetation. He was the husband-brother of Ishtar (Asherah, fertility goddess). Tammuz supposedly died every autumn when he departed to the underworld; from there he was recovered by the disconsolate Ishtar. His reappearance marked the bursting forth of life in the springtime. The fourth Babylonian month, July, was named in honor of Tammuz, which name was applied in later postbiblical times by Jews to their fourth month, June-July. Tammuz is equated with the Greek Adonis and the Egyptian Osiris. Allusions to the worship of Tammuz cults seem to be referred to in Jer. 22:18 and Amos 8:10. The worship of this god was widespread throughout the Fertile Crescent from Babylonia-Assyria to Palestine-Syria. The rites of Tammuz included a divine marriage of the king annually to the fertility goddess in the person of a temple priestess. Tammuz worship was especially notorious at Byblos (biblical Gebal) on the Mediterranean. M.F.U.

Tar'tak (tar'tak). A heathen deity mentioned with *Nibhaz* (which see) as introduced into Samaria by the Avvite settlers (2 Kings 17:31).

Zeus (zūs). In Greek mythology, king of the gods and of men. He is identical with the Roman Jupiter, not only in nature but also in name, for Jupiter is compounded of *Iōuvis* and *pater*. As in the course of time the Roman god Jupiter became identified with the Greek, he was regarded as a son of Saturn and of Ops, corresponding with the Greek Uranus and Rhea respectively. From Zeus came all that appears in the heavens; he was the bringer of light, the cause of the dawn as well as of the full moon. He controlled all weather, sent the lightning and rain, was the giver of victory, watched over justice and truth, and was therefore the most ancient and important god of oaths.

Zeus is mentioned in Acts 14:11-12, where it is recorded that the people cried: " 'The gods have become like men and have come down to us.' And they began calling Barnabas, Zeus, and Paul, Hermes, because he was the chief speaker." Barnabas was probably identified with Zeus because of his majestic appearance; Paul with Hermes because of his eloquence. The temple of Zeus is said to have been "just outside the city" (v. 13), as was frequently the custom.

BIBLIOGRAPHY: C. Gordon, *The Loves and Wars of Anat* (1943); E. O. James, *Concept of Deity* (1951); J. Finegan, *Archaeology of World Religions* (1952); A. Kapelrud, *Baal in the Ras Shamra Texts* (1952); B. Branston, *Gods of the North* (1955); E. O. James, *Myth and Ritual in the Ancient Near East* (1958); id., *Cult of the Mother-Goddess* (1959); id., *The Ancient Gods* (1960); T. H. Gaster, *Thespis* (1961); S. N. Kramer, *Mythologies of the Ancient World* (1961); id., *Sumerian Mythology* (1961); E. G. Parrinder, *Worship in the World's Religions* (1961); E. O. James, *Worship of the Sky God* (1963); N. C. Habel, *Yahweh Versus Baal* (1964); E. O. James, *The Tree of Life* (1966); W. F. Albright, *Yahweh and the Gods of Canaan* (1966); S. Piggott, *The Druids* (1968); A. S. Kapelrud, *The Violent Goddess: Anat in the Ras Shamra Texts* (1969); S. N. Kramer, *The Sacred Marriage Rite* (1969); E. E. Barthell, Jr., *Gods and Goddesses of Ancient Egypt* (1970); E. A. S. Butterfield, *The Tree at the Navel of the Earth* (1970); L. Campbell, *Religion in Greek Literature* (1970); G. W. Carter, *Zoroastrianism and Judaism* (1970); J. Ferguson, *Religions of the Roman Empire* (1970); E. O. James, *Origins of Sacrifice* (1970); *The Laws of Manu* (1970); C. de Loverdo, *Gods with Bronze Swords* (1970); W. J. Perry, *The Origin of Magic and Religion* (1970); H. O. Thompson, *Mekal: The God of Beth-Shan* (1970); U. Cassuto, *The Goddess 'Anat: Canaanite Epics of the Patriarchal Age* (1971); M. Jastrow, *Aspects of Religious Belief and Practice in Babylonia and Assyria* (1971); R. E. Witt, *Isis in the Greco-Roman World* (1971); T. R. Glover, *The Conflict of Religions in the Early Roman Empire* (1974); L. Spence, *Myths and Legends of Babylonia and Assyria* (1975); T. Jacobsen, *The Treasures of Darkness* (1976); L. W. King, *Babylo-nian Religion and Mythology* (1976); O. R. Gurney, *Some Aspects of Hittite Religion* (1977); H. W. F. Saggs, *The Encounter with the Divine in Mesopotamia and Israel* (1978); M. Boyce, *Zoroastrians: Their Beliefs and Practices* (1979).

GOG (gog).

1. Son of Shemaiah and father of Shimei, and one of the descendants of Reuben (1 Chron. 5:4).

2. The prince of Rosh, Meshech, and Tubal ("the chief prince of Meshech and Tubal," KJV), who, Ezekiel said, would invade the restored land of Israel from the far distant northern land by the appointment of God in the last times, with a powerful army of numerous nations (Ezek. 38:1-9) and with the intention of plundering Israel, now dwelling in security (vv. 10-16). When Gog shall fall upon Israel, he is to be destroyed by a wrathful judgment from the Lord, that the nations may know that God is the Lord (vv. 17-23). On the mountains of Israel Gog, with all his hosts and nations, will succumb to the judgment of God (39:1-8).

Ezekiel 38-39, which deal with Gog, the prince, and Magog, his land, describe the actual invasion of Palestine by a great northern confederacy, ostensibly headed by Russia. The scene depicts a gigantic outburst of anti-Semitism and a colossal attempt to overrun Palestine and annihilate the Jews. Russia and the northern powers have been persecutors of dispersed Israel, and it is consonant with the covenants and promises of Israel, which are yet to be fulfilled (cf. Gen. 15:18-21; Deut. 33), that divine destruction should be precipitated at the climax of the last attempt to destroy the remnant of Israel in Jerusalem and Palestine. The entire prophecy belongs to the "Day of the Lord" (cf. Isa. 2:10-22; Rev. 19:11-21) and evidently precedes the actual battle of Armageddon by a number of years. The prophetic perspective concerning Gog, however, includes the final revolt of the nations at the close of the mediatorial messianic kingdom (20:6-9). M.F.U.

GOIIM (gōy'im). A Heb. word for "nations," or "peoples," rendered by the NASB and NIV as a proper noun in Gen. 14:1, 9.

GO'LAN (gō'lan). One of the three cities of refuge on the E of the Jordan, the others being Bezer and Ramoth (Deut. 4:43; cf. Josh. 20:8; 21:27; 1 Chron. 6:71). It became the head of the province of Gaulanitis, one of the four provinces into which Bashan was divided after the Babylonian captivity, and possibly identical with modern Sahem el-Jolan, about seventeen miles E of the Sea of Galilee, in western Hauran.

GOLD. A unit of money and a mineral. *See* Metrology; Mineral Kingdom.

GOLDEN CITY (Heb. *madhēbâ*). A term applied in the KJV to Babylon (Isa. 14:4; NASB and NIV, see marg.) and occurring nowhere else. "Not one of the early translators ever thought of deriving this word from the Aramaean *dehab* (gold), but translated the word as if it were *marhebah* (haughty, violent treatment). We understand it, according to *madmenah* (dunghill) in chap. 25:10, as denoting the place where they were reduced to pining away, i.e., as applied to Babylon as the house of servitude where Israel had been wearied to death" (Delitzsch, *Com.*, ad loc.). The NASB and NIV render "fury."

GOLDSMITH. *See* Handicrafts.

GOL'GOTHA (gol'go-tha; "place of a skull"). The gospels and tradition disagree as to its locality. John 19:41-42 locates the place by saying that "in the place where He was crucified there was a garden; and in the garden a new tomb, in which no one had yet been laid." Here Jesus was laid, for it was close by, and it was the Jews' preparation day. The Scripture references place the spot outside the city, and from Matt. 27:33 and Mark 15:29 it is to be concluded that the place of crucifixion was on the public road. The traditional site of Calvary, within the Church of the Holy Sepulcher, is now within the city walls, which were built by the Turkish ruler Suleiman the Magnificent in the sixteenth century. But the area of the church was evidently outside the walls in Jesus' day. *See* Calvary.   H.F.V.

BIBLIOGRAPHY: C. C. Dobson, *The Garden Tomb and the Resurrection* (n.d.); C. Marston, *The Garden Tomb, Jerusalem* (1945); A. Parrot, *Golgotha and the Church of the Holy Sepulcher* (1957); K. M. Kenyon, *Digging up Jerusalem* (1974), pp. 226-34, 261-67.

Traditional site of the garden tomb

GOLI'ATH (go-li'ath). Goliath, although repeatedly called a Philistine, was probably descended from the old Rephaim, of whom a scattered rem-

nant took refuge with the Philistines after their dispersion by the Ammonites (Deut. 2:20-21; 2 Sam. 21:22).

The only mention made of Goliath is his appearance as the champion of the Philistines, and his death at the hands of David (1 Sam. 17), c. 1010 B.C. The Philistines had ventured upon another inroad into the country and had taken up a firm position on the slope of a mountain, Ephes-dammim, between Socoh and Azekah, in western Judah. Israel encamped over against them on the slope of a second mountain, at a place called the valley of the Terebinth, and between the two camps lay a deep, narrow valley, which seemed destined as a field on which the warriors of either side might exercise their valor. From the Philistine camp there advanced a champion, Goliath of Gath, six cubits and a span high (which, taking the cubit at 18 inches, would make him 9½ feet tall), with a bronze helmet, clothed in a coat of mail the weight of which was 5,000 shekels, and with a spear like the shaft of a weaver's beam. For forty days he terrified the people by challenging, morning and evening, to single combat any of Israel's warriors. David had been sent to his brothers with provisions and, hearing the challenge of Goliath, inquired its meaning. Upon being told, he offered to become Israel's champion and went forward armed with a sling and five smooth stones. He answered the scornful taunt of the giant with, "This day the Lord will deliver you up into my hands." He struck Goliath in the forehead and, slaying the fallen champion, cut off his head. "When the Philistines saw that their champion was dead, they fled" and were pursued by the Israelites, who slaughtered them.

Skeletons recovered in Palestine attest to the fact that men as tall as Goliath once lived in that general region. Critics commonly reject the historical reliability of the David-Goliath narrative, adducing contradictions in the account. An alleged contradiction is 2 Sam. 21:19, which reports that "Elhanan . . . killed Goliath the Gittite," whereas 1 Sam. 17:50-51 (cf. 19:5; 21:9; 22:10, 13) asserts that David did so. Moreover, 1 Chron. 20:5 reports that "Elhanan the son of Jair killed Lahmi the brother of Goliath the Gittite." If this glaring error was in the original the final redactors of Samuel were guilty of a most obvious and stupid blunder and must be considered as incredibly incompetent. Rather, the explanation of the apparent discrepancy is that the passage in 2 Samuel has suffered corruption in the course of transmission. A careful study of the original suggests that the reading both in Samuel and Chronicles originally was either, "And Elhanan the son of Jair killed Lahmi and the brother of Goliath," or, "Elhanan the son of Jair the Bethlehemite killed the brother of Goliath." In the original it is obvious that both passages substantiate that David killed Goliath and Elhanan killed "the brother of Goliath."

BIBLIOGRAPHY: Y. Yadin, *The Act of Warfare in Bible Lands* (1963), 1:13-45, 48-49, 80-85; 2:248-50, 265-66; R. K. Harrison, *Introduction to the Old Testament* (1969), p. 704; C. J. Barber and J. D. Carter, *Always a Winner* (1977), pp. 85-104.

GO'MER (gō'mer).

1. The eldest son of Japheth and father of Ashkenaz, Riphath, and Togarmah (Gen. 10:2-3). The name afterward occurs as that of a tribe (*see* Ezek. 38:6), probably the Cimmeranians, who dwelt, according to Herodotus, on the Maeotis, in the Taurian Chersonesus (K. & D., *Com.*).

2. The name of the daughter of Diblaim, a harlot who became the wife or concubine (according to some, in vision only) of the prophet Hosea (Hos. 1:3), about 785 B.C.

GOMOR'RAH (go-mor'ra; apparently meaning "submersion"; cf. Arab. *ghamara*, to "overflow, inundate"). The city in the Jordan Valley (Gen. 10:19; 13:10) that, with Sodom, became a type of intolerable wickedness and was destroyed by fire (19:24-28). Like Sodom, its ruler was vanquished by a Mesopotamian confederacy that invaded the Jordan Valley in the time of Abraham (14:8-11). The biblical notices point out that the district of the Jordan where Sodom, Gomorrah, Admah, Zeboiim, and Zoar were located was exceedingly productive and well populated around 2054 B.C., but that not long afterward it was abandoned. This circumstance is in full agreement with archaeological findings. (*See* W. F. Albright, *The Archaeology of Palestine and the Bible*, pp. 133ff.). These cities were located in the valley of Siddim (14:3). Probably this was the area at the southern end of the Dead Sea, now covered with water. Somewhere in the vicinity of 2050 B.C. this region was overwhelmed by a great conflagration. The country was said to have been "full of tar pits" (14:10). Bitumen deposits are still to be found in that area. Being on the fault-line forming the Jordan Valley, the Dead Sea, and the Arabah, this region has been the scene of earthquakes throughout history. The biblical account sets forth the miraculous elements, but geological activity was doubtless a factor. The salt and free sulfur of this area, now a burned-out region of oil and asphalt, were mingled by an earthquake to form a violent explosion. Evidently salt and sulfur were blasted red-hot into the sky so that literally it rained fire and brimstone over the whole plain (19:24, 28). Lot's wife being turned into a pillar of salt is reminiscent of "the Mount of Sodom" known to the Arabs as Jebel Usdum, a five-mile-long salt mass stretching N and S at the southeastern end of the Dead Sea. Somewhere under the slowly rising water of the southern part of the lake the five cities of the plain are to be found. According to Tacitus's *History* 5.7 and Josephus's *Wars* 4.8.4, their ruins were still visible in classical and NT times, not yet being covered with water.   M.F.U.

BIBLIOGRAPHY: W. F. Albright, *Bulletin of the American Schools of Oriental Research* 14 (1924): 5-7; id., *Annual of the American Schools of Oriental Research* 6 (1924-25): 58-62; J. P. Harland, *Biblical Archaeologist* 5 (1941): 17-32; id., *BA* 7 (1943): 41-54.

GOODLY TREES. *See* Beautiful Trees.

GOODMAN. In the NT, a KJV term from Gk. *oikodespotēs* referring to a "landowner" (so NASB, Matt. 13:27; 20:1,11), the "head of the house" (so NASB, Matt. 10:25; 24:43; Luke 13:25; 14:21), or the "owner of the house" (so NASB, Mark 14:14; Luke 22:11). The NIV translates "owner" (Matt. 13:27; 24:43; Luke 13:25; 14:21; 22:11), "landowner" (Matt. 20:1, 11; 21:33), "head of the house" (Matt. 10:25), and "owner of the house" (Mark 14:14). In the KJV *oikodespotēs* is also rendered "master of the house" and "householder." The OT appearance of "goodman" (Prov. 7:19, KJV) is the rendering of Heb. *'îsh*, "man," i.e., husband. The NASB gives "the man," and the NIV, "husband."

GOODNESS. In some places *kindness* seems more especially meant; e.g., "the earth is full of the goodness [NASB, lovingkindness; NIV, "unfailing love"] of the Lord" (Ps. 33:5, KJV). In others it expresses the supreme benevolence, holiness, and excellence of the divine character, sum of all God's attributes. "I Myself will make all My goodness pass before you" (Ex. 33:19). In common use *goodness* is the opposite of *badness*, the quality of character that makes its possessor lovable; excellence more particularly of a religious kind, virtue, righteousness.

GOPHER WOOD. *See* Vegetable Kingdom.

GO'SHEN (gō'shen).

1. A northeastern section of the Egyptian Delta region usually called "the land of Goshen," "country of Goshen" (Gen. 45:10; Josh. 10:41), or simply "Goshen" (Gen. 47:27) and "the land of Rameses" (47:11; cf. Ex. 12:37). In this region the Israelites under Jacob settled during the time Joseph was prime minister (Gen. 46:28-34). This was a fertile section of Egypt, excellent for grazing and certain types of agriculture, but apparently not particularly inviting to the pharaohs because of its distance from the Nile irrigation canals. It extends thirty or forty miles in length, centering in Wadi Tumilat, and reaches from Lake Timsa to the Nile. It was connected with the name of Rameses because Rameses II (c. 1290-1224 B.C.) built extensively in this location at Pithom (Tell el Retabah) and Rameses (Tell ed-dab'a). Tanis was called the House of Rameses (c. 1300-1100 B.C.). Therefore, the term *Raamses* in Ex. 1:11 must be construed as being a modernization of an archaic place name and as having reference to an earlier city Zoan-Tanis, where the Israelites labored centuries earlier.   M.F.U.

2. A district of southern Palestine lying between Gaza and Gibeon, its name probably being given in remembrance of Egypt (Josh. 10:41; 11:16). In the latter passage the maritime plain of Judah, the Shephelah, is expressly mentioned, and if Goshen was any part of that rich plain, its fertility may have suggested its name.

3. A town mentioned in company with Debir, Socoh, and others, as being in the mountains of Judah (Josh. 15:51), in the group on the SW part of the hills.

BIBLIOGRAPHY: A. H. Gardiner, *Journal of Egyptian Archaeology* 5 (1918): 218-23; id., *JEA* 10 (1924): 28-32, 94; E. Naville, *JEA* 10 (1924): 18-39.

GOSPEL (Anglo-Saxon, *godspel,* "good story"). Good news, and employed as the equivalent of the Gk. *euaggelion.* This word in the earlier Gk. language signified "a present given to one who brought good tidings," or "a sacrifice offered in thanksgiving for such good tidings having come." In later Gk. it was employed for the good tidings themselves. It is used to signify:

1. The good news of the death, burial, and resurrection of Christ as provided by our Lord and preached by His disciples (1 Cor. 15:1-4). The gospel then is full and free deliverance from sin on the basis of simple faith in Jesus Christ, the vicarious sin-Bearer (Eph. 2:8-10). In this aspect the gospel has two phases: one, to the unsaved —Christ died for me (John 3:16; Acts 16:30-31); second, to the saved—I died in Christ (Rom. 6:2-10), with a key to the experiential realization of this fact in the life furnished by Rom. 6:11.

2. Forms of the gospel to be differentiated. Many Bible teachers make a distinction in the following: (1) *The Gospel of the Kingdom.* The good news that God's purpose is to establish an earthly mediatorial kingdom in fulfillment of the Davidic covenant (2 Sam. 7:16). Two proclamations of the gospel of the kingdom are men-

tioned, one already past, beginning with the ministry of John the Baptist, carried on by our Lord and His disciples, and ending with the Jewish rejection of the Messiah. The other preaching is yet future (Matt. 24:14), during the Great Tribulation, and heralding the second advent of the King. Closely connected, although perhaps not identical in its emphasis with the gospel of the kingdom, is the everlasting gospel (Rev. 14:6) preached to those on earth during the latter part of the Tribulation. (2) *The Gospel of God's Grace* (*see* no. 1 above). Paul calls this gospel of the grace of God "my gospel" (Rom. 2:16) because the full doctrinal content based upon the gospel of the grace of God embraces the revelation of the result in the outcalling of the church, her relationship, position, privileges, and responsibility. This distinctive Pauline truth, honeycombing Ephesians and Colossians, is interwoven in all of the Pauline writings.

3. "A different gospel" (Gal. 1:6; 2 Cor. 11:4) "which you have not accepted." This consists of any denial or perversion of the gospel of the grace of God. Its essential stamp is that it denies the full efficacy of God's grace alone to save, keep, and perfect, and introduces some sort of human merit. In Galatia it was legalism. Its teachers are under God's terrible anathema. The relation of the gospel to the law of Moses has been a source of much confusion. Under grace the Ten Commandments are all presented, except that involving the observance of the seventh day. However, they are to be operative not to find favor with God but because the redeemed one has already found favor and eternal life and possesses the indwelling Spirit to work them out in daily conduct.

4. The four stories of our Lord's life published by Matthew, Mark, Luke, and John. The writers are called evangelists. These accounts are "gospels" because they recite the events in the life, death, resurrection, and ascension of the Lord and predicted bestowment of the Spirit, making possible "the gospel."   M.F.U.

GOSPELS. *See* Bible, Books of.

GOSPELS, THE FOUR. The term *gospel* stems directly from the Anglo-Saxon *godspel,* meaning "god-message." Ultimately, however, the earlier form of the expression went back to *god-spel,* signifying "a good message," a phrase apparently invented to reflect exactly the Gk. *euaggelion.* The gospels find no parallel in world literature. Negatively they are not romances or folk tales, since they catalog historical events. Neither are they biographies in any strict sense, nor memoirs. They are not even in the strict sense of the word literary works. None of the evangelists, not even Luke, is dominated by literary aspirations. Perhaps the gospels can be best described as portraits of Jesus, the promised Messiah.

Matthew delineates the prophesied coming One as a King; Mark presents Him as a Servant;

493

Luke, as a Man; John, as God. They thus give a fourfold portraiture of One who is in His person and work set forth as the Savior and Redeemer.

The gospels are thus written in a unique literary genre developed to present the divine message of salvation. In these four portraits of the Savior are immortalized the church's memory and testimony concerning Jesus. All four are concerned with what Jesus was and said and did. Each evangelist has his peculiar style and his contribution is indispensable to the picture of the Christ that we get from the fourfold presentation.

Written in the simple, compelling language of the common people, the four gospels inimitably present Jesus as no biography, history, or other similar type of literary form could make Him known. Table 11, "The Life of the Lord Jesus," summarizes the events in Christ's life and gives the relevant Scripture passages in the four gospels.

The term *gospel* as used of these four pictures of Jesus is of later development. Nowhere in the NT is it employed of the books we now know as gospels. It is rather applied to the message of free and gracious salvation offered to sinners through the finished work of Jesus Christ (Rom. 1:1). Justin Martyr apparently first used the term *memoirs* to describe these books. However, beginning with the second half of the second century the title, later universally used, may be distinctly traced.

Writers of the Gospels. The authors of the four gospels were Matthew, Mark, Luke, and John (*see* under specific names). They were not all fishermen, as is often supposed, but were from different secular occupations and from various parts of the country.

Patristic testimony regarding both the authors and the order of the several gospels is conclusive. Matthew wrote at Jerusalem, before starting out to evangelize the nations; Mark wrote at Rome, before starting out to establish the faith in Egypt; Luke wrote in Greece, or while sharing Paul's imprisonment at Caesarea; John wrote at Ephesus after his exile at Patmos. Clement of Alexandria (A.D. 150) affirms that Matthew continued his stay at Jerusalem with the other apostles, busy with his own countrymen for a period of twelve years after the crucifixion (*Strōmateis* 6.5.53). Eusebius says, "The Holy Apostles and disciples of our Savior, being scattered over the whole world, Thomas, according to tradition, received Parthia as his allotted region; Andrew received Scythia, and John Asia, where, after continuing for some time, he died at Ephesus. Peter appears to have preached through Pontus, Galatia, Bithynia, Cappadocia, and Asia, to the Jews that were scattered abroad; who also, finally coming to Rome, was crucified with his head downward, having requested of himself to suffer in this way" (*Ecclesiastical History* 3.1).

Matthew. Theodore of Mopsuestia says, "For a

good while the apostles preached chiefly to Jews in Judea. Afterward Providence made way for conducting them to remote countries. Peter went to Rome; the rest elsewhere; John, in particular, took up his abode in Ephesus. About this time the other evangelists, Matthew, Mark, and Luke, published their gospels, which were soon spread abroad all over the world" (cited by Lardner, 5:299). The author of the *Imperfect Work* (about A.D. 560) wrote, "The occasion of Matthew's writing is said to be this: There was a great persecution in Palestine, so that there was danger lest all the faithful should be dispersed. That they might not be without teaching, though they should have no teachers, they requested Matthew to write for them a history of all Christ's words and works, that wherever they should be, they should have with them the ground of their faith" (Lardner, 5:300). Exactly when Matthew's gospel was written is at present indeterminate. Ancient writers differ in dates. Theophylact, of the eleventh century, and Euthymius, of the twelfth, state that it was produced "eight years after the ascension," which would be about A.D. 41 or 42 of our current chronology. But more ancient writers give a later date. The Paschal Chronicle of the seventh century says it was written "about fifteen years after our Lord's ascension," with which Nicephorus Callisti, of the fourteenth century, agrees. This would be about A.D. 48. But Irenaeus, Bishop of Lyons, in the second century, says, "Matthew indeed produced a gospel written among the Hebrews in their own dialect, whilst Peter and Paul proclaimed the gospel and founded the church at Rome. After the departure [death] of these, Mark, the disciple and interpreter of Peter, also transmitted to us in writing that which had been preached by Peter. And Luke, the companion of Paul, committed to writing the gospel preached by him [Paul]. Afterward John, the disciple of our Lord, the same that lay in his bosom, also published the gospel while he was yet in Ephesus, in Asia" (Eusebius *E. H.* 5.8). In no case could this have been earlier, but probably was later, than A.D. 61, the year Paul arrived at Rome a prisoner. Epiphanius, Bishop of Cyprus, in A.D. 367, who is accounted high authority in these matters, says that Matthew wrote first (of the four evangelists) and Mark soon after, being a companion of Peter at Rome; that Mark and Luke were both of the seventy disciples sent out to the Gentiles; that both were offended at Christ's words recorded in John 6:44; that Peter recovered Mark, and Paul recovered Luke to the Christian faith afterward; that Mark wrote the second gospel and Luke the third, and John wrote the fourth and last gospel (*see* Lardner, 4:187-88).

By whom the gospel of Matthew was given in our present Gk. form is unknown, but it was probably by himself. The consensus of critical scholars is that it is not a mere translation but an

Table 11
The Life of the Lord Jesus

Time	No.	Event	Matt.	Mark	Luke	John
B.C.		*Preliminary facts*				
	1	Luke's preface to his gospel			1:1-4	
6	2	Prediction to Zacharias of John the Baptist's birth			1:5-25	
5	3	Gabriel's annunciation to Mary of Messiah's birth			1:26-38	
5	4	Mary visits Elizabeth and her prophetic hymn			1:39-56	
5	5	Birth of John and Zacharias's prophetic hymn			1:57-80	
5	6	Joseph's dream respecting Mary's chastity	1:18-25			
		Birth and boyhood of Jesus				
	7	Genealogy of Christ's royal and natural ancestry	1:1-17		3:23-38	
4	8	The Lord's birth at Bethlehem	1:18,25		2:1-7	1:1-14
4	9	The angel's revelation in song to the shepherds			2:8-20	
4	10	The infant Jesus receives His name at His circumcision			2:21	
4	11	Child presented at the Temple for legal redemption			2:22-39	
4	12	Visit of the Magi to Herod at Jerusalem	2:1-12			
4	13	Herod's consternation and inquiries	2:3-7			
4	14	The Magi visit the village of Bethlehem	2:10-12			
3	15	Herod's jealousy and resentment aroused	2:7,8,16			
3	16	Flight of Joseph and family into Egypt	2:13-15			
3	17	Herod massacres the male infants of Bethlehem	2:16-18			
2	18	Recall of the holy family from Egypt	2:19-21			
1	19	Returning, they fear Herod Archelaus the ethnarch	2:22			
		[Here follow about ten years of silent history.]				
A.D.						
9	20	Jesus at twelve, with the Sanhedrists in the Temple			2:40-52	
		[Here follow about eighteen years of silent history.]				
26	21	John the Baptist inaugurates his ministry	3:1-12	1:2-8	3:1-18	
27	22	Inauguration of Jesus Christ to His ministry	3:13-17	1:9-11	3:21-23	
27	23	Jesus made subject to the temptations of Satan	4:1-11	2:12-13	4:1-13	
27	24	John the Baptist witnesses that Jesus is the Son of God				1:19-36
27	25	Two of John's disciples leave him and follow Christ				1:35-42
27	26	Philip and Nathanael now also become His disciples				1:43-51
27	27	The first miracle wrought by Jesus Christ in Cana				2:1-12
		From the first to the second Passover				
27	28	Traders' animals expelled from the Temple with scourge				2:13-22
27	29	Interview of Nicodemus with Jesus by night				3:1-21
27	30	John the Baptist witnesses the second time for Christ				1:15-34
27	31	Christ's disciples baptize other followers				3:22
27	32	The imprisonment of John the Baptist by Antipas	14:3-5	6:17-20	3:19-20	
27	33	Jesus thereupon leaves Judea for Galilee	4:12	1:14-15	4:14-15	4:1-13
27	34	Jesus converses with Samaritan woman at the well				4:4-42
27	35	Jesus opens His public ministry in Galilee	4:12	1:14-15	4:14-15	4:43-45
27	36	The nobleman seeks Jesus at Cana to heal his son				4:46-54
		From the second to the third Passover				
28	37	Jesus visits Jerusalem during the Passover				5:1
28	38	Healed an infirmity of thirty-eight years				5:2-9
28	39	Jews dispute Christ's right to heal on Sabbath				5:10-17
28	40	Jews affirm that Christ claimed equality with God				5:18-47
28	41	Returns to Nazareth and proves His Messiahship			4:15-22	
28	42	Rejected at Nazareth, He dwells at Capernaum	4:13-16		4:23-31	
28	43	Resumes public teaching here and works miracles	4:17-25	1:21-22	4:31-32	
28	44	Miracle of fishes; calls Peter, Andrew, James, and John	4:18-22	1:16-22	5:1-11	
28	45	Jesus casts out an unclean spirit in synagogue		1:22-28	4:33-37	
28	46	Peter's wife's mother miraculously cured of fever	8:14-17	1:29-34	4:38-41	
28	47	Christ's first circuit in Galilee with disciples	4:23-25	1:35-39	4:42-44	
28	48	He cures a leper who gives Him great fame	8:2-4	1:40-45	5:12-16	
28	49	Returning to Capernaum, He heals the paralytic	9:2-8	2:1-12	5:17-26	
28	50	Call of Matthew and the feast at his house	9:9-13	2:13-17	5:27-32	
28	51	Discussion with Jews about the disciples' fasting	9:14-17	2:18-22	5:33-39	
28	52	Disciples pluck ears of grain on the Sabbath	12:1-8	2:23-28	6:1-5	
28	53	Jesus healed the man's withered hand on Sabbath	12:9-14	3:1-6	6:6-11	
28	54	Our Lord heals multitudes at the seaside		3:7-12		
28	55	After a night of prayer, Jesus chooses the twelve	10:1-42	3:13-19 {4:21-25}	6:12-19	
28	56	Jesus preaches on the mountains of Galilee	5-7	{9:43-48}	6:20-49	
28	57	Centurion's servant healed miraculously by Christ	8:5-13		7:1-10	
28	58	The widow's son of Nain restored to life			7:11-17	
28	59	John the Baptist's inquiry from his prison at Machaerus	11:2-6		7:18-23	
28	60	Christ's eulogy upon His cousin, John the Baptist	11:7-19		7:24-35	
28	61	He upbraids cities where He had wrought miracles	11:20-30			
28	62	Woman anoints His feet in the Pharisee's house			7:36-50	
28	63	Second circuit of two days' preaching in Galilee			8:1-3	
28	64	Returning to Capernaum, He heals the demoniac	12:22-37	3:22-30	11:14-26	
28	65	His mother and relatives think Jesus to be insane	12:46-50	3:20-21	8:19-21	

Time	No.	Event	Matt.	Mark	Luke	John
28	66	From a boat He preaches seven parables	13:1-52	4:1-34	8:4-18	
28	67	Asleep at sea, He awakens and stays the storm	8:23-27	4:35-41	8:22-25	
28	68	Jesus cures two demoniacs among the Gadarenes	8:28-34	5:1-20	8:26-40	
28	69	Return to west shore, He raises Jarius' daughter	9:18-25	5:21-43	8:40-55	
28	70	Heals woman of issue of blood twelve years	9:20-22	5:25-34	8:43-48	
28	71	Christ rejected the second time at Nazareth	13:54-58	6:1-6		
28	72	Third circuit of Jesus' preaching in Galilee	9:35-38	6:6		
28	73	The twelve are sent forth to work miracles	10:1-42	6:7-13	9:1-6	
28	74	Herod Antipas beheads John at Machaerus	14:1-12	6:14-29	9:7-9	
28	75	The twelve returning report their successes		6:30	9:10	
28	76	Crosses Galilean Sea and feeds five thousand	14:13-21	6:31-44	9:10-17	
28	77	Returning, He meets the sea in storm and night	14:22-36	6:45-56		6:15-21
28	78	The five thousand fed, find Jesus at Capernaum				6:22-71
29	April.	*From the third to the fourth Passover*				
29	79	Jesus delays going to the Feast of Booths (Tabernacles)				7:1-10
29	80	Many cures by Christ on Gennesaret plain	14:34-36	6:53-56		
29	81	Pharisees refuted about washing hands	15:1-20	7:1-23	6:39	
29	82	Visits Tyre and Sidon; cures the Syrophoenician's daughter	15:21-28	7:24-30		
29	83	Returns by Decapolis making many cures	15:29-31	7:31-37		
29	84	Jesus feeds four thousand on the mountain	15:29-38	8:1-9		
29	85	He recrosses Galilean Sea to Magadan (West)	15:39	8:10		
29	86	Sails to Bethsaida-Julias (E of Jordan)	16:1-4	8:13,22		
29	87	Cures blind man who saw men as trees walking		8:22-26		
29	88	Passes into regions of Caesarea Philippi	16:13	8:27-30		
29	89	Jesus asks the disciples their opinion of Him	16:13-20	8:27-30	9:18-21	
29	90	Jesus begins now to predict His own death	16:21	8:31	9:22	
29	91	Christ's transfiguration on Mt. Hermon	17:1-13	9:2-13	9:28-36	
29	92	Descending He casts out a demon	17:14-21	9:14-29	9:37-43	
29	93	Jesus again predicts His own death and rising	17:22-23	9:30-32	9:44-45	
29	94	Stater provided in the fish's mouth	17:24-27			
29	95	Disciples contend who shall be greatest	18:1-35	9:33-50	9:41-50	
29	Oct.	*Feast of Booths (Tabernacles) six months after Passover*				
29	96	Jesus goes to Jerusalem and teaches in Temple				7:1-14
29	97	Puts severest test to human consciousness				7:17
29	98	The people are divided as to Christ's doctrine				7:11-44
29	99	Nicodemus defends Jesus before the Sanhedrin				7:45-53
29	100	Christ, the Jews, and the adulteress				8:1-11
29	101	Jesus now claims to be the Light of the World				8:12-20
29	102	His preexistence before Abraham was				8:42,56-58
29	103	Jesus escapes from the stoning of the Jews				8:59
29	104	He gives sight to the beggar born blind				9:1-41
29	105	He announces himself the Good Shepherd				10:1-16
29	106	He again calls Himself the Son of God	26:63-64			{ 9:35-37 { 10:36
29	107	Christ finally leaves Galilee			9:51-56	
29	108	Requisites for discipleship to Christ			9:51-56	
29	109	Seventy disciples sent forth to work			10:1-16	
29	110	They return rejoicing in their success			10:17-24	
29	111	Tempting lawyer and the Good Samaritan			10:25-37	
29	112	Jesus visits Martha and Mary (Bethany)			10:38-42	
29	113	Teaches disciples the Lord's Prayer	6:5-13		11:1-4	
29	114	Miracles on demoniacs ascribed to Beelzebul			11:14-26	
29	115	Disciples admonished as to Pharisees			12:1-3	
29	116	Dangers and duties of discipleship			12:3-53	
29	117	He declines arbitrating an inheritance			12:13-21	
29	118	Counsels, parables, and predictions			12:22-59	
29	119	A woman's spirit of infirmity cured			13:10-17	
30	120	Christ at the Feast of Dedication				10:22-30
30	121	Test question before stoning Jesus				10:31-38
30	122	Jesus escapes and goes to Perea				10:39-42
30	123	Lazarus sick, He returns to Bethany				11:1-16
30	124	Christ describes Antipas as a fox			13:22	
30	125	He miraculously cures the man afflicted with dropsy			13:31-32	
30	126	The parables of the guests and of the great supper			14:1-6	
30	127	The perils of discipleship			14:7-24	
30	128	The lost sheep; lost silver; the lost son			14:25-35	
30	129	The unjust steward; the rich man and Lazarus			15:3-32	
30	130	Miracle of the resurrection of Lazarus			16:1-31	11:17-46
30	131	Sanhedrin conspires against Christ's life				11:47-53
30	132	Leaving Jerusalem He goes to Ephraim				11:54
		Christ's last journey to Jerusalem through Samaria				
30	133	Cures ten lepers on borders of Samaria			17:11-19	
30	134	The judge and the importunate widow			18:1-8	
30	135	The self-righteous Pharisee and the tax-gatherer			18:9-14	
30	136	Jesus goes to Jerusalem by Perea	19:1-2	10:1		
30	137	Pharisees question Jesus about divorce	19:3-12	10:2-12		
30	138	Christ's love and blessing for little children	19:13-15	10:13-16	18:15-17	
30	139	The rich young ruler and discipleship	19:16-30	10:17-31	18:18-30	
30	140	Compensation of the laborers in the vineyard	20:1-16			
30	141	Jesus foretells his death a third time	20:17-19	10:32-34	18:31-34	
30	142	Request of a special favor for James and John	20:20-28	10:35-45		
30	143	Bartimaeus and another blind man cured	20:29-34	10:46-52	18:35-43	
30	144	Zaccheus called down from a sycamore tree			19:2-10	
30	145	Men thought the kingdom of God was now near			19:11	
30	146	Jesus counsels by the nobleman and his money			19:12-27	

Time	No.	Event	Matt.	Mark	Luke	John
		Last Jewish Sabbath beginning at sunset Friday				
30	147	A woman anoints Christ's head and feet (Bethany)	26:6-13	14:3-9		12:1-8
30	148	At Jerusalem Jews seek for Jesus' life				11:55-57
30	149	Crowds visit Bethany to see Lazarus and Jesus				12:9-11
		Last week of Passover ending with the crucifixion				
		First Day, Sunday				
30	150	Christ's triumphal entrance into Jerusalem	21:1-11	11:1-11	19:29-40	12:12-19
30	151	Approaching nigh the city, He weeps over Jerusalem			19:41-44	
30	152	Jesus enters the Temple inspecting its affairs		11:11		
30	153	He retires to Bethany to spend the night	21:17	11:11		
		Second Day, Monday				
30	154	Returning the next day hungry He curses the fig tree	21:18-22	11:12-14		
30	155	He cleanses the Temple again at end of His ministry	21:12-13	11:15-18	19:45-46	
30	156	Jesus heals the blind and lame in the Temple	21:14			
30	157	At evening Jesus leaves the city for Bethany		11:19		
		Third Day, Tuesday				
30	158	Returning He explains the lesson of the fig tree	21:20-22	11:20-26		
30	159	Duty to forgive in order to be forgiven		11:25-26		
30	160	The duty and power of faith in God urged	21:21-22	11:22-24		
30	161	Daily Jesus teaches the people in the Temple			19:47	
30	162	The Sanhedrists challenge His authority to teach	21:23-27	11:27-33	20:1-18	
30	163	Responds: Parable of two sons and a vineyard	21:28-32	12:1-16		
30	164	The Sanhedrists seek to lay hands on Jesus	21:45-46	12:12	19:47-48	8:37
30	165	Parable of a landowner (or king), his son, and his vineyard	21:33-44	12:1-14		
30	166	Parable of the Marriage Feast	22:1-14			
30	167	Herodians and Pharisees try to trap Him through His words	22:15-22	12:13-17	20:19-26	
30	168	Sadducees cavil about the resurrection	22:23-33	12:18-27	20:27-40	
30	169	Jesus with the lawyer and the great commandment	22:35-40	12:28-34		
30	170	If David's son, how does David call Him Lord?	22:41-46	12:35-37	20:41-44	
30	171	Warnings and woes for scribes and Pharisees	23:1-36	12:38-40	20:45-47	
30	172	Christ's tearful prediction respecting Jerusalem	23:37-39		13:34-35	
30	173	A poor widow's offering appreciated by Jesus		12:41-44	21:1-4	
30	174	Some Greeks desire to see Jesus Christ				12:20-22
30	175	Jesus prays and the Father answers from heaven				12:27-30
30	176	From Mount Olivet Jesus predicts downfall of Jerusalem	24:1-41 24:42-51	13:1-37	21:5-37	
30	177	Christ's answer concerning the Judgment Day	25:1-46			
30	178	Judas Iscariot conspires against Christ's life	26:1-16	14:1-11	22:1-6	
30	179	But many of the Sanhedrin believed on Christ				12:42
		Fourth Day, Wednesday, Day of Silence				
		Fifth Day, Thursday				
30	180	Jesus sends forth two disciples for Passover	26:17-19	14:12-16	22:7-13	
30	181	Jesus observes Passover at sunset	26:20-25	14:17-31	22:14-23	
30	182	Strife of the disciples who should be greatest			22:24-30	
30	183	Thereupon Jesus Himself washes disciples' feet				13:1-20
30	184	Jesus institutes and administers the Lord's Supper	26:26-29	14:22-25	22:15-20	
30	185	Jesus foretells and designates His betrayer	26:20-25	14:17-21	22:21-23	13:21-29
30	186	Judas after the supper withdraws to betray Him				13:27-30
30	187	Jesus predicts the scattering of the twelve	26:31-35	14:27-31	22:31-38	13:36-38 14:4,25-31
30	188	Farewell words of Christ with His disciples				16:1-33
30	189	He enters into prayer and agony in Gethsemane	26:36-46	14:32-42	22:39-46	18:1
30	190	Judas now identifies and betrays Jesus	26:47-50	14:42-46	22:47-51	18:2-9
30	191	Peter cuts off Malchus's ear, which Jesus healed	26:51-56	14:47-50	22:49-53	18:10-11
		Sixth Day, Friday				
30	192	Jesus before Annas at night, and Caiaphas at dawn	26:57-68	14:53-54	22:54	18:13,24
30	193	Three times Peter denies that he knows the Lord	26:69-75	14:66-72	22:54-62	18:25-27
30	194	Jesus avows that He is the Christ of God	26:59-68	14:55-65	22:63-71	18:19-24
30	195	Christ before Pilate for sentence to death	27:1-14	15:1-5	23:1-5	18:28-38
30	196	Pilate send Jesus to Herod Antipas of Galilee			23:6-12	
30	197	Herod and soldiers mock Jesus with robe, crown, and reed	27:27-31	15:16-20		
30	198	Pilate exonerates Jesus, but the people require Barabbas	27:15-26	15:6-15	23:13-25	18:39-40 19:1-16
30	199	Judas remorsefully returns his reward	27:3-10		Acts 1:16-20	
30	200	Jesus bears his cross, relieved by Simon	27:31-33	15:21	23:26	19:16-17
		Particulars related to Christ's crucifixion and resurrection				
30	201	The place of crucifixion was called Golgotha	27:33	15:22	23:33	19:17-18
30	202	He was crucified between two robbers	27:38	15:27	23:32-33	19:18
30	203	The three hours of preternatural darkness	27:45	15:33	23:44-45	
30	204	His garments divided among the Roman soldiers	27:35	15:24	23:34	19:23-24

Time	No.	Event	Matt.	Mark	Luke	John
30	205	The jeers and gibes of enemies unto Christ	27:39-44	15:29-32	23:35-43	
30	206	Tenderness and sympathy manifested by friends	27:36-56	15:40-41	23:47-49	19:25-27
30	207	The tearing of the veil of the Temple	27:51	15:38	23:45	
30	208	The splitting of the rocks by an earthquake	27:51			
30	209	The resurrection of the bodies of the saints	27:52-53			

The seven sayings of Jesus on the Cross

Time	No.	Event	Matt.	Mark	Luke	John
30	210	Prayer for His murderers: "Father forgive them"			23:34	
30	211	Promise to the penitent thief: "Today you shall be with Me"			23:42-43	
30	212	Jesus commits His mother to John: "Behold your son"				19:26-27
30	213	Jesus' warning cry of thirst: "I thirst"	27:48	15:36		19:28-30
30	214	His loud outcry of agony: "Eloi, Eloi, lama, sabachtani"	27:46	15:34-37	23:46	
30	215	Christ's final word touching His mission: "It is finished"				19:30
30	216	He commends His spirit unto God: "Father, into Thy hands"	27:50	15:37	23:46	
30	217	Having completed His sufferings, Jesus dies	27:50	15:37	23:46	19:30
30	218	Treatment by soldiers of Christ's dead body				19:31-37
30	219	Officer of the day testifies that Jesus "was the Son of God"	27:54			
30	220	Christ's friends lay His body in the tomb	27:57-61	{15:42-47 16:1}	23:50-56	19:38-42

Seventh Day, Saturday, April 8

Time	No.	Event	Matt.	Mark	Luke	John
30	221	Custody of Christ's body after its burial	27:62-66			

FROM CHRIST'S RESURRECTION TO HIS ASCENSION

First day's appearance, Easter, April 9

Time	No.	Event	Matt.	Mark	Luke	John
30	222	Women at dawn, with spices, find an empty tomb	28:1-2	16:1-6	24:1-8	20:1
30	223	Mary Magdalene runs to tell Peter and John				20:2
30	224	The others stay at the sepulcher and talk with the angels	28:2-7	16:5-7	24:4-8	
30	225	Peter and John run to the empty sepulcher			24:12	20:3-10
30	226	Christ's first appearance is to Mary Magdalene		16:9		20:11-17
30	227	His second appearance is to Mary, Salome, and Joanna	28:8-10	16:8	24:9-10	
30	228	The guards report to chief priests the facts known	28:11			
30	229	The guards take a bribe to falsify the facts	28:12-15			
30	230	His third appearance is to Peter, first Sabbath			24:34	1 Cor. 15:5
30	231	Fourth appearance is to two going to Emmaus		16:12-13	24:13-35	
30	232	Fifth appearance that day to disciples, Thomas being absent		16:14	24:36-49	20:19-23

Appearance of Christ after the first day

Time	No.	Event	Matt.	Mark	Luke	John
30	233	Sixth appearance to the ten, Thomas present				20:24-29
30	234	Seventh appearance to eleven on a mountain in Galilee	28:16-20	16:15-18		
30	235	Eighth appearance to seven fishing in Galilee				21:1-24
30	236	Ninth appearance to five hundred on a mountain of Galilee	28:16			1 Cor. 15:6
30	237	Tenth appearance to James, place not noted				1 Cor. 15:7
30	238	He was seen, not now and then, but literally, *"through forty days"* namely, in every one of the forty days (Acts 1:3-9). He was also seen by Paul when he was converted near Damascus (I Cor. 15:8), and by Stephen when he saw "the Son of Man standing at the right hand of God" (Acts 7:56), and by the apostle John again in the apocalyptic vision (Rev. 1:9-16)				

original composition. Socrates, the historian, states that Matthew went to Ethiopia, where he is said to have died a natural death. Eusebius says that Pantaenus, the philosopher, who afterward became a Christian and was placed at the celebrated school at Alexandria, penetrated as far as the Indies, and "there found his own arrival anticipated by some who there were acquainted with the gospel of Matthew, to whom Bartholomew, one of the apostles, had preached, and left them the gospel of Matthew in Hebrew, which was also preserved until this time" (see Eusebius *E. H.* 5.10).

Mark. Mark is the evangelist who wrote the second gospel. Papias, Bishop of Hierapolis in the first half of the second century, furnished the earliest notice of this gospel. He says, "Mark, having been the interpreter of Peter, wrote down accurately whatever he remembered, without however recording in order what was either said or done by Christ. *For neither did he hear the Lord, nor did he follow him* (as did the Twelve). . . . So, then Mark committed no error in thus writing down such details as he remembered; for he made it his own forethought not to omit or misrepresent any details that he heard [from Peter]" (Eusebius *E. H.* 3.39). Jerome observes of Mark that "taking his gospel which himself had composed, he went to Egypt and at Alexandria founded a church of great note"; and in his *Book of Illustrious Men* says, "Mark, the disciple and interpreter of Peter, at the desire of the brethren at Rome, wrote a short gospel according to what he had heard related by Peter, which, when Peter knew it, he approved and authorized it to be read in the churches" (*see* Lardner, 5:334). Universal testimony agrees that Mark wrote down in his gospel as best he could the substance of Peter's preaching; and the gospel itself confirms by internal evidence the testimony of the Fathers in many respects. For while it details in a graphic manner important facts, it is at once the briefest and least complete of the four gospels. Nevertheless, it represents fairly the impulsive and energetic Peter, and the very omissions and additions indicate the style of the apostle. Justin Martyr, who wrote about A.D. 140-50 and was born before the death of the apostle John, cites from the *Memoirs of Peter* the names given to James and John by Jesus, who called them "Boanerges," or sons of thunder; a circumstance mentioned only in Mark's gospel (3:17). Jerome, after mentioning Mark as having composed his gospel and gone to Egypt, founding a notable church at Alexandria, states that this evangelist "died in the eighth year of the reign of Nero." As Nero ruled the empire A.D. 54-68, this would place the death of Mark in the year 62 (Lardner, 5:331).

Three things are made evident as related to Mark's gospel by these patristic citations: (1) that Mark composed his gospel of the substance preached by Peter; (2) that Peter "knew" of the fact, and both approved and authorized his gospel to be read in the several churches; (3) that all this was accomplished before the death of Peter at Rome.

Luke. By common consent, Luke is regarded as the writer of the third gospel and of Acts. Even such writers as the Frenchman Renan, known as hostile to Christianity, concede this fact as incontestable. The third gospel is derived from different sources, but all legitimate authorities, as it is confessedly due to those apostles who "from the beginning were eyewitnesses and servants of the word" (prologue of chap. 1). Nevertheless, it is the most complete gospel of them all, and the only one that observes a strictly historical method, the first three gospels being biographical sketches or, as designated by Justin Martyr "Memoirs of the Apostles." It is to be remarked that both Luke's gospel and Acts are dedicated to one Theophilus (friend of God), which was a custom in those days, obligating those thus receiving a copy as a gift to exert themselves to give the work circulation (Lee).

John. John is the author of the fourth gospel. After extraordinary research and testing, the criticism of the best scholarship of the age ascribes this work to that apostle "whom Jesus loved." No classic writing of equal antiquity is so well attested by both external and internal evidence as John's gospel. It has been said, so peculiar and marked is this writing, that if we did not know who its author was, we should have to imagine a personage of such character for its authorship.

Designations of the Writers. The terms *evangelist* and *synoptist* are associated with the gospel writers.

Evangelists. In organizing the workers for the kingdom of Christ, "He gave some as apostles, and some as prophets, and some as evangelists . . . for the equipping of the saints" (Eph. 4:11-12). Evangelists appear to have been appointed to a certain *work,* rather than to be a specific order in the apostolic church. They were afterward known as *evangelistai,* "evangelists," whose function was that of missionary preachers, about whom Eusebius says, "leaving their country they performed the office of evangelists to those who proclaim Christ; they also delivered to them the books of the holy gospels. The Holy Ghost also wrought many wonders through them, so that as soon as the gospel was heard men voluntarily gathered in crowds and eagerly embraced the true faith with their whole minds." The evangelists were "bringers of good tidings given to the heralds of salvation through Christ, who are not apostles" (Thayer). In the time of Chrysostom the term was applied to "the writers of the gospels" (Cremer).

Synoptists. The writers of the first three gospels are known as synoptists in distinction from the fourth gospel; and the first three gospels are called the synoptic gospels; from *sun,* "together," and *opsis,* "view." The reference is to the parallel narratives in the facts recorded and the statements made by Matthew, Mark, and Luke. John's gospel is different in character, being intentionally supplementary to the accounts given by the synoptists. Clement of Alexandria says, "The three gospels previously written, having been distributed among all, and also handed down to him [i.e., John], they say that he admitted them, giving his testimony to their truth; but that there was only wanting in the narrative the account of the things done by Christ, among the first of his deeds, and at the commencement of the gospel. . . . For it is evident that the other three evangelists only wrote the deeds of our Lord for one year after the imprisonment of John the Baptist, and intimated this in the very beginning of their history. . . . [The] Apostle John, it is said, being entreated to undertake it, wrote the account of the time not recorded by the former evangelists, and the deeds done by our Savior, which they have passed by (for these were the events that occurred before the imprisonment of John), and this very fact is intimated by him when he says [2:11]: 'This beginning of miracles Jesus made' " (Eusebius *E. H.* 3.24). Clement elsewhere says, "But John, last of all, perceiving that what had reference to the body in the gospel of our Savior was sufficiently detailed, and being encouraged by his familiar friends and urged by the Spirit, wrote a spiritual gospel" (Eusebius *E. H.* 6.14).

The Synoptic Gospels. Matthew, Mark, and Luke are termed the "synoptic" gospels because, in marked contrast to John, they present a "common view" of the facts about Jesus implied in the Gk. word *sunopsis,* "a blended view." Critics maintain that Matthew and Luke contain substantial additions to material common to all three synoptics, and in these additions differ considerably from each other. Yet comparison shows that the framework regarding time and place is common to all three. In addition, many events and some teachings are related in all. More striking is the similarity of language employed. These likenesses are so well recognized and so numerous that the idea prevails that the first three gospels are not three independent compositions. This is the practically unanimous critical opinion. In addition to the agreements, remarkable disagreements also occur. The resulting "Synoptic Problem" has occupied unflagging critical labors for more than a century and a half. Scholars spend their energies attempting to discover a hypothesis that will plausibly explain the phenomena. The principal solutions offered are (1) an oral gospel underlying all three; (2) mutual dependence one upon another; (3) the hypothesis of a written source or sources.

Hypothesis of Oral Tradition. This hypothesis assumes that the evangelists wrote independently of one another, each describing the circumstances of his gospel from oral narratives of the words and deeds of Jesus rather than from written documents. It is held that this oral tradition as a result of repetition had come to have a relatively fixed form. This is asserted to be sufficient reason to account for the similarities and dissimilarities of the synoptic gospels. Beginning with Gieseler in 1818 this oral hypothesis, with variation, has had advocates to the present.

Mutual-Hypothesis Theory. This theory, as held by Augustine, maintains the use of one of the gospels by one of the other two. Numerous variations of the theory have been presented. The hypothesis of sources has been held by numerous scholars in the twentieth century. At the beginning of the century there was critical consensus of opinion that behind Matthew's and Luke's gospels lay two written sources. First, the gospel of Mark and a document commonly designated "Q," consisting principally of the logia of Jesus. Under this so-called Two-Document Theory, "Q" is discovered first upon examination of the material not contained in Mark's gospel that is common to Matthew and Luke. The suggestion that each center of Christianity had a different version of "Q," and that the writer of Matthew had one form and the writer of Luke another, has not won general support.

Proto-Luke Theory. B. H. Streeter (*The Four Gospels,* 4th ed. rev. [1930]) and V. Taylor (*Behind the Third Gospel* [1926]) have proposed this theory. It holds that someone, perhaps Luke, collected into one document previously unwritten teachings and events, particularly parables. This document was called "L." Luke then combined "L" with "Q." The result was Proto-Luke. Subsequently Luke inserted large portions of Mark into Proto-Luke to form a third gospel.

Four-Document Theory. Streeter later held that a Jewish Christian document "M" underlies Matthew, whose sources would thus be Mark, "Q," and "M." This resulted in the Four-Document Theory, which maintains that underlying Matthew and Luke, besides minor oral and written sources, were four documents, namely, Mark, "Q," "M," and "L," embodying traditions of various Christian centers: Mark reflecting Rome; "Q," Antioch; "M," Jerusalem; and "L," Caesarea. This theory had wide acceptance for a time.

M. S. Enslin (*Christian Beginnings* [1938]) and others, however, have vigorously challenged this theory. Enslin rejects even "Q" and maintains that the writer of Luke used Matthew as one source. A number of scholars have held that a primitive gospel or *Grundschrift* underlies our gospel, such as B. W. Bacon (*The Gospel of Mark: Its Composition and Date* [1925]), W. Bussmann (*Synoptische Studien,* 3 vols. [1925-31]), F. C. Grant (*The Growth of the Gospels* [1933]).

Multiple Source Theory. This theory has been espoused by some scholars in views somewhat similar to Streeter's hypothesis. Like the higher criticism of the OT, higher criticism of the gospels forms an intellectually titillating occupation for scholars with changing fads and fancies but does not provide a final solution.

Floyd V. Filson says, "The following statements seem warranted: The writers of Matthew and Luke used Mark; they used at least one other written source; we cannot determine conclusively the exact number and extent of such written sources; each writer, in using his sources, felt free to conform his style and wording somewhat to his own literary habits; possibly short written sources lay behind Mark" (*Schaff-Herzog Ency. of Religious Knowledge* [1955], pp. 470-71. Cf. also Filson, *Origins of the Gospels* [1938]).

The Relation of the Gospel of John to the Synoptics. Critical difficulties of the book of John relate mainly to the book taken by itself. However, its unlikeness to the synoptic gospels is so great that it is not unusual that some critics have thought that to accept its authenticity is to deny that of the synoptics. But careful study of many of the superficial difficulties causes them to lose their apparent significance, such as the mention of three Passovers in John and but one in the other gospels. This circumstance does not imply discrepancy in the length of Jesus' public ministry. The fragmentary character of the gospel reports is adequate explanation that the other Passover feasts were not mentioned or included. The process of harmonizing the order of events between John and the synoptics is now less easy and certain than was formerly thought because of the fragmentary character of all reports. On the other hand, the same fragmentariness makes it less easy to assert with confidence that the gospel of John and the synoptic gospels are contradictory or even inconsistent.

Grouping of the Four Gospels. Luke's prologue gives plain indication that there were in existence at that time various narratives concerning Jesus that apparently had gained some currency. The apocryphal gospels are certainly much later, but apparently the so-called "gospel of the Hebrews" and "gospel of Peter" found considerable acceptance for some time. Gradually these and other narratives were set aside in favor of what we now know as the four gospels. By the middle of the second century Tatian's *Diatessaron*, which is a single narrative formed by combining the four gospels that we now have, shows that the order was by that time established. It seems clear that it was so established for quite some time in Asia Minor. Perhaps at Ephesus, where the first three gospels had been taken and where the fourth was written, the present grouping of narratives that we now have was made. According to Papias, long before the middle of the second century this process was taking place, if not already consummated. The accepted group of the gospels has always consisted of the same four books. Their order, however, varies greatly in the various manuscripts. Almost every possible arrangement can be found. The order Matthew, John, Luke, Mark is found only less often than the order that finally prevailed.

Possible Aramaic Originals of the Gospels. The fact that the mother tongue of Jesus and the apostles was Aram. but that the gospels were written in Gk. has led some recent scholars to defend Aram. originals of the four gospels. Papias's testimony in the first half of the second century is to the effect that Matthew composed the "logia" in the Heb., or as the word may connote, "Aramaic." Jerome, around A.D. 400, was acquainted with a gospel in the language of the Jews. Are scholars sound in giving credence to these traditional clues, and will internal evidence support the theses of Aram. originals? The vague references of the church Fathers are of little significance. What about the character of the Gk. of the gospels? As early as the nineteenth century, scholars such as Marshall and Wellhausen had argued that one or more of the Gk. gospels was originally translated from an Aram. work.

C. F. Burney in 1922 set forth the thesis that John's gospel was penned at Syrian Antioch in Aram. around A.D. 75 (*The Aramaic Origin of the Fourth Gospel* [1922]). C. C. Torrey had previously claimed an Aram. origin for the gospels. His views were aired in a series of studies and essays (*The Four Gospels* [1933], 2d ed. [1947]; *Our Translated Gospels* [1936]; *Documents of the Primitive Church* [1941]). The embarrassing impediment to this view, however, is that no Aram. originals are extant. Argument proceeds on the contention that the style is Semitic and that the Gk. employs idioms that parallel Aram. idioms, which in passages cited are contended to make no clear sense. Especially, the passages that are alleged to make no clear sense in Gk. may be understood as mistranslations of the original Aram. The view, however, is plagued by vagueness concerning which precise passages contain mistranslations. A. T. Olmstead held the view

that a comprehensive Aram. gospel underlies our present gospels, but he did not maintain that they were translations of Aram. originals ("Could an Aramaic Gospel Be Written?" *Journal of Near Eastern Studies* 1 [1942]: 41-75). M. Black has more recently outlined the case. His collocation of linguistic evidence is cautious and careful (*An Aramaic Approach to the Gospels and Acts* [1946], 2d ed. [1952]).

Approaching the view of Aram. originals for the gospels, a number of scholars such as E. J. Goodspeed (*New Chapters in N.T. Study* [1937]); D. W. Riddle (*The Gospels: Their Origin and Growth* [1939]); E. C. Colwell (*The Greek of the Fourth Gospel* [1931]) have attacked C. C. Torrey and his followers. It is pointed out that numerous idioms supposed to be Semitic are paralleled in Gk. literature. Alleged mistranslations turn out to be passable Gk. More important still, the fact is adduced that no Aram. gospels are extant. It is quite obvious that the critical notion of Aram. originals behind the gospels has not presented an approved case. It is possible that Aram. sources were used in the composition of our present gospels, but evidently they were composed originally in Gk. However, their linguistic traits demonstrate an early Semitic tradition stemming from Palestine.

The Synoptic Gospels and Form Criticism. The twentieth century has witnessed a growth in what has been called form criticism. Form criticism has been especially applied to the analysis of the synoptic gospels. The German term is *Formgeschichte,* denoting "history of form." This literary method analyzes literary forms that contain earlier traditions. It maintains that the earlier oral tradition produced a number of literary forms that appear in the finished written record. In other words, it holds that the earlier oral tradition shaped the final literary product. It devotes itself to the analysis of these forms. This method of criticism maintains that the synoptic gospels are composed of numerous separate units whose form in the final written records was affected by later editorial arranging. The resultant product does not catalog actual events in Jesus' ministry in sequential order. Form criticism classifies the separate units of tradition in accordance with their varying forms. It speaks frequently of *Sitz im Leben,* or "life situation." By analysis of form it is believed that the particular situation in the church that formed this unit of tradition can be traced. It thus becomes evident, it is asserted, that the synoptic gospels have only limited value in telling us who Jesus was or what He said or did. They rather furnish information about the thinking and reactions of the early church. The form criticism method has appeared in the works of M. Dibelius (*Formgeschichte des Evangeliums* [1919]) and R. Bultmann (*Die Geschichte der synoptischen Tradition* [1921], 2d ed. [1931]). Also in the works of K. L. Schmidt

(*Der Rahmen der Geschichte Jesu* [1919]) the form critical method has been given clear-cut expression. The question may be asked as to whether the form critics allow that the gospels give us a true portrayal of the historical Jesus. To this question it may be said that most of them would assert that they rather give us first of all testimony to the life and teaching of the early church. The gospels are of value, under this view, in preserving tradition as it developed by use in instruction, worship, and other activities of the early church.

Is Form Criticism Sound? Conservative scholars have pointed out the inability of form criticism to deal adequately with the historical background of the gospels as well as the intelligence and integrity of the disciples of Jesus. In its recognition of the topical arrangement of much of the gospel material it overreaches itself in casting aspersion upon the general framework of Jesus' life and ministry. In addition, it fails to account for the glowing faith in the face of stubborn doubt that transfigured the early disciples after the resurrection. It fails to see how important the qualification and conviction of an eye-witness are in shaping the early tradition.

There is a sense in which form criticism is correct in stressing the importance of the early oral period, but it comes short of attaching proper significance to the fact that within two decades or so the composition of the written gospels began. Such a comparatively short period of early tradition does not allow for the assumptions form criticism normally makes concerning the lack of reliability and historicity of the gospel narratives. This school of criticism has been signally unable to assign all the gospel material to plausible forms. It lists types of gospel tradition such as the passion story, stories about Jesus, miracle tales, parables, and sayings, and what V. Taylor has termed "The pronouncement story." This latter, however, is held to begin with a difficulty, a dispute, or a miracle, and to eventuate in a word or pronouncement of Jesus.

Form Criticism of the Gospel of John. The fourth gospel has not come under the influence of form criticism as have the synoptics. Because it is obviously the work of one writer, it can scarcely be regarded as a product of oral tradition. Acts has been subject to the form critical method, but here the success of this critical method has been merger.

When the Gospels Were Written. A precise dating of the gospels has always been a difficult matter and, despite progress of twentieth-century research, still remains uncertain. Perhaps the greatest strides have been made in dating the gospel of John. The discovery of the Rylands Papyrus Fragment of the gospel of John, dating around A.D. 130, has made more untenable a middle second-century date for the fourth gospel. The Qumran Literature of the Dead Sea Scrolls

is rendering great service to NT criticism. Its evidence is disposing of radical late-dating of John that separated it from the authentic apostolic tradition. This used to be done on the basis of the alleged Gnostic influence upon the gospel. Heretical Gnosticism of the second to fourth centuries featured God as Light and Life. Since this terminology is typical of the gospel of John, critics used to assert plausibly that the fourth gospel was penned by a later writer who was not himself a Gnostic but used Gnostic terminology in opposing Gnostic error. New archaeological finds at Chenoboskion in Upper Egypt, consisting of forty Gnostic treatises written in the Coptic language and dating from the third and fourth centuries A.D., have shown that Gnosticism is much later than the gospel of John, although the Gnostics based much of their teachings on the gospel. The Dead Sea Scrolls themselves prove that the alleged Gnosticism in John is in reality a dualism (light against darkness). This dualism is prominent in the literature from Qumran and was popular in pre-Christian Palestine. Archaeology clearly demonstrates the Palestinian background and authentic origins of the fourth gospel. Perusal of the Qumran scrolls and the gospel of John can lead only to the conclusion that both authors lived in the same age and environment. There is now no necessity for dating the gospel of John any later than the last decade of the first century. *See* Merrill F. Unger, *The Dead Sea Scrolls* (1957), pp. 41-46; J. A. T. Robinson, *Redating the New Testament* (1976).

Although the synoptic gospels cannot be dated precisely, numerous scholars date Mark A.D. 65-75, Luke A.D. 85, Matthew A.D. 85 or 90; and John A.D. 90 or somewhat later. C. C. Torrey dates Mark A.D. 40, Matthew only slightly later, and Luke and John not beyond A.D. 60. This extreme early dating has not found wide acceptance, however. More scholars follow A. Harnack's view (cf. *The Sayings of Jesus* [1908]; *The Date of the Acts and the Synoptic Gospels* [1911]), that Luke is to be dated before A.D. 60 and Mark somewhat earlier.

The tendency today is to date the Synoptic Gospels before the destruction of Jerusalem in A.D. 70 and the gospel of John in the last decade or two of the century. An indication of what has been happening in the field is seen in the work of John A. T. Robinson, lecturer in theology at Trinity College, Cambridge. Though a liberal theologian, he concluded in his *Redating the New Testament* and his *Can We Trust the New Testament?* (both produced in the late 1970s) that all the NT books were written between about A.D. 47 and 70. He thinks Mark may date as early as 45, Luke within ten or fifteen years after that, and Matthew at least by 70. Then he pleads for not separating John from the other gospels and for dating its composition prior to the fall of Jerusalem. Admittedly Robinson has not brought about a revolutionary redating of the gospels, but he has been part of the scholarly trend to earlier dating of them.

Are the Gospels Myth? Prominent in twentieth-century biblical criticism has been the concept of myth. The rationalism and deism of the eighteenth and nineteenth centuries discounted the biblical stories as myth. In the NT itself myths are contrasted with truth (2 Tim. 4:4; Titus 1:14) and with history (2 Pet. 1:16). They are denounced as incompatible with true religion and God's revelation (1 Tim. 1:4; 4:7). Although commentators are in disagreement as to what constitutes the NT concept of myth, whether fanciful elaboration of the OT stories by rabbinical teachers, allegorical exegesis of the Philo type or pre-Gnostic Jewish speculations, it is quite certain that according to NT revelation myths are human inventions as contrasted to the Word of God.

In recent times numerous critics have insisted on the demythologization of the NT, particularly the gospels. Rudolf Bultmann of Germany in 1941 published a widely circulated article, "Neues Testament und Mythologie." Barth and Brunner had spoken of "Christian myth" in contrast to pagan myth, but Bultmann's radical and original concept of myth stirred up a critical hornet's nest. Bultmann insisted that the gospel records are historically unreliable and inquired what relevancy they had for our present-day life and faith. Persuaded that form criticism had demonstrated that the historical nucleus was completely vitiated by the religious interpretation that the early church gave to the life and work of Jesus, Bultmann not only branded the miracle stories as mythological but declared that the gospels in their entirety were myths, out of line with modern man's scientific tradition. The whole account of Jesus was a Christological myth, as well as eschatological beliefs in heaven or hell, the return of Christ, etc.

Bultmann advocated a demythologizing of the gospels, contending that the true objective of the gospel stories was never to describe supernatural events taking place in space and time. Rather, their purpose was to announce God's coming to a human soul, or self, and the conversion taking place thereby. Thus Bultmann was not willing to give up Christianity altogether. This demythologizing criticism spearheaded by Bultmann has had a wide influence in contemporary study of the gospels. However, it fails completely to meet the requirements the NT lays down for Christianity: namely, faith in the revealed person and work of Jesus of the gospels. According to the gospel definitions of faith and the Pauline and Petrine interpretations of the life and work of the Messiah, Bultmann's advice can only be categorized as thoroughgoing rejection of historical Christianity. His rationalism fails completely to explain the historical fact that immediately after Jesus' death primitive Christians should have given such an interpretation to Christ's life unless His life, death, resurrection, and ascension had given them incontrovertible evidence that He was the Messiah, the Son of God, promised in the OT. No rationalization of Barth, Brunner, or Bultmann can explain the faith of the early Christians, nor the phenomenon of the NT, nor the efficacy of the Christian gospel. Bultmann's view strikes at the essence of the Christian message of God's becoming man and dying for the sins of the world. This criticism ignores the particular emphasis all NT writers put upon the necessity of a Redeemer who is human as well as divine. Bultmann's disdain of eschatology demonstrates the spiritual bankruptcy of his views (cf. Gustave Staehlin, "Mythos," in Kittel's *Theologisches Woerterbuch zum Neuen Testament* 4:769ff.).   M.F.U.

BIBLIOGRAPHY: B. F. Westcott, *An Introduction to the Study of the Gospels* (1895); F. L. Godet, *Introduction to the New Testament: The Collection of the Four Gospels and the Gospel of St. Matthew* (1899); R. K. Bultmann and K. Kundsin, *Form Criticism* (1934); F. V. Filson, *Origins of the Gospels* (1938); V. Taylor, *The Gospels: A Short Introduction* (1945); B. C. Butler, *The Originality of St. Matthew* (1951); M. C. Tenney, *The Genius of the Gospels* (1951); V. Taylor, *The Formation of Gospel Tradition* (1953); D. E. Nineham, ed., *Studies in the Gospels* (1955); F. C. Grant, *The Gospels: Their Origin and Growth* (1957); R. K. Bultmann, *History of the Synoptic Tradition* (1963); N. B. Stonehouse, *Origins of the Synoptic Gospels* (1963); W. R. Farmer, *The Synoptic Problem* (1964); C. J. G. Montefiore, *The Synoptic Gospels*, 2 vols. (1967); J. C. Hawkins, *Horae Synopticae* (1968); D. B. J. Campbell, *The Synoptic Gospels* (1969); J. A. T. Robinson, *Redating the New Testament* (1976); C. M. Talbert, *What Is a Gospel?* (1977); R. P. Martin, *International Standard Bible Encyclopedia* (1982), 2:529-32.

GOURD. *See* Vegetable Kingdom: Castor Oil Plant.

GOURDS (Heb. *peqā'îm, paqqūōt*). Ornamentation shaped like gourds is referred to in the description of the decoration of the Temple (1 Kings 6:18) and the bronze sea (7:24). *See* Laver; Sea, Bronze; Tabernacle.

Wild gourds were among the ingredients of Elisha's poisonous stew (2 Kings 4:38). *See* Vegetable Kingdom: Castor Oil Plant; Gourds, Wild.

GOURDS, WILD. *See* Vegetable Kingdom.

GOVERNMENT OF GOD. *See* Theocracy; Israel.

GOVERNMENT OF ISRAEL. *See* Israel.

GOVERNOR. One who rules by authority delegated from a supreme ruler to whom he is responsible. Gedaliah was "appointed over" and therefore governor for Nebuchadnezzar II in Palestine after the fall of Jerusalem in 587 B.C. (Jer. 40:5; 41:2). Persian governors had administration over the Jews after the captivity. Zerubbabel and Nehemiah, although Jews by birth, were Persian administrators (Neh. 5:14, 18; Hag. 1:14). At the time of our Lord, although Pontius

Pilate's Roman title was procurator, he was actually the governor of Judea at the time of the crucifixion and is so named (Matt. 28:14). *See also* Ruler.

GOYIM (gō'yim). The name of a place in Gilgal defeated by Joshua and the Israelites in the conquest (Josh. 12:23, NIV; the NASB renders "Goiim").

GO'ZAN (gō'zan). A northeastern Mesopotamian city located on the Habor River, a tributary of the Euphrates. It lay E of the important patriarchal city of Haran and NW of the great Assyrian metropolis of Nineveh. The Assyrians deported the Israelites to Gozan after the capture of the capital of Samaria (2 Kings 17:6; 18:11; 19:12; 1 Chron. 5:26). The Assyrians called Gozan "Guzanu." It is the Gauzanitis of Ptolomey. Baron von Oppenheim discovered a new culture at Tell Halaf, ancient Gozan, in 1911 and 1913. Halafian pottery, now proverbial for its beauty, dates from c. 4000 B.C.   M.F.U.

GRACE. "Grace is what God may be free to do, and indeed what he does, accordingly, for the lost after Christ has died on behalf of them" (Lewis Sperry Chafer, *Systematic Theology*, 7:178). It is thus apparent that God's grace is to be distinguished from His mercy and love (Eph. 2:4-5), "But God, being rich in mercy, because of His great love with which He loved us, even when we were dead in our transgressions, made us alive together with Christ (by grace you have been saved)." Mercy is therefore the compassion of God that moved Him to provide a Savior for the unsaved. Had God been able to save even one soul on the ground of His sovereign mercy alone, He could have saved every person on that basis, as Lewis Sperry Chafer points out, and the death of Christ would not have been a necessity. Divine love on the other hand is the motivating plan behind all that God does in saving a soul. But since God is holy and righteous, and sin is a complete offense to Him, His love or His mercy cannot operate in grace until there is provided a sufficient satisfaction for sin. This satisfaction makes possible the exercise of God's grace. Grace thus rules out all human merit. It requires only faith in the Savior. Any intermixture of human merit violates grace. God's grace thus provides not only salvation but safety and preservation for the one saved, despite his imperfections. Grace perfects forever the saved one in the sight of God because of the saved one's position "in Christ." Grace bestows Christ's merit and Christ's standing forever (Rom. 5:1-2; 8:1; Col. 2:9-10); "for in Him all the fulness of Deity dwells in bodily form, and in Him you have been made complete." Grace thus obviates any obligation to gain merit, and the law as a merit system is no longer applicable to a believer, since he is no longer "under law, but under grace" (Rom. 6:14). The problem

of a holy life is met in the gospel of grace by the fact that the saved one has an entirely new position in grace instead of in Adam (5:12-20). And being baptized "into Christ" (6:1-11), he is "dead to sin, but alive to God." Knowledge of and faith in this glorious in-Christ position (6:11) is the key that makes it actual in the believer's everyday experience. Rewards for faithfulness and practical holiness of life are to be dispensed, but this is a truth not to be confused with an unforfeitable and unmerited salvation.

BIBLIOGRAPHY: J. Watson, *The Doctrines of Grace* (1900); L. S. Chafer, *Grace* (1922); J. Moffat, *Grace in the New Testament* (1931); J. N. D. Anderson, *Law and Grace* (1954); J. Murray, *The Covenant of Grace* (1954); C. R. Smith, *The Biblical Doctrine of Grace and Related Doctrines* (1956); C. C. Ryrie, *The Grace of God* (1963).

GRACE AT MEALS. A short prayer at mealtime, returning thanks to God for food provided and asking the divine blessing upon it. The propriety of such an act is evident from the injunction (Rom. 14:6; 1 Cor. 10:31; 1 Tim. 4:4) and from the example of our Lord (Mark 8:6-7; Luke 24:30). Among the Jews "grace" was said both before and after meals, and also by women, slaves, and children. Regulations were made down to the pettiest detail, namely, what form was to be used for the fruits of the trees; what for wine; what for the fruits of the ground; for bread; for vegetables; for vinegar; for unripe fallen fruit; for locusts, milk, cheese, eggs; and scholars contended as to when this and that form was suitable. When such restriction was laid upon prayer by the legal formula, it could not but be chilled into an external performance (Schürer, *History of the Jewish People*, div. 2, 2:117ff.).

GRAFT (Gk. *egkentrizō*, to "prick in"). Grafting is the process in horticulture by which a portion of a plant is made to unite with another plant, whether of the same kind or of another variety or species. The plant upon which the operation is performed is called the stock; the portion inserted or joined with it, the scion or graft. The usual process is to take shoots or buds from approved trees and to insert them into others where, with proper care, they continue to grow. Thus fruit is kept from degenerating, for the grafts receive nourishment from the stocks, but always produce fruit of the same sort as the tree from which they were taken.

The apostle Paul makes use (Rom. 11:17-24) of this figure in a striking manner: he compares the Jewish theocracy to a good olive tree, the Gentiles to a wild one, of which a branch is engrafted upon the former, and which by that means it acquires fruitfulness.

GRAIN (Heb. *seror*, "packed," i.e., "kernel"; Gk. *kokkos*, "kernel"). Used (Amos 9:9; 1 Cor. 15:37; etc.) in the singular and not as we do in a collective sense. *See also* Vegetable Kingdom: Corn.

GRANARY. *See* Storehouse.

GRAPES. *See* Vegetable Kingdom: Vine.

GRASS. *See* Vegetable Kingdom.

GRASSHOPPER. *See* Animal Kingdom: Locust.

GRATING. A bronze network, movable by a bronze ring at each corner and placed below the top of the great altar (Ex. 27:4; 35:16; 38:4-5, 30; 39:39). *See* Altar.

GRAVE.

Egyptian. The Egyptians were distinguished above other peoples of the ancient biblical world for their attention to burial and the afterlife. Believing in a future existence that was a higher form of their earthly life, they interred all sorts of physical comforts with the deceased. Besides food and drink, household pets were embalmed and placed in the tomb, and often happy scenes from the life of the deceased were painted on the sarcophagi or on the tomb walls. (*See* John Garstang, *Burial Customs of Ancient Egypt,* and Steindorff and Seele, *When Egypt Ruled the East.*) The poor were simply interred without clothing and uncoffined beneath the sand, but even in this extremity food and water were placed alongside the deceased. People of wealth were buried in a mastaba during the early dynasties. This was a development from the simple trench into which the body had been lowered and a pile of dirt heaped upon it. The mastaba consisted of a rectangular structure of brick or stone placed over the grave. In the vicinity of the great pyramids at Gizeh and at Saqqarah numberless mastabas of the nobility have been uncovered. In the case of royalty the pyramid was used, as the Great Step Pyramid at Saqqarah, belonging to the Third Dynasty. This and other pyramids developed from the mastaba when several of these structures were placed one on top of another. Still further developments were the colossal pyramids at Gizeh. King Zoser of the Third Dynasty was interred in the Step Pyramid at Saqqarah. Khufu, Khafre, and Menkaure were honored by the great Gizeh pyramids. The pyramids at the other eight pyramid fields were much smaller. In the splendid New Kingdom, when Egypt ruled the East, the mastaba and pyramid had become outmoded. The style for rock-cut tombs was in vogue. Examples of these are the tombs of Rameses VI and Amenhotep II. The story of the sumptuous tomb of *Tutankhamen* (which see) reads like a fairy tale. Reliefs were carved on the walls; paintings made in bright colors depicted happy scenes from the earthly life of the deceased in the case of the queens and nobles. But the kings, who were supposed to be divine, were pictured in the company of the gods or in transit from this life to the next.

Mesopotamian and Persian. Much is now known of graves from the Royal Tombs at Ur. Sumerian royalty, like the Egyptians, desired creature comforts to follow them in death, so courtiers and horses and servants were drugged and buried alive or poisoned before burial. This is indicated by the tomb of Queen Puabi (*see* articles Burial; Grave) and others and her husband at Ur. She was buried in great splendor with twenty-five servants and a great variety of belongings. Babylonians at a considerably later date practiced cremation like the Romans, placing the ashes of the deceased in artistic glazed crematory urns. The great kings of Persia—Darius, Xerxes, and Artaxerxes—cut their tombs out of solid rock near Persepolis. Those of Darius I and Artaxerxes I have a column-adorned facade. Darius is pictured worshiping Ahura Mazda in front of a fire altar. The tomb of Cyrus the Great was built near Parsargadae, NE of Persepolis.

Hellenistic tomb in the Kidron Valley, Jerusalem

Greek. Early pre-Hellenic Greek tombs of the Mycenean period were shaped like beehives. Later, lavish tombs such as that of King Mausolus of Caria (c. 350 B.C.) became the prototype of succeeding mausoleums. Greek sarcophagi were also handsomely executed. Tomb reliefs are in the highest tradition of Hellenic art. At Marathon, the so-called Soros, is an artificial mound thrown up little by little to mark the spot where almost 200 Athenians fell in 490 B.C., heroically defending their democratic land against the invasion of Persia. This constitutes the unique "community tomb."

Roman. Early Romans practiced cremation, placing the ashes of the deceased in columbaria ("pigeon lodgings"). Such columbaria were found near Virgil's tomb at Naples, at Rome's seaport of Ostia, at Pompeii, in many Roman cities of the Middle East, and even at Masada. Many of these were artistically carved. Well-known cities of first-century Rome had a "Street of the Sepulchres." When Paul came into Rome over the Appian Way, he passed hundreds of tombs of wealthy Romans of the Imperial Period, some consisting of flat slabs, others standing pillars, mausoleums, and some towers. Burial in the catacombs was common in Rome of the early Christian era. Compartments in the rock received the bodies and were shut with panels inscribed with the name of the deceased along with an emblem of the sacred monogram, the fish, the shepherd, or a praying man.

Hebrew. Among the Jews, graves were sometimes mere cavities dug out of the earth (Gen. 35:8; 1 Sam. 31:13); natural caves or grottoes (23:17); artificial tombs hewn out of the rock, provided with galleries and chambers, preference being given to places outside cities (Luke 7:12; John 11:30). Only kings and prophets (1 Kings 2:10; 16:6; 1 Sam. 25:1; 28:3) were buried in cities. The rich had, no doubt, family burying places (Gen. 23:20; Judg. 8:32; 2 Sam. 2:32; 1 Kings 3:22), while the poorer classes doubtless had their public ones (Jer. 26:23; 2 Kings 23:6; cf. Matt. 27:7). Graves hewn in the rock or laid out in natural caves were closed with large flat stones (27:60; 28:2; John 11:38). Monuments were set up in early times on or over graves (Gen. 35:20; cf. 2 Sam. 18:18; Job 21:32), which afterward took the form of magnificent mausoleums with pyramids and many kinds of emblems (1 Macc. 13:27-30).

Probably there were burying places attached to each village in ancient times, as we find in the case of Nain, where the graveyard remains to this day.

In postexilic times it was sought to restore and adorn the graves of the prophets and other holy persons, and this was particularly affected by the Pharisees to testify their reverence for the prophets (cf. Matt. 23:30-32).

Flat stones laid upon graves had upon them a marking to warn passersby lest they should contract uncleanliness by touching the grave. For this end also the tombs were whitewashed every year on the 15th of Adar.

There are scriptural traces of the popular idea that graves were the residence of demons (cf. 8:28), who were, perhaps, connected with soothsaying (Acts 16:16); while others refer such allusions to the supernatural notions respecting offering to the souls of the departed. *See* Tomb.

M.F.U.

BIBLIOGRAPHY: *See* Burial.

GRAVECLOTHES (Gk. *keiria,* "winding sheet"). From early times the body was washed (Acts 9:37), then wrapped in a linen cloth (Matt. 27:59), or the limbs separately wound with strips of linen (John 11:44).

GRAVED, GRAVER. *See* Handicrafts: Carver.

GRAVEN IMAGE (Heb. *pesel,* or *pāsîl,* a "carving"). A figure made of wood or stone (Ex. 20:4; Deut. 27:15, both KJV; marg., NASB, for "idol"), meant to represent Jehovah. *See* Idol; Image Worship.

GRAY. *See* Hair.

GREASE. *See* Fat.

GREAT LIZARD. *See* Animal Kingdom: Lizard, Great.

GREAT OWL. *See* Animal Kingdom: Owl.

GREAVES. *See* Armor, Arms.

GRECIA. *See* Greece.

GRECIANS. *See* Greeks.

GREECE. Properly that country in Europe inhabited by the Greeks (1 Macc. 1:1), but in Acts 20:2 apparently designating only that part of it S of the Roman province of *Macedonia* (which see). Greece is sometimes described as a country containing the four regions of Macedonia, Epirus, Achaia (or Hellas), and Peloponnesus, but more commonly only the latter two are to be understood as comprised in it. There seems to have been little contact between Greece and the Hebrews until the Macedonian conquest of the East; hence the few references in the OT. Greece is mentioned in Gen. 10:2, 4 under the name *Javan* (which see); the Jews and Greeks are said to have met in the slave market (Joel 3:6); and Greece is spoken of as "the shaggy goat" by Daniel (Dan. 8:21).

At the beginning of the Christian era those territories that now form the Republic of Greece formed the Roman province of Achaia, with the proconsuls residing at Corinth, Macedonia, and Thrace. As a place of learning, however, Athens held the first rank, and study there was held indispensable to a Roman youth wishing to distinguish himself. Her schools of grammar, rhetoric, dialectics, and philosophy were crowded.

Christianity was first planted in Greece by Paul, who visited Philippi (Acts 16:12), then Thessalonica, Berea, Athens, and Corinth (chaps. 17-18). Dionysius the Areopagite, who was converted through the apostle's address on Mars' Hill, is said to have become the Bishop of Athens. *See* Greeks; Paul.

BIBLIOGRAPHY: W. Smith, ed., *Dictionary of Greek and Roman Biography and Mythology,* 3 vols. (1864); J. B. Bury, *A History of Greece to the Death of Alexander the Great* (1913); E. Hamilton, *The Greek Way* (1930); G.

Mediterranean Sea

Murray, *Five Stages of Greek Religion* (1955); H. D. F. Kitto, *The Greeks* (1964); E. Melas, ed., *Temples and Sanctuaries of Ancient Greece* (1970).

GREEK. An inhabitant of Greece.

GREEKS. In the OT, inhabitants of Greece and the coastlands and islands belonging to the Greek race; in the NT, Hellenists, or Greek-speaking Jews.

In the OT Javan (Heb. *yāwān*) is translated "Greece" (cf. Dan. 10:20; 11:2, marg.); in Joel 3:6, *yᵉwānîm* is translated "Greeks" (marg., "Sons of Javan"). In the NT the versions distinguish between *Hellēnes*, "Greeks" by birth, as opposed to *Ioudaioi*, "Jews," whence *Hellēnes* is sometimes applied to Gentiles in general; and *Hellēnistai*, "Grecians," i.e., Greek-speaking Jews, as opposed to *Hebraioi*, home Jews dwelling in Palestine (cf. Acts 6:1; 9:29). The differences among the Scripture versions in Acts 11:20 and 17:17 results from a difference in the Gk. texts that they followed.

In NT times, Greeks or Hellenists were foreign Jews who spoke Gk., which the conquests of Alexander had made the language of the educated throughout the Near East, and also the language of the masses in the great centers of commerce. Some would include under the name *Hellenists*, proselytes of Greek birth.

There are legends of early Jewish settlements in Arabia, Ethiopia, and Abyssinia. Indeed, the natural overflow of a vigorous people inheriting the business energy of their father Jacob would have united with the varying fortunes of war to carry numbers of Jews far beyond the limits of Palestine at a remote period. Of the influence of the Jews who were scattered abroad in these early ages it is impossible to form an estimate. Theirs was not professedly a missionary religion; but wherever the faithful Jew went he carried the knowledge of the true God, as did Naomi (Ruth 1:15-16; 2:12), or, indirectly, Naaman's maid (2 Kings 5:3-4); and, as far as his influence extended, he carried that combination of religion and lawful commerce that the great missionary explorer Livingstone thought so desirable.

But the Dispersion, as a distinct element influencing the entire character of the Jews, dates from the Babylonian Exile. Its limits had been extended by the Greek conquests in Asia, by the colonizing policy of some of the successors of Alexander the Great, and by the persecutions of Antiochus, so that at the beginning of the Christian era the Dispersion was divided into three great sections—the Babylonian, the Syrian, and the Egyptian.

From Babylon the Jews spread throughout Persia, Media, and Parthia; but the settlements in China belong to a modern date. Nisibis, in NE Mesopotamia, became a colonizing center. In Armenia the Jews arrived at the greatest dignities. We find them throughout Asia Minor even to its western coast. They were numerous in Cyprus and were important enough in Delos and in Cos to receive religious recognition from the Romans. The Jews of the Syrian provinces gradually formed a closer connection with their new homes, and together with the Gk. language adopted in many respects Greek ideas. Hence arose Hellenism.

This Hellenizing tendency, however, found its most free development at *Alexandria* (which see). The Jewish settlements established there by Alexander and Ptolemy I became the source of the African dispersion, which spread over the N coast of Africa and perhaps inland to Abyssinia. At Cyrene and Berenice (Tripoli) they formed a considerable portion of the population. It was Jason of Cyrene who wrote " 'in five books' a history of the Jewish war of liberation, which supplied the chief materials for the second book of the Maccabees."

The Jewish settlements in Rome either resulted from "the occupation of Jerusalem by Pompey, 63 B.C. or were largely increased by that event. Under the favor of the early emperors they increased, until in the time of Claudius they had become formidable on account of their numbers and dissensions, and were banished from the city" (cf. Acts 18:2 and Suetonius *Claudius* 25, *"Judoeos impulsore Chresto assidue tumultuantes Roma expulit"*). But they soon flowed back and were quite numerous (28:17, 23-25,

29-30) and conspicuous (Martial *Epigrams* 11.94; Juvenal *Satire* 3.14).

Thus at the Day of Pentecost there were at Jerusalem devout Jews out of every nation under heaven (Acts 2:5), for although scattered throughout so many remote lands, the Dispersion was still bound together in itself and to its mother country by religious ties. The Temple was the acknowledged center of Judaism, and the faithful Jew everywhere contributed the half shekel toward its maintenance. But, while the fires of patriotism burned unquenched and unquenchable throughout the Jewish world, it was impossible to maintain pharisaic strictness and rigor in these remote lands. Egypt, for example, was beyond the reach of the beacon fires that signaled the time of appearance of the new moon, and beyond the Sabbath reading of the Heb. Scriptures. The influence of the Dispersion on the rapid proclamation of Christianity can scarcely be overrated. The course of the apostolic teaching followed in regular progress the line of Jewish settlements. This we can see by following the travels of Paul in the Acts. Throughout the apostolic journeys the Jews were the class to whom "it was necessary that the word of God should be spoken . . . first" (13:46); and they in turn were united with the mass of the population by the intermediate body of "the devout," which had recognized in various degrees the faith of the God of Israel.

The Hellenistic system was so widely diffused as to form an excellent preparation for a world religion. It was strong enough to give the new faith a good start, yet too weak to restrain its growth or to smother its free spirit in a mass of Judaic details and reduce it to the position of an advanced Judaism. The steadfast adhesion of the Hellenistic system to the historic faith, with its comparative freedom from pharisaic narrowness, well qualified it to be the nurse of a new religion that was to be an expanded but not enfeebled development of the old. The purely outward elements of the national life were laid aside with a facility of which history offers few examples, while the inner character of the people remained unchanged.

The LXX version of the OT had given the Hellenists a Bible in the universal language of the NT world. In the fullness of time, when the great message came, a language was prepared to receive it; and thus the dialect of the NT forms a great lesson in the true philosophy of history, becoming in itself a monument of the providential government of mankind.   w.h.

GREEN. *See* Color.

GREEN HERBS, GREEN GRASS, GREEN THING. *See* Vegetable Kingdom: Grass.

GREETING. *See* Salutations.

GREYHOUND. *See* Animal Kingdom.

GRIND. *See* Mill.

Figurative. To oppress the poor by exaction (Isa. 3:15, "grinding the face of the poor").

The expression "May my wife grind for another" (Job 31:10) means, "Let her become another's menial" (cf. Ex. 11:5; Isa. 47:2).

GROVE. Mentioned in Judg. 15:5 in connection with torches being tied to the tails of foxes, which Samson released into the Philistines' "standing grain . . . thus burning up both the shocks and the standing grain, along with the vineyards and groves."

In the KJV *grove* is the incorrect rendering of two Heb. words: (1) *'ashērâ*, the Canaanite goddess, a wooden idol generally set up beside the altars of Baal; (2) *'ēshel* (Gen. 21:33), actually the *tamarisk tree* (which see, Vegetable Kingdom).

BIBLIOGRAPHY: W. L. Reed, *Asherah in the Old Testament* (1949); W. F. Albright, *From the Stone Age to Christianity* (1957), pp. 231, 310; K. G. Jung, *International Standard Bible Encyclopedia,* 1:317f.

GUARANTEE (Gk. *'egguos*). In the highest sense the term is applied to Christ, who, in His character as mediator, is represented as "the guarantee of a better covenant" (Heb. 7:22), having made Himself responsible for all that in this covenant was required to be accomplished for the salvation of those who were to share in its provisions.

GUARD.

1. Heb. word for a "cook" (*ṭabbāḥ*); as butchering fell to the lot of the cook in Eastern countries it gained the secondary sense of "executioner" and is applied to the guard of the king of Babylon (2 Kings 25:8); also rendered "bodyguard" (Gen. 37:36; Jer. 39:9; 41:10; Dan. 2:14).

2. Heb. word for a "runner" (*rāṣ*), the ordinary term employed for the attendants of the Jewish kings, whose office it was to run before the chariot (2 Sam. 15:1; 1 Kings 1:5) and to form a military guard (1 Sam. 22:17; 2 Kings 10:25; 11:6; 2 Chron. 12:10; see marg., NASB, where the literal meaning of "guard" is given as "runners").

3. The Heb. words for "watch" (*mishmeret, mishmār*), express properly the *act* of *watching* but are occasionally transferred to the persons who kept watch (Neh. 4:9, 22; 7:3; Job 7:12; the NIV renders "guard" in all these passages).

GUARDIAN ANGELS. *See* Angels.

GUDGO'DAH (gud-gō'da; "cutting, cleft"). The fortieth station of the Israelites, between Mt. Hor and Jotbathah (Deut. 10:7). The name appears to be preserved in the present Wadi Ghudhagidh. Same as Hor-haggidgad (Num. 33:32).

GUEST. *See* Hospitality.

GUEST ROOM (Gk. *kataluma,* to "break up," i.e., a "journey"). Any room used for the entertainment of guests (Mark 14:14; Luke 22:11); rendered "inn" in 2:7. *See* House.

GUILT. *See* Sin.

GULF. *See* Chasm.

GULL. *See* Animal Kingdom: Sea Gull.

GU'NI (gū'ni; "colored, dyed").

1. One of the sons of Naphtali, perhaps about 1870 B.C., but not necessarily born before the migration to Egypt (Gen. 46:24; Num. 26:48; 1 Chron. 7:13). His descendants are called Gunites (Num. 26:48).

2. Father of Abdiel and grandfather of Ahi, who was head of the Gileadite Gadites (1 Chron. 5:15).

GU'NITE (gū'nīt). A general name of the descendants of *Guni* (which see), of the tribe of Naphtali (Num. 26:48).

GUR (gur; a "whelp" as "abiding" in the lair). An ascent near Ibleam, on the road from Jezreel to Beth-haggan, where the servants of Jehu overtook and slew Ahaziah the king (2 Kings 9:27). It has not been identified.

GUR-BA'AL (gur-bā'al; "sojourn of Baal"). A place in Arabia captured by Uzziah (2 Chron. 26:7); not identified.

GUTTER (Heb. *ṣinnôr*). Drinking troughs (thus NIV, Ex. 2:16), into which Jacob placed peeled rods when the sheep came to drink (Gen. 30:38, 41). For the use of the term *gutter* in the KJV of 2 Sam. 5:8, *see* Water Tunnel. The NIV translates "Water shaft."

HAAHASH'TARI (hā-a-hash'ta-ri). The last mentioned of the four sons of Naarah, the second wife of Ashhur, of the tribe of Judah (1 Chron. 4:6).

HABA'IAH (hab'ā-ya); also **Hoba'iah** (ho-bā'ya; "Jehovah has hidden"). A priest whose descendants returned from the captivity with Zerubbabel but were removed from the priesthood, not being able to trace their genealogy (Ezra 2:61; Neh. 7:63), about 536 B.C.

HABAK'KUK (ha-bak'ūk; "embrace," or perhaps the name of a plant, cf. Akkad. *hambakuku*). The eighth in order of the twelve minor prophets. Nothing certain is known as to the circumstances of Habakkuk's life, as we have only apocryphal and conflicting accounts. In the headings to his book (1:1; 3:1) Habakkuk is simply described as a man who held the office of prophet. From the conclusion to the psalm in chap. 3, "For the choir director, on my stringed instruments" (v. 19), we learn that he was officially qualified to take part in the liturgical singing of the Temple and therefore belonged to one of the Levitical families who were charged with the maintenance of the Temple music, and, like the prophets Jeremiah and Ezekiel, who sprang from priestly households, belonged to the tribe of Levi. This is supported by the superscription of the apocryphon of Bel and the Dragon, "Habakkuk the son of Joshua of the tribe of Levi" (K. & D., *Com.*).

HABAK'KUK, BOOK OF. The prophecy is named from its evident author (1:1), of whom practically nothing is known. From the reference "For the choir director on my stringed instruments" (3:19), combined with the reference to Habakkuk as "the son of Jesus of the tribe of Levi" in the apocryphal legend of Bel and the Dragon, some scholars such as S. Mowinckel have come to the conclusion that the prophet was a Levitical member of the Temple choir.

Time of Composition. The book is evidently to be placed in the general period of the rise of the neo-Babylonian Empire around 620 B.C., since allusion is made to the Chaldean invasion (1:5-6). The preferred date of many critics is in the latter portion of Josiah's reign (c. 625-608 B.C.) or in the reign of Jehoiakim (608-597 B.C.). B. Duhm, E. Sellin, and C. C. Torrey unwarrantedly change Kasdim, that is, Chaldeans, in 1:6 to Kittim (Cypriotes), declaring that the prophecy was aimed at Alexander the Great, and date the book that late.

Criticism. Literary critics have handled the book of Habakkuk harshly. Karl Marti leaves only seven verses of the entire book intact. B. Duhm, who is scarcely to be called conservative, says that Marti treats the book as cruelly as Yahweh is said to treat the house of the ungodly (3:13): "Thou didst strike the head of the house of the evil to lay him open from thigh to neck." Critics differ considerably with regard to the unity of chaps. 1-2. Chapter 3 is more commonly derived from chaps. 1-2 and dated in the fourth or third century B.C. (Pfeiffer). However, the theme of both is the same, and both contain linguistic likenesses. Chapter 3 is specifically called a prayer of Habakkuk (v. 1). The technical musical terms contained in it need not be relegated to a postexilic period, for they were evidently in use in preexilic times in the psalter.

Content.

I. Prophet's twofold complaint (1:1–2:20)
  A. The first complaint (1:1-11)
    1. Israel's sin and God's silence (1:2-4)
    2. God's reply: the Chaldean invasion (1:5-11)
  B. The second complaint (1:12–2:20)
    1. Chaldean cruelty and God's silence (1:12–2:1)
    2. God's response: Israel's salvation;

woes upon the Chaldeans (2:2-20)
II. Prayer of the prophet (3:1-19)
A. Title (3:1)
B. Initial request (3:2)
C. A theophany (3:3-15)
D. An unperturbable faith (3:16-19)

Canonicity. The book is quoted prominently in the NT, and the references there give Habakkuk significance theologically (cf. Acts 13:41 with Hab. 1:5; Rom. 1:17; Gal. 3:11; and Heb. 10:38 with Hab. 2:4). Both Jewish and Christian thought have accorded the book canonical authority. From the Qumran caves came a commentary on the first two chapters of Habakkuk that interpreted the prophecy in terms of the history of the Qumran community.

BIBLIOGRAPHY: G. A. Smith, *The Book of the Twelve Prophets* (1928), 2:115-61; E. B. Pusey, *The Minor Prophets* (1962); R. K. Harrison, *Introduction to the Old Testament* (1969), pp. 931-38; 2:165-223; F. E. Gaebelein, *Four Minor Prophets* (1970), pp. 141ff.; C. L. Feinberg, *The Minor Prophets* (1976), pp. 205ff.; F. A. Tatford, *The Minor Prophets* (1982), 2:5:11-63; C. J. Barber, *Habakkuk and Zephaniah* (1985); F. E. Gaebelein, ed., *Expositor's Bible Commentary* (1985), 7:493-534.

HABAZZINI'AH (hab-a-zî-ni'a). The father of one Jeremiah and grandfather of the chief Rechabite, Jaazaniah (whom the prophet Jeremiah tested with the offer of wine in the Temple; Jer. 35:3), about 607 B.C.

HABITATION. In the KJV, the rendering of several Heb. and Gk. words, and used in the general sense of a place to dwell in (Pss. 69:25; 104:12; Acts 1:20; etc). The NASB and NIV often render "dwelling" or "dwelling place."

Figurative. In the NASB God is called "a rock of habitation" (Ps. 71:3; "refuge" in the NIV); and in 132:13 He is said to have "chosen Zion . . . for His habitation" ("dwelling," NIV). In the KJV God is called the habitation of His people (Ps. 91:9). Justice and judgment are the habitations of His throne (89:14), since all His acts are founded on them (117:2). God is said to "inhabit the praises of Israel" (22:3), i.e., Jehovah is the object of and graciously receives the praises of His people. Eternity is represented as His habitation (Isa. 57:15), i.e., the eternally dwelling One, whose life lasts forever and is always the same. *See* House; Tent.

HA'BOR (hā'bor; "joining together"). A river of Mesopotamia, identified with the modern Khabur. It flows S through Gozan and after a course of 190 miles meets the E branch of the Euphrates. Deported Israelites from Samaria were settled on its banks by Tiglath-pileser III of Assyria (745-727 B.C.; 1 Chron. 5:26) and by Sargon II (721-705 B.C.; 2 Kings 17:6; 18:11).

HACALI'AH, HACHALI'AH (hak-a-lî'a). The father of Nehemiah, the governor after the captivity (Neh. 1:1; 10:1; "Hachaliah," KJV), before 446 B.C.

HACHI'LAH, or **Hakilah** (ha-ki'la; "dark"). A hiding place of David at the time the Ziphites proposed betraying him to Saul (1 Sam. 23:19; 26:1, 3). Hachilah appears to have been the long ridge, now called El Kôlah, where there is a high hill with a ruin, called Yûkîn.

HACH'MONI (hak'mō-ni; "wise, skillful"). A man known only as the father (or ancestor, cf. 1 Chron. 27:2) of Jashobeam, the chief of David's warriors (11:11, where *son of Hachmoni* is rendered "Hachmonite"; the parallel passage in 2 Sam. 23:8 has "Tahchemonite"), and also of Jehiel, the companion of the princes in the royal household (1 Chron. 27:32), considerably before 1000 B.C. Hachmon or Hachmoni was, no doubt, the founder of a family to which these belonged. The actual father of Jashobeam was Zabdiel (27:2), who belonged to the Korahites (12:6); possibly the Levites descended from Korah (McClintock and Strong, *Cyclopedia*).

HACHMONITE (hak'mo-nīt). *See* Hachmoni; Jashobeam.

HA'DAD (hā'dad; "sharp, fierce"). Probably an official title, like Pharaoh, and the names of several men. It is found occasionally in the altered form, Hadar.

1. One of the sons of Ishmael (Gen. 25:15; "Hadar," KJV; 1 Chron. 1:30), after c. 1900 B.C.

2. The son of Bedad and king of Edom. He gained an important victory over the Midianites on the field of Moab. He was the successor of Husham and established his court at Avith (Gen. 36:35; 1 Chron. 1:46).

3. Another king of Edom, successor of Baal-hanan. The name of his city was Pai (Pau), and his wife's name Mehetabel (1 Chron. 1:50). He is called Hadar in Gen. 36:39 (*see* NIV marg.), where his death is not mentioned.

4. An Aramaean deity identified with the weather god Rammon (Heb. Rimmon). Adad (Hadad) was an ancient Mesopotamian deity, god of the storm and thunder. The name *Hadad* occurs in many compound names of Aramaeans, such as Hadadezer and Ben-Hadad ("son of Hadad").

5. A prince of the royal house of Edom. In his childhood he escaped the massacre under Joab and fled with some followers into Egypt. Pharaoh treated him kindly and gave him his sister-in-law in marriage. By her he had a son, Genubath, who was brought up in the palace with the sons of Pharaoh. After David's death Hadad resolved to recover his dominion. Pharaoh opposing him, he left Egypt and returned to his own country (1 Kings 11:14-25). It does not appear from the text, as it now stands, what the result of this attempt was, other than that he was one of the troublers of Solomon's reign (v. 14). Our version makes v. 25 refer to Rezon, but the LXX has, "This is the evil which Adar did." The meaning then will be, This same kind of mischief (incur-

sions in the land of Israel like those of Rezon) was also wrought by Hadad.

HADADE'ZER (hā-dad-ē'zer; "Adad his help"). Son of Rehob, and king of the Aramaean state of Zobah. His name is sometimes given as Hadarezer in the KJV (2 Sam. 10:16, 19; 1 Chron. 18:3; 19:16, 19). While on his way to establish his dominion (about 984 B.C.) he was defeated in the neighborhood of the Euphrates (2 Sam. 8:3). From 10:7, we learn that Joab commanded the forces of Israel. Hadadezer made preparations for the campaign of the following year on a far larger scale. When David heard that Hadadezer was gathering great armies on the Euphrates, he determined to anticipate his attack. He marched in person with his troops over the Jordan to the NE, and at Helam, a place unknown to us, a decisive battle was fought. The Aramaeans from both sides of the Euphrates were completely routed (8:4; 10:18), and Hadadezer's power was so thoroughly broken that all the small tributary princes seized the opportunity of throwing off his yoke.

BIBLIOGRAPHY: T. H. Robinson, *A History of Israel* (1951), 1:201, 237-38; M. F. Unger, *Israel and the Aramaeans of Damascus* (1957), pp. 42-48.

HADADRIM'MON (hā-dad-rim'on; two Syrian deities). A place in the plain of Megiddo (Zech. 12:11). The lamentation on account of the death of the good king Josiah, who lost his life in battle here, was so great as to pass into a proverb (2 Chron. 35:22-25).

HA'DAR (hā'dar; perhaps "chamber").
1. In the KJV, one of the "sons of Ishmael" (Gen. 25:15), given in 1 Chron. 1:30 as *Hadad* (which see).
2. An Edomite king who succeeded Baal-hanan (Gen. 36:39). The name of his city and the name and genealogy of his wife are given. In the parallel list in 1 Chron. 1:50-51, he appears as Hadad. We know from another source (1 Kings 11:14) that Hadad was one of the names of the royal family of Edom. *See* Hadad, no. 3.

HADARE'ZER. *See* Hadadezer.

HAD'ASHAH (had'a-sha; "new"). A city in the valley of Judah (Josh. 15:37), between the hilly region and the Philistine border.

HADAS'SAH (ha-das'sa; "myrtle"). The earlier Jewish name of Esther (Esther 2:7). *See* Esther.

HADATTAH. *See* Hazar-hadattah.

HA'DES (Gk. *hadēs,* "unseen"). This word occurs several times in the original and in the NASB and NIV, although KJV renders "hell" (Matt. 11:23; 16:18; Luke 10:15; 16:23; Acts 2:27, 31; Rev. 1:18; 6:8; 20:13-14; *hadēs* is behind KJV "grave" in 1 Cor. 15:55; but the true reading is *thanatos,* "death," which the NASB and NIV follow).

The ancient Greek view of Hades, and the Ro-

man view of Orcus, or Inferna, is that of a place for all the dead in the depth of the earth; dark, dreary, cheerless, shut up, inaccessible to prayers and sacrifices, ruled over by Pluto. This presiding god was the enemy of all life, heartless, inexorable, and hated accordingly by gods and men.

The Heb. *Sheol* (which see) is the equivalent for Hades and is likewise the subterranean abode of all the dead until the judgment. It was divided into two departments, paradise or Abraham's bosom for the good, and Gehenna or hell for the bad.

In the NT, as will be seen above, the term *Hades* is of comparatively rare occurrence; in our Lord's own discourses it is found only three times, and on two of the occasions by way of contrast to the region of life and blessing. From a consideration of the various passages the following may be a just conclusion: "It seems as if in the progress of God's dispensations a separation had come to be made between elements that originally were mingled together, so that Hades was henceforth appropriated, both in the name and in the reality, to those who were reserved in darkness and misery to the great day; and other names, with other and brighter ideas, were employed to designate the intermediate resting place of the redeemed. These latter pass immediately upon death into the presence of their Lord (John 14:2-3; Phil. 1:23). Such being the nature of the scriptural representation on the subject, one must condemn the fables that sprung up amid the Dark Ages about the limbus, or antechamber of hell, and the purgatorial fires, in which it was supposed even redeemed souls had to complete their ripening for glory" (*Imp. Dict.,* s.v.).

Luke 16:19-31, which sets forth the account of the rich man and Lazarus (and which, strictly speaking, is not a parable), indicates a difference in Hades after the ascension of Christ. Before this far-reaching event it seems clear that Hades was in two compartments, the residence respectively of saved and unsaved spirits. "Paradise" and "Abraham's bosom," both common Jewish terms of the day, were adopted by Christ in Luke 16:22 and 23:43 to designate the condition of the righteous in the intermediate state. The blessed dead, being with Abraham, were conscious and "comforted" (16:25). The dying thief was on that very day to be with Christ in "Paradise." The unsaved were separated from the saved by a "great chasm fixed" (16:26). The rich man, who is evidently still in Hades, is a representative case and describes the unjudged condition in the intermediate state of the wicked. As to his spirit, he was alive, fully conscious, in exercise of his mental faculties, and also tormented. It is thus apparent that insofar as the unsaved dead are concerned, no change in their abode or state is revealed in connection with the ascension of Christ. At the sinners' judgment of the great white throne, Hades will surrender the wicked. They will be judged and cast into the lake of fire (Rev. 20:13-14; *see* Lake of Fire). However, with regard to the state of the righteous and the location of paradise, Christ's ascension has evidently worked a drastic change. The apostle Paul was "caught up to the third heaven . . . into Paradise" (2 Cor. 12:1-4). Paradise, therefore, now denotes the immediate presence of God. When Christ "ascended on high" He "led captive a host of captives" (Eph. 4:8-10). Since it is immediately added that He "descended into the lower parts of the earth," evidently the paradise division of hades, He set free the saved spirit denizens of the underworld. Thus during the present church age, the redeemed who die are "absent from the body . . . at home with the Lord." The wicked, by contrast, are in hades. Both are awaiting resurrection: one the resurrection to life and the other the resurrection to condemnation. *See* Intermediate State; Gehenna; Lake of Fire.   M.F.U.

BIBLIOGRAPHY: A. T. Pierson, *The Inevitable Alternative* (n.d.); W. E. Clark, *The Gates of Hades* (1927); J. J. Müller, *When Christ Comes Again* (1956), pp. 65-76; T. F. Glasson, *Greek Influence on Jewish Eschatology* (1961); J. H. Gerstner, *Jonathan Edwards on Heaven and Hell* (1980); W. G. T. Shedd, *The Doctrine of Endless Punishment* (1980).

HA'DID (ha'did; "sharp, pointed"). A place in Benjamin, 725 of whose inhabitants returned from captivity (Ezra 2:33; Neh. 7:37, where some copies read 721; 11:34). Located at Haditheh, three miles ENE of Lydda.

HAD'LAI (had'li; "ceasing, resting"). The father of Amasa, which latter was one of the Ephraimites who opposed the captives of Judah in the civil war between Pekah and Ahaz (2 Chron. 28:12), about 735 B.C.

HADO'RAM (ha-dō'ram).
1. The fifth of the thirteen sons of Joktan (Gen. 10:27; 1 Chron. 1:21), and supposed to be progenitor of a tribe in Arabia Felix. It is impossible to identify the tribe in question.
2. The son of Toi (Tou), king of Hamath, sent by his father (with valuable presents of gold, silver, and bronze) to congratulate David on his victory over their common enemy, Hadadezer, king of Syria (1 Chron. 18:10), about 984 B.C. In the parallel narrative of 2 Sam. 8:9-10, the name is given as Joram. This, being a contraction of Jehoram, which contains the name of Jehovah, is peculiarly an Israelite appellation (Smith, s.v.).
3. Chief officer of the tribute in the time of Rehoboam, son of Solomon. He was stoned to death by the people of the northern tribes when sent by the king to collect the usual taxes (2 Chron. 10:18), about 934 B.C. Probably the same person as Adoniram (thus NIV in 2 Chron. 10:8) in 1 Kings 4:6 and 5:14.

HA'DRACH (hā'drak). The name of a country mentioned by Zechariah (9:1). It occurs in the late Assyrian monuments as Hatarrika and is identified with Tell Afis, about twenty-eight miles SW of Aleppo.

HA'ELEPH (ha'e-lef; "ox"). One of the towns allotted to Benjamin and mentioned in the second group of fourteen towns (Josh. 18:28; "Eleph," KJV). "Robinson (ii, p. 139), is, no doubt, correct in supposing it to be the present Neby Samvil (i.e., prophet Samuel), two hours NW of Jerusalem" (K. & D., *Com.*).

HAFT. A handle, as of a dagger (so NASB, Judg. 3:22).

HA'GAB (ha'gab; "a locust"). One of the Temple servants whose descendants returned from Babylon under Zerubbabel (Ezra 2:46), before 536 B.C.

HAG'ABA (hag'a-ba; "a locust"). One of the Temple servants whose descendants returned from the captivity with Zerubbabel (Neh. 7:48), before 536 B.C.

HAG'ABAH (hag'a-bah; Ezra 2:45). Another form of the preceding.

HA'GAR (hā'gar; derivation uncertain). A native of Egypt, servant of Abraham (Gen. 21:9-10), and handmaid of Sarah (16:1).

Sarah, continuing childless for so long a time, determined to become a mother by proxy (not uncommon in the East) through her maid, whom she gave to Abraham as a secondary wife (Gen. 16), c. 2050 B.C. No sooner did Hagar find herself likely to become the mother of her master's heir than she openly triumphed over her less favored mistress; "her mistress was despised in her sight." Sarah, deeply wounded, complained to Abraham, who gave her power to act as she thought best toward Hagar.

Sarah made Hagar feel her power by treating her "harshly," and Hagar fled, doubtless intending to return to Egypt by a road used from time immemorial running from Hebron past Beersheba "on the way to Shur." There the angel of the Lord found her by a spring and directed her to return to her mistress and submit to her, promising her the birth of a son and numerous descendants.

Obedient to the heavenly visitor and having distinguished the place by the name of Beer-lahai-roi, Hagar returned again to the tent of Abraham, where in due time she had a son. Abraham called him, as directed by the angel (v. 11), Ishmael, "God hears." About fourteen years later Isaac was born, and when he was weaned, two or three years later, Ishmael greatly offended Sarah by mocking her son. Sarah insisted upon his expulsion from the family, together with Hagar (21:1-10).

Abraham, though displeased, consented, being divinely instructed to follow Sarah's advice. Hagar and her son were sent away. In the desert the strength of Ishmael gave way and, having no more water, Hagar laid him down under one of the stunted shrubs of that region. She withdrew about a bow shot's distance, unwilling to see his suffering, and wept. The angel of the Lord appeared with a comforting promise of her son's increasing greatness and directed her to a well, from which she filled the bottle and gave her son to drink (21:11-19). We have no account of Hagar's subsequent history beyond what is involved in that of Ishmael, who established himself in the wilderness of Paran, in the neighborhood of Sinai, and was married to an Egyptian woman (vv. 20-21). In Gal. 4:24 the apostle Paul, in an allegory, makes Hagar represent the Jewish Dispensation, which was in bondage to the ceremonial law. Sarah represents the true church of Christ, which was free from this bondage.

BIBLIOGRAPHY: C. E. Macartney, *Chariots of Fire* (1951), pp. 60-66; J. A. Thompson, *Archaeology and the Old Testament* (1982), pp. 33-36.

HAGARENES. *See* Hagrites.

HAGERITE, JAZIZ THE. *See* Jaziz; Hagrites.

HAGERITES. *See* Hagrites.

HAG'GAI (hag'gaī; "festal"). The tenth in order of the twelve minor prophets, and the first of the three who, after the return of the Jews from the Babylonian Exile, prophesied in Palestine. Of the place and year of his birth and of his descent nothing is known. He commenced to prophesy in the second year of Darius Hystaspes (Hag. 1:1). Together with Zechariah he urged the renewal of the building of the Temple, which had been suspended after the reign of Cyrus, and obtained the permission and assistance of the king (Ezra 5:1; 6:14). Animated by the high courage of these devoted men, the people went about their work with vigor, and the Temple was completed and dedicated in the sixth year of Darius, 516 B.C.

HAGGAI, BOOK OF. Haggai lived at the same time as Zechariah and, as an older man, labored with the younger man to encourage the returned Babylonian exiles to finish rebuilding the Temple. Work on this structure had been started in the second year of Cyrus, late in 536 B.C., but had been abandoned because of difficulties and opposition.

Occasion. In the second year of the Persian monarch Darius (520 B.C.), Haggai (Heb. "festal") preached his four prophetic messages. Excerpts of these sermons compose the canonical book. The first prophetic utterance (1:1-15) was preached in August-September 520 B.C., the second (2:1-9) in September-October 520 B.C., the third (2:10-19) in November-December 520 B.C., and the fourth (2:20-23) in November-December.

Outline.

I. Plea to finish the Temple (1:1-15)

II. Prophecies of the millennial Temple (2:1-9)

III. Promise of present blessing upon finishing the Temple (2:10-19)

IV. Prophecy of the future destruction of Gentile world power (2:20-23)

Authorship. Since the addresses of the prophet, as we now possess them, are severely curtailed resumés, and since the prophet is always spoken of in the third person, critics such as Oesterly and Robinson deny that the book as it now stands is from Haggai's hand. They claim that it is to be attributed, in all probability, to a contemporary who wrote down the salient points of the prophet's sermons. The arguments of brevity and use of the third person, however, are not convincing reasons that the entire book may not have been written by Haggai himself. If Haggai wrote under inspiration, there is no reason why he might not have used short excerpts from his larger discourses or have employed the third person.

BIBLIOGRAPHY: W. Kelly, *Lectures Introductory to the Study of the Minor Prophets* (n.d.), pp. 386-430; G. A. Smith, *The Book of the Twelve Prophets* (1928), 2:225-54; T. F. K. Laetsch, *The Minor Prophets* (1956), pp. 383-402; T. V. Moore, *A Commentary on Haggai and Malachi* (1960); E. B. Pusey, *The Minor Prophets* (1961), 2:293-321; R. K. Harrison, *Introduction to the Old Testament* (1969), pp. 944-48; F. E. Gaebelein, *Four Minor Prophets* (1970), pp. 199-246; J. Baldwin, *Haggai, Zechariah, Malachi* (1972); H. C. von Orelli, *The Twelve Minor Prophets* (1977), pp. 281-300; F. A. Tatford, *The Minor Prophets* (1982), 3:2:1-75.

HAGGEDO'LIM (hag-ge-do'lim). The father of Zabdiel, the chief officer of the priests who were chosen by lot to live in Jerusalem following Nehemiah's appointment as governor of Judah (Neh. 11:14).

HAG'GERI. *See* Hagri.

HAG'GI (hag'i; "festive"). The second of the seven sons of the patriarch Gad (Gen. 46:16) and progenitor of the family of Haggites (Num. 26:15).

HAGGI'AH (hag-gi'a; "festival of Jehovah"). A Levite of the family of Merari, apparently the son of Shimea and the father of Asaiah, which last seems to have been contemporary with David (1 Chron. 6:30).

HAG'GITES (hag'īts). The family title of the descendants of *Haggi* (which see), the son of Gad (Num. 26:15).

HAG'GITH (hag'gith; "festive"). A wife of David, known only as the mother of Adonijah (2 Sam. 3:4; 1 Kings 1:5, 11; 2:13; 1 Chron. 3:2). She was probably married to David after his accession to the throne, 1000 B.C.

HAGIOG'RAPHA (hag-i-og'ra-fa; "holy writings"). A name sometimes applied to the third division of the Scriptures, called "The Writings" by the Jews and consisting of the Psalms, Proverbs, Job, Daniel, Ezra, Nehemiah, Ruth, Esther, Chronicles, Song of Solomon, Lamentations, and Ecclesiastes. This division was so arbitrary that it was never accepted as proper by the church.

BIBLIOGRAPHY: A. Bentzen, *Introduction to the Old Testament* (1948), 1:25-26.

HA'GRI (ha'gri; a "Hagrite"). "Mibhar the son of Hagri" was one of the mighty men of David's guard, according to 1 Chron. 11:38 ("Haggeri," KJV). The parallel passage (2 Sam. 23:36) has "Bani the Gadite," though the NIV reads "the son of Hagri."

HA'GRITES (ha'grīts; often rendered "Hagarenes" or "Hagarites" in other versions). A nation living E of Palestine which was dispossessed by Reuben, Gad, and eastern Manasseh, in the days of Saul. First Chron. 5:10 refers to this time. Verses 18-22 seem at first sight to refer to the days of Jotham and Jeroboam II, but we are inclined to think that v. 18 is a resumption of the narrative of v. 10, which is interrupted by the genealogy of Gad (vv. 11-17); the more because Pekah, in whose reign the first captivity took place (2 Kings 15:29), was contemporary with Jotham (15:32), so that little time would be left for the occupation by Israel (1 Chron. 5:20-22).

The power of the Hagrites is shown by the force sent against them (1 Chron. 5:18) and their wealth in flocks and herds by the spoil (v. 21). Their subsequent hostility appears from Ps. 83:6, where they are mentioned next to Moab. The NIV, however, reads "descendants of Hagar" rather than "Hagrites." In 1 Chron. 27:31, Jaziz the Hagrite keeps the flocks of David, likely in his ancestral regions. In 11:38 Mibhar "the son of Hagi" may equally well mean "son of a Hagrite." We need find no discrepancy between this and 2 Sam. 23:36, "Bani the Gadite," since the two accounts are connected with different periods of David's life, about thirty years apart, and it is not likely that the persons about him were exactly the same.

It is generally supposed that the Hagrites were the descendants of Hagar. This is favored by the fact that of the three names, Jetur, Naphish, and Nodab, which are mentioned in 1 Chron. 5:19, apparently as names of Hagrite tribes or chiefs, Jetur and Naphish appear in Gen. 25:15 as names of sons of Ishmael. In Ps. 83:6 Ishmaelites are distinguished from Hagrites; but it may be as a general and special term, as Parisians might be distinguished from the French in one passage and in another all might be called French, or, as among the seven nations of Canaan, one was called especially Canaanites.

Smith (*Bib. Dict.*) believes the name and location of the Hagrites may be represented by *Hejer*, the Agrae of Ptol. v.19.2, and Strabo xvi.767. Gesenius (12th ed.) believes that the *agraioi* of Strabo were probably another section of the same race. We know them only by the land taken from them E of Gilead; but as a pastoral tribe they no doubt traversed at different times a good deal of territory. Jetur is thought to be represented by Iturea.   W.H.

HA'I. *See* Ai.

HAIL.

1. Gk. *chaire,* "be cheerful, rejoice." A salutation conveying a wish for the welfare of the person addressed (Luke 1:28); continued among our Saxon forefathers in "Joy to you" and "Health to you."

2. Congealed rain (Heb. *bārād;* Gk. *chalaza*) with which God defeated an army of Canaanites (Josh. 10:11, "the Lord threw large stones from heaven on them as far as Azekah, and they died"). This phenomenon, which resembled the terrible hail in Egypt (Ex. 9:24), was manifestly a miraculous occurrence produced by the omnipotent power of God, for the hailstones did not injure the Israelites who were pursuing the enemy. In Palestine, "hail is common, and is often mingled with rain and with thunder storms (cf. Pss. 18:12-13, etc.), which happen at intervals through the winter, and are frequent in the spring" (Smith, *Hist. Geog.,* p. 64).

As a hailstorm is generally accompanied by lightning, we find in Scripture hail and fire (i.e., lightning) mentioned together (Ex. 9:23; Pss. 78:48; 105:32; etc.).

Figurative. Hail is the symbol of divine vengeance upon kingdoms and nations, as the enemies of God and His people (Isa. 28:2, 17; 32:19; Hag. 2:17).

HAILSTONE (Heb. *'eben bārād*). A stone of hail (Josh. 10:11). *See* above.

HAIR (properly Heb. *śē'ar;* Gk. *thrix*). The customs of ancient nations regarding the hair varied considerably.

Of the Head.

Egyptians. According to Herodotus, the Egyptians "only left the hair of their head and beard grow in mourning, being at all other times shaved." This agrees perfectly with the authority

Egyptian women's manner of wearing the hair

of the sculptures and of Scripture, where Joseph is said to have "shaved himself," when sent for from prison by Pharaoh (Gen. 41:14). Love of cleanliness seems to have been the motive for this custom, and the priests carried this so far that they shaved the whole body every three days. Even the heads of young children were shaved, certain locks being left at the front, sides, and back. Women always wore their own hair, and they were not shaved even in mourning, or after death. Wigs were also worn, though rather by women than by men.

Assyrian. In the Assyrian sculptures the hair always appears long, combed closely down upon the head and falling in a mass of curls upon the shoulders. Herodotus testifies that the Babylonians wore their hair long. The very long hair, however, that appears in the figures on the monuments is supposed to have been partly false, a sort of headdress to add to the effect of the natural hair.

Greeks. The Greeks of the oldest times regarded long hair in man as an ornament and cut it only as a sign of mourning. At Athens, down to the Persian wars, the hair was worn long and fastened up into a knot by a needle in the form of a grasshopper. A free Athenian citizen did not wear his hair short, or he would have been mistaken for a slave. The Greek women, to judge from existing monuments, followed an extraordinary variety of fashions, but all of them sought to cover the forehead as much as possible. Hairpins (made of ivory, bronze, silver, and gold), headbands, and nets were used in dressing the hair. Both Greek and Roman ladies tried by artificial means to lighten their dark hair.

Grecian manner of wearing the hair (Alexander the Great)

Hebrews. The Hebrews bestowed special care on the hair and beard (*see* below), regarding thick, abundant hair as an ornament, whereas the bald head was exposed even to insults (2 Kings 2:23). Long flowing hair was worn only by youths in more ancient times (2 Sam. 14:26; Song of Sol. 5:11) and by Nazirites during the term of their vow (Num. 6:5). Women always wore their hair long (Song of Sol. 4:1; Luke 7:38; John 11:2; 1 Cor. 11:15) and put up in plaits (2 Kings 9:30); as did the Nazirites (Judg. 16:13, 19). Fashionable ladies were in the habit of curl-

ing artificial locks (cf. Isa. 3:24). The fashionable braided hair, in which the Jewish women of a later time probably imitated the style of Roman ladies, is censured by the apostles as unsuitable for Christian women (1 Tim. 2:9; 1 Pet. 3:3). Even men began at that time to curl their hair, a practice that was generally condemned (Josephus *Ant.* 14.9.4), the usual custom for men being to cut the hair from time to time with a razor (Ezek. 44:20) but without shaving it bare. Female hairdressers, who are first mentioned in the rabbinical writers, may have existed in more ancient times, for barbers are mentioned in 5:1.

Roman manner of wearing the hair (Tiberius Caesar)

The Beard.

Customs. Western Asiatics have always cherished the beard as the badge of the dignity of manhood and attached to it the importance of a feature, e.g., the eye or nose. The Egyptians, on the contrary, shaved the hair of the face and head and compelled their slaves to do the like. The enemies of the Egyptians, probably including many of the nations of Canaan, Syria, and Armenia, etc., are nearly always represented bearded. In the Ninevite monuments is a series of battle views from the capture of Lachish by Sennacherib, in which the captives have beards very like some of those in Egyptian monuments. There is, however, an appearance of conventionalism both in Egyptian and Assyrian treatment of the hair and beard on monuments, which prevents our accepting it as characteristic.

Hebrew Regulations, etc. Among the Hebrews the beard was considered an ornament and was not shaven, only trimmed (2 Sam. 19:24). The dressing, trimming, anointing, etc., of the beard were performed with much ceremony by persons of wealth and rank (Ps. 133:2). The removal of the beard was a part of the ceremonial treatment proper to a leper (Lev. 14:9). Size and fullness of beard are said to be regarded, at the present day, as a mark of respectability and trustworthiness.

Beard of Assyrian

The beard is the object of an oath, and that on which blessings or shame are spoken of as resting. The custom in mourning was and is to shave or pluck out it and the hair (Isa. 15:2; 50:6; Jer. 41:5; 48:37; Ezra 9:3), to neglect it in seasons of permanent affliction (2 Sam. 19:24), and to regard any insult to it as the last outrage that enmity can inflict (10:4-5). The beard was an object of salutation (20:9), and it was a custom to swear by it (Matt. 5:36). The law forbade the deforming of the head by cutting away the hair

Beard of Assyrian: Tiglath-Pileser

around it, and of the beard by cutting the corners (Lev. 19:27). This is understood to mean that the hair was not to be cut in a circle from one temple to another, as among the Arabs; neither might that portion of the face where the beard and hair met be shaved. These regulations are thought by some to have reference to the fact that among some nations these customs are part of idolatrous worship.

Figurative. Hair was a symbol of that which was of the *least value* in man's person (1 Sam. 14:45; 2 Sam. 14:11; 1 Kings 1:52; Matt. 10:30; Luke 12:7; 21:18); of *great number* (Pss. 49:12; 69:4); a *minute distance* (Judg. 20:16). White or gray hair is the symbol of honor or authority and is thus entitled to respect (Lev. 19:32; Prov. 16:31; Dan. 7:9; Rev. 1:14); sometimes of approaching decay, as of Israel (Hos. 7:9). To cover the beard (NASB, "mustache"), i.e., to cover the face up to the nose, is a sign of mourning (Lev. 13:45), of trouble and shame (Ezek. 24:17; Mic. 3:7), and is really equivalent to covering the head (Jer. 14:4; Esther 6:12).

HAKILAH. *See* Hachilah.

HAK′KATAN (hak′a-tan, "little or junior"). A descendant (or native) of Azgad, and father of Johanan, which last returned with 110 male retainers from Babylon with Ezra (Ezra 8:12), before 457 B.C.

HAK′KOZ (hak′oz). The head of the seventh division of priests according to the arrangement of David (1 Chron. 24:10), about 975 B.C. He is probably the one whose descendants were excluded by Nehemiah from the priesthood because of defective pedigree (Ezra 2:61; Neh. 7:63; both "Koz," KJV). To the same family seems to have belonged Meremoth, who repaired two portions of the walls of Jerusalem, one portion of which extended from the door of the high priest's house to the end of it (3:4, 21).

HAKU′PHA (ha-kū′fa; "crooked, bent," cf. Arab. *ḥakafa,* "to be curved"). One of the Temple servants who returned from Babylon with Zerubbabel (Ezra 2:51; Neh. 7:53), about 538 B.C.

HA′LAH (ha′la). The district in the Assyrian Empire into which the captive Israelites were taken by the Assyrian kings (2 Kings 17:6; 18:11; 1 Chron. 5:26) and situated on the banks of the Khabour, evidently near Gozan.

HA′LAK (hā′lak; "bare"). The Smooth or Bald Mountain mentioned in the description of Joshua's conquests in Canaan (Josh. 11:17; 12:7). Doubtless this ridge is referred to in Num. 34:3-4; Josh. 15:2-3, under the name "ascent of Akrabbim." It is now located NNE of Abdeh, which is on the Wadi el-Marra.

HALF SHEKEL, HALF OF A SHEKEL. A *beka,* a weight and a unit of money. *See* Metrology.

HAL'HUL (hal'hūl). A town in the highlands of Judah, in which, tradition says, Gad the seer of David was buried (Josh. 15:58); the modern Hal-hûl, about four miles N of Hebron.

HA'LI (ha'li; "jewel"). One of the towns assigned to Asher (Josh. 19:25), not definitely located.

HALL. See House.

HAL'LEL (hal'el; Heb. *hallēl*, Gk. *humnos*, "praise"). The name of a particular part of the hymnal service chanted at certain festivals. This service received the designation "hallel" because it consists of Pss. 113-18, which are psalms of praise and begin with "Hallelujah." It is also called the "Egyptian Hallel," because it was chanted in the Temple while the Passover lambs were slain. This Hallel was also chanted after the morning sacrifice on the feast of Pentecost, the eight days of the feast of Tabernacles, and the eight days of the feast of Dedication. It was chanted in private families on the first evening of Passover. The Great Hallel was so called because of the reiterated response after every verse, "For His lovingkindness is everlasting" (Ps. 136). It was recited on the first evening of the Passover, at the supper, by those wishing to have a fifth cup, i.e., one above the enjoined number. The hymn sung by Jesus and His disciples after the Last Supper (Matt. 26:30) is supposed to have been part of this Hallel.

HALLELU'JAH (hal-e-lū'ya; Heb. *hallᵉlū-yâ;* "praise ye Jah," i.e., Jehovah; Gk. *allēlovia*). Evidently a common form of adoration and thanksgiving in Jewish worship, as appears from its frequent employment at the beginning and close of many of the psalms (see Pss. 106, 111-13, 117, 135). In the great hymn of triumph in heaven over the destruction of Babylon the large multitude in chorus, like the voice of mighty thunderings, burst forth, "Hallelujah! For the Lord our God, the Almighty, reigns," in response to the voice from the throne saying, "Give praise to our God, all you His bond-servants" (Rev. 19:1-6).

BIBLIOGRAPHY: R. deVaux, *Ancient Israel: Its Life and Institutions* (1961), pp. 510-12.

HALLO'HESH (ha-lō'hesh; "the whisperer, enchanter"). The father of Shallum, which latter assisted Nehemiah in repairing the walls of Jerusalem (Neh. 3:12; "Halohesh," KJV). He was one of the popular chiefs who covenanted with Nehemiah (Neh. 10:24), 445 B.C.

HALLOW, HALLOWED (Heb. *qādash*, to "set apart, consecrate," KJV; Gk. *hagiazō*, to "make sacred," KJV, NASB, and NIV). Although the term *hallowed* appears but twice in the NASB and NIV (Matt. 6:9; Luke 11:12; both in the Lord's Prayer) and the term *hallow* not at all (in contrast to the KJV, where it appears frequently), the concept is present in the terms *consecrate, dedicate, sanctify,* and *holy,* all of which are used at one time or another in the NASB and NIV to replace KJV *hallow* or *hallowed.* See Consecrate; Sanctify.

HALO'HESH. See Hallohesh.

HALT. See Diseases: Lame, Lameness.

HAM (ham; *hot*). One of Noah's three sons (Gen. 5:32). Like his brothers he was married at the time of the Deluge, and with his wife was saved from destruction in the ark (7:13). After the Deluge he provoked the wrath of his father by an act of indecency toward him that occasioned a far-reaching prophecy (9:21-27). A list of his descendants is given in 10:6-18.

Cush, Mizraim, and Put were the progenitors of the tribes that peopled Africa, and Canaan became the father of those that principally occupied Phoenicia and Palestine (see table 12, "The Descendants of Ham").

The Hamitic peoples are presented in Gen. 10:8-10 as developing earthly imperial power in their first appearance in human history. This power, moreover, is implied to be evil. Nimrod is said to have been "a mighty hunter before the Lord" (10:9). The simple construction of this passage, so commonly misinterpreted, is that Yahweh took note of his royal character as that of a "hunter," which was the exact opposite of the divine ideal of a king—that of a shepherd (cf. 2 Sam. 5:2; 7:7; Rev. 2:27). A hunter gratifies

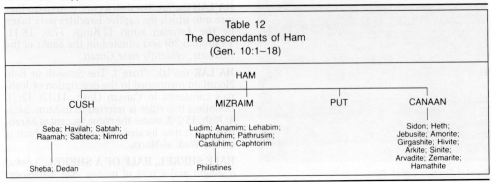

Table 12
The Descendants of Ham
(Gen. 10:1–18)

	HAM		
CUSH	MIZRAIM	PUT	CANAAN
Seba; Havilah; Sabtah; Raamah; Sabteca; Nimrod	Ludim; Anamim; Lehabim; Naphtuhim; Pathrusim; Casluhim; Caphtorim		Sidon; Heth; Jebusite; Amorite; Girgashite; Hivite; Arkite; Sinite; Arvadite; Zemarite; Hamathite
Sheba; Dedan	Philistines		

himself at the expense of his victim. On the other hand, a shepherd spends himself for the good of the subjects of his care. Hamitic imperial power is said to have begun in Babel, Erech, Accad, and Calneh (Gen. 10:10). The cities of Babylon, Erech, and Accad are now well known. They were among the earliest great capitals of the civilized world and were located "in the land of Shinar." This term denotes the entire alluvial plain of Babylon between the Tigris and the Euphrates, in approximately the last two hundred miles of these great rivers as they flowed in ancient times. This region was divided according to the cuneiform accounts into the northern portion called Accad in which Babel (Akkad. *Babilu*, signifying gate of god) and the city of Accad (Agade) were situated. The southern portion was called Sumer, in which Erech, ancient Uruk, modern Warka, was located. This, the cradle of ancient civilization, was the first center of imperialism under the Hamitic peoples.

The name of Ham, alone of the three sons of Noah, if our identification be correct, is known to have been given to a country (Pss. 78:51; 105:23; 106:22).

HA'MAN (hā'man). The son of Hammedatha the Agagite, and prime minister of Ahasuerus, the Persian king (Esther 3:1), after 486 B.C. As Agag was a title of the kings of the Amalekites, it is supposed that Haman was descended from the royal family of that nation. Either he or his father probably found his way to Persia as captive or hostage. His intrigues against Mordecai and the Jews, the discovery of his plot, and his own execution are graphically delineated in the book of Esther.

HA'MATH (hā'math; "fortress"). An ancient city-state, capital of the upper Syria in the valley of the Orontes, and a most important town, as Shalmaneser claims to have captured eighty-nine towns belonging to it. Originally a Canaanite colony (cf. Gen. 10:18), in the time of Hezekiah it was taken by the Assyrians (2 Kings 18:34) and was annexed to the Assyrian empire, 720 B.C. It was located in a fertile and well-watered valley at the foot of Lebanon. The city kingdom of Hamath was prominent in OT history from the time of David onward and is well known from the Assyrian monuments. Its site (seventy-five miles S of Aleppo) has been extensively excavated, revealing a distinctive Hittite occupation. In the famous Battle of Karkar in 853 B.C., Hamath was prominently joined with Ben Hadad of Damascus and Ahab, king of Israel, against the encroachments of Shalmaneser III of Assyria. Despite this valiant stand, Hamath later succumbed to the Assyrians. Citizens of Hamath were transplanted into the Northern Kingdom when Israel fell (2 Kings 17:24, 30). Some Israelites were also transplanted to Hamath (Isa. 11:11). In later Assyrian histo-

ry Hamath became a province of Syria and subsequently of Persia in the time of Nehemiah.

M.F.U.

BIBLIOGRAPHY: D. Baly, *The Geography of the Bible* (1957), p. 162; W. D. Davies, *The Gospel and the Land* (1974), pp. 16-17 n.3.

HAM'ATHITE (ham'a-thīt). The inhabitants (Gen. 10:18; 1 Chron. 1:16), or rather founders of *Hamath* (which see).

HA'MATH-ZO'BAH (hā'moth-zō'ba; 1 Chron. 8:3). Supposed to be the same as *Hamath* (which see). Some believe it different and distinguished from it by the suffix "zobah." It is, however, most likely to be identical with the well-known city of Hamath on the Orontes; Hadadezer's empire was large in extent and in all likelihood comprehended the region of Hamath, captured by Solomon (2 Chron. 8:3).

HAMITES (1 Chron. 4:40). The Simeonites, wishing to extend their territory, "went to the entrance of *Gedor*" (which see) and there found these Hamites who "lived there formerly." They may have been Egyptian Cushites or even Canaanites (1:8). Only this is certain, that they were a peaceful shepherd people, dwelling in tents and therefore nomads.

HAM'MATH (hām'ath; "warm springs").

1. One of the fortified cities in the territory alloted to Naphtali (Josh. 19:35). It is not possible from this list to determine its position, but the notices of the Talmudists leave no doubt that it was near Tiberias, one mile distant—in fact, that it had its name *Chammath*, "hot baths," because it contained those of Tiberias. Josephus mentions it under the name *Emmaus* as a village not far from Tiberias. The Hummâm, at present three in number, still send up their hot and sulfureous water at a spot rather more than a mile S of the modern town. In the list of Levitical cities given out of Naphtali (21:32), the name of this place seems to be given as Hammoth-dor, and in 1 Chron. 6:76 it is further altered to Hammon. Now located at Hamman Tabariyeh, two miles S of Tiberias.

2. A Kenite, ancestor of the Rechabites (1 Chron. 2:55; "Hemath," KJV).

HAMMEDA'THA (ham-e-da'tha). Father of the infamous Haman and commonly designated as "the Agagite" (Esther 3:1, 10; 8:5; 9:24), though also without the title (9:10).

HAM'MELECH (ham'e-lek; "the king"). In the KJV, the father of Jerahmeel, which latter was one of those commanded by Jehoiakim to arrest Jeremiah and Baruch (Jer. 36:26), before 605 B.C. It is uncertain whether this was the same as Hammelech the father of Malchijah, into whose dungeon Jeremiah was afterward cast (Jer. 38:6), before 589 B.C. Others, however, as in the NASB and NIV, which render only "the king," regard

519

the word in both cases as an appellative, referring in the first passage to Jehoiakim and in the latter to Zedekiah. *See* Hammoleketh.

HAMMER. An implement described by four Heb. words in the OT. A heavy wooden mallet used for driving in tent pegs was called a *halmût* (Judg. 5:26). Another type of heavy maul was called a *kêlap* (Ps. 74:6; NIV, "hatchets"). A smaller tool suitable for the gold beater (Isa. 41:7) and the quarrymen (Jer. 23:29) was called a *paṭṭîsh*. A tool evidently similar to the *paṭṭîsh,* and doubtless a pointed hammer of the stonecutter and smith (1 Kings 6:7; Isa. 44:12), and in general a workman's hammer (Judg. 4:21), was called a *maqqābâ.*   M.F.U.

HAMMOL'EKETH (ha-mol'e-keth; "the queen"). A woman introduced in the genealogies of Manasseh as daughter of Machir and sister of Gilead (1 Chron. 7:17-18), and as having among her three children Abiezer, from whose family sprang the great judge Gideon. The Jewish tradition is that "she used to reign over a portion of the land that belonged to Gilead," and that for that reason her lineage has been preserved. *See* Hammelech.

HAM'MON (ham'on; "glowing, warm").
1. A town in the territory of Asher (Josh. 19:28), apparently midway between Naphtali and Sidon. Probably Umm el-Awamid, about ten miles S of Tyre.
2. A Levitical city of Naphtali assigned to the Gershonites (1 Chron. 6:76) and answering to the similar names of *Hammath* and *Hammoth-dor* (which see).

HAM'MOTH-DOR (ham'mōth-dōr; "hot springs of Dor"). A city of Naphtali (Josh. 21:32); probably the same as *Hammath* (which see).

HAMMU'EL (ha-mū'el; "heat or anger of God"). The son of Mishma and (apparently) father of Zaccur, of the tribe of Simeon (1 Chron. 4:26; "Hamuel," KJV).

HAMMURA'BI (ham-u-rā'bi). The sixth king of the famous First Dynasty of Babylon, formerly identified with Amraphel of Gen. 14:1. This identification is now no longer possible as a result of the thousands of clay tablets recovered from the middle Euphrates city of Mari in 1937, and information based upon the Khorsabad List. New sources of information enable us to place Hammurabi's reign c. 1728-1686 B.C. (Albright). This is at least three centuries subsequent to the age of Abraham. Hammurabi exalted Babylon as his capital. His city had a ziggurat. He adorned the cities of Asshur and Nineveh. His reign was one of great prosperity, advance in astronomy, architecture, mathematics, and literature. The creation and Flood epics were edited in his day and have descended to us in the form that they took under his reign. Copies of these epics, dating

about 640 B.C., were found in the library of Ashurbanipal at Nineveh. Hammurabi's black stela from the city of Ur was inscribed in both the Semitic and Sumerian languages. Hammurabi is famous in large part for his code of laws discovered in 1901-2 by Jacques de Morgan at Susa, where it had been carried by Elamite raiders. This famous code offers interesting parallels to pentateuchal laws, preceding them by at least three centuries and adapted to an urban irrigation culture in contrast to the simple agrarian culture of Palestine.   M.F.U.

BIBLIOGRAPHY: G. R. Driver and J. Miles, *The Babylonian Laws* (1952); C. H. Gordon, *Hammurapi's Code* (1957); H. W. F. Saggs, *The Greatness That Was Babylon* (1962); D. J. Wiseman, *Journal of Semitic Studies* 7 (1962): 161-72; L. W. King, *A History of Babylon* (1969), pp. 84-86, 89-90, 99ff., 103, 128-30; 153-58.

The Code of Hammurabi found at Susa, c. 1780 B.C.

HAM'ONAH (ham'ō-na; "multitude"). The figurative name of the place in the valley in which the burial of Gog and his forces are prophetically announced to take place (Ezek. 39:16).

HA'MON-GOG (ha'mon-gog; "multitude of Gog"). The name given by the prophet Ezekiel (39:11) to the valley in which the slaughtered army of Gog are described as being buried. *See* Gog.

HA'MOR (ha'mōr; a "he-ass"). A Hivite from whom (or his sons) Jacob purchased the plot of ground in which Joseph was afterward buried (Gen. 33:19; Josh. 24:32; Acts 7:16; in the latter verse "Emmor" in the KJV), and whose son, Shechem, seduced Dinah (Gen. 34:2). As the latter appears to have founded the city of Shechem, Hamor is also named as the representative of its inhabitants (Judg. 9:28) in the time of Abimelech. Neither his character and influence nor his judicious behavior in the case of his son saved him from the indiscriminate massacre by Dinah's brothers.

HAM'RAN (ham'ran; "fair"). A son of Dishon and descendant of Esau (1 Chron. 1:41; "Amram," KJV; "Hemdan," NIV). In Gen. 36:26 he is called more correctly Hemdan (which see).

HAMSTRING (Heb. *'āgar;* to "extirpate"). The method employed to render useless the captured horses of the enemy (Josh. 11:6; 2 Sam. 8:4; 1 Chron. 18:4), since the Israelites were forbidden to use that animal (Deut. 17:16). It consisted in severing the achilles tendon of the hind legs. The KJV term is *hough* (pronounced "hock").

HAMUEL. *See* Hammuel.

HA'MUL (ha'mūl; "pitied, spared"). The second of the two sons of Perez, son of Judah (1 Chron. 2:5). He could not have been born, however, before the migration of Jacob into Egypt (as appears to be stated in Gen. 46:12), since Perez was not at that time grown up (38:29).

HA'MULITES (ha-mū-līts). The descendants (Num. 26:21) of Hamul.

HAMU'TAL (ha-mū'tal; "kinsman of the dew"). Daughter of Jeremiah of Libnah, wife of King Josiah and mother of King Jehoahaz (2 Kings 23:31; 24:18; Jer. 52:1), 639 B.C.

HANAM'EL (ha-nam'el; "God has compassion"). The son of Shallum and cousin of Jeremiah to whom, while Jerusalem was besieged, he sold a field in Anathoth (Jer. 32:6-12), about 590 B.C. The prohibition to sell Levitical estates applied merely to their alienating them from the tribe. "The transaction was intended to evince the certainty of restoration from the impending exile by showing that possessions, which could be established by documents, would be of future value to the possessor" (vv. 13-15).

HA'NAN (hā'nan; "merciful").
1. One of the sons (or descendants) of Shashak, one of the chief men of Benjamin, residing at Jerusalem (1 Chron. 8:23).
2. The last named of the six sons of Azel the Benjamite (1 Chron. 8:38; 9:44).
3. Son of Maacah and one of David's mighty men (1 Chron. 11:43), 1000 B.C.
4. One of the Temple servants whose posterity were among those who returned from the captivity with Zerubbabel (Ezra 2:46; Neh. 7:49), 536 B.C.
5. One of the Levites who assisted Ezra in expounding the law to the people (Neh. 8:7), 445

B.C. He also sealed the covenant made by Nehemiah (10:10). He is probably the same as the one mentioned in 13:13 as the son of Zaccur, who, on account of his integrity, was appointed to distribute the Levitical revenues among his brethren.
6. A leader of the people who subscribed to the covenant drawn up by Nehemiah (Neh. 10:22). The same name occurs in v. 26.
7. The son of Igdaliah and an officer of the Lord's house. Into the chamber of his sons Jeremiah brought the Rechabites in order to test their temperance (Jer. 35:3-6), about 607 B.C.

HANAN'EL, TOWER OF (ha-nan'el; "God has favored"). A tower that formed part of the N wall of Jerusalem (Neh. 3:1; 12:39). From these two passages, particularly from the former, it might almost be inferred that Hananel was but another name for the Tower of the Hundred; at any rate they were close together and stood between the Sheep Gate and the Fish Gate. This tower is further mentioned in Jer. 31:38. The remaining passage in which it is named (Zech. 14:10) also connects this tower with the Corner Gate, which lay on the other side of the Sheep Gate.

BIBLIOGRAPHY: M. Avi-Yonah, *Israel Exploration Journal* 4 (1954): 241-42.

HANA'NI (ha-na'ni; "gracious").
1. One of the sons of Heman, appointed by lot in the time of David for the service of song in the sanctuary. Hanani had charge of the eighteenth division (1 Chron. 25:4, 25), after 1000 B.C.
2. A prophet or "seer" who rebuked Asa, king of Judah, for seeking help from the king of Syria against Baasha, king of Israel. In punishment for his defection from the true God, Hanani threatened him with wars during the remainder of his reign. Enraged at the prophet's boldness, the king put him in prison (2 Chron. 16:7-10), 879 B.C. This Hanani is probably the same as the father of the prophet Jehu who denounced Baasha (1 Kings 16:1, 7) and King Jehoshaphat (2 Chron. 19:2; 20:34).
3. One of the sons (or descendants) of Immer, who had taken a foreign wife during the captivity (Ezra 10:20).
4. One of the "brothers" of Nehemiah who, with others, went from Jerusalem to Susa, probably sent by Ezra, and brought information concerning the condition of the returned Jews. Their information probably led to the mission of Nehemiah (Neh. 1:2). Hanani returned to Judah and, together with one Hananiah, was placed in charge of the gates of Jerusalem, to see that they were opened and shut at the proper hours, morning and evening (7:2), 445 B.C.
5. A priest, one of the musicians who officiated in the ceremony of purifying the walls of Jerusalem when they had been rebuilt (Neh. 12:36), 445 B.C.

HANANI'AH (han-a-nī'a; "Jehovah was favored").

1. One of the sons of Zerubbabel who was of the family of David (1 Chron. 3:19). His sons are given as Pelatiah and Jeshaiah (v. 21).

2. One of the sons of Shashak and a leader of the tribe of Benjamin (1 Chron. 8:24).

3. A son of Heman, appointed by David to take charge of the sixteenth division of Levitical musicians (1 Chron. 25:4, 23), about 1000 B.C.

4. "One of the king's officers" in the army of Uzziah, king of Judah (2 Chron. 26:11), after 783 B.C.

5. An Israelite of the family of Bebai who renounced his Gentile wife after the captivity (Ezra 10:28), 456 B.C.

6. "One of the perfumers" (or makers of the sacred ointments and incense, Ex. 30:22-38) who repaired part of the wall of Jerusalem (Neh. 3:8), 445 B.C. Possibly the same as no. 5.

7. The son of Shelemiah (Neh. 3:30) and one of the priests who repaired the wall of Jerusalem opposite their houses, from "above the Horse Gate" (v. 28), 445 B.C.

8. The "commander of the fortress" and the person who was associated with Nehemiah's brother, Hanani, in charge of the gates of Jerusalem. He is described as "a faithful man" and one who "feared God more than many" (Neh. 7:2), 445 B.C. His office seems to have been one of authority and trust and perhaps the same as that of Eliakim, who was "over the household" in the reign of Hezekiah (2 Kings 19:2).

9. The name of one of the "leaders of the people" who sealed the covenant made by Nehemiah and the people to serve the Lord (Neh. 10:23), 445 B.C.

10. A priest, apparently son of Jeremiah, after the captivity (Neh. 12:12); probably the same as one of those who celebrated the completion of the walls of Jerusalem (v. 41), 445 B.C.

11. Son of Azzur, a prophet of Gibeon, who uttered false prophecies in the fourth year of Zedekiah, king of Judah. He publicly prophesied in the Temple that within two years Jeconiah and his fellow captives, with the vessels of the Lord's house, which Nebuchadnezzar had taken away to Babylon, should be brought back to Jerusalem. He sought to uphold his prophecy by taking off from the neck of Jeremiah the yoke that he wore by divine command (Jer. 27:2), in token of the subjection of Judah and the neighboring countries to the Babylonian Empire. Jeremiah was told to go and tell Hananiah that for the wooden yokes that he had broken he should make yokes of iron, "that they may serve Nebuchadnezzar." Jeremiah also added this rebuke and denunciation: "Listen now, Hananiah, the Lord has not sent you, and you have made this people trust in a lie. Therefore thus says the Lord, 'Behold, I am about to remove you from the face of the earth. This year you are going to die, because you have

counseled rebellion against the Lord.' So Hananiah the prophet died in the same year in the seventh month" (28:1-17), about 593 B.C. "The history of Hananiah is of great interest, as throwing much light upon the Jewish politics of that eventful time, divided as parties were into the partisans of Babylon on one hand, and Egypt on the other. It also exhibits the machinery of false prophecies, by which the irreligious party sought to promote their own policy in a very distinct form" (McClintock and Strong, *Cyclopedia*).

12. The father of Zedekiah who was one of the officials to whom Micaiah reported Baruch's reading of Jeremiah's prophecies (Jer. 36:12), about 604 B.C.

13. The grandfather of Irijah, the captain of the guard at the Gate of Benjamin who arrested the prophet Jeremiah upon the supposition that he intended to desert to the Chaldeans (Jer. 37:13), 597 B.C.

14. The original name of Shadrach, one of the three Hebrew children, by which latter name he is better known (Dan. 1:6-7, 11, 19; 2:17).

HAND (Heb. *yād*, the "open" palm; *kap*, the "hollow" of the hand; Gk. *cheir*).

Figurative. Being the part of the body that is chiefly employed in active service, the *hand* is used in Scripture with a great variety of applications: (1) Hands are the symbols of human action; *pure* hands represent pure actions and *unjust* hands injustice, whereas "hands covered with blood" denote actions stained with cruelty, etc. (Job 9:30; Ps. 90:17; Isa. 1:15; 1 Tim. 2:8). (2) *Washing* the hands was a symbol of innocence (Deut. 21:6-7; Ps. 26:6; Matt. 27:24). (3) The hand, in general, was the symbol of *power* and *strength*, especially the *right* hand (Ex. 15:6; Ps. 17:7). (4) *Holding by the right hand* was expressive of support (73:23; Isa. 41:13); *standing at the right hand* indicated *protection* (Pss. 16:8; 109:31; 110:5); *to lean upon* the hand of another was a mark of *familiarity*, as well as of *superiority* (2 Kings 5:18; 7:17); to give the hand, as to a master, was a sign of *submission* (2 Chron. 30:8, marg.); pouring water on another's hands signified to serve him (2 Kings 3:11); to "seal the hand" is to prevent one from working, e.g., by reason of the cold (Job 37:7); to withdraw the hand is to withhold support (Ps. 74:11), while to cut it off was an example of extreme self-denial (Matt. 5:30). (5) The open hand is figurative of liberality (Deut. 15:8; Ps. 104:28), the closed hand a lack of it (Deut. 15:7). (6) The right hand was used to indicate the S, and the left the N (1 Sam. 23:19; 2 Sam. 24:5; Job 23:9). (7) The right hand was the place of honor (1 Kings 2:19) and power (Mark 14:62). (8) "I will also turn My hand against you" (Isa. 1:25) signifies a movement of the hand, hitherto at rest, either for the purpose of inflicting punishment upon the person named (Ps. 81:14; Jer. 6:9; Ezek. 38:12; Amos

1:8, marg.), or, though this is seldom the case, for the purpose of saving one (Zech. 13:7).

Customs. Men lifted up their hands in prayer (Job 11:13; 1 Tim. 2:8), also in taking an oath (Gen. 14:22, marg.; etc.); put the hands together over the head as a gesture of extreme grief (2 Sam. 13:19; Jer. 2:37); the accuser stood at the right hand of the accused in a trial (Ps. 109:6; Zech. 3:1); the thumb of the right hand of the priest was touched with blood of the consecration ram (Ex. 29:20; Lev. 8:23-24). The Jews washed their hands before eating (Matt. 15:2; Mark 7:3) or after touching an unclean person (Lev. 15:11); servants were directed by movements of the hand of master or mistress (Ps. 123:2); treaties were made and sureties entered into by joining hands (2 Kings 10:15; Job 17:3, marg.; Prov. 6:1, marg.; 17:18, marg.); the hand was placed under the thigh of a person to whom an oath was made (Gen. 24:2-4, 9; 47:29); joy was shown by clapping the hands (2 Kings 11:12; Ps. 47:1), whereas striking and clapping them together expressed extreme anger (Num. 24:10; Ezek. 21:14, 17).

HANDBREADTH. *See* Metrology: Linear Measures.

HANDFUL. *See* Metrology: Dry Measures of Capacity.

HANDICRAFTS. The word *handicraft* is not found in Scripture, and yet it is appropriate, inasmuch as most of the mechanical work of ancient times was performed by hand.

Archaeological discoveries have revealed remarkable evidences left by the non-Semitic Sumerians who arrived in the Plain of Shinar in lower Babylonia sometime before 4000 B.C. The excavations of Abram's city of Ur have uncovered exquisite jewels, many of which may be seen in the University Museum of Philadelphia. The hoard of jewels recovered from the Royal Tombs is especially valuable. Queen Puabi's tomb (dating to about 2500 B.C.) was fabulously adorned. Apparently demonstrating complete loyalty to the beautiful queen, twenty-five of her court ladies had walked alive into the tomb or had been drugged and carried there. In full regalia, the royal sepulcher remained untouched until 1927 when retrieved by Sir Leonard Woolley. The artistic skill of the workmen of that day is revealed in the queen's diadem of minute beads, palmettes, flowerettes, rosettes, and exquisitely thin rolled gold. This splendor furnished the background for carved stags, antelopes, and bearded bulls. The queen wore a jeweled cap of gold, its silver bands adorned with beech leaves. Heavy gold earrings were in her ears. She was also bedecked with a necklace, gold pins, and fish-shaped amulets. Several other tombs of the period were also filled with magnificent pieces. Another remarkable example of Sumerian art was a solid gold helmet of a warrior. Also found were finely wrought golden tumblers, dainty cosmetic boxes, a paint cup, and a silver toiletry box with a lid carved from seashells showing a lion attacking a goat. At Tepe Gawra, an ancient city mound in northern Mesopotamia, objects of gold, silver, and their alloys were dug up. Also found were ivory combs banded with gold and studded with precious stones.

Jewels go back to early times in Egypt and seem only to have been preceded by the Sumerians. Stone necklaces and bracelets from the Badarian civilization (c. 3500 B.C.) have been found. Pre-Dynastic Egyptian artists developed fine styles. By the Twelfth Dynasty (2000-1750 B.C.), Egyptian craftsmanship in jewelry reached a high mark in beauty, color, and design. Egyptian jewelry is noted for its good taste and its fine execution. Sumerian and early Egyptian artists are also known for their skill in wood, leather, stone, and various other materials.

When they left Egypt, the Hebrews had among them skilled workmen in gold, silver, brass, wood, and leather, as is evident from the building of the Tabernacle. But when these artists died, the development of the mechanical arts seemed to have come to a standstill (Judg. 5:8; 1 Sam. 13:19). Even in the time of Solomon the Hebrews needed the teaching of the Phoenicians (1 Sam. 5:11; 1 Kings 5:1-9, 21; 7:13-14).

Manual labor was generally held in low esteem by the Greeks, and in later times many free citizens declined to engage in it at all. The Romans also seem to have thought that there was something objectionable in mechanical labor, and in many wealthy homes this was mostly done by slaves. To pursue a trade was not, at least in later times, considered degrading among the Jews. Indeed, at this time all the rabbinical authorities were working at some trade, and it became the fashion to enjoy hard labor: the great Hillel was a woodcutter; his rival, Shammai, a carpenter; and among the celebrated rabbis of later times we find shoemakers, tailors, carpenters, sandal makers, smiths, potters, builders, etc. They were not ashamed of their manual labor. It was a rabbinical principle that "whoever does not teach his son a trade, is as if he brought him up to be a robber."

Apothecary. *See* Perfumer, below; article Perfume.

Armorer. In 1 Sam. 8:12 it is recorded that Samuel told the Israelites that if they chose a king he would take their sons and set them to make his "weapons of war," i.e., to be engaged in the arts of warfare rather than in those of peace. As to the work of the armorer, it can be better understood by consulting the article *Armor.*

Baker (Heb. *'āpâ,* to "cook"). Makers of bread and pastry, a department then more varied than that of cook (Gen. 40:1-2, 5, 16-22; 41:10; Hos. 7:4). In Jer. 37:21 it is stated that bread was brought daily "from the bakers' street," a bakers'

An Egyptian model of grain store

bazaar that would indicate that bakers formed a guild.

In Egypt the bakery profession was one of great importance. A biblical reminiscence of this was the unfortunate baker who was placed in prison. The baker's dream recounts all sorts of fancy baked food (Gen. 40:16-17). Egyptian bakers were required to give strict account of their stocks of materials to the overseer of granaries. Miniature models of such scenes have come down to us from excavated tombs. Closely associated with the baker was the miller. Mother and daughter had this task among the common people. The job consisted in turning with wooden handles the heavy grinding stones, sometimes a foot and a half in diameter. In more primitive times the grain was simply crushed in a curvature of the rock with a small hand stone. Public millers had a busy trade and used donkeys to turn the stones. At Ostia, the port of Rome, and at Pompeii archaeologists have recovered mills that

indicate a booming business requiring large storehouses. The Bible refers frequently to the miller or "grinder" (Ex. 11:5; Judg. 16:21; Matt. 24:41; Luke 17:2).　M.F.U.

Brick Maker. Brick making, a mere manual occupation with nothing to stimulate the clever workmen to creative craftsmanship, was only followed by the members of the community who had not even the satisfaction of working for themselves. Thus the Israelites were forced to this occupation in Egypt. Brickmaking was a government monopoly. The pay was a small remuneration for the laborious drudgery. Egypt and Babylonia, with mighty rivers and alluvial silt, excelled in brick construction. (*See* Brick.) However, these lowly workmen were essential to building trades in biblical lands. Guilds or unions of brick makers traveled in groups throughout the country ready to perform service where needed. An example of large-scale brick making and bricklaying comes to us from the splendid reign of Thutmose III (c. 1483-1450 B.C.). The tomb of the great officer of Thutmose's court, Rekhmire, near Thebes, is adorned with scenes and inscriptions describing his career. In one of these pictures Rehkmire leans on a staff and inspects stonecutters, brick makers, sculptors, and builders who toil before him. Brick making in ancient Egypt was a process involving the breaking up of the Nile mud with mattocks, moistening it with water, and then mixing it with sand and chopped straw (Ex. 5:6-19). Then placed in molds, it was put in the sun to bake. Semitic foreigners appear on the tomb making and laying bricks, working on the temple of Amon. The bricklayers say: "He supplies us with bread, beer and every good sort" while the taskmaster says to the builders: "The rod is in my hand; be not idle" (cf. P. E. Newberry, *The Life of Rekhmara;* James Breasted, *Ancient Records of Egypt*, 1906-7, vol. 2, sec. 758ff.). This reference to brick making is all the more significant inasmuch as Thutmose III (according to the Masoretic chronology) was the pharaoh of the oppression.

Builder. Besides brick making and bricklay-

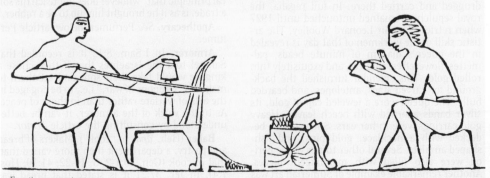

Egyptian carpenters

ing, carpentry and stonemasonry were important trades in the ancient world.

Carpenters. The Egyptian carpenter was more important than the Palestinian. There were palaces and wealthy houses to beam and trim, wooden mummy cases to cut out, furniture to make, irrigation pumps (*shadufs*) to erect, large river-going vessels and smaller boats to make, and implements of various sorts to fashion. Especially noteworthy are the large barges that transported huge blocks of limestone and sandstone and giant obelisks; also, such large works as pillars, gates, temple, and palace doors. Carpenters' tools such as adzes, ax heads, and chisels have been recovered. Palestinian carpenters in early Israel did not develop a high degree of skill. Palestinian dwellings, even of the peasantry, were of mud brick or stone so that woodwork for construction purposes was minimal. Solomon, therefore, had to import Phoenician craftsmen to build his royal palaces and the Temple. After the Solomonic era, however, carpentry was cultivated. Nebuchadnezzar II carried away carpenters (Jer. 24:1, KJV; NASB and NIV, "craftsmen"). The Palestinian carpenter must have had tools similar to those used in Egypt. Sandstone served as a plane, saws with flint teeth were mounted on a frame, and a heavy stone served as a hammer. The adz was an all-purpose tool. At the time of Isaiah, carpenters developed great skill not only in common construction work but in idol making (cf. Isa. 44:12-17).

Stonemasons. The worker in stone was indispensable in Palestine, as in the land of the Nile. The vast palaces, tombs, pyramids, temples, and obelisks required consummate skill on the part of a multitude of stone workers. The mighty pyramids with their minute constructional accuracy testify to the high development of the art of construction in early Dynastic Egypt. In early Israel before the prosperity of the Davidic-Solomonic era, stone houses among the Israelites were not common; Hiram of Tyre's craftsmen, however, increased stonemasonry. There were building trades in Jerusalem during the Hebrew monarchy. When public buildings or the Temple fell into disrepair, money was raised by public subscription, and it was paid out "to the carpenters and the builders, who worked on the house of the Lord; and to the masons and the stonecutters, and for buying timber and hewn stone to repair the damages to the house of the Lord" (2 Kings 12:11-12). Timber was cut by men especially qualified for this work. Solomon boasted that the Sidonians were expert timber cutters. Solomon's Temple was built out of fine quarry-chiseled marble (1 Kings 7:9-12). Jesus stressed the importance of a solid building foundation in a country where heavy rains might occur (Matt. 7:24-27).

M.F.U.

Calker. A KJV term referring to one who repaired the seams of ships (Ezek. 27:9, 27). The original Heb. term appears also in other passages, as for example in 2 Kings 12:8; 22:5; Neh. 3:4-32, in connection with the repair of the Temple and, following the Exile, Jerusalem.

Carpenter. *See* Builders, above; Woodworkers, below.

Carver. The rendering of six Heb. words meaning to engrave, sculpture, and carve. Carving was carried on to a great extent by the Egyptians both upon buildings and furniture. The arts of carving and engraving were much in demand in the building of the Tabernacle and the Temple (Ex. 31:5; 35:33; 1 Kings 6:18, 35; Ps. 74:6) as well as in the ornamentation of the priestly dresses. Carving of wood is mentioned (Ex. 31:5), and a detailed description of the process of idol making is given in Isa. 44:13. In the KJV and NASB the terms *graved* and *graver* sometimes appear in place of *carved*. The NIV usually reads "engraved," or "engraver."

Confectioner. *See* Perfumer, below; and also the articles Oils and Ointment; Perfume; Perfumer.

Dyer. This word does not occur in Scripture, but we have mention of dyed skin and of various colored curtains in the Tabernacle (Ex. 25:4-5; 26:14; etc.), and of Lydia, a seller of purple (Acts 16:14). The dyeing of purple was actively carried on, especially in Thyatira, and an inscription found there particularly mentions the guild of dyers of that place.

Nomadic society in Bible lands not only wove its own textiles but dyed them; however, commercial guilds of specialists existed in this field. Fragments of wooden looms and dyeing vats were found at Lachish in southern Judah. Clay loom weights were unearthed in some of the homes destroyed by Nebuchadnezzar. Long before Abraham's time Canaanites wove and dyed fine textiles. At Tell Beit Mirsim (Kiriath-sepher) many loom weights were recovered along with an elaborate setup for cloth production. In Syria, at Ugarit, remains of a dyeing establishment were recovered. The Canaanites were especially skillful in extracting purple dyes from murex shells. Byblos on the Mediterranean was noted not only for its papyrus production but for its cloth manufacture. Weavers and dyers in ancient Sumer went through a long period of apprenticeship. Egypt was noted early for its superb linen. Fine awnings of blue, yellow, and light green were exported. Weavers' beams (1 Sam. 17:7) have been found in biblical sites. Hebrews were more skillful at dyeing than almost any other art-craft. They used Tyrian murex shells, yielding purple reds, and vegetable dyes. Vegetable matter and indigo were employed from remote times. Pomegranate bark supplied black. Almond leaves yielded yellow. Potash, lime, and grape treacle yielded indigo.

M.F.U.

Embalming (from Heb. *ḥānaṭ*, "to spice"). The

process of preserving a corpse by means of spices (Gen. 50:2-3, 26) was a distinct craft.

Egyptians. Egyptians preserved the body to keep it in a fit state to receive the soul that once inhabited it. The soul was thought to depend on the body for its future fortunes. Physical decomposition robbed the soul of some part of itself and was even thought to cease existence when the corpse had entirely disappeared. Hence the Egyptians made every possible effort to preserve the body. There were various kinds of mummification, determined by the financial ability of the deceased. During the Old Kingdom the internal organs were removed to canopic jars of marble or alabaster. The lids of those jars were shaped like an animal deity who was supposed to watch over the body. During the seventy-day process of mummification the brain was removed and a resinous paste inserted into the cranial cavity. The body was then entwined elaborately in linen. After bandaging, the body was put into a papyrus carton that was painted with elaborate religious symbols. Nobles were encased in three coffins. A mummy of a great pharaoh, like Tutankhamen, was inserted into a series of precious containers. That particular monarch was entombed in incredible splendor. The inner case of solid gold was inlaid with lapis lazuli, carnelian, and enamel. Gorgeous jewels and scarabs bearing a royal seal of the ruler were placed in early Egyptian tombs. Occasionally a scepter was placed in the hands of the deceased king. For a discussion of the process of mummification, see A. Lucas, *Ancient Egyptian Materials and Industries.* pp. 307-90.) Herodotus tells of a kind of embalming adopted by the poor. In this process they cleansed the body by an injection of *syrnoea* and salted it for seventy days, after which time it was returned to the people who brought it.

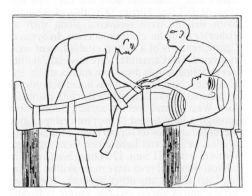

Swathing or wrapping bandages around a mummy

Hebrew. Joseph's and Jacob's embalming after the manner of the Egyptians was exceptional (Gen. 50:2, 26). However, wealthy people did anoint the bodies of their loved ones with costly oil (John 12:7), and they wound them in linen with aromatic spices (19:39). *See* Burial. M.F.U.

Embroiderer. Weaving, plain sewing, and artistic needlework were practiced among the Hebrews as well as among their neighbors (Ex. 28:39; 35:35; 38:23; Judg. 5:30; Ps. 45:14). Long before Abraham's time the Canaanites wove fine textiles and had a flair for vivid colors. Remains of a dyeing establishment have been uncovered at Ugarit. Byblos and other Phoenician coastal cities were famous for their woven cloth and garments. From murex shells purple-red dye was extracted. Tell Beit Mirsim has yielded ample evidence of developed weaving, dyeing, and artistic work on the loom. Mesopotamian mantles were commonly known for their beauty. Long before the time of Abraham, a Babylonian ruler might have his own private factory for weaving materials. Egypt was famous not only for its fine linen, which Flinders Petrie said was as fine in the First Dynasty (c. 2900 B.C.) as our modern linen, but also for exquisitely embroidered garments and tapestries. The Israelites first learned the art of embroidery in Egypt, and it would appear that certain families were distinct in the arts of weaving and embroidering, especially in the tribes of Judah and Dan (Ex. 35:30, 35; 1 Chron. 4:21). The OT especially refers to a high degree of artistic development in the priests' garments, the ephod, and the gold, blue, scarlet, and fine twined linen of the Tabernacle covering. Assyrian and Babylonian garments were mentioned as early as the time of Joshua (7:21) and were cited as articles of commerce by Ezekiel (27:24). *See also* Needlework; Weaving. M.F.U.

The high priest's garments were artistically embroidered

Engraver. *See* Carver.

Fining Pot. A refining pot. *See* Metalworker; Refiner, below.

Founder. *See* Metalworker, below.

Fuller. *See* Launderer, below.

Gardener. *See* the articles Garden; Agriculture.

Glassworker. The Egyptians and Phoenicians made opaque glass early and developed the art of making vases, jewelry, bottles, etc. *See* the article Glass.

Goldsmith. The Hebrews called this technician "a refiner" (*ṣōrēph;* Mal. 3:2-3), a melter of gold (Neh. 3:8, 32; Isa. 40:19; 46:6; Jer. 10:9, 14; 51:17). From early times gold has been used in jewels.

Egyptian. Gold was known long before silver in Egypt. Silver came much later from Asia Minor and was known as "white gold" by Egyptian jewelers. Gold was dug from the eastern desert and the Egyptian wadis; its shining splendor attracted men before they knew how to write. Gold was commonly used in Egypt, even being covered with inlay of stones or enamel. King Tutankhamen's solid coffin and his death mask inlaid with precious stones and enamel are well-known examples of Egyptian extravagance in the use of this metal. The pendant of King Senwosret (c. 1887-1849 B.C.), found in the tomb of his daughter, Princess Sit Hat Hor Yunet, near her father's pyramid at el Lahun, is of gold lavishly inlaid with precious stones. The cartouche of the king is at the center. This was likely the pharaoh who occupied the throne when Israel entered Egypt.

Babylonian. The headdress of Queen Puabi of Sumerian Ur (c. 2500 B.C.), recovered from the Royal Tombs by Woolley, is a superb illustration of the work of Sumerian-Semitic artists who were executing their finest work in gold during

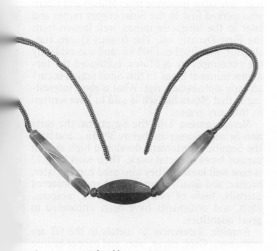

Sumerian man's headdress, c. 2500 B.C.

the third millennium B.C. The gold flowers springing from the "Spanish comb," the band of golden leaves, the heavy golden earrings, and the various necklaces done in semiprecious stones give us a good idea of the wonderful skill of the Sumerian goldsmiths. Also, glyptic artists or engravers produced solid gold cylinder seals with fine intaglio designs. These show exquisite artistic beauty as well as a vast variety of golden cups, helmets, and other objects. Gold and electrum (pale gold) objects from Mesopotamia and Tepe Gawra would grace any artistic display of the present day. In ancient oriental kingdoms special quarters were given over to the goldsmiths, who created fashionable articles for the court and sacred vessels for the temples.

Biblical. In the OT, anklets, bracelets, diadems, necklaces, nose rings, earrings, finger rings, crowns, coronets, camel crescents, gold hair nets, pendants, perfume boxes, jewelry boxes, and amulets are mentioned. Solar discs and lunar crescents (cf. Isa. 3:18) have been excavated at Ras Shamra, ancient Ugarit. Amulets or magical pendants to ward off evil spirits were common. The Jewish priest's ephod (Ex. 39) had four rows of three stones each, one gem representing each of the twelve Israelite tribes. Mentioned in the first row are "ruby, topaz, and emerald," in the second row "a turquoise, a sapphire and a diamond," in the third row "a jacinth, an agate, and an amethyst," and in the fourth row "a beryl, an onyx, and a jasper." They were enclosed in settings of gold filigree. Gems of gold fastened the splendid breastplate to the high priest's ephod at the shoulders (39:20-21). The lavish jewel finds at Ur, the home of Abraham, and other Mesopotamian cities make the account in Exodus thoroughly credible. The golden calf (chap. 32) wrought out of the people's "articles of silver and articles of gold" is another example of the art of the goldsmith among the Hebrews. Rebekah's jewelry consisted of a "gold ring weighing a half-shekel and two bracelets for her wrists weighing ten shekels in gold" (Gen. 24:22, 30). Saul and Jonathan had jewels of beauty. In 2 Sam. 1:10 the Amalekite says concerning the slaying of Saul: "And I took the crown which was on his head and the bracelet which was on his arm, and I have brought them here to my lord." David's royal jewels included not only a crown but buckles, shields, and spears. His vast bounty, a result of his conquests, enabled him to accumulate a fortune in jewels and gave his son Solomon a start on his splendid reign (cf. 1 Chron. 28-29). To the vast wealth in gold and precious stones inherited from his father, Solomon added great quantities of metal and precious stones acquired by tribute, exploitation, marriage dowries, and his own business enterprises in spice trade, horses, copper mining in the Arabah, and trade at Ezion-geber. A vast influx of gold especially characterized his reign. M.F.U.

Figurative. The skill of a goldsmith lies in the *subtlety* of his art, and with this the use of the word in Prov. 6:18 agrees: "A heart that *devises* wicked plans" (cf. 1 Sam. 23:9; lit., to "forge"). In the verse, "Behold, I have inscribed you on the palms of My hands" (Isa. 49:16), there is an allusion to the ancient custom of puncturing ornamental figures and mementoes upon the hand, arm, and forehead, and coloring the punctures with indigo, cypress, etc. This gives us the figure of Zion being as close to God as He is to Himself, and facing Him amid all the emotions of His divine life.

Graved, Graver. *See* Carver, above.

Launderer (Heb. *kābas*, to "wash"; Gk. *gnapheus*, a clothes "dresser"). The art of the launderer is of great antiquity and seems to have, at an early period, reached a comparative degree of perfection. Many persons, both men and women, were engaged in cleaning cloths and items of various kinds, and the occupations of the launderer form some of the subjects of Egyptian sculptures. It is probable that they were only a subdivision of the dyers. The trade of the launderers, so far as it is mentioned in Scripture, appears to have consisted chiefly in cleansing garments and whitening them (Mark 9:3; KJV renders "fuller"). The process of cleansing cloth consisted in treading or stamping on the garments with the feet or with bats in tubs of water, in which some alkaline substance (soap) had been dissolved. In early times before and even after the invention of soap, potash, niter, and several earths were employed for cleaning cloths, as well as various herbs, many of which are still in use among the Arabs. The "fuller's field" (2 Kings 18:17; Isa. 7:3; 36:2, *see* marg.) was near Jerusalem, and its mention would seem to indicate that it was a well-known resort of this craft. The KJV renders "fuller" in place of NASB "launderer." *See also* the articles Fuller's Field; Soap; Mineral Kingdom: Niter.

Biblical leatherworker

Leatherworker (Heb. *'ôr;* Gk. *dermatinos,* Matt. 3:4). The probability is that the Israelites obtained much of their knowledge of the making of leather from the Egyptians. Part of the process of curing skins is introduced in the sculptures, and that of dyeing them is mentioned in the Bible (Ex. 25:5). In one instance a man is represented dipping the hide into a vase, probably containing water, in which it was left to soak, preparatory to lime's being applied to remove the hair, a process similar to that adopted at the present day in the East. The tanning and preparation of leather was also a branch of art in which the Egyptians displayed considerable skill; the leather cutters constituted one of the principal subdivisions of the fourth class, and a district of the city was exclusively appropriated to them in the Libyan part of Thebes. Of leather they made thongs, shoes, sandals, the coverings and seats of chairs or sofas, bow cases, and most of the ornamental furniture of the chariot; harps were also adorned with colored leather, and shields and numerous other things were covered with skin prepared in various ways. Reference is made (2 Kings 1:8; Matt. 3:4) to girdles of leather.

Mason. *See* Stoneworker, below; and also the article House in the general listing.

Metalworker. There were workers in metal throughout the ancient world.

Egyptian. Metal working and mining developed early in Egypt. In the Pyramid Age (c. 2900-2450 B.C.) skilled metal workers were producing ingenious bronze rip saws, often six feet in length, for heavy woodwork. The huge pyramid stone blocks were cut by special saws. Vast quantities of gold for Egypt's skillful goldsmiths were imported from E African Punt. Egyptian craftsmen made wide use of copper, perhaps unintentionally alloyed at the earlier periods. As early as the First Dynasty, Egyptians pioneered in the copper-rich Sinai Peninsula. They developed skill in copper smelting and compounding metals, evidently knowing the value of alloys. Egyptians had slave labor imported from Midian and Edom who worked first in the Sinai copper mines and later in the turquoise mines, well known from the First Dynasty on. The famous Queen Hatshepsut, who lived c. 1500 B.C. and was evidently the contemporary of Moses, cultivated the turquoise mines of Sinai. In this Sinai region occurs an early alphabetic script. What is most interesting is that Moses himself is said to have written in this very region.

Mesopotamian. Like the Egyptians, the early non-Semitic Sumerians before 3000 B.C. and later the Semitic Babylonians developed high skill in various types of metal work. Their work in gold is now well known. They also used copper; later, bronze; and finally, iron. Sacred and nonsacred utensils, tools of every description, weapons, idols, and ornaments have been uncovered in great quantities.

Israelite. References to metals in the OT are numerous. Gold, silver, iron, and copper-bronze appear frequently on its pages. Gold, silver, and copper were used in the Tabernacle. David took vast quantities of copper in war.

Iron was introduced into Israel in the period of Saul who, as a result of his victories over the Philistines, broke their tight monopoly on this important metal (1 Sam. 13:19-20). The iron-smelting formula became public property, and metal was popularized in Israel. This worked an economic revolution in Palestine, making possible a higher standard of living. It is not surprising, therefore, to read that in amassing materials supplied to Solomon for the building of the Temple, "David prepared large quantities of iron to make the nails for the doors of the gates and for the clamps" (1 Chron. 22:3). Mention is also made of saws, sharp instruments, and axes (20:3). For the working of metals, three different trades were developed early in Israel: that of the worker in iron (Isa. 44:12; 2 Chron. 24:12), the worker in bronze (1 Kings 7:14), and the worker in gold and silver (Judg. 17:4; Jer. 10:9, 14). We read of axes and other iron instruments (Num. 35:16; Deut. 19:5; 27:5), whereas vessels and cooking utensils were of copper. The working (hammering) of iron was known to the patriarchs. In later times arms and other things formerly made of copper, such as chains, bolts, and armor, were made of iron (cf. Judg. 16:21 with Job 20:24; Pss. 107:16; 149:8; Isa. 45:2). Copper working apparently was not older than that of iron, both originating with Tubal-cain (Gen. 4:22). Copper ore, found more frequently solid in large masses and easier to work than iron ore, was more widely spread in earlier ages. Smelted ore was in use by at least 2500 B.C. in the Ararat region. Bronze was used for all sorts of vessels, weapons, armor, mirrors (Ex. 38:8), and statues (Dan. 5:4, 23). Casting was certainly known and practiced among the Hebrews (Judg. 17:4; 1 Kings 7:46; 2 Chron. 4:17). In the last two passages we are told that the workmen employed by Solomon cast the metal vessels, etc., of the Temple in the clay soil of Jordan. *See also* Refiner, below.

Needlework (Heb. *riqmâ,* Judg. 5:30; Ps. 45:14, "embroidered work"; *rōqēm,* Ex. 26:36; 27:16; 28:39; 36:37; 38:18). It is best to understand this as *colored weaving,* i.e., stuff woven from yarn of different stripes or cubes; as distin-

guished from "the work of a skillful workman," i.e., artistic weaving in which figures, flowers, and in some instances gold thread were woven (26:1, 31; 28:6, etc.). *See* Embroiderer; Weaver.

Perfumer. A person whose business it was to compound ointments in general was called an apothecary or *perfumer* (Neh. 3:8). The work was sometimes carried on by women (1 Sam. 8:13). Originally the "anointing oil" was prepared by Bezalel (Ex. 31:11; 37:29), after which it was probably prepared by one of the priests. Not least in importance of the duties of an ancient perfumer was the mixing of medicinal herbs. Babylonia, Egypt, and other areas of the Bible world developed the medical arts early. A clay tablet excavated in Nippur in lower Babylonia between the Tigris and the Euphrates gives a formula for a balsam salve prescribed for a metal worker who lived centuries before Abraham and suffered from burns. Perfumers also prepared spices for burials (2 Chron. 16:14).

The perfumes used in the religious services and in later times in the funeral rites of monarchs imply specialized knowledge and practice in the art of the perfumers, who appear to have formed a guild or association (Ex. 30:25, 35; Neh. 3:8; 2 Chron. 16:14; Eccles. 10:1). *See* Ointment; Perfume in the general listing.

The orientals delighted in perfumes and cosmetics. Especially in Egypt a knowledge of fragrant spices and oils was cultivated. The carved back of the chair of King Tutankhamen in the Cairo Museum shows the queen placing the finest perfume on the shoulder of the young king. From the ornate tomb of Queen Puabi of Ur, during the third millennium B.C., on down to noble ladies of many lands, examples survive of the perfumer's art, and toiletry sets from the dressing rooms of many ancient queens have survived to illustrate the development of the beautician's art. The spice and frankincense trade of the ancient world built up enormous wealth. Moses and the Israelites learned much from the perfume industry of Egypt.

Sacred Incense. Moses, in giving the formula for incense to be used exclusively in the Tabernacle, specified as follows: "Take . . . spices, stacte and onycha and galbanum, spices with pure frankincense; there shall be an equal part of each.

Egyptian metalworkers

And with it you shall make incense, a perfume, the work of a perfumer, salted, pure, and holy" (Ex. 30:34-36). Stacte was a gum resin exuded from the storax tree. Onycha was probably related to benzoin. Galbanum was a brown-yellowish resin exuded from a carrotlike plant found in the ancient East. Frankincense was a white aromatic gum secreted from trees related to the terebinth, found in SW Arabia, Abyssinia (Ethiopia), and India.

Sacred Anointing Oil. In the holy anointing oil (used in the Tabernacle) the "finest of spices" were enumerated in Ex. 30:22-25 as "flowing myrrh," "fragrant cinnamon," "fragrant cane," "cassia," "and of olive oil a hin. And you shall make of these a holy anointing oil, a perfume mixture, the work of a perfumer; it shall be a holy anointing oil." Myrrh was made from an aromatic resin exuded from a balsamlike shrub that grows in parts of the Arabian desert or from Syrian-Palestinian rock roses. Punt, in E Africa, had groves of myrrh trees. Queen Hatshepsut's sailors from Egypt in the fifteenth century B.C. were amazed to see native huts built among those groves. Sweet cinnamon was made from the bark of a tree known in the Solomonic era in Palestine and in Babylonia. Cassia was a type of cinnamon. Calamus, or sweet cane, came from a far country (Jer. 6:20). It is mentioned as a sweet smelling plant in the Song of Solomon (4:14). It is evidently of the flag family and thrives in damp places, as does the iris.

Other Perfumes. Spikenard (Syrian nard) was a highly valuable ingredient of ointments. It may have come from the pasturelands of the Himalayas. At any rate, it was extremely expensive. Judas criticized the extravagance of Mary when she anointed Christ's feet with it (John 12:3-8). Henna, or camphire, a yellow-flowered shrub furnishing ancient dyeing matter for finger- and toenails, was often mixed with spikenard. Aloes may be Indian sandalwood or, as believed by some, the gum of the eagle tree of India. Mixed with myrrh and cinnamon, it was a highly valued perfume (Ps. 45:8; Prov. 7:17).

Plasterer. *See* articles House; Plaster.

Potter. Pottery making is one of the oldest crafts of civilized man. The art of ceramics was invented at the close of the Late Stone Age in the Near East, perhaps as early as 5000 B.C. The simple pottery fragments that have survived the millennia tell a story of the tastes and destinies of nations. Recovered pottery fragments are one of the best allies of the archaeologist in dating ancient civilizations and identifying strata of culture from varied mounds. Archaeologists identify ancient cultures by the type of pottery unearthed. For example, in Mesopotamia the exquisite Halafian ware (c. 4500-4000 B.C.) from Tell Halaf marks a specific culture. Samarran ware, found at Samarra on the Tigris, dates c. 3800 B.C. Characteristic Obeidan pottery from Tell Obeid near

Ur marks civilization c. 3500 B.C. Warkan ware from Erech (Uruk) dates around 3200 B.C. Jemdet Nasr ware dates c. 3200-3000 B.C. The invention of the pottery wheel marked a revolution in ancient cultures and paralleled the beginning of the historical period in Egypt (c. 3000 B.C.). At Lachish in S Judah a potter's workshop with a simple pottery wheel dating from c. 1500 B.C. was unearthed. Pottery found at Jericho, at Ugarit, at Megiddo, and practically all other Palestinian sites illustrates the biblical notices of this ancient craft. The Israelites, of course, had pottery in the wilderness. Biblical references to this craft occur in Isa. 45:9 and Jer. 18:3-6. At Jerusalem there was a royal establishment of potters (1 Chron. 4:23) from whose employment, and from the fragments cast away in the process (Isa. 30:14), the Potter's Field perhaps received its name (Matt. 27:7, 10).

Biblical potter at work

Figurative. There are several allusions to both the potter and his products. The breaking of pottery is used, from its fragile nature, to illustrate the ease with which God punishes the wicked (Ps. 2:9; Isa. 30:14; Jer. 19:11); from its cheapness, the depreciation of good men (Lam. 4:2). The thorough acquaintance of the potter with both the clay and the vessel that he made from it is used to illustrate God's knowledge of humanity. The power of the potter in molding the clay is used to illustrate the absolute power of God in molding the destinies of men (Rom. 9:21). To place one's self as clay in the hands of God, as the potter, is a striking figure of complete trust and surrender (Isa. 64:8). The phrase "throw it to the potter" (Zech. 11:13) is apparently a proverbial expression for contemptuous treatment, although we have no means of tracing its origin satisfactorily. "As the words read, they can only be understood as signifying that the potter was in the house of Jehovah when the money was thrown to him: that he had either some work to do there, or that he had come there to bring some earthenware for the temple kitchens" (*see* 14:20; K. & D., *Coms,* ad loc.).   M.F.U.

Refiner. Refining in Scripture was of liquids and metals, and the processes were quite different. In respect to liquids the primary idea was that of straining or filtering, the word for which was *zāqaq;* but in respect to metals it was that of melting, and for this the word was *ṣārap*. But the first word also, in course of time, came to be used of gold or other metals to denote their refined or pure state (1 Chron. 28:18; 29:4). The refiner's art was essential to the working of the precious metals. It consisted in the separation of the dross from the pure ore, which was effected by reducing the metal to a fluid state by the application of heat and by the aid of solvents, such as alkali (Isa. 1:25) or lead (Jer. 6:29), which, amalgamating with the dross, permitted the extraction of the unadulterated metal. The instruments required by the refiner were a crucible or furnace and a bellows or blow pipe. The workman sat at his work (Mal. 3:3); he was thus better enabled to watch the process and let the metal run off at the proper moment. The Egyptians carried the working of metals to an extraordinary degree of perfection; and there is no doubt that the Hebrews derived their knowledge of those arts from this source, though there is evidence that the art of working in copper and iron was known before the Flood (Gen. 4:22). *See also* Metalworker, above.

Rope. Ropes and various kinds of twine were made by the ancients of flax and other materials. For large ropes of ordinary quality and for common purposes, the fibers of the date tree were employed by the Egyptians as at the present day, and many specimens of these durable materials have been found in the excavations of Upper and Lower Egypt. In a tomb at Thebes, of the time of Thutmose III, is represented the process of twisting thongs of leather, which is probably the same as that adopted in rope making.

The Scripture references to rope are but few: the binding of Samson with ropes by Delilah (Judg. 16:11-12); in Ahithophel's counsel to drag down with ropes the supposed place of David's retreat (2 Sam. 17:13); the servants of the defeated Syrian king, Ben-hadad, coming to Ahab with ropes around their necks (1 Kings 20:31-32) as a sign of absolute surrender; and in the account of Paul's shipwreck (Acts 27:32).

Figurative. Isaiah directs a woe against those guilty of impiety: "Woe to those who drag iniquity with the cords of falsehood, and sin as if with cart ropes" (5:18). "There is a bitter sarcasm involved in the bold figure employed. They were proud of their unbelief, but this unbelief was like a halter with which, like beasts of burden they were harnessed to sin, and therefore to the punishment of sin, which they went on drawing farther and farther, in ignorance of the wagon behind them" (Delitzsch, *Com,* ad loc.).

Shipbuilder. The Hebrews were not a seafaring or shipbuilding people but seafaring occupations were prominent in the great empires on the Nile, Tigris-Euphrates, and the Phoenician coastal cities.

Egyptian. The Egyptians were the earliest Mediterranean boat builders, with the Phoenicians of Byblos running a close second. Small flat-bottomed boats were useful for fishing and fowling in the Delta marshes. Large barges transported stone from Upper Egypt. Trading boats toured the river, as well as funeral barges that carried mummies and tomb adornments along the river. Some of the barges were sacred to the sun god. During the third millennium B.C. the Egyptians sailed oceangoing vessels to Phoenicia regularly, especially to obtain forest products.

Wooden model of Egyptian ship

Phoenician. The Phoenicians developed early a reputation for their boats and skill in manning them. Although these were often no larger than coastal New England fishing boats, they carried on extensive trade over all the Mediterranean. With masts of cedar, flooring of fir, oars of oak, rowing benches of ivory inlaid with boxwood, and sailcloth made in the looms of Egypt, these vessels put out from Sidon, Arvad, and Tyre. In the Solomonic era (c. 960 B.C.) Phoenician boat builders and mariners were employed by the Hebrew monarch to develop a fleet at Ezion-geber to carry goods to S Arabian and N African ports.

Mesopotamian. At an early period the Sumerians, and later the Babylonians, built boats of reed basketwork caulked with bitumen. The Assyrians constructed skin boats and rafts of timber by the eighth century B.C. These were precursors to the *guffahs,* which still sail the Euphrates. The seaborne traffic for Babylon, which arrived through the Persian Gulf from India and Africa bringing exotic spices and luxury articles, consisted of wooden boats not drastically different from the Phoenician and Egyptian craft.

Greek. By 600 B.C. the Greeks were developing distinctive boats, making improvements on Egyptian and Phoenician models. Bow and stern were turned up. Corinthian warships were double-decked, one deck for rowers and the other for fighters. Their ships were large, requiring anchors and employing slave labor.

Biblical. The tribe of Dan apparently had ships (Judg. 5:17). Solomon's fleet (1 Kings 9:26-28) takes a prominent place, but it was an unusual feature of Solomon's prosperity and splendor. Ferryboats crossing the Jordan are mentioned (2 Sam. 19:15, 18, KJV). The Galilean fishing boats in which Jesus went back and forth across the sea of Galilee are prominent in the gospels. The ships in which the apostle Paul sailed in his Mediterranean missionary journeys are mentioned conspicuously in the book of Acts. M.F.U.

Shoemaker. *See* Leatherworker, above.

Silversmith. *See* Metalworker, above.

Stonecutter. *See* Stoneworker, below.

Stonemason. *See* Builders; Stoneworker; and also the article House in the general listing.

Stoneworker. Stone work of various kinds was familiar in the ancient world.

Egyptians. The Egyptians, at a remote period, used stone implements; and we find that stone-tipped arrows continued to be used occasionally for hunting long after the metal head had been adopted. Examples of stone knives used for certain religious purposes have also been found in excavations and tombs.

"The most ancient buildings in Egypt were constructed of limestone, hewn from the mountains bordering the valley of the Nile; but so soon as the durability of sandstone was ascertained the quarries of Silsilis were opened, and these materials were universally adopted. Immense blocks of stone were quarried here and transported to their destined localities. The obelisks transported from the quarries of Syene, at the first cataracts, to Thebes and Heliopolis, vary in size from seventy to ninety-three feet in length. Small blocks of stone were sent from the quarries by water to their places of destination in boats or on rafts, and if any land carriage was required, they were placed on sledges and rollers; but those of very large dimensions were dragged the whole way by men, overland. . . . The immense weight of stone shows that the Egyptians were well acquainted with mechanical powers and the mode of applying a locomotive force with the most wonderful success. . . . The hieroglyphics on obelisks and other granite monuments are sculptured with a minuteness and finish which is surprising, even if they had used steel as highly tempered as our own" (Wilkinson, *Ancient Egyptians,* 2:156, 300ff.).

Hebrews. Stone work among the Hebrews consisted of the hewing and smoothing of stones and marble for great buildings. They were also skillful in cutting and engraving precious stones for ornaments (Ex. 35:33). From the fact that David secured masons from Hiram (2 Sam. 5:11;

1 Chron. 14:1), we infer that the Hebrews were not as skillful as the Tyrians.

As will be seen from the above, the ancients employed substantially the same appliances as are used in working stone today, and the great pyramids, temples, aqueducts, etc., of the East testify to the workmen's skill.

Tailor. *See* the article Dress in the general listing.

Tanner. A dresser of hides (Acts 9:43). The art of treating skins of animals was widely cultivated in antiquity. It was known by the Hebrews (Ex. 25:5). The Egyptians were adept at it. Ancient Egyptian literature gives an insight into the process of tanning. A three-day treatment with salt and flour cleansed the skins from foreign matter. Lime was used to remove the hair. The acrid juices of desert plants or oak bark were also used. The skin was dried for several days and treated with acid barks and leaves such as sumac. Hebrews and Egyptians and other ancient peoples used leather for various purposes—for tent coverings (26:14), for water containers (Gen. 21:14), for milk (Judg. 4:19, *see* marg.) and wine (Matt. 9:17), for oil and other liquids. It was also used for shields, the leather being oiled to keep it soft and pliable (2 Sam. 1:21; Isa. 21:5). Various articles of clothing were also made of leather. Elijah and John the Baptist wore leather garments (2 Kings 1:8; Matt. 3:4). Sandals, shields, and helmets were also prepared. Another common use was leather finely treated for writing parchment. The art of tanning, although necessary, was a malodorous task and one that was regarded as unclean by many who recognized certain animals as unclean. Thus, under Judaism, tanners had to live outside the city, often near the water, like Simon the tanner who lived by the seashore at Joppa (Acts 10:6). It is highly significant in the context of 9:43 and 10:9-23 that Peter lodged with Simon the tanner. This is an element in the narrative showing the divine dealing with the apostle of the circumcision in overcoming the Judaistic horror of the ceremonially unclean. The entire Acts narrative displays God's working with Peter to break down his prejudices against the Gentiles and to prepare him for the scene and sermon in Cornelius's house when the gospel was opened to the Gentiles. *See* Leatherworker.

Tools. Metalworkers used the anvil, hammer (Isa. 41:7), tongs, chisel or graving tool (Ex. 32:4), bellows (Jer. 6:29), melting or refining pot (Prov. 17:3), and for large castings, the furnace (Ezek. 22:18).

Weaver, Weaving. Weaving was common in almost every home in Palestine in Bible times. Families wove their own textiles, from common articles of dress to coarse tent cloth. Woolen looms and dyeing vats were uncovered in excavation at Lachish in southern Judea and other places. The Canaanites, long before the arrival of the Hebrews, wove and dyed their own fabrics.

Evidence of the weaver and dyer's art came from Tell Beit Mirsim, Ugarit, and Byblos, which was particularly famous for its woven materials, as well as many other places. Samson's "thirty linen wraps and thirty changes of clothes" (Judg. 14:12-13) indicate the activity of the weaving arts in the time of the Judges. Carpet looming was also common (Prov. 7:16).

The weaving of the common, coarser, and finer woolen, linen, cotton, and hair cloths into garments, covers, tent curtains, etc., was the business of the wives, as was the spinning of flax, wool, cotton, goat's and camel's hair (Ex. 35:25-26, 35; 2 Kings 23:7; Prov. 31:13, 19). But the art of weaving (Ex. 27:16), ornamented with flowers and figures, was performed by men, as well as the weaving of fine linen in which the sons of Shelah were engaged even in Egypt (1 Chron. 4:21). Hence the particular manipulations of this business were so generally known that in figurative language we often read of the weavers' beam (1 Sam. 17:7; 2 Sam. 21:19), the shuttle (Job 7:6), warp and woof (Lev. 13:47-59), etc. *See also* Embroiderer; Needlework, above. M.F.U.

Weaver

Woodworker. Carpentry was employed in many ways by the Egyptians and the Israelites.

Egyptian. Carpenters and cabinetmakers were a numerous class of workmen, and their occupations form one of the most important subjects in the paintings that represent the Egyptian trades. From these we learn that the Egyptians used wood to make furniture (boxes, tables, sofas, chairs, etc.) and various parts of houses (doors, etc.). With the carpenters may be mentioned the wheelwrights, makers of coffins, and the coopers; and this subdivision of one class of artisans shows that they had systematically adopted the division of labor. The makers of chariots and traveling carriages were of the same class. Palanquins, canopies, and wooden chests for traveling and religious purposes were the work of cabinetmakers or carpenters; but the makers of coffins were distinct from both of these. The boat builders and basket makers were subdivisions of workers in

wood. The occupation of the cooper was comparatively limited in Egypt, where water and other liquids were carried or kept in skins and earthenware jars; and the skill of the cooper was only required to make wooden measures for grain, which were bound with hoops of either wood or metal. Among the many occupations of the carpenter, that of veneering is noticed in the sculptures of Thebes as early as the time of the New Kingdom, about 1450 B.C.

Egyptian woodworking tools

Israelites. As among the Egyptians the carpenter, joiner, carver, sculptor, wagon maker, and basket maker all worked in wood. These trades were probably never strictly separated from one another. Mention of the first three is made in connection with the building of the Tabernacle (Ex. 25:9-28; 35:30-35; 37:1, 10, 15, 25). The Israelite leaders had covered wagons in the desert, which they probably brought from Egypt (Num. 7:3), and baskets are mentioned (Num. 6:15, 17, 19; Deut. 26:2, 4); but coopering is not mentioned at all.

Tools. Among the Egyptians, the usual tools of the carpenter were the ax, adz, handsaw, chisels of various kinds, the drill, and two sorts of planes (one resembling a chisel, the other, apparently of stone, acting as a rasp on the surface of the wood, which was afterward polished by a smooth body, probably of stone); and these, with the ruler, plummet, right angle (square), a leather bag containing nails, the hone, and the horn of oil, constituted the principal, and perhaps the only, implements used.

Among the Israelites the following tools for carpenters and joiners are incidentally mentioned: the ax, hatchet, saw, plane, level, compass (cf. Isa. 44:13), hammer, and pencil (or red lead).

BIBLIOGRAPHY: I. Mendelsohn, *Bulletin of the American Schools of Oriental Research* 89 (1943): 25ff.; R. J. Forbes, *Studies in Ancient Technology*, (1955-64), pp. 1-8; G. E. Wright, *Biblical Archaeology* (1957), pp. 191-98; H. Frankfort, *Art and Architecture of the Ancient Orient* (1959); A. Lucas, *Ancient Egyptian Materials and Industries* (1962); L. S. de Camp, *The Ancient*

Engineers (1963); D. Strong and D. Brown, Roman Crafts (1976).

Embalming. L. Cottrell, Life Under the Pharaohs (1960), pp. 221-36; E. A. T. W. Budge, The Mummy: Chapters on Egyptian Funereal Archaeology (1964); B. Mertz, Temples, Tombs and Hieroglyphs (1964), pp. 64-113.

Embroiderer: H. F. Lutz, Textiles and Costumes Among the Peoples of the Ancient Near East (1923).

HANDKERCHIEF (Gk. soudarion, "sweat-cloth"). A cloth used for wiping the perspiration from the face and for cleaning the nose (Luke 19:20; Acts 19:12). A similar "face-cloth" was also used for swathing the head of a corpse (John 11:44; 20:7).

HANDLE (Heb., plural kappôt, lit., "hands"). The thumb pieces or knobs of the bolt or latch to a door (Song of Sol. 5:5). See Lock.

HANDMAID, HANDMAIDEN. See Maid.

HANDS, LAYING ON OF. This occurs in Scripture as a patriarchal usage, as with Jacob's laying his hands upon the heads of Joseph's children (Gen. 48:14). It also occurs in later times, as when Jesus placed His hands upon children presented to Him for His blessing (Matt. 19:15). The laying on of hands formed part of the ceremony observed at the appointment and consecration of persons, such as of Joshua by Moses (Num. 27:18-23; Deut. 34:9). It sometimes attended the healing of persons by a prophet, although in one instance (2 Kings 4:34) Elisha placed his hands upon the hands of the child. In the gospel age the action was, undoubtedly, used in connection with the bestowal of supernatural gifts, or the miraculous effects of the Holy Spirit (Mark 5:23, 41; 7:32), although our Lord extended His hands over the apostles when blessing them at the Mount of Olives (Luke 24:50). The apostles laid their hands upon the sick and healed them (Matt. 9:18; Mark 6:5, 13, etc.), and at times also laid their hands upon the baptized, that they might receive the special gifts of the Spirit (Acts 8:15-18; 19:6). A quite natural extension of this practice was to apply it to those who were set apart to the sacred office in the church—the men already possessed of delegated power and authority proceeding, like Moses in respect to Joshua, to put some of their own honor upon those chosen to the same responsible and dignified position (14:3; 1 Tim. 4:14). "Not that the mere act could confer any special spiritual power, but it was employed as a fit and appropriate symbol to denote their full and formal consent to the bestowal of the divine gift; and, being accompanied by prayer to Him who alone can really bestow it, might ordinarily be regarded as a sign that the communication had actually taken place."

Ecclesiastical Uses. In the rites of the early church the laying on of hands was used in confirmation, which generally was an accompaniment of baptism and symbolized the reception of the Holy Spirit. It was also practiced in ordination (which see). In the modern church Roman Catholics use the laying on of hands in the ceremonies that precede extreme unction, in ordination, and in confirmation (in both of which services it has received a sacramental efficacy). In the mass, previous to the consecration of the elements, the priest extends his hands over the people in blessing. The Church of England and the Protestant Episcopal churches employ it as a symbolical act in baptism and confirmation. The Methodist, the Presbyterian, and the Congregational churches employ it only in ordination.

HANDSTAVES (Heb. maqqēl, a "rod" or "staff"). A KJV term replaced in the NASB and NIV by "war clubs" (Ezek. 39:9). See Armor.

HANDWRITING. See Certificate of Debt.

HA'NES (ha'nez). A place in Egypt mentioned only in Isa. 30:4: "For their princes are at Zoan, and their ambassadors arrive at Hanes." Hanes has been supposed by Vitringa, Michaelis, Rosenmüller, and Gesenius to be the same as Heracleopolis Magna in the Heptanomis. This identification depends on the similarity of the two names. Other scholars, however, are inclined to identify Hanes with Tapanhes, a fortified town on the eastern frontier. This is the identification of the Aram. paraphrase on the passage.

HANGING. See Punishment.

HAN'IEL. See Hanniel, no. 2.

HAN'NAH (han'a; "grace, favor"). Wife of Elkanah (a Levite of Ephratah) and mother of Samuel. Although childless, she was much beloved by her husband. But she was greatly distressed by the insults of Elkanah's other wife, Peninnah, who had children. On one of her visits to Shiloh she vowed before the Lord that if He would give her a son, she would devote him to His service. Her manner, speaking in an inaudible tone, attracted the attention of the high priest, Eli, who suspected her of drunkenness. From this suspicion she easily vindicated herself, received a blessing from Eli, and returned to her home with a lightened heart. Before the end of the year Hannah became the mother of a son, whom she named Samuel, about 1106 B.C. When Samuel was old enough to be weaned Hannah took him to Shiloh and presented him, with due form, to the high priest (1 Sam. 1:1-28). The joy of Hannah found expression in an exulting song of thanksgiving. It is especially remarkable that in this song (2:10) is the first mention in Scripture of the word anointed or Messiah, and, as there was no king in Israel at the time, it seems the best interpretation to refer it to Christ. There is also a remarkable resemblance between this song and that of Mary (Luke 1:46-55). Hannah came up to Shiloh every year to visit Samuel and to bring him a coat. She received the kindly notice of Eli and, blessed of God, gave birth to three other sons and two daughters (2:21).

BIBLIOGRAPHY: C. J. and A. A. Barber, *You Can Have a Happy Marriage* (1985), pp. 55-66.

HAN'NATHON (han'a-thon; probably "favored"). A place on the northern boundary of Zebulun (Josh. 19:14), apparently about midway between the Sea of Galilee and Mt. Carmel, perhaps at Tell el-Bedeiwiyeh.

HAN'NIEL (han'i-el; "grace of God").

1. The son of Ephod, leader of the tribe of Manasseh, and one of those appointed by Moses to divide the land among the several tribes (Num. 34:23).

2. One of the sons of Ulla and a leader of the tribe of Asher (1 Chron. 7:39; "Haniel," KJV).

HA'NOCH (ha'nok; dedicated, "initiated").

1. The third son of Midian and grandson of Abraham and Keturah (Gen. 25:4; 1 Chron. 1:33), after 1950 B.C.

2. The oldest son of Reuben (Gen. 46:9; Ex. 6:14; 1 Chron. 5:3), from whom came "the family of the Hanochites" (Num. 26:5), perhaps about 1850 B.C.

HA'NOCHITES (ha'no-kīts). *See* Hanoch, no. 2.

HA'NUN (ha'nun; "favored").

1. The son and successor of Nahash, king of the Ammonites (2 Sam. 10:1-5; 1 Chron. 19:2-6). David, who had received kindness from Nahash, sent an embassy to console Hanun on the death of his father, about 984 B.C. The young king, led by his courtiers, misapprehended the object of the mission and treated the ambassadors shamefully. Their beards were *half* shaven and their garments cut off at the middle, and in this plight they were sent back to David. After news was brought to the king of the affront, he commanded the ambassadors to remain in Jericho until their beards grew. He vowed vengeance, and Hanun, anticipating war, called to his aid the Syrians. The power of the Syrians, however, was broken in two campaigns, and the Ammonites were left to their fate.

2. A Jew who was associated with the inhabitants of Zanoah in repairing the Valley Gate of Jerusalem after the captivity (Neh. 3:13), 445 B.C.

3. The sixth son of Zalaph, who repaired part of the walls of Jerusalem (Neh. 3:30), 445 B.C.

HAPHARA'IM (haf-a-ra'yim; "double pit"). A place near the borders of Issachar, mentioned as between Shunem and Shion (Josh. 19:19). Probably et-Taiyibeh, eight miles NW of Bethshan.

HAPPIZZEZ (hap'piz-zez). The head of the eighteenth division of the priests as established by David (1 Chron. 24:15).

HA'RA (hā'ra). A province of Assyria, mentioned (1 Chron. 5:26) as one of the localities to which Tiglath-pileser deported the 2½ trans-Jordanic tribes. Being joined with Hala, Habor, and the river of Gozan, all situated in western Assyria between the Tigris and Euphrates, we may safely conclude that Hara was in their neighborhood.

HAR'ADAH (har'a-da; "place of terror"). The twenty-fifth station of the Israelites in the desert (Num. 33:24); perhaps at the head of the valley NE of Jebel Araif en Nakah.

HA'RAN (ha'ran; cf. Akkad. *ḥarrānu*, "road caravan route").

1. One of the three sons of Terah, brother of Abraham, and the father of Lot, Milcah, and Iscah. He died in his native place (Ur) before his father, Terah (Gen. 11:26-29), probably before 2250 B.C.

2. The son of Ephah, a concubine of Caleb, and father of Gazez (1 Chron. 2:46), after 1440 B.C.

3. (Hebrew same as no. 1). One of the three sons of Shimei, a Gershonite, who was appointed by David to superintend the offices at the Tabernacle (1 Chron. 23:9), about 960 B.C.

BIBLIOGRAPHY: W. F. Albright, *Journal of Biblical Literature* 43 (1924): 385-93; S. Lloyd and W. Brice, *Anatolian Studies* 1 (1951): 77-111; D. S. Rice, *Anatolian Studies* 2 (1952): 36-84; C. J. Gadd, *Anatolian Studies* 8 (1958): 35-92.

HA'RAN, CITY OF. An ancient and still-existing northern Mesopotamian commercial city on the Balikh River, sixty miles from its entrance into the Euphrates. It was located in Paddan-aram ("field of Aram"). The city was on the busy caravan road connecting with Nineveh, Asshur, and Babylon in Mesopotamia, and with Damascus, Tyre, and Egyptian cities in the W and S. It was a natural stopping place for Terah and Abraham on their trek to Palestine. Interestingly, Haran, like Ur, was a center of the moon god cult. Whether Terah was a worshiper of the moon god

Well near Haran

Sin and refused to break with his idolatry is an open question (Gen. 11:31-32). At any rate, when Terah died at Haran, Abraham and his nephew Lot and their families continued their migration SW into Canaan, passing through the hill country of Shechem and on to Bethel. Abraham and his clan kept in touch with Haran. Isaac's wife, Rebekah, was brought from Nahor, a neighboring city of Haran (chap. 24). Jacob's wife Rachel also came from this region (chap. 29), where Jacob himself spent twenty years. The Mari Tablets, unearthed in excavations at Mari by the Musée du Louvre under the leadership of André Parrot, mention Nahor. These tablets belong to the eighteenth century B.C. Haran was also a flourishing city in the nineteenth and eighteenth centuries B.C., as is known from frequent references to it in cuneiform sources. Cuneiform tablets from Nuzu, a small Assyrian town SW of Kirkuk, greatly illuminate the patriarchal age. Such social usages as the deathbed blessing (chap. 27) and the use of concubines to ensure heirs (16:3) are referred to in the Nuzu Letters. The city of Haran remained important throughout the centuries. Here the Assyrians made their last stand (609 B.C.), and three years later the city fell to the Medes, who destroyed it and drove the Assyrians back across the Euphrates.   M.F.U.

HA'RARITE (ha'ra-rīt). The designation of three of David's guard: Agee (2 Sam. 23:11), Shammah (2 Sam. 23:33), and Sharar (2 Sam. 23:33, "the ararite") or Sacar (1 Chron. 11:35), the father of Ahiam, another member of the guard.

HARBO'NA (har-bō'na; Avestan, "the bald man"). One of the seven chamberlains of King Ahasuerus, commanded by him to exhibit the beauty of Queen Vashti to his courtiers (Esther 1:10). He also suggested to the king the hanging of Haman (7:9, "Harbonah"), about 478 B.C.

HARBO'NAH (har-bō'na; Esther 7:9). *See* Harbona.

HARDEN. "To harden one's face" (Prov. 21:29, KJV); is to put on an impudent, shameless face; the NASB expression is "shows a bold face," and the NIV, "puts up a bold front." "To harden the neck" (Prov. 29:1, NASB, KJV; "stiffened their neck," 2 Kings 17:14; Neh. 9:29, KJV) is to be stubborn, self-willed.

HARDNESS OF HEART (Matt. 19:8; Mark 3:5). Indicates a destitution of feeling, insensitivity to spiritual things, persistence in wrongdoing, wickedness; in common use—stinginess, solidity, firmness. In Ezek. 3:7 (see marg.) the reference is evidently to a moral hardening. To "harden" or "stiffen the neck" (2 Kings 17:14; Neh. 9:29; Prov. 29:1; etc.) is to be stubborn, self-willed.

BIBLIOGRAPHY: W. Barclay, *A New Testament Wordbook* (n.d.), pp. 100-102.

HARE. *See* Animal Kingdom: Rabbit.

HA'REPH (ha'ref; "reproachful"). The "father" of Beth-gader and "son" of Caleb of Judah by one of his legitimate wives (1 Chron. 2:51), about 1190 B.C.

HA'RETH. *See* Hereth.

HARHA'IAH (har-ha'ya). The father of Uzziel, "of the goldsmiths," which latter repaired part of the walls of Jerusalem after the captivity (Neh. 3:8), 445 B.C.

HAR'HAS (har'has; 2 Kings 22:14). Given in 2 Chron. 34:22 as *Hasrah* (which see).

HAR'HUR (har'hur). One of the Temple servants whose posterity returned from Babylon with Zerubbabel (Ezra 2:51; Neh. 7:53), before 536 B.C.

HA'RIM (hā'rim; perhaps "consecrated, devoted, or flat-nosed").
1. The head of the third course of priests as arranged by David (1 Chron. 24:8), after 1000 B.C.
2. An Israelite whose descendants, to the number of 320 males, or 1,017 in all, returned from Babylon with Zerubbabel (Ezra 2:32, 39; Neh. 7:35, 42), before 536 B.C. Among these some are enumerated (Ezra 10:21) as priests in the corresponding lists of those who renounced their Gentile wives and others (10:31) as ordinary Israelites. Others consider Harim to be a place and identify it with the village Charim, situated eight miles NE of Jaffa (McC. and S., *Cyc.*).
3. The father of Malchijah, who repaired part of the wall of Jerusalem (Neh. 3:11), before 445 B.C.
4. One of the priests who signed the covenant of Nehemiah (Neh. 10:5), 445 B.C.
5. One of the leaders of the people who signed the covenant (Neh. 10:27), 445 B.C.
6. One of the priests who returned from Babylon (Neh 12:15). In the former list the name is changed to Rehum (v. 3), about 536 B.C.

HA'RIPH (hā'rif; "autumnal").
1. An Israelite whose descendants (or possibly a place whose inhabitants), to the number of 112, returned from Babylon with Zerubbabel (Neh. 7:24), probably the same as Jorah (Ezra 2:18), before 536 B.C.
2. A leader of the people who gave his hand to the covenant made by Nehemiah (10:19), 445 B.C.

HARLOT, WHORE. Terms used for several Heb. words having similar connotations.
1. Harlot (Heb. *zônâ;* Gk. *pornē*). Any woman, married or single, who practices unlawful sexual indulgence, whether for gain or lust (Gen. 34:31; Judg. 19:2; Prov. 23:27; Matt. 21:31-32; Luke 15:30; 1 Cor. 6:15-16). The term is usually rendered "prostitute" in the NIV. From Gen. 38:15 it would appear that such women were marked by a veil or by some peculiarity of its size or the method of wearing it; although Jahn (*Bib. Arch.,*

p. 141) thinks that all such women went without the veil and that Tamar assumed one for the purpose of concealing herself from her father-in-law. The representation given by Solomon shows that in his time prostitutes practiced their trade upon the "streets" (Prov. 7:6-23; 9:13-18).

2. Temple Prostitute (Heb. *q^edēshâ*, "to consecrate"). In the three passages (Gen. 38:21-22; Deut. 23:17; Hos. 4:14), one "set apart to a sacred purpose," according to the infamous rites in use among the worshipers of certain deities in Canaan and neighboring countries. Herodotus refers to the custom of the Babylonians, who compelled every native female to attend the temple of Venus once in her life and to prostitute herself in honor of the goddess. Such prostitution was forbidden by the law of Moses (Lev. 19:29; 21:9), yet it seems to have been assumed that the harlot class would exist, and the prohibition of Deut. 23:18 forbidding offerings from the wages of such sin is perhaps due to the influence of the heathen example. It is interesting to note that men were not excluded from the practice of temple prostitution (23:18, marg.).

3. Foreigner (Heb. *nokrîyyâ*, 1 Kings 11:1; Prov. 5:20; 7:5). There are different possibilities as to why there is a connection between foreign or "strange" (KJV) women and harlotry. One account seems to be that it refers to a man's leaving his own rightful wife for another, who ought to be strange to him (Prov. 5:17-18, 20). Another explanation is that the earliest and most frequent offenders against purity were foreigners like the Midianite woman in the days of Moses (Num. 25), the Canaanites, and other Gentiles (Josh. 23:12-13).

Figurative. The term *harlot,* or *prostitute,* is used figuratively for idolatress (Isa. 1:21; Jer. 2:20; 3:2; Ezek. 16:13-63; Rev. 17:1, 5, 15; 19:2). *See* Adultery; Fornication.

BIBLIOGRAPHY: D. J. Wiseman, *Tyndale House Bulletin* 14 (1964): 8ff.; M. Astour, *Journal of Biblical Literature* 85 (1966): 185-96; E. Yamauchi, *Orient and Occident,* ed. H. Hoffner (1973), pp. 213-22; D. W. Wead, International Standard Bible Encyclopedia (1981), 2:616f.

HARMON (har'mon). A place name otherwise unknown or, more likely, a term to be translated "mountain of oppression" (Amos 4:3, marg.).

HARNE'PHER (har-ne'fer). One of the sons of Zophah, a leader of the tribe of Asher (1 Chron. 7:36).

HARNESS, HARNESSED. The act of fastening animals to a cart or vehicle, e.g., *yoking* cattle (1 Sam. 6:7, 10, "hitched") or horses (Jer. 46:4). From the monuments we see that the harness of the Egyptian war chariots was of leather, richly decorated, many-colored, and studded with gold and silver.

HA'ROD (ha'rod; "trembling or terror"). The spring at which the test of drinking was applied

before the battle of Israel with the Midianites (Judg. 7:1, 4-7). The well bursts out of the source "some fifteen feet broad and two feet deep, from the very foot of Gilboa." It is identical with the present fountain *'Ain Jalud,* a mile E of Jezreel, and opposite Shunem. The Israelis have built a beautiful park at the site.

Harod valley viewed from Mt. Gilboa

HA'RODITE (ha'ro-dīt). Shammah and Elika, two of David's heroes (2 Sam. 23:25), were so called probably from their being natives of *Harod* (which see). In 1 Chron. 11:27 an error in writing gives us Harorite.

HAR'OEH (har'ō-e; 1 Chron. 2:52). *See* Reaiah.

HA'RORITE (ha'ro-rīt; 1 Chron. 11:27). Another form for *Harodite* (which see), an epithet of Shammoth, one of David's heroes.

HARO'SHETH-HAGGO'YIM (ha-rō'sheth-ha-goy'im). A city in the N of Palestine, the home of Sisera (Judg. 4:2, 13, 16). Harper thinks the name signifies "forests" and says "there still are the densely wooded slopes." Easton says "the name in the Hebrew is *Harosheth ha Gojim,* i.e., 'the smithy of the nations,' probably so called because here Jabin's iron war chariots, armed with scythes, were made." Jabin's great army gathered here preparatory to battle and defeat. It has been located at Tell 'Amar on the northern bank of the Kishon, sixteen miles NNW of Megiddo, but excavations indicate that it was not occupied until the tenth century B.C. The KJV renders "Harosheth of the Gentiles."

HARP. *See* Music.

HARROW (Heb. *hōrēsh*). The verb rendered "to harrow" (Job 39:10) expresses apparently the "breaking of the clods" (Isa. 28:24; Hos. 10:11), and is so far analogous to our harrowing, but whether done by any such machine as we call "a harrow" is doubtful.

The term *harrow* appears in the KJV of 2 Sam. 12:31; 1 Chron. 20:3; it is replaced in the NASB by *sharp iron instruments,* and in the NIV by *iron picks.*

HAR'SHA (har'sha; possibly "silent, dumb"). One of the Temple servants whose descendants returned from Babylon with Zerubbabel (Ezra 2:52; Neh. 7:54), before 536 B.C.

HART. *See* Animal Kingdom: Deer.

HA'RUM (ha'rūm; "exalted"). The father of Aharhel, the "families" of which latter are enumerated among the posterity of Coz, of the tribe of Judah (1 Chron. 4:8).

HARU'MAPH (ha-rū'maf; "snub-nosed"). "Father" of Jedaiah, which latter was one of the priests who repaired part of the walls of Jerusalem (Neh. 3:10), 445 B.C.

HAR'UPHITE (har'ū-fīt). A patronymic applied to Shephatiah (1 Chron. 12:5), which denotes either one descended from Haruph, or a native of *Hariph* (which see).

HA'RUZ (ha'ruz; "gold," or cf. S. *Arab;* "be covetous or eager"). A citizen of Jotbah and father of Meshullemeth, who became the wife of King Manasseh and mother of King Amon (2 Kings 21:19), before 641 B.C.

HARVEST (Heb. *qāṣîr,* "a cutting"). The crops in the southern parts of Palestine and in the plains come to maturity about the middle of April, but in the northern and mountainous sections they do not become ripe until three weeks later, or more. The harvest began with the barley and the festival of the Passover (Lev. 23:9-14; Ruth 2:23; 2 Sam. 21:9-10) and ended with the wheat (Gen. 30:14; Ex. 34:22) and the festival of Pentecost (Lev. 23:16). *See* Agriculture.

Figurative. Harvest is a figurative term for *judgment* (Jer. 51:33; Hos. 6:11; Joel 3:13; cf. Rev. 14:15); a season of *grace* (Jer. 8:20); a time when many are ready to receive the gospel (Matt. 9:37-38; John 4:35); and, as the harvest is considered the *end* of the season, so our Lord says, "The harvest is the *end* of the age" (Matt. 13:39). *Dew* in harvest, causing the plants to ripen with rapidity and luxuriance, is a symbol of God's fostering care (Isa. 18:4); *cold* in harvest is refreshing, like a faithful messenger (Prov. 25:13); whereas *rain* in harvest, being untimely, is a symbol of honor given to a fool (26:1).

HASADI'AH (has-a-dī'a; "favored by Jehovah"). One of the five sons of Zerubbabel mentioned in 1 Chron. 3:20.

HASENU'AH (has-e-nū'a). An Israelite of the tribe of Benjamin, whose descendants dwelt in Jerusalem after the captivity (1 Chron. 9:7), before 536 B.C.

HASHABEI'AH (hash-a-bī'a; "Jehovah reckons, imputes").

1. The son of Amaziah and father of Malluch, of the family of Merari (1 Chron. 6:45).

2. The son of Bunni and father of Azrikam, of the family of Merari (1 Chron. 9:14; Neh. 11:15), before 445 B.C.

3. The fourth of the six sons of Jeduthun (1 Chron. 25:3), who had charge of the twelfth course of singers (v. 19), after 1000 B.C.

4. A Hebronite, appointed by David on the W side of Jordan "for all the work of the Lord and the service of the king" (1 Chron. 26:30), after 1000 B.C.

5. Son of Kemuel and chief officer of the Levites in David's time (1 Chron. 27:17), perhaps the same as no. 4.

6. One of the chief Levites who made voluntary offerings of victims for the Passover kept by King Josiah (2 Chron. 35:9), about 639 B.C.

7. One of the Levites who responded to the invitation of Ezra to act as a minister in the house of the Lord (Ezra 8:19), about 457 B.C.

8. One of the chief priests into whose care Ezra entrusted the silver, gold, and other valuables for the sacred vessels at Jerusalem (Ezra 8:24). He is probably the same whose father, Hilkiah, is mentioned in Neh. 12:21, 457 B.C.

9. The son of Mattaniah and father of Bani (Neh. 11:22), before 445 B.C.

10. A chief of the Levites (Neh. 12:24) who repaired part of the walls of Jerusalem (3:17) and subscribed the covenant of fidelity to Jehovah (10:11), 445 B.C.

HASHABIAH. *See* Hashabeiah.

HASHAB'NAH (ha-shab'na; probably for Hashabiah). One of the leaders of the people who subscribed Nehemiah's covenant (Neh. 10:25), 445 B.C.

HASHABNEI'AH (ha-shab-nī'a; "Jehovah has taken account").

1. The father of Hattush, which latter repaired part of the walls of Jerusalem (Neh. 3:10), before 445 B.C.

2. A Levite who was among those who officiated at the solemn fast under Ezra and Nehemiah when the covenant was sealed (Neh. 9:5), 445 B.C.

HASHBAD'DANA (hash-bad'da-na). One of those who stood at Ezra's left hand while he read the law to the people (Neh. 8:4), 445 B.C.

HA'SHEM (ha'shem). The sons of Hashem the Gizonite are named among the members of David's guard (1 Chron. 11:34; the Jashen of 2 Sam. 23:32), before 1047 B.C.

HASHMO'NAH (hash-mo'na). The thirtieth station of the Israelites in the wilderness (Num.

32:29-30), near Mt. Hor. It was located, apparently, near the intersection of Wadi el-Jerafeh with Wadi el-Jeib, in the Arabah.

HA'SHUB. *See* Hasshub.

HASHU'BAH (ha-shū'ba; "esteemed"). One of the five sons of Zerubbabel (Keil, *Com.*), but according to some authorities the son of Pedaiah, the descendant of David (1 Chron. 3:20).

HA'SHUM (ha'shūm).
1. An Israelite whose posterity (or perhaps a place whose inhabitants), to the number of 223, came back from Babylon with Zerubbabel (Ezra 2:19), or 328 in all (Neh. 7:22). Seven men of them married foreign wives, from whom they separated (Ezra 10:33), before 536 B.C.
2. One of those who stood up with Ezra while he read the book of the law to the people (Neh. 8:4), about 445 B.C.
3. The head of a family who sealed the covenant made by Nehemiah and the people (Neh. 10:18), 445 B.C.

HASHU'PHA. *See* Hasupha.

HAS'RAH (has'ra). The father (or mother) of Tikvah or Tokhath and grandfather of Shallum, which last was husband of Huldah the prophetess (2 Chron. 34:22). The parallel passage (2 Kings 22:14) gives the name, probably by transposition, in the form Harhas. Hasrah is said to have been "keeper of the wardrobe," perhaps the sacerdotal vestments, before 639 B.C.

HASSENA'AH (has-en-a'a). A Jew whose sons rebuilt the Fish Gate during the repair of the walls of Jerusalem (Neh. 3:3), before 445 B.C. In Ezra 2:35; Neh. 7:38 the name is given without the article—*Senaah* (which see).

HASSENUAH. *See* Hasenuah.

HAS'SHUB (ha'shūb). The name of several OT persons. Except for 1 Chron. 9:14, the name is rendered "Hashub" in the KJV.
1. The son of Pahath-moab, and one of those who repaired part of the walls of Jerusalem (Neh. 3:11), 445 B.C. Perhaps he is the same person mentioned (10:23) as one of the Israelite leaders who joined in the sacred covenant of Nehemiah.
2. Another who assisted in the building of the wall of Jerusalem (Neh. 3:23), 445 B.C.
3. A Levite, son of Azrikam and father of Shemaiah, which last was one of those living in the "villages of the Netophathites," and having general oversight of the Temple (1 Chron. 9:14; Neh. 11:15), before 445 B.C.

HAS'SOPHERETH (ha'sō-fe-reth). One whose "sons" were a family who returned from Babylon with Zerubbabel, among the descendants of Solomon's servants, about 536 B.C. Called Sophereth in the KJV of Ezra 2:55 and in the KJV, NIV, and NASB of Neh. 7:57.

HASU'PHA (ha-sū'fa). One of the Temple servants whose descendants returned from Babylon with Zerubbabel (Ezra 2:43; Neh. 7:46), before 536 B.C.

HAT (Dan. 3:21, KJV). A cap (so NASB) or type of headwear. The NIV renders "turban." *See* Dress.

HA'TACH. *See* Hathach.

HATE (Heb. *śānē';* Gk. *miseō*). In the root of the Heb. word is the idea of ugliness, deformity; hence to regard with feelings contrary to love; to abhor, to loathe, to cherish dislike to. In both the Heb. and Gk. words we find the above meaning in some places (e.g., 2 Chron. 18:7; Ps. 45:7; Matt. 24:10; etc.); whereas in others the meaning is "to regard with less love" (e.g., Prov. 13:24; Mal. 1:3; Rom. 9:13).

The requirement to hate father and mother, wife and children, and one's own life (Luke 14:26) means that all earthly ties and love must be subordinate to love for Christ.

God's hatred is toward all sinful thoughts and ways. It is a feeling of which all holy beings are conscious in view of sin, and is wholly unlike the hatred that is mentioned in the Scriptures among the works of the flesh (cf. Gal. 5:19-21).

BIBLIOGRAPHY: J. Denny, *Expository Times* 20 (1909): 41-42; K. Stendahl, *Harvard Theological Review* 55 (1962): 343-55.

HA'THACH (hā'thak). A eunuch in the palace of Ahasuerus, appointed to wait on Esther, and who acted for her in her communications with Mordecai (Esther 4:5-6, 9-10), about 478 B.C.

HA'THATH (hā'thath; "terror," as in Job 6:21). Son of Othniel and grandson of Kenaz, of the tribe of Judah (1 Chron. 4:13), consequently also grandnephew and grandson of Caleb (v. 15; cf. Judg. 1:13), probably after 1170 B.C.

HATI'PHA (ha-ti'fa; Aram., "captive"). One of the Temple servants whose posterity returned from Babylon with Zerubbabel (Ezra 2:54; Neh. 7:56), before 536 B.C.

HAT'ITA (hat'ī-ta; Aram., "dug up, furrowed"), or **Hati'ta** (há-tī'tá). One of the gatekeepers whose descendants returned from Babylon (Ezra 2:42; Neh. 7:45), before 536 B.C.

HAT'TIL (hat'il). One of the descendants of "Solomon's servants" whose posterity returned from Babylon with Zerubbabel (Ezra 2:57; Neh. 7:59), before 536 B.C.

HAT'TUSH (hat'ush; derivation uncertain).
1. One of the sons of Shemaiah, among the posterity of Zerubbabel (1 Chron. 3:22), after 536 B.C.
2. A descendant of David who accompanied Ezra to Jerusalem (Ezra 8:2), 457 B.C.
3. Son of Hashabneiah, and one of those who

rebuilt the walls of Jerusalem (Neh. 3:10), 445 B.C. Perhaps identical with no. 2.

4. One of the priests who united in the sacred covenant with Nehemiah (Neh. 10:4), about 445 B.C.

5. A priest who returned from Babylon with Zerubbabel (Neh. 12:2), 536 B.C.

HAURAN' (how-ran'; "hollow" or "black land of basaltic rock"). A mound-dotted extinct volcanic plateau E of the Sea of Galilee and S of Damascus and Mt. Hermon. This region has roughly the same boundaries as OT Bashan. The region is extremely fertile and forms a natural granary. Numerous ghost towns exist in its area, some of them constructed of basalt and called "the giant cities of Bashan." In later Greco-Roman times the area, smaller than formerly, was known as Auranitis. This was one of the four provinces that Augustus gave to Herod the Great (c. 23 B.C.). Subsequently it formed a part of Philip's tetrarchy. Ezek. 47:16-18 envisions Hauran as a boundary for restored Israel.

HAVEN. The rendering of two Heb. and one Gk. word, and having the meaning of our words *port* or *harbor.*

HAV'ILAH (hav'i-la; perhaps "sandy," cf. Heb. *ḥôl,* "sand").

1. A region encompassed by the Pishon branch of Eden's river. It is represented as richly producing gold, onyx, and bdellium—an aromatic gum (Gen. 2:11-12). This region is not to be confused with the Havilah of the Joktanites (10:29; 25:18; 1 Sam. 15:7) or of the Kushites (Gen. 10:7; 1 Chron. 1:9). It evidently skirted Babylonia and was on the boundary "as one goes toward Assyria."

2. A district evidently N of Sheba in Arabia, between Ophir and Hazarmaveth. Its people were nomads (Ishmaelites, Gen. 25:17-18). Apparently its boundaries were fluid and reached into N Arabia, as is indicated by the narrative of Saul's warfare with the Amalekites (1 Sam. 15:7).

3. The second son of Cush (Gen. 10:7; 1 Chron. 1:9).

4. The twelfth named of the thirteen sons of Joktan (Gen. 10:29; 1 Chron. 1:23).   M.F.U.

HAV'VOTH-JA'IR (ha'voth-jā-ir; "huts or hamlets of jair"). A district of villages in Bashan, E of the Jordan, which the son of Manasseh took and called by his name (Num. 32:41).

Deut. 3:14 says that "Jair . . . took all the region of Argob as far as the border of the Geshurites and the Maachathites, and called it . . . Bashan, after his own name, Havvoth-jair" ("Bashan-havoth-jair," KJV). In Judg. 10:4 it is recorded that Jair the Gileadite and judge had thirty cities called Havvoth-jair.

HAWK. *See* Animal Kingdom: Hawk; Night Hawk.

HAY. *See* Vegetable Kingdom.

HAZ'AEL (haz'a-el; "God beholds, i.e., cares for"). An officer of Ben-hadad, king of Syria, whom Elijah was commanded to anoint to be king (1 Kings 19:15).

When Elisha was at Damascus, Hazael was sent by his master, then ill, to consult the prophet respecting his recovery (2 Kings 8:7-13), about 843 B.C. The answer was that he "shall surely recover." "But," the prophet added, "the Lord has shown me that he will certainly die." He then looked steadily upon Hazael until he became ashamed, upon which the man of God wept. Upon Hazael's asking, "Why does my lord weep?" Elisha replied, "Because I know the evil that you will do to the sons of Israel," etc. Hazael exclaimed, "But what is your servant, who is but a dog, that he should do this great thing?" The prophet responded, "The Lord has shown me that you will be king over Aram."

Hazael returned and told Ben-hadad the prophet's answer. The next day he took a cloth, dipped it in water, and spread it over the face of the king, who, in his feebleness and probably in his sleep, was smothered and died what seemed a natural death (2 Kings 8:15).

Hazael ascended the throne and was soon engaged in hostilities with Ahaziah, king of Judah, and Jehoram, king of Israel, for the possession of Ramoth-gilead (2 Kings 8:28). A text from Asshur mentions the significant dynastic change at Damascus and strikingly confirms the biblical account of Hazael's accession: "Adadidri forsook his land [i.e., died violently or was murdered]. Hazael, son of nobody, seized the throne." Evidence from the *stela* of Ben-hadad from the region of Aleppo in N Syria, discovered in 1940, indicates that the Adadidri of this account is none other than Ben-hadad I and that the Ben-hadad in the biblical account is neither an error nor a gloss for Adadidri, as E. J. Kraeling surmises (*Aram and Israel,* pp. 77, 79, n. 1), but is the same person (Albright, *Bulletin of the Am. Schools of Oriental Research* 87:26).

Hazael was soon confronted by Jehu of Israel (c. 842-815 B.C.), a dangerous usurper like himself. Jehu incurred the implacable hatred of Hazael by submitting to Shalmaneser III in the Assyrian invasion of 841 B.C. rather than joining the Syrian coalition to resist the enemy's advance. Shalmaneser's Black Obelisk shows Jehu, or his emissary, kneeling before the Assyrian emperor presenting "tribute of Iaua [Jehu], son of Omri." Hazael single-handedly stemmed the Assyrian invasion of 841 B.C. and was able at least to ward off a crushing blow. Until 837 B.C., which marked Shalmaneser's final effort to subdue central and southern Syria, Hazael was free to satisfy his lust for territorial expansion. He began relentlessly to thresh Gilead and Bashan "with implements of sharp iron" (2 Kings 10:32-33; Amos 1:3-4).

Hazael renewed his relentless attacks upon Israel at Jehu's death (815 B.C.) and reduced his son Jehoahaz (815-801 B.C.) to an extreme stage of abasement (2 Kings 13:1-9, 22, 25). Hazael became so powerful that he took possession of the Philistine plain, destroyed Gath, and besieged Jerusalem. He was bought off by the payment of a large sum raised by stripping the Temple (12:17-18).

In extending his sway to the S, Hazael became the most powerful of the Aramean conquerors who ruled at Damascus. In fact, he became the chief power in all Syria. However, the reappearance of Assyria in the W under Adadnirari III (807-782 B.C.) demonstrated that Hazael's empire, built on brute force, lacked intrinsic solidarity. Whereas a unified Syria had met and checked Shalmaneser's advance under Ben-hadad I at Karkar in 853 B.C., Adadnirari's westward push gave no proof at all of such solidarity. Damascus did escape actual destruction but was put under an oppressive tribute. According to the Saba stela discovered in 1905, Adadnirari says, "To march against Aram I gave command. Mari' [Hazael] I shut up in Damascus, his royal city. One hundred talents of gold, 1000 talents of silver . . . I received" (D. D. Luckenbill, 2, sec. 735). Even such countries as Bit Humri (Israel) and Palastu (Philistia) revolted in the crisis and sent tribute to Assyria. From the upper portion of a slab found at Nimrud (Calah), the cuneiform inscription of Adadnirari lists among other countries "Tyre, Sidon, Humri [Omriland, Israel], Edom, Palastu [Philistia]" as lands that he says "I brought into submission to my feet. Tribute and tax I imposed upon them" (Luckenbill, op. cit., sec. 739).

After an extended rule of at least forty years, Hazael died in 801 B.C., or slightly later. Adadnirari III, for the year 802 B.C. and likely several years earlier, names Mari' as a king at Damascus. This circumstance must be accounted for under the supposition that the term is a second name of Hazael and is merely a popular title of the kings of Damascus. According to Albright, it is an abbreviation of a name like Mari-hadad—"Hadad is my lord" (*Bulletin of the American Schools of Oriental Research* 87:28, n. 16). An inscription from an ivory recovered from the site of Arslan Tash in N Syria carries the name "Our lord Hazael" and dates from the time of Adadnirari III (F. Thureau-Dangin, A. Barrois, G. Dossin, and M. Dunand, *Arslan Tash*, 1931, pp. 135-38). It is significant in computing the date of Hazael's death. Other similar ivories found at Nimrud are dated somewhat later since an Assyrian tablet of inventory lists them as booty from Damascus at the time of Hazael's successor (*see* C. C. McCown, *The Ladder of Progress in Palestine*, 1943, p. 198).   M.F.U.

BIBLIOGRAPHY: C. C. McCown, *The Ladder of Progress in Palestine* (1943), p. 198; M. F. Unger, *Israel and the Aramaeans of Damascus* (1957), pp. 75-82, 160-63; D. W. Thomas, ed., *Documents from Old Testament Times* (1958), pp. 46-52, 242-50; K. A. Kitchen, *The Bible in Its World* (1977), p. 111.

HAZA'IAH (ha-za'ya; "Jehovah beholds"). Son of Adaiah and father of Col-hozeh, a descendant of Perez (Neh. 11:5), before 536 B.C.

HA'ZAR (ha'zar; an "enclosure"). A term frequently prefixed to geographical names in order to indicate their dependence as *villages* upon some town or noted spot. Gesenius (*Heb. Lex.,* s.v.) says that Hazar is "spoken also of the movable villages or encampments of nomadic tribes, who usually pitch their tents in a circle, or so as to form an inclosure." The African Arabs, who originally emigrated from Arabia, have retained many of their ancestral customs. When these Arabs are in a region where they are liable to attacks from enemies, they pitch their tents in a circle, with their cattle and goods in the center. The whole is then fenced in with a low wall of stones, in which are inserted thick bundles of thorny acacia, the tangled branches and long needlelike spikes forming a perfectly impenetrable hedge around the encampment. *See* Hazaraddar, etc.

HA'ZARAD'DAR (ha'zar-ad'ar; "village of Addar"). A place in the southern desert part of Palestine, between Kadesh-barnea and Azmon (Num. 34:4; Josh. 15:3, where it is simply "Addar," or "Adar," KJV).

HA'ZAR-E'NAN (ha'zar-ē'nan; "village of fountains"). A village named as a boundary place (Num. 34:9-10; Ezek. 47:17; 48:1), probably located seventy miles ENE of Damascus and identified as Qaryatein on the road to Palmyra. "And the boundary shall extend from the sea to Hazar-enan at the border of Damascus" cannot have any other meaning than that the northern boundary, which started from the Mediterranean Sea, stretched as far as Hazar-enan, the frontier city of Damascus (Keil, *Com.*, Ezek. 47:17).

HA'ZAR-GAD'DAH (ha'zar-gad'a; "village of fortune"; Josh. 15:27). A town in the extreme S of Judah. Perhaps identified with Khirbet Ghazza.

HA'ZAR-HATTICON. See Hazer-hatticon.

HA'ZARMA'VETH (ha'zar-ma'veth; "village of death"). One of the sons of Joktan (Gen. 10:26; 1 Chron. 1:20), or a district of Arabia Felix that was settled by him.

HA'ZAR-SHU'AL (ha'zar-shū'al; "village of jackals"). A town, the identifications of which are all supposition; some locate it at Khirbet el-Meshash, fifteen miles E of Beersheba. It was upon the S border of Judah (Josh. 15:28; Neh. 11:27) but afterward included in the territory of Simeon (Josh. 19:3; 1 Chron. 4:28).

HAZAR SUSAH (hā'zar su'sa). A town of unknown location included in the territory of Benjamin (Josh. 19:5).

HAZAR SUSIM (hā'zar su'sim). Another form of *Hazar Susah* (which see; 1 Chron. 4:31).

HAZ'AZON-TA'MAR (haz'a-zon-ta'mar). The ancient name of Engedi (Gen. 14:7; "Hazezon-tamar," KJV; 2 Chron. 20:2).

HAZEL. *See* Vegetable Kingdom: Almond.

HA'ZER-HAT'TICON (ha'zer-hat'i-kon; "middle village"). Named in the prophecy of Ezekiel (47:16; "Hazar-hatticon," KJV) as the ultimate boundary of the land. Its location has not been ascertained.

HAZE'RIM (ha-ze'rim; "villages"). In the KJV, the name of a place (Deut. 2:23); or, perhaps, a general designation of many towns by the name of Hazor, or Hagar, found among the *Avites* (which see), in NW Arabia Petraea.

HAZE'ROTH (ha-ze'roth; "villages"). The sixteenth station of the Israelites and their second after leaving Sinai (Num. 11:35; 12:16; 33:17-18; Deut. 1:1). At Hazeroth the people "remained" (Num. 11:35), and here occurred the sedition of Miriam and Aaron (chap. 12), after which Israel moved to "the wilderness of Paran."

HA'ZIEL (ha'zī-el; "vision of God"). A "son" of the Gershonite Shimei, and head of the family of Ladan (1 Chron. 23:9), about 960 B.C.

HA'ZO (ha'zō). One of the sons of Nahor by Milcah (Gen. 22:22), after 2100 B.C. He must, in all likelihood, be placed in Ur of the Chaldees, or the adjacent countries.

HA'ZOR (hā'zor; "enclosure, village").

1. A chief city of N Palestine (Josh. 11:10), near Lake Huleh, and the seat of Jabin, a powerful Canaanite king who sent out a summons to the neighboring kings to assist him against Joshua (11:1-5). Like other strong places in Palestine, it stood on a mound or tell (v. 13), but the surrounding country was suitable for chariot maneuvers (*see* vv. 4, 6, 9; Judg. 4:3). Another Jabin king of Canaan, oppressed Israel, from whose yoke deliverance was obtained by Deborah and Barak; Hazor remained in possession of the Israelites and belonged to the tribe of Naphtali (Josh. 19:36; Judg. 4; 1 Sam. 12:9). It was one of the places that Solomon fortified and for which he made a tax levy (1 Kings 9:15). Its inhabitants were carried off to Assyria by Tiglath-pileser (2 Kings 15:29; Josephus *Ant.* 9.11.1). Hazor is mentioned in the Amarna Letters (227:3 and 228:23).

Hazor was located nine miles N of the Sea of Galilee at Tell el-Qedah. It was the largest city in Palestine in OT times. At its peak in the fifteenth

Excavations at Hazor, which have revealed more than twenty layers of ruins

to fourteenth centuries B.C., it may have had a population of 40,000. Hazor consisted of a bottle-shaped mound about 130 feet high and covering 25 to 30 acres and a lower city of 175 to 200 acres. John Garstang excavated there briefly in 1928, and Yigael Yadin led a Hebrew University dig there from 1955 to 1958 and in 1968. The lower city was found to have had five levels of occupation. First settled in the mid-eighteenth century B.C., it was finally destroyed in about 1230 B.C. The last destruction Yadin dated to Joshua's days. In passing, it must be asked why Deborah and Barak could not have been responsible for the 1230 destruction and Joshua for an earlier destruction during the Amarna Period in the fourteenth century.

Settlement on the tell was found to begin in the twenty-seventh century. After the destruction of the Canaanite city in the thirteenth century, Yadin concluded that Israelites resettled the site. An unfortified town of the eleventh century was followed by Solomonic construction of walls and a gate during the tenth century. The gate complex is similar to those that Solomon built at Gezer and Megiddo. After Solomon's city was destroyed by fire, the House of Omri rebuilt the site in the ninth century, erecting a strong citadel and a number of public buildings. One of the latter, a large storehouse with two rows of pillars in the center, was mistakenly interpreted by Garstang as stables of Solomon's day. A large underground water system, on the same plan and larger than the one at Megiddo, was discovered on the mound's southern edge. This consisted of a vertical shaft with a rock-cut staircase dug one hundred feet into the tell where it entered an eighty-two-foot tunnel that led to water. The Omride citadel continued in use until the conquest and destruction by Tiglath-pileser in 732 B.C.   H.F.V.

2. A city in the S of Judah (Josh. 15:23), perhaps Hezron, near Kadesh-barnea (v. 3). This is believed to have been the central town of that name, the other Hazors, Hazor-hadattah, etc., being so called probably for distinction's sake.

3. "The kingdoms of Hazor" (Jer. 49:28-33); probably a district of Arabia. "It may be a collective name, and refer to settled, not wandering Arabs, dwelling in strong farmsteads. The tents of these nomads, and the insignificant Bedouin villages, without doors and bars, present a strange contrast to the great cities of Syria, with their magnificent palaces (vv. 23-27); and yet even the former contain precious goods, tempting the foreigner's greed" (Orelli, Com., ad loc.).

4. A city inhabited by the Benjamites after the captivity (Neh. 11:33); possibly the modern Khirbet Hazzur, four miles NNW of Jerusalem. From the places mentioned with it, such as Anathoth, Nob, etc., it would seem to have been a little N of Jerusalem.

BIBLIOGRAPHY: *Archaeological Discoveries in the Holy*

Land (1967), pp. 57-66; M. Avi-Yonah, ed., *Encyclopedia of Archaeological Excavations in the Holy Land* (1976), 2:474-95; A. F. Rainey, *International Standard Bible Encyclopedia* (1982), 2:636-38.

HA′ZOR-HADAT′TAH (hā′zor-ha-dat′a; "New Hazor," Josh. 15:25). One of the extreme southern towns of Judah; apparently el-Hudeira, SE of Tuwāni toward the Dead Sea.

HAZZELELPO′NI (haz-e-lel-pō′ni), or rather, **Zelelpo′ni** (ze-lel-pō′ni). The sister of Jezreel and others of the sons of Etam, a descendant of Judah (1 Chron. 4:3).

HAZZOBEBAH (hazōbē′ha). A descendant of Judah and son of Coz (or Koz) and grandson of Helah (1 Chron. 4:8).

HE (ה) (hā). The fifth letter of the Heb. alphabet, pronounced like English "h." In the Heb. of Ps. 119:33-40 each verse begins with this letter.

HEAD. This part of the body has generally been believed to be the seat of intelligence, whereas the heart, or the parts near it, were the place of the affections (Gen. 3:15; Ps. 3:3; Eccles. 2:14). In Scripture the *head* is sometimes used for the whole person (Gen. 49:26; Prov. 10:6), or for life itself (Dan. 1:10).

Customs. In *grief* the head was covered (2 Sam. 15:30; Esther 6:12), shorn (Job 1:20), sprinkled with dust (Josh. 7:6; Job 2:12) or ashes (2 Sam. 13:19), or the hands placed on it (13:19; Jer. 2:37). *Shaving* the head was forbidden to the priests and Nazirites (Lev. 21:5, 10; Num. 6:5). Lepers always went with the head uncovered (Lev. 13:45), and women generally covered the head in public (Gen. 24:65; 1 Cor. 11:5-6). The heads of criminals and enemies slain in war were often cut off (Judg. 5:26; 1 Sam. 17:51, 57; 31:9; Matt. 14:10). The KJV suggests that the head was bowed in worshiping God (Gen. 24:26; Ex. 4:31) and as a token of respect (Gen. 43:28).

Diseases. The head was liable to leprosy (Lev. 13:42-44), scabs (Isa. 3:17), and internal disease (2 Kings 4:19; Isa. 1:5). *See* Diseases.

Figurative. The head is illustrative of God (1 Cor. 11:3), of Christ (11:3; Eph. 1:22; Col. 2:19); of *rulers* (1 Sam. 15:17; Dan. 2:38), of *chief men* (Isa. 9:14-15); of the *chief city* of a kingdom (7:8). The *covered* head is a symbol of defense and protection (Ps. 140:7), or of subjection (1 Cor. 11:5, 10); *made bald* signifies heavy judgments (Isa. 3:24; 15:2; 22:12; Mic. 1:16); *lifted up*, of joy and confidence (Ps. 3:3; Luke 21:28); of *exaltation* (Gen. 40:13; Ps. 27:6); *anointed*, of joy and prosperity (23:5); *shaking or wagging the head* is a gesture of mockery at another's fall (Isa. 37:22) or misfortune (Ps. 22:7; Jer. 18:16; Matt. 27:39). According to Scripture the head is the noblest part of man. Because the human organism culminates in the head, Christ is called the "head of the church"; and for the same reason the head is the general metaphorical designation of him who is most exalted, the most excellent, the chief. He who blesses lays his hand upon the head of the person to be blessed, and he who consecrates on the head of the person to be consecrated. Precisely for the same reason tongues of fire are distributed on the heads of the apostles, as it was a heavenly laying on of hands.

BIBLIOGRAPHY: N. Turner, *Christian Words* (1982), p. 201.

HEADBAND (Heb. plural, *qishshūrîm*). The Heb. term is translated "attire" (Jer. 2:32) and "sashes" (Isa. 3:20) in the NASB. The NIV renders "wedding ornaments" and "sashes," respectively. *See* Dress.

HEADDRESS. *See* Dress.

HEAD OF THE CHURCH. On account of the intimate union that exists between Christ and the church He is called the head (Eph. 4:15; 5:23) and the church His Body (4:12; Col. 1:24), inseparably united. Not only does the church, as a Body, stand in need of Christ (Eph. 4:15-16; Col. 2:19), but the apostle ventures the bold expression that Christ also needs the church, as that which belongs to His completeness. Believers are baptized by the Holy Spirit into Christ (Rom. 6:3-4; Gal. 3:27) and into His Body. The figure of body and head is used more than any other to represent the service and manifestation of Christ through His redeemed people of this age. Christ is not only head of His mystic Body, the church, He is also head of the bride (Eph. 5:23-33). This last figure again presents the church in the unique relationship it sustains to Christ, which will be realized after its glorification and the marriage of the Lamb.

HEADSTONE. In Zech. 4:7 (KJV; NASB, "top stone"; NIV, "capstone") Christ, under the symbolism of a stone, is presented as the head of the corner (Acts 4:11; 1 Pet. 2:7). The whole company of believers is viewed as a building of God, composed of living stones, Christ being the cornerstone (Eph. 2:19-22). In the millennial age, toward which the golden candlestick of Zech. 4:1-7 points, Christ will be manifested also as the corner or headstone of the Temple of His restored covenant people Israel, the golden candlestick of 4:2 more specifically speaking of converted Israel as the light of the world in the Kingdom age. *See* Cornerstone.

HEAL. *See* Diseases, Treatment of.

HEART (Heb. mostly *lēb;* Gk. *kardia*). According to thorough investigation and evidence of Scripture in all its parts, the heart is the innermost center of the natural condition of man. The heart is: (1) the center of the bodily life, the reservoir of the entire life-power (Ps. 40:8, 10, 12) and indeed in the lowest physical sense, for eating and drinking, as strengthening of the heart (Judg. 19:5-6, 8-9; 1 Kings 21:7; Acts 14:17; etc.), becomes the strengthening of the whole man; (2)

the center of the rational-spiritual nature of man; thus when a man determines upon anything, it is called to "presume" in his heart to do so (Esther 7:5, marg.); when he is strongly determined, he "stands firm in his heart" (1 Cor. 7:37); what is done gladly, willingly, and of set purpose, is done "obedient from the heart" (Rom. 6:17). The heart is the seat of love (1 Tim. 1:5) and of hatred (Lev. 19:17). Again, the heart is the center of thought and conception; the heart knows (Deut. 29:4; Prov. 14:10), it understands (Isa. 44:18; Acts 16:14), and it reflects (Luke 2:19). The heart is also the center of the feelings and affections: of joy (Isa. 65:14); of pain (Prov. 25:20; John 16:6); all degrees of ill will (Prov. 23:17; James 3:14); of dissatisfaction from anxiety (Prov. 12:25) to despair (Eccles. 2:20, KJV); all degrees of fear, from reverential trembling (Jer. 5:24) to blank terror (Deut. 28:28; Ps. 143:4); (3) the center of the moral life; so that all moral conditions, from the highest love of God (Ps. 73:26) even down to the self-deifying pride (Ezek. 28:2, 5-6), darkening (Rom. 1:21), and hardening (Isa. 6:10; 63:17; Jer. 16:12; 2 Cor. 3:15) are concentrated in the heart as the innermost life circle of humanity (1 Pet. 3:4). The heart is the laboratory and origin of all that is good and evil in thoughts, words, and deeds (Matt. 12:34; Mark 7:21); the rendezvous of evil lusts and passions (Rom. 1:24); a good or evil treasure (Luke 6:45); the place where God's natural law is written in us (Rom. 2:15), as well as the law of grace (Isa. 51:7; Jer. 31:33); the seat of conscience (Heb. 10:22; 1 John 3:19-21); the field for the seed of the divine word (Matt. 13:19; Luke 8:15). It is the dwelling place of Christ in us (Eph. 3:17); of the Holy Spirit (2 Cor. 1:22); of God's peace (Col. 3:15); the receptacle of the love of God (Rom. 5:5); the closet of secret communion with God (Eph. 5:19). It is the center of the entire man, the very hearth of life's impulse.

BIBLIOGRAPHY: G. C. Berkouwer, *Man: The Image of God* (1962), pp. 194-278; R. Dentan, *Knowledge of God in Ancient Israel* (1968), pp. 37-38; E. Hatch, *Essays in Biblical Greek* (1970), pp. 94-109; R. Jewett, *Paul's Anthropological Terms* (1971), pp. 305-33.

HE ASS. *See* Animal Kingdom: Donkey.

HEATH. *See* Vegetable Kingdom: Juniper.

HEATHEN (Heb. *gôyim*, "troop"). At first the word *gôyim* denoted generally all the nations of the world (Gen. 18:18; cf. Gal. 3:16), but afterward the Jews became a people distinguished from the other nations. They were a separate people (Lev. 20:23; 26:14-38), and the other nations were heathen. With these nations the Israelites were forbidden to associate (Josh. 23:7; 1 Kings 11:2), to intermarry (Josh. 23:12), or to worship their gods. Owing to its position these nations penetrated into Palestine, and the advance of heathen culture could not be prevented. For that reason the lines of defense against all illegality were only the more strictly and carefully drawn by the vigilance of the scribes. "Two points especially were not to be lost sight of in guarding against heathen practices—heathen idolatry and heathen non-observance of the Levitical law of uncleanness. With respect to both the pharisaism of the scribes proceeded with extreme minuteness. For the sake of avoiding even an only apparent approximation of idolatry, the Mosaic prohibition of images (Ex. 20:4; Deut. 4:16-18; 27:15) was applied with the most relentless consistency." Not only did they declare themselves ready to die rather than to allow a statue of Caligula in the Temple (Josephus *Ant.* 18.3.1), but the Jews also repudiated pictorial representations in general, such as the trophies in the theater or the eagle at the gate of the Temple. Minute and exact regulations were made to prevent any encouragement of idolatry or contact with it: e.g., an Israelite was not to have any business transaction with a Gentile during the three days preceding or the three days following a heathen festival, and on the festival itself an Israelite was to hold no kind of interaction with the town; all objects possibly connected with idolatrous worship were forbidden, wood taken from an idol grove was prohibited, and bread baked by it could not be eaten, or if a weaver's shuttle was made of such wood its use was forbidden, as well as cloth woven with it. A Gentile—as a nonobserver of the laws of purification—was unclean, and all dealings with him were defiling, including his house and all objects touched by him (John 18:28). Provisions coming from the heathen were not to be eaten by Jews, although they were allowed to trade in them. A strictly legal Israelite could not at any time eat at a Gentile table (Acts 11:3; Gal. 2:12; Schurer, div. 2, 1:51ff.). *See* Gentile.

HEAVE OFFERING. *See* Sacrificial Offerings.

HEAVE SHOULDER. *See* Sacrificial Offerings.

HEAVEN. The rendering of several Heb. and Gk. words:

Material. (1) *The sky* (Heb. *shāmayim,* "lofty"), by far the most frequent designation of *heaven* in the Heb. Scriptures, and meaning the firmament, which appears like an arch spread out above the earth, and represented as supported on foundations and pillars (2 Sam. 22:8; Job 26:11), with the rain descending through its gates or windows (Ps. 78:23; cf. Gen. 28:17). We find such expressions as "toward the heavens," "reaching to heaven" (Gen. 15:5; 28:12); "under heaven," i.e., on earth (Eccles. 1:13; 2:3); "under the *heavens,*" i.e., the whole earth (Gen. 7:19; Deut. 2:25; Job 28:24; etc.); "the heavens and the earth," i.e., the universe (Gen. 1:1; 2:1). Akin to this word is *height* (Heb. *mārôm,* "elevation"), which, though not rendered "heaven," has doubtless a celestial signification (Pss. 68:18; 93:4; 102:19),

rendered "on high," "height." (2) *A wind* (Heb. *galgal,* "a wheel"), rendered "heaven" in Ps. 77:18 (KJV), but meaning a *whirlwind* (as in NASB and NIV). (3) *Clouds* (Heb. *shahaq,* "cloudy dust, vapor"), the *skies* or heavens; serene (Job 37:18) or covered with clouds (37:16); from which descend the rain and dew (36:28; Prov. 3:20), and manna (Ps. 78:23; cf. Isa. 45:8), and whence the thunder is heard (Ps. 77:17-18). Closely connected with (3) is (4) *Celestial expanse* (Heb. *rāqîa',* "that which is spread out"), i.e., firmament (which see). (5) Of the Greek terms, *ouranos* signifies the *heights* and therefore the vaulted expanse of the sky; the region where clouds and tempests gather (Matt. 16:2-3; Luke 4:25); also heaven, the region above the sky, the seat of things eternal and perfect where God and the other heavenly beings dwell (Matt. 5:34; 23:22; etc.). Paul (2 Cor. 12:2) seems to designate this heaven the third heaven.

Spiritual. Scripture evidently specifies three heavens, since "the third heaven" is revealed to exist (2 Cor. 12:2), and it is logical that a third heaven cannot exist without a first and second. Scripture does not describe specifically the first and second heaven. The first, however, apparently refers to the atmospheric heavens of the birds (Hos. 2:18, "sky") and of clouds (Dan. 7:13). The second heaven may be the stellar spaces (cf. Gen. 1:14-18). It is the abode of all supernatural angelic beings. The third heaven is the abode of the Triune God. Its location is unrevealed. It is the divine plan at present to populate the third heaven. It is a place (John 14:1-3). It is called "glory" (Heb. 2:10); those who enter it will be perfected forever (10:14) and made partakers of Christ's fullness (John 1:16), which is all fullness (Col. 1:19) and which comprehends the very nature of the Godhead bodily (2:9). The apostle John was called into heaven (Rev. 4:1). The apostle Paul was caught up to the third heaven (2 Cor. 12:1-9). He was prohibited, however, from revealing what he saw and heard. Heaven is a place of beauty (Rev. 21:1–22:7), of life (1 Tim. 4:8), service (Rev. 22:3), worship (19:1-3), and glory (2 Cor. 4:17-18).

The Heavenly City. In Rev. 21:9–22:7 the apostle John describes the New Jerusalem, the heavenly city. Prophetic students have given this various interpretations. Seiss, Scott, Kelly, Darby, and Jennings maintain it describes the Millennium. Ottman, Larkin, Govett, and others hold that it describes the eternal state. J. Dwight Pentecost (*Things to Come,* 1958, p. 572) correctly proposes that it describes *the eternal habitation of the resurrected saints during the Millennium.*

The city is a *literal city.* From Heb. 12:23-23 we learn that the inhabitants of the city (besides its being the abode of the Triune God) consist of: (1) The bride, the Lamb's wife, the church, referred to as "the general assembly and church of the first-born who are enrolled in heaven." (2)

The redeemed saints of the OT. These are referred to as "the spirits of righteous men made perfect." (3) "Myriads of angels," i.e., unfallen angels. Our Lord referred to this city in John 14:2-3 when He said He would go away and would come again and that He was preparing "a place" for His disciples.

Entrance to the city will be by translation (glorification) or resurrection, both in the case of the church saints and the saved OT saints. As J. Dwight Pentecost correctly says, "Thus all the redeemed of the ages who enter this city may do so by resurrection. The city thus becomes the abode of all the resurrected saints who enter it at the time of their resurrection" (*Things to Come*, p. 577).

With regard to *the relation of this heavenly eternal city to the earth,* it may be said that the resurrected saints of all ages in that city will be in their eternal state and possessed of eternal blessings, although this will not be true of things on the millennial earth. Concerning *the relationship of this heavenly city to eternity,* it may be said that at the end of the Millenium, after the earth has been renovated by fire, this dwelling place is removed. Afterwards, however, it will find its place and will be the connecting link between the new heaven and the new earth in the eternal state.

The *description of the heavenly city* by the apocalyptic seer is lavishly magnificent. It is said to possess "the glory of God" (Rev. 21:11), with a "brilliance . . . like a very costly stone, as a stone of crystal-clear jasper" (v. 11). Its twelve gates, inscribed with the names of the twelve tribes of sons of Israel, indicate Israel's portion in the city; that is, the redeemed of Israel. The twelve foundations of the city's wall will have in them the names of the twelve apostles of the Lamb (v. 14). The city is called "the bride, the wife of the Lamb" (v. 9). This shows its connection with the church, the bride, being called "wife" here because the symbolism of marriage is viewed as consummated, indicating that Christ is joined gloriously with His redeemed people of this age from Pentecost to the translation.

The foundations of the walls of the city are described as garnished with all manner of precious stones such as jasper, sapphire, chalcedony, emerald, sardonyx, sardius, chrysolite, beryl, topaz, etc. The twelve gates are set each one so that they consist of one huge pearl. The seer's city is said to be pure gold. No temple is there because the Triune God is unveiled in all of His glory. No light is needed because the unobscured glory of God is revealed in the city.

In the heavenly city paradise is restored, and the river of the water of life flows freely. The reference in 22:2 to "the tree of life" yielding its "fruit" monthly and its leaves being for "the healing of the nations" has reference to the city during the millennial period. Evidently, after the millennial period as the city merges into the eternal state all traces of the curse will be removed and there will be no need for healing as there will be no sickness. But sickness will prevail during the Millennium.

This picture of the heavenly city brings to a close the revelation of the glorious future for the redeemed of the ages. *See also* Jerusalem, New.

M.F.U.

BIBLIOGRAPHY: E. M. Bounds, *Heaven: A Place—A City—A Home* (1921); W. M. Smith, *The Biblical Doctrine of Heaven* (1968); N. Turner, *Christian Words* (1982), pp. 202-5.

HE'BER (hē'ber; Heb. *ḥeber,* "fellowship").

1. Son of Beriah and grandson of Asher (Gen. 46:17; 1 Chron. 7:31-32). His descendants are called Heberites (Num. 26:45).

2. "A descendant of *Hobab* (which see); whose wife, Jael, slew Sisera (Judg. 4:17-22). He is called Heber the Kenite (4:11, 17; 5:24), which seems to have been a name for the whole family (1:16). Heber appears to have lived separate from the rest of the Kenites, leading a patriarchal life. He must have been a person of some consequence from its being stated that there was peace between the house of Heber and the powerful King Jabin. At the time the history brings him under our notice his camp was in the plain of Zaanaim, near Kedesh, in Naphtali" (Kitto).

3. Probably a son of Mered (of Judah) by his "Jewish wife" (*see* Jehudijah); and father or founder of Soco (1 Chron. 4:18).

4. One of the sons of Elpaal and a head of the tribe of Benjamin (1 Chron. 8:17).

5. For KJV "Heber" in 1 Chron. 5:13; 8:22, *see* Eber.

BIBLIOGRAPHY: C. E. Macartney, *Ancient Wives and Modern Husbands* (1934), pp. 105-21.

HE'BREW LANGUAGE. The language of the Hebrews and of the OT Scriptures, with the exception of a few chapters written in Aram. It is not called Heb. anywhere in Scripture, but this is not surprising when we remember how rarely that name is employed to designate the Israelites. It is called "the language of Canaan" (Isa. 19:18), as distinguished from that of Egypt; and "Judean" (2 Kings 18:26, 28), as distinguished from Aramaean. Heb. belongs to the Semitic or Shemitic group of languages.

Characteristics. (1) Heb. has a predominance of guttural *sounds*—at least four, if not five; the use of strong letters, which may be represented by *tt, ts, kk* (or *kh*); and the vowels are kept in strict subordination to the consonants, it being a rare and exceptional case when a word or syllable begins with a vowel. (2) Like other Semitic languages, Heb. is characterized by the three-letter *root.* This is expanded into a variety of conjunctional forms expressing intensity, reflexiveness, causation, etc., modifications of the root idea being indicated not by additions to the root but by changes within the root. (3) It has a peculiar use of the *plural,* not only denoting plurality but likewise extension, in space or time. (4) In *composition* the Heb. is simple, pictorial, and poetical.

History. Heb. was already in spoken and written use when Moses and the Israelites came up out of Egypt (c. 1440 B.C.). The evidence of the Pentateuch and the witness of archaeology support this fact. The proto-Semitic script discovered by Petrie early in the twentieth century, and the discovery of a simple alphabetic Semitic script closely akin to Heb. at Ras Shamra-Ugarit on the N Syrian coast, 1929-37, added new evidence that Heb. was available as a literary vehicle for Moses, the first inspired penman of Scripture. "Ugaritic," belonging to the Amarna Age, late fifteenth and fourteenth centuries B.C. (cf. Cyrus Gordon, *The Living Past* [New York, 1941], pp. 103-35), was contemporary with the Mosaic age. Although there is not the slightest need to suppose that Moses wrote in any other script than the primitive prong-shaped alphabet of early Heb., yet as one brought up in the Egyptian court (Ex. 2:10) and well versed in Egyptian sciences and hieroglyphics (Acts 7:22), he could have written in Egyptian. Besides, he was likely familiar with Akkad., the *lingua franca* of all SW Asia at the time, a fact proved by the Amarna Letters. See David Diringer, "Early Hebrew Writing" in *The Biblical Archaeologist* 13, no. 4 (1950): 74-95.

Origin. Heb. originated from the old Phoenician alphabet from which all alphabets in current use, Semitic and non-Semitic, were ultimately derived. The origin of this proto-Semitic alphabet is still unclear, although an early example of the rude script was discovered at Serabit el Khadem in the Sinaitic Peninsula in 1904-5. Albright dates this script in the early fifteenth century (*Bulletin of the Am. Schools of Oriental Research* 110 [April 1948]: 22). It is of more than passing interest that this proto-"Sinai-Hebrew Script" was discovered in the very area in which Moses was commanded to write (Ex. 17:8-14), but early Heb. goes back to the time of Abraham. The question is, Did the patriarch import it from Haran or find it in Palestine? The patriarchs evidently used an Aram. dialect in Mesopotamia, but when they came into Canaan they adopted a local Canaanite dialect that was not identical with the standard speech of the sedentary Canaanites, as may be linguistically demonstrated (W. F. Albright, *From the Stone Age to Christianity,* p. 182). The Canaanite origin of Heb. is attested by Ugaritic and Phoenician. Numbers of important Canaanite inscriptions have been recovered, notably the Sarcophagus of Ahiram of Byblos, eleventh century B.C. Later Phoenician inscriptions from Cyprus, Sardinia, Carthage, and other colonies of the Mediterranean show the Canaanite affinities of Heb. The Gezer Calendar (c. 925 B.C.) written in perfect classical Heb., followed by the Moabite Stone (c. 850 B.C.) written in the language of Moab, which was closely akin to Heb., as well as later inscriptions from Samaria from the time of Jeroboam II help to trace the development of Heb. as a closely aligned Canaanite dialect. Other important early Heb. materials include the Siloam Inscription (c. 701 B.C.) cut in Hezekiah's rock conduit, and notably the Lachish Letters, which give us the Heb. spoken and written at the time of Jeremiah.

Written Hebrew. The rounded letters of present-day Heb. Bibles are evidently a modification of Aram. characters. The famous Dead Sea Scrolls from the second century B.C. are written in this type of letter, as is the Nash Papyrus, dated c. 125 B.C. The vowel points in modern Heb. Bibles were not added until A.D. 600-800 and were the work of Masoretic scholars, notably at Tiberias in Palestine.　　　　　　　　　　　　M.F.U.

BIBLIOGRAPHY: J. Barr, *Comparative Philology and the Text of the Old Testament* (1968); R. K. Harrison, *Introduction to the Old Testament* (1969), pp. 201-10; E. Ullendorf, *Is Biblical Hebrew a Language?* (1977).

HEBREWS. The first person in the Bible called a Hebrew is Abram (Gen. 14:13). Thereafter his descendants through Isaac and Jacob were known as "Hebrews" (40:15; 43:32; Ex. 2:11). The origin of the name *Hebrew* offers a difficult problem. The term may be derived from the prominent Semitic progenitor, Eber, the ancestor of Abraham (Gen. 10:21). Again "Abram the Hebrew" (14:13) may be "Abram who crossed the river," that is, the Euphrates (Josh. 24:2-3). Accordingly, the LXX translates "Abram, the Hebrew" *hā 'Ibhrî,* from *'ābar,* "to cross over." Gen. 14:13 has *ho peratēs,* "the one who crossed over." Another archaeological and linguistic possibility is the widely discussed question whether or not the Habiru, featured in the Nuzian-Hittite and Amarna documents of the fifteenth and fourteenth centuries B.C., are not to be identified, at least in part, with the Hebrews. For the scholar who follows the underlying chronology of the MT and places the Exodus c. 1440 B.C., the identification Hebrew (Habiru) may fit historically, but its linguistic affiliation is doubtful. The Habiru in central Palestine, reflected in the Amarna Letters, do not seem to have been the same as biblical Hebrews.

BIBLIOGRAPHY: H. Cazelles, *Peoples of Old Testament Times,* ed. D. J. Wiseman (1973), pp. 1-28.

HEBREWS, EPISTLE TO. This magnificent epistle, from the standpoint of doctrinal contribution and literary excellence, is in many ways without peer among NT books. This book is of unparalleled importance in expounding the transition from the old Levitical economy to Christianity. It eloquently sets forth the foundation Judaism furnished Christianity in messianic type, symbolized in prophecy.

Attestation and Authorship. External evidence unmistakably attests the early existence of the epistle. Clement of Rome, Polycarp, Justin Martyr, Dionysius of Alexandria, and Theophilus of Antioch quote from it. However, Marcion and the Muratorian Fragment do not recognize it. Eusebius, Origen, Athanasius, and others held that it was written by Paul, but the authorship has remained uncertain. The writer of the epistle does not mention his name, which is contrary to the custom of the apostle. Moreover, the writer to the Hebrews uses the LXX throughout except possibly at 10:30, whereas Paul employs both the Heb. text and the LXX. The style and vocabulary are not particularly Pauline.

Occasion and Date. It seems clear that the Temple was still in existence and the ritual still continued. The present tense is repeatedly used in this connection (8:4, 13; 9:4-9; 10:1-10; 13:10-11). The readers had evidently been Christians for a long time and had suffered severely. A date A.D. 67-69 would seem to fit the internal evidence.

Purpose. The writer aims to establish the supremacy of Christ and Christianity (1:1–10:18) and to warn those who accepted Christ of the dangers of apostasy (6:4-8; 10:26-31; 13:14-17). In view of the outmoded nature of Judaism the writer also exhorts his readers to make a complete break with it (12:18–13:17). To accomplish this purpose the writer in closely knit argument establishes the superiority of Christ over angels, over Moses and Joshua, and over OT priesthood and ritual.

Outline.

I. Introduction (1:1-4)

II. The Son superior to the angels (1:5–2:18)
- A. OT proof (1:5-14)
- B. Resulting obligation (2:1-4)
- C. Reasonableness of the Son's humiliation (2:5-18)

III. The Son superior to Moses and Joshua (3:1–4:16)
- A. To Moses (3:1-6)
- B. Failure under Moses and Joshua (3:7–4:2)
- C. Provided rest (4:3-10)
- D. Necessity of attaining this rest (4:11-13)
- E. Christ's triumph as High Priest our incentive to draw near (4:14-16)

IV. The superiority of Christ's high priesthood (5:1–7:28)
- A. His high priestly qualifications (5:1-10)
- B. Necessity of comprehending spiritual truth (5:11–6:20)
- C. Melchizedek aspect of Christ's high priesthood (7:1-25)
- D. Christ's high priesthood contrasted with the Levitical (7:26-28)

V. The superiority of Christ's high priestly ministry (8:1–10:18)
- A. The circumstances (8:1-13)
- B. Contrast of sanctuary and service under the two covenants (9:1-28)
- C. Contrast of Levitical sacrifices and Christ's sacrifice (10:1-18)

VI. Practical application (10:19–12:29)
- A. Plea for faithfulness (10:19-39)
- B. Call to achieve by others' example (11:1–12:4)
- C. Consolation by fact of sonship (12:5-13)
- D. Warning against apostasy (12:14-17)
- E. Argument from the higher position of the Christian (12:18-29)

VII. Conclusion: Social and religious obligations, personal instructions (13:1-25)

M.F.U.

BIBLIOGRAPHY: B. F. Westcott, *The Epistle to the Hebrews* (n.d.); J. Moffatt, *The Epistle to the Hebrews*, International Critical Commentary (1924); W. R. Newell, *Hebrews, Verse by Verse* (1947); W. H. G. Thomas, *Hebrews: A Devotional Commentary* (1962); F. F. Bruce, *The Epistle to the Hebrews*, New International Commentary on the New Testament (1964); A. Murray, *The Holiest of All* (1965); P. E. Hughes, *A Commentary on the Epistle to the Hebrews* (1977); R. Anderson, *Types in Hebrews* (1978); F. J. Delitzsch, *Commentary on the Epistle to the Hebrews*, 2 vols. (1978); W. Milligan, *The Theology of the Epistle to the Hebrews* (1978); A. B. Bruce, *The Epistle to the Hebrews* (1980); W. Goudge, *Commentary on Hebrews* (1980); T. C. Edwards, *Epistle to the Hebrews* (1982); D. Guthrie, *Letter to the Hebrews* (1983); J. F. MacArthur, Jr., *Hebrews*, The MacArthur New Testament Commentary (1983); L. L.

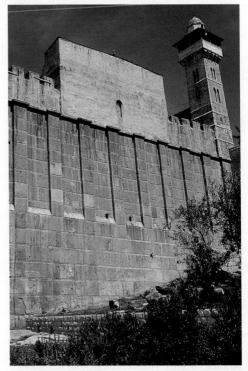

The mosque of Hebron which stands over the cave of Machpelah

Morris, *Hebrews* (1983); A. Saphir, *The Epistle to the Hebrews,* 2 vols. in 1 (1984).

HE'BRON (hē'bron; a "community"; "alliance").

1. A town in the mountains of Judah, about three thousand feet above the Mediterranean Sea, and between Beersheba and Jerusalem, being about twenty miles from each. It was named Kiriath-Arba (Gen. 23:2; Josh. 14:15; 15:13). About two miles to the N is *Mamre* (which see), after Mamre the Amorite (Gen. 13:18; 35:27), which is now called el-Khalil ("the friend"). Among those who lived there were the Canaanites and the Anakim (23:2; Josh. 14:15; 15:13), Abraham (Gen. 13:18), Isaac and Jacob (35:27). David made it his royal residence (2 Sam. 2:1-4; 5:5; 1 Kings 2:11); as did Absalom (2 Sam. 15:10). Sarah was buried here (Gen. 23:17-20); Joshua took Hebron (Josh. 10:36-37; 12:10), and Caleb retook it (14:14). The Romans also captured and destroyed it.

The traditional site of the cave of Machpelah, burial place of some of the patriarchs, is currently marked by the mosque of Hebron, which was formerly a Crusader church and that stands on the site of a church erected by the emperor Justinian in the sixth century. Cenotaphs in the mosque memorialize Abraham and Sarah, Isaac and Rebekah, and Jacob and Leah, who are presumed to have been buried in the cave below.

H.F.V.

2. The third son of Kohath and a grandson of Levi; a younger brother of Amram, father of Moses and Aaron (Ex. 6:18; Num. 3:19; 1 Chron. 6:2, 18; 23:12), before 1440 B.C. His descendants are called *Hebronites* (Num. 3:27; etc.).

3. The son of Mareshah and, apparently, grandson of Caleb, of the posterity of Judah (1 Chron. 2:42-43), after 1400 B.C.

BIBLIOGRAPHY: M. Avi-Yonah, *The Holy Land* (1972), pp. 13, 16-18, 54, 96, 128, 224.

HE'BRONITE (hē'bron-īt). A descendant of Hebron, the third son of Kohath (Ex. 6:18; Num. 3:19, cf. v. 27; 1 Chron. 26:23, 30-31). We find them settled in Jazer, in Gilead, "men of outstanding capability," seventeen hundred in number, who were superintendents for King David (26:31-32), whereas twenty-seven hundred others held the same position over the 2½ tribes (v. 30).

HEDGE. See Vegetable Kingdom.

HEDGEHOG. See Animal Kingdom.

HEG'AI (heg'ī). The eunuch having charge of the harem of Ahasuerus, and the preparation of the females sought as concubines for him (Esther 2:3, 8, 15), about 478 B.C.

HEIFER. See Animal Kingdom: Ox, and also the article Sacrifices.

Figurative. As the heifer, or young cow, was not used for plowing, but only for treading out the grain, when it ran without any headstall, the expression a "stubborn heifer" (Hos. 4:16) is used for resisting authority. To "plow" with another man's heifer (Judg. 14:18) is to take an unfair advantage of another. A heifer that "loves to thresh" (Hos. 10:11) is figurative of one choosing pleasant, productive, and profitable labor, because in threshing the animal was allowed to eat at pleasure (Deut. 25:4). "A pretty heifer" is figurative of the beauty and wealth of Egypt (Jer. 46:20); to "skip about like a threshing heifer," of the luxurious Chaldeans (50:11).

HEIFER, RED. See Sacrificial Offerings.

HEIR. See Inheritance.

HE'LAH (hē'la). One of two wives of Ashhur (1 Chron. 4:5, 7), a descendant of Judah, and the mother of *Coz* (which see), or Koz.

HE'LAM (hē'lam; 2 Sam. 10:16-17). Memorable as the place located between the Euphrates and the Jordan, where David routed the Syrians under Hadadezer. The town named Alema (1 Macc. 5:26), modern 'Alma in the Hauran, is the probable location.

HEL'BAH (hel'ba; "fatness"). A town of Asher not far from Sidon, and one of the places from which the Canaanites were not expelled (Judg. 1:31). Identified with Mahalib of the Assyrian monuments, four miles NE of Tyre. It still exists in the village of Halbun, a place with many ruins eighteen miles N of Damascus in the midst of a valley by the same name.

HEL'BON (hel'bon; "fat," i.e., fertile). A place named only in Ezek. 27:18, where "the wine of Helbon" is mentioned among the commodities furnished by Damascus to the great market of Tyre. "It still exists in the village of *Helbon,* a place with many ruins three and a half miles N of Damascus in the midst of a valley of the same name" (Keil, *Com.,* ad loc.).

HEL'DAI (hel'dī). See Heleb; Helem.

HE'LEB (he'leb; "fat, fatness"). Son of Baanah the Netophathite and one of David's warriors (2 Sam. 23:29); elsewhere more correctly called Heled (1 Chron. 11:30), or, better still, Heldai (1 Chron. 27:15).

HEL'ECH (hel'ek). A place otherwise unknown whose men provided protection to the walls of Tyre according to the lament-song of Ezekiel (Ezek. 27:11).

HE'LED (he'led). Son of Baanah, a Netophathite, and one of David's warriors (1 Chron. 11:30), called in the parallel passage (2 Sam. 23:29) Heleb, but more accurately Heldai (1 Chron. 27:15).

HE'LEK (he'lek; a "portion"). The second son of Gilead, of the tribe of Manasseh, whose descendants were called Helekites (Num. 26:30; Josh. 17:2).

HE'LEM (he'lem).

1. The brother of Shemer and great-grandson of Asher (1 Chron. 7:34-35), probably before 1440 B.C. Perhaps the same as Hotham (v. 32).

2. One assisting Zechariah in typical crowning of the high priest (Zech. 6:14), probably by erroneous transcription for Heldai (v. 10).

HE'LEPH (he'lef). A city mentioned as the starting point of the northern border of Naphtali, beginning at the W (Josh. 19:33). Khirbet Arbathsh, NE of Mt. Tabor, has been suggested as its location.

HE'LEZ (he'lez; perhaps, "strength").

1. One of David's mighty men (2 Sam. 23:26), an Ephraimite of Pelon (1 Chron. 11:27), and captain of the seventh monthly course (27:10), about 970 B.C.

2. Son of Azariah and father of Eleasah, of the tribe of Judah (1 Chron. 2:39).

HE'LI (he'li). The father-in-law of Joseph and maternal grandfather of Christ (Luke 3:23, KJV; NASB marg.). Also rendered Eli.

HELIOPOLIS ("city of the sun"). The Gk. name for several biblical cities. *See* Baalbek; Beth-shemesh, no. 4; City of Destruction; On, no. 2; Sun, Worship of.

HEL'KAI (hel'kī; probably a shortened form of Hilkiah). Son of Meraioth and one of the chief priests in the time of the high priest Joiakim (Neh. 12:15), after 536 B.C.

HEL'KATH (hel'kath; "portion, field"). A town assigned to the tribe of Asher on the eastern border (Josh. 19:25) and one of the Levitical cities (21:31). In 1 Chron. 6:75 Hukok is an old copyist's error.

HEL'KATH-HAZ'ZURIM (hel'kath-haz'ū-rim; "smoothness of the rocks," others, "field of the sharp edges"). The name given to the plain near the pool of Gibeon because of the deadly combat of twelve of the adherents of Ish-bosheth with as many of David's, which appears to have brought on a general engagement, resulting in the defeat of the men of Israel (2 Sam. 2:12-17).

HELL. A term that in common usage designates the place of future punishment for the wicked. Other meanings in many instances are expressed by this term, which must be recognized to prevent mistakes and confusion, In some cases it refers to the grave, in others to the place of disembodied spirits without any necessary implication as to their happiness or unhappiness. This fact, however, does not affect the correctness of the belief indicated by the common use of the term, a belief supported by many passages of Scripture.

Scripture Terms. The words of the original Scriptures rendered "hell" in English are three in number. With a solitary exception (2 Pet. 2:4, *tartaroō*, to "incarcerate") they are the only words thus translated. These, however, are not the only terms, as we shall see, in which the idea of a place of future penal suffering for the wicked is clearly and strongly expressed. The three words are as follows:

Sheol. Without entering into the discussion as to the derivation or root meaning of this term in the OT, it may be sufficient to say that it occurs several times in Scripture. The general idea is "the place of the dead"; and by this is meant, not the grave, but the place of those who have departed from this life. The term is thus used with reference to both the righteous and the wicked: of the righteous (Pss. 16:10; 30:3; Isa. 38:10; etc.), of the wicked (Num. 16:33; Job 24:19; Ps. 9:17; etc.). This is in accordance with the general character of the OT revelation, which presents much less clearly and strongly than the NT the doctrine of the future life with its distinct allotments of doom. But there are many hints, and more than hints, of the difference in the conditions of the departed. The psalmist prays: "Do not drag me away with the wicked and with those who work iniquity" (28:3; see also Isa. 33:14; 66:24; Dan. 12:2).

Hades. One of the NT terms rendered "hell." Like the OT "sheol," it is comprehensive and has a quite similar significance. It refers to the underworld, or region of the departed, the intermediate state between death and the resurrection. It occurs several times in the NT, namely: Matt. 11:23; 16:18; Luke 10:15; 16:23; Acts 2:27, 31; Rev. 1:18; 6:8; 20:13-14. The KJV renders this word "hell" in every case, with the exception of 1 Cor. 15:55 in the KJV only, where it gives "grave" (the NASB and NIV at this point read "death," from *thanatos,* not *hadēs*). The NIV usually renders "depths," or "grave," for *hades.* The distinction thus recognized between "hades" and "hell" as a place of misery is a valid one. Nevertheless it is equally plain that our Lord, certain of His words, associated judgment and suffering with the condition of some of the inhabitants of "hades" (e.g., Matt. 11:23-24; Luke 16:23-27). *See* Hades.

Gehenna. The valley of Hinnom. A place where the Jewish apostasy, the rites of Molech, were celebrated (1 Kings 11:7). It was converted by King Josiah into a place of abomination, where dead bodies were thrown and burned (2 Kings 23:13-14). Hence the place served as a symbol, and the name was appropriated to designate the abode of lost spirits. In this way the term was used by our Lord.

The word occurs in the NT, and in every case it is properly translated "hell," denoting the eternal state of the lost after resurrection. That is, the meaning of the English word is particularly the meaning of Gehenna (Matt. 5:22, 29-30; 10:28;

18:9; 23:15, 33; Mark 9:43, 45, 47; Luke 12:5; James 3:6).

The distinction between hades (the intermediate state) and Gehenna (eternal hell) is of importance, not only because it is necessary to the understanding of quite a large number of passages in the NT, but it may also prevent misconstruction and remove uncertainty as to Christ's teaching with regard to the future state of the wicked. It also has important bearing upon the doctrine of "Christ's descent into hell" (hades) and that of the intermediate state.

Scripture Synonyms. The Bible doctrine of hell is by no means confined to the terms above mentioned and to the passages in which they appear. There are many phrases in which the overshadowing idea is presented with great distinctness, such as "unquenchable fire," "black darkness," "furnace of fire," "fire and brimstone," "the smoke of their torment," "the lake of fire which burns with brimstone," "where their worm does not die," "the eternal fire which has been prepared for the devil and his angels." Van Oosterzee does well to remark: "There is no doubt that Holy Scripture requires us to believe in a properly so-called *place* of punishment, in whatever part of God's boundless creation it is to be sought. That the different images under which it is represented cannot possibly be taken literally will certainly need no demonstration; but it is perhaps not unnecessary to warn against the opinion that we have to do here with mere imagery. Who shall say that the reality will not infinitely surpass in awfulness the boldest pictures of it?"

For theological treatment of the doctrine, *see* Punishment; Gehenna.

BIBLIOGRAPHY: H. Buis, *The Doctrine of Eternal Punishment* (1957); J. N. D. Kelly, *Early Christian Doctrines* (1978), pp. 473, 483f.; W. G. T. Shedd, *The Doctrine of Eternal Punishment* (1980).

HEL′LENIST (hel′en-ist). A term employed of a person who spoke Gk. but was not racially of the Greek nation. The expression is especially used of Jews who adopted the Gk. language and, to some extent, Greek customs and culture (Acts 6:1; 9:29).

HELMET. *See* Armor, Arms.

HE′LON (he′lon; "valorous, strong"). The father of Eliab, which latter was head of the tribe of Zebulun at the Exodus (Num. 1:9; 2:7; 7:24; 10:16), 1440 B.C.

HELP. Besides its usual meaning of *assistance*, a technical application is given the term in 1 Cor. 12:28 (Gk. *antilēpsis;* a "laying hold of"), where it is used in connection with the ministrations of the deacons who have care of the sick, and refers to *helpers.*

Another Gk. term, *boētheia,* is behind the word *helps* in Acts 27:17 and refers to apparatus for securing a leaking vessel by means of ropes, chains, etc., forming a process of undergirding. The NASB gives "supporting cables," whereas the NIV reads "ropes."

HELPER (Heb. *'ēzer kenegdô;* a "help as his counterpart"). An aid "suitable for him," such as the man stood in need of (Gen. 2:18). KJV renders "a help meet for him."

HELPER (Gk. *paraklētos,* "summoned, called to one's side"; "Paraclete," KJV). In the Gk., this word refers to one who pleads another's cause before a judge; the word is rendered "advocate" in 1 John 2:1 where it is applied to Christ. The NIV translates, "one who speaks . . . in our defense." When Jesus promised to His sorrowing disciples to send them the Holy Spirit as a "Helper," He took the title to Himself: "I will ask the Father, and He will give you *another* Helper" (John 14:16; *see* marg.). The Gk. *paraklētos* applies well to both Jesus and the Spirit. Jesus was eminently a helper to His disciples, teaching, guiding, strengthening, and comforting them; and now that He has gone the Spirit is His substitute to carry on His work in us. In this present age it is, therefore, evident that the Holy Spirit is the believer's *paraklētos* on earth, indwelling and helping him, whereas Christ is his *paraklētos* in heaven, interceding for him at the Father's right hand. *See* Advocate; Holy Spirit.

HELVE (Heb. *'ēs,* "wood"). An obsolete term (Deut. 19:19, KJV) for the handle of an axe. *See* Ax, Axe.

HEM OF A GARMENT. The extremity, border of the outer garment (Ex. 28:33; 39:24-26; cf. Matt. 9:20; 14:36). The importance that the later Jews, especially the Pharisees, attached to this portion of the dress (Matt. 23:5) was founded upon the regulation in Num. 15:38-39. The fringe did not owe its origin to this regulation but was originally the ordinary mode of finishing the robe; the ends of the threads composing the woof being left in order to prevent the cloth from unraveling.

BIBLIOGRAPHY: F. J. Stephens, *Journal of Biblical Literature* 50 (1931): 59-70; J. B. Pritchard, ed., *Ancient Near Eastern Texts* (1969), pp. 560-62; R. A. Brauner, *Journal of the Ancient Near Eastern Society* 6 (1974): 35-38.

HE′MAM (hē′mam). The son of Lotan, the eldest son of Seir (Gen. 36:22). The same as *Homam* (which see).

HE′MAN (hē′man; "faithful").

1. One of the four persons celebrated for their wisdom, to which that of Solomon is compared (1 Kings 4:31). He is probably the same as the son of Zerah and grandson of Judah (1 Chron. 2:6). The mention of these men together as famous for their wisdom does not at all require that we should think them contemporaries.

2. Son of Joel and grandson of Samuel the

prophet; one of the "sons of the Kohathites," and one of the leaders of the Temple music as organized by David (1 Chron. 6:33, where singer should better be rendered *musician;* 15:17; 16:41-42), about 970 B.C. This, probably, is the Heman to whom the eighty-eighth psalm is ascribed. He had fourteen sons and three daughters. "Asaph, Heman, and Jeduthun are termed 'seers' (2 Chron. 35:15), which refers rather to their genius as sacred musicians than to their possessing the spirit of prophecy (1 Chron. 15:19; 25:1; 2 Chron. 5:12), although there is not wanting evidence of their occasional inspiration" (McClintock and Strong, *Cyclopedia*).

HE'MATH. For the city (1 Chron. 13:5; Amos 6:14), *see* Hamath, the NASB and NIV spelling; for the man, *see* Hammath.

HEM'DAN (hem'dan; "pleasant"). The first named of the four "sons" of Dishon, which latter was a son of Seir, and one of the Horite "chiefs" in Mt. Seir (Gen. 36:26). In 1 Chron. 1:41 the name is given as Amram in the KJV and as Hamran in the NASB.

HEMLOCK. *See* Vegetable Kingdom: Wormwood.

HEMORRHAGE. *See* Diseases: Issue.

HEMORRHOIDS. *See* Diseases.

HEN. *See* Animal Kingdom: Cock.

HEN (hen; favor, "grace"). The son of Zephaniah, to whom the prophet was sent with a symbolical crown (Zech. 6:14); probably a figurative name for Josiah (v. 10). "By the LXX and others the words are taken to mean 'for the favor of the son of Zephaniah' " (Smith, *Dict.*).

HE'NA (hē'na; signification unknown). A city, probably in Mesopotamia, mentioned in connection with Hamath, Arpad, etc., as having been overthrown by Sennacherib before his invasion of Judea (2 Kings 18:34; 19:13; Isa. 37:13). It is probably the city of Ana on the Euphrates.

HEN'ADAD (hen'a-dad; "favor of Hadad"). A Levite whose sons were active in the restoration after the captivity (Ezra 3:9). Two of the latter, Bavai and Binnui, are named (Neh. 3:18, 24; 10:9), before 536 B.C.

HENNA. *See* Vegetable Kingdom.

HE'NOCH. *See* Enoch.

HE'PHER (he'fer; a "pit, well").

1. The younger son of Gilead and great-grandson of Manasseh (Num. 27:1). He was the father of Zelophehad (26:33; 27:1; Josh. 17:2-3), and his descendants were called Hepherites (Num. 26:32), before 1400 B.C.

2. The second son of Asshur (a descendant of Judah) by one of his wives, Naarah (1 Chron. 4:6), after 1440 B.C.

3. A Mecherathite, one of David's heroes, according to 1 Chron. 11:36. The name does not appear in the list given in Samuel and is supposed to be an interpolation, or identical with Eliphelet of 2 Sam. 23:34.

4. A royal city of the Canaanites, taken by Joshua (12:17) and used by Solomon for commissary purposes (1 Kings 4:10). It is to be sought for in the neighborhood of Socoh, in the plain of Judah. Some identify it with Hafireh, about two miles E of Arubboth.

HEPH'ZIBAH (hef'zi-bah; "my delight is in her").

1. The queen of Hezekiah and mother of King Manasseh (2 Kings 21:1), before 690 B.C.

2. In the KJV and NIV, a symbolical name given to Zion by Isaiah (62:4). Zion had been called "Forsaken" but now is called Hephzibah, i.e., "My delight is in her," as the object of God's affection. This prophetic identification will find fulfillment in the future conversion and millennial blessing of the nation Israel.

HERALD (Heb. *kārōzā'*, only in Dan. 3:4). A crier, from an old Persian word *khresii* (Keil, *Com.*, ad loc.). The several Gk. words usually rendered "preach" in the NT have the meaning of to proclaim as a herald, whereas the word *preacher* (1 Tim. 2:7; 2 Tim. 1:11; 2 Pet. 2:5) would be more correctly rendered *herald*.

HERB. *See* Vegetable Kingdom: Grass.

HERBS, BITTER (Heb. *merōrîm*). The Israelites were commanded to eat "bitter herbs" with the Passover bread (Ex. 12:8; Num. 9:11) in remembrance of the bitterness of their bondage in Egypt (Ex. 1:14). "The *Mishnah* mentions these five as falling within the designation of 'bitter herbs,' viz., lettuce, endive, succory, what is called 'Charchavina (urtica, beets?), and horehound' " (Edersheim, *The Temple*, p. 204).

HERD (Heb. *bāqār;* Gk. *agelē*). "The herd was greatly regarded both in the patriarchal and Mosaic period. The ox was the most precious stock next to horse and mule. The herd yielded the most esteemed sacrifice (Num. 7:3; Ps. 69:31; Isa. 66:3); also flesh meat and milk, chiefy converted, probably, into butter and cheese (Deut. 32:14; 2 Sam. 17:29), which such milk yields more copiously than that of small cattle. The full-grown ox was hardly ever slaughtered in Syria; but, both for sacrificial and convivial purposes, the young animal was preferred (Ex. 29:1). The agricultural and general usefulness of the ox, in plowing, threshing, and as a beast of burden (1 Chron. 12:40; Isa. 46:1), made such a slaughtering seem wasteful. The animal was broken to service probably in his third year. In the moist season, when grass abounded in the waste lands, in the 'south' region, herds grazed there. Especially was the eastern table land (Ezek. 39:18;

Num. 32:4) 'a place for cattle.' Herdsmen, etc., in Egypt were a low, perhaps the lowest caste; but of the abundance of cattle in Egypt, and of the care there bestowed on them, there is no doubt (Gen. 47:6, 17; Ex. 9:4, 20). So the plague of hail was sent to smite especially the cattle (Ps. 78:48), the firstborn of which also were smitten (Ex. 12:29). The Israelites departing stipulated for (10:26), and took 'much cattle' with them (12:38). Cattle formed thus one of the traditions of the Israelitish nation in its greatest period, and became almost a part of that greatness. When pasture failed, a mixture of various grains (Job 6:5) was used, as also 'chopped straw' (Gen. 24:25; Isa. 11:7; 65:25), which was torn in pieces by the threshing machine and used probably for feeding in stalls. These last formed an important adjunct to cattle keeping, being indispensable for shelter at certain seasons (Ex. 9:6, 19)" (Smith, *Bib. Dict.*).

HERDMAN, HERDSMAN. (Heb. *bôqēr*, a tender of oxen; in distinction from *rō'î*, a feeder of sheep). The rich owners of herds placed them in charge of herdsmen, who watched the cattle to keep them from straying, to protect them from wild beasts, and lead them to suitable pasture. Usually they carried a staff furnished with a point of iron (*see* Goad) and a wallet or small bag for provisions, etc. (1 Sam. 17:40; Ps. 23:4; Mic. 7:14; cf. Matt. 10:10; Luke 9:3-4). They wore a cloak, with which they could envelop the entire body (Jer. 43:12); and their food was always simple, sometimes only the chance fruit they might find (Amos 7:14; Luke 15:15-16). Their wages consisted of the products of the herd, especially of the milk (Gen. 30:32-33; 1 Cor. 9:7). The occupation of herdsman was honorable in early times (Gen. 47:6; 1 Sam. 11:5; 1 Chron. 27:29; 28:1). Saul himself resumed it in the interval of his cares as king; also Doeg, "the chief of Saul's shepherds," was certainly high in his confidence (1 Sam. 21:7). Pharaoh put some of Joseph's brothers in charge of his livestock (Gen. 47:6). David's herdmasters were among his chief officers of state. The prophet Amos at first followed this occupation (Amos 1:1; 7:14). *See* Shepherd.

HE'RES (he'rez; "mountain of the sun").

1. A city of Dan, near Aijalon, which the Amorites continued to hold (Judg. 1:35), but as tributaries. Keil (*Com.,* ad loc.) believes it is only another name for *Ir-shemesh,* i.e., Beth-shemesh.

2. A mountain pass in the Transjordan near Succoth by which Gideon returned from his conquest of the Midianite chiefs (Judg. 8:13).

HE'RESH (he'resh; "silent, dumb"). One of the Levites who lived in the "villages of the Netophathites," near Jerusalem, on the return from captivity (1 Chron. 9:15), 536 B.C.

HERESY (Gk. *hairesis,* a "choice"). Means, in the NT: (1) a chosen course of thought and action; hence one's chosen opinion, tenet, and so a sect or party, as the Sadducees (Acts 5:17); the Pharisees (15:5; 26:5); and the Christians (24:5, 14; 28:22); (2) dissensions arising from diversity of opinions and aims (Gal. 5:20, marg.; 1 Cor. 11:19, KJV; NASB, "factions"; NIV, "differences"); (3) doctrinal departures from revealed truth, or erroneous views (Titus 3:10, KJV; 2 Pet. 2:1); the apostles vigorously warned the church against such departures (Acts 20:29; Phil. 3:2).

In the apostolic age we find three fundamental forms of heresy, which reappear with various modifications in almost every subsequent period.

Judaistic. "The Judaizing tendency, the heretical counterpart of Jewish Christianity, so insists on the unity of Christianity with Judaism, as to sink the former to the level of the latter, and make the Gospel merely a perfected law. It regards Christ also as a mere prophet, a second Moses, and denies, or at least wholly overlooks, his priestly and kingly offices, and his divine nature in general. The Judaizers were Jews in reality, and Christians only in appearance and name. They held circumcision and the whole moral and ceremonial law of Moses to be still binding, and the observance of them necessary to salvation. Of Christianity as a new, free, and universal religion, they had no conception. The same heresy, more fully developed, appears in the 2d century under the name of *Ebionism.*"

The Paganizing or Gnostic Heresy. "This exaggerates the Pauline view of the distinction of Christianity from Judaism, sunders Christianity from its historical basis, resolves the real humanity of the Saviour into a Docetistic illusion (i.e., the heavenly Being, whose nature is pure light, suddenly appearing as a sensuous apparition). The author of this baptized heathenism, according to the uniform testimony of Christian antiquity, is Simon Magus, who unquestionably adulterated Christianity with pagan ideas and practices, and gave himself out, in pantheistic style, for an emanation of God. This heresy, in the 2d century, spread over the whole Church, east and west, in various schools of *gnosticism.*"

Syncretistic Heresy. As attempts had already been made, before Christ, by Philo and others to blend the Jewish religion with heathen philosophy, especially that of Pythagoras and Plato, so now, under the Christian name, there appeared confused combinations of these opposing systems, forming either a paganizing Judaism or a Judaizing paganism, according as the Jewish or the heathen element prevailed.

"Whatever their differences, however, all these three fundamental heresies amount at last to a more or less distinct denial of the central mystery of the Gospel—the incarnation of the Son of God for the salvation of the world. They make Christ either a mere man or a mere superhuman phantom; they allow, at all events, no real and abiding union of the divine and human natures in the person of the Redeemer."

Heresy disturbed the unity of doctrine and of fellowship in the early church, which was therefore forced to exclude those holding false doctrine from its communion. Once excluded, they formed societies of their own. This was the case with the Novatians, Gnostics, Donatists, etc.

BIBLIOGRAPHY: J. H. Blunt, ed., *Dictionary of Sects, Heresies, Ecclesiastical Parties and Schools of Religious Thought* (1874); J. W. C. Wand, *The Four Great Heresies* (1950); J. H. Gerstner, *Theology of the Major Sects* (1960); H. Davies, *Christian Deviations* (1965); W. R. Martin, *The Kingdom of the Cults* (1985).

HE'RETH (he'reth; "thicket"). The place in the wooded mountains to which David fled from Saul (1 Sam. 22:5). Possibly the scene of the incident narrated in 2 Sam. 23:14-17; 1 Chron. 11:16-19.

HERETIC. *See* Heresy.

HERITAGE. *See* Inheritance.

HER'MAS (hūr'mas; Gk. *Hermas,* "Mercury"). A Christian resident of Rome to whom Paul sent greeting (Rom. 16:14). Irenaeus, Tertullian, and Origen attributed to him the work called *The Shepherd,* but that is highly unlikely because *The Shepherd* was written about A.D. 150. He is celebrated as a saint, in the Roman calendar, on May 9.

HER'MES (hūr'mēz; the Greek name of Mercury).

1. A man mentioned (Rom. 16:14) as a disciple in Rome. "According to the Greeks he was one of the seventy disciples and afterward Bishop of Dalmatia" (Calmet, *Dict.,* s.v.).

2. Messenger god of the Greeks (Acts 14:12). The Roman name and KJV rendering is Mercury. *See* Gods, False: Mercury.

HERMOG'ENES (hūr-moj'ē-nēz; "Mercury-born"). A disciple in Asia Minor mentioned by the apostle Paul, along with Phygelus, as having deserted him, doubtless from fear of the perils of the connection (2 Tim. 1:15). Nothing more of him is known.

HER'MON (hūr'mon; "sacred mountain"). A mountain that formed the northernmost boundary (Josh. 12:1) of the country beyond the Jordan (11:17), which Israel took from the Amorites (Deut. 3:8). It must, therefore, have belonged to Anti-Libanus (1 Chron. 5:23; cf. Deut. 4:48; Josh. 11:3, 17; etc.). It is identified with the present Jebel es-Sheikh, i.e., Sheikh's Mountain, situated thirty miles SW of Damascus and forty miles NE of the Sea of Galilee. Its height is 9,101 feet above the Mediterranean Sea. In Deut. 4:48 it is called Mt. Sion, i.e., a high mountain, being by far the highest of all mountains in or near Palestine. The ancient inhabitants of Canaan had sacred places

The foothills of Mt. Hermon

on the high mountains and the hills. We need not wonder, then, that Hermon should have been selected for the altar and the sacred fire. Hermon was the religious center of primeval Syria. Its Baal sanctuaries not only existed but gave it a name, before the Exodus (Josh. 11:17). The view from the perpetually snow-clad Hermon is magnificent. From the torrid Dead Sea region its cooling snows can be seen 120 miles distant; its melting snows form the main source of the Jordan and the rivers that water the Damascus plateau. The psalmist speaks (133:3) of the "dew of Hermon." The snow on the mountain condenses the vapors during the summer so that abundant dews descend upon it while the surrounding country is parched. One of its tops is called Abu-Nedy, i.e., "father of dew."

It has been widely held that the Hermon region was the scene of our Lord's transfiguration. If so, Christ traveled from Bethsaida, on the NW shore of the Sea of Galilee, to the coasts of Caesarea Philippi; from there He led His disciples "up to a high mountain by themselves. And He was transfigured before them." Afterward He returned, going toward Jerusalem through Galilee (cf. Matt. 16:13; Mark 8:22-28; 9:2-13, 30-33).

HER'MONITES (hūr'mon-īts). Properly "the Hermons," with reference to the three summits of Mt. Hermon ("peaks of Hermon," NASB, Ps. 42:6).

HER'OD (her'ud). This was not a personal name but the family or surname. It belonged alike to all the generations of the Herodian house as known to the Scriptures; much confusion has arisen from not having recognized that simple fact. Hence some have even questioned the accuracy of Luke in that he called Herod Antipas "Herod," when Josephus uniformly calls him "Antipas." But the point assumed is itself a mistake. For Luke mentions him as "Herod," and "Herod the tetrarch," and "the tetrarch of Galilee" in the same chapter (3:1, 19); and Josephus repeatedly calls him "Herod the tetrarch," and "Herod the tetrarch of Galilee," and "that Herod who was called Antipas" (*Ant.* 18.2.3; 18.7.1; *Wars* 2.9.1). The identification therefore is perfect as regards the person, the official title, and the political geography; Luke's mention is strictly historical. All the descendants of Herod the Great down to the fourth generation, who were identified with the government of Palestine and are mentioned in the NT, are known in history by the surname Herod: Herod Archelaus, Herod Antipas, Herod Philip II, Herod Agrippa I, and Herod Agrippa II.

Her'od the Great (37-4 B.C.)

History. The father of Herod the Great was a man of Idumaean blood named Antipater. The Idumaeans were of the Edomite stock, descendants from Esau (Josephus *Ant.* 14.1.3). They occupied a southern district of Palestine known as the Negeb, located between the Mediterranean and the Dead Sea and southward. By conquest John Hyrcanus brought the Idumaeans into the Jewish state about 130 B.C., and as they conformed to the Jewish rite of circumcision they embraced the Jewish religion (*see* table 13, "Herod and the Hasmonaeans"). However, the Jews regarded the Idumaeans with considerable suspicion and prejudice, calling them "half Jews" (*Ant.* 14.15.2). Josephus records that Herod was appointed procurator of Galilee when he was only twenty-five years of age (*Ant.* 14.9.2; *see* Whiston's note ad loc). Mark Antony gave Herod a tetrarchy (*Ant.* 14.13.1-2; *Wars* 1.12.5), and af-

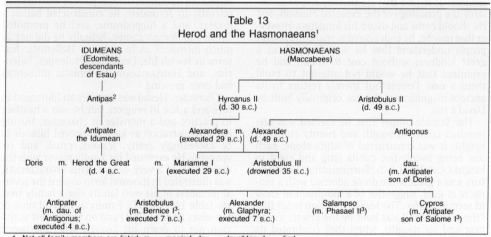

Table 13
Herod and the Hasmonaeans[1]

IDUMEANS (Edomites, descendants of Esau)		HASMONAEANS (Maccabees)	
Antipas[2]		Hyrcanus II (d. 30 B.C.)	Aristobulus II (d. 49 B.C.)
Antipater the Idumean	Alexandera m. Alexander (executed 29 B.C.) (d. 49 B.C.)		Antigonus
Doris m. Herod the Great (d. 4 B.C.)	m. Mariamne I (executed 29 B.C.)	Aristobulus III (drowned 35 B.C.)	dau. (m. Antipater son of Doris)
Antipater (m. dau. of Antigonus; executed 4 B.C.)	Aristobulus (m. Bernice I[3]; executed 7 B.C.)	Alexander (m. Glaphyra; executed 7 B.C.)	Salampso (m. Phasael II[3]) Cypros (m. Antipater son of Salome I[3])

1. Not all family members are listed; m. = married; dau. = daughter; d. = died.
2. Not the Antipas of Scripture; for that person, see table 14, "Herod's Family."
3. Herod the Great's brothers were Phasael I (son, Phasael II), Pheroras, and Joseph II (son, Joseph III; Joseph I was Herod's and Salome's paternal uncle and Salome I's first husband); his sister was Salome I (dau., Bernice I; son, Antipater).

terward he persuaded the Roman senate to make Herod a king (*Ant.* 14.14.4). The great Roman historian Tacitus affirms that Herod was placed on the throne by Mark Antony and that Augustus (Caesar) enlarged his privileges (*Histories* 5.9). But Herod did not succeed in asserting his royal rights over Palestine until he had captured Jerusalem, 37 B.C. Nevertheless, his coronation by Caesar was made an occasion of great magnificence (*Wars* 1.20.3).

Remains of buildings at Herod's fortress at Masada

Architecture. Herod had a passion for pretentious display in magnificent architecture and monuments, as had all his ruling descendants after him. To conciliate the Jews, who had been alienated by his cruelties, he proposed to reconstruct their ancient Temple that Solomon had originally built, though it has been shrewdly suspected that he entertained the sinister motive to possess himself of the public genealogies collected there, especially those relating to the priestly families. It is said that he thereby hoped to destroy the genealogy of the expected Messiah, lest He should come and usurp his kingdom. However that may be, he endeavored to make the Jewish people understand that he was doing them a great kindness without cost to them, and he promised that he would not attempt to build them a new Temple but merely restore to its ancient magnificence the one originally built by David's son.

The Temple proper that he erected was one hundred cubits in length and twenty cubits in height. It was constructed of white stone, each one being twenty-five cubits long and eight in height (*Ant.* 15.11.2-3). Surmounting this structure was a great white dome adorned with a pinnacle of gold, suggestive of a mountain of snow as seen from afar. The Jewish tradition holds that "the temple itself was built by the priests in one year and six months, when they celebrated its completion with Jewish feast and sacrifices; but that the cloisters and outer inclosures were eight years in building." However that may be, addi-

tions were made continually from year to year; so that though Herod began the rebuilding in 20 B.C., as a whole it was literally true that the Temple was "built in forty-six years," as the Jews so asserted to Jesus (John 2:20). But the end was not yet, for the work was really continued until A.D. 64, just six years before the final destruction of the Temple by the Roman soldiers of Titus. Even then, when the Romans under Vespasian made incursion into Palestine in 66, Herod's greatgrandson, Herod Agrippa II, was making expensive preparations to "raise the holy house twenty cubits higher" (*Wars* 5.1.5).

The destruction of the Temple occurred on the Jewish Sabbath, August 10, in the year 70. When Jerusalem was captured, the Temple was burned, the Jewish people were expatriated; and never since has sacrifice been offered up to God on Jewish altars.

At about the same time Herod rebuilt the Temple at Samaria, "out of a desire to make the city more eminent than it had been before, but principally because he contrived that it might at once be for his own security and a monument of his magnificence" (*Ant.* 15.8.5). He is also credited with having erected a monument over the royal tombs at Jerusalem, after having attempted to rob the dead of their sacred treasures, such as "furniture of gold, and precious goods that were laid up there" (*Ant.* 16.7.1).

Herod was Palestine's greatest builder. He built a magnificent new Greco-Roman capital and port at Caesarea with its impressive breakwaters and a temple to the divine Augustus. He rebuilt Samaria and renamed it Sebaste (the Greek form of Augustus). The city was equipped with a theater and forum, and crowning the heights was a temple to Augustus. At Masada, Jericho, the Herodium near Bethlehem, and in Jerusalem he built luxurious palaces and fortified retreats. In Jerusalem he constructed baths, a theater, and a hippodrome, and he promoted Greek and Roman games. Actually he did not so much introduce as to promote Hellenistic features in Jewish life. Under the Ptolemies, Seleucids, and Hasmonaeans Hellenistic influences had been growing.

Character. Herod was not only an Idumaean in race and a Jew in religion, but he was a heathen in practice and a monster in character. During his administration as king he proved himself to be exceedingly crafty, jealous, cruel, and revengeful. He exercised his kingly power with the disposition of a very despot. This characteristic was illustrated in its worst form toward the several members of his own family (for a family tree, *see* table 14, "Herod's Family"). He had nine or ten wives (*Wars* 1.28.4) and on the merest suspicion put to death his favorite wife, Mariamne (*Ant.* 15.7.1-7), and also her sons, Aristobulus and Alexander (*Wars* 2.11.6., closing sentence; cf. *Ant.* 16.10.1-16.11.7), and at last, when on his

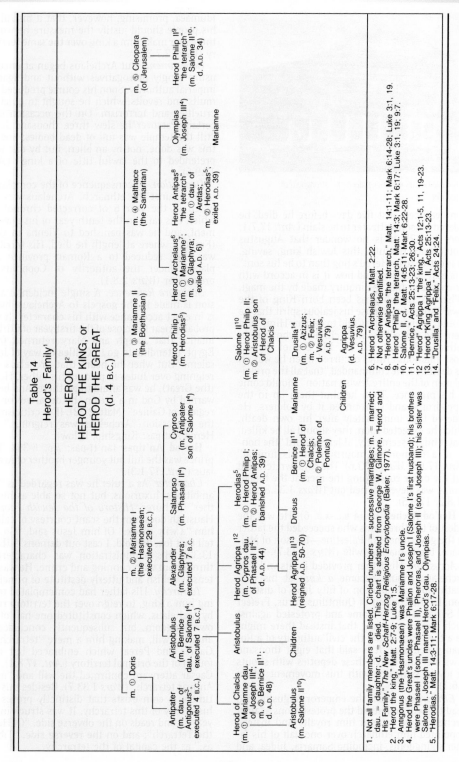

Table 14
Herod's Family[1]

HEROD I[2]
HEROD THE KING, or
HEROD THE GREAT
(d. 4 B.C.)

m. ① Doris:
- Antipater (m. dau. of Antigonus[3]; executed 4 B.C.)

m. ② Mariamne I (the Hasmonaean; executed 29 B.C.):
- Aristobulus (m. Bernice I[4] dau. of Salome I[4]; executed 7 B.C.)
  - Herod of Chalcis (m. ① Mariamne dau. of Joseph II[4]; m. ② Bernice II[11]; d. A.D. 48)
    - Aristobulus (m. Salome II[10])
  - Herod Agrippa I[12] (m. Cypros dau. of Phasael II[4]; d. A.D. 44)
    - Drusus
    - Bernice II[11] (m. ① Herod of Chalcis; m. ② Polemon of Pontus)
    - Mariamne
    - Herod Agrippa II[13] (reigned A.D. 50-70)
    - Drusilla[14] (m. ① Azizus; m. ② Felix; d. Vesuvius, A.D. 79)
  - Herodias[5] (m. ① Herod Philip I; m. ② Herod Antipas; banished A.D. 39)
- Alexander (m. Glaphyra; executed 7 B.C.)
  - Salampso (m. Phasael II[4])
  - Cypros (m. Antipater son of Salome I[4])

m. ③ Mariamne II (the Boethusian):
- Herod Philip I (m. Herodias[5])
  - Salome II[10] (m. ① Herod Philip II; m. ② Aristobulus son of Herod of Chalcis)
    - Children

m. ④ Malthace (the Samaritan):
- Herod Antipas[8] "the tetrarch" (m. ① dau. of Aretas; m. ② Herodias[5]; exiled A.D. 39)
- Herod Archelaus[6] (m. ① Mariamne[7]; m. ② Glaphyra; exiled A.D. 6)
- Olympias (m. Joseph III[4])
  - Mariamne

m. ⑤ Cleopatra (of Jerusalem):
- Herod Philip I[9] "the tetrarch" (m. Salome II[10]; d. A.D. 34)

Agrippa (d. Vesuvius, A.D. 79); Children

1. Not all family members are listed. Circled numbers = successive marriages; m. = married; dau. = daughter; d. = died. This chart is adapted from George W. Gilmore, "Herod and His Family," *The New Schaff-Herzog Religious Encyclopedia* (Baker, 1977).
2. "Herod the king," Matt. 2:7-9; Luke 1:5.
3. Antigonus (the Hasmonaean) was Mariamne I's uncle.
4. Herod the Great's uncles were Phalion and Joseph I (Salome I's first husband); his brothers were Phasael I (son, Phasael II), Pheroras, and Joseph II (son, Joseph III); his sister was Salome I. Joseph I. Joseph II married Herod's dau. Olympias.
5. "Herodias," Matt. 14:3-11; Mark 6:17-28.
6. Herod "Archelaus," Matt. 2:22.
7. Not otherwise identified.
8. "Herod Antipas "the tetrarch," Matt. 14:1-11; Mark 6:14-28; Luke 3:1, 19.
9. "Herod "Philip" the tetrarch, Matt. 14:3; Mark 6:17; Luke 3:1, 19; 9:7.
10. Salome II, cf. Matt. 14:6-11; Mark 6:22-28.
11. "Bernice," Acts 25:13-23; 26:30.
12. "Herod" Agrippa I "the king," Acts 12:1-5, 11, 19-23.
13. "Herod "King Agrippa" II, Acts 25:13-23.
14. "Drusilla" and "Felix," Acts 24:24.

Herod the Great's summer palace and stronghold at Herodium

own deathbed, just five days before he died, he ordered his son Antipater to be slain (*Ant.* 17.7.1; *Wars* 1.33.7). It is no wonder that Augustus should have ridiculed this Jewish king, saying, "It is better to be Herod's hog than to be his son!" It is easy to understand how it is in accord with his character that the inquiry made by the magi, "Where is He who has been born King of the Jews?" should so arouse his jealous spirit that he should "search for the Child to destroy Him," and "sent and slew all the male children who were in Bethlehem" (Matt. 2:2, 13, 16). One of Herod's most infamous crimes occurred when he was on his deathbed. He commanded "that all the principal men of the entire Jewish nation" should come to his presence. Then he shut them up in the hippodrome and surrounded it by soldiers. He ordered that immediately after his own death, which he expected soon, they should all be killed, that it might seemingly, at least, afford "the honor of a memorable mourning at his funeral" (*Ant.* 17.6.5; *Wars* 1.33.6). The royal wretch died but the order concerning the men at the hippodrome was never carried out (*Wars* 1.33.8; *Ant.* 17.8.2; 17.9.5).

Her′od Archela′us (4 b.c.-a.d. 6). He was the eldest of the three sons who succeeded the father in the government of Palestine—the son of Malthace, the Samaritan wife (*Wars* 1.33.7).

Accession. His father provided in his will that Archelaus should become *a king* at his own death; but a deputation of fifty Jews of distinction, by the consent of Quintilius Varus, Prefect of Syria, sailed to Rome and protested against such measure, urging that instead there might be a theocracy under the civil authority of a Roman procurator. It is said that eight thousand Jews met and hailed these deputies with shouts of joy in sympathy with this movement (*Wars* 2.6.1).

Ethnarchy. When the emperor Augustus had read the will and heard the protestations against Archelaus, he refused him royalty and instead appointed him ethnarch over one-half of his father's kingdoms, including Samaria, Judea, and Idumaea, promising, however, that if his ruling his people should justify the measure he would thereafter make him a king over the same territory (*Wars* 2.7.3).

Government. But Archelaus began at once to usurp kingly prerogatives without and against imperial authority. Soon his course produced tumults and revolts, which he sought to quiet by cruelties and terrorism. On the occasion of a certain Passover he slew three thousand Jews, "till the temple was full of dead bodies: and all this was done, not by an alien, but by one who pretended to the lawful title of a king" (*Ant.* 17.9.5).

Deposition. In consequence of the complaints made against the ethnarch, Archelaus was deposed in the year 6 of corrected chronology, which was early in the tenth year of his government, and he was banished to Vienna in Gaul (France), where at length he died. His territory was then reduced to a Roman province and placed under the authority of Coponius as procurator (*Wars* 2.8.1).

Scripture Reference. A single incidental allusion is made in the gospels to Archelaus, but it is in exact accordance with his character. It was probably near the close of the first year of Christ's infancy that Joseph and Mary returned from Egypt, intending to go to Galilee by way of Jerusalem. "But when he heard that Archelaus was reigning over Judea in place of his father, Herod (the Great), he was afraid to go there. And being warned by God in a dream, he departed for the regions of Galilee" (Matt. 2:22). (For criticism on the expression "Archelaus was reigning," *see* Herod Antipas: Kingship, below).

Her′od An′tipas (ăn′tĭ-pås; a.d. 6-39). This prince was the full but younger brother of Archelaus (*Ant.* 17.1.3).

Character. As a ruler he was regarded as "sly, ambitious, luxurious, but not so able as his father" (Schürer, *History of the Jewish People*). Hausrath does him the scant courtesy of calling him "a wily sneak." Of him Jesus said, "Go and tell that fox, 'Behold, I cast out demons' " (Luke 13:32). His administration was characterized throughout with cunning and crime. He was intensely selfish and utterly destitute of principle.

Tetrarchy. His father had contemplated making him a king, to reign over the territory ruled by Archelaus, which constituted one-half of his own kingdom, but subsequently concluded to alter his will, making him a mere "tetrarch" of Galilee and Perea, which embraced but onefourth of the original territory (*Ant.* 17.8.1), and Caesar afterward confirmed the will and "made Antipas tetrarch" (*Wars* 1.33.7). Besides this testimony a coin exists that distinctly proves the historicity of this tetrarchy. It was struck in the year 33 and reads on the obverse side, "Of Herod the Tetrarch"; and on the reverse side, "Tiberias," as the capital of the tetrarchy.

Marriages. Herod Antipas was first married to the daughter of Aretas, an Arabian king of Petraea. Nevertheless he was intrigued with Herodias, the wife of his half-brother, Philip I, who was a tetrarch of noble standing, in whose house Antipas was a guest. The two eloped, although both were married at the time (*Ant.* 18.5.1). Now Herodias was granddaughter of Herod the Great and sister of Herod Agrippa I, and the wife and niece of Herod Philip I.

John and Antipas. The scandalous conduct of Herod Antipas and Herodias is cited in the first three gospels in connection with the reproof administered by John the Baptist to Herod Antipas, and is treated quite at large by Josephus (Matt. 14; Mark 6; Luke 3; *Ant.* 18.7.1). For John had been saying to Herod, "It is not lawful for you to have your brother's wife" (Mark 6:18). Luke added, "But when Herod the tetrarch was reproved by him on account of Herodias, his brother's wife, and on account of all the wicked things which Herod had done, he added this also to them all, that he locked John up in prison" (Luke 3:19-20).

The first two gospels mention "the daughter of Herodias," but neither gives her name. Josephus says that her name was Salome (*Ant.* 18.5.4). The occasion referred to by both evangelists and historian, in which so much interest centers, was a festive party of the nobles who assembled at the tetrarch's palace to celebrate his birthday. Salome first appears in sacred history in this scene. On the mother's side she was granddaughter of Simeon, the high priest. Now the fact that a child was born to Philip and Herodias by the first marriage of the mother was a bar to her second marriage under Jewish law. Her marriage to Antipas, while her proper husband and his proper wife were still living, was aggravating to the Jews because she was a Jewess and belonged to the royal family; and their evil reputation was the more conspicuous in that Herod Antipas was the ruler of the Jews and had shamelessly defied the Jewish laws (Lev. 18:18; 20:21).

This anniversary was the occasion, and this daughter, Salome, was made the guilty person by whom Herodias secured revenge for the reproof given her husband for living with her unlawfully. After Salome danced before the nobles to the great fascination and gratification of Herod, he promised her anything she might ask of him, to the half of his kingdom. Herodias saw her opportunity and induced her daughter to request the head of John the Baptist, who was then in the nearby prison. "And although he was grieved, the king commanded it to be given because of his oaths, and because of his dinner guests" (Matt. 14:1-10). The executioner was sent to the prison at once, and the ghastly gift was given. John the Baptist was beheaded, the man who "among those born of women there has not arisen anyone greater" (11:11; Luke 7:28). The voice of one

crying in the wilderness was at last silenced. "And his disciples came and took away the body and buried it; and they went and reported to Jesus" (Matt. 14:12).

The place of John the Baptist's prison was anciently known as Machaerus, but the modern name is Mkaur. It is located in the mountain fastnesses with a deep ravine below, on the eastern shore of the Dead Sea, between Abarim and Pisgah, not far from the northern extreme of the sea. It is said that the rock-hewn dungeon was beneath the splendid banquet hall in which the nobility were entertained when the swordsman was sent to bring in the prisoner's head. Here in the same mountains in which Israel sought for the grave of her first prophet (Moses), the last prophet (John) was entombed.

Treacheries. It was now the thirty-ninth year of our chronology when Caius Caligula had been upon the imperial throne at Rome for two years. He soon discovered the real character of Herod Antipas. Ascertaining that the tetrarch was plotting with a Roman officer of the army named Sejanus, had been cooperating with the king of Parthia against the Roman Empire, and had laid in store arms for seventy thousand men of war, Caligula soon called Antipas to judgment. Meantime Herodias was most urgent that the tetrarch should go to Rome and make request that he might receive a crown as king. Moreover, Antipas was extremely jealous of his nephew Herod Agrippa I, who had already received a kingdom. Antipas had deeply offended Agrippa by insulting reflections on his condition of poverty before he had had royalty bestowed on him. Agrippa was on intimate terms with the emperor and kept him posted as to these movements of his uncle Antipas. At length Antipas unwillingly was constrained to go to Rome and request that the first will of his father might be granted him by the emperor. Herod Agrippa I immediately sent his freedman named Fortunatus to Rome with the necessary documents to prove his accusations against his uncle, and Agrippa himself followed in a few days to confront Antipas with the facts and proofs in person. Antipas was just having his first interview with the emperor when Fortunatus entered and handed the letters at once to the emperor. When Agrippa had also arrived, and all the accusations against Antipas were understood by Caligula, the emperor challenged Antipas to deny the charges preferred against him of treachery toward the imperial government, in alliance with Sejanus and with Artabanus, king of Parthia, and the secret storing up arms. The tetrarch could not deny these accusations and so confessed his guilt.

Antipas Deposed. Thereupon Caligula deprived Herod Antipas of his tetrarchy "and gave it by way of addition to Agrippa's kingdom," confiscated his money, and sent him and his wife into perpetual banishment in Lyons, Gaul (France), and eventually in Spain, where he died (*Ant.* 18.7.1-2; *Wars* 2.9.6). Dion Cassius also relates that "Herod the Palestinian, having given a certain occasion by reason of his brothers (nephew) was banished beyond the Alps, and his estates of the government confiscated to the state" (book 55, *Caesar Augustus,* 27).

Jesus and Antipas. It is now in place to consider the relationships of our Savior and this tetrarch during the week of the crucifixion, which occurred six years before Herod Antipas was deposed and exiled. From the time that this Herod had slain John the Baptist, this crime had haunted his conscience. When then he heard of the deeds done by Jesus, "he was greatly perplexed, because it was said by some that John had risen from the dead. . . . And Herod said, 'I myself had John beheaded; but who is this man about whom I hear such things?' " (Luke 9:7, 9). And he said, "This is John the Baptist; he has risen from the dead; and that is why miraculous powers are at work in him" (Matt. 14:2).

We find Herod Antipas at Jerusalem when Jesus was before Pilate on trial for His life. When Pilate understood that Jesus was from Galilee, the territory of Antipas, he sent him to Herod as belonging to his jurisdiction. "Now Herod was very glad when he saw Jesus; for he had wanted to see Him for a long time, because he had been hearing about Him and was hoping to see some sign performed by Him." Nevertheless, as Christ did not reply to his questions of curiosity, he was offended, and "Herod with his soldiers, after treating Him with contempt and mocking Him, dressed Him in a gorgeous robe and sent Him back to Pilate. Now Herod and Pilate became friends with one another that very day, for before they had been at enmity with each other" (Luke 23:6-12; cf. Acts 4:27).

Kingship of Antipas. Criticism has found difficulty in understanding how the evangelists mention that *"Archelaus was reigning* over Judea in place of his father Herod (the Great)" as if he were *a king,* whereas Archelaus was but an ethnarch, and his father ruled a *kingdom* (Matt. 2:22). So also Herod Antipas is repeatedly called *"a king"* in the first two gospels when his principality was merely a tetrarchy (14:1, 9; Mark 6:14, 22-27). Alford says, "Herod was not king properly, but only a tetrarch." Westcott states that "he was called king by courtesy." Whedon says that he was so called "in compliance with custom"; and Farrar, "It is only popularly that he is called king." The determining argument, however, is fatal to all these conjectural opinions and is based upon the *uses* of the word *king* at the time the evangelists employed it, and not in its *modern* restricted sense. We now apply the term absolutely and exclusively to *royalty,* but in the time of Augustus and afterward, it was applicable not only to a sovereign ruler but "in a general and lower sense applied equally to *a prince, ruler,*

viceroy, and the like" (Robinson's *Greek Dictionary of the New Testament,* on Basileus, and also Basileuō). The designation was applied "to a chief, a captain, a judge . . . *to a king's son, a prince, or anyone sharing in the government;* generally a lord, a master, a householder, *and after Augustus, to any great man"* (Liddell and Scott, *Greek Dictionary* [1883], on Basileus). Josephus (born A.D. 37), who lived in the time of the apostles, confirms this usage when he relates that Herod the Great altered his will, *"and therein made Antipas king,"* when in fact he was merely made tetrarch (*Wars* 1.32.7).

Her'od Phil'ip II (4 B.C.-A.D. 34), **Philip the Tetrarch.** *See also* Philippi. This Herod was also the son of Herod the Great and Cleopatra of Jerusalem. He should not be confused with a half-brother of the same name, who was the son of Mariamne the Boethusian, and known as Philip I. By his father's will Philip I was excluded from all government rights on account of the supposed treachery by his mother toward her husband (*Wars* 1.30.7). He married his niece Herodias, who afterward eloped with her husband's half-brother Herod Antipas. Philip I and Herodias had a daughter named Salome, who played a role in the death of John the Baptist. Philip II, the tetrarch, married this Salome.

Tetrarchy. With characteristic accuracy, Luke (3:1) refers to this "Philip" and is confirmed in all particulars by Josephus and contradicted in none. This Jewish historian gives us definitely the countries included in Philip's tetrarchy. He mentions (*Ant.* 17.11.4; cf. 17.8.1) how Herod the Great by will provided that his own kingdom should be divided among his three sons. Archelaus was to take half the territory, as has already been described, to be ruled as an ethnarch. The remaining half was to be divided into two parts, to be called tetrarchies, meaning each a fourth part, to be given to Philip II and Antipas: Philip's tetrarchy was to include Batanea, Trachonitis, Auranitis (i.e., Gaulonitis, and part of Jamia; Antipas's tetrarchy was to include Perea and Galilee. These regions were located in northeastern Palestine. There is in existence a coin struck by the authority of Philip II, in the reign of the Emperor Tiberius, which bears the following superscription:

Obverse: *Tiberios Sebastos Kaiser* ("Tiberius Augustus Caesar").

Reverse: *Philippou tet [rarches]* ("Of Philip Tetrarch").

Philip's subjects were mostly Syrians and Greeks. He had a peaceful rule for thirty-seven years.

Conduct. This tetrarch was altogether the best of all the Herods. He is described as "a person of moderation and quietness in the conduct of his life and government," whose consideration for his subjects was remarkable; When he traveled among them he was careful to have "his tribunal

. . . on which he sat in judgment, [follow] him in his progress; and when any one met him who wanted assistance, he made no delay, but had his tribunal set immediately, wheresoever he happened to be; and sat down upon it, and heard his complaint" (*Ant.* 18.4.6). Moreover, he left monuments of himself worthy of his name in improvements for his people. At Paneas, at the base of Mt. Hermon, in the N, at the principal source of the Jordan, he built a new city called Caesarea Philippi (*Ant.* 18.2.1; cf. Matt. 16:13). It is now a ruin. This city must be distinguished from Caesarea on the Mediterranean Sea. He also erected Bethsaida to the rank of a city, whose site was a little N of the Sea of Galilee on the upper Jordan, and he gave it the name Julias, after Julia, "Caesar's daughter" (*Ant.* 18.2.1; *Wars* 2.9.1).

Death. After a long rule distinguished for its moderation and equity, this worthy tetrarch died A.D. 34, which was "in the thirtieth year of the reign of Tiberius" (*Ant.* 18.4.6). He was greatly beloved by his people. He had married Salome, the daughter of Herodias, but they left no children. Upon his death his territory was annexed to the Roman province of Syria. "When he was carried to [the] monument which he had already erected for himself beforehand, he was buried with great pomp" (*Ant.* 18.4.6).

Philip and the Gospels. He is mentioned by Luke as "tetrarch of the region of Ituraea," which is the Gk. name for the country lying at the base of the Lebanon mountains (Luke 3:1). "When Jesus came into the district (Mark, Gk. *tas kōmas,* "the villages") of Caesarea Philippi, He began asking His disciples, saying, 'Who do people say that the Son of Man is. . . . But who do you say that I am?' And Simon Peter answered and said, 'Thou art the Christ, the Son of the living God.' And Jesus answered and said to him, 'Blessed are you, Simon Barjona, because flesh and blood did not reveal this to you, but My Father who is in heaven' " (Matt. 16:13-17; Mark 8:27-30). It was in this region that Jesus began to teach them that "the Son of Man must suffer many things, and be rejected by the elders and chief priests and scribes, and be killed, and be raised up on the third day" (Luke 9:22). "But they did not understand this statement, and they were afraid to ask Him" (Mark 9:32).

Thus the second generation of the Herodians known to the gospels passes out of history.

We come now to the third generation of the Herods.

Her'od Agrip'pa I (A.D. 37-44).

Princely Life. This Agrippa was the son of Bernice and Aristobulus, a son of Herod the Great, who killed him. He was born 10 B.C. and died A.D. 44. He was the child of two first cousins and was himself married to another first cousin, who again was married to an uncle! Josephus mentions him as "Agrippa" and "Agrippa the Great" (*Wars* 1.28.1; *Ant.* 17.2.2; 18.5.4). In the NT he

is called either by his surname "Herod" or "Herod the king" (Acts 12:1, 6, 11, 19-21). He was brought up and educated at Rome, as were most of the Herodian princes. Agrippa appears to have been a man of gracious manners, of kindly spirit, gifted with extraordinary powers of eloquence, and quite vain. In religion he was a zealous rather than a devout Jew, attentive to "tithe mint and dill and cummin," but neglectful of "the weightier provisions of the law: justice and mercy and faithfulness." He was keenly fond of popularity and possessed much personal magnetism (*Ant.* 19.6.1-2; 19.7.3).

Reverses. Agrippa and Caius (Gaius) Caligula, the heir apparent to the imperial throne, in early life became warm personal friends, a fact that afterward was greatly to the advantage of this prince, for out of this intimacy came some remarkable surprises and reverses of fortune to Agrippa. One day these friends were riding out together in a chariot, and Eutychus, a freedman, was their charioteer. In the course of conversation, Agrippa enthusiastically stretched out his hands and said confidingly to Caligula that he wished that old Tiberius would die, that Caius Caligula might assume the purple and the throne. The freedman, overhearing the remark, reported it to the emperor Tiberius, who at once peremptorily ordered Agrippa to be put in chains and then imprisoned. The order was executed, and wearing his robe of distinction, Agrippa was placed among the criminals of the state. This humiliation was endured, however, but six months, when Tiberius died, and Caligula at once became emperor (*Ant.* 18.6.5-6; *Wars* 2.9.5-6).

Kingship. A few days after the imperial funeral Agrippa was summoned to appear at the new emperor's palace—the palace of Caligula. Having shaved and changed his garment, he presented himself hopefully in the presence of the new emperor, his friend, who immediately proceeded to "put a diadem upon [Agrippa's] head, and appointed him to be king of the tetrarchy of [his uncle] Philip [and that of] Lysanius." He also "changed his iron chain for a gold one of equal weight," which he hung about his neck (*Ant.* 18.6.10). Afterward this golden chain was "hung up within the limits of the temple [at Jerusalem], over the treasury, that it might be a memorial of the severe fate he had lain under, . . . that it might be a demonstration how the greatest prosperity may have a fall, and that God sometimes raises what is fallen down: for this chain thus dedicated, afforded a document to all men, that King Agrippa had once been bound in a chain for a small cause, but recovered his former dignity once again; . . . and was advanced to be a more illustrious king than he was before" (*Ant.* 19.6.1). The Senate at Rome also gave him the honorary position of praetor.

Assumes Government. In the second year of Caligula's reign Agrippa requested leave of the emperor to return home to Palestine and take possession of his kingdom (*Ant.* 18.6.11). Accordingly he sailed on the Mediterranean, in the usual course, to Alexandria in Egypt. At this time the Jews and Greeks of the city were in unpleasant relations with each other. When the Greeks saw this Jewish king, accompanied by his bodyguard and making much use of gold and silver, they spitefully took occasion to mock him with the meanest insults. They even took a poor, naked, idiot boy named Carabas, who was the butt of the street boys, placed a crown of paper on his head, clothed him in mat cloth, gave him a stick for a scepter and the gamin of the city for a bodyguard, and thrust him out onto the public stage in mockery of the new king (see Philo of Alexandria *Against Flaccus* 5.8). But when Agrippa reached his subjects in Palestine the Jews were astonished to see him returning as a king, and he was received with apparent satisfaction.

Memorable Services. Having organized and established his kingdom in accordance with his promise on leaving the emperor at Rome, King Agrippa I returned to the imperial capital. It was about this time that Caligula developed unmistakable indications of insanity and, among other things, demanded that he should be universally deified and adored as a god and that all men should swear by his name. He filled his Jewish subjects with the utmost horror when he ordered Petronius, governor of Syria, to place a gilded statue of the emperor in the Holy of Holies of the Temple at Jerusalem to be worshiped, because when they had submitted to become subjects of the empire they were guaranteed all their own national and religious rights. A similar attempt at Alexandria had occasioned both tumults and massacres. A delegation composed of Jews, who were the principal men among them, was organized, with the eminent Philo at their head, to persuade Caligula to desist from this inexpressible wrong. But when they went to the emperor he refused them his presence and bade Philo, "Begone!" Petronius meantime marched with an army to Jerusalem. At Ptolemais "many ten thousands of Jews" flocked to petition the Syrian prefect not to compel them to "violate the law of their forefathers"; but that, if he persisted in carrying out the imperial order, to first kill them, and then do what he was resolved upon (*Ant.* 18.8.1-2). Petronius was touched with this loyalty to their faith and, dismissing the Jews, promised to send to Rome in their interests in this matter (18.8.3-6). Meantime Agrippa, who was at this time at Rome, furnished in honor of Caligula a magnificent banquet. When the emperor was full of wine, and Agrippa had toasted his health, Caligula generously proposed in return everything that might contribute to Agrippa's happiness and that so far as was in the emperor's power, he should be at his service. With admirable tact and address Agrippa declined to receive

anything on his own behalf, as he had already received so much; but, on behalf of his brethren at home, he said, "My petition is this, that thou wilt no longer think of the dedication of that statue which thou hast ordered to be set up in the Jewish temple by Petronius." Caligula thereupon "as a favour to Agrippa" rescinded the order (*Ant.* 18.8.7-8). Nevertheless, because Petronius so far disobeyed Caligula's orders as to make representations and so delay executing his orders, the emperor ordered the prefect to commit suicide (18.8.9); but the order was delayed at Rome, and soon Caligula died by the dagger of the assassin Chaerea, whom the emperor had outrageously insulted. This was in A.D. 41.

Enlarged Kingdom. Claudius now became emperor through the friendly offices of Herod Agrippa I, who with great diplomacy used his influence with the Senate favorably for this man. As a return for being elevated to the imperial succession in the house of the Caesars and the empire of the world, Claudius published edicts in favor of the Jews and greatly enlarged the dominions of Agrippa by adding Judea, Samaria, and Abilene, so that his realm was now almost as extensive as that of his grandfather King Herod the Great, lacking only Idumaea (*Ant.* 9.5.1; *Wars* 2.11.5). Evidence of the historicity of this account is furnished in a coin struck by Herod Agrippa I, at Caesarea. It reads:

Obverse: *Basileus megas Agrippa Philokaiser* ("Agrippa the Great, Lover of Caesar").

Reverse: *Kaisar ē Sebastō Aimeni* ("Caesar on Port Sebastus").

Sebaste is the standing Greek word for Augustus, the title assumed by several emperors. "Cumanus took one troop of horsemen, called the troop of Sebaste, out of Caesarea" (*Wars* 2.12.5).

Humiliations Imposed. Though having received royalty, with the added heritage of his grandfather's kingdom, Herod Agrippa was made to feel that his dominion was after all a mere dependency upon the Roman power that dominated the nations included in the Empire. Being of Idumaean origin, it is related that on one occasion, before his kingdom had been enlarged by Claudius, when the feast of Tabernacles (or Booths, NASB) was observed, the lesson from the law for the day was read: "You shall surely set a king over you whom the Lord your God chooses, one from among your countrymen . . . you may not put a foreigner over yourselves who is not your countryman" (Deut. 17:15). Remembering that he was of foreign stock and was so recognized by his brethren, Agrippa, from bitter anticipations, burst into tears before them all; but the people, sympathizing with him, exclaimed, "Fear not, Agrippa, thou art our brother!" For the law required also, "You shall not detest an Edomite, for he is your brother. . . . The sons of the third generation who are born to them may enter the assembly of the Lord" (Deut. 23:7-8). Agrippa thus was clearly entitled to this consideration; he was at least the third generation removed from the Idumaeans or Edomites.

Now Agrippa resided mostly at Jerusalem, and he began the building of impregnable walls to fortify the city (*Ant.* 19.7.2). But Marsus Vibius, prefect of Syria, ordered the constructions discontinued on the mere grounds of suspicion. The king, like his ancestors, was fond of pretentious display. He had once invited a number of petty kings contiguous to his own realm to be his guests and accept his hospitality at the city Tiberias, where royal spectacles were to be witnessed. Marsus Vibius came also from Syria. Agrippa and the five kings, thinking to do him honor, went forth in a chariot about seven furlongs to meet the prefect. But Marsus, being suspicious of the meaning of the hospitable popularity and display of the public games, offered a great affront to all concerned when he ordered the five kings to proceed at once and quietly to their respective homes (*Ant.* 19.8.1).

Christian Persecutions. Herod Agrippa I is known in the NT simply as "Herod." He was the only Herod who had royalty bestowed upon him and who governed all Palestine after the death of his grandfather Herod the Great, who died soon after the birth of Jesus. He is mentioned only in the book of Acts, where he is named twice in the same chapter in connection with two different events (chap. 12). Although usually a gracious man, he was exceedingly ambitious to please his Jewish subjects, and this passion led him to become a persecutor of the Christians in the little community at Jerusalem. The record reads: "Now about that time Herod the king laid hands on some who belonged to the church, in order to mistreat them. And he had James the brother of John put to death with a sword. And when he saw that it pleased the Jews, he proceeded to arrest Peter also," with a view of slaying him after the Passover was ended (Acts 12:1-3). But Peter was delivered at night by the intervention of an angel. Now this procedure was exactly in agreement with the Jewish Talmud in the Mishna, which reads thus: "The ordinance of putting to death by the sword is this, the man's head is cut off with a sword, as is accustomed to be done *by royal command*" (Lomby, *Com.,* ad loc.).

Death. Agrippa and his deputies and other dignitaries of the land assembled at Caesarea, at the seaside, to celebrate the games at a festival and to offer vows for the safety and prosperity of the emperor Claudius. Early in the morning of the second day of the celebration the king presented himself to the people clad in "a garment made wholly of silver, and of a texture truly wonderful." When the sun's rays touched his dress the reflections "shone out after a surprising [splendor]." Josephus says that the people exclaimed that "he was a god" and that "the king did neither

rebuke them nor reject their impious flattery" (19.8.2; cf. Acts 12:19-23). After five days the king "departed this life, being in the fifty-fourth year of his age, and in the seventh of his reign; for he reigned four years under Caius [Caligula] Caesar, three of them were over Philip's tetrarchy only, and on the fourth he had that of Herod [Antipas] added to it; and he reigned besides those, three years under the reign of Claudius Caesar" (*Ant.* 19.8.2).

Her'od Agrip'pa II (A.D. 50-70).

Identification. Much confusion and difficulty have been experienced in trying to identify these two historical personages—father and son—as they bear exactly the same name. Nevertheless, they are known in both profane and sacred history by different names. Outside of Scripture the elder is called Herod Agrippa I and the younger Herod Agrippa II. But in the NT the father is named either "Herod," as he is repeatedly called in the same chapter (Acts 12:6, 11, 19-21), or "Herod the king" (12:1); whereas the son, in contrast to the father, is called either "Agrippa" (25:22-23; 26:32) or "King Agrippa" (25:26; 26:27). True, both were kings and bore the same name, but they were not both rulers at the same time, and their kingdoms were different. So far as appears in Scripture, Herod Agrippa I was king of all Palestine proper during the period A.D. 41-44, whereas Herod Agrippa II was king of perhaps one-third of that country, lying to the N and NE, during the period A.D. 52-70, when his government was utterly destroyed by the Roman-Jewish war and the Jewish nation ceased to exist. As to scriptural incidents associated with each, it was Herod Agrippa I who beheaded James, the brother of John, and also imprisoned Peter at Jerusalem (12:1-3); but it was Herod Agrippa II who went to Caesarea, whom Paul called "King" or "King Agrippa" in his defense at Caesarea (26:2, 7, 13, 19, 26-27) and whom Luke calls either "Agrippa" or "King Agrippa" in narrating the same occasion (25:13, 22-24, 26; 26:28, 32).

Youth. When Herod Agrippa I died in A.D. 44, he left this son and three daughters, named Bernice, Mariamne, and Drusilla (*Ant.* 18.5.4; 19.9.1). Agrippa II, who was born A.D. 27, was only seventeen years old at his father's death and was resident at the imperial capital, receiving his education under the patronage of the emperor. "Now Agrippa, the son of the deceased, was at Rome, and brought up with Claudius Caesar" (*Ant.* 19.9.2). This emperor at first contemplated placing young Agrippa immediately upon his father's throne to rule all Palestine; but better counsel prevailing, he concluded that it would be "a dangerous experiment" for "so very young a man," who was without any experience, to undertake to govern so large a kingdom (*Ant.* 19.9.2). So Claudius made the country a Roman province, and "sent Cuspius Fadus to be procurator of Judea, and the entire kingdom" (*Ant.* 19.9.2; *Wars* 2.11.6).

Royalty. When his uncle, Herod king of Chalcis, died in A.D. 48, Agrippa was twenty-one. Claudius now appointed him to be governor of that vacant kingdom. At the same time he was made superintendent of the Jewish Temple at Jerusalem and manager of its treasury, with full power to remove the high priests from office at will, an authority that he frequently exercised, as did his uncle before him (*Ant.* 20.1.3; 20.8.11; 20.9.1, 4, 6). These frequent changes of the high priesthood for political reasons made Herod Agrippa II quite unpopular with the Jews.

It is not clear whether royalty was conferred upon this Agrippa when he was appointed at Chalcis over his uncle's vacant kingdom, but it is quite certain he had this distinction at least when he was transferred to another and greater kingdom. His royal residence was finally established at Caesarea Philippi, at the southwestern base of Mt. Hermon, which is at the principal source of the Jordan River.

Kingdom. Josephus remarks: "Now after the death of Herod, king of Chalcis, Claudius set Agrippa, the son of Agrippa, over his uncle's kingdom, while Cumanus took upon him the office of procurator of the rest [of the territory], which was a Roman province" (*Wars* 2.12.1). He also mentions that about the year 53, "when [Claudius] had completed the twelfth year of his reign, he bestowed upon Agrippa [II the two former tetrarchies of Philip and Lysanius]; but took from him Chalcis, when he had been governor thereof four years" (*Ant.* 20.7.1; *Wars* 2.12.1), "and removed [him] into a greater kingdom" (*Wars* 2.12.8). His realm was now situated in the N and NE of Palestine, but the regions known as Peraea, Judea, Samaria, and Galilee, which belonged to the kingdom of his father, were never included in the kingdom of King Herod Agrippa II. A coin exists, struck by the authority of the second Herod, at Caesarea Philippi, the capital of his new kingdom, in the imperial reign of Nero, which reads thus:

Obverse: "Nero Caesar."

Reverse: "By King Agrippa, Neronias."

That is, the city Caesarea Philippi is renamed "Neronias" in honor of Nero, the reigning emperor at that time.

End. Herod Agrippa II, unlike his father, was never popular with his subjects. It appears to have been the purpose of the procurator, Florus, to goad the Jews into revolt and war with the whole Roman Empire by his own official and infamous conduct toward those people. The "multitude of Jews . . . addressed themselves to the king [Agrippa II] and to the high priests, and desired they might have leave to send ambassadors to Nero against Florus" (*Wars* 2.16.3). But Agrippa, in a public address, endeavored to dissuade the Jews from their warlike purpose, an appeal that ended in tears and greatly moved the impassioned people addressed. But when Agrippa saw that the inevitable had come, he joined his forces with those of the Romans and made war upon his abused and aggrieved subjects (*Wars* 2.16.4–2.17.4). In a battle before Gamala he was wounded in the elbow by a stone but continued in command of his own troops until the Romans had destroyed both his kingdom and the Jewish commonwealth. The war closed in the capture of Jerusalem in the year 70. Agrippa then retired to Rome, where at length he died at the age of seventy-three, A.D. 100, and in the third year of the reign of the emperor Trajan.

Josephus makes special note that Titus, the Roman general, affixed his signature to the history of the Roman-Jewish war, as written by himself, and authenticated its statements as being historical, and, moreover, when he was emperor, ordered the publication of his books; and that Josephus then had in his possession sundry letters from Herod Agrippa II attesting the truth of his historical narrative as one who was an eyewitness of the facts stated therein (*Life* 65).

Princesses of the House of the Herods. The Herodian princesses were not themselves Jewish rulers but were married to those who were. They belonged to the royal family by birth. Though there were others, Herodias, Bernice, and Drusilla are the only Herodian princesses mentioned in the NT.

Hero'dias (he-rō'di-as; feminine of Herod). The daughter of Aristobulus—one of the sons of Mariamne and Herod the Great—and sister of Herod Agrippa I. *See* above, under Herod Antipas: John and Antipas.

Berni'ce (ber-nî'se). Bernice was the eldest daughter of Agrippa I, by his wife Cypros, and the sister of Herod Agrippa II, Mariamne, and Drusilla. She was espoused to Marcus, the son of Alexander, and upon his death was married to her uncle Herod, king of Chalcis, by whom she had two sons (Josephus *Ant.* 18.5.4; 19.5.1). After the death of Herod she lived for some time with her brother, Agrippa II, probably in an incestuous relationship. She was afterward married to Polemon, King of Cilicia, but soon deserted him and returned to her brother. With him she visited Festus on his appointment as procurator of Judea, when Paul defended himself before them all (Acts 25:13, 23; 26:30). She afterward became the mistress of Vespasian and his son Titus.

Drusil'la. Herod Agrippa I left three daughters, named Bernice, Mariamne, and Drusilla, in that order (*Ant.* 18.5.4). When the father died in A.D. 44, Drusilla was only six years old. As she grew into womanhood she became a celebrated beauty and was the envy of even her sister Bernice.

Being a Jewess of a family of distinction, she accepted in marriage Azizus, king of Edessa (Emesa), on the express condition that he would conform to the required ceremony of becoming a Jew, but when "Felix was procurator of Judea, he saw this Drusilla, and fell in love with her; for she did indeed excel all other women in beauty." Felix sent a Jew "to persuade her to forsake her present husband, and marry him; and, [he] promised, that if she would not refuse him, he would make her a happy woman." She accepted this offer and was "prevailed upon to transgress the laws of her forefathers, and to marry Felix; and when he had a son by her, he named him Agrippa" (*Ant.* 20.7.1-2). This son and mother died in the eruption of Mt. Vesuvius in A.D. 79.

Claudius Felix was a man of low origin and instinct. He "had been a slave [in Rome], in the vilest of all positions, at the vilest of all epochs, in the vilest of all cities" (Farrar). Tacitus says that as a procurator "Antonius Felix exercised the prerogatives of a king, with the spirit of a slave, rioting in cruelty and licentiousness"; a man who "supposed he might perpetrate with impunity every kind of villainy" (*Annals* 12.54). Suetonius remarks that "in consequence of his elevation [to be procurator of Judea], he became the husband of three queens" (*Claudius* 28).

During the procuratorship, "Felix arrived with Drusilla, his wife who was a Jewess, and sent for Paul, and heard him speak about faith in Christ Jesus. And as he was discussing righteousness, self-control, and the judgment to come, Felix became frightened and said, 'Go away for the present, and when I find time, I will summon you.'" He hoped that bribe money would be given him to release Paul and accordingly sent for him often, but when he was to be succeeded by the honorable Porcius Festus, "Felix left Paul imprisoned" to please the Jews (Acts 24:24-27). Thus closed the scene and the procuratorship of Felix at Caesarea.   H.F.V.

BIBLIOGRAPHY: F. W. Farrar, *The Herods* (1898); A. H. M. Jones, *The Herods of Judea* (1938); S. Perowne, *Light and Times of Herod the Great* (1956); id., *The Later Herods* (1958); F. F. Bruce, *Annual of Leeds University Oriental Society* 5 (1963-65): 6-23; S. Sandmel, *Herod: Profile of a Tyrant* (1967); M. Grant, *Herod the Great* (1971); H. W. Hoehner, *Herod Antipas* (1972); M. Stern, *The Jewish People in the First Century,* ed. S. Safari and M. Stern (1974), 1:216-307; R. T. France, *Novum Testamentum* 21 (1979): 98-100.

HERO'DIANS (he-rō'di-anz). A party among the Jews of the apostolic age, and keenly opposed to Jesus (Matt. 22:16; Mark 3:6; 12:13); but of which no explicit information is given by any of the evangelists. The party was probably formed under Herod the Great and appears to have held that it was right to pay homage to a sovereign who might be able to bring the friendship of Rome and other advantages, but who had personally no title to reign by law and by religion. On this question they differed from the Pharisees (Matt. 22:16-17), although they joined forces with them in disguised opposition, or in open union against Jesus, in whom they saw a common enemy. The

Herodians were obviously something more than a political party and something less than a religious sect.

BIBLIOGRAPHY: B. W. Bacon, *Journal of Biblical Literature* 39 (1920): 102-12; H. H. Rowley, *Journal of Theological Studies* 41 (1940): 14-27; C. Daniel, *Revue Biblique* 6 (1967): 31-55; 261-77; id., *Revue Biblique* 7 (1969): 45-79; id., *Revue Biblique* 7 (1970): 397-402; H. W. Hoehner, *Herod Antipas* (1972), pp. 331-42; W. J. Bennett, *Novum Testamentum* 17 (1975): 9-14.

HERO'DIAS. See Herod: Herod Antipas; Princesses of the House of the Herods.

BIBLIOGRAPHY: Josephus, *Ant.* 18.5.1; 18.7.1-2; id., *Wars* 9.6; E. Schürer, *History of the Jewish People in the Time of Jesus,* ed. N. N. Glatzer (1961); 1:167-76, 355-57; J. D. M. Derrett, *Biblische Zeitschrift* 9 (1965): 49-59, 233-46.

HERO'DION (he-rō'di-on; derived from "Herod"). A Christian at Rome to whom Paul sent a salutation as his kinsman (Rom. 16:11).

HERON. See Animal Kingdom.

HE'SED. The father of one of Solomon's deputies, *Ben-hesed* (which see).

HESH'BON (hesh'bon; "reckoning"). Originally a Moabite town, but when the Israelites arrived from Egypt it was ruled over by Sihon, called both "king of the Amorites" and "king of Heshbon." It was taken by Moses (Josh. 13:21, 26) and became a Levitical city (21:39; 1 Chron. 6:81) in the tribe of Reuben (Num. 32:37; Josh. 13:17), but being on the border of Gad, is sometimes assigned to the latter (Josh. 21:39; 1 Chron. 6:81). Heshbon, now Hesbân, is twenty miles E of Jordan and four thousand feet above that stream as it enters the Dead Sea. It is the site of an excellent spring that made it an extremely desirable location. Its extensive ruins, particularly from the Roman period, are still visible.

Siegfried Horn of Andrews University excavated at Heshbon in 1968 and 1971, and Lawrence Geraty (also of Andrews) worked there in 1974 and 1976. A cut through part of the tell revealed that it had an occupational history extending from the twelfth century B.C. to the fourteenth century A.D., and excavations do not support existence of a town on the site in the days of Sihon. In spite of some searching in the area, no other candidate for the Heshbon of Sihon has yet been found.

Figurative. In Song of Sol. 7:4 the eyes of the Shulammite are likened to "the pools in Heshbon, by the gate of Bath-rabbim." The bright pools in the stream that runs beneath Hesbân on the W are probably intended (Harper).   H.F.V.

BIBLIOGRAPHY: M. Avi-Yonah, ed. *Encyclopedia of Archaeological Excavations in the Holy Land* (1976), 2:510-14; R. S. Boraas and L. T. Geraty, *Archaeology* 32 (1979): 10-20.

HESH'MON (hesh'mon). A town in the S of Judah (Josh. 15:27), perhaps the same as Azmon (v. 4).

HES'LI (hes'li). Son of Naggai and father of Nahum of the maternal ancestry of Christ after the Exile (Luke 3:25; "Esli," KJV and NIV). He is probably the same as *Elioenai* (which see), the son of Neariah and father of Johanan (1 Chron. 3:23-24).

HETH (heth). The forefather of the nation of the *Hittites* (which see) called "sons of Heth" (Gen. 23:3, 5, 7, 10, 16, 18, 20; 25:10; 49:32). Once we hear of the "daughters of Heth" (27:46). In the genealogical tables of 10:15-18 and 1 Chron. 1:13-16 Heth is named as a son of Canaan, younger than Sidon, the firstborn, but preceding the Jesbusite, Amorite, and other Canaanite families. The Hittites were, therefore, a Hamitic race. The NIV renders all references to the "sons of Heth" as "the Hittites."

HETH (ח) (hāth). The eighth letter of the Hebrew alphabet, cf. Ps. 119:57-64.

HETH'LON (heth'lon). The name of a place on the northern border of Palestine (Ezek. 47:15; 48:1). In all probability the "way of Hethlon" is the pass of the northern end of Lebanon and is thus identical with "Lebo-hamath," i.e., "the entrance of Hamath" in Num. 34:8, KJV, marg. It may, however, be identified with Heitela, NE of Tripoli in Syria.

HEWING. The Gibeonites, having deceived Joshua, were sentenced to serve as "hewers of wood and drawers of water for the whole congregation" (Josh. 9:21), a service that was performed by the lowest class of the people (Deut. 29:11). In 1 Kings 5:15 it is recorded that Solomon had "80,000 hewers of stone in the mountains." The NIV refers to them as "stonecutters."

HEZ'EKI. *See* Hizki.

HEZEKIAH (hez-i-kī'a). The name of a king (which see) of Judah and of two other persons.

1. An ancestor of Zephaniah the prophet (Zeph. 1:1), 630 B.C. rendered "Hizkiah" in KJV.

2. One of those who sealed the covenant with Ezra and Nehemiah (Neh. 10:17; "Hizkijah," KJV). Some believe that the name should be taken with that preceding and it should be read as "Ater-Hezekiah," a name given (KJV) in the lists of those who returned from Babylon with Zerubbabel (cf. Ezra 2:16; Neh. 7:21; Smith, s.v.).

HEZEKIAH, KING (hez-i-kī'a; "Jehovah is strength").

The twelfth sovereign (excluding Athaliah), of the separate kingdom of Judah. His co-regency lasted from 728 to 715 B.C. and his sole regency from 715 to 686 B.C. He was the son of Ahaz and Abi of Abijah, born 736 B.C. (2 Kings 18:1-2; 2 Chron. 29:1).

Reformer. As a godly king his first act was to purge, repair, and reopen the Temple, which had been neglected and polluted during the idolatrous reign of his weak father, Ahaz. His task consisted of rooting out Canaanite fertility cults and other pagan contaminations. Hezekiah's reformation was so thorough that he did not even spare "the high places." These centers of contaminated worship on hilltops "he removed . . . and broke down the sacred pillars and cut down the asherah" (2 Kings 18:3-7; 2 Chron. 29). A still more decisive act was the destruction of the bronze serpent of Moses (cf. Num. 21:9), which had become an idolatrous object. His great reformation was followed by the celebration of the Passover (chap. 30), to which not only all Judah was summoned but also the remnant of the ten tribes.

Warrior.

War with Philistines. Early in his reign (c. 714 B.C.) Hezekiah assumed an aggressive war against the Philistines. He not only retook the cities that his father had forfeited (2 Chron. 28:18-19) but even dispossessed the Philistines of their own cities except Gaza (2 Kings 18:8) and Gath (Josephus *Ant.* 9.13.3). Accordingly, he came to rule as a sort of feudal overlord of the Philistine cities, and Ashdod under its Greek prince was induced to lead them in the revolt against Assyria.

Early Relations with Assyria. Hezekiah inherited the Assyrian menace from his father, who mortgaged the Judean kingdom to "the giant of the Semites." From 715 B.C., the beginning of his own independent rule, Hezekiah faced a series of Assyrian invasions that dominated his reign. As a wise and godly ruler, he made every attempt to build up his country that he might eventually throw off the Assyrian yoke his father had saddled upon it by alliance (2 Kings 16:7-9). The purport of his reform was to fortify the moral and spiritual defenses of his country. He also built up the national economy and the military. Agriculture and trade expanded by the establishment of warehouses and stock yards at strategic places (2 Chron. 32:27-29). A national system of defenses was inaugurated (32:5-7), and Jerusalem was assured an adequate water supply in the event of siege (32:30). Ample warning was granted Judah of the Assyrian peril. In Hezekiah's fourth co-regnal year (724 B.C.)—undoubtedly his regency is meant—Shalmaneser V had begun, and by the beginning of 721 B.C. Sargon II had completed, the siege of Samaria (2 Kings 18:9-11). In the ensuing interval the Assyrian menace moved ever nearer. In 711 B.C. Sargon claimed the credit of a campaign against Ashdod. The Assyrian record (Isa. 20:1) clearly outlines that it was the Assyrian commander-in-chief "tartan" (Assyrian *turtannu*, "second in rank") who actually conducted the campaign. *See* W. F. Albright, *O.T. Commentary*, Philadelphia (1948), p. 161.

Sennacherib and Hezekiah. Early in the reign of Sennacherib, Hezekiah revolted against Assyria. The Assyrian preoccupation in lower Mesopotamia with the irrepressible Chaldeans of the sea lands under Merodach-baladan, king of Babylon, coupled with Hezekiah's consciousness of his own prosperity, were prime factors in the revolt. It was the same Merodach-baladan who, pretending to congratulate Hezekiah upon his recovery from a serious illness, tried with lavish gifts to win over Judah into a coalition that was being secretly formed against Assyria (Isa. 39:1-8). This Merodach-baladan was twice ruler of Babylon (722-710 B.C., 703-702 B.C.), and his embassy to Judah was apparently dispatched in the latter part of the earlier period of his reign. Hezekiah manifested egotistical folly in showing Merodach-baladan's emissaries all his treasures. Isaiah, foreseeing the future strengthening of the Chaldeans, severely rebuked Hezekiah for his foolishness. In 701 B.C. the Assyrian emperor launched his great western campaign as a punitive measure against Hezekiah and other Palestinian-Syrian rebels. This important campaign is not only vividly described in the biblical record but is also contained in the annals of Sennacherib, which were recorded on clay cylinders, or prisms. The edition of these annals is found on the so-called Taylor Prism of the British Museum, with a copy on a prism of the Oriental Institute of the University of Chicago. In detail Sennacherib depicts his third campaign, which included the siege of Jerusalem. After the subjugation of Philistine coastal towns and Philistine strongholds, together with Moabite, Edomite, and other cities, he refers to a victorious battle near Altaku (Eltekeh), where Palestinian forces were reinforced by Egyptian bowmen and chariotry. Then Sennacherib makes a lengthy reference to his attack on Hezekiah's realm. "As for Hezekiah, the Jew, who did not submit to me, all 46 of his strong walled cities as well as the small cities in their neighborhood . . . I besieged and took. 200,150 people, great and small, male and female, horses, mules, asses, camels, cattle and sheep without number I brought away from them and counted as spoil. Himself, like a caged bird, I shut up in Jerusalem, his royal city. Earth works I threw up against him—the one coming out of his city gate I turned back to his misery. The cities of his which I had despoiled I cut off from his land and to Mitinti, king of Ashdod, Padi, king of Ekron, and Sili-bel, king of Gaza, I gave them." Sennacherib goes on to tell that the "terrifying splendor" of his majesty overcame Hezekiah. This Assyrian monarch boasts placing Hezekiah under a large tribute, carrying away gems, antimony, jewels, couches of ivory, elephant hides, maple, boxwood, and all kinds of valuable treasures as well as his daughters, his harem, and his musicians. The account of Sennacherib's western campaign recorded on the Taylor Prism is evidently the same as that described in 2 Kings 18:13–19:37; 2 Chron. 32:1-12; and Isa.

36:1–37:37. There are numerous striking points of agreement, as well as some difficulties. For example, when Sennacherib invaded Palestine he is said to have captured many of the fortified Judean cities (2 Kings 18:13) and to have threatened Jerusalem with a great army dispatched from Lachish under "Tartan and Rab-saris and Rabshakeh" (v. 17). A sculpture recovered at Nineveh shows Sennacherib sitting upon his chair throne at Lachish and receiving rich spoils while prisoners are tortured. These details fit well into the biblical account. Moreover, it is now known from the monuments that Tartan (Assyrian *turtannu*, "second in rank"), Rabshakeh (Assyrian *rab-shaqu*, "chief officer"), and Rab-saris (Assyrian *rabu-sha-reshi*, originally "chief eunuch") were titles of high Assyrian officials and not personal names at all (Millar Burrows, *What Mean These Stones?* New Haven [1941], p. 43f.). Hezekiah's tribute is placed at thirty talents of gold in both sources but at only three hundred talents of silver in 18:14, as compared with eight hundred that the Assyrian king mentions. E. Schrader reconciles the two differences on the basis of the Babylonian light and Palestinian heavy talent, whereas George Barton suggests a textual corruption (*Archaeology and the Bible,* 7th ed. [1937], p. 473).

Sickness and Death. The Assyrians, despite their boasts, were not able to take Jerusalem. Toward the end of his reign Hezekiah became dangerously ill (2 Kings 20:1; 2 Chron. 32:24; Isa. 38:1). His kingdom was still in a perilous state from the Assyrian menace. Having no heir at the time, Hezekiah prayed that his life might be spared. He was granted a fifteen-year extension of life and died a natural death peacefully (686 B.C.).

Builder.

Siloam Tunnel. Hezekiah is famous for the steps he took to supply fresh water within the city walls of Jerusalem. "He made the pool and the conduit, and brought water into the city" (2 Kings 20:20). In Chronicles it is appended that "it was Hezekiah who stopped the upper outlet of the waters of Gihon and directed them to the west side of the city of David" (2 Chron. 32:30). The intermittent spring of Gihon, Jerusalem's most ancient water supply, was located below the steep eastern hill (Ophel) in the deep Kidron Valley. It was thus exposed to enemy attack. Hezekiah completely covered over this ancient spring and diverted it through a conduit 1,777 feet long and hewn out of solid rock into a reservoir within the city walls. Tunnels at Megiddo and Gezer are similar to this amazing engineering feat of Hezekiah's workmen.

Siloam Reservoir. In addition to the tunnel, Hezekiah built a larger reservoir, called the Pool of Siloam. The pool measures about 20 × 30 feet. In Jesus' day the blind man who was healed was

The Pool of Siloam

directed to go and wash in this pool (John 9:7-11).

The Siloam Inscription. Hezekiah's tunnel was made famous by its remarkable inscription, discovered accidentaly in 1880 by a boy wading in the pool. The six-line memorial, beautifully cut on the wall of the conduit in classical Heb. characters about nineteen feet from the Siloam end of the aqueduct, has paleographic value on a par with the Moabite Stone. The inscription is translated: "The boring through is completed. Now this is the story of the boring through. While the workmen were still lifting pick to pick each toward his neighbor and while three cubits remained to be cut through, each heard the voice of the other who called his neighbor, since there was a crevice in the rock on the right side. And on the day of the boring through the stone cutters struck, each to meet his fellow pick to pick; and there flowed the waters to the pool for 1200 cubits and 100 cubits was the height of the rock above the heads of the stone cutters."

BIBLIOGRAPHY: J. Finegan, *Light from the Ancient Past* (1946), pp. 170-82; K. A. Kitchen, *Ancient Orient and Old Testament* (1966), pp. 82-84; J. B. Pritchard, ed., *Ancient Near Eastern Texts* (1969), pp. 287-88; E. R. Thiele, *Mysterious Numbers of the Hebrew Kings* (1983), pp. 35-38, 120, 135-36, 168-69, 174-77.

HE'ZION (he'zi-on; "vision"). The father of Tabrimmon and grandfather of Ben-hadad I, to whom Asa sent silver and gold from the sacred treasury to secure his aid against Baasha (1 Kings 15:18), before 915 B.C. In the absence of all information, the natural suggestion is that he is the same person as Rezon, the contemporary of Solomon (11:23). The two names are similar in Heb. and even more so in the versions (Smith).

HE'ZIR (he'zir; "swine, boar").

1. The head of the seventeenth course of priests as established by David (1 Chron. 24:15), after 1000 B.C.
2. One of the heads of the people who sealed the solemn covenant with Nehemiah (Neh. 10:20), 445 B.C.

HEZ'RO (hez'rō). One of David's elite heroes known as "the thirty" (2 Sam. 23:35; 1 Chron. 11:37). He was a Carmelite, i.e., a native of the town of Carmel in the mountains of Judah. *See* Carmel.

HEZ'RON (hez'ron).

1. The third son of Reuben (Gen. 46:9; Ex. 6:14; 1 Chron. 4:1; 5:3). His descendants were called *Hezronites* (Num. 26:6).
2. The elder of the two sons of Perez and grandson of Judah (Gen. 46:12; Ruth 4:18-19; 1 Chron. 2:5, 9, 18, 21, 24-25; cf. Matt. 1:3; Luke 3:3, where the KJV renders "Esrom," and the NASB and NIV, "Hezron").
3. A place on the southern boundary of Judah, W of Kadesh-barnea (Josh. 15:3, 25). In the latter passage it is called Kerioth-hezron and is identified with *Hazor* (which see).

HID'DAI (hid'ay). One of the "thirty" heroes of David, "of the brooks of Gaash" (2 Sam. 23:30). In 1 Chron. 11:32 he is given as *Hurai* (which see).

HID'DEKEL (hid'e-kel; Heb. *Hiddekel;* Sumerian, *Igna;* Babylonian, *Idigla, Diglat;* Old Persian, *Tigra;* Gk. Tigris). The Hiddekel is thus the ancient name of the Tigris (Gen. 2:14, see marg.; Dan. 10:4, marg.), a name used by the NIV. Modern Arabs still call it Diglah. The Pishon and the Gihon mentioned in connection with the rivers of Eden (Gen. 2:10-14) are presumably canals, called rivers in Babylonia, which connected the Tigris and Euphrates as ancient river beds. Biblical notices thus place the Garden of Eden somewhere in the Tigris-Euphrates country, evidently in the easternmost third of Breasted's "Fertile Crescent." The Tigris has its chief source in central Armenia, originating on the southern slope of the Anti-Taurus. Two eastern sources rise out of Lake Van. As the river flows ESE through the Kurdistan Mountains, it is gradually augmented by various tributaries such as the Upper and Lower Zab and the Dyalah. In ancient times the Tigris entered separately into the Persian Gulf; now it joins the Euphrates and mingles with its waters for more than one hundred miles in the Shatt al-Arab before entering the Persian Gulf. The entire length of the Tigris to the junction of the Euphrates is 1,146 miles and is only slightly more than half the length of the latter stream. On the banks of the Tigris were located Nineveh and the ancient Assyrian city of Ashur.

HI'EL (hi'el; perhaps "God liveth"). A native of Bethel, who rebuilt Jericho in the reign of Ahab

(1 Kings 16:34), and in whom was fulfilled the curse pronounced by Joshua (Josh. 6:26), after 875 B.C.

HIERAP'OLIS (hē-er-ap'o-lis; city of the mythical Amazon queen Hiera). This important center of Christian influence was situated near Colossae and Laodicea in the Lycus River valley of Phrygia. It is referred to only in Col. 4:13 (cf. Acts 19:10, marg.). Paul evidently did not preach there. Other of the early Christians did, possibly Philip the Evangelist and John. The hot baths of Hierapolis, noted for their medicinal benefits, drew patrons of the Plutonium ("Entrance to Hades"). The city was a wealthy dyeing center. It was a cosmopolitan city with a considerable Jewish population. In 1887 Karl Humann led a German archaeological team in preliminary excavations at Hierapolis. Italian archaeologists under the supervision of Paolo Verzone worked at the site in 1957, 1958, 1961, and 1962. The main street, more than a mile long, was built during the reign of Domitian near the end of the first century A.D. An arch of Domitian and a Byzantine gate also stand on that section of roadway. N of town may be seen ruins of a second century bath converted into a Christian church in the fifth century. Beyond that sprawls a necropolis with tombs dating from Hellenistic to Christian times. In the south end of town stand a greater bath complex dating from the second century A.D., a well-preserved theater from the same century, a temple of Apollo of the third century, and a Christian basilica of the sixth century. From dates indicated, it is evident that what has been excavated so far does not date to NT times.   H.F.V.

BIBLIOGRAPHY: S. E. Johnson, *Biblical Archaeologist* 13 (1950), 12-17; W. M. Ramsay, *The Historical Geography of Asia Minor* (1972), pp. 15, 49, 73, 83-84, 91, 130-35; G. L. Borchert, *International Standard Bible Encyclopedia* (1982) 2:707-8.

HI'EROGLYPH'ICS (hī'er-o-glif'iks; from Gk. *hieros*, "sacred," and *gluphein*, to "carve"). Pictures of such objects as an animal, tree, bird, etc., representing a word, syllable, or single sound and intended to convey a meaning. The name was first applied to the engraved marks and symbols found on the monuments and other records of ancient Egypt. The key to these inscriptions was the Rosetta Stone, which Champollion successfully deciphered. The Egyptian hieroglyphics were generally engraved but in old temples are found in high relief. They are generally read from right to left either vertically or horizontally. They ceased to be written about A.D. 300. *See* Writing.

HIGGAI'ON (hi-gī'yon). Possibly a musical note. It is transliterated in Ps. 9:16; translated "resounding music" in 92:3 and "meditation" in 19:14.

HIGHEST (Heb. *'elyôn*, "elevated"; Gk. *hupsistos*). A title ascribed to Jehovah (Ps. 18:13; 87:5;

The Rosetta Stone

KJV only; NASB and NIV, "Most High") and, in the NT, to our Savior as being of the highest region, i.e., *heaven* (Matt. 21:9; Mark 11:10; Luke 2:14; etc.). *See also* Most High.

HIGH PLACE (from Canaanite *bāmâ*, plural, *bāmôt*, "ridge"; Heb. "elevation of land"). Localities chosen as places of worship of God or idols. The high places were features of Canaanite religion, and the conquering Israelites were commanded to destroy them when they entered Canaan (Num. 33:52; Deut. 33:29). Israel came in contact with the high places of the Moabites before they entered the land (Num. 21:28; 22:41). Being defiled by Canaanite fertility cults and other paganistic pollutions, the high places were often connected with licentiousness (Hos. 4:11-14) and immorality (Jer. 3:2). One of the best known high places is the "Conway High Place" at Petra. (*See* W. F. Albright, *The Archaeology of Palestine*, pp. 161-65.) The Ugaritic tablets of the late fifteenth century B.C. from Ras Shamra show that animals were sacrificed in the high places of Baal in North Syria. Always contiguous to the rock altar was a sacred pillar, *maṣṣēbâ*, a sacred pole having phallic associations capped with a symbol of the *'ashērâ*, evidently denoting female fertility. Male prostitutes, *qedēshîm*, and sacred courtesans, *qedēshôt* (1 Kings 14:23-24; 2 Kings 23:7), maintained chambers for cultic prostitution in honor of the heathen deity. At Gezer firstborn babies were slain and their bodies placed in jars near the high place (cf. Isa. 57:5). Early shrines indicate that the elevation was intended to display impressiveness. Babylonians devised artificial hills called ziggurats. The Greeks loved their lofty Mt. Olympus and their Acropolis. The worship of Jehovah, contrary to the law of Moses, which specified one altar for all Israel, was often conducted on high places. The Mosaic prescription was a safeguard to protect the people from idolatrous associations and corruption. The worship of the God of Israel at other altars was allowable only in times of great stringency, as after the fall of Shiloh, when the Temple had not yet been erected (1 Kings 3:2-4; 2 Chron. 1:3). High places were legitimate also in the Northern Kingdom, when access to the Jerusalem Temple was no longer possible. After Solomon, who grievously sinned in erecting high places for his heathen wives (1 Kings 11:1-8), this heathenistic institution prevailed among many kings of the Davidic line. Jehoram, Jehoshaphat's son, made high places in the mountains of Judah (2 Chron. 21:11), as did Ahaz. Hezekiah broke them down (2 Kings 18:4, 22); Manasseh, in his idolatrous orgy, re-erected them (21:3). They were again destroyed by Josiah (23:5, 8, 13). The prophets denounced the high places (Ezek. 6:3). Emphasis was placed on the fact that Zion was the place to worship (Isa. 2:2-3; 8:18; Joel 2:1; 3:17; Amos 1:2; Micah 4:1-2).   M.F.U.

BIBLIOGRAPHY: W. F. Albright, *Archaeology and the Religion of Israel* (1953), pp. 103-7; M. Dothan, *Israel Exploration Journal* 6 (1956): 14-25; W. F. Albright, *Supplements to Vetus Testamentum* 4 (1957): 242-58; S. Iwry, *Journal of Biblical Literature* 76 (1957): 225-32; P. H. Vaughan, *The Meaning of 'Bama' in the Old Testament* (1974).

HIGH PRIEST. *See* Priest, High.

HIGHWAY (usually Heb. $m^e sillâ$). An embanked road or raised causeway. *See* Roads.

HI'LEN (hi'len; 1 Chron. 6:58). *See* Holon.

HILKI'AH (hil-kī'a; *portion of Jehovah*).

1. The father of Eliakim, who was overseer of the household in the time of Hezekiah (2 Kings 18:18, 26, 37; Isa. 22:20; 36:3, 22), 715 B.C.

2. High priest in the reign of Josiah. According to the genealogy in 1 Chron. 6:13 (*see* Neh. 11:11) he was son of Shallum and, from Ezra 7:1, apparently the ancestor of Ezra the scribe. His high priesthood was rendered particularly illustrious by the great reformation effected under it by King Josiah (2 Kings 23:4; 24; 2 Chron. 34:9, 14-22), by the solemn Passover kept at Jerusalem in the eighteenth year of the king's reign (35:1-19), and, above all, by the discovery that he made in the house of the Lord of a book called "the book of the law" (2 Kings 22:8) and "the book of the covenant" (23:2), 639 B.C. The contents of this book are unknown.

3. A Merarite Levite, the son of Amzi and father of Amaziah (1 Chron. 6:45).

4. The second son of Hosah, a Merarite, ap-

pointed by David as gatekeeper of the Tabernacle (1 Chron. 26:11), about 995 B.C.

5. One of those who stood at the right hand of Ezra while he read the law to the people (Neh. 8:4), about 445 B.C.

6. One of the chief priests who returned from Babylon with Zerubbabel and Jeshua (Neh. 12:7). His son, Hashabiah, is mentioned in v. 21, 536 B.C.

7. A priest of Anathoth and father of the prophet Jeremiah (Jer. 1:1), before 626 B.C.

8. Father of Gemariah, who, with Elasah, was sent by Zedekiah with a message to the captives at Babylon (Jer. 29:3), before 599 B.C.

HILL. The rendering of several words in the original.

1. "Hill" (Heb. *gib'â;* "high"), from a root that seems to indicate curvature or humpishness, peculiarly applicable to the rounded hills of Palestine (Ex. 17:9; 1 Sam. 7:1; etc.).

2. "Mountain" (Heb. *har*). Our translators have also employed the English word "hill" for the very different term *har*, which has a much more extended sense than *gib'â*, meaning a whole district rather than an individual eminence, and to which our word *mountain* answers with tolerable accuracy. For instance, the "hill country" of Deut. 1:7; Josh. 9:1; 10:40; 11:16 is the elevated district of Judah, Benjamin, and Ephraim, which would more correctly be called "the mountain." In 2 Kings 1:9 and 4:27, the use of the word *hill* obscures the allusion to Carmel, which in other passages on the life of the prophet (e.g., 1 Kings 18:19; 2 Kings 4:25) has the term *Mount* correctly attached to it.

3. In the NT the Gk. word *bounos* ("hillock") is rendered "hill" (cf. Luke 3:5; 23:30), whereas *oros* (to "rise" or "rear") is sometimes rendered "hill" and sometimes "mountain" (cf. Matt. 5:1 to 5:14; Luke 4:29 to 9:37; etc.).

HILL COUNTRY. The rendering in the OT (Josh. 21:11) of *har* (*see* Hill, no. 2; and Bethel, Mount of); and in the NT of the Gk. *oreinos,* "mountainous" (Luke 1:39, 65); and meaning Mt. Ephraim. The rendering "hill country" is misleading. "With their usual exactness the Hebrews saw that these regions (i.e., the mountains of Judah, Ephraim, and Naphtali) formed part of one range, the whole of which they called not by a collective name, but singularly—the mountain" (Smith, *Hist. Geog.,* p. 53).

HIL'LEL (hil'lel; "praising"). A Pirathonite and father of the judge Abdon (Judg. 12:13, 15), before 1070 B.C.

HIN. *See* Metrology: Liquid Measures of Capacity.

HIND. The female of Hart. *See* Animal Kingdom: Deer.

HINGES. The rendering of two Heb. words,

namely, *ṣîr,* to "open," Prov. 26:14, and *pōth* literally an "interstice," 1 Kings 7:50 (NIV, "sockets"). Doors in the East turn on pivots rather than on what we call hinges. They were sometimes made of metal (e.g., Solomon had hinges in the Temple made of gold) or at least plated with it, but generally they were of the same material as the door itself. These pivots worked in sockets—above and below—in the door frame. With the weight of the door resting on the lower pivot, the door would open with much less ease than one working on our hinges, especially when the lower socket became worn (cf. Prov. 26:14).

The Judean hills

HINNOM, VALLEY OF (hin'om). Otherwise called "the valley of the son of Hinnom," or "the valley of Benhinnom"; a deep and narrow ravine with steep, rocky sides to the S and W of Jerusalem, separating Mt. Zion to the N from the "Hill of Evil Counsel," and the sloping rocky plateau of the "valley of Rephaim" to the S. The earliest mention of the valley of Hinnom is in Josh. 15:8; 18:16, where the boundary line between the tribes of Judah and Benjamin is described as passing along the bed of the ravine. On the southern brow, overlooking the valley at its eastern extremity, Solomon erected high places for Molech (1 Kings 11:7), whose horrid rites were revived from time to time in the same vicinity by the later idolatrous kings. Ahaz and Manasseh made their children "pass through the fire" in this valley (2 Kings 16:3; 2 Chron. 28:3; 33:6), and the fiendish custom of infant sacrifice to the fire-gods seems to have been kept up in Topheth at its southeast extremity for a considerable period (Jer. 7:31; 2 Kings 23:10). To put an end to these abominations the place was polluted by Josiah, who rendered it ceremonially unclean by spreading over it human bones and other corruptions (2 Kings 23:10, 13-14; 2 Chron. 34:3-5). From that time it appears to have become the common cesspool of the city, into which its sewage was conducted to be carried off by the waters of the Kidron, as well as a laystall, where all its solid filth was collected. From its ceremonial defilement and from the detested and abominable fire of Molech, if not from the supposed everburning funeral piles, the later Jews applied the name of this valley Ge Hinnom, "Gehenna," to denote the place of eternal torment. The name by which it is now known is Wâdi Jehennam, or Wâdi er Rubêb. *See* Gehenna; Hell.

BIBLIOGRAPHY: G. A. Smith, *Jerusalem* (1907), 1:170-80; J. Simons, *Jerusalem in the Old Testament* (1952), pp. 10-12, 52; D. Baly, *The Geography of the Bible* (1957), p. 162.

The valley of Hinnom, Jerusalem

HIP AND THIGH. In KJV a proverbial expression for a "great slaughter" (Judg. 15:8), similar to the Arab. "war in thigh fashion" or the German "cutting arm and leg in two."

HIPPOPOTAMUS. *See* Animal Kingdom: Behemoth.

HI'RAH (hī'ra). An Adullamite and friend of Judah (Gen. 38:1, 12; cf. v. 20).

HI'RAM (hī'ram; probably shortened from *'aḥiram,* "exalted brother," Heb. and Phoenician). Generally in the Chronicles "Huram"; and "Hirom" in 1 Kings 5:10, 18, marg. Hiram (Ahiram) was a common Phoenician royal name, as is attested by the inscriptions, notably that discovered on the sarcophagus of Ahiram at Byblos (biblical Gebal, Ps. 83:7; Ezek. 27:9), discovered in 1923-24 by a French expedition under M. Montet and dating probably from the eleventh century B.C. (*See* W. F. Albright, *Archaeology and the Religion of Israel,* p. 40.) However, we cannot definitely identify Hiram of Tyre with Ahiram of Byblos.

1. King of Tyre, who sent an embassy to David after the latter had conquered the stronghold of Zion and taken up his residence in Jerusalem. It seems that the dominion of this ruler extended over the western slopes of Lebanon; and when

David built himself a palace, Hiram materially assisted the work by sending cedar wood from Lebanon and skillful workmen to Jerusalem (2 Sam. 5:11; 1 Chron. 14:1). He reigned c. 970-936 B.C., and was the same prince who sent an embassy of condolence and congratulation when David died and Solomon ascended the throne. In consideration of large quantities of grain, wine, and oil sent him by Solomon, Hiram furnished from Lebanon the timber required for the Temple, delivering it at Joppa, the port of Jerusalem (1 Kings 5:1-12, 18; 9:11-14, 27; 2 Chron. 2:3, 11-12). He also supplied large quantities of gold and received from Solomon in return twenty towns in Galilee (1 Kings 9:11-14). When he came to inspect them, they pleased him so little that he applied to them a name of contempt (*Cabul*) and returned them to Solomon (1 Kings 9:11-13; 2 Chron. 8:2). It does not, however, appear that the good understanding between the two kings was broken by this unpleasant circumstance. It was after this that he admitted Solomon's ships to a share in the profitable trade of the Mediterranean (1 Kings 10:22); and Jewish sailors, under the guidance of Tyrians, were taught to bring the gold of Ophir (9:26-28) to Solomon's two harbors on the Red Sea. Dius, the Phoenician historian, and Menander of Ephesus assign to Hiram a prosperous reign of thirty-four years and relate that his father was Abibal and his son and successor Baleazar. Others (later writers, as Eusebius, after Tatian, *Proep. Ev.* 10.11) relate that Hiram, besides supplying timber for the Temple, gave his daughter in marriage to Solomon. Some have regarded this Hiram as a different person from the friend of David, arguing from the long reign necessary if he was the same one who helped David build his house. Hiram I was evidently a powerful ruler, since at this era southern Phoenicia was consolidated under one king who ruled at Tyre but who was officially called "King of the Sidonians."

Another Hiram, king of Tyre, is mentioned in the royal records of the great Assyrian conqueror Tiglath-pileser III (744-727 B.C.).

2. The son of a widow of the tribe of Naphtali and of a Tyrian father. He was sent by King Hiram to execute the principal works of the interior of the Temple and the various utensils required for the sacred services (1 Kings 7:13-14, 40). It is probable that he was selected for this purpose by the king with the notion than his half-Hebrew blood would render him the more acceptable at Jerusalem, about 960 B.C. He is known as *Huram* (which see) in the NIV.

HIRE. *See* Wages.

HIRED MAN, HIRED SERVANT (Heb. *śākîr;* Gk. *misthōtos*). A laborer employed on hire for a limited time (Job 7:1; 14:6; Mark 1:20), as distinguished from one belonging to his master. Naturally, as a temporary laborer, he would feel much less interest than would the shepherd or permanent keeper of the flock (John 10:12-13, "hireling"). *See* Service.

HISS (Heb. *shāraq,* to "whistle"). This term usually expresses insult and contempt (Job 27:23) or mingled astonishment and contempt, as by beholders of the ruined Temple (1 Kings 9:8). The Heb. term may also be translated *whistle* (which see).

HISTORY, NEW TESTAMENT AND EARLY CHRISTIANITY. The fifty years from the birth of Christ to the accession of the last of the Herods—Herod Agrippa II—is a period of unparalleled changes and complications in the government and political geography of Palestine.

Table 15 (pp. 573-75) synchronizes the reign of the Roman emperors of the first Christian century, the numerous high priests of the Jews, and the different political governments of that country, with the Christian history of the same period.

Table 16 (p. 576) lists and gives dates for the high priests who served from 4 B.C. to A.D. 67 and slightly after, and it compares the dates assigned to the successive procurators of Judea by various critics (Schürer, Lewin, Whitehouse, and McClintock and Strong).

BIBLIOGRAPHY: P. Schaff, *History of the Apostolic Church* (1853); J. Orr, *Progress of Dogma* (1901); F. C. Grant, *An Introduction to New Testament Thought* (1950); R. M. Grant, *A Historical Introduction to the New Testament* (1963); O. W. Heick, *A History of Christian Thought* (1965); F. F. Bruce, *New Testament History* (1969); W. W. Gasque and R. P. Martin, *Apostolic History and the Gospel* (1970); W. Fairweather, *Background to the Gospels* (1977); id., *Background to the Epistles* (1977); N. A. Dahl, *Studies in Paul* (1977); J. N. D. Kelly, *Early Christian Doctrines* (1978).

HISTORY, OLD TESTAMENT. To write an OT history would require careful analysis of the entire biblical narrative. Such a task is impossible here. Therefore, table 17 (pp. 577-79), summarizing the correlation of OT events with contemporary history, is presented (*see also* Chronology.) In locating such pivotal events as Abraham's entrance into Canaan, the Exodus, and the conquest in the frame of contemporary history, the author adheres to the numbers preserved in the MT of the Heb. OT, thus placing Abraham's birth c. 2161 B.C., his entrance into Palestine c. 2086 B.C., the Egyptian sojourn c. 1871-1441 B.C., the Exodus c. 1441 and the conquest c. 1400 B.C. Scholars who do not hold to the OT chronological scheme place Abraham anywhere from 2000 B.C. to 1600 B.C., the Egyptian sojourn not until 1720 B.C. or later, and the Exodus 1290 B.C. in the reign of Rameses II or in the reign of Merneptah (1230 B.C.) or even later toward the close of the thirteenth century B.C. These views, however, cannot be reconciled with the general chronological scheme underlying Genesis through Kings,

Table 15
The New Testament and First-Century Christianity

Date	Emperors	Christian History	High Priest[1]	Palestinian Rulers
4 B.C.	Augustus (Octavius)	Probable date of the birth of Jesus Christ	Eleazar appointed by Archelaus. Jesus ben Joazar (second time)	Death of Herod the Great, March 13 Three sons succeed him: (a) Herod Archelaus, ethnarch of one half of the territory: Samaria, Judea, and Idumea (b) Herod Antipas, tetrarch of one fourth: Galilee and Perea (c) Herod Philip, tetrarch of Panias, Auranitis, Batania, and Trachonitis. Quirinius (Cyrenius) registers the Jewish population
A.D. 6	Augustus		Annas (Hanan)	Archelaus deposed and banished; his territory becomes a Roman province Coponius, procurator of Judea, A.D. 6-9, under the governor of Syria Quirinius registers Jewish property
A.D. 9	Augustus	Jesus visits Jerusalem (Luke 2)		Marcus Ambivius, procurator of Judea, A.D. 9-12
A.D. 12	Augustus			Annius Rufus, procurator of Judea, A.D. 12-15
A.D. 14	Augustus dies Aug. 19; Tiberius succeeds, A.D. 14-37			
A.D. 15	Tiberius		Ishmael ben Phabi	Valerius Gratus, procurator, A.D. 15-26
A.D. 16	Tiberius		Eleazar ben Hana	
A.D. 17	Tiberius		Simon ben Kamhith	
A.D. 18	Tiberius		Joseph Kaiaphas ("Caiaphas"), A.D. 18-36	
A.D. 26	Tiberius	Ministry of John the Baptist		Pontius Pilate, procurator, A.D. 26-36
A.D. 27	Tiberius	Baptism of Jesus; His ministry begins. First Passover, March 22. First Galilean circuit (Matt. 4; Mark 1; Luke 4)	Caiaphas	Pontius Pilate, procurator
A.D. 28	Tiberius	Christ's second Passover. Second Galilean circuit (Matt. 13; John 5)	Caiaphas	Pontius Pilate, procurator
A.D. 29		Third Passover. Third Galilean circuit (Matt. 9-10; Mark 6; Luke 9) Oct., Feast of Booths (John 7) Dec., Feast of Dedication (John 10)	Caiaphas	Pontius Pilate, procurator
A.D. 30	Tiberius	Christ at Bethany. Fourth Passover week Christ betrayed Thursday night The crucifixion, Friday The resurrection, Sunday The ascension, forty days later Pentecost, fifty days after the resurrection First miracle by the apostles (Acts 3); Sanhedrin imprison Peter and John (Acts 4)	Caiaphas	Pontius Pilate, procurator
A.D. 31	Tiberius	Ananias and Sapphira die; the apostles imprisoned, but delivered by an angel; they are summoned before Sanhedrin; Gamaliel interposes; the Apostles beaten (Acts 5)	Caiaphas	Pontius Pilate, procurator
A.D. 34	Tiberius		Caiaphas	Pontius Pilate, procurator; Philip, the tetrarch, dies. Vitellius, legate of Syria
A.D. 36	Tiberius	Saul leads in persecutions. Ethiopian converted by Philip (Acts 8).	Jonathan ben Hannan by Vitellius	Pontius Pilate deposed. Marcellus succeeds, A.D. 36

Date	Emperors	Christian History	High Priest[1]	Palestinian Rulers
A.D. 37	Tiberius dies March 16; Caligula succeeds, A.D. 37-41	Stephen martyred; Saul converted and spends three years in Arabia (Acts 9; Gal. 1:18)	Theophilus by Vitellius	Caligula gives Herod Agrippa I tetrarchies of Philip and Lysanius. Maryllus sent to Judea as hipparch
A.D. 39	Caligula			Herod Antipas deposed; Publius Petronius, governor of Syria. March 16, Caligula attempts to put his statue in the Temple at Jerusalem
A.D. 40	Caligula	Paul visits Jerusalem; plots made against his life; he goes to Tarsus (Acts 9) Christianity passes to the Gentiles; Cornelius converted and baptized (Acts 10-11)		
A.D. 41	Caligula dies Jan. 24; Claudius succeeds	Gentile Christians multiply at Antioch, Syria, and are first called Christians in Antioch (Acts 11)	Simon Kantheras by Agrippa I	Herod Agrippa I made king over Samaria, Abilene, and Judea by Caligula and Claudius, A.D. 41-44
A.D. 42	Claudius	Barnabas brings Paul from Tarsus to Antioch. Agabus predicts a great famine (Acts 11)	Matthias ben Hanan by Agrippa I	Herod Agrippa I, king of Palestine, A.D. 41-44
A.D. 43	Claudius		Elionaeus ben Kantherus by Agrippa I	
A.D. 44	Claudius	James beheaded by Agrippa I; Peter released from prison by an angel (Acts 12)	Joseph ben Kamhith by Herod of Chalcis	Herod Agrippa I exploits at Caesarea in the theater and dies five days after, aged fifty-four (Acts 12); Claudius makes Cuspius Fadus procurator of Judea
A.D. 45	Claudius	Paul and Barnabas sent on first missionary journey to the Gentiles (Acts 13-14)		Theudas executed
A.D. 46	Claudius			Tiberius Alexander, procurator, A.D. 46-48
A.D. 47	Claudius		Ananias by Herod of Chalcis	
A.D. 48	Claudius	Judaizers visit Antioch; Paul and Barnabas sent to Jerusalem; Council decrees liberty to Gentiles (Acts 15)		Ventidius Cumanus, procurator of Judea. Herod of Chalcis dies, and Claudius gives his principality to Herod Agrippa II, son of Herod Agrippa I
A.D. 50	Claudius	Paul and Silas's second missionary journey to Gentiles (Acts 15-17)	Ishmael ben Phabi (younger) by Agrippa II	
A.D. 51	Claudius	Paul and Silas visit cities in Asia Minor and Europe. The Macedonian vision. Paul and Silas at Philippi are whipped and imprisoned. Paul goes to Athens; preaches his memorable discourse on Mars' Hill		
A.D. 52	Claudius	Paul meets Aquila and Priscilla. Writes the first epistle to the Thessalonians		Antonius Claudius Felix, procurator of Judea, A.D. 52-60 King Agrippa II pleads for Jews at Rome
A.D. 53	Claudius	Paul before Gallio at Achaia; leaves Corinth and visits Ephesus (Acts 18). Writes the second epistle to the Thessalonians		
A.D. 54	Claudius. dies; accession of Nero, A.D. 54-68.	Paul visits Jerusalem again. Makes third missionary journey		
A.D. 55	Nero	Paul is two years at Ephesus; meets Apollos (Acts 18). A tumult arises; town clerk quiets the people (19). Paul goes to Macedonia and Greece (20)		
A.D. 57	Nero	Paul writes both epistles to the Corinthians, also to the Galatians. Goes to Corinth staying three months		

Date	Emperors	Christian History	High Priest[1]	Palestinian Rulers
A.D. 58	Nero	Paul writes the epistle to the Romans; with Luke leaves Corinth for Macedonia, Troas, and Miletus, returning to Jerusalem via Tyre and Caesarea Agabus illustrates prediction with Paul's girdle; Philip's four daughters prophesy A tumult at Jerusalem; Paul is assaulted, but rescued by the Roman captain; addresses the mob; is sent to Caesarea by night; Paul's defense before Felix (20-24)		
A.D. 59	Nero	Paul imprisoned at Caesarea for two years (24)		
A.D. 60	Nero	Paul defends himself before Festus and King Herod Agrippa II at Caesarea (25-26) His voyage to Rome; shipwrecked at Melita (Malta); spends winter there (27-28)		Portius Festus, procurator of Judea, A.D. 60-62
A.D. 61	Nero	Voyage resumed, Paul lands at Puteoli; thence to Rome afoot; is delivered to Burrus, the pretorian prefect of Nero; lives for two years in his own rented house (28)	Joseph Kabi, by Agrippa II	
A.D. 62	Nero	Paul writes to Philemon, and to the Colossians, the Philippians, and the Ephesians	Hanan ben Hanan, and Jesus ben	
		Acts of the Apostles closes	Damnai, by Agrippa II	
		Conybeare and Howson conjecturally trace Paul's life further as follows:		
A.D. 63	Nero		Jesus ben Gamaliel, by Agrippa II	
A.D. 64	Nero	Rome burns and Nero persecutes the Christians for his own crime		Gessius Florus, procurator
A.D. 65	Nero	Paul travels to Spain	Matthias ben Theophilus, by Agrippa II	
A.D. 66	Nero	Paul visits churches in Asia Minor		
A.D. 67	Nero	Paul writes the first epistle to Timothy and also the epistle to Titus	Phannias appointed by the people	
A.D. 68	Nero commits suicide; Galba succeeds	Paul is martyred at Rome		Marcus Antonius Julianus, procurator. (Josephus Wars 5.4.3)
A.D. 69	Successively Galba, Otho, and Vitellius	Apostles go abroad to evangelize the nations		
A.D. 70	Vespasian			Titus destroys Jerusalem and the Temple
A.D. 79	Vespasian dies; Titus succeeds, A.D. 79-81			
A.D. 81	Titus dies; Domitian succeeds	Domitian persecutes Christians		
A.D. 96	Domitian dies; Nerva succeeds			
A.D. 98	Trajan	The apostle John dies		
A.D. 100	Trajan			Herod Agrippa II dies at Rome in Trajan's reign at the age of seventy-three, having ruled twenty-two years and survived the war thirty years.

1. The dates for the high priests given above, the conclusions of Ewald and Schürer, are not claimed to be exact, but closely approximate.

despite alleged archaeological evidence offered in their support.

BIBLIOGRAPHY: G. H. A. von Ewald, *The History of Israel,* 5 vols. (1874); H. P. Smith, *Old Testament History* (1903); G. F. Owen, *Abraham to the Middle East Crises* (1957); R. K. Harrison, *History of Old Testament Times* (1962); E. H. Merrill, *Historical Survey of the Old Testament,* (1966); L. J. Wood, *Survey of Israel's History* (1970); J. H. Hayes and J. M. Miller, eds., *Israel and Judaean History* (1977); R. de Vaux, *The Early History of Israel* (1978); J. H. Raven, *The History of the Religion of Israel* (1979).

HITT′ITES (hit′īts; Heb. *Ḥittî, Ḥittîm, Ḥēt*).

Old Testament References. A people mentioned frequently in the OT, forty-seven times under their own name and fourteen times as descendants of Heth (Gen. 10:15). In the days of Abraham a group was located in the neighborhood of Hebron (chap. 23), from whom the patriarch bought a burial place. Esau married Hittite wives (26:34; 36:2); the spies sent out by Moses found Hittites located in the hill country (Num. 13:29). Hittites were among the dwellers of Canaan at the time of the conquest and offered

opposition to Israel (Josh. 9:1-2; 11:3). They were located near a territory held by Israel, for the inhabitants of Luz built a new city in Hittite territory (Judg. 1:26). As the land was gradually conquered, the Hittites were not driven out by Israel but remained and in some cases intermarried. They appear in various ways at later times. Hittites were among David's followers (1 Sam. 26:6). Uriah, whom David put to death, was a Hittite (2 Sam. 11:3). Solomon had Hittite women in his harem (1 Kings 11:1). Hittites, among others, were used as forced labor (9:20-21). The various biblical references to the Hittites used to be treated with great skepticism, but thanks to our ability through archaeology to resurrect an ancient people, today the Hittites and Hittite culture are well known.

Archaeological Discovery. It is now known that the center of Hittite power was in Asia Minor. There an empire that once vied with Egypt and Assyria, but had been long forgotten, has been discovered by modern archaeologists. A missionary at Damascus named William Wright and the orientalist A. H. Sayce were among the

Table 16
High Priests[1] and Procurators of Judea

High Priests	Date	Procurator	Dates Assigned by Critics			
			Schürer	Lewin	White-House	McClintock & Strong
	B.C.		B.C.	B.C.	B.C.	B.C.
Joazar ben Boethus	4	Archelaus as ethnarch	4	4	3	4
Eleazar		Herod Antipas as tetrarch	4	4	3	4
Jesus ben Joazar (second time)	4	Philip II as tetrarch	4	4	3	4
	A.D.		A.D.	A.D.	A.D.	
ANNAS (Hanan)[2]	6	Archelaus is deposed	6	6	7	6
		Coponius, procurator	6	6-9	7-9	6-9
		Marcus Ambivius	9	9-12	9-12	9-12
		Annius Rufus	12	12-15	12-15	12-15
Ishmael ben Phabi	15	Valerius Gratus	14	15-26	15-26	15-26
Eleazar ben Hanan						
Simon ben Kamithus	17					
JOSEPH CAIAPHAS (KAIAPHAS)[3]	18					
	34					
Jonathan ben Hanan	36	Marcellus	36		36-38	36-38
Theophilus ben Hanan	37	Maryllus (hipparch)	37	37	39	37-40
	39	Herod Antipas deposed				
Simon Kantheras	41	Herod Agrippa I king	39	41-44		41-44
Matthias ben Hanan						
Elionaeus ben Kantheras						
Joseph ben Kamydus	44	Cuspius Fadus	44	44-46	44-46	45-46
		Tiberius Alexander	46	46-48	46-48	47-49
Ananias ben Nebaeaus	47	Ventidius Cumanus	48	48-50	48-51	49-53
Jonathan						
Ishmael ben Phabi (Junior)	50	Antonius Claudius Felix	52	50-58	51-60	53-55
		Portius Festus	60	58-60	60-62	55-62
Joseph Kabi ben Simon	61					
Hanan ben Hanan (Ananus)	62	Florus Albinus	62	60-64	62-64	
Jesus ben Damni	62					
Jesus ben Gamaliel	63					
		Gessius Florus	64	64		65
Matthias ben Theophilus	65					
Phannias ben Samuel	67					
		Marcus Antonius Julianus[4]				69-70

1. The names of the high priests specifically mentioned in the NT are given in capitals.
2. Luke 3:2; John 18:13, 24; Acts 4:6.
3. Matt. 26:3, 57; Luke 3:2; John 11:49; 18:13-14, 24, 28; Acts 4:6.
4. Josephus *Wars* 6.4.3.

Table 17
Old Testament Events Correlated with Contemporary History

Date	Biblical History			Contemporary History
Dateless Past	Creation of the world			
Probably B.C. 10,000	Creation of man Development of Cainite civilization			Farming, domestication of animals, crude arts, first villages founded
Probably Before B.C. 5000	The Flood			
c. B.C. 5000	Development into nations of the descendants of Noah—Shem, Ham, and Japheth			Early Chalcolithic Age, pottery developed, copper introduced. Badarian, Amratian cultures in Egypt
c. B.C. 4700	Tower of Babel erected Confusion of tongues			First great buildings erected in Babylonia. Earliest levels of Nineveh, Tepe Gawra, Tell ed-Judeideh, etc.
c. B.C. 4500-3000	Development of urban cultures in Babylonia			Halafian culture (c. 4500), Obeidan culture (c. 3600) at Tell Obeid near Ur. Warkan (Uruk, Erech) (c. 3200); writing invented, earliest cylinder seals; Jemdet Nasr culture (c. 3000)
c. B.C. 3500				Rise of Ebla empire
c. B.C. 3000-2700		Noah to	Continuous spiritual declension and lapse of	Union of Egypt, Dynasties I, II (c. 2900-2700). Early dynastic or Sumerian period in Babylonia (c. 2800-2360)
c. B.C. 2700-2200		Abraham	Noah's descendants into idolatry	Egyptian Old Kingdom (Pyramids), Dynasties III-VI (c. 2700-2200) First Semitic Dynasty (Sargon I)(c.2360-2180)
c. B.C. 2250-2200	Terah born			First intermediate period or dark age in Egypt (c. 2200-1989)
c. B.C. 2161	Birth of Abraham			Gutian rule in Babylonia (c. 2180-2070) Sumerian revival under Third Dynasty of Ur (c. 2070-1960)
c. B.C. 2086	Abraham's entrance into Canaan			Ur-Nammu, Dungi, Bur-Sin, Gimil-Sin, and Ibi-Sin rule in power at Ur, Abraham's birthplace
c. B.C. 2075	Invasion of Mesopotamian kings			
c. B.C. 2050	Destruction of Sodom and Gomorrah			
c. B.C. 1950	Isaac			Fall of Ur (c. 1960). Elamite princes in Isin and Larsa in lower Babylonia. Small Amorite and Elamite states in Babylonia
c. B.C. 1871	Israel's entrance into Egypt			Strong Middle Kingdom in Egypt (Dynasty XII)
	Joseph's prime ministry			Amenemes I-IV, Senwosret I-III (c. 1989-1776 B.C.)
c. B.C. 1780	Israel in Egypt			First Dynasty of Babylon (c. 1850-1550). Hammurabi, (c. 1728-1689). Mari Age. Hyksos period of foreign domination in Egypt (c. 1720-1570)
c. B.C. 1520	Moses born			New Empire, Dynasty XVIII (c. 1570-1150). Kamose, Thutmose I, II, Queen Hatshepsut (c. 1520-1482)
c. B.C. 1485	Final phase of Israelite oppression			Thutmose III (c. 1482-1436)
c. B.C. 1441	Exodus from Egypt			Amenhotep II (c. 1436-1425)
c. B.C. 1441	Israel in the wilderness			Thutmose IV (c. 1425-1412)
c. B.C. 1401	Fall of Jericho			Amenhotep III (c. 1412-1387); Amarna period
c. B.C. 1400 to 1361	Conquest of Canaan Period of Joshua and elders			Invasion of Palestine by Habiru Amenhotep IV (Aknaton) (c. 1387-1366). Advance of Hittites
c. B.C. 1361	Oppression of Cushan-rishathaim			Tutankamen in Egypt (c. 1366-1357)
c. B.C. 1353	Othneil's deliverance—forty years peace			Harmhab—decline of Egyptian influence in Palestine
c. B.C. 1313	Oppression by Eglon of Moab			Seti I, pharaoh (c. 1314-1290)
c. B.C. 1295	Ehud's deliverance			Rameses II (c. 1290-1224)—brilliant reign
c. B.C. 1295	Peace for eighty years			Hittite advance into Syria Merneptah's stela mentions Israel in Palestine
c. B.C. 1215	Jabin's oppression			Weak kinglets on throne of Egypt—Amenmose, Siptah, Seti II
c. B.C. 1195-1155	Deborah's exploit Forty-year peace			Rameses III (c. 1198-1167). Invasion of Sea Peoples repulsed Greek history: the Trojan War (c. 1200)
c. B.C. 1155	Midianite oppression			Decline of Egyptian power—weak reign of Rameses IV and V
c. B.C. 1148	Gideon's victory and judgeship			Egypt power in Palestine practically nil

Date	Biblical History			Contemporary History
c. B.C. 1148	Forty-year peace after Gideon			
c. B.C. 1108	Abimelech king at Shechem			Peleset (Philistines) increase in power
c. B.C. 1105	Ammonite oppression, Jephthah judge			
c. B.C. 1099	Philistine ascendancy			
c. B.C. 1085	Samson is judge			
c. B.C. 1065	Eli is judge			
c. B.C. 1050	Battle of Ebenezer; Philistines take the Ark			Great empires on Tigris-Euphrates, Halys, and Nile decline, leaving Syria-Palestine open for conquests of David (c. 1004-
c.B.C. 1020	Saul and the beginnings of the monarchy			965). The splendor of Solomon's reign (c. 965-926).
c. B.C. 1004	David king of Judah			
c. B.C. 998	David king of all Israel			
c. B.C. 965	Solomon			
c. B.C. 926	Division of the monarchy			Rezon seizes power in Damascus (c. 930)
	Kingdom of Judah	*Kingdom of Israel*		
c. B.C. 926	Rehoboam	Jeroboam I		Shishak's invasion (c. 921)
c. B.C. 913	Abijam (Abijah)			
c. B.C. 910	Asa			Aramean Kingdom of Damascus expands under Hezion and Tabrimmon
c. B.C. 909		Nadab		
c. B.C. 908		Baasha		
c. B.C. 900				Aramaeans of Damascus ascendant under Hezion
c. B.C. 886		Elah		
c. B.C. 885		Zimri, Tibni Omri		Ben-hadad I of Damascus
c. B.C. 874		Ahab		
c. B.C. 873	Jehoshaphat		Elijah	Rise of Assyria: Ashurbanipal II (883-859) Conquests of Shalmaneser III (859-824)
c. B.C. 853	Jehoram	Ahaziah Jehoram (852)		Battle of Qarqar: Syrian coalition vs. Assyria (853)
c. B.C. 841	Ahaziah Athaliah	Jehu		Jehu surrenders to Assyrians
c. B.C. 835	Jehoash		Elisha	Shamshi-Adad V (823-811) Adad-nirari III (810-783)
c. B.C. 814		Jehoahaz		
c. B.C. 798		Joash		
c. B.C. 796	Amaziah			Decline of Assyria
c. B.C. 793	Uzziah (792)	Jeroboam II	Amos Hosea	
c. B.C. 753		Zechariah		Tiglath-pileser III (745-727) overruns Syria-Palestine
c. B.C. 752		Shallum Menahem Pekah		
c. B.C. 742		Pekahiah		
c. B.C. 750	Jotham (co-regency)			
c. B.C. 740		Isaiah Micah		
c. B.C. 735	Ahaz			
c. B.C. 732		Hoshea		Damascus falls to Assyria (732)
c. B.C. 728	Hezekiah (co-regency)			Shalmaneser V (727-722) beseiges Samaria
c. B.C. 723		Samaria falls		Sargon II (722-705) takes Samaria (723/722)
	Kingdom of Judah			
c. B.C. 701				Sennacherib (705-681) invades Judah
c. B.C. 696	Manasseh's idolatrous reign			
				Sennacherib's death (681) Esarhaddon's reign (681-669); conquers Egypt
c. B.C. 642	Amon			Ashurbanipal (669-626)

Date	Biblical History		Contemporary History
c. B.C. 640	Josiah		
			Asshur falls to Medes (614)
			Nineveh falls to Medes and Babylonians (612)
c. B.C. 609	Josiah slain by Neco		Defeat of Assyrians and Egyptians by Neco (609)
c. B.C. 609	Jehoahaz		
	Jehoiakim		
c. B.C. 605	Daniel carried to Babylon	Jeremiah	Nebuchadnezzar defeats Neco (609)
			Nabopolassar's death (605)
			Nebuchadnezzar II (605-562)
c. B.C. 597	Jehoiachin		Jehoiachin and Ezekiel, etc. carried to Babylon (598)
	Zedekiah		
			Lachish Letters (c. 589)
c. B.C. 586	Fall of Jerusalem		Jerusalem destroyed (587)
	Daniel's career in Babylon		Nebuchadnezzar's conquests (Egypt)
	Ezekiel prophesies to exiles		Evil-Merodach, liberation of Jehoiachin (c. 561)
			Neriglissar (560-556)
			Nabunaid (Nabonidus) (556-539)
c. B.C. 539	Fall of Babylon		Belshazzar (co-regent with Nabunaid)
c. B.C. 538	Edict of Cyrus		
c. B.C. 536	Return of a remnant. Rebuilding of the Temple begun		Rule of Cyrus, founder of Persian Empire, until his death (530)
			Cambyses king of Persia (530-522)
c. B.C. 522			Darius I (522-486)
c. B.C. 520	Ministry of Haggai and Zechariah		
	Building of the Temple resumed		
c. B.C. 515	Temple completed by Zerubbabel		
			Defeat of Persians at Marathon (490)
			Xerxes I (Ahasuerus) (486-465)
			Persian defeat at Salamis (480)
c. B.C. 479	Esther queen		
c. B.C. 458	Ezra's return. Revival of the law		Artaxerxes I (465-424)
c. B.C. 444	Nehemiah's return to rebuild walls		Periclean Age in Greece (460-429)
			Herodotus, Socrates, Plato
c. B.C. 432	Malachi prophesies		See Chronology, OT.

first scholars to piece together the picture of this ancient imperial people from scattered monuments (Wright, *The Empire of the Hittites* [1884]; A. H. Sayce, *The Hittites, the Story of a Forgotten Empire*, rev. ed. [1925]). Knowledge was vastly increased when a German professor named Hugo Winckler discovered thousands of cuneiform tablets at Boghaz-keui, the Hittite capital located on the great bend of the Halys River, ninety miles E of Ankara. This phenomenal discovery was made in 1906-7 and 1911-12. A Czech scholar, Friedrich Hrozny, and other linguists have deciphered Hittite cuneiform used

Hittite relief

between 1900 and 1100 B.C. This accomplishment has opened up a vast Hittite literature consisting of their annals, religious texts, and myths in Sumero-Akkadian characters received from the Hurrians (Horites). Portions of Hittite legal codes have also been discovered. Though many Hittite excavations have been conducted, pride of place goes to the work at Boghaz-keui, the four-hundred-acre capital of the Hittite empire. From 1931 to 1939, Kurt Bittel led German Oriental Society digs there and resumed them again in 1952. Since then annual excavations have been conducted at the site.

Periods of Hittite Power. Two chief periods of Hittite power are to be distinguished. The first (1800-1600 B.C.) refers back to the time of the First Dynasty of Babylon; the second comprises the new Hittite kingdom, which was powerful in the years 1380-1200 B.C. This latter kingdom was consolidated by a powerful ruler at Boghaz-keui named Suppiluliuma. This mighty conqueror incorporated into his empire the Mesopotamian kingdoms of Mitanni and of the Hurri and pushed his army southward into Syria to the very confines of Palestine. The king of Mitanni, whom he conquered, was named Tushratta, well-known from his correspondence with Amenhotep III and IV of Egypt (J. A. Knudtzon, *Die el-Amarna Tafeln*). Tushratta gave his daughter to be the wife of Amenhotep III. Suppiluliuma was followed by Arandash and then Arandash's brother; Mershilish was followed by his son Muwatallish. The latter clashed with Rameses II in the famous Battle of Kadesh and almost defeated the proud pharaoh. The brother and second king after Muwatallish was Hattushilish, who signed a non-aggression pact with Rameses II. This agreement was sealed by the marriage of the Hittite king's daughter to Rameses II. Around 1200 B.C. Egyptian power went into temporary eclipse, and the Hittite empire came to its end. The capital at Boghaz-keui fell. However, Hittite kingdoms continued to exist at Senjirli, Carchemish, Sakjegeuzi, Hamath, and other places. Evidently Hittites from these city states filtered S into Palestine and even entered the Hebrew armed forces. One such person, Uriah the Hittite, was the husband of Bathsheba.

Language and Culture. The Hittites were non-Semitic, probably Aryan, the first Indo-Europeans to cross the Caucasus into Armenia and Cappadocia. They brought with them pre-Indo-European language, the harbinger of Sanskrit, Greek, Latin, Slavonic, and Teutonic tongues. They formed a cultural tie between Europe and Mesopotamia.

Aggressiveness. Many scholars consider the Hittites to be the third most influential of ancient peoples of the Middle East, rivaling the Egyptians and the Mesopotamians. Hebrews dreaded them as well as the empires on the Tigris and Euphrates. About 1750 they destroyed the Babylonian capital of the great Hammurabi. Their aggressiveness is demonstrated also in their commercial activities, which included an extensive trade in horses with Solomon. Clay tablets reveal that like the Hyksos, the Mitanni, and other peoples of Western Asia, the Hittites were noted for fine horses. The Hittites also kept secret their ironsmelting formula when iron was regarded to be almost as valuable as silver and gold. Not until two centuries later did the Philistines come into this knowledge and not until the Saul-Davidic era did Israel learn it.

Religion. Hittite religion contains a grand medley of Egyptian and Babylonian deities. The Hittites transported Ishtar of Nineveh as far W as Asia Minor. Marduk, the patron god of Babylon, is said on one tablet to have gone to the land of the Hittites where he sat upon his throne for twenty-four years. They also assimilated Egyptian deities with the gods of Syria and Asia Minor. Hittites dwelt in what later became prominent centers of early Christianity: Tarsus, Iconium, Lystra, etc. The famous Ephesian goddess Diana may have been a Hittite Artemis. Hittite gods are frequently depicted astride the backs of animals or enthroned between them. However, they are not actually presented as animals. This was evidently the arrangement in Jeroboam's cultic calves at Dan and Bethel, with Jehovah invisibly enthroned.   M.F.U.; H.F.V.

BIBLIOGRAPHY: J. Garstang, *The Land of the Hittites* (1910); O. R. Gurney, *The Hittites* (1964); C. W. Ceram, *The Secret of the Hittites* (1967); H. A. Hoffner, Jr., *Tyndale Bulletin* 20 (1969): 29-55.

HI'VITES (hī'vīts; cf. Heb. *ḥawwâ*, "tent village," *Arab. ḥiwa'*, "collection of tents," Heb. "the Hivite"). One of the seven nations of Canaan who were to be destroyed by the Israelites (Deut. 7:1, and elsewhere; cf. Gen. 10:17). The focus of the Hivites seems to have been in the N. In Josh. 11:3 the Hivites dwelt "at the foot of Hermon in the land of Mizpeh"; in Judg. 3:3 they "lived in Mount Lebanon, from Mount Baal-hermon as far as Lebo-hamath"; in 2 Sam. 24:7 "all the cities of the Hivites" are numbered apparently near Tyre. And all these seem to be in some sense official locations of the Hivite race, rather than mere chance settlements. But the name *Hivite* may be a descriptive term like *Amorite* (which see) and not a local name, for we find Hivites in other localities. Hamor, the father of Shechem, was a Hivite. The whole story (Gen. 34:2-31) shows them to have been warmhearted, impulsive, and overconfident (v. 23), as well as overly trustful (v. 21) and given to trade and to the multiplication of flocks and herds rather than to war. It is hinted that the absence of any attempt at revenge confirms this impression of unwarlike character, as does the ease with which Abimelech took the city, though indeed at last not without hard fighting (Judg. 9:22-49) and by the "unmilitary character" of his slayer and of her weapon (v. 53). Perhaps the name of their god, Baal-berith, "Baal of the league," may confirm this impression of their unwarlike character. In Josh. 9:7, 17 we find Hivites occupying four confederate cities (Gibeon, Chephirah, Beeroth, and Kiriath-jearim) in the western half of the territory assigned. Here we find the same foresighted keenness and disposition to gain their ends by diplomacy rather than by arms; their craft this time is less self-confident and more successful.

The Hivite form of government is not described, but the mention of "our elders and all the inhabitants of our country" (Josh. 9:11) certainly indicates one in which the people had considerable voice, since the sending of an embassy of unconditional peace is one of the highest acts of sovereignty. Hamor and Shechem "spoke to the men of their city" (Gen. 34:20-24) and reasoned but did not attempt to command.

There is confusion between Hivite and Horite (Hurrian) in the original text of Gen. 36:2, 20, 29 and Josh. 9:7, LXX. It is possible that the Hivites were an ethnic subdivision of the Horites (Hurrians). *See* Horite.

BIBLIOGRAPHY: H. A. Hoffner, Jr., *Tyndale Bulletin* 20 (1969): 27-37.

HIZ'KI (hiz'kî; "my strength"; or perhaps an abbreviation for Hezekiah). One of the "sons" of

Elpaal; one of the chief residents of Jerusalem (1 Chron. 8:17-18; "Hezeki," KJV).

HIZKI'AH, HIZKI'JAH. A son of Neariah and descendant of Jehoiachin and thus part of the post-exilic royal line (1 Chron. 3:23). *See* Hezekiah.

HOAR FROST. *See* Frost.

HO'BAB (hō'bab; "beloved"). The son of Reuel the Midianite (Num. 10:29; Judg. 4:11), 1440 B.C. He has usually been identified with Jethro (Ex. 18:5, 27; cf. Num. 10:29); but it is rather his father, Reuel, to whom the title "Moses' father-in-law" is intended to apply in 10:29. That Jethro and Reuel were names of the same person seems evident from Ex. 2:18, 21; 3:1. Hobab would, therefore, be the brother-in-law of Moses. When Jethro returned to his home (18:27), Moses prevailed upon Hobab to remain (as seems implied by the absence of any refusal to his second request in Num. 10:29-32) and act as guide through the desert. We find his descendants among the Israelites (Judg. 4:11).

HO'BAH (hō'ba). A place N of Damascus to which Abraham pursued the kings who had pillaged Sodom (Gen. 14:15). Location uncertain, possibly Tell el-Salihiye, about ten miles E of Damascus.

HOBA'IAH. *See* Habaiah.

HOD (hod; "majesty"). One of the sons of Zophah, of the tribe of Asher (1 Chron. 7:37).

HODA'IAH. *See* Hodaviah.

HODAVI'AH (hod-a-vī'a; "praise of Jehovah").
1. The first named of the seven sons of Elioenai, of the descendants of Zerubbabel (1 Chron. 3:24), probably a brother of Nahum (Luke 3:25; "Naum," KJV).
2. One of the chief men of the tribe of Manasseh, E of Jordan at the time of the Assyrian captivity (1 Chron. 5:24).
3. Son of Hasennuah and father of Meshullam, of the tribe of Benjamin (1 Chron. 9:7), before 536 B.C.
4. A Levite whose descendants (seventy-four in number) returned from Babylon with Zerubbabel (Ezra 2:40), before 536 B.C. In the parallel passage (Neh. 7:43) his name is written Hodevah. He is probably the same as Judah (Ezra 3:9).

HO'DESH (hō'desh; "a month"). One of the wives of Shaharaim, of the tribe of Judah, several of whose children are enumerated (1 Chron. 8:9), in v. 8 more correctly *Baara* (which see).

HODE'VAH (ho-dē'va; "majesty of Jah," Neh. 7:43). *See* Hodaviah, no. 3.

HODI'AH (ho-dī'a; "majesty of Jehovah").
1. A man referred to in 1 Chron. 4:19. The KJV interpreted *Hodiah* as a female name, and spoke of "the sons of his wife" as being "the father of

Keilah the Garmite, and Eshtemoa the Maacathite." The KJV reading, "the sons of his wife Hodiah the sister of Naham," is probably in error; *see* the NASB of 1 Chron. 4:17-19. The NIV reads, "the sons of Hodiah's wife, the sister of Naham." The Heb. grammatical structure supports the interpretation that it is the wife of Hodiah who is in view, for otherwise the words "Hodiah" and "wife of" should be reversed in line with normal appositional structure.
2. One of the Levites who assisted Nehemiah in expounding the law (Neh. 8:7; 9:5). From the association of his name in 10:10 with some of those mentioned in connection with his in 8:7, we conclude that they are the same person, 445 B.C.
3. Another Levite mentioned in Neh. 10:13 as one of those who signed the covenant with Nehemiah.
4. One of the Israelites who joined in signing the covenant with Nehemiah (Neh. 10:18).

HOG'LAH (hog'la; perhaps "partridge," cf. Arab. *hajal,* "partridge"). The third of the five daughters of Zelophehad the Gileadite to whom, in the absence of male heirs, portions were assigned by Moses (Num. 26:33; 27:1; 36:11; Josh. 17:3).

HO'HAM (hō'ham; derivation uncertain). The king of Hebron who joined the league against Gibeon but was overthrown in battle by Joshua and slain after being captured in the cave of Makkedah (Josh. 10:3), after 1400 B.C.

HOLD. *See* Stronghold.

HOLIDAY (Heb. *hănāhâ,* "quiet"). It has been related that when Ahasuerus took Esther to be his wife he "made a holiday for the provinces" (Esther 2:18; "release," KJV). The exact nature of this holiday or "quiet" is not known, but the LXX and Aram. understand it as immunity from taxes.

HOLINESS (Heb. *qōdesh;* Gk. *hagiōsunē;* in both cases "separation," or "setting apart," holy, from Saxon, "halig," "whole," "sound"). Holiness is a general term used to indicate sanctity or separation from all that is sinful, impure, or morally imperfect; i.e., it is moral wholeness. The term is used with reference to persons, places, and things.

Holiness of God. Holiness is one of the essential attributes of the divine nature. It is, on the one hand, entire freedom from moral evil and, on the other, absolute moral perfection. The Scriptures lay great stress upon this attribute of God (Ex. 15:11; 1 Sam. 2:2; Pss. 71:22; 99:9; 111:9; Isa. 6:3; Hab. 1:12; Rev. 15:4; etc.). Of great consequence in this connection is the revelation of God's holiness in the character and work of Jesus Christ. (Regarding the sinlessness of Christ, *see* the discussion "The Uniqueness of Christ as a Person" in the article Jesus Christ; and also the article Atonement).

By the holiness of God, it is not implied that He is subject to some law or standard of moral excellence external to Himself, but that all moral law and perfection have their eternal and unchangeable basis in His own nature. He is the One in whom these eternal sanctities reside, who is Himself the root and ground of them all. In this sense it is said without qualification, "There is none holy like the Lord" (1 Sam. 2:2); "Thou alone art holy" (Rev. 15:4).

The holiness of God is set before us in the Scriptures as of great practical consequence. (1) It is the special ground of reverence, awe, and adoration (Pss. 71:22; 111:9; Isa. 6:3; etc.). (2) It is the standard of all holiness (Matt. 5:48; 1 Pet. 1:6; etc.). (3) It implies necessarily the divine opposition to, and condemnation of, all sin (Hab. 1:13; 1 Sam. 6:20; Isa. 6:5; etc.). (4) The contemplation of this attribute is accordingly peculiarly adapted to awaken or deepen human consciousness of sin. See Scriptures above referred to. (5) It is revealed to men, nevertheless, as setting before them the highest end of their aspiration, hope, and endeavor (Ex. 19:6; Lev. 20:7; Heb. 12; 1 Pet. 1:16).

Holiness in Moral Creatures Generally. The Scriptures represent the unfallen angels as "holy" (Matt. 25:31; Mark 8:38); men are also in many instances represented thus (2 Kings 4:9; 2 Chron. 35:3; Ezra 8:28; Mark 6:20; 1 Pet. 2:5).

But in all such cases the following distinctions are to be borne in mind: (1) Holiness of the most exalted type in the creature, as in the holy angels, is less than the holiness of God. Their holiness is perfect conformity to the will of God, One infinitely superior to themselves. The holiness of God is absolute; its law is in the perfection of His own Being. (2) God is in the most complete sense separate from evil. In Him is no possibility of sin. With infinite comprehension He perfectly measures the enormity of sin and hates it with a perfect hatred. The angels are finite in their capacities, and, however holy, there exists for them at least the abstract possibility of sinning. For this reason it is written, "There is no one holy like the Lord" (1 Sam. 2:2); "He puts no trust even in His servants; and against His angels He charges error" (Job 4:18), and, "Behold, he puts no trust in his holy ones, and the heavens are not pure in His sight" (15:15). In connection with the last passage, Dillmann says, "In comparison with the all-transcending holiness and purity of God, the creatures which ethically and physically are the purest are impure."

Holiness in Man. We may note: (1) In many cases the holiness ascribed to men in the Scriptures is simply ceremonial and formal. They are persons "separated," "set apart," or dedicated to holy services. They were expected or required along with this outward dedication, however, to lead holy lives and to be inwardly dedicated, a requirement frequently overlooked. Thus the

priests and the Levites are spoken of in the OT as "holy." (2) The holiness predicated or required of men, upon which the Scriptures everywhere lay almost exclusive stress, is that of character and conduct. (3) Man appears before us in the Scriptures as a fallen being, by nature unholy and sinful. Created in the image of God, he has lost one of the most essential features of that image—holiness. (4) Holiness, so far as it appears in man, is an outcome of God's gracious work in salvation and yet not without the proper exertion of one's own free will and the putting forth of strenuous effort (Eph. 4:22-24). (5) Exalted attainments in holiness are possible for men and often realized in this life (Luke 1:75; 2 Cor. 7:1; 1 Thess. 3:13). (6) The whole tone of Scripture accords with the weighty exhortation "Pursue peace with all men and the sanctification without which no one will see the Lord" (Heb. 12:14). (6) The NT teaches that the believer was sanctified positionally when he was saved by virtue of his being presented "in Christ" (1 Cor. 1:2, 30), that he is being sanctified experientially as he reckons upon his position in Christ (Rom. 6:11), and that he will be ultimately sanctified in the sense of full conformity to Christ in glorification (Rom. 8:30). See Sanctification.

Holy Place, Things, etc. The Scriptures also ascribe holiness to places (e.g., the Temple and the "Holy of Holies") and to things such as altars and other accessories of worship. By holiness in such instances is meant "separation" or dedication to holy uses, and of course there is implied no moral quality or inherent sanctity in the objects themselves. They were to be treated with reverence, as should churches and accessories of worship in these days, because of the holiness of God to whose service they are dedicated. See Holiness, Ceremonial.

BIBLIOGRAPHY: R. Otto, *The Idea of the Holy* (1929); N. H. Snaith, *Distinctive Ideas of the Old Testament* (1944), pp. 21-50; J. C. Ryle, *Holiness* (1952); S. Charnock, *The Existence and Attributes of God* (1958), pp. 440-532; S. Neill, *Christian Holiness* (1960); W. Eichrodt, *Theology of the Old Testament* (1961), 1:270-82; O. R. Jones, *The Concept of Holiness* (1961); G. von Rad, *Old Testament Theology* (1962), 1:203-12, 272-79; R. C. Sproul, *The Holiness of God* (1985).

HOLINESS, CEREMONIAL. Jehovah had called Israel to be "a kingdom of priests and a holy nation" (Ex. 19:6), having placed them in covenant fellowship with Himself. In this covenant relationship He established an institution of salvation, which furnished the covenant people with the means of obtaining the expiation of their sins and securing righteousness before God and holiness of life with Him (see also Lev. 11-15; 17-18; Deut. 14:1-21). This holiness was shown in certain ceremonies and laws:

1. The dedication of the firstborn (Ex. 13:2, 12-13; 22:29-30; etc.) and the offering of all firstlings and firstfruits (Deut. 26:2, 10; etc.).

2. The distinction between clean and unclean food (Lev. 11; Deut. 14).

3. Provision for purification (Lev. 12-15; Deut. 23:1-14). *See* Purification.

4. Laws against disfigurement (Lev. 19:28; Deut. 14:1-2) and against excessive scourging (25:3).

5. Laws against unnatural marriages and lusts (Lev. 18, 20).

6. Holiness of priests (which see), *Levites* (which see), and sacred places. *See* Tabernacle; Temple.

7. Of times. *See* Festivals.

HOLM OAK. *See* Vegetable Kingdom: Cypress.

HO'LON (hō'lon; "sandy").

1. A town in the mountains of Judah (Josh. 15:51), given to the priests (21:15). Sometimes identified with Khirbet 'Alin, ten miles NW of Hebron.

2. A city in the plain of Moab upon which judgment was pronounced by Jeremiah (Jer. 48:21). Not identified although named in connection with Jahzah, Dibon, and other known places.

HOLYDAY (Heb. *ḥāgag*, to "dance"; Gk. *heortē*). A KJV term better rendered "festival" (so NASB and NIV, Ps. 42:4; Col. 2:16) or "feast."

HOLY GHOST. *See* Holy Spirit.

HOLY GHOST, SIN AGAINST. *See* Sin: The Unpardonable Sin.

HOLY OF HOLIES. *See* Tabernacle.

HOLY ONES. *See* Godly Ones; Saints.

HOLY PLACE. *See* Tabernacle, Temple.

HOLY SPIRIT. The third Person in the Trinity.

Scriptural Designations (Heb. *rûaḥ, 'ĕlohîm* "Spirit of God," or *rûaḥ, YHWH*, "Spirit of Jehovah"; Gk. *to pneuma to hagion,* "the Holy Ghost," or "the Holy Spirit"). Frequently the term is simply "the Spirit," or "the Spirit of the Lord," or "the Spirit of God," or "the Spirit of Jesus Christ" (Matt. 3:16; Luke 4:18; John 14:17; Acts 5:9; Phil. 1:19).

Theological Statements. The doctrine of the Holy Spirit has about it the difficulty that belongs to that of the Trinity or the existence of God as a purely spiritual being—the difficulty that arises from the narrow limits of human understanding. Nevertheless, the Scriptures bring to us their definite representations of truth, and with these Christian thought must concern itself. The chief topics of theology respecting the Holy Spirit are: (1) His personality; (2) His deity; (3) His relation to the Father and to the Son; and (4) His office or work.

Personality. The historic and prevailing doctrine of the Christian church, in accordance with the Scriptures, has been that the Holy Spirit is a person distinct from the Father and the Son, though united to both in the mysterious oneness of the Godhead. He is not simply a personification or figurative expression for the divine energy or operation, as some have held at various periods of the history of the church (Anti-Trinitarians), but He is an intelligent agent, possessed of self-consciousness and freedom. In proof of this it is justly said: (1) that the Scriptures that ascribe distinct personality to the Father and the Son with equal explicitness ascribe distinct personality to the Holy Spirit. Prominent illustrations of this are found in Matt. 3:16-17; 28:19; John 14:16-17; 15:26. (2) The pronouns used with reference to the Holy Spirit are invariably personal pronouns, e.g., John 16:13-14; Acts 13:2. (3) The attributes of personality, self-consciousness, and freedom are ascribed to the Holy Spirit (1 Cor. 2:10; 12:11). (4) The relations described as existing between the Holy Spirit and mankind are such as to emphasize His personality. The Spirit strives with man (Gen. 6:3). He instructs, regenerates, sanctifies, and comforts believers (John 3:5-6; 14:16-17; 16:13-14; 1 Pet. 1:2). We are warned not to "blaspheme against," "not to resist," not to "grieve," nor to "quench" the Holy Spirit (Matt. 12:31-32; Acts 7:51; Eph. 4:30; 1 Thess. 5:19).

Deity. The deity of the Holy Spirit has been but little disputed in the church by those who have admitted His personality. The Arian heresy of the fourth century, which represented the Holy Spirit as the earliest of all the creatures of the created Son, is the chief exception to the general rule. The Scriptures that establish the personality of the Holy Spirit in many cases, as must have been noted, also establish His deity. Beyond this, attention is commonly called to the following sure indications of Holy Scripture: (1) The Holy Spirit is distinctly called God, and names are given to Him that properly belong to God (Acts 5:3-4; Acts 28:25-27; Heb. 10:15-17; 2 Cor. 3:17-18). (2) Divine attributes, such as knowledge, sovereignty, and eternity, are ascribed to the Holy Spirit (1 Cor. 2:11; 12:11; Heb. 9:14). (3) Divine works, such as creation and the new birth, are attributed to Him (Gen. 1:2; Job 26:13; John 3:3-8). (4) Worship and homage such as belong only to God are paid to the Holy Spirit (Acts 28:25-27; 2 Cor. 13:14). And harmonious with this is the fact that the sin against the Holy Spirit is the unpardonable sin (Matt. 12:31-32). *See* Sin: The Unpardonable Sin.

Relation to Trinity. The relation of the Holy Spirit to the Father and to the Son is a subject with respect to which the faith of the church developed slowly. The controversies of the first four centuries related principally to the Son. The Council at Nicaea, A.D. 325, gave forth simply this clause respecting the third Person in the Trinity: "And we believe in the Holy Spirit." The second Council at Constantinople, A.D. 381, added the words "the Lord and Giver of life who proceeds from the Father, who is to be worshiped and glorified with the Father and the Son, and who spake through the prophets." At the third Synod of Toledo, A.D. 589, the words *"filio que"* ("and the Son") were added, so as to assert the procession of the Holy Spirit from the Son as well as the Father. This was a principal cause of the division between the Western and Eastern churches, the former maintaining, the latter denying, that the Holy Spirit proceeds from both the Father and the Son (*see* Shedd, *Hist. of Doctrine*, 1:355-62). The prevailing doctrine may be thus summed up: (1) The Holy Spirit is the same in substance and equal in power and glory with the Father and the Son. (2) He is, nevertheless, as to His mode of subsistence and operation, subordinate to both the Father and the Son, as He proceeds from them and is sent by them, and they operate through Him (John 15:26; 16:13-15; 14:26; Phil. 1:19; Acts 11:15-17).

Office. Van Oosterzee does well to say, "Happily, not the sounding the depths of the Holy Spirit's nature, but the receiving and possessing of the Holy Spirit himself, is for us, even as Christian theologians, the main point." Hence, without detracting from the value of what has preceded, of paramount importance is the office and work of the Holy Spirit. This is indicated as follows: (1) The Spirit is the immediate source of all life, physical and intellectual (Ps. 104:30; Isa. 32:15; Job 33:4; Gen. 2:7, KJV; Ex. 31:3; Num. 11:17; etc.). (2) He bore an important part in the coming of Christ in the flesh and the qualifying of His human nature for His work (Luke 1:35; John 3:34; 1:32-33). (3) He is the revealer of all divine truth. The Scriptures are especially the product of the Holy Spirit (Mic. 3:8; John 14:26; 16:13; 1 Cor. 2:10-13). (4) He moves upon the hearts and consciences of all men, attending revealed truth with His power wherever it is known and even where it is not known, affording some measure of divine light and gracious influence (Acts 2:17; John 16:7-11; 1 Cor. 2:4). (5) He convicts men of sin; graciously aids them in repentance and faith; regenerates, comforts, and sanctifies believers; bears witness to their acceptance with God and adoption as God's children; and dwells in them as the principle of a new and divine life. In addition to Scripture quoted above, *see* Rom. 8:14-16; 1 Cor. 6:19; 2 Cor. 3:17-18 (*see* Witness of Spirit). (6) He also exercises guidance in the ministrations of the church, calling men to various offices and endowing them with qualifications for their work (Acts 13:2, 4; 1 Cor. 12:4-11).

Special Work in the Believer. The Holy Spirit in this particular age from Pentecost to the outtaking and glorification of the church, the Body of Christ, performs a special work in every believer the moment he exercises saving faith in Christ. Simultaneously with regenerating him the Spirit baptizes the believer into union with other believers in the Body (1 Cor. 12:13) and into union with Christ Himself (Rom. 6:3-4). This is a unique and distinctive ministry of the Spirit during this age. The Holy Spirit also dwells perpetually within every believer (John 14:17; Rom. 8:9-14; 1 Cor. 6:19-20) and seals every believer for the day of redemption (Eph. 4:30). In addition, the Holy Spirit fills every believer when special conditions of filling are met (5:18).

Dispensational Ministry. According to the prophetic announcement of John the Baptist of the Spirit's baptizing work (Matt. 3:11-12; Mark 1:8; Luke 3:16-17; John 1:32-33), the death, resurrection, and ascension of Christ were to inaugurate the new age of the Holy Spirit's ministry. Our Lord prophetically announced a drastic change in the Holy Spirit's operation in the age that was to begin. At Pentecost the Holy Spirit came as the ascension gift. He came, moreover, in a sense in which He was not here before and to perform all the ministries delegated to Him in this age; namely, regenerating, baptizing, sealing, and indwelling every believer with the added privilege of each believer's being filled with the Spirit, if he meets the conditions of filling. The distinctive ministry of the Spirit for this age is His baptizing work. This occurred for the first time in Acts 2 (cf. 1:5; 11:15-16). The first occurrence of the baptizing work of the Spirit in chap. 2 marked the birthday of the Christian church. In chap. 8 the racially mongrel Samaritans were admitted to gospel privilege and granted the gift of the Holy Spirit, which included the Spirit's baptizing work, placing them in the church, the Body of Christ. In chap. 10 the Gentiles were likewise admitted. This latter instance marks the normal course of the age. Every believer, upon the simple condition of faith in Christ, is regenerated, baptized into the Body, indwelt perpetually, sealed eternally, and given the privilege of being continuously filled. The experiences of OT saints and all pre-Pentecost believers came short of these tremendous blessings that are the heritage of every genuine believer in this age.

BIBLIOGRAPHY: A. Kuyper, *The Work of the Holy Spirit* (1941); W. H. G. Thomas, *The Holy Spirit of God* (1950); E. H. Bickersteth, *The Holy Spirit: His Person and Work* (1959); J. Owen, *The Holy Spirit, His Gifts and Power* (1960); J. E. Cumming, *Through the Eternal Spirit* (1965); C. C. Ryrie, *The Holy Spirit* (1965); J. F. Walvoord, *The Holy Spirit* (1965); J. Buchanan, *The Office and Work of the Holy Spirit* (1966); F. D. Bruner, *The Theology of the Holy Spirit* (1970); M. F. Unger, *The Baptism and Gifts of the Holy Spirit* (1974); E. M. B. Green, *I Believe in the Holy Spirit* (1975); H. C. G. Moule, *The Person and Work of the Holy Spirit* (1977); C. F. D. Moule, *The Holy Spirit* (1979); E. Schweizer, *The Holy Spirit* (1980).

HOLY SPIRIT, SIN AGAINST. *See* Sin: The Unpardonable Sin.

HO'MAM (hō'mam; cf. Heb. *hāmam*, "confuse, make a noise"). One of the sons of Lotan and grandson of Seir the Horite (1 Chron. 1:39). In the parallel passage (Gen. 36:22) his name is written Hemam.

HOME. *See* Family; Household.

HOMER. *See* Metrology: Dry Measures of Capacity.

HONESTY. "Honest" is generally rendered "honorable" and "right." Gk. *semnotēs* has the meaning of "gravity, probity, purity" (1 Tim. 2:2, KJV; "dignity," NASB; "holiness," NIV). "Honesty" (Rom. 13:13; 1 Thess. 4:12, KJV) is the rendering of the Gk. *euschēmonōs* and means "seemly, properly, with propriety" ("decently," NIV). In general, honesty stands for upright disposition, integrity in dealing with others, probity, purity. In Gen. 42:11 and Luke 8:15, mention is made of "honest men" and an "honest heart" (NIV, "noble heart").

HON'EY. A sweet, thick fluid manufactured by bees from flowers and fruits and placed in the cells of the comb (Judg. 14:8; Ps. 19:10). In the East honey was much esteemed as food (Gen. 43:11; 2 Sam. 17:29). It was often eaten directly from the honeycomb or prepared in various ways (Ex. 16:31; 1 Sam. 14:26). Canaan is often described as a land "flowing with milk and honey" (Ex. 3:8, 17; etc.). This graphic figure portrays the fertile land supplying rich pasture for cattle, which give milk so abundantly that the land is said to flow with it, and producing many kinds of flowers, which provide food to honey-producing bees. Wild honey was frequently deposited in rocks (Deut. 32:13), in trees (1 Sam. 14:25-26), and, upon occasion, in the carcasses of animals (Judg. 14:8). It was sought for making pastries and condiments. Honey was produced not only from bees but also artificially from dates and grapes (Arab. *dibs;* Josephus *Wars* 4.8.3). Honey was excluded from the offerings made by fire to the Lord (Lev. 2:11), apparently because, like leaven, it produces fermentation. Honey was often presented as a gift (Gen. 43:11; 1 Kings 14:3). John the Baptist had "wild honey" as an important part of his diet (Matt. 3:4). Honey in general supplied the place of sugar. For example, three hundred pounds of grapes produced one hundred pounds of *dibs* and, when diluted with a little water, furnished a kind of sugar (Ex. 16:31).

Figurative. Honey and milk are used to denote sweet discourse (Song of Sol. 4:11). The Word of God is compared to honey and described as spiritually delectable (Pss. 19:10; 119:103), and honey taken in appropriate quantities is used to illustrate pleasure in moderation (Prov. 25:16, 27). *See also* Animal Kingdom: Bees.   M.F.U.

HONOR. The rendering of several Heb. and Gk. words, meaning: (1) respect paid to superiors, such as to God (John 5:23; Rev. 5:12); to parents and kings, including submission and service (Ex. 20:12; Matt. 15:4; 1 Pet. 2:17); the esteem due to

virtue, wisdom, glory, reputation, and probity (Prov. 15:33; 22:4; 29:23); (2) the reward, emolument, position given to subjects (Num. 22:17, 37; 2 Chron. 1:11-12) and the final reward of righteousness (John 5:44, marg.; Rom. 2:7; Heb. 2:7; 2 Pet. 1:17).

HOOD (Heb. *ṣānîp*). A KJV expression (Isa. 3:23). *See* Diadem; Dress; Turban.

HOOF (Heb. *parsâ*, to "split, divide"). The cleft or "split" foot of cattle (Ex. 10:26; Lev. 11:3; etc.), and also of the horse, though not cloven (Isa. 5:28; Jer. 47:3). The parting of the hoof is one of the main distinctions between clean and unclean animals. *See also* Claw; Nail.

HOOK.

1. A ring, such as we place in the nose of a bull to lead him about (2 Kings 19:28; Isa. 37:29; Ezek. 29:4; etc.); an allusion in the first two passages to the absolute control of Jehovah over Sennacherib. A similar method was adopted for leading captives, such as Manasseh (2 Chron. 33:11).

2. A peg, or pin, upon which the curtains were hung in the *Tabernacle* (which see; Ex. 35:11; etc.).

3. A vinedresser's pruning hook (Isa. 2:4; Mic. 4:3; Joel 3:10).

4. Forked pegs, upon which the carcasses of beasts were hung for flaying (Ezek. 40:43).

5. A *fleshhook* or *fork* (both which see).

HOOPOE. *See* Animal Kingdom.

HOPE. In the NT the "expectation of good" (Gk. *elpis*). This original word denotes a joyful and contented expectation of eternal salvation (Acts 23:6; 26:7; Rom. 5:4-8; 1 Cor. 13:13). Because of God's manifested salvation in Christ, and because He is the source of all the believer's expectations, He is called the "God of hope" (Rom. 15:13). Paul calls his converts his *hope,* not as the cause but as objects of his hope. In the OT hope is expressed by several different words meaning "safety, security, trust" (Heb. *beṭaḥ,* Pss. 16:9; 22:9, both KJV; etc.). Another Heb. word denoting "refuge," in the sense of firm and certain expectation, is *mibṭaḥ* (Pss. 42:5; 71:5). In KJV hope is used in the sense of "refuge," or "shelter" (Heb. *maḥāseh,* Jer. 17:7, 17; Joel 3:16). Another expression denotes something "waited for" (Heb. *miqweh,* Ezra 10:2). In Zech. 9:12 still another term is employed (Heb. *tiqwâ;* "the prisoners of hope"); those described here cherishing expectation of deliverance. The fountainhead of hope is the death, burial, and resurrection of Christ (1 Pet. 1:3). "Christ in you" is the "hope of glory" (Col. 1:27). In the NT hope is also marked by an eschatological significance, for example, in Titus 2:13, where the coming of the Lord is called "the blessed Hope," that is, the expectation giving joy to the Christian in promise of future glorification.   M.F.U.

BIBLIOGRAPHY: C. F. D. Moule, *The Meaning of Hope* (1963); D. L. Moody, *The Hope of Glory* (1964); W. Zimmerli, *Man and His Hope in the Old Testament* (1968).

HOPH'NI (hof'nī). The first named of the two sons of the high priest Eli (1 Sam. 1:3; 2:34), who fulfilled their hereditary sacerdotal duties at Shiloh. Their brutal greed and lust, which increased with their father's age (2:12-17, 22), filled the people with indignation and provoked the curse that was pronounced against their father's house, first by an unknown prophet (vv. 27-36) and then by the youthful Samuel (3:11-14). Both were slain on the day the Ark was captured by the Philistines (4:10-11), about 1050 B.C., at the battle of Ebenezer. The Scriptures call them "sons of Belial" (2:12, see marg.).

HOPH'RA (hof'ra). *See* Pharaoh, Hophra.

HOR, MOUNT (hōr; "the mountain"). The name of two mountains.

1. The mountain on which Aaron died (Num. 20:25, 27). The word *Hor* is regarded by lexicographers as an archaic form of Har, the usual Heb. term for "mountain." The few facts given us in the Bible regarding Mt. Hor are soon told. It was "by the border" (20:23) or "at the edge" (33:37) of the land of Edom. It was the next halting place of the people after Kadesh (20:22; 33:37), and they left it for Zalmonah (33:41) on the road to the Red Sea (21:4). It was during the encampment at Kadesh that Aaron was "gathered to his people." The once commonly accepted site of Mt. Hor is E of the 'Arabah, the highest and most conspicuous of the whole range of the sandstone mountains of Edom, having close beneath it on its E side the mysterious city of Petra. The tradition has existed from the earliest date. It is now the Jebel Nebi-Harûn, "the mountain of the Prophet Aaron." This identification does not, however, meet the full requirements of the narrative. "There is a mountain which fully meets the requirements of the Bible text, and the natural demands of the narrative, as to the Mount Hor where Aaron died and was buried. That mountain is Jebel Madurah, near the western extremity of Wady Feqreh, a little to the SW of the passes es-Sufâh and el-Yemen. Its formation, its location, its name, go to identify it with the place of Aaron's burial, and there is even a smack of tradition in its favor. . . . In its location, Jebel Madurah stands at a triangular site, where the boundaries of Edom, of Canaan, and the Wilderness of Zin meet. It is at the extremest NW boundary of Edom, yet it is not within that boundary line. It is on the very verge of the land of promise, yet it is not within the outer limits of that land" (Trumbull, *Kadesh-Barnea*, p. 129).

2. A mountain named only in Num. 34:7-8 as one of the marks in the northern boundary of the land of promise. Its identification is difficult. The Mediterranean was the western boundary; the first point was Mt. Hor and the second the entrance of Hamath, or "Lebo-hamath." R. A. S. Macalister equates it with Mt. Hermon. The reference is evidently to the whole Lebanon range or a prominent peak of the range.

HO'RAM (ho'răm). The king of Gezer, who, coming to the relief of Lachish, was overthrown by Joshua (Josh. 10:33), after 1400 B.C.

HO'REB (ho'rĕb; "dryness, desert," Ex. 3:1; 17:6; 33:6; Deut. 1:2, 6, 19; etc.; 1 Kings 8:9; 19:8; 2 Chron. 5:10; Ps. 106:19; Mal. 4:4). In the opinion of some a lower part or peak of Sinai from which one ascends, towards the S, the summit of Sinai (Jebel Musa); but according to others a general name of the whole mountain of which Sinai was a particular summit. *See* Sinai.

BIBLIOGRAPHY: B. Bernstein, *Sinai: The Great and Terrible Wilderness* (1979).

HO'REM (hō'rem). One of the "fortified cities" of Naphtali (Josh. 19:38), between Migdal-el and Beth-anath. Exact location not known.

HOR'ESH (hor'esh). A place in the wilderness of Ziph where David fled from Saul and where Jonathan met him to provide him support (1 Sam. 23:15, 16, 18, 19). *See* Ziph.

HOR-HAGGID'GAD (hor'-ha-gid'gad). The thirty-third station of Israel in the desert (Num. 33:32-33), probably the same as their forty-first station, *Gudgodah* (which see; Deut. 10:7).

HO'RI (hō'ri). *See* Horite.

1. A son of Lotan, and grandson of Seir (Gen. 36:22; 1 Chron. 1:39).

2. A Simeonite, whose son Shaphat was the commissioner or "spy" of his tribe, sent by Moses to explore the land of Canaan (Num. 13:5), c. 1401 B.C.

3. The expression "of Hori" in the KJV of Gen. 36:30 is rendered "descended from the Horites" in the NASB and NIV.

HORIM. *See* Horites.

HO'RITE (hō'rīt; Heb. *Ḥōrî*, plural, *Ḥōrîm*).
   Biblical References. In the Pentateuch a number of references to an enigmatic people called Horites. These people were defeated by Chedorlaomer and the invading Mesopotamian army (Gen. 14:6). They were governed by chieftains (36:29-30) and are described as having been exterminated or destroyed by Esau's descendants (Deut. 2:12, 22). This unknown people used to be thought of as a local and restricted group of cave dwellers, the name *Horites* being thought of as derived from Heb. *ḥōr*, "cave." Other than this alleged etymological description, the Horites remained completely obscure, not appearing in the Bible outside the Pentateuch or in extrabiblical literature.

Archaeological Discoveries. In recent decades, however, archaeology has brought to light evidences of the Hurrians (whom many equate with the biblical Horites, but others question the identification), who now occupy a prominent place on the stage of ancient history. This ethnic group is now known not only to have existed but to have played a far-reaching role in ancient Near Eastern cultural history. As a result of the recovery of the Hurrian civilization, the popular etymology that connects them with early cave dwellers has generally been abandoned. Excavations at Mari on the middle Euphrates, about seven miles N of Abou Kemal, conducted since 1933 by the Musée du Louvre, have unearthed numerous Hurrian tablets. To this early phase of Hurrian literature (c. 2400-1800 B.C.) belong some of the Hurrian religious texts found at the ancient Hittite capital of Hattushash (Boghaz-keui) in Asia Minor. But the most important discovery regarding the Hurrians comes from Nuzi, present-day Yorgan Tepe, a dozen miles SW of modern Kirkuk. In the old Akkadian period (c. 2360-2180 B.C.) this city was known as Gasur and had a predominantly Semitic population. But before the eighteenth century B.C. the city had become an important center of the Hurrians. It was known as Nuzi. At this period the Hurrians were a dominant ethnic element throughout the Middle East. Thousands of clay tablets were uncovered at Nuzi. These were inscribed by Hurrians in the Babylonian language but contained many native Hurrian words. A large number of these tablets are to be dated in the fifteenth century B.C., and they give much information concerning the life of the Hurrian people. Remarkable parallels from Nuzi tablets concerning marriage,

"Horns" on the altar of incense

adoption, and social customs, such as those that prevailed in the patriarchal period of Genesis, occur. Scholars are still busy translating thousands of clay tablets shedding light on the Hurrians and other peoples of western Asia. As this material becomes accessible, the puzzle of the biblical Horites is becoming solved.

National Affiliations. The Hurrians were non-Semites, who before the second millennium B.C. migrated into northern Mesopotamia. Their homeland was evidently the region S of the Caucasus. They appear first upon the pages of history c. 2400 B.C. in the Zagros Mountain region E of the Tigris. After the Gutian victory over the last kings of Akkad, the Hurrians seem to have inundated northern Mesopotamia, especially the E Tigris country. Hurrian names were common even in southern Mesopotamia during the Third Dynasty of Ur (c. 1960 B.C.), and they continued to be numerous under the First Dynasty of Babylon (c. 1830-1550 B.C.).

BIBLIOGRAPHY: E. A. Speiser, *Annual of the American Society for Oriental Research* 13 (1933): 26-31; W. F. Albright, *From the Pyramids to Paul*, ed. L. Leary (1935), pp. 9-26; E. A. Speiser, *Journal of the American Oriental Society* 68 (1948): 1-13; J. C. L. Gibson, *Journal of Near Eastern Studies* 20 (1961): 217-38; R. de Vaux, *Revue Biblique* 74 (1967): 481-503; F. W. Bush, *International Standard Bible Encyclopedia* (1982), 2:756-57.

HOR'MAH (hor'ma; "a devoted place, destruction"). The chief town of a Canaanite king in the S of Palestine (Josh. 12:14), near which the Israelites were overcome by the Amalekites when against the advice of Moses they attempted to enter Canaan by that route (Num. 14:45; cf. 21:1-3; Deut. 1:44). It was afterward taken by Joshua and assigned to Judah (Josh. 15:30) but finally fell to Simeon (19:4; 1 Chron. 4:30). Hormah has not been positively identified, and several leading scholars have their candidates.

HORN, HORNS (Heb. *qeren*, "projecting"; Gk. *keras*). Horns are mentioned in Scripture in several ways.

1. Trumpets were at first merely horns perforated at the tip, such as are still used for calling laborers to meals. Later they were made of metal, such as the silver trumpets of the priests (Num. 10:1; etc.). Those used at the overthrow of Jericho (Josh. 6:4, 6, 13) were probably large horns or instruments in the shape of a horn, which gave a loud, far-sounding note (see Lev. 23:24; 25:9). *See also* Music.

2. Horns, being hollow and easily polished, have been used in ancient and modern times for drinking and kindred purposes, such as a *flask* or vessel to hold oil (1 Sam. 16:1, 13; 1 Kings 1:39) or antimony for blacking the eyelashes. *See* Inkhorn.

3. The projections of the altar of burnt offering (Ex. 27:2) and of the altar of incense (30:2) at

their four corners were called "horns." By laying hold of these horns of the altar of burnt offering, a criminal found safety (1 Kings 1:50; 2:28) if his offense was accidental (Ex. 21:14).

4. The peak or *summit* of a hill was called a *horn* (Isa. 5:1, NASB, marg.).

5. In the KJV of Hab. 3:4, "he had horns coming out of his hand," the context implies *rays* of light (so NASB and NIV; cf. Deut. 33:2).

Figurative. Two principal applications of this metaphor will be found—*strength* and *honor*. Horns being the chief source of attack and defense with the animals to which God has given them, they are employed in Scripture as emblems of the power of God (Ps. 18:2), of Christ (Luke 1:69; Rev. 5:6), of Ephraim (Deut. 33:17), of the wicked (Pss. 22:21; 75:10), and of the righteous, of kingdoms (Dan. 7:7-8, 24; 8:3, 5-6, 20), and of anti-Christian powers (Rev. 13:1; 17:3, 7).

The *budding* or *sprouting* of horns is figurative of the commencement or revival of a nation or power (Ps. 132:17; Ezek. 29:21); *raising up,* of arrogance (Ps. 75:4-5) and also of glory (v. 10); *exalting,* of increase of power and glory (1 Sam. 2:1, 10; Pss. 89:17, 24; 92:10; 112:9); *pushing with,* of conquests (Deut. 33:17; 1 Kings 22:11; Mic. 4:13); *bringing down,* of degradation (Job 16:15, I have "thrust," i.e., laid low, "my horn in the dust," as a wounded animal); *cutting off,* of destruction of power (Ps. 75:10; Jer. 48:25; Lam. 2:3, see marg.).

BIBLIOGRAPHY: R. de Vaux, *Ancient Israel: Its Life and Institutions* (1961), p. 414.

HORNET. See Animal Kingdom.

HORONA'IM (hōr'o-na'im; "double cave"). A city of Moab, on the mountain slope of Luhith, along the route of the invading Assyrians (Isa. 15:5; Jer. 48:3, 5, 34). It is probably el-'Arak.

HOR'ONITE, THE (hōr'o-nit). An epithet of Sanballat (only in Neh. 2:10, 19; 13:28). Fürst and Gesenius derive it from Beth-horon, whereas Strong's *Exhaustive Concordance* and Robinson's Gesenius take it from Horonaim. On the latter supposition Sanballat was a Moabite, and this would accord well with his connection with Tobiah the Ammonite. But if the term is from Beth-horon, he was probably a Samaritan or related to the Samaritans. This would agree with Josephus, who says: "He was a Cuthean by birth, of which stock were the Samaritans also" (*Ant.* 11.7.2).   W.H.

HORSE. See Animal Kingdom: Horse; Dromedary; and also the article Horses, Horsemen in the general listing.

Figurative. On account of the strength of the horse, he has become the symbol of war (Deut. 32:13; Ps. 66:12; Isa. 58:14; Zech. 9:10; 10:3); of conquest, as in Song of Sol. 1:9, where the bride advances with her charms like a "mare among the chariots of Pharaoh." The war horse rushing

into battle is figurative of the impetuosity of the wicked in sin (Jer. 8:6). In Zech. 6:2-7 the prophet mentions horses that were red, black, white, and dappled. The red horses symbolize war, the black pestilence, and the dappled famine, whereas the white points to the glorious victories of the ministers of the divine judgment.

BIBLIOGRAPHY: V. Møller-Christian and K. Jørgensen, *Encyclopedia of Bible Creatures* (1965); G. S. Crandall, *Animals of Bible Lands* (1970).

HORSE GATE. A gate in the old wall of Jerusalem at the W end of the bridge leading from Zion to the Temple (Neh. 3:28; Jer. 31:40; 2 Chron. 23:15), perhaps so called because the "horses which the kings of Judah had given to the sun" (2 Kings 23:11) were led through it for idolatrous worship.

HORSELEECH. See Animal Kingdom: Leech.

HORSES, HORSEMEN. In antiquity the Hittites cultivated horses. This animal seems to have been introduced from inner Asia. Horses were bred by the fierce Mitanni, who wrote about them in Hittite cuneiform. Even as a cart horse it was apparently unknown in Egypt even in the great Pyramid Age (2800-2400 B.C.). Egyptian wall reliefs depict asses and donkeys but no horses at the earlier periods. From the Hyksos the Egyptians acquired a taste for horse-drawn chariots such as those that pursued the fleeing Israelites (Ex. 14:9, 26-29). The introduction of the horse into lower Mesopotamia is still obscure. When Israel entered Palestine, they found people of the plains equipped with horses and chariots made of iron (Judg. 1:19). Not until the period of the monarchy, after 1020 B.C., did the hill-dwelling Israelites possess horse-drawn chariots such as their neighbors owned. David hamstrung the horses he captured from his enemies, doubtless in obedience to Deut. 17:16: "Moreover, he shall not

Chariot horses

multiply horses for himself, nor shall he cause the people to return to Egypt to multiply horses." Solomon, disregarding the Deuteronomic injunctions, equipped his army with thousands of horses and chariots (2 Chron. 9:25). Solomon also had as one of his pet commercial projects horse-and-chariot trade between Egypt and Asia Minor, bringing handmade chariots (and evidently horses, too) from Egypt and shipping fine horses from Cilicia. In early Israel mules were traditionally royal mounts (2 Sam. 18:9; cf. Zech. 9:9; Matt. 21:5). Kings of Judah and Israel had numerous horses, and Ahab of Israel is mentioned on the Assyrian monuments as furnishing a sizable contingent of horses and chariotry in the Syrian coalition against Shalmaneser III at Karkar (853 B.C.). The Assyrians were great horse-lovers, Assyrian monarchs often using them for lion hunting. Persian kings made large use of horses as couriers (cf. Zech. 1:8-11; 6:1-8). Romans employed cavalry escorts for important prisoners, such as for Paul enroute to Antipatris (Acts 23:23-32). Chariot racing was a favorite diversion in their amphitheaters. In Bible times horses were unshod and driven with bit and bridle. They were often sumptuously adorned, frequently with bells (Zech. 14:20).   M.F.U.

BIBLIOGRAPHY: *See* article Horse, above.

HO'SAH (hō'sa; "hopeful").

1. A city of Asher, at a point on the boundary line where it turned from the direction of Tyre toward Achzib (Josh. 19:29); location unknown.

2. A Levite of the family of Merari who, with thirteen of his relatives, was appointed gatekeeper to the Ark after its arrival in Jerusalem (1 Chron. 16:38; 26:10-11, 16). In the latter distribution the gate of Shallecheth, on the W side of the Temple, fell to him, about 988 B.C.

HOSANNA (Gk. *hosannah,* from Heb. *hōshî'ânâ',* "save now"). The cry of the multitude as they joined in our Lord's triumphal procession into Jerusalem (Matt. 21:9, 15; Mark 11:9-10; John 12:13). The psalm from which it was taken (Ps. 118) was one with which they were familiar from being accustomed to recite verses 25 and 26 at the feast of Tabernacles. On that occasion the *Hallel,* consisting of Pss. 113-18, was chanted by one of the priests, and at certain intervals the multitudes joined in the responses, waving their branches of willow and palm and shouting "Hallelujah," or, "Hosanna," or, "O Lord, we beseech Thee, do send now prosperity" (118:25). On each of the seven days during which the feast lasted, the people thronged the court of the Temple and went in procession about the altar, setting their boughs bending toward it, the trumpets sounding as they shouted, "Hosanna." It was not uncommon for the Jews in later times to employ the observances of this feast, which was preeminently a feast of gladness, to express their feelings on other occasions of rejoicing (1 Macc. 13:51; 2 Macc. 10:6-7). *See* Hallel.

The early Christian church adopted this word into its worship. It is found in the apostolical constitutions connected with the great doxology "Glory be to God on high" and was frequently used in the Communion service, during which the great doxology was sung.

BIBLIOGRAPHY: F. C. Burkitt, *Journal of Theological Studies* 17 (1916): 139-49; J. S. Kennard, *Journal of Biblical Literature* 67 (1948): 171-76; J. J. Petuchowski, *Vetus Testamentum* 5 (1955): 226-71.

HOSE, HOSEN (Aram. *paṭîsh,* Dan. 3:21). The KJV rendering of the Aram. term. The NASB reads "coats," marg., "cloaks," and the NIV, "trousers."

HOSE'A (Heb. *hōshēa,* "deliverer"). The son of Beeri, and the first of the minor prophets.

Time. In the first verse of his prophecy it is stated that the word of the Lord "came to Hosea the son of Beeri, during the days of Uzziah, Jotham, Ahaz, and Hezekiah, kings of Judah, and . . . of Jeroboam the son of Joash, king of Israel." J. F. McCurdy dates the beginning of Hosea's public life at 748 B.C. and Hezekiah's death at 690 B.C., which would make the prophet's ministry extend over a period of about fifty-eight years. The book furnishes strong presumptive evidence in support of this chronology.

Place. There seems to be a general consent among commentators that the prophecies of Hosea were delivered in the kingdom of Israel and that he was a subject of that kingdom. This is favored not only by the fact that his prophetic addresses are occupied throughout with the ten tribes but also by the peculiar style and language of his prophecies, which have here and there an Aramean coloring, and still more by the intimate acquaintance with the circumstances and localities of the Northern Kingdom (5:1; 6:8-9; 12:12), which even goes so far as to call the Israelite kingdom "the land" (1:2), and the king of Israel "our king" (7:5). It has been conjectured that Hosea, having long appealed in vain to his countrymen, retired to Judah, and that there his prophecy was committed to writing in its present form.

The Prophet's Family Relations. It is recorded in 1:2-9 that Hosea, at the command of God, took a harlot (Gomer the daughter of Diblaim) as his wife and had by her two sons (Jezreel and Lo-ammi) and one daughter (Lo-ruhamah), and in 3:1-2 that by divine command he purchased an adulteress. These statements have given rise to much discussion as to their literal or allegorical interpretation. Strong (McClintock and Strong, *Cyclopedia,* s.v.) expresses the opinion that "there were two marriages by the prophet: first in chaps. 1, 2, of a woman (probably of lewd inclinations already) who became the mother of three children, and was afterward repudiated for her adultery; and the second in chap. 3, of a woman at least attached formerly to another, but evidently reformed to a virtuous wife. Both these women represented the Israelitish nation, especially the northern kingdom, which, although unfaithful to Jehovah, should first be punished and then reclaimed by him." Keil (*Com.*, ad loc.) says, "No other course is left to us than to picture to ourselves Hosea's marriages as internal events, i.e., as merely carried out in that inward and spiritual intuition in which the word of God was addressed to him; and this removes all the difficulties that beset the assumption of marriages contracted in outward reality."

HOSE'A, BOOK OF. The span of Hosea's ministry is indicated in the superscription to the book: "During the days of Uzziah [c. 792-740 b.c.], Jotham [c. 750-742 b.c.], Ahaz [c. 735-715 b.c.], and Hezekiah [c. 715-686 b.c.], kings of Judah, and during the days of Jeroboam [II, c. 793-753 b.c.] . . . , king of Israel" (1:1). The prophetic ministry of Hosea extended well beyond Jeroboam II's death into the period of civil war in which Zachariah (c. 753-752), Shallum (c. 752), Menahem (c. 752-742), Pekahiah (c. 742-740), Pekah (c. 752-732), and Hoshea (c. 732-723) reigned, until the fall of Samaria. For this reason some scholars, such as R. Pfeiffer (*Introduction to the O.T.* [1940], p. 566), view the reference to Hezekiah and other Judean kings in 1:1 as an interpolation. This is not necessitated since the recorded prophecies of Hosea are obviously only a compendium of his activity that extended into the early years of Hezekiah's reign. Whether the prophet was carried into Assyrian captivity is not known. Like Jeremiah of Judah, he was the prophet of doom to the Northern Kingdom.

Purpose. Hosea is the prophecy of God's unchanging love for Israel. Despite their contamination with Canaanite paganism and fertility cults, the prophet bent every effort to warn the people to repent in the face of God's perpetual love for them. His theme is fourfold: Israel's idolatry, wickedness, captivity, and restoration. Throughout the entire book, however, he weaves the theme of the love of God for Israel. Israel is depicted prophetically as Jehovah's adulterous wife, shortly to be put away but eventually to be purified and restored. These events are set forth in the divine command that the prophet marry a harlot. The offspring of that union are given names symbolic of Hosea's chief prophecies: Jezreel, "the dynasty of Jehu is to be extirpated"; Lo-ruhamah, "not shown mercy," a prophecy of the Assyrian captivity; Lo-ammi, "not my people," temporary rejection of Israel (cf. Rom. 11:1-24). In 2:1 Hosea is commanded to "say, to your brothers, 'Ammi,' and to your sisters, 'Ruhamah,' i.e., "my people" and "shown mercy," pointing to final restoration of the nation (cf. 11:25-27) in the end time (Hos. 1:2-2:23).

Contents.
I. Israel, Jehovah's faithless wife, repudiated and restored (1:1-3:5)
   A. The first marriage (1:1-2:23)
      1. Israel rejected, birth of Jezreel, Lo-ruhamah, Lo-ammi (1:1-9)
      2. Israel comforted (1:10-11)
      3. Israel chastised (2:1-13)
      4. Israel restored (2:14-23)
   B. The second marriage (3:1-5)
      1. The marriage itself (3:1-3)
      2. The symbolic meaning (3:4-5)
II. Israel, the object of God's love, reestablished as a repentant and restored nation (4:1-14:9)
   A. Israel's guilt (4:1-19)
   B. The Divine displeasure (5:1-15)
   C. The repentant remnant's cry (6:1-3)
   D. Jehovah's response (6:4-13:8)
   E. Final restoration (13:9-14:9)

Authorship and Genuineness. The book is unquestionably written by "Hosea, the son of Beeri" (1:1). Even the critical school commonly admits this unity. Two types of passages were sometimes denied to Hosea by late nineteenth-century criticism, namely those dealing with Judah and those promising restoration and blessing. Actually, there is no compelling reason for not attributing to Hosea any of the prophecy. More recent criticism tends to deny fewer passages as later interpolations (Aage Bentzen, *Introduction to the O.T.* [1949], 2:33, and Oesterley and Robinson, *Introduction to the Books of the O.T.*, p. 349). While granting the "possibility, even the probability" that certain passages in which Judah is mentioned may be later interpolations, critics by no means insist upon that and, regarding the passages on restoration, assert that the evidence "does not justify us in dogmatically asserting that they are not the work of Hosea himself." Divine authority and authenticity of the book are indicated by quotations from the prophet found in the NT (cf. Hos. 11:1 and Matt. 2:15; Hos. 6:6 and Matt. 9:13, 12:7; Hos. 10:8 and Luke 23:30; Hos. 2:23 and Rom. 9:25; Hos. 13:14 and 1 Cor. 15:55; Hos. 1:9-10, 2:23 and 1 Pet. 2:10).   M.F.U.

BIBLIOGRAPHY: N. H. Smith, *Mercy and Sacrifice* (1953); G. Oestborn, *Yahweh and Baal: Studies in the Book of Hosea* (1956); E. B. Pusey, *The Minor Prophets* (1961), 1:9-142; H. H. Rowley, *Men of God* (1963), pp. 66-97; J. L. Mays, *Hosea, a Commentary* (1969); G. C. Morgan, *Hosea: The Heart and Holiness of God* (1974); H. W. Wolff, *Hosea* (1974); H. C. von Orelli, *The Twelve Minor Prophets* (1977), pp. 9-72; F. I. Andersen and D. N. Freedman, *Hosea.* Anchor Bible (1980); F. A. Tatford, *The Minor Prophets* (1982), 1:1:7-172; J. M. Boice, *The Minor Prophets* (1983), 1:13-95; C. J. and A. A. Barber, *You Can Have a Happy Marriage* (1984), pp. 119-31.

HOSHA'IAH (hō-sha'ya; "Jah has saved").
   1. A man who assisted in the dedication of the

wall of Jerusalem after it had been rebuilt by Nehemiah (Neh. 12:32), 445 B.C.

2. The father of a certain Jezaniah, or Azariah, who was a man of note after the destruction of Jerusalem by Nebuchadnezzar. He wanted Jeremiah to favor the flight of the remnant of the Jews into Egypt (Jer. 42:1; 43:2), 586 B.C.

HOSHA'MA (hō-sha'ma), or **Hosh'ama** (hōsh'a-ma; "Jah has heard"). One of the sons of King Jehoiachin, born during his captivity (1 Chron. 3:18), after 597 B.C.

HOSHE'A (hō-shē'a; Heb. same as Hosea).

1. The original name of Joshua, the son of Nun (Num. 13:8, 16; Deut. 32:44, marg.). Moses changed his name when he sent the spies into the land of Canaan.

2. The son of Elah, and last king of Israel. He conspired against and killed his predecessor, Pekah (2 Kings 15:30), "in the twentieth year of Jotham." Tiglath-pileser set up Hoshea as the nominal king of Samaria, his personal representative (about 732 B.C.). He did not become established on the throne till after an interval of at least eight years, in the twelfth year of Ahaz (17:1). It is declared of him that "he did evil in the sight of the Lord, only not as the kings of Israel who were before him" (v. 2). Shortly after his accession he submitted to the supremacy of Shalmaneser, who appears to have entered his territory with the intention of subduing it by force if resisted (v. 3), and indeed seems to have stormed the strong caves of Beth-arbel (Hos. 10:14). Discovering that Hoshea had entered into negotiations with So, king of Egypt, prompted Shalmaneser to return and punish the rebellious king with imprisonment for withholding tribute (2 Kings 17:4). He was probably released by the payment of a large ransom, but a second revolt soon after provoked the king of Assyria to march an army into the land of Israel. After a three years' siege Samaria was taken and destroyed, and the ten tribes were carried away beyond the Euphrates, 721 B.C. (2 Kings 17:5-6; 18:9-12). Of the subsequent fortune of Hoshea we know nothing.

3. Son of Azaziah and leader of the tribe of Ephraim in the time of David (1 Chron. 27:20), about 1000 B.C.

4. One of the leaders of Israel who joined in the sacred covenant with Nehemiah after the captivity (Neh. 10:23), 445 B.C.

HOSPITALITY. In biblical times it was believed to be a sacred duty to receive, feed, lodge, and protect any traveler who might stop at one's door. The stranger was treated as a guest, and men who had thus eaten together were bound to each other by the strongest ties of friendship, which descended to their heirs and was confirmed by mutual presents. Hospitality was a religious duty for the Greeks as well as for the He-

brews, who were enjoined by the law of Moses (Lev. 19:34). The present practice of the Arabs is still similar to ancient Hebrew hospitality. A traveler may sit at the door of a perfect stranger and smoke his pipe until the master welcomes him with an evening meal, may tarry a limited number of days without inquiry as to his purposes, and may then depart with a simple "God be with you" as his only compensation. As the Hebrews became more numerous, inns were provided, but they did not entirely supersede *home hospitality*. The OT gives illustrations of it in Gen. 18:1-8; 19:1-3; 24:25, 31-33; etc. Job says (31:32), "The alien has not lodged outside, for I have opened my doors to the traveler." Neglect of the law of hospitality is illustrated in the case of the rich man and Lazarus (Luke 16:19-25).

The spirit of *Christian* hospitality is taught in the NT (Luke 14:12-14). The Gk. *philoxenos* (a "lover of strangers") is the word used for hospitable in Titus 1:8; 1 Pet. 4:9; and *philoxenia* ("love of strangers") for hospitality in Rom. 12:13; Heb. 13:2.

BIBLIOGRAPHY: D. W. Riddle, *Journal of Biblical Literature* 57 (1938): 141-54; J. Pedersen, *Israel, Its Life and Culture* (1940), 1-2:356-58; R. de Vaux, *Ancient Israel, Its Life and Institutions* (1962), pp. 10, 74-76, 160-63.

HOST.

1. In a social sense, literally a "stranger" (Gk. *xenos*), i.e., one who receives and entertains hospitably. *See* Rom. 16:23, where "and to the whole church" is added; meaning that Gaius received all the members of the church who crossed his threshold or kindly permitted the church to worship in his house.

2. "One who receives all comers," an *innkeeper* (so NASB and NIV) or *host* (so KJV), from Gk. *pandocheus* (Luke 10:35).

3. In a military sense ("host," KJV; "army," NASB), *see* Army.

HOST OF HEAVEN ("army of the skies," Gen. 2:1; etc.). The sun, moon, and stars, under the symbol of an army, in which the sun is considered king, the moon his viceregent, and the stars and planets their attendants (cf. Judg. 5:20). The worship of the host of heaven was one of the earliest forms of idolatry (which see) and was common among the Israelites in the times of their turning away from the pure service of God (Deut. 4:19; 2 Kings 17:16; 21:3, 5; Jer. 19:13; Zeph. 1:5; Acts 7:42).

The "host of heaven" referred to in Dan. 8:10-12 appears to be figurative for "the holy people," i.e., Israel (see 8:24). The comparison of Israel to the "host of heaven" has its root in the fact that God, the King of Israel, is called the God of hosts ("the Commander of the host," v. 11). The *hosts* are generally understood as stars or angels, but the tribes of Israel, who were led by God out of Egypt, are also called "the hosts of the Lord" (Ex. 7:4; 12:41; NIV, "divisions"). As in heaven the angels and stars form the host of God, so on earth the sons of Israel are His host. This comparison serves, then, to characterize the insolence of Antiochus (the "horn," Dan. 8:9) as a wickedness against heaven and the heavenly order of things (Keil, *Com.,* ad loc.).

Jehovah is frequently mentioned as "the Lord, the God of hosts," i.e., of the celestial armies (Jer. 5:14; 38:17; 44:7; Hos. 12:5; etc.). The Heb. *Sabaoth,* "hosts," is used by the apostles Paul and James (Rom. 9:29; James 5:4). The NIV frequently renders "the Lord, the God of hosts" as "the Lord God Almighty."

BIBLIOGRAPHY: S. N. Kramer, *Mythologies of the Ancient World* (1961).

HOSTAGE (Heb. *ta'ărūbâ;* "suretyship"). One delivered into the hand of another as security for the performance of a pledge or engagement. In ancient times it was usual for conquered kings or nations to give hostages for the payment of tribute and of continuance in subjection. Thus Jehoash, king of Israel, exacted hostages from Amaziah, king of Judah (2 Kings 14:14; 2 Chron. 25:24).

HO'THAM (hō'tham; a "seal ring"). One of the sons of Heber, the grandson of Asher (1 Chron. 7:32; 11:44). He is probably the same as Helem, whose sons are enumerated in v. 35 and grandsons in vv. 36-37.

HO'THAN (hō'than; Heb. same as Hotham). An Aroerite, father of Shama and Jeiel, two of David's "mighty men" (1 Chron. 11:44), about 1000 B.C.

HO'THIR (hō'thîr). The thirteenth son of *Heman* (which see), who, with eleven of his kinsmen, had charge of the twenty-first division of Levitical singers (1 Chron. 25:4, 28), after 1000 B.C.

HOUGH. *See* Hamstring.

HOUR. *See* Time.

HOUSE (Heb. *bayit;* Gk. *oikia*). The beginning of house building is lost in the darkness of primeval times and reaches back in the sacred record to the days of Cain (Gen. 4:17). Although the Israelites did not become dwellers in cities until their sojourn in Egypt and after the conquest of Canaan (cf. Gen. 47:3; Ex. 12:7; Heb. 11:9), the Canaanites, the Assyrians, and the Egyptians were from an early period builders of houses and cities. Of course, houses would vary according to the climate, tastes, and condition of the people. And yet we find some leading characteristics in the oriental house, distinguishing it from that of northern latitudes.

Material. The material for house building is determined partly by what is to be had in the locality, partly by the object of the buildings, and partly by the means of the builders. The houses of the rural poor in Egypt, as well as in most parts

of Syria, Arabia, and Persia, are for the most part mere huts of mud or sunburnt bricks. Those of the Israelites were probably mostly made of brick burned or merely dried in the sun, or of lime and sandstone. Only houses of the rich and palaces were built of hewn stone (1 Kings 7:9; Isa. 9:10) or white marble (1 Chron. 29:2). For mortar, clay or lime or gypsum (Isa. 33:12; cf. Deut. 27:4) and asphalt (Gen. 11:3) were used. The beams, doorposts, doors, windows, and stairs were commonly of sycamore (Isa. 9:10). In more ornamental buildings they were of olive, cypress, cedar, and sandal (1 Kings 7:2; Jer. 22:14).

Exterior. In earlier times it appears that only large palaces were built of more than one story. Such were the palace of Solomon, the house of Lebanon (1 Kings 7:2-12), and the three-story side chambers of Solomon's Temple (6:5-10). There is no other mention in Scripture of any house in Palestine with more than one story, for Acts 20:9 refers to Troas.

(1) *The walls* were whitewashed outside and inside with lime or gypsum; palaces were painted bright red (Jer. 22:14). The exterior of a dwelling house of the better kind in Palestine was for the most part plain and unattractive, having not more than the doorway and two or three latticed windows.

(2) *The roof* was usually flat, without any chimneys, and did not overhang the external walls. In the poorer class of houses the roofs were made of earth, stamped and rolled upon a foundation of boughs or rafters. The nature of these roofs readily explains the transaction referred to in Mark (2:4) and Luke (5:19). The bearers of the paralytic probably broke up the simple materials of the roof and through the aperture let him down into the presence of Jesus. The better class of houses had their roofs laid with tiles and stone. The outer edge was provided with a parapet or latticelike railing to prevent falling (Deut. 22:8). The roof is one of the most important parts of an Eastern house, as various kinds of business and

Eastern house, partly cutaway

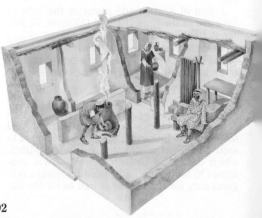

amusement occurred upon it. Rahab hid the spies beneath the stalks of flax laid on the roof to dry (Josh. 2:6). The roof was used for confidential communing (1 Sam. 9:25), for sleeping (v. 26), for lamentation (Isa. 15:3; Jer. 48:38), and for watching the approach of an enemy (Isa. 22:1) or the bearer of tidings (2 Sam. 18:24, 33). Booths were built upon the roof (Neh. 8:16) and altars for idolatrous worship (2 Kings 23:12; Jer. 19:13; Zeph. 1:5). Upon the roof, as in a most public place, Absalom spread the tent for his father's concubines, to indicate the unalterable estrangement between himself and David (2 Sam. 16:21-22). Announcements were made from the roof (Matt. 10:27; Luke 12:3). It was usual to have two flights of steps to ascend to the roof, one within the house and one in the street, which would afford a more ready escape than through the house (Matt. 24:17).

(3) *The porch* (Heb. *'ûlām*, "vestibule") was not uncommon in Egyptian houses, but was an unusual feature in the houses of ancient Palestine; no reference to it is found in the OT, except in the case of the Temple and Solomon's palace (1 Kings 7:6, 12; 2 Chron. 15:8; Ezek. 40:7). In the KJV and NIV "porch" (Judg. 3:23, Heb. *misderôn*) is incorrect and is better rendered "roof chamber," as in NASB. Again in KJV we read of a porch attached to the high priest's palace (Matt. 26:71, Gk. *pulōn*), which was the gate or entrance to the house from the street, as elsewhere (Acts 10:17; 12:14; 14:13; Rev. 21:12). In John 5:2 we read of a portico, that is, a porch or colonnade often at the entrance of a building.

(4) *Doors* were commonly made of wood, the more expensive being of cedar (Song of Sol. 8:9). But doors made of single slabs of stone, some inches thick, occasionally ten-feet high, and turning on stone pivots, are found in the old houses and sepulchers in Syria. The doorways of Eastern houses were sometimes richly ornamented, although they were generally plain in appearance even when belonging to sumptuous dwellings. The doorway from the street into the court was usually guarded from sight by a wall or some arrangement of passages and had a stone seat for the porter and other servants. The Israelites were directed to write sentences from the law and place them over the door (Deut. 6:9).

(5) *The court* (Heb. *ḥāṣer*, "inclosed") was one of the common characteristics of Eastern houses, the latter being built to inclose one, two, and even three courts. If there was only one court, it was an open space or quadrangle, around which the apartments for the inhabitants, and in country places also the sheds for the cattle, were arranged. A house of a somewhat better description usually consisted of the court, three or four storerooms on the ground floor, with a single chamber above, from which a flight of stairs led to the court. The houses of men of rank and also palaces were usually built with a roomy court,

surrounded with porticoes and galleries, paved, and provided with a well (2 Sam. 17:18) and baths (11:2), probably planted with trees, and forming the reception room of the house. If there were three or more courts, all except the outer one were alike in size and appearance. But the outer one, being devoted to the more public life and contact with society, was materially different from all the others. Into this court the principal apartments looked and were either open to it in front or were entered from it by doors. Over the doorway leading from the street was a projecting window with a lattice more or less elaborately wrought, which, except in times of public celebrations, was usually closed (2 Kings 9:30). An awning was sometimes drawn over the court and the floor strewn with carpets on festive occasions. The stairs to the upper apartments were usually in a corner of the court. Around part, if not the whole, of the court was a veranda, often nine- or ten-feet deep, over which, when there was more than one floor, ran a second gallery of like depth with a balustrade. If there were more than three courts the second was for the use of the master of the house, where he was attended by his eunuchs, children, and wives; he saw only those whom he called from the third court, where they lived. It was into this court that Esther came to invite the king to visit her part of the palace, but she would not on any account have gone into the outer court.

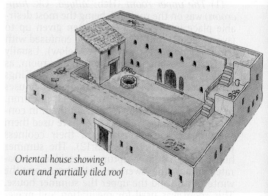

Oriental house showing court and partially tiled roof

(6) *The window* of an Eastern house had no glass, consisted generally of an aperture inclosed with latticework, and was small so as to exclude the heat. The windows usually looked onto the court, but in every house one or more looked onto the street, making it possible for a person to observe the approach of another without himself being visible (Judg. 5:28; 2 Sam. 6:16; Prov. 7:6; Song of Sol. 2:9). Where houses were built against the city wall it was not unusual for them to have projecting windows surmounting the wall and looking out into the country. From such a window the spies escaped from Jericho (Josh. 2:15) and Paul from Damascus (2 Cor. 11:33).

Daniel's room had several windows, and his lattices were open when his enemies found him at prayer (Dan. 6:10). The projecting nature of the window and the fact that a couch or raised seat encircled the interior so that persons sitting at the window were near the aperture, easily explain the falls of Ahaziah and Eutychus (2 Kings 1:2; Acts 20:9).

(7) *The pillar* formed an important feature in oriental buildings, partly, perhaps, as reminiscent of the tent with its supporting poles, and partly from the use of flat roofs. Pillars were used to support flat roofs or awnings as well as to support curtains (Ex. 26:32). The circumstance of Samson's pulling down the house by means of the pillars may be explained by the fact that the company was assembled on tiers of balconies above each other, supported by central pillars on the basement. When these were pulled down the whole of the upper floors also fell (Judg. 16:26-30).

(8) These ancient houses did not have *chimneys;* the word so rendered (Hos. 13:3) means a hole through which the smoke escaped. They were used only in the poorer houses, where wood was used for fuel. In the better class of houses the rooms were warmed by charcoal in braziers (Jer. 36:22; Mark 14:54; John 18:18) or by a fire in the open court at night (Luke 22:55).

Interior.

(1) *The upper room* (Heb. *'ăliyyâ,* Gk. *huperōon*) was on the roof and, being the most desirable place in the house, was often given up to favored guests, but it must not be confused with the *guest chamber* (which see, below). Usually the Scriptures mention but one upper room, as if there were only one (1 Kings 17:19; 2 Kings 4:11; Acts 9:39; 20:8), but in the larger houses there were several (1 Chron. 28:11; 2 Chron. 3:9). Frequent mention is made of them in connection with kings, who seem to have used them as summer houses because of their coolness (Judg. 3:20; 2 Kings 1:2; 23:12). The summer house spoken of in Scripture was seldom a separate building; the lower part of the house was the winter house and the upper the summer house. This room was used for meditation and prayer (Mark 14:15; Luke 22:12), was set apart for the

Eastern house with threshing floor in front

prophets (1 Kings 17:19; 2 Kings 4:10), and, because of its size and coolness, was a place of meeting (Acts 1:13; 20:8). For similar reasons the dead were laid out in it (9:39). An upper room appears to have been built over the gateways of towns (2 Sam. 18:33).

(2) *The guest chamber* (Heb. *lishkâ,* Gk. *kataluma*) was placed opposite the entrance onto the court and was used by the master of the house for the reception of all visitors. It was often open in front and supported in the center by a pillar and was generally on the ground floor but raised above the level of the court. This would seem to have been the guest chamber where our Lord ate His last Passover (Mark 14:14-15; Luke 22:11), being not the "upper room" but an elevated ground-floor room. Before entering, the guests took off their shoes; so our Lord is thought to have had His feet bare when the woman washed them (Luke 7:38).

(3) *Other rooms.* There are seldom any special bedrooms in Eastern houses, except in those of the wealthy (2 Kings 11:2; Eccles. 10:20; 2 Sam. 4:7). In Egypt there were such rooms (Gen. 43:30; Ex. 8:3), as also in Syria (2 Kings 6:12). Generally a low divan, raised around the sides of the room, served for seats by day, and on it were placed the beds for sleeping during the night. The *ceilings* of the principal apartments were adorned with much care and often at great expense. The *kitchen,* when there was an inner court, was always attached to it, as the cooking was performed by the women. The furniture of this apartment consisted of a sort of raised platform of brick, with receptacles on it for fire, answering to the "boiling places" of Ezekiel (46:23). The fuel used was usually charcoal, and the food was cooked in pots and chafing dishes.

(4) The *furniture* in ancient Eastern houses was generally simple, owing probably to the people's spending so much time outdoors. And though we have no exact information respecting the furniture of houses in Palestine, it is probable that they indulged, as did surrounding nations, in many luxuries, as wealth permitted. For the furnishing of an apartment the Israelites appear to have held the following articles as indispensable: a bed, table, chair, and lampstand (2 Kings 4:10). To these were added, for the complete furnishing of a house, the necessary cooking, eating, and drinking vessels. In the houses of the wealthy these articles were not only provided in great abundance but were also costly and luxurious. The rooms were furnished with cushions and couches, which served also as beds, and were covered with costly carpets (Prov. 7:16) and soft pillows. The bedsteads were inlaid with ivory (Amos 6:4), and the tables and stools, which were much more in use among the Israelites than at present in the East (2 Kings 4:10; Prov. 9:14), were artistically wrought. The eating and drink-

ing vessels were of gold and silver, and the wardrobes and chests were equally ornate.

Figurative. The word *house* is often used in Scripture in the sense of lineage or family; thus Joseph was of the house of David (Luke 1:27, marg.; 2:4); offspring (2 Sam. 7:11); household (Gen. 43:16; Isa. 36:3). Heaven is the house of God (John 14:2); the grave is the house appointed for all living (Job 30:23; Isa. 14:18, marg.); the body is called a house (2 Cor. 5:1-2).

BIBLIOGRAPHY: A. C. Bouquet, *Everyday Life in New Testament Times* (1954); E. W. Heaton, *Everyday Life in Old Testament Times* (1956); W. A. Corswant, *Dictionary of Life in Bible Times* (1960).

HOUSEHOLD.

1. The rendering generally of the same Heb. and Gk. words as are rendered "house," and meaning the members of a family living in the same dwelling, including servants and dependents (Isa. 36:3). The expression "those of Caesar's household" (Phil 4:22) seems to refer to some of the servants of the emperor.

2. One of the divisions of the Hebrews, such as tribes, families, households, etc. *See* Israel, Constitution of.

HOUSETOP. The flat roof of an Eastern *house* (which see).

Figurative. Some of these roofs were covered with earth rolled hard, which, softened by rain, would afford nourishment for grass seeds. When the returning drought and heat came the grass soon withered, a proper illustration of momentary prosperity followed by ruin (2 Kings 19:26; Ps. 129:6; Isa. 37:27).

HOWLER. *See* Animal Kingdom: Owl, no. 8.

HUB (Heb. ḥishshûr). The central part of the wheel, where the spokes unite. In the KJV of 1 Kings 7:33 the Heb. term is incorrectly translated "spoke." Cf. Nave; Spoke; Rims.

HUB'BAH (hub'a). One of four sons of Shomer, a descendant of Asher (1 Chron. 7:34).

HUK'KOK (hūk'ok). A city on the southern border of Naphtali, near Aznoth-tabor (Josh. 19:34). Robinson and Van de Velde identify it with Yakuk, five miles W of the site of Capernaum, and that is now generally accepted. There is another Hukkok (1 Chron. 6:75; NASB and NIV, "Hukok") in Asher. In Josh. 21:31 it is called Helkath instead of Hukkok, a case in which two names are applied to one place.

HU'KOK (hū'kok; 1 Chron. 6:75). *See* Hukkok.

HUL (hūl; "circle"), the second son of Aram, and grandson of Shem (Gen. 10:23; 1 Chron. 1:17). The geographical location of the people whom he represents is not positively known. Identification either with Huleh around Lake Merom or with Hūli'a in the Mt. Massius regions mentioned by Ashurnasirpal seems quite probable.

HUL'DAH (hul'da; "mole, weasel"). A prophetess, the wife of *Shallum* (which see), who was keeper of the wardrobe (2 Kings 22:14). She dwelt, in the reign of Josiah, in that part of Jerusalem called the Mishneh (the "Second Quarter"). To her the king sent Hilkiah the priest, Shaphan the scribe, and others to consult respecting the denunciations in the lately found book of the law. She then delivered an oracular response of mingled judgment and mercy, declaring the near destruction of Jerusalem but promising Josiah that he should be taken from the world before these evil days came (22:14-20; 2 Chron. 34:22-28), about 639 B.C. Huldah is known only from this circumstance.

HUMAN SACRIFICE. *See* Sacrifice.

HUMAN SOUL. *See* Soul.

HUMANITY OF CHRIST. *See* Christ, Incarnation of.

HUMILIATION OF CHRIST. An expression that refers to the earthly life of the Lord Jesus Christ and contrasts His condition during that period, on the one hand, with the glory of His pre-existent state and, on the other, with His subsequent exaltation. The fact, the constituent features, the end, and the ethical significance of Christ's humiliation are all matters of explicit Scripture teaching.

(1) *The fact* was more than suggested in certain utterances of the Lord Himself (John 3:13; 6:62; 16:28; 17:5). In deepest harmony with such utterances, as well as with the declared facts of our Lord's earthly history, was apostolic teaching; e.g., Paul said, "He humbled Himself" (Phil. 2:8; *see also* 2 Cor. 8:9; Heb. 2:9-10, 17-18). According to the importance of these and other passages, the humiliation of Christ began with His incarnation, culminated in His death upon the cross, and came to its end in His exaltation to the right hand of God.

(2) *Nature.* An examination of the Scripture bearing upon this subject shows that the humiliation consisted (*a*) in His voluntary incarnation; (*b*) in His not only entering into union with human nature but also in assuming a manhood that, though sinless, was still subject to the infirmities of man's moral condition (*see* Rom. 8:3); (*c*) in that He was "born under the Law" (Gal. 4:4-5), i.e., subjected to legal measures and obligations appropriate only for human beings; (*d*) in His standing as the representative of sinners (2 Cor. 5:21); (*e*) in His sacrificial death; (*f*) in that His humiliation was made more conspicuous by poverty, persecutions, and the scorn and cruelties that He suffered at the hands of blind and sinful men.

(3) *The end* of His humiliation was (*a*) in a subordinate sense, the fulfillment of certain types and predictions of the OT dispensation (*see* Matt. 2:23; 27:9-10; John 12:38); (*b*) chiefly, that

Christ might come in the most complete sense into oneness with mankind and thus accomplish human redemption (2 Cor. 5:21; 8:9; etc.).

(4) *Its ethical import* appears in that (*a*) Christ sets before the world the most perfect example of usefulness (*see* Matt. 20:28; 2 Cor. 8:9); (*b*) likewise of patience and humility (Matt. 10:24-25; 11:29; Heb. 12:2-3).

BIBLIOGRAPHY: A. B. Bruce, *The Humiliation of Christ* (1914); E. H. Gifford and S. J. Andrews, *The Incarnation of Christ*, 2 vols. in 1 (1981).

HUMILITY (Heb. *'ānāwâ*, "gentleness, affliction," also from *'ānâ*, "to be bowed down"; Gk. *tapeinophrosunē*, "lowliness of mind," *praotēs*, "gentleness"). Humility in the spiritual sense is an inwrought grace of the soul that allows one to think of himself no more highly than he ought to think (Eph. 4:1-2; Col. 3:12-13; cf. Rom. 12:3). In contrast, the moralists considered humility (from *humus*, "earth") to be meanness of spirit. The exercises of it are first and chiefly toward God (Matt. 11:29; James 1:21). It requires us to feel that in God's sight we have no merit and to in honor prefer others to ourselves (Rom. 12:10; cf. Prov. 15:33). It does not demand undue self-depreciation but rather lowliness of self-estimation and freedom from vanity. The Gk. term *praotēs*, "gentleness" (rendered "meekness" in KJV) expresses a spirit of willingness and obedience and a lack of resistence to God's dealings with us. But humility must also be expressed towards those who wrong us, in order that their insults and wrongdoing might be used by God for our benefit (*see* Acts 20:18-21). It is enjoined of God (Ps. 25:9; Col. 3:12; James 4:6, 10) and is essential to discipleship under Christ (Matt. 18:3-4).

BIBLIOGRAPHY: R. C. Trench, *Synonyms of the New Testament* (1953), pp. 148-57.

HUM'TAH (hum'ta). One of the cities in the hill country allotted to Judah following Israel's conquest of Canaan (Josh. 15:54).

HUNCHBACK. *See* Diseases.

HUNDREDS. One of the groups (Ex. 18:21) into which Moses divided the people of Israel. *See* Israel, Classification of.

HUNDRED, TOWER OF THE (*mē'â*, "a hundred"). One of the towers on the wall of Jerusalem, rebuilt by Nehemiah (3:1; 12:39), near the Sheep Gate. The KJV gives Tower of Meah.

HUNGER (Heb. *rā'ēb*). The rendering of the same Heb. and Gk. words that are sometimes rendered *famine* (which see).

Figurative. Our Lord, in the Sermon on the Mount (Matt. 5:6), uses hunger as symbolic of deep and earnest longing after righteousness.

HUNT, HUNTER, HUNTING (Heb. *ṣayid*, to "lie in wait"; *rādap*, to "run after"). Naturally, the pursuit and capture of wild animals early became a means of both sustenance and pleasure.

Egyptians. In Egypt the desert had its perils and resources; the lion, leopard, panther, and other dangerous beasts were found there. The nobles, like the pharaohs of later times, regarded as their privilege or duty the stalking and destroying of these animals. The common people hunted the gazelle, oryx, mouflon sheep, ibex, wild ox, the ostrich, and such humbler game as the porcupine and the long-eared hare. To scent and retrieve the game, the hyena ran side by side with the wolf-dog and the lithe Abyssinian greyhound. When the Egyptian wished to procure animals without seriously hurting them, he used the net for birds, and the lasso and the *bola* for quadrupeds, these being less injurious than the spear and arrow. The *bola* was made of a single rounded stone, attached to a strap about five yards long. When the stone was thrown the cord twisted around the legs, muzzle, or neck of the animal, and the hunter was able to bring down his prey.

Chaldeans. Among this people the chase was a favorite pastime and afforded substantial additions to the food supply. It was, however, essentially the pastime of the noble, who hunted the lion and bear in the wooded covers or the marshy thickets of the river bank, and the gazelle, ostrich, and bustard on the elevated plains or rocky tablelands of the desert. Recovered reliefs show that Assyrian kings especially delighted in hunting lions. Ashurbanipal is presented most vividly in his chariot spearing a leaping lion.

Assyrian relief of dying lioness

Biblical. The chase is mentioned as being pursued as early as the time of Nimrod, who was "a mighty hunter before the Lord" (Gen. 10:9); but it does not appear to have formed a special occupation among the Israelites. It was practiced by farmers and shepherds, partly for the sake of food (Gen. 27:3-5, 30-31; Prov. 12:27), partly in defending their flocks against beasts of prey (1 Sam. 17:34-35).

Hunters used the bow and arrow (Gen. 27:3), slings (1 Sam. 17:40), nets, snares, and pits, especially for larger animals, such as antelopes (Isa. 51:20) and lions (2 Sam. 23:20; Ezek. 19:3-4).

The following regulations are given in the Mosaic law: (1) The products of the land in the Sabbatic year were to be left, in part to serve the wants of the beasts of the field (Ex. 23:11; Lev.

25:7). (2) If eggs or young birds were taken from a nest, the mother was allowed to escape (Deut. 22:6-7). (3) Israelites and any strangers among them were required to let the blood flow from edible wild beasts and birds taken in the hunt and to cover it with earth (Lev. 17:13) because, containing the life, it was considered holy.

HU'PHAM (hū'fam). Apparently one of the sons of Benjamin (Num. 26:39) and founder of the family of the Huphamites. He is supposed to be the same as Huppim. From 1 Chron. 7:12, 15, it would appear that Huppim was a grandson of Benjamin.

HU'PHAMITES (hū'fam-īts). The descendants (Num. 26:39) of *Hupham* (which see).

HUP'PAH (hūp'a; "covering, protection"). A priest in David's time, having charge of the thirteenth of the twenty-four classes into which the king divided the priests (1 Chron. 24:13), 1000 B.C.

HUP'PIM (Gen. 46:21; 1 Chron. 7:12, 15). *See* Hupham.

HUR (hūr; a "hole, prison"). The name of five men.

1. A man who is mentioned in connection with Moses and Aaron on the occasion of the battle with Amalek at Rephidim, when he and Aaron held up the hands of Moses (Ex. 17:10, 12). He is mentioned again in connection with Aaron in 24:14 as being left in charge of the people by Moses during his ascent of Sinai, c. 1440 B.C. He was, according to Josephus (*Ant.* 3.2.4), the husband of Miriam, the sister of Moses.

2. The grandfather of Bezalel, the chief artificer of the Tabernacle—"the son of Uri, son of Hur, of the tribe of Judah" (Ex. 31:2; 35:30; 38:22). In the lists of the descendants of Judah in 1 Chronicles the pedigree is more fully preserved. Hur there appears as one of the great family of Perez. He was the firstborn son of Caleb, the son of Hezron, by a second wife, Ephrath (2:19-20; 2:50; 4:4; cf. 2:5, also 4:1), and the father, besides Uri (2:20), of three sons, who founded the towns of Kiriath-jearim, Bethlehem, and Beth-gader (v. 51), before 1440 B.C. (Smith, *Dict.*).

3. The fourth named of the five kings of Midian who were slain (with Balaam) by the Israelites, under the leadership of Phinehas (Num. 31:8), about 1401 B.C. In a later mention of them (Josh. 13:21) these five Midianites are called "dukes of Sihon," properly, "vassals."

4. A person whose son (Ben-hur) was the first named of Solomon's twelve deputies. His district was in Mt. Ephraim (1 Kings 4:8), about 960 B.C.

5. Father of Rephaiah, which latter is called "the official of half the district of Jerusalem" after the captivity and who assisted in repairing its walls (Neh. 3:9), before 445 B.C.

HU'RAI (hū'rī). A native of the valleys ("brooks")

of Mt. Gaash and one of David's mighty men (1 Chron. 11:32), called less correctly (2 Sam. 23:30) *Hiddai* (which see), 953 B.C.

HU'RAM (hū'ram). Another form of *Hiram* (which see).

1. A Benjamite, son of Bela, the firstborn of the patriarch (1 Chron. 8:5).

2. The form in which the name of the king of Tyre in alliance with David and Solomon—and elsewhere given as Hiram—appears in Chronicles (2 Chron. 2:3, 11-12; 8:2, 18; 9:10, 21). The NIV, however, renders "Hiram" in Chronicles.

3. The same change occurs in Chronicles in the name of Hiram the artificer, which is given as Huram (2 Chron. 4:11) and Huram-abi (2:13; 4:16).

HU'RI (hū'ri). The son of Jaroah and father of Abihail, of the descendants of Gad in Bashan (1 Chron. 5:14).

HUSBAND. *See* Marriage.

HUSBANDMAN, HUSBANDMEN. The KJV rendering for several Heb. terms (*'îsh 'ǎdāmâ*, "man of the ground"; *'ikkār; 'ebed; yôgēb*) and one Gk. one (*geōrgos*). Replaced in the NASB and the NIV by *farmer, tiller of the ground, plowman,* and *vinedresser.* The term *husbandry* appears in the KJV of 2 Chron. 26:10 (Heb. *'ǎdāmâ*) and 1 Cor. 3:9 (Gk. *geōrgos*). The NASB and NIV readings are "soil" and "field" respectively. *See* Farmer; Plowman.

HUSBANDRY. *See* Husbandman.

HU'SHAH (hū'sha; "hurry; haste"). Son of Ezer and descendant of Hur, of the family of Judah (1 Chron. 4:4), and probably from where the patronymic *Hushathite* (which see) came (2 Sam. 21:18; 1 Chron. 11:29; 20:4). He seems to be the same as Shuhah in 1 Chron. 4:11.

HU'SHAI (hū'shī; "hasty"). An Archite and a prominent actor in the history of Absalom's rebellion. When David fled from Jerusalem Hushai joined him, but, at David's suggestion, he returned to the city for the purpose of serving his master, as occasion might offer (2 Sam. 15:32-37). Accordingly, he offered his allegiance to Absalom (16:16-19) and was invited by him to a conference that would decide the prince's action. Hushai advised delay in the pursuit of the king until more ample preparation had been made, thus defeating the counsel of Ahithophel (17:5-22). The immediate result was the suicide of the defeated Ahithophel (v. 23) and the ultimate consequence was the crushing of the rebellion, about 997 B.C. He is called the "friend" of David (1 Sam. 15:37; 1 Chron. 27:33). Baana, Solomon's deputy in Asher (2 Kings 4:16), was doubtless his son.

BIBLIOGRAPHY: W. G. Blaikie, *David, King of Israel* (1981), pp. 259-67; F. W. Krummacher, *David, the King of Israel* (1983), pp. 401-19.

HU'SHAM (hū'sham; "hastily"). A Temanite, the son of Bedad and successor of Jobab, among the native princes of Mt. Seir before the usurpation of the Edomites (Gen. 36:34-35; 1 Chron. 1:45-46).

HU'SHATHITE, THE (hū'sha-thīt). The designation of one of the heroes of David's guard, Sibbecai (2 Sam. 21:18; 1 Chron. 11:29; 20:4; 27:11). Josephus, however, calls him a Hittite. In 2 Sam. 23:27 he is called Mebunnai, a corruption of Sibbecai. *See* Hushah.

HU'SHIM (hū'shim; "hasters").

1. The son of Dan (Gen. 46:23), given as Shuham in Num. 26:42.

2. A name given as that of "the *sons* of Aher," or Aharah, the third son of Benjamin (1 Chron. 7:12; cf. 8:1), and therefore only a plural form for *Shuham,* as a representative of his brethren.

3. One of the wives of Shaharaim, a Benjamite, in the country of Moab, by whom he had Abitub and Elpaal (1 Chron. 8:8, 11).

HU'SHITES (hu'shīts). *See* Hushim, no. 2.

HUSK. *See* Vegetable Kingdom: Pods.

HUT (Heb. *mᵉlûnâ,* Isa. 1:8, NASB and NIV; Heb. *sūkkâ,* Job 27:18, NASB and NIV). The "hut" in Isa. 1:8 (NASB and NIV) was a shed or *lodge* (so KJV) for the watchman of a garden: "The daughter of Zion is left like a shelter in a vineyard, like a watchman's hut in a cucumber field." It was usually built on an elevation of ground, with room for only one person, who in solitude watched the ripening crop. "So did Jerusalem stand in the midst of desolation reaching far and wide—a sign, however, that the land was not entirely depopulated" (Delitzsch, *Com.,* ad loc.).

For the "hut" in Job 27:18, *see* Cottage; Booth.

HUZ. *See* Uz.

HUZ'ZAB (hūz'ab; Heb. *nāṣab,* to "establish"). This word is erroneously rendered in KJV (Nah. 2:7) as a proper name. The meaning appears to be as follows: the prophet has been declaring that "the gates of the river are opened,/And the palace is dissolved," and then he cries out, as if against objectors, "And it is fixed" (so NASB), or "decreed" (so NIV), i.e., it is determined (by God).

HYACINTH. *See* Mineral Kingdom: Jacinth.

HYENA. *See* Animal Kingdom: Hyena; Jackal.

HYK'SOS (hik'sōs; Egyptian for "rulers of foreign lands"). A mixed race, predominantly NW Semitic, which gradually infiltrated Egypt and finally took control (c. 1720-1550 B.C.). They reigned during Dynasties XV and XVI. Their capital was at Zoan-Tanis in the Delta. Archaeological excavations have uncovered many Hyksos remains. They introduced the horse and chariot into Egypt, as well as the composite bow. These implements of war made possible the New Em-

pire of Egypt after 1550 B.C. and the expulsion of the Hyksos. The Hyksos Dynasties of Egypt were brought to an end when Khamose and Ahmose expelled them from the Delta (c. 1600-1550 B.C.). Amenhotep I inaugurated the splendid strong Eighteenth Dynasty (c. 1546-1319 B.C.). Although many scholars maintain that the Exodus took place under the Nineteenth Dynasty, the chronological data preserved in the MT undeniably places this event in the Eighteenth Dynasty. The Hyksos erected large earthen enclosures for their horses. This type of construction can be seen at Jericho, Shechem, Lachish, and Tell el-Ajjul. They also erected many temples to Baal. There are evidences of the worship of the mother goddess. Common in Hyksos levels are cultic objects such as nude figurines, serpents, and doves, showing their complete devotion to a degrading worship. Hyksos burial customs are distinctive, as is their chariotry.   M.F.U.

BIBLIOGRAPHY: H. E. Winlock, *Rise and Fall of the Middle Kingdom in Thebes* (1947), pp. 150-70; W. G. Waddell, *Manetho.* Loeb Classical Library (1948); J. van Seters, *The Hyksos: A New Investigation* (1966).

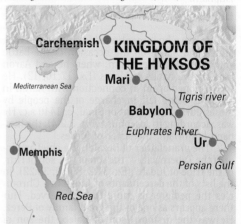

HYMENAE'US (hī-men-ē'us; "pertaining to Hymen, god of marriage"). A person in Ephesus twice named in the epistles of Timothy, who, with Alexander (1 Tim. 1:20) and Philetus (2 Tim. 2:17), had departed from the truth in faith and practice.

Error. The chief doctrinal error of these persons consisted in maintaining that "the resurrection has already taken place" (2 Tim. 2:18). The precise meaning of this expression is by no means clearly ascertained; the most general and perhaps best founded opinion is that they understood the resurrection in a figurative sense of the great change produced by the gospel dispensation. Thus he stands as one of the earliest of the Gnostics.

Sentence. "Whom I have delivered over to Satan" (1 Tim. 1:20). The exact meaning of this formula has been much discussed. Some believe it means simply excommunication; others, supernatural infliction of corporeal punishment; others, a combination of both. Elliott (*Com.*, ad loc.) says, "We conclude, then, with Waterland, that 'delivery over to Satan' was a form of Christian excommunication, declaring the person reduced to the state of a heathen, *accompanied with* the authoritative infliction of bodily disease or death." Satan was held to be the instrument or executioner of all these visitations (cf. 1 Cor. 5:5; 1 John 5:16).

BIBLIOGRAPHY: R. C. H. Lenski, *Interpretation of St. Paul's Epistles to the Colossians, to the Thessalonians, to Timothy* (1937), pp. 543-46, 811-13; E. K. Simpson, *The Pastoral Epistles* (1957), pp. 38-39, 137-38; H. P. Liddon, *Explanatory Analysis of St. Paul's First Epistle to Timothy* (1978), pp. 8-9; P. Fairbairn, *The Pastoral Epistles* (1980), pp. 106-10, 345-46.

HYPOCRISY (Heb. from *ḥānap*, to "defile," cf. Jer. 3:9, "polluted"; Gk. *hupokrisis*, "an answer, to play a part"). Dissimulation of one's real character or belief; a false assumption of character or belief. The Gk. word signifies the part taken by an actor; hence, outward show. Hypocrisy is professing to be what one is not and is generally applied to religious character. It is forbidden to the Christian (James 3:17).

HYPOCRITE. The hypocrite is a double person, natural and artificial. The first he keeps to himself, and the other he puts on, as he does his clothes, to make his appearance before men. Hypocrites have been divided into four classes: (1) The *wordly* hypocrite, who makes a profession of religion and pretends to be religious, merely from worldly considerations (Matt. 23:5). (2) The *legal* hypocrite, who relinquishes his vicious practices, in order thereby to merit heaven, while at the same time having no real love for God (Rom. 10:3). (3) The *evangelical* hypocrite, whose religion is nothing more than a bare conviction of sin; who rejoices under the idea that Christ died for him, and yet has no desire to live a holy life (Matt. 13:20). (4) The *enthusiastic* hypocrite, who has an imaginary sight of his sins and of Christ and talks of remarkable impulses and high feelings, etc., while living in the most scandalous practices (2 Cor. 11:14).

HYSSOP. In some of the sacrifices the relation between the shed blood and the transgressor was made manifest by the sprinkling on him of part of the blood. This was done using a bunch of hyssop. The first record of this use of hyssop is in connection with the Exodus, when the Israelites employed it to sprinkle the doorposts with the blood of the paschal lamb (Ex. 12:22). It was also used in connection with the ceremony of purifying lepers (Lev. 14:4-7) and in sprinkling blood on the leprous house (vv. 48-53). Hyssop was also used in the peculiar ordinance appointed for the purification of ceremonial uncleanness contracted by touching a dead body (Num. 19:14-18). *See* Sacrificial Offerings: Heifer, The Red.

The simplest form of the hyssop sprinkler is the "bunch," which each father in Israel hastily prepared before leaving Egypt. In the Mosaic ritual the bunch of hyssop was tied with a scarlet thread (19:6). In the account of the crucifixion (John 19:28-29) it is recorded, "they put a sponge full of the sour wine upon a bunch of hyssop, and brought it to His mouth." In the parallel passages of Matthew and Mark no reference is made to the hyssop, but it is said that the sponge was put upon a reed. Some explain the difference of statement by the supposition that the hyssop was fastened to a reed; others that the Gk. term rendered "reed" was a long stalk of hyssop; others, as Haley (*Alleged Discrepancies*, p. 235), believe that drink was twice offered to our Lord.

Figurative. The psalmist, having in view the frequent use of hyssop in the ceremonial law as a means by which the virtue of the sacrifice was transferred to the transgressor, applies it figuratively to the purification of the soul from guilt when he prays, "Purify me with hyssop, and I shall be clean" (Ps. 51:7). In alluding to Solomon's botanical knowledge it is said, "He spoke of trees, from the cedar tree that is in Lebanon even to the hyssop that grows on the wall" (1 Kings 4:33). The tall cedar and the humble hyssop at once suggests the most extensive range in the vegetable world. *See* Vegetable Kingdom. David at the time the Ziphites proposed betraying him to Saul (1 Sam. 23:19; 26:1, 3). Hachilah appears to have been the long ridge, now called El Kôlah, where there is a high hill with a ruin, called Yûkîn.

HACH'MONI (hak'mō-ni; "wise, skillful"). A man known only as the father (or ancestor, cf. 1 Chron. 27:2) of Jashobeam, the chief of David's warriors (11:11, where *son of Hachmoni* is rendered "Hachmonite"; the parallel passage in 2 Sam. 23:8 has "Tahchemonite"), and also of Jehiel, the companion of the princes in the royal household (1 Chron. 27:32), considerably before 1000 B.C. Hachmon or Hachmoni was, no doubt, the founder of a family to which these belonged. The actual father of Jashobeam was Zabdiel (27:2), who belonged to the Korahites (12:6); possibly the Levites descended from Korah (McClintock and Strong, *Cyclopedia*).

I AM (*'ehyeh 'āsher 'ehyeh,* "I am Who I am"). The name God gave Himself when speaking to Moses from the midst of the burning bush (Ex. 3:14; lit., God *is He who is*); the absolute *I,* the self-existent *One.*

BIBLIOGRAPHY: S. Charnock, *Existence and Attributes of God* (1977), pp. 78-80.

IBEX. *See* Animal Kingdom.

IB'HAR (ib'har; "choice"). One of the sons of David, born to him in Jerusalem (2 Sam. 5:15; 1 Chron. 3:6; 14:5), after 1000 B.C.

IB'LEAM (ib'lē-am). A city—with suburban towns—within the natural boundaries of Asher but assigned to Manasseh (Josh. 17:11); one of the towns from which Manasseh failed to expel the Canaanites (v. 12). It is called *Bileam* (1 Chron. 6:70), a Levitical city (cf. Josh. 21:25, where it is called Gath-rimmon). Probably preserved in the ruins of Khirbet-belameh, about ten miles SE of Megiddo.

IBNE'IAH (ib-nē'ya; "built by Jah"). A son of Jeroham, who, with other Benjamites, returned to Jerusalem after the captivity (1 Chron. 9:8), after 536 B.C.

IBNI'JAH (ib-nī'ja; "building of Jah"). The ancestor of Meshullam, a Benjamite, who settled in Jerusalem after the return from Babylon (1 Chron. 9:8), after 536 B.C.

IB'RI (ib'ri; an "Eberite," or "Hebrew"). The last of the sons of Merari by Jaaziah, apparently a descendant of Levi in the time of David (1 Chron. 24:27).

IB'SAM (ib'sam; "fragrant, pleasant"). One of the "sons" or descendants of Tola, the son of Issachar, in David's army (1 Chron. 7:2; "Jibsam," KJV), about 1000 B.C.; or he may have been a son of Tola, with descendants in the army of David.

IB'ZAN (ib'zan). The tenth judge of Israel (Judg. 12:8-10). He was of Bethlehem, probably the Bethlehem of Zebulun (so Michaelis and Hezel) and not of Judah (as Josephus says). He governed seven years, probably after 1080 B.C. The prosperity of Ibzan is marked by the great number of his children (thirty sons and thirty daughters) and his wealth by their marriages, for they were all married.

ICE (Heb. *qeraḥ,* "smooth," Job 6:16; 38:29; Ps. 147:17; sometimes "hail," NIV). "On the Central Range (in Palestine) snow has been known to reach a depth of nearly two feet, and the pools at Jerusalem have sometimes been covered with ice. But this is rare" (Smith, *Hist. Geog.,* p. 65).

ICH'ABOD (ik'a-bad; "where is the glory? inglorious"). The son of Phinehas and grandson of Eli. The wife of Phinehas was about to give birth when she heard that her husband was slain in battle, that Eli was dead, and that the Ark of God had been taken by the Philistines. Under such circumstances her labor proved fatal to her. When she was lying at the point of death, the women standing about tried to cheer her, saying, "Do not be afraid, for you have given birth to a son." She replied only by naming the child Ichabod, adding, "The glory has departed from Israel, for the ark of God was taken" (1 Sam. 4:19-22), about 1050 B.C. The only other mention of Ichabod is in 14:3, where it is stated that his brother Ahitub was father of *Ahijah* (which see), who acted as high priest for Saul.

BIBLIOGRAPHY: J. Kitto, *Daily Bible Illustrations* (1981), 1:612-13.

ICO'NIUM (ī-kō'ni-um). A celebrated city of Asia Minor, visited probably three times by the apostle Paul (Acts 13:51; 14:1, 19, 21; 16:2), the present Konya, having a population of 200,000.

BIBLIOGRAPHY: W. M. Ramsay, *Cities of St. Paul* (1960), pp.

317-84; E. M. Blaiklock, *Cities of the New Testament* (1965), pp. 27-30.

ID′ALAH (id′a-la). A city of Zebulun, near its western border, mentioned between Shimron and Bethlehem (Josh. 19:15). It is identified with Khirbet et Huwara about one-half mile S of Beit Lahm.

ID′BASH (id′bash; "honeyed"). A descendant of Judah who, with his two brothers (and a sister), are said to be "the sons of Etam" (1 Chron. 4:3), probably meaning of the lineage of the founder of the place, or perhaps that they themselves were its settlers.

ID′DO (id′o).

1. The father of Ahinadab, Solomon's deputy in the district of Mahanaim (1 Kings 4:14), before 960 B.C.

2. A Gershomite Levite, son of Joah and father of Zerah (1 Chron. 6:21); perhaps more correctly called Adaiah in v. 41.

3. Son of Zechariah, and ruler of the half tribe of Manasseh in Gilead (1 Chron. 27:21), 960 B.C.

4. Heb. same as no. 2, a seer whose "visions" against Jeroboam incidentally contained some of the acts of Solomon (2 Chron. 9:29). He appears to have written a chronicle relating to the life and reign of Abijah (13:22), which he seems to have called a midrash (*see* marg.), or "exposition," and also a book concerning genealogies, in which the acts of Rehoboam were recorded (12:15), after 934 B.C. These books are lost, but they may have formed part of the foundation of the existing books of Chronicles.

5. The father of Berechiah and grandfather of the prophet Zechariah (Zech. 1:1, 7), although in other places Zechariah is called "the son of Iddo" (Ezra 5:1; 6:14; Neh. 12:16). Iddo returned from Babylon with Zerubbabel (12:4), 536 B.C.

6. The "leading man" of the Jews established at Casiphia. It was to him that Ezra sent for Temple servants to join his company. Thirty-eight Levites and 220 Temple servants responded to his call (Ezra 8:17-20), 457 B.C. It would seem from this that Iddo was a chief person of the Temple servants and also that this is one of the circumstances that indicate that Jews, in their several colonies under the Exile, were still ruled by the heads of their nation and allowed the free exercise of their worship (Kitto).

IDLE. This word appears in Matt. 12:36, KJV, with the meaning of *unprofitable* or *pernicious*. The NASB renders "careless," marg. "useless." The meaning of the term in Luke 24:11, KJV, is *nonsensical, absurd.* The NASB reads "as nonsense."

IDOL, IMAGE. These are the rendering of a large number of Heb. and Gk. words and may be divided as follows: (1) abstract terms, which, with a deep moral significance, express the degradation associated with, and stand out as a protest of the

language against, the enormities of idolatry; (2) those that apply to the idols or images as the outward symbols of the deity who was worshiped through them; (3) terms relating to material and workmanship.

Abstract Terms. Seven of these terms were used.

1. An empty thing (Heb. *'āwen*), rendered elsewhere "trouble," "iniquity," "vanity," "wickedness," "sorrow," etc., and only once "idol" (Isa. 66:3). The primary idea of the root seems to be emptiness, nothingness, as of breath or vapor; and, by a natural transition, in a moral sense, wickedness in its active form of mischief, and then, as the result, sorrow and trouble. Hence *'āwĕn* denotes a vain, false, wicked thing, and expresses at once the essential nature of idols and the consequences of their worship.

2. A nonentity (Heb. *'ĕlîl*, good for "nothing") is thought by some to have a sense akin to that of "falsehood" and would therefore much resemble no. 1, as applied to an idol. It is used of the idols or "images" of Memphis (Ezek. 30:13). It appears in strong contrast with Jehovah in Pss. 96:5; 97:7.

3. A terrifying thing (Heb. *'êmim*), so-called from the terror they inspired in their devotees (Jer. 50:38, "fearsome idols," NASB; "idols that go mad with terror," NIV). In this respect it is closely connected with no. 4.

4. A horrible thing (Heb. *mipleṣet*), rendered "horrid image" and applied to the idol of Maacah, probably of wood, which Asa cut down and burned (1 Kings 15:13; 2 Chron. 15:16; "repulsive Asherah pole," NIV) and which was unquestionably a phallus, the symbol of the productive power of nature and the nature-goddess Ashera.

5. A shameful thing (Heb. *bōshet*, "shame," Jer. 11:13; Hos. 9:10), applied to Baal or Baal-peor, as characterizing the obscenity of his worship.

6. Logs, blocks (Heb. *gillûlîm*), such as are rolled (*gālal*) like helpless logs (Ezek. 30:13). The expression is applied, principally in Ezekiel, to false gods and their symbols (Deut. 29:17; Ezek. 8:10; etc.). It stands side by side with other contemptuous terms in 16:36; 20:8; as, e.g., *sheqeṣ*, "filth," "abomination," "detestable things" (8:10). The NIV renders merely "idols" here.

7. A detestable thing (Heb. *shiqqûṣ*, "filth, impurity"), especially applies to that which produced ceremonial uncleanness (Ezek. 37:23; "vile images," NIV). As referring to the idols themselves, it primarily denotes the obscene rites with which their worship was associated and hence, by metonymy, is applied both to the objects of worship and also to their worshipers (8:10; 16:36; 20:8).

Names of Idols. These terms applied more directly to the images or idols as the outward symbols of the deity who was worshiped through them.

1. A likeness (Heb. *semel* or *sēmel*, "semblance"), rendered "idol" (2 Chron. 33:7, 15; Ezek. 8:3, 5); "figure" (Deut. 4:16). It corresponds to the Lat. *simulacrum*.

2. A representation (Heb. *ṣelem*, a "shadow"). It is the "image" of God in which man was created (Gen. 1:27; cf. Wisd. of Sol. 2:23), distinguished from "likeness," as the "image" from the "idea" that it represents, although it would be rash to insist upon this distinction. But whatever abstract term may best define the meaning of *ṣēlēm*, it is unquestionably used to denote the visible forms of external objects and is applied to figures of gold and silver (Num. 33:52; Dan. 3:1), such as the golden image of Nebuchadnezzar, as well as to those painted upon walls (Ezek. 23:14). "Image" perhaps most nearly represents it in all passages. Applied to the human countenance it is rendered "expression" (Dan. 3:19).

3. An appearance (Heb. *t'mûnâ*, rendered "form" (Job 4:16; cf. Deut. 4:12) and "likeness" (5:8).

4. Something formed or fashioned (Heb. *'āṣāb*, *'eṣeb*) (Jer. 22:28, KJV) or *'ōṣeb* (Isa. 48:5), all derived from a root *'āṣab*, "to work," or "fashion," are terms applied to idols as expressing that their origin was due to the labor of man.

5. A form (Heb. *ṣîr*) applied only once to an idol (Isa. 45:16). The word signifies "a form" or "mold," and hence an "idol."

6. Stone monument (Heb. *maṣṣēbâ*), anything "set up," such as a "pillar" (Gen. 28:18; 31:45; 35:14). Such were the stones set up by Joshua after the passage of the Jordan (Josh. 4:9), at Shechem (24:26), and by Samuel when victorious over the Philistines (1 Sam. 7:12). When solemnly dedicated they were anointed with oil, and libations were poured upon them. The word is applied to the obelisks that stood at the entrance to the temple of the Sun at Heliopolis (Jer. 43:13). The Palladium of Troy, the black stone in the Kaaba at Mecca said to have been brought from heaven by the angel Gabriel, and the stone or "image which fell down from heaven" at Ephesus (Acts 19:35) are examples of the belief, so common in ancient times, that the gods sent down their images to earth.

7. Incense altar (Heb. *ḥammānîm* from *hmm*, "be hot, stand for heating, brazier"), often mentioned in connection with the statues of Astarte (Lev. 26:30; Isa. 17:8; 27:9; Ezek. 6:4, 6; 2 Chron. 14:5; 34:7); while from 34:4 it appears that they stood upon the altars of Baal.

8. Figured stone (Heb. *maśkît*, with the root apparently from *śākâ*, "to look at, behold," Lev. 26:1 ["carved stone," NIV]; Num. 33:52; cf. Ezek. 8:12). The general opinion appears to be that *'eben maśkît* signifies a stone with figures carved upon it.

9. Teraphim. Household deities. *See* Teraphim.

Material. Terms relating to the material and workmanship of the idol.

1. An artistically executed likeness (Heb. *pesel*), graven or carved images, rendered "idols" in Judg. 3:19, 26. The verb is employed to denote the fine work of the stone worker (Ex. 34:4; 1 Kings 5:18). The term *pesel* was applied to images of metal and wood, as well as those of stone (Deut. 7:25; Isa. 30:22; 40:19; Hab. 2:19).

2. A metal-cast idol. Heb. *nēsek, nesek,* and *massēkâ* are evidently synonymous in later Hebrew (Isa. 41:29; 48:5; Jer. 10:14) and denote a molten image, the last term often being used in distinction from *pesel* (Deut. 27:15; Judg. 17:3; etc.).

Forms of Idols. Among the earliest objects of worship regarded as symbols of deity were meteoric stones, then rough, unhewn blocks, and later stone columns or pillars of wood in which the divinity worshiped was supposed to dwell. The Bible does not give us many traces of the forms of idolatrous images. *Dagon* (which see), god of the Philistines, had a figure partly human, terminating in a fish. *See* idolatry.

BIBLIOGRAPHY: J. B. Pritchard, *Palestinian Figurines in Relation to Certain Goddesses Known Through Literature* (1944); H. H. Rowley, *Faith of Israel* (1956), pp. 74ff.; T. C. Vriezen, *The Religion of Ancient Israel* (1963), pp. 22-78; T. W. Overholt, *Journal of Theological Studies* 16 (1965): 1-12; F. M. Cross, *Canaanite Myth and Hebrew Epic* (1973).

IDOLATRY. In a general sense idolatry is the paying of divine honor to any created thing; the ascription of divine power to natural agencies. Idolatry may be classified as follows: (1) the worship of inanimate objects, such as stones, trees, rivers, etc.; (2) of animals; (3) of the higher powers of nature, such as the sun, moon, stars; and the forces of nature, as air, fire, etc.; (4) hero-worship or of deceased ancestors; (5) *idealism*, or the worship of abstractions or mental qualities, such as justice. Another classification is suggestive: (1) the worship of Jehovah under image or symbol; (2) the worship of other gods under image or symbol; (3) the worship of the image or symbol itself. Each of these forms of idolatry had its peculiar immoral tendency. *See* Gods, False; Idol.

Idolatry of Israel's Neighbors. In the course of her history Israel adopted many idolatrous practices from her heathen neighbors.

Egyptian. The Egyptians had a bewildering conglomeration of deities. It is impossible to list all the gods sacred to them. Every aspect of nature, every object looked at, animate as well as inanimate, was viewed as indwelt by a spirit that could select its own form, occupying the body of a cow, a crocodile, a fish, a human being, a tree, a hawk, etc. In their hieroglyphic inscriptions and their tomb paintings ancient Egyptian artists have left impressions of literally thousands of deities. The Pyramid Texts mention some 200.

The Book of the Dead catalogs 1,200. The great deity, the sun-god Amun-Re, was one of the principal deities. Many of the pharaohs were believed to incarnate Amun-Re. Akhenaton, around 1380 B.C., switched from the worship of Amun as the state religion to the solar disc, Aton (and approached monotheism). An entire shake-up in the religious constitution of the nation followed. When Tutankhamen went back to Amun worship there was a similar political upheaval. Egypt venerated her fertility gods, and her Isis, a counterpart of Astarte, was adopted as far W as Italy. In Pompeii the ruins of a little temple of Isis is extant. Egyptians venerated Osiris, an agricultural deity, consort of Isis and the father of young Horus, who became successor of Osiris when the latter became the underworld god. Osiris was immensely influential. He was associated with the life-giving waters of the Nile River. At Heliopolis, biblical On, gods worshiped included Nut, Seb, Isis, Set, Osiris, Temu, Tefnut, Shu, and others, besides a lesser group of deities. The sight of animal- and bird-headed Egyptian deities such as Ptah, Knum, Hathor, Set, Sobek, etc., must have been thoroughly repulsive to the Hebrews, and yet the splendor and attraction of Egyptian cults must have been dazzling to the less spiritually minded.

The Egyptian agricultural deity Osiris was associated with the life-giving waters of the Nile River

Canaan. Fertility cults nowhere controlled people more completely than in Canaan. When Israel entered Palestine, the Canaanites were in the last stages of degradation as the result of centuries of worshiping degrading deities. The only safe recourse for the Israelites was complete separation and annihilation of the Canaanites and their religion. Orgiastic nature worship, fertility cults in the form of serpent symbols, unbounded license, and moral abandon could only be met with a severe code of ethics. El, a heartless, unbridled tyrant, had three wives or con-

sorts who were patrons of sex and war. Baal was the great NW Semitic god of the storm. At Tyre, Melcarth was honored. Koshar was the Vulcan of the Canaanite; Hauron, the shepherd god. Mot was the god of death. The Ras Shamra texts speak of a sun goddess, Shapash. In the worship of these various deities prostitution was glorified. Veneration of Astarte continued for many centuries until the Christian emperor Theodosius, in the fourth century A.D., destroyed the Venus and the Adonis cult centers. There were also various pillar cults that had a degrading cultic significance, such as at Gezer and Ader in Moab.

Babylonia and Assyria. Early inhabitants of Mesopotamia paid homage to fertility gods. There the famous goddess of propagation, Ishtar, was thought of as descending to the underworld to seek her young husband, Tammuz. Other gods of production were Dagon, who in the W became father of Baal and brother of the virgin goddess of fertility, Anath. Babylonians also worshiped the sky god, Anu; En-lil, the wind god; Enki, earth and water god; Ningal, the mother goddess; Dumuzi (Tammuz of the Bible); Utu, the sun-god; Nannar, the moon god; Marduk, another form of the sun-god who later became the chief god of Babylon; and Ashur, the principal god of the Assyrians. Along with Ishtar, their immoral goddess of love, they worshiped Nabu, patron of learning; Nergal, god of war and the underworld; and Nusqu, the god of fire. The later Chaldeans especially revered the gods of fire and of the heavens as a result of their interest in astrology. Perhaps Babylonia exerted a greater influence upon Israelite religion than either Canaan or Egypt. However, Abraham, by his divine call, was brought out of paganism; and although he knew the many gods at Ur, particularly the moon god Sin, who was also worshiped at Haran, his vision of the "God of glory" (Acts 7:2) purged out the intermixture of idolatry. Along with the moon god, the sun god Shamash was greatly venerated among the Babylonians and Assyrians. Numerous cuneiform tablets depict scenes of Shamash worship. The cuneiform and monumental finds of the Sumerian-Akkadian peoples in Mesopotamia give us richer archaeological information of Mesopotamian religion than the records of Egypt. Stone and clay inscriptions, literary tablets unearthed in such temple libraries as those at ancient Nippur, SE of Babylon, the Tell Farah tablets from central Babylonia, and the thousands of clay tablets from Lagash (twenty-sixth century B.C.) yield a great fund of religious information. Tablets from the royal library of King Sargon II of Assyria (721-705 B.C.), augmented by Sennacherib and Esarhaddon, give further information. The phenomenal finds from the great library of Ashurbanipal (668-633 B.C.) have shown how potent a factor Sumero-Akkadian religion was in the ancient biblical world.

Idolatrous Usages. Mountains and high places

Relief of protective spirit of the Assyrians

were chosen spots for offering sacrifice and incense to idols (1 Kings 11:7; 14:23), and the seclusion of gardens and the thick shade of woods offered great attractions to their worshipers (2 Kings 16:4; Isa. 1:29; Hos. 4:13). The host of heaven was worshiped on the housetop (2 Kings 23:12; Jer. 19:13; 32:29; Zeph. 1:5). The priests of the false worship are sometimes designated Chemarim, a word of Aramaic origin, to which different meanings have been assigned. It is applied to the non-Levitical priests who burned incense on the high places (2 Kings 23:5), as well as to the priests of the calves (Hos. 10:5). In addition to the priests there were other persons intimately connected with idolatrous rites and the impurities from which they were inseparable. Both men and women consecrated themselves to the service of idols: the former as *kedêshîm,* for which there is reason to believe the KJV (Deut. 23:17; etc.) has not given too harsh an equivalent; the latter as *kedêshôth,* who wove shrines

High place at Megiddo

for Astarte (2 Kings 23:7). The same class of women existed among the Phoenicians, Armenians, Lydians, and Babylonians (Epist. of Jer., v. 43). They are distinguished from the public prostitutes (Hos. 4:14) and are associated with the performances of sacred rites. Besides these accessories there were the ordinary rites of worship that idolatrous systems had in common with the religion of the Hebrews. Offering burnt sacrifices to the idol gods (2 Kings 5:17), burning incense in their honor (1 Kings 11:8), and bowing down in worship before their images (19:18) were the chief parts of their ritual; and from their very analogy with the ceremonies of true worship were more seductive than the grosser forms.

Idolatry Among the Israelites. Although of a family that worshiped strange gods (Josh. 24:2), Abraham still worshiped the one true God when He revealed Himself to him and called him to leave his native land for Canaan (Gen. 12:1). The household idols that Rachel took with her (31:19) were an inferior kind of god, which might be combined with the worship of the one supreme God. Hence we find no idolatry in the strict sense either among the patriarchs or Israelites in Egypt and under Moses, but only solitary traces of idolatry and image worship, whereby the knowledge and worship of God was polluted but not supplanted (30:27; 31:53). The traces of idolatry that have been sought in Ex. 17:7; Num. 25:2; Josh. 24:14; Ezek. 20:7; and Amos 5:25-36 prove nothing more than disturbances of pure Jehovah worship by image worship, heathen superstition, and proneness to fleshly sins. The golden calf (Ex. 32) was intended to be a representation of Jehovah after an Egyptian pattern. Amos (Amos 5:25) in his rebuke seems to have in view image worship but not the service of the Assyrian idols Sikkuth and Kiyyun. The worship of Baal-peor was a temporary apostasy, brought about by the temptations to licentious indulgence offered by the rites of that deity.

The people of Israel were first seduced into apostasy from Jehovah into heathen idolatry by the Canaanites, who had not been rooted out. This apostasy took place during the time of the Judges. The various gods to whose service the Israelites gave themselves were Canaanite; after the invasion of Palestine by the Assyrians, Assyrian idols were added. After the death of Joshua and the elders who outlived him, Israel "forsook the Lord and served Baal and the Ashtaroth" (Judg. 2:13); and from this time its history becomes little more than a chronicle of the inevitable sequence of offense and punishment (2:12-14). Idolatry became the national sin, even Gideon, the judge, giving occasion to, or assisting in, idolatrous worship. In later times the practice of secret idolatry was carried to greater lengths. Images were set up on the grain floors, in the wine vats, and behind the doors of private houses (Isa. 57:8; Hos. 9:1-2); and to check this tendency the statute in Deut. 27:15 was originally proclaimed. Under Samuel's administration a fast was held and purificatory rites performed to mark the public renunciation of idolatry (1 Sam. 7:3-6), but in the reign of Solomon all this was forgotten. Each of his many foreign wives brought with her the gods of her own nation, and the gods of Ammon, Moab, and Sidon were openly worshiped.

Among the Ten Tribes. Jeroboam, fresh from his recollections of the bovine worship of Egypt, erected golden calves at Bethel and at Dan and by this crafty state policy effectively severed the kingdoms of Judah and Israel (1 Kings 12:26-33). But Jeroboam's calves were doubtless intended to fasten the worshiper's attention upon Yahweh, thought of as invisibly represented above the animals, astride their backs. The deity astride a bull was a common conception illustrated by ancient Near-Eastern iconography. The successors of Jeroboam followed in his steps, until Ahab, who married a Sidonian princess, at her instigation (21:25) built a temple and altar to Baal and revived all the abominations of the Amorites (v. 26). Henceforth Baal worship became so completely identified with the Northern Kingdom that it is described as walking in the way or statutes of the kings of Israel (2 Kings 16:3; 17:8), as distinguished from the sin of Jeroboam. The conquest of the ten tribes by Shalmaneser was for them the last scene of the drama of abominations that had been enacted uninterruptedly for upward of 250 years. In the Northern Kingdom no reformer arose to vary the long line of royal apostates; whatever was effected in the way of reformation was done by the hands of the people (2 Chron. 31:1).

Idolatry in Judah. Rehoboam, the son of an Ammonite mother, perpetuated the worst features of Solomon's idolatry (1 Kings 14:22-24); and in his reign the great schism in the national religion was made. The first act of Hezekiah on ascending the throne was the restoration and purification of the Temple, which had been dismantled and closed during the latter part of his father's life (2 Chron. 28:24; 29:3). This purging of idols was not confined to Judah and Benjamin but spread throughout Ephraim and Manasseh (31:1), and to all external appearance idolatry was extirpated. But the reform extended little below the surface (Isa. 29:13). With the death of Josiah the last effort to revive a purer ritual, if not a purer faith, among the people ended. Idolatry spread fearfully in the last times of the kingdom of Judah, until it brought down on the people the punishment of captivity in Babylon. This exile bore wholesome fruit, for in captivity the Jews wholly gave up idolatry, with the exception of certain of those who had returned to Palestine, marrying pagan wives and sharing their worship, which departure was corrected by Ezra (Ezra 9-

10). Later a new danger presented itself in Greek influence brought into Asia by Alexander, and some place-hunting Jews were base enough to adopt Greek idolatry. The nation was so far from showing any inclination to idolatry that the attempt of Antiochus Epiphanes was utterly rejected by the Jews (1 Macc. 2:23-26). The erection of synagogues has been assigned as a reason for the comparative purity of the Jewish worship after the hatred for images acquired by the Jews in their intercourse with the Persians.

Idolatry and the Law. Israel had entered into a solemn compact with Jehovah, accepting Him as the one true God and pledging themselves faithfully in service to Him (Ex. 19:3-8; 20:2-5). Idolatry, therefore, was a state of offense to an Israelite (1 Sam. 15:23), a political crime of the gravest nature, high treason against his king. It was a transgression of the covenant (Deut. 17:2-5), "evil" preeminently in the eyes of Jehovah (1 Kings 21:25). Idolatry was also a great wrong because of the licentious rites associated with it (Rom. 1:26-32), thus debauching the morals of its adherents. Regarded in a moral aspect, false gods are called a "stumbling block" (Ezek. 14:3), "lies" (Amos 2:4; Rom. 1:25), "abominations" (Deut. 29:17; 32:16), "guilt" (Amos 8:14); and with a profound sense of the degradation consequent upon their worship, they were characterized by the prophets as "shameful" and "shame" (Jer. 11:13; Hos. 9:10); "strange gods" (Deut. 32:16); "new gods" (Judg. 5:8); "demons . . . not God" (Deut. 32:17; 1 Cor. 10:20-21); and as denoting their foreign origin, gods "which were beyond the River" (Josh. 24:14-15). Their powerlessness is indicated by describing them as gods "who cannot save" (Isa. 45:20); "that did not make the heavens" (Jer. 10:11); "nothing" and "no such thing" (Isa. 41:24; 1 Cor. 8:4); "wind and emptiness" (Isa. 41:29); "vain things" (Acts 14:15).

Many customs associated with idolatry were forbidden by the law. Maimonides tells us that the prohibition against sowing a field with mingled seeds and wearing garments of mixed material was because some idolaters attributed a kind of magical influence to the mixture (Lev. 19:19). It was also forbidden to interchange the garments of the sexes (Deut. 22:5); to cut the flesh for the dead (Lev. 19:28; cf. 1 Kings 18:28), or to shave the forehead (Deut. 14:1), these things being associated with the idolatrous rites. Eating of things offered was a necessary appendage to sacrifice (cf. Ex. 18:12; 32:6; 34:15; Num. 25:2). Printing upon one's person was forbidden to the Israelites (Lev. 19:28), because idolaters branded upon their flesh some symbol of the deity they worshiped, such as the ivy leaf of Bacchus (3 Macc. 2:29).

Penalties. The first and second commandments are directed against idolatry of every form. Individuals and communities were equally amenable to the rigorous code. The individual offender was given over to destruction (Ex. 22:20); his nearest relatives were not only bound to denounce him and deliver him up to punishment (Deut. 13:6-10), but their hands were to strike the first blow when, on the evidence of at least two witnesses, he was stoned (17:2-7). To attempt to seduce others to false worship was a crime of equal enormity (13:6-10). An idolatrous nation shared a similar fate.

Figurative. The term *idolatry* is used to designate *covetousness*, which takes mammon for its god (Eph. 5:5; Col. 3:5; cf. Matt. 6:24; Luke 16:13). *Appetite* or gluttony is also included under idolatry (Phil 3:19; cf. Rom. 16:18; 2 Tim. 3:4). *See* Gods, False. M.F.U

BIBLIOGRAPHY: A. H. Sayce, *Lectures on the Origin and Growth of Religion as Illustrated by the Ancient Babylonians* (1891); W. M. Adams, *The Book of the Master of the Hidden Places* (1898); M. H. Pope, *El in the Ugaritic Texts* (1955); J. Adam, *The Religious Teachers of Greece* (1965); L. J. R. Ort, *Mani: A Religio-Historical Description* (1967); E. A. T. W. Budge, *The Gods of the Egyptians*, 2 vols. (1969); U. Oldenberg, *The Conflict Between El and Ba'al in Canaanite Religion* (1969); J. Ferguson, *The Religions of the Roman Empire* (1970); R. E. Witt, *Isis in the Graeco-Roman World* (1971); P. Green, *The Shadow of the Parthenon* (1972); T. R. Glover, *The Conflict of Religions in the Early Roman Empire* (1974); V. J. Walters, *The Cult of Mithras in the Roman Provinces of Gaul* (1974); G. Herm, *The Phoenicians* (1975), pp. 94-123; S. K. Heyob, *The Cult of Isis Among Women in the Graeco-Roman World* (1975); E. G. Parrinder, *Mysticism in the World's Religions* (1976); J. G. Griffiths, *The Origins of Osiris and His Cult* (1980); C. Downing, *The Goddesses* (1981); R. MacMullen, *Paganism in the Roman Empire* (1981); F. M. Kotwal and J. W. Boyd, eds., *A Guide to Zoroastrian Religion* (1982); M. H. van Voos, et al., *Studies in Egyptian Religion* (1982); S. Benko, *Pagan Rome and the Early Christians* (1984).

IDOLOMANCY. *See* Magic: Various Forms.

IDUME'A (id-u-mē'a; Gk. "pertaining to Edom"). This is a term employed by Greeks and Romans for the country of Edom (Mark 3:8 and in KJV only, Isa. 34:5-6; Ezek. 35:15; 36:5). After the fall of Jerusalem (587 B.C.) the Edomites began to advance northward (36:5). By 312 B.C. the Nabataeans, who established themselves in Edom, drove them from Petra. The Edomites were gradually pushed into the southern half of Judea, including the region around Hebron, an area that the Greeks later called Idumea. Judas Maccabaeus warred against them and a half century later John Hyrcanus completely subdued them, imposed the rite of circumcision, and invoked the old Jewish law of assembly (Deut. 23:7-8). Julius Caesar in 47 B.C. appointed an Idumean, Antipater, procurator of Judea, Samaria, and Galilee. Herod, son of Antipater, was crowned king of the Jews in 37 B.C. When Titus besieged Jerusalem in A.D. 70, the Idumeans joined the Jews in rebellion against Rome. Josephus says that 20,000 Idumeans were admitted as defenders of the Holy City. Once within, they proceeded to rob and kill, but these traitors received the same fate as the few surviving Jews when Rome took over Jerusalem. Idumea, or Edom, ceased to be. M.F.U.

IE'ZER (yē'zer; "helpless"; abridged for Abiezer). A son of Gilead of Manasseh (Num. 26:30), elsewhere (Josh. 17:2; etc.) called *Abiezer* (which see).

IE'ZERITES (yē'zer-īts). The descendants (Num. 26:30) of Iezer.

I'GAL (ī'gal; He [God] redeems).
1. The son of Joseph, and agent from Issachar sent to spy out the land of Canaan (Num. 13:7), 1441 B.C.
2. The son of Nathan of Zobah, and one of David's mighty warriors (2 Sam. 23:36), about 962 B.C. In the parallel list (1 Chron. 11:38) the name is given as "Joel the brother of Nathan."
3. One of the sons of Shemaiah, of the descendants of Zerubbabel (1 Chron. 3:22), after 536 B.C.

IGDALI'AH (ig-da-lī'a; "great is the Lord"). The father of Hanan, into whose chamber Jeremiah brought the Rechabites to propose the test of their temperance (Jer. 35:4), about 600 B.C.

I'GEAL. *See* Igal.

IGNORANCE. The term implies "error, going astray" (cf. Lev. 4:2, "If a person sins unintentionally"). In the NT the Greek means "want of knowledge"; sometimes simple, excusable want of information (Acts 17:30); sometimes inexcusable (Eph. 4:18); sometimes moral blindness or *sinful* ignorance (Acts 3:17).

I'IM (i'im; "heaps, ruins"). A city in the extreme S of Judah (Josh. 15:29), and doubtless included within the territory of Simeon, as the associated places were (cf. 19:3). It is probably to be identified with the ruins of Deir el-Ghawi, near Ummin Deimneh. *See also* Iye-abarim; Iyim.

I'JE-AB'ARIM. *See* Iye-abarim.

I'JON (i'jon; "a ruin"). A frontier town in the N of Palestine, in the hills of Naphtali—a store city. It was captured in the days of Asa by Ben-hadad (1 Kings 15:20; 2 Chron. 16:4), and later by Tiglath-pileser (2 Kings 15:29). It is thought to be Tell el-Dibbin, in the fertile valley of Merj 'Ayûn ("the meadow of springs"), NW of Dan.

IK'KESH (ik'kesh; "crooked, perverse"). The father of Ira, a Tekoite who was one of David's famous warriors (2 Sam. 23:26; 1 Chron. 11:28), and captain of the sixth regiment of his troops (27:9), 1000 B.C.

I'LAI (ilâ-ī). An Ahohite, and one of David's heroes (1 Chron. 11:29), called Zalmon in the parallel list (2 Sam. 23:28), 1000 B.C.

ILLUMINATED. *See* Enlightened.

ILLYR'ICUM (i-lir'i-kum). A region lying between Italy, Germany, Macedonia, and Thrace, having on one side the Adriatic Sea and on the other the Danube. It answers to the present Dalmatia; by which name, indeed, the southern part of Illyricum itself was known, and where Paul informed Timothy that Titus had gone (2 Tim. 4:10). It is of uncertain dimensions, being understood differently by Greek and Roman writers. It is mentioned only once in the NT and that simply as the extreme limit to which, in the direction of Rome, Paul carried the gospel message (Rom. 15:19). It is difficult to ascertain the exact meaning of this passage. The expression "round about" may be joined with Jerusalem and signify its *neighborhood* (as Alford); or it may be joined with "as far as Illyricum" and denote the *circuit* of the apostle's journey, an expression warranted by the indefinite phrase of Luke, "those districts" (Acts 20:2).

IMAGE. *See* Form, Likeness.

IMAGE, NEBUCHADNEZ'ZAR'S (Heb. *şelem,* a "resemblance"). Nebuchadnezzar saw in his dream a great metallic image that was terrible to look upon. It was not an idol image but a *statue* and from the description given was evidently in human form. The image appeared divided as to its material into five parts—the head of fine gold, breast and arms of silver, the "belly [the abdomen] and its thighs" (loins) of bronze (i.e., copper), the legs and upper part of the thighs of iron, and the feet of clay (Dan. 2:32-33). Thus it can be seen that the material became inferior from the head downward, finally terminating in clay. While Nebuchadnezzar was contemplating this statue a "stone was cut out without hands" (v. 34), broke loose from the mountain, struck against the lowest part of the image, broke the whole of its pieces, and ground all of its material into powder. The expression "without hands" signifies without human help.

Nebuchadnezzar's dream, as unraveled by Daniel, describes the course and end of "the times of the Gentiles" (Luke 21:24; cf. Rev. 16:19); that is, of the Gentile world power to be destroyed at the second coming of Christ. "The stone . . . cut out without hands" symbolizes Christ returning as "King of kings and Lord of lords" to set up His millennial kingdom. The four empires represent Babylon, Media-Persia, Greece under Alexander, and Rome. The latter power is seen divided first into two legs, fulfilled in the eastern and western Roman empires, and then into ten toes (cf. Dan. 7:26). The ten-toed form will be the condition of Gentile world domination at the time of the returning striking stone (2:34-35). The Gentile world system will be destroyed by a sudden crushing blow, not by a gradual process. At the first advent of Christ neither the sudden crushing blow took place nor did the ten-toed condition occur.

In Daniel (chap. 3) is an account of a golden image set up by Nebuchadnezzar in the plain of Dura. It probably represented his patron god, Bel-merodach, and adoration of it was a test of loyalty. As its height was out of proportion to its breadth (six cubits) ten to one, it is probable that a tall pedestal is included in its measurement.

M.F.U.

IMAGE OF GOD.

As Borne by Man (Heb. *şelem,* "resemblance"; accompanied in Gen. 1:26; 5:1 by *demût,* "likeness"). Attempts have been made by modern as well as ancient writers to base important distinctions upon the use of the two words, but such attempts are regarded generally as instances of overrefined or fantastic exegesis. The double expression is for the purpose of giving strength and emphasis to the idea of godlikeness in man as set forth in these passages. Likeness added to image tells us that the divine image that man bears is one corresponding to the original pattern.

The conception of man as created after the image of God is justly held to be of great importance and fundamental in theology. It is foremost among the Bible representations of man; it is bound up in the account of his creation; it appears in striking relation elsewhere, sometimes with the same, at others with different, expressions (Gen. 9:6; Ps. 8; Eph. 4:24; Col. 3:10; James 3:9; cf. Matt. 5:48; Luke 6:36; Acts 17:28-29; 1 Pet. 1:15-16; 2 Pet. 1:4, where the exalted capacity and nature of man are assumed).

Significance of the Idea. This has been a favorite battleground of theologians, partly due to the brevity of the Scripture statements and more largely to the different theological presuppositions with which the subject has been considered. An outline of the history of speculation or of doctrine upon this point cannot be given here. Evidently the Scriptures proclaim resemblance of a most important character between the constitution of man and the divine nature. Man is exalted above all the other creatures of the earth, as the account shows, in that he is a copy of the Creator. And, what is also of great importance according to the representations of Scripture, this image survived the Fall and, though blurred, still exists. The sacredness of human life is based upon this fact (Gen. 9:6). The cursing tongue as well as the violent hand must for the same reason be restrained (James 3:9). As to the effect of the Fall and man's sinful history upon God's image in man, the Scriptures are almost wholly silent. Paul (Rom. 3:23) declares that "all have sinned and *fall short* of the glory of God," a statement equivalent to saying that the glorious image is, because of sin, less than it once was. There are also recognitions of loss through sin in this respect, where, in the famous passages of Eph. 4:24; Col. 3:10, the apostle speaks of the "new self," or one's renewal. But, as the best theologians commonly agree, the representations of Scripture are such as to create the impression that in some lofty sense the divine image is inalienable from man. As to what constituted this image originally and as to what it still constitutes, it should be said that a too frequent mistake has been to concentrate attention upon some single feature instead of comprehending all those excellent characteristics that, according to the Scriptures, belonged or belong to man and that constitute his likeness to his Maker. Also the effort has been made to distinguish too sharply between what in the likeness has been lost through sin and what is permanent. Man's nature has generally suffered loss from sin, but even in those respects in which the loss has been greatest, "in righteousness and holiness," the loss is not such as to render him incapable of divine renewal. With these preliminaries in view, the chief significance of the idea or the contents of the divine image, may be summarized as follows: (1) *Spirituality.* Man's likeness to God is not, as some of the early Latin Fathers fancied, a bodily likeness. God is Spirit, and the first great point of resemblance between man and his Creator is found in man's spiritual nature. His life is inbreathed from God—a distinguishing fact in his creation (*see* Gen. 2:7; Job 32:8). With this stands connected the fact of man's immortal nature and destiny, for God is the Eternal Spirit. The general teaching of Scripture is that this feature survives. (2) *Personality.* God is a person; He is conscious of His own existence. He is the Supreme Intelligence. He is free. Man is also self-conscious; he is endowed with intelligence, rationality, and freedom. And at this point, despite sin, there still may be discerned in man wonderful vestiges of his inherent greatness and likeness to the divine. (3) *Holiness.* God is the Holy One. Man was created pure, with no inherent tendency to sin; with such qualities in his nature that he was after the image and likeness of the righteous and holy God. (4) *Love.* God is love. The cardinal virtue, or moral excellence, proclaimed for man in the

Scriptures is love. Man originally bore, and again may bear, the divine likeness in this respect. But here, as elsewhere, we see the necessity for restoration. (5) *Dominion.* God is sovereign. He created man to rule (*see* Gen. 1:26; Ps. 8:6; etc.). Whether the place assigned to man in the creation is to be considered a feature of his likeness to the divine or in the consequence of that likeness, is a question that has been much discussed. The latter is the more exact view, as reference here is to his position rather than to his nature. And yet man's royalty in the natural world is still so great that it must suggest his original complete fitness for it. For related topics, *see* Righteousness; Sin, Original; Grace; Immortality.

Christ the Image of God. In two passages of the NT Christ is thus designated. In Col. 1:15 He is "the image of the invisible God"; in Heb. 1:3 He is "the radiance of His glory," "the exact representation of His nature" (cf. John 1:1; 17:25-26).

Ellicott remarks, "The Son is the Father's image in all things, save only in being the Father." Christ has appeared in the world as the perfect manifestation of God. And that He called Himself "the Son of man" is not opposed to this fact. For if man in his original state bore the divine image, certainly He must bear it who is not only perfect in His human nature but is also the "only begotten Son" of God. What this designation of Christ may convey to us as to the eternal relations between the Father and the Son is a deep matter that cannot be considered here. But it should be noted that this "second man," this "Son from heaven," this eternal "Word," this "image of the invisible God," appears in the NT as the Author of salvation. And the end of this salvation is conformity to His image. In the OT man appears created after the image of God; in the NT "the Son is the prototype of redeemed or renewed humanity" (Rom. 8:29; Col. 3:10-11; cf. Rom. 8:19 with 1 John 3:2; Phil. 3:21; 2 Cor. 3:18; 1 Cor. 15:47, 49).   E.MCC.

BIBLIOGRAPHY: D. Cairns, *The Image of God in Man* (1953); G. C. Berkouwer, *Man: The Image of God* (1962); E. E. Sauer, *The King of the Earth* (1962); R. L. Harris, *Man: God's Eternal Creation* (1971); C. J. Barber, *Theological Students Fellowship Bulletin 7* (1975): 17-20; J. Laidlaw, *The Biblical Doctrine of Man* (1983).

IMAGERY. *See* Images.

IMAGE WORSHIP. *See* Idol; Idolatry.

IMAGES (Heb. *maśkît,* an "image," Lev. 26:1; "picture," Num. 33:52). "The room of his carved images" ("the chambers of his imagery," KJV; NIV has "idol") is an expression found in Ezek. 8:12 in the description given by the prophet of the vision shown him of the Temple. The prophet appears to have been conducted out of the inner court through its northern gate into the outer court and placed in front of the northern gate, which led into the open air. There was a hole in the wall, and on breaking through the wall by the command of God, he came to a door. Entering it, he saw all kinds of figures of animals portrayed on the wall; in front of these, seventy of the elders of Israel were standing and praying reverently to the images of the beasts with burning incense. The vision was a revelation of what was going on throughout the whole of Israel. The secret chamber is figurative of the idolatry secretly practiced by the people; the number seventy represents the whole nation. The pictures on the walls, representing animal worship, showed the great degradation of the nation's religion, which was justified by the elders under the delusion that "the Lord does not see us; the Lord has forsaken the land"; that is to say, not that "He does not trouble Himself about us," but that "He does not know what we do; and has withdrawn His presence and help." Thus they denied God's omniscience and omnipresence. "Room of his carved images" is a term applied to the rooms or closets in the homes of the people in which idolatrous images were set up and worshiped.

IMAGINATION. The image-making, pictorial faculty of the mind, reproducing and recombining former thoughts and experiences. It illustrates, adorns, and illuminates our speech and writing by presenting new views and applications of things, truths, and conceptions. It is the artist's great qualification and the supreme talent of the inventor, finding expression in painting and sculpture, new machinery, architecture, landscape gardening, etc.

In KJV "imagination" is the rendering of the Heb. *sherîrût*, "firmness," generally in a bad sense; i.e., "hardness of heart" (Deut. 29:19; frequently in Jeremiah); *yēṣer*, "form, conception" (Gen. 6:5; 8:21; Deut. 31:21; etc.); Gk. *dialogismos*, "deliberating with one's self " (cf. Rom. 1:21); *dianoia*, "way of thinking" (cf. Luke 1:51).

IMITATOR (Gk. *mimētēs*). Paul urges Christians to be "imitators of me"; etc., meaning that they were to be like him in all good things (1 Cor. 4:16; 11:1; etc.); also to take God as an example (Eph. 5:1). In Phil. 3:17 he exhorts the brethren to "join in following my example, and observe those who walk according to the pattern you have in us," i.e., to be co-imitators. KJV renders "followers."

IM'LA (im'la; "full"). The father of Micaiah, which latter was the prophet who ironically foretold the defeat of the allied kings of Judah and Israel against Ramoth-gilead (2 Chron. 18:7-8). In the parallel passage (1 Kings 22:8-9) his name is written Imlah. The NIV renders "Imlah" in both passages.

IM'LAH. *See* Imla.

IMMAN'UEL (i-man'u-el; "God with us"; i.e., "savior"). A name given to Christ by Matthew

(1:23) after Isa. 7:14. According to orthodox interpretation the name denotes the same as God-man (*theanthrōpos*) and has reference to the personal union of the human nature and the divine in Christ.

IMMATERIALITY. Not consisting of matter. This quality is predicated of God and the human soul. "Finite and passive matter, with its divisibility, is not in his essence. The absolute Being is thoroughly one with itself, and is not composite; the composite is divisible, the divisible is finite and material; thus all this cannot be applied to God" (Dorner, *Christ. Doctrine*, 1:238). God is also free from the limitations to which matter is subject, i.e., from the limits of space and time. The immateriality of God is therefore the basis of the qualities of eternity, omnipresence, and unchangeableness.

The immateriality of the soul includes simplicity as another of its qualities, but it is not superior to the limitations of space and time, since the soul needs the body as a necessary organ of its life.

IM'MER (im'er; "sheep, lamb"). The name of several priests.

1. The father of Meshillemith (1 Chron. 9:12), or Meshillemoth (Neh. 11:13), some of whose descendants took a conspicuous part in the sacred duties at Jerusalem after the Exile. His descendants, to the number of 1,052, returned from Babylon with Zerubbabel (Ezra 2:37; Neh. 7:40). He is probably the same as mentioned in Ezra 10:20, some of whose descendants divorced their Gentile wives, long before 536 B.C. By some he is identified with nos. 4 and 5.

2. A priest in the time of David, and head of the sixteenth sacerdotal division (1 Chron. 24:14).

3. One who accompanied Zerubbabel from Babylon but was unable to prove his Israelite descent (Ezra 2:59; Neh. 7:61), 536 B.C. "It does not clearly appear, however, that he claimed to belong to the priestly order, and it is possible that the name is only given as that of a place in the Babylonish dominions from which some of those named in the following verses came" (McClintock and Strong, *Cyclopedia*, s.v.).

4. The father of Zadok, which latter repaired part of the walls of Jerusalem (Neh. 3:29), before 445 B.C.

5. The father of Pashhur, which latter "had Jeremiah the prophet beaten, and put him in the stocks" (Jer. 20:1-2), before 605 B.C.

IMMORTALITY. "Exemption from death and annihilation"; with reference to man, unending personal existence beyond the grave.

Scripture Doctrine. Viewed strictly, the idea of man's future life is not altogether identical with that of his immortality. And yet practically the question, "If a man die shall he live again?" covers the whole matter.

The Old Testament. The idea of individual immortality is not as prominently and emphatically set forth in the OT as in the NT. It was the purpose and method of the OT writers to present, not so much the contrast between the present and the future, as that between the chosen people and the heathen nations. It is national life, and not that of individuals, that occupies the foremost place. Nevertheless, the assertion, made even by certain Christian writers, that the doctrine of the future life is not taught in the OT Scriptures, is unwarranted. And the supposition, which has sometimes been entertained, that the patriarchs and prophets and the Jewish people generally held no such doctrine is unreasonable and opposed to fact. It is to ascribe to them lower views of man's nature and future destiny than prevailed among the nations with which they came in contact. It is to regard the recipients and custodians of special revelation as less enlightened than others to whom such privileges had not been afforded. That the Jews, with the exception of the Sadducees, universally believed in man's immortal nature when Christ came is beyond dispute. And there is sufficient evidence to show that such had been their belief during the preceding centuries of their history. For example, such common expressions as "was gathered to his people," along with the prohibition of necromancy, or invocation of the dead, clearly testify to the popular Hebrew belief in continued conscious existence beyond the grave. If the number of passages in the OT explicitly affirming this doctrine is not large, it should not, therefore, be a matter of trivial objection. The fact of life after death is taken for granted. Its recognition pervades the general drift or spirit of these ancient Scriptures. Thus man is represented as created in the image of God and therefore a creature whose chief existence is spiritual, not to be obliterated by the death of the body. His highest good is constantly set before us, as found in the divine favor and fellowship. All temporal good is insignificant in comparison with this. "The prosperity of the wicked" is not to be envied, because of the "end" that is realized in "the sanctuary." In the same place of clear and holy light is seen the contrasted condition and prospect of the righteous. "I am continually with Thee; Thou hast taken hold of my right hand. With Thy counsel Thou wilt guide me, and afterward receive me to glory" (Ps. 73). Thus the whole drift or tendency is to turn the thoughts of the people from the present toward the future. And besides, there are several places in the OT where the doctrine of a future life is plainly asserted. The sixteenth psalm, especially as connected with the apostolic comments (Acts 2:27; 13:35), is a case in point (*see* also Ps. 17:15; Isa. 26:19; Dan. 12:2-3).

The New Testament. In 2 Tim. 1:10 Paul speaks of Christ, "who abolished death, and brought life and immortality to light through the gospel." Literally the phrase "brought . . . to light" means "has illuminated," or "shed light upon." It is certainly not implied here that the doctrine of immortality was unknown to the world before Christ came, for some sort of belief in that doctrine had been common, if not universal, among the Gentile nations as well as among the Jews. It means that "the gospel pours light upon and discloses the author, origin, and true nature of life and immortality to our view" (*see* Whedon, *Com.,* on above passage). It should be added that not only among the Jews had some (particularly the Sadducees) cast away the belief and hope of a future life, but also false philosophy and prevailing corruption had weakened or destroyed the faith of many among the Gentiles. The mission of Christ, therefore, was not only to "shed light upon immortality" by means of definite and authoritative instruction but also by His life and death and resurrection to make it possible for men to attain to an immortality that should be blessed. Accordingly, we find explicit utterances from Christ in large number with respect to this subject. He argued with the Sadducees against their unbelief. And His argument is significant as showing not only His own affirmation of a future deathless life but also His affirmation of that doctrine as taught in the OT (*see* Luke 20:27-38). He taught the doctrine plainly, illustrating it with parables; it ran as a solemn undertone through all His teachings (*see* Matt. 5:12; 8:11-12; 12:32; 13:36, 43; 18:8-9; 22:11-13; 25:1-13, 31-46; Mark 8:35-37; Luke 12:4-5; 13:24-29; 16:19-31; 18:29-30; John 3:16; 5:39-40; 6:47-58; 10:28; 11:25; 14:1-6; etc.). It should be noted that, in the passages referred to, Christ speaks of the future, not only of the righteous but also of the wicked; also, that He speaks of a blessed immortality as attainable only through Himself. The teachings of the apostles, as found in other parts of the NT, are as we might expect, equally explicit with those of Christ. It is unnecessary to cite illustrations. As it has well been said, "the obligation which even in this respect the world owes to the Gospel of the Cross is one which cannot be overrated" (Van Oosterzee).

Theological. By immortality theologians frequently mean the survival of the spiritual part of man after physical death. However, it must be clearly kept in mind that immortality is not mere existence after death. Death does not end human life, whether in the case of the saved or unsaved. In fact, the tenet of the immortality of the soul alone is unknown in Scripture. The Bible does not look at this disembodied existence as life or completed happiness. The biblical concept of immortality is a deathlessness of the whole person, the body particularly as united to the soul and spirit. Therefore, it may be said that immortality refers to the body, the material part of man, but as this affects the whole man including soul and spirit. Immortality, then, is not simply a future conscious condition, however prolonged, but a state of deliverance, of bliss, due to redemption and the possession of a glorified body united to the soul and the spirit. It therefore includes resurrection and a perfected life in body, soul, and spirit.

Immortality and Eternal Life. Immortality is not identical with the gift of eternal life, which all believers in Christ possess. Believers who possess eternal life, as well as unbelievers, suffer death. The only possibility of a believer's not dying is the coming of the Lord and the instantaneous glorification of his human body (1 Cor. 15:51-53; 1 Thess. 4:13-17). The possession of eternal life guarantees a future immortal body either by translation or resurrection, but the body of the saved person is only potentially immortal (Rom. 8:22-23; 2 Cor. 5:1-5). All who have eternal life are thus guaranteed the future immortality of the body, that is, they are promised either resurrection unto life or translation unto glory. In either case the result is the same—namely, a glorified body that is immortal, deathless, painless, and sinless, united to the redeemed soul and spirit. This fully redeemed personality is what the Bible means by immortality. Unsaved people who do not possess eternal life possess a mortal body that will never be immortal. Their soul and spirit will go on existing forever but their body, raised for judgment, will suffer "the second death" at the sinner's judgment of the white throne (Rev. 20:14). This is not annihilation. This is eternal conscious existence in separation from God, and thus torment and what is called "fire which burns with brimstone." Apparently the term "second death" implies the dissolution or corruption of the resurrected body of the unsaved whose personality does not possess immortality. Only those who believe on Christ, "who alone possesses immortality and dwells in unapproachable light; whom no man has seen or can see" (1 Tim. 6:16), obtain that same immortality that Christ, as the Firstfruit, secured by His death and resurrection. Immortality, then, is brought "to light through the gospel" (2 Tim. 1:10). The heathen concept of the immortality of the soul is not biblical. Immortality belongs to the realm of the body as it affects the whole redeemed man.

Immortality and the Believer's Hope. No believer yet has an immortal body. Christ alone, who did not see corruption (Ps. 16:10; Acts 2:31), possesses such a body as the glorified Son of Man in heaven. He put on immortality over a mortal body, that is, His body that died on the cross. By His redemptive work on the cross and His resurrection He "brought life and immortality to light through the gospel" (2 Tim. 1:10). The cross of Christ guaranteed the glorification of the human body of the believer, whether by translation or resurrection. No unbeliever has this hope. Although the Christian's body may suffer dissolution, as the body of the unsaved person's does, yet only the believer in Christ can look forward to an immortal body joined to a deathless soul and spirit. Thus Christ's redemption extends to the entire personality. It is not a shadowy, disembodied existence in Sheol or Hades. It is a full deliverance. Thus it may be said that immortality cannot be correctly used of the soul. It must be posited of the incorruption or incorruptibility of the body as it affects the whole man. The destiny of the believer is to be transformed "into conformity with the body of His glory" (Phil. 3:21). This body will be suitable for our "citizenship" in heaven (3:20). All Christians will see the dissolution of the human body, except those who will be living at the end of the age when Christ returns. They will be translated without seeing death. This is what the apostle means in 2 Cor. 5:4: "while we are in this tent, we groan, being burdened, because we do not want to be unclothed, but to be clothed, in order that what is mortal may be swallowed up by life." All other Christians will see corruption, or death (that is, the separation of the body from the soul and spirit). They, however, will receive immortality or be clothed with immortality by resurrection. Resurrection may be defined as the reunion of the soul and spirit with the body in the glorified form; deathless, sinless, painless, fatigueless.

BIBLIOGRAPHY: J. Orr, *The Christian View of God and the World* (1947); L. S. Chafer, *Systematic Theology* (1948), 2:152-53, 155; C. Hodge, *Systematic Theology* (1950), 3:716ff.; L. Boettner, *Immortality* (1956); R. Martin-Achard, *From Death to Life* (1960); G. C. Berkouwer, *Man: The Image of God* (1962), pp. 234-78; D. Winter, *Hereafter* (1973); R. A. Morey, *Death and the Afterlife* (1984); H. D. F. Salmond, *The Biblical Doctrine of Immortality* (1984).

IMMUTABILITY. The divine attribute of unchangeableness. The Scripture declarations of this attribute are most clear and emphatic. It is indicated in the title under which God made Himself known to Moses, "I Am," "I Am Who I Am" (Ex. 3:14; *see* Num. 23:19; 32:11; Mal. 3:6; James 1:17).

From this it is to be understood that God is eternally the same in His essence, in the mode of His existence, in His perfections, and in the principles of His administration.

This attribute is essential to deity. To think of God otherwise than as unchangeable is to think of Him otherwise than as perfect.

Immutability is not, however, to be confounded with immobility. God acts, and His actions vary with reference to different ends. His affections toward the same persons change according to the changed attitude of those persons toward Him. Thus, according to the representations of Scripture, the God who "is not a man, that he should repent" (1 Sam. 15:29, KJV) nevertheless does "repent," an accommodation of language to express the truth above stated. In reality such changes in the divine operations and affections are illustrations of the fact and character of divine immutability (*see* Num 23:19; Ps. 90:13; Ezek. 33:7-19; Jonah 3:9-10).

The proper conception of God's unchangeableness is to be derived only from the Scriptures, and the sublimity of the conception given there is one of the indications of divine revelations.

BIBLIOGRAPHY: S. Charnock, *Existence and Attributes of God* (1977), pp. 98-143.

IM'NA. The son of Helem, a descendant of Asher (1 Chron. 7:35).

IM'NAH (im'na; cf. Arab. *yumnah,* "good luck, fortune").

1. The first named of the sons of Asher (Gen. 46:17; Num. 26:44; 1 Chron. 7:30), about 2000 B.C. The name is given as Jimnah in the KJV of Gen. 46:17 and as Jimna in the KJV of Num. 26:44.

2. The father of Kore, which latter, a Levite, had charge of the E gate of the Temple and was appointed by Hezekiah over the freewill offerings (2 Chron. 31:14), 715 B.C.

IMPERISHABLE. The rendering in the NASB and NIV of two Gk. words to describe something as ever-enduring, unchanging.

1. Gk. *aphtharsia* is applied in 1 Cor. 15:42, 50, 53-54 to the body of a man as exempt from decay after the resurrection (the KJV reads "incorruption"). The same Gk. word is rendered "immortality" in Rom. 2:7; 2 Tim. 1:10; it is given as "incorruptible" in Eph. 6:24 (NASB; "in sincerity," KJV; "undying," NIV).

2. The "wreath" ("crown," KJV) of the saints is imperishable (Gk. *aphthartos,* 1 Cor. 9:25; "incorruptible," KJV; "that will last forever," NIV), as is their inheritance (1 Pet. 1:4). *See also* 1 Cor. 15:52; 1 Pet. 1:23.

IMPORTUNITY (Gk. *anaideia*). Persistence (Luke 11:8; cf. 18:1; 1 Thess. 5:17).

IMPOSITION OF HANDS. See Hands, Laying on of.

IMPOTENT. In the KJV, a general term indicating disablement. The NASB renders "sick" (John 5:3, 7; Acts 4:9; the NIV has "invalid" and "cripple" respectively) and "without strength" (14:8; NIV, "crippled").

IMPRECATION. *See* Curse.

IMPRECATORY PSALMS. *See* Psalms.

IMPURITY. *See* Uncleanness.

IMPUTATION. One of the major doctrines of Christianity. It has produced a great deal of theological controversy (*see* Hagenbach and Shedd, *History of Doctrine*). The actual word *impute* means to "reckon over unto one's account." The case of the apostle's writing to Philemon concerning whatever his runaway slave Onesimus

might owe him gives a perfect scriptural illustration of the meaning of the phrase: "charge that to my account" (Philem. 18). Three major imputations are expounded in Scripture:

Of Adam's Sin to the Race. This is the clear teaching of Rom. 5:12-21. Verse 12 clearly indicates that death has come upon all men "because all sinned." The tense of the verb *sinned* is the aorist and does not therefore concern the sin of men in their daily experience. But the passage clearly indicates that all men sinned when Adam sinned and thereby incurred upon themselves the penalty of physical death as a consequence. In demonstrating that this passage does not have reference to personal sins, we call attention to the apostle's observation that between the time of Adam and Moses, before the Mosaic law was instituted, all died. Likewise all irresponsible persons such as infants and imbeciles died, although they were never guilty of willful sin as in the case of Adam. Many theologians object to this teaching of real imputation, that is, of reckoning to each person that which is antecedently his own. But Scripture furnishes a close parallel in the record of Levi, who was supported by tithes and is specifically said to have paid tithes while being in the loins of his great-grandfather Abraham (Heb. 7:9-10), that is, when Abraham paid tithes to Melchizedek.

Of the Sin of the Human Race to Christ. This involves a judicial imputation inasmuch as the sin was never antecedently Christ's and when laid upon Him became His in a fearful sense. The truth of the gospel lies in this grand fact. Although the theological term *impute* is not employed with regard to the laying of the sin of Adam's race upon the Sin Bearer, the idea is obviously contained in such expressions as "caused the iniquity of us all to fall on Him," "He Himself bore our sins," and "made Him who knew no sin to be sin" (Isa. 53:5-6; 1 Pet. 2:24; 2 Cor. 5:21).

Of the Righteousness of God to the Believer. The great theme of the book of Romans has to do with the doctrinal expression of imputation of the righteousness of God to the believer as it pertains to his salvation. It is quite obvious, therefore, that this truth is of great consequence to the Christian's salvation. The Pauline epistles in general clearly show that this phase of imputation is the groundwork of the Christian's acceptance and standing before an infinitely holy God. Only this righteousness can find acceptance for salvation, and through it alone one may enter heaven. The pregnant phrase *"the righteousness of God"* (Rom. 1:17; 3:22; 10:3) signifies not merely that God Himself is righteous but that there is a righteousness that proceeds from God. Since no human being in God's eyes is righteous (3:10), it is clear that an imputed righteousness, the righteousness of God Himself, is sinful man's only hope of acceptance with the Holy One. Possessing this righteousness is the only thing that fits one for the presence of God (Phil. 3:9; Col. 1:12). When this righteousness is imputed by God to the believer, it becomes his forever by a judicial act, since it was not antecedently the believer's. It is thus patent that this demands a righteousness that is made over to the believer, just as Christ was made to be sin for all men (2 Cor. 5:21). By the believer's baptism by the Spirit "into Christ" this righteousness is made a legal endowment by virtue of the death of Christ. Indeed, imputed righteousness becomes a reality on the basis of the fact that the believer is "in Christ." As hitherto one was "in Adam" (Rom. 5:12-21), so by the Spirit's baptism (6:3-4) he is now placed in the resurrected Christ and is a recipient of all that Christ is, even of the "righteousness of God" that Christ is. It is a transcendent truth that Christ is made to the believer the righteousness "from God" (1 Cor. 1:30), and, being "in Christ," the believer "might become the righteousness of God in Him" (2 Cor. 5:21). The glory of this "in Christ" position is beyond description or human comprehension, "for by one offering He has perfected for all time those who are sanctified" (Heb. 10:14). The "fulness" of Christ (John 1:16; Col. 1:19; 2:9-10) becomes the believer's portion in Christ, "for in Him all the fulness of Deity dwells in bodily form, and in Him you have been made complete." The basis of the legality of such imputation, resulting in such a position for the believer, resides in the fact that Christ offered Himself "without blemish" to God (Heb. 9:14). This means that Christ not only was made a sin offering, but His death (by which remission of sin is made legally possible on the basis that He substituted for those who believe and presented Himself as an offering well-pleasing to God) also made possible a release of all that He is in infinite merit, bestowing this merit on the meritless. When others did not possess and could not gain a standing and merit before God, He released His own self in infinite perfection for them (see 2 Cor. 8:9). As the cross furnishes the legal basis for the remission of sin, so it furnishes likewise the legal basis for the imputation of righteousness. Both aspects of a sweet savor and a non-sweet savor in the estimation of the Father are typically expounded in the five offerings of Lev. 1-5. There was that in the death of Christ that was a non-sweet savor to God manifested in the terrible words "My God, My God, why hast Thou forsaken Me?" (Ps. 22:1; Matt. 27:46). The character of the perfect, sinless Lamb of God (Heb. 9:14) suggests the sweet savor aspect. Thus the sweet savor aspect of Christ's offering, and its accomplishment in the believer by his union with Christ through the work of the Holy Spirit, is the legal ground for the imputation of God's righteousness to the believer. Foundational to essential Christian teaching and the essence of the gospel are these three imputations. They are typi-

cal in the Mosaic system; antitypical in the Christian era.   M.F.U.

BIBLIOGRAPHY: L. S. Chafer, *Systematic Theology* (1948), 2:296-315; 3:243-44; 5:143-44; 7:191-94; W. G. T. Shedd, *Dogmatic Theology* (1952), 2:148-257; J. Murray, *The Imputation of Adam's Sin* (1959); C. Hodge, *Commentary on the Epistle to the Romans* (1965), pp. 221-99; G. C. Berkouwer, *Sin* (1971), pp. 436-65; H. Bavinck, *Our Reasonable Faith* (1978), pp. 224-30, 240-46; F. B. Westcott, *The Biblical Doctrine of Justification* (1983), pp. 165-82, 188-209.

IM'RAH (im'ra; "he, i.e., God, resists"). One of the sons of Zophah, of the tribe of Asher (1 Chron. 7:36). *See* Hotham.

IM'RI (im'ri).

1. The son of Bani and father of Omri of Judah (1 Chron. 9:4), before 536 B.C.

2. The father of Zaccur, which latter repaired part of the wall of Jerusalem (Neh. 3:2), before 445 B.C.

INABILITY. Scripture represents fallen man as utterly lost and unable to please God or to save himself. The divine revelation is that God has "already charged that both Jews and Greeks are all under sin" (Rom. 3:9). God's final verdict is that the whole world is guilty before Him (vv. 10-20). Justification by faith in Christ crucified is the one and only remedy for sinners (3:21–5:11). God enables men to believe; and when they believe they receive a new life and a new nature, in addition to the indwelling Spirit, who imparts the dynamic for holy living and service that is pleasing to God.   M.F.U.

INCANTATION. *See* Magic.

INCARNATION (Lat. *in* and *caro,* "flesh"). The act of assuming flesh; in theology, the gracious voluntary act of the Son of God in assuming a human body and human nature.

The Christian Doctrine. The doctrine of the incarnation, briefly stated, is that the Lord Jesus Christ is one person with two natures indissolubly united, the one nature being that of the eternal Son of God, the other that of man, in all respects human, "yet without sin." It includes the miraculous conception and birth of Christ. The incarnation is absolutely without parallel in history. The fabled incarnations of pagan religions are at most only indications of the vague longing of humanity for union with the divine and are thus in some sense imaginative anticipations of the Christian reality. The incarnation is also to be distinguished from theophanies, or those appearances of a divine person in human form (often bearing the title "the angel of the Lord," "angel of God"), of which the OT gives instances (see Gen. 16:7; 21:17; Ex. 3:2; 14:19; Judg. 6:11-22; etc.). These are to be regarded as preintimations or occasional prophetic manifestations of that which was to be permanently realized in Christ.

Scripture Teachings. In addition to the gospel record of the miraculous conception and birth of Christ (see Luke 1:26-35; 2:1-14, cf. with Matt. 2:1-15), the Scriptures disclose this doctrine in several ways:

1. In the OT prophecies, which represent Christ as a person both human and divine, He is set forth in "the seed" of the woman, a descendant of Abraham, of Judah, and of David, "a man of sorrows." But He is also called "the Mighty God," "the Eternal Father," "the Son of God," "the Lord [Jehovah] our righteousness." Although these familiar Scriptures do not formally state the doctrine of the incarnation, they logically suggest or lead up to it.

2. Also in the NT there are many passages that present the elements of this doctrine separately—Christ is represented as a man with a human body and a rational human soul; physically and mentally He is truly human. The designation "the Son of man" occurs more than eighty times in the gospels. But elsewhere this same person claims for Himself, and has ascribed to Him, the attribute of deity.

3. There are numerous instances in which these two elements of Christ's personality are combined in the statement, or in which they are brought without hesitation or reserve close together (e.g., Matt. 16:27; 22:42-45; 25:31-46; Mark 14:60-62; Luke 9:43-44; John 3:31; Rom. 5:15, 21; 1 Cor. 15:47).

4. Although the doctrine does not rest for its authority upon isolated proof texts, but rather upon the Scripture revelation as a whole, still there are certain utterances of great weight in which the truth is distinctly, and we may say even formally, stated (see John 1:1-14, cf. 1 John 1:1-3; 4:2-3; Rom. 1:2-5; Phil. 2:6-11; 1 Tim. 3:16; Heb. 2:14). The only way in which the force of these teachings can be set aside or lessened is by proving lack of authority on the part of the Scriptures. It should be added that the only way in which the Scriptures can be understood or intelligently interpreted is in the light of the essential facts of the incarnation.

Theological Development of the Doctrine. The early centuries of the history of the church were marked in an unusual degree by speculations concerning the Person of Christ. The representation of Scripture raised many questions among thinkers and led to numerous attempts to give scientific form and elaborateness to the doctrine of the incarnation. These speculations were affected in some instances by Jewish opinions and prejudices held by members of the Christian community but more frequently by one form or another of pagan philosophy. It is not surprising, therefore, that various styles of error, heresies that became historic, appeared, and were overthrown, during those centuries. Among the prominent heresies were the following, namely:

1. Ebionism, or the doctrine of the Ebionites,

a Jewish sect that existed even in the time of the apostles. This error arose from mistaken Jewish preconceptions concerning the Messiah and consisted in the denial of the divine nature of Christ.

2. Gnosticism, a name indicating the assumption of superior capacity for knowledge (Gk. gnōsis, "knowledge"). Gnosticism in its diverse forms received its impulse, and in the main its guidance, from pagan philosophy. In different ways it denied the humanity of Christ, even to the extent of denying the reality of His human body.

3. Sabellianism, which at bottom was a denial of the tri-personality of God, denied, accordingly, the existence of the Son of God as a distinct person before the incarnation. The union between the divine and human natures in Christ was held to be but temporary.

4. Arianism denied that the Son was of the same essence with the Father but held that the essence in both was similar, hence reaching the conclusion that Christ was created, though the greatest of all creatures. In connection with this heresy was the fierce contention over homoousios, "same substance," and homoiousios, "similar substance," a discussion to which uninformed persons, who do not realize the importance of the issue involved, sometimes sneeringly refer.

5. Apollinarianism, resting upon the platonic distinction between body, soul, and spirit as three distinct elements in man, viewed Christ as having a human body and soul, or animal life, but not a human spirit having rationality and intelligence, in place of which was the divine nature of Christ. Thus Christ was not completely human.

The study of the heresies of early church history is especially valuable because the errors of modern times, such as Socinianism, Unitarianism, and Rationalism, are simply these ancient and oft-refuted heresies revived. It would be a mistake to suppose that during those centuries the faith of the Christian church was reduced to confusion. As has been said with much force, "the faith of the common people is determined by the word of God, by the worship of the sanctuary, and by the teachings of the Spirit. They remain in a great measure ignorant of, or indifferent to, the speculations of theologians."

The Importance of the Doctrine. Lewis Sperry Chafer (Systematic Theology [1948], 7:194) correctly places the incarnation as one of the seven greatest events that have occurred in the history of the universe: (1) the creation of the angels, (2) creation of material things, including all life on the earth, (3) the incarnation, (4) the death of the Incarnate One, (5) His resurrection, (6) His coming again, (7) His reign on the earth forever. That God in the Person of the Son should identify Himself completely with the human race, become a kinsman of the human family, and as the Kinsman-Redeemer lay down His life for their redemption from sin, as in the book of Ruth (cf.

Lev. 25:49; Isa. 59:20), is in itself an event of immeasurable importance.

Present-Day Thinking. The early twentieth century saw an interest in the humanity of Jesus. Christology was severely neglected. A. Harnack in his *What Is Christianity?* (1904) apparently differentiated between the gospel *about* Jesus and that *of* Jesus. Numerous studies of the human aspects of the Person of our Lord were made. Albert Schweitzer in his *Quest of the Historical Jesus* (English translation 1910) showed the invalidity of the stress on the humanity of Jesus without the Christological element. Neo-orthodox theologians have also led a strong reaction against the mere human view of our Lord. Emil Brunner as well as Karl Barth held that the revelation of God centers not in the historical coming of Jesus but only in the Christ who is discerned by the eye of faith. Notorious, however, has been neo-orthodox Christology in neglecting the historical words of Jesus as well as His deeds (cf. W. L. Sperry, *Jesus Then and Now* [1949]). Emil Brunner is of the opinion that to give any adequate statement of the union of the divine and human natures of Christ in one person exceeds man's intellectual capacity.

William Temple (*Christus Veritas* [1924]) made an attempt to place the incarnation within the realm of the evolutionary idea of the universe. Lionel Thornton in *The Incarnate Lord* (1928) tried to orientate the doctrine of the incarnation in the framework of the organic philosophy of the period. In these studies, however, Christ is given the place not of a divine Savior from sin but rather the role of a cosmic principle. W. R. Matthews in his *The Problem of Christ in the Twentieth Century* (1950) has wrestled with the psychological aspects of Christ's Person. John Knox (*On the Meaning of Christ* [1947]) regards the ancient creeds as metaphysically inaccurate and believes that they are to be correctly evaluated as attempts to set forth in symbol the divine revelatory act in Christ. Both Reinhold Niebuhr and Paul Tillich question the orthodox statements of Christ's Person and His atoning work on the ground that they come close to logical nonsense. Only in symbolical terms can the presence of the Eternal from beyond the historical context be expressed historically (cf. Paul Tillich, *The Interpretation of History* [1936]; id., *Systematic Theology* 1 [1951]; Reinhold Niebuhr, *The Nature and Destiny of Man* [1943]).   M.F.U.

BIBLIOGRAPHY: P. T. Forsyth, *The Person and Place of Jesus Christ* (1910); R. H. MacIntosh, *The Doctrine of the Person of Christ* (1912); J. K. Moseley, *The Doctrine of the Incarnation* (1936); R. Bultmann, *Jesus and the Word* (1929); E. Brunner, *The Mediator* (1927); L. F. Thornton, *The Incarnate Lord* (1928); W. M. Horton, *Our Eternal Contemporary* (1942); W. N. Pittenger, *Christ and Christian Faith* (1941); John Knox, *On the Meaning of Christ* (1947); Otto Piper, *God in History* (1939). A. E. J. Rawlinson, *The New Testament Doctrine of Christ* (1926); W. D. Davies, *Paul and Rabbinic Judaism* (1948); K. Barth, *Church Dogmatics* (1956), 1:122-202; L. Morris, *The Lord from Heaven* (1958); D. M. Baillie, *God Was in Christ* (1961); J. McIntyre, *The Shape of Christology* (1966); G. W. Bromiley, *International Standard Bible Encyclopedia* (1966), 1:663-66; E. H. Gifford and S. J. Andrews, *The Incarnation of Christ* (1981).

INCENSE (Heb. usually *qeṭôret*, once applied to the "fat" of rams, the part always burned in sacrifice; once *qiṭṭēr*, Jer. 44:21, marg., both from the Hebrew, to "smoke"; sometimes *lebônâ*, Isa. 43:23; 66:3; Jer. 17:26; 41:5). *Frankincense* (Isa. 60:6; Jer. 6:20; NIV, "incense" in both passages), an aromatic compound that gives forth its perfume in burning. Its most general use in Scripture is that perfume that was burned upon the Jewish altar of incense (*see* Tabernacle). Among both the Hebrews and Egyptians we find no other trace of incense than in its sacerdotal use, but in Persian sculptures we see it burned before the king.

Material. The incense employed in the service of the Tabernacle was called "incense of the aromas" (Heb. *qeṭôret sammîm*), the ingredients of which are given in Ex. 30:34-35. These consisted of: (1) *stacte* (Heb. *naṭāp*), i.e., "not the juice squeezed from the highly fragrant myrrh tree, but probably a species of *gum storax* resembling myrrh"; (2) *onycha* (Heb. *sheḥēlet*, lit., a "scale"), the shell of the perfumed mollusk, *blatta byzantina*, found in the Mediterranean and Red seas and yielding a musky odor when burned; (3) *galbanum* (Heb. *ḥelbenâ*, lit., "fat"), a gum that is obtained by making incisions in the bark of a shrub growing in Syria, Arabia, and Abyssinia; and (4) *pure frankincense* (Heb. *lebônâ*, lit., "white"), a pale yellow, semitransparent, pungent resin, which, when burned, is fragrant; it is grown in Arabia and Judea.

Preparation. The KJV says "of each there shall be a like *weight*," i.e., equal parts of the various ingredients, but Abarbanel, Ibn Ezra, and others think that the meaning is that each ingredient was, in the first place, to be pounded by itself, and then mixed with the rest, for it is possible that the ingredients were not all pounded to the same extent. Besides, it was to be *salted* (KJV, "tempered"), was to be "pure, and holy," i.e., unadulterated with any foreign substance, and was to be reserved exclusively for sacred use, any other application of it being forbidden on pain of being "cut off from [one's] people."

Sacred Use. The person selected to burn incense upon the altar of incense was Aaron, but in the daily service of the second Temple the office devolved upon the inferior priests, from among whom one was chosen by lot (Luke 1:9). King Uzziah was punished for presuming to infringe upon this prerogative of the priests (2 Chron. 26:16, 21). The times of offering incense were in the morning, at the time of trimming the lamps, and in the evening, when the lamps were lighted

(Ex. 30:7-8). On the Day of Atonement (*see* Festivals) the high priest offered the incense.

Censers

Figurative. Incense in Scripture is the symbol of prayer; "May my prayer be counted as incense before Thee" (Ps. 141:2; *see* Isa. 60:6). In Rev. 5:8; 8:3-4 we meet with the same idea. But "it is not prayer alone that is expressed by incense. . . . A good or evil savor was to Israel the symbol of a good or godless life; and when, therefore, the sanctuary of God was kept continually filled with fragrance, they beheld in this the sweet savor, not of prayer alone, but of that life to which, as a priestly nation, they were called" (W. Milligan, *Bib. Ed.,* 3:226). *See* Tabernacle; Temple.

BIBLIOGRAPHY: M. Haran, *Vetus Testamentum* 10 (1960): 113-29; R. de Vaux, *Ancient Israel: Its Life and Institutions* (1961), pp. 286, 411, 423, 430-32; G. van Beek, *Biblical Archaeologist Reader,* ed. E. Campbell and D. N. Freedman (1964), 2:99-126; N. Glueck, *Translating and Understanding the Old Testament,* ed. H. Frank and W. Reed (1970), pp. 325-39.

INCEST. The crime of cohabitation with a person within the degrees forbidden by the Levitical law (Lev. 18:1-18). The prohibition of incest and similar sensual abominations is introduced with a general warning as to the licentious customs of the Egyptians and Canaanites and an exhortation to walk in the judgments and ordinances of Jehovah. Intercourse is forbidden (1) with a mother; (2) with a stepmother; (3) with a sister or half-sister; (4) with a granddaughter, the daughter of either son or daughter; (5) with the daughter of a stepmother; (6) with an aunt, sister of either father or mother; (7) with the wife of an uncle on the father's side; (8) with a daughter-in-law; (9) with a sister-in-law, or brother's wife; (10) with

a woman and her daughter, or a woman and her granddaughter; (11) with the sister of a living wife. No special reference is made to sexual intercourse with a daughter, being a crime regarded as not likely to occur; with a full sister, i.e., the daughter of one's father and mother, being included in number 3; or with a mother-in-law, included in number 10. Those mentioned in nos. 1, 2, 3, 8, and 10 were to be followed by the death of the criminals (20:11-12, 14, 17), on account of their being accursed crimes (Deut. 23:1; 27:20, 22-23); whereas the punishment of those guilty of nos. 6, 7, and 9 was to bear their iniquity and die childless (Lev. 20:19-21). *See* Marriage.

BIBLIOGRAPHY: L. M. Epstein, *Marriage Laws in the Bible and the Talmud* (1942), see index pp. 356-57; E. Neufeld, *Ancient Hebrew Marriage Laws* (1944), pp. 211-12; id., *Hittite Laws* (1951), p. 128; G. R. Driver and J. C. Miles, *The Babylonian Laws* (1952), 1:206, 318-22; W. G. Cole, *Sex and Love in the Bible* (1959), pp. 169, 289, 382, 386, 390ff.; S. Mendelsohn, *Criminal Jurisprudence of the Ancient Hebrews* (1968), pp. 26-27; D. Bakan, *And They Took Themselves Wives* (1979), pp. 20, 67-70; M. Lamm, *The Jewish Way in Love and Marriage* (1980), pp. 26-27, 39-41, 43, 65, 69, 71-80, 88-89, 94, 162.

INCONTINENCY (Gk. *akrasia,* "want of self-control"). A KJV term referring to an inability to restrain sexual indulgence. The NASB and NIV render "lack of self-control" (1 Cor. 7:5; cf. 2 Tim. 3:3).

INCORRUPTIBLE. This word appears in both the KJV and the NASB but in different places.

In the NASB the term is the translation of Gk. *aphthartos* in Rom. 1:23 (NIV, "immortal") and of Gk. *aphtharsia* in the benediction to the Ephesians (6:24): "Grace be with all those who love our Lord Jesus Christ with a love incorruptible." The NIV here has "undying."

In the KJV the term appears in 1 Cor. 9:25; 15:52; 1 Pet. 1:4, 23 as the rendering of Gk. *aphthartos;* it is replaced in the NASB by *imperishable* (which see).

INCORRUPTION. See Imperishable.

INDEPENDENCE OF GOD. God is absolute and not dependent upon any thing or person outside of Himself for His existence. "His being and perfections are underived, and not communicated to him, as all finite perfections are by him to the creature." He is independent (1) as to His knowledge (Isa. 40:13-14); (2) in power (Job 36:23); (3) as to His holiness, His bounty, and His goodness (Rom. 9:18).

INDIA (Heb. *hōdû*). The limit of the territories of Ahasuerus in the East (Esther 1:1; 8:9). The country so designated is not the peninsula of Hindustan, but the region through which the Indus River flowed—the Punjab.

INFANT BAPTISM. *See* Baptism.

INFANT SALVATION. *See* Salvation.

INFINITY. Unlimited extent of space or duration or quantity. As designating an essential attribute of God the term refers to His unlimited existence, capacity, energy, and perfections.

The word *infinity* does not occur in the Scriptures, and yet, properly understood, it is an appropriate term and necessary to express certain revelations of Scripture concerning God. God is not subject to the limitations of time or space. Thus infinity expresses both His eternity and His immensity. His power and knowledge and other perfections also exist in unlimited fullness.

This idea of God, necessary to our conception of Him, can be held by us only in a negative form, this being due to the finite nature of our understanding. It is nevertheless a positive idea and represents the actual fact that God in His being and attributes transcends not only our comprehension, but also all limits that must everywhere else be recognized. God is the only infinite existence.

Care must, however, be exercised not to conceive of the infinity of God in a material manner. God is the infinite Spirit. His presence pervades and fills all space, but not necessarily to the exclusion of other and finite existences. The mistake of Spinoza, and Pantheists generally, has been that of applying to God the material conception of infinity. And upon the principle of the impenetrability of matter, or that two bodies cannot occupy the same space at the same time, the conclusion has been reached that the being of God includes all things, or that all things are parts or manifestations of God. The idea of infinity brought forward by Mansel in *The Limits of Religious Thought* is also essentially of the same character, although he avoids the Pantheistic conclusion by appealing from philosophy to faith for the right conception of God. It must be borne in mind that the infinity of God is that of spirit, and to spirit the ideas of extension and impenetrability do not apply, as they do to matter. And further, the infinite Spirit is necessarily one capable of creating finite existences. And withal there must ever be the proper acknowledgment of the incapacity of the human mind to argue adequately upon this and certain other subjects.

E.M.

BIBLIOGRAPHY: L. S. Chafer, *Systematic Theology* (1948), 1:215-16; 7:199-200; C. Hodge, *Systematic Theology* (1950), 1:380ff.; A. Hodge, *Outlines of Theology* (1972), pp. 104ff.

See also God.

INFIRMITY (Gk. *astheneia*), NASB, KJV, NIV; Gk. *astheneia, nosos;* Heb. *maḥăleh* and others, KJV). This word is used once in the NASB and NIV in a passage referring to Jesus: "In order that what was spoken through Isaiah the prophet might be fulfilled, saying 'He Himself took our infirmities, and carried away our diseases'" (Matt. 8:17; cf. Isa. 53:4). The term (Heb. *mak'ōb*) encompasses not only disease but also suffering and sorrow.

The expression is much more common in the KJV and is used there to denote a disability of one kind or another. It is most often replaced in the NASB and NIV by the term *weakness,* but other terms (*diseases, sickness, menstruation,* and *grief*) appear also. The Gk. *nosos* is rendered "sickness, disease" (Luke 7:21; etc.). Romans 15:1 states that those "who are strong ought to bear the weaknesses of those without strength." The KJV often renders this word "infirmity."

INFLAMMATION. *See* Diseases.

INGATHERING, FEAST OF. *See* Festivals: Booths (or Tabernacles), feast of.

INHERITANCE. The following laws prevailed among several nations:

Greek. If a person died without a will, leaving sons, all of equal birthright and none of them disinherited, the sons inherited the property in equal parts, the eldest probably receiving the same as the rest. Daughters were provided with dowries, which went back to the remaining heirs in case the daughter was divorced or left childless after marriage. If a man had no son, he usually adopted one to continue the family and its religious worship; and if he had daughters he would marry one of them to the adopted son, in which case the chief share of the inheritance fell to his daughter and her husband, the rest receiving dowries. If only daughters survived, the succession passed to them, and the next of kin had a legal right to one of the heiresses and could claim to marry her, even though she had married another before receiving the inheritance. A man marrying an heiress was bound by custom and tradition, if he had sons, to name one as heir to the property coming with his wife and thus restore the house of his son's maternal grandfather. Children born out of wedlock were illegitimate and had no claim to the estate of the father. If a man died without a will, leaving no biological or adopted heirs, his nearest relatives in the male line inherited and, in default of these, those in the female line as far as children of first cousins.

Roman. If a man died without a will, leaving a wife and biological or adopted children, they were his heirs. This did not apply, however, to daughters who had passed into the hands of their husbands, or of children who had been freed by emancipation from the power (*potestas*) of their father. If a man left no wife or children, the *agnati,* or relatives of the male line, inherited, according to the degree of their kinship. If there were no *agnati,* and the man was a patrician, the property went to his *gens.* The relatives in the female line (*cognati*) were generally not entitled to inherit by the civil law.

Hebrew. The Hebrew institutions relative to inheritance were of a simple character. Under the patriarchal system the property was divided among the sons of the legitimate wives (Gen. 24:36; 25:5), a larger portion being assigned to one, generally the eldest, on whom devolved the duty of maintaining the females of the family. The sons of concubines were portioned off with presents (25:6). At a later period the exclusion of the sons of unlawful wives was rigidly enforced (Judg. 11:1-2).

The possession of land, which Israel received by lot from God, was to remain the inalienable property of the several families. According to an old-standing custom, the father's property went to his sons, the firstborn receiving a double portion, the other sons single and equal portions—i.e., of five sons the firstborn got two-sixths, and each of the others one-sixth of the father's entire property. In consideration of this division, the firstborn, as head of the family, had to provide food, clothing, and other necessities in his house, not only for his mother but also for his sisters until they married. This custom was more precisely defined by Moses: the father could not deprive his firstborn of his birthright by mere whim (Deut. 21:15-17), but it might be taken away because of a trespass against the father, as in the case of Reuben (Gen. 49:4; 1 Chron. 5:1). See Firstborn.

If there were no sons, the property went to the daughters (Num. 27:8) on the condition that they did not marry out of their own tribe (Num. 36:6-9; Tobit 6:12; 7:13), otherwise the patrimony was forfeited. If there were no daughters, it went to the brother of the deceased; if no brother, to the paternal uncle; and, failing these, to the next of kin (Num. 27:9-11). In the case of a widow's being left without children, the nearest of kin on her husband's side had the right of marrying her, and in the event of his refusal, the next of kin (Ruth 3:12-13); with him rested the obligation of redeeming the property of the widow (4:1-10) if it had been either sold or mortgaged. If none stepped forward to marry the widow, the inheritance remained with her until her death and then reverted to the next of kin. The land being thus so strictly tied up, the notion of *heirship*, as we understand it, was hardly known to the Jews. See Table 18, "The Hebrew Order of Succession as Heirs."

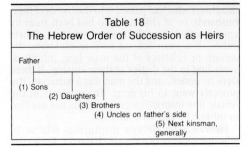

Table 18
The Hebrew Order of Succession as Heirs

Father
(1) Sons
   (2) Daughters
      (3) Brothers
         (4) Uncles on father's side
            (5) Next kinsman, generally

If the deceased possessed what we call *personal property*—i.e., flocks and herds, garments, precious metals, or jewels, which last, in oriental countries, is still the favorite mode of investment—the portions of the younger children, as well as gifts or dowers for the daughters, were usually provided from this source. The strict law of entail with regard to land did not at all restrain the deceased in the disposition of his personal property. It was to this latter that the request of the younger son in Jesus' parable referred. He asked that the third part of the movable property, which would naturally come to him at his father's death, should be granted him now (Luke 15:12).

See also Wills.

BIBLIOGRAPHY: E. Neufeld, *Ancient Hebrew Marriage Laws* (1944), pp. 259-65; R. de Vaux, *Ancient Israel: Its Life and Culture* (1961), pp. 53-55, 166; G. H. Dalman, *The Words of Christ* (1981), pp. 125-27.

INHERITANCE, SPIRITUAL. "The metaphor of the spiritual 'inheritance' is peculiarly, though not exclusively, Pauline. St. Peter employs it twice (1 Pet. 1:4; 3:9), St. James once (2:5, KJV; NASB, "heirs"), but St. Paul in a multitude of instances. It is closely interwoven with the substance of the longest and most intricate arguments in his epistles; it appears in the reports of his sermons in the Acts; he alone of all the sacred writers employs it in what may be described as the most daring of all theological conceptions—that which is embodied in the celebrated definition of believers as 'heirs of God and joint heirs with Christ.' To our minds heirship involves no more than the idea of the acquisition of property by succession, and the idea of succession is manifestly inapplicable with reference to the eternal God. That the heirship to which St. Paul alludes is Roman and not Hebrew is evident not only from the accompanying reference to adoption, but also from the fact that it is a joint and equal heirship."

Sir Henry Maine writes (*Ancient Law*): "The notion (among the Romans) was that though the physical person of the deceased had perished, his legal personality had survived and descended unimpaired to his heirs or co-heirs, in whom his identity (so far as the law was concerned) was continued" (p. 181). "The testator lived on in his heir or in the group of his co-heirs. He was in law the same person with them" (ibid., p. 188). "In pure Roman jurisprudence the principle that a man lives on in his heir—*the elimination, so to speak, of the fact of death*—is too obvious for one to mistake the center round which the whole law of testamentary and intestate succession is circling" (ibid., p. 190). Contrary to the well-known maxim of English law, *Nemo est heres viventis* ("No one is heir of the living"), according to Roman law, the moment a child was born he was his father's heir. Paul the Jurist (third century A.D.) observes that there is a species of copartnership between a father and his children; "when, therefore, the father dies, it is not so correct to say that they succeed to his property, as that they acquire the free control of their own."

"In the light of the theories of Roman jurisprudence incongruity disappears from the great Pauline metaphor, and we discern in it a new sublimity. Instead of the death of the ancestor being essentially connected with the idea of inheritance, we find this circumstance 'eliminated.' The heir has not to wait for the moment of his father's decease. In and through his father he is already a participator in the family possessions. The father does not die, but lives on forever in his family. Physically absent, he is spiritually present, not *with* so much as *in* his children. In this phrase, 'the heirs of God,' there is presented a most vivid view of the intimate and eternal union between the believer and God, and of the faithful soul's possession in present reality, and not merely in anticipation of the kingdom of God on earth and in heaven" (W. E. Ball, *Mag. of Christ. Lit.*, p. 344).

INIQUITY. The translation of several Gk. and Heb. terms.

1. Heb. *'awôn,* perversity, depravity, sin (Gen. 4:13, "punishment," etc.); guilt contracted by sinning (Ex. 20:5; etc.); anything unjustly acquired (Hos. 12:8); penalty of sin (Isa. 5:18); calamity, misery (Ps. 31:10).

2. Heb. *'āwel* (Job 34:10, "commit iniquity," KJV; "do wrong," NASB and NIV) and Heb. *'awlâ* (2 Chron. 19:7, "iniquity," KJV; "unrighteousness," NASB; "injustice," NIV) means perverseness.

3. In the NT the Gk. words are very expressive. Thus *adikia,* rendered "unrighteous," "unrighteousness," "iniquity," "iniquities," "wickedness" (and other similar terms) in the NASB means that which is not just (Acts 8:23; Heb. 8:12); *anomia* (Matt. 23:28, "iniquity," KJV; "lawlessness," NASB; "wickedness," NIV; *see also* 2 Thess. 2:7) and *paranomia* (2 Pet. 2:16, "iniquity," KJV; "transgression," NASB; "wrongdoing," NIV) mean "without law" and "transgression of the law"; whereas *ponēria* (Matt. 22:18; Luke 11:39; Rom. 1:29; 1 Cor. 5:8; etc.) signifies depravity, wickedness, malice.

In ordinary usage the term *iniquity* means absence of equity, wickedness, sin. *See* Lawlessness, Transgression.

INJURIES. *See* Law, Offenses.

INK (Heb. *dᵉyô,* Jer. 36:18; Gk. *melan,* "black," 2 Cor. 3:3; 2 John 12; 3 John 13). The ink of the ancients was composed of powdered charcoal, lampblack, or soot mixed with gum and water. It was intensely black and would retain its color for a long time but was easily erased from the parchments with sponge and water (*see* Num. 5:23). When needed for use, some of the dry preparation

was mixed with water until about the consistency of modern printer's ink. Both the Egyptians and the Hebrews made use of different colors for writing, some of the books of the latter having been written, according to Josephus, in red, blue, purple, gold, and silver tints.

INKHORN (Heb. *qeset,* a round "vessel"). This consists of a long tube for holding pens, sometimes made of hard wood but generally of metal—brass, copper, or silver. It is about nine or ten inches long, one and a half or two inches wide, and half an inch deep. To the upper end of this case the inkstand is attached. This is square or cylindrical, with a lid moving on hinges and fastening with a clasp. The inkhorn was carried in the girdle.

INN (Heb. *mālôn,* Gen. 42:27; 43:21; Ex. 4:24, NASB and NIV, a "lodging place"; the Gk. *kataluma* is used for an "inn," Luke 2:7; or "guest room" as in Mark 14:14; Luke 22:11). In the East hospitality was religiously observed, and therefore, in our sense of the term, inns were not known. Khans, or caravansaries, are the representatives of European inns and were only gradually established. It is doubtful whether there is any allusion to them in the OT, the meaning of "lodging place" in Gen. 42:27, Ex. 4:24, and Jer. 9:2 being only the *station,* the place of rest for the night, either under a tent or in a cave. The first place of an inn may be found in Jer. 41:17, KJV, "the habitation of Chimham" (Heb. *gērût;* NASB, marg., "the lodging place of Chimham"). The NIV describes the place itself as Geruth Kimham. The *pandocheion* (Luke 10:34) probably differed from the *kataluma* (2:7) in having a "host" or "innkeeper" (10:35), who supplied a few of the necessary provisions and attended to the needs of travelers left to his charge. In these inns, bazaars

Site of the Inn of the Good Samaritan, halfway between Jerusalem and Jericho

and markets were held, animals killed and meat sold, along with wine and cider; so that they were much more public places than might at first be imagined.

The origin of inns is unknown. Perhaps they were established at first by traders who regularly passed the same road. Now they are spread over the whole of the East, being found in cities, villages, and even the open highway. They consist of large buildings of stone arranged in a square, which enclose a spacious court. They are frequently of two stories, the lower containing stores and vaults for goods and stalls for cattle, the upper being used for travelers. They also contain a well or a large reservoir.

It appears that houses of entertainment were sometimes, as in Egypt (Herodotus *History* 2:35), kept by prostitutes. But the inference that the women mentioned in Josh. 2:1; Judg. 16:1; 1 Kings 3:16 were innkeepers seems rather forced.

INNOCENCE (Heb. *niqqāyôn*, lit., "clearness," Gen. 20:5; Pss. 26:6; 73:13; Hos. 8:5; *zākû*, "purity," Dan. 6:22). The Hebrews considered innocence as consisting chiefly in an exemption from external faults, but this is a different standard of morality from that of the gospel (*see* Matt. 5:28; John 3:25) or even of the OT (Ps. 51:7). Innocence is sometimes used as an exemption from punishment, as in Jer. 46:28, where the expression "I shall . . . by no means leave you unpunished" is more literally rendered "I will not treat you as one innocent" (from Heb. *nāqî*, "blameless," "innocent"; cf. Nah. 1:3; Ps. 18:26).

INNOCENTS, SLAUGHTER OF (*see* Matt. 2:16). The slaying of the young children of Bethlehem, by order of Herod, in the hope of killing Jesus. *See* Herod I.

"INQUIRE OF THE LORD." A phrase often found in early Scripture history. Rebekah is represented as going "to inquire of the Lord" (Gen. 25:22). During Jethro's visit to Moses we find the lawgiver vindicating his judicial office in these words: "Because the people come to me to inquire of God," etc. (Ex. 18:15-16). In the tribal war against the Benjamites "the sons of Israel inquired of the Lord" (Judg. 20:27). We read also of this being done in the times of Saul, David, and Samuel (1 Sam. 9:9; 10:22; 2 Sam. 2:1; 5:19, 23; 1 Chron. 14:10, 14). This longing of humanity for some material representation of divine direction and decision was responded to by Jehovah, who in different ways made known His counsel and guidance to those who "inquired" of Him. This was done through the pillar of cloud, the Shekinah, the Urim and the Thummim, and prophecy.

INSCRIPTION (Gk. *epigraphē*, "written upon"). A superscription, title, in the NT referring to writing in black letters upon a lighter tablet, perhaps surfaced with wax. Pilate wrote a trilin-

gual inscription and had it placed on the cross (Luke 23:38; John 19:19). Inscriptions also appeared on coins (Matt. 22:20; Mark 12:16; Luke 20:24). *See also* Writing.

INSPECTION GATE (Heb. *mipqād;* "appointment, census"). The name of a gate of Jerusalem, opposite the house of the Temple servants and the merchants, between the Horse Gate and the angle of the old wall near the Sheep Gate (Neh. 3:31 "the gate Miphkad," KJV); probably identical with the Gate of the Guard (12:39 "the prison gate," KJV). Some identify it with the upper Benjamin Gate (Jer. 20:2) and locate it at the W end of the bridge; but that gate was probably situated elsewhere. In Ezek. 43:21 *mipqād* is rendered "the appointed place" of the house, referring to the place set apart for burning the sin offering.

INSPIRATION. The doctrine of the inspiration of Scripture is of immense importance. This is at once apparent when one considers that all evangelical Christian doctrines are developed from the Bible and rest upon it for authority. L. Boettner is correct when he calls the biblical teaching of inspiration "the mother and guardian of all the others" (*Studies in Theology* [1947], p. 48). An unsound view of inspiration of Scripture is bound to countenance unsound views, produce distorted teachings or serious gaps in essential doctrinal systematization, or offer a temptation to too easy subscription to plausible but unsound scientific or philosophic theorizings.

The Scriptural Definition of Inspiration. In defining divine inspiration in the distinctive sense in which it is employed in the Holy Scriptures, the difference in meaning of this expression from revelation and illumination must be carefully comprehended.

Revelation. Revelation, which may be oral or written, may be defined as an operation of God communicating to man truth that otherwise man could not know. Since man was created in God's image and endowed with capacity to know God, it is rational to expect that God would communicate Himself and His mind to man. If unfallen man, being a finite creature, needed divine revelation and instruction (Gen. 2:16-17; 3:8), how much more is fallen man completely incapacitated by sin.

Inspiration. "A supernatural influence exerted on the sacred writers by the Spirit of God, by virtue of which their writings are given Divine trustworthiness" (B. B. Warfield, "Inspiration," *Int. Stand. Bible Ency.*, p. 1473). In defining scriptural inspiration three factors must be kept in mind: first, the primary efficient *Cause,* the Holy Spirit, who acts upon man; second, the subject of inspiration, man, the *agent* upon whom the Holy Spirit acts directly; third, the *result* of inspiration, *a written revelation, given once for all, thoroughly accredited and tested by miracle and fulfilled prophecy* (cf. J. E. Steinmueller, *Companion to Scripture Studies* [1941], 1:5, 14).

Illumination. Illumination is a ministry of the Holy Spirit that enables all who are in right relation with God to understand the objective written revelation. Thus, revelation involves *origin,* inspiration, *reception* and *recording,* and illumination, *understanding* or *comprehending* the written objective revelation. In other words, revelation comprehends God's *giving* truth. Inspiration embraces man under divine control accurately *receiving* the truth thus given. Illumination deals with man's *understanding* the God-given, inspired revelation (1 Cor. 2:14). Revelation as it concerns Holy Scripture had a specific time period involving the inspiration of certain sovereignly chosen individuals as the recipients of the revelation. It is plain that both of these divine operations have ceased. In contrast, illumination is continuously operative in all those who qualify for this ministry of the Holy Spirit.

The Scriptural Doctrine of Inspiration.

The Fact of Inspiration Stated. Second Tim. 3:16-17 says, "All Scripture is inspired by God and profitable for teaching, for reproof, for correction, for training in righteousness; that the man of God may be adequate, equipped for every good work." Five great truths of inspiration are herein taught: first, the plenary inspiration of the Bible, "all"; second, the plenary inspiration specifically of the OT, plainly implying the entire NT as well, that is, "all Scripture"; third, the divine authorship of Scripture—"inspired by God" ("God-breathed"); fourth, the supreme value of all Scripture to the spiritual life, "profitable for teaching, for reproof, for correction, for training in righteousness"; fifth, the holy purpose of Scripture, "that the man of God may be adequate, equipped for every good work."

The Fact of Inspiration Implied. The sacred authors were prophets and apostles of God's Word in the highest sense of the term. Scripture is filled with such expressions as "Now the Word of the Lord came . . . saying" (1 Kings 16:1); "Thus the Lord said to me . . ." (Jer. 13:1); "The word of the Lord came expressly to Ezekiel" (Ezek. 1:3). The apostle Paul and others claimed to speak by direct revelation (Eph. 3:1-10; etc.). Prophets spoke of future events (such as Moses' foretelling the coming of the great Prophet, Christ) and have had their predictions verified during succeeding centuries. David (Ps. 22) and Isaiah (Isa. 53) minutely prophesied the sufferings, death, and resurrection of Christ. Daniel previewed the rise of Persia, Greece, and Rome (Dan. 2:37-40; 7:4-7). Some prophets, such as Moses, Elijah, and Elisha, had their messages authenticated by miracle. Others had an irresistible compulsion to speak, such as Jeremiah (20:9). They were often commanded to write their utterances or wrote under divine leading (Ex. 24:4; Deut. 27:8; Isa. 30:8; Jer. 30:2; Luke 1:1-3; etc.).

Nature of Inspiration. "But know this first of all, that no prophecy of Scripture is a matter of one's own interpretation, for no prophecy was ever made by an act of human will, but men moved by the Holy Spirit spoke from God" (2 Pet. 1:20-21). This pivotal passage deals with the question of *how* Scripture was inspired. First, it declares how it did not originate—it is not "a matter of one's own interpretation," that is, it is not the result of human research nor the product of the writer's own thought. It did not come into being by the will of man. Man did not propose to write it, decide its subject matter, or outline its arrangement. Second, this passage tells how the Scriptures did originate. "Men," that is, certain divinely selected men, "spoke from God," the source. These inspired men were borne, or carried along, by the Holy Spirit, the message being *His, not theirs.* Accordingly, if it can be demonstrated that we have the words they spoke and wrote transmitted substantially in identical form with the original documents, and the science of textual criticism enables this to be done, then a charge of error is a charge against God, not against men except, of course, where the supposed "error" may be due to textual corruption in the long course of transmission. Where the text has unquestionably suffered in transmission, the labors of devoted scholars are directed to its restoration. This is done through ancient versions, textual variants, and other linguistic and historical evidence continuously being made available by archaeology and various other phases of sound biblical research.

Other Scriptural Proofs of the Inspiration of the Scriptures. God spoke through OT prophets (Heb. 1:1-2). The OT Scriptures are inviolable (John 10:34-36). The indefectability and certainty of promise and prophecy are clearly seen in the oft-recurring expression "that what was spoken . . . might be fulfilled" (Matt. 1:22; 2:15, 23; 8:17; 12:17; etc.) and in such Scriptures as 24:35, "Heaven and earth will pass away, but My words shall not pass away." Jesus quoted the OT as authoritative (4:4, 7, 10). The Holy Spirit in the prophets equipped them for their ministry (1 Pet. 1:10-11), and the Spirit of God spoke through David (2 Sam. 23:1-2) and other prophets. Besides the scriptural proofs, unbroken Jewish and Christian tradition attest the inspiration of Scripture.

The True Biblical Doctrine of Inspiration. Scripture nowhere fully explains the precise *modus operandi* of inspiration, yet it is possible to formulate a doctrine that is in agreement with all the plain and sufficient scriptural revelation vouchsafed to us. This doctrine, almost universally rejected today on the basis of alleged philosophic, scientific, historical, archaeological, and linguistic difficulties involved, is called *verbal,* *plenary inspiration.* It is sometimes called the *dynamic view.* This view holds that the superintendency of the Holy Spirit rendered the writers of Scripture infallible in their communications of truth and inerrant in their literary productions. Yet it leaves room for the fullest play of the personality, style, and background of the individual authors. By verbal inspiration is signified that in the *original writings* the Holy Spirit led in the choice of each word used (cf. 1 Cor. 2:13; John 10:34-36). Compare Gal. 3:16, where the problem turns upon the singular or plural of a word. By plenary inspiration is meant that the accuracy that verbal inspiration insures is extended to every portion of the sacred revelation, so that it is as a whole and in all its constituent parts infallible as to truth and final as to divine authority. This is the traditional teaching of the church and is that doctrine set forth by Christ and the apostles. This teaching preserves the dual authorship of Scripture (the divine and the human) in perfect balance, ascribing to each the consideration that is accorded in the Bible.

Results of Inspiration. The Bible having been brought into existence by the supernatural action of the Holy Spirit upon the sacred writers, the question is, What is the result of this divine process in the product itself?

The Absolute Inerrancy of the Autographa. Absolute freedom from error must be attributed to the original copies of the inspired writings. It is unthinkable that inaccuracy and mistake can coexist with inspiration. Can God who is Supreme Truth speak that which is untrue? The claim of verbal, plenary inspiration for the original writings, however, does not extend to the multitudinous transcriptions and various translations, both ancient and modern. Inerrancy applies to transcriptions such as the Masoretic-Hebrew text, the Greek NT text, and the translations such as the Septuagint, Vulgate, Syriac, Luther's Bible, and various English versions only insofar as they reproduce exactly the original autographic manuscripts. Since none of the original manuscripts are in existence, critics commonly reject the inerrancy of the autographa as "an assumption for which there is no warrant in sound reason" (G. Maines, *Divine Inspiration,* p. 109). But the fact and the truth rest not upon "reason" but upon the clear revelation of the Scriptures themselves (2 Tim. 3:16; 2 Pet. 1:20-21).

Providential Preservation of Scripture with Regard to Its Substance. The Holy Spirit, it is reasonable to conclude, also had a definite ministry in preserving the inspired Scriptures through millennia of transmission. Possible errors that have crept in as a result of copyists' slips, glosses, etc., are the domain of lower criticism and here the Christian scholar may find a worthy task for his labors. The high development of NT textual criticism as the result of many manuscript finds has given us the transmitted text in a high degree

of purity. Lack of manuscript evidence in the OT field has seriously curtailed textual criticism and hence there are many more unresolvable textual difficulties in the OT than in the NT. Recent phenomenal manuscript finds such as the Dead Sea Scrolls (notably the Isaiah Manuscript) are tending to alleviate this condition regarding the OT text.

Scriptural Inerrancy Embraces Scientific Features. In this realm, although serious problems exist, there are no proved facts of science that necessitate abandonment of the scriptural doctrine of inspiration. Many scientific theorizings would seem to suggest this; but when the Bible is correctly placed in the prescientific era in which it had its birth, its alleged scientific inaccuracies are much less formidable than the liberal or neo-orthodox interpreter would have us believe.

Scriptural Inerrancy Embraces Historical and Literary Features. In no field has the Bible been more seriously challenged than in the historical. While it is true that many serious historical problems still remain, such as the existence of the Philistines in patriarchal times, the date of the Exodus, and the identity of Darius the Mede in the book of Daniel, archaeology has made colossal contributions toward resolving many of these problems. The existence of Sargon II, the Hittites and the Horites (the Hurrians), the religion of the Canaanites, the historicity of the patriarchs, and many other serious problems have been cleared up. Although there is almost universal rejection of a thoroughly sound teaching of biblical inspiration in our day, the conservative scholar with an abundance of this new apologetic material at his disposal may well hesitate before abandoning this solid foundation of true biblical exposition and theological systematization.

BIBLIOGRAPHY: F. S. R. L. Gaussen, *The Inspiration of the Holy Scriptures* (n.d.); J. Orr, *Revelation and Inspiration* (1952); R. L. Harris, *Inspiration and Canonicity of the Bible* (1957); E. J. Young, *Thy Word Is Truth* (1960); M. C. Tenney, ed., *The Bible—Living Word of Revelation* (1968), pp. 103-64; B. B. Warfield, *The Inspiration and Authority of the Bible* (1970); J. W. Montgomery, ed., *God's Inerrant Word* (1973), pp. 63-94, 115-42, 201-18, 242-62; J. M. Boice, ed., *The Foundation of Biblical Authority* (1978), pp. 23-60, 85-102; R. L. Saucy, *The Bible: Breathed from God* (1978); N. L. Geisler, ed., *Inerrancy* (1979); B. H. Carroll, *Inspiration of the Bible* (1980); R. Nicole and J. R. Michaels, eds., *Inerrancy and Common Sense* (1980), pp. 49-118; J. D. Woodbridge, *Biblical Authority* (1982); D. A. Carson and J. D. Woodbridge, eds., *Scripture and Truth* (1983), pp. 173-98, 287-302, 325-58; J. M. Boice, *Standing on the Rock* (1985); R. Haldane, *The Authenticity and Inspiration of the Holy Scriptures* (1985).

INSTANT, INSTANTLY. In addition to the usual use of the word (i.e., a particular point of time), several Gk. words are used in the NT. These words imply *to be urgent, urgently,* or *fervently,* as will be seen from the NASB and NIV of the following passages (Luke 7:4; 23:23; Acts 26:7; Rom. 12:12). In 2 Tim. 4:2 (KJV) we find "be instant in season, out of season." The literal sense is "stand ready"—"be alert" for whatever may happen — and is translated "be ready" in the NASB. The NIV, close to the KJV, translates, "be prepared in season and out of season."

INSTRUCTION. *See* Education; Children; Schools.

INSTRUMENT (Heb. *k⁰lî,* something "prepared"). A general term for any *apparatus,* such as an implement, utensil, weapon, vessel, article of furniture, etc. The expression "instruments of unrighteousness" (Rom. 6:13; Gk. *hopla adikias*) is a part of a figure in which sin as a ruling power would employ the members of the body as *weapons* against holiness.

INSULT. Such treatment of another, in word or deed, as expresses contempt. It is not definitely noticed in the Mosaic law; only the reviling of a ruler was forbidden (Ex. 22:28, "curse") but without any special penalty attached. The severity with which disrespect toward sacred persons was regarded appears from 2 Kings 2:23-24.

INTEGRITY (Heb. *tōm,* "completeness"). The term has various shades of meaning: *simplicity* or *sincerity* (Gen. 20:5; Pss. 25:21; 78:72); *entirety* as represented by Job when under grievous trial (Job 2:3, 9; 27:5; 31:6; cf. Pss. 26:1; 41:12; etc.).

INTENTION. Purpose, design. The deliberate exercise of the will with reference to the consequences of an act attempted or performed.

It is one of the fundamental principles of ethics that the moral quality of an action is in the intention. This is a general principle, however, to be guarded by the fact that no one is at liberty to do evil that good may come.

In the doctrine of the Roman Catholic church the idea of intention plays a peculiarly important part in connection with the efficacy of the sacraments. Thus the efficacy of baptism depends upon the intention of the priest. "He must have the intention to baptize indeed, i.e., to do what the Church does, or what Christ has ordained" (Deharbe, *Catechism,* p. 251). Also, more generally, in the decrees of the Council of Trent (eleventh canon, sec. 7) it is stated: "If anyone shall say that in ministers, while they effect and confer the sacraments, there is not required the intention at least of doing what the Church does, let him be anathema." In opposition to this is the 26th Article of Religion of the Church of England, which declares that the unworthiness or wickedness of ministers "hinders not the effect of the sacraments . . . which be effectual because of Christ's institution and promise, although they be ministered by evil men." *See* Sacraments.

INTERCESSION (Heb. *pāga',* to "come upon";

Gk. *entunchanō,* to "meet with, to come between").

Intercession of Christ. This belongs to the office of Christ as Priest (*see* Jesus Christ, Offices of) and refers generally to the aid that He extends as mediator between God and mankind (*see* Mediation). In a particular sense Christ is represented as drawing near to God and pleading in behalf of men (Rom. 8:27; Heb. 7:25), and thus, in harmony with the idea of intercession, He is called our Advocate (1 John 2:1). The prayers and praises of believers are acceptable to God through Christ's intercession (*see* Heb. 4:14-16; 13:15; 1 Pet. 2:5; Rev. 8:3).

The objects of Christ's intercession are (1) the world, the whole of humanity, which He represents. On no other ground can we understand how a guilty race could be permitted to extend its existence upon the earth under the moral government of God. In the broadest meaning of the term Isaiah says He "interceded for the transgressors" (Isa. 53:12). (2) The great body of His people. In a special and peculiarly appropriate and emphatic sense Christ pleads the cause of those who are savingly united to Him. He prays for them as "not of the world" (*see* John 17). (3) Individuals, and particularly those who penitently put their trust in Him. "Christ is the head of every man" (1 Cor. 11:3). "If anyone sins, we have an Advocate with the Father" (1 John 2:1).

Intercession of the Holy Spirit. In one important and moving passage (Rom. 8:26) the Spirit's intercession is mentioned in particular and refers to the aid of the Holy Spirit given to believers that their prayers may be received by God.

Intercession of Christians. Roman Catholics believe in the intercession of the saints, i.e., of canonized departed spirits. This is rejected by Protestants as unscriptural because it derogates from the character of Christ, who is the only and sufficient mediator between God and man, and also because of the supposition involved that there exists a class of glorified human beings who have personal merits of their own, on account of which they may plead effectually for others. A great truth is to be recognized, however, in that it is the privilege and duty of all Christians to pray effectively for others. This is intercession in a subordinate although still important sense. The propriety and validity of such human intercession is illustrated in the Scriptures of both Testaments (*see* 1 Sam. 12:23; 1 Kings 18:36-37; Matt. 5:44; 1 Tim. 2:1; etc.).

INTEREST. *See* Usury.

INTERMARRIAGE. *See* Marriage.

INTERMEDIATE STATE. A phrase employed in theology in two ways: first, it is sometimes used to designate the interval between the death and resurrection of Christ. This is Van Oosterzee's exclusive use of the term. Second, the use that is by far more general refers the term to the condition of mankind after death and before the resurrection and final judgment. The following discussion, therefore, embraces these two distinct though importantly related subjects.

Of Christ. The condition or situation of the God-man during the period in which His body lay in the grave may be a matter for reverent inquiry but not one for dogmatic statement, as there is not sufficient Scripture basis for the latter.

1. We may look upon our Lord at this point as affording another illustration of His acceptance of human conditions in that He existed for a time as a disembodied spirit and for a time awaited His resurrection and glorification. The words spoken to Mary, "I have not yet ascended to the Father" (John 20:17), would seem to indicate that His spirit, which had been disembodied, had not attained the final blessedness. On the other hand, His promise to the penitent thief certainly had a glorious meaning (Luke 23:43; cf. 2 Cor. 12:2-4; Rev. 2:7).

2. At the same time the intermediate state may be regarded as the transition between our Lord's humiliation and exaltation. In one sense, it was the beginning of His exaltation, for though He "died . . . and . . . was buried" (1 Cor. 15:3, 4), even in death He triumphed over death, in that His body "did not undergo decay" (Acts 2:27; 13:37). Also, it is held that in entering the world of spirits our Lord did so triumphantly and took possession of the kingdom of the dead. Reference is made to this in Rom. 10:7; 14:9; Eph. 4:8-10; Col. 2:15; 1 Pet. 3:18-19; but the precise character of Christ's activity during this interval is one of those obscure matters upon which speculation has been abundant and has often gone beyond the proper warrant of Holy Scripture.

3. Christ's descent "into hell" is a phrase the proper meaning of which has been a subject of endless controversy. That the phrase should continue to be used is, in view of its ambiguity and liability to abuse, at least open to question.

The Apostles' Creed contains in its fifth article the words "He descended into hell." But it is universally conceded that they did not appear in that creed or any other before the fourth century. The purpose for which the clause was introduced is in dispute. It remains in the Apostles' Creed as used by the Roman, Greek, and Lutheran churches and the Church of England. The Protestant Episcopal church prefaces the creed with a note permitting the substitution of the words "He went into the place of departed spirits," as meaning the same as the words of the creed. The Methodist church omits the words altogether. *See* Creeds; also *Westminster Catechism,* answer to question 50.

The phrase "descended into hell," or any proper equivalent, does not appear in the NT. The words quoted by Peter (Acts 2:25-31), and much relied upon, are quoted also by Paul (13:34-35),

but in such a way as to show that both apostles had in mind solely the resurrection of our Lord as preceded by His actual death and burial. But for the exposition of these and other passages (as Eph. 4:8-10; 1 Tim. 3:16, and especially 1 Pet. 3:18-21; 4:6), the meanings of which are disputed, reference must be made to the works of Scripture exegetes.

It would be vain to attempt to outline here the history of speculation in connection with this subject. It should be said, however, that the view that Christ's activity during His intermediate state embraced the preaching of His gospel was held by quite a considerable number of the early church Fathers. The advantages of this preaching were regarded as offered to both Jews and Gentiles in Hades. This view, as is well known, has been revived and brought into considerable prominence within recent years. But that this gospel proclamation by our Lord in the world of spirits has ever been repeated (if it ever existed), or that others have been commissioned to similar work, must certainly remain a matter of pure and perilous conjecture. Upon the inference taken from this view of probation and the offer of salvation beyond the grave, further remark will be made in the second part of this article.

The Roman Catholic view of the descent is interwoven with the peculiar ideas of the Roman church as to the various divisions of the world of spirits. The purpose of Christ in the descent was to deliver the saints of Israel and others from the *limbus patrum* and conduct them to heaven (*see Cat. Council Trid.,* art. v.).

The doctrine of the Greek church represents Christ as descending into Hades for the purpose of offering redemption "to those who were subject to Satan on account of original sin, releasing believers, and all who died in piety under the Old Testament dispensation."

The Lutheran doctrine has presented considerable variations. But prominent amid the conflict of opinions is the view of the later Lutheran theologians, which regards the "descent into hell" as taking place not before but immediately after the resurrection. The period of the intermediate state was passed in Paradise. Early on Easter morning before the risen Lord manifested Himself to men, He went soul and body to hell, the abode of the lost, and there proclaimed His power over the devil and his angels. The "descent," according to this view, belonged emphatically to Christ's exaltation. The greatest extravagance of opinion upon this subject was that taught by Johannes Hoch in the sixteenth century, namely, that the soul of Christ descended into hell to suffer punishment while His body lay in the grave. That such a thought could find any measure of acceptance is, as has been said, "the opprobrium of one of the darkest chapters of historical theology."

Without going further, sufficient example has

been presented to illustrate the sentence quoted by Van Oosterzee: "On this subject also it is wiser, after David's fashion (Ps. 139:18) to meditate on one's couch than to write thereupon." *See* Hell.

Of Mankind. This likewise is a subject upon which the light of the Scripture is not abundant. There is, however, a progress to be noted when we compare the revelations of the NT with those of the OT. That the human spirit continues to exist consciously after the death of the body is a fact most clearly established upon a biblical basis, to say nothing of the strength of philosophical arguments upon the matter (*see* Immortality). That a most powerful contrast is declared between the state of the righteous and that of the wicked, not only after the final judgment but also during the interval between that event and the death of the body, should also be regarded as beyond question. But still the precise condition or situation in which the departed spirit finds itself immediately after death is another matter, upon which even the teachings of the NT are not full or always explicit. Accordingly speculation has been rife and has frequently illustrated the peril of attempting to be "wise above that which is written." It is not feasible here to do more than to indicate by the most general outline the various theories that have found their advocates and, besides this, to suggest the conclusions that may be derived fairly from the Scriptures.

1. The belief has been held by many at different times in the history of the church that during the intermediate state the soul is unconscious. Strictly speaking, the theory has sometimes gone beyond this and denied the existence of any spiritual principle in man that may survive the disorganization of the body. A modification of the theory of the unconscious state, or sleep of the soul, has appeared in the speculation that the soul, while disembodied, can take no note of the succession of events, and thus no note of time; and therefore, so far as consciousness is concerned, the moment of death is practically identical with that of resurrection. In criticizing these speculations upon philosophic grounds, it may be sufficient to say that in all its forms the theory in question is opposed to the picture of conscious life given by our Lord in the account of the rich man and Lazarus, as well as to the general representations of the Apocalypse. The fact upon which stress is often laid, that in the NT the dead are sometimes spoken of as sleeping, and the saints as "asleep in Jesus" (1 Thess. 4:14), proves nothing in favor of the theory. For this is simply a figurative expression with reference to the resemblance that death bears to sleep; and, besides this, sleep is one thing and utter unconsciousness is another.

2. In contrast with the preceding is the theory that obliterates the intermediate state by representing human beings as entering at the moment of their death upon their final condition. Re-

demption, according to this condition (that of Gnosticism), accomplishes its final triumph in the deliverance of the spirit from the body, whereas Paul represents the final triumph as the resurrection, the "redemption of our body" (Rom. 8:19-23; 1 Cor. 15). This theory also ignores the final judgment as represented in the Scriptures.

3. The theory of a purgatory, or the intermediate state of suffering between heaven and hell for the discipline and purification of those who finally are to enter heaven, belongs to the Roman church. It is part of an elaborate system of doctrine concerning the souls of the departed developed by medieval theology. It has no foundation in Scripture and is even opposed by such Scriptures as pronounce those "who die in the Lord" as "blessed" or "with Christ." It dishonors the perfect atonement of our Lord and has led to the great abuse of the sale of masses for the dead.

4. Within recent years has been presented, sometimes with great apparent force, the theory that regards the intermediate state as one of probation and opportunity to choose the righteous way of life, particularly for those who, from no fault of their own, have not in the present world known the gospel. This theory rests for its Scripture support mainly upon 1 Pet. 3:19-21; 4:6, those controversial passages to which reference has already been made. Interwoven with this theory are what may be regarded as overstrained conceptions of the necessity of probation in every case for the development of moral life, and of the necessity of an intellectual apprehension of the historic Christ in order to secure salvation (*see* Faith; also Arminian view of the application of the benefits of atonement in article on *Election*). It should be said that many, if not most, of the advocates of this view guard it, or attempt to guard it, in such a way as not to encourage men in the rejection of the gospel, for they admit, as all must, that the whole tone of Scripture, at least for those who hear the gospel, is to this effect: "Behold, now is 'the acceptable time,' behold, now is 'the day of salvation' " (2 Cor. 6:2; *see also* Luke 16:25-31).

5. From what is revealed in the Scriptures it may reasonably be concluded (*a*) that the intermediate state is not for the wicked that of their final misery, nor for the righteous that of their completed and final blessedness. They await the resurrection and the judgment of the great day (*see* Matt. 25:31-46; John 5:28-29) (*see* Resurrection; Judgment). (*b*) The state of those "who die in the Lord" is, even for this period, pronounced "blessed." It is so, for the reason that though they wait for the final consummation, they are "with Christ" (Rev. 14:4, 13; *see* Phil. 1:23; John 14:1, 3; Luke 23:43; etc.). (*c*) For those who have willfully rejected the offer of salvation through Christ there is no ground of hope based upon Scripture that after death that offer will be re-

newed. It is proper to emphasize this statement in view of the spirit of presumption fostered by conjectural dealing with this most awful of all themes. *See* Hell; Hades; Gehenna; Lake of Fire; Punishment.   E.MCC.

BIBLIOGRAPHY: L. Boettner, *Immortality* (1958), pp. 91-159.

INTERPRETATION OF SCRIPTURE. *See* Inspiration.

IOB (yôb). The third named of the sons of Issachar (Gen. 46:13; "Job," KJV), called Jashub (Num. 26:24; 1 Chron. 7:1). *See* Jashub.

IPHDEI'AH (if-dē'ya; "Jehovah redeems"). One of the "sons" of Shashak, and a leader of the tribe of Benjamin, resident at Jerusalem (1 Chron. 8:25), before 588 B.C.

IPH'TAH (if'ta; "he will open"). A city in the lowland district of Judah (Josh. 15:43), not positively identified, but located by some at Tarqumiya, about six miles NW of Hebron.

IPH'TAHEL (if'ta-el; "God will open"), **Iph'tah El** (NIV). A valley located at the intersection of the line between Asher and Naphtali, with the northern boundary of Zebulun (Josh. 19:14, 27). It is probably "no other than the large Wady *Abilîn*, which takes its rise in the hills in the neighborhood of Jefât" (Robinson, *Bib. Res.,* p. 107).

IR (ir; a "city"). The father of Shuppim (Shephupham) and Huppim (Hupham), of the tribe of Benjamin (1 Chron. 7:12); probably identical with one of the sons of Benjamin (Gen. 46:21) and, therefore, not as is often supposed, the same as "Iri" (1 Chron. 7:7).

I'RA (ī'ra). The name of three of David's favorite officers.
    1. A Jairite, and "a priest to David" (2 Sam. 20:26), after 1000 B.C.
    2. A Tekoite, son of Ikkesh, and one of David's thirty warriors (2 Sam. 23:26; 1 Chron. 11:28). He was afterward placed in charge of the sixth division of troops, 993 B.C.
    3. An Ithrite, one of David's mighty men (2 Sam. 23:38; 1 Chron. 11:40), about 993 B.C.

I'RAD (ī'rad). One of the antediluvian patriarchs of the Cainite line, son of Enoch and father of Mehujael (Gen. 4:18).

I'RAM (ī'ram). The last named of the Edomite chiefs in Mt. Seir, apparently contemporary with Horite kings (Gen. 36:43; 1 Chron. 1:54).

IR-HAHA'RES. *See* City of Destruction.

I'RI (i'ri) The last named of the five sons of Bela, son of Benjamin (1 Chron. 7:7).

IRI'JAH (i-rī'ja; "Jehovah sees or provides"). Son of Shelemiah, and a captain of the guard at the Gate of Benjamin. He arrested the prophet

Jeremiah on the pretense that he was deserting to the Chaldeans (Jer. 37:13-14), about 597 B.C.

IR-NA'HASH (ir-na'hash; "city of a serpent," 1 Chron. 4:12, marg., "the city of Nahash") **Ir Na'hash** (NIV). Thought by some to be a city founded (rebuilt) by Tehinnah. It apparently would be better rendered "city of copper" (cf. 4:14) and connected with Nahas (Copper Ruin), located near the N end of the 'Arabah.

IRON. *See* Mineral Kingdom.
    Figurative. Iron is used in Scripture as the symbol of *strength* (Dan. 2:33; etc.), of *stubbornness* (Isa. 48:4); of severe *affliction* (Deut. 4:20; Ps. 107:10, marg.); of a *hard, barren soil* (Deut. 28:23); of harsh exercise of *power* (Ps. 2:9; Rev. 2:27).

I'RON. *See* Yiron.

IR'PEEL (ir'pe-el; "God will heal"). A city of the tribe of Benjamin (Josh. 18:27). From the associated names it would seem to have been located in the district W of Jerusalem.

IRRIGATION. There is a reference to artificial irrigation by conduits in the statement "who has cleft a *channel* for the flood" (Job 38:25; Prov. 21:1). Besides, they were well known to the Israelites from Egypt (Deut. 11:10), for there water is brought from the Nile, its canals and reservoirs, to the higher-lying regions in various ways: sometimes by *draw wells* with a long lever (now called *shaduf*); sometimes by large *dredge wheels* moved by the foot, over which passes a long endless rope with earthen jars fixed to it such as are still in use (11:10), though the phrase "water it with your foot" may refer to pushing aside the soil between one furrow and another, so as to allow the flow of water; sometimes by more complex machines moved by oxen; sometimes by carrying it on the shoulder in buckets.

BIBLIOGRAPHY: M. S. Drower, *A History of Technology*, ed. O. Singer (1965), 1:520-27; R. J. Forbes, *Ancient Technology* (1965), 2:1-79.

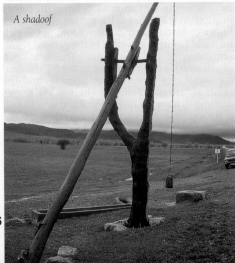

A shadoof

IR-SHE'MESH (ir-she'mesh; "city of the sun"), **Ir She'mesh** (NIV). A city of Dan, on the border between Eshtaol and Shaalabbin (Josh. 19:41), the same as Beth-shemesh (1 Kings 4:9).

I'RU (i'ru). The first named of the sons of Caleb, the son of Jephunneh (1 Chron. 4:15), after 1440 B.C.

I'SAAC (ī'zak; Heb. *yiṣḥāq*, "laughter," i.e., "mockery"). The only son of Abraham by Sarah. The name Isaac was fitly chosen by Jehovah in commemoration of the child's miraculous birth (Gen. 17:19) and of the *laughing* joy it occasioned.

Early Life. The birth of Isaac occurred (about 2061 B.C.) when Abraham was a hundred years old and Sarah ninety (Gen. 21:5; cf. 17:17). He was circumcised when he was eight days old, and his mother's skeptical laughter was turned into exultation and joy. The next event recorded of Isaac is his weaning, probably (according to Eastern custom) when he was two years old (21:8). In honor of the occasion Abraham made a great feast, as an expression, no doubt, of his joy. This happiness was naturally shared by the mother and the friends of the parents. But *Ishmael* (which see) saw no occasion for gladness to him—being supplanted in the more peculiar honor of the house by this younger brother. He mocked Isaac and so angered Sarah that she insisted upon his being sent away (vv. 9-14).

Offering. We are next informed of the event connected with the command of God to offer Isaac up as a sacrifice on a mountain in the land of Moriah (chap. 22), perhaps 2045 B.C. He was probably about sixteen years of age; according to Josephus (*Ant.* 1.13.2), twenty-five. It appears from the narrative that Isaac was not aware that he was to be offered until the act was in process of being accomplished (*see* vv. 7-8) and then offered no resistance. His conduct proved him to be a fitting type of Him who came to do not His own will but the will of Him that sent Him.

Marriage. A long gap occurs in the narrative of Isaac's life, and we hear nothing of him until his marriage to Rebekah. We may reasonably infer that a period of twenty years or more elapsed since the last event recorded concerning him; for his marriage took place after his mother's death, which occurred when Isaac was thirty-seven years old. In obedience to the command of Abraham, a trusted servant went to Mesopotamia to take, under divine direction, a partner from among his own kin for Isaac. Rebekah was chosen and became the wife of Isaac when he was forty years of age (chap. 24), about 2021 B.C.

Death of Abraham. Previous to his death Abraham made a final distribution of his property, leaving to Isaac his possessions, whereas the sons of Hagar and Keturah were sent away with presents into the E country (Arabia). Isaac and Ishmael buried their father in the cave of Machpelah, and Isaac took up his residence "by Beer-lahai-roi" (25:5-11).

Children. After about twenty years (about 2001 B.C.), and in answer to prayer, Rebekah gave birth to two sons, Jacob and Esau (25:21-26). As the boys grew, Isaac "loved" Esau, perhaps for his robust character, while Jacob, "a peaceful man, living in tents," was the favorite of his mother.

Denies His Wife. Although a famine in the land compelled Isaac to seek food in some foreign land, he was admonished by God not to go down to Egypt but to continue in the Promised Land. At this time the Lord renewed His promise to Isaac and to his seed and confirmed the promise made to his father, Abraham. Isaac did not fully trust the divine protection, though, but was led by his fears into a lie. While dwelling in the neighborhood of Gerar he had the weakness to call Rebekah his sister, afraid that the people might kill him if they knew her to be his wife. Upon learning the truth Abimelech, the Philistine king, rebuked Isaac for his lie but allowed him to remain in the land (26:1-11).

Later Life. Isaac remained in the land of the Philistines, cultivated a portion of ground, and in the same year reaped "a hundredfold." His flocks and herds grew so large that he became rich, which so excited the envy of the Philistines that they drove him from their territory. He then reopened the wells that his father had dug and that the Philistines had filled up, digging also several new ones, which they claimed as theirs. Withdrawing from one after another, he finally dug one that he was allowed to keep unmolested; and, in token of his satisfaction at the peace he enjoyed, he called it Rehoboth, "broad places" or "room" (26:12-22). He then returned to Beersheba, where the Lord appeared to him and repeated the covenant blessing. Abimelech also sought and obtained from Isaac a covenant of peace (26:24-31). It was when Esau was forty years of age, and Isaac a hundred, that the former married Judith and Basemath, daughters of Canaan, "and they brought grief to Isaac and Rebekah" (vv. 34-35).

Isaac's Blessing. The last prominent event in the life of Isaac is the blessing he gave to his sons (27:1-40). Being old and dim of sight and supposing that his death was near at hand, Isaac called Esau and requested him to take venison and to make him "a savory dish" that he might eat and bless him before he died. Rebekah, hearing his request, sought to frustrate his intention and to secure the blessing for Jacob. While Esau was absent, Rebekah prepared the dish, and Jacob, disguised so as to resemble his hairy brother, deceived his father and obtained the blessing. Upon discovering the deception Isaac, remembering, no doubt, the prediction that "the older shall serve the younger," declined to revoke the words he had uttered but bestowed an inferior blessing upon Esau. This so angered Esau that he seems to have looked forward to Isaac's death as affording an opportunity for taking vengeance upon his brother. The aged patriarch was therefore induced, at his wife's entreaty, to send Jacob into Mesopotamia, that he might take a wife "from the daughters of Laban" (27:41–28:6).

Death. After some time Jacob returned and found his father "at Mamre of Kiriath-arba (that is, Hebron), where Abraham and Isaac had sojourned." Here Isaac died at the age of 180, "and was gathered to his people, . . . and his sons Esau and Jacob buried him" (35:27-29), about 1881 B.C.

As a Type. Many Bible students teach that Isaac in his various relations presents a type of Christ. Those who hold such a view see Isaac in his surrender and submission to the sacrifice on Moriah (Gen. 22) as a type of Christ "obedient to the point of death" (Phil. 2:5-8). Abraham is set forth as a type of the Father who "did not spare His own Son, but delivered Him up for us all" (John 3:16; Rom. 8:32). The ram miraculously caught in the thicket and sacrificed instead of Isaac is a type of substitutionary atonement— Christ offered as a burnt offering in the place of sinners (Heb. 10:5-10). Abraham saying, "I and the lad will go yonder; and we will worship and return to you" (Gen. 22:5) prefigures resurrection (Heb. 11:17-19). In Gen. 24 Isaac again appears as a type of Christ as the bridegroom, Rebekah being a type of the church, the *ecclesia,* the virgin bride of Christ (Gen. 24:16; 2 Cor. 11:2; Eph. 5:25-32). Again, Abraham appears as a type of the Father, and the unnamed servant a type of the Holy Spirit, who "will not speak on His own initiative" but takes the gifts of the bridegroom to woo the bride (John 16:13-14). Thus the servant enriches the bride (cf. 1 Cor. 12:7-11; Gal. 5:22) and conducts her to the bridegroom.

Isaac and Archaeology. The name *Isaac,* like that of Jacob, is an abbreviated name whose full form would be Yitshaq-'el (cf. Ya'qub'el). These names belong to types now well known in the environment from which the early Hebrews sprang. The name *Abraham* has also been found in Mesopotamia, showing that it was a name actually in use at the time. The name *Jacob* occurs in tablets of the eighteenth century B.C. from Chagar Bazar in northern Mesopotamia and also as a place name in Palestine in the fifteenth century B.C. in Thutmose III's list. The Nuzi Letters, excavated between 1925 and 1941 not far from modern Kirkuk, not only illustrate patriarchal customs and life in general but give an example of the circumstances of the birth of Ishmael (Gen. 16:1-6). Nuzi marriage regulations stipulate that if a wife is barren she must furnish her husband with a slave wife. Later, when Sarah had herself given birth to Isaac and determined that Hagar and her child be disinherited, the patriarch's reluctance to comply with her demand was readily comprehensible in the light of the common practice at Nuzi. There the law stipulated that in case the slave wife should bear a son, that son must not be expelled. It is clear in the light of Nuzian parallels why Abraham was loath to agree with Sarah's illegal demand, and doubtless he would have refused to do so, despite his concern for Isaac, had not a divine dispensation overridden the law.   M.F.U.

BIBLIOGRAPHY: G. Rawlinson, *Isaac and Jacob: Their Lives and Times* (1890); H. C. Leupold, *Exposition of Genesis* (1942), 2:594-770, 929-31; W. H. G. Thomas, *Genesis: A Devotional Commentary* (1946), pp. 183-246, 341-44; F. J. Delitzsch, *New Commentary on Genesis* (1978), 2:65-158; W. G. Blaikie, *Heroes of Israel* (1981), pp. 138-99; G. Bush, *Notes on Genesis* (1981), 1:335 –2:104.

ISA'IAH (ī-zā'ya; "Jehovah saves"). Little information has come to us respecting the history of Isaiah. His father's name was Amoz (Isa. 1:1), but we do not know of what tribe. Isaiah is thought to have lived in Jerusalem, near the Temple (chap. 6) and to have married a prophetess, by whom he had a son named Maher-shalal-hash-baz (8:3); another son, Shear-jashub, being mentioned in 7:3. His dress was suitable to his vocation (20:2), probably a coarse linen or hairy overcoat of a dark color, such as was worn by mourners.

1. Time of the Prophet. Isaiah prophesied under the reigns of Uzziah, Jotham, Ahaz, and Hezekiah, kings of Judah. The first period of his ministry was in the reigns of Uzziah (792-740 B.C.) and Jotham (750-738 as regent, 738-732 as sole ruler), in which he called for repentance without success, and consequently had to announce judgment and banishment. The second period extended from the commencement of the reign of Ahaz (735-715) to that of the reign of Hezekiah; the third from the accession of Hezekiah (c. 715) to the fifteenth year of his reign. After this Isaiah took no further part in public affairs, but he lived till the commencement of Manasseh's reign when, according to a credible tradition, he suffered martyrdom by being sawn apart. To this Heb. 11:37 is supposed to be an allusion.

2. Writings. Isaiah was the author of a biography of King Uzziah (2 Chron. 26:22) and of Hezekiah (32:32), as well as of the sublime prophecies that bear his name. Both biographies have been lost, together with the annals of Judah and Israel into which they had been inserted. He is by general consent the greatest of all Hebrew writers, and so fully does he describe the Person and offices of the Messiah, that from the time of Jerome he has been known as the evangelical prophet.

3. Position. Isaiah appears to have held a high rank in Jerusalem, for Hezekiah, when sending a deputation to him, chose his highest officers and the elders of the priests (2 Kings 19:2). It is exceedingly probable that he was the head of the prophetic order, holding in Jerusalem the same rank that Elisha had held in the prophetic schools in Israel. His authority greatly increased after the fulfillment of his prophecies by the Babylonian Exile, the victories of Cyrus, and the deliverance of the covenant people. Even Cyrus was induced (Josephus *Ant.* 40.1.1 and 2) to set the Jews at liberty by the prophecies of Isaiah concerning himself.

Concerning the opinion of a "second Isaiah," *see* Isaiah, Book of. *See* Jesaiah.

BIBLIOGRAPHY: A. H. Sayce, *The Life and Times of Isaiah* (1896); S. J. Schultz, *The Prophets Speak* (1968), pp. 102-12; L. J. Wood, *The Prophets of Israel* (1979), pp. 297-314.

ISAIAH, BOOK OF. Isaiah (Heb. *Yᵉsha'yāhû*, "Jehovah is salvation") was the greatest of the Hebrew prophets. His general prophecies are without equal as far as beauty of style, versatility of treatment, brilliance of imagery, and splendor of diction are concerned. He has often been called "the Prince of OT Prophets" (cf. B. A. Copass, *Isaiah, Prince of O.T. Prophets* [1944]). His book is the first among the so-called "latter prophets," and his name has been given to his prophetic collection.

Time of Prophecy. He resided and ministered in Jerusalem from c. 740 B.C., in "the year of King Uzziah's death," until c. 700 B.C. or somewhat later. He thus prophesied during the kingships of Uzziah, Jotham, Ahaz, and Hezekiah, kings of Judah (1:1). He was married to a prophetess (8:3) and had two sons: Shear-jashub (7:3), "a remnant will return," and Maher-shalal-hash-baz (8:3), "swift is the booty, speedy is the prey." Thus the name of the first child held a promise of mercy; the second, one of judgment.

The Purpose. Isaiah in his ministry emphasized the spiritual and the social. He struck at the root of the nation's trouble in its apostasy and idolatry and sought to save Judah from its moral and political and social corruption. He failed, however, to turn the nation Godward. His divine commission carried the warning that this would be the case (6:9-12). Thereupon he boldly declared the inevitable crash of Judah and the preservation of a small godly remnant (6:13). However, gleams of hope radiate throughout his prophecy. Through this small remnant worldwide redemption would eventuate through the Messiah at His first advent (9:2, 6; 53:1-12; etc.). At the second advent national salvation and restoration for Israel would result (2:1-4; 9:7; 11:1-16; 35:1-10; 54:11-17). The theme that Israel would one day be a messianic nation to the world and a medium of universal blessing (yet to be fulfilled), with which the prophecies of Isaiah are imbued, has given him the name of messianic prophet.

Outline.

I. Prophecies from the standpoint of the prophet's own time (1:1–35:10)
   A. Prophecies concerning Judah and Jerusalem (1:1–13:6)
      1. General introduction (1:1-31)
      2. Millennial blessing through cleansing (2:1–4:6)
      3. Israel's reproof for her sins (5:1-30)
      4. The prophet's call and commission (6:1-13)
      5. Immanuel's prophecy (7:1-25)
      6. Prophecy of Assyrian invasion (8:1-22)
      7. Messianic prediction (9:1-21)
      8. Assyrian punishment (10:1-34)
      9. Millennial restoration (11:1-16)
      10. Millennial worship (12:1-6)
   B. Prophecies against foreign nations (13:1–23:18)
      1. Babylon (13:1–14:23)
      2. Assyria (14:24-27)
      3. Philistia (14:28-32)
      4. Moab (15:1–16:14)
      5. Damascus (17:1-14)
      6. Land beyond the rivers of Ethiopia (18:1-7)
      7. Egypt (19:1-25)
      8. Assyria's conquest (20:1-6)
      9. Desert areas (21:1–22:25)
      10. Tyre (23:1-18)
   C. Prophecy of kingdom establishment (24:1–27:13)
      1. The Great Tribulation (24:1-23)
      2. Character of the kingdom (25:1-12)
      3. Restored Israel (26:1–27:13)
   D. Prophecies concerning Judah and Assyria (28:1–35:10)
      1. Danger and deliverance (28:1–33:24)
      2. The Day of the Lord (34:1-17)
      3. Full millennial blessing (35:1-10)
II. Historical interlude (36:1–39:8)
   A. Sennacherib's invasion (36:1–37:38)
   B. Hezekiah's sickness and recovery (38:1-22)
   C. Arrival of Babylonian envoys; prophecy and captivity (39:1-8)
III. Prophecies of redemption and restoration from the idealistic standpoint of the Babylonian Exile (40:1–66:24)
   A. Comfort to the exiles, the promise of restoration (40:1–48:22)
      1. Message of comfort: promise of messianic restoration (40:1-11)
      2. Basis of comfort: God's character (40:12-31)
      3. The reason for comfort: Jehovah's vindication against idolators by raising up Cyrus, the deliverer (41:1-29)

4. The comforter—Jehovah's servant (42:1-25)
5. The result of the comfort: a nation restored (43:1–45:25); the downfall of the Babylonian idols (46:1-12) and Babylon itself (47:1-15)
6. Exhortation of comfort to those yet to be delivered from captivity (48:1-22)
B. Comfort to the exiles in the prophecy of the Messiah-Redeemer (49:1–57:21)
1. His call and work (49:1-26)
2. His obedience (50:1-11)
3. His redemption (51:1–52:12)
4. His atonement and exaltation (52:13–53:12)
5. His guarantee of Israel's restoration (54:1-17)
6. Worldwide salvation (55:1-13)
7. His warnings and promises (56:1–57:21)
C. Comfort in the prophecy of Israel's future glory (58:1–66:24)
1. Obstacles to Israel's restoration removed (58:1–59:21)
2. Jerusalem's exaltation in the messianic age (60:1-22)
3. Messiah's ministry for Israel and the world (61:1-11)
4. God's concern for Jerusalem (62:1-12)
5. Messiah's conquest of Israel's enemies (63:1-14)
6. The remnant's prayer (63:15–64:12)
7. Jehovah's response (65:1-25)
8. Kingdom blessing (66:1-24)

Date and Authorship. Until about the middle of the eighteenth century the traditional view that Isaiah wrote the entire prophecy was almost universally held. However, since 1775, when J. C. Doederlein denied Isaiah's authorship of chaps. 40-66, it has been common for critics to speak of a "second Isaiah." This unknown writer allegedly wrote in the period immediately before the end of the Babylonian captivity (c. 550-539 B.C.). B. Duhm went a step further and denied the unity of chaps. 40-66, and he invented a "third Isaiah" for chaps. 55-66. Duhm is followed notably by K. Elliger and E. Sellin. Other critics divide the third Isaiah into a school of writers, rather than attribute it to an individual. In 1928 C. C. Torrey, in his book entitled *The Second Isaiah,* advanced the hypothesis that chaps. 34-66 (36-39 excluded) were by one author living in Palestine. He thus presented strong evidence for the unity of this section.

Rejection of Three Critical Claims. The critical view, that Isaiah could not have written the entirety of the book that bears his name, is summarized in three claims, each of which can be refuted. The first critical claim is that the standpoint

of the writer of chaps. 40-66 is exilic and consequently precludes Isaiah's authorship on the basis of the historic function of prophecy. The argument is not that the standpoint of the writer is exilic. This is freely admitted. The question is whether under the influence of the spirit of prophecy, a prophet might not be naturally transported into the future to describe coming events to a future generation. Critics who rule out the supernatural and admit at most a premonition or "brilliant intuition" (cf. Robert Pfeiffer, *Introduction,* p. 423) are compelled to deny the possibility of such an occurrence as supernatural projection into the future and, accordingly, must refuse Isaiah's authorship of the second part of the book. But the critical arguments are inconclusive, and to therefore reject the unity of the book on the basis of the *analogy of prophecy (see* S. R. Driver, *Introduction,* 9th ed., pp. 236-43), maintaining that a prophet never projects himself into an ideal standpoint in the future except when the transference to that state is transient (for example Isa. 5:13-15; 9:1-6; 23:1, 14), is not correct. Actually examples occur in Ezekiel (Ezek. 40:2). This prophet was transported from Babylon during the captivity "into the land of Israel" to behold from the idealistic future standpoint of the Millennium the extended vision of the millennial Temple and Israel in the land during the future Kingdom age (Ezek. 40-48). Similarly, Ezekiel is brought out "by the Spirit of the Lord" and set down in the midst of a valley "full of bones" (37:1). In this case the prophet is projected into the ideal standpoint of Israel's final worldwide dispersion and regathering. John was evidently similarly projected into the future Day of the Lord (Rev. 1:10) to behold the protracted events of that future period (4:1–19:21). Paul was caught up to the third heaven (2 Cor. 12:2-4). Accordingly, to reject the unity of chaps. 40-66 on the basis that Isaianic authorship violates the "historic function of prophecy" is unsustained. The prophet, says Driver (ibid., p. 237), "speaks always, in the first instance, to his own contemporaries; the message which he brings is intimately related to the circumstances of his time; his promises and predictions, however far they reach into the future, nevertheless rest upon the basis of the history of his own age, and correspond to the needs which are then felt." However, it is open to serious doubt whether the words of consolation of the so-called "second Isaiah" were not appropriate for the faithful, persecuted believers in the early reign of Manasseh. The fall of Jerusalem and Sennacherib's invasion were events that brought the possibility of exile close and for all that was revealed, such an exile may have taken place almost immediately. Critics fail to see that the essential notion of prophecy involving the direct operation of the Holy Spirit upon the faculties of man cannot be circumscribed by time or space or comprehended to any extent apart from the supernatural. If critics admit a transient projection into the future, why may there not be an extended projection?

The second critical claim is that the differences in style between the two sections of the book preclude Isaiah's authorship of chaps. 40-66. This argument is extremely precarious and highly subjective, failing to take into consideration that an author of Isaiah's versatility may change his style in the course of a long literary career of possibly over forty years. Then too, critics are impressed by similarities of style between the two. Some even assert that the similarities led later redactors to append this second section to Isaiah's genuine prophecy.

The third critical claim is that differences in theological concepts of the two sections indicate separate authorship. This is the weakest of all. In the first Isaiah, God's majesty is supposedly emphasized; by the second Isaiah, God's infinity. Also the prominent idea of a remnant in the first part is supposedly unemphasized in the second part. But such arguments reveal the essential unsoundness of the entire critical view.

Argument from the Unity of the Book. To the weakness of the critical arguments must be added other reasons supporting the unity of the book of Isaiah that commend themselves to conservative scholars.

The NT witness. The weight of this argument cannot be dismissed by contending that biblical writers do not concern themselves with points of technical introduction. This may be true, but the manner of quotation, as in John 12:38-41, is so direct and personal that the actual author is indicated. (*See* also Luke 3:4-6; John 1:23, also Matt. 8:17; 12:18-21; John 12:38-41; and Paul's quotation, Rom. 9:27-33; 10:16-21).

Implicit reference to Isaiah. Illustrations in the exilic prophets that are taken from the second part of Isaiah point to Isaiah's authorship (cf. Nah. 1:15 with Isa. 52:7; Jer. 31:35 with Isa. 51:15; Jer. 10:1-16 with Isa. 41:7 and 44:12-15; Zeph. 2:15 with Isa. 47:8, 10).

The voice of tradition. The Isaiah Manuscript, the Dead Sea Scrolls, the LXX evidence, Jewish tradition, Josephus, the Apocrypha, the church Fathers, and the general witness of Christians down to the middle of the eighteenth century are against the idea of a second and third Isaiah. The general testimony of the greatness of the second Isaiah from a literary and prophetic point of view involves the critical contention in difficulty. If this writer was the greatest of the prophets, why did his reputation dwindle so rapidly that by the second century B.C. he was almost an anonymity and his great prediction confused with that of a much lesser light, Isaiah the son of Amoz, whose stature had so phenomenally increased that Ecclesiasticus gives him such high praise?

Palestinian authorship. Evidence that the author of Isa. 40-66 was a native Palestinian favors Isaianic unity of the entire prophecy. C. C. Torrey's second Isaiah, although arguing for a different author for the second section, presents a favorable defense of the unity of chaps. 40-66 and its Palestinian authorship.

BIBLIOGRAPHY: G. A. Smith, *The Book of Isaiah,* Expositor's Bible, 2 vols. (1908); G. B. Gray and A. S. Peake, *A Critical and Exegetical Commentary on the Book of Isaiah,* International Critical Commentary, 2 vols. (1912); O. T. Allis, *The Unity of Isaiah* (1950); C. R. North, *Isaiah 40-55* (1964); C. R. Erdman, *The Book of Isaiah* (1954); R. D. Culver, *The Sufferings and Glory of the Lord's Righteous Servant* (1958); E. J. Young, *The Book of Isaiah,* 3 vols. (1965-72); J. A. Alexander, *Commentary on the Prophecies of Isaiah* (1962); H. C. Leupold, *Exposition of Isaiah,* 2 vols. (1968-71); R. K. Harrison, *Introduction to the Old Testament* (1969), pp. 764-800; O. Kaiser, *Isaiah 1-12* (1972); id., *Isaiah 1-39* (1974); R. N. Whybray, *Isaiah 40-66* (1975); H. C. von Orelli, *The Prophecies of Isaiah* (1977); W. Kelly, *Exposition of the Book of Isaiah* (1979); R. E. Clements, *Isaiah 1-39* (1980); J. A. Alexander, *Isaiah: Translated and Explained,* 2 vols. (1981); A. Martin and J. A. Martin, *Isaiah: The Glory of the Messiah* (1983); J. Ridderbos, *Isaiah,* Bible Student's Commentary (1985).

IS'CAH (is'ka). The daughter of Haran and sister of Milcah and Lot (Gen. 11:29; cf. v. 31). Jewish tradition, as in Josephus (*Ant.* 1.6.5), Jerome, and the Targum Pseudo-Jonathan, identifies her with *Sarah* (which see).

ISCAR'IOT (is-kar'i-ot; probably from Heb. *'ish qᵉrîôth,* "man of Kerioth"). A surname of *Judas* (which see) the traitor, to distinguish him from others of the same name (Matt. 10:4; etc.).

ISH'BAH (ish'ba; "he will praise"). A descendant of Judah and founder ("father") of Eshtemoa (1 Chron. 4:17). He is perhaps the same as Ishi (v. 20).

ISH'BAK (ish'bak; "leaving"). A son of Abraham and Keturah (Gen. 25:2; 1 Chron. 1:32); after 2030 B.C., and the progenitor of a tribe of northern Arabia.

ISH'BI-BE'NOB (ish'bi-be'nob). One of the Rephaim, a gigantic warrior "the weight of whose spear was three hundred shekels of bronze," and who attacked David but was slain by Abishai (2 Sam. 21:16), about 970 B.C.

ISH-BO'SHETH (ish-bo'sheth; "man of shame"). The youngest of Saul's four sons (2 Sam. 2:8; 1 Chron. 8:33; 9:39; in the two later passages his name is given as *Eshbaal,* "the man of Baal"). The name evidently offers an example of rendering the "Baal" element by *"bōshet,"* Heb. for "shame," showing the abhorrence with which heathen gods were held.

Succeeds Saul. Ishbosheth was the only son who survived his father, his three brothers being slain with Saul in the battle of Gilboa, about 1000 B.C. Being the oldest of the royal family, he was, according to the law of oriental succession, the heir to the throne. His uncle Abner loyally espoused his cause, but the whole kingdom was in ruins, and hardly a single city W of the Jordan either could or would acknowledge the rule of the house of Saul. Abner, therefore, took Ish-bosheth beyond the Jordan to the city Mahanaim and announced him as Saul's successor (2 Sam. 2:8-9). Abner appears to have first undertaken to reunite under his protection the country of the east and then reconquer the territory subdued by the Philistines. The order in which these districts were retaken seems to be indicated in v. 9. While Abner was making these efforts some five years probably elapsed, leaving the length of Ish-bosheth's reign two years (v. 10). He was forty years old when he began to reign. Even the semblance of authority that he possessed he owed to the will and influence of Abner, who kept the control of affairs in his own hands, carrying on all wars and negotiations with David (2:12; 3:6-12).

Breaks with Abner. At length Ish-bosheth accused Abner (whether justly or not is not stated) of cohabiting with Rizpah, his father's concubine, which according to oriental custom, was considered treason. When Ish-bosheth accused him of this, Abner fell into a rage and announced his intention of handing over the kingdom to David. Ish-bosheth made no reply, "because he was afraid of him" (2 Sam. 3:7-11). Soon after, Abner made proposals to David, and the latter demanded Michal, his former wife. Ish-bosheth forced Paltiel to give her up (vv. 12-16). While carrying on negotiations with David, Abner fell a victim to the resentment of Joab for the death of Asahel (v. 17-27).

Death. When Ish-bosheth heard that Abner was dead, "he lost courage"; he was soon after murdered by Rechab and Baana while taking his midday rest, probably to revenge a crime of his father or in the hope of obtaining a reward from David. They met with a stern reaction from that king, who rebuked them for the cold-blooded murder and ordered them to be executed. The head of Ish-bosheth was buried in the sepulcher of Abner in Hebron (4:1-12), about 996 B.C.

I'SHHOD (i'shod; "man of renown"). A son of Hammolecheth and, from his near connection with Gilead, probably an important person (1 Chron. 7:18; "Ishod," KJV).

ISH'I (ish'i; "salutary").

1. The son of Appaim and father of Sheshan, and a descendant of Judah (1 Chron. 2:31).

2. Another descendant of Judah, but through what line is not known (1 Chron. 4:20); his sons were Zoheth and Ben-zoheth.

3. A Simeonite, four of whose sons led their brethren in the invasion of Mt. Seir and the dispossession of the Amalekites (1 Chron. 4:42), before 715 B.C.

4. One of the chiefs of Manasseh east, who were "mighty men of valor, famous men, heads of their fathers' households" (1 Chron. 5:24), about 720 B.C.

ISHI'AH. *See* Isshiah, no. 1.

ISHI'JAH. *See* Isshijah.

ISH'MA (ish'ma). A descendant of Judah, given as one of the "sons of Etam" (1 Chron. 4:3).

ISHMAEL (ish'ma-el; "God will hear"). The name of the eldest son (which see) of Abraham and of several other men.

1. Son of Azel, a descendant of Saul through Merib-baal, or Mephibosheth (1 Chron. 8:38; 9:44), before 588 B.C.

2. A man of Judah, whose son (or descendant), Zebadiah, was "ruler of the house of Judah" under Jehoshaphat (2 Chron. 19:11), about 875 B.C. The office of "ruler," etc., was that of lay president of the supreme court in Jerusalem.

3. Son of Johanan of Judah, and captain of "hundreds," who assisted Jehoiada in restoring Joash to the throne (2 Chron. 23:1), 836 B.C.

4. One of the "sons" of Pashhur, who relinquished his Gentile wife after the Exile (Ezra 10:22), 456 B.C.

5. Murderer of Gedaliah, who was the superintendent, under the king of Babylon, of the province of Judea. His full description is "Ishmael the son of Nethaniah, the son of Elishama, of the royal family" of Judah (Jer. 41:1; 2 Kings 25:25). "Whether he was actually a son of Zedekiah or a king, or more generally, that he had royal blood in his veins—we cannot tell."

During the siege of Jerusalem he, like many others of his countrymen (cf. Jer. 40:11), fled across the Jordan, where he found a refuge at the court of Baalis, then king of Bene-Ammom (Josephus *Ant.* 10.9.2). Gedaliah had taken up his residence at Mizpah, a few miles N of Jerusalem, where the prophet Jeremiah resided with him (Jer. 40:6). Ishmael had been instigated by Baalis to slay Gedaliah (v. 14), and his intention was made known by Johanan, who offered to put Ishmael to death. To this Gedaliah would not consent (vv. 15-16), and a short time later Ishmael and ten companions, "princes of the king" (KJV), came and were entertained by him at a feast. He returned the kindness shown him by murdering Gedaliah and all his attendants, including some Chaldean soldiers (41:1-3). So secretly was the deed executed that for two days it remained undiscovered. On the second day Ishmael saw a party of eighty devotees bringing incense and offerings to the Temple, who, at his invitation, turned aside to the residence of Gedaliah. As they passed into the city he closed the gates and killed all but ten, who escaped by the offer of heavy ransoms. He then carried off the daughters of King Zedekiah and the people of the town, and started for the country of the Ammonites. The massacre was soon made known, and Ishmael was quickly followed by Johanan and his companions, who "found him by the great pool that is in Gibeon" (vv. 4-12), 588 B.C. Ishmael, with eight of his men, escaped and went to the Ammonites. Nothing more is recorded of him.

ISH'MAEL (ish'ma-el; "God will hear"). The eldest son of Abraham by Hagar, his Egyptian concubine (Gen. 16:15-16). He was born when the patriarch was eighty-six years old, fourteen years before the birth of Isaac (21:5), c. 2076 B.C. The place of his birth was Mamre.

Circumcision. The next recorded event of his life is his circumcision, which occurred when he was thirteen years of age (Gen. 17:25). It was at this time that the Lord renewed to Abraham in more definite terms the promises made respecting Ishmael (v. 20). Up to this time Abraham appears to have considered Ishmael as the heir of promise and to have had great affection for him (vv. 17-18).

Expulsion. Ishmael is not mentioned again until the weaning of Isaac, when Ishmael was probably between fifteen and sixteen years of age (Gen. 21:8; see further comment below). During the festivities of the occasion, Ishmael, doubtless angered by his blighted hopes, apparently mocked Isaac. Sarah, overhearing him, became angry and said to Abraham, "Drive out this maid and her son, for the son of this maid shall not be an heir with my son Isaac." Grieved at the demand of Sarah, Abraham yielded only when influenced by a divine admonition. The beautiful and touching picture of Hagar's departure and journey is recorded in vv. 14-16: "So Abraham rose early in the morning, and took bread and a skin of water, and gave them to Hagar, putting them on her shoulder, and gave her the boy, and sent her away. And she departed, and wandered about in the wilderness of Beersheba. And the water in the skin was used up, and she left the boy under one of the bushes. Then she went and sat down opposite him, about a bowshot away, for she said, 'Do not let me see the boy die.' And she sat opposite him, and lifted up her voice and wept." The Lord appeared to Hagar, opened her eyes, and she saw a well of water, and thus saved the life of the boy. Again the cheering promise was renewed to her of her son, "I will make a great nation of him" (v. 18).

Age at the Time of the Expulsion. The age of Ishmael at the time of his expulsion has given occasion to considerable discussion. He was doubtless thirteen years of age (Gen. 17:25) at the time of his circumcision, and the time of his expulsion was about two or three years later (21:5-8). The translation of 21:14, which seems to speak of Ishmael as an infant, is not an appropriate expression. It is unnecessary to assume that the child was put on Hagar's shoulder; the construction of the Hebrew not requiring it; and the sense of the passage rendering it highly improbable. Hagar carried "them," i.e., the bread

and the skin of water, on her shoulder. The fact of the lad's being overcome by thirst and fatigue before his hardy Egyptian mother is not remarkable, especially when we remember God's miraculous interposition in her behalf.

Marries. Thus miraculously preserved, Ishmael grew and dwelt in the wilderness (Paran) and became an archer. It would seem to have been his mother's wish to return to Egypt, but this being prevented, she took him an Egyptian wife (21:21), who gave him twelve sons (25:13-15) and one daughter. This daughter being called the "sister of Nebaioth" (28:9), the limitation of the parentage of the brother and sister seems to point to a different mother for Ishmael's other sons.

Later Life. Of this we know little. Ishmael was present with Isaac at the burial of Abraham (Gen. 25:9). We are given a list of his twelve sons and told that Esau married his daughter, Mahalath (28:9). Ishmael died when he was "one hundred and thirty-seven years; and he breathed his last . . . and was gathered to his people. And they settled from Havilah to Shur which is east of Egypt as one goes toward Assyria; he settled in defiance of all his relatives" (25:17-18).

Character. Ishmael appears to have been a wild and wayward child, and doubtless the perfect freedom of desert life and interaction with those who looked upon him as heir-apparent of their great chief tended to make him impatient of restraint and overbearing in his temper. His harsh treatment by Sarah, his disappointment in not becoming the heir of Abraham, and the necessity of earning a scanty living by his sword and bow would naturally wound his proud spirit and make him what the angel had predicted: "a wild donkey of a man; his hand will be against everyone, and everyone's hand will be against him" (16:12).

BIBLIOGRAPHY: J. Montgomery, *Arabia and the Bible* (1934); J. J. Davis, *Paradise to Prison* (1975), pp. 188-93, 213-14, 231-32.

ISH'MAELITE (ish'ma-el-īt). A descendant of Abraham's son Ishmael. The term is probably sometimes used as a general name for all the Abrahamic peoples from Egypt to the Euphrates and perhaps to the Persian Gulf, their headquarters being in W Arabia. In Gen. 37:25, 27-28 the name *Ishmaelites* may have been applied in general to the caravan, which included a body of Midianite traders. The same relation may exist in Judg. 8:22, 24; in v. 24 that kind of traders may have been called "Ishmaelites" in the same way that the name *Canaanites* (which see) was used for merchants, since the Ishmaelites were caravan traders from the remotest times.

Muhammad claimed descent from Ishmael. Although in the confusion of the Arab genealogies the names are lost beyond the twenty-first generation before the prophet, the claim is probable enough, since the pre-Muhammadan law of blood revenge, which required everyone to know his ancestors for four generations back, would prevent all confusion in regard to race. And, after making due allowance of mixture with Joktanites and Keturahites, we may fairly regard the Arabs as essentially an Ishmaelite race.

In 2 Sam. 17:25 Amasa, Absalom's commander-in-chief, was the son of "Ithra the Israelite," but in 1 Chron. 2:17 "the father of Amasa was Jether the Ishmaelite." "Ishmaelite" is more likely the correct reading (so NIV), inasmuch as the fact of Amasa's father being an Israelite would be too common to demand special mention. But, "according to Jardri, Jether was an Israelite, dwelling in the land of Ishmael, and thence acquired his surname, like the house of Obed-edom the Gittite." Or, as there were Israelites who bore the name of Ishmael (*see* especially 1 Chron. 8:38; 9:44; also 2 Chron. 19:11; 23:1; Ezra 10:22; 2 Kings 25:23-25; Jer. 40:8, 14-16; 41:1-15), it might well be that Jether or Ithra was descended from some Israelite named Ishmael.   w.h.

ISHMA'IAH (ish-ma'ya; "Jehovah hears," or "Jehovah will hear").

1. A Gibeonite, and one of the chiefs of the warriors who joined themselves to David when he was at Ziklag (1 Chron. 12:4; "Ismaiah," KJV), about 1000 B.C. He is called "a mighty man among the thirty, and over the thirty," i.e., David's bodyguard, but his name does not appear in the lists of the guard in 2 Sam. 23 or 1 Chron. 11. Possibly he was killed in some encounter before David reached the throne (Smith).

2. Son of Obadiah, and ruler of the tribe of Zebulun in the time of David (1 Chron. 27:19), 1000 B.C.

ISH'MEELITE. *See* Ishmaelite.

ISH'MERAI (ish'me-rī). One of the family of Elpaal, a chief Benjamite residing at Jerusalem (1 Chron. 8:18), before 588 B.C.

I'SHOD. *See* Ishhod.

ISH'PAH (ish'pa). One of the "sons" of Beriah, a chief Benjamite (originally from the neighborhood of Aijalon) living in Jerusalem (1 Chron. 8:16; "Ispah," KJV), before 588 B.C.

ISH'PAN (ish'pan). One of the "sons" of Shashak, a chief Benjamite residing at Jerusalem (1 Chron. 8:22), before 588 B.C.

ISH-TOB. This proper name in the KJV of 2 Sam. 10:6, 8 is more correctly "men [from Heb. *ish*] of Tob." *See* Tob.

ISH'UA, ISH'UAH. *See* Ishvah.

ISH'UAI. *See* Ishvi.

ISH'UI. *See* Ishvi.

ISH'VAH (ish'va). The second named of the sons of Asher (Gen. 46:17; "Ishuah," KJV; 1 Chron. 7:30; "Isuah," KJV). He appears to have left no descendants (cf. Num. 26:44).

ISH'VI (ish'vi).

1. The third son of Asher (Gen. 46:17; "Isui," KJV; 1 Chron. 7:30; "Ishuai," KJV), and founder of the Ishvites (Num. 26:44; "Jesui," KJV).

2. The second named of Saul's sons by Ahinoam (1 Sam. 14:49-50; "Ishui," KJV). In the list of Saul's genealogy, in 1 Chron. 8-9, his name is omitted. Some, therefore, claim that he died young. In 1 Sam. 31:2 his place is occupied by Abinadab, with whom others identify him.

ISLAND, ISLE. (Heb. *i*). Although island is a word commonly found in KJV, the Heb. *i* is usually rendered "coastlands" by the NASB and NIV; Isa. 11:11, where it is said that "the Lord will again recover . . . the remnant of His people . . . from the islands of the sea," is an exception in the NASB and NIV. *See* Coastland.

ISMACHI'AH, or **Ismaki'ah** (is-ma-kī'a; "Jah will sustain"). One of the Levites charged by Hezekiah with overseeing the sacred offerings under the general direction of the high priest and others (2 Chron. 31:13), about 719 B.C.

ISMAKI'AH. *See* Ismachiah.

ISMA'IAH. *See* Ishmaiah.

IS'PAH. *See* Ishpah.

IS'RAEL (iz'rā-el; "having power with God, or God's fighter").

1. Jacob, the name conferred by the angel of Jehovah upon *Jacob* (which see) at Peniel (Gen. 32:28); "for you have striven with God and with men and have prevailed."

2. Israelites, i.e., the whole people of Israel, the twelve tribes; called *all Israel* (Josh. 3:17; 7:25; Judg. 8:27) *the sons of Israel* (Jer. 3:21); the *house of Israel* (Ex. 16:31; 40:38); *in Israel* (1 Sam. 9:9); and *the land of Israel* (1 Sam. 13:19; 2 Kings 6:23). Sometimes the whole nation is represented as one person: "Israel is My son" (Ex. 4:22); *My servant* (Isa. 41:8, cf. 42:1; 44:1; 49:3); *your brother* (Num. 20:14). Cf. also Isa. 42:24; 43:1, 15; 44:5. Israel is sometimes put emphatically for the *true Israelites,* the faithful, those distinguished for piety and virtue (Ps. 73:1; Isa. 45:17; John 1:47; Rom. 9:6; 11:26; Gal. 6:16). In the expression (Isa. 49:3) "You are My Servant, Israel," Christ is undoubtedly referred to.

Israelites was the name used for the twelve tribes, from their leaving Egypt until after the death of Saul, but after their defection, the ten tribes arrogated to themselves the name of the whole nation, Israel, i.e., the Northern Kingdom, in contrast with Judah, the Southern Kingdom (2 Sam. 2:9-10, 17, 28; 3:10, 17; 1 Kings 12:1; etc.). The kings of the ten tribes were called *kings of Israel,* and the descendants of David, who ruled over Judah and Benjamin, were known as *kings of Judah;* and in the prophets of that period Judah and Israel are put in opposition (Hos. 4:15; 5:3, 5; 6:10; 7:1; 8:8-9; Amos 1:1; 2:4-6; Mic. 1:5; Isa.

5:7). Yet in Isa. 8:14 the two kingdoms are called the "houses of Israel."

KINGDOM OF JUDAH

After the Babylonian captivity the returned exiles, though mainly of Judah, resumed the name of Israel as the designation of their nation, but as individuals they are called Jews in the Apocrypha and NT. The expression "to all Israel in Judah and Benjamin" (2 Chron. 11:3) characterizes all who had remained true to the house of David as Israel, i.e., those who walked in the footsteps of their progenitor Israel (Jacob) (Keil, *Com.*, ad loc.).

Israel is a term that seems to have been used to distinguish laymen from priests, Levites, and other ministers (Ezra 6:16; 9:1; Neh. 11:3).

ISRAEL, CLASSIFICATION. *See* Israel, Constitution of.

ISRAEL, CONSTITUTION OF. To properly understand this subject it must be remembered that the Israelites are sometimes spoken of as one of the nations, with a *civil* constitution, while at other times they are mentioned as the people adopted into covenant with Jehovah, when reference is made to the *theocratic* constitution.

The Civil Constitution. This had respect to the classification of the people, succession and right of *inheritance* (which see) *land and property* (which see).

Classification. The nation, in virtue of its descent from the twelve sons of Israel, formed a great family called "the house of Israel." Genea-

logically it was divided (Josh. 7:14, 16-18) into:

1. Tribes (Heb. *maṭṭeh*, or *shēbeṭ*, both meaning "branch," the former term being applied to the tribe in its genealogical branches, the latter as being under one scepter). Tribal divisions are found among many ancient peoples, such as the Edomites, Ishmaelites, Arabs, etc. The Hebrew tribes were founded by the twelve sons of *Jacob* (which see) as the tribal fathers of the people. An exception to this rule was made in the case of Joseph's sons Ephraim and Manasseh, they being raised to the position of heads of tribes, having been adopted by Israel as his sons (Gen. 48:5). This would make, strictly speaking, thirteen tribes, but only twelve are uniformly reckoned (*see* Ex. 24:4; Josh. 4:2; etc.), because Levi, as entrusted with the service of worship, occupied a mediatorial position between Jehovah and Israel; consequently no special tribal territory was allotted to them (13:14, 33), but they dwelt in towns scattered throughout all the other twelve tribes. When the Levites were so reckoned, Ephraim and Manasseh were included together as the tribe of Joseph (Num. 26:28; cf. v. 57; Josh. 17:14, 17). This tribal organization was still further established and completed by the giving of the land of Canaan to the Israelites according to their tribes, clans, and fathers' houses. Such a firm root did this organization take that it survived the troublesome times of the judges and was not dissolved by the introduction of the monarchy. We find the heads of tribes exercising great influence on the election of kings (1 Sam. 8:4-5; 10:20-24; 2 Sam. 3:17; 5:1-3), consulted by them on all important state affairs (1 Kings 8:1; 20:7-8; 2 Kings 23:1), and sometimes asserting their influence with great energy (1 Kings 12). Though the tribal organization lost its firm basis with the carrying away of the people into exile, the elders maintained the internal administration and guidance of the people both in and after the Exile (Jer. 20:1; Ezek. 14:1; 20:1). In the prophetic vision that Israel had of the future condition of his sons (Gen. 49:3-28), he thus enumerates them: *Reuben*, the "first-born"; *Simeon* and *Levi*, "implements of violence"; *Judah*, whom his "brothers shall praise"; *Zebulun*, dwelling "at the seashore"; *Issachar*, "a strong donkey"; *Dan*, the "judge"; *Gad*, whom "raiders shall raid"; *Asher*, whose "food shall be rich"; *Naphtali*, a "doe let loose," giving "beautiful words"; *Joseph*, "a fruitful bough"; *Benjamin*, "a ravenous wolf." In this enumeration it is remarkable that the subsequent division of the tribe of Joseph into the two branches of Ephraim and Manasseh is not yet alluded to. Respecting the question of the territory occupied by the several tribes, *see* Land; Palestine.

2. Families or Clans (Heb. *mishpāḥôt*, "circle of relatives"), the first subdivision under tribes, founded from the beginning by Jacob's grandchildren (the sons of his own or adopted sons)

and also by grandchildren and great-grandchildren of the twelve heads of the tribes. Of the fifty-seven families into which the twelve tribes were divided in the last year of their wilderness travels (Num. 26), two belonging to Judah were formed by his grandchildren (v. 21); to Manasseh one family founded by his grandson Gilead, and six by Gilead's sons or Manasseh's great-grandsons (vv. 29-34); to Ephraim, a family founded by his grandson Eran (v. 36); to Benjamin, two families by his grandchildren, the sons of Bela (v. 40); and to Asher, two families by his grandchildren, the sons of Beriah (v. 45). The principle according to which not only sons but grandsons and great-grandsons were raised to be founders of families is unknown.

3. Households (Heb. *bayit*, "house"; *bêth'āb*, "house of father"), a technical expression denoting the larger subdivisions or family groups into which the "families" (clans) fell. "Father's house" also denotes that family having the primacy in every tribe or family, or that house belonging to the father of a tribe or his representative in each division of the people.

4. Men (Heb. *geber*, a "person"), fathers with wife and children.

Government. "According to patriarchal custom, the fathers, standing by right of birth (primogeniture) at the head of the several tribes and divisions of tribes, regulated the relations of the tribes and clans, directed their common affairs, settled disputes as they arose, punished offenses and crimes, and administered law and equity. By founding clans grandchildren were often put on an equality with sons; the heads of clans and fathers' houses gradually attained to almost equal authority and standing with the heads of tribes, for each governed within his own circle, as far as was possible in that state of servitude to which the Israelites were gradually reduced in Egypt. Thus from the heads of tribes, clans, and families proceeded *elders* (which see), who, even before the time of Moses, formed the superiors of the people" (Keil, *Arch.,* 2:312).

Theocratic Constitution. As we have already seen, the Israelites possessed the elements of a state in their tribal constitution, and it was not until their adoption into covenant with Jehovah, the Lord of the whole earth (Ex. 19:5), that they received through Moses the laws and ordinances for the kingdom that they were to establish in Canaan. This constitution is called a *theocracy* (Gk. *theokratia,* "rule of God") and has its root in the peculiar relation into which Jehovah entered with the people of Israel, whom He chose to carry out His purposes of redemption (Ps. 44:4; Isa. 43:14-15). According to Keil (*Arch.,* pp. 320-21), the theocracy "consists essentially in these three things: (*a*) God himself, as Lawgiver, orders or modifies the relations of the religious and common life of the people by immediate revelation given to Moses. (*b*) He takes into his

own hand the control and government of the Israelitish state or kingdom, in that he is ever really present to his people, makes known his will in important state affairs by the Urim and Thummim, by prophets, and, when necessary, interposes in a miraculous way, judging, punishing, blessing. (*c*) Finally he raises up for the people the needed leaders and rulers, and furnishes them with the power required for their office. Thus all the human superiors of the Israelites were, in the strictest sense of the word, servants and representatives of God, who had only to carry out his law, to execute his will. The one Lord and sovereign as Jehovah, the covenant God, who, as Lawgiver, supreme Judge and Ruler of his people, united in himself all the powers constituting the state, and directed them by his servants."

Under the theocracy we find that Jehovah called Moses to be the instrument of His will in the *giving of the law;* that the *judicial power* was entrusted to the leaders of the tribes and elders of the congregation (*see* Classification, above; Elders); the *executive* was held sometimes by the leaders of the tribes, sometimes by men called by Jehovah in extraordinary cases to lead and govern the people, and invested with sovereign power; the *priesthood,* with the high priest at its head, stood between the congregation or its individual members and Jehovah in religious matters; and, last, as a check to the overstraining of priestly power and to all hierarchal ambition, were the *prophets,* who, with divine authority and power, and without respect of persons, admonished all ranks to keep within the limits of the law.

BIBLIOGRAPHY: E. W. Hengstenberg, *History of the Kingdom of God* (1881), 1:234-469; A. J. McClain, *The Greatness of the Kingdom* (1959), pp. 91-95; R. J. Rushdoony, *Institutes of Biblical Law* (1973); R. D. Culver, *Toward a Biblical View of Civil Government* (1974), pp. 126-81.

ISRAEL, KINGDOM OF. An earthly kingdom was not incompatible with the *theocracy* (which see), if the kings submitted unconditionally to the will of Jehovah and, as earthly representatives of His sovereignty, wished only to execute His laws and judgments. It was not the original intention of Jehovah to leave His people as sheep without a shepherd, but to set over them a man who should lead them (Num. 27:16-17), as He gave them Moses and Joshua and afterward judges from Othniel to Samuel. Knowing that Israel would long for a king, God gave a promise to the patriarchs that "kings shall come forth from you" (Gen. 17:6, 16; 35:11); this promise was renewed by Moses (Deut. 28:36), along with a law given relating to the king (17:14-20), whereby the earthly kingdom was incorporated in the theocracy.

Law of Kingdom. This law (Deut. 17:14-20) does not prescribe an earthly kingdom but only arranges for such if desired by Israel. It provides that (1) one of their own people, and not a stranger, shall be chosen; (2) he shall not "multiply horses," i.e., strengthen his power by a standing army; (3) "neither shall he multiply wives," which would serve to gratify lust and give splendor to his court (cf. 1 Kings 11:3); (4) he shall carefully study the law, a copy of which was to be given him, and guide his rule by it. This law "of the kingdom" was proclaimed by Samuel, written "in the book and placed . . . before the Lord" (1 Sam. 10:25).

Still further, the king set by Jehovah over His people was not a constitutional prince elected by the people, but was independent. He owed his selection to God, was dependent upon Him alone, and was bound to carry out the Mosaic law, and follow the will of Jehovah as made known by His prophets (1 Sam. 10:24; 13:13; 15:26, 28-29, 35; 16:1, 13). Thus Saul and afterward David were chosen by Jehovah to be princes over Israel, and anointed by Samuel to their office.

The kingdom was not firmly established under truly theocratic meaning by Saul. He unduly exalted himself and was rejected because of his opposition to the will of Jehovah (see Saul). *David* (which see), on the contrary, was always faithful to the theocratic idea and carefully watched over its institutions. Thus the earthly kingdom became the visible representation of Jehovah's sovereignty over Israel.

The kingdom, although intended to be hereditary as among other peoples (Deut. 17:20; cf. 1 Sam. 13:13), first became so under David in virtue of the divine promise (2 Sam. 7:12-16). The law of succession was that the eldest, or firstborn, son followed his father on the throne (2 Chron. 21:3), though not without exceptions (2 Kings 23:34; 2 Chron. 11:22). If the successor was a minor, a regency intervened, or the queen mother acted as sovereign (1 Kings 15:13), or the high priest became guardian (2 Kings 12:2).

Administration. Kings, as "the Lord's anointed," were considered by the people to be holy persons (1 Sam. 24:6-10; 26:11, 16, 23; 2 Sam. 1:16) without being deified or becoming inaccessible to their subjects. In the highest cases of appeal they pronounced sentence personally (15:2; 1 Kings 3:9, 16-28), usually led the army in war (2 Sam. 5:6; etc.), and publicly arranged for and conducted festivals (1 Sam. 6; 1 Kings 8).

Officials. As a bodyguard the kings had the *Cherethites* (which see) and *Pelethites* (which see), who also executed the sentences pronounced by them (2 Sam. 15:18; 20:7; etc.). They were supported in their administration by many officials (1 Kings 4:2) who served as counselors. In 2 Sam. 8:16-18, 20:23-26, 1 Chron. 27:32-34, and 1 Kings 4:1-6 the following officials are named: (1) the head of the army, or commander-in-chief; (2) the commander of the Cherethites and Pelethites; (3) the recorder, probably the keeper of the state archives; (4) the secretary, or scribe; (5) the high priest; (6) privy counselors

(*Cohanim,* or friends of the king), called also "chiefs at the king's side" (1 Chron. 18:17), "elders who had served his father Solomon" (1 Kings 12:6), "the king's advisors" (2 Kings 25:19; Jer. 52:25); (7) the overseers, or "deputies," of public works (1 Kings 5:16); (8) those having charge of the royal storehouses, of agriculture, vineyards, flocks, herds, etc. (1 Chron. 27:25-31) besides deputies who acted as chief tax collectors (1 Kings 4:7-19); (9) the person placed over the deputies (v. 5). There were also the cupbearers (10:5), the keeper of the wardrobe (2 Kings 10:22), and inferior servants.

In addition, although at variance with the law, (Deut. 17:17), there were a large number of wives and concubines (2 Sam. 5:13; 1 Kings 11:3; 2 Chron. 11:21), who, on the death of the king, became the property of his successor (2 Sam. 12:8).

Revenue. Revenue was derived from the following sources: (1) voluntary gifts from subjects (1 Sam. 10:27; 16:20) and from foreign visitors (1 Kings 10:10, 25; 2 Chron. 32:23); (2) regular contributions made by subjects (1 Kings 4:7; cf. 1 Sam. 17:25, marg.); (3) tribute paid by subject peoples (2 Sam. 8:2; 2 Kings 3:4; Isa. 16:1); (4) the share of spoil taken in war (2 Sam. 8:10; 12:30); (5) the produce of the royal domains, i.e., of the fields, vineyards, flocks, etc. (1 Chron. 27:25-31; 2 Chron. 26:10), and the gain by commerce, etc. (1 Kings 10:11, 14-15, 22).

Continuance. Israel, as the legitimate kingdom, lasted until the destruction of the state by the Chaldeans, but the apostate ten tribes, revolting under the lead of Jeroboam, perished much earlier (see Chronology). Respecting Israel as a separate kingdom, see History, OT.

BIBLIOGRAPHY: A. J. McClain, *The Greatness of the Kingdom* (1959), pp. 104-19; R. D. Culver, *Toward a Biblical View of Civil Government* (1974), pp. 165-81; L. J. Wood, *Israel's United Monarchy* (1979).

ISSACHAR (is'a-kar; "he will bring reward"). The name of the ninth son of Jacob (see article immediately below) and also the name of one of the Korahite Levites, who was the seventh son of Obed-edom and one of the gatekeepers of the house of the Lord (1 Chron. 26:5).

IS'SACHAR (is'a-kar; "he will bring reward"). The ninth son of Jacob and the fifth of Leah (Gen. 30:18), about 1925 B.C. He was born at Paddan-aram, and but little is recorded of him.

The Tribe of Issachar. At the descent into Egypt four sons are ascribed to Issachar; these sons founded the four chief families of the tribe (Gen. 46:13; Num. 26:23-25; 1 Chron. 7:1). The number of fighting men, when the census was taken at Sinai, was 54,400, ranking the tribe *fifth* (Num. 1:28-29); at the second census the number had increased to 64,300, ranking it *third* (26:25).

Position. Issachar's place during the journey to

Canaan was on the E of the Tabernacle, with his brothers Judah and Zebulun (2:3-8). At this time the captain of the tribe was Nethanel the son of Zuar (1:8). He was succeeded by Igal the son of Joseph, who went as one of the spies (13:7), and he again by Paltiel the son of Azzan, who assisted Joshua in apportioning the land of Canaan (34:26).

Territory. The allotment of Issachar lay above that of Manasseh. The specification of its boundaries and contents is contained in Josh. 19:17-23.

Subsequent History. Jacob's prophecy "Issachar is a strong donkey, lying down between the sheepfolds. When he saw that a resting place was good . . . he bowed his shoulder to bear burdens, and became a slave at forced labor" (Gen. 49:14-15) was fulfilled by Issachar's paying tribute to the various marauding tribes attracted to its territory by the richness of the crops.

ISSHI'AH (is-shī'a; "lent by Jehovah"). The name of three men.

1. One of the sons of Izrahiah, and a great-great-grandson of Issachar (1 Chron. 7:3). The KJV renders "Ishiah."

2. The first of the sons of Rehabiah, and great-grandson of Moses (1 Chron. 24:21; cf. 26:25, where he is called Jeshaiah).

3. The second son of Uzziel (grandson of Levi), and father of Zechariah (1 Chron. 23:20; "Jesiah," KJV; 24:25).

ISSHI'JAH (ish-ī'ja; Heb. same as above). One of the "sons" of Harim, who renounced his Gentile wife after the captivity (Ezra 10:31; "Ishijah," KJV and NIV), 456 B.C.

ISSUE.

1. In Isa. 22:24 this term carries the meaning of anything ignoble, worthless, and is applied to the large and hitherto ignoble family of Eliakim, who would "hang on him all the glory of his father's house."

2. The emission of a horse (stallion), to whom the idolatrous paramours of Judah are compared (Ezek. 23:20).

3. In the KJV, the term has the meaning of offspring (Gen. 48:6; Matt. 22:25), as it is rendered in NASB. The NIV translates "children."

4. A KJV term used medically to describe hemorrhage (Lev. 12:7; Matt. 9:20) and other discharges (Lev. 15:2) rendering the victims unclean. *See* Diseases.

IS'UAH. *See* Ish'vah.

IS'UI. *See* Ishvi, no. 1.

ITAL'IAN (ital'i-an; "of or from Italy," Acts 10:1). This only mention of the name in Scripture is in connection with the cohort to which Cornelius belonged. It was probably composed of Italians separate from the legionary soldiers and not of the Italian Legion.

IT'ALY (it'a-li). The name occurs five times in Scripture (Acts 18:2; 27:1, 6; Heb. 13:24). From these passages we have testimony respecting the Jewish colony in Italy, the commerce between it and Asia, and the Testament denotes the whole natural peninsula between the Alps and the Straits of Messina.

ITCH. *See* Diseases.

ITH'AI (ith'ī; 1 Chron. 11:31). *See* Ittai.

ITH'AMAR (ith'a-mar; "palm-coast," Gesenius). The fourth and youngest son of Aaron (Ex. 6:23; Num. 3:2; 1 Chron. 6:3), before 1440 B.C. He was consecrated to the priesthood along with his brothers (Num. 3:3); after the death of Nadab and Abihu, who left no children (3:4), he and Eleazar took the places they had held in the priestly office (Lev. 10:6, 12; Num. 3:4; 1 Chron. 24:2). We learn nothing more of Ithamar, save that the property of the Tabernacle (the curtains, hangings, pillars, cords, and boards) was under his charge (Ex. 38:21) and that he superintended its removal by the Gershonites and Merarites (Num. 4:28, 33). Ithamar and his descendants occupied the position of common priests until the high priesthood passed into his family in the person of Eli, under circumstances of which we are ignorant. Abiathar, whom Solomon deposed, was the last high priest of that line, and the pontificate reverted to the elder line of Eleazar in the person of Zadok (1 Kings 2:27, 35). A priest by the name of Daniel, of Ithamar's posterity, returned from Babylon (Ezra 8:2).

ITH'IEL (ith'i-el; perhaps, "God with me").

1. The son of Jeshaiah and father of Maaseiah, a Benjamite, one of whose posterity returned from Babylon (Neh. 11:7), long before 536 B.C.

2. A person mentioned along with Ucal in Prov. 30:1, to whom the words of Agur's prophecy were addressed.

ITH'LAH (ith'la; "a hanging of lofty place"). A city on the borders of the tribe of Dan, mentioned only in Josh. 19:42 ("Jethlah," KJV). It is probably Beithul, three miles E of Yalo (Aijalon).

ITH'MAH (ith'ma; bereavement, "orphanhood"). A Moabite and one of David's mighty men (1 Chron. 11:46), 950 B.C.

ITH'NAN (ith'nan). One of the cities of S Judah (Josh. 15:23), not identified.

ITH'RA (ith'ra). An Israelite (but more correctly an Ishmaelite, according to 1 Chron. 2:17, where he is called Jether), and father of Amasa (David's general) by Abigail, David's sister (2 Sam. 17:25; 1 Kings 2:5), before 1000 B.C. The NIV renders the name as Jether in all three passages.

ITH'RAN (ith'ran; "abundance, excellence").

1. One of the sons of Dishon, grandson of Seir the Horite (Gen. 36:26; cf. v. 30; 1 Chron. 1:41).

2. One of the sons of Zophah, the great-grand-

son of Asher (1 Chron. 7:37). Perhaps the same as Jether in v. 38.

ITH'REAM (ith're-am; "residue of the people"). David's sixth son, born of Eglah at Hebron (2 Sam. 3:5; 1 Chron. 3:3), about 1000 B.C.

ITH'RITE (ith'rīt). The descendants of a Jether living in Kiriath-jearim (1 Chron. 2:53). Two of David's mighty men, Ira and Gareb (11:40; 2 Sam. 23:38), belonged to the family of *Jether* (which see).

IT'TAH-KA'ZIN. *See* Eth-kazin.

IT'TAI (it'ī).

1. "Ittai the Gittite," i.e., a native of Gath, a Philistine in the army of David who first appeared on the morning of David's flight from Absalom and Jerusalem. The king saw him coming with those who remained faithful, and recognizing him as "a foreigner and also as an exile," and as one who had but recently joined his service, urged him to return and not ally himself to a doubtful cause. But Ittai declared, "As the Lord lives, and as my lord the king lives, surely wherever my lord the king may be, whether for death or for life, here also your servant will be." He was allowed to proceed and passed over the Kedron with the king and his company (2 Sam. 15:18-23), 970 B.C. When David organized and numbered the army at Mahanaim, Ittai was given command of a third part of the force, and seems to have enjoyed equal rank with Joab and Abishai (18:2, 5, 12).

2. The son of Ribai, a Benjamite of Gibeah, one of David's thirty mighty men (2 Sam. 23:29; the NIV reads "Ithai"). In the parallel list of 1 Chron. 11:31 the name is given as Ithai.

ITURAE'A, ITURE'A (it-ū-rī'a). A small province on the northeastern border of Palestine, lying along the base of Mt. Hermon and a portion of the tetrarchy of Philip (Luke 3:1). It lies NE of the Sea of Galilee, E of the sources of the Jordan River.

Jetur, the son of Ishmael, gave his name, like the rest of his brethren, to the little province he colonized (*see* Gen. 25:15-16). Ituraea, with the adjoining provinces, fell into the hands of a chief called Zenodorus; but about 20 B.C. they were taken from him by the Roman emperor and given to Herod the Great, who bequeathed them to his son Philip (*see* Luke 3:1). Caligula gave Ituraea to Herod Agrippa I. When Herod Agrippa died, Ituraea was incorporated into the province of Syria under procurators.

I'VAH. *See* Ivvah.

IVORY. Imported into Tyre by "sons of Dedan" (Ezek. 27:15) and "ships of Tarshish" (1 Kings 10:22), ivory was used in ornamenting houses, constructing furniture, etc., as in the present day in the East. "Ivory tusks" are mentioned in Ezek. 27:15.

A considerable amount of ivory has been found in Near Eastern excavations. For example, at Megiddo in a stratum dating to the thirteenth century B.C. Canaanite carvings of figurines, plaques, combs, and small boxes came to light. Innumerable pieces of ivory used for inlay were found in the excavation of Samaria, illustrating Amos's condemnation of the luxury of the place. Excavations at Calah (Nimrud) turned up a fine collection of carved ivory pieces produced in the Assyrian Empire during the ninth century B.C.

Ivory carving

The Canaanites, Phoenicians, and Syrians were especially skilled in the carving of ivory and the use of it in inlay. Their sources of supply were the elephant herds of the upper Euphrates region and, by trade, Africa and India. Hiram of Tyre and Solomon cooperated in commercial ventures launched from Ezion-geber to Ophir through the Red Sea. Their ships returned with ivory in their holds (cf. 1 Kings 9:26-28; 10:22; and 2 Chron. 9:21).   H.F.V.

IV'VAH (ī'va). One of the cities of the Assyrians (2 Kings 18:33-34; 19:13; Isa. 37:13) from which they brought colonists to repopulate Samaria (2 Kings 17:24, where it is rendered *Avva*, [which see]; the KJV is "Ava").

IVY. *See* Vegetable Kingdom.

I'YE-ABARIM (ī'ye-ab'a-rim; "ruins of Abarim"). The forty-seventh station of the Israelites in the wilderness, "at the border of Moab" (Num. 33:44; "Ije-abarim," KJV) or "opposite Moab, to the east" (21:11; "toward the sunrising," KJV).

I'YIM (ī'yim). A contracted form (Num. 33:45; "Iim," KJV) of Iye-abarim (which see).

IZ'EHARITES. *See* Izharites.

IZ'HAR (iz'har; "anointing").

1. The son of Helah, wife of Ashhur, the father (founder) of Tekoa (1 Chron. 4:7; "Jezoar," KJV; "Zohar," NIV).

2. The second son of Kohath, the son of Levi and father of Korah (Ex. 6:18, 21; Num. 3:19; 16:1; 1 Chron. 6:2, 18, 38; 23:12, 18). His descendants are called *Izharites* (which see), about 1440 B.C.

IZ'HARITES (iz'har-its). A family of Kohathite Levites descended from Izhar the son of Kohath (Num. 3:27; 1 Chron. 24:22; 26:23, 29.

IZLI'AH (izlī'a; cf. Arab. *yazalīy*, "eternal; unceasing"). One of the "sons" of Elpaal, and apparently a chief Benjamite living in Jerusalem (1 Chron. 8:18; "Jezliah," KJV); probably about 588 B.C.

IZRAHI'AH (iz-ra-hī'a; "Jehovah will bring

forth"). The son of Uzzi and great-grandson of Issachar (1 Chron. 7:3).

IZ'RAHITE (iz'ra-hīt). A patronymic epithet of Shamhuth, one of David's commanders (1 Chron. 27:8); probably so called as being descended from Zerah, Judah's son.

IZ'RI (iz'ri; the "Jezerites"). The leader of the fourth division of Levitical singers under David (1 Chron. 25:11); probably the same as *Zeri* (which see), of the sons of Jeduthun, mentioned in v. 3, 1000 B.C.

IZZI'AH (iz-ī'a; "whom Jehovah sprinkles"). An Israelite of the "sons" of Parosh, who put away his Gentile wife after the Exile (Ezra 10:25; "Jeziah," KJV), 456 B.C.

JA'AKAN (ja'a-kan). The son of Ezer and grandson of Seir (1 Chron. 1:42; "Jakan," KJV). The ancestor of the Bene-jaakan, around whose well the children of Israel encamped after they left Moseroth (Num. 33:30-32) and again in a reverse direction after they left Kadesh-barnea, before they reached Mt. Hor or Moserah (Deut. 10:6), before 1440 B.C. In Gen. 36:27 the name appears in the simple form *Akan*.

JAA'KANITES. *See* Jaakan.

JAAKO'BAH (ja-a-kō'ba; another form of Jacob). One of the prosperous descendants (*nᵉśi'îm*, "princes") of Simeon that emigrated to the valley of Gedor in the time of Hezekiah (1 Chron. 4:36), about 710 B.C.

JA'ALA (jā'a-la; "wild goat"). One of "Solomon's servants," whose descendants (or perhaps a place whose former inhabitants) returned from the captivity with Zerubbabel (Neh. 7:58); called (by the KJV and the NASB) in the parallel passage (Ezra 2:56) by the equivalent name Jaalah, before 536 B.C.

JA'ALAH (ja'a-la; Ezra 2:56). *See* Jaala.

JA'ALAM. *See* Jalam.

JAANAI. *See* Janai.

JA'AR (jā'ar). According to the NIV margin of Ps. 132:6, a short form of *Kirjath-Jearim* (which see).

JA'ARE-OR'EGIM (ja'a-rā-ōr'e-jim). The father of *Elhanan* (which see), a Bethlehemite, who killed Goliath the Gittite (2 Sam. 21:19), but in 1 Chron. 20:5 it is stated that "Elhanan the son of Jair killed Lahmi the brother of Goliath." The reading in Chronicles is probably the correct one, the word *Oregim* having crept in from the next line through oversight of the copyist.

JAARESHI'AH (ja'a-re-shi'a; origin uncertain).

One of the "sons" of Jeroham, a chief man of the Benjamites residing at Jerusalem (1 Chron. 8:27).

JAA'SIEL (ja-a'si-el; "God makes").
1. A Mezobaite and one of David's bodyguards (1 Chron. 11:47); about 1000 B.C.
2. The son of Abner and leader of the tribe of Benjamin in the time of David (1 Chron. 27:21). He is identified by some with no. 1.

JA'ASU (ja'a-su; "they will do"). An Israelite of the "sons" of Bani who renounced his Gentile wife after the return from Babylon (Ezra 10:37), 456 B.C.

JAAZANI'AH (ja-az-a-ni'a; "Jehovah hears").
1. The son of Jeremiah (not the prophet) and a chief man of the Rechabites, whom the prophet tested as to their obedience to Jonadab, their founder, by offering them wine (Jer. 35:3-19), 606 B.C.
2. A Maacathite, son of Hoshaiah, and one of the "captains" who accompanied Johanan when he paid his respects to Gedaliah at Mizpah (2 Kings 25:23; Jer. 40:8) and after his assassination asked for Jeremiah's advice (42:1). He appears to have assisted Johanan in recovering the prey from Ishmael (41:11-16) and to have gone to Egypt with the rest (43:4-5). In Jer. 40:8; 42:1 the name is changed to Jezaniah. He is doubtless the person called Azariah in Jer. 43:2, 588 B.C.
3. The son of Shaphan and leader of the seventy elders of Israel, seen by Ezekiel in his vision offering idolatrous worship at Jerusalem (Ezek. 8:11), 592 B.C.
4. The son of Azzur, one of the leaders among the twenty-five men seen (in a vision) by Ezekiel at the E gate of the Temple devising mischief and giving "evil advice" (Ezek. 11:1-2), 592 B.C.

JA'AZER. *See* Jazer.

JAAZI'AH (ja-a-zī'a; "comforted by Jehovah").

Apparently the third son or descendant of Merari the Levite and founder of an independent house in that family (1 Chron. 24:26-27). Neither he nor his descendants are mentioned elsewhere (*see* 23:21-23; Ex. 6:19). The word *Beno,* which follows Jaaziah, should probably be translated "his son," i.e., the son of Merari (McC. and S.).

JAA'ZIEL (ja-a'zi-el; "comforted by God"). A Levitical musician among those of the "second rank" (1 Chron. 15:18); the same as the Aziel who was one of those "with harps tuned to alamoth" (v. 20), after 1000 B.C.

JA'BAL (jā'bal). The son of Lamech and Adah and the brother of Jubal (Gen. 4:20-21). He is described as "the father of those who dwell in tents and have livestock." This obviously means that Jabal was the first to adopt the nomadic life still followed by many Arabian and Tartar tribes in Asia.

JAB'BOK (jab'ok). A stream E of the Jordan, which empties into that river nearly midway between the Dead Sea and the Sea of Galilee, or about forty-five miles S of the latter. Its headwaters rise on the edge of Moab, only about eighteen miles E of the Jordan. The river flows at first toward the desert under the name of Ammân, past Rabbath-Ammon; there turns N, fetches a wide compass NW, cuts the Gilead range in two, and flows in a very winding channel WSW to the Jordan. Its whole course, counting its windings, is over sixty miles. It is shallow and always fordable, except where it breaks between steep rocks. Its valley is fertile and has always been a frontier and a line of traffic. It was once the border of the Ammonites (Num. 21:24; Deut. 2:37; 3:16) and afterward became the boundary between the kingdoms of Sihon and Og (Josh. 12:2, 5). The earliest notice of it precedes the accounts of the mysterious struggle of Jacob with Jehovah and the interview with his brother, Esau (Gen. 32:22), both of which took place on Jabbok's southern bank. The Jabbok is now called Zerka, "the blue river."

BIBLIOGRAPHY: D. Baly, *The Geography of the Bible* (1957),

The Jabbok River

p. 229; Y. Aharoni, *The Land of the Bible* (1979), pp. 9, 12, 34, 37-39, 54, 62, 111, 207-9, 265, 314, 317, 327.

JA'BESH (ja'besh; "dry, parched").
1. The father of *Shallum* (which see) who killed Zechariah, king of Israel, and reigned only a month (2 Kings 15:10, 13-14), before 742 B.C.
2. The short form of *Jabesh-gilead* (which see).

JA'BESH-GIL'EAD (ja-besh-gil'e-ad; "Jabesh of Gilead"). A town of Gilead beyond Jordan, a night's journey from Bethshan (1 Sam. 31:11; 2 Sam 2:4) and lying within the territory assigned to the eastern half tribe of Manasseh (Num. 32:29, 40). Its inhabitants were severely punished because they did not respond to the call against Benjamin (Judg. 21:8-14), every man being put to the sword and 400 virgins being given to the Benjamites.

The city survived the loss of its males and is next heard from as being besieged by Nahash the Ammonite. He offered to spare its inhabitants if they would agree to have their right eyes put out (to render them unfit for military service). Being allowed seven days to ratify the treaty, they appealed to Saul, who raised a large army and defeated the Ammonites (1 Sam. 11:1-11).

This service was gratefully remembered, and when Saul and his sons were slain on Mt. Gilboa (1 Sam. 31:8) the men of Jabesh, after a night march, took down their corpses, burned them, and buried their ashes "under the tamarisk tree at Jabesh" (v. 13). For this act David sent his blessing (2 Sam. 2:5).

Its site is not defined in Scripture. Josephus (*Ant.* 6.5.1) calls Jabesh the metropolis of Gilead. Robinson (*Bib. Res.,* p. 320) supposed it to be the ruins of ed-Deir in the Wadi Yabis.

Nelson Glueck however, located it about ten miles SE of Bethshan on twin mounds, Tell el-Meqbereh and Tell Abu Kharaz, on the Wadi Yabis (Jabesh) flowing into the Jordan S of the Sea of Galilee.

BIBLIOGRAPHY: N. Glueck, *The River Jordan* (1947), pp. 159-69.

JA'BEZ (ja'bez; "son of pain").
1. A descendant of Judah, but of what family is not apparent. The only mention made of him is this remarkable account: "And Jabez was more honorable than his brothers, and his mother named him Jabez saying, 'Because I bore him with pain.' Now Jabez called on the God of Israel, saying, 'Oh that Thou wouldst bless me indeed, and enlarge my border, and that Thy hand might be with me, and that Thou wouldst keep me from harm, that it may not pain me! And God granted him what he requested" (1 Chron. 4:9-10). Keil (*Com.,* ad loc.) supposes that this is a record of a vow made by Jabez, the conditions only being given. "The reason of this is, probably, that the vow had acquired importance sufficient to make it worthy of being handed down only from God's

having so fulfilled his wish that his life became a contradiction of his name, the son of pain having been free from pain in life, and having attained to greater happiness and reputation than his brothers."

2. A place inhabited by "the families of scribes" (1 Chron. 2:55), apparently in Judah. It is not mentioned anywhere else.

JA'BIN (ja'bin; "he [God] understands"). Probably a royal title at Hazor, like Agag among the Amalekites.

1. A king of Hazor who organized a confederacy of the northern kings against the Israelites. These assembled with their hosts near the waters of Merom, where Joshua surprised this vast army and overthrew it. He then took Hazor and killed Jabin (Josh. 11:1-14), about 1370 B.C.

2. Another king of Hazor and probably a descendant of the former. He is called "king of Canaan" (Judg. 4:2) in distinction from the kings of other nations, such as Moab, Mesopotamia, etc. (Keil, *Com.*). He seems to have had unusual power, as he is credited with 900 iron chariots. The idolatry of the Israelites lost them divine protection, they became subject to Jabin, who "oppressed the sons of Israel severely for twenty years" (4:3). From this they were delivered by the great victory won by Barak over the forces of Jabin, commanded by Sisera (vv. 3-16), about 1215-1195 B.C. The war still continued until it ended in the overthrow of Jabin. His name is mentioned in Ps. 83:9.

JAB'NEEL (jab'nîl; "God builds, causes to build").

1. A town on the northern boundary of Judah (Josh. 15:11), probably the same as *Jabneh* (which see). Known as Jamnia during the Hellenistic period, it was renamed Ibelin by the Crusaders and is the modern Israeli town of Yebna. At this site in A.D. 90 a Jewish assembly met to make decisions concerning the canon.

2. A city on the border of Naphtali (Josh. 19:33), probably the modern Yemma, about four miles SW of the Sea of Galilee.   H.F.V.

JAB'NEH (jab'ne; "he [God] causes to be built"). Probably the same as Jabneel no. 1, a point on the northern boundary of Judah between Mt. Baalah and the Mediterranean Sea. There was a constant struggle between the Danites and the Philistines, and it is not surprising that we find Jabneh in the hands of the latter. Uzziah captured this place along with Gath and Ashdod (2 Chron. 26:6). Josephus calls it Jamnia. It still exists as a good-sized village under the name of Jebuah, about two miles from the sea, seven miles S of Joppa.

JA'CAN (ja'kan). One of seven chief Gadite "kinsmen" living in Bashan (1 Chron. 5:13).

JA'CHIN, JA'KIN (ja'kin; "he [God] establishes").

1. The fourth son of Simeon (Gen. 46:10; Ex. 6:15), called Jarib in 1 Chron. 4:24. He was the founder of the Jachinites (Num. 26:12).

2. One of the priests residing in Jerusalem after the captivity (1 Chron. 9:10; Neh. 11:10).

3. Head of the twenty-first division of priests in the time of David (1 Chron. 24:17).

4. Jachin and Boaz were the names of two pillars of bronze set in the porch of Solomon's Temple (1 Kings 7:15-22; 2 Chron. 3:17). *See* Temple. It has been convincingly shown that the names of these two columns stood for the initial words of dynastic oracles that were inscribed upon them (R. B. Y. Scott, *Journal of Biblical Literature* 58 [1939]: 143f.; cf. Paul Garber, *Biblical Archaeologist* [Feb. 1951]: 8f.). The Jachin formula may have been, "Yahweh will establish (*yakin*) thy throne forever," or something similar, and the "Boaz" oracle may have run, "In Yahweh is the king's strength." Frequently Jachin and Boaz have been interpreted as sacred obelisks similar to those erected beside great Egyptian temples at Thebes and Heliopolis or beside the temple of Melcarth at Tyre. This view is possible, since Solomon did, apparently, make concessions to the architectural fads of his day. Sometimes they have been viewed as stylized trees or again as cosmic pillars, like the Pillars of Hercules. The best interpretation seems to be that put forth by Robertson Smith, who viewed them as "gigantic cressets or fire altars." W. F. Albright adopted Robertson Smith's essential view that Jachin and Boaz were immense fire altars, adducing proof from the painted tombs of Marisa in southern Palestine, where similar incense burners appear. Albright presented added evidence from the Egyptian Djed Pillar, a sacred emblem of Osiris that bears certain affinities to these structures. The most important fact is that each of the shafts of the two pillars is represented as being crowned with an oil basin or a lampstand, Heb. *gūllâ* (1 Kings 7:41; cf. Zech. 4:3) (W. F. Albright, *Archaeology and the Religion of Israel*, pp. 144-48; id., *Bulletin of the American Schools of Oriental Research* 85 [1942]: 18-27). Thus imitating Phoenician models, these immense incense stands illuminated the facade of the Temple. They doubtless caught the first glint of the Jerusalem sunrise or were wrapped in mists of the Kidron Valley. With their blazing, smoking wicks, they recalled to worshipers the fiery, cloudy pillar that led Israel of old through the wilderness. The N Syrian shrine uncovered at Tell Tainat, like Solomon's edifice, had two columns situated at its portico. Such pillars flanking the main entrance of temples were common in Syria, Phoenicia, and Cyprus in the first millennium B.C. Spreading eastward, they came into vogue in Assyria. They are to be found in Sargon's temple at Khorsabad, late eighth century B.C.,

and westward to the Phoenician colonies in the western Mediterranean. *(See* Boaz.)   M.F.U.

JACINTH. *See* Mineral Kingdom.

JACKAL. *See* Animal Kingdom.

JACOB (ja'kob). The name of the father of Joseph the husband of Mary the mother of Jesus (Matt. 1:15-16), before 40 B.C.; and of the patriarch (*see* article below).

JA'COB (ja'kob; "heel-catcher, supplanter"; by popular etymology, but perhaps "he whom God protects," from Arab. and Ethiopic *'akaba,* "guard, keep").

The second born of the twin sons of Isaac and Rebekah, their conception being supernatural in answer to Isaac's prayer. Jacob was born when his father was sixty years old, probably at Beer-la-hai-roi (Gen. 25:21-26; cf. v. 11), about 2001 B.C.

Personal History. It is recorded that Jacob grew up to be "a peaceful man, living in tents," preferring the quiet of a homelife to the active, dangerous career of a hunter. He was the favorite of his mother, whereas Isaac showed partiality toward Esau.

Buys Esau's Birthright. The first incident mentioned is his purchase of Esau's birthright for the paltry sum of a pot of stew, thus making use of his brother's hunger to advance his own interests. "The birthright consisted afterward in a double portion of the father's inheritance (Deut. 21:17); but with the patriarchs it embraced the chieftainship, rule over the brethren and the entire family (Gen. 27:29), and the title to the blessing of promise (27:4, 27-29), which included the future possession of Canaan and of covenant fellowship with Jehovah (28:4)" (K. & D., *Com.*).

Obtains Isaac's Blessing. Isaac, now aged, was about to pronounce his blessing upon Esau, his elder son, but was thwarted by the deception practiced upon him by Rebekah and Jacob. Jacob impersonated Esau and added direct falsehood to the fraud. Thus Jacob received his father's blessing (27:1-29).

Flight from Esau. Esau hated his brother because of his deception and its success and resolved to slay him, only delaying until a sufficient time after the probably near death of his father. Rebekah, informed of Esau's purpose, advised Jacob to flee to her brother Laban in Haran, obtaining Isaac's consent by saying that she wished Jacob to marry one of his kinswomen and not a daughter of Canaan. Isaac blessed Jacob again and sent him away (27:41–28:5). Jacob's age is arrived at as follows: Joseph was thirty years old when introduced to Pharaoh, and, allowing for seven years of plenty and two of famine (45:6), Joseph was 39 years old when Jacob went to Egypt, at which time Jacob was 130 years of age. Therefore Joseph was born before Jacob was 91. His birth occurred in the fourteenth year of

Jacob's sojourn in Mesopotamia (30:25; 29:18, 21, 27), which would mean Jacob's flight took place in his seventy-seventh year.

Dream at Bethel. On his journey to Laban he stopped at Luz for the night and was given the vision of the ladder and the ascending and descending angels. God there confirmed to him the promises given to his fathers and promised him protection on his journey and a safe return to his home. In recognition of the divine presence Jacob called the place Bethel and made a vow dedicating to Jehovah a tenth of all God gave him (28:10-22). *See* Ladder.

Serves Laban. Arriving at Haran, Jacob met Rachel, Laban's daughter, by whom Jacob's coming was made known to her father. After a month Laban inquired what wages Jacob desired for his services, and he asked for Rachel on the condition of seven years' service. At the expiration of the time, which seemed to Jacob "but a few days because of his love for her," Laban availed himself of the customs of the country and substituted his elder daughter, Leah, for Rachel. Upon the discovery of the deception, Laban excused himself saying: "It is not the practice in our place, to marry off the younger before the first-born." Another seven years' service gained for Jacob his beloved Rachel. Leah became the mother of Jacob's firstborn, Reuben, and three other sons, Simeon, Levi, and Judah, following in succession. Rachel, having borne no children, gave to Jacob her maid, Bilhah, who bore Dan and Naphtali. Two other sons, Gad and Asher, were born of Leah's maid, Zilpah. Leah then bore two more sons, Issachar and Zebulun, and a daughter, Dinah. At length Rachel became the mother of a son, whom she called Joseph (29:1–30:24). A number of years later Benjamin was born. (*See* table 19, "The Children of Jacob.") After Jacob's fourteen years had expired he was induced by Laban to remain six years longer, and, by a hardly honorable artifice, he increased greatly in wealth. This displeased Laban, so that a separation was deemed advisable (30:25–31:16).

Flees from Laban. Gathering together his family and property, he set out for Canaan, about 1900 B.C. On the third day Laban learned of Jacob's departure and followed after him but was warned by God not to hinder his return. After much reproach and recrimination peace was restored, and Laban returned to his home (31:17-55). Shortly after the departure of Laban, Jacob met a company of angels and called the place, in honor of them, Manhanaim ("two hosts").

News from Esau. Jacob sent messengers to Esau with a friendly greeting. They returned with word that his brother was on the way to meet him with 400 men. Greatly alarmed and distressed, he divided his people, with the flocks and herds, into two companies, so that if one was attacked the other might escape. Jacob also prepared a present

644

for Esau, sending it ahead; hoping thus to pacify his brother (32:1-23).

Wrestling. Then came a night of prayer, during which the angel of the Lord wrestled with him. In attestation of his power with God, through faith, his name was changed from Jacob to Israel ("wrestler with God"). His request, that he might know the name of the person with whom he wrestled, was denied him, but Jacob named the place Peniel, "the face of God" (32:24-30).

Reconciled to Esau. In the morning Jacob saw Esau approaching with his army and sent forward first his women servants, then Leah and her children, and last Rachel and Joseph. Esau's bitter feelings gave way at the sight of his brother, his liberal gifts, and earnest entreaties. They embraced as brothers, and, for all we know, maintained friendly relations for the rest of their lives. Jacob remained for a while on the other side of Jordan, at Succoth. He then came to Shechem, camped there, and, purchasing a plot of ground, "erected there an altar, and called it El-Elohe-Is-

Jacob's Well

rael," i.e., "Mighty one, God of Israel" (33:1-20). Here is located "Jacob's well" (John 4:6).

Goes to Bethel. Having been brought into collision with the people of Shechem because of the violation of Dinah and the revenge taken by her brothers, Jacob was commanded to go and dwell in Bethel. He took the strange gods found in his family and buried them "under the oak which was near Shechem." There God appeared to Jacob again and blessed him, renewing the Abrahamic covenant (Gen. 34:1–35:15).

Bereavement. While journeying from Bethel to Ephrath his beloved wife Rachel died giving birth to her second son, Benjamin (35:20). Not long after that Jacob lost his beloved son Joseph, who was sold by his brothers to Midianite traders (chap. 37).

Egypt. With the great famine predicted by Joseph being felt in Canaan, Jacob sent his sons down into Egypt to purchase grain. He retained Benjamin, his youngest son, afraid that harm might come to him. His sons returned with a good supply of food and told him that they had been taken for spies and could only disprove the charge by carrying Benjamin to the "lord of the land." Jacob's credulity was greatly tested when his sons came home the second time with the news that "Joseph is still alive." Convinced, however, of the truth of their story, he decided to go and see him before he died. On his way he was encouraged by a vision at Beersheba. He came to Egypt and was affectionately received by Joseph (chaps. 42-46), about 1871 B.C. Joseph presented his father to Pharaoh, and he and his family located in Goshen (42:1–47:1-12). This pharaoh was doubtless one of the powerful rulers of the splendid Twelfth Dynasty (2000-1780 B.C.).

Death. After living seventeen years in Egypt "the time for Israel to die drew near," and, calling Joseph to him, Jacob acquainted him with the divine promise of the land of Canaan and took from him a pledge that he would bury him with his fathers. He then adopted Joseph's sons, Ephraim and Manasseh, as his own and pronounced his benediction upon his sons. And when Jacob had finished blessing his sons, he "drew his feet into the bed and breathed his last" (49:33), dying at the ripe age of 147 (47:27–49:33) about 1854 B.C. His body was embalmed, carried with great care and pomp into

Table 19 The Children of Jacob			
By Leah	By Rachel	By Bilhah	By Zilpah
(1) Reuben	(12) Joseph	(5) Dan	(7) Gad
(2) Simeon	(13) Benjamin	(6) Naphtali	(8) Asher
(3) Levi			
(4) Judah			
(9) Issachar			
(10) Zebulun			
(11) Dinah			

the land of Canaan, and deposited with his fathers and his wife Leah in the cave of the field of Machpelah (50:1-13). His descendants were led out from Egypt by Moses and entered Canaan under the leadership of Joshua. The twelve tribes of which the nation was composed were named after his sons, with the exception that Joseph was represented by his sons Ephraim and Manasseh. The list of Jacob's descendants (46:8-27) was probably made up at the time of his death, as we find mentioned sons of Benjamin, who was a mere youth when he went to Egypt.

Scripture References. "Hosea, in the latter days of the kingdom, seeks (12:3-4, 12) to convert the descendants of Jacob from their state of alienation from God, by recalling to their memory the repeated acts of God's favor shown to their ancestor. And Malachi (1:2) strengthens the desponding hearts of the returned exiles by assuring them that the love which God bestowed upon Jacob was not withheld from them. Besides the frequent mention of his name in conjunction with those of the other two patriarchs, there are distinct references to events in the life of Jacob in four books of the history of Jacob's birth to prove that the favor of God is independent of the order of natural descent. In Heb. 12:16, and 11:21, the transfer of the birthright and Jacob's dying benediction are referred to. His vision at Beth-el and his possession of land at Shechem are cited in John 1:51, and 4:5, 12. And Stephen in his speech (Acts 7:12, 16) mentions the famine which was the means of restoring Jacob to his lost son in Egypt, and the burial of the patriarch in Shechem" (Smith, *Bib. Dict.*).

Character. Jacob appears to have inherited the gentle, quiet, and retiring character of his father along with a selfishness and a prudence that approached cunning. These showed themselves in his reprehensible deception of his father, his dealings with Esau, and the means that he employed to make his bargain with his uncle (Laban) work to his own enrichment. We must remember, however, that he was accustomed to caution and restraint in the presence of a more vigorous brother, that he was secretly stimulated by a belief that God designed for him some superior blessing, that he was compelled to leave home to preserve his life, and that he was obliged to cope with an avaricious and crafty uncle. But "God revived the promise over which he had brooded for sixty years, since he learned it in childhood from his mother. Angels conversed with him. Gradually he felt more and more the watchful care of an ever-present spiritual Father. Face to face he wrestled with the representative of the Almighty. And so, even though the moral consequences of his early transgressions hung about him, and saddened him with a deep knowledge of all the evil of treachery, and domestic envy, and partial judgment, and filial disobedience, yet the increasing revelations of God en-

lightened the old age of the patriarch; and at last the timid 'supplanter,' the man of subtle devices, waiting for the salvation of Jehovah dies, the 'soldier of God,' uttering the messages of God to his remote posterity" (Smith, *Bib. Dict.*).

Figurative. The "God of Jacob" (Ex. 3:6; 4:5; 2 Sam. 23:1; Ps. 20:1; Isa. 2:3); simply "Jacob" (Ps. 24:6) where the term *'ĕlōhê,* God, appears to have been dropped from the text, and "Mighty One of Jacob" (132:2), are titles of Jehovah as the national deity. For the house or family of Jacob, i.e., the Israelites, we have the "house of Jacob" (Ex. 19:3; Isa. 2:5-6; 8:17; etc.), "offspring of Jacob" (Isa. 45:19), "descendants of Jacob" (Jer. 33:26), "sons of Jacob" (1 Kings 18:31; Mal. 3:6), "assembly of Jacob" (Deut. 33:4), and simply "Jacob" (Num. 23:7, 10, 23; 24:5, 17, 19; etc.), and the expression "in Jacob" (Gen. 49:7; Lam. 2:3), i.e., among the Jewish people.

Archaeological Light. The Nuzi Letters, excavated 1925-41 on the ancient site of Nuzi, SE of Nineveh, shed great light on the patriarchs, particularly Jacob. One of the tablets parallels to some extent the relationship between Jacob and Laban (Gen. 29-31). Although the element of adoption, which is present in the Nuzi document, is absent in the biblical story, in the case from Nuzi a man adopts another as his son, giving him his daughter for a wife and making him and his children heirs, unless the adopter should later have a son of his own. In the Nuzi account, the adopted son was to receive an equal share of the estate with the actual son. However, the son's children would in this instance forfeit any right (C. H. Gordon, *Biblical Archaeologist* 3 [Feb. 1940]: 2f.). It is also specified that the adopted son would not be entitled to take another wife in addition to the daughter of his adopted father.

Esau's selling of his birthright to Jacob (Gen. 25:27-34) is also illustrated by the rites of primogeniture at Nuzi. There a legal arrangement existed whereby the privileges of the first-born could be transferred to another. In one case they were transferred to one who was not actually a brother but was adopted as a brother. In another case, actual brothers were involved, as Esau and Jacob, and the one who surrendered his rights received three sheep in return, to some extent at least comparable to the meal that Esau got.

The household gods that Rachel stole from Laban (Gen. 31:34) are also illustrated from the Nuzi information. These implied leadership of the family and, in the case of a married daughter, ensured her husband the right of the property of her father (Gordon, *Revue Biblique* 44 [1935]: 35f.). Since Laban evidently had sons of his own when Jacob left him, they alone had the right to their father's gods, and the theft of these household idols by Rachel was a serious offense (31:19, 30, 35) aimed at preserving for her husband, Jacob, the chief title to Laban's estate (cf. Jack

Finegan, *Light from the Ancient Past* [1946], p. 55). It is also interesting to note that Jacob, which stands evidently for *Ya'qub-'el*, "May El protect," occurs in tablets of the eighteenth century B.C. from Chagar Bazar in N Mesopotamia (C. J. Gadd, *Iraq* [1949], p. 38, n. 5). The name *Jacob* likewise occurs as a Palestinian place-name in Thutmose III's list of the fifteenth century B.C. Subsequent scholarship has questioned the nature and importance of the teraphim ("household gods").   M.F.U.; R.K.H.

BIBLIOGRAPHY: G. Rawlinson, *Isaac and Jacob: Their Lives and Times* (1890); F. B. Meyer, *Israel: A Prince with God* (1909); W. H. Thomson, *Life and Times of the Patriarchs* (1912), pp. 179-250; W. H. G. Thomas, *Genesis: A Devotional Commentary* (1946), pp. 223-495; A. R. Millard, *Archaeology and the Life of Jacob* (1962); J. M. Holt, *The Patriarchs of Israel* (1964); I. Hunt, *The World of the Patriarchs* (1966); J. J. Davis, *Paradise to Prison* (1975), pp. 241-60, 287-304; R. S. Candlish, *Studies in Genesis* (1979), pp. 435-817; F. J. Delitzsch, *A New Commentary on Genesis* (1979), 2:132-403; W. G. Blaikie, *Heroes of Israel* (1981), pp. 204-26, 266-80; G. Ch. Aalders, *Genesis*, Bible Students' Commentary (1981), 2:76-294.

JACOB'S WELL. See Jacob.

JA'DA (ja'da; "knowing"). The last named of the two sons of Onam, a descendant of Judah through Jerahmeel; his two sons are likewise mentioned (1 Chron. 2:28, 32).

JA'DAH (ja-da). The NIV reading for *Jarah* (which see).

JA'DAI (ja'dī; "knowing"). One of the sons of Nebo who divorced his Gentile wife after the Exile (Ezra 10:43).

JA'DDAI (ja'dī). See Jadai.

JADDU'A (ja-dū'a; "knowing").
1. One of the leaders of the people who signed the covenant made by Nehemiah (Neh. 10:21), 445 B.C.
2. The son of Jonathan (Neh. 12:11) and the last high priest mentioned in the OT (v. 22). This is all that we learn of him from Scripture, but we gather that he was a priest in the reign of the last Persian king, Darius Codommanus, and that he was still priest after the Persian dynasty was overthrown, i.e., in the reign of Alexander the Great. Josephus (*Ant.* 11.8.3-6) makes Jaddua high priest when Alexander invaded Judea, but the balance of his story does not deserve credit.

JA'DON (ja'don; "judge"). A Meronothite who assisted in reconstructing the walls of Jerusalem after the return from Babylon (Neh. 3:7), 445 B.C.

JA'EL (jā'el; "ibex, wild goat"). The wife of Heber the Kenite and slayer of Sisera. Sisera took refuge, after the defeat of the Canaanites by Barak, in the tent of Jael, there being peace between the house of Heber and Jabin, king of Hazor. He probably would not have so openly violated all ideas of oriental propriety by entering a woman's apartments but for Jael's earnest invitation. She covered him with a rug and gave him milk to drink. Fearing discovery by his pursuers, he exacted a promise from her to preserve the secret of his concealment and fell into a heavy sleep. Jael took one of the great wooden pegs that fastened down the cords of the tent and "drove the peg into his temple. . . . So he died." Barak, coming up in his pursuit of Sisera, was met by Jael, who showed him the deed she had performed (Judg. 4:17-22), about 1195 B.C.

BIBLIOGRAPHY: C. E. Macartney, *The Way of a Man with a Maid* (1931), pp. 141-52; id., *Ancient Wives and Modern Husbands* (1934), pp. 105-22.

JA'GUR (ja'ger). A town of southern Judea on the border of Edom, mentioned (Josh. 15:21) as part of the portion of Judah. Probably Tell Gur, ten miles E of Beersheba.

JAH. See Yah.

JA'HATH (ja'hath).
1. Son of Reaiah (or Haroeh), of the posterity of Hezron, and father of two sons, Ahumai and Lahad (1 Chron. 4:2).
2. A son of Shimei, grandson of Gershom, and great-grandson of Levi (1 Chron. 23:10). Considerable confusion occurs respecting *Shimei* (which see) and his sons. In v. 9 the three sons of Shimei are by some error (probably the transposition of the latter clause) attributed to his brother Laadan, whereas in v. 11 Jahath is stated to have been "first" (i.e., most numerous in posterity) of the *four* sons of Shimei. A similar disagreement appears in the parallel passage (1 Chron. 6) where Jahath (v. 43) occurs as the son of Gershom, and again (v. 20) as a son of Libni (i.e., Laadan), instead of Shimei.
3. One of the sons of Shelomoth, an Izharite of the family of Kohath appointed by David o a prominent place in the sacred services (1 Chron. 24:22), about 960 B.C.
4. A Merarite Levite, and one of the overseers of the Temple repairs carried on by King Josiah (2 Chron. 34:12), 639 B.C.

JA'HAZ (ja'haz). A town in the tribe of Reuben, mentioned in connection with Moab (Josh. 13:18; 21:36; Isa. 15:4). It was called Jahzah in 1 Chron. 6:78. Sihon the Amorite was defeated here (Num. 21:23-24; Deut. 2:32-34). On the Moabite stone, lines 19 and 20, the name is spelled like the shorter Heb. form and the place is given as a fortress, seemingly near Dibon, although its exact location is not known. In the KJV it was also called *Jahaza* (Josh. 13:18) and *Jahazah* (21:36; 48:21).

JA'HAZA, JAHA'ZAH. See Jahaz.

JAHAZI'AH. See Jahze'iah.

JAHA'ZIEL (ja-haz'i-el; "God sees").
1. One of the Benjamite warriors who deserted

Saul and came to David when he was at Ziklag (1 Chron. 12:4), shortly before 1000 B.C.

2. One of the priests in the reign of David, appointed with Benaiah to blow the trumpet before the Ark when it was brought to Jerusalem (1 Chron. 16:6), about 986 B.C.

3. The third "son" of Hebron, the grandson of Levi through Kohath (1 Chron. 23:19; 24:23).

4. Son of Zechariah, a Levite of the family of Asaph who was inspired by Jehovah to prophesy to Jehoshaphat his victory over the Moabites and others who were invading the country (2 Chron. 20:14-18), about 875 B.C.

5. The father of a son who was head of "the sons of Shecaniah," and returned with Ezra from Babylon with 300 males (Ezra 8:5), 457 B.C.

JAH'DAI (ja'dī). A descendant, apparently of Caleb, of the family of Hezron; his sons' names are given, but his own parentage is not stated (1 Chron. 2:47).

JAH'DIEL (ja'di-el). One of the heroes of the tribe of Manasseh E of Jordan (1 Chron. 5:24).

JAH'DO (ja'dō). A Gadite, son of Buz and father of Jeshishai, of the descendants of Abihail, resident in Gilead (1 Chron. 5:14), before 771 B.C.

JAH'LEEL (ja'lîl. The last named of the three sons of Zebulun (Gen. 46:14; Num. 26:26). His descendants are called Jahleelites (26:26), before 1640 B.C.

JAH'LEELITES (ja'lîl-its). The descendants of *Jahleel* (which see).

JAH'MAI (ja'mī). One of the "sons" of Tola, grandson of Issachar (1 Chron. 7:2).

JAH'ZAH (1 Chron. 6:78; Jer. 48:21). *See* Jahaz.

JAH'ZEEL (ja'ze-el; "allotted by God"). The first named of the sons of Naphtali (Gen. 46:24). His descendants are called Jahzeelites (Num. 26:48). In 1 Chron. 7:13 and Gen. 46:24 (NIV) the name is written *Jahziel* (which see).

JAH'ZEELITES (ja'zîl-īts; Num. 26:48). The descendants of *Jahzeel* (which see).

JAHZE'IAH (ja'ze-ī-a). Son of Tikvah, apparently a priest who, along with Jonathan the son of Asahel, opposed the proposal that the Jews who had married foreign wives during the Exile appear before the assembly in order to appease "the fierce anger of our God" (Ezra 10:14-15), 457 B.C.

JAH'ZERAH (ja'ze-ra). The son of Meshullum and father of Adiel, a priest (1 Chron. 9:12), long before 536 B.C. He is probably the same as Azarel (Neh. 11:13).

JAH'ZIEL (ja'ze-el; 1 Chron. 7:13; Gen. 46:24 [NIV]). *See* Jahzeel.

JAILER (Gk. *desmophulax*, Acts 16:23). A *keeper of a prison* (which see).

JA'IR (jā'ir; "he enlightens").

1. The son of Segub, who was descended from Judah on his father's side (1 Chron. 2:22) and from Manasseh on his mother's side. Moses reckons Jair as belonging to Manasseh (Num. 32:41; Deut. 3:14; *see also* 1 Kings 4:13), probably because of his exploits and possessions in Gilead (1 Chron. 2:23). He settled in the part of Argob bordering on Gilead, where we find the small towns taken (retaken) by him named collectively Havvoth-jair, or "the towns of Jair" (Num. 32:41; Deut. 3:14; 1 Kings 4:13; 1 Chron. 2:22). They are said to have numbered *twenty-three* (1 Chron. 2:22), *thirty* (Judg. 10:4), and *sixty* (Josh. 13:30; 1 Kings 4:13; 1 Chron. 2:23). Perhaps the entire sixty were captured by Jair and his relatives, and twenty-three of them were assigned to him, others being added afterward (McClintock and Strong, *Cyclopedia*).

2. The eighth judge of Israel, a Gileadite in Manasseh (Josephus *Ant.* 5.7.6) and probably a descendant of the preceding. He ruled twenty-two years, and his opulence is thus recorded: "And he had thirty sons who rode on thirty donkeys, and they had thirty cities in the land of Gilead that are called Havvoth-jair to this day." The twenty-three villages of the more ancient Jair were probably among the thirty that this Jair possessed. He was buried in Kamon, probably in the same region (Judg. 10:3-5).

3. The father of Elhanan, who killed Lahmi, the brother of Goliath (1 Chron. 20:5), before 1018 B.C. In the parallel passage (2 Sam. 21:19) we find Jaare-oregim.

4. A Benjamite, son of Shimei and father of Mordecai, Esther's uncle (Esther 2:5), before 518 B.C.

JA'IRITE, THE (jā'ir-īt; 2 Sam. 20:26). *See* Ira.

JA'IRUS (ja'i-rus). A ruler of a synagogue, probably at Capernaum, whose only daughter Jesus restored to life (Mark 5:22-23, 35-42; Luke 8:41-42, 49-55; cf. Matt. 9:18), A.D. 27. Some have wrongfully inferred from our Savior's words "The child has not died, but is asleep," that the girl was only in a swoon (H. Olshausen, *Biblical Commentary on the Gospels and on the Acts of the Apostles* 1:321; Neander, *Leben Jesu*, p. 347; McClintock and Strong, *Cyclopedia*).

BIBLIOGRAPHY: G. C. Morgan, *The Great Physician* (1963), pp. 165-72.

JA'KAN. *See* Jaaken.

JA'KEH (ja'ke; "pious," cf. Arab. *waka*, "preserve, be pious"). The father of Agur, whose sayings are given in Prov. 30. Beyond the mention in v. 1 we have no clue as to the existence of either person. There is great difference of opinion as to the person intended. The traditional view gives the word a figurative import (*yᵉqāhâ*, "obedience") and applies it to David. Others understand a real name of some unknown Israelite to be intended, which seems most likely.

JA'KIM (ja'kim; "God sets up").

1. One of the "sons" of Shimei, a Benjamite living in Jerusalem (1 Chron. 8:19).

2. Head of the twelfth division of priests as arranged by David (1 Chron. 24:12), about 970 B.C.

JAKIN. *See* Jachin.

JA'LAM (ja'lam). The second named of Esau's three sons by Oholibamah (Aholibamah, KJV) in Canaan (Gen. 36:5, 14; 1 Chron. 1:35; "Jaalam," KJV).

JA'LON (ja'lon). The last named of the four sons of Ezrah, of the tribe of Judah and, apparently, of a family related to that of Caleb (1 Chron. 4:17).

JAM'BRES (jam'brez). A person mentioned by Paul as opposing Moses (2 Tim. 3:8). *See* Jannes.

JAMES (jāmz), more correctly **Jacobus** (jà-kō'bŭs; Gk. *Iakōbos*—Jacob).

1. The son of Zebedee (Matt. 4:21; Mark 1:19; Luke 5:10) and Salome (cf. Matt. 27:56; Mark 15:40; 16:1), and the elder brother of John the evangelist (Mark 5:37).

James appears first in the sacred narrative as a fisherman, he and his brothers being partners with Simon Peter (Luke 5:10). When called by our Lord to be His followers in the spring or summer (A.D. 27), James and his brother responded with an eagerness that renders them models of obedience (Matt. 4:21-22; Mark 1:19-20). We find him named among the twelve who received (A.D. 28) a call to apostleship (Matt. 10:2; Mark 3:14, 17; Luke 6:13-14; Acts 1:13). These brothers and Peter seemed for some reason to be especially fitted to live in close intimacy with the Master and were with Him on several interesting occasions. They alone were present at the transfiguration (Matt. 17:1; Mark 9:2; Luke 9:28), at the raising of Jairus's daughter (Mark 5:37; Luke 8:51), and at the Garden of Gethsemane during our Lord's agony (Matt. 26:37; Mark 14:33). With Andrew they listened to the Lord's private discourse on the fall of Jerusalem (13:3). Through mistaken views of the Messiah's kingdom and an ambition to share in its glory, they joined in the request made to Jesus by their mother (Matt. 20:20-23; Mark 10:35-40). James was the first of the apostles to suffer martyrdom, being slain with a sword at the command of Herod (Acts 12:2), A.D. 44.

From the desire to punish the inhabitants of a certain village in Samaria because they declined to receive Jesus (Luke 9:52-54), we infer that James and John were warm and impetuous in temperament. They were called by our Lord (Mark 3:17) "Boanerges"—*sons of thunder*—probably because of their boldness and energy in discharging their apostleship.

2. James the Less (another of the twelve apostles.) He was the son of Alphaeus (Matt. 10:3; Mark 3:18; Luke 6:15; Acts 1:13) and Mary, the sister of our Lord's mother (Matt. 27:56; Mark 15:40; Luke 24:10; John 19:25), and was called James the Less (*hō mikros*, "the little"), either because he was younger than James the son of Zebedee or on account of his short stature (Mark 15:40; *see* marg.). His mother is supposed by some to have been called sister, i.e., sister-in-law, of Mary the mother of Jesus, because of their marriage to two brothers, Clopas and Joseph (*see* John 19:25; Clopas, or Cleopas, KJV, is believed by scholars to be the same person as Alphaeus). It has also been supposed that Alphaeus died without offspring and that his wife was espoused by Joseph, on which account James is perhaps the legal son of Alphaeus and the reputed half brother of our Lord. James had a brother, Joses or Joseph (Matt. 27:56). In KJV Luke 6:16 mentions "Judas the brother of James," whereas NASB and NIV render "the son of James."

3. The brother of the Lord. The natural interpretation of the passages Matt. 13:55; Mark 6:3 indicates that James and his brothers and sisters were sons and daughters of Joseph and Mary, the mother of Jesus. He was not one of the twelve apostles (Matt. 10:2-4), or at first a believer in Jesus (John 7:5). From Acts 1:13-14 we conclude that his former skepticism had passed away, as it is stated there that "His brothers" continued with the apostles and others in the "upper room" after the ascension. Although he was not one of the twelve, he was included among those who saw a vision of the risen Lord (1 Cor. 15:5, 7). Like Paul and Barnabas, he received the title of apostle (Gal. 1:19) and was recognized by the zealots of the law as their leader (2:12). He occupied a prominent, if not the chief, place in the church at Jerusalem (v. 9), was president of the first council (Acts 15:13), and, with the elders, received Paul upon his return from his third missionary tour (21:18), A.D. 57. He was the author of the epistle that bears his name. Eusebius tells us that James was surnamed "the Just" by the ancients on account of his eminent virtue.

BIBLIOGRAPHY: W. Barclay, *The Master's Men* (1959), pp. 82-86, 100-104; J. B. Lightfoot, *The Epistle of Paul to the Galatians* (1966), pp. 19, 95, 100ff.; C. J. Barber, *God Has the Answer* . . . (1974), pp. 61-71; J. D. Jones, *The Apostles of Christ* (1982), pp. 46-68.

JAMES, EPISTLE OF. The chief of the five epistles called "catholic" or "general" in their titles (James, 1 and 2 Peter, 1 John, and Jude). These epistles were addressed not to individual churches, as were most of the Pauline epistles, but to Christians in general.

Nature and Purpose. The book is a homily written to the twelve tribes "who are dispersed abroad," that is, to Jewish Christians of the Dispersion. The author's aim was to rally Christians from their worldliness to the practical privileges of their profession. The epistle has been called the most Jewish book in the NT. Some would even go so far as to ascribe it to a non-Christian Jew and maintain that it was later adapted to Christian use by two or three phrases containing the name of Christ (1:1; 2:1). However, the Christianity of the epistle is seen not so much in its subject matter as in its spirit. It is an interpretation of the OT law and the Sermon on the Mount in the light of the Christian gospel. The author shows acquaintanceship with the books of the Apocrypha and was evidently especially influenced by two, Ecclesiasticus and the Wisdom of Solomon.

Attestation. Not until toward the end of the fourth century (the Third Council of Carthage, A.D. 397) did the epistle of James become generally recognized as canonical. Eusebius classed it among the antilegomena, yet quotes 4:11 as Scripture. It is omitted in the Muratorian canon, yet the epistle was more widely known in the first three centuries than has been supposed. The Old Syriac Version included it. Hermas evidently used it. James is frequently referred to in the Testaments of the Twelve Patriarchs. Ignatius evidently knew it, as well as Polycarp, but none of these shows certain dependence upon James. However, Origen, Cyril of Jerusalem, Athanasius, Jerome, and Augustine recognized the epistle as Scripture. The internal evidence is stronger than the external. The epistle thoroughly harmonizes with what we know of this James from Josephus (*Ant.* 20.9.1) and the book of Acts (15:13-21; 21:17-25) and from Galatians (1:19; 2:9-10), as well as with the well-known circumstances of Jewish Christians in the Dispersion. The supposed opposition to Paul is purely imaginary. Properly interpreted, the opposition disappears. In the absence of doctrinal content, if there had been a forger, he would most assuredly have chosen the name of some well-known apostle and not the more or less obscure name of James, the Lord's brother.

Authorship. *See* James, no. 3.

Destination. James evidently intended his epistle for the large number of Christian Jews scattered throughout the Roman Empire. He may have slanted it with particular reference to the eastern Dispersion, since Peter addresses the Diaspora in Asia Minor where the epistle of James, it is conjectured, would be less likely known. The book of Acts records that there were Jews in almost every city where Christianity was planted, as at Jerusalem on the Day of Pentecost (Acts 2:9-11). Many of these were converted to Christianity and carried the message back home with them. It was to these Jewish believers that James addressed his letter.

The Date. The epistle of James may be presumed to be very early, possibly the first epistle to Christians. This is indicated by the early mar-

tyrdom of James, according to tradition in the year A.D. 62. Much more substantial reasons, however, are adduced from the internal evidence. The epistle shows no trace of the distinctive references concerning the new age, the outcalling of the church, the features of grace, or of the relationship of Gentile converts to the law of Moses, which resulted in the Jerusalem Council of Acts 15, over which James presided. The general absence of doctrine in the epistle, its Palestinian atmosphere, and its OT flavor combine to substantiate this view. The epistle shows no evidence of the fall of Jerusalem.

The Plan. The apostle undertakes to deal with the needs of his fellow Christian believers in the Dispersion. After a brief greeting (1:1) he (1) exhorts his readers to take the proper attitude toward testings and trials (1:2-18); and (2) warns them to react properly toward the Word of God (1:19-27); (3) he rebukes a demonstration of carnal partiality (2:1-13); (4) he expounds the uselessness of faith apart from works (2:14-26); (5) he speaks strongly against the sin of an uncontrolled tongue (3:1-12); (6) he expounds true and false wisdom (3:13-18); (7) he advises them against quarrelsomeness, worldliness, and pride (4:1-10); (8) he emphasizes brotherly consideration (4:11-12); (9) he criticizes the spirit of their business activity (4:13–5:6); (10) he calls them to patient endurance of life's misfortunes (5:7-12); (11) he shows them what to do when afflicted (5:13-18); and (12) he stresses the need for restoring a person who has gone astray (5:19-20).

Outline. James deals with the mature believer (3:2).

I. Salutation (1:1)
II. The mature believer's reaction toward trials (1:2-18)
III. His reception of the Word (1:19-27)
IV. His treatment of others (2:1-13)
V. His genuine faith (2:14-26)
VI. His control of the tongue (3:1-12)
VII. His attitude toward true wisdom (3:13-18)
VIII. His amiableness, spirituality, humility (4:1-10)
IX. His concern for his fellows (4:11-12)
X. His discretion in business (4:13–5:6)
XI. His patient endurance (5:7-12)
XII. His conduct when afflicted (5:13-18)
XIII. His concern for a straying brother (5:19-20)   M.F.U.

BIBLIOGRAPHY: C. L. Mitton, *The Epistle of James* (1966); S. Zodhiates, *The Behavior of Belief* (1970); J. B. Adamson, *The Epistle of James,* New International Commentary on the New Testament (1976); J. B. Mayor, *The Epistle of St. James* (1977); R. Johnstone, *Lectures Exegetical and Practical on the Epistle of James* (1978); D. E. Hiebert, *The Epistle of James* (1979); P. H. Davids, *The Epistle of James,* New International Greek Testament Commentary (1982); E. R. Stier, *Commentary on James* (1982).

JA'MIN (ja'min; "right hand").

1. The second son of Simeon (Gen. 46:10; Ex. 6:15; 1 Chron. 4:24), about 1871 B.C. He was founder of the family of the Jaminites (Num. 26:12).

2. The second son of Ram, the fourth in descent from Judah (1 Chron. 2:27).

3. One of the priests who expounded the law to the people when read by Ezra (Neh. 8:7), about 445 B.C.

JA'MINITES, THE (jā'min-īts). The descendants of Jamin, the son of Simeon (Num. 26:12).

JAM'LECH (jam'lek; "whom *God* makes king"). A leader of the tribe of Simeon, apparently one of those whose family invaded the valley of Gedor in the time of Hezekiah (1 Chron. 4:34), about 715 B.C.

JA'NAI (ja'nī). One of the chief Gadites living in Bashan (1 Chron. 5:12; the name is given as *Jaanai* in the KJV).

JANGLING. A KJV expression replaced in the NASB by "fruitless discussion" and in the NIV by "meaningless talk" (1 Tim. 1:6); the phrase "empty talkers" (Titus 1:10, NASB) comes from a similar Gk. word.

JA'NIM (ja'nim). NIV for *Janum* (which see).

JAN'NAI (jan'ī; "Janna," KJV). The son of Joseph and father of Melchi, the sixth in ascent from Christ on His mother's side (Luke 3:24), about 200 B.C.

JAN'NES (jan'ez). Jannes and Jambres are two of the Egyptian magicians who attempted by their enchantments to counteract the influence on Pharaoh's mind of the miracles wrought by Moses (2 Tim. 3:8; cf. Ex. 7-8).

JANO'AH, JANO'HAH (ja-nō'a; "quiet"). Jano'hah (ja-nō'ha; Heb. same as Janoah).

1. A place apparently in the N of Galilee, or the "land of Naphtali," one of those taken by Tiglath-pileser in his first incursion into Palestine (2 Kings 15:29).

2. A place on the boundary of Ephraim (Josh. 16:6-7; "Janohah," KJV). Eusebius gives it as twelve miles E of Neapolis. A little less than that distance from Nablus, and about SE in direction, two miles from Akrabeh, is the village of Yanûn, seven miles SE of Shechem, doubtless the ancient Janoah, but now a small village with extensive ruins of antiquity.

JA'NUM (ja'num; "asleep"). A town of Judah in the mountain district, apparently not far from Hebron (Josh. 15:53), possibly Beni Na'im, four miles E of Hebron.

JA'PHETH (jā'feth; "widespreading"). One of the three sons of Noah (Gen. 5:32; 6:10; 7:13; 9:18; 10:1; 1 Chron. 1:4-5). Although he is mentioned last in these passages, we learn from Gen. 10:21 (cf. 9:24) that he was the eldest of the

three. He and his wife were among those who entered the Ark (Gen. 7:7; 1 Pet. 3:20). He had seven sons (Gen. 10:2; 1 Chron. 1:5), and his descendants occupied the "coastlands of the nations" (Gen. 10:5), i.e., of the Mediterranean Sea in Europe and Asia Minor. His act of filial piety when with Shem he covered his father's nakedness is recorded in 9:20-27.

JAPHI'A (ja-fī'a; "may he [i.e., God] cause to be bright").

1. The king of Lachish who, with three other kings, joined Adoni-zedek, king of Jerusalem, against Joshua, but was defeated and slain after hiding in the cave of Makkedah (Josh. 10:3-27), about 1395 B.C.

2. One of the sons of David, born to him at Jerusalem by one of his wives, whose name is not given (2 Sam. 5:15; 1 Chron. 3:7; 14:6), after 1000 B.C.

3. A town on the eastern part of the southern boundary of Zebulun, situated on the high ground between Daberath and Gath-hepher (Josh. 19:12). Robinson (*Researches,* 3:194) identifies it with modern Yafa, about 1½ miles SW of Nazareth. This undoubtedly is the correct site.

JAPH'LET (jaf'let; "he [i.e., God] will rescue"). A son of Heber and great-grandson of Asher, and father of three sons and a daughter (1 Chron. 7:32-33). Some think it to have been a branch of his descendants (Japhletites) that are mentioned in Josh. 16:3 as having settled along the border between Ephraim and Dan, but that is improbable.

JAPH'LETITES (jaf'le-tīts). Their territory is mentioned (Josh. 16:3) as one of the landmarks on the S boundary of Ephraim. Although some consider the name to be representative of the descendants of *Japhlet* (which see), Smith (*Bib. Dict.*) believes that the name perhaps preserves the memory of some ancient tribe who at a remote time dwelt on these hills.

JA'PHO. *See* Joppa.

JAR. A general description of vessels made of fired clay, although applied infrequently to mineral, stone, or metal containers. Several Heb. terms are translated by "jar" in the NASB and NIV, probably indicating several different sizes and shapes of containers.

The *kad* (Gen. 24:14-18, 20, 43-46) was a small water jug that could also be used for storing flour (1 Kings 17:12). A larger container of the same variety was the *nēbel* (Jer. 13:12; Lam. 4:2), which probably stood about two feet in height and had a capacity of about five gallons. It was probably twice the size of the *kad* and could be closed with some form of stopper. The *baqbūq* (1 Kings 4:3; Jer. 19:1, 10) may have been a type of decanter that produced a gurgling noise when being emptied. The *'āsûk* (2 Kings 4:2), mentioned only once in the Heb. Bible, was apparently a storage jar for oil with a special spout for filling small vessels such as lamps. Another rare word, *şinşenet* (Ex. 16:33), described a container for manna.

The term *şappaḥat* probably denoted two vessels of quite different sorts. In 1 Sam. 26:11-16, the reference is to a water canteen, whereas in 1 Kings 17:12 a small jug seems to be indicated. Of uncertain shape and size are the *keli* of 1 Kings 17:10; Jer. 32:14 and the *merqāḥâ* of Job 41:31. The latter has been interpreted as a container for ointment (so KJV, NASB, RSV, NIV). The rare term *'eşeb* (Jer. 22:28) has been rendered "jar" or "vessel" by some translators, and "idol" by others.

Şelōḥît, another rare word, probably describes a flat cooking pan (*see* Cruse).

In the NT the Gk. term *hudria* described a water jar that could be either large (John 2:6) or small (4:28). The *keramion* was evidently a portable water jar, whereas the *alabastron* (Matt. 26:7) was a small alabaster jug containing expensive perfume.   R.K.H.

BIBLIOGRAPHY: R. Amiran, *Ancient Pottery of the Holy Land* (1970).

JA'RAH (ja'ra; "honey"; 1 Chron. 9:42). *See* Jehoadah and Jadah.

JA'REB (ja'reb; "he will contend; contentious"). Occurs as a proper name in Hos. 5:13; 10:6, where a "King Jareb" is spoken of as the false refuge and final subjugator of the kingdom of Israel. It is a figurative title for the king of Assyria. The NIV renders the word *yārēb* (Jareb) as "great king."

JA'RED (ja'red; perhaps "descent"). A pre-Flood patriarch, the fifth from Adam. He was the son of Mahalalel and father of Enoch (Gen. 5:15-20; 1 Chron. 1:2; Luke 3:37).

JARESI'AH. *See* Jaareshiah.

JAR'HA (jar'ha). The Egyptian slave of Sheshan, a descendant of Jerahmeel. He was married to the daughter of his master, and, in consequence, obtained his freedom. Because Sheshan had no sons, his descendants were traced through this connection (1 Chron. 2:34-41).

JA'RIB (ja'rib; "he will contend, contender").
1. A son of Simeon (1 Chron. 4:24), given in Gen. 46:10 as *Jachin* (which see) or Jakin (NIV).
2. One of the leading men sent by Ezra to secure a priest "for the house of our God" on the return from Jerusalem (Ezra 8:16-17), about 457 B.C.
3. A priest of the "sons" of Jeshua, who divorced his Gentile wife after the captivity (Ezra 10:18), 456 B.C.

JAR'MUTH (jar'muth; "elevation, height").

1. A town in the low country of Judah (Josh. 15:35), and the seat of the Canaanite king Pirim. He was one of the five who conspired to punish Gibeon for having made an alliance with Israel (10:3, 5), and who were routed at Beth-horon and put to death by Joshua at Makkedah (v. 23). It is identified with the modern Yarmuk (about eight miles NE of Beit Jibrin), a village with the remains of walls and cisterns of early date.
2. A Levitical (Gershonite) city in the tribe of Asher (Josh. 21:29), also called Remeth (19:21) and Ramoth (1 Chron. 6:73).

Fired clay jar from Hazor

JARO'AH (ja-rō'a; cf. Arab. *wariha,* "to be soft"). A chief man of the tribe of Gad living in Bashan (1 Chron. 5:14), before 740 B.C.

JA'SAU. *See* Jaasu.

JA'SHAR, BOOK OF. *See* Jasher, Book of.

JA'SHEN (ja'shen; "sleeping"). A person several of whose "sons" are named as among David's famous bodyguard (2 Sam. 23:32), called (1 Chron. 11:34) Hashem the Gizonite. The discrepancies between the two passages may, perhaps, best be reconciled by understanding the two brave men referred to as being Jonathan Ben-shammah (or Ben-shagee) and Ahiam Ben-sharar (or Ben-sacar), grandsons of Jashen (or Hashem) of Gizon, in the mountains of Judah—hence called Hararites, before 1000 B.C.

JA'SHER, BOOK OF (ja'sher; RV and RSV, Ja'sher, the "book of righteous"; NASB and NIV, "book of Jashar" [Josh. 10:13; 2 Sam. 1:17-18]). The book of the upright or righteous man, that is to say, of the true members of the theocracy, or godly men. From the two references given it has been justly inferred that the book was a collection of odes in praise of certain heroes of the theocracy, interwoven with historical notices of their achievements. That the passage in Joshua quoted from this work is extracted from a song is evident enough, both from the poetical form of the composition and also from the parallelism of the sentences. The reference in 2 Sam. 1:18 is to an elegy upon Saul and Jonathan in the book of Jasher. Some suppose the book of Jasher to have perished in the captivity.

BIBLIOGRAPHY: L. Goldschmidt, *The Book of Jashar* (1923).

JASHO'BEAM (ja-shō'be-am; "let the people return").

1. A Hachmonite, one of David's warriors, and the first named in the two lists given of them (2 Sam. 23:8, "Josheb-basshebeth a Tahchemonite"; "The Tachmonite," KJV; 1 Chron. 11:11, "the son of a Hachmonite"). The former passage attributes to him the defeat of 800 Philistines, the latter of 300. This is accounted for by Kennicott (*Diss.*, 1:95-96) as follows: ". . . the initial letter of the Hebrew words for *three* and *eight*, being used as an abbreviation, a mistake arose." Strong (J. McClintock and J. Strong, *Cyclopedia*, s.v.) inclines to the supposition that "Jashobeam, or Josheb-bash-shebeth (2 Sam. 23:8) was the name or title of the chief, Adino and Eznite being descriptive epithets, and Hachmonite the patronymic of the same person." The exploit of breaking through the host of the Philistines to procure water from the well of Bethlehem is ascribed to the three chief heroes, and therefore to Jashobeam, the first of the three (23:13-17), before 1000 B.C.

2. One of the Korhites who joined David at Ziklag (1 Chron. 12:6), before 1000 B.C.

3. One who commanded 24,000 and did duty in David's court in the month Nisan (1 Chron. 27:2). He was the son of Zabdiel.

JA'SHUB (ja'shub; "he returns").

1. The third son of Issachar and founder of the family of the Jashubites (Num. 26:24; 1 Chron. 7:1). He is called Iob (Gen. 46:13; "Job," KJV), perhaps by contraction, corruption, or substitution, before 1871 B.C.

2. One of the sons of Bani, a layman in the time of Ezra who had to put away his foreign wife (Ezra 10:29), 456 B.C.

JASHU'BI-LE'HEM (ja-shu'bi-le'hem; "returner of bread"). Either a person or a place named among the descendants of Shelah, the son of Judah (1 Chron. 4:22). It is probably a place, and we should infer that it lay on the western side of the tribe, in or near the Shefelah.

JA'SHUBITES, THE (ja'shu-bīts). The family founded by Jashub, the son of Issachar (Num. 26:24).

JA'SIEL. See Jaasiel.

JA'SON (jā'sun; "healing"). He was the man of Thessalonica who entertained Paul and Silas in that city. The mob, in consequence, assaulted his house and, not finding his guests, dragged Jason before the ruler, who released him on security (Acts 17:5-9). He is probably the same as the Jason mentioned in Rom. 16:21 as a kinsman of Paul, and probably accompanied him to Corinth (A.D. 54).

BIBLIOGRAPHY: N. H. Snaith, *The Jews from Cyrus to Herod* (1950), pp. 35f.; J. Bright, *History of Israel* (1961), pp. 403-5.

JASPER. See Mineral Kingdom.

JATH'NIEL (jath'ni-el; "God bestows"). The fourth son of Meshelemiah, a Korhite Levite, one of the gatekeepers of the Temple (1 Chron. 26:2), about 960 B.C.

JAT'TIR (jat'ir). A city in the mountains of Judah (Josh. 15:48), and, with its pasturelands, assigned to the priests (Josh. 24:14; 1 Chron. 6:57). David was accustomed to visiting Jattir and sent to his friends gifts taken from his enemies (1 Sam. 30:27). According to Eusebius and Jerome it was in their time a large place inhabited by Christians, twenty miles from Eleutheropolis; now known as Khirbet 'attin, thirteen miles SW of Hebron.

JA'VAN (ja'van; Heb. *yāwān;* Arab. *yunan;* "Greece, Greeks").

The fourth named of the sons of Japheth and father of Elishah, Tarshish, Kittim, and Dodanim (Gen. 10:2, 4; 1 Chron. 1:5, 7).

The name appears in Isa. 66:19 (as Greece in the NIV), where it is coupled with Tarshish, Put, Lud, Meshech, and Rosh, and more particularly with Tubal and the "distant coastlands," as representatives of the Gentile world; in Ezek. 27:13 (Greece, NIV) as being among the places where the Syrians obtained articles of trade; and in the Heb. text of Dan. 8:21; 10:20 (cf. 11:2; Zech. 9:13). The English translation of the term in Daniel and Zechariah is "Greece," and a comparison of the passages where the Heb. word occurs leaves no doubt that Javan was the name given to Greece by the Hebrews and believed to be the country settled by Javan's posterity. Javan refers more precisely to the Ionians who inhabited the coasts of Lydia and Caria and whose cities were important commercial centers two centuries before those on the Peloponnesus. Sargon II (721-705) first mentions them in Assyrian records as the result of an encounter with them in naval battle.

JAVELIN. See Armor, Arms.

JAW (Heb. usually *leḥî,* rendered "jaws," Ps. 22:15; "jaw teeth," Prov. 30:14; "teeth," Joel 1:6). The jawbone of a donkey was the weapon with which Samson performed great slaughter (Judg. 15:15). See Cheek.

JA'ZER (ja'zer; "helpful"; sometimes "Jaazer," KJV). A town E of Jordan, in or near Gilead (Num. 32:1, 3). It was taken by Israel from the Amorites (21:32), was assigned to the tribe of Gad (32:1, 3,

35), and was constituted a Levitical city (Josh. 21:39; 1 Chron. 26:31). It must have been a place of importance, as it gave its name to a district and its dependent towns (Num. 21:32). From its being mentioned as lying between Dibon and Nimrah, it would seem to have been located on the high plain of Heshbon. Jazer is mentioned in connection with the census taken under David (2 Sam. 24:5; 1 Chron. 26:31), and also in the prophecies of Isaiah (16:8-9) and Jeremiah (48:32). It has been identified with Khirbet Jazzir, about ten miles W of Amman.

JA'ZIZ (ja'ziz). A Hagrite and overseer of David's flocks (1 Chron. 27:31), which were probably pastured E of Jordan where the forefathers of Jaziz had lived for ages (cf. vv. 19-22).

JEALOUSY (Heb. *qin'â;* Gk. *zēlos*). Properly, suspicion of a wife's purity (Num. 5:14-15); often used of Jehovah's sensitive regard for the true faith of His people (Ex. 20:5; etc.; 2 Cor. 11:2); used for anger or indignation, or intense interest for the welfare of another (Ps. 79:5; Zech. 1:14; 8:2; 1 Cor. 10:22). "I, Jehovah thy God, am a jealous God, who will not transfer to another the honor that is due to himself (Isa. 42:8; 48:11), nor tolerate the worship of any other god (Ex. 34:14), but who directs the warmth of his anger against those who hate him (Deut. 6:15) with the same energy with which the warmth of his love (Song of Sol. 8:6) embraces those who love him, except that love in the form of grace reaches much farther than wrath" (K. & D., *Com.,* ad loc.). When speaking of the jealousy of God, we are to understand this language to be employed to illustrate rather than represent the emotions of the divine mind. The same causes operating upon the human mind would produce what we call anger, jealousy, repentance, grief, etc.; therefore, when these emotions are ascribed to the mind of God, this language is used because such emotions can be represented to us by no other.

BIBLIOGRAPHY: G. F. Oehler, *Theology of the Old Testament,* 2 vols. in 1 (1978), 1:165-68.

JEALOUSY, IDOL OF (Heb. *sēmel haqqin'â*). The image seen by Ezekiel in the vision of the abominations of Jewish idolatry (Ezek. 8:3, 5). The idolatrous object was such as to excite the *jealousy* (which see) of Jehovah; probably Baal or Asherah, whose image had already been placed in the Temple by Manasseh (2 Kings 21:7). "As the God of Israel, Jehovah cannot tolerate the image and worship of another god in *his* temple. To set up such an image in the temple of Jehovah was a practical renunciation of the covenant, a rejection of Jehovah on the part of Israel as its covenant God" (Keil, *Com.,* ad loc.).

JEALOUSY OFFERING (Heb. *minhat q^enā'ōt,* lit., "offering of jealousies," an intensive plural). If a man suspected his wife of adultery without

her having been caught in the act, or without his having witnesses to prove her supposed guilt, then he was required to bring her to the priest, along with an offering (Num. 5:12-31). It consisted of a tenth of an ephah of barley meal, without oil or incense, called "a grain offering of jealousy, a grain offering of memorial." The priest set her before Jehovah, poured holy water (Ex. 30:18) into an earthen basin, and put dust into it from the floor of the sanctuary. Uncovering her head, he put the offering into her hand; and holding the water in his hand, he pronounced a solemn oath of purification before her, to which she responded, "Amen, Amen."

The dust was strewn upon the water as an allusion to the fact that dust was eaten by the serpent as a curse of sin (Gen. 3:14) and therefore as a symbol of a state deserving a curse, a state of the deepest humiliation and disgrace (Ps. 72:9; Isa. 49:23; Mic. 7:17). On the very same ground an earthen vessel was chosen, that is to say, one quite worthless in comparison with a copper one. The loosening of the hair of the head is to be regarded here as a removal or loosening of the female headdress and a symbol of the loss of the proper ornament of female morality and marital fidelity. The priest, as a representative of God, held the vessel in his hand, with the water in it, which was called the "water of bitterness that brings a curse," inasmuch as, if the crime imputed to her was well-founded, it would bring upon the woman bitter suffering as the curse of God.

The priest wrote these curses, those contained in the oath, in a roll, and washed them with the bitter water, i.e., washed the writing in the vessel, so that the words of the curse should pass into the water, and be imparted to it; a symbolical act intended to set forth the truth that God imparted to the water the power to act injuriously upon a guilty body, though it would do no harm to an innocent one.

After all this was done he gave her the water to drink (Num. 5:11-31), although, according to v. 26, not till after the presentation of the sacrifice and the burning of the memorial upon the altar.

It cannot be determined with any certainty what the nature of the disease threatened in the curse was; but the idea of the curse seems to have been properly enunciated by Theodoret, who said, "The punishment shall come from the same source as the sin." The punishment was to answer exactly to the crime and to fall upon those bodily organs that had been the instruments of the woman's sin, namely, the organs of childbearing.

BIBLIOGRAPHY: A. C. Welsh, *Prophet and Priest in Old Israel* (1953), pp. 61ff.

JEALOUSY, WATERS OF. *See* Jealousy Offering.

JE'ARIM (je'a-rim; "forests"). A mountain

named in specifying the northern boundary of Judah (Josh. 15:10), having *Chesalon* (which see), modern Kesla (ten miles W of Jerusalem), upon it as a landmark.

JEATH'ERAI (je-ath'e-rī). A Levite of the family of Gershom (1 Chron. 6:21), generally thought to be the same called Ethni in v. 41.

JEBERECHI'AH, JEBEREKI'AH (je-ber-e-kī'a; "Jehovah blesses"). The father of Zechariah (not the prophet), which latter Isaiah took as one of the witnesses of his marriage with "the prophetess" (Isa. 8:2), or, as Delitzsch thinks (*Com.*, ad loc.), as witnesses of the writing upon the tablet, about 742 B.C.

JE'BUS (je'bus). The name of Jerusalem under Jebusite control (Judg. 19:10; also "Jebusi," KJV, Josh. 18:16, 28). Jebusite Jerusalem, which David captured (2 Sam. 5:8; 1 Chron. 11:4-5), has been shown by archaeological excavation to have been the SE hill, and to have been fortified by stout walls, which have been uncovered. The Jebusite city was S of the Temple area on Moriah. *See* Jerusalem.

BIBLIOGRAPHY: J. Simons, *Jerusalem in the Old Testament* (1952), pp. 60-61, 246-47; M. F. Unger, *Archaeology and the Old Testament* (1954), pp. 92-93, 206-9.

JEB'USITE, JEB'USITES (jeb'ū-sīt; Heb. always sing. *hayebūsî*, 2 Sam. 5:6; 24:16, 18; 1 Chron. 21:18, and *yebûsî* in 2 Sam. 5:8; 1 Chron. 11:6; Zech. 9:7). One of the Canaanite peoples who were to be dispossessed by Israel. In the list of the doomed nations the Jebusites always come last, except in Ezra 9:1; Neh. 9:8. But this was not because they were of no account. They were mountaineers, living in the "hill country" (Num. 13:29; Josh. 11:3). Their city was Jerusalem (15:63), "that is, Jebus" (1 Chron. 11:4), which was also known as "the Jebusite" (Josh. 15:8; 18:16, 28). Their warlike character is seen throughout their entire history. It was Adonizedek, king of Jerusalem, who raised the confederacy against Gibeon (10:1-4). The Jebusites were summoned to take part in the confederacy headed by Jabin, king of Hazor (11:1, 3). The king of Jerusalem was among those smitten by Joshua (12:10), and from 12:7 we might infer that Israel had taken their territory. But they still retained at least their royal city (Judg. 1:21) until the time of David (2 Sam. 5:6-8; 1 Chron. 11:4-6). Living on the border between Judah and Benjamin, the Jebusites dwelt with Judah (Josh. 15:63) and with Benjamin (Judg. 1:21), to which tribe Jerusalem belonged (Josh. 18:28). It is presumably implied that neither tribe was able to dislodge them.

The only appearance of Jebusites after this is in the story of Araunah (2 Sam. 24:16-24), or Ornan (1 Chron. 21:14-28), the Jebusite. Neh. 9:8 is a historical reminiscence, and probably Zech. 9:7; but Ezra 9:1 certainly seems to imply the existence of the Jebusites as a distinct heathen tribe.

JEBUSITES AND ARCHAEOLOGY. Archaeology has shown that Jebusite Jerusalem lay on the eastern hill S of the higher ground that in the tenth century B.C. became Solomon's Temple area. The Jebusites did not select the better location because this high place above the Kidron was already occupied by a Canaanite temple, which the Jebusites did not care to displace. The site they developed as an impregnable stronghold was a tiny triangle bounded by the Kidron, Tyropoeon, and Zedek valleys. Its bold rock escarpments made an ideal fortification site, and its water supply from the Gihon spring made it secure. When David took the city of the Jebusites, it was named Davidsburg, or city of David. As a result of the labors of such persons as Sir Charles Warren, Clermont-Ganneau, Hermann Guthe, F. Bliss, Capt. R. Weill, John Garstang, J. W. Crowfoot, and Kathleen Kenyon, the ancient limits of the city of David have been determined. Portions of the Jebusite city wall and fortifications were uncovered, including the great western gate. In part these probably go back to 2000 B.C. Evidence brought to light shows that the city that David captured was shaped like a huge human footprint with a total area of about eleven acres. Its stout walls and elevated position and perennial water supply made it virtually impregnable. David's prowess, however, took it by storm.

BIBLIOGRAPHY: G. E. Wright, *Biblical Archaeology* 28, no. 1 (1965): 22, 127-29.

Portion of the Jebusite wall at Jerusalem

JECAMIAH. *See* Jekamiah.

JECHILIÁH, JECHOLIÁH. *See* Jercoliah.

JECHONI'AS. *See* Jeconiah.

JECOLI'AH (jek-ō-li'a; "able through Jehovah"). Wife of Amaziah, king of Judah, and mother of Azariah, or Uzziah (2 Kings 15:2), about 797 B.C. In 2 Chron. 26:3 her name is Jechiliah (Jecoliah in the NIV). In the KJV she is known as *Jecholiah* and *Jecoliah.*

JECONI'AH (jek-ō-nī'a). An altered form of the name of King *Jehoiachin* (which see), found in some versions in 1 Chron. 3:16-17; Esther 2:6; Jer. 24:1; 27:20; 28:4; 29:2; Matt. 1:11-12.

JEDA'IAH (je-da'ya; "Jehovah has been kind," cf. Arab. *yadā*, "to do good").
  1. (Heb. *yᵉdāyâ*). The son of Shimri and father of Allon, of the ancestors of Ziza, a chief Simeonite who migrated to the valley of Gedor (1 Chron. 4:37), before 715 B.C.
  2. (Heb. same as no. 1). Son of Harumaph and one of those who repaired the walls of Jerusalem (Neh. 3:10), 445 B.C.
  3. (Heb. *yᵉdā'yâ;* "Jehovah knows"). The chief of the second division of priests as arranged by David (1 Chron. 24:7), about 960 B.C.
  4. (Heb. same as no. 3). A priest officiating in Jerusalem after the captivity (1 Chron. 9:10; Neh. 11:10); in the latter passage called the son of Joiarib (probably a corrupt reading). He seems to have belonged to the family of Jeshua; 973 of his relatives accompanied him from Babylon (Ezra 2:36; Neh. 7:39). A Jedaiah is mentioned in Neh. 12:6-7, 19, 21, but whether it is the same person or not is difficult to decide, some (Smith, *Bib. Dict.*) holding that there were two priestly families of this name. He is probably identical with the Jedaiah whom the prophet was directed to crown with the symbolical wreath (Zech. 6:10-14), 536-517 B.C.

JEDI'AEL (je-di'a-el; "known of God").
  1. One of the "sons" of Benjamin, ancestor of many Benjamite families, numbering, according to David's census, 17,200 warriors (1 Chron. 7:6, 10-11). He is usually identified with Ashbel (1 Chron. 8:1) but may have been a later descendant of Benjamin, who reached the first rank by reason of the fruitfulness of his house and the decadence of older branches.
  2. The son of Shimri and one of David's heroes (1 Chron. 11:45), and, perhaps, the chief of Manasseh who joined David at Ziklag (12:20), before 1000 B.C.
  3. The second son of Meshelemiah and a Korhite of the Levitical family of "the sons of Asaph." He was appointed a gatekeeper of the Tabernacle by David (1 Chron. 26:2), about 960 B.C.

JEDI'DAH (je-di'da; "beloved"). The daughter of

Adaiah of Bozkath, wife of King Amon and mother of Josiah (2 Kings 22:1), 640 B.C.

JEDIDI'AH (je-di-dī'a; "beloved by Jehovah"). The name given by God through Nathan to Solomon (2 Sam. 12:25).

JEDU'THUN (je-du'thun; "praise, praising"). A Merarite, and one of the masters of the sacred music appointed by David (1 Chron. 16:42; 25:1, 3; etc.), about 960 B.C. From a comparison of 15:17, 19 with 16:41-42; 25:1, 3, 6; 2 Chron. 35:15, some identify him with Ethan. In 35:15 he is called the "king's seer." His sons appear sometimes as exercising the same office (1 Chron. 25:1, 3), at others as gatekeepers (16:38). His descendants are mentioned (2 Chron. 29:14) as taking part in purifying the Temple in the reign of Hezekiah, and later still (Neh. 11:17; 1 Chron. 9:16) as involved in the singing. His name is used (2 Chron. 35:15) instead of Jeduthunites (sons of Jeduthun). Jeduthun also appears in the titles of Pss. 39, 77.

JEEZER. *See* Iezer.

JEEZERITES. *See* Iezerites.

JE'GAR-SAHADU'THA (je'gar-sa-had-ū'tha; Aram., "heap of testimony"). The Aramean name given by Laban the Syrian to the heap of stones that he erected as a memorial of the compact between Jacob and himself, whereas Jacob commemorated the same by setting up a pillar (Gen. 31:47), as was his custom on several other occasions, and naming it Galeed, a "witness heap."

JEHALE'HEEL, JEHAL'ELEL. *See* Jahall'elel.

JEHALL'ELEL (je-hal'e-lel; "praiser of God").
  1. Descendants of Judah whose own immediate parentage is not known. Four of his sons are enumerated (1 Chron. 4:16).
  2. A Merarite Levite whose son, Azariah, took part in the restoration of the Temple in the time of Hezekiah (2 Chron. 29:12), 719 B.C.

JEHDE'IAH (je-dē'ya).
  1. A descendant of Shubael, or Shebuel, of the family of Gershom, and head of a division of the Levitical Temple attendants arranged by David (1 Chron. 24:20; cf. 23:16), about 960 B.C.
  2. A Meronothite who had charge of the royal donkeys under David (1 Chron. 27:30), 1000 B.C.

JEHEZ'KEL (je-hez'kel; "God will strengthen"). The head of the twentieth division of priests under David (1 Chron. 24:16). *See* Ezekiel.

JEHI'AH (je-hī'a; "Jehovah liveth"). A Levite associated with Obed-edom as "gatekeepers for the ark" when brought by David to Jerusalem (1 Chron. 15:24), 982 B.C. Called Jeiel in v. 18.

JEHI'EL (je-hī'el).
  1. A Levite "of the second rank," appointed by David to play "with harps tuned to alamoth" on the occasion of the removal of the Ark to Jerusa-

lem (1 Chron. 15:18, 20). In the former passage he and those with him are called "gatekeepers." He is apparently the *Jehiah* (which see) of v. 24. By some he is identified as the Gershonite leader of the "sons of Ladan" in the time of David (23:8) who had charge of the treasurers (29:8). If so, his descendants were called Jehielites (26:21), 982 B.C.

2. Son of Hachmoni (or a Hachmonite), who "tutored the king's sons" (1 Chron. 27:32). The mention of Ahithophel (v. 33) seems to fix the date before the revolt, perhaps about 976 B.C.

3. The second named of the six brothers of Jehoram, and son of King Jehoshaphat (2 Chron. 21:2). These brothers were all murdered by Jehoram upon his accession (v. 4), 850 B.C.

4. One of the descendants ("sons") of Heman the singer, who assisted King Hezekiah in his reformations (2 Chron. 29:14), and probably the same person who was appointed one of the overseers of the sacred offerings (31:13), 719 B.C.

5. One of the "officials of the house of God" who contributed liberally toward the Temple sacrifices in the time of King Josiah (2 Chron. 35:8), 639 B.C.

6. The father of Obadiah, which latter returned with 218 males of the sons of Joab from Babylon with Ezra (Ezra 8:9), before 457 B.C.

7. A priest, one of the "sons" of Harim, who divorced his Gentile wife after the Exile (Ezra 10:21), 457 B.C.

8. One of the "sons" of Elam, who put away his Gentile wife after the captivity (Ezra 10:26), and probably the father of Shecaniah, who proposed that measure (v. 2), 457 B.C.

See also Jeiel.

JEHI'ELI (je-hi'e-li; "Jehielite"). A Gershonite Levite of the family of Ladan. His sons had charge of the treasures of the Lord's house (1 Chron. 26:21-22), before 960 B.C.

JEHI'ELITES (je-hi'e-lits). The descendants (1 Chron. 26:21) of *Jehiel,* no. 1 (which see).

JEHIZKI'AH (je-hiz-kī'a; same as *Hezekiah,* "Jehovah strengthens"). The son of Shallum, one of the leaders of Ephraim, who, at the insistence of Oded the prophet, demanded the liberation of the captives brought into Samaria by the army under Pekah in the campaign against Judah (2 Chron. 28:12; cf. vv. 8, 13, 15), about 741 B.C.

JEHO'ADAH, JEHOADDAH (je-hō'a-da; "whom Jehovah adorns"). Son of Ahaz, the great-grandson of Jonathan, the son of Saul (1 Chron. 8:36), called *Jarah* (which see) in 1 Chron. 9:42.

JEHOAD'DAN (je-hō-ad'an). **Jehoad'din** (je-hō-ad'in; perhaps "Jehovah delights"). A woman of Jerusalem, queen of Joash and mother of Amaziah (2 Kings 14:2; 2 Chron. 25:1), 825 B.C.

JEHO'AHAZ (je-hō'a-haz; "Jehovah has laid hold of," abbrev., Jo'ahaz).

1. The son and successor of Jehu, the twelfth king of Israel after the division of the kingdom (2 Kings 10:35). He reigned seventeen years, 814-798 B.C. Following the sins of Jeroboam his forces were defeated by the Syrians until they were reduced to fifty horsemen, ten chariots, and ten thousand footmen. In his humiliation he besought Jehovah, and a deliverer was granted to Israel, probably in the person of *Jehoash* (which see), his son, who expelled the Syrians and re-established the affairs of the kingdom (13:1-9, 25).

2. The third son of Josiah by Hamutal, called *Shallum* (which see) in 1 Chron. 3:15, where he is given as the fourth son, but by a comparison of 2 Kings 23:31 and 2 Chron. 36:11, we find that Zedekiah was the younger. After his father had been slain in resisting the progress of Pharaoh Neco, Jehoahaz was raised to the throne, at the age of twenty-three, in preference to his elder brother, Jehoiakim (2 Kings 23:31, 36). He was anointed at Jerusalem (v. 30) and found the land full of trouble but free from idolatry (cf. v. 24). He is described as an evildoer (v. 32) and an oppressor (cf. Ezek. 19:3), but seems to have been lamented by the people (Jer. 22:10; Ezek. 19:1). Pharaoh Neco, upon his return from the Euphrates, removed him from the throne, and put Jehoiakim in his place. Jehoahaz was taken first to Riblah in Syria, and then to Egypt, where he died. His reign lasted only three months, 609 B.C.

3. The name given (2 Chron. 21:17; 25:23) to the youngest son of Jehoram, king of Judah; usually called *Ahaziah* (which see).

BIBLIOGRAPHY: T. Kirk and G. Rawlinson, *Studies in the Books of Kings,* 2 vols. in 1 (1983), 2:224-29; E. R. Thiele, *Mysterious Numbers of the Hebrew Kings* (1983), pp. 57, 105-11, 182.

JEHO'ASH (je-hō'ash; "Jehovah has given," cf. Arab. *'asa, 'awasa,* "to bestow"; sometimes called Joash).

1. The eighth king of Judah and son of King Ahaziah (2 Kings 11:2), by Zibiah (12:1; 2 Chron. 24:1). He was born about 843 B.C. His aunt, Jehosheba, saved him from the massacre by *Athaliah* (which see), hiding him "with her in the house of the Lord six years." At the age of seven years he seems to have been the only living descendant of Solomon and was then brought into the Temple and anointed king. *Jehoiada* (which see), the high priest, thought the time ripe for overthrowing the power of Athaliah, the usurper, and secured the cooperation of the royal bodyguard. The noisy greeting that was accorded Jehoash brought Athaliah to the Temple, where she was seized and slain, about 835 B.C. Jehoash behaved well as long as Jehoiada, his uncle, lived. Excepting that the high places were still resorted to for incense and sacrifice, pure religion was

restored, and the Temple was repaired. But after the death of his aged counselor, evil advisers led him into sin; the law was neglected, idolatry prevailed, and God's anger kindled against him. Prophets were sent to warn him, but the ungrateful king responded by putting to death Zechariah, the son and successor of his benefactor Jehoiada. In about a year Hazael, king of Syria, came against him, overcame his forces, and, appearing before Jerusalem, was bought off with the treasures of the Temple. Jehoash also suffered from a painful malady and was at length slain by his own servants, about 796 B.C. He was buried in the city of David, but not in the sepulcher of the kings (2 Kings 11-12; 2 Chron. 24). He is one of the three kings omitted in the genealogy of Christ (Matt. 1:8). He is called Joash consistently in the NIV.

2. The son and successor of Jehoahaz, king of Israel. He became viceroy to his father (2 Kings 13:10), reigning thirteenth over the separate kingdom sixteen years, including his viceroyship, 798-782 B.C. According to the scriptural account, Jehoash "did evil in the sight of the Lord; he did not turn away from all the sins of Jeroboam the son of Nebat, with which he made Israel sin, but he walked in them" (2 Kings 13:11). Josephus says (*Ant.* 9.8.6) that "He was a good man, and in disposition was not at all like his father." The statement in Kings is supposed by some to refer to the first part of his reign, while that of Josephus relates to the latter part, after a restoration.

Jehoash held Elisha in great respect, and when he heard of the prophet's last illness he went to his bedside, wept over him, and said, "My father, my father, the chariots of Israel and its horsemen!" The prophet promised him deliverance from the Syrian yoke in Aphek, and bade him strike the ground. The king struck three times and then stopped, whereupon the prophet rebuked him for stopping and limited his victories over Syria to three. These promises were accomplished after the prophet's death, Jehoash in three successive victories overcoming the Syrians and retaking from them the towns that Hazael had torn from Israel (2 Kings 13:14-25).

The success of Jehoash appears to have made Amaziah, king of Judah, jealous, and he sought a quarrel with him. Jehoash replied with a parable, but Amaziah was determined in his purpose, and a war ensued in which Jehoash was victorious. Having defeated Amaziah in Beth-shemesh in Judah, he advanced against Jerusalem, broke down the walls to the extent of 400 cubits, and carried away the treasures both of the Temple and the palace, together with hostages for the future good behavior of Amaziah (2 Kings 14:8-14; 2 Chron. 25:17-24). Jehoash, soon after his victory, died in peace and was buried in Samaria.

BIBLIOGRAPHY: D. W. Thomas, ed., *Documents from Old Testament Times* (1958), p. 50; T. Kirk and G. Rawlinson, *Studies in the Books of Kings*, 2 vols. in 1 (1983),

2:119-24, 129-34; E. R. Thiele, *Mysterious Numbers of the Hebrew Kings* (1983), pp. 35, 52-53, 62, 111-16, 120, 180-81, 206.

JEHOHA'NAN (je-hō-ha'nan; "Jehovah is favorable"). Jehohanan and Johanan appear in the KJV, NIV, and NASB but not always in the same verses. *Jehohanan* is in the KJV, NIV, and NASB of Ezra 10:28; Neh. 12:13, 42; it is in the NASB and NIV of Ezra 10:6; Neh. 6:18, where it replaces KJV *Johanan;* and it is in the KJV and NIV of 1 Chron. 26:3; 2 Chron. 17:15; 23:1, where it is replaced in the NASB by *Johanan* (which see). The material below follows the NASB usage.

1. A priest, the "son" of Eliashib, into whose chamber Ezra retired to mourn over the marrying of Gentile wives by the Jews (Ezra 10:6). He is identified with the Johanan mentioned in Neh. 12:22-23.

2. An Israelite of the family of Bebai who divorced his Gentile wife after the Exile (Ezra 10:28), 456 B.C.

3. The son of Tobiah the Ammonite, and married to the daughter of Meshullam, the priest (Neh. 6:18), 445 B.C.

4. A leading priest, descendant of Amariah, who later returned with Zerubbabel. He was contemporary with Joiakim (Neh. 12:13; cf. vv. 2, 12), considerably after 536 B.C.

5. A priest who took part in the musical services at the dedication of the walls of Jerusalem by Nehemiah (Neh. 12:42), 445 B.C.

JEHOI'ACHIN (je-hoy'a-kin; "Jehovah will establish"). Son of Jehoiakim, king of Judah, and Nehushta, daughter of Elnathan of Jerusalem; called also Jeconiah.

He succeeded his father as the nineteenth king over the separate kingdom and reigned three months and ten days, 597 B.C. His age at his accession was eighteen years, according to 2 Kings 24:8, but eight years according to 2 Chron. 36:9. (The usual explanation of this difference is that he reigned ten years in conjunction with his father. This would make him eight at the beginning of his joint reign and eighteen when he began to reign alone.) Jehoiachin "did evil in the sight of the Lord" and probably opposed the interests of the Chaldean empire, for in three months after his accession we find Nebuchadnezzar laying siege to Jerusalem, as Jeremiah had predicted (Jer. 22:18-30). Immediately after Jehoiachin's succession the Egyptians were completely driven out of Asia, the fortresses S of Jerusalem were encircled, and numbers of the inhabitants of the lowlands carried away as prisoners. Jerusalem was at the time quite defenseless, and in a short time Jehoiachin surrendered (with the queen-mother and all his servants, captains, and officers) to Nebuchadnezzar, who carried them, with the eunuchs and harem, to Babylon (24:1). The number of captives is given in

2 Kings 24:14 as 10,000, including warriors, craftsmen, and others. Nebuchadnezzar also took the treasures found in the palace and Temple (v. 13) and placed Mattaniah, the only surviving son of Josiah, on the throne, changing his name to Zedekiah (24:14-17).

Jehoiachin was placed in prison in Babylon, where he remained for thirty-six years until the death of Nebuchadnezzar, when Evil-merodach not only released him but gave him a seat at his own table and an allowance for his support (2 Kings 25:27-30; Jer. 52:31-34), 561 B.C. We learn from 28:4 that four years after he had gone to Babylon there was an expectation at Jerusalem of Jehoiachin's return, but Jeremiah accuses Hananiah, who thus prophesied, of falsehood (v. 15). The tenor of Jeremiah's letter to the elders of the captivity (chap. 29) would seem to indicate that there was a party among the captivity who were looking for the overthrow of Nebuchadnezzar and the return of Jehoiachin. Neither Daniel nor Ezekiel makes any further allusion to him, except that Ezekiel dates his prophecies by the year "of King Jehoiachin's exile" (1:2; 8:1; 24:1; etc.), the latest date being the twenty-seventh year (29:17).

The archaeologist's spade has given remarkable minute corroboration of the biblical notices of Jehoiachin's captivity. In excavations near the Ishtar Gate of Babylon almost 300 clay tablets dating from 595-570 B.C. were recovered from some fourteen rooms. These important documents contain receipts of barley, oil, and other supplies that had been rationed to captive artisans and workmen exiled from many lands. King Jehoiachin appears as "Yaukin, king of the land of Yahud [Judah]" as the recipient of some of these rations. Moreover, the cuneiform tablets carry the names of Jehoiachin's five sons and their Jewish attendant, named Kenaiah. These tablets, discovered by E. F. Weidner, point to the fact that several of the sons were born before 592 B.C., with the eldest, Shealtiel, father of Zerubbabel, born c. 598 B.C. at the latest, which makes Zerubbabel at the time of the reconstruction of the second Temple (c. 520-516 B.C.) older than had been commonly supposed. In addition, three clay jar handles dug up at Beth-shemesh and Kiriath-Sepher (see Debir) were impressed with a seal in old Phoenician script "belonging to Eliakim, steward of Yaukin." This indicates that the crown property was in charge of Eliakim during Jehoiachin's exile and that Zedekiah, expecting a possible return of his royal nephew, did not seize the property of the rightful ruler (see Biblical Archaeologist 5, no. 4, [Dec. 1942]).

BIBLIOGRAPHY: W. F. Albright, Journal of Biblical Literature 51 (1932): 77, 84, 91-103; id., Biblical Archaeologist 5 (1942): 49-55; A. Honeyman, JBL 67 (1948): 13-15; D. Freedman, BA 19 (1956): 56-58; E. R. Thiele, Bulletin of the American Schools of Oriental Research 143 (1956): 22-27; id., Mysterious Numbers of the Hebrew Kings (1983), pp. 35, 186-89, 206; E. Auerbach, Vetus Testamentum 9 (1959): 113-15.

JEHOI'ADA (je-hoya-da; "Jehovah knows").

1. The father of Benaiah, one of David's chief warriors (2 Sam. 8:18; 20:23; 23:20, 22; 1 Kings 1:8, 26, 32; etc.), before 1000 B.C. He is probably the same person mentioned as leader of 3,700 Aaronites who assisted David at Hebron (1 Chron. 12:27). In 27:34 his name seems to have been transposed with that of his son, although Keil (Com., ad loc.) suggests that the Jehoiada mentioned there was a grandson of this Jehoiada.

2. The high priest at the time of Athaliah's usurpation, about 842 B.C., and during most of the reign of Jehoash. He married Jehosheba, daughter of King Jehoram and sister of King Ahaziah. When Athaliah (which see) killed the royal family, Jehoiada with his wife stole and secreted Jehoash and after six years placed him on a throne. In this revolution Jehoiada showed great tact and ability. He waited until public sentiment seemed ripe for a change and then entered into secret alliance with the chief partisans of the house of David and of the true religion. He gathered at Jerusalem the Levites from the different cities and concentrated a large concealed force in the Temple by the expedient of not dismissing the old divisions of priests and Levites when their successors came to relieve them. These were armed by means of the shields and armor deposited in the Temple treasury by David, divided into three bands, and posted at the principal entrances. The courts were filled with people favorable to the cause, and then Jehoiada produced the young king, crowned and anointed him, and presented him with a copy of the law, according to Deut. 17:18-20. Nor did Jehoiada forget the sanctity of the Temple. None but the priests and ministering Levites were allowed to enter, and strict orders were given that Athaliah should not be slain within its precincts. The new reign was inaugurated by a solemn covenant between himself, as high priest, and the people and king to renounce the worship of Baal, which was followed by the destruction of the altar and temple of Baal and the death of his priest, Mattan. His influence over the young king was beneficial, and Jehoash ruled well and prosperously during Jehoiada's lifetime. The restoration of the Temple in the twenty-third year of Jehoash's reign was carried on under Jehoiada's supervision. For an account of this work see 2 Kings 11-12 and 2 Chron. 22:11–24:14. At length he died at the age of 130 (24:15-16) and, as a signal honor, was buried "in the city of David among the kings," perhaps 798 B.C. He is, doubtless, the same as Berechiah (Matt. 23:35); his son, Zechariah, was slain by command of the king (2 Chron. 24:20-22).

3. The son of Paseah, apparently one of the

chief priests who, with Meshullam, repaired the Old Gate of Jerusalem (Neh. 3:6), 446 B.C. The NIV renders the name *Joiada* (which see).

4. A priest who was in Jerusalem when the Jews were led into captivity, but who was displaced. Zephaniah was put in his stead (Jer. 29:26).

BIBLIOGRAPHY: T. Kirk and G. Rawlinson, *Studies in the Books of Kings*, 2 vols. in 1 (1983), pp.115-22.

JEHOI'AKIM (je-hoy'a-kim; "Jehovah raises up"). The eighteenth king of the separate kingdom of Judah. His original name was Eliakim, but its equivalent, Jehoiakim, was given him by Pharaoh Neco, the Egyptian king. He was the second son of Josiah by Zebidah, the daughter of Pedaiah of Rumah (2 Kings 23:36), born about 633 B.C.

Made King. Jehoiakim's younger brother, Jehoahaz, or Shallum (Jer. 22:11), was made a king at the death of his father, Josiah. The intention, probably, was for him to follow up his father's policy in siding with Nebuchadnezzar against Egypt. Pharaoh Neco, having overcome all resistance with his victorious army, deposed Jehoahaz, made him a prisoner in Riblah, and afterward took him to Egypt. He set Eliakim upon the throne, 609 B.C., changing his name to Jehoiakim, and charged him with collecting a tribute of one hundred talents of silver and a talent of gold (nearly $200,000; 2 Kings 23:33-35; 2 Chron. 36:3-4).

Made a Vassal. After the battle of Carchemish, Nebuchadnezzar captured Jerusalem and, taking the king prisoner, "bound him with bronze chains to take him to Babylon." He also took "some of the articles of the house of the Lord" and carried them to the temple of Bel (his god) in Babylon (2 Chron. 36:6-7). Nebuchadnezzar for some reason seems to have abandoned his intention of conveying Jehoiakim to Babylon, and restored him to his throne as a vassal (2 Kings 24:1; Jer. 25:1).

Destroys the Roll. In the fourth year of Jehoiakim's reign the prophet Jeremiah caused a collection of his prophecies to be written out by Baruch and publicly read in the Temple. This came to the knowledge of the king. He sent for it and had it read before him. He listened to only a small portion of it, then took the roll, and, cutting it in pieces, burned it in the fire. But Jeremiah was bidden to take another roll and write upon it the same words, with the addition of another and an awful denunciation (Jer. 36).

Rebellion and Death. After three years of subjection Jehoiakim, deluded by the Egyptian party in his court (cf. Josephus *Ant.* 10.6.2), withheld his tribute and rebelled against Nebuchadnezzar (2 Kings 24:1). This step was taken against the earnest protestation of Jeremiah and in violation of his oath. We are not informed as to what moved Jehoiakim to rebel, but it may be that seeing Egypt entirely severed from the affairs of

Syria since the battle of Carchemish and Nebuchadnezzar wholly occupied with distant wars, he hoped to make himself entirely independent. His reign was now turbulent and unhappy. Bands of Chaldeans, Syrians, Moabites, and Ammonites came against him and cruelly harassed the country. It was perhaps at this time that the great drought occurred, as described in Jer. 14 (cf. chap. 15 with 2 Kings 24:2-3). In the closing years of his reign the Ammonites appear to have overrun the land of Gad (Jer. 49:1), and other nations ravaged Israel (Ezek. 25). Jehoiakim came to his end, as was predicted, in a violent manner, and his body was thrown over the wall, perhaps to convince the enemy of his death. It was afterward taken away and given an unhonored burial (Jer. 22:18-19; 36:30; 2 Kings 24:3-4), 597 B.C.

Character. Jehoiakim was a vicious and irreligious man, and one who encouraged the abominations of idolatry (Jer. 19, supposed to refer to his reign). The vindictive pursuit of *Uriah* (which see) and the indignities offered to his corpse by the king's command are samples of his irreligion and cruelty (26:20-23). His daring impiety is shown by his treatment of the roll containing Jeremiah's prophecy; and his selfishness is shown by his spending large sums in building magnificent palaces for himself when the land was impoverished by the tributes laid upon it by Egypt and Babylon (22:14-15).

BIBLIOGRAPHY: J. Bright, *Biblical Archaeologist* 12 (1949): 46-52; W. F. Albright, *Journal of Biblical Literature* 71 (1952): 31, 253; J. Hyatt, *JBL* 75 (1956): 27784; D. Freedman, *BA* 19 (1956): 50-60; E. R. Thiele, *Bulletin of the American Schools of Oriental Research* 143 (1956): 22-27; id., *Mysterious Numbers of the Hebrew Kings* (1983) pp. 182-86; E. Auerbach, *Vetus Testamentum* 9 (1959): 113-21; T. Kirk and G. Rawlinson, *Studies in the Books of Kings*, 2 vols. in 1 (1983), 2:224-30.

JEHOI'ARIB (je-hoy'a-rib; "Jehovah will contend"). Head of the first of the twenty-four divisions of priests, as arranged by David (1 Chron. 24:7), about 961 B.C. Some of his descendants returned from the Babylonian captivity (1 Chron. 9:10; Neh. 11:10, "Joiarib"). Jewish tradition asserts that only four of the divisions returned from Babylon, namely, Jedaiah, Immer, Pashhur, and Harim, and that they were subdivided into six each, to keep up the old number of twenty-four. But we find that other of the priestly divisions are mentioned as returning (Neh. 10:2-8), and in the list (12:1-7) that of Jehoiarib, or *Joiarib* (which see), as the name is abbreviated, is expressly mentioned.

JEHON'ADAB (je-hon'a-dab), **Jonadab** (jon'a-dab; "Jehovah is magnanimous").

1. The son of Shimeah, nephew of David, and a friend of Amnon. He gave the latter the wicked advice that resulted in the ensnaring of Amnon's sister, Tamar (2 Sam. 13:3-5), about 974 B.C.

When Amnon was murdered by Absalom, and the exaggerated report reached David that all the princes were slaughtered, Jonadab was aware of the facts, and, being with the king, assured him that Amnon alone was slain (vv. 32-33, 35).

2. A son (or descendant) of Rechab, the founder of a peculiar tribe who bound themselves to abstain from wine and never to relinquish the nomadic life. This mode of life, partly monastic, partly Bedouin, was adhered to from generation to generation, and when, many years after the death of Jehonadab, the Rechabites were forced to take refuge from the Chaldean invasion within the walls of Jerusalem, nothing would induce them to transgress the rule of their ancestor (Jer. 35:19). The single occasion in which Jehonadab appears before us in the historical narrative is in 2 Kings 10:15-16, about 842 B.C. Jehu was advancing, after the slaughter of Beth-eked, on the city of Samaria, and met Jehonadab. Upon being assured that he was in sympathy with the king, he was taken up into the chariot and entrusted with the king's secret, namely, the destruction of the Baalites. He then proceeded to Samaria in the royal chariot. It may be that Jehonadab had been commissioned by the people of Samaria to meet the king on the road and appease him. If so, his venerable character, his rank as head of a tribe, and his neutral position well qualified him for the task. No doubt he acted with Jehu throughout, but the only occasion in which he is expressly mentioned is when he went with Jehu through the temple of Baal to turn out any "servants of the Lord" who might happen to be in the mass of pagan worshipers (10:23).

JEHO'NATHAN (je-hō'na-than; "Jehovah has given"). The full Heb. form of the name *Jonathan* (which see), the eldest son of King Saul, and the name of several other biblical characters.

1. The name of one of the Levites sent by Jehoshaphat through the cities of Judah to teach the law to the people (2 Chron. 17:8), 875 B.C.

2. The name of a priest (Neh. 12:18), and a representative of the family of Shemaiah (v. 6) in the days of Joiakim, after 536 B.C.

3. In the KJV of 1 Chron. 27:25, the name of the son of Uzziah, and superintendent of certain of King David's storehouses. The NASB and NIV read "Jonathan."

JEHO'RAM (je-hō'ram), **Jo'ram** (jo'ram; "Jehovah is high").

1. The son of Ahab and Jezebel, and successor of his brother Ahaziah, who died childless. He was the ninth king on the separate throne of Israel and reigned twelve years (2 Kings 1:17; 3:1), about 852-841 B.C. In 2 Kings 8:16 (NASB, KJV, NIV) and elsewhere in the KJV he is called Joram the son of Ahab king of Israel.

After the death of Ahab the Moabites, who had been tributary to Israel, asserted their independence; and their king, *Mesha* (which see), with-

held his tribute of 100,000 lambs and the wool of 100,000 rams. Thereupon Jehoram asked and obtained the help of Jehoshaphat (king of Judah) in a war against the revolting Moabites. While marching through the wilderness of Edom the armies were in great danger due to lack of water. Jehoshaphat suggested an inquiry of some prophet of Jehovah, and Elisha was found. He severely rebuked Jehoram, and bade him inquire of the prophets of Baal, but afterward predicted a great victory over the Moabites. The king was directed to have many ditches dug in the valley and was assured that they would be filled immediately with water. The Moabites, advancing, saw the water reddened like blood with the rays of the morning sun, and concluding that the allies had fallen out and slain each other, advanced incautiously. They were put to rout, and their land utterly ravaged (2 Kings 3:1-25).

A little later war again broke out between Syria and Israel, and we find Elisha befriending Jehoram. The king was made acquainted with the secret counsels of the Syrian king and was thus enabled to defeat them; and the blinding of the Syrian soldiers by God stopped the invasion (2 Kings 6:8-23).

When the Syrian inroads ceased, it seems probable that Jehoram felt less dependent upon the aid of the prophet and relapsed into idolatry. He was most likely rebuked by Elisha and threatened with a return of the calamities from which he had escaped. When he refused to repent, a fresh invasion by the Syrians and a close siege of Samaria actually came to pass, according, probably, to the word of the prophet. Hence, when the terrible incident arose in consequence of the famine of a woman's boiling and eating her own child, the king immediately attributed the evil to Elisha, the son of Shaphat, and determined to take away his life. The providential interposition by which both Elisha's life was saved and the city delivered is narrated in 2 Kings 7, and Jehoram appears to have restored his friendship with Elisha (8:4).

It was soon after the events mentioned above that Elisha went to Damascus and predicted the revolt of Hazael and his accession to the throne of Syria. Jehoram seems to have thought the revolution in Syria, which immediately followed Elisha's prediction, a good opportunity to pursue his father's favorite project of recovering Ramoth-gilead from the Syrians. He accordingly made an alliance with his nephew Ahaziah, who had just succeeded Joram on the throne of Judah, and the two kings proceeded to occupy Ramoth-gilead by force. The expedition was an unfortunate one. Jehoram was wounded in battle and obliged to return to Jezreel to be healed of his wounds (2 Kings 8:29; 9:14-15), leaving his army under Jehu to hold Ramoth-gilead against Hazael. Jehu and the army under his command, however, revolted from their allegiance to Jehoram (chap. 9) and, hastily marching to Jezreel, surprised Jehoram, wounded and defenseless as he was. Going out to meet him, Jehoram fell pierced by an arrow from Jehu's bow on the very piece of ground that Ahab had wrested from Naboth the Jezreelite, thus fulfilling to the letter the prophecy of Elijah (1 Kings 21:21-29). The death of Jehoram ended the dynasty of Omri. Jehoram, like his father, was an idolater, laying aside his worship of Baal, probably after his rebuke by Elisha, but still clinging to the abominations of Jeroboam (12:26, 31-32).

2. Eldest son and successor of Jehoshaphat, and fifth king on the separate throne of Judah. He was crowned at the age of thirty-two; his sole regency lasted about eight years, 849-841 B.C. (2 Kings 8:16; 2 Chron. 21:1-6). Jehosheba, his daughter, was wife to the high priest Jehoiada. As soon as he was fixed on the throne he put his six brothers to death, with many of the chief nobles of the land. He then, probably due to the influence of his wife, Athaliah, the daughter of Ahab, proceeded to establish the worship of Baal (2 Kings 8:18-19). A prophetic writing from the aged prophet Elijah (2 Chron. 21:12-15) failed to produce any good effect upon him. This was in the first or second year of his reign. The remainder of it was a series of calamities. First the Edomites, who had been tributary to Jehoshaphat, revolted from his dominion and, according to old prophecies (Gen. 27:40), established their permanent independence. Next Libnah, one of the strongest fortified cities in Judah (2 Kings 19:8), rebelled against him. Then followed invasions by armed bands of Philistines and Arabians, who stormed the king's palace, put his wives and all his children except his youngest son, Ahaziah, to death (2 Chron. 22:1), or carried them into captivity, and plundered all his treasures. He died of a terrible disease (21:19-20) early in the twelfth year of his brother-in-law Jehoram's reign over Israel.

Jehoram was an impious and cruel tyrant, manifesting his impiety by the setting up of Baal worship in the high places and prostituting the daughters of Judah to the infamous rites of Ashteroth; and showing his cruelty by the murder of all his brothers —the first example of that abominable practice of avoiding a disputed succession.

3. One of the priests sent by Jehoshaphat to instruct the people in the law (2 Chron. 17:8), after 875 B.C.

BIBLIOGRAPHY: T. Kirk and G. Rawlinson, *Studies in the Books of Kings*, 2 vols. in 1 (1983), 2:90-100.

JEHOSHAB'EATH (je-hō-shab'e-ath; "Jehovah is an oath"). The form in which the name of *Jehosheba* (which see) is given in 2 Chron. 22:11. It is stated here, but not in Kings, that she was the wife of Jehoiada, the high priest.

JEHOSH'APHAT (je-hosh'a-fat; "Jehovah

judged"). The name of a king (*see* article below) of Judah and of other persons in the Bible.

1. Son of Ahilud, who filled the office of recorder or annalist in the courts of David (2 Sam. 8:16; 20:24; 1 Chron. 18:15) and Solomon (1 Kings 4:3), 985-984 B.C.

2. Son of Paruah, one of the twelve deputies of King Solomon (1 Kings 4:17). His district was Issachar, about 960 B.C.

3. Son of Nimshi and father of King Jehu (2 Kings 9:2, 14), before 842 B.C.

4. One of the priests appointed to blow trumpets before the Ark when it was carried from the house of Obed-edom to Jerusalem (1 Chron. 15:24), about 982 B.C. *See* Joshaphat.

JEHOSHAPHAT (je-hosh'a-fat; "Jehovah judged"). The fourth king of the separate kingdom of Judah, the son of Asa (by Azubah), whom he succeeded on the throne when he was thirty-five years old, and reigned twenty-five years (about 873-848; 1 Kings 22:42; 2 Chron. 20:31). His history is to be found among the events recorded in 1 Kings 15:24; 2 Kings 8:16, or in the continuous narrative in 2 Chron. 17:1–21:3. He was contemporary with Ahab, Ahaziah, and Jehoram.

Strengthens Himself. Jehoshaphat first strengthened himself against Israel by fortifying and garrisoning the cities of Judah and the Ephraimite conquests of Asa (2 Chron. 17:1-2). But soon afterward the two Hebrew kings, perhaps appreciating their common danger from Damascus and the tribes on their eastern frontier, formed an alliance. Jehoshaphat's eldest son, Jehoram, married Athaliah, the daughter of Ahab and Jezebel.

Resists Idolatry. In his own kingdom Jehoshaphat showed himself a zealous follower of the commandments of God; he tried, although it would seem not quite successfully, to put down the high places and groves in which the people of Judah burned incense (1 Kings 22:43; 2 Chron. 17:6; 20:33). In his third year he sent out certain officials, priests, and Levites to go through all the cities of Judah, teaching the people out of the book of the law (17:7-9). Riches and honors increased around him. He received tribute from the Philistines and Arabians, and kept up a large standing army in Jerusalem (17:10-19).

Alliance with Ahab. He went to Samaria to visit Ahab and become his ally against the Syrians. Desirous of consulting the Lord, Jehoshaphat had the prophet Micaiah sent for; but he did not make the impression upon Jehoshaphat that might have been expected, or else the king felt bound in honor not to recede. He came very near falling a victim to the plan that Ahab had laid for his own safety, but instead he escaped and returned to Jerusalem in peace (1 Kings 22:1-44; 2 Chron. 18:1–19:1). There he met the just reproaches of the prophet Jehu and went himself through the people, "from Beersheba to the hill country of Ephraim," reclaiming them to the law of God (2 Chron. 19:2-4).

Further Reforms. He tried to remedy the many defects in the local administration of justice. He appointed judges in every city, and a supreme council at Jerusalem composed of priests, Levites, and "the heads of the fathers' households," to which difficult cases were referred and appeals brought from the provincial tribunals (2 Chron. 19:5-11).

Commerce. Turning his attention to foreign commerce, he built at Ezion-geber, with the help of Ahaziah, a navy designed to go to Ophir; but it was wrecked at Ezion-geber. He afterward, through the advice of Eliezer the prophet, declined the cooperation of the king of Israel, and the voyage prospered. The trade was, however, soon abandoned (2 Chron. 20:35-37; 1 Kings 22:49).

Wars. After the death of Ahaziah king of Israel, Jehoram, his successor, persuaded Jehoshaphat to join him in an expedition against Moab. The allied armies were saved by a miraculous supply of water and were afterward victorious over the enemy (2 Kings 3:4-27). Another war, and to Jehoshaphat a much more dangerous one, was kindled by this. The Moabites turned their wrath against him and induced the Ammonites, the Syrians, and the Edomites to unite with them. Jehoshaphat, believing that his help was to come from God, proclaimed a fast, and the people assembled in Jerusalem to implore divine assistance. "Then Jehoshaphat stood in the assembly of Judah and Jerusalem, in the house of the Lord before the new court, and he said, 'O Lord, the God of our fathers, . . . O our God, wilt thou not judge them? For we are powerless before this great multitude who are coming against us; nor do we know what to do, but our eyes are on Thee.' " After he ceased praying Jahaziel, a Levite, pronounced deliverance in the name of the Lord, assuring Judah of the overthrow of the enemy without a blow from them. And so it happened; the allies quarreled among themselves and destroyed each other. This great event was recognized by the surrounding nations as the act of God, and they allowed Jehoshaphat to close his life in quiet (2 Chron. 20). During the last years of his reign his son *Jehoram* (which see) was associated with him in the government. His name occurs in the ancestral list of our Lord (Matt. 1:8).

Character. The character of Jehoshaphat is summed up thus: "Jehoshaphat, who sought the Lord with all his heart" (2 Chron. 22:9). His good talents, the benevolence of his disposition, and his generally sound judgment are shown not only in the great measures of domestic policy that distinguished his reign, but by the manner in which they were executed. No trace can be found

in him of the pride that dishonored some and ruined others of the kings who preceded and followed him.

BIBLIOGRAPHY: C. E. Macartney, *The Woman of Tekoah* (1955), pp. 37-49; T. Kirk and G. Rawlinson, *Studies in the Books of Kings*, 2 vols. in 1 (1983), 2:78-85; E. R. Thiele, *Mysterious Numbers of the Hebrew Kings* (1983), pp. 55, 58, 63, 86-100.

JEHOSH'APHAT (je-hosh'a-fat), **Valley of.** The name given to the valley situated between Jerusalem and the Mount of Olives, which in modern times has been used by the Jews as a burying ground. This is a typical use of the word, in a sense of divine judgments upon the enemies of God and His people (Joel 3:2, 12). In this valley Jehoshaphat overthrew the united enemies of Israel (2 Chron. 20:26, "valley of Beracah").

From about the fourth century A.D. the valley of Jehoshaphat has been identified with the Kidron. This identification is based on Joel 3:2, 12 and particularly Zech. 14, but since no actual valley bore this name in pre-Christian antiquity, Joel's prophetic employment of it is figurative of the place where the judgment of the nations will take place prior to Christ's second advent and the setting up of the millennial kingdom.

JEHOSH'EBA (je-hosh'e-ba; "Jehovah her oath," that is, worshiper of Jehovah). The daughter of Joram, sister of Ahaziah, aunt of Joash, all kings of Judah, and wife of Jehoiada the high priest (2 Kings 11:2). Her name in the Chronicles (2 Chron. 22) is sometimes given as *Jehoshabeath*. As she is called (2 Kings 11:2) "the daughter of King Joram, sister of Ahaziah," it has been conjectured that she was the daughter, not of Athaliah, but of Joram by another wife. By her the infant Joash was rescued from the massacre of the royal seed by Athaliah, and he and his nurse hid in the palace and afterward in the Temple (2 Kings 11:2-3; 2 Chron. 22:11-12).

JEHO'VAH. *See* (The) Lord.

JEHO'VAH-JI'REH. *See* (The) Lord Will Provide.

JEHO'VAH-NIS'SI. *See* (The) Lord Is My Banner.

JEHO'VAH-SHA'LOM. *See* (The) Lord Is Peace.

JEHO'VAH-SHAM'MAH. *See* (The) Lord Is There.

JEHOZ'ABAD (je-hoz'a-bad; "Jehovah endowed").

1. The son of Shomer (or Shimrith), a Moabitess, and one of the two servants who assassinated King Jehoash of Judah in that part of Jerusalem called Millo (2 Kings 12:21; 2 Chron. 24:26), about 797 B.C.

2. A Korahite Levite, second son of Obed-edom, and one of the gatekeepers of the S gate

of the Temple and of the storehouse appointed by David (1 Chron. 26:4, 15), about 967 B.C.

3. The last named of Jehoshaphat's generals, who had the command of 180,000 troops (2 Chron. 17:18), about 875 B.C.

JEHOZ'ADAK (je-hoz'a-dak; "Jehovah has justified," contracted "Jozadak" in Ezra and Nehemiah and as "Josedech" in the KJV of Haggai and Zechariah). Son of the high priest Seraiah at the time of the Babylonian captivity (1 Chron. 6:14), 588 B.C. Whether he succeeded to the high priesthood after the slaughter of his father (2 Kings 25:18-21) is not known, but if he did he had no opportunity of performing the functions of his office, as he was carried to Babylon by Nebuchadnezzar (1 Chron. 6:15). He probably died in exile, as his son Joshua (Jeshua) was the first high priest who officiated after the return from captivity (Ezra 3:2, 8; 5:2; 10:18; Neh. 12:26; Hag. 1:1, 12, 14; 2:2, 4; Zech. 6:11).

JE'HU (jē'hū; Gesenius, "Jehovah is He"). A king of Israel (*see* article below) and four other persons in the Bible.

1. The son of Hanani; a prophet of Judah, but whose ministrations were chiefly directed to Israel. His father was probably the seer who rebuked Asa (2 Chron. 16:7). He must have begun his career as a prophet when young. He first denounced Baasha (1 Kings 16:1, 7) and then, after an interval of thirty years, reappeared to reprove Jehoshaphat for his alliance with Ahab (2 Chron. 19:2-3). He survived Jehoshaphat and wrote about his life (20:34), about 879-850 B.C.

2. The son of Obed and father of Azariah, of the tribe of Judah (1 Chron. 2:38).

3. A Simeonite, son of Joshibiah, and one of the leading Simeonites who moved into the valley of Gedor in search of pasture during the reign of Hezekiah. They attacked and dispossessed the original inhabitants (1 Chron. 4:35, 39-41), about 713 B.C.

4. An Anathothite, one of the chief of the slingers of Benjamin, who joined David at Ziklag (1 Chron. 12:3), before 1000 B.C.

JEHU (jē'hū; Gesenius, "Jehovah is He"). The eleventh king of the separate kingdom of Israel. He was the son of Jehoshaphat (2 Kings 9:2) and the grandson of Nimshi, although sometimes called the latter's son (1 Kings 19:16). The first appearance of Jehu is his memory of riding with Bidkar, now his officer, behind Ahab on the journey from Samaria to Jezreel (2 Kings 9:25). Elijah was commanded at Horeb to anoint him king, but, for unknown reasons, did not do so (1 Kings 19:16-17).

Anointed King. Jehu meantime, in the reigns of Ahaziah and Jehoram, had risen to importance. He was under the last named king, captain of the armed forces in the siege of Ramoth-gilead. While Jehu was in the midst of the officers of the besieging army, a wild-looking youth suddenly entered and insisted on a private inteview with him. They retired into a secret chamber. The youth uncovered a vial of sacred oil, poured it over Jehu's head, and after announcing to him the message from Elisha—that he was appointed to be king of Israel and destroyer of the house of Ahab —rushed out of the house and disappeared. Jehu's countenance as he reentered the assembly of officers showed that some strange tidings had reached him. He tried at first to evade their questions but then revealed the situation in which he found himself placed by the prophetic call. In a moment the enthusiasm of members of the army took fire. They threw their garments under his feet so as to form a rough carpet, then blew the royal salute on their trumpets, and thus ordained him king (2 Kings 9:1-13), c. 841 B.C.

Slays the Kings. Jehu accepted the kingdom and immediately began to make it secure. He cut off all communicaton between Ramoth-gilead and Jezreel and set off at full speed with Bidkar, whom he had made captain of his army. Jehoram was there (suffering from wounds received at the hands of the Syrians), as well as Ahaziah, king of Judah, who had come to see him. The watchman told of the coming of a company, and as it neared the city he announced to the kings that "the driving is like the driving of Jehu, ... for he drives furiously." When near the city the alarm was taken, and the two kings hastened out and met Jehu in the field of Naboth. In answer to the question of Jehoram, "Is it peace, Jehu?" the latter replied, "What peace, so long as the harlotries of your mother Jezebel and her witchcrafts are so many?" Then he drew his bow and shot Jehoram, while his followers pursued and mortally wounded Ahaziah. Jehu advanced to Jezreel and fulfilled the divine warning on Jezebel. The queen appeared at the palace window as if to welcome Jehu, but he shouted, "Who is on my side? Who?" Two eunuchs appeared, and at his command they threw her from the window (2 Kings 9:14-37).

Destroys House of Ahab. Jehu then sent a letter to the rulers, challenging them to set up one of the young princes as king and fight out the matter. They replied that they were ready to submit to him; whereupon he ordered them to appear the next day with the heads of all the royal princes of Samaria, which they did. He explained that he must be regarded as the appointed minister of the divine decrees against the house of Ahab and proceeded to slay all the officers of the late government who would most likely disturb his own reign (2 Kings 10:1-11). Proceeding to Samaria he met forty-two sons (or nephews) of Ahaziah, king of Judah, and put them to the sword (10:12-14; 2 Chron. 22:8).

Destroys Baalites. On his way to Samaria he met Jehonadab, the Rechabite, to whom he confided his purpose of exterminating the Baalites.

Arriving at Samaria, he announced that he was to be even more enthusiastic in the service of Baal than Ahab had been and summoned the Baalites to come and sacrifice to that god. When they were assembled in the temple, clad in their sacerdotal garments, Jehu offered the chief sacrifice; Jehonadab joined in the deception. At a concerted signal the eighty trusted guards fell upon and massacred the worshipers and thus at one blow exterminated the heathen population of Israel. The temple and image of Baal were demolished, and the sanctuary became a latrine (2 Kings 10:15-28).

Sin and Punishment. Jehu sinned against God in not overturning the golden calves worshiped in Bethel and Dan, and thus continued in the sin of Jeroboam. For this it was foretold that his dynasty should only extend to four generations.

His Wars. After his violent political and religious purge in Israel, Jehu incurred the implacable hatred of *Hazael* (which see) of Damascus by submitting to Shalmaneser III, king of Assyria, in the Assyrian invasion of 841 B.C., rather than joining Syria in a coalition against the encroachments of "the giant of the Semites." The Black Obelisk of Shalmaneser III, which Austen Layard found in the imperial palace at Nimrod, displays Jehu, or his deputy, actually prostrating himself before the Assyrian emperor. The accompanying inscription reads: "Tribute of Iaua (Jehu), son of Omri. Silver, gold, a golden bowl, a golden beaker, golden goblets, pitchers of gold, lead, staves for the hand of the king. Javelins I received from him" (D. D. Luckenbill, *Ancient Records of Assyria and Babylonia,* (1927), vol. 1, sec. 590). But Assyrian withdrawal for the time from the west and Hazael's growing power must have made Jehu lament his Assyrian appeasement policy. The Aramaeans began to thresh Gilead and Bashan "with implements of sharp iron" (2 Kings 10:32-33; Amos 1:3-4) before Jehu died, around 814 B.C.   M.F.U.

Character. Jehu was a positive and ambitious character; quick to decide upon a plan of action and equally ready in execution. He was prudent, calculating, and passionless. The narrative justifies us, we think, in judging that his zeal for God was regulated much by God's zeal for him. "He must be regarded, like many others in history, as an instrument for accomplishing great purposes rather than as great or good in himself. In the long period during which his destiny, though known to others and perhaps to himself, lay dormant; in the ruthlessness with which he carried out his purposes; in the union of profound silence and dissimulation with a stern, fanatic, wayward zeal, he has not been without his likenesses in modern times" (Smith, *Dict.,* s.v.).

BIBLIOGRAPHY: T. Kirk and G. Rawlinson, *Studies in the Books of the Kings,* 2 vols. in 1 (1983), 2:103-13; E. R. Thiele, *Mysterious Numbers of the Hebrew Kings* (1983), pp. 36-37, 56-57, 76-77, 103-4.

JEHUB'BAH (je-hub'a; "hidden"). A man of Asher, son of Shemer, or Shomer, of the house of Beriah (1 Chron. 7:34). The NIV reads Hubbah for Jehubbah.

JEHU'CAL (je-hū'kal; "Jehovah is able"). The son of Shelemiah, and the person who was sent with Zephaniah by King Hezekiah to Jeremiah to request that he would pray to the Lord on behalf of the kingdom (Jer. 37:3). He afterward joined with his associates in requesting the death of the prophet because of his unfavorable response (38:4), in which verse he is called one of the "officials." In 38:1 his name is given in the abbreviated form Jucal.

JE'HUD (jē'hud; "praise"). A town on the border of Dan, named between Baalath and Bene-berak (Josh. 19:45). The modern site is Yazūr, five miles SE of Joppa.

JEHU'DI (je-hū'di; "a man of Judah, a Jew"). The son of Nethaniah, sent by the officials of Jehoiakim's court to bring Baruch to read Jeremiah's denunciation (Jer. 36:14), and then by the king to fetch the volume itself and read it to him (vv. 21, 23), 608 B.C.

JEHUDI'JAH (je-hū-di'ja; "Jewess"). Probably the wife of Mered (1 Chron. 4:18). The KJV rend-

Panel of Black Obelisk showing Jehu, or his deputy, paying tribute to Shalmaneser III

ers this word as a proper name, whereas it most likely refers merely to the fact that she was a Jewess (NASB, "his Jewish wife"). She is the mother of Jered, Heber, and Jekuthiel.

JE'HUSH. See Jeush, no. 3.

JEI'EL (je-i'-el).

1. A Reubenite of the house of Joel at the time of the taking of some census, apparently on the deportation of the trans-Jordanic tribes by Tiglath-pileser (1 Chron. 5:7), about 740 B.C.

2. A Benjamite, apparently the founder ("father"), as well as a resident, of Gibeon, and the husband of Maacah. A number of his sons are named (1 Chron. 8:29-31, where the name is supplied by the NASB and NIV translators; 9:35-37, where the name replaces KJV *Jehiel*).

3. The son of Hothan, an Aroerite, and one of David's mighty men (1 Chron. 11:44; the name replaces KJV *Jehiel*), 993 B.C.

4. A Merarite Levite appointed by David to assist in the removal of the Ark to Jerusalem (1 Chron. 16:5). He is probably the same as the one mentioned in the same verse as a performer on "instruments of music, harps, lyres," and identical with the gatekeeper (15:18) and musician (v. 21), about 982 B.C.

5. A Levite, and great-grandfather of Jehaziel, who predicted success to Jehoshaphat against the Ammonites and Moabites (2 Chron. 20:14), considerably before 875 B.C.

6. The scribe who, with others, kept the account of the numbers of King Uzziah's troops (2 Chron. 26:11), about 769 B.C.

7. A Levite of the sons of Elizaphan who assisted in the restoration of the Temple under King Hezekiah (2 Chron. 29:13), 719 B.C.

8. One of the chief Levites in the time of Josiah who assisted in the rites of the great Passover (2 Chron. 35:9), about 639 B.C.

9. An Israelite of the "sons" of Nebo who had taken a foreign wife and had to relinquish her (Ezra 10:43), 457 B.C.

10. In the KJV of Ezra 8:13, one of those who returned with Ezra from Babylon to Jerusalem. See Jeuel.

JEKAB'ZEEL (je-kab'zēl; "God will gather"). A town in Judah (Neh. 11:25), probably identical with *Kabzeel* (which see).

JEKAME'AM (jek-a-mē'am; "the people will rise"). A Levite, the fourth in rank of the "sons" of Hebron in the Levitical arrangement established by David (1 Chron. 23:19; 24:23), about 960 B.C.

JEKAMI'AH (jek-a-mī'a; "Jehovah will rise").

1. The son of Shallum and father of Elishama, of the descendants of Sheshan of Judah (1 Chron. 2:41), probably about 588 B.C.

2. The fifth named of the sons of King Jeconiah

(1 Chron. 3:18; "Jecamiah," KJV), born to him during the captivity, after 597 B.C.

JEKU'THIEL (jekū'thi-el; "God will support," cf. Arab. *qata*, to "sustain, nourish"). A man recorded in the genealogies of Judah (1 Chron. 4:18) as the son of Mered by his Jewish wife (see Jehudijah), and in his turn the father, or founder, of the town of Zanoah.

JEMI'MA (je-mī'ma; a "pigeon, dove"), **Jemimah** (NASB and NIV). The name of the first of the three daughters born to Job after his restoration to prosperity (Job 42:14).

JEM'UEL (jem'ū-el; "day of God"). The eldest son of Simeon (Gen. 46:10; Ex. 6:15); elsewhere (Num. 26:12) called Nemuel.

JEPH'THAH (jef'tha; "he will open"). The ninth judge of Israel, the illegitimate son of Gilead.

A Marauder. In consequence of his illegitimacy, he was banished from his father's house and took up his residence at Tob, a district of Syria, not far from Gilead (Judg. 11:1-3). It was here that he became head of a marauding party, and when a war broke out between the Israelites and the Ammonites, he probably made a name for himself.

Leader of Israel. This induced the Israelites to seek his aid as commander; and though at first he refused in consequence of their ill-treatment of him, yet on their solemn covenant to regard him as their leader, he consented. In this capacity he was successful and, in a war that soon followed, the Ammonites were defeated with great loss (11:3-33). On the eve of the battle he made a vow (vv. 30-31) that whatever should come forth from his house first to meet him on his return home he would devote to God. This turned out to be his daughter, an only child, who welcomed his return with music and dancing (see below).

Quarrel with Ephraimites. His victory over the Ammonites was followed by a quarrel with the Ephraimites, who challenged his right to go to war without their consent and used threatening language toward him. Jephthah remonstrated with them and then, gathering his forces, fought and defeated them in battle. The Gileadites then seized the fords of Jordan and made those attempting to cross pronounce the word *Shibboleth;* but if anyone pronounced it "Sibboleth," they knew him to be an Ephraimite and killed him on the spot (12:1-6).

Rule and Death. The remainder of Jephthah's rule seems to have been peaceful, lasting about six years (c. 1105-1099 B.C.). He was buried in his native region, in one of the cities of Gilead (12:7).

Character. Jephthah appears to have been a daring, fearless man, skilled in war, quick to avenge injuries, and ready to defend the helpless as well as to forgive wrong. He does not seem to have been rash and impetuous, notwithstanding his vow, for he did not take up the sword at once, but waited until negotiations with the king of the Ammonites had been without effect.

His Vow. Volumes have been written on what is generally termed "Jephthah's rash vow"; the question is whether, in doing to his daughter according to his vow, he actually offered her as a sacrifice. That he really did so is a horrible conclusion but one that it seems impossible to avoid. The following may be taken as a summary of the arguments on both sides.

In favor of actual sacrifice, the following arguments are urged: (1) The express terms of the narrative, "I will offer it up as a burnt offering," and he "did to her according to the vow." (2) The fact that Jephthah was half heathen and that the circumstances took place where the heathen dwelt in great numbers and where human sacrifices were not unknown. (3) That Jephthah's excessive grief on seeing his daughter come forth to meet him can only be accounted for on the supposition that he considered her devoted to death. (4) That the mourning for Jephthah's daughter for four days in the year can be reconciled only with the supposition that she was an actual sacrifice. (5) That there is nothing in the history to show that his conduct was sanctioned by God.

In opposition it is urged: (1) By translating the Heb. prefix (which is rendered *and* in our version) to *or,* all difficulty will be removed. His words would then read, "shall be the Lord's, *or* I will offer it up as a burnt offering"; and not infrequently the sense requires that the Heb. should be thus rendered (Lev. 27:28) where there is a similar meaning of the conjunctive *waw.* (2) He cannot be understood as declaring an intention to offer a burnt offering whatever might come forth to meet him, since he might have been met by what no law or custom permitted to be so offered. (3) The sacrifice of children to Molech is expressly forbidden and declared an abomination to the Lord (Lev. 20:2-3); and it would be a yet higher insult to offer them to the Lord. (4) There is no precedent for such an offering. (5) No father by his own authority could put even an offending child to death, much less one that was innocent (Deut. 21:18-21; 1 Sam. 14:24-45). (6) It is said he did to her "according to the vow which he had made," and "she had no relations with a man," which conveys the idea that she was devoted to a life of celibacy; and that what the daughters of Israel bewailed was not her death, but her celibacy, for she "wept in the mountains because of her virginity" (Judg. 11:38-40). There appears to have been a class of women devoted exclusively to the Temple service who were Nazirites (Ex. 38:8); to this company of females reference is made in 1 Sam. 2:22 (*see also* Luke 2:37). To such a company of devoted women Jephthah's daughter might be set apart. One of the strongest points on this side of the

argument is that the Heb. word *lethanoth,* rendered "wept," rather meant "to celebrate." Therefore, these daughters of Israel went yearly, not to lament, but with songs of praise to celebrate the daughter of Jephthah. The prominence given to the daughter's virginity, as an argument against Jephthah's sacrifice, we think is hardly warranted. It is probably mentioned to give greater force to the sacrifice, as it would leave him without descendants, which in the East was considered a special misfortune (G. H. A. von Ewald, *Hist. of Israel;* K. & D., *Com.;* Robertson, *Early Religion of Israel;* McClintock and Strong, *Cyclopedia;* Smith, *Bib. Dict.;* and others).

BIBLIOGRAPHY: H. Levy, *Orientalia* 9 (1940): 262ff.; H. H. Rowley, *Bulletin of the American Schools of Oriental Research* 85 (1942): 28ff.; L. J. Wood, *Distressing Days of the Judges* (1975), pp. 278-301; A. R. Fausset, *A Critical and Expository Commentary on the Book of Judges* (1977), pp. 186-208.

JEPHUN'NEH (je-fun'e; "he is ready").

1. The father of Caleb, which latter was a faithful explorer of Canaan with Joshua, and a Kenizzite (Num. 13:6; 14:6, 30, 38; 26:65; 32:12; 34:19; Deut. 1:36; Josh. 14:6, 13-14; 15:13; 21:12; 1 Chron. 4:15; 6:56), before 1414 B.C.

2. One of the sons of Jether, of the descendants of Asher (1 Chron. 7:38), probably before 1017 B.C.

JE'RAH (je'ra; "moon, month"). The fourth son of Joktan (Gen. 10:26; 1 Chron. 1:20). "God will" be "compassionate."

JERAH'MEEL (je-ra'mēl; "God will" be "compassionate").

1. The firstborn son of Hezron, son of Perez, son of Judah (1 Chron. 2:9). His descendants were called Jerahmeelites (1 Sam. 27:10; 30:29).

2. A Merarite Levite, the representative of the family of Kish, probably the son of Mahli (1 Chron. 24:29; cf. 23:21), about 960 B.C.

3. In the NASB and NIV, "the king's son" employed by Jehoiakim, after he had burned the roll of Jeremiah's prophecy, to make Jeremiah and Baruch prisoners (Jer. 36:26), about 608 B.C. In the KJV this person is described as the son of Hammelech.

JERAH'MEELITE (je-ra'mēl-īt; 1 Sam. 27:10; 30:29). Descendants of Jerahmeel, no. 1.

JE'RED (je'red; "descent"). A son, apparently, of Mered, of the tribe of Judah, by his Jewish wife (*see Jehudijah*). He is named as the father (founder) of Gedor (1 Chron. 4:18), perhaps about 1640 B.C.

See also Jared, for the person named in 1 Chron. 1:2.

JER'EMAI (jer'e-mī; "high"). One of the "sons" of Hashum who divorced his wife after the return from Babylon (Ezra 10:33), 457 B.C.

JEREMI'AH (jer-e-mī'a; "Jehovah will lift up,

exalt," or "will rise"). The name of the great prophet (*see* article below) and of eight other persons in the Bible.

1. An inhabitant of Libnah, the father of Hamutal, wife of Josiah, and mother of Jehoahaz and Zedekiah (2 Kings 23:31; 24:18; Jer. 52:1), before 608 B.C.

2. One of the chief men of the tribe of Manasseh E, apparently about the time of its deportation by the Assyrians (1 Chron. 5:24), about 727 B.C.

3. One of the Benjamite warriors who joined David at Ziklag (1 Chron. 12:4), before 1000 B.C.

4 and 5. The fifth and tenth in rank of the Gadite adventurers who joined David's troops in the wilderness (1 Chron. 12:10, 13), before 1000 B.C.

6. One of the priests who signed the sacred covenant along with Nehemiah (Neh. 10:2); probably the same as one of those who followed the princes in the circuit of the newly repaired walls with the sound of trumpets (12:34), 445 B.C.

7. A priest who accompanied Zerubbabel from Babylon to Jerusalem (Neh. 12:1). It is probably himself or his division that is mentioned in v. 12, 536 B.C.

8. The son of Habazziniah and father of Jaazaniah, which last was one of the Rechabites whom the prophets tested with the offer of wine (Jer. 35:3), before 626 B.C.

JEREMI'AH (jer-e-mī'a; "Jehovah will lift up, exalt," or "will rise").

The second of the greater prophets of the OT. He was the son of Hilkiah, a priest of Anathoth, in the land of Benjamin (Jer. 1:1). Many writers, both ancient and modern, have supposed that his father was the Hilkiah mentioned in 2 Kings 22:8. Against this hypothesis, however, there have been urged (Keil, Ewald, Orelli, and others) the following facts: (1) that the name is too common to be a ground of identification; (2) that the manner in which Hilkiah is mentioned is inconsistent with the notion of his having been the high priest of Israel; (3) that neither Jeremiah himself nor his opponents allude to him; and (4) that the priests who lived at Anathoth (1 Kings 2:26) were of the house of Ithamar, while from Zadok down they were of the line of Eleazar.

Early Life. The word of the Lord came to Jeremiah while he was still young (Jer. 1:6) and happened in the thirteenth year of the reign of King Josiah (626 B.C.), while the prophet still lived in Anathoth. He appears to have remained in his native city until he was obliged to leave in order to escape the persecution of his fellow townsmen (11:21) and even of his own family (12:6). He then took up his residence at Jerusalem.

Under Josiah. He probably assisted King Josiah in the reformation effected during his reign (2 Kings 23:1-2). The movement on behalf of true religion ceased as soon as the influence of the

court was withdrawn, and the prophet bewailed the death of this prince as the precursor of the divine judgments for the national sins (2 Chron. 35:25).

Under Jehoahaz. The short reign —three months —of this king gave little scope for prophetic action, and we hear nothing of Jeremiah during this period.

Under Jehoiakim. The king (608-597 B.C.) had come to the throne as the vassal of Egypt, and for a time the Egyptian party was dominant in Jerusalem. Jeremiah appeared as the chief representative of the party that favored the supremacy of the Chaldeans as the only way of safety. In so doing he had to expose himself to the suspicion of treachery, and was interrupted in his ministry by "the priests and the prophets," who, with the populace, brought him before the civil authorities, urging that capital punishment should be inflicted on him for his prophecies (Jer. 26). The officials of Judah endeavored to protect him and appealed to the precedent of Micah the Moresheth, who had uttered a similar prophecy in the reign of Hezekiah; and so for a time he escaped. Ahikam, the son of Shaphan, seems to have had some influence in securing the prophet's safety. In the fourth year of Jehoiakim Jeremiah was commanded to write the predictions that he had been given (chap. 36). Probably as a measure of safety he was, as he says, "restricted," and could not himself go to the house of the Lord. He therefore enlisted Baruch to write the predictions and to read them publicly on the fast day. Baruch was summoned before the officials, who advised that both he and Jeremiah should conceal themselves while they endeavored to influence the mind of the king by reading the roll to him. Jehoiakim read the three or four leaves and then destroyed the roll. He gave orders for the immediate arrest of Baruch and Jeremiah, who, however, were preserved from the angry king. The prophet, at the command of God, rewrote the roll, adding "many similar words" (v. 32). To this period is assigned the prophecy in the valley of Ben-hinnom (chap. 19) and his ill treatment at the hand of *Pashhur* (which see).

Under Jehoiachin. We still find Jeremiah uttering his voice of warning during the closing days of the reign of Jehoiakim and the short reign of his successor, Jehoiachin (598 B.C.; Jer. 13:18; cf. 2 Kings 24:12; Jer. 22:24-30). He sent a letter of counsel and condolence to those who shared the captivity of the royal family (chaps. 29-31).

Under Zedekiah. In the fourth year (594 B.C.) of this monarch's reign Hananiah prophesied that the power of the Chaldeans would be destroyed and the captives restored from Babylon (Jer. 28:3); he corroborated his prophecy by taking off from the neck of Jeremiah the yoke that he wore by divine command (v. 10; cf. 27:2). Jeremiah was told to "go and speak to Hananiah, saying, 'Thus says the Lord, "You have broken the yokes of wood, but you have made instead of them yokes of iron." For thus says the Lord of hosts, the God of Israel, "I have put a yoke of iron on the neck of all these nations, that they may serve Nebuchadnezzar king of Babylon" ' " (28:13-14). It was probably not until the latter part of the reign of Zedekiah that the prophet was put in the confinement, as we find that "they had not yet put him in the prison" when the army of Nebuchadnezzar commenced the siege of Jerusalem (37:4-5). Jeremiah had declared what the fatal issue would be (chap. 24) and was incarcerated in the court of the prison adjoining the palace, where he predicted the certain return from the impending captivity (32:37). Jeremiah's suffering reached its climax under this king, especially during the siege of Jerusalem. The approach of the Egyptian army and the consequent withdrawal for a time of the Chaldeans brightened the prospects of the Jews, and the king entreated Jeremiah to pray to the Lord for them. The answer received from God was that the Egyptians would go to their own land and that the Chaldeans would return and destroy the city (37:7-8). This irritated the officials, who made the departure of Jeremiah from the city the pretext of accusing him of deserting to the Chaldeans. In spite of his denial, he was cast into prison where he would doubtless have perished but for the intervention of Ebed-melech, one of the royal eunuchs (37:12–38:13). The king seems to have been favorably inclined toward the prophet, but, for fear of the officials, consulted with him secretly (38:14-28). In one of these secret interviews Jeremiah obtained a milder imprisonment in the guardhouse belonging to the royal citadel where he was given "a loaf of bread daily from the baker's street, until all the bread in the city was gone" (37:17-21). While in prison he bought, with all requisite formalities, the field at Anathoth that his kinsman Hanamel wished to get rid of (32:6-9), thus showing his faith in his country's future.

Under Nebuchadnezzar. Nebuchadnezzar took the city (586 B.C.; Albright's date, 587), and gave a special charge to his captain, Nebuzaradan, to free Jeremiah and to obey his request (39:11-12). He was, accordingly, delivered from the prison and the choice given him either to go to Babylon or remain with his own people. He chose the latter and went to Mizpah with Gedaliah, who had been appointed governor of Judea. After the murder of Gedaliah he advised Johanan, the recognized leader of the people, to remain in the land (42:7-22). The people refused to heed his advice under the plea that he was acting in the interest of the Chaldeans, went to Egypt "as far as Tahpanhes," and took Jeremiah and Baruch with them (43:6-7). While there he still sought to turn the people who had so long rebelled against the Lord back to Him (chap. 44). His writings give us

no further information respecting his life, but it is probable that he died in Egypt soon after.

Traditions. There is a Christian tradition that Jeremiah was stoned to death by the Jews at Tahpanhes. An Alexandrian tradition reported that his bones had been brought to that city by Alexander the Great. On the other hand, there is the Jewish statement that, on the conquest of Egypt by Nebuchadnezzar, he, with Baruch, made his escape to Babylon and died there in peace.

Archaeology. In 1935 J. L. Starkey discovered eighteen ostraca with Heb. writing in the ancient Phoenician script in a guardroom adjoining the outer gate of the city of Lachish (cf. Harry Torczyner, *Lachish I: The Lachish Letters*, 1938; W. F. Albright, *Bulletin of the American Schools of Oriental Research* 70 [April 1938]: 11-17). Additional ostraca were found in the last campaign in 1938. These letters were written by a certain Hoshaiah, who was at some military outpost, to a man named Jaosh, evidently the high commanding officer at Lachish. Nebuchadnezzar had attacked and partly burned Lachish about a decade previously in Jehoiachin's reign. These letters, however, belong to the layer of ashes representing the final destruction of the city and are to be dated early in 588 B.C. when Nebuchadnezzar was beginning his final siege of Jerusalem together with that of Lachish and Azekah. These so-called Lachish Letters have immense paleographic value and shed much historical light on the time of Jeremiah. The Heb. names and expressions used, such as "weakening the hands of the people," remind us of Jer. 38:4.   M.F.U.

Character. "In every page of Jeremiah's prophecies we recognize the temperament which, while it does not lead the man who has it to shrink from doing God's work, however painful, makes the pain of doing it infinitely more acute, and gives to the whole character the impress of a deeper and more lasting melancholy. He is preeminently 'the man that hath seen afflictions' " (Lam. 3:1). He reveals himself in his writings "as a soul of gentle nature, yielding, tenderhearted, affectionate, with almost a woman's thirst for love, with which certainly the iron, unbending firmness, and immovable power of resistance belonging to him in his prophetic sphere are in strange contrast" (Orelli, *Com.*, p. 11).

BIBLIOGRAPHY: F. B. Meyer, *Jeremiah: Priest and Prophet* (n.d.)

JEREMIAH, BOOK OF. The prophesies of Jeremiah are named after the prophet himself, Yirmeyahu or Yirmeyah. His ministry extended over the last tragic forty years of the kingdom of Judah to the destruction of Jerusalem and the deportation of its inhabitants to Babylon.

Purpose. The prophetic oracles of Jeremiah constitute a stern warning to Judah and its capital city, Jerusalem, to abandon idolatry and apostasy in order to escape the inevitable consequence of the seventy-year Babylonian captivity (25:1-14). The prophet's sermons met with intense opposition from a society fanatically addicted to idolatry. The brave prophet, however, discharged his ministry despite continual persecution and danger of death. The tense three-sided contest for world dominion between Assyria, Egypt, and Babylon forms the background of his prophetic career. Because he predicted the triumph of Babylon and the consequent captivity of Judah, with repeated warning against a useless alliance with Egypt, he incurred almost universal disfavor. A note of doom dominates his message. Against this dark background, passages setting forth messianic hope flash through his prophecies. These great foregleams of a better day (cf. 23:5-7; 30:4-11; 31:31-34; 33:15-18) point to the final restoration of Israel. This is not to be confused, however, with the restoration from Babylon, but points to a period of unparalleled tragedy (30:3-10) and the manifestation of David's "righteous Branch . . . The Lord our Righteousness" (23:5-6; 30:9). These great messianic prophecies are yet to be fulfilled (Acts 1:7; 15:14-18) in the future millennial kingdom (Rom. 11:15-29).

Outline.

I. Introduction: The prophet's call (1:1-19)
II. Prophetic oracles against Jerusalem and Judah (2:1–45:5)
   A. In the reign of Josiah and Jehoiakim (1:1–20:18)
      1. First oracle—national sin and ingratitude (2:1–3:5)
      2. Second oracle—destruction from the north (3:6–6:30)
      3. Third oracle—threat of exile (7:1–10:25)
      4. Fourth oracle—the broken covenant and the sign of the waistband (11:1–13:27)
      5. Fifth oracle—the drought (14:1–15:21); the sign of the unmarried prophet (16:1–17:18); warning regarding the Sabbath (17:19-27)
      6. Sixth oracle—sign of the potter's house (18:1–20:18)
   B. During various periods until Jerusalem's destruction (21:1–39:18)
      1. Zedekiah and the people's punishment (21:1–29:32)
      2. Future messianic kingdom (30:1–33:26)
      3. Sin of Zedekiah; the loyalty of the Rechabites (34:1–35:19)
      4. Jehoiachin's opposition (36:1-32)
      5. Jerusalem's experiences during the siege (37:1–39:18)
   C. After the fall of Jerusalem (40:1–45:5)

1. Jeremiah's ministry to the remnant in the land (40:1–42:22)
2. Jeremiah's ministry in Egypt (43:1–44:30)
3. Jeremiah's message to Baruch (45:1-5)
III. Prophecies against the nations (46:1–51:64)
   A. Against Egypt (46:1-28)
   B. Against Philistia (47:1-7)
   C. Against Moab (48:1-47)
   D. Against Ammon (49:1-6)
   E. Against Edom (49:7-22)
   F. Against Damascus (49:23-27)
   G. Against Arabia (49:28-33)
   H. Against Elam (49:34-39)
   I. Against Babylon (50:1–51:64)
IV. Historical appendix
   A. Judah's fall and captivity (52:1-30)
   B. Jehoiachin's liberation (52:31-34)

Authorship and Authenticity. Numerous arguments support the fact that Jeremiah, "the son of Hilkiah, of the priests who were in Anathoth in the land of Benjamin" (Jer. 1:1), is the author of the book.

Internal Evidence. The prophet dictated to his secretary, Baruch, all his prophecies in the beginning of his ministry to the fourth year of Jehoiakim. This material consists of well over half the prophet's ministry. When this roll was destroyed by King Jehoiakim (36:23), the prophet dictated another edition, which included much new material (36:32). This is not the present book, because many portions of the book of Jeremiah bear a later date in his prophetic career (e.g., 21:1; 24:1; etc.), and still others show evidence of being composed in the later portion of his ministry. Internal evidence demonstrates that the prophet wrote the entire book. Chapter 52 is a possible exception. This was possibly appended to his prophecies from 2 Kings 24:18–25:30, with which it is practically identical.

External Proof. OT references to the prophecies are explicit (cf. Daniel's allusion to the prediction of the seventy years' captivity, Dan. 9:2; Jer. 25:11-14; 29:10). Second Chron. 36:21 and Ezek. 1:1 confirm this prophecy and the general period of Jeremiah. Extracanonical evidence adds its voice. Ecclus. 49:6-7 traces the destruction of Jerusalem to the rejection of Jeremiah's warning and the prophecies. Josephus (*Ant.* 10.5:1) and the Talmud confirm the same fact. In the NT, Matt. 2:17-18 quotes Jer. 31:15; Matt. 21:13, Mark 11:17, and Luke 19:46 quote from Jeremiah 7:11; Rom. 11:27 has reference to Jer. 31:33-34, and Heb. 8:8-13 also quotes from this passage. Christian tradition also adds its testimony to the Jeremian authenticity of the prophecy.

Apparent Composite Character of the Book. This is explained by the fact that the book was written in stages. The earlier edition was destroyed. It was reissued later with additions. Subsequent prophecies were collated and doubtless edited by Baruch. For this reason the contents are not always in systematic order or chronological sequence. The wide divergence between the LXX and the Masoretic Heb. is difficult to account for and seems to comprehend two different forms of the book.

Modern Criticism Fails to Disprove Jeremian Authenticity. Critical theories are to a large extent subjective. Robert Pfeiffer conjectures that Baruch combined the prophet's book with his own, redoing many of the prophetic speeches in his own "deuteronomistic style" (*Intr.* [1940], p. 55). It is contended that even Baruch's book was later extensively revised with both prose and poetic editions. But such a procedure on the part of a pious disciple like Baruch is unreasonable. A. Bentzen rejects the idea that Baruch wrote the "deuteronomistic sections." Bentzen thinks that Jeremiah was used by "deuteronomistic zealots" (*Intr.* [1949], p. 119). H. Birkeland assumes that the book contains several complexes of traditions (*Zum hebraeischen Traditionswesen* [1938], p. 42), but the old idea of a nucleus of traditions subsequently expanded is without factual foundation. Critical theories are bereft of any valid substitute for Jeremian authorship of the prophecy.

BIBLIOGRAPHY: T. F. K. Laetsch, *Bible Commentary: Jeremiah* (1952); E. A. Leslie, *Jeremiah: Chronologically Arranged, Translated and Interpreted* (1954); J. Bright, *Jeremiah,* Anchor Bible (1965); I. L. Jensen, *Jeremiah: The Prophet of Judgment* (1966); R. K. Harrison, *Introduction to the Old Testament* (1969), pp. 801-82; W. L. Holladay, *Jeremiah: Spokesman Out of Time* (1974); H. C. von Orelli, *The Prophecies of Jeremiah* (1977); J. A. Thompson, *The Book of Jeremiah,* New International Commentary on the Old Testament (1980); C. L. Feinberg, *Jeremiah, a Commentary* (1982).

JEREMIAS (je-re-mī'as). A Gk. form of the name *Jeremiah,* the prophet, and the KJV rendering in Matt. 16:14.

JER'EMOTH (jer'e-mōth; "tall"; cf. Arab. *warima,* "to be thick, tall, swollen").

1. One of the "sons" of Becher (1 Chron. 7:8) and head of a Benjamite house that existed in the time of David, about 1017 B.C. The KJV renders "Jerimoth."

2. A Benjamite chief, a son of the house of Beriah and Elpaal (1 Chron. 8:14). His family dwelt at Jerusalem, apparently about 588 B.C.

3. A Merarite Levite, son of Mushi (1 Chron. 23:23), called Jerimoth in 1 Chron. 24:30, about 960 B.C.

4. Son of Heman, head of the thirteenth division of musicians in the divine service (1 Chron. 25:22); called Jerimoth in v. 4 (and by the NIV in v. 22), about 960 B.C.

5. Son of Azriel, leader of the tribe of Naphtali in the reign of David (1 Chron. 27:19), about 1000 B.C. The KJV and NIV render "Jerimoth."

6. One of the "sons" of Elam, who put away his foreign wife after the captivity (Ezra 10:26), 456 B.C.

7. One of the "sons" of Zattu who had taken Gentile wives and put them away after the return from Babylon (Ezra 10:27), 456 B.C.

8. One of the "sons" of Bani, who also put away his Gentile wife (Ezra 10:29), 456 B.C. The KJV renders "Ramoth."

JERI'AH (jer'i'a). The eldest son of Hebron (1 Chron. 23:19; 24:23). He is called Jerijah in the KJV and NASB of 1 Chron. 26:31.

JER'IBAI (jer'i-bī; "Jehovah contends"). The second named of the sons of Elnaam, and one of David's bodyguard (1 Chron. 11:46), after 1000 B.C.

JER'ICHO (jer'i-kō; possibly "place of fragrance" or "moon city"). An ancient city in the wide plain where the Jordan Valley broadens between the Moab mountains and the western precipices, and situated on the route of Israel after they crossed the Jordan under Joshua (Josh. 3:16). The first mention of Jericho in Scripture is in connection with the advance of Israel to Canaan; they "camped in the plains of Moab beyond the Jordan opposite Jericho" (Num. 22:1). From the manner and frequency in which it is referred to it would seem to have been the most important city of the Jordan Valley at that time (31:12; 34:15; 35:1; etc.). The spies sent by Joshua were entertained in Jericho by *Rahab* (which see), for which they promised her protection when the city would be destroyed (Josh. 2:1-21; 6:25). The miraculous capture of Jericho, the sin and punishment of Achan, and the curse pronounced upon anyone who should attempt to rebuild it are graphically recorded (6:1–7:26). Jericho was given to the tribe of Benjamin (18:21), "and from this time a long interval elapsed before Jericho appeared again upon the scene. It is only incidentally mentioned in the life of David in connection with his embassy to the Ammonite king (2 Sam. 10:5). And the solemn manner in which its second foundation under Hiel, the Beth-elite, is recorded (1 Kings 16:34) would certainly seem to imply that up to that time its site had been uninhabited. It is true that mention is made of 'a city of palm trees' (Judg. 1:16; 3:13) in existence apparently at the time when spoken of. However, once actually rebuilt, Jericho rose again slowly into consequence. In its immediate vicinity the sons of the prophets sought retirement from the world: Elisha 'healed the spring of the waters;' and over against it, beyond Jordan, Elijah 'went up by a whirlwind into heaven' (2 Kings 2:1-22). In its plains Zedekiah fell into the hands of the Chaldeans (25:5; Jer. 39:5). In the return under Zerubbabel the 'children of Jericho,' three hundred and forty-five in number, are comprised (Ezra 2:34; Neh. 7:36); and it is even implied that they removed thither again, for the 'men of Jericho' assisted Nehemiah in rebuilding that part of the wall of Jerusalem that was next to the sheep-gate (3:2). The Jericho of the days of Josephus was a distant one hundred and fifty stadia from Jerusalem and fifty from the Jordan."

In the NT Jericho is mentioned in connection with Jesus' restoring sight to the blind (Matt. 20:29-30; Mark 10:46; Luke 18:35) and His being entertained by Zaccheus (19:1-8). And finally, it was introduced in the parable of the Good Samaritan (Luke 10:30), which, if not a real occurrence, derives interest from the fact that robbers have ever terrorized the road from Jerusalem to Jericho.

The ancient strategic fortress commanding the entrance to Canaan from the E is represented by the modern mound known as Tell es-Sultan. The springs at this site yield a plentiful supply of water. Through the excavations of Ernst Sellin and the Deutsche Orientgesellschaft (1907-9), those of John Garstang (1930-36), and of Kathleen Kenyon (1952-58) the occupational history of the ancient city has been determined.

Excavations at Old Testament Jericho

The site was occupied in Mesolithic times during the eighth millennium B.C. Kathleen Kenyon dated a great defense tower and houses of the earliest village to that millennium. Garstang assigned alphabetic names to later cities that occupied the site. City A was dated about 3000-2500 B.C.; City B, 2500-1700; City C, belonging to the Hyksos period, 1700-1500; City D, captured by

Joshua, 1500-1400. Garstang claimed that the walls of Joshua's day were double. The outer wall was six feet thick and the inner one twelve feet thick, and there was a rubble-filled space of about fifteen feet between them. He believed that the outer wall slid down the slope of the mound and caused the inner wall to collapse as well. The destruction he dated to about 1400 B.C.. Then City E belonged to the time of Ahab (c. 860 B.C.) when Hiel the Bethelite rebuilt the town (1 Kings 16:34). Advocates of the late date of the Exodus and the conquest, who would put the fall of Jericho around 1250 B.C., tried to repudiate Garstang's conclusions; but he stood by them.

When Kathleen Kenyon took up her work at Jericho, she concentrated on the Neolithic and Mesolithic levels at Jericho, but she did give some attention to the Joshua question. She concluded that there never was a double wall at Jericho. The inhabitants had moved the wall farther down the slope to give more protected space and had left the foundation of the inner wall, giving the appearance of a double wall. Moreover, this wall she dated to the Early Bronze Age (3000-2000 B.C.) and suggested that the wall of Joshua's day had probably eroded away during the half millennium when Jericho had been uninhabited between the time of Joshua and Hiel. Probably it had been made of mud brick. The city of Joshua's day (measuring about 8½ acres) she believed fell about 1350-1325 B.C. On the basis of the work done, it seems necessary to conclude that Garstang was in error about the walls of Jericho, but it is not necessary to abandon his dating of the fall of the city because he worked with quantities of material from the Late Bronze (1500-1200 B.C.) tombs of Jericho. These do not seem to have been used after about 1400.

NT or Herodian Jericho stood on both sides of the Wadi Qelt almost two miles SW of Tell es-Sultan; there Herod the Great built his winter palace. Work was begun at the site by James L. Kelso and Dimitri Baramki in 1950 for the American Schools of Oriental Research and Pittsburgh-Xenia Theological Seminary and continued by James Pritchard in 1951 and by Ehud Netzer for the Hebrew University since 1974. South of the Wadi Qelt stood an artificial mound with a pavilion on top of it. South of the artificial mound was a wing of the palace, which is now covered over. Steps led from the artificial mound to the Wadi Qelt. At the foot of the mound on the E was a large pool, and on the W was a sunken garden backed by a grand facade with forty-eight statuary niches. A bridge led across the Wadi Qelt to the N wing of the palace, which consisted of a reception hall, two open courtyards, a bath complex, and other rooms. Nearby, Hasmonaean palaces and a monumental swimming pool have been discovered but are only partially excavated.

H.F.V.

BIBLIOGRAPHY: J. Garstang and J. B. E. Garstang, *The Story of Jericho* (1948); J. L. Kelso, *Biblical Archaeologist* 14 (1951): 34-43; J. B. Pritchard, *Bulletin of the American Schools of Oriental Research* 123 (Oct. 1951): 8-17; J. L. Kelso and D. C. Baramki, *Annual of the American Schools of Oriental Research* 29-30 (1955); K. M. Kenyon, *Digging Up Jericho* (1957); id., *Excavations at Jericho*, 2 vols. (1960-65); id., *Archaeology in the Holy Land* (1960); L. J. Wood, *Survey of Israel's History* (1970), pp. 94-99, 170-75; M. Avi-Yonah, ed., *Encyclopedia of Archaeological Excavations in the Holy Land* (1956): 2:558-75; E. Netzer, *BASOR* 228 (Dec. 1977): 1-13; E. Netzer and E. Meyers, *BASOR* 228 (Dec. 1977): 15-27.

View of the excavated mound, Tell Jericho

JER′IEL (jer′i-el; "God sees"). A man of Issachar, one of the six heads of the house of Tola mentioned in the census in the time of David (1 Chron. 7:2), perhaps after 1000 B.C.

JERI′JAH (jer′i′ja). A different form (1 Chron. 26:31, KJV, NASB) of the name *Jeriah* (which see).

JER′IMOTH (jer′i-moth; cf. **Jeremoth**).

1. The fourth named of the four sons of Bela, son of Benjamin and founder of a Benjamite house that existed in the time of David (1 Chron. 7:7; cf. v. 2), after 1689 B.C.

2. One of the Benjamite archers and slingers who joined David at Ziklag (1 Chron. 12:5), before 1000 B.C.

3. The last named of the sons of Mushi, the son of Merari (1 Chron. 24:30); elsewhere called Jeremoth.

4. One of the sons of Heman, head of the fifteenth ward of musicians (1 Chron. 25:4, 22); called Jeremoth in the latter verse, about 960 B.C.

5. Son of King David, whose daughter Mahalath was the first wife of Rehoboam, her cousin Abihail being the other (2 Chron. 11:18), before 974 B.C. He is not named in the list of David's children (1 Chron. 3; 14:4-7), and it is probable that he was the son of a concubine. The passage 2 Chron. 11:18 is not quite clear, since the word *daughter* is a correction of the q^ere; the original text had *bēn*, i.e., "son."

6. A Levite and one of the overseers of the Temple offerings in the reign of Hezekiah (2 Chron. 31:13), 729 B.C.

7. In the KJV, one of the sons of Becher (1 Chron. 7:8); the NASB and NIV give *Jeremoth*.

8. In the KJV and NIV, a son of Azriel (1 Chron. 27:19); the NASB gives *Jeremoth*.

JE′RIOTH (je′ri-oth; "tent curtains"). Apparently the second wife of Caleb, the son of Hezron (1 Chron. 2:18), about 1440 B.C. The Vulg. renders this as the son of Caleb by his first-mentioned wife, and father of the sons named; but this is contrary to the Heb. text, which is closely followed by the LXX. Perhaps the connective *waw* should be rendered by *even,* thus making Jerioth another name for Azubah.

JEROBO′AM I (jer-o-bō′am; "the people multiplied"). Jeroboam was the name of the first (this article) and fourteenth (*see* article below) kings of Israel. The first king of Israel by this name was the son of Nebat, an Ephraimite, by a woman named Zeruah (1 Kings 11:26).

Noticed by Solomon. At the time when Solomon was constructing the fortifications of Millo underneath the citadel of Zion, he discovered the strength and activity of the young Ephraimite who was employed on the works, and he raised him to the rank of superintendent over the taxes and labors exacted from the tribe of Ephraim (1 Kings 11:28), after 960 B.C.

Future Foretold. On one occasion when leaving Jerusalem, he encountered Ahijah, "the prophet" of the ancient sanctuary of Shiloh. Ahijah stripped off his new outer garment and tore it into twelve pieces, ten of which he gave to Jeroboam with the assurance that, on obedience to His laws, God would establish for him a kingdom and dynasty equal to that of David (vv. 29-39).

Flight into Egypt. Jeroboam probably began to form plots and conspiracies, for Solomon sought to take his life. He fled to Egypt, where he received the protection of Pharaoh Shishak. He remained there until the death of Solomon (v. 40), about 926 B.C.

Revolt of Israel. Upon the accession of Rehoboam, Jeroboam appears to have headed a deputation that asked for a redress of grievances. The harsh answer of Rehoboam inevitably caused a revolution, and Jeroboam was called to be "king over all Israel" (12:1-20).

As King. He selected Shechem as his capital, but for some unknown reason moved the seat of government to Penuel, E of Jordan. He later returned to the W of Jordan and took up his permanent residence at Tirzah (1 Kings 12:25; cf. 15:21, 33; 16:6-8; Josh. 12:24). The policy of Jeroboam was to bring about a religious as well as political disruption of the kingdom. He therefore sought to discourage the yearly pilgrimages to the Temple at Jerusalem. To this end he established shrines at Dan and Bethel, sanctuaries of venerable antiquity, and at the extremities of the kingdom. He set up "two golden calves," doubtless thought of, according to a widespread Semitic custom of viewing deities enthroned on the backs of animals, as representing Jehovah's invisible presence, and established a priesthood for his crown (1 Kings 12:26-33). While he was officiating at the altar, a man of God appeared and prophesied the coming of King Josiah, who would one day burn the bones of its ministers upon that altar. Jeroboam attempted to arrest the man. When the arm that he stretched forth was dried up, in answer to the prayer of the man of God he was healed (13:1-10). Jeroboam continued his idolatrous practices, making "priests of the high places from among all the people" (13:33), and his rebellion soon brought about the extinction of his dynasty. His son Abijah fell sick, and Jeroboam sent his wife in disguise to the prophet Ahijah, who, however, recognized her and predicted her son's death. She returned to Tirzah, and "as she was entering the threshold of the house, the child died." Jeroboam never recovered from the blow and died soon after, having reigned about twenty-two years (14:1-20), c. 931-909 B.C. Jeroboam waged constant war with the house of Judah, but the only act distinctly recorded is a battle with Abijah, the son of Rehoboam, in which he was defeated. For the time being he lost the important cities of Bethel, Jeshanah, and Ephron of Ephraim (2 Chron. 13:1-19).

Character. Although he was the founder of a new kingdom, Jeroboam was a less remarkable man than we might expect. His government exhibited one idea—that of raising a barrier against the reunion of the tribes. He was a slave and victim to that idea; and although the barrier that he raised was effective, it only showed his weakness in needing such a barrier for his protection.

BIBLIOGRAPHY: T. Kirk and G. Rawlinson, *Studies in the Books of Kings* (1983), 2:14-27, 140-48; E. R. Thiele, *Mysterious Numbers of the Hebrew Kings* (1983), 36-38, 53, 78, 106-9, 111-16.

JEROBOAM II. This Jeroboam was the son of the successor of Jehoash and the fourteenth king of Israel, c. 793-753 B.C. Even though he followed the example of the first Jeroboam in keeping up the idolatry of the golden calves, the Lord had pity upon Israel. Jeroboam brought to a successful end the wars that his father had undertaken and delivered Israel from the Syrian yoke (cf. 2 Kings 13:4; 14:26-27). He took the chief cities of Damascus (14:28; Amos 1:3-5) and Hamath, and he restored the ancient eastern limits, from Lebanon to the Dead Sea, to Israel (2 Kings 14:25; Amos 6:14). He reconquered Ammon and Moab (1:13; 2:1-3) and restored to the trans-Jordanic tribes their territory (2 Kings 13:5; 1 Chron. 5:17-22). But it was merely an outward

restoration. The sanctuary at Bethel was kept up in royal state (Amos 7:13), but drunkenness, licentiousness, and oppression prevailed in the country (Hos. 4:12-14; Amos 2:6-8; 4:1; 6:6). Idolatry was united with the worship of Jehovah (Hos. 4:13; 13:6). Amos prophesied the destruction of Jeroboam and his house by the sword (Amos 7:9, 17), and Hosea (Hos. 1:1) denounced the crimes of the nation.

Excavations at Samaria, the capital of the Northern Kingdom, have confirmed its popularity and splendor in the eighth century B.C. Jeroboam II refortified the city with a double wall. In exposed sections, this reached as much as thirty-three feet in width, constituting fortifications so substantial that the mighty Assyrian army took three years to capture the city (2 Kings 17:5). The splendid palace of limestone with a strong rectangular tower and extensive outer court, hitherto assigned to the Ahab era, almost certainly belongs to Jeroboam II (J. Finegan, *Light from the Ancient Past* [1946], p. 55). The jasper seal discovered by Schumacher at Megiddo and inscribed "Shema, servant of Jeroboam," is to be connected with Jeroboam II rather than Jeroboam I, as is now epigraphically certain. The blossoming of art in this prosperous era is demonstrated by the lifelike and magnificently executed lion that appears on the seal.

Amos's prophecies shed light on the increase of commerce and wealth in Jeroboam's realm and its consequent luxury and moral deterioration. Increased tribute poured in, creating a wealthy class that was utterly selfish and unscrupulous (Amos 2:6; 8:6). Simple dwellings of unburned brick gave way to "houses of well-hewn stone." Ahab's ivory palace (evidently referring only to decorations) was imitated by many of the wealthy landowners (1 Kings 22:39; Amos 3:15; 5:11). Loose feasting was the order of the day (6:4-6). Religion degenerated into mere ritualism devoid of righteousness and morality (4:4; 5:5; 8:14). The evils of the time called for divine retribution. Jeroboam's house was to be visited with the sword (7:9). Somewhere around 753 B.C. Jeroboam died a natural death, but his son and successor, Zechariah, after a six-month reign, was assassinated by a usurper, inaugurating a period of decline and civil strife.   M.F.U.

BIBLIOGRAPHY: *See* Jeroboam I.

JERO'HAM (je-ro'ham; "compassionate").

1. The son of Elihu and father of Elkanah, the father of Samuel (1 Sam. 1:1; 1 Chron. 6:27, 34), before 1171 B.C.

2. The father of several Benjamite leaders residing at Jerusalem (1 Chron. 8:27), before 536 B.C.

3. The father of Ibneiah, a Benjamite leader who was a resident of Jerusalem (1 Chron. 9:8), probably before 536 B.C. Perhaps the same as no. 2.

4. A priest whose son Adaiah was one of the priests residing at Jerusalem (1 Chron. 9:12), before 536 B.C. The same names are given as father and son in Neh. 11:12 and are probably identical.

5. An inhabitant of Gedor and father of Joelah and Zebadiah who joined David at Ziklag (1 Chron. 12:7), before 1000 B.C.

6. A Danite whose son (or descendant) Azarel was ruler over his tribe in the time of David (1 Chron. 27:22), before 1000 B.C.

7. Father of Azariah, which latter was one of the "captains of hundreds" by whose assistance Jehoiada placed Joash on the throne of Judah (2 Chron. 23:1), before 836 B.C.

JERUBBA'AL (jer-ub-bā'al; "Baal will contend"). A surname given by his father to Gideon, the judge of Israel, because he destroyed the altar of Baal (Judg. 6:32; 7:1; 8:29, 35; 9:1-2, 5, 16, 19, 24, 28, 57; 1 Sam. 12:11).

JERUBBE'SHETH (jer-ub-be'sheth; "contender with shame," i.e., "idol"). A name for Jerubbaal in which Baal is branded *bōshet* (*beshet*), the Heb. word for "shame." This epithet of Gideon (2 Sam. 11:21) was given to avoid pronouncing the name of the false god Baal.

JERU'EL (je-rū'el; "founded by God"). "The wilderness of Jeruel" is mentioned (2 Chron. 20:16) by Jahaziel as the place where Jehoshaphat would

meet the Moabites and Ammonites and overcome them. This "wilderness" was, doubtless, a part of the great stretch of flat country, bounded on the S by Wadi el Ghâr and extending from the Dead Sea to the neighborhood of Tekoa. It is now called el Hasasah.

JERU'SALEM (je-rū'sa-lem). The first city of Palestine, and the "holy city" for three great world religions: Christianity, Judaism, and Islam.

Name. The etymology of the name is not certain; it is apparently of Semitic origin. An Egyptian notice from the third quarter of the nineteenth century B.C. mentions Urusalimum. The Tell el Amarna correspondence of the fourteenth century B.C. refers to the town as Urusalim. The Assyrians called it Ursalimmu. Modern scholars take these names to mean "founded by the god Shalem," a god of the Amorites (Jerusalem is said to have been founded by Amorites and Hittites; Ezek. 16:3, 45). In time, however, the second part of the name became associated with *shalom* ("peace") in Hebrew minds, and Jerusalem came to mean "city of peace." Romans and Greeks called it Hierosolyma. To the Arabs it is El Kuds, meaning "holy town."

Location. The "holy city" is located fourteen miles W of the Dead Sea, thirty-three miles E of the Mediterranean. Bethlehem lies about five

View of the Old City of Jerusalem from the Mount of Olives

675

miles to the SE. The city is situated on an uneven rocky plateau at an elevation of 2,550 feet. It is 3,800 feet above the level of the Dead Sea. It is poetically called "beautiful in elevation, the joy of the whole earth" (Ps. 48:2). Its location has helped to give it prestige. It was exclusive, with no river frontage like Babylon, Thebes, Rome, or Memphis, and with no harbor like Tyre, Sidon, or Alexandria. It was off the main highways between Asia Minor and Egypt. It possessed a good water supply from the ancient *Gihon spring* (which see) (The Virgin's Fountain) in the Kidron and *En Rogel* (which see) or Job's well at the junction of the Kidron and the Hinnom valleys. It was centrally located and ideal for the capital of the united kingdom of Israel, in the Davidic-Solomonic era (c. 1000-930 B.C.), and Judah (c. 930-587 B.C.). Jerusalem stands at a point where three steep-sided little wadis join to form one valley. They are the Kidron, Tyropoeon, and Hinnom valleys. The Kidron runs N and S and lies on the E of the city. Between it and the Tyropoeon Valley (also N-S) a long, narrow spur extends southward; on this stood the Jebusite town conquered by David. Then a western hill (now known as Zion) stands between the Tyropoeon and the Hinnom, which runs N and S and then curves in an easterly direction to join the other two valleys. To the E of the Kidron rises the Mount of Olives.

Climate. Being high in elevation and fanned by the afternoon breeze from the Mediterranean, Jerusalem has a mean annual temperature of 63 degrees. However, the temperature can mount to 100 degrees in summer and drops to 25 degrees in the winter. Snow occasionally falls, sometimes to a depth of one foot, but does not last long.

General Boundary of David's City. Jebusite Jerusalem of David's day was located on the SE hill and was shaped somewhat like a gigantic human footprint. The enclosed area was about eleven acres, as excavations by Kathleen Kenyon (1961-67) have demonstrated. David built north-ward, constructing a new palace for himself in the area known as Ophel and buying the thresh-ing floor of Araunah the Jebusite (2 Sam. 24:18). On the latter Solomon was later to build the Temple. Then, as Nahman Avigad has shown in his excavations in the Jewish Quarter since 1969, Israelite settlement expanded onto the western hill in the eighth–seventh centuries B.C. After Nebuchadnezzar's destruction of Jerusalem (586 B.C.), Nehemiah rebuilt the walls in 444 B.C. These evidently encompassed the Temple area, Ophel, and most of the old City of David. But excavations have shown that the eastern wall followed the crest of the hill instead of standing partway down the slope, as the Jebusite wall had. The western part of the city was not included in Nehemiah's reconstruction.

The walls and gates of Jerusalem of Nehemi-ah's time are minutely described. The gates at Jerusalem include the following: Sheep Gate, Fish Gate, Old Gate, Valley Gate, Refuse Gate, Fountain Gate, Water Gate, Horse Gate, and East Gate. Towers include that of Hammeah, of Hana-nel, and of Furnaces. The walls include the Broad Wall, the wall of the Pool of Shelah (i.e., Siloam), and the wall of Ophel. Jerusalem again spread to the western ridge in the second century B.C., and a new N wall was built in the second or first century B.C. It is now known that there was a jog in that wall and that the area covered by the Church of the Holy Sepulcher lay outside that wall. Thus Calvary could have been located there. A new N wall, N of the modern wall, was begun by Herod Agrippa I (A.D. 41-44) and finished just before the outbreak of the Jewish war in A.D. 66.

The walls and gates as seen in Jerusalem today are due in large part to the construction of Sulei-man the Magnificent, sixteenth century A.D. The present walls of Jerusalem have thirty-five towers and eight gates: the Damascus Gate, Herod's Gate, Stephen's Gate, the Refuse Gate, the Zion Gate, the Jaffa Gate, the New Gate, and the Gold-en Gate.

The Golden Gate, Jerusalem

History. The history of Jerusalem from the time of Joshua to its destruction by Titus—a period of fifteen centuries—is a succession of changes, revolutions, sieges, surrenders, and famines. Each is followed by restoration and re-building. The city's greatest glory was reached under the reign of King Solomon, who built the Temple and a royal palace besides greatly enlarg-ing and strengthening the walls of the city. Jeru-salem's possibly greatest humiliation was reached under the reign of Antiochus Ephi-phanes, 175-165 B.C., when the most violent and cruel efforts were made to destroy the Jews and their religion.

For the earliest record of Jerusalem we must

go to the description of the boundaries of Judah and Benjamin (Josh. 5, 18). Until David captured the entire city from the Jebusites (2 Sam. 5:7; 1 Chron. 11:5), these ancient inhabitants had always been in possession of a part of it. From the time when David brought the Ark of God into the city (2 Sam. 6:2-17) until the destruction by Nebuchadnezzar, the metropolis was continually added to and embellished. Notable improvements included Hezekiah's vast structures for aqueduct and water supply and the enclosing with an outside wall of Zion and the City of David. During the years immediately succeeding the capture of the city by Nebuchadnezzar, it lay in ruins. Cyrus the Great decreed the return of the captive Jews to their city and the rebuilding of the walls, which by Nehemiah's time had been broken down for 140 years (Neh. 4:7-22). Under Nehemiah the city regained much of its former glory. Alexander the Great in 332 B.C. showed much favor to the Jews, exempting them in some degree from tribute. In 320 B.C., because the Jews refused to fight and defend themselves on the Sabbath day when Ptolemy Soter attacked the city, it was captured, and many of its inhabitants were removed to Africa. The Seleucids (Syrians) wrested control of Palestine from the Ptolemies in 198 B.C. Their campaign against Jewish religion, as ordered by Antiochus Epiphanes, terminated in an order for the cessation of Jewish worship and their observance of the Sabbath and in the desecration of the

The Citadel, Jerusalem

Temple in 168 B.C. A Maccabean revolt launched in that year was ultimately successful in erecting an independent Jewish state, which continued from 142 to 63 B.C. Eventually, bickering among factions in the Jewish state led to an invitation to the Roman general Pompey to intervene to settle the quarrel in 63 B.C. In this way the Romans gained control of Palestine. During the civil wars involving Pompey and Julius Caesar and Mark Antony and Octavian, Palestine was caught in the cross fire. After Octavian (Augustus) established himself as ruler of the Roman world and restored order to the Empire and after Herod the Great established himself as king in Jerusalem, the city soon again became restored to much of its former grandeur. Under Herod the Temple was enlarged and beautified. It was in this state that Christ found the city. Under Herod the city was given a better water supply. Under Herod's grandson, Herod Agrippa, in A.D. 41, the area inside the city wall was doubled. Bad government by Roman procurators, appointed over Judea as a Roman province, led to discontent and rebellion, however; and finally Titus laid siege to the city and destroyed it in A.D. 70, sacrificing one million lives.

The Early Church. After the death and resurrection of Christ, Jerusalem became the scene of the most stirring events connected with Christianity, beginning with the Day of Pentecost and including much of the history contained in Acts. The gospel was first proclaimed in strict obedience to the command of Christ (Acts 1:4). The church increased rapidly (chap. 5). Stephen, the first martyr, was sacrificed (chap. 7). Paul sat at the feet of Gamaliel and later preached. He was taken to Caesarea and Rome. In Jerusalem the great council was held, at which the question of the rite of circumcision was discussed, and during which addresses were made by Peter, Barnabas, Paul, and James, the half brother of Jesus. James was the president of the council, occupying a prominent place, if, indeed, not the first place in the church (chap. 15). Herod Agrippa killed the apostle James, the brother of John, by beheading him (12:1-2). The extreme severity of the persecutions tended to scatter the Christians, which resulted in the dissemination of the gospel throughout the world.

The City After A.D. 70 In A.D. 70 the Romans destroyed the city and massacred its inhabitants. Under Hadrian the Romans began to refortify Jerusalem as a Gentile city and hold it against its former inhabitants. The Jewish revolt (A.D. 132-35) under Bar Cocheba was evidently due to this circumstance. It was suppressed, and the rebuilding of the city resumed and completed. The new city was called Colonia Aelia Capitolina. This name described it as a Roman colony. Aelia was in honor of Hadrian, whose first name was Aelius, and Capitolina indicated that it was dedicated to

Jupiter Capitolinus. A temple was dedicated to this heathen god where the former Jewish Temples had stood on Mt. Moriah. The name of Aelia continued for several centuries. Constantine removed the ban against Jews entering the Holy City. Both Constantine and his mother built churches in the city. In A.D. 614 the Persians under Chosroes II captured Jerusalem and massacred the inhabitants. From 637 to 1917 the city remained in Muslim hands except for the brief periods when the Crusaders held Jerusalem.

Archaeology. An account of scientific exploration of Jerusalem normally begins with Captain Charles Warren, a British mining engineer. From 1867 to 1870 he tried to follow the line of the ancient wall by excavations, shafts, and tunnels. He is especially known for the discovery of "Warren's Shaft," the means that he identified as being used by Joab in the conquest of Jerusalem from the Jebusites (2 Sam. 5:8). This was the ancient water system of Jerusalem. It consisted of a horizontal tunnel leading from the spring Gihon into the hill on which the Jebusite city was built. The tunnel ended in a cave that served as a cistern. Above the cave rose a 32-foot vertical shaft, which connected with a sloping passageway 127 feet long. The entrance to this passageway was inside the city wall. Women could then descend the sloping passage to the vertical shaft and lower their water skins into the cave to procure a water supply. Joab supposedly discovered this water system, ascended the passageway, and entered the city at night, delivering it into the hands of David. At the SE corner of the Temple area Warren found what he believed was the wall of Ophel, which continued S along the eastern slope. Thus he turned the attention of archaeologists to the area of the city of David and the Jebusite city, presently S of the Temple area. Because this region was outside the walls and largely unoccupied, it could be investigated more easily than other parts of Jerusalem.

Numerous others were to engage in archaeological or exploratory work during subsequent decades. A partial list would include Clermont-Ganneau and H. Guthe (1881), F. J. Bliss and A. C. Dickie (1894-97), Montague Parker and L.-H. Vincent (1909-11), Raymond Weill (1913-14, 1923-24), R. A. S. Macalister and J. Garrow Duncan (1923-25), J. W. Crowfoot and G. M. Fitzgerald (1927-28), E. L. Sukenik and L. A. Mayer (1925-27), and C. N. Johns (1934-40). There is not room here to note the discoveries or theses of these men; moreover, many of their views have had to be modified by more recent discoveries.

A new chapter in the rediscovery of Jerusalem began in 1961 when Kathleen Kenyon and Roland de Vaux directed annual campaigns (until 1967) to investigate a number of areas in the city, using the most up-to-date stratigraphic techniques. They were especially interested in the Jebusite wall and the size of Davidic Jerusalem. They showed that the wall stood farther down the slope than previously thought and that the Jerusalem of David was about eleven acres in size.

Since the Six-Day War in 1967, Israeli archaeologists have had access to the entire Jerusalem area. A team under the leadership of Benjamin Mazar has been working S and SW of the Temple. It is now known that "Robinson's Arch" was not a bridge between the Temple Mount and the Upper City but a span supporting a monumental stairway leading down from the Temple Mount. It is now known too that there was only one bridge across the Tyropoeon Valley—that of "Wilson's Arch," N of the Western Wall plaza. Mazar also found remains of a paved street that ran along the Temple's southern wall. From this street a monumental stairway some 64 meters (210 feet) wide led up to the Huldah Gates.

The Western, or Wailing, Wall

Excavations also were conducted in the Jewish Quarter of the Old City (SW of the Temple Mount) from 1969 to the present under the leadership of N. Avigad for the Hebrew University and the Israel Department of Antiquities. This work has been possible because large parts of the Jewish Quarter were destroyed during the 1948 war; and since the 1967 reunification, demolition and rebuilding of some areas has taken place. Houses of the Herodian period, some with fine mosaic floors and wall frescoes with geometric patterns, were found to be built directly over the Israelite strata. Among Avigad's most significant discoveries are the main street of Byzantine Jerusalem and the Nea Church, built by the emperor Justinian in 543.

Excavations in the Armenian Garden (S of the Citadel) under the leadership of D. Bahat and M. Broshi (1970-71) and in the Jerusalem Citadel by Ruth Amiran and A. Eitan uncovered part of the foundation platform on which Herod's palace had been built. In 1971 and 1972 M. Broshi, E. Netzer, and Mrs. Yael Yisrael, on behalf of the Armenian Patriarchate, excavated in the courtyard of the Armenian Monastery at the "House of Caiaphas" just outside the Zion Gate. Excavations at the Pool of Bethesda (John 5:2-4) since 1956 show that the traditional pools went out of use before Jesus' day. The miracle performed at this pool by Jesus is now ascribed to a cave E of the traditional pools. A restudy of the fortress of Antonia by P. Benoit has led him to the conclusion that the fortress was not a large structure with four towers as previously thought. Moreover, he has come to believe that the pavement identified as the Gabbatha (John 19:13) had nothing to do with the crucifixion but was a pavement from a forum laid by Hadrian when he rebuilt Jerusalem in the second century. The arch over the pavement in the Sisters of Zion Convent is certainly Hadrianic. Benoit thinks the Antonia stood in the narrow area between the Temple Mount and the Via Dolorosa. A. Mazar and Y. Cohen carried out a survey of the ancient aqueducts of Jerusalem in 1969 on behalf of the Israel Academy of Sciences and Humanities.

The Via Dolorosa

Especially exciting in recent years has been the work of Yigal Shiloh, who began excavating the city of David in 1978. He traced the history of the city from the Chalcolithic period to the days of the Maccabees. Among his more interesting dis-

coveries is a stepped-stone structure used by David and Solomon as a supporting rampart for the citadel of the monarchy period and the walls of the second century B.C., built along the crest of the hill and on the same line as Nehemiah's wall. For a report on Shiloh's successes, one should consult Yigal Shiloh, *Excavations at the City of David, 1978-1982 Interim Report of the First Five Seasons.* Other important works on Jerusalem archaeology include Nahman Avigad, *Discovering Jerusalem;* Kathleen Kenyon, *Digging Up Jerusalem* and *Jerusalem, Excavating 3000 Years of History;* Benjamin Mazar, *The Mountain of the Lord;* an Israel Exploration Society publication entitled *Jerusalem Revealed—Archaeology in the Holy City 1968-1974,* and Michael Avi-Yonah, ed., *Encyclopedia of Archaeological Excavations in the Holy Land,* vol. 2.

The Modern City. The modern city occupies the site of the ancient ruin and extends far beyond it to the N and W. The site of the former magnificent Temples (of Solomon, Zerubbabel, and Herod) is occupied by a Muslim mosque, the Dome of the Rock, built by Abd el-Melik in A.D. 686. In World War I Palestine was conquered by the British under General Allenby, and Jerusalem surrendered Dec. 9, 1917. Since that time Palestine has undergone remarkable growth. Zionism has flourished, the State of Israel has emerged (1948) as a result of United Nations action, and Jerusalem is a flourishing city. Jerusalem was divided by Jew and Arab from 1948 to 1967 and has since been united under Israeli control.

Prophecy. Prophetic Scripture outlines a brilliant future for Jerusalem. During the Millennium it is to be the capital of the earth (Isa. 60; Zech. 14; Ezek. 40-48). The second coming of Christ will eventuate in the destruction of Israel's enemies, the judgment of the nations, the deliverance of the Israelite remnant, and the establishment of the kingdom. But before that great event Israel will go through the time of the Great Tribulation (Jer. 30:7) under the terrible rule of the Antichrist. Only as the remnant looks upon Him whom they have pierced will they be converted (Zech. 12:10–13:1) and at last recite the penitential strains of Isa. 53.   M.F.U.; H.F.V.

BIBLIOGRAPHY: G. A. Smith, *Jerusalem,* 2 vols. (1907-8); L.-H. Vincent, *Jerusalem Antique* (1912); L.-H. Vincent and F.-M. Abel, *Jerusalem Nouvelle,* 3 vols. (1914-26); F.-M. Abel, *Géographie de la Palestine* (1933), 1:181-84; G. H. Dalman, *Sacred Sites and Ways* (1935); L.-H. Vincent and A. Steve, *Jerusalem de l'Ancient Testament,* 3 vols. (1954-56); M. Join-Lambet, *Jerusalem* (1958); M. Avi-Yonah, *Jerusalem* (1960); K. M. Kenyon, *Jerusalem: Excavating 3000 Years of History* (1967); J. Jeremias, *Jerusalem in the Time of Jesus* (1969); K. M. Kenyon, *Digging Up Jerusalem* (1974); T. Kollek and M. Pearlman, *Jerusalem, Sacred City of Mankind* (1974); B. Mazar, *Mountain of the Lord* (1975); M. Avi-Yonah, *Encyclopedia of Archaeological Excavations in the Holy Land* (1976), 2:579-647; Y. Yadin, ed., *Jerusalem Revealed* (1976); R. M. Mackowski, *Jerusa-*

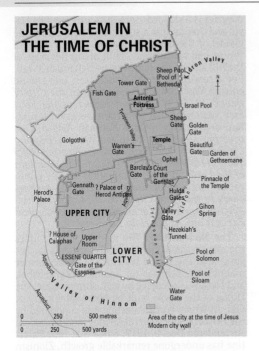

JERUSALEM IN THE TIME OF CHRIST

Kidron Valley

Sheep Pool
(Pool of
Bethesda)

Tower Gate

Fish Gate

Antonia
Fortress

Israel Pool

Tyropoeon Valley

Sheep
Gate

Golden
Gate

Golgotha

Temple

Warren's
Gate

Beautiful
Gate

Garden of
Gethsemane

Ophel

Barclay's Court
Gate of the
Gentiles

Pinnacle of
the Temple

Gennath ? Palace of
Gate Herod Antipas

Herod's
Palace

Hulda
Gates

Kidron

UPPER CITY

Valley
Gate

Gihon
Spring

Hezekiah's
Tunnel

? House of
Caiaphas

Upper
Room

LOWER
CITY

ESSENE QUARTER

Gate of the
Essenes

Pool of
Solomon

Tyropoeon Valley

Valley

of

Hinnom

Pool of
Siloam

Water
Gate

Aqueduct

Aqueduct

0   250   500 metres

Area of the city at the time of Jesus

0   250   500 yards

Modern city wall

lem: *City of Jesus* (1980); N. Avigad, *Discovering Jerusalem* (1984); J. Wilkinson, *The Jerusalem Jesus Knew* (1985).

JERU'SALEM, NEW. This is the city of God that comes down out of heaven, as described in Rev. 21:2, 10. This city is the one "which has foundations" and that Abraham saw by faith (cf. Heb. 11:8-10). It is described in Heb. 12:22-24. Christ makes mention of it in His message to the church in Philadelphia (Rev. 3:12). In full correspondence with the description as given in Heb. 12:22-24, the church is present; the angels are present; a company of "righteous men made perfect," to which Israel would belong, is present; and Christ the Mediator and God the Father are present. Taking the measurements of the city literally, the breadth and height are equal, being 12,000 furlongs, which would be 1,500 miles each way. The glory of the eternal city is described in terms of being pure gold. The city descends from heaven and is doubtless to be considered as something distinct from heaven. It is named for the bride of Christ, the church, evidently because she has some superior right to it or forms the chief body of redeemed humanity to occupy it. However, other peoples and beings enter her gates, making it clearly a cosmopolitan center. It must be clearly remembered that when the last two chapters of the Bible describe the future eternal state of all things, they differentiate at least four different abodes: (1) the new heaven, (2) the new earth, (3) the bridal city, and (4) "outside," which is evidently identical with

the lake of fire, or the second death (Rev. 22:15, cf. 20:14-15; 21:8). But in this changed situation with its different dwelling places the place of residence is no longer subject to change. This is the consummation of revelation in which time merges into eternity.   M.F.U.

JERU'SHA (je-rū'sha; "taken in marriage, possessed"). The daughter of Zadok and queen of Uzziah. She was the mother of Jotham, king of Judah (2 Kings 15:33), 738 B.C. Also called *Jerushah* (which see).

JERU'SHAH (je-rū'sha). Another form (2 Chron. 27:1) of the name *Jerusha* (which see).

JESAI'AH. *See* Jeshaiah.

JESARE'LAH. *See* Jesharelah.

JESHA'IAH (je-shā'ya; "Jehovah saves").
1. The second named of the sons of Hananiah, the son of Zerubbabel (1 Chron. 3:21), after 536 B.C. The KJV renders "Jesaiah."
2. One of the sons of Jeduthun, appointed to play the harp (1 Chron. 25:3) at the head of the eighth division of Levitical musicians (v. 15), after 1000 B.C.
3. The son of Rehabiah, of the Levitical family of Eliezer. His descendant Shelomoth was over the sacred treasury in the time of David (1 Chron. 26:25; cf. 24:21, where he is called Isshiah), after 1000 B.C.
4. Son of Athaliah, and head of the family of Elam. He returned from Babylon with seventy males (Ezra 8:7), about 457 B.C.
5. A Levite of the family of Merari, who, in company with Hashabiah, met Ezra at Ahava, on the way from Babylon to Palestine (Ezra 8:19), about 457 B.C.
6. Father of Ithiel, a Benjamite, whose descendant Sallu resided in Jerusalem after the Exile (Neh. 11:7), before 445 B.C. The KJV renders "Jesaiah."

JESH'ANAH (jesh'a-na; "old").
1. One of the cities of Israel that was taken with its suburbs from Jeroboam by Abijah, king of Judah (2 Chron. 13:19). It is probably to be identified with Burj el-Isaneh, three miles N of Jifneh.
2. One of the gates of Jerusalem in Nehemiah's time, referred to as the "Old Gate" by the NASB (Neh. 3:6; 12:39).

JESHARE'LAH (jesh-a-rē'la; perhaps, "upright toward God"). Head of the seventh division of the Levitical musicians (1 Chron. 25:14). He was a son of Asaph (v. 2, where his name is given as Aharelah). The NIV renders Jesarelah.

JESHEB'EAB (je-sheb'-e-ab; perhaps, "father's seat"). The head of the fourteenth division of priests as arranged by David (1 Chron. 24:13), before 960 B.C.

JE'SHER (je'sher; "uprightness"). One of the

sons of Caleb, the son of Hezron, by his wife Azubah (1 Chron. 2:18), about 1440 B.C.

JESHIAH. *See* Isshiah.

JESH'IMON (jesh'i-mon; "a waste, a desolation," Num. 21:20; 23:28, KJV, NIV, and NASB marg.; 1 Sam. 23:19; etc.). "In the OT the wilderness of Judea is called the Jeshimon, a word meaning devastation, and no term can better suit its haggard and crumbling appearance. It covers some thirty-five miles by fifteen . . . short bushes, thorns, and succulent creepers were all that relieved the brown and yellow barrenness of the sand, the crumbling limestone, and scattered shingle. Such is Jeshimon, the wilderness of Judea. It carries the violence and desolation of the Dead Sea Valley right up to the heart of the country, to the roots of the Mount of Olives, to within two hours of the gates of Hebron, Bethlehem, and Jerusalem" (Smith, *Hist. Geog.*).
BIBLIOGRAPHY: G. A. Smith, *The Historical Geography of the Holy Land* (1906), pp. 312-14; D. Baly, *The Geography of the Bible* (1957), pp. 35-38, 88, 156, 164, 192, 206.

JESHI'SHAI (je-shi'shī; "aged"). The son of Jahdo and father of Michael, one of the ancestors of the Gadites who dwelt in Gilead (1 Chron. 5:14), long before 740 B.C.

JESHOHA'IAH (je-shō-ha'ya). A leader of the Simeonites and one of those who emigrated to Gedor (1 Chron. 4:36), about 715 B.C.

JESH'UA, JESH'UAH (jesh'ū-a; a later form of Joshua, "Jehovah is salvation").
1. A priest in the reign of David, to whom the ninth division fell by lot (1 Chron. 24:11; "Jeshuah," KJV), about 960 B.C. Perhaps the same as the one mentioned in Ezra 2:36 and Neh. 7:39, whose descendants returned from Babylon.
2. A Levite appointed with others by Hezekiah to distribute the sacred offerings among their brothers (2 Chron. 31:15), 719 B.C.
3. Son of Jehozadak, first high priest of the third series, namely, of those after the Babylonian captivity, and ancestor of the fourteen high priests who were his successors down to Joshua or Jason, and Onias or Menelaus, inclusive. Jeshua, like his contemporary Zerubbabel, was probably born in Babylon, where his father, Jehozadak, had been taken captive while young (1 Chron. 6:15). He came up from Babylon in the first year of Cyrus with Zerubbabel (Ezra 2:2; Neh. 7:7; 12:1, 7, 10) and took a leading part with him in the rebuilding of the Temple and the restoration of the Jewish commonwealth (Ezra 3:2, 8-9; 4:3; 5:2), 536-446 B.C. Besides the great importance of Jeshua as a historical character from the critical times in which he lived and the great work that he accomplished, his name Jesus, his restoration of the Temple, his office as high priest, and especially the two prophecies concerning him in Zech. 3 and 6:9-15, point him out

as an eminent type of Christ. He is also called Joshua (Hag. 1:1, 12; 2:2, 4; Zech. 3:1, 3, 6, 8-9; 6:11).
4. A descendant (or native) of Pahath-moab, mentioned with Joab as one whose posterity, numbering 2,812 (Ezra 2:6) or 2,818 (Neh. 7:11), returned from Babylon, before 536 B.C.
5. A Levite named along with Kadmiel as one whose descendants ("sons of Hodaviah"), numbering 74, returned from Babylon (Ezra 2:40; Neh. 7:43), before 436 B.C.
6. The father of Jozabad, which latter was appointed by Ezra as one of the receivers of the offering for the sacred service (Ezra 8:33), about 457 B.C.
7. A Jew whose son, Ezer, repaired the part of the wall ("in front of the ascent of the armory") under Nehemiah (Neh. 3:19), 445 B.C.
8. A Levite, probably a son of Azaniah (Neh. 10:9), who assisted in explaining the law to the people under Ezra (Neh. 8:7; 9:4-5; 12:8), about 445 B.C.
9. Joshua, the son of Nun (Neh. 8:17, KJV).
10. Son of Kadmiel, one of the Levites who served in the Temple, "to praise and give thanks" after the restoration in the time of Eliashib (Neh. 12:24), about 406 B.C. Perhaps, however, "son" here is a transcriber's error for "and," in which case this Jeshua will be the same as no. 5 (McClintock and Strong, *Cyclopedia*).
11. A city of Judah inhabited after the captivity (Neh. 11:26), perhaps Tell es-Sa'weh.

JESH'URUN (jesh'ū-run; "upright"). An honorable surname given to Israel (Deut. 32:15; 33:5, 26; Isa. 44:2; in the latter, "Jesurun" in the KJV) and representing Israel as a nation of just or upright men. The epithet *righteous nation*, as we may render Jeshurun, was intended to remind Israel of its calling and involved the severest reproof of its apostasy.

JESI'AH. *See* Isshiah.

JESIM'IEL (je-sim'i-el; "God will place"). One of the thirteen Simeonite leaders who, in the time of Hezekiah, migrated to the valley of Gedor for purposes of conquest (1 Chron. 4:36).

JES'SE (jes'e). A son (or descendant) of Obed, the son of Boaz and Ruth (Ruth 4:17, 22; 1 Chron. 2:12; Matt. 1:5-6; Luke 3:32). He had eight sons (1 Sam. 17:12), the youngest of whom was David. Jesse's wealth consisted chiefly of sheep, for whom David acted as shepherd (16:11; 17:34-35). The last historical mention of Jesse is in relation to the asylum that David procured for him from the king of Moab (1 Sam. 22:3-4), before 1000 B.C.
Although Jesse was of prominent lineage, yet he himself was unknown and of modest station in life. In such great messianic passages as Isa. 11:1, 10, allusion is made to this fact. After Saul had become estranged from David, he contemp-

tuously called him "the son of Jesse," thereby displaying his scorn toward him (1 Sam. 20:31; 22:7; 25:10).   M.F.U.

JEST. The expression "Against whom do you jest?" (Isa. 57:4; "sport," KJV) may well be rendered, "Against whom do you make yourselves merry?"

JESTING (Gk. *eutrapelia*, "pleasantry, humor, facetiousness"). This term is used in a bad sense (Eph. 5:4), as scurrility, ribaldry, low jesting.

JES'UI. See Ishvi.

JES'UITES. See Ishvites.

JES'URUN. See Jeshurun.

JE'SUS CHRIST (jē'zus krīst). In order to understand the life of the Lord, recourse should first be had in brief to the broad teachings of the NT respecting the character, relations, and claims of Jesus Christ. He is the one subject whose history fills the four gospels. We should properly *apprehend,* although we cannot *comprehend,* the divine personality set forth in these Scriptures; that personality whose words, deeds, and sufferings, and whose *revealing names and titles,* are recorded for our learning.

Names Assigned to the Lord. Matthew opens his gospel as "the book of the genealogy of Jesus Christ, the son of David." Both designations are used here as a personal name, although usually "Christ" is a term employed rather as an appellative, or common name.

His Personal Name. The Lord's personal name was Jesus, which signifies *Savior.* It is carefully accented by repetitions in the record as being highly important. (1) He was so called prospectively by Gabriel to Mary: "And behold, you will conceive in your womb, and bear a son, and you shall name Him *Jesus*" (Luke 1:31, italics added). (2) He was so named by the angel to Joseph in his supernatural dream respecting Mary and the child: "And she will bear a Son; and you shall call His name Jesus, for it is He who will save His people from their sins" (Matt. 1:21). (3) He was so called on the day of His birth: "She gave birth to a son; and he called His name Jesus" (Matt. 1:25). (4) He was so called when His name was officially bestowed at circumcision: "His name was then called Jesus, the name given by the angel before he was conceived in the womb" (Luke 2:21).

His Official Name. His official appellative was *Christ,* which means *the Anointed One.* Here the Messiah and the Christ of the Scriptures meet and identify themselves in the personality of Jesus, who was anointed of God as the Prophet, Priest, and King (*Christos* = Christ = *the Anointed*; Heb. *Māshîah, Messiah* = *the Anointed*). "You know, Jesus of Nazareth, how God anointed Him with the Holy Spirit and with power, and how He went about doing good, and heal-

ing all who were oppressed by the devil; for God was with Him" (Acts 10:38). Andrew, who had been one of John the Baptist's disciples, when he turned to follow Jesus, "found first his own brother Simon, and said to him, 'We have found the Messiah' (which translated means *Christ)*" (John 1:41, italics added). "It had been revealed" to the just and devout Simeon "by the Holy Spirit that he would not see death before he had seen *the Lord's Christ*" (Luke 2:25-26, italics added). Peter, answering the Lord's question, said, "*Thou art the Christ, the Son of the living God*" (Matt. 16:16, italics added).

Other Titles. The Jehovah of the OT is the Jesus of the NT. (1) Jesus is called "the Son of Man" (*ho huios tou anthrōpou*). With this formula Jesus usually addressed Himself to the apprehension of His disciples. The reasons are obvious: Jesus was in His condition of humility; He was, as yet, thus best known to His followers in His humanity. He was to be known as the promised "seed" of the woman. He was a perfect man whose unique mission into this world was to be the Redeemer of lost mankind. (2) Jesus is called distinctively "the Son of God" (*ho huios tou theou*). This title expresses the deity of the Lord Jesus as distinguished from His humanity. In Scripture this designation is never applied to His miraculous birth, or exclusively to His messiahship, which, however, is included, but invariably to His original relation to the Father as He was in His preexistence before He assumed humanity. Our Lord declared Himself to be the Son of God, and included His messiahship as based upon His proper oneness and equality with God, either by direct expression or indirectly by implication. That relation made the messiahship possible, as expressed in "God . . . sending His own Son in the likeness of sinful flesh" (Rom. 8:3). The reference is not to the incarnation or miraculous conception of Christ but to His oneness with God in the glory that He had with the Father before the world was created (John 17:5). Jesus said to the Jews, "Do you say of Him, whom the Father sanctified and sent into the world, 'You are blaspheming,' because I said, 'I am the Son of God'?" (John 10:36; cf. 9:35-37; Matt. 26:33, 64). The Jews understood that Jesus made this high claim and wanted to stone Him because He, being a man, had made Himself God (John 10:33). Paul reaffirms the claim when he represents Jesus Christ as He "who, although He existed in the form of God, did not regard equality with God a thing to be grasped. . . . That at the name of Jesus every knee should bow, of those who are in heaven, and on earth, and under the earth, and that every tongue should confess that Jesus Christ is Lord, to the glory of God the Father" (Phil. 2:6-11). (3) Jesus is called "God our Savior" (*ho Sōtēros hēmōn Theos*). These passages express Christ's unity and identity with God, illustrating the character of the preexistence of Jesus. Hence, the apostle Paul speaks of "the commandment of God our Savior" (1 Tim. 1:1; Titus 1:3); of "the kindness of God our Savior and His love" (Titus 3:4); of that which "is good and acceptable in the sight of God our Savior" (1 Tim. 2:3); and that men should "adorn the doctrine of God our Savior in every respect" (Titus 2:10), "looking for the blessed hope and the appearing of the glory of our great God and Savior, Christ Jesus" (2:13).

Ground of Christian Belief. The four gospels are occupied in furnishing facts illustrative of Jesus Christ and His work as related to mankind; also in teaching His relation to God. As these Scriptures derive all their character and significance from His personality and life—without which they would have no occasion to exist— our faith in their teaching rests on the following propositions: (1) the absolutely unique and perfect manhood of Jesus Christ among men; (2) the realization in Him of all the messianic predictions of Scripture; (3) all His miracles (*see* Table 20, "The Miracles of Jesus"), being restorative, were part of His redemptive plan; (4) the resurrection of Jesus from the dead, an absolute historical fact; (5) the transformation secured in the character of the individual believer; (6) the Spirit's witness to personal adoption in Christian consciousness; and (7) the preeminence of the Christian nations as seen on the atlas of the world.

The Uniqueness of Christ as a Person. As a result of form critics of the twentieth century, such as K. L. Schmidt, M. Dibelius, and R. Bultmann, and the consequent common critical view that the gospel accounts of Jesus' life and work are strongly mythological, there has been a strong tendency to strip Jesus Christ of the uniqueness ascribed to Him in the four gospels. The question may well be asked, In what sense was Jesus Christ unique?

Unique in His Birth. Was Jesus born like all other children by natural generation? Was Joseph His physical father? Is the doctrine of His virgin birth a myth effectually disposed of by form criticism and completely unhistorical? Whatever modern criticism may say, the record of the birth of Jesus as catalogued in the gospels presents the eternal Word who "was with God" and "was God" (John 1:1), becoming flesh (1:14) in a virgin's womb by the Holy Spirit and under the overshadowing "power of the Most High" (Luke 1:35).

Scripture gives a chaste, exalted story of the nativity. The gospels present Jesus as if He was divine. If God was actually becoming incarnate, conception in other than a virgin's womb would have been pure nonsense. No birth in all history was so simple and sublimely beautiful. If it is quasi-legendary and must be demythologized, why the absence of the fanciful and fantastic? Conception by the Holy Spirit, the virgin birth,

Table 20
The Miracles of Jesus

No.	Miracles	Matthew	Mark	Luke	John
1	Turning water into wine				2:1-11
2	Healing a nobelman's son at Cana				4:46-54
3	Healing a lame man at the pool of Bethesda				5:1-9
4	First miraculous catch of fish			5:1-11	
5	Delivering a synagogue demoniac		1:23-28	4:31-36	
6	Healing Peter's mother-in-law	8:14-17	1:29-31	4:38-39	
7	Cleansing a leper	8:2-4	1:40-45	5:12-16	
8	Healing a paralytic	9:2-8	2:3-13	5:18-26	
9	Healing a man with a withered hand	12:9-14	3:1-5	6:6-11	
10	Healing a centurion's servant	8:5-13		7:1-10	
11	Raising a widow's son			7:11-17	
12	Healing a blind and dumb demoniac	12:22		11:14	
13	Stilling a storm	8:18, 23-27	4:35-41	8:22-25	
14	Delivering the Gadarene demoniacs	8:28-34	5:1-20	8:26-39	
15	Healing a woman with an issue of blood	9:20-22	5:25-34	8:43-48	
16	Raising Jairus' daughter	9:18-19, 23-26	5:22-24, 35-43	8:41-42, 49-56	
17	Healing two blind men	9:27-31			
18	Delivering a dumb demoniac	9:32-33			
19	Feeding the 5,000	14:14-21	6:35-44	9:12-17	6:4-13
20	Walking on the water	14:24-33	6:45-52		6:16-21
21	Delivering a Syrophoenician's daughter	15:21-28	7:24-30		
22	Healing a deaf mute in Decapolis		7:31-37		
23	Feeding the 4,000	15:32-39	8:1-9		
24	Healing a blind man at Bethsaida		8:22-26		
25	Delivering a demon-possessed boy	17:14-18	9:14-29	9:38-43	
26	Finding the tribute money	17:24-27			
27	Healing a man born blind				9:1-7
28	Healing a crippled woman on the Sabbath			13:10-17	
29	Healing a man with dropsy			14:1-6	
30	Raising of Lazarus				11:17-44
31	Cleansing ten lepers			17:11-19	
32	Healing blind Bartimaeus	20:29-34	10:46-52	18:35-43	
33	Cursing the fig tree	21:18-19	11:12-14		
34	Restoring Malchus' ear			22:49-51	(18:10)
35	Second miraculous catch of fish				21:1-14

the angelic choir on Judean hills, and the wise men's star present a marvelous blending of the simple and the sublime, the humanly inscrutable and the spiritually satisfying. If the incarnation was God become man, as the gospels present, and not merely God entering *a* man, as modern criticism teaches, the miraculous would be expected. If the critic conveniently labels these details in the nativity as myth and succeeds in demythologizing it, the result is a divine man but not a God-man. The resulting creation of the critics is an historical misfit not dovetailing with OT prophecies, NT doctrine, apocalyptic, general church history, and human experience. Besides, it crashes head-on with the rest of the gospel accounts of the life, death, and resurrection of Christ, which are of one piece with the nativity story. If we believe the gospels, we shall find ourselves bowing at the manger cradle of the Christ Child and adoring Him.

Unique in His Life. Was Jesus' earthly life unique? Was He compassed with sin, afflicted with error and frailty common to all other men? Did He have a genuine messianic consciousness? Did He know who He was and what He had come into the world to do, or was He an apocalyptic enthusiast dominated by grandiose dreams, deluding Himself and His followers? Criticism of the life of Christ in the early part of this century tended to deny Him ethical flawlessness (cf. such liberal interpretations as Benjamin W. Bacon, *Jesus the Son of God* [1930]; Harry E. Fosdick, *The Manhood of the Master* [1913]; id., *The Man from Nazareth* [1950]; Sherwood Eddy, *A Portrait of Jesus* [1943]; Ralph W. Sockman, *Paradoxes of Jesus* [1936]; Ernest F. Tittle, *Jesus After Nineteen Centuries* [1932]). Whatever such criticism might conclude concerning the interpretation of the life of Jesus Christ, it is inescapable that He is presented in the gospels as sinless in life. A unique life is indicated as subsequent to a unique birth. With wonderful clarity the evangelists present a sinless Savior against the backdrop of a sinful world. He is portrayed as a Savior who came to save sinners and was able to save them because He Himself was sinless.

Although He was presented as sinless, He had the keenest sensitivity to sin. He was never conscious of sin in Himself. He never confessed sin. He is always depicted in the gospel accounts as acting and speaking apart from sin. John, the disciple closest to His affection, declares, "In Him there is no sin" (1 John 3:5). Peter says He "committed no sin, nor was any deceit found in His mouth" (1 Pet. 2:22). Paul pens the fact that He "knew no sin" (2 Cor. 5:21). Enemies were constrained to confess the same fact. Pilate confessed Him to be a righteous man (Matt. 27:24) and declared, "I find no guilt in Him" (John 18:38). Judas had to own that he had betrayed "innocent blood" (Matt. 27:4).

The gospels are filled with the fascination of a sinless and selfless Christ who cultivated unbroken fellowship with the Father in full obedience to the divine will, even to the death of the cross. Moreover, men who refuse to exercise faith in the gospel accounts and who view the sinlessness of Jesus as a pious fiction of the early church are confronted with the poignant beauty and power of Christ as the dominating character of the gospels.

Men like Wilhelm Wrede (*Das Messiasgeheimnis in den Evangelien* [1901]) denied the mystic consciousness of Jesus in the synoptic gospels, particularly in Mark. Wrede contended that mystery attaches to the problem of Jesus' messiahship, and he used the term "Mystic Secret." He declared this was a dogmatic invention of the primitive church. He held that the church had no real proof that Jesus Himself held to or declared Himself to be the Messiah. Consequently Wrede maintained it superimposed this dogmatic invention upon the traditional account of Christ's life in order to explain the silence of tradition on the subject. Wrede forgot that the phenomena he cited are explainable as simple historical facts rather than an artificial invention forced upon the accounts. Works in a general sense favorable to Wrede's position, with variations, are A. Schweitzer, *The Quest of the Historical Jesus,* 2d ed. (1911); M. Dibelius, *From Tradition to Gospel* (1935); C. C. McCown, *The Search for the Real Jesus* (1940); R. Bultmann, *Theology of the N. T.,* vol. 1 (1951). More conservative interpretations are found in J. W. Bowman, *The Intention of Jesus* (1943); W. Manson, *Jesus, the Messiah* (1943); V. Taylor, *The Gospel According to St. Mark* (1952).

Unique in His Death. Were the sufferings of Jesus radically different from those of the saints and martyrs? Was His death unparalleled, or was it merely the martyrdom of a misguided zealot rather than the redemptive act of the Savior of the world? Was it vicarious, redemptive, and substitutionary, or was it purely an example and ethically influential?

The theological thinking of the past century has been dominated by the spirit of relativism. This view, a product of the History of Religions school of the nineteenth century, professes to find elements similar to Christianity in the various great ethnic faiths. Its tendency is more and more to refuse to speak in absolutes, denying the uniqueness of Christianity and Christ and thus to put the birth, life, and death of Jesus Christ on a general par with the experience of other great and good men. The present-day question of relativism in relation to the uniqueness of Christ and Christianity presents one of the most profound problems of our present ecclesiastical climate. Only by walking the way of faith will contemporary relativizing scholarship correct itself. Contemporary biblical criticism must realize that faith in the uniqueness of Christ and the absoluteness of Christianity is not an attainment of human intellect or human brilliance. It is gained rather through the enlightenment of the Spirit of God.

Looking at the gospel accounts, we discover that the sufferings of Christ are presented as entirely different from those of any other human being. The agony in the Garden and the sweat that "became like drops of blood" (Luke 22:44) were the result not merely of extreme mental and physical anguish on the human plane but were occasioned by the sinless soul of the Son of God coming in contact with the weight of the world's sin. Apart from this explanation the gospel accounts of the darkness of Gethsemane's anguish are unexplainable. The sufferings of Calvary are more than the excruciating pain of crucifixion or body-racking thirst. Other men have endured as much or more. The cross of Christ is a travesty unless He who hung there knew no sin but was made a sacrifice for sin "that we might become the righteousness of God in Him" (2 Cor. 5:21). The sinless One coming in contact with the sin of the world and enduring the wrath of God against sin are the only sensible explanations of the unique sufferings of Christ. Without a sinless life and a virgin birth as antecedents, such a death is impossible and meaningless.

Contemporary scholarship develops the life of Christ under various presentations based on the assumption that Jesus differed only by degree from other people. Some, realizing the obvious fact that the gospels would never have been penned unless Jesus was an eminent personality, stress this element (cf. S. J. Case, *The Historicity of Jesus* [1912]; also the works of Browne and Ray O. Miller). Others highlight His character, such as Martin J. Scott. Others, His spiritual insight (F. W. Lewis) or His spiritual life (cf. Rittelmeyer, E. Irvine, and Steer). Others emphasize His strength of character and spiritual eminence (cf. David Smith, Wendling, and Coates). Others dwell upon the everyday naturalness of Jesus and His love of outdoor life (Bruce Barton and Kagawa). Albert Schweitzer held that Jesus reacted as a fanatic believer in an apocalyptic program (*The Quest of the Historical Jesus* [1910]; *The Psychiatric Study of Jesus* [1948]). The flaw of all of those treatments of the life of Christ is that our Lord differed only in degree from other men, whereas the gospels present Him as God become flesh, deity and humanity united in one Person.

Unique in His Resurrection. Is the bodily resurrection of Christ historically and experientially defensible, or is it a mere myth dreamed up by excited followers? Rationalism has always questioned the resurrection of Christ on the grounds of the miraculous, but this aspect of His Person and work is inseparable from His supernatural birth, life, and death. If Jesus was He whom the gospels portray Him to be and He whom He Himself claimed to be, resurrection was the vin-

dicating event of His sinless life and redemptive death. More than this, it was an absolute necessity.

The prevailing problem in modern thinking is the difficulty of fitting the resurrection into the scientific atmosphere of our day that assumes that the universe is shut up to the rigid and irrefutable rule of natural law. But natural law is not a body of regulations that forces compliance. Rather, it is merely an observation of how things have been known to occur in the space-time universe. An adequate view of natural law does not preclude the possibility of divine intervention in the space-time universe any more than it rules out human exercise of mind over matter. By their abilities, men violate the laws of nature constantly.

Numerous writers in this scientific age labor to explain away Christ's physical resurrection. For example, Shirley Jackson Case maintains that the early Christian believers were compelled to outstrip their heathen rivals by attributing to their "hero" a resurrection that was already believed in by devotees of Osiris, Hercules, Dionysius, Adonis, and Attis (cf. S. J. Case, *Experience with the Supernatural in Early Christian Times* [1929]; *The Origins of Christian Supernaturalism* [1946]). Old writers such as K. H. Venturini at the beginning of the nineteenth century held the absurd position that Jesus did not really die but merely swooned, revived in the tomb, and was rescued by His disciples. D. F. Strauss, another noted rationalist, saw the ridiculousness of this view and supplanted it by a mystical theory (1835). Similarly C. H. Weisse, after the middle of the nineteenth century, refused to allow that the resurrection had to do with the outward corporeal existence but merely touched the spiritual and psychic life. Adolf Harnack accepted the Easter message of the soul's survival after death but rejected the Easter event.

Despite the unbelief of the naturalists the Christian church has hung tenaciously to the resurrection. The Lord's Day, the climax of the church calendar in Easter Sunday, and the experiential assurance of myriads of regenerated believers all attest the importance of this doctrine in Christian conviction. J. S. Stewart (*A Faith to Proclaim* [1953], pp. 106f.) speaks clearly of this as a "cosmic event" and as "the shattering of history by a creative act by God Almighty." This, Stewart says, was God "doing something comparable only with what He had done at the first creation."

All who clearly evaluate the resurrection see its inseparable connection with other unique features of the Person and work of Christ. Disbelievers in the resurrection of Christ must realize that this truth, like any other spiritual truth, becomes experiential on the basis of faith. Those who walk with the risen Christ, like the Emmaus disciples, will receive the revelation that they received. The present spiritually adrift age, dazzled by man's scientific progress and ensnared by towering intellectual pride, must realize that the resurrection of Jesus Christ is a great experienced reality that makes intelligible all the other realities of the Person and work of Christ. Men are blundering today by thinking that science can speak *ex cathedra* on such a matter as Christ's resurrection. The voice of science is authoritative and often unquestioned in the natural realm, but regarding the life of Christ science cannot speak because it is confined to the natural and the life of Jesus of Nazareth spans both time and eternity and embraces the natural as well as the supernatural.

However, as an actual event of history, the resurrection of Christ on purely naturalistic grounds is as well attested an event as any happening of ancient times. The glowing faith of the hitherto unbelieving disciples, the establishment of the Christian church, the production of the NT Scriptures, and the history of the redemptive touch of the risen Christ upon the human heart are all phenomena that are unexplainable to the rationalistic denier of the historicity of the resurrection. Such a resurrection saga as confronts us in the NT, not only in the gospels but in all the other books, in itself is an eloquent contradiction of man's proud unbelief.

Unique in His Redemptive Touch. In the resurrection was fulfilled Christ's incipient announcement of the purpose of His coming into the world. "I came that they might have life, and might have it abundantly" (John 10:10). Down through the ages those who have rested their faith in a crucified and risen Redeemer have experienced the regenerating touch of God upon their lives. No change is quite so wonderful as that which takes place in the person who begins to have faith in Jesus Christ. Those who know His redemptive touch and make their quest the supreme goal of knowing Him (Phil. 3:10), such as the apostle Paul did, have moved and are moving the world for God and for good. Not only does the believing soul receive life but fullness of life. The whole magnificent theology of Paul is based on the believer's union with the resurrected Christ. This exalted position Paul contends is transferred into experiential reality on the basis of faith. The believer in the resurrected Christ is "dead to sin, but alive to God in Christ Jesus" (Rom. 6:11). This high position is transferred into his everyday experience when he believes. Thus the resurrection power of Jesus Christ manifested in fullness of life is on a faith basis.

Those who do not exercise faith cannot hope to understand or interpret the life of Jesus, appreciate His personal work, or have any knowledge of the life or fullness of life He came to bring. They are shut up, if intellectually honest, to explaining away the miraculous and supernatural elements of His Person and unique work, which make Him what He is, and form the basis of what He accomplished. Thomas believed because he saw. But millions since his day and because of Christ's redemptive touch have been "blessed . . . who did not see, and yet believed" (John 20:29). It remains a thrilling fact that Christians, not only the ignorant and unlearned but the philosophical and learned, have this as a treasure, that they know the living Christ. Through the channel of faith His life has flowed into their being. Although they have never seen Him with the physical eye, He is no less real to the spiritual perception.

Because Jesus was unique in birth, in life, in sufferings, in death, and in resurrection, He is the basis of the good news, or gospel, that Christians have received and that they proclaim, by which gospel, Paul says, "you stand, by which also you are saved. . . . For I delivered to you as of first importance what I also received, that Christ died for our sins according to the Scriptures, and that He was buried and that He was raised on the third day according to the Scriptures" (1 Cor. 15:1-3).

It is thus apparent that apart from the many-sided uniqueness of the Person and work of Christ there can be no Christian gospel. The gospel centers in Christ. The gospel is Christ. The gospel brings to men redemption. Men who reject the Christ of the four gospels cut away the foundation of the Christian gospel. This may not seem a tragedy to those with superficial views of sin and the necessity of God's grace. But souls awakened to the depravity of sin and the lostness of the human soul apart from God's mercy, see in the rejection of the supernatural Christ a catastrophe of first magnitude. Without the Christ of the gospels fulfilling the messianic prophecies of the OT and furnishing the gospel as expounded by the apostle Paul, Christianity is an empty shell, a mere corpse overlaid with elaborate ritual and costly trappings, but spiritually meaningless. Christ is the life of Christianity and its very heart. If the heart is rejected, the life is forfeited. Jesus must remain the absolute One or the greatest unanswered riddle of history.   M.F.U.

BIBLIOGRAPHY: E. R. Stier, *The Words of the Lord Jesus*, 8 vols. (1855); J. Orr, *The Virgin Birth of Christ* (1927); J. W. Shepard, *The Christ of the Gospels* (1939); G. A. Ogg, *The Chronology of the Public Ministry of Jesus* (1940); T. W. Manson, *The Servant-Messiah* (1953); H. E. W. Turner, *Jesus, Master and Lord* (1953); V. Taylor, *The Life and Ministry of Jesus* (1955); A. Edersheim, *The Life and Times of Jesus the Messiah*, 2 vols. (1962); G. C. Morgan, *The Crises of the Christ* (1963); id., *The Teaching of Christ* (1965); J. G. Machen, *Virgin Birth of Christ* (1967); E. F. Harrison, *A Short Life of Christ* (1968); C. C. Anderson, *Critical Quests of Jesus* (1969); J. F. Walvoord, *Jesus Christ Our Lord* (1969); C. H. Dodd, *The Founder of Christianity* (1970); D. Guthrie, *A Shorter Life of Christ* (1970); J. Reumann, *Jesus in the Church's Gospels* (1970); W. M. Chandler, *The Trial of Jesus* (1972); R. G. Gromacki, *The Virgin*

Birth (1974); R. D. Culver, *The Life of Christ* (1976); H. W. Hoehner, *Chronological Aspects of the Life of Christ* (1977); I. H. Marshall, *I Believe in the Historical Jesus* (1977); W. Pannenberg, *Jesus: God and Man* (1977); J. N. D. Anderson, *The Mystery of the Incarnation* (1978); R. Anderson, *The Lord from Heaven* (1978); J. M. Boice, *God the Redeemer*, vol. 2, Foundations of the Christian Faith (1978); A. M. Hunter, *Christ and the Kingdom* (1978); J. Jeremias, *The Prayers of Jesus* (1978); J. Lawlor, *When God Became Man* (1978); T. W. Manson, *The Sayings of Jesus* (1979); P. Toon, *Jesus Christ Is Lord* (1979); H. P. Liddon and J. Orr, *The Birth of Christ* (1980); W. Milligan, *The Ascension of Christ* (1980), H. C. G. Moule and J. Orr, *The Resurrection of Christ* (1980); G. H. Dalman, *The Words of Jesus* (1981); E. H. Gifford and S. J. Andrews, *The Incarnation of Christ* (1981); J. Denney, *The Death of Christ* (1982); F. W. Farrar, *The Life of Christ* (1982); A. T. Innes and J. Powell, *The Trial of Christ* (1982); E. R. Stier, *Words of the Risen Savior* (1982); F. J. Delitzsch and P. J. Gloag, *The Messiahship of Christ* (1983); W. G. Blaikie, *The Public Ministry of Christ* (1984); J. Harris, *The Teaching Methods of Christ* (1984); P. Toon, *The Ascension of Our Lord* (1984); W. E. Vine, *The Divine Sonship of Christ* (1984); A. Maclaren and H. B. Swete, *The Post-Resurrection Ministry of Christ* (1985).

JE′SUS, OFFICES OF. "Jesus is, in virtue of his incarnation, anointed mediator between God and man. His work was the fulfillment and consummation of the ancient prophetical, priestly, and regal functions to which the typical servants of God under the old economy were anointed. These offices he began to discharge on earth, and continues to discharge in heaven. While considering them as distinct, it is important to remember that they are one in the mediatorial work" (Pope, *Christ. Theol.*, p. 196).

The Prophetic Office. We call Christ our highest Prophet because He is the perfect revealer of the counsel and will of God for the salvation of sinners. As such He comes with supreme credentials, the Truth and the Light of men. The Lord not only speaks of Himself as a prophet (Matt. 13:57; John 4:44) but also receives this name from others (Matt. 21:11; John 3:2; 4:19; 6:14; 9:17) and declares that He is come into the world in order to bear witness of the truth (John 18:37). His disciples call Him prophet and apostle (Luke 24:19; Acts 3:22-24; Heb. 1:1-2; 3:1; 2 Pet. 1:18-19; Rev. 1:5).

Christ came as the greatest prophet, priest, and king. As revealed in God *par excellence* He fulfilled Deut. 18:15: "The Lord your God will raise up for you a prophet like me from among you, from your countrymen, you shall listen to him."

Priestly Office. Here on earth our Lord was a priest in a preeminent sense, both in His sacrifice of Himself for the sins of the world and in His intercession. He is also our present High Priest, interceding for us in heaven. Jesus' baptism in Jordan was evidently a divine setting-apart of the Messiah for His threefold office of Prophet,

Priest, and King, especially as a priest, for therein was the essence of His work manifested in human redemption. *See* Intercession; Mediation; Propitiation.

Kingly Office. All the OT prophecies concerning the kingdom have in view Christ's kingly office. (1) Christ will in the future occupy David's throne as David's heir (2 Sam. 7:16; Ps. 89:20-29; Isa. 11:1-16; Jer. 33:19-21). (2) He was born as a king (Matt. 2:2). (3) He came into the world as a king (Luke 1:32-33). (4) He was rejected as a king (Mark 15:12-13; Luke 19:14). (5) He died as a king (Matt. 27:37). (6) He is coming again as a king (Rev. 19:16). Christ is never called "King of the church," although the term is used in the worship of the church (1 Tim. 1:17). He is "King of the Jews" (Matt. 2:2) and "head over all things to the church" (Eph. 1:22-23). At His second coming Christ will set up the Davidic mediatorial kingdom and reign as King-Priest (Zech. 6:11-13). His millennial reign will be mediatorial in the sense that God will reign through Christ. The mediatorial kingdom will continue until all enemies, angelic and human, will be put down (1 Cor. 15:25-28). However, Christ's kingly reign is eternal (2 Sam. 7:16; Ps. 89:36-37; Isa. 9:6-7) inasmuch as Christ goes on reigning by the same authority of the Father (1 Cor. 15:28). *See* Kingdom of God.

BIBLIOGRAPHY: J. Garbett, *Christ, As Prophet, Priest, and King*, 2 vols. (1842); H. R. Mackintosh, *The Doctrine of the Person of Christ* (1914); H. E. Brunner, *The Mediator* (1934); L. S. Chafer, *Systematic Theology* (1948), 1:357-58; 3:17-26, 30, 37; 4:64-65, 300, 392; 5:82-83, 93-169, 317-76; 7:20, 223, 256; B. B. Warfield, *The Person and Work of Christ* (1950); G. C. Berkouwer, *The Person of Christ* (1954); P. T. Forsyth, *The Person and Place of Jesus Christ* (1964); G. C. Berkouwer, *The Work of Christ* (1965); H. P. Liddon, *The Divinity of Our Lord* (1978); A. M. Hunter, *Christ and the Kingdom* (1980).

JE′THER (je′ther; "eminence, abundance, surplus").

1. Jethro, the father-in-law of Moses (Ex. 4:18, marg.).

2. The firstborn of Gideon's sons, who, when called upon to execute the captured Midianite kings, Zebah and Zalmunna, "was afraid, because he was still a youth" (Judg. 8:20). According to 9:18 he was killed, with sixty-nine of his brothers, at the hand of Abimelech.

3. The father of Amasa, commander of Absalom's army (1 Kings 2:5, 32). Jether is merely another form of Ithra (2 Sam. 17:25), the latter probably being a corruption. He is described in 1 Chron. 2:17 as an Ishmaelite, which again is more likely to be correct than the "Israelite" of the Heb. in 2 Sam. 17 or the "Jezreelite" of the LXX and Vulg. in the same passage (K. & D., *Com.*, ad loc.). Kimchi suggests "that in the land of Ishmael Jether was called the Israelite from his nationality, and in that of Israel they called him

the Ishmaelite on account of his living in the land of Ishmael."

4. The son of Jada, a descendant of Hezron, of the tribe of Judah (1 Chron. 2:32).

5. The son of Ezrah, whose name occurs in a dislocated passage in the genealogy of Judah (1 Chron. 4:17).

6. The head of a family of warriors of the line of Asher, and father of Jephunneh (1 Chron. 7:38). He is probably the same as Ithran (v. 37).

JE'THETH (je'theth; derivation uncertain). One of the "chiefs" who were descended from Esau (Gen. 36:40; 1 Chron. 1:51).

JETH'LAH. *See* Ithlah.

JETH'RO (jeth'rō; "excellence, superiority"). A priest or prince of Midian, both offices probably being combined in one person. Moses spent the forty years of his exile from Egypt with him and married his daughter Zipporah (Ex. 3:1; 4:18; 18:1-7), c. 1475 B.C. At the advice of Jethro, Moses appointed deputies to judge the congregation and share the burden of government with him (18:13-26). On account of his local knowledge he was entreated to remain with the Israelites throughout their journey to Canaan (Num. 10:29-32). It is said in Ex. 2:18 that the priest of Midian whose daughter Moses married was Reuel. But in 3:1 he is called Jethro, as in 4:18 and chap. 18, and in Num. 10:29 he is called "Hobab the son of Reuel the Midianite" (cf. Judg. 4:11). Jethro and Reuel were probably different names of Moses' father-in-law (the former being either a title or a surname showing the rank of Reuel in his tribe), and the son, Hobab, was probably his brother-in-law.

JE'TUR (je'tur). One of the twelve sons of Ishmael (Gen. 25:15; 1 Chron. 1:31). His name stands also for his descendants, the Ituraeans (5:19), living E of the northern Jordan (Luke 3:1).

JEU'EL (je-ū'el).

1. A descendant of Zerah who, with 690 of his relatives, dwelt in Jerusalem after the captivity (1 Chron. 9:6), 536 B.C.

2. One of the "last" sons of Adonikam who, with sixty males, formed part of the caravan of Ezra from Babylon to Jerusalem (Ezra 8:13; "Jeiel," KJV), about 457 B.C.

JE'USH (je'ush).

1. The first of the three sons of Esau by Oholibamah, born in Canaan, but afterward a chief of the Edomites (Gen. 36:5, 14, 18; 1 Chron. 1:35), after 1950 B.C.

2. The first named son of Bilhan, the grandson of Benjamin (1 Chron. 7:10), considerably after 1900 B.C.

3. A son of Eshek, a remote descendant of Saul (1 Chron. 8:39; "Jehush," KJV).

4. A Levite, one of the four sons of Shimei, of

the Gershonites. He and his brother Beriah, not having many sons, were reckoned as the third branch of the family (1 Chron. 23:10-11), about 960 B.C.

5. The first named of the three sons of Rehoboam, apparently by Abihail, his second wife (2 Chron. 11:19), after 926 B.C.

JE'UZ (je'uz; "counselor"). The head of a Benjamite house, one of the sons of Shaharaim, born of his wife Hodesh in Moab (1 Chron. 8:10).

JEW (jū; Heb. *yᵉhûdî*). A Jehudite, i.e., descendant of Judah; Gk. *Ioudaios,* a name formed from that of the patriarch Judah and applied first to the tribe or country of Judah or to a subject of the kingdom of Judah (2 Kings 25:25; Jer. 32:12; 38:19; 40:11, 41:3; 52:28) in distinction from the seceding ten tribes, the Israelites. From the time of the Babylonian captivity, as the members of the tribe of Judah formed by far the larger portion of the remnant of the covenant people, *Jews* became the appellation of the whole nation (2 Macc. 9:17; John 4:9; 7:1; Acts 18:2, 24). The original designation of the Israelite people was the *Hebrews,* as the descendants of Abraham. Thus Paul was appropriately called a Hebrew, and still later the terms *Hebrew* and *Jew* were applied with little distinction. *See* Israel; Hebrew.

JEWEL, JEWELRY. In all ages and among all peoples the love of ornament has expressed itself in the making and wearing of objects of beauty in such forms as were attainable. Very early, as soon indeed as the use of metals was known, the making of jewelry, in our sense of the word, began. In the prehistoric Bronze Age we find multitudes of objects for personal adornment made of that material. Articles of silver and gold set with stones are preserved for us from the very dawn of history. The almost universal practice of burying such treasures with the remains of their owners has been a priceless boon both to history and archaeology in revealing to us the arts, the commerce, the culture, and the migrations of perished races and civilizations.

Uses. The uses of jewelry in Scripture have been various: mere personal adornment (Ex. 11:2; Isa. 3:18-21); gifts and tokens of friendship or affection (Gen. 24:22, 53; Ezek. 16:11-13); emblems of office in secular and religious ceremonials (Gen. 41:42; Dan. 5:7, 16, 29); and priestly insignia (Ex. 28, 39). The royal jewels and the insignia of orders of nobility in Europe and the ecclesiastical jewelry of the Greek and Roman Catholic churches are modern examples of office emblems and priestly insignia. In addition to these uses it may be noted that in ancient times, and still in the East, where money could not be invested as it is with us, precious stones and elaborate jewelry formed one of the safest and most convenient ways of preserving great wealth in small bulk—easy to transport and to conceal.

Scripture Terms. Four Heb. words are commonly used in reference to jewels or jewelry: (1) *S͏eḡullâ,* "shut up, treasure," rendered "possession," is connected with the idea and habit referred to in no. 4, immediately below (*see* Mal. 3:17, marg.) and is often used figuratively (Ex. 19:5; Ps. 135:4). (2) *K͏elî,* is something "wrought" or "prepared," an article of silver or gold (Gen. 24:53; Ex. 3:22; 11:2; 12:35; Num. 31:50-51), and more generally refers to jewels (Isa. 61:10; Ezek. 16:39). This is also an indefinite term, often, perhaps, meaning vessels or implements, at other times decorations or trappings. (3) *Ḥelyâ,* an ornament or trinket (Hos. 2:13), again general in character. (4) *Nezem,* a "ring," the only term that is at all specific, generally rendered "earring," and clearly so in Gen. 35:4; Ex. 32:2, 3; Ezek. 16:12; but sometimes meaning a "nose ring" (Prov. 11:22; Isa. 3:21). In many other cases (Gen. 24:22, 30, 47; Num. 31:50-51; Judg. 8:24-26; Prov. 25:12; etc.), although the former is the rendering, the latter may very probably be the original sense. The nose ring is sometimes two or two-and-a-half inches in diameter (as in Arabia, especially in the Nejed) or less (as with the women of Anatolia), and sometimes, as in the region of Damascus, is reduced to a mere jeweled stud, like our earrings within the last generation.

Other forms of jewelry need but brief reference. Bracelets and necklaces are familiar in all ages and nations, but in ancient times they were largely worn by men, as is conspicuously shown in the Assyrian sculptures and implied in Scripture passages such as Num. 31:50; Dan. 5:7, 16, 29. The large, massive golden bracelets of both men and women were sometimes made hollow, as is now done, and filled with sulphur, partly to lighten their weight and partly to save material. This has been proved by Phoenician examples and was probably frequent. Some of the ancient necklaces were very beautiful; much use was not made of precious stones, but glass and glazed earthenware were used, especially in Phoenician jewelry, in ornaments of beads, and pendants mingled with gold.

The passage "Your cheeks are lovely with ornaments, your neck with strings of beads" (Song of Sol. 1:10) probably refers to a style of ornament seen in many Cypriote figures, a series of coins, hung by small chains or links from behind the ears and coming down by the sides of the face in pendant "rows."

Egyptian. The art of manufacturing jewelry had reached great perfection in Egypt at an early date. Nothing in ancient gilt or gem work, and scarcely anything now, can surpass in elegance the jewelry found with mummies of the royal family of the Twelfth Dynasty. The jeweled treasuries of Tutankhamen of the resplendent Eighteenth Dynasty were incredibly magnificent. His tomb, when opened in 1922, was intact. The tombs were systematically violated and robbed in ancient times, but a few escaped intact, and in them were found the mummies of several princesses, with their jewels. Among these were necklaces, bracelets, etc., exquisitely wrought and set with pearls, carnelian, emerald, and lapis lazuli. Other articles were inlaid with these same stones somewhat in the manner of *cloisonne* enamel, including two very remarkable crowns like delicate wreaths, the one encrusted with flowers of gems and bearing a fanlike spray of similar flowers, with stems and leaves of gold; the other a lacelike garland of gold with forget-me-nots of gems and beads of lapis lazuli (cf. Ezek. 16:12). The most familiar form of Egyptian jewelry is that of the so-called scaraboid seals. Many of them, doubtless, were used more as ornaments than as actual seals, though they were frequently employed for the latter purpose.

Rings from Palestine from the first century A.D.

Assyrian. The jewelry of Assyria and Babylonia may be characterized generally as large, heavy, and showy but not graceful or delicate. The form best known to us, however, is that of the peculiar "Chaldean cylinders," or rolling seals, which, like the Egyptian scarabs, were largely worn as ornaments and charms. Herodotus mentions a cylinder seal, a staff, and some other articles as forming part of the regular outfit of a Babylonian gentleman for all dress occasions; with this may be compared the much more ancient account of Judah (Gen. 38:18). Sumerian jeweled wealth is lavishly illustrated by the royal tomb of Queen Puabi, discovered by Woolley at ancient Ur.

Phoenician. With regard to the Phoenician artisans in Judea, it is not necessary to suppose that they resided there, except perhaps in the principal cities, but they probably traveled through the country doing a little business from place to place. Some writers observe that this custom may still be seen in the East; the itinerant goldsmith and jeweler comes with his small portable furnace, crucible, and stock in trade, and sets up business for a day or two. The women bring their treasured coins to be fashioned into bracelets, bangles, or rings, and the artificer deducts a little percentage for his work. This method is probably very ancient and widespread. Excavations in the Royal Tombs of Byblos have yielded abundant evidences of Phoenician jewel-craft. In the National Museum of Lebanon gleaming objets d'art displaying Phoenician skill can be seen today.

Hebrew. Or course, the most interesting and important articles of Hebrew jewelry are those connected with the worship of the Tabernacle, especially the high priest's breastpiece, of which such specific descriptions are given. The style of workmanship must have been Egyptian in character; the Israelites had been living there for generations and must have been familiar with the art of that country, while long cut off from association with Mesopotamia. At a later period of their history they came under Assyrian and Babylonian influence. In art matters, they were largely influenced by their Phoenician neighbors. We have seen how the latter borrowed and mingled the art styles of Egypt and Mesopotamia, developing no originality, though much of skill and delicacy in treatment. It would seem, therefore, that the influences dominating Hebrew art in jewelry must have been first Egyptian, then Phoenician, and finally Chaldean.

At this point a few words should be said as to the differences between ancient and modern jewelry. The whole method of cutting stones in facets is modern and European —Eastern and ancient jewelry is quite different. In ancient times the stones were dressed *en cabochon,* as modern jewelers call it, i.e., made in rounded forms with smooth or polished convex surfaces. This mode we still employ for opaque and translucent gems, such as turquoises, opals, moonstones, and "carbuncle" garnets, but anciently it was universal. This method gives none of the brilliant flashing effect now so highly esteemed, which results from the internal reflection and refraction of the rays of light from the numerous facets. Hence the ancients seem to have cared less for transparency than we do, and to make up for the loss of beauty in this regard they paid more attention to engraving gems than the moderns. Any collection of ancient jewelry will show a large proportion of opaque and semitransparent stones, all *en cabochon,* rounded, and many beautifully sculptured with cameos, intaglios, or inscriptions. In this work the ancients excelled, and the fineness, sharpness, and boldness of their gem engraving

cannot be surpassed, indeed, can scarcely be equaled by modern workmen with the best of tools and magnifiers (*see* Anklets; Bracelets; Precious Stones; Ring).   D.S.M.; M.F.U.

BIBLIOGRAPHY: J. S. Harris, *Annual of the Leeds University Oriental Society* 4 (1962-63): 49-83; id., *Annual of the Leeds University Oriental Society* 5 (1963-65): 40-62; C. Aldred, *Jewels of the Pharaohs* (1971); J. I. Packer, M. C. Tenney, and W. White, Jr., eds., *The Bible Almanac* (1980), pp. 214-20.

JEW'ESS, (jū'es). A woman of Hebrew extraction, without distinction of tribe (Acts 24:24). This passage refers to Drusilla, wife of Felix and daughter of Herod Agrippa I, but in 1 Chron. 4:18 Mered's "Jewish wife" (NIV, "Judean") is mentioned, and in Acts 16:1 Timothy is called "the son of a Jewish woman."

JEWISH (Gk. *Ioudaïkos*). Of or belonging to Jews. The apostle Paul warns his young brother against Jewish myths, i.e., the rabbinical legends (Titus 1:14).

JEZANI'AH (jez-a-nī'a; Jer. 40:8; 42:1). *See* Jaazaniah, no. 1.

JEZ'EBEL (jez'e-bel; perhaps "noncohabited, un-husbanded"). The daughter of Ethbaal, king of Tyre and Sidon, and queen with Ahab. Her father had formerly been a priest of Astarte, but had violently dispossessed his brother Phelles of the throne. The first mention of Jezebel in Scripture is her marriage with Ahab (1 Kings 16:31), about 871 B.C.

Introduces Idolatry. The first effect of her influence was the immediate establishment of the Phoenician worship on a grand scale at the court of Ahab. At her table were supported no less than 450 prophets of Baal and 400 of Astarte (1 Kings 16:31-32; 18:19), whereas the prophets of Jehovah were slain by her orders (18:13; 2 Kings 9:7).

Opposes Elijah. When at last the people, at the instigation of *Elijah* (which see), rose against her ministers and slaughtered them at the foot of Carmel, and when Ahab was terrified into submission, she alone retained her presence of mind; and when she received, in the palace of Jezreel, the tidings that her religion was all but destroyed, she vowed to take the life of the prophet (1 Kings 19:1-2).

Secures the Death of Naboth. When Jezebel found her husband cast down by his disappointment at being thwarted by *Naboth* (which see), she took the matter into her own hands. She wrote a warrant in Ahab's name, which was to secure the death of Naboth. To her, and not Ahab, was sent the announcement that the royal wishes were accomplished, and she bade her husband go and take the vacant property (1 Kings 21:1-16). On her, accordingly, fell the prophet's curse, as well as on her husband (v. 23).

Influence. Her policy was so triumphant that there were at last but seven thousand people who had not bowed the knee to Baal or kissed the hand of his image. Through her daughter Athaliah, queen of Judah, the same policy prevailed for a time in that kingdom. Jezebel survived Ahab fourteen years and maintained considerable ascendency over her son Jehoram.

Death. When Jehu entered Jezreel, Jezebel was in the palace, which stood by the gate of the city, overlooking the approach from the E. She determined to face the destroyer of her family, whom she saw rapidly advancing in his chariot. She painted her eyelids in the Eastern fashion with antimony, so as to give a darker border to the eyes and make them look larger and brighter, possibly in order to induce Jehu, after the manner of Eastern usurpers, to take her, the widow of his predecessor, for his wife, but more probably as the last act of regal splendor. She adorned her head, and, looking down upon him from the high latticed window in the tower, she met him by an allusion to a former act of treason in the history of her adopted country. Jehu looked up from his chariot. Two or three officials of the royal harem showed their faces at the windows and, at his command, threw her down from the chamber. She fell in front of Jehu's chariot. When, afterward, he wished to show respect to her corpse as that of "a king's daughter," nothing was found of her but "the skull and the feet and the palms of her hands," thus fulfilling the prophecy of Elijah (2 Kings 9:30-37), about 841 B.C.

Character. Jezebel was a woman in whom were united the sternest and fiercest qualities inherent in the Phoenician people. The wild license of her life and the magical fascination of her arts and of her character were known throughout the nation (2 Kings 9:22). Long afterward her name lived as the byword for all that was detestable. In Rev. 2:20 she is used as a type of those who encourage immorality and false teaching, in the same way that she engulfed Israel in idolatry.

BIBLIOGRAPHY: N. Avigad, *Israel Exploration Journal* 14 (1964): 274-76; F. I. Andersen, *Journal of Biblical Literature* 85 (1966): 46-57.

JE'ZER (je'zer; "form, purpose"). The third named of the sons of Naphtali (Gen. 46:24; Num. 26:49; 1 Chron. 7:13) and the progenitor of the Jezerites (Num. 26:49), before 1870 B.C.

JE'ZERITES (je'zer'its; Num. 26:49). *See* Jezer.

JEZI'AH. *See* Izzi'ah.

JE'ZIEL (je'zi-el). A "son" of Azmaveth and one of the Benjamite archers who joined David at Ziklag (1 Chron. 12:3), before 1000 B.C.

JEZLI'AH. *See* Izliah.

JEZO'AR. *See* Izhar.

JEZRAHI'AH (jez-ra-hī'a; "Jehovah will shine"). He was the superintendent leader of the singers

at the dedication of the walls of Jerusalem after the Exile (Neh. 12:42), 445 B.C.

JEZ'REEL (jez'rēl; "God sows").
1. A descendant of the father (or founder) of Etam, of the line of Judah (1 Chron. 4:3).
2. The oldest son of the prophet Hosea, so called because of the great slaughter predicted by his father (Hos. 1:4-5), about 748 B.C. *See* "The bloodshed of Jezreel," in no. 3, below.
3. The name of a city in Issachar (Josh. 19:18), and the plain in which it was located (1 Sam. 29:1; Hos. 1:5). It was situated about fifty-five miles N of Jerusalem and is identified with the present Zer'in, about seven miles N of Jenin. Here the kings of Israel had a palace (2 Sam. 2:8-9), and here the court often resided (1 Kings 18:45-46; 2 Kings 10:11). In or near the town was a temple of Baal and an Asherah (1 Kings 16:32-33). The palace of Ahab was on the eastern side of the city, forming part of the city wall (cf. 1 Kings 21:1; 2 Kings 9:25, 30, 33). The palace in which Jezebel lived was on the city wall, with windows facing to the E (2 Kings 9:30). Nearby was the vineyard of Naboth, coveted by King Ahab, and secured by Jezebel through the cruel death of its owner (1 Kings 21:1-16).

"The bloodshed of Jezreel" ("I will punish the house of Jehu for the bloodshed of Jezreel," Hos. 1:4) is generally understood to be put for the murders perpetuated by Ahab and Jehu at this place. But the divine vengeance is to be visited upon the house of Jehu and would seem, therefore, to be because of his acts. This may be, not because of his extermination of the house of Ahab, in which he fulfilled the divine command, but by reason of the motives that actuated Jehu. That he was moved by evil and selfish motives is evident (*see* 2 Kings 10:29, 31).

The "District of Jezreel" refers to the fortification or entrenchment surrounding the city, outside of which Naboth was executed (1 Kings 21:23).

The "Spring of Jezreel" ("The spring which is in Jezreel," 1 Sam. 29:1) is mentioned as the spot near which the Israelites pitched their camp in one of their campaigns against the Philistines. At present it is called Ain Jalûd (or Ain Jalût), i.e., Goliath's fountain, probably because it was regarded as the scene of Goliath's defeat. It is a very large spring issuing from the foot of the mountain on the NE border of Gilboa.

"The Property of Jezreel" (also called the "territory of Jezreel," 2 Kings 9:10), is the field or country adjacent to the city, where the crime of Ahab occurred (2 Kings 9:10, 21, 36; etc.).

The "Tower in Jezreel" was one of the turrets or bastions guarding the entrance of the city, and where the watchman was stationed (2 Kings 9:17).

The "Valley of Jezreel" lies on the northern side of the city between the ridges of Gilboa and

Moreh. Its name was afterward extended to the whole plain of Esdraelon (Josh. 17:16; Judg. 6:33; Hos. 1:5). Smith suggests that the "word for 'vale,' '*ēmeq*, literally *deepening*, is a highlander's word for a valley as he looks *down* into it, and is never applied to any extensive plain away from hills."

4. A town in the mountains of Judah, mentioned between Juttah and Jokdeam (Josh. 15:56, and probably the native place of Ahinoam, one of David's wives (1 Sam. 25:43; 27:3); the site has not yet been discovered.

BIBLIOGRAPHY: E. Robinson, *Biblical Researches* (1856), 2: 318-25; R. A. S. Macalister, *Palestine Exploration Quarterly* 41 (1909): 175; S. Yeivin, *Bulletin of the Israel Exploration Society* 14 (1948): 89; D. Baly, *The Geography of the Bible* (1957), pp. 148-54.

JEZ'REELITE (jez'rēl-īt). An inhabitant of *Jezreel* (which see) in Issachar (1 Kings 21:1, 4, 6-7, 15-16; 2 Kings 9:21, 25).

JEZ'REELITESS (jez'rēl-ī-tes; 1 Sam. 27:3, 30:5; 2 Sam. 2:2, 3:2; 1 Chron. 3:1). A woman of Jezreel in Judah, mentioned in connection with David's wife Ahinoam.

JIB'SAM. *See* Ibsam.

JID'LAPH (jid'laf; "he weeps"). The seventh named of the eight sons of Nahor (Abraham's brother) by Milcah (Gen. 22:22), perhaps about 2100 B.C.

JIM'NA, JIM'NAH. *See* Imnah.

JIPH'TAH. *See* Iphtah.

JIPH'THAL-EL. *See* Iphtahel.

JOAB (jō'ab). The name of one of David's captains (see article below) and of several other men in the Bible.

1. In 1 Chron. 2:54 there is mention of "Atroth-beth-joab." Which Joab is meant is uncertain.

2. The son of Seraiah (son of Kenaz), a Judaite and progenitor of the inhabitants of Ge-harashim, who were craftsmen (1 Chron. 4:14).

3. The head of a family whose descendants, with those of Jeshua, to the number of 2,812 (Ezra 2:6) or 2,818 (Neh. 7:11) returned from Babylon with Ezra. It is not certain whether Jeshua and Joab were sons of Pahath-moab, or whether, in the registration of those returned, the descendants of Jeshua and Joab were represented by the sons of Pahath-moab. The Joab mentioned in Ezra 8:9 is probably the same person; 445 B.C.

JO'AB (jō'ab; "Jehovah is father"). A "captain of the host" of David. He was one of the three sons of Zeruiah, the sister of David. His father is not named in the Scriptures, but Josephus (*Ant.* 7.1.3) gives his name as Suri. He seems to have resided at Bethlehem, and to have died before his sons, as we find mention of his tomb at the place (2 Sam. 2:32).

First Appearance. Joab's first appearance was in connection with his brothers, Abishai and Asahel, in command of David's army, when they went against Abner, who was championing the claims of Ish-bosheth to the throne. The armies met at the pool of Gibeon, and Abner was defeated in battle. In his flight he killed Asahel, who was pursuing him (2 Sam. 2:13-32), about 1000 B.C.

Avenges Asahel. Joab was greatly angered at

View of the Jezreel Valley from Megiddo

the death of his brother, but postponed his revenge. Abner, quarreling with Ish-bosheth, came to David in Hebron in order to enlist in his service. Returning from a raid, Joab was informed of Abner's visit. He chided the king, accused Abner of treachery, and then sent messengers after Abner, who returned at once and was killed by Joab and his brother Abishai. David reproved the act, but seems to have been in fear of his able and intrepid nephew (2 Sam. 3:8-39).

In Chief Command. At the siege of Jerusalem Joab succeeded in scaling the height upon which the fortress stood and was made "chief" of the army of all Israel, of which David was then king (2 Sam. 5:6-10; 1 Chron. 11:5-8). He immediately undertook, in conjunction with David, the fortification of the city (2 Sam. 5:9; 1 Chron. 11:8). He had a chief armor-bearer of his own, Naharai, a Beerothite (2 Sam. 23:37; 1 Chron. 11:39), and ten attendants to carry his equipment and baggage (2 Sam. 18:15). He was in charge of giving the signal by trumpet for advance or retreat (18:16). He was called "lord" (11:11), "the commander of the king's army" (1 Chron. 27:34). His usual residence was in Jerusalem, but he had a house and property, with barley fields adjoining, in the country (2 Sam. 14:30), in the "wilderness" (1 Kings 2:34), probably on the NE of Jerusalem (cf. 1 Sam. 13:18; Josh. 8:15, 20), near an ancient sanctuary, called from its nomadic village "Baal-hazor" (2 Sam. 13:23; cf. 14:30), where there were extensive sheepwalks.

Military Achievements. Joab's military exploits were conducted by him in person and may be divided into three campaigns: that against the allied forces of Syria and Ammon, that against Edom, and that against the Ammonites.

In the campaign against the allied forces of Syria and Ammon, Joab attacked and defeated the Syrians, while his brother did the same to the Ammonites. The Syrians rallied with their kindred beyond the Euphrates and were finally routed by David himself (2 Sam. 10:7-14).

In the campaign against Edom the decisive victory was gained by David himself in the "Valley of Salt" and celebrated by a triumphal monument (8:13). But Joab had the charge of carrying out the victory and remained for six months, completely destroying the male population, whom he then buried in the tombs of Petra (1 Kings 11:15-16).

In the third campaign the Ammonites were again left to Joab (2 Sam. 10:7-19). The Ark was sent with him at the siege of Rabbah, and the whole army was encamped in booths or huts around the beleaguered city (11:1, 11). After a sortie of the inhabitants, which caused some loss to the Jewish army, Joab took the lower city on the river and then sent to urge David to come and take the citadel, that the glory of the capture might be the king's (12:26-28).

Services to David. Joab served David faithfully, both in political and private relations, and he showed himself to be truly devoted to the king's interests. (1) During the Ammonite war Joab lent himself to the king's passion and secured the death of Uriah the Hittite (2 Sam. 11:14-25). (2) When Absalom accomplished the death of Amnon, Joab effected Absalom's return by means of the widow of Tekoah. When Absalom revolted, Joab's former closeness to the prince did not impair his fidelity to the king. He followed Absalom beyond the Jordan and in the final battle of Ephraim, in spite of David's injunction to spare him and when no one else had courage to act so decisive a part, killed the prince (2 Sam. 18:2, 11-15). (3) When David resolved to number the people, Joab tried to dissuade him from his purpose. Unsuccessful in this, Joab performed the task slowly in order to give the king an opportunity to reconsider the matter (24:1-9).

Murder of Amasa. David, to conciliate the powerful party that had supported Absalom, offered the command of the army to Amasa. Joab was grievously offended by this act of the king, and when Amasa tarried longer than the time allowed him to assemble his forces, Joab had an opportunity of displaying his superior resources. Abishai was ordered to pursue the revolting Sheba (perhaps with Joab in command, K. & D.), and when Amasa came up to meet them at Gibeon he was treacherously killed by Joab (2 Sam. 20:4-13).

Joins Adonijah. Shortly before the death of David a demonstration was made in favor of his eldest surviving son, Adonijah, instead of Solomon, and Joab joined this party. The prompt measures taken rendered Adonijah's demonstration abortive, and Solomon was declared king (1 Kings 1:7-39).

Death. Hearing of the death of Adonijah, Joab fled for refuge to the altar. Solomon, hearing of this, sent Benaiah to put him to death, and, as he refused to come forth, Benaiah killed him. His body was buried in the wilderness of Judah (1 Kings 2:5, 28-34), about 962 B.C.

Character. Joab was a man of great military prowess, valiant, and capable. He was revengeful, and not above treachery in order to gratify his vengeance. Although he treated his king with little ceremony he was, nevertheless, truly devoted to his interests. His principles did not prevent his serving his master's vices as well as his virtues. Altogether he appears in history as one of the most accomplished and unscrupulous warriors that Israel ever produced.

BIBLIOGRAPHY: R. O. Corvin, *David and His Mighty Men* (1970), pp. 69-86; W. G. Blaikie, *David, King of Israel* (1981), pp. 135-54, 285-96.

JO'AH (jō'a; "Jehovah is brother").

1. Son of Asaph and "recorder" of King Hezekiah, and one of the messengers sent to receive the

insulting message of Rabshakeh (2 Kings 18:18, 26, 37; Isa. 36:3, 22), about 719 B.C.

2. A Levite of the family of Gershom, son of Zimnah and father of Iddo (1 Chron. 6:20-21). He is probably the same person who, with his son Eden, assisted Hezekiah in the reformation of the Temple worship (2 Chron. 29:12), about 719 B.C. He is identified with Ethan, mentioned in 1 Chron. 6:42.

3. The third son of Obed-edom, one of the gatekeepers (porters, KJV) for the Tabernacle in the time of David (1 Chron. 26:4), after 1000 B.C.

4. Son of Joahaz and recorder for King Josiah. He was appointed one of the superintendents of the Temple repairs (2 Chron. 34:8), 639 B.C.

JO'AHAZ (jō'a-haz; "Jehovah holds"). The father of Joah, a recorder in the reign of Josiah (2 Chron. 34:8), 639 B.C.

JOA'NAN (jō-a'nan). The son of Rhesa and grandson of Zerubbabel, in the lineage of Christ (Luke 3:27; "Joanna," KJV).

JOAN'NA (jō-a'na; Gk., probably feminine of *Jōannēs,* John). The wife of Chuza, the steward of Herod Agrippa (Luke 8:3). She, with other women, was either cured of disease by Jesus or received material benefits from Him and afterward ministered to Him and His disciples. She was also one of the women to whom Christ appeared after the resurrection (Luke 24:10).

For the name in Luke 3:27, *see* Joanan.

JO'ASH (jō'ash; Heb. *Yô'āsh,* "Jehovah has given"; Arab. *'asa,* "to give").

1. The father of Gideon, who, although himself an idolater, ingeniously screened his son from those desiring to avenge his overthrow of the altar of Baal (Judg. 6:11, 29-31; 7:14; 8:13, 29). He was buried in Ophrah, where he lived (8:29-32).

2. A person who was ordered by King Ahab to imprison Micaiah the prophet for denouncing the allied expedition against Ramoth-gilead (1 Kings 22:26; 2 Chron. 18:25), about 853 B.C. In both passages he is called "the king's son," which is usually taken literally. Some, however, suggest that the title may merely indicate a youth of princely stock; others, that Melek, translated "king," is a proper name.

3. King of Judah (2 Kings 11:2; 12:19-20; 13:1, 10; 14:1, 3, 17, 23; 1 Chron. 3:11; 2 Chron. 22:11; 24:1-2, 4, 22, 24; 25:23, 25). *See* Jehoash, no. 1.

4. King of Israel (2 Kings 13:9, 12-14, 25; 14:1, 23, 27; 2 Chron. 25:17-18, 21, 23, 25; Hos. 1:1; Amos 1:1). *See* Jehoash, no. 2.

5. A descendant of Shelah, son of Judah, mentioned among those "who ruled in Moab" (1 Chron. 4:22). The Hebrew tradition, quoted by Jerome and Jarchi, applies it to Mahlon, the son of Elimelech, who married a Moabitess.

6. A son of Shemah (or Hasmath), the Gibeath-

ite, who, with his brother Ahiezer and other "mighty men," joined David at Ziklag (1 Chron. 12:3).

BIBLIOGRAPHY: T. Kirk and G. Rawlinson, *Studies in the Books of the Kings,* 2 vols. in 1 (1983), 2:119-24, 129-34; E. R. Thiele, *Mysterious Numbers of the Hebrew Kings* (1983), pp. 57, 104.

JO'ASH (Heb. *Yô'āsh,* "Jehovah has come, hastened").

1. One of the "sons" (descendants) of Becher, son of Benjamin, and a leader of his family (1 Chron. 7:8).

2. The person having charge of the "stores of oil" under David and Solomon (1 Chron. 27:28), after 1000 B.C.

JO'ATHAM. See Jotham, no. 2.

JOB. For the character in the book that bears his name, *see* Job, Book of; for the Job referred to in the KJV of Gen. 46:13, see the article Jashub.

JOB, BOOK OF. This splendid dramatic poem belongs to the Wisdom Literature of the OT. It is universally recognized as superb literature. The poem takes its name from its chief character, Job, *'iyyôb.* Interestingly enough, the name occurs in the Berlin Execration Texts as the name of a certain prince in the region of Damascus in the nineteenth century B.C. (*Bulletin of the American Schools of Oriental Research* 82 [1941]: 36). The name is also found in the Amarna correspondence dating c. 1400 B.C. referring to a prince of Pella. Job of the biblical story was a dweller in the land of Uz (Job 1:1), which evidently lay somewhere between Damascus on the N and Edom on the S; that is, in the steppes E of Palestine-Syria.

Subject. The book of Job revolves around the perplexing question of why the righteous suffer and how their suffering can be reconciled with the infinite goodness and holiness of God. Job loses family, wealth, and his own health, and then sits "among the ashes," where he is visited by three friends who come to mourn with him and to offer their explanations of his misfortune. Job's three friends offer practically the same answer (chaps. 3-31), implying that suffering is always the outcome of sin. Job desperately asserts his innocence and at times appears almost delirious under the unjust insinuations. He borders upon accusing God of injustice, but he recoups his confidence in the divine goodness and protests that he will be finally vindicated. At this juncture Elihu comes on the scene and appears with the divine message elaborated in the NT, that sufferings are very often the medium of refining the righteous, the chastisements of a Father who loves His children, and by no means the action of a vindictive or implacable God (chaps. 32-37). Then God speaks to Job out of the whirlwind, humbling him and bringing him to a realization that he, himself, is to be abhorred before God's presence (42:1-6). His self-abnegation and spiritual refining are a prelude to his restoration (42:7-17).

Outline.

I. Prologue: Testing of Job (1-2)
II. Job falsely comforted by his friends (3-31)
   A. First cycle of speeches:
      Job's speech followed by those of his three friends, each in turn answered by Job (3-14)
   B. Second cycle of speeches:
      Each friend speaks to Job and is answered by him (15-21)
   C. Third cycle of speeches:
      Eliphaz and Bildad speak until answered by Job (22-31)
III. Speeches of Elihu (32-37)
   A. First Speech: Purpose of affliction (32-33)
   B. Second Speech: God vindicated (34)
   C. Third Speech: The advantages of piety (35)
   D. Fourth speech: God's greatness and Job's ignorance (36-37)
IV. Speeches of God and Job's response (38:1-42:6)
   A. First speech: Creation declares God's all-power; Job's conversion (38:1-40:5)
   B. Second speech: Power of God and human weakness; Job's humility (40:6-42:6)
V. Epilogue: Job's friends rebuked; Job restored (42:7-17)

Time and Composition. Great disagreement prevails as to the composition. Critics date the composition of the book anywhere from patriarchal times (Ebrard) to as late as 400 B.C. (Eissfeldt; Volz) or even the third century B.C. (Cornill). Probably the most likely date is the Solomonic era, (Franz Delitzsch; Keil), because it bears evidence of the creative beginning period of Wisdom Literature. It comprehends ideas similar to parts of Proverbs (cf. Job. 15:8 and chap. 28 with Prov. 8).

Authenticity. It is customary among critics to deny the authenticity of (1) the prologue and epilogue; (2) chap. 28, the poem of Divine Wisdom; (3) the description of leviathan and behemoth (40:10-41:25); and (4) the discourses of Elihu (32:1-37:24). No valid reason can be brought forward for ascribing the prologue and epilogue to a later author. "The dialogue cannot have had any independent existence," as A. Bentzen correctly observes. "In 8:4-29:5 it presupposes the description of Job's illness as given in the narrative" (*Intr.*, 2:175). Chapter 28 cannot be proved to be extraneous, although the passage is admittedly loosely connected with the context, but so are other choice literary pieces of the book. If, as is certainly true, "the finest literary masterpieces are to be found among these incidental pieces and in digressions rather than in the argumentative scaffolding of the book," as

Pfeiffer admits, why reject this passage and retain others when "to remove even some of them would greatly reduce the value of the original poem and imply that the poetic genius of the supplementers was equal, if not superior, to that of the original poet?" (*Intr.*, p. 686). The same answer may be given to the critical contention that the descriptions of leviathan (crocodile) and behemoth (hippopotamus) in 40:15-41:34 are a subsequent insertion. The language and ideas of this passage are similar to the remainder of the book (cf. 40:15 and 39:15 with 5:23; 41:9 with 3:9; etc.). Elihu's speeches are rejected because he does not appear in the prologue or epilogue. He is not merely a loquacious interrupter. He adds a momentous truth that affliction of the righteous is disciplinary (33:16-18, 27-30; 36:10-12). Elihu's speeches answer Job's problem and get him ready for Jehovah's appearance and words from the whirlwind. There would be a genuine lack in the book if the Elihu sections were omitted. He does not appear in the epilogue because, unlike Job's friends, he did not merit rebuke. His contribution to the solution of the problem of the book invalidates the rejection of this portion.

BIBLIOGRAPHY: S. Cox, *Commentary on the Book of Job* (1880); A. B. Davidson, *The Book of Job*, Cambridge Bible for Schools and Colleges (1903); R. Gordis, *The Book of God and Man* (1965); M. H. Pope. *Job*, Anchor Bible (1965); R. K. Harrison, *Introduction to the Old Testament* (1969), pp. 1022-46; F. I. Andersen, *Job*, Tyndale Old Testament Commentaries (1976); E. C. S. Gibson, *The Book of Job* (1978); R. B. Zuck, *Job*, Everyman's Bible Commentary (1978); W. H. Green, *The Argument of the Book of Job Unfolded* (1979); H. H. Rowley, *Job*, New Century Bible (1980); E. Dhorme, *Commentary on the Book of Job* (1984).

JO'BAB (jō'bab; "howler, one who calls shrilly").
1. The last in the order of the sons of Joktan (Gen. 10:29; 1 Chron. 1:23).
2. Son of Zerah of Bozrah, and one of the "kings" of Edom (Gen. 36:33-34; 1 Chron. 1:44-45), probably before 1440 B.C.
3. The king of Madon, a royal city of the Canaanites. He assisted Jabin, king of Hazor, against Joshua; they were both overcome by him (Josh. 11:1), after 1370 B.C.
4. A Benjamite, and the first named of the sons of Shaharaim by his wife Hodesh (1 Chron. 8:9).
5. One of the "sons" (probably descendants) of Elpaal, a chief of Benjamin at Jerusalem (1 Chron. 8:18), probably about 588 B.C.

JOCH'EBED (jok'ē-bed; "Jehovah her glory"). The wife of Amram and mother of Miriam, Aaron, and Moses (Num. 26:59), c. 1520 B.C. In Ex. 6:20 it is expressly declared that she was the sister of Amram's father, and, consequently, her husband's aunt. It was contrary to the law for persons thus related to marry, and several attempts have been made to prove a more distant relationship. Kitto says, "The fact seems to be that where this marriage was contracted there was no law forbidding such alliances, but they must in any case have been unusual, although not forbidden; and this, with the writer's knowledge that they were subsequently interdicted, sufficiently accounts for this one being so pointedly mentioned." So K. and D. (*Com.*, ad loc.).

JO'DA (jō'da). The son of Joanan and father of Josech, listed among the maternal ancestors of Christ (Luke 3:26, NASB and NIV; "Juda," KJV).

JO'ED (jō'ed; "Jehovah his witness"). The son of Pedaiah and grandfather of Sallu, who was one of the Benjamites chosen to dwell in Jerusalem after the captivity (Neh. 11:7), before 536 B.C.

JO'EL (jō'el; "Jehovah is God").

1. The eldest of the two sons of Samuel, appointed by him as judges in Beersheba. By the taking of bribes and perversion of judgment they led to the popular desire for a monarchy (1 Sam. 8:2-3; 1 Chron. 6:28), before 1030 B.C. He is named as the father of Heman, the Levitical singer (6:33; 15:17).

2. A descendant of Simeon, one of those whose families emigrated to the valley of Gedor (1 Chron. 4:35), about 715 B.C.

3. A descendant of Reuben, but by what line or in what degree of proximity is uncertain (1 Chron. 5:4, 8).

4. A chief of the Gadites living in Bashan (1 Chron. 5:12), perhaps about 782 B.C.

5. A Kohathite Levite, son of Azariah and father of Elkanah (1 Chron. 6:36). He is probably the Joel who assisted Hezekiah in his restoration of the Temple services (2 Chron. 29:12), 719 B.C.

6. The third named of the four sons of Izrahiah, a chief of the tribe of Issachar in the time of David (1 Chron. 7:3), about 1000 B.C.

7. Brother of Nathan and one of David's mighty men (1 Chron. 11:38), about 1000 B.C. He is called "Igal the son of Nathan" in 2 Sam. 23:36. Kennicott decides in favor of the former as most likely to be the genuine text (*Dissertations*, pp. 212-14).

8. A Levite, head of the family of Gershom, who, at the head of 130, was appointed by David to assist in removing the Ark (1 Chron. 15:7, 11), after 1000 B.C. He is probably the same as the third of the "sons" of Ladan (23:8), and also with the son of Jehieli, who was one of those in charge of the "treasures of the house of the Lord" (26:22) (Keil).

9. Son of Pedaiah, and prince in the time of David, of the half tribe of Manasseh west (1 Chron. 27:20), about 1000 B.C.

10. One of the "sons" of Nebo, who put away his Gentile wife after the return from Babylon (Ezra 10:43), 456 B.C.

11. Son of Zichri and "overseer" of the Benjamites living in Jerusalem after the captivity (Neh. 11:9), about 536 B.C.

12. Son of Pethuel, and second of the twelve minor prophets (Joel 1:1; Acts 2:16). Nothing is known of his life, and all that can be inferred with any certainty from his writings is that he lived in Judah and probably prophesied in Jerusalem. The date of his ministry is also a disputed point; some make him contemporary with Amos and Isaiah during the reign of Uzziah, about 770 B.C., others (Keil, *Com.*) assign him to the first thirty years of Jehoash.

JOEL, BOOK OF. Joel, the writer of the book of Joel, was a prophet of the Southern Kingdom. His name means "Jehovah is God." His frequent addresses to the priesthood would seem to indicate that he himself was a priest.

Purpose. The prophet's purpose was to warn the nation to repent in the light of approaching judgment, as well as to stir up the faithful among the people to believe the promises of God involving coming salvation and the destruction of the enemies of God's kingdom. In the prophecy a terrible plague of insects is made the occasion of great prophetic significance (Joel 1:13-14), foreshadowing the Day of the Lord. Chapter 2 demonstrates this fact when the scourge of locusts fades out of the picture and the future Day of Jehovah comes into full view. The prophetic imagery refers to the end time of the present age, the period of the "times of the Gentiles" (Luke 21:24; Rev. 16:14). The Battle of Armageddon is also prefigured, as well as the regathering of Israel and the Kingdom blessing. Joel presents the following order of events: (1) The invasion of Palestine by Gentile nations under the leadership of the Beast and the false prophet (Joel 2:1-10; cf. Armageddon, Rev. 16:13-14). (2) Decimation of the invading hordes by the Lord's host (Joel 2:11; cf. Rev. 19:11, 21). (3) Judah's conversion in the land (Joel 2:12-17). (4) The Lord's promise of deliverance (Joel 2:18-27). (5) The pouring out of the Holy Spirit preceding the Kingdom age (Joel 2:28-29). (6) The second advent of Christ with the establishment of the mediatorial Kingdom (Joel 2:30-32; cf. Acts 15:15-17). (7) The judgment of the nations (Joel 3:1-16). (8) Realization of full millennial conditions (Joel 3:17-21; cf. Zech. 14:1-21).

Outline.

I. The Day of the Lord in prophetic type (1:1-20)
   A. The prophet (1:1)
   B. The locust plague (1:2-7)
   C. Repentance and prayer of the afflicted people (1:8-20)

II. The Day of the Lord itself in prophecy (2:1-32)
   A. The invaders (2:1-10)
   B. The Lord's host at Armageddon (2:11)
   C. Repentant remnant in Palestine (2:12-27)

D. The Lord's response to the remnant (2:28-29)
E. Signs of the Day of the Lord (2:30-32)
III. The judgment of the nations in prophecy (3:1-16)
  A. Israel reinstated (3:1)
  B. The nations judged (3:2-3)
  C. Phoenicia and Philistia condemned (3:4-8)
  D. The call to arms and the judgment (3:9-16)
IV. Millennial blessing in prophecy (3:17-21)
  A. Jerusalem's ascendancy (3:17)
  B. Judah's prosperity (3:18)
  C. Egypt and Edom's desolation (3:19)
  D. Explanation of Jerusalem's exaltation (3:20-21)

Authorship. As early as 1872, M. Vernes denied the Joel authorship (cf. 1:1). Vernes maintained that chap. 3 was not written by the same person as chaps. 1 and 2. Such critics as J. W. Rothstein, Sievers, B. Duhm, and Paul Haupt also deny the unity of the book. These views have not met with wide acceptance, however (cf. L. Dennefelt, *Les Problemes du Livre de Joel* [1926]; J. Smith, W. H. Ward and J. Bewer, *Joel* in International Critical Commentary [1911]; A. S. Kapelrud, *Joel Studies* [1948]; R. K. Harrison, *Introduction to the Old Testament* [1969], pp. 874-82).

Date. Critics commonly date Joel's prophecy anywhere from the division of the kingdom (c. 932 B.C.) to the time of Malachi (c. 400 B.C.) or even later. The safest date seems to be preexilic. The reign of Joash (835-796 B.C.) is most appropriate for the prophecy.

Several lines of argument would seem to indicate that Joel's prophecy is early. Its style and general spirit are dissimilar to that of Haggai, Zechariah, and Malachi, postexilic prophets. Its language and style rather belong to the period of Hebrew classical literature. Joel's diction seems reminiscent of Amos, who himself seems to have made use of Joel (cf. Joel 3:16 with Amos 1:2; Joel 3:18 with Amos 9:13). Perhaps most significant is the lack of the mention of a king in the book. Joash was a minor and for a long time under the guardianship of Jehoida the high priest. Then too, Israel's enemies were the Phoenicians and Philistines (Joel 3:4), the Egyptians and Edomites (3:19), and the Assyrians and the Babylonians who harassed Israel from the time of Amos to the Exile. Cornill, Oesterley and Robinson, Merx, and S. R. Driver agree for a postexilic date but their evidence is inconclusive. Joel 3:2 is supposed to allude to the Exile but this is clearly a predictive passage of the nation's present-day scattering and by no means needs to refer to the Babylonian captivity. The mention of the Javanim or "Ionians" does not necessitate a date after the Exile. These people are alluded to in the Assyrian records of the eighth century B.C. Arguments based on the silence with regard to a king or

idolatrous places of worship in the Northern Kingdom are pointless. Such mention is also lacking in Nahum, Jonah, Zephaniah, and Obadiah.

BIBLIOGRAPHY: A. S. Kapelrud, *Joel Studies* (1948); E. B. Pusey, *The Minor Prophets* (1961), 1:143-221; R. K. Harrison, *Introduction to the Old Testament* (1969), pp. 874-82; G. W. Ahlström, *Joel and the Temple Cult of Jerusalem* (1971); L. C. Allen, *The Books of Joel, Obadiah, Jonah, and Micah,* New International Commentary on the Old Testament (1976); H. C. von Orelli, *The Twelve Minor Prophets* (1977), pp. 73-102; F. A. Tatford, *The Minor Prophets* (1982), 1:2:9-87; J. M. Boice, *The Minor Prophets* (1983), 1:99-132.

JOE′LAH (jō-e′la, "furthermore"). One of the two sons of Jeroham of Gedor who joined David at Ziklag (1 Chron. 12:7), before 1000 B.C.

JOE′ZER (jō-ē′zēr; "Jehovah his help"). One of the Korahites who united themselves to David at Ziklag (1 Chron. 12:6), before 1000 B.C.

JOG′BEHAH (jog′be-ha; "hillock"). One of the "fortified cities" rebuilt by the Gadites (Num. 32:35). It is mentioned (Judg. 8:11) as in the route of Gideon while pursuing the Midianites. Its name still exists in Jubeihah, six miles NW of Rabbath Amman.

JOG′LI (jog′li; "exiled"). The father of Bukki, the man appointed from the tribe of Dan to the commission for dividing the land of Canaan (Num. 34:22), about 1380 B.C.

JO′HA (jō′ha; probably "Jehovah revives").
1. One of the sons of Beriah the Benjamite, and a leader of his tribe residing at Jerusalem (1 Chron. 8:16), perhaps about 588 B.C.
2. A Tizite who, with his brother Jediael, was one of David's mighty men (1 Chron. 11:45), 1000 B.C.

JOHA′NAN (jō-ha′nan; contracted form of Jehohanan, "God is gracious"). In all but a few passages *Johanan* appears in the same verses in the KJV, NIV, and NASB. The exceptions are 1 Chron. 26:3; 2 Chron. 17:15; 23:1, where NASB *Johanan* replaces KJV and NIV *Jehohanan* (which see); and Ezra 10:6; Neh. 6:18, where NASB and NIV *Jehohanam* (which see) replaces KJV *Johanan.* The material below is based on NASB usage.

1. The son of Kareah, one of the Jewish leaders who rallied around Gedaliah on his appointment as governor (2 Kings 25:23; Jer. 40:8). He also warned the governor of Ishmael's intention to assassinate him and offered to kill Ishmael, but Gedaliah refused to listen to his advice (40:13-16). After the murder of Gedaliah, Johanan led in the pursuit of the assassin and rescued the people he had taken captive (41:11-16). He then consulted with Jeremiah as to what course the remnant of the people should pursue, but when he was told by the prophet to remain in the land he and his associates refused and moved (taking Jeremiah with them) to Tahpanhes, in Egypt (43:1-7).

From this time we lose sight of him and his fellow captains, and they doubtless shared the threatened punishment (vv. 11-12), 586 B.C.

2. The eldest son of Josiah, king of Judah (1 Chron. 3:15). He probably died early, as Scripture makes no further mention of him, after 639 B.C.

3. The fifth son of Elioenai, one of the descendants of Zerubbabel (1 Chron. 3:24), probably after 400 B.C. He is identified by some with Nahum, mentioned (Luke 3:25) among the ancestry of Christ.

4. Son of Azariah, and father of Azariah, high priests (1 Chron. 6:9-10), and by some thought to have been the same as Jehoiada (2 Chron. 24:15).

5. One of the mighty men who joined David at Ziklag (1 Chron. 12:4), before 1000 B.C. He was probably a Benjamite.

6. The eighth named of the Gadite warriors who rallied to the support of David in the stronghold in the wilderness (1 Chron. 12:12), before 1000 B.C.

7. A Korahite and the head of the sixth division of the Levitical Temple gatekeepers (1 Chron. 26:3; "Jehohanan," KJV, NIV), about 960 B.C.

8. The second named of the commanders of Jehoshaphat, king of Judah. This person was commander of 280,000 men (2 Chron. 17:15; "Jehohanan," KJV and NIV) and was, probably, the same whose son Ishmael supported Jehoiada in the restoration of prince Jehoah (23:1), about 875 B.C.

9. The father of Azariah, the man who insisted upon sending home the captives taken from Judah (2 Chron. 28:12; NIV, "Jehohanan"), about 735 B.C.

10. The son of Hakkatan, of the "sons" of Azgad, who returned with 110 men from Babylon with Ezra (Ezra 8:12), about 457 B.C.

11. A priest mentioned in the KJV, NIV, and NASB of Neh. 12:12 as *Johanan,* but identified with the *Jehohanan* (which see) of Ezra 10:6 ("Johanan," KJV).

12. In the KJV of Neh. 6:18, the son of Tobiah the Ammonite. *See* Jehohanan.

JOHN (jon; Gk. *'Iōannēs;* from Heb. *Yôḥānān,* "Jehovah is gracious"). The name of the apostle (*see* article following); of the baptizer and forerunner (*see* article following) of Jesus Christ; and of several other biblical personages.

1. The father of the apostle Peter (John 1:42; 21:15-17).

2. One of the family of the high priest, who, with Annas and Caiaphas, sat in the council before whom the apostles Peter and John were summoned for their cure of the lame man and for preaching in the Temple (Acts 4:6). "Lightfoot identifies him with Rabbi Johanan ben Zaccai, who lived forty years before the destruction of the Temple, and was president of the great syna-

gogue after its removal to Jabne, or Jamnia. Grotius merely says he was known to rabbinical writers as 'John the priest' " (Smith, *Dict.*).

3. The Heb. name of the evangelist Mark, who throughout the narrative of the Acts is thus designated (Acts 12:12, 25; 13:5; 15:37).

JOHN THE APOSTLE (jon; Gk. *'Iōannēs;* from Heb. *Yôḥānān,* "Jehovah is gracious"). The son of Zebedee, a fisherman on the Sea of Galilee, (Mark 1:19-20; Luke 5:10), and Salome (Matt. 27:56; cf. Mark 15:40). We have no information respecting the religious character or personal participation of Zebedee in the events of the gospel history, but John's mother was one of the women who followed Jesus even to His crucifixion.

Early Life. John was probably the younger brother of James (Matt. 4:21). The mention of the "hired servants" (Mark 1:20); of the "private means" of those women who supported Jesus, which probably included Simone, John's mother (Luke 8:3); of "his own household" (John 19:27), and of his acquaintance with Caiaphas the high priest (18:15) implies a position of at least considerable influence and means. His mother, who manifested an earnest desire for the welfare of her sons (Matt. 20:20), probably instructed him in religious things. His trade of fisherman was adapted to holy meditation, since it frequently required him to pass whole nights in stillness upon the water.

Introduction to Jesus. The incident recorded in John 1:35-39 would seem to indicate that John had first become a disciple of John the Baptist. His mention of Andrew only by name is consistent with his usual manner of naming himself as "the other disciple," the disciple "whom Jesus loved." John was probably among the disciples who followed their new Teacher to Galilee (1:43), were with Him at the marriage feast of Cana (2:2), journeyed with Him to Capernaum and thence to Jerusalem (2:12, 23), and came back through Samaria (4:5). He then returned to his former occupation.

As Apostle. At last the time came when the disciples were to enter into closer relation to Jesus and become His apostles. John, with his brother James, Simon, and Andrew, were called at the same time to be "fishers of men" (Mark 1:17-20; Luke 5:10). John, with Peter and James, was distinguished above the other apostles, entering more fully into the Master's feelings and plans, and receiving in return His confidence and love. Mention is made of John at the restoration of Peter's mother-in-law (Mark 1:29-31); at the ordination of the twelve apostles (3:17), where he and his brother received the surname Boanerges ("sons of thunder") from Jesus; at the raising of Jairus's daughter (5:35-37; Luke 8:51); at the transfiguration (Matt. 17:1; Mark 9:2; Luke 9:28); rebuking one who cast out devils in the Lord's name because he was not one of their company (9:49); seeking to call down fire from heaven upon a village of the Samaritans (9:54); joining with his mother and James in asking for the highest places in the kingdom of the Master (Matt. 20:20-28; Mark 10:35-45); with Jesus upon the Mount of Olives when He foretold the destruction of Jerusalem (13:3); sent by the Master to prepare, with Peter, the Passover (Luke 22:8); asking Jesus, at the Last Supper, who would betray Him (John 13:23-26); with Peter and James in Gethsemane (Mark 14:32-33). When the betrayal occurred, Peter and John followed from a distance and, through the personal acquaintance between the latter and Caiaphas, gained admittance into the palace (John 18:15-16). John was the only disciple present at the crucifixion and was appointed by Jesus to care for Mary (19:26-27).

Friendship for Peter. Notwithstanding the denial of Peter, he and John continued to be friends and are afterward often mentioned together. To them Mary Magdalene first ran with the news of the empty tomb (20:2). They were the first to reach the tomb and look inside (20:4-8). For at least eight days they remained in Jerusalem (20:26), after which they returned to the Sea of Galilee, pursuing their old trade (21:1). John was the first to recognize the risen Lord; Peter was the first to plunge into the water and swim toward the shore where Jesus stood (21:7). Peter's affection and anxiety for John are shown in his question, "Lord, and what about this man?" (21:21).

History of Acts. The same union continues in Scripture between Peter and John. Together they witnessed the ascension and shared in the election of Matthias and the baptism at Pentecost. Together they entered the Temple as worshipers (Acts 3:1), were imprisoned, and protested against the threats of the Sanhedrin (4:3-21). They were also sent together to preach to the Samaritans (8:14). John and the rest of the apostles remained at their post despite the persecution of Saul (cf. 8:1). He did not meet Paul when the latter came back to Jerusalem as a convert (Gal. 1:19); but this, of course, does not make the inference necessary that he had left Jerusalem. During the persecution under Herod Agrippa he lost his brother, James, by martyrdom (Acts 12:2), while his friend Peter sought safety in flight (12:18-19). Fifteen years after Paul's first visit he was still at Jerusalem (Conybeare and Howson, *Life and Epistles of Paul*). He was one of the "pillars" of the church and took part in settling the controversy between the Jewish and Gentile Christians (15:6-13; Gal. 2:9). We have only the slightest trace of the work of the apostle during this period.

After His Departure from Jerusalem. John probably remained in Judea till the death of Mary released him from his promise. When this took place we can only speculate. There are no signs of his being at Jerusalem at the time of Paul's last visit (Acts 21). "Assuming the authorship of the epistles and Revelation to be his, the facts which the New Testament writings assert or imply are: *1.* That, having come to Ephesus, some persecution drove him to Patmos (Rev. 1:9). *2.* That seven churches in Asia Minor were the special objects of his affectionate solicitude (1:11); that in his work he had to encounter men who denied the truth on which his faith rested (1 John 4:1; 2 John 7), and others who disputed his authority (3 John 9-10)." If we add to this that he must have outlived all, or nearly all, of those who had been the friends and companions of even his maturer years; that this lingering age gave strength to an old impression that his Lord had promised him immortality (John 21:23); that, as if remembering the actual words that had been thus perverted, the longing of his soul gathered itself up in the cry, "Come, Lord Jesus" (Rev. 22:20), we have stated all that has any claim to the character of historical truth. Tradition tells us that he was shipwrecked off Ephesus and arrived there in time to check the progress of the heresies that sprang up after Paul's departure; that in the persecution under Domitian he was taken to Rome and that the boiling oil into which he was thrown had no power to hurt him; that, returning to Ephesus, he attested to the truth of the first three gospels, writing the fourth to supply what was wanting; that he introduced the Jewish mode of celebrating the Easter feast; and that, when all capacity to work and teach was gone—when there was no strength even to stand—he directed himself to be carried to the assemblage of believers, and simply said, with a feeble voice, "Little children, love one another."

Writings. The following books of the NT are generally accepted as having been written by the apostle John: the gospel, the three epistles bearing his name, and the Revelation.

BIBLIOGRAPHY: J. M. MacDonald, *The Life and Writings of St. John* (1877); J. H. Bernard, *The Gospel According to St. John*, International Critical Commentary (1929), 1:34-78; W. H. G. Thomas, *The Apostle John: Studies in His Life and Writings* (1953); W. Barclay, *The Master's Men* (1959), pp. 28-39; P. J. Gloag, *The Life of St. John* (1950); C. J. Barber, *Searching for Identity* (1975), pp. 13-22; J. D. Jones, *The Apostles of Christ* (1982), pp. 69-86.

JOHN, FIRST EPISTLE OF. The first epistle of John is in the nature of a family letter from the heavenly Father to His "little children" who are in the world. The great theme of the epistle is fellowship in the family of the Father. The intimacy of the epistle has always had great attraction for the people of God.

Occasion and Date. The epistle was apparently written to compete with various forms of error, particularly Cerinthian Gnosticism. False teachers of this cult had denied the essential truth of the incarnation, that Christ had come in the flesh, maintaining that matter was evil. The writer also combated false mysticism that denied the reality of the sin nature in the Christian. He also railed against those who violated Christian fellowship and rejected Christian morality and love. The first epistle of John is in a sense a moral and practical application of the gospel. The time between the two could not have been long. It was probably written a little later than the gospel, around A.D. 90 or 95.

Purpose. The apostle plainly refutes the false ideas of the errorists. He does this positively, giving fresh interpretation and application of the gospel to the urgent demands of his time. He shows the reality of the fellowship with the Father and that believers possess eternal life now in this world. He stresses the close connection of the possession of eternal life with the manifestation of love, right conduct, and sound morality. The apostle apparently does not develop this thought in progressive fashion but in what has been called a "spiral" manner, treating a number of related topics and interweaving them. For this reason outlining the epistle is difficult and to some extent arbitrary. The book is commonly divided into two principal parts.

Outline:
- I. Family fellowship (1:1–3:24)
    - A. The incarnation the basis of this fellowship (1:1-3)
    - B. Family fellowship with the Father and the Son (1:3-4)
    - C. Conditions of family fellowship (1:5–3:24)
        1. Walking in the light (1:5-7)
        2. Realization of the indwelling sin nature (1:8)
        3. Forgiveness by confession (1:9-10)
        4. Christ's advocacy maintains fellowship (2:1-2)
        5. The tests of fellowship, obedience, and love (2:3–3:24)
- II. Family fellowship in the world (4:1–5:21)
    - A. Warning against false teachers (4:1-6)
    - B. Description of God's true child (4:7-10)
    - C. Manifestations of life of love (4:11-21)
    - D. Faith as a conquering principle in the world conflict (5:1-21) M.F.U.

BIBLIOGRAPHY: J. H. A. Ebrard, *Biblical Commentary on the Epistles of St. John* (1860); P. J. Gloag, *Introduction to the Johannine Writings* (1891); C. H. Dodd, *The Johannine Writings* (1946); R. S. Candlish, *The First Epistle of John* (1955); L. Strauss, *The Epistles of John* (1962); J. R. W. Stott, *The Epistles of John*, Tyndale New Testament Commentaries (1964); B. F. Westcott, *The Epistles of St. John* (1966); R. Law, *The Tests of Life* (1968); F. F. Bruce, *The Epistles of John* (1970); G. G. Findlay, *Fellowship in the Life Eternal* (1977); I. H. Marshall, *The Epistles of John*, New International Commentary on the New Testmament (1978); J. M. Boice, *The Epistles of John* (1979); R. C. Stedman, *Expository Studies in I John* (1980); J. J. Lias, *First Epistle of John* (1982); J. Morgan and S. Cox, *The Epistles of John*, 2 vols. in 1 (1982); D. W. Burdick, *The Letters of John the Apostle* (1985).

JOHN, SECOND AND THIRD EPISTLES OF.

These two letters are extremely short. Each was sent by "the elder" (2 John 1; 3 John 1). They were written in the province of Asia probably between A.D. 95 and 100. Second John is addressed to a Christian mother and her family, called "the chosen lady and her children." The second epistle, as in the first, gives prominence to the commandment of love. It warns against false teachers (v. 7). These heretics were to be treated with sternness and shown no hospitality. The key phrase of the second epistle is "the truth," by which John means the body of revealed truth, the Scriptures. The epistle is divided into three parts.

Outline:
- I. "The truth" and love are joined together in true Christian life (1-6)
- II. The danger of unscriptural ways (7-11)
- III. A superscription (12-13)

The third epistle of John, like the second, was written by the apostle probably around A.D. 95. The aged apostle arraigned the church for permitting one Diotrephes to exercise dominating authority. In the primitive church such a thing was incredible. This domineering individual had rejected the apostolic authority. Historically this small epistle outlines the commencement of the clericalism and priestly arrogation of authority that in later centuries was to develop in such evil proportions. The believer's resource in such a day of declension is also given. John does not write as an apostle but as an elder, and the letter is addressed not to a church but to a faithful man in the church, to comfort and sustain those who were adhering to the simplicity of earlier times. The third letter of John stresses personal responsibility in a day of deterioration.

Outline:
- I. Personal greetings to "the beloved" Gaius (1-4)
- II. Instructions concerning ministers (5-8)
- III. Warning against the power-loving Diotrephes (9-11)
- IV. The praiseworthy Demetrius (12-14) M.F.U.

BIBLIOGRAPHY: *See under* John, First Epistle.

JOHN, THE GOSPEL OF.

The fourth gospel, regarded by many as the deepest and most wonderful book in the NT. Although in one sense it is simple, direct, penetrating, and to be understood by common people, yet in another respect it is a sublimely profound revelation fathomed only by spiritual scholars. Some have called it "the greatest book in the world."

Purpose. The aim of the gospel of John is spiritual. Although many different opinions have been advanced, the purpose is stated clearly and unequivocally in 20:30-31: "Many other signs therefore Jesus also performed in the presence of the disciples, which are not written in this book; but these have been written that you may believe that Jesus is the Christ, the Son of God; and that believing you may have life in His name." It is evident from this statement that the author's intent was to conduct men to saving faith in Christ as the Son of God and so enable them to obtain eternal life. The deity of Christ is thus proved by miraculous signs consisting of a selective group of miracles, which he enumerates as demonstrating Christ's messiahship. A careful reading of the gospel will also disclose that the author seeks to accomplish this in various other ways by presenting the true Person and work of the Savior and by a variety of telling figures describing Christ as the Bread of Life, the Light of the World, the Good Shepherd, the Truth, the Way, the Life, and the Vine. To accomplish his spiritual aim, John records eight miracles. All but two —the feeding of the five thousand (6:4-14) and the walking on the water (6:15-21)—are peculiar to John. This wondrous book has a literary unity; the miracles, the discourses, the imagery, and the figures are all selected in order to attain its purpose. In the synoptic gospels the miraculous works of Jesus are frequently performed out of mercy, but in the gospel of John they are presented as attestations of His messiahship.

Outline:

I. Prologue: The deity and glory of the Son of God (1:1-5)

II. The incarnation and reception of the Son of God (1:6-18)

III. The Son of God revealed to Israel (1:19–12:50)

IV. The Son of God instructing His disciples (13-17)

V. The Son of God glorified in His passion (18-19)

VI. The Son of God revealed in resurrection power and glory (20-21)

Author. Internal evidence that the author is "the disciple whom Jesus loved," who also leaned on His breast at supper (21:20, cf. 21:7), and that this is the apostle John, is supported by numerous lines of evidence. (1) *He was a contemporary of the events described.* The writer was known to the high priest and entered the high priest's residence in company with Jesus (18:15). He alone narrates the fact that it was the high priest's servant whose ear Peter cut off (18:10). He deals with questions about the period before the destruction of Jerusalem and not with controversies of the second century when Gnostic and Ebionite defections were active (cf. 6:15; 11:47-50). Numerous other details point to the contemporary scene. (2) *He was a Jew of Palestine.* He shows acquaintance with Heb., as is shown by the book's opening words (cf. Gen. 1:1). Three times

he quotes from the Heb. (12:40; 13:18; 19:37). He knows intimately the Hebrew festivals, that of Passover (21:13, 23; 6:4; 13:1; 18:28), the Feast of Booths (7:2; Tabernacles, KJV), and the Feast of Dedication (10:22). Jewish customs and habits of thought are familiar to him, such as questions of purification (3:25; 11:55), marriage customs, especially the way of arranging waterpots (2:1-10); Jewish burial customs (11:38, 44; 19:31, 40). He shows firsthand knowledge of Palestine, that there is a descent from Cana to the Sea of Galilee (2:12) and that Jacob's well is deep (4:11). He is familiar with such places as Ephraim (11:54), Aenon (3:23), Mt. Gerizim (4:20), Jerusalem and the Kidron (18:1), Bethesda and Siloam (5:2; 9:7), and Golgotha (19:17; etc.). (3) *He was John, the beloved apostle.* This is a general deduction sustained from the above facts. He indicates the hours of events recounted (1:39; 4:6, 52; 19:14). He reports quotations of Philip (6:7; 14:8), Thomas (11:16; 14:5), Judas (14:22), and Andrew (6:8-9). He leaned on Jesus' breast at the Last Supper (13:23-25) and was numbered among the three, Peter, James, and John. Moreover, Peter is distinguished from the author by name, as in 1:41-42; 13:6, 8, and James had suffered martyrdom long before the writing of the gospel (Acts 12:2). He characteristically introduces himself (John 13:23; 19:26; 20:2; 21:7, 20). These general facts make it difficult to escape the conclusion that John the apostle wrote the fourth gospel.

Authenticity. External evidence for the early date and apostolic authorship of the gospel of John is as substantial as that for any NT book. Early evidence is found in the epistle of Barnabas. Tatian quotes the fourth gospel in his *Diatessaron*, as well as Theophilus of Antioch. The Muratorian Canon says, "John, one of the disciples, wrote the fourth book of the gospels." From the time of Irenaeus the evidence becomes indisputable. He frequently quotes the gospel and in such a way as to show it had been used for a long time in the churches. This testimony is perhaps most important considering he was a pupil of Polycarp, and Polycarp was a friend of the apostle John. Clement of Alexandria and Tertullian of Carthage often quote from the gospel of John.

Date. The date of the fourth gospel is to be assigned between A.D. 85 and 95. A papyrus bit containing two verses of the gospel of John has been discovered; it belongs to the Papyrus Rylands and is dated c. A.D. 140. This bit of evidence suggests that the fourth gospel was in existence as early as the first half of the second century and at that time was already in wide use.   M.F.U.

BIBLIOGRAPHY: F. L. Godet, *Commentary on the Gospel of John*, 2 vols. (n.d.); S. Lathes, *The Witness of St. John to Christ* (1870); C. E. Luthardt, *St. John the Author of the Fourth Gospel* (1875); id., *St. John's Gospel Described and Explained* ... , 3 vols. (1876-78); T. Whitelaw, *The Gospel of St. John* (1888); G. B. Stevens, *The Johannine Theology* (1894); W. F. Howard, *The*

Fourth Gospel in Recent Criticism and Interpretation (1935); id., *Christianity According to St. John* (1943); M. C. Tenney, *John: The Gospel of Belief* (1948); B. F. Westcott, *The Gospel According to St. John* (1950); J. C. Ryle, *Expository Thoughts on the Gospels* (1951), vols. 3-4; W. Hendricksen, *A Commentary on the Gospel of John* (1953); R. H. Lightfoot, *St. John's Gospel, a Commentary* (1956); R. Brown, *The Gospel According to John,* Anchor Bible, 2 vols. (1966); J. Marsh, *Saint John* (1968); L. L. Morris, *Studies in the Fourth Gospel* (1969); id., *The Gospel According to John* (1971); H. A. Kent, Jr., *Light in the Darkness* (1974); J. M. Boice, *The Gospel of John,* 5 vols. (1975-79); C. K. Barrett, *The Gospel According to St. John* (1978); W. R. Cook, *The Theology of John* (1979); C. K. Barrett, *Essays on John* (1982); A. Jukes, *Four Views of Christ* (1982), pp. 90-110; R. Govett, *Govett on John* (1984); J. H. Bernard, *The Central Teaching of Christ, John 14-17* (1985).

JOHN THE BAPTIST, "John the baptizer." The forerunner of Jesus Christ. He and his mission were foretold by Isaiah (Isa. 40:3; cf. Matt. 3:3) and by Malachi (Mal. 3:1). John was of the priestly tribe by both of his parents, his father, Zacharias, being a priest of the division of Abijah, and his mother, Elizabeth, being "from the daughters of Aaron" (Luke 1:5). His birth—through the miraculous interposition of almighty power, by reason of his parents' extreme age—was foretold by an angel sent from God, who at the same time assigned to him the name of John. He was born in the hill country (where his mother had gone, probably for the sake of privacy) six months before the birth of our Lord (perhaps 5 B.C.).

Early Life. On the eighth day he was brought to be circumcised, and friends of his parents proposed to call him Zacharias, after his father. But his mother required that he should be called John, a decision that his father, still speechless, confirmed by writing on a tablet. He was set apart as a Nazirite, according to the angelic injunction (Luke 1:15; cf. Num. 6:1-21). All that we know of the period between this time and the beginning of his ministry is contained in a single verse: "The child continued to grow, and to become strong in spirit, and he lived in the deserts until the day of his public appearance to Israel" (Luke 1:80).

Beginning of Ministry. At length, in the fifteenth year of the reign of Tiberius Caesar (A.D. 25), John began to preach, and he attracted a great multitude from "Jerusalem . . . and all Judea, and all the district around the Jordan" (Matt. 3:5). To them he proclaimed the near approach of "the kingdom of heaven" and administered the rite of baptism "for repentance." His birth, his hard, ascetic life, and the general expectation that some great one was about to appear served to attract this great multitude, for "John performed no sign" (John 10:41).

Meeting with Jesus. Before long Jesus presented Himself to John in order to receive baptism at his hand, which John declined to administer until the Lord declared that "in this way it is fitting for us to fulfill all righteousness" (Matt. 3:15).

Subsequent Ministry. With the baptism of Jesus, John's special office ceased. The King had come, and there was little further need of the herald. We learn that John and his disciples continued to baptize some time after our Lord entered upon His ministry (John 3:23; 4:1). John also instructed his disciples in certain moral and religious duties, such as fasting (Matt. 9:14; Luke 5:33) and prayer (11:1). We also learn that he still continued to be a witness to Jesus, so confidently pointing Him out as the Lamb of God that two of his own disciples were led to accept Jesus as the true Messiah and became His followers (John 1:29-39).

Imprisonment and Death. Shortly after this, John's public ministry was violently brought to a close. Herod Antipas had taken Herodias, his brother Philip's wife. When John reproved him for this and other sins (Luke 3:19), Herod cast him into prison in the castle of Machaerus on the eastern shore of the Dead Sea. While confined there John sent two of his disciples to Jesus with the inquiry, "Are You the Expected One?" This was doubtless in order to assist his disciples in transferring their allegiance to Jesus, as Jesus Himself bore testimony to the steadfastness of John (7:19-28). Herodias, embittered against John, determined to have him killed but was prevented by Herod's conviction that John was a just man (Mark 6:19-20) and by his fear of the people (Matt. 14:5). But at last her opportunity arrived, and, taking advantage of a promise given by Herod to her daughter, Herodias ordered the head of John the Baptist. The king reluctantly complied and sent an executioner, who beheaded him in the prison. John's disciples, when they heard of his death, buried his body and went and told the Lord (Matt. 14:3-12; Mark 6:17-29).

John's Acquaintance with Jesus. Much discussion has arisen concerning the apparent contradiction between Matt. 3:13-14 and John 1:31-33. In the former John evidently knew Jesus, while in the latter he says, "I did not recognize Him." The truth seems to be that John knew Jesus but was not certain of His messiahship. It was necessary for him, before asserting positively that Jesus was the Christ, to have undoubted testimony of the fact. This was given him in the descent of the Holy Spirit in the form of a dove, as John himself declared (John 1:33).

Character. The nature of John the Baptist was full of impetuosity and fire—a second Elijah. His life, however, was characterized by the graces of self-denial, humility, and holy courage. His abstinence was so great that some thought him possessed and said, "He has a demon!" In his humility he declined the honors that an admiring multitude almost forced upon him and declared himself to be *no one*—merely a voice—calling upon the people to prepare for the reception of the One whose sandal he was not worthy to remove. And when that One came, he recommended his own disciples to attach themselves to Him, furnishing an example of gracefully accepting the fact that "He must increase, but I must decrease." For his courage in speaking the truth he went a willing victim to prison and to death. BIBLIOGRAPHY: J. Feather, *The Last of the Prophets* (1894); W. J. Sparrow-Simpson, *The Prophet of the Highest* (1895); A. T. Robertson, *John the Loyal* (1911); F. B. Meyer. *John the Baptist* (1954); M. L. Loane, *John the Baptist as Witness and Martyr* (1968).

JOI'ADA (joy'a-da; "Jehovah knows").

1. A contraction of *Jehoiada* (which see), the son and successor of Eliashib in the high priesthood who was succeeded by his son Jonathan (Neh. 12:10-11, 22). Another of his sons married a daughter of Sanballat, on which account he was banished by Nehemiah (Neh. 13:28), before 445 B.C.

2. One of the repairers of the Jeshanah (or Old) Gate of Jerusalem under Nehemiah's direction (Neh. 3:6). *See* Jehoiada, no. 3.

JOI'AKIM (joy'a-kim; "Jehovah establishes"). A contraction of *Jehoiakim* (which see), a high priest, son of Jeshua and father of Eliashib (Neh. 12:10, 12, 26), before 445 B.C.

JOI'ARIB (joy'a-rib; "Jehovah will contend").

1. A teacher, and one of those with whom Ezra consulted upon the subject of obtaining a company of Levites to return with him to Jerusalem (Ezra 8:16). This conference took place at the river Ahava (v. 15) and resulted in sending a delegation to "Iddo the leading man at the place Casiphia," who responded with a large number of the desired ministers (vv. 17-20), about 457 B.C.

2. A descendant of Judah, son of Zechariah, and father of Adaiah, probably through Shelah (Neh. 11:5), before 445 B.C.

3. The founder of one of the divisions of priests and the father of Jedaiah (Neh. 11:10). It is thought that there is some error in the list by which he is given as the father of Jedaiah, for in 1 Chron. 9:10 (where his name is given in full, Jehoiarib), he ranks with Jedaiah and Jachin as heads of divisions of priests (*see* Keil, ad loc.).

4. A priest who returned with Zerubbabel from Babylon (Neh. 12:6). His son, Mattenai, was a contemporary of the high priest Joiakim (v. 19), 536 B.C.

JOININGS (1 Chron. 22:3, KJV). Clamps.

JOK'DEAM (jok'de-am). A city of Judah in the hill country (Josh. 15:56), apparently S of Hebron. Perhaps it is to be identified with Khirbet Raqa' near Ziph.

JO'KIM (jōkim; contraction of "Joiakim"). A descendant of Shelah, the son of Judah (1 Chron. 4:22). *See* Joiakim.

JOK'MEAM (jok'me-am). One of the places given, with its suburbs, to the Levites (1 Kings 4:12;

1 Chron. 6:68). It is in the Jordan Valley. Its name is given as Kibzaim in Josh. 21:22.

JOK'NEAM (jok'ne-am). A city in Palestine on the border of Zebulun's allotted portion (Josh. 12:22; 19:11; 21:34). Called also Jokmeam in the KJV and NASB (1 Kings 4:12; 1 Chron. 6:68). It is modern Tell Qeimun or Tel Yoqneam, twelve miles SW of Nazareth.

JOK'SHAN (jok'shan). The second son of Abraham and Keturah (Gen. 25:2-3; 1 Chron. 1:32). His sons Sheba and Dedan are the ancestors of the Sabaeans and Dedanites that populated a part of Arabia Felix.

JOK'TAN (jok'tan). Second named of the two sons of Eber, a descendant of Shem. His brother was Peleg (Gen. 10:25-26, 29; 1 Chron. 1:19-20, 23).

JOK'THEEL (jok'thīl).

1. A city in the low country of Judah, mentioned between Mizpeh and Lachish (Josh. 15:38).

2. The name given by King Amaziah to Sela —the stronghold of the Edomites—after he captured it from them (2 Kings 14:7; cf. 2 Chron. 25:11-13). Possibly Petra.

JO'NA (jō'na). The KJV term in John 1:42 for John the father of the apostle Peter. *See* John, no. 1.

JON'ADAB (jon'a-dab; "Jehovah gives"). A shortened form of the name *Jehonadab* (which see).

1. The son of Shimeah and nephew of David (2 Sam. 13:3, 32, 35).

2. The Rechabite whose followers refused to drink the wine that Jeremiah, at the Lord's command, offered to them (Jer. 35:6, 8, 10, 14, 16, 18-19).

JO'NAH (jō'na; "dove"). The fifth in order of the minor prophets, the son of Amittai. He was born in Gath-hepher, in the tribe of Zebulun (2 Kings 14:25).

Personal History. Jonah flourished probably in or before the reign of Jeroboam II (c. 782-753 B.C., Thiele's dates) and predicted the successful conquests, enlarged territory, and brief prosperity of the Israelite kingdom under that monarch's sway (2 Kings 14:25). What else we know of Jonah's history is to be gathered from the book that bears his name. He was commissioned by Jehovah to go and prophesy to the Ninevites, but because as a partisan Israelite he did not want to see Israel's great enemy spared, he was reluctant to obey and attempted to flee to Tarshish. He went to Joppa and there embarked upon a ship. A violent storm arose, and the captain of the vessel called upon Jonah to pray to his God to save them. As the storm did not abate, the sailors proceeded to cast lots, believing that some per-

son on board the ship had caused the anger of
God, as manifested in the tempest. Jonah was
singled out as the culprit, and at his suggestion
they unwillingly cast him into the sea. By the
appointment of God he was swallowed by a great
fish, which upon the third day cast him out upon
dry land. Jonah was again commanded to go to
Nineveh and immediately obeyed. The people repented, a fast was appointed, and the city was not
destroyed. Provoked at the sparing of Nineveh,
Jonah in his displeasure prayed to Jehovah to
take his life because his proclamation had not
been fulfilled. God taught him, by means of the
rapidly growing and speedily decaying plant, that
it was proper for Him to exercise mercy toward
the repentant city (Jonah 1:1–4:11).

Jonah and the Fish. Much objection has been
urged against the truth of the story of Jonah and
the fish. It is simply said, "The Lord appointed a
great fish to swallow Jonah." The species of marine animal is not defined, and the Greek *ketos*
is often used to specify not the genus whale but
any large fish or sea monster. All objection to its
being a whale that lodged Jonah in its stomach,
from the narrowness of throat or rareness of
haunt in the Mediterranean, are thus removed.
Since the days of Bochart it has been a common
opinion that the fish was of the shark species,
Lamia canis carcharias, or "sea dog." Entire human bodies have been found in some fish of this
kind. Still, granting all these facts, the narrative
is miraculous, and nothing is impossible with
God.

The Sign of the Prophet. Various interpretations are given of "the sign of Jonah the prophet"
(Matt. 12:39). Keil (*Com.,* ad loc.) says: "The
mission of Jonah was a fact of symbolical and
typical importance, which was intended not only
to enlighten Israel as to the position of the Gentile world in relation to the kingdom of God, but
also to typify the future adoption of such of the
heathen as should observe the word of God, into

*Mosque at the traditional site of the grave of Jonah at
Gath-hepher.*

the fellowship of the salvation prepared in Israel
for all nations." Whedon (*Com.,* ad loc.) explains:
"Our Lord, even in refusing a *sign,* gives a sign.
His prophecy of his burial, after the manner of
the swallowing of Jonah, was in itself a miracle
of foreknowledge, and so a proof of his Messiahship."

BIBLIOGRAPHY: F. E. Gaebelein, *The Servant and the Dove*
(1946), pp. 52-143; H. Martin, *The Prophet Jonah: His
Character and Mission* (1958); P. Fairbairn, *Jonah, His
Life, Character and Mission* (1964), pp. 3-81.

JONAH, BOOK OF. Jonah is listed among the
minor prophets and is unique in that it is not a
collection of Jonah's prophecies but is a biographical account of his ministry in Nineveh. It
teaches the lesson that God's grace went beyond
the boundaries of Israel to embrace the nations.
It is placed among the minor prophets because
the experience and the career of Jonah are prophetic of the death, burial, and resurrection of
Christ and the consequent blessing upon the
Gentiles.

Literary Character. Critics commonly view the
book as being either legend, myth, or parable,
but it is correctly evaluated as history. There is
not the slightest reason to stumble over the miraculous and to brand it as legend or myth. The
miracles of the book of Jonah are a piece with
those that honeycomb all Scripture, particularly
the Pentateuch. The storm, Jonah's being swallowed by the sea monster, the conversion of the
Ninevites, and the fast-growing plant are no
more incredible than the dividing of the Red Sea,
the cloudy and fiery pillar, manna from heaven,
water out of the flint, or the resurrection of
Christ. The latter is directly connected with Jonah's experience in the great fish (Matt.
12:39-41; Luke 11:29-32). The book is certainly
designed to be viewed as historical. There is nothing in it to suggest otherwise. To assert that our
Lord's words regarding Jonah did not imply His
belief in the historicity of events is highly artificial and arbitrary. Ancient Jewish opinion looked
upon the account as historical (Josephus *Ant.*
9.10.2). The general Jewish and Christian tradition has followed the same view. But although
the book is historical, it is more than history. Its
right to the position in the twelve minor prophets
is due to the fact that it is *predictive* or *typical*
history. In its prophetic aspects the book of Jonah
has important ramifications. In one sense of the
word, Jonah in his ministry prefigures Christ in
His specific character as the Sent One, being
buried, raised from the dead, and carrying salvation to the nations. In another aspect of his ministry, Jonah portrays Israel nationally, outside of
its own land, as since A.D. 70, a serious trouble to
the Gentiles, yet meanwhile witnessing to them.
Finally they are cast out by the Gentiles, but
preserved through their future tribulation at the
end of this age (Dan. 12:1). At the time of the

second advent of Christ they will find salvation and deliverance (Rom. 11:25-26), becoming worldwide witnesses to the Gentiles in the future earthly Davidic millennial kingdom (Zech. 8:7-23).

Author and Date. It is by no means impossible that Jonah himself was the author of this book in the eighth century B.C. This is the predominating tradition. It is true there are Aramaisms in the book. This is made mention of by the critics. But such forms occur in early as well as in late OT books and are to be found in the Ras Shamra epics from Ugarit, dating c. 1400 B.C. Robert Pfeiffer imagines that an historical blunder occurs in the designation of the Assyrian emperor as the "king of Nineveh" (3:6) and the description of Nineveh as "an exceeding great city, a three days' walk" (3:3). Pfeiffer, moreover, asserts that it is "physiologically improbable" for a man to survive three days within a fish. But the expression "Nineveh *was* an exceedingly great city" does not imply a date after 600 B.C., but merely points to the dimensions of the city as Jonah found them. Luke 24:13 constitutes a parallel. This verse states that Emmaus *"was* about seven miles from Jerusalem." In answer to Pfeiffer's rationalistic position, it should be noted that Christ believed in the historicity of the miracle narrated in Jonah (Matt. 12:39-41; Luke 11:29-30). To deny the miraculous in Jonah is to limit God, who is certainly able to preserve a man for three days in a fish. The term "king of Nineveh" can scarcely be dismissed. The Israelites normally spoke of the ruler of Assyria as king, as in similar references to surrounding kings (cf. 1 Kings 20:43; 21:1; 2 Kings 3:9, 12; 2 Chron. 24:23). The universalistic ideas of the book are not a late and strange development but appear early (cf. Gen. 9:1-10). To assert that such teaching was confined to the postexilic era is arbitrary. The period of Jonah can be fitted into historical conditions at Nineveh under Semiramis, the queen regent, and her son Adad-Nirari III (810-782 B.C.). The god Nebo was worshiped and constituted an approach to monotheism reminiscent of Amenophis IV of Egypt in the fourteenth century B.C. Jonah preached in Nineveh either in the closing years of this reign or earlier in the reign of Assurdan III (771-754 B.C.). This period was favorable for Jonah's ministry. Whether the plagues recorded in Assyrian history in 765 and 759 B.C. and the total eclipse of 763 B.C., regarded as portents of divine wrath, prepared the Ninevites for his message is not known.

How the reference to a "great city of three days' walk" is to be understood is not clear. Excavations reveal that the wall of Nineveh was 8 miles in circumference (compare Babylon at 11 miles, Ur at 2½ miles, and the Jerusalem of David at 11 acres), and there was a suburban area outside the walls. It would not have taken more than about one day to walk around the urban area. One suggestion is that the city was so large it would have taken three days to stop at all its significant squares and major buildings and proclaim the judgment of God.

Outline.
I. The prophet's first call and disobedience (1:1–2:10)
  A. The divine commission and his flight (1:1-3)
  B. The storm (1:4-7)
  C. The confession (1:8-12)
  D. The prophet's being thrown in the sea (1:13-17)
  E. His intercession and salvation (2:1-10)
II. The prophet's second call and his obedience (3:1–4:11)
  A. He goes to Nineveh (3:1-4)
  B. The Ninevites repent (3:5-9)
  C. The city is saved (3:10)
  D. Jonah is angered (4:1-4)
  E. Jonah is reproved (4:5-11)

Unity of the Book. Critics commonly reject the psalm in chap. 2, but if this psalm is removed, the symmetry of the book is undeniably destroyed. The book obviously falls into two halves, the first half including chaps. 1-2 and the second half including chaps. 3-4. Moreover, 1:1-3*a* is practically identical with 3:1-3*a*. Also, it is to be noted that 2:2 and 4:2 both mention Jonah's praying. In one case there is a complaint and in the other a song of thanksgiving. The rejection of 2:2-9 accordingly destroys the basic symmetry of the book. Critics assert that in 2:1 it is said that Jonah prayed, but what follows is not a prayer but a song of praise for deliverance. But such a critical censure is pointless, displaying ignorance of the fact that thanksgiving is the very heart of prayer. In addition, critics maintain that the song of thanksgiving for deliverance occurs prior to the deliverance, but not until v. 10 is it said that Jonah was cast upon the dry land. Julius Wellhausen even went so far as to say that the mention of weeds in 2:5 exploded the idea that Jonah was in the fish's belly. His remark that "weeds do not grow in a whale's belly" (*Die Kleinen Propheten* [1898], p. 221) has become proverbial, but Edward J. Young (*Introduction to the O.T.* [1949], p. 257) shows clearly that Wellhausen and other objectors to the genuineness of 2:2-9 miscomprehend the meaning of the psalm completely. Says Young, "Of course weeds do not grow in whales' bellies. But this is not a psalm of thanksgiving *for deliverance from a whale's belly.* It is rather a song of thanksgiving for *deliverance from drowning.* The figures of speech employed in this psalm have reference to drowning, not to a whale's belly. Furthermore, there is not one scintilla of evidence which makes this psalm purport to have reference to deliverance from the belly of a fish. The school of negative criticism has unjustly imputed to this psalm a meaning which it was never intended to bear."

705

BIBLIOGRAPHY: G. C. Aalders, *The Problem of the Book of Jonah* (1948); E. B. Pusey, *The Minor Prophets* (1961), 1:371-427; R. K. Harrison, *Introduction to the Old Testament* (1969), pp. 904-18; F. E. Gaebelein, *Four Minor Prophets* (1970), pp. 57-140; L. C. Allen, *The Books of Joel, Obadiah, Jonah, and Micah,* New International Commentary on the Old Testament (1976); H. C. von Orelli, *The Twelve Minor Prophets* (1977), pp. 167-84; R. T. Kendall, *Jonah: An Exposition* (1978); F. A. Tatford, *The Minor Prophets* (1982), 2:2:11-86; J. M. Boice, *The Minor Prophets* (1983), 1:211-50; F. E. Gaebelein, ed., *The Expositor's Bible Commentary* (1985), 7:361-91.

JO'NAM (jō'nam). The son of Eliakim and father of Joseph, among the maternal ancestors of Christ (Luke 3:30; "Jonan," KJV). He is not mentioned in the OT.

JO'NAN. *See* Jonam.

JONAS. The KJV term in Matt. 12:39-41; 16:4; Luke 11:29-30,32 for the prophet Jonah and the KJV term in John 21:15-17 for John the father of the apostle Peter. *See* John, no. 1; Jonah.

JO'NATH E'LEM REHO'KIM (jō'nath-e'lem-re-hō'kim). A term in the title of Ps. 56.

JON'ATHAN (jon'a-than; a contracted form of *Jehonathan,* "Jehovah has given").

1. The son (or descendant) of Gershom the son of Manasseh (Judg. 18:30). Jonathan, who was a Levite, resided at Bethlehem and, leaving that place to seek his fortune, came to Mt. Ephraim to the home of Micah. This person made Jonathan an offer to receive him into his house as priest, an offer that he accepted (17:7-13). Not long after, five Danite spies, looking for a suitable place for settlement, came to the house of Micah and inquired of Jonathan regarding the success of their journey. He replied, "Go in peace; your way in which you are going has the Lord's approval." Afterward, when a company of 600 Danites were on their way to occupy Laish, they went to Micah's house, appropriating the graven image, the ephod, the household idols, and the molten image. Jonathan accepted their invitation to accompany them and became their priest. This office remained in his family until "the day of the captivity of the land" (18:1-30).

2. The eldest son of Saul, king of Israel. This Jonathan first appears in history some time after his father's accession, being at that time at least thirty. In the war with the Philistines, commonly called from its locality "the war of Michmash," he commanded 1,000 men of the 3,000 that composed Saul's standing army. He was encamped at Gibeah, and he "smote the garrison of the Philistines" in Geba (1 Sam. 13:2-3), c. 1020 B.C. Saul and the whole population rose, but unsuccessfully, and the tyranny of the Philistines became harsher than ever. From this oppression Jonathan resolved to deliver his people, and, unknown to any but his armor-bearer, he attacked the garrison at Michmash (14:1, 4-14). A panic

seized the garrison, spread to the camp, and thence to the surrounding bands. This was increased by an earthquake and by the combined assault of various bodies of Israelites hidden in the mountains. Saul and his band joined in the pursuit of the Philistines, the king having forbidden any to taste food until the evening. Ignorant of this command and its accompanying curse, Jonathan ate some honey while passing through the forest. Saul would doubtless have fulfilled his vow and have sacrificed Jonathan, but the people interfered in his behalf (14:16-45).

Jonathan is next introduced to us as the bosom friend of David. Their friendship began on the day of David's return from the victory over Goliath and was confirmed by a solemn covenant, which was ratified by Jonathan's giving his friend his robe, sword, bow, and belt (18:1-4). Shortly after this he pleaded with his father on behalf of David and secured a reversal of the royal decree against the latter's life (19:1-7). The king's madness soon returned, however, and David fled. The friends met by the stone of Ezel and entered into a second covenant, pledging themselves to strive for each other's safety, and David swearing to show kindness to the family of Jonathan when he should be delivered of his enemies. Jonathan again pleaded with his father to spare David, which so enraged the king that he "hurled his spear at him," with the evident intention of taking his life. The next day Jonathan communicated the failure of his mission to David, and they parted to meet only once more (20:1-42). This last meeting was in the wilderness of Ziph, during Saul's pursuit of David. Jonathan gave expression to his confidence in his friend's elevation to the throne. "The two of them made a covenant before the Lord" and parted to meet no more (23:15-18).

We hear no more of Jonathan until the battle of Gilboa, when, with his father and his two brothers, he was slain by the Philistines (31:2, 8). His remains were carried to Jabesh-gilead and buried there (vv. 11-13) but were afterward moved, with those of his father, to Zela in Benjamin (2 Sam. 21:12-14). Jonathan left one son, Mephibosheth, who was five years old at the time of his death (4:4), about 1000 B.C.

Jonathan was a man of daring who was not afraid to place himself in the greatest danger for the sake of his country. But his most noticeable characteristic was his ardent and unselfish devotion to his friends, which led him to give up his hopes of the throne and even expose himself to death for the sake of those he loved. Notwithstanding that his affection for his father was repelled by the latter, owing to the king's insanity, he cast his lot with his father's decline, and "in their death they were not parted."

3. Son of Abiathar, the high priest, who adhered to David during the rebellion of Absalom (2 Sam. 15:27, 36). He remained at En-rogel to

report to his master the proceedings in the camp of the insurgents but, being discovered, fled to Bahurim and escaped by hiding in a well (17:17-21), about 970 B.C. Later his loyalty to the house of David was shown when he announced to the ambitious Adonijah the forestallment of his measures by Solomon's succession to the throne (1 Kings 1:42-43), c. 966 B.C.

4. The son of Shimei and nephew of David who slew a gigantic relative of Goliath and became one of David's chief warriors (2 Sam. 21:21; 1 Chron. 20:7). He is probably the same who is mentioned as one of David's counselors (27:32, where *dōd* is translated "uncle").

5. The son of Shagee the Hararite, and one of David's famous warriors (2 Sam. 23:32; 1 Chron. 11:34).

6. The second son of Jada, the grandson of Jarahmeel, of the family of Judah. Jether dying without sons, this branch of the line was continued through Jonathan's two sons, Peleth and Zaza (1 Chron. 2:32-33).

7. The son of Uzziah who was in charge of King David's storehouses "in the country, in the cities, in the villages, and in the towers" (1 Chron. 27:25; "Jehonathan," KJV), after 1000 B.C.

8. Father of Ebed, which latter was an Israelite of the "sons" of Adin, who returned with Ezra from Babylon with fifty males (Ezra 8:6), before 457 B.C.

9. Son of Asahel, employed with Jahzeiah in separating the people from their Gentile wives (Ezra 10:15), 457 B.C.

10. Son of Joiada and father of Jaddua, Jewish high priests (Neh. 12:11); elsewhere (12:22) called *Johanan* (but see discussion at *Jehohanan,* no. 1). Josephus relates (*Ant.* 11.11.2) that he murdered his own brother, Jesus, in the Temple, because Jesus was endeavoring to get a high priesthood from him through the influence of Bagoses, the Persian general.

11. A priest, the descendant of Malluchi, in the time of Joiakim (Neh. 12:14), between 536 and 549 B.C.

12. Son of Shemaiah, and father of Zechariah, a priest who blew the trumpet at the dedication of the wall (Neh. 12:35), after 536 B.C. He is probably the same as Jehonathan (v. 18).

13. A scribe in the time of King Zedekiah, in whose house Jeremiah was imprisoned by the officials of Judah (Jer. 37:15, 20; 38:26), 589 B.C.

14. One of the sons of Kareah, who, with others, held a conference with Gedaliah, the Babylonian governor of Jerusalem (Jer. 40:8), 588 B.C.

BIBLIOGRAPHY: A. P. Stanley, *Scripture Portraits* (n.d.), pp. 63-68; S. Cox, *The Expositor* (1896), 1:416-27; C. J. Barber and J. D. Carter, *Always a Winner* (1977), pp. 115-25; W. G. Blaikie, *David, King of Israel* (1981), pp. 67-71; J. Kitto, *Daily Bible Illustrations* (1981), 1:705-7; W. J. Deane and T. Kirk, *Studies in the First Book of Samuel,* 2 vols. in 1 (1983), 1:167-80; 2:165-74.

JOP′PA (jop′pa; Heb. *yāpô,* "beauty"). An old city on the Mediterranean, about thirty miles NW of Jerusalem. It is supposed to have got its name from the mass of sunshine that its houses reflected. It is an ancient city, appearing in the lists of the great conqueror Thutmose III (fifteenth century B.C.) and occurring in the Amarna Letters of the early fourteenth century. It was included in the portion assigned to Dan (Josh. 19:46; "Japho," KJV). Its harbor naturally made it the port of Jerusalem. It was to Joppa that Hiram floated down from Tyre the fir trees of Lebanon (2 Chron. 2:16), and, later, Zerubbabel, acting on the edict of Cyrus, caused to be brought here cedar trees from the same mountains (Ezra 3:7). Here Jonah embarked for Tarshish (Jonah 1:3). In Joppa Peter wrought the miracle on Tabitha (Acts 9:36), resided for quite a time with Simon the tanner (v. 43), saw the vision of the great sheet let down from heaven (10:8-16), and received the summons from Cornelius (vv. 17-23). Jonathan Maccabeus captured Joppa in 148 B.C. (1 Macc. 10:76). Simon, suspecting its inhabitants, set a garrison there (12:34) and upon the restoration of peace established it again as a haven (14:5). The city was destroyed twice by the Romans and changed hands several times during the Crusades. In the fourth century it was made the seat of a bishopric. The city (Yâfa) now comprises the S part of the Tel Aviv-Jaffa municipality.

Boats in the harbor at Jaffa, ancient Joppa

Y. Kaplan for the Tel Aviv Museum conducted excavations at Joppa from 1955 to 1966. Remains documented all periods from the sixteenth century B.C. to Byzantine and Arab times. In confirmation of an Egyptian papyrus of the thirteenth century describing an Egyptian fort at Joppa, the excavators found the fort and its gate with an inscription bearing the titles of Rameses II. The Philistines wrought destruction there during the twelfth century. At the end of the eighth century the town evidently became part of the Assyrian empire. In the fifth century it was under the control of Sidon, as a Sidonian fort there attests. The excavations also revealed the destruction of Joppa by Vespasian at the time of the destruction of Jerusalem in A.D. 70.   R.K.H.; H.F.V.

BIBLIOGRAPHY: S. Talkowsky, *The Gateway of Palestine: A History of Jaffa* (1925); M. Avi-Yonah, ed., *Encyclopedia of Archaeological Excavations in the Holy Land* (1976), 2:532-41.

JO'RAH (jō'ra). A man whose descendants (or place whose former inhabitants), numbering 112, returned from the Babylonian captivity (Ezra 2:18). Called Hariph in Neh. 7:24, about 536 B.C.

JO'RAI (jō'ra-ī; same as "Jorah"). The fourth named of seven Gadite leaders (1 Chron. 5:13), the place of whose residence is not given, unless, as Keil conjectures (*Com.*, ad loc.), v. 16 mentions it. In that case they lived in Gilead, in Bashan, perhaps about 782 B.C.

JO'RAM (jō'ram; "Jehovah is high," a shortened form of *Jehoram,* which see).

1. Son of Toi, king of Hamath, who was sent by his father to congratulate David upon his victory over Hadadezer (2 Sam. 8:9-10), about 986 B.C. He is called Hadoram in 1 Chron. 18:10.

2. One of the descendants of Eliezer (1 Chron. 26:25).

3. Jehoshaphat's son *Jehoram* (which see; in Matt. 1:8 the name is given as Joram).

4. The name of Ahab's son according to the NIV, usually rendered *Jehoram* (which see) in other versions.

JOR'DAN, RIVER OF (Heb. generally with article *hayyardēn,* "the descender," probably from the rapid descent of the stream). It is now called El Urdan, or Esh-Sheri'ah, or the watering-place, and is the chief river of Palestine.

JOR'DAN (Jor'dan) **VALLEY** (Heb. *'Arābâ*; rendered "the Arabah," Deut. 11:3; Josh. 18:18; Ezek. 47:8). Its modern name is El Ghor, For convenience we treat both the river and valley together.

The Jordan Valley is a rift more than 160 miles long, counting from just below Lake Huleh, where the dip below sea level begins, to the point on the Arabah S of the Dead Sea where the valley rises again to sea level. It is from 2 to 15 miles broad and falls as deep as 1,292 feet below sea level at the surface of the Dead Sea, whereas the bottom of the Dead Sea is 1,300 feet deeper still. In this valley is the Jordan River, two great lakes—Galilee and the Dead Sea—respectively 13 and 50 miles long, and large tracts of arable land, especially about Gennesaret, Bethlehem, and Jericho. Actually the Jordan rift is part of a geological fault that extends from Mt. Hermon down into E Africa.

Geologists claim this valley is due to volcanic action's forcing up two long folds of limestone running N and S, with a diagonal ridge shutting off the Dead Sea from the Red Sea and enclosing a part of the old ocean bed. "There then followed a period of great rains, with perpetual snow and glaciers on Lebanon, during which the valley was filled with fresh water to an extent of two hundred miles, or one long lake from the Sea of Galilee to some fifty miles S of the present end of the Dead Sea. How the valley passed from that condition to its present state is not clear. . . . In this valley are six distinct sections: the Beka'a, or valley between the Lebanons; the Upper Jordan, from its sources at the foot of Hermon through Lake Huleh to the Lake of Galilee; this lake itself; the lower Jordan to its mouth at Jericho; the Dead Sea; and thence to the Gulf of 'Akaba, the Wady 'Arabah" (Smith, *Hist. Geog.,* pp. 470-71).

The Upper Jordan. "The great valley of Palestine, as it runs out from between the Lebanons, makes a slight turn eastward round the foot of Hermon, so that Hermon not only looks right down the rest of its course, but is able to discharge into this three fourths of the waters which gather on its high and ample bulk" (Smith). Four streams that unite before entering Lake Huleh contest the honor of being considered as the source of Jordan: (1) the Nahr Bareighit, which comes down the Merj 'Arun; (2) the Nahr Hasbany, which springs half a mile to the N of Hasbeya, from a buttress of Hermon, and flows down between Hermon and the Jebel Dahar, the longest of the four but having much less water than the two following; (3) the Nahr Leddân, the shortest but heaviest, springing from Tell-el-Qadi in the bosom of the valley itself; and (4) Nahr Banias, rising in the very roots of Hermon and having the largest number of tributaries. These last two have generally been considered as the sources of Jordan.

This whole district was given (20 B.C.) to Herod the Great by Augustus, and the town he built was known as Caesarea Philippi. To this region Jesus went to avoid Jewish hostility, and it is this district that is referred to in Ps. 42. It was, from a military point of view, the northern gate of Palestine; and here in Dan lay the limit of the land of Israel. At the lower end of this district lay Lake Huleh, about five miles NE of Hazor, without doubt the Lake Semechonitis of Josephus (*Ant.* 5.5.1; *Wars* 3.10.7) and probably also the waters of Merom of the book of Joshua (11:5-6). From the lower end of the lake the Jordan River enters the Great Rift below the level of the sea, falling 680 feet in less than nine miles, and then glides quietly into the Lake of Galilee.

It is hard for the modern tourist to visualize what the upper Jordan looked like in biblical times because Israeli engineers have deepened and straightened the riverbed and have drained the malarial swamps of Huleh and converted the area into about fifteen thousand acres of magnificent farmland.

The Jordan River betweeen Galilee and the Dead Sea

The Lower Jordan. The Jordan Valley between the Lake of Galilee and the Dead Sea is sixty-five miles long. On the W are the mountains of Galilee and Samaria, with the break between them of the valley of Jezreel. On the E are the flat hills of Gilead, some two thousand feet above the Jordan, broken by the valleys of the Yarmuk and Jabbok. Between these ranges of hills the valley is from three to fourteen miles wide. Much of this valley is fertile, vegetation being extremely abundant, especially in the spring. There is, however, much poor land, jungle, obtrusive marl, and parched hillsides, all justifying the name of desert. Down this broad valley there curves and twists the deeper, narrower riverbed, from 200 yards to a mile broad. This is the breadth to which the Jordan rises when in flood, once a year (Josh. 3:4; Eccles. 24:26). Farther on we come to the Jordan itself, from 90 to 100 feet broad, rapid and muddy. The depth varies from 3 feet at some fords to 10 or 12. In the 65 miles the descent is 610 feet, an average of 14 feet a mile. But few towns have been built in the Jordan Valley for the following reasons: from early spring to late autumn the heat is intolerable, the temperature rising as high as 130 degrees in August; in ancient times the valley was infested with wild beasts, and there were frequent incursions of Arabs. The importance of the Jordan in Scripture would seem to arise from its being a boundary (Gen. 32:10; Deut. 3:20; 27:4; Num. 34:10-12; Josh. 1:2) and a military frontier (Judg. 7:24; 12:5). To pass the Jordan was figurative of decision, like crossing the Rubicon. Many of the most remarkable names and events of Scripture are associated with the Jordan: Joshua leading Israel into the Promised Land, the parting of Elijah and Elisha, Naaman being healed in its waters, David crossing it to escape from the rebellious Absalom, and the baptism of Jesus by John.

With the partition of Palestine in 1948, much of the Jordan Valley came under the control of the Hashemite Kingdom of Jordan, with its capital at Amman. After 1967 it became the boundary between the state of Jordan and the Israeli-occupied West Bank.   H.F.V.

BIBLIOGRAPHY: D. Baly, *The Geography of the Bible* (1959), pp. 111-15, 193-202; id., *Geographical Companion to the Bible* (1963), pp. 13, 31, 41-49, 72, 81-88; G. L. Harding, *Antiquities of Jordan* (1967); N. Glueck, *The River Jordan* (1968); id., *The Other Side of Jordan* (1970); K. Prag, *Levant* (1974), pp. 69-116; C. M. Bennett, *Archaeology in the Levant,* ed. P. R. S. Moorey and P. J. Parr (1978), pp 164-71.

JO'RIM (jō'rim). The son of Matthat and father of Eliezer, maternal ancestors of Jesus (Luke 3:29).

JOR'KEAM (jor'kē-am). The son of Raham, descendant of Caleb; or the name of a place in the tribe of Judah (1 Chron. 2:44; "Jorkoam," KJV).

JOS'ABAD. *See* Joazabad, no. 1.

JOS'APHAT. A Gk. form (Matt. 1:8, KJV) of the name of a king of Judah. *See* Jehoshaphat.

JO'SE. *See* Joshua, no. 4.

JO'SECH (jō'zek). The son of Joda and father of Semein, among Christ's maternal ancestors (Luke 3:26; "Joseph," KJV).

JOS'EDECH. *See* Jehozadak.

JOSEPH (jō'zef). The name of the elder son (*see* article below) of Jacob and Rachel, and of several other persons in the Bible.

1. The father of Igal, the spy delegated from Issachar to explore Canaan (Num. 13:7), 1440 B.C.

2. One of the sons of Asaph who were appointed leaders of the first division of sacred musicians by David (1 Chron. 25:2, 9), about 960 B.C.

3. A Jew of the family of Bani who divorced his Gentile wife after the captivity (Ezra 10:42), 456 B.C.

4. Son of Shebaniah, and one of the chief priests after the captivity (Neh. 12:14), after 536 B.C.

5. The husband of Mary and foster-father of our Lord. By Matthew (who gives the line of royal descent) he is said to have been the son (i.e, son-in-law) of Jacob, whose lineage is traced through David up to Abraham. Luke (giving the line of natural descent) represents him as the son of Eli and traces his origin back to Adam. Only a few statements respecting Joseph appear in Scripture. While living at Nazareth (Luke 2:4) he became engaged to Mary (1:27), but before he took her home as his wife he proved to be with child. Grieved at this and yet not wishing to make a public example of Mary, Joseph "desired to put her away secretly." He was dissuaded from taking this step by the assurance of the angel that Mary had conceived under divine influence (Matt. 1:18-23). Joseph obeyed the divine command and took Mary as his wife (1:24). Shortly after, he was obliged by the decree of enrollment from Augus-

tus Caesar to leave Nazareth with his wife and go to Bethlehem, where Jesus was born. When the shepherds came he was there with Mary and her baby. He went with them to the Temple to present the infant according to the law and, warned by an angel, took them down to Egypt, where he remained until he was directed by a heavenly messenger to return to the land of Israel. His intention to reside in Bethlehem was changed through fear of Archelaus, and he settled in Nazareth (2:1-23), where he carried on his trade of carpenter. When Jesus was twelve years old Joseph took Him and Mary to Jerusalem to keep the Passover and upon their return to Nazareth continued to act as His father (Luke 2:41-51). Scripture furnishes no additional information respecting Joseph, and the origin of all the earliest stories and assertions of the Fathers concerning him is to be found in the apocryphal gospels.

6. The son of Mattathias and father of Jannai, maternal ancestors of Jesus (Luke 3:24).

7. A maternal ancestor of Christ, given as *Josech* (which see) in the NASB and NIV (Luke 3:26).

8. The son of Jonam and father of Judah, among Christ's maternal ancestors (Luke 3:30).

9. Of Arimathea, "a prominent member of the Council, who himself was waiting for the kingdom of God," and was a secret disciple of Jesus. The crucifixion seems to have wrought in him positive convictions, for, upon learning of the death of our Lord, he "gathered up courage and went in before Pilate, and asked for the body of Jesus." Pilate, having learned from the centurion who had charge of the execution that Jesus was actually dead, gave the body to Joseph, who took it down from the cross. After it had been embalmed at the cost of Nicodemus, another secret disciple (John 19:38-39), Joseph had the body wrapped in linen and deposited it in a new tomb belonging to himself and located in a garden "in the place where He was crucified" (Matt. 27:58-60; Mark 14:43-46; Luke 23:50-53; John 19:38-42). Luke describes Joseph as "a good and righteous man" and adds that "he had not consented to their plan and action," i.e., of the Jewish authorities. From this remark it seems to be evident that he was a member of the Sanhedrin.

10. Surnamed Barsabas, one of the two persons whom the early primitive church nominated immediately after the resurrection of Christ, praying that the Holy Spirit would show which one should be named an apostle in place of Judas. When the lots were cast Matthias was chosen (Acts 1:23-25). Joseph also bore the name of Justus and was one of those who had accompanied the apostles and Jesus "beginning with the baptism of John, until the day that He was taken up from us" (vv. 21-22).

11. A Levite of Cyprus (Acts 4:36), surnamed *Barnabas* (which see) by the apostles.

See also Joses.

BIBLIOGRAPHY: For *Joseph the Husband of Mary,* see: A. T. Robertson, *The Mother of Jesus* (1925), pp. 21-32; C. J. and A. A. Barber, *You Can Have a Happy Marriage* (1984), pp. 133-45.
For *Joseph of Arimathea,* see: A. Deane, *New Testament Studies* (1909), pp. 109-22.
For *Joseph Barsabbas,* see: A. Deane, *New Testament Studies* (1909), pp. 16-28.

JOSEPH (jō'zef; "may he," i.e., Jehovah, "add"). The eldest son of Jacob and Rachel, born while his father was still serving Laban (Gen. 30:22-25), about 1910 b.c. After his birth Joseph is mentioned in connection with his father's flight from Laban (Gen. 33:2, 7) and then no more until he was seventeen years of age.

Position in the Family. As the child of Rachel, "son of his old age" (37:3), and doubtless also for his excellence of character, his father loved him more than all his brothers. This, together with the fact that he reported to his father the evil conduct of the sons of Bilhah and Zilpah, caused his brothers to hate him. Their jealousy was aggravated by Jacob's showing his preference in presenting Joseph with a coat, probably a long tunic with sleeves, worn by youths of the richer class (37:2-4). A still greater provocation was the telling of his dreams, that seemed to foreshow his preeminence in the family (vv. 5-11).

Sold into Slavery. Such was Joseph's relation to his brothers when his father sent him from the valley of Hebron to Shechem to inquire concerning their welfare. They were not at Shechem but were found by Joseph in Dothan. His appearance aroused their hatred, and, with the exception of Reuben, they resolved to kill him. Reuben interfered on Joseph's behalf and persuaded them to cast him into a pit, intending "to restore him to his father." This they accordingly did, after stripping him of his tunic. While they were eating a company of Arabian merchants (Ishmaelites) appeared, and, at the suggestion of Judah and in the absence of Reuben, Joseph was sold to them for twenty shekels of silver. Dipping Joseph's tunic in the blood of a goat, they sent it to Jacob, so that he might believe that his favorite had been torn to pieces by some wild beast. Their trick succeeded, and Joseph was mourned as dead. The merchants sold Joseph to Potiphar, an officer of Pharaoh, and he became an Egyptian slave (37:12-36), about 1897 b.c.

Slave Life. Joseph behaved himself so discreetly in the service of Potiphar, and was so led of God, that he found great favor with his master, who gave him the direction of all his affairs. Refusing, however, to gratify the improper request of his master's wife, he was accused by her of unchastity and thrust into prison. Here, also, God was with Joseph, granting him favor in the eyes of the governor of the prison, so that he entrusted all the prisoners to his care, leaving everything to his supervision (39:1-23). While in prison Joseph interpreted correctly the dreams of two of his fellow prisoners—Pharaoh's chief cupbearer and baker—disclaiming any human skill and acknowledging that the interpretations were of God. These interpretations were fulfilled three days afterward, on the king's birthday (chap. 40).

Exaltation. After two years Pharaoh had two prophetic dreams that the magicians and wise men of Egypt were unable to interpret. The cupbearer, calling to mind the service rendered him by Joseph, advised his royal master to put his skill to the test. Joseph was sent for and interpreted the dreams as foretelling seven years of plenty to be followed by seven years of famine. He followed up this interpretation by advising Pharaoh to "look for a man discerning and wise, and set him over the land of Egypt." This counsel pleased Pharaoh and his ministers, who believed that Joseph possessed the spirit of supernatural insight and wisdom. Joseph was appointed ruler over Pharaoh's house and over all the land; in other words, becoming next to Pharaoh in authority in Egypt. Pharaoh called him Zaphenath-paneah ("savior of the world") and married him to Asenath, daughter of Potipherah, the priest of On. This promotion took place when Joseph was thirty years of age (41:1-46), about 1883 b.c. During the seven years of plenty Joseph prepared for the years of famine to follow by carefully husbanding the grain, which was so abundant as to be beyond measurement. During these years his two sons, Manasseh and Ephraim, were born (41:47-52). When scarcity began, Joseph was in a condition to supply the wants of Egypt and also of surrounding nations. He put all Egypt under Pharaoh—first the money, then the cattle, the land (excepting the priests'), and eventually the Egyptians themselves became the property of the crown. The people were distributed according to the cities in which the grain was stored and were instructed to pay a tax to the crown of one-fifth of the product of the soil (41:53-57; 47:14-26).

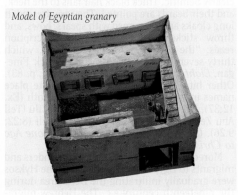

Model of Egyptian granary

Joseph and His Brothers. Early in the time of famine the brothers of Joseph, except Benjamin,

went to Egypt to buy food. Applying to Joseph, who had supreme control over the stores of Egypt, they did not recognize him, but he knew them and seems to have resolved to make them feel and acknowledge the wrong they had done him. He acted as a foreigner toward them, spoke harshly to them, inquired whence they had come, and accused them of being spies. This charge they denied and told him specifically about their family. After putting them in prison for three days he sent them home to bring back their youngest brother as proof of their veracity, keeping Simeon as hostage. Having with great difficulty secured Jacob's permission, they returned with Benjamin, a present, and double money to repay the sum placed by order of Joseph in each man's sack. The presence of his younger brother assured Joseph of the truth of his father's welfare, and, yielding to his natural impulses, he made himself known to his brothers. He inquired again concerning his father; told them not to grieve because of the sin they had committed in selling him, as God had overruled it for their welfare; charged them to return to Canaan and bring Jacob and their families to Egypt, saying that he would provide for them during the five remaining years of famine. These events reached the ear of Pharaoh; he approved all that Joseph had done and commanded that Jacob and his family should forthwith come into Egypt (42:1–45:24).

Welcomes Israel. Israel, convinced that Joseph still lived, went to Egypt, where he was tenderly welcomed, provided for, and placed in the land of Goshen. When he died he was embalmed by order of Joseph and carried by him to Canaan and laid in the cave of Machpelah (45:25; 50:13).

Remaining History. Upon their return from Canaan Joseph found his brothers in fear lest, their father being dead, he would punish them. He assured them that this was not his purpose and promised to still nourish them and their little ones. Joseph lived to be 110 and, dying, made his brothers promise that they would carry up his bones to the land of promise. After his death he was embalmed and "placed in a coffin in Egypt" (50:14-26), about 1800 b.c. The promise was religiously kept, for "Moses took the bones of Joseph with him" (Ex. 13:19), and they were at length put in their final resting place at Shechem (Josh. 24:32).

Character. In Joseph we recognize the elements of a noble character—piety, pure and high morality, simplicity, gentleness, fidelity, patience, perseverance, an iron will, and indomitable energy.

Chronology. The Joseph story, according to the biblical chronology preserved in the Masoretic Heb. text, is to be placed c. 1871 b.c., i.e., during the splendid Twelfth Dynasty. However, many scholars have concluded that it would be an

Cave of Machpelah, Hebron, site of Joseph's tomb

"historical misinterpretation" (Alexis Mallon, "Les Hebreux en Egypte," *Orientalia* 3 [1921]: 67) to imagine that a young Semitic foreigner would have been lifted up to such power under native Egyptian dynasties. This would be more likely, it is claimed, under the Hyksos-Semitic conquerors of Egypt. It is unfortunate that this period of the Hyksos infiltration is to a large extent unknown. Everybody agrees, however, that Israel was in Egypt during this period of confusion and turmoil (c. 1750-1550) and that the notice that an oppressor called "a new king . . . who did not know Joseph" (Ex. 1:8) refers to one of the pharaohs of the New Empire, after the hated Asiatic Hyksos were expelled from Egypt. This tallies with the fact that the Israelites were in residence in the plain of Tanis, called "the field of Zoan" (Ps. 78:12). This was the Hyksos capital of Egypt.

Archaeology. That Jacob and his sons went down into Egypt under Joseph's prime minister-ship has been denied by some of the more radical critics (cf. Leroy Waterman, *Journal of the American Oriental Society* 57: 375-80; id., *American Journal of Semitic Languages and Literatures* 55: 25-43). But this historical tradition is so inextricably woven into the fabric of Jewish history that it "cannot be eliminated without leaving an inexplicable gap" (W. F. Albright, *From the Stone Age to Christianity* [1940], pp. 183ff.). In addition to this general conclusion, numerous evidences of Israel's sojourn in Egypt appear in the Genesis-Exodus part of the Pentateuch. Most astonishing are the surprising number of Egyptian personal names showing up in the Levitical genealogies (Theophile Meek, "Moses and the Levites," *American Journal of Semitic Languages and Literatures* 56: 117ff.). Unquestionably Egyptian are such names as Moses, Hophni, Phinehas, Merari, Putiel (first element), and Assir. First Sam. 2:27 further corroborates this fact. Critics unwarrantedly, however, deny that the other tribes sojourned in

Egypt on the basis that the Egyptian names are apparently confined to the Levitical tribe. Another evidence of the Egyptian sojourn is the authentic local coloring that appears in numerous aspects of the Pentateuchal account. Many bits of Egyptian coloring exist "which are beautifully illustrated by Egyptological discoveries" (W. F. Albright in *Young's Analytical Concordance,* 20th ed. [1936], p. 27). When the writer, for instance, mentions the title of Egyptian officials such as the "chief cupbearer" and "chief baker" (Gen. 40:2), they are those of bona fide palace officials mentioned in Egyptian documents. (*See* G. E. Wright and F. Filson, *Westminster Historical Atlas to the Bible* [1945], p. 28b). Other examples occur in 39:4; 41:40, 42-43. Such striking examples as the famines of Egypt (cf. chap. 41) are illustrated by at least two Egyptian officials who give a resume of their charities on the walls of their tombs, listing dispensing food to the needy "in each year of want." One inscription from c. 100 B.C. actually mentions the famine of seven years' duration in the days of Pharaoh Zoser of Dynasty III about 2700 B.C. Such items as dreams, the presence of magicians (cf. 41:8), mummification (50:2, 26), and Joseph's life span of 110 years (50:22), the traditional length of a happy, prosperous life in Egypt, are all well illustrated by the monuments. The family of Jacob, some seventy persons (46:26-27), were settled down in Goshen (vv. 28-34). This area has been identified with the eastern part of the Delta around the Wadi Tumilat. The region around this wadi, especially N of it, was one of the most fertile parts of Egypt, "the best of the land" (47:11). A fine archaeological parallel is the representation of a group of W Semitic immigrants going down to Middle Egypt around the year 1900 B.C. The scene is sculptured on the tomb at Beni Hasan of one of Senwosret II's officials named Khnumhotep. A party bringing barter products from SW Asia appears under the leadership of "Sheik of the highlands, Ibshe." The name and the faces are clearly Semitic. Thick black hair falls to the neck, and their beards are pointed. They are dressed in long cloaks and are armed with spears, bows, and throw sticks. The accompanying inscription reads: "the arrival, bringing eye paint, which thirty-seven Asiatics bring to him" (Jack Finegan, *Light from the Ancient Past* [1946], p. 83). Other bits of evidence are the Canaanite place names in the Delta. These include Succoth (Ex. 12:37), Baal-zephon and Migdol (14:2), Zilu (Tell Abu Zeifah), and very likely Goshen itself (8:22; 9:26). (*See* W. F. Albright, *From the Stone Age to Christianity* [1940], p. 184.)

Moreover, in addition to Canaanite traders and migrants to Egypt, we now know that the Hyksos were gradually infiltrating the Delta area during the nineteenth century B.C. The Hebrew migration may be seen as part of that general movement. It is also interesting to see how the biblical account of the famine may fit into Egyptian history. The Middle Kingdom began with the nobles enjoying considerable power as feudal lords. However, the pharaohs were able to reestablish the absolute power over Egypt that they had enjoyed during the Old Kingdom period (the pyramid age) at just about the time Joseph as prime minister would have been enslaving the people in return for food, if one follows the Masoretic chronology.   R.K.H.; H.F.V.

BIBLIOGRAPHY: J. M. Taylor, *Joseph the Prime Minister* (1886); T. Kirk, *The Life of Joseph* (1900); F. B. Meyer, *Joseph: Beloved, Hated, Exalted* (1955); J. B. Pritchard, ed., *Ancient Near Eastern Texts* (1969), pp. 553-54; K. A. Kitchen, *The Joseph Narrative* ... (1970); G. Lawson, *The History of Joseph* (1972).

JO'SES (jō'sēz; Gk. form of Joseph).

1. A brother of Jesus (Mark 6:3).

2. Son of Mary and brother of James the Less. Their mother was present at Christ's crucifixion and visited His grave (Mark 15:40, 47). Some regard this Joses and the brother of Jesus as one and the same person.   R.K.H.

JO'SHAH (jō'sha). Son of Amaziah and one of the leaders of Simeon, the increase of whose family led them to move to the valley of Gedor, from which they expelled the Hamites (1 Chron. 4:34, 38-41), about 711 B.C.

JOSH'APHAT (josh'a-fat; "Jehovah judges"). A Mithnite, and one of David's mighty men (1 Chron. 11:43), about 1000 B.C.

JOSHAVI'AH (josh-a-vī'a). A son of Elnaam, and, with his brother Jeribai, one of David's mighty men (1 Chron. 11:46), 1000 B.C.

JOSHBEK'ASHAH (josh-bek'a-sha; perhaps "he," i.e., God, "returns a hard fate"). A son of Heman, and leader of the seventeenth division of the Temple musicians (1 Chron. 25:4, 24), about 960 B.C.

JOSHEB-BASSHE'BETH (jō'sheb-bash'e-beth; "sitting in the council"; "Josheb-basshe'-beth," KJV). The Tachemonite, the "chief of the captains" among David's mighty men (2 Sam. 23:8). He is called *Jashobeam* (which see) in 1 Chron. 11:11.

JOSHIBI'AH (jo-shi-bī'a; "dweller with Jehovah"; "Josibiah," KJV). The son of Seraiah, of the tribe of Simeon. His son Jehu was one of those who migrated to Gedor (1 Chron. 4:35), before 711 B.C.

JOSHUA (josh'ū-a). The name of the assistant and successor of Moses (*see* article below), and of four other persons in the Bible.

1. A native of Beth-shemesh, an Israelite, the owner of the field into which the cart that bore the Ark came on its return from the land of the Philistines (1 Sam. 6:14, 18), about 1076 B.C.

2. The governor of Jerusalem at the time of the

reformation by Josiah (2 Kings 23:8), 621 B.C.

3. The son of Jehozadak (Hag. 1:1, 12, 14), a high priest in the time of Haggai and Zechariah. In Zechariah (3:1-10) Joshua, as high priest, represents the people dressed in the garb of slaves and, afterward, clothed with the new and glorious garments of deliverance. This symbolic action prefigures the future national cleansing of Israel at the second advent of Christ and her reconstitution as a nation in the millennial kingdom. When messengers came to Jerusalem, from the remnant of the captivity in Babylon, to offer presents of gold and silver to the Temple, the prophet was directed to have some of their offerings made into crowns for Joshua, as a symbol of the priestly and royal crowns of Israel that were to be united on the head of the Messiah (Zech. 6:10-11). For further discussion, *see* Jeshua, no. 3.

4. One of the maternal ancestors of Jesus (Luke 3:29; "Jose," KJV), not mentioned in the OT.

JOSH'UA (josh'ūa); (Heb. *yᵉhôshūa‘*, "Jehovah is salvation"), changed by Moses (Num. 13:16) from *Hoshea*, "salvation" (13:8). The assistant and successor of Moses. He was the son of Nun, the son of Elishama, head of the tribe of Ephraim (Ex. 33:11; Num. 1:10).

In Battle. In the Bible Joshua is first mentioned as the victorious commander of the Israelites in their battle against the Amalekites at Rephidim (Ex. 17:8-16), 1440 B.C.

On Mount Sinai. When Moses ascended Sinai to receive the two tables for the first time (Ex. 24:13), Joshua, who is called his servant, accompanied him part of the way and was the first to meet him on his return (32:17).

In Charge of Tabernacle. After the defection of Israel and their worship of the golden calf, Moses moved the Tabernacle outside the camp and, returning to the congregation, left it in charge of Joshua (33:11).

An Unwise Request. When it was told Moses that Eldad and Medad prophesied in the camp, Joshua asked Moses to forbid them, to which Moses replied, "Are you jealous for my sake? Would that all the Lord's people were prophets, that the Lord would put His Spirit upon them!" (Num. 11:27-29).

A Spy. Soon after, Joshua was appointed as one of the twelve chiefs sent to explore the land of Canaan (13:8, 16-17). He and *Caleb* (which see) were the only ones to give an encouraging report of their journey, and they exhorted the people to go up and possess the land (14:6-9).

Appointed Ruler. When the forty years of wandering had almost passed, Joshua, because of his faithfulness, was one of the few survivors (Num. 26:65). Moses, by direction of God (27:18-23), invested him solemnly and publicly with authority, in connection with Eleazar, over the people (Deut. 3:28).

With Moses in the Tabernacle. It was revealed to Moses that he was soon to die and that he should appear with Joshua in the Tabernacle. While in the presence of God, Moses gave his faithful minister a commission from God: "Be strong and courageous, for you shall bring the sons of Israel into the land which I swore to them, and I will be with you" (Deut. 31:14, 23).

Assumes Charge of Israel. Under the commission of God, again renewed (Josh. 1:1-9), Joshua, "filled with the spirit of wisdom" (Deut. 34:9) assumed the command of the people, c. 1400 B.C. From Shittim he sent spies into Jericho, where they were given lodging and were hidden by *Rahab* (which see). They returned to Joshua with an account of the fear of the people because of the Israelites (Josh. 2).

Entrance into Canaan. The next morning after their return, Joshua broke camp at Shittim and moved down to the edge of Jordan, which at this season, the harvest (April), overflowed its banks (Josh. 3:15). On the third day the officers instructed the people in the order of the march, and Joshua ordered them to sanctify themselves for the next day. In the morning the priests advanced in front of the people, bearing the Ark, and when their feet touched the water the river was divided. They took their position in the midst of the riverbed and remained there until the people had all passed over. Meanwhile, twelve chosen men, one from each tribe, took twelve stones from the spot where the priests stood, leaving in their place twelve other stones taken from the dry land. When all this was done Joshua commanded the priests to come up out of the Jordan, and as soon as they reached dry ground the waters of the Jordan returned and overflowed its banks as before (4:1-18).

It need not be assumed that there was only a narrow dry path on which the multitude of Israelites might pass over. The waters of the Jordan were blocked by a mud slide at Adam and Zarethan, some sixteen miles north of Jericho (Josh. 3:16). Thus the bed of the Jordan would have been dry for some twenty miles between Adam and the Dead Sea, and the time needed for the Israelites to cross would have been minimal. A narrow pathway would have required so much time for passage that the whole upper valley of the Jordan would have been submerged.

In Canaan. The host encamped that night at Gilgal, in the plains of Jericho, and there Joshua set up the twelve stones taken from the Jordan as a perpetual memorial of the dividing of its water (4:19-24). At the command of God, Joshua caused the people to be circumcised, a rite that seems to have been neglected in the case of those born after the Exodus (5:5). Four days after the crossing of Jordan the Passover was celebrated; the Israelites ate the next day of bread made from the grain of the land, and the manna ceased (5:10-12).

Capture of Jericho. As Joshua stood by Jericho, he saw a warrior with a drawn sword in his hand, who, in reply to Joshua's challenge, announced himself as the "captain of the host of the Lord" and gave the divine plan for the capture of the city (vv. 13-14). The men of war and the priests carrying the trumpets and the Ark were to circle the city once each day for six days, and seven times on the seventh day, when the walls of the city would fall. Joshua followed the directions he was given, watched the fall of the city, put the inhabitants to death, and destroyed the property found within it. The Israelites spared only Rahab and her household and the silver and gold and vessels of brass and iron, which they placed in the sacred treasury (chap. 6).

The First Defeat. The next undertaking was the capture of *Ai* (which see), which the spies informed Joshua would be easily accomplished. Only 3,000 men were sent to take it—so sure seemed victory. They were repulsed and chased to Shebarim, with a loss of thirty-six men. Asking the Lord as to the reason for the defeat of Israel, Joshua was told of the taking of spoil from Jericho by one of the Israelites. A lot was ordered, which resulted in fixing the crime upon *Achan* (which see) and the destruction of himself, family, and property (chap. 7).

Taking of Ai. Joshua then formed a plan for taking Ai by stratagem, which met with complete success. The city was destroyed with all its inhabitants; its king was hanged on a tree and buried under a great heap of stones, the only memorial of the city (8:1-29). After this Joshua caused the law to be engraved upon stones on Mt. Ebal and read to the people stationed upon that mountain and Mt. Gerizim (8:30-35).

Craft of the Gibeonites. When the kings of the Hittites and other nations W of Jordan heard of the fall of Ai, they armed themselves against Joshua. But the Gibeonites, a confederacy of several cities not far from the encampment of the Israelites, sent ambassadors in torn clothes, with old sacks and dry bread, pretending that they had come from a distant country and wished to make a covenant with Israel. They obtained a treaty, which was respected by Joshua, and were made "hewers of wood and drawers of water for the whole congregation" (chap. 9).

Battle of Gibeon. Alarmed by the defection of the Gibeonites, Adoni-zedek, king of Jerusalem, became an ally of the kings of Hebron, Jarmuth, Lachish, and Eglon and laid siege to Gibeon. Joshua hastened to the aid of the cities, marching by night from Gilgal and, taking the Amorites by surprise, defeated them near Beth-horon. Joshua was helped in this battle by an unprecedented hailstorm, which killed more than fell by the sword, and by a miraculous lengthening of the day, which enabled him to pursue the fugitives to Makkedah (Josh. 10:1-14).

The lengthening of the day of the battle of

Gibeon has elicited much skepticism and called forth many theories. The miraculous event may have consisted in the expansion of the rotary motion of the earth or in an extraordinary refraction of the light so as to be visible over the whole globe. Keil suggests that the day merely seemed lengthened because the work accomplished by the Israelites was so great.

Subsequent Conquests. This great battle was followed by the conquest of Makkedah, Libnah, Lachish, Gezer, Eglon, Hebron, and Debir. In this one campaign Joshua subdued the southern half of Palestine from Kadesh-barnea to Gaza, the eastern and western limit of the southern frontier; and he led the people back to Gilgal (Josh. 10:15-43). In another campaign he marched to Lake Merom, where he met and overthrew a confederacy of the Canaanite kings of the N under Jabin, king of Hazor; and in the course of the war led his victorious soldiers to the gates of Sidon (Zidon, KJV) and into the valley of Lebanon, under Mt. Hermon, but left the cities standing, with the exception of Hazor. In six years Joshua was master of the whole land from Mt. Halak, at the ascent of Mt. Seir on the S, to Baal-gad, under Mt. Hermon on the N. His conquests were six nations, with thirty-one kings, including the Anakim, the old terror of Israel (11:1–12:24).

The severe treatment of the Canaanites has provoked considerable comment. That Joshua was right because he acted under the command of Jehovah has been justified by (1) the excessive wickedness of the Canaanites (Lev. 18:21-24) and (2) the contamination of their example (Deut. 7:1-5). Archaeology has corroberated the wickedness and utter debilitating effect of Canaanite cults. Religious literature excavated at Ras Shamra (1929-37) presents the Canaanite pantheon as utterly immoral. The chief god, El, was a monster of wickedness. His son, Baal, great NW Semitic god of the thunder, was no better. The three famous goddesses, Asherah, Anath, and Ashtoreth, were patronesses of sex and war, and their bloodiness and lustfulness must have reduced Canaanite civilization to extremely sordid depths. This archaeological picture of Canaanite religion fully supports Philo of Byblos's estimate of the utter corruption of Canaanite cults and removes critical doubt of the authenticity of Philo's material.

Dividing the Inheritance. Joshua, in conjunction with Eleazar and the heads of the tribes, now proceeded to apportion the Promised Land, including the part yet unconquered, asking for his portion Timnath-serah, a city of the hill country of Ephraim (chaps. 13-19). After the inheritance of five of the tribes had been determined Joshua moved to Shiloh, where he set up the Tabernacle and assembled the people (18:1). Seven tribes had not received their inheritance, and Joshua reproved them for not taking possession of the

land. Three men were appointed from each tribe to survey the rest of the land and to divide it into seven portions, which, with their cities, they described in a book. When the survey was finished, Joshua cast lots for the seven portions before the Tabernacle in Shiloh (18:2-10). Six cities of refuge were appointed by the people themselves, three on the W of Jordan and three on the E (chap. 20). The Levites, having claimed the right given to them by Moses, received forty-eight cities and their surrounding villages, which were given up by the several tribes in proportion to the cities they severally possessed (chap. 21; cf. Num. 35:1-8). The warriors of the trans-Jordanic tribes were then dismissed in peace to their homes (Josh. 22).

Old Age and Death. After an interval of rest Joshua called all Israel to an assembly and delivered to them two solemn addresses concerning the marvelous fulfillment of God's promises to their fathers. He warned them of the conditions upon which their property depended and caused them to renew their covenant with God at Shechem. He died at the age of 110 years and was buried in his own city, Timnath-serah (24:1-31), about 1365 B.C.

Character. It is difficult to form an estimate of Joshua's character, because the man is overshadowed by the greatness of the events in which he was placed. And yet this is not a dishonor to him, but a glory; a lesser man would have been seen and heard more. His life, though recorded with fullness of detail, shows no stain. By the faithful serving of his youth he was taught to command as a man; as a citizen he was patriotic in the highest degree; as a warrior, fearless and blameless; as a judge, calm and impartial. He was quite equal to every emergency under which he was to act—valiant without temerity, active without precipitation. No care, no advantage, no duty was neglected by him. He ever looked up for and obeyed divine direction with the simplicity of a child and wielded the great power given him with calmness, unostentation, and without swerving, to the accomplishment of a high, unselfish purpose. He earned by manly vigor a quiet, honored old age and retained his faith and loyalty, exclaiming, in almost his dying breath, "As for me and my house, we will serve the Lord."

M.F.U.; H.F.V.

BIBLIOGRAPHY: T. Smith, *History of Joshua* (1870); W. J. Deane, *Joshua: His Life and Times* (1889); W. S. LaSor, *Great Personalities of the Old Testament* (1959), pp. 69-77; G. A. Getz, *Joshua: Defeat to Victory* (1979); W. G. Blaikie, *Heroes of Israel* (1981), pp. 433-37.

JOSHUA, BOOK OF. The name, meaning "Jehovah saves," well describes the character of Joshua's military career.

Purpose. The book of Joshua demonstrates God's faithfulness to His promise by leading Israel into the land of Canaan as He had previously led them out of Egypt (Gen. 15:18-21; Josh. 1:2-6). The account of the conquest is highly selective and abbreviated. Those events that are enumerated are deemed sufficient for the purposes the author had in mind.

Typical Meaning. According to 1 Cor. 10:11 events of the Exodus, the wilderness wandering, and the conquest of Canaan are highly typical. "Now these things happened to them as an example," literally, "as types." Accordingly, Joshua is a type of Christ as our conquering commander. The redemption out of Egypt and the passage of the Red Sea typify our being baptized by the Holy Spirit into union with Christ (cf. 10:2): "And all were baptized into Moses in the cloud and in the sea." This redemptive experience prefigures the position the Christian has by virtue of being in Christ by the Spirit's baptizing work (12:13; Rom. 6:2-3; Col. 2:9-12). The crossing of Jordan is a type of our death with Christ *experientially,* as the crossing of the Red Sea is a type of our *positional* death in Christ. Claiming by faith our experience based upon our position is set forth by the crossing of the Jordan and the entering the land of conflict and victory (cf. Eph. 6:10-20). Canaan is not a type of heaven but a type of our meeting our spiritual enemies in victorious Christian living. It is considering ourselves "to be dead to sin, but alive to God in Jesus Christ" (Rom. 6:11). Every believer is positionally "dead to sin" and "alive to God." The difference is that when he reckons it true, it becomes experientially actual. The Canaanites, Perizzites, Hivites, and others like them may typify our spiritual enemies (Eph. 6:12).

Outline.

I. Conquest of the land (1:1–12:24)
   A. Commission of Joshua (1:1-9)
   B. Preparation to cross the Jordan (1:10–2:24)
   C. The Jordan crossed (3:1–4:24)
   D. Israel circumcised and Passover observed at Gilgal (5:1-15)
   E. Capture of Jericho and Ai (6:1–8:29)
   F. Altar on Mt. Ebal erected (8:30-35)
   G. Deception of Gibeonites (9:1-27)
   H. Conquest of southern Canaan (10:1-43)
   I. Conquest of northern Canaan (11:1-15)
   J. Summary of the conquest (11:16–12:24)
II. Division of the land (13:1–22:34)
   A. Instruction of Joshua (13:1-7)
   B. Eastern tribes assigned (13:8-33)
   C. Western tribes assigned (14:1–19:51)
   D. Cities of refuge provided (20:1-9)
   E. Levitical towns chosen (21:1-45)
   F. Eastern tribes sent away (22:1-34)
III. Joshua's farewell address and death (23:1–24:33)

Authorship and Date. The book is anonymous. That the book, however, was composed in substance by Joshua himself or by an inspired writer

soon after his death is supported by the following facts: (1) The account has the vividness of an eye-witness (Josh. 5:1, 6). Such events as the sending out of the spies (chap. 2), the crossing of Jordan (chap. 3), the capture of Jericho and Ai (chaps. 6-8), and so forth, are described with great vividness of detail. (2) Parts of the book, at least, are written by Joshua (cf. 18:9; 24:26). (3) The narrative was written very early. Rahab, the harlot, was still alive (6:25). That the Jebusites were living "with the sons of Judah at Jerusalem until this day" (15:63) points to a pre-Davidic date (cf. 2 Sam. 5:5-9). References such as those mentioning the Canaanites' dwelling at Gezer (Josh. 16:10) are pre-Solomonic, because the pharaoh of Egypt killed the Canaanite inhabitants and gave the cities as a present to his daughter, Solomon's wife. Jerusalem was not yet an Israelite capital (18:16, 28). Archaic names of cities appear, such as Baalah, later Kiriath-jearim (15:9). The Gibeonites were still "hewers of wood and drawers of water" (9:27), whereas in Saul's day they suffered massacre and their status had been changed (2 Sam. 21:1-9). (4) Although the book is early and doubtless written by Joshua himself, minor details in the present form of the work cannot be assigned to Joshua's original work, for example the account of his death (Josh. 24:29-31) and the strange use of the term "from all the hill country of Judah and from all the hill country of Israel" (11:21). The reference in Joshua to the book of Jashar (10:13) is similar to a reference to Jashar that occurs in 2 Sam. 1:18, and as a consequence some have argued that the book of Joshua was written during David's reign or later, but that is not a legitimate argument. Almost nothing is known of the book of Jashar, which may have been an anthology of national heroes, expanded from century to century to include contemporary celebrities.

Relation to the Pentateuch. Denying that the book of Joshua is a literary unit, the critics weave it into their theory of the Pentateuch and have coined the unsound critical term "Hexateuch" to fit their hypothesis. The sources J (Jehovistic) and E (Elohistic) are claimed to be the two primary sources of chaps. 1-12, revised later by Deuteronomic writers. Chapters 13-22 are said to be from a priestly source (P) and were added to JED around 400 B.C. That the "Hexateuch" is purely a critical invention is proved from the following reasons: (1) It is of a piece with the documentary hypothesis of the Pentateuch and is founded upon the same false literary, historical, and religious philosophical presuppositions. (2) Certain pronounced linguistic peculiarities that appear in the Pentateuch are absent from the book of Joshua. (3) There is no historical evidence that Joshua was ever thought of as forming a unit with the Pentateuch. The Samaritans took only the Pentateuch, which would have been inconceivable had Joshua at that time formed a

"Hexateuch," and especially so when the book apparently favors the Samaritans by its references to Shechem (24:1, 32).

Authenticity and Credibility of the Book. To the believing student the book of Joshua by its own internal evidence, the implicit and explicit references to it in the NT (Heb. 11:30-31), and the intimate fashion in which its typology is interwoven in the NT revelation of God's redemption in Christ (3:7–4:11; cf. 4:8) stamp it as genuine. Moreover, a detailed geographical and archaeological study of references and events recorded in the book lends credence to its historicity.   M.F.U.

BIBLIOGRAPHY: Y. Kaufmann, *The Biblical Account of the Conquest of the Land* (1953); G. E. Mendenhall, *Law and Covenant in Israel and the Ancient Near East* (1955); J. Gray, *Joshua, Judges, Ruth,* New Century Bible (1967); J. A. Soggin, *Joshua, a Commentary* (1972); G. Bush, *Notes on Joshua* (1976); W. G. Blaikie, *The Book of Joshua* (1978); J. Garstang, *Joshua-Judges: The Foundations of Biblical History* (1978); W. G. Scroggie, *Joshua in the Light of the New Testament* (1981); M. Woudstra, *The Book of Joshua,* New International Commentary on the Old Testament (1981).

JOSI'AH (jō-sī'a). The name of a king of Judah (*see* article below) and of the son of Zephaniah, residing in Jerusalem after the captivity, in whose house Zechariah was to crown the high priest Joshua (Zech. 6:10), 519 B.C.

JOSI'AH (jō-sī'a; perhaps, "Jehovah heals," cf. Arab. '*asa,* "cure, nurse"; "Josias," Matt. 1:10-11, KJV). The name of a son of Zephaniah (*see* article above) and of the sixteenth king of the separate kingdom of Judah; this king was the son of King Amon and his wife Jedidah. Josiah, at the early age of eight years, succeeded his father on the throne of Judah (2 Kings 21:26; 22:1; 2 Chron. 34:1), c. 640 B.C.

Idolatry Overthrown. In the eighth year of his reign "he began to seek the God of his father David" (2 Chron. 34:3) and manifested that enmity to idolatry in all its forms that distinguished his character and reign. In the twelfth year of his reign "he began to purge Judah and Jerusalem of the high places, the Asherim, the carved images, and the molten images" (34:3). So strong was his detestation of idolatry that he ransacked the sepulchers of the idolatrous priests of former days and burned their bones upon the idol altars before they were overthrown. He did not confine his operations to Judah but went over a considerable part of Israel, with the same object in view. At Bethel, in particular, he executed all that the prophet (1 Kings 13:2) had foretold (2 Kings 23:1-20; 2 Chron. 34:3-7).

Temple Repaired. In the eighteenth year of his reign Josiah proceeded to cleanse and repair the Temple. The task was committed to Shaphan, the scribe; to Maaseiah, an official of the city; and to Joah. All parties engaged in the work displayed such fidelity that the money could be given to them without reckoning (2 Kings 22:3-7; 2 Chron. 34:8-13).

Finding of the Law. In the course of this pious labor the high priest Hilkiah discovered in the sanctuary "the book of the law," by Moses. He reported his discovery to Shaphan, who conveyed the volume to the king and read it in the royal presence. Alarmed by the penalties threatened in the law, Josiah sent several of his chief counselors to consult with the prophetess Huldah, who replied that although these dread penalties would be inflicted, he would be gathered to his fathers in peace before the days of punishment came. Perhaps with a view of averting the threatened doom, Josiah convened the people at Jerusalem and, after the reading of the law, made a solemn covenant with Jehovah (2 Kings 22:8–23:3; 2 Chron. 34:14-32). To ratify the renewal of the covenant Josiah appointed the Passover to be held at the legal time, which was accordingly celebrated on a scale of unexampled magnificence. But it was too late; the hour of mercy had passed, for "the Lord did not turn from the fierceness of His great wrath" (2 Kings 23:21-23, 26; 2 Chron. 35:1-19).

Death. Not long after this Pharaoh Neco, king of Egypt, sought passage through Josiah's territory on his way to fight against Carchemish, on the Euphrates. Josiah, disguising himself, went out to battle and was mortally wounded by a random arrow and taken to Jerusalem, where he died (609 B.C.). "Then Jeremiah chanted a lament for Josiah. And all the male and female singers speak about Josiah in their lamentations to this day"; i.e., in the lamentation that they were wont to sing on certain fixed days, they sang also the lamentation for Josiah (2 Kings 23:29-30; 2 Chron. 35:20-25). Both Jeremiah and Zephaniah mention Josiah in their prophecies.

BIBLIOGRAPHY: F. M. Cross and G. E. Wright, *Journal of Biblical Literature* 75 (1956): 203-19; D. Freedman, *Biblical Archaeologist* 19 (1956): 50-60; J. B. Pritchard, *Hebrew Inscriptions from Gibeon* (1959), pp. 18ff.; J. Naveh, *Israel Exploration Journal* 10 (1960): 129-39; H. H. Rowley, *Men of God* (1963), pp. 159-67; T. Kirk and G. Rawlinson, *Studies in the Books of Kings* 2 vols. in 1 (1983), 2:216-23; E. R. Thiele, *Mysterious Numbers of the Hebrew Kings* (1983), pp. 35, 52-53, 180-81, 206.

JOSI'AS. The name of a king of Judah in the KJV of Matt. 1:10-11. *See* Josi'ah.

JOSIBI'AH. *See* Joshibiah.

JOSIPHI'AH (jōs-i-fi'a; "Jehovah will increase, add"). One of the family of Shelomith, whose son led 160 men under Ezra to Jerusalem from Babylon (Ezra 8:10), about 457 B.C.

JOT. Rather, iota. The smallest letter of the Gk. alphabet (ι), from the Heb. *yôd* (י), and answering to the *i* or *y* of the European languages. It is used figuratively in KJV to express the smallest of trifles (Matt. 5:18; NASB and NIV, "smallest letter"), just as *alpha* and *omega* are used to express the beginning and the end.

JOT'BAH (jot'ba; "goodness, pleasantness"). The city of Haruz, whose daughter Meshullemeth was the mother of King Amon (2 Kings 21:19). It is possibly to be identified with Jotapata (Khirbet Jefāt), seven miles N of Sepphoris.

JOT'BATH. *See* Jotbathah.

JOT'BATHAH (jot'ba-tha; "goodness, pleasantness"). One of the Israelite encampments (Num. 33:33-34; Deut. 10:7; "Jotbath," KJV).

JO'THAM (jō'tham; "Jehovah is upright").

1. The youngest of Gideon's seventy legitimate sons, and the only one of them who escaped the massacre ordered by Abimelech (Judg. 9:5), perhaps about 1108 B.C. After Abimelech had been made king by the Shechemites, Jotham appeared on Mt. Gerizim and protested against their act in a beautiful parable, in which the trees are represented as bestowing upon the bramble the kingly honor that had been refused by the cedar, the olive, and the vine (vv. 7-12). We hear no more of him but are informed that three years later the curse that he uttered was accomplished (v. 57).

2. The eleventh king of Judah, and son of King Uzziah by Jerushah, daughter of Zadok. After his father was struck with leprosy Jotham conducted the government for him until his death (about thirteen years), when he ascended the throne, being then twenty-five years of age (2 Kings 15:5, 32-33; 2 Chron. 27:1), about 740 B.C. Jotham reigned in the spirit and power of his father and avoided any assumption of the priestly function that proved so disastrous to his father. He was unable, however, to correct all of the corrupt practices of the people. He built the upper gate of the Temple—i.e., the northern gate of the inner court—and continued the fortifying of Jerusalem that his father had begun. He also built "cities in the hill country of Judah" and "fortresses and towers on the wooded hills" (27:2-4). He waged war successfully against the Ammonites, who seem to have refused to pay to Jotham the tribute which they paid to Uzziah (2 Chron. 26:8). For three years after their defeat he compelled them to pay one hundred talents of silver and ten thousand measures each of wheat and barley (27:5). After a reign of eighteen years, including his joint reign with Uzziah, Jotham died and was buried in the sepulcher of the kings (2 Kings 15:38; 2 Chron. 27:8-9), about 732 B.C.

The KJV of Matt. 1:9 describes this person as Joatham the son of Ozias.

3. A descendant, apparently, of Caleb, and one of the six sons of Jahdai (1 Chron. 2:47).

JOURNEY, DAY'S; SABBATH DAY'S. *See* Metrology: Measures of Length.

JOY. Usually some form of Heb. *gîl*, to "leap," or

"spin around" with pleasure; a stronger term than *śimḥâ* (Ps. 30:5; etc.); *māśôś* (Job 8:19; etc.), rejoicing; Gk. *chara* (Matt. 2:10), gladness; the cause or occasion of joy (Luke 2:10; 1 Thess. 2:20).

1. Joy is a delight of the mind arising from the consideration of a present or assured possession of a future good. When moderate it is called *gladness;* raised suddenly to the highest degree it is *exultation* or *transport;* when the desires are limited by our possessions it is *contentment;* high desires accomplished bring *satisfaction;* vanquished opposition we call *triumph;* when joy has so long possessed the mind that it has settled into a temper, we call it *cheerfulness.* This is natural joy.

2. There is a *moral joy,* which is a self-approbation, or that which arises from the performance of any good actions; this kind of joy is called peace, or serenity of conscience; if the action be honorable, and the joy rise high, it may be called *glory.*

3. *Spiritual joy* is called a "fruit of the Spirit" (Gal. 5:22); "joy in the faith" (Phil. 1:25). Its objects are God Himself (Ps. 43:4; Isa. 61:10); the promises (Phil. 3:3; 1 Pet. 1:8); the gospel (Ps. 89:15); the prosperity of Christ's kingdom (Acts 15:3; Rev. 11:15, 17); the happiness of a future state (Ps. 16:9-11; Rom. 5:2; 15:13). This spiritual joy is permanent (John 16:22; Phil. 4:4) and unspeakable (1 Pet. 1:8).

BIBLIOGRAPHY: J. B. Payne, *Theology of the Older Testament* (1962), pp. 417-19; W. Morrice, *Joy in the New Testament* (1984).

JOZ'ABAD (joz'a-bad; contraction of Jehozabad, "Jehovah endowed").

1. An inhabitant of Gederah, and one of the famous Benjamite archers who came to David at Ziklag (1 Chron. 12:4; "Josabad," KJV), before 1000 B.C.

2, 3. Two of the "captains" of Manasseh having this name who joined David when retreating to Ziklag (1 Chron. 12:20), before 1000 B.C.

4. One of the subordinate overseers, under Colnaniah and Shimei, who had charge of the contributions, tithes, and consecrated gifts in the time of Hezekiah. He was probably a Levite (2 Chron. 31:13), about 719 B.C.

5. One of the Levite officers who contributed offerings at the renewal of the Passover by Josiah (2 Chron. 35:9), about 621 B.C.

6. A Levite, the son of Jeshua, employed with others by Ezra to weigh the silver and gold and vessels brought from Babylon for the sanctuary (Ezra 8:33), about 457 B.C. He is probably the same as the chief Levite who afterward was "in charge of the outside work of the house of God" (Neh. 11:16), 445 B.C.

7. One of the priests, of the "sons" of Pashhur, who put away his Gentile wife after the captivity (Ezra 10:22), 456 B.C.

8. A Levite who also divorced his Gentile wife (Ezra 10:23), 456 B.C. Perhaps identical with no. 9.

9. One of the Levites who assisted Ezra in expounding the law to the people (Neh. 8:7), about 445 B.C.

JOZ'ACAR (joz'a-kar; "Jehovah has remembered"). The son of Shimeath, an Ammonitess, and one of the two servants of Joash, king of Judah, who formed a conspiracy against him and killed him in Millo (2 Kings 12:21; 2 Chron. 24:25-26; in the former passage the KJV term is *Jozachar* and the NIV *Jozabad;* in the latter it is *Zabad* in the KJV and NIV), 839 B.C.

JOZ'ADAK (joz'a-dak; Ezra 3:2, 8; 5:2; 10:18; Neh. 12:26). *See* Jehozadak.

JU'BAL (jū'bal). The second son of Lamech by Adah, a descendant of Cain. He is called "the father of all those who play the lyre and pipe" (Gen. 4:21). According to Josephus (*Ant.* 1.2.2), he "exercised himself in music; and invented the psaltery and the harp."

JUBILEE. *See* Festivals: Septenary Festivals.

JU'CAL (jū'kal). An abbreviated form (Jer. 38:1) of *Jehucal* (which see).

JU'DA (jū'da). An incorrect English form. *See* Judah; Judas; Joda.

JU'DAH (jū'da). The name of the patriarch and fourth son (*see* article below) of Jacob and Leah, and of several other persons in the Bible.

1. A Levite who returned to Jerusalem with Zerubbabel (Neh. 12:8), about 536 B.C. He is perhaps the same person whose sons aided in rebuilding the Temple (Ezra 3:9), although the latter may be the same as Hodaviah (2:40).

2. The son of Hassenuah, a Benjamite, and "second in command of the city" of Jerusalem. Strong (McClintock and Strong, *Cyclopedia* s.v.) maintains that the true translation is "over the second city" and that Judah was prefect over Acra, or the Lower City (Neh. 11:9), 445 B.C.

3. One of those (priest or Levite is not stated) who followed the Jewish princes around the southern portion of the rebuilt wall of Jerusalem (Neh. 12:34), 445 B.C. He is perhaps identical with the musician named in v. 36.

4. The son of Joseph and father of Simeon, listed among the maternal ancestors of Christ (Luke 3:30; "Juda," KJV).

JU'DAH (jū'da; Heb. *Yehûdâ,* "may he," i.e., God, "be praised"; "Judas" in the KJV of Matt. 1:2-3). The patriarch and fourth son of Jacob and Leah, and whole brother to Reuben, Simeon, and Levi, older than himself, and Issachar and Zebulun, who were younger (Gen. 29:35), about 1950 B.C.

Personal History. It was by Judah's advice that his brothers sold Joseph to the Ishmaelites in-

stead of taking his life. By the light of his subsequent conduct we see that his action on this occasion arose from a generous impulse, although the form of the question he put to them suggests an interested motive: "What profit is it for us to kill our brother and cover up his blood? Come and let us sell him" (Gen. 37:26-27).

Moves to Adullam. After the sale of Joseph, Judah moved to Adullam and married the daughter of a Caananite, by whom he had three sons, Er, Onan, and Shelah. Er married a woman whose name was Tamar, but he died childless. Judah then gave Tamar to his second son, Onan, who also died without children. Judah was reluctant to bestow his only surviving son upon this woman and told her to wait until the boy became of marriageable age (38:1-11).

Judah's Sin. Upon learning that Judah was going to Timnah, Tamar disguised herself as a harlot and, sitting along the roadside, met Judah and became pregnant by him. The result was the birth of two sons, Zerah and Perez (38:12-30).

Becomes Leader. Though not the firstborn, Judah "prevailed over his brothers" (1 Chron. 5:2), and we find him subsequently taking a decided lead in all the affairs in the family. When it became necessary to go a second time into Egypt for food, he remonstrated with Jacob for not allowing Benjamin to go with them and agreed to be responsible for his safety (Gen. 43:3-10). When the cup was found in Benjamin's sack and punishment from Joseph seemed imminent, Judah's earnest prayer for his father and brothers and his offer of himself as slave so moved Joseph that he could no longer retain his secret (44:16-34). It was also Judah who was sent by Jacob to smooth the way for him in the land of Goshen (46:28). We hear nothing more of him till he received, along with his brothers, the final blessing of his father (49:8-12).

The Tribe of Judah. When Judah went into Egypt he had three sons, but so greatly did this family increase that at the first census it numbered 74,600, being first in population of all the tribes. At the second census it numbered 76,500, still retaining its rank. Its representative among the spies, and also among those appointed to partition the land, was Caleb the son of Jephunneh (Num. 13:6).

Position. During the march through the desert Judah's place was on the E side of the Tabernacle toward the sunrise, with his kinsmen Issachar and Zebulun (2:3-9; 10:14). According to rabbinical authority, Judah's standard was green, with the symbol of a lion (Keil).

Portion in Canaan. Judah was the first tribe to receive its allotted possessions W of the Jordan, and this territory included fully one-third of the whole land. When the land was again distributed by actual survey, a portion of Judah's land was given to Simeon. The boundaries and contents of the territory allotted to Judah are given at great length (Josh. 15:1-12, 20-63).

Relation to Other Tribes. During the rule of the judges, Judah maintained an independent spirit toward the other tribes; and although they acquiesced in the Benjamite Saul's appointment as king, it could hardly have been with very good grace, as may be inferred from the small contingent they supplied to that monarch's army against Amalek (1 Sam. 15:4).

As a Kingdom. When Judah established David as king and moved the sanctuary to Jerusalem, the Ephraimites were dissatisfied and seized the first opportunity of setting up an independent kingdom. Then the history of Judah as a tribe lapsed into that of Judah as a kingdom. What followed was a varied history of wars, vassalage, and occasional prosperity. Against Judah were arrayed Israel, Egypt, and Syria, and finally the country was ravaged by the king of Babylon. Jerusalem was burned with fire, the holy Temple laid in ashes, the people taken away into captivity. The nation Judah was no more (2 Kings 24-25; Jer. 34-41).

BIBLIOGRAPHY: R. K. Harrison, *A History of Old Testament Times* (1957); L. J. Wood, *A Survey of Israel's History* (1970); J. H. Hayes and J. M. Miller, eds., *Israelite and Judean History* (1977); E. R. Thiele, *Mysterious Numbers of the Hebrew Kings* (1983), pp. 79-192.

KINGDOM OF ISRAEL

JUDAH, KINGDOM OF. *See* History, Old Testament; Judah.

JU'DAS (jū'das; Gk. form, *'Ioudas,* of Heb. *Judah*). In the KJV of Matt. 1:2-3, the term refers to the patriarch *Judah* (which see). More generally, the name refers to the betrayer of Christ, Judas Iscariot (*see* article below) and to five other biblical characters.

1. Judas, mentioned with James, Joseph, and Simon, as a son of Mary and brother of Jesus (Matt. 13:55; Mark 6:3).

2. Judas, surnamed Thaddeus (cf. Matt. 10:3, where his name is given in the KJV as Lebbaeus; Mark 3:18). The Gk. of Luke (6:16) simply designates him "Judas of James," which probably means that he was the son of James, as the NASB and NIV render it (6:16; Acts 1:13), or perhaps the brother of *James the Less* (which see). We find mention of Judas among the twelve apostles (Matt. 10:3; Mark 3:18; Luke 6:16), besides which the only circumstance recorded of him in the gospels consists in the question put by him to our Lord (John 14:22): "Judas (not Iscariot) said to Him, 'Lord, what then has happened that You are going to disclose Yourself to us and not to the world?' " Nor have we any account of his activities after the resurrection, for the traditions respecting him are lacking in authority, associating him with the founding of the church at Edessa.

3. Judas of Galilee, who stirred up a sedition among the Jews soon after the birth of Jesus (Acts 5:37). According to Josephus, he was born in Gamala, and the sedition occurred in A.D. 6. He was destroyed and his followers scattered by Cyrenius, proconsul of Syria and Judea.

4. A Jew who lived in Damascus on the street called Straight, probably the "Street of Bazaars." Ananias went there by direction of God and recovered Saul from his blindness (Acts 9:11). The so-called "House of Judas" is still shown in an open space called "the Sheyk's Place," a few steps out of the Street of Bazaars.

5. Judas, surnamed Barsabbas, a disciple, and one of the deputation sent to confirm the Syrian Christians. The epistle having been read to the church assembled at Antioch, Judas and Silas exercised their prophetical gifts for the confirmation of the believers, after which Judas returned to Jerusalem (Acts 15:22, 27, 32).

JU'DAS ISCAR'IOT (Gk. *'Ioudas,* from Heb. *Judas; 'Iskariotēs,* "inhabitant of Kerioth"). The son of Simon and one of our Lord's twelve apostles.

His Call. We learn nothing of Judas previous to his call (Matt. 10:4; Mark 3:19; Luke 6:16), and yet the appearance of his name in the lists of the apostles would seem to indicate that he had previously declared himself a disciple. It does not seem necessary to speculate upon the motives that influenced Judas to become a disciple, or to attempt a solution of the question why such a man was chosen for the office of an apostle.

As Treasurer. When the twelve became an organized body, traveling, receiving money and other offerings, distributing to the poor, it became necessary that someone should act as steward; we learn that this duty fell to Judas and also that "he was a thief, and as he had the money box, he used to pilfer what was put into it" (John 12:4-6; 13:29).

Treachery Foretold. Some time previous to the betrayal of Jesus "many of His disciples withdrew, and were not walking with Him anymore" (John 6:66), probably influenced by the disappointment of their earthly expectations or fearful of coming evil. In deep sadness of heart Jesus asked His disciples the question, "You do not want to go away also, do you?" Receiving assurance of faithfulness from the disciples through Peter, "Jesus answered them, 'Did I Myself not choose you, the twelve, and yet one of you is a devil?' Now He meant Judas the son of Simon Iscariot, for he, one of the twelve, was going to betray Him" (vv. 67-71). The scene at Bethany, which in John (12:3-9) indicates that it was Judas who protested Mary's use of the costly perfume to anoint Jesus' feet (cf. Matt. 26:6-13; Mark 14:3-9), points to the smallness of spirit that would lead him to betray his Lord.

Betrayal of Jesus. Previous to the feast of the Passover Judas had gone to "the chief priests and officers," agreeing to betray Jesus to them for a sum of money (Matt. 26:14-16; Mark 14:10-11; Luke 22:3-6). He seems to have concealed his treachery, however, for we find him still with the disciples. At the beginning of the Last Supper he was present, his feet were washed, and he heard the fearful words, "You are clean, but not all of you," and the Master's teaching of the meaning of the act (John 13:2-15). Reclining near Jesus, he heard Him tell the disciples, "One of you will betray Me," and he asked with the others, "Surely not I, Lord?" And then, fully given over to Satan, he heard Jesus say to him, "What you do, do quickly." Judas rose from the feast (Matt. 26:20-25; John 13:26-30), and shortly afterward he completed the betrayal. He knew the garden where Jesus and the disciples often went, and he came accompanied by a band of officers and servants, to whom he made known his Master by a kiss (Matt. 26:47-49; Mark 14:43-45; Luke 22:47-48; John 18:1-5). Jesus replied to that kiss with words of stern, sad reproach, "Judas, are you betraying the Son of Man with a kiss?" (Luke 22:48).

Remorse and Death. When Judas saw that Jesus was condemned, he was conscience stricken. Returning to the priests, he confessed his crime and hurled down the money, which they refused to take (Matt. 27:3-5). Feeling, perhaps, that there was for him no restoration, that he was, indeed, "the son of perdition" (John 17:12), "he went away and hanged himself" (Matt. 27:5). He went "to his own place" (Acts 1:16-25).

Between two passages that describe these events (Matt. 27:5; Acts 1:16-25) there appears at first sight a discrepancy. In Matthew it is stated "he threw the pieces of silver into the sanctuary and departed; and he went away and hanged himself." In Acts (chap. 1) another account is given. There it is stated: (1) that instead of throwing the money into the Temple he bought a field with it; (2) that instead of hanging himself, "falling headlong, he burst open in the middle and all his bowels gushed out"; (3) that for this reason, and not because the priests had bought it with the price of blood, the field was called "Hakeldama . . . Field of Blood." The fact would seem to be that Judas hanged himself, probably with his girdle or belt, which either broke or became untied, and threw him heavily forward upon the jagged rocks below, thus inflicting the wound mentioned by Peter in the Acts. The apparent discrepancy in the two accounts as to the disposition of the money may be thus explained: "It was not lawful to take into the temple treasury, for the purchase of sacred things, money that had been unlawfully gained. In such case the Jewish law provided that the money was to be restored to the donor, and, if he insisted on giving it that he should be induced to spend it for something for the public weal. By a fiction of law the money was still considered to be Judas's, and to have been applied by him in the purchase of the well-known 'potter's field' " (Edersheim, *Life and Times of Jesus the Messiah,* 2:575).

Character. The strongest element in the character of Judas was doubtless avarice, and there is no vice at once so absorbing, so unreasonable, and so degrading as the vice of avarice. The disappointment of every expectation that had first drawn him to Jesus, the intolerable rebuke of that sinless life, and, lastly, the sight of Mary's lavish sacrifice, which brought no gain to himself, increased his alienation, so that Judas became capable of the deed that has given his name an everlasting stain.

BIBLIOGRAPHY: S. Cox, *The Expositor* (1896), 1:331-63; C. E. Macartney, *The Wisest Fool and Other Men of the Bible* (1949), pp. 180-91; E. F. Harrison, *Meditations on the Gospel of John* (1949), pp. 175-91; C. J. Barber, *Searching for Identity* (1975), pp. 96-107.

JUDE. The "brother of James" (Jude 1) and the author of the last of the general epistles, usually identified with the Judas who was the half brother of Jesus or with the Judas who was surnamed Thaddeus (but see the discussion below of the epistle of Jude, under "Authorship").

JUDE, EPISTLE OF. One of the general letters dealing primarily with false teachers (Jude 4-6) and in this respect resembling 2 Peter. Jude expresses affectionate solicitude for the Christians (1-3, 20-25) and urges them to contend "for the faith which was once for all delivered to the saints." His language is extremely stern toward heretics. He denounces and threatens them rather than refuting them. Although the epistle deals with conditions that were incipient in the writer's time, nevertheless the scope of the book comprehends conditions at the end of the age and so has a suitable place before the book of Revelation.

Authorship. According to the testimony of the book itself, it was written by "Jude, a bond-servant of Jesus Christ, and brother of James" (v. 1). Since James was one of the brothers of Jesus, Jude was likewise one of His brothers. Matthew 13:55 and Mark 6:3 ("Judas" in both places in the NIV) indicate that Jesus had a brother by that name. Six other Judes or Judases are referred to in the NT, but the writer of this epistle is not to be confused with any of them. He differentiated himself from others of the same name by the mention of his brother, rather than his father. The reason for this is that his brother was much better known among his readers. Jude was not an apostle, as indicated by the omission of the apostolic title. Almost nothing is known about the life of Jude. He was apparently convinced of the deity of Christ after the resurrection.

Authenticity. Hermas, Polycarp, Athenagoras, Theophilus of Antioch, Tertullian, Clement of Alexandria, and Eusebius give early attestation to the authority of the book. Jude is more strongly attested than 2 Peter. This is somewhat astonishing when one considers its lack of apostolic authorship, its shortness, its polemic character, and its alleged reference to apocryphal literature. Clement of Alexandria, Tertullian, Augustine, Jerome, and other church Fathers maintained that Jude actually made reference to the Apocrypha. For this reason many early Fathers rejected it as authentic. Verse 9 was thought to have been a quotation from the Assumption of Moses and vv. 14-15 were supposed to be taken from the book of Enoch. It is possible that Jude quoted a passage from a known uncanonical book, not by way of endorsement, but because he used this particular statement as divinely given.

Background. The general character of the epistle does not permit a certain determination of the locality of its composition or its destination. It may be that the letter was intended for the same people as those to whom James addressed his letter.

Occasion and Date. The inroads of apostasy and heretical doctrine stirred up the author to write and to warn the faithful Christians against this danger. The author cites important examples of defection in the OT and their result, notably the defection of the Israelites when they came up out of Egypt; defection among angelic beings, evidently in connection with the Flood (v. 6); and the apostasy of Sodom and Gomorrah. Jude gives an eloquent and impassioned polemic against the apostate teachers (vv. 8-19). He concludes his epistle with comfort to Christians by reminding them of their first duty. The date is undetermina-

ble; any time from A.D. 66 to A.D. 75-80 could be possible. It is commonly dated around A.D. 75 by Zahn and others.

Outline.
  I. Introduction (1-2)
 II. The occasion of the letter: Apostasy (3-4)
III. Historical examples of apostasy (5-7)
      A. Of Israel (5)
      B. Of angelic beings (6)
      C. Of Sodom and Gomorrah (7)
 IV. Description of false teachers (8-13)
  V. Authoritative declarations of God's judgment of the wicked (14-19)
 VI. Encouragement of true believers and their full duty to Christ (20-23)
      A. Edification and prayer in the Holy Spirit (20)
      B. Preservation in the love of God and expectation of divine mercy (21)
      C. Exhortation to soul-winning (22-23)
VII. Conclusion: Benediction (24-25)   M.F.U.

BIBLIOGRAPHY: C. Bigg, *A Critical and Exegetical Commentary on the Epistles of St. Peter and St. Jude*, International Critical Commentary (1961); E. M. B. Green, *Second Epistle General of Peter and the General Epistle of Jude*, Tyndale New Testament Commentaries (1968); J. N. D. Kelly, *A Commentary on the Epistles of Peter and Jude*, Harper New Testament Commentaries (1969); G. L. Lawlor, *Translation and Exposition of the Epistle of Jude* (1972); F. A. Tatford, *Jude's Apostates* (1975); W. Jenkyn, *An Exposition upon the Epistle of Jude* (1976); T. Manton, *An Exposition of the Epistle of Jude* (1978); J. B. Mayor, *The Epistle of St. Jude and 2 Peter* (1978); J. F. MacArthur, Jr., *Beware the Pretenders* (1979).

JUDE'A (jū-dī'a). The name of the southernmost Roman division of Palestine. Judea is very small, for if you include the whole maritime plain and the desert, it does not amount to more than 2,000 square miles. But it never included the whole of the plain. Apart from the Shephelah and the plain, Judea was 55 miles long, from Bethlehem to Beersheba, and from 25 to 30 miles broad, about 1,350 square miles, of which nearly one-half was desert. On the E was the Jordan and its valley, and coming W, the desert, then the "hill country," then the Shephelah (or low hills), and, finally, the maritime plain. On the N Judea was bounded by Samaria and on the S by the desert.

The wilderness of Judea extends from the beach of the Dead Sea to the very edge of the central plateau (or hill country), thus obliging travelers from the E to journey from five to eight hours through a waterless desert. Three well-watered spots are on its eastern edge, Jericho, 'Ain Feshka (10 miles to the S), and 'Ain Jidi (or Engedi, 18 miles farther). Three roads into Judea begin at Jericho; another road into Judea begins at 'Ain Feshka; and still another begins at Engedi. The roads from Jericho run NW to Ai and Bethel, SW to Jerusalem, and SSW to the lower Kidron and Bethlehem. Just after this last road crosses the Kidron it is joined by the road from 'Ain Feshka. The road from Engedi breaks into two branches, one running NW to Bethlehem and Jerusalem, a wild and difficult road never used by caravans, the other branch turning SW to Yuttah and Hebron.

Smith (*Hist. Geog.*, p. 310) says that the three features of Judea's geography that are most significant in her history are "her pastoral character, her neighborhood to the desert, her singular unsuitableness for the growth of a great city." Two, at least, of the prophets were born in the face of the wilderness of Judea—Amos at Tekoa, and Jeremiah at Anathoth. The wilderness was the scene of David's refuge from Saul; here John the Baptist prepared for his mission; and here our Lord suffered His temptation.

Although physically the most barren and awkward, Judea was morally the most famous and powerful of the provinces of Syria. Her character and history are thus summed up: "At all times in which the powers of spiritual initiative or expansion were needed, she was lacking, and so in the end came her shame. But when the times required concentration, indifference to the world, loyalty to the past, and passionate patriotism, then Judea took the lead, or stood alone in Israel, and these virtues even rendered brilliant the hopeless, insane struggles of her end. Judea was the seat of the one enduring dynasty of Israel, the

site of their temple, the platform of their chief prophets. After their great exile they rallied round her capital, and centuries later they expended upon her fortresses the last efforts of their freedom. It is, therefore, not wonderful that they should have won from it the name which is now more frequent than either their ancestral designation of Hebrews or their sacred title of Israel" (Smith, *Hist. Geog.*, pp. 259-60).

JUDGE. For judge in the general sense of magistrate, *see* Law, Administration of.

JUDGES. There is a restricted sense of the word *judge*, in which it refers to that person who presided over the affairs of the Hebrews in the period between Joshua and the accession of Saul.

Age of the Judges. "In those days there was no king in Israel; every man did what was right in his own eyes" (Judg. 17:6; 18:1; 19:1; 21:25). This sentence, frequently and earnestly repeated, gives us the keynote of the whole book of Judges. Each tribe took thought for itself how best to secure and maintain an adequate territory, so that separate interests of all sorts soon became prevalent and regard for the general welfare was more and more forgotten. This separation of the parts of the nation was aided by the early disunion and jealousies of the several tribes, no one of which held preeminence. The consequences of this internal discord were so threatening that it

The hills of Judea

became a grave question whether the nation would be able to hold even the soil on which its peculiar religion and culture were to attain their full development. Then, too, the ancient inhabitants still retained their hold on large tracts or on important positions throughout the country. The neighboring powers still looked upon the newcomers as an easy prey to incursion and devastation, if not to actual subjugation. Nor did Israel escape the pernicious influence of idolatry, both of Canaan and the surrounding countries. The following is a review of the period of the judges: The children of Israel did evil against Jehovah, though He had manifested special favor to them; He therefore sold them into the hand of various enemies; they then cried to Him in their trouble; He raised up a deliverer who saved them; the land had a period of rest; again the people sinned; and the same cycle was repeated.

The Judges. Under the circumstances mentioned above the people were left an easy prey to idolatrous influences. They seemed incapable of grasping the idea of a divine and invisible King; therefore God allowed them judges who acted, for the most part, as agents of the divine will, regents of the invisible King, holding their commission directly from Him or with His sanction. They would thus be more inclined to act as dependent vassals of Jehovah than as kings, who would naturally have notions of independent rights and royal privileges. In this greater dependence of the judges upon the divine King we see the secret of their institution. As to the nature of the office, it appears to have resembled that of the Roman dictator, to which it has been compared, with this exception, that the dictator laid down his power as soon as the crisis that had called for its exercise had passed away; but the Hebrew judge remained invested with his high authority throughout his life (1 Sam. 4:18; 7:15). Sometimes these judges commenced their career with military exploits, but this was not always the case. Eli and Samuel were not military men; Deborah judged Israel before she planned the war against Jabin; and of Jair, Ibzan, Elon, and Abdon, it is at least uncertain whether they ever held any military command. The origin of their authority must in all cases be traced ultimately to Jehovah, owing to the very nature of the theocracy, yet this did not prevent differences of detail in the manner of their appointment. In Judg. 2:16 it is distinctly stated that "the Lord *raised up* judges" (italics added; cf. 3:10; 6:34; 11:29; 13:25). One, Barak, was named by the prophetess Deborah, who was herself acknowledged as a judge of Israel (4:5-6). Of others it is simply said that they *arose* (10:1, 3), although Jephthah furnishes a clear instance of *popular election* (10:18; 11:5-6).

Name and Function. The name in Heb. is the participle of *shāpaṭ,* "to judge, pronounce" judgment. The judges were men (excepting Deborah)

who procured justice or right for the people of Israel, not only by delivering them from the power of their enemies but also by administering the laws and rites of the Lord (Judg. 2:16-19). *Judging* in this sense was different from the administration of civil jurisprudence and included the idea of government such as would be expected from a king (*see* 1 Sam. 8:5-6; 2 Kings 15:5). Alongside the extraordinary rule of the judges, the ordinary administration of justice and government of the commonwealth still remained in the hands of the heads of the tribes and the elders of the people.

Chronology of the Period. The following are the data of this period as we find them in the book of Judges:

	Event or Period	Years
1.	Oppression by Cushan-rishathaim (3:8)	8
	Deliverance by Othniel and period of rest (3:9-12)	40
2.	Oppression by the Moabites (3:14)	18
	Deliverance by Ehud and period of rest (3:15-30)	80
	Shamgar as judge (3:31)	
3.	Oppression by King Jabin (4:2-3)	20
	Deliverance by Deborah and Barak and period of rest (4:4-5:31)	40
4.	Oppression by the Midianites (6:1-7)	7
	Deliverance by Gideon and period of rest (6:8-8:28)	40
	Abimelech's reign (9:22)	3
	Tola, judge (10:1-52)	23
	Jair, judge (10:3)	22
5.	Oppression by the Amorites (10:7-8)	18
	Deliverance by Jephthah, judge (11:1-12:7)	6
	Ibzan, judge (12:8-10)	7
	Elon, judge (12:11-12)	10
	Abdon, judge (12:13-15)	8
6.	Oppression by the Philistines (13:1)	40
	Samson judged Israel during this period (15:20; 16:31) twenty years	
	Total	390
	If we add to this:	
(a)	The time of Joshua, not distinctly mentioned	20
(b)	The time of Eli, judge (1 Sam. 4:18)	40
		450
	And adding still further:	
(c)	The times of Samuel and Saul combined	40
(d)	The reign of David (2 Sam. 5:4; 1 Kings 2:11)	40
(e)	The reign of Solomon to the building of the Temple (1 Kings 6:1)	3
	The whole time from the entrance of Israel into Canaan to the building of the Temple	533
	Add forty years for wandering in the desert, and we have	573

But according to 1 Kings 6:1, the Temple was built in the 480th year after the Israelites left Egypt. The apostle Paul says: "And after these things He gave them judges until Samuel the prophet" (Acts 13:20). There can be but little doubt that some of the rulers were contemporaneous, which would greatly reduce the length of the period. *See* Chronology, History, Old Testament.

BIBLIOGRAPHY: Y. Kaufmann, *Biblical Account of the Conquest of Palestine* (1953); R. de Vaux, *Ancient Israel: Its Life and Institutions* (1961), pp. 143-63; N. Gottwald, *The Tribes of Yahweh* (1979); L. H. Wiseman, *Practical Truths from Judges* (1985).

JUDGES, BOOK OF. The book of the OT that carries on the history of God's chosen people through the era intervening from the death of Joshua (c. 1375 B.C.) to the era of Samuel (c. 1075 B.C.), a period of roughly three centuries.

Purpose. The book of Judges aims to demonstrate that defection from Jehovah incurs severe punishment and servitude. Only by turning back to God can restoration be enjoyed. Thus the judges were charismatic leaders, raised up by God to deliver His theocratic people. Only by heeding their Spirit-directed message and following them in deliverance against their enemies could restoration be accomplished. The OT judges performed two functions. By divine power and Spirit-anointed leadership they delivered the people from enemy oppression. Having accomplished this, they ruled over them and administered government in the name of Israel's God. In their governmental capacity they correspond roughly to the *shufetim* of Phoenicia and the *sufetes* of Carthage, who were akin to the Roman consuls. (*See* Zellig Harris, *A Grammar of Phoenician Language* [1936].) The events illustrating the spiritual principle of restoration upon repentance are selective. Often they are coeval rather than chronological in sequence. Evidently long periods are passed over without comment. Quite a few of the judges are mentioned by name only, without any word about their particular deliverance. Since the book reports seven apostasies, seven servitudes to seven heathen nations, and seven deliverances, it is evidently put in a symmetrical form. A parallel in church history is found in the professing church since the apostolic age, in which the rise of numerous sects and the forfeited sense of the unity of the Spirit and of one body appear.

Critical View of Literary Composition and Date. The prevailing literary view of Judges, though not intimately connected with Pentateuchal criticism, is built on many of the same fallacies. It construes the book of Judges as a collection of old hero tales that were taken from two chief sources labeled J and E. These two documentary strata were supposed to have been fused in the latter half of the seventh century B.C. into one with a few small additions, such as the minor judges, to form substantially the present book (10:1-5; 12:8-15). A Deuteronomist somewhat later supposedly gave a pragmatic religious interpretation to the whole that, according to Julius Bewer (*The Literature of the O.T.* [1933], p. 230) was "distorted and wrong" from "an historical point of view." It is also maintained that the book did not attain its precise present form until around 200 B.C.

Conservative View of Literary Composition and Date. The evidence of the book itself coupled with tradition indicates that it was written sometime during the early years of the Hebrew monarchy, probably in the era of Saul, around 1020 B.C. Samuel, as a member of the prophetic school, may well have been the author-compiler. This is supported by the following evidence: (1) The author was undoubtedly a compiler to a large extent. This is necessitated by the simple consideration that the events extended over several centuries. The compiler, for example, selected the prose account of the deliverance of Deborah in chap. 4, and the early poem The Song of Deborah, in chap. 5. More prominence was accorded the stories of Gideon and Samson. This is evidently explained by their high didactic value. (2) The book displays the unity of one author-editor. Its symmetrical development and unified plan are the result of the early influence of the book of Deuteronomy as a genuine Mosaic composition. In this important book, blessing in Canaan is promised on the terms of obedience to the divine law, and punishment is threatened upon the breaking of it (Deut. 28:1-68). Critics who reject the Mosaic authenticity of Deuteronomy explain this intense pragmatic interpretation as the work of a so-called Deuteronomistic Work of History (cf. Aage Bentzen, *Introduction to the O.T.,* 2:87), but this is the result of an unsound assumption and a false view of the date and genuineness of the book of Deuteronomy. (3) The book evidently belongs to the period of Saul (cf. the statement in Judg. 1:21 that "the Jebusites have lived with the sons of Benjamin in Jerusalem to this day." This notice could not have been penned after David's conquest of Zion in the seventh year of his reign (c. 996 B.C.; 2 Sam. 5:6-8). The statement "in those days there was no king in Israel" (Judg. 17:6; 18:1; 19:1; 21:25) points to the early period of the monarchy. (4) Hebrew tradition names Samuel as the author. The internal evidence and Hebrew tradition lend their voice to a position that is defended by many Christian conservative scholars.

Outline.

I. Introduction to the period (1:1–2:5)
   A. Political conditions (1:1-36)
   B. Religious conditions (2:1-5)
II. The period of the judges (2:6–16:31)
   A. Religious condition of the entire period (2:6–3:6)
   B. The judges (3:7–16:31)
     1. Othniel (3:7-11)
     2. Ehud (3:12-30)
     3. Shamgar (3:31)
     4. Deborah and Barak (4:1–5:31)
     5. Gideon and Abimelech (6:1–9:57)
     6. Tola (10:1-2)
     7. Jair (10:3-5)
     8. Jephthah (10:6–12:7)
     9. Ibzan (12:8-10)
     10. Elon (12:11-12)
     11. Abdon (12:13-15)
     12. Samson (13:1–16:31)
III. The double appendix (17:1–21:25)
   A. The idolatry of Micah and the Danites (17:1–18:31)
   B. The crime at Gibeah and its punishment (19:1–21:25)　　　　　M.F.U.

BIBLIOGRAPHY: C. F. Burney, *The Book of Judges* (1930); C. A. Simpson, *Composition of the Book of Judges* (1957); A. E. Cundall and L. L. Morris, *Judges and*

Ruth, Tyndale Old Testament Commentaries (1967); R. K. Harrison, *Introduction to the Old Testament* (1969), pp. 680-94; A. D. H. Mayes, *Israel in the Period of the Judges* (1974); R. G. Boling, *Judges,* Anchor Bible (1975); L. J. Wood, *Distressing Days of the Judges* (1975); G. Bush, *Notes on Judges* (1976); A. R. Fausset, *A Critical Commentary on the Book of Judges* (1977); J. Garstang, *Joshua-Judges: The Foundations of Bible History* (1978).

JUDGMENT. In this article we treat of judgment: (1) right of private; (2) judgments of men; (3) judgments of God; and (4) judgment, the final.

Judgment, Right of Private. Important considerations regarding the right of private judgment are (1) the Protestant-Catholic split; (2) the position held within Protestant denominations; and (3) the obligation a private citizen has to the state.

Protestant-Catholic Split. The right of individuals to interpret the Scriptures for themselves or to form their own judgments as to the meaning of the Scriptures is an issue principally between Roman Catholics and Protestants. It is asserted by the Roman Catholic church that the church is the divinely authorized and infallible interpreter of Scripture revelation. It is admitted that many questions of details in connection with the study of the Bible should be left to scientific research. But still it is held that in all controversies with respect to the meaning of particular passages, as well as to the general doctrine of the Scriptures, the decision of the church is final. The only course that is safe or right for the people is to submit unreservedly to the judgment of the church.

In opposition to this Protestants generally hold that the Bible is a book for the people. It is God's message to be received and read and, in its great general meaning, to be apprehended directly by the people themselves. The prophets of the OT spoke to the people. The gospels and the epistles were for popular use and instruction. And while parts of Holy Scripture are difficult or impossible to understand without skilled interpretation, still the truth essential to salvation is within the reach of all. Christ has not appointed any class or body of men in the church as interpreters of the Scriptures in any such sense as to make their interpretation final or supreme before the conscience and intelligence of the people. The responsibility for religious faith and conduct belongs to the individual. One does not have the obligation to submit blindly in these respects to the guidance of others. It is to be maintained, however, that everyone is bound to exercise diligence and to use all proper means for the right understanding of moral truth, to pay respect to the judgment of those wiser than oneself, and especially to pay heed to those interpretations of the Scriptures that have generally prevailed or have been universal in the history of the Christian church.

Private Judgment in Churches not Professing Infallibility. The claim of the church of Rome to infallibility covers not only the interpretation of Scripture but other matters resting professedly upon tradition, with respect to which the church has rendered formal decision. Protestants meet this twofold assumption with their historic watchword "The Bible the only and sufficient rule of faith and practice." And yet the extent to which private judgment may be rightfully exercised in Protestant churches is a question by no means settled. At the one extreme are those who hold that the church should present very few, if any, doctrinal tests of membership; reliance should be placed upon vigorous Christian institutions as most likely to lead to a real and general Christian belief. This is the view of the Broad church party in the Church of England and others of so-called liberal tendencies. At the other extreme are those who would impose upon the membership of Protestant churches not only a detailed system of doctrine but also ethical regulations that are not supported by the Scriptures. With this is strictly asserted the obligation of membership in these churches. The more moderate position holds that churches for their very existence must have a basis of general doctrine that rests unmistakably upon the Scriptures and must prescribe a line of conduct resting upon the same authority. The difficulties, both theoretical and practical, grow out of a lack of proper conception of the church and of the churches. For discussion of this we refer to the article in this work, Church.

Liberty of Private Judgment in Relation to the State. Civil government is clearly recognized by the Scriptures as resting upon divine authority. Obedience to the state may therefore be said, in general terms, to be a divine requirement (*see* Rom. 13:1-7; 1 Pet. 2:13-15). But it is equally clear that in order to justly exact obedience from citizens or subjects the state must confine its action within its proper sphere. The function of the state is to protect life and property and to preserve social order. When civil government attempts to enforce assent to religious doctrines or to enact laws that require disobedience to the commandments of God, then the right of private judgment must be asserted. "We must obey God rather than men." There are other cases, into which we cannot here enter, in which a perversion or abuse of civil power must be met by the exercise of individual conscience. This is a principle, nevertheless, that in a free and popular government needs to be carefully guarded. For discussion of this point, see Hodge, *Systematic Theology,* 3:356-60; Lieber, *Political Ethics.*

Judgments of Men. The Scriptures recognize it to be necessary that, under proper limitations, men should form and express judgments relative to their fellowmen.

There is the necessity of private, unofficial

judgment. We must constantly form estimates of the conduct and character of others for our own guidance and safety and usefulness. "You will know them by their fruits." The prohibition of judging in Matt. 7:1 is not opposed to this, as can be seen in vv. 6-7 of the same chapter. We are forbidden to usurp God's place as judge, or to pass rash and unjust and uncharitable and needless judgments.

It is also necessary that men should judge officially. Human government is divinely authorized. And the exercise of judicial functions is essential to all government. All judges, however, are to remember that they are subject to the judgment of God, and to exercise their office equitably and with due moderation. (*See* Rom. 13:1-5; 1 Pet. 2:13-15.)

BIBLIOGRAPHY: L. L. Morris, *The Biblical Doctrine of Judgment* (1960); W. Förster, *Palestinian Judaism in New Testament Times* (1964).

JUDGMENTS. Theologians have often maintained that there is one general judgment. This is a tenet strongly entrenched in Christian theology. But a careful inductive study of all the Scriptures involved demonstrates that there are at least eight distinct judgments described in the Bible.

The Judgment of the Cross. This is the judgment upon sin effected by Christ when He said, "It is finished" (John 19:30). It is the basis of the believer's salvation when he believes. Christ has borne the sinner's guilt and in Him, as a substitute for all on behalf of whom He died, sin has been judged. The one who believes on Christ has been released from judgment, and "there is therefore now no condemnation" (John 5:24; Rom. 8:1; Gal. 3:13; Heb. 9:26-28; 1 Pet. 2:24).

The Judgment of Believers. This takes the form of divine correction and chastisement (1 Cor. 11:30-32; Heb. 12:3-13; John 15:1-9). The apostle Paul says: "But if we judged ourselves rightly, we should not be judged. But when we are judged, we are disciplined by the Lord in order that we may not be condemned along with the world" (1 Cor. 11:31-32). This, then, involves God's disciplinary action against a sinning saint. "The sin leading to death" (1 John 5:16; cf. 1 Cor. 5:1-5; Acts 5:1-11) occurs when the believer, through deliberate continued sin, brings reproach upon the name of Christ and upon his salvation by free grace, and forfeits his physical life "that his spirit may be saved in the day of the Lord Jesus."

The Believer's Works. This judgment concerns only Christians, and it is not a matter of judgment for sins that have been judged at the cross and with which the believer will not again be faced (John 5:24; Rom. 8:1); it involves instead the divine appraisal of the Christian's works and service. This will entail reward or loss of reward

(2 Cor. 5:10; Rom. 14:10, 12; Eph. 6:8; 2 Tim. 4:8). *See* Judgment Seat of Christ.

The Judgment of Self. This is referred to in 1 Cor. 11:31-32. It has reference to stern criticism of a Christian of his own ways with accommodation to the divine will and immediate confession of and turning away from all sin (1 John 1:7-9). True confession is equivalent to self-judgment and involves immediate cleansing and restoration to fellowship and walking "in the light."

Judgment of the Nations. This judgment is referred to in Matt. 25:31-46. It involves divine dealing with the nations on the basis of their treatment of Israel. The "goat" nations on the left hand involve those peoples who are sent to the lake of fire. The "sheep" nations on the right hand enter the millennial kingdom. The peculiar basis of this judgment is the way all nations have dealt with Israel during the Tribulation period preceding the second advent of Christ. OT prophecy is clear in its prediction that some Gentile nations will enter the coming kingdom of Israel (cf. Isa. 60:3; 61:6; 62:2). These nations will be subordinate to Israel. As the millennial state merges into the eternal state, Gentile nations are still asserted to be on the earth when the heavenly Jerusalem descends from heaven (Rev. 21:24, 26).

The Judgment of Israel. Ezekiel 20:33-44 clearly teachs that Israel must come into judgment before being restored in the millennial kingdom. This OT teaching has confirmation in the NT from the parable of the ten virgins (Matt. 25:1-13 (*see* Joel 3:11-15). Prophecy seems to teach that there will be a general resurrection of all truly regenerated Israelites of the past dispensation to be judged. Those who had a kingdom hope are to arise and enter the earthly glory (cf. Ezek. 37:1-14; Dan. 12:1-3).

The Judgment of Angels. These are fallen angels and are evidently judged in connection with the great white throne (1 Cor. 6:3; 2 Pet. 2:4; Jude 1:6).

The White Throne Judgment. This last great judgment comprehends the judgment of all unsaved of all ages (Rev. 20:11-15). The basis will be works, which evidently suggests differences and degrees of punishment. All who are not found in "the book of life" are cast into "the lake of fire." This is called "the second death," which means final and complete cutting off from God's presence and a sin-cleansed universe.

For theologians who object to these various judgments, a simple choice must be made between following traditional theology or the plain teachings of the Scripture inductively formulated. The author considers that the doctrine of a general judgment is incompatible with inductive logic in handling the Scriptures.   M.F.U.

JUDGMENT HALL (Gk. *praitorion*, "headquarters" in a Roman camp; the palace of a governor). *See* Praetorium.

JUDGMENT SEAT (Gk. *bēma*, a "step"). A raised place mounted by steps; used of the official seat of a judge (Matt. 27:19; John 19:13; Acts 18:12, 16-17; 25:6, "seat on the tribunal"); of the judgment seat of God (Rom. 14:10); Christ (2 Cor. 5:10); and of the structure, resembling a throne, that Herod built in the theater of Caesarea, from which he used to view the games and make speeches to the people (Acts 12:21, marg.).

BIBLIOGRAPHY: A. N. Sherwin-White, *Roman Society and Roman Law in the New Testament* (1965), pp. 24-27.

JUDGMENT SEAT OF CHRIST. This judgment is spoken of in 2 Cor. 5:10: "For we must all appear before the judgment seat of Christ, that each one may be recompensed for his deeds in the body, according to what he has done, whether good or bad." The manifestation of the believer's works is in question in this judgment. It is most emphatically not a judgment of the believer's sins. These have been fully atoned for in the vicarious and substitutionary death of Christ, and remembered no more (Heb. 10:17). It is quite necessary, however, that the service of every child of God be definitely scrutinized and evaluated (Matt. 12:36; Rom. 14:10; Gal. 6:7; Eph. 6:8; Col. 3:24-25). As a result of this judgment of the believer's works, there will be reward or loss of reward. In any event, the truly born-again believer will be saved (1 Cor. 3:11-15). The judgment seat, literally *bēma,* evidently is set up in heaven previous to Christ's glorious second advent to establish His earth rule in the millennial kingdom (Matt. 16:27; 2 Tim. 4:8; Rev. 22:12). The out-taking of the church, according to 1 Thess. 4:13-18; 1 Cor. 15:51-58, must first be fulfilled. The judgment seat of Christ is necessary for the appointment of places of rulership and authority with Christ in His role of "King of kings and Lord of lords" at His revelation in power and glory.

M.F.U.

JUDGMENTS OF GOD. *See* Judgment.

JU'DITH (jū'dith; "Jewess"). The daughter of Beeri, the Hittite, and one of Esau's two wives (Gen. 26:34). She is elsewhere called *Oholibamah* (which see; in the KJV her name is given as Aholibamah).

BIBLIOGRAPHY: M. S. Enslin and S. Zeitlin, *The Book of Judith* (1972).

JUG (Heb. *ṣappaḥat; nēbel; nō'd*). In the NASB and NIV "jug" replaces KJV "cruse" in 1 Sam. 26:11-12,16 and in the NASB "jug" replaces "bottle" in 1 Sam. 1:24; 10:3; 16:20; 25:18; Jer. 13:12. The NIV renders "skin" in 1 Sam. 1:24; 10:3; 16:20; and 25:18; and "wineskin" in Jer. 13:12. *See also* Bottle; Cruse.

JU'LIA (jū'li-a; feminine of "Julius"). A female

disciple at Rome to whom Paul sent salutations (Rom. 16:15).

JU'LIUS (jū'li-us). The centurion who conducted Paul to Rome. At Sidon he allowed Paul to visit his friends and treated him courteously throughout the voyage (Acts 27:1, 3, 43), A.D. 62.

JU'NIA, JU'NIAS (jū'ni-a; jū'ni-as).

Junias. A Christian at Rome to whom Paul sent a salutation in connection with Andronicus as "my kinsmen, and my fellow prisoners, who are outstanding among the apostles, who also were in Christ before" himself (Rom. 16:7), A.D. 60. From his calling them kinsmen it is supposed that they were of Jewish extraction.

JUNIPER. *See* Vegetable Kingdom: Juniper.

JU'PITER. *See* Gods, False: Zeus.

JU'SHAB-HE'SED (ju'shab-he'sed; "returner of kindness"). According to some, the son of Pedaiah (1 Chron. 3:20); but according to Keil (*Com.,* ad loc.), the last named of the sons of Zerubbabel. Keil thinks that the two groups of sons (vv. 19-20) are mentioned separately because they had different mothers.

JUSTICE, IN ETHICS. A term referring both to disposition and to conduct. For various Heb. and Gk. words rendered justice or righteousness in the Scriptures, we refer to Young's or Strong's concordance. The Lat. word *"iustitia"* is defined by Cicero as *"animi affectio suum cuique tribuens"* (*De Finibus* 5.23.65). This definition he expands elsewhere so as to have justice include religion, filial affection, fidelity, lenity in moderating punishment, and kindly benevolence (*Partitiones Orat.* 22.78). Thus the term is used in a general sense for "what is right, or as it should be." The NT conception of justice thoroughly accords with this. Justice is not only respect for the rights of one's fellowmen, as of life, property, and reputation; in the broadest sense it includes the proper recognition of man's duty toward God. It begins with that (*see* Matt. 22:21, 37-38, and many other places). With respect to man's relation to man, it includes several details often forgotten as items of justice. Thus charity or love is an obligation of righteousness (Rom. 13:8), and respect for human nature is enjoined in the precept "Honor all men" (1 Pet. 2:17). Thus also is courtesy and hospitality (3:8-9; 4:9). In short, man in his relation to man is to reflect the justice or righteousness of God; with the exception, considered below, that man, as an individual, is not to administer retributive justice. The public administration is a most important part of social ethics and, as just noted, entirely distinct from the ethics of individual life. Here it is to be borne in mind that in human courts where just laws are properly administered, they are reflections, at least, of the distributive justice, that is, of divine justice (*see* Judgments of Men). The judicial function of the state, must, however, be confined within its proper limits, taking cognizance of only external conduct, and this so far as it relates to the protection of life, property, reputation, and social order. And yet justice is not to be administered merely upon grounds of social expediency but because it is justice (*see* Punishment).

E.MCC.

JUSTICE OF GOD (Heb. *ṣedeq*, "right, rightness"). In theology, as in the Scriptures, the terms justice and righteousness are used synonymously. The justice of God is both an essential and a relative attribute of the divine existence. It is a necessary outflow from the holiness of God. It is that in positive form that is negatively described as holiness, or separateness from evil. And, further, it is the holiness of God as manifested and applied in moral government. *See* Holiness of God.

The justice or righteousness of God is proclaimed emphatically in the Scriptures of the OT and NT (e.g., Gen. 18:25; Ps. 11:7; John 17:25; Heb. 6:10). In accordance with the Scripture, divine justice, i.e., perfect justice, is everywhere in the divine administration. God is the righteous Governor of the world. His laws are equitable and practicable. This is legislative or rectoral justice. God is also the righteous Judge. The sentences He pronounces, the rewards He bestows, and the penalties He inflicts are all righteous. This is the judicial or distributive justice (*see* Deut. 32:3-4; Pss. 19:7-10; 36:6; 97:2; 119:142; Isa. 33:22; Acts 10:34; Rom. 2:11; Rev. 15:3; 16:7; et al.).

The relation of the justice to the grace of God cannot be considered here fully. It should be remarked, however, that the revelation of His highest grace in Christ was "to demonstrate His righteousness" (Rom. 3:25-26; *see* Grace; Atonement). Also, the rewards graciously apportioned to the eternally saved vary in measure and have respect to the individual character and deeds of those who receive them. The righteousness or justice of God, also like His holiness, is communicable to men. It is the work of divine grace to impart to men rightness by renewal "in righteousness and holiness of truth" (Eph. 4:23, 24; Isa. 46:13; 51:5; 56:1; Rom. 10:3). *See* Image of God.

There is no warrant for the statement that the OT magnifies the justice of God more than does the New. The NT brings to light most distinctly the economy of grace, but by no means has it been lost sight of in the Old. But, at the same time, it reveals most fully the triumph of the righteous kingdom of God, culminating in the final judgment.

E.MCC.

JUSTIFICATION. Justification is a divine act whereby an infinitely Holy God judicially declares a believing sinner to be righteous and acceptable before Him because Christ has borne the sinner's sin on the cross and has become "to us . . . righ-

teousness" (1 Cor. 1:30; Rom. 3:24). Justification springs from the fountain of God's grace (Titus 3:4-5). It is operative as the result of the redemptive and propitiatory sacrifice of Christ, who has settled all the claims of the law (Rom. 3:24-25; 5:9). Justification is on the basis of faith and not by human merit or works (3:28-30; 4:5; 5:1; Gal. 2:16). In this marvelous operation of God the infinitely holy Judge judicially declares righteous the one who believes in Jesus (Rom. 8:31-34). A justified believer emerges from God's great courtroom with a consciousness that another, his Substitute, has borne his guilt and that he stands without accusation before God (8:1, 33-34). Justification makes no one righteous, neither is it the bestowment of righteousness as such, but rather it declares one to be justified whom God sees as perfected once and forever in His beloved Son. As Lewis Sperry Chafer says: "Therefore, this may be stated as the correct formula of justification: The sinner becomes righteous in God's sight when he is in Christ: he is justified by God freely, all without a cause, because thereby he is righteous in His sight" (*Systematic Theology*, 7:222).

M.F.U.

Throughout the whole history of this doctrine the principal point of difference and dispute has been as to whether faith is the only condition of justification or whether good works in connection with faith are also to be regarded as an instrumental cause. Upon this question opinion has run to opposite extremes—from antinomianism to the doctrine of penances and works of supererogation. A chief cause of error has been an undue magnifying of the intellectual element in faith at the expense of the element that is moral and practical. Even in the earliest days of Christianity the tendency was to regard faith as merely a mental assent to Christian doctrine. The possessor of such faith deemed himself as having fully met the gospel requirement, though regardless of the claims of Christian service and even of ordinary morality. Passages in the epistles of Paul and James were written to correct this antinomian error (e.g., Rom. 6:1; Gal. 5:16-25; James 2:14-26). Partly as a recoil from this error the demand arose that, in addition to good works as evidences of true faith in believers, the sins of believers should be expiated by penances. And still further came the false idea of the character of good works. Instead of the clear recognition of the only relative and imperfect character of the righteousness of even the best Christians, the distinction was made between the divine commands and the divine counsels, and the belief obtained footing that by keeping both, men might do more than meet the divine requirements. Thus the scriptural doctrine of justification by faith became, to a considerable extent, beclouded in the early period of the history of the church. The abuses that later became prevalent in the Roman Catholic church through the fail-

729

ure to maintain the Scripture conception of faith and through the false conception of good works are well known. Without entering in detail into the views of this or of the Greek church, it must suffice us to emphasize the fact that the rescuing of the Scripture doctrine upon this subject, largely, though not wholly, lost sight of for a long time, was the work of the Reformation of the sixteenth century. Justification by faith is a fundamental doctrine of Protestant and evangelical Christianity. It stands opposed to those rationalistic conceptions of sin, and the attitude of God toward it, that reduce justification to a nullity, and to those views of Christian merit, cherished by Romanism, that derogate from the efficacy of Christ's atonement; at the same time it holds before men the great hope of the gospel and lays deep the foundation of Christian morality.

E.MCC.; M.F.U.

BIBLIOGRAPHY: J. Bennett, *Justication as Revealed in Scripture* (1840); G. C. Berkouwer, *Faith and Justification* (1954); A. M. Hunter, *Interpreting Paul's Gospel* (1954); J. Buchanan, *The Doctrine of Justification* (1955); L. L. Morris, *Apostolic Preaching of the Cross* (1955); H. Küng, *Justification* (1964); L. S. Chafer, *Salvation* (1965); F. B. Westcott, *The Biblical Doctrine of Justification* (1983).

JUS'TUS (jus'tus; "just").

1. The surname of Joseph, also called Barsabbas, who, with Matthias, was selected by the apostles as a candidate for the place made vacant by the apostasy of Judas Iscariot (Acts 1:23).

2. The name in the KJV, NASB and NIV of Titius Justus, a disciple living at Corinth, in whose house, near the synagogue, Paul preached to the Gentiles (Acts 18:7), A.D. 54.

3. Called also Jesus, a Jewish Christian mentioned in connection with Mark by Paul as being his "only fellow workers" at Rome when he wrote to the Colossians (Col. 4:11), A.D. 64.

JUT'TAH (jū'ta; "inclined"). A Levitical city in the mountains of Judah (Josh. 15:55; 21:16). It was allotted to the priests, but in the catalog (1 Chron. 6:57-59) the name has escaped (*see* NIV margin). It is supposed to have been the residence of Zacharias and Elizabeth, and the birthplace of John the Baptist (cf. Luke 1:39). It is doubtless the present Jutta, or Jitta, about five miles S of Hebron.

KAB, CAB. A Hebrew dry measure equal to about two quarts (2 Kings 6:25). *See* Metrology.

KAB′ZEEL (kab′zîl; "God has gathered"). A city in the S of Judah, the birthplace of Benaiah (Josh. 16:21; 2 Sam. 23:20; 1 Chron. 11:22). In Neh. 11:25 it is called *Jekabzeel* (which see). Perhaps it was located at Khirbet Hora, about ten miles NE of Beersheba.

KA′DESH (kā′desh; "consecrated"). More fully **Ka′desh-bar′nea** (ka′desh-bar′nē-a). A spot where the Israelites encamped twice while journeying from Egypt to Palestine, their nineteenth and thirty-seventh station. Its original name seems to have been *Rithmah* (which see), becoming Kadesh when the Tabernacle rested there; *En-mishpat* (Gen. 14:7), "Fountain of Judgment," when judgment was passed upon the Israelites; and *Meribah* (which see) when it became the place of murmuring and strife.

From Kadesh-barnea Moses sent messengers to explore the Promised Land. There the people rebelled and prepared to choose a captain to lead them back to Egypt (Num. 14:4). Consequently, Kadesh, the "sanctuary," became En-mishpat, a "Fountain of Judgment," when the rebellious people were sentenced to complete forty years of wandering. Israel determined to obtain possession of Canaan (14:39-40) and pushed into the S country (the Negeb), that is, the high land between the desert and Canaan proper. They were, however, defeated by the Amorites (Deut. 1:44) and the Amalekites (Num. 14:45).

Scripture References. The first mention of Kadesh-barnea is in connection with the devastating march of *Chedorlaomer* (which see), king of Elam, in the days of Abraham (Gen. 14:1-16). Kadesh is mentioned in connection with the flight of Hagar, where it is recorded that she rested by "the spring on the way to Shur" (16:7), between Kadesh and Bered (v. 14). Again it is recorded that Abraham moved from Hebron and sojourned at a point "between Kadesh and Shur" (20:1). Some believe that the rebellion of Korah and his company occurred at Kadesh, that it was there "the earth opened its mouth and swallowed them up" (Num. 16:1-32). It was certainly at Kadesh that Miriam died and was buried (20:1), and it was there that Moses struck the rock when he had been told only to speak to it (vv. 2-11). This was the third time that it became the "Fountain of Judgment" by Jehovah's passing judgment upon Moses for his impatience, presumption, and lack of reverent obedience (vv. 12-24). Then Kadesh, "consecrated (place)" or "sanctuary," became Meribah, or "strife" (v. 13).

A long halt at Kadesh followed (Deut. 1:46), and it appears that the Israelites scattered in the valleys of the desert, leading a nomadic life. All this time Kadesh was the northernmost limit of their roving and, in a peculiar sense, the center of their occupancy, the pivot of their wanderings. Thirty-seven years passed, during which time Israel did not advance one single step toward the occupancy of the Promised Land. Then "the whole congregation" (Num. 20:1; Deut. 2:1) came together in Kadesh, as if it was the rendezvous and rallying point of the scattered nation.

From Kadesh Moses sent messengers to the king of Edom with the request that Israel might pass through his country on the way to Canaan (Num. 20:14-21), and he also sent a similar request to the king of Moab (Judg. 11:16-17).

Location. This has been successfully identified with 'Ain Kadeis or 'Ain el Qudeirat, about fifty miles S of Beersheba in the NE part of the Sinai Peninsula. The determining factor of the location was water (Num. 20:2). With the region some five or six miles to the N, which was also well watered, Israel acquired the most livable part of the Sinai Peninsula. This circumstance offers the reason for their extended stay at this place. T. E. Law-

731

rence and C. L. Woolley examined 'Ain Kadeis in 1914 on behalf of the Palestine Exploration Fund and drew up a plan of a fortress on the site. In 1956 M. Dothan excavated the fortress under the auspices of the Israel Department of Antiquities and found that it dated to the tenth century B.C. No remains of the Mosaic period have been located there, but none should be expected—given the nature of the Hebrew encampment. Moreover, excavation or even exploration of the site is incomplete.

BIBLIOGRAPHY: H. C. Trumbull, *Kadesh-Barnea: Its Importance and Probable Site* (1884); C. L. Wooley and T. E. Lawrence, *The Wilderness of Zin* (1936); L. J. Wood, *A Survey of Israel's History* (1970), pp. 137-38, 155-61.

KAD'MIEL (kad'mi-el; "God is in the front").

1. One of the Levites who, with his family, returned from Babylon with Zerubbabel. Apparently he was a representative of the descendants of Hodaviah, or, as he is elsewhere called, Hodevah or Judah (Ezra 2:40; Neh. 7:43; 12:8, 24). He assisted in the various reforms of that period (Ezra 3:9), 536 B.C.

2. A Levite who assisted in leading the devotions of the people after they were taught the law by Ezra (Neh. 9:4-5). He also signed the covenant (10:9), 445 B.C. He is thought to have been a son of no. 1.

KAD'MONITE (kad'mon-it). A tribe mentioned only in Gen. 15:19 as one of the nations to be dispossessed by Israel. As an adjective the name means "eastern," or "ancient." Quite probably, therefore, the Kadmonites were "bene-kedem" (Judg. 6:33, "sons of the east"), i.e., tribes who roamed in the barren areas E and SE of Palestine.

W.H.; M.F.U.

KAIN (kān). A city of the low country of Judah (Josh. 15:57; "Cain," KJV), Khirbet Yagin, three miles SE of Hebron.

KAL'LAI (kal'ī; "swift, light"). Son of Sallai and a chief priest in the time of the high priest Joiakim (Neh. 12:20), after 635 B.C.

KA'MON (ka'mon). The place of the judge Jair's burial (Judg. 10:5; "Camon," KJV). Josephus (*Ant.* 5.7.6) states that Kamon was a city of Gilead. Eusebius and Jerome place it on the great road, six Roman miles N of Legio, on the plain of Jezreel or Esdraelon. Polybius (doubtlessly correct) mentions it among other cities of Gilead (*History* 5.70.12).

KA'NAH (ka'na; "place of reeds").

1. A stream or "brook" that empties into the Mediterranean between Caesarea and Joppa after serving as a boundary between Ephraim and Manasseh (Josh. 16:8; 17:9). It is identified by some as the river Aujeh.

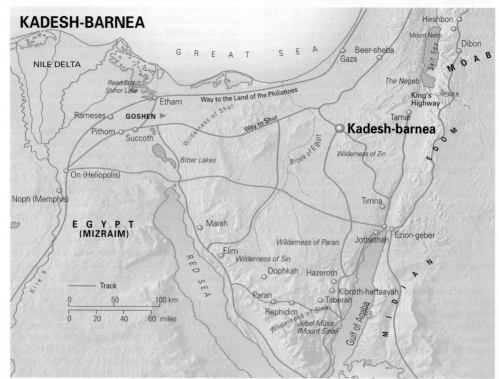

KADESH-BARNEA

2. A town N of Asher (Josh. 19:28), identified with modern Qana, about six miles SE of Tyre.

KAPH (כ) (kaf; Heb. *kap*, "palm of hand"). Eleventh letter of the Heb. alphabet (cf. Ps. 119:81-88, where this letter begins each verse in the Heb.).

KARE'AH (ka-rē'a; "bald"). The father of Johanan and Jonathan, Jewish leaders in the time of Gedaliah, the Babylonian-appointed governor of Jerusalem (Jer. 40:8, 13, 15-16; 41:11, 13-14, 16; 42:1, 8; 43:2, 4-5). He is called Careah in 2 Kings 25:23, KJV.

KAR'KA (kar'ka; "ground, floor"). A place named in the description of Judah's lot, lying between the Mediterranean and the Dead Sea (Josh. 15:3; "Karkaa," KJV). Perhaps to be located at 'Ain el-Qeseimeh, three miles NW of Kadesh-Barnea.

KAR'KOR (kar'kor; cf. Arab. *karkar*, "soft, level ground"). A place E of the Jordan where Gideon's 300 men, "weary yet pursuing," captured Zebah and Zalmunna (Judg. 8:4, 12). Its location cannot be determined with accuracy, but some would place it at Qarqar in the Wadi Sirham, 120 miles SE of Amman.

KARNA'IM (karna'yim). A place mentioned in Amos 6:13 as either a literal city or district of unknown location or a figurative place whose meaning is "horns." The prophet then would be ridiculing wicked Israel for having overcome the "horns," a symbol of strength, by strength.

KAR'TAH (kar'ta; "city"). A town in the tribe of Zebulun, assigned (Josh. 21:34) to the Levites of the family of Merari.

KAR'TAN (kar'tan; "town, city"). One of the cities of refuge in Naphtali, belonging to the Gershonite Levites, not far from the Sea of Galilee (Josh. 21:32; "Kiriathaim," 1 Chron. 6:76). It is present-day Khirbet el-Kureiyeh, fifteen miles SE of Tyre.

KAT'TAH (kat'ta). One of the towns of Zebulun (Josh. 19:15; "Kattath," KJV), probably the same as Kitron (Judg. 1:30).

KATYDID. *See* Animal Kingdom: Locust.

KEBAR. *See* Chebar.

KE'DAR (kē'der; Heb. *qādar*, "to be dark," but cf. Arab. *qadara*, "to be able, mighty").
1. The second son of Ishmael and father of the tribe bearing his name (Gen. 25:13; 1 Chron. 1:29). Little is known of Kedar, but his descendants are frequently mentioned (see no. 2).
2. Kedar, in the stricter sense, was a nomadic tribe of Ishmaelites that wandered as far as the Elanitic gulf. But this term is usually used in Scripture as the collective name of the Arab tribes (Bedouin) in general (Song of Sol. 1:5; Isa. 21:16-17; 42:11; 60:7; Jer. 2:10; 49:28; Ezek.

27:21). In Ps. 120:5 Kedar and Meshech represent uncivilized tribes.

KED'EMAH (ked'e-ma; "eastward"). The last named son of Ishmael, and probably head of an Arab tribe of the same name (Gen. 25:15; 1 Chron. 1:31).

KED'EMOTH (ked'e-mōth; "eastern places"). A city of Reuben, assigned with its pastureland to the Levites of the Merari family (Josh. 13:18; 21:37; 1 Chron. 6:79). "From the wilderness of Kedemoth" Moses sent a deputation to Sihon, king of the Amorites, with a request to pass through his land (Deut. 2:26). Site uncertain.

KE'DESH (kē'desh; "sacred place, sanctuary").
1. A city in the extreme S of Judah (Josh. 15:23), and probably the same as *Kadesh-barnea* (which see).
2. A city in the tribe of Issachar, given to the Levites of the family of Gershom (1 Chron. 6:72; called "Kishion," Josh. 19:20; 21:28). Perhaps Tell Abu Qudeis, about two miles SE of Megiddo.
3. A "fortified city" of Naphtali (Josh. 19:37) and one of the cities of refuge (20:7). Its king was slain by Joshua (12:22). It was the residence of Barak (Judg. 4:6), was captured by Tiglath-pileser (2 Kings 15:29), and was a well-known place after the captivity (1 Macc. 11:63-74). Probably to be identified with Khirbet Qedish, about two miles S of Tiberias.

KE'DESH-NAPH'TALI (kā'desh-naf'ta-lī; Judg. 4:6).

KEDORLAOMER. *See* Chedorlaomer. *See* Kedesh no. 3.

KEHELA'THAH (ke-he-la'tha; "assembly convocation"). One of the stations (twenty-third) of the children of Israel in the desert (Num. 33:22-23).

KEI'LAH (kē'la). A city in the plains of Judah that David once relieved from a siege by the Philistines, but its inhabitants were false and sought to deliver him up to Saul (1 Sam. 23:1-13). The site is satisfactorily identified with Khirbet Qila, about 8½ miles NW of Hebron. In the time of Nehemiah Keilah was so considerable that it had two prefects who assisted in repairing the walls of Jerusalem (Neh. 3:17-18).

KELA'IAH (ke-la'ya). One of the Levites who divorced his Gentile wife after the captivity (Ezra 10:23, "that is, Kelita").

KELAL. *See* Chelal.

KEL'ITA (kel'i-ta; perhaps "dwarf"; cf. Arab. *qulāt*). One of the Levites who put away his Gentile wife after the captivity (Ezra 10:23), assisted Ezra in expounding the law (Neh. 8:7), and signed the covenant made by Nehemiah (10:10), 456 B.C.

KELUB. *See* Chelub.

KELUHI. *See* Chelluhi.

KEM'UEL (kem'ū-el; "assembly of God").

1. One of the sons of Abraham's brother Nahor (Gen. 22:20-21), about 2150 B.C.

2. The son of Shiphtan and representative of Ephraim in the partition of the land of Canaan (Num. 34:24), about 1375 B.C.

3. The father of Hashabiah, who was leader of the Levites in the time of David (1 Chron. 27:17), about 1000 B.C.

KENAANAH. *See* Chenaanah.

KE'NAN (kē'nan). The son of Enos and great-grandson of Adam. He was born when his father was 90 years old. He lived 70 years and became the father of Mahalalel, after which he lived 840 years (Gen. 5:9-14). He is also mentioned in 1 Chron. 1:2.

KENANI. *See* Chenani.

KE'NATH (kē'nath; "possession"). A city in Gilead that was taken with "its villages" from the Canaanites by Nobah, and afterward called by his name (Num. 32:42). It is mentioned (1 Chron. 2:22-23) apparently as taken by Jair. Kenath is now Kanawat, a ruined town E of Bashan and about fifty miles SE of Damascus, on the W side of the Hauran Mountains. It overlooks a vast region and is surrounded by a cluster of cities, all within a distance of a half hour to two hours. The number of ruined buildings of all kinds is considerable.

KE'NAZ (kē'naz).

1. One of the sons of Eliphaz, the firstborn of Esau. He became chief of one of the Edomite tribes of Arabia Petraea (Gen. 36:11, 15; 1 Chron. 1:36). Genesis 36:42 and 1 Chron. 1:53, according to Keil and Delitzsch (*Com.,* ad loc.), include a list, not of persons, but of capital cities of the several kingdoms.

2. A brother of Caleb and father of Othniel who took Kiriath-Sepher and received Caleb's daughter Achsah as a reward (Josh. 15:17; Judg. 1:13; 3:9, 11; 1 Chron. 4:13), about 1400-1370 B.C.

3. The son of Elah and grandson of Caleb (1 Chron. 4:15).

KE'NITES (kē'nīts; "pertaining to copper-smiths"). A group of metalsmiths who traveled throughout the mineral-bearing region in the Wadi Arabah. They are first mentioned in Gen. 15:19 as one of the nations to be "given" to Israel. They descended from the Midianites and developed extraordinary skill in metalwork. They settled down early along the SW shore of the Dead Sea, SE of Hebron (Judg. 1:16). Hobab, the son of Reuel, was a Kenite and acted as a guide to Israel in the wilderness (1:16; 4:11). Their nomadism is suggested in the OT by numerous individual Kenites described as living in various places. Besides their residence SE of Hebron, they were found in the Wadi Arabah (Num. 24:21), in Naphtali (Judg. 4:11) and in the Davidic-Solomonic era they are mentioned in southern Judah (1 Sam. 15:6; 27:10). Heber, mentioned in Judg. 4:11 and 5:24, was a Kenite, and the ascetic Rechabites mentioned in 1 Chron. 2:55 were also of Kenite extraction.   M.F.U.

BIBLIOGRAPHY: W. F. Albright, *Catholic Biblical Quarterly* 25 (1963): 1-11; L. J. Wood, *A Survey of Israel's History* (1970), pp. 137, 217; J. A. Thompson, *The Bible and Archaeology* (1982), p. 71.

KEN'IZZITE (ken'i-zīt; Heb. *haqqᵉnizzî*). The Kenizzites are mentioned in Gen. 15:19, where they are named between the Kenites and the Kadmonites among the nations to be dispossessed by Israel. They probably dwelt somewhere in the southern part of Canaan. They were related to the Kenites and like them were skilled metal-workers of the copper-rich Jordan Valley and the Arabah (*see* Kenite). In Gen. 36:11, 15 Kenaz is a son of Eliphaz, the son of Esau, and in 36:42 Kenaz appears among the "chiefs" of Edom. This might lead us to believe that the Kenizzites were an Edomite tribe, if they had not been mentioned so long before. The case is similar to that of *Amalek* (which see); but the occurrence of the name *Kenaz* in vv. 15, 42 makes it appear that Kenaz may have been a more common name than Amalek. In Num. 32:12; Josh. 14:6, 14 the same Heb. ("Kenezite," KJV) is an epithet of Caleb or of Jephunneh in the phrase "Caleb the son of Jephunneh the Kenizzite." It is quite probable that Caleb was descended from the Edomite Kenaz. This is argued from 15:13, "Now he gave to Caleb the son of Jephunneh a portion among the sons of Judah," and 14:14, "Hebron became the inheritance of Caleb the son of Jephunneh, the Kenizzite until this day, because he followed the Lord God of Israel fully." The same is indicated by Edomite and Horite names in the genealogy of Caleb. Thus, besides Kenaz (Gen. 36:11, 15), we find Shobal (cf. 1 Chron. 2:52 with Gen. 36:20), Manahathites (1 Chron. 2:52; cf. Manahath, Gen. 36:23), Korah (cf. Gen. 36:14, 16, 18 with 1 Chron. 2:43), the Ithrites (1 Chron. 2:53; cf. Ithran, Gen. 36:26), Elah (1 Chron. 4:15; cf. Gen. 36:41), and Jephunneh, who has been compared with Pinon (Gen. 36:41).   W.H.; M.F.U.

KENO'SIS (ke-nō'sis; Gk. *kenōsis*, "an emptying"). A Gk. word used in theology with reference to the self-denial of the Son of God in becoming incarnate and entering into His state of humiliation. This use of the term is based upon Phil. 2:7, where the phrase *heauton 'ekenōse,* "emptied Himself," occurs. The same idea of self-deprivation, or the laying aside of something that Christ possessed as a divine person in His pre-existent state, finds expression in other places in the Scriptures. For example, in John 17:5 the Lord speaks of the glory that He had with the Father "before the world was." Paul says of Christ, "though He was rich, yet for your sake He became poor" (2 Cor. 8:9).

The profound and difficult question naturally raised is, In what sense did the Son of God lay aside His divine riches in becoming the God-man? Of what "glory" did He divest Himself? What are we to understand by the kenosis, or "emptying of Himself"? The question is inwoven with the mystery of the incarnation. And the inquiry soon leads to depths that are unfathomable because of the incomprehensibility of God and the inability of the human mind to conceive adequately the divine mode of existence. And yet, fidelity to the Scriptures and the proper demands of the intellect foster the attempt to penetrate the mystery as far as possible, even though the result may fall far short of the full solution.

A brief survey of the fluctuations of doctrine and conjecture on this subject will be helpful. Historically, the question has presented many phases, among them these: Was the Son of God during His earthly sojourn in the flesh self-deprived in any measure of His divine attributes? If He still retained them fully in His possession, was their exercise or use for the time surrendered? If so, to what extent? Under what regulating principles? Was the consciousness of our Lord simply human—the divine consciousness for the time nonexistent or awakening in Him only gradually—or was His consciousness throughout that of the God-man?

The ancient church, with but few exceptions, taught that the Son did not retain the divine glory for Himself, for His own advantage, while yet He did not cease even in the flesh to be what He eternally was. "That emptying," said Hilary, "is by no means the annihilating of the heavenly nature." The theology of the Middle Ages so honored the divine nature of Christ as to overlook all limitations assumed in the union of that nature with the human. Thomas Aquinas admitted only an outward development in age and wisdom as in the sight of men.

The kenosis became the subject of much controversy between the theologians of Giessen and Tübingen early in the seventeenth century, the former (Menzer and Feurborn) maintaining that if Christ did not during His humiliation actually divest Himself of His attributes, such as omnipotence and omniscience, and so on, He did lay aside their use. The latter (Haffenreffer, Thummius, Nicolai, Oriander) contend that the kenosis was only a concealment or veiling of their use. Later Thomasius (*Person and Work of Christ*) took the ground positively of self-abdication of the divine attributes on the part of Christ, assuming a sleeplike unconsciousness of the divine nature of the Son during this earthly life, and the exclusion of the Son from the Trinity during that period. Gess (*Die Lehre von der Person Christi*) and Georg Ludw. Hahn (*Theologie der N. T.*) take substantially the same ground. This scanty out-

line is sufficient to show the perilous paths that are followed when the attempt is made to push speculation too far in this direction. Likewise it must be apparent that the conclusion reached should be such as not to deny the absolute unchangeableness of God, nor the constant completeness of the divine nature in the Son even in the days of His humiliation; while, on the other hand, the reality of His loving self-abasement in His entrance into fellowship with humanity should be duly recognized. All reflection upon this subject, as upon many others, must be under the guidance of, and within the limits of, Scripture teaching.

That the "Word made flesh" was truly God, as well as man, with divine nature and attributes undiminished, cannot be doubted by anyone who believes the first chapter of John's gospel, to say nothing of the force of other Scriptures.

Whether the consciousness of His divine nature was from the very outset possessed by our Lord is a matter upon which the Scriptures are silent. Luke, however, furnishes a glimpse that is suggestive when the child Christ says, "Did you not know that I had to be in My Father's house?" (Luke 2:49). And certainly He clearly expresses this consciousness during the years of His ministry (e.g., John 8:58; 10:30; 14:9-11; 17:25).

As to the divine attributes in Christ, the distinction seems valid between their full possession and their constant exercise. That He constantly possessed the attributes of deity is inseparable from faith in His divine, and therefore unchangeable, nature. And yet the use of these same properties appears to have been in some way limited. This must be manifest to anyone who attentively reads the gospels. And the law of this limitation is found in the love and self-sacrifice that led our Lord to the complete acceptance of His human and earthly lot. He who "emptied Himself" took "the form of a bond-servant." The two expressions are mutually explanatory. Thus He who was "in the form of God" and "did not regard equality with God a thing to be grasped," placed Himself in relation to the Father in the lowly position of a servant (Matt. 26:39; John 4:34; 5:30; 14:28; 17:4, 18); He was also the servant of mankind (Matt. 20:28; Luke 22:26-27); He never wrought miracles for Himself, but often did so for others (cf. Matt. 4:3-4; 14:15-21; 15:32-39); He admitted and asserted a limitation to His knowledge with respect to one matter but manifested and declared Himself to be possessed of divine knowledge with respect to other matters—even the highest. And here the fullness of His knowledge was always at the service of His love (cf. Matt. 11:27; Mark 13:32; John 3:12-13; 17:25-26). He neither exercised His omnipotence nor exhibited His omniscience for His own advantage and glory but for the performance of His saving work among men.

Two other expressions in the same passage

(Phil. 2:5-8) throw light upon the kenosis. Before the kenosis Christ was "in the form of God"; afterward He was "made in the likeness of men," "found in appearance as a man." Here the contrast is between the *manifestations of being* and *character* that naturally belonged to the Son of God, and the veiling of the divine glory that came to pass when He became incarnate. What the "form of God" was that the Son laid aside, the apostle does not tell us; but evidently it was such manifestation of the divine being as was befitting to Him who "did not regard equality with God a thing to be grasped." Paul elsewhere writes that God "dwells in unapproachable light" (1 Tim. 6:16). In strongest contrast with this was all the outward appearance of the earthly life of our Lord. He left the companionship of angels for that of men. The angels are the servants of God. Though on special occasions they were sent to minister to Him (Matt. 4:11; Luke 22:43), Christ never called for them (*see* Matt. 26:53).

Two features of the incarnate life of the Son of God are emphasized by Paul for ethical purposes in connection with the kenosis: first, self-sacrificing love (Phil. 2:3-5); second, obedience (2:8, 12-13). The sequence, the exaltation of Christ (vv. 9-11), has the gloriously hopeful suggestion and promise for all His followers. *See* Incarnation; Humiliation of Christ.

BIBLIOGRAPHY: A. B. Bruce, *The Humiliation of Christ* (n.d.), pp. 134-92, 357-65; P. T. Forsyth, *The Person and Place of Jesus Christ* (n.d.), pp. 291-320; H. R. Macintosh, *The Doctrine of the Person of Christ* (1914), pp. 141-284; H. E. Brunner, *The Mediator* (1934), pp. 316-27, 343, 349, 431; L. S. Chafer, *Systematic Theology* (1948), 1:373-89; 6:257-58; 7:57, 78-80, 194-96; J. F. Walvoord, *Jesus Christ Our Lord* (1969), pp. 138-45; J. B. Lightfoot, *St. Paul's Epistle to the Philippians* (1970), pp. 110-15, 127-32; R. Johnstone, *Lectures on the Epistle to the Philippians* (1977), pp. 145-61; J. M. Boice, *God the Redeemer*, Foundations of the Christian Faith 2 (1978): 121-60; J. D. G. Dunn, *Christology in the Making* (1980), pp. 114-21.

KEPHAR AMMONI. *See* Chephar-Ammoni.

KEPHIRAH. *See* Chephirah.

KERAN. *See* Cheran.

KERCHIEF. *See* Dress.

KERE' (ke-ra', ke-rā) (Aram. passive part. *qⁿerē*, signifying "what is to be read"). This is a marginal reading in the traditional Hebrew MT. In the opinion of the Jewish scholars (Masoretes) this was the superior reading and was to be substituted or read for what was written in the text, called the *kethib* (which see). Actually the vowel pointings of the *kethib* were to be read with the *kere*.

KER'EN-HAP'PUCH (ker'en-hap'uk; "paint-horn," i.e., "cosmetic box"). The name given to the youngest daughter of Job after his restoration to prosperity (Job 42:14).

KER'ETHITES. *See* Cherethites.

KE'RIOTH (kē'rī-ŏth; "cities"). A city of Moab mentioned by Jeremiah (Jer. 48:24, 41) and Amos (Amos 2:2; "Kirioth," KJV) in their prophecies of its overthrow by the Babylonians. It occurs on the Moabite Stone (line 13).

KE'RIOTH-HEZ'RON (ke'ri-ŏth-nez'ron). A city of southern Judah and probably included with Simeon (Josh. 15:25; "Kerioth, and Hezron," KJV), and identified with *Hazor* (which see). It seems to be the place alluded to in the name of Judas Iscariot, a native of Kerioth. It is called simply Hezron in 15:3. The city has been identified with Khirbet el-Karyathein, about 4½ miles S of Tell Mā'in.

KE'RITH. *See* Cherith.

KE'ROS (ke'ros). One of the Temple servants whose descendants returned with Zerubbabel to Jerusalem after the captivity (Ezra 2:44; Neh. 7:47), before 536 B.C.

KER'UB. *See* Cherab.

KES'ALON. *See* Chesalon.

KE'SED. *See* Chesed.

KE'SIL. *See* Chesil.

KESUL'LOTH. *See* Chesulloth.

KETHIB (ke-thîb', also written *kethiv, ke-thēve*, an Aram. passive part. *kⁿa-thîb*, "written"). The *kethib* was the reading actually occurring in the Heb. text and represented, even though an inferior reading in the opinion of the Masoretic scholars, an ancient traditional reading deserving of some credence. The vowels on the *kethib* were meant to be superimposed upon the marginal, or *kere*, reading (*see* Kere). The *Kethib Kere* device proves the high veneration of Masoretic scholars for the traditional readings and for sacred regard of the text together with their extreme unwillingness to change it, even in the case of an inferior traditional reading. M.F.U.

KETTLE (Heb. *dûd*, "boiling"). A large pot for cooking (1 Sam. 2:14; 2 Chron. 35:13; elsewhere rendered "pot," Job 41:20; "basket," Ps. 81:6). From 1 Sam. 2:14 it is evident that this vessel was used in preparing the peace offerings: "All that the fork brought up the priest would take for himself."

KETU'RAH (ke-tū'ra; "incense"). The second wife (or concubine, 1 Chron. 1:32) of Abraham (Gen. 25:1, 4). By Abraham she had six sons, who, after they grew to manhood, were sent "to the land of the east" so that they would not interfere with Isaac. It is generally supposed that she was married to Abraham after the death of Sarah; but against this it is urged that it is improbable that six sons should have been born to Abraham by one woman, and that, too, after he was 140 years old, and that he then should have lived to see them arrive at an adult age. It has therefore been suggested that Keturah had been Abraham's secondary or concubine wife before the death of Sarah, and that she was raised to the dignity of a full wife after that event. Through the offspring of Keturah Abraham became the "father of a multitude of nations."

BIBLIOGRAPHY: J. A. Montgomery, *Arabia and the Bible* (1934), pp. 37-53; G. Ch. Aalders, *Genesis,* Bible Student's Commentary (1981), 2:72-73.

KEY. As an instrument for fastening, *see* Lock.

Figurative. Because of its power to open to, or exclude from, all treasures of a city or house, the key is often used in Scripture as a symbol of *power* and *authority,* whether in church or state. Thus Isaiah speaks (22:22) of the key of David being given to Eliakim as the most influential adviser of the king. The power of the keys consisted not only in the supervision of the royal chambers, but also in deciding who was and who was not to be received into the king's service.

With reference to the administration of the house of David in the higher sense, our Lord is represented as having the key of David (Rev. 3:7), receiving and excluding whom He pleases, and committing to His apostles—to Peter first as the most prominent member of the apostolic body —the keys of the kingdom (Matt. 16:19; 18:18). *See* Peter.

"The key of knowledge" (Luke 11:52) of spiritual things is the Scriptures, which the scribes reserved exclusively for themselves. The figure used by our Lord is that of *knowledge* being a temple into which the scribes should have led the people, but whose gate they closed, and holding the key with jealous care, even their commentaries hiding rather than revealing knowledge.

KEZI'AH (ke-zī'a; "cassia"). Job's second daughter born to him after his adversity (Job 42:14; "Kezia," KJV).

KE'ZIB. *See* Chezib.

KE'ZIZ. *See* Emek-keziz.

KHAN (kan). The more common Arab. name for the establishments that correspond to our *inn* (which see).

KIB'ROTH-HATTA'AVAH (kib'rōth-ha-ta'a-va; "the graves of lust"). One of the stations of the Israelites, probably in Wadi Murrah, about thirty miles NE of Sinai. It was the scene of murmuring and discontent, followed by most severe punishment (Num. 11:34-35; 33:16-17; Deut. 9:22; cf. Ps. 78:30-31).

KIB'ZAIM (kib'za-im; a "double heap"). A city of Ephraim, assigned to the Kohathite Levites (Josh. 21:22), called *Jokmeam* (which see) in 1 Chron. 6:68. Its site is not ascertained.

KID. The young of the goat. *See* Animal Kingdom: Goat; Sacrificial Offerings.

KIDNAP (Heb. *gānab,* to "steal, secretly carry away"). The kidnapping of a freeborn Israelite, either to treat him as a slave or to sell him into slavery, was by the law of Moses punished by death (Ex. 21:16; Deut. 24:7). In 1 Tim. 1:10 Paul denounces kidnappers (Gk. *andrapodistēs;* NIV, "slave traders") among other ungodly or profane men.

KIDNEY (Heb. *kilyâ;* Gk. *nephros*).

The kidney with its surrounding fat was part of the burnt offering (Ex. 29:13, 22; Lev. 3:4, 10, 15; 4:9; 8:16, 25; etc.). *See* Sacrificial Offerings.

Figurative. To the Hebrews, the kidneys, because of their sensitivity, were believed to be the seat of desire. Scripture contains many eloquent passages referring to this, although the NASB and NIV have rendered them in such a way as to make them understandable to us. When a man suffers deep within himself, he is "pierced within" (in the kidneys, Ps. 73:21); when he rejoices, it is with his "inmost being" (kidneys, Prov. 23:16); and when he earnestly longs, his "heart [kidneys] faints within" (Job 19:27). The kidneys also seem to provide knowledge and understanding, as in Ps. 16:7 and Jer. 12:2, where the word is rendered "mind" (i.e., "my mind [kidneys] instructs me in the night"). Job complains that God has split his "kidneys open" (Job 16:13, cf. Lam. 3:13, marg.).

KI'DON. *See* Chidon.

KID'RON (kid'ron; "turbid, dusky, gloomy"; Gk. *Kedrōn;* "Cedron," John 18:1, KJV). The brook that flows through the valley of Jehoshaphat. The name was also applied to its bed, the *valley* of Kidron. It is thus described by Smith (*Hist. Geog.,* p. 511): "To the north of Jerusalem begins the torrent-bed of the Kidron. It sweeps past the Temple Mount, past what were afterward Calvary and Gethsemane. It leaves the Mount of Olives and Bethany to the left, Bethlehem far to the right. It plunges down among the bare terraces, precipices, and crags of the wilderness of Judea—the wilderness of the scapegoat. So barren and blistered, so furnace-like does it [the valley] become as it drops below the level of the sea, that it takes the name of Wady-en-Nar or the Fire Wady. At last its dreary course brings it to the precipices above the Dead Sea, into which it shoots its scanty winter waters; but all summer it is dry." The valley is only 20 miles long but has a descent of 3,912 feet. The place where it enters the Jordan is a narrow gorge about 1,200 feet deep.

The Kidron was the brook crossed by David when he fled from Absalom (2 Sam. 15:23). Solomon fixed it as the limit of Shimei's walks (1 Kings 2:37); beside it Asa destroyed and burned his mother's idol, or Asherah (15:13); here Athaliah was executed (Josephus, *Ant.* 9.7.3; cf. 2 Kings 11:16). It then became the regular receptacle for the impurities and abominations of the idol worship when removed from the Temple and destroyed by the adherents of Jehovah (23:4, 6, 12; 2 Chron. 29:16; 30:14); and in the time of Josiah this valley was the common cemetery of Jerusalem (2 Kings 23:6; Jer. 26:23; 31:40).

BIBLIOGRAPHY: D. Baly, *The Geography of the Bible* (1957), pp. 167-68; G. E. Wright, *Biblical Archaeology* (1957), pp. 126, 221.

The Bene Hezir tomb and the tomb of Zechariah, located in the Kidron Valley

KIL'EAB. *See* Chileab.

KIL'ION. *See* Chilion.

KIL'MAD. *See* Chilmad.

KIM'HAM. *See* Chimham.

KIN. *See* Kindred.

KI'NAH (kî'na; "lamentation dirge"). A city in the extreme S of Judah toward Edom (Josh. 15:22). Kinah is located at the head of Wadi el Keini.

KINDNESS and **Loving-Kindness** (Heb. *ḥesed,* "desire, zeal"). Zeal toward another in a good sense: (1) Of men, as shown in doing mutual favors, benefits (Gen. 21:23; 2 Sam. 10:2); compassion for the afflicted (Job 6:14; "pity," KJV). The formula to "show kindness" is frequent in Scripture (2 Sam. 3:8; 9:1, 7), and in 2 Sam. 9:3 there is the expression "to whom I may show the kindness of God," i.e., "like that of God," or "for the sake of God." (2) Of God toward men, as shown in *mercies, benefits,* and so on (Pss. 31:21; 107:43; 117:1; etc.). Kindness is also the rendering of the Gk. *chrēstotēs,* "moral goodness," and so "benignity" (Rom. 2:4; Gal. 5:22; 2 Cor. 6:6; Eph. 2:7; Col. 3:12).

BIBLIOGRAPHY: C. H. Dodd, *The Bible and the Greeks* (1935), pp. 59-62; L. H. Marshall, *The Challenge of New Testament Ethics* (1947), pp. 305-8; N. Glueck, *Hesed in the Bible* (1967); K. Sakenfeld, *The Meaning of Hesed in the Bible* (1978); C. J. Barber, *Ruth: An Expositional Commentary* (1983), pp. 52-54, 77-84, 118-32.

KINDRED, KINSMAN. This is a general heading

expressing the variety of family relations that are found in Scripture. The following are commonly found Heb. and Gk. words and their translations dealing with this topic:

1. *Family* (Heb. *mishpāḥâ,* usually so rendered). This word corresponds to our word *clan* and is used of the different tribes of Canaanites (Gen. 10:18); a subdivision of the Israelites (Ex. 6:14; Num. 1:20; etc.); figuratively for a nation (Jer. 5:9; 8:3; 25:9; 20:32; Mic. 2:39); and of a specific house (Ruth 2:3; Job 32:2). It is also rendered "relatives" (Gen. 24:41; Josh. 6:23). In all of these it refers to relationship, to *consanguinity,* more or less remote.

2. *Lineage* (Heb. *môledet*). Hence a *person born, a child* (Gen. 28:9; Lev. 18:9, 11); persons of the *same family* or *lineage,* a "relative" (Gen. 12:1; 24:4; 31:3; 43:7; Num. 10:30); also rendered "kindred" (Esther 2:10; 8:6). In some of these instances the relation is only that of common nationality.

3. *Acquaintance* (Heb. *môda'at,* rendered "kinsmen," Ruth 3:2, *see* marg.). Used to express blood relationship.

4. *Near relative* (Heb. *gô'ēl* "near of kin"). This term is applied to one who is so related as to possess the rights and obligations of a *kinsman* (which see), an *avenger* (which see). It is generally used to denote the nearest kinsman, able to redeem; "the closest relative" (Ruth 4:1; 3:12).

5. *Brother* (Heb. *'āḥ*). This term occurs as "kinsmen" only in 1 Chron. 12:29 (KJV), but occurs frequently elsewhere in a wide sense, including all collateral relationships, whether by consanguinity, affinity, or simple relationship. From this term comes *brotherhood.* The Hebrews also expressed consanguinity by such words and phrases as *flesh* (Gen. 37:27; Isa. 58:7); *bone and flesh* (Gen. 29:14; Judg. 9:2; 2 Sam. 5:1; etc.); *"blood relative"* (Lev. 18:6; 25:49).

6. In the NT the following Gk. words refer to kindred: *genos,* the most general and frequent term, our "kin," i.e., blood relationship; its derivative, *suggeneia,* "corelationship"; *patria,* "families" (Acts 3:25), descent in a direct line (Luke 2:4; Eph 3:15), *phulē,* "offshoot," a "tribe" (Rev. 5:9; 7:9; 11:9; 13:7; etc.). Of the names denoting special relations, the principal will be found explained under their proper headings *Father, Brother,* and so on. It will be seen there that the words denoting near relation in the direct line are also used for the superior or inferior degrees in that line, such as grandfather, grandson, and so on. The words expressing collateral consanguinity are *uncle, aunt, nephew, niece* (not in KJV), *cousin.* The terms of affinity are *father-in-law, mother-in-law, son-in-law, daughter-in-law, brother-in-law, sister-in-law.* The domestic and economic questions arising out of kindred may be classed under the headings *Family, Marriage, Inheritance,* and *Blood Revenge.*

KINE. The KJV term for NASB and NIV "cows." For a discussion of the figurative use of the term *cows,* see the entry in the general listing. *See also* the discussion of the ox in the article Animal Kingdom.

KING (Heb. and Aram. *melek,* "ruler"; Gk. *basileus*).

General Use of Term. This term is used with considerable latitude in Scripture and is often applied where some inferior epithet would correspond better with modern ideas. Thus, when we read of the king of Sodom, of Gomorrah, of Admah, of Zeboiim, and of Bela (Gen. 14:2)—all towns lying within a limited distance—it is important that we understand the term *king* in the sense of a local ruler. This and many similar notices show a prevailing tendency in early times toward monarchical government. Whenever the people of a district settled down and formed themselves into a regular community it was under the presidency of a regal head. Not in Egypt alone, but in Salem, in Gerar, in all the little towns to which the patriarchs came, a king invariably appears on the scene. Thus, in so small a country as Canaan *thirty-one kings* were conquered by Joshua (Josh. 12:9, 24), while Adonibezek speaks of having subdued *seventy* (Judg. 1:7).

Hebrew Use of the Term. Among the Israelites the title *king* was applied to the supreme head of the nation from about 1020-587 B.C.

Occasion. The immediate occasion for the substitution of a regal form of government for that of the *judges* (which see) seems to have been the siege of Jabesh-gilead by Nahash, king of the Ammonites (1 Sam. 11; 12:12), and his refusal to make a covenant with the inhabitants of that town except on humiliating and cruel conditions (11:2, 4-6). The Israelites seem to have been convinced that they could not succeed against their formidable enemies unless, like other nations, they placed themselves under the rule of a king. Probably another influencing cause was the disgust excited by the corrupt administration of affairs by the sons of Samuel and the desire for a radical change (8:3-6). Accordingly, the original idea of a Hebrew king was twofold: first, that he should lead the people to battle in time of war, and second, that he should execute judgment and justice for them in war and peace (8:20).

Powers. Besides being commander in chief of the army, supreme judge, and absolute master of the lives of his subjects, the king exercised the power of imposing taxes and of exacting personal service and labor from his subjects. The degree to which the exaction of personal labor might be carried on a special occasion is illustrated by King Solomon's requirements for building the Temple. The king of Israel, as the viceregent of Jehovah, also had another claim to respect and obedience (1 Sam 10:1; 16:13) and was, as it were, His son, if just and holy (2 Sam. 7:14; Pss.

89:26-27; 2:6-7). Set apart as a consecrated ruler and anointed with the holy oil (Ex. 30:31; 1 Kings 1:39), he became "the Lord's anointed."

Court. A ruler who had so much authority, both human and divine, was naturally distinguished by outward honors and luxuries. Thus, gradually, he came to have a magnificent court. When the kingdom was at its height he sat on a throne of ivory, covered with pure gold, at the feet of which were two figures of lions. He was dressed in royal robes (1 Kings 22:10; 2 Chron. 18:9); his insignia were a golden crown perhaps with gems (2 Sam. 1:10; 12:30; 2 Kings 11:12; Ps. 21:3) and a royal scepter. He was treated with the utmost consideration; those who approached him bowed to the ground (1 Sam. 24:8). He had a more or less extensive harem, guarded by eunuchs (2 Sam. 20:3; 1 Kings 11:3; etc.).

Succession. The law of succession to the throne is somewhat obscure, but it seems most probable that the king named his successor during his lifetime. This was certainly the case with David (1 Kings 1:30; 2:22) and with Rehoboam (2 Chron. 11:21-22). At the same time, if no partiality for a favorite wife or son intervened, there would always be a natural bias of affection in favor of the eldest son.

Officers. These were the recorder, or chronicler, whose duty it was to write the annals of the king's reign; the scribe, or secretary (2 Sam. 8:17; 20:25; 2 Kings 12:10; etc.); the chief steward "in charge of the royal household" (Isa. 22:15; 36:3); the king's friend (1 Kings 4:5) or companion; the keeper of the wardrobe (2 Kings 10:22); the captain of the bodyguard (2 Sam. 20:23); officers over the king's treasure, storehouses, laborers, vineyards, olive trees, sycamore trees, camels, herds, and flocks (1 Chron. 27:25-31); the commander in chief of the army (2 Sam. 11:1; 20:23; 1 Chron. 27:34); the royal counselors (1 Chron. 27:32; Isa. 3:3; 19:11, 13).

Revenue. The following sources are mentioned: the cornfields, vineyards, and olive gardens; the produce of the royal flocks (1 Sam. 21:7; 2 Sam. 13:23; 2 Chron. 26:10; 1 Chron. 27:25-31); a nominal tenth of the produce of grain lands and vineyards and of sheep (1 Sam. 8:15, 17); a tribute from merchants who passed through Hebrew territory (1 Kings 10:14-15); presents made by his subjects (1 Sam. 10:27; 16:20; 1 Kings 10:25; Ps. 72:10). In the time of Solomon the king had trading vessels of his own at sea (1 Kings 10:22). It is probable that Solomon and some other kings may have derived some revenue from commercial ventures (1 Kings 9:28); the spoils of war taken from conquered nations and the tribute paid by them (2 Sam. 8:2, 7-8, 10; 1 Kings 4:21; 2 Chron. 27:5); and last, an undefined power of exacting compulsory labor, to which reference has been already made (1 Sam. 8:12-13, 16).

New Testament Use of Term. Owing to the

peculiar political relations of the Jews, the title *king* has different significations: the Roman *emperor* (1 Pet. 2:13, 17); and so the "seven kings" (Rev. 17:10) are thought to be the first seven Caesars; Herod Antipas (Matt. 14:1-9; Mark 6:14-27), although he was only *tetrarch* (cf. Luke 3:19); the ten provincial representatives of the Roman government (Rev. 17:12), as being supreme each in his own jurisdiction.

Figurative. "King" is used symbolically to signify the possessor of supreme power (Prov. 8:15-16); it is applied to God as the sole proper sovereign and ruler of the universe (1 Tim. 1:17); to Christ as the sole head and governor of his church (6:15-16; Matt. 27:11; Luke 19:38; John 1:49; 18:33, 37); to men, as invested with regal authority by others (Luke 22:25; 1 Tim. 2:1-2; etc.). The people of God are called *kings* and *priests* (Rev. 1:6, KJV; NASB and NIV, "a kingdom," Ps. 49:14; Dan. 7:22, 27; Matt. 19:28; Luke 22:29-30; 1 Cor. 6:2-3; etc.); death, the "king of terrors" (Job 18:14); the *Leviathan* (which see), "king over all the sons of pride" (41:34). *See* History, Old Testament; Israel, Kingdom of.

BIBLIOGRAPHY: I. Engnell, *Studies in Divine Kingship in the Ancient Near East* (1943); H. Frankfort, *Kingship and the Gods* (1948); A. R. Johnson, *Sacral Kingship in Ancient Israel* (1955); G. E. Mendenhall, *Law and Covenant in Israel and the Ancient Near East* (1955); K. W. Whitelaw, *The Just King* (1979); L. Rost, *The Succession to the Throne of David* (1982).

KINGDOM OF GOD, KINGDOM OF HEAVEN. The "kingdom of God" is evidently a more comprehensive term than the "kingdom of heaven" and embraces all created intelligences, both in heaven and on earth, who are willingly subject to God and thus in fellowship with Him. The "kingdom of heaven"—more precisely the "kingdom of the heavens"—is a term descriptive of any type of rulership God may assert on the earth at a given period. As a predicted kingdom it has reference to the establishment of the kingdom of Israel on the earth (Acts 1:6) and is the subject of extended glowing prophecies in the OT (cf. Pss. 2:6; 72:1; Isa. 11:1; 32:1; 65:17; Jer. 33:15; Dan. 7:13-14; Mic. 4:1; Zech. 9:10; 12:1; 14:9). As a covenanted kingdom the kingdom of heaven becomes the national hope of Israel (2 Sam. 7:4-17). John the Baptist, Christ, and the apostles announced that the kingdom of national Israel was "at hand." That offer was rejected. As a result the "kingdom of heaven" in its earthly manifested form was postponed until Christ's second advent. Widespread attempts to "bring in the kingdom" on the basis of Christ's first advent are misplaced. According to the clear teaching of the Bible it will be realized only in connection with the second advent. The testimony of Scripture agrees completely with this fact. According to Matt. 13 the present gospel age represents the mystery form of the kingdom. "Since the kingdom of heaven is no other than the rule of God

on the earth, He must now be ruling to the extent of full realization of those things which are termed 'the mysteries' in the NT and which really constitute the new message of the NT" (Lewis Sperry Chafer, *Systematic Theology*, 7:224). The "kingdom of the heavens," that is, the manifested rule of God on the earth in the mediatorial Davidic kingdom, will not be realized until the future millennial period. The kingdom of God and the kingdom of heaven, as Chafer points out, are not identical despite the fact that "Matthew employs the terminology of the kingdom of heaven" and Mark and Luke, when presenting practically the same teaching, employ the phrase "kingdom of God." According to Scripture the "sons of the kingdom shall be cast out" (Matt. 8:12; 24:50-51; 25:28-30). This fate cannot be applied to the kingdom of God and its members (John 3:18). The parable of the wheat and the tares (Matt. 13:24-30, 36-43) and the parable of the good and bad fish (13:47-50) are only spoken of in connection with the kingdom of heaven. The parable of the leaven, however (13:33; Luke 13:20-21), is applied to both kingdoms. "Leaven represents evil doctrine rather than evil persons, and evil doctrine may and does corrupt both kingdoms" (op. cit., pp. 224-25).   M.F.U.

BIBLIOGRAPHY: L. S. Chafer, *The Kingdom in History and Prophecy* (1919); J. Bright, *The Kingdom of God* (1953); W. G. Kümmel, *Promise and Fulfillment* (1957); G. N. H. Peters, *The Theocratic Kingdom of Our Lord Jesus Christ*, 3 vols. (1957); A. J. McClain, *The Greatness of the Kingdom* (1959); G. Lundstrom, *The Kingdom of God in the Teaching of Jesus* (1963); G. E. Ladd, *Jesus and the Kingdom* (1964); J. F. Walvoord, *The Millennial Kingdom* (1965); G. H. Dalman, *The Words of Christ* (1981), pp. 91-155, 234-332.

KINGDOM OF ISRAEL. *See* Israel, Kingdom of; Constitution of.

KINGDOM OF JUDAH. *See* Judah, Kingdom of.

KINGLY OFFICE OF CHRIST. *See* Jesus, Offices of.

KINGS, 1 AND 2, BOOKS OF. These books are named from the opening word of 1 Kings in the Hebrew text, *wᵉhammelek*, meaning "and the king," and from the fact that this section of Scripture deals with the kings of Israel and Judah in their historical setting, in one case to the fall of Samaria (722-721 B.C.) and in the other case to the Babylonian captivity. In the LXX and the Vulg. it is recorded as 3 and 4 Kings. In modern Hebrew Bibles it appears as 1 and 2 Kings after 1 and 2 Samuel. The book was originally single-volumed like Samuel.

Scope. As a historical narrative the books of Kings carry on the recital of the history of Israel where 1 and 2 Samuel leave off, just prior to the death of David. The historical narrative is carried forward to the fall of Samaria in the case of the Northern Kingdom and until the thirty-seventh year of King Jehoiachin's captivity in Babylon. The time span is c. 972-560 B.C.

Chronology. The task of harmonizing the synchronous reigns of the kings of Judah and Israel has been a difficult problem, exercising the ingenuity of scholars for many years. More recent chronologists include F. X. Kugler, *Von Moses bis Paulus*, 1922; J. Begrich, *Die Chronologie der Koenige von Israel und Judah*, 1929; S. Mowinckel, *Die Chronologie der israelitischen und jeudischen Koenige*, 1932; M. Vogelstein, *Biblical Chronology*, Part 1, 1944. Numerous factors complicate the chronology of the monarchic period such as coregencies, ancient calendar reckonings, synchronisms, and so on. Edwin R. Thiele's *The Mysterious Number of the Hebrew Kings* (1951) is enlightening. W. F. Albright has also made valuable contributions to the chronological study of this period in his article "The Chronology of the Divided Monarchy," in *Bulletin of the American Schools* 100:16-22. Albright observes coregencies and synchronisms but reduces the reigns of Judahite kings as well as the number of Israelite kings, especially in the case of the Omrides. These and other studies have somewhat reduced vexing problems, yet few of the dates of this period are absolutely fixed, although in most cases are perhaps not more than five years wrong.

Authorship. The Talmud (*Baba Bathra*, 14b) names Jeremiah as the author of these books. J. E. Steinmueller (*A Companion to Scripture Studies*, 2: 98f.) espouses this view. He maintains that the Jeremian authorship does not rule out the composition of the book at Babylon, since tradition holds that Nebuchadnezzar carried Jeremiah to Babylon after the former had conquered Egypt in his thirty-seventh year (568 B.C.). In Babylon Jeremiah died as an aged man past ninety. Under this view Jeremiah wrote 2 Kings 25:27-30 in Babylon, although the remainder of the book may have been compiled long before that time.

Sources. The writer, whether he was Jeremiah or not, was in all probability a contemporary of Jeremiah and also a prophet who was deeply distressed at the spiritual declension of Judah. The author makes free mention of sources that he evidently used extensively. He refers to the book of the acts of Solomon (1 Kings 11:41). The book of the chronicles of the kings of Israel is mentioned seventeen times. The book of the chronicles of the kings of Judah is referred to fifteen times.

Critical View. Higher critics commonly place the original edition of the book of Kings shortly after the death of Josiah, somewhere between 609 and 600 B.C. The claim is made that the writer was the first to use historical materials derived from the recently discovered book of Deuteronomy, which initially is alleged to have appeared in 621 B.C. The book is supposed to be a religious and not a historical work. Critics call it a Deuteronomistic history (cf. Pfeiffer, *Introduction*, p. 380). The unique law of the central sanctuary appearing in Deut. 12 is supposed to be the guiding principle for evaluating each king. Thus, authentic history is ruled out. It is also maintained that in c. 550 B.C., during the exilic period, a second Deuteronomist added the history to the liberation of King Jehoiachin (2 Kings 25:27-30) and made various additions to the book. Wellhausen critics assume as well that this Deuteronomist also redid the Pentateuchal books, except Leviticus, together with Joshua, Judges, and Samuel. Supposedly a few additions were finally made by a priestly writer until the time it was canonized (c. 200 B.C.).

Repudiation of the Critical Position. This critical view must be rejected because it is unsound and of one piece with the partitioning of the Pentateuch. The same erroneous philosophical, historical, and literary suppositions underlie the notion of a Deuteronomistic work of history as underlie the unsound partitioning of the Pentateuch. The objectionable theory is that the book discovered in the eighteenth year of Josiah's reign (2 Kings 22:3-8) was Deuteronomy and that alone, and that this book was composed shortly before its discovery and passed off as the law of Moses. It is a far sounder view to accept early Pentateuchal evidences of the existence of Deuteronomy rather than to invent this artificial theory and to reject all such inferences as later glosses or redactional additions. Moreover, the critical theory must be rejected because the Deuteronomic stamp is no less original with other OT books than it is with the book of Kings. It is pure supposition to view Joshua, Judges, and Samuel as originally written without the background of the Deuteronomic laws. It must not be denied, however, that the author of Kings had a pragmatic and religious motive. He was not supplanting existing histories but writing a religious history. This history is not to be accounted as distorted or arbitrary simply because it deals with the rulers of the theocratic kingdoms on the basis of their loyalty to the Word of God.

Outline.

I. The reign of King Solomon (1 Kings 1:1–11:43)
   A. His accession (1:1-53)
   B. His charge (2:1-46)
   C. His marriage (3:1)
   D. His wisdom (3:2-28)
   E. His administration (4:1-34)
   F. His buildings (5:1–8:66)
   G. His splendor (9:1–10:29)
   H. His apostasy (11:1-43)

II. The reigns of contemporaneous kings (1 Kings 12:1–2 Kings 17:41)
   A. Rehoboam in Judah (1 Kings 12:1-24; 14:21-31)
   B. Jeroboam in Israel (12:25–14:20)

C. Abijam in Judah (15:1-8)
D. Asa in Judah (15:9-24)
E. Nadab in Israel (15:25-31)
F. Baasha in Israel (15:32–16:7)
G. Elah in Israel (16:8-14)
H. Zimri in Israel (16:15-20)
I. Omri in Israel (16:21-28)
J. Ahab in Israel (16:29–22:40)
K. Jehoshaphat in Judah (22:41-50)
L. Ahaziah in Israel (1 Kings 22:51–2 Kings 1:18)
M. Jehoram in Israel (3:1–8:15)
N. Jehoram in Judah (8:16-24)
O. Ahaziah in Judah (8:25-29)
P. Jehu in Israel (9:1–10:36)
Q. Athaliah in Judah (11:1-16)
R. Jehoash in Judah (11:17–12:21)
S. Jehoahaz in Israel (13:1-9)
T. Jehoash in Israel (13:10-25)
U. Amaziah in Judah (14:1-20)
V. Jeroboam II in Israel (14:23-29)
W. Azariah in Judah (14:21–15:7)
X. Zechariah in Israel (15:8-12)
Y. Shallum in Israel (15:13-15)
Z. Menahem in Israel (15:16-22)
AA. Pekahiah in Israel (15:23-26)
BB. Pekah in Israel (15:27-31)
CC. Jotham in Judah (15:32-38)
DD. Ahaz in Judah (16:1-20)
EE. Hoshea in Israel (17:1-41)
III. The reigns of the Judahite kings (2 Kings 18:1–25:30)
A. Hezekiah (18:1–20:21)
B. Manasseh (21:1-18)
C. Amon (21:19-26)
D. Josiah (22:1–23:30)
E. Jehoahaz (23:31-35)
F. Jehoiakim (23:36–24:7)
G. Jehoiachin (24:8-17; 25:27-30)
H. Zedekiah (24:18–25:26)   M.F.U.

BIBLIOGRAPHY: C. F. Burney, *Notes on the Hebrew Text of the Books of Kings* (1903); J. A. Montgomery, *The Book of Kings,* International Critical Commentary (1951); J. Ellul, *The Politics of Man and the Politics of God* (1972); F. W. Farrar, *The First Book of Kings* (1981); id., *The Second Book of Kings* (1981); T. Kirk and G. Rawlinson, *Studies in the Books of Kings* (1983); E. R. Thiele, *Mysterious Numbers of the Hebrew Kings* (1983); H. Vos, *First and Second Kings* (1989).

KING'S DALE, KING'S VALLEY. See Shaveh, Valley of.

KIN'NERETH. See Chianereth.

KINSMAN (Heb. *gô'ēl,* "redeemer"). This Heb. term for kinsman is used to imply certain obligations arising out of that relationship, and has for its primary meaning "coming to the help or rescue" of one. The *gô'ēl* among the Hebrews was the nearest living male blood relative ("close relative," Ruth 3:12; 4:1), and on him devolved certain duties to his next of kin.

Blood Avenger. The most striking office of the kinsman *gô'ēl* was that of blood avenger (*see* Blood, Avenger of). Although the word is peculiar to the Heb. language, the institution that it represents is common to several branches of the Semites. The unit of Semitic society is the clan, a body of persons united to one another by blood, a family on a somewhat enlarged scale. The members of the clan, closely bound by blood ties to one another, feel a mutual responsibility for one another. A wrong done to a single member is a crime against the entire clan. The obligation, therefore, rests upon the clan to punish the wrongdoer. In the case of murder it is a positive obligation to seek not vengeance but avengement. The blood of the murdered person cries up from the ground, and the cry is heard loudest by that member of the clan who stands nearest to the dead. The crime consists in the spilling of the blood —its waste—rather than in the extinction of life. The son is enjoined to avenge the blood of his father; the brother is obliged to punish a crime committed against his sister. "Lynch law" is the most primitive form of justice; and *gô'ēl* is the "avenger," legitimately constituted as such and recognized by the verdict of ancient Semitic society. If the killing was accidental the *gô'ēl* had no claim, unless the slayer left the city of refuge before the death of the high priest in whose reign the crime was committed. *See* Cities of Refuge.

Redeemer. It was the duty of a kinsman (i.e., "redeemer") to redeem the paternal estate that his nearest relative might have sold through poverty (Lev. 25:25; Ruth 4:4), to ransom his kinsman who may have sold himself (Lev. 25:47-49), and to act as go-between in case a person wished to make restitution to a relative. If there was no kinsman then the compensation went to the priest as representing Jehovah, the king of Israel (Num. 5:6-8). From Ruth (chaps. 3-4) it has been inferred that among the duties of kinsman *gô'ēl* was that of marrying the widow of a deceased kinsman. But the Levirate law expressly limits the obligation to a brother. The nearest kinsman had the right to redeem the land, which, perhaps, involved marrying the widow of the deceased owner, according to usage. See Marriage, Levirate; Redeemer.

BIBLIOGRAPHY: D. Jacobson, *The Social Background of the Old Testament* (1942); A. Malamat, *Journal of the American Oriental Society* 82 (1962): 143-50; F. I. Andersen, *Bible Translator* 29 (1969): 29-39; J. H. Hayes and J. M. Miller, eds., *Israelite and Judean History* (1977), pp. 70-120.

KI'OS. See Chios.

KIR (kir; "wall"). The place to which Tiglath-pileser led captive the people of Damascus (2 Kings 16:9), according to the prophecy of Amos (1:3-5), and from which at some time the Arameans emigrated to Syria (9:7). Delitzsch (*Com.,* on Isa. 22:6) identifies the Kir in this passage with that mentioned in Kings and Amos. It seems to have been situated on the river Kur (*Kuros*), which takes its rise in Armenia.

KIR OF MOAB (kir of Mō'ab). One of the two strongly fortified cities of Moab (Isa. 15:1), the other being Ar. It is probably the same as *Kir-hareseth* (which see).

KIR-HAR'ESETH (kir-har'e-seth; "city of pottery," some read "new city," 2 Kings 3:25; Isa. 16:7, 11; "Kir-heres," Jer. 48:31, 36; and "Kir of Moab," Isa. 15:1). A strongly fortified city of Moab, which is now known as Kerak and lies about fifty miles from Jerusalem. Joram, king of Israel, took the city and destroyed all but its walls (2 Kings 3:25). King Mesha endeavored to fight his way through the besiegers with 700 men, but when this attempt failed, in desperation he took his firstborn son, who was to succeed him as king, and offered him as a sacrifice upon the wall. From the other passage cited it would appear to have been restored before Isaiah's time and ravaged by the Babylonians.

KIR'IATH (kir'yath; "city"). A city belonging to Benjamin (Josh. 18:28; "Kirjath," KJV). By some it is identified with Kiriath-jearim, but this is disputed.

KIRIATHA'IM (kir'yath-tha'im; "double city"; sometimes "Kirjathaim," KJV).

1. A city of refuge in Naphtali (1 Chron. 6:76); elsewhere (Josh. 21:32) called *Kartan* (which see).

2. An ancient town E of Jordan, from which the gigantic *Emim* (which see) were expelled by the Moabites (Gen. 14:5, "Shaveh-kiriathaim," cf. Deut. 2:9-10). It was next held by the Amorites, from whom it was taken by the Israelites and assigned to Reuben (Num. 32:37; Josh. 13:19). During the Babylonian Exile the Moabites again took possession of this and other towns (Jer. 48:1; Ezek. 25:9). *See* Moabite Stone, line 10. Harper and others identified Kiriathaim with the ruins of El Kūreiyât, about six miles NW of Dibon.

KIR'IATH-AR'BA (kir'yath-ar'ba; "city of Arbah"; "Kir'jath-arba," KJV). A city in the mountains of Judah, named after Arba the Anakite (Gen. 23:2; Josh. 14:15; 15:54; 20:7; Judg. 1:10; Neh. 11:25), but better known as *Hebron* (which see).

KIR'IATH-A'RIM (Ezra 2:25; "Kirjath-arim," KJV). *See* Kiriath-jearim.

KIR'IATH-BA'AL (kir'yath-ba'al; "city of Baal"), another name (Josh. 15:60; 18:14) for *Kiriath-jearim* (which see). Rendered "Kir'jath-ba'al," KJV.

KIR'IATH-HU'ZOTH (kir'yath-hu'zōth; "city of streets"; "Kir'jath-hu'zoth," KJV). A city of Moab to which Balak took Balaam to offer up sacrifice (Num. 22:39). Balak undoubtedly expected through these offerings to propitiate Jehovah and secure His favor to the Moabites.

KIR'IATH-JE'ARIM (kir'yath-je'a-rim; "city of forests"; "Kirjath-jearim," KJV), or **Kiriath-arim** (kĭr'iăth-ā'rĭm; contracted form, Ezra 2:25; "Kirjath-arim," KJV). A Gibeonite town (Josh. 9:17), first assigned to Judah (15:60) but afterward to Benjamin (18:28). It was called Baalah (15:9) and Kiriath-baal (v. 60). Modern Deir al 'Azar, it was located about eight miles N of Jerusalem and just W of Abu Ghosh. Kiriath-jearim lay on the western border of Benjamin; once the Ark was set there, it was off the debatable plain of the Shephelah and within Israel's proper territory. Here the Ark rested until David brought it to Jerusalem (2 Sam. 6:2-3, marg., 12; 1 Chron. 15; cf. Ps. 132).

BIBLIOGRAPHY: Y. Aharoni, *The Land of the Bible* (1979), pp. 59, 110, 212, 244, 248, 253-56, 282n, etc.

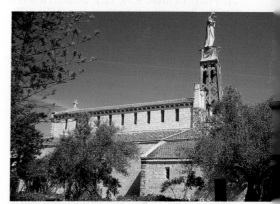

Present-day site of biblical Kiriath-jearim

KIR'IATH-SAN'NAH (kir'yath-sa'na; "Kirjath-sannah," KJV); called also **Kiriath-sepher** (kir'yath-sef'er) or "city of books," and later, **Debir** (which see, no. 2; Josh. 15:15-16, 49). This southern Judah city of the hill country has been identified with Tell Beit Mirsim, some thirteen miles WSW of Hebron. Melvin Grove Kyle and W. F. Albright excavated the site from 1926 to 1932. The results were most satisfactory, revealing clear strata with occupation from c. 2200 B.C. to 586 B.C., when Nebuchadnezzar destroyed it for the last time. At this place masonry of the Canaanites, Egyptians, Hyksos, and Hebrews can be seen. This site has greatly increased knowledge of Hebrew craftsmanship, particularly pottery making, building, and dyeing. Here a jar handle was recovered marked "Belonging to Eliakim, steward of Yaukin" (Jehoachin). Othniel took Debir (Kiriath-seper) and received Caleb's daughter Achsah as a reward (15:7, 15-16). The city was given over to the descendants of the priesthood (21:15).   M.F.U.

KIR'IATH SEPH'ER. *See* Kiriath-Sannah.

KIR'IOTH (kir'yōth) (Amos 2:2, KJV). *See* Kerioth.

KIR'JATH. *See* Kiriath.

KIR'JATHA'IM. *See* Kiriathaim.

KIR'JATH-AR'BA. *See* Kiriath-arba.

KIR'JATH-A'RIM. A KJV term replaced in the NASB by Kiriath-arim and in the NIV by Kiriath Jearim. *See* the discussion at Kiriath-jearim.

KIR'JATH-BA'AL. *See* Kiriathbaal.

KIR'JATH-HU'ZOTH. *See* Kiriath-huzoth.

KIR'JATH-JE'ARIM. *See* Kir'iath-jearim.

KIR'JATH-SANNAH. *See* Kir'iath-sannah.

KISH (kish).
1. The father of King Saul (1 Sam. 9:3; 10:11, 21; 14:51; 1 Chron. 9:39; 12:1; 26:28). He was a wealthy Benjamite, the son of Ner (8:33; 9:39) and grandson of Abiel the "son" of Zeror (1 Sam. 9:1), being used in the general sense of male descendant. No incident respecting him is mentioned with the exception of his sending Saul after the lost donkeys (9:3) and that he was buried in Zela (2 Sam. 21:14), about c. 1025 B.C. He is mentioned in Acts 13:21.
2. The third son of Jeiel (of Gibeon) and Maacah, a Benjamite of Jerusalem (1 Chron. 8:29-30; 9:35-36).
3. The second son of Mahli (grandson of Levi). His sons married their cousins, the daughters of his brother Eleazar (1 Chron. 23:21-22; 24:29), probably before 1440 B.C.
4. Another Levite, also of the family of Merari. He was the son of Abdi and assisted Hezekiah in cleansing the Temple (2 Chron. 29:12), 719 B.C.
5. A Benjamite, and great-grandfather of Mordecai (Esther 2:5), considerably before 478 B.C.
6. An ancient lower Mesopotamian city eight miles E of Babylon. Excavated palaces, temples, canals, and *ziggurats* (temple towers) give much information on Babylonian life before Abram's residence at Ur. Sargon I (c. 2380 B.C.) was a native of Kish. Hammurabi (c. 1700 B.C.) adorned the city.
BIBLIOGRAPHY: W. F. Albright, *From Stone Age to Christianity* (1957), pp. 184ff.; C. J. Barber and J. D. Carter, *Always a Winner* (1977), pp. 46-54; W. G. Blaikie, *The First Book of Samuel* (1978), pp. 121-32.

KISH'I (kish'i; 1 Chron. 6:44). *See* Kushaiah.

KISH'ION (kis'yon; "hard ground"). A city of Issachar (Josh. 19:20) assigned to the Levites of the family of Gershon and as a city of refuge (21:28; "Kishon," KJV). It is erroneously transcribed Kedesh (1 Chron. 6:72).

KI'SHON (ki'shon; "ending, winding"; and "Kison," Ps. 83:9, KJV). Also known as the "waters of Megiddo" (Judg. 5:19), a torrent or winter stream in central Palestine (cf. Ps. 83:9). It rises in the hills about Tabor and Gilboa and, running in a NE direction through the plains of Esdraelon and Acre, empties into the Mediterranean Sea at the foot of Mt. Carmel. The two channels of the stream unite a few miles N of Megiddo. The channel of the united stream is deep and miry here, the ground for some distance on each side is low and marshy; the fords during winter are difficult, and often, after heavy rain, impassable. Yet in summer the whole plain and riverbed are dry and hard. Indeed, during the greater part of the year the stream is confined to a few miles next to the sea. The modern name is Nahr el Mukatta', i.e., "the river of slaughter" (cf. 1 Kings 18:40). In the song of Deborah (Judg. 5:21) it is spoken of as "the ancient torrent."

The Kishon River near Haifa

It was a little to the S of Kishon, namely, at Megiddo, that *Sisera* (which see) was defeated. While the battle raged, a violent storm of wind and rain came (5:20-21), and the plain became a marsh and the dry riverbed a foaming torrent. This, of course, greatly interfered with the fighting of Sisera's cavalry and charioteers. Kishon was also the scene of the destruction of the prophets of Baal. Their slaughter doubtless took place near the foot of Carmel.

BIBLIOGRAPHY: D. Baly, *The Geography of the Bible* (1957), pp. 148-54; W. F. Albright, *The Archaeology of Palestine* (1960), pp. 117-18; Y. Aharoni, *The Land of the Bible* (1979), pp. 9, 17, 22-24, 50, 111, 152, 224-25, 257-58.

KIS'LEV. *See* Chislev.

KIS'LON. *See* Chislon.

KIS'LOTH TABOR. *See* Chisloth-Tabor.

KIS'ON *See* Kishon.

KISS. Kissing the lips by way of affectionate salutation was customary among near relatives of both sexes, both in patriarchal and in later times (Gen. 29:11; Song of Sol. 8:1). Between individuals of the same sex, and in a limited degree between those of different sexes, the kiss on the cheek as a mark of respect or an act of salutation has at all times been customary in the East. In the Christian church the "holy kiss" or "kiss of love" was practiced not only as a friendly salutation but as an act symbolical of love and Christian brotherhood (Rom. 16:16; 1 Cor. 16:20; 2 Cor. 13:12; 1 Thess. 5:26; 1 Pet. 5:14). It was embodied in the earlier Christian offices and has been continued in some of those now in use. Among the Arabs the women and children kiss the beards of their husbands or fathers. The husband or father returns the salute by a kiss on the forehead. In Egypt an inferior kisses the hand of a superior, generally on the back, but sometimes, as a special favor, on the palm also. To testify abject submission, and in asking favors, the feet are often kissed instead of the hand. The written decrees of a sovereign are kissed in token of respect; even the ground is sometimes kissed by orientals in the fullness of their submission (Gen. 41:40, *see* marg.; 1 Sam. 24:8; Ps. 72:9; etc.). Kissing is spoken of in Scripture as a mark of respect or adoration given to idols (1 Kings 19:18; Hos. 13:2; Smith, *Bib. Dict.,* "Kiss").

KITE. *See* Animal Kingdom.

KITH'LISH. *See* Chitlish.

KIT'LISH. *See* Chitlish.

KIT'RON (kit'ron; "figurative, knotty"). A city in Zebulun, from which the Israelites did not expel the Canaanites (Judg. 1:30), probably the same as *Kattath* (which see). A. Alt locates it at Tell el-Far about 7½ miles SE of Haifa.

KIT'TIM, CHIT'TIM (kit'im). A general name (such as our Levant) applied to the islands and coasts of the Mediterranean in a loose way without fixing the particular part, though particular and different parts of the whole are probably in most cases to be understood. According to Josephus (*Ant.* 1.6.1) it is an ancestral name. "Chethimus possessed the island Chethima; it is now called Cyprus." By the Greeks the name was retained for the city Citium, a Phoenician colony of unknown antiquity on the southern coast, while "by the Hebrews all islands and most of the seacoasts are called Chethim." Modern scholars hold that the name was extended first from Citium to all Cyprus and afterward to the coasts and islands, especially of Greece, though sometimes it was carried as far as Italy. In Maccabees, Chittim is Macedonia. The Vulg. in Numbers and the Vulg. and the Aram. Targum in 1 Chron. 1:7 have "Italy," and in Ezek. 27:6 the Targum has "Apulia."

Among the Phoenicians *Kitti* meant Cyprians. Among the Hebrews we may say that the writers

who showed most interest in and acquaintance with the maritime operations of Tyre, as Isaiah (*see* chap. 23), Jeremiah (25:22; 47:4), and Ezekiel (chaps. 26-28), used almost entirely the longer and more accurate form *Kittiyim,* as Isa. 23:1, *kethibh* (but in 23:12 it is *kittim*); Jer. 2:10; whereas authors more remote in space or time have the shorter form *Kittim* (Gen. 10:4; Num. 24:24; 1 Chron. 1:7; Dan. 11:30).

The name *Chittim,* being once given to these regions, might continue as a geographical term without regard to changes in population; but the association of Kittim in Gen. 10:4 with Javan and Elishah points to Greeks and Carians rather than to Phoenicians. If in Gen. 10:4 we read Rodanim (as in 1 Chron. 1:7) instead of Dodanim, we may with plausibility liken Javan, Elishah, Kittim, and Rodanim to Ionia, Elis, Citium, and Rhodes.

Cyprus was visited by Sargon I, about 2380 B.C. It paid tribute to Thutmose III in the fifteenth century B.C.; seven of its kings sent ambassadors to Sargon II, 709 B.C., who erected a monolith at Citium; ten of its kings sent envoys to Esar-haddon at the close of the war against Abdimiljuti and Sanduarri, 676 B.C. *See* Cyprus.

KIY'YUN (ki'un). A word occurring in the Bible only in Amos 5:26. It is generally revocalized Kaiwan or Kewan, i.e., Saturn (Ninib). Apparently the Masoretes gave the vocalization of Shiqquṣ ("a detestable thing," whence Kiyyun). KJV uses the word *Chiun;* RSV translates "Kaiwan your star god." The NIV renders "the pedestal of your idols" for "Kaiwan your idols" (*see* marg.). Stephen quotes "the star of the god Rompha" (Acts 7:43), the Kiyyun of Amos being read by the LXX translators Rephan, evidently the Egyptian name for Saturn. *See* Gods, False.   M.F.U.

KNEAD. The preparation of dough by working it into a mass with the hands; a task usually performed by women (Gen. 18:6; 1 Sam. 28:24; 2 Sam. 13:8; etc.) but sometimes by men (cf. Hos. 7:4).

KNEADING BOWL. The vessel in which the dough was mixed and leavened and then left to rise (Ex. 8:3; 12:34; and Deut. 28:5, 17, where the KJV has "store"). For this purpose the Arabs use a piece of leather that can be drawn up into a bag by running a cord along the border, in which they often prepare and carry their dough. It is not probable that the bowls used by the Hebrews in the references above were like these, as they were not a nomadic people. *See* Bread.

KNEE. The expression "knelt" or "kneeling on his knees," "falling on his knees," has for its primary notion that of *breaking down,* and then to *invoking God, to bless* (2 Chron. 6:13; Ps. 95:6; Dan. 6:10; Matt. 17:14). To kneel signifies also to give or receive a blessing, because the person blessed kneels. In this sense it refers to: (1) the benediction of dying parents (Gen. 27:4, 7, 10,

19); (2) of the priest to the people (Lev. 9:22, 23); (3) of a prophet (Num. 24:1; Deut. 33:1). It also signifies "to salute," which is connected with blessing (2 Kings 4:29).

The expression "and he made the camels kneel down" (Gen. 24:11) means that they were to rest.

To "bow" the knee is to perform an act of worship (1 Kings 19:18; Isa. 66:3, where the rendering is "blesses an idol").

Kneeling in prayer was a practice of great antiquity, and references are made to it in both the OT and NT (2 Chron. 6:13; Ps. 95:6; Dan. 6:10; Luke 22:41; Acts 7:60; 9:40; 21:5; Eph. 3:14).

Figurative. Knees are used symbolically for *persons* (Job 4:4; Heb. 12:12).

KNIFE (Heb. *ma'ăkelet, śakkîn, ta'ar*). The knives of the Egyptians, and of other nations in early times, were probably only of hard stone, and the use of the flint or stone knife was sometimes retained for sacred purposes after the introduction of iron and steel. Herodotus (2.86) mentions knives both of iron and of stone used in different stages of the same process of embalming. The same may perhaps be said to some extent of the Hebrews.

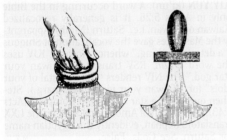

Egyptian knives

Lachish yielded an inscribed Hyksos knife. Hittite daggers have been recovered at Beth-shan from about 1470 B.C. Till the time of Saul and David iron and "steel" knives with ivory handles were rare, being monopolized by the iron-smelting Philistines.

In their meals the Jews, like other orientals, made little use of knives, but they were required both for slaughtering animals either for food or sacrifice, as well as for cutting up the carcasses (cf. Lev. 7:2; 8:15, 20, 25; 9:8-15; 1 Sam. 9:24; etc.). Smaller knives were in use for paring fruit and for sharpening pens (Jer. 36:23). The razor was often used for Naziritic purposes, for which a special chamber was reserved in the Temple (Num. 6:5, 9, 19; Ezek. 5:1; etc.). The pruning "hooks" of Isa. 18:5 (KJV) were probably curved knives. The lances of the priests of Baal were pointed knives (1 Kings 18:28), and the suffering caused by cutting themselves with these knives was supposed to secure from Baal a favorable hearing. The knives that, with other articles of Temple furniture, were brought back from Babylon were doubtless used for killing and dissecting the sacred offerings (Ezra 1:9, *see* marg.).

BIBLIOGRAPHY: D. Corswant, *Dictionary of Life in Bible Times* (1956), p. 164.

KNOCK (Heb. *dāpaq;* Gk. *krouō,* Song of Sol. 5:2; Judg. 19:22, "pounding"; Matt. 7:7; Rev. 3:20; etc.). "Though [some Eastern people] are very jealous of their privacy, yet they never knock when about to enter your room, but walk in without warning or ceremony. It is nearly impossible to teach [some] servants to knock at your door. They give warning at the outer gate, or entrance, either by calling or knocking. To stand and *call* is a very common and respectful mode; and thus it was in Bible times, and to it there are many very interesting allusions. Moses commanded the holder of a pledge to stand without, and call to the owner thereof to come forth (Deut. 24:10-11). This was to avoid the insolent intrusion of cruel creditors. Peter stood knocking at the outer gate door (Acts 12:13-16), and so did the three men sent to Joppa by Cornelius (10:17-18). The idea is that the guard over your privacy is to be placed at the entrance to your premises" (Thomson, *Land and Book,* 1:191). The expression "Ask . . . seek . . . knock" (Matt. 7:7; Luke 11:9) depicts the fervor of an earnest prayer.

KNOPS. An archaic translation of two Heb. words, one denoting the spherodial decorations of the seven-branched candlestick in the Tabernacle (Heb. *kaptōr;* Ex. 25:31-36; NASB, "bulbs," NIV, "buds") and one denoting the ornamentation of the Temple (Heb. *peqā'îm;* 1 Kings 6:18; NASB and NIV, "gourds") and of laver in it (1 Kings 7:24; NASB and NIV, "gourds"). *See* Bulbs; Laver; Sea, Bronze; Tabernacle of Israel.

KNOWLEDGE. The expression "to know" sometimes means *to approve* of and take delight in (Ps. 1:6; Rom. 8:29); to cherish (John 10:27); to experience (Eph. 3:19). In Job 7:10 it is used of an inanimate object: "He will not return again to his house, nor will his place know him anymore." By a euphemism "to know" frequently denotes sexual intercourse (Gen. 4:1, KJV).

Knowledge may be partial (1 Cor. 13:9). It implies discovery, detection; as "through the Law comes the knowledge of sin" (Rom. 3:20). Knowledge is spoken of as an emblematical person, and as the gift of God (Prov. 1:29; 8:10; etc.). Knowledge may be perverted and thus become the medium of evil (Isa. 47:10; Rom. 1:28; 1 Cor. 8:1). Respecting divine knowledge, *see* Omniscience.

KO'A (kō'à). This word occurs only in Ezek. 23:23 in the prophetic announcement of punishment to the Jewish people from the various nations whose idolatries they had adopted: "The Babylonians and all the Chaldeans, Pekod and Shoa and Koa, and all the Assyrians with them."

The Koa are evidently to be equated with Kutu (Ku), located E of the Tigris and S of the lower Zab.

KO'HATH (kō'hath). The second son of Levi (Gen. 46:11), and the father of Amram, Izhar, Hebron, and Uzziel (Num. 3:19). Of his personal history we know only that he went down to Egypt with Levi and Jacob (Gen. 46:11), that his sister was Jochebed (Ex. 6:20), and that he lived to the age of 133 (6:18), about 1871 B.C. His descendants, the *Kohathites* (which see), formed one of the three great divisions of the Levites and contained the priestly family descended from Aaron (6:18-20). In the service of the Tabernacle their duty was to bear the Ark and the holy objects (Num. 4:15; 7:9). The inheritance of the Kohathites who were not priests lay in the half tribe of Manasseh in Ephraim (1 Chron. 6:61-70) and in Dan (Josh. 21:5, 20-26).

KO'HATHITES (kō'ha-thīts). The descendants of Kohath, the second of the three sons of Levi (Gershon, Kohath, Merari), from whom the three principal divisions of the Levites derived their name (Gen. 46:11; Num. 3:27; 2 Chron. 34:12; etc.). *See* Levites: Classification.

KOLA'IAH (ko-lī'ya; "voice of Jehovah").
1. A Benjamite and remote ancestor of Sallu, which latter dwelt in Jerusalem after the captivity (Neh. 11:7), long before 445 B.C.
2. The father of Ahab, which latter was a false prophet denounced by Jeremiah (Jer. 29:21), about 626 B.C.

KO'RAH (kō'ra).
1. The third son of Esau by his Canaanite wife Oholibamah (Gen. 36:5, 14, 18; 1 Chron. 1:35), about 1950 B.C. He was born in Canaan before Esau migrated to Mt. Seir (Gen. 36:5-9), and became the chief of an Edomite tribe (36:18). "Korah, in Gen. 36:16 has probably been copied by mistake from v. 18" (K. & D., *Com.*, ad loc.).
2. The Levite who conspired with Dathan and Abiram against Moses. Korah was the son of Izhar, the brother of Amram, the father of Moses and Aaron, making him cousin to these leaders of Israel (Ex. 6:21; Num. 16:1-49). About all that we know of Korah is in connection with the conspiracy of which he was one of the leaders.

Korah was probably influenced by jealousy because the high honors and privileges of the priesthood had been exclusively appropriated by the family of Aaron. Moses having supreme authority in civil affairs, the whole power over the nation would seem to have been taken by him and Aaron. The particular grievance that rankled in the minds of Korah and his company was their exclusion from the office of priesthood and their being confined—those among them who were Levites—to the inferior service of the Tabernacle.

Having joined to himself Dathan and Abiram

and 250 "leaders of the congregation," Korah appeared with them before Moses and Aaron and charged them with usurpation of privileges and offices rightfully belonging to others. Moses no sooner heard this charge than he "fell on his face," as if to refer the matter to the Lord (cf. Num. 14:5) and declared that the decision should be left to Jehovah. He told them to appear the next day with censers and incense.

The next day the rebels presented themselves before the Tabernacle, along with Moses and Aaron, and the whole congregation gathered at the instigation of Korah. The Lord appeared, and a voice commanded Moses and Aaron to separate themselves from the congregation, that they might not share in its destruction for making common cause with the conspirators. The two leaders prayed that the people might be spared and that Jehovah would confine His wrath to the leaders of the rebellion. The congregation, instructed by Moses, withdrew, and after Moses had appealed to what was about to happen as a proof of the authority by which he had acted, the earth opened and then closed over the fallen tents of Korah, Dathan, and Abiram. The other 250 rebels, who were probably in front of the Tabernacle, were then consumed by fire "from the Lord," about 1430 B.C. The incense burners of the rebels were made into plates to form an outer covering to the altar, a warning of the just judgment of God (vv. 38-40). The next morning the whole congregation murmured against Moses and Aaron and charged them with having slain the people of Jehovah. Notwithstanding the prayers of Moses and his brother, they could not avert the bursting forth of wrathful judgment. A plague destroyed 14,700 (vv. 41-50), and the high priesthood of Aaron was confirmed (chap. 17). As the descendants of Korah afterward became eminent in the Levitical service, it is clear that his sons were spared. They were probably living in separate tents or had separated themselves from the conspirators at the command of Moses. He is referred to in Num. 26:9-11; 1 Chron. 6:22, 37. In Jude 11 Korah is coupled with Cain and Balaam, and is held up as a warning to presumptuous and self-seeking teachers.
3. Son of Hebron. The eldest of the four sons of Hebron, of the family of Caleb and tribe of Judah (1 Chron. 2:43), considerably after 1380 B.C.

BIBLIOGRAPHY: R. K. Harrison, *Introduction to the Old Testament* (1969), pp. 628-30.

KO'RAHITE (kō'ra-hīt; Ex. 6:24; Num. 26:58; 1 Chron. 9:19, 31; the KJV sometimes renders "Korhites," or "Korathites"). That portion of the Kohathite Levites who were descended from *Korah* (which see). *See* Levites: Classification.

KOR'AZIN. *See* Chorazin.

KO'RE (kō're; "crier" or "partridge").

1. A Levite, the son of Ebiasaph, and father of Shallum, who was one of the "keepers of the thresholds of the tent" (1 Chron. 9:19). In 26:1 Kore is named as the father of Meshelemiah (or Shelemiah), a Temple gatekeeper, 960 B.C.

2. Son of Imnah, a Levitical keeper of the eastern gate, appointed by Hezekiah to receive the freewill offerings and distribute them to the priests (2 Chron. 31:14), 719 B.C.

3. Mistaken translation in 1 Chron. 26:19, KJV. Should read "Korah."

KOUM. See Kum.

KOZ (koz; "thorn"). In the NASB and NIV, the father of Anub and others of the posterity of Judah (1 Chron. 4:8; "Coz," KJV); where, however-

er, his own parentage is not stated, unless he is a son or brother of Ashhur (v. 5).

The term appears in the KJV in Ezra (2:61) and Nehemiah (3:4,21; 7:63); in those verses it is replaced in the NASB and NIV by *Hakkoz* (which see).

KU'E. (kū'e). A place from which Solomon imported horses (1 Kings 10:28; 2 Chron. 1:16), usually identified with Cilicia (see NIV, marg.).

KUM (kūm; Gk. from Aram. *qûmî;* "cumi," KJV). "Arise" (Mark 5:41).

KUSHA'IAH (ku-shā'ya). A Merarite Levite whose son Ethan was appointed a chief assistant of Heman in the Temple music by David (1 Chron. 15:17), 975 B.C. In 1 Chron. 6:44 he is called Kishi.

LA'ADAH (la'a-da; meaning uncertain). The second son of Shelah (son of Judah) and "father" (founder) of Mareshah (1 Chron. 4:21).

LAADAN. *See* Ladan.

LA'BAN (lā'ban; "white").

1. The son of Bethuel (Gen. 28:5), grandson of Nahor, Abraham's kinsman, and brother of Rebekah (Gen. 24:15, 29); an Aramean herd owner of Mesopotamia. He united with his father, according to the usual custom, in consenting to the marriage of Rebekah to Isaac (24:29-33, 50-59), about 1920 B.C. When their son Jacob became of marriageable age his parents directed him to take a wife from the daughters of Laban, and Jacob complied (28:2, 5). Laban arranged with his nephew to give him Rachel on condition of seven years' service, but on the wedding night led Leah, his eldest daughter, into the bridechamber. When Jacob complained to him Laban made the weak excuse, "It is not the practice in our place, to marry off the younger before the first-born." But, to satisfy Jacob, he promised to give him Rachel in a week if he would serve him seven years longer. To this Jacob consented, and eight days later he was wedded to the woman he loved (29:15-30). At the end of the second period of seven years Jacob desired to return to Canaan, but Laban persuaded him to remain, making a contract with him to keep his flocks. By a cunning artifice Jacob made this bargain result greatly to his own advantage (30:25-43) and at the end of six years left stealthily for his former home (31:1-21). Three days later, Laban, hearing of Jacob's flight, started in pursuit and overtook him on the seventh day at Mt. Gilead. The night before Laban was warned by God in a dream not to speak to Jacob "either good or bad," that is, not to threaten or persuade him to return. Laban confined himself to bitter reproaches. He told Jacob that he had power to do him harm if God

had not forbidden him and accused him of stealing his household gods. Finally a covenant of peace was established and was celebrated with a feast, and the next morning Laban departed to his own place (31:22-55).

2. A place in the desert, on the route of the Israelites (Deut. 1:1), probably identical with Libnah (Num. 33:20).

BIBLIOGRAPHY: F. Josephus, *Antiquities of the Jews,* 1.6.5; 1.19.1-11; W. H. G. Thomas, *Genesis: A Devotional Commentary* (1946), pp. 269-307; G. Ch. Aalders, *Genesis,* Bible Student's Commentary (1981), 2:65-69, 113-37.

LABOR. This English term is the rendering of a large number of Hebrew and Greek terms. The teaching of Scripture (Gen. 2:15) is that man, even in his state of innocence, was to lead a life of activity, which was different, however, from the trouble and restlessness of the weary toil into which he was plunged by sin. Exercise of some kind was essential to his well-being (cf. Eccles. 5:12). In consequence of the Fall, the earth no longer yielded spontaneously the fruits requisite for man's maintenance, but he was obliged to secure the necessities of life by labor and strenuous exertion (Gen. 3:19).

"*Work,* as distinguished from *labor,* is not so much a term denoting a lighter kind of labor as a general and comprehensive term applied to the performance of any task, whether easy or severe. *'Ăbōdâ* is the execution of a definite daily task, whether in field labor (Ps. 104:23) and mechanical employment (Ex. 39:32) on the one hand, or priestly service and the duties connected with the worship on the other (12:25-26; Lev. 23:7-8), i.e., such occupations as came under the denomination of labor, business, or industrial employment" (K. & D., *Com.,* on Ex. 20:8).

That labor was held in high respect we gather from such expressions as, "Do you see a man skilled in his work? He will stand before kings"

(Prov. 22:29; cf. 10:4; 12:24, 27). When Nebuchadnezzar carried the Jews away into captivity he found among them a 1,000 craftsmen and smiths (2 Kings 24:14-16; Jer. 29:2).

The ancient rabbis regarded manual labor as honorable and urged it upon all as a duty. In the Talmud we find such sayings as the following: "He who does not teach his son a craft is, as it were, bringing him up to robbery"; "Labor is greater to be prized, for it elevates the laborer, and maintains him."

The following values of labor are given by F. R. Conder (*Bib. Ed.*, 3: 223ff.): "The *denarius,* which was the Roman equivalent for a quarter shekel, was a day's pay of a Roman soldier. This was in exact accordance with the price, mentioned in the parable of the laborers in the vineyard, of a penny a day. The limit between the proper subject for alms for the purpose of support and the independent man was fixed by the oral law at the receipt of two hundred *zuzae,* that is to say, to one shekel per week. . . . This was considered by the law of Moses to be the lowest rate at which life was to be supported." *See* Handicrafts; Service.

BILIOGRAPHY: C. L. Mitton, *The Epistle of James* (1966), pp. 175-83; F. J. Delitzsch, *A New Commentary on Genesis* (1978), 1:165-76; G. Bush, *Notes on Exodus* (1981), 1:85-94; J. I. Packer, M. C. Tenney, and W. White, eds., *The Bible Almanac* (1980), pp. 263-70, 280-91.

LA'CHISH (lā'kish). A royal Canaanite city and one of the chief fortresses of Judah, identified with the large twenty-two-acre mound now known as Tell ed-Duweir. It is situated thirty miles SW of Jerusalem, fifteen miles W of Hebron. It is of immense strategic importance, dominating the old road from the Palestinian highland to the Nile valley. The site was excavat-

Assyrian relief showing invaders taking booty from Lachish

ed by the Wellcome-Marston Archaeological Expedition beginning in 1933. The work was supervised by J. L. Starkey until his murder by bandits early in 1938. The excavation of this site, ranking in importance with Bethshan and Megiddo, was thereafter carried on by Charles H. Inge and Lankester Harding. Yohanan Aharoni led Israeli digs there in 1966 and 1968, and David Ussishkin of Tel Aviv University has been excavating there since 1973.

The city was occupied several millennia before Abraham and was an important city still standing when the Israelites invaded Palestine. Its king, Japhia, joined a confederacy against Joshua (Josh. 10:3, 5) but was captured by the Israelites (10:31-35; 12:11). It was rebuilt or fortified by Rehoboam (2 Chron. 11:9) and had a reputation for strength. Amaziah fled there and was slain (2 Kings 14:19; 2 Chron. 25:27). Lachish fiercely resisted the siege of Sennacherib when on his way to Egypt (2 Kings 18:13-17; 2 Chron. 32:9; Isa. 36:2; 37:8) but ultimately capitulated in 701 B.C. Sennacherib portrayed the event on the walls of his palace at Nineveh. The city experienced two destructions by Nebuchadnezzar, one in 598 B.C. when Jehoiachin and the Jerusalem citizens were carried into captivity (2 Kings 24) and another in 589/88 B.C. when the city was reduced to ashes. After the Exile it was reoccupied (Neh. 11:30). Micah (1:13) denounced Lachish because it was the first to admit the iniquities of Israel into Judah, i.e., the idolatry of the image worship of the ten tribes. (*See* Mic. 1:5; Amos 3:14). Numbers of inscriptions have been found at the site, notably a broken bowl written in Egyptian, apparently by an Egyptian tax collector enumerating certain wheat deliveries. This is dated in the "year 4" of a certain pharaoh. Also found in a Late Bronze Age temple at Lachish were a bowl and a jar inscribed in an early Canaanite script. This script is identical with that of the proto-Semitic inscriptions found at Serabit el-Khadem on the Sinai Peninsula and in similar levels at Shechem, Gezer, and Beth-shemesh. Most important of all of the Lachish discoveries are the so-called Lachish Letters. These priceless documents, of vast epigraphic importance, illustrate the Hebrew current in the time of Jeremiah. They are to be dated between the two Babylonian sieges of Lachish (598-589/88 B.C.). Eighteen of these pieces of ancient inscribed pottery were found in 1935, to which three more were added in 1938. Practically all of these ostraca were written by a certain Hoshaiah, who was thought to be stationed at a military outpost, to a man named Jaosh, believed to be the high commanding officer at Lachish. This traditional interpretation has been disputed by Yigael Yadin, who concluded that the letters were first drafts of letters sent by Hoshaiah, the commander at Lachish, to Jaosh, his superior in Jerusalem. In any event, they give a sense of "you are there" at the destruction of Judah by Nebuchadnezzar. Other significant finds at the site include the 105-foot-square platform on which David built a government house, a Late Bronze temple, the walls of Rehoboam, a mass grave of 1,500 bodies probably dating to the Assyrian attack, the gate complex, and an Assyrian siege ramp and a Judean counter-ramp.   H.F.V.

BIBLIOGRAPHY: H. Horezyner, ed., *Lachish IV: The Bronze Age* (1958); Jack Finegan, *Light from the Ancient Past* (1965), p. 162; Y. Aharoni, *Lachish V* (1975); M. Avi-Yonah and E. Stern, eds., *Encyclopedia of Archaeological Excavations in the Holy Land* (1977), 3:735-53.

LA'DAN (lā'dan).

1. An Ephraimite, the son of Tahan and grandfather of Elishama, which latter was head of his tribe at the Exodus (1 Chron. 7:26), before 1440 B.C.

2. The first named of the two sons of Gershon, the son of Levi (1 Chron. 23:7-9; 26:21). Keil (*Com.,* ad loc.) believes that Ladan was a later descendant of Gershon than Libni, and that the Shimei of v. 9 was a descendant of Libni.

LADDER (Heb. *sullām;* "staircase"). This word occurs only in the account of Jacob's dream at Bethel (Gen. 28:12, "and behold, a ladder was set on the earth with its top reaching to heaven," etc.). By many the rendering "staircase" (NIV, "stairway") is preferred, and is supposed to apply to the rocky mountainside. The vision that Jacob saw of angels ascending and descending teaches the fact of communication between heaven and earth, and the ministry of angels. To us there is a deeper meaning since the incarnation. The true staircase by which heavenly messengers ascend and descend is the Son of Man. It is He who really bridges the interval between heaven and earth, God and man. However, the true fulfillment of Jacob's vision will not take place until the millennial age when the covenant with Abraham con-

firmed in Isaac and Jacob will be realized (John 1:49-51).

LA'EL (lā'el; "to, belonging to God," i.e., devoted to Him). The father of Eliasaph, who was leader of the Gershonites at the time of the Exodus (Num. 3:24), 1210 B.C.

LA'HAD (lā'had; "oppression," cf. Arab. *lahada,* "to press down, overburden"). The second of the two sons of Jahath, a descendant of Judah (1 Chron. 4:2), after 1210 B.C.

LAHAI'ROI. See Beer-lahai-roi.

LAH'MAS (lā'mas). A city in the plain of Judah (Josh. 15:40; Lahmam, KJV), perhaps among the Philistines W of the highlands of Judea. It is thought to be represented by the ruins of el-Lahm, about two miles E of Lachish.

LAH'MI (lā'mi). Named as the brother of Goliath and slain by Elhanan (1 Chron. 20:5). Strong (McClintock and Strong, *Cyclopedia,* s.v.) considers this an incorrect reading for Bethlehemite, as is found in the parallel passage (2 Sam. 21:19). Winer, Keil, Deutsch, Grove, and others maintain that Chronicles gives the true reading. *See* Goliath.

LA'ISH (lā'ish; a "lion").

1. A native of Gallim, a Benjamite, to whose son, Palti, Saul gave David's wife Michal (1 Sam. 25:44; 2 Sam. 3:15), about 1015 B.C.

2. A place in the N of Palestine (Judg. 18:7, 14), about four miles from Paneas, at the head of the Jordan. It was taken by the restless Danites and included within their territory. It is called also Leshem and Dan (Josh. 19:47, *see* marg.; Judg. 18:29; Jer. 8:16), now identified with Tell el-Qadi, "the mound of the judge," to the N of the waters of Merom (cf. Josh. 11:5). *See also* Dan; Laishah.

Artist's impression of the siege of Lachish

LA'ISHAH (lā'ish-a). A place mentioned in Isa. 10:30, thought by some to be the modern el-Isawîyeh, about a mile NE from Jerusalem. KJV, Laish.

LAKE (Gk. *limnē*, a "pool"). A term used in the NT only of the lake of Gennesaret (Luke 5:1-2; 8:22-23, 33) and the "lake of fire" (Rev. 19:20; 20:10, 14-15; 21:8). *See* Gehenna.

LAK'KUM (lak'um; "an obstruction," cf. Arab. *lakama*, "to obstruct a roadway"). A place in the NE of Naphtali (Josh. 19:33; "Lakum," KJV). Probably Khirbet el-Mansurah, W of the Jordan near where it flows out of the Sea of Galilee.

LA'MA (lā'ma). A term signifying "why," quoted from Ps. 22:1 by our Savior on the cross (Matt. 27:46; Mark 15:34).

LAMB. Lambs and young rams form an important part of almost every sacrifice in the OT (Lev. 4:32; Num. 6:14). *See* articles Animal Kingdom; Sacrifice. *Lamb of God* is a term used typically of Christ as the Sin-bearer of the world (John 1:29, 36; cf. Acts 8:32; 1 Pet. 1:19). In these passages Christ is likened to a sacrificial lamb on account of His death, innocently and patiently endured to expiate sin. "Lamb" was evidently a term used early to describe the redemption to be brought by the long-awaited Messiah (Isa. 53:7). The sheep speaks eloquently of the coming Redeemer and Sin-bearer. The lamb as the symbol of Christ was typified by the Paschal lamb and will be travestied by the Antichrist, who sets himself up as the true Christ, professing to imitate the Redeemer, and whose false prophet is described as "another beast coming up out of the earth; and he had two horns like a lamb" (Rev. 13:11). Especially significant is the use of the figure of the lamb as a symbol of Christ in the Apocalypse. There the lion-lamb portrays Christ in His future victory as crowned because of His redemptive work (5:12-13; 7:9; 22:1, 3). The term "marriage of the Lamb" (19:7-9) symbolizes the union of Christ and His church in glory previous to His second coming to earth to destroy His enemies, cast out satanic power, and set up the long-awaited mediatorial kingdom of Israel (19:11-17). In the Revelation John beheld "a Lamb standing, as if slain, having seven horns and seven eyes, which are the seven Spirits of God, sent out into all the earth" (5:6), i.e., invested with the attributes of God, omnipotence and omniscience, and sharing the universal empire and homage of the universe.

BIBLIOGRAPHY: C. H. Dodd, *The Interpretation of the Fourth Gospel* (1953), pp. 230-38; L. L. Morris, *The Apostolic Preaching of the Cross* (1965), pp. 129-85; N. Turner, *Christian Words* (1980), pp. 251-52.

LAME. A general term referring to imperfect limbs, either by birth or injury. Lameness is mentioned among the bodily imperfections that would exclude a son (descendant) of Aaron from entering the Holy Place or offering sacrifices. A person thus afflicted might, however, eat of the sacrifices, like other priests (Lev. 21:17-23). *See also* Diseases.

LA'MECH (lā'mek).

1. The fifth in descent from Cain, being the son of Methushael and the father of Jabal, Jubal, Tubal-cain, and the latter's sister, Naamah (Gen. 4:18-22). Lamech took two wives, Adah and Zillah, and was thus the first to practice polygamy. To the narrative of Lamech we are indebted for the only example of antediluvian poetry (vv. 23-24):

"Adah and Zillah,
Listen to my voice,
You wives of Lamech,
Give heed to my speech,
For I have killed a man for wounding me;
And a boy for striking me;
If Cain is avenged sevenfold,
Then Lamech seventy-sevenfold."

Many views have been entertained as to the meaning of these words. Keil (*Com.*, ad loc.) says that "in the form of pride and arrogance Lamech celebrates the inventions of Tubal-cain"; and the idea of the song is, "Whoever inflicts a wound or stripe on me, whether man or youth, I will put to death; and for every injury done to my person I will take ten times more vengeance than that with which God promised to avenge the murder of my ancestor Cain." Turner (*Companion to Genesis*, p. 209) says "that he had slain a young man, not in cold blood, but in consequence of a wound or bruise he had himself received; and on the ground, apparently, of a difference between his case and that of Cain's—viz., that he had done *under* provocation what Cain had done *without* it—he assures himself of an interest in the divine guardianship greater than that granted to Cain."

2. The son of Methuselah and father of Noah. He lived to be 777 (Gen. 5:25-31; 1 Chron. 1:3; Luke 3:36).

BIBLIOGRAPHY: R. S. Candlish, *Studies in Genesis* (1979), pp. 108-10.

LA'MED (ל) (lā'med; "oxgoad"). Letter 12 of the Heb. alphabet corresponding to Gk. *lambda*. (λ), English "L." It stands before the twelfth section of Ps. 119 in which each verse of the Heb. begins with this letter.

LAMENT. *See* Mourning.

LAMENTATIONS, BOOK OF. One of the so-called Megilloth, or Rolls, found in the third part of the Heb. canon. The work consists of five elegiac poems lamenting the destruction of Jerusalem at the time of the Babylonian captivity. It is termed *Ekah* (How!) in the Heb. from its initial word. The Gk. rendering in the LXX is *Threnoi*, rendered Lamentations in the Lat. Jeremiah is usually appended as the traditional author.

Purpose. Lamentations portrays the reaction of a devout Israelite toward the destruction of the theocracy. The tragic scene presents God's people as so corrupt that Jehovah has forsaken His sanctuary and abandoned it to enemies. The poet celebrates the Lord's righteousness but bewails the iniquity of the nation and calls upon the inhabitants to repent. The whole note is one of deep tragedy. The Lord's people, from whom salvation would eventually come, have become so vile as to be fit only for destruction.

Form. The first four elegiac poems are alphabetic. In the first two (chaps. 1 and 2) a new letter of the Heb. alphabet opens each verse, which has three parts. In the third lamentation (chap. 3) three verses are allotted to each of the twenty-two letters of the alphabet, and every verse in each group of three begins with the same letter. In the fourth dirge, one verse composed of two members is distributed to each letter. The last dirge is not alphabetic but consists of twenty-two verses. The meter is what is known as *qinah,* a special elegiac arrangement. The first member of the verse is longer than the second and is sometimes called the "limping verse." Instead of being balanced and reinforced by the second, it is faintly echoed, giving the effect of the whole dying away in a plaintive cadence.

Authorship. Many scholars such as Chaney, Ewald, Eissfeldt, Pfeiffer, and others dismiss authorship by Jeremiah. The main reason given in support of this is that the tradition is unreliable, being removed by three centuries from the age of the prophet. Internal evidence in comparison with Jeremiah's other writings, and several historical allusions, are used as alleged evidence. In reply it may be said that if Jeremiah is not the author, no other contemporaneous writer fits the qualifications of authorship any better. Denying Jeremiah's authorship, critics are cast into complete confusion concerning the question of who the author was. The long-sustained tradition of Jeremiah's authorship could hardly have arisen without solid basis. Argument from differences in vocabulary are extremely precarious. Supporting Jeremiah's authorship is a strong and persistent tradition dating from the time of the Greek version. The Vulg. and the Targum of Jonathan, as well as many of the church Fathers and numerous later commentators, follow this tradition. Internal evidence is also suggestive. The scenes are lifelike in their portrayal and suggest an eyewitness. A comparison of the Lamentations with Jeremiah's other writings also shows points of similarity, and the sensitive temperament of the great prophet is reflected in the elegiac poems. (*See* S. R. Driver, *Introduction* [1913], p. 462 for similarities.)   M.F.U.

BIBLIOGRAPHY: N. K. Gottwald, *Studies in the Book of Lamentations* (1954); B. Albrektson, *Studies in the Text and Theology of the Book of Lamentations* (1963); R. K. Harrison, *Jeremiah and Lamentations,* Tyndale Old Testament Commentaries (1973); R. Gordis, *The Song of Songs and Lamentations* (1974); W. C. Kaiser, Jr., *A Biblical Approach to Personal Suffering* (1982).

LAMP (Heb. *nēr lappîd,* "torch"; Gk. *lampas*). Although lamps are frequently mentioned in Scripture, no indication is given of their form and structure. The natural supposition is that they were similar to those employed in surrounding countries, especially Egypt, to which in matters of art and comfort the Israelites were closely related. The following are the references to lamps:

1. That part of the golden lampstand that bore the light; also of the ten golden lampstands ("candlesticks," KJV) in the Temple of Solomon (Ex. 25:37; 1 Kings 7:49; 2 Chron. 4:20; 13:11; Zech. 4:2).

Eastern lamp: oil was poured into the center hole and the wick burned in the end hole

2. A torch, such as were carried by the soldiers of Gideon (Judg. 7:16, 20), and, perhaps, similar to those that Samson tied to the foxes' tails (15:4). *See* Torch.

3. Lamps for domestic use. The form of these is known from the numerous excavations in Palestine and elsewhere in the Near East, and the shapes varied with the various periods of history. During most of the OT period in Palestine a lamp was simply a small clay saucer for oil with a pinched lip to hold the wick; olive oil was used for illumination. Normally lamps had a single wick, but sometimes they had four or even more. During the Roman period the common lamp was a small, oblong, covered saucer that could be held in the palm of the hand. Normally it had one wick but it could have two or more.

4. The use of lamps fed with oil in marriage processions is alluded to in the parable of the ten virgins (Matt. 25:1). These probably were similar to the modern Egyptian lantern, called *fanoos,* a sort of folding lantern.

Figurative. Lamp is used as symbolical of: the Word of God (Ps. 119:105; Prov. 6:23); salvation of God (Gen. 15:17; Isa. 62:1, rendered "torch" in both places); God's guidance (2 Sam. 22:29; Ps. 18:28); spirit of man (Prov. 20:27); ministers and wise rulers (2 Sam. 21:17; John 5:35); completely put out, the destruction of him who curses his parents (Prov. 20:20).

BIBLIOGRAPHY: R. H. Smith, *Biblical Archaeologist* 27 (1964): 1-31; 101-24; id., *BA* 29 (1966): 1-27.

LAMPSTAND, GOLDEN. See Tabernacle.

LANCES (Heb. *rōmah*, to "hurl," 1 Kings 18:28; cf. Job 39:23; 41:29, NIV). This word is elsewhere rendered and appears to mean a javelin, or light spear. It may mean the iron point or head of a lance. See Armor: Spear, Javelin, Dart.

LAND. Respecting the cultivation of land by the Hebrews, *see* Agriculture.

LAND AND PROPERTY.

Distribution. The patriarchs were promised for their posterity the possession of Canaan on the W of Jordan. But owing to the opposition of the Amorites, who had formed two large kingdoms on the E of Jordan, the Israelites were compelled first to wage war with Sihon of Heshbon and Og of Bashan. They were defeated by Israel, and their territory was taken and divided by Moses, who gave it to the tribes of Reuben and Gad, and the half tribe of Manasseh. They were allowed to enter upon their possession, however, only after having fulfilled their promise of sending all their men of war in aid of their brothers over the Jordan (Num. 32; Deut. 2:26–3:20; Josh. 13:15-32).

Joshua had charge of the taking and dividing of Canaan, and, having defeated thirty-one kings and taken their cities, he proceeded, by divine command, to divide the whole of that land among the remaining tribes, according to the boundaries fixed by Moses (Num. 34:1–35:8). The portion of each tribe was fixed by lot, that is, it was decided by lot where each tribe was to be located (26:52-56; 33:54). Then the compass, size, and boundaries of the several territories were settled and regulated by the commission appointed for the purpose, consisting of Eleazar the priest, Joshua, and twelve leaders of the tribes mentioned by name (Num. 34:16-29; Josh. 14:1-2). Naturally the extent of territory assigned to each tribe depended upon its number (Num. 33:54). A committee was formed of three men out of each tribe to survey the land (Josh. 18:4-9), that is not to measure it geometrically but to have it described according to the number of its cities and villages, its soil, and so on. The land was subdivided, so that every clan and father's house received an inheritance for itself. All the land was not immediately taken possession of, for the Canaanites were not exterminated. In the course of time the Canaanites left in the land were subdued, and their land became the property of the Israelites. As to the division of the cities, towns, and villages, the OT does not give any clear account.

Israel was taught that she had conquered Canaan only by the help of Jehovah (Ps. 44:3), and that the land was and remained the property of Jehovah, the covenant God (Lev. 25:23). Though the land was promised to the children of Israel for an everlasting possession (Gen. 13:15-16), yet their retaining it was conditional on their faithful fulfillment of its covenant obligations (Lev. 26:32-45; Deut. 4:26-30), and even the ground did not become Israel's property in such a way that the possessor could dispose of it as he willed.

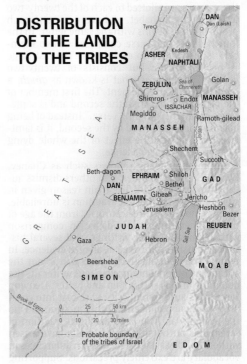

DISTRIBUTION OF THE LAND TO THE TRIBES

Probable boundary of the tribes of Israel

Laws. There were laws concerning the rest, redemption, and consecration of the land.

Rest. That Israel might be constantly reminded of the condition upon which it held the land, a year of rest for the ground was to be observed every seventh year, "a sabbath to the Lord" (Lev. 25:4); and every fiftieth year was to be a Jubilee, in which everyone returned to his property (25:10, 13).

The land was not to be sold in perpetuity, but there was a provision for redeeming the land by the seller or next of kin (25:23-24); and if not redeemed before, the land reverted without payment in the Jubilee year to its original possessor or his heir (v. 28). Thus every sale of land became a lease, since only its produce was sold, until the Jubilee (25:15-16).

Redemption. In case the owner or his next of

kin wished to redeem the land, then the years that had elapsed since the sale were reckoned, and the buyer received only as much purchase money as would be due for the time remaining until the next Jubilee (25:25-27). This right of redemption in the Jubilee held *absolutely* for (1) property in lands and houses in villages and unwalled places, and (2) for the houses of the Levites in the cities allotted for them, and the attached fields (25:31-34). In a *limited* way it held (1) for the dwelling house in walled cities; for them the right of redemption lasted only a full year from the day of sale (vv. 29-30); and (2) for the fields vowed unto the Lord, with the limitation that if they were not recovered for the prescribed valuation, but were sold to another, they did not revert in the Jubilee to their original possessor or his heir, but as being holy to Jehovah like a devoted field, became the property of the priests (27:14-21). Houses in walled cities were not so closely connected with the land, which the Lord gave to His people for an inheritance, that they could be regarded as inalienable.

Consecration. A bought field could be consecrated to the Lord by the buyer only so far as it had become his property. Strictly speaking, he had only bought its produce until the Jubilee and could, therefore, vow only this to Jehovah. If he ransomed it, he ransomed it for himself until the Jubilee; if he did not ransom it, the sanctuary had the use of it for this interval, after which the field reverted in either case without payment to the original owner (Lev. 27:22-24). An hereditary owner could vow a portion to Jehovah, who had given him all. In such a case ransom was allowed until the Jubilee by the payment of the value of the harvests until this date with an added fifth. Then the field remained his property, and from the Jubilee onward its produce again belonged to him cost free. If not redeemed it was understood that he had given it wholly to Jehovah, and it became the property of the priests (27:16-21).

BIBLIOGRAPHY: H. Danby, trans., *The Mishnah* (1933), pp. 374-452; D. Daube, *Studies in Biblical Law* (1947); G. Mendenhall, *Law and Covenant in Israel and the Ancient Near East* (1955); W. A. Whitehouse, *The Biblical Doctrine of Justice and Law* (1955); Z. Falk, *Hebrew Law in Bible Times* (1964); J. B. Pritchard, ed., *Ancient Near Eastern Texts* (1969), pp. 159-98.

LANDMARK. See Boundary Mark.

LANE. See Street.

LANGUAGES. The ancient biblical world was a thorough mixture of several languages. Important was Sumerian, a non-Semitic pictograph and sign language current in southern Babylonia previous to 3000 B.C. The Semitic Babylonians brought in Akkadian, written in cuneiform characters. The great family of Semitic languages included its Eastern branch, Assyrian-Babylonian (Akkad.); NW Semitic, Aramaic, Ugaritic, Hebrew, and Phoenician; S Semitic, Arabic, Ethiop-

ic, and Amharic. The language of the Philistines still remains obscure. The Moabites spoke a dialect similar to Hebrew, as shown by the Moabite Stone discovered in 1868. The Gezer Calendar (c. 925 B.C.), the Siloam Inscription (c. 702 B.C.), and the Lachish Letters (c. 589 B.C.) give us epigraphic evidence of the development of Hebrew. (*See* Hebrew Language.) The Ugaritic Tablets from Ras Shamra (1929-37) have greatly illuminated Canaanite dialects and, being closely associated with Hebrew, have shed much light on the language of the OT. As a cultural bridge between the great Egyptian Empire and the empires on the Halys in Asia Minor and on the Tigris-Euphrates in Mesopotamia, the ancient Hebrews came constantly in contact with various languages. Now well known are Hittite, Hurrian, and Semitic dialects spoken in antiquity. Excavations at Boghaz-Keui, Mari on the Middle Euphrates, and at Nuzi in the Tigris country have yielded a whole vast cuneiform literature in Hittite and Hurrian. At the end of the OT period (c. 400 B.C.) Hebrew began to fade out, and Aramaic became the *lingua franca* of SW Asia as Akkadian had been in the Amarna Period (c. 1400 B.C.). By the time of Jesus, Aramaic was the vernacular in Palestine with *koine* Greek a universal language since Alexander's conquests in the fourth century B.C. The Latin of the Roman Empire also became a kind of *lingua franca*. The superscription on the cross was hence written in Greek, Latin, and Hebrew (Aram.; Luke 23:38, KJV).   M.F.U.

BIBLIOGRAPHY: G. L. Archer, *New Perspectives on the Old Testament*, ed. J. B. Payne (1970), pp. 160-69; M. Black, *An Aramaic Approach to the Four Gospels and Acts* (1953); G. Mussies, *The Morphology of Koine Greek* (1971). See *The Minister's Library* (1985), pp. 130-31, 167-69.

LANGUAGES, CONFUSION OF (Gen. 11:1-9). The biblical account of this event begins with the statement "Now the whole earth used the same language and the same words" (v. 1). The author of the book of Genesis conceived the unity of the human race to be of the most rigid nature—not simply a generic unity, nor again simply a specific unity, but a specific based upon a numerical unity, the species being nothing else than the enlargement of the individual. Unity of language is assumed by the sacred historian, apparently as a corollary of the unity of race. No explanation is given of the origin of speech, but its exercise is evidently regarded as coeval with the creation of man. Speech, being inherent in man as a reflecting being, was regarded as handed down from father to son by the same process of imitation by which it is still perpetuated. The original unit of speech was restored in Noah. Disturbing causes were, however, early at work to dissolve this twofold union of community and speech. The human family endeavored to check the tendency to separation by the establishment of a great central edifice, and a city that should serve as a metropolis of the whole world (vv. 3-4). The project was defeated by the interposition of Jehovah, who determined to "confuse their language, that they may not understand one another's speech" (vv. 5-7). *See also* Babel, Tower of.

The desire for renown and the purpose to maintain their unity were thus manifested, revealing pride and the loss of spiritual unity and brotherly love. "Consequently the undertaking, dictated by pride, to preserve and consolidate by outward means the unity which was inwardly lost, could not be successful, but could only bring down the judgment of dispersion" (K. & D., *Com.*). By the firm establishment of an ungodly unity the wickedness and audacity of men would have led to fearful enterprise. Therefore God determined, by confusing their language, to prevent the heightening of sin through ungodly association, and to frustrate their design.

The nature of the confusion of language has been variously understood. It is unnecessary to assume that the judgment inflicted on the builders of Babel amounted to a loss, or even a suspension, of articulate speech. The desired object would be equally attained by a miraculous forestallment of those dialectical differences of language that are constantly in a process of production. The elements of the one original language may have remained, but were so disguised by variations of pronunciation, and by the introduction of new combinations, as to be practically obliterated.

"When it is stated, first of all, that God had resolved to destroy the unity of lips and words by a confusion of the lips, and then that he scattered the men abroad, this act of divine judgment cannot be understood in any other way than that God deprived them of the ability to comprehend one another, and thus effected their dispersion. The event itself cannot have consisted merely in a change of the organs of speech produced by the omnipotence of God, whereby speakers were turned into stammerers who were unintelligible to one another" (K. & D., *Com.*, ad loc.).

BIBLIOGRAPHY: G. Smith, *Chaldaean Account of Genesis* (1880), p. 17; S. L. Caiger, *Bible and Spade* (1936), p. 29; J. J. Davis, *Paradise to Prison* (1975), pp. 144-51; G. Bush, *Notes on Genesis* (1979), 1:177-87; R. S. Candlish, *Studies in Genesis* (1979), pp. 175-80; F. J. Delitzsch, *A New Commentary on Genesis* (1979), 1:346-56.

LANTERN (Gk. *phanos,* "shining"). This word occurs only in John 18:3, where it is recorded that the party that went to Gethsemane was provided "with lanterns and torches and weapons." A lantern is simply a lamp with a covering of some sort to protect it from the wind and other violence. Therefore too sharp a distinction between it and a lamp should not be drawn, and not infrequently either term might be indifferently used. The torches, for example, of Gideon's band, were probably lanterns rather than lamps in the

ordinary sense, and when the psalmist speaks of "a lamp to my feet" (Ps. 119:105), we naturally conclude that he refers to some kind of lantern.

LAODICE'A (lā-od-i-sē'a). Of the several cities named Laodicea in Syria and Asia Minor, only one is mentioned in the Scriptures, namely, the one situated in the confines of Phrygia and Lydia, on the banks of the Lycus, and about ninety miles E of Ephesus—not far from Colossae. After having been successively called Diosopolis and Rhoas, it was named Laodicea in honor of Laodice, the wife of Antiochus II (261-246 B.C.), who rebuilt it. It was destroyed by an earthquake (A.D. 66, or earlier) and rebuilt by Marcus Aurelius. It was the seat of a Christian church (Col. 2:1; 4:13, 15-16; Rev. 1:11). It is now a heap of ruins, called by the Turks *Eski-hissar,* or "old castle."

The town was located on a flat-topped hill. A wall (about a kilometer long on each of its four sides) surrounded the crown of the hill. Gates pierced this wall on the N, E, and NW. At the SW edge of the plateau stood a stadium, built and dedicated to Vespasian in A.D. 79. Near the stadium was a stone aqueduct, five miles long and probably dating to the second century A.D. Adjacent to the stadium on the N is a structure probably to be identified as baths and built during the reign of Hadrian (A.D. 117-38). Remains of two rather badly ruined theaters stand on the NE of Laodicea. Ruins of numerous other unidentified structures may be seen at the site.

BIBLIOGRAPHY: W. M. Ramsay, *The Cities and Bishoprics of Phrygia* (1895), 1:32-83; D. Magie, *Roman Rule in Asia Minor* (1950), 1:127; J. S. Rudd and E. M. B. Green, *Expository Times* 69 (1957-58): 176-78; C. J. Hemer, *Buried History* 11 (1975): 175-90; W. M. Ramsay, *The Letters to the Seven Churches of Asia* (1978), pp. 413-33.

LAODICE'A, CHURCH AT. Among the residents of this city at the time of the apostles were many Jews; and it is probably owing to this fact that a Christian church was planted here at so early a date. It appears from the epistle to the Colossians (4:15-16) that Paul never visited Laodicea, but hearing, most probably, from Epaphras of the false doctrines spread in that city, he wrote to the Colossians desiring that his epistle to that church should also be read in Laodicea. The message of the Spirit (Rev. 3:14-22) to the church of Laodicea was an awful warning. *See* Laodiceans, Epistle to.

The Laodicean condition describes the spiritual lukewarmness and worldliness that will prevail in the professing church of Christ at the end of the age. Rich, cultured, religiously ritualistic —this church will have become so self-satisfied and worldly as to have ostracised Christ completely. He is represented prophetically as standing on the outside knocking for admission (Rev. 3:20). No longer is He admitted by the corporate body, but stands outside extending an invitation

Ruins at Laodicea

to individuals. The awful spiritual condition, so utterly abhorrent to God, calls forth one of the boldest figures used in the NT. "So because you are lukewarm, and neither hot nor cold, I will spit you out of My mouth" (3:16; cf. 2 Tim. 3:1-8 for the spiritual and moral conditions at the end of the church age).   M.F.U.

LAODICE′ANS, EPISTLE TO. In Col. 4:16 Paul desires that the letter from Laodicea be read at Colossae. From this it has been supposed that Paul wrote an epistle to the Laodiceans, which is no longer extant. Jerome and Theodoret mention such an epistle, and it was also referred to at the second council of Nicaea. The epistle assuming to be that in question, and which is generally condemned as spurious, is found in some copies of the NT printed in Germany; and Calmet in his dictionary gives a full translation of it. Some (Conybeare and Howson) have thought that the epistle to the Ephesians is the one alluded to by the apostle. Another explanation of the passage is that Paul intended the letter of the Laodiceans *to him,* conveyed by Epaphras, to be read in the church of Colossae, together with the apostolic epistle to the Colossians themselves; and that as the epistle to the Colossians was in some sense an answer to the Laodiceans, it would be necessary that both should be read in the church of Laodicea (*Imperial Bible Dictionary,* s.v.).

LAP.

1. Heb. *beged,* 2 Kings 4:39, a "garment" (*ḥêq,* Prov. 16:32, the "bosom"). The fold of the garment in which the Israelites were accustomed to carrying articles in lieu of pockets; thus one of the sons of the prophets gathered "his lap full of wild gourds" (2 Kings 4:39). *See* Dress. The psalmist prayed, "Return to our neighbors sevenfold into their bosom ("laps," NIV) the reproach" (Ps. 79:12); the same allusion in Luke 6:38, "Give, and it will be given to you; good measure, pressed down, shaken together, running over, they will pour into your lap."

2. Heb. *lāqaq,* to "lick" up, as a dog (cf. 1 Kings 21:19). Drinking the water "as a dog laps" was the test given to Gideon's men (Judg. 7:5-6), those who knelt and lapped the water, that is, brought the hand to the mouth so rapidly as to resemble a dog's tongue, were retained for service, presumably as evidence that they were fit for active service.

LAPIS LAZULI. *See* Mineral Kingdom: Sapphire.

LAPPETH. *See* Lap.

LAP′PIDOTH (lap′i-doth; "torches"). The husband of the prophetess Deborah (Judg. 4:4), about 1195 B.C.

LAPWING. *See* Animal Kingdom: Hoopoe.

LASCIVIOUSNESS (Gk. *'aselgeia,* that which "excites disgust"). A KJV term referring to unbridled lust, licentiousness, wantonness. *See* Sensuality.

LASE′A (la-sē′a). A city of Crete, near Fair Havens (Acts 27:8). If the vessel in which Paul was sailing stopped for any length of time it is probable that Paul visited Lasea. Its ruins are located near Cape Leonda, about five miles from Lasea.

LA′SHA (la′sha). One of the places named in defining the border of the Canaanites (Gen. 10:19). Jerome, Jonathan, and the Jerusalem Targum identify it with Calirrhoe, a place with sulphur baths E of the Dead Sea, in Wadi Zerka Ma'in.

LASHA′RON (la-sha′ron; "of or to Sharon"; signification unknown). One of the thirty-one Canaanite towns, W of Jordan, struck by Joshua (Josh. 12:18). Perhaps the LXX preserves the original reading "the king of Aphek [which belongs] to Sharon."

LAST DAY. *See* Judgment.

LAST TIME. *See* Eschatology.

LATCHET (Heb. *śerôk,* "thong"; Gk. *himas,* "strap," i.e., "tie"). The KJV term for the strap or thong used by the orientals to fasten the sandal upon the foot (Isa. 5:27; Mark 1:7; Luke 3:16; John 1:27).

LAT'IN (lat'in). The vernacular language of the Romans, although most of them in the time of Christ also spoke Gk.

LATRINE. *See* Draught House.

LATTICE. The rendering of the following words:

1. A lathed aperture (Heb. *'eshnāb*), a lattice window through which the cool breezes pass (Judg. 5:28; Prov. 7:6).

2. A net (Heb. *śebākâ*, 2 Kings 1:2), probably a screen before a window.

3. A window lattice (Heb. *ḥerek*, Song of Sol. 2:9).

The object of the lattice is to keep the apartments cool by intercepting the direct rays of the sun and at the same time permit a free circulation of the air through the trellis openings. Perhaps the network through which Ahaziah fell and received his mortal injury was on the parapet of his palace (2 Kings 1:2).

LAUGH. (Gk. *katagelaō*, to deride, laugh down; KJV, "laughed to scorn"). Elements of rejection, disbelief, and mockery are combined (Matt. 9:24; Mark 5:40; Luke 8:53).

LAUNDERER. *See* Handicrafts; Fuller's Field; Mineral Kingdom: Nitre; Soap.

LAUGHTER. "In Scripture it usually expresses joy (Gen. 21:6; Ps. 126:2; Eccles. 3:4; Luke 6:21); sometimes mockery (Gen. 18:13; Eccles. 2:2; James 4:9); also security (Job 5:22). When predicated of God (Pss. 2:4; 59:8; Prov. 1:26) it signifies that he despises or pays no regard to the person or subject" (McClintock and Strong, *Cyclopedia*, s.v.).

LAVER (Heb. *kikkār*, something "round," a "basin"). The basin (so usually in the NIV) in which the priests washed their hands and feet while engaged in their public ministrations. The Tabernacle laver differed from that of the Temple.

Tabernacle Laver. This was made by divine direction of bronze (Ex. 30:18) out of the mirrors of the Hebrew women (38:8). It was placed between the Tabernacle and the great altar, so as to be convenient for the priests' use when going from the altar to the Tabernacle (30:20-21; 40:32). It consisted of two parts, the laver proper and the stand, or pedestal. Neither the form nor size is given. Regarding its shape, something may be deduced from the etymology of the Heb. term and its use in other passages. *Kikkār* "is derived from a root that seems primarily to mean *excavation by hammering,* and this would naturally yield a semi-globular hollow, which form is confirmed by the convenience for a lavatory, like a washbowl or basin, and by the similar shape of the molten sea and the smaller lavers, which took its place in the temple (1 Kings 7:38, 40, 43, etc.), and which are denoted by the same word. The laver proper was probably used as the receptacle

for the water, which was allowed to run down upon the hands and feet of those washing."

The laver of the Tabernacle

The stand (Heb. *kēn*, "support") was, doubtless, circular in shape and formed another basin. It was evidently an expansion of the shaft, probably with a turned-up rim. As no mention is made of a vessel in which the parts of the animals offered in sacrifice were washed, the laver probably served this purpose. No direction is given as to the kind of water to be used, but the Jewish commentators state that any kind might be employed, provided that it be renewed daily. "In the account of the offering by the woman suspected of adultery there is mention made of 'holy water' mixed with dust from the floor of the tabernacle, which the woman was to drink according to certain rites (Num. 5:17). Most probably this water was taken from the laver. Perhaps the same should be said of the 'water of purifying' (8:7), which was sprinkled on the Levites on the occasion of their consecration to the service of the Lord in the tabernacle" (Fairbairn). Like other sacred vessels, the laver was consecrated with oil (Lev. 8:10-11). No mention is made in the Heb. text of the mode of transporting the laver, but in Num. 4:14, a passage is added in the LXX agreeing with the Samaritan version, which prescribed the method of packing it, namely, in a purple cloth, protected by a skin covering.

Temple Basins (Lavers). Owing to the increased number of priests and victims in Solomon's Temple, greater facilities were needed for washing: ten smaller lavers or "basins" were used for the sacrifices, and a large cast metal "sea" was used for the ablutions of the priests (2 Chron. 4:6). Of these we have more minute descriptions than of the Tabernacle laver.

The Cast Metal Sea (Heb. *yām*, "sea"; KJV, "molten sea"). This was a huge round basin, five cubits high, ten cubits in diameter at the brim, "and thirty cubits in circumference" (1 Kings 7:23-26). Perhaps the circumference measurement was of the bowl at the water line and did not include the projected rim. It was made of strong bronze, a handbreadth in thickness. "Its brim was bent outward in a cuplike form, and made to resemble the flower of the lily, while underneath two rows of 'knops' (coloquintidas, i.e., wild cucumbers or apples), ten to every cubit, ran around the sea for ornament." In 2 Chron. 4:3 we have "figures like oxen" instead of "knops" or "buds." It is possible that *bakarim,* oxen, may be a corruption of *pekaim* (Clark, *Com.* ad loc.). The capacity of this huge basin was 2,000 baths (one bath equaled 7½ gallons). The "3,000 baths" of 2 Chron. 4:5 is thought to be an error of a transcriber. The water was doubtless drawn from this basin by means of faucets. This laver was supported by twelve oxen, three looking toward each point of the compass, although it is probable that they all stood upon one and the same base of metal.

Solomon's "molten sea"

The Ten Lesser Basins, or Lavers. In order to convey water to any part of the courts where it might be needed for washing such things as they offered for the burnt offering (2 Chron. 4:6), ten basins held in beautifully ornamented stands of bronze were prepared, five of them being placed on the S and five on the N side of the altar (1 Kings 7:38-39; 2 Chron. 4:6; for a full description of the stands and the basins, *see* 1 Kings 7:27-39).

The stands were all alike in form, size, and casting and were square chests, four cubits long, the same wide, and three cubits high. They were constructed with flat panels ("borders") supported by frames that were ornamented with figures of lions, oxen, and cherubim. Each stand had four bronze wheels and bronze axles, and the four feet had supports (7:30). The meaning seems to

be that the chests had feet at each corner, and that these rested upon the axles in such a manner as to raise the chest above the rim of the wheels (v. 32), the four wheels being under the borders. Keil supposes that the supports ran up each corner from the foot and reached to the lower side of the small basin, or laver, thus helping to support it ("beneath the basin were cast supports with wreaths at each side," v. 30). The wheels were 1½ cubits high, in construction resembling that of chariot wheels, and their axles, rims, spokes, and hubs were cast in bronze.

The top portions of the stands were constructed for the purpose of holding the basins. They were made with plates and borders, like the sides, but appear to have been arched so as to rise in the center, terminating in a circular receptacle, ½ cubit high by 1½ cubits in diameter, for the basin. These plates and borders were engraved with cherubim, lions, and palm trees. The basins themselves were four cubits in diameter, corresponding with the stands, narrowing down at the base to 1½ cubits, and held forty baths (about 440 gallons), just 1/50 of the capacity of the great laver.

Some have thought that the stands were made of so great a height in order to bring the basin near the height of the altar. It may be that these chests (stands) opened at the sides, and were actually tanks for washing the sacrifices in, the water coming into them from the basins by means of a pipe. After use they could be wheeled away and cleaned.

Basin (Laver) in the Second Temple. In the postexilic or second Temple, there appears to have been only one laver of bronze, with twelve instead of two pipes, and a machine for raising water and filling it.

Typical Meaning of the Laver. The laver or basin is a type of Christ, cleansing the believer-priest from the defilement of sin (John 13:2-10; Eph. 5:25-27). The priests, after serving at the bronze altar (itself a type of Christ's cross on which He, as our whole burnt offering, purchased our redemption), could not enter the Holy Place of God's manifested presence until their hands and feet were cleansed.

BIBLIOGRAPHY: W. F. Albright, *Archaeology and the Religion of Israel* (1946), pp. 152-54; G. E. Wright, *National Geographic Magazine* 112 (1957): 844. *See also* Tabernacle.

LAW (Heb. *tôrâ,* "teaching, instruction"; Gk. *nomos*). A term employed almost 200 times in the Bible and signifying the revealed will of God with respect to human conduct. It includes all the divine commands and precepts for regulating man's moral life without and within. It is used in six different senses in Scripture.

That Which Is Enacted by Man. (Gen. 9:6; Matt. 10:15; Luke 20:22; 1 Tim. 1:8-10; 2 Tim. 2:5.) Law in this aspect embraces that which established human government requires of those under its jurisdiction.

The Law of Moses. The law of Moses was a divinely instituted rule of life mediated through Moses to govern God's covenant people, Israel, in Canaan. It regulated their common, everyday conduct and was a covenant of works (Ex. 19:5-6). They were never able to keep this covenant, and it has been superseded by a new covenant (Jer. 31:31-34; Heb. 8:8-13). The Mosaic code of laws included the commandments (Ex. 20:1-17), the ordinances stipulating the Israelites' social life (21:1–23:33), and those directing Israel's worship (25:1–31:18). This Mosaic system, including the Ten Commandments as a way of life, came to an end with the death of Christ (John 1:17; Rom. 10:4). The Mosaic age was preceded (Ex. 19:4) and followed (John 1:17) by grace. In the gracious dispensation inaugurated as the result of the atonement of Christ, all the Ten Commandments appear in the epistles except that one regarding the seventh day, and are operative not as stern "you shall nots" but as gracious duties and privileges of a redeemed people possessing the dynamic of the Holy Spirit, willingly and effectively carrying out the commandments' injunctions. The Mosaic law was thus a temporary divine administration in effect only until Christ should come. It had the definite ministry of imparting to sin the character of transgression (Rom. 5:13; Gal. 3:19).

Leather Scroll

The Law of Grace. The law of grace includes the doctrines and precepts of grace addressed to the redeemed child of God in this age. It must be carefully noted that the Christian is not under law; grace has imparted to him all the merit that he could ever need (John 1:16; Rom. 5:1-2; 8:1-2; Col. 2:9-10). Being "in-lawed" to Christ (1 Cor. 9:20-21) does not mean that the Christian is without law, but it does mean, as one redeemed by grace, that he has the duty, or rather gracious privilege, of not doing that which is displeasing to God and of fully discharging that which is well pleasing to Him on the basis of a manifestation of spontaneous gratitude for his salvation in grace.

God's Will. The revealed will of God in any situation becomes a law to the Christian, although it embraces all God's revealed pleasure for any people at any time. Thus the word *law* in the book of Romans is sometimes used in referring to something other than the law of Moses (Rom. 7:15-25; 8:4).

Natural Law Written on the Heart. Natural law written on the heart is closely connected with the revealed will of God, but it is to be distinguished in that it is what God requires of all His creatures. "For when Gentiles who do not have the Law do instinctively the things of the Law, these, not having the Law, are a law to themselves, in that they show the work of the Law written in their hearts, their conscience bearing witness, and their thoughts alternately accusing or else defending them" (Rom. 2:14-15).

The Kingdom Rule of Life. This is the aspect of law that will be in force in the future Millennium. Matthew 5:1–7:29 gives a summary of it. It seems unthinkable to many theologians that there will be a reinstatement of law after the age of grace. But that such is the case is clearly taught in Ezekiel's great prophecy of millennial conditions described in chaps. 40-48. The legal administration of the Millennium will be an exalted and spiritualized economy and will operate under ideal conditions with Satan bound, a large ministry and operation of the Holy Spirit, and the personal presence of Christ.   M.F.U.

BIBLIOGRAPHY: W. S. Plumer, *The Law of God as Contained in the Ten Commandments* (1864); C. H. Dodd, *Gospel and Law* (1953); E. F. Kevan, *The Evangelical Doctrine of Law* (1955); G. Mendenhall, *Law and Covenant in Israel and the Ancient Near East* (1955); Z. Falk, *Hebrew Law in Bible Times* (1964); M. Noth, *The Laws of the Pentateuch and Other Studies* (1966); J. D. M. Derrett, *Law in the New Testament* (1970); A. Phillips, *Ancient Israel's Criminal Law* (1970); D. J. Wiseman, *Vox Evangelica* 8 (1973), 5-21; B. N. Kaye and G. J. Wenham, eds., *Law, Morality and the Bible* (1978); P. Fairbairn, *The Revelation of Law in Scripture* (1979); J. D. M. Derrett, *Studies in the New Testament*, 3 vols. (1977-82).

LAW, ADMINISTRATION OF.

Judges and Courts. Early courts, local courts, local senates, and the Sanhedrin administered the law in biblical times.

Early Courts. In patriarchal times the head of

the house had the judicial power over his household, even over life and death (Gen. 38:24). With the increase of families this power passed over to the heads of tribes and clans; but after the Exodus those who sought justice naturally turned to Moses (Ex. 18:13-16). Moses, unable to keep up with the demands made upon him and acting on Jethro's advice, chose from among the elders "able men who fear God, men of truth, those who hate dishonest gain." These he appointed as rulers over thousands, hundreds, fifties, and tens, who should act as judges in all small matters, while the more difficult matters were brought to Moses for decision (18:17-26; Deut. 1:13-18). The relation of these judges to one another is not exactly defined in Scripture; but it may have consisted in the fact that the judges over thousands were appointed to settle the disputes between the tribes and chief clans of the people; the judges over hundreds, and so on, the quarrels and the different contentions between the larger and smaller divisions of the clans and families.

Local Courts. After the entrance into Canaan the same general rules remained in force. For this period there is only the quite general command: "You shall appoint for yourself judges and officers [*shōterim*] in all your towns which the Lord your God is giving you, according to your tribes, and they shall judge the people with righteous judgment" (Deut. 16:18). These officials were the *local justices,* who, in the several cities, pronounced finally on all minor controversies, that is, such as were easy to decide by law, and punished the guilty. For more difficult cases, such as those that had been referred to Moses, a *higher court* was appointed, having its seat at the place of the sanctuary and consisting of priests and judges; with the high priest and a (secular) supreme judge (Deut. 17:8; 19:16-21). In this court the lay judge conducted the investigation (19:18), while the priest gave guidance from the law (Lev. 10:6-11); finally the judge pronounced sentence.

Senate. Besides these local courts, the elders of every city formed a *senate* or *magistracy,* whose duty it was, as representatives of the congregation, to remove the evil from among their midst. This senate decided various simple family matters that required no deeper judicial investigation, punished the guilty even with death, and delivered up the deliberate manslayer to the avenger of blood (Deut. 19:12). Among the cases that came under the jurisdiction of this senate were a rebellious son (21:18-21), a husband's charge against the virgin chastity of his wife (22:13-21), and the refusal in the matter of *levirate marriage* (which see). These matters belonged rather to the department of government than to the administration of justice in the strict sense; and the elders took up these cases as the upholders of good order.

David, after his wars, arranged the affairs of his kingdom; and among the other appointments set apart 6,000 Levites to be *shoterim* and judges (1 Chron. 23:4; cf. 26:29). It is doubtful if these Levites were associated with the local courts, the probability being that they were appointed to administer the payments of the people for the sanctuary, to watch over them, and in disputed cases to give judicial decisions. Jehoshaphat, desirous of spreading the knowledge of the law (2 Chron. 17:7-9), put judges in all the fortified cities (19:5-7) and provided a supreme tribunal in Jerusalem, consisting of Levites, priests, and heads of tribes, presided over by the high priest (for the interest of Jehovah) and the prince of the house of Judah (for the king's interest), with functions of an exclusively judicial character. In postexilic times the functions of the local courts were expanded. Josephus (*Wars* 2.14.1) mentions local courts that discharged judicial functions; and local Sanhedrins are referred to as those to whom the believers would be delivered (Matt. 10:17; Mark 13:9). These lesser courts were empowered to deal with criminal cases of a serious nature, even to the sentencing of murderers. We may also regard as belonging to the same category those courts that in Matt. 5:22 are assumed to be inferior to the high court of the Sanhedrin; and similarly with regard to the "elders" of Capernaum (Luke 7:3). The most subordinate of these courts consisted of seven persons; although three judges were considered sufficient to decide certain cases. There is a statement in the Mishna to the effect that an inferior Sanhedrin consisted of twenty-three persons, and that one of this sort was assigned to every town with a population of at least 120, or, according to R. Nehemiah's view, of at least 230, in order that there might be a judge for every ten inhabitants.

The Sanhedrin. The Sanhedrin was the great council in latter times (*see* Sanhedrin).

Judicial Procedure in the Courts. The course of justice was simple. The judges appointed by Moses were to judge the people "at all times" (Ex. 18:22), while the lawgiver himself sat with Aaron and the leaders of the congregation before the Tabernacle (Num. 27:2; cf. Ex. 18:19-23). Judges in the cities, after the custom of the ancient East, had their seat at the gate (Deut. 21:19; 22:15; Prov. 22:22; Amos 5:11, 15) and in the open squares. Before them the litigants appeared, and presented their case orally (Deut. 1:16; 25:1); and the accused who did not appear was summoned (25:8). Counsel was unknown in the OT. The supreme judges of the people administered justice in public; for example, Deborah under a palm tree (Judg. 4:5), the kings in the gate or court of the palace (2 Sam. 15:2-6; cf. 14:4; 1 Kings 3:16); Solomon at a porch hall of judgment in his palace (7:7). Later the princes sat for judgment at the entrance of the New Gate of the Temple (Jer. 26:10-11). The judge was bound to hear and examine closely (Deut. 1:16-17; 13:14). The *proof* varied according to circumstances. It might be a simple oath (Ex. 22:11), the word of the accuser if a parent (Deut. 21:18-21), a token (22:15, 17). Generally the declarations of witnesses were taken, and those of two or three were required to make the testimony valid (19:15), especially in criminal cases (Num. 35:30; Deut. 17:6). Witnesses were to be rigidly questioned, and if a witness was found to be false he was to be punished with the punishment that would have fallen upon the accused (19:18-19). From Prov. 16:33 and 18:18 it would appear that, other evidence lacking, the lot was applied, though it is not mentioned in the Pentateuch but only in Josh. 7:14 and 1 Sam. 14:40-42 as an immediate divine decision. Sentence was pronounced orally, although under the kings the judges seem to have written their sentences (Isa. 10:1). Punishment was executed without delay (Num. 15:36; Deut. 22:18-19, 21; etc.) and was administered before the judge (25:2-3), probably by the officers of the court; if capital, it was stoning by the whole congregation (Num. 15:36) or by the people of the city (Deut. 22:21), the witnesses being the first to cast a stone (13:9; 17:7), which could hardly be expected of a witness who was not fully satisfied as to the truth of his testimony; or by the avenger of blood (Num. 35:19). After the introduction of the king, punishment was administered by his servants (2 Sam. 1:15) or by the royal guard in case of state or treasonable offenses (1 Kings 2:25, 34, 46; 2 Kings 10:25).

BIBLIOGRAPHY: C. R. Smith, *Biblical Doctrine of Society* (1920); Z. Falk, *Hebrew Law in Bible Times* (1964); W. Beyerlin, *Origins and History of the Oldest Sinaitic Traditions* (1965); W. F. Albright, *New Horizons in Biblical Research* (1966); A. Alt, *Essays on Old Testament History and Religion* (1968), pp. 101-71; R. D. Culver, *Toward a Biblical View of Civil Government* (1974), pp. 61-268. *See also* Law; Law of Moses.

LAWLESSNESS (Gk. *anomia;* Matt. 7:23; 13:41; and elsewhere, NASB). *See* Iniquity.

LAW OF MO'SES (Heb. *tôrah môsheh*). Signifies the whole body of Mosaic legislation (1 Kings 2:3; 2 Kings 23:25; Ezra 3:2); called with reference to its divine origin *the law of the Lord* (Pss. 19:8; 37:31; Isa. 5:24; 30:9). In the latter sense it is called by way of eminence *this law* (Heb. *hattôrâ*, Deut. 1:5; 4:8, 44; 17:18-19; 27:3, 8). The law is especially embodied in the last four books of the Pentateuch. Respecting the question of the *origin* of the Mosaic law, we quote from J. Robertson, *Early Religion of Israel,* pp. 335ff.: "It occurs at once as a striking thing that the uniform tradition is, that Moses gave laws and ordinances to Israel; and that it is not a blind ascription of everything to some great ancestor may be gathered from the fact that there are ordinances and customs which are not traced to him. The Sabbath is made as old as the creation; circumcision is a mark of the covenant with Abraham;

sacrifices are pre-Mosaic; and the abstaining from the sinew that shrank is traced to the time of Jacob. The body of laws, however, that formed the constitution of Israel as a people is invariably referred to Moses. The persistence with which it is represented that law, moral and ceremonial, came from Moses, and the acceptance of the laws by the whole people as of Mosaic origin, proves at least that it was a deeply-seated belief in the nation that the great leader had given some formal legal constitution to his people. . . . The testimony of a nation is not so lightly to be set aside; it is the work of criticism to explain and account for tradition, not to give it the lie."

For a more recent study see George E. Mendenhall, "Law and Covenant in Israel and the Ancient Near East," in *Biblical Archaeologist* 17, no. 2 (May 1954): 26-46; no. 3 (Sept. 1954): 49-76.

Principles. At the root of the Mosaic code lies (1) the principle of strict but righteous retribution, the intention being to eliminate evil and produce reverence for the righteousness of the holy God in the heart of the people; (2) the principle that punishment should correspond to the heinousness of the offense, that there shall fall upon the culprit what he has done to his neighbor; and that the punishment is to be limited to the guilty party and not be extended to his children (Deut. 24:16); (3) the principle that all presumptuous disobedience to God and to His holy ordinances should be punished with unsparing severity; and (4) the threat of "a curse and severe punishments from God, the avenger of all evil, for offenses which either escape the eye of civil justice, or which, like apostasy from the Lord to idolatry, may prevail to such a degree that the arm of the earthly magistrate is overpowered and paralyzed by the spirit of the time."

Division. In analyzing the Mosaic code we adopt the divisions usual in systems of law—civil, criminal, judicial, constitutional, ecclesiastical, and ceremonial.

Civil. Civil law regulated the daily life of the Israelites and had provisions regarding persons and possessions.

Of Persons. The authority of the father was to be sacred; cursing, striking (Ex. 21:15, 17; Lev. 20:9), or stubborn and willful disobedience were to be considered as capital crimes; but punishment of death was vested only in the congregation (Deut. 21:18-21); also the vow of a daughter was conditional upon consent of her father (Num. 30:3-5).

The right of the *firstborn* to a double portion of the inheritance was not to be set aside by partiality (Deut. 21:15-17); inheritance was allowed to daughters in default of sons, if the heiress married within her own tribe (Num. 27:6-8; cf. chap. 36); *unmarried daughters* were entirely dependent upon their fathers (30:3-5).

The power of the husband over his wife was

such as to make the wife dependent even to the fulfilling of an engagement before God, as in the case of a vow (30:6-25); but a widow or divorced wife became independent and was bound by any vow she may have made (v. 9); upon marriage the husband was excused from war or public duties for one year (Deut. 24:5); *marriages* within certain degrees were forbidden (Lev. 18:1-24); *divorce* for "indecency" was allowed, but the divorced wife could not be taken back after marriage to another (Deut. 24:1-4); *slander* against a wife's virginity was punishable by fine and by deprival of power of divorce, but if the wife was proved guilty she was put to death (22:13-21); *a slave wife,* bought or captive, was not to be actual property, or to be sold; if ill-treated, was to be freed (Ex. 21:7-9; Deut. 21:10-14); *raising up of seed* (Levirate law) was a right to be claimed by widows with a view to preserving the family (25:5-10).

The *power of the master over the slave was limited,* so that the slave's death under chastisement was punishable (Ex. 21:20), and maiming gave liberty (vv. 26-27). The *Hebrew slave* was freed at the Sabbatical year (his wife and children, if they entered bondage with him, were to go out with him), unless he formally consented to remain in perpetual servitude (21:1-6; Deut. 15:12-18); but in any case he seems to have received his freedom and that of his children at the Jubilee (Lev. 25:10); if a slave was sold to a resident alien ("stranger"), he was always redeemable, at a price proportional to the distance from the Jubilee (25:47-54). *Foreign slaves* were held and inherited as property forever (25:45-46), and fugitive slaves from other nations were not to be given up (Deut. 23:15).

Strangers seem never to have been *sui juris,* or able to protect themselves; kindness toward them was enjoined as a duty (Ex. 22:21; Lev. 19:33-34).

Of Possessions. All land was considered as belonging to Jehovah, with its holders as His tenants (Lev. 25:23); *sold land,* therefore, was to return to its original owners at the Jubilee, the price of sale to be calculated accordingly and redemption on equitable terms to be allowed at all times (25:25-28); a *house sold* was to be redeemed within one year, and if not, to pass to the purchaser altogether (25:29-30); land was to rest in Sabbatic and Jubilee years, and spontaneous growth of these years was to be for the poor, the stranger, and so on (23:22; Deut. 24:19-21). The *houses of the Levites,* or those in unwalled villages, were to be redeemed at any time, in the same way as land, and Levitical suburbs were inalienable (Lev. 25:31-34). *Sanctified* land or houses, tithes, or unclean firstborn animals might be redeemed at the addition of one-fifth their value (reckoned by a priest according to the distance from the Jubilee), if devoted and unredeemed by the owner, to be hallowed at the Jubilee forever and given to the priests (27:14-

33). Regarding *inheritance* (which see), the following were the regulations respecting *losses:* if two men fought together, and as a result one was disabled from work, the other was to pay for the lost time (Ex. 21:18-19); claims for losses from trespass, or for any lost thing, were to be brought before the judges, and adverse judgment was followed by double payment to the other (22:9); a man finding any lost thing, and denying it, was obliged, when he wished to present a trespass offering, to restore the lost thing with an added fifth to the one to whom it belonged (Lev. 6:3-5). The general principle upon which these enactments were based was that an Israelite's fellow countrymen were his brothers, and he was always to act the brotherly part. Therefore, whenever he found anything that was lost he was commanded to care for it and to make diligent search for its owner with a view of restoration (Deut. 22:1-4).

All *debts* to an Israelite were to be released at the Sabbatical year, but they might be exacted of strangers (Deut. 15:1-11); *interest* from an Israelite was not to be taken (Ex. 22:25-27; Deut. 23:19-20); *pledges* were not to be insolently or ruinously exacted (Deut. 24:6, 10-13, 17-18).

Taxation included *census money.* A poll tax (of a half shekel) was to be paid for the service of the Tabernacle (Ex. 30:12-16). *Spoil* in war was to be divided equally between combatants and the congregation; of the combatant's half 1/500, and of the people's 1/50, was to be given as a heave offering unto the Lord (Num. 21:26-30). *Tithes* (which see) included *poor laws* providing for the legal right of the poor to *glean* fields and vineyards (Lev. 19:9-10; Deut. 24:19-22); for the hungry to eat of grain, and so on, on the spot (23:24-25); for daily payment of wages (24:15); and for the *maintenance of priests. See* Priest.

Criminal. Criminal law dealt with crimes and their punishment.

Offenses Against God. Offenses against God that were considered treason were all forbidden, in principle, by the Ten Commandments. The *first commandment* prohibited the acknowledgment of false gods (Ex. 22:20) and all idolatry (Deut. 13; 17:2-5). The *second commandment* prohibited witchcraft and false prophecy (Ex. 22:18; Deut. 18:9-22; Lev. 19:31). The *third commandment* prohibited blasphemy (Lev. 24:15-16). The *fourth commandment* prohibited breaking the Sabbath (Num. 15:32-36). Punishment in all cases was death by stoning. Idolatrous cities were to be utterly destroyed.

Offenses Against Man. The *fifth commandment* prohibited disobedience to, the cursing of, or the striking of parents (Ex. 21:15, 17; Lev. 20:9; Deut. 21:18-21); it also prohibited disobedience to a priest or supreme judge. Punishment was death by stoning (cf. 1 Kings 21:10-14; 2 Chron. 24:20-21). The *sixth commandment* prohibited the wrongful taking of life. (1) Murder was punished without sanctuary, reprieve, or satisfaction (Ex. 21:12, 14; Deut. 19:11-13). If in a quarrel a pregnant woman was struck, and she lost her child, fine was exacted; but if she suffered other injury, full retribution (Ex. 21:22-23). Death of a slave by striking with a rod was to be punished (21:20-21). (2) Death by an ox known to gore was punishable by the death of the ox and its owner, but as this was not an intentional crime the owner was allowed to redeem his forfeited life by expiation money (Ex. 21:28-30). (3) In the case of accidental homicide, the guilty party could escape the avenger by fleeing to a city of refuge until death of the high priest (Num. 35:9-28; Deut. 4:41-43; 19:4-20). (4) Death at the hands of an unknown person was to be expiated by formal disavowal and sacrifice by elders of the nearest city (Deut. 21:1-9).

The *seventh commandment* pertained to the marriage relationship. (1) *Adultery* was punished by the death of both offenders; the *rape* of a married or betrothed woman, by the death of the offender (22:22-27). (2) The rape or seduction of an unbetrothed virgin was to be compensated by marriage, with a dowry (fifty shekels) and without power of divorce; or, if she was refused, by payment of a full dowry (Ex. 22:16-17; Deut. 22:28-29). (3) Unlawful marriages (incestuous, etc.) were to be punished, some by death, some by childlessness (Lev. 20).

The *eighth commandment* dealt with theft or trespass. (1) If stolen property found with the thief was an ox, donkey, or sheep, the thief had to make twofold restoration; if he had killed or sold the property, he had to make fivefold restoration for an ox and fourfold for a sheep (Ex. 22:1, 4). If the thief was unable to make restitution, he might be sold (v. 3); if he was killed while breaking in his death was unavenged (v. 2). (2) *Trespass,* injury to things, or money lent was to be compensated (22:5-15). (3) Perversion of justice by bribes, threats, and so on, was strictly forbidden (23:6-9). (4) Kidnapping was to be punished by death (Deut. 24:7).

The *ninth commandment* prohibited false witness and slander. (1) A false witness was punished with that which he wished done to the one against whom he testified (Ex. 23:1-3; Deut. 19:16-21). (2) Slander of a wife's chastity was punished by a fine and the loss of the power of divorce (Deut. 22:13-19).

The *tenth commandment* forbade coveting and was applied in the criminal law in various ways. It was forbidden to remove boundary lines, under penalty of a curse (Deut. 27:17); a neighbor's straying animal was to be returned (Ex. 23:4-5), or helped if in trouble (Deut. 22:1-4); injury done to the field or vineyard of another by animal or fire was to be compensated by the best of one's own (Ex. 22:5-6); the killing of an animal was to be made good, animal for animal (Lev. 24:18); a blemish caused to another was to be

punished by *lex talionis,* or damages (Ex. 21:18-19, 22-25; Lev. 24:19-20).

Judicial. See Law, Administration of.

Constitutional. See Israel, Constitution of.

Ecclesiastical and Ceremonial. Ecclesiastical and ceremonial law pertained to sacrifice and offerings and to holiness. For these, *see* the articles Sacrificial Offerings; Holiness, Ceremonial.

Mosaic and Near Eastern Laws. As a result of archaeological excavations, especially of the past three decades, the law of Moses appears in a much clearer context. The Code of Hammurabi, dating from c. 1700 B.C., and discovered at ancient Susa (biblical Shushan) in 1901-2 has been classic in illuminating and illustrating Mosaic law. Now, however, Sumerian, Babylonian, Assyrian, Hittite, and Canaanite codes are shedding their light on the Mosaic legislation. Especially must be mentioned the laws of Lipit-Ishtar, king of Isin, in central Babylonia, dating c. 1875 B.C., and even the earlier laws of Eshnunna, an ancient city NE of modern Baghdad. (*See* Francis R. Steele, *American Journal of Archaeology* 3 [1948]: 445-50; Albrecht Goetze, *Sumer* 4 [1948]: 63-102; P. A. Pohl, *Orientalia* 18 [1949]: 126-29.) In this context the famous Code of Hammurabi appears as a comparative latecomer in Babylonia. The Code of Eshnunna, antedating Hammurabi's code by almost two centuries, contains the first exact parallel to any biblical law, namely, that concerning the division of oxen after a fatal combat between the animals (Ex. 21:35). In addition to these codes must be mentioned the old Babylonian and Assyrian tablets from Kanish in Cappadocia (nineteenth century B.C.). A wealth of legal material (fifteenth century B.C.) has also been recovered at Nuzi, near modern Kirkuk, since 1925. Assyrian laws have been recovered by the Germans in the city of Ashur on the Tigris, much of it coming from the period of Tiglath-pileser I (c. 1110 B.C.). Hittite laws have also come to light and date a century or two earlier than the laws of Tiglath-pileser. In comparison with these various laws "the Book of the Covenant exhibits a combination of simplicity in economic life and ethical humanitarianism in human relations which could have arisen only in early Israel" (W. F. Albright, *The O.T. in Modern Study* [1951], pp. 39f.).

Mosaic Law and the Code of Hammurabi. This famous seven-foot-tall piece of black diorite that regulated the commercial, domestic, social, and moral life of the Hammurabi period (c. 1728-1676 B.C.) constitutes one of the most astonishing legal finds in history. It antedates the Mosaic legislation by three centuries. This famous legal code illuminates the Mosaic laws. As a result of the careful study of the two bodies of material, it will be found that the Mosaic code is neither borrowed from nor dependent upon the Babylonian, but is unique in those specific features that suited Israel's need as an elect, theocratic nation.

In comparing the two it might be observed (1) that the Mosaic and Hammurabic codes are different in content, the Mosaic laws containing numerous ritual regulations and religious stipulations, Hammurabic laws being almost purely civil; and (2) the two codes regulate different societies, Hammurabi's laws governing an urban, commercial, thickly settled, irrigation culture; the Mosaic laws governing a simple agricultural, pastoral people not urbanized or commercially developed but conscious of their divine calling.

The two codes vary in their morality. Alfred Jeremias succinctly states the essential contrast of the two bodies of laws, noting that the Babylonian code is characterized by significant limitations: "(1) There is no control of lust. (2) There is no limitation of selfishness through altruism. (3) There is nowhere to be found a postulate of charity. (4) There is nowhere to be found the religious motif which recognizes sin as the destruction of the people because it is in opposition to the fear of God. In the Hammurabic Code every trace of religious thought is absent; behind the Israelite law stands ever the ruling will of the Holy God; it bears throughout a religious character" (*The O.T. in the Light of the Ancient East* [*1911*], 2:112). It may be fairly said that the resemblances or the likenesses between the two codes are traceable to similarity of antecedents and general intellectual and cultural heritage.

M.F.U.

BIBLIOGRAPHY: A. Alt, *Die Ursprünge des israelitischen Rechts* (1934); S. Mendenhall, *Criminal Jurisprudence Among the Ancient Hebrews* (1968); D. Daube, *Studies in Biblical Law* (1947); J. B. Pritchard, ed., *Ancient Near Eastern Texts* (1969), pp. 159-223, 531-47; B. N. Kaye and G. J. Wenham, *Law, Morality and the Bible* (1978).

See also Law; Ten Commandments.

LAWGIVER (Heb. *mᵉḥōqēq;* Gk. *nomothetēs*). Used in the usual sense of lawgiver (Isa. 33:22); of God as the Supreme Lawgiver and Judge (James 4:12); but elsewhere as a "scepter," a badge of power (Ps. 60:7; Gen. 49:10).

LAWYER (Gk. *nomikos,* according to "law"). A term used to signify one who was *conversant with the Mosaic law* (Matt. 22:35; Luke 7:30; 10:25; 11:45; 14:3; Titus 3:13), and probably applied to a *scribe* (which see) in his practical administration of the law in the pronouncement of legal decisions. It is not by accident that the expression is so frequently used by Luke. He purposes by this repetition to make clear to his Roman readers the character of the Jewish scribes.

LAYING ON OF HANDS. *See* Hands, Laying on of.

LAZ'ARUS (laz'a-rus; abridged form of Heb. "Eleazar").

1. A beggar named in the story of the rich man (Luke 16:20-31), whose patient piety in this world was rewarded with bliss in the next. This is the only instance of a proper name appearing in a parable.

2. A man of Bethany and the brother of Mary and Martha. He was a personal friend of Jesus, by whom he was raised from the dead four days after his burial (John 11:1-44). Later, when a supper was given to our Lord, Lazarus was present, and many people gathered through a desire to see the resurrected man. Such convincing evidence of Jesus' power was distasteful to the chief priests, and they "took counsel that they might put Lazarus to death also" (12:1-11). This they probably did not do, but satisfied themselves with the death of Jesus. According to an old tradition in Epiphanius (*Hoer* 66.34, p. 652), Lazarus was thirty years old when restored to life and lived thirty years after.

BIBLIOGRAPHY: J. D. Jones, *The Lord of Life and Death* (n.d.), pp. 7-20; S. Cox, *The Expositor* (1896), 1:428-41; C. J. Barber, *Searching for Identity* (1975), pp. 75-83.

LEAD. *See* Mineral Kingdom.

LEAF. Fig leaves are mentioned as forming the first covering of Adam and Eve (Gen. 3:7).

Figurative. Leaves, as the outward manifestation of life in the tree, are often used symbolically. A bright, fresh-colored leaf, showing that the tree was richly nourished, is figurative of prosperity (Ps. 1:3; Jer. 17:8); a faded leaf, on the contrary, shows a lack of moisture and nourishment and becomes an emblem of adversity and decay (Job 13:25; Isa. 64:6). In Ezekiel's vision of the holy waters the blessings of the Messiah's kingdom are spoken of under the image of trees growing on a river's bank and with fadeless leaves (Ezek. 47:12), which were for "the healing of the nations" (Rev. 22:1-2).

Leaves of a Door. Three Heb. terms are so translated: *ṣelā',* a "side," 1 Kings 6:34; *qela',* 1 Kings 6:34; and *delet,* Ezek. 41:24. Keil (*Com.* ad loc.) thinks that the term refers to doors made in two sections, like "Dutch doors," that could be open either above or below. Their height in this case would be sufficient to allow the priests to pass through with only the lower half open. In Isa. 45:1, the "leaved gates" (KJV) or "doors" (NASB) refer to a double gate.

Leaves of a Book. *See* Columns of a Book.

LEAGUE. *See* Covenant.

LE'AH (lē'a). The oldest daughter of Laban, who by the deceit of her father became the wife of Jacob (Gen. 29:16-23). She was not beautiful like her sister Rachel, having weak eyes, which is probably the reason of Jacob's preference for her younger sister. Leah had six sons, Reuben, Simeon, Levi, Judah (29:32-35), Issachar, and Zebulun (30:17-20), and a daughter, Dinah (v. 21). She probably died in Canaan, as she is not mentioned in the migration to Egypt (46:6), and was buried in Hebron (49:31).

BIBLIOGRAPHY: H. F. Stevenson, *A Galaxy of Saints* (1957), pp. 25-31.

LEATHER. *See* the articles Handicraft; Writing.

LEAVEN. A substance added to dough to cause it to rise, from Lat. *levamen*, that is, "that which rises," from *lavere*, "to raise."

Terms. The Heb. term *śe'ōr* occurs only five times in Scripture, in four of which (Ex. 12:15, 19; 13:7; Lev. 2:1-11) it is translated "leaven" and in the fifth (Deut. 16:3) "leavened bread." The NIV translates "yeast" in each of these references. This probably denotes the small portion of dough left from the preceding baking that had fermented and turned acidic. Its distinctive meaning is *fermented* or *leavened mass*. The Heb. expression *maṣṣâ*, "sweet," means without leaven (Lev. 10:12); thus the Heb. terms for the meaning of fermented or sour. The Gk. term is *zumē* and has the same latitude of meaning as the general Heb. words for leaven.

Preparation. In early times leaven was made from fine white bran kneaded with mold or with the meal of certain plants such as fitch or vetch, or from barley mixed with water and then allowed to stand until it turned sour. In later times it was made from bread flour kneaded without salt and kept until it passed into a state of fermentation.

Levitical Regulations. The Mosaic law strictly forbade the use of leaven in the priestly ritual (Lev. 2:11). Typically this signified that the offering was to be a type of purity, and leaven, which causes disintegration and corruption, symbolized evil and the energy of sin. To the Hebrew mind, whatever was in a decayed state suggested the idea of uncleanness and corruption. Amos (4:5), in the light of the prohibitions of the law, ironically commands the Jews of his day to "offer a thank offering also from that which is leavened." In two instances, however, the law permits its use—with the offering of the new loaves presented at Pentecost (Lev. 23:17) and in connection with the peace offering (7:13). The reason for the exception at Pentecost is that the two wave loaves of fine flour typify the NT church brought into being by the baptism of the Holy Spirit (Acts 2:1-4; 1 Cor. 12:12-13). The two wave loaves typifying the church contain leaven because there is evil in the church; but it is to be carefully noted that the loaves with leaven were baked; that is, the manifested evil in the Body of Christ, the church, was judged in the death of Christ. Leaven, then, is symbolic or typical of evil, always having this implication in the OT (cf. Gen. 19:3; Ex. 12:8, 15-20, 34, 39). In the NT its symbolic meaning is also clear. It is "malice and wickedness" as contrasted with "sincerity and truth" (1 Cor. 5:6-8). It represents evil doctrine (Matt. 16:12) in its threefold manifestation of Phariseeism, Sadduceeism, and Herodianism (16:6; Mark 8:15). Religious externalism constituted the leaven of the Pharisees (Matt. 23:14, 16,

28), while a skeptical attitude toward the supernatural was the leaven of the Sadducees (22:23, 29), and the spirit of worldly compromise was the leaven of the Herodians (22:16-21; Mark 3:6). The parable of the leaven "which a woman took, and hid in three pecks of meal, until it was all leavened" (Matt. 13:34) is in agreement with the unvarying scriptural meaning of leaven. M.F.U.

BIBLIOGRAPHY: O. T. Allis, *Evangelical Quarterly* 19 (1947): 254-73; J. Jeremias, *The Parables of Jesus* (1955), pp. 89-90; N. Turner, *Christian Words* (1980), p. 255.

LEB KA'MAI (leb ka'mī). A cryptic name for Babylonia or Chaldea (Jer. 51:1, NASB and NIV marg.).

LEBA'NA (le-ba'na; Neh. 7:48). *See* Lebanah.

LEB'ANAH (leb'a-na), **Leba'nah** (le-ba'na; "white," poetically "the moon"). A Temple servant whose descendants returned from Babylon with Zerubbabel (Ezra 2:45; Neh. 7:48), about 536 B.C.

LEB'ANON (leb'a-non; "white," from the snow on its peaks). The loftiest and best-known mountain range of Syria, forming the northern boundary of Palestine. It is really a branch running southward from the Caucasus, and at its lower end forking into two parallel ranges—the *eastern*, or Anti-Lebanon, and the *western*, or Lebanon proper. The mountain chain of Lebanon begins at the great valley connecting the Mediterranean with the plain of Hamath ("Lebo-Hamath," Num. 34:8) and runs SW until it sinks into the plain of Acre and the low hills of

The mountains of Lebanon viewed from Upper Galilee

Galilee. Its extreme length is 110 miles, and the average breadth at its base about 20 miles. Its average height is from 6,000 to 8,000 feet; the highest peak—Jebel Mukhmel—is about 10,200 feet, and the Sannin about 9,000 feet. The highest peaks are covered with perpetual ice and snow, and the line of cultivation reaches to the height of about 6,000 feet. In the mountain recesses wild beasts range, as of old (2 Kings 14:9; Song of Sol. 4:8). Lebanon is remarkable for the grandeur and beauty of its scenery, and it supplied the sacred writers with many expressive similes (Pss. 72:16; 104:16-18; Song of Sol. 4:15; Isa. 2:13; 35:2; 60:13; Hos. 14:5). It was noted for its cedars (Ps. 29:5; Song of Sol. 5:15), its wines (Hos. 14:7), and its cool waters (Jer. 18:14).

The *eastern* range, or Anti-Lebanon, has its center at Mt. Hermon, from which a number of ranges radiate like the ribs of a half-opened fan. The first runs NE, parallel to Lebanon, from which it is separated by the valley of Coele-Syria, or the Beqa', whose average breadth is about six miles. Its elevation is not more than 4,500 feet. As it advances northward its features become wilder and grander, and the elevation increases until, above the plain of Zebedâny, it attains an elevation of about 7,000 feet. There is little change until it reaches the parallel of Ba'albek, when it begins to fall and declines gradually until at length it sinks down into the plain of Hamath. The lowest and last of the Anti-Lebanon ranges runs nearly due E along the plain of Damascus, continuing onward to Palmyra. Its average elevation is not more than 3,000 feet, and, with the exception of a few peaks, it does not rise more than 700 feet above the plain.

Climate. The climate of Lebanon varies greatly. In the plain of Dan, at the source of the Jordan, the heat and vegetation are almost tropical. The coast along the western base of Lebanon, though sultry during the summer months, is not unhealthy. The sea breeze setting in the evening keeps the night comparatively cool, and the air is dry and free from malaria. In the plains of Coele-Syria and Damascus snow falls, sometimes eight inches deep. The main ridges of both ranges are generally covered with snow from December to March. During the summer the higher parts of the mountain are cool and pleasant, rain seldom falling between June 1 and September 20.

History. Lebanon is first mentioned (Deut. 1:7; 11:24) as a boundary of the country promised to Israel; and to those who had lived in Egypt or the desert Lebanon must have seemed a paradise. It was originally inhabited by a number of independent, warlike tribes, some of whom Joshua conquered near Lake Merom (Josh. 11:2-18). They are said to have been of Phoenician stock (Pliny 5.17; Eusebius *Onom.*, s.v.; cf. 1 Kings 5). Farther N were the Hivites (Judg. 3:3), the Giblites, and the Arkites. The Israelites never completely subdued them, but the Phoenicians ap-

pear to have had them under their power, as they supplied themselves and Solomon with timber from their forests (1 Kings 5:9-11; Ezek. 27:9). Still later the king of Assyria felled its timber for his military engines (Isa. 14:8; 37:24; Ezek. 31:16). In the fourth century B.C. the whole country was incorporated with the country or kingdom of the Seleucids. Today the Republic of Lebanon embraces much of what was ancient Phoenicia.

Figurative. Lebanon is used to symbolize that which is great, strong, beautiful, as: (1) the army of Asshur (Isa. 10:34); (2) a proud people (Isa. 29:17); (3) the Jews (Jer. 22:6, 23; Hab. 2:17); (4) perhaps of the Temple, in which was timber from Lebanon; (5) the mourning of Lebanon, of deep affliction (Ezek. 31:15).

BIBLIOGRAPHY: P. K. Hitti, *History of Syria* (1951); id., *Lebanon in History* (1957); M. K. Khayat and M. C. Keatinge, *Lebanon, Land of the Cedars* (1967); J. P. Brown, *Lebanon and Phoenicia* (1969).

REGION OF LEBANON

LEBA'OTH (le-bā'oth; Josh. 15:32). *See* Beth-le-baoth.

LEBBE'US (le-bē'us; "courageous"). In KJV a surname of Judas (Matt. 10:3), one of the twelve apostles. He was called also Thaddaeus, which Meyers (*Com.* in loco.) believes was his regular apostolic name.

LE'BO HA'MATH (lē'bō hā'math). The NASB

and NIV name for *Hamath* (which see). The KJV translates Lebo literally as "entrance" and thus the full name as "entrance to Hamath."

LEBO'NAH (le-bō'na; "frankincense"). A town near Shiloh, N of the spot where the young men of Benjamin were directed to capture the Shilonite maidens at the yearly festival (Judg. 21:19). It is, doubtless, the same as *Lubban,* three miles NW of Shiloh.

LE'CAH (le'ka). A place in the tribe of Judah founded by Er (1 Chron. 4:21), not elsewhere mentioned.

LEECH. See Animal Kingdom.

LEEKS. See Vegetable Kingdom.

LEES (Heb. *shēmer,* something "preserved"). "Wines on the lees" are wines that have been left to stand upon their lees after the first fermentation is over, which have thus thoroughly fermented, have been kept a long time, and are then filtered before drinking. Hence the wine was both strong and clear; in which case it was used figuratively for the full enjoyment of blessedness in the perfected kingdom of God (Isa. 25:6, "aged wine, ... refined, aged wine," see marg.). Allowed to remain upon the lees, the wine became thick and syrupy, and symbolized the sloth, indifference, and gross stupidity of the ungodly (Jer. 48:11; Zeph. 1:12, marg.). To drink the lees ("dregs," Ps. 75:8; and elsewhere in the NIV) was an expression for the endurance of extreme punishment.

LEFT. The left hand was esteemed of ill omen, hence the term *sinister* as equivalent to unfortunate. This was especially the case among the Greeks and Romans. The Greek term was used in taking auguries; but those omens were euphemistically called *euōnuma,* which in fact were regarded as unlucky, that is, which came *from the left, sinister* omens (for which a *good name* was desired). Among the Hebrews the left hand indicated the *north* (Gen. 14:15, see marg.; Job 23:9), the person's face being supposed to be turned toward the East.

LEFT-HANDED (Heb. *'iṭṭēr yad-yᵉmînô,* "shut" as to "his right hand"). A term applied to one who is unable to use skillfully his right hand (Judg. 3:15; 20:16). It can hardly mean ambidexterity, since the expression "shut as to his right hand" would preclude the fact of one's ability to use both hands alike. An instance of using both hands dexterously is given in 1 Chron. 12:2. Perhaps this power of using the left hand may have come through practice.

LEG. The bones of the legs of crucified persons were broken to hasten death (John 19:31). See Crucifixion.

LEGION. A main division of the Roman army, nearly equivalent to our regiment. It comprised a much larger number of men, running from

3,000 men to about 6,000 at the time of Christ. See Army.

Figurative. The word *legion* came to mean a great number or multitude, for example, of angels (Matt. 26:53) and of evil spirits (Mark 5:9, 15).

BIBLIOGRAPHY: H. M. D. Parker, *The Roman Legions* (1928).

LEHA'BIM (le-ha'bim). A people reckoned among the Midianite stock (Gen. 10:13; 1 Chron 1:11). The Lehabim are undoubtedly the fairhaired, blue-eyed Libyans, who as far back as the nineteenth and twentieth dynasties had been incorporated into the Egyptian army. At one time they occupied much the same place in Egyptian history as was subsequently occupied by the Lydians, and the Twenty-second Dynasty, that of Shishak, was of Libyan extraction and owed its rise to power to the influence of the Libyan troops.

LEHA'BITES. See Lehabim.

LE'HI (le'hi; a "cheek, or jawbone"). The place in Judah where Samson killed the Philistines with a jawbone (Judg. 15:9, 14, 16). In v. 19 we read of "the hollow place that is in Lehi." The spring in the hollow place he called En-hakkore, "fountain of him that prayed."

LEM'UEL (lem'u-el, belonging "to God"). A person of whom nothing is known, except that to him the admonitory apothegms of Prov. 31:2-9 were addressed by his mother. The rabbinical commentators identify Lemuel with Solomon, which seems the most likely conjecture. Others (such as Grotius) refer the epithet to Hezekiah, while yet others (such as Gesenius) believe that it refers to some neighboring petty Arabian prince.

LEND. See Loan.

LENGTH, MEASURES OF. See Metrology.

LENTIL. See Vegetable Kingdom.

LEOPARD. See Animal Kingdom.
Figurative. The leopard is illustrative of God in His judgments (Hos. 13:7); of the Macedonian kingdom (Dan. 7:6); of the Antichrist (Rev. 13:2); *tamed,* of the wicked subdued by truth and grace (Isa. 11:6).

LEPER (Heb. *ṣāra',* "smite"). A peson suffering from leprosy. The nature of leprosy is discussed in the article Diseases. Mosaic regulation of leprosy is discussed below, in the article Leprosy and the Mosaic Law.

LEPROSY AND THE MOSAIC LAW (Heb. *ṣāra'at,* "a smiting," "a scourge"). Here will be considered the Mosaic regulations respecting the existence of leprosy and the purification from it. The law for leprosy treats leprosy in man, in a house, and in fabrics:

Leprosy in Man. The priest was to decide

whether the leprosy was in its dangerous forms when appearing on the skin (Lev. 13:2-28), on the head and beard (vv. 29-37); in harmless forms (vv. 38-39); and when appearing on a bald head (vv. 40-44); and he was to give instructions concerning the removal of the leper from social contact (vv. 45-46). When he was thus excluded the leper was to wear mourning costume, rend his clothes, leave the hair of his head disordered, keep the beard covered, and cry, "Unclean! Unclean!" that everyone might avoid him for fear of being defiled (cf. Lam. 4:15). As long as the disease lasted he was to dwell outside the camp (Lev. 13:45-46; Num. 5:2-4; 12:15; etc.) Respecting the symptoms the priest was to decide as to whether they indicated leprosy or some other disease.

The ceremony prescribed for the purification of persons cured of leprosy is based on the idea that this malady is the bodily symbol not so much of sin merely as of death. Accordingly the rite of purification resolved itself into two parts. The first part of the rite had to do with the readmission of the sufferer (Lev. 14:1-9), who had been looked upon as dead, into the society of the living, and the preparation for his return to fellowship with the covenant people. This ceremony, therefore, took place outside the camp. The officiating priest caused two clean and living birds, along with some cedar wood, scarlet wool, and hyssop, to be brought. One of the birds was killed over running water, that is, water from a spring or stream, in such a way that the blood would flow into the water. He then dipped into this the living bird, the cedar, the scarlet wool, and the hyssop—the symbol of duration of life, vigor of life, and purity. He then sprinkled it seven times upon the leper, after which the living bird was set free, thus symbolizing that the leper was at liberty to return to society. The slain bird, though not having a sacrificial character, seems intended to show that the leper was saved from death by the intervention of divine mercy. The sprinkling was repeated *seven* times. The symbolical cleansing was followed by the shaving off of the hair, which was peculiarly liable to be affected by the leprosy, bathing the body in water, and washing the clothes.

The second part of the rite had to do with readmission of the former leper to the camp (Lev. 14:10-32), that he might resume living in his tent. This privilege was obtained after a second cleansing, on the eighth day. On this day the priest presented the candidate, with the necessary offerings, before the Lord. These offerings were two male lambs, one ewe lamb, three-tenths of an ephah of flour mingled with oil, and one log of oil. The priests waved one of the male lambs and the log of oil for a trespass offering. The lamb was then slain, and some of the blood was put upon the tip of the ear, the hand, and the foot of the person. These same organs were afterward anointed with oil, and after the priest had sprin-

kled some of the oil seven times before the Lord the remainder was poured upon the head of the person to be dedicated. The ewe lamb was then offered for a sin offering, for the purpose of making atonement (v. 19), after which the burnt and meat offerings were presented. In case the person was poor he offered one lamb, two turtledoves, or two young pigeons (vv. 21-22). Thus the restored leper was admitted again to communion with the altar and with Israel.

Leprosy in a House. The law concerning leprosy in a house was made known to Moses, as intended for the time when Israel should possess Canaan and dwell in houses. This leprosy manifested its presence by depressions of a greenish or reddish color on the walls, and was of vegetable formation. When these indications were observed the owner of the house reported to the priest, who directed that the whole contents of the house should be taken out, in order to prevent everything within it from becoming unclean. The priest then examined the walls of the house, and if he saw symptoms of the plague he ordered the house closed for seven days. If on the seventh day the leprosy gave evidence of spreading he ordered the affected stones to be removed, the inside of the house to be scraped, the removed parts replaced by others, and the walls plastered with fresh mortar. If, after these precautions, the evil should reappear, the leprosy was pronounced to be of a malignant type, and the house was pulled down, its stones, timber, and rubbish being removed to an unclean place outside the city. Any person entering the house, who ate or slept in it, was accounted unclean and was required to wash his clothes. If it was found that the plague had not spread after the house was plastered, the priest declared it free from disease, and after sprinkling it seven times with the same kind of sprinkling water as was used in the case of human leprosy, he purified it and made atonement for it that it might be clean (Lev. 14:33-53).

Leprosy in Fabrics. The leprosy in woolen or linen fabrics and in leather was probably the result of damp or ill ventilation, causing the material to rot, and was also indicated by greenish or reddish spots upon them. The presence of these was reported to the priest, who ordered the affected article to be shut up for seven days. If the spots had spread by the eighth day, the article was burned; if not, it was ordered washed and shut up another seven days. If similar spots then appeared, the article or material was burned; but if the leprous spot had yielded to the washing but left a stain, the stained portion was cut out and the remainder pronounced clean. In case no further indication of the disease appeared, the material was washed the second time and pronounced clean (Lev. 13:47-59). The Jewish laws exempted dyed material from liability to leprosy.

BIBLIOGRAPHY: H. Danby, trans., *The Mishnah* (1933), pp. 474, 483, 676-97; G. M. Lewis, *Practical Dermatology*

(1952); G. C. Sauer. *Manual of Skin Diseases* (1959).

LE'SHEM (le'shem). A city in N Palestine (Josh. 19:47), elsewhere called *Laish* (which see).

LE'THEK. A unit of dry measure of about ten bushels (Hos. 3:2). *See* Metrology.

LETTER. Used both as an alphabetical character and correspondence (*see* Writing and Epistle). The words of the apostle (Gal. 6:11), "See with what large letters I am writing to you with my own hand," is thus explained by Meyer (*Com.,* ad loc.): "In accordance with his well-known manner in other passages, *Paul adds to the letter, which up to this point he had dictated, the conclusion from verse 11 onward in his own handwriting.* . . . But this close of our epistle was intended to catch the eyes of the readers as *something so especially important, that from verse 12 to the end the apostle wrote with very large letters,* just as we, in writing and printing, distinguish by letters of a larger size anything that we wish to be considered as peculiarly significant."

Figurative. The "letter" of the law is used by the apostle Paul in opposition to the spirit (Rom. 2:27, 29; 7:6; 2 Cor. 3:6-7). In general *letter* is used to denote the Mosaic law, and mere external obedience to it.

LETU'SHIM (le-tū'shim; "hammered, oppressed"). The second son of Dedan, grandson of Abraham by Keturah (Gen. 25:3), considerably after 1950 B.C. The plural form of the three sons of Dedan would seem to indicate *tribes* descended from him. *See* Dedan.

LETU'SHITES. *See* Letushim.

LEUM'MIM (le-um'im; "nations, peoples"). The last of the three sons of Dedan, grandson of Abraham by Keturah (Gen. 25:3), or more probably a tribe descended from Dedan, among whose descendants they appear as third. Some have identified them with the Alumeotai of Ptolemy (6.7.24); but the Alumeotai of central Arabia have been quite as probably thought to correspond to Almodad. In the Sabaean inscriptions, however, the forms *l'mm* and *l'mym* occur.

LEUM'MITES. *See* Leummim.

LE'VI (lē'vī; a "joining").

1. The third son of Jacob and Leah (Gen. 29:34), probably 1945 B.C. One fact alone is recorded in which Levi appears prominent. His sister *Dinah* (which see) was seduced by Shechem, and, according to the rough usage of the times, the stain could only be washed out by blood. Simeon and Levi took this task upon themselves. Covering their scheme with fair words and professions of friendship, they committed a cowardly and repulsive crime (Gen. 34). Levi shared in the hatred that his brothers bore to Joseph (37:4) and joined in the plot against him carried out at Dothan (37:12-32). Years lat-

er, with his three sons—Gershon, Kohath, and Merari—Levi went down into Egypt (46:11), and as one of the four oldest sons we may think of him as among the five specially presented to Pharaoh (47:2). Finally, Jacob, on his deathbed, recalled Levi's old crime and expressed his abhorrence of it (49:5-7). *See* Levites.

2. Father of Matthat and son of Melchi, third preceding Mary among the ancestors of Jesus (Luke 3:24) considerably before 22 B.C.

3. The father of another Matthat, and son of Simeon, in the maternal line between David and Zerubbabel (Luke 3:29), after 876 B.C.

4. An apostle. *See* Matthew.

BIBLIOGRAPHY: W. F. Albright, *Archaeology and the Religion of Israel* (1942), pp. 109, 204-5; T. J. Meek, *Hebrew Origins* (1950), pp. 123-24.

LEVIATHAN. *See* Animal Kingdom.

LEVIRATE MARRIAGE (from Lat. *levir,* a "husband's brother"). The name applied to the custom among the Hebrews that when an Israelite died without leaving male issue, his nearest relative should marry the widow and continue the family of his deceased brother through the firstborn son of their union, he becoming the heir of the former husband. If the brother did not choose to marry the widow she subjected him to gross insult. *See* Marriage, Levirate.

BIBLIOGRAPHY: S. A. Cook, *The Laws of Moses and the Code of Hammurabi* (1903); R. H. Kennett, *Ancient Hebrew Life and Social Custom* (1933); M. Burrows, *The Basis of Israelite Marriage* (1938); id., *Journal of Biblical Literature* 59 (1940): 23-33, 448, id., *Bulletin of the American Schools of Oriental Research* 77 (1940): 2-15; E. Neufeld, *Ancient Hebrew Marriage Laws* (1944), pp. 23-55; H. H. Rowley, *Harvard Theological Review* 40 (1947): 77-79; D. A. Leggett, *Levirate and Goel Institutions in the Old Testament* (1974); C. J. Barber, *Ruth: An Expositional Commentary* (1983), pp. 54-59, 96-102, 107-25.

LE'VITES (lē'vīts; *Heb. beênêlēwî,* "sons of Levi," or simply *lēwî,* "Levites"). A patronymic title that, besides denoting all the descendants of Levi (Ex. 6:25; Lev. 25:32; Josh. 21:3, 41), is also the distinctive title of that portion of the tribe that was set apart for the service of the sanctuary and subordinate to the priests (Num. 8:6; Ezra 2:70; John 1:19; etc.). We sometimes read of "the Levitical priests" (Josh. 3:3; Ezek. 44:15).

Appointment. No reference is made to the consecrated character of the Levites in Genesis. Tracing its descent from Leah, the tribe would naturally take its place among the six chief tribes sprung from the wives of Jacob and share with them a superiority over those who bore the names of the sons of Bilhah and Zilpah. The work of Aaron and his greater brother Moses would give prominence to the family and tribe to which they belonged. And again the tribe stood separate and apart as the champions of Jehovah after the sin of making the golden calf. If the Levites had been sharers in the sin of the golden calf, they were, at any rate, the foremost to rally around their leader when he called on them to help him in stemming the progress of the evil. But we are told that the tribe of Levi was specially chosen by God for the purpose of entrusting to it the care and administration of holy things (Num. 3:5-13; 8:14-19). They were consecrated to Jehovah as His peculiar property, instead of the *firstborn* (which see) of the whole nation, these latter being replaced by the Levites, while all over and above the number required were ransomed at the rate of five shekels a head (18:15-16).

Division. Different functions were assigned to the separate houses of the Levitical branch of the tribe, as can be seen in table 21, formulated from Ex. 6:16-25 and Num. 3:17-20, italicizing the priestly branch.

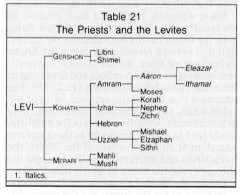

Table 21
The Priests[1] and the Levites

1. Italics.

In Num. 3:21, Libni and Shimei are mentioned as fathers of families, as in Hebron in v. 27. The design of the genealogy appears to be to give the pedigrees of Moses and Aaron and some other principal heads of the family of Aaron (*see* Ex. 6:25).

Age and Qualifications. A Levite's period of service was from twenty-five to fifty years of age (Num. 8:24-25); after the latter age he ceased from work and merely "assisted" his brothers. The age of thirty years mentioned in Num. 4:3-49 has been variously explained, some thinking it to have arisen from an error of the copyist, others that it referred to the time of transporting the Tabernacle, others that the first selection of Levites was those from twenty-five to fifty, but that *all future* Levites had to commence service at thirty. The LXX solves the difficulty by uniformly reading twenty-five instead of thirty. No other qualification than that of age is mentioned, although the regulations in force among the priests respecting deformity and cleanness doubtless applied also to the Levites.

Duties. The functions of the whole tribe of Levi were to preserve the law of Jehovah in all its integrity and purity, to see that its requirements

were duly complied with, to dispense justice in accordance with its enactments, and to transmit it to posterity (Lev. 10:11; Deut. 17:18; 31:9-13; 33:10; cf. 2 Chron. 17:8-9; Neh. 8:9; Ezek. 44:23; Mal. 2:7-8). The Levites, apart from their priestly portion, were to act as assistants to the sons of Aaron "for all the service of the tent" (Num. 18:4), but they were forbidden to touch any sacred furniture or the altar until it had been covered by the priests (4:5-15). As the Tabernacle was the sign of the presence among the people of their unseen King, so the Levites may be compared to a royal guard. When the people settled in Canaan it was the duty of the Levites, acting as police, to guard the sanctuary, to open and close it, to look after the cleaning of it and the furniture, to prepare the bread of the Presence and to do whatever other baking was needed in connection with the sacrifices, to lead the *music* (which see) during worship, to assist the priests in slaughtering and skinning the animals for sacrifice, to examine the lepers according to law, to look after the Temple supplies, and so on. For the heavier and more menial duties of their office, the Levites were assisted by Temple slaves. Thus the Gibeonites had been appointed to act as hewers of wood and drawers of water (Josh. 9:21). David and other kings presented persons to the sanctuary to perform services of such a nature (Ezra 8:20), probably prisoners of war who had become proselytes, called after the captivity *Temple servants* (which see).

Classification. The better to systematize their service, Moses divided the Levites into three sections by their respective descent from the sons of Levi, namely, Gershon, Kohath, and Merari. They were under the general supervision of Eleazar, the son of Aaron, with aides having charge of a section (Num. 3:32).

Kohathites. Elizaphan was leader (Num. 3:30). At the building of the Tabernacle they numbered 8,600 men (3:28), with 2,750 qualified for active service (4:36). They camped on the S side of the Tabernacle (3:29). Their duty was to have charge of the Ark, the table of the bread of the Presence, the lampstands, the altars of burnt offering and of incense, the sacred vessels used in the service, and the veil (3:31; 4:4-15).

Gershonites. Eliasaph was leader (Num. 3:24). They numbered 7,500 men, with 2,630 qualified for active service (3:22; 4:40). They camped on the W side of the Tabernacle (3:23). Their duty was to have charge of curtains, the tent (i.e., above the planks), the coverings and the hanging for the door of the Tabernacle, the hangings of the court and the court entrance, their cords and instruments of service, also the work of taking down and setting these up (3:25-26; 4:22-28).

Merarites. Zuriel was leader (Num. 3:35). They numbered 6,200 men, with 3,200 qualified for active service (3:34; 4:44). They camped on the N side of the Tabernacle (3:35). Their duty was to have charge of the frames, bars, pillars, and sockets of the Tabernacle; also the pillars of the court, their sockets, pegs, cords, and tools pertaining thereto (3:36-37; 4:29-32). Owing to the heavy nature of the materials they had to carry, four wagons and eight oxen were assigned to them; and in the march both they and the Gershonites followed immediately after the standard of Judah, and before that of Reuben, that they might set up the Tabernacle before the arrival of the Kohathites (7:8).

Consecration. The consecration of the Levites began with sprinkling them with the "purifying water" (marg., "water of sin"), followed by shaving off the hair of the entire body, washing the clothes, and accompanied by the sacrifice of two bulls, fine flour, and oil (Num. 8:6-15). The purifying water is thought by some to be the same as that used in the purification for leprosy (Lev. 13:6, 9, 13), whereas others understand it to be the water in the laver, provided for the purpose of cleansing the priests for the performance of their duties. After this purification they were brought before the door of the Tabernacle and set apart for service by the laying on of the hands of the elders.

Revenues and Residence. Chosen from among the whole people to be Jehovah's peculiar possession, the Levites did not obtain, like the rest of the tribes, any inheritance in the land of Canaan. Their portion was to be Jehovah Himself (Num. 18:20; Deut. 10:9; etc.), who ordained that they should have set apart for them four cities out of every tribe, along with the necessary pasture for their cattle (Num. 35:1-8). Besides this they received the tithes due to Jehovah from the fruits of the fields, from the flocks and herds (Lev. 27:30-33; cf. Num. 18:21-24), of the firstfruits (Ex. 23:19; Lev. 2:14; 23:17; etc.), of the firstborn (Ex. 13:12-13; Lev. 27:26; Num. 18:15-17; Deut. 15:19), as well as certain portions of the sacrificial offerings of the people (Num. 18:8-11, 19). Of the tithes the Levites had to turn over a tithe to the priests (18:26-32). The Levites lived for the greater part of the year in their own cities and came up at fixed periods to take their turn of work (1 Chron. 25-26). How long that term lasted we have no sufficient data for determining.

History. The history of the Levites occurs in distinctive segments.

Until the death of Solomon. We have seen that the Levites were to take the place of the earlier priesthood of the firstborn as representatives of the holiness of the people; that they acted as the royal guard, waiting upon Jehovah; and that they alone bore the Tabernacle and its sacred furniture. Failing to appreciate their holy calling, members of the section of Levites whose position brought them into contact with the tribe of Reuben conspired with it to reassert the old patriarchal system of a household priesthood. However, they were severely punished by divine interposi-

tion (Num. 16:1-40). Joshua, the successor of Moses, faithfully planned to continue the Mosaic ideal of the Levites as the priestly caste, providing them with cities to dwell in and servants from the conquered Hivites. During the period of the Judges we have only scanty material respecting the Levites, but the conduct of the people would seem to indicate that either the Levites failed to bear witness to the truth or had no power to enforce it. The shameless license of the sons of Eli may be looked upon as the result of a long period of decay affecting the whole order. Samuel, himself a Levite (1 Chron. 6:28, 33), infused new life into the organization. His rule and that of his sons, and the prophetical character now connected with the tribe, tended to give them the position of a ruling caste; and perhaps the desire of the people for a king was a protest against the assumption of the Levites of a higher position than that originally assigned them.

David definitely recognized their relation to the priesthood and publicly admitted their claim to be the bearers of the Ark (15:2). In the procession that entered Jerusalem bringing the Ark to its final resting place, the Levites were conspicuous, wearing their linen ephods and appearing in their new character as minstrels (15:27-28). The education that the Levites received for their peculiar duties, no less than their connection, more or less intimate, with the schools of the prophets, would tend to make them, so far as there was any education at all, the teachers of the others, the transcribers and interpreters of the law, and the chroniclers of the times in which they lived.

During the Divided Kingdom. Smith observes: "The revolt of the ten tribes, and the policy pursued by Jeroboam, led to a great change in the position of the Levites. They were the witnesses of an appointed order and a central worship. He wished to make the priests the creatures and instruments of the king, and to establish a provincial and divided worship. The natural result was that they left the cities assigned to them in the territory of Israel, and gathered round the metropolis of Judah (2 Chron. 11:13-14). In the kingdom of Judah they were, from this time forward, a powerful body, politically as well as ecclesiastically. We find them prominent in the war of Abijah against Jeroboam (13:10-12). They are sent out by Jehoshaphat to instruct and judge the people (19:8-10). The apostasy that followed on the marriage of Jehoram and Athaliah exposed them for a time to the dominance of a hostile system; but the services of the temple appear to have gone on, and the Levites were again conspicuous in the counter revolution effected by Jehoiada (chap. 23), and in restoring the temple to its former stateliness under Joash (24:5). The closing of the temple under Ahaz involved the cessation at once of their work and of their privileges (28:24). Under Hezekiah they again became prominent, as consecrating themselves to the special work of cleansing and repairing the temple (29:12-15); and the hymns of David and of Asaph were again renewed. Their old privileges were restored, they were put forward as teachers (30:22), and the payment of tithes, which had probably been discontinued under Ahaz, was renewed (31:14). The genealogies of the tribe were revised (v. 17), and the old classification kept its ground. The reign of Manasseh was for them, during the greater part of it, a period of depression. That of Josiah witnessed a fresh revival and reorganization (34:8-13). In the great Passover of his eighteenth year they took their places as teachers of the people, as well as leaders of their worship (35:3, 15). Then came the Egyptian and Chaldean invasions, and the rule of cowardly and apostate kings. Then the sacred tribe showed itself unfaithful. They had, as the penalty of their sin, to witness the destruction of the temple and to taste the bitterness of exile" (*Dict. of the Bible*).

After the Captivity. After the captivity, Smith notes, the "position taken by the Levites in the first movements of the return from Babylon indicates that they had cherished the traditions and maintained the practices of their tribe. It is noticeable that, in the first body of returning exiles, they were present in a disproportionately small number (Ezra 2:36-42). Those who do come take their old parts at the foundation and dedication of the second temple (3:10; 6:18). In the next movement under Ezra their reluctance was even more strongly marked. None of them presented themselves at the first great gathering (8:15). The special efforts of Ezra did not succeed in bringing together more than thirty-eight, and their places had to be filled by two hundred and twenty of the Nethinim (v. 20). Those who returned with him resumed their functions at the feast of tabernacles as teachers and interpreters (Neh. 8:7), and those who were most active in that work were foremost also in chanting the hymnlike prayer which appears in ch. 9 as the last great effort of Jewish psalmody. They are recognized in the great national covenant, and the offerings and tithes which were their due are once more solemnly secured to them (10:37-39). They take their old places in the temple and in the villages near Jerusalem (12:29), and are present in full array at the great feast of the dedication of the wall. The two prophets who were active at the time of the return, Haggai and Zechariah, if they did not belong to the tribe, helped it forward in the work of restoration. The strongest measures were adopted by Nehemiah, as before by Ezra, to guard the purity of their blood from the contamination of mixed marriages (Ezra 10:23); and they are made the special guardians of the holiness of the Sabbath (Neh. 13:22). The last prophet of the Old Testament sees, as part of his vision of the latter days, the time when the Lord 'shall purify the sons of Levi'

(Mal. 3:3). The guidance of the Old Testament fails us at this point, and the history of the Levites in relation to the national life becomes consequently a matter of inference and conjecture" (*Dict. of the Bible*).

In the New Testament. The Levites appear but seldom in the history of the NT. Where we meet with their names it is as the type of a formal, heartless worship, without sympathy and without love (Luke 10:32). The mention of a Levite at Cyprus in Acts 4:36 shows that the changes of the previous century had carried that tribe also into "the Dispersion among the Greeks."

BIBLIOGRAPHY: J. Orr, *The Problem of the Old Testament* (1906), pp. 163, 308-10, 313, 328, 376; G. B. Gray, *Sacrifice in the Old Testament* (1925), 179-270; J. Pedersen, *Israel, Its Life and Culture* (1940), 3-4: 150-97; J. H. Kurtz, *Sacrificial Worship in the Old Testament* (1980).

LEVITICAL CITIES. As the Levites were to "have no inheritance in their land" (Num. 18:20), Moses commanded the children of Israel, that is, the rest of the tribes, to give towns to the Levites to dwell in of the inheritance that fell to them for a possession, with pasturage around the cities for their cattle (35:2-5). The pasturage was to "extend from the wall of the city outward a thousand cubits around. You shall also measure outside the city on the east side two thousand cubits." These dimensions have caused great difficulty because of the apparent contradiction in the two verses, as specifying first 1,000 cubits and then 2,000.

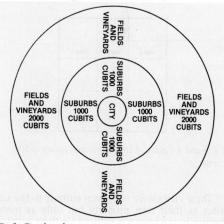

Fig 2. Circular plan

Of the many explanations given of these measurements, two seem most probable. The Talmud (*Erubin,* 51a) assumes that the cities were circular in form, the space measured from the wall 1,000 cubits around being used as "suburbs," and the space measured outside the city 2,000 cubits around being used for fields and vineyards, that is, as "the fields of the suburbs" (fig. 2). Keil & Delitzsch (*Com.*, Num. 35:1-8), following J. D. Michaelis, assume that "the towns and surrounding fields *were* squares, the pasturage stretching 1,000 cubits from the city wall in every direction, ... the length of each outer side [being] 2,000 cubits, apart from the length of the city wall: so, that, if the town itself occupied a square of 1,000 cubits (fig. 3), the outer side of the town fields would measure 2,000 + 1,000 cubits in every direction; but if each side of the city was only 500 cubits long (fig. 4), the outer side of the town fields would measure 2,000 + 500 cubits in every direction." Of these cities six were to be *cities of refuge* (which see), and thirteen were allotted to the priests' portion of the tribe. Which cities belonged to the priests, which to the nonpriestly portion of the tribe, and how they were distributed among the other tribes (Josh. 21:3-42), is shown in table 22, "Distribution of the Levitical Cities."

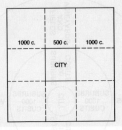

Fig. 3 and 4. Square of 1000 cubits and square of 500 cubits

These cities were not given entirely to the Levites as their own property but only as many houses in the towns as sufficed for their necessities. These could be redeemed if sold at any time, and reverted to them without compensation in the year of Jubilee, even if not redeemed before (Lev. 25:32-33); but such portion of the city as was not taken possession of by them, together with the fields and villages, continued to be the property of those tribes to which they had been assigned by lot.

Table 22 Distribution of the Levitical Cities		
Levitical Family	Tribal Location	No. of Cities
Kohathites:		
Priests	Judah and Simeon	9
	Benjamin	4
	Ephraim	4
Not priests	Dan	4
	Half Manasseh (W)	2
	Half Manasseh (E)	2
Gershonites	Issachar	4
	Asher	4
	Naphtali	3
	Zebulun	4
Merarites	Reuben	4
	Gad	4
	Total	48

BIBLIOGRAPHY: W. F. Albright, *Archaeology and the Religion of Israel* (1942), pp. 121-24; id., *Louis Ginzberg Jubilee Volume* (1945), pp. 49-73.

LEVITICUS. As Exodus is the book of redemption, Leviticus is the book of the cleansing, worship, and service of the redeemed people.

Name. The name describes its contents, for it deals with the law of the priests, the sons of Levi, Leviticus being taken from the Vulgate *Leviticus* (through the LXX *Leueitikon*). The designation sets forth the book as a manual of the OT priesthood (Heb. 7:11). The Jews, however, commonly designate the book from its opening phrase *wayiqra*, "and He called." Leviticus sets forth the way of the priestly approach to God. Its inspired NT commentary, the epistle to the Hebrews, describes the same approach in the dispensation of grace. Being a handbook of Levitical directions, it has little narrative, and such brief passages as the episode of the strange fire offered by Nadab and Abihu (10:1-2) are most intimately connected with the illustrations of the law given.

Literary Character. The book incontrovertibly claims Mosaic authorship. Some fifty-six times in twenty-seven chapters the claim is made that these laws were divinely given through Moses. This is the traditional view. However, higher pentateuchal criticism denies the Mosaic authenticity of Leviticus. Critics commonly assign it to the so-called Priest Code, abbreviated P, which is frequently dated about 500 B.C. or a little later. Some critics believe that Leviticus 17-27 is distinct enough from P to be designated H ("Holiness Code"), which is assumed to be combined with P to form our present book. Thus the critics can hardly escape making the book of Leviticus a pious forgery.

Weakness of the Critical Theory. The hypothesis of an exilic date (S. R. Driver) or postexilic date (Julius Bewer) for the so-called Priestly Code is filled with serious objections for the conservative. Morally it involves the dishonesty of passing off as Mosaic what was not Mosaic at all. This procedure is manifestly inconsistent with the moral standards of a prophet or any adequate view of inspiration. There is also the historical absurdity of getting so late a concoction of laws accepted at all or, what is even more incredible, approved as directly mediated by God to Moses. In addition, there is the legal inanity that is manifested in foisting the code in its Mosaic dress and wilderness framework on a postexilic economy. Critics describe the purpose of Leviticus as arousing the postexilic community to organize "a theocracy which was to be symbolized and realized in a hierocracy" (Julius Bewer, *The Literature of the O. T.*, 7th ed. [1947], p. 259), but this is highly artificial, arbitrary, and against internal evidence of the book itself. Moreover, archaeological discoveries have shown that codification of law in the Near East came early, rather than late, as critics used to assert. There is therefore no objective reason for dating OT legislation late. *See* Law of Moses: Mosaic and Near Eastern Laws.

Contents.

I. Directions for coming to God (1:1–16:34)
  A. Directions for priestly sacrifices (1:1–7:38)
  B. Directions for priestly consecration (8:1–9:24)
  C. Directions for priestly violation (10:1-20)
  D. Directions for priestly purification (11:1–15:33)
  E. Directions for the Day of Atonement (16:1-34)
II. Directions for fellowship with God (17:1–27:34)
  A. Directions preserving holiness (17:1–22:33)
  B. Directions governing religious feasts (23:1-44)
  C. Directions for lamps, bread of the Presence, etc. (24:1-23)
  D. Directions for Sabbath and Jubilee (25:1–26:2)
  E. Promises and warnings (26:3-46)
  F. Directions concerning vows and tithes (27:1-34)

BIBLIOGRAPHY: R. K. Harrison, *Introduction to the Old Testament* (1969), pp. 589-613; G. Bush, *Notes on Leviticus* (1976); M. Noth, *Leviticus: A Commentary* (1977); S. H. Kellogg, *The Book of Leviticus* (1978); G. J. Wenham, *The Book of Leviticus*, New International Commentary on the Old Testament (1979); R. K. Harrison, *Leviticus, an Introduction and Commentary*, Tyndale Old Testament Commentaries (1980).

LEVY (Heb. *mas*, "tribute"). The term applied to a company of 30,000 Israelites raised by Solomon (1 Kings 5:13). They were free Israelites who to pay tribute (or tax) worked four months in the year, felling trees under the direction of subjects of Hiram. Another *levy* was of Canaanites, who were assigned to tributary labor (9:15), in this case for the erection of buildings. The NIV translates *mas* as "forced labor."

LEWD, LEWDNESS (Heb. *zimmâ*, etc., "badness"). Evil or wicked in a moral sense, licentiousness (Judg. 20:6; Ezek. 16:43, 58; etc.). The word is also used once in Hos. 2:10 and refers to the "parts of shame" (Heb. *nablût*).

LIBATION. The act of pouring wine on the ground in divine worship. Sometimes other liquids have been used, such as oil, milk, water, and honey, but mostly it has been wine. Among the Greeks and Romans it was an essential part of solemn sacrifices. Libations were also in use among the Hebrews, who poured a hin of wine on the sacrifice after it was killed, and the several pieces of the sacrifice were laid on the altar ready to be consumed in the flames. *See* Offerings.

LIBERTINES. *See* Freedmen, Synagogue of the.

LIBERTY, CHRISTIAN. Also called evangelical liberty, this is a phrase that covers several NT representations of the Christian life.

1. Believers are emancipated from the bondage of Satan, the domination of sin, guilt, and the fear of death (*see* John 8:31-36; Acts 26:17-18; Rom. 7:24-25; 8:15; Heb. 2:14-15). Spiritual union with Christ, involving the service of Christ, is compatible with perfect freedom; inasmuch as we are thus restored to the right relationship to God and brought into harmony with His will (*see* Matt. 11:28-30; James 1:25).

2. Christians are not under obligation to observe the distinctly Jewish regulations. Circumcision, the sign of the Old Covenant, with the whole body of ceremonial and economic requirements essential to the chosen nation during the period that was preparatory to the gospel, under the gospel is set aside. These features of religion, once imposed by special revelation, were annulled by the incoming of the new dispensation. They were not in keeping with the proper magnifying of the grace of Christ, the dignity and inward liberty of redeemed souls, their moral elevation and illumination, or their relationship as children of God. Nor were they adapted to Christianity as designed to be the universal religion of the world (*see* John 4:20-24; Acts 15:1-29; Gal. 2:1-21; 5:1-6; Heb. 8:10, 13).

3. The phrase also refers to the privilege of Christians to regulate their lives as individuals with respect to matters that are morally indifferent. The NT instructions upon this point were developed for the most part on account of the attempt to impose Jewish regulations upon converts of Christianity, but the principles set forth are of much broader application and are still of great importance (*see* Rom. 13; 14:14; 1 Cor. 7:8; also Scriptures referred to above). With respect to such things as are not commanded or forbidden in the Word of God, Christian liberty may be exercised and should be allowed. Actions are not to be pronounced sinful that are not sinful. Nonessentials are not to be elevated to the place

of essential virtues. Proper room must be left for the exercise of individual judgment or of enlightened Christian conscience. But this liberty with respect to things indifferent is not absolute. Its exercise is under the limitations of the laws of self-preservation, of expediency, of duty, or of love. Concession should be made for the sake of "the weak," though care should be taken not to make them in such a way, or to such an extent, as to perpetuate their weakness or to promote superstition. If the former is not done "the weak" are needlessly injured. If the latter is omitted the principle of evangelical liberty is violated, Christians are reduced to un-Christian slavery, and the progress of Christ's kingdom is obstructed.

BIBLIOGRAPHY: M. C. Tenney, *Galatians: Charter of Christian Liberty* (1973).

LIB'NAH (lib'na; "whiteness").

1. The twenty-first station of the Israelites in the wilderness (Num. 33:20-21); not identified.

2. A city of the Canaanites, near Lachish, captured by Joshua (Josh. 10:29-32; 12:15); the birthplace of Josiah's queen, Hamutal (2 Kings 23:31). It was strongly fortified when Sennacherib laid siege to it, and the Assyrian army was cut off (19:8-9, 35). It was a Levitical city in the tribe of Judah (Josh. 21:13) and has been identified with the modern Tell es Safi, but today commonly is identified with Tell Bornat, about five miles N of Lachish.

LIB'NI (lib'ni; "white").

1. The first son of Gershon, the son of Levi (Ex. 6:17; Num. 3:18; 1 Chron. 6:17, 20), after 1900 B.C. His descendants are called Libnites (Num. 3:21; 26:58).

2. The son of Mahli, son of Merari (1 Chron. 6:29). It is probable that he is the same as the preceding and that something has been omitted from the text (Smith, *Dict.*, s.v.).

LIB'NITE (lib'nīt; "white"). A descendant of Libni, the Levite (Num. 3:21; 26:58).

LIB'YA (lib'ya). The country of the Lubim (Gen. 10:13), the tract lying on the Mediterranean between Egypt and Carthage (Ezek. 30:5; Acts 2:10). Cyrene was one of its cities. *See* Lubim.

LICE. *See* Animal Kingdom.

LIE. A lie is the utterance by speech or act of that which is false, with intent to mislead or delude. In Scripture the word is used to designate all the ways in which men deny or alter the truth in word or deed, as also evil in general. Good is designated as truth and evil as its opposite. Hence the Scriptures most expressly condemn lies (John 8:44; 1 Tim. 1:9-10; Rev. 21:27; 22:15). The Bible mentions instances of good men telling lies but without approving them, as that of Abraham (Gen. 12:13-19; 20:2-13), Isaac (26:7-9), Jacob (chap. 27), the Hebrew midwives (Ex. 1:15-19), Michal (1 Sam. 19:11-17), David (chap. 20).

BIBLIOGRAPHY: H. C. Trumbull, *A Lie Never Justifiable* (1893); J. Murray, *Principles of Conduct* (1957), pp. 123-48.

LIEUTENANTS. *See* Satraps.

LIFE. As used in the Bible, life denotes both physical, or natural, life, eternal life, and absolute life.

Physical, or Natural, Life. This is mere animal life (Gen. 6:17; 7:15). It thus often has reference to man's bodily life upon the earth, its relative value, and transient duration (e.g., Ex. 1:14; Pss. 17:14; 63:3; James 4:14). This form of life propagated by human generation is subject to physical death. Nevertheless, as it involves the whole man, this life is endless in every human being, saved or unsaved. Natural life has a beginning but no end. For the saved it involves eternal life or endless union and fellowship with God. For the unsaved it involves eternal existence in separation from God.

Eternal Life. This is the gift of God as a result of faith in Jesus Christ (Eph. 2:8-10). It must not be confused with mere endless existence, which is true of the unsaved. It involves the endless continuance and perfection of blessedness and communion with God entered upon by the saved on the earth (cf. Matt. 18:8-9; Luke 18:30; John 3:15-16; 6:40; 17:3; Rom. 2:7). (*See* Immortality.) Thus John writes, "He who has the Son has the life; he who does not have the Son of God does not have the life" (1 John 5:12; cf. John 10:10 with Col. 1:27).

Absolute Life. God in Christ, as self-existent or absolute life, is the source of all life (John 4:26; 14:6; Col. 3:4; 1 John 1:1-2; 5:20).

Manner of Life. This is referred to in Luke 8:14; Eph. 4:18; 1 Tim. 2:2; 1 John 2:16. M.F.U.

BIBLIOGRAPHY: J. Orr, *The Christian View of God and the World* (1897); E. D. Burton, *Spirit, Soul and Flesh* (1918); J. Pedersen, *Israel, Its Life and Culture* (1940), 1-2: 99-181; O. Cullmann, *Immortality of the Soul* (1958); C. E. B. Cranfield, *Reconciliation and Hope*, ed. R. Banks (1974), pp. 224-30; R. H. Gundry, *Sōma in Biblical Theology* (1976).

LIFT (Heb. *nāśā'* Gk. *airō*). Besides the general meaning of raising, this word has figurative meanings:

1. To *lift up the hands* is, among the orientals, a common part of taking an oath (Gen. 14:22; Ex. 6:8, *see* marg.). To lift up one's hand *against* another is to attack, to fight him (2 Sam. 18:28; 1 Kings 11:26-27, *see* marg.).

2. To lift up one's *face* in the presence of another is to appear boldly in his presence (2 Sam. 2:22; Ezra 9:6).

3. *To lift up one's hands, eyes, soul,* or *heart to the Lord,* are expressions describing the sentiments and emotion of one who prays earnestly or ardently desires something.

LIGHT (mostly Heb. *'ôr;* Gk. *phōs*). Light is declared by the Scriptures to have come into existence by the express decree of the Almighty and to have been in existence long before man or animals or vegetables had their being (Gen. 1:3).

Of all the benefits that we, as inhabitants of this lower world, have received from God, there are few more remarkable than the possession of light, along with an ability to make use of it. By it we come to possess much of our knowledge, many of our comforts and necessities; to say nothing of its wonderful purity, delicacy, and variety of colors that it reveals to the eyes of men. It is not at all surprising, therefore, that it should exercise a vast influence over the imagination of mankind and lead to its worship. Such being the case, we find many instances in the Word where such tendency is discouraged. *See* Sun, Worship of.

Figurative. The Almighty Himself is frequently spoken of as connected with the idea of light. Thus "God is light" (1 John 1:5); the "Father of lights" (James 1:17). God is addressed as "covering Thyself with light as with a cloak" (Ps. 104:2) and as One "who alone possesses immortality and dwells in unapproachable light" (1 Tim. 6:16). Great sublimity is introduced by the combination of figures of darkness and light, and by making them mutually enhance each other (Ps. 18:11-12; Ex. 24:15-17). Jesus, as the One who brings the true knowledge of God, is called "the light of men" (John 1:4; *see* also Matt. 4:16; John 1:9; 8:12; 12:35-36). Light is continually used as figurative of holiness and purity (Prov. 6:23; Isa. 5:20; Rom. 13:12). Light also, as might naturally be expected, is frequently used for spiritual illumination, especially that illumination that is effected in the soul by the indwelling Spirit of God (2 Cor. 4:6; Eph. 5:14; 1 Pet. 2:9). Again, light is used as the figure in general for that which cheers or renders prosperous, and is applied with much force to spiritual joy arising from the happy influences of the Spirit of peace. Hence the frequent use of the expressions "the light of Thy countenance" (Ps. 4:6); "the Lord is my light and my salvation" (27:1); and "light is sown like seed for the righteous, and gladness for the upright in heart" (97:11). A striking variety is given in Job 37:21: "Men do not see the light which is bright in the skies," their trouble so oppressing them that all seems dark, and they observe not the happier times in store for them. The Word of God is compared to a "lamp" (Ps. 119:105). Light is also applied to the heavenly state (Isa. 60:19-20; Col. 1:12; Rev. 21:23-25; 22:5). Finally, the figure is applied to Christians in general (Matt. 5:14; Eph. 5:8) and to holy men, such as John the Baptist (John 5:35). *See* Lamp.

BIBLIOGRAPHY: C. H. Dodd, *The Interpretation of the Fourth Gospel* (1954), pp. 201-12; D. Flusser, *Aspects of the Dead Sea Scrolls*, eds., C. Rabin and Y. Yadin (1958), pp. 215-66; L. Sibum, *The Bible on Light* (1966).

LIGHTNING (Heb. *bārāq*, "gleam"; Gk. *'astrapē*). In Syria lightning is frequent in autumn, seldom a night passing without a great deal of it, sometimes accompanied by thunder. A squall of wind and clouds of dust usually precede the first rains.

Figurative. Lightning is used as a symbol of God's glorious and awful majesty (Rev. 4:5); such as His edicts, enforced with destruction to those that oppose Him (Pss. 18:14; 144:6; Zech. 9:14); and, accompanied with thunder and hail, of great plagues, so that men blasphemed on account of it.

LIGN ALOES. *See* Vegetable Kingdom: Aloes, Lign Aloes.

LIGURE. *See* Mineral Kingdom: Jacinth.

LIKENESS. *See* Form.

LIK'HI (lik'hi). The third named of the four sons of Shemidah, son of Manasseh (1 Chron. 7:19), after 1876 B.C.

LILY. *See* Vegetable Kingdom.

LILY BLOSSOM (Heb. *peraḥ shōshān).* In the NASB and NIV of 1 Kings 7:26 this term is used in connection with the decoration of the brim of the large cast metal sea in Solomon's Temple. The KJV reads "flowers of lilies." *See* Laver: Temple Basins; Sea, Bronze.

LILY DESIGN. Part of the ornamentation of the two pillars that were erected (2 Chron. 3:15) before the (Temple) house. The pillars were surmounted by capitals, and these were covered to a depth of four cubits with sculpture in the form of flowering lilies, below which was a cubit of network and pomegranates (1 Kings 7:19, 22).

LILY OF THE COVENANT. *See* Shushan Eduth.

LIME. *See* Mineral Kingdom.

LINE. The rendering of several Heb. words and one Gk. word, with various meanings. Thus we have a line such as our measuring line (2 Sam. 8:2; Isa. 34:17; Ezek. 40:3; 47:3; Amos 7:17), a cord (Josh. 2:18, 21; etc.). There can be little doubt that the Hebrews acquired the art of measuring land from the ancient Egyptians, who were early acquainted with it. The language of Josh. 18:9, "So the men went and passed through the land, and described it by cities in seven divisions in a book," evidently indicates that a survey of the whole country had been made.

Figurative. The word *line*, as a string of a musical instrument, is used for *sound* (Ps. 19:4). In Isa. 28:10, 13, the expression "line on line, line on line" ("rule on rule, rule on rule," NIV), and so on, is a sneer intended to throw ridicule upon the smallness and irritating character of the prophet's interminable and uninterrupted chidings. The word also means a *portion* as described by measurement (Ps. 16:6).

LINEAGE (Gk. *patria*, paternal "descent," "families," Acts 3:25; Eph. 3:15; family or race, Luke 2:4). *See* Genealogy.

LINEAR MEASURES. *See* Metrology.

LINEN. Linen was well known in the ancient biblical world. The Egyptians were especially famous for their fine linen. The flax was planted in Egypt in November and gathered almost four months later. It had to be separated from its seeds, bunched, retted, laid in the sun, and immersed in water to bleach and soften it for crushing. The flax fibers were beaten out of the woody portions, and it was drawn by a comblike implement into thread for weaving on looms. Palestine as well as Egypt developed dexterity in weaving fine linens. Flax prospered in the tropical climate around Jericho. Rahab is said to have had dried flax on the top of her roof. Blooming flax is a common sight in biblical lands. The Hebr. word *pishtim* is rendered "linen" in some versions in Lev. 13:47; Deut. 22:11; Jer. 13:1; etc., and "flax" in Josh. 2:6; Judg. 15:14; Prov. 31:13; Isa. 19:9; Ezek. 40:3; Hos. 2:5, 9. This expression refers not only to flax (Judg. 15:14) but also to the plant itself (2:6) and what is manufactured from it. It was used for nets (Isa. 19:8-9), waistbands (Jer. 13:1), measuring lines (Ezek. 40:3), as well as priestly dress (44:17-18). (*See* Flax.) The Heb. expression *bûs* from a root signifying "to be white" (Akkad., *busu*) is apparently a late word for fine linen and appears to be identical with Gk. *bussos*. It was employed for the attire of the Levitical choir (2 Chron. 5:12), for the loose upper garment worn by kings over the close-fitting tunic (1 Chron. 15:27), and for the veil for the Temple, embroidered by the skill of Tyrian craftsmen (2 Chron. 3:14). Mordecai was arrayed in robes of "fine linen and purple" (Esther 8:15) when honored by the Persian monarch, and the dress of the rich man in Luke 16:19 was "purple and fine linen" (*bussos*). The merchandise of mystical Babylon contained as one of its commodities fine linen (Rev. 18:12). The Heb. word *shêsh*, an Egyptian word denoting linen of *byssus*, is used of the linen brought to Tyre (Ezek. 27:7), which was also one of the offerings brought out of Egypt by the Israelites (Ex. 25:4; 35:6). It seems apparent that *shêsh* is identical with Heb. *bûs*. It is used to describe the garments of Joseph (Gen. 41:42), of priests (Ex. 28:5; 39:2-3, 5; etc.), and also of the curtains and veil of the Tabernacle (26:1, 31, 36; 27:9, 16, 18; etc.). Linen was extensively used in wrapping the dead, as in the burial of our Lord. This practice was evidently of Egyptian influence. In the land of the Nile mummy wrappings were of incredible proportions and were exclusively of linen. Laodicea in Asia Minor was an important center of linen weaving. Such cities as Byblos, Tyre, and Beth-shan were famous as linen-manufacturing cities as late as the fourth century A.D. *See also* Dress.

M.F.U.

Figurative. Linen is used as an emblem of moral purity (Rev. 15:6) and of luxury (Luke 16:19).

BIBLIOGRAPHY: L. M. Wilson, *Ancient Textiles from Egypt* (1933); A. E. Bailey, *Daily Life in Bible Times* (1943); A. Bellinger, *Bulletin of the American Schools of Oriental Research* 118 (1950): 9-11; G. M. Crowfoot, *Palestine Exploration Quarterly* 83 (1951): 5-31.

LINTEL (Heb. *mashqôp*, "overhanging"). The beam that forms the upper part of the framework of a door (Ex. 12:7, 22-23). This the Israelites were commanded to mark with the blood of the Paschal lamb on the memorable occasion when the Passover was instituted.

LI'NUS (lī'nus). One of the Christians at Rome whose salutations Paul sent to Timothy (2 Tim. 4:21), A.D. 64.

LION. *See* Animal Kingdom.

Figurative. The strength (Judg. 14:18; 2 Sam. 1:23), courage (17:10; Prov. 28:1; etc.), and ferocity (Gen. 49:9; Num. 24:9) of the lion was proverbial. Hence the lion was symbolical of Israel (24:9), of the tribe of Judah (Gen. 49:9), of Gad (Deut. 33:20) and Dan (33:22, "a lion's whelp"), of Christ (Rev. 5:5), of God in protecting His people (Isa. 31:4), of God in executing judgments (38:13; Lam. 3:10; Hos. 5:14; 13:8), of the boldness of the righteous (Prov. 28:1), of brave men (2 Sam 1:23; 23:20), of cruel and powerful enemies (Isa. 5:29; Jer. 49:19), of persecutors (Ps. 22:13; 2 Tim. 4:17), of Satan (1 Pet. 5:8), of imaginary fears of the slothful (Prov. 22:13; 26:13). The *tamed* lion is symbolical of the natural man subdued by grace (Isa. 11:7; 65:25), while the roaring of a lion is used to characterize a king's wrath.

LIP (Heb. *šāpâ*, with the idea of "termination"). In addition to its literal meaning the word is often used in the original for an edge or border, as of a cup, a garment, the sea, and so on. It is often put as the organ of speech, thus to "open His lips" is to begin to speak (Job 11:5; 32:20); to "restrain my lips" is to keep silence (Ps. 40:9; Prov. 10:19). The "fruit of our lips" (Hos. 14:2; Heb. 13:15) is a metaphor for *praise,* a thank offering. "The lips of strangers" stands in Scripture for language or dialect (1 Cor. 14:21). The moral quality of speech is represented by "lying lips," i.e., *falsehood* (Prov. 10:18; 17:7), *wickedness* (Ps. 120:2; cf. Prov. 17:4), or *truth* (12:19). Ardent professions are represented by "burning lips" (26:23). To "separate with the lip" (Ps. 22:7) has always been an expression of the utmost scorn and defiance; so "unclean lips" are used to express an unfitness to impart or receive divine communications (Isa. 6:5, 7), and the touching of the lip with a "burning coal" is figurative for cleansing it.

LITTER (Heb. *ṣāb*, Isa. 66:20; "wagon," NIV). A

covered and curtained couch provided with shafts, and borne by men or animals, that was in general use as a conveyance throughout the East.

LITTLE OWL. *See* Animal Kingdom: Owl.

LIVER (Heb. *kābēd,* "heavy, weighty," as the "heaviest" of the internal organs). The word often occurs in the natural sense, as indicative of a vital organ in the animal system, especially with reference to the part of animals slain in sacrifice ("the lobe of the liver," Ex. 29:13, 22; Lev. 3:4, 10, 15; 4:9; etc.). *See* Sacrificial Offerings. The liver was used by the ancients for the purpose of *divination* (which see), and such use was not unknown to the Jews, though it is only once referred to in the Scriptures, and then with reference to the conduct of a heathen prince (Ezek. 21:21). In common with other ancient peoples, the Israelites were inclined to identify the liver more with the source and center of life than we do and sometimes put *liver* where we would put *heart* (*see* Prov. 7:23; Lam. 2:11, *see* marg.).

LIVING BEINGS (Ezek. 1, 3, 10). **Living Creatures** (Rev. 4:6-9). Both are identical with *cherubim* (which see).

LIZARD. *See* Animal Kingdom: Lizard; Great Lizard; and Sand Lizard.

Figurative. In Prov. 30:28 the lizard is introduced as one of the instances of instinctive discernment and providence; tolerated, even in palaces, to destroy flies.

LOAVES OF BREAD (Heb. *kikkār,* "circle"; Gk. *'artos;* sometimes only *lehem,* "bread"). Round cakes or biscuits, the usual form of bread among the orientals (Ex. 29:23, "cake of bread"; Judg. 8:5; 1 Sam. 10:3; 1 Chron 16:3; Matt. 14:17; Mark 6:38; etc.). *See* Bread, Offering.

LO-AM'MI (lō'am-i; "not my people"). The figurative name given by the prophet Hosea to his second son by Gomer, the daughter of Diblaim (Hos. 1:9), to denote the rejection of the kingdom of Israel by Jehovah. Its significance is explained in vv. 9-10.

LOAN. The law of Moses did not contemplate any raising of money by loans to obtain capital; and bankers and sureties, in the commercial sense (Neh. 5:3; Prov. 22:26), were unknown in the early ages of the Hebrews. The law made the following provisions respecting loans.

Interest. It strictly forbade any interest to be taken for a loan to any poor person, and at first, as it seems, even in the case of a foreigner; but this prohibition was afterward limited to the Hebrews only, from whom, of whatever rank, not only was no usury on any pretense to be exacted, but relief to the poor by way of loan was enjoined, and excuses for evading this duty were forbidden (Ex. 22:25; Lev. 25:35-37; Deut. 15:1-3, 7-10; 23:19-20).

As commerce increased, the practice of usury, and so also of suretyship, grew; but the exaction of it from a Hebrew appears to have been regarded to a late period as discreditable (Ps. 15:5; Prov. 6:1; 11:15; 17:18; 20:16; Jer. 15:10; Ezek. 18:5-17; 22:12). Systematic breach of the law in this respect was corrected by Nehemiah after the return from captivity (Neh. 5:1-13). The money changers, who had seats and tables in the Temple, were traders whose profits arose chiefly from the exchange of money with those who came to pay their annual half shekel.

Pledges. In making loans no prohibition is pronounced in the law against taking a *pledge* of the borrower, but certain limitations are prescribed in favor of the poor. (1) The outer garment, if taken in pledge, was to be returned before sunset. (2) The prohibition was absolute in the case of (*a*) the widow's garment (Deut. 24:17) and (*b*) a millstone of either kind (24:6). (3) A creditor was forbidden to enter a house to reclaim a pledge, but was to stand outside until the borrower should come forth to return it (24:10-11). (4) The original Roman law of debt permitted the debtor to be enslaved by his creditor until the debt was discharged; and he might even be put to death by him. The Jewish law, although it did not forbid temporary bondage in the case of debtors, did forbid a Hebrew debtor to be detained as a bondsman longer than the seventh year, or, at furthest, the year of Jubilee (Ex. 21:2; Lev. 25:39-42; Deut. 15:9).

BIBLIOGRAPHY: *See* Debt.

LOCK (Heb. verb *nā'al,* to "fasten"; noun *man'ûl*). The doors of the ancient Hebrews were secured by bars of wood or iron, the latter generally used in the entrances of fortresses, prisons, and towns (*see* Isa. 45:2). The locks are usually of wood and consist of a partly hollow bolt from fourteen inches to two feet long for external doors or gates, or from seven to nine inches for interior doors. The bolt passes through a groove in a piece attached to the door into a socket in the doorpost. In the groove-piece are from four to nine small iron or wooden sliding pins or wires, which drop into corresponding holes in the bolt, and fix it in its place (Neh. 3:3, 6, 13-15). The key has a certain number of iron pegs at one end, which correspond to the holes in the bolt of the lock, into which they are introduced to open the lock; the former pins being thus pushed up, the bolt may be drawn back. These keys were from seven inches to two feet in length, and so heavy as sometimes to be as much as a man could conveniently carry. It is to a key of this description that the prophet probably alludes: "Then I will set the key of the house of David on his shoulder" (Isa. 22:22). But it is not difficult to open a lock of this kind even without a key, namely, with the finger dipped in paste or some other adhesive substance. The passage in Song of Sol. 5:4-5, is thus probably explained.

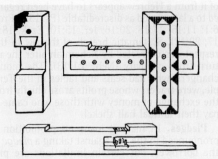

Egyptian wooden lock and key

LOCUST. *See* Animal Kingdom.

Figurative. The locust is used in Scripture as a symbol of *destructive enemies* (*see* the highly poetical description in Joel 1:4, 6-7; 2:2-9) and also of armed men (Nah. 3:17).

LOD (lod, 1 Chron. 8:12; Ezra 2:33; Neh. 7:37; 11:35). The city of Lydda (Acts 9:32; etc.). *See* Lydda.

LO-DE'BAR (lō-de'bar; "no pasture"). Probably identical with Debir (Heb. *Lidebir,* Josh. 13:26, *see* marg.), in Gilead, N of the brook Jabbok, not far from Mahanaim. It was the residence of Ammiel, whose son Machir entertained Mephibosheth (2 Sam. 9:4-5) and afterward sent supplies to David (17:27). The place is identified with Ummed-Dabar, S of the Wadi el-'Arab, E of the Jordan.

LODGE (Heb. *lîn* or *lûn,* to "stop over night," and several Gk. words). In the general sense of stopping for rest, or the place of lodging (Gen. 24:23; Josh. 4:3; Ruth 1:16; etc.). *See also* Hut; Inn.

LOG. (1) Used for building purposes (Matt. 7:3-5; Luke 6:41-42). In the passages referred to reference is made to a common proverb among the Jews respecting those who, with greater sins, reproved the lesser faults of others. The KJV renders "beam," and the NIV "plank." *See* Speck. (2) A liquid measure of capacity. *See* Metrology.

LOGOS (Gk. *ho logos,* "the Word"). A term used by the apostle John conveying most expressively the mission of Jesus as the revealer of the Godhead (John 1:1, 14). The title declares Christ's eternity and absolute deity ("In the beginning was the Word, and . . . the Word was God") as well as His assumption of humanity for man's salvation ("and the Word became flesh"). Words are the vehicle for the revelation of the thoughts and intents of the mind to others. In the Person of the incarnate Logos, God made Himself fully known to man. Nothing knowable by man concerning

God is undisclosed by incarnate deity. Christ as the Word constitutes the complete and ultimate divine revelaton. God has spoken with finality in "His Son" (Heb. 1:1-2), who was Himself God, coequal and coeternal with the Father. Only such a Being coming forth from "the bosom of the Father" could, as a distinct Person of the Godhead, "explain" the Father—literally "show Him forth" (John 1:18). The question of whether John was influenced by Philo and Alexandrian Greek speculation is frequently debated. It is preferable to see the origin of his thought in the OT where the Word of God is the divine agent in creation and the revelation of God's will to men. Moreover, studies in the Dead Sea Scrolls have led a number of scholars to the conclusion that the background of John is Jewish rather than Hellenistic. John further discourses profoundly on the Person and work of "the Word" in his first epistle (1:1, 5, 7), and finally in Rev. 19:13.   M.F.U.

BIBLIOGRAPHY: G. Vos, *Princeton Theological Review* 11 (1913): 557-602; O. Cullmann, *Christology of the New Testament* (1959), pp. 249-69; G. H. Dalman, *The Words of Christ* (1981), pp. 229ff.

LOINS. Literally, the parts of the back and sides of the human or animal body that parallel the spine on each side and extend between the ribs and the hips. In Heb., the main word, *motnayim* (Gen. 37:34; Ps. 66:11), and related words, *kesel* (Ps. 38:7), *ḥalāṣayim* (Job 40:7), *mayim* (Isa. 48:1), and *yerek* (Ex. 1:5), are sometimes also translated back, hips, waist, thighs, sides, and, in the KJV, flanks (Lev. 3:4, 10, 15; 4:9; 7:4; Job 15:27). The one Gk. term is *osphus* (Eph. 6:14; Heb. 7:10; NIV, "waist"). Ancient people commonly used "loins" figuratively for the center of emotions such as pain or terror (Deut. 33:11; Job 40:16). It is used by euphemism for the reproductive power (Gen. 35:11; 2 Chron. 6:9; both KJV). The loins were especially dressed with sackcloth symbolizing a mourning heart (1 Kings 20:31, 32). The loose and flowing garments of the orientals required that they be gathered and belted at the waist before one engaged in any exertion or enterprise; hence, "to gird up the loins" (1 Kings 18:46; Job 38:3; 40:7) is used as a picture for vigorous effort.

LO'IS (lō'is; perhaps "agreeable"). The maternal grandmother of Timothy, his father being a Greek (Acts 16:1). She was commended by the apostle Paul for her faith (2 Tim. 1:5).

LONGSUFFERING. *See* Patience.

LOOKING GLASS. *See* Mirror.

LOOP. The curtains of the Tabernacle were fastened by loops to their corresponding clasps. They were probably made of goat's hair cord and were dyed blue (Ex. 26:4-6, 10-11; 36:11-13, 17-18). *See* Tabernacle.

LORD. The rendering of several Heb. and Gk. words, which have different meanings:

1. *Jehovah* (*yahweh;* Heb. *YHWH,* "self-existent"). This is used as a proper name of God and should have been retained in that form by the translators. *See* (The) LORD; Yahweh.

2. *Lord* (Heb. *'Adôn*), an early word denoting ownership; hence, absolute control. It is not properly a divine title, being used of the owner of slaves (Gen. 24:14, 27; 39:2, 7, rendered "master"), of kings as the lords of their subjects (Isa. 26:13, "master"), of a husband as lord of the wife (Gen. 18:12). It is applied to God as the owner and governor of the whole earth (Ps. 114:7). It is sometimes used as a term of respect (like our *sir*) but with a pronoun attached ("my lord"). It often occurs in the plural.

3. *Adonai* (Heb. *'ădônāy*), emphatic, "the Lord"; many regard it as the plural of no. 2. It is used chiefly in the Pentateuch—always where God is submissively and reverently addressed (Ex. 4:10, 13; Josh. 7:8) and also when God is spoken of (1 Kings 13:9; 22:6; etc.). The Jews, out of a superstitious reverence for the name *Jehovah,* always pronounce *Adonai* where *Jehovah* is written. The similar form, *with the suffix,* is also used of men, as of Potiphar (Gen. 39:2, "master") and of Joseph (42:30, 33).

4. *Lord, Master* (Gk. *kurios,* "supreme"), he to whom a person or thing belongs, the master, the one having disposition of men or property, as the *"owner* of the vineyard" (Matt. 20:8; 21:40; Mark 12:9; Luke 20:15, *see* marg.); the "Lord of the harvest" (Matt. 9:38; Luke 10:2); the "master of the house" (Mark 13:35, see marg.); "Lord of the Sabbath" (Matt. 12:8; Mark 2:28; Luke 6:5), as having the power to determine what is suitable to the Sabbath, and of releasing himself and others from its obligation. The term is also a title of honor sometimes rendered "sir" and is expressive of the respect and reverence with which servants salute their master (Matt. 13:27; Luke 13:8; 14:22; etc.); employed by a son in addressing his father (Matt. 21:29); by citizens toward magistrates (27:63); by anyone wishing to honor a man of distinction (8:2, 6, 8; 15:27; Mark 7:28; Luke 5:12; etc.); by the disciples in saluting Jesus, their teacher and master (Matt. 8:25; 16:22; Luke 9:54; John 11:12; etc.). This title is given to *God,* the ruler of the universe, both with the article *ho kurios* (Matt. 1:22; 5:33; Mark 5:19; Acts 7:33; 2 Tim. 1:16, 18; etc.) and without the article (Matt. 21:9; 27:10; Mark 13:20; Luke 2:9, 23, 26; Heb. 7:21; etc.). The title is also applied to Jesus as the Messiah, since by His death He acquired a special ownership of mankind and after His resurrection was exalted by a partnership in the divine administration (Acts 10:36; Rom. 14:8; 1 Cor. 7:22; 8:6; Phil. 2:9-11).

5. *Baal* (Heb. *ba'al,* "master"), applied only to heathen deities, or to the man as husband, and so on, or to one specially skilled in a trade or profession. *See* Baal.

6. Other and less important words in the original are rendered "Lord," such as *mārē',* "master" (Acts 2:47), an official title, and *seren,* a Philistine term found in Joshua, Judges, and 1 Samuel, where "the *lords* of the Philistines" are mentioned.

BIBLIOGRAPHY: E. Lohmeyer, *Kyrios Christos* (1928); W. Bousset, *Kyrios Christos* (1935).

(THE) LORD; KJV, "Jehovah" (je-hō'va; Heb. YHWH, LXX; usually *ho Kurios*). The name of God most frequently used in the Hebrew Scriptures but commonly represented—we cannot say rendered—in the KJV and NIV by LORD.

Pronunciation. The true pronunciation of this name, by which God was known to the Hebrews, has been entirely lost, the Jews themselves scrupulously avoiding every mention of it and substituting in its stead one or other of the words with whose proper vowel points it may happen to be written, usually the name *Adonai.* They continued to write YHWH, but read *Adonai.* Where God is called "My Lord Jehovah" (Heb. *Adonai* YHWH), Elohim was substituted to avoid the double Adonai. When the vowel points were added to the Heb. text the rule, in the case of words written but not read, was to attach to these words the vowels belonging to the words read in place of them. Thus they attached to *YHWH* the points of *'ădônāy;* hence the form *Yehôwāh* and the name Yeh'v'h. The strong probability is that the name *Jehovah* was anciently pronounced *Yāhwēh,* like the *Iabe* of the Samaritans. This custom, which had its origin in reverence, and has almost degenerated into a superstition, was founded upon an erroneous rendering of Lev. 24:16, from which it was inferred that the mere utterance of the name constituted a capital offense. According to Jewish tradition, it was pronounced but once a year by the high priest on the Day of Atonement when he entered the Holy of Holies; but on this point there is some doubt.

For the LeClerc-Haupt-Albright view that *Yahweh* was originally a causative finite verb *see* Yahweh.

Import. The passage in Ex. 3:14 seems to furnish designedly a clue to the meaning of the word. When Moses received his commission to be the deliverer of Israel, the Almighty, who appeared in the burning bush, communicated to him the name that he should give as the credentials of his mission: "God said unto Moses, *I am that I am* [Heb. *'ehyeh 'ăsher 'ehyeh*]: and he said, Thus shalt thou say unto the children of Israel, *I am* hath sent me unto you" (KJV).

In both names *'ehyeh* and YHWH, the root idea is that of *underived existence.* When it is said that God's name is *He Is,* simple being is not all that is affirmed. *He is* in a sense in which no other being *is. He is,* and the cause of His being is in

Himself. *He is because He is.* But compare the etymology that Yahweh means "He causes to be"—"He creates" (P. Haupt and W. F. Albright's view). *See* Yahweh.

When Made Known. The notice in Ex. 6:3, "By my name Jehovah was I not known to them" (KJV), does not imply that the patriarchs were completely ignorant of the existence or the use of the name. It simply means that previous to their deliverance from Egyptian bondage they had no *experiential knowledge* of such redemption. Under Moses they were to experience such deliverance and have the redemptive power of God made real to them and the redemptive name of God vouchsafed to them. Previously, as shepherds in Palestine, Abraham, Isaac, and Jacob had known God as *El Shaddai* ("the Almighty," Gen. 17:1, KJV), proving His power, but not in redemption as such.

BIBLIOGRAPHY: W. Eichrodt, *Theology of the Old Testament* (1975), 1:187-92; J. Kitto, *Daily Bible Illustrations* (1981), 1:372-74.

(THE) LORD IS MY BANNER. KJV, **Jeho'vah-Nis'si** (je-hō'va-nis'i; "Jehovah my banner"). The name given by Moses to an altar that he erected upon the hill where he sat with uplifted hands during the successful battle against the Amalekites (Ex. 17:15). Nothing is said about sacrifices being offered upon the altar, and it has been suggested that the altar with its expressive name was merely to serve as a memorial to posterity of the gracious help of Jehovah.

(THE) LORD IS PEACE. KJV, **Jeho'vah-Sha'-lom** (je-hō'va-sha'lom; "Jehovah-peace"). The name given to an altar erected by Gideon in Ophrah after the Lord had given him the commission to deliver Israel from the Midianites, confirming it by miracles and a message of peace (Judg. 6:24; marg., *"Yahweh-shalom"*). As it was a time of backsliding, Gideon gave expression to his surprise and gratitude by erecting this altar as a monument to Jehovah as the God of peace.

(THE) LORD IS THERE. KJV, **Jeho'vah-Sham'mah** (je-hō'va-sham'a; "Jehovah is there"). The figurative name given by Ezekiel (48:35; NASB, NIV, and KJV, "The Lord is there") to millennial Jerusalem seen by him in his vision. The expression signifies that Jehovah has turned His favor once more to Jerusalem, which will enjoy great prosperity as the capital of the earth in the Kingdom age.

(THE) LORD WILL PROVIDE. KJV, **Jeho'vah-Ji'reh** (je-hō'va-jī're; "Jehovah will see," i.e., "provide"). The name given by Abraham to the mountain on which the angel of the Lord appeared to him and not only arrested the sacrifice of Isaac but provided a ram in his place (Gen. 22:14; marg., *"YHWH-jireh"*). *See* Moriah.

THE LORD'S DAY. This, the first day of the week in the Christian order, commemorates the new creation with Christ Himself as its resurrected head. It is not a mere changeover from the Sabbath but a new day marking a new dispensation. The Sabbath related to the old creation (Ex. 20:8-11; 31:12-17; Heb. 4:4). There are prophetic foreshadowings of the Lord's Day in the OT (Ps. 118:22-24; cf. Acts 4:11-12; Lev. 23:11; cf. Matt. 28:1). The term "Christian Sabbath" is scarcely biblically defensible. This day of grace marks the beginning of the week with a day of privilege, whereas the Sabbath came at the end of a week of labor, an order expected under the law. It must carefully be remembered that the Lord's Day, the term *Sunday* (which see) being of pagan origin, is strictly a Christian institution. It is not for all men, and it is scarcely justifiable to attempt to legislate its observance upon unsaved people. As Lewis Sperry Chafer points out, "Men are not justified in returning to the rules provided for the Sabbath in order to secure directions for the observance of the Lord's Day. When Christ came from the grave, He said to His friends, 'Rejoice' (cf. Ps. 118:24), and, 'Go tell . . .' (Matt. 28:9-10, literal rendering). These words may well be taken as a wise direction respecting observance of the day. The Lord's Day, moreover, can be extended to all days whereas the Sabbath could not be (cf. Rom. 14:5-6)" (*Systematic Theology*, 7:229).

M.F.U.

BIBLIOGRAPHY: W. Rordorf, *Sunday, the History of the Day of Rest and Worship in the Earliest Centuries of the Church* (1968); P. K. Jewett, *The Lord's Day* (1971); R. T. Beckwith and W. Stott, *This Is the Day* (1978); D. A. Carson, ed., *From Sabbath to Lord's Day* (1982).

THE LORD'S PRAYER. This prayer is in reality a prayer for the kingdom and in the kingdom (Matt. 6:8-15; 7:7-11). "Thy kingdom come. Thy will be done, on earth as it is in heaven" can only be realized in its contextual meaning in the coming millennial kingdom. There is no doubt that this prayer, so universally recited and often sentimentally entrenched in human affections because of childhood training, was nevertheless evidently not intended as a ritual prayer for this age. Its petitions, however, are remarkably comprehensive, and it has served as a vehicle of blessing for countless millions. The prayer is not given as a set form that is to be slavishly followed but rather as setting forth the general sentiments and desires that are acceptable to Him to whom we pray.   M.F.U.

BIBLIOGRAPHY: M. Dods, *The Prayer That Teaches Us to Pray* (1893); E. F. Scott, *The Lord's Prayer* (1951); J. C. Macaulay, *After This Manner* (1952); T. Watson, *The Lord's Prayer* (1960); J. Jeremias, *The Prayers of Jesus* (1967); A. Saphir, *The Lord's Prayer* (1984).

LORD'S SUPPER (Gk. *kuriakon deipnon*, a "meal belonging to the Lord").

Name. The meal established by our Lord (1 Cor. 11:20) and called "Supper" because it was instituted at suppertime. Synonymous with this is the phrase "the table of the Lord" (10:21), where we also find the term "the cup of the Lord." Other terms were introduced in the church, such as *Communion* (Gk. *koinōnia*, "participation," i.e., a festival in "common," 1 Cor. 10:16) and *Eucharist* ("a giving of thanks") because of the hymns and psalms that accompanied it.

Origin. Of this we have the accounts recorded by Matthew (26:26-29), Mark (14:22:25), Luke (22:19-20, 30), and Paul (1 Cor. 11:24-26), whose words differ little from those of Luke. The only difference between Matthew and Mark is that the latter omits the words "for forgiveness of sins." Paul declares (1 Cor. 11:23) that the account that he wrote to the Corinthians he "received from the Lord," which would seem to imply a communication made to himself personally by the Lord, contrasting it with the abuse among them.

Jesus instituted the supper while He was observing the Passover with His disciples, so some reference to that feast should be given. The following order of observing the Passover prevailed at the time of Christ: (1) Where the celebrants met, the head of the household, or celebrant, blessed a cup of wine, of which all partook. (2) The hands were then washed, this act being accompanied by a benediction. (3) The table was then set with the Paschal lamb, unleavened bread, bitter herbs, and sauce. (4) The celebrant first, and then others, dipped a portion of the bitter herbs into the sauce and ate them. (5) The dishes were removed and a cup of wine brought, followed by an interval for asking questions as to the meaning of this strange procedure, and then the wine was passed. (6) The table being again set, the celebrant then repeated the commemorative words that opened what was strictly the Paschal supper—a solemn thanksgiving and reading of Pss. 103-104. (7) Then came a second washing of hands with a short blessing, the breaking of one of the two cakes of unleavened bread, with thanks. The bread was then dipped, with the bitter herbs, into the sauce, and eaten. (8) Meat was eaten with the bread, accompanied by another blessing, a third cup of wine known as the "cup of blessing," and then (9) a fourth cup, with the recital of Pss. 115-18, from which this cup was known as the cup of the *Hallel* (which see), of the Song of Sol. (10) There might be, in conclusion, a fifth cup, provided that the Great Hallel was sung over it (possibly Pss. 120-38).

"Comparing the ritual thus gathered from rabbinic writers with the New Testament, and assuming (1) that it represents substantially the common practice of our Lord's time; and (2) that the meal of which he and his disciples partook was either the Passover itself or an anticipation of it, conducted according to the same rules, we are able to point, though not with absolute certainty, to the points of departure which the old

practice presented for the institution of the new. To 1 or 3, or even to 8, we may refer the first words and the first distribution of the cup (Luke 22:17-18); to 2 or 7, the dipping of the sop (John 13:26); to 7, or to an interval during or after 8, the distribution of the bread (Matt. 26:26; Mark 14:22; Luke 22:19; 1 Cor. 11:23-24); to 9 or 10 ('after supper,' Luke 22:20), the thanksgiving and distribution of the cup, and the hymn with which the whole was ended." (Bennett, *Christian Archaeology*, p. 416).

Observance. The Passover was an annual festival, but no rule was given as to the time and frequency of the new feast, although the command "Do this, as often as you drink it" (1 Cor. 11:25) suggests a more frequent observance. It would appear that the celebration of the Lord's Supper by the first disciples occurred daily in private houses (Acts 2:46), in connection with the agape, or love feast, to indicate that its purpose was the expression of brotherly love. The offering of thanks and praise (1 Cor. 10:16; 11:24) was probably followed with the holy kiss (Rom. 16:16; 1 Cor. 16:20). It was of a somewhat festive character, judging from the excesses that Paul reproved (1 Cor. 11:20), and was associated with an ordinary meal, at the close of which the bread and wine were distributed as a memorial of Christ's similar distribution to the disciples. From the accounts in the Acts (2:42, 46) and from Paul's letter to the Corinthians (11:20-21) it is safely inferred that the disciples each contributed a share of the food necessary for the meal, thus showing a community of love and fellowship. To this unifying power of the Eucharist Paul evidently refers (10:16-17). From the account given in 11:17-34 it is evident that each person ate of that which he brought and held therein his own private meal in place of the Lord's Supper. There was not a proper waiting for the distribution of the elements by a church officer, and there seems to be no evidence that a priestly consecration and distribution of the bread and wine were regarded as necessary to the validity of the sacrament. It is true that a blessing was spoken over the cup (1 Cor. 10:16), but every Christian would probably offer this blessing at that time, when the arrangements of church life as regards public worship were as yet so little reduced to fixed order.

Early Church. In the earliest notices of the Lord's Supper a simple and almost literal imitation of the meal as instituted by Christ is prevalent. In the "Teaching of the Twelve" the instructions for celebrating the Eucharist are as simple and archaic as those respecting baptism. In Justin Martyr's account of the Lord's Supper is noticed an almost like simplicity as in the "Teaching." A change is in the fact that special celebrants or officers are now recognized: "There is brought to the president of the brethren bread and a cup of wine mixed with water." The deacons distribute the consecrated elements and carry away a portion to those who are absent. In Tertullian's account there is scarcely more formality.

In ante-Nicene times the following order was observed: the prayers, the kiss of peace between man and man, and woman and woman; the offerings for the feast, the poor, and the clergy; and the communion of the partaking of the consecrated elements. The wine was mingled with water, and the communicants, standing, received both elements in the hands of the officiating deacons. Portions of the sanctified bread were sometimes borne to their homes by the members, where the family Communion was repeated in kind. The custom of the apostolic church for all communicants to make offerings of bread and wine and other things, to supply the elements of the Eucharist and gifts to the poor, was continued through all the early history of Christianity and in a modified form until the twelfth century.

As church government and discipline developed, the ceremonies connected with the Eucharist became more formal and involved.

At the institution of the Lord's Supper Christ used *unleavened bread.* The early Christians carried with them the bread and wine for the Eucharist and took the bread in common use, which was leavened. When this custom ceased the Greeks retained leavened bread, while in the Latin church unleavened bread became common since the eighth century.

We have no evidence as to whether the wine used by Christ was pure, mixed with water, fermented, or unfermented; although general practice, as well as other facts, would lead to the conclusion that it was fermented.

Essential Nature. There is controversy concerning the essential nature of the Lord's Supper.

Transubstantiation. Transubstantiation is the view held by the Roman Catholic church. The Council of Trent teaches that after the consecration the body and blood, together with the soul and divinity of our Lord Jesus Christ, are contained "truly, really, and substantially in the sacrament of the most holy eucharist," and it anathematizes those who say that Christ's body and blood are there in sign and figure only. Furthermore, the Roman Catholic church teaches "that the worship of sacrifice was not to cease in the Church, and the Council of Trent defines that in the eucharist or mass a true and proper sacrifice is offered to God" (*Cath. Dict.,* s.v.).

Consubstantiation. The Lutheran church rejects transubstantiation, while insisting that the body and blood of Christ are mysteriously and supernaturally united with the bread and wine, so that they are received when the latter are. This is called *consubstantiation.*

Spiritual Presence View. According to this view, "this hallowed food (the bread and wine), through concurrence of divine power, is in verity and truth, unto faithful receivers, *instrumentally*

a cause of that mystical participation whereby I make myself wholly theirs, so I give them in hand an actual possession of all such saving grace as my sacrificial body can yield, and as their souls do presently need, this is to them, and in them, my body" (Hooker, *Eccles. Polity,* book 5, p. 167). "The body of Christ is given, taken, and eaten in the supper only after a heavenly and spiritual manner. And the means whereby the body of Christ is received and eaten in the supper is faith" (*Discipline, Methodist Church,* Art. 18).

Symbolic, or Zwinglian, View. According to this view, partaking of the supper merely commemorates the sacrificial work of Christ, and its value to the participant consists only in the bestowal of a blessing.

BIBLIOGRAPHY: A. J. B. Higgins, *The Lord's Supper in the New Testament* (1952); J. Jeremias, *The Eucharistic Words of Jesus* (1955); E. F. Kevan, *The Lord's Supper* (1966); W. Barclay, *The Lord's Supper* (1967); E. Schweizer, *The Lord's Supper According to the New Testament* (1967); M. Chemnitz, *The Lord's Supper* (1979); I. H. Marshall, *Last Supper and Lord's Supper* (1980).

LO-RUHA'MAH (lō-rū-ha'ma; "not pitied, not favored"). The name divinely given to the second child (a daughter) of the prophet Hosea (1:6) to indicate that the Lord would not continue to show compassion toward the rebellious nation, as He up to this time had done under Jeroboam II (2 Kings 13:23). In Hos. 2:23 the expression is translated "her who had not obtained compassion." A *daughter* is named to represent the effeminate period that followed the overthrow of the first dynasty, when Israel was at once degradated and irreverent. When God restored His favor to the people her name was changed to *Ruhamah* (which see).

LOSS. See Law of Moses: Civil.

LOT. 1. (Heb. *gôrāl,* a "pebble"; *ḥebel,* "measuring line, portion"; Gk. *lanchanō,* to "cast lots," Luke 1:9; *klēros,* "pebble, bit of wood"; to cast lots with, Acts 1:26). The custom of deciding doubtful questions by lot is one of great extent and high antiquity, recommending itself as a sort of appeal to the Almighty, secure from all influence of passion or bias, and is a sort of divination employed even by the gods themselves (Homer *Iliad* 22.209; Cicero *De divinatione* 1.34; 2.41). Among the Jews also the use of lots with a religious intention, direct or indirect, prevailed extensively. The religious estimate of them may be gathered from Prov. 16:33. The following historical or ritual instances are: (1) choice of men for an invading force (Judg. 1:1-3, *see* marg.; 20:9); (2) partition of the land of Palestine among the tribes (Num. 26:55; Josh. 18:10), of Jerusalem, that is, probably its spoil or captives among captors (Obad. 11), of the land itself in a similar way (1 Macc. 3:36); apportionment of possessions, or spoil, or of prisoners, to foreigners or captors

(Joel 3:3; Nah. 3:10; Matt. 27:35); (3) settlement of doubtful questions (Prov. 16:33; 18:18), a mode of divination among heathen by means of arrows, two inscribed and one without mark (Ezek. 21:21), detection of a criminal (Josh. 7:14), appointment of persons to offices or duties, such as the priests (Luke 1:9); also successor to Judas (Acts 1:26); selection of the scapegoat on the Day of Atonement (Lev. 16:8, 10). *See* Urim and Thummim.

2. That which falls to one by lot, as a *portion* or *inheritance* (Deut. 32:9; Josh. 15:1; 1 Chron. 16:18; Pss. 105:11; 125:3, marg.; Isa. 17:14; 57:6; Acts 8:21; cf. Acts 13:19).

LOT (lot). The son of Haran and nephew of Abraham. The genealogy given in table 23 exhibits Lot's family relations (Gen. 11:27-32). After the death of his father (Gen. 11:28), Lot was left in the charge of his grandfather Terah, with whom he migrated to Haran (11:31), c. 2120 B.C. Following the death of Terah, Lot accompanied Abraham to Canaan (12:4-5), c. 2086 B.C., thence to Egypt, and back again to Canaan (12:10; 13:1).

Separation. The flocks and herds of both increased so greatly that the land did not furnish enough pasture, and consequently disputes arose between their herdsmen. To put an end to strife Abraham proposed a separation and magnanimously left the choice of territory to his nephew, who selected the plain of Jordan and fixed his home at Sodom (13:5-12).

A Prisoner. A few years after, Lot was carried away by Chedorlaomer, along with other captives from Sodom, but was rescued and brought back by Abraham (14:12:8-16), c. 2060 B.C.

Escape from Sodom. When Jehovah had determined to destroy Sodom, Lot was still residing there and, sitting at the city gate, met the messengers (angels) of the Lord. He pressed them to pass the night at his house, and they yielded to his entreaty. While they were at supper the house was beset by a number of the inhabitants, who demanded, with the basest violation of hospitality, that the strangers should be delivered up to them for sexual relations. Lot went out to them, shut the door behind him to protect his guests,

and resisted the demands of the crowd. This enraged them still more, and they were about to break in the door when the angels pulled Lot into the house, shut the door, and struck the people with blindness. Lot was then informed of the coming destruction of the city and exhorted to remove his family. In the morning he was hastened away by the angels. Instead of cheerfully obeying the commandment to flee to the mountain, Lot entreated that he might be allowed to take refuge in Zoar, the smallest of the cities of the plain. While on their way Lot's wife, disobedient to the divine command "Do not look behind you" lingered behind, probably from a longing for her home and earthly possessions, and "became a pillar of salt." Lot, moved by fear, soon left Zoar and moved to a cave in the neighboring mountains (19:1-30).

Daughters' Crime. While there his daughters, dreading the extinction of their family, resolved to procure children through their father. This they succeeded in doing by making him drunk with wine and in that state seducing him into an act of which he would not in soberness have been guilty. The son of the elder daughter was Moab, progenitor of the Moabites, and of the younger Ben-ammi, "the father," that is, ancestor of the Ammonites (19:31-38). Lot is not mentioned again in the OT, and the time and place of his death are unknown. He is alluded to in 2 Pet. 2:7-8, being described as "righteous," that is, a type of the carnal worldly believer in contrast to Abraham, the man of faith.

BIBLIOGRAPHY: W. H. G. Thomas, *Genesis: A Devotional Commentary* (1946), pp. 122-26, 169-76; C. J. Barber, *Dynamic Bible Study* (1981), pp. 115-38.

LO'TAN (lōʹtan). The first named son of Seir, the Horite, and a chief of Edom prior to the ascendency of the Esauites (Gen. 36:20, 29; 1 Chron. 1:38). His sons were Hori and Hemam (or Homam; Gen. 36:22; 1 Chron. 1:39), and through his sister, Timna, he was related to Eliphaz, Esau's son (Gen. 36:12).

LO'TUS (Heb. *ṣeʾel*). A marshy plant that provided shelter and a hiding place for the behemoth

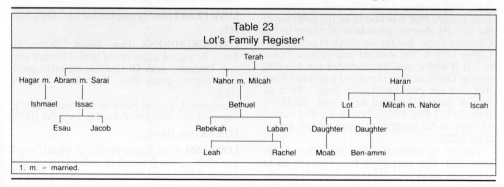

Table 23
Lot's Family Register[1]

		Terah							
Hagar m. Abram m. Sarai			Nahor m. Milcah			Haran			
Ishmael	Issac			Bethuel		Lot	Milcah m. Nahor		Iscah
Esau	Jacob		Rebekah		Laban	Daughter	Daughter		
			Leah		Rachel	Moab	Ben-ammi		

1. m. = married.

(Job 40:21-22). The KJV translates "shady trees." *See* Vegetable Kingdom.

LOVE (Heb. *'ahăbâ;* Gk. *'agapē*). Chiefly represented in the Scriptures as an attribute of God and as a Christian virtue. Its consideration, therefore, belongs to both theology and ethics.

An Attribute of God. According to the Scriptures, God has feeling, affection, although rationalistic theologians (e.g., Schleiermacher, Bruch) have asserted the contrary. We must derive our conceptions of God from the special revelation that He has given of Himself, and this declares His love as strongly as His existence. It is held by some to be inadequate to speak of love as a divine attribute. "God is love" (1 John 4:8, 16). The Scriptures contain no equivalent statements with respect to other qualities of the divine nature. Love is the highest characteristic of God, the one attribute in which all others harmoniously blend. The love of God is more than kindness or benevolence. The latter may be exercised toward irrational creatures, but love is directed toward rational, personal beings. The eternal love of God has never been without its object, a fact upon which we receive some light from the Scripture revelation of the threefold personality of God (*see* Trinity; *see* also Matt. 3:17; John 15:9; 17:23-26). The gracious love of God to men, even to sinful men, is most strongly declared in both the OT and NT (e.g., Ex. 34:6; Isa. 63:9; Jer. 31:3; John 3:16; 1 John 4:10). The love of God underlies all that He has done and is doing, although many facts exist that we cannot reconcile with His love on account of our limited understanding. The highest disclosure and most complete proof of divine love is in redemption (*see* Rom. 5:8; 8:32-39; 1 John 4:9-10). The reality and power of this love are properly apprehended only under the influence of the Holy Spirit. "The love of God has been poured out within our hearts through the Holy Spirit who was given to us" (Rom. 5:5).

A Christian Virtue. Love (Gk. *'agapē;* NASB and NIV, "love"). The only word in the Bible translated *charity* means *love*. It is affection, tender and passionate attachment, a sentiment of our nature excited by qualities in a person or thing that command our affection; a virtue of such efficacy that it is said to be the fulfilling of the law. Its absence invalidates all claim to the Christian name. It is the antithesis of selfishness. Luther calls it "the shortest and longest divinity." It is active, and dissatisfied if not blessing others. Christian love is piety, the greatest boon that God can give, for "God is love." "In it all human duty is summed up" (Matt. 22:37-40; Rom. 13:8; 1 Cor. 13:13). Love is the first named element in the composite "fruit of the Spirit" (Gal. 5:22).

Charity, in modern speech, has other meanings: first, that sentiment that prompts us to think and speak well of others, judge their acts kindly, and make them happy; second, generosity to the poor; third, that which is thus given; and fourth, a benevolent foundation.

Love is the preeminent virtue inculcated and produced by Christianity. The whole law is summed up in love, not in the sense of rendering all other requirements as inconsequential, but in the sense that love is fundamental, expresses the spirit of all others, and with enlightenment will lead to the observance of all others (Matt. 22:37-39; 5:43-48; John 14:15, 21; 15:12-14; Rom. 13:8; 1 Cor. 13; Gal. 5:14). Accordingly, love is declared to be the chief test of Christian discipleship (John 13:35; Matt. 5:44; 1 John 3:14). Also, love is the highest motive or ground of moral actions. Without this all other motives fall short of furnishing the true stimulus of Christian living. As all sin roots itself in selfishness, so all virtue springs out of love; and yet the love that is presented in the NT as the mainspring of holy living is grateful love as distinct from the love that is wholly disinterested. "We love, because He first loved us" are words that rightly express the whole matter (1 John 4:19; *see also* 2 Cor 5:14; Rom. 12:1-2). The contention of Fenelon that true Christian love should be disinterested, that we must love God exclusively on account of His perfection, so that if He did not bless us, but were to cast us off, we would love Him still, finds no support in the Scriptures. It contains a measure of truth inasmuch as it emphasizes the warning that we are certainly not to love the gifts of God more than the Giver and that we are not to love God wholly on account of His gifts. In reality, grateful love includes adoring love, or that which loves God for His own sake. Christian love, it is also important to note, is made possible only by divine grace. It is one of the fruits of the Spirit (Gal. 5:22; *see also* 1 John 3:14).   E. MCC.

BIBLIOGRAPHY: B. J. Bamberger, *Hebrew Union College Annual* 6 (1929): 39-53; J. Moffat, *Love in the New Testament* (1929); N. H. Snaith, *The Distinctive Ideas of the Old Testament* (1944), pp. 94-142; D. M. Baillie, *God Was in Christ* (1948), pp. 184-89; A. Nygren, *Agape and Eros* (1953); D. E. Trueblood, *Company of the Committed* (1961), pp. 96-113; V. P. Furnish, *The Love Command in the New Testament* (1972); L. L. Morris, *Testaments of Love* (1981).

LOVE FEAST. *See* Agape; Eucharist; Lord's Supper.

LOVINGKINDNESS (Heb. *hesed,* "desire, ardor"). In a good sense *hesed* is zeal toward anyone, *kindness, love.* Of God toward men, *goodness, mercy, grace* (Pss. 17:7; 26:3; 36:7, 10; etc.).

BIBLIOGRAPHY: N. Glueck, *Hesed in the Bible* (1967); K. Sakenfeld, *The Meaning of Hesed in the Bible* (1978).

LOWER *See* Depths.

LOWLAND (Heb. *hashshᵉpēlâ*). A broad, swelling tract of many hundred miles in area that sweeps gently down from the mountains of Judah toward the Mediterranean. It is referred to in Deut. 1:7; Josh. 9:1; 10:40; 11:2, 16; etc.). *See also* Shephelah. The NIV usually translates "foothills."

LU'BIM (lū'bĭm; Nah. 3:9; 2 Chron. 12:3; 16:8; cf. Dan. 11:43). An African race, the primitive Libyans (always the translation of *lubim* in the NIV). They are always mentioned in connection with Egyptians and Ethiopians. They formed part of the armies of Shishak (2 Chron. 12:3) and of Zerah (16:8), and they helped No-amon, or Thebes (Nah. 3:9). In Dan. 11:43 they pay court to a northern conqueror. The Lubim were probably the Rebu, or Lebu, of the Egyptian monuments, a fair race of Semitic type, warlike but not able to stand against Merneptah and Rameses II. Their home appears to have been on the N coast of Africa, W of Egypt. They doubtless belonged to the oldest stream of colonization that flowed westward along the northern coast of Africa. The territory of the Lubim and their kindred tribes may be likened to that of the great Arab tribe of the Benee 'Alee, which extends "from Egypt to Morocco." "Reduced by the Egyptians about 1250 B.C., and afterward driven inland by the Phoenician and Greek colonists, they still remain on the northern confines of the great desert, and even within it and in the mountains, while their later Semitic rivals pasture their flocks in the rich plains." Probably the Mizraite Lehabim (Gen. 10:13; 1 Chron. 1:11) are the same as the Lubim. *See* Libya.   W.H.; M.F.U.

LU'CIFER (lū'si-fer; Heb. *hēlēl*, "brightness"). This designation, referring to Satan, is the KJV rendering of NASB, "star of the morning," that is, "bright star" (Isa. 14:12-14), probably what we call the "morning star" (so NIV). As a symbolical representation of the king of Babylon in his pride, splendor, and fall, the passage goes beyond the Babylonian prince and invests Satan, who, at the head of this present world-system is the real though invisible power behind the successive world rulers of Tyre, Babylon, Persia, Greece, and Rome. This far-reaching passage goes beyond human history and marks the beginning of sin in the universe and the fall of Satan and the pristine, sinless spheres before the creation of man. Similarly Ezekiel (28:12-14), under the figure of the king of Tyre, likewise traces the fall of Satan and the corruption of his power and glory. In the Ezekiel passage Satan's glorious and splendid unfallen state is described. In Isa. 14:12-14 his fall is depicted. In both passages representation is not of Satan as confined to his own person but working in and consummating his plans through earthly kings and rulers who take to themselves divine honors and who, whether they actually know this or not, rule in the spirit and under the aims of Satan. Daniel 10:13 and Eph. 6:12 show that there are human as well as superhuman agencies in world governments in the satanic

world system.   M.F.U.

BIBLIOGRAPHY: Merrill F. Unger, *Biblical Demonology*, 2d ed. (1953), pp. 181-92; id., "Demonism and World Governments," pp. 192-200. *See also* Devil; Satan.

LU'CIUS (lū'shi-us; for Lat. *Lucius*). Of Cyrene, one of the "prophets and teachers" at Antioch who, at the command of the Holy Spirit, ordained Barnabas and Saul (Acts 13:1; Rom. 16:21), A.D. 45.

LUD (lud; Gen. 10:22; 1 Chron. 1:11, NASB and NIV; 1:17; Isa 66:19; Ezek. 27:10; Ezek. 30:5, NASB only). The NIV renders Lydians in Isa. 66:19; Ezek. 27:10; 30:5. *See* Ludim.

LUDIM (lu'dim; Gen. 10:13; 1 Chron. 1:11, KJV and NIV), **Lydia** (Ezek. 30:5, KJV and NIV), **Lydians** (Jer. 46:9).

The Lud of Gen. 10:22 and 1 Chron. 1:17 was the fourth son of Shem; the Ludim of Gen. 10:13 and 1 Chron. 1:11 (KJV only; "people of Lud," NASB; "Ludites," NIV) were the first mentioned among the descendants of Mizraim, the second son of Ham. In Jer. 46:9 ("the Lydians") and Ezek. 30:5 ("Lud," NASB; "Lydia," KJV and NIV), Lud and Ludim are associated with African nations, and partly so in Isa. 66:19 and Ezek. 27:10. Our first impulse would be to refer all these prophetic passages, especially Jer. 46:9 and Ezek. 30:5, to the Mizraite tribe. It is hinted, however, that the Lud and Ludim of the prophets may have been the Ionian and Carian mercenaries that were employed in the Egyptian army from the time of Psammethichus I to the final subjugation of the country. This might explain the ambiguous manner in which they are associated with both Asiatic and African nations. In the time of the prophets Lydia might well be taken to represent the western part of Asia Minor.

Lydia was a kingdom in western Asia Minor that was wealthy and powerful in the seventh and sixth centuries B.C. As a result of their extensive trade with the Greeks, they invented the coinage of gold and silver money. Their smeltery/mint has been excavated at *Sardis* (which see), their great capital. *Cyrus the Great* (which see) of Persia brought an end to the Lydian kingdom and the reign of its famous king Croesus in 546 B.C. Under the Persians Sardis was the western terminus of the great trunk line that extended from Susa to Sardis (about fifteen hundred miles). Later Lydia became part of the kingdom of Pergamum, which entered the Roman Empire as the province of Asia in 133 B.C. Three of the cities of Revelation—Thyatira, Sardis, and Philadelphia (Rev. 2:18–3:13)—were located in Lydia.

LU'HITH (lū'hith; Jer. 48:5; Isa. 15:5). A Moabite town situated upon an ascent, to which the people fled from the invading Babylonians.

LUKE (lūk; Gk. *Loukas;* Lat. *Lucanus*). The evangelist and author of the gospel bearing his name and the Acts of the Apostles. *See* Gospels; Bible, Books of.

The materials found in Scripture referring to the life of Luke are scanty and seem to yield the following results: (1) Luke was of Gentile origin. This is inferred from the fact that he is not reckoned among those "who are from the circumcision" (Col. 4:11; cf. v. 14). When and how he became a physician is not known. (2) He was not one of the "eyewitnesses and servants of the word" (Luke 1:2). (3) On the supposition of Luke's being the author of the Acts we gather from those passages in which the first person *we* is employed that he joined Paul's company at Troas and sailed with them to Macedonia (Acts 16:10-11). He accompanied Paul as far as Philippi (16:25–17:1) but did not share his persecution or leave the city, for here the third person *they* is used. The first person *we* does not reappear until Paul comes to Philippi at the end of his third journey (20:6), from which it is inferred that Luke spent the intervening time—a period of seven or eight years—in the city or neighborhood; and as the *we* continues to the end of the book, that Luke remained with Paul during his journey to Jerusalem (20:6–21:18), was that apostle's companion to Rome (27:1), sharing his shipwreck (28:2), and reaching the imperial city by way of Syracuse and Puteoli (28:12-16). According to the epistles he continued to be one of Paul's "fellow workers" till the end of his first imprisonment (Philem. 24; Col. 4:14). The last glimpse of the "beloved physician" discovers him to be faithful amid general defection (2 Tim. 4:11). Tradition since the time of Gregory of Nazianzus makes Luke a martyr, yet not unanimously, since accounts of a natural death slip in. *Where* he died remains a question; certainly not in Rome with Paul, for his writings are far later (Meyer, *Com.*, on Luke, in introduction).

LUKE, GOSPEL OF. The third synoptic gospel, a work of high literary quality ascribed by almost universal Christian tradition to Luke, the beloved physician and traveling companion of Paul.

Characteristics. Renan viewed Luke's gospel as "the most beautiful book that has ever been written." The subject matter as well as the author's literary talent combine to give the book an interesting appeal and polish conspicuous in the NT. The elevated subject matter was a challenge to the author's literary endeavor. Whereas Matthew presents Christ as King, Mark presents Him as Servant, John presents Him as the Son of God, and Luke presents Him as the Son of man, the human-divine One in contrast to John's divine-human One. The term "Son of Man" acts as a key phrase, and 19:10 is commonly taken as the key verse: "For the Son of Man has come to seek and to save that which was lost." In agreement with his purpose, Luke narrates those events that demonstrate the humanity of Christ. The divine

genealogy is traced to Adam. A detailed account of Christ's mother and of His infancy and childhood is presented. The parables included by Luke have a human touch. Although Luke beautifully sets forth the humanity of the divine One he carefully shields His deity and kingship (1:32-35). It has truly been said that Luke is the gospel of "a man whose name is Branch" (Zech. 6:12). Luke is distinctive in that it catalogs much material that is not included in the other evangels. This new material amounts to more than 50 percent of its content. For example, Luke has a joyous note and records five great outbursts of song—Elizabeth's *Beatitude*, Mary's *Magnificat*, Zachariah's *Benedictus*, the angels' *Gloria in Excelsis*, and Simeon's *Nunc Dimittis*. His gospel is emphatically "good news of a great joy."

Purpose. The evangelist proposes to write in order that Theophilus might know the "exact truth" of the things wherein he had been instructed (Luke 1:4). Theophilus seems to have been a Gentile, and the epithet *kratistos*, often given to persons of rank (Acts 23:26; 24:3; 26:5), suggests that he was an individual of eminence, most likely a recent convert. Some believe that he was a *patronos libri* and acted as a patron for the production of the book. Everyone is of the opinion that the gospel was intended for people at large, especially the Greek-speaking world.

Date. Since the book was written before the Acts, which is to be dated c. A.D. 61, it was likely written while Paul was at Caesarea. Since internal evidence that Luke wrote both the gospel and the book of Acts (and he divulges the fact that the gospel was written first, Acts 1:1), it must be concluded that the gospel was penned prior to A.D. 61. Luke was in Caesarea where Paul was in prison (Acts 27:1). This circumstance would furnish him opportunity for the research he mentions with such fine literary style and classical flourish in Luke 1:1-4.

Attestation. External evidence is strong concerning the early existence and use of Luke. Justin Martyr quotes 22:44; 23:46. The Muratorian Fragment calls the third gospel "Luke." Heggesippus, Tatian, the unbeliever Celsus, Marcion, Clement of Alexandria, and Tertullian all refer to "Luke." Robertson's statement in the *International Standard Bible Encyclopedia* on Luke sums up the evidence: "Surely the general use and acceptance of the third gospel in the early second century is beyond reasonable doubt. It is not easy to decide when the actual use began, because we have so little data from the first century."

Outline.

I. Introduction (1:1-4)
II. The Son of Man in His human relationships (1:5–2:52)
III. The Son of Man in His baptism, ancestry, and testing (3:1–4:13)

IV. The Son of Man in His ministry as Prophet-King in Galilee (4:14–9:50)
V. The Son of Man's journey from Galilee to Jerusalem (9:51–19:44)
VI. The Son of Man offered as Israel's King, His rejection, and sacrifice (19:45–23:56)
VII. The Son of Man in resurrection, ministry, and ascension (24:1-53)   M.F.U.

BIBLIOGRAPHY: A. Plummer, *A Critical and Exegetical Commentary on the Gospel According to St. Luke,* International Critical Commentary (1896); J. M. Creed, *The Gospel According to St. Luke* (1930); P. Parker, *The Gospel Before Mark* (1931); F. L. Godet, *A Commentary on the Gospel of St. Luke* (1957); I. H. Marshall, *Luke: Historian and Theologian* (1970); L. L. Morris, *The Gospel According to St. Luke,* Tyndale New Testament Commentary (1974); I. H. Marshall, *The Gospel of Luke,* New International Greek New Testament (1978); J. A. Fitzmyer, *The Gospel According to Luke,* Anchor Bible (1982).

LUNACY, LUNATIC. *See* Demoniac; Diseases: Madness.

LUST. The rendering of several Heb. and Gk. words with various meanings.

1. In the KJV the term is sometimes used simply to express intense longing and desire; in those cases the NASB and NIV replace the word with various terms as appropriate ("desire," or "want," Ex. 15:9; Deut. 12:15; "greedy," Num. 11:34; etc.).

2. In the ethical sense *lust* is used to express sinful desire—sinful either in being directed toward forbidden objects or in being so violent as to overcome self-control and to engross the mind with earthly, carnal, and perishable things.

"By lusts Paul, like Peter and James, understands, not the natural appetites of the body, but the sinful, godless inclinations (Rom. 1:24), whether these be of a sensuous or of a spiritual nature. He purposely quotes the Old Testament commandment against sinful lust (Ex. 20:17; Deut. 5:21) in such a manner that it is not any definite objects of lust, but the longing for them as such that he calls forbidden (Rom. 7:7, *see* margin). In his sense every lust is a product of sin (v. 8), which compels us to obey the lusts of the body (6:12); every natural appetite may be perverted by sin into lust (13:14)" (Weiss, *Theology of the N.T.,* 1:328).

LUTE. *See* Music.

LUZ (luz; "almond tree").

1. The ancient (Canaanite) name of Bethel (Gen. 28:19; 35:6; 48:3), or a town that formerly stood upon or near the latter city (*see* Bethel). In Josh. 16:2 "Luz is distinguished from Beth-el because the reference is not to the town of Beth-el, but to the southern range of mountains belonging to Beth-el, from which the boundary ran out to the town of Luz, so that this town, which stood upon the border, was allotted to Benjamin (18:13)" (K. & D., *Com.*).

2. A town in the land of the Hittites, built by an inhabitant of the former Luz. He was spared when the latter was destroyed by the Benjamites (Judg. 1:23-26). Luweiziyeh, a ruin 4½ miles NW of Banias, is suggested as the site by Conder.

LYCAO'NIA (līk-a-ō'ni-a). A small Roman province of Asia Minor, bounded N by Galatia, E by Cappadocia, S by Isauria, and W by Phrygia. It is not fertile, though level, and therefore adapted to pasturage. Its cities are Derbe, Iconium, and Lystra. The "Lycaonian language" (Acts 14:11) was a corrupt Greek mingled with Assyrian. Paul preached in this region (14:1-6) and then revisited it (cf. 16:1-2).

LY'CIA (lī'si-a). A mountainous province in SW Asia Minor belonging to Rome. Patara and Myra are its towns, which were visited by Paul (Acts 21:1; 27:5). It is a part of the region now known as *Tekeh.*

The mountains of Lycia

LYD'DA (lid'a). A town about eleven miles SE of Joppa, called Lod in the OT (1 Chron. 8:12), and modern Israelis have reverted to the OT name. It is located in the midst of a rich and fertile plain. It was one of the most westernly of the Jewish settlements after the Exile, the site of which is described as Ge-haharashim, the valley of the smiths or craftsmen. It was here that Peter healed the paralytic and secured many converts (Acts 9:32-35). It was not Jewish, but pagan, under the name *Diospolis. See* Lod.

LYD'IA (lid'i-a). A seller of purple of the city of *Thyatira* (which see) who dwelt in Philippi. She sold the purple-dyed garments from Thyatira in Philippi and traded in both the cheap and expensive merchandise. As her husband is not mentioned and she was a householder, she was probably a widow. She was not by birth a Jewess, but a proselyte, as the phrase "a worshiper of God" suggests. Converted by the preaching of Paul and baptized by him, she pressed upon him the use of her house so earnestly that he was constrained to accept (Acts 16:14-15, 40). Whether she was one of the women who "shared" Paul's struggle as a fellow Christian (Phil. 4:3) is impossible to say.

BIBLIOGRAPHY: W. M. Ramsay, *St. Paul the Traveller and Roman Citizen* (1960), pp. 214-15; D. E. Hiebert, *Personalities Around Paul* (1973), pp. 171-77.

LYDIA, LYDIANS (lid'i-à, lid'i-anz). The rendering of *ludim* in Jer. 46:9 and, in the KJV and NIV, the rendering of *lud* in Ezek. 30:5. *See* Lud; Ludim.

LYE. *See* Mineral Kingdom: Nitre.

LYRE. *See* Music.

LYSA'NIAS (lī-sā'ni-us). A tetrarch or governor of the region known as Abilene. This country was drained by the Abana River and located between Baalbek on the N side of Mt. Hermon and Damascus. This Lysanias ruled in the time of John the Baptist (Luke 3:1) in the fifteenth year of Tiberias. So critics insist that Lysanias, the son of Ptolemy who reigned in Chalcis in Coelesyria (40-34 B.C.), gave the name to this tetrarchy and that Luke has made a historical blunder. Lysanias, however, who ruled Chalcis is never called tetrarch nor does Abila appear in his kingdom. In A.D. 37 the emperor Caligula appointed Herod Agrippa king of the tetrarchy of Philip and added Lysanias to the tetrarchy. The tetrarchy of Lysanias, with its capital at Abila some eighteen miles NW of Damascus, was distinct from the kingdom of Chalcis (Josephus *Ant.* 19.5.1; 20.7.1). In the time in which Luke writes, the region about Abila was ruled by the tetrarch Lysanias, and therefore Luke is correct.   M.F.U.

LYS'IAS (lis'I-as).
1. *Claudius,* the "commander" of the Roman troops in Jerusalem who rescued Paul from the fury of the Jews (cf. Acts 22:24-30) and sent him under guard to the procurator Felix at Caesarea (2317-30; 24:7, 22), A.D. 55.

2. A general under Antiochus Epiphanes and Antiochus Eupator (1 Macc. 3:32-37). *See* Maccabees, the.

LYS'TRA (lis'tra). A town of *Lycaonia* (which see), where Paul preached after being driven from Iconium (Acts 14:2-7). Here he healed a lame man and because of this was taken by the inhabitants to be the god Hermes (vv. 8-12). Through the influence of Jews from Antioch and Iconium the tide was turned, and Paul was nearly stoned to death (v. 19; 2 Tim. 3:11). Paul left for Derbe but soon returned (Acts 14:21). It is not definitely stated that he ever visited Lystra again but the route of his third missionary journey (18:23) makes that probable. Lystra was a Roman colony located on a hill about one mile NW of Khatyn Serai, which is situated eighteen miles SSW of Iconium.

BIBLIOGRAPHY: E. M. Blaiklock, *Cities of the New Testament* (1965), pp. 31-34; A. H. Jones, *The Cities of the Eastern Roman Provinces* (1971), pp. 134-35.

The countryside around the site of Lystra

MA'ACAH (ma'a-ka; "oppression"; sometimes "Maachah," KJV).

1. The last named of the four children of Nahor by his concubine Reumah (Gen. 22:24). Whether this child was a son or daughter is not stated.

2. One of David's wives and the mother of Absalom. She was the daughter of Talmai, king of Geshur (2 Sam. 3:3). Geshur lies to the N of Judah between Hermon and Bashan.

3. A city and small Syrian kingdom at the foot of Mt. Hermon, near Geshur (Josh. 13:13, "Maacath"; 2 Sam. 10:6, 8; 1 Chron. 19:7). The kingdom embraced the southern and eastern descending slopes of Hermon, and a portion of the rocky plateau of Iturea. The Israelites included this territory in their grant but never took possession of it (Josh. 13:13). Its king contributed 1,000 men to the Syrian alliance against David (2 Sam. 10:6-8), which was defeated (v. 19).

4. The father of Achish, king of Gath, to whom Shimei went in pursuit of two runaway servants and by so doing forfeited his life by going beyond the limits prescribed by Solomon (1 Kings 2:39).

5. The mother of King Abijam. She was the daughter (granddaughter) of Abishalom, and wife of Rehoboam (1 Kings 15:2), about 926 B.C. In v. 10 she is called the "mother" of Asa, but there the term is used in a loose sense and means "grandmother." The following seem to be the facts: Maacah was the granddaughter of Absalom (Abishalom), and the daughter of Tamar (Absalom's only daughter) and Uriel of Gibeah (2 Chron. 11:20-22; 13:2, where she is called "Micaiah"). Because of the abuse of her power as "queen mother" in encouraging idolatry, Asa removed her from her position as queen (1 Kings 15:10-13; 2 Chron. 15:16).

6. The second named of the concubines of Caleb (son of Hezron) and the mother by him of several children (1 Chron. 2:48).

7. The sister of Huppim and Shuppim and wife of Machir, by whom he had two sons (1 Chron. 7:15-16).

8. The wife of Jeiel and mother of Gibeon (1 Chron. 8:29; 9:35).

9. The father of Hanan, one of David's valiant men (1 Chron. 11:43).

10. The father of Shephatiah, military chief of the Simeonites in the time of David (1 Chron. 27:16), c. 1000 B.C.

MAAC'ATH (mā-ak'a-th; Josh. 13:13). See Maacah, no. 3, above.

MAAC'ATHITES (ma-ak'a-thīts). Inhabitants of Maacah (Josh. 13:13), a small kingdom S of Mt. Hermon, located in the northern part of the Golan Heights, bounded on the S by the kingdom of Geshur. There were Maacathite warriors among the mighty men of Israel. One was apparently the father of Ahasbai in 2 Sam. 23:34; one was the father of Jezaniah, or Jaazaniah (2 Kings 25:23; Jer. 40:8); another, Eshtemoa (1 Chron. 4:19), may have taken the title from Maacah, Caleb's concubine (2:48). Indeed, Maacah was so common as a personal name that other Maacathites may have received the epithet in the same way. It is possible that the kingdom of Maacah may have taken its name from the Maacah of Gen. 22:24. The Maacathites are mentioned in Joshua in connection with the Geshurites as bordering the territory of Og, king of Bashan (12:5; cf. 13:11) but not dispossessed by Israel.

MA'ACHAH. See Maacah.

MAADA'I (ma-a-dī). A Jew of the family of Bani who divorced his Gentile wife after the captivity (Ezra 10:34), 456 B.C.

MAADI'AH (ma-a-dī'a; "ornament of Jehovah"). One of the priests who returned from Babylon with Zerubbabel (Neh. 12:5), about 536 B.C. He is thought to be the same as Moadiah (v. 17).

MAA'I (ma-ī). One of the priests appointed to perform the music at the celebration of the completion of the walls of Jerusalem after the Exile (Neh. 12:36), 445 B.C.

MAAL'EH-ACRAB'BIM. *See* Akrabbim, Ascent of.

MA'ARATH (ma'a-rath; "desolation"). A place in the mountains of Judah (Josh. 15:59), not positively identified, perhaps Beit Ummar, about seven miles N of Hebron.

MAAS'AI (ma-as'ī; "work of Jehovah"). The son of Adiel, descendant of Immer, and one of the priests residing at Jerusalem after the captivity (1 Chron. 9:12), probably after 536 B.C.

MAASE'IAH (ma-a-se'ya; "work of Jehovah").

1. One of the Levites of the second class of appointed musicians "with harps tuned to alamoth," at the bringing of the Ark from the house of Obed-edom (1 Chron. 15:18, 20), about 982 B.C.

2. One of the "captains of hundreds" who assisted the high priest Jehoiada in raising Joash to the throne of Judah (2 Chron. 23:1), 836 B.C.

3. An official who assisted Jeiel the scribe in arranging the army of King Uzziah (2 Chron. 26:11), about 783 B.C.

4. A person slain by Zichri, an Ephraimite hero, in the invasion of Judah by Pekah, king of Israel (2 Chron. 28:7), about 735 B.C. Maaseiah is called the "king's son," but this should probably not be interpreted literally, "for in the first years of his reign, in which this war arose, Ahaz could not have had an adult son capable of bearing arms, but" Maaseiah was likely "a royal prince, a cousin or uncle of Ahaz" (Keil, *Com.*, ad loc.).

5. An "official of the city," appointed by King Josiah to cooperate with Shaphan and Joah in repairing the Temple (2 Chron. 34:8), 621 B.C. He is probably the same as Mahseiah, the father of Neriah, and grandfather of Baruch and Seraiah (Jer. 32:12; 51:59).

6. One of the priests of the descendants of Jeshua who divorced his Gentile wife after the captivity (Ezra 10:18), 456 B.C.

7. Another priest of the "sons" of Harim who put away his Gentile wife after the Exile (Ezra 10:21), 456 B.C. He is probably the one who belonged to the chorus that celebrated the completion of the walls (Neh. 12:42), 445 B.C.

8. A priest of the "sons" of Pashhur who divorced his Gentile wife after the return from Babylon (Ezra 10:22), 456 B.C. Perhaps the same as one of the trumpeters who joined in celebrating the building of the walls of Jerusalem (Neh. 12:41), 445 B.C.

9. An Israelite, descendant of Pahath-moab who put away his Gentile wife after the Exile (Ezra 10:30), 456 B.C.

10. A Jew, whose son Azariah repaired a portion of the walls of Jerusalem after the return from Babylon (Neh. 3:23), 445 B.C.

11. One of those who stood at the right hand of Ezra while he read the book of the law to the people (Neh. 8:4), about 445 B.C.

12. One of the priests who, with the Levites, expounded the law as it was read by Ezra (Neh. 8:7), about 445 B.C.

13. One of the "leaders of the people" who joined in the covenant with Nehemiah (Neh. 10:25), 445 B.C.

14. The son of Baruch and one of the descendants of Judah who dwelt in Jerusalem after the captivity (Neh. 11:5), about 536 B.C. In 1 Chron. 9:5 the same person is probably listed as *Asaiah* (which see).

15. The son of Ithiel, a Benjamite, and one whose descendants resided in Jerusalem after the return from Babylon (Neh. 11:7), before 536 B.C.

16. A priest whose son Zephaniah was sent by Zedekiah, king of Judah, to inquire of the prophet Jeremiah during the invasion by Nebuchadnezzar (Jer. 21:1; 29:21, 25; 37:3), before 589 B.C.

17. The son of Shallum, and a doorkeeper of the Temple, with a chamber in the sacred edifice (Jer. 35:4), about 607 B.C.

MAAS'IAI. *See* Maas'ai.

MA'ATH (ma'ath). A person named as the son of Mattathias, and father of Naggai in the maternal ancestry of Jesus (Luke 3:26). As no such name appears in the OT genealogies, it is thought that this name has been accidentally interpolated from Matthat (v. 24).

MA'AZ (ma'az; "anger"). The first named of the three sons of Ram, the firstborn of Jerahmeel, of the descendants of Judah (1 Chron. 2:27), after 1440 B.C.

MAAZI'AH (ma-a-zī'a; "Jehovah is a refuge").

1. The head of the last (twenty-fourth) division of priests as arranged by David (1 Chron. 24:18), before 960 B.C.

2. One of the priests who sealed the covenant made by Nehemiah (Neh. 10:8), about 445 B.C.

MAC'BANNAI. *See* Machbannai.

MAC'CABEES, THE (mak'a-bēz). The Hasmonaean family, distinguished in Jewish history, from 167 B.C. until the time when Judea became a province of Rome, were called Maccabees from Judas, a distinguished member of the house, whose surname was Maccabaeus.

Name. The etymology of the word *Maccabee* is uncertain. Some have maintained that it was formed from the combination of the initial letters of the Hebrew sentence, "Who is like Thee among the gods, O Lord?" (Ex. 15:11), which is supposed to have been inscribed upon the banner of the patriots. Another derivation has been proposed, which, although direct evidence is lacking, seems satisfactory. According to this, the word is formed from *Maqqābâ*, "a hammer," giving a sense not altogether unlike that in which the Frankish ruler Charles Martel derived a surname from his favorite weapon, the hammer (*martel,* in French). Although the name Maccabees has gained the widest currency, that of Hasmonaeans, or Asmonaeans, is the proper name of the family. This name probably came from Chasmon, the great-grandfather of Mattathias.

Pedigree. The relation of the various members of the family will be seen in table 24.

History. The Maccabees first came to prominence through the terrible persecution of the Jews under Antiochus Epiphanes. His accession was immediately followed by desperate efforts of the hellenizing party at Jerusalem to assert its ascendency. Jason, brother of Onias III, the high priest, secured the high priesthood and bought permission (2 Macc. 4:9) to carry out his design of habituating the Jews to Greek customs (4:7, 20). Three years later Menelaus supplanted Jason by a larger bribe, and the latter fled to the Ammonites (4:23-26). During the absence of Antiochus on his second invasion of Egypt, he was reported as dead, and Jason seized the opportunity of recovering his office, took the city, and inflicted all manner of cruelties on the inhabitants. Antiochus, on hearing of this, and supposing that there was a general revolt of the Jews,

hastily returned to Jerusalem, laid siege to the city, put 40,000 of its inhabitants to death, and sold as many more into slavery. He despoiled the Temple of its precious vessels and furniture and returned to Antioch laden with the treasure. On the occasion of his fourth and last invasion of Egypt, he was arrested by the Roman ambassadors and ordered to leave the country on pain of the wrath of the Roman Senate. On his way home he passed through Palestine and vented his wrath upon the Jews, commissioning his lieutenant Apollonius, with an army of 22,000 men, to destroy Jerusalem. Taking advantage of the Sabbath, he came upon the people assembled in their synagogues, massacred the men, and made the women and children captives. He burned the city and erected a fort on an eminence commanding the Temple, so that the worshipers approaching it were slain. The place itself was defiled with every abomination; and the daily sacrifice was made to cease, according to the prediction of Daniel (Dan. 8:9-12; 11:31). Matters were brought to a height by the famous decree of Antiochus, commanding that all the people should conform to the religion of the sovereign on pain of death. This brought about the Maccabaean war.

Mattathias. At the time of the great persecution Mattathias was already advanced in years, and the father of grown-up sons. He was a priest of the division of Joarib, the first of the twenty-four divisions (1 Chron. 24:7), and, conse-

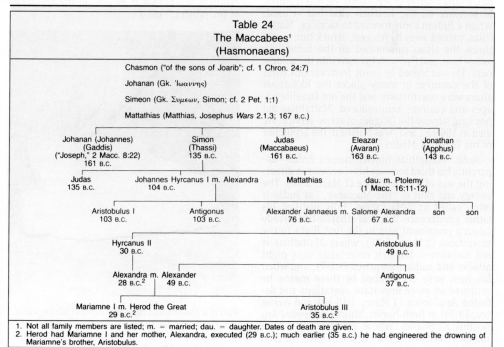

Table 24
The Maccabees[1]
(Hasmonaeans)

Chasmon ("of the sons of Joarib"; cf. 1 Chron. 24:7)

Johanan (Gk. Ἰωάννης)

Simeon (Gk. Συμεών, Simon; cf. 2 Pet. 1:1)

Mattathias (Matthias, Josephus *Wars* 2.1.3; 167 B.C.)

Johanan (Johannes) (Gaddis) ("Joseph," 2 Macc. 8:22) 161 B.C.	Simon (Thassi) 135 B.C.	Judas (Maccabaeus) 161 B.C.	Eleazar (Avaran) 163 B.C.	Jonathan (Apphus) 143 B.C.

Judas 135 B.C.	Johannes Hyrcanus I m. Alexandra 104 B.C.	Mattathias	dau. m. Ptolemy (1 Macc. 16:11-12)

Aristobulus I 103 B.C.	Antigonus 103 B.C.	Alexander Jannaeus m. Salome Alexandra 76 B.C. 67 B.C.	son	son

Hyrcanus II 30 B.C.	Aristobulus II 49 B.C.

Alexandra m. Alexander 28 B.C.[2] 49 B.C.	Antigonus 37 B.C.

Mariamne I m. Herod the Great 29 B.C.[2]	Aristobulus III 35 B.C.[2]

1. Not all family members are listed; m. = married; dau. = daughter. Dates of death are given.
2. Herod had Mariamne I and her mother, Alexandra, executed (29 B.C.); much earlier (35 B.C.) he had engineered the drowning of Mariamne's brother, Aristobulus.

KINGDOM OF THE MACCABEES AT ITS GREATEST EXTENT (100 B.C.)

Independent Judea after Jonathan's campaigns, 142 BC
Land conquered by Simon, 142-135 BC
John Hyrcanus I, 128-104 BC
Aristobulus I, 104-103 BC
Alexander Jannaeus, 103-76 BC
Boundary of Hasmonean kingdom, 76 BC
Hellenistic city

Lysias organized an expedition against Judas; but his army, a part of which had been separated from the main body to effect a surprise, was defeated by Judas at Emmaus with great loss, 166 B.C. (3:43–4:25); in the next year Lysias himself was routed at Bethsura. After this success Judas was able to occupy Jerusalem, except the "tower" (6:18-19), and he purified the Temple (4:36, 41-53) on the 25th of Chislev, exactly three years after its defilement (1:59). The next year was spent in wars with frontier nations (chap. 5); but in spite of continued triumphs the position of Judas was still precarious. In 163 B.C. Lysias laid siege to Jerusalem. The accession of Demetrius brought with it fresh troubles to the patriot Jews. A large party of their countrymen, with Alcimus at their head, gained the ear of the king, and he sent Nicanor against Judas. Nicanor was defeated, first at Capharaslama, and again in a decisive battle at Adasa, near the field of Beth-horon (161 B.C.), on the 13th of Adar (1 Macc. 7:49; 2 Macc. 15:36), where he was slain. This victory was the greatest of Judas's successes, and practically decided the question of Jewish independence; but it was followed by an unexpected reverse. A new invasion under Bacchides took place. Judas was able to gather only a small force to meet the sudden danger. Of this a large part deserted him on the eve of the battle; but the courage of Judas was unshaken, and he fell at Eleasa, the Jewish Thermopylae, fighting at desperate odds against the invaders. His body was recovered by his brothers and buried at Modin "in the sepulcher of his fathers," 161 B.C.

quently, of the noblest blood. He retired to Modin, a little town W of Jerusalem. He was required to sacrifice on the heathen altar but refused. When a Judean came forward to sacrifice, Matthathias, carried away by his zeal, struck him, overthrew the altar, summoned all the faithful to follow him, and fled with his sons into the wilderness. He was joined by many from various parts of the country; in many places the idolatrous altars were overthrown, and the old Israelite usages and customs reintroduced. Mattathias did not long survive the fatigues of active service. He died in 166 B.C., and "was buried in the sepulcher of his father at Modin."

Judas. Mattathias himself named Judas—apparently his third son—as his successor in directing the war of independence (1 Macc. 2:66). The energy and skill of "the Maccabee," as Judas is often called in 2 Maccabees, fully justified his father's preference. It appears that he had already taken a prominent part in the first flight to the mountains (2 Macc. 5:27), where Mattathias is not mentioned. His first enterprises were night attacks and sudden surprises (8:6-7); and when his men were encouraged by these means he ventured on more important operations and defeated Apollonius (1 Macc. 3:10-12) and Seron (vv. 13-24) at Beth-horon. Shortly afterward Antiochus Epiphanes, whose resources had been impoverished by the war (vv. 27-31), left the government of the Palestinian provinces to Lysias.

Part of a Hasmonaean coffin discovered at Modin, site of the sepulcher of Judas

Jonathan. After the death of Judas the patriotic

party seems to have been for a short time wholly disorganized, and it was only by the pressure of unparalleled sufferings that they were driven to renew the conflict. For this purpose they offered the command to Jonathan, surnamed Apphus ("the wary"), the youngest son of Mattathias. He retired to the lowlands of the Jordan (1 Macc. 9:42), where he gained some advantage over Bacchides (161 B.C.), who made an attempt to hem in and destroy his whole force. After two years Bacchides again took the field against Jonathan, 158 B.C. This time he seems to have been but feebly supported, and after an unsuccessful campaign he accepted terms that Jonathan proposed. After his departure Jonathan "judged the people at Michmash" (v. 73) and gradually extended his power. The claim of Alexander Balas to the Syrian crown gave a new importance to Jonathan and his adherents. The success of Alexander led to the elevation of Jonathan, who assumed the high-priestly office (10:21); and not long afterward he placed the king under fresh obligations by the defeat of Apollonius, a general of the younger Demetrius (chap. 10). After the death of Alexander, Jonathan attached himself to Antiochus VI. He at last fell victim to the treachery of Tryphon, 144 B.C. (1 Macc. 11:8–12:4).

Simon. As soon as Simon, the last remaining brother of the Maccabaean family, heard of the detention of Jonathan in Ptolemais by Tryphon, he placed himself at the head of the patriot party. His skill in war had been proved in the lifetime of Judas (1 Macc. 5:17-23), and he had taken an active share in the campaigns of Jonathan (11:59). Tryphon, after carrying Jonathan about as a prisoner for some little time, put him to death and then, having murdered Antiochus, seized the throne. Simon made overtures to Demetrius II, 143 B.C., which were favorably received, and the independence of the Jews was at length formally recognized. The long struggle was now triumphantly ended, and it remained only to reap the fruits of victory. This Simon hastened to do. The prudence and wisdom for which he was already distinguished at the time of his father's death (2:65) gained for the Jews the active support of Rome (15:16-21), in addition to the confirmation of earlier treaties. After settling the external relations of the new state upon a sure basis, Simon regulated its internal administration. With two of his sons he was murdered at Dok by Ptolemaeus, 135 B.C. (1 Macc. 16:11-16).

John Hyrcanus. Having been unanimously proclaimed high priest and ruler at Jerusalem, John Hyrcanus marched against Jericho to avenge the death of his father and brothers. The threats of Ptolemy against the mother of Hyrcanus caused him to protract the siege, until the sabbatical year obliged him to lift it. But Ptolemy, after killing her and her sons, fled to Philadelphia. Antiochus soon after invaded Judea and, besieging Jerusalem, reduced Hyrcanus to great extremity. At the feast of Passover, however, he granted a truce for a week, supplied the besieged with sacrifices, and ended with conceding a peace on condition that the Jews surrendered their arms, paid tribute for Joppa and other towns, and gave him 500 talents of silver and hostages. Ewald (*History of Israel,* 5:344) says that "John sought relief in his financial difficulties by opening the tomb of David. The treasures which he found there enabled him not only to pay the required redemption money, but also to enlist foreign mercenaries." John himself immediately accompanied the king to Parthia, where Antiochus was killed. Hyrcanus availed himself of the opportunity to shake off the Syrian yoke and establish the independence of Judea, which was maintained until it was subjugated by the Romans. He also captured several towns beyond the Jordan; destroyed the Samaritan temple on Mt. Gerizim; captured the towns of Dora and Marissa in Idumaea and forced the rite of circumcision upon the people; renewed a treaty, offensive and defensive, with Rome, and amassed great wealth. His sons, Antigonus and Aristobulus, conducted a campaign against the Samaritans; and when Antiochus Cyzicenus came to the relief of the Samaritans, he was defeated by Aristobulus. After a year or so Samaria fell into the hands of Hyrcanus. Soon after, being exposed to some indignity from a Pharisee, he openly left that sect and joined the Sadducees. He passed the rest of his days in peace, built the castle of Baris on a rock within the fortifications of the Temple, called by Herod "Antonia." His reign lasted from 135 to 104 B.C.

Aristobulus. Aristobulus succeeded his father, John Hyrcanus, as high priest and governor. He was the first since the captivity to assume the title of king. He starved his mother to death and imprisoned three of his brothers. He reigned only one year.

Alexander Jannaeus. Aristobulus was succeeded by his brother Alexander Jannaeus, who killed one brother who displayed ambition but left the other alone. After varying fortunes, he found himself at the head of 60,000 men, and he marched in triumph to Jerusalem. After a reign of twenty-seven years he died, 76 B.C.

Alexander was succeeded by his widow Alexandra (76-67). Her eldest son, Hyrcanus II, became high priest. Her abler and more energetic second son, Aristobulus II, she kept in check. Her reign was peaceful and prosperous. By building up the army and defenses, she escaped attack. Before the death of his mother, Aristobulus II (67-63) had taken measures to rule after her. In the civil war that followed her death, Aristobulus had the support of his father's veterans and soon subdued his brother, who was allowed to retire peacefully to private life. But Antipater, the military governor of Idumaea, saw an opportunity to advance his own cause and persuaded the weak Hyrcanus to fight once again; with the help of Aretas, king of the Nabataeans, he defeated his brother. At this point the brothers' appeals to the Roman general Pompey brought Rome into Jewish politics. Pompey annexed Palestine to the Roman Empire in 63 B.C., but it was decades before peace came to the area. Aristobulus and his sons fought the Romans with great ferocity but ultimately were defeated and destroyed. The situation was complicated by the Roman civil war between the forces of Pompey and Caesar. Hycanus managed to achieve sovereignty in Palestine but Antipater, governor of Idumaea (southern province of the Maccabaean kingdom) and father of Herod the Great, enjoyed the real power. The two went over to the side of Caesar in the civil war, and Rome subsequently made Herod king of the Jews.

Hyrcanus, who previous to this had been incapacitated for the priesthood by having his ears cut off, was put to death in his eightieth year, 30 B.C. Thus perished the last of the males of the Maccabaean line. Herod married Mariamne, in whom the line of the Hasmonaeans came to an end and by her marriage passed into the Idumaean line of the Herodians.

Two of the first generation of Maccabees, though they did not, like their brothers, attain to leadership, shared their fate—Eleazar, by a noble act of self-devotion; John, apparently the eldest brother, by treachery. Probably history affords no parallel to the courage with which this band of men dared to face death, one by one, in a holy cause. "The Maccabees inspired a subject-people with independence; they found a few personal followers, and they left a nation" (McClintock and Strong, *Cyclopedia;* Smith, *Bib. Dict.;* Ewald, *History of Israel*). See Apocrypha; Herod.

BIBLIOGRAPHY: E. R. Bevan, *Jerusalem Under the High Priests* (1904), pp. 69-108; E. Bickerman, *From Ezra to the Last of the Maccabees* (1947), pp. 93-145; W. R. Farmer, *Maccabees, Zealots, and Josephus* (1956), pp. 47-158; D. S. Russell, *The Jews from Alexander to Herod* (1967), pp. 1-57; B. I. Reicke, *The New Testament Era* (1968), pp. 42-62.

MAC'BENAH. *See* Machbenah.

MACEDO'NIA (mas-e-dō'ni-a). A country lying N of Greece, whose rivers were the Strymon and the Axius, and whose mountains included Olympus and Athos. Some of its chief cities were Amphipolis, Apollonia, Berea, Neapolis, Philippi, and Thessalonica. It was conquered by the Romans, 168 B.C. Under the famous Philip II and his son, Alexander the Great, it attained the summit of its power (359-323 B.C.). Paul was summoned to preach in Macedonia by a vision (Acts 16:9; 20:1). The history of his journey through Macedonia is given in detail in Acts (16:10–17:15). He again passed through this province (20:1-6) and, after many years, probably visited it for a third time (Phil. 2:24; 1 Tim. 1:3). *See* Paul.

BIBLIOGRAPHY: *Cambridge Ancient History* (1927), 6:200-

271, 352-504; id. (1928), 7: 75-108, 197-223; id. (1930), 8: 241-78; id. (1932), 9: 441-42; id. (1936), 11: 566-70.

Roman road in Macedonia

MACHAE'RUS (ma-ke'rus; "the Black Fortress"). A strong fortress of Perea, and the place, according to Josephus (*Ant.* 18.5.2), of John the Baptist's beheading. It was built by Alexander Jannaeus as a check against Arab marauders (Josephus *Wars* 7.6.2), demolished by Gabinius when he made war against Aristobulus, and rebuilt by Herod. It was situated in the gorge of Callirhoe, one of the valleys E of the Dead Sea, 3,860 feet above the sea, 2,546 feet above the Mediterranean, and eighteen miles SE of the mouth of the Jordan River. *See* John the Baptist.

MACH'BANNAI (mak'ba-nī). The eleventh of the Gadite warriors who joined themselves to David in the wilderness (1 Chron. 12:13), about 1002 B.C. *See* Macbannai.

MACHBE'NAH (mak-bē'na). If a man, the son of Sheva, and the one after whom the place of the same name was called (1 Chron. 2:49). *See* Macbenah.

MA'CHI (ma'ki). The father of Geuel, who represented the tribe of Gad among the explorers of Canaan (Num. 13:15), c. 1440 B.C. *See* Maki.

MA'CHIR (ma'kīr; "sold").

1. The eldest son of Manasseh (Josh. 17:1), who had children during the lifetime of Joseph (Gen. 50:23), after 1876 B.C. He was the founder of the family of the *Machirites* (which see; Num. 26:29), who settled in the land taken from the Amorites (32:39-40; Deut. 3:15; Josh. 13:31; 1 Chron.

2:23). Because Machir's grandson Zelophehad had only daughters, a special enactment was made regarding their inheritance (Num. 27:1-11; 36:1-12; Josh. 17:3-6). His daughter became the wife of Hezron and mother of Segub (1 Chron. 2:21). Machir's mother was Aramaean, and by his wife, Maacah, he had several sons (7:14-16).

2. A descendant of the former, a son of Ammiel residing at Lo-debar who took care of the lame son of Jonathan until he was provided for by David (2 Sam. 9:4-5), and afterward hospitably entertained the king himself at Mahanaim (17:27-29), about 984-967 B.C. *See* Makir.

MA'CHIRITES (ma'kir-īts; "the Machirites," only in Num. 26:29). Descendants of Machir, who was son of Manasseh by an Aramite concubine. His wife and children are named in 1 Chron. 7:16-17; but the statement in v. 17, "These were the sons of Gilead the son of Machir, the son of Manasseh," with the declaration that Machir was "the father of Gilead" (v. 14) would add Gilead to the list of Machir's sons. At the same time the enumeration of the Gileadites by families in Num. 26:29-32, together with the account of the inhabiting of Gilead in 32:39-40, gives some credibility to the opinion that if Machir was the father of Gilead, Gilead is used collectively for the inhabitants of Gilead, in the same way that Moab is used for the Moabite nation, and that what is meant is that Machir was the ancestor of the Gileadites. The wife of Machir, who seems to have been of the tribe of Benjamin, was Maacah, the sister of Huppim and Shuppim (1 Chron. 7:12, 15-16). And Abiah (2:24) was the last wife of Hezron (v. 21), son of Perez (v. 5), son of Judah (v. 4). Thus did the Machirites connect Manasseh with both Judah and Benjamin. The daughters of Zelophehad, whose story is told in Num. 26:33; 27:1-11; 36:1-12; Josh. 17:3-6, were Machirites. The law that prevented confusion of inheritances by tribal intermarriages was first made in regard to this case (Num. 36:1-12), and was not in existence at the time of the before-mentioned intermarriages. *See also* Manassites.   w.h.

MACHNADE'BAI (mach-na-de'bī; "what is like the liberal?"). An Israelite of the "sons" of Bani who put away his Gentile wife after the captivity (Ezra 10:40), 456 B.C. *See* Macnadebai.

MACHPE'LAH (mak-pe'la; perhaps "double"). A field containing the cave bought by Abraham for a burial place (Gen. 23:9, 17) and where he buried Sarah (v. 19). Abraham himself was buried there (25:8-9), along with Isaac and Rebekah, his wife, and Leah, the wife of Jacob (49:30-31), and later Jacob also (50:13). This is the last biblical mention of the cave of Machpelah; and there is no reason to believe that any building was erected on the spot before the captivity. The cave was in *Hebron* (which see), and is now marked by a Muslim mosque, in which are shown the so-

called tombs. Muslim and Christian have together held this sanctuary for 600 years. Much of the structure as it stands today dates to the reign of Herod the Great.

BIBLIOGRAPHY: E. J. H. MacKay and F. M. Abel, *Hebron, le Haram el Kahlil, sepulture des Patriarchs* (1923); M. Lehmann, *Bulletin of the American Schools of Oriental Research* 129 (1953): 15-18.

MAC'NADEBAI. *See* Machnadebai.

MAD. *See* the article Madness in the general listing; and also Diseases: Madness.

MADA'I (mad'ī; a "Mede"). The third son of Japheth (Gen. 10:2; 1 Chron. 1:5), from whom the Medes descended. We hear of Madai upon the Assyrian monuments, about 840 B.C., where they are called Amadâ and found by the Assyrian army in Media Atropatênê.

MA'DIAN. *See* Midian.

MADMAN'NAH (mad-man'a; "dunghill"). A town in the extreme S of Judah (Josh. 15:31), afterward assigned to Simeon. From 1 Chron. 2:49 it appears to have been founded or occupied by Shaaph, the son of Maacah, Caleb's concubine. It is possibly to be identified with Miniay, or Minieh, S of Gaza.

MAD'MEN (mad'men; "dunghill"). A town in Moab threatened with the sword from the Babylonian invasion (Jer. 48:2), identified as Khirbet Dimneh, 2½ miles NW of Rabba.

MADME'NAH (mad-mē'na; "dunghill"). A town (Isa. 10:31) named on the route of the Assyrian invaders, N of Jerusalem, between Nob and Gibeah. The same word in Isa. 25:10 is rendered "manure pile," but the verse may mean "that Moab will be trodden down by Jehovah as straw is trodden to fragments on the threshing floors of Madmenah." Its location is uncertain.

MADNESS. Besides its proper meaning of mania (*see* Diseases), madness, along with various other words of similar import, is used in Scripture of a violent disturbance of the mental faculties: (1) from overstudy (Acts 26:24-25); (2) from sudden and startling intelligence (12:15); (3) of false prophets (Isa. 44:25; Hos. 9:7); (4) as the result of drunkenness (Jer. 25:16; 51:7); (5) in derision, with reference to the ecstatic utterances of the prophets when in a state of holy exaltation (2 Kings 9:11; Jer. 29:26); (6) from furious passion, as possesses a persecutor (Ps. 102:8; Acts 26:11); (7) idolatrous hallucination (Jer. 50:38), or wicked and extravagant revelry (Eccles. 2:2); (8) a reckless state of mind (10:13), bordering on delirium (Zech. 12:4), whether induced by overstrained mental effort (Eccles. 1:17; 2:12) or depraved tempers (Eccles. 7:25; 9:3; 2 Pet. 2:16).

MA'DON (ma'don; "strife"). A Canaanite city in the N of Palestine, ruled by a king named Jobab (Josh. 11:1) and captured by Joshua (12:19). It is probably to be identified with the village of Madîn, near Hattin, W of the Sea of Galilee.

MAG'ADAN (mag'a-dan; Aram. *migdᵉlā'*; "tower"). A small town in Galilee, on the W shore of the Sea of Galilee, between Capernaum and Tiberias, mentioned only in Matt. 15:39 ("Dalmanutha" in the parallel passage, Mark 8:10), and may be the same as Migdal-el (Josh. 19:38). It was the birthplace of Mary Magdalene, i.e., the Magdalene (John 19:25; 20:1, 18). It is now probably the small village of el-Mejdel, three miles NW of Tiberias.

BIBLIOGRAPHY: W. F. Albright, *Annual of the American Schools of Oriental Research* 2-3 (1923): 29-46.

MAG'BISH (mag'bish; probably "sturdy, strong," cf. Akkad. *gabshu*, "massive, powerful"). The name of a man (or place) whose descendants, numbering 156, returned to Palestine with Zerubbabel (Ezra 2:30).

MAG'DALA. See Magadan.

MAG'DALEN (mag'da-len), or **Magdale'ne** (mag-da-lē'ne). The surname of one of the Marys.

MAG'DIEL (mag'di-el). One of the chiefs of Edom, descended from Esau (Gen. 36:43; 1 Chron. 1:54).

MA'GI (mā'jī, Gk. *magoi* singular, *magos* from Old Persian *magav*). The KJV renders "wise men" in Matt. 2:1, 7, 16.

In the Old Testament. In the Heb. text of the OT the word occurs but twice, and then only incidentally. Among the Chaldean officers sent by Nebuchadnezzar to Jerusalem one had the name or title of Rab-mag (Jer. 39:3, 13). This word has been interpreted as equivalent to "chief of the magi." However, it seems here simply to mean "great prince," from Akkad. *rab* ("great") and *mugi* ("prince"). The term *magi* was used as the name for priests and wise men among the Medes, Persians, and Babylonians. These persons were supposed to be adept in that secret learning that in remote antiquity had its seat in Egypt, and later in Chaldea, from which latter fact they were often called "Chaldeans" (Dan. 2:2, marg., "master astrologers," 4-5, 10; 4:7; 5:7, 11, 30). They formed five classes: the *Hartummim,* expounders of sacred writings and interpreters of signs; the *Ashaphim,* conjurers; the *Mekashephim,* exorcists, soothsayers, magicians, diviners; the *Gozerim,* casters of nativities, astrologists; and the *Kasdim,* Chaldeans in the narrower sense. The magi took their places among "the astrologers, those who prophesy by the stars, those who predict by the new moons." It is with such men that we have to think of Daniel and his fellow exiles as associated. They are described as "ten times better than all the magicians and conjurers"

The shore of the Sea of Galilee where the village of Magadan once stood

(1:20). The office that Daniel accepted (5:11) was probably identical with that of the Rab-mag who was first mentioned.

Later Meaning. We find that the word *magi* presented itself to the Greeks as connected with a foreign system of divination and the religion of a foe whom they had conquered; it soon became a byword for the worst form of imposture. The swarms of impostors that were to be met with in every part of the Roman Empire, known as "Chaldei," "Mathematici," and the like, bore this name also. We need not wonder, accordingly, to find that this is the predominant meaning of the word as it appears in the NT. The noun and the verb derived from it are used by Luke in describing the impostor, who is therefore known distinctively as Simon Magus (Acts 8:9). Another of the same class (Bar-jesus) is described as having, in his cognomen Elymas, a title that was equivalent to Magus (13:6-8). In one memorable instance, however, the word retains its better meaning. In the gospel of Matthew, written according to the general belief of early Christian writers for the Hebrew Christians of Palestine, we find it, not as embodying the contempt that the fraud of impostors had brought upon it, but in the sense that it had of old, as associated with a religion they respected, and of an order of which one of their own prophets had been the head. Thus, the evangelist would probably see in them men who were at once astronomers and astrologers, but not mingling any conscious fraud with their efforts after a higher knowledge (Matt. 2:1). The indefinite expression "from the east" (*see* also 8:11; 24:27; Luke 13:29; Rev. 21:13) leads us to assume that the writer himself had no more precise information at his command. "It is entirely baseless to determine their *number* from the *threefold* gifts, and to regard them as *kings* on account of Pss. 68:30, 32; 72:10; Isa. 49:7; 60:3, 10." From an early period the church has believed the magi to be the first Gentile worshipers of the Christ. "The expectations of the Jews, that their Messiah was to rule over the *world*, might at that period have been sufficiently disseminated throughout the foreign countries of the E to lead heathen astrologers, for the object in question, to the Jewish capital" (Meyer, *Com.*, ad loc.; Smith, *Bib. Dict.*, s.v.). *See* Star.

BIBLIOGRAPHY: S. V. McCasland, *Journal of Biblical Literature* 51 (1932): 323-35; M. S. Enslin, *JBL* 59 (1940): 317-38; S. V. McCasland, *JBL* 76 (1957): 149-52.

MAGIC, MAGICIANS (from Heb. *ḥereṭ*, to "engrave," and so to "draw magical lines or circles"). The art or science of working wonders beyond the ordinary powers of man. "Magic may be divided into two classes—natural or scientific, and supernatural or spiritual—the one attributed its wonders to a deep, practical acquaintance with the powers of nature; the other to celestial or infernal agency. But both systems seem to have

taken their origin in traditional accounts of early miracles—in attempts to investigate how such miracles were performed, and whether it were possible or not to imitate them. The theory of atoms held by the Epicureans appears to have been the basis of most magical speculations. It may be expressed somewhat after this manner: All changes in nature take place by the operation of atoms and must *ultimately*, therefore, be effected by mechanical action. Wherever man can substitute artificial action of the same kind, he can produce the same effects as those of nature. It required, in the first place, a knowledge of the mode in which nature acted; and, second, the power of applying the same agencies. On the other hand, the spiritual or geotic (literally 'terrestrial,' and so *superstitious*) magic relied entirely on the powers of spiritual beings; it demanded no knowledge of nature, and rarely required any moral or intellectual preparation. Its works were understood to be purely miraculous; and those who practiced it claimed the wonder-working power only by means of mighty and unseen intelligences in obtaining communion with and authority over whom their science consisted" (*Imperial Bible Dictionary*, s.v.). As stated in the article *Magi*, classes who were expert in magical arts were among the Egyptians, Babylonians, and so on. We will refer to these before calling attention to the Scripture accounts.

Egypt. The god Thot, having pointed out evil to men, gave to them at the same time the remedy. The magical arts, of which he was the repository, made him virtual master of the other gods. Their mystic names, their secret weaknesses, the perils they most feared, ceremonies by which they could be subdued, prayers that they must grant under penalty of misfortune or death, were all known to him. This wisdom, transmitted to his worshipers, gave them the same authority in heaven, earth, or the nether-world. Thus, they could bind or loose Osiris, Sit, Anubis, or even Thot himself; send them forth, recall them, constrain them to work or fight for them.

Naturally, this great power exposed the magicians to temptations, being often led to use it to the detriment of others, to satisfy spite, or gratify their grosser appetites. Many made a gain of their knowledge, putting it at the service of the ignorant who would pay for it. They pretended to be able to bring on sicknesses, deceptive or terrifying dreams, specters, or to constrain the wills of men, cause women to be victims of infatuation, and so on. Magic was not supposed to be all powerful against destiny; thus, fate decreed that the man born on the twenty-seventh of Paophi would die of a snakebite, but magic might decide as to the year in which his death would occur. Still more efficacious were the arts of magic in combating the influences of secondary deities, the evil eye, and the spells of man. After expelling the hurtful deity it was necessary to restore the health of the victim, and the magician was naturally led to the study of medicine. Magic was also invoked against magic, and thus rivalry arose among magicians.

Among the officers of distinction in the royal household were the "masters of the secrets of heaven," those who saw what is in the firmament, on the earth, and in hades; those who knew all the charms of the soothsayers, prophets, or magicians. The laws of the seasons and the stars, propitious months, days, or hours, presented no mysteries to them, drawing, as they did, their inspiration from the magical books of the god Thot. They understood the art of curing the sick, interpreting dreams, invoking or obliging the gods to aid them, and so on. The great lords themselves somewhat reluctantly agreed to become initiated into the occult sciences, and were invested with these formidable powers; sorcery was not considered incompatible with royalty, and the magicians of Pharaoh often took Pharaoh himself as a pupil. The Egyptians believed "that everything that happened was owing to the action of some divinity. They believed, therefore, in the incessant intervention of the gods; and their magical literature is based on the notion of frightening one god by the terrors of a more powerful divinity, either by prayer placing a person under the protection of his divinity, or by the person's actually assuming its name and authority. Sometimes threats are uttered against a god; or rather, as an Egyptian priest (Abammom by name) said, the daimones, i.e., subordinate ministers of the gods" (Maspero, *Dawn of Civilization,* pp. 212, 281-82; Renouf, *Religion of Ancient Egypt,* pp. 219ff.).

Chaldea. The Chaldeans believed that the operations of nature were not carried on under impersonal and unswerving laws but by voluntary and rational agents, swayed by an inexorable fate against which they dared not rebel but still free enough and powerful enough to avert by magic the decrees of destiny, or at least to retard their execution. "From this conception of things each subordinate science was obliged to make its investigations in two perfectly distinct regions; it had first to determine the material facts within its competence—such as the position of the stars, for instance, or the symptoms of a malady; it had then to discover the beings which revealed themselves through these material manifestations, their names and characters. When once it had obtained this information, and could lay its hand upon them, it could compel them to work on its behalf; science was thus nothing else than the application of magic to a particular class of phenomena . . . . Chaldea abounded with soothsayers no less than with astrologers, to whom the sick were confided, as expert in casting out demons and spirits. Consultations and medical treatment were, therefore, religious offices, in which were involved purifications, offerings, and

a whole ritual of mysterious words and gestures. The use of magical words was often accompanied by remedies, which were for the most part grotesque and disgusting in their composition; [these] filled the possessing spirits with disgust, and became the means of relief owing to the invincible horror with which they inspired the persecuting demons . . . . The neighboring barbaric peoples were imbued with the same ideas as the Chaldeans regarding the constitution of the world and the nature of the laws which governed it. They lived likewise in perpetual fear of those invisible beings whose changeable and arbitrary will actuated all visible phenomena. . . . In the eyes of these barbarians, the Chaldeans seemed to be possessed of the very powers which they themselves lacked" (Maspero, *Dawn of Civilization,* pp. 780ff.).

Scripture Accounts. The household idols or "teraphim" were consulted by the Israelites for oracular answers (*see* Judg. 18:5-6; Zech. 10:2). The only account of divining by teraphim is in the record of Nebuchadnezzar's advance against Jerusalem (Ezek. 21:19-22).

In Gen. 44:5, referring to the cup found in Benjamin's sack, we read: "Is not this the one from which my lord drinks, and which he indeed uses for divination?" (*see* Cup, no. 4). It is certainly not to be inferred that Joseph actually adopted this superstitious practice. The intention of the statement may simply have been to represent the goblet as a sacred vessel, and Joseph as acquainted with its common divinatory use.

In the histories of Joseph and Moses the magicians are spoken of as a class. When Pharaoh's officers were troubled by their dreams, being in prison, they were at a loss for an interpreter. Before Joseph explained the dreams he disclaimed the power of interpreting save by divine aid, saying, "Do not interpretations belong to God? Tell it to me, please" (Gen. 40:8). In like manner, when Pharaoh had his two dreams, we find that he had recourse to those who professed to interpret dreams. Joseph, being sent for on the report of the chief of the cupbearers, was told by Pharaoh that he had heard that he could interpret a dream. From the expectations of the Egyptians and Joseph's disavowals, we see that the interpretation of dreams was a branch of the knowledge to which the ancient Egyptian magicians pretended.

The Bible narrative of the events immediately preceding the Exodus introduces the magicians. When the rod of Aaron was changed into a serpent, it is said that Pharaoh called his magicians, and they also "did the same with their secret arts" (Ex. 7:11). The same is said of their imitation of the first and second plagues (7:22; 8:7). But when they attempted to imitate Moses in the plague of the gnats, they were unsuccessful, for it is recorded that "the magicians tried with their secret arts to bring forth gnats, but they could not"

(8:18). Whether the magicians really did what they appeared to do, or only performed a clever trick, has been a question of much dispute. Some contend that they did produce the same sort of miracle as that wrought through Moses, and that this was through demoniacal influence. It would seem the writer's intention to intimate that the Egyptian magicians considered Moses to be one of their own profession—what he did, that they claimed to be able to do also—he worked by the same means and only exceeded them in degree. And this was unquestionably the opinion of the king himself. That they could not produce gnats is not conclusive proof against their having acted through supernatural agency. It is quite evident from Scripture that satanic and demonic power, although great, is definitely limited and can go only so far. They admitted that this plague was from Jehovah, and the next plague (boils) attacked them and caused them embarrassment and perplexity.

Balaam (see Num. 22:5-41; Josh. 13:22) furnishes us another case of a man accustomed to using incantations; and it is evident that Balak believed, in common with the whole ancient world, in the power and operation of the curses, anathemas, and incantations pronounced by priests, soothsayers, and so on.

Saul attempted to obtain a knowledge of the future in ungodly ways and commanded his servants to seek for a woman who was a medium —the mistress of a conjuring spirit with which the dead were conjured up for the purpose of making inquiry concerning the future (1 Sam. 28:7-14; see Necromancy, below). The supernatural terror running throughout the account cannot, however, be proved to be due to this art; for it has always been held by sober critics that the appearing of Samuel was permitted for the purpose of declaring the doom of Saul, and not that it was caused by the medium's incantations. She is no more than a bystander after the first; she sees Samuel, and that is all.

The prophets, through their condemnation of them, tell us that magical practices prevailed among the Hebrews in the later days of the two kingdoms. Isaiah (Isa. 2:6) says that the people were "soothsayers like the Philistines," understood by Delitzsch (Com., ad loc.) to mean "cloud-gatherers," or "storm-raisers." In another place (8:19) he reproves the people for consulting "the mediums and the spiritists who whisper and mutter"; whereas in 47:12-13 the magic of Babylon is characterized by the prominence given to astrology. Micah (Mic. 3:5-7) refers to the prevalence of divination among those who were such pretended prophets as the opponents of Jeremiah, not avowed prophets of idols as Ahab's seem to have been.

Jeremiah was constantly opposed by false prophets who pretended to speak in the name of the Lord, saying that they had dreamed, but they told false visions and practiced various magical arts (Jer. 14:14; 23:25-32; 27:9-10).

From Ezekiel (Ezek. 8:7-12) we learn that fetishism was among the idolatries that the Hebrews, in the latter days of the kingdom of Judah, had adopted from their neighbors. The passage in 13:18 is thought by some to refer to the making of amulets; whereas others believe that it is figurative of hiding the truth.

Daniel, when taken captive, was instructed in the learning of the Chaldeans and placed among the wise men of Babylon (Dan. 1:4-6), by whom we are to understand the *magi* (which see), for the term is used as including magicians, conjurers, sorcerers, and Chaldeans, the last being apparently the most important class (2:2, 4-5, 10; cf. 1:20). As in other cases the true prophet was put to the test with the magicians, and he succeeded where they utterly failed.

After the captivity it is probable that the Jews gradually abandoned the practice of magic. Zechariah speaks indeed of the deceit of teraphim and diviners (Zech. 10:2), and foretells a time when the very names of idols should be forgotten and false prophets should have virtually ceased (13:1-4), yet in neither case does it seem certain that he is alluding to the usages of his own day. In the Apocrypha we find indications that in the later centuries preceding the Christian era magic was no longer practiced by educated Jews.

In the NT we read little of magic. Philip the deacon found in Samaria Simon, a famous magician, known as *Simon Magus* (which see), who, while having great power with the people, is not said to have been able to work wonders. At Paphos, Elymas, a Jewish sorcerer and false prophet, was struck blind for a time at the word of Paul (Acts 13:6-12); while at Ephesus, Jewish believers abandoned their practice of the magical arts. We have also the remarkable case of Paul casting out a "spirit of divination" from a slave girl "who was bringing her masters much profit by fortunetelling" (16:16-18). "Our examination of the various notices of magic in the Bible gives us this general result: They do not, as far as we can understand, once state positively that any but illusive results were produced by magical rites. They therefore afford no evidence that man can gain supernatural powers to use at his will."

Magic Forbidden. The law contains distinct prohibitions against all magical arts. Besides several passages condemning them, in one place there is a specification that is so full that it seems evident that its object is to include every kind of magical art. The Israelites are commanded not to learn the abominations of the peoples of the Promised Land. Then follows this prohibition: "There shall not be found among you anyone who makes his son or his daughter pass through the fire, one who uses divination, one who practices witchcraft, or one who interprets omens, or a sorcerer" (Deut. 18:10). It is added that these phenomena of demon-inspired paganism are abominations, and that because of them the Canaanites were driven out from before the Israelites.

Various Forms. As stated in the article *Divination* (which see), there were forms of ascertaining the divine will and future events that were taken in good sense and, therefore, not forbidden. Two other classes of divination are mentioned in Scripture—those forbidden and those without special sanction or reprobation. We group these together for greater convenience in the study of the subject:

Astrologers. Called by the Hebrews "dividers of the heavens," they are mentioned with "those who prophesy by the stars" (Isa. 47:13). They apparently "cut up the heavens" into certain sections in order to trace the course of them, making an effort to foretell the future. They were a part of the court of Nebuchadnezzar II (Dan. 2:2, marg.) and were characteristic of such ancient courts as that of Babylon and Chaldea. Astrology was widely practiced among heathen nations but was accounted illegitimate among the Hebrews, being considered inconsistent with the worship of Jehovah and classified (as in Isa. 47:12-13) with occultism and demon-inspired paganism.

Belomancy. This is divination by arrows. It is said of the king of Babylon that "he shakes the arrows" (Ezek. 21:21), more strictly, the quiver with the arrows. On this practice itself Jerome writes: "He consults the oracle according to the custom of his nation, putting his arrows into a quiver, and mixing them together, with the names of individuals inscribed or stamped upon them, to see whose arrow will come out, and which state shall be first attacked." In this case Jerusalem was the ill-fated object of this divination, as we learn from the next verse, "Into his right hand came the divination 'Jerusalem.' " The arrow lot of the ancient Greeks was similar to this; also that of the ancient Arabs. Another kind of arrow lot was by shooting. Three suitors of an Eastern princess decided their claims by each shooting an arrow inscribed with his own name. The arrow taking the longest flight indicated the name of the successful competitor. This sort of divination is not to be confounded with the arrow shot by Jonathan, which was an understood sign; nor the shooting of the arrows by Joash, king of Israel, at the command of the prophet, in which we have a symbolical prophecy.

The Chaldeans. Among others consulted by the king of Babylon respecting his dream were the Chaldeans. Among an Aramaic people the priests in a stricter sense were called Chaldeans, from the fact of the ancient supremacy of the Chaldean people in Babylonia. These Chaldeans sought their greatest glory in the study of astrology and also possessed the knowledge of divination from omens, of expounding of dreams and

prodigies, and of skillfully casting horoscopes (Keil, *Com.,* on Dan. 2:2). *See also* the articles Chaldean Astrologers; Magi.

Charmers (Heb. *lāhash,* to "whisper"), a word used to express *serpent charming* (Ps. 58:5; Jer. 8:17; Eccles. 10:11). In the first of these passages *lāhash* occurs in connection with the Heb. word *ḥeber,* meaning a "confederacy" (i.e., with the spirits of the other world), which is rendered in the same manner and has a similar meaning. It is certain that from time immemorial some people of the East have exercised remarkable power over even the most poisonous of serpents (*see* Serpent Charmer). The "charmer" mentioned in the KJV of Deut. 18:11 is one who pronounced a ban, probably referring to the custom of binding or banning by magical knots, or one who casts a spell (so NIV). Another reference to character is found in Isa. 19:3 (Heb. *'iṭṭîm,* "mutterers").

Divination, Diviners. Generally speaking, "divination differs from prophecy in that the one is a human device while the other is a divine gift —the one an unwarranted prying into the future by means of magical arts, superstitious incantations, or natural signs, arbitrarily interpreted; the other a partially disclosed insight into the future by the supernatural aid of Him who sees the end from the beginning" (*Imperial Bible Dictionary,* s.v.). In Scripture the diviners were *false* prophets, and divination was allied to witchcraft and idolatry (Deut. 18:10; Josh. 13:32; 1 Sam. 15:23; Jer. 27:9; etc.), and energized by demon power (cf. 1 Cor. 10:20-21). *See also* Divination in the general listing.

Dreams, Divination by. The Hebrews, along with other Easterners, greatly regarded dreams and applied for their interpretation to those who undertook to explain them. Such diviners were called *oneirocritics,* and the art itself *oneiromancy.* Dreams were looked upon from the earliest antiquity as premonitions from their idol gods to future events. Opposed to this was the command of Jehovah forbidding His people from observing dreams and from consulting explainers of them. Those who pretended to have prophetic dreams and to foretell future events, even though what they foretold came to pass, if they had any tendency to promote idolatry, were put to death (Deut. 13:1-4). In opposition to the word of God no prophets were to be received, although they rained signs and wonders—not even an angel from heaven (Gal. 1:8).

Enchantment. The practice of conjurers and exorcists in employing incantations or magic, ritual procedures in enlisting the aid of evil spirits to effect some design or in purportedly setting free the demonized from their torments (cf. Dan. 1:20; 2:2, 10, 27). It appears as the heathen counterpart of prayer. *See* Divination; Enchantment; Sorcery.

Exorcist (Gk. *'exorkistēs,* "one who exacts an oath"). One who employs a formula of conjuration for expelling demons (Acts 19:13). The use of the term *exorcists* in this passage, as the designation of a well-known class of persons to which the individuals mentioned belonged, confirms what we know from other sources as to the common practice of exorcism among the Jews. Among all the references to exorcism, as practiced by the Jews, in the NT (Matt. 12:27; Mark 9:38; Luke 9:49-50) we find only one instance that affords any clues as to the means employed (Acts 19:13). In this passage it is said that "some of the Jewish exorcists, who went from place to place, attempted to name over those who had the evil spirits the name of the Lord Jesus, saying, 'I adjure you by Jesus whom Paul preaches.' " *See* Demon; Exorcism.

Familiar Spirits, Consulter with. See Familiar Spirit in the general listing.

Idolomancy. Consulting with images, literally *teraphim.* These household gods of the Semitic nations are often mentioned in the OT from the time of Laban (Gen. 31:19, *see* marg.). They were wooden images (1 Sam. 19:13, 16) consulted as "idols," from which the excited worshipers fancied that they received oracular responses (Ezek. 21:21; Zech. 10:2).

Magician. A general term including all those who worked wonders beyond the ordinary powers of man. *See* head of this article.

Medium. See Necromancer, Spiritist, below; and also the articles Familiar Spirit; Necromancer; and Spiritist in the general listing.

Necromancer (Heb. *dōrēsh 'el hammēthîm,* "one who inquires of the dead"). One who pretends to be able by incantations to call up the dead to consult them respecting things unknown to the living, often called in Scripture "mediums and spiritists." A few, such as Cicero (*Tusculanae Disputationes* 1.16.37), scoffed at the idea, but the practice has held its ground in pagan and even Christian lands until the present. The Eastern magi were especially famed for necromantic skill. The necromancer was supposed to be the possessor of a conjuring spirit, i.e., of a spirit with which the dead were conjured up for the purpose of making inquiry concerning the future (*see* Lev. 19:31). Such a person was the medium of Endor, to whose incantations the ghost of Samuel responded (*see* Saul). It is evident from her exclamation that she was surprised at this appearance, and that she was not able to conjure up departed spirits or persons who had died. The spirit was supposed to be granted to the necromancer as a servant or attendant, and to be bound to him by the ties or obligations of witchcraft. To the spirits of the departed thus evoked the necromancer lent a low, soft, almost whispering voice (Isa. 8:19; cf. 19:3), as seemed natural for such beings. It is not certain that these mutterings and whisperings were produced by ventriloquism, although this may be the case, as ventriloquism was one of the arts of ancient jug-

glers. "In most parts of Greece necromancy was practiced by priests or consecrated persons in the temples: in Thessaly it was the profession of a distinct class of persons called Psychagogoi (evokers of spirits)." Necromancy was forbidden to the Israelites as a heathen superstition (Lev. 19:31), and those who disobeyed were threatened with death (20:6; Deut. 18:10-14). Still, it found its way among them, especially when idolaters occupied the throne (2 Kings 21:6; 2 Chron. 33:6; Isa. 8:19; 29:4; cf. 19:3, where the Egyptian enchantments are mentioned). *See also* Spiritists, this entry; and the articles Familiar Spirit; Necromancer in the general listing.

Prognosticators (Heb. *môdî'îm lehŏdāshîm,* "making known as to the months"). These are mentioned in Isa. 47:13, where the prophet enumerates the astrological superstitions of the Chaldeans, who foretold the future by observing the phases of the moon. *See* Astrology.

Rabdomancy (Gk. *hrabdos,* a "staff," and *manteia,* "divination"). Divination by rods. Cyril of Alexandria calls this an invention of the Chaldeans and describes it as consisting in this, that two rods were held upright and then allowed to fall while forms of incantation were being uttered. The oracle was inferred by the way in which the rods fell, whether forward or backward, to the right or to the left. This custom is referred to in Hos. 4:12: "And their diviner's wand informs them," and is evidence of the tendency of Israel to idolatry.

Soothsayer, Soothsaying. The soothsayer (diviner) was the pagan counterpart of the prophet, prognosticating future events, or professing to do so (Josh. 13:22) by various arts. Actually, diviners were energized by evil powers, as the prophet of the Lord was under the control of the Holy Spirit.

Sorcery (Heb. from *kāshap,* to "whisper"; Gk. *mageia,* Acts 8:11; *pharmakeia,* "medication"). A sorcerer was one who professed to tell the lot of others, to have power with evil spirits (Isa. 47:9, 12; Dan. 2:2), and was severely denounced (Mal. 3:5; Rev. 9:21; 18:23; 21:8; 22:15). This art was also practiced in connection with pharmacy, the mixing of drugs and medical compounds. *See* Sorcery.

Spiritist (Heb. *yidde'ōnî,* a "knowing" one). A term denoting a person pretending to be wise but usually employed in connection with mediums. A spiritist might employ any of the magical arts (Lev. 19:31; 20:27; 1 Sam. 28:3, 9), and the Israelites were forbidden to consult any such person (Deut. 18:11).

Splanchnomancy. The term refers to divination by inspection of entrails. Splanchnomancy was practiced in Rome by the Etrurian soothsayers and frequently referred to by Greek and Latin writers. Cicero (*De divinatione* 2.15) mentions the importance of the *liver* in divination of this kind. One example of this is contained in Scripture (Ezek. 21:21), where it is said that the king of Babylon "looks at the liver," when deciding future course. Liver-divination was especially widespread in Assyria-Babylonia, and thousands of clay tablets dealing with omens and incantations have been dug up.

Stargazer (Heb. *hōzeh,* "beholder," and *kôkāb,* "star"). One who attempts to foretell what will happen by observing the stars (Isa. 47:13). *See* Astrology, above.

Witch, Witchcraft. Generally the KJV rendering of the same original words translated "sorcery," "sorcerer" (*see* above). Witchcraft (functioning as a medium, NIV) is mentioned in Deut. 18:11 as being forbidden to the Israelites.

Wizard. The KJV term *wizard* is replaced in the NASB and NIV by *spiritist* (*see* above; and also the article Spiritist).

BIBLIOGRAPHY: L. W. King, *Babylonian Magic and Sorcery* (1896); T. W. Davies, *Magic, Divination and Demonology Among the Hebrews and Their Neighbors* (1899); R. C. Thompson, *The Reports of the Magicians and Astrologers of Nineveh and Babylon,* 2 vols. (1900); id., *The Devils and Evil Spirits of Babylonia,* 2 vols. (1903-4); A. Guillaume, *Prophecy and Divination* (1938); M. F. Unger, *Biblical Demonology* (1952).

MAGISTRATE. The rendering of several Heb. and Gk. words, and referring to a public civil officer. Among the Hebrews, Greeks, and Romans the corresponding term had a much wider signification than the term *magistrate* with us.

1. "Magistrates and judges" (Ezra 7:25) ought to be rendered "judges and rulers."

2. *Archōn,* "first," rendered "magistrate" (Luke 12:58), signifies *one first in power.* Similar in derivation and meaning is Gr. *archē* (12:11; Titus 3:1, "rulers"). *Archōn* is also used of the Messiah as "the ruler of the kings of the earth" (Rev. 1:5), and of Moses as the judge and leader of the Israelites. It is spoken of magistrates of any kind, e.g., the high priest, civil judges, a ruler of the synagogue, and so on.

3. General (Gk. *stratēgos*) properly signifies the *leader of an army, commander;* but in the NT a *civic commander* (Acts 16:20, 22, 35-36, 38). In Roman colonies and municipal towns the chief magistrates were usually two in number (called *duumviri*). These had the power of administering justice in the less important cases. *See* Israel, Constitution of.

MA'GOG (mā'gog; "region of Gog"). Mentioned in Gen. 10:2; 1 Chron. 1:5 as the second son of Japheth, but understood by some to be the name of a people. Magog is associated with Gomer in Genesis, with Gog in Ezekiel (38:2; 39:6, cf. v. 1). Gog is described by the prophet as belonging to "the land of Magog," the situation of which is defined by its proximity to the isles of the Aegean. It is clear that Lydia is meant, and that by Magog we must understand "the land of Gog." Scholars have sought to identify Gog with Gugu (Gyges),

king of Lydia, and with Gagaia of the Amarna Letters. *See* Gog.

MA'GOR-MIS'SABIB (mā'gor-mis'a-bib; "terror round about"). The name given by Jeremiah to *Pashhur* (which see), symbolic of his fate (Jer. 20:3-6).

MAG'PIASH (mag'pi-ash). One of the chief Israelites who signed the covenant made by Nehemiah (Neh. 10:20), 445 B.C.

MAHA'LAH. *See* Mahlah, no. 2.

MAHA'LALEEL. *See* Mahalalel, no. 1.

MAHA'LALEL (ma-ha'la-lel; "praise of God").
1. The son of the patriarch Kenan, the grandson of Seth. Born when his father was 70, he himself became the father of Jared at the age of 65 and died when he was 895 (Gen. 5:12-17; 1 Chron. 1:2; both Mahalaleel, KJV; Luke 3:37, Maleleel, KJV, Mahalaleel, NASB).
2. An Israelite of the tribe of Judah and family of Perez (Pharez), and ancestor of Athaiah, who resided in Jerusalem after the captivity (Neh. 11:4), before 536 B.C.

MA'HALATH (ma'ha-lath; "sickness").
1. The daughter of Ishmael and third wife of Esau (Gen. 28:9; 36:3; in the latter passage called Basemath).
2. The granddaughter of David, daughter of Jerimoth, and wife of Rehoboam (2 Chron. 11:18), 926 B.C.
3. Part of the title of Pss. 53 and 88. *See* Musical Terms.

MA'HALI. *See* Mahli.

MAHANA'IM (ma-ha-na'im; "double camp" or "double host," so called because the host of God joined that of Jacob as a safeguard). A place beyond the Jordan, N of the brook Jabbok, where the angels of God appeared to Jacob (Gen. 32:1-2). The name was afterward given to the town then existing, or afterward founded, in the neighborhood. It was on the boundary of Gad and Manasseh, as well as of Bashan (Josh. 13:26, 30), and was a city of the Levites (21:38; 1 Chron. 6:80). Here Ish-bosheth reigned and was assassinated (2 Sam. 2:8, 12; 4:5-8). Many years after David went to Mahanaim and was entertained by Barzillai (17:24, 27; 1 Kings 2:8). Near this the battle between the forces of David and Absalom appears to have been fought (2 Sam. 18). It was named as the station of one of the twelve officers who had charge, in monthly rotation, of the provisions for Solomon's establishment (1 Kings 4:14). It has not been positively identified, but it may be represented by a ruined site under the name of Maneh, 2½ miles N of Ajlun.

MA'HANEH-DAN (ma'ha-ne-dan; "camp of Dan").
1. A place at which 600 Danites once encamped before the capture of Laish (Judg. 18:11-13). It

was to the W of Kiriath-jearim and was called "Dan, after the name of Dan their father" (18:29).

2. In the NASB and NIV, it is also the place where the Spirit of God began to move upon Samson (Judg. 13:25). *See* Dan, Camp of.

MAHAR'AI (ma-har'ī; "swift, hasty"). The Netophathite who was one of David's mighty men (2 Sam. 23:28; 1 Chron. 11:30) and was appointed captain, for the tenth month, of a contingent of 24,000 men (27:13), about 975 B.C.

MA'HATH (ma'hath).

1. A Kohathite, son of Amasai and father of Elkanah, in the ancestry of Heman (1 Chron. 6:35), before 1000 B.C.

2. Another Kohathite, who, with his brother Levites, took part in the restoration of the Temple under Hezekiah (2 Chron. 29:12) and was afterward appointed one of the overseers of the sacred offerings (31:13), c. 715 B.C.

MA'HAVITE (ma'ha-vīt). Apparently a partial designation of Eliel, one of David's guards (1 Chron. 11:46). Because no place or person called *Mahavah*, or *Mahavai*, is anywhere else alluded to from which the title could have been derived, a corruption in the text is supposed. Bertheau suggests that it should read "he of Mahanaim."

MAHA'ZIOTH (ma-ha'zi-oth; "visions"). One of the fourteen sons of Heman the Levite (1 Chron. 25:4) and appointed by lot as leader of the twenty-third division of Temple musicians (v. 30), before 960 B.C.

MA'HER-SHAL'AL-HASH'-BAZ (ma'her-shal'-al-hash'baz; "spoil hastens, prey speeds"). Words that Isaiah was commanded to write "in ordinary letters," and afterward was given as a symbolical name to a son to be born to him (Isa. 8:1, 3). In v. 1 the word is rendered "swift is the booty, speedy is the prey" (*see* marg.). The KJV is Maher-Shal-Hash.

MAH'LAH (ma'la; "disease").

1. The eldest of the five daughters of Zelophehad, of the tribe of Manasseh, who married among their kindred and so kept their inheritance (Num. 26:33; 27:1; 36:11; Josh. 17:3).

2. The name of a child, whether son or daughter is uncertain, of Hammolecheth, the sister of Gilead, a Manassite (1 Chron. 7:18).

MAH'LI (ma'li; "weak, sickly").

1. The eldest son of Merari and grandson of Levi (Ex. 6:19; Num. 3:20; 1 Chron. 6:19; 23:21; 24:26; Ezra 8:18). He had three sons, named Libni (1 Chron. 6:29), Eleazar, and Kish (23:21; 24:28), and his descendants were called *Mahlites* (Num. 3:33; 26:58).

2. A son of Mushi, a son of Merari, and therefore nephew of the preceding (1 Chron. 23:23;

24:30). He had a son, Shamar (6:46-47), before 1440 B.C.

MAH'LITES (ma'līts). Descendants of *Mahli* (which see), the son of Merari (Num. 3:33; 26:58).

MAH'LON (ma'lon; "sickly"). The elder of the two sons of Elimelech the Bethlehemite and Naomi. Having moved to Moab with his parents, Mahlon married Ruth the Moabitess, and died without offspring (Ruth 1:2, 5; 4:9-10), before 1070 B.C.

MA'HOL (ma'hol; a "dance"). A person who seems to have been the father of Heman, Calcol, and Darda, men renowned for their wisdom before the time of Solomon (1 Kings 4:31). If these are the same as those given (1 Chron. 2:6) as the sons of Zerah, the word must be taken, as elsewhere, to denote simply their pursuit as musical composers, an art connected with dancing.

MAHSE'IAH (ma-se'yah). The grandfather of Baruch, the scribe and attendant of Jeremiah (Jer. 32:12; 51:59).

MAID, MAIDEN. In English, "maid" can have a sexual connotation (virgin, spinster) and also a social one (domestic servant, attendant). Although "maiden" can be used in the same sexual sense as "maid," it has considerably wider social usage.

The KJV and NASB render *shibḥâ* "(hand)maid" (Gen. 30:7; Ps. 123:2; etc.) to describe a maidservant, and *na'ărâ* is used in 2 Kings 5:2-4; Prov. 9:3 of a similar relationship. In Gen. 30:3; Ex. 21:20; Lev. 25:6, *'āmâ* described a general concubine/slave relationship. In Judg. 5:30, *raḥam* was the term applied to females captured in war. Whereas the KJV rendered *bᵉtûlâ* by "maid(ens)" in Judg. 19:24; Job 31:1; Ps. 78:63; etc., the NASB and the NIV (in Judg. 19:24) translated it by "virgin(s)." This is an unfortunate error, because *bᵉtûlâ* means basically "a woman of marriageable age," who may or may not be a virgin. Thus in Joel 1:8, a widowed *bᵉtûlâ* (or *bethula*) was weeping for the husband of her youth (i.e., her young husband). In the NT, *paidiske*, an enlarged form of *pais*, "child," was used of a female servant (Mark 14:66; Luke 22:56).

MAIL, COAT OF. *See* Armor.

MAIMED (from Heb. *ḥāraṣ*, to "wound," Lev. 22:22). To be deprived by violence of some necessary member. Such sacrifices were not allowed to be offered. *See* Lame; Sacrifices; and Diseases: Maimed.

MAINSAIL. *See* Ship.

MA'KAZ (ma'kaz; "end, boundary"). One of the places in the district under the supervision of Ben-deker, i.e., the son of Deker (1 Kings 4:9), one of Solomon's purveyors. Its situation is unknown.

MAKER. A term usually applied to God as creator (Job 4:17; 36:3; Ps. 95:6; Prov. 22:2; Isa. 17:7; etc.; Hos. 8:14). It is used of *man* in Hab. 2:18. The NASB and NIV of Isa. 1:31 replace KJV "maker" with "work," the former reading, "The strong man will become tinder, his work also a spark." Delitzsch (*Com.,* ad loc.) observes: "The fire of judgment need not come from without. Sin carries the fire of indignation within itself, and an idol is, as it were, an idolater's sin embodied and exposed to the light of day."

MAKHE'LOTH (mak-e'lōth; "assemblies"). The twenty-sixth station of Israel in the wilderness, between Haradah and Tahath (Num. 33:25-26); present location unknown.

MA'KI. *See* Machi.

MA'KIR. *See* Machir.

MAKKE'DAH (mak-e'da; "herdsman's place"). A royal Canaanite city in the low country of Judah (Josh. 12:16), located near the place at which Joshua put to death five kings who had fought against Israel (10:10-29). It was afterward assigned to Judah (15:41). George Smith identifies this place with el-Mughâr, "the caves," to the SW of Ekron, yet admits that placement as doubtful.

MAK'TESH. *See* Mortar.

MAL'ACHI (mal'a-kī; "messenger"). The last of both the minor prophets and OT writers (Mal. 1:1). The circumstances of Malachi's life are unknown, except for what may be inferred from his prophecies. He seems to have been contemporary with Nehemiah, if we may judge from the agreement found between them in the reproof administered for the marriage of Gentile wives (2:11-14 with Neh. 13:23-29) and negligent payment of tithes (Mal. 3:8-10 with Neh. 13:10-14), 432 B.C.

MALACHI, BOOK OF. The last of the OT books and last of the minor prophets.

Name. Malachi (Mal. 1:1) means "my messenger" in Heb. It is common in critical circles to deny that Malachi was a historical person and to make the prophecy anonymous. It is claimed that Malachi is merely an appellative or symbolical expression suggesting the mission of the real author. The reference to "My messenger" in 3:1 is supposed later to have suggested the name. The Gk. version renders 1:1 "by the hand of his messenger" but uses the title *Malachias.* The Targum of Jonathan ben Uzziel assumes that by Malachi, Ezra the scribe is referred to. It is better to take the name *Malachi* as an abbreviated form of Malakiyah, "the messenger of Jehovah." It is highly unreasonable to assume the anonymity of the book. None of the other major or minor prophets is anonymous. Nor is it necessary to suppose that 1:1 is connected with 3:1.

Author and Date. The book is obviously a unit, the work of one man. Practically nothing is known of the life of Malachi except what suggestions may be gleaned from the book itself. Certain evidence, however, enables one to fix upon the approximate date of the prophecy. A Persian governor was in authority in Jerusalem, and is called a *pehah* (1:8). The Temple had been completed for some time, and the religious ritual was practiced for a long time (1:7-10; 3:8). It is patent from these elements of internal evidence that the prophecy is to be dated after Haggai and Zechariah. Religious zeal had waned and enough time had elapsed for abuses to become evident. Personal piety, especially of the priests, had degenerated (1:6-8), foreign marriages flourished (2:10-14), and paying tithes for Temple support had fallen into neglect. The book is reminiscent of the era of Ezra-Nehemiah. A date around 455 B.C. or later would be probable.

Unity and Authenticity. Critics have been in general agreement as to the unity of the book. Editorial additions are taken to be inconsequential. Chapter 2:11-12 is looked upon by Cornill and Marti as being a later interpolation. Chapter 4:4-6 (Heb. text 3:22-24) is sometimes construed to be an interpretation of 3:1 and, according to A. Bentzen, "probably a later commentary." But all of these critical contentions are pure conjecture. The NT fully attests the canonical and doctrinal authority of Malachi (cf. Mal. 4:5-6 with Matt. 11:10, 14; 17:11-12; Mark 9:10-11; Luke 1:17; cf. Mal. 3:1 with Matt. 11:10 and Mark 1:2; Mal. 1:2-3 with Rom. 9:13). (For a critical discussion *see* C. C. Torrey, "The Prophecy of Malachi," *Jour. Bibl. Lit.* [1898]: 1-15; J. M. P. Smith, "The Book of Malachi," *International Critical Commentary* [1912]).

Outline.
I. Introductory appeal: God's love for Israel (1:1-5)
II. Warning against priests' sins (1:6–2:9)
   A. Their carelessness and their ritual functions (1:6–2:4)
   B. Their slovenly teaching (2:5-9)
III. Forewarning against the people (2:10–4:3)
   A. First warning: against treachery (2:10-16)
   B. Second warning: of judgment (2:17–3:6)
   C. Third warning: to repent (3:7-12)
   D. Fourth warning: God's condemnation (3:13 – 4:3)
IV. Concluding solemn warning (4:4-6)
   A. To observe the Mosaic law (4:4)
   B. To have in mind the (second) coming of Christ (4:5-6)   M.F.U.

BIBLIOGRAPHY: G. C. Morgan, *Wherein Have We Robbed God?* (1898); R. K. Harrison, *Introduction to the Old Testament* (1968), pp. 958-62; F. A. Tatford, *The Minor Prophets* (1982), 3: 3: 1-171; F. E. Gaebelein, ed., *Expositor's Bible Commentary* (1985), 7: 701-25; W. C. Kaiser, Jr., *Malachi: God's Unchanging Love* (1985).

MAL'CAM (mal'kām; "their king"). A Benjamite

and fourth named of the seven sons of Shaharaim by his wife Hodesh (1 Chron. 8:9).

MAL'CHAM. *See* Gods, False.

MALCHI'AH. *See* Malchijah, Malkijah.

MAL'CHIEL (mal'kī-el; "God is my king"), **Malkiel** (NIV). The younger son of Beriah, the son of Asher (Gen. 46:17), about 2000 B.C. His descendants were called Malchielites (Num. 26:45), and he himself was the "father" (founder) of Birzaith (1 Chron. 7:31).

MAL'CHIELITE (mal'kī-el-īt). A descendant of *Malchiel* (Num. 26:45).

MALCHI'JAH (mal-kī'ja; "Jehovah is King"; sometimes "Malchi'ah," KJV), **Malkijah** (NIV).
1. A Gershonite Levite in the ancestry of Asaph (1 Chron. 6:40).
2. A priest, the father of Pashhur, which latter King Zedekiah sent to Jeremiah to inquire of the Lord when Nebuchadnezzar made war against him (1 Chron. 9:12; Neh. 11:12; Jer. 21:1; 38:1), before 589 B.C.
3. The head of the fifth division of the sons of Aaron as arranged by David (1 Chron. 24:9), before 967 B.C.
4. An Israelite, formerly resident (or descendant) of Parosh, who put away his Gentile wife after the captivity (Ezra 10:25), 456 B.C.
5. Another Israelite of the same place (or parentage) who did the same as no. 4 (Ezra 10:25), 456 B.C.
6. A Jew of the family (or town) of Harim who divorced his Gentile wife (Ezra 10:31), 456 B.C. He also assisted in repairing the walls of Jerusalem (Neh. 3:11), 445 B.C.
7. The son of Rechab, an official of part of Beth-haccherem, who repaired the Refuse Gate of Jerusalem under Nehemiah (Neh. 3:14), 445 B.C.
8. The "goldsmith" ("son of," *see* marg.) who assisted in repairing the walls of Jerusalem (Neh. 3:31), about 445 B.C.
9. One of those who stood by Ezra when he read the book of the law to the people (Neh. 8:4), about 445 B.C.
10. One of the priests who signed the sacred covenant with Nehemiah (Neh. 10:3), 445 B.C.
11. One of the priests appointed, probably as singers, to assist in celebrating the completion of the walls of Jerusalem (Neh. 12:42), 445 B.C.

MALCHI'RAM (mal-kī'ram; "exalted is the king," i.e., God), **Malkiram** (NIV). The second son of King Jeconiah (Jehoiachin), born to him during his captivity (1 Chron. 3:18, cf. 2 Kings 24:12), after 597 B.C.

MALCHI-SHU'A (mal-ki-shu'a; "the king," i.e., God is "salvation"; sometimes Melchi-shua, KJV), **Malki-Shua** (NIV). One of the four sons of Saul, probably by Ahinoam (1 Sam. 14:49;

1 Chron. 8:33; 9:39). He was slain, with his father, at the battle of Gilboa (1 Sam. 31:2; 1 Chron. 10:2), c. 1004 B.C.

MAL'CHUS (mal'kus; Gk. *malchos*, from Heb. *melek*, "king"). The servant of the high priest whose ear was cut off by Peter at the arrest of Jesus in the Garden of Gethsemane (John 18:10). Caiaphas is doubtless the high priest intended, for John, who was personally acquainted with him (18:15), is the only evangelist who gives the name of Malchus.

MALEFACTOR. An evildoer, rebel, insurgent.

MALE'LEEL. *See* Mahalelel, no. 1.

MALICE (Gk. *kakia*, "badness," 1 Cor. 5:8; Eph. 4:31; Col. 3:8; Titus 3:3; 1 Pet. 2:1). This Gk. word denotes a vicious disposition, evilness, or wickedness. A kindred word is in Rom. 1:29 (Gk. *kakoētheia*, "bad character"), given by Paul in his long list of Gentile sins and implying malignant subtlety or malicious craftiness. Aristotle defines malice as "taking all things in the evil part" (*Rhetoric* 2.13), as the Geneva version of the Scriptures likewise renders it. It is "that peculiar form of evil which manifests itself in a malignant interpretation of the actions of others, an attributing of them all to the worst motive" (Trench, *Synonyms of the NT*, p. 11).

MALIGNITY. *See* Malice.

MALKI-SHU'A. *See* Malchi-shua.

MAL'KIEL. *See* Malchiel.

MALKI'JAH. *See* Malchijah.

MALKI'RAM. *See* Malchiram.

MAL'LOTHI (mal'ō-thi). One of the sons of Heman (1 Chron. 25:4), appointed by David as head of the nineteenth division of Temple musicians (25:26), before 960 B.C.

MALLOWS. *See* Vegetable Kingdom.

MAL'LUCH (mal'uk; "reigning" or "counselor").
1. A Levite of the family of Merari and an ancestor of Ethan the musician (1 Chron. 6:44).
2. One of the descendants of Bani who divorced his Gentile wife after the return to Jerusalem (Ezra 10:29), 456 B.C.
3. A Jew of the family of Harim who put away his Gentile wife after the captivity (Ezra 10:32), 456 B.C.
4. One of the priests who signed the covenant made by Nehemiah and the people to serve Jehovah (Neh. 10:4), 445 B.C. The associated names would seem to indicate that he was one who returned with Zerubbabel from Babylon (12:2), 536 B.C.
5. One of the "chief of the people" who signed the covenant made by Nehemiah (Neh. 10:27), 445 B.C.

MAL'LUCHI (mal'uk-i). A chief priest whose

house was represented in the time of Joiakim by Jonathan (Neh. 12:14; "Melicu," KJV; "Malluch," NIV).

MAL'TA (mal'ta; "Melita," KJV). An island about seventeen miles long, nine miles wide, and about sixty miles in circumference. Paul's ship was wrecked here (Acts 27:27–28:1). The Phoenicians colonized it, the Greeks conquered it, the Carthaginians took it from the Greeks in 528 B.C., and the Romans took it from the Carthaginians in 242 B.C. It has been an independent state since 1964. St. Paul's Bay is shown at the NE of the island as the spot where his shipwreck took place and seems to meet all the requirements of the Acts narrative.   H.F.V.

BIBLIOGRAPHY: James Smith, *The Voyage and Shipwreck of St. Paul* (1978).

MAM'MON (mam'un; Gk. from Aram. *māmônā'*, "wealth"). A term signifying *riches* (Luke 16:9, 11) but personified and spoken of as opposed to God (Matt. 6:24; Luke 16:13). The phrase "make friends for yourselves by means of the mammon of unrighteousness," and so on, is interpreted as follows by Godet (*Com.*, Luke 16:9): "Instead of hoarding up or enjoying, hasten to make for yourselves, with the goods of another (God's), personal friends, who shall then be bound to you by gratitude, and share with you their well-being." According to Meyer and Ewald the "friends" are the angels, but Godet prefers to understand them as "men who have been succored by one on earth."

MAM'RE (mam're).

1. The Amorite who, with his brothers Aner and Eschol, was an ally to Abraham (Gen. 14:13, 24), about 2065 B.C.

2. The name of Abraham's dwelling place near Hebron (Gen. 23:17, 19; 35:27). Here Abraham entertained three angels and was promised a son (18:1, 10, 14). The cave of Machpelah lay "before

Ancient oak at Mamre

[probably to the east of the grove of] Mamre" (23:17, 19; 25:9; 49:30; 50:13). Mamre is now located two miles N of Hebron. There Herod the Great built a wall around the well of Abraham, enclosing an area 150 by 200 feet. Destroyed by Vespasian in A.D. 68, this enclosure was rebuilt by Hadrian in the second century and made the center of a pagan cult dedicated to Hermes-Mercury. Constantine removed Hadrian's pagan altar from the supposed site of Abraham's altar and erected a church. Within Hadrian's enclosure today one may see ruins of this church and Abraham's well.   H.F.V.

BIBLIOGRAPHY: M. Avi-Yonah and E. Stern, eds., *Encyclopedia of Archaeological Excavations in the Holy Land* (1977), 3:776-78.

MAN, MEN.

Names. Several words are used with as much precision as terms of equal importance in other languages. (1) *Adam* (Heb. *'ādām*, perhaps "red earth," occurring also in Ugaritic and Arab., presents man of the earth, earthy, Gen. 1:26). (a) The proper name of the first man (Luke 3:38; Rom. 5:14; 1 Tim. 2:13-14; Jude 14); *see* also the remarkable use of it in 1 Cor. 15:45: "the first man, Adam." (b) The generic name of the human race as originally created, and afterward, like our *man*, a person, whether man or woman (Gen. 1:26-27; 5:1; Deut. 8:3). (c) Man in opposition to woman (Gen. 3:12). (d) Used rarely for those who maintain the dignity of human nature (Eccles. 7:28), that is, who manifest true uprightness. (e) The more degenerate and wicked portion of mankind (Gen. 6:2). (f) Men of inferior rank as opposed to those of higher rank (Isa. 2:9; 5:15; Ps. 62:9). (2) *Man, as distinguished from a woman* (Heb. *'îsh;* Gk. *anēr*), presents him with immaterial and personal existence (1 Sam. 21:4; Matt. 14:21); as a *husband* (Gen. 3:16 rendered "husband," Hos. 2:16, *see* marg.); and in reference to excellent mental qualities (Jer. 5:1, "roam to and fro through the streets of Jerusalem . . . and seek . . . if you can find a *man,"* etc.). (3) *Enosh* (Heb. *'ĕnôsh,* "mortal"), also occurring in Ugaritic, describes man as transient, liable to sickness, and so on. "Let not man prevail against Thee" (2 Chron. 14:11). (4) *Geber* (Heb. *geber*) connects man with human strength. It is applied to man as distinguished from woman, for example, "nor shall a man put on a woman's clothing" (Deut. 22:5); as distinguished from children (Ex. 12:37); to a male child in opposition to a female (Job 3:3, *see* marg.), the birth of a male child being a matter of joy in the East, rather than that of a female. It is used often in poetry (14:10; 22:2; Pss. 34:8; 40:4; Prov. 6:34; etc.). (5) *Methim* (Heb. *mĕtîm,* "men," males). The singular is to be traced in the pre-Flood proper names Methushael and Methuselah. Perhaps it may be derived from the root *mût,* "to die," in which case its use would be appropriate in Isa. 41:14. If this conjecture is to be admitted, this word would correspond to *brotos* and might be read "mortal." Other Heb. words rendered *man* are *nepesh*, a "breathing" creature (2 Kings 12:4), an animate being, *ba'al*, "master" or "husband" (Prov. 22:24; 23:2; 29:22); *gūlgōlet*, "skull" (Ex. 16:16), corresponding to our *poll*. The Gk. words properly rendered *man* are: *anthrōpos*, "man-faced," and so a "human" being, and *'anēr*, a "male," as distinguished from a woman.

It is noteworthy that the title *Son of Man*, which Christ applied to Himself, refers to man in this broadest and most comprehensive sense, and thus expresses the relationship He bears to every human being. For fuller presentation of terms and their force see Young's *Concordance*, also lexicons of Gesenius, Liddell and Scott, and so on. It is to be borne in mind, however, that although the precise force of these terms must be understood for accurate interpretation, the Bible doctrine concerning man is so presented that its most general and important features may be otherwise easily discovered.

Origin. Man came into existence by a distinct act of creation. He originally bore, and in an important sense still bears, the image and likeness of God. Although with respect to his bodily organism he belongs to the animal world, he possesses a spiritual nature that gives him an exalted rank above all animals. He alone of all creatures upon earth is truly a rational and moral and religious being, and is capable of communion with God. He alone is represented as sinful, yet the object of redemption. Before him is the certainty of future judgment and an immortal destiny (*see* Gen. 1:26-28; 9:6; Ex. 4:11; Job 35:10; Pss. 8:4-8; 94:9; Matt. 6:29-33; 12:12; 25:31-46; Rom. 5:12-21; etc.). *See* Creation; Image of God; Immortality; Atonement; Judgment.

Unity. Man's original unity, or that the whole of mankind has descended from one human pair, is one of the obvious teachings of Scripture (*see* Gen. 1:27; 2:21-25; Matt. 19:4; Acts 17:26; Rom. 5:12; 1 Cor. 15:21, 47-49). Although denied by certain natural philosophers, this doctrine is generally accepted not only by orthodox theologians but by such distinguished scientists as Buffon, Linnaeus, Blumenbach, A. Von Humboldt, and many others. This doctrine is of religious and ethical importance inasmuch as it is related to man's noble origin, the reality of human brotherhood, the universality of sin and of redemption.

Antiquity. With respect to the antiquity of man, the Scripture chronology appears to date his origin to at least 6,000 years, perhaps several thousand years earlier, since the genealogies of Genesis 5 and 11 cannot legitimately be used for chronological purposes (*see* the article Genealogies). To what extent our understanding of the Scriptures at this point is beset with difficulties, and how such difficulties should be treated, is not practical to consider here. It is to be noted, never-

theless, that natural science agrees with the Scriptures in regarding man as the most recent in origin of all creatures dwelling upon the earth.

BIBLIOGRAPHY: J. Orr, *God's Image in Man* (1905); H. W. Robinson, *The Christian Doctrine of Man* (1911); J. G. Machen, *The Christian View of Man* (1937); H. E. Brunner, *Man in Revolt* (1930); A. R. Johnson, *The Vitality of the Individual in the Thought of Ancient Israel* (1949); C. R. Smith, *The Biblical Doctrine of Man* (1951); D. Cairns, *The Image of God in Man* (1953); K. Barth, *Christ and Adam* (1956); L. Koehler, *Hebrew Man* (1956); K. Barth, *Church Dogmatics* (1958), 3: 1: 176-211, 235-49; W. G. Kummel, *Man in the New Testament* (1963); R. Scroggs, *The Last Adam* (1966); W. Pannenberg, *What Is Man?* (1970); R. Jewett, *Paul's Use of Anthropological Terms* (1971); H. W. Wolff, *Anthropology of the Old Testament* (1975); G. Carey, *I Believe in Man* (1977); J. Laidlaw, *The Biblical Doctrine of Man* (1983).

MAN, SON OF (Gk. *ho huios tou anthrōpou*). This title, evidently taken from Dan. 7:13 where everlasting dominion is ascribed to the Messiah, was assumed by Christ and occurs sixty-one times in the gospels referring only to Him. It is found once in the Acts (7:56), where Stephen sees heaven open and Christ, whom he calls "the Son of Man," standing at the right hand of God. In the light of the corresponding term "the Son of God," which stresses Christ's deity, the term "Son of Man" emphasizes His divine humanity. Whereas the gospel of John presents Christ as the Son of God, the gospel of Luke presents Him as the Son of Man. The term "Son of Man" is Christ's racial name as a representative man (cf. 1 Cor. 15:45-47). The term "Son of David" delineates His kingly Jewish name, as "Son of God" denotes His divine name. This term "Son of Man" was widely used by our Lord to demonstrate that His mission (Matt. 11:19; Luke 19:10), His death and glorious resurrection (Matt. 12:40; 20:18; 26:2), and His second coming in power (Matt. 24:37-44; Luke 12:40) went far beyond all mere Jewish limitations. Nathaniel, in confessing Him as "King of Israel," received the reply "You shall see greater things . . . the angels of God ascending and descending on the Son of Man" (John 1:50-51). Under the name *Son of Man*, universal judgment is given to Christ (5:22-27). Under this designation is fulfilled in Christ the OT prophecies of blessing through the seed of the woman and the coming God-Man (Gen 1:26; 3:15; 12:3; Pss. 8:4; 80:17; Isa. 7:14; 9:6-7; Zech. 13:7). The term "Son of Man" is used by the Lord ninety-one times in addressing Ezekiel the prophet. As a term in the case of our Lord, denoting His racial name, as a representative man, it implies transcendence, not mere blessing to the Jews. Somewhat the same thought is involved in the use of the term referred to in Ezekiel. In Ezekiel's day Israel had forsaken her divine mission (5:5-8). Although Israel is in exile, Jehovah will not forsake His people. On the other hand, He would have them to remember that they are but a small part of the entire race about whom He is concerned. There is therefore natural emphasis upon the word *man,* as the cherubim that Ezekiel saw in his vision "had human form," and when the prophet glimpsed the throne of God he saw "a figure with the appearance of a man" (1:26).

M.F.U.

BIBLIOGRAPHY: C. H. Kraeling, *Anthropos and the Son of Man* (1927); G. S. Duncan, *Jesus, Son of Man* (1947); G. H. Dalman, *The Words of Christ* (1981), pp. 234-67.

MAN OF LAWLESSNESS, THE (Gk. *ho anthrōpos tēs hamartias,* 2 Thess. 2:3; "man of sin," KJV). This is the devil-indwelt "man of lawlessness . . . the son of destruction" who "opposes and exalts himself against every so-called god or object of worship, so that he takes his seat in the temple of God [at Jerusalem], displaying himself as being God" (2 Thess. 2:3-4). Power will be given him "over every tribe and people and tongue and nation" (Rev. 13:7). A worldwide reign of terror, blasphemy, and murder will be inaugurated by him. "He will speak out against the Most High and . . . will intend to make alterations in times and in law" (Dan. 7:25). It will be his supreme attempt to be "like the Most High" (Isa. 14:14). "He will even oppose the Prince of princes" (Dan. 8:25). His brief but horrible career will be brought to an end by the second coming of Christ (Rev. 19:11-21). He is the Antichrist, the first Beast of Rev. 13:1-10 (J. A. Seiss, *The Apocalypse* II, pp. 388-412; Clarence Larkin, *The Book of Revelation,* pp. 103-26; *Dispensational Truth,* pp. 115-23). Prophetic teaching has been thrown into considerable confusion by identifying the second Beast of 13:11-18 with the Antichrist (W. Scott, *Exposition of Revelation,* p. 280; W. Kelly, *The Revelation Expounded,* pp. 159-64; A. C. Gaebelein, *Annotated Bible,* 4:242-43; C. I. Scofield, *Reference Bible,* p. 1342). But the first Beast and not the second is the Antichrist of Scripture. This is well demonstrated by W. R. Newell (*The Book of Revelation,* pp. 195-201). Satan indwells this monstrous person and through him will strike his final furious blows at the Jewish remnant of the last days, who will be proclaiming "this gospel of the kingdom" (Matt. 24:14), and at the Gentiles, who will believe the good news of the imminent setting up of the millennial kingdom. As a man of lawlessness, the Antichrist will be the consummation of human opposition to God's will and rule. *See* Antichrist.

M.F.U.

MAN'AEN (man'a-en; Gk. form of Menahem). A Christian prophet or teacher who had been an associate *suntrophos* ("one brought up with") of Herod the tetrarch in his youth and was one of those who assisted at Antioch in ordaining Paul and Barnabas (Acts 13:1).

MAN'AHATH (man'a-hath; "resting place"). The

second of the five sons of Shobal, the son of Seir the Horite (Gen. 36:23; 1 Chron. 1:40).

MANA'HATHITES (ma-na'hath-īts; sometimes "Manahethites," KJV). A term usually taken to mean inhabitants of Manahath, which is commonly identified with a town in Judah. But in 1 Chron. 8:6, where only Manahath is mentioned, it is in connection with Benjamite genealogies. The expression "they carried them into exile," however, may imply a removal beyond the circle of Benjamin towns; cf. v. 8, where the land of Moab is mentioned. The tribal lines were not always sharply drawn in the early ages, as we have seen under *Machirites* (which see). And the hostility between Judah and Benjamin included the other tribes as well as Judah and must have been largely ignored from simple necessity, since Benjamin could not live alone and intermarriages with other tribes must have been frequent for a time. We incline, therefore, to the ordinary view, which is favored by Gesenius (Heb. *Lex.,* 12th ed.). But the difference in the Heb. pointing is hard to explain, and some identify the town with the *Menûḥâ* of Judg. 20:43 (*see* KJV, "with ease"; NIV, "easily"; RV, "at their resting place," marg., "at Menuhah"). It may be that 1 Chron. 2:52 and 54 refer to entirely different persons. In Gen. 36:23 and 1 Chron. 1:40 Manahath is son of Shobal, son of Seir. The Manahathites in both verses are among the posterity of Caleb, and this is interesting in connection with the possible Edomite descent of Caleb noticed under "Kenizite."

W.H.; M.F.U.

MANAS'SEH (ma-nas'e; "causing to forget"). The name of the fourteenth king of Judah (*see* article below) and other biblical persons.

1. The elder son of Joseph and his Egyptian wife, Asenath (Gen. 41:51; 46:20), about 1885 B.C. Manasseh and his brother were both adopted by Jacob upon his deathbed, who, however, gave the first place and the birthright blessing to Ephraim (chap. 48). Nothing is known of Manasseh's personal history. His wife's name is not mentioned, nor is it certain that he had one. Machir, the son of an Aramitess concubine (1 Chron. 7:14), was probably his only son and sole founder of his house. *See* Manassites.

2. Given in some versions of Judg. 18:30 as the father of Gershom, whose son Jonathan acted as priest to the Danites when they set up a graven image. It is generally thought that the reading is suspicious and that it should be rendered "Moses," as in the Vulg., many copies of the LXX, and the NIV.

3. A descendant (or resident) of Pahath-moab, who put away his Gentile wife after the captivity (Ezra 10:30), 456 B.C.

4. An Israelite of the family of Hashum, who did the same as no. 3 (Ezra 10:33), 456 B.C.

MANAS'SEH. The fourteenth king of Judah, and

other biblical personages (*see* article above). Manasseh was the son of King Hezekiah by his wife Hephzibah and ruled for a total of fifty-five years, from 696 to 642 B.C., (2 Kings 21:1; 2 Chron. 33:1). Of Manasseh few facts are given, although his was the longest reign in the annals of Judah.

Sin. Ascending the throne at the early age of twelve, he yielded to the influence of the idolatrous, or Ahaz, party and became in time a determined and even fanatical idolater. As he grew up he took delight in introducing into his kingdom the superstitions of every heathen country. The high places were restored, the groves replanted, the altars of Baal and Asherah rebuilt, and the sun, moon, and all the host of heaven were worshiped. The gods of Ammon, of Moab, and of Edom were zealously worshiped everywhere. Babylonian and Egyptian paganism was common; incense and offerings rose on the roofs of the houses to the fabled deities of the heights; wizards practiced their enchantments, and the valley of Hinnom was once more disgraced by the hideous statue of Molech, to whom parents offered up their children as burnt sacrifices. In the very Temple of the Lord stood an image of Asherah, and white horses harnessed to a splendid chariot sacred to the sun were placed in the entrance of the court. This apostasy did not go unrebuked by the prophets, whom the king endeavored to silence by the fiercest persecution recorded in the annals of Israel (2 Kings 21:2-16; 24:3-4). Fuller particulars are preserved by Josephus, who says that executions took place every day (*Ant.* 10.3.1). According to rabbinical tradition Isaiah was sawn asunder by order of Manasseh, and after his death the prophetic voice was heard no more until the reign of Josiah.

Retribution. The crimes of Manasseh were not long left unavenged. The Philistines, Moabites, and Ammonites, who had been tributary to Hezekiah, seem to have revolted during Manasseh's reign (Zeph. 2:4-9; Jer. 47-49). But the great blow was inflicted by Assyria, from whence an army came to Judea and, taking Manasseh prisoner, conveyed him to Babylon (2 Chron. 33:11).

Archaeology. In the Assyrian inscriptions of Esarhaddon there is a direct reference to Manasseh that illuminates the account of the wicked king's being carried away to Babylon, his repentance, and subsequent restoration to the throne. According to 2 Chron. 33:10-13 Jehovah brought upon the idolatrous Manasseh and his people "the commanders of the army of the king of Assyria, . . . and they captured Manasseh with hooks, bound him with bronze chains, and took him to Babylon." There is no direct confirmation of this notation by the chronicler in Assyrian literature, but Esarhaddon's inscriptions do relate the forced visit of Manasseh to the great Assyrian capital of Nineveh about the year 678 B.C. "At that time the older palace of Nineveh which the kings who went before, my fathers, had

built . . . had come to seem too small to me, and the people of the lands my arms had despoiled I made to carry the basket and the hod . . . that small palace I tore down in its totality . . . and I commanded the kings of Syria and those across the sea—Baalu, king of Tyre; Manasseh, king of Judah; Kaushgabri, king of Edom; Mussurri, king of Moab . . . Milkiashapa, king of Gabail (Byblos), etc., etc. . . . twenty kings in all. I gave them their orders" (D. D. Luckenbill, *Ancient Records of Assyria and Babylonia,* vol. 2, sec. 690). It had been commonly supposed by critics that Manasseh's captivity in Babylon was a mistake for Nineveh. Assyrian cuneiform tablets, however, prove that Esarhaddon did in fact reconstruct the ancient city destroyed by his father Sennacherib. "At the beginning of my rule in the first year of my reign when I took my seat upon the royal throne in might there appeared favorable signs in the heaven and on earth. . . . Through the soothsayers' rites encouraging oracles were disclosed and for the rebuilding of Babylon and the restoration of Esagila (temple of the gods) they caused the command to be written down" (Luckenbill, sec. 646). Esarhaddon gives the following description of his building of Babylon: "I summoned all my artisans and the people of Babylonia in their totality. I made them carry the basket and laid the head pad upon them. Babylon I built anew, I enlarged, I raised aloft, I made magnificent" (sec. 647). It is enlightening that with such a trophy of his reign, Esarhaddon would have allowed Manasseh and the more than a score of kings whom he compelled to come to Nineveh to return to their countries without seeing this evidence of his splendor. Moreover, on the Senjirli Stela of Esarhaddon, Baalu, king of Tyre, appears lifting manacled hands in supplication to Esarhaddon, and beside him Tirhakah, king of Ethiopia, is shown with a hook through his lips and fastened by a rope to Esarhaddon's hand.

Reformation. Manasseh was brought to repentance and "humbled himself greatly before the God of his fathers." God heard his prayer and restored him to his kingdom at Jerusalem. His captivity is supposed to have lasted about a year, and after his return Manasseh took measures to secure his kingdom, especially the capital, against hostile attacks. He removed the idols and the statues from the house of the Lord and caused the idolatrous altars that he had built upon the Temple hill and in Jerusalem to be cast forth from the city. He repaired the altar of Jehovah and called upon the people to serve the Lord God of Israel. But the people still sacrificed on the high places, "although only to the Lord their God" (2 Chron. 33:12-19). The last Scripture mention of Manasseh is his death and burial in the garden of Uzza (2 Kings 21:18; 2 Chron. 33:20), 642 B.C.

BIBLIOGRAPHY: R. H. Charles, *The Apocrypha and Pseudepigrapha of the Old Testament* (1913), 1:612-24;

Assyrians deport prisoners, often cruelly treated

2:155-62; J. B. Pritchard, ed., *Ancient Near Eastern Texts* (1969), pp. 291, 294; T. Kirk and G. Rawlinson, *Studies in the Books of Kings*, 2 vols. in 1 (1983), 2:203-11; E. R. Thiele, *Mysterious Numbers of the Hebrew Kings* (1983), pp. 64, 174-78.

MANAS'SES. *See* Manasseh.

MANAS'SITES (ma-nas′īts). Descendants of Manasseh, the elder son of Joseph. The relation between Manasseh and Ephraim seems to have been a little like that between Jacob and Esau, the younger brother having priority of influence, while the elder retained the birthright of material prosperity. The great national leader Joshua was an Ephraimite. The territory of Ephraim was rich and well situated for traffic and communication, and, besides Joshua's inheritance, it contained Ebal, Gerizim, Shiloh, Shechem, and Samaria. Samuel, though a Levite, was a native of Ramah in Mt. Ephraim, and Saul belonged to a tribe closely allied to the family of Joseph (*see* Machirites); so that during the priesthood of the former and the reign of the latter the supremacy of Ephraim may be said to have been practically maintained. And after the division of the kingdom Ephraim formed the essential part of the Northern Kingdom.

Manasseh's population was also great. In the first census at Sinai, Manasseh numbered 32,200 (Num. 1:10, 35; 2:20-21; 7:54-59) and Ephraim 40,500. But fifty years later (26:34, 37) Manasseh took its place in the catalog as the eldest, and numbered 52,700 to Ephraim's 32,500. When David was crowned at Hebron, while Ephraim sent 20,800 men, western Manasseh alone sent 18,000, and eastern Manasseh with Reuben and Gad sent 120,000, "with all kinds of weapons of war for the battle," out of a total muster of about

350,000 for the whole country (1 Chron. 12:23-38).

The tribe of Manasseh was divided, probably on account of difference of habit and occupation. One section was devoted to the pursuits of husbandry; they sought a quiet, peaceful region, with rich soil and genial climate, and they found these in the fertile valleys and plains of central Palestine. Another, and apparently much larger, section was pastoral in its tendencies. It was also warlike—trained to arms and accustomed to fatigue. *Manasseh east*—The descendants of Machir, son of Manasseh, invaded northern Gilead and Bashan, ruled by King Og, drove out the Amorites, and occupied the whole kingdom (Num. 32:29-42; Deut. 3:13-15). *Manasseh west*—This territory was small and not fully defined in the Bible. It lay on the N side of Ephraim and included the northern section of the hills of Samaria, a region of great beauty and fertility.

The children of Manasseh, Machir (Josh. 17:1), Jair (Deut. 3:14), and probably Nobah (Num. 32:42, cf. v. 41) were mighty men of war, of whom it is nowhere hinted that they were unable to drive out the inhabitants of any land that they chose to attack. "The district which these ancient warriors, east of Jordan, conquered was among the most difficult, if not the most difficult, in the whole country. It embraced the hills of Gilead with their inaccessible heights and impassable ravines, and the almost impregnable tract of Argob, which derives its modern name of *Lejeah* from the secure 'asylum' it affords to those who have taken 'refuge' within its natural fortifications" (Smith, *Bib. Dict.*, s.v. "Manasseh").

In general it was Ephraim that mingled in public affairs; yet of fifteen judges Manasseh furnished four: Gideon, Abimelech, Jair, and Jephthah. Gideon has been believed to be the greatest of the judges, and he might have been a king and the founder of a dynasty if he had been willing (Judg. 8:22-23). But being detached from the great body of Israel, the Manassites probably spread themselves like desert nomads over the wide regions whence they had expelled the Hagrites (1 Chron. 5:19). Thus they fell into idolatry (v. 25). Whether their fall was more rapid or deeper than that of western Israel does not appear, for perhaps their exposed position might explain the fact that they were carried away in the first captivity (v. 26). The notices of Manasseh in the reforms of Asa (2 Chron. 15:9), Hezekiah (30:1, 10-11, 18; 31:1), and Josiah (34:6, 9) leave rather a favorable impression, but they seem to refer to W Manasseh only.   w.h.

MANDRAKE. *See* Vegetable Kingdom.

MA'NEH (ma′ne). The rendering in Ezek. 45:12 of the Heb. *māneh,* a measure of weight, elsewhere translated "minas." *See* Metrology: Mina.

MANGER (Heb. *'ēbûs,* Job 39:9; Prov. 14:4; Isa.

1:3; Gk. *phatnē,* Luke 2:7, 12; 13:15, "stall"). The Heb. term can mean "manger" or "stall." It is rendered "crib" in the KJV and "manger" in the NASB and NIV. The Gk. term as well means both stall and manger, from which cattle were fed. Probably it refers here to that portion of the inn that was used as a stable. In the East the cattle were shut up in an open yard enclosed by a rough fence of stones or other material. Poor travelers, or those excluded from the house through lack of room, would share these humble quarters with the animals. Several of the Christian Fathers assert that the stable itself was a cave.

Traditional site of the Bethlehem manger

MANNA (Heb. *mān,* "what?"; Gk. *manna*). The name given by the Israelites to the miraculous food furnished them during their wanderings in the desert. When they saw it lying on the ground "they said to one another, 'What is it?' For they did not know what it was" (Ex. 16:15). The most important passages in the OT on this topic are the following: Ex. 16:14-36; Num. 11:7-9; Deut. 8:3, 16; Josh. 5:12; Ps. 78:24-25; Wisd. of Sol. 16:20-21. From these passages we learn that the manna came every morning, except the Sabbath, in the form of a small round seed resembling frost lying on the ground. It had to be gathered early, before the sun melted it; it had to be gathered every day, except the Sabbath. An attempt to lay aside for a succeeding day, except on the day immediately preceding the Sabbath, failed by the substance's becoming wormy and offensive. It was prepared for food by grinding and baking, it tasted like fresh oil, like wafers made with honey, equally agreeable to all palates. The whole nation subsisted upon it for forty years, and it suddenly ceased when they first got the new grain of the land of Canaan. It was always regarded as a miraculous gift directly from God and not as a product of nature.

The author of Hebrews (9:4) includes a "golden jar holding manna" among the contents of the Ark of the Covenant for a memorial. It was a constant tradition of the Jews that the Ark, the tables of stone, Aaron's rod, the holy anointing oil, and the jar of manna were hidden by Josiah when Jerusalem was taken by the Chaldeans, and that these shall be restored in the days of the Messiah. *See* Vegetable Kingdom.

For a discussion of the tamarisk-manna in the light of archaeology see F. S. Bodenheimer, "The Manna of Sinai," *The Biblical Archaeologist* 10, no. 1 (1947): 2-6; F. S. Bodenheimer and O. Theodor, *Ergebnisse der Sinai-Expedition 1927* (1929), pp. 45-88.

Figurative. Manna is the symbol of immortality: "to him I will give some of the hidden manna" (Rev. 2:17; cf. John 6:3-13).

MANO'AH (ma-nō'a; "rest, quiet"). The father of Samson, a Danite of Zorah. When his wife told him of the announcement that a son should be born to them, Manoah prayed to the Lord that He would send the messenger again to teach them how they should treat him. This prayer was granted; but when he knew that it was God's angel, Manoah feared that he and his wife would die, because they had "seen God." His wife quieted his fears, assuring him of God's pleasure by His acceptance of their sacrifice (Judg. 13:2-23), before 1070 B.C. We hear of Manoah once again in connection with the marriage of Samson, when both parents protested their son's choice of a wife, but to no avail (14:2-3). They accompanied him to Timnah, both at the bethrothal and the wedding (vv. 5, 10) but are not named. Manoah probably did not survive Samson, who was buried "between Zorah and Eshtaol in the tomb of Manoah his father" (16:31).

BIBLIOGRAPHY: G. Bush, *Notes on Judges* (1981), pp. 174-91; J. M. Lang and T. Kirk, *Studies in the Book of Judges,* 2 vols. in 1 (1983), 1:64-80; 2:3-67.

MANSERVANT. *See* Service.

MANSLAYER. One who by accident strikes another so as to kill (Num. 35:6, 12). The cases mentioned of manslaughter appear to be a sufficient sample of the intention of the lawgiver: (1) Death by a blow in a sudden quarrel (Num. 35:21). (2) Death by a stone or missile thrown at random (vv. 22-23). (3) By the head of an ax flying from its handle (Deut. 19:5). (4) Whether the case of a person killed by falling from a roof unprovided with a parapet involved the guilt of manslaughter on the owner is not clear, but the law seems intended to prevent the imputation of malice in any such case by preventing as far as possible the occurrence of the fact itself (22:8). In all these and similar cases the manslayer was allowed to retire to a *city of refuge* (which see). Besides these the following may be mentioned as cases of homicide: (1) An animal not known to be vicious causing death to a human being was to be put to death and regarded as unclean. But if it was known to be vicious the owner also was liable to fine, or even death (Ex. 21:28-32). (2) A thief overtaken at night in the act might lawfully be put to death, but if the sun had risen the act of killing him was to be regarded as murder (22:2-3). *See* Murder.

MANTLE. *See* Beautiful Mantle from Shinar; Dress.

MANUSCRIPTS. *See* Dead Sea Scrolls; Versions of the Scripture; Scripture Manuscripts: Old Testament; Scripture Manuscripts: New Testament.

MA'OCH (ma'ok; perhaps, "oppression"). The father of Achish, the king of Gath, to whom David fled from Saul (1 Sam. 27:2), about 1004 B.C.

MA'ON (ma'on; "abode, dwelling").
1. The son of Shammai, of the family of Caleb and tribe of Judah. He was the "father" (founder) of Bethzur (1 Chron. 2:45).
2. An elevated town in the tribe of Judah, seven miles S of Hebron, where David hid himself from Saul (1 Sam. 23:24-25), and near Nabal's possessions (25:2-3); probably now Tell Main, a small heap of ruins.

MA'ONITES (ma'on-īts; same form as Maon). Oppressors of Israel, mentioned only in Judg. 10:12, where they are named in connection with the Egyptians, Amorites, sons of Ammon, Philistines, Sidonians, and Amalekites. The name agrees well with the plural, *Meunim* (which see), but no mention is made of any previous invasion of Israel by the Meunim. And Midian, whose yoke had been so heavy and so lately borne, is not mentioned in the list. These facts have led some to receive the reading "Midian," which is given in both the great manuscripts of the LXX. If the reading "Maonites" is to be retained, we may suppose Maon in Judah to have been originally occupied by this people and to have taken its name from them. Maon was mentioned in connection with Ziph and Carmel. The modern Maîn is seven miles S of Hebron.   w.h.

MA'RA (ma'ra; "bitter"). The name chosen for herself by Naomi as being more appropriate to her by reason of her afflictions than her former name, which signifies "my delight" (Ruth 1:20).

MA'RAH (ma'ra; "bitterness"). The sixth station of the desert wandering of Israel (Ex. 15:23; Num. 33:8-9). Here the waters were miraculously sweetened by casting a tree into them, as directed by God (Ex. 15:24-25). It is identified as 'Ain Hawârah, forty-seven miles from 'Ayûn Mousa.

MAR'ALAH (mar'a-la; "trembling, earthquake"). A place four miles from Nazareth, on the southern boundary of Zebulun (Josh. 19:11), apparently within the bounds of Issachar, W of Sarid and E of Dabbesheth.

MARANATH'A (mar-an-ath-a; Gk. from Aram. *māranā' tā',* "our Lord cometh"). An expression used by Paul at the conclusion of his first epistle to the Corinthians: "If anyone does not love the Lord, let him be accursed. Maranatha" (16:22;

see NIV marg.). It is thought to have been used as a watchword, common to all believers in the first age. Coupled here with an anathema, or curse (*see* marg.), it is the Christian's reminder as he waits the advent of the judge to execute the anathema.

MARBLE. *See* Mineral Kingdom.

MAR'CUS. *See* Mark.

MAR'DUK. *See* Gods, False: Merodach.

MARE'SHAH (ma-re'sha; "summit, chief place").
1. A person named as the "father" of Hebron, among the descendants of Judah. From the position his name occupies he is supposed to be the brother of Mesha, Caleb's firstborn (1 Chron. 2:42), about 1380 B.C.
2. A son of, or, more probably, a city founded by, Laadah, of the family of Shelah (1 Chron. 4:21).
3. A town of Judah mentioned with Keilah and Achzib (Josh. 15:44), rebuilt by Laadah (1 Chron. 4:21) and fortified by Rehoboam (2 Chron. 11:8). It was the native place of the prophet Eliezer (20:37) and near the valley of Zephathah, where the Ethiopians under Zerah were defeated (14:9-13). It was inhabited by Edomites in the Greek period and known as Marisa. It figured prominently in the Maccabaean war (1 Macc. 5:66; 2 Macc. 12:35), being destroyed by the Parthians in 40 B.C.

Mareshah is identified with Tell Sandahannah, about one mile S of Beit Jibrin. R. A. S. Macalister and F. J. Bliss excavated at the site in 1900 for the Palestine Exploration Fund. Though they found some Iron Age materials, most of what they discovered concerned the Hellenistic stratum, which contained a city wall about 500 feet on a side, within which was a town laid out on the grid plan with streets intersecting at right angles. In 1902, 1925, and 1962 some fine rock-cut and

Tell Mareshah

elaborately painted Hellenistic tombs were found there. H.F.V.

BIBLIOGRAPHY: W. F. Albright, *Archaeology and the Religion of Israel* (1942), pp. 146-47; id., *Archaeology of Palestine* (1960), pp. 152-53.

MA'RI (ma'ri). An ancient city on the Middle Euphrates, represented today by Tell Hariri, about six miles N of Abou Kemal. André Parrot conducted excavations sponsored by the Musée du Louvre at the site, 1933-39 and 1951-56; other French teams have worked there in recent years. These diggings have been most successful in revealing a brilliant civilization of this city in the second millennium B.C. Among the outstanding discoveries were a temple of Ishtar and a ziggurat (temple tower). Most famous of all the buildings uncovered in Mari was the royal palace, a sprawling edifice of about 260 rooms covering more than six acres. It consisted of royal apartments, administrative offices, and even a school for scribes. It was ornamented with great wall paintings, some of which were still preserved. From the palace archives more than twenty thousand tablets were recovered. Many of these cuneiform tablets record diplomatic correspondence by the last king of Mari, Zimri-lim, with the great Hammurabi of Babylon. The Mari Letters have helped to date Hammurabi (c. 1728-1626 B.C.), thus settling a difficult point in biblical chronology. In fact, the Mari documents have been a major discovery and have completely revised current knowledge of history, linguistics, and historical background of the OT during the first quarter of the second millennium B.C. The June 1984 issue of the *Biblical Archaeologist* is devoted to Mari and its legacy. *See* Scripture Manuscripts: Old Testament; Scripture Manuscripts: New Testament; Dead Sea Scrolls. M.F.U.

BIBLIOGRAPHY: A. Parrot, *Syria* 16 (1935): 1-28, 117-40; id., 17 (1936): 1-31; id., 18 (1937): 54-84, 325-54; id., 19 (1938): 1-29; id., 20 (1939): 1-22; id., 21 (1940): 1-29; G. E. Mendenhall, *Biblical Archaeologist Reader* 2 (1964): 3-20; G. Roux, *Ancient Iraq* (1964), pp. 164-77, 189-201; A. L. Oppenheim, *Letters from Mesopotamia* (1967).

MARK (Gk. *Markos*). The evangelist who was probably the same as "John who was also called Mark" (Acts 12:12, 25). He was the son of a certain Mary in Jerusalem (12:12) and was, therefore, presumably a native of that city. He was of Jewish parentage, his mother being a relative of Barnabas (Col. 4:10). It was to her house that Peter went when released from prison by the angel (Acts 12:12). That apostle calls him his son (1 Pet. 5:13), probably because he was converted under his ministry. He accompanied Paul and Barnabas on their first journey (Acts 12:25; 13:5) but left them at Perga and returned to Jerusalem (13:13). Whatever the reason for this act, it seems to have been sufficient in Paul's estimation to justify his refusing to allow Mark to accompany

him on his second journey. Barnabas was determined to take him, and thus Mark was the cause of a "sharp disagreement" between them and a separation (15:36-39). This did not completely estrange him from Paul, for we find Mark with the apostle in his first imprisonment at Rome (Col. 4:10; Philem. 24). Later he was at Babylon and united with Peter in sending salutations (1 Pet. 5:13). He seems to have been with Timothy at Ephesus when Paul wrote to him during his second imprisonment and urged him to bring Mark to Rome (2 Tim. 4:11), A.D. 66. Tradition states that Mark was sent on a mission to Egypt by Peter, that he founded the church of Alexandria, of which he became bishop, and suffered as a martyr in the eighth year of Nero. In the gospel of Mark his record is emphatically "the gospel of Jesus Christ, the Son of God" (Mark 1:1), living and working among men and developing the mission more in acts than by words.

MARK. Several uses of the term appear in Scripture.

1. God commands the man with writing materials to "put a mark on the foreheads" of all persons in Jerusalem, that they might be spared in the time of judgment (Ezek. 9:4, 6). The Heb. letter *tau*, the last of the alphabet, was used as a mark or "signature" (Job 31:35, *see* marg.), and in early times was written in the form of a cross. The mark (Gk. *charagma*, "stamp") is to be stamped on the right hand or the forehead as the badge of the followers of Antichrist (Rev. 13:16-17; 14:9, 11; 16:2; 19:20; 20:4).

2. The *goal* or *end* one has in view, from the Gk. *skopos*, something "watched" (Phil. 3:14).

3. In Lev. 19:28 we find two prohibitions of an unnatural disfigurement of the body: "You shall not make any cuts in your body for the dead, nor make any tattoo marks on yourselves." The latter (Heb. *qa'àqa'*, "incision") has no reference to idolatrous usages, but was intended to implant upon the Israelites a proper reverence for God's creation (K. & D., *Com.*, ad loc.).

4. In Gal. 6:17 Paul writes, "From now on let no one cause trouble for me, for I bear in my body the brand-marks of Jesus," that is, the brand of my Master, Jesus Christ. The Gk. *stigma* is the common word for the brand or mark with which masters marked their slaves. "From the very numerous records [on fragments of marble] of manumissions at Delphi and other shrines in Greece we have learned the legal process by which a slave gained his own liberty. He went to the temple of the god, and there paid his money to the priests; they then with his money bought the slave from his master, on the part of the god. He became for the rest of his life a slave to the god, which meant practically freedom, subject to certain periodical duties. If at any time his master or his master's heirs sought to reclaim him he had the record of the transaction in the temple.

"But on one point these documents are silent: If he traveled, if he were far away from home and were seized as a runaway slave, what security could he have? I believe St. Paul gives us the solution. When liberated at the temple, the priest, if he desired it, branded him with the 'stigmata' of his new master. Now St. Paul's words acquire a new and striking application. He had been the slave of sin; but he had been purchased by Christ, and his new liberty consisted in his being the slave of Christ. Henceforth, he says, let no man attempt to reclaim me; I have been marked on my body with the brand of my new master, Jesus Christ. Probably he referred to the many scars he bore of his persecutions" (Mahaffy, *Christian Work*).

MARK, GOSPEL OF. The second gospel by order in the English Bible.

Theme. In all the gospels one unique personality dominates. In Mark we have Christ as a Servant, just as He appears as King in Matthew, Man in Luke, and God in John. But Mark's Servant is also King, Man, and God. In Mark, Jesus is seen as the Mighty Worker, rather than as the Great Teacher. It is preeminently the gospel of Jehovah's Servant, "the Branch" (Zech. 3:8). Chapter 10:45 describes the scope of the book, "For even the Son of Man did not come to be served but to serve." No genealogy is included, for such is not important for a servant. In this gospel Christ appears as a lowly servant who, "although He existed in the form of God, . . . emptied Himself, . . . being made in the likeness of men" (Phil. 2:6-8). This lowly Servant was nevertheless the mighty God (Isa. 9:6). In keeping with the servant character, the gospel is one of deeds rather than of words.

Outline.

I. The Servant's preparation (1:1-13)
II. The Servant's Galilean ministry (1:14–7:23)
III. The Servant's ministry north and east of Galilee (7:24–9:50)
IV. The Servant's ministry enroute to Jerusalem (10:1-52)
V. The Servant's ministry in Jerusalem (11-13)
VI. The Servant's submission to death (14-15)
VII. The Servant's triumphant resurrection and ascension (16)

Attestation—External Evidence. The gospel circulated early among Christians. By the middle of the second century it was included by Tatian in his Diatessaron, or "Harmony of the Four Gospels" (c. A.D. 168). It is quoted by Irenaeus in the last quarter of the second century as being Mark's. Others before him, such as Papias, assert that Mark was both Peter's disciple and interpreter. Mark's close association with Peter is corroborated by numerous details of internal evidence, suggesting eyewitness testimony. But Mark evidently used other sources besides Peter. Quite a bit of material reveals Aramaic coloring. Rome is fixed by tradition as the place where the gospel was written by Mark. If so, it must be dated around A.D. 65-68, but if Luke's gospel was written before A.D. 63, Mark must be dated still earlier.

Author. Internal evidence agrees with the traditional Markan authorship. The writer is clearly a Christian Jew. He knows Jewish thought and life. He is acquainted with Aramaic. He writes with a thorough knowledge of Palestine.

Sources. Recent criticism accords this shortest and simplest of the four gospels a place of priority in time and primacy of importance. The reason for this is that it is now viewed as a basic source for Matthew and Luke, and especially underlies John. But in early traditional lists it appears in second, third, and fourth places, never in the first. Until Lachmann's "discovery" of the priority of Mark in 1835 the gospel had little interest in critical circles. But this critical view is unsound and is not to be accepted without stern challenge. There is, however, a sense in which Mark is dependent not upon any canonical gospel but upon Peter the apostle. *See* Attestation.   M.F.U.

BIBLIOGRAPHY: V. Taylor, *The Gospel According to St. Mark* (1952); C. E. B. Cranfield, *The Gospel According to St. Mark.* Cambridge Greek Testament Commentary (1959); R. A. Cole, *The Gospel According to St. Mark.* Tyndale New Testament Commentaries (1961); C. F. D. Moule, *The Gospel According to Mark* (1965); D. E. Hiebert, *Mark: A Portrait of the Servant* (1974); W. L. Lane, *The Gospel According to Mark.* New International Commentary on the New Testament (1974); W. Hendriksen, *Exposition of the Gospel According to Mark* (1975); E. Trocme, *The Formation of the Gospel According to Mark* (1975); H. B. Swete, *Commentary on Mark* (1977); H. Vos, *Mark* (1978); J. A. Alexander, *Commentary on the Gospel of Mark* (1980).

MARKET (Heb. *ma'ărāb*). In the NT the Gk. word *'agora* is rendered "market place" and

The agora (market place) at Smyrna

generally denotes any place of public resort in towns or cities where trials are held (Acts 16:19), where citizens resort (17:17), and where commodities are displayed for sale (Mark 7:4). From this is derived *'agoraios*, "relating to the market place," and rendered "wicked men from the market place" (Acts 17:5). It is rendered "courts" in Acts 19:38, where it refers to judicial days or assemblies. Agoras in the cities of Greece or Greek cities of Asia Minor were more than markets; they were centers of life. There one might find temples, law courts, and government offices, as well as commercial facilities. Markets in the East were held at or near the gates of cities, where goods were displayed either in tents or the open air (2 Kings 7:18).   H.F.V.

MA'ROTH (ma'rōth; "bitterness"). A town W of Judah, not far from Jerusalem, on the route of the invading Assyrian army from Lachish (Mic. 1:12).

MARRIAGE. The rendering of several words and phrases in the Heb. and Gk., meaning to be "master"; to "take," that is, a wife; to "magnify" or "lift up" a woman; to "contract"; to "dwell together"; to "perform the duty of a brother"; to "become," that is, the wife of one. In all the Heb. Scriptures there is no single word for the estate of marriage or to express the abstract idea of *wedlock*.

Origin. Marriage is a divine institution designed to form a permanent union between man and woman that they might be helpful to one another (Gen. 2:18). Moses presents it as the deepest corporeal and spiritual unity of man and woman, and monogamy as the form of marriage ordained by God (2:24; cf. Matt. 19:5). Without the marital tie the inhabitants of this world would have been a mixed multitude. The family circle, family instruction, and parental love and care would have been altogether unknown.

Temporary Reactions. At an early period the original law, as made known to Adam, was violated through the degeneracy of his descendants, and concubinage and polygamy became common. The patriarchs themselves took more than one wife. Abraham, at the instigation of Sarah, took her maid as his subordinate wife. Jacob was tricked, through the duplicity of Laban, into taking Leah first, and then Rachel, to whom he had been betrothed. Afterward, through the rivalry of the sisters, he took both their handmaids. From these facts it has been inferred that polygamy was not wrong in ancient times, nor at all opposed to the divine law as revealed to the Jews. But this is an unwarranted conclusion. It is indeed true (respect being had to the state of religious knowledge, the rude condition of society, and the views prevalent in the world) that the practice could not infer, in the case of individuals, the same amount of criminality as would necessarily adhere to it now, amid the clear light of gospel

times. But still, all along it was a departure from the divine law.

For the reasons given above it was tolerated but never with God's approval. Jesus told the Jews, "Because of your hardness of heart, Moses permitted you to divorce your wives; but from the beginning it has not been this way" (Matt. 19:3-8). The Mosaic law aimed at mitigating, rather than removing, evils that were inseparable from the state of society in that day. Its enactments were directed to the discouragement of polygamy; to prevent the injustice frequently consequent upon the exercise of the rights of a father or a master; to bring divorce under some restriction; and to enforce purity of life during the maintenance of the matrimonial bond.

Laws of Intermarriage. An important feature of the law of Moses is the restraint that it imposes upon marriage within certain degrees of relationship and affinity:

Between an Israelite and a Foreigner. The only distinct prohibition in the Mosaic law refers to the Canaanites, with whom the Israelites were not to marry, on the ground that it would lead them to idolatry (Ex. 34:15-16; Deut. 7:3-4). The legal disabilities resting upon the Ammonites and the Moabites (23:3) totally forbade marriage between them and Israelite women but permitted that of Israelites with Moabite women (Ruth 1:4). The prohibition against marriages with the Edomites and Egyptians was less stringent, as a male of those nations received the right of marriage on his admission to full citizenship in the third generation of proselytism (Deut. 23:7-8). Thus the prohibition was *total* in regard to Canaanites on either side, *total* on the side of males in regard to the Ammonites and Moabites, and *temporary* on the side of males in regard to the Edomites and Egyptians. In the case of wives, proselytism was not necessary, but it was so in the case of husbands.

Between Israelites and Israelites. The law began (Lev. 18:6-8) with the general prohibition against marriage between a man and "any blood relative." This was followed by special prohibitions against marriage with a (1) mother, (2) stepmother, (3) sister or half-sister, (4) granddaughter, (5) daughter of a stepmother, (6) aunt, (7) wife or uncle on the father's side, (8) daughter-in-law, (9) brother's wife (unless he died childless; *see* Marriage, Levirate), (10) a woman and her daughter, whether both together or in succession, or a woman and her granddaughter, (11) two sisters at the same time, (12) mother-in-law. The case of a daughter being taken in marriage is not mentioned, simply because it was regarded as unlikely to occur; that of a full sister is included in no. 3, and of a mother-in-law in no. 10. Breaches of nos. 1, 2, 3, 8, and 12 were to be followed by the death or extermination of the offender (Deut. 27:20, 22-23), whereas the threat held out against nos. 6, 7, and 9 was that the guilty parties should "bear their sin" and "die childless" (Lev. 20:19-21). These prohibitions were based upon moral propriety, heathen practices, and social convenience.

In addition to the above, there were special prohibitions: (1) The high priest was forbidden to marry anyone except a virgin selected from among his own people (Lev. 21:13-14). (2) The priests were forbidden to marry prostitutes and divorced women (21:7). (3) Heiresses were prohibited from marrying outside of their own tribe (Num. 36:5-9; cf. Tobit 7:10). (4) Persons defective in physical powers were not to intermarry with Israelites (Deut. 23:1). A wife divorced by her husband and married to another man, if her second husband died or divorced her, could not revert to her first husband (Deut. 24:1-4). Such a marriage would lower the dignity of the woman and make her appear too much like property. Such prohibition was also intended to prevent a frivolous severance of the marriage tie and to fortify the marital bond. In the Christian church we find that bishops and deacons are prohibited from having more than one wife, probably referring to a second marriage of any kind. A similar prohibition applied to those entered upon the church records as *widows* (which see). They must have been the wife of one man, that is, probably, not remarried.

Marriage Customs.

Age of Marriage. With regard to age, no restriction is pronounced in the Bible. Early marriage is spoken of with approval in several passages (Prov. 2:17; 5:18; Isa. 62:5), and, in reducing this general statement to the more definite one of years, we must take into account the early age at which persons arrive at puberty in oriental countries. The Talmudists forbade marriage in the case of a man under thirteen years and a day, and in the case of a woman under twelve years and a day. The usual age appears to have been higher, about eighteen years.

Selection of Bride. Perhaps in imitation of the Father of the universe, who provided Adam with a wife, fathers from the beginning considered it their duty and prerogative to secure wives for their sons (Gen. 24:3-4; 38:6; etc.). In the absence of the father the responsibility of selection was passed to the mother (21:21). In some cases the proposal was made by the father of the girl (Ex. 2:21). Occasionally the whole business of selecting the wife was committed to a friend.

The Betrothal. The selection of the bride was followed by the espousal, which was not altogether like our "engagement" but was a formal proceeding, undertaken by a friend or legal representative on the part of the bridegroom and by the parents on the part of the bride. It was confirmed by oaths and accompanied with presents to the bride. These presents were described by different terms, that to the bride by "a dowry" (Heb. *mōhar*) and that to the relatives by "a

present" (Heb. *mattān*). Thus Shechem offered "ever so much bridal payment and gift" (Gen. 34:12), the former for the bride and the latter for the relatives. It has been supposed, indeed, that the *mohar* was a price paid to the father for the sale of his daughter. Such a custom undoubtedly prevails in certain parts of the East at the present day, but it does not appear to have been the case with free women in patriarchal times. It would undoubtedly be expected that the *mohar* should be proportioned to the position of the bride and that a poor man could not on that account afford to marry a rich wife (1 Sam. 18:23). A "settlement," in the modern sense of the term, that is, a written document securing property to the wife, did not come into use until the post-Babylonian period: the only instance we have of one is in Tobit 7:14, where it is described as an "instrument." The Talmudists called it a *ketubah* and have laid down minute directions as to the disposal of the sum secured in a treatise of the Mishna expressly on that subject. The act of betrothal was celebrated by a feast, and among the more modern Jews it is the custom in some parts for the bridegroom to place a ring on the bride's finger. Some writers have endeavored to prove that the rings mentioned in the OT (Ex. 35:22; Isa. 3:21) were nuptial rings, but there is not the slightest evidence of this. The ring was nevertheless regarded among the Hebrews as a token of fidelity (Gen. 41:42) and of adoption into a family (Luke 15:22).

Marriage Ceremonies. Before the time of Moses, when the proposal was accepted, the marriage price paid, and the gifts distributed, the bridegroom was at liberty to move the bride at once to his own home (Gen. 24:63-67). Isaac and Rebekah's experience was an unusual case, because of the bride's being secured at a distance, while the bridegroom remained at home. Usually the marriage took place at the home of the bride's parents and was celebrated by a feast to which friends and neighbors were invited and which lasted seven days (Gen. 29:22, 27). The word *wedding* does not occur in the OT; but it is probable that some ratification of the espousal with an oath took place (*see* Prov. 2:17; Ezek. 16:8; Mal. 2:14) and that a blessing was pronounced (Gen. 24:60; Ruth 4:10-12). But the essence of the ceremony consisted in the removal of the bride from her father's house to that of the bridegroom or his father. There seems, indeed, to be a literal truth in the Heb. expression "to take" a wife (Gen. 21:21; 24:3, 38; 26:34; *see* marg.), for the ceremony appears to have mainly consisted in the taking. After putting on festive dress, placing a "garland" on his head (Isa. 61:10; "crown," Song of Sol. 3:11, marg., "wreath"), the bridegroom set forth from his house, attended by his groomsmen (cf. Judg. 14:11; Matt. 9:15), preceded by a band of musicians or singers (Gen. 31:27; Jer. 7:34; 16:9; 1 Macc. 9:39), and accompanied by persons bearing lamps (2 Esd. 10:2; Matt. 25:7; cf. Jer. 25:10; Rev. 18:23). Having reached the house of the bride, who with her companions anxiously expected his arrival (Matt. 25:1, 6), he conducted the whole party back to his own or his father's house, with every demonstration of gladness (Ps. 45:15). On their way back they were joined by a party of young girls (virgins), friends of the bride and bridegroom, who were in waiting to catch the procession as it passed (Matt. 25:6). The inhabitants of the place pressed out into the streets to watch the procession (Song of Sol. 3:11). At the house a feast was prepared, to which all the friends and neighbors were invited (Gen. 29:22; Matt. 22:1-10; Luke 14:8; John 2:2), and the festivities were protracted for seven or even fourteen days (Judg. 14:12; Tobit 8:19). The guests were provided by the host with wedding clothes (Matt. 22:11), and the feast was enlivened with riddles (Judg. 14:12) and other amusements. The bridegroom now entered into direct communication with the bride, and the "friend of the bridegroom . . . rejoices greatly" at hearing the voice of the bridegroom conversing with her (John 3:29), which he regarded as a satisfactory testimony of the success of his share in the work. The last act in the ceremony was the conducting of the bride to the bridal chamber (Heb. *ḥeder,* Judg. 15:1; Joel 2:16), where a canopy, named a *ḥūppâ,* was prepared (cf. Ps. 19:5; Joel 2:16). The bride was still completely veiled, explaining the deception practiced on Jacob (Gen. 29:23, 25). A newly married man was exempt from military service, or from any public business that might draw him away from his home, for the space of a year (Deut. 24:5). A similar privilege was granted to one who was betrothed (20:7).

A Jewish wedding feast

Marriage Relation. In considering the social and domestic conditions of married life among the Hebrews, we must, in the first place, take into account the position generally assigned to women in their social scale. There is abundant evidence that women, whether married or unmarried, went about with their faces unveiled (Gen. 12:14; 24:16, 65; 29:11; 1 Sam. 1:13). Women not infrequently held important offices. They took their part in matters of public interest (Ex. 15:20; 1 Sam. 18:6-7); in short, they enjoyed as much freedom in ordinary life as the women of our own country. If such was her general position, it is certain that the wife must have exercised an important influence in her own home. She appears to have taken her part in family affairs and even to have enjoyed a considerable amount of independence (2 Kings 4:8; Judg. 4:18-22; 1 Sam. 25:14, 18-37; Prov. 31:10-31; etc.).

Dependence of the Wife. And yet the dependence of the wife on her husband is shown by the Heb. appellation for husband (*ba'al,* Ex. 21:3, 22), lit., "lord, master," and is seen in the conduct of Sarah, who speaks of her husband Abraham as "my lord" (Gen. 18:12). From this mastery of the husband over the wife arose the different standard of virtue that existed in married life. The wife, subject to her husband as master, was obliged to regard the sanctity of the marriage relation, and any unchastity on her part was visited with death. The husband could take any unmarried woman he chose and violate the laws of chastity, as we understand them, with impunity (38:24). This absolute sanctity of marriage on the part of the wife was acknowledged by other nations of antiquity, such as Egypt (12:15-19) and Philistia (20:1-18; 26:7-11). Arising from the previously existing inequality of husband and wife and the prevailing notion that the husband was lord over his wife, Moses could neither impose the same obligation of fidelity nor confer the same rights on both. This is evident from the following facts: (1) The husband in the case of the wife's infidelity could command her death as well as that of her lover (Lev. 20:10; Deut. 22:22; Ezek. 16:38-41; John 8:3-5). (2) If he became suspicious of his wife he could bring her to the priest and have administered to her the "water of bitterness" (Num. 5:12-31). But if the husband was guilty of criminal intercourse with an unmarried woman, no statute enabled the wife to arraign him for a breach of marriage or infringement of her or their rights. Should he sin with a married woman, it was the injured husband that could demand the death of the seducer, not the wife of the criminal. (3) If the wife vowed anything to the Lord, or imposed upon herself voluntary obligations to Jehovah, her husband could nullify them (Num. 30:6-8). (4) The husband could divorce his wife if it so pleased him (Deut. 24:1-4).

Protection of the Wife. The woman was protected by the following laws: (1) The daughter of an Israelite sold by her father as a maidservant (i.e., housekeeper and concubine), who did not please her master, was not to be treated as were menservants, namely, be sent away free at the end of six years; but she was provided for as follows: She could be redeemed, that is, another Israelite could buy her for a concubine, but she could not be sold to an alien (Ex. 21:7-8). She might be given to her purchaser's son, in which case she was to be treated as a daughter. If he gave the son an additional wife, he was not to "reduce her food, her clothing, or her conjugal rights" (vv. 9-10). If these three things were not provided, then she was to "go out for nothing, without payment" (v. 11). (2) If her husband maliciously charged a newly married woman with lack of chastity, he was to be scourged and lost his right of divorce (Deut. 22:13-19). (3) If she had children they were to render equal obedience to her as to the father (Ex. 20:12; Deut. 27:16). (4) As has already been stated, the husband was not to vex his wife by marrying her sister (Lev. 18:18). (5) The husband was forbidden to transfer the primogeniture from the son of a less beloved wife to the child of his favorite wife. (6) If her husband disliked her, he was not arbitrarily to dismiss her but to give her a "certificate of divorce" (Deut. 24:1). (7) If divorced, or if her husband died, the woman was free and at liberty to marry another (Deut. 24:2).

Social and Domestic Conditions. In early times the oriental woman appears to have enjoyed much freedom. She, whether married or single, went about with her face unveiled (Gen. 12:14; 24:16, 65; 29:11; 1 Sam. 1:13); she might meet and converse with men, even strangers, in a public place (Gen. 24:24-25, 45-47; 29:9-12; 1 Sam. 9:11-13); she might be found alone in the country without any reflection on her character (Deut. 22:25-27), or she might appear in a court of justice (Num. 27:1-2). If such was her general position, we can readily accord her a considerable amount of independence and influence at home. Thus we find her entertaining guests (2 Kings 4:8), sometimes in the absence of her husband (Judg. 4:18), and even against his wishes (1 Sam. 25:14, 18-19); she conferred with her husband respecting the marriage of her children (Gen. 27:46) and even sharply criticized his conduct (1 Sam. 25:25; 2 Sam. 6:20). The ideal relations between husband and wife appear to have been those of tenderness and affection, frequent reference being made to his love for her (Gen. 24:67; 29:18). The wife was the husband's consolation in bereavement (24:67), and her grief at his loss presented a picture of the most abject woe (Joel 1:8). Polygamy, of course, produced jealousies and quarrels (Gen. 30:1-24; 1 Sam. 1:2, 6), and the purchase of wives and the small liberties allowed daughters in the choice of husbands must

have resulted in many unhappy unions. In the NT the mutual relations of husband and wife are a subject of frequent exhortation (Eph. 5:22-33; Col. 3:18-19; Titus 2:4-5; 1 Pet. 3:1-7).

Duties. In a Hebrew household the wife had general superintendence of the domestic arrangements, such as cooking (Gen. 18:6; 2 Sam. 13:8-9), the distribution of food at the meals (Prov. 31:15), and the manufacture of cloth and clothing (31:13, 21-22).

Figurative. Marriage is illustrative of Jehovah's relation with Israel (Isa. 54:5; 62:4-5; Jer. 3:1; Hos. 2:16-20). In the NT the image of the bridegroom is transferred from Jehovah to Christ (Matt. 9:15; John 3:29) and that of the bride to the church (2 Cor. 11:2; Eph. 5:23-24, 32; Rev. 19:7; 21:2, 9; 22:17).

BIBLIOGRAPHY: W. Smith and S. Cheetham, *A Dictionary of Christian Antiquities* (1880), 2:1092-115; W. R. Smith, *Religion of the Semites* (1894); id., *Kinship and Marriage in Early Arabia* (1903); E. A. Westermark, *The History of Human Marriage*, 3 vols. (1922); M. Burrows, *The Basis of Israelite Marriage* (1938); W. Goodsell, *A History of Marriage and the Family* (1939), pp. 1-53; E. Neufeld, *Ancient Hebrew Marriage Laws* (1944); D. R. Mace, *Hebrew Marriage* (1953); H. N. Granquist, *Marriage Conditions in a Palestinian Village*, 2 vols. (1975).

MARRIAGE, CHRISTIAN. Christianity confirms, simplifies, and vindicates from abuse the original and sacred ordinance of marriage. The stability and purity of the church and state have been proportionate to the popular and legal stability of the marriage relationship. The original appointment of monogamy is confirmed (Matt. 19:6; Mark 10:6-8). The presence of Jesus at the wedding in Cana happily illustrates the feeling and teaching of Christianity respecting marriage. Christ taught the divine origin and sacredness of this institution. It is more than filial duty; it is unifying. The husband and wife become one through the purity and intensity of mutual love; common interests are necessitated by common affection (Matt. 19:5-6; Eph. 5:31), only one ground for divorce being lawful (Matt. 19:9). The utmost that may be inferred from the expression "who made themselves eunuchs for the sake of the kingdom of heaven" (19:12) is that marriage is not binding upon every member of the race, and that devotion or discretion may make it expedient to renounce or defer it. The example of Peter (Matt. 8:14; Mark 1:30; Luke 4:38) and the express teaching of NT writers (1 Tim. 4:3; 5:14; Heb. 13:4) are in harmony with the conduct of Christ respecting the sanctity of the marriage relationship. The counsel of Paul to the Corinthian church (1 Cor. 7), evidently in reply to their request, is entirely consistent with the general doctrine of the NT. He guards marriage so carefully that even to those who are joined to unbelievers the advice is given not to disturb their relationship except by mutual consent and for mutual good. "According to the principles thus laid down, marriage is not merely a civil contract; the Scriptures make it the most sacred relation of life; and nothing can be imagined more contrary to their spirit than the notion that a personal agreement, ratified in a human court, satisfies the obligation of this ordinance."

Matrimony was elevated to the dignity of the sacrament in the Roman Catholic church mainly on the ground of the apostle's words "This mystery is great; but I am speaking with reference to Christ and the church" (Eph. 5:32); in the Vulg. the Gk. being rendered *sacramentum*. However "it is not this that is conveyed by the passage, as indeed, in general, marriage 'has from Christ neither a sacramental *institution*, nor *form*, nor *substance*, nor *end*,' but it is rather the sacredly ideal and deeply moral character, which is forever assured to marriage by this typical significance in the Christian view" (Meyer, *Com.*, ad loc.; Pope, *Christian Theology*, 3:237-43, 308).

MARRIAGE, LEVIRATE (from Lat. *levir*, a "brother-in-law"). The marriage of a man with his deceased brother's widow, in the event of the brother's dying childless. The first instance of this custom occurs in the patriarchal period, where Onan is called upon to marry his brother Er's widow (Gen. 38:8). The Levirate marriage was not peculiar to the Jews; it has been found to exist in many Eastern countries, particularly in Arabia and among the tribes of the Caucasus. The Mosaic provision was as follows: If brothers (on the father's side) lived together, that is, in the same place, and one of them died childless, the wife was not to go outside and marry a stranger; but the surviving brother was to take her as his wife. The firstborn son by her took the name of the deceased, thus continuing his name in the family register, that it might not perish out of Israel. In case the brother-in-law did not wish to marry the widow, she might cite him legally before the elders of the place. If, after conference with them, he still persisted in declaring his unwillingness, he was not compelled to do the duty of a brother-in-law. But he was obliged to submit to the humiliation of having his sandal pulled off by his sister-in-law in the presence of the elders and of having his face spat upon. The one act denoted that he thus gave up all claim to his deceased brother's estate; the other was an act expressive of contempt (Deut. 25:5-10). From Ruth 4:1-10 it would appear that in the case of the refusal of the brother-in-law to take the widow, then the next male relative had the right to do so. The divine sanction that the Mosaic law gave to Levirate marriage is not to be regarded as merely an accommodation to a popular prejudice. Such marriage was not strictly commanded, but it was considered a duty of love, the nonfulfillment of which brought reproach and ridicule on the man and his house. It did not abolish the general prohibition of marriage with a brother's wife but proceeded from one and the same principle with it. By the *prohibition* the brother's house was preserved in its integrity; by this *command* it was raised to a permanent condition. In both cases the dead brother was honored and fraternal love preserved as the moral foundation of his house. Based upon such a marriage as this was the ground for the question asked of our Lord by the Sadducees (Matt. 22:23-30). The rabbis taught that in the next world a widow who had been taken by her brother-in-law reverted to her first husband at the resurrection. Christ answered both parties by the declaration that "in the resurrection they neither marry, nor are given in marriage."

BIBLIOGRAPHY: M. Epstein, *Marriage Laws in the Bible and the Talmud* (1942), pp. 86-99; D. A. Leggett, *Levirate and Goel Institutions in the Old Testament* (1974); C. J. Barber, *Ruth: An Expositional Commentary* (1983), pp. 52-60, 95-116.

MARROW. The soft oily substance contained in the hollow bones of animals (Heb. *mōaḥ*, Job 21:24; Gk. *muelos*, Heb. 4:12).

Figurative. "Choice pieces with marrow" (Isa. 25:6; NIV, "best of meats") is an expression symbolizing the full enjoyment of blessedness in the perfected kingdom of God. "Marrow" in Heb. 4:12 is used figuratively for the most secret thoughts of a person.

MAR'SENA (mar'se-na; cf. Avestan marshanā, "forgetful man"). Perhaps *nobleman*, one of the "seven princes [satraps or viziers] of Persia and Media" in the time of Ahasuerus (Esther 1:14), about 479 B.C.

MARSH (Heb. *gebe'*, a "reservoir," Ezek. 47:11). A swamp or wet piece of land. The place referred to by Ezekiel is the "Valley of Salt," near the Dead Sea; for there the Kidron, the course of which the prophet describes the holy waters as following, empties.

MARS' HILL (Gk. *Aries Pagos*, "hill of Aries," Greek god of war, Roman Mars, Acts 17:22, KJV). Another name for the *Areopagus* (which see).

MAR'THA (mar'tha; Gk. from Aram., "lady, mistress"). The sister of Lazarus and Mary, who all resided in the same house at Bethany (Luke 10:38-41; John 11:1-39; 12:2). Martha appears to have been at the head of the household (Luke 10:38) and from that circumstance has been thought to have been a widow. This is, however, uncertain, and it is generally supposed that the two sisters (unmarried) managed the household for their brother. The incident narrated by Luke (10:38-42) shows that Jesus was intimate with the family and was at home in their house. It also brings out the contrary dispositions of the two sisters. Martha hastens to provide suitable entertainment for their friend and His followers, while Mary sits at His feet listening to His gracious discourse. The busy, anxious Martha, annoyed at the inactivity of Mary, complains impatiently to Jesus, "Lord, do You not care that my sister has left me to do all the serving alone? Then tell her to help me." This brought from the Master the often-quoted reply, "Only a few things are necessary, . . . for Mary has chosen the good part, which shall not be taken away from her." At the death of Lazarus their respective characters are portrayed: Martha active, Mary meditative; Martha reproachful and objecting, Mary silent but immediately obedient to the summons of Jesus; Martha accepting Jesus as the Christ and sharing in the belief of a resurrection but not believing, as Mary did, in Jesus as "the life." All that is recorded of Martha in addition is that at a supper given to Jesus and His disciples at Bethany, at which Lazarus was present, she, as usual, busied herself with serving.

BIBLIOGRAPHY: J. D. Jones, *The Lord of Life and Death* (n.d.), pp. 93-107; J. N. Sanders, *New Testament Studies* (1954-55), pp. 29ff.

MARTYR (Gk. *martus,* so rendered only in KJV, Acts 22:20; Rev. 2:13; 17:6; and in the NIV only in Acts 22:20). A *witness* (which see), and generally so given. The meaning of the word *martyr,* which has now become the most usual, is one who has proved the strength and genuineness of his faith in Christ by undergoing a violent death. *Stephen* (which see) in this sense was the first martyr, and the spiritual honors of his death tended in no small degree to raise to the most extravagant estimation, in the early church, the value of the testimony of blood. Eventually a martyr's death was supposed, on the alleged authority of the following texts, to cancel the sins of the past life (Mark 10:39; Luke 12:50), to answer for baptism, and at once to secure admission into paradise (Matt. 5:10-12).

BIBLIOGRAPHY: H. B. Workman, *Persecution in the Early Church* (n.d.); F. J. Foakes-Jackson and K. Lake, *The Beginnings of Christianity* (1933), 5:30-37; N. Turner, *Christian Words* (1980), pp. 272-74.

MA'RY (māˈri; Gk. *Maria* or *Mariam;* from Heb. *miryām,* "obstinacy, rebellion").

The Mother of Jesus. Mary was the daughter of Eli or Heli, of the tribe of Judah and of the lineage of David, hence in the royal line (Luke 3:23).

The Annunciation. In the summer of the year known as 5 B.C. Mary, a virgin betrothed to Joseph, was living at Nazareth. At this time the angel Gabriel came to her with a message from God and announced that she was to be the mother of the long-expected Messiah—that by the power of the Holy Spirit the everlasting Son of the Father should be born of her (Luke 1:26-38; cf. Rom. 1:3).

Visit to Elizabeth. Informed by the angel that her cousin Elizabeth was within three months of delivering a child, Mary set off to visit her, either

at Hebron or Juttah. Immediately upon her entrance into the house "Elizabeth heard Mary's greeting, the baby leaped in her womb; and Elizabeth was filled with the Holy Spirit. And she cried out with a loud voice, and said, 'Blessed among women are you, and blessed is the fruit of your womb!' " Mary stayed with her cousin about three months, then returned to her own house (1:36-56).

Married to Joseph. In a few months Joseph found that Mary was with child, and he determined to "put her away secretly" (*see* Deut. 24:1) instead of yielding her up to the law to suffer the penalty he supposed she had incurred (22:23-24). But being assured of the truth by an angel, he took her as his wife (Matt. 1:18-25).

Mother of Jesus. Soon after Joseph and Mary went to Bethlehem to be enrolled for the taxing, and while there Jesus was born and laid in a manger (Luke 2:1-7). On the eighth day Jesus was circumcised. On the fortieth day after the nativity—until which time Mary could not leave the house (Lev. 12:2-4)—she presented herself with her baby for their purification in the Temple. The poverty of Joseph and Mary is alluded to in the mention of their offering, "a pair of turtle-doves, or two young pigeons." There she met Simeon and the prophetess Anna and heard their thanksgiving and prophecy (Luke 2:21-38). Returning to Bethlehem, Mary and Joseph were warned of the purpose of Herod and fled to Egypt. Returning the next year, they went to Nazareth (Matt. 2:12-23). At the age of twelve Jesus accompanied His family to Jerusalem, and Mary was temporarily separated from Him (Luke 2:42-50), A.D. 8. Jesus continued to increase "in wisdom and stature," and Mary "treasured all these things in her heart."

Was Mary the Mother of Any Children Other Than Jesus? The question whether or not Mary was the mother of any children other than Jesus has caused almost endless controversy. Of course, the advocates of her perpetual virginity assert that she was not. From the accounts in Matt. 13:55-56 and Mark 6:3, it would seem more than likely that she had a number of children. This presumption is increased by the fact that the persons named as the "brothers" of Jesus are mentioned in connection and in company with His *sisters* and *mother.* Indeed, the denial of the natural interpretation of these passages owes its origin, in all probability, to the tradition of perpetual virginity, the offspring of the false notion of the superior sanctity of celibacy.

Subsequent Mention of Mary. Mary is mentioned only four more times after our Lord's ministry commenced. These four occasions are: *the marriage at Cana,* where Jesus solemnly withdraws Himself from her authority (John 2:1-4); *at Capernaum,* where at a public gathering Mary desires to speak to Jesus, and He seems to refuse to admit any authority on the part of His relatives, or any privilege on account of their relationship (John 2:12; Matt. 12:46-50); *at the crucifixion,* where Christ, with almost His last words, commends His mother to the care of the disciple whom He loved, and from that hour John assures us that he took her into his home (John 19:25-27); *after the ascension,* engaged in prayer in the upper room in Jerusalem, with other faithful followers of the Lord (Acts 1:14).

Tradition. Tradition and Roman Catholic speculation have viewed Mary as guarded from actual sin by divine grace. This notion, which prevailed from the twelfth century, was developed into a papal decree of December 8, 1854. On November 1, 1950, the bull *Munificentissimus Deus* declared the dogma of the Assumption of Mary. This dogma asserts "that the Virgin Mary, the Immaculate Mother of God, when the course of her life was finished, was taken up, body and soul, into the glory of heaven" (*Acta Apostolicae Sedis,* 32 [1950], pp. 753-73).

Character. "Her faith and humility exhibit themselves in her immediate surrender of herself to the divine will, though ignorant how that was to be accomplished (Luke 1:38); her energy and earnestness in her journey from Nazareth to Hebron (v. 39); her happy thankfulness in her song of joy (v. 48); her silent, musing thoughtfulness in her pondering over the shepherds' visit (2:19), and in her keeping her Son's words in her heart (v. 51), though she could not fully understand their import. In a word, so far as Mary is portrayed to us in Scripture, she is, as we should have expected, the most tender, the most faithful, humble, patient, and loving of women, but a *woman* still" (Smith, *Dict.*).

Mary Magdale'ne (mag-da-lē'ne, or commonly mag'da-len; "of Magdala").

Name. Of this there are four explanations: (1) The most natural is that she came from the town of *Magadan* (which see; the name of the town is frequently given as Magdala; it means "tower," or "fortress"), probably situated on the western shore of Lake Tiberias, and the same as that of the modern village of El-Mejdel. (2) The Talmudists make mention of a Miriam Megaddela: "Miriam with the braided locks," which Lightfoot considers as identical with "the woman who was a sinner" (Luke 7:37). (3) Jerome sees in her name and that of her town the old *Migdol* ("watchtower") and says that the name denotes the steadfastness of her faith. (4) Origen, taking the more common meaning of *gādal* (to "be great"), "sees in her name a prophecy of her spiritual greatness as having ministered to her Lord and been the first witness of the resurrection."

Personal History. Mary Magdalene enters the gospel narrative, with certain other women, as ministering to Jesus "out of their private means" (Luke 8:2-3); all of them being moved by gratitude for their deliverance from "evil spirits and sicknesses." Of Mary it is said that "seven demons

[*daimonia*] had gone out" of her (v. 2; Mark 16:9). This life of ministration brought Mary Magdalene into companionship of the closest nature with Salome, the mother of James and John (15:40), and also with Mary the mother of the Lord (John 19:25). They "were standing at a distance, seeing these things" (Luke 23:49), during the closing hours of Christ's agony on the cross. The same close association that drew them together there is seen afterward. She remained by the cross till Jesus' death, and she waited till the body was taken down and wrapped in the linen cloth and placed in the tomb of Joseph of Arimathea (Matt. 27:61; Mark 15:47; Luke 23:55). She, with Salome and Mary, the mother of James, "brought spices, that they might come and anoint" the body (Mark 16:1). The next morning, accordingly, in the earliest dawn (Matt. 28:1; Mark 16:2), they came to the tomb. Mary Magdalene had been to the tomb, had found it empty, and had seen the angels (Matt. 28:5; Mark 16:5). She went with her cry of sorrow to Peter and John (Luke 24:10; John 20:1-2) and, returning with them, tarried after they went back. Looking into the tomb, she saw the angels, and she replied to their question as to her reason for weeping, "They have taken away my Lord, and I do not know where they have laid Him." Turning back, she saw Jesus, but did not at first recognize Him. Recalled to consciousness by His utterance of her name, she exclaimed, "Rabboni" (Teacher) and rushed forward to embrace His feet. Jesus' response was to teach her a spiritual dependence upon Christ that could live without His visible presence: "Stop clinging to Me, for I have not yet ascended to the Father." Mary then went to the disciples and told them what she had seen and heard (John 20:11-18).

Mary Magdalene has long been in popular tradition equivalent to "Mary the sinner" and has been identified with the penitent woman who anointed Jesus. There were probably two anointings recorded in the gospels, the acts of two different women: one in some city unnamed, during our Lord's Galilean ministry (Luke 7:37-38), and the other at Bethany, before the last entry into Jerusalem (Matt. 26:7; Mark 14:3; John 12:3), by the sister of Lazarus. There is no reliable evidence to connect Mary Magdalene with either anointing. (1) When her name appears in Luke 8:2 there is not one word to connect it with the history immediately preceding. (2) The belief that Mary of Bethany and Mary Magdalene are identical is more startling. The epithet *Magdalene,* whatever may be its meaning, seems chosen for the express purpose of distinguishing her from the other Marys. No one evangelist gives the slightest hint of identity. Nor is this lack of evidence in the NT itself compensated by any such weight of authority as would indicate a really trustworthy tradition (Smith, *Dict.,* s.v.).

Mary, Sister of Lazarus. The facts about her are few. She and her sister Martha appear in Luke 10:38-42 receiving Christ in their house. Mary sat listening eagerly for every word from the divine Teacher and was commended by Jesus as having "chosen the good part," the one thing necessary, while "Martha was distracted with all her preparations." The next mention of Mary is in connection with the raising of Lazarus (John 11:1-45). She sat still in the house until Martha came to her secretly and said, "The Teacher is here, and is calling for you." She arose hastily to go to meet Him. At first she gave way to complaint: "Lord, if You had been here, my brother would not have died." But her great joy and love revived upon her brother's return to life, and found expression in the anointing at the last feast of Bethany (Matt. 26:6-13; Mark 14:3-9; John 12:1-8). Matthew and Mark do not mention her by name. Of her subsequent history we know nothing; the ecclesiastical traditions about her are based on the unfounded hypothesis of her identity with Mary Magdalene.

Mary, the Wife of Clopas (Gk. *Maria hē tou Klōpa*, KJV "of Cleophas"). In John's gospel we read that "there were standing by the cross of Jesus His mother, and His mother's sister, Mary the wife of Clopas, and Mary Magdalene" (John 19:25). The same group of women is described by Matthew as consisting of "Mary Magdalene, along with Mary the mother of James and Joseph, and the mother of the sons of Zebedee" (Matt. 27:56) and by Mark as "Mary Magdalene, and Mary the mother of James the Less and Joses, and Salome" (Mark 15:40). From a comparison of these passages it appears that Mary of Clopas and Mary the mother of James the Less and Joseph are the same person and that she was the sister of Mary the mother of Jesus. In answer to the alleged improbability of two sisters having the same name, it may be said that Miriam, the sister of Moses, may have been the holy woman after whom Jewish mothers called their daughters. This is on the hypothesis that the two names are identical, but on a close examination of the Greek text we find that it is possible that this was not the case. The virgin Mary is Mariam; her sister is Maria. Mary of Clopas was probably the elder sister of the Lord's mother. She is brought before us for the first time on the day of the crucifixion—in the parallel passages already quoted from Matthew, Mark, and John. In the evening of the same day we find her sitting desolately at the tomb with Mary Magdalene (Matt. 27:61; Mark 15:47), and at the dawn of Easter morning was again there with sweet spices, which she had prepared on Friday night (Matt. 28:1; Mark 16:1; Luke 23:56), and was one of those who had "a vision of angels, who said that He was alive" (Luke 24:23). It is probable that Clopas was dead and that the two widowed sisters lived together in one house.

Mary, Mother of Mark. Also sister to Barnabas (cf. Col. 4:10). It would appear from Acts 4:37 and 12:12 that while the brother disposed of his property for the benefit of the church, the sister gave up her house as one of the places of meeting. The fact that Peter went to that house on his release from prison indicates that there was some special intimacy between them, and this is confirmed by the language he uses toward Mark as being his "son" (1 Pet. 5:13). "It has been surmised that filial anxiety about her welfare during the persecutions and the famine that harassed the church at Jerusalem was the chief cause of Mark's withdrawal from the missionary labors of Paul and Barnabas."

A Christian woman at Rome to whom Paul sent greetings, as to one "who has worked hard for you" (Rom. 16:6).

BIBLIOGRAPHY: For *Mother of Jesus*, see: W. M. Ramsay, *The Education of Christ* (1898); A. T. Robertson, *The Mother of Jesus* (1963); W. M. Ramsay, *Was Christ Born in Bethlehem?* (1978).

For *Mary Magdalene*, see: S. J. Andrews, *The Life of Our Lord upon the Earth* (1978).

For *Mary, Sister of Lazarus*, see: J. D. Jones, *The Lord of Life and Death* (n.d.), pp. 123-37; M. L. Loane, *Mary of Bethany* (1949).

For *Mary, the Wife of Clopas*, see: J. R. Mackay, *Expository Times* 40 (1928-29): 319-21; E. F. F. Bishop, *Expository Times* 65 (1953-54): 382-83.

MASH (mash). One of the sons of Aram, the son of Shem (Gen. 10:23). In 1 Chron. 1:17 (and in Gen. 10:23 in the NIV) the name appears as Meshech.

MA'SHAL (ma'shal). A Levitical town in Asher (1 Chron. 6:74). It was assigned to the Gershonite Levites. Called Mishal in Josh. 19:26 (NASB and NIV; KJV is Misheal); 21:30 (NASB, KJV and NIV).

MAS'KIL (mas'kil). Appears in the titles of Pss. 32, 42, 44, 45, 52-55, 74, 78, 88, 89, 142; meaning uncertain.

MASON. *See* Handicrafts: Builder; Stoneworker; and also the article House.

MAS'REKAH (mas're-ka; "vineyard"). A city in Edom, and the native place of Samlah, an Edomite king (Gen. 36:36; 1 Chron. 1:47). It is Jebel el-Mushrak, twenty-two miles SW of Ma'an.

MAS'SA (mas'a; "burden"). A son of Ishmael (Gen. 25:14; 1 Chron. 1:30). His descendants were not improbably the *Masani,* who are placed by Ptolemy E of Arabia, near the borders of Babylonia. The Assyrian inscriptions name Massa with Tema and Nebaioth.

MAS'SAH (mas'a; "trial, temptation"). A name given to the place where the Israelites murmured for want of water (Ex. 17:7; Deut. 6:16; 9:22; 33:8); called also *Meribah* (which see).

MAST. *See* Ship.

MASTER.

1. A man who rules, governs, or directs. A possessor, owner (Heb. *'ādôn*), e.g., the "owner" of the hill of Samaria (1 Kings 16:24); a master of servants (Gen. 24:14, 27; 39:2, 7); of kings, as lords of their subjects (Isa. 26:13); also rendered "lord," as of a husband as lord of a wife (Gen. 18:12) or a ruler to whom honor is due (45:8); or one to whom respect is due, as a brother (Num. 12:11).

2. Gk. *kurios*, one who is "supreme" in authority, as in "no one can serve two masters" (Matt. 6:24; Mark 13:35; Luke 14:21-23; 16:13; Acts 16:16, 19; etc.), elsewhere rendered *lord* (which see).

3. A superintendent or overseer in a general sense, rendered by the Gk. *epistatēs*, "appointed over." This expression is used for *rabbi* (which see) by the disciples when addressing Jesus (Luke 5:5; 8:24; 9:33, 49; 17:13).

See also Chief; Head.

MASTICH. *See* Vegetable Kingdom.

MA'TRI (ma'trī). *See* Matrite.

MA'TRITE (ma'trīt; "rainy").

Benjamite family to which Saul the king of Israel belonged (1 Sam. 10:21), considerably before 1020 B.C.

MAT'TAN (mat'an; a "gift").

1. The priest of Baal slain before his altars in the idol temple at Jerusalem (2 Kings 11:18; 2 Chron. 23:17), 836 B.C. He probably accompanied Athaliah, the queen mother, from Samaria.

2. The father of Shephatiah, one of the officials who charged Jeremiah with treason and afterward cast him into prison (Jer. 38:1-6), before 588 B.C.

MAT'TANAH (mat'a-na; a "gift"). The fifty-third station of Israel, on the N side of Arnon (Num. 21:18-19). Probably to be identified with Khirbet el-Medeiyineh.

MATTANI'AH (mat-a-nī'a; "gift of Jehovah").

1. The original name of *Zedekiah* (which see), king of Judah, which was changed when Nebuchadnezzar placed him on the throne instead of his nephew Jehoiachin (2 Kings 24:17).

2. A Levite singer of the family of Asaph residing at Jerusalem after the captivity (1 Chron. 9:15), about 440 B.C. He is described as the son of Mica (Neh. 11:17; 12:35) and after the return from Babylon lived in the villages of the Netophathites (cf. 1 Chron. 9:16; Neh. 12:28), which the singers had built in the neighborhood of Jerusalem (12:29). As leader of the Temple choir after its restoration (11:17; 12:8) in the time of Nehemiah, he took part in the musical service that accompanied the dedication of the wall of Jerusalem (12:35). We find him among the Levites of the second rank, who were gatekeepers (12:25).

3. One of the fourteen sons of Heman, whose office it was to blow the horns in the Temple service as appointed by David. He had charge of the ninth division of musicians (1 Chron. 25:4, 16), about 975 B.C. He is possibly the same as the father of Jeiel, descendant of Asaph and ancestor of Jahaziel the Levite in the reign of Jehoshaphat (2 Chron. 20:14).

4. A descendant of Asaph, the Levite singer, who assisted in the purification of the Temple in the reign of Hezekiah (2 Chron. 29:13), c. 715 B.C.

5. An Israelite "of the sons of Elam" who divorced his Gentile wife after the Exile (Ezra 10:26), 456 B.C.

6-8. Three Israelites—one a descendant (or resident) of Zattu (Ezra 10:27), another "of the sons" (i.e., inhabitants) of Pahath-maob (10:30), and still another a descendant (or resident) of Bani (10:37)—who put away their Gentile wives after the captivity, 456 B.C.

9. A Levite, father of Zaccur and grandfather of Hanan, the latter of which had charge of the offerings for the Levites in the time of Nehemiah (Neh. 13:13), considerably before 444 B.C.

MAT'TATHA (mat'a-tha; "gift of Jehovah"). The son of Nathan and grandson of David, among the ancestry of our Lord (Luke 3:31).

MAT'TATHAH. *See* Mattatha; Mattattah.

MATTATHI'AS (mat-a-thī'as). Gk. form of Heb. Mattathiah ("gift of Jehovah").

1. The son of Amos and father of Joseph, in the genealogy of our Lord (Luke 3:25).

2. The son of Semein in the same catalog (Luke 3:26). "As no such name appears in the parallel passages of the Old Testament, and would here unduly protract the interval limited by other intimations of the generations, it is probably interpolated from No. 1" (Strong, *Harmony and Exposition of the Gospels*, p. 16).

MAT'TATTAH (mat'a-ta). An Israelite of the "sons" (inhabitants) of Hashum who put away his foreign wife after the Exile (Ezra 10:33; "Mattathah," KJV), about 456 B.C.

MATTENA'I (mat-te-nī; "liberal," probably a contraction of Mattaniah).

1, 2. Israelites, one a son (or citizen) of Hashum (Ezra 10:33), and the other of Bani (10:37), who put away their foreign wives after the captivity, 456 B.C.

3. A priest of the family of Joiarib, who lived in the time of Joiakim the son of Jeshua (Neh. 12:19), after 536 B.C.

MAT'THAN (math'an). The son of Eleazar and father of Jacob, which last was father of Joseph, "the husband of Mary" (Matt. 1:15-16), considerably before 40 B.C.

MAT'THAT (math'at; "gift," i.e., "of God").

1. The son of Levi and father of Eli, who was

the father of the virgin Mary (Luke 3:24), before 22 B.C.

2. The son of another Levi and father of Jorim (Luke 3:29).

MAT'THEW (math'u; contraction of Mattathias, "gift of Jehovah"). The son of a certain Alphaeus, surnamed Levi (Mark 2:14; Luke 5:27). It is not known whether his father was the same as the Alphaeus named as the father of James the Less, but he was probably another.

Residence and Profession. Matthew's residence was at Capernaum, and he was a publican or "tax-gatherer." There was at that time a large population surrounding the Lake of Gennesaret; its fisheries supplied a source of livelihood, and its surface was alive with busy navigation and traffic. A customhouse was established at Capernaum by the Romans, where Matthew was tax collector. The publicans proper were usually Romans of rank and wealth, who farmed out the business of collecting to resident deputies called *portitors*. It was to this class that Matthew belonged.

Call. While Matthew was thus occupied, "sitting in the tax office," Jesus said to him, "Follow Me!" He probably already knew Jesus, for he immediately "rose, and followed Him" (Matt. 9:9; Mark 2:14; Luke 5:27-28). Shortly after this Matthew "gave a big reception for Him in his house" (Luke 5:29; cf. Matt. 9:10; Mark 2:15) and perhaps as a farewell to his old associates, for "many tax-gatherers and sinners came and were dining" (Matt. 9:10). After this we find no mention of him except in the catalogs of the apostles (Luke 6:15) and his presence in the "upper room" in Jerusalem after our Lord's ascension (Acts 1:13). The gospel that bears his name was written by this apostle, according to the testimony of all antiquity. Tradition relates that Matthew preached in Judea after the ascension for twelve or fifteen years and then went to foreign nations.

BIBLIOGRAPHY: E. J. Goodspeed, *The Twelve* (1957), pp. 25-28, 41-43; id., *Matthew, Apostle and Evangelist* (1959); W. Barclay, *The Master's Men* (1960), pp. 58-68; J. D. Jones, *The Apostles of Christ* (1982), pp. 150-71.

MATTHEW, GOSPEL OF. The first book of the NT. It was undoubtedly placed first in the category of the four gospels because at an early date it was received as authentic and presented the life of Jesus Christ particularly as it affected Jews converted to Christianity.

Theme. The subject of the book is outlined in the first verse. The gospel of Matthew is "the book of the genealogy of Jesus Christ, the son of David, the son of Abraham" (Matt. 1:1). In this introduction our Lord is related to two of the most important OT covenants, the Davidic (2 Sam. 7:8-16) and the Abrahamic (Gen. 15:18). Matthew, accordingly, describes Jesus Christ in this twofold character. In line with the scope indicated in v. 1 of chap. 1 he sets forth first the King the son

of David, then the son of Abraham in His obedience unto death. In this book the covenant King of Israel, David's "righteous Branch" (Jer. 23:5; 33:15) is presented. The first twenty-five chapters deal with the King of the Davidic covenant; His royal birth in Bethlehem, fulfilling Mic. 5:2; the ministry of John the Baptist, the King's forerunner, fulfilling Mal. 3:1; the ministry of the King Himself, His rejection by the nation Israel, and His predictions of His second coming in power and great glory. S. Lewis Johnson says, "The theme of Matthew, then, is the presentation of the King and His kingdom to the nation in fulfillment of the OT prophecy" (*Bibliotheca Sacra* 112 [April 1955]: 144). Not until the closing part of the book (chaps. 26–28), does Matthew revert to the Abrahamic covenant. He then records the propitiatory death of the son of Abraham. To determine the "structure" and purpose of the gospel, one must take this division in 1:1 into consideration. The book is peculiarly the gospel for Israel, but as proceeding from the atonement of Christ, a gospel of world outreach.

The traditional site of the Mount of the Beatitudes

Outline.
  I. The King, the son of David, offered to Israel (1:1–25:46)
    A. The genealogy and birth of the King (1:1-25)
    B. The infancy and concealment of the King (2:1-23)
    C. The kingdom presented to Israel and rejected (3:1–11:1)

D. The revelation of the King's new program (11:2–13:52)
E. The ministry of the rejected King (13:53–23:39)
F. The rejected King's promise to return in power and glory (24:1–25:46)
II. The King, the son of Abraham, put to death and raised again (26:1–28:8)
III. The King in resurrection ministry to His disciples (28:9-20)

Author. This gospel was incontestably written by the apostle Matthew, whose original name was Levi. He was a Jew whose father's name was Alphaeus. As he was a tax collector under the Romans at Capernaum and thus a hated publican, it is unthinkable that his name would have been attached to the first gospel had he not been the actual writer of it. Moreover, seventeen independent witnesses of the first four centuries attest its genuineness.

Original Language. Despite the critical claim that Matthew originally wrote the gospel in Aram., this contention has never been proved. If there was an Aram. original, it disappeared at an early date. The Gk. gospel, which is now the church's heritage, was almost beyond doubt written in Matthew's lifetime. The Jewish historian Josephus furnishes an illustration of the fate of the Heb. original of Matthew, if such ever existed. The celebrated historian himself tells us that he penned his great work "The History of the Jews' Wars" originally in Aram., his native tongue, for the benefit of his own nation and that he subsequently rendered it in Gk.

Date. The book of Matthew, like the other synoptics and the book of Acts, does not report the fall of Jerusalem and the Temple but describes these events as still future. These books had been written either before this tragedy or a long time after it. It would be indeed rash to put them long after A.D. 70. Therefore, they must have been penned before that date. Since Luke's gospel is earlier than Acts, and Matthew is certainly earlier than Luke, it seems entirely probable that if he wrote an Aram. original he did so around A.D. 40-45. This would place the Gk. Matthew around the middle of the first century A.D.

Purpose. Matthew seems definitely to have written to confirm persecuted Jewish believers in their faith and to reconcile them in their thinking that the gospel was not a rejection of OT prophecies but rather an outworking of the great promises of the Abrahamic and Davidic covenants. The Jews needed clear demonstration of the Messiah's Person and work and to have objections removed that hindered unbelieving Jews. The writer accomplishes this purpose by proving the kingship of the predicted divine-human Messiah; that He fulfilled OT predictions in His Person and work; that He produced the credentials of Israel's King and announced teachings of the kingdom; and His Person and work were rejected by the nation; that He announced a new program, His death, resurrection, and second advent; and that after this present age of His building the church, He will return to set up His kingdom. It is thus uniquely the gospel for the Jews.   M.F.U.

BIBLIOGRAPHY: J. A. Broadus, *Commentary on the Gospel of Matthew* (1886); A. C. Gaebelein, *The Gospel of Matthew* (1910); A. H. M'Neile, *The Gospel According to St. Matthew* (1915); C. R. Erdman, *The Gospel of Matthew* (1920); R. C. H. Lenski, *The Interpretation of St. Matthew's Gospel* (1943); A. Plummer, *The Gospel According to St. Matthew* (1956); W. Kelly, *Lectures on the Gospel of Matthew* (1959); W. Hendriksen, *Exposition of the Gospel According to Matthew* (1973); J. F. Walvoord, *Matthew: Thy Kingdom Come* (1974); J. A. Alexander, *The Gospel According to Matthew* (1979); H. Vos, *Matthew* (1979); S. D. Toussaint, *Behold the King* (1980); J. Morison, *A Practical Commentary on the Gospel According to St. Matthew* (1981).

MATTHI'AS (ma-thī'as; evidently a variant of Mattathias, "gift of Jehovah"). Of the family of Matthias no account is given, and of his life we have no account, excepting the incident narrated in Acts 1:15-26, where he is chosen as an apostle. The 120 were assembled at Jerusalem, waiting for the advent of the Holy Spirit and, at the suggestion and under the supervision of Peter, proceeded to fill the place among the twelve left vacant by the defection and death of Judas Iscariot. Peter laid down the essential qualification for the apostolic office—his having been one of the companions of Christ from His baptism by John till His ascension—and declared the object of the election to be "a witness with us of His resurrection" (1:21-22). Two such men were chosen, but the ultimate decision was referred to God Himself by the sacred trial of the lot, accompanied by prayer. The two were Joseph, called Barsabbas, and surnamed Justus; and Matthias, upon whom the lot fell. He was immediately numbered among the apostles. Nothing reliable is recorded of his later life. He is not mentioned again in the NT. Eusebius and Epiphanius believed him to be one of the seventy disciples. One tradition says that he preached the gospel in Judea and was then stoned to death by the Jews. Others make him a martyr—by crucifixion—in Ethiopia or Colchis. An apocryphal gospel was published under his name, and Clement of Alexandria quotes from the Traditions of Matthias (Kitto; Smith).

The Lot. According to Grotius, this was taken by means of two urns. In one they placed two rolls of paper, with the names of Joseph and Matthias written within them, and in the other two rolls, one with the word "apostle" and the other blank. One roll was drawn from each urn simultaneously. Clarke (*Com.*) believes that the selection was by ballot, the Lord directing the mind of the majority to vote for Matthias. In the case of selection by lot there was no chance, for "the lot is cast into the lap [properly *urn*], but its every decision is from the Lord" (Prov. 16:33).

MATTHITHI'AH (mat-i-thī'a; "gift of Jehovah").

1. A Levite, the eldest son of Shallum the Korahite, who had charge of the baked offerings, "things which were baked in pans" (1 Chron. 9:31), probably after the Exile, about 445 B.C.

2. One of the sons of Jeduthun, a Levite appointed chief of the fourteenth division of the Temple musicians by David (1 Chron. 25:3, 21). He is probably the same as the one appointed to assist in the musical service at the removal of the Ark to Jerusalem and to act as gatekeeper (15:18, 21; 16:5), about 988 B.C.

3. An Israelite, of the "sons" (residents) of Nebo, who put away his Gentile wife after the Exile (Ezra 10:43), 456 B.C.

4. One of those who stood at the right hand of Ezra when he read the law to the people (Neh. 8:4), about 445 B.C.

MATTOCK. An agricultural implement like a pickax, with a wide point for grubbing up and digging out roots and stones (1 Sam. 13:20-21). Until the time of Saul, the Philistines had a monopoly on the smelting of iron, and Israelites had to take their tools to them for sharpening.

Although the *mattock* appears in the KJV, the NIV, and the NASB, different Heb. words are behind the term in the three versions. *See* Coulter; Plowshare.

MAUL. A club (so NASB and NIV, Prov. 25:18).

MAW. The stomach of a sacrificial animal (so NASB, Deut. 18:3).

MAZ'ZAROTH (maz'a-rōth). Only in Job 38:32, KJV (marg., NASB; the NIV reads "morning star," marg.), and referring to the twelve signs of the zodiac, which were imagined as *menazil,* i.e., lodging houses, or *burug,* strongholds, in which, one after another, the sun lodges as it completes the circle of the year. The question, "Can you lead forth a constellation [*mazzaroth*] in its season?" means, Can you lead forth the zodiacal sign for each month, so that it becomes visible after sunset as it is visible before sunset? To these signs priests offered incense and were abolished by Josiah (2 Kings 23:5).

ME JARKON. *See* Me-Jarkon.

ME-ZAHAB. *See* Mezahab.

ME'AH. *See* Hundred, Tower of the.

MEAL.

1. (Heb. *qemaḥ,* "marrow"). The fatness of wheat, or barley, i.e., its ground substance (Num. 5:15; 1 Kings 4:22; etc.).

2. Fine meal (Matt. 13:33; Luke 13:21), the finest portion of *flour* (which see).

MEALS, MEALTIME. *See* Food.

MEA'RAH (me-a'ra; a "cave"). A place between Tyre and Sidon (Josh. 13:4). Possibly only a cave,

although extensive ruins are thought by Robinson possibly to be those of "Mearah of the Sidonians." The NIV renders "from Arah," taking the *me* as the prefixed preposition, "from." *See* Arah.

MEASURE. *See* Metrology.

MEASURING LINE. *See* Metrology: Linear Measures.

MEASURING ROD OR REED. *See* Metrology, Linear Measures.

MEAT. This word does not appear in the KJV in the sense of animal food, which is denoted uniformly by "flesh." Perhaps "savoury meat" (Gen. 27:4) and "corn and bread and meat" (45:23) would be exceptions (the NASB renders "savory dish" and "grain and bread and sustenance"). The only real and inconvenient ambiguity caused by the change that has taken place in the meaning of the word is in the case of the "meat-offering," which consisted solely of flour and oil, sacrifices of flesh being confined to the other offerings. The NASB and NIV read "grain offering" (Lev. 6:14).

Several other words, distinct in the original, are rendered "meat" in the KJV; these are generally replaced in the NASB and NIV by "food." None presents any special interest except Heb. *ṭerep* (something *torn*). This word is rendered "food" in the NASB, with a marginal reading of "prey." In the NT a variety of Gk. words are rendered "meat" in the KJV; in the NASB and NIV such expressions as "at the table," "something to eat," and "food" are used instead.

MEAT OFFERING. A KJV expression referring to a particular *grain offering,* the NASB and NIV rendering of the Heb. *See* Sacrifices.

MEBUN'NAI (me-bun'i; "built, constructed"). In this form appears, in one passage only (2 Sam. 23:27), the name of one of David's guard, who is elsewhere called Sibbecai (21:18; 1 Chron. 11:29; 20:4; 27:11).

MECHE'RATHITE (me-ke'rath-īt), **Meke'rathite** (NIV). A native or inhabitant of Mecherah (1 Chron. 11:36); from 2 Sam. 23:34 it would appear to be a corruption for Maacathite.

MECO'NAH (me-kō'na; "a base or foundation"; "Mekonah," KJV). A town situated near Ziklag in the south of Palestine and inhabited by men of Judah after the captivity (Neh. 11:28).

ME'DAD (mē'dad; "beloved, friend"). One of the seventy elders chosen to assist Moses in the government of the people. He and Eldad remained behind in the camp and were not among the rest of the seventy at the Tabernacle. When the Spirit came upon these, He descended also upon Medad and Eldad, so that they prophesied. A lad reported the matter to Moses, who did not forbid them, as requested by Joshua, but replied, "Would that all the Lord's people were prophets" (Num. 11:26-29), c. 1441 B.C.

ME'DAN (mē'dan). The third son of Abraham and Keturah (Gen. 25:2; 1 Chron. 1:32), after 2050 B.C.

MED'EBA (med'ē-ba; "water of quiet"). A city of great antiquity in Moab (Num. 21:30), belonging to Reuben (Josh. 13:16). It was a sanctuary of the Moabites in the days of Ahaz and is named as one of the cities of Moab in the prophetic curse recorded in Isa. 15:2. When the Ammonites were defeated by Joab they found refuge in Medeba (1 Chron. 19:1-15). The ruins, about eighteen miles E of the Dead Sea, were fairly extensive in the nineteenth century, but little remains today. Most important of the antiquities is a sixth-century Byzantine floor mosaic discovered in the Greek Orthodox church at Medeba late in the nineteenth century when a new church was being constructed at the site. Though much of it was destroyed, the section representing Jerusalem is virtually intact; the map has now been incorporated into the pavement of the church. *See* M. Avi-Yonah, *The Madaba Mosaic Map*, Israel Exploration Society, 1954.

MEDES (mēds). Inhabitants of *Media* (which see; 2 Kings 17:6; 18:11; Isa. 13:17; Dan. 5:28, 31).

ME'DIA (mē'di-a). An ancient Asiatic country situated S of the Caspian Sea, N of Elam, E of the Zagros Mountains, and W of Parthia. It extended about 150,000 square miles, being about 600 miles in length and 250 miles in breadth. In the heyday of its power it stretched far beyond these confines. The country was noted for its horses. Its original inhabitants were subjugated by an Indo-European race called in the Heb. *māday* (Gen. 10:2; 1 Chron. 1:5). The country is called Media (Esther 1:3, 14, 18; 10:2; Isa. 21:2; Dan. 8:20). Darius is referred to in 5:31 as "the Mede." Ezra 6:2 also refers to Media; as elsewhere "the Medes" are alluded to. Media comes into historical perspective in the ninth century B.C., being encountered in the inscriptions of Shalmaneser III (c. 836 B.C.), who conducted a campaign against these peoples in the Zagros Mountain region. The "Amadai" (Medes) are listed among those who paid tribute to the Assyrian Shamshi-Adad (825-812 B.C.). Adad-Nirari III (812-782 B.C.) continued contact with these people. The mighty Tiglath-pileser III (745-727 B.C.) invaded Media and added districts of it to the Assyrian Empire. Sargon II, after capturing Samaria (721 B.C.), deported Israelites into the towns of the Medes (2 Kings 17:6; 18:11). Later, around 710 B.C., Sargon more completely subdued the Median people and forced them to pay tribute in the form of horses. Sargon's successor, Sennacherib, likewise put the Medes under heavy tribute.

In the succeeding years the Medes increased in power. About 614 B.C. they advanced down the Tigris and captured Asshur, the ancient capital of Assyria. In 612 B.C., Cyaxares, in an alliance with the Chaldeans under Nabopolassar and the Scythian hordes, captured Nineveh. This great event marked the crash of the Assyrian Empire. Cyaxares received as his part of the victor's spoil Assyria proper and the neighboring countries toward the N and NW. Nabopolassar's son Nebuchadnezzar married Cyaxares' daughter. This event strengthened the alliance between Media and Babylonia. It was in the era of Nebuchadnezzar (c. 605-562 B.C.) that the Median kingdom reached the apex of its power. In this period the empire included what is today part of Iraq, Iran, Anatolian Turkey, and Armenia. It embraced Ecbatana, present-day Hamadan, and Rhagae, modern Tehran.

Sacks of meal and pulses at Beersheba market

Persia was dominated by Media until the rise of Cyrus II, founder of the mighty Persian Empire. About 549 B.C. he subdued Media, establishing his capital in Pasargadae. Under the Persians, however, Media remained an important province and the dual name Medes and Persians long described the empire (Dan. 5:28; Esther 1:19). The expression "the laws of the Medes and Persians" was reminiscent of the unchangeable character of Median law, which even a king could not alter without the consent of his government. Medo-Persia, in a sense a dual nation, became a mighty empire that lasted until the conquests of Alexander the Great (330 B.C.). After Alexander's decease, it became a part of Syria (1 Macc. 6:56), or the Seleucid Empire. Subsequently it was part of the Parthian and Bactrian empires, and of the Neo-Persian Empire of the Sassanids (A.D. 226-641).   M.F.U.; H.F.V.

BIBLIOGRAPHY: G. G. Cameron, *History of Early Iran* (1968); D. J. Wiseman, ed., *Peoples of Old Testament Times* (1973), pp. 313-57.

ME'DIAN (mē'di-an). Darius, "the son of Ahasuerus, of Median descent" (Dan. 9:1), also called "the Mede" (5:31; 11:1).

MEDIATION, MEDIATOR. A term, the proper use of which in theology refers to the work of

Christ in establishing the gospel dispensation, and in its continuance to the end.

Scriptural Basis. In several passages Christ is called the Mediator, i.e., "the mediator of a new covenant" (*mesitēs*, "middleman, mediator"; *see* 1 Tim. 2:5; Heb. 8:6; 9:15; 12:24). The Scriptures present Christ as the One through whom is effected reconciliation between God and men, and through whom the moral and spiritual harmony of the world, broken by sin, shall ultimately be restored (e.g., 2 Cor. 5:18-20; Col. 1:21-22; Heb. 2:17; 1 Cor. 15:24-28).

Theological. The following features of doctrine are of chief importance: (1) The necessity for mediation arises from the holiness of God and the sinfulness of man. The reconciliation wrought by Christ, therefore, is represented as having two phases, that of God to man, and that of man to God (*see* 2 Cor. 5:18-20). It should always be borne in mind, however, that the whole provision of the mediatorial economy arises from the love of God (John 3:16; Rom. 5:8). (2) Christ is the only Mediator (in addition to Scriptures above cited, *see* Acts 4:12; Gal. 2:12; 3:21). In His work of mediation His atoning death is central (*see* Matt. 20:28; 26:28; Rom. 5:6; 1 Cor. 1:18; 2:2; 1 Pet. 2:24; 3:18; etc.). But more generally the whole work of Christ as Prophet, Priest, and King is embraced in His own work of mediation. The teachings of the Scriptures leave no room for the Roman Catholic view that priests and saints and angels, and especially the virgin Mary, are mediators, a view that is based upon a false doctrine of the prerogative of the priesthood and also a false conception of human merit. But still it is admissible and proper to recognize the real, though subordinate, sense in which all believers are members of " a royal priesthood" (1 Pet. 2:9). The mediation of Christ, however, is supreme, and in its principal features stands entirely alone. (3) In Christ are found the necessary qualifications for this work. (*1*) He is the God-man. It was essential that the mediator should be divine; otherwise His sacrifice could not have availed to take away sins; He could not be the perfect revelation of God to men, or be the source of spiritual and eternal life to believers, or control all events for the final consummation of His kingdom (Heb. 9:14; Rom. 8:3; John 10:10; 1 Cor. 15:25). It was necessary that He should also be human; otherwise He could not have died to redeem us, or stood as our representative before God's law, or partaken in human experiences, or be united with us in a common nature (Heb. 2:11-16; 4:15; Rom. 8:3; Phil. 2:7). (*2*) He was without sin. As under the law the sacrifice laid upon the altar must be without blemish, so the "Lamb of God who takes away the sin of the world" (John 1:29) must Himself be free from sin, otherwise His sacrifice would not have been acceptable; He could not have access to God or be the source of holy life for His people (Heb. 7:26; 4:15-16; 1 Pet. 1:19;

2:22). *See* Atonement; Intercession; Jesus Christ; Jesus, Offices of; Kingdom of God.

BIBLIOGRAPHY: H. B. Swete, *The Ascended Christ* (1916), pp. 87-100; H. E. Brunner, *The Mediator* (1934); V. Taylor, *Jesus and His Sacrifice* (1937); L. S. Chafer, *Systematic Theology* (1948), 5:252, 261-73; 7:19-20, 81-82, 234-35; V. Taylor, *The Names of Jesus* (1954), pp. 110-13.

MEDIATOR. *See* Atonement; Intercession.

MEDICINE. *See* Diseases, Treatment of.

MEDITATION. "A private devotional act, consisting in deliberate reflection upon some spiritual truth or mystery, accompanied by mental prayer and by acts of the affection and of the will, especially formation of resolutions as to future conduct" (*Cent. Dict.,* s.v.). Meditation is a duty that ought to be attended to by all who wish well to their spiritual interests. It should be *deliberate, close,* and *continuous* (Pss. 1:2; 119:97). The *subjects* that ought more especially to engage the Christian mind are: the works of creation (19:1-6); the perfections of God (Deut. 32:4); the character, office, and work of Christ (Heb. 12:2-3); the office and operations of the Holy Spirit (John 15-16); the dispensations of Providence (Ps. 97:1-2); the precepts and promises of God's words (Ps. 119); the value, powers, and immortality of the soul (Mark 8:36); the depravity of our nature, and the grace of God in our salvation, etc.

MEDIUM. *See* Familiar Spirit; Necromancy (in both the general listing and the article Magic); Spiritist.

MEEKNESS. *See* Humility.

MEGID′DO (me-gid′ō; "place of troops"). One of the royal cities of the Canaanites (Josh. 12:21), first assigned to Issachar (17:11) but afterward belonging to Manasseh (Judg. 1:27). Megiddo did not become firmly occupied by the Israelites until the time of Solomon, who placed one of his twelve deputies over Taanach and Megiddo (1 Kings 4:12) and erected some costly works there (9:15). The valley of Megiddo was a part of the Plain of Esdraelon. It figured as a battlefield, and here *Barak* (which see) gained a notable victory over the king of Hazor, whose commanding general was Sisera (Judg. 4:15). To this place Ahaziah king of Judah fled, and there he died (2 Kings 9:27). But the chief historical interest of Megiddo is concentrated in the death of Josiah. He endeavored to stop Pharaoh Neco of Egypt, while the Egyptian was passing through the glens of Carmel into the plain of Megiddo. He was defeated, as he fled was shot by the Egyptian archers and died on the road to Jerusalem (23:29-30; 2 Chron. 35:20-24; Zech. 12:11). In the last passage the mourning mentioned is on account of Josiah's death.

Megiddo is marked by the modern site Tell el Mutesellim. It has been extensively excavated and forms one of the most important archaeological sites of Palestine. In 1903-5 its remarkable archaeological history began when G. Schumacher of the Deutsche Orientgesellschaft first began examining it. However, by far the greatest work on the site was done by the Oriental Institute of the University of Chicago. Begun under the direction of Clarence S. Fisher in 1925, this work was continued in subsequent years by P. L. O. Guy and Gordon Loud. The site was occupied in the late Stone Age, long before 4500 B.C. Around 3500 B.C. the first city at this site, commanding the strategic Plain of Esdraelon, was built. This city was surrounded by a massive wall originally some thirteen feet thick and later buttressed to twice that thickness. A brick wall and gate of c. 1880 B.C. are known. Thutmose III of Egypt captured the Canaanite city c. 1468 and held it briefly, but the Canaanites held the important strategic center until dispossessed by the Israelites (c. 1100 B.C.). It is not known whether or not David erected any construction at Megiddo. Solomon, however, reconstructed the city as one of his chariot towns (1 Kings 9:15; cf. 10:26-29). He also made it the center of one of his administrative districts. Shishak of Egypt (1 Kings 14:25; 2 Chron. 12:9), who overran Jerusalem and Judea in the fifth year of Rehoboam, apparently took Megiddo c. 925 B.C. He left evidence in an inscribed stela.

Tell el-Mutesellim, the site of ancient Megiddo

University of Chicago teams continued to excavate at Megiddo from 1925 to 1939, according to a plan to strip the entire mound down to bedrock. They took away a Persian town from Stratum I, an unwalled town of the time of King Josiah in the seventh century B.C. (Stratum II), an Assyrian governor's headquarters of the same century (Stratum III), and uncovered Stratum IV, which they identified as Solomonic. In that level they found two great stable compounds, a governor's palace, walls, and the city gate. Then in 1960 Yigael Yadin of the Hebrew University worked at Megiddo and modified the Chicago conclusions, assigning the walls, the city gate, and the palace

to the time of Solomon and the stables to the days of Ahab. Moreover, the great water system, formerly dated to the twelfth century, Yadin reassigned to Solomon's day. Yadin's reinterpretations have generally been followed, but Yohanan Aharoni of Tel Aviv University defended the University of Chicago dating of Stratum IV as Solomonic.   M.F.U.; H.F.V.

BIBLIOGRAPHY: E. Robinson, *Biblical Researches* (1867), 2:329-30; A. Malamat, ed., *The Kingdoms of Israel and Judah* (1961), pp. 66-109; D. W. Thomas, ed., *Archaeology and Old Testament Study* (1967), pp. 309-28; Y. Yadin, *Hazor* (1972), pp. 147-64; M. Avi-Yonah and E. Stern, eds., *Encyclopedia of Archaeological Excavations in the Holy Land* (1977), 3:830-56.

MEGID'DON. *See* Megiddo.

MEHET'ABEEL. *See* Mehetabel, no. 2

MEHET'ABEL (me-het'a-bel; "God benefits").
1. The daughter of Matred and wife of Hadad (or Hadar), the last known king of Edom (Gen. 36:39; 1 Chron. 1:50). *See* Hadad.
2. The father of Delaiah and grandfather of Shemaiah, which latter had been hired by Tobiah and Sanballat to intimidate Nehemiah (Neh. 6:10; "Mehetabeel," KJV), before 445 B.C.

MEHI'DA (me-hī'da). A person whose descendants (or a place whose inhabitants) were among the Temple servants who returned from Babylon with Zerubbabel (Ezra 2:52; Neh. 7:54), before 536 B.C.

ME'HIR (me'hēr; "hire, price"). The son of Chelub and father (founder?) of Eshton, of the family of Judah (1 Chron. 4:11).

MEHO'LAH. *See* Meholathite.

MEHO'LATHITE (me-hō'la-thīt). Probably a native of *Abel-meholah* (which see; 1 Sam. 18:19; 2 Sam. 21:8).

MEHU'JAEL (me-hū'ja-el). The son of Irad (grandson of Cain) and father of Methushael (Gen. 4:18).

MEHU'MAN (me-hū'man; perhaps "faithful"). One of the seven eunuchs whom Ahasuerus commanded to bring Queen Vashti into the royal presence (Esther 1:10), about 478 B.C.

ME-JAR'KON (me-jar'kon; "waters of yellowishness"). A town near Joppa in the tribe of Dan (Josh. 19:46), which probably received its name from a nearby spring.

MEKO'NAH. *See* Meco'nah.

MELATI'AH (mel-a-ti'a; "Jehovah has delivered"). A Gibeonite who assisted in repairing the wall of Jerusalem after the return from Babylon (Neh. 3:7), 445 B.C.

MEL'CHI (mel'ki; "my king"), **Mel'ki** (NIV).
1. The son of Jannai and father of Levi, fourth

graved upon the jewels of his breastplate (v. 29). The sacrifice in the case of jealousy was called a memorial because it brought iniquity to remembrance (Num. 5:15). A memorial was also a *record* (Ex. 17:14; "book of remembrance," Mal. 3:16). The act of Mary in anointing the feet of Jesus was to be spoken of in "memory of her" (Matt. 26:13; KJV and NIV, "memorial"; Mark 14:9; cf. Acts 10:4).

Stepped pyramid of Saqqarah

MEM'PHIS (mem'fis). An important ancient Egyptian capital situated on the Nile River some fifteen miles S of Cairo. The Hebrews were acquainted with Memphis under the name Noph (Isa. 19:13, KJV) and Moph (Heb. text of Hos. 9:6). The city goes back to the time of Menes, founder of the First Dynasty (c. 3100 B.C.). Herodotus asserts that Menes built the city on a strip of land reclaimed from the Nile. Manetho considered Dynasties III-V and VII-VIII to be Memphite. King Djoser embellished the city, and Imhotep, his renowned architect, constructed a step pyramid, a splendid monument in the Memphis acropolis at Saqqarah. This famous funerary structure is accounted the oldest extant stone structure in Egypt. Ptah was adored at this city. Memphis continued to be a famous metropolis even after the rise of Thebes and did not lose its importance until overshadowed by Alexandria, Alexander the Great's brilliant city. Memphis existed down to the Middle Ages, but the ruins of its ancient buildings were carried away to build Cairo. Practically all that remains now of importance are a score of pyramids and the celebrated Sphinx, mute memorials of Memphis's ancient glory. Jeremiah refers to the city's outrages (Jer. 2:16). The weeping prophet also predicted Nebuchadnezzar's Egyptian victories and that the people of Israel residing in Memphis would be carried away as captives (46:14-19). The prophet Ezekiel also made predictions concerning the city (Ezek. 30:13, 16).

Memphis was a huge metropolitan complex in its heyday. Besides its residential quarters, it had numerous temples and palaces and commercial districts with wharves, warehouses, workshops, and business establishments. It may have extended as much as twelve miles along the Nile and apparently consisted of residential complexes built around the royal palaces, with suburbs inhabited by populations of various origins. A clue to the size of greater Memphis may be derived from the sprawling chain of pyramids and mastabas that stretch for about twenty miles along the Nile W of the ancient site.   M.F.U.; H.F.V.

BIBLIOGRAPHY: W. M. F. Petrie, *Memphis*, 3 vols. (1909-10); M. Dimick, *Memphis, the City of the White Wall* (1956).

MEMU'CAN (me-mū'kan). One of seven princes, or royal counselors, at the court of Ahasuerus, at whose suggestion Queen Vashti was divorced (Esther 1:14, 16, 21), about 478 B.C.

MEN'AHEM (men'a-hem; "comforter"). The seventeenth king of the Northern Kingdom, Israel. He was the son of Gadi, and probably one of the generals of King Zechariah. When he heard of the conspiracy of Shallum, his murder of the king, and his usurpation of the throne, he went up from Tirzah and killed the usurper in Samaria. Menahem in turn usurped the throne and reduced Tiphsah because it refused to recognize him as king. He continued the calf worship of Jeroboam and contributed to the ungodliness, demoralization, and feebleness of Israel, a melancholy picture of which has been left by the contemporary prophets Hosea and Amos. During his reign the hostile forces of Assyria first appeared on the NE frontier of Israel. Tiglath-pileser III (Pul) received from Menahem a gift of one thousand talents of silver, exacted from Israel by an assessment of fifty shekels a head, and became his ally. Menahem's reign lasted ten years, about 752-742 B.C. He left the throne to his son Pekahiah (2 Kings 15:14-22).

BIBLIOGRAPHY: M. F. Unger, *Israel and the Aramaeans of Damascus* (1957), pp. 97ff.; D. W. Thomas, ed., *Documents from Old Testament Times* (1958), pp. 53-57; H. Tadman, *Scripta Hierosolymitana* 8 (1961): 248-66; E. R. Thiele, *Mysterious Numbers of the Hebrew Kings* (1983), pp. 108, 120-29, 139-62, 199.

ME'NAN. *See* Men'na.

ME-NE, ME-NE, TE-KEL, UPHAR-SIN. The words of an inscription supernaturally written upon the wall in Belshazzar's palace (Dan. 5:5-28). The words are Chaldee, and their meaning is given in the text; *mᵉne'*, "numbered"; *tᵉqēl*, "weighed"; *ûparsîn*, from *pāras*, "divided," i.e., "dissolved, destroyed." "In all the three words there lies a double sense, which is brought out in the interpretation.... Daniel interprets mene: thus God had numbered thy kingdom, i.e., its duration, and has finished it, i.e., its duration is so counted out that it is full, that it now comes to an end. . . . The interpretation of tekel presents this double meaning: Thou art weighed in the balances and found too light, i.e., deficient in moral worth. In upharsin, 'thy kingdom is divided,' the meaning is not that the kingdom was to be divided into two equal parts; but *peras* is to divide into pieces, to dissolve the kingdom" (Keil, *Com.,* ad loc.).

It is recorded that the wise men could not "declare the interpretation of the message" and that it must have required a supernatural endowment on the part of Daniel—a conclusion confirmed by the exact coincidence of the event with the prediction.

BIBLIOGRAPHY: A. H. Sayce, *Higher Criticism and the Verdict of the Monuments* (1895), pp. 530ff.; E. G. Kraeling, *Journal of Biblical Literature* 58 (1944): 11-14; D. N. Freedman, *Bulletin of the American Schools of Oriental Research* 145 (1957): 31-32.

ME'NI (mē'nī). *See* Gods, False.

MEN'NA (men'a). The son of Mattatha and father of Melea in the ancestry of Jesus (Luke 3:31; "Menan," KJV).

MEON'ENIM, PLAIN OF. The NASB of Judg. 9:37 replaces the KJV expression with "the diviners' oak," marg. "terebinth." The NIV has "soothsayers' tree."

MEON'OTHAI (me-on'o-thī; "my dwellings"). Apparently the brother of Hathath, the son of Othniel, and father of Ophrah (1 Chron. 4:14), after 1440 B.C.

MEPH'AATH (mef'a-ath; "illuminative"). A Levitical city (Josh. 21:37; 1 Chron. 6:79) in the tribe of Reuben (Josh. 13:18). According to Eusebius, a garrison was stationed here as a defense against the inhabitants of the desert. It seems originally to have been a dependency of the Amorites (Num. 21:26) but afterward to have belonged to Moab (Jer. 48:21). Perhaps Tell Jawa, six miles S of 'Amman.

MEPHIB'OSHETH (me-fib'o-sheth; "exterminator of shame," i.e., "idols").

1. The son of Saul by his concubine Rizpah, the daughter of Aiah. He and his brother Armoni were among the seven victims who were surrendered by David to the Gibeonites and by them slain before Jehovah, to avert a famine from which the country was suffering (2 Sam. 21:8-9), about 996 B.C.

2. The son of Jonathan, and grandson of Saul. When his father and grandfather were slain at Gilboa, Mephibosheth was a child five years of age, living under the care of his nurse, probably at Gibeah. When the tidings of the disaster came to the royal household the nurse fled, carrying the child upon her shoulder. In her haste she let him fall, and Mephibosheth was crippled for life in both feet (2 Sam. 4:4), about 1000 B.C. After the accident Mephibosheth seems to have

found a refuge in the house of Machir, a Gadite sheikh at Lo-debar, near Mahanaim, by whom he was brought up (Josephus *Ant.* 7.5.5). He married and was living there when David, having conquered his enemies, had leisure to make endeavors to fulfill his oath to Jonathan by the stone Ezel that he would not cut off his loving-kindness from his house forever (1 Sam. 20:15). From Ziba he learned of the existence and whereabouts of Mephibosheth, and brought him and his son Micah (2 Sam. 9:1-5; cf. 1 Chron. 9:40) to Jerusalem. The interview was characterized by fear and reverence on the part of Jonathan's son and by kindness and liberality on that of David. All the property of his grandfather was conveyed to Mephibosheth, and Ziba was commanded to cultivate the land in his interest. Mephibosheth took up his residence in Jerusalem and was a daily guest at the royal table (2 Sam. 9:6-13), about 984 B.C.

The next mention of Mephibosheth respects his behavior upon the revolt of Absalom. Of this there are two accounts—his own (2 Sam. 19:24-30) and that of Ziba (16:1-4)—and they naturally differ. Ziba, because of his loyalty and kindness, was rewarded with the possessions of his master. Mephibosheth met David a few days after and told his story, namely, that he had desired to flee with his benefactor but was deceived by Ziba, so that he was obliged to remain behind. He had, however, done all that he could to evidence his sympathy with David, having gone into the deepest mourning for his afflicted friend. From the day the king left he had allowed his beard to grow ragged, his feet to be unwashed, and his linen unchanged. David doubtless believed his story and revoked his judgment given to Ziba so much as to have the land divided between the two. Mephibosheth's answer was, "Let him even take it all, since my lord the king has come safely to his own house," 967 B.C. We hear no more of Mephibosheth, except that the king did not let him be included in the vengeance that the Gibeonites were allowed to execute upon the house of Saul (21:7).

BIBLIOGRAPHY: W. G. Blaikie, *David, King of Israel* (1981), pp. 211-18, 270-73, 299-300.

ME'RAB (me'rab; "increase"). The eldest daughter of King Saul (1 Sam. 14:49), whom, in accordance with the promise made before the death of Goliath (17:25), Saul had betrothed to David (18:17), about 1015 B.C. David's hesitation looks as if he did not much value the honor—at any rate, before the marriage Merab's younger sister, Michal, had displayed her attachment for David, and Merab was then married to Adriel the Meholathite, to whom she bore five sons (2 Sam. 21:8), who were given up to the Gibeonites by David.

MERA'IAH (mer-ī'ya; "rebellion"). A chief priest contemporary with the high priest Joiakim (Neh. 12:12).

MERA'IOTH (mer-ī'oth; "rebellious").

1. The son of Zerahiah, a high priest of the line of Eleazar (1 Chron. 6:6-7, 52; Ezra 7:3). Lightfoot (*Temple Service,* 4:1) thinks that he was the immediate predecessor of Eli in the office of high priest and that at his death the high priesthood changed from the line of Eleazar to that of Ithamar. The same person is doubtless meant in 1 Chron. 9:11; Neh. 11:11, but placed by copyist's mistake between Zadok and Ahitub, instead of before the latter.

2. A chief priest whose house was represented in the time of Joiakim by Helkai (Neh. 12:15). The NIV renders the name Meremoth.

MERA'RI (mer-a-ri; "bitter, sad"). The third named of the sons of Levi, probably born in Canaan (Gen. 46:11; Ex. 6:16; Num. 3:17; 1 Chron. 6:1, 16, 19; etc.), about 1890 B.C. All that is known of his personal history is the fact of his birth before the migration of Jacob to Egypt and of his being one of the seventy persons who accompanied him there (Gen. 46:8, 11). He became the head of the third division of the Levites, that is, the Merarites.

MERA'RITES (me-ra'rīts). *See* Levites.

MERATHA'IM (mer-a-thā'im; "twofold" or "double rebellion," Jer. 50:21). The name given to Babylon. "The dual expresses intensity, without two rebellions of Babylon being supposed. The allusion is to rebellious defiance of the Lord (v. 24). The summons is addressed to the avenger described in v. 3" (Orelli, *Com.,* ad loc.).

MERCHANDISE, MERCHANT. *See* Commerce.

MERCURY. *See* Hermes.

MERCY (Heb. *hesed,* "kindness"; Gk. *eleos,* "compassion"). "Mercy is a form of love determined by the state or condition of its objects. Their state is one of suffering and need, while they may be unworthy or ill-deserving. Mercy is at once the disposition of love respecting such, and the kindly ministry of love for their relief" (Miley, *Systematic Theology,* 1:209-10). Mercy is a Christian grace and is very strongly urged toward all men (Matt. 5:7; 23:23; James 3:17; etc.). *See* Grace, Love.

BIBLIOGRAPHY: N. Turner, *Christian Words* (1980), pp. 277-80.

MERCY SEAT. *See* Tabernacle.

ME'RED (me'red; "rebellion"). The second son of Ezrah, of the tribe of Judah (1 Chron. 4:17-18).

MER'EMOTH (mer'e-mōth; "heights," i.e., "exaltations").

1. A priest, son of Uriah (Urijah), who was appointed to weigh and register the gold and silver vessels brought to Jerusalem (Ezra 8:33), about 457 B.C. He repaired two sections of the wall of Jerusalem under Nehemiah (Neh. 3:4, 21), 445 B.C.

2. A layman of the "sons" (inhabitants?) of Bani, who divorced his Gentile wife after the captivity (Ezra 10:36), 456 B.C.

3. A priest, or a family of priests, who signed the covenant with Nehemiah (Neh. 10:5). The latter supposition is more probable, as in 12:3 the name occurs among those who returned with Zerubbabel a century before.

4. The NIV reading for *Meraioth,* no. 2 (which see). The NIV thus identifies this Meremoth with that of Neh. 12:3.

ME'RES (me'rez). One of the seven princes of Persia and Media in the days of Ahasuerus (Esther 1:14), about 478 B.C.

MER'IBAH (mer'i-ba; "quarrel, strife").

1. The latter of two names that Moses gave to a fountain because of the complaints of the people of Israel. It was near Rephidim, in the wilderness of Sin, probably in the Wadi Feiran on the western gulf of the Red Sea (Ex. 17:1-7), and called also "Massah" (v. 7).

2. There is another Meribah near Kadesh (Num. 27:14, Meribah of Kadesh; Deut. 32:51, Meribah-kadesh), generally distinguished from the first by adding the word "waters" to it (Pss. 81:7; 106:32, "waters of strife"; 95:8, "provocation"). It was at this place that Moses struck the rock and offended God by his impatience (Num. 20:10-13), near the close of the desert wanderings (Deut. 32:51).

MER'IBAH-KA'DESH (mer'i-ba-ka'desh; Deut. 32:51). *See* Meribah, no. 2.

MER'IB-BA'AL (mer'ib-ba'al; "contender with Baal"). The son of Jonathan (1 Chron. 8:34; 9:40), who in 2 Samuel is called *Mephibosheth* (which see) by substitution of Heb. *bōshet* ("shame") for the false god.

MERO'DACH (me-ro'dak). *See* Gods, False.

MERO'DACH-BAL'ADAN (me-ro'dak-bal'a-dan; Akkad. "Marduk has given a son"). The name of a king of Babylon, contemporary with Hezekiah king of Judah (Isa. 39:1). He is mentioned also with the name Berodach-baladan (2 Kings 20:12), which form is due to a confusion of two Heb. characters that are much alike in their old forms.

Leader of the Chaldeans. Merodach-baladan was by race a Chaldean, and though the Chaldeans were almost certainly Semites they were nevertheless quite a distinct people (*see* Chaldeans). The Chaldeans were divided into a number of small tribes settled, for the most part, about the head of the Persian Gulf. They all envied the Babylonians their superior position and their vastly greater wealth, and again and again made efforts to win ascendency and secure political control in the Euphrates valley. Had all these separate Chaldean tribes been united under one leader this might have been achieved long before the eighth century. The leadership was not secured until Merodach-baladan had made himself chief of the tribe of Bit Yakin, which had its seat in the marshes close by the head of the Persian Gulf. Even under so masterful a spirit as his, the Chaldeans would hardly have united but for his success in winning power in Babylonia. The prize of power in Babylonia had long been so highly esteemed among the Chaldeans that whoever won it was sure of leadership in all the Chaldean tribes as well as in his own. If the chief of the tribe of Bit Yakin became lord of Babylon he was certain to be called lord of the tribes of Bit Dakkuri, Bit Amukkani, and of every other Chaldean clan. In the year 732, Ukinzir, prince of the tribe of Amukkani, made himself king of Babylon in defiance of the Assyrian king who had been the ruler of Babylonia. That made him a sort of leader of all the Chaldeans, though they were not yet united enough to support him to the bitter end when the Assyrians were ready to attack him. When Tiglath-pileser III (*see* Tiglath-pileser) came into Babylonia to reconquer it, the Chaldean states submitted one after another without a struggle. Of all those chiefs who thus sent presents and acknowledged themselves as subjects of the Assyrians there was none so significant as Merodach-baladan, who presented (729 B.C.) an immense gift of gold, precious stones, choice woods, embroidered robes, cattle, and sheep. It was the first time that he had ever made submission to the Assyrians. The submission was for a time only—he would soon be in the full tide of rebellion. During the short reign of Shalmaneser V no attempt appears to have been made by Merodach-baladan or by any other Chaldean prince to gain ascendency in Babylonia, or even complete freedom from Assyrian overlordship. But as soon as he was dead, in 722, the opportunity came and was speedily embraced. The successor of Shalmaneser was Sargon II, who had tremendous difficulties to face in the far west and would therefore presumably have but little time or energy to devote to Babylonia.

King of Babylon. Without any great difficulty Merodach-baladan took southern Babylonia and then the city of Babylon itself. On New Year's Day in 721 he was proclaimed the ruler of Babylon. That he dared this much is proof of the stuff of which he was made. Sargon, of course, had to meet this challenge and immediately entered Babylonia with his army. At Dur-ilu he met Merodach-baladan accompanied by Elamite allies. In later inscriptions Sargon claims a victory—that was the usual custom of writing royal documents—but it is perfectly clear from the sequel that it must have been a very small victory indeed. Merodach-baladan was left in possession of the city of Babylon, where he had enough wealth to satisfy him for the present and enough difficulties with priests and people to tax his highest powers. He was not likely to attempt to conquer

northern Babylonia under the conditions that now prevailed, and Sargon let him operate freely, while he went to meet continually recurring rebellions elsewhere.

Merodach-baladan was now practically king of Babylon and naturally also head of all the Chaldean states. He had achieved much indeed, but he was left in a position of enormous difficulty—a position that would test his qualities of statesmanship, without which no king becomes really great.

Reverses. His statesmanship was not equal to his generalship, and he was soon in a turmoil. His Chaldean followers wanted plunder, as did his Aramaean and Elamite allies, and all these were consumed with mutual jealousies. He doubtless desired to govern well, for by so doing it was possible to win cordial allegiance from the Babylonian people and a firm hold upon the throne. But some concession had to be made to his hungry followers, so he gradually ventured on a career of plunder. The chief property owners of Sippar, Nippur, Babylon, and Borsippa were moved into Chaldea, and their possessions handed over to his followers. This act lost for him the allegiance of the priesthood and of the wealthy classes, and these now turned longingly to Sargon as a possible deliverer from the rapacious Chaldean. An army was dispatched southward from Assyria, which soon cut off Merodach-baladan from his Elamite allies. He was powerless to meet this Assyrian army and therefore had to flee into the land from which he had come, after ruling Babylon for eleven years. Sargon pursued him into Chaldea, where he was wounded and fled into Elam. There he waited for a favorable opportunity, which did not come until Sargon was dead and Sennacherib was on his throne.

King for the Second Time. Then came a rebellion in Babylonia against him under the leadership of a certain Marduk-zakir-shumu, who is called the son of a slave. When he had reigned only one month Merodach-baladan appeared and in 702 was again proclaimed king of Babylon. It was probably at just this time that Merodach-baladan sent his embassy to Hezekiah (2 Kings 20:12-19; 2 Chron. 32:31; Isa. 39:1-8), though the date of it is obscure and doubtful. This embassy was sent nominally to congratulate Hezekiah upon his recovery from illness but was probably an attempt to get Hezekiah to join in a rebellion in the west against the Assyrian king. Such a diversion as that would have greatly helped Merodach-baladan's position in Babylonia. The plan failed, for Sennacherib invaded Babylonia, and Merodach-baladan saved his life only by precipitate flight into his old homeland.

Final Reverses. Sennacherib then attacked the west, and while thus engaged, a new rebellion began in Babylonia in which, naturally enough, Merodach-baladan was ready to participate. It was, however, of very short duration, for Sennacherib entered the land again. Once more Merodach-baladan had to flee. He put his goods, his people, and his gods upon boats, floated them down the Euphrates to the Persian Gulf, and settled on its eastern shores in a part of Elam, where Sennacherib dared not follow. There in exile he soon died. His career is without a parallel among his people. It was filled with contradictions. No man before him of that race had held power so great for so long a time. He had failed ultimately, but his followers would in a later day succeed far beyond his dreams.   R.W.R.; M.F.U.

BIBLIOGRAPHY: G. Roux, *Ancient Iraq* (1964), pp. 258-66.

ME'ROM (me'rom; "height, or upper waters"). Often identified with Lake Huleh, this is a triangular-shaped body of water, about 4½ miles in length by 3½ wide. It is 270 feet below the level of the Mediterranean Sea. The Jordan passes through it, and it was where Joshua won a great victory over the Canaanites (Josh. 11:5-8). It is in the upper part of Palestine, in a level plain at the foot of the hills of Naphtali that touch the roots of Hermon, itself 10,000 feet in height. Most of the Huleh region has now been drained by Israeli engineers, and it has been converted to productive farmland. The only reference to Merom in Scripture (Josh. 11:5-9) gives it as the scene of the third and last great victory gained by Joshua over the Canaanites. Some scholars, however, identify Merom with present-day Meiron, located at the base of Jebal Jermak W of Safed, where there is an important spring. Thutmose III (c. 1480 B.C.) refers to Mrm. Other scholars would locate Merom at Khirbet el-Bijar near Marun er-Ras, where there is also an abundance of spring water.   H.F.V.

MERON'OTH. See Meronothite.

MERON'OTHITE (me-ron'o-thīt). The native of a place probably called Meronoth, of which, however, no further traces have yet been discovered. Two Meronothites are named in the Bible: (1) Jehdeiah, who had the charge of the royal donkeys of King David (1 Chron. 27:30); and (2) Jadon, one of those who assisted in repairing the wall of Jerusalem after the return from the captivity (Neh. 3:7).

ME'ROZ (mē'roz). A place in northern Palestine, referred to in Scripture in connection with a curse in the song of Deborah (Judg. 5:23; cf. 21:8-10; 1 Sam. 11:7). It would seem as if its people might have helped in the campaign against Sisera but failed to do so. It has been satisfactorily identified with Khirbet Mārūs some 7½ miles S of Kadesh of Naphtali.

ME'SECH (Ps. 120:5, KJV only). *See* Meshech, no. 1.

ME'SHA (mē'sha).
1. A place in Arabia, the western limit of the children of Joktan (Gen. 10:30) and possibly

identical with Massa and Mash. However that may be, there is frequent mention of the latter country in the cuneiform inscriptions. It corresponds roughly with the Arabia Petraea of the geographers. It was the desert district that stretched away westward and southward of Babylon.

2. King of Moab and tributary to Ahab. At the death of Ahab (c. 853 B.C.) Mesha endeavored to shake off the yoke of Israel and free himself from the burdensome tribute of 100,000 lambs and the wool of 100,000 rams. When Jehoram became king he secured the assistance of Jehoshaphat in reducing the Moabites to their former condition of tributaries. The two armies marched by a circuitous route around the Dead Sea and were joined by the forces of the king of Edom. The Moabites were defeated and driven from their stronghold, from which the king and 700 fighting men made an attempt to break through the besieging army. Beaten back, he withdrew to the wall of the city, upon which he offered up his firstborn son and heir to the kingdom as a burnt offering to Chemosh, the fire god of Moab. His bloody sacrifice had the effect of inducing the besiegers to retire, with much spoil, to their own land (2 Kings 3:4-27), c. 851 B.C. The exploits of "Mesha, son [i.e., "votary"] of Chemosh, king of Moab," are recorded in the inscription on the Moabite Stone, discovered by M. Ganneau at Dibon in Moab.

3. The eldest son of Caleb (brother of Jerahmeel and son of Hezron) and "father" (founder) of Ziph (1 Chron. 2:42), about 1390 B.C.

4. A son of the Benjamite Shaharaim by his wife Hodesh (1 Chron. 8:9).

BIBLIOGRAPHY: For *King of Moab*, see: N. Glueck, *Annual of the American Schools of Oriental Research* 14 (1933-34); D. J. Wiseman, ed., *Peoples of Old Testament Times* (1973), pp. 235, 275. *See also* Moabite Stone.

ME'SHACH (mē'shak). The name given to Mishael, one of the companions of Daniel, by the commander of the officials of the Babylonian court. He and Daniel and two other captive youths were selected to be trained as personal attendants and advisers of the king (Dan. 1:7; etc.), about 604 B.C. *See* Shadrach.

ME'SHECH (mē'shek).
1. A Japhetic people alluded to in Gen. 10:2. Ezekiel refers to them as allied with Tubal and associated with Gog, "the prince of Rosh, Meshech, and Tubal" (Ezek. 32:26; 38:2-3; 39:1). Ezekiel also mentions them as engaged in commerce in the emporia of Tyre, dealing in slaves and bronze vessels (27:13). In the records of Tiglath-pileser I (c. 1110 B.C.) and Shalmaneser III (860-825 B.C.) the land of Musku (Meshech) is mentioned and situated in the mountains on the northern boundary of Assyria and bordering on Tabal, biblical Tubal, in the west. The Moschoi and Tibarenoi are referred to by Herodotus as

living in the mountains SE of the Black Sea (3.94; 7.78). Both Strabo and Pliny refer to Moschoi.

2. Another name (1 Chron. 1:17) for *Mash* (which see).   M.F.U.

MESHELEMI'AH (me-shel-e-mī'a; "Jehovah remunerates"). A Levite of the family of Kore. He and his seven sons and brothers were gatekeepers of the Tabernacle in the time of David (1 Chron. 9:21; 26:1-2, 9), before 975 B.C. They were all assigned to the E gate, except Zechariah (v. 14), who had the N gate.

MESHEZ'ABEL (me-shez'a-bel; "God delivers"). The grandfather of Meshullam, who assisted in repairing the wall of Jerusalem (Neh. 3:4), and one of the "leaders of the people" who signed the covenant with Nehemiah (10:21), and father of Pethahiah the Zerahite of Judah (11:24), before 445 B.C. Probably the same person is referred to in all the passages.

MESHIL'LEMITH (me-shil'e-mith; 1 Chron. 9:12). *See* Meshillemoth.

MESHIL'LEMOTH (me-shil'e-mōth; "deeds of recompense").

1. A priest, the son of Immer and father of Meshullam (1 Chron. 9:12, where he is called Meshillemith). He is said (Neh. 11:13) to be the son of Immer and father of Ahzai, before 440 B.C.

2. The father of Berechiah, one of the leaders of Ephraim who protested against the attempt of the Israelites to make slaves of their captive brothers of Judah (2 Chron. 28:12), before 735 B.C.

MESHO'BAB (me-shō'bab; "returned, restored"). A leader of the tribe of Simeon, whose family so increased that he migrated to Gedor in the time of Hezekiah (1 Chron. 4:34), about 719 B.C.

MESHUL'LAM (me-shul'am; "repaid, rewarded").

1. The grandfather of Shaphan, the scribe who was sent by King Josiah to take charge of the money collected for the repairs of the Temple (2 Kings 22:3), before 639 B.C.

2. The eldest named of the children of Zerubbabel (1 Chron. 3:19), about 536 B.C.

3. A Gadite, and one of the leaders of the tribe residing in Bashan, whose genealogies were taken in the time of Jeroboam and of Jotham (1 Chron. 5:13), 783-738 B.C.

4. A Benjamite, and one of the descendants of Elpaal living in Jerusalem after the captivity (1 Chron. 8:17).

5. A Benjamite, son of Hodaviah (1 Chron. 9:7), or Joed (Neh. 11:7), and father of Sallu, who resided at Jerusalem after the captivity, before 445 B.C.

6. Another Benjamite (son of Shephatiah) who lived at Jerusalem after the Exile (1 Chron. 9:8), about 445 B.C.

7. A priest (son of Zadok) whose descendants lived in Jerusalem (1 Chron. 9:11; Neh. 11:11), before 445 B.C. He is probably the same as *Shallum* (which see).

8. The son of Meshillemith and ancestor of Maasai (1 Chron. 9:12), or Amashsai (Neh. 11:13), long before 445 B.C.

9. A Levite of the family of Kohath and one of the overseers of the Temple repairs in the reign of Josiah (2 Chron. 34:12), 639 B.C.

10. One of the "leading men" sent by Ezra to Iddo to gather together the Levites to join the caravan about to return to Jerusalem (Ezra 8:16), about 557 B.C.

11. A leader in the time of Ezra, probably a Levite, who assisted Jonathan and Jahzeiah in abolishing the marriages that some of the people had contracted with foreign wives (Ezra 10:15), 457 B.C. He is probably the Temple gatekeeper mentioned in Neh. 12:25, which last is also called Meshelemiah (1 Chron. 26:1), Shelemiah (v. 14), and Shallum (Neh. 7:45).

12. One of the "sons" (descendants) of Bani who divorced his Gentile wife after the captivity (Ezra 10:29), 456 B.C.

13. The son of Berechiah who repaired a portion of the walls of Jerusalem after the captivity (Neh. 3:4, 30), 445 B.C. It was his daughter who married Jehohanan, the son of Tobiah the Ammonite (6:18).

14. The son of Besodeiah; he, with Joiada, repaired the Old Gate of Jerusalem (Neh. 3:6), 445 B.C.

15. One of the principal Israelites who stood at Ezra's left hand when he read the law to the people (Neh. 8:4), about 445 B.C. He is, perhaps, one of those who signed the sacred covenant (10:20).

16. One of the priests who signed the covenant made by Nehemiah and the people to serve the Lord (Neh. 10:7).

17. A priest in the days of Joiakim, the son of Jeshua, and representative of the house of Ezra (Neh. 12:13), after 536 B.C.

18. A priest at the same time as no. 17 above, and a son of Ginnethon (Neh. 12:16).

MESHUL'LEMETH (me-shul'e-meth; form of *Meshullam* which see). The daughter of Haruz of Jotbah, wife of Manasseh, king of Judah, and mother of his successor, Amon (2 Kings 21:19), about 690 B.C.

MESI'AS. *See* Messiah.

MESO'BAITE. *See* Mezobaite.

MESOPOTA'MIA (mes-ō-po-tā'mi-a). "The country between the rivers," the ordinary Gk. rendering of the Heb. *Aram-naharaim,* meaning "Aram," or "Syria of the two rivers" (Gen. 24:10; Deut. 23:4; Judg. 3:8, 10; *see* Roger T. O'Callaghan, *Aram-Naharaim* [1948]). Mesopotamia is now known as Iraq. The two great rivers of the of the region are the Tigris and Euphrates. The term *Mesopotamia* refers to the upper part of the valley of the two rivers known today by Arabs as Al Jazira, or "the island." In modern usage Mesopotamia embraces also the lower part of the valley. The Tigris and the Euphrates were the lifeblood of this region in antiquity. These mighty rivers, which cradled ancient civilization, have sources in the 10,000-foot peaks of the Armenian mountains. Here they gain sufficient water from melting snows to feed streams that flow through the arid regions to the south. The silt-retaining waters of these rivers built the plain of Babylonia over the millennia and produced a region of extreme fertility that, with irrigation, produces wheat, barley, figs, dates, pomegranates, corn, and many other commodities. A network of irrigation canals honeycombed this region in antiquity, and it was capable of supporting a dense population and a very high degree of civilization. Great kings like Rim-Sin of Larsa and Hammurabi of Babylon took pride in their great irrigation projects, as did many other of those early rulers. Today this region lies scorched and almost uninhabitable with blistering heat and fine wind-driven sand. This territory was overrun by Muslims in the seventh century A.D. and the Mongols in the thirteenth, and its vast irrigation culture vanished. It was under Turkish rule until 1917, when the British took Baghdad. Since then British rule has been succeeded by the Iraqi government. Efforts are currently being made to restore the irrigation network of ancient times. These efforts are doomed to limited success because of the increasing salinity of the soil.

M.F.U.; H.F.V.

BIBLIOGRAPHY: C. H. Gordon, *Hebrew Union College Annual* 26 (1955): 43-108; J. J. Finkelstein, *Journal of Near Eastern Studies* 21 (1962): 73-92.

MESS, MESSES (from Heb. *maś'at,* a "raising"). The Heb. denotes the uplifting of hands in prayer (Ps. 141:2), the rising of a flame (Judg. 20:38, 40), or a "portion" (NASB and NIV) or "mess" (KJV) of food (Gen. 43:34; 2 Sam. 11:8).

MESSI'AH (Heb. *māshîaḥ,* "anointed"; rendered in the LXX by the Gk. equivalent *Christos*).

The word *Christ* is therefore almost invariably used instead of Messiah in the NT as the official designation of our Lord. In the OT priests are referred to as the "anointed" (e.g., Lev. 4:3; 8:12; Ps. 105:15), as are kings (e.g., 1 Sam. 24:7-11; 2 Sam 23:1; 1 Kings 19:16). We also read (19:16) of anointing to the office of prophet. But along with these subordinate uses of the term, which undoubtedly foreshadowed the three great offices of Christ as Prophet, Priest, and King, its highest use was employed to designate the One promised of God as the great Deliverer, and who was to be in a preeminent and altogether unique sense the Anointed, or the Messiah, of God. The subject is therefore extensive, and offers to the student an immense field for investigation not only in the OT and NT Scriptures but also in Jewish and Christian literature.

The Messianic Idea. The OT messianic revelation appears not merely in particular predictions. The whole of the OT is rather to be looked upon as bearing a prophetic character. The idea underlying the whole development of these Scriptures and the life dealt with therein is that of God's gracious manifestation of Himself to men and the establishment of His kingdom on the earth. This idea becomes more and more distinct and centralizes itself more and more fully in the Person of the coming King, the Messiah. The creation and Fall of man and the growing sinfulness of the race make clear the need for deliverance. The preservation of a part of mankind from the Flood, and the continuance of human history, have great suggestion of promise. The call of Abraham, with the promise "in your seed all the nations of the earth shall be blessed" revealed the divine purpose, which had been previously indicated, yet more distinctly (*see* Gen. 22:18; cf. 12:3; 9:26; 3:15). The founding of the Jewish nation, its theocratic character, its institutions, its ritual, and its history all center on this one idea. The sinfulness of sin, the possibility of a divinely appointed method of deliverance from sin, and the realization of a kingdom of righteousness lie at the very basis of the Jewish economy. Moreover, the chosen nation bore its peculiar character not merely for its own sake, but also for the sake of the world. Upon condition of fidelity to the covenant the promise was given: "You shall be to Me a kingdom of priests and a holy nation" (Ex. 19:6). The devout wish of Moses was significant also in the same direction, "Would that all the Lord's people were prophets" (Num. 11:29). But the highest glory of Israel was that from the nation One was to come in whom these noble relations to God and man, only to a large extent symbolized by the nation itself, should be perfectly fulfilled. The actual "Son" and "Servant" of God, the true Prophet, Priest, and King, was to be the Messiah. This is the key to the whole body of the OT Scriptures.

Designations. That various designations were

given to the Messiah was only natural, and to have been expected. Among them are the "seed" of Abraham, "son of David," "Son of Man," "My Son," "My Servant," "My chosen one," "the Branch," "Wonderful Counselor, Mighty God, Eternal Father, Prince of Peace" (*see* Gen. 22:18; 2 Sam. 23:5; Ps. 2:7; Isa. 9:6-7; 42:1; Zech. 3:8; 6:12; Dan. 7:13-14; 10:16-18).

Prophetic Passages. The number of passages in the OT regarded by the Jews in pre-Christian times as prophetic of the Messiah is much larger than that of the special predictions to which Christians have commonly appealed. It is stated by Edersheim to be more than 456, of which 75 are from the Pentateuch, 243 from the Prophets, and 138 from the Hagiographa. "But comparatively few of these," he adds, "are what would be termed verbal predictions." This harmonizes, however, with what has already been said with regard to the general character of the OT revelation. (For a complete list of passages messianically applied in the rabbinic writings, *see* Edersheim's *Life and Times of Jesus,* Appendix 9.) The predictions to which Christians as well as Jews have attached special importance embrace the following: Gen. 3:15 (the protoevangelium); 9:27; 12:3; 22:18; 49:8, 10; Deut. 18:18; 2 Sam. 7:11-16; 23:5; Pss. 2, 16, 22, 40, 110; Isa. 2, 7, 9, 11, 40, 42, 49, 53; Jer. 23:5-6; Dan. 7:27; Zech. 12:10-14; Hag. 2:9; Mal. 3:1; 4:5-6. For an exposition of these and other passages, reference may profitably be made to the OT commentaries, both Jewish and Christian.

Jewish Views of the Messiah. Two questions can be asked of the Jews: What Messiah did they expect? and, What should the OT revelation have led them to expect? While Jewish expectation had been deepening and in some respects becoming more definite and true during the centuries preceding the Christian era, so that at the time of our Lord's appearing it seemed to await its immediate fulfillment, yet the Jewish people were not prepared to recognize Jesus as the Christ. The reason is found in the rabbinical and popularly received ideas of the Messiah. The fatal mistake of the Jews was not in rejecting the Scriptures but in giving to them a narrow and unspiritual interpretation. Jesus truly said, "You search the Scriptures, because you think that in them you have eternal life; and it is these that bear witness of Me; and you are unwilling to come to Me, that you may have life" (John 5:39-40). Their interpretation was far from being wholly false, as Edersheim shows with reference to the list of rabbinic interpretations noted above. It embraced "such doctrines as the premundane existence of the Messiah; his elevation above Moses, and even above the angels; his representative character; his cruel sufferings and derision; his violent death, and that for his people; his work in behalf of the living and of the dead; his redemption and restoration of Israel; the opposition of

the Gentiles, their partial judgment and conversion; the prevalence of his law; the universal blessings of the latter days; and his kingdom." But this same interpretation left out certain elements of greatest and governing importance. The doctrines of original sin, and of the sinfulness of man's whole nature, were greatly reduced from their Scripture meaning and were practically omitted from the prevalent Jewish teaching. Consequently the deepest thought of the messiahship, the salvation of the world from sin, was lacking. In keeping with this, the priestly office of the Messiah was also lost sight of, as was the prophetic office of the Messiah. The all-absorbing ideas were those of kingship and deliverance. And these were chiefly of national significance. The restoration of national glory was the great hope of Israel. All else was subordinate to that. Of modern Jewish views our space permits only a few observations. Although the denial has been constant that Jesus is the Christ, and although during many centuries the Jews almost universally continued to look for their national deliverer (and their hope was again and again stimulated and disappointed by the appearance of more than a score of false Messiahs), marked changes have taken place within recent years in Jewish opinions and belief upon this subject. (1) The relatively small and diminishing class known as Orthodox Jews adheres to the ancient expectation. (2) The Reform Jews, embracing many of the most learned and influential, have laid this expectation aside. With this class the whole conception of the Messiah has become dim and confused. It is doubted as to whether the Messiah refers to a person or a time; also as to whether or not the person or time has arrived. (3) The main body of modern Jews still looks forward to the ingathering of the Jews and their restoration to national glory in the land of their forefathers, and along with this they expect an era of universal peace and harmony among men. But still there is great diversity of opinion as to the method and means by which these results are to be accomplished. The Messiah may mean a particular person born of the Jewish race, or the term may stand for a conjunction of events brought about by the Jewish people. A feature made prominent at present in Jewish denial of the messiahship of our Lord is that, in their view, the OT prophecies predict the full and blessed results of the messianic reign as coming at once with the advent of the Messiah, and such results have not come; and they can find no prediction of a second advent. To us as Christians this objection has no force, in view of the comprehensiveness and, at the same time, the gradual and incomplete development of OT prophecy. The prophecies of the old dispensation do indeed look forward to the ripened results of Christ's reign. But the prophecies of the NT supplement those of the OT in unfolding the gradual methods by which these results are to be reached, and in predicting the final glorious coming of Christ.

The Messianic Realization. The question, Is Jesus the Christ? is plainly of greatest importance, not to Jews only but to all races of mankind. This question is answered affirmatively because Jesus distinctly claimed to be the Messiah, a claim reconcilable with His character only upon the supposition that His claim was valid. The conception of messiahship that Jesus held and promulgated was unspeakably above the prevailing Jewish conception, and yet in reality was that of OT prophecy. The gospel of Matthew gives important revelation concerning the Messiah's kingdom. The phrase "kingdom of heaven," literally, "of the heavens," is peculiar to Matthew and denotes the messianic rule on the earth of Christ as the son of David. The designation is appropriate because it is the rule of the heavens over the earth (Matt. 6:10). The phrase is derived from the OT (Dan. 2:34-36, 44; 7:23-27), and it is said that the "God of heaven" will set up this kingdom covenanted to David's posterity (2 Sam 7:8-16) after the destruction of Gentile world powers by the returning Christ, the stone "cut out without hands." This kingdom was confirmed in regard to the Son of God through the angel Gabriel (Luke 1:31-33). In Matthew's gospel the kingdom of heaven is described in three ways: (1) as being *at hand,* from the beginning of John the Baptist's preaching (Matt. 3:2) to the rejection of the King and the announcement of His new message (12:46-50), (2) *in the seven "mysteries of the kingdom of heaven"* now being consummated in this present age, and (3) *in the future prophetic aspect* when the kingdom will be established at the return of Christ in glory (Matt. 24-25; Acts 15:14-18). Of this future messianic glory our Lord had full consciousness in His earthly public ministry. *See* Prophecy; Christ; Son of Man.

BIBLIOGRAPHY: W. Manson, *Jesus the Messiah* (1943); H. H. Rowley, *The Servant of the Lord* (1952); B. B. Warfield, *Biblical and Theological Studies* (1952), pp. 79-126; T. W. Manson, *The Servant Messiah* (1953); A. R. Johnson, *Sacral Kingship in Ancient Israel* (1955); E. J. Young, *Daniel's Vision of the Son of Man* (1958); O. Cullmann, *The Christology of the New Testament* (1959), pp. 111-36; F. Hahn, *The Titles of Jesus in Christology* (1969); R. N. Longenecker, *The Christology of the Early Jewish Christianity* (1970); G. H. Dalman, *The Words of Christ* (1981), pp. 289-323; F. J. Delitzsch and P. J. Gloag, *The Messiahship of Christ* (1983).

METALS. All the principal metals were familiar to the Hebrews and are mentioned in Scripture. For knowledge of metals in the ancient world, *see* Handicrafts: Goldsmith; Metalworker; Mineral Kingdom.

METALWORKER. *See* Handicrafts.

METEYARD. A linear measure. *See* Metrology.

ME'THEG-AM'MAH (me'theg-am'a; "bridle of the mother," i.e., "mother city"). The figurative term for a chief city of the Philistines, namely, Gath. To give up one's bridle to another is equivalent to submitting to him (2 Sam. 8:1), and "bridle of the mother city" means the jurisdiction or power of the metropolis. The NASB replaces Metheg-ammah with "chief city."

METHU'SAEL. *See* Methushael.

METHU'SELAH (me-thū'ze-la; "man of the dart"). The son of Enoch and grandfather of Noah. At the age of 187 he became the father of Lamech, after whose birth he lived 782 years and died at the advanced age of 969 (Gen. 5:21-22, 25-27; 1 Chron. 1:3).

METHU'SHAEL (me-thū'sha-el; "man of God"). The son of Mehujael and father of Lamech, of the family of Cain (Gen. 4:18; "Methusael," KJV).

METRETES. A foreign measure of capacity. *See* Metrology.

METROLOGY. The science of weights and measures.

Linear Measures. The names of the most common smaller linear measures are taken from members of the human body, because, in nearly all nations, these were at first used to measure lengths. As men's bodies differed in size these measures varied. But the progress of art and commerce gradually brought them to a uniform standard. The linear measurements were:

Finger or Digit (Heb. *'eşba').* The smallest measure among the Hebrews, and equal to the breadth of the human finger (about 0.75 inch). We find the thickness of the solid parts of Solomon's pillars measured by *fingers* (Jer. 52:21).

Handbreadth (Heb. *tepah,* between three and four inches, 2 Chron. 4:5; Ps. 39:5; *ţōpaḥ,* Ex. 37:12). The width of the four fingers closely pressed together. The handbreadth was in common use in early Hebrew times (25:25; 1 Kings 7:26; etc.). It is used as an architectural term (1 Kings 7:9, "coping") and is thought to mean the *corbels* upon which the roof beams rest.

Span (Heb. *zereth*). The width from the end of the thumb to that of the little finger, when these were extended. This measure was in use among the Hebrews in very early times (Ex. 28:16; *see* 39:9; 1 Sam. 17:4). It was about nine inches.

Cubit (Lat. *cubitum,* "elbow, cubit"; Heb. *'ammâ;* Gk. *pēchus,* the "forearm"). An important and constant measure among the Hebrews (Ex. 25:10, 17, 23; etc.; 1 Kings 7:24, 27, 31; etc.; Ezek. 40:5; etc.), and other ancient nations. It was commonly reckoned as the length of the arm from the point of the elbow to the end of the middle finger, about eighteen inches.

Egyptian Cubit. This was six handbreadths or palms, about 17.72 inches, but the royal Egyptian cubit was a palm longer (20.67 inches), evidence for this being found in measuring sticks recovered from tombs.

Babylonian Cubit. Herodotus states that the "royal" exceeded the "moderate" cubit by three digits. The majority of critics, however, think that Herodotus is speaking of the ordinary Greek cubit, though the opposite view is affirmed by Grote. Bockh estimates the Babylonian royal cubit at 20.806 inches.

Hebrew Cubit. The Hebrews, like the Egyptians and Babylonians, had two cubits, the common and apparently older cubit (Deut. 3:11; 2 Chron. 3:3), and a cubit that was a handbreadth longer (Ezek. 40:5; 43:14). The common Hebrew cubit was 17.72 inches and the long cubit 20.67 inches, apparently the same as the Egyptian royal cubit.

Pace (Heb. *ṣa'ad,* 2 Sam. 6:13). Equal to a "step," and so translated elsewhere. The above passage is the only one in which the term can be used as a measure of distance and, if so, would answer to our yard.

Measuring Rod or Reed (Heb. *qāneh,* "reed"). Properly the calamus, or sweet cane, which, probably from its shape and length, came to be used for a measure (Ezek. 40:3, 5; 42:16-19). Its length is given (40:5) as six times a cubit, plus six handbreadths, nearly eleven feet.

Furlong. See Mile, below.

Mile (Gk. *milion,* Matt. 5:41). Equal to 1,618 English yards, and thus 142 yards less than the English statute mile. The *mile* was derived from the Roman system of measurement and was in common use in our Lord's time. The Gk. *stadion,* "established," rendered "mile," is rendered "furlong" in the KJV and was 600 Greek feet, or 625 Roman feet, i.e., 606.75 English feet.

Sabbath Day's Journey (Gk. *sabbatou hodos,* Acts 1:12). A very limited distance, such as would naturally be regarded as the immediate vicinity of any locality. It is supposed to have been founded on the command "Let no man go out of his place on the seventh day" (Ex. 16:29). This measure was fixed by the Jewish legislators at 2,000 cubits. It is supposed to have been suggested by the space between the Ark of God and the people (Josh. 3:4), or the extent of the suburbs of Levitical cities (Num. 35:5). The strict observance of the Sabbath day's journey was evaded by the "connection of boundaries." He who desired to go farther than 2,000 cubits had only, before the beginning of the Sabbath, to deposit somewhere within this limit, and therefore perhaps at its end, food for two meals. He thus declared, as it were, that here would be his place of abode, and he might then, on the Sabbath, go not merely from his actual to his legal abode, but also 2,000 cubits from the latter. Even such particular preparation was not necessary in all cases. If, for example, anyone should be on the road when the Sabbath began, and see at a distance of 2,000 cubits a tree or a wall, he might declare it to be his Sabbath home and might then go not only 2,000 cubits to the tree or wall, but 2,000 cubits farther (Schürer, *History of the Jewish People,* div. 2, 2:121-22).

Some Distance (Heb. *kibrat-hā'āreṣ,* Gen. 35:16; 48:7; 2 Kings 5:19). This seems to indicate some definite distance, but it is impossible to state with precision what that distance was. The LXX renders it "a horse's race," i.e., as the Arabs inform us, a *parasang* (thirty furlongs), about four English miles.

Day's Journey (Heb. *derek yôm*). The most usual method of calculating distance in traveling in the East (Gen. 30:36; 31:23; Ex. 3:18; etc.; once in NT, Luke 2:44). Of course, it was not an exact measure, varying as the journey would according to the circumstances of the travelers, the country traveled, and so on. The ordinary day's journey among the Jews was twenty to thirty miles, but when traveling in company, only ten miles.

Meteyard (mēt'yard; Heb. *middâ*). A general term for measure, archaic for *measuring stick* (Lev. 19:35, KJV). The term does not appear in the NASB and NIV.

Dry Measures of Capacity. Dry measures of capacity are given below in ascending order of size. Note that some dry measures are also used as liquid measures.

Handful (Heb. *qōmeṣ,* Lev. 2:2; 5:12). Probably never brought to any greater accuracy than the natural capacity of the human hand. It was also used as a liquid measure.

Kab (Heb. *qab,* "hollow," 2 Kings 6:25). This was, according to the rabbis, equal to one-sixth of a seah (*see* below). It is equal to about two quarts.

Omer (Heb. *'ōmer,* a "heap," Ex. 16:16-36; "sheaf," Lev. 23:10). An ancient Hebrew measure. Its relative value was one-tenth of an ephah (Ex. 16:36), and it held about 5.1 pints. It contained the portion of manna assigned each individual for his daily food (16:16-20).

Seah (Heb. *se'â,* "measure"; rendered "measure" in Gen. 18:6; 1 Sam. 25:18; 2 Kings 7:16, 18; *ephah,* Judg. 6:19). It was a common household measure. According to the rabbis, it was equal to one-third of an ephah and was, perhaps, identical with "measure," *'shālîsh,* in Isa. 40:12.

Ephah (Heb. *'ēpâ*). A measure of Egyptian origin and in very common use among the Hebrews. It contained ten omers (Ex. 16:36), about three pecks and three pints, and was equivalent in capacity to the liquid measure, *bat.* According to Josephus (*Ant.* 8.2.9), the ephah contained seventy-two sextarii.

Bushel. Though the bushel appears in the KJV, NIV, and NASB, there was no exact equivalent to the bushel in ancient times. The term appears in the NASB of Amos 8:5 to replace KJV "ephah." It appears in the KJV of Matt. 5:15; Mark 4:21; Luke 11:33, and in those verses is replaced in the NASB with "peck-measure." It appears in the NIV in Luke 16:7 in place of NASB "measures." *See* Homer.

Homer (Heb. *hōmer,* "heap," Lev. 27:16; Num. 11:32; Ezek. 45:13; *kōr,* 1 Kings 4:22; 5:11; 2 Chron. 2:10; 27:5; Gk. *koros,* "measure," Luke 16:7, *see* marg.). According to Fuerst, the *homer* was originally a donkey load and hence a measure of like capacity. It was supposed to have been called *kor* because of its being a circular measure. The homer contained ten ephahs (Ezek. 45:11), nearly eight bushels. The half-homer was known as *lĕthĕk (see* Hos. 3:2).

Liquid Measures of Capacity. The liquid measures of capacity given below are in ascending order of size.

Log (Heb. *lōg,* "hollow," Lev. 14:10; etc.). This term originally signified a *basin.* The rabbis reckoned it equal to six hen's eggs, their contents being measured by the amount of water they displaced, thus making it the one-twelfth of a *hin.*

Hin (Heb. *hin,* of Egyptian origin, Ex. 29:40; 30:24; Num. 15:4, 7, 9; Ezek. 4:11; etc.). This held one-sixth bath, nearly six pints.

Bath (Heb. *bat,* "measured"). This was the largest of the liquid measures; first mentioned in 1 Kings 7:26; equal to the ephah, and so to one-tenth of a homer (Ezek. 45:11). Its capacity would thus be seven and a half gallons.

Foreign Measures of Capacity. In the NT we find the following foreign measures, given in ascending order of size.

Sextarius or Xestes (Gk. *chēstēs*). A Greek measure with no Hebrew equivalent, holding about a pint (Josephus *Ant.* 8.2.9). Also any small vessel, such as a cup or pitcher, whether a sextarius or not (Mark 7:8; KJV, "pot").

Choenix (Gk. *choenix,* only in Rev. 6:6, NASB and NIV, "quart"). A dry measure, containing two sextarii, or about one quart.

Modius (Gk. *modius*). A dry measure holding sixteen sextarii, i.e., about one peck. It occurs three times in the NT and is rendered "peck-measure" (Matt. 5:15; Mark 4:21; Luke 11:33). In each case it is accompanied by the Gk. article, intimating that it was in use in every household.

Saton (Gk. *saton,* Matt. 13:33; Luke 13:21, "peck"). A dry measure, supposed to be identical with the Hebrew seah, and to contain one peck.

Metretes (Gk. *metrētēs,* "measure," John 2:6, *see* marg.). Known as *amphora,* it was used for measuring liquids and contained seventy-two sextarii (*see* above), or somewhat less than nine English gallons.

Coros (Gk. *koros,* Luke 16:7, "measure"; NIV, "bushel"). The same as the homer.

Measures of Weight. The Jewish rabbis estimated weights according to the number of grains of barley, taken from the middle of the ear, to which they were equivalent. In describing the

weights used by the Hebrews we begin with the shekel, because it is the base of all the calculations of these weights.

Shekel (Heb. *sheqel,* "weight"). Equal to twenty *gerahs* (Ezek. 45:12) or ten English pennyweights. Of all the Jewish weights none is so accurately marked as the shekel, from the fact that half a shekel was ordered by God to be paid by each Israelite as a ransom for his soul (Ex. 30:13). The circumstances of the captivity do not warrant the idea that the Hebrews lost their knowledge of their weights, least of all the shekel. The poorer classes were left in Canaan (2 Kings 24:15-16; 25:11-12), and they probably continued the use of the ancient weights and money; while the upper classes, who were carried into captivity, would likely have retained some of them, especially the shekel. Then, too, we find the shekel in use in Jerusalem in the time of Zerubbabel. Although in very early times there may have been but one shekel (Gen. 23:15), it appears certain that from the period of the Exodus there were at least two shekels—one used in all ordinary transactions (Ex. 38:29; Josh. 7:21; 2 Kings 7:1; Amos 8:5; etc.); the other used in the payment of vows, offerings, and for other religious purposes (Ex. 30:13; Lev. 5:15; Num. 3:47) and called the "shekel of the sanctuary." It is a matter of much conjecture as to what, if any, difference existed between these two shekels, and also the shekel "by the king's weight" (2 Sam. 14:26). Jahn (*Biblical Archaeology,* sec. 116) identifies the common and sacred shekels and thinks that "the king's shekel" did not "amount to more than a fourth, perhaps not to more than the fifth or sixth part of the legal shekel." Keil (*Biblical Archaeology,* 2:231) thinks there was a common shekel, which was only the half of the holy one, or equal to the *beka* (Ex. 38:26). He arrives at this conclusion by comparing 1 Kings 10:17 with 2 Chron. 9:16, according to which 3 minas equal 300 common shekels; i.e., the mina contained 100 shekels, whereas it contained only 50 holy, or Mosaic, shekels. He also identifies the shekel "by the king's weight" with the "shekel of the sanctuary." After the captivity, the probability is that only the holy shekel was in use. The passage in Ezek. 45:12, written when a considerable portion of the captivity was passed, directs that on the return home there should be but one uniform standard. That standard was to be the holy shekel, being composed of 20 gerahs (Ex. 30:13). Other evidence of this is furnished in the fact that whereas in the earlier Scriptures reference was made to a difference of standard, no such distinction occurs after the captivity; the shekel coins of that period were all nearly of a weight.

Beka or *Half shekel* (Heb. *beqa',* a "fraction"; mentioned only twice, Gen. 24:22; Ex. 38:26). In the latter passage it is said to equal one-half of a holy shekel. It was the weight in silver that was

Israelite shekels

paid for each Israelite numbered (Ex. 38:26) and was equal to the tribute (cf. Matt. 17:24).

Gerah (Heb. *gērâ*, "kernel," a "bean" or "grain"). The smallest of the Hebrew weights, and the equivalent of the twentieth part of the holy shekel (Ex. 30:13; Lev. 27:25; Num. 3:47; 18:16; Ezek. 45:12).

Mina (Heb. *māneh*, a "portion," the original of the Lat. *moneta* and our *money*; 1 Kings 10:17; Ezra 2:69; Neh. 7:71-72; Ezek. 45:12, "maneh"; Gk. *mna*, Luke 19:13-25). From Ezek. 45:12 it appears that there were 60 holy shekels in a mina, whereas from the passages in Kings and Chronicles it is evident that a mina was equivalent to 100 shekels. These latter Keil thinks were the common shekels, 100 of which would make only 50 holy (i.e., Mosaic) shekels. Sixty minas formed a talent.

Talent (Heb. *kikkār*, "circle"; Gk. *talanton*, a "balance"). The name given to this weight, perhaps from its having been taken as "a round number" or sum total. It was the largest weight among the Hebrews, being used for metals, whether gold (1 Kings 9:14; 10:10; etc.), silver (2 Kings 5:22), bronze (Ex. 38:29), or iron (1 Chron. 29:7). The talent was used by various nations and differed considerably. It is perhaps impossible to determine whether the Hebrews had one talent only or several of different weights. From Ex. 38:24-29 we infer that the talent of gold, silver, and bronze was a talent of the same weight, and the evidence favors but one weight of that denomination, which contained 3,000 shekels. Estimating a shekel at 10 pennyweight, the talent would be equal to 93 pounds 12 ounces avoirdupois, or 125 troy weight. A talent seems to have been a full weight for an able man to carry (2 Kings 5:23). In the NT the talent occurs in a parable (Matt. 25:15) and as the estimate of a stone's weight, "about one hundred pounds each" (Rev. 16:21, *see* marg.).

In addition to the above, which we can with certainty call Hebrew weights, both the OT and NT refer to other weights, probably introduced from foreign nations. Of these we give the following brief account:

Daric or *Drachma* (Heb. *'adarkôn*, 1 Chron. 29:7; Ezra 8:27; *dark^emôn*, Ezra 2:69; Neh. 7:70; etc.). Thought by some to be identical to each other. Others conclude from 1 Chron. 29:7 that the *'adarkôn* was less than three-tenths of a shekel.

Pound (Gk. *mna*, "mina," Luke 19:13, NASB and NIV; Gk. *litra*, "pound," John 12:3; 19:39, KJV, NASB; "pint," NIV). Probably a Greek weight, used as a money of account, of which 60 went to the talent. It weighed 100 drachmae, or 15 ounces 83¾ grains. The "pound" in John 12:3; 19:39 (Gk. *litra*) refers to a Roman pound of 12 ounces.

The expression "ten pounds" appears in the KJV of Luke 19:13, but it is replaced in the NASB and NIV by "ten minas."

Measures of Value, or Money. The necessity of some kind of money arose very early in civilization. The division of labor required some measure of value; and commerce took a more convenient, if more complicated, form by making this common measure to serve as a circulating medium. Men decided early that the precious metals formed by far the most convenient material for such a medium, although it is probable that they were first introduced in their gross and unpurified state. Money in ancient times was both uncoined and coined.

It is well known that ancient nations that were without a coinage weighed the precious metals, a practice represented on the Egyptian monuments, on which gold and silver are shown to have been kept in the form of rings. It is uncertain whether any of these rings had a government stamp to denote their purity or value. Gold when brought as tribute was often in bags, which were deposited in the royal treasury. Though sealed and warranted to contain a certain quantity, they were weighed unless intended as a present or when the honesty of a person was beyond suspicion. The Egyptians had also unstamped copper money called "pieces of brass," which, like the gold and silver, continued to be taken by weight even in the time of the Ptolemies. Gradually the Greek coinage did away with the old system of weighing. The gold rings found in the Celtic countries have been thought to have had the same use.

The pecuniary transactions recorded in the Bible were all, we can scarcely doubt, effected by bullion. Silver was weighed out by the patriarchs, who used it not only to buy grain from Egypt (Gen. 42:25-28; 43:15, 18-23; 44:1-8), but land from the Canaanites (23:15-16). The narrative of the purchase of the burial place from Ephron gives us further insight into the use of money at that time (23:3-16). Here a currency is clearly indicated like that which the monuments of Egypt show to have been there used in a remote era. A similar purchase is recorded of Jacob, who bought a parcel of a field at Shalem for a hundred "pieces" (*kesitahs*) of money (33:18-19). Throughout the history of Joseph we find evidences of the constant use of money in prefer-

Weighing money

ence to barter (43:21; 47:13-17). Under the Mosaic law it was in silver shekels that money was paid to the sanctuary for the ransom of male Israelites (Ex. 30:13-16), compensations and fines (21:22; Lev. 5:15; Deut. 22:19, 29), and the priestly valuations (Lev. 27:3-25; Num. 18:16), and all exchange and sales reckoned. Half shekels are mentioned (Ex. 30:13, 15), which were called *bekas* (38:26), as well as quarter shekels (1 Sam. 9:8).

Very large sums were reckoned by the largest weight of the Israelites, the *talent,* a *round thing,* a name that indicates that there were lumps of silver in the form of thick round discs or rings, weighing 3,000 shekels. We may thus sum up our results respecting the money mentioned in Scripture written before the return from Babylon. From the time of Abraham silver money appears to have been in general use in Egypt and Canaan. This money was weighed when its value had to be determined, and we may therefore conclude that it was not of a settled system of weights. Because the money of Egypt and that of Canaan are spoken of together, we may reasonably suppose they were of the same kind. It is even probable that the form in both cases was similar or the same, since the ring money of Egypt resembles the ordinary ring money of the Celts, among whom it was probably first introduced by Phoenician traders.

Coined money was invented by the Lydians in Anatolia. Taking advantage of the abundance of gold and silver in their country, they turned out a great deal of coined currency. By the end of the seventh century B.C. coined money was plentiful in the Aegean world. Cyrus the Great, who conquered the fabulously opulent Croesus and his capital city of Sardis by 546 B.C., introduced coins into the mighty Persian Empire that he founded. Darius the Great (522-486 B.C.) made extensive use of this notable aid to commerce. He coined

silver and gold and this, with many other commercial advantages, was the explanation of the might and grandeur of Persian power. The discovery of coinage was a great stride in commercial progress. It seems such a simple thing and doubtless Egyptians and Greeks, who came in contact with it through the Anatolian Lydians, must have wondered why they had not hit upon this brilliant idea earlier.   M.F.U.

The earliest coins mentioned in the Bible are the gold coins called drachmas, 538 B.C. It is thought by some that Jewish silver shekels and half shekels were introduced under Ezra (about 458 B.C.); but it is most probable that they were issued under Simon Maccabaeus (*see* 1 Macc. 15:6), and copper coins were struck by the Hasmonaean and Herodian family, 140 B.C. The following alphabetical list embraces all the denominations of money mentioned in the OT and the NT.

Beka (Heb. *beqa‘,* a "half"). A Jewish weight of a half shekel's value (Ex. 38:26). As a coin it may have been issued at any time from Alexander until the earlier period of the Maccabees. *See* Shekel.

Bronze. (1) Heb. *nᵉḥōshet,* "copper"; Ezek. 16:36, "lewdness." In the expression "Because your lewdness was poured out," *nᵉḥōshet* probably means bronze or copper in the general sense of money. The only objection raised to this is that the Hebrews had no copper coin. But all that can be affirmed with certainty is that the use of copper or bronze as money is not mentioned elsewhere in the OT. We cannot infer with certainty from this that it was not then in use. As soon as the Hebrews began to stamp coins, bronze or copper coins were stamped as well as the silver shekels, and specimens of these are still in existence from the time of the Maccabees. Judging from their size, these coins were in all probability worth a whole, a half, and a quarter gerah. (2) In Matt. 10:9 (Gk. *chalkos,* rendered "money" in Mark 6:8; 12:41, *see* marg.) "copper" is used, apparently of a small Roman or Greek copper coin, of about the value of one-half cent. The copper coins of Palestine are so minute, and so irregular in their weight, that their value, like that of the English copper coinage of the present day, was chiefly legal, or conventional, and did not represent the relative value of the two metals—silver and copper.

Cent. Two names of coins in the NT are rendered by this word. (1) Gk. *kodrantēs;* Lat. *quadrans* (Matt. 5:26; Mark 12:42), a coin current in Palestine in the time of our Lord. It was equivalent to two *lepta* (KJV, "mites"). The name *quadrans* was originally given to the quarter of the Roman *as,* or piece of three *unciae,* therefore also called *teruncius.* The value was what one might earn in ten or fifteen minutes of work. Its value was about 3.8 mills. (2) Gk. *'assarion* (Matt. 10:29; Luke 12:6), properly a small *as, assarium,* but in the time of our Lord used as the Gk. equivalent of the Lat. *as*. The rendering of the Vulg. in Luke 12:6 makes it probable that a single coin is intended by two *assaria*. The *'assarion* is what one might earn in an hour or less.

Daric or Drachma (Heb. *'ădarkón*, 1 Chron. 29:7; Ezra 8:27; *darkᵉmôn*, Ezra 2:69; Neh. 7:70-72). The *daric* is usually thought to mean the *daric* of the Persians and seems to be etymologically connected with the Greek *drachma*. The drachma is of interest as the earliest coined money that we can be sure was known to and used by the Jews. It must have been in circulation among the Jews during the captivity and was extensively circulated in Greece. The coin was stamped on one side with the figure of a crowned archer, with one knee bent; on the other side a deep, irregular cleft. The two darics in the British Museum weigh 128.4 grains and 128.6 grains respectively.

The *drachma*, as a silver coin (Luke 15:8-9, *see* marg.), was very common among the Greeks and Hebrews. At the time of Luke's writing this Greek coin was of about the same weight as the Roman *denarius* (*see* below) and was almost superseded by it. The author of the Chronicles uses the words that in his time designated the current gold coins. He did not intend to assume that darics were in use in the time of David. Probably the sum in darics is the amount contributed in gold pieces received as coins, whereas the talents represent the weight of the vessels and other articles brought as offerings.

Denarius (Gk. *dēnarion*, Matt. 18:28; 20:2, 9, 13; 22:19; Mark 6:37; 12:15; 14:5; Luke 7:41; 10:35; 20:24; John 6:7; 12:5; Rev. 6:6). This was a Roman silver coin, in the time of Jesus and the apostles. It took its name from its being first equal to ten "donkeys," a number afterward increased to sixteen. The earliest specimens are from approximately the start of the second century B.C. From this time it was the principal silver coin of the commonwealth. In the time of Augustus eighty-four denarii were struck from a pound of silver, which would make the standard weight about sixty grains. This Nero reduced by striking ninety-six from the pound, which would give a standard weight of about fifty-two grains, results confirmed by the coins of the periods, which are, however, not exactly true to the standard. In Palestine, in the NT period, evidence points to

Coin of Nero

the denarii as mainly forming the silver currency. The denarius was the daily wage of a laborer. The only way to compute the value of NT coins in current values is to consider what a laborer might earn in a day in various countries of the world (*see* Matt. 20:2, 4, 7, 9, 10, 13).

Didrachma. See Tribute Money in the general listing.

Fourth of a Shekel (Heb. *rebă'*, "fourth," 1 Sam. 9:8). The money that Saul's servant gave to Samuel as a present.

Gerah (Heb. *gērâ*, a "kernel," Ex. 30:13; Lev. 27:25; Num. 3:47; 18:16; Ezek. 45:12). The smallest weight and also the smallest piece of money among the Hebrews. It represented the twentieth part of a shekel, weighed 13.7 Paris grains, and was worth less than one-fifth of a day's wage.

Gold. There is no positive mention of the use of *gold money* among the Hebrews; it probably was circulated by weight (1 Chron. 21:25). The gold coinage current in Palestine in the NT period was the Roman imperial *aureus*, which passed for twenty-five denarii.

Half of a Shekel. See Beka.

Mina (Gk. *mna*, Luke 19:13-25). A value mentioned in the parable, as is the talent in Matt. 25:14-30. The reference appears to be to a Greek pound, a weight used as a money of account, of which 60 went to the talent, the weight depending upon the weight of the talent. The *mina* contained 100 drachmas.

Piece of Money. This expression represents two kinds of money in the OT: (1) *Kesitah* (Gen. 33:19). "The kesitah was a weighed piece of metal, and to judge from Gen. 23:16; Job 42:11, of considerably higher value than the shekel; not an unstamped piece of silver of the value of a lamb," as supposed by the old interpreters (Keil, *Arch.*, 2:24). These silver pieces, with their weight designated on them, are the *most ancient money* of which we have any information. It is clear that they circulated singly, because the worth of the article bought was given in the *number* of them. (2) *Stater* (*see* below).

Piece of Silver. Generally speaking, the word has been supplied for a word understood in the Heb. The phrase is always "a thousand" or the like "of silver" (Gen. 20:16; 45:22; etc.). In similar passages the word "shekels" occurs in the Heb., and there is little if any doubt that this is the word understood in all these cases. There are, however, two exceptional passages where a word equivalent to "piece" or "pieces" is found in the Heb. The first occurs in 1 Sam. 2:36, where "piece" is the rendering of the Heb. *'ăgôrâ*, something "gathered." It may be the same as the *gērâ* (*see* above). The second is in Ps. 68:30, "Trampling under foot the pieces of silver." "Pieces" here is the translation of the Heb. *răṣ*, which occurs nowhere else in Scripture. Gesenius thinks pieces of uncoined silver is meant. In the NT "pieces" is the rendering of the Gk. *argurion* (Matt. 26:15; 27:3, 5-6, 9) in the account of the betrayal of our Lord for "thirty pieces of silver." These are often taken to be denarii, but on insufficient ground. The parallel passage in Zechariah (11:12-13) is rendered "thirty shekels of silver." This was the sum payable as compensation for a slave that had been killed (Ex. 21:32), and also the price of a bondslave (Hos. 3:2). By paying thirty shekels (about ninety denarii) they therefore gave him to understand that they did not estimate his services higher than the labor of a purchased slave. These shekels were probably tetradrachms of the Attic standard of the Greek cities of Syria and Phoenicia. These tetradrachms were common at the time of our Lord, and of them the *stater* was a specimen. The value put upon the conjuring books, doubtless by the conjurors themselves, was 50,000 pieces of silver (Acts 19:19). The Vulg. has accurately rendered the phrase *denarii,* as there is no doubt that these coins are intended.

Shekel (Heb. *sheqel,* "weight"). The shekel was properly a certain *weight,* and the *shekel weight* of silver was the unit of value through the whole age of Hebrew history down to the Babylonian captivity. It is now generally agreed that the oldest Jewish silver coins belong to the period of Simon Maccabaeus, 140 B.C. They are the *shekels* and *half shekels,* weighing 220 and 110 grains, with several pieces in copper. The shekel presents on the obverse the legend SHEKEL OF ISRAEL; a cup or chalice, above which appears the date of Simon's government in which it was struck. On the reverse side appears JERUSALEM THE HOLY, with a triple lily or hyacinth. It is generally believed that the devices on this coin are intended to represent the pot that held manna and Aaron's rod that budded. The half shekel resembles the shekel, and they occur with the dates of the first, second, third, and fourth year of Simon. The value of the gold shekel is about 55 denarii, $5.50; the silver about 3.67 denarii. Of copper, we have parts of the copper shekel —the half, the quarter, the sixth.

Small Copper Coin (Gk. *lepton,* Mark 12:42; Luke 12:59, "cent"; 21:2). A coin current in Palestine in the time of our Lord. It seems in Palestine to have been the smallest piece of money, being the half of the kodrantēs or quadrans (*see* Cent). From Mark's explanation, "two small copper coins, which amount to a cent" (12:42), it may perhaps be inferred that the cent or *quadrans* was the more common coin. In the Greco-Roman coinage of Palestine, the two smallest coins of which the assarion is the more common, seem to correspond to these two coins, the larger weighing about twice as much as the smaller.

Stater (Gk. *statēr*). (1) The term *stater* is held to signify a coin of a certain weight, but perhaps means a standard coin. The gold staters were didrachms of the later Phoenician and the Attic talents, which in this denomination differ only about four grains troy. Of the former talent were the Daric staters or darics; of the latter, the stater of Athens. The electrum staters were coined by the Greek towns of the W coast of Asia Minor. They were three parts of gold to one of silver. Thus far the stater is always a didrachm. In silver the term is applied to the tetradrachms of Athens, which was of the weight of two gold staters of the same currency. There can therefore be no doubt that the name stater was applied to the standard denomination of both metals and does not positively imply either a didrachm or a tetradrachm. (2) In the NT the stater is mentioned once as a "two-drachma" (Matt. 17:24-27). The stater must here mean a silver tetradrachm; and the only tetradrachms then current in Palestine were of the same weight as the Hebrew shekel. And it is observable, in confirmation of the minute accuracy of the evangelist, that at this period the silver currency in Palestine consisted of Greek imperial tetradrachms, or staters, and Roman denarii of a quarter their value, didrachms having fallen into disuse (Smith, *Dict.*).

Talent (Heb. *kikkār,* a "circle"; Gk. *talanton,* a "balance"). The largest weight among the Hebrews, the talent was used for metals, whether gold, silver, and so on. In the NT this word occurs (1) in the parable of the unmerciful servant (Matt. 18:24); (2) in the parable of the talents (25:14-30). At this time the Attic talent prevailed in Palestine; sixty minas went to the talent and fifty shekels to the mina.

Tribute Money. See Tribute, in the general listing.

BIBLIOGRAPHY: R. de Vaux, *Ancient Israel: Its Life and Institutions* (1961), pp. 178-206; J. I. Packer, M. C. Tenney, and W. White, eds., *The Bible Almanac* (1980), pp. 214-22, 271-301, 330-39.

MEU'NIM (me-ū'nim; Neh. 7:52). *See* Meunites.

MEU'NITES (me-ū'nīts). Plural of the gentilic adjective *me'ūnī,* "from Maon," referring to the people of Maon. A people who lived in Mt. Seir (2 Chron. 20:1), they evidently had their capital at Ma'on, a dozen miles SE of Petra. The Simeonites near Gedar attacked them as foreigners (1 Chron. 4:39-41). Second Chron. 26:7 mentions them with the Philistines and the Arabians. After the captivity, some of their descendants served as servants in the Jerusalem Temple (Ezra 2:50; Neh. 7:52), where they are called "the sons of Meunim." They are identified by the Gk. version with the Minaeans. If such an identification is correct, they formed probably the northernmost section of that S Arabian people.

MEZ'AHAB (mez'a-hab; "water of gold"), **Me-Zahab** (NIV). The father of Matred and grandfather of Mehetabel, who was the wife of Hadar, or

Hadad, the last named king of Edom (Gen. 36:39; 1 Chron. 1:50).

MEZO'BAITE (me-zō'bīt). A designation of Jaasiel, the last named of David's heroes (1 Chron. 11:47; "Mesobaite," KJV), probably meaning "from Zobah."

MI'AMIN. See Mijamin.

MIB'HAR (mib'har; "elite, choice"). The son of Hagri, and one of David's heroes (1 Chron. 11:38).

MIB'SAM (mib'sam; "sweet odor, balsam").

1. The fourth named of the sons of Ishmael (Gen. 25:13; 1 Chron. 1:29).

2. The son of Shallum and grandson of Shaul, the sixth son of Simeon (1 Chron. 4:25).

MIB'ZAR (mib'zar; "fortress"). One of the chiefs of Edom descended from Esau (Gen. 36:42; 1 Chron. 1:53).

MI'CA (mī'ka; "who is like Jehovah?"; "Micha," KJV).

1. A son of Mephibosheth (2 Sam. 9:12), given in 1 Chron. 8:34-35 as *Micah* (which see).

2. The son of Zabdi and father of Mattaniah, of the family of the Levite Asaph (Neh. 11:17, 22), and probably the same one who joined in the sacred covenant with Nehemiah (10:11), about 445 B.C. See Micah.

MI'CAH (mī'ka; a contraction of Micaiah, "who is like Jehovah?").

1. A man of Mt. Ephraim who lived, probably, in the time of the elders who survived Joshua, about 1360 B.C. He had stolen 1,100 shekels of silver from his mother; but, impelled by the fear of her curse, he had confessed and restored the money. Thereupon she put 200 shekels into a goldsmith's hands to make an image (or images) for the semi-idolatrous establishment set up by Micah. At first Micah installed one of his sons as priest but afterward appointed a wandering Levite named Jonathan at a yearly stipend (Judg. 17:1-13). When the Danites were on their journey northward to settle in Laish they took away both the establishment and priest of Micah, who, upon overtaking the Danite army, found it too powerful for him to attack and returned to his home (18:1-26).

2. The son of Shimei, father of Reaiah, and one of the descendants of Joel the Reubenite (1 Chron. 5:5), before 782 B.C.

3. The son of Merib-baal (or Mephibosheth) and grandson of Jonathan (1 Chron. 8:34-35; 9:40-41), after 1000 B.C.

4. The first in rank in the Kohathites of the family of Uzziel, as arranged by David (1 Chron. 23:20), about 966 B.C. His son's name was Shamir, and a brother Isshiah is mentioned (24:24-25).

5. The father of Abdon (2 Chron. 34:20). See Micaiah, no. 2.

6. A prophet, a native of Moresheth of Gath (Mic. 1:1, 14-15). He is thus distinguished from a former prophet, Micaiah (1 Kings 22:8). The period during which Micah exercised the prophetical office is stated in the superscription to his prophecies (1:1) to have extended over the reigns of Jotham, Ahaz, and Hezekiah, kings of Judah, about 738-690 B.C. This would make him contemporary with Hosea, Amos, and Isaiah. One of his prophecies (Jer. 26:18) is distinctly assigned to the reign of Hezekiah and was probably delivered before the great Passover that inaugurated the reform in Judah. Very little is known of the circumstances of Micah's life. He was probably of the kingdom of Judah. For rebuking Jehoram for his impieties, Micah, according to Pseudo-Epiphanius, was thrown from a precipice and buried at Morathi, in his own country, near the cemetery of Enakim.

BIBLIOGRAPHY: L. J. Wood, *Distressing Days of the Judges* (1975), pp. 38, 147-50; J. M. Lang and T. Kirk, *Studies in the Book of Judges*, 2 vols. in 1 (1983), 1:21-33.

MICAH, BOOK OF. One of the books of the minor prophets, named after the prophet Micah, Heb. *mîkâ*, an evident shortening of *Mikayahu*, signifying "Who is like the Lord?" The LXX renders his name *Michaias* and the Vulg. *Michaeas*.

The Prophet. Micah was a native, apparently, of Moresheth (Mic. 1:14), a Judean town near Gath, and at intervals a dependency of the Philistines. His prophetic ministry flourished in the reigns of Jotham (750-732 B.C.), Ahaz (c. 735-715), and Hezekiah (c. 715-686). He was a simple villager, but a prophet of social righteousness. Like Amos, the herdsman, he defended the cause of the poverty-stricken masses. Like Hosea, Amos, and Isaiah, Micah foretold the fall of the Northern Kingdom and the taking of Samaria (1:5-7), and he warned of the coming desolation of Judah (vv. 9-16). His prophetic oracles had special reference to Judah; nevertheless he envisioned all Israel (vv. 1, 5-7).

Outline.

I. Prediction of approaching judgment (1:1–2:13)
   A. Upon Samaria (1:2-8)
   B. Upon Judah (1:9-16)
   C. Upon cruel oppressors (2:1-11)
   D. Upon a remnant (2:12-13)
II. Prediction of the messianic kingdom (3:1–5:15)
   A. Preliminary judgments (3:1-12)
   B. Description of the kingdom (4:1-5)
   C. Establishment of the kingdom (4:6-13)
   D. Rejection of the King at His first coming (5:1-2)
   E. Interval between the royal rejection and return (5:3)
   F. The Messiah's second coming (5:4-15)

III. The divine controversy and final mercy (6:1–7:20)
    A. The people's ingratitude and sin (6:1–7:6)
    B. Prophetic intercession (7:7-20)

Prophetic Style. Micah writes in simple yet eloquent language. He is outspoken and fearless in denouncing iniquity (cf. 1:5; 2:1-2). He is logical in his development but often abrupt in transition from one subject to another. He makes considerable use of metaphor (1:6; 3:2-3, 6; 4:6-8, 13; 6:10-11) and paronomasia, or play upon words (cf. chap. 1), and is fond of rhetorical interrogation (cf. 1:5; 2:7; 4:9; etc.). He shows how God requires justice and loves mercy but requires these characteristics also in His followers.

Literary Composition. Negative criticism has attacked the unity of Micah. Robert Pfeiffer is characteristic of modern criticism. According to him the first three chapters are authentic; however, section 4:1–5:15 is regarded as an interpolation, whereas 6:1–7:6 is said to be a later anonymous prophet's work, having its own editorial appendix (7:7-20). However, the expression "hear" (1:2; 3:1; 6:1) is an element of style suggesting unity of authorship. Moreover, there are a number of parallels in chaps. 4-7 with writings contemporary with Micah or written near his time (*see* R. K. Harrison, *Introduction to the Old Testament* [1969], p. 924). Critics claim that the argument of the book is not closely knit. The fact that the book consists of various discussions delivered by the prophet over an extended period of time and under various circumstances is sufficient explanation of its lack of logical order. Critical views against Micah are weakened by the unsound theory of the evolutionary development of religious concepts in Isaiah, Micah's contemporary. This view erroneously insists that certain theological ideas found in Micah did not come into developed form until a later date. This is purely supposition. There is no objective evidence to prove that such ideas, particularly concerning salvation, had not crystallized in Micah's day.

BIBLIOGRAPHY: T. Laetsch, *The Minor Prophets* (1956), pp. 245-92; L. C. Allen, *The Books of Joel, Obadiah, Jonah and Micah*, New International Commentary on the Old Testament (1976), pp. 239-403; J. L. Mayes, *Micah: A Commentary* (1976); H. C. von Orelli, *The Twelve Minor Prophets* (1977), pp. 185-222; H. W. Wolff, *Micah the Prophet* (1981); F. E. Gaebelein, ed., *Expositor's Bible Commentary* (1985), pp. 395-445.

MICA′IAH (mi-ka′ya; "who is like Jehovah?").

1. The son of Imlah, a prophet of Samaria, who, in the last year of the reign of Ahab king of Israel predicted his defeat and death, 853 B.C. Three years after the great battle with Ben-hadad, Ahab proposed to Jehoshaphat that they should jointly go up to battle against Ramoth-gilead. Jehoshaphat consented but suggested that they should "inquire first for the word of the Lord."

Ahab gathered together four hundred prophets in an open space at the gate of the city of Samaria, who gave the unanimous response "Go up, for the Lord will give it into the hand of the king." Among them Zedekiah the son of Chenaanah made horns of iron as a symbol and announced, as from Jehovah, that with those horns Ahab would push the Assyrians until he consumed them. Jehoshaphat was dissatisfied with the answer and asked if there was no other prophet of Jehovah at Samaria. Ahab replied that there was still one—Micaiah, the son of Imlah; but he added, "I hate him, because he does not prophesy good concerning me, but evil." Micaiah, however, was sent for and urged to agree with the other prophets "and speak favorably." He at first expressed an ironical concurrence and then openly foretold the defeat of Ahab's army and the death of Ahab himself. He declared that the other prophets had spoken under the influence of a lying spirit. Upon this Zedekiah struck Micaiah upon the cheek, and Ahab ordered him to be taken to prison and fed bread and water until his return (1 Kings 22:1-28; 2 Chron. 18:2-27). We hear nothing further from the prophet in the sacred story, but Josephus narrates that Micaiah was already in prison when sent for to prophesy before Ahab and Jehoshaphat; that it was Micaiah who had predicted death by a lion to the son of a prophet, under the circumstances mentioned in 1 Kings 20:35-36; and that Micaiah had rebuked Ahab, after his brilliant victory over the Syrians, for not putting Ben-hadad to death.

2. The father of Achbor, which latter was sent by Josiah to consult with the prophetess Huldah (2 Kings 22:12; "Michaiah," KJV). In the parallel passage (2 Chron. 34:20) he is called *Micah* (which see).

3. The mother of King Abijah (2 Chron. 13:2; "Michaiah," KJV; "Maachah," NIV); elsewhere (2 Chron. 11:20) called *Maacah* (which see).

4. One of the princes of Jehoshaphat, whom he sent to teach the law of Jehovah in the cities of Judah (2 Chron. 17:7; "Michaiah," KJV), about 870 B.C.

5. A priest of the family of Asaph, whose descendant Zechariah took part in the dedication of the walls of Jerusalem after the captivity (Neh. 12:35), before 445 B.C.

6. One of the priests who took part in the same ceremony (Neh. 12:41; "Michaiah," KJV), 445 B.C.

7. The son of Gemariah, and the person who, having heard Baruch read the terrible predictions of Jeremiah, went and declared them to all the officials assembled in King Jehoiakim's house (36:11-13; "Michaiah," KJV); and the officials immediately sent for Baruch to read the prophecies to them (37:11-14), about 606 B.C.

BIBLIOGRAPHY: C. E. Macartney, *The Wisest Fool* (1949), pp. 99-107.

MICE. *See* Animal Kingdom.

MI'CHA. *See* Mica.

MI'CHAEL (mī'kel; "who is as or like God?").

1. "One of the chief princes" or archangels (Dan. 10:13; cf. Jude 9), described (Dan. 10:21) as the "prince" of Israel and (12:1) as "the great prince who stands" in time of conflict "over the sons of your people." As special guardian of the Jews, Michael will defend them in their terrific time of trouble (Jer. 30:5) during the Great Tribulation when the remnant will be delivered and established in the millennial kingdom. As Gabriel represents the ministration of the angels toward men, so Michael is the type and leader of their strife, in God's name and His strength, against the power of Satan. In the OT, therefore, he is the guardian of the Jewish people in their antagonism to godless power and heathenism. In the NT (Rev. 12:7-9), he fights in heaven against the dragon—"the serpent of old who is called the devil and Satan, who deceives the whole world," and so takes part in that struggle that is the work of the church on earth. There remains still one passage (Jude 9; cf. 2 Pet. 2:11) in which we are told that "Michael the archangel, when he disputed with the devil . . . about the body of Moses, did not dare pronounce against him a railing judgment, but said, 'The Lord rebuke you.' " The reference seems evidently to be to Moses' appearance in glorified form on the mount of transfiguration (Matt. 17:1-8) as the representative of the redeemed who have passed through death into the kingdom (13:43; Luke 9:30-31).

2. The father of Sethur, which latter represented the tribe of Asher among the explorers of Canaan (Num. 13:13), 1440 B.C.

3. A leader of the tribe of Gad, mentioned among those who settled in the land of Bashan (1 Chron. 5:13).

4. Another Gadite and ancestor of Abihail (1 Chron. 5:14). Perhaps the same as no. 3.

5. The son of Baaseiah and father of Shimea, and a Gershonite Levite among the ancestors of Asaph (1 Chron. 6:40).

6. One of the four sons of Izrahiah, a descendant of Issachar (1 Chron. 7:3).

7. A Benjamite of the sons of Beriah (1 Chron. 8:16).

8. A captain of the "thousands" of Manasseh who joined David at Ziklag (1 Chron. 12:20).

9. The father of Omri, whom David appointed leader of the tribe of Issachar (1 Chron. 27:18).

10. One of the sons of Jehoshaphat king of Judah, whom he portioned before his death and who were slain by their brother Jehoram upon his accession (2 Chron. 21:2-4), 850 B.C.

11. A "son" (or descendant) of Shephatiah, whose son Zebadiah, with eighty-two males, came with Ezra from Babylon (Ezra 8:8), before 457 B.C.

BIBLIOGRAPHY: A. C. Gaebelein, *Gabriel and Michael, the*

Archangels, Their Prominence in Bible Prophecy (1945).

MI'CHAH. *See* Micah.

MICHA'IAH. *See* Mica'iah, nos. 2-7.

MI'CHAL (mī'kal; evidently a shortened form of Michael, "who is like God?"). Saul's younger daughter (1 Sam. 14:49), probably by Ahinoam (v. 50). After David had slain Goliath, Saul proposed to give him his eldest daughter, Merab, but when the time arrived for the marriage she was given to Adriel the Meholathite (18:17-19). The pretext under which Saul broke his promise is not given, but it appears to have been that Merab had no love for David.

Marriage. It was told Saul that his daughter Michal loved the young hero, and he seized the opportunity of exposing David to the risk of death. He asked no dowry of him save the slaughter of a hundred Philistines. Before the appointed time David doubled the number of victims, and Michal became his wife (18:20-28), about 1010 B.C.

Saves David's Life. Another great defeat inflicted by David upon the Philistines so excited the jealousy of Saul that he endeavored to kill David. Failing in the attempt, he sent watchers to David's house to put him to death in the morning. Michal aided David's escape by letting him down through a window, and then dressed the bed as if still occupied by him. She took the household idol (teraphim), laid it upon the bed, its head enveloped with a goat's hair netting, as if to protect it from gnats, and the rest of the figure covered with clothes. Saul's messengers forced their way into the room, despite Michal's declaration that David was sick, and discovered the deception. When Saul was informed he was so enraged that Michal fabricated the story of David's threatening to kill her (19:11-17).

Second Marriage. Saul probably doubted Michal's story of David's escape, and when the rupture between the two men became incurable, Michal was married to Palti (or Paltiel) of Gallim (25:44; 2 Sam. 3:15).

Restored to David. When Abner revolted to David, the king consented to make a league with him only on this condition: "But I demand one thing of you, namely, you shall not see my face unless you first bring Michal, Saul's daughter, when you come to see me." Ish-bosheth was requested to deliver up Michal, and, having done so, she was taken to the king by Abner, who ordered her weeping husband to return to his home (2 Sam. 3:13-16).

Rupture with David. On the day of David's greatest triumph, namely that of bringing the Ark of the Lord to Jerusalem, the king appeared in the procession, dancing and leaping. When he returned to his own house, Michal, who had seen him from her window, met him with scornful words. She was offended that the king had lowered himself to the level of the people. She availed herself of the shortness of the priest's shoulder dress to make a contemptuous remark concerning David's dancing. David's retort was a tremendous one, conveyed in words that once spoken could never be recalled. It gathered up all the differences between them that made sympathy no longer possible, and we do not need the assurance of the sacred writer that "Michal . . . had no child to the day of her death," to feel quite certain that all intercourse between her and David must have ceased from that date (2 Sam. 6:16-23), 992 B.C. In the KJV her name appears once again (21:8) as the mother of five sons, but the probable presumption is that Michal has been, by the mistake of the transcriber, substituted for Merab, the wife of Adriel. The NASB and NIV read "Merab."

BIBLIOGRAPHY: C. E. Macartney, *Ancient Wives and Modern Husbands* (1934), pp. 89-94; C. J. and A. A. Barber, *You Can Have a Happy Marriage* (1984), pp. 67-79.

MICH'MAS (mik'mas), **Mich'mash, Mic'mash** (mik'mash; "something hidden"). A town of Benjamin about seven miles NE of Jerusalem. Here Saul and the Philistines contended for the upper hand, Saul taking his position with 2,000 men and placing the other 1,000 at Gibeah with his son Jonathan. Jonathan struck the Philistine garrison that was at Geba, and the Philistines hastened to avenge the defeat. They collected an innumerable army of foot soldiers, besides 30,-000 chariots and 6,000 horsemen, and encamped before Michmash. Saul retreated down the valley to Gilgal, near Jericho, to rally the Israelites (1 Sam. 13:1-7). Jonathan resolved to attack the outpost of the Philistines at the pass of Michmash, and God gave him a great victory (14:1-14). Michmas is mentioned as the place whose inhabitants returned from captivity (Ezra 2:27; Neh. 7:31; 11:31). It is the present Mukhmas, a village in ruins on the northern ridge of the Wadi Suweinit (cf. Isa. 10:28).

The area near Michmash

MICH'METHATH (mik'me-tha), **Mic'methath** (NIV). A town on the border of Ephraim and Manasseh, W of the Jordan (Josh. 16:6; 17:7), present Khirbet Juleijil.

MICH'RI (mik'ri), **Mic'ri** (NIV). Ancestor of Elah, one of the heads of the fathers of Benjamin after the captivity (1 Chron. 9:8), before 536 B.C.

MICH'TAM. *See* Mikhtam.

MIC'MASH. *See* Michmas.

MICMETHATH. *See* Michmethath.

MIC'RI. *See* Michri.

MIDDAY (Heb. *ṣohŏrayim,* "double light," 1 Kings 18:29; *maḥăṣît hayyôm,* "half of the day," Neh. 8:3; Gk. *hēmera mesos,* "middle day," Acts 26:13). *See* Time.

MID'DIN (mid'in). A town W of the Dead Sea, mentioned only in Josh. 15:61. Its location is unknown.

MIDDLE WALL. *See* Dividing Wall, Barrier of.

MID'IAN (mid'i-an; "strife"). The fourth named of the six sons of Abraham by Keturah (Gen. 25:2; 1 Chron. 1:32). Beyond the fact of his having four sons (Gen. 25:4; 1 Chron. 1:33), nothing is recorded concerning him.

MID'IANITES (mid'i-an-īts). A race dwelling S and E of Palestine, in the desert N of the Arabian peninsula. There are no trustworthy accounts of Midian outside the Bible. In Scripture, Midian appears in connection with (1) Abraham, (2) Joseph, (3) Moses, (4) Balaam, and (5) Gideon.

1. In Gen. 25:1-2 Midian is the fourth son of Abraham by Keturah, and evidently one of those who were sent away into the east country with gifts by Abraham during his lifetime (v. 6). According to the Arab account, "Medyen are the offspring of Shu'eyb, and are the offspring of Medyán (Midian), son of Abraham, and their mother was Kantoor Ga, the daughter of Yukt Aan (Joktan) the Canaanite." "Medyen is the city of the people of Shu'eyb," who is "generally supposed to be the same as Jethro, the father-in-law of Moses," though some deny it.

2. In the time of Joseph we find the Midianites associated with the Ishmaelites so closely that it is hard to define their relationship; perhaps there was a company of Midianite merchantmen in the Ishmaelite caravan (Gen. 37:25, 27-28, 36). In all likelihood the descendants of Ishmael, and Midian, as well as of other exiled children of Abraham, had intermarried. In Judg. 8:24 the Midianites seem to be called Ishmaelites. But this latter term may have come to be applied generally to traders of that particular kind, such as *Canaanite* (which see), which came to mean merchant.

3. In the early life of Moses (Ex. 2:15) after killing the Egyptian he fled for refuge to the land of Midian. Here he married the daughter of Jeth-

ro, the priest of Midian, whose sheep he kept for forty years (2:16-21; 3:1; Acts 7:29). At the time of his call he was at Horeb, in the peninsula of Sinai (Ex. 3:1). As the Midianites were mostly nomads, this peninsula can have been only a temporary station for pasturage, unless, as is quite possible, it was then more fertile than now. But, according to the Arabians and Greeks, the city of Midian was on the Arabian side of the Arabian Gulf, where in all probability lay the true land of Midian.

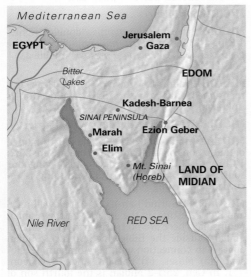

Mediterranean Sea
EGYPT
Jerusalem
Gaza
Bitter Lakes
EDOM
Kadesh-Barnea
SINAI PENINSULA
Marah   Ezion Geber
Elim
Mt. Sinai LAND OF
(Horeb)   MIDIAN
Nile River   RED SEA

4. In the time of Balaam, Moab (then ruled by Balak son of Zippor) conferred with the elders of Midian in regard to Israel, and the resulting embassy to Balaam consisted of elders both of Moab and Midian (Num. 22:1-7). In the chapters that relate the prophecies of Balaam (23-24) only Moab is mentioned. In 25:1 it is the daughters of Moab who entice Israel; but in 25:6-15 it is Midian, and in vv. 16-18; 31:1-12 vengeance is executed on Midian. In 31:8-9 it is among the Midianites that Balaam perishes. We may therefore conclude that Midian had a prominent part in the transaction. (For connection of Moab with Midian, see Moabites.)

5. In the time of Gideon, Midian appears again (Judg. 6:1–8:28), but not as an organized army of warriors or as a nation powerful enough to bring the Israelites under its despotic sway. Israel by idolatry lost the divine protection and the national cohesion that would have protected the nation against such marauders. The Midianites united with the Amalekites and the sons of the east—men, women, and children, as we suppose—with their belongings and certainly with their cattle (6:5), forming an innumerable horde of camel-riding nomads. They apparently were the first

people to employ the domesticated camel on a large scale. This gave them greatly increased desert mobility, c. 1150 B.C. They oppressed Israel, not by a strong military despotism backed by chariots of iron, as did Jabin and Sisera (4:2-3), but by coming up when the harvest was ripe, "like locusts," destroying "the produce of the earth." The story is best read in the inimitable language of the Bible itself. The whole account, from the Midianite invasion at the beginning, to the panic and rout, to their final disappearance at the end, is the story of a mob, formidable from its numbers and its hunger. This ends the story of Midian. Henceforth it is hardly mentioned, except as a historical reminiscence (but see Isa. 60:6; Hab. 3:7). Certainly Midian is never again mentioned as a source of terror. It is probable that from the beginning they had intermarried with the Ishmaelites and that in the end they were merged with the roving peoples of the northern part of the Arabian desert, under the general name *Arabs.* Midian has been called the Judah of the Arabians.   W.H.; M.F.U.

BIBLIOGRAPHY: F.-M. Abel, *Géographie de la Palestine* (1933), 1:285-87, 392-93; J. Montgomery, *Arabia and the Bible* (1934), pp. 9-10, 43-47, 52, 186; W. F. Albright, *From the Stone Age to Christianity* (1940), pp. 120, 194-96, 200, 219; id., *Archaeology and the Religion of Israel* (1953), pp. 60, 100, 132, 206.

MIDNIGHT. *See* Time.

MIDWIFE. A woman assisting at childbirth. *See* Diseases, Treatment of.

MIG'DAL E'DER (mig'dal ē'der). *See* Eder.

MIG'DAL-EL (mig'dal-el; "tower of God"). A fortified city that fell to Naphtali (Josh. 19:38). A number of places are claimed as the original site. Possibly Mujeidil about twelve miles NW of Kades (Kedesh) is the location.

MIG'DAL-GAD (mig'dal-gad; "tower of fortune"). A town in the plain of Judah, between the hilly region and the territory held by the Philistines (Josh. 15:37). Its site is not positively known, but it is in the *Shephelah* (which see), perhaps near Lachish. Possibly it is to be located at Mejdad, twenty-four miles W of Hebron.

MIG'DOL (mig'dol).

1. This was the encampment of Israel during the Exodus from Egypt. It was near the Red (Reed) Sea (cf. Ex. 15:4, 22; Deut. 11:4). It is also said to be before Pi-hahiroth and before Baal-zephon (Ex. 14:2; Num. 33:7). Since Migdol is the ordinary Canaanite word for "watchtower," this site may have been a military outpost. The place is an example of Canaanite names in the Delta. An extended Semitic occupation of the NE Delta before the New Egyptian Empire (c. 1546-1085 B.C.) is indicated from other such Canaanite place names as Succoth (Ex. 12:37), Baal-zephon (14:2), Zilu (Tell Abu Seifah), and most likely

Goshen itself (8:22; 9:26) (W. F. Albright, *From the Stone Age to Christianity* [1940], p. 184).

2. A place referred to in Jer. 44:1; 46:14. Here Jews fled to Egypt and took up their residence after the destruction of Jerusalem by Nebuchadnezzar. The place was in the north of Egypt and is probably to be equated with the *Magdali* of the el-Amarna Tablets. It is modern Tell el Heir, almost a dozen miles S of Pelusium. In Ezek. 29:10, cf. 30:6, the expression occurs "from Migdol to Syene and even to the border of Ethiopia," evidently indicating extreme limits N and S in Egypt.   M.F.U.

MIGHTY MEN (Heb. *gibbōr*, "powerful"; sometimes "mighties," KJV). The title given to the three great captains of David and meaning "warrior," i.e., leader in war (2 Sam. 23:8-9, 16-17, 22; 1 Chron. 11:10-12, 24).

MIGRATION OF BIRDS. *See* Animal Kingdom: Bird.

MIG'RON (mig'ron; "precipice"). A town of Benjamin, apparently on the route of the invading Assyrian army southward (Isa. 10:28). From Michmash a narrow valley extends northward out of and at right angles to what has been identified as the passage of *Michmash* (which see). Saul was stationed at the further side of Gibeah, "under the pomegranate tree which is in Migron" (1 Sam. 14:2). Gibeah is at Tell el-Ful.

MIJ'AMIN (mij'a-min; "from the right hand," i.e., the side of good luck).

1. The head of the sixth division of priests in the time of David (1 Chron. 24:9), before 960 B.C.

2. A layman of Israel, of the family of Parosh, who divorced his Gentile wife after the captivity (Ezra 10:25; "Miamin," KJV), 456 B.C.

3. One of the priests who signed the covenant made by Nehemiah and the people to serve Jehovah (Neh. 10:7), 445 B.C. It is probable that he is the same as no. 4 below. *See* Miniamin, no. 2.

4. One of the priests who came to Jerusalem with Zerubbabel from Babylon (Neh. 12:5), about 536 B.C. He is probably the same person who is called Miniamin in v. 17, and thus may be the same as no. 3 above.

MIKH'TAM (mik'tam; a "writing," especially a "psalm"). This word occurs in the titles of six psalms (16, 56-60; "Michtam," KJV; "Miktam," NIV), all of which are ascribed to David. Meaning uncertain.

MIK'LOTH (mik'lōth; "rods").

1. One of the sons of Jeiel, "the father" (or head) of Gibeon, and father of Shimeah (or Shimeam). He was one of the Benjamite residents of Jerusalem (1 Chron. 8:29, 32; 9:35, 37-38), about 536 B.C.

2. The chief officer of the second division of the army under Dodo, in the reign of David (1 Chron. 27:4), after 1000 B.C.

MIKNE'IAH (mik-ne'ya; "possession of Jehovah"). A Levitical gatekeeper of the Temple and one of the musicians "with lyres tuned to the sheminith" appointed by order of David (1 Chron. 15:18, 21), about 966 B.C.

MILALA'I (mil-al-ī; "eloquent"). One of the priests' "kinsmen" who took part in the dedication of the walls of Jerusalem (Neh. 12:36), about 536 B.C.

MIL'CAH (mil'ka, "counsel, advice").

1. The daughter of Haran, and the wife of Nahor, by whom she had eight children. One of these, Bethuel, was the father of Rebekah (Gen. 11:29; 22:20, 23; 24:15, 24, 47), about 1950 B.C.

2. The fourth named of the five daughters of Zelophehad of the tribe of Manasseh, to whom, as they had no brothers, an inheritance was given in the division of the land (Num. 26:33; 27:1; 36:11; Josh. 17:3), about 1375 B.C.

MIL'COM (mil'kom). A false god (Zeph. 1:5; NIV marg., "Malcom"). *See* Gods, False.

MILDEW. Properly a species of fungus or parasitic plant generated by moisture and corrosive of the surface to which it adheres. In Arabia the mildew of grain is produced by a warm wind, by which the green ears are turned yellow, so that they bear no grain (Deut. 28:22). *See* Vegetable Kingdom.

MILE. *See* Metrology: Linear Measures.

MILE'TUS (mī-lē'tus). A town on the coast of Asia Minor, thirty-six miles S of Ephesus. It was the most important of the Ionian cities and became a great center of culture during the sixth century B.C. For example, Thales of Miletus around 600 B.C. led in the development of philosophy. Miletus led an Ionian revolt against the Persians in 499 B.C. When the Persians subjugated the area once more, they destroyed Miletus as a punishment for her rebelliousness. The famous Hippodamus of Miletus laid out the new city on the grid plan, with streets intersecting at right angles. The "Hippodamian" plan has been used in many places in many eras ever since. The city was a great and prosperous center in Hellenistic and Roman times. Theodor Wiegand launched a Berlin Museum excavation at Miletus in 1899 and continued the work until 1914. Prof. Karl Weichert supervised another dig there in 1938 and returned from 1955 to 1957. In 1959 Prof. G. Kleiner took charge of the excavations, and currently the work is conducted by Prof. Müller-Wiener, director of the German Archaeological Institute in Istanbul. Gradually a picture of the magnificence of Miletus is emerging. Its great theater with seating for 15,000, its council chamber, baths, agoras, gymnasia, harbor facilities, stadium, and much more have been uncovered. Paul stopped at Miletus on his third missionary journey and addressed the people (Acts 20:15-

17). Some think the Miletus where Paul left Trophimus sick (2 Tim. 4:20) was in Crete, but there seems to be no need for such a conclusion. For archaeological diggings *see Türk Arkeloji Dergesi* 8, no. 1 (1958): 31-32.

BIBLIOGRAPHY: D. Magie, *Roman Rule in Asia MInor* (1950), pp. 73-74.

MILK. The rendering of two Heb. words and one Gk. word:

Sweet Milk (Heb. *hālāb,* "fat"; Gk. *gala*). This was in extensive use among the Hebrews, as well as other nations. They used not only the milk of cows but also that of sheep (Deut. 32:14), of camels (Gen. 32:15), and of goats (Prov. 27:27). It was not regarded as a mere adjunct in cooking but as substantial food adapted to all ages and classes. The Scriptures frequently mention it in connection with honey as a delicacy (Ex. 3:8; 13:5; Josh. 5:6; Jer. 11:5).

Curdled Cheese (Heb. *hem'â*). This seems to mean both butter and curdled milk. Curdled sour milk still forms, after bread, the chief food of the poorer classes in Arabia and Syria. Nor is it wanting on the tables of the well-to-do and is brought to market in large quantities. It is carried by travelers, mixed with meat and dried, and then dissolved in water to make a refreshing drink. It was this curdled milk that Abraham set before the angels (Gen. 18:8) and Jael gave to Sisera (Judg.

4:19). If kept long enough in this state it acquired a slightly intoxicating property. It is rendered "curds" (Isa. 7:22), and its use in connection with honey is figurative of scarcity. Bread and wine would be unattainable, so thickened milk and honey would be eaten instead. A very striking allusion to milk is that which forbids a kid to be boiled in its mother's milk (Ex. 23:19; 34:26; Deut. 14:21). *See* Kid.

Figurative. Milk occurs as a sign of abundance (Gen. 49:12; Ezek. 25:4; Joel 3:18; etc.), but more frequently with honey. "Milk and honey" is a phrase that occurs about twenty times in Scripture. Milk is also illustrative of the blessings of the gospel (Isa. 55:1; Joel 3:18), the first principles of God's Word (1 Cor. 3:2; Heb. 5:12; 1 Pet. 2:2), edifying discourse (Song of Sol. 4:11), and the wealth of the Gentiles (Isa. 60:16).

MILL. *See* Millstones.

MILLENNIUM. From Lat. *mille,* "thousand," *annum,* "year"; a theological term based upon Rev. 20, indicating the thousand-year period of Christ's future reign on the earth in connection with the establishment of the kingdom over Israel (Acts 1:6). Basically, however, it is more accurate to employ the term *kingdom,* which has far-reaching roots in the OT, rather than a term signifying merely a time during which the kingdom continues. Three common millennial views

The theater at Miletus

are held: postmillennialism, amillennialism, and premillennialism.

Postmillennialism. This interpretation maintains that present gospel agencies will root out evils until Christ will have a spiritual reign over the earth, which will continue for 1,000 years. Then the second advent of Christ will initiate judgment and bring to an end the present order. This theory, largely disproved by the progress of history, is no longer popular, but it has enjoyed some resurgence in recent years. Postmillennialism was promulgated by the teaching in England of Daniel Whitby, 1638-1726.

Amillennialism. Advocates of this view maintain that no Millennium is to be looked for except that which, it is claimed, is in progress now in this gospel age. This theological interpretation spiritualizes or, rather, gives a mystical meaning to the vast kingdom promises in the OT. Zion is construed not to mean Zion but to refer to the Christian church. It makes no trenchant differentiation between Israel and the church, a distinction that evidently underlies John the Baptist's prophecy of the baptism of the Spirit and Jesus' reference to this in Acts 1:5. This spiritual ministry formed the church (Acts 2; cf. 1 Cor. 12:13). The apostle Paul apparently makes a clear distinction between Israel and the church in 10:32, and he also outlines a future for Israel in Rom. 11. Amillennialism does not seem to take full account of these facts. Moreover, the view contends that Satan is at present bound, a position that premillennialists maintain is hardly justified by conditions in the present age.

Premillennialism. This interpretation teaches that the age will end in judgment at the second coming of Christ, who will restore the kingdom to Israel and reign for at least 1,000 years. The criticism that such a view of the Millennium is based on an obscure passage in Rev. 20 is not allowed by premillennialists since this reference, they say, embraces all the kingdom promises of the OT as well as the Day of the Lord, which is prominent in Scripture and connects with the kingdom, or Millennium. Most of the opposition to premillennialism comes from the assumption that an earthly kingdom with Israel at the head would involve a retrogression from the spirituality brought in by Christ through His death, resurrection, and ascension. But premillennialists hold that the promise of the fulfillment of the covenants and promises to Israel in the OT demand such an earthly kingdom. The Millennium will be the last of the ordered ages of time. Eternity will not dawn until the Millennium is complete (Isa. 65:17; 66:22; 2 Pet. 3:13; Rev. 21:1). The Millennium will be characterized by the binding of Satan and the severe limitation of sin. The perfect sinless state, however, will occur in the eternal state after the Millennium.   M.F.U.

BIBLIOGRAPHY: *Postmillennial:* D. Brown, *Christ's Second Coming* (1919); L. Boettner, *The Millennium* (1957).

Amillennial: F. E. Hamilton, *The Basis of the Millennial Faith* (1942); G. L. Murray, *Millennial Studies* (1948); O. T. Allis, *Prophecy and the Church* (1964).

Premillennial: N. West, *The Thousand Years in Both Testaments* (n.d.); D. H. Kromminga, *The Millennium in the Church* (1945); J. F. Walvoord, *The Millennial Kingdom* (1965).

MILLET. *See* Vegetable Kingdom.

MILLO (Heb. "the filling"). Always with an article, evidently a rampart consisting of two walls with the space between them filled in.

1. In the KJV of Judg. 9:6, 20, the name of the citadel of Shechem, the garrison of which joined in proclaiming Abimelech as their king. The NASB reads, "Beth-millo," and the NIV, "Beth Millo."

2. The Millo at *Jerusalem* (which see) was such a fortification, the definite article before the name indicating that it was a well-known fortress, probably one that had been built by the Jebusites. "And David built all around from the Millo [NIV, "terraces"] and inward" (2 Sam. 5:9; 1 Chron. 11:8), as did Solomon (1 Kings 9:15; 11:27). It formed a prominent part of the fortifications by which Hezekiah prepared for the approach of the Assyrians (2 Chron. 32:5). The same place is likely meant by "the house of Millo" (NIV, "Beth Millo") where Joash was killed (2 Kings 12:20-21). Jebusite, Davidic, and Solomonic Jerusalem have been explored. Masonry at the N end of the city of David on Ophel apparently corresponds to Millo.   M.F.U.

BIBLIOGRAPHY: J. Simons, *Jerusalem in the Old Testament* (1952), pp. 131-44.

MILLSTONE. The mill for grinding grain had not wholly superseded the *mortar* (which see) in the time of Moses (Num. 11:8); but fine flour, i.e., meal ground or pounded fine, is mentioned as early as the time of Abraham (Gen. 18:6); hence mills and mortars must have been previously known. The mills of the ancient Hebrews probably differed but little from those in present use in the East. These consist of two circular stones, about eighteen inches or two feet in diameter, the lower of which is fixed and has its upper surface slightly convex, fitting into a corresponding concavity in the upper stone. The latter, called by the Hebrews *rekeb*, "chariot," and by the Arabs *rekkab*, "rider," has a hole in it through which the grain passes, immediately above a pivot or shaft that rises from the center of the lower stone, and about which the upper stone is turned by means of an upright handle fixed near the edge. It is worked by women, sometimes singly and sometimes two together, who are usually seated on the bare ground (Isa. 47:1-2), "facing each other; both have hold of the handle by which the upper is turned round on the 'nether' millstone. The one whose right hand is disengaged throws in the grain as occasion requires through the hole in the upper stone. The proverb of our Saviour (Matt. 24:41) is true to life, for *women* only grind. I cannot recall an instance in which men were at the mill" (Thomson, *Land and Book,* chap. 34). The labor is very hard, and the task of grinding in consequence is performed only by the lowest servants (Ex. 11:5) and captives (Judg. 16:21; Job 31:10; Isa. 47:1-2; Lam. 5:13). So essential were millstones for daily domestic use that they were not to be taken in pledge (Deut. 24:6; Josephus *Ant.* 4.8.26) in order that a man's family might not be deprived of the means of preparing their food. The hand mills of the ancient Egyptians appear to have been of the same character as those of their descendants and, like them, were worked by women. They also had a large mill on a very similar principle, but the stones were of far greater power and dimensions, and this could only have been turned by cattle or donkeys, like those of the ancient Romans and of the modern Cairenes. It was the millstone of a mill of this kind, driven by a donkey, that is alluded to in Matt. 18:6. With the movable upper millstone of the hand mill the women of Thebez broke Abimelech's skull (Judg. 9:53).

BIBLIOGRAPHY: W. M. Thomson, *The Land and the Book* (1907), 3:218-19, 455.

A handmill

MINA. The rendering in Luke 19:13 of Gk. *mna,* which was both a weight and a unit of money. *See* Metrology.

MINCING (Heb. *ṭāpap,* Isa. 3:16). To take short steps, just putting the heel of one foot against the toe of the other. The women whom the prophet Isaiah rebuked could take only short steps because of the chains by which the costly foot rings worn above the ankles were connected. Tripping is a child's step. Although well versed in sin and old in years, the women of Jerusalem tried to maintain a youthful, childlike appearance. They therefore tripped along with short, childlike steps.

MINERAL KINGDOM. For the sake of continuous study we give the different objects in the mineral kingdom in alphabetical order. *See also* Metals; Precious Stones.

Adamant. *See* Diamond.

Agate (Gk. *achatēs,* from the river of that name in Sicily; Heb. *shebô; kadkōd*). This name is applied to those varieties of semitransparent quartz (chalcedony) that have the general character of being clouded, banded, or lined in several shades or colors. When the layers are even, and black and white, the quartz is properly called *onyx;* and when red and white, *sardonyx,* though the terms are often used somewhat loosely. In these latter cases the cutting down from one layer to another gives the beautiful cameo effect of a raised device of one color upon a ground of another. All the agates were favorite stones with the ancients and are abundant in collections of classical and oriental jewelry, being hard enough to take and retain a high polish and not too hard to be cut and engraved readily by means of corundum points.

The term appears four times in the KJV and twice in the NASB and NIV. In the KJV, NIV, and NASB of Ex. 28:19; 39:12 it is the rendering of Heb. *shebô* in the accounts of the breastpiece made for Aaron. The LXX gives *achtēs* and may be taken as correct in the modern sense.

In the other two appearances of the term in the KJV, Isa. 54:12 and Ezek. 27:16, "agate" is the rendering of Heb. *kadkōd,* "striking fire, sparkling," and is probably incorrect. The NASB and NIV of the two passages give "rubies."

Alabaster (Gk. *alabastron,* Matt. 26:7; Mark 14:3; Luke 7:37; Heb. *shēsh, shayish,* 1 Chron. 29:2; Song of Sol. 5:15, NASB, but "marble" in the KJV and NIV). Identified with the substance now called oriental (or Egyptian) alabaster, also "onyx marble" and "Mexican onyx," this is a variety of carbonate of lime, usually stalagmitic in origin, with a layered structure due to its deposition from water, giving it a banded aspect of slightly varying shades and colors, often very delicate and beautiful. This banded character has led to its frequently being called onyx among the ancients, and onyx marble and Mexican onyx among ourselves, although it is very different from true onyx, which is a variety of agate and very hard. Today the name *alabaster* is applied to a still softer stone, the compact variety of gypsum, or sulphate of lime, used for small statuettes, paper weights, and little ornaments of no great value. The *alabastrites* of Theophrastus,

Pliny, and the ancients generally was largely quarried and worked at Alabastron, a well-known locality near Thebes, and was the favorite material for the little flasks and vases for ointment and perfumery that are so abundant in Egyptian tombs and almost all ancient collections. Such articles were called *alabastra;* but by a frequent change of usage the word was transferred to any perfume flask, or the like, without special regard to its material or to its source; as "a piece of delft" or "china" (originally Delft ware or China ware) now signifies any article of crockery (cf. the LXX of 2 Kings 21:13). Horace (*Odes* 4.12.17) uses *onyx* for a perfume flask, and other classical writers do the same thing.

Amber. A KJV term from Heb. *ḥashmal* (LXX *'ēlektron*). It appears only in Ezek. 1:4, 27; 8:2. The NASB and NIV render "glowing metal," with NASB marg. *electrum.*

Amethyst (Heb. *'aḥlāmâ;* Gk. *amethustos,* the Gk. name alluding to a notion that the amethyst prevented *intoxication;* used only in Ex. 28:19; 39:12; Rev. 21:20). This is one of the few cases in which there is little doubt as to the correctness of the rendering, the name having been used from Theophrastus's day to the present for the purple or violet variety of quartz. It was a favorite stone among the ancients, often finely cut or carved in intaglio. Though not rare enough to be of great value, it is still used in fine jewelry because of its rich and almost unique color; there are few purple gemstones. The Heb. name signifies "dream stone," as though it was supposed to induce, or to interpret, dreams.

Bdellium (Heb. *bedōlāḥ;* Gen. 2:12; Num. 11:7). A fragrant gum obtained from a tree found in Arabia, Babylonia, Media, and India. It is said to have had the same color as manna (Num. 11:7). In Gen. 2:12 it is listed with gold and the onyx stone, or beryl, as products of the land of Havilah. The LXX renders it *anthrax* (carbuncle or ruby) in Gen. 2:12 and *krystallos,* rock crystal, in Num. 11:7. The NIV translates "aromatic resin" in Gen. 2:12 and "resin" in Num. 11:7.

M.F.U.

Beryl (Gk. *bērullos,* Rev. 21:20, for Heb. *tarshîsh*). The modern name designates the pale-colored varieties of silicate of glucina, the deep-green variety being emerald. In Rev. 21:20 beryl is no doubt correct, but in the OT all is uncertain. The NASB gives "beryl" in repeated instances; but in some of these, at least, this rendering cannot be correct. *Tarshîsh* occurs in Ex. 28:20, in which there appears to be some confusion as to the places of the stones in the breastplate; in Song of Sol. 5:14; Ezek. 1:16; and Dan. 10:6, it is rendered without translation by the LXX (English "beryl"; marg. of Dan. 10:6 gives "yellow serpentine"). In the NASB of Ezek. 10:9, the wheels in the vision of the cherubim are said to appear "like the gleam of a Tarshish stone" (marg. "beryl"); and in both 10:9 and

28:13 the LXX gives *lithos anthrakos* as *anthrax.* Here there is a strange confounding of this with a deep-red stone such as *anthrax* (or carbuncle), as appears also in regard to *emerald* (which see), indicating the uncertainty of the Greek translators as to the meaning of *tarshîsh;* as does also their merely transliterating the word in other cases, as noted above. But Jerome's rendering of Ezek. 1:16—*"quasi visio maris"* (Vulg.), almost establishes the impression of a green or blue-green stone like beryl, or, as Luther suggests, turquoise, rather than anything red or yellow. The NIV translates Heb. *bāreqet* as "beryl" in Ex. 28:17; 39:10; Ezek. 28:13. It renders *tarshish* as "chrysolite" (which see). The NASB takes *bāreqet* to be "emerald" (which see). *See* Emerald.

Brass. *See* Bronze.

Brick. *See* article Brick in the general listing.

Brimstone (Heb. *goprît,* from *gōper,* "gopher wood," Gen. 6:14). At first sight the connection of brimstone and the gopher tree seems farfetched, but if *gōper* means resinous trees, their inflammable yellow exudations may not inaptly be compared with sulfur or brimstone.

In the OT *brimstone* is repeatedly used to convey the idea of barrenness and desolation, evidently from its association with the Dead Sea; so, definitely, Deut. 29:23, also Isa. 34:9, and probably Job 18:15. The NIV invariably uses "sulfur" rather than "brimstone." Tristram, Lynch, and others describe its occurrence around the lake and in the valleys leading into it, and also on both sides of the Jordan Valley, where there are many hot sulfurous springs. These springs deposit sulfur, and pieces of it are scattered over the flats around portions of the lake. In some places it occurs with tar, for which the Dead Sea region is noted from very early times (Gen. 14:10)—an unusual association, but known also near Bologna, Italy. Some of the hot sulfur springs in Judea have been much esteemed for the treatment of rheumatic diseases, and so are to this day; some show ruins of Roman baths. Sulfur also occurs in connection with bands of gypsum (sulfate of lime) in the cliffs and terraces along the lower Jordan Valley, which go back to a former period of much greater height and extension of the Dead Sea. Sulfur is also referred to in the OT in the combination "fire and brimstone" in connection with violent storms (Gen. 19:24; Ps. 11:6; Ezek. 38:22). The idea here has, no doubt, been justly interpreted as referring to lightning—as is clear in Isa. 30:33—perhaps from the popular idea, alluded to even by Pliny and Seneca, of a sulfurous odor (probably the ozone odor) after a discharge of lightning. The same combination (*pur kai theion*) recurs in the NT (Luke 17:29; Rev. 9:17; 14:10; 19:20; 20:10; 21:8), the translation of a familiar Heb. phrase.

Bronze (Heb. *neḥōshet;* Gk. *chalchos;* Lat. *aes*). Bronze, the alloy of copper and tin, was used to an enormous extent in ancient times. It was the principal material for all manner of articles, both of ornament and use, as far back as the Chalcholithic Age (3500-3000 B.C.), a period characterized by the transition from stone to copper. Great interest has arisen as to the source of the tin so largely used in the manufacture of the ancient bronzes, as tin occurs in but few localities. Most of it is understood to have been brought from the great tin mines of the Cornwall peninsula and the Scilly Islands by the Phoenicians, who maintained for many centuries steady commerce by sea. The bronze articles then manufactured in the Punic cities and colonies were exported all over the world in exchange for the products of every region, to enhance the wealth of Tyre and Carthage. The bronze, however, varied a great deal in composition, and some contained an admixture of zinc, approaching brass. Such may have been the "fine shiny bronze, precious as gold" (Ezra 8:27, NASB; 1 Esd. 8:57). The zinc mines at Laurium, in Greece, were extensively worked in ancient times; and it seems probable that various proportions of the three metals were employed, giving alloys all the way from bronze to brass; but the former is much the more ancient and frequent. *See* Tin.

Palestine archaeology distinguishes several Bronze Ages: Early (3000-2000 B.C.); Middle (2000-1500 B.C.); and Late Bronze Age (1500-1200 B.C.), followed by the Iron Age (1200-300 B.C.). Bronze was thus abundant among the Hebrews and their neighbors from early times (Ex. 38; 2 Sam. 8:8; 1 Chron. 18:8; 22:3, 14; 29:7, "brass"). The last passage is interesting as showing that in David's time iron was yet more abundant and that the "bronze age" was entirely past before 1000 B.C. so far as Palestine was concerned. The NIV, however, never translates *nᵉḥōshet* as "brass" but always "bronze." The word occurs in both a literal and figurative sense. As in Ezra 8:27, so in 1 Kings 7:45; 2 Chron. 4:16; Ezek. 1:7; and Dan. 10:6 it seems probable that brass is meant. To the many other passages describing various objects such as mirrors (Ex. 38:8), weapons and armor (1 Sam. 17:5-6, 38; 2 Sam. 8:8, 10; 21:16; etc.), the "bronze serpent" (Num. 21:9; 2 Kings 18:4), or the furnishings of the Tabernacle (Ex. 26:11, 37) or Temple (1 Kings 7:14; 2 Chron. 4; Jer. 52:17, 22); etc., the preceding remarks as to bronze and mixed alloys will apply.

In the NT the word *chalkolibanon* (Rev. 1:15; 2:18) is much disputed as to its meaning. There seems to be an evident reference to Dan. 10:6 or to Ezek. 1:7, 27, but the term itself is obscure to us, though doubtless familiar at the time. Very probably it was the name for some bright-colored alloy, bronze or brass, employed for handsome articles and highly esteemed. It may be a reference to *orichalcum,* the alloy of copper and gold; or to *electrum,* gold and silver, which is the LXX

rendering of *ḥashmal* of Ezek. 1:4, 27; 8:2. *See* Copper.

Figurative. The word appears in many metaphors, such as for a hot, rainless sky (Deut. 28:23) or parched soil (Lev. 26:19); for baseness as contrasted with the precious metals (Isa. 60:17; Jer. 6:28—here also with the opposite idea of value, as compared with wood); and constantly to express conceptions of physical strength, power, durability, etc. (Job 6:12; 40:18; 41:27; Ps. 107:16; Isa. 45:2); or of moral qualities, such as firmness (Jer. 1:18), obstinacy (Isa. 48:4), and the like.

Carbuncle. The term *carbuncle,* which appears in the KJV as the translation of the Heb. terms *bāreqet* and *'eqdāḥ,* does not appear in the NASB or NIV but is instead replaced by *crystal* and *emerald,* respectively.

Chalced'ony (kal-sēd'o-ni; Gk. *chalkedōn,* occurring only in Rev. 21:19). The modern chalcedony—light-colored, noncrystalline quartz—was probably the ancient *iaspis* (*see* Jasper). King's *chalcedonius* was a blue-green stone, not readily identified by us; he speaks of it as resembling *callais,* i.e., turquoise, and as found at certain copper mines at Chalcedon; which points together suggest the modern chrysocolla—silicate of copper.

Chalk Stones (Heb. *'abnê-gir,* "stones of boiling," Isa. 27:9, lit., "stones of lime," i.e., limestone, from an obsolete root, *gîr,* to "boil, effervesce," such as lime in slaking). The making of lime by roasting limestone in kilns, and preparing mortar, cement, and whitewash from it, is one of great antiquity. Palestine is largely a country of limestone, chiefly cretaceous; and there are gypsum beds along portions of the Jordan Valley (*see* Brimstone); so that material for both lime and plaster was abundant. Tristram describes the extensive use of these substances in the East for lining cisterns, tombs, etc.—the former fairly honeycombing some portions of the country, especially among the hills, and fed by gutters or channels of cement laid along the edges of the terraces. The material remains hard and waterproof even after 3,000 years. The ancient limekiln was a pit or depression three or four feet deep, like a saucer in form, wherein were placed alternate layers of fuel (brushwood, etc.) and lime rock, broken up small by a wheel like that of an oilpress (alluded to in Isa. 27:9). The fuel was then kindled and the pit covered with sod, much as we do a charcoal heap, leaving only an opening for draft. *See also* Plaster.

Figurative (Isa. 27:9). The sense of the passage is given thus by Delitzsch—that Israel's repentance would be shown by the destruction of idolatrous altars, the stones of which would be broken to pieces, calcined, and slaked for mortar. In Amos 2:1 the burning of human bones into lime is denounced as an act of sacrilege on the part of Moab (cf. also the defiling of the idolatrous altars in this manner by Josiah, 2 Kings 23:16, 20; 2 Chron. 34:5, as predicted in 1 Kings 13:2). *See* Lime.

Chrys'olite (krĭs'ō-līt; "gold stone"). It was plainly our topaz. The Gk. name is definite as to color and included not only yellow topazes, but other gems of similar tint, such as the occasional yellow or "golden" beryls, some zircons, etc. The only distinct reference is Rev. 21:20; but the LXX employs the word for *tarshîsh* (Ex. 28:20; 39:13; indefinitely Ezek. 28:13). This word and *topazion* have changed meanings between the Gk. and the English, the ancient topaz being our chrysolite, and *vice versa*. The modern chrysolite—silicate of magnesia with some iron—is a rich yellow-green gem, also called olivine and peridot, but in nowise described as "golden."

Chrysop'rase (kris-op'race; Gk. *chrusoprasis,* "greenish yellow," only in Rev. 21:20). The identity is entirely uncertain. The modern chryso-prase, a light green chalcedony, was probably included in the ancient *iaspis* (*see* Jasper), and does not agree with the classical descriptions of the stone then so called. Pliny's account of *chrysoprasus*—bright green with gold spots—fails to correspond with any mineral that we know; and the attempt to identify this stone must be altogether conjectural.

Clay. This term is applied differently in scientific and in popular usage. In the former it denotes a definite compound, chiefly silicate of alumina, arising from the decomposition of certain feldspathic rocks and forming whitish chalky-looking beds. In this pure condition it is highly valuable for fine grades of pottery. But it is generally much contaminated with other substances; all ordinary clays contain more or less oxide of iron, which causes pottery and bricks made from them to be yellow or red after burning. Most clays also contain silica and other foreign materials and so graduate into common soil, or earth. To all of these impure mixtures the term *clay* is applied, in distinction from sandy, gravelly, or calcareous soils. Two Heb. words occur in the OT for clay:

1. *Tît,* rendered "mire," "mud," for the fine deposit left from the evaporation of water (Ps. 69:14; Jer. 38:6) or washed up on the shore (Isa. 57:20) is used in the sense of clay for bricks or pottery (Isa. 41:25; Nah. 3:4).

2. *Hōmer* is properly clay for bricks or pottery (Isa. 29:16; 45:9; Jer. 18:4; etc.). In Job 4:19 *hōmer* seems to indicate a mud hut, from the idea of being perishable. The distinction seems usually to be in the thought of the material as wrought or unwrought, though this is not always borne out (*see* 30:19; Isa. 10:6, where the word is rendered "mire" or "mud"), but its usual meaning is in connection with human arts or processes (Job 10:9; 38:14, and passages cited above).

3. *Pēlos* is the NT Gk. word used in all the meanings for clay (John 9:6, 11, 14-15; Rom. 9:21). The passage "But we have this treasure in earthen vessels" (2 Cor. 4:7) is a striking allusion to the custom of keeping gold or silver in earthen jars, contrasting the precious contents with the humble receptacle.

Vessels and utensils of baked clay are, of course, often alluded to (2 Sam. 17:28; Jer. 18:3-4; 19:1), and fine pottery was made in Mesopotamia and Egypt from before 5000 B.C. onward. Pottery remains in ancient excavated biblical sites constitute the greatest ally of the scientific archaeologist for recognizing and dating ancient cultures.

Figurative. Clay is often used as a type of fragility (Ps. 2:9; etc.). The words usually employed are Heb. *kelî yôṣēr,* "earthenware," marg. "potter's ware."

Besides being used for making pottery and *brick* (which see), clay has been employed in Palestine and throughout the East for sealing doors and earthen jars (cf. Jer. 32:14) in order to secure them. Sepulchers were thus sealed, as our Lord's probably was (Matt. 27:66). Another important use of clay in the East was for tablets and cylinders used for records (Ezek. 4:1) and even for ordinary correspondence. Quantities of these have been found in Assyria and Babylonia, and their cuneiform writings interpreted. The Chaldean traditions of the creation, the Fall, and the Flood have thus been recovered. Great discoveries of cuneiform literature inscribed on clay tablets include the Amarna Letters (1886), the Hittite monuments at Boghaz-Keui (1906), the Ras Shamra Tablets (1929-37), the Mari Letters, and the Lachish Ostraca (on pottery; 1935-38).

Copper (Heb. *nehōshet*). This metal, though abundantly familiar to the Hebrews, is seldom named in the KJV, the word being generally translated "bronze." It is correctly rendered "copper" in Deut. 8:9 and Job 28:2. Copper was known and worked in the Orient very early. For the most part it was alloyed with tin to form bronze and probably later to some extent with zinc to form brass, the favorite modern alloy. Its use preceded that of iron, as is clearly shown in prehistoric archaeology and asserted by Hesiod and Lucretius. Homer describes it in connection with the shield of Achilles (*Illiad* 18.474); and at ancient Troy Schliemann found both copper and bronze objects, with the stone molds used in casting them. In the Near East copper was introduced c. 4500 B.C., with the Chalcolithic (copper-stone) Age c. 4500-3000 B.C., the Early Bronze Age c. 3000-2000 B.C., the Middle Bronze Age c. 2000-1500 B.C., and Late Bronze Age c. 1500-1200 B.C. The Iron Age dates c. 1200-300 B.C. Up until the Iron Age (1200-300 B.C.) copper was the most practical metal in the OT era, as bronze was used for all kinds of utensils, weapons, and knives (cf. Ex. 38:3; Num. 16:39; Jer. 52:18). Deuteronomy 8:9 gives a graphic picture of the iron-and-copper-rich Arabah: "A land where you shall eat food without scarcity, in which you shall not lack anything; a land whose stones are iron, and out of whose hills you can dig copper." Nelson Glueck uncovered copper smelting and mining centers in the Arabah region in the 1930s, and Benno Rothenberg worked there in the 1960s. Copper was also a well-known metal in Egypt, and Egyptians worked the copper mines of the Sinai Peninsula and the Arabah.

It is impossible to determine the exact meaning of *nehōshet* in its many OT occurrences; the word was applied to copper and to its alloys, bronze and brass, so far as the latter was known. As to the abundance of it among the Hebrews, *see* Bronze; also the interesting records of the source, use, and final disposal of the Tabernacle bronze (1 Chron. 18:8; 2 Chron. 4:9-18; also 1 Kings 7:13-47 and 2 Kings 25:13-17). The sources of the great amount of copper used for the ancient bronzes, etc., are vaguely known. The mining of copper is mentioned in the OT (Deut. 8:9; Job 28:2; and probably Gen. 4:22). The Egyptians obtained it from Arabia, in the Sinaitic peninsula. Modern travelers have described the vestiges still remaining of extensive and very ancient operations, especially at and near the place known as Wadi Maghâra: these include shafts in the sandstone rock and ruins of reservoirs for water, of miners' settlements, of furnaces, with heaps of slag, etc., and hieroglyphic inscriptions going back as far as the Fourth Dynasty. By Homer's time, and doubtless long before, the copper mines of Cyprus identified with the very name of the island were familiar and celebrated. In the *Odyssey* (1.181), Athéné appears in the disguise of a merchant, taking iron to Temese, in Cyprus, to exchange for copper. Many accounts in classical authors allude to the importance and value of the copper of Cyprus, to the mines as a source of revenue to Cypriote kings, and of gifts from them to other monarchs or to temples, etc. They were worked extensively until recent years. Eusebius refers to copper mines in Palestine, saying that under Diocletian's persecution Christians were sentenced to labor in them (8.15.17) at a place called Phreno, which Jerome locates in Idumea, between Petra and Zoar. In the NT the Gk. word *chalchos* is rendered "copper" in one instance (Matt. 10:9); elsewhere "money" (Mark 6:8; 12:41).

Figurative. This word is translated "lewdness" (Ezek. 16:36), as referring to the preceding verses (33-34) for disgraceful pay or hire; somewhat like the more general idea of *aischrokerdēs* (1 Tim. 3:3, 8), as applied to "sordid gain."

Coral (Heb. *rā'mâ,* Job 28:18; Ezek. 27:16, KJV, NIV, and NASB; "corals" from Heb. *peninîm,* Lam. 4:7, NASB). The Heb. term *ra'mâ,* something "high" in value, is rather obscure, but the idea of something *high* (growing upward) is strongly suggestive of coral. The Heb. term

peninîm is translated "rubies" in the KJV (Job 28:18; Prov. 3:15; 8:11; 31:10; Lam. 4:7), but as "corals" (Lam. 4:7), "jewels" (usually marg. "corals," Prov. 3:15; 8:11; 20:15; 31:10), or "pearls" (Job 28:18) in the NASB. The NIV renders all the preceding Proverbs passages with "ruby" or "rubies." The passage in Lam. 4:7 is the only one that indicates redness; the others denote merely beautiful and precious objects, are employed solely for comparison, and are in every case plural. From these facts, and from the resemblance to the Arab. name, the suggestion is strongly in favor of pearls as the meaning of *peninîm.* The rendering "red coral" is favored by Gesenius and others and is compared with the Arab. *panah,* a "branch"; but this is vague. An apt suggestion has been made in connection with the fact that pink pearls are occasionally obtained from the Red Sea shell known to naturalists as *pinna.* These pink pearls are highly prized and, doubtless, have been so from antiquity. If these were meant in the passage in Lamentations, the various renderings would be greatly harmonized. Possibly too, the name may have included not only pearls but beads of coral, red carnelian, garnet, etc., or strung gems in general (*see* Pearls). The red coral of the Mediterranean and the Red Sea has been gathered and valued from the earliest times and is frequent in Egyptian jewelry. The small branches, polished, with beads made from it, have been used for ages, as they are today. Coral is, of course, not a precious stone, but is the calcareous skeleton or framework secreted by a connected community of small polyps, which enclose and conceal it entirely during life. Coral fishery is still an important industry of the eastern Mediterranean.

Crystal (Gk. *krustallos,* "ice"; Heb. *zekûkît,* KJV and NIV; *gābîsh, qerah, 'eqdāh,* Isa. 54:12, NASB). This word, among the ancients and even down to recent times, has been used simply to denote any hard material of great transparency and without marked color. Thus it was applied to glass and to the clear colorless varieties of quartz now designated as rock crystal. This latter substance was largely regarded by the ancients as a permanently solidified form of water and was prized and admired for articles of ornament, as it is by the modern Europeans and Japanese, whose "crystal balls" and carved objects of *vertu* are so much valued in our art collections. The scientific application of the word is wholly different, modern, and technical, denoting the geometrical forms assumed by various substances in passing into the solid state and with no reference to transparency. Of course the Scripture use of the word is entirely in the former sense, being of some clear and brilliant substance like ice or glass. Cf. Job 28:18; Ezek. 1:22 where the Heb. words *gābîsh* and *qerah* both denote "ice" or "crystal" (although the KJV of Job 28:18 renders "pearls" for *gābîsh*). In Isa. 54:12 Heb. *'eqdāh* is given as "crystal" in the NASB, "sparkling jewels" in the NIV, "carbuncle" in the KJV. The NIV translates "crystal" only once in the OT, a rendering of zᵉkōkît (Job 28:17).

Diamond, Adamant. With regard to these words there is little reason to think that the diamond was known to the Hebrews or even to the ancient Greeks. The first definite reference to it is apparently found in the Latin poet Manilius, about A.D. 12; Pliny describes it unmistakably in his great work on natural history, which appeared some two years before his death, A.D. 79. The stone that the Greeks, and after them the Romans, called *adamas,* "the invincible," as being harder than anything else, was probably some of the forms of corundum, the next hardest of minerals. Diamond, or adamant, in the OT is represented by two distinct Heb. words, which divide themselves into two sets of three each; the first set relates to some stone of value and brilliancy and the second to something very hard. In the two descriptions of the breastplate (Ex. 28:18; 39:11), and in Ezekiel's account of the Tyrian treasures (Ezek. 28:13), the word is *yahălōm* (which can be rendered "jasper" or "precious stone"; *see also* Emerald). The other three passages represent the word *shāmîr,* a hard "point." The reference in Jer. 17:1, "The sin of Judah is written down with an iron stylus; with a diamond point," is of course a simple figurative expression in which a stylus tipped with some hard mineral is contrasted with one of iron or steel. The substance employed for such engraving on stone was doubtless a small flake or pointed chip of corundum in some of its forms, which would easily cut or drill into any other mineral. This "adamantine claw," as the LXX gives it, was no doubt perfectly familiar to those for whom Jeremiah wrote. The passage "Like emery harder than flint I have made your forehead" (Ezek. 3:9, marg. "corundum"; "firmer than a rock"; cf. Isa. 50:7), is even more completely figurative. The third passage, "They made their hearts like flint" (Zech. 7:12, marg. "corundum") is not rendered by any noun in the LXX, "they adamantenized their hearts." In all these cases the allusion is undoubtedly to corundum as the hardest substance known to the ancients and used for all purposes of drilling and engraving other stones; and it is of interest to notice the widespread use of a similar word in other languages for the same idea.

Dross. This general term includes, in the OT, several distinct kinds of impurities present in metals and necessary to be removed in order to obtain them in a useful and valuable state. The admixtures may be either: (1) mechanical, of rocky or earthy material intermingled with the ore; (2) chemical, the substances united with the metal in the ore; or (3) other metallic elements present as alloys. Three words are employed in the Heb.; of these the most frequent is *sîg* (Ps. 119:119; Prov. 25:4; Isa. 1:25; Ezek. 22:18-19;

etc.). In other cases *'ereṣ,* "earth," is employed, as in Ps. 12:6, where Gesenius well explains the phrase *lā'āreṣ* in the sense of "from," or "as to," earth, i.e., earthy mixture. A third word is *bᵉdîl,* properly and usually *tin* but employed in the sense (no. 3) above, for a metallic admixture or alloy (Isa. 1:25), and there to be rendered, not *tin,* but *alloy,* a common impurity in silver, often removed by cupellation, of which there seems to be a hint in Jer. 6:29.

Emerald. With regard to this word the confusion seems absolutely hopeless. The stone itself was of course well known and highly valued, as it has been among almost all peoples from the remotest times. It is familiar in early Egyptian jewelry, and the ancient mines where it was procured have been rediscovered in Upper Egypt, at Mt. Zabarah. The Hebrews, of course, must have known it in their Egyptian sojourn, and would have carried away emeralds with them among the "spoil" of jewelry given them at their departure. But what word represents this gem in the OT is extremely doubtful.

As a consequence of this confusion, the emerald, carbuncle, and turquoise are closely related in the KJV, NIV, and NASB. In the KJV, Heb. *nōpek* is rendered "emerald," whereas in the NASB and NIV the same Heb. word is translated *"turquoise"* (which see). Similarly, except for Isa. 54:12, where a different Heb. word is involved, KJV "carbuncle," from Heb. *bāreqet* is regularly replaced in the NASB by "emerald," and in the NIV by "beryl."

The situation is simpler in the NT. The Gk. word *smaragdos* denotes our emerald, from the time that Theophrastus so fixed its use; but it also comprises other precious stones of similar color—e.g., the deeper varieties of beryl, which graduate into true emerald; also green tourmalines, peridots, malachite, etc. It is curiously confused in the LXX, however, with *anthrax,* which like its Lat. equivalent *carbunculus,* a glowing coal, denotes a red gem with deep fiery reflections. Both *anthrax* and *carbunculus* included true ruby (so far as it was known), spinel ruby, several varieties of red garnet, and other gems of similar crimson color, such as occasional red tourmalines, zircons, etc. Theophrastus speaks of engraving upon *anthrax,* which suggests garnet, a favorite engraved stone among the ancients. In the two passages (Rev. 4:3; 21:19), the original is *smaragdos,* and the English translation "emerald" is without question correct. The same is true for passages in the Apocrypha.

Flint. This term is often loosely applied to any very hard, compact rock; in strictness it belongs only to the fine-grained and nearly opaque varieties of noncrystalline or cryptocrystalline quartz or silica, of dull color and luster, that occur, not as forming rock masses themselves, but in nodules and concretions in other rocks, especially limestone and chalk. But, as stated above, it is commonly used in a general sense, implying hardness and fine texture. In the OT it is thus represented by the word *hallāmîsh,* perhaps "hardness," of rather obscure derivation, which appears in such passages as Deut. 8:15; 32:13; Ps. 114:8; and figuratively in Isa. 50:7. In 5:28; Ezek. 3:9, the word rendered "flint" is *sûr,* "rock," and in Zech. 7:12 *shāmîr,* elsewhere "diamond" or "adamant" (so KJV), is rendered "flint." Flint proper was the material employed almost everywhere in early prehistoric time for edge tools and weapons, prior to the use of metals. Its hardness, and the peculiar sharpness of its edges when broken or "flaked," rendered it all-important for such purposes; and hence the science of prehistoric archaeology has dealt very largely with the study of flint implements in their wide distribution, their varied forms, and their stages of development from ruder to more finished types. All this lies back of any OT references; but a persistence in the use of stone implements for certain sacred purposes, long after metal tools were in common use, is alluded to by classical writers and appears in Ex. 4:25 and Josh. 5:2-3 ("flint knives," NASB and NIV). For further information on this subject *see* introductory remarks on Metals.

Glass. *See* article on Glass in the general listing.

Gold. A precious metal widely used in the ancient world and obtained in the OT from Havilah (Gen. 2:11); Sheba (1 Kings 10:1, 2); and Ophir (9:28). Several Heb. and Gk. terms are employed to name it.

1. *Zāhāb* ("yellow, golden"), from unused roots having the idea of shining, being bright (Gen. 2:11-12). In Job 37:22 it is used figuratively for a brilliant sky, "golden splendor"; possibly there may be a reference to the aurora borealis, a rare phenomenon in the latitude of Palestine, but one that might occasionally be seen and would produce a strong impression. In Zech. 4:12, "golden oil," it is applied to a clear yellow liquid. The root ideas are of luster and color.

2. *Beser* ("clipping, dug out"), properly metal in a crude state, "golden ore." In Job 22:24, the righteous man shall prosper temporally and acquire gold and silver in abundance, but his richest possession, his treasure (v. 25) and his delight (v. 26), shall be in God Himself. In 28:19 it is again rendered *gold. Beser* seems to stand in contrast with *pāz* (no. 3), as implying native gold, whether found in placer deposits, in grains and nuggets, or as occurring in rocks, to be smelted out; whereas the other word has the idea of gold that has been refined.

3. *Pāz* (to "separate, purify," as metals from the ore). This noun occurs in Pss. 19:10; 21:3; 119:127; Prov. 8:19; Song of Sol. 5:11; Isa. 13:12; and Lam. 4:2. It is usually rendered "fine gold," "much fine gold," etc. In Ps. 19:10 the familiar line of Watts "gold that has the furnace passed"

is probably exact, although the LXX renders the word by Gk. *lithos timios* and *chrusion apuros* as though native gold, a signification that belongs more properly to the preceding noun.

4. *Segôr* ("closed, shut up," i.e., a thing kept closed, a treasure), means treasured or precious gold (1 Kings 6:20-21; 7:49-50; 10:21; 2 Chron. 4:20, 22; 9:20; Job 28:15).

The above four Heb. terms, therefore, present the idea of gold as (1) the bright yellow metal, which is (2) gathered from the soil or taken from the rock, in a condition in which it may be used to some extent as it is, either hammered or melted, but is (3) purified and refined for choicer purposes, while in any of its forms it is (4) treasured with care. Two other Heb. words occur that are poetical in their use.

5. *Kethem* ("golden store," or "hoard"), kindred in meaning to no. 4. This root idea appears in Job 31:24; but usually the word seems to have only the general sense of gold (28:16, 19; Ps. 45:9; Prov. 25:12; Lam. 4:1; Dan. 10:5). In Song of Sol. 5:11, it is joined with no. 3, in the phrase *kethem pāz,* "a store of gold."

6. *Hārûs.* The word is frequent as a simple name for gold (Ps. 68:13, "glistening gold"; Prov. 3:14; 8:10; 16:16; Zech. 9:3 render "choice," "fine," etc.).

7. Gk. *chrusos* occurs in many NT passages.

Gold, from its color, its malleability, its durability, and its occurrence native in the metallic state was doubtless the first metal to attract the attention of early man. In prehistoric archaeology, however, it does not appear much, or at all, until well into the Bronze Age. But once within the historic period it assumes great prominence, both in early remains and later in the accounts of ancient writers, and seems to have been long used with an abundance unknown to the modern world. A large part of the gold now known exists in the form of coin or bullion and is thus withdrawn from use in the arts; anciently it was not so much employed as the "medium of exchange," but rather as an article of value and beauty. Gold coinage, in our sense, is late. Egyptian representations show gold as weighed out in the form of rings (1 Chron. 21:25; Ezra 8:25-26) and make many similar references to payment by weight, both in gold and silver. Genesis 13:2; 24:22; etc., give us early references to wealth in gold. In Ex. 12:35; 32:3-4; 35:22; chap. 37; Num. 31:50-54; etc., we see great abundance of gold jewelry and other objects at later periods; in the time of David and Solomon the accounts are surprising (1 Kings 6:21-22; chap. 10; 1 Chron. 22:14, 16; 2 Chron. 1:15; chaps. 3, 9), but not more so than those given by classical authors as to the enormous amounts of gold possessed by ancient monarchs, and the lavish use of it for decorations and furniture in the temples and palaces. With the accounts of Solomon and the queen of Sheba may be compared that of the funeral pyre of Sardanapalus, as given by Athenaeus, which was made of perfumed woods, with enormous quantities of gold, and kept burning for fifteen days. Exploration is constantly bringing to light treasures of goldwork throughout the ancient lands of the East, besides all that is already preserved in museums and collections and all that has been captured, destroyed, and remelted through centuries of war and pillage. See Handicrafts: Goldsmiths.

The gold of the ancient world must represent, in the first place, a great amount of "placer" deposits, accumulated during Tertiary and Quaternary time, from the erosion of rock sources, perhaps not very rich but sufficient to yield considerable amounts at many points by this natural process of concentration long undisturbed. Most of these deposits must have been worked out at an early day; others lasted down to classical times but have now long been exhausted. At present, the regions covered by the ancient civilizations yield but the merest fraction of the world's supply of gold, which comes chiefly from the Americas and Australia, and next from South Africa, the Urals, and Siberia. These latter lands may have yielded, at times, portions of their gold to the ancient world; Herodotus refers to it among the Scythians, an indefinite term for the peoples of N and W Asia. The biblical sources—Sheba, Ophir, Uphaz, etc.—have been endlessly discussed; and though good arguments exist for both India and Arabia, there can be little doubt that Ophir was in the former, from the thoroughly East Indian character of the associated products mentioned as brought from there in 1 Kings 10:11, 22; and 2 Chron. 9:10, 21 (almug or algum being generally regarded as sandalwood), and from the length of the time occupied by the trips made, which suggests a much farther country than the neighboring Arabia. On the other hand, Sheba is SW Arabia, a region that yielded many rich products in ancient times. Both Diodorus and Strabo refer to Arabia as furnishing gold, though it is not found there now; the placers are doubtless exhausted, and their sources undiscovered or lost. Diodorus (3.12, 14) describes the gold mines at a place known as Eshuranib, in the Bisharee District, worked by captives and convicts under strict military guard. Here the process was much the same as our quartz mining, but with very simple appliances; the rock was broken into small pieces with hammers, pounded in stone mills or troughs with iron pestles, then washed on inclined tables, and the gold thus separated was afterward refined in crucibles. The OT has much to say of "beaten" gold, "hammered" gold, and "overlaying" with gold. The ancients knew the art of gilding, much like ours; but we find many articles of Assyrian and other work that are heavily plated with gold; and there are objects of later Indian manufacture now in England that show this same style, e.g.,

a life-size tiger's head, part of a support of a throne belonging to Tippoo Saib, made of wood and covered with thick, hammered gold, now in Windsor Castle (cf. Solomon's lion throne, 1 Kings 10:18-20; 2 Chron. 9:17-19). So the great image in the plain of Dura (Dan. 3:1) must evidently have been "golden" only in thin exterior plating, probably over wood. This idea was afterward taken up in Greece by Phidias and applied to his celebrated works. That such was the usual construction of smaller "golden" and "silver" idols also is implied in Isa. 41:7; 44:12-13 and repeatedly stated in the "Epistle of Jeremiah" (Baruch 6:39, 50, 57, 70), in the vivid account given there of the Chaldean images of the gods.

Hyacinth. See Jacinth.

Iron (Heb. barzel). This word is undisputed and is, of course, frequent, both literally and in metaphors of strength, etc. In its first occurrence (Gen. 4:22) the reference is in all probability to meteoric iron. This seems an inescapable conclusion in the light of the immense priority of the use of copper and bronze to that of iron, as clearly shown in prehistoric archaeology. But the expression is simple enough in its general sense, describing Tubal-cain as the pioneer in metallurgical arts, without implying his personal acquaintance with their later advances. Iron was apparently known and worked to a small extent long before it became frequent in the Iron Age, 1200-300 B.C. The readiness with which iron perishes by oxidation would obliterate the evidences of its earlier limited use. Iron was familiar to the civilized nations of the ancient world. Homer has many references to it, though with an association of value that indicates it as still somewhat rare and choice. It was freely used among the Etruscans, Egyptians, and Assyrians, as shown by explorations, and among the Canaanites, as seen in the OT records. Layard found Assyrian articles of iron coated with bronze, which generally crumbled on exposure to the air. It would seem that its use was especially for tools and weapons of attack, whereas bronze and the copper alloys were for defensive armor and objects that did not need hardness and sharpness of edge and point. Thus Goliath was clad in bronze armor, like Homer's Achaioi Chalkochitōnes, but his spearhead was of iron (1 Sam. 17:5-7). By the time of David's later years it was not only abundant (1 Chron. 22:3; 29:2) but had come to be more so than bronze (29:7; Isa. 60:17). This was due to Saul and David's conquests over the Philistines, who held the secret of smelting iron (1 Sam. 13:19-22). The Philistines probably obtained the secret from the Hittites, whose monopoly on this important metal was not broken till about 1200 B.C. Sir Flinders Petrie found abundant confirmation of Philistine domination of iron smelting at Gerar, where iron furnaces and iron instruments were recovered. The industrial revolution of the Davidic-Solomonic era was due in large part to the "steel boom" in Israel. In Isa. 44:12, and more fully detailed in Eccles. 10:10, we find vivid and familiar pictures of the forge and the smith. The OT references to iron are varied; thus it appears in general among the spoils of war (Num. 31:22; 2 Sam. 8:8), for chariots—probably sheathed or plated with it (Josh. 17:16, 18; Judg. 1:19; 4:3, 13)—King Og's bedstead (Deut. 3:11), the huge spearhead of Goliath (1 Sam. 17:7), for axes and axheads (Deut. 19:5; cf. Num. 35:16; 2 Kings 6:5-6, see marg.; Isa. 10:34), for stone-cutting tools (Deut. 27:5), saws, harrows, etc. (2 Sam. 12:31); Tabernacle vessels (Josh. 6:19, 24); idols (Dan. 5:4), a stylus for engraving (Job 19:24; Jer. 17:1), and often for bonds or fetters (Pss. 105:18; 107:10, see marg.; 149:8); also as a figure of strong dominion, an iron scepter or mace (2:9), etc. In these latter and other similar passages, such as Deut. 28:48, the literal and figurative uses of the word blend into each other so as not always to be readily distinguished. Thus it is not clear whether the "iron furnace" (4:20; 1 Kings 8:51; and Jer. 11:4) has an actual or metaphorical reference to the servitude in Egypt.

Archaeologists are of the opinion that the earliest iron in Bible lands was meteoric, containing a small amount of nickel. Both the Egyptian name of iron and the cuneiform ideogram suggest that it was a "metal of heaven." This may be the explanation of the reference to iron among the descendants of Cain in Gen. 4:22. Moreover, excavations have shown that iron ores were occasionally smelted in Mesopotamia at an early date. At Tel Asmar (ancient Eshnunna) Henri Frankfort unearthed evidence of an iron blade from an occupational level belonging to c. 2700 B.C. (*Oriental Institute Commissions 18*, pp. 59-61). A small steel ax has also been recovered from Ur (Millar Burrows, *What Mean These Stones?* [1951], p. 158). However, for some inexplicable reason the discovery of iron was not pursued and did not come into general use on an industrial scale, as we have seen, until after 1200 B.C.

M.F.U.

Figurative. In clearly figurative uses it is often applied to ideas of physical strength, endurance, etc. (Deut. 33:25; Mic. 4:13; Job 40:18; Dan. 7:7, 19), and in mixed symbols (1 Kings 22:11; 2 Chron. 18:10; and the striking similes of Dan. 2:32-45); and likewise to purely moral qualities, in either good or bad senses—firm, unyielding (Jer. 1:18; Isa. 48:4); with the last compare the epithet so frequently applied to Israel, "an obstinate [*stiff-necked*] people" (Ex. 32:9; 33:3, 5; Deut. 9:6, 13; 2 Chron. 30:8; etc.). In Deut. 28:23 it is used with great vividness to depict the parched and hardened ground in a protracted drought, and so of a rainless sky (Lev. 26:19). In Ezek. 4:3 the "iron plate" to be used by the prophet as a sign against Jerusalem of the coming siege is compared with the portable screens for archers, etc., represented on Assyrian sculptures.

Jacinth, Hyacinth. This name is now applied to the orange-red and red-brown varieties of zircon (silicate of zirconia); but the classical *huakinthos* (Rev. 21:20; *huakinthinos,* Rev. 9:17, "hyacinth") appears rather to have been our blue sapphire. Yet there is some uncertainty regarding it, as Pliny speaks of it as golden-colored; generally, however, the classical *hyacinthus* was blue. In Rev. 21:20 (Gk. *huakinthos*) it no doubt means sapphire. In the NASB and NIV (Ex. 28:19; 39:12) it is used instead of KJV "ligure" for Heb. *leshem* in the account of the breastpiece, and in these cases apparently a deep yellow gem is meant, possibly our zircon-hyacinth. Yet as the LXX uses *huakinthos* (for *tekēlet*) in all the descriptions of the Tabernacle furnishings, where *blue* is employed in the English versions, and evidently meant, and as various ancient writers mention the *hyacinthus* as being some shade of blue, there can be little question of its being our sapphire. *See also* Sapphire.

Jasper (Heb. *yāshepēh;* Gk. *iaspis*). Great uncertainty surrounds the meaning of the word *iaspis* among the ancients. The name is now limited to the richly colored and strictly opaque varieties, many of which are fine ornamental stones and were largely used for seals, cylinders, etc., by the ancients, but are totally remote from any idea of great preciousness or great brilliancy. As near as we can gather from Pliny's descriptions, the stone that he called *iaspis*—following Theophrastus—seems to have included several kinds of delicately colored translucent varieties of quartz (the chalcedonies); he especially mentions blue, green, and rosy tints. If so, what is now called chrysoprase would be included here. But these also, however beautiful, are lacking in the elements of brilliancy and rarity. Probably some other minerals were also classed by Pliny as *iaspis,* perhaps the delicate green jades and other semitransparent stones of rich, light colors. Doubtless we should translate the phraseology of John in Rev. 21:11, 18 not as a specific assertion of certain optical properties belonging to the stone named, but rather as an attempt to illustrate from various combined sources conceptions too glorious for description. "Her brilliance was like a very costly stone, as a stone of crystal-clear jasper"—a light more beautiful than words can depict, with the rich sky-blue (or green or rosy or mingled opaline) hues of an *iaspis* and the transparency of crystal.

Lapis Lazuli. *See* Sapphire.

Lead (Heb. *'ōperet*). The Heb. term very plainly indicates this metal, from its heaviness (Ex. 15:10) and its ready dissipation by oxidizing at high temperatures (Jer. 6:29; cf. Ecclus. 22:14 and 47:18); a very heavy metal, less valuable than tin. It was used for weights (Zech. 5:7-8) and for filling in inscriptions cut in rock (Job 19:24; also

Num. 31:22; Ezek. 22:18, 20; 27:12). The word translated "plumb line" (Amos 7:7-8) is *'ănāk* and like the English rendering implies a probable, though not necessary, idea of lead as the material of the weight. In Zech. 4:10 the word "plumb line" is *'eben bedîl*, a weight of tin, literally, "stone of tin"; whereas in Zech. 5:8 the "lead weight" is *'eben hā'ōperet*, "stone of lead." It is needless to seek specific details of composition in such references. Any heavy substance may thus be employed; but it is interesting to remember that the most common ores of these two metals, cassiterite or tinstone (oxide of tin) and galena (sulfide of lead), are very heavy minerals, and a piece of either of them would serve well to suspend a plumb line. But the use of *'eben,* "stone," in the sense of a weight, is early and familiar in Heb.; thus Isa. 34:11, "plumb line of emptiness" (marg. "stones of void"), and better rendered by Gesenius as "plummet of desolation," and so in various references. Other ancient uses of lead were for making solder (41:7), for tablets for writing, and, in very early buildings, for fastening or filling in between rough stonework, so noted at Nineveh by Layard. Oxide of lead has also been found in the glaze upon both Egyptian and Assyrian pottery, as among the moderns. Lead is a metal of somewhat frequent occurrence, the only workable ore being the sulfide galena. Lead mines at Jebel e' Rossas, near the Red Sea, between Kosseir and Berenice, were well known.

Ligure. See Jacinth.

Lime (Heb. *śîd,* to "cover" or "plaster" with lime). In Deut. 27:2, 4 to "coat" with lime is mentioned (cf. Josh. 8:32); in Isa. 33:12 and Amos 2:1 lime is referred to as the substance bones turn into after being burned. The process of burning lime (*see* Chalk Stones) was familiar; but it is not possible to say just what the Hebrew modes of using it were or how far they distinguished lime from other substances, such as plaster. Our modern chemistry enables us to understand the nature and behavior of these substances, theoretically, far better than the ancients; but they certainly knew them practically and used them well. Carbonate of lime (limestone), when heated, loses its carbonic acid and passes to caustic or unslaked lime (calcium oxide); this, on contact with water, combines with it with great heat, forming calcium hydrate (slaked lime), which gradually takes up carbon dioxide again from the air and passes back to carbonate. If slaked lime is mixed with sand, mortar results, which hardens into an artificial stone consisting of grains of sand embedded in a mass of carbonate of lime—very hard and enduring. Sulfate of lime (gypsum, alabaster) contains a quantity of water held in the condition known as "water of crystallization"; by heating, this water is driven off, and the anhydrous sulfate may then be pulverized, this being plaster; on contact with water the latter is again taken up, and the

material suddenly solidifies or "sets." Various combinations and applications of these two great lime products have been used for ages and in many lands. Admixtures of clay with mortar yield certain forms of cement, and the hydraulic cement used for masonry under water is made from argillaceous limestone. Stucco consists essentially of a mixture of plaster with pulverized marble and becomes hard and capable of polish far beyond simple plaster. Whitewash is slaked lime (hydrate) mixed with a large quantity of water, so as to be spread thinly and evenly over walls, etc. Probably all these materials were known to the Hebrews; but it does not appear possible to distinguish any precise terms for them.

Lye. See Niter.

Marble (Heb. *shēsh, shayish,* "white"; Gk. *marmaros;* Esther 1:6; Rev. 18:12). The term *marble* is used loosely for any fine-grained building or ornamental stone, not very hard, white or of delicate color, and taking a handsome polish. Strictly, it refers to crystalline limestones possessing these qualities, but other varieties and even other stones are often included in the term. Palestine is a limestone country; and the word, as used in the Bible, has its ordinary meaning and requires no discussion. From 1 Kings 5:15, 18; 7:10 it would seem as though the material was the white or cream-colored Jurassic limestone of Lebanon, of which the sun temple at Baalbek is constructed. In Herod's Temple true white crystalline marble was largely employed. In the passage in Esther 1:6, several other words are also used, including porphyry and alabaster.

Mortar. This term for building is distinguished from the apparatus for grinding (Heb. *hēmar,* Gen. 11:3; Ex. 1:14; etc. The root (*hāmar*) is properly to "boil" or "foam," though it has some secondary meanings; but this primitive sense vividly suggests the slaking of lime in our ordinary making of mortar. In ancient buildings we find some without any fastening material at all, the stones merely fitted together accurately; in some cases lead was used and in others iron clamps; but most frequently we find either tar (Gen. 11:3, and many existing ruins in Mesopotamia), clay, or some form of cement or mortar prepared for the purpose, and often mixed with straw, as we use hair. Other references to the mixing or "treading" of mortar, in this case plainly not our lime mortar, are Isa. 41:25 and Nah. 3:14; here *hōmer* has apparently its frequent meaning of clay, and the rendering "mortar" in our versions is not applicable.

Another word, *'āpār,* properly "dust" or "dry earth" (so KJV, Lev. 14:41), is in some places rendered "mortar" (KJV) or "plaster" (NASB), especially Lev. 14:42, 45, and refers to clay (so NIV) used for filling interstices in walls or for coating them. In Ezek. 13:10-15; 22:28 the word *mortar* (KJV, from Heb. *'āpār*) or *whitewash* (NASB and NIV, from Heb. *tāpēl*) may imply some form of stucco or cement, used to protect *adobe* houses from the action of the weather. *See* Brick, in the general listing; Lime, Plaster, in this article.

Figurative: See Mortar in general listing.

Niter (Heb. *neter;* Gk. *nitron*). A term found in the KJV but not the NASB and NIV. It is a name for native carbonate of soda, or natron, including also the closely related minerals thermonatrite and trona. The name *niter* is now applied to an entirely different substance—saltpeter or nitrate of potash. Natron occurs in nature only in solution; it contains ten molecules (more than 60 percent) of water, and is essentially the same material as that commonly known as "washing soda." By exposure to the air and by heat more or less of this water is lost, and several other sodium carbonates are thus produced, with varying proportions of water, and even the anhydrous salt. Thermonatrite and trona (abbreviated from natrona) are compounds of this kind, containing about 14 and 20 percent of water respectively, and occurring in the evaporated crusts and deposits from alkaline lakes in dry regions. The principal ancient source was at the "soda lakes" of Egypt, described by Pliny and Strabo, as well as by explorers. There are nine of these lakes, the largest being about five miles long and a mile and a half wide, others much smaller; they are situated some sixty miles NW of Cairo, in the desert of St. Macarius. Beneath the general surface of sand lies a heavy bed of dark clay impregnated with salt, gypsum, and carbonate of lime; the water leached from this clay is strongly charged with salt and with sulfates and carbonates of soda. In the dry season the smaller lakes evaporate to solid crusts, the larger concentrate and deposit beds of these salts, variously mixed in composition but rich in sodium carbonates. The crusts are dug and broken with spades and poles, dried in the sun on the banks, taken to the Nile—some thirty miles—and there shipped on boats to Alexandria. Large amounts are sent to Crete for use in soap making, and the material is also widely employed in the East to soften the hard limestone waters for drinking. Similar deposits occur in other regions of the Old World, and largely in Nevada and California, especially Mono Lake and Owen's Lake. At the latter important soda works have been established.

The ancients employed these natural carbonates for washing, mixed with oil so as to form a true soap; and this primitive though effective method is still in use. They also made artificial vegetable alkalies of the same kind by burning plants and leaching the ashes with water; these were designated in Heb. as *bōr* and *bōrît;* so Mal. 3:2. The effect of pouring acid upon such a carbonate, producing violent effervescence, was evidently familiar, from Prov. 25:20, where the rendering of *neter* in the NASB and NIV is "soda" in place of KJV "nitre"—a vivid comparison to the revulsion of one in sorrow against untimely mirth. The two words *neter* and *bōrît* occur together in Jer. 2:22, where the former is rendered "nitre" in the KJV, "soda" in the NIV, and "lye" in the NASB, and the latter is given as "soap" in all three versions. *Lye* and *soap* appear elsewhere in the Bible, "lye" being the rendering in the NASB and "soda" in the NIV of Heb. *bōr* in Job 9:30, and "soap" being the rendering of Heb. *bōrît* in the KJV, NIV, and NASB of Mal. 3:2. *See also* Soap, below.

Onyx (Gk. *onux*, generally for Heb. *shōham*). This term probably in most cases is the stone still so named (Gen. 2:12; Ex. 25:7; etc.). The word denotes the varieties of that stone that show somewhat even bands or layers of black or dark tints, and white. When cut parallel to the layers the semitransparent white bands show the darker bands through them, and suggest the fingernail, whence the name *onux*. The same word has also been used, both anciently and among us, for other translucent banded stones, such as "Mexican onyx" (*see* Alabaster). The word *shōham* occurs quite often and is variously rendered by the LXX, indicating great uncertainty as to its meaning. References to the Arab. *sahum,* "paleness," and *sachma,* "blackness," made by various writers, give little aid, though strongly against any of the bright-colored stones above named. Josephus, however, states clearly that the stone on the breastplate was onyx and the shoulder-pieces of the ephod sardonyx—the variety of onyx with bands of dark red (sardine or sardius). This testimony, from one personally familiar with the priestly vestments, is incontestable and goes far to establish the same meaning for the other cases in which *shōham* occurs. *See* Agate.

Pearls. These cannot be strictly classed among precious stones, yet they have always been associated with gems in connection with jewelry and so may be treated here. Pearls are formed by secretion in the bodies of many kinds of molluscan shellfish and consist of the same material and possess the same color as the interior layers of the shell in which they occur. This material is partly mineral matter (carbonate of lime) and partly organic matter. Most commercial pearls are yielded by the so-called "pearl oysters," which occur widely distributed along all the shores of the Indian and South Pacific oceans. The scientific name of the chief pearl-yielding species is *Meleagrina margaritifera.* The ancient pearl fisheries were chiefly in the Red Sea and the Persian Gulf; the latter still retain great importance, but the former have ceased to be worked for a long time. Ceylon and the north Australian coast now furnish large quantities.

The references to pearls in the Scriptures are curiously few, and in the OT uncertain, although we know from ancient jewelry that pearls were familiar from very early times. Those in Egypt are presumably from the Red Sea, where they were sought and found as late as the Roman period. In the Red Sea occurs also the large delicate *pinna,* or "wing shell," which occasionally yields translucent pink pearls, greatly prized for their beauty and rarity. It seems probable, partly from the resemblance to the Arab. name and partly from the manner of expression, that the Heb. word *penînîm*—always plural and variously rendered by OT translators (in the NASB OT, "jewels," Prov. 3:15; 8:11; 20:15; 31:10; "corals," Lam. 4:7; "pearls," Job 28:18; in the KJV OT appearing but once [Job 28:18], and then as the translation of Heb. *gābîsh; see* Crystal; in the NIV OT, "ruby") —actually refers to Pearls. This is the view of the rabbis and many commentators, yet the passage in Lamentations (4:7) implies redness and has made the rendering problematical. Gesenius would adopt *pearls* but for this, and he inclines to the meaning *red coral,* deriving the word from *pārad,* to "divide" or "separate" (as in branching corals). But the precious pink pearls yielded by the Red Sea pinnas, Gk. *pinna,* would seem to solve the apparent difficulty. The very name in the Gk. is almost identical, and perhaps the derivation may be found in connection with *penîmâ* and *penîmî,* "within, inner," formed in and taken from the interior of a shellfish. It is also possible, as the LXX and Vulg. renderings of the passages in Proverbs would suggest, that this word may have possessed an indefinite meaning, including pearls and strung jewels or beads, such as of red coral, garnet, carnelian, etc. A feminine singular form, *penînnâ,* occurs once (1 Sam. 1:2, 4) as the name of the other wife of Elkanah, just as we use Pearl, and many European nations Marguerite, etc. The same name is still in use among Arabic-speaking people, in almost the identical form of 1 Sam. 1.

The NT references (Matt. 13:45; Rev. 17:4; 21:21) are perfectly simple renderings of Gk. *margaritēs,* a "pearl."

Pitch. The rendering of two (NASB) or three (KJV) Heb. terms. In the NASB, NIV, and KJV Heb. *kōper* (Gen. 6:14) and *zepet* (Ex. 2:3; Isa. 34:9) are translated "pitch." In the KJV an additional Heb. word, *kāpar,* from *kōper,* is also given as "pitch," although the NASB renders "cover." Isaiah 34:9 shows the use of *zepet* for mineral pitch (asphalt) to depict a barren, desolate region, like the shores of the Dead Sea.

Mineral pitch or asphalt was of great utility in sealing objects against water and moisture. It was employed to caulk the seams of boats, notably Noah's ark (Gen. 6:14), which was significantly covered with pitch. It is noteworthy that *kappēr* is the same expression rendered "atonement" in Lev. 17:11; etc., for it is atonement that keeps out the waters of judgment and makes the believer's position "in Christ" safe. The ark is typical of the place of the believer "in Christ" (Eph. 1:1-14) and constitutes a type of our Lord as the refuge of His people from judgment (Heb. 11:7). Pitch was also

used to cover the basket in which the baby Moses was concealed among the reeds of the Nile (Ex. 2:3). Ancient deposits of pitch existed at Hit on the Euphrates River above Babylon, and other places in Mesopotamia. It was widely used in ziggurat construction, as in the *Tower of Babel* (which see; Gen. 11:3), in Babylonia, and also in constructional decoration to hold tablets of limestone or lapis lazuli, as these recovered architectural embellishments attest. *See also* Tar.

M.F.U.

Plaster. Plaster, made from gypsum by heating it and mixing the dehydrated and powdered product with water, must have been known to the Hebrews, as gypsum occurs in the terraces along the Jordan and Dead Sea valleys. The Egyptians seem to have used it freely, with colors, and overlaid it with varnish in their interior wall paintings. Several Heb. terms are given as "plaster" in the KJV, NIV, and NASB.

1. In Deut. 27:2, 4, the noun *śîd,* from *śîd,* "to cover with lime," is rendered "plaster" in the KJV and NIV, but it is plainly lime, from Isa. 33:12 and Amos 2:1, and is so translated in the NASB.

2. Another more general word, *ṭîaḥ,* appears in Ezek. 13:12 and is translated as "daubing" in the KJV, "whitewash" in the NIV, and "plaster" in the NASB. The Heb. term is derived from the word *ṭûaḥ,* given as "plaster" (KJV and NIV) and "replaster" (NASB) in Lev. 14:42, 43, 48 (cf. 1 Chron. 29:4 for the use of *ṭûaḥ* to refer to the "overlay" of silver plating on the walls of the Temple).

3. The word *'āpār,* "powdered," appears in Lev. 14:41, 45, where it is rendered "dust" and "mortar" in the KJV and "plaster" in the NASB and NIV (*see also* Gen. 2:7, and elsewhere, for the use of the Heb. term with the sense of "dust").

4. In Dan. 5:5 the Heb. word for plaster is *gîrā,* Aram. form for ordinary Heb. *gîr,* properly lime, here probably stucco ("plaster," NIV) gypsum slabs (alabaster) were probably much used for wall facings at Nineveh, but not so much at Babylon, where the scene referred to occurred. *See also* Lime; Mortar.

Figurative. See Mortar in the general listing.

Ruby, Rubies. The English term *ruby,* from Heb. *'ōdem,* does not appear in the KJV, though it is present in the NASB and NIV (Ex. 28:17; 39:10; Ezek. 28:13). The KJV gives *sardius* (which see).

The term *rubies* appears in the KJV, NIV, and the NASB but not for the same Heb. words. In the KJV and NIV, "rubies" is the rendering for Heb. *penînîm* in Job 28:18 ("pearls," NASB) and Lam. 4:7 ("corals," NASB). In the NASB and NIV, "rubies" is the translation of Heb. *kadkōd,* "striking fire, sparkling," and appears in Isa. 54:12 and Ezek. 27:16 (both "agate," KJV).

Salt (Heb. *melaḥ,* powder; *hals*). This is the common substance—sodium chloride—familiar in various applications, in the Bible as with us.

Beds of rock salt occur at many points around the Dead Sea, called the "Salt Sea" (Heb. *yām hammelaḥ,* Gen. 14:3; Num. 34:12; Deut. 3:17; Josh. 3:16; 12:3; 15:2, 5; 18:19), the Mediterranean being the "Great Sea" (Josh. 15:12) or the "sea." The flats at the southern end of the Dead Sea are coated with salt in the dry season; these or similar spots are alluded to (Deut. 29:23; Zeph. 2:9; and Jer. 17:6); and some locate here the "Valley of Salt" (2 Sam. 8:13; 2 Kings 14:7; Ps. 60, title). The waters of the Dead Sea are intensely salty and bitter from the large amount of magnesium salts that they contain, having the composition of "a half-exhausted mother-liquor" (Le Conte) from which most of the sodium salts have been deposited, as well as the lime salts, during a long and extreme concentration since the time when the lake extended over the greater part of the Jordan Valley to hundreds of feet above its present level. The preserving properties of salt were well known; its use by the Phoenicians in curing fish is plain from Neh. 13:16; this salt they evidently made from Mediterranean water, as they had doubtless done for ages.

Figurative. In the East salt has long been regarded as possessing a certain sacred character, so that partaking of it together was regarded as a pledge of friendship and faithfulness (2 Chron. 13:5); this idea appears in a strictly religious sense, as between God and men (Num. 18:19), and hence in the offering of all sacrifices salt was essential (Lev. 2:13; Ezra 6:9; Ezek. 43:14; and Mark 9:49).

In a figurative sense for purifying and preserving influences, it is spoken of in Matt. 5:13; Mark 9:50; Luke 14:34; Col. 4:6. In these references there is an allusion to a popular belief that salt can lose its virtue; Pliny seems to recognize this idea (31.39, 44) in speaking of *sal tabescens.* This belief might arise from the use of impure rock salt or mixed saline and earthy deposits from the Dead Sea flats, etc., from which the salt would dissolve out, leaving only a tasteless and useless residue.

In Judg. 9:45 is a reference to the custom of strewing salt over the ruins of a captured town, thus figuratively devoting it to desolation. In 2 Kings 2:20-21 the idea of purification is again seen in Elisha's "healing" of the spring. These two symbolic acts illustrate two contrasted associations connected with salt in the Eastern mind.

Sapphire (Heb. *sappîr;* Gk. *sappeiros*). The sapphiros of the ancients was not our sapphire, the transparent blue corundum, but usually the opaque stone known to us as lapis lazuli (so NASB of Lam. 4:7; Ezek. 1:26; 28:13; elsewhere KJV, NASB, NIV, "sapphire"), varying from ultramarine to dark violet blue. With this were doubtless included some other blue stones, especially the rich blue chalcedony now called sapphirine quartz and perhaps occasionally cyanite and even

possibly some true sapphires. Lapis lazuli is frequent in ancient Egyptian and Babylonian jewelry and was evidently familiar and highly prized. Sapphirine quartz was much employed for Babylonian cylinder seals. Both of these stones are good material for engraving upon, whereas true sapphire is too hard for any ordinary tools. The objection raised by some that the remarkable passage in Ex. 24:10—the vision of God as seen by Moses and the elders of Israel—implies transparency, does not apply to "a pavement of sapphire, as clear as the sky itself." The words are plainly an attempt to describe an intense depth and beauty of color resembling, but surpassing, that of the sky; and there is no more implication from this comparison that the sapphire was a transparent stone than there is regarding gold in the similar case in Rev. 21:21 where John describes the heavenly city as "pure gold, like transparent glass."

As far as we can judge, the modern sapphire was the hyacinth (or jacinth) of the ancients. Greek mythology tells of Hyacinthus, who was transformed into a flower bearing his name. This was not our hyacinth, but apparently the blue reed; or, some have thought, the larkspur. The name was then transferred to a clear blue gem; and hence we may so understand the biblical hyacinth or jacinth—certainly at least in Rev. 21:20. The stone now so called is entirely different, comprising the orange-red and red-brown varieties of zircon. See Jacinth.

Sardine, Sardius, Sardonyx (Heb. *'ōdem;* Gk. *sardios*). The name *sard,* derived from Sardis in Lydia, is applied to the deep red or brownish red varieties of carnelian (i.e., *chalcedony,* which see), which have always been favorite stones for engraving seals and like purposes, examples being abundant in collections of ancient gems. The *sardius* (sardonyx, NIV) of Rev. 21:20 doubtless means this stone; the *lithos sardinos* of Rev. 4:3 is less certain. In the OT *sardion* and *lithos sardiou* are used variously, but always implying red gems. In Ex. 25:7 and 35:9, where the LXX uses this word for *shōham* (onyx), it seems probable that *sardonyx* (which see) was included under *shōham* on the one hand and *sardiou* on the other.

Sardonyx (Gk. *sardonux*). The variety of onyx in which some of the layers are of red carnelian (sard). The name has long been used with little change. The stone was a favorite among the ancients, as it still is, for the cameo effects produced by cutting designs in one layer with a background of another differently colored. In Rev. 21:20 this is doubtless the stone meant. In the OT it is probable (as suggested above) that it is included in some of the references to both *onux* and *sardios*. Josephus says that the shoulder clasps of the ephod were sardonyxes, adding that these are "needless to describe, as being known to everyone" (Ex. 28:9). As these were engraved with the names of the tribes (six upon each), they were doubtless large red-and-white sardonyx plates, perhaps two inches long, with the names cut in intaglio in the contrasted colors. This particular account of the engraving, with Josephus's statement, disposes of the idea that *shōham* can mean beryl or emerald, which could rarely furnish pieces of such size or be carved advantageously in such ways.

Silver. This precious metal was employed as a medium of commercial exchange from early antiquity (Gen. 23:16; 37:28). It was not coined until the time of Croesus of Lydia and the introduction of coinage into the Persian Empire by Cyrus the Great in the sixth century B.C. In early times it was weighed out in lumps (Job 28:15; Isa. 46:6). It was used in patriarchal times for personal ornaments (Gen. 24:53 and later Ex. 3:22; Song of Sol. 1:11). Royal crowns (Zech. 6:11), musical instruments, i.e., trumpets (Num. 10:2), and drinking cups of the nobility (Gen. 44:2) were made of it. The metal was used extensively in the Tabernacle and Temple for sockets (Ex. 26:19), hooks, fillets of the pillars (Ex. 27:10; 38:19), platters, and bowls (Num. 7:13). Idols were made of silver (Ps. 115:4; Acts 19:24). Silver was used by the Sumerians in the third millennium B.C.; the artisans of Ur fashioned many silver art objects and silver jewelry. Egyptians knew the metal in the Old Kingdom. Silver was especially prominent under the New Empire after 1450 B.C. Great quantities of silver jewelry and other objects from this period show that the Egyptians evidently imported large quantities at this time. Centuries before this, silver figures prominently in the Joseph narratives (cf. Gen. 44:2, 5, 12, 16; 45:22). The refining of silver is often referred to in the OT (Prov. 17:3; Isa. 48:10; Zech. 13:9; Mal. 3:3; etc.). An exquisite silver Persian bowl, now in the Metropolitan Museum of Art, comes from the reign of Artaxerxes I (464-424 B.C.).

Homer describes elegant articles of silver work, e.g., the *crater,* offered as a prize by Achilles at the funeral games of Patroclus (*Iliad* 22.704-45), "which was unrivaled on earth for beauty," wrought by Sidonians and brought by Phoenician merchants as a present to Thoas; and also a similar *crater,* given to Menelaus by a Sidonian king (*Odyssey* 4.615; 15.115). From these and many other ancient references we learn of great use of silver for articles of value and elegance; but little has come down to us. Greek objects in silver are rare and were so even in Roman times. Pliny and others give accounts of celebrated Greek silversmiths; but the few examples of their work then existing were of extreme value. Their favorite style was that of designs embossed on bands of silver, which were then soldered on the vase or patera itself. The work was so delicate and elaborate that it could not be molded for casts; and in his time, Pliny says, there were no artists capable of reproducing it.

The designs were largely mythological or Homeric, occasionally of domestic life. We have some fine specimens of Phoenician and Cypriote silver work of early date, such as those found among the Curium treasures in Cyprus (Metropolitan Museum of Art, New York—Cesnola collection), but all darkened and altered so as to possess none of their original beauty. The Phoenician work is widely distributed in the ancient world, and it is easily recognized by experts from its conventional and nonoriginal character— Egyptian and Assyrian patterns and motifs being constantly and curiously mingled. The Phoenicians were great imitators, adapters, and traders and possessed fine mechanical skill, but lacked originality. Their style of work was largely a combination of *repoussé* with chasing, the patterns being first hammered into relief from below and then finished with a graver on the outer or upper side.

Among the many OT references to silver only a few distinctions need be made. It is spoken of literally in several ways:

1. As a precious metal for objects of beauty or value (*see* Joseph's cup, Gen. 44:2); for royal or sacred vessels, especially in connection with the Tabernacle or the Temple (*see* Ex. 26:19, 21; 1 Chron. 18:10; 28:14-17; 29:2-5; 2 Chron. 24:14; Ezra 1:6, 11; 5:14; 8:26; Dan. 5:2); of dishes (Num. 7); often as the material of idols, either cast or plated (*see* Gold; also Ex. 20:23; Judg. 17:3; Pss. 115:4; 135:15; Isa. 2:20; 31:7; Hos. 13:2; Jer. 10:9), imported in plates or sheets for overlaying images.

2. As metal being "smelted or wrought" (Job 28:1; Ps. 12:6; Prov. 17:3; 25:4; Ezek. 22:18-22).

3. As "money," in payment of fines, tribute, gifts, etc., weighed out by shekels or talents (Gen. 23:15-16; Lev. 27:3, 16, 25; Deut. 22:19, 29; Judg. 17:2, 4, 10; 2 Sam. 18:11-12; 1 Kings 20:39; 2 Kings 5:22-23; 15:20; Jer. 32:9-10; Amos 8:6, marg.).

The word *kesep* is simply rendered "money" in many passages, such as Gen. 42:25-35; 43:12-23; Ex. 21:34; 22:7; 30:16; Num. 3:48-51; Jer. 32:25, 44; and so generally, also with frequent allusions to its estimation by weight. Coins were not known among the Jews until late (cf. 1 Macc. 15:6); the earlier forms must have been more like our bullion, small bars or flat pieces, or perhaps the ring money depicted upon some of the Egyptian remains, as weighed in scales.

The NT references are simple and need little comment. By that time coins were familiar (Matt. 26:15; 27:3-9—"pieces of silver," *argurion,* a silver coin), rendered "silver coins" in Luke 15:8 for *drachmē,* perhaps an allusion to the almost universal custom among Eastern women of wearing coins as ornaments on headdresses, bracelets, etc.— at times imitated among ourselves. In many cases *argurion* is simply rendered "money" (Matt. 28:12; Mark 14:11; Luke 9:3; 22:5; Acts

24:26); while it is translated "silver" in 8:20; 20:33; 1 Pet. 1:18. Conversely, *arguros,* the general name for the metal or treasure consisting of it (so Acts 17:29; James 5:3; Rev. 18:12) is used for silver coins in Matt. 10:9.

The sources of ancient silver are but little known. Diodorus speaks (1.33) of mines on the island of Meroe, together with gold, copper, and iron. An important source was Spain (cf. 1 Macc. 8:3); Strabo and others speak of it as yielding large amounts, chiefly from Tartessus and Carthago Nova. Jeremiah's statement (Jer. 10:9) may have a like reference, if Tartessus is the same as Tarshish, as has been often supposed.

Figurative. Silver is used figuratively of God's words (Ps. 12:6); the tongue of the just (Prov. 10:20); saints purified by affliction (Ps. 66:10; Zech. 13:9); "rejected silver," i.e., impure, as compared to wicked men (Jer. 6:30); also the *dross* of silver (Isa. 1:22; Ezek. 22:18). Wisdom is declared to be more valuable than silver (Job 28:15; Prov. 3:14; 8:10, 19; 16:16).

Slime. See Pitch; Tar.

Soap (Heb. *bōrît*). The Heb. *bōrît* is a general term for any substance of *cleansing* qualities. As, however, it appears in Jer. 2:22, in contradistinction to Heb. *nether,* which undoubtedly means "natron" (mineral alkali), it is fair to infer that *bōrît* refers to vegetable alkali or some kind of potash, which forms one of the usual ingredients in our soap. It occurs in Mal. 3:2, but there is nothing to tell us whether it was obtained from the vegetable or mineral kingdom. But *bōr* (Job 9:30, "lye," NASB; "washing soda," NIV) denotes a vegetable alkali used for washing. Numerous plants, capable of yielding alkalies, exist in Palestine and the surrounding countries; we may notice one named Hubeibeh (the *Salsola kali* of botanists) found near the Dead Sea, the ashes of which are called el-Kuli, from their strong alkaline properties; and the Ajram, found near Sinai, which, when pounded, serves as a substitute for soap. Modern travelers have also noticed the *Saponaria officinalis* and the *Mesembryanthemum nodiflorum,* both possessing alkaline properties, as growing in Palestine. *See* Niter, above.

Soda. *See* Niter.

Steel. *See* Iron.

Sulfur. *See* Brimstone in this article; and also Sodom; Gomorrah in the general listing.

Tar (Heb. *ḥēmār,* "boiling up," to be "red"; Gen. 11:3; 14:10; Ex. 2:3; *zepet,* "flowing" or "fluid," Ex. 2:3; Isa. 34:9). Much of the tar or asphalt of ancient times came from the Dead Sea, which was called Lacus Asphaltites. The use of it as a cement for bricks at Babylon is described by Herodotus and other ancient writers, and may be seen in great ruins to this day, e.g., the so-called wall of media, not far from Babylon.

Tin (Heb. *bedîl;* Gk. *kassiteros*). This metal, though rare in its occurrence, was very early

discovered and smelted and played a most conspicuous part in the art and commerce of the ancient world. It is a remarkable fact that though its only ore, cassiterite or tinstone (the oxide), has no metallic aspect and occurs at but few and remote points, tin should have become known so early and its alloy with copper (bronze) become the great metal for all purposes of arts, arms, and ornaments during the entire extent of the Bronze Age of archaeology—3000-1200 B.C. The source of the main supply is judged to have been Cornwall, where the Phoenicians procured it through many centuries (*see* under Bronze), but its use was widespread even in far earlier times. Stone molds are found at many points in Europe, showing that bronze articles were cast as well as procured by commerce. Either reduced tin, therefore, or the ore itself must have been a very early article of trade throughout prehistoric Europe. There are tin mines in both Saxony and Bohemia and a few in the Iberian peninsula, but otherwise we know of no Old World sources between Cornwall and Malacca. To these extreme points of the Eurasian continent we must look for the main supply. There are evidences of important Phoenician tin traffic by sea with Cornwall, but the prehistoric use of bronze must probably go back to Indian sources and to the earliest migrations from eastern and southern Asia, while Europe was yet in the Neolithic Age. Arrian found tin abundant in Arabia, but Smith has shown that at that period it came there from Egypt and not from the East. After the time of Julius Caesar, British tin was brought overland via Marseilles.

The OT references are Num. 31:22; Ezek. 22:18, 20; 27:12. In Isa. 1:25, the rendering "alloy" (NASB; "tin," KJV; "dross," NIV) should be *lead,* frequently in connection with silver ores; and this passage, together with Zech. 4:10 (*see* under Lead), shows that the word *bedîl* was used rather loosely. Ecclesiasticus 47:18 gives tin a rank above lead in value: "You gathered gold like tin and amassed silver like lead."

Classical references are frequent, so Homer, in the Shield of Achilles (*Iliad* 18.474) and elsewhere in the *Iliad.* Pliny seems to have designated lead and tin respectively as *plumbum nigrum* and *plumbum candidum;* whereas his *stannum* was apparently an alloy of the two metals (Beckmann), a sort of hard pewter. It seems probable that tin and lead were not very clearly discriminated by the ancients, as indicated in the passages cited above from Isaiah and Zechariah.

Topaz (Gk. *topazion,* for Heb. *piṭdâ,* a "gem"; Ex. 28:17; 39:10; Job 28:19; Ezek. 28:13). This word has changed meanings exactly with chrysolite in ancient and modern usage. (*See* Chrysolite.) The Gk. *topazion* was apparently our chrysolite—the yellow-green gem called by jewelers peridot and by mineralogists olivine. Some of these are very rich olive greens and have even been confounded with emeralds, though of a different shade; such are the reputed emeralds in the chapel of the Three Magi in the cathedral of Cologne. The history of these splendid peridots is not known, but they are thought to have been brought from the East at the time of the Crusades. The "topaz" of Rev. 21:20 is probably a peridot, and the OT references, though less certain, may be fairly taken as the same.

Turquoise (Heb. *nōpek;* Ex. 28:18; 39:11; Ezek. 28:13, all NASB and NIV; KJV, "emerald"). The turquoise does not appear in the KJV, nor is it recognizable among the descriptions of Theophrastus, though plainly in Pliny, as *callais* and *callaina*. But as a peculiarly oriental gem from Khorassan and Turkestan, anciently from Arabia, and largely used in Egyptian jewelry from very early times, it must have been well known to the Hebrews; and there can hardly be any doubt that some of the obscure and disputed names of the OT must refer to turquoise. Famous Egyptian turquoise mines were located at Serabit in the Sinai Peninsula, where this blue or blue-green mineral containing copper and iron was obtained. As early as the Third Dynasty and again during the strong Twelfth Dynasty and particularly during the period of the New Empire (c. 1550-1230 B.C.) the Serabit mines yielded turquoise for jewelry, amulets, and sumptuous household furnishings. At Serabit El-Khadem Sir Flinders Petrie discovered important alphabetic inscriptions (1904-5).

Whitewash (Ezek. 13:10-15; 22:28; Matt. 23:27). See Mortar.

BIBLIOGRAPHY: W.M.F. Petrie, *Researches in Sinai* (1906); R. J. Forbes, *Metallurgy in Antiquity* (1950); J. Kelso, *Bulletin of the American Schools of Oriental Research* 122 (1951); J. Perrot, *Israel Exploration Journal* 5 (1955): 185-89; J. R. Harris, ed., *Ancient Egyptian Minerals and Industries* (1962); A. Guillaume, *Palestine Exploration Quarterly* 94 (1962): 129-32; H. Hodges, *Technology in the Ancient World* (1970); R. F. Tylecote, *A History of Metallurgy* (1976).

MINES, MINING. It is evident from many allusions to it that mining was familiar to the Hebrews (*see* the remarkable description of ore mining in Job 28:1-11). Mining has been carried on from an early date in the Sinaitic peninsula. The Monitu, who frequented this region from the dawn of history, discovered at an early period in the sides of the hills rich veins of metals and strata bearing precious stones. From these they learned to extract iron, oxides of copper, and manganese, and turquoises which they exported to the Delta. (*See* Turquoise.) The fame of these riches excited the pharaohs, who fitted out expeditions that established themselves by main force in the districts where the mines lay. In the Wadi Magharah ("the Valley of the Cave") are still traces of the Egyptian colony of miners who settled there for the purpose of mining copper and left their hieroglyphic inscriptions upon the face of the rock. The ancient furnaces are still to be seen, and on the coast of the Red Sea are found the piers and wharves from which the miners shipped their metal in the harbor of Abu Zelimeh.

The copper mines of Phaeno in Idumea, according to Jerome, were between Zoar and Petra, in which during the persecution of Diocletian the Christians were condemned to work. There are traces or records of gold-working in Egypt. Those in the Bishárce desert have been discovered. Ruins of the miners' huts still remain at Serabit el-Khadem. Copper and iron were both native products of Palestine and were worked also in the island of Meroe, at the mouth of the Nile. The island of Cyprus is also mentioned as a source of copper.

MINGLED PEOPLE (Heb. *'ēreb,* "mixture"). The non-Egyptian settlers in the land, e.g., Phoenicians, especially Greek, Ionian, and Carian troops who had been settled there since the days of Psammetichus, father of Neco (Jer. 25:30; Ezek. 30:5).

The "mingled people" in the midst of Babylon (Jer. 50:37, KJV) were probably the foreign soldiers or mercenary troops, who lived among the native population, as the Targum takes it.

MIN'IAMIN (min'ya-min; "from" the "right" hand).

1. One of the Levites who had charge of the distribution to his brothers of the sacred offerings in the time of Hezekiah (2 Chron. 31:15), 715 B.C.

2. One of the priests who came from Babylon with Zerubbabel (Neh. 12:17), and perhaps one of the trumpeters at the dedication of the wall of Jerusalem (12:41; "Mijamin," NIV), 536-445 B.C. The name is elsewhere given as "Mijamin" (10:7; 12:5; both NASB and NIV) or Miamin (12:5, KJV).

MINISTER. This term is used to describe various officials of a religious and civil character.

Old Testament. In the OT two terms are used.

1. Heb. *mᵉshārēt,* which is applied to the *attachés* of a royal court (2 Chron. 22:8; cf. Ps. 104:4); to the priests and Levites (Isa. 61:6; Ezek. 44:11; Joel 1:9, 13; Ezra 8:17; Neh. 10:36). Elsewhere rendered "servant."

2. Heb. *pālaḥ,* to "serve," appears in Ezra 7:24 with reference to those who served in the house of God. The KJV reads "ministers," the NASB and NIV, "servants."

New Testament. In the NT we have three terms, each with its distinctive meaning:

1. *Leitourgos,* a "public servant," answers most nearly to the Heb. *mᵉshārēt* and is usually employed in the LXX as its equivalent. It speaks of a subordinate public administrator (Rom. 15:16; Heb. 8:2) and in Rom. 13:6 it is rendered "servants." In all these instances the original and special meaning of the word as used by the Athenians, one who performs certain gratuitous public services, is preserved.

2. *Hupēretēs* differs from the two others in that it contains the idea of actual and personal attendance upon a superior. Thus it is rendered "attendant" in Luke 4:20, where it refers to the *chazen* of the Talmudists whose duty it was to open and close the synagogue, to produce and replace the books employed in the service, and generally to wait on the officiating priest or teacher. The idea of *personal attendance* comes prominently forward in Acts 26:16, as well as in Luke 1:2, where it is rendered "servants." In all these cases the etymological sense of the words *hupo eretēs* (lit., a "sub-rower," one who rows under command of the steersman) comes out.

3. *Diakonos* is usually employed in relation to the ministry of the gospel: its application is twofold, in a general sense to indicate ministers of any order, whether superior or inferior, and in a special sense to indicate an order of inferior ministers (*see* Deacon). Our Lord Himself is called a minister, with reference to the holy service He had to perform as the Great High Priest of His people's profession (Heb. 8:2).

BIBLIOGRAPHY: J. B. Lightfoot, *The Christian Ministry* (1901); T. W. Manson, *The Church's Ministry* (1948); J. K. S. Reid, *The Biblical Doctrine of Ministry* (1955); L. L. Morris, *Ministers of God* (1964); T. M. Lindsay, *The Church and Its Ministry in the Early Centuries* (1977).

MIN'NI (min'i). A kingdom named (Jer. 51:27) along with Ararat and Ashkenaz, "the Minyai of Nicholas of Damascus (Josephus *Ant.* 1.3.8); the Mannai of the inscriptions. Shalmaneser III of Assyria overran the country of the Minni in 830 B.C. In 715 the king of Minni revolted but was subdued to the Assyrian yoke. The Minni gave Ashurbanipal (669-626) a great deal of trouble, till they finally sided with the Medes and others to bring about the fall of Nineveh and the Assyrian Empire (612 B.C.). The territory of the Minni was in Armenia in the Lake Van and Lake Urmia region."

MIN'NITH (min'ith). An Ammonite town E of the Jordan, to which the terrible carnage of Jephthah reached (Judg. 11:33); celebrated for its excellent wheat, which was exported to the markets of Tyre (Ezek. 27:17). It was probably located about four Roman miles E of Heshbon, where there are traces of terraces and walls.

MINSTREL (Heb. *menaggēn,* one "striking" the lyre). This word occurs twice in the KJV (2 Kings 3:15; Matt. 9:23), once in the NASB (2 Kings 3:15), and not at all in the NIV. In the NASB and NIV the expression in Matthew is changed to "flute-players." In 2 Kings 3:15 Elisha, in the presence of the confederate kings of Judah, exclaims, "But now bring me a minstrel." The NIV translates "harpist." It may be that through the music he expected "to collect his mind from the impressions of the outer world, and by subduing the self-life and life in the external world to be-

come absorbed in the intuition of divine things" (Keil, *Com.,* ad loc.). The word "flute-players" (Gk. *aulētēs;* Matt. 9:23) refers to a dirge or lament for the dead daughter of the ruler of the synagogue. Minstrels were common in royal courts at Babylon and in Assyria, Egypt, and Palestine.

MINT. *See* Vegetable Kingdom.

MIPHKAD. *See* Inspection Gate.

MIRACLES (Lat. *miraculum,* from *mirari,* to "wonder"). Wonderful events, distinguished from events that only seem to be, or are merely, wonderful. The term *miracle* is etymologically inadequate and indicates only one, and that not the most important, feature of the proper conception. In general terms miracles may be defined as supernatural manifestations of divine power in the external world, in themselves special revelations of the presence and power of God; and in connection with other special revelations to which they are subservient, as aiding in their attestation, establishment, and preservation.

Biblical Doctrine. The Scripture representations of miraculous events in the OT and NT furnish the primary grounds for their consideration.

Biblical Names of Miracles. Of deepest significance among these are the words that literally mean "powers" and "signs" (e.g., Mark 9:39; Acts 2:22; 19:11, cf. Ex. 9:16; 15:6; Luke 23:8; John 2:11, cf. Num. 14:22; Deut. 11:3). Miracles are also called "wonders" (e.g., Ex. 15:11; Dan. 12:6). It is to be noted, however, that in the NT they are never referred to simply under that name; some other term, such as "signs," is used to bring out the deeper meaning (e.g., John 4:48; Acts 4:30; 2 Cor. 12:12). As "wonders," miracles are out of the ordinary course of events. They produce astonishment as being outside the ordinary operations of cause and effect. Thus far the aspect is chiefly negative. But miracles are also "powers" (often translated "mighty works," "wonderful works," "miracles"). As such they are manifestations of the power of God. Whoever the agent is in their accomplishment, the power is of God. They are wrought by "the Spirit of the Lord"; in them is seen "the finger of God" (Luke 4:18; 11:20; cf. Acts 3:12). As "signs," miracles point to something beyond themselves. They indicate the near presence of God. They reveal the connection of the one who works them with the spiritual world and are thus seals attending his authority as a messenger from God (John 2:18, 23; 3:2; Matt. 12:38; Acts 14:3; 2 Cor. 12:12).

Another name of beautiful significance is that which the apostle John applies to the miracles of the Lord. He frequently uses simply the term "works," not indeed exclusively with reference to the miracles of Christ and yet often with particular reference to them, as if miraculous works were only the natural and appropriate works of one who was Himself miraculous (John 5:36; 7:21, *see* marg.; 10:25, 32, 38; 14:11-12; 15:24). (For full discussion of this part of the subject see Trench, *Notes on the Miracles,* Preliminary Essay.)

Supernatural Character of Miracles. The Bible recognizes a divinely established order in nature (Gen. 8:22; James 5:7), but also a special series of facts brought about by the direct intervention of God; and such facts are miracles (Deut. 11:13-17). The Bible does not, however, represent nature or natural law as something independent or separate from God. The universe is not a vast mechanism that God has created and left to itself. The power that continually works therein is His power. What we call natural law, according to the biblical conception, is only the order of God's ordinary working in the natural world (Pss. 19:1-6; 104; John 5:17; Heb. 1:3). A miracle, therefore, is a putting forth of the same power in the natural world in an extraordinary or supernatural manner. Thus we see why and in what sense miracles are "wonders." They are such not because the usual exhibitions of God's power in the natural world are in themselves less wonderful but because of their unusual and supernatural character. In the biblical view the whole world is wonderful (Job 26; etc.). To him who has eyes to see, nature everywhere is full of marvels. And therefore it is sometimes said that in the sense of being wonderful the whole system of things is miraculous, and accordingly we have no right to distinguish any fact or event as being in any special sense a miracle. And thus, to say everything is miraculous often becomes only another way of saying "nothing is miraculous." A miracle is not only wonderful, but it is so in the sense of being a "new thing" (Num. 16:30) and therefore peculiarly fitted to awaken the feeling of wonder. And further, miracles are "powers" not in the sense of being greater, but different, manifestations of divine power than are usually exhibited. They are special acts of power and therefore have special impressiveness. To produce a harvest implies power as great as to feed a multitude with a few loaves and fishes. But the manifestation is different. In the one case the power is often overlooked; in the other it is recognized (Rom. 1:20; Acts 14:17; Luke 9:43; John 6:14). Likewise miracles are "signs" in the sense of being supernatural indications of the near presence and power of God. They declare the supremacy and perfect freedom of God even in the natural world. They are also "signs" of special grace from God because of their essential connection with that special revelation that centers in Jesus Christ, whose mission it is to release and restore the world from the disorder and dominion of sin.

It is not in place, nor is it practicable, to discuss here philosophically the relation between the natural and supernatural and the meanings to be attached to these terms. But it should be said that to speak of miracles as contrary to nature is not to speak in harmony with the Scriptures. Nietzsche properly says "miracles belong to the higher order of things, which is a higher nature also." We may say that they lie beyond or outside the ordinary method of God's working in the natural world to which our observation is confined; but still we must think of them as having their appropriate place in the one great plan and purpose of Him whose will is law and who fills the universe with His presence.

Purpose. The end for which miracles are wrought has already in some measure been indicated. But further statement and illustration are necessary.

The miracles of the Bible serve the great end of God's gracious revelation. They are revelations in themselves but are inwrought with the history of special revelation. Accordingly we find them confined to the great epochs or critical periods of that history.

The theophanies of ante-Mosaic times were not strictly miracles; i.e., they are to be distinguished from miraculous works wrought by the instrumentality of man. They were divine manifestations but not authentications of God's messengers. Moses appears in the OT as the first great miracle worker. And the reason for that is evident when we remember his unique position in the religious history of mankind, the greatness of his work, and the obstacles he encountered (Ex. 10:1-2; 14:21-31; 20:1-21; etc.). One common purpose unites and explains all the miracles in connection with the deliverance of the chosen people from the land of bondage and their secure settlement in the land of promise; that is the founding of a monotheistic religion, the worship of the true God in the midst of an idolatrous world. The next great displays of miraculous power were centuries later and gathered about the persons of Elijah and Elisha when the cause of true religion was threatened with destruction. And again, after a long interval came another, and in some senses remarkable, renewal of miracles with new messages from God to revive the sinking faith of the chosen nation during the captivity.

The coming of Christ marked the greatest of all epochs in religious history. The revelation He brought, which centered in Himself, was that for which all preceding revelations were preparatory. Coming to offer such new matters for faith, and to ask from men such complete submission to His authority and such complete trust in His power and grace, it was necessary that He should exhibit the signs of His character and mission. All that was miraculous in His history and activity was subservient to the great purpose of His coming. And these signs of His heavenly nature were all the more essential because of the state of humiliation into which He had entered. The NT

Scriptures, therefore, especially abound in miracles. Chief among them is the resurrection of our Lord. Space does not here permit comparison between the miracles of Christ and the miracles of the OT. But it should be noted that as a whole His were upon a grander scale, and, with a single exception, never works of judgment and destruction. The withering of the barren fig tree was the destruction of an insensate object, and the underlying purpose of even that act was merciful. The power to work miracles was given to the apostles and was exercised by them for the purpose of carrying forward the work of establishing Christianity, committed to them by the ascended Lord (Rom. 15:18-19; 2 Cor. 12:12).

Thus throughout the Bible record we find the same end in view. Miracles are to arrest the attention of men and aid in winning their acceptance of revealed truth. And so far as the sacred record shows us they were wrought only when most needed—in the great crises of revealed religion.

Bible Criteria of Miracles. The Scriptures are careful to note the distinction between true miracles and those that are false and to furnish the tests by which judgment is to be formed. At many times in the past, men have appeared who have professed to work miracles and have exhibited marvelous powers. Such was the case in the contests between Moses and the Egyptian magicians (Ex. 7-8) and between the apostles and Elymas and Simon Magus (Acts 13:6-12; 8:9-24), not to specify others of later date. Christ and the apostle Paul both left their predictions that deceivers of this kind would arise "with all power and signs and false wonders" (2 Thess. 2; cf. Matt. 24:24); the "false wonders" in many cases were, no doubt, mere tricks of expert jugglers. And yet in some instances it would be consistent with the view of the Scriptures to regard them as worked by the aid of evil spiritual powers, Satan and his angels. Thus Trench regards the works wrought by the Egyptian magicians and others referred to in Acts 13:8; Matt. 24:24; 2 Thess. 2:9; Rev. 13:13. In any event, it is a matter of great importance to distinguish between such acts of deception and actual miracles—i.e., works wrought by the power of God in connection with the history of revelation. *See* C. F. Dickason, *Angels, Elect and Evil* (1975) for the role of Satan and demons in miracle and deception.

The tests presented by the Scriptures are mainly two, namely, the character of the agent and the end for which the supernatural event is wrought. False prophets can work no true miracles, and the wonders they may work are to be tried also by the teaching they seek to establish (Deut. 13:1-3; Matt. 24:24; 2 Thess. 2:9). This is not, as may seem if viewed superficially, circular. It simply takes cognizance of the fact that man is a moral being and has in him some measure of power to at least intuitively recognize truth. True miracles appeal not merely to the senses but also to the heart and conscience. And besides that, there are some events—the resurrection of Christ, for example—that so far transcend the effects of all created power as to leave no proper occasion for doubt.

Importance of Miracles. The Scriptures would guard us at this point against two extremes. We are not to attach to miracles an exaggerated value or importance. They are not the highest evidence of truth. That is found rather in the truth itself. Miracles are not demonstrations of truth, certainly not in the sense of compelling those who behold them to accept the truth in connection with which they stand. Many who witnessed the divine works of the Lord refused to believe in Him. And He declared faith that was founded upon His words to be of higher value than that which was based upon His miracles (John 4:48; 14:11; 20:29). On the other hand, we are not at liberty to underrate their importance. Christ did not work miracles needlessly. He appealed to them as among the evidences of His authority (Matt. 11:4-5, 20-24; 12:28, 39-40; John 5:36; 20:25, 27-28; 14:11; 15:24); and many were led to faith by the aid of these means (e.g., 11:45). Miracles are acts of condescension and special grace to unbelieving men. And though their ultimate effect depends upon the inner bent of those who behold them, still they are in this respect like the truth itself with which they stand connected. They are not only tests of character, but also divine means for awakening attention and reverent reflection, and then leading those who are receptive to recognition and acceptance of the truth (3:19, 21; 18:37; etc.).

The question often raised—whether, on the whole, miracles are helps or hindrances to faith—here finds its answer. Much depends upon the person whose faith it is proposed to establish and much also upon the kind of faith it is sought to establish. With the true faith of the gospel, miracles are bound up as an indispensable element and are in thorough harmony with those supernatural measures and operations in man's spiritual life upon which the gospel concentrates chief attention.

Theological Considerations. Under this head space permits only a few suggestions and references.

Possibility. The possibility of miracles is not a matter of question for one who believes in a personal God. The denial of such possibility is at bottom pantheistic or atheistic (e.g., Spinoza, Renan).

Credibility. The credibility of miracles has been subjected to frequent assaults from various standpoints. For a compact history and refutation of them we refer to Trench, *Notes on the Miracles.*

To appreciate rightly the truth in this matter, we must not view miracles as isolated facts but view them in their actual relationships. The scriptural concept of God and of man, and of the purpose and work of God in saving man, furnish the explanation that outweighs all theoretical objections. And, practically, whoever realizes the proper effect of the gospel, the renewing power of the Holy Spirit, has an inner witness to the power of God and the reality of divine revelation that leave no room for doubt concerning the external acts of God with which the history of revelation is interwoven. (Cf. Num. 16:30; 2 Cor. 5:17; Col. 3:10.)

Continuance. The question of the continuance of miracles beyond the apostolic age must be one of history. As conservative a theologian as Charles Hodge declares that "there is nothing in the New Testament inconsistent with the occurrence of miracles in the postapostolic age of the Church." At the same time, however, he discredits the miracles claimed by the Roman Catholic church to have been wrought by her saints, as well as the distinctive claim of that church to power in that direction. Trench regards it as a strong presumption against the continuance of this power in the Christian church that in the earlier history of God's dealings with His people miracles were only at great and critical periods. The necessity for miracles no longer exists. And further, the professed miracles of later times will not bear the tests of genuineness. (For valuable discussion of this point and comparison of biblical with extrabiblical miracles we refer to Trench.) The passage in Mark 16:17-18, which has been interpreted by some (e.g., Grotius, Lavater, Hess) in a wide sense and extending to all times, has been taken in a restricted sense by others (e.g., Augustine and Protestant theologians generally).

The promise of miraculous power, it is held, was completely fulfilled in the early period of the church, when such power was needed for the establishment of Christianity.

It is proper to say that the portion of Mark's gospel in which this passage occurs (16:9-20) is regarded by some eminent Christian scholars (notably Meyer) as a later addition from some unknown source. The NASB contains in the margin the note: "Some of the oldest mss. do not contain vv. 9-20."

It is important to remember that the craving for miracles manifest in some directions at the present day may spring not from faith but from the lack of it and from failure to recognize the great spiritual works that God is constantly accomplishing.

BIBLIOGRAPHY: B. F. Westcott, *Characteristics of the Gospel Miracles* (1859); B. B. Warfield, *Counterfeit Miracles* (1918), reprint, *Miracles: Yesterday and Today* (1953); C. S. Lewis, *Miracles, A Preliminary Study* (1947); G. H. Clark, *The Philosophy of Science and Belief in God* (1964); C. F. D. Moule, ed., *Miracles* (1965); W. M. Taylor, *Miracles of Our Savior* (1975); A. B. Bruce, *The Miracles of Christ* (1980); C. Brown, *Miracles and the Critical Mind* (1984); J. Laidlaw, *Studies in the Miracles of Our Lord* (1984).

MIRAGE (Heb. *shārāb,* "parched ground"). An optical illusion common in the East; directly referred to by Isaiah in Isa. 35:7 ("scorched land," marg. "mirage," NASB; "parched ground," KJV; "burning sand," NIV); 49:10 ("scorching heat," NASB; "heat," KJV; "desert heat," NIV).

MIR′IAM (mir′i-am; "obstinacy, rebellion").

1. The daughter of Amram and Jochebed and sister of Moses and Aaron. She is probably (Josephus *Ant.* 2.9.4) the sister who was stationed near the river Nile to watch over her infant brother (Ex. 2:1-8).

The first mention of Miriam by name is when, after the passage of the Red Sea, she led the chorus of women who replied to the male chorus with timbrels and dancing. She is here called "Aaron's sister," probably to point out the position she was to occupy in the congregation as ranking not with Moses but with Aaron and, like him, subordinate to Moses. She is the first person of that household to whom prophetic gifts are ascribed. "Miriam the prophetess" is her acknowledged title (Ex. 15:20-21), c. 1440 B.C.

The exalted position of Moses aroused a feeling of envy in the minds of his brother and sister, and they at length disputed the preeminence of his special calling. Miriam instigated the open rebellion and was followed by Aaron. An occasion was found for their manifestation of discontent in the Cushite wife whom Moses had taken. "Has the Lord indeed spoken only through Moses? Has He not spoken through us as well?" Summoned to the Tabernacle by Jehovah, they were administered a stern rebuke, and Miriam, the instigator of the rebellion, was struck with leprosy. When Aaron saw his sister, he said to Moses, "Oh, my lord, I beg you, do not account this sin to us." And Moses prayed unto Jehovah, "O God, heal her, I pray!" God heard his prayer, though not without inflicting deep humiliation upon Miriam. She was shut outside of the camp, excluded from the congregation for seven days, after which restoration and purification from her leprosy were promised. During her seclusion the people did not journey any farther (Num. 12:1-15), c. 1439 B.C. This stroke, and its removal, which took place at Hazeroth, form the last public event of Miriam's life. She died toward the close of the wanderings, at Kadesh, and was buried there (20:1), c. 1401 B.C. Her tomb was shown near Petra in the days of Jerome. According to Josephus she was married to the famous Hur and, through him, was grandmother of the architect Bezaleel. In the Koran (chap. iii) she is confounded with the virgin Mary; hence the holy family is there called the family of Amram, or Imram.

2. Probably the first named of the sons of Mered, of the family of Caleb, by Bithia, the daughter of Pharaoh (1 Chron. 4:17). *See* Mered.

MIR'MAH (mir'ma; "deceit"). The last of the seven sons of Shaharaim by Hodesh; born in the land of Moab (1 Chron. 8:10), after 1440 B.C.

MIRROR. Two Heb. words, *mar'â* (Ex. 38:8) and *re'î* (Job 37:18). The Hebrew women on coming out of Egypt probably brought with them mirrors like those that were used by the Egyptians. These were made of a mixed metal, chiefly copper, wrought with such admirable skill that they were capable of a luster that has even been partially revived in some of those discovered at Thebes, though they had been buried in the earth for many centuries. The mirror itself was nearly round, inserted into a handle of wood, stone, or metal, whose form varied according to the taste of the owner. Some presented the figure of a female, a flower, a column, or a rod ornamented with the head of Hathor, a bird, or a fancy device. Sometimes the face of a Typhonian monster was used to support the mirror, serving as a contrast to the features whose beauty was displayed within it. The metal of which the mirrors were composed, being liable to rust and tarnish, required care to be kept constantly bright (Wisd. 7:26; Ecclus. 12:11). This was done by means of pounded pumice-stone, rubbed on with a sponge, which was generally suspended from the mirror. The obscure image produced by a tarnished or imperfect mirror appears to be alluded to in 1 Cor. 13:12 (Smith, *Bib. Dict.*). See Glass.

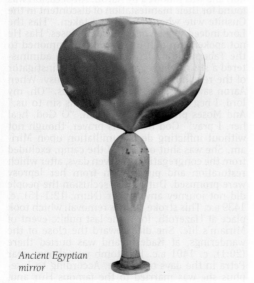

Ancient Egyptian mirror

MIS'GAB (*miśgāb*, "high place," "refuge"). The Heb. expression is transliterated in the KJV of Jer. 48:1; it is frequently translated "stronghold" in the NASB and NIV.

MISH'AEL (mish'a-el; "who is like God?")
1. The first named son of Uzziel (son of Ko-

hath), the uncle of Aaron (Ex. 6:22). When Nadab and Abihu died, Mishael and his brother Elzaphan, at the command of Moses, removed their bodies from the sanctuary (Lev. 10:4-5), about 1439 B.C.
2. One of those who supported Ezra on the left when he read the law to the people after the captivity (Neh. 8:4), about 445 B.C.
3. One of the three Jewish youths trained with Daniel at the Babylonian court and who "entered the king's personal service" (Dan. 1:6, 11, 19). His court name was Meshach (v. 7). With the other two he assisted Daniel in solving the dream of Nebuchadnezzar (2:17-18) and was "appointed over the administration of the province of Babylon" (3:12). The three were afterward cast into the fiery furnace for not worshiping the image set up by the king, but, being miraculously preserved, they were promoted by royal decree (3:13-30), perhaps after 586 B.C.

MI'SHAL (mī'shal). A city of Asher (Josh. 19:26; "Misheal," KJV), assigned to the sons of Gershon of the Levites (21:30); also called Mashal (1 Chron. 6:74). Location uncertain.

MI'SHAM (mī'sham; "fleet, swift." Arab. *sa'ama,* "to trot swiftly," as a camel). A son of Elpaal, a Benjamite, and one of the builders of Ono, Lod, and their suburbs (1 Chron. 8:12), after 1170 B.C.

MI'SHEAL. *See* Mishal.

MISH'MA (mish'ma; "hearing").
1. The fifth son of Ishmael, and head of an Arabian tribe (Gen. 25:14; 1 Chron. 1:30), about 1800 B.C.
2. The son of Mibsam, of the tribe of Simeon, and father of Hammuel (1 Chron. 4:25-26), perhaps about 1300 B.C.

MISHMAN'NAH (mish-man'a; "fatness"). One of the twelve Gadite warriors who joined David at Ziklag (1 Chron. 12:10), before 1000 B.C.

MISH'RAITES (mish'ra-īts, only in 1 Chron. 2:53). The fourth of the four families of Kiriath-jearim. It is usual to assume that Kiriath-jearim, whose father was Shobal (v. 52), was the city of that name and that the four families were its colonies. This is quite probable, but not certain. Sometimes the name of a person is the same as that of a place. Thus Ephrath in Gen. 35:16, 19 is the name of a place, whereas in 1 Chron. 2:19 it is the name of Caleb's second wife. In 2:42-43 the familiar name Hebron is used as the name of a person, as is Haran in v. 46.
"There is a Jewish tradition, embodied in the Targum of Rabbi Joseph, that the families of Kirjath-jearim were the sons of Moses whom Zipporah bare him, and that from them were descended the disciples of the prophets of Zorah and Eshtaol" (Smith, s.v. "Puhites"). But it is probable that the Mishraites, etc., were either colonies or leading families of Kiriath-jearim and that

Shobal was called its "father," as having founded or greatly improved it. The latter is more probable, since the statement is made of Shobal, as an entirely independent fact, that he "had sons" (2:52), and the name of Kiriath-jearim is not among them. w.h.

MISPAR. See Mispereth.

MIS'PERETH (mis'pe-reth). One of those who returned with Zerubbabel from Babylon (Neh. 7:7), about 445 B.C. He is called Mispar in Ezra 2:2.

MIS'REPHOTH-MA'IM (mis're-fōth-ma'im; "hot springs," lit., "burning of waters"). Understood by the Greek translators "as a proper name, though the rabbins and some Christian commentators render it in different ways, such as *salt pits, smelting huts,* or *glass huts*" (K. & D., *Com.*). It is mentioned (Josh. 11:8) as a place between Sidon and the valley of Mizpeh where Joshua pursued the allied Canaanites after the defeat of Jabin (cf. 13:6). It is now frequently identified with Khirbet el-Musheirifeh, eleven miles N of Acre at the base of Ras en-Naqurah.

MIST (Heb. *'ēd*). A rising vapor, or cloud, which again distills upon the ground (Gen. 2:6; Job 36:37). The reference in Genesis probably refers to a perennial stream (so NIV) or an underground canal.

MITE. A mite (KJV) or small copper coin (NASB) was a unit of money. See Metrology.

MITH'CAH. See Mithkah.

MITH'KAH (mith'ka; "sweetness"). The twenty-ninth station of the Israelites in the desert, mentioned between Terah and Hashmonah (Num. 33:28-29), perhaps Wadi Abu Takiyeh.

MITH'NITE (mith'nīt). The designation of Joshaphat, one of David's guard in the catalog of 1 Chron. 11:43.

MITH'REDATH (mith're-dath; "gift of Mithra"). A Persian god of the light between heaven and hell.
1. The treasurer of Cyrus, king of Persia, to whom the king gave the vessels of the Temple to be transferred by him to the hands of Sheshbazzar, the prince of Judah (Ezra 1:8), 536 B.C.
2. A Persian officer, stationed in Samaria, who joined in writing a letter to Artaxerxes in opposition to the Jews (Ezra 4:7), 522 B.C.

MITRE. A KJV term for the headdress worn by the high priest. See Dress: Garment; and also the article Turban.

MITYLE'NE (mit-i-lē'ni). The chief city on the island of Lesbos, in the Aegean Sea between Chios and Assos, famous for riches and literary character and for having the privileges of a free city. It was a favorite resort area for Roman aristocrats. Sappho, Alcaeus, Pittacas, and Theophrastus were natives of Mitylene. Paul touched there overnight (Acts 20:14-15). The name was given to the entire island. See Paul.

MIXED MARRIAGES. Marriages between Jews and Gentiles were strictly prohibited by the Mosaic law. See Marriage: Laws of Intermarriage.

MIXED MULTITUDE (Heb. *'ēreb,* "mixture"). With the Israelites who journeyed from Rameses to Succoth, the first stage of the Exodus from Egypt, there went up (Ex. 12:38) "a mixed multitude" ("many other people," NIV), who have not hitherto been identified. During their residence in Egypt, marriages were naturally contracted between the Israelites and the natives. This hybrid race is evidently alluded to by Rashi and Aben Ezra and is most probably that to which reference is made in Exodus. That the "mixed multitude" is a general term, including all those who were not of pure Israelite blood, is evident; more than this cannot be positively asserted. In Exodus and Numbers it probably denotes the miscellaneous hangers-on of the Hebrew camp, whether they were the issue of spurious marriages with Egyptians or were themselves Egyptians or belonging to other nations. The same happened on the return from Babylon, and in Neh. 13:3 (cf. 10:28) a slight clue is given by which the meaning of the "mixed multitude" may be more definitely ascertained. According to Deut. 29:11 they seem to have occupied a very low position among the Israelites and to have furnished them with hewers of wood and drawers of water. See Mingled People.

MI'ZAR (mī'zar). A mountain that cannot be identified unless, as seems likely, it is an alternative name for Mt. Hermon (Ps. 42:6).

MIZ'PAH (miz'pa; "watchtower"), or **Miz'eh** (miz'pe). The name of several places.
1. The heap of stones raised by Jacob as a witness of the covenant made by him and Laban (Gen. 31:49). Laban called it, in the language of Aram, Jegar-sahadutha, and Jacob called it Galeed, in the language of Canaan. Both names have the same meaning, "the heap of witness." Jacob and Laban made a covenant not to pass beyond Mizpah to the harm of the other. The place was in Gilead, E of the Jordan, and in later times was known from afar by its mizpah, or "watchtower," whose garrison kept watch upon the Aramaean tribes of the Hauran.
2. Another place E of the Jordan, called Mizpah of Gilead, where *Jephthah* (which see) lived (Judg. 11:34) and where the Israelites assembled under him against the Ammonites (10:17; 11:11). It is probably the same as the Ramath-mizpeh of Gad (Josh. 13:26).
3. "The land of Mizpeh" (Josh. 11:3) was a district in Gilead inhabited by Hivites, the country below Hasbeya, between Nahr Hashbany on the E and Merj Ayûn on the W, with the village

of Mutelleh or Mtelleh, at present inhabited by Druses, which stands upon a hill more than 200 feet high and from which there is a splendid view over the Huleh basin. It is from this that it has derived its name (*see* Robinson, *Biblical Researches*, p. 272).

4. A city of Benjamin, named in the list of the allotment between Beeroth and Chephirah and in apparent proximity to Ramah and Gibeon (Josh. 18:26, "Mizpeh"). Its connection with the two last named towns is also implied in the later history (1 Kings 15:22; 2 Chron. 16:6; Neh. 3:7). It was one of the places fortified by Asa against the incursions of the kings of Northern Israel (1 Kings 15:22; 2 Chron. 16:6; Jer. 41:10). After the destruction of Jerusalem, it became the residence of the superintendent appointed by the king of Babylon (40:7; etc.) and was inhabited after the captivity (Neh. 3:7, 15, 19). Robinson (*Biblical Researches*, 2:139) supposes it to be the present Neby Samwīl (i.e., prophet Samuel), 4½ miles NW of Jerusalem, but it is more likely Tell en-Naṣbeh about 8 miles distant.

W. F. Badé, on behalf of the Pacific School of Religion in Berkeley, California, excavated there in 1926, 1927, 1929, and 1935. He found that Mizpeh was inhabited as early as the third millennium B.C., but the place was insignificant before the Hebrew period (c. 1100-400 B.C.). The wall of the early Hebrew period was weak, but about 900 B.C. it was replaced by a formidable system of fortifications. The new wall, probably built by Asa, was more than a mile in circumference, thirteen feet thick, and had ten projecting towers. There was only one city gate, on the NE, inside of which was an open space interpreted as a marketplace.   H.F.V.

The site of ancient Mizpeh

5. A city of Judah (Josh. 15:38, "Mizpeh") in the district of the Shephelah, or maritime lowland. Van de Velde suggests its identity with the present Tell es-Sâfiyeh—the Blanchegarde of the Crusaders.

6. A town of Moab to which David moved his parents when threatened by Saul (1 Sam. 22:3). It was probably a mountain fastness on the high land that bounded the Arboth-Moab, E of the Dead Sea, and that could be easily reached from Bethlehem by crossing the Jordan near its entrance into the Dead Sea.

BIBLIOGRAPHY: F.-M. Abel, *Géographie de la Palestine* (1933), 2:388-90; C. C. McCown, *Excavations at Tell En-Nasbeh*, 2 vols. (1947).

MIZ′RAIM (miz′ra-im; Heb. *miṣrayim*). In Gen. 10:6, 13-14 and 1 Chron. 1:8, 11-12, Mizraim is the second son of Ham and the father of "the people of Lud, Anam, Lehab, Naphtuh, Pathrus, Casluh, from which the Philistines came, and Caphtor." But elsewhere *miṣrayim* is the standing name of Egypt, in which sense it occurs nearly eighty-seven times, the only exception being that in 1 Sam. 30:13 "a young man of Egypt" is, in Heb., "a young man an Egyptian."

It is very generally believed that Mizraim is a dual form, properly and originally signifying the two Egypts, Upper and Lower. (*See* Egypt.) In Isa. 11:11 the origin is left out of view, the name no doubt being mostly used for that part of Egypt that was nearest and most familiar, and Mizraim is Lower Egypt in distinction from Pathros, which is Upper Egypt. The same may be the case in Jer. 44:1, 15; Ezek. 29:14; 30:14. But in Jeremiah Egypt may possibly be the whole of which Pathros is a part, and in Ezekiel the use of the two names may be a poetic variation. So Robinson and Gesenius. Some, with Gesenius's twelfth German edition, think the ending of Mizraim local instead of dual. The singular *māṣôr* is found only in 2 Kings 19:24; Isa. 19:6; 37:25; Mic. 7:12.

The names of Mizraim and the descendants of Mizraim in Gen. 10:13-14 and 1 Chron. 1:11-12 all appear to be names of nations rather than of individuals, and they include far more than Egypt. "Mizraim, therefore, like Cush, and perhaps Ham, geographically represents a center whence colonies went forth in the remotest period of postdiluvian history." "We regard the distribution of the Mizraites as showing that their colonies were but a part of the great migration that gave the Cushites the command of the Indian Ocean, and which explains the affinity the Egyptian monuments show us between the pre-Hellenic Cretans and the Carians (the latter no doubt the Seleges of the Greek writers) and the Philistines" (Smith, s.v. "Mizraim").

MIZ′ZAH (miz′a). The fourth and last of the sons of Reuel the son of Esau, by Basemath (Gen. 36:13; 1 Chron. 1:37), and a petty Edomite chief (Gen. 36:17).

MNA'SON (nā'son; perhaps "reminding"). A Christian with whom Paul lodged the last time he was in Jerusalem (Acts 21:16), A.D. 60. He was a native of Cyprus and may have been acquainted with Barnabas, who was a Cyprian (4:36).

MO'AB (mō'ab; perhaps "from father"). The name of the son whom Lot's eldest daughter bore to him after the destruction of Sodom, and founder of the Moabites (Gen. 19:30-37), about 2055 B.C.

MO'ABITE, MO'ABITES (mō'a-bīt). Descendants of the elder of Lot's two surviving daughters, as the Ammonites are of the younger. The starting point of both was in the vicinity of Zoar. Thence the roving Ammonites went to the NE (*see* Ammonites), whereas the more peaceful Moabites remained near their ancestral home, displacing the Emim (Deut. 2:10-11; cf. Gen. 14:5).

Territory. According to Smith (s.v. "Moab"), the territory of Moab at its greatest extent included three parts: (1) The "land of Moab" (Ruth 1:1-2), a tract enclosed by natural fortifications; on the N by the chasm of the Arnon, on the W by the cliffs that rise almost perpendicularly from the shore of the Dead Sea, on the S amd E by a semicircle of hills that opens only for the Arnon and another Dead Sea torrent. (2) The "land of Moab," the more open country from the Arnon north to the hills of Gilead. (3) The so-called "plains of Moab" (Num. 22:1), "the sunk" district in the tropical depths of the Jordan Valley. Before the arrival of Israel, Sihon, king of the Amorites, had taken from "the former king of Moab," very

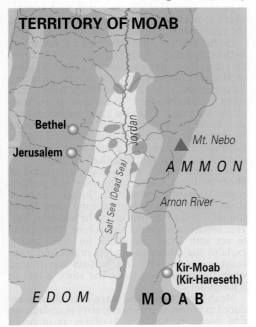

TERRITORY OF MOAB

Bethel
Jerusalem
Jordan
Mt. Nebo
AMMON
Salt Sea (Dead Sea)
Arnon River
Kir-Moab
(Kir-Hareseth)
EDOM   MOAB

possibly Zippor the father of Balak (22:2), all the land "from the Arnon to the Jabbok" (21:26). Thus Moab was *penned up* in the closely fenced "land of Moab" mentioned above (no. 1).

Coming up from Egypt the Israelites approached Moab through the desert facing Moab, outside the bordering circle of hills on the SE. They were forbidden to molest the Moabites in the enjoyment of the land that they had taken from the Emim (Deut. 2:9-11). They therefore applied for permission to pass through the territory of Moab and, being refused, went around its borders.

Moab and Israel.

Refuses Passage. From Deut. 2:29 it would appear at first sight that both Moab and Edom granted the request of Israel to be allowed to pass through their territory, whereas Num. 20:18-21 and Deut. 23:3-4 seem to show that both Moab and Edom utterly refused. But more careful reading removes the difficulty and gives us a clear idea of the whole transaction. Israel's request in Num. 20:17 is to be allowed to *cross* the territory of Edom by the royal highway. This the martial Edomites refused, with a display of force, standing on their national dignity and declining to show any hospitality for relationship's sake. From Jephthah's statement in Judg. 11:17 it appears that the more timorous Moabites took the same course. But it nowhere appears that they showed any further signs of hostility. Indeed Jephthah (11:25-26) makes the special point that Moab did not fight against Israel while they were neighbors for 300 years. In Deut. 23:4, 7 there is no complaint of hostility on the part of either Edom or Moab, but only of want of hospitality on the part of Moab and Ammon and the hiring of Balaam to curse Israel. There is not the slightest hint that either nation made any attempt to hinder the Israelites from passing along the edge of its territory, trading with the people as they are said to have done in 2:28-29. For in "You shall not pass through us" in Num. 20:18, "through" must be taken in the sense of "by way of " ("via"). The Heb. is *lō' ta'ăbōr bî.* So far from being hostile, the Moabites were only too friendly, sending their daughters to cultivate friendly relations with the Israelites and then to entice them to their idolatrous services. For in Num. 25:2 "they invited" is feminine, referring to the daughters. Thus the conduct of Moab and Edom stood in strong contrast with the aggressive attitude assumed by Sihon, king of the Amorites. Moses could, therefore, truthfully make use of the peaceful conduct of those nations in his message to Sihon (Deut. 2:26-29), and so could Jephthah in his dealings with the sons of Ammon (Judg. 11:15-27).

The peaceful character and rich possessions of Moab may account for the terror of Balak at the approach of the Israelites and for the special means that he took to guard against them. Instead of flying to arms, like Sihon, he first consulted with the elders of Midian. Moab and Midian were kin by virtue of their common descent from Terah (Gen. 11:27; 19:36-37; 25:2; *see also* table 25, "Kinship of Moab and Midian").

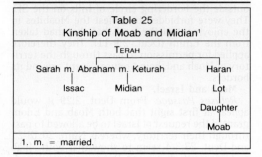

Table 25
Kinship of Moab and Midian[1]

TERAH

Sarah m. Abraham m. Keturah	Haran
Issac Midian	Lot
	Daughter
	Moab

1. m. = married.

So the tradition in Targum (Pseudo-Jonathan on Num. 22:4) that up to this time Moab and Midian had been one nation, with kings alternately taken from Midian and Moab, and that Balak was a Midianite may have at its foundation a fact.

The result of the conference was that the two nations united in sending for Balaam. If we are right in understanding Mic. 6:5-7 as a quotation from Balaam, it would seem that Balak in his desperation contemplated a sacrifice like that made by a later king of Moab (2 Kings 3:26) and that he was restrained by Balaam in words of remarkable depth and truth that have been compared with those of our Lord (Matt. 9:13; 12:7; cf. Hos. 6:6).

"It is remarkable that Moses should have taken his view of the promised land from a Moabite sanctuary, and been buried in the land of Moab. It is singular, too, that his resting place is marked in the Hebrew records only by its proximity to the sanctuary of that deity to whom in his lifetime he had been such an enemy" (Smith). "He buried him in the valley in the land of Moab, opposite Beth-peor," i.e., the abode of Baal-peor (Deut. 34:6; cf. Ps. 106:28).

Exclusion of Moab. The exclusion of Moabites (and Ammonites) from the congregation of the Lord to the tenth generation was not on account of any active hostility but, as is expressly said (Deut. 23:3-4), on account of their want of hospitality and of the hiring of Balaam. We may well believe that the ingenuity that made the daughters of Moab the means of enticing the Israelites into drawing the curse upon themselves made the exclusion of Moab more rigorous. The principal share in the transaction seems, however, to have belonged to *Midian* (which see). Indeed, Moab is named in connection with the affair only in Num. 25:1. *See* Marriage: Laws of Intermarriage.

The defeat of Midian in the field of Moab by the

Edomite Hadad (Gen. 36:35) is sometimes understood to refer to a war between Moab and Midian, but it looks rather like a defeat of the allied Midianites and Moabites by Edom. This accords well with what is otherwise known of the martial character of Edom and the unwarlike disposition of Moab and Midian (*see* above, and also Midian, especially no. 5).

Time of Judges. After the conquest Moab oppressed Israel once for eighteen years, but, as if recognizing the general unmilitary character of Moab, the text significantly says, "The Lord strengthened Eglon the king of Moab against Israel. . . . And he gathered to himself the sons of Ammon and Amalek; and he went and defeated Israel," etc. (Judg. 3:12-13).

Time of the Kingdom. Of Saul we read simply that he fought against Moab (1 Sam. 14:47). But the early relations of Moab and Israel seem on the whole to have been friendly, as shown by the book of Ruth. Ruth brought a Moabite element into the line of David and, hence, on the human side, into the ancestry of our Savior. Thus David, when pressed by Saul, entrusted his father and mother to the keeping of the king of Moab (22:3-4). But twenty years or more afterward, from some cause unknown to us, he treated the Moabites with great rigor (2 Sam. 8:2), and their spoil, with that of other nations, went to swell the treasure amassed for the Temple. The Moabites became tributary, and when we again hear of them they are acting for Solomon the same part that they had acted for the Israelites in Balaam's time— sending their daughters to lead him astray.

In the days of Ahab they still paid tribute, which shows both the severity of Israel's yoke and the resources of the country (2 Kings 3:4-5).

On the death of Ahab they revolted. According to the chronology of our English Bible (2 Chron. 20:1-25), their first step was to collect an army of Moabites, Ammonites, and others, including Edomites (vv. 1, 10, 23), and attack Judah, then ruled by Jehoshaphat. Judah met them with prayer and praise. By divine interposition, dissension broke out in the camp of the invaders, the Moabites and Ammonites first slaughtering the Edomites and then each other, so that nothing was left for Israel but to gather the spoil.

The consequence was a counter-invasion of Moab by Israel (eager to humble and perhaps regain a revolted province), Judah (ready to strike down a dangerous enemy), and Edom (mindful of the trap into which he had been led). This sequence of events shows how Edom came to act with Israel and Judah for once, and it explains the otherwise unaccountable and inexcusable severity with which Moab was treated when the victory was won. The story is told in 2 Kings 3:4-27.

Moab for a time must have been greatly reduced in power, so that nearly sixty years later we find predatory bands of Moabites as of Arabs

(13:20). But later, in the days of Isaiah, about the time of the death of Ahaz, "Moab has regained all and more than all of his former prosperity, and has besides extended himself over the district which he originally occupied in the youth of the nation, and which was left vacant by the removal of Reuben to Assyria" by Tiglath-pileser (18:11; 1 Chron. 5:26).

Prophecies. Isaiah, in his "oracle concerning Moab" (Isa. 15-16; cf. 25:10), predicts, in poetic lamentation, the fall of Moab from his high estate and his reduction to a small and feeble remnant (16:14). Jeremiah (Jer. 48) 140 years later (600 B.C.) echoes the lament of the older prophet, whose prophecy he had no doubt read, and gives Moab a gleam of hope at the last (48:47). These prophecies refer naturally to injuries to be inflicted by Assyria and Babylon. But they are especially interesting from their allusions, which show clearly the condition of Moab. The nation appears in them as high-spirited, wealthy, populous, and even to a certain extent civilized, enjoying a wide reputation and popularity. Outside the towns lie the fields and vineyards, the gardens of "summer fruits"; the harvest an "abundance which they have acquired and stored up." These characteristics contrast favorably with any traits recorded of Ammon, Edom, Midian, Amalek, the Philistines, or the Canaanite tribes. Since the descriptions of Isaiah and Jeremiah agree, they seem to represent the nation as permanently flourishing.

In Josiah's time Zephaniah threatens Moab and Ammon with vengeance for their reviling words against Israel but mentions no act of hostility. In 2 Kings 24:2 we find marauding bands of Moabites and Ammonites, along with Aramaeans and Chaldeans, harassing Judah in the time of Jehoiakim.

Jeremiah (Jer. 27:3) warned Edom, Moab, Ammon, Tyre, and Sidon, as he warned Judah, not to resist Nebuchadnezzar, into whose hand God had delivered those countries for the time, but to serve him and remain in their lands. It is to be presumed that they profited by his advice, since it appears from 40:11 that these countries had been a refuge to many of the Jews when the storm finally broke.

After the Captivity. Sanballat, who in Nehemiah's time was associated with Tobiah the Ammonite and Geshem the Arab against the Jews (Neh. 2:10, 19; etc.), was a Horonite. If this name is derived from Horonaim, Sanballat was a Moabite, as he is quite often regarded. If from Beth-horon, he was probably a Samaritan. *See* Horonite.

In Judith, shortly after the captivity (4:3) Moab and Ammon occupy their ancient seats. The Maccabees do not mention Moab or any towns south of the Arnon. In the time of Josephus (*Ant.* 1.11.5), the Moabites were "even still a great nation." The name remained to the time of Eusebius (A.D. about 380), and at the time of the Council of Jerusalem, A.D. 536, it formed the see of a bishop under the name Charak-Moba (Smith).

Language and Worship. The language of Moab was merely a dialect of Hebrew, differing from biblical Hebrew only in some comparatively trifling details.

The national deity of the Moabites was *Chemosh* (which see), mentioned only in Num. 21:29; Judg. 11:24; 1 Kings 11:7, 33; 2 Kings 23:13; Jer. 48:7, 13, 46.

BIBLIOGRAPHY: F.-M. Abel, *Géographie de la Palestine* (1933), 1:278-81; N. Glueck, *The Other Side of Jordan* (1940), p. 150; A. H. van Zyl, *The Moabites* (1960); G. L. Harding, *The Antiquities of Jordan* (1967); J. A. Sanders, ed., *Near Eastern Archaeology in the Twentieth Century* (1970), pp. 284-95; D. J. Wiseman, ed., *Peoples of Old Testament Times* (1973), pp. 229-58.

MO'ABITE STONE. One of the important memorials of alphabetic writing is the famous Moabite Stone, erected by Mesha king of Moab as a record of his successful revolt from Israel and in honor of his god *Chemosh* (which see), to whom his successes are ascribed. It was set up c. 850 B.C. The stone was discovered in 1868 by a German missionary, the Rev. F. Klein. He was on a visit to Moab and was informed by an Arab sheikh that at Dhiban, the ancient Dibon, was lying a stone inscribed with old characters. On examining it he found that it was a stela of black basalt, rounded at the top and measuring nearly four feet in length and two in width. It was covered with thirty-four lines of an inscription in the letters of the Phoenician alphabet. Mr. Klein had little idea of the importance of the discovery he had made and contented himself with noting down a few words and compiling an alphabet out of the rest. On his return to Jerusalem he informed the Prussian consulate of the discovery, and measures were taken at once to secure the stone.

In the spring of the following year M. Clermont-Ganneau, the dragoman of the French consulate, heard that the stone was still lying at Dhiban with its inscribed face exposed to the weather, and he determined to get possession of it for France. Natives were accordingly sent to take squeezes of the inscription and to offer a large sum of money for the monument. The natives quarreled in the presence of the Arabs, and it was with some difficulty that a half-dried squeeze was carried off safely by Selim el-Oari, M. Clermont-Ganneau's agent, and delivered to the French consulate. It is upon this squeeze, now preserved in the Louvre, that we are largely dependent for our knowledge of the contents of the text. The largeness of the sums offered and the rival bidding of the two European consulates naturally aroused in the minds of both Moabite and Turkish officials an exaggerated idea of the stone's value. The governor of Nablus accordingly demanded the splendid prize for himself, and the Arabs, rather than lose it for nothing, lighted

Artist's impression of the Moabite Stone

a fire under it, poured cold water over it, and so shivered it into fragments. The pieces were distributed among different families and placed in their granaries, in order to act as charms in protecting the corn from blight. A considerable number of fragments have since been recovered, but without the squeeze that was taken while the stone was intact, it would have been impossible to fit many of them together, and for the missing portions of the text it is our only authority.

The work of restoration and interpretation was ably performed by Clermont-Ganneau, by way of amends for the overhasty zeal that brought about the destruction of the monument. The latest and best edition of the text, however, is that which was published in 1886 by the two German professors, Smend and Socin, after weeks of study of the squeeze preserved in the Louvre.

The inscription on this stone in a remarkable degree supplements and corroborates the history of King Mesha recorded in 2 Kings 3:4-27. It affords evidence of the knowledge of alphabetic writing in the lands of the Jordan. "The art of writing and reading can have been no new thing. As soon as Mesha has shaken off the yoke of the foreigner, he erects an inscribed monument in commemoration of his victories. . . . It is the first and most natural thing for him to do, and it is taken for granted that the record will have numerous readers. . . . Moreover, the forms of the letters as they appear on the Moabite Stone show that alphabetic writing must have been long practiced in the kingdom of Mesha. They are forms which presuppose a long acquaintance with the art of engraving inscriptions upon

stones, and are far removed from the forms out of which they must have developed. Then, again, the language of the inscription is noteworthy. Between it and Hebrew the differences are few and slight. It is a proof that the Moabites were akin to the Israelites in language as well as in race, and that like their kinsfolk they had adopted the ancient 'language of Canaan.' The likeness between the languages of Moab and Israel extends beyond the mere idioms of grammar and syntax. It is a likeness which exists also in thought" (Sayce, *Higher Crit. and the Mon.*, p. 364).

BIBLIOGRAPHY: G. A. Cooke, *A Text-Book of North-Semitic Inscriptions* (1903), pp. 1-14; D. W. Thomas, ed., *Documents from Old Testament Times* (1958), pp. 195-98; F. I. Andersen, *Orientalia* 35 (1966): 81-120; D. J. Wiseman, ed., *Peoples of Old Testament Times* (1973), pp. 229, 247.

MO'ABITESS (mō'a-bī-tes; feminine of "Moabite"). A Moabite woman (Ruth 1:22; 2:2, 21; 4:5, 10; 2 Chron. 24:26).

MOADI'AH (mō-a-dī'a; Neh. 12:17). *See* Maadiah.

MOCK (Heb. *qālas*, to "disparage," Hab. 1:10; "scoff," KJV and NIV; and other Heb. and Gk. words). To ridicule, make light of, as of a fortification or an enemy.

MOCKERS (Gk. *empaiktes*). One who *trifles*, and so *derides* (2 Pet. 3:3); "scoffers," KJV and NIV.

MODERATION. Better, "forbearing spirit" (Phil. 4:5, NASB), "gentleness" (Phil. 4:5), or "patience." In 1 Tim. 3:3; Titus 3:2; 1 Pet. 2:18, the Gk. is rendered by the word "gentle."

MODIUS. A foreign measure of capacity. *See* Metrology.

MOL'ADAH (Heb. *môlādâ*, "origin, birth"). A town in the southern part of Judah, probably about twenty miles S of Hebron, named in connection with Kedesh and Beersheba (Josh. 15:26). It was afterward assigned to Simeon (19:2; 1 Chron. 4:28) and was occupied after the Exile (Neh. 11:26). Later it was called Malada, an Idumaean fortress (Josephus *Ant* 18.6.2), which Eusebius and Jerome located about twenty Roman miles S of Hebron.

MOLDY. *See* Mouldy.

MOLE. *See* Animal Kingdom.

MOLECH (mō'lek). *See* Gods, False.

MO'LID (mō'lid; "begetter"). The son of Abishur by his wife Abihail, and a descendant of Jerahmeel (1 Chron. 2:29).

MOLOCH (mō'lok). *See* Gods, False.

MOLTEN IMAGE. *See* Calf, Golden.

MOLTEN SEA. *See* Laver.

MOMENT (Heb. *regaʿ*, "wink," Ps. 30:5; etc.; Gk. *atomas*, "indivisible," 1 Cor. 15:52; *stigmē*, a "point," Luke 4:5). An instant (as in Num. 16:21, 45; "at once," NIV), the smallest interval of time. *See* Time.

MONEY. *See* Metrology: Measures of Value, or Money.

MONEY CHANGER (Gk. *kollubistēs,* "a coin dealer"; *kermatistēs,* "money broker," from *kerma,* a "small coin").

1. Bankers who sat in the Court of the Gentiles (or in its porch) and for a fixed discount changed all foreign coins into those of the sanctuary. Every Israelite, rich or poor, who had reached the age of twenty was obliged to pay into the sacred treasury, whenever the nation was numbered, a half shekel as an offering to Jehovah (Ex. 30:13-15). This tribute was in every case to be paid in the exact Hebrew half shekel. The money changers assessed a fixed charge for their services. This charge must have brought in a large revenue, since not only many native Palestinians might come without the statutory coin, but a vast number of foreign Jews presented themselves on such occasions in the Temple. In addition to the tribute, those who came to worship at the Temple needed money for other purposes. Most sacrifices for the feasts were bought within the Temple area. It was easier to get the right money from the authorized changers than to have disputes with the dealers. Thus the immense offerings of foreign Jews and proselytes to the Temple passed through the hands of the money changers. Indeed, they probably transacted all business matters connected with the sanctuary.

2. The Gk. *trapezitēs* (Matt. 25:27, marg.), "bankers," is a general term for a money changer, broker, banker; one who exchanges money for a fee and pays interest on deposits. The fact that this occupation had become characterized by avarice may account for the strong language and vigorous action of Jesus in Matt. 21:12 and Mark 11:15.

MONEY, LOVE OF (Gk. *philarguria,* 1 Tim. 6:10). Avarice or covetousness.

MONEY, PIECE OF (Gen. 33:19; Job 42:11; etc.). *See* Metrology.

MONEY PURSES. *See* articles Dress; Purse.

MONITOR. *See* Animal Kingdom: Chameleon.

MONSTERS (Heb. *tannîm*). The context of Lam. 4:3 requires jackal (so NASB and NIV), but the Heb. term is given other translations in the various passages where it appears. *See* Animal Kingdom: Dragon; Jackal; Whale; Wolf.

MONTH. *See* Time.

MOON. The terms that were used to designate the moon contain no reference to its office or essential character; they simply describe it by the accidental quality of color—*yārēaḥ* signifying "pale" or "yellow," *lᵉbānâ,* "white." The moon held an important place in the kingdom of nature as known to the Hebrews. In the history of the creation (Gen. 1:14-16) it appears simultaneously with the sun and is described in terms that imply its independence of that body so far as its light is concerned. Conjointly with the sun it was appointed "for signs, and for seasons, and for days and years"; though in this respect it exercised a more important influence, if by the "seasons" we understand the great religious festivals of the Jews, as is particularly stated in Ps. 104:19 and Ecclus. 43:6-7. Besides this it had its special office in the distribution of light; it was appointed "to govern the night," as the sun was to govern the day, and thus the appearance of the two founts of light served "to separate the day from the night." The inferiority of its light is occasionally noticed, as in Gen. 1:16; Song of Sol. 6:10; Isa. 30:26. The worship of the moon was extensively practiced by the nations of the East. Ur in lower Mesopotamia, Abraham's birthplace, was an important center of the worship of Sin, the moon god, as was Haran in Upper Mesopotamia, where Abram and Terah emigrated. In Egypt the moon was honored under the name Isis and was one of the only two deities that commanded the reverence of all the Egyptians. In Syria the moon was represented by one of the Ashtaroth surnamed "Karnaim," from the horns of the crescent moon by which she was distinguished. There are indications of the early introduction into the countries adjacent to Palestine of a species of worship distinct from any that we have described, namely, the direct homage of the heavenly bodies—sun, moon, and stars—characteristic of Sabianism. The first notice we have of this is in Job 31:26-27, and it is observable that the warning of Moses (Deut. 4:19) is directed against this nature worship rather than against the form of moon worship that the Israelites must have witnessed in Egypt. At a later period, however, the worship of the moon in its grosser form of idol worship was introduced from Syria, probably through Aramaic influence. In 2 Kings 23:5 we read that Josiah did away with those "who burned incense to Baal, to the sun and to the moon," etc. Manasseh appears to have been the great patron of this form of idolatry, for he "worshiped all the host of heaven" (21:3, 5). From his reign down to the captivity, moon worship continued to prevail among the Jews, with the exception of a brief period under Josiah. Jeremiah has several references to it (Jer. 7:18; 8:2; 44:17). In the first of those references the prophet gives us a little insight into the manner of worship accorded to the moon: "The children gather wood, and the fathers kindle the fire, and the women knead dough to make cakes for the queen of heaven." These cakes were probably intended as gifts, in acknowledgment of a supposed influence exercised by the moon on the affairs of the world or, more specially, on the products of the soil.

Figurative. In the figurative language of Scripture the moon is frequently seen presaging events of the greatest importance, such as the second coming of Christ, through the temporary or permanent withdrawal of its light (Isa. 13:10; Joel 2:31; Matt. 24:29; Mark 13:24). The moon's becoming "like blood" (Rev. 6:12) points to approaching judgments.   M.F.U.

MOON, NEW. *See* Festivals.

MO'RASTHITE. The KJV expression in Jer. 26:18; Mic. 1:1). It is replaced in the NASB and NIV with "Micah of Moresheth" to distinguish him from the elder prophet Micaiah son of Imlah. *See* Moresheth-gath.

MOR'DECAI (mor'de-kī; possibly from Akkad. *Marduk*, patron god of Babylon). The name of two biblical characters.

1. Esther's cousin, the son of Jair, a descendant of Kish the Benjamite. He resided at Susa, the metropolis of Persia, at the time when Ahasuerus (Xerxes) desired a successor to Queen Vashti. Mordecai had under his care his adopted daughter, Hadassah (Esther) (Esther 2:5-7). Among the fairest women of the land who were gathered at the palace was Esther, upon whom the king's choice fell.

Mordecai sat in the king's gate in those days (that is, probably, held some office in or about the palace), and became aware of the plot of two of the king's officials against the king's life, which, through Esther, was made known to the monarch. Although the conspirators were punished, no reward seems to have been bestowed upon Mordecai (2:21-23), about 478 B.C.

Some years later, the king promoted Haman, and Mordecai alone refused to manifest the customary signs of homage to the royal favorite. Some think his refusal to bow before Haman arose from religious scruples, as if such salutation as was practiced in Persia were akin to idolatry; others, as seems far more probable, that he refused, from a stern unwillingness as a Jew, to bow before an Amalekite. Haman's indignation was aroused, and he determined upon revenge. Remembering the avowed enmity of the Israelites against his people, he resolved upon their extermination and obtained from the king a decree for the slaughter of all the Jews in the empire. When Mordecai learned what had been done he "tore his clothes, put on sackcloth and ashes, and went out into the midst of the city and wailed loudly and bitterly." Esther, having been informed of this through her servants, sent Hathach, one of the king's eunuchs, to learn the cause of Mordecai's grief. He sent word to the queen of the decree of extermination against the Jews, and an exhortation for her to interfere in behalf of herself and their people. Esther was equal to the occasion and, seizing a favorable opportunity, presented herself unbidden before Ahasuerus and secured his consent to come with Haman to a banquet on the following day (3:1-5:8).

That night the monarch could not sleep and commanded that the records be read to him. Providentially part of them that was read referred to the conspiracy frustrated by Mordecai. In answer to his question, "What honor or dignity has been bestowed on Mordecai for this?" the king's attendants replied, "Nothing." He then asked, "Who is in the court?" and they said, "Behold, Haman is standing in the court." The king said, "Let him come in," and then asked him, "What is to be done for the man whom the king desires to honor?" Haman, supposing that he was the person alluded to, named the highest and most public honor he could conceive of, and received the astounding answer, "Do so for Mordecai the Jew, who is sitting at the king's gate." The next day Esther appealed to the king on behalf of her people, and Haman was hanged on the gallows that he had prepared for Mordecai (chaps. 6-7). Mordecai was summoned into the royal presence and was promoted to the position so recently held by Haman (8:1-2, 15), "and his fame spread throughout all the provinces" (9:4). The first use he made of his power was to counteract as far as possible the decree obtained by Haman, which could not be recalled, as the kings of Persia had no power to rescind a decree once issued. The Jews were permitted to defend themselves and so were preserved from destruction. The feast of Purim (*see* Festivals) was instituted in memory of this deliverance, and is observed to this day (9:20-32). Mordecai is supposed to be the author of the book of Esther, which contains the narrative.

2. A leading man among the Israelites who returned from Babylon to Jerusalem with Zerubbabel (Ezra 2:2; Neh. 7:7), 536 B.C. Perhaps the same as no. 1.

BIBLIOGRAPHY: C. E. Macartney, *Chariots of Fire* (1951), pp. 169-80; A. Raleigh, *The Book of Esther* (1980), pp. 69-87, 134-54, 242-43.

MO'REH (mō're; "teacher, teaching").

1. The "oak of Moreh" (Gen. 12:6), to which Abraham came when he entered Canaan, where the Lord appeared to him, and where he built an altar. The "oaks of Moreh" (Deut. 11:30) are mentioned by Moses when addressing the Israelites before entering Canaan. They are situated about 1½ miles from Shechem. It is thought by some that Moreh was an early Canaanite and that the oaks were named after him.

2. The "hill of Moreh," in the valley of Jezreel on the N side of the spring of Harod, near which the Midianites were encamped when attacked by Gideon (Judg. 7:1); probably the same as Little Hermon (Jebel Dahy) some eight miles NW of Mt. Gilboa.

BIBLIOGRAPHY: D. Baly, *The Geography of the Bible* (1957), pp. 21, 38-39, 149-51, 173-74, 189.

The Temple was built on Mt. Moriah

MO'RESHETH-GATH (mo'resh-eth-gath; "possession of Gath," i.e., "nearby Gath"). Apparently the birthplace or residence of the prophet Micah (Mic. 1:14). Jerome (*Onomast*) places it a short distance E of Eleutheropolis, from which Robinson (*Researches*, 2:423) concludes that it must have been near Mareshah. Possibly to be identified with Tell ej-Judeideh, about five miles W of Gath.

MORI'AH (mo-rī'a). "The land of Moriah" is named (Gen. 22:2) as the place where *Abraham* (which see) went to offer up Isaac. It is thought to be the same as "Mount Moriah," one of the hills of Jerusalem on which Solomon built the Temple, on the spot once occupied by the threshing floor of Ornan the Jebusite (2 Chron. 3:1). The Jews themselves believe that the altar of burnt offerings in the Temple stood upon the very site of the altar on which Abraham intended to offer up his son.

BIBLIOGRAPHY: F. -M. Abel, *Géographie de la Palestine* (1933), 1:374-75.

MORNING (Heb. *bōqer*, Gen. 1:5; etc.; Gk. *prōia*, Matt. 21:18). The early part of the day after sunrise. *See* Dawn; Time.

Figurative. Morning is illustrative of a nearby time, as "the upright shall rule over them in the morning," i.e., speedily (Ps. 49:14). Christ is called the "morning star" (Rev. 22:16), as He introduced the light of gospel day; the reward of saints (2:28), stars being an emblem of lofty position; the morning cloud, as speedily disappearing before the sun, is figurative of the short-lived profession of hypocrites (Hos. 6:4).

MORNING SACRIFICE. *See* Sacrifice.

MORNING WATCH. *See* Watch.

MORSEL. The translation of several Heb. and Gk. terms.

1. Heb. *pat*, "bit." A term answering to our *bit*, and usually referring to food (Prov. 17:1), sometimes rendered "piece," i.e., of bread (*see* the NASB of Judg. 19:5; Ruth 2:14; 1 Sam. 28:22; 1 Kings 17:11).

2. Heb. *mitlahămîn*, "bits greedily swallowed." The Heb. expression appears only in Prov. 18:8; 26:22. It is given as "morsels" in the NASB and NIV. The KJV rendering, "wounds," is less apt.

3. Gk. *psōmion*, "fragment." A piece of bread "dipped" into the sauce (John 13:26-30; "sop," KJV). In the East meat is so thoroughly cooked as to be easily separated by the fingers. When, however, the food is in a semifluid state, or so soft that the fingers cannot conveniently hold it, it is conveyed to the mouth by means of a thin piece of bread. It is customary for the host to honor a guest by thus passing to him any dainty morsel. Jesus' dipping the morsel of bread and handing it to Judas would indicate that his place at the table must have been near to the Lord.

4. Gk. *brōsis*, "eating," "food." The Gk. term appears in Heb. 12:16 as part of a reference to the price for which Esau sold his birthright: "a morsel of meat," KJV; "a single meal," NASB and NIV.

MORTAL, MORTALITY. A term used for a human being, as frequently with us. The Gk. *thnētos* ("liable to die") is applied to man's natural body in contrast with the body that shall be (Rom. 6:12; 1 Cor. 15:53, 54; 2 Cor. 4:11; 5:4).

MORTAR.

1. Heb. *medōkâ*, Num. 11:8; *maktēsh*, "hollow," Prov. 27:22, a hollow vessel of wood, stone, or metal, used to pulverize grain or other substances. The most ancient mention of its use is in the account of the manner in which the Israelites prepared the manna in the desert: "The people would go about and gather it and grind it between two millstones or beat it in the mortar" (Num. 11:8).

Pounding various substances in stone mortars with metal pestles

Figurative. "Though you pound a fool in a mortar with a pestle along with crushed grain, yet his folly will not depart from him" (Prov. 27:22). Grain may be separated from its husk and all its good properties preserved by such an operation. But the fool's folly is so essentially a part of himself that no such process can remove it from him.

2. The word descriptive of any cement used in building, and the rendering of the Heb. word *hōmer,* "mire" or "clay." Thus the builders of the tower of Babel "used brick for stone, and they used tar ['slime,' KJV] for mortar" (Gen. 11:3). *Mortar* in Ex. 1:14 is thought by some to mean the *clay* from which the bricks were made; as also in Isa. 41:25, "He will come upon rulers as upon mortar"; and Nah. 3:14. *See* Mineral Kingdom: Clay; Tar.

Another Heb. word translated "plaster" is *'āpār* (*powdered,* usually rendered *dust*), used in the account of the treatment of a leprous house (Lev. 14:41-45). Here the mortar scraped from the walls is called "plaster" ("dust," KJV), while the fresh material placed upon the walls is called "plaster" also ("mortar," KJV). *See* Mineral Kingdom: Lime; Mortar; Plaster.

In Ezekiel (13:10-16) the figure is introduced of the people building a wall which the false prophets plastered (Heb. *tāpēl;* NIV "whitewash"). The meaning of the figure is intelligible enough. The people build up false hopes, and the prophets not only paint these hopes for them in splendid colors, but even predict their fulfillment, instead of denouncing their folly. The plastering is therefore a figurative description of deceitful flattery or hypocrisy (*see* Matt. 23:27; Acts 23:3). The same word occurs in the sense of that which is unsavory (Job 6:6) or foolish (Lam. 2:14).

MORTGAGE (Heb. *'ārab,* to "give security," Neh. 5:3). A lien upon real estate for debt (Gesenius reads the passage, "We must pawn our houses"). In Prov. 17:18 it is rendered "pledge."

MORTIFICATION (Gk. *thanatoō,* to "kill," Rom. 8:13; *nekroō,* to "deaden," Col. 3:5). The term *mortify* appears in the KJV of Rom. 8:13; Col. 3:5, with the sense of "put to death," or "consider as dead," the NASB readings of those

passages. The NIV renders "put to death" in both passages.

MOSE'RA, MOSE'RAH (mo-se'ra; a "bond"). The thirty-ninth station of the Israelites in the desert, between Beeroth Bene-Jaakan and Gudgodah (Deut. 10:6); evidently near Mt. Hor, since Aaron is said to have died there (cf. Num. 33:37-38). The exact location is uncertain.

MOSE'ROTH (mo-se'rōth; "correction"). A station of the Israelites named between Hashmonah and Bene-jaaken (Num. 33:30-31); probably the same as Moserah.

MO'SES (mō'zez). The deliverer, leader, lawgiver, and prophet of Israel. The name in Heb. is *mōsheh* ("drawn out"), but the original is Egyptian *ms',* a "child," a "son," reflecting that Pharaoh's daughter simply named him "child" (cf. Thutmose, Ahmose, etc., in which the same element appears frequently in Egyptian names). Thutmose = "Son of Thot," etc. Moses belonged to the tribe of Levi, and was the son of Amram by his wife Jochebed. The other members of the family were Aaron and Miriam, his elder brother and sister. His immediate pedigree is given in table 26, "The Family Register of Moses."

The life of Moses is divided into three equal portions of forty years each (Acts 7:23, 30, 36): his life in Egypt, exile in Arabia, and government of Israel.

Life in Egypt. Here took place his birth, adoption, and the avenging of his countrymen.

Birth. Moses was born about 1520 B.C. and, according to Manetho (Josephus *Against Apion* 1.26; 2.2), at Heliopolis; his birth, according to Josephus (*Ant.* 2.9.2-4), having been foretold to Pharaoh by the Egyptian magicians, and to his father by a dream. At the time of Moses' birth the decree commanding the slaying of all male children was in force (Ex. 1:10, 16), but his mother was by some means able to conceal him and hid him away for three months. When concealment was no longer possible she placed him in a small

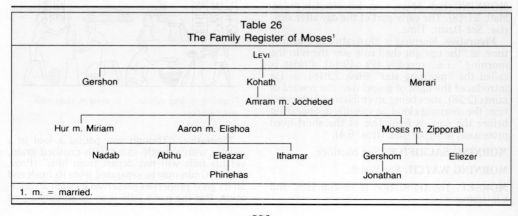

Table 26
The Family Register of Moses[1]

LEVI

Gershon	Kohath	Merari

Amram m. Jochebed

Hur m. Miriam	Aaron m. Elishoa	Moses m. Zipporah

Nadab	Abihu	Eleazar	Ithamar	Gershom	Eliezer

Phinehas   Jonathan

1. m. = married.

boat or basket of papyrus—perhaps from an Egyptian belief that the plant is a protection from crocodiles. She placed him among the reeds of the Nile and left his sister to watch the result. The daughter of Pharaoh, who may well have been the famous Queen Hatshepsut, and who herself a little later assumed the throne of Egypt, came to the river to bathe, saw the basket, and had it brought to her. It was opened, and the cry of the child moved the princess to compassion. She determined to rear it as her own. The sister was then at hand to recommend as a Hebrew nurse the baby's mother, who was hired by the princess (2:1-9).

Adoption. The child was adopted by the king's daughter, and from this time for many years Moses must be considered as an Egyptian (2:10). In the Pentateuch this period is a blank, but in the NT he is represented as "educated in all the learning of the Egyptians" and as "a man of power in words and deeds" (Acts 7:22). The discovery of the tablets of el-Amarna shows how extensive were the knowledge and use of writing throughout the East in the time of Moses and that the young prince could write—doubtless in Egyptian hieroglyphics, Akkad. cuneiform, and in alphabetic cuneiform such as Ugaritic, which was almost identical with the Heb. of the day. *See* Babylonia; Egypt.

Avenges His Countrymen. When he was forty years old (Acts 7:23) Moses resolved to cast in his lot with his brethren (Heb. 11:24-26), and seeing an Israelite being beaten by an Egyptian, and thinking that they were alone, he killed the Egyptian and buried the corpse in the sand. The next day he endeavored to act as peacemaker between two Hebrews, but his offices were refused and he became aware that his act of the preceding day was known. It became evident to him that safety was to be found only in flight (Ex. 2:11-15).

Exile in Arabia. Here took place the middle years of Moses' life, culminating in his return to Egypt as a prophet of God.

Marriage. Moses fled, about 1480 B.C., at the beginning of the reign of the famous Thutmose III (if we follow the Masoretic chronology), into Midian, in or near the peninsula of Sinai, and rested himself by a well, where he helped some young women to water their sheep. Because of this they returned to their home earlier than usual, and when they told their father, Jethro, the reason, he had Moses called in, and Moses consented to live with him, later taking his daughter Zipporah as his wife and assuming charge of his father-in-law's flock (Ex. 2:16-21; 3:1).

Call. In the seclusion of this shepherd life Moses received his call as a prophet. The traditional scene of this event is in the valley of Shoeib, on the N side of Jebel Musa, but we are unable to fix the spot with any certainty. It was "to the west side of the wilderness" at Horeb (3:1); to which

the Heb. adds, while the LXX omits, "the mountain of God." Upon the mountain was the well-known acacia, the thorn tree of the desert, spreading out its tangled branches, thickset with white thorns, over the rocky ground. The angel of the Lord appeared to Moses in a flame of fire in the midst of the bush, the dry branches of which would naturally have burned in a moment, but that remained unconsumed. The twofold revelation was made to Moses of the eternal self-existence of the one God and of his mission to deliver his own people. Two signs attested to him his divine mission—the staff that turned into a serpent, and the hand of Moses made leprous and afterward cleansed. Should these be disbelieved by the people a third was promised, that the waters of the Nile thrown by Moses upon the land would be turned into blood. The objection of Moses, "I am slow of speech and slow of tongue," was answered by the promise of Jehovah's assistance. Moses' difficulties were now all exhausted and removed by the assurances of God; but since he was still unwilling to undertake the mission, Aaron was allowed to be his spokesman, and Moses consented (3:2–4:17).

Return to Egypt. He then returned to the home of his father-in-law and received permission to visit his brethren. God appeared to him and assured him of the death of all those in Egypt who sought his life, c. 1440 B.C. Moses then set out upon his journey with his wife and sons. On the way Moses, threatened with death by Jehovah, was spared upon the circumcision of his son. It would seem to have been in consequence of this event, whatever it was, that the wife and her children were sent back to Jethro and remained with him until they joined Moses at Rephidim (18:2-6). He once more received a token of divine favor in the arrival of Aaron, who met him at the "mountain of God," went with him to Egypt, and communicated to the people of Israel the words of Jehovah (chap. 4)

Government of Israel. The history of Moses henceforth is the history of Israel for forty years, c. 1440-1400 B.C. He and Aaron appeared before Pharaoh to demand permission for the children of Israel to go to the wilderness and sacrifice to Jehovah. Then followed the contest between these two men and the king, and the plagues sent by Jehovah (chaps. 5-12).

Exodus. On the night of the deliverance Moses took the decisive lead, and after that he is usually mentioned alone. Under divine direction he did not lead the people by the nearest way to the Promised Land, i.e., through the country of the Philistines, lest, being opposed by this warlike people, the Israelites should turn back into Egypt. "Hence God led the people around by the way of the wilderness to the Red Sea" (13:17-18), through which the Israelites passed in safety while the hosts of Pharaoh perished in its waves.

Journey to Sinai. From the Red Sea Moses led

Israel through Marah, where the bitter waters were sweetened (15:23); Elim, where there were twelve springs of water and seventy palm trees (15:27); the wilderness of Sin, where the people murmured for want of bread and were supplied with quail and manna (chap. 16); Rephidim, where the smitten rock of Horeb gave forth water (17:1-7), where the hands of Moses, upheld by Aaron and Hur, inspired the Israelites with courage, so that they defeated the Amalekites (17:8-16), and where Jethro, Moses' father-in-law, brought to him his wife and two sons (chap. 18).

At Sinai. Arriving at Sinai, Moses responded to the call of Jehovah and, going up into the mountain of God, received the message to the people to prepare for divine communications (19:1-13). He led the people to the foot of the mountain on the third day, where he received the Ten Commandments (19:14–20:17); conducted the ceremony of ratifying the covenant (24:1-8), reading all the "words of the Lord" (24:3) and all the "ordinances" (chaps. 21-23); stayed forty days and nights on the mountain (24:18), receiving the details of the plan of the sanctuary and worship of God (chaps. 25-31), and the two tablets of stone (31:18). In chap. 32 we have a vivid description of the righteous indignation of Moses at the sin of Israel in the worship of the golden calf, which led him to destroy the tablets of stone and call for volunteers to kill the idolaters (vv. 1-29); and we see his no less earnest zeal in the capacity of mediator (32:30–33:16). The glory of Jehovah was revealed to him (33:17-23), and the tablets of the law were renewed (34:1-4). A covenant was made with Israel (vv. 10-27), and after a second stay of forty days upon the mountain Moses returned to the people, his shining face covered with a veil (vv. 28-35). Moses then superintended the erection of the Tabernacle and its preparation for worship (chaps. 35-40), received the statutes of Israel for the congregation of Jehovah (Lev. 1-7), and consecrated Aaron and his sons for the priesthood (chaps. 8-9). Judgment was executed upon Nadab and Abihu (chap. 10), and further regulations were given (chaps. 11-27). After this Moses numbered the people (Num. 1); arranged the order of the tribes in the camp and on the march (chap. 2); numbered the Levites and arranged for their special calling (chaps. 3-4); gave directions respecting unclean persons, trespasses, Nazirites, etc. (chaps. 5-6); received the dedicatory gifts from the princes of the tribes (chap. 7); consecrated the Levites (chap. 8); and prepared for the onward journey (9:1–10:10).

Journey. On the twentieth day of the second month of the second year the cloud lifted from the Tabernacle, announcing that the time to leave Sinai had come. Moses accordingly gave the order to march, and the people moved forward (Num. 10:11-33). Mention is made of Moses' securing, by prayer, the quenching of the fire at Taberah (11:1-3); the story records his complaint

of the burden of his duties and the subsequent appointment of seventy elders to assist him (11:10-30); the sedition of Miriam and Aaron (chap. 12); the sending out of the spies (chaps. 13-14); the rebellion of Korah, Dathan, and Abiram (chap. 16); the deaths of Miriam and Aaron, and the striking of the rock at Meribah (chap. 20); the plague of serpents (chap. 21); the appointment of Joshua by Moses as his successor (chap. 27); the assignment of their inheritance to the Reubenites and Gadites (chap. 32); the appointment of commissioners to divide the Promised Land (chap. 34); and Moses' farewell address (Deut. 1-33).

Death. For forty years the care and burden of the Israelites had been upon the mind and heart of Moses. The people were camped in Moab, awaiting the command to pass over the Jordan into the land of promise. Moses had sinned at Meribah in not sanctifying Jehovah in the eyes of the people (Num. 20:12) and had thereby forfeited the privilege of entering Canaan. At the command of God he blessed the people and then ascended Mt. Nebo, a peak of Pisgah, which gave a view of the land promised to Abraham, Isaac, and Jacob. After this favor had been granted him Moses died and was buried by Jehovah "in the valley in the land of Moab, opposite Beth-peor," in an unknown sepulcher (Deut. 34:1-6), c. 1400 B.C.

Character. "Moses was in a sense peculiar to himself the founder and representative of his people. And in accordance with this complete identification of himself with his nation is the only strong personal trait which we are able to gather from his history (Num. 12:3). The word *meek* is hardly an adequate reading of the Hebrew *'ānāw,* which should rather be *much enduring.* It represents what we should now designate by the word *disinterested.* All that is told of him indicates a withdrawal of himself, a preference of the cause of his nation to his own interests, which makes him the most complete example of Jewish patriotism" (Smith, *Dict.,* s.v.). He joins his countrymen in their degrading servitude (Ex. 2:11; 5:4) and forgets himself to avenge their wrongs (2:14). He desires that his brother should be leader instead of himself (4:13); and when Jehovah offers to destroy the people and make of him a great nation (32:10), he prays for their forgiveness—"If not, please blot me out from Thy book which Thou hast written!" (v. 32).

Moses and Archaeology. The story of Moses being found in a papyrus ark among the reeds by the riverside has many parallels in ancient lore. To the classical examples of Romulus and Remus, Bacchus, and Perseus, must now be added account of the great Sargon I of Akkad (c. 2400 B.C.). The cuneiform legend of the ninth century B.C. thus speaks of Sargon: "My humble mother conceived me; she bore me in secret, placed me in an ark of bulrushes, made fast my door with pitch and gave me to the river which did not overwhelm me. The river lifted me up and carried me to Akki, the irrigator . . . Akki, the irrigator, hauled me out . . . took me to be his son and brought me up" (Hugo Gressmann, *Altorientalische Texte and Bilder zum Alten Testament* [1909], 1:79). There is certainly no necessity to postulate a common origin for such simple, natural romances, but "if one must do so, the episode of Moses (sixteenth century B.C.) may have been the inspiration of them all (S. Caiger, *Bible and Spade* [1936], p. 68). Archaeology sheds light on Moses' name, which is apparently nothing more than Egyptian *mase*, pronounced *mose* after the twelfth century B.C., and meaning "the child." This Egyptian word is preserved in such composites as Ahmose ("son of Ah," the god of light) and Thutmose ("son of Thot") (cf. Alan H. Gardiner, *Journal of Egyptian Archaeology* 5 [1918]: 193). Pharaoh's daughter evidently did not endow this unknown infant, a child of an alien race, with a special name. She simply contented herself to call him "the child." The sacred penman, however, as a result of an unusual coincidence of sound and circumstance, connects the name with the Heb. root *māshâ*, "to draw out," because Pharaoh's daughter "drew him out of the water" (Ex. 2:10). The presence of a Nubian element in Moses' family is another fact attested to by his own name and those of his kinsmen. "Then Miriam and Aaron spoke against Moses because of the Cushite [Ethiopian or Nubian] woman he had married (for he had married a Cushite woman)" (Num. 12:1). The name of Moses' brother Aaron's grandson, Phinehas, means "Nubian" in Egyptian and "is interesting as providing an independent but an absolutely reliable confirmation" of the circumstance (W. F. Albright, *From the Stone Age to Christianity*, p. 193).

Writings. Although much controversy has been carried on respecting the extent of the authorship of Moses, it is probable that there should be attributed to him the Pentateuch (as far as Deut. 31:23), the song of Moses (32:1-43), the blessing of Moses on the tribes (33:1-29), and Ps. 90. The evidence of Moses' being the author of the Pentateuch is thus summed up by Keil (*Introduction to the Old Testament*, pp. 160ff.): (1) In Ex. 17:14 (*see* marg.), after the victory over the Amalekites, Moses receives the divine command to write in *the* book (*bāsēpĕr*), as a memorial, the will of God that Amalek should be utterly blotted out. According to 24:3-4, Moses wrote the words of the covenant and the "ordinances" of Israel (20:2-17; chaps. 21-23) in "the book of the covenant." According to Num. 33:2 he wrote down the camping stations of the Israelites in the wilderness by divine command. (2) According to Deut. 31:9-11, Moses wrote the law and gave it to the priests, with the command to read it before all Israel at the Feast of Booths (vv. 24-26): "And it came about, when Moses finished writing the

words of this law in a book until they were complete, that Moses commanded the Levites, . . . 'Take this book of the law and place it beside the ark of the covenant of the Lord your God, that it may remain there as a witness against you.' " To this double testimony we must add 17:18, that the future king who should be chosen was to write "a copy of this law" for himself, and was to read it every day; cf. 27:1-8, where Moses commands the people to set up on Mt. Ebal great stones coated with lime, and to write upon these all the words of this law, which was actually done (Josh. 8:30-35); Deut. 28:58, 61; 29:19-20, 27, where Moses threatens if they do not obey the law *written in this book;* and 30:10, where he promises blessings if they "keep His commandments and His statutes which *are written in this book of the law*" (italics added). *See also* Gleason L. Archer, *A Survey of Old Testament Introduction*, rev. ed., pp. 109-18.

As a Lawgiver. "It occurs at once as a striking thing that the uniform tradition is, that Moses gave laws and ordinances to Israel. . . . The *body* of laws that formed the constitution of Israel as a people is invariably referred to Moses. The persistence with which it is represented that law, moral and ceremonial, came from Moses, and the acceptance of the laws by the whole people as of Mosaic origin, proves at least that it was a deeply-seated belief in the nation that the great leader had given some formal legal constitution to his people" (Robertson, *Early Religion of Israel*, p. 335).

Later Scripture Reference. In the OT the name of Moses does not occur as frequently, after the close of the Pentateuch, as might be expected. In Judges (18:30) the name is given as "Manasseh" in the Heb. copies in order to avoid the admission that the great lawgiver's grandson was the first idolatrous priest among them. In the Psalms and the Prophets, however, Moses is frequently named as the chief of the prophets. Smith observes: "In the New Testament he is referred to partly as the representative of the law, especially in the vision of the transfiguration, where he appears side by side with Elijah. As the author of the law he is contrasted with Christ, the Author of the Gospel: 'The law was given by Moses' (John 1:17). The ambiguity and transitory nature of his glory is set against the permanence and clearness of Christianity (2 Cor. 3:13-18), and his mediatorial character against the unbroken communication of God in Christ (Gal. 3:19). His 'service' of God is contrasted with Christ's sonship (Heb. 3:5-6). 1. Moses is, as it would seem, the only character of the Old Testament to whom Christ expressly likens himself—'Moses wrote of me' (John 5:46). It suggests three main points of likeness: (*a*) Christ was, like Moses, the great prophet of the people—the last, as Moses was the first. (*b*) Christ, like Moses, is a lawgiver: 'Him shall ye hear.' (*c*) Christ, like Moses, was a prophet out of the midst of the nation—'from their brethren.' As Moses was the entire representative of his people, feeling for them more than for himself, absorbed in their interests, hopes, and fears, so, with reverence be it said, was Christ. 2. In Heb. 3:1-19; 12:24-29; Acts 7:37, Christ is described, though more obscurely, as the Moses of the new dispensation—as the Apostle, or Messenger, or Mediator of God to the people—as the Controller and Leader of the flock or household of God. 3. The details of their lives are sometimes, though not often, compared (Acts 7:24-28, 35). In Jude 9 is an allusion to an altercation between Michael and Satan over the body of Moses. It probably refers to a lost apocryphal book, mentioned by Origen, called the 'Ascension, or Assumption, of Moses' " (*Bib. Dict.*, s.v.).

BIBLIOGRAPHY: G. Rawlinson, *Moses: His Life and Times* (1887); M. G. Kyle, *Moses and the Monuments* (1912); F. B. Meyer, *Moses: The Servant of God* (1953); W. M. Taylor, *Moses: The Law Giver* (1961); J. P. Free, *Archaeology and Bible History* (1962), pp. 84-110; H. H. Rowley, *Men of God* (1963), pp. 1-36; D. M. Beegle, *Moses, the Servant of Yahweh* (1972); J. J. Davis, *Moses and the Gods of Egypt* (1971); J. Hamilton, *Moses, The Man of God* (1984).

MOSES, BOOKS OF. *See* Moses; Pentateuch.

MOSES, LAW OF. *See* Law of Moses.

MOST HIGH (Heb. *'elyôn*, "elevated"; Gk. *hupsistos*). A title ascribed to God (Pss. 18:13; 87:5; Luke 1:32, 35, 76; 6:35), indicative of His rank as Supreme Being. In Matt. 21:9; Mark 11:10; Luke 2:14; 19:38, *hupsistos* is rendered "in the highest," referring to heaven as the highest place He could be. *See also* Highest.

MOTE. *See* Speck.

MOTH.

Figurative. The moth is a figure employed to represent destructive power. Apparently an insignificant figure, it is in reality a terrible one, inasmuch as it points to a power of destruction working imperceptibly and slowly, yet effecting the destruction of the object selected with all the greater certainty (*see* Job 4:19; 27:18, marg.; Isa. 50:9; 51:8; Hos. 5:12; Matt. 6:19; etc.). *See* Animal Kingdom.

MOTHER (Heb. *'ēm;* Gk. *mētēr*).

General Use. The mother among the Israelites occupied a higher position in the family than was accorded to her by many other nations (*see* Family). When the father had more than one wife, the son appears to have confined the title "mother" to his real mother, by which he distinguished her from his father's other wives (Gen. 43:29). When precision was not required the stepmother was sometimes called mother (37:10, where Jacob speaks of Leah as Joseph's mother). The stepmother was often distinguished from one's own mother by the name of "father's wife." "Mother," like brother, father, etc., was employed in a

somewhat wider sense than is usual among us, such as grandmother (1 Kings 15:10); of any female ancestor (Gen. 3:20); of a benefactress (Judg. 5:7); of any intimate relationship (Job 17:14).

Mosaic Code. The Mosaic code had several regulations respecting treatment of parents, even animals. Thus the young animal was to be with its mother ("dam," KJV) seven days after birth before it could be sacrificed (Ex. 22:30; Lev. 22:27); a lamb was not to be seethed in its mother's milk (Ex. 23:19); a mother bird was not to be taken with her young (Deut. 22:6-7).

Figurative. As in English so in Heb., a nation was considered as a mother, and individuals as her children (Isa. 50:1; Jer. 50:12; Ezek. 19:2; Hos. 4:5). Large and important cities are called mothers (2 Sam. 20:19), such as "Babylon the great, the mother of harlots" (Rev. 17:5). A place where two ways part has the designation of "mother of the way" (Ezek. 21:21, marg.), because out of it two ways arise as daughters. In Job (1:21) the earth is represented as the common mother, to whose bosom all must return. The sentiment, at once so mild and tender, which is felt by a true mother for her child, is used to illustrate the love of God for His people (Isa. 44:1-8; 66:6-14; 1 Cor. 3:1-2; 1 Thess. 2:7).

MOTIONS OF SIN. The word *motions* in this KJV expression is from Gk. *pathēma* and refers to the passions through which the sins are brought about, of which the sins are the actual consequence. When the Gk. term refers to an external state, it signifies suffering, misfortune, and calamity and is generally translated "suffering" or "sufferings" in the KJV, NIV, and NASB.

MOULDY (Heb. *niqqūd*, "crumbled," Josh. 9:5, 12). The Heb. term refers to crumbs of bread and not to moldiness, a meaning which the NASB reading, "had become crumbled," reflects.

MOUNT. Though normally used with the sense of *mountain, hill country,* or *to ascend,* in the KJV this word sometimes has the meaning of *siegeworks* or *siege* (*see* Isa. 29:3; Jer. 6:6).

MOUNT E'PHRAIM. *See* Ephraim.

MOUNT OF ASSEMBLY. *See* Assembly, Mount of.

MOUNT OF BEATITUDES. This was the name given to the mountain mentioned in Matt. 5:1, probably the place known as the "Horns of Hattin," Kurun Hattîn, near Capernaum, and on the W of the Lake of Galilee. Hattin is the name of the village above which are the two elevations now called "the horns." Its situation is central both to the peasants of the Galilean hills and the fishermen of the Galilean lake, between which it stands, and would therefore be a natural resort both to Jesus and His disciples when they retired from the shores of the sea for solitude, and also to the crowds who assembled from Galilee, from Decapolis, from Jerusalem, from Judea, and from beyond Jordan. None of the other mountains in the neighborhood could answer as well to this description, inasmuch as they are merged into the uniform barrier of hills around the lake; whereas this stands separate, "the mountain" that alone could lay claim to a distinct name, with the exception of Tabor, which is too distant to answer the requirements. The hospice and church of the Italian Franciscan sisters now crown the traditional site adjacent to the Sea of Galilee.

MOUNT OF CORRUPTION. *See* Corruption, Mount of.

MOUNT OF THE AM'ALEKITES. *See* Hill Country of the Amalekites.

MOUNT OF THE CONGREGATION. *See* Assembly, Mount of.

MOUNT OF THE VALLEY. Better "hill of the valley" (so NASB and NIV, Josh. 13:19).

MOUNTAIN.
    Figurative. Mountain is used as symbolical of strength, stability. Thus when David says, "O Lord, by Thy favor Thou hast made my mountain to stand strong" (Ps. 30:7), he means to express the stability of his kingdom. In like manner the kingdom of the Messiah is depicted as a mountain (Isa. 2:2; Dan. 2:35), as is also the Chaldean monarchy (Jer. 51:25; Zech. 4:7). Mountains are frequently used to signify places or sources of strength (Jer. 3:23); the righteousness of God (Ps. 36:6); persons in authority (Ps. 72:3); difficulties (Isa. 40:4; Zech. 4:7; Matt. 17:20); proud and haughty persons (Isa. 2:14); a burning mountain, of destroying enemies (Jer. 51:25). A threshed mountain is used for heavy judgments (Isa. 41:15); a mountain laid waste is figurative of desolation (42:15; Mal. 1:3); singing mountains, of great joy (Isa. 44:23; 55:12), of dropping new wine, of abundance (Amos 9:13).

MOUNTAIN SHEEP. *See* Animal Kingdom.

MOURN. The rendering of quite a number of Heb. and Gk. words.
    Occasions. Mourning is frequently referred to in Scripture as an expression of grief for the dead. Thus Abraham mourns for Sarah (Gen. 23:2); Jacob for Joseph, thinking him dead (37:34-35); the Egyptians for Jacob (50:3, 10); the Israelites for Aaron (Num. 20:29), for Moses (Deut. 34:8), and for Samuel (1 Sam. 25:1); David for Abner (2 Sam. 3:31-32, 35); Mary and Martha for Lazarus (John 11:31). There is mourning on account of calamities, either endured or impending, e.g., Job under his many afflictions (Job 1:20-21; 2:11), Israel under the threatening of divine dis-

The Mount of Beatitudes

pleasure (Ex. 33:4), the Ninevites in view of threatened destruction (Jonah 3:5). There is as well mourning in repentance of sin (3:6-9), and the mourning of the Israelites on the Day of Atonement (Lev. 23:27; cf. Zech. 12:10-11).

Jews lament and mourn at the Western Wall

Modes. The modes of expressing grief were numerous and varied.

Weeping. Weeping, as the general name for the expression of mourning, was one of the chief of these. The tree under which Deborah, Rebekah's nurse, was buried was called Allon-bacuth, the "oak of weeping" (Gen. 35:8, marg.), on account of the lamentation made for her. The children of Israel wept "each man at the doorway of his tent" for flesh to eat (Num. 11:10). Tears are repeatedly referred to (Pss. 42:3; 56:8; etc.). In fact the orientals seem to have had tears at their command and could weep at pleasure.

Lamentation. Loud lamentation was another method of expressing sorrow (Ruth 1:9; 2 Sam. 3:31-34; 13:36), often with wailing and howls of grief, even amid the solemnities of worship (Joel 1:13; Mic. 1:8). The Egyptians were vociferous in their grief: "there was a great cry in Egypt" at the death of the firstborn (Ex. 12:30). Not only did the relatives of the deceased give utterance to loud cries, but hired mourners were often engaged to swell the lamentation with screams and noisy utterances (2 Chron. 35:25; Eccles. 12:5). *See* Dead, Burial of.

Personal Disfigurement. Such action was doubtless resorted to that the public might be convinced of the greatness of the mourner's grief. Among the particular forms were rending the clothes (Gen. 37:29, 34; 44:13; 2 Chron. 34:27; Isa. 36:22; Jer. 36:24; Matt. 26:65; Mark 14:63; etc.); dressing in sackcloth (Gen. 37:34; 2 Sam. 3:31; 21:10; Ps. 35:13; Isa. 37:1; Joel 1:8, 13; Amos 8:10; Job 16:15; etc.); wearing black or other somber-colored garments (2 Sam. 14:2); covering the face or head (2 Sam. 15:30; Jer. 14:4; Ezek. 24:17); sitting in or sprinkling ashes

or dust upon the person (2 Sam. 13:19; 15:32; Josh. 7:6; Esther 4:1, 3; Job 2:12; 42:6; Isa. 61:3; Jer. 6:26; Rev. 18:19); the removal of ornaments or the neglect of one's person (Ex. 33:4; Deut. 21:12-13; 2 Sam. 14:2; 19:24; Ezek. 26:16; Dan. 10:3; Matt. 6:16-17); laying bare some part of the body (Isa. 20:2, 4; 47:2; 50:6; Jer. 13:22, 26; Nah. 3:5; Mic. 1:8, 11); shaving the head, cutting the hair short, or plucking out the hair of the head or beard (2 Sam. 19:24; Ezra 9:3; Job 1:20; Jer. 7:29; 16:6); fasting (2 Sam. 1:12; 3:35; 12:16, 22; Ezra 10:6; Ezek. 24:17); diminution in offerings to God, and the prohibition against partaking of sacrificial food (Deut. 26:14; Hos. 9:4; Joel 1:9, 13, 16); sitting or lying in silence (Gen. 23:3; Judg. 20:26; 2 Sam. 12:16; Job 1:20; Ezra 9:3; Lam. 2:10); lifting up the hands (Ezra 9:5; Lam. 1:17).

Forbidden Modes. Some of the expressions of mourning that were usual among the heathen were forbidden to the Israelites: cutting the flesh (Lev. 19:28; Deut. 14:1), shaving the forehead (14:1, i.e., the eyebrows and eyelids and the forepart of the head—an idolatrous custom). Priests were not to defile themselves for the dead by any outward expression of mourning, except for near relatives (Lev. 21:1-2); and the high priest not even for these (21:10-11), under which restriction the Nazirites also came (Num. 6:7).

BIBLIOGRAPHY: R. de Vaux, *Ancient Israel: Its Life and Institutions* (1961), pp. 56-61.

MOUSE. *See* Animal Kingdom.

MOUTH (Heb. properly *peh;* Gk. *stoma*). In addition to its ordinary applications the Hebrews used the following idiomatic phrases: a mouth "smoother than butter" (Ps. 55:21), i.e., a flattering mouth; a "deceitful mouth" (109:2).

Notice the following remarkable phrases: To speak "mouth to mouth," i.e., in person, without an interpreter or third party (Num. 12:8; cf. 1 Kings 8:15; Jer. 32:4, marg.); with "one mouth," i.e., with universal consent (Josh. 9:2, marg.; cf. 1 Kings 22:13; 2 Chron. 18:12); "to put words in his mouth," i.e., to suggest what someone else shall say (Ex. 4:15; Num. 22:38; 23:5, 12; 2 Sam. 14:19). To "be in your mouth" is to be frequently spoken of (Ex. 13:9; Ps. 34:1). To "put your hand over your mouth" is to be silent (Judg. 18:19; Job 21:5; 40:4), for silence is enjoined by placing the finger upon the lip. To write "from the mouth of" anyone is to do so from his dictation (Jer. 36:4, marg., cf. vv. 27, 32; 45:1, marg.). To inquire at "the mouth of the Lord" (Josh. 9:14, marg.) is to consult with Him; while to set one's mouth "against the heavens" (Ps. 73:9) is to speak arrogantly, blasphemously against God. God's word is called "the rod of His mouth" (Isa. 11:4). The mouth is sometimes used for that which one speaks, as well as for the speaker himself (Ex. 4:16; Num. 3:16, marg.; Jer. 15:19, marg.).

MOWING (Heb. *gēz*, lit., "fleece," something cut; rendered "mown grass" in Ps. 72:6). Mowing can scarcely be said to exist in Palestine, unless we understand by it cutting with a sickle. The climate is too hot and dry to allow grain to grow sufficiently tall to need a scythe to cut it. The Heb. term refers to "grass ready for mowing."

The "king's mowing" (Amos 7:1) may refer to some royal right of early pasturage, or tyrannical exaction from the people (NIV, "king's share").

MO'ZA (mō'za; "going forth").
1. The second son of Caleb by his concubine Ephah (1 Chron. 2:46), about 1380 B.C.
2. Son of Zimri, and descendant of Saul (1 Chron. 8:36-37; 9:42-43), perhaps about 850 B.C.

MO'ZAH (mō'za). A town of Benjamin connected with Mizpeh and Chephireh (Josh. 18:26). Its location is unknown, but it may be identified with Koloniyeh almost five miles NW of Jerusalem on the Jaffa Road.

MUFFLER (Heb. *re'ālâ*, "veil"). Long fluttering veils, more expensive than ordinary ones (Isa. 3:19, "veil," NASB).

MULBERRY TREE. *See* Vegetable Kingdom.

MULE. *See* Animal Kingdom.

MUP'PIM (mup'im). A Benjamite, and one of the fourteen descendants of Rachel who belonged to the original colony of the sons of Jacob in Egypt (Gen. 46:21). In Num. 26:39 the name is written Shephupham; in 1 Chron. 7:12, 15 it is Shuppim; in 8:5 it is Shephuphan.

MURDER (Heb. *rāṣaḥ*, to "kill"). From the very beginning of human history murder has been considered one of the greatest of crimes. The principle on which the act of taking the life of a human being was regarded by the Almighty as a capital offense is stated on its highest ground as an outrage on the likeness of God in man, to be punished even when caused by an animal (Gen. 9:5-6; *see* also John 8:44; 1 John 3:12, 15). Its secondary or social ground appears to be implied in the direction God gave Noah to replenish the earth, which immediately follows His statement about the shedding of man's blood (Gen. 9:7). The postdiluvian command was limited by the law of Moses, which, while it protected accidental homicide, defined with additional strictness the crime of murder. It prohibited compensation or reprieve of the murderer, or his protection if he took refuge in the refuge city, or even at the altar of Jehovah (Ex. 21:12, 14; Lev. 24:17, 21; 1 Kings 2:5, 6, 31-34). Bloodshed, even in warfare, was held to involve pollution (Num. 35:33-34; Deut. 21:1-9; 1 Chron. 28:3). It is not certain whether a master who killed his slave was punished with death (Ex. 21:20). No punishment is mentioned for attempted suicide, nor does any special re-

striction appear to have attached to the property of the suicide (2 Sam. 20:23). Striking a pregnant woman so as to cause her death was punishable with death (Ex. 21:22-23). If an animal known to be vicious caused the death of anyone, not only was the animal destroyed, but the owner also, if he had taken no steps to restrain it, was held guilty of murder (21:29, 31). The duty of executing punishment on the murderer is in the law expressly laid on the "avenger of blood"; but the question of guilt was to be previously decided by the Levitical tribunal. In regal times the duty of execution of justice on a murderer seems to have been assumed to some extent by the sovereign, as well as the privilege of pardon (14:7-11; 1 Kings 2:31-34). It was lawful to kill a burglar taken at night in the act, but unlawful to do so after sunrise (Ex. 22:2-3).

MURRAIN. *See* Diseases.

MUSE (Heb. *śiaḥ*, to "ponder," Ps. 143:5). To meditate, reflect; pertaining to delighting, as an old man, in memories. In Luke 3:15 the KJV reading "muse" (from *dialogizomai*) is replaced in the NASB and NIV by "wondering" (NASB marg., "reasoning" or "debating").

MU'SHI (mū'shi). A son of Merari, son of Kohath (Ex. 6:19; Num. 3:20; 1 Chron. 6:19, 47; 23:21, 23; 24:26, 30). His offspring were called Mushites (Num. 3:33; 26:58).

MU'SHITES (Num. 3:33; 26:58). *See* Mushi.

MUSIC. Music was a prominent art in ancient biblical times and played a vital role both in Israel and adjacent lands.

Vocal. Hebrew music was primarily vocal. The lyre was an instrument commonly used to accompany the human voice. When singing first appears in the Bible, it is as a familiar part of merrymaking in connection with sending away guests and loved ones (Gen. 31:27). As a religious ceremony, vocal music first appears in Ex. 15:1, 20 in the antiphonal song led by Miriam in celebration of the passage through the Red Sea. Two other responsive songs are probably found in Ps. 136 and 1 Sam. 18:7. The digging of the well ("Beer") was celebrated by a song (Num. 21:17-18). Moses taught Israel some of his last warnings in a song (Deut. 32:1-4). Deborah and Barak celebrated their triumph in song (Judg. 5:1-31). David was received with song by Israel's women after his victory over Goliath (1 Sam. 18:6-7). Barzillai mentioned "singing men and women" among social pleasures (2 Sam. 19:35). Solomon was a song writer, composing 1,005 songs (1 Kings 4:32). Singing was common in ancient Israel. David's trained choir numbered 288. It continued under Solomon (2 Chron. 5:12-13; 9:11), Jehoshaphat (20:21-22), Joash (23:13, 18), Hezekiah (29:27-30), Josiah and after him (35:15, 25), Ezra (Ezra 2:41; 3:11; 7:24) and Nehemiah

(Neh. 7:44; 10:28; etc.). The "songs of Zion" were famous (cf. Ps. 137:3).

Instrumental. Instrumental music as well as vocal was common in ancient Israel. Saul was influenced by it (1 Sam. 10:5), and David's skill in playing upon the lyre had a profound effect upon Saul when he was demonized (16:23). David was not only a great warrior but a skilled musician and singer. Instrumental music certainly figured largely in Solomon's Temple (1 Chron. 25). "Male and female musicians" are specifically mentioned in the prism of Sennacherib (691 b.c.) as being part of the tribute the Judean Hezekiah had to render to Sennacherib. These musicians were certainly not mediocre to be mentioned in connection with the Assyrian court. In Elisha's day a minstrel was easily procurable (2 Kings 3:15). At the time of the Exile, the Israelites are said to have hung their harps on the trees and refused to sing the songs of Zion (Ps. 137). Instrumental music and singing were common in the postexilic period (Ezra 3:10-11; Neh. 12:27-47).

Tambourine, Timbrel, Tabret. The Heb. *tōp* is most often translated "tambourine," sometimes "timbrel." The KJV often uses the term "tabret." Some scholars think it was a drum, like a tom-tom, made "of a wooden hoop and very probably two skins, without any jingling contrivance or sticks" (see Kurt Sachs, *A History of Musical Instruments* [1940]; Sol B. Finesinger, "Musical Instruments in the O.T.," *Hebrew Union College Annual* 3 [1926]: 21-75). It was associated with

Harp

merrymaking or praise (cf. Ex. 15:20; Judg. 11:34; 1 Sam. 18:6; Ps. 68:25). This instrument played an important part from patriarchal times through the period of the restoration.

Lyre, Harp, Lute, Psaltery, Trigon, Stringed

Lyre

Instrument, Sackbut(?). The main Heb. word for this kind of instrument is *kinnôr,* which is translated "lyre" and "harp" (1 Chron. 13:8; Neh. 12:27; Isa. 23:16). By its translation in the LXX and the Vulgate, *kinnôr* may be definitely identified as a species of lyre and was called *kithara* by the Greeks and Romans.

Several archaeological illustrations give a good idea of what the Israelite lyre was. On a Beni Hasan monument to be dated around 1900 b.c., one of the Semites entering Egypt is depicted performing on a lyre. Inasmuch as lyres were unknown in ancient Egypt in Old-Kingdom monuments, they were introduced by Asiatics coming from Palestine. According to rabbinic sources, to make the lyre strings the small intestines of sheep were stretched across a sounding board over a blank space and attached to a crossbar. The performer apparently drew a plectrum across the strings with his right hand and deadened the strings with his left. Pictures on Assyrian monuments portray the lyre in similar fashion, as on the Black Obelisk of Shalmaneser III and the musicians appearing before Sennacherib at Lachish, although the players in this case seem to be drawing the index fingers over the strings instead of using a plectrum. David played with his hand before Saul (1 Sam. 16:23).

Another Heb. term often translated "harp" is *nēbel* (Pss. 33:2; 144:9; Amos 6:5). The KJV also renders this word "psaltery" and "viol"; the NIV, "lyre" or simply "musical instrument." The word normally means "a skin bottle," but in twenty-seven cases it refers to a musical instrument. The LXX and Vulg. both often translate this term "psaltery." Since the psaltery is plainly a harp, which has more and longer strings than the lyre, and since this instrument was common both in Egypt and Mesopotamia from very ancient times, the Hebrew instrument seems to be therefore correctly defined as a harp. The rabbinic tradition asserts that the harp was called *nēbel* because it was shaped like a skin bottle, the body being rounded out and covered with skin.

Qitrōs, a Heb. word of Gk. origin, is translated "lyre" (Dan. 3:5, 7, 10, 15; "harp," KJV). *'Aśôr*, a Heb. form that literally means "ten," is used together with *nēbel* (Pss. 33:2; 144:9), translated "harp of ten strings." When used alone (Ps. 92:3) it is translated "ten-stringed lute" (NASB) or "instrument of ten strings" (KJV, NIV). Sachs considers this instrument to be a zither of ten strings. Phoenicians played this instrument, but apparently it was not used in Egypt or Mesopotamia.

Pesanterîn is a transliteration from the Gk. found only in Dan. 3:5, 7, 10, 15 and translated "psaltery," a kind of harp or lyre (so NIV). In this same Daniel passage, the Aram. word *śabbekā'* is translated "trigon," probably referring to a small triangular harp of four or more strings and a high pitch. Some claim it may have been a large, many-stringed harp. In either case, it was not a "sackbut" (KJV), which was probably a wind instrument.

Minnîm is translated "stringed instruments" in its few occurrences (Pss. 45:8; 150:4) and probably refers to another form of harp, if not simply a generic term.

Trumpet, Horn, Cornet. Trumpets consisted of the horn (*qeren*) of the ram or goat. This term is used scores of times in the OT for either animal anatomy or musical instruments made from animal parts (Dan. 3:5, 7, 10, 15; "cornet," KJV) as the context dictates. Most often, "trumpet(s)" is the translation of *shôpār*, the Heb. word referring to a ram's horn wind instrument. It was used for giving of signals for war, as in the case of

Stringed instruments and tambourine ("timbrel")

Joshua, Ehud, Gideon, and Joab. It announced the year of Jubilee and also approaching danger (Jer. 4:5; Ezek. 33:3; Joel 2:1). It heralded the appearance of the new moon and full moon (Ps. 81:3).

Another type of trumpet was of metal. Moses was instructed to prepare two trumpets of silver (Num. 10:2). These were called *ḥaṣōṣerâ* (Neh. 12:35; Ps. 98:6) and were in pairs, as Moses' two trumpets and the two trumpets on the Arch of Titus, as well as on Jewish coins. Doubtless two priests blew on the trumpets simultaneously.

The Heb. word *yôbēl* is sometimes translated "horn" (Ex. 19:13) or "trumpet," but most often "jubilee," signifying the festival introduced by this trumpet's prolonged blast. *Tāqôa'* is "trumpet" (Ezek. 7:14).

Flute, Pipe, Organ. The flute referred to in Nebuchadnezzar's band (Dan. 3:5, 7, 10, 15) is from the Heb. *mashrôqî*, which was often used as a whistle. It could also refer to any of the instruments of wood that were blown. The term *'ûgāb* was probably a kind of flute that was later used to describe woodwind instruments in general. It is translated "flute" (Job 21:12) and "pipe" (Gen. 4:21; "flute," NIV); "organ" in both places by the KJV. The word *ḥālîl* ("pipe," KJV) is commonly considered to be a flute and is so translated by the NASB and the NIV (Isa. 30:29; Jer. 48:36). Sachs, however, considers it to be an oboe since at the time the instrument appears (the era of Saul) the double oboe was in common vogue. It too may have been used at times for woodwind instruments in general.

Flutes occur in prehistoric, Old Kingdom, and Middle Kingdom Egyptian drawings. It is inconceivable to think the flute was not known among the Israelites, being simply a reed indented with holes and blown. Flutes are still common in the Middle East.

Cymbals. The Heb. words for cymbals are onomatopoetic (names that imitate the instruments' sounds). The more common is *meṣiltayim* (1 Chron. 15:16, 19; Ezra 3:10; etc.). The other is *ṣelṣelîm* (2 Sam. 6:5; Ps. 150:5). Cymbals are seen on Assyrian reliefs where two types appear: one is beaten horizontally; one, vertically. This instrument occurs for the first time in the list of instruments upon which David played on the occasion of bringing up the Ark of God to Jerusalem from the house of Abinadab.

Castanets, Cornet. The Heb. term *mena'āna'* is translated "castanets" in its only occurrence (2 Sam. 6:5; "cornets," KJV; "sistrums," NIV). The word is derived from a root verb meaning *to shake*. Sachs and Finesinger are both of the opinion that this instrument was the sistrum, an instrument common in Egypt and early Babylonia. It was a rattle-type noisemaker composed of a handle with a metal loop at one end. The metal circle was perforated by holes through which wires were positioned and loosely secured by bent ends. These wires jingled when the instrument was shaken. Excavations at Bethel in 1934 yielded a sistrum containing a carving of the Egyptian goddess Hathor.

Bagpipe, Dulcimer. The Aram. word, *sûmpōnyâ,* found in the Bible only in Dan. 3:5, 7, 10, 15, is best translated "bagpipe," a wind instrument, rather than "dulcimer" (KJV), a stringed instrument.

Generic "Instruments." Shālîshîm (1 Sam. 18:6) and *keli* (2 Chron. 23:13) are both general terms simply translated "instruments of music."

It should be noted that the verses from Dan. 3, so often referred to in earlier paragraphs, list six instruments found in Babylon. In this list *qeren* (horn) and *mashrôqî* (flute) are *Semitic.* The other four are of Gk. derivation: *qîtrōs* (lyre); *śabbekā* (trigon); *pesanterîn* (psaltery). The Greek influence in Babylonian linguistics is accountable by early commercial connections between Greece and Assyria long before Daniel's time.

What sort of music scale the Hebrews used or how their music sounded is not known for certain. Authorities such as Sachs speculate that the scale was pentatonic.

BIBLIOGRAPHY: C. H. Cornill, *Music in the Old Testament* (1909); J. Stainer, *The Music of the Bible* (1914); S. B. Finesinger, *Hebrew Union College Annual* 3 (1926): 21-75; K. Sachs, *A History of Musical Instruments* (1940); P. Gradenwitz, *The Music of Israel* (1949); A. Z. Idelsohn, *Jewish Music in Its Historical Development* (1967); R. K. Harrison, *New International Dictionary of Biblical Archaeology* (1983), pp. 322-23.

MUSTARD. *See* Vegetable Kingdom.

MUTTER (Heb. *hāgâ,* Isa. 8:19). Ancient wizards ("spiritists," NASB and NIV; *see* Magic) imitated the chirping of bats, which was supposed to proceed from the shades of Hades, and uttered their magical formulas in a whispering tone.

MUZZLE (Heb. *hāsam;* Gk. *phimoō,* to "stop the mouth"). In the East grain was threshed by oxen trampling upon it; and the command was not to muzzle the ox when threshing (Deut. 25:4). This was not intended to apply merely to the ox employed in threshing, but to be understood in the general sense in which the apostle Paul used it (1 Cor. 9:9; 1 Tim. 5:18), that a laborer was not to be deprived of his wages.

MY'RA (mī'ra). One of the chief cities of Lycia in Asia Minor. It was situated about two miles from the sea, upon rising ground, at the foot of which flowed a navigable river with an excellent harbor. It was at Myra that Paul, on his voyage to Rome, was transferred from the ship that had brought him from Cilicia to the ship from Alexandria (Acts 27:5). To be seen at Myra today are fascinating rock-cut Lycian tombs, a Roman theater, a Roman bath, a Hellenistic fortress, and at the harbor area the ruins of a temple, a sixth-century church, and a granary of Hadrian. In the nearby town of Demre is the famous Church of St. Nicholas, who was martyred in 655. He is the St. Nicholas connected with Christian legend.

H.F.V.

MYRRH. *See* Vegetable Kingdom.

MYRTLE. *See* Vegetable Kingdom.

MYS'IA (mish'i-a). A province in the NW of Asia Minor, and separated from Europe only by the Propontis and Hellespont. Paul passed through this province and embarked at its chief port, Troas, on his first voyage to Europe (Acts 16:7-8).

MYSTERY (Gk. *mustērion*). The NT use of the term "mystery" has reference to some operation or plan of God hitherto unrevealed. It does not carry the idea of a secret to be withheld, but of one to be published (1 Cor. 4:1; "secret things," NIV). Paul uses the word twenty-one times. The term mystery, moreover, comprehends not only a previously hidden truth, presently divulged, but one that contains a supernatural element that still remains in spite of the revelation. The more important biblical mysteries are the following:

1. The mysteries of the kingdom of heaven (Matt. 13:3-50).

2. The mystery of the translation of the living saints at the end of the church age (1 Cor. 15:51-52; 1 Thess. 4:14, 17).

3. The mystery of the church as the Body of Christ, composed of saved Jews and Gentiles of this age (Eph. 3:1-11; 6:19; Col. 4:3).

4. The mystery of the church as the bride of Christ (Eph. 5:28-32).

5. The mystery of "Christ in you, the hope of glory" (Gal. 2:20; Col. 1:26-27).

6. "God's mystery, that is, Christ Himself" (Col. 2:2, 9; 1 Cor. 2:7). This involves Christ as the fullness of the Godhead in bodily form.

7. The mystery of lawlessness (2 Thess. 2:7; Matt. 13:33).

8. The mystery of the operation by which man is restored to godliness (1 Tim. 3:16).

9. The mystery of Israel's blindness during the gospel age (Rom. 11:25).

10. The mystery of the seven stars (Rev. 1:20).

11. The mystery of Babylon, the harlot (Rev. 17:5, 7).

BIBLIOGRAPHY: N. Turner, *Christian Words* (1980), pp. 281-87.

NA'AM

NA'AM (nā'am; "sweetness, pleasantness"). One of the sons of Caleb, the son of Jephunneh (1 Chron. 4:15), about 1375 B.C.

NA'AMAH (nā'a-ma; "sweetness, pleasantness").

1. One of the four women whose names are preserved in the records of the world before the Flood, all except Eve being Cainites. She was the daughter of Lamech and Zillah and sister of Tubal-cain (Gen. 4:22).

2. Wife of Solomon and mother of King Rehoboam (1 Kings 14:21, 31; 2 Chron. 12:13). On each occasion she is distinguished by the title "the [not "an," as in the KJV] Ammonitess." She was, therefore, one of the foreign women whom Solomon took into his establishment (1 Kings 11:1), after 960 B.C.

3. A city in the plain of Judah, mentioned between Beth-dagon and Makkedah (Josh. 15:41), not definitely located.

NA'AMAN (nā'a-man; "pleasantness").

1. One of the family of Benjamin who came down to Egypt with Jacob (as read in Gen. 46:21) or, more correctly, born in Egypt. According to the LXX version of that passage, he was the son of Bela, which is the parentage assigned to him in Num. 26:40. In the enumeration of the sons of Benjamin, he is said to be the son of Bela and head of the family of the Naamites. He is also reckoned among the sons of Bela (1 Chron. 8:3-4), after 1876 B.C.

2. "The Syrian" was commander of the armies of Ben-hadad II (Josephus *Ant.* 8.15.5), king of Damascene Syria. He is described in 2 Kings 5:1 as "a great man with his master, and highly respected, . . . a valiant warrior." He was, however, a leper; and when a captive Hebrew girl spoke of a prophet in Samaria who could cure her master of leprosy, Ben-hadad furnished him with a letter to King Joram. But when the king read the letter to the effect that Naaman had been sent to him

to be cured, he tore his clothes, suspecting that the object was a quarrel. Elisha the prophet, hearing of this, sent for Naaman, who came to his house, not being permitted as a leper to enter. Elisha sent a messenger to him saying, "Go and wash in the Jordan seven times, and your flesh shall be restored to you and you shall be clean." Naaman was indignant at the apparent incivility and would doubtless have returned to Syria without a cure but for the entreaties of his servants. He bathed in the Jordan and was cleansed of his leprosy. Returning to Elisha, he acknowledged that Jehovah was above all gods, and he declared his intention of worshiping Him alone. He asked permission to take home two mules' loads of earth, probably to set up in Damascus an altar to Jehovah. He desired to bestow valuable gifts upon Elisha, but the prophet refused to accept anything. His servant, Gehazi, coveting some of the riches proffered his master, hastened after Naaman and asked, in his master's name, for a portion. Naaman granted him more than he had asked (5:2-23), about 848 B.C.

"Naaman's appearance throughout the occurrence is most characteristic and consistent. He is every inch a soldier, ready at once to resent what he considers a slight cast either on himself or the natural glories of his country, and blazing out in a moment into sudden 'rage,' but calmed as speedily by a few good-humored and sensible words from his dependents, and after the cure has been effected evincing a thankful and simple heart, whose gratitude knows no bounds, and will listen to no refusal" (McClintock and Strong, *Cyclopedia,* s.v.).

The expression "because by him the Lord had given victory to Aram" (v. 1) seems to point to services such as were incidentally to serve the divine purposes toward Israel and may on this account have been ascribed to Jehovah.

Naaman's request to be allowed to take away

two mules' loads of earth is not easy to understand. The natural explanation is that, with a feeling akin to that which prompted the Pisan invaders to take away the earth of Aceldama for the Campo Santo at Pisa, the grateful convert to Jehovah wished to take away some of the earth of His country to form an altar. But in the narrative there is no mention of an altar.

BIBLIOGRAPHY: C. E. Macartney, *The Wisest Fool* (1949), pp. 169-79.

NA'AMATHITE (nā'a-ma-thīt). An epithet of Zophar, one of Job's friends, found only in Job 2:11; 11:1; 20:1; 42:9 and always in the phrase "Zophar the Naamathite." There are several towns from which it might have been derived, such as "Noam, a castle in the Yemen, and a place on the Euphrates; Niameh, a place belonging to the Arabs; and Noamee, a valley in Tihameh," not to mention the common Naaman. The LXX calls Zophar the Minaean and the king of the Minaeans. But of the real meaning of the term nothing is known.   W.H.

NA'AMITE (nā'a-mīt). One of the family descended from Naaman (Num. 26:40), a Benjamite. The name is a contraction seldom occurring in Heb. and is rendered "the Naamanites" by the Samaritan codex.

NA'ARAH, NA'ARATH (na'a-ra; "a girl").
1. The second named of the two wives of Ashhur of the tribe of Judah, and the mother by him of four sons (1 Chron. 4:5-6), about 1440 B.C.
2. A town named (Josh. 16:7; "Naarath," KJV) as one of the southern landmarks of Ephraim. It was in the Jordan Valley and N of Jericho. Probably the same as Naaran (1 Chron. 7:28).

NA'ARAI (na'a-rī). The son of Ezbai, and one of David's heroes (1 Chron. 11:37), about 1000 B.C. In 2 Sam. 23:35 he is called "Paarai," probably through a scribal error.

NA'ARAN (na'a-ran). A town in Ephraim, between Bethel and Jericho (1 Chron. 7:28), and possibly the same as Naarah (Josh. 16:7). It is evidently Noorath mentioned by Eusebius, five Roman miles N of Jericho, to be identified with Tel el-Jisr.

NA'ARATH. *See* Naarah.

NA'ASHON. *See* Nahshon.

NA'ASSON. *See* Nahshon.

NA'BAL (nā'bal; "foolish"). A descendant of Caleb, who lived in Maon (Tell Ma'in about 1½ miles S of Carmel of Judah and 8½ miles S of Hebron) when David, with his followers, was on the southern borders of Palestine (1 Sam. 25:2), about 1004 B.C. He was a man of great wealth, having 3,000 sheep and 1,000 goats, which he pastured in Carmel (not the promontory of that name but the present Kurmul, on the mountains of Judah). When David heard in the desert (v. 1)

that Nabal was shearing his sheep, which was generally accompanied with festivities, he sent ten young men to Nabal and instructed them to wish him peace and prosperity, to remind him of David's friendly services, and to solicit a present for himself and his people. The services alluded to were doubtless protection afforded by David and his men to Nabal's shepherds and flocks against the Bedouin Arabs. Nabal refused the petitioners in a churlish manner: "Who is David? And who is the son of Jesse? There are many servants today who are each breaking away from his master. Shall I then take my bread and my water and my meat that I have slaughtered for my shearers, and give it to men whose origin I do not know?" (vv. 10-11). Thus, in order to justify his covetousness, he set down David as a worthless vagrant. David was enraged at this reply and started with four hundred men to take vengeance upon Nabal. In the meantime one of Nabal's servants told Abigail, his intelligent and godly wife, what had taken place. As quickly as possible she took a bountiful present of provisions (v. 18) and, sending it to David, followed herself to appease his wrath. They met, and Abigail, throwing herself at David's feet, sought his forgiveness. David's anger was appeased, and in his reply he praised Jehovah for having sent Abigail to meet him and congratulated her upon her understanding and acts, which had kept him from bloodshed (vv. 32-33). He received her gifts and dismissed her with the assurance that he had granted her request (v. 35). All this had occurred without the knowledge of Nabal. When Abigail returned and found him in a drunken stupor she told him nothing until the next morning. Conscious of the danger that had threatened him, and either angry at the loss he had sustained or vexed because his wife had humbled herself in such a manner, Nabal collapsed: "his heart died within him so that he became as a stone" (v. 37). It was as if a stroke of paralysis fell upon him. He seems not to have changed in his nature by his affliction, for ten days later "the Lord struck Nabal, and he died" (v. 38). David not long after took Abigail for his wife (vv. 40-42).

BIBLIOGRAPHY: C. E. Macartney, *Ancient Wives and Modern Husbands* (1934), pp. 123-40; W. G. Blaikie, *The First Book of Samuel* (1978), pp. 378-90.

NABATAE'ANS (nab-a-tē'anz). These remarkable people were originally Arabians. Between the sixth and fourth centuries B.C. they pushed northward and seized the fortresses of Edom and Moab. Gaining control of the great caravan routes of the Middle East, they developed a remarkable civilization. They came into their greatest glory between 200 B.C. and A.D. 100. In the year A.D. 106 they were annexed to Rome as a province of Arabia. The great fortress of Petra, sixty miles S of the Dead Sea, became their capital. This remarkable rose-colored city was unknown to the West until 1812. Petra, known in the OT as Sela (Isa. 16:1), contained notable "high places," or outdoor religious sanctuaries. Petra's great high place was discovered by G. L. Robinson in 1900. The Conway High Place, found by Agnes Conway Horsefield, flourished in the first century b.c. The Nabataeans honored both sun and moon. Their chief deities were Dusares, that is, Dionysus, and the female goddess Alat. Numerous other deities are found in their pantheon. In the first century A.D., Nabataea was located S of Idumaea, reaching to the Mediterranean Sea S of Gaza. It also extended through the Arabah almost to Syrian Damascus. The Nabataean king Aretas IV (9 b.c.-a.d. 40) appointed an ethnarch of Damascus, who plotted to arrest Paul when the apostle escaped from the city by a basket let over the wall. The Nabataeans were ingenious. They built dams, reservoirs, and aqueducts at the rock city of Sela, NW of Buseirah, known in the Bible as Bozrah (Isa. 63:1).   M.F.U.

BIBLIOGRAPHY: G. L. Harding, *The Antiquities of Jordan* (1959); N. Glueck, *Deities and Dolphins* (1966); J. I. Lawlor, *The Nabataeans in Historical Perspective* (1974).

NABONI'DUS (nab-o-ni'dus). The last ruler of the Neo-Babylonian Empire (556-539 b.c.), he is called Nabunaid in the cuneiform records. His son Belshazzar, who figures prominently in Dan. 5, was associated with him legally from his third regnal year to the capture of Babylon by Cyrus the Great, founder of the Persian Empire (539 b.c.). He was the last Babylonian ruler to repair the ziggurat of the moon god Sin at Ur. One of his daughters was a devotee of the moon god temple at Ur. No Babylonian document actually affirms that Nabunaid's son Belshazzar was present at the fall of Babylon, yet there is no positive evidence against his participation in these events. Indeed, "of all known Babylonian records dealing with the situation at the close of the Neo-Babylonian Empire, the fifth chapter of Daniel ranks next to cuneiform literature in accuracy so far as outstanding events are concerned" (R. P. Doughterty, *Nabonidus and Belshazzar* [1929], p. 200). Joseph Free (*Archaeology and Bible History* [1950], p. 235) says: "The matter concerning Belshazzar, far from being an error in the Scriptures, is one of the many striking confirmations of the Word of God which have been demonstrated by archaeology."   M.F.U.

BIBLIOGRAPHY: R. P. Doughterty, *Nabonidus and Belshazzar* (1929); J. Lewy, *Hebrew Union College Annual* 19 (1946): 405-89; J. B. Pritchard, ed., *Ancient Near Eastern Texts* (1969), pp. 221, 301, 305-6, 308-16, 560-62, 566; C. J. Gadd, *Anatolian Studies* 8 (1958): 35-92.

NABOPOLAS'SAR (na-bō-po-las'ar). A Chaldean who laid the foundations of the new Babylonian Empire by revolting against Assyria in 625 b.c. He was able to start reconstruction of the city of Babylon. In 612 b.c., in alliance with Cyaxares the Mede and the Scythians he took Nineveh, the Assyrian capital (cf. Nah. 3:1-3). Nabopolassar was Nebuchadnezzar II's father, and the son succeeded to the royal power after the battle of Carchemish, when Egypt was defeated (605 b.c.).   M.F.U.

BIBLIOGRAPHY: D. J. Wiseman, *Chronicles of the Chaldaean Kings* (1956), pp. 5-21; G. Roux, *Ancient Iraq* (1964), 312-14.

NA'BOTH (nā'both; cf. Arab. *nabata,* to "sprout, grow," hence probably "a sprout"). An Israelite of Jezreel and the owner of a small portion of ground (2 Kings 9:25-26) that lay on the eastern slope of the hill of Jezreel. He also had a vineyard (1 Kings 21:1), the location of which is not certain. The royal palace of Ahab was close to the city wall at Jezreel. According to both texts, it immediately adjoined the vineyard, and it thus became an object of desire to the king, who offered either an equivalent in money or another vineyard in exchange. Naboth, in the independent spirit of a Jewish landholder, refused. "The Lord forbid me that I should give you the inheritance of my fathers." Ahab was cowed by this reply; but the proud spirit of Jezebel was roused. She took the matter into her own hands. She wrote letters in Ahab's name to the elders and nobles of Jezreel, directing them to proclaim a fast and place Naboth at the head of the services. Two men of worthless character accused him of having "cursed God and the king," and he and his children (cf. 2 Kings 9:26) were stoned to death. Jezebel then informed Ahab of the death of Naboth, whereupon he took possession of the land. The perpetration of this crime brought upon Ahab and Jezebel the severest punishment (1 Kings 21), about 853 B.C.

BIBLIOGRAPHY: F. I. Andersen, *Journal of Biblical Literature* 85 (March 1966): 46-57; T. Kirk and G. Rawlinson, *Studies in the Books of Kings,* 2 vols. in 1 (1983), 2:62-63, 73-75.

NA′CHON. See Na′con.

NA′CHOR. See Nahor.

NA′CON (nā′kon; "prepared"). A name for the threshing floor near which Uzzah was slain (2 Sam. 6:6; "Nachon," KJV). It is uncertain whether this is the name of the owner or merely an epithet applied to it, i.e., *the prepared floor.* In 1 Chron. 13:9 it is called the "threshing floor of Chidon," which is supposed by some to be another name of the owner. Eventually it was known by the name of Perez-uzzah (2 Sam. 6:8).

NA′DAB (nā′dab; "spontaneous, liberal").
1. The eldest son of Aaron and Elisheba (Ex. 6:23; Num. 3:2). He, his father and brother, and seventy old men of Israel were led out from the midst of the assembled people (Ex. 24:1) and were commanded to stay and worship God "at a distance," below the lofty summit of Sinai, where Moses alone was to come near to the Lord, c. 1439 B.C. Nadab and his brothers Abihu, Eleazar, and Ithamar were anointed, with their father, to be priests of Jehovah (28:1). He and Abihu, in offering incense, kindled it with "strange" fire, that is, fire not taken from that which burned perpetually on the altar (cf. Lev. 6:13) and for this offense were struck dead before the sanctuary by fire from the Lord (10:1-2; Num. 3:4; 26:61). On this occasion, as if to mark more decidedly the divine displeasure, Aaron and his surviving sons were forbidden to observe the usual mourning ceremonies for the dead. It seems likely from the injunction (Lev. 10:9-10) that the brothers were in a state of intoxication when they committed the offense.
2. King Jeroboam's son, who succeeded to the throne of Israel, about 909 B.C., and reigned two years (1 Kings 15:25-31). He followed the idolatrous policy of his father (cf. 15:3 and 12:30). At the siege of Gibbethon a conspiracy broke out in the midst of the army, and the king was slain by Baasha, a man of Issachar.
3. A son of Shammai (1 Chron. 2:28), of the tribe of Judah, and father of two sons (v. 30).
4. A son of Jeiel, the "father" (founder) of Gibeon (1 Chron. 8:29-30; 9:35-36), of the tribe of Benjamin.

NAG′GAI (nag′ī). An ancestor of Jesus in the maternal line, the son of Maath and father of Hesli (Luke 3:25; "Nag′ge," KJV).

NAG′GE. See Naggai.

NA′HALAL (na′ha-lal; "pasture"). A city in Zebulun on the border of Issachar (Josh. 19:15; "Nahallal," KJV), but inhabited by Canaanites tributary to Israel (Judg. 1:30; "Nahalol," KJV). It was given, with its pasture lands, to the Merari family of Levites (Josh. 21:35). It is evidently modern Tel en-Nahl, S of Acre.

NAHA′LIEL (na-hā′li-el; "wadi" or "torrent, valley of God"). One of the encampments of Israel when in the wilderness (Num. 21:19), between Mattanah and Bamoth. It was near Pisgah, north of Arnon. Its exact location is conjectural.

NAHALLAL. See Na′halal.

NA′HALOL (nā′ha-lol). Another form (Judg. 1:30) of *Nahalal* (which see).

NA′HAM (nā′ham; "solace, consolation"). A brother of the wife of Hodiah; Hodiah's sons were Keila the Garmite and Eshtemoa the Maacathite (1 Chron. 4:19, NASB). Both the KJV and NASB readings at this point are difficult; but the NASB and NIV, which indicate that Hodiah is a man, are probably the more accurate.

NAHAMA′NI (na-ha-ma′ni; "compassionate"). A leading man among those who returned from Babylon with Zerubbabel (Neh. 7:7), about 445 B.C.

NA′HARAI (nā′ha-rī; "snorting"). The Beerothite, one of David's mighty men and the armor bearer of Joab (1 Chron. 11:39; 2 Sam. 23:37), about 975 B.C.

NA′HASH (nā′hash; "serpent").
1. "Nahash the Ammonite," king of Ammon at the foundation of the monarchy in Israel, c. 1020 B.C. He was directing an assault against Jabesh-gilead, and when the inhabitants asked him to make a treaty with them he dictated the cruel alternative of the loss of their right eyes or slavery, arousing the swift wrath of Saul and causing the destruction of the Ammonite force (1 Sam. 11:1-11). He is probably the same as Nahash the father of Hanun, who had rendered David some special and valuable service, which David was anxious for an opportunity of requiting (2 Sam. 10:2).
2. A person mentioned only once (2 Sam. 17:25), in stating the parentage of Amasa, the commander in chief of Absalom's army. Amasa is there said to have been the son of a certain Ithra by Abigail "the daughter of Nahash, sister to Zeruiah." By the genealogy of 1 Chron. 2:16 it appears that Zeruiah and Abigail were sisters of David and the other children of Jesse. The question then arises, How could Abigail have been at the same time daughter of Nahash and sister to the children of Jesse? To this three answers may be given: (a) The universal tradition of the rabbis, that Nahash and Jesse were identical. (b) The

explanation first put forth by Stanley, that Nahash was the king of the Ammonites and that the same woman had first been his wife or concubine—in which capacity she had given birth to Abigail and Zeruiah—and afterward wife to Jesse and the mother of his children. (c) A third possible explanation is that Nahash was the name not of Jesse, nor of a former husband of his wife, but of his wife herself (Smith, *Bib. Dict.,* s.v.).

NA'HATH (nā'hath; "rest, quiet").

1. One of the chiefs in the land of Edom, eldest son of Reuel, the son of Esau (Gen. 36:13, 17; 1 Chron. 1:37).

2. A Kohathite Levite, son of Zophai (1 Chron. 6:26). He is the same as Toah (v. 34) and Tohu (1 Sam. 1:1) and was an ancestor of Samuel.

3. A Levite in the reign of Hezekiah and an overseer of the sacred offerings in the Temple (2 Chron. 31:13).

NAH'BI (na'bi; "concealed, hidden"). The son of Vophsi, a Naphtalite; he was one of the twelve spies (Num. 13:14), c. 1441 B.C.

NA'HOR (nā'hor; "snorting, snoring"; sometimes "Na'chor," KJV).

1. The son of Serug, father of Terah, and Abraham's grandfather (Gen. 11:22-24; Luke 3:34-35). He lived 148 years, before 2200 B.C.

2. Grandson of the preceding, a son of Terah and brother of Abraham (Gen. 11:26; Josh. 24:2), about 2200 B.C. He married Milcah, his brother Haran's daughter, by whom he had eight children (Gen. 11:29; 22:20-23), and had as concubine Reumah, who bore him four children (v. 24). When Abraham and Lot migrated to Canaan Nahor remained in Haran, where his descendants were certainly living two generations later (24:10; 29:5). It was to the family descended from Nahor and Milcah that Abraham and Rebekah in turn had recourse for wives for their sons. The city of Nahor (24:10) is frequently mentioned in the Mari Letters of the eighteenth century B.C., when it was ruled by an Amorite prince. It also is named in the Middle Assyrian documents. It was situated below Haran in the Balikh Valley of Upper Mesopotamia.

NAH'SHON (nā'shon). The son of Amminadab and leader of Judah when first numbered in the desert (Ex. 6:23, "Naashon," KJV; Num. 1:7; 1 Chron. 2:10-11), 1439 B.C. His sister Elisheba was wife to Aaron (Ex. 6:23), and his son Salmon married Rahab after the taking of Jericho (Matt. 1:4-5, "Naashon," KJV). In the encampment (Num. 2:3), in the offering of the princes (7:12, 17), and in the order of the march (10-14), the first place is assigned to him as captain of Judah's host. We have no further particulars of his life, but we know that he died in the wilderness (26:64-65). His name occurs in Matt. 1:4; Luke 3:32 (in both references, "Naasson,"KJV), in the genealogy of Christ, where his lineage is evidently copied from Ruth 4:18-20; 1 Chron. 2:10-12.

NA'HUM (nā'hum; "compassionate").

1. The seventh of the minor prophets. Of himself little is known. The book is titled simply "The book of the vision of Nahum the Elkoshite" (1:1). The site of the village is disputed. According to Jerome, it was in Galilee, and only insignificant ruins remained in his day. Toward the end of the sixteenth century the idea arose that Nahum was born at Alkosh, a town near Mosul, where a modern tomb is also pointed out as the place of his burial.

2. The son of Hesli and father of Amos, in the maternal ancestry of Christ (Luke 3:25; "Naum," KJV). He is probably the same as Johanan, the son of Elioenai (1 Chron. 3:24).

NAHUM, BOOK OF. One of the books of the minor prophets. Nahum was an accomplished poet who devoted his great talent to a moving description of the destruction of Nineveh, the mighty capital of the Assyrian Empire. He foresees in this a manifestation of God's punitive justice. The book stands seventh in the order of the minor prophets. Nahum's prophetic ministry occurred between the conquest of No-Amon (Thebes) in Egypt (3:8), regarded as a past event, one that occurred in 661 B.C. under Ashurbanipal, and the destruction of Nineveh in 612 B.C. The prophet confines himself to one theme, the destruction of Nineveh, "the bloody city" (3:1).

Outline.

I. An ode to God's majesty (1:1–2:2)
  A. Superscription (1:1)
  B. God's vengeance (1:2-11)
  C. Judah's restoration (1:12–2:2)
II. An ode on Nineveh's destruction (2:3–3:19)
  A. The prophecy of Nineveh's fall (2:3-13)
  B. The cause of Nineveh's fall (3:1-19)

Subject. Nahum's preview of Nineveh's destruction (chaps. 2-3) foresees the crash of the Assyrian Empire. In 612 B.C. Cyaxares the Mede in league with Nabopolassar of Babylon commenced the siege. The terrifying aspect of Nineveh's fall is depicted as a just recompense of the powerful and cruel city. Nahum was a seventh-century prophet who lived at the same time as Zephaniah, Habakkuk, and Jeremiah. In the destruction of Nineveh, Nahum sees the punishment of the horrible cruelty of the Assyrian world power.

Authorship. Since the latter part of the nineteenth century critics have customarily denied 1:2–2:2 in substance to Nahum. Nahum 1:2-10 is regarded as the remnant of a postexilic acrostic poem that was later prefixed to Nahum's prophetic oracle concerning Nineveh. Robert Pfeiffer considers chaps. 2:3–3:19 to be Nahum's triumphal ode and the intervening material (1:11–2:22) has in part a redactional and in part an original section of the poem. The redactional portion was allegedly inserted about 300 B.C. In characteristic negative fashion, Pfeiffer denies the prophetic character of the book and avers that Nahum's poem on the fall of Nineveh was erroneously viewed as a prophecy and preserved as a result of this misapprehension. An example of critical subjectivity, Pfeiffer's view is to be rejected. If the introductory song was considered written by a redactor, why could it not have been originally written by Nahum? The acrostic idea is based on violent emendations and upon the assumption that the redactor wrote it from a faulty memory. If the acrostic arrangement could be proved, the question still remains, Why refuse to attribute it to Nahum?

BIBLIOGRAPHY: P. Haupt, *Journal of Biblical Literature* 26 (1907): 1-53, 151-64; A. Haldar, *Studies in the Book of Nahum* (1947); W. A. Meier, *The Book of Nahum* (1959); R. K. Harrison, *Introduction to the Old Testament* (1969), pp. 926-30; F. E. Gaebelein, ed., *Expositor's Bible Commentary* (1985), 7: 449-89.

NAIL. The translation of a number of words in the original languages; the English term is used in several ways.

1. An ordinary peg, or a tent peg (Heb. *yātēd*). Nail appears in this sense only in the KJV; it is replaced in the NASB and NIV by *peg* (which see).

2. Ordinary and ornamental nails (Heb. *masmēr*). Those mentioned in 1 Chron. 22:3 and 2 Chron. 3:9 were partly for pivots upon which the folding doors turned, partly in the construction of the doors. Those used for fastening the gold plates upon the planks were also probably of gold.

Figurative. In the proverb "The words of wise tions are like goads, and masters of these collections are like well-driven nails" (Eccles. 12:11), we are taught that truth sinks deeply into the mind as a nail well pointed does when driven into the wall. In a collection of 206 Oriental proverbs, made by Lydia Einsler and published in the *Journal of the German Palestine Society* 19, no. 2, is the following, " 'She now has a house and nail in the wall,' referring to a woman who was of a low station socially but had attained a higher. It was often used of a poor girl who had made a good marriage. The nail in the wall is typical of something firm and strong, able to support heavy burdens."

Nails are mentioned in the accounts of the crucifixion (John 20:25; Col. 2:14).

3. Nail of the finger (Heb. *sipporēn;* Deut. 21:12). Like cutting the hair, the paring of the nails—both signs of purification—was a symbol of a slave woman passing out of slavery and being received into fellowship with the covenant nation.

In Jeremiah 17:1, "stylus" ("tool," NIV) is the rendering of the same Heb. term and means the "point" of a stylus or metal pin.

4. Claws of a bird or beast. In Dan. 4:33 Nebu-chadnezzar's nails (Aram. *ṭepar*) are said to have grown like the claws of a bird; the *nails* (KJV), or *claws* (NASB), of the fourth beast are mentioned in 7:19. This use of *claws* is distinct from Heb. *parsâ*, "hoof," NASB; but variously "claws" or "hoof," KJV (e.g., Deut. 14:6, where *parsâ* is both "claws" and "hoof"). *See* Claws; Hoof.

NA'IN (nā'in; "pleasantness, beauty"). The city at the gate of which Jesus raised the widow's son to life (Luke 7:11-15). Robinson found a hamlet named Neïn, six miles SW of Nazareth, standing on a bleak, rocky slope of the northern descending slope of Jebel ed-Duhy (the "hill of Moreh" of Scripture) in the Valley of Jezreel. In this locality Eusebius and Jerome place the city of Nain.

The village of Nain

NA'IOTH (nā'oth; "dwellings"). Or, more fully, "Naioth in Ramah," the place in which Samuel and David took refuge after the latter's escape from Saul (1 Sam. 19:18). Saul followed them there after having sent three companies of men to take David. When he came to Secu, near Ramah, the Spirit of the Lord came upon him, so that he went along prophesying until he came to Naioth; there he took off his clothes and prophesied before Samuel, lying upon the ground all day and night (vv. 20-24). Keil and Delitzsch (*Com.*) believe Naioth to be a proper name applied to the common dwelling of the pupils of the prophets, who had assembled around Samuel in the neighborhood of Ramah.

NAKED (Heb. *'erwâ*, "nudity"; Gk. *gumnos*). Absolute nakedness (Job 1:21; Eccles. 5:15; Amos 2:16; Mic. 1:8), but elsewhere in the sense of ragged, poorly clad (Isa. 58:7; Matt. 25:36). In John 21:7 the meaning is "clad in the undergarment only" (the outer garment being cast aside).

Figurative. "Naked" is used figuratively to signify *stripped* of *resources, disarmed;* thus "I have stripped Esau bare" (Jer. 49:10) signifies the destruction of Edom. The "nakedness of a land" (Gen. 42:9, KJV) signifies the weak and ruined parts of it where the country lies most open and exposed to danger. "Naked" is also used for discovered, made manifest (Job 26:6; cf. Heb. 4:13).

In Ezek. 16:36-39 nakedness symbolizes the stripping from one of his righteousness through idolatry.

NAMES (Heb. *shēm;* Gk. *onoma*). Names are designed to distinguish objects and originally expressed the distinct impressions that objects made upon one or the special relations in which they stood to the person. Thus God brought the beasts to Adam, and from the impression they made upon him he assigned names to them (Gen. 2:19). Some names were given prophetically, such as the name of Jesus, the Savior (Matt. 1:21). Often the name of a natural object was given to a child, such as Jonah (dove), Tamar (palm tree), and Tabitha (gazelle). Sometimes a name preserved the memory of a national event, such as Ichabod (1 Sam. 4:21). From a comparison of the roots of many names with the same roots in the cognate dialects it is evident Heb. was in early days much more closely allied to Arab. than when it became a literary tongue. Much use might be made of the study of Heb. proper names for the better understanding of the history of that people.

Play On. The Israelites were fond of playing on names. The name to them was a *sign* of something quite outward. Hence names rarely became hereditary in Heb.; they still retained their significance, being proper personal names, seldom passing into the unmeaning surname. They generally expressed some personal characteristic, some incident connected with the birth, some hope or wish or prayer of the parent; and henceforth the child embodied it, and for the parents' sake felt it like a personal vow and made his life an effort to realize it. This tendency to play on names and find analogies or contrasts in them is seen throughout the Bible (*see* Ruth 1:20; 1 Sam. 25:3, 25). So we have "Dan [*judge*] shall judge his people" (Gen. 49:16) and many other instances.

Personal Names. These may be divided into two classes: those given at birth and those imposed in later life.

Those given at birth. At such times the slightest event was considered to be of importance—a chance word, a sly intimation by the gossip at the bedside, a pious or hopeful ejaculation by the mother; and, where names were sought for, any well-omened word was hastily seized and attached to the newcomer. Sometimes the name would express the *time* of birth, e.g., Shaharaim (the "dawn"), Hodesh (the "new moon"); sometimes the *place,* as Zerubbabel ("born in Babylon"). The condition of the mother is often indicated; thus Rachel dying in childbirth named her son Ben-oni ("son of my pain"), whereas Leah ("exhausted") and Mahli ("sick") are names that hint of much weakness, if not death. Sometimes the name indicates a peculiarity of the child, such as Esau ("hairy"), Edom ("red"), Korah ("bald").

Or the feeling of the parent found expression —Eve called her firstborn Cain ("acquisition"), but she came to know that a mother's feelings are made up more of sadness than of joy, and she called her second son Abel ("vanity"). The strong affection of Hebrew women for their children is sometimes shown in the names they gave them, e.g., Adah ("ornament"), Peninnah ("pearl"), Rachel ("dove"), Susanna ("lilies"), etc. Religious names were frequently given, the most simple being expressive of thanks to God for the gift of a child, such as Mahalalel ("praise to God"), and of wonder at God's liberality, such as Zabdiel ("bountifully given") and Zechariah ("God has remembered"). A name may express some great longing of the parent. Rachel named her first son Joseph ("adding," i.e., may God add to me another child). A name may also express resignation and trust, such as Elioenai ("toward Jehovah are my eyes"). The name was generally given by the parents, but sometimes a number of their kinsmen and friends would agree in bestowing one (Ruth 4:17; Luke 1:59).

Change of name. Often the name given at birth was changed for a new one, or a new one was added to the original name and gradually took its place. Thus Abram's name was changed to *Abraham* (which see) when he renewed his covenant with Jehovah (Gen. 17:5); Jacob (the "supplanter") became Israel ("prince") after his successful struggle with the angel (32:28). Princes often changed their names on their accession to the throne (2 Kings 23:34; 24:17). This was also done in the case of private persons on entering upon public duties of importance (Num. 13:16; cf. John 1:42; Acts 4:36). So the prophet Nathan, on assuming the charge of Solomon's education, gave him the name *Jedidiah* (2 Sam. 12:25). Children frequently received names expressive of relationship such as Abimelech ("father of the king"), or one of the several divine names is coupled in the same manner with another element, such as Nathanael, with the divine name *El,* or Jonathan, with the divine name *Jehovah* (contracted *Jo*) and the verb *gave.* The word *El* enters early in the composition of names, whereas those compounded with the name *Jehovah* do not appear until the Mosaic era; and not until the time of Samuel are names compounded with this name of God common.

Figurative. The *name* in Heb. is sometimes used to signify the collected attributes or characteristics of the object named. This is particularly the case with the divine name (Ex. 34:5-6). Our Lord says, "I manifested Thy *name,*" etc. (John 17:6), where *name* embraces the whole divine nature revealed by the Son. The expression "name of God" indicates the entire administration of God by which He reveals Himself and His attributes to men; the glory and power of God displayed in nature (Ps. 8:1); God's revelation of Himself to His people (Zech. 10:12); and when

God announces His mighty presence it is said, "Thy name is near"(Ps. 75:1). In the NT the name of Christ refers to all that Jesus is to men (Luke 24:47; Acts 9:15); to "believe in His name" (John 1:12), "there is no other name under heaven . . . by which we must be saved" (Acts 4:12), "life in His name" (John 20:31) all refer to the saving and life-giving power in Christ, which is communicated to the believer. The expression "let everyone who names the name of the Lord" (2 Tim. 2:19) means everyone who acknowledges Him to be what His name means, *the Lord.*

BIBLIOGRAPHY: J. Pedersen, *Israel, Its Life and Culture* (1940), 1-2: 245-59; A. F. Key, *Journal of Biblical Literature* 83 (1964): 55-59; J. Barr, *Bulletin of the John Rylands Library* 52 (1969-70): 11-29; R. de Vaux, *Proclamation and Presence,* ed. J. I. Durham and J. R. Porter (1970), pp. 44, 48-75.

NAO′MI (nā-ō′mi; "my pleasantness, delight"). A woman of Bethlehem, in the days of the judges, whose history is interwoven with that of her daughter-in-law Ruth (Ruth 1-4), about 1322-1312 B.C. Her husband's name was Elimelech, and her two sons were Mahlon and Chilion. With them, because of a famine in her own country, she went to Moab, where they died. Returning to her native land, she was accompanied by Ruth, who became the wife of Boaz. Upon her return she replied to those asking her, "Is this Naomi?" "Do not call me Naomi; call me Mara, for the Almighty has dealt very bitterly with me" (1:19-20).

BIBLIOGRAPHY: C. E. Macartney, *The Woman of Tekoah* (1955), pp. 102-11; C. J. Barber, *Ruth: An Expositional Commentary* (1983), pp. 39-60, 95-98, 110, 112, 127-34.

NA′PHISH (nā′fish). The eleventh son of Ishmael (Gen. 25:15; 1 Chron. 1:31). The tribe descended from Nodab was subdued by the Reubenites, the Gadites, and the half tribe of Manasseh, when "they made war against the Hagrites, Jetur, Naphish, and Nodab" (1 Chron. 5:19). The tribe is not found again in the sacred records, nor is it mentioned by later writers. It has not been identified.

NA′PHOTH (na′fōth). A town assigned to the tribe of Manasseh but located in the territory of Asher (Josh. 17:11). Called elsewhere Naphoth Dor (Josh. 11:2; 12:23; 1 Kings 4:11) because of its association with the coastal city or plain of *Dor* (which see).

NAPH′TALI (naf′ta-lī; "my wrestling").

The sixth son of Jacob. Naphtali was the second son of Bilhah, Rachel's maid, and brother to Dan. Of the personal history of Naphtali we know nothing, as up to the time of Jacob's blessing the twelve patriarchs his name is mentioned only in the two public lists (Gen. 35:25; 46:24).

The Tribe of Naphtali.

Numbers. When Israel went down into Egypt

Naphtali had four sons (Gen. 46:24; 1 Chron. 7:13). While in Egypt Naphtali increased with wonderful rapidity, numbering at the first census 53,400 (Num. 1:43), ranking *sixth.* The number decreased during the wilderness journey, for at the second census the adult males amounted to only 45,400, ranking *eighth* (26:50).

Position. During the march through the wilderness Naphtali occupied a position on the N of the sacred tent with Dan and Asher (2:25-31).

Territory. In the apportionment of the land the lot of Naphtali was not drawn till the last one. Their portion lay at the northern angle of Palestine and was inclosed on three sides by that of other tribes —Zebulun (S), Asher (W), trans-Jordanic Manasseh (E).

Subsequent history. Naphtali had its share in the incursions and molestations by the surrounding pagans. One of these, apparently the severest struggle of all, fell with special violence on the N of the country, and the leader by whom the invasion was repelled—Barak, of Kedesh-naphtali —was the one great hero whom Naphtali is recorded to have produced (Judg. 4:6). Naphtali was also the first tribe captured by the Assyrians under Tiglath-pileser (2 Kings 15:29). But though the history of the tribe ends here, yet under the title of Galilee the district that they formerly occupied became in every way far more important than it had ever been before.

NAPHTALI, HILL COUNTRY OF. The mountainous district that formed the main part of the territory of Naphtali (Josh. 20:7), similar to that of Ephraim and Judah.

BIBLIOGRAPHY: Y. Aharoni, *The Settlement of the Israelite Tribes in Upper Galilee* (1947).

NAPH′TUHIM (naf′tū-him). A Mizraite nation or tribe, mentioned only as descendants of Noah (Gen. 10:13; 1 Chron. 1:11), and who probably settled at first, or when Gen. 5 was written, either in Egypt or immediately W of it.

NAPH′TUHITES. *See* Naphtuhim.

NAPKIN. *See* Handkerchief.

NARCIS′SUS (nar-sis′us; a well-known flower). A person at Rome to some of whose household (or friends) Paul sent salutation (Rom. 16:11). He cannot be the celebrated favorite of the Emperor Claudius, as that person was put to death before the epistle was written.

NARD. *See* Vegetable Kingdom.

NA′THAN (nā′than; "He, i.e., God, has given").

1. A son of David; one of the four who were born to him by Bath-Shua (Bathsheba; 1 Chron. 3:5; cf. 14:4 and 2 Sam. 5:14), about 987 B.C. Nathan appears to have taken no part in the events of his father's or his brother's reigns. To him are to be referred, probably, the words of Zech. 12:12. He appears as one of the forefathers

of Mary in the genealogy of Luke (Luke 3:31).

2. The Hebrew prophet who lived in the reigns of David and Solomon. The first mention of him is in a consultation with David, in which he advises him to build the Temple (2 Sam. 7:2-3); but after a vision he informed David that he was not to carry out his intention (vv. 4-17), about 984 B.C.

About a year after David's sin with Bathsheba and the death of Uriah, Nathan comes forth to reprove him. The reason for this delay seems to be set forth by David in Ps. 32, where he describes the state of his heart during this period and the sufferings he endured while trying to conceal his crime. To insure success Nathan resorted to a parable of a rich man taking from a poor man his "one little ewe lamb." The parable was selected so that David could not suspect that it had reference to him and his sin. With all the greater shock, therefore, did the prophet's words "You are the man" come to the king (2 Sam. 12:1-15), about 977 B.C. At the birth of Solomon, Nathan came to David, according to Jehovah's instructions, and named the child Jedidiah, because "the Lord loved him" (vv. 24-25).

In the last years of David, Nathan, with Bathsheba, secured the succession of Solomon (1 Kings 1:11-30), and at the king's request assisted at his inauguration (vv. 32-38, 45), about 960 B.C. He assisted David by his advice when he reorganized the public worship (2 Chron. 29:25). His son Zabud succeeded him as the "king's friend," and another son, Azariah, was "over the deputies" in Solomon's time (1 Kings 4:5). He left two works behind him—the Acts of David (1 Chron. 29:29) and the Acts of Solomon (2 Chron. 9:29). The last of these may have been incomplete, as we cannot be sure that he outlived Solomon. His grave is shown at Halhul, near Hebron.

3. An inhabitant of Zobah in Syria, and the father of Igal, one of David's mighty men (2 Sam. 23:36), about 984 B.C. In 1 Chron. 11:38 it is given as Joel, the brother of Nathan.

4. A descendant of Judah, being the son of Attai and father of Zabad (1 Chron. 2:36).

5. One of the leading Jews who were sent by Ezra from his encampment at the river Ahava to the Jews' colony at Casiphia, to obtain "ministers . . . for the house of our God" (Ezra 8:15-17), about 457 B.C. He is perhaps the same as the Nathan who put away his Gentile wife (10:39).

BIBLIOGRAPHY: C. E. Macartney, *The Woman of Tekoah* (1955), pp. 133-47; W. G. Blaikie, *David, King of Israel* (1981), pp. 229-39.

NATHAN'AEL (na-than'ā-el; Gk. from Heb. "God has given"). A disciple of our Lord, of whose life we have no particulars save the references in John's gospel. It appears that after Jesus was proclaimed by John the Baptist to be the Lamb of God, He went to Galilee. Having called Philip

to follow him, the latter hastened to Nathanael to inform him that the Messiah had appeared. Nathanael expressed his distrust that any good could come from so small and insignificant a place as Nazareth. He accompanied Philip, however, and upon his approach was saluted by Jesus as "an Israelite indeed, in whom is no guile." This elicited the inquiry from Nathanael as to how he had become known to Jesus. The answer, "Before Philip called you, when you were under the fig tree, I saw you," satisfied him that Jesus was more than man, and "Nathanael answered Him, 'Rabbi, You are the Son of God; You are the King of Israel'" (John 1:43-51), A.D. 25. We meet with the name of Nathanael only once more, and then simply as one of a small company of disciples at the Sea of Tiberias to whom Jesus showed Himself after His resurrection (21:2). From this reference we learn that Nathanael was a native of Cana of Galilee. "It is very commonly believed that Nathanael and Bartholomew are the same person. The evidence for that belief is as follows: John, who twice mentions Nathanael, never introduces the name of Bartholomew at all. Matthew (10:3), Mark (3:18), and Luke (6:14) all speak of Bartholomew, but never of Nathanael. It may be, however, that Nathanael was the proper name and Bartholomew (son of Tholmai) the surname of the same disciple, just as Simon was called Bar-jona, and Joses, Barnabas. It was Philip who first brought Nathanael to Jesus, just as Andrew had brought his brother Simon; and Bartholomew is named by each of the first three evangelists immediately after Philip, while by Luke he is coupled with Philip precisely in the same way as Simon with his brother Andrew, and James with his brother John" (Smith, *Bib. Dict.,* s.v.).

BIBLIOGRAPHY: W. Barclay, *The Master's Men* (1960), pp. 111-16; C. J. Barber, *God Has the Answer . . .* (1974), pp. 51-60; J. D. Jones, *The Apostles of Christ* (1982), pp. 130-49.

NA'THAN-MEL'ECH (nā'than-mel'ek; "given of the king"). An official (i.e., eunuch) from before whose chamber at the Temple entrance King Josiah removed the horses dedicated to the sun by the king of Judah (2 Kings 23:11), 624 B.C.

NATIVITY OF CHRIST. See Christmas; Jesus.

NATURAL. The rendering of two Gk. words:

1. *Phusikos* ("produced by nature"), thus "the natural function" (Rom. 1:26-27) means that which is aggreeable to nature. "Natural branches" (11:21, 24) are those growing naturally as opposed to ingrafted branches.

2. *Psuchikos* ("having the nature and characteristics of the principle of animal life") that which men have in common with animals; thus the "natural body" (1 Cor. 15:44, 46), and equivalent to "flesh and blood" (v. 50). In the expression the "natural man does not accept the things of

the Spirit" (2:14), the meaning refers to the unregenerate man governed by his sensuous nature with its subjection to appetite and passion.

NATURAL HISTORY. In dealing with the natural history of the Bible we should be governed by principles similar to those that we use in determining the allusions to nature in other ancient and most modern books. Nothing like a scientific classification of animals and plants can be detected in the Bible any more than in Homer or Horace or Shakespeare or Wordsworth. Natural objects are grouped with reference to their more obvious characteristics. Thus plants are divided into trees and herbs. Yet even in speaking of the knowledge of the vegetable kingdom that Solomon possessed, it is said that "he spoke of trees, from the cedar that is in Lebanon even to the hyssop that grows on the wall" (1 Kings 4:33). All plants are here characterized as trees. Solomon seems to have divided the animal kingdom into four classes, corresponding to the modern classes of the vertebrates—"he spoke also of animals and birds and creeping things and fish" (4:33). The last class doubtless includes most or all of the aquatic creatures not included in the modern class of fish, while "creeping things" includes reptiles and amphibians. It is plain that in this classification of Solomon no notice is taken of insects, coelenterata, etc. Worms were probably included among "creeping things." Moses seems to have recognized a somewhat similar division. In the ceremonial law a classification into clean and unclean was based on the correlation of certain organs and functions, such as cleft hoofs and rumination, and in the case of aquatic creatures the presence or absence of fins and scales. According to this, water mollusks, coelenterata, and scaleless fish were in one class and other fish in a second.   G.E.P.

NATURE.

1. (Gk. *genesis;* elsewhere, as Rom. 11:24; 1 Cor. 11:14, *phusis,* "genus"). The following are the uses of these terms: (a) the law of the natural or moral world (Rom. 11:24); (b) birth, origin, natural descent, e.g., "Jews by nature" or (NIV) "birth" (Gal. 2:15), "which by nature are no gods" (4:8); (c) *genus,* "kind": "for every species (marg. "nature") of beasts," etc. (James 3:7).

2. (Gk. *homoiopathēs*), used in the expressions "men of the same nature as you" (Acts 14:15; "human like you," NIV) and "a man with a nature like ours" (James 5:17; "a man just like us," NIV) and meaning "suffering like" another, "of like feelings or affections."

NAUGHTINESS. A KJV term appearing in 1 Sam. 17:28 (Heb. *rôa',* "badness"), Prov. 11:6 (Heb. *hawwâ,* "calamity," "wickedness," "evil desire"), and James 1:21 (Gk. *kakia,* "malice," "ill will," "vicious disposition"). The NASB and NIV translations are "wickedness" or "wicked" or

"evil" (1 Sam. 17:28; James 1:21) and "greed" or "evil desires" (Prov. 11:6).

NA'UM. *See* Nahum.

NAVE (Heb. *gab,* "hollow" or "curved"). Sometimes defined as the hub of a wheel, the central part into which the spokes are inserted. The NASB and NIV, however, render the word as the *rim* of a wheel (1 Kings 7:33). Cf. Hub; Spoke; Rims.

Church of the Annunciation, Nazareth

NAVEL (Heb. *shōr,* "twisted," as a string). The umbilical connection of the fetus with the mother (Ezek. 16:4), hence the abdomen where it is attached (Song of Sol. 7:2).

NAVY. *See* Fleet.

NAZ'ARENE (naz'a-rēn). An inhabitant or native of Nazareth, as Matt. 21:11; etc., and rendered "from Nazareth." The term *Nazarene* (Gk. *Nazōraios*) occurs in Matt. 2:23; Mark 14:67; 16:6; Luke 24:19; Acts 2:22; 24:5; etc., and should have been rendered *Nazoraean* in English. At first it was applied to Jesus naturally and properly, as defining His residence. In the process of time its population became mixed with other peoples, its dialect rough, provincial, and strange, and its people seditious, so that they were held in little consideration. "The name of Nazareth was but another word for *despised one.* Hence, although no prophet has ever said anything of the word Nazarene, yet all those prophecies describing the Messiah as a *despised one* are fulfilled in His being a *Nazarene.* But we are convinced that something more than this is intended. The Heb. word for Nazareth was Netzer, a *branch,* or rather *germ.* . . . Nazareth is called a germ from its insignificance, yet it shall through Him, fill the earth with its importance" (Whedon, *Com.,* ad loc.). The Christians were called "Nazarenes" (Acts 24:5), a contemptuous appellation, as the followers of Jesus, whose presumed descent from Nazareth stamped Him as a false Messiah.

BIBLIOGRAPHY: W. O. E. Oesterley, *Expository Times* 52 (1940-41): 410-12; W. F. Albright, *Journal of Biblical Literature* 65 (1946): 397-99; M. Black, *An Aramaic Approach to the Gospels and Acts* (1946), pp. 143-46; P. Winter, *New Testament Studies* 3 (1957): 138, n. 1.

NAZ'ARETH (naz'a-reth). The home of Joseph and Mary.

Location. Nazareth is situated on the most southern of the ranges of lower Galilee, about ten miles from the plain of Esdraelon. "You cannot see from Nazareth the surrounding country, for Nazareth lies in a basin; but the moment you climb to the edge of this basin . . . what a view you have. Esdraelon lies before you, with its twenty battlefields—the scenes of Barak's and of Gideon's victories, of Saul's and Josiah's defeats, of the struggles for freedom in the glorious days of the Maccabees. There is Naboth's vineyard and the place of Jehu's revenge upon Jezebel; there Shunem and the house of Elisha; there Carmel and the place of Elijah's sacrifice. To the E the valley of Jordan, with the long range of Gilead; to the W the radiance of the Great Sea. . . . You can see thirty miles in three directions" (Smith, *Hist. Geog.*, p. 432). Across the plain of Esdraelon emerged from the Samaritan hill the road from Jerusalem and Egypt. The name of the present city is en-Nâzira, the same as of old.

Modern Nazareth

Scripture Mention. Nazareth is not mentioned in the OT or by Josephus. It was the home of Joseph and Mary (Luke 2:39); there the angel announced to Mary the birth of the Messiah (1:26-28), and there Joseph brought Mary and Jesus after the sojourn in Egypt (Matt. 2:19-23); there Jesus grew up to manhood (Luke 4:16) and taught in the synagogue (Matt. 13:54; Luke 4:16). His long and intimate association with this village made Him known as "Jesus of Nazareth" (18:37; John 1:45; etc.). The disrepute in which Nazareth stood (John 1:46) has generally been

attributed to the Galileans' lack of culture and rude dialect; but Nathanael, who asked, "Can any good thing come out of Nazareth?" was himself a Galilean. It would seem probable that "good" must be taken in an ethical sense and that the people of Nazareth had a bad name among their neighbors for irreligion or some laxity of morals.

Present Condition. Modern Nazareth is a bustling city with a population of some forty to fifty thousand, composed largely of Muslims and Christians. A Jewish community has settled on the heights above the city. Tourism is an especially important basis of the economy. The chief attraction of Nazareth is the new Church of the Annunciation (1966) built on the traditional site of Mary's house, which is shown under the church. This church replaced an earlier one built in 1730, which in turn was constructed on the site of a twelfth-century Crusader church. Nearby is the Church of St. Joseph (consecrated in 1914), which stands on the traditional site of Joseph's carpenter shop (shown below the church). Between the two churches is a Franciscan monastery. Not far away is Mary's well, which has certainly provided water for the village from the first century to the present.

BIBLIOGRAPHY: M. Avi-Yonah and E. Stern, eds., *Encyclopedia of Archaeological Excavations in the Holy Land* (1977), 3: 919-22; E. M. Blaiklock, *The Archaeology of the New Testament* (1984), pp. 3, 22, 31, 70-74, 150.

NAZ'IRITE. One of either sex who was bound by a vow of a peculiar kind to be set apart from others for the service of God. The obligation was either for life or for a defined time.

Name (Heb. *nāzîr*, and *nᵉzîr 'elōhîm*, "Nazirite of God"). The term comes from the verb *nāzar*, to "separate," and denotes in general one who is separated from certain things and unto others, and so distinguished from other persons and consecrated unto God (cf. Gen. 49:26; Deut. 33:16). According to others, the word *nēzer*, a "diadem," contains the original idea of *nāzar*, which will then radically signify "to crown," and the hair is regarded as a crown to the person. In accordance with this view the Nazirite is a "crowned one," because "his separation to God is on his head" (Num. 6:7), evidently in allusion to the mass of uncut hair, which was considered an ornament (6:5; cf. 2 Sam. 14:25-26).

Origin. The origin of the custom is obscure. The prescriptions in Num. 6 presuppose it to have been an institution already in existence and merely regulate it so as to bring it into harmony with the whole Mosaic legislation. There are no conclusive analogies tending to show that the custom was derived from a heathen source, especially from Egypt.

The Nazirite Vow. This vow consisted in the person's consecrating his life to God for a fixed period. The Mosaic law speaks of such consecration as being limited to a particular time that was probably fixed by the one making the vow; yet instances occur of children being dedicated by their parents before their birth to be Nazirites all their lives, e.g., Samson (Judg. 13:5, 12-14), Samuel (1 Sam. 1:11), and John the Baptist (Luke 1:15). According to the Mishna the usual time was thirty days, but double vows for sixty days and triple vows for a hundred days were sometimes made. The vow of the apostle Paul seems also to have been a kind of Nazirite vow, in fulfillment of which he shaved his head at Cenchrea (Acts 18:18), although according to the law (Num. 6:9, 18) and the Talmud the shaving of the head was required to be done at the door of the Temple.

The Law of the Nazirite (Num. 6:1-21). The Nazirite, during the term of his consecration, was bound to abstain from wine, grapes, every product of the vine, and from every kind of intoxicating drink. He was forbidden to cut his hair or to approach any dead body, even that of his nearest relative. If a Nazirite incurred defilement by accidentally touching a dead body, he had to undergo certain rites of purification and to recommence the full period of his consecration. There is nothing whatever said in the OT of the duration of the period of the vow of the Nazirite of days. When the period of the vow was fulfilled he was released from it and was required to offer a ewe lamb for a burnt offering, a ewe lamb for a sin offering, and a ram for a peace offering, with the usual accompaniments of peace offerings (Num. 6:13-20) and of the offering made at the consecration of priests (Ex. 29:2; Num. 6:15), "unleavened bread and unleavened cakes mixed with oil, and unleavened wafers spread with oil." He also brought a meat offering and a drink offering, which appear to have been presented by themselves as a distinct act of service (v. 17). He was to cut off his "dedicated head of hair" (i.e., the hair that had grown during the period of his consecration) at the door of the Tabernacle and to put it into the fire under the sacrifice on the altar. The priest then placed upon his hands the boiled left shoulder of the ram, with one of the unleavened cakes and one of the wafers, and then took them again and waved them for a wave offering. These, as well as the breast and the heave, or right, shoulder (to which he was entitled in the case of ordinary peace offerings, Lev. 7:32-34) were given to the priest. The Nazirite also gave him a present proportioned to his circumstances (Num. 6:21). From this the custom afterward grew up that, when poor persons took the Nazirite's vow upon them, those who were better off defrayed the expenses of the sacrifices (cf. Acts 21:23-24). When all the service was concluded the late Nazirite was again at liberty to drink wine (Num. 6:20).

Meaning of the Vow. As the name means, it was an act of consecrating oneself to Jehovah (Num. 6:2), negatively "by renouncing the world with its pleasures—that are so unfavorable to sanctification—and all its defiling influences"; and positively, by giving a certain complexion to the life as being specifically devoted to the Lord. Consequently, the Nazirite was "holy to the Lord" (v. 8). Abstinence from the fruit of the vine was meant not merely to secure the sobriety that is necessary to qualify one for the service of the Lord but to serve as a symbol of the renunciation of those weaknesses of the flesh that tend to endanger a man's sanctification.

The long, uncut hair of the Nazirite was the symbol of strength and abundant vitality (*see* 2 Sam. 14:25-26) and was worn in honor of the Lord as a sign that he belonged to the Lord and dedicated himself to His service with all his vital powers. Then, too, a luxurious growth of long hair was looked upon as imparting a somewhat handsome appearance, an ornament, and, in the case of the Nazirite, was the diadem of the head consecrated to God.

The time that the Nazirite vow lasted was not a lazy life, involving a withdrawal from the duties of citizenship, but it was perfectly reconcilable with the performance of all domestic and social duties, the burial of the dead alone excepted. "The position of the Nazirite, as Philo, Maimonides, and others clearly saw, was a condition of life consecrated to the Lord, resembling the sanctified relation in which the priests stood to Jehovah, and differing from the priesthood solely in the fact that it involved no official service at the sanctuary and was not based upon a divine calling and institution, but was undertaken spontaneously for a certain time and through a special vow. The object was simply the realization of the idea of a priestly life, with its purity and freedom from all contamination from everything connected with death and corruption, a self-surrender to God stretching beyond the deepest earthly ties. In this respect the Nazirite's sanctification of life was a step toward the realization of the priestly character which had been set before the whole nation as its goal at the time of its first calling (Ex. 19:5); and although it was simply the performance of a vow, and therefore a work of perfect spontaneity, it was also a work of the Spirit of God which dwelt in the congregation of Israel, so that Amos could describe the raising up of Nazirites along with prophets as a special manifestation of divine grace" (K. & D., *Com.*, ad loc.).

BIBLIOGRAPHY: R. de Vaux, *Ancient Israel: Its Life and Institutions* (1961), pp. 465-67.

NE'AH (nē'a). A town of Zebulun, on the southern border of Rimmon (Josh. 19:13). As it is stated to have been not far from Rimmon, it lay perhaps at the modern site *Nimrin,* a little W of Kurn Hattin.

NEAP'OLIS (Gk. *ne-ap'o-lis,* "new city"). A place in northern Greece and a seaport town of Philippi, ten miles away. The modern city of more than fifty thousand inhabitants covers the site of the NT city; so there is little to see dating to the biblical period. Remains of a Roman aqueduct still stand. It was the place where Paul first landed in Europe (Acts 16:11) and the terminus of the great Egnatian Road. Its modern name is Kavalla.

Harbor at Neapolis, modern Kavalla

NEARI'AH (nî-a-rī'a; "servant of Jehovah").

1. One of the six sons of Shemaiah in the line of the royal family of Judah after the captivity (1 Chron. 3:22-23). Some identify him with *Naggai* (which see).

2. A son of Ishi and one of the captains of the five hundred Simeonites who, in the days of Hezekiah, drove out the Amalekites from Mt. Seir (1 Chron. 4:42), about 715 B.C.

NE'BAI (ne'bī). A family of the heads of the people who signed the covenant with Nehemiah (Neh. 10:19), 445 B.C.

NEBA'IOTH (ne-bī'oth; "Neba'joth," KJV). The eldest son of Ishmael (Gen. 25:13; 1 Chron. 1:29) and father of a pastoral tribe named after him (Isa. 60:7; cf. Gen. 17:20). This Arabian clan was a neighbor to the people of Kedar, and its name occurs in the records of Ashurbanipal (669-626 B.C.). They seem to be the forerunners of the later *Nabataeans* (which see).

NEBA'JOTH. *See* Neba'ioth.

NEBAL'LAT (ne-bal'at). A place occupied by the Benjamites after the captivity (Neh. 11:34). Identified with Beit Nabāla, four miles NE of Lydda.

NE'BAT (nî-bat; "He [i.e., God] has regarded"). The father of Jeroboam, whose name is only preserved in connection with that of his distinguished son (1 Kings 11:26; 12:2, 15; etc.), before 934 B.C. He is described as an Ephraimite of Zereda.

NE'BO (nê'bo). As a geographical name may signify an elevated place, answering to Arabic *naba'a* ("to be high"), or refer to a center of the worship of Nebo, a Babylonian deity.

1. A town E of Jordan, situated in the fertile country asked for by Reuben and Gad (Num. 32:3), taken possession of and rebuilt by Reuben (v. 38), although it does not occur in the catalogue of the towns of Reuben in the book of Joshua (Josh. 13:15-22), which may be because the Israelites gave it another name. Although rebuilt by the Reubenites (Num. 32:37-38; 33:47; 1 Chron. 5:8), it reverted to Moab (*Moabite Stone,* 14, *see* Moabite Stone). Its modern site is on or near Mt. Nebo.

2. The mountain from which Moses saw the Promised Land (Deut. 32:49; 34:1), and in a ravine of which he was buried (32:50; 34:6). It was the head or summit of *Mt. Pisgah* (which see), a portion of the general range of the "mountains of Abarim." Josephus says of Abarim (*Ant.* 4.8.48) that it "is a very high mountain, situated over against Jericho, and one that affords a view of much of the excellent land of Canaan." This is corroborated by Eusebius and Jerome. The mountains of Abarim are a mountain range forming the Moabite tableland, which slope off into the steppes of Moab.

3. A man whose fifty-two descendants are mentioned among those of Judah and Benjamin who returned from Babylon with Zerubbabel (Ezra 2:29; Neh. 7:33). Seven of them put away their foreign wives (Ezra 10:43).

4. A Babylonian god (Isa. 46:1). *See* Gods, False.

NE'BO-SAR'SEKIM. *See* Samgar-nebo.

NEBUCHADNEZ'ZAR (neb-ū-kad-nez'er; Akkad. *Nabu-kudduriuṣur,* "Nebo, defend the boundary"). The form of the name as commonly given is due to dissimilation, and in Heb. the name is more correctly represented in the form Nebuchadrezzar, than in the form Nebuchadnezzar. Nebuchadnezzar was the son of Nabopolassar and was in all probability of Chaldean race and not of pure Babylonian (*see* Babylonia). When the Assyrian power was tottering to its fall, the Chaldeans, who lived in the S near the Persian Gulf, saw an opportunity of again seizing power in the much coveted city of Babylon. The signs of decay were evident in the reign of Ashurbanipal (*see* Assyria), and Nabopolassar seized the throne in 625 as soon as Ashurbanipal had ceased to reign in Assyria. But Nabopolassar was not accounted king at once by the Assyrians and numerous conflicts must have occurred during his reign between the successors of Ashurbanipal and the new Chaldean king in Babylon. Nabopolassar followed the ancient Babylonian custom of building temples and attending to the internal affairs of his kingdom.

In the Field. Nabopolassar's son Nebuchadnezzar was destined to be his successor and was his representative in the field. He probably began his military service against the later Assyrian kings and soon achieved distinction. Toward the end of the reign of Nabopolassar, the fall of Nineveh became imminent, and the Babylonian king determined to gain not only his own complete independence of Assyria but also as much as possible of the former Assyrian possessions. He allied his own family to that of the Medes, who were threatening to overthrow Assyria, by marrying his son Nebuchadnezzar to the daughter of Cyaxares. This alliance, as well as the vigilance and ability of Nebuchadnezzar as a warrior, was completely successful. When the Medes delivered the final blow that forever ended the Assyrian commonwealth, they secured Nineveh and the northern and northwestern provinces of the Assyrian Empire, while Nabopolassar secured all of southern Assyria and as much of the vast western provinces as were still in Assyrian control. All this territory, however, was but loosely held together during the latter part of the Assyrian control, and much of it was already lost to Egypt.

Opposes Egypt. It was quite natural that Egypt should early seek to profit by the weakening of Assyrian power. Palestine and Syria had belonged to Egypt by right of conquest during the reign of Thutmose III, and as late as the days of Amenophis III and Amenophis IV the governors of Syrian cities were accustomed to address the Egyptian kings as their lords and even as their gods. When Neco II succeeded his father, Psammetichus I, as king of upper and lower Egypt, he promptly began the reconquest of Syria and Palestine. In 608 B.C. he left Egypt and marched up the seacoast, penetrating inland to the plain of Esdraelon at Megiddo. There Josiah, king of Judah, vainly opposed him and was killed (2 Kings 23:29). Neco was soon able to count himself master of the whole country. It was now his purpose to move eastward to the Euphrates and cross the great valley to seize what might fall to his share when the Assyrian Empire met its end. He reached Carchemish, on the Euphrates, in 605, and there was confronted by Nebuchadnezzar at the head of his father's armies. The battle that ensued was one of the greatest in all history, judged simply by its immediate historic results. Neco was utterly and disastrously defeated and fled homeward closely pursued by the victor. That one blow made Nebuchadnezzar the presumptive holder of all the valuable territory of Syria and Palestine. He pursued Neco to the borders of Egypt.

Becomes King. At that critical moment, 605 B.C., Nebuchadnezzar's father died at Babylon, and he had to return immediately to take over the government. Otherwise he would probably have invaded Egypt. Had he dared to do so his success would have been almost certain, and he and his father would have made in twenty years an empire as vast as that achieved by the Assyrians after centuries of relentless conflict. The first years of the reign of Nebuchadnezzar were devoted to the establishing and ordering of his rule in Babylonia. The warlike enterprises that follow he has unfortunately not described for us. Following the example of the earlier Babylonian kings, Nebuchadnezzar has left to us records almost exclusively of his building operations and proofs of his zeal in the worship of the gods and of care in conserving their sanctuaries. From the OT and from the classical historians we secure the necessary information for following his campaigns with reasonable fullness. The Egyptians had been defeated in their plan of securing by the sword possession of Syria and Palestine, but they had not given up the hope of attaining their desires in some other way. Apries, who is called Hophra (Egyptian Mah-ab-Rē) in the OT, was now king of Egypt, and he set himself to arrange rebellions in Palestine that should culminate in the loss of this territory to Nebuchadnezzar.

Mythical beast depicted on tiles on the Ishtar Gate, Babylon

Western Campaign. Evidently in the first year of his reign Nebuchadnezzar led a force into Palestine and subdued the Jews, carrying off numerous captives (including Daniel, 2 Kings 24:1-

9; Dan. 1:1-7). Then Zedekiah of Judah, in the first year of his reign (597), rebelled again, and Nebuchadnezzar invaded once more, taking additional captives (including Ezekiel, 2 Kings 24:10-20; Ezek. 1:1-3). Finally Nebuchadnezzar faced another rebellion and this time besieged Jerusalem (588-586) and destroyed it along with the Temple, bringing to an end the kingdom of Judah (2 Kings 25:1-21). In these acts of rebellion Edom, Moab, Tyre, Sidon, and Ammon had also joined, and these all were punished by Nebuchadnezzar. The punishment of Tyre was more difficult and less successful than that of the other partners. Nebuchadnezzar besieged it from 585 to 572 B.C. and finally destroyed the mainland city of Tyre. But the island city survived because the Babylonians had no navy with which to reduce it. Tyre continued to enjoy prosperity until finally wiped out by Alexander the Great in 332 B.C. The punishment of Egypt for inciting the Palestinian states was undertaken and successfully carried through in 568. Nebuchadnezzar himself has left us no account of this important campaign, but an Egyptian inscription proves that he marched the whole length of Egypt proper to Syene (the modern Aswân). As the direct result of this single campaign, Egypt became subject to Babylonia during the reign of Amasis II, who had dethroned Hophra and succeeded him on the throne. To hold the advantage thus gained Nebuchadnezzar had to invade Egypt again, and one of his own inscriptions mentions the sending of an expedition there in the thirty-seventh year of his reign. Nebuchadnezzar also carried on a war (Jer. 49:28-33) against the Arabs of Kedar, but we have no other account of it than that preserved in the OT. With this ends our knowledge of the warlike undertakings of Nebuchadnezzar. There is every reason to believe that he fought many a campaign of which we know nothing. He would not have been able to hold this great empire together without frequent recourse to the sword. By force he had achieved power and only by force would it have been successfully maintained. It is curious and interesting to notice that on at least one occasion Nebuchadnezzar played the part of peacemaker. When the Medes, who had overthrown Assyria, pushed westward, they came into conflict with the Lydians. On May 25, 585 B.C., during a fierce battle on the Halys, an eclipse of the sun separated the combatants. Nebuchadnezzar interposed and made peace among them. A selfish desire to prevent too great success of his former allies doubtless contributed to this undertaking, but the deed may be nevertheless accounted good.

Works of Peace. If we were to accept Nebuchadnezzar's own estimate of his life and work, we would conclude that he had little interest in his campaigns and that his real concern was the glory of Babylon and its gods. The chief concern of Nebuchadnezzar was for the great temple of Bel-Marduk at Babylon, known under the name *E-sagila*. This he rebuilt and greatly adorned and beautified. To the Nebo temple of E-zida at Borsippa he also gave unstinted means and time. Besides these two temples he carried on works of repair and construction in bewildering number and variety at Ur, Larsa, Sippar, Erech, and Kutha. The city of Babylon (*see* Babylon) he also greatly beautified and strengthened. In it he built new streets and greatly strengthened its walls, so that the city was deemed impregnable. The worldwide glory of Babylon owed more to Nebuchadnezzar than to any other man. After a prosperous and eventful reign of forty-three years (604-562 B.C.), Nebuchadnezzar died and was succeeded by his son, Evil-merodach (Amel-Marduk; cf. 2 Kings 25:27). Taking Nebuchadnezzar's reign as a whole, it may safely be regarded as one of the strongest as it was clearly one of the most glorious in all the long history of Babylon as a world center. A man of great force and decision of character, not severe in his dealings beyond the custom of his age, a man who could plan and execute great and daring movements, he may surely be regarded as one of antiquity's greatest men. Many insights into Nebuchadnezzar's character and culture are portrayed in Daniel 2-4, including his sinful pride and his humiliation and restoration by God.

Nebuchadnezzar and Archaeology. Nebuchadnezzar's Babylon was extensively excavated from 1899 to 1914 by Robert Koldewey and the Deut-

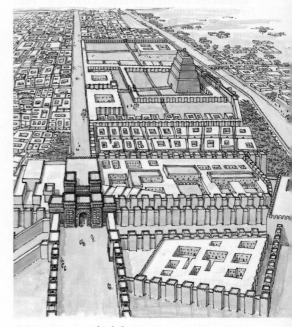

Artist's impression of Babylon

sche Orientgesellschaft (see Koldewey's, *Das wieder erstehende Babylon,* 4th ed., 1925). Among the tremendous complex of ruins was the great Ishtar Gate, beautifully decorated with a series of bulls and dragons in enameled, colored brick. (For further results *see* Babylon.) Archaeology has shown the complete suitability, albeit egocentricity, of Nebuchadnezzar's words recorded in Dan. 4:30: "Is this not Babylon the great, which I myself have built as a royal residence by the might of my power and for the glory of my majesty?" In fact, an extensive inscription, now in the British Museum, details the various construction projects of Nebuchadnezzar at Babylon.

BIBLIOGRAPHY: A. Malamat, *Israel Exploration Journal* 6 (1956): 246-56; D. J. Wiseman, *Chronicles of the Chaldaean Kings* (1956), pp. 18, 37, 64-75.

NEBUCHADREZ'ZAR (neb-ū-kad-rez'er). Another form of *Nebuchadnezzar* (which see).

NEBUSHAZ'BAN (neb-û-shaz'ban). A *rab-saris* (which see) or officer of the Babylonian occupation force who delivered Jeremiah from confinement and allowed him to return home (Jer. 39:13). The NIV calls him "a chief officer."

NEBUZARA'DAN (neb-û-zar-a'dan; Akkad. *Nābū-zēr-id-dina,* "Nebo has given offspring"). The "captain of the bodyguard" (Jer. 39:10; etc.), a high officer in the court of Nebuchadnezzar, apparently the person next to the monarch. He appears not to have been present during the siege of Jerusalem, but as soon as the city was actually in the hands of the Babylonians he arrived, and from that moment everything was completely directed by him, 586 B.C. Only one act is referred directly to Nebuchadnezzar—the appointment of the governor or superintendent of the conquered district. All this Nebuzaradan seems to have carried out with wisdom and moderation. He appears to have left Judea for this time when he took down the chief people of Jerusalem to his master at Riblah (2 Kings 25:8-20). In four years he again appeared (Jer. 52:12). Nebuchadnezzar in his twenty-third year made a descent on the regions E of Jordan, including the Ammonites and the Moabites, who had escaped when Jerusalem was destroyed. From there he proceeded to Egypt, and, either on the way there or on the return, Nebuzaradan again passed through the country and carried off 745 more captives (52:30).

NECHO. *See* Neco.

NECK. This part of the human frame is used by the sacred writers with considerable variety and freedom in figurative expressions. Thus, "Your neck is like the tower of David built with rows of stones" (Song of Sol. 4:4), and "like a tower of ivory" (7:4), with reference to the graceful ornament that the neck is, especially to the female

figure. "Who for my life risked their own necks" (Rom. 16:4) is a strong expression for hazarding one's life. "Neck" is also used to represent that part of the building at which the roof or gable rests upon the wall (Hab. 3:13). To "put your feet on the necks" (Josh. 10:24) is a usual expression in the East for triumphing over a fallen foe. A common reference was to a beast of burden, which bore upon his neck the yoke and thus became an emblem of man in relation to a true or false service (cf. Matt. 11:29). A stiff or hardened neck is a familiar expression for a rebellious spirit (Ps. 75:5, marg.; Prov. 29:1; Isa. 48:4, "your neck is an iron sinew," i.e., inflexible; Acts 7:51). *See* Yoke.

Placing the foot on the neck of a captive

NECKLACE (Heb. *rābîd,* "binding"). The word *necklace* is not found in the NASB, but in early times, as now, necklaces were common in the East. They were sometimes made of silver or gold (Ex. 35:22), sometimes of jewels or pearls strung on a ribbon (Song of Sol. 1:10), hanging to the breast or even to the girdle. To these were attached crescent ornaments (Judg. 8:21; Isa. 3:18). *See* Dress; Jewelry.

NE'CO (nî'ko; 2 Chron. 35:20, 22; 36:4; "Necho," KJV). A name applied to one of the *pharaohs* (which see).

NECROMANCER (from Gk. *nekros,* "the dead," and *manteia,* "divination"; Heb. *dōrēsh el-hammētîm,* "one who inquires of the dead"). In many ancient nations there were those who pretended to be able by incantations to call up the dead and consult with them on the mysteries of the present and future. The Mosaic law forbade consultation with the necromancer (Deut. 18:11). Another method of consulting the dead was by examining the viscera of one newly dead or slain, in order to draw out omens.

The most famous instance of necromancy in Scripture is Saul and the medium of Endor, recounted in 1 Sam. 28:1-25. It is an unequivocal divine condemnation of all traffic in occultism and a glaring exposé of the fraudulency of spiritism. This practice of consulting the dead, common among the heathen nations, was strictly forbidden to any Israelite. The reason is simple. It was a recourse to a medium who was under the control of a divining demon; in fact, the woman of Endor was identical with the modern spiritistic medium. She is called "a woman that hath a familiar spirit," literally, "a woman controlled or mastered by a divining demon" (vv. 7-8, KJV). In the episode, the spirit of Samuel was actually brought back from the spirit world, as the circumstances of the account indisputably prove. However, the seer's spirit was not brought back by the medium's power but by divine power, to pronounce doom upon Saul and to expose the fraud of spiritism, its traffic in evil power, and its complete inconsistency with the worship of Israel's God. Neither ancient nor modern spiritism can recall or have communion with the spirits of the departed dead, as the medium's fear in the narrative shows (vv. 12-13). What spiritistic mediums can do, however, is to impersonate the spirits of the departed dead and give superhuman knowledge by reason of their superior powers as evil spirit beings. Necromancy is also discussed in the articles Magic; Familiar Spirit. *See* Merrill F. Unger, *Biblical Demonology,* 2d ed. (1953), pp. 143-64.   M.F.U.

NEDABI'AH (ne-da-bī'yah). A son of Jehoiachin, king of Judah, about whom nothing else is known (1 Chron. 3:18).

NEEDLE (Gk. *hraphis*). This term occurs in Scripture only in proverb. "It is easier for a camel to go through the eye of a needle," etc. (Matt. 19:24; Mark 10:25; Luke 18:25). *See* Camel.

NEEDLEWORK. *See* Handicrafts: Embroiderer; Needlework; Weaving.

NEGEV (neg'ev). "The south," the little-watered region situated S of Judea and, in the present-day, a part of the Israeli state. In the biblical era grazing was its principal industry (Gen. 20:14). The Negev is about 3,600 square miles in area and contains important biblical sites such as Kadesh-barnea and Beersheba. The modern boundaries of Israel are larger and taper down to the site of Ezion-geber on the Gulf of Aqabah. In 1959 Nelson Glueck completed his monumental archaeological survey of Transjordan, the Jordan Valley, and the Negev (Southern Palestine). The results of his detailed surface surveys in the Negev, begun in 1951, appear in *Rivers in the Desert: A History of the Negeb* (1959). Compare also Glueck, "The Negeb," in *The Biblical Archaeologist* 22 no. 4 (1959): 82-97.

BIBLIOGRAPHY: F.-M. Abel, *Géographie de la Palestine* (1933); C. L. Woolley and T. E. Lawrence, *The Wilderness of Zin* (1936); Y. Aharoni, *Israel Exploration Journal* 8 (1958): 26ff.; id., *IEJ* 10 (1960): 23ff., 97ff.; N. Glueck, *Rivers in the Desert* (1959); A. Negev, *Cities of*
the Desert (1966); Y. Aharoni, *The Land of the Bible* (1979).

The dry, mountainous region of the Negev

NEGINOTH. (neg'i-nōth). A term appearing in the KJV of the titles of Pss. 4,6,54,67,76 and meaning "stringed instruments" (so NASB and NIV).

NEHEL'AMITE (ne-hel'a-mīt; "dreamed," only in Jer. 29:24, 31-32). A patronymic or patrial of unknown origin and significance, applied to the false prophet Shemaiah. No such name of person or place as Nehelam is known. The Targum gives the name as Helam. A place named Helam, between the Jordan and Euphrates, is mentioned in 2 Sam. 10:16-17. This may be identical with Ptolemy's Alamatha, W of the Euphrates and not far from Nicephorium and Thapsacus. Possibly the mention of "Nehelamite" contains a punning allusion to the dreams (*ḥalōmîm*) of the false prophets (*see* Jer. 23:25-28, 32, and other passages).

NEHEMI'AH (nē'he-mi'a; "Jehovah consoles").

1. The second named of "the people of the province . . . whom Nebuchadnezzar the king of Babylon had carried away," and who returned with Zerubbabel from Babylon (Ezra 2:2; Neh. 7:7), 536 B.C.

2. The son of Azbuk, official of Beth-zur, in the mountains of Judah, and one who was prominent in rebuilding the walls of Jerusalem (Neh. 3:16), 445 B.C.

3. Governor of the Jews. The genealogy of Nehemiah is unknown, except that he was the son of Hacaliah (Neh. 1:1) and brother of Hanani (7:2; cf. 1:2). All that we know for certain of Nehemiah is found in the book bearing his name.

He first appears at Susa as cupbearer to King Artaxerxes Longimanus (Neh. 1:11–2:1), about 446 B.C. In that year he was informed of the deplorable condition of his countrymen in Judea, and determined to go to Jerusalem to endeavor to better their condition.

Three or four months later he presented his request to the king to be allowed to go and rebuild Jerusalem. His royal master granted his request and appointed him *Tirshathá*, "governor." Accompanied by a troop of cavalry and letters from the king to the different governors through whose provinces he was to pass, as well as to Asaph, the keeper of the king's forests (to supply him with timber), he started upon his journey, being under promise to return to Persia within a given time (2:1-10).

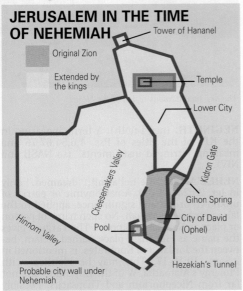

JERUSALEM IN THE TIME OF NEHEMIAH

- Tower of Hananel
- Original Zion
- Extended by the kings
- Temple
- Lower City
- Cheesemakers Valley
- Kidron Gate
- Gihon Spring
- Hinnom Valley
- Pool
- City of David (Ophel)
- Probable city wall under Nehemiah
- Hezekiah's Tunnel

Nehemiah, without a moment's unnecessary delay, began the restoration of the city walls, which was accomplished in the wonderfully short time of fifty-two days (6:15), 444 B.C. In this he was opposed by Sanballat and Tobiah, who not only poured out a torrent of abuse and contempt upon all engaged in the work but actually made a conspiracy to fall upon the builders with an armed force and put a stop to the undertaking. The project was defeated by the vigilance and prudence of Nehemiah. This armed attitude was continued from that day forward (chap. 4). He also reformed abuses, redressed grievances (chap. 5), introduced law and order (chap. 7), and revived the worship of God (chap. 8). Various stratagems were then resorted to in order to get Nehemiah away from Jerusalem and, if possible, take his life. But that which most nearly succeeded was the attempt to bring him into suspicion with the king of Persia, as if Nehemiah intended to set himself up as an independent king as soon as the walls were completed. The artful letter of Sanballat so far wrought upon Artaxerxes that he issued a decree stopping the work until further orders (Ezra 4:21).

In these reforms Nehemiah enjoyed the coop-

eration of Ezra, who had preceded him to Jerusalem, and who is named as taking a prominent part in public affairs (Neh. 8:1, 9, 13; 12:36). Nehemiah refused to receive his lawful allowance as governor during the whole term of his office because of the people's poverty but entertained for twelve years, at his own cost, 150 Jews and welcomed any who returned from captivity (13:14-18).

Nehemiah, after twelve years' service, returned to Babylon (5:14; 13:6), 434 B.C. It is not known how long he remained there, but "after some time" he obtained permission to again visit Jerusalem, where his services were needed because of new abuses that had crept in. When he arrived, Nehemiah enforced the separation of the mixed multitude from Israel (13:1-3), expelled Tobiah the Ammonite from the Temple chamber (vv. 4-9), and made better arrangements for the support of the Temple service (vv. 10-14) and for the observance of the Sabbath (vv. 15-22). His last recorded act was an effort to put an end to mixed marriages, which led him to drive away a son of Joiada, the high priest, because he was son-in-law to Sanballat the Horonite (vv. 23-28). It is supposed that Nehemiah remained in Jerusalem until about 405 B.C., toward the close of the reign of Darius Nothus, mentioned in 12:22. The time and place of his death is unknown. To Nehemiah is credited the authorship of the book that bears his name.

Nehemiah's character seems almost without a blemish. He was a man of pure and disinterested patriotism, willing to leave a position of wealth, power, and influence in the first court of the world and share the sorrows of his countrymen. He was not only noble, high-minded, and of strict integrity, but he was also possessed of great humility, kindness, and princely hospitality. In nothing was he more remarkable than in his piety, walking before his God with singleness of eye, seeking divine blessing and cooperation in prayer, and returning thanks to him for all his successes.

BIBLIOGRAPHY: H. H. Rowley, *Men of God* (1963), pp. 211-44; C. J. Barber, *Nehemiah and the Dynamics of Effective Leadership* (1976).

NEHEMIAH, BOOK OF. A postexilic book taking its name from its main character and traditional author, said to be "the words of Nehemiah the son of Hacaliah" (Neh. 1:1). The book occurs in the third section of the Heb. canon and constitutes one of the historical books of that group.

Purpose. It is closely linked with Ezra and together with that book shows God's faithfulness in the restoration of His exiled people to their own land. God's purpose is seen to work through great monarchs of the Persian Empire such as Cyrus, Darius I the Great, and Artaxerxes. God is also seen to operate through the agency of His own anointed servants, such as Ezra, Nehemiah,

Artist's impression of Nehemiah rebuilding the Temple

Zerubbabel, Joshua, Haggai, and Zechariah. The book narrates the rebuilding of the walls of Jerusalem and the establishment of civil authority under Nehemiah as governor. The book of Nehemiah is more civil and secular than Ezra, but it also contains a priestly slant.

Date and Authority. Nehemiah is commonly regarded as the work of the so-called chronicler. This priest-historian is supposed to have written 1 and 2 Chronicles and the book of Ezra-Nehemiah long after the time of these leaders. The date is customarily put at the beginning of the Greek period, around 330 B.C. These arguments, however, are unsound. It is better to regard the book as belonging to the latter half of the fifth century B.C. Whether Ezra precedes Nehemiah or Nehemiah, Ezra is disputed by critics. Since Jewish tradition and the title of the book assign the authorship to Nehemiah, section 1:1–7:5 is to be looked upon as an excerpt from the author's memoirs, as the first person indicates. This material is inserted apparently without change. Other passages evidently taken from Nehemiah's memoirs are 11:1-2; 12:27-43; 13:4-31. The work also consists of earlier documents that were incorporated into the author's work, such as 7:6-73a. The remainder of the book is based upon historical sources.

Outline.

I. Restoration of the walls (1:1–7:73)
   A. The initial circumstances (1:1–2:20)

B. The actual construction (3:1–6:19)
C. The later census (7:1-73)
II. Reformation of the faith (8:1–13:31)
   A. The Covenant renewed (8:1–10:39)
   B. The nation revived (11:1–13:13)
   C. The violations remedied (13:14-31)

BIBLIOGRAPHY: J. M. Myers, *Ezra, Nehemiah,* Anchor Bible (1965); L. H. Brockington, *Ezra, Nehemiah and Esther,* New Century Bible (1969); R. K. Harrison, *Introduction to the Old Testament* (1969), pp. 1145-51; D. Kidner, *Ezra and Nehemiah,* Tyndale Old Testament Commentaries (1979); W. Adeney, *Ezra and Nehemiah* (1980); F. C. Fensham, *The Books of Ezra and Nehemiah,* New International Commentary on the Old Testament (1982); H. Vos, *Ezra, Nehemiah, Esther* (1987).

NE'HILOTH (ne'hi-lōth). The title of Ps. 5 (KJV); it means *wind instruments.* The NASB reads: "for flute accompaniment," with a marg. note: "Or, *according to a lower octave.*" The NIV translates "for flutes."

NE'HUM (ne'hum; "consoled," i.e., by God). One of those who returned from Babylon with Zerubbabel (Neh. 7:7), about 445 B.C.

NEHUSH'TA (ne-hush'ta; "bronze"). The daughter of Elnathan of Jerusalem, wife of Jehoiakim, and mother of Jehoiachin, kings of Judah (2 Kings 24:8), about 616 B.C.

NEHUSH'TAN (ne-hush'tan; a piece of "brass," bronze). The name given by King Hezekiah to the *bronze serpent* (which see) when he broke it into pieces because the people had made it an object of worship (2 Kings 18:4, *see* marg.).

NEI'EL (ne-i'el). A place mentioned as a landmark of Asher (Josh. 19:27), possibly Neah (v. 13). It has been associated with Khirbet Ya'hîn, about two miles N of Kabūl on the edge of the plain of Acre; at the S of the valley of Jiphtah-el.

NEIGH (Heb. *ṣāhal,* to "sound" clear, Jer. 8:16; 13:27; 50:11). The neighing of a horse, a sign of excessive wantonness; used figuratively of men: "each one neighing after his neighbor's wife" (Jer. 5:8).

NEIGHBOR (Heb. *rēa',* "associate"; Gk. *plēsion,* "near"). Generally a person near, one connected by bonds of humanity, and whom natural regard would lead to treat with kindness and equity (Ex. 20:16-17; Deut. 5:20). The construction placed upon "neighbor" (Lev. 19:18) was that of *friend* as opposed to enemy; therefore, it was held that to hate one's enemy was not forbidden by the law (Matt. 5:43). But Jesus, in the parable of the Good Samaritan (Luke 10:29-37), taught that all the world were neighbors. Moreover, the Pharisees used the term *neighbor* in an exclusive sense, namely, one who observed the law in the strictest manner. They called themselves neighbors; therefore the question, "Who is my neighbor?"

BIBLIOGRAPHY: A. C. Knudson, *Principles of Christian Eth-*

ics (1943), pp. 118-56; P. E. Johnson, *Christian Love* (1951), pp. 23-48.

NE'KEB. *See* Adami-nekeb.

NEKO'DA (ne-kō'da; "distinguished, speckled").

One of the Temple servants whose descendants returned to Jerusalem after the captivity (Ezra 2:48; Neh. 7:50), 536 B.C. The sons of Nekoda were among those who went up after the captivity from Tel-melah, Tel-harsha, and other places, but they were unable to prove their descent from Israel (Ezra 2:60; Neh. 7:62).

NEM'UEL (nem'ū-el; or perhaps for Jemuel, "day of God").

1. The first named son of Eliab, a Reubenite, and brother of Dathan and Abiram (Num. 26:9), about 1438 B.C.

2. The eldest son of Simeon (1 Chron. 4:24), from whom were descended the family of the Nemuelites (Num. 26:12). In Gen. 46:10 he is called *Jemuel* (which see).

NEM'UELITES (nem'ū-el-īts; Num. 26:12). Descendants of *Nemuel,* no. 2 (which see), of the tribe of Simeon.

NE'PHEG (ne'feg).

1. One of the sons of Izhar, the son of Kohath (Ex. 6:21).

2. One of David's sons, born to him in Jerusalem (2 Sam. 5:15; 1 Chron. 3:7; 14:6), after 1000 B.C.

NEPHEW, NEPHEWS. In the KJV the rendering of the second instance of the Heb. term *bēn* (normally "son") in Judg. 12:14; of the Heb. term *neked* in Job 18:19; Isa. 14:22; and of the Gk. term *'ekgonon* in 1 Tim. 5:4.

In the NASB and NIV *nephew* appears only in Gen. 12:5; 14:12 as the replacement for KJV *brother's son.* Elsewhere *nephew* (or *nephews*) is replaced by *posterity* or *descendants* (Job 18:19; Isa. 14:22), *grandsons* (Judg. 12:14), or *grandchildren* (1 Tim. 5:4), terms that fully reflect the Heb. and Gk. expressions.

NEPH'ILIM (nef'i-lim; Gen. 6:4; Num. 13:33). *See also* Giant. The Nephilim are considered by many to be giant demigods, the unnatural offspring of the "daughters of men" (mortal women) in cohabitation with the "sons of God" (angels; cf. Gen. 6:1-4). This utterly unnatural union, violating God's created order of being, was such a shocking abnormality as to necessitate the worldwide judgment of the Flood. Another view of the Nephilim is that they were particularly violent (the name is from a root, "to fall," i.e., on other people), strong ("mighty"), and infamous ("men of renown") people who predated the marriages of v. 2. This viewpoint often explains the unions as intermarriage of the godly line of Seth (described in 4:25–5:32) with the ungodly line of Cain (4:1-24).

NE'PHISH (ne'fish; 1 Chron. 5:19, KJV). *See* Naphish.

NEPHISH'ESIM (ne-fish'e-sim; Neh. 7:52, KJV). *See* Nephisim.

NEPHI'SIM (ne-fi'sim). The head of a family of Temple servants who returned with Zerubbabel from Babylon (Ezra 2:50), about 536 B.C. The parallel text (Neh. 7:52) has Nephushesim. The NIV reads Nephussim in both places.

NEPH'THALIM (nef'tha-lim; Matt. 4:13, 15; Rev. 7:6, KJV). *See* Naphtali.

NEPHTO'AH, THE WATERS OF (nef-tō'a; "an opening"). The spring or source of the water, or (inaccurately) waters of Nephtoah, was one of the landmarks in the boundary line that separated Judah from Benjamin (Josh. 15:9; 18:15). It lay two miles NW of Jerusalem, in which direction it seems to have been satisfactorily identified in 'Ain Lifta, a spring situated a little distance above the village of the same name. Nephtoah was formerly identified with various springs—the spring of St. Philip ('Ain Haniyeh) in the Wadi el Werd; the 'Ain Yalo in the same valley, but nearer Jerusalem; the 'Ain Karim, or Fountain of the Virgin of medieval times, and even the so-called Well of Job at the western end of the Wadi 'Aly.

NEPHUSH'ESIM (ne-fush'e-sim, Neh. 7:52). *See* Nephisim.

NEPHUSSIM. *See* Nephisim.

NER (nēr; *light,* "lamp"). A Benjamite, father of Kish and Abner and grandfather of King Saul (1 Sam. 14:50; 26:5; 2 Sam. 2:8; 1 Chron. 8:33), about 1100 B.C. The statement in 1 Chron. 9:36, that Kish and Ner were both sons of Jeiel, is explained by the supposition of an elder Kish, uncle of Saul's father or, rather, Ner's grandfather.

NE'REUS (ne're-us; Lat. from Gk., the name of a sea god). A Christian at Rome saluted, with his sister, by the apostle Paul (Rom. 16:15), A.D. 60 (55). A legendary account of him is given in *Acta Sanctorum,* from which may be gathered the tradition that he was beheaded at Terracina, probably in the reign of Nerva. His ashes are said to be deposited in the ancient church of *SS. Nereo et Archileo* at Rome.

NER'GAL (ner'gal). One of the chief Assyrian deities. *See* Gods, False.

NER'GAL-SHARE'ZER (ner'gal-sha-rē'zer; Akkad; *Nergal-shar-uṣur,* "Nergal, protect the king"). The name of two princes, the one Assyrian, the other Babylonian.

1. In the biblical description of the end of the reign of Sennacherib he is said to have been killed by his two sons, Adrammelech and Sharezer (2 Kings 19:37; Isa. 37:38). There is little doubt that the name *Sharezer* is simply the latter part

of the name *Nergal-sharezer.* The name is given by Abydemus as Nergilos, so that the OT has preserved the latter half of his name and the Greek historian the first half. Abbreviations of names in this manner are common among Assyrians and Babylonians. The Assyrian story of the death of Sennacherib is much more brief in its details and does not mention the names of his murderers. It is as follows: "On the twentieth day of Tebet Sennacherib, king of Assyria, was killed by his son during an insurrection. . . . From the twentieth day of Tebet to the second day of Adar the insurrection continued, and on the eighteenth day of Sivan (of the following year) Esarhaddon ascended the throne." It will be observed that in this account the death of Sennacherib is ascribed to the act of one son, and not to two, as in the OT. It is a probable conjecture that the death of the Assyrian king was due to the jealousy felt by his son Esarhaddon, who succeeded him.

2. The name of one of the Babylonian princes belonging to the attendants of Nebuchadnezzar (Jer. 39:3, 13, given as "Nergal-sar-ezer"). He held the office of *Rab-mag* and is the Nergal-sharusur, Gk. Neriglissar, who married one of Nebuchadnezzar's daughters, murdered Evil-merodach (which see), his brother-in-law, and ascended the throne, reigning from 560 to 556.

BIBLIOGRAPHY: D. J. Wiseman, *Chronicles of the Chaldaean Kings* (1956), pp. 37ff.

NE'RI (ne'ri). The son of Melchi and father of Shealtiel, in the genealogy of Christ (Luke 3:27).

NERI'AH (ne-rī'a; "lamp of Jehovah"). The son of Mahseiah and father of Baruch, Jeremiah's scribe (Jer. 32:12, 16; 36:4, 8, 14, 32; 43:3, 6; 45:1; 51:59). He is probably the same as Neri.

NE'RO (nē'rō; 2 Tim., *subscription,* KJV). A Roman emperor, born at Antium, probably December 15, A.D. 37, the son of Cneius Domitius Ahenobarbus by Agrippina, the sister of Caligula, his original name being Lucius Domitius Abenobarbus. When he was twelve years old his mother married her uncle, the emperor Claudius, who four years afterward gave his daughter Octavia to Nero in marriage, having formally adopted him under the name of Nero Claudius Caesar Drusus Germanicus. He succeeded Claudius, A.D. 54, and for five years showed clemency and justice, though his private life was extremely licentious. During his early years he was especially under the influence of the great Seneca. When he disposed of Seneca, he seemed to rule without restraint. Later he caused the death of Britannicus, the son and heir of Claudius. In A.D. 59 he procured from the Senate an order for the death of his mother to please his mistress, Poppaea, the wife of Otho. This was soon followed by the divorce of Octavia and Nero's marriage to Poppaea. In A.D. 64 a dreadful conflagration raged in Rome, said to have been started by Nero, who is reported to

have watched the progress of the flames from the top of a high tower, chanting to his own lyre verses on the destruction of Troy. The truth of this story is doubtful, but it was believed at the time, and Nero sought to assign the blame for the disastrous fire on the Christians, many of whom were put to death. Having killed Poppaea by a kick when she was with child, Nero proposed to marry Antonia, his adopted sister, and on her refusal ordered her to be put to death. He then married Statilia Messalina, whose husband Vestinus he had assassinated for marrying Messalina after the emperor had cohabited with her.

The jurist Longinus was exiled, and the most virtuous citizens were put to death. In the midst of these sad events Nero's ambition seemed to be to excel in circus games. He went to Greece to show his ability as musician and charioteer in the Olympian games, returning to Rome in great pomp as victor. The formidable insurrection that broke out in Gaul alarmed Nero, and, deserted by the praetorian guard and condemned to death by the Senate, he committed suicide.

Bust of Nero

It was during Nero's reign that the war commenced between the Jews and Romans, which terminated in the destruction of Jerusalem by Titus. Nero was the emperor before whom Paul was brought on his first imprisonment at Rome; and in the persecution of the Christians by Nero Paul and Peter are supposed to have suffered martyrdom. The early Christians believed Nero would return as the Antichrist; and many modern writers find his name in the mystic number of the Apocalypse (Rev. 13:18).

BIBLIOGRAPHY: J. H. Bishop, *Nero: The Man and the Legend* (1964); B. H. Warmington, *Nero: Reality and Legend* (1969); M. Grant, *Nero* (1970).

NEST (Heb. *qēn,* from *qānan,* to "build;" Gk. *kataskēnōsis,* "encampment, a perch"). The law (Deut. 22:6-7) directs that if anyone found a bird's nest by the road upon a tree or upon the ground, with young ones or eggs, and the mother sitting upon them, he was to let the mother go. The eagle's preference for localities removed from man and commanding a wide view is referred to in Job 39:27-28. "Is it at your command that the eagle mounts up, and makes his nest on high?" The loftiness of the eagle's nest was proverbial; it was "among the stars" (Obad. 4). The rock dove in Palestine often builds a nest on cliffs over deep ravines or gorges (Jer. 48:28).

See also Animal Kingdom: Bird.

Figurative. "I shall die in my nest" (Job 29:18) seems to mean in the bosom of one's family, with children to succeed him. To "make your nest as high as an eagle's" was a phrase by which the prophets reproved the pride and ambition of men (Jer. 49:16; Hab. 2:9). The figure of the partridge "that hatches eggs which it has not laid" (Jer. 17:11) is applied to one who gathers riches unlawfully; the robbing of a nest in the absence of the parent birds is symbolic of an easy victory (Isa. 10:14); the dominion exercised over the surrounding nations by Assyria is symbolized under the figure of a cedar of Lebanon, in whose boughs all the birds of heaven made their nests (Ezek. 31:3-6; cf. Dan. 4:21).

NET. The rendering of several Heb. and Gk. words. The frequency of images derived from them show that nets were much used by the Hebrews for fishing, fowling, and hunting.

Fishing Nets. Of fishing nets among the Hebrews we have no direct information, but it is likely that they were similar to those of the Egyptians. These used two kinds. The drag net had floats on the upper edge and leads on the lower edge to keep it close to the bottom (Isa. 19:8). It was sometimes let down from a boat, while those who pulled it usually stood on the shore. In lake fishing the net is cast from and drawn into the

Fishing nets at Akko

boat, except in case of a large draught, when the fishermen dragged the net after their boats to the shore (John 21:6, 8). A smaller net was sometimes used for fishing in shallow water. It was furnished with a pole on either side; and the fisherman, holding a pole in each hand, thrust it below the surface of the water, awaiting the moment when the fish passed over it. This, or a smaller landing net, was used to land fish wounded with a spear or caught by a hook.

Fowling Nets. The Egyptians used the trap and the clap-net. "The trap was generally made of network, strained over a frame. It consisted of two semicircular sides or flaps of equal size, one or both moving on the common bar, or axis, upon which they rested. When the traps were set the two flaps were kept open by means of strings, probably of catgut, which, the moment the bait that stood in the center of the bar was touched, slipped aside, and allowed the two flaps to collapse, thus securing the bird. Another kind, which was square, appears to have closed in the same manner; but its construction was different, the framework running across the center, and not, as in the others, round the edges of the trap. The clap-net was of different forms, though on the same general principle as the traps. It consisted of two sides, or frames, over which the network was strained; at one end was a short rope, which was fastened to a bush or a cluster of reeds, and at the other was one of considerable length, which, as soon as the bird was seen feeding in the area of the net, was pulled by the fowlers, causing the two sides to collapse" (Wilkinson, *Ancient Egyptians,* 2:180, 182).

Hunting Nets. These were of universal use among the Hebrews and were probably like those of the Egyptians, of two kinds — one, a long net, furnished with several ropes, and supported on forked poles, varying in length to correspond with the inequalities of the ground over which it was extended. The other was smaller and used for stopping gaps and is probably alluded to in Job 19:6; Ps. 140:5; Isa. 51:20.

Figurative. The spreading of the net is an appropriate image of the subtle devices of enemies (Pss. 9:15; 10:9; 25:15; etc.) "Fish caught in a treacherous net" (Eccles. 9:12) is figurative of men suddenly overtaken by evil, the unexpected suddenness of the capture being the point of comparison. "An antelope in a net" (Isa. 51:20) is the figure of one exhausted with ineffectual attempts to release himself. Being caught in a net represents the unavoidable vengeance of God (Lam. 1:13; Ezek. 12:13; Hos. 7:12). In Hab. 1:14-16 "hooks" and "nets" are great and powerful armies by which the Chaldeans gained dominion over lands and peoples and brought home the spoil. To "sacrifice to their net" (v. 16) is to attribute to the means that he has employed the honor due to God.

Fishing on Galilee with a net

Fishing on Galilee from a boat

NETA'IM (ne-ta'im). A town inhabited by potters who were descendants of Shelah son of Judah (1 Chron. 4:23). Its location is unknown but it was evidently near *Gederah* (which see).

NETHAN'EL (ne-than'el; "God gives").

1. The son of Zuar and head of the tribe of Issachar at the Exodus (Num. 1:8; 2:5; 7:18, 23; 10:15), 1440 B.C.

2. The fourth son of Jesse, David's father (1 Chron. 2:14), about 1026 B.C.

3. One of the priests who "blew the trumpets before the ark" when it was brought from the house of Obed-edom (1 Chron. 15:24), about 989 B.C.

4. A Levite, "the scribe and father of" Shemaiah (1 Chron. 24:6).

5. The fifth son of Obed-edom and one of the gatekeepers of the Temple appointed by David (1 Chron. 26:4), before 960 B.C.

6. One of the officials commissioned by King Jehoshaphat to teach in the cities of Judah (2 Chron. 17:7), about 870 B.C.

7. One of the chief Levites who made offerings when the observance of the Passover was renewed by King Josiah (2 Chron. 35:9), about 621 B.C.

8. A priest of the family of Pashhur, in the time of Ezra, who had married a foreign wife (Ezra 10:22), 456 B.C.

9. The representative of the priestly family of Jedaiah in the time of Joiakim, the son of Jeshua (Neh. 12:21), before 445 B.C.

10. A Levite, of the sons of Asaph, who took part in the dedication of the wall of Jerusalem (Neh. 12:36).

NETHANI'AH (neth-a-nī'a; "Jehovah bestows").

1. The son of Elishama and father of Ishmael, who murdered Gedaliah (2 Kings 25:23, 25; Jer. 40:8, 14-15; 41:1-2, etc.). He was of the royal family of Judah, before 586 B.C.

2. One of the four sons of Asaph the singer (1 Chron. 25:2). He was head of the fifth division of the Temple musicians (v. 12), about 961 B.C.

3. One of the Levites appointed by Jehoshaphat to accompany the officials who were to teach the law in the cities of Judah (2 Chron. 17:8), 869 B.C.

4. The father of Jehudi, which latter was sent by the officials to request Baruch to read the scroll to them (Jer. 36:14), about 606 B.C.

NETH'INIM (neth'i-nim; Ezra 7:24). The Heb. and KJV rendering of *Temple servants* (which see).

NETO'PHAH (ne-to'fa; "dripping, distillation"). A place in Judah, near Bethlehem, fifty-six of whose people returned with Zerubbabel from captivity (Ezra 2:22; Neh. 7:26). Maharai and Heleb (or Heldai), two of David's guard, were from Netophah (2 Sam. 23:28-29; 1 Chron. 27:13, 15), as well as one of the captains who remained under arms near Jerusalem after its destruction by Nebuchadnezzar (9:16).

NETO'PHATHITES (ne-to'fa-thīts; "the Netophathite," Neh. 12:28; "Netophathi," KJV). Inhabitants of Netophah, which was near Bethlehem or connected with it (Neh. 7:26; cf. 1 Chron. 2:54), and seems to have belonged to Judah, since Maharai the Netophathite was a Zerahite (2 Sam. 23:28; 1 Chron. 27:13; cf. Josh. 7:17) and Heldai the Netophathite was "of Othniel" (2 Sam. 23:29; 1 Chron. 27:15; cf. Judg. 1:8-13). Netophah itself is mentioned only in Ezra 2:22; Neh. 7:26; but as two of David's men, Maharai and Heldai, mentioned above, were Netophathites, the town must have existed long before. The Jewish authors have a tradition "that the Netophathites slew the guards which had been placed by Jeroboam on the road leading to Jerusalem, to stop the passage of the first fruits from the country villages to the temple. . . . Jeroboam's obstruction, which is said to have remained in force till the reign of Hoshea. . . . was commemorated by a fast on the 23d Sivan," which is said to be still retained in the Jewish calendar. The Mishna mentions "oil of Netophah" and the valley of "Beth Netophah." The site is now identified with Khirbet Bedd Faluh, about 3½ miles S of Bethlehem.

NETTLES. *See* Vegetable Kingdom.

NETWORK.

1. Heb. *reshet*. The grate of the altar of burnt offering (Ex. 27:4; 38:4).

2. Heb. *śᵉbākâ* ("twined"), applied to latticework, especially around the capitals of columns such as the two court pillars of the Temple (1 Kings 7:18, 20, 41-42; 2 Kings 25:17; 2 Chron. 4:12-13), which, according to Keil (*Com.*, ad loc.), was formed of seven cords plaited together in the form of festoons (cf. Jer. 52:22-23). The word is used once to refer to the "lattice" before a window or balcony (2 Kings 1:2).

NEW BIRTH. The technical expression frequently used for *regeneration* (which see).

NEW MOON. See Festivals.

NEWNESS (Gk. *kainotēs*). A new state of spirit or life in which the Spirit places the believer (Rom. 6:4; 7:6).

NEW TESTAMENT. The NT or "New Covenant" is a term describing a portion of the Bible revealed in fulfillment of the OT and dealing with the nativity, ministry, life, death, resurrection, and ascension of the predicted Messiah and the inauguration of the new dispensation of the Christian church on the Day of Pentecost.

The ministry of Christ is set forth in the four gospels. These gospels record selections from the events of Christ's life; taken together they set forth a Personality, not a biography. The twenty-nine formative years of the Messiah are passed over silently. This silence is broken only once or twice. The gospels do not present everything the Son of God did, but they introduce in a wonderful way "the Doer."

The gospels are elucidated by the OT. The foreview of Christ, presenting and including His Person, work, and kingdom, are indispensable requisites to opening up the gospels. To understand the gospels one must not confuse the kingdom, which was offered to Israel, and the church of Jesus Christ. The throne of David (Luke 1:32) must not be made identical with "My Father on His throne" (Rev. 3:21), nor must the house of Jacob (Luke 1:33) be construed as the church of Jesus Christ. It must also be remembered that the mission of the Messiah was primarily to the Jewish nation (Matt. 10:5-6; John 1:11). He was "a servant to the circumcision" (Rom. 15:8). He fulfilled the law, died under the law, and set us free from the law (cf. Gal. 4:4-5).

Therefore, to understand the gospels one must expect to be on legal ground up to the time of the cross (Matt. 10:5-6; 15:22-28; Mark 1:44). The Sermon on the Mount must be seen to be law, not grace. It demands a perfect character that grace alone through divine power can produce. In understanding the NT it also must be borne in mind that the full-orbed revelation concerning grace is to be found in the epistles, not in the gospels, and that Christ by His life, death, and resurrection made possible the operation of divine grace. The gospels do not present the doctrine of the church. Not until the Messiah was rejected as King and Savior by the Jews did He begin to announce a "mystery," until that moment "hidden in God" (Eph. 3:3-10). His great new announcement was "I will build My church" (Matt. 16:16-18).

This church was still future, for it was to be based upon a wholly new operation of the Spirit—His baptizing work (Matt. 3:11; Mark 1:8; Luke 3:16-17; cf. Acts 1:5; 11:16). A study of those Scriptures reveals that the baptism of the Spirit occurred between Acts 1:5 and 11:16; that is, in the pivotal new beginning inaugurated on the Day of Pentecost. On this day the Holy Spirit came to perform His baptizing work for the first time and consequently to give birth to the Christian church.

Following the gospels and Acts, numerous epistles deal with the great Pauline revelation governing this new Body, and the rest of the NT books give practical teaching for this period.

The book of Revelation outlines the future and destiny of the church (chaps. 2-3), as well as the destiny of Israel after her tribulation and establishment of the kingdom (chaps. 4-20). The final two chapters present the eternal state. Since the dispensation of grace was not begun until the cross, when "the veil of the temple was torn in two from top to bottom" (Matt. 27:51), the term *New Testament* is a popular accommodation to describe the latter portion (less than one-third) of divine revelation rather than a strictly accurate usage. See Covenant.   M.F.U.

BIBLIOGRAPHY: G. B. Stevens, *Theory of the New Testament* (1918); C. K. Barrett, *The New Testament Background* (1956); C. C. Ryrie, *Biblical Theology of the New Testament* (1959); W. C. van Unnik, *The New Testament* (1962); R. M. Grant, *An Historical Introduction to the New Testament* (1963); B. M. Metzger, *The New Testament, Its Background, Growth, and Content* (1965); L. L. Morris, *Apostolic Preaching of the Cross* (1965); M. C. Tenney, *New Testament Times* (1965); D. Guthrie, *New Testament Introduction* (1968); F. F. Bruce, *New Testament History* (1969); J. Finegan, *Archaeology of the New Testament* (1969); H. D. McDonald, *Living Doctrines of the New Testament* (1970); R. G. Gromacki, *New Testament Survey* (1974); D. E. Hiebert, *Introduction to the New Testament*, 3 vols. (1975); D. Tidball, *The Social Context of the New Testament* (1984). For additional information see *The Minister's Library* (1985), pp. 104-9, 114-16, 119-20, 125-27, 165-229.

NEW YEAR, SEVENTH NEW MOON, FEAST OF TRUMPETS. See Festivals: Feast of Trumpets.

NEZI'AH (ne-zī'a; "illustrious"). One of the Temple servants whose descendants accompanied Zerubbabel from Babylon (Ezra 2:54; Neh. 7:56), about 536 B.C.

NE'ZIB (ne'zib; a "statue," or "idol"). A town on the lowland of Judah, mentioned between Ash-nah and Keilah (Josh. 15:43). It is to be located at Khirbet Beit Neṣib, about 2¼ miles S of Khirbet Ḳila

NIB'HAZ (nib'haz). An Avvite deity (2 Kings 17:31). *See* Gods, False.

NIB'SHAN (nib'shan). A town in the wilderness of Judah, on the shore of the Dead Sea, near Engedi (Josh. 15:62), but its location is not definite.

NICA'NOR (ni-kā'nor; Gk. "victorious"). A deacon of the church at Jerusalem (Acts 6:5).

NICODE'MUS (nik-ō-dē'mus; Gk. "victor over the people"). His family is unknown, though some recognize him as Nicodemus Ben Gorion, the brother of Josephus the historian. This Nicodemus was a member of the Sanhedrin and was counted one of the three richest men of Jerusalem. But it was said that he afterward became poor, and his daughter was seen gathering barleycorn for food from under the horses' feet. Some have conjectured that this was the result of the persecutions he received for having embraced Christianity (Whedon, *Com.*, John 3:1).

Interview with Jesus. Nicodemus was a Pharisee and a member of the Sanhedrin. Being convinced by His miracles that Jesus was a teacher "come from God," he sought an interview with Him; but fear of the Jews and a regard for his reputation, no doubt, influenced him to make the visit by night. He opened the conversation by an announcement of his belief in Christ's divine mission and was answered by a declaration of the wonderful doctrine of the new birth (John 3:1-10). Jesus also maintained that this doctrine of regeneration should be accepted upon His own divine authority (vv. 10-13), and He insisted upon the doctrine of responsibility for unbelief (vv. 18-21).

Defends Jesus. When, upon a later occasion, the officers sent to apprehend Christ returned without Him and were reproached by the rest of the Sanhedrin, Nicodemus said to them, "Our Law does not judge a man, unless it first hears from him and knows what he is doing, does it?" His words were answered by the taunt, "You are not also from Galilee, are you? Search, and see that no prophet arises out of Galilee" (7:45-52).

At Christ's Burial. Perhaps encouraged by the example of Joseph of Arimathea, Nicodemus assisted at the burial of Jesus. He brought a mixture of myrrh and aloes, about a hundred pounds' weight, to anoint the body, and he assisted in its embalming and burial (19:39-42). Nothing further is known of Nicodemus from Scripture. Tradition adds that after he had thus publicly declared himself a follower of Jesus, and had been baptized by Peter, he was displaced from his office and expelled from Jerusalem.

Character. "A constitutional timidity is observable in all that the Gospel tells us about Nicodemus; a timidity which could not be wholly overcome even by his honest desire to befriend and acknowledge one whom he knew to be a prophet, even if he did not at once recognize in him the promised Messiah" (F. W. Farrar, *Life of Christ*, p. 92).

BIBLIOGRAPHY: E. F. Harrison, *Meditations on the Gospel of John* (1949), pp. 65-74.

NICOLA'ITANS (nik-ō-lā'i-tanz). A sect or party that arose in the apostolic period of the church, mentioned twice by name in the book of Revelation (2:6, 15). In the former passage it is said, to the credit of the church in Ephesus, that she shared in the feelings of the Lord concerning the Nicolaitans, viewing them with the hatred they deserved. The charge is made that some in Pergamos (v. 15) held to teachings of the Nicolaitans, who are compared to those who "hold the teaching of Balaam," etc. "The general voice of antiquity accuses them of holding the lawfulness of eating things offered to idols, and of mixing in and encouraging idolatrous worship; and as they are charged with denying God to be the creator of the world, and attributing its existence to other powers, they could unquestionably, on such grounds, permit themselves so to act, and thus far it is probable that the accusation is not ill-founded. The community of women was another doctrine which they are said to have adopted, and their conduct seems to have been in the highest degree licentious" (*Imperial Bible Dictionary*, s.v.). The origin of the sect will perhaps never be ascertained with certainty. *See* Nicolas.

NIC'OLAS (nik'ō-las; Gk. "victor over the people"). A native of Antioch who had become a proselyte to the Jewish faith. He was afterward converted to Christianity and was elected one of the first seven deacons (Acts 6:5). By some it has been believed that the sect of the Nicolaitans was founded by this Nicolas, but of this there is no positive evidence.

NICOP'OLIS (ni-kop'o-lis; "city of victory"). A city to which Paul refers (Titus 3:12) as the place where he intended to pass the following winter. Titus was at this time in Crete (1:5). There were several cities of this name, which leaves some doubt as to the one about which Paul wrote. Of the three, one was in Thrace, another in Cilicia, and a third in Epirus; the latter seems the most likely to have been meant. This was built by Augustus Caesar in 30 B.C. in honor of a victory at Actium, which was only four miles distant.

NI'GER (nī'jer; "black"). Of Antioch (Acts 13:1). *See* Simeon, no. 5.

NIGHT. *See* Time.

Figurative. The expression "Morning comes but also night" (Isa. 21:12) is interpreted by Delitzsch (*Com.*, ad loc.): "Even if the morning dawns, it will be swallowed up again directly by night. And the history was quite in accordance with such an answer. The Assyrian period of judgment was followed by the Chaldean, and the Chaldean by the Persian, the Persian by the Grecian, and the Grecian by the Roman." The phrase "songs in the night" (Job 35:10; Ps. 77:6) uses night to represent trials and suffering. Thus night stands for a period of distress or trouble and, by a natural extension, also for *death* or the *grave* (John 9:4). Sons "of night" (1 Thess. 5:5) are those who practice the deeds of depravity. Night is also used for a time of ignorance and helplessness (Mic. 3:6).

NIGHT HAWK. *See* Animal Kingdom: Hawk; Night Hawk; Owl.

NIGHT MARCHES. From Num. 9:21, "If it remained in the daytime and at night, whenever the cloud was lifted, they would set out," it is evident that the Israelites made *night marches*. Such marches might have been made either to escape heat or to avoid their enemies—the Amalekites, Edomites, or Ammonites.

NIGHT MONSTER (Heb. *lilît,* Isa. 34:14). In Assyr., Lilith was "a night demon," and the biblical reference is apparently to a demonic creature, something seen in the night by special divine revelation. Respecting Dan. 2:19, "Then the mystery was revealed to Daniel in a night vision," Keil (*Com.,* ad loc.) says: "A vision of the night is not necessarily to be identified with a dream. It is possible, indeed, that dreams may be, as the means of a divine revelation, dream visions, and as such may be called visions of the night, but in itself a vision of the night is a vision simply which anyone receives during the night while he is awake."

See also Animal Kingdom: Owl.

NIGHT WATCH. *See* Watch.

NILE. The one great river of Egypt, navigable for most of its four-thousand-mile course. It is the longest river in the world. The name *Nile,* from the Gk. *Neilos,* Lat. *Nilus,* probably means "dark blue" (cf. Arab., *En-nil*). The river is known to modern Egyptians as *El Bahr,* "the sea" (cf. Nah. 3:8). The Heb. term is *yeʾōr,* which in the plural refers to the Nile River system (cf. Isa. 7:18, marg.). The ancient Egyptians deified it as *Hapi.* Hecataeus of Miletus (fifth century B.C.), accurately described Egypt as "the gift of the river." The geographer Ptolemy in the second century A.D. believed that the Nile River had its source in the heart of Africa at the base of "the Mountains of the Moon." Henry Stanley's discovery in 1888 proved the ancient geographer substantially correct. Stanley first caught sight of a cloud-wrapped mountain at the equator, which he called "the Rain Maker." The Duke of Abruzzi in the early part of the twentieth century explored the 16,791-foot summit of the mountain and demonstrated that the Nile does rise in the Mountains of the Moon. Rains and melting snows from this mountain pour into the waters of Victoria, Albert, and Edward lakes, from which the Nile springs. The main part of the upper river is known as the White Nile. The White Nile is joined by the Blue Nile at Khartoum. The only other tributary is the Atbara, flowing in from the SE. The Nile is furnished a never-failing supply of water by almost daily equatorial rains.

The marvel of the Nile is its annual inundation. Occurring regularly, it overflowed its banks extensively before the dams were completed at Aswan (1902, 1971). At the beginning of June it commences its annual rise. Between July 15 and 20 it rises rapidly. Toward the last part of September the water stops rising and remains constant for twenty to thirty days. In October it rises again, attaining its greatest height, then receding. The fields dry off in January, February, and March, and the soil, softened and fertilized, bears splendid crops. Occasionally inundation failed to take place. Under the famous Dynasty XII, a certain Egyptian official in the reign of Sesostris I speaks of unfruitful years when he did not collect unpaid debts of the field due after short payment. In Joseph's time there was a serious seven-year famine (Gen. 41:54) because of the failure of the inundation. There was likewise a recorded failure for seven years in the reign of the Caliph el-Mustansir. The famine at that time reached serious proportions in A.D. 1070. In pharaonic times the agricultural year consisted of three seasons: the inundation period—June to October; spring (or planting)— October to February; summer (or harvest)— end of February to June. Today the great dam at Aswan gives Egypt a greater cultivatable area than in ancient times.

Between Khartoum at the confluence of the Blue and White Nile and Aswan (ancient Elephantine) there are six cataracts. From the first cataract at Aswan to Memphis, near modern Cairo, is a distance of 600 miles and was known as Upper Egypt. In the course of its last 125 miles from Memphis to the Mediterranean, the Nile branches out into the Delta, so-called because it is shaped like the Gk. letter, and is called Lower Egypt. The Delta forms a great triangle of fertile land cut through by the numerous mouths of the Nile, the most important of which are the Rosetta and Damietta. At the former the famous Rosetta Stone was uncovered, proving to be the key to the reading of ancient Egyptian hieroglyphics and inaugurating the modern science of Egyptology. In Upper Egypt the Nile Valley is mostly a narrow ribbon, usually not more than a dozen miles across, a thread of green wedged in between crags, shelves, and the relentless sands of the desert. The peculiar isolation and the advantages of the almost never-failing river gave Egypt an ideal locale for an early and advanced stage of culture. Egypt in a definite sense was the Nile.

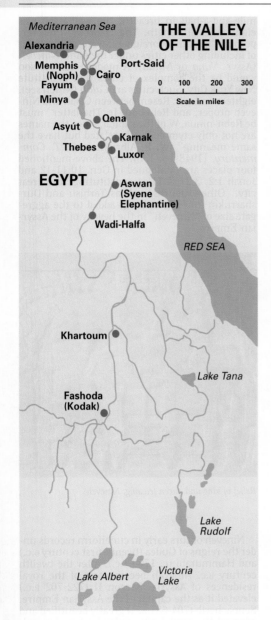

THE VALLEY OF THE NILE

Mediterranean Sea

Alexandria

Memphis (Noph)
Cairo
Port-Said
Fayum
Minya

0   100   200   300
Scale in miles

Asyút
Qena
Karnak
Thebes
Luxor

EGYPT
Aswan (Syene Elephantine)

Wadi-Halfa

RED SEA

Khartoum

Lake Tana

Fashoda (Kodak)

Lake Rudolf

Lake Albert
Victoria Lake

In the OT the Nile is famous as the river in which Moses' mother laid him in a papyrus boat by the river's brink (Ex. 2:3). The waters of the river were turned into blood at the time of the Exodus (7:20-21, 24-25). The river of Egypt was famous for papyrus production (Isa. 19:7). Goshen was the NE area of the Delta, nearest Palestine. In patriarchal times, evidently under the famous Twelfth Dynasty, Abraham migrated

there to escape famine in the land of Canaan (Gen. 12:10–13:1). Joseph was sold into Egypt by his brothers, and Jacob and his family settled there in a similar time of famine (46:3 –50:26). Hebrews during their captivity built such store cities as Pithom and Rameses (cf. Ex. 1:11). It was to Egypt that Joseph and Mary fled with the Christ child, when endangered by the unscrupulous Herod (Matt. 2:13-21). Egypt was a site of ancient cities whose monumental remains constitute great archaeological discoveries, such as Memphis, Amarna, Thebes, and Heliopolis.

M.F.U.

BIBLIOGRAPHY: J. Ball, *Contributions to the Geography of Egypt* (1939); H. E. Hurst, *The Nile* (1952); A. Moorehead, *The White Nile* (1960); id., *The Blue Nile* (1962).

NIM'RAH (nim'ra; "limpid"). A place mentioned by this name in Num. 32:3 only, among those that formed the districts of the "land of Jazer and the land of Gilead." It is the same as Beth-nimrah (v. 36), which belonged to the tribe of Gad. It is located near the Wadi Sha'ib.

NIM'RIM (nim'rim; "limpid waters" or [waters of] "the leopards"). A fertile tract in Moab, SE of the Dead Sea, probably in Wadi Nemeirah. Springs existed near Beth-nimrah. These waters were cursed (Isa. 15:6; Jer. 48:34).

NIMROD (Heb. "rebel"). The son of Cush and founder of the kingdom of Babylon (Gen. 10:8-9). In Micah 5:6 Babylon is designated as "the land of Nimrod." In the Bible Nimrod appears as a great personality in whom earthly imperial power first appears in human history. That this character is evil appears from several observations.

1. Earthly kingship initially comes into existence among the Hamitic peoples, upon one branch of which a prophetic curse was pronounced and in the entire family of which there is an absence of divine blessing (Gen. 9:25-27).

2. Nimrod is represented as the establisher of Babylon (Gen. 10:8-12), which is invariably outlined in Scripture both in type and prophecy as a religiously and morally evil system (Isa. 21:9; Jer. 50:24; 51:64; Rev. 16:19; 17:5; 18:2-3).

3. Nimrod's name "no doubt suggested to the Israelites the idea of 'rebel' . . . against God" (A. Dillmann, *Genesis* [1897], 1:350). The name *Nimrod* in the divine account is definitely meant to suggest the concept of rebellion as descriptive of the character of this first world empire-builder, despite the fact that the original name in Hamitic speech did not have this meaning.

Nimrod has been explained plausibly as Sumerian (early non-Semitic Babylonian) *Ninmaradda*, "lord of Marad," a town SW of Kish (W. F. Albright, in *O. T. Commentary* [1948], p. 138). If, however, Babylonian Cush is to be connected with the exceedingly ancient city kingdom of Kish (founded c. 3200 B.C.), from whence the Babylonian emperors of the third millennium

B.C. took their title "kings of the world," archaeological light is thrown on the primeval imperial period preserved in the name of Nimrod. The dynasty of Kish, consisting of twenty-three kings, is significantly enumerated first in the Mesopotamian dynasties that were established just after the Flood (cf. Jack Finegan, *Light from the Ancient Past* [1946], p. 31; Thorkild Jacobsen, *The Sumerian King List*, Assyriological Studies, no. 11 [1939]). Then, too, Nimrod is said to have been "a mighty hunter before the Lord" (Gen. 10:9). The simple meaning of this statement is that Nimrod was the exact opposite of the divine ideal of a king—that of a shepherd (cf. 2 Sam. 5:2; 7:7; 1 Pet. 5:4). Whereas a hunter gratifies himself at the expense of his victim, the shepherd expends himself for the good of the subjects of his care. Nimrod has been connected with the legendary name of Gilgamesh, the demi-god king of Uruk (biblical Erech, Gen. 10:10), modern Warka, in SW Sumer. Although the beginning of Nimrod's kingdom is said to be "Babel and Erech and Accad and Calneh, in the land of Shinar," there is nothing to prove that Gilgamesh is a reflection of Nimrod. Others imagine that Nimrod is the Babylonian Merodach (Marduk) in human form. The existence in Mesopotamia of many cities preserving the name *Nimrod* is evidence of his widespread popularity in antiquity (cf. Birs Nimrud; Tell Nimrud, near Baghdad; and Nimrud [ancient Calah], about twenty miles S of Nineveh). Nimrod's designation as a "hunter" clearly connects him with the founding of the military state based on absolute force. However, Babylonian and Assyrian art picturing wild animals in hunting scenes may point to Nimrod also as a literal hunter, which in the Heb. account is given a religious connotation.   M.F.U.

BIBLIOGRAPHY: E. A. Speiser, *Eretz Israel* 5 (1958): 32-36.

NIMRUD. *See* Calah; Nimrod.

NIM'SHI (nim'shi). The grandfather of Jehu (2 Kings 9:2, 14), but he is also called his father (9:20; 2 Chron. 22:7).

NIN'EVE (nin'e-ve). The Gk. form (Luke 11:32, KJV) of *Nineveh* (which see).

NIN'EVEH (nin'e-ve). A famous and ancient city situated on the eastern bank of the Tigris River opposite the modern city of Mosul. The Bible names Nimrod as the founder of Nineveh (Gen. 10:8-11). In 612 B.C. the ancient splendid city and capital of the Assyrian Empire was so completely obliterated, according to its prophesied decimation by Hebrew prophets, that it became like a myth until its discovery by Sir Austen Layard and others in the nineteenth century. The site has now been extensively excavated. Its occupational levels reach back as far as prehistoric times. Excavated pottery indicates Sumerian origin. The actual walled city has been outlined to indicate an area three miles in length and less than a

mile-and-a-half in breadth; the wall itself was eight miles in length. The Hebrews, however, perhaps like other foreigners, were in the habit of including other cities under the name *Nineveh* (Assyr. *Nuna* or *Ninua*). A modern comparison would be the complex of cities that constitute New York City. Such cities are *Calah* (which see), eighteen miles S; Resen, between Calah and Nineveh proper; and Rehoboth-Ir. The latter "must be Rebit-ninua, W of the capital, since the names are not only etymologically related but have the same meaning" (W. F. Albright in *O. T. Commentary*, [1948], p. 138). The above-mentioned four places are catalogued in Gen. 10:11-12 and Jonah 1:2; 3:27; 4:11 as constituting "the great city." Other suburbs such as Tarbisu and Dursharrukin (or Sargonsburg) added to the aggregate size of "Nineveh" in the heyday of the Assyrian Empire.

Relief of king and queen feasting, Nineveh

Nineveh occurs early in cuneiform records under the reigns of Gudea (twenty-first century B.C.) and Hammurabi (c. 1700 B.C.). After the twelfth century B.C. Nineveh became one of the royal residences of Assyria. Sargon II (722-702 B.C.) elevated it as the capital of the Assyrian Empire. Sennacherib (704-681 B.C.) greatly beautified and adorned the capital city. Splendid temples, palaces, and fortifications made it the chief city of the empire (2 Kings 19:36). Sennacherib built a massive wall forty to fifty feet high that extended for two-and-a-half miles along the Tigris and eight miles around the inner city. The defenses of the capital can still be traced. Sennacherib also built a water system containing the oldest aqueduct in history at Jerwan, across the Gomer River. Austen Layard did the first successful digging in 1847, uncovering the splendid royal residence of Sennacherib in 1849-51. He unearthed the seventy-one-room palace with walls lined with sculptured slabs. The remains of Nineveh are a silent witness to the glory of Assyria under Sennacherib and his successors Esarhaddon (681-669 B.C.) and Ashurbanipal (669-626 B.C.). The Kuyunjik Mound yielded not only the vast palace of Sennacherib but also the royal residence and famous library of Ashurbanipal in which were housed 22,000 inscribed clay tablets. These are important for their accounts of the creation and Flood and because they furnish scholars with invaluable background material for OT studies.

An alliance of Medes, Babylonians, and Scythians destroyed Nineveh in August 612 B.C., after a two-month siege. This great victory was due in part to the releasing of the city's water supply and the inundation of the Koser River, dissolving the sun-dried brick of which much of the city was built. Nahum prophesied the fall of the "bloody city" (Nah. 2:1–3:19; cf. Zeph. 2:13-15). Nineveh is a site so huge that perhaps it never will be completely excavated. A modern village covers one of the larger palaces. Cemeteries that cannot be disturbed cover other areas. Excavators have to bore through thirty to forty feet of debris before Assyrian strata are reached. (For Nineveh's repentance *see* Jonah, Book of). The nearby mound of Nebi Yunus, that is, "Mound of the Prophet Jonah," contains the palace of Esarhaddon. The popular tradition is that Jonah is buried beneath the mosque at Nebi Yunas.   M.F.U.

BIBLIOGRAPHY: A. H. Layard, *Nineveh and Its Remains* (1849); id., *Discoveries in the Ruins of Nineveh and Babylon* (1853); J. Bonomi, *Nineveh and Its Palaces* (1853); R. C. Thompson and R. W. Hutchinson, *A Century of Exploration at Nineveh* (1929); R. C. Thompson, *Iraq* 1 (1954), 95-104; R. C. Thompson and R. W.

NINEVEH

Hutchinson, et al., *Liverpool Annals of Archaeology and Anthropology* 18 (1931), 55-116; id., 19 (1932), 55ff.; id., 20 (1933), 71-186; A. Parrot, *Nineveh and the Old Testament* (1955).

NIN'EVITE (nin'e-vīt; Luke 11:30). The "men of Nineveh" (Matt. 12:41).

NI'SAN (nī'san; Heb. *nîsān,* from Akkad. *nisanu,* "beginning, opening"). The first month of the sacred year, called Abib in the Pentateuch, for which it is substituted only in the time of the captivity (Neh. 2:1; Esther 3:7). *See* Calendar; Time.

NIS'ROCH (nis'rok; 2 Kings 19:37; Isa. 37:38). An Assyrian God. *See* Gods, False.

NITER. *See* Mineral Kingdom.

NO, or **No-A'mon.** *See* Thebes.

NOADI'AH (nō-a-dî'a; "Jehovah convenes").
1. One of the Levites who, with Meremoth, Eleazar, and others weighed the silver, gold, and utensils of the Temple brought back from Babylon (Ezra 8:33), about 457 B.C.
2. A professed prophetess, who seems to have joined Tobiah and Sanballat in opposition to Nehemiah (Neh. 6:14), about 445 B.C.
3. One of the five daughters of Zelophehad of the tribe of Manasseh (Num. 26:33), c. 1435 B.C. As their father had died leaving no son, the daughters applied for an inheritance in the Promised Land in their father's right. Moses, under divine direction, granted their request (27:1-7), and this promise was redeemed by Joshua (Josh. 17:3-4).
4. Also the name of the well-known pre-Flood patriarch (which see below).

NO'AH (nō'a; "rest, quiet"). The son of Lamech and tenth in descent from Adam (Gen. 5:28-29). Beyond the record of his birth the Scriptures tell us nothing of Noah until he was 500 years old, when it mentions his three sons, Shem, Ham, and Japheth (5:32; 6:10).

As Preacher. The wickedness of the human race had for a long time provoked the wrath of God. A cause of their unrighteousness was the intermarriage of the "sons of God" and the "daughters of men." Jehovah resolved to destroy the human race, but He allowed a respite of 120 years, during which time Noah sought to bring the people to repentance (Gen. 6:1-9; 1 Pet. 3:20; 2 Pet. 2:5). Thus Noah was "a preacher of righteousness," exercising faith in the testimony of God and condemning the world by the contrasted excellence of his conduct.

In the Ark. At length the cup of man's shocking iniquity, manifested in the breaking down of the divinely established orders of created beings (*see* Giants; Nephilim), was full, and the time of their destruction was near at hand. Noah, because of his righteousness, was exempted from

925

extermination and was saved by means of the ark, constructed according to divine direction (Gen. 6:14-22). He entered the ark when he was 600 years old, and the Flood (*see* The Flood), which commenced on the seventeenth day of the second month (7:6, 11), kept rising for 40 days (vv. 12, 17) and only began to abate after 150 days (8:3). On the seventeenth day of the seventh month the ark rested on Ararat; after 40 days Noah sent forth a raven and, at intervals of seven days (or a week), a dove. Finally, on the first day of the first month of his 601st year, Noah removed the covering of the ark; and on the twenty-seventh day of the following month he returned again to dry land (8:4-19).

Noah's Sacrifice. The first thing that Noah did after leaving the ark was to build an altar and to offer sacrifice. He took his offerings from every clean beast and every clean fowl, such animals as were destined for man's food. God accepted the sacrifice and promised no more to waste the earth with a plague of waters but to continue without interruption the regular alternations of day and night and of the seasons of the year (8:20-22). Jehovah blessed Noah and his sons and pronounced his superiority over the inferior creation. All living creatures were given to man for food, with the prohibition against eating blood. Provision was made for the security of human life against animals as well as men. To give Noah and his sons a firm assurance of the prosperous continuance of the human race, God established a covenant with them and gave them as a sign the "bow in the cloud" (9:1-17).

Intoxication. After this Noah entered upon agricultural pursuits and began to cultivate the vine. Whether in ignorance of its properties or not we do not know, but Noah drank wine until intoxicated and shamefully exposed himself in his tent. Ham, seeing the nakedness of his father, displayed a lascivious bent of character and told his brothers, who reverently covered their father with a garment, walking backward that they might not see his nakedness. For this they received their father's blessing, whereas Ham reaped for his son Canaan a prophetic curse (9:20-27).

Conclusion. After this we hear no more of the patriarch but the sum of his years: "Noah lived three hundred and fifty years after the flood. So all the days of Noah were nine hundred and fifty years, and he died" (9:28-29).

Character. The character of Noah is given in a few words descriptive of him in Gen. 6:9: "Noah was a righteous man, blameless in his time; Noah walked with God." That is, he was *righteous* in his moral relations to God and *blameless* in his character and conduct. His righteousness and integrity were manifested in his walking with God.

Noah and Archaeology. In the Sumerian account of the Flood the flood hero appears under the name *Ziusudra* and in the Babylonian version as Utnapishtim. The Babylonian account is contained in the eleventh chapter of the famous Gilgamesh Epic. Of all ancient traditions that bear upon the OT, the Babylonian flood story, revolving around Utnapishtim, manifests the most striking and detailed similarity to the Bible. Both Noah and his Babylonian counterpart are divinely warned of the Flood and are instructed to build a boat, pitch it with pitch, and preserve human and animal life in it. Both accounts tell of the landing place of the boat and describe the sending out of birds. In both, sacrifices are offered with the idea of the gods or the one true God smelling the sacrifice. Both speak of rewards after the Flood.   M.F.U.

BIBLIOGRAPHY: M. F. Unger, *Archaeology and the Old Testament* (1954), pp. 46-71; A. Heidel, *The Gilgamesh Epic and Old Testament Parallels* (1949); J. B. Pritchard, ed., *Ancient Near Eastern Texts* (1969), p. 42.

NO-AMON. *See* Thebes.

NOB (nob). A priestly city in Benjamin, situated on an eminence near Jerusalem. It would seem from Isa. 10:28-32 that it was on one of the roads leading from the N and within sight of the city. Here David applied to Ahimelech for bread after he fled from Saul (1 Sam. 21:1-6), from which it appears that the Ark was then located there before being moved to Jerusalem (2 Sam. 6:1-2). A company of the Benjamites settled here after the return from the exile (Neh. 11:32). But the event for which Nob was most noted in the Scripture annals was a frightful massacre that occurred there in the reign of Saul (1 Sam. 22:17-19). All trace of the name has long ago disappeared from the country. Jerome states that nothing remained in his time to indicate where it had been. Geographers are not agreed as to the precise spot with which we are to identify the ancient locality. Père Abel locates it on Scopus at Räs Umm et-Tala.

Noah and his family after the Flood

NO'BAH (nō'ba; a "barking").

1. An Israelite whose family is not named but who probably belonged, like Jair, to one of the families of Machirites of the tribe of Manasseh (cf. Num. 32:39-41). He took the town of Kenath and its villages (Heb. "daughters") and gave it his own name, Nobah (v. 42).

2. The name given by the above to the town of Kenath, after being taken by him (Num. 32:42).

NOBLES. *See* Princes.

NOD (nod; "wandering, exile"). A place, the location of which is dependent upon that of Eden. The inhabitants of Bussorah and of Bushire claim that the land of Nod lay between these two cities on the NE of the Persian Gulf. It was the retreat of Cain after the murder of Abel (Gen. 4:16). *See* Eden.

NO'DAB (nō'dab; "nobility"). The name of a Bedouin tribe mentioned (1 Chron. 5:19 only) in the account of the war of the Reubenites, Gadites, and the half-tribe of Manasseh against the Hagrites. Nothing more is definitely known respecting them.

NO'E (nō'e). The Gk. form (Matt. 24:37-38; Luke 3:36; 17:26-27; all KJV) of Noah (which see).

NO'GAH (nō'ga; "brilliance, luster"). One of the sons of David who was born to him in Jerusalem by a wife other than Bathsheba (1 Chron. 3:7, 9; 14:3, 6), after 1000 B.C.

NO'HAH (nō'ha; "rest"). The fourth named of the sons of Benjamin and the head of a family (1 Chron. 8:2).

NON (non). Once (1 Chron. 7:27) for *Nun* (which see; Heb. *nun,* "fish"), the father of Joshua.

NOON. *See* Time.

NOPH (nof). The Heb. name of the Egyptian city *Memphis* (which see), the capital of Lower Egypt and of all Egypt during the Old Kingdom. Its ruins have been carried away over the millennia and its stones used in buildings elsewhere. Not much is to be seen there today. In Hos. 9:6 the Heb. name is Moph, and it is translated Memphis, which is its Gk. and Lat. form.

NO'PHAH (no'fa). One of the Moabite cities occupied by Amorites (Num. 21:30), probably the same as Nobah (Judg. 8:11), according to which passage it was near Jogbehah, not far from the eastern desert, and still existing in the ruined place called Nowakis, NW of Amman.

NORTH.

1. (Heb. *mĕzārîm,* "scatterer," Job 37:9). The north wind, so called as dispersing clouds and bringing clear, cold weather. Among the Hebrews the cardinal points of the heavens were considered with reference to the E. Thus to a man facing the E, the N would be at his left hand (Gen. 14:15, *see* marg.; Job 23:9). Land lying to the N was considered as *higher* and to the S as *lower;*

hence to travel northward was to "go up" (Gen. 45:25; Hos. 8:9; Acts 18:22; 19:1), whereas to travel southward was to "go down" (Gen. 12:10; 26:2; 1 Sam. 25:1; 26:2; 30:15-16).

2. (Heb. *ṣāpôn,* "hidden"), the northern quarter of the heavens, called the "hidden," because the ancients regarded the N as the seat of gloom and darkness, in contrast to the bright and sunny S. Thus the phrase "out of the north comes golden splendor" (Job 37:22), i.e., "fair weather." Delitzsch (*Com.,* ad loc.) believes that a contrast is made between the "gold" mined in the N and "the terrible majesty of Jehovah." The reason that Babylonia, Chaldea, Assyria, and Media were said to be N of Palestine (Jer. 1:14; 46:6; etc.; Ezek. 26:7; Zeph. 2:13) is that the kings of most of these countries, in order to avoid the deserts, invaded Palestine chiefly from the N side by way of Damascus and Syria; that is, by way of the so-called fertile crescent. By "the chiefs of the north" (Ezek. 32:30) some understand the Tyrians and their allies (26:15) joined with the Zidonians. "The families of the north" (Jer. 25:9) may indicate kings who were dependent on Babylon; whereas "the king of the North" is the king of Syria, opposed to the king of the S, namely, Egypt (Dan. 11:6-15, 40). The Heb. word is applied to the N wind (Prov. 27:16; Song of Sol. 4:16).

NOSE, NOSTRILS (Heb. *'ap;* dual *'appayim,* properly "breathing place," Num. 11:20). The same Heb. word sometimes means *anger* (Prov. 22:24), as shown in the breathing.

Figurative. "I will put My hook in your nose" (2 Kings 19:28; Job 41:2; Isa. 37:29) is a figurative expression taken from the custom of restraining wild animals, and means to control, humiliate. "For behold, they are putting the twig to their nose" (Ezek. 8:17) appears to be a proverbial expression variously interpreted. Some understand it as the barsom, which the Pharisees while praying held in front of the mouth as a magical mode of driving demons away. Two other explanations may be given — that it is a proverbial expression, "to apply the twig to anger," in the sense of adding fuel to the fire. The second, that of Hitzig, "They apply the sickle to their nose," i.e., by seeking to injure me they injure themselves (Keil, *Com.,* ad loc.).

The phrase "they will remove your nose and your ears" (Ezek. 23:25) is not to be interpreted, as the earlier expositors suppose, from the custom prevalent among the Egyptians and other nations of cutting off the nose of an adulteress, but rather it depicts the mutilation of prisoners.

NOSE RING. A ring worn in or on the nose as an adornment (Gen. 24:47; Isa. 3:21; Ezek. 16:12). The KJV renders the word "earring" and "nose jewel." *See* Jewelry.

NOVICE (Gk. *neophutos,* "newly planted"). One

lately converted, not yet matured in Christian experience (1 Tim. 3:6, KJV only). Later the term came to be applied to converts to Christianity preparing for baptism.

NU'BIANS. The NIV rendering of KJV and NASB "Ethiopians" in Dan. 11:43. *See* Ethiopia.

NUMBER. The rendering of several Heb. and Gk. words.

Mode of Expressing Numbers. Like most oriental nations, it is probable that the Hebrews in their written calculations made use of the letters of the alphabet. That they did so in post-Babylonian times we have conclusive evidence in the Maccabaean coins; and it is highly probable that this was the case also in earlier times. But, though on the one hand it is certain that in all existing manuscripts of the Heb. text of the OT the numerical expressions are written at length, yet on the other hand the variations in the several versions among themselves and from the Heb. text, added to the evident inconsistencies in numerical statement among certain passages of that text itself, seem to prove that some shorter mode of writing was originally in vogue, liable to be misunderstood, and in fact misunderstood by copyists and translators. These variations appear to have proceeded from the alphabetic method of writing numbers.

Arithmetic. Although we know little of the arithmetic of the Hebrews, they must have made considerable progress in the science. Thus we find reference made to *addition* (Num. 1:26), *subtraction* (Lev. 27:18), *surplus* (25:27; Num. 3:46, 48), *multiplication* (Lev. 27:16), *division* (25:50), and *fractions* (Gen. 47:24; Lev. 5:16; 6:5; Num. 15:4; Ezek. 4:11; 45:13). The proportions of the measurements of the Temple in Ezekiel presuppose a considerable proficiency in mathematics.

Scripture Numerics. Many interpreters of Scripture are persuaded that numbers in the Bible have a symbolic meaning. *See* F. W. Grant, *The Numerical Bible, The Pentateuch,* pp. 11-20, for an interpretation of the spiritual meaning of Bible numbers.

BIBLIOGRAPHY: J. J. Davis, *Biblical Numerology* (1968); M. J. Harris and C. Brown, *New International Dictionary of New Testament Theology* (1976), 2:683-704.

NUMBERS, BOOK OF. The fourth book of the Pentateuch, continuing the redemptive history of Israel where Exodus leaves off. As Genesis is the book of origins, Exodus the book of redemption, and Leviticus the book of worship and fellowship, Numbers is the book of the service and walk of God's redeemed people.

Name. The LXX title *Arithmoi* (numbers) was rendered *Liber Numeri* in the Vulg., which appears in English as the book of Numbers or simply Numbers. The book is so designated because it makes a double reference to taking a census of the Jewish people (chaps. 1-3 and chap. 26). As was usual, the Jews named the book from its opening word *wayyᵉdabbēr* ("and He [Jehovah] said"), or more often from the fifth word *bᵉmidbar* ("in the wilderness").

Aim. Numbers continues the journey commenced in the book of Exodus, beginning with the events of the second month of the second year (Num. 10:11) and ending with the eleventh month of the fortieth year (Deut. 1:3). The thirty-eight years of wandering deal with the failure of the redeemed people in the face of every divine provision for their welfare and success. The book is typically significant in warning against the dangers of unbelief. The people disobeyed at Kadesh-barnea (Num. 14) and suffered repeated defeat and eventual death in the desert (20:1–33:49).

Outline.
I. Departure from Sinai (1:1–10:10)
   A. Numbering of the people (1:1-54)
   B. Arranging of the camp (2:1-34)
   C. Instructing priest and Levite (3:1–4:49)
   D. Protecting from defilement (5:1-31)
   E. Giving the Nazirite law (6:1-27)
   F. Enumerating gifts of the leaders (7:1-89)
   G. Lighting of the Tabernacle lamps (8:1-4)
   H. Cleansing of the Levites (8:5-26)
   I. Observing the Passover (9:1-14)
   J. Guiding the camp (9:15-23)
   K. Signals for calling and moving the camp (10:1-10)
II. Journey to Moab (10:11–21:35)
   A. From Sinai to Kadesh-barnea (10:11–14:45)
   B. The desert wandering (15:1–19:22)
   C. From Kadesh-barnea to Moab (20:1–22:1)
III. Encampment by Jordan (22:2–36:13)
   A. Balaam's oracles (22:1–25:18)
   B. Instructions (26:1–31:54)
   C. Territorial distribution E of the Jordan (32:1-42)
   D. Itinerary from Egypt (33:1-56)
   E. Instruction before entering the land (34:1–36:13)

Critical Theory. Critics who deny Mosaic authorship divide Numbers into P (Priestly Code) and JE (Jehovistic-Elohistic narrative). Chapters 1:1–10:28 are supposedly a long extract from P, while JE is interwoven in the book. This criticism of Numbers, of a piece with Pentateuchal higher criticism in general, is based upon the same erroneous philosophic, literary, and religious presuppositions. It is a product of rationalistic scepticism that attempted to reconcile prevailing modes of thinking of the nineteenth century with the testimony of the Mosaic books.

BIBLIOGRAPHY: G. B. Gray, *A Critical and Exegetical Commentary on Numbers.* International Critical Commentary (1903); J. H. Greenstone, *Numbers*. The Holy Scriptures with Commentary (1939); N. H. Snaith, *Leviticus and Numbers*. New Century Bible (1967); R. K. Harrison, *Introduction to the Old Testament* (1969), pp. 614-37; G. Bush, *Notes on Numbers* (1983).

NUN (nun; a "fish," as prolific).

1. An Ephraimite who was the father of Joshua (Ex. 33:11; Num. 11:28; 13:8, 16; 14:6, 30, 38; 26:65; 27:18; 32:12, 28; etc.). There is no account given of his life.

2. The fourteenth letter (נ or ן) of the Hebrew alphabet (Ps. 119:105-112).

NURSE, NURSING (Heb. *yānaq*, to "give milk," once *'āman*, to "support, foster," Ruth 4:16). It is clear, both from Scripture and from Greek and Roman writers, that in ancient times the position of the nurse was one of honor and importance (*see* Gen. 24:59; 35:8; 2 Sam. 4:4; 2 Kings 11:2). The same term is applied to a foster father or

mother, e.g., Num. 11:12; Ruth 4:16; Isa. 49:23. In great families male servants, probably eunuchs in later times, were entrusted with the charge of the boys (2 Kings 10:1, 5).

NURTURE (Gk. *paideia*, Eph. 6:4, KJV). The whole training and education of children that relates to the cultivation of mind and morals. For this purpose commands and admonitions are sometimes used and at other times, reproofs and punishments. It includes also the care and training of the body. It also is a term describing God's dealing with His children under grace.

NUTS. *See* Vegetable Kingdom.

NUZI. *See* Jacob.

NYM'PHA (nim'na; "nymph-given"). A prominent Christian in Laodicea, whose house was used as a place of worship (Col. 4:15).

OAK, WORSHIP OF. Oak groves in early times were used as places of religious concourse; altars were set up in them (Josh. 24:26); Jacob buried idolatrous images under an oak (Gen. 35:4), probably because, since the oak was a consecrated tree, no one would disturb them there. Idolatry was practiced under oaks (Isa. 1:29; 57:5; Ezek. 6:13), and idols were made of oak (Isa. 44:14). *See* Vegetable Kingdom.

Figurative. The oak is a symbol of Israel (Isa. 6:13) and of strong and powerful men (Amos 2:9). *Fading oaks* are a symbol of the wicked under judgment (Isa. 1:30).

OAR. *See* Ship.

OATH. Two terms are employed in the OT to express what we understand by *an oath,* to *take an oath,* or to *swear.* (1) Heb. *'ālâ,* "imprecation," according to Gesenius, from El, the name of God, and so "to call upon God." Hence the word quite naturally passed over to the sense of *imprecation, cursing,* as it is frequently rendered (Num. 5:23; Isa. 24:6; Zech. 5:3; etc.). It also means *a sworn covenant* (Gen. 26:28; 2 Sam. 21:7) and *an oath,* as an appeal to God in attestation of the truth of a statement (Ex. 22:11; Neh. 10:29). (2) *sheᵇû'â,* from the Heb. *sheba',* "seven," the sacred number. To "seven one's self," or to do by sevens, was to act after the manner of God—to give what was done a peculiarly sacred character—hence to make an oath or swear. Solemn agreements, or oaths, were often accompanied by a sevenfold action of some sort, e.g., the giving of seven ewe lambs by Abraham to Abimelech (Gen. 21:30).

Nature of Oath. Every oath contains two elements, namely, an affirmation, or promise, and an appeal to God as omniscient and the punisher of falsehoods. (1) The principle on which an oath is held to be binding is incidentally laid down in Heb. 6:16: "For men swear by one greater than

themselves, and with them an oath given as confirmation is an end of every dispute." The Almighty is represented as promising or denouncing with an oath, i.e., doing so in the most positive and solemn manner. (2) On the same principle that oath has always been held most binding that appealed to the highest authority both as regards individuals and communities. (*a*) Thus believers in Jehovah appealed to Him both judicially and extrajudicially. (*b*) Appeals of this kind to authorities recognized respectively by adjuring parties were regarded as bonds of international security and their infraction as being not only grounds for international complaint but also offenses against divine justice. (3) As a consequence of this principle, (*a*) appeals to God's name on the one hand, and to heathen deities on the other, are treated in Scripture as tests of allegiance (Ex. 23:13; Deut. 29:12; etc.). (*b*) So also the sovereign's name is sometimes used as a form of obligation (Gen. 42:15; 2 Sam. 11:11; 14:19). (4) Other forms of oath, serious or frivolous, are mentioned, some of which are condemned by our Lord (Matt. 5:33; 23:16-22; cf. James 5:12), yet He did not refuse the solemn adjuration of the high priest (Matt. 26:63-64).

Occasions. The Hebrews used oaths under the following circumstances: (1) Agreement or stipulation for performances of certain acts (Gen. 14:22; 24:2-3, 8-9; etc.). (2) Allegiance to a sovereign or obedience from an inferior to a superior (Eccles. 8:2; 2 Chron. 36:13; 1 Kings 18:10). (3) Promissory oath of a ruler (Josh. 6:26; 1 Sam. 14:24, 28; etc.). Priests took no oath of office (Heb. 7:21). (4) Vows made in the form of an oath (Lev. 5:4). (5) Judicial oaths. Public or judicial oaths were required on the following occasions: (*a*) A man receiving a pledge from a neighbor was required, in case of injury happening to the pledge, to clear himself by oath of the blame of damage (Ex. 22:10-11; 1 Kings 8:31; 2 Chron.

6:22). (b) A person suspected of having found or otherwise come into possession of lost property was to vindicate himself by an oath (Lev. 6:3). It appears that witnesses were examined on oath; a false witness, or one guilty of suppression of the truth, was to be severely punished (Lev. 5:1; Deut. 19:16-19; cf. Prov. 29:24). (c) A wife suspected of infidelity was required to clear herself by oath (Num. 5:19-22). But this ordeal does not come under the civil administration of justice.

Forms of Oaths. As to the forms of oaths, the Jews appealed to God with or without an imprecation in such phrases as "God do this to me and more also," etc. (1 Sam. 14:44); "as the Lord lives" (14:39; 19:6; 2 Sam. 15:21; 1 Kings 18:10); "as the Lord lives and as your soul lives" (1 Sam. 20:3); "the Lord is between you and me forever" (20:23); "the God of Abraham judge between us" (Gen. 31:53). The Jews also swore "by heaven," "by the earth," "by Jerusalem," "by the temple" (Matt. 5:34-35; 23:16), "by the angels" (Josephus *Wars* 2.16. 4), and by the lives of distinguished persons (Gen. 42:15-16; 1 Sam. 1:26; 17:55; 2 Sam. 11:11; 14:19). The *external manner* of an oath was as follows: (1) Originally the oath of a covenant was taken by solemnly sacrificing *seven* animals, or it was attested by *seven* witnesses or pledges, consisting either of so many animals presented to the contracting party or of memorials erected to testify to the act (Gen. 21:28-31). (2) Lifting up the hand. Witnesses laid their hands on the head of the accused (Gen. 14:22; Lev. 24:14; Isa. 3:7). (3) Putting the hand under the thigh of the person to whom the promise was made. It has been explained (a) as having reference to the covenant of circumcision; (b) as containing a principle similar to that of phallic symbolism, i.e., the genital organ the symbol of the Creator; (c) as referring to the promised Messiah. (4) Oaths were sometimes taken before the altar or, as some understand the passage, if the persons were not in Jerusalem, in a position looking toward the Temple (1 Kings 8:31; 2 Chron. 6:22). (5) Dividing a sacrifice and passing between or distribution of the pieces (Gen. 15:10, 17; Jer. 34:18). In every case the oath taken before a judgment seat seems to have consisted of an adjuration by the judge, responded to by the persons sworn with an *amen* (Heb. *'āmēn,* "truly," 1 Kings 22:16; Gk. *su eipas,* "you have said," Matt. 26:63-64).

Sanctity. As the sanctity of oaths was carefully inculcated by the law, so the crime of perjury was strongly condemned; and to a false witness the same punishment was assigned that was due for the crime to which he testified (Ex. 20:7; Lev. 19:12; Deut. 19:16-19; Ps. 15:4; Jer. 5:2; 7:9; Ezek. 16:59; Hos. 10:4; Zech. 8:17).

Christian. The Christian practice in the matter of oaths was founded in great measure on the Jewish. Thus oath-taking on the gospels was an imitation of the Jewish practice of placing the hands on the book of the law. The meaning of our Lord's interdiction of swearing (Matt. 5:33-37) was that "Christianity should know no oath at all. To the consciousness of the Christian, God should always be so vividly present that, to him and others in the Christian community, his yea and nay are, in point of reliability, equivalent to an oath. His yea and nay are oath enough" (Meyer, *Com.,* ad loc.). The prohibition of swearing does not refer to official oaths but to private conduct, for none of the oaths referred to by our Lord are judicial oaths. The orientals were great swearers, and the secondary oaths forbidden by our Lord are just the ordinary profanities of their conversation. In these they avoided the use of God's name, and they supposed that the breaking of these oaths did not constitute perjury.

BIBLIOGRAPHY: J. E. Tyler, *Oaths: Their Origin, Nature, and History* (1835); S. A. B. Mercer, *The Oath in Babylonian and Assyrian Literature* (1912); D. Daube, *Studies in Biblical Law* (1947); M. G. Kline, *Westminster Theological Journal* 27 (1964): 1-20; G. F. Oehler, *Theology of the Old Testament* (1978), pp. 176, 230, 248-50.

OBADI'AH (ō-ba-dī'a; "servant of Jehovah").

1. An officer of high rank in the court of Ahab, who is described as "over the household," i.e., apparently, lord high chamberlain or mayor of the palace (1 Kings 18:3), about 870-850 B.C. Notwithstanding his position, he "feared the Lord greatly," and during the persecution of the prophets by Jezebel he concealed 100 of them in a cave, supplying them with food. In the third year of the terrible famine that visited Samaria, Ahab and Obadiah divided the land between them to search for pasture. While on his journey he unexpectedly met Elijah, who commanded him to tell the king of the prophet's appearance. Obadiah hesitated, fearing death at Ahab's hands, but when Elijah insisted he had no choice but to obey (vv. 5-16).

2. A man referred to in 1 Chron. 3:21 in an obscure manner. Keil (*Com.,* ad loc.) and Smith (*Dict.,* s.v.) believe the passage clearly corrupt. Strong (McC. and S., *Cycl.,* s.v.) considers that Obadiah was a son of Arnan, as the LXX and Vulg. have, reading "his son" instead of "sons of," and identifies him with Joda (Luke 3:26) and Abiud (Matt. 1:13) of Christ's genealogy.

3. According to the received text, one of the five sons of Izrahiah, a descendant of Issachar, and a leader of his tribe (1 Chron. 7:3).

4. One of the six sons of Azel, a descendant of Saul (1 Chron. 8:38; 9:44).

5. A Levite, son of Shemaiah, who dwelt in one of the villages of the Netophathites, near Jerusalem (1 Chron. 9:16). He is named as one of the Temple gatekeepers (Neh. 12:25), about 445 B.C.

6. The second named of the eleven Gadite warriors of renown who joined David at Ziklag (1 Chron. 12:9), before 1000 B.C.

7. The father of Ishmaiah, who was chief officer of the tribe of Zebulun in David's reign (1 Chron. 27:19).

8. One of the officials whom Jehoshaphat employed to teach in the cities of Judah (2 Chron. 17:7), about 870 B.C.

9. A Levite of the family of Merari, who was one of the overseers of Temple repairs ordered by King Josiah (2 Chron. 34:12), 622 B.C.

10. The son of Jehiel, of the sons of Joab, who came up with a company of 218 male kinsmen in the second caravan with Ezra (Ezra 8:9), about 457 B.C.

11. One of the priests who signed the covenant with Nehemiah (Neh. 10:5), 445 B.C.

12. The prophet. As to the person and circumstances of Obadiah nothing certain is known; and the traditional accounts of him in the rabbis and Fathers, some of whom identify him with Ahab's pious commander, others with the third captain sent by Ahaziah against Elisha (2 Kings 1:13), are evidently false.

OBADIAH, BOOK OF. One of the minor prophets, constituting the smallest book of the OT. The name *Obadiah,* the prophet and traditional author of the oracle, means "the servant or worshiper of Jehovah."

Subject. The prophetic oracle is taken up wholly with the denunciation of Edom for its unbrotherly conduct toward Judah, presenting a foreview of its complete decimation and Judah's deliverance in the Day of the Lord.

Contents.

 I. Edom's destruction prophesied (vv. 1-9)
  A. Her fortifications conquered (vv. 1-4)
  B. Her possessions consumed (vv. 5-9)
 II. Edom's destruction explained (vv. 10-14)
 III. Edom's destruction completed (vv. 15-21)
  A. Her sin judged (vv. 15-16)
  B. Her victim saved (vv. 17-20)
  C. Her kingdom replaced (v. 21)

The Date. The prophecy is variously dated by critics. Oesterley and Robinson view the book as a group of oracles from "almost anytime between the end of the sixth and middle of the second centuries B.C." (*Introduction,* p. 370). Critics generally ascribe the prophecy to the Chaldean period after the destruction of Jerusalem in 587 B.C. and deny the unity of the book. Robert Pfeiffer was of the opinion that the original oracle against Edom is preserved in two editions, Obadiah 1-9 and Jeremiah 49:7-22. He dated Obadiah 1-15 about 460 B.C. and 16-21, which he regarded as "apocalyptic fancy," even later. There is no genuine reason to deny the unity of the prophecy or to refuse it a place in the reign of Jehoram (c. 848-841 B.C.). During Jehoram's reign the Philistines and Arabians overran Judah and plundered Jerusalem (2 Chron. 21:16-17; cf. Joel 3:3-6; Amos 1:6). At that time the Edomites were particularly hostile to Judah (2 Kings 8:20-22;

2 Chron. 21:8-20). All the requirements of the prophecy are satisfied in this historical context. In support of this view it may be said that the prophet Amos (c. 760) had an acquaintance with Obadiah (cf. Obad. 4 with Amos 9:2; Obad. 9-10, 18 with Amos 1:11-12; Obad. 14 with Amos 1:6, 9; Obad. 19 with Amos 9:12; and Obad. 20 with Amos 9:14). Jeremiah, too, doubtless used the prophecies (cf. Obad. 1-6 with Jer. 49:7-22). Moreover, the position of Obadiah in the minor prophets after Amos suggests a preexilic origin. (For critical literature *see* T. H. Robinson, "The Structure of the Book of Obadiah," *Jour. of Theol. Studies* 17 [1916]: 402-8; G. W. Wade, *Obadiah* in the *Westminster Commentaries* [1925].)

BIBLIOGRAPHY: J. D. W. Watts, *Obadiah: A Critical, Exegetical Commentary* (1969); R. K. Harrison, *Introduction to the Old Testament* (1969), pp. 898-903; L. C. Allen, *The Books of Joel, Obadiah, Jonah and Micah,* New International Commentary on the Old Testament (1976); F. E. Gaebelein, ed., *Expositor's Bible Commentary* (1985), 7: 335-57.

O'BAL (ō'bal). A son of Joktan, and founder of an Arabian tribe (Gen. 10:28). The locality (called Ebal in 1 Chron. 1:22; *see* NIV marg.) where they settled is unknown.

O'BED (ō'bed; "serving").

1. The son of Boaz and Ruth and father of Jesse the father of David (Ruth 4:17; 1 Chron. 2:12), about 1070 B.C. The name *Obed* occurs only in Ruth 4:17 and in the four genealogies (Ruth 4:21-22; 1 Chron. 2:12; Matt. 1:5; Luke 3:32).

2. A descendant of Jarha, the Egyptian slave of Sheshan, in the line of Jerahmeel. He was grandson of Zabad, one of David's mighty men (1 Chron. 2:37-38), after 1015 B.C.

3. One of David's mighty men (1 Chron. 11:47), about 1000 B.C.

4. One of the gatekeepers of the Temple, son of Shemaiah, the firstborn of Obed-edom (1 Chron. 26:7), before 960 B.C.

5. Father of Azariah, one of the captains of hundreds who joined Jehoiada in the revolution by which Athaliah fell (2 Chron. 23:1), c. 842 B.C.

O'BED-E'DOM (ō'bed-ē'dom; "servant of Edom").

1. A Levite of the family of Korhites and belonging to the class of gatekeepers (1 Chron. 15:18, 24). He is called a Gittite, or Gathite, from his birthplace, the Levitical city of Gath-rimmon in the tribe of Dan. After the death of Uzzah, the Ark, which was being conducted from the house of Abinadab in Gibeah to the city of David, was carried aside into the house of Obed-edom, where it remained three months, during which time Obed-edom was greatly prospered (13:14). It was brought from that place by David (1 Chron. 15:25), about 986 B.C. It was Obed-edom the Gittite who was appointed to play "with lyres tuned to the sheminith" (1 Chron. 15:21; 16:5, 38). He

is probably the same person mentioned in 26:4-8.

2. The son of Jeduthun and one of the Temple gatekeepers (1 Chron. 16:38), before 960 B.C.

3. A person who had charge of the utensils of the sanctuary in the time of Amaziah, king of Judah (2 Chron. 25:24), about 783 B.C.

OBEDIENCE. As a branch of Christian ethics, obedience is to be viewed not only with respect to the relations existing between God and man and between man and society but also with respect to the example of Christ and man's relation to Him.

1. Perfect obedience to the commandments of God must be the object of our constant endeavor. The imperfect results of even our most strenuous efforts, however, reveal the necessity of God's grace in Christ. Nothing less than entire self-surrender to God and reverent trust can make this grace available (*see* 1 John 1:6-10; 2:1-6; Rom. 3:20; 5:1; 6:1-2; etc.). *See* Law; Atonement; Faith.

2. Christian obedience also includes that of children to their parents (*see* Luke 2:51; Eph. 6:1-2); of servants to their masters (*see* Titus 2:9-10; Col. 3:23; Eph. 6:6); proper respect to civil authority (*see* Matt. 22:21; Rom. 13:1-7); also proper recognition of the authority of the church, or the obligations of Christian fellowship (Matt. 18:17; 2 Cor. 6:14-18). But *see,* further, Judgment, Right of Private.

BIBLIOGRAPHY: W. Mundle, *New International Dictionary of New Testament Theology* (1976), 2:172-80; P. Toon, *Free to Obey* (1979).

OBEDIENCE OF CHRIST. This embraces not only the holy life of our Lord, His complete conformity to the divine law to which He was subject as a man, but also His voluntary acceptance of His sacrificial suffering and death as the Savior of mankind (*see* John 8:46; 17:4-6; Matt. 3:15; Rom. 5:18; Gal. 4:4-5; Phil. 2:7-8). The distinction between the active and passive obedience of Christ, however, has been too sharply drawn by many theologians and made the basis of artificial theorizing. Thus, while to the death of Christ is ascribed the blessing of pardon, to what is called His active obedience is referred the imputation of Christ's perfect righteousness to believers, in the stead of imperfect righteousness (*see* Imputation). But, as Van Oosterzee observes, "The very doing of the Lord was to a certain extent a suffering; his suffering on the other hand, in some respects his highest form of action." The holy life of Christ is essentially connected with human salvation because: (1) Although His atonement centers in His death, His whole life was sacrificial, and the offering of Himself even in death could not have been acceptable without the spotless life that preceded (*see* 1 Pet. 1:18-19). (2) Christ thus became in Himself the perfect manifestation of truth and righteousness and thus, in His self-denial and love, the perfect ideal of righ-

teousness for mankind (*see* John 14:6-9; 13:14-15; 1 Pet. 2:21; 1 Cor. 11:1; Phil. 2:4-12). (3) He is also thus fitted to be the "second Adam," the source of spiritual life and strength to His people (*see* John 10:10; 15:4; Acts 3:15; 1 Cor. 15:45). (4) Thus also Christ achieved His exaltation to the throne of His mediatorial kingdom (*see* Phil. 2:9-11; Heb. 2:16-18).

BIBLIOGRAPHY: G. C. Berkouwer, *The Person of Christ* (1953), pp. 314-27.

O'BIL (ō'bil). An Ishmaelite who was in charge of the herds of camels in the reign of David (1 Chron. 27:30).

OBLATION. See Offering.

O'BOTH (ō'both). The forty-sixth station of the Israelites in their journey from Egypt to Canaan, near Moab (Num. 21:10-11; 33:43-44), probably the oasis el-Weiba.

OBSCURITY. See Gloom.

OBSERVED (Gk. *paratērēsis,* that which may be seen; "without outward show"). In the expression "the kingdom of God is not coming with signs to be observed" (Luke 17:20), the meaning is, "The coming of Messiah's kingdom is not so conditioned that this coming could be *observed* as a visible development; or that it could be said, in consequence of such observation, that here or there is the kingdom" (Meyer, *Com.,* ad loc.).

OBSERVER OF TIMES. See Magic.

OCH'RAN, OC'RAN (ok'ran). Ochran (Ocran, KJV and NIV) was the father of Pagiel, the latter being the leader of the tribe of Asher, who assisted Moses in the numbering of the people (Num. 1:13; 2:27; 7:72, 77; 10:26), 1438 B.C.

O'DED (ō'ded; "reiteration").

1. The father of Azariah the prophet who met Asa on his return from defeating the Ethiopians (2 Chron. 15:1), before 905 B.C. The address is in v. 8 (*see* marg.) ascribed to Oded, probably through a mistake of the copyists.

2. A prophet of the Lord in Samaria in the time of Pekah's invasion of Judah (about 735 B.C.). He met the victorious army returning with their booty and prisoners (200,000) and pointed out to them their cruelty and guilt, exhorting them to turn away the anger of God by sending back their prisoners (2 Chron. 28:9). His speech made a deep impression, and, according to the advice of some of the leaders of Ephraim, the captives were fed, clothed, anointed, and returned to Jericho.

ODOR. See Aroma.

OFFENSE. The English rendering of several Gk. and Heb. words. In the OT, "offense" or "offenses" appears in the NASB in Gen. 41:9; Eccles. 10:4 for Heb. *ḥēṭ',* with the meaning of "crime or its penalty"; in Lev. 19:7 for Heb. *piggûl,* "an offense" ("abomination," KJV; "impure," NIV);

and in Ezra 10:19 for Heb. *'āshēm,* with the meaning of "guilt." In the KJV, *ḥēṭ'* (Eccles. 10:4), *mikshôl* (1 Sam. 8:14), and *'āshām* (Hos. 5:15) are behind the English terms. The NIV translates *'āwôn* as "responsibility for offenses" (Num. 18:1) and it renders *ḥaṭṭā't* "offense" (Deut. 19:15) as well as its cognate *ḥēṭ'* (Deut. 21:22).

In the NT, Gk. *skandalon,* "the movable stick of a trap," i.e., an impediment, "a rock of offense" (Rom. 9:33) is frequently translated "offense," although the NASB and NIV are more likely to use *stumbling block* (Matt. 16:23; 18:7; Luke 17:1; Gal. 5:11), *hindrances,* or obstacles, (Rom. 16:17). The "offence of the cross" (Gal. 5:11, KJV and NIV) was the offense that the Jews took at Christianity, because faith in a crucified Savior —faith without legal observances—was alone offered as the means of salvation. "Offense" is the KJV and NASB translation of *proskomma* and *proskopē* in Rom. 14:20; 2 Cor. 6:3. The NIV renders "causes to stumble" and "stumbling block" respectively.

In Rom. 4:25; 5:15-20, another Gk. term, *paraptōma,* to "fall beside" or "near," a "lapse" or "deviation from the truth" is given as "offense" in the KJV and "transgression" in the NASB. The NIV translates "sins" in 4:25 and "trespass" in 5:15-20. The reverse is the case with *parabasis* in Rom. 5:14. *Offended,* or *offend,* appears as the KJV translation of *hamartanō* in Acts 25:8, of *skandalizō* in Matt. 13:57; 17:27; Mark 6:3, and of *ptaiō* in James 2:10; 3:2, although the NASB uses the terms *offense* and *stumble.* The NIV translates "do wrong" in Acts 25:8; "take offense" in Matt. 13:57 and Mark 6:3; "offend" in Matt. 17:27; and "stumbles" or "stumble" in James 2:10 and 3:2. *See* Abomination; Stumbling Block; Transgression.

BIBLIOGRAPHY: W. Barclay, *New Testament Wordbook* (1955), pp. 111-14; N. Turner, *Christian Words* (1980), pp. 294-98.

OFFERING.

1. *An offering presented* (Heb. *qorbān,* brought near), usually of the meat offerings (Lev. 2:4; 7:14, 29).

2. *A heave-offering* (Heb. *t͏erûmâ,* heave), a portion *lifted* or taken by a person from his property as an offering to God; consequently, everything that was offered by the Israelites, either voluntarily or in consequence of a command from the Lord, for the erection and maintenance of the sanctuary and its officials (Isa. 40:20; Ezek. 44:30; 45:1; etc.).

3. *A present* (Heb. *minḥâ,* a donation), especially of a bloodless offering (Isa. 19:21; 66:3; Dan. 9:21, 27).

4. *A libation* (Heb. *massākâ,* pouring), in worship a *libation,* but it is to be taken in Dan. 2:46 in the general sense of sacrifice. *See* First Fruits; Sacrifice; Sacrificial Offerings.

OFFICE. The rendering of numerous Heb. and Gk. words, with some variety of meaning: *position* (Gen. 41:13; 1 Chron. 23:28); the *priestly fraternity* (Luke 1:9; Heb. 7:5); *pastoral oversight* (1 Tim. 3:1). In the KJV this translation also means *responsibility* (Num. 4:16; 2 Chron. 24:11; Ps. 109:8); *priestly service* (Luke 1:8); *function,* as of a member of the body, or of the church (Rom. 12:4).

OFFICER. It is obvious that most, if not all, of the Heb. words rendered "officer" are either of an indefinite character or are synonymous terms for those who serve in functions known under other and more specific names such as "scribe," "eunuch," etc.

1. *Eunuch* (Heb. *sārîs,* to "castrate," Gen. 37:36; 39:1; cf. 40:2), usually (but not in the NIV) rendered *eunuch* (which see).

2. *Prefect* (Heb. *shōṭēr,* properly a "writer"), from the use of writing in judicial administration, a *magistrate;* the "taskmasters" ("slave drivers," NIV) set over the Israelites in Egypt (Ex. 5:6-19); those appointed with the elders to administer public affairs among the Israelites (Num. 11:16; Deut. 20:5, 8-9; 29:10; Josh. 1:10; etc.); magistrates in the cities and towns of Palestine (Deut. 16:18; 1 Chron. 23:4; 26:29; etc.), and apparently a military chief (2 Chron. 26:11).

3. *One appointed* (Heb. *niṣṣāb,* "fixed," 1 Kings 9:23, *see* marg.), elsewhere "deputy," general receivers of taxes, or chief tax collectors, who levied the king's duties or taxes, consisting in the East, for the most part, of the produce of the land, and were delivered at the royal kitchen.

4. *A superintendent* (KJV only), either civil, military, or ecclesiastical (Heb. *pāqēd,* Gen. 41:34; Judg. 9:28; Esther 2:3; etc.).

A Roman lictor

5. The two words so rendered in the NT each bear in ordinary Gk. a special sense. In the case of *hupēretēs* (Matt. 5:25; John 7:32, 45-46; 18:3, 12, 18, 22; Acts 5:22, 26), this is of no definite kind, but the word is used to denote an inferior officer of a court of justice, a messenger or bailiff, like the Roman lictor. *Praktores* (Luke 12:58, KJV), at Athens, were officers whose duty it was to register and collect fines imposed by courts of justice; to "deliver to the officer" means, to give in the name of the debtor to the officer of the court.

OFFICES OF CHRIST. The three offices of Christ as Prophet, Priest, and King.

Biblical View. This division of the saving work of Christ is derived from the Scriptures inferentially. The OT term *Messiah* is generally, though not universally, held to have this threefold significance (*see* Messiah). Also the work ascribed by prophecy to Christ had this threefold character (*see* particularly Deut. 18:15; Isa. 49:7; chap. 53). Moreover, the divinely appointed economy of Judaism, with the three great offices of prophet, priest, and theocratic king, was typical of Christ. In the NT we find that Christ spoke of Himself most distinctly as king. He referred to Himself but indirectly as prophet (e.g., Matt. 13:57) and never called Himself priest. His reserve may be explained by His words in John 16:12-13. We find, however, from the gospels that His work in a large measure was actually that of a prophet; and as the time drew near for His great sacrifice He spoke of it in a way that clearly indicated His priestly character (*see* Matt. 26:26-28; John 10:11, 17-18). This fullness of Christ's work, as might be expected, is more clearly set forth in Acts and in the epistles (*see* Acts 2:22, 33, 38; 4:12; 5:31; 7:37, 52; Heb. 1:2-3; 2:9-11; 7:22-28; etc.).

Christ is Prophet because more than all others He has declared to men the truth and will of God. He is Himself the revelation of God (*see* John 14:9; 17:25-26; Heb. 1:1-2; etc.). He is Priest not only because of His holy character and mediatorial position, but also, and emphatically, because of His sacrificial work (*see,* besides Scriptures already cited, 1 John 2:1-2; Rev. 5:9). *See* Atonement.

He is King not only by virtue of His divine nature but also because as the God-man He is the divinely appointed head of the mediatorial kingdom, who in His second advent as "King of kings" (Rev. 19:16) will restore the kingdom to Israel (Acts 1:6) and fulfill the Davidic covenant and the OT promises made to Israel (2 Chron. 7; Isa. 60; Zech. 8; etc.).

It is important in the highest degree that each one of these forms of the work of Christ should be duly recognized. Otherwise we fail to obtain the right conception of Christ and of His relations to mankind.

Historical. The division of Christ's mediatorial work in three offices, based upon Scripture, was formally stated in the early church, as indicated in the writings of Eusebius, Cyril of Jerusalem, and Augustine.

In the Middle Ages it was elaborated by Thomas Aquinas. It was introduced into the theology of the Lutheran and Calvinistic churches. Through the influence of T. A. Ernesti, in 1773, and others, this form of statement fell to a large extent into disuse. It was revived by Schleiermacher and others, who in this respect followed in his footsteps. It is now currently employed in the theology of the evangelical churches of Europe and America.

BIBLIOGRAPHY: J. Garbett, *Christ, As Prophet, Priest, and King,* 2 vols. (1842); L. S. Chafer, *Systematic Theology* (1948), 1:357-58; 3:17-26, 30, 33; 4:64-65, 300, 392; 5:82-83, 93-169, 317-76; 7:20, 223, 250; A. J. McClain, *The Greatness of the Kingdom* (1959); I. H. Marshall, *The Work of Christ* (1969); W. Milligan, *The Ascension of Christ* (1980).

OFFSCOURING (Heb. *sᵉḥî,* "refuse," as "swept" off). A figurative term for something vile (Lam. 3:45). The apostles were looked upon by some in their day in this way (Gk. *peripsēma,* 1 Cor. 4:13, KJV; "scum," NIV).

OG (og). An Amorite, king of Bashan (Num. 21:33; 32:33; Deut. 4:47; 31:4), who ruled over sixty cities (Josh. 13:30), the chief of which were Ashtaroth and Edrei (v. 12) at the time of the occupation of Canaan, c. 1400 B.C. He was defeated by the Israelites at Edrei and, with his children and people, was exterminated (Num. 21:33-35; Deut. 1:4; 3:1-13; 29:7; Josh. 2:10). His many walled cities were taken (Deut. 3:4-10), and his kingdom was assigned to the trans-Jordanic tribes, especially the half tribe of Manasseh (3:13; Josh. 9:10; 13:12, 30). He was a man of giant stature, and Moses speaks of his iron bedstead (or sarcophagus, some scholars believe), nine cubits long by four broad, which was preserved as a memorial in Rabbath (Deut. 3:11). He was one of the last representatives of the giant race of Rephaim.

O'HAD (ō'had; "unity"). The third named of the sons of Simeon (Gen. 46:10) and head of a family in Israel (Ex. 6:15).

O'HEL (ō'hel; "tent"). One of the children of Zerubbabel (1 Chron. 3:20).

OHO'LAH (ōhō'la; "her own tent"). The name of a probably imaginary harlot, used by Ezekiel (23:4-5, 36, 44; "Aholah," KJV) as a symbol of the idolatry of Samaria, the apostate branch of Judah being designated by Oholibah ("Aholibah," KJV). The terms indicate respectively that, whereas the worship of Samaria had been self-invented and never sanctioned by Jehovah, at Jerusalem it was divinely instituted but was now degraded and abandoned for foreign alliances. They are both graphically described as lewd women, adulteresses prostituting themselves to the Egyptians and Assyrians, in imitating their abominations and idolatries; as such the allegory is an epitome of the history of the Jewish people.

OHO'LIAB (ōhō'li-ab; "tent of his father"; "Aholiab," KJV). The son of Ahisamach, of the tribe of Dan, an expert workman in precious metals and other materials and, together with Bezalel, appointed to superintend the preparation of such articles for the Tabernacle (Ex. 31:6; 35:34; 36:1-2; 38:23), c. 1440 B.C.

OHOL'IBAH (ōhō'li-ba; "my tent is in her"; "Aholibah," KJV). A symbolical name given to Jerusalem (Ezek. 23:4, 11, 22, 36, 44), under the figure of an adulterous harlot, as having once contained the true worship of Jehovah and having prostituted herself to foreign idolatries. *See* Oholah.

OHOLIBA'MAH (ōhōl-i-ba'ma; "tent of the height"; "Aholibamah," KJV).
1. The granddaughter of Zibeon the Hivite and one of the wives of Esau (Gen. 36:2). In a previous narrative (26:34) Oholibamah is called Judith the daughter of Beeri the Hittite. The probable explanation is that her proper name was Judith and that Oholibamah was the name that she received as the wife of Esau and founder of the three tribes of his descendants.
2. One of the chiefs who sprang from Esau (Gen. 36:41; 1 Chron. 1:52). The list of names in which this is included is probably of places, not of persons. This would seem to be evident from the expression in the heading, "according to their families and their localities, by their names" (Gen. 36:40,) as compared with v. 43, "according to their habitations in the land of their possession" (Keil, ad loc.; Smith, *Dict.,* s.v.).

OIL. The following original words are rendered "oil": (1) Most generally oil is the rendering of the Heb. *shemen,* "grease." Sometimes rendered "ointment" in the KJV. (2) Heb. *yiṣhār,* "shining, clear olive oil" (Num. 18:12; Deut. 7:13; 11:14; 12:17; etc.). (3) Aram. *mᵉshah,* an "unguent" (only in Ezra 6:9; 7:22). (4) Gk. *elaion,* neuter of word meaning "olive."

Of the numerous substances, animal and vegetable, that were known to the ancients as yielding oil, the olive berry is the one the Scriptures mention most frequently. The best oil is made from fruit gathered about November or December, when it has begun to change color but before it has become black. The berry in the more advanced state yields more oil, but it is of an inferior quality.

Harvesting. In order not to injure either the crop or the tree, great care is necessary in gathering, either by hand or shaking the fruit off carefully with a light stick. It is then carefully cleaned and carried to press, which is considered best; or, if necessary, laid on tables with hollow trays made sloping, so as to allow the first juice to flow into other receptacles beneath, care being taken not to heap the fruit too much and so prevent the free escape of the juice, which is injurious to the oil though itself useful in other ways.

Olive trees on the Mount of Olives

Manufacture. In order to make oil, the fruit was either bruised in a mortar, crushed in a press loaded with wood or stones, ground in a mill, or trodden with the feet. The "beaten" oil of Ex. 27:20; 29:40; Lev. 24:2; Num. 28:5 was probably made by bruising in a mortar. The berries are bruised in a crude mill consisting of a round stone resembling a millstone but much larger, usually six to eight feet in diameter. This stone is laid flat on the ground. Its upper surface is depressed about three inches, except at its edge. The center of this stone is bored through, and an upright pole is fastened in it, projecting about three feet above it. Another stone disk, five or six feet in diameter and a foot or eighteen inches thick, is set on edge in the depression on the top of the other. Through the center of this stone passes a long pole, one end of which has a ring attached to it, which fits over the end of the upright in the other disk, while the other end is attached to a whiffletree, by which a horse or mule draws it round and round the mill. The berries are placed in the cavity on the face of the horizontal stone, and the upright stone moves around the edge of the cavity, crushing the berries as it goes. A part of the oil thus expressed is drawn off by a hole in the elevated rim of the stone. The refuse is then transferred to baskets, which are piled on top of one another in the space between two grooved upright posts. A lever, weighted at its distal end with heavy stones, compresses these baskets and expresses the crude oil. This is run into large stone reservoirs, in which it becomes clarified and is kept for use or sale. From these the oil was drawn out for use in horns or other small vessels, which were stored in cellars or storehouses, of which special mention is made in the inventories of royal property and revenue (1 Sam. 10:1; 16:1, 13; 1 Kings 1:39; 17:16; 2 Kings 4:2, 6; 9:1, 3; 1 Chron. 27:28; 2 Chron. 11:11; 32:28; Prov. 21:20). A supply of oil was always kept in the Temple (Josephus *Wars* 5.13.6), and an oil treasure was among the stores of the Jewish kings (2 Kings 20:13; 2 Chron. 32:27-28). Oil of Tekoa was reckoned the best. Trade in oil was carried on with the Tyrians, by whom it was probably often re-exported to Egypt, whose olives do not for the most part produce good oil (2 Chron. 2:10). Direct trade in oil was also carried on between Egypt and Palestine (Ezra 3:7; Isa. 57:9; Ezek. 27:17; Hos. 12:1).

Olive press

Uses.

As Food. Oil is now, as formerly, in general use as food throughout western Asia, taking the place of butter and animal fat in various preparations (cf. Ezek. 16:13). Indeed, it would appear that the Hebrews considered oil one of the prime necessities of life (Sirach 39:31; cf. Jer. 31:12; 41:8; Luke 16:6). It is frequently mentioned with honey (Ezek. 16:13, 19; 27:17), and its abundance was a mark of prosperity (cf. Joel 2:19).

Cosmetic. As is the case generally in hot climates, oil was used by the Jews for anointing the body, e.g., after the bath, and giving to the skin and hair a smooth and comely appearance, e.g., before an entertainment. At Egyptian entertainments it was usual for a servant to anoint the head of each guest as he took his seat (Deut. 28:40; 2 Sam. 12:20; 14:2; Ruth 3:3).

Funereal. The bodies of the dead were anointed with oil by the Greeks and Romans, probably

as a partial antiseptic, and a similar custom appears to have prevailed among the Jews.

Medicinal. As oil is in use in many cases in modern medicine, it is not surprising that it should have been much used among the Jews and other nations of antiquity for medicinal purposes. Celsus repeatedly speaks of the use of oil, especially old oil, applied externally with friction in fevers, and in many other cases. Josephus mentions that among the remedies employed in the case of Herod, he was put into a sort of oil bath. The prophet Isaiah (Isa. 1:6) alludes to the use of oil as ointment in medical treatment; and it thus furnished a fitting symbol, perhaps also an efficient remedy, when used by our Lord's disciples in the miraculous cures that they were enabled to perform (Mark 6:13). With similar intention, no doubt, its use was enjoined by James (5:14).

Light. Oil was in general use for lamps, being still used in Egypt with cotton wicks twisted around straw, the receptacle being a glass vessel into which water is first poured (Matt. 25:1-9; cf. Luke 12:35).

Ritual. Oil as poured on or mixed with the flour used in offering (*see* Sacrificial Offerings), excepting the sin offering (Lev. 5:11) and the offering of jealousy (Num. 5:15). The use of oil in sacrifices was indicative of joy or gladness; the absence of oil denoted sorrow or humiliation (Isa. 61:3; Joel 2:19; Rev. 6:6). Kings, priests, and prophets were anointed with oil or ointment. Tithes of oil were also prescribed (Deut. 12:17; 2 Chron. 31:5; Neh. 10:37, 39; 13:12; Ezek. 45:14).

Figurative. Oil was a fitting symbol of the Spirit or spiritual principle of life, by virtue of its power to sustain and fortify the vital energy; and the anointing oil, which was prepared according to divine instructions, was therefore a symbol of the Spirit of God, as the principle of spiritual life that proceeds from God and fills the natural being of the creature with the powers of divine life. Anointing with oil, therefore, was a symbol of endowment with the Spirit of God for the duties of the office to which a person was consecrated (Lev. 8:12; 1 Sam. 10:1, 6; 16:13-14; Isa. 61:1). Oil was symbolic of abundance (Deut. 8:8; Ezek. 16:13); lack of oil was a figure for want, poverty (Deut. 28:40; Joel 1:10); to "suck honey from the rock, and oil from the flinty rock" (Deut. 32:13) is a figure derived from the fact that Canaan abounds in wild bees, which make their hives in clefts of the rock and in olive trees that grow in a rocky soil. The expression suggests the most valuable productions out of the most unproductive places, since God so blessed the land that even the rocks and stones were productive. "The oil of gladness" is a figure for the consolations of the gospel (Isa. 61:3; Heb. 1:9); "oil upon the head" (Ps. 141:5) is a figure for kind reproof. "His words were softer than oil" (55:21) is used to

Ancient olive tree in the garden of Gethsemane

express the hypocritical pretense of a false friend (cf. Prov. 5:3). *See* Vegetable Kingdom: Olive.

BIBLIOGRAPHY: H. N. and A. L. Moldenke, *The Plants of the Bible* (1952), pp. 97-98, 158-60; A. Goor and M. Nurock, *The Fruits of the Holy Land* (1968), pp. 89-120; M. Zachary, *Plants of the Bible* (1982), pp. 56-57, 87, 193, 198-208.

OIL, HOLY, ANOINTING. The mode of preparing this oil is prescribed (Ex. 30:22-25). It was a compound consisting of one hin (about one gallon) of olive oil, 500 shekels of pure myrrh, 250 shekels of cane, 250 shekels of fragrant cinnamon, and 500 shekels of cassia (the aromatic bark of a shrub that grows in Arabia). The proportions in which these ingredients were mixed compels us to assume that the cinnamon, calamus, and cassia were not mixed with the oil in their dry form but as prepared spices, say in the shape of cinnamon cane and cassia ointment; or it may have been, as the rabbinical writers assure us, that the dry substances were steeped or boiled in water to extract the strength or virtue out of them; then to the liquid thus obtained the oil was added, and both were put upon the fire to boil till the whole of the watery element should evaporate. The preparing of the anointing oil was superintended by Bezalel, the perfumer (37:29).

OILS AND OINTMENTS.

Name. Although the term *ointment* is frequent in the KJV, it is rare in the NASB and NIV, usually being replaced there by *oil* (sometimes alone, at other times not, e.g., "holy anointing oil," Ex.

30:25; "precious oil," 2 Kings 20:13; Is. 39:2; "perfumer's oil," Eccles. 10:1), or *perfume* (Matt. 26:7, 9; Mark 14:3-4; Luke 7:37, 38, 46; 23:56; John 12:3, 5). The Heb. terms include *shemen, rōqēaḥ, mishḥâ,* and *mirqaḥat; muron* is the Gk. original.

Nature and Preparation. The ointments and oils used by the Israelites were generally composed of various ingredients. Olive oil was combined with sundry aromatics, chiefly foreign (1 Kings 10:10; Ezek. 27:22), particularly spices, myrrh, and nard. Being costly, these ointments were a much-prized luxury (Amos 6:6). The ingredients, and often the prepared oils and resins ready for use, were imported from Phoenicia in small alabaster boxes, in which the delicious aroma was best preserved. The preparation of these required peculiar skill and formed a particular trade, sometimes carried on by women (1 Sam. 8:13; *see* Handicrafts: Perfumers). The better kinds of ointments were so strong, and the different substances so perfectly amalgamated, that they have been known to retain their scent for centuries. One of the alabaster vases at Alnwick Castle contains some ancient Egyptian ointment that has retained its fragrance between 2,000 and 3,000 years.

Uses. The practice of producing agreeable odors by burning incense, anointing the person with aromatic oils and ointments, and sprinkling the dress with fragment waters originated in, and is mostly confined to, warm climates. In such climates the perspiration is profuse, and much

A clay flask from biblical times containing balsamic oil, found at Qumran

care is needed to prevent offensive results. It is in this necessity that we find a reason for the use of perfumes, particularly at feasts, weddings, and on visits of persons of rank. The following are the uses of ointments in Scripture:

Cosmetic. The Greek and Roman practice of anointing the head and clothes on festive occasions prevailed also among the Egyptians and appears to have had place among the Jews (Ruth 3:3; Prov. 27:9, 16; Eccles. 7:1; 9:8; etc.). Oil of myrrh, for like purposes, is mentioned (Esther 2:12). Egyptian paintings represent servants anointing guests on their arrival at their entertainer's house, and alabaster vases exist that retain the traces of the ointment that they were used to contain.

Funereal. Perfumes as well as oil were used to anoint dead bodies and the clothes in which they were wrapped (Matt. 26:12; Mark 14:3, 8; Luke 23:56; John 12:3-7; 19:40).

Medicinal. Ointment formed an important feature in ancient medical treatment (Isa. 1:6). The mention of balm of Gilead and of eye salve (*collyrium*) points to the same method (Isa. 1:6; John 9:6; Jer. 8:22; Rev. 3:18; etc.).

Ritual. Besides the oil used in many ceremonial observances, a special ointment was used in consecration (Ex. 29:7; 30:23-25; 37:29; 40:9, 15). Strict prohibition was issued against using this ointment for any secular purpose, or on the person of a foreigner, and against imitating it in any way whatsoever (30:32-33). The weight of the oil in the mixture would be twelve pounds eight ounces in English measure. A question arises: In what form were the other ingredients, and what degree of solidity did the whole attain? According to Maimonides, Moses, having reduced the solid ingredients to powder, steeped them in water till all the aromatic qualities were drawn forth. He then poured in the oil and boiled the whole till the water evaporated. The residue thus obtained was preserved in a vessel for use. Another theory

Egyptian mode of anointing

supposes all the ingredients to have been in the form of oil or ointment. The measurement by weight of all except the oil seems to imply that they were in some solid form, but whether in an oily state or in that of powder cannot be ascertained. A process of making ointment consisting, in part at least, in boiling, is alluded to (Job 41:31).

See also Anointing; Oil; Oil, Holy, Anointing.

BIBLIOGRAPHY: R. J. Forbes, *Studies in Ancient Technology* 3 (1955): 1-49; R. K. Harrison, *Healing Herbs of the Bible* (1966), pp. 49-54.

OIL TREE (Isa. 41:19, KJV). *See* Vegetable Kingdom: Olive.

OINTMENT. *See* Oils and Ointments.

OLD. *See* Elders.

OLD GATE. The name (Neh. 3:6; 12:39) of a gate in *Jerusalem* (which see), probably the gate on the NE corner. The NIV renders "Jeshanah [i.e., "old"] Gate." *See also* Gate.

OLD TESTAMENT. The part of the Bible extending from Genesis to Malachi.

Designation. This portion of revealed truth consists of thirty-nine books, which make up about 8/13 of the content of the whole Bible. The thirty-nine books of the Protestant canon are identical with the ancient Hebrew canon. Roman Catholics have a larger canon, consisting of eleven of the fourteen apocryphal, called deuterocanonical books. These books, however, have no legitimate place in the canon. The OT bears a vital and inseparable relation to the NT. It is fundamental and preparatory. The NT is enfolded in the OT, and the OT is unfolded by the NT. It is a mistake to separate the two testaments. In rejecting Christianity and the NT revelation, Judaism makes this blunder. The terms *Old Testament* and *New Testamant* were popularized by the Latin Fathers and did not come into vogue until the Christian Scriptures were complete. The term *Old Testament* was used as a device to distinguish the Christian Scriptures from the "Jewish Scriptures." In one sense of the word, the terms *Old Testament* and *New Testament* are inaccurate, since the Old or Mosaic Covenant overlaps and was in force until the crucifixion of Christ and the veil of the Temple was torn in two from top to bottom. The New Covenant is based upon the death, resurrection, and ascension of Christ, and the Jew who would now enjoy salvation must come by "a new and living way" (Heb. 10:20), that is, Christ (John 14:6).

Origin and Preservation. The NT expressly declares the inspiration of the OT books (2 Tim. 3:16; 2 Pet. 1:20-21). Likewise, everywhere in the OT the Hebrew Scriptures are presented as the divinely revealed Word of God. God is everywhere set forth implicitly and explicitly as its principal Author. The sacred writers are represented as receiving or recording the divine message in its fullness and with divine accuracy. Internal evidence of its inspiration abounds everywhere. The sacred authors repeatedly prefix their messages with such commanding expressions as "Thus says the Lord" (Ex. 4:22) and "Hear the word of the Lord" (Isa. 1:10). Prophets such as Isaiah, Jeremiah, and Daniel have had their predictions verified by time.

Almost as unique as the inspiration of the OT is its preservation. Many other books besides Scripture existed (Eccles. 12:12). Echoes of ancient literary pieces survive in the Scripture references to the book of Jasher (Josh. 10:13; 2 Sam. 1:18) and "the Book of the Wars of the Lord" (Num. 21:14). Human writings apparently contested with inspired documents. Divine intervention assured the giving, reception, and recording of Holy Scripture as well as its miraculously meticulous and accurate preservation through the centuries—an almost incredible phenomenon at a time when each manuscript had to be executed by hand.

Position and Purpose in the Canon. The OT comes before the NT because it is introductory both historically, typically, and redemptively to all that is enfolded there. The central unifying theme is the Person and work of Christ. From the proto-evangelium (Gen. 3:15) to Malachi's "Sun of righteousness," Christ is the interwoven and inseparable subject of all the OT. The OT does not present the church of the NT (except typically), which was a mystery hidden in God (Eph. 3:1-9) and was first revealed to the apostle Paul. The OT, however, fully presents the first advent of Christ, leaving the gap between the two comings to be filled in by the NT church. The OT in amazing detail presents the coming of the Redeemer to work out man's salvation (cf. Isa. 53:1-12) and also with great elaboration sets forth the second coming of Christ and the establishment of the millennial kingdom, involving the restoration of Israel. The disciples' question in Acts 1:6, "Lord, is it at this time You are restoring the kingdom to Israel?" finds the fullest elucidation in the OT, not in connection with the church, but in connection with the Great Tribulation and the cataclysmic second coming of Christ, as set forth in the book of the Revelation (chaps. 4-19).

Value of the OT. Although the OT Scriptures were given to one small nation, its message is for all time. In no sense is it confined to Palestine or to the Jews, but because of its world outreach becomes vital to all peoples of every land and age. The target of relentless critical attack stigmatized by unbelief, it continues with the NT to meet man's deepest needs and to lead the human race to the fountain of salvation and dynamic inspiration for right living.   M.F.U.

BIBLIOGRAPHY: D. Baly, *The Geography of the Bible* (1957); R. de Vaux *Ancient Israel: Its Life and Institutions* (1961); W. F. Albright, *The Biblical Period from Abra-*

ham to Ezra (1963); D. W. Thomas, ed., *Archaeology and the Old Testament* (1967); R. K. Harrison, *Introduction to the Old Testament* (1969); L. J. Wood, *A Survey of Israel's History* (1970); D. J. Wiseman, ed., *Peoples of Old Testament Times* (1973); G. L. Archer, Jr., *Survey of Old Testament Introduction* (1974); W. C. Kaiser, Jr., *Toward an Old Testament Theology* (1978); Y. Aharoni, *The Land of the Bible* (1979); E. Würthwein, *The Text of the Old Testament* (1979); W. G. Blaikie, *Heroes of Israel* (1981); E. M. Blaiklock and R. K. Harrison, eds., *The New International Dictionary of Biblical Archaeology* (1983). For further information see *The Minister's Library*, 2 vols. (1985, 1987), pp. 65-163.

OLIVE. *See* Vegetable Kingdom: Oil.

OLIVES, MOUNT OF. The ridge of hills east of Jerusalem, separated from it by the Jehoshaphat Valley.

Name. Its descriptive appellation is "the Mount of Olives" (Heb. *har hazzêtîm*, only in Zech. 14:4; Gk. *to oros tou elaiov*, the mount on which the olive grew; Matt. 21:1; 24:3; 26:30; Mark 11:1; Luke 19:37; John 8:1). It is referred to (2 Sam. 15:30) as "the ascent of the Mount of Olives"; "the mountain which is east of Jerusalem" (1 Kings 11:7); "the mount of destruction" (2 Kings 23:13), from the heathen altars erected there by Solomon (cf. 1 Kings 11:7); "the hills" (Neh. 8:15), and "the mount called Olivet" (Acts 1:12). The hill has now two names, Jebel et-Tûr, i.e., "the Mount," and Jebel et-Zeitûn, "Mount of Olives."

Physical Features. The Mount of Olives is a limestone ridge, rather more than a mile in length, running in general direction N and S and covering the whole eastern side of the city of Jerusalem. At the N the ridge bends to the W, enclosing the city on that side also. At the N about a mile intervenes between the city walls, while on the E the mount is separated only by the valley of Kidron. It is to the latter part that attention is called. At a distance its outline is almost horizontal, gradually sloping away at its southern end; but when seen from below the eastern wall of Jerusalem, it divides itself into three or perhaps four independent summits or natural elevations. Beginning at the N they are: Galilee or *Viri Galilaei*, from the address of the angel to the disciples (Acts 1:11); Mount of Ascension, now distinguished by the minaret and domes of the Church of the Ascension, in every way the most important; Mount of the Prophets, subordinate to the former; and Mount of Offense. Three paths lead from the valley to the summit. The first passes under the N wall of the enclosure of Gethsemane and follows the line of the depression between the center and the northern hill. The second parts from the first about fifty yards beyond Gethsemane and, striking off to the right up the very breast of the hill, surmounts the projection on which is the traditional spot of the lamentation over Jerusalem and thence proceeds directly upward to the village of Bethany. The third leaves the other two at the NE corner of Gethsemane and, making a considerable detour to the S, visits the so-called "Tombs of the Prophets" and, following a slight depression that occurs at that part of the mount, arrives in its turn at Bethany. Every consideration is in favor of the first path being that which David took when fleeing from Absalom, as well as that usually taken by our Lord and His disciples in their morning and evening walks between Jerusalem and Bethany, and that also by which the apostles returned to Jerusalem after the ascension. Tradition assigns many sacred sites to the Mount of Ascension, Gethsemane, and the place of lamentation. The third of the traditional spots mentioned— that of the lamentation over Jerusalem (Luke 9:41-44)—has been shown to have been badly chosen and that the road of our Lord's "triumphal entry" was not by the short and steep path over the summit but the longer and easier route around the southern shoulder of the southern of the three divisions of the mount.

The Mount of Olives viewed from Jerusalem

Scripture Notices. The Mount of Olives is mentioned in connection with the flight of David from Absalom (2 Sam. 15:30); with the building there of high places by Solomon (2 Kings 23:13); and with the vision of the Lord's departure from Jerusalem (Ezek. 10:4, 19; 11:23), in which last passage the prophet said, "And the glory of the Lord went up from the midst of the city, and stood over the mountain which is east of the city." The command to "go out to the hills, and bring olive branches," etc. (Neh. 8:15), indicates that the mount, and probably the valley at its base, abounded in various kinds of trees. In the

time of Jesus the trees were still numerous (Mark 11:8). The only other OT mention of the Mount of Olives is in Zechariah's prophecy of the destruction of Jerusalem and the preservation of God's people (Zech. 14:4). The NT narrative makes Olivet the scene of four remarkable events in the history of Jesus: the triumphal entry—its scene being the road that winds around the southern shoulder of the hill from Bethany to Jerusalem (Matt. 21:1, 8-10; Mark 11:1, 8-10; Luke 19:29, 36-37, 41); the prediction of Jerusalem's overthrow (Mark 13:1-2); Gethsemane—after the institution of the Lord's Supper, Jesus led His disciples "over the ravine of the Kidron" and "out to the Mount of Olives," to a garden called Gethsemane (John 18:1; Matt. 26:30, 36); and the *ascension* (which see).

BIBLIOGRAPHY: D. Baly, *The Geography of the Bible* (1957), pp. 41, 156, 162, 196.

OLIVET *See* Olives, Mount of.

OLIVET DISCOURSE. This great prophetic pronouncement of our Lord extends from Matt. 24:1 to 25:46, cf. Luke 21:5-38. In this far-reaching eschatological pronouncement Jesus in a sense gives a farewell message to Israel through His disciples in the role of representative Israelites and outlines the future of the nation previous to the millennial kingdom. In this prophetic statement concerning Israel, no mention is made of the church, her beginning, her course, her destiny, or her sojourn in the world. Likewise, no reference is made to the Person or work of the Holy Spirit as each occurs in this age. If the course and character of this present age are reflected, it is only in a general sense apart from the distinctive character and destiny of the church (cf. 24:6-7).

The disciples' threefold question recorded in Matt. 24:3 is answered as follows: "When will these things be?" that is, the destruction of the city and Temple in A.D. 70. Luke 21:20-24 answers that. The second and third questions: "And what will be the sign of Your coming and of the end of the age?" are answered in Matt. 24:4-33. Christ spoke of Israel's cataclysmic time of trouble at the end of the age and warned concerning it (vv. 9-28). The glorious appearing of the Messiah to Israel is described in 24:29–25:30, exhortations to watch in 24:36–25:13, and judgments upon Israel in 24:45–25:30. The prophecy concludes with the judgment of the nations in regard to their treatment of Israel (25:31-46). Thus the Olivet discourse in Matthew and Luke gives us the eschatological future of the nation Israel and, except for the destruction of Jerusalem in A.D. 70, deals with the fate of Israel in Daniel's Seventieth Week after the glorification of the church. *See* the articles Seventy Weeks; Daniel, Book of.

M.F.U.

BIBLIOGRAPHY: A. C. Gaebelein, *The Olivet Discourse* (n.d.); J. D. Pentecost, *Things to Come* (1985), pp.

275ff.; J. F. Walvoord, *Matthew: Thy Kingdom Come* (1974), pp. 179-204; S. D. Toussaint, *Behold the King* (1980), pp. 266-94.

OLYM'PAS (ō-lim'pas). The name of an individual, apparently in Rome, to whom Paul sent greetings (Rom. 16:15).

O'MAR (ō'mar). A descendant of Esau through his son Eliphaz (Gen. 36:11, 15; 1 Chron. 1:36).

OME'GA (Ω) (ō-me'ga). The last letter of the Gk. alphabet, as alpha is the first.

Figurative. Omega is used metaphorically to denote the *end* of anything. "I am the Alpha and the Omega, the first and the last, the beginning and the end" (Rev. 1:8, 17; 21:6; 22:13; cf. Isa. 41:4; 44:6).

OMER. A Hebrew dry measure. *See* Metrology.

OMNIPOTENCE. Exclusively an attribute of God and essential to the perfection of His being. It is declared in such Scriptures as Gen. 17:1; Ex. 15:11-12; Deut. 3:24; Pss. 62:11; 65:6; 147:5; Jer. 32:17; Matt. 6:13; 19:26; Eph. 3:20; Rev. 19:6. By ascribing to God absolute power, it is not meant that God is free from all the restraints of reason and morality, as some have taught, but that He is able to do everything that is in harmony with His wise and holy and perfect nature (*see* Matt. 23:19; Heb. 6:18). The infinite power of God is set before us in the Scriptures in connection with His work of creation (Gen. 1:1; Rom. 1:20), His work of upholding the world (Heb. 1:3), the redemption of mankind (Luke 1:35, 37; Eph. 1:19), the working of miracles (Luke 9:43), the conversion of sinners (1 Cor. 2:5; 2 Cor. 4:7), and the complete accomplishment of the great purpose of His kingdom (Matt. 6:13; 13:31-32; 1 Pet. 1:5; 1 Cor. 15; Rev. 19:6). For fuller exposition *see* works of systematic theology, elsewhere referred to, particularly Hodge, Dorner, Van Oosterzee.

E. MCC.

BIBLIOGRAPHY: L. S. Chafer, *Systematic Theology* (1948), 1:209-11, 305-8; K. Barth, *Church Dogmatics* (1957), 2.1.522-607; S. Charnock, *The Existence and Attributes of God* (1979), 2:5-107.

OMNIPRESENCE. An attribute of God alone, by which is meant that God is free from the laws or limitations of space (*see* Ps. 139:7-10; Jer. 23:23-24; Heb. 1:3; Acts 17:27-28; etc.). It is essential to the right conception of God in this respect that we avoid all materialistic notions of His presence that confuse God with everything and thus lead to *pantheism* (which see). God is Spirit, and His infinite presence is to be regarded in the dynamical sense rather than in the sense of a substance infinitely extended. He is distinct from all His works while His power and intelligence and goodness embrace and penetrate them all. The omnipresence of God is also to be regarded as compatible with various manifestations of His presence according to the spheres of life in which

He exists and operates. Thus in the most exalted sense He is "Our Father . . . in heaven" (*see* Matt. 6:9; etc.).

BIBLIOGRAPHY: L. S. Chafer, *Systematic Theology* (1948), 7:243-44; K. Barth, *Church Dogmatics* (1957), 2.1.461-90; S. Charnock, *The Existence and Attributes of God* (1979), 1:363-405.

OMNISCIENCE. The divine attribute of perfect knowledge. This is declared in Pss. 33:13-15; 139:11-12; 147:5; Prov. 15:3; Isa. 40:14; 46:10; Acts 15:18; 1 John 3:20; Heb. 4:13, and in many other places. The perfect knowledge of God is exclusively His attribute. It relates to Himself and to all beyond Himself. It includes all things that are actual and all things that are possible. Its possession is incomprehensible to us, and yet it is necessary to our faith in the perfection of God's sovereignty. The revelation of this divine property like that of others is well calculated to fill us with profound reverence. It should alarm sinners and beget confidence in the hearts of God's children and deepen their consolation (*see* Job 23:10; Pss. 34:15-16; 90:8; Jer. 17:10; Hos. 7:2; 1 Pet. 3:12-14). The Scriptures unequivocally declare the divine prescience and at the same time make their appeal to man as a free and consequently responsible being.

BIBLIOGRAPHY: L. S. Chafer, *Systematic Theology* (1948), 1:192-200; 7:244-45; K. Barth, *Church Dogmatics* (1957), 2.1.71, 130, 189f.; id. (1958), 3.1.156ff., 243ff., 344ff.; id. (1961), 4.3.146f.; S. Charnock, *The Existence and Attributes of God* (1979), 1:406-96.

OM'RI (om'ri).

1. The seventh king of Israel, originally commander of the armies of Elah king of Israel, and engaged in the siege of Gibbethon when informed of the king's death and the usurpation of Zimri.

Proclaimed king by his army, Omri left Gibbethon and besieged Zimri in Tirzah. In despair Zimri burned himself in his palace (1 Kings 16:16-18), 885 B.C. Another competitor appeared in the person of Tibni, the son of Ginath. After a civil war of four years Omri was left undisputed master of the throne (vv. 21-22), c. 880 B.C. Having resided six years in Tirzah, he moved to the hill Samaria, which he bought from Shemer for two talents of silver. He seems to have been a vigorous and unscrupulous ruler, anxious to strengthen his dynasty by connections and alliances with foreign states. He made a treaty with Ben-hadad I of Damascus, surrendering to him some foreign cities (20:34), among them, probably, Ramoth-gilead (22:3), and admitted into Samaria a resident Syrian embassy, which is described by the expression "you shall make streets for yourself in Damascus, as my father made in Samaria" for Ben-hadad. He united his son in marriage to the daughter of a principal Phoenician prince, which led to the introduction of Baal worship into Israel. Of Omri it is said: "Omri did evil in the sight of the Lord, and acted more wickedly than all who were before him. For he walked in all the way of Jeroboam the son of Nebat and in his sins which he made Israel sin, provoking the Lord God of Israel with their idols" (16:25-26). This worldly and irreligious policy is denounced by Micah (Mic. 6:16) under the name of "the statutes of Omri." He died c. 874 B.C. and was succeeded by his son Ahab. His daughter Athaliah was the mother of Ahaziah, king of Judah (2 Kings 8:26).

The Moabite Stone attests the military prowess of Omri, mentioning his military successes over Moab, lines 4-9. "Now Omri had taken possession of all the land of Medeba." Years later Mesha, a wealthy sheep-owning king of Moab, was paying wool tribute to Israel (2 Kings 3:4). Assyrian records also attest the political and military importance of Omri; a century after Omri's reign the Assyrians were still referring to Israel as "the land of the House of Omri." Jehu, a later Israelite usurper, is styled "Mar Humri" ("son," i.e., royal successor, of Omri). The Samaritan Ostraca unearthed at the "ostraca house" in Samaria bear the names of both Yahweh and Baal, corroborating Omri's apostasy (1 Kings 16:25-26).

2. One of the sons of Becher the son of Benjamin (1 Chron. 7:8).

3. A descendant of Perez the son of Judah (1 Chron. 9:4).

4. Son of Michael and head of the tribe of Issachar in the reign of David (1 Chron. 27:18).

BIBLIOGRAPHY: J. B. Pritchard, ed., *Ancient Near Eastern Texts* (1969), pp. 280-85, 320; J. P. Lewis, *Historical Backgrounds of Bible History* (1971), pp. 61, 63, 93-97, 115, 176.

ON (on; "strength").

1. The son of Peleth and one of the leaders of the tribe of Reuben who took part with Korah, Dathan, and Abiram in their revolt against Moses (Num. 16:1). His name does not appear in the narrative of the conspiracy; neither is he alluded to when reference is made to the final catastrophe. There is a rabbinical tradition to the effect that he was prevailed upon by his wife to withdraw from his accomplices.

2. A city of Egypt, the residence of Potiphera, whose daughter Asenath became the wife of Joseph (Gen. 41:45, 50; 46:20). The city was devoted to the worship of the sun god Ra, and thus was known also as Heliopolis, Gk. for "sun city" (*see* Jer. 43:13, NASB; in the KJV the place name is given as Beth-shemesh, from Heb. *bêt shemesh,* "sun temple," or "house of the sun god"; the NIV reads "temple of the sun"). On was situated ten miles NE of Cairo and was the chief city of Egyptian science. Herodotus speaks of it as one of the four great cities, noted for religious festivals in honor of the sun. Its magnificent ruins have become the richest adornments of other cities, like Rome and Constantinople. Two magnificent red

Syene granite obelisks set up by the great Thutmose III (c. 1490-1450 B.C.) in front of the temple of Ra in Heliopolis now adorn the Thames Embankment in London and Central Park in New York. A single obelisk remains in Heliopolis, that set up by Senwosret I (c. 2000 B.C.) in honor of Re-Horus of the Horizon. This is a remnant of the glory of ancient On. The ancient city was famous for the worship of the sun, and many sun cults operated there. It was the religious capital of early Egypt around 2900 B.C. *See also* City of Destruction for discussion of a place given in some ancient manuscripts as City of the Sun.

M.F.U.

BIBLIOGRAPHY: A. Rowe, *Palestine Exploration Quarterly* 94 (1962): 133-42.

O'NAM (ō'nam).

1. A descendant of *Seir* (which see) the Horite through his son *Shobal* (which see). Gen. 36:23; 1 Chron. 1:40.

2. A son of Jerahmeel's second wife Atarah and thus a descendant of Judah through Hezron (1 Chron. 2:26, 28). See Jerahmeel, no. 1.

O'NAN (ō'nan; "strong"). The second son of Judah by the daughter of Shua the Canaanite (Gen. 38:4; 46:12; Num. 26:19; 1 Chron. 2:3), about 1925 B.C. When his brother Er, Judah's firstborn, was put to death by Jehovah on account of his wickedness, Onan refused, in defiance of the ancient custom, to produce offspring by his widow, Tamar. For this he was punished by death (Gen. 38:8-10).

ONES'IMUS (o-nes'i-mus; Gk. "useful, profitable"). The servant (or slave) in whose behalf Paul wrote the epistle to Philemon. He was a native, or certainly an inhabitant, of Colossae, since Paul, in writing to the church there, speaks of him (Col. 4:9) as "one of your number." Fleeing from his master Philemon to Rome, he was there led to embrace the gospel through the instrumentality of the apostle (Philem. 10). After his conversion the most happy and friendly relationship sprang up between the teacher and the disciple; and so useful had he made himself to Paul that he desired to have Onesimus remain with him. This, however, he forbore in view of the relations of Onesimus and his master's right to his services. Onesimus, accompanied by Tychicus, left Rome with not only this epistle but with that to the Colossians (Col. 4:9), A.D. 60.

BIBLIOGRAPHY: C. E. Macartney, *The Woman of Tekoah* (1955), pp. 148-60; D. E. Hiebert, *Personalities Around Paul* (1973), pp. 178-83.

ONESIPH'ORUS (on-e-sif'o-rus; "benefit-bringing, profit-bearing"). A Christian of Ephesus who not only ministered to the apostle there (2 Tim. 1:18) but who, being in Rome during Paul's second imprisonment, "was not ashamed" of his "chains," sought out Paul, and "often refreshed" him (1:16-17), A.D. 60. In his epistle the apostle expressed his appreciation for the services rendered by Onesiphorus and sent salutations to his household (4:19).

BIBLIOGRAPHY: D. E. Hiebert, *Personalities Around Paul* (1973), pp. 184-89.

ONION. *See* Vegetable Kingdom.

ONLY BEGOTTEN (Gk. *monogenēs*, "single of its kind"). This term is used of Christ (John 1:14, 18; etc.) to denote that in the sense in which He is the Son of God He has no brothers or sisters. *See* Sonship of Christ.

O'NO (ō'no; "strong"). A city of Benjamin built (or restored), apparently, by Shemed (1 Chron. 8:12). Some of the inhabitants of Ono returned after the captivity (Ezra 2:33; Neh. 7:37). The valley in which it was located was known as "the plain of Ono" (6:2), probably the same as "the valley of craftsmen" (11:35), and in any case a part of the extension of the *Vale of Sharon* (which see). It is commonly identified with Kefr 'Ana, SE of Joppa.

ON'YCHA (on'I-ka). An ingredient of the holy incense (Ex. 30:34) used in the Tabernacle ritual. It was likely obtained from a mollusk. *See also* Animal Kingdom.

ONYX. *See* Mineral Kingdom.

O'PHEL (ō'fel; "mound" or "tower").
1. The ridge of Jerusalem extending S of the Temple mount between the Kidron Valley on the E and the Tyropoeon Valley on the W. This was

Mt. Ophel, Jerusalem

the location of the original city of Jerusalem, which was occupied by the Jebusites when David captured it and made it the capital of the Hebrew kingdom (2 Chron. 27:3; 33:14). David fortified and enhanced the city in various ways. Later, after the Babylonian destruction, Nehemiah rebuilt the wall around Ophel. Kathleen Kenyon excavated the ancient fortification of Ophel in the 1960s, and Yigal Shiloh worked there in the 1970s and 1980s. *See* Jerusalem.

2. The place in central Palestine in which was the house where Gehazi deposited the presents that he took from Naaman (2 Kings 5:24, rendered "hill" in the NIV, *see* marg. of the NASB; "tower," KJV). It was probably near the city of Samaria.

O'PHIR (ō'fir).
1. One of the sons of Joktan, the son of Eber, a great-grandson of Shem (Gen. 10:29; 1 Chron. 1:23).

2. The famous gold-producing region prominent in the OT. It is believed to have been located in SW Arabia in what is now known as Yemen. It may have included a part of the adjacent African seaboard. Yemen was famous for its gold mines, which are known to have still existed in the ninth century B.C. Ophir was visited by the trading fleet of Solomon and the Phoenicians. Solomon's navy was fitted out at Ezion-Geber, then traveled to Ophir, taking "four hundred and twenty talents of gold from there" (1 Kings 9:26-28; 22:48; 2 Chron. 8:17-18; 9:10). At the northern end of the Gulf of Aqabah, Ezion-Geber (modern Tell el Keleifeh) was excavated by Nelson Glueck. Solomon used the copper of the Arabah, smelted at Ezion-Geber, as a stock-in-trade. His *tarshish* or "refinery" fleet sailed down the Red Sea and spent part of three years to make the trip, explainable by long hauls in excessively hot weather. In exchange for copper, Solomon's refinery fleet brought back not only the fine gold of Ophir but silver, apes, ivory, and peacocks (1 Kings 10:22). Gold of Ophir garnished Solomon's armor, throne, Temple, and house of the forest of Lebanon (10:14-19). M.F.U.

OPH'NI (of'ni). A town NE of Benjamin (Josh. 18:24), perhaps the Gophna of Josephus and the Bethgufnin of the Talmud, which still survives in the modern Jifna, or Jufna, 2½ miles NW of Bethel. A palace of the Roman period was discovered on this site.

OPH'RAH (of'ra; "fawn, hind").
1. A city of Benjamin (Josh. 18:23; cf. 1 Sam. 13:17), probably the same as Ephron (2 Chron. 13:19), Ephraim (John 11:54), and Apherema (1 Macc. 11:34).

2. A town of Manasseh, W of the Jordan and six miles SW of Shechem (Judg. 6:11, more fully Ophrah of the Abiezrites, 8:27, 32). It was the

native place of Gideon (6:11), his residence after his ascension to power (9:5), and the place of his burial (8:32). Robinson was doubtless correct in locating it at et-Taiyibeh, four miles NE of Bethel. Because of the ephod's having been deposited there it was a place of pilgrimage.

Jebusite wall, Mt. Ophel

3. A Judaite, a son of Meonothai (1 Chron. 4:14), although it is more than likely that "became the father of" here means to found, and that Ophrah is the name of a village.

ORACLE (Heb. *d^ebîr,* from *dābar,* to "speak"; Gk. *logion,* "utterance" of God). The divine communications given to the Hebrews. The manner of such utterances was various: God speaking sometimes face to face, as with Abraham and Moses; sometimes by dreams and visions, as with Joseph and Pharaoh; sometimes by signs and tokens, as with Gideon and Barak; sometimes by word of prophecy; and sometimes by a regularly organized system of communication, as with *Urim* and *Thummim* (which see). These last were distinctly Hebrew and were always accessible, as in the case of David's inquiring whether it would be safe for him to take refuge with the men of Keilah (1 Sam. 23:9-12; cf. 30:7-8). The earliest oracle on record, probably, is that given to Rebekah (Gen. 25:22-23), whereas the most complete is that of the child Samuel (1 Sam. 3).

Heathen oracles are mentioned in Scripture, a celebrated case being that of Baal-zebub at Ekron, where inquiry was made respecting the recovery of King Ahaziah (2 Kings 1:2). Other oracular means in Palestine were the teraphim, such as that of Micah (Judg. 17:5, *see* marg.); the ephod of Gideon (8:27; etc.); the false gods of Samaria, with their false prophets, and consequently their oracles. Israel is reproached by Hosea for consulting wooden idols (Hos. 4:12), and also by Habakkuk (Hab. 2:19).

ORATION. *See* Orator.

ORATOR. The rendering in the KJV of Heb. *lāḥash* in Isa. 3:3 and Gk. *rhētor* in Acts 24:1. The Heb. term means "a whispering, charming" and is translated "skillful enchanter" in the NASB and NIV of the passage. The Gk. term has the meaning of "professional advocate" and is applied to Tertullus, who acted as the attorney (so NASB) or lawyer (so NIV) for the Jewish persecutors of Paul. He was a forensic speaker, a class common in Rome.

The *oration* (Gk. *dēmēgoria*) or "address" (NASB and NIV) delivered by Herod (Acts 12:21) was a rhetorical effort addressed to the populace for the sake of popularity.

ORCHARD (Heb. *pardēs,* "park"). A garden planted with trees (Song of Sol. 4:13, cf. Eccles. 2:5; rendered "forest" in Neh. 2:8).

ORDINANCES, CHRISTIAN. These are "outward rites prescribed by Christ to be performed by His Church" (Charles Ryrie). For most evangelical Protestants, ordinances are symbolic in nature and neither contain in themselves nor convey to others the grace of God. Many, however, call ordinances *sacraments,* a term that usually includes the idea of imparting grace. In either case, the faith within the soul of the participant can be encouraged and motivated by prayerful meditation on the divine meaning of the form.

Nearly all Christians practice baptism (Matt. 28:19) and the Lord's Supper (1 Cor. 11:23-29). Baptism means identification with the Holy Trinity in general and with the death, burial, and resurrection of Christ in particular (Rom. 6:3-4). Christians are divided over two main issues: the mode of baptism (sprinkling, Heb. 9:10; pouring, Heb. 6:2; immersion, Acts 8:38-39) and the time of baptism (in infancy, Col. 2:11-12; after belief, Acts 2:41).

The Lord's Supper means the remembrance of the sacrifice of the body and blood of the Lord Jesus for man's sin. It apparently was the focal point for worship in the early church (Acts 2:42). Christians are divided here too over two main issues: the nature of the Lord's Supper (transubstantiation, Roman Catholics; consubstantiation, Lutherans; spiritual presence, Calvin; memorial only, most evangelicals), and the frequency of the Lord's Supper (daily, Acts 2:46; weekly, 20:7; monthly; annually).

Besides the two common ordinances, some Christians include the following: footwashing (John 13:1-14), love feast (1 Cor. 11:17-22), laying on of hands (Acts 8:15-18), holy kiss (1 Thess. 5:26), and anointing of the sick with oil (James 5:14-15). Roman Catholics believe in seven sacraments including confirmation, penance, matrimony, extreme unction, and holy orders. Some dispensationalists teach that physical ordinances are transitional from Israel to the church, and that either baptism or both baptism and the Lord's Supper are not for this age of grace.

For further study *see* these related articles: Sacrament; Baptism; Agape; Eucharist; Lord's Supper; Anointing; Ablution; Kiss; Ordination.

ORDINATION. In the limited and technical sense ordination is the ceremony by which a person is set apart to an order or office; but in a broader, and in fact its only important sense, ordination signifies the appointment or designation of a person to a ministerial office, with or without attendant ceremonies.

Bible Usage. Uses in the OT and NT appear.

Old Testament Ordination. Ordination was practiced early in Bible times. The Hebrew priests, Levites, prophets, and kings were solemnly ordained for their several offices (*see* under their several articles). Moses thus, i.e., by laying on of hands, appointed *Joshua* (which see) as his successor (Num. 27:18-20, 22-23; Deut. 34:9).

Example of Christ. In the introduction of the Christian dispensation no exterior act of ordination was practiced by Christ. The calling, appointing, and commissioning of the twelve apostles was His personal act, unattended, so far as the record shows, with any symbolic act or ceremony. In the account (Mark 3:14) of His appointing "twelve, that they might be with Him, and that He might send them out to preach," the Gk. word is *epoiēse,* "he made," i.e., he "appointed" them for the purposes named. The word rendered "appointed" (John 15:16; Gk. *ethēka*) means "I have set, or placed." In no ordination of His disciples to their ministerial or apostolic office is it recorded that He *laid His hands upon them.* But just before His ascension, our Lord, in blessing His disciples and breathing upon them the Holy Spirit, "lifted up His hands" (Luke 24:50). In so doing He illustrated the nature of the spiritual influence that was to come upon them in its full manifestation at Pentecost. In this connection He uttered the words so often grossly perverted, "If you forgive the sins of any, their sins have been forgiven them; if you retain the sins of any, they have been retained" (cf. John 20:22-23). A literal and materializing construction of this passage, with those relating to the keys and the power of binding and loosing (Matt. 16:19; 18:18), became early in the history of the church a great fountain of error in reference to the office and power of the clergy (*see* Peter).

In the Apostolic Church. In the appointment of Matthias to the vacant apostleship, the principal interest appears to have centered on ascertaining whom the Lord had chosen (Acts 1:21-26); in this case there is no evidence of the imposition of hands.

Deacons. The first ordination in the Christian church was that of the seven deacons, in which

case the apostles set them apart by prayer and the laying on of hands (6:5-6).

Barnabas and Paul. Paul, although he had been called and set apart by Christ, submitted to the laying on of hands (13:1-3). "The simplest interpretation is that the Church as a whole held a special service for this solemn purpose. *Codex Bezae* makes all clear by inserting the nominative 'all.' . . . Further, there is no sign in 13:2, 3 that this 'consecration' by the Church was more efficacious than the original divine call; the ceremony merely blessed Barnabas and Saul for a special work, which was definitely completed in the next three years" (Ramsay, *St. Paul the Traveller,* pp. 66-67).

Elders. It is recorded (Acts 14:23) that Paul and Barnabas "appointed elders for them in every church." In this narrative the Gk. word *cheirotoneō* is used for the first time. Unfortunately its meaning is by no means certain. Originally it meant *to elect by popular vote,* yet it came to be used in the sense *to appoint* or *designate.* Apparently, the votes and voice of each congregation were considered. The term is obviously used in that way by Paul (2 Cor. 8:19). As to the ceremonies used in these ordinations, the components of prayer, fasting, and commending the persons ordained to the Lord are mentioned.

Principles. In reviewing the scriptural instances of ordination we note the following: (1) Christ ordained in the sense of appointing His disciples to ministerial service by His own authority and without employing any ceremony. (2) In the election of Matthias to fill the place of Judas, it was deemed sufficient to learn by prayer and the lot whom the Lord had chosen, then without any ceremony to number him with the eleven. (3) The laying on of hands as a ceremony of ministerial ordination was first practiced by the apostles in the case of the seven deacons. (4) It was also practiced in the case of Paul and Barnabas and elders of the NT church. (5) We have no account of anyone's having been ordained to the office of bishop in distinction from that of elder; still less is there any intimation that bishops were or were to become the only officers competent to ordain ministerial candidates; whereas elders were frequently, if not always, associated even with apostles in the act of ordination.

Meaning of Ordination. Ordination in the early church seems to have been regarded as a formal induction into the ministerial office and as having more significance than a mere bestowment of the authority of the church. The clergy were at first elected by the people; and Clement of Rome speaks of them as having been appointed by other distinguished men, with the approbation of the whole church. But the fact that the special ordination of the presbyters or the bishop was considered necessary seems to imply that a special efficacy was associated with the rite.

Augustine, however, distinctly exclaims, "What else is the imposition of hands than a prayer over a man?" With the growing importance of the episcopal office, and the sanctity associated with it and the clergy in general, the rite of ordination assumed the character of a sacramental act in which special grace was conferred, and that could only be performed by the bishop. The ordination of clergymen was as early as the fourth or fifth century admitted into the number of the sacraments. It is so held now by the Roman Catholic and Greek churches. In the Church of England and the Episcopal church of the United States ordination has not the significance of a sacrament; and the view of the English Reformers was not that the laying on of hands, as such, conferred any grace. Only bishops can ordain, and any other than episcopal ordination is invalid. The Lutheran and Reformed churches have always acknowledged and practiced ordination; but their confessions and theologians have justly laid stress upon the necessity of the divine call to the ministry. The Moravians confine to their bishops the right to ordain but recognize the validity of the ordination by other Protestants. The Disciples of Christ, Quakers, and Plymouth Brethren do not recognize any human rite of ordination. The Discipline of the Methodist church (¶ 163) provides for the ordination of deacons by the bishop, whereas an "elder is constituted by the election of the Annual Conference, and by the laying on of hands of a bishop and some of the elders who are present" (Dis., ¶ 166). The following note in the Discipline (¶ 449) sets forth the Methodist view as to bishops: "This service is not to be understood as an ordination to a higher order in the Christian ministry, beyond and above that of elders or presbyters, but as a solemn and fitting consecration for the special and most sacred duties of superintendency in the Church."

BIBLIOGRAPHY: A. R. Hay, *New Testament Order for Church and Missionary* (n.d.); J. B. Lightfoot, *The Christian Ministry* (1879); id., *Ordination Addresses* (1891); A. R. Hay, *The Woman's Ministry in Church and Home* (1962); R. L. Saucy, *The Church in God's Program* (1972); R. H. Fuller, ed., *Toward a New Theology of Ordination* (1976); M. Warkentin, *Ordination, a Biblical-Historical View* (1982).

O'REB (ō'reb; "a raven"). One of the leaders of the Midianite host that invaded Israel and was defeated and driven back by Gideon. He was killed, not by Gideon himself or the people under his immediate conduct, but by the men of Ephraim, who rose at his entreaty and intercepted the flying horde at the fords of the Jordan (Judg. 7:24-25), about 1200 B.C. The terms in which Isaiah refers to it (Isa. 10:26) are such as to imply that it was a truly awful slaughter. He places it in the same rank with the two most tremendous disasters recorded in the history of Israel—the destruction of the Egyptians in the Red Sea and of the army of Sennacherib (cf. Ps. 83:11).

BIBLIOGRAPHY: J. M. Lang and T. Kirk, *Studies in the Book of Judges*, 2 vols. in 1 (1983), 1:154-67.

O'REB, ROCK OF (ō'reb; the "raven's crag"). The place at which Gideon slew Oreb (Judg. 7:25; Isa. 10:26), believed by some to be E of Jordan. Keil and Delitzsch say (*Com.*, ad loc.) that it was "west of Jordan, where the Ephraimites had taken possession of the waters of the Jordan in front of the Midianites."

O'REN (ō'ren). The third named of the sons of Jerahmeel, of the tribe of Judah (1 Chron. 2:25), about 1190 B.C.

ORGAN. See Music.

ORI'ON (o-ri'on). The celestial constellation composed of myriads of stars, most of which are invisible without a telescope. It was early imagined to resemble the form of a hunter who, according to ancient legend, was put to death by Artemis after his pursuit of the Pleiades. Job attributed the creation of Orion, Arcturus, and Pleiades to God (Job 9:9; 38:31). This constellation is located S of Taurus and Gemini. It includes the giants Betelgeuse and Rigel.   M.F.U.

ORNAMENT (Heb. generally *'ădî*, "trapping"). The number, variety, and weight of the ornaments ordinarily worn upon the person form one of the characteristic features of oriental costume, both in ancient and modern times. The monuments of ancient Egypt exhibit wealthy ladies loaded with rings, earrings of great size, anklets, armlets, bracelets of the most varied character, richly ornamented necklaces, and chains of various kinds. There is sufficient evidence in the Bible that the inhabitants of Palestine were equally devoted to finery. The Midianites appear to have been as prodigal as the Egyptians in the use of ornaments (Num. 31:50-52; Judg. 8:24-26).

Male. From the most ancient times two ornaments pertained to men: a staff in the hand (Gen. 38:18) and a seal worn by a ribbon on the breast or in a ring on the right hand (41:42; Jer. 22:24; Esther 3:10; 8:2). *Earrings,* which were worn by the Midianites (Judg. 8:24-26) and other orientals, seem also to have been worn by men among the Israelites (Ex. 32:2-3). Gold necklaces do not appear as a male ornament among the Israelites, as they do among the Persians and Medes; neither does the custom of the Egyptians and Medo-Persians, whose kings adorned their highest ministers with gold chains as insignia of office or tokens of their favor (Gen. 41:42; Dan. 5:7).

Female. Much more varied were the ornaments and jewelry of Israelite women. In the OT Isaiah (Isa. 3:18-23) supplies us with a detailed description of the articles with which the luxurious women of his day were decorated, and the picture is filled up by incidental notices in other places. The notices that occur in the early books of the Bible imply the weight and abundance of the ornaments worn at that period. *Earrings* were worn by Jacob's wives, apparently as charms, for they are mentioned in connection with idols: "So they gave to Jacob all the foreign gods which they had, and the rings which were in their ears" (Gen. 35:4). *Nose rings* were worn in the right or left nostril, perhaps also in the division of the nose (24:47; Isa. 3:21; Ezek. 16:12). *Necklaces* were made of metal, of jewels, or of pearls, strung on a ribbon (Song of Sol. 1:10), hanging down to the breast or girdle. To these were attached golden *crescents* (Judg. 8:21; Isa. 3:18), perhaps also *amulets* and *perfume boxes* (3:20). *Armlets* or *bracelets* (Gen. 24:22; Num. 31:50; Isa. 3:19) were worn by women and also by men of rank (2 Sam. 1:10). There also were *anklets* (Isa. 3:18), fastened with *chains* (3:20), which women used to make a tinkling as they tripped along (3:16). These trinkets were made of gold in the case of women of rank; as, in addition, were hand mirrors of metal (Ex. 38:8; Isa. 3:23), probably carried in the hand as ornaments. The poetical portions of the OT contain numerous references to the ornaments worn by the Israelites in the time of their highest prosperity. The appearance of the bride is thus described in the Song of Solomon (1:10-11; 4:4, 9).

BIBLIOGRAPHY: H. Frankfort, *The Art and Architecture of the Ancient Orient* (1954); K. R. Maxwell-Hyslop, *Western Asiatic Jewelry* (1971).

Ostriches

OR'NAN (or'nan). The form given (1 Chron. 21:15, 18, 20-25, 28; 2 Chron. 3:1) to *Araunah* (which see).

ORON'TES (o-ron'tez). A historically famous river of Syria taking its source in the elevated Beq'a Valley. It runs N through Syria and then W into the Mediterranean Sea at the port of ancient Antioch-on-the-Orontes, named Seleucia Pieria. Antioch was a famous NT center of early Christianity (Acts 11:20-26; 13:1-3). Riblah appears prominently in 2 Kings and Jeremiah in connection with Zedekiah of Judah and Nebuchadnezzar (2 Kings 25:20-21; Jer. 39:5-6; 52:9-10). Other

important centers on the Orontes were Hamath, a Hittite stronghold, Kadesh, where Rameses II clashed with the Hittites, and Homs (Emessa), a center of early Christianity.   M.F.U.

OR'PAH (or'pa; "neck"). A Moabitess and wife of Chilion, the son of Naomi. At first she was disposed to accompany her mother-in-law to Canaan but afterward she decided to remain among her own people. She gave Naomi the kiss of farewell and returned "to her people and her gods" (Ruth 1:4, 14-15).

ORPHAN (Heb. *yātôm,* "lonely," Jer. 5:28; Lam. 5:3). One deprived of one or both parents. But the Heb. word, as well as the Gk. (*orphanos,* John 14:18), is used figuratively for one bereft of a teacher, guide, guardian. In this sense the Gk. word *aporphanizō* (1 Thess. 2:17) is used, referring to one *bereft of* connections with society.

O'SEE (ō'zē). A less correct way (Rom. 9:25) of Anglicizing the name of the prophet *Hosea* (which see).

OSHE'A (o-shē'a; "deliverer"). Another form (Num. 13:8, 16, sometimes "Hoshea") of the name *Joshua* (which see).

OSNAPPAR (os'nap-er), or **Osnapper.** The name of a king mentioned only in Ezra 4:10 and called there the "great and honorable Osnappar" ("Asnappar," KJV; "Ashurbanipal," NIV), an Aram. form of the Assyrian Ashurbanipal (Gk., Sardanapallos; Lat., Sardanapalus). He followed his father, Esarhaddon, on the throne of Assyria and ruled 668-633. He completed the Assyrian conquest of Egypt, ravaged Elam when it proved to be a threat to him, and savagely put down a rebellion in Babylon. He was a terribly ruthless and vindictive king, who has been described as "barren in political insight." He is important to the Bible student, however, because he collected a great library of texts from all over Mesopotamia. Containing tens of thousands of texts written on clay tablets, it was discovered in the main by Hormuzd Rassam for the British Museum in 1853. This library has been said to "form the foundations of the science of Assyriology." Among other things, it contained copies of the Babylonian accounts of the creation and the Flood.   H.F.V.

OSPRAY, OSPREY. *See* Animal Kingdom: Buzzard; Vulture.

OSSIFRAGE. *See* Animal Kingdom: Vulture.

OS'TIA (os'ti-a). A famous seaport of Rome at the mouth of the Tiber. The port connected with the city proper by the Ostian Way. Paul's ship landed at Puteoli (Acts 28:13), another port accommodating heavily laden grain ships, because harbor facilities at Ostia were not yet completed. Claudius (A.D. 41-54) and Trajan in 104 completed harbor facilities at Ostia so it was no longer necessary to unload goods at Puteoli 138 miles away and haul them overland. In the second century A.D. Ostia reached its peak and may have had a population in excess of 100,000. Systematic excavations began at Ostia in 1909 and have continued more or less uninterruptedly to the present. About half of the 160 acres of the ancient city have now been excavated, revealing tremendous granaries and warehouses, a theater, numerous sanctuaries of the Mithra cult and other temples, a Jewish synagogue, and blocks of apartment houses and shops. The Ostian excavations have revealed a great deal about the wealth, commerce, and religious sects in Rome at the time of Paul.   M.F.U.

OSTRICH. *See* Animal Kingdom.

Figurative. In Lam. 4:3 the ostrich is used as a symbol of the unnatural cruelty of the Jews in their calamity; in companionship the ostrich (Job 30:29) is a figure of extreme desolation, taken from the isolated life of that bird in the desert.

OTH'NI (oth'ni; apocopated from Othniel). One of the sons of Shemaiah, and a gatekeeper of the Tabernacle (1 Chron. 26:7).

OTH'NIEL (oth'ni-el; "God is might").

1. "The son of Kenaz, Caleb's younger brother" (Judg. 3:9). The probability is that Kenaz was the head of the tribe (Judah) and that Othniel, as the son of Jephunneh, was one of the descendants of Kenaz.

The first mention of Othniel is on the occasion of the taking of Kiriath-sepher, or *Debir* (which see), as it was afterward called. Caleb, to whom the city was assigned, offered as a reward to its captor, his daughter Achsah. Othniel won the prize (Josh. 15:16-17; Judg. 1:12-13), about c. 1380 B.C.

Israel "forgot the Lord their God, and served the Baals and the Asheroth." As a punishment for their idolatry the Lord delivered them into the hands of *Cushan-rishathaim* (which see), king of Mesopotamia, whom they were obliged to serve for eight years. In this oppression the Israelites cried unto the Lord, and He raised them up a deliverer in the person of Othniel the Kenizzite. "The Spirit of the Lord came upon him, and he judged Israel. When he went out to war . . . he prevailed over Cushan-rishathaim. Then the land had rest forty years. And Othniel the son of Kenaz died" (Judg. 3:7-11), about 1360 B.C.

2. An Othniel is mentioned (1 Chron. 27:15) as an ancestor of Heldai, the head of a family of Netophathites and probably the same person as above.

BIBLIOGRAPHY: J. M. Lang and T. Kirk, *Studies in the Book of Judges,* 2 vols. in 1 (1983), 1:34ff.

OUCH (ouch; pl. "ouches," Heb. *mishbe̱sôt,* "woven together" in filigree fashion). An archaic term referring to the gold work, which not only served to fasten the stones upon the woven fabric of the ephod but formed at the same time clasps or brooches, by which the two parts of the ephod were fastened together. The NASB and NIV read "filigree" (Ex. 28:11-25; 39:6-18). *See* High Priest, Dress of.

OUTER TUNIC. *See* Dress.

OUTLANDISH (Heb. *nēkār,* Neh. 13:26). "Foreign," as the women of other nations that caused Solomon to sin.

OUTRAGEOUS (Heb. *she̱tep,* to "gush out," Prov. 27:4). Whence the metaphor, anger is an *outpouring,* or *flood* (so NASB).

OVEN (Heb. *tannûr,* "fire pot"; Gk. *klibanos,* "earthen pot"). There are four kinds of ovens or places for baking, in the East:

1. Mere sand, heated by a fire, which was afterward removed. The raw dough was placed upon it, and in a little while turned; and then, to complete the process, covered with warm ashes and coals. Unless turned they were not thoroughly baked (Hos. 7:8).

2. An excavation in the earth lined with pottery. This is heated, the dough spread on the sides, and so baked.

3. A large stone jar, about three feet high, open at the top and widening toward the bottom, with a hole for the extraction of the ashes. Each household possessed such an article (Ex. 8:3); and it was only in times of extreme need that the same oven sufficed for several families (Lev. 26:26). It was heated with dry twigs and grass (Matt. 6:30), and the loaves were placed both inside and outside of it.

Oven

4. A plate of iron, placed upon three stones; the fire was kindled beneath it, and the raw cakes placed upon the upper surface. No doubt bakers had a special oven in ancient times (Hos. 7:4, 6), such as are now public in oriental cities.

Figurative. "Ten women will bake your bread

in one oven" (Lev. 26:26) is a figurative expression for scarcity; for in ordinary times each woman would have enough baking for an oven of her own. "You will make them as a fiery oven" (Ps. 21:9; "furnace," NIV) is a figure taken from the intense heat of an oven being prepared for baking; hence speedy destruction (cf. Hos. 7:4, 6-7). "Our skin has become as hot as an oven" (Lam. 5:10), i.e., as an oven is scorched and blackened with fire, so hunger dries up the pores till the skin becomes as if scorched by the sun.

OVERLIVE (Josh. 24:31). Another form for *outlive*.

OVERPASS (Heb. *'ābar,* to "cross over," Jer. 5:28, KJV; "excel," NASB; "no limit," NIV). To excel, to go beyond; here in badness.

OVERSEER (Heb. usually *pāqîd,* a "visitor"; Gk. *episkopos,* a "bishop," Acts 20:28). An officer having the superintendence of a household, such as Joseph (Gen. 39:4-5; cf. 41:34); a superintendent, either civil, military, or ecclesiastical (Judg. 9:28; 2 Chron. 31:13; Esther 2:3). *See* Elder.

OVERSHADOW (Gk. *episkiazō,* to "envelop in a shadow"). From a vaporous cloud that casts a shadow the word is transferred to a shining cloud surrounding and enveloping persons with brightness (Matt. 17:5; Luke 9:34).
   Figurative. It is used of the Holy Spirit's extending creative energy upon the womb of the virgin Mary and impregnating it; a use of the word that seems to have been drawn from the familiar OT idea of a cloud as symbolizing the immediate presence and power of God.

OWL. *See* Animal Kingdom.

OX. A castrated male of the *Bos taurus* family, valued in the OT period as a patient, heavy draft animal. *See* Animal Kingdom.
   Figurative. "As the ox licks up the grass" (Num. 22:4) is a figure of easy victory. For an ox to "low over his fodder" (Job 6:5) is to complain without cause. "As an ox goes to the slaughter" is used in connection with a rash youth (Prov. 7:22). To "let out freely the ox and the donkey" (Isa. 32:20; lit., let the ox and the donkey roam in freedom) is a figure of copious abundance, inasmuch as the cattle would not have to be watched lest they should stray into the grainfields. "A fattened ox" (Prov. 15:17) represents sumptuous living. Oxen not muzzled in treading corn (1 Cor. 9:9-10) is figurative of the minister's right to support.

OXGOAD. *See* Goad.

OX, WILD. *See* Animal Kingdom: Wild Ox.

O'ZEM (ō'zem; probably "strength").
   1. The sixth son of Jesse and next eldest above David (1 Chron. 2:15), about 1060 B.C.
   2. One of the sons of Jerahmeel (1 Chron. 2:25), about 1190 B.C.

OZI'AS (ō-zī'as). Another form of the name of Uzziah king of Judah (Matt. 1:8-9).

OZ'NI (oz'ni; "cared, i.e., attentive"). The fourth son of Gad and the founder of the family of Oznites (Num. 26:16).

OZ'NITES (oz'nīts; "having" quick "ears"). The descendants of *Ozni* (which see) or Ezbon (Gen. 46:16). One of the families of the tribe of Gad (Num. 26:16).

PA'ARAI (pa'a-ri). "The Arbite," one of David's valiant men (2 Sam. 23:35), called *Naarai* (which see) in 1 Chron. 11:37.

PACE (Heb. *ṣa'ad*, a "step," as elsewhere rendered). This was not a formal measure but was taken in the general sense (2 Sam. 6:13). *See* Metrology: Linear Measures.

PAD'DAN (pa'dan; Heb. *paddān*, "plain, field"). Mentioned in Gen. 48:7. *See* Paddan-aram.

PAD'DAN-A'RAM (pad'an-a'ram; "plain or field of Aram," i.e., Syria). The name given to the country of Rebekah (Gen. 25:20) and the home of Laban (28:2-7); called "the land of Aram" by Hosea (Hos. 12:12). It was a district of *Mesopotamia* (which see), the large plain surrounded by mountains, in which the town of Haran was situated. Paddan-aram was intimately associated with the history of the Hebrews. Abraham's family had settled there, and there he sent his servant to secure a wife for Isaac (Gen. 24:10, *see* marg.; 25:20); and later Jacob went there and married (28:2; 41:18).

BIBLIOGRAPHY: D. J. Wiseman, ed., *Peoples of Old Testament Times* (1973), pp. 134-35. *See also* Haran.

PADDLE (Heb. *yātēd*). Literally a tent peg (so NASB and NIV, Judg. 4:21), or a stake or pin, but in Deut. 23:13 (KJV), a small shovel.

PA'DON (pa'don; "redemption, ransom, deliverance"). The name of one of the Temple servants whose descendants returned from Babylon (Ezra 2:44; Neh. 7:47), about 536 B.C.

PA'GIEL (pa'gi-el; "meeting or rendezvous" with God). The son of Ochran and leader of the tribe of Asher at the time of the Exodus (Num. 1:13; 2:27; 7:72; 10:26), c. 1440 B.C.

PA'HATH-MO'AB (pa'hath-mō'ab; "governor of Moab"). The head of a leading family of Judah, whose 2,812 descendants returned to Jerusalem after the captivity (Ezra 2:6; Neh. 7:11 says 2,818), and another company, of 200 males, under Ezra (Ezra 8:4). Hasshub the Pahath-moabite is named among the builders of the walls of Jerusalem (Neh. 3:11). In Ezra 10:30, eight of the "sons" of Pahath-moab are named as putting away their foreign wives. That this family was of high rank in the tribe of Judah we learn from their appearing *fourth* in order in the two lists (Ezra 2:6; Neh. 7:11) and from their leader having signed *second* among the lay princes (Neh. 10:14).

PA'I (pa'i; 1 Chron. 1:50). *See* Pau.

PAINTING. A form of art that played an important role in antiquity.

Palestine. Ancient painting as early as the fourth millennium B.C. showed remarkable vitality. The most popular type of work of this kind was done on cave walls or plastered surfaces. Early paintings have been found at such sites as Megiddo and Jericho. Egyptian and Mesopotamian art of this type also flourished. The wealth and ease afforded by these irrigation cultures fostered leisure and supplied the means for the cultivation of the arts. Famous in Palestine are the paintings on cave walls in the Hellenistic city of Marisa (Beit Jibrin) dating from the third century B.C.

Egypt. Egyptian belief in life after death manifested itself in bright colors and cheerful paintings that adorn the walls of rock-cut tombs as at Thebes and Saqqarah. The Egyptians were skillful in designing objects of everyday life, the lotus with bud and leaf, the animals and birds of the Nile Valley, and lifelike people and events. In fine colors they portrayed on sarcophagi and mummy cases festal meals and social pastimes, scenes from city life and farm life. The Egyptians ground their paints on stones worn smooth by constant use. These relics of an ancient art may be seen in many museums.

Egyptian wall painting

Crete. Knossos in Crete shows famous painted frescoes executed between 1900 and 1750 B.C. Minoan Crete, explored by Sir Arthur Evans, has given us much information of paintings in the House of the Frescoes and on sarcophagi. Such frescoes as the "Saffron Gatherer" and the "Toreador and His Horse" are notable for their artistic execution.

Rome. Fresco painting was widely popular in the time of Jesus and in the apostolic age. Excavations at Pompeii in the Villa of the Mysteries have yielded elaborate cultic rites executed in fresco paintings. Such paintings come from all parts of the Roman world.   M.F.U.

BIBLIOGRAPHY: A. Lucas, *Ancient Egyptian Materials and Industries* (1948), pp. 391-413; R. J. Forbes, *Studies in Ancient Technology* 3 (1956): 202-55.

PAINTING THE EYES. *See* Eyes, Painting of.

PALACE. The dwelling of a king or important official. All over the biblical world palaces figure prominently.

In Israel. Saul's austere palace-fortress has been excavated at Gibeah by W. F. Albright and displays stout masonry, cyclopean walls, and rustic construction. David's first palace was at Hebron and must have been a crude edifice compared with his more lavish dwelling at Jebusite Jerusalem, which he captured. Hiram of Tyre sent him cedar trees and carpenters and artisans to build him a house (2 Sam. 5:11). David's palace must have been simple but nevertheless evidently showed evidence of Phoenician artistry. Solomon's palace was much grander. This was indeed a lavish building, as we may gather from 1 Kings, but unfortunately nothing survives of it. The vast wealth of Solomon, along with the skilled Phoenician workers, doubtless produced a fabulous structure. Herod the Great's palace at Jerusalem in the first century B.C. was also magnificent. At the city of Samaria Omri and his son Ahab, in the first quarter of the ninth century B.C., built lavish palaces, as did also Jeroboam II in the following century. Much later Herod also

built at Sebastieh (the name of Samaria in the Roman period). Herod built other palaces at Masada, Jericho, and in Herodion (near Bethlehem).

In Egypt. All of the pharaohs of Egypt's thirty dynasties had ornate and expensive palaces. Knowledge of these has come down through tomb reliefs and other forms of art. Especially well known is the palace of Merenptah, the son of Rameses II, about 1230 B.C. This palace was destroyed by fire, which left traces of painted frescoes; walls were brick, the roof of wood. The throne room opened at the end of a colonnaded court. The room was supported by six huge columns of white limestone, twenty-five feet high. The king's cartouche appears on the bronze door fastenings. The palace of Amenhotep III at Thebes has also been excavated by the Metropolitan Museum of Art. (*See* its bulletins for 1916-18.) The palace of Amenhotep IV (c. 1385-1366 B.C.) is also well known. It was built at Akhetaten, or Amarna, where the famous Amarna Letters were discovered. The king's palace was designated the "castle" of Aton. The palace was surrounded by an extensive complex of buildings. A double wall (with fortified passages) ran around the palace. The queen, the famous Nofretete, had her own palace. The royal residence also had priestly quarters situated near the Chapel of Aton, as well as large servants' quarters and a place for craftsmen.

In Mesopotamia. Both the Assyrians and Babylonians had splendid palaces. The palaces of Sargon II (722-705 B.C.) and of his son Sennacherib are well known for their size and lavish decorations. Nebuchadnezzar's palace at Babylon in the sixth century B.C. is also famous. The throne room of Nebuchadnezzar II was adorned with enamel bricks done in artistic geometrical lines. Bulls and dragons in enameled, colored bricks were favorite decorative motifs in the Babylon of this era, which was world-famous for its many buildings, including temples, ziggurats, wide processional streets, hanging gardens, and other architectural wonders. Nebuchadnezzar's palace fitted in with the splendor of its surroundings. A notable royal palace was uncovered at Mari on the Middle Euphrates. Dating from around 1700 B.C., this tremendous structure covers more than 7½ acres, including not only royal apartments but administrative offices and even a school for scribes. It was adorned with great mural paintings, portions of which are still in a fair state of preservation, containing depictions of sacrifice and a scene in which the king of Mari receives from Ishtar, the goddess of propagation, the emblematic staff and ring symbolic of his royal power (cf. A. Parrot in *Syria* 18 [1937], pp. 325-54. Also copies of *Syria* [1935-39]). The palaces of the great Persian monarchs at Persepolis are also noteworthy for their vastness and extravagance. The palaces of ancient Susa, which have been excavated by Jacques de Morgan, illustrate the story of Nehemiah, who refers to the time when he was "in Susa the capital" acting as cupbearer to Artaxerxes, the king. It also reminds us of Dan. 8:2.

Relief of Darius

Elsewhere in the Biblical World. The palaces excavated at Knossos, Phaestos, Mallia, and elsewhere on Crete display the glory of the Minoan culture, especially during the period from about 1600 to 1400 B.C. Palace fortresses uncovered at Mycenae, Pylos, Tiryns, and elsewhere on the Greek mainland demonstrate the power and wealth of the Myceneans between about 1400 and 1200 B.C. The palaces of the Hittite kings found at Boghazköy and other centers in Asia Minor and Syria likewise show the power of those biblical people. Studies of palaces of Cyprus, Syria, and of the Caesars at Rome help to round out our knowledge of the Bible world.   M.F.U.; H.F.V.

BIBLIOGRAPHY: I. Benzinger, *Bulletin of the American Schools of Oriental Research* 120 (December 1950): 11-22; id., *BASOR* 123 (October 1951): 8-17; id., *Israel Exploration Journal* 7, no. 1 (1957): 1-60; A. Badawy, *Architecture of Egypt and the Near East* (1966); G. Turner, *Iraq* 32 (1970): 177-213; D. Ussishkin, *Biblical Archaeologist* 36 (1973): 78-105.

PA'LAL (pa'lal; "He," i.e., God, "judges"). The son of Uzai, and one of those who assisted in rebuilding the walls of Jerusalem (Neh. 3:25), 445 B.C.

PALESTINA (Ex. 15:14; Isa. 14:29, 31, all KJV). Palestine.

PALESTINE. Palestine, as the scene of ancient biblical events, is the region of SW Asia extending S and SW of the Lebanon ranges, NE of Egypt and N of the Sinai Peninsula. The "river" or "brook of Egypt" (Gen. 15:18; 2 Chron. 7:8), the modern Wadi el-Arish, is its SW boundary. On the W its boundary is the Mediterranean plain and on the E the Arabian Desert. It formed a tiny bridge between the ancient empires on the Tigris-Euphrates rivers in Mesopotamia, on the Halys River in Asia Minor, and the mighty civilization of

Egypt on the Nile. It constitutes the westernmost extremity of Breasted's "Fertile Crescent."

The Name. The name *Palestine* as a geographical designation was most probably derived from an Egyptian group, the *prst* (or *plst*) which migrated from the Delta region to southern Canaan at the beginning of the Proto-dynastic period (2900-2700 B.C.). Evidence of migrations from Egypt at this period have been furnished by excavations at Arad, En-gedi, and elsewhere. The *prst* (spelled this way because there was no letter *l* in Egyptian) evidently gave their name to the area where they settled, which was known as the "land of the Philistines" in Abraham's day (Gen. 21:32-34). It was these same people with whom Isaac also had dealings (Gen. 26:1). About 1200 B.C. a group of the Aegean Sea People, who conquered the Hittites and Phoenicians, settled ultimately in the coastal areas of southern Canaan and became known in the OT by the name of the land in which they were living. Philistia was subsequently rendered *hē Palaistinē* in Greek, a form which Herodotus (fifth century B.C.) was apparently the first to use. The Romans called it Palestina. Palestine as an official designation did not come into usage, however, until the second century A.D., first describing the SW plain of Phoenicia and subsequently applied to all Palestine W of the Jordan. *Canaan* (which see) is the older name of Palestine, the former seemingly derived from Hurrian, meaning "belonging to the land of red purple." By the fourteenth century B.C. this geographical designation came to be employed of the region in which the "Canaanites," or Phoenician traders, exchanged red-purple dye from murex shells on the Mediterranean coast for other commodities. In the Amarna Letters "the land of Canaan" is applied to the Phoenician coast, and the Egyptians called all western Syria by this name. The "holy land" is referred to only in Zech. 2:12. This name differentiates the country as Jehovah's and the people who possessed it in covenant relation with Him. After the OT period in the Hellenistic-Roman era (333 B.C.–A.D. 300) the country was called Judea, a term that at first described only the region around Jerusalem after the Babylonian Exile.

Size. It averages about 70 miles in width and its greatest width is some 90 miles. "Dan to Beersheba," an expression denoting the extremity of the ancient N-S boundaries at their fullest extent, is a distance of only about 150 miles. OT Palestine was never much more than 10,000 sq. miles with barely 6,000 miles W of the Jordan and less than 4,000 E of it. In the Davidic-Solomonic era the boundaries roughly extended to the Euphrates and to the borders of Egypt, but this included tributary peoples, a population of about 2 million or possibly more than 3 million counting tributary peoples. In NT times Palestine consisted of Roman Judea, composed of Galilee, our Lord's home province in the N; Samaria, occupying the central highlands; and Judea extending on the S to the borders of Edom.

Geography. From the Mediterranean to the Arabian Desert two mountain ranges separate the land into four bands running N and S. These consist of the level coastal Maritime Plain, the Central Range or southerly spur from Mt. Lebanon, the Ghor or deep valley of the Jordan, and Eastern Palestine, consisting of a long plateau extending from Mt. Hermon to Mt. Hor in Edom.

Maritime Plain. This runs from the river Leontes on the N, five miles N of Tyre, to the desert beyond Gaza on the S. Mt. Carmel interrupts the valley, N of Carmel is the Plain of Acre. From Carmel S to Joppa the area is known as the Plain of Sharon, and S of Joppa is the Philistine Plain.

Central Range. The Central Range as a continuation of the Lebanon Mts. consists of Galilee, Samaria, and Judea. In Upper Galilee rise a number of hills, some 2,000 to 3,000 feet in height and a few to almost 4,000 feet. Lower Galilee is triangular, bounded by the Sea of Galilee and the Jordan to Beth-shan on its eastern border and the Plain of Esdraelon on the SW side. It consists of ranges running E and W with elevations much less than upper Galilee. Hills of lower Galilee usually have an altitude of 400-600 feet, although Mt. Tabor reaches 1,843 feet, and Mt. Gilboa has one peak 1,698 feet and another 1,648 feet. The Plain of Esdraelon intercepts the central region; S of Esdraelon the range is interrupted by many wadis. Mt. Ebal rises 3,077 feet and Gerizim 2,849 feet. Samaria was located in this region. From Bethel to Hebron, in Judea, the range has an average height of 2,200 feet. Bethel reaches 2,930 feet, Jerusalem 2,598, Bethlehem 2,550, and Hebron 3,300.

Jordan Valley. The Jordan Valley consists of a deep gorge. At the foot of Mt. Hermon it is 1,700 feet above sea level. From there it descends rapidly to the Dead Sea, where it is 1,290 feet below sea level. The bottom of the Dead Sea reaches 1,300 feet still lower than its surface, recognized as the lowest point on the earth's surface and being a part of an amazing geological fault running S to the Red Sea and into East Africa.

Eastern Palestine. A large, fertile plateau, much of eastern Palestine more than 3,000 feet above sea level. It included ancient Bashan, Gilead, and Moab. This general territory is divided naturally into four parts by four rivers. There is the Yarmuk with Bashan to the N and the Jabbok with Gilead to the N and S; the Arnon, S of which was Moab; and the river Zered, with Edom located southward. The Yarmuk and Jabbok are tributaries of the Jordan. The Arnon and the Zered flow into the Dead Sea; S of the Dead Sea lies the deep copper-rich Arabah stretching to Ezion-geber at the head of the Red Sea.

Climate. Because of the diversity in elevation from Hermon's snowy 9,101 feet to the Dead

Sea's tropical 1,290 feet below sea level, a great variety of plant and animal life is found. In the hill country prevailing W winds create adequate rains from October to April; E winds from the desert bring intense heat and discomfort (Job 1:19; Jer. 18:17; Ezek. 17:10). Two seasons characterize Palestine: winter—moist, rainy, and mild, lasting from November to April; summer—hot and rainless, lasting from May to October.

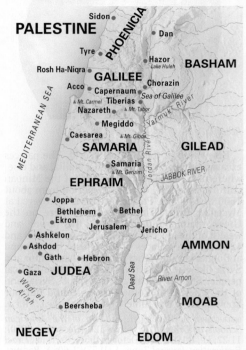

Biblical Archaeology. Archaeologists claim important finds in Palestine long before the biblical period (e.g., Carmel Man). In the Chalcolithic Age (c. 4500-3000 B.C.) early Palestinian cultures appear at Teleilat Ghassul just N of the Dead Sea, not far from Jericho. At this early period mudbrick houses were adorned with amazing mural paintings. Artistic frescoes survive. The Bronze Age (c. 3000-2000 B.C.) is marked by the discovery of the earliest Canaanite sanctuaries at Megiddo, Jericho, and Ai. The Middle Bronze Age (c. 2000-1500 B.C.) is marked at the beginning by Abraham's entrance into Palestine, which in this period was thinly settled in the heavily forested highland regions. Archaeology has fully corroborated the general background of the patriarchal period. The Middle Bronze Age cities were stoutly fortified with high walls, towers, moats, and Cyclopean masonry. In the Late Bronze Age (1500-1200 B.C.) came the Israelites. Their conquest of Palestine took place around 1400 B.C. (Masoretic chronology). At this period City D of

Jericho was built upon three earlier predecessors. It was this city that eventually fell to Joshua and the Israelites. During the period of Israelite conquest Ai and Bethel figure prominently, as well as Lachish. These cities have all been excavated. The situation at Ai particularly offers difficulty because et-Tell, identified as Ai, was unoccupied in 2000-1050 B.C. But there is serious question as to whether this identification is correct.

Numerous Iron Age or Hebrew monarchy sites have been excavated too. Among some of the more significant are Megiddo, Beth-Shan, Gezer, Hazor, Lachish, Samaria, and Jebusite Jerusalem. Excavations relating to NT study have not been so numerous as those connected with the OT. Especially significant for NT study has been the work at Caesarea, Capernaum, Samaria, Herodian Jericho, and excavations in the Temple area in Jerusalem. A detailed treatment of archaeological finds in Palestine would be impossible in a one-volume work of this type. See the individual Palestinian biblical sites for discussion of archaeological discoveries at each.

The story of the rediscovery of Palestine could begin in almost any of the early modern centuries. But a complete revolution in the surface exploration of Palestine came with the work of Edward Robinson of Union Theological Seminary of New York in 1838. His *Biblical Researches* (1841) marked an important milestone in Palestinian studies. Another significant development during the foundational period of Palestinian archaeology was the establishment of the Palestine Exploration Fund in 1865. An important project of the fund was the plotting of an inch to a mile survey of Western Palestine under the leadership of C. R. Conder and H. H. Kitchener.

The advent of scientific archaeology in Palestine may be said to have occurred in 1890, when the British scholar W. M. Flinders Petrie developed his pottery chronology method of dating at the mound of Tell el Hesy. There his work was confirmed and refined by American excavator F. J. Bliss. Between 1890 and 1914 the Palestine Exploration Fund sponsored work at several sites in the Shephelah. Of special importance was R. A. S. Macalister's work at Gezer (1902-9). German scholars also began to work in Palestine. The German Palestine Society was organized in 1877 and the German Oriental Society in 1898. The latter worked on the Capernaum synagogue, at Jericho, and at Shechem. The American Schools of Oriental Research was founded in 1900 and conducted five minor excavations before World War I. The great American expedition before World War I was at Samaria (1908-10) under the leadership of G. A. Reisner. His work marked the beginning of scientific excavation in Palestine.

During the years between the wars a new beginning of sorts came to Palestinian archaeology in 1920 when the British set up in Palestine a modern Department of Antiquities headed by an experienced archaeologist. The first major excavation in this period was the University of Pennsylvania Museum dig at Beth-Shan (1921-33). But the greatest single undertaking was the Oriental Institute of the University of Chicago excavation at Megiddo (1925-39), originally designed to take down the entire tell, stratum by stratum, and to serve as a model of stratigraphic technique. The American Schools of Oriental Research initiated or participated in several excavations between the wars. These included Gibeah of Saul, Tell Beit Mirsim, Tell en-Nasbeh, Beth-Zur, Jerash, Bethel, and Tell el-Kheleifeh, identified as Solomon's seaport of Ezion-geber. W. F. Albright and Nelson Glueck especially led in ASOR projects. Also Elihu Grant excavated at Beth-Shemesh (1928-33), and the Harvard dig at Samaria continued (1931-33, 1935). The British Palestine Exploration Fund worked at Lachish (1933-38); John Garstang dug at Jericho (1930-36); and Judith Marquet-Krause excavated at Et-Tell (1933-35). In 1925 and 1928 British excavators also made discoveries connected with Palestinian prehistory in Galilee and Carmel caves.

Agitation connected with the division of Palestine and the establishment of the State of Israel effectively stopped archaeological work between 1938 and 1949. After 1949 resumption of excavation was under quite different conditions from the earlier period. On the Israeli side there was a strong nationalistic spirit and historical consciousness that gave rise to a desire to unearth the past. The Israelis built several large universities with departments of archaeology where they could train personnel to conduct the various digs. The Hebrew University, founded in 1925, had already produced qualified archaeologists by 1948. On the Jordanian side there was no such strong national scholarship, and foreign scholars and teams were welcome. The greatest excitement in the archaeological world at the time of the United Nations division of Palestine focused on the Dead Sea Scrolls. Numerous excavations were conducted in caves and at Qumran.

In Jordan and on the West Bank in the 1950s important digs were conducted at Dhiban (Dibon), NT Jericho, OT Jericho, Dothan, Bethel, Gibeon, Shechem, Beth-Zur, and Petra. Momentum built up in the 1960s with work on Jebusite Jerusalem, Gibeah, Taanach, Et-Tell, on Mt. Gerizim, at the Herodium, and elsewhere. Israeli archaeologists first attacked the site of Tell Qasile in 1949 and went on to work at Dor, Ramat Rahel, Hazor, Joppa, Acre, Caesarea, and elsewhere during the 1950s. During the following decade they continued at Caesarea and worked at Megiddo, En-Gedi, Tiberias, Arad, Chorazin, Masada, Timna, Dan, and elsewhere.

The Six-Day War in 1967 brought a new era to biblical studies. Now, with Israeli control of the West Bank, many of the key sites from the Bible were in Israeli hands. Dead Sea Scrolls scholars on both sides of the "Middle East Curtain" now had access to each other, and Israelis had access to the Old City with opportunity to excavate there. The Israelis tried to assure Western archaeologists that they were welcome to return to the West Bank; a few did. Joseph Callaway went back to Et-Tell. The Drew-McCormick Harvard Expedition returned to Shechem, and the Danes excavated again at Shiloh. Israeli archaeologists have continued work in Israeli territory, at places like Beersheba, Hazor, Lachish, Chorazin, Dan, and Tell Qasile. And they have dug in occupied territory at such places as the Herodium and Megiddo. Consortiums of schools have also excavated at Tell el Hesi, Aphek, and Caesarea. The Franciscans have done a lot of work at Capernaum. But some of the most exciting archaeological investigation since the war has gone on in the Old City. Benjamin Mazar has directed the excellent work in the Temple area. Excavations in the Jewish Quarter, in the Armenian Garden, the Citadel, and on the City of David also have been rewarding.

Over in Jordan archaeological work has been undertaken at Heshbon, the Amman citadel, at Petra, and elsewhere. Surveys of sites have been conducted in the E Jordan Valley and S of the Dead Sea. Changed conditions have forced a change in the administration of the American Schools of Oriental Research in Jerusalem. The school now has an Amman Center of Oriental Research and an Albright Institute in Jerusalem, both autonomous.

With all that has been done and is now in progress in Palestine, it can confidently be stated that work there has scarcely begun. Of the approximately 5,000 known archaeological sites in the land, only about 10 percent have been excavated to any significant degree, and only about fifty have been the scene of major digs.

History. The first glimpse of the history of Palestine is found in Genesis (10:15-20). Canaan, the son of Ham, is the father of Sidon, i.e., the Phoenician stock; Heth, i.e., the Hittites; the Jebusites, a local tribe in and about Jerusalem; the Amorites, men of the hills; the Girgashites, an unknown stock; the Hivites, peasantry or fellahîn; the Arkites, citizens of Arka, in northern Phoenicia; the Sinites, people from some locality near Arka; the Arvadites, inhabitants of the island of Arvad off Tartos; the Zemarites, inhabitants of Sumra, and the Hamathites, the inhabitants of Hamath. "And afterward the families of the Canaanite were spread abroad. And the territory of the Canaanite extended from Sidon as you go toward Gerar, as far as Gaza; as you go toward Sodom and Gomorrah and Admah and Zeboiim, as far as Lasha" (vv. 18-19). These boundaries are substantially those of Canaan and later those of Palestine. Some of the primitive inhabitants of Canaan are called Rephaim— *giants* (Deut. 2:11,

20; 3:11; cf. Num. 13:33). The Amorites appear to belong to this race, as also the Emim, the Zamzummim or Zuzim, Ammon or Ham, and the Anakim, who are described as redoubtable giants. They inhabited the hill country, both E and W of the Jordan. The term *Amorite* is equivalent to "highlander." Although Canaan is represented as the father of all Palestine, the Canaanites ("lowlanders") are one family or group of the seed of Canaan. They inhabited the Philistine plain and the Jordan Valley. The Horites were the aborigines of Edom. The Amalekites were a Bedouin stock, inhabiting the 'Arabah, the Tîh, and Sinai, where their descendants still live a more or less predatory life. The Hittites proceeded from the Taurus, extending their conquests southward to Hamath and Carchemish and finally to southern Canaan. Some of them were in Hebron in Abraham's day. Ezekiel said (Ezek. 16:3) that the father of Jerusalem was an Amorite and the mother was a Hittite. During the Eighteenth and Nineteenth Dynasties of Egypt the Egyptians vainly attempted to break the Hittite power. Rameses II finally made a treaty with them. Eventually, in the time of Sargon II of Assyria (709 B.C.), the last of the Hittite city-states in Syria were brought under Assyrian control.

The earliest mention of Palestine in Babylonian records is its conquest by Naram-sin, son of Sargon of Akkad, about 2350 B.C. It was called then "the land of the Amorites." His conquests extended also to Cyprus. Other Babylonian records show that an extensive commerce existed between Babylonia and Palestine. The inference is almost inevitable that it depended upon the maintenance of the ancient overlordship of Babylon. Babylonian science and writing existed in Palestine during the early second millennium B.C., and relics of them have been found there and in el-Amarna. Not until the reign of Thothmes III was Palestine finally conquered by Egypt, 1481 B.C., in a great battle near Megiddo. The el-Amarna tablets give many details of the Egyptian occupation of Palestine.

About 1400 B.C. the Hittites began to conquer large portions of Syria and Palestine, and the Amorites and Canaanites began to regain their independence from Egypt. Edom had never submitted to the Egyptian yoke. Under Rameses II Palestine and Syria were temporarily reconquered.

During the sojourn of the patriarchs in Palestine they doubtless found both the Hebrew and Babylonian languages a medium of polite intercourse, and the political affinities of the land a sure protection. When Jacob's sons went into Egypt the Hyksos, an Asiatic people with Babylonian culture, were infiltrating the land; in subsequent decades they gradually rose to power there. Under the circumstances it was not strange for Joseph to be made prime minister. Then from about 1720 to 1580 the Hyksos ruled Egypt. A native Egyptian dynasty overthrew the Hyksos and destroyed foreign control in about 1580 B.C. So when the Israelites were oppressed it was by a king of African descent "who did not know Joseph" and hated all that belonged to the Asiatics. When the Israelites came to Canaan, both Egyptian and Babylonian overlordship were at an end, and the Hebrews did not have to contend with mighty empires but only with numerous discordant tribes of the natives, a circumstance that greatly facilitated their conquest. Canaan was an agricultural and commercial country, not a center of conquering power. Its religion was of Babylonian origin.

The history of the Israelites from the Exodus, c. 1440 B.C. (Masoretic chronology), to the captivity is given with so much detail in the Bible that it is unnecessary to present more than the leading outlines. After forty years in the wilderness the Israelites entered Canaan. In a few years they conquered most of eastern and western Palestine. They failed, however, to subdue part of the Philistine plain, all of Phoenicia, Lebanon, and Anti-Lebanon, even part of the highlands of Judea, including Jerusalem, the future capital, and all of Edom and Moab. In the time of Saul and David the kingdom was consolidated from the Mediterranean to the Euphrates and from Phoenicia to the Red Sea. In the days of Rehoboam the kingdom was divided, and Judah and Benjamin and sometimes Edom formed the kingdom of Judah, and northern and eastern Palestine that of Israel, with ten tribes. Jeroboam tried to draw away the hearts of Israel from Jerusalem as a religious center by establishing a focus of idolatry at Bethel, a few miles to the N. At first this effort was only partially successful. And even late into the history of the divided commonwealth the pious Israelites turned to the Temple and worship at Jerusalem with an irrepressible yearning. At last, however, the whole people seems to have been corrupted, and in 721 B.C. Samaria was taken and the ten tribes deported to Assyria. For a while longer some of the kings of Judah resisted the idolatry that had ruined Israel, but in 586 B.C. Jerusalem was taken by Nebuchadnezzar, and the best of the people were carried away captive to Babylon.

For seventy years Palestine remained a ruined country; the poor who remained were subjected to the worst type of oriental despotism. In 536 B.C. the first installment of the Jews returned to Jerusalem under Zerubbabel. Later, under Ezra and Nehemiah, others of the more enterprising of the exiles followed. The immense majority of the Hebrew people, however, remained in Assyria, Arabia, and other parts of the East. Wherever they retained their national identity they were thoroughly cured of idolatry. To this day Judaism, although formal and pharisaical, is in no part of the world idolatrous.

From the time of the restoration until the conquest of Alexander, 332 B.C., Palestine continued to be a province of Persia. Subsequently it was ruled by the Ptolemies of Egypt (301-198 B.C.). During the period of the Seleucids (198-167) it was under the Greek yoke. In 167 B.C. Mattathias led a revolt that resulted in the independence of Judea under the Hasmonaean dynasty (143 B.C.), which lasted until 63 B.C., when Pompey took Jerusalem and made Judea a vassal kingdom under Herod. Roman covetousness ultimately brought about a rebellion, which was finally ended by Vespasian and Titus, who destroyed Jerusalem and reduced Judea to a simple Roman province, A.D. 70. Hadrian rebuilt Jerusalem about A.D. 130, calling it Aelia Capitolina. Soon afterward the rebellion of Bar Kochba broke out but was put down with immense slaughter, A.D. 135. It was at this time that the Romans changed the name of Judea, which became hateful to them, to Syria Palestina. Jerusalem was made a heathen city, and Jews were forbidden to set foot in it on pain of death. Thenceforward Palestine remained a part of the Byzantine or continuing Roman Empire in the East until, in the early part of the seventh century, it fell into Muslim hands. During the eleventh and twelfth centuries it was the scene of the Crusades until, in A.D. 1187, it was conquered by Saladin. In A.D. 1517 it succumbed to the Turks, who held it until 1917, when it was liberated and passed under British protectorate. The State of Israel was established May 14, 1948, but controlled only part of Palestine. Israel gained control of the West bank and Gaza Strip during the Six-Day War in 1967. As part of the peace talks with the Palestinian Authority, Israel has relinquished control of the Gaza Strip and parts of the West Bank.

M.F.U.; H.F.V.

BIBLIOGRAPHY: G. H. Dalman, *Sacred Sites and Ways* (1935); D. Baly, *The Geography of the Bible* (1957); id., *Geographical Companion to the Bible* (1963).

PAL'LU (pal'ū; "distinguished"). The second named of the sons of Reuben (Gen. 46:9; Ex. 6:14; Num. 26:5, 8; 1 Chron. 5:3) and founder of the Palluites (Num. 26:5), about 1900 B.C.

PAL'LUITE (pal'ū-īt). A descendant of *Pallu* (which see), of the tribe of Reuben (Num. 26:5).

PALM TREE. *See* Vegetable Kingdom.

Figurative. The straightness and beauty of the palm would naturally suggest giving its name to women; and we have the comparison "Your stature is like a palm tree" (Song of Sol. 7:7). The palm is a figure of the righteous enjoying their deserved prosperity (Ps. 92:12), doubtless with reference to the greenness of its foliage, its symmetry, its fruit, etc. Palm branches are a symbol of victory (Rev. 7:9).

The early church used the palm to express the triumph of the Christian over death through the resurrection; and on the tombs the palm is generally accompanied by the monogram of Christ, signifying that every victory of the Chris-

Palms at Jericho

tian is because of this divine name and sign. The palm is especially the sign of martyrdom, as this was considered in the light of victory. *See also* Vegetable Kingdom.

PALM TREES, CITY OF. *See* Jericho.

PALMERWORM. *See* Animal Kingdom: Locust.

PALSY. *See* Diseases: Paralysis.

PAL'TI (pal'ti; "delivered").
1. The son of Raphu, of the tribe of Benjamin, and appointed to represent that tribe among the twelve spies (Num. 13:9), c. 1440 B.C.
2. The son of Laish of Gallim, to whom Saul gave Michal in marriage after he had driven away David (1 Sam. 25:44; "Phalti," KJV; "Paltiel," NIV), before 1004 B.C. The only other reference to him is when Michal was restored to David and "her husband went with her, weeping as he went, and followed her as far as Bahurim. Then Abner said to him, 'Go, return.' So he returned" (2 Sam. 3:15-16, where he is called Paltiel), about 977 B.C.

PAL'TIEL (pal'ti-el; "God delivers").
1. The son of Azzan and leader of the tribe of Issachar (Num. 34:26). He was one of the twelve appointed to divide the land of Canaan among the tribes, c. 1440 B.C.
2. The son-in-law of Saul (1 Sam. 25:44;

2 Sam. 3:15); elsewhere in the NASB he is called Palti ("Phalti," KJV; *see* article above).

PAL'TITE (pal'tīt; i.e., sprung from Beth-pelet, in the S of Judah, Josh. 15:27). The same as *Palti* (which see) and the Gentile name of Helez, chief of the seventh division of David's army (2 Sam. 23:26), called the Pelonite in 1 Chron. 11:27; 27:10.

PAMPHYL'IA (pam-fil'i-a; "of every race"). "One of the coast regions in the S of Asia Minor, having Cilicia on the E and Lycia on the W. In the Persian war, while Cilicia contributed one hundred ships and Lycia fifty, Pamphylia sent only thirty. The name probably then embraced little more than the crescent of comparatively level ground between Taurus and the sea. The Roman organization of the country, however, gave a wider range to the term Pamphylia. In St. Paul's time it was not only a regular province, but the Emperor Claudius had united Lycia with it, and probably also a good part of Pisidia. It was in Pamphylia that St. Paul first entered Asia Minor, after preaching the Gospel in Cyprus. He and Barnabas sailed up the river Cestrus to Perga (Acts 13:13). We may conclude, from Acts 2:10, that there were many Jews in the province; and possibly Perga had a synagogue. The two missionaries finally left Pamphylia by its chief seaport, Attalia. Many years afterward St. Paul sailed near the coast (27:5)" (Smith, *Bib. Dict.*, s.v.).
BIBLIOGRAPHY: A. H. M. Jones, *Cities of the Eastern Roman Empire* (1971), pp. 124ff.; E. D. S. Bradford, *Paul the Traveller* (1974), pp. 112, 115-16, 123, 134, 141.

The theater at Perga in the region of Pamphylia

PAN. A number of Heb. words are given as "pan" or "pans" in the KJV, NIV, and NASB. One of them, *marheshet*, "frying pan" in the KJV and NIV (Lev. 2:7; 7:9), is more likely a deep, lidded, cooking pan (*see* marg., NASB). Another term,

Heb. *maḥăbat,* "pan" in the KJV, is usually translated "griddle" in the NASB and NIV (cf. Lev. 2:5; 1 Chron. 23:29). Still another, Heb. *kap,* appears frequently in discussions of the Tabernacle and the Temple, referring there to containers for incense, described as "spoons" in the KJV, "spoons" or "pans" in the NASB, and "ladles" in the NIV.

PAN'NAG (pan'ag). In the account of the commerce of Tyre, it is stated (Ezek. 27:17), "Judah and the land of Israel, they were your traders; with the wheat of Minnith, cakes, honey, oil," etc. The Heb. for "cakes" is *pannag* (cf. marg.), the meaning of which cannot be definitely ascertained. Some understand confectionery, sweetmeats made from honey (thus the NIV "confections"). Some kind of sweetmeat is evidently intended. Cf. Akkad. *pannigu,* a variety of cake. *See also* Vegetable Kingdom.

PAPER. *See* Writing; Papyrus; Gebal.

PA'PHOS (pa'fos; "heated"). A city of Cyprus and its capital. It was famous for the worship of Venus, whose great temple was at "Old Paphos." Here Paul's convert Sergius Paulus was secured (Acts 13:6-13; *see* Conybeare and Howson's *Life of St. Paul*). Old Paphos was settled by Greek or Phoenician colonists late in the second millennium B.C. New Paphos, about ten miles NW of Old Paphos, was the port of the old city, and it gradually became the more important of the two. New Paphos was the capital of Cyprus in Paul's day. Excavations in the 1960s uncovered some of the public buildings of Roman New Paphos: an odeon with an agora in front of it, next to the odeon a temple (possibly dedicated to Asklepios), a theater, and two rather luxurious villas (one of which was believed to have been the palace of the Roman governor).   H.F.V.

BIBLIOGRAPHY: F. F. Bruce, *Paul: Apostle of the Heart Set Free* (1977), p. 162.

PAPYRUS. A plant growing along the Nile in Egypt during the biblical period. It no longer is found in the Nile marshes of Lower Egypt, but it grows in the Sudan. It is also found in the region around Lake Huleh in Galilee. In the ancient world papyrus, Lat. *cyperus papyrus,* from which we get our word *paper,* was a common writing material. To prepare the writing product the outer covering of the stem of the plant was removed and the inner fibers were cut into thin strips. Some of these were placed vertically. Superimposed upon them were soaked fibers laid horizontally. These two layers were stuck together with an adhesive substance, pressure applied, and the strips dried. The result was a yellowish piece of papyrus paper. Often the exterior was rubbed smooth to accommodate a finer type of writing with ink. Papyrus rolls were used in ancient Egypt during the Old Kingdom (c. 2800-2250 B.C.) and perhaps even earlier. Egyptian papyrus

rolls are still in existence from the end of the third millennium B.C. According to the Story of Wenamon (11:41), about the twelfth century B.C. papyrus rolls were exported from Egypt to Gebal in Phoenicia. For this reason the Greeks later called this city "Byblus," meaning "papyrus," later "book." The largest ordinary papyrus roll in common use was about 30 feet long and some 10 inches high, adequate for the nonvocalized Heb. text of Isaiah. Egyptians upon occasion employed such huge rolls as the Papyrus Harris, 133 feet in length, and the Book of the Dead, 123 feet in length. Among the Jews the common use of the standard size papyrus rolls necessitated the division of some books such as the Torah of Moses into five books. The books of Samuel, Kings, and Chronicles, and perhaps others, were partitioned into two books when translated into Gk. because Gk. included the vowels, requiring more space than the consonantal Heb. text. Evidently Baruch wrote on papyrus as Jeremiah dictated to him, using pen and ink. The reed or calamus made from the hollow stalk of coarse grass or rush was cut diagonally with a knife and split in the end like a modern pen, hence the term "scribe's knife" (Jer. 36:23). Ink was commonly made of soot or lamp black and gum mixed in water. Ancient Egyptians also employed papyrus for constructing boats (Isa. 18:2, cf. Moses' "wicker basket," Ex. 2:3, *see* marg.). The papyrus was the symbol of Lower Egypt, and the Egyptians made a notable discovery when they made use of this vegetable membrane as an excellent writing material.

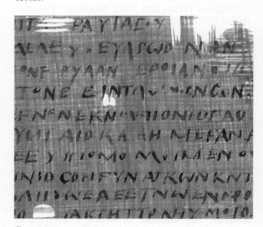

Egyptian papyrus paper

Because the climate of Egypt is so dry, even fragile papyrus has been preserved in quantity. Though some papyri came to light earlier, they were found in quantity during the latter part of the nineteenth century and the early twentieth. Some of them were discovered accidentally by workers, but many were excavated during archaeological campaigns. Space limitations permit only a summary of the results of those finds. Though the papyri were written in several languages, the majority were produced in Gk. during the period just before, during, and after the time when the NT was written, and they are extremely valuable for NT study.

1. They show (as a result of studies in historical grammar) that the NT was written during the first Christian century instead of later, as critics often have asserted.

2. They demonstrate that the NT was written in the language of the people instead of in a Gk. coined by biblical writers.

3. They show further that the grammar of the NT is good grammar, judged on the basis of contemporary usage instead of on the basis of classical usage.

4. They help to give clarity to meanings of NT words not previously well understood.

5. The biblical papyri, dating from the second century and following, underscore the fact that the Gk. text we have had all along has been remarkably preserved in transmission. There is incredibly little difference between these early texts and those from later centuries, and not one doctrine is affected in the variations that do occur.

H.F.V.

BIBLIOGRAPHY: J. Černý, *Paper and Books in Ancient Egypt* (1952); I. J. Gelb, *A Study of Writing* (1963).

PARABLE. A word derived from the Gk. verb *paraballo*, to "lay by the side of," to "compare"; and so a "likeness, similitude."

Original Terms and Their Meaning. "Parable" is the rendering of the following Heb. and Gk. terms:

1. Heb. *māshāl*, a "similitude." Most commonly rendered "discourse" or "oracle," in Ps. 78:2 "parable" is the rendering, and an obscure or mysterious saying appears to be meant; whereas in other instances it signifies a fictitious narrative, invented for the purpose of conveying truth in a less offensive or more engaging form than that of direct assertion, such as that by which Nathan reproved David (2 Sam. 12:1-4), that in which Jotham exposed the folly of the Shechemites (Judg. 9:7-15), and that addressed by Jehoash to Amaziah (2 Kings 14:9-10), although these latter two are more properly classified as "fables."

2. Gk. *parabolē*, a "placing one thing beside another," an example by which a doctrine or precept is illustrated (Luke 14:7); a pithy and instructive saying involving some likeness or comparison, and having preceptive or admonitory force; an aphorism, a maxim (Matt. 15:15; Luke 5:36; 6:39; a proverb, and so rendered in 4:23.

3. Gk. *paroimia*, a saying out of the usual course; any dark saying that shadows forth some didactic truth, a symbolic or figurative saying

(John 16:29, rendered "figure of speech"; "proverb," *see* marg.); an allegory, i.e., extended and elaborate metaphor (10:6).

Definition and Distinctions. In the NT the term *parable* is not confined to those lengthened narratives to which alone we now usually apply it. Thus, "And He said to them, 'No doubt you will quote this proverb to Me, "Physician, heal yourself!" ' " (Luke 4:23). The word is frequently used, either by the evangelists or by the disciples of Jesus, with reference to instructions of Christ, which we would simply call figurative, metaphorical, or proverbial. In Luke 6:39 we read, "And He also spoke a parable to them: 'A blind man cannot guide a blind man, can he? Will they not both fall into a pit?' " (cf. Matt. 15:14-15). In all these sayings of our Lord, however, it is obvious that the germ of a parable is contained. We have only to work upon the hint given us, and we have the perfect story.

Trench (*Notes on the Parables*, p. 9) says: "In the process of distinguishing it [the parable] from those forms of composition with which it is most nearly allied, and therefore most likely to be confounded, and justifying the distinction, its essential properties will come before us much more clearly than I could hope to bring them in any other way." In defining the difference between the parable and the *fable*, he writes, "The parable is constructed to set forth a truth spiritual and heavenly; this the *fable*, with all its value, is not; it is essentially of the earth, and never lifts itself above the earth. It never has a higher aim than to inculcate maxims of prudential morality, industry, caution, foresight; and these it will sometimes recommend even at the expense of the higher self-forgetting virtues. . . . Yet again there is another point of difference between the parable and the fable. While it can never be said that the fabulist is regardless of truth, since it is neither his intention to deceive, when he attributes language and discourse by reason to trees, and birds, and beasts, nor is anyone deceived by him; yet the severer reverence for truth, which is habitual to the higher moral teacher, will not allow him to indulge even in this sporting with the truth, this temporary suspension of its laws, though upon agreement, or, at least, with tacit understanding. . . . The great Teacher, by parables, therefore, allowed himself in no transgression of the established laws of nature, in nothing marvelous or anomalous; he presents to us no speaking trees or reasoning beasts, and we should be at once conscious of an unfitness in his so doing."

He says that "the parable is different from the *myth*, inasmuch as in the *myth* the truth, and that which is only the vehicle of the truth, are wholly blended together. . . . The mythic narrative presents itself not merely as the vehicle of the truth, but as itself being the truth; while in the parable there is a perfect consciousness in all minds of the distinctness between form and essence, shell and kernel, the precious vessel and yet more precious wine which it contains."

Again he says, "The parable is also clearly distinguishable from the *proverb,* though it is true that in a certain degree the words are used interchangeably in the NT, and as equivalent the one to the other. Thus, 'Physician, heal thyself' (Luke 4:23) is termed a parable, being more strictly a proverb. It is not difficult to explain how this interchange of the two words should have come to pass. Partly from the fact of there being but one word in the Hebrew to signify both parable and proverb; which circumstance must have had considerable influence upon writers accustomed to think in that language, and itself arose from the parable and proverb being alike enigmatical and somewhat obscure forms of speech, 'dark sayings,' speaking a part of their meaning, and leaving the rest to be inferred."

The parable differs from the allegory "in form rather than in essence: there being in the allegory an interpenetration of the thing signifying and the thing signified, the qualities and properties of the first being attributed to the last, and the two thus blended together, instead of being kept quite distinct and placed side by side, as is the case in the parable. The allegory needs not, as the parable, an interpretation to be brought to it from without, since it contains its interpretation within itself, and, as the allegory proceeds, the interpretation proceeds hand in hand with it, or at least never falls far behind it." "I am the true vine," etc. (John 15:1-8) is an allegory, whereas 10:1-16 contains two allegories.

The Parable as a Means of Teaching. Two characteristics of the parable render it eminently useful in teaching. It is illustrative, assisting to make truth intelligible, or, if intelligible before, to present it more vividly to the mind. The parable "does not indeed contain direct proof of the doctrine which it unfolds, but it associates with it all the force of that proof which is given by the exhibition of the universal prevalence of any principle. Growth, for example, we know to be a law of nature. Let us set out, therefore, with the conviction that the kingdom of grace corresponds with the kingdom of nature—the conviction, it is to be borne in mind, which constitutes the foundation of the parable; and, in a story calling our attention to that growth, we have not only an illustration, but a proof, that the same growth which appears in the natural must also appear in the spiritual world. The analogy convinces us that it must be so, and is therefore so far a proof" (Wm. Milligan, *Imperial Bible Dictionary,* s.v.).

Again, "the mind takes a natural delight in this manner of teaching, appealing as it does not to the understanding only, but to the feelings, to the imagination, in short to the whole man, calling as it does the whole man, with all its powers and faculties, into pleasurable activity; and all things thus learned with delight are those longest remembered." The Scriptures are full also of *acted* parable, for every type is a *real* parable. The whole Levitical constitution, with its sacred precincts, its priesthood, its sacrifices, and all its ordinances, is a parable, and is so declared (Heb. 9:9). The wandering of Israel in the desert has ever been regarded as a parable of spiritual life.

Whedon (*Com.,* on Matt. 13:1ff.) thus happily sums up the advantages of the parable as a means of teaching: "The sacred parable was a wonderful vehicle of truth to serve three distinct purposes, viz.: to *reveal,* to *conceal,* and to *perpetuate.* It *revealed* the sacred truth by the power of analogy and illustration. It *concealed* the truth from him who had not, by proper sympathy or previous instruction, the true key to its hidden meaning. To such a one it was a riddle or a tale. And so our Lord could give to his disciples in this method the deepest secrets of his kingdom for ages, while the caviler, who would have abused the truth, heard without understanding (v. 11). But the truth thus embodied in narrative was, as it were, materialized and made fit for *perpetuation.* It had a form and body to it by which it could be preserved in tangible shape for future ages."

Interpretation of Parables. It has been urged by some writers, by none with greater force or clearness than by Chrysostom, that there is a scope or purpose for each parable and that our aim must be to discern this, not to find a special significance in each circumstance or incident. It may be questioned, however, whether this canon of interpretation is likely to lead us to the full meaning of this portion of our Lord's teaching. It must be remembered that in the great patterns of interpretation that He Himself has given us there is more than this. Not only the sower and the seed and the several soils have their counterparts in the spiritual life, but the birds of the air, the thorns, and the scorching heat have each of them a significance. It may be inferred from these two instances that we are, at least, justified in looking for meaning even in the seeming accessories of a parable. The very form of the teaching makes it probable that there may be, in any case, more than one legitimate explanation. A parable may be at once ethical and in the highest sense of the term prophetic. There is thus a wide field open to the discernment of the interpreter. There are also restraints upon the fertility of his imagination: (1) The analogies must be real, not arbitrary. (2) The parables are to be considered as parts of a whole, and the interpretation of one is not to override or encroach upon the lessons taught by others. (3) The direct teaching of Christ presents the standard to which all *our* interpretations are to be referred, and by which they are to be measured. (4) And, finally, the parable may not be made the first source of doctrine. Doctrines otherwise and already grounded may be illustrated, or indeed further confirmed by them, but it is not allowable to constitute doctrine first by their aid.

Classification. Tables 27 and 28 classify the parables in the Scriptures. In addition to the parables, we call attention to the allegories of (1) the vine and its branches (John 15:1-8) and (2) the sheep and shepherd (10:1-16). We have also several sayings of our Lord that obviously contain the germ of a parable, such as: the houses on the rock and on the sand (Matt. 7:24-27; Luke 6:46-49); children in the marketplace (Matt. 11:16-17; Luke 7:32); the unclean spirit (Matt. 12:34-45; Luke 11:24-26); the city (Matt. 5:14); the lamp (Matt. 5:15; Mark 4:21; Luke 8:16); the householder (Matt. 13:52); the attendants of the bridegroom (Matt. 9:15; Mark 2:19-20; Luke 5:34-35); the patched garment (Matt. 9:16; Mark 2:21; Luke 5:36); old and new wineskins (Matt. 9:17; Mark 2:22; Luke 5:37); the harvest and lack of workmen (Matt. 9:37-38; Luke 10:2); the opponent (Matt. 5:25; Luke 12:58); the narrow gate, etc. (Matt. 7:13-14; Luke 13:24); building a tower (14:28-30); the king going to war (14:31-32); the fig tree (Matt. 24:32-35; Mark 13:28-31; Luke 21:29-33); the watching servants (Mark 13:34-37); the faithful and the unfaithful servants (Matt. 24:45-51); and the watching householder (Matt. 24:43; Luke 12:39).

BIBLIOGRAPHY: G. C. Morgan, *The Parables and Metaphors of Our Lord* (1943); J. A. Findlay, *Jesus and His Parables* (1950); G. H. Lang, *Pictures and Parables* (1955); A. M. Hunter, *Interpreting the Parables* (1960); J. Jeremias, *The Parables of Jesus* (1964); W. M. Taylor, *The Parables of Our Saviour* (1975); A. B. Bruce, *The Parables of Christ* (1980); W. Arnot, *The Parables of Our Lord* (1982); J. Laidlaw, *Studies in the Parables of Christ* (1984).

PARACLETE. *See* Advocate; Helper; Holy Spirit.

PARADISE (Gk. *paradeisos*, "park"). This term has been applied to *Eden* (which see). In the later books of the OT it appears in the sense of a *park* or *pleasure ground* (Heb. *pardēs*, rendered "forest," Neh. 2:8; "parks," Eccles. 2:5; "orchard," Song of Sol. 4:13). It first appears in Gk. as coming straight from Persia. Greek lexicographers classify it as a Persian word. Modern linguists accept the same conclusion with hardly a disagreement. In Xenophon the word occurs frequently, and we receive vivid pictures of the scene that it implied. A wide open park, enclosed against injury, yet with its natural beauty unspoiled, with stately trees, many of them bearing fruit, watered by clear streams on whose banks roamed large herds of antelope or sheep—this was the scenery that connected itself in the mind of the Greek traveler with the word *paradeisos* and for which his own language supplied no precise equivalent. Through the writings of Xenophon and through the general mixture of orientalism in the later Gk. after the conquests of Alexander, the word gained a recognized place, and the LXX writers chose it for a new use that gave it higher worth and secured for it a more enduring life. They used the same word whenever there was any allusion, however remote, to the fair region that had been the first blissful home of man. It was natural, however, that this higher meaning should become the exclusive one and be associated with new thoughts. Paradise, with no other word to qualify it, was the bright region that man had lost, which was guarded by the flaming sword. Paradise, or the Garden of Eden, became to the later Jews a common designation for the state of bliss that awaits the righteous after death—by which they meant that delights like those of Eden are enjoyed by the departed —they are in a paradise-like state. With reference to this use of the term, but with a deeper insight into the spiritual relation of things and the connection between the past and future, it is employed in the NT to indicate the destiny and experience of the redeemed (Luke 23:43; cf. Rev. 2:7; 22:2, 14). It is quite difficult to locate paradise as mentioned by Paul (2 Cor. 12:4). Whedon (*Com.,* ad loc.) believes it nearer to earth than the third heaven (v. 2). Meyer (*Com.,* ad loc.) says, "The *paradise* is here not the *lower,* i.e., the place of *Sheol,* in which the spirits of the departed righteous are until the resurrection, but the *upper,* the paradise of God (Rev. 2:7) in heaven, where God's dwelling is."

BIBLIOGRAPHY: N. Turner, *Christian Words* (1980), pp.

Table 27
Parables Recorded in the Old Testament

SPOKEN BY	CONCERNING	SPOKEN AT	RECORDED IN
Balaam	The Moabites and Israelites	Mt. Pisgah	Num. 23:24
Jotham	Trees making a king	Mt. Gerizim	Judg. 9:7-15
Nathan	The poor man's ewe lamb	Jerusalem	2 Sam. 12:1-4
Woman of Tekoa	Two brothers striving	Jerusalem	2 Sam. 14:5-7
A young prophet	The escaped prisoner	Near Samaria	1 Kings 20:35-42
Jehoash	The thorn bush and the cedar	Jerusalem	2 Kings 14:9
Isaiah	The vineyard yielding wild grapes	Jerusalem	Isa. 5:1-7
Ezekiel	The eagles and the vine	Babylon	Ezek. 17:3-10
	The lion's cubs	Babylon	Ezek. 19:2-9
	Israel, a vine planted by water	Babylon	Ezek. 19:10-14
	The boiling pot	Babylon	Ezek. 24:3-5, 10-14

308-12; S. D. F. Salmond, *The Biblical Doctrine of Immortality* (1984), p. 346.

PA'RAH (pa'ra; "young cow, heifer"). One of the towns of Benjamin (Josh. 18:23), identified as Farah, 5½ miles NE of Jerusalem.

PARALYTIC. *See* Diseases: Paralysis.

PARAMOUR (Heb. *pîlegesh,* Ezek. 23:20). Applied to the male lover in this passage but elsewhere rendered *concubine* (which see).

PA'RAN (pa'ran). A wilderness located in the E central region of the Sinai Peninsula. This region bordered the Arabah and the Gulf of Aqaba on the E and apparently comprised the wilderness of Zin, Kadesh-barnea, and Elath in its borders on the W.

Paran is first noticed in connection with the expedition of the eastern kings against Sodom (Gen. 14:6; "El Paran," NIV). We then learn that Ishmael dwelt in the wilderness of Paran (21:21); that after Israel left Sinai they camped in Paran (Num. 10:12; 12:16); that the spies were sent from Paran into Canaan (13:3) and returned to "the wilderness of Paran, at Kadesh" (v. 26). Its

Table 28
Parables Recorded in the Gospels

	PARABLES	IMPORT	OCCASION	SCRIPTURE
1.	The Sower	The relation between the preached truth and its hearers	Sermon on the seashore	Matt. 13:3-8; Mark 4:3-8; Luke 8:5-8
2.	The Tares	Present intermixture of good and bad	Sermon on the seashore	Matt. 13:24-30
3.	The Mustard Seed	The remarkable outward growth of the kingdom	Sermon on the seashore	Matt. 13:31-32; Mark 4:31-32; Luke 13:19
4.	The Leaven	The inward working of evil in the kingdom	Sermon on the seashore	Matt. 13:33; Luke 13:20-21
5.	The Hidden Treasure	Israel's present condition in the kingdom	To the disciples alone	Matt. 13:44
6.	The Pearl of Great Price	The church in the kingdom	To the disciples alone	Matt. 13:45-46
7.	The Dragnet	The future separation of the good and bad	To the disciples alone	Matt. 13:47-50
8.	The Unmerciful Servant	The gospel law of forgiveness illustrated	In answer to Peter's question. How often shall I forgive?	Matt. 18:23-35
9.	The Laborers in the Vineyard	An answer to Peter's question and a warning against the hireling spirit	Teaching the self-righteous	Matt. 20:1-16
10.	The Two Sons	Obedience better than profession	The chief priests demand His authority	Matt. 21:28-32
11.	The Landowner and the Wicked Vinegrowers	Guilt and rejection of Israel	The chief priests demand His authority	Matt. 21:33-46; Mark 12:1-12; Luke 20:9-19
12.	Marriage of the King's Son	The long-suffering and goodness of God; the rejection of those despising it; and necessity of purity	In answer to remark of a self-righteous guest	Matt. 22:1-14
13.	The Ten Virgins	Israel's preparation for the Lord's coming	In prophesying the second advent	Matt. 24:1-13
14.	The Talents	Duty of working while the day lasts	At the house of Zaccheus	Matt. 25:14-30
15.	The Seed Growing Secretly	The invisible energy of the Word	Sermon on the seashore	Mark 4:26-29
16.	The Two Debtors	Love proportioned to grace received	At Simon the Pharisee's self-righteous reflection	Luke 7:41-43
17.	The Good Samaritan	Love is to know no limits, spare no pains	The lawyer's question. Who is my neighbor?	Luke 10:25-37
18.	The Friend at Midnight	Perseverance in prayer	Disciples ask a lesson in prayer	Luke 11:5-8
19.	The Rich Fool	Vanity of riches without religion	Brothers ask him to divide an inheritance	Luke 12:16-21
20.	The Barren Fig Tree	The longsuffering and severity of God regarding Israel	Informed of the execution of the Galileans	Luke 13:6-9
21.	The Great Supper	Exclusion of those declining the invitation	In answer to one dining with Him	Luke 14:7-24
22.	The Lost Sheep	Christ's peculiar love for sinners	Answer to the murmuring of the Pharisees and scribes	Matt. 18:12-14; Luke 15:4-7
23.	The Lost Coin	Christ's peculiar love for sinners	Answer to the murmuring of the Pharisees and scribes	Luke 15:8-10
24.	The Prodigal Son	Christ's peculiar love for sinners	Answer to the murmuring of the Pharisees and scribes	Luke 15:11-32
25.	The Unjust Steward	Christian prudence commended	To the disciples	Luke 16:1-9
26.	The Rich Man and Lazarus	Unbelief punished. faith rewarded	Rebuking the covetousness of the Pharisees	Luke 16:19-31
27.	The Unprofitable Servants	Service without love not meritorious	Teaching self-righteous ones	Luke 17:7-10
28.	The Unjust Judge	Encouragement to constant prayer	Teaching the disciples	Luke 18:1-8
29.	The Pharisee and the Tax-gatherer	Humility in prayer	Teaching the self-righteous	Luke 18:10-14
30.	The Minas	Patient waiting and working for Christ	At the house of Zaccheus	Luke 19:12-27

mountainous nature and its rugged passes seem to have impressed the Israelites, accustomed to the level country of Egypt (Deut. 1:19), and they feared to enter these passes until they were found to be open (v. 22). To Paran David went at the death of Samuel (1 Sam. 25:1), probably because he could not find support for himself in the desert of Judah. Hadad the Edomite, when he revolted from Solomon, went to Egypt by way of Paran (1 Kings 11:18).

PAR'BAR (par'bar; "suburb"). A part of the city of Jerusalem connected with the Temple (2 Kings 23:11, "precincts," NASB, but "suburbs," KJV; 1 Chron. 26:18; NIV, "court"). As to the meaning of the name, the rabbis generally agree in translating it "the outside place," whereas modern authorities accept it as equivalent to the *parwārîm* in 2 Kings 23:11 (KJV, "precincts"; NIV, "court"). In accepting this interpretation, there is no difficulty in identifying the Parbar with the suburb mentioned by Josephus in describing Herod's Temple, as lying in the deep valley that separated the W wall of the Temple from the city opposite it, in other words the southern end of the Tyropoeon. Parbar is possibly an ancient Jebusite name. Keil (*Com.*, 1 Chron. 26:18) believes it to have been the name of a separate building on the W side, the back of the outer court of the Temple by the door *Shallecheth,* which contained cells for storage of goods and furniture (*see* marg.).

PARCHED CORN. *See* Roasted Grain.

PARCHED LAND. *See* Scorched Land.

PARCHED PLACES (Heb. *ḥārēr,* Jer. 17:6, KJV). Arid land. The NASB reads "stony wastes."

PARCHMENT. *See* Writing.

PARDON. *See* Forgiveness; Justification.

PARE THE NAILS. *See* Nail.

PARENT (Gk. *goneus*). The fifth commandment (Ex. 20:12; cf. Lev. 19:3; Deut. 5:16) enjoined devotion to parents as a religious duty; and as the law was declared more fully the relation of children to parents was more accurately defined and more firmly established in society. A child who cursed (Ex. 21:17; Lev. 20:9; cf. Deut. 27:16; Prov. 20:20) or struck his parents was punishable with death. Obstinate disobedience on the part of sons was, upon judicial investigation, punished with stoning (Deut. 21:18-21). But such crimes seem to have been almost unknown. According to the rabbinical ordinances a son was considered independent when he could make his own living; and, although a daughter remained in the power of her father till marriage, she could not after she was of age be given away without her own express and full consent. A father might chastise his child but only while young, and even then not to such an extent as to destroy self-respect. But to beat a grown-up son was forbidden on pain of excommunication; and the apostolic injunction "Fathers, do not provoke your children to anger" (Eph. 6:4) finds an almost literal counterpart in the Talmud (Edersheim, *Sketches of Jewish Social Life in the Days of Christ,* p. 99). According to the law a father married his sons (Gen. 24; Ex. 21:9; Judg. 14:2-3) and daughters (Gen. 29:16-29; 34:12) at his pleasure; and he might sell the latter as concubines (Ex. 21:7). Much value was attached to the blessing of a parent, whereas the curse of a parent was accounted a great misfortune (Gen. 27:4, 12; 49:1-28).

BIBLIOGRAPHY: E. Neufeld, *Ancient Hebrew Marriage Laws* (1944), pp. 250-71.

PARLOUR. Archaic rendering of several Heb. terms. In 1 Chron. 28:11 Heb. *ḥeder* refers to the *inner rooms* (so NASB and NIV) of the Temple porch and holy place. Hebrew *'aliyyâ* in Judg. 3:20-28 refers to a "cool roof chamber" (NASB) or "upper room" (NIV) upon the flat roof of a house. It was open to currents of air and as such offered relief from the heat.

The "parlour" in 1 Sam. 9:22, Heb. *lishkâ,* was the chamber or *hall* (so NASB and NIV) in which Samuel ate the sacrificial meal with Saul.

PARMASH'TA (par-mash'ta; Old Persian, "the very first"). The seventh named of the sons of *Haman* (which see), slain by the Jews (Esther 9:9).

PAR'MENAS (par'me-nas). One of the seven deacons, "men of good reputation, full of the Spirit and of wisdom" (Acts 6:3, 5). There is a tradition that he suffered martyrdom at Philippi in the reign of Trajan, A.D. 98-117. Hippolytus said that he was at one time bishop of Soli. He is commemorated in the calendar of the Byzantine church on July 28.

PAR'NACH (par'nak). Father of Elizaphan, leader of the tribe of Zebulun at the close of the Exodus (Num. 34:25), c. 1440 B.C.

PA'ROSH (pa'rōsh; "a flea"). The 2,172 descendants of Parosh who returned from Babylon with Zerubbabel (Ezra 2:3; Neh. 7:8). Another detachment of 150 males, with Zechariah at their head, accompanied Ezra (Ezra 8:3). Seven of the family had married foreign wives (10:25). They assisted in the building of the wall of Jerusalem (Neh. 3:25) and signed the covenant with Nehemiah (10:14), before 536 B.C.

PARSHANDA'THA (par-shan-da'tha; Old Persian, "inquisitive, inquiring"). The eldest of Haman's ten sons, who were slain by the Jews at Susa (Esther 9:7).

PAR'SIN. *See* Mene.

PAR'THIANS (par'thi-anz). They are mentioned as being present in Jerusalem on the Day of Pentecost (Acts 2:9). They were a people of NW Persia

(Iran) who lived in the general region SE of the Caspian Sea. The ancient Parthians are called a "Scythic" race and probably belonged to the great Turanian family. Nothing is known of them till about the time of Darius Hystaspes, when they are found in the district that so long retained their name. They appear as faithful subjects of the Persian monarchs. Herodotus speaks of them as contained in the sixteenth satrapy of Darius. In the final struggle between the Greeks and Persians they remained faithful to the latter, serving at Arbela; but they offered only a weak resistance to Alexander when, on his way to Bactria, he entered their country. In the division of Alexander's dominions they fell to the share of Eumenes, and Parthia for some time was counted among the territories of the Seleucidae. About 256 B.C., however, they revolted and, under Arsaces, succeeded in establishing their independence.

Parthia, in the mind of the writer of the Acts, would designate the great empire the Parthians built up, which extended from India to the Tigris and from the Chorasmian desert to the shores of the southern ocean. Hence the prominent position of the name *Parthians* in the list of those present at Pentecost. Parthia was a power almost rivaling Rome—the only existing power that had tried its strength against Rome and not been defeated in the encounter. The Parthian dominion lasted for nearly five centuries, commencing in the third century before Christ. The Parthians seized Jerusalem in 40 B.C., and Rome made Herod king of Judea at that time to check the formidable westward push of the Parthian Empire.

BIBLIOGRAPHY: G. Rawlinson, *Parthia* (n.d.); N. C. Debevoise, *Parthia* (1938); M. A. R. Colledge, *The Parthians* (1967).

PARTIAL, PARTIALITY. The translation of several terms in the original. Heb. *nākar* means "to scrutinize" and therefore to care for, or respect; it is used with *pānîm*, "face," to convey the idea of showing partiality toward someone (Deut. 1:17; 16:19; Prov. 24:23; 28:21). Heb. *nāśā'*, to "lift," is similarly used in combination with *pānîm* to mean "be partial" (Lev. 19:15). The Gk. verb *prosōpolēmpteō* (James 2:9) is derived from two others meaning to "accept the face"; and both have the idea of partiality. This is contrary to the Bible, for God commanded that the judges should pronounce judgment without partiality ("respect of persons," KJV; *see* Lev. 19:15; Deut. 1:17; 16:19). God is declared to be impartial or without favoritism (*prosōpolēptes*, Acts 10:34; *prosōpolēmpsia,* Rom. 2:11; Eph. 6:9; Col. 3:25); and Christians are warned against partiality (*prosōpolēmpsia,* James 2:1; *epiblepō,* 2:3; *prosōpolēmpteō,* 2:9; cf. Prov. 24:23; 28:21).

Undue inclination toward one or another party (Gk. *prosklisis*) is cautioned against in 1 Tim. 5:21.

PARTITION, MIDDLE WALL OF. *See* Dividing Wall, Barrier of.

PARTRIDGE. *See* Animal Kingdom.

PARU'AH (pa-rū'a; "blossoming" or "increase"). The father of the Jehoshaphat who was Solomon's deputy in Issachar (1 Kings 4:17), 960 B.C.

PARVA'IM (par-va'im). The name of a place rich in gold, from which it was brought to adorn Solomon's Temple (2 Chron. 3:6). The name does not occur elsewhere and has never been satisfactorily explained. Gesenius and other authorities regard it as a general term signifying the East and corresponding to our "Levant."

PARZITE. *See* Perez.

PA'SACH (pa'sak; to "divide"). The first named of the sons of Japhlet, of the tribe of Asher (1 Chron. 7:33), about 1390 B.C.

PASDAM'MIM (pas-dam'im). A place mentioned (2 Sam. 23:9 [NIV; *see* marg.]; 1 Chron. 11:13; Ephes-dammim, 1 Sam. 17:1) as the scene of a fierce conflict with the Philistines. It was between Socoh and Azekah. *See* Ephes-dammim.

PASE'AH (pa-se'a; "lame").
1. One of the sons of Eshton, among the descendants of Judah, described as "the men of Recah" (1 Chron. 4:12).
2. The head of a family of Temple servants who returned with Zerubbabel (Ezra 2:49; Neh. 7:51). His "son" (or descendant) Joiada assisted in restoring one of the gates of the city (3:6), probably before 536 B.C.

PASH'HUR (pash'her).
1. The son of Immer the priest. He was chief officer of the Temple (Jer. 20:1), and when he heard the prophecies of Jeremiah he had Jeremiah beaten and put in the stocks. The next day he released Jeremiah, who informed him that his name had been changed to Magor-missabib (i.e., "terror on every side") and that he and all his house would be carried to Babylon and would die there (20:2-6), about 605 B.C. Nothing more is known of him.
2. Another priest, the son of Malchijah, who in the reign of Zedekiah was one of the chief officers of the court (Jer. 38:1). He was sent, with others, by Zedekiah to Jeremiah at the time when Nebuchadnezzar was preparing his attack upon Jerusalem (chap. 21), about 589 B.C. Again, somewhat later, Pashhur joined with others in petitioning the king to have Jeremiah put to death because of his denunciations. In the time of Nehemiah this family appears to have become a chief house and its head the head of a division (1 Chron. 9:12; Ezra 2:38; Neh. 7:41; 10:3; 11:12).
3. The father of Gedaliah, which latter took part with Jucal and the Pashhur in no. 2 in the accusation and imprisonment of Jeremiah (Jer. 38:1), 589 B.C.

PASSENGER (Prov. 9:15; Ezek. 39:11, 14, 15, KJV). Those who pass by, or who pass through the land (*see* NASB).

PASSION OF CHRIST (Gk. *to pathein*, "suffering"). A term employed in Acts 1:3, KJV (NASB and NIV, "suffering"), with reference to the crucifixion of the Lord. For the chief points of the history of the event, *see* Jesus Christ.

PASSIONS, LIKE (Gk. *homoiopathēs*). Used in the KJV in the expressions "men of like passions with you" (Acts 14:15) and "a man subject to like passions as we are" (James 5:17). It means "men of the same nature," "man with a nature like ours" (so NASB) or "men, human like you" (NIV).

PASSOVER, FEAST OF. See Festivals.

PASTOR (Heb. *rō'eh*, "shepherd," and usually so rendered; Gk. *poimēn*, "shepherd"). The rendering "pastor" in the KJV of the OT is confined to several passages in Jeremiah (2:8; 3:15; 10:21; 12:10; 17:16; 22:22; 23:1-2) and reflects the translation of those passages in the Geneva Bible. The NASB and NIV renderings, "shepherd," "shepherds," or, in 2:8 only, "ruler," or "leaders," lit., "shepherd," are to be preferred. The Gk. term *poimēn* (Eph. 4:11) is elsewhere rendered "shepherd."

PASTOR, CHRISTIAN (lit., "shepherd"). Paul's pastoral epistles contain the sum and substance of NT teaching on this subject. He laid down three functions: (1) The ministration in divine service includes the ordering of worship, administering the sacraments, and preaching the Word. Here the pastor is appropriately termed *minister*. (2) The responsibility of the pastoral care springs out of no. 1. The feeding of the flock is the instruction of its members, but it is also the vigilant distributive attention to all its interests in the whole economy of life. The shepherds must imitate the chief shepherd, who "calls his own sheep by name." (3) This pastoral relation passes naturally into what we have scriptural authority for calling the spiritual government of the church. Its ministers are called *rulers* (Gk. *hēgoumenoi*) or *presidents* (Gk. *proestōtes*), and all its members are bidden to *obey them that have the rule*. The design of the Lord's gift of pastors and teachers, as supplementary to that of apostles and evangelists, is "the equipping of the saints for the work of service, to the building up of the body of Christ" (Eph. 4:12). Pastors are to be watchful (Heb. 13:17; 2 Tim. 4:5), gentle and affectionate (1 Thess. 2:7-8), and should exhort, warn, and comfort (2:11; 1 Cor. 4:14-15).

PASTURE. See Shepherd.

PASTURELANDS (Heb. *migrāsh;* "suburbs," KJV). A place where cattle are driven to graze; especially the open country set apart for pasture around the *Levitical cities* (which see; Num. 35:2; Josh. 21:11; 1 Chron. 6:55). It also meant an open area around a city or building (Ezek. 27:28; cf. 45:2; 48:17).

PAT'ARA (pat'a-ra). A seaport where Paul changed ships during his third missionary journey (Acts 21:1-2). Located on the coast of Lycia, it was a city of magnificence and large population in Paul's time. Its ruins are impressive, though unfortunately nearly everything to be seen there today dates after the time of Paul (e.g., the handsome gate of c. A.D. 100; the baths of Vespasian, A.D. 69-79; the granary of Hadrian, second century; the theater with its second-century stage building). Christianity had a footing in the city, and it was the residence of a bishop.   H.F.V.

BIBLIOGRAPHY: A. H. M. Jones, *The Cities of the Eastern Roman Provinces* (1937), pp. 98-102.

PATH.
   Figurative. The dispensations of God are called His paths (Pss. 25:10; 65:11), as are also His precepts (17:5); the phenomena of nature are also paths of God (77:19; Isa. 43:16).

PATH'ROS (path'ros; Egyptian, "Southland"). The name of upper Egypt as distinguished from Matsor, or lower Egypt (Isa. 11:11; Jer. 44:1, 15; Ezek. 30:14). It was the country that was called Thebais by the classic geographers and Paturissu in the cuneiform texts. Colonies of Jews were settled there.

PATH'RUS (path'rus; 1 Chron. 1:12). See Pathros.

PATHRU'SIM (path-rū'sim). The fifth in order of the sons (i.e., descended tribes) of Mizraim (Gen. 10:14; 1 Chron. 1:11-12, where they are called the people of Pathrus), believed to have been inhabitants of Pathros, Egypt, and from it to have taken their name. See Pathros.

PATHRU'SITES. See Pathrusim.

PATIENCE.
   1. Gk. *makrothumia*. Endurance, constancy, forbearance, long-suffering.
   2. Gk. *hupomonē*. "A remaining under," steadfastness, constancy, a patient waiting for.
   The difference between these two terms is given by Trench (NT *Syn.*, 2:14): "*Makrothumia* will be found to express patience in respect of persons, *hupomonē* in respect of things. . . . We should speak, therefore, of the *makrothumia* of David (2 Sam. 16:10-13), the *hupomonē* of Job (James 5:11)." Patience is that calm and unruffled temper with which the good man bears the evils of life, whether they proceed from persons or things. It also manifests itself in a sweet submission to the providential appointments of God and fortitude in the presence of the duties and conflicts of life. This grace saves one from discouragement in the face of evil (Luke 21:19), aids

in the cultivation of godliness (2 Pet. 1:6), aids the development of the entire Christian character (James 1:4), and, continued till the end, will terminate in reward in the life to come (Rom. 2:7; James 5:7-8).

Patience of God. Respecting the patience of God, Trench says (vol. 2, p. 15), "While both graces [the two forms mentioned above, namely, with persons and with things] are possessed by men only the former is an attribute of God. Men may tempt and provoke him, and he does display patience in regard to them (Ex. 34:6; Rom. 2:4; 1 Pet. 3:20); there may be a resistance to God in *men,* because he respects the wills with which he created them, even when those wills are fighting against him. But there can be no resistance to God, nor burden upon him, the Almighty, from *things;* therefore *patience of things* is never ascribed to him." The "God who gives perseverance" (*hupomonē*) means that God is the Author of patience in His servants (Rom. 15:5).

PAT'MOS (pat'mos). A small, rocky island belonging to the group called "Sporades," in that part of the Aegean known as the Icarian Sea. On account of its rocky, barren, and desolate nature the Roman government used the island as a place of banishment for criminals. The prisoners were compelled to work the mines of the island. The emperor Domitian banished the apostle John to this island (Rev. 1:9), A.D. 95. Patmos was the locale for the far-reaching apocalyptic visions of the book of the Revelation. The fifty-mile-square Aegean island has magnificent scenery and the white crags of the shoreline and the beauty of the open ocean furnish an example of a geographical background that aids the biblical interpreter to expound the events and experiences of the revelator who was banished to its shores.   M.F.U.

PATRIARCH (Gk. *patriarchēs, patēr,* "father," *archēs,* "head"). The founder of a tribe, a progenitor. It is applied in the NT to Abraham (Heb. 7:4), to the sons of Jacob (Acts 7:8-9), and to David (2:29). In common usage the title *patriarch* is assigned especially to those whose lives are recorded in Scripture previous to the time of Moses.

PATRIARCHAL AGE, THE. The period of Abraham, Isaac, and Jacob. If one follows the Masoretic chronology and the general chronological scheme underlying the Heb. Bible, Abraham was born c. 2161 B.C. and entered Canaan 2086 B.C. The patriarchal period would extend in this case from 2086 to 1871 B.C. and the Egyptian sojourn from 1871 to 1441 B.C. (cf. 1 Kings 6:1 with Ex. 12:40-41). Scholars for the most part reject the numbers underlying the biblical chronology and place Abraham's migration from Ur anywhere from 1900 to 1750 B.C. and the patriarchal period itself anywhere from 1750 to 1500 B.C. However, following the simple biblical chronology, Abra-

ham is placed, insofar as his early Mesopotamian connections are involved, just prior to the new Sumero-Akkadian empire of Ur-Nammu, the founder of the famous Third Dynasty of Ur (c. 2080-1960 B.C.), who assumed the new title "king of Sumer and Akkad." The mightiest work of this monarch was the erection of the great ziggurat at Ur, which is well preserved today. The patriarch thus left Ur just before it entered the heyday of its power. On the other hand, the patriarchal age in Palestine would be coterminous with numerous smaller Elamite and Amorite states of Mesopotamia with strong city-states existing at Isin, Larsa, and Eshnunna, whose princes took over the heritage of the Third Dynasty of Ur after its collapse. As far as Egypt is concerned the patriarchal age marked the strong Middle Kingdom under the Twelfth Dynasty (c. 2000-1780 B.C.). Abraham went down to Egypt evidently in the early years of this dynasty. Joseph became prime minister of and Jacob stood before one of the powerful pharaohs of this dynasty, Amenemes I-IV or Senwosret I-III.

The Ur of Abraham's age has been excavated, showing a remarkably rich commercial emporium, the center of the important cult worshiping the moon god Sin. Archaeology has given support to the position that Abraham, Isaac, and Jacob were historical figures and not mere legendary creations, mythological heroes, or personification of clans or tribes. (*See* R. P. DeVaux, *Revue Biblique* 53 [1949]: 321-28.) The old critical view of the unhistoricity of the patriarchal narratives has been almost completely discredited by recent archaeological discoveries at Nuzi between 1925 and 1941. The Nuzi Tablets furnish many illustrations of patriarchal customs such as adoption, marriage laws, rights of primogeniture, and the teraphim. Since 1933 the Mari Letters from Tell Hariri have added their weight of confirmation. Such names as Abraham, Isaac, and Jacob occur extrabiblically in the cuneiform tablets. Moreover, Abraham's sojourns at Haran (Gen. 11:31; 12:5), a town that is still in existence on the Balikh River sixty miles W of Tell Halaf, have been made more believable. Cuneiform sources of the nineteenth and eighteenth centuries B.C. mention Haran frequently. The name appears in Assyrian documents as *Harranu* (meaning "road"), likely describing the trade flowing through this city from Damascus, Carchemish, and Nineveh. Haran, like Ur, was the center of the worship of the moon god Sin. The city of Nahor, Rebekah's home (24:10), occurs frequently in the Mari Tablets discovered in 1935 and belonging to the eighteenth century B.C. Another support for Abraham's residence in Aram-Naharaim is the names of Abraham's forefathers in Assyrian times: Serug (Assyr. *Sarugi*), Nahor, and Terah (*Til Turakhi,* "mount of Terah"). Moreover, the general situation in Canaan at the time of Abraham's arrival in the Middle

Bronze Age (2000-1500 B.C.) is thoroughly in agreement with the representations in Genesis. Archaeology has exploded the critical idea that the stories of the patriarchs are mostly regressions from the time of the dual monarchy (ninth and eighth centuries B.C.). Places that are named in the patriarchal narratives, moreover, are not the towns and holy sites of later periods, such as Mizpeh and Gibeah, but are nearly all known from archaeological explorations to have existed in the patriarchal period. Examples are Dothan, Gerar, Jerusalem, Bethel, Shechem, and Beersheba. Also, the general historical background of the remarkable chapter 14 of Genesis has been essentially corroborated by modern archaeology. Although certain conclusions may need to be modified somewhat (cf. J. Van Seters, *Abraham in History and Tradition* [1975]), there can be no doubt that archaeology has in recent decades performed a splendid service in vindicating the essential historicity of the patriarchal period of Genesis, besides marvelously illustrating its background.   M.F.U.

BIBLIOGRAPHY: C. F. Pfeiffer, *The Patriarchal Age* (1961); T. L. Thompson, *The Historicity of the Patriarchal Narratives* (1974), pp. 157-273; J. van Seters, *Abraham in History and Tradition* (1975); J. H. Hayes and J. M. Miller, eds., *Israelite and Judean History* (1977), pp. 70-120; R. de Vaux, *Early History of Israel* (1978).

PATRIMONY. The produce of the property that a *Levite* (which see) possessed according to his family descent (Deut. 18:8, "fathers' estate"). Thus a Levite who went to the sanctuary might either rent his property in the Levitical town and draw the yearly income, or sell the house that belonged to him there.

PAT'ROBAS (pat'ro-bas; "life of his father"). One of the Christians at Rome to whom Paul sent salutations (Rom. 16:14).

PA'U (pa'u; "bleating"). A place in Edom (Gen. 36:39), the capital of Hadar, king of Edom. Its position is unknown. It is called Pai in 1 Chron. 1:50 (Pau in the NIV).

PAUL. The great apostle (Gk. *Paulos*, "little"; *Saulos*, perhaps from Heb. *shā'ûl*, "asked").

Name. The name *Paul*, which was used for the first time by the historian in Acts 13:9, "Saul, who was also known as Paul," has given rise to much discussion. The usual theory is that the apostle had a Jewish name, Saul, and a Roman name, Paul. Ramsay says (*St. Paul the Traveller*, etc., p. 81), "It was the fashion for every Syrian, Cilician, or Cappadocian who prided himself on his Greek education and his knowledge of the Greek language to bear a Greek name; but at the same time he had his other name in the native language by which he was known among his countrymen in general." But it is best to understand that Saul's name was changed as a matter of course *when he became a Christian*, that the word *Paul* means "little," and that Paul wanted to be known as the "Little One" in Christ's service; such changes in the cases of Abram, Gideon, Naomi, etc., are to be noted.

Personal History. Paul was a native of Tarsus, a city of Cilicia (Acts 21:39; 22:3), and was of pure Jewish descent, of the tribe of Benjamin (Phil. 3:5). There is no mention of his mother, and the information respecting his father is meager, namely, that he was a Pharisee (Acts 23:6) and that from him Saul inherited the rights of Roman citizenship (22:28). "The character of a Roman citizen superseded all others before the law and in the general opinion of society, and placed him amid the aristocracy of any provisional town" (Ramsay, p. 31). It will help to better understand the apostle's life and teaching to remember that he was (1) a Roman citizen; (2) a Tarsian, a citizen of no humble city (*see* Tarsus); (3) a Hebrew; and (4) a Pharisee. The date of his birth is unknown, although an ancient tradition places it as the second year after Christ.

Previous to Conversion. Because it was the custom among the Jews that all boys learn a trade, Paul learned "tent-making," "the material of which was haircloth supplied by the goats of his native province and sold in the markets of the Levant by the well-known name of *cilicium*" (Coneybeare and Howson, *Life and Epistles of St. Paul*). At the proper age (probably about thirteen) he went to Jerusalem to pursue his studies in the learning of the Jews. Here he became a student of Gamaliel, a distinguished teacher of the law (Acts 22:3). He grew more and more familiar with the outward observances of the law, gaining that experience of the "spirit of slavery," which would enable him to understand himself and to teach others the blessing of the "spirit of adoption." Paul is first introduced to us in connection with the martyrdom of Stephen and the persecution that followed, A.D. 36. "Stephen, full of grace and power, was performing great wonders and signs among the people" (6:8). The learned members of the foreign synagogues endeavored to refute his teachings by argument or by clamor. As the Cilician synagogue is mentioned among them, we can readily believe that Saul was one of the disputants. In this transaction he was, if not an assistant, something more than a mere spectator, for "the witnesses laid aside their robes at the feet of a young man named Saul" (7:58). He is described as a young man (*neanias*) but was probably at least thirty. After Stephen's burial Saul continued his persecution of the church, as we are told again and again in Luke's narrative and in Paul's own speeches and epistles. He "began ravaging the church," invading the sanctuaries of domestic life, "entering house after house" (8:3). Those whom he thus tore from their homes he committed to prison. And not only did men thus suffer at his hands, but women also, a fact three times repeated as a great aggravation of his cruelty (8:3). These persecuted people were even "punished . . . often in all the synagogues" (26:11). Stephen was not the only one to suffer death, as we may infer from the apostle's own confession, "I persecuted this Way to the death, binding and putting both men and women into prisons . . . also when they were being put to death I cast my vote against them" (22:4; 26:10). He even endeavored to cause them "to blaspheme" (26:11). His fame as an inquisitor was notorious far and wide. Even at Damascus Ananias had heard "how much harm" he had done to Christ's "saints at Jerusalem" (9:13). It was not without reason that in his later years he remembered how he had persecuted "the church of God beyond measure" (Gal. 1:13).

Saul's Conversion. Owing to the persecution of the church the believers were scattered abroad and went everywhere preaching the word. "And Saul, still breathing threats and murder against the disciples of the Lord," determined to follow them. "Being furiously enraged at them," he persecuted them "even to foreign cities" (Acts 26:11; cf. 8:3; Gal. 1:13; 1 Tim. 1:13). He went to the high priest "and asked for letters from him to the synagogues at Damascus," where he had reason to believe that Christians were to be found. While on his journey to that city his wonderful conversion took place, changing the proud and persecuting Saul into the loving, helpful Paul. We hesitate to enlarge upon the words of Scripture, referring to the narrative of Luke (Acts 9:3-9). The conflict of Saul's feelings was so great and his remorse so piercing and deep, that during this time he neither ate nor drank. He could have had no contact with the Christians, for they had been terrified by the news of his approach; and the unconverted Jews could have no true sympathy with his present state of mind. But he called upon God, and in his blindness a vision was granted him—a vision soon to be realized—of his being restored to sight by Ananias. After his restoration he was baptized, communed with the disciples, and "immediately he began to proclaim Jesus in the synagogues, saying, 'He is the Son of God' " (9:20), A.D. 37. Conscious of his divine mission, he never believed that it was necessary to consult those who were apostles before him, but he went into Arabia (Gal. 1:17). Of the time thus spent we learn further from himself (v. 18) that it was three years, which may mean either three full years or one year with parts of two others. We are not told to what district he retired, or for what purpose—perhaps for seclusion, meditation, and prayer. After he returned to Damascus (v. 17) the Jews took counsel to slay him, but the disciples took him by night and let him down by the wall in a basket (Acts 9:25). According to Paul (2 Cor. 11:32) it was the ethnarch under Aretas the king who watched for him, desiring to apprehend him.

First Visit to Jerusalem. Preserved from destruction at Damascus, Paul turned his steps toward Jerusalem. His motive for the journey, as he himself tells us, was "to become acquainted with Cephas [Peter]" (Gal. 1:18). He tried to join the disciples; but "they were all afraid of him, not believing that he was a disciple" (Acts 9:26). Barnabas became his sponsor to the apostles and the church, assuring them of the facts of Paul's conversion and subsequent behavior at Damascus. Barnabas's introduction quieted the fears of the apostles, and Paul "was with them moving about freely in Jerusalem" (v. 28). It is not strange that the former persecutor was singled out from the other believers as the object of murderous hostility. He was therefore again urged to flee, and, by way of Caesarea, he went to his native city, Tarsus. The length of his stay in Jerusalem was fifteen days (1:18), A.D. 39.

At Antioch. While Paul was at Tarsus a movement was going on at Antioch that raised that city to an importance second only to that of Jerusalem in the early history of the church. A large number believed there through the preaching of the disciples driven from Jerusalem, and when this was reported at Jerusalem, Barnabas was sent on a special mission to Antioch. Needing assistance, he went to Tarsus to seek Saul, A.D. 44. Ramsay believes (p. 46) that Paul's stay in Tarsus was ten years. After Paul returned with Barnabas to Antioch, they labored together for "an entire year." As new converts in vast numbers came in from the ranks of the Gentiles the church began to lose its ancient appearance of a Jewish sect and to stand as a self-existent community. They were, therefore, first at Antioch distinguished as "Christians"—they that are connected with Christos. While Barnabas and Saul were evangelizing the Syrian capital, certain prophets came down from Jerusalem to Antioch. One of them, named Agabus, announced that a time of famine was at hand (probably A.D. 46). No time was lost in preparing for the calamity. All the Antioch Christians, according to their ability, "determined to send a contribution for the relief of the brethren living in Judea. And this they did, sending it in charge of Barnabas and Saul to the elders" (Acts 11:22-30). This was the occasion of Paul's *second visit* to Jerusalem. Having fulfilled their mission they returned to Antioch, bringing with them another helper, John, whose surname was Mark (12:25). "And while they were ministering to the Lord and fasting, the Holy Spirit said, 'Set apart for Me Barnabas and Saul for the work to which I have called them.' Then, when they had fasted and prayed and laid their hands on them, they sent them away" (13:1-3).

First Missionary Journey. The date of their departure is variously fixed between A.D. 45 and 50, probably 47-48, lasting perhaps two years.

Cyprus. Their first point of destination was the island of Cyprus, the native place of Barnabas. Reaching Salamis, they preached the word of God

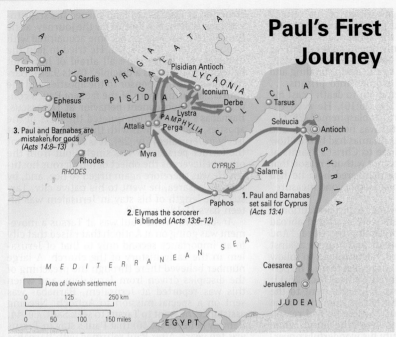

Paul's First Journey

Pergamum

Sardis

Ephesus

Miletus

PHRYGIA

GALATIA

Pisidian Antioch

LYCAONIA

Iconium

CILICIA

PISIDIA

Derbe

Tarsus

Lystra

Seleucia

Attalia · Perga

PAMPHYLIA

Antioch

3. Paul and Barnabas are mistaken for gods (Acts 14:8–13)

Rhodes

Myra

RHODES

CYPRUS

SYRIA

Salamis

Paphos

1. Paul and Barnabas set sail for Cyprus (Acts 13:4)

2. Elymas the sorcerer is blinded (Acts 13:6–12)

Caesarea

Jerusalem

JUDEA

M E D I T E R R A N E A N   S E A

Area of Jewish settlement

0   125   250 km

0   50   100   150 miles

EGYPT

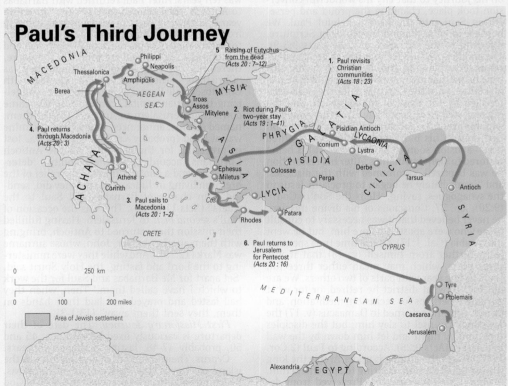

Paul's Third Journey

MACEDONIA

Philippi

Neapolis

5. Raising of Eutychus from the dead (Acts 20 : 7–12)

1. Paul revisits Christian communities (Acts 18 : 23)

Thessalonica

Amphipolis

Berea

AEGEAN SEA

MYSIA

Troas

Assos

Mitylene

PHRYGIA

GALATIA

Pisidian Antioch

LYCAONIA

2. Riot during Paul's two-year stay (Acts 19 : 1–41)

Iconium

Lystra

4. Paul returns through Macedonia (Acts 20 : 3)

ACHAIA

Athens

Corinth

Ephesus

Miletus

Colossae

PISIDIA

Perga

Derbe

CILICIA

Tarsus

Antioch

3. Paul sails to Macedonia (Acts 20 : 1–2)

LYCIA

Cos

Rhodes

Patara

6. Paul returns to Jerusalem for Pentecost (Acts 20 : 16)

CRETE

CYPRUS

SYRIA

0   250 km

0   100   200 miles

Area of Jewish settlement

M E D I T E R R A N E A N   S E A

Tyre

Ptolemais

Caesarea

Jerusalem

Alexandria   EGYPT

Paul's Second Journey

5. Riot after Paul's preaching in synagogue (Acts 17:1–9)

4. Baptizing of Lydia and imprisonment of Paul and Silas

3. Paul's vision of the mission to Macedonia

MACEDONIA

Philippi
Thessalonica
Neapolis
Berea
SAMOTHRACE
Apollonia
Amphipolis
Troas
AEGEAN
SEA   Pergamum
MYSIA
BITHYNIA AND PONTUS

GALATIA
PHRYGIA
LYCAONIA
Antioch
Iconium
CILICIA
Cilician Gates

ACHAIA
Athens
Sardis
Thyatira
Ephesus
ASIA
PISIDIA
Corinth
Cenchreae

Colossae
Miletus
Rhodes

Lystra
PAMPHYLIA
Derbe
Perga

Tarsus
Antioch

1. Paul departs with Silas

7. Paul works with Aquila and Priscilla (Acts 18:1–4)

6. Paul disputes with philosophers at the Areopagus (Acts 17:16–34)

RHODES

2. Timothy joins Paul and Silas

CYPRUS
Salamis

Paphos

SYRIA

CRETE

MEDITERRANEAN SEA

Area of Jewish settlement

0   250   500 km

0   100   200   300 miles

Caesarea
Jerusalem

EGYPT

Paul's Trip to Rome

Rome
ITALIA
Puteoli
ADRIATIC SEA

AEGEAN SEA

5. Paul awaits trial before Caesar

Rhegium

SICILIA

Syracuse

Athens

Cnidus

LYCIA
Myra

PAMPHYLIA

CILICIA
Tarsus

Antioch

SYRIA

MALTA

4. Shipwrecked on Malta (Acts 28)

Fair Havens
Phoenix   CRETE
CAUDA   Lasea
Salmone

RHODES

CYPRUS

2. Trials before Felix and Festus; Paul appeals to Caesar (Acts 24, 25)

Sidon

Caesarea
Antipatris
Jerusalem

3. Strong winds make navigation difficult (Acts 27)

MEDITERRANEAN SEA

SYRTIS

0   250   500 km

0   100   200   300 miles

Area of Jewish settlement

Alexandria
EGYPT

1. Paul arrested (Acts 21 : 33)

in the synagogues of the Jews; and John also ministered with them. From Salamis they traveled to Paphos, at the other extremity of the island, the residence of the Roman governor, Sergius Paulus, who, hearing of the arrival of Barnabas and Saul, sent for them, desiring to hear the word of God. Attached to the governor was a Jew named Bar-Jesus, or Elymas, a false prophet and magician, who, fearful of the influence of the apostles, withstood them, "seeking to turn the proconsul away from the faith." Paul rebuked Bar-Jesus, denounced him in remarkable terms, declaring against him God's sentence of temporary blindness. "Immediately a mist and a darkness fell upon him, and he went about seeking those who would lead him by the hand." The proconsul, moved by the scene and persuaded by the teaching of the apostle, became a believer (13:4-12). From this point of the apostolic history Paul appears as the great figure of every event. He now entered on his work as the preacher to the Gentiles, and simultaneously his name was suddenly changed. Nothing is said to explain the change of name, although we find many conjectures among writers (*see* above).

Perga and Antioch. From Paphos Paul and his company set sail for Perga in Pamphylia, where they remained a short time. An event occurred there that was attended with painful feelings at the time and involved the most serious consequences: "John left them and returned to Jerusalem" (Acts 13:13). This abandonment of the expedition by John was doubtless because of a change of plan and made a deep and lasting impression upon Paul (cf. 15:38). From Perga they traveled to Antioch in Pisidia. Here, on the Sabbath, "they went into the synagogue and sat down." Being invited to speak after the reading of "the Law and the Prophets," Paul stood and addressed the people (13:16-41). The discourse made a deep and thrilling impression upon the audience, and the apostles were requested to repeat their message on the next Sabbath. During the week so much interest was stirred up that on the Sabbath "nearly the whole city assembled to hear the word of God." Filled with envy because of the desire of the Gentiles to hear, the Jews "began contradicting the things spoken by Paul, and were blaspheming." The apostles turned to the Gentiles and boldly proclaimed salvation to them. Opposition increased, and the apostles left Antioch (13:42-51) and came to Iconium.

Iconium. This city belonged at different times to Phrygia and Lycaonia. Ramsay (*St. Paul the Traveller*, p. 109) believes it was at this time in the former. Here they went first to the synagogue, and the effect of their discourses was such that great numbers, both of Jews and Greeks, believed the gospel. Persecution was raised by the unbelieving Jews, but the apostles persevered and lingered in the city for a considerable time, encouraged by the miracles that God worked

through them. Learning the intention of the hostile Gentiles and their Jewish instigators to raise a riot and stone them, Paul and his company fled (13:51-14:6).

Lystra and Derbe. These cities of Lycaonia were now reached. Here their mission was attested by a miracle—the cure of a cripple. The people of the city ascribed the work to a deity and exclaimed, "The gods have become like men and have come down to us." They identified Paul with Hermes and Barnabas with Zeus and were about to pay them divine honors. From this the apostles with difficulty dissuaded them. The people in general were disappointed at the repulse of the honors they had offered. The easy step from blind worship to rapid persecution was soon taken, at the instigation of certain Jews who came from Antioch and Iconium. Paul was stoned and dragged out of the city for dead; but as the new disciples stood around him he revived and returned into the city. He and Barnabas departed the next day for Derbe, where they gained many disciples (14:7-21).

Return. Paul revisited Lystra, Iconium, and Antioch, "strengthening the souls of the disciples, encouraging them to continue in the faith." The apostles also ordained elders in every church for their teaching and guidance. They then passed through Pisidia and Perga (in Pamphylia) to Attalia. They embarked for Antioch in Syria, where they related the successes that had been granted to them, especially the opening of the "door of faith to the Gentiles." And so ended the first missionary journey (14:21-27).

The Council at Jerusalem. (Acts 15; Gal. 2.) While Paul and Barnabas were abiding at Antioch, certain men came down from Judea and taught the brethren that it was necessary for the Gentile converts to be circumcised. The older converts in Antioch had all entered through the synagogue and had necessarily accepted certain prohibitions as a rule of life. But in Galatia there were many who became Christians without any connection with the synagogue. Paul does not seem to have imposed upon them any preliminary compliance; and even Peter had no scruple in associating freely with Antioch Christians in general. It appears that Peter, having come to Antioch, fellowshiped with the Gentile converts until the arrival of some Jewish brethren, when he withdrew and separated himself from them. Paul, seeing this, rebuked Peter "in the presence of all" and "opposed him to his face" (Gal. 2:11-14). Because this doctrine was vigorously opposed by the two apostles, it was determined to refer the question to the apostles and elders at Jerusalem. Paul and Barnabas themselves and certain others were selected for the mission. In Gal. 2:2 Paul says that he went up "because of a revelation." On their way to Jerusalem they announced to the brethren in Phoenicia and Samaria the conversion of the Gentiles. Arriving at

Jerusalem, Paul had private interviews with the more influential members of the Christian community (2:2). The apostles and the church in general, it appears, would have raised no difficulties; but certain believers, who had been Pharisees, thought fit to maintain the same doctrine that had caused the disturbance at Antioch. A formal decision became necessary. After considerable discussion Peter addressed the council, followed by Paul and Barnabas with a statement of facts. Then James gave his decision, which was adopted by the apostles, elders, and brethren. They wrote to the Gentiles in Antioch and Syria and Cilicia, disavowing the men who "have disturbed you with their words, unsettling your souls," and bearing emphatic testimony to Paul and Barnabas as the "beloved" who "have risked their lives for the name of our Lord Jesus Christ." Having been dismissed, the apostles returned to Antioch and read the epistle to the gathered multitude, who "rejoiced because of its encouragement." The apostles continued at Antioch, preaching the word. Soon after, Paul expressed a desire to revisit the cities where he had preached and founded churches. Barnabas determined to take John Mark with them, and "there arose such a sharp disagreement that they separated from one another" (Acts 15:24-39).

Second Missionary Journey. Paul chose Silas for his companion, and the two went together through Syria and Cilicia, visiting the churches, and so came to Derbe and Lystra. At the latter place they found *Timothy* (which see), whom Paul desired to take with him and therefore circumcised him because of the Jews. Paul then passed through the regions of Phrygia and Galatia. Avoiding, by direction of the Spirit, Asia and Bithynia, he came with his companions by way of Mysia to Troas, on the borders of the Hellespont (Acts 15:40; 16:8).

Macedonia. Paul saw in a vision a man of Macedonia who besought him, saying, "Come over to Macedonia and help us." The vision was understood to mean that "God had called us to preach the gospel to them." They traveled N with the intention of entering Bithynia, but "the Spirit of Jesus did not permit them." So they passed by Mysia without preaching there (16:6-8). It is at this point that the historian, speaking of Paul's company (v. 10), substitutes "we" for "they." He says nothing of himself. We can only infer that Luke, to whatever country he belonged, became a companion of Paul at Troas. The party immediately set sail from Troas, touched at Samothrace, passed on to Neapolis, and from thence journeyed to Philippi (16:9-12).

Philippi. The first convert in Macedonia was Lydia, a woman of Thyatira, who already worshiped God. She made a profession of her faith in Jesus and was baptized. So earnest was she in her invitation that Paul and his company made her house their home while at Philippi. A female slave, who brought gain to her masters by her powers of prediction when she was in the possessed state, harassed Paul and his company. Some believe that the young woman was a *ventriloquist;* Plutarch so understands the word and states that in his time such persons were called *puthōnes* (the Gk. word used in v. 16). Paul, in the name of Jesus, cast the spirit out of the girl, whereupon her masters, seeing their hope of gain was gone, dragged Paul and Silas before the magistrates. They yielded to the clamor of the multitude and ordered the apostles to be beaten and cast into prison. This cruel wrong was the occasion of the signal appearance of the God of righteousness and deliverance. The narrative tells of the earthquake, the jailer's terror, his conversion and baptism, and also of the anxiety of the rulers when they learned that those whom they had beaten and imprisoned without trial were Roman citizens (16:13-40).

Thessalonica. Leaving Philippi, Paul and Silas traveled through Amphipolis and Apollonia and stopped at Thessalonica, where there was a Jewish synagogue. For three Sabbaths Paul proclaimed Christ in the synagogue, and as a result some of the Jews, with many devout Greeks "and a number of the leading women," joined with Paul and Silas. But the envy of the unbelieving Jews was excited, and, gathering a mob, they assaulted the house of Jason, with whom Paul and Silas were staying as guests. "And the brethren immediately sent Paul and Silas away by night" (17:1-10). How long they stayed in Thessalonica is uncertain, but the success of their work and the language of 1 Thess. 1-2 would indicate quite a length of time.

Berea. The next point reached was Berea, where the apostles found Jews more noble than those of Thessalonica had been. Accordingly they gained many converts, both Jews and Greeks. When the Thessalonian Jews heard of this they came and stirred up the people. A riot was avoided only by Paul's departure for the coast, whence he set sail for Athens, leaving Silas and Timothy behind (17:10-15). Some of "the brethren" went with Paul as far as Athens, where they left him, carrying back "a command for Silas and Timothy to come to him as soon as possible."

Athens. Paul was left in Athens alone (1 Thess. 3:1), August A.D. 51. As he looked about him he "saw the city full of idols," and "his spirit was being provoked within him." According to his custom, he sought out his brethren of the scattered race of Israel, declaring to them that the Messiah had come. He also began to discourse daily in the Agora (marketplace) with them that met with him, among whom were philosophers of the Epicurean and Stoic schools. His teachings were received partly in pity, partly in contempt, and yet anyone with a novelty was welcome, for "all the Athenians and the strangers visiting there used to spend their time in nothing other than telling or hearing something new." They therefore brought him to the Areopagus, that he might make to them a formal exposition of his doctrine. Here the apostle delivered that wonderful discourse reported in Acts 17:22-31. Beginning by complimenting them on their carefulness in religion, he, with exquisite tact and ability, exposed the folly of their superstitions and unfolded the character and claims of the living and true God. But when Paul spoke of the resurrection the patience of his audience failed; some mocked him, and others, believing they had heard enough of his subject for the time, promised him another audience. So Paul departed from among them. But some believed, among whom was Dionysius the Areopagite and a woman named Damaris (17:34). We are not informed how long Paul remained in Athens or for what cause he left.

Corinth. From Athens Paul proceeded to Corinth, where, as at Thessalonica, he chose to earn his own subsistence by working at his trade of tent-making. This brought him into an acquaintance with Aquila and Priscilla, with whom he made his home. "And he was reasoning in the synagogue every Sabbath and trying to persuade Jews and Greeks" (18:4). While he was thus engaged Silas and Timothy came from Macedonia and joined him. The first epistle to the Thessalonians was probably written at this time, drawn out from Paul by the report given him of the church in Thessalonica (1 Thess. 3:1-2). Their coming greatly encouraged him, for he acknowledged himself to have been "in weakness and in fear and in much trembling" (1 Cor. 2:3). This was doubtless that period of pressing want from which he was relieved by the arrival of "the brethren" (Silas and Timothy) from Macedonia with contributions (2 Cor. 11:9). Rejected by the Jews, he turned to the Gentiles and worshiped in the house of a proselyte named Titius Justus. Encouraged by the conversion of Crispus, the chief ruler of the synagogue, and by a vision of the Lord, he remained in Corinth, teaching the word, a year and six months. During this period he probably wrote the second epistle to the Thessalonians. The Jews then made an unsuccessful attempt against Paul but were defeated by the calmness of Gallio, the deputy.

Return. After this long stay at Corinth he departed into Syria, taking with him Priscilla and Aquila (Acts 18:1-18). The apostle's destination was Jerusalem, since he desired to be there on the Day of Pentecost (20:16). He journeyed by the way of Ephesus, leaving his friends Aquila and Priscilla there. This visit seems to have been a brief one, the only record of it being "And when he had landed at Caesarea, he went up and greeted the church [at Jerusalem], and went down to Antioch" (18:22). He thus completed his second missionary journey in the early summer of A.D. 54 (Conybeare and Howson) or September A.D. 53

(Lewin). Ramsay makes it early in the spring of 53, as Passover in that year fell on March 22.

Third Missionary Journey. After a considerable stay at Antioch, Paul departed and went over all the country of Galatia and Phrygia, "strengthening all the disciples" (Acts 18:23) and giving directions for the collection in behalf of the poor saints in Jerusalem (1 Cor. 16:1-2).

Ephesus. He then came to Ephesus (probably October A.D. 53), where he found about twelve disciples who had received the instructions of Apollos. Upon inquiry Paul found that they had received only John's baptism and were ignorant of the advent of the Spirit and all the ministries committed to Him in this age. He thereupon explained the mission of John as a teacher of repentance to prepare men's minds for Christ, who is the true object of faith. They believed and were baptized, having been introduced into the spiritual blessings of the new age. Entering upon his public ministry, for three months he spoke boldly in the synagogue. Being opposed he withdrew to the school of one Tyrannus, where he discoursed daily for two years. "And God was performing extraordinary miracles by the hands of Paul," so that many from among the exorcists became converts and burned their books of magic to the value of about ten thousand dollars. At about this time (according to Conybeare and Howson) he paid a visit to Corinth and, returning to Ephesus, wrote the first epistle to the Corinthians. The religious change was becoming so great that the craftsmen who gained their living by making models of the statue of Artemis (Diana) became alarmed and raised an insurrection (see Demetrius; Gods, False: Artemis). The danger increased, and the apostle and his companion left the city (Acts 18:1–20:1), January A.D. 56.

Troas and Macedonia. On leaving Ephesus Paul went first to Troas, where he preached with great success, though much dejected by the nonarrival of Titus, who had been sent to Corinth (2 Cor. 2:12-13). The necessity of meeting Titus urging him forward, he sailed to Macedonia and, landing at Neapolis, proceeded immediately to Philippi. Here he was "comforted . . . by the coming of Titus" (7:6) and was probably rejoined by Timothy (1:1). Titus was sent to Corinth with the second epistle to the Corinthians and to finish the collection he had begun there (8:6, 16-18). Hearing that Judaizing teachers had been corrupting the church of Galatia, Paul wrote the epistle to the Galatians, powerfully refuting the errors in question. Paul traveled through Macedonia, perhaps to the borders of Illyricum (Rom. 15:19), and then he carried out the intention of which he had spoken so often and arrived at Corinth, where he probably remained three months (Acts 20:2-3). Here he wrote the epistle to the Romans, about January A.D. 57. Leaving Europe, Paul now directed his course toward Jerusalem, accompanied by Luke. At Troas he restored *Eutychus* (which see) to life. Paul journeyed by land to Assos, where he took ship for Miletus. By invitation the elders of the church at Ephesus met him here and were bidden an affectionate farewell (20:3-38). The voyage was then resumed by the way of Cos, Rhodes, and Patara, to Tyre. Here Paul and his company remained seven days and then sailed to Ptolemais, stopping one day, and reached Caesarea. In opposition to the entreaties of Philip (the evangelist) and others, as well as the prophetic intimations of danger from Agabus, Paul determined to go on to Jerusalem, which he probably did on horseback (21:1-17), May 20, A.D. 57.

Arrest at Jerusalem. This fifth visit of Paul to Jerusalem since his conversion is the last of which we have any certain record. He was gladly received by the brethren and the following day had an interview with James and the elders, relating "one by one the things which God had done among the Gentiles through his ministry." The charge had been brought against him that he taught "all the Jews who are among the Gentiles to forsake Moses, telling them not to circumcise their children nor to walk according to the customs." In order to dispel this impression he was asked to do publicly an act of homage to the law. They had four men who were under the Nazirite law, and Paul was requested to put himself under the vow with these and to supply the cost of their offerings. When the seven days were almost ended some Jews from Asia stirred up the people against him on the charge of bringing Greeks into the Temple to pollute it. The whole city was moved, the apostle was dragged out of the Temple, and they were about to kill him. The appearance of soldiers and centurions sent by the commander of the Roman troops stopped their blows. The commander ordered Paul to be chained and, not able to learn who he was or what he had done, sent him to "the barracks." He obtained leave to address the people (Acts 21:40; 22:1-21) and delivered what he himself called his "defense." At the mention of his mission to the Gentiles they shouted, "Away with such a fellow from the earth, for he should not be allowed to live!" Seeing that a tumult was imminent, the commander sent him within the barracks, ordering him to be scourged. From this outrage the apostle protected himself by mentioning his Roman citizenship. The next day he was taken before the Sanhedrin; no conclusion was arrived at. A dissension between the Sadducees and Pharisees arose. The life of the apostle was in danger, and he was removed again to the barracks. That night he was cheered by a vision, in which he was told to "take courage" for he must "witness at Rome also." The conspiracy of forty Jews to kill him was frustrated by news brought by Paul's sister's son, and it was determined to send him to Caesarea to Felix, the governor of Judea (22:21–23:24).

Before Felix. In charge of a strong guard of soldiers, he was taken by night as far as Antipatris; the cavalry alone went with him to Caesarea. Felix simply asked Paul of what province he was, promising him a hearing when his accusers should come (23:23-35). Five days later the high priest Ananias and certain members of the Sanhedrin appeared, with Tertullus as their attorney. The charges made against Paul were denied by him, and Felix delayed proceedings until Lysias, the commander, should arrive, commanding that Paul should be treated with indulgence and his friends allowed to see him. After several days Felix sent for Paul, influenced probably by the desire of Drusilla, his wife, to hear him, she being a Jewess. Felix trembled under his preaching but was unrepentant, shutting his ears to conviction and neglecting his official duty, hoping that he might receive a bribe from Paul for his liberation. Not receiving this he retained Paul as a prisoner without a hearing two years, until the arrival of Festus (chap. 24), A.D. 59.

Before Festus. As soon as the new governor, Festus, came to Jerusalem, the Jews requested him to send for Paul. He replied that Paul should be kept at Caesarea, to which place he ordered his accusers to accompany him. After ten days he returned, and on the next day Paul was brought before the tribunal. When asked if he was willing to be tried at Jerusalem, the apostle, aware of his danger, replied that he stood at Caesar's judgment seat. He then uttered the words *"Caesarem appello"* ("I appeal unto Caesar"), which a Roman magistrate dared not resist. Festus conferred with his council and replied, "You have appealed to Caesar, to Caesar you shall go" (25:1-12).

Before Agrippa. While waiting for an opportunity to send Paul to Rome, Festus desired to prepare an account of the trial to be sent to the emperor. This was a matter of some difficulty, as the information elicited at the trial was so vague that he hardly knew what statement to insert; and it seemed "absurd" to send a prisoner and not to signify the crime laid against him. About this time King Agrippa II, with his sister Bernice, came on a complimentary visit to the new governor. To him Festus recounted the case, confessing his own ignorance of Jewish theology, whereupon Agrippa expressed a desire to hear the prisoner. The next day Agrippa and Bernice came "amid great pomp," with a retinue of military officers and chief men of Caesarea. Paul was brought, and, permission having been given him to speak, he pronounced one of his greatest apologies for the Christian truth. When he spoke of the resurrection Festus exclaimed, "Paul, you are out of your mind! Your great learning is driving you mad." This Paul courteously denied, and, turning to the Jewish voluptuary, he made the appeal to him, "King Agrippa, do you believe the Prophets? I know that you do," to which the king ironically responded, "In a short time you will persuade me to become a Christian." The reply of Paul concluded the interview, and it was decided that he had done nothing worthy of death, and he might have been set free except for his appeal to Caesar. There was no retreat, and nothing remained but to wait for a favorable opportunity of sending the prisoner to Rome (25:13–26:32).

Voyage to Rome. At length (August A.D. 59, Ramsay; A.D. 60, Conybeare and Howson) Paul, under the care of Julius, a centurion of the Augustan cohort who had charge of a convoy of prisoners, set sail in a coasting vessel belonging to Adramyttium. The next day they touched at Sidon, "and Julius treated Paul with consideration and allowed him to go to his friends and receive care." The next port reached was Myra, a city of Lycia, where they found a ship of Alexandria bound for Italy; and to this vessel Julius transferred his prisoners. Leaving behind the harbor of Cnidus and doubling Salmone, the headland of Crete, they beat up with difficulty under the shelter of the island as far as Fair Havens, near Lasea, which still bears its ancient name. "The ship reached Fair Havens in the latter part of September, and was detained there by a continuance of unfavorable winds until after October 5" (Ramsay, p. 322). Contrary to the warning of the apostle that it would be perilous to continue the voyage at that season of the year, it was decided not to remain. The hope was to reach Phoenix and winter there. Overtaken by the "Euraquilo," a violent wind, they were unable to bear up and, letting the ship drive, were carried under the protecting shelter of a small island named Clauda. The storm raged with unabated fury, and the ship was drifting in the Adriatic Sea, when, on the fourteenth night after their departure from Clauda, they found themselves near land. In the morning they ran aground, and they all escaped safely to the land, which they found to be Malta (*Melita,* KJV; Acts 27), about November. The people of the island treated them kindly and were deeply impressed with Paul's shaking off a viper from his hand, believing him to be a god. The company remained three months on the island, and Paul performed miracles of healing. They then departed from Malta in February on an Alexandrian ship, "which had the Twin Brothers for its figurehead," and came, by the way of Syracuse and Rhegium, to Puteoli, in Italy. Here they found Christian brethren, with whom they remained seven days, and so went toward Rome, being met by brethren from that city at "the Market of Appius and Three Inns" (28:11-15), spring A.D. 60.

At Rome. Upon his arrival in Rome the apostle was allowed to dwell in his own rented house (under the care of a soldier) and to receive visitors (Acts 28:16, 30). After three days he invited the chief men among the Jews to come to him

and explained his position. He had committed no offense against the holy nation; he came to Rome not to accuse his countrymen but was compelled to appeal to Caesar by their conduct. "For I am wearing this chain for the sake of the hope of Israel," he concluded. They replied that they had received no letters concerning him and that none of the brethren coming from Jerusalem had spoken evil of him. They expressed also a desire to hear further concerning his religious sentiments. The day for the hearing was set. They came in large numbers, and he expounded and testified to them the kingdom of God, endeavoring to persuade them by arguments from their own Scriptures, "from morning until evening." Some believed, and others did not, and separating, they had "a great dispute among themselves" (vv. 17-29). Paul remained in his own house under military custody. He was permitted to preach "the kingdom of God" and teach those things "concerning the Lord Jesus Christ" (v. 31). This imprisonment lasted two years (v. 30), from spring A.D. 60 to spring A.D. 62. Here closes the account as given in the book of Acts, but we gather from his epistles that during this time he wrote the letters of Philemon, Colossians, Ephesians, and Philippians.

Release and Subsequent Labors. It is the general opinion that at the end of the two years Paul was granted a trial before Nero, which resulted in his acquittal and liberation. He then probably fulfilled his intention, lately expressed (Philem. 22; Phil. 2:24), of traveling eastward through Macedonia, on to Ephesus, and from there to Colossae and Laodicea. From Asia Minor he went to Spain (disputed by many), where he remained two years. Returning to Asia Minor and Macedonia, he wrote the first epistle to Timothy; to Crete, epistle to Titus; wintered at Nicopolis; was arrested there and sent to Rome for trial. This is the scheme as given by Conybeare and Howson. Lewin (*Life of St. Paul*) gives the following scheme: Paul sailed for Jerusalem and went thence by Antioch and Asia Minor. He visited Colossae, Ephesus, Crete, Macedonia, and Corinth. He wintered at Nicopolis, made his traditional journey to Spain, and was probably arrested at Ephesus and taken to Rome. Ramsay says (p. 360) that "the hints contained in the Pastoral Epistles hardly furnish an outline of his travels, which must have lasted three or four years, A.D. 62-65."

Second Imprisonment and Death. This imprisonment was evidently more severe than the first one. Now he was not only chained but treated "as a criminal" (2 Tim. 2:9). Most of his friends left him, many, perhaps, like Demas, "having loved this present world" (4:10), others from necessity; and we hear the lonely cry, "Only Luke is with me" (4:11). So perilous was it to show any public sympathy for him that no Christian ventured to stand by him in the court of justice. As the final stage of his trial approached he looked forward to death as his final sentence (4:6-8). Probably no long time elapsed after Paul's arrival before his case came up for hearing. He seems to have successfully defended himself from the first (4:17) of the charges brought against him and to have been delivered from immediate peril and from a painful death. He was sent back to prison to wait for the second stage of the trial. He probably believed that this would not come up, or at least the final decision would not be given, until the following winter (4:21), whereas it actually took place about midsummer. We are not left to conjecture the feelings with which he awaited this consummation, for he himself expressed them in that sublime strain of triumphant hope that is familiar to the memory of every Christian and that has nerved the heart of a thousand martyrs: "I have fought the good fight, I have finished the course, I have kept the faith; in the future there is laid up for me the crown of righteousness, which the Lord, the righteous Judge, will award to me on that day" (4:7-8). The presence of Luke still consoled him, and Onesiphorus sought him out and visited him in prison, undeterred by the fear of danger or of shame (1:16). He longed, however, for the presence of Timothy, to whom he wrote the second epistle, urging him "to come before winter" (4:21). We do not know if Timothy was able to fulfill these last requests; it is doubtful whether he reached Rome in time to receive Paul's parting commands and cheer his latest sufferings. The only intimation that seems to throw any light upon the question is the statement in the epistle to the Hebrews (13:23) that Timothy had been liberated from imprisonment in Italy. We have no record of the final stage of the apostle's trial and know only that it ended in martyrdom, summer A.D. 68 (or 67). He died by decapitation, according to universal tradition, "weeping friends took up his corpse and carried it for burial to those subterranean labyrinths (Clement *Rom.* 1.5) where, through many ages of oppression, the persecuted Church found refuge for the living, and sepulchers for the dead."

Character. Although we learn much concerning the character of Paul from his life and labors—his burning zeal, untiring industry, singleness of aim, patient suffering, and sublime courage—it is in his letters that we must study his true life, for in them we learn "what is told of Paul by Paul himself " (Gregory Nazianzen). "It is not only that we there find models of the sublimest eloquence, when he is kindled by the visions of the glories to come, the perfect triumph of good over evil, the manifestation of the sons of God, and the transformation into God's likeness; but in his letters, besides all this which is divine, we trace every shade, even to the faintest, of his human character also. Here we see that fearless independence with which he ' withstood Peter to the face, because he was to be blamed'

(Gal. 2:11); that impetuosity which breaks out in his apostrophe to the 'foolish Galatians' (3:1); that earnest indignation which bids his converts 'beware of dogs, beware of the concision' (Phil. 3:2), and pours itself forth in the emphatic 'God forbid' (Rom. 6:2; 1 Cor. 6:15), which meets every Antinomian suggestion; that fervid patriotism which makes him 'wish that he were himself accursed from Christ for his brethren, ... who are Israelites' (Rom. 9:3); that generosity which looked for no other reward than 'to preach the glad tidings of Christ without charge' (1 Cor. 9:18, 25) and made him feel that he would rather 'die than that any man should make this glorifying void'; that dread of officious interference which led him to shrink from 'building on another man's foundation' (Rom. 15:20); that delicacy which shows itself in his appeal to Philemon, whom he might have commanded, 'yet for love's sake rather beseeching him' (Philem. 9); that scrupulous fear of evil appearance which 'would not eat any man's bread for naught, but wrought with labor and travail night and day, that he might not be chargeable to any of them' (1 Thess. 2:9); that refined courtesy which cannot bring itself to blame till it has first praised (cf. 1 Cor. 1:5-7; 2 Cor. 1:6-7, with the latter part of these epistles), and which makes him deem it needful almost to apologize for the freedom of giving advice to those who are not personally known to him (Rom. 15:14-15); that self-denying love which 'will eat no flesh while the world standeth,' lest he make his 'brother to offend' (1 Cor. 8:13); that impatience of exclusive formalism with which he overwhelms the Judaizers of Galatia, joined with a forbearance so gentle for the innocent weakness of scrupulous consciences (1 Cor. 8:12; Rom. 14:21); that grief for the sins of others which moved him to tears when he spoke of the enemies of the cross of Christ, 'of whom I tell you even weeping' (Phil. 3:18); that noble freedom from jealousy with which he speaks of those who, out of rivalry to himself, preach Christ even of envy and strife, supposing to add afflictions to his bonds, 'What then? notwithstanding every way, whether in pretense or in truth, Christ is preached; and I therein do rejoice, yea, and will rejoice' (1:18); that tender friendship which watches over the health of Timothy, even with a mother's care (1 Tim. 5:23); that intense sympathy in the joys and sorrows of his converts which could say, even to the rebellious Corinthians, 'Ye are in our hearts, to die and live with you' (2 Cor. 7:3); that longing desire for the intercourse of affection, and that sense of loneliness when it was withheld, which perhaps is the most touching feature of all, because it approaches most nearly to a weakness" (Conybeare and Howson).

Paul's Citizenship. It is a mistake to suppose that Paul's citizenship, which belonged to the members of the family, came from their being natives of Tarsus. Although it was a "free city" (*urbs libera*), enjoying the privileges of being governed by its own magistrates, and was exempted from the occupation of a Roman garrison, its citizens did not necessarily possess the *civitas* of Rome. The Roman commander (Acts 21:37-39; 22:25-27) knew that Paul was a Tarsian, without being aware that he was a citizen. This privilege had been granted, or descended, to his father as an individual right perhaps for some services rendered to Caesar during the civil wars (Conybeare and Howson; Bloomfield, *New Testament*).

Member of the Sanhedrin. "There are strong grounds for believing that if Paul was not a member of the Sanhedrin at Stephen's death he was elected into that powerful senate soon after; possibly as a reward for the zeal he had shown against the heretic. He himself says that in Jerusalem he not only exercised the power of imprisonment by commission from the high priest, but also, when the Christians were put to death, *gave his vote* against them (Acts 26:10). From this expression it is natural to infer that he was a member of that supreme court of judicature. If this inference is well founded, and the qualification for members of the Sanhedrin was that they should be the fathers of children, Saul must have been a married man, and the father of a family. If so it is probable that his wife and children did not long survive; for otherwise some notice of them would have occurred in the subsequent narrative, or some allusion to them in the epistles" (Conybeare and Howson).

Conversion. Some regard the circumstances of the case as by no means miraculous but as produced solely by certain terrific *natural phenomena*, which they suppose had such an effect on the high-wrought imagination, and so struck the alarmed conscience of Saul, as to make him regard as reality what was merely produced by fancy. "Paul, however ardent might be his temperament and vivid his imagination, *could not* so far deceive himself as to suppose that the *conversation* really took place if there had been no more than these commentators tell us. Besides he is so minute in his description as to say it was in the *Hebrew language*" (Bloomfield, *New Testament*). The seeming discrepancies found in the several accounts (Acts 9, 22, 26) have been differently explained. "The Greek 'akouo,' like our word 'hear,' has two distinct meanings—*to perceive sound* and *to understand*. The men who were with Saul heard the sound, but did not understand what was said to him. As to the fact that one passage represents them as 'standing,' the other as having 'fallen to the earth,' the word rendered 'stood' also means *to be fixed, rooted to the spot*. Hence the sense may be, not that they stood erect, but that they were rendered *motionless*, or *fixed to the spot*, by overpowering fear. Or, perhaps, when the light with such exceeding brilliancy burst upon them,

they all 'fell to the earth,' but afterward rose and 'stood' upon their feet" (Haley, *Alleged Discrepancies of the Bible*).

"Saul, Who Was Also Known as Paul" (Acts 13:9). "The invariable use in the Acts of Saul at this point, and Paul afterward, and the distinct mention by St. Luke himself of the transition, is accounted for by the desire to mark the turning-point between Saul's activity among his own countrymen and his new labors as the apostle of the Gentiles" (Smith). "We are inclined to adopt the opinion that the Cilician apostle had this Roman name, as well as his other Hebrew name, in his earlier days, and even before he was a Christian . . . yet we cannot believe it accidental that the words which have led to this discussion occur at this point of the inspired narrative. The heathen name rises to the surface at the moment when St. Paul visibly enters on his office as the apostle to the heathen" (Conybeare and Howson *Life and Epistles of Paul*, 1:152-53).

Journeys to Jerusalem. In the book of Acts we are informed of five distinct journeys made by the apostle to Jerusalem after the time of his conversion. In the epistle to the Galatians Paul speaks of two journeys to Jerusalem—the first being "three years" after his conversion, the second "fourteen years" later (Gal. 1:18; 2:1). The question arises whether the second journey of the epistle must be identified with the second, third, or fourth of the Acts, or whether it is a separate journey, distinct from any of them. It is agreed by all that the fifth cannot possibly be intended. Paley and Schrader have resorted to the hypothesis that the Galatian visit is some supposed journey not recorded in the Acts at all. Conybeare and Howson (*Life and Epistles of Paul*) identify it with the third journey of Acts 15.

Vow at Cenchrea (Acts 18:18). The impression on the reader's mind is that Paul himself shaved his head at Cenchrea. Eminent commentators hold the view that the ceremony was performed by Aquila; also that the vow was not one of *Nazirite* but a *votum civile,* such as was taken during or after recovery from sickness, deliverance from any peril, or on obtaining any unexpected good. In case of a Nazirite vow the cutting of the hair, which denoted that the legal time had expired, could take place only in the Temple in Jerusalem, or at least in Judea (Conybeare and Howson; Bloomfield, *New Testament*).

Reply to Ananias (Acts 23:3-5). "God is going to strike you," etc. Some consider these words as an outburst of natural indignation and excuse it on the ground of the provocation, as a righteous denouncing of an unjust ruler. Others believe them a prophetic denunciation, terribly fulfilled when Ananias was murdered in the Jewish wars (Josephus *Wars* 2.17.9). "I was not aware, brethren, that he was high priest." These words are variously explained. "Some think that St. Paul meant to confess that he had been guilty of a want of due reflection; others that he spoke ironically, as refusing to recognize a man like Ananias as high priest; others have even thought that there was in the words an inspired reference to the abolition of the sacerdotal system of the Jews and the sole priesthood of Christ. Another class of interpreters regards St. Paul as ignorant of the fact that Ananias was high priest, or argues that Ananias was not really installed in office. And we know from Josephus that there was the greatest irregularity in the appointments about this time. Lastly, it has been suggested that the imperfection of St. Paul's vision was the cause of his mistake" (Conybeare and Howson).

Charge Against Paul Before Felix (Acts 24:5-6). Paul was accused of a threefold crime: first, with causing factious disturbances among all the Jews throughout the empire (which was an offense against the Roman government and amounted to *lese majeste,* or treason against the emperor); second, with being a ringleader of the sect of the Nazarenes (which involved heresy against the law of Moses); and third, with an attempt to profane the Temple at Jerusalem (an offense not only against Jewish but also Roman law, which protected the Jews in the exercise of their worship; Conybeare and Howson, 2:282).

Thorn in the Flesh (2 Cor. 12:7). "The best commentators are, with reason, agreed that the word *skolops* (thorn) must be taken in the natural sense, as denoting some very painful order or mortifying infirmity; *grievous afflictions* being, in all languages, expressed by metaphors taken from the piercing of the flesh by thorns or splinters. Various acute *disorders* have been supposed to be meant, as the headache" (Jerome, Tertullian), earache, impediment of speech (10:10), or a malady affecting the eyesight. "But it should rather seem that some *chronic* distemper or infirmity is meant, and probably such as was exceedingly mortifying as well as painful; otherwise the apostle would scarcely have felt such anxiety to have it removed. A most probable conjecture is that it was a *paralytic* and *hypochondriac affection,* which occasioned a distortion of countenance, and many other distressing effects, which would much tend to impair his usefulness" (Bloomfield, *New Testament*). Dr. Ramsay suggests (p. 94) that the malady was a species of chronic malarial fever, with its regularly recurring weakness, producing sickness and trembling.

Message. The preaching of the apostle Paul as reflected in his epistles was distinctive. The OT, as well as the gospel accounts up to the crucifixion, looked forward to the cross and primarily envisioned Israel and the blessing to the earth by means of the kingdom through Israel. The death, burial, resurrection, and ascension of Christ, together with the gift of the Holy Spirit at Pentecost in Acts 2, initiated the church period wherein the work accomplished by Christ became experientially effective in the early Christians. This experience of Christ's finished work is narrated principally in the book of Acts.

However, with the Pauline epistles we are given the theological exposition of what the finished work of Christ and the consequent giving of the Holy Spirit purchased for men. "Hidden in God" (Eph. 3:9) was the revelation given to the apostle, consisting first of the fact that the interval of time between the crucifixion and the resurrection of Christ and His return in glory was unrevealed; second, that during this era the out-calling of the *ecclesia,* the church, which is Christ's Body, was to occur. The Lord prophetically announces the church in Matt. 16, but leaves unrevealed its formation, its call, its position, its relationships, its privileges, and its duties. In the Upper Room discourse in John 14-17, the Lord gives preliminary teaching concerning this future entity, principally with regard to the work of the Holy Spirit, who would come at Pentecost. With the coming of the Holy Spirit the church was formed and began its existence. However, all through the book of Acts the precise doctrine that would govern the church was unrevealed. Neither Peter nor any of the other disciples was given the revelation distinctively concerning the church.

Two periods in the life of the apostle after his conversion are passed over in silence. One is his sojourn in Arabia, from which he came forth in full possession of the gospel revelation as set forth in Galatians and Romans. In the two silent years in prison at Caesarea between his arrest in the Temple at Jerusalem and his deportation to Rome he likely received other revelation. At any rate, the doctrine, position, walk, and destiny of the church appear in his writings alone. This was given to him by divine revelation. In his epistles to seven Gentile churches (Thessalonica, Corinth, Galatia, Ephesus, Philippi, Colossae, and Rome) the "mystery which for ages has been hidden in God" (Eph. 3:9) is fully set forth. These letters give full instructions concerning the unique place of the church in this age and in the counsels and purposes of God.

The central message of the apostle is the church as one body (1 Cor. 12:13) formed by the baptizing work of the Holy Spirit. This ministry of the Holy Spirit of baptizing, which was prophetic in the gospels with John the Baptist (Matt. 3:11; Mark 1:8; Luke 3:16; Acts 1:5), became historic in Acts 2 and in the experience of the church in the book of Acts, and was given its doctrinal exposition through the revelation of Paul in the epistles.

The baptism of the Spirit, according to Paul, places one "in Christ." This vital organic oneness of the people of this age with Christ and with one another in Him (Rom. 6:3-4; Gal. 3:27; Col. 2:8-10) forms the central core of the Pauline revelation. This "in Christ" position wrought by the giving of the Holy Spirit subsequent to the ascension of Christ makes real in the believer all that Christ purchased for him on the cross. Thus Paul becomes the expositor theologically of the finished work of Christ on the cross.

Although all centers in the new entity, the church, the mystery hid in God, and the connection of this new entity with the present age, to Paul was also committed the unfolding of the doctrines of grace that were latent in the teachings of Jesus Christ. To Paul was given the revelation concerning the precise relationship and purpose of the law to the new entity, the church. He unfolds the believer's justification, sanctification, and glory. He is distinctively the witness to a glorified Christ, head over all things to the church, which is Christ's Body. He thus places in his theological approach the believer in closest union with Christ, identified with Him by the Spirit's baptizing work in death, burial, resurrection, ascension, and coming glory.

The mystery "hidden in God" according to the Pauline revelation was a divine purpose to make of Jew and Gentile a wholly new thing, the church, which is Christ's Body, formed by the baptism of the Holy Spirit (1 Cor. 12:12-13) in which the earthly distinction of Jew and Gentile disappears (Eph. 2:14-16). The revelation of this mystery, which was foretold by our Lord (Matt. 16:18), was revealed to Paul. Failure to see the apostle's distinctive revelation and to enter into his differentiation between law and grace, the church and Israel, the present age as distinguished from other ages, and the present purpose of God in distinction to His OT purpose for His yet-future kingdom purpose have caused untold confusion in the Christian world.

Paulinism and Contemporary Thought. Modern scholarship has signally failed to catch the unique revelatory emphasis of the apostle's theology. Albert Schweitzer, for example, found in apocalyptic literature (as the result of increased knowledge of first-century Judaism) the explanation of Paulinism, particularly in the idea of a close union of the saved with the Messiah (*The Mysticism of Paul the Apostle* [Eng. trans., 1931]). Schweitzer stressed the social implications of the phrase "in Christ." In contrast to Schweitzer, Deissmann correctly emphasizes the central importance of the term "in Christ," which he said indicated "the most intimate possible fellowship of the Christian with the living Christ" (*Paul: A Study in Social and Religious History* [Eng. trans., 1926]). C. A. A. Scott interpreted the thought of salvation as the explanation of Paul's theology (*Christianity According to Saint Paul* [1927]). R. Bultmann stressed Pauline terminology as the explanation of his theological concepts. This study is of course important, but it is hardly the answer to the explanation of Paul's theological thought. Kittel (*Theologisches Wörterbuch zum N. T.* [1933]) has given impetus to this stress on terms employed.

Numbers of scholars in Germany have, in this century, contended that the ancient mystery religions had a peculiar influence on the apostle. Cf. Loisy (*La Naissance du Christianisme* [1933]), Bousset (*Kyrios Christos* [1913, 1921]), Reitzenstein (*Die hellenistischen Mysterienreligionen*, 3d ed. [1927]). The idea of mystery-religion influence upon the apostle Paul has not been popular outside of Germany, however. Critics like Kennedy and Schweitzer disfavored such influence (cf. Kennedy's *St. Paul and the Mystery Religions* [1913] and Schweitzer's *Paul and His Interpreters* [Eng. trans., 1912]). Critics such as W. D. Davies emphasized Paul's Judaistic background and saw a large influence of his rabbinic training in his preaching and teaching (*Paul and Rabbinic Judaism* [1948]).

Modern treatment of the apostle has stimulated realization of the vast theological importance of Paulinism, which extends far beyond the elementary concept of justification by faith (Karl Barth, *The Epistle to the Romans* [Eng. trans., 1933]). Arthur Darby Nock has written a satisfying biography of Paul (*St. Paul* [1938]). With regard to the Pauline epistles there is a tendency in present-day criticism to approve in many cases traditional datings and authorship.

BIBLIOGRAPHY: G. Lyttleton, *Observations on the Conversion and Apostleship of St. Paul* (1800); H. S. Seekings, *The Men of the Pauline Circle* (1914); T. R. Glover, *Paul of Tarsus* (1925); G. A. Deissmann, *Paul: A Study in Social and Religious History* (1926); A. H. McNeile, *St. Paul: His Life, Letters, and Christian Doctrine* (1932); C. H. Dodd, *The Mind of Paul* (1934); J. Stalker, *The Life of St. Paul* (1950); D. G. Miller, *Conqueror in Chains* (1951); W. J. Conybeare and J. S. Howson, *The Life and Epistles of Paul* (1953); W. D. Davies, *Paul and Rabbinic Judaism* (1956); S. Sandmel, *The Genius of Paul* (1958); E. White, *St. Paul: The Man and His Mind* (1958); C. E. Macartney, *Paul: The Man* (1961); R. N. Longenecker, *Paul, Apostle of Liberty* (1964); O. E. Moe, *The Apostle Paul* (1968); G. Ogg, *The Chronology of the Life of Paul* (1968); R. N. Longenecker, *Ministry and Message of Paul* (1971); H. N. Ridderbos, *Paul: An Outline of His Theology* (1975). F. F. Bruce, *Paul: Apostle of the Heart Set Free* (1977); J. Eadie, *The Words of the Apostle Paul* (1985).

PAU'LUS (paw'lus). *See* Sergius Paulus.

PE (ᴆ) (pā). The seventeenth letter of the Heb. alphabet, heading the seventeenth section of Ps. 119, in which each verse of the original begins with this letter.

PEACE (Heb. *shālôm*, "peace, health"; Gk. *eirēnē*, "unity, concord"). A term used in different senses in the Scriptures. (1) Frequently with reference to outward conditions of tranquility and thus of individuals, of communities, of churches, and of nations (e.g., Num. 6:26; 1 Sam. 7:14; 1 Kings 4:24; Acts 9:31). (2) Christian unity (e.g., Eph. 4:3; 1 Thess. 5:13). (3) In its deepest application, spiritual peace through restored relations of harmony with God (e.g., Isa.

9:6-7; 26:3; Luke 2:14; John 14:27; Acts 10:36; Rom. 1:7; 5:1; Gal. 5:22; etc.). *See* Atonement; Faith; Pardon; Adoption; Holy Spirit.

BIBLIOGRAPHY: W. Barclay, *Flesh and Spirit* (1962), pp. 83-90; N. Turner, *Christian Words* (1980), pp. 320-21.

PEACE OFFERING. *See* Sacrifices; Sacrificial Offerings.

PEACOCK. *See* Animal Kingdom.

PEARL. *See* Mineral Kingdom.

PECULIAR (Heb. *segūllâ;* Gk. *periousios*). The Heb. term signifies personal property, something treasured. The NASB and NIV readings declare Israel to be the Lord's own, or treasured, possession (Ex. 19:5; Deut. 14:2; 26:18; Ps. 135:4). David speaks of giving his treasure of gold and silver "to the house of . . . God" (1 Chron. 29:3). The Gk. term has the meaning of "that which is peculiarly one's own"; thus KJV "peculiar people" in Titus 2:14; 1 Pet. 2:9 is replaced in the NASB by a reference to a people for the Lord's "own possession," and in the NIV by "people that are his very own."

PED'AHEL (ped'a-hel). A leader of the tribe of Naphtali who was charged with the task of helping to apportion the land of Canaan after the conquest (Num. 34:28).

PED'AHZUR (ped'a-zur). The father of Gamaliel, a leader of Manasseh who was responsible for numbering his tribe in preparation for the march from Sinai (Num. 1:10; 2:20; 7:54, 59; 10:23).

PEDAI'AH (ped-ī'yah).
1. The grandfather of Jehoiakim king of Judah (2 Kings 23:36).
2. The third son of Jehoiachin king of Judah and father of Zerubbabel (1 Chron. 3:18-19).
3. The father of Joel, an officer placed by David over the half tribe of Manasseh (1 Chron. 27:20).
4. A leader under Nehemiah who helped build a portion of the wall of Jerusalem (Neh. 3:25).
5. A leader of Judah who stood to the left of Ezra as the latter read the law of Moses to the people (Neh. 8:4). Perhaps the same as no. 4.
6. A Benjamite whose descendant Sallu was selected by lot to live in the city of Jerusalem under Nehemiah's governorship (Neh. 11:7).
7. A Levite whom Nehemiah appointed to be in charge of the Temple storerooms (Neh. 13:13).

PEEP (Heb. *ṣāpap;* Isa. 8:19). Better, "whisper." *See* Magic.

PEG (Heb. *yātēd*).
1. Similar to a nail and usually made of wood (Isa. 22:25; Ezek. 15:3; both "pins" in the KJV).
2. The bronze pegs driven into the ground to hold the cords of the Tabernacle court (Ex. 27:19; 35:18; 38:20, 31; all are "pins" in the KJV) or for any other purpose or material (Judg. 4:21-22; 5:26; 16:14, "pin," KJV, NASB, NIV, although

Heb. is *yātēd*; Ezra 9:8, "nail," KJV, "firm place," NIV; Ezek. 15:3, "pin," KJV, "pegs," NIV).

Figurative. A tent peg was used as a general designation for national rulers (Zech. 10:4, "nail," KJV), who stand in relation to the commonwealth as a tent peg to the tent, which it holds firmly and keeps upright (Isa. 22:23, "nail," KJV). The figure in this passage is changed, so that Eliakim, instead of being honored, is likened to a peg driven into the wall and upon which his family hung. When the nail fell, all that hung upon it (his family) shared the same fate (v. 25). A similar use of peg is found in Ezra 9:8 ("nail," KJV), where the returned captives are spoken of as having "a peg in His holy place."

PE'KAH (pē'ka; God "has opened" the eyes). The eighteenth king of Israel. He is introduced into Scripture history as the son of Remaliah and captain of King Pekahiah, whom he murdered and succeeded to the throne (2 Kings 15:25), c. 740 B.C. Because fifty Gileadites were with him in the conspiracy it has been conjectured that he was a native of Gilead. Under his predecessors Israel had been much weakened through the payment of enormous tribute to the Assyrians (*see* especially 15:20) and by internal wars and conspiracies. Pekah steadily applied himself to the restoration of its power. For this purpose he sought for the support of a foreign alliance and fixed his mind on the plunder of the sister kingdom of Judah. He must have made the treaty by which he proposed to share its spoils with Rezin, king of Damascus, when Jotham was still on the throne of Jerusalem (15:37), but its execution was long delayed, probably in consequence of that prince's righteous and vigorous administration (2 Chron. 27). When, however, his weak son Ahaz succeeded to the crown of David, the allies no longer hesitated and besieged Jerusalem. The history of the war is found in 2 Kings 16 and 2 Chron. 28. It is famous as the occasion of the great prophecies in Isa. 7-9. Pekah was despoiled of at least half of his kingdom and fell into the position of an Assyrian vassal (2 Kings 15:29), c. 733 B.C. About a year later Hoshea conspired against him and put him to death (v. 30). Of his character and reign it is recorded, "He did evil in the sight of the Lord."

BIBLIOGRAPHY: T. Kirk and G. Rawlinson, *Studies in the Books of Kings* (1983), 2:161-65; E. R. Thiele, *Mysterious Numbers of the Hebrew Kings* (1983), pp. 64, 108, 128-29, 134-37, 174, 200.

PEKAHI'AH (pēk-a-hī'a; "Jehovah has opened [the eyes]," "Jehovah has observed"). The seventeenth king of Israel, being the son and successor of Menahem. After a brief reign of scarcely two years, 742-740 B.C., a conspiracy was organized against him by Pekah, who, at the head of fifty Gileadites, attacked him in his palace, murdered him and his friends Argob and Arieh, and seized the throne (2 Kings 15:23-26). His reign was an idolatrous one, as he followed in the sinful practices of Jeroboam.

PE'KOD (pē'kod). A strong Aramaean tribe (the Puqudu) dwelling in the plain E of the Tigris near its mouth. In Ezekiel's day these people were a part of the Chaldean Empire (Jer. 50:21; Ezek. 23:23).

PELAI'AH (pel-ī'yah).

1. A son of Elioenai and descendant of King Jehoiachin through Zerubbabel, Hananiah, and Shecaniah. He lived after the Exile (1 Chron. 3:24).

2. A Levite who assisted Ezra in interpreting the law to the throngs gathered to hear it read (Neh. 8:7). He also is likely the Levite who signed the covenant presented by Nehemiah (Neh. 10:10).

PELALI'AH (pel-a-li'yah). The grandfather of Adaiah, one of the priests assigned by lot to live in Jerusalem under Nehemiah's governorship (Neh. 11:12).

PELATI'AH (pel-a-tī'yah).

1. A descendant of King Jehoiachin through Zerubbabel and Hananiah (1 Chron. 3:21).

2. A Simeonite leader who helped in the defeat of the Amalekites in the days of Hezekiah (1 Chron. 4:42).

3. One of the leaders of the Judean people who signed the covenant offered by Nehemiah (Neh. 10:22).

4. Son of Benaiah and one of the leaders of Judah whom Ezekiel saw in vision as responsible for Judah's apostasy just before Jerusalem's fall to the Babylonians (Ezek. 11:1, 13).

PE'LEG (pe'leg; "division"). The son of Eber and fourth in descent from Shem. His brother's name was Joktan and his son's Reu (Gen. 10:25; 11:16-19; 1 Chron. 1:25). His name is said to have been given him because "in his days the earth was divided" (Gen. 10:25; 1 Chron. 1:19). The "division" referred to is enigmatic and may point to the scattering of Noah's descendants (Gen. 11:8).

PEL'ET.

1. A descendant of Caleb son of Hezron (1 Chron. 2:47). *See* Caleb, no. 2.

2. A Benjamite who joined David at Ziklag (1 Chron. 12:3).

PEL'ETHITE (pel'i-thīt; 2 Sam. 8:18; 15:18). The term is equivalent to *courier*, as one portion of the officials had to convey the king's orders to distant places (2 Chron. 30:6). Some believe the Pelethites and *Cherethites* (which see) to have been foreigners (Philistines, Ewald, *History of Israel*, 1:246; 3:143); but the evidence is meager.

PELICAN. *See* Animal Kingdom.

PEL'ONITE. Any citizen of Pelon, a place so far not identified (1 Chron. 11:27, 36; 27:10).

PELU'SIUM (pe-lū'si-um). A fortified city in the NE delta of Egypt and the name of the easternmost mouth of the Nile River (Ezek. 30:15-16, NIV; marg., NASB, for Sin).

PEN. *See* Writing.

PENCE. Replaced in the NASB by *denarii. See* "Denarius" in Metrology: Measures of Value, or Money.

PENI'EL (pe-ni'el; Gen. 32:30). *See* Penuel.

PENIN'NAH (pe-nīn'na). The wife of Elkanah who, unlike Hannah, was able to bear children (1 Sam. 1:2, 4).

PENNY. *See* "Denarius," in Metrology: Measures of Value, or Money.

PENTATEUCH. From Gk. *penta,* "five," *teuchos,* "a tool" or "implement"; a later Gk. term applied to the five books of Moses, which in their ancient scroll form were kept in sheaths or cases for protection. The Gk. term first appears in the second century A.D. and was later employed by Origen (J. E. Steinmueller, *Companion to Scripture Studies* [1942], 2:7).

Contents. The Pentateuch is the first of the three divisions of the ancient Hebrew canon, called earlier the law or Torah. It catalogs the giving of those religious and civil institutions that form the basis of ancient Israel's theocratic national life. This section of the Heb. Bible, introductory to the other two sections of the Prophets and the Writings, is composed of five books: Genesis, Exodus, Leviticus, Numbers, and Deuteronomy. Moses is the traditional author. It is by no means impossible that the original five-volume arrangement was executed by Moses himself. These books, especially Genesis, Leviticus, and Deuteronomy, are natural units in themselves. We may, therefore, conclude with Edward J. Young "that the five-volume division was the work of the original author of the Law, namely, Moses" (*Introduction to the O. T.* [1949], p. 48). If, however, such a five-volume division was not in effect from the beginning and the five books were originally one book, such a five-volume division was necessitated in later times for liturgical reasons to facilitate the reading of the law in the synagogue services. The explanation of this is that ancient books were in the cumbersome form of rolls or scrolls. A scroll 30 feet long would ordinarily accommodate the Heb. text of Genesis or Deuteronomy. If the length was longer than this, they became difficult to handle. The Hebrews were accustomed to employing the standard 30-foot size. It is true that the Egyptians sometimes used extremely long rolls like the Papyrus Harris, 133 feet long, and the Book of the Dead, 123 feet long. But these were definitely exceptions and antiquarian relics and not intended for everyday use. It can plainly be seen why the division of the Pentateuch would be necessitated. The five-volume division of the Pentateuch is attested by both Philo and Josephus in the first century A.D., and its existence goes back to LXX times (third century B.C.), and probably to the time of Ezra-Nehemiah.

Names. In the OT the Pentateuch is variously designated by names descriptive of its contents. It is called the "law" or "Torah" (Josh. 1:7), more fully "the book of the law of Moses" (8:31); "the book of the law" (8:34); "the book of the law of God" (24:26); "the law of Moses" (1 Kings 2:3); and "the book of the law of the Lord" (2 Chron. 17:9). The NT calls it "the book of the law" (Gal. 3:10); "the law of Moses" (Luke 2:22); "the Law of the Lord" (2:23); or simply "the Law" (Matt. 5:17; Luke 10:26).

Importance. The Pentateuch is of religious, historical, and cosmic importance.

Religious Importance. The Pentateuch is the foundation of all subsequent divine revelation. Both Christianity and Judaism rest on the inspired revelation of the Pentateuchal books. The Pentateuch describes the beginning of the cosmic universe, of man, of human sin, of human civilization, of the nations, and of God's redemptive program in type (Gen. 3:21) and prophecy (3:15). The three primary names of Deity—Jehovah, Elohim, and Adonai—and five of the most important compound names occur in the opening book of the Pentateuch. This volume initiates the program of progressive self-revelation of God culminating in Christ. Christ is the central theme of the Pentateuch. This portion is honeycombed with the miraculous and with typical, symbolic, and prophetic elements dealing with the Person and work of the coming divine Redeemer (cf. 1 Cor. 10:11).

Historical Importance. The Pentateuch is most intimately bound up with history and archaeology. The Pentateuch is not history in the strict sense of the term, however, but a highly specialized history of redemption, or almost a philosophy of the history of redemption. It has an all-pervading purpose to include only such historical background as is essential for introducing and preparing the stage for the Redeemer. In other words, the Pentateuch is history but more than history; it is history wedded to prophecy, a Messiah-centered history combining with a Messiah-centered prophecy. To consummate the redemptive plan it initiates, it has been called the philosophy of Israel's history (cf. Herbert C. Alleman, *O. T. Commentary* [1948], p. 171). In such a character, the Pentateuch catalogs the events concerning the origin of the Israelite people and their constitution as a theocratic nation. It interprets the old in the light of the nation's relationship to Jehovah and His redemptive purpose for the world. Archaeology has shed abundant light on the Pentateuch. Babylonian cuneiform tablets illustrate the creation and particularly the Flood, yielding amazing parallels of detail. The longevity

of the patriarchs is illustrated by the Sumerian king list. The Table of the Nations (Gen. 10) is shown by archaeological discoveries to be an amazing document. The patriarchal age is set in the framework of authentic history and the Egyptian sojourn, the Exodus, and the conquest are now much better understood as the result of the triumphs of scientific archaeology since 1800.

Cosmic Importance. The Pentateuchal account of the creation of the world and man stands unique in all ancient literature. All nonbiblical creation legends by their polytheistic crudity stand in striking contrast to Gen. 1:1–2:3. The unifying principle of the universe in one omnipresent and omniscient God is revealed through inspiration in the majestic Genesis account. Ancient Mesopotamian writers blindly groped after this principle. The Pentateuch is all the more striking against the background of a world grossly ignorant of the first principles of causation. The discovery of secondary causes and the explanation of the *how* of creation in its ongoing operation is the achievement of science. Revelation alone can sense the *why* of creation. The Bible alone discloses that the universe exists because God made it and has a definite redemptive purpose in it. Regarding its account of creation as outlined in Gen. 1, the "sequence of created phases" that it stipulates is "so rational that modern science cannot improve on it, given the same language and the same range of ideas in which to state its conclusions." In fact, "modern scientific cosmogonies show such a disconcerting tendency to be short-lived that it may be seriously doubted if science has yet caught up with the Biblical story" (W. F. Albright, *O. T. Commentary* [1948], p. 135). In its account of the Flood, the Pentateuch is also incomparably superior to the crudities and inconsistencies of the polytheistic account preserved in the eleventh book of the Assyro-Babylonian classic *The Epic of Gilgamesh.* For a summary of the higher criticism of the Pentateuch and its authorship, *see* Gleason Archer, *Survey of O. T. Introduction,* rev. ed. (1974), pp. 81-119.   M.F.U.

BIBLIOGRAPHY: F. Josephus *Antiquities of the Jews* 1.1.–4.8.49; W. H. Green, *Higher Criticism of the Pentateuch* (1906); M. G. Kyle, *Moses and the Monuments* (1920); id., *The Deciding Voice of the Monuments in Biblical Criticism* (1924); O. T. Allis, *The Five Books of Moses* (1949); W. J. Martin, *Stylistic Criteria and the Analysis of the Pentateuch* (1955); W. H. G. Thomas, *Through the Pentateuch Chapter by Chapter* (1957); U. Cassuto, *The Documentary Hypothesis and the Composition of the Pentateuch* (1961); L. J. Wood, *Survey of Israel's History* (1970), pp. 27-167; G. H. Livingstone, *The Pentateuch in Its Cultural Environment* (1974); D. J. A. Clines, *The Theme of the Pentateuch* (1978); R. de Vaux, *The Early History of Israel* (1978); W. G. Blaikie, *Heroes of Israel* (1981).

PENTECOST (pen'te-kost). *See* Festivals. As to the leading events of *the* Pentecost, namely, that which followed the death of our Lord, see Tongues, Gift of.

PENU'EL (pe-nu'el; "face of God").

1. The name of the place at which Jacob wrestled with God (Gen. 32:24-32; "Peniel," v. 30). The exact site is not known. It is placed not far from Succoth, E of the Jordan and N of the Jabbok. The people of Penuel seem to have treated Gideon scornfully when he pursued the Midianites across the Jordan, for which he threatened to destroy their tower (probably castle, Judg. 8:8-9, 17), which was rebuilt by Jeroboam (1 Kings 12:25).

2. A son of Hur, grandson of Judah, and father (i.e., founder) of Gedor (1 Chron. 4:4).

3. The last named of the eleven sons of Shashak, a leading man residing in Jerusalem (1 Chron. 8:25).

PE'OR (pē'or; "opening, cleft").

1. A mountain in Moab, to the top of which Balak led the prophet *Balaam* (which see), that he might see and curse the host of Israel (Num. 23:28, where it is written, "Peor which overlooks the wasteland," i.e., the wilderness on either side of the Dead Sea). Mt. Peor was one peak of the northern part of the mountains of Abarim by the town of Beth-peor and opposite to where Israel encamped in the steppes of Moab (Deut. 3:29; 4:46).

2. In four places (Num. 25:18, twice; 31:16; Josh. 22:17) Peor occurs as a contraction for Baal-peor (cf. Num. 25:3, 5, margs.).

3. The "Peor" referred to in Num. 25:18; 31:16 is the god *Baal-peor*. See Gods, False.

PERATH (pe-rath'). The Heb. word for the *Euphrates* (which see) and the term used in the NIV of Jer. 13:4-7 ("Parah," marg., NASB, 13:4).

PERA'ZIM (per-ā'zim). Another name (Isa. 28:21) for *Baal-perazim* (which see).

PERDITION, SON OF (Gk. *huios tēs apoleias*). The Gk. *apoleia*, a "perishing, destruction," is rendered "perdition" in the NASB only in John 17:12, where Jesus calls Judas Iscariot "the son of perdition" and refers to his end as the fulfillment of Scripture. The Jews frequently expressed a man's destiny by calling him "the son" of the same. Elsewhere, KJV "perdition" is rendered in the NASB and NIV by "destruction" (cf. 2 Thess. 2:3; 1 Tim. 6:9; Heb. 10:39; 2 Pet. 3:7; Rev. 17:8, 11). The best commentary on this statement is made by Peter (Acts 1:20).

PE'RES (pe'res; Aram. *peras*, to "split up"). One of the three words of the writing on the wall interpreted by Daniel (Dan. 5:28), being the singular of the word rendered "Upharsin" (v. 25). The meaning of the verb is to "divide into pieces," to "dissolve" the kingdom.

PE'RESH. A son of Machir (Makir, NIV) and his

wife Maacah of the tribe of Manasseh (1 Chron. 7:16). *See* Machir, Makir, no. 1.

PE'REZ (pe'rez, "breach"; sometimes "Phares," or "Pharez," KJV). A twin son (with Zarah) of Judah by Tamar (his daughter-in-law; Gen. 38:29; 1 Chron. 2:4). Little is known of his personal history, although his family is often mentioned. He and his brothers were numbered among the sons of Judah (Gen. 46:12), and after the death of Er and Onan he is named as the second son (Num. 26:20). His family was numerous, as is shown in Ruth 4:12: "May your house be like the house of Perez whom Tamar bore to Judah." His descendants were notable in the time of David (1 Chron. 27:2-3) and after the captivity (1 Chron. 9:4; Neh. 11:4-6).

PE'REZ-UZ'ZAH, PE'REZ-UZZA (pe'rez-uz'a; "the breach of Uzzah," 2 Sam. 6:8; 2 Chron. 13:11). A place also called Nacon (2 Sam. 6:6) and Chidon (1 Chron. 13:9), the place where *Uzzah* (which see) died as a result of touching the Ark of God (2 Sam. 6:6-8). About a mile and a half or two miles from the site of Kiriath-jearim on the road to Jerusalem is a small village still called Khirbet el-Uz, or "the ruins of Uzzah." This seems to be Perez-uzzah.

PERFECTER (Gk. *teleiōtēs,* "completer"). Spoken of Jesus (Heb. 12:2, NASB and NIV) as one who in His own person raised faith to its perfection and so set before us the highest example of faith. The KJV renders "finisher."

PERFECTION, PERFECT. The rendering of several Heb. and Gk. words. The fundamental idea is that of completeness. Absolute perfection is an attribute of God alone. In the highest sense He alone is complete, or wanting nothing. His perfection is eternal and without defect. It is the ground and standard of all other perfection (*see* Job 36:4; 37:16; Matt. 5:48). A relative perfection is also ascribed to God's works. It is also either ascribed to men or required of them. By this is meant complete conformity to those requirements as to character and conduct that God has appointed. But this, it is constantly to be borne in mind, has reference to the gracious government of God that takes account of man's present debilitated condition (*see* Gen. 6:9; 17:1; Job 1:1, 8; 2:3; Matt. 5:48; Phil. 3:15; James 3:2; 1 Pet. 5:10; etc.). The term *perfection* as applied to man's present moral life has been a subject of much contention. The propriety of using the word as in any sense of actual description has even been denied. But fidelity to the Scriptures requires us to believe that, in some important sense, Christians may be perfect even in this life, although they still must wait for perfection in a larger sense in the life that is to come. This important sense in which the Bible presents man's present perfection relates to the believer's *position* in union with Christ by the Spirit's baptizing work (Rom. 6:3-4; Gal. 3:27; Col. 2:10-12; 1 Cor. 12:13). Being placed "in Christ," the Christian acquires a perfect position, because the Father sees him in the Son's perfection. As far as his actual experience is concerned, however, the Christian realizes his *perfect position* only in proportion as he believes in what he is "in Christ." He is what he is "in Christ" ("perfect," i.e., "complete," Col. 2:9-10), whether he reckons on it or not. The difference is that his *position of perfection* becomes *experiential* as he believes himself to be what he *is* "in Christ" (Rom. 6:11). For fuller discussion of this we refer to articles in this work. *See* Sanctification; Sin.

BIBLIOGRAPHY: J. Wesley, *A Plain Account of Christian Perfection* (1777); B. B. Warfield, *Perfectionism* (1931), 1:113-341; R. N. Flew, *The Idea of Perfection in Christian Theology* (1934), pp. 1-117; L. S. Chafer, *He That Is Spiritual* (1965); J. Fletcher, *The Works of the Rev. John Fletcher* (1974), 1:270-71, 381-82, 589; 2:492-526, 554-643, 658-59; N. Turner, *Christian Words* (1980), pp. 324-29.

PERFUME. Such passages as the following: "Oil and perfume make the heart glad" (Prov. 27:9); "All Thy garments are fragrant with myrrh" (Ps. 45:8); "What is this coming up from the wilderness like columns of smoke, perfumed with myrrh and frankincense?" (Song of Sol. 3:6); "And you have journeyed to the king with oil and increased your perfumes" (Isa. 57:9), and others, give abundant and striking evidence of the use and love of perfume in the East. In hot climates the use of perfumes is a sanitary necessity. They not only mask bad smells but correct them and are wonderfully reviving to the spirits from the depression that they fall into in crowded places. There can be but little doubt, from what may be observed in the East, that the use of sweet odors in religious rites generally has originated in sanitary precautions. Being but little acquainted with soap, their chief substitutes for it were ointments and other preparations of gums, woods, etc. The Hebrews manufactured their perfumes chiefly from spices imported from Arabia, among which the following are mentioned in Scripture: *Algum* (2 Chron. 2:8; 9:10-11) or *almug* (1 Kings 10:11-12); *balm* (Gen. 37:25; 43:11; Jer. 8:22; 46:11; etc.); *bdellium* (Gen. 2:12; Num. 11:7); *frankincense* (Ex. 30:34; Lev. 2:1-2; 24:7; etc.); *galbanum* (Ex. 30:34); *myrrh* (30:23; Ps. 45:8; Prov. 7:17; Song of Sol. 1:13; Matt. 2:11; John 19:39; etc.); *onycha* (Ex. 30:34); *saffron* (Song of Sol. 4:14); *nard* (Mark 14:3; John 12:3); and *stacte* (Ex. 30:34). These perfumes were generally in the form of *ointments* (which see), *incense* (which see), or extracted by some process of boiling and then mixed with oil. Perfumes entered largely into the Temple service, in the two forms of incense and ointment (30:22-38). Nor were they less used in private life; not only were they applied to the person but to garments (Ps. 45:8; Song of Sol. 4:11) and to articles of furniture, such as beds (Prov. 7:17). On the arrival of a guest the same compliments were probably paid in ancient as in modern times (Dan. 2:46). When a royal personage went abroad in his litter (covered and curtained couch carried by shafts), attendants threw up "columns of smoke" about his path (Song of Sol. 3:6). The use of perfumes was omitted in times of mourning, whence the allusion in Isa. 3:24.

BIBLIOGRAPHY: A. Lucas, *Journal of Egyptian Archaeology* 27 (1937): 27-33; id., *Ancient Egyptian Materials and Industries* (1948), pp. 353-55, 359-64; G. W. van Beek, *Journal of the American Oriental Society* 41 (1958): 141-52.

PERFUME BOXES. *See* Dress.

PERFUMER (*rāqah,* to "perfume," Ex. 30:25; 37:39; Eccles. 10:1). *See* Handicrafts: Perfumer; Oils and Ointment; Perfume.

PER'GA (per'ga). The capital of Pamphylia, located on the river Cestrus, about seven miles from its mouth, was visited by Paul when on his first missionary journey (Acts 13:13-14). It was celebrated for the worship of Artemis (Diana), whose temple stood on a hill outside the town. (*See* Artemis; Gods, False.) Arif Mansel of Istanbul University conducted excavations at Perga in 1946, 1953-1957, and from 1967 to his death in 1975 on behalf of the Turkish Historical Society. Jale Inan of Istanbul University has been excavating there since 1975. The city consists of an acropolis on its N side and the major part of the city that lay at its feet on the S. The city was divided into four quarters by two colonnaded streets. Most of the city wall dates to the Hellenistic period, but a later addition on the S dates to the fourth century A.D. Outside the wall on the S stand the theater and stadium and inside the walls numerous structures, including baths, a palestra, an agora, two churches, and a fountain.

H.F.V.

BIBLIOGRAPHY: W. M. Ramsay, *St. Paul the Traveller and Roman Citizen* (1960), pp. 89ff., 98f., 123f., 135f.;

Fragments from the ruins at Perga

E. D. S. Bradford, *Paul the Traveller* (1974), pp. 115-17, 123, 132.

PER'GAMUM (per'ga-mum). A city of Mysia in Asia Minor, about three miles N of the river Bakyrtchai (the ancient Caicus) and about twenty miles from the sea. It had a vast library of 200,000 volumes, which was moved by Antony to Egypt and presented to Cleopatra. In this town was first discovered the art of making parchment, which was called *pergamena*. The city was greatly addicted to idolatry, and its grove, which was one of the wonders of the place, was filled with statues and altars. Antipas met martyrdom here (Rev. 2:13), and here was one of the seven churches of Asia (v. 12). The wealth of the Attalic princes had raised Pergamum to the rank of the first city in Asia as regards splendor. It was a sort of union of a pagan cathedral city, a university town, and a royal residence, embellished during a succession of years by kings who all had a passion for expenditure and ample means of gratifying it.

The acropolis of the city seems to have been well fortified as early as the fourth century B.C. Attalos I (241-197 B.C.) began to construct the magnificent buildings that were to earn the city a pristine place among ancient Greek centers. Eumenes II (197-159) erected the most magnificent structures of the acropolis. Systematic study of Pergamum began in 1878 after the German engineer Carl Human (now buried on the Pergamum acropolis) discovered the great altar of Zeus (believed by some to be Satan's seat, Rev. 2:13), now in East Berlin. Major archaeological campaigns have been conducted there: 1878-86, 1900-1913, 1927-36, 1957-72, and 1975 to the present. Most of the structures on the acropolis have now been laid bare, as has the famous asclepion, or hospital complex, in the lower city of the Roman period. I. U. Rombock of the German Ar-

Ruins at Pergamum

chaeological Institute has been directing restoration of the temple of Hadrian on the acropolis since 1976.   H.F.V.

BIBLIOGRAPHY: A. H. M. Jones, *The Cities of the Eastern Roman Empire* (1937); W. Barclay, *Letters to the Seven Churches* (1958); F. A. Tatford, *The Patmos Letters* (1969); W. M. Ramsay, *The Seven Letters to the Churches of Asia* (1975).

PERI'DA (pe-rī'da; Neh. 7:57). *See* Peruda.

PERISHABLE (Gk. *phthartos; phthora;* also *'apollumi,* lit., "perishes"). Paul uses this word (1 Cor. 15:42, 50, 53-54, NASB and NIV) in connection with the body and in contrast with the word *imperishable* (Gk. *'aphtharsia; 'aphthartos*) when describing the resurrection of the dead; i.e., what is perishable belongs to this life and to the unresurrected, whereas the imperishable is equated with a new life and immortality. The same thought is expressed in 9:25, where Paul speaks of receiving the imperishable rather than the perishable wreath ("crown," KJV). Except for 1 Pet. 1:7 (Gk. *'apollumi*), where the KJV uses *perisheth,* the NASB and NIV term *perishable* replaces KJV *corruptible,* or *corruption.*

PER'IZZITES (per'i-zīts; Heb. always *happerîzî*). "The Perizzite," one of the nations whose land was given to Israel. They are not named in Gen. 10, and their origin is not known. They first appear (13:7) as dwelling in the land together with the Canaanites in Abram's day (34:30). In Judg. 1:4-5 they dwell in the land given to Judah, in southern Palestine, Bezek being apparently the stronghold of the Canaanites and Perizzites, though it may have been merely a rallying point. In Josh. 17:15-18 the Perizzites and *Rephaim* (which see) dwell in the "hill country" near Mt. Ephraim, in the land of Ephraim and West Manasseh. They appear as late as the time of Solomon, who made them, with other Canaanite tribes, tributary to Israel (1 Kings 9:20; 2 Chron. 8:7). A late echo is in 2 Esd. 1:21, where "the Canaanites, the Perezites, and the Philistines" are named as the original inhabitants of the land. The "unwalled towns" (*'ārê happerāzî,* Deut. 3:5) and the "country villages" (*kōphĕr happerāzî,* 1 Sam. 6:18) are translated by the LXX as referring to the Perizzites, whence it has been suggested that Perizzite may mean "a dweller in an unwalled village," as does *pārūz* in the Mishna. We may compare the Arab. word meaning *low ground between hills* (where the unwalled villages would grow up). The LXX probably read *happerîzî.*   W.H.; M.F.U.

PERJURY. *See* Oath: Sanctity.

PERSEVERANCE. A term used both in ethics and theology. In ethics it denotes the duty and privilege of a Christian to continue steadfastly in obedience and fidelity to Christ, not in order to inherit eternal life but to demonstrate love and gratitude to Christ for His great salvation (1 Cor. 15:58; Rev. 3:2). Arminian views stipulate this faithfulness to inherit eternal life, but Calvinists hold that the NT teachings testify to the safety and security of the believer as a result of his faith in Christ and his resulting position in Christ (Rom. 8:28-39; Eph. 1:1-14; 2:8-10; etc.). The Christian's fidelity and obedience will be rewarded at the judgment seat of Christ. His salvation is not affected by lack of human faithfulness, but his rewards are. Calvinists teach that final perseverance is a result of the doctrine of unconditional election. Thus the Westminster Confession says, "This perseverance of the saints depends not upon their own free will but upon the immutability of the decree of election flowing from the free and unchangeable love of God the Father. . . ." In other words, those who are real Christians cannot fall away or be eternally lost. Their position in Christ by the baptizing work of the Holy Spirit assures their eternal salvation. When men begin to interject human faithfulness and human works into the question of their eternal salvation, they take it off the rock of Christ's finished work and place it upon a flimsy basis. If getting to heaven depended upon human merit or faithfulness in any degree, no human being would ever get there or claim merit for entrance. Christ will abundantly reward faithfulness in His redeemed children, but He can never accept their faithfulness as merit for salvation. Failure to distinguish between salvation and rewards has confused this subject in theological thinking and this is, accordingly, a much disputed doctrine.

M.F.U.

PERSIA. A world empire that flourished from 539 to 331 B.C.

The Early History. The original native name

Parsa, or Persia, was descriptive of the homeland of the Persians in the western and larger part of the Iranian plateau that extended from the Indus on the E to the Tigris on the W. Iran was another native designation of the land. This name was officially restored in 1935 by the Persian government and means "the [land] of the Aryans." It is descriptive of the people of Aryan language who came into the highland (c. 1500 B.C.). The Amadai, or Medes, and the inhabitants of the land of Parsua W of Lake Urmia, or Persians, were the two Aryan tribes that were to come into the greatest prominence. The Medes occupied the NW portion of the territory. Their capital city was Hagmatana, later Ecbatana, modern Hamadan. Cyaxares, the Mede, was confederate with Nabopolassar in the fall of Nineveh in 612 B.C. Gradually the Persians migrated southward and settled in Anshan in a portion of country that they called Parsamash, in recollection of their old homeland of Parsua. Around 700 B.C. their leader was named Achaemenes. This name prevailed in the later Persian kings. About the middle of the seventh century B.C. the king of Parsamash was called Tiespes. He was a notable conqueror and increased the territories of the Persians E of Anshan and N of the Persian Gulf. This extended country became known as Parsa or Persian Land.

Cyrus II, The Great. The founder of the mighty Persian Empire ascended the throne of Anshan c. 559 B.C. Astyages, the Mede, was conquered by Cyrus who took Ecbatana. Henceforth Cyrus grew greater and greater with Parsa taking the lead, Media coming second, and Elam third. The supremacy of the Persians was hereafter established, although the Medes continued to be held in high esteem. Reference is made in Scripture to "Persia and Media" (Esther 1:19), as well

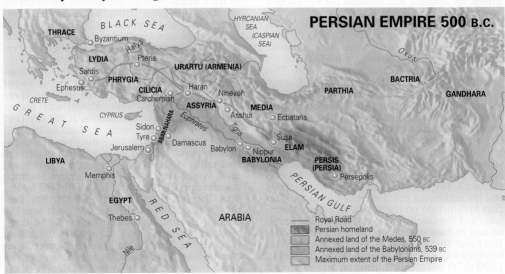

PERSIAN EMPIRE 500 B.C.

Royal Road
Persian homeland
Annexed land of the Medes, 550 BC
Annexed land of the Babylonians, 539 BC
Maximum extent of the Persian Empire

as "the Medes and Persians" (Dan. 5:28). With lightning-like rapidity Cyrus extended his conquests, defeating Croesus of Lydia (c. 546 B.C.) and Babylon (539 B.C.), thus establishing the mighty Persian Empire. Cyrus was a remarkably humane leader (cf. Isa. 45:1-4). It was he who issued the decree restoring the Jews to their homeland (2 Chron. 36:22-23; Ezra 1:2-4). Archaeology has demonstrated that Cyrus's concession to the exiles was not an isolated account of generosity but a general policy of a remarkably beneficent leader of winning the favor of his new subjects by showing consideration for their religious beliefs. Cyrus's capital was Pasargadae in the land of Parsa. On his ruined palace can still be read the repeated words, "I, Cyrus the king, the Achaemenid." Cyrus was killed in battle in 530 B.C. His body was returned to Pasargadae and buried in a tomb that is still extant. Plutarch (c. A.D. 46-120) says the inscription on the tomb ran thus: "O man, whosoever thou art and whensoever thou comest, for I know that thou wilt come, I am Cyrus and I won for the Persians their empire. Do not, therefore, begrudge me this little earth which covers my body."

Cambyses II (530-522 B.C.) was Cyrus's son, who conquered Egypt. Shortly after his Egyptian triumphs civil war broke out, evidently led by his brother Bardiya or Smerdis. Cambyses is believed to have suffered a self-inflicted wound as he leaped on his horse in a hurry and in an excited state to ride off to deal with the insurrection. Reportedly the chape of Cambyses' dagger sheath came off, and he accidently stabbed himself in the thigh and died about three weeks later somewhere in Syria. The Persian Empire almost collapsed in the confusion that followed; but Darius seems to have assassinated Bardiya, won the throne for himself, and subdued the revolts that broke out in the various provinces.

Darius I, The Great (522-486 B.C.). This powerful ruler put down the rebellion, saved the empire, and recorded his victory over his enemies on the famous Rock of Behistun, visible from the old caravan road from Ecbatana to Babylon. This pivotal monument, with its trilingual inscriptions describing Darius's quelling of the insurrection, furnished the key to the decipherment of Akkad. cuneiform, just as the Rosetta Stone opened up the ancient language of the Nile River. Darius ruled a vast empire. The closing years of his reign saw the outbreak of the Graeco-Persian wars and the defeat of Persia at Marathon (490 B.C.), a precursor to the later defeat at Salamis (480 B.C.). The mighty empire over which Darius and his successors ruled extended from the Grecian Archipelago on the W, the Caucasus Mountains and the Caspian Sea on the N, to the Arabian and Nubian deserts on the S (cf. Esther 1:1; 10:1) and the Indus River on the E. This vast territory was nearly 3,000 miles long and 500 to 1,500 miles wide, constituting an area of some 2 million square miles. In this huge kingdom Judah was a tiny dependency practically lost in the vast stretch of empire.

Xerxes (485-465 B.C.). Xerxes followed his father Darius on the Persian throne. This king, as well as his father, was devoted to Ahura-Mazda. Xerxes is evidently the Ahasuerus of the book of Esther. Esther did not become queen until the seventh year of Xerxes' reign (478 B.C.), after his return from his defeat in Greece (480 B.C.) when Herodotus states that he paid attention to his harem (9.108). Although the queen at this time is said to have been Amestris, certainly Xerxes, from what we know of him, may well have had other wives.

Artaxerxes I Longimanus (464-423 B.C.). Artaxerxes I succeeded Xerxes. In his reign Nehemiah was cupbearer and visited Jerusalem (Neh. 2:1). The Elephantine Papyri, discovered in 1903 on the island of Elephantine at the First Cataract of Egypt, shed important light on the Artaxerxes-Nehemiah era. Ezra 7:1-8 specifies that Ezra journeyed to Jerusalem in Artaxerxes' seventh year. This was 458 B.C., if Artaxerxes I is meant. In such a case Ezra precedes Nehemiah. However, some construe Artaxerxes to be Artaxerxes II, the seventh year of whose reign would be 398 B.C. (cf. Ezra 10:6).

Later Kings. Following Artaxerxes I the splendid Persian throne was occupied by Darius II (423-404 B.C.), Artaxerxes II Mnemon (404-359 B.C.), Artaxerxes III Ochus (359-338 B.C.), Arses (338-335 B.C.), and Darius III (335-331 B.C.), when the far-flung Persian Empire fell to the conquests of Alexander the Great.

Persia and Archaeology. Persian archaeology may be said to have had its beginning in 1835, when Henry C. Rawlinson, with the British army in Iran, began to copy the famous Behistun inscription, the great trilingual inscription (Persian, Akkad., and Elamite) cut by Darius on a cliff about five hundred feet above a plain W of Ecbatana. Rawlinson himself was to decipher the Persian and Akkad. parts of this inscription.

Actual excavation began at Susa (biblical Shushan) in 1854 when the British archaeologist W. K. Loftus sank the first trial trenches there and identified it as Susa. Marcel and Jeanne Dieulafoy conducted excavations at the site (150 miles N of the head of the Persian Gulf) from 1884 to 1886. Then in 1897 the French Delegation in Persia started work at Susa under the leadership of Jacques de Morgan and continued until World War I. R. de Mequenem assumed directorship after the war, to be followed by Roman Ghirshman and since 1967 by M. Jean Perrot. One of de Morgan's greatest finds was the Code of Hammurabi, which turned up in three pieces in December 1901 and January 1902. Susa is a large site. Four gigantic mounds, covering an area of 300 acres, stand on the E bank of the Shaur River, and a smaller mound rises W of the river. For details of discovery *see* article Susa. Between World Wars I and II Persian archaeology was put on a more firm footing. In 1927 the Iranian Archaeological Service was established, and national activity began in the field of archaeology. André Godard, a distinguished French archaeologist, directed the service from 1931 to 1960.

Though many sites have been attacked by domestic and foreign teams, the two sites most important for the present study are Pasargadae and Persepolis. Cyrus the Great established his main capital at Pasargadae, about forty-five miles NE of the later complex at Persepolis. Pasargadae is said to have been founded on the site of Cyrus's victory over Astyages the Mede, which gave him control over the empire. The first archaeological soundings were made at Pasargadae in the first decade of the twentieth century by Ernst Herzfeld. Ali Sami, the director of the Archaeological Institute at Persepolis, began a five-year dig in 1949. David Stronach, director of the British Institute of Persian Studies in Tehran, excavated there from 1961 to 1963. At the SW edge of Pasargadae stands the tomb of Cyrus. Its stepped stone base measures about forty-five by thirty-eight feet and the tomb chamber itself about seventeen by seventeen feet and nineteen feet high. Its gabled roof stands to a height of about thirty-five feet from the ground. About a half mile to the NE of the tomb is a complex of palaces: an audience hall, a garden pavilion, a gatehouse, and a residential palace. These structures were built of black and white limestone. The residential palace consisted of a central hall with thirty stone columns on black and white square subbases. Another half mile to the NE lay the citadel area of Pasargadae.

Persepolis (thirty miles NE of Shiraz in central western Iran) was built between about 520 and 450 B.C., not so much as a political capital as a ceremonial shrine for the celebration of the Persian new year festival. Although some archaeological work was done there as early as 1878, the first definitive and major excavation at the site was carried on by the Oriental Institute of the University of Chicago under the leadership of Ernst Herzfeld and Erich Schmidt (1931-39). The Iranian Archaeological Service continued work there during and after World War II. Persepolis is a great complex built at an elevation of 5,800 feet on a massive stone platform 40 feet high and covering 33 acres. Darius I constructed the platform and worked out the master plan for the structures in advance. He also built a stairway up to the platform, his private palace, and the treasury, and began the Apadana or audience hall. Xerxes completed the Apadana, a monumental gateway, his own palace, and the so-called harem. Artaxerxes I completed the Throne Hall and may have constructed a private palace. The great Apadana was 197 feet square and its roof was

supported by 36 65-foot columns, 13 of which remain standing. About 6 miles N of Persepolis is Naksh-i Rustam, a rock cliff with royal tombs cut into it. These are commonly believed to be of Darius II, Artaxerxes I, Darius I, and Xerxes I.

M.F.U.; H.F.V.

BIBLIOGRAPHY: G. G. Cameron, *The History of Early Iran* (1936); id., *Persepolis Treasury Tablets* (1948); A. T. Olmstead, *History of the Persian Empire* (1948); D. J. Wiseman, ed., *Peoples of Old Testament Times* (1973), pp. 312-57; J. M. Cook, *The Persian Empire* (1983).

Persepolis

PER'SIS (per'sis; Gk. *Persian*). A Christian woman at Rome to whom Paul sent salutations (Rom. 16:12).

PERSONALITY. In theology as in metaphysics, personality is that which constitutes a person. Says Locke: "A person is a thinking, intelligent being that has reason and reflection, and can consider itself as itself, the same thinking thing in different times and places." In other words, the distinguishing marks of personality are self-consciousness and freedom.

1. According to the Scriptures, God is a person. He is not merely an eternal substance but the one eternal free and self-conscious Being. He says "I" and teaches men to say "thou." The Bible doctrine of God is therefore not opposed only to atheism, which denies His existence, but also to pantheism, which merges His existence in that of the universe. It is objected, as by Mansel, e.g., that personality implies limitation and therefore implies a contradiction in our thought of God, thus illustrating the limits of religious thought. This objection is ably answered by Hodge (*Systematic Theology*, vol. 1, chaps. 4-5), where he shows that it is founded upon an arbitrary definition of the absolute and infinite. Also Mansel himself, a Christian theist, says upon this sub-

ject: "It is our duty to think of God as personal, and it is our duty to believe that he is infinite." Further, Hodge suggests, with respect to the objection that "without a thou there can be no I," that according to the Scriptures and the faith of the church, there are in the unity of the Godhead three distinct Persons—the Father, the Son, and the Holy Spirit, "so that from eternity the Father can say I and the Son thou." The personality of God as a fact apprehended by our faith is essential to religion. "We do not worship a law, however simple and fruitful it may be; we do not worship a force if it is blind, however powerful, however universal it may be; nor an ideal, however pure, if it be an abstraction. We worship only a Being who is living perfection, perfection under the highest form—Thought, Love." *See* Trinity; Freedom.

2. Man is also a person. In this respect he is distinct from things and from animals. This is one of the features of his likeness to his Creator. Here is the basis of his moral obligation. *See* Image of God; Freedom.   E. MCC.; M.F.U.

BIBLIOGRAPHY: Various theories of personality are found in T. Leary, *Interpersonal Diagnosis of Personality* (1957); R. Ruddock, ed., *Six Approaches to the Person* (1972); J. W. Thomas, *Bi/Polar: A Positive Way of Understanding People* (1978); R. M. Ryckman, *Theories of Personality* (1982); C. S. Hall and G. Lindsey, *Theories of Personality* (1978); B. R. Hagenhahn, *Introduction to Theories of Personality* (1980); S. Maddi, *Personality Theories* (1980).

PERU'DA (pe-rū'da; "divided, separated"). The name of one of "Solomon's servants," whose descendants returned with Zerubbabel from Babylon (Ezra 2:55), before 536 B.C. In Neh. 7:57 he is called Perida.

PERVERSE, PERVERSITY. Habitually disobedient (Deut. 32:20, KJV, "froward"); deceit, falsehood (Prov. 2:12; 6:14; etc.).

PESTILENCE (Heb. *deber;* Gk. *loimos*). The Heb. term seems to have originally meant "destruction" but is regularly applied to that common oriental epidemic the *plague* (which see). The prophets usually connect sword, pestilence, and famine (2 Sam. 24:15). *See also* Disease.

PESTLE (Heb. *'elî,* "lifted"). The instrument used for grinding in a mortar (Prov. 27:22) in order to separate the grain from the husk.

PE'TER (pē'ter; Gk. *petros,* "a rock"). Formerly Simon. Peter was the son of Jonas (John 1:42; 21:15-16) and probably a native of Bethsaida in Galilee (1:44).

Occupation. Peter and his brother Andrew were fishermen on the Sea of Galilee (Matt. 4:18; Mark 1:16) and partners of James and John (Luke 5:10). Although his occupation was a humble one, it was not incompatible with some degree of mental culture and seems to have been quite profitable.

Meets Jesus. With his brother Andrew, Peter was a disciple of John the Baptist; and when their teacher pointed out Jesus to Andrew as the Lamb of God, Andrew went to Peter and told him, "We have found the Messiah." He brought him to Jesus, who looked upon him and said, "You are Simon the son of John; you shall be called Cephas" (John 1:36-42). This interview resulted in no immediate change in Peter's external position. He returned to Capernaum and continued his usual vocation, waiting for further instruction.

Call. This was received on the Sea of Galilee, where the four partners were engaged in fishing. The people were pressing upon Jesus to hear the word, and He entered Peter's boat. At Christ's request the boat was thrust out a little from the land so He could discourse with the multitude. After this He wrought the miracle of the great haul of fish, foreshadowing the success of the apostles as fishers of men (Luke 5:1-7). Peter and Andrew immediately accepted the call and, leaving all, were soon after joined by James and John, who also received a call to follow the Master (Matt. 4:18-22; Mark 1:16-20; Luke 5:8-11), A.D. 27. Immediately after this Jesus wrought the miracle of healing on Peter's wife's mother (Matt. 8:14-15; Mark 1:29-31; Luke 4:38-40), and Peter for some time attended upon our Lord's ministry in Galilee, Decapolis, Perea, and Judea, returning at intervals to his own city. During this period he was selected as one of the witnesses of the raising of Jairus's daughter (Mark 5:22, 37; Luke 8:41, 51).

Apostle. The special designation of Peter and his eleven fellow disciples took place some time afterward, when they were set apart as the Lord's immediate attendants (Matt. 10:2-4; Mark 3:13-19; Luke 6:13-16). They appear then first to have received formally the name of apostles, and from that time Simon bore publicly, it would seem almost exclusively, the name *Peter,* which had up to this time been used rather as a characteristic term than as a proper name.

Walks on the Sea. On one occasion a boat, in which were a number of the disciples, was in the midst of the sea, tossed with waves. Jesus appeared walking on the sea, much to the alarm of the disciples, who said, "It is a ghost!" Hearing His words of encouragement, Peter put the Master to the test by saying, "Lord, if it is You, command me to come to You on the water." Jesus replied, "Come!" and Peter, obeying, walked for a while on the surface of the sea. But losing his confidence because of the tempest, he began to sink, and he uttered the cry "Lord, save me!" The Master took him by the hand and accompanied him to the ship. When safe in the boat Peter fell down at His feet and declared, "You are certainly God's Son!" (Matt. 14:25-33).

We find him asking the meaning of our Lord's parable of the blind leading the blind (15:15).

Confession. In a conversation with His disciples as to men's declarations concerning Himself, Jesus asked, "But who do you say that I am?" Peter promptly replied, "Thou art the Christ, the Son of the living God." In His reply the Master made the declaration, so often commented upon, "You are Peter, and upon this rock I will build My church," etc. (Matt. 16:13-19; Mark 8:27-29; Luke 9:18-20).

Rebukes Jesus. Our Lord on one occasion began to inform His disciples of His coming sufferings and death. "Peter took Him aside and began to rebuke Him, saying, 'God forbid it, Lord!' "But Jesus turned and said to Peter, "Get behind Me, Satan!" etc. (Matt. 16:21-23; Mark 8:31-33). The Lord seems to have been calling Peter Satan. Not quite so. But He recognized Satan speaking in the words that Peter uttered.

Mount of Transfiguration. Peter, with James and John, was a witness of the Lord's transfiguration and in the ecstasy of the hour exclaimed, "Lord, it is good for us to be here; if You wish, I will make three tabernacles here, one for You, and one for Moses, and one for Elijah" (Matt. 17:1-4; Mark 9:2-5; Luke 9:28-33).

Mention is made of Peter's inquiry as to forgiveness (Matt. 18:21); declaration of having left all for Jesus' sake (19:27; Mark 10:28; Luke 18:28); asking the meaning of the parable of the overturning of the Temple (Mark 13:3) and of the servant watching for his master (Luke 12:41); and calling the Master's attention to the withered fig tree (Mark 11:21).

The Last Supper. When Jesus would keep the Passover He commissioned Peter and John to make proper preparation (Luke 22:8). All being ready for the supper, Jesus began to wash the disciples' feet; but when He came to Peter he, in his presumptuous humility, declared, "Never shall You wash my feet!" But upon the Master's replying, "If I do not wash you, you have no part with Me," Peter consented, with the request that the washing might include also hands and head (John 13:3-9). When our Lord declared that one of them would betray Him, Peter beckoned to John that he should ask of whom He spoke (13:24). Still later he stoutly asserted that under no circumstances would he ever leave his Master, to which Jesus replied by saying, "Simon, Simon, behold, Satan has demanded permission to sift you like wheat," and told him of his speedy denial (Luke 22:31-34; Matt. 26:33-35; Mark 14:29-31; John 13:36-38).

At Gethsemane. Peter and the two sons of Zebedee accompanied Jesus to Gethsemane (Matt. 26:36-37; Mark 14:32-33), and when Judas came with his company to apprehend the Lord, Peter drew his sword and cut off the right ear of Malchus, a slave of the high priest, for which he was promptly rebuked (Matt. 26:51-52; John 18:10-11).

Denial. When Jesus was apprehended, Peter, along with John, followed Him at a distance to the palace of Caiaphas and entered into his court. While he was there a slave girl said to him, "You are not also one of this man's disciples, are you?" Peter answered, "I am not" (John 18:15-17; Matt. 26:58, 69-70; Mark 14:66-68; Luke 22:55-57). Peter's *second* denial occurred on the porch, to which he had withdrawn. Another servant girl declared to those who were standing about, "This man was with Jesus of Nazareth." Peter, with an oath, denied even an acquaintance with Jesus (Matt. 26:71-72; Mark 14:69-70; Luke 22:58, where the accuser was a man; John 18:25). His *third* denial was uttered after a while (Luke says *an hour*) and was in reply to some who charged him with being one of the disciples of Jesus, saying, "The way you talk gives you away." Peter probably made some remark in his Galilean dialect. He cursed and swore, then declared, "I do not know the man!" The crowing of the cock and the look of our Lord awakened Peter to a sense of his guilt, "and he went out and wept bitterly" (Matt. 26:73-75; Mark 14:70-72; Luke 22:59-62; John 18:26-27).

At the Sepulcher. On the morning of the resurrection, the women, finding the stone removed from the door of the sepulcher, hastened to tell the disciples. Mary Magdalene outran the rest and told Peter and John, who immediately ran toward the spot. John arrived before Peter but did not enter the sepulcher. Peter went in and saw the linen cloths and the face cloth laid carefully away, showing that there had been no violence or pillage. John now entered and believed that his Lord had risen, but Peter departed "marveling at that which had happened" (Luke 24:10-12; John 20:1-8).

Restoration. "We are told by Luke (24:34) and by Paul that Christ appeared to him first among the apostles. It is observable, however, that on that occasion he is called by his original name, Simon, not Peter; the higher designation was not restored until he had been publicly reinstituted, so to speak, by his Master. That reinstitution took place at the Sea of Galilee (John 21), an event of the very highest import. Slower than John to recognize their Lord, Peter was the first to reach him: he brought the net to land. The thrice repeated question of Christ, referring doubtless to the three protestations and denials, was thrice met by answers full of love and faith. He then received the formal commission to feed Christ's sheep, rather as one who had forfeited his place, and could not resume it without such an authorization. Then followed the prediction of his martyrdom, in which he was to find the fulfillment of his request to be permitted to follow the Lord. With this event closes the first part of Peter's history" (Smith, *Bib. Dict.* [which see]).

After the Ascension. After this Peter stands forth as the recognized leader of the apostles, although it is clear that he does not exercise or claim any authority apart from them, much less over them. It is he who points out to the disciples the necessity of filling the place of Judas and the qualifications of an apostle (Acts 1:15-22).

Pentecost. On the Day of Pentecost Peter, as the spokesman of the apostles, preached a remarkable sermon that resulted in the conversion of about three thousand people (2:14-41).

First Miracle. Peter and John went up to the Temple to pray, and as they were about to enter, a lame man, who was lying at the entrance of the gate called Beautiful, accosted them, asking alms. Peter said to him, "Look at us! . . . I do not possess silver and gold, but what I do have I give to you: In the name of Jesus Christ the Nazarene—walk!" When the people ran together to Solomon's porch, Peter preached Jesus to them. For this the apostles were imprisoned, and the next day they were brought before the Sanhedrin to answer the question, "By what power, or in what name, have you done this?" Peter replied with boldness, and they were dismissed (Acts 3:1–4:23).

Ananias and Sapphira. In this miracle of judgment Peter acted simply as an instrument, not pronouncing the sentence, but denouncing the sin, and that in the name of his fellow apostle and of the Holy Spirit (5:1-11).

In Prison. Many miracles of healing were performed by the apostles, and they were thrust into prison; "but an angel of the Lord during the night opened the gates of the prison" and commanded them to go to the Temple and preach the words of "Life." They were brought before the high priest and rebuked for their preaching, but Peter declared it to be their purpose to "obey God rather than men," and he charged the rulers of the people with being guilty of the murder of Jesus. Angered at his words, they sought to slay the apostles but were restrained by the wise counsel of Gamaliel (5:14-40).

In Samaria. After Philip had preached a while in Samaria, Peter and John were sent down to confirm the converts; and while there Peter rebuked Simon the sorcerer, showing him that, though professedly a believer, he was still "in the gall of bitterness and in the bondage of iniquity" (8:14-24).

Meets Paul, etc. Acts 9:26 and Gal. 1:17-18 record the first meeting of Peter and Paul about three years later. This interview was followed by other events marking Peter's position—a general apostolic tour of visitation to the established churches (Acts 9:32), in the course of which two great miracles were wrought on Aeneas and Tabitha, and in connection with which the most signal transaction after the Day of Pentecost is recorded, the baptism of Cornelius (9:32–10:48). Peter's conduct gave great offense to his countrymen (11:2), and it needed all his authority, corroborated by a special manifestation of the Holy

Spirit, to induce his fellow apostles to recognize the propriety of this great act.

Miraculous Deliverance. A few years later (A.D. 44), Herod, having found that the murder of James pleased the Jews, arrested Peter and put him in prison. He was kept under the care of "four squads of soldiers," who relieved one another on the watch. Two were stationed at the gate, while the other two were attached to Peter by chains. Notwithstanding these precautions, an angel delivered the apostle, who reported himself at the house of Mary, the mother of John Mark, where many of the church were gathered praying for his safety (12:2-17). His miraculous deliverance marks the close of this second great period of his ministry. The special work assigned to him was completed. From that time we have no continuous history of him. It is quite clear that he retained his rank as the chief apostle; equally so, that he neither exercised or claimed any right to control the proceedings of the others. He left Jerusalem, but it is not said where he went. Certainly not to Rome, where there are no traces of his presence before the latter part of his life. Some years later (A.D. 51) we find him in Jerusalem at the convention of apostles and elders, assembled to consider the question whether converts should be circumcised. Peter took the lead in the discussion, contending that salvation comes through grace, which is received through faith; and that all distinction between believers is thereby removed (15:7-11). His argument was enforced by James, and the question was at once and finally settled. A painful collision occurred between Peter and Paul at Antioch. Peter had eaten there with Gentiles; but when certain Jews sent by James came from Jerusalem, he, fearful of offending them (representing as they did the circumcision), withdrew from all social connection with the Gentiles. Paul, apprehensive of disastrous consequences and believing that Peter was infringing upon a great principle, said that he "opposed him to his face, because he stood condemned" (Gal. 2:11-14). This controversy did not destroy their brotherly communion, which continued to the end of Peter's life (2 Pet. 3:15-16).

Peter was probably employed for the most part in building up and completing the organization of Christian communities in Palestine and the adjoining districts. There is, however, strong reason to believe that he visited Corinth at an early period. The name of Peter as founder or joint founder is not associated with any local churches save those of Corinth, Antioch, or Rome, by early ecclesiastical tradition. From 1 Pet. 5:13-14, it is probable that Peter either visited or resided for some time at Babylon, and that Mark was with him there when he wrote that epistle. It may be considered as a settled point that he did not visit Rome before the last year of his life. The evidence for his martyrdom there is complete, while there is a total absence of any contrary statement in the writings of the early Fathers. Clement of Rome, writing before the end of the first century, speaks of it but does not mention the place, that being, of course, well known to his readers. Ignatius, in the undoubtedly genuine epistle to the Romans (chap. 4), speaks of Peter in terms that imply a special connection with their church. In the second century Dionysius of Corinth, in the epistle to Soter, bishop of Rome (following Eusebius, *Ecclesiastical History* 2.25), states, as a fact universally known and accounting for the intimate relations between Corinth and Rome, that Peter and Paul both taught in Italy and suffered martyrdom about the same time. In short, the churches most nearly connected with Rome and those least affected by its influence, which was as yet inconsiderable in the East, concur in the statement that Peter was a joint founder of that church and suffered death in that city. The time and manner of the apostle's martyrdom are less certain. The early writers imply, or distinctly state, that he suffered at or about the same time as Paul, and in the Neronian persecution. All agree that he was crucified. Origen says that at his own request he was crucified with his head downward.

Character. Among the leading characteristics of Peter were: "Devotion to his Master's person (John 13:37), even leading him into extravagance (13:9), and an energetic disposition, which showed itself sometimes as boldness (Matt. 14:29) and temper (John 18:10). His temperament was choleric, and he easily passed from one extreme to another (13:8-9)" (McClintock and Strong, *Cyclopedia,* s.v.). "The contrast between Peter of the gospels—impulsive, unsteadfast, slow of heart to understand the mysteries of the kingdom—and the same apostle as he meets us in the Acts, firm and courageous, ready to go to prison and to death, the preacher of the faith, the interpreter of Scripture, is one of the most convincing proofs of the power of Christ's resurrection and the mighty working of the pentecostal gift" (E. H. Plumptre, *Bible Educator,* 4:129).

Prominence as an Apostle. By consulting Matt. 17:1; Mark 9:2; 14:33, we learn that Peter was among the most beloved of Christ's disciples. Sometimes he speaks in the name of the twelve (Matt. 19:27; Luke 12:41); sometimes he answers when questions are addressed to them all (Matt. 16:16; Mark 8:29); sometimes Jesus addresses him in place of them all (Matt. 26:40). His eminence among the apostles depended partly on the fact that he was chosen among the first, and partly on his own peculiar traits. This position became more decided after the ascension of Jesus and perhaps in consequence of the saying in John 21:15-19. The early church regarded him as the representative of the apostolic body—a very distinct theory from that which makes him their head or governor in Christ's stead. Peter held no

distinct office (*Primus inter pares*) and certainly never claimed any powers that did not belong equally to all of his fellow apostles (McClintock and Strong, *Cyclopedia,* s.v.).

The Rock. "You are Peter, and upon this rock I will build My church," etc. "The expression *this rock* upon which *I will build my church,* has received very different interpretations . . . in various ages. The first is the construction given by the Church of Rome. . . . It affirms that the rock is Peter individually, that the commission constituted him supreme apostle, with authority, inherited from him by the bishops of Rome. Other constructions are more convincing. First, as may be shown, not Peter alone, but each apostle, was a *rock* and a recipient of the *keys,* and all were coequal in powers. Second, were the authority conveyed to Peter alone and personally, it must still be shown that this personal prerogative was among the successional attributes conferred upon him. Third, that Peter was ever bishop of Rome is without historical foundation; and the pretense of a succession from him by the Roman bishop is a fable. It is to be clearly noted that Peter was not given the keys of the church but of 'the kingdom of heaven' as a sphere of Christian profession (cf. Matt. 13). Since a key signifies power and authority (Isa. 22:22; Rev. 3:7), the book of Acts gives the infallible commentary on Peter's use of this special prerogative. It was Peter who opened the door of Christian opportunity to Israel at Pentecost (Acts 2:38-40), to the Samaritans (Acts 8:14-17), and to the Gentiles in Cornelius's abode (Acts 10:34-46). After gospel opportunity was introduced to this age to Jew (Acts 2), Samaritan (Acts 8), and Gentile (Acts 10), there was no assumption whatever by Peter of any other authority (Acts 15:7-11). The power of binding and loosing (Matt. 18:18; John 20:23) was shared with the other disciples. It is preposterous to make this refer to human destiny, as Rev. 1:18 explains."   M.F.U.

BIBLIOGRAPHY: W. M. Taylor, *Peter the Apostle* (1876); F. B. Meyer, *Peter: Fisherman, Disciple, Apostle* (1953); W. Barclay, *The Master's Men* (1960), pp. 15-27; O. Cullmann, *Peter: Disciple–Apostle–Martyr* (1962); H. Martin, *Simon Peter* (1967); R. E. Brown, K. P. Donfried, and J. Reumann, eds., *Peter in the New Testament* (1973); F. F. Bruce, *Peter, Stephen, James, and John* (1979); J. R. MacDuff, *The Footsteps of Peter* (1982); W. H. G. Thomas, *The Apostle Peter* (1985).

PETER, FIRST EPISTLE OF. One of the general, or catholic, epistles written by the apostle Peter.

Purpose and Message. This is a letter of hope in the midst of suffering and testing. Peter was writing to "those who reside as aliens, scattered throughout Pontus, Galatia, Cappadocia, Asia, and Bithynia" (1:1). The keynote of the book is suffering and glory. About seven words of suffering occur in it. The sufferings of Christ are used as an example (1:11; 2:21; 4:1-2; 5:1). Suffering is to be looked for (4:12); it represents the will of God (4:19); it is to be borne patiently (2:23; 3:9); rejoicingly (4:13); others were suffering (5:9); suffering has value (1:6-7; 2:19-20; 4:14). The practical note dominates the epistle rather than the doctrinal.

Occasion and Date. The epistle is probably to be dated around A.D. 65, and the Neronian persecutions apparently furnish its background. The provinces of Asia also mistreated their Christian citizens and residents. The apostle shows acquaintance with early epistles such as James, 1 Thessalonians, Romans, Colossians, Ephesians, and Philippians. Accordingly it was most probably written after the prison epistles. Many commentators consider the "Babylon" of 5:13 to have reference to the literal Babylon of the Euphrates (*see* Calvin, Alford, Mayor, Moorehead). The majority of writers, however, make it a symbolic reference to Rome, but Alford thinks "we are not to find an allegoric meaning in a proper name thus simply used in the midst of simple matter-of-fact sayings" (*Greek Testament,* 4:129).

Authorship. The early church presented almost unanimous agreement on the Petrine authorship. No other book has stronger attestation of authenticity than 1 Peter. Second Peter 3:1 is the earliest acknowledgment of the first epistle. The book seems to be alluded to in the epistle of Barnabas and in Clement's epistle to the Corinthians. Polycarp quotes it in his epistle to the Philippians. Irenaeus is the first to quote it by name. Internal evidence likewise agrees with the external. The writer calls himself Peter (1:1). He was a witness of the sufferings of Christ (5:1). The vocabulary reminds us of the Peter of the gospels and the Acts. There is a similarity between Peter's speeches in the Acts and his words in the epistle (cf. Acts 10:34 with 1 Pet. 1:17; Acts 2:32-36, 10:40-41 with 1 Pet. 1:21; Acts 4:10-11 with 1 Pet. 2:7-8).

Outline.
I. Salutation (1:1-2)
II. Suffering and the certainty of future inheritance (1:3-12)
III. Suffering and personal life (1:13–2:10)
IV. Suffering and social and domestic life (2:11–3:12)
V. Faith and right conduct and suffering (3:13–4:6)
VI. Right conduct in the light of the end (4:7-19)
VII. Suffering and right relationship between elders and the congregation (5:1-11)
VIII. Conclusion (5:12-14)

BIBLIOGRAPHY: J. Brown, *Expository Discourses in the First Epistle of the Apostle Peter,* 3 vols. (n.d.); C. Bigg, *A Critical and Exegetical Commentary on the Epistles of St. Peter and St. Jude,* International Critical Commentary (1903); A. M. Stibbs and A. F. Walls, *The First Epistle General of Peter,* Tyndale New Testament Commentaries (1960); E. G. Selwyn, *First Epistle of St. Peter* (1961); J. N. D. Kelly, *A Commentary on the Epistles of Peter and Jude,* Harper New Testament Commentaries (1969); J. H. Jowett, *The Epistles of St. Peter* (1970); E. Best, *I Peter,* New Century Bible (1971); R. Leighton, *Commentary on First Peter* (1972); J. Lillie, *Lectures on the First and Second Epistles of Peter* (1978); F. J. A. Hort, *Expository and Exegetical Studies* (1980).

PETER, SECOND EPISTLE OF. A second general, or catholic, epistle, written by the apostle Peter.

Subject Matter. Peter's second epistle may be viewed as a complement to his first. It deals with the second coming of Christ and the evils preceding this great event. The first epistle also speaks of the second coming but does not deal with the conditions prior to that prophetic event. Stern warning is given of coming apostasy, when monetary considerations would sway church leaders. As a result loose morality and general iniquity would abound. In chap. 1 Peter expounds certain precious promises of God's Word; in chap. 2 he inveighs against false teachers; in chap. 3 he deals with the certainty of the coming of the Lord and the prevailing skepticism of the end time.

Authorship. The writer of the epistle strongly affirms himself to be Simon Peter (1:1). The book thus represents itself to be the genuine production of the apostle Peter, who claims to have been present at the transfiguration of Christ (1:16-18) and to have been warned by our Lord of his impending death (1:14). Despite these clear claims, numerous modern critics consider the work written by a pseudonymous author in the postapostolic period. The writer is supposed to have assumed Peter's name a century or so after Peter's death. Supposed differences in style between First and Second Peter are alleged to indicate that the books were by different authors. Although there are confessedly some differences in vocabulary, it has been shown by Zahn (*Introduction to the O. T.,* 2:289ff.) that there are some striking likenesses. One may also ask whether a forger would run the risk of detection by failing to pay more attention to the style and language of First Peter. Second Peter, however, lacks any proved evidence of forgery. The autobiographical allusions are true to fact. No new material is added. There is nothing romantic or indisputably anachronistic about the second epistle. This is in striking contrast to the apocalyptic "Gospel of Peter" and the "Apocalypse of Peter." A claim is also made that the epistle was penned at a period when the Pauline letters were made use of by heretics to promulgate their teachings (3:15-16). This reference to Paul's letters, however, does not imply that they had been already collected or even that they had already all been written. The reference may merely refer to such as Peter had come to know. It cannot be shown that Peter deals with a more advanced stage of apostasy than Paul dealt with. Against the charge of spuriousness is the apostolic tone, the Christian earnestness, the genuineness of the autobiographical allusions, and the absence of the fantastic. It ought, therefore, to be accepted as a genuine work of the apostle Peter.

Attestation. Although it is true that Peter's second epistle has less historical support of its genuineness than any other NT book, it bears points of resemblance to a number of writings during the period of A.D. 90-130. It is not mentioned in the Muratorian Fragment, nor does it occur in the Old Syriac and Old Latin versions. All this is doubtless explainable on the basis of the brevity of the epistle, its containing no striking new material, and its not being addressed to any specific person or church. According to Zahn, the epistle of Jude gives an early attestation of it, and therefore we need no other.

Occasion and Date. Antinomian Gnosticism had begun to manifest itself. The false teachings spread with its immoral tendencies. The apostle wrote to correct this evil and to forewarn of conditions at the end of the age. There is no decisive evidence that Second Peter was not written shortly after First Peter. It was penned probably in A.D. 66-67, which date would meet all requirements.

Purpose and Plan. The epistle is the second in which the apostle proposes to stir up the "sincere" minds of his readers "by way of reminder" (3:1). To this end he urges upon them growth in Christian grace (1:5-15), warns against false teachers (chap. 2), and urges believers to patient expectation of the Lord's return (3:1-14).

Outline.
  I. Introduction (1:1-4)
  II. Exhortation to Christian growth (1:5-11)
  III. Apostolic authority (1:12-21)
  IV. The peril of apostate teachers (2:1-22)
  V. Conduct in the light of the Lord's return (3:1-18)   M.F.U.

BIBLIOGRAPHY: B. B. Warfield, *Southern Presbyterian Journal* 33 (1882): 45-75; C. E. B. Cranfield, *I and II Peter and Jude* (1960); E. M. B. Green, *The Second Epistle General of Peter and the General Epistle of Jude,* Tyndale New Testament Commentaries (1968); J. B. Mayor, *The Epistle of Jude and the Second Epistle of Peter* (1978); J. Brown, *Parting Counsels: An Exposition of 2 Peter 1* (1980). *See also* 1 Peter.

PETHAHI'AH (peth-a-hī'a; "Jehovah opens," i.e., the womb).

1. A priest, head of the nineteenth division in the reign of David (1 Chron. 24:16), about 970 B.C.

2. A Levite in the time of Ezra who had married a foreign wife (Ezra 10:23). He is probably the same person mentioned in Neh. 9:5, about 445 B.C.

3. The son of Meshezabel and descendant of Zerah, who was counselor of King Artaxerxes in matters relating to the Jews (Neh. 11:24), 445 B.C.

PE'THOR (pe'thor). A town in Mesopotamia where Balaam resided (Num. 22:5; Deut. 23:4). It was probably a noted seat of Babylonian magi, because those wise men were accustomed to congregate in particular localities. Shalmaneser II of Assyria captured this place from the Hittites, who called it Pitru. Still earlier, it appears in the lists of the great Egyptian conqueror Thutmose III (fifteenth century B.C.). The town was located on the W bank of the Euphrates a few miles S of Carchemish.

PETHU'EL (pe-thū'el). The father of the prophet Joel (Joel 1:1), eighth century B.C.

PETITION. *See* Prayer.

PE'TRA (pe'tra). The capital of Edom and subsequently of *Nabataea* (which see) about fifty miles S of the Dead Sea. The name is from the Gk. word *petra,* "rock," Heb. *sela'.* The rock-cut city of Petra was a noted pagan center. It was also a notable fortress and stronghold. Many identify Petra with OT Sela. Sela is referred to in 2 Kings 14:7-10; 2 Chron. 25:11-12; Isa. 16:1; Jer. 49:16-17; Obad. 3-4. Whether or not the OT refers to Petra, the NT indirectly refers to it. Aretas IV, king of Petra (9 B.C.-A.D. 40) ruled Damascus during the days of Paul's conversion and earliest witness and sought to apprehend the apostle there (2 Cor. 11:32-33). The site is about a mile long and a half mile wide. Its dominant natural feature is the 950-foot acropolis known as Umm

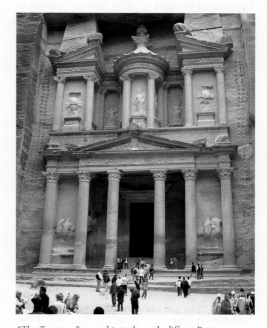

"The Treasury," carved into the rock cliffs at Petra

el-Biyara. Its high place is an excellent example of the high places referred to and condemned in the OT. Petra is striking even in ruins. Some of its structures are rose red and others a dark red ochre shade of sandstone with bands of yellow, gray, and white. These buildings and tombs are almost all cut into the rock cliffs of the area. Among the most exciting remains are the Khazneh (often called "the Treasury," with a facade 92 feet wide and 130 feet high); a Roman theater capable of seating 4,000, and Ed Deir (a temple with a facade 165 feet wide, 148 feet high, and a door 23 feet high). H.F.V.

BIBLIOGRAPHY: Ian Browning, *Petra* (rev. ed.).

PEUL'LETHAI (pe-ūl'le-thī). The eighth son of Obed-Edom, the Korathite, and a gatekeeper of the Solomonic Temple (1 Chron. 26:5). *See* Obed-Edom, no. 1.

PHA'LEC (fā'lek; Luke 3:35, KJV). *See* Peleg.

PHAL'LU (fal'ū; Gen. 46:9, KJV). *See* Pallu.

PHAL'TI (1 Sam. 25:44), **Phal'tiel** (2 Sam. 3:15). Renderings in the KJV of the name *Palti* (which see, no. 2).

PHAN'UEL (fan'ū-el). The father (Luke 2:36) of the prophetess *Anna* (which see).

PHA'RAOH (fār'o). The title of Egyptian kings. It is the Heb. form of the Egyptian title "the great house." During the early dynasties the expression was an honorific title for the chief Egyptian ruler, but from the powerful Eighteenth Dynasty when Egypt ruled the East (c. 1550-1320 B.C.), it was in common use as the official title of the kings of Egypt. (*See* Jack Finegan, *Light from the Ancient Past* [1946], p. 88.) Of the many pharaohs (thirty dynasties in all), the following are among those alluded to in the Bible:

The Pharaoh of the Patriarchs. If one subscribes to the chronology embedded in the MT, Abraham was born in 2161 B.C. and entered Canaan in 2086 B.C. This would make the patriarchal period in Palestine coeval with the strong Middle Kingdom in Egypt under the Twelfth Dynasty (2000-1780 B.C.). Abraham visited one of the earlier kings of this dynasty, and Joseph became prime minister of one of these powerful rulers, either Amenemes (I-IV) or Senwosret (I-III). Many scholars, however, make the pharaoh of Joseph one of the Hyksos kings (Dynasties XV-XVII) resident at Avaris-Tanis (c. 1720-1550 B.C.). This, however, is contrary to the Masoretic chronology.

The Pharaoh of the Oppression. If the early date of the Exodus (c. 1441 B.C.) is subscribed to, Thutmose III (c. 1482-1450 B.C.) furnishes an ideal figure for the pharaoh of the oppression. According to the Bible, Moses waited for the death of the great oppressor before returning to Egypt from his refuge in Midian (Ex. 2:23). However, late-date theorists commonly identify Seti

I (c. 1319-1301 B.C.) as the pharaoh of the oppression, disregarding the Masoretic chronology.

The Pharaoh of the Exodus. Amenhotep II (c. 1450-1425 B.C.), son of the famous empire-builder Thutmose III, likely was the pharaoh of the Exodus. There are no references, of course, in the contemporary records of this pharaoh to such national disasters as the ten plagues or the destruction of the Egyptian army in the Red (Reed) Sea, much less to the escape of the Hebrews. This is not amazing, however, as Egyptians were loathe to catalog their disasters. If Amenhotep II was the pharaoh of the Exodus, his eldest son was slain in the tenth plague (Ex. 12:29). It seems clear that Thutmose IV (c. 1425-1412 B.C.) was not Amenhotep II's eldest son. He could, therefore, have fitted into the historical situation. Many scholars make Rameses II (c. 1301-1234 B.C.) the pharaoh of the Exodus. This, however, is not proved.

The Father-in-Law of King Solomon (c. 960-922 B.C.). Solomon married this Egyptian ruler's daughter. He was a firm ally of the Hebrew monarch (1 Kings 3:1; 7:8).

Pharaoh Shishak, a member of the Twenty-second or Libyan Dynasty, who appears on the Egyptian monuments as Sheshonk I and overran Judah and Jerusalem during the reign of Solomon's successor, Rehoboam (1 Kings 14:25) of Judah (c. 926 B.C.). Late in the reign of Solomon, Jeroboam, who was subsequently to become king of Israel, took refuge in the court of Shishak (11:40; 2 Chron. 10:2).

Zerah the Ethiopian, evidently Osorkon I, Shishak's successor. This pharaoh was defeated in southern Palestine in Asa's reign (c. 910-869 B.C.; cf. 2 Chron. 14:9-15; 16:8).

So (c. 732-724 B.C.), whom Hoshea, king of Israel, tried to align against Assyria. He was possibly a powerful general or *tartan* of Egypt rather than a pharaoh (2 Kings 17:4).

Tirhakah of the Twenty-fifth Dynasty. He conducted a military campaign against Sennacherib of Assyria (2 Kings 19:9). His name on the Egyptian monuments is rendered Taharka.

Neco of the Twenty-sixth Dynasty, who killed Josiah of Judah at Megiddo (2 Kings 23:29-30). Neco was conquered by Nebuchadnezzar, who built the Chaldean Empire on defeated Egypt.

Hophra. Called also Apries (c. 588-569 B.C.), he ruled during the ministry of Jeremiah, who, with others, fled to Egypt. The prophet foretold that this pharaoh would be defeated by his enemies (Jer. 44:30). The Bible refers to other unnamed pharaohs (1 Kings 11:14-22; 2 Kings 18:21). *See* Egypt. M.F.U.

BIBLIOGRAPHY: H. Frankfort, *Kingship and the Gods* (1948); C. J. Gadd, *Ideas of Rule in the Ancient Near East* (1948). For books on a popular level, see: L. Cottrell, *The Lost Pharaohs* (1950); id., *The Mountains of Pharaoh* (1956); etc.

Pharaoh Amenhotep I, from Thebes

PHA'RES (fa'rez; Matt. 1:3; Luke 3:33; all KJV). *See* Perez.

PHA'REZ. *See* Perez.

PHAR'ISEES (far'i-sēz; Gk. from Aram. *pᵉrīshā'*, "separated").

Name. The name *Separatists* is thought by some to have been derived from that separation that took place in the time of Zerubbabel and then again in the time of Ezra, when Israel separated from the pagans dwelling in the land and from their uncleanness (Ezra 6:21; 9:1; 10:11; Neh. 9:2; 10:29). But this is correctly objected to on the ground that their name must have come to the Pharisees in consequence of their stricter view of the notion of uncleanness, not only from the uncleanness of the heathen but from that with which they believed the great portion of Israel to have been affected. This seems to have been the sense in which they were called the *separated* or the *separating,* and they might have been so called from either praise or blame. It is not probable that they took the name themselves, but that their adversaries called them "the separatists." They called themselves *Ḥaberîm* (Aram. *ḥābar,* "associate"), this term being in the language of the Mishna and of ancient rabbinical literature in general exactly identical with *Perushim;* a Haber in them meaning one who associates himself with the law in order to observe it strictly in opposition to the encroachments of Hellenism.

Origin. The *priests* and *scribes* determined the inner development of Israel after the captivity. Virtually identical in Ezra's time, they became more and more separated, until, in the Maccabaean period, two parties sharply contrasted with each other were developed from them. The *Sadducean* party came from the ranks of the priests, the party of the *Pharisees* from the scribes. The characteristic feature of the Pharisees arises from their *legal tendency,* that of the Sadducees from their *social position.* When once the accurate observance of the ceremonial law was regarded as the true essence of religious conduct, Pharisaism already existed, but not as a distinct sect or party. It appears that during the Greek period, the chief priests and rulers of the people took up an increasingly low attitude toward the law; the Pharisees united themselves more closely into an association that made a duty of the law's punctilious observance. They appear in the time of John Hyrcanus under the name of "Pharisees," no longer indeed on the side of the Maccabees but in hostile opposition to them. The reason for this was that the Maccabaeans' chief object was no longer the carrying out of the law but the maintenance and extension of their political power. The stress laid upon religious interests by the Pharisees had won the bulk of the nation to their side, and Queen Alexandra, for the sake of peace with her people, abandoned the power to the Pharisees. Their victory was now complete; the whole conduct of internal affairs was in their hands. All the decrees of the Pharisees done away with by Hyrcanus were reintroduced, and they completely ruled the public life of the nation. This continued in all essentials even during subsequent ages. Amid all the changes of government under Romans and Herodians the Pharisees maintained their spiritual authority. Consistency with principle was on their side, and this consistency procured them the spiritual supremacy. Although the Saducean high priests were at the head of the Sanhedrin, the decisive influence upon public affairs was in the hands of the Pharisees. "They had the bulk of the nation as their ally, and women especially were in their hands. They had the greatest influence upon the congregations, so that all acts of public worship, prayers, and sacrifices were performed according to their injunctions. Their sway over the masses was so absolute that they could obtain a hearing even when they said anything against the king or the high priest, consequently they were the most capable of counteracting the design of the kings. Hence, too, the Saducees, in their official acts, adhered to the demands of the Pharisees, because otherwise the multitude would not have tolerated them" (Schürer, *History of the Jewish People in the Time of Christ*, div. 2, 2:28).

Teachings. Pharisaism thus represented the effect of Hellenism on normative Judaism; many of the differences between it and Saduceeism were the result of their respective reactions toward Greek culture (cf. W. F. Albright, *From the Stone Age to Christianity* [1941], pp. 272-73).

Immortality. The Pharisees taught "that every soul is imperishable, but that only those of the righteous pass into another body, while those of the wicked are, on the contrary, punished with eternal torment" (Josephus *Wars* 2.8.14); or "they hold the belief that an immortal strength belongs to souls, and that there are beneath the earth punishments and rewards for those who in life devoted themselves to virtue or vileness, and that eternal imprisonment is appointed for the latter, but the possibility of returning to life for the former" (Josephus *Ant.* 18.1.3). The above is merely the Jewish doctrine of retribution and resurrection (Dan. 12:2), testified to by all subsequent Jewish literature, and also by the NT, as the common possession of genuine Judaism.

Angels. The Pharisees also taught the existence of angels and spirits, whereas the Saducees denied them (Acts 23:8); in this respect they also represented the general standpoint of later Judaism.

Providence, Human Freedom. The Pharisees "make everything depend on fate and on God, and teach that the doing of good is indeed chiefly the affair of man, but that fate also cooperates in every transaction" (Josephus *Wars* 2.8.14). "They assert that everything is accomplished by faith. They do not, however, deprive the human will of spontaneity, it having pleased God that there should be a mixture, and that to the will of fate should be added the human will with its virtue or

baseness" (Josephus *Ant.* 18.1.3). "If we strip off its Greek form, from what Josephus says, it is nothing more than this, that according to the Pharisees *everything* that happens takes place through God's providence, and that consequently in human actions also, whether good or bad, a cooperation of God is to be admitted. And this is a genuine OT view" (Schürer, div. 2, 2:15).

Political. "In politics the standpoint of the Pharisees was the genuinely Jewish one of looking at political questions not from a political, but from a religious point of view. The Pharisees were by no means a 'political' party, at least not directly. Their aim, viz., the strict carrying out of the law, was not political, but religious. So far as no obstruction was cast in the way of this, they could be content with any government. It was only when the secular power prevented the practice of the law in that strict manner which the Pharisees demanded, that they gathered together to oppose it, and then really became in a certain sense a political party, opposing even external resistance to external force. To politics as such they were always comparatively indifferent." We must consider the Pharisee as acting under two different *religious* views: (1) The idea of the *Divine Providence* might be made the starting point. From this concept resulted the thought that the sway of the heathen over Israel was the will of God. Hence, this chastisement of God must be willingly submitted to; a heathen and, moreover, a harsh government must be willingly borne, if only the observance of the law was not thereby prevented. (2) *Israel's election* might be placed in the foreground. Then the rule of the heathen over the people of God would appear as an abnormality whose abolition was by all means to be striven for. Israel must acknowledge no other king than God alone and the ruler of the house of David, whom He anointed. The supremacy of the heathen was illegal and presumptuous. From this standpoint it was questionable, not merely whether obedience and payment of tribute to a heathen power was a duty, but whether it was lawful (Matt. 22:17-21; Mark 12:14-17; Luke 20:22-25).

Practices. As an Israelite avoided as far as possible all contact with a pagan, lest he should thereby be defiled, so did the Pharisee avoid as far as possible contact with the non-Pharisee, because the latter was to him included in the notion of the unclean Amhaarez (i.e., Israelites other than Pharisees). When, then, the gospels relate that the Pharisees found fault with the free interaction of Jesus with "tax-gatherers and sinners," and with His entering into their houses (Mark 2:14-17; Matt. 9:9-13; Luke 5:27-32), that criticism agrees exactly with the standpoint here described. The Pharisees, according to the Talmud, were of seven kinds: (1) *the Shechemite Pharisee,* who simply kept the law for what he could profit thereby, as Shechem submitted to circumcision to obtain Dinah (Gen. 34:19); (2) *the Humbling Pharisee,* who to appear humble always hung down his head; (3) *the Bleeding Pharisee,* who in order not to see a woman walked with his eyes closed, and thus often met with wounds; (4) *the Mortar Pharisee,* who wore a mortar-shaped cap to cover his eyes that he might not see any impurities or indecencies; (5) *the What-am-I-yet-to-do Pharisee,* who, not knowing much about the law, as soon as he had done one thing, asked, "What is my duty now? and I will do it" (cf. Mark 10:17-22); (6) *the Pharisee from Fear,* who kept the law because he was afraid of future judgment; (7) *the Pharisee from Love,* who obeyed the Lord because he loved Him with all his heart (Delitzsch, *Jesus und Hillel*).

Pharisaism and Christianity Compared. (1) In relation to the OT dispensation it was the Savior's great effort to unfold the principles that had lain at the bottom of that dispensation and carry them out to their legitimate conclusions, to fulfill the law (Matt. 5:17), to "fulfill," not to confirm, as too many suppose it to mean. The Pharisee taught such a servile adherence to the letter of the law that its remarkable character, as a pointing forward to something higher than its letter, was completely overlooked, and its moral precepts, intended to elevate men, were made rather the instruments of contracting and debasing their ideas of morality. Thus, strictly adhering to the letter, "You shall not commit murder," they regarded anger and all hasty passion as legitimate (5:21-22). (2) Whereas it was the aim of Jesus to call men to the law of God itself as the supreme guide of life, the Pharisees multiplied minute precepts and distinctions to such an extent, upon the pretense of maintaining it intact, that the whole life of Israel was hemmed in and burdened on every side by instructions so numerous and trifling that the law was almost, if not wholly, lost sight of (*see* Matt. 12:1-13; 23:23-30; Mark 3:1-6; 7:1-13; Luke 13:10-17; 18:9-14). (3) It was a leading aim of the Redeemer to teach men that true piety consisted not in forms, but in substance; not in outward observances, but in an inward spirit; not in small details, but in great rules of life. The whole system of Pharisaic piety led to exactly opposite conclusions. Under its influence "the weightier provisions of the law: justice and mercy and faithfulness" (Matt. 23:23; Luke 11:42) were undervalued and neglected; the idea of religion as that which should have its seat in the heart disappeared (11:38-42); the most sacred obligations were evaded (Mark 7:11-13); vain and trifling questions took the place of serious inquiry into the great principles of duty (Matt. 19:3; etc.); and even the most solemn truths were handled as mere matters of curious speculation or means to entrap an adversary (22:35-36; Luke 17:20). (4) The lowliness of piety was, according to the teaching of Jesus, an inseparable concomi-

tant of its reality, but the Pharisees sought mainly to attract attention and excite the admiration of men (Matt. 6:2-4, 16-18; 23:5-7; Luke 14:7-11; 18:11-14). (5) Christ inculcated compassion for the degraded, helpfulness to the friendless; liberality to the poor, holiness of heart, universal love, and a mind open to the truth. The Pharisees regarded the degraded classes of society as classes to be shunned, not to be won over to the right (Luke 7:39; 15:2; 18:11), and pushed from them such as the Savior would have gathered within His fold (John 7:47-48). They made a prey of the friendless (Matt. 23:14); with all their pretense to piety they were in reality avaricious, sensual, and dissolute (Matt. 23:25-28; John 8:7), and devoted their energies to making converts to their own narrow views (Matt. 23:15). The exclusiveness of Pharisaism certainly justifies its being called a sect (Gk. *hairesis,* Acts 15:5; 26:5). Their number, which was comparatively small, was about six thousand.

BIBLIOGRAPHY: R. T. Herford, *The Pharisees* (1924); G. F. Moore, *Judaism in the First Centuries of the Christian Era,* 3 vols. (1927-30); L. I. Finkelstein, *The Pharisees* (1962); I. Abrahams, *Studies in Pharisaism and the Gospels* (1967); W. D. Davies, *Introduction to Pharisaism* (1967); J. Neusner, *The Rabbinic Traditions About the Pharisees Before 70,* 3 vols. (1971); W. Fairweather, *Background to the Gospels* (1977).

PHA'ROSH (fa'rosh; Ezra 8:3, KJV). *See* Parosh.

PHAR'PAR (far'par; "swift," cf. Arab. *farbar,* "haste"). One of the two rivers of Damascus mentioned by Naaman: "Are not Abanah and Pharpar, the rivers of Damascus, better than all the waters of Israel?" (2 Kings 5:12), the same as the "Awaj," a little S of Damascus. Its total length is forty miles, and it is but one-fourth the volume of the Barada, or Abana. It flows through the Wadi el-Ajam, "the valley of the Persians."

PHAR'ZITE (far'zīt). *See* Perez.

PHASE'AH (fa-se'a). *See* Paseah.

PHE'BE (fē'bē). *See* Phoebe.

PHE'NICE (fe'nis). *See* Phoenicia (Acts 11:19; 15:3) and Phoenix (Acts 27:12).

PHENIC'IA (fe-nish'i-a). *See* Phoenicia.

PHI-BE'SETH (fi-be'seth). *See* Pi-beseth.

PHI'COL (fī'kol). Commander of the army of Abimelech, the Philistine king of Gerar (Gen. 21:22, 32; 26:26), about 1980 B.C.

PHILADEL'PHIA (fil-a-del'fi-a; "brotherly love"). A city in Lydia of Asia Minor, containing one of "the seven churches that are in Asia" (Rev. 1:4, 11; 3:7). It was built by Attalus II Philadelphus, whose name it bore. It was situated on the lower slopes of the Tmolus, about twenty-eight miles SW of Sardis and 100 miles W of Smyrna (Izmir). Its elevation is 952 feet above the sea. A Roman town until A.D. 1379, it fell, after persistent resistance, into the hands of the Turks. It has been several times almost destroyed by earthquakes. Its name now is Alasehir, "City of God." Today all that one can see there dating to the Christian history of the city are a section of Byzantine wall and a couple of brick pillars of the Church of St. John dating to the eleventh century. The town is an unimportant place of fifteen to twenty thousand people. H.F.V.

BIBLIOGRAPHY: W. Barclay, *Letters to the Seven Churches* (1958); F. A. Tatford, *The Patmos Letters* (1969); W. M. Ramsay, *Letters to the Seven Churches of Asia* (1975).

PHILE'MON (fī-lē'mon; "affectionate"). A member of the church of Colossae, who owed his conversion to the apostle Paul, for such is the interpretation generally assigned to the words "You owe to me even your own self as well" (Philem. 19). To him Paul addressed his epistle in behalf of Onesimus. His character, as given in that letter, was one of great nobility. The apostle commends his faith and love, his benevolence and hospitality, and his docile, sympathizing, and forgiving spirit. His house at Colossae was shown in the time of Theodoret. Tradition represents him as bishop of that city and as having suffered martyrdom.

PHILEMON, EPISTLE TO. A brief epistle of Paul to Philemon, a Christian slave owner, whose slave Onesimus had run away from him.

Object. Onesimus had fled to Rome, and he seems to have defrauded his master (v. 18). At Rome he was converted under the ministry of Paul and was induced by the great apostle to return to his master. The exquisite epistle to Philemon recommends the converted runaway slave to Philemon's favorable reception. Paul urges that the new convert be no longer considered a mere servant but also a brother in Christ. Paul also requests Philemon to prepare him a lodging, as he expects to visit Colossae shortly. Philemon is also addressed to a certain "Apphia," perhaps Philemon's wife, and to "Archippus," a minister in the Colossian church (cf. Col. 4:17).

Place of Writing. Philemon is closely connected with Colossians. Onesimus carried both epistles. However, Tychicus is joined with Onesimus in the epistle to the Colossians (4:9). Paul and Timothy stand in the greetings of Paul. Paul is named as a prisoner in both (Philem. 9; Col. 4:18); and in both Archippus is addressed (Philem. 2; Col. 4:17). It seems evident, therefore, that both epistles were written in about the same time and place—at Rome during Paul's first imprisonment, A.D. 61 or 62.

Authenticity. Origen cites the epistle as a Pauline letter addressed to Philemon concerning Onesimus. Tertullian refers to the brevity of this epistle as the "sole cause of its escaping the falsifying hands of Marcion" (*Against Marcion* 5.21). Eusebius refers to it as one of the "universally acknowledged Epistles of the canon" (*Ecclesias-*

tical History 3.25). Jerome and Ignatius also allude to it. It is quoted infrequently by the Fathers, evidently because of its brevity. Its coincidences with the Colossian epistle attest to its authenticity.

Its Style. This short epistle is a masterpiece of Christian tactfulness and politeness. In fact, it has been called "the polite epistle." Its politeness, however, has no trace of insincerity, often found in the urbanity of the world. As Luther noted, the epistle exhibits "a right noble, lovely example of Christian love." Verses 17 and 18 of the epistle present a forceful illustration of imputation: "Accept him as you would me," that is, reckon to him my merit; "if he has wronged you in any way, or owes you anything, charge that to my account," that is, reckon to me his demerit.

Outline.
I. Salutation (1-3)
II. Appreciation of Philemon's character (4-7)
III. Pleading in behalf of Onesimus (8-21)
IV. Paul's personal affairs (22-24)
V. Benediction (25) M.F.U.

BIBLIOGRAPHY: W. H. G. Thomas, *Studies in Colossians and Philemon* (1973); H. C. G. Moule, *Studies in Colossians and Philemon* (1977); W. G. Scroggie, *Studies in Philemon* (1977). *See* also Colossians.

PHILE'TUS (fī-lē'tus; "beloved"). An apostate Christian named in connection with Hymenaeus (2 Tim. 2:17) as holding false views regarding the resurrection. The apostle does not state their opinions, concerning which there have been many dissertations. Dean Ellicott (*Com.,* ad loc.) says: "The false asceticism which is so often tacitly alluded to and condemned in these epistles led very probably to an undue contempt for the body, to false views of the nature of death, and thence to equally false views of the resurrection. Death and resurrection were terms which had with these false teachers only a *spiritual* meaning and application; they allegorized the doctrine, and turned all into figure and metaphor." The names of Philetus and Hymenaeus occur separately among those of Caesar's household whose relics have been found in the Columbaria at Rome.

PHIL'IP (fil'ip; Gk. *Philippos,* "lover of horses"). The name of two Herodian rulers, Herod Philip I (or Philip I; Matt. 14:3) and Herod Philip II ("the tetrarch"; Luke 3:1; *see* discussion at Herod: Herod Philip II) and of an apostle and an evangelist.

1. Philip the Apostle. This Philip was of the city of Bethsaida, in Galilee (John 1:44; 12:21), but of his family we have no information. Little is recorded of Philip in the Scriptures.

He had probably gone with Andrew and Peter to hear the preaching of John the Baptist. They had, without doubt, spoken to him of Jesus as the long-expected Savior, for on the next day after Andrew brought his brother Simon to Jesus,

Philip unhesitatingly complied with the Master's request to follow Him (1:41-43). He was thus the fourth of the apostles who attached themselves to Jesus.

The first act of Philip was to invite Nathanael to "come and see" Jesus, saying, "We have found Him of whom Moses in the Law and also the Prophets wrote, Jesus of Nazareth, the son of Joseph" (1:45-47). His ready acceptance of Jesus, and what he said to Nathanael, seem to imply much acquaintance with the Word.

When the twelve were specially set apart for their office, Philip was numbered among them (Matt. 10:3; Mark 3:18; Luke 6:14).

When Jesus was about to feed the 5,000 He asked Philip, "Where are we to buy bread, that these may eat?" And it is added, "And this He was saying to test him" (John 6:5-7). Bengel and others suppose that this was because the duty of providing food had been committed to Philip, whereas Chrysostom and Theodore of Mopsuestia rather suppose it was because this apostle was weak in faith. The answer of Philip agrees well enough with either supposition. Certain Greeks, desiring to see Jesus, made application to Philip for an introduction. Philip, uncertain at first whether to comply with their request or not, consulted with Andrew, who went with him and mentioned the circumstance to Jesus (12:21-22). Scripture adds only the remark of Philip, "Lord, show us the Father, and it is enough for us" (14:8), and refers to his presence at Jerusalem with the church after the ascension (Acts 1:13). The later traditions concerning this apostle are vague and uncertain; but there is nothing improbable in the statement that he preached the gospel in Phrygia and that he met his death at Hieropolis in Syria.

2. Philip the Evangelist. Of his family nothing is known. We first hear of this Philip in his appointment as one of the seven deacons, his name following Stephen in the list (Acts 6:5). They were appointed to superintend the daily ministration of food and alms and so to remove all suspicion of partiality. The persecution that followed the death of Stephen stopped the daily ministrations of the church. The teachers who had been most prominent were compelled to take flight, and Philip was among them.

Philip found his way to the city of Samaria, where Simon Magus practiced sorcery. The latter was held in great reverence because of the wonders he wrought. Philip performed many substantial miracles and thus drew away from the sorcerer the attention of the people, who listened gladly to the gospel. Simon himself seems to have regarded Philip as in league with some superhuman being and looked upon baptism as the initiatory rite through which he might obtain the same powers; he solicited and obtained baptism from the evangelist (8:5-13).

After Peter and John had come to Samaria to complete the work begun by Philip, he was directed by the angel of the Lord to proceed to Gaza. On the way he met a court official of Candace, queen of Ethiopia, who had come to Jerusalem to worship. The eunuch was reading Isa. 53 when Philip drew near to his chariot and asked him if he understood that which he read. Upon invitation Philip took a seat and expounded the Scripture, preaching Jesus, the result of which was the conversion and baptism of the eunuch. Upon the return from the water in which the baptism occurred "the Spirit of the Lord snatched Philip away; and the eunuch saw him no more" (Acts 8:39). Philip continued his work as a preacher at Azotus (Ashdod) and among the other cities that had formerly belonged to the Philistines and, following the coastline, came to Caesarea (8:26-40).

PHILIP'S TRAVELS IN PALESTINE

Philip preaches from Azotus to Caesarea (Acts 8:40)

MEDITERRANEAN SEA

Plain of Sharon

Caesarea

SAMARIA

Sebaste (Samaria)

Jordan

Joppa   Antipatris

Philip preaches in Samaria (Acts 8:5)

Lydda
Jamnia

Philip converts Ethiopian eunuch (Acts 8:26-39)

Azotus   Jerusalem

JUDEA

Gaza

DEAD SEA

Route of Philip

For a number of years (estimated from fifteen to nineteen) we lose sight of the evangelist. The last glimpse we have of him in the NT is in the account of the apostle Paul's journey to Jerusalem. At his house the great apostle and his companions stayed for many days. The four virgin daughters of Philip, "who were prophetesses," and Agabus, who prophesied of Paul's danger from the Jews, are mentioned in the narrative (21:8-14). The traditions concerning Philip are conflicting and uncertain. The Greek martyrologies make him to have been bishop of Tralles, in Lydia; but the Latins make him end his days in Caesarea.

BIBLIOGRAPHY: W. M. Ramsay, *Cities and Bishoprics of Phrygia* (1895-97), 2:552; M. R. James, *The Apocryphal New Testament* (1924), pp. 439-53; H. F. Stevenson, *A*

Galaxy of Saints (1957), pp. 75-78; J. D. Jones, *The Apostles of Christ* (1982), pp. 109-29.

PHILIP'PI (fi-lip'ī; "lover of horses, warlike"). A town of Macedonia, anciently known as Krenides (Strabo 7.331). It was situated about nine miles from the Aegean Sea, NW of the island of Thasos. King Philip II took it from the Thracians and gave it his own name. The area of Philippi was then important for its gold mines, but the economy was bolstered by the fertility of the soil as well. The Philippi that the apostle Paul visited was a Roman colony founded by Augustus. The position of the city on the main road from Rome to Asia, the Via Egnatia, made it strategically important.

The fertile plain of Philippi was the battlefield between Mark Antony and Octavian and Brutus and Cassius, in which the former conquered and the Roman Republic was overthrown in 42 B.C. In celebration of the victory the city was made a Roman colony with the special privileges this involved. Paul and Silas were imprisoned here on the second missionary journey (Acts 16:9-40). The Philippian church was especially generous and beloved by Paul (2 Cor. 8:1-6; 11:9; Phil. 1:1-8), and his epistle to this congregation has always been a favorite of Christians. The second epistle to the Corinthians may have been written in this city. The first church in Europe was planted here.

Ruins of an early church at Philippi

Excavations at Philippi were conducted by the

Traditional site of the Philippian prison

French School of Athens 1914-38, and since World War II to the present they have been carried on by the Greek Archaeological Service. Dominating the site is the forum, a rectangle 330 by 165 feet, which in its present form dates to about A.D. 175. Apparently, however, the form of it is about the same as in Paul's day. On the N side of the forum is a bema where Paul probably stood before the magistrates (Acts 16:19-21). A stretch of the Via Egnatia (Egnatian Way) may be seen adjacent to the N side of the forum. South of the forum are remains of a sixth-century Christian basilica (Basilica B). North of the forum across the modern road are excavated remains of a fifth-century basilica (Basilica A). Next to that the modern visitor is shown what is identified as the prison into which Paul and Silas were cast. Actually a Roman cistern, it seems to have dubious support for having been the place where Paul was held. On the slope of the acropolis just to the NE of Basilica A is a well-preserved theater, which in its original form probably dated from the time of Philip II in the fourth century B.C.   H.F.V.

BIBLIOGRAPHY: W. A. McDonald, *Biblical Archaeologist* 3 (1940): 18-24; A. N. Sherwin-White, *Roman Society and Roman Law in the New Testament* (1963), pp. 93-95; E. M. Blaiklock, *Cities of the New Testament* (1965), pp. 39-44.

PHILIP'PIANS, EPISTLE TO. A letter of the apostle Paul addressed to the church at Philippi. It was the first city of the district called Macedonia Prima, correctly rendered "a leading city of the district of Macedonia, a Roman colony" (Acts 16:12). It was made a Roman colony by Augustus in honor of his celebrated victory over Brutus and Cassius. As a colony it was "a little Rome" itself, transplanted to the provinces. Its inhabitants were Roman citizens who had the privilege of voting and were governed by their own senate and legislature.

Purpose. The epistle is general, correcting no disorders, false doctrines, or disturbances, but exhorting the Philippians to consistency of Christian living. The immediate occasion was the expression of thanks for a contribution sent by Epaphroditus, who was now returning to take back the apostle's letter. The only disturbance behind it was a lack of lowliness of mind among some with resulting disputing and friction between two women, Euodia and Syntyche.

The Outline.

I. Salutation (1:1-2)

II. The believer's joy in spite of suffering (1:3-30)

III. The believer's example in Christ of joyous and loyal service (2:1-30)

    A. Exhortation to unity and meekness (2:1-4)

    B. Christ's humiliation (2:5-8)

    C. Christ's exaltation (2:9-11)

    D. Manifestation of practical salvation (2:12-16)

    E. Paul's example (2:17-30)

IV. Christ, the source of the believer's joy (3:1-21)

    A. Warning against legalism, the enemy of joy (3:1-6)

    B. Trusting Christ, the source of joy (3:7-21)

V. Christ, the believer's joy, giving victory over worry (4:1-22)

    A. Exhortation to united joy (4:1-4)

    B. The peace of God, the key to joy (4:5-7)

    C. The presence of God in practical joy (4:8-22)

VI. Benediction (4:23)

Background and Date. The Philippian church had been established by the apostle Paul on his second missionary journey (Acts 16:9-40). The vision at Troas induced him to cross over into Europe and to visit the city of Philippi. There was apparently no synagogue in the city, and the church began by the riverside. Lydia, a seller of purple from Thyatira, was converted. As a result of Paul's experience with a demon-possessed slave girl, he was cast into prison, miraculously delivered, and saw other converts in the Philippian jailor and his house. After this experience, he had to leave the city, but Luke remained at Philippi. This is obvious because from that point onward Luke uses the third person in speaking of the party. The small church established here was a nucleus of a work of God. The church was loyal to Paul and twice sent a contribution while he was at Thessalonica (Phil. 4:15-16). The church also sent him a gift at Corinth (2 Cor. 11:8-9; cf. Acts 18:5). To thank the Philippians and to send them instruction and comfort, Paul wrote the letter, since Epaphroditus was about to return to Philippi (Phil. 2:28). The epistle was manifestly penned from Rome (cf. 1:13; 4:22) and very likely near the end of Paul's two years there (Acts 28:30-31). The general background would suggest that Philippians is the last of the four so-called prison

epistles. The first three of those epistles were written about A.D. 60; therefore, Philippians must be dated at the close of the year A.D. 61. M.F.U.

BIBLIOGRAPHY: H. C. G. Moule, *Philippian Studies: Lessons in Faith and Love* (n.d.); J. B. Lightfoot, *St. Paul's Epistle to the Philippians* (1897); J. H. Jowett, *The High Calling* (1909); K. Barth, *The Epistle to the Philippians* (1962); W. Hendriksen, *A Commentary on the Epistle to the Philippians* (1962); J. A. Motyer, *Philippian Studies* (1966); J. Eadie, *A Commentary on the Greek Text of the Epistle of Paul to the Philippians* (1977); R. Johnstone. *Lectures on the Epistle to the Philippians* (1977); H. C. G. Moule, *Studies in Philippians* (1977); C. J. Vaughan, *Epistle to the Philippians* (1985).

PHILIS'TIA (fil-is'ti-a). The land of the *Philistines* (which see), as it is usually called in poetry (Ex. 15:14; Isa. 14:29-31; Pss. 60:8; 87:4; 108:9).

PHILISTINES. A powerful sea people who settled in the coastal strip in SW Palestine, extending along the Mediterranean from Joppa to S of Gaza. Taking advantage of the fruitful, well-watered Maritime Plain about fifty miles long and fifteen miles wide, they developed into a strong rival of Israel.

Origin. The second millennium B.C. Philistines are said to have come from Caphtor (Amos 9:7; Jer. 47:4; cf. Deut. 2:23) usually believed to be Crete. The monuments show that the Peleste, or Philistines, invaded Palestine with other "sea peoples" at the time of Rameses III (1195-1164 B.C.) of Egypt. This Egyptian monarch repulsed them in several battles, but some of the invaders survived in Syria and eventually reached SE Palestine. There they settled and became known by the name of the country, Philistia, derived from an Egyptian word *prst* (or *plst*). This was evidently the name of a Delta group which had migrated from Egypt to southern Canaan at the time when Menes of Thinis was ruling over a unified Egypt (c. 2900 B.C.), and whose descendants were known to Abraham as Philistines. Genesis 10:13-14 records that their ancestor Casluhim was born in Egypt, but his offspring apparently left during the Proto-dynastic period (2900-2700 B.C.). Other contemporary Egyptian groups settled in the Aegean in Crete and elsewhere, establishing the Minoan civilization. The migrants to Canaan, who gave their Egyptian name to the land, lived in the interior around Gerar and Beersheba. They were agriculturalists, and not belligerent maritime people as were the Aegean invaders of Palestine in the second millennium B.C. The reference in Gen. 10:14 to Philistine origins is thus correct for the third millennium B.C. Philistines. By contrast, the references in Amos 9:7 and Jer. 47:4 are to the second millennium B.C. group which formed part of the Sea People. To be consistent historically, the prophets should have used the name *Caphtorim* to describe them, as in the much earlier source (Deut. 2:23). But this was archaic, since the Caphtorim had long been known as Philistines.

In the days of the judges and the Hebrew monarchy, the Philistines, like later Mycenaean rulers of Crete, were quite warlike.

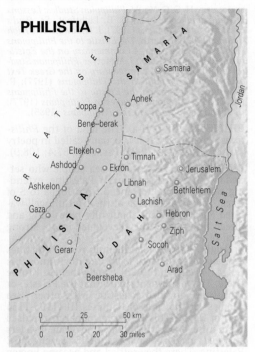

PHILISTIA

Race. The Philistines were a non-Semitic people. The fact that they were uncircumcised figures prominently in the OT. They were apparently Aryans, viewed by some scholars as Indo-Europeans. Rameses III's temple at Medinet Habu contains reliefs depicting the Philistines. They appear as a tall, Hellenic-looking people.

Government. Their power and threat to Israel was due to a large extent to their political organization. It consisted of a league of five great cities. The famous Philistine pentapolis was composed of (1) Gaza, strategically located a few miles from the Mediterranean and controlling the Maritime Plain and caravan routes to Egypt and Arabia; (2) Ekron, a wealthy market in the valley of Sorek, close to Danite territory; (3) Ashdod, on the main road to Joppa and lying east of Lydda; (4) Ashkelon, a strong fort on the coast, controlling principal caravan routes; (5) Gath, NE of Gaza and bordering on the Shephelah. The effective political organization was headed by five Philistine lords, who are called in Heb., *seranim.* In numerous instances they are simply called *sarim,* the normal Heb. word for "princes." Some scholars have connected *seranim* with a dialectal variation of *sar,* Heb. "prince." It has also been connected with Gk. *tyrant.* At the time of Joshua these five lords seem to have been joined in a confederacy.

Military Might. Besides their warlike nature, effective political organization, and economic power, the Philistines posed a continual threat to Israel because of their early control of the iron monopoly. Iron came into use in Palestine around 1200 B.C. The Philistines knew the secret of smelting it, which they evidently got from the Hittites. They were able to import, smelt, and forge iron and make use of various iron military weapons. By enforcing a rigid monopoly over Israel, the Philistines were able to make great strides in military encroachments upon Israelite territory. This Philistine iron monopoly is described in 1 Sam. 13:19-22. Sir Flinders Petrie at Tell Jemmeh, apparently ancient Gerar, found abundant evidence of iron manufacture. An iron smeltery and sword factory with furnaces and numerous iron weapons were discovered. Also iron-rimmed chariots were depicted on pottery.

Religion. The Philistines were intensely religious. They celebrated their victories in the "house of their idols" (1 Sam. 31:9). They often carried their idol gods into battle (2 Sam. 5:21). Dagon (Heb. *dāgôn*), a diminutive of *dāg,* "fish," was a grain deity who was represented with the hands and face of a man and the tail of a fish (1 Sam. 5:4). To his temple the captive Ark was carried (5:2), and to him they offered thanksgiving when they had taken Samson (Judg. 16:23-24). They also worshiped Ashtaroth (1 Sam. 31:10). This is the ancient Assyrian goddess of propagation, Ishtar. At Ekron there was a sanctuary to Baal-zebub, "lord of habitation," who was sufficiently well known as the "god of Ekron" to attract the patronage of Ahaziah (2 Kings 1:2-3). His name in Greek became Beelzebub, "the ruler of the demons" (Matt. 12:24).

Philistine-Israelite Struggle. In Judg. 3:3 the Philistines are left to prove Israel. Shamgar (Judg. 3:31) is said to have slain 600 Philistines with an oxgoad. The tribe of Dan had to move to the NE because of the Philistine advance (18:2). In 13:1, just previous to the time of Samson, Israel was overrun by the Philistines for forty years. Samson, the Israelite hero, produced great victories over the Philistines but eventually met death in the Philistine temple of Dagon (chaps. 13-16). About 1050 B.C., at the battle of Ebenezer, the Philistines again overran the whole country, destroying Shiloh and carrying away the Ark (1 Sam. 4:4). The sacred relic of Israel, however, caused untold suffering to the Philistines, who returned it after seven months (5:6-12). About two decades later Israel recovered her territory under Samuel (7:1-14).

Hebrew Domination. Jonathan defeated the Philistines at Michmash (1 Sam. 13-14), and David won signal victories over them (chaps. 17-18). During the Davidic era the Philistines were completely subjugated and were among the tributary peoples under Solomon.

Under the Judahite Kings. The divided monarchy caused some resurgence of Philistine power. Nadab, around 909 B.C., and other Judahite monarchs invaded Philistia (1 Kings 15:27; 16:15). The Philistines paid tribute to Jehoshaphat (c. 873-848 B.C.; 2 Chron. 17:11), but their power increased during the reigns of Jehoram (c. 853-841 B.C.) and Ahaz (c. 735 B.C.; 2 Chron. 21:16; 28:18). Uzziah and Hezekiah attacked them (26:6-7). They suffered under Egyptian and Assyrian attacks in the eighth and seventh centuries B.C. because of their exposed position on the great highways between Egypt and the Euphrates. Philistine studies are still in their infancy. To date only one Philistine temple has been excavated in Palestine, at Tell Qasile at the northern city limits of Tel Aviv, in 1972.

BIBLIOGRAPHY: R. A. S. Macalister, *The Philistines, Their History and Civilization* (1914); W. F. Albright, *The Archaeology of Palestine* (1949), pp. 110-22; G. E. Wright, *Biblical Archaeologist* 29 (1966): 70-86; Edward Hindson, *The Philistines and the Old Testament* (1971); D. J. Wiseman, ed., *Peoples of Old Testament Times* (1973), pp. 53-78; Trude Dothan, *The Philistines and Their Material Culture* (1982).

PHILOL'OGUS (fi-lol'o-gus; "fond of talk"). A Christian at Rome to whom Paul sends his salutation (Rom. 16:15). Pseudo-Hippolytus makes him one of the seventy disciples and bishop of Sinope. His name is found in the Columbarium "of freedmen of Livia Augusta" at Rome, which shows that there was a Philologus connected with the imperial household at the time when it included many Julias.

PHILOSOPHY (Gk. *philosophia*, "love of wisdom"). This term is used in Gk. writings of either zeal for, or skill in, any art or science or other branch of knowledge. It occurs only once in the NT to describe the theology of certain Jewish Christian ascetics who busied themselves with refined and speculative inquiries into the nature and classes of angels and to the ritualism of the Mosaic legislature and the traditional Jewish regulations respecting practical living (*see* Col. 2:8).

M.F.U.

PHIN'EHAS (fin'i-as; Egyptian, "the Nubian"). The name of several biblical personages.

1. The grandson of Aaron and son of Eleazar by his wife, "one of the daughters of Putiel" (Ex. 6:25). He first appears in biblical history at the time of the licentious idolatry, where his zeal and action secured the end of the plague that was destroying the nation (Num. 25:7-8), c. 1435 B.C. For this he was rewarded by the special praise of Jehovah and by a promise that the priesthood should remain in his family forever (vv. 10-13). He was appointed to accompany as priest the expedition by which the Midianites were destroyed (31:6). Seven years later he also headed the party dispatched from Shiloh to protest the altar that the trans-Jordanic tribes were reported to have built near the Jordan (Josh. 22:13-32). In the partition of the country he received an allotment of his own—a hill on Mt. Ephraim. Here his father was buried (24:33). Phinehas appears to have been the ruler of the Korahites, or Korhites (1 Chron. 9:20). After the death of Eleazar he became high priest (the third of the series), in which capacity he is introduced as giving the oracle to the nation during the whole struggle with the Benjamites on the matter of Gibeah (Judg. 20:28). The verse that closes the book of Joshua is ascribed to Phinehas, as the description of the death of Moses at the end of Deuteronomy is to Joshua. The tomb of Phinehas, a place of great resort to both Jews and Samaritans, is shown at Awertah, four miles SE of Nablus.

The narrative of the Pentateuch presents Phinehas as an ardent and devoted priest, whereas in one of the psalms (106:30-31) he is commemorated in the identical phrase that is consecrated forever by its use in reference to the great act of faith of Abraham—"and it was *reckoned to him as righteousness*" (Rom. 4:3; cf. Gen. 15:6).

2. The second son of Eli (1 Sam. 1:3; 2:34; 4:4, 11, 17, 19; 14:3). This Phinehas was killed with his brother by the Philistines when the Ark was captured, about 1050 B.C.

3. A Levite of Ezra's time (Ezra 8:33), unless the meaning be that Eleazar was of the family of the great Phinehas.

PHLE'GON (fle'gon; "burning"). A Christian at Rome to whom Paul sent salutations (Rom. 16:14). Pseudo-Hippolytus states that he was one of the seventy disciples and bishop of Marathon.

PHOE'BE (fē'bē; "radiant"). A "servant" (deaconess, *see* marg.) of the church at Cenchrea, commended by Paul to the church of Rome, who had been a recipient of her kindness (Rom. 16:1-2). She seems to have been on her way to Rome on some important business, the nature of which is not known.

PHOENIC'IA (fe-nish'i-a). The narrow coastland stretching along the NE Mediterranean. It is bordered on the E by the Lebanon Mountains and on the SE by the hills of Galilee. It is famous in history for such great commercial emporia as *Tyre* and *Sidon* (both which see), Byblos (*see* Gebal), and *Arvad* (which see). It was a part of OT Canaan. At present it consists of the Republic of Lebanon and South Latakia. The boundary generally extended from Arvad southward over 120 miles to the Ladder of Tyre. At some periods the territory was included from Mt. Carmel to the Orontes River. In NT times Phoenicia extended as far S as Dor, sixteen miles S of Tyre. It was thus a narrow ribbon of coastland at its greatest extent some two hundred miles long. For references to Phoenicia *see* Acts 11:19; 15:3; 21:2.

BIBLIOGRAPHY: G. Rawlinson, *History of Phoenicia* (1889).

PHOENICIANS. The inhabitants of Phoenicia. The name *Phoenician* is evidently derived from

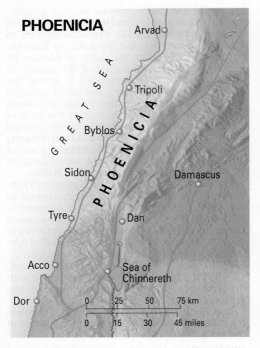

PHOENICIA

Arvad

GREAT SEA

Tripoli

PHOENICIA

Byblos

Sidon

Damascus

Tyre

Dan

Acco

Sea of
Chinnereth

Dor

0   25   50   75 km

0   15   30   45 miles

Gk. *phoinos,* meaning "blood red." Three possible explanations are available. (1) *Phoinos* refers to the reddish sunburned skin of Phoenician seamen or, more likely, (2) to the reddish purple dye from the mollusks-murex, widely exported by Phoenicians and widely used as a coloring material in antiquity. (3) However, it may be safest to derive the name *Phoenician* from *phoinix,* "the date palm." It would then signify the land of palms, like Palmyra.

Race. The Phoenicians were Semitic and were known as Canaanites as long as the Phoenician cities were important for their commercial activity. In the table of nations (Gen. 10:8-12), Canaan denotes the descendants of Ham, who settled in the land later known as Palestine and from whom the country took its original name. Thus originally Hamitic according to the table of nations, the Canaanites settled in a small country that was like a bridge between Egypt and the great Semitic empires that flourished on the Fertile Crescent. At an early date they must have succumbed to the pressure of racial and linguistic intermixture with Semites with the loss of their own ethnic predominance. This is doubtless the explanation as to why anthropologically and ethnologically the evidence is that the Canaanites were predominantly Semitic rather than Hamitic. Such explanations as that the terms used in Gen. 10 "[express] not race but empire or civilization" (J. A. Montgomery, *Record and Revelation* [1938], p. 2), or that Canaan is called a son of

Ham "on account of the long domination of the land of Canaan by Egypt" (H. S. Gehman, *Westminster Dictionary of the Bible* [1944], p. 89), are scarcely satisfactory, especially in view of the stress laid upon the Hamitic origin of Canaan (9:22-27).

Factors in Phoenician Commercialism. Three outstanding reasons account for the world-famous commercial activities of the Phoenicians. (1) Their conquest by the Israelites around 1380 B.C. deprived them of most of Palestine and crowded them on the narrow ribbon of coastland extending from Accho N of Mt. Carmel to Ras Shamra-Ugarit more than 200 miles N. Shortly thereafter the Aramaeans took the hinterland of Syria E of Mt. Lebanon. Thus hemmed in to the coast of northern Palestine and southern Syria, they took to the sea and became one of the most distinguished seafaring peoples of history, founding commercial colonies on the shores and islands of the Mediterranean as far W as Spain. In the ninth century they established Carthage. They also founded centers at Tartessus and at Gades in Spain. They seem to have gone past the Pillars of Hercules to secure tin from Cornwall, Britain. (2) The mountains that approach close to the narrow coastal strip further confined the Phoenicians and were a factor in their seafaring exploits. (3) Another circumstance was the plentiful yield of pine, cypress, and cedar trees for shipbuilding. The men of Byblos (OT Gebal) were noted shipbuilders (Ezek. 27:9), and the Sidonians were expert in timber felling (1 Kings 5:6). The two greatest ports were Tyre and Sidon, although Byblos, Arvad, Arka, Zarepath, and Ugarit were famous.

Religion. Canaanite religion is now well known as the result of the recovery of the religious epic literature from ancient Ugarit. These priceless documents reveal the chief gods and goddesses of the numerous Canaanite cities in various periods. The important deities were El, the supreme Canaanite deity, and his son, Baal, the reigning king of the gods who dominates the Canaanite pantheon. In Ugaritic literature, Baal is given the epithet of Aliyan, "the one who prevails." Both of these gods are utterly immoral in their actions, as are the three goddesses, Anath, Astarte, and Ashera. These three are patronesses of sex and war and reveal the barbarity and licentiousness of Canaanite cults (*see* John Gray, *The Canaanites* [1964]). These Canaanite deities periodically exerted an extremely debilitating influence on Israel. Such degeneracy is illustrated in the Ahab-Jezebel apostasy (1 Kings 18-19). The gross idolatrous lapse of Solomon (11:5) is another example. Solomon suffered from the degenerating influence of the licentious cultic ritual of the Phoenician religion. The prophetic curse upon Canaan (Gen. 9:25-27) was principally religious and refers to the religious depravity and moral degeneracy of Canaanite cults. This was a prime reason for their extermination by the conquering Israelites under divine orders.

Art. From an early period Canaanites played a conspicuous role in the cultural history of civilization. By the end of the fourth millennium important cities such as Jericho, Gezer, Megiddo, Beth-shan, Byblos, Hamath, Jerusalem, and Ai were already in existence. Literature, music, religion, art, and science developed on the busy bridge between great civilizations. The Canaanites were in a position to absorb from other peoples, and it is hard to distinguish what they copied or assimilated from what they invented. The invention of the alphabet, which is attributed to the Canaanites, was adopted by the Greeks. In fact, the Greeks learned so much about writing and writing materials from the Canaanites that their word for book, *biblion* ("Bible"), was connected with the Phoenician city *Byblos*. Phoenicians early knew the art of glassmaking, if they did not actually make the discovery themselves; the Sumerians probably were the ones who first discovered that art. The Phoenicians had great artistic ability in working fine metals for jewelry. The Canaanites also possessed literary skill, as the Ugaritic epic literature attests. Even though their religion degenerated morally, it nevertheless had many artistic and aesthetic elements. In architecture the Phoenicians also excelled, as the account of Solomon's building activities, particularly of the Temple in Jerusalem, attest (cf. 1 Kings 5-10).

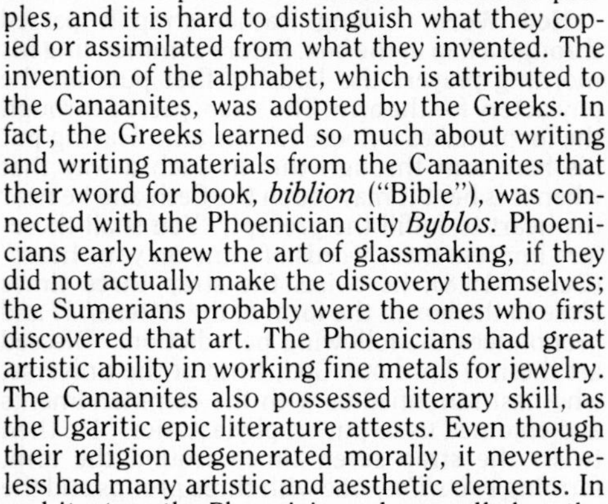
k y t ch z v h d g b a
t sh r k tz p e s n m l

The Phoenician alphabet

History. During the Egyptian Old Kingdom period (c. 2700-2200 B.C.), Phoenicia fell under Egyptian influence. Phoenician Gebal was the port through which trade with Egypt especially flowed. Again during the Egyptian Middle Kingdom (c. 2000-1776) Egypt effectively dominated Phoenicia, at least by means of economic imperialism and perhaps with the stationing of troops there. Then when Egypt built her empire (c. 1580-1100) she controlled the Lebanese coast as part of that empire. Thutmose III, the great "Napoleon of ancient Egypt," mentioned conquests in Phoenicia and claimed this part of Canaan as a vassal dependency. As the Egyptian and Hittite empires passed off the scene, Phoenicia was free to develop on her own. During her period of independence (c. 1100-900 B.C.) Tyre established dominance over the rest of Phoenicia; and her king Hiram enjoyed favorable commercial relations with David and Solomon, helping the former build a palace and the latter to build a palace, a seaport and merchant marine, and the Temple. Later, King Ethbaal of Tyre married his daughter Jezebel to Ahab of Israel, and as a result Baal worship entered the Northern Kingdom. After about 900 B.C. Phoenicia fell under the sway of Assyria, but at first at least this was not severely restrictive for the Phoenicians because the Assyrians were willing to give them considerable freedom as long as they paid their tribute. In fact, being part of the great Assyrian Empire was commercially advantageous to the Phoenicians. During this period the Phoenicians established colonies in the western Mediterranean, transmitted the alphabet to western lands, and traded their high quality timber and dye and fabrics and other commodities with far places. After the fall of the Assyrian Empire, Nebuchadnezzar incorporated Phoenicia into his empire. Tyre, like Jerusalem, incurred the displeasure of Nebuchadnezzar. After Nebuchadnezzar destroyed Jerusalem in 586, he launched a twelve-year siege of Tyre (585-572), at the end of which time he destroyed mainland Tyre, leaving the island city relatively secure and prosperous. Later Alexander the Great determined to conquer Tyre and during a siege of seven months (332 B.C.) built a road to the island and took the great commercial emporium, destroying it utterly. Subsequently Tyre was rebuilt and repopulated with Greeks. Phoenicia was again prosperous during the Hellenistic and Roman empires. M.F.U.; H.F.V.

BIBLIOGRAPHY: D. B. Harden, *The Phoenicians* (1962); S. Moscati, *The World of the Phoenicians* (1968); D. J. Wiseman, ed., *Peoples of Old Testament Times* (1973), pp. 259-86; G. Herm, *The Phoenicians: Purple Empire of the Ancient World* (1975).

PHOE'NIX (fē'nix). A harbor of Crete "facing southwest and northwest" (Acts 27:12, marg., "possibly, northeast and southeast"). Paul and his fellow passengers on the ship going to Adramyttium hoped to winter there. The harbor is in the southern part of the island. M.F.U.

PHRYG'IA (frij'i-a). An inland province of Asia Minor. Once it seemed to include the greater part of the peninsula of Asia Minor, then it was divided into Phrygia Major and Minor, and the Romans again divided it into three parts, Phrygia Salutaris on the E, Phrygia Pacatiana on the W, and Phrygia Katakekaumene ("the burned") in the middle, for this part was volcanic. The country was fertile, and its rich pastures made it famous for its breeds of cattle. Paul crossed this province twice in the course of his missionary journeys. It is the Greater Phrygia that is referred to in the NT. The towns of Antioch in Pisidia (Acts 13:14), Colosse, Hierapolis, Iconium, and Laodicea were situated in it. In the passages (16:6; 18:23) Phrygia is mentioned in a manner not intended to be precise, the former referring to Paul's second missionary journey and the latter to the third. Neither is 2:10 inconsistent with this view. By Phrygia we must understand an extensive district, which contributed portions to several Roman provinces, and varying portions at different times.

BIBLIOGRAPHY: W. M. Ramsay, *The Cities and Bishoprics of Phrygia*, 2 vols. (1897); A. H. M. Jones, *Cities of the Eastern Roman Provinces* (1937); D. Magie, *Roman Rule in Asia Minor*, 2 vols. (1950).

PHU'RAH. *See* Purah.

PHUT. *See* Put.

PHU'VAH. *See* Puvvah.

PHYGE'LUS (fi-je'lus; "a fugitive"; 2 Tim. 1:15; "Phygellus," KJV). A Christian connected with those in Asia of whom Paul speaks of as having turned away from himself. It is open to question whether their repudiation of the apostle was joined with a falling away from the faith, and whether the open display of the feeling of Asia took place—at least so far as Phygelus and Hermogenes were concerned—at Rome. Phygelus may have forsaken the apostle at some critical time when his support was expected (*see* 4:16), or he may have been a leader of some party of nominal Christians at Rome, such as the apostle describes at an earlier period (Phil. 1:15-16) as opposing him there.

PHYLACTERY.
   Name. (Gk. "safeguard, amulet," so-named because it was thought to ward off evil spirits and ill fortune.) Neither the LXX nor the other Gk. versions have this term in their translations of the passages that enjoin this token. Even Josephus does not use the word *phylactery*, though he mentions the custom. The Jews in Christ's time and to this day call phylacteries *tepîlîn* (Heb. for "prayer bands").
   Form and Use. A phylactery, or *frontal* (which see), was a strip of parchment with four passages of Scripture written upon it in the following order: Deut. 11:13-22; 6:4-9; Ex. 13:11-16; 13:1-10. Each strip was rolled up, tied with the white hairs of a calf's or a cow's tail, and placed in one of the compartments of a small box. During prayer these phylacteries were worn by the male Israelites firmly attached with leather straps to the forehead between the eyebrows, and on the left arm, so as to be near the heart. This practice—regarding the origin of which only this much is certain, that it was in existence in our Lord's time (Matt. 23:5; Josephus *Ant.* 4.8.13)—is founded upon a literal interpretation of Ex. 13, where, with reference to the enactments as to the observance of the Passover and the sanctifying of the firstborn, we read: "And it shall serve as a sign to you on your hand, and as a reminder on your forehead" (v. 9), and "as phylacteries on your forehead" (v. 16); and Deut. 6:8; 11:18, where the injunction, so far as the latter part of it is con-

cerned, is repeated, and that with reference to the whole of the commandments. Of course the injunction was intended to be taken figuratively.

The boxes for the head phylactery and for the arm were ordinarily 1½ inches square; the former having on the outside to the right the three-pronged letter *shin*, which is designed as an abbreviation of the divine name *Shaddai*, "the Almighty," whereas on the left side it had a four-pronged *shin*, the two constituting the sacred number seven.

How Worn. A long leather strap is passed through a flap in the box. Before commencing his morning prayers the Israelite first puts on the phylactery for the arm. The strap, passed through the loop, makes a noose for the arm. Having put his bare arm through this in such a way that when it is bent it may touch the flesh and be near the heart to fulfill the precept, "You shall therefore impress these words of mine on your heart" (Deut. 11:18), he twists the strap three times close to the box in the form of the letter *shin* and pronounces the following benediction: "Blessed art thou, O Lord our God, King of the universe, who hast sanctified us with the commandments and enjoined us to put on phylacteries." He then twists the strap seven times around the arm, forming two *shins*, one with three prongs and the other with four.

He next puts on the head phylactery, placing it exactly in the center between the eyes so as to touch the spot where the hair begins to grow (Deut. 11:18) and pronounces the following benediction before he secures it: "Blessed art thou, O Lord our God, King of the universe, who hast sanctified us with thy commandments, and enjoined upon us the command about phylacteries."

To "broaden their phylacteries" (Matt. 23:5) was to make the strips wider, requiring a larger box, thus making them more conspicuous. Some believe that this means having wider straps.

The real meaning of phylacteries is equivalent to amulets or charms. The rabbinists regarded and treated them as such, even though they otherwise disclaimed all connection with heathen views and fear of demons.

PHYSICIAN. The exclamation "Physician, heal yourself!" (Luke 4:23) was delivered by Jesus as part of a rebuke of the worshipers at the synagogue in Nazareth and represented what those worshipers wanted to say to Him. In earlier quoting Isa. 61:1 and applying it to Himself, Jesus had implied both that His listeners needed a physician and that they would find one in Him. They resented the implication, leading to the rejoinder from Jesus that in effect said, "You are going to turn into ridicule even what you have just heard and are going to say to Me, 'You who pretend to save humanity from its misery, begin by delivering Yourself from Your own misery,'" namely, from the lack of esteem or consideration that was attached to Him.

The saying "It is not those who are well who need a physician" (5:31) was quoted to the scribes and Pharisees who objected to Jesus' eating with Levi. So far as the statement conceded to the Pharisees that they were perfectly well (and thus had no need of Him as a physician), it was irony. On the other hand it was calculated to raise serious doubts in their minds as to whether their point of view was correct (Godet, *Com.,* ad loc.). *See* Diseases, Treatment of.

PI-BE'SETH (pī-be'seth; Egyptian, "house of the goddess Bast"). The Gk. rendering is Boubastos; the Egyptian Pi-Pasht, i.e., the place of Pasht, was so-called from the cat-headed Bubastis or Bast, the Egyptian Artemis, which was worshiped there in a splendid temple. It was situated on the royal canal leading to Suez, not far from its junction with the Pelusiac arm of the Nile. It was the chief seat of the Nomas Bubastiles, was destroyed by the Persians, who demolished its walls (Diodorus Siculus *Bibliotheca historica* 16.51), and has entirely disappeared, with the exception of some ruins that still bear the name of Tell Basta. The prophet Ezekiel (Ezek. 30:17) declared that the young military men of Pi-beseth would fall by the sword and the population of the city go into exile. The NIV renders the name "Bubastis."

PICTURES. Images were strictly forbidden (Heb. *maskît,* "figure"), as were idolatrous representations, either independent images, or more usually stones sculptured in low relief, or engraved and colored (Num. 33:52; cf. Ezek. 23:14, "portrayed"). Pictures, movable as with us, were probably unknown to the Jews; but colored sculpture and drawings on walls or wood, such as mummy cases, must have been familiar to them in Egypt.

The "pictures of silver" referred to in the KJV of Prov. 25:11 were probably cornices with carvings (the NASB and NIV read "settings of silver"), and the "apples of gold" representations of fruits or flowers, such as Solomon's flowers and pomegranates (1 Kings 6-7).

PIECE of Gold, Money, Silver. *See* Metrology: Measures of Value, or Money.

PIETY. The term occurs only in the exhortation "Let them first learn to practice *piety* in regard to their own family" (1 Tim. 5:4; Gk. *eusebeia*), better toward their own "household." The NIV renders, "put their religion into practice." It translates Heb. *yir'āh* as "piety" in Job 4:6; 15:4; 22:4. Toward *God* the Gk. word means reverence, toward *man,* due and proper respect.

PIG. *See* Animal Kingdom: Swine.

PIGEON. *See* Animal Kingdom: Dove; and the article Sacrificial Offerings.

PI-HAHI'ROTH (pi-ha-hī'roth). The place before or at which the Israelites encamped at the close of their third march from Rameses. It was "between Migdol and the sea.... in front of Baal-zephon" (Ex. 14:2, 9; Num. 33:7; v. 8, "Hahiroth") and is not identified beyond dispute. But Père Abel placed it in the swamps of Jeneffeh at the extremity of the pass between the mountain and the Bitter Lake.

PI'LATE (pī'lat). The Roman procurator of Judea, A.D. 26-36.

Name. Pilate's family name, Pontius (pon'shus), indicates that he was connected, by descent or adoption, with the clan of Pontii. His surname, Pilatus, may have been derived from *pilatus,* armed with *pilum* (or javelin), or *pileatus,* the *pileus* (or cap) being the badge of freed slaves.

Personal History. Information regarding Pilate is available in the Scriptures and in Josephus and the early church Fathers; less reliable material is provided in traditions and legends.

Early History. The early history of Pilate is unknown, save some unreliable traditions. A German legend relates that he was an illegitimate son of Tyrus, king of Mayence, who sent him to Rome as a hostage. There he committed a murder and was sent to Pontus, where he subdued the barbarous tribes, receiving in consequence the name of Pontius, and was sent to Judea.

Procurator. Pilate was appointed governor of Judea by Tiberius (A.D. 26) and immediately offended the Jews by moving the headquarters of his army from Caesarea to Jerusalem. The soldiers, of course, took their standards—which bore the image of the emperor—with them into the holy city. The sight of the standards planted within sight of the Temple greatly enraged the people, who declared themselves ready to submit to death rather than to this idolatrous innovation. Pilate yielded to their demands and ordered the standards to be returned to Caesarea (Josephus *Ant.* 18.3.1-2; *Wars* 2.9.2-4). On two other occasions Pilate nearly drove the Jews to insurrection; the first, when he hung in his palace on Mt. Zion golden shields inscribed with the names of deities. The shields were removed only by an order from the emperor. The second was when he appropriated the revenue of the Temple, arising from the redemption of vows, for the building of an aqueduct. To these acts must be added the slaughter of certain Galileans (Luke 13:1), who seem to have been slain while they were offering sacrifices in the Temple.

His Connection with Jesus. It was the custom for the procurators to reside at Jerusalem during the great feasts in order to preserve order, and, accordingly, at the time of our Lord's last Passover Pilate was occupying his official residence in Herod's palace. It was to the gates of this palace that Jesus, condemned on the charge of blasphemy, was brought early in the morning by the chief priests and officers of the Sanhedrin, who were unable to enter the residence of a Gentile, lest they should be defiled and unfit to eat the Passover (John 18:28). Pilate, therefore, came out to learn their purpose and demanded the nature of the charge. At first they seem to have expected that he would have carried out their wishes without further inquiry and therefore merely described our Lord as a disturber of the public peace; but as the Roman procurator had too much respect for justice, or at least understood his business too well, to consent to such a condemnation, they were obliged to devise a new charge and therefore interpreted the Lord's claims in a political sense, accusing Him of assuming the royal title, perverting the nation, and forbidding the payment of tribute to Rome (Luke 23:3, an account plainly presupposed in John 18:33). It is evident that from this moment Pilate was distracted between two conflicting feelings —a fear of offending the Jews and a conscious conviction that Jesus was innocent. Moreover, this last feeling was strengthened by his own hatred of the Jews, whose religious scruples had caused him frequent trouble, and by a growing respect for the calm dignity and meekness of the sufferer. First he examined the Lord privately and asked Him whether He was a king. At the close of the interview he came out to the Jews and declared the prisoner innocent. To this they replied that His teaching had stirred up all the people from Galilee to Jerusalem. The mention of Galilee suggested to Pilate a new way of escaping from his dilemma by sending on the case to Herod Antipas; but Herod, though pacified by this act of courtesy, declined to enter into the matter. So Pilate was compelled to come to a decision, and, first having assembled the chief priests and also the people, he announced to them that the accused had done nothing worthy of death; but, at the same time, in hopes of pacifying the Sanhedrin, he proposed to scourge Him before he released Him. But as the accusers were resolved to have His blood, they rejected this concession, and therefore Pilate had recourse to a fresh expedient. It was the custom for the Roman governor to grant every year, in honor of the Passover, pardon to one condemned criminal. Pilate therefore offered the people their choice between two—the murderer Barabbas and the prophet whom a few days before they had hailed as the Messiah. To receive their decision he ascended the *Bema,* a portable tribunal placed on the *Gabbatha,* a mosaic pavement in front of the palace. As soon as he was seated he received a message from his wife, who had "suffered greatly in a dream because of Him" (Matt. 27:19), urging him not to condemn the Just One. But he had no alternative, as the mob, urged by the priests, chose Barabbas for pardon and clamored for the death of Jesus. Insurrection seemed imminent,

and Pilate yielded. Before issuing the fatal order he washed his hands before the multitude, as a sign that he was innocent of the crime, in imitation, probably, of the ceremony enjoined in Deut. 21. As it produced no effect, Pilate ordered his soldiers to inflict the scourging preparatory to execution; but the sight of unjust suffering so patiently borne seems again to have troubled his conscience and prompted a new effort in favor of the victim. But the priests only renewed their clamors for His death, and, fearing that the political charge of treason might be considered insufficient, returned to their first accusation of blasphemy. They quoted the law of Moses (Lev. 24:16), which punished blasphemy with stoning, declared that He must die, "because He made Himself out to be the Son of God" (John 19:7). But this title augmented Pilate's superstitious fears, already aroused by his wife's dream; he feared that Jesus might be one of the heroes or demigods of his own mythology. He took Him again into the palace and inquired anxiously into His descent ("Where are You from?") and His claims (John 19:9). The result of this interview was one last effort to save Jesus by a fresh appeal to the multitude; but now arose the formidable cry, "If you release this Man, you are no friend of Caesar" (19:12); and Pilate, to whom political success was as the breath of life, again ascended the tribunal and finally pronounced the desired condemnation. So ended Pilate's share in the greatest crime that has been committed since the world began.

Later History. Scripture gives us no further information concerning Pilate, but we learn from Josephus that his anxiety to avoid giving offense to Caesar did not save him from political disaster. The Samaritans were noisy and rebellious. Pilate led his troops against them and defeated them easily enough. The Samaritans complained to Vitellius, now president of Syria, and he sent Pilate to Rome to answer their accusations before the emperor. When he reached it he found Tiberius dead and Caius (Caligula) on the throne, A.D. 36. Eusebius adds that soon afterward, "wearied with misfortunes," he killed himself. As to the scene of his death, there are various traditions. One is that he was banished to Vienna Allobrogum (Vienne on the Rhone), where a singular monument—a pyramid on a quadrangular base, fifty-two feet high—is called Pontius Pilate's tomb. Another is that he sought to hide his sorrows on the mountain by the Lake of Lucerne, now called Mt. Pilatus; and there, after spending years in its recesses in remorse and despair rather than penitence, he plunged into the dismal lake that occupies its summit. We learn from Justin Martyr, Tertullian, Eusebius, and others that Pilate made an official report to Tiberius of our Lord's trial and condemnation; and in a homily ascribed to Chrysostom, though marked as spurious by his Benedictine editors (*Homilies* 8, in

Pasch., 8:968, D), certain *hupomnēmata (Acta,* or *Commentarii Pilati)* are spoken of as well-known documents in common circulation. The *Acta Pilati,* now extant in Gk., and two Lat. epistles from him to the emperor, are certainly false. Confirmation of the existence of Pilate and of his chronological placement came with the work of A. Frova, who conducted an Italian Archaeological Mission dig in the theater of Caesarea (1959-63). There he found an inscription mentioning Pontius Pilate and the Emperor Tiberius.

BIBLIOGRAPHY: F. Josephus *Ant.* 18.3.3; Tacitus *Annals* 15.44; Philo Judaeus *De Virtutibus et Legatione ad Gaium* 38; P. L. Maier, *Pontius Pilate* (1968).

PIL'DASH (pil'dash; derivation uncertain). One of the eight sons of Nahor, Abraham's brother, by his wife and niece, Milcah (Gen. 22:22), about 2080 B.C.

PIL'FERING (Gk. *nosphizō,* "to set apart, divide"). Secretly appropriating and setting apart for one's self the property of another, as of a servant thus misusing the property of his master (Titus 2:10; "purloining," KJV; "to steal," NIV). The same Gk. term is used of the act of Ananias in apparently giving all his property to the church and then appropriating part of the purchase money for his own use (Acts 5:2-3).

PIL'HA (pil'ha). One of the leaders of the people who signed the covenant with Nehemiah (Neh. 10:24), 445 B.C.

PILLAR. The rendering of nine Heb. words and one Gk. word.

1. The essential notion of a pillar is of a shaft or isolated pile either supporting or not supporting a roof. Pillars form an important feature in oriental architecture, partly, perhaps, as a reminiscence of the tent with its supporting poles, and partly also from the use of flat roofs, in consequence of which the chambers were either narrower or divided into portions by columns. The general practice in oriental buildings of supporting flat roofs by pillars, or of covering open spaces by awnings stretched from pillars, led to an extensive use of them in construction. At Nineveh the pillars were probably of wood, and it is likely that the same construction prevailed in the "house of the forest of Lebanon," with its hall and porch of pillars (1 Kings 7:2, 6). The "capitals" (vv. 16-20; "chapiters," KJV) of the two pillars, Jachin and Boaz, resembled the tall capitals of the columns at Persepolis.

2. Perhaps the earliest application of the pillar was the votive or monumental. This in early times consisted of nothing but a single stone or pile of stones (Gen. 28:18; cf. 31:46; etc.). The stone *Ezel* (1 Sam. 20:19) was probably a terminal stone or a roadside marker. The monument set up by Saul (15:12) is explained by Jerome to be a trophy. The word used is the same as that

Pillars from the Parthenon, Athens

for Absalom's pillar. So also Jacob set up a pillar over Rachel's grave (Gen. 35:20). The monolithic tombs and obelisks of Petra are instances of similar usage. Absalom set up a pillar "to preserve" his name (2 Sam. 18:18).

Figurative. The figurative use of the word *pillar,* in reference to the cloud and fire accompanying the Israelites on their march, or as in Rev. 10:1, is plainly derived from the notion of an isolated column not supporting a roof. In poetry we read of pillars on which earth and heaven rest (Job 9:6; 26:11; Ps. 75:3); and the comparison is made of a man, or his limbs, with pillars, for strength and firmness (Song of Sol. 5:15; Jer. 1:18; Gal. 2:9; Rev. 3:12; 10:1). In 1 Tim. 3:15, we have the metaphorical expression "the pillar and support of the truth."

PILLAR OF CLOUD AND FIRE. In Ex. 13:18 it is stated that "God led the people around by the way of the wilderness"; in v. 21 (cf. 14:24; Num. 14:14; Neh. 9:12-19) it is said that "the Lord was going before them in a pillar of cloud by day to lead them on the way, and in a pillar of fire by night to give them light, that they might travel by day and by night," etc., that they might march at all hours. To this sign of the divine presence and guidance there was a natural similarity in the caravan fire, which consisted of small iron vessels or grates with wood fires burning in them, fastened at the end of long poles and carried as a guide in front of caravans, by which the direction of the road was indicated in the daytime by the smoke and at night by the light of the fire. A still closer analogy is found in the custom of the ancient Persians of carrying fire, which they called "sacred and eternal," in silver altars in front of the army. The pillar of cloud and fire must not, however, be confounded with any such caravan or army fire, or set down as nothing more than a mythical conception or a dressing up of this natural custom. The cloud was not the result of a caravan fire, nor was it a mere symbol of the divine presence; it had a miraculous origin and supernatural character.

1. There was but one pillar of both cloud *and* fire (Ex. 14:24), for even when shining in the dark it is still called the pillar of cloud (14:19) or the cloud (Num. 9:21), so that it was a cloud covering the fire. By day it appeared as a cloud in contrast with the light of the sun, but by night as a fiery splendor (9:15-16).

2. When this cloud went before the army of Israel it assumed the form of a column; but when it stood still above the Tabernacle or came down upon it, it most probably took the form of a round globe of cloud. When it separated the Israelites from the Egyptians at the Red Sea, we imagine it spreading out like a cloud bank, forming, as it were, a dividing wall.

3. In this cloud Jehovah, i.e., the visible representation of the invisible God under the OT, was present with Israel and spoke to them. In this, too, appeared "the glory of the Lord" (Ex. 16:10; 40:34). The fire in the pillar was the same as that in which the Lord revealed Himself in the burning bush and afterward descended upon Sinai amid thunder and lightning in a thick cloud (19:16-18). It was a symbol of the zeal of the Lord and therefore was enveloped in a cloud that protected Israel by day from heat, sunstroke, and pestilence (Isa. 4:4-5; 49:10; Pss. 91:5-6; 121:6). At night it lighted up Israel's path by its splendor and defended it from terror and calamity (Pss. 27:1-3; 91:5-6). It also threatened destruction to those who murmured against God (Num. 17:10), sending out fire against the rebels and consuming them (Lev. 10:2; Num. 16:35).

PILLOW. The KJV term *pillow* does not appear in the NASB and NIV, being replaced there by several different words. Heb. *kābîr,* "something netted," appears in the NASB of 1 Sam. 19:13-16 as a "quilt" of goats' hair, and in the NIV as a "garment." Heb. *mᵉra'ashôt* is behind the expression *at its head* in those verses; and a similar expression, *under his head,* is used for the Heb. word in Gen. 28:11, 18 (*see also* Bolster). The "pillows" of KJV Ezek. 13:18, 20, from Heb. *keset,* are replaced in the NASB reading by "magic bands," and in the NIV by "magic charms."

The "pillow" on which the Lord rested His head (Mark 4:38, KJV), from Gk. *proskephalaion,* was a rower's bench or its cushion (so NASB and NIV).

PILOT (Heb. *hōbēl,* a "steersman"). Also rendered "captain" in Jonah 1:6, but in Ezek. 27:8 "pilots" seems to be used in a figurative sense for the chief men of Tyre. Keil (*Com.,* on Ezek.) believes the meaning to be that the chief men in command of the ships (captains and pilots) were as a rule citizens of Tyre. The NIV translates Gk. *kubernētēs* as "pilot" in Acts 27:11 and *euthunontos* similarly in James 3:4.

PIL'TAI (pil'ti; "my deliverances"). The representative of the priestly house of Moadiah or Maadiah, in the time of Joiakim, the son of Jeshua, and apparently one of the priests who returned with Zerubbabel to Jerusalem (Neh. 12:17), 536 B.C.

PIN. For the nominal use of this word, *see* Peg.

PINE TREE. *See* Vegetable Kingdom: Box Tree.

PINNACLE (Gk. *pterugion,* a "wing, any pointed extremity," Matt. 4:5; Luke 4:9). The NIV translates, "highest point." It is impossible to decide definitely what portion of the Temple is referred to as the pinnacle. The use of the definite article makes plain that it was not *a* pinnacle but *the* pinnacle. Much difference of opinion exists respecting it, but it may be that it was the *battlement* ordered by law to be added to every roof.

PI'NON (pī'non). One of the "chief" men (i.e., head or founder of a tribe) of Edom (Gen. 36:41; 1 Chron. 1:52), about 1440 B.C.

PINT. A unit of measure in John 12:3 usually rendered "pound." *See* Metrology: Measures of Weight: Pound.

PIPE. *See* Music.

PI'RAM (pī'ram; perhaps wild ass). The Amorite king of Jarmuth who, with four confederate kings, made war against Gibeon and was defeated by Joshua. The kings fled to the cave at Makkedah, from which they were brought at the close of the battle and pursuit and hanged. Their bodies were taken down and cast "into the cave where they had hidden themselves" (Josh. 10:3-27), c. 1375 B.C.

PIR'ATHON (pir'a-thon; "height, summit," cf. Arab. *far'*, "top"). The dwelling place of Abdon, who died after holding the office of judge for eight years and was buried there (Judg. 12:13-15). It is also mentioned (2 Sam. 23:30; 1 Chron. 11:31) as the home of Benaiah, the hero. It was in the land of Ephraim, on the mountains of the Amalekites. Fer'ata, on a height some 7½ miles W by S of Shechem, is the plausible identification by Robinson.

PIR'ATHONITE (pir'a-thon-īt). The native of, or dweller in, *Pirathon* (which see). Two such are named in the Bible, Abdon the son of Hillel (Judg. 12:13, 15), and "Benaiah the Pirathonite of the sons of Ephraim" (1 Chron. 27:14).

PIS'GAH (pis'ga; Rash es-Siyâghah.) The headland of the rugged Abarim range in Jordan (ancient Moab), breaking through the ridge and skirting the NE end of the Dead Sea by Jericho (Deut. 34:1). Although Pisgah is often considered as identical to or a part of a neighboring peak, Mt. Nebo, it is actually slightly NW of Nebo.

From the top or head of Pisgah Moses took his survey of the Promised Land. The particular peak upon which he stood was near Nebo (Num. 21:20; 23:14; Deut. 3:27; 34:1).

Upon Pisgah Balaam offered sacrifices (Num. 23:14), so that it was probably one of the ancient "high places" of Moab (33:52). The exact identification of Pisgah was long a problem, until the Duc de Luynes (1864) and Professor Paine, of the American Palestine Exploration Society (1873), independently identified it with Jebel Siyâghah, the extreme headland of the range of Abarim, of which the highest summit is Nebo. Respecting the view from this point Smith writes (*Hist. Geog.*, p. 563): "The whole of the Jordan valley is now open to you, from Engedi, beyond which the mists become impenetrable, to where, on the N, the hills of Gilead seem to meet those of Ephraim. The Jordan flows below. Jericho is visible beyond. Over Gilead, it is said, Hermon can be seen in clear weather, but the heat hid it from

us. The view is almost that described as the last on which the eyes of Moses rested, the higher hills of West Palestine shutting out all possibility of a sight of the [Mediterranean] sea."

PI'SHON (pī'shon). One of the four rivers said to "flow out of Eden to water the garden" (Gen. 2:10-14). The Pishon and the Gihon were presumably canals (called "rivers" in Babylonia), which connected the Tigris and Euphrates as ancient riverbeds. Some scholars identify it with the Pallakottos Canal near the ancient Sumerian town of Eridu, not far from Abraham's city of Ur.

M.F.U.

PISID'IA (pi-sid'i-a). A mountainous district in Asia Minor, N of Pamphylia, twice visited by the apostle Paul, and in which he was probably in "dangers from robbers" (2 Cor. 11:26; cf. Acts 13:14; 14:21-24). It was overrun with desperate bands of men who resisted the power of Rome. Antioch was in Pisidia, as distinguished from the more renowned Antioch in Syria.

BIBLIOGRAPHY: E. M. Blaiklock, *Cities of the New Testament* (1965), pp. 22-26.

Ruins of Antioch in the region of Pisidia, now a part of modern Turkey

PISON. *See* Pishon.

PIS'PA (pis'pa). The second named of the sons of Jether, of the tribe of Asher (1 Chron. 7:38).

PISTA'CHIO. *See* Vegetable Kingdom: Nuts.

PIT. The rendering of several Heb. and two Gk. words, and used in the sense of a deep hole dug, in the first instance, for a well or cistern. When these were without water they were used as (1) *a place of burial* (Pss. 28:1; 30:3, 9; Isa. 38:18) and (2) a place of *destruction* (Zech. 9:11).

Figurative. To "go down to the pit" (Pss. 28:1; 30:3, 9; etc.), a phrase of frequent occurrence, is sometimes employed to denote dying without hope, but more commonly it refers simply to going to the place of the dead. To dig a pit (7:15; 57:6; Prov. 26:27) is to plot mischief. The pit, as a place of great discomfort and probable starvation, naturally suggested a place of punishment (Rev. 9:1-2).

PITCH. *See* Mineral Kingdom.

PITCHER. The translation of a variety of Heb. and Gk. terms. Rebekah used a *kad,* a small jug, for carrying water (Gen. 24:14-18, 20, 43-46; "jar," NASB and NIV); and the widow of Zarephath stored flour in such a container (1 Kings 17:12-16, marg., NASB, for "bowl"; "barrel," KJV; "jar," NIV). The same Heb. term is employed in 1 Kings 18:33 of the barrels (so KJV) of water used by Elijah on Mt. Carmel ("pitchers," NASB; "jars," NIV) in Judg. 7:16-20 ("jars," NIV) of the pitchers used by Gideon's 300 men; and in Eccles. 12:6 of the pitchers (so NIV) shattered by the well.

The "pitchers" (KJV), "pot" (NIV), or "earthen jars" (NASB) in Lam. 4:2 was a *nēbel,* a container about twice the size of the *kad* and having a capacity of about five gallons; it could be closed with a stopper.

The *qaśwâ* (1 Chron. 28:17; "cups," KJV; "pitchers," NIV) was a kind of jug; the *gābia* (Jer. 35:5; "pots," KJV), a "bowl" (so NIV).

The *keramion* (Mark 14:13; Luke 22:10) was a portable water jar; the *xestēs* (Mark 7:4, "pitchers," NASB and NIV; "pots," KJV) was a sextarius, which held about a pint.

See also Jar.

Figurative. The "pitcher" shattered "by the well" (Eccles. 12:6) is used figuratively for the end of life. "Earthen pitchers" ("jars," NASB; "pots," NIV), as contrasted with "fine gold" (Lam. 4:2), represent the enemy's estimate of the worth of Israel's sons.

Clay water jars or pitchers

PI'THOM (pi'thom). A storage city of Egypt mentioned in Ex. 1:11 in connection with the bondage of the children of Israel, who were said to have built it and Raamses. It is located in the NE part of Egypt in the land referred to as Goshen. It was SW of Succoth and identified with Tell el-Retabah. The name seems to be derived from Egyptian Pi-Tum, signifying the "house or dwelling of Tum," the solar deity. Excavations at this site reveal constructions made of bricks without straw (cf. 5:10-15). Extensive brickwork in the site constituted large storage spaces. Together with Rameses (Qantir), Pithom was alleged to have been built by Rameses II (c. 1290-1224 B.C.), but in the light of Rameses II's notorious practice of taking credit for achievements wrought by his predecessors, those cities were evidently merely rebuilt or enlarged by him. Inasmuch as Tanis was called the house of Rameses only for a couple of centuries (c. 1300-1100 B.C.), the reference of 1:11 must be to the older city, Zoan, where the oppressed Israelites labored centuries earlier. It is probable, therefore, that the name *Raamses* in 1:11 (same as Rameses) is to be construed as a modernization of an archaic occupational area, Avaris, once a flourishing city before the expulsion of the Hyksos (c. 1570 B.C.). If that is true, both Pithom and Rameses (Avaris/Qantir) were built by the enslaved Israelites long before the time of Rameses II. However, many scholars refer 1:11 to the reign of Seti I or Rameses II.

PI'THON (pi'thon). The eldest son of Micah, the grandson of Jonathan, the son of Saul (1 Chron. 8:35; 9:41), after 1000 B.C.

PLAGUE. A judgment or calamity that God sends upon men (Gen. 12:17; Ex. 11:1; Ps. 106:29-30). The Heb. word *nega'* means "stroke," "plague," or "disease." Another common Heb. word denoting calamities afflicted by God is *makkâ,* also meaning "blow," "sound," or "slaughter," but sometimes translated "plague," or "plagues" (Lev. 26:21; Num. 11:33; Deut. 28:59; 1 Sam. 4:8; etc.). Another original term denoting divine judgment, mostly of a final decision, is *negep,* also from a root to "strike," and is translated "plague," or "plagues" in many places (Ex. 12:13; 30:12; Num. 8:19; etc.). A variation of this is the term *maggēpâ,* also referring to fatal disease, as a divine judgment (Ex. 9:14; 1 Sam. 6:4; etc.). The Gk. term *plēgē* denotes "a blow" and is a word used for public calamity and heavy affliction sent by God as a punishment ("plagues," Rev. 9:18, 20; 11:6; 15:1; 16:9; etc.).

PLAGUES OF E'GYPT. The term usually employed in speaking of the divine visitations of wrath with which Jehovah punished the Egyptians because they would not allow the Israelites to leave.

History. Moses, with Aaron as spokesman, appeared before Pharaoh to convey to him the divine command to allow the departure of the Israelites. In attestation of their authority Aaron cast down his staff before the king, and it became a serpent. This miracle, having been performed, or simulated, by his magicians, "Pharaoh's heart was hardened" (Ex. 7:13) against Jehovah; he refused the desired permission, and thus produced the occasion for the ten plagues. Although it is distinctly stated that the plagues prevailed throughout Egypt, their descriptions seem principally to apply to that part of Egypt that lay nearest to Goshen, and more especially to "the field of Zoan," or the tract about that city, since it seems almost certain that Pharaoh dwelt in the Delta, and that territory is especially indicated in Ps. 78:43. The descriptions of the first and second plagues seem especially to refer to a land abounding in streams and lakes, which is more characteristic of the Delta than Upper Egypt. Still we must not forget that the plagues evidently prevailed throughout the land. There is nothing in the biblical account of the plagues to fix the length of time occupied in their infliction. Although some scholars contend that the plagues took place over the space of a year, the basis of their reasoning seems to be that so long a period of time enables them to compare the plagues with certain natural phenomena occurring at fixed seasons of the year in Egypt. The biblical historian asserts that each plague lasted only a short time; and unless we suppose an interval of several weeks between each, a few months, or even weeks, would afford sufficient time for the happening of the whole.

The Plagues.

Blood (Ex. 7:19-25). Pharaoh having hardened his heart against the first sign, Moses and Aaron were empowered to enforce the release of Israel by a series of punishing miracles. In the morning they met Pharaoh near the Nile and made another demand for the people's release. Upon his refusal Aaron lifted up the staff over "the waters of Egypt," and "all the water that was in the Nile was turned to blood" (vv. 19-20). Keil and Delitzsch observe: "The changing of the water into blood is to be interpreted in the same sense as in Joel 2:31, where the moon is said to be turned into blood; that is to say, not as a chemical change into real blood, but as a change in the color, which caused it to assume the appearance of blood (cf. 2 Kings 3:22). The reddening of the water is attributed by many to the red earth which the river brings down from Sennaar, but Ehrenberg came to the conclusion, after microscopical examinations, that it was caused by cryptogamic plants and infusoria [secretions of decaying organic matter]. This natural phenomenon was here intensified into a miracle, not only by the fact that the change took place immediately in all branches of the river at Moses's word and through the smiting of the Nile, but even more by a chemical change in the water, which caused the [fish] to die, the stream to stink, and what seems to indicate putrefaction, the water to become undrinkable" (*Com.*, ad loc.). The plague

appears to have extended throughout Egypt, embracing "their rivers," or different arms of the Nile; "their streams," or Nile canals; "their pools," or standing lakes formed by the Nile; and all "their reservoirs of water," or the standing lakes left by the overflowings of the Nile. The "vessels of wood" and the "vessels of stone" were those in which was kept the water for daily use, those of stone being the reservoirs in which fresh water was kept for the poor. "The Egyptians dug around the Nile for water to drink" (v. 24), as it probably purified itself by filtering through the banks. The miracle was imitated by the magicians, but where they got water is not stated. On the supposition that the changing of the Nile water took place at the time when the river began to rise, and when the reddening generally occurs, many expositors fix upon the month of June or July for the time of this plague, in which case all the plagues would be confined to the space of about nine months. Perhaps a more likely date was September or October, that is to say, after the yearly overflow of the Nile. This plague was humiliating, inasmuch as the Egyptians were so dependent upon the Nile for water that they worshiped it as a god, as well as some of its fish.

Frogs (Ex. 8:1-15). The second plague also proceeded from the Nile and consisted of unparalleled numbers of frogs. These were the small Nile frog, called by the Egyptians *dofda*. As foretold to Pharaoh, the frogs not only penetrated into the houses and inner rooms and crept into the domestic utensils, the beds, the ovens, and the kneading troughs, but they even got upon the men themselves. This miracle was also imitated by the Egyptian magicians, who made "frogs come up on the land of Egypt" (v. 7). Whether the Egyptian augurs really produced frogs by means of some evil occult power or only simulated the miracle is not stated. One thing is certain: they could not remove the evil, for Pharaoh was obliged to send for Moses and Aaron to intercede with Jehovah to take them away. This request of Pharaoh, coupled with the promise to let the people go, was a sign that he regarded Jehovah as the author of the plague. Upon the morrow God removed the plague and the frogs died, the odor of their putrefaction filling the land. This plague must have been aggravating to the Egyptians, for the frog was included among their sacred animals, in the second class of local objects of worship. It was sacred to the goddess Hekt, who is represented with the head of this animal. Then, too, the fertilizing water of Egypt had twice become a plague.

Gnats (Ex. 8:16-19). Gnats creep into the eyes and nose, and they have a sting that causes a painful irritation. After the harvest they rise in great swarms from the inundated rice fields. The plague was caused by Aaron's smiting the dust of the ground with his staff; all the dust throughout the land of Egypt thereupon turned into gnats, which were upon man and beast. We are not able, nor is it necessary for us, to assert whether this miracle consisted in calling creatures into existence or in a sudden creative generation and supernatural multiplication, for in either case we have a miracle. The failure of the magicians in this instance is believed to have been because of God's restraint of the demoniac powers, which the magicians had before made subservient to their purpose. Their declaration, "This is the finger of God" (v. 19), was not to glorify God but simply to protect their own honor, that Moses and Aaron might not be considered as superior to themselves in virtue or knowledge. It was merely equivalent to saying, "It is not by Moses and Aaron that we are restrained, but by a *divine power*, possibly some god of Egypt."

Insects (Ex. 8:20-32). The fourth plague was foretold to Pharaoh in the morning as he came out to the water, doubtless for worship. It consisted of swarms of insects, probably dog flies. They are more numerous and annoying than gnats, and when enraged they fasten themselves upon the human body, especially the edges of the eyelids, and become a dreadful plague. As the Egyptian magicians only saw in the plague the work of some deity they could not imitate, a distinction between the Israelites and the Egyptians was made in the plagues that followed. Jehovah placed a "division" (v. 23), i.e., a redemption, or deliverance, between the two peoples. Thus Pharaoh was to be taught that Israel's God was the author of the plagues; that He had authority over Egypt; indeed, that He possessed supreme authority. Pharaoh called Moses and told him to sacrifice to God in the land. This Moses declined to do, on the ground that by so doing the Israelites would be an abomination in the eyes of the Egyptians. The abomination would not have consisted in their sacrificing animals that the Egyptians considered holy, for the cow was the only animal offered in sacrifice that the Egyptians so regarded. The abomination would rather be that the Israelites would not observe the sacrificial *rites* of the Egyptians. The probability is that the Egyptians would have looked upon such sacrifice as an insult to their gods and, enraged, would stone the Israelites. Pharaoh, therefore, promised to let the Israelites go if he were released from the plague, but he hardened his heart as soon as the plague was taken away.

Pestilence (Ex. 9:1-7). This plague consisted of a severe disease that killed the cattle of the Egyptians that were in the field, those of the Israelites being spared. A definite time was fixed for the plague, in order that, whereas diseases occasionally occur in Egypt, Pharaoh might see in this one the judgment of Jehovah. That the loss of cattle seems to have been confined to those in the field must be understood from v. 3 and from the fact that there were beasts to be killed by the hail

(v. 25). Again this plague was an insult to the gods of Egypt, for the cow, the calf, and the bull were all worshiped there. The heart of Pharaoh still remained hardened.

Boils. The sixth plague was of boils breaking forth in sores (Ex. 9:8-12). Moses and Aaron took soot or ashes from a smelting furnace or lime kiln and threw it toward heaven. This flew like dust throughout the land and became *boils* (which see, Diseases). The magicians appear to have tried to protect the king by their secret arts but were attacked themselves. The king's heart remained hardened, and he refused to let the people go.

Hail (Ex. 9:17-35). In response to the continued hardness of Pharaoh, Jehovah determined to send such hail as had not been known since Egypt became a nation (vv. 18, 24). A warning was sent out for all God-fearing Egyptians to house their servants and cattle, thus showing the mercy of Jehovah. The hail was accompanied by thunder and lightning, the latter coming down like burning torches, and multitudes of men and beasts were slain, trees and plants destroyed. Terrified by the fierceness of the storm, Pharaoh called for Moses and Aaron and said, "I have sinned this time; the Lord is the righteous one, and I and my people are the wicked ones" (v. 27). Moses promised to pray to Jehovah on behalf of the Egyptians that the storm cease; but as soon as the storm ceased Pharaoh again hardened his heart and refused permission to Israel. "The account of the loss caused by the hail is introduced (vv. 31-32) to show how much had been lost, and how much there was still to lose through continued refusal. According to Pliny the barley is reaped in the sixth month after the sowing time, the wheat in the seventh. The barley is ripe about the end of February or beginning of March, the wheat at the end of March or beginning of April. The flax is in flower at the end of January. Consequently the plague of hail occurred at the end of January, or at the latest in the first half of February; so that there were at least eight weeks between the seventh and tenth plague" (K & D., *Com.,* ad loc.). The havoc caused by this plague was greater than any of the earlier ones; it destroyed men, which others seem not to have done.

Locusts (Ex. 10:1-20). Pharaoh still persisted in resisting the command of Jehovah. Moses was directed to announce another plague. He appeared before the king and put the question, "How long will you refuse to humble yourself before Me?" and added the command "Let My people go, that they may serve Me" (v. 3). A compromise was suggested, by which the men should be allowed to go and worship, but that the women should remain, Pharaoh knowing full well that in such a case the men would return. This compromise was rejected, and Moses and Aaron were driven from the king's presence. Moses lifted up his staff, and the Lord brought an E wind, which the next day brought *locusts* (which see, Animal Kingdom). They came in such dreadful swarms as Egypt had never known before, nor has experienced since; "they covered the surface of the whole land, so that the land was darkened. . . . Thus nothing green was left on tree or plant of the field through all the land of Egypt" (v. 15). The fact that the wind blew a day and a night before bringing up the locusts showed that they came from a great distance, and therefore proved to the Egyptians that the omnipotence of God reached far beyond the borders of Egypt and ruled over every land. Another miraculous feature of the plague was its unparalleled extent, that it was over all Egypt, whereas ordinary swarms are confined to particular districts. In this respect the judgment had no equal either before or afterward (v. 14). In response to Pharaoh's entreaty the Lord "shifted the wind to a very strong west wind" (v. 19), which took away the locusts and cast them into the Red Sea. Pharaoh's promise to allow the Israelites to depart was no more sincere than those he had made before.

Darkness (Ex. 10:21-29). As the king still continued to be defiant, a continuous darkness came over all Egypt, with the exception of Goshen (v. 23). It is described as a "thick darkness" (v. 22). The combination of two words or synonyms gives the greatest intensity to the thought. The darkness was so great that they could not see one another, and no man rose from his place. The Israelites alone "had light in their dwellings" (v. 23). This does not refer to their houses but means that their part of the land was not visited by the plague. The cause of this plague is not given in the text, but most commentators agree that it was the *chamsin*, a wind that generally blows in Egypt before and after the vernal equinox, and lasts two or three days. It rises suddenly, and fills the air with fine dust and coarse sand; the sun is obscured, and the darkness following is greater than the thickest fog. Men and animals hide themselves from this storm, and the inhabitants shut themselves up in the innermost rooms of their houses till it is over, for the dust penetrates even through well-closed windows. "The darkness which covered the Egyptians, and the light which shone upon the Israelites were types of the wrath and grace of God" (Hengstenberg). Again the theology of Egypt was attacked; the sun-god was blotted out by the thick darkness. Pharaoh proposed another compromise, that the Israelites, men, women, and children, should go, but that the flocks and herds should remain. But Moses insisted upon the cattle's being taken for the purpose of sacrifices and burnt offerings, saying, "Not a hoof will be left behind" (v. 26). This firmness Moses defended by saying, "We ourselves do not know with what we shall serve the Lord." At this Pharaoh was so enraged that he not only dismissed Moses but threatened him with death if he should come into his presence again.

Moses answered, "You are right; I shall never see your face again!" (v. 29). God had already told Moses that the last blow would be followed by the immediate release of the people, and there was no further necessity for him to appear before Pharaoh. This announcement to Moses is recorded in 11:1.

Death of the Firstborn (Ex. 11:1–12:30). The brief answer of Moses (10:29) was followed by an address (11:4-8) in which he announced the coming of the last plague and declared that there should be "a great cry in all the land of Egypt, such as there has not been before and such as shall never be again" (v. 6), and that the servants of Pharaoh would come to Moses and entreat him to go with all the Israelites. "And he went out from Pharaoh in hot anger" (v. 8). Then Moses commanded the Israelites to ask from the Egyptians articles of silver and gold, and the Egyptians readily "let them have their request" (v. 36). The Passover (*see* Festivals) was instituted, and the houses of the Israelites sprinkled with the blood of the victims. The firstborn of the Egyptians were struck at midnight, as Moses had forewarned Pharaoh. The clearly miraculous nature of this plague, coming as it did without intervention on the part of Moses, taking only the firstborn, and sparing those of the Israelites, must have convinced Pharaoh that he had to deal with the One who inflicted this punishment by His own omnipotence. That very night Pharaoh sent for Moses and Aaron and gave them permission to depart with their people, their children, and their cattle, even urging haste. *See* Exodus.

General Considerations. The nature of the plagues, their ultimate objective, and Egyptian imitation of the plagues all deserve particular attention.

Miraculous Nature of the Plagues. Whether the plagues were exaggerations of natural evils or not, they were evidently of a miraculous character. They formed the chief part of the miraculous side of the great deliverance of the Israelites from Egyptian bondage. The historian obviously intends us to regard them as miraculous, and they are elsewhere spoken of as the "wondrous acts among them, and miracles in the land of Ham" (Ps. 105:27), i.e., in Egypt (106:7), "signs and wonders" that He sent into the midst of Egypt (135:9). Even if we admit them to have been of the same kind as phenomena natural to the country, their miraculous character would be shown by the unparalleled degree to which the affliction reached; in their coming and going at the command of Moses as the agent of Jehovah; and in the exemption of the Israelites from the general calamity.

Design. As we have already said, the plagues had for their ultimate object the liberation from Egypt; but there were probably other ends contemplated: (1) On Moses, tending to educate and discipline him for the great work on which he was about to enter; to give him confidence in Jehovah, and courage in obeying Him. (2) Upon the Israelites, impressing them with God's care for them and His great power exercised in their behalf. (3) Upon the Egyptians, convincing them of the advantage of casting in their lot with Israel. (4) In demonstrating to Egypt, Israel, and other nations the vanity of Egypt's gods (Ex. 12:12).

The Egyptian Imitations. The question arises as to whether these imitations were miracles performed through the agency of evil spirits or tricks by sleight of hand. It is certainly more conformable to scriptural modes of expression—and therefore more likely to be true—to consider these miracles real; and that the magicians were the instruments of supernatural powers of evil, which at any crisis in the history of redemption always condense their energies. On the other hand, it may be said that the magicians did nothing more than the jugglers of India easily do today. It must be noted that they failed to perform a miracle on the instant, as in the case of the plague of the lice, when no time was allowed them. They were also unable to remove the infliction, or even exempt themselves from it. *See* Moses; Pharaoh.

BIBLIOGRAPHY: T. S. Millington, *Signs and Wonders in the Land of Ham* (1873)—some editions of this work carry the title *The Plagues of Egypt;* J. Pedersen, *Israel, Its Life and Culture* (1940), 3-4: 725-37; J. J. Davis, *Moses and the Gods of Egypt* (1972).

PLAIN. A level stretch of land. The Heb. *biq'â* denotes a wide expanse of level land, usually between mountain ranges, such as the "plain in the land of Shinar" (Gen. 11:2); the plain of Megiddo (2 Chron. 35:22; Zech. 12:11); and the plain of Ono (Neh. 6:2). The uniform word for plain (or "plateau" in the NIV) is *mîshôr* (Josh. 13:9, 16-17, 21; Zech. 4:7; etc.), which in Deut. 3:10 is rendered "tableland" (NIV, "plateau"). A similar word, Heb. *kikkār,* "circle," denotes an entire region, as in Gen. 13:10-12, where Lot sees "all the valley of the Jordan" (*see* marg.).

Plain of Armageddon

PLAITING (1 Pet. 3:3, KJV). *Braiding* the hair.

PLANE (Heb. *maqṣū'â,* a "scraper"). A carpenter's tool, perhaps a *chisel* (so NIV) or *carving* tool (Isa. 44:13). *See* Handicrafts.

PLANE TREE. *See* Vegetable Kingdom.

PLANKS. In the KJV *planks* occurs for Heb. *sēla'* in 1 Kings 6:15; Heb. *'ēs* in Ezek. 41:25; and Heb. *'āb* in 41:26; the NASB renders the terms respectively as *boards, wood,* and *threshold,* with a marginal note giving *canopy* or *canopies* as a possible substitute for *threshold* or *thresholds.* The NIV translates them "planks," "wooden overhang," and "overhangs," respectively.

PLANT. *See* articles Agriculture; Garden; Vegetable Kingdom.

PLASTER. Several uses of plaster are mentioned in Scripture.

1. When a house was infected with "leprosy" the priest was to take away the part of the wall infected and, putting in other stones, replaster the house with fresh plaster (Lev. 14:42, 48).

2. The words of the law were ordered to be engraved on Mt. Ebal on stones that had previously been coated with lime (Deut. 27:2, 4; Josh. 8:32). The process was probably similar to that adopted in Egypt for receiving bas reliefs. The wall was first made smooth and its interstices, if necessary, filled up with plaster. When the figures had been drawn and the stone adjacent cut away so as to leave them in relief, a coat of lime whitewash was laid on, followed by one of varnish after the painting of the figures was complete.

3. It was probably a similar coating of cement on which the fatal letters were traced by the mystic hand "on the plaster of the wall" of Belshazzar's palace at Babylon (Dan. 5:5). *See* Lime, Mortar, Plaster in article Mineral Kingdom.

PLASTERER. *See* House; Mineral Kingdom; Plaster.

PLATTER.
Figurative. To "clean the outside of the cup and of the *platter*" while it remained unclean within (Luke 11:39) is a symbol of hypocrisy. *See* Dish.

PLAY. *See* Games; Music.

PLEDGE. *See* Hostages; Loan.

PLE'IADES (plē'ya-dēz; *kîmâ,* "heap, cluster," Job 9:9; 38:31; Amos 5:8). A constellation of seven large and other smaller stars in the eastern sky, found in Taurus (the Bull), more particularly in the shoulder of the animal.

PLOW. Egypt, probably legitimately, claims the honor of inventing the plow. It was entirely of wood, of simple form, as it is still in that country. It consisted of a share, two handles, and a pole or beam, the last being inserted into the lower end of the stilt, or the base of the handles, and was strengthened by a rope connecting it with the heel. It had no coulter but was probably shod with metal. It was drawn by two oxen, guided and driven by the plowman with a long goad.

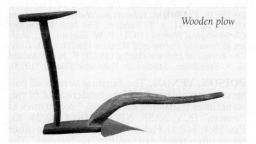

Wooden plow

The plow now used in Palestine differs in some respects from that described above. It is lightly built, with the least possible skill or expense, consisting of two poles, which cross each other near the ground. The pole nearer the oxen is fastened to the yoke, whereas the other serves, the one end as the handle, the other as the plowshare. With these frail plows and tiny oxen, the farmer must wait until the ground is saturated and softened (cf. Jer. 14:4), however late the season may be. Then they cannot sow and plow in more than half an acre per day, and few average so much (Thomson, *Land and Book,* 1:208). Thomson believes that the twelve pairs of oxen (1 Kings 19:19) were each yoked to a plow.

Figurative. Plowing was a symbol of repentance (Jer. 4:3), peace and prosperity (Isa. 2:4; Mic. 4:3), desolation (Jer. 26:18), and the labor of ministers (1 Cor. 9:10). "The plowers plowed upon my back" (Ps. 129:3) is a figure of scourging; keeping the hand upon the plow, a sign of constancy (Luke 9:62).

PLOWMAN. In the KJV, the Heb. terms *harash* and *'ikkār* are behind the English term; in the NASB, those two Heb. terms as well as Heb. *yāgab* and Gk. *arotriaō* are the source of the English expression. Heb. *'ikkār* is not only a plowman, but a *farmer* in general. In some instances NASB *plowman* replaces KJV *husbandman. See* Farmer; Farmers; Farming.

PLOWSHARE. The iron tip of the plow where it enters the earth. To beat a plowshare into a sword is symbolic of war; the reverse of peace.

In the KJV, NIV, and NASB *plowshare* appears in Isa. 2:4; Joel 3:10; Mic. 4:3 as the translation of Heb. *'ēt.* In the NASB and NIV the term appears in 1 Sam. 13:20-21 as the translation of Heb. *maḥăreshet.*

See also Coulter; Mattock.

PLUMB LINE (Heb. *'ănāk*), or **Plummet** (Heb. *mishqelet*). A line, to one end of which is attached a weight. Its use by masons was early known to

the Egyptians and is ascribed to their king Menes about 2900 B.C.

Figurative. A wall built with a plumb line is a perpendicular wall, a wall built with mechanical correctness and solidity. The wall built with a plumb line is a figurative representation of the kingdom of God in Israel, as a firm and well-constructed building. To hold a plumb line to a building may represent the act of construction; or it may be applied to a building in judgment as to the propriety of destroying it (2 Kings 21:13; Amos 7:7-8). The expression "And I will make justice the measuring line, and righteousness the level" (Isa. 28:17) refers to the process of using a plumb line, this being a figure by which what Jehovah is about to do is depicted as a building that He is erecting, and which He will carry out, so far as His despisers are concerned, with a plan of strict retribution. To carry a plumb line in the hand (Zech. 4:10) is a sign of being engaged in the work of building or of superintending the erection of a building.

POCH'ERETH-HAZZEBA'IM (pok'e-reth-ha-ze-ba'im; "binder of the gazelles"), **Pok'ereth-Hazzeba'im** (NIV). A man whose sons were among "Solomon's servants" who returned from the captivity with Zerubbabel (Ezra 2:55, 57; Neh. 7:57, 59), before 536 B.C. The KJV reads "Pochereth of Zebaim."

PO'CHERETH OF ZABA'IM. *See* Pocherethhazzebaim.

PODS. *See* Vegetable Kingdom.

POET (Gk. *poiētēs,* a "performer"). This term occurs in Acts 17:28, in which Paul quotes from Aratus of Cilicia, in the third century, and Cleanthes of Mysia, "For we also are His offspring." From this he argues the absurdity of worshiping idols. The NIV translates Heb. *mōshelîm* as "poets" in Num. 21:27.

POETRY, OLD TESTAMENT. Modern scholarship has shown that large sections of the Heb. Bible are poetic besides the three poetical books—Psalms, Proverbs, and Job —recognized by the Masoretes. Many scholars have studied Heb. versification in the past 200 years. These studies have been aided by extensive archaeological findings in Assyrian, Egyptian, Babylonian, and Canaanite (Ugaritic) poetic literature. This considerable nonbiblical literature has furnished an illuminating background for the study of Bible poetry and demonstrates that the poetry of the Hebrews shares many of the same forms and features of the poetry of neighboring peoples.

Nature of Hebrew Poetry. Hebrew verse is characterized by parallelism. This is a type of sense rhythm constituting thought arrangement rather than word arrangement. This basic phenomenon of Heb. versification was first clearly set forth by Robert Lowth in 1753. (*See* Lowth's

De sacra poesi Hebraeorum praelectiones academicae [English trans., 1847]). Lowth distinguished three chief types of parallelism: synonymous, antithetic, and synthetic.

Synonymous Parallelism is a repetition of the same thought with equivalent expressions, the first line or stich reinforcing the second, giving a distich or couplet:

He who sits in the heavens laughs,
The Lord scoffs at them. (Ps. 2:4)

Antithetic Parallelism consists of the repetition of a contrasting thought in the second line to accentuate the thought of the first:

The young lions do lack and suffer hunger;
But they who seek the Lord shall not be in want of any good thing. (Ps. 34:10)

Synthetic Parallelism is a building up of thought, with each succeeding line adding to the first:

And he will be like a tree firmly planted by streams of water,
Which yields its fruit in its season,
And its leaf does not wither;
And in whatever he does, he prospers. (Ps. 1:3)

This basic pattern of Heb. poetry conveys thoughts pleasing to the mind and produces a musical cadence pleasing to the ear. There are numbers of variations in parallelism discovered since Lowth's day, such as *inverted parallelism* (Pss. 137:5-6; 30:8-10). This occurs in a quatrain when the first line is parallel to the fourth instead of the second and the intervening lines are parallel. G. B. Gray in his *Forms of Hebrew Poetry* (1915) made important advances in the study of parallelism. He distinguished many complete and incomplete parallelisms.

Hebrew Poetry Is Highly Figurative. The Heb. language itself is resonant, rhythmic, and musical, even in prose. Its vocabulary is vivid. It abounds in figures of speech such as alliteration, personification, hyperbole, metaphor, simile, metonymy, and assonance. The difference between Heb. prose and poetry is not always easy to define. In poetry the rhythms are confined within certain limits, whereas in prose they are absolutely free.

Hebrew Poetry Is Rhythmic. Scholarly researchers have shown that Heb. versification is not qualitative; that is, it does not count syllables but depends upon a number of accents. Scholars have differentiated *lyric meter* to be two plus two as in the Song of Solomon; *epic* or *didactic,* three plus three, as in Job or Proverbs; *dirge* or *qinah,* three plus two, as in Lamentations. However, too often scholars have assumed that the ancient Hebrews had definite poetic laws and have superimposed such an artificial prosody on Heb. poetry. This mistake has resulted in wholesale corrections. It must be concluded that Heb. poetry is rhythmical but not strictly metrical. Hebrew poets did not bind themselves by rigid rules. There is evidence also of stanzas or strophes, but

scholars need to beware of superimposing their own artificial divisions upon ancient Heb. poetry. Research in this field promises to yield more light on Heb. verse.

BIBLIOGRAPHY: C. F. Burney, *The Poetry of Our Lord* (1925); W. F. Albright, *Yahweh and the Gods of Canaan* (1968), pp. 1-41; J. T. Sanders, *The New Testament Christological Hymns* (1971); P. W. Skehan, ed., *Studies in Israelite Poetry and Wisdom* (1971); G. B. Gray, *The Forms of Hebrew Poetry* (1972); F. M. Cross and D. N. Freedman, *Studies in Yahwistic Poetry* (1973).

POISON, VENOM. The burning venom of poisonous serpents is the Heb. rendering of *hēmâ,* sometimes translated as "poison," sometimes as "venom" (KJV, NASB, NIV; *see* Deut. 32:24, 33; Pss. 58:4; 140:4). Heb. *rō'sh* and *merōrâ* are other terms often translated "poison" or "venom." The Gk. word *ios* is used to refer to the serpent's poisonous venom (Rom. 3:13; James 3:8). For other uses of Heb. *rō'sh* and *merōrâ*, *see* Gall.

POK'ERETH-HAZZEBA'IM. *See* Pochereth-Hazzebaim.

POLE. *See* Standard.

POLICEMAN (Gk. *hrabdoukos*). A rod holder, i.e., a Roman lictor, a public servant who bore a bundle of rods before the magistrates of cities and colonies as insignia of their office, and who executed the sentences that they pronounced (Acts 16:35).

POLL (Heb. *gūlgōlet,* a "skull," and so rendered in Judg. 9:53; 2 Kings 9:35). The *head* (Num 3:47, NASB); sometimes a *census* (Num. 1:2; 1 Chron. 23:3, 24). Cutting the hair or shaving the head is rendered (in the NASB) by the verbs *trim* (Heb. *kāsam,* Ezek. 44:20), *cut off* (Heb. *gāzaz,* Mic. 1:16), and *cut* (*gālaḥ,* 2 Sam. 14:26). The NIV translates the respective verbs by "trim," "shave," and "cut."

POLL TAX (Gk. *kensos*). A register and valuation of property in accordance with which taxes were paid, the tax or tribute levied on individuals, and to be paid yearly (Matt. 17:25; 22:17; Mark 12:14). The KJV renders this term "tribute," and the NIV, "taxes."

POLLUTION. *See* Contamination.

POL'LUX (pol'uks). *See* Gods, False: Castor and Pollux.

POLYGAMY. *See* Marriage.

POMEGRANATE. Representations of pomegranates, in blue, purple, and scarlet, ornamented the hem of the robe of the ephod (Ex. 28:33-34; *see* High Priest, Dress of), and carved figures of the pomegranate adorned the tops of the pillars in Solomon's *Temple* (which see). The "spiced wine . . . from the juice of my pomegranates" (Song of Sol. 8:2) is made at the present day in the East as it was in the days of Solomon. *See* Vegetable Kingdom.

Figurative. The liquid ruby color of the pulp of this fruit is alluded to in the figurative description of the beautiful complexion of the bride (Song of Sol. 4:3).

POMMEL (Heb. *gūllâ,* "round"). The ball or round ornament on the capital of a column (2 Chron. 4:12, KJV; "bowl," NASB; "bowl-shaped," NIV; *see also* 1 Kings 7:41-42, KJV, NASB, NIV).

PON'TIUS PI'LATE (pon'shus pī'lat). *See* Pilate.

PON'TUS (pon'tus; the "sea"). A large district in the N of Asia Minor, extending along the coast of the Pontus Euxinus, from which circumstance the name was derived. It is three times mentioned in the NT (Acts 2:9-10; 18:2; 1 Pet. 1:1). All these passages agree in showing that there were many Jewish residents in the district. As to the annals of Pontus, the one brilliant passage of its history is the life of the great Mithridates, a dynasty of kings that ruled from c. 337 to 63 B.C. Under Nero the whole region was made a Roman province, bearing the name *Pontus.*

POOL. The translation of several terms in the original.

1. A *collection* or *gathering* of water (Ex. 7:19, from Heb. *miqweh;* in this verse, "pools," KJV, "reservoirs," NASB and NIV).

2. Heb. *'agam,* a *marsh* or *pond* (Ex. 7:19; Isa. 35:7, cf. 14:23, NASB, "swamps of water").

3. Heb. *berēkâ,* "a pool," or "pond" (Eccles. 2:6; Isa. 36:2; Nah. 2:8). "Pools" in the KJV of Ps. 84:6, from a slightly different Heb. word, is more appropriately "blessings" (so NASB).

4. Heb. *mayim,* "waters" (*see* Gen. 1:10), given

The Towers' Pool in Jerusalem, built by Herod the Great to hold water piped in from a spring south of Bethlehem

as "pool" in the NASB and NIV of Jer. 41:12. *See* Water; Well, no. 3.

5. Gk. *kolumbēthra,* a "diving place," given as "pool" in John 5:2, 4, 7; 9:7; cf. 9:11, KJV.

The following are the principal pools (*reservoirs* mentioned in Scripture:

Pool of Hezekiah (2 Kings 20:20). The pool of Hezekiah was a basin opened by King Hezekiah in the city and fed by a water course. In 2 Chron. 32:30 it is stated that "it was Hezekiah who stopped the upper outlet of the waters of Gihon and directed them to the west side of the city of David," i.e., by a subterranean channel into the city of David. This pool, called by the Arabs Birket el-Hammâm, is pointed out by tradition in the NW part of the modern city, not far E of the Jaffa gate.

The Upper and Lower Pool. The "upper" pool (Isa. 7:3; 36:2; 2 Kings 18:17) is one lying near the fuller's field and on the road to it, outside the city. The lower pool is named in Isa. 22:9. They are generally known as the upper and lower pools of Gihon. Support for the identification of the pools of Gihon with "the upper and lower pools" arises from there being no other similar or corresponding reservoirs in the neighborhood; and the western position of the upper pool suits well the circumstances mentioned in Scripture (36:2). It may be added that a trustworthy tradition places the fuller's field W of the city.

The Old Pool (Isa. 22:11). The "old pool" was not far from the two walls. The two walls were near the king's garden (2 Kings 25:4; Jer. 39:4), which must be sought in the SE of the city, near the fountain ("pool") of Siloam (Neh. 3:15).

The King's Pool (Neh. 2:14). The king's pool is thought to be the Fountain of the Virgin Mary, E of Ophel (Robinson, 2:102, 149) and is perhaps the same as the pool of Solomon. *See* Gibeon; Samaria; Solomon; Bethesda; and Siloam for the pools under those names.

POOR. In the Heb. and Gk., as in the English language, there were a number of words used to express the condition of being in need. The Scriptures frequently mention the poor, and they teach that no inconsiderable part of the duty required of believers under both Testaments has respect to the treatment accorded to the poor. No merit, however, is given to the assumption of poverty; and the Mosaic law takes every precaution to prevent poverty. Its extreme form of want and beggary was ever represented as the just recompense of profligacy and thriftlessness (Ps. 37:25; Prov. 20:4; 24:34).

Mosaic Enactments. It was stated from the first that there would be those among the covenant people who would be in circumstances calling for sympathy and aid (Deut. 15:11). Negatively, the poor man was to have no advantage over others on the ground of his poverty (Ex. 23:3); but neither, on the other hand, was his judgment on that account to be wrested from him (v. 6). Among the special enactments in his favor the following must be mentioned: (1) The right of gleaning (Lev. 19:9-10; Deut. 24:19-21). (2) The custom of giving the poor and the stranger their portion of the produce of the land in sabbatical years (Ex. 23:11; Lev. 25:6). (3) The reversion of land to the owner in the Jubilee year, with the year-long right of redemption as to town homes (Lev. 25:25-30). (4) The prohibition of usury and the limitation on what could be retained as a pledge (Lev. 25:35-37; cf. Ex. 22:25-27; etc.). (5) The forbidding of permanent bondage and the enjoinment to free Hebrew bondmen or bondwomen in the sabbatical and Jubilee years (Deut. 15:12-15; cf. Lev. 25:39-42, 47-54). (6) The requirement that portions from the tithes be shared by the Levites and then the poor (Deut. 14:28; 26:12-13). (7) The right of the poor to partake in entertainments at the feasts of Weeks and Booths (Deut. 16:11-14; see Neh. 8:10). (8) The requirement that wages be paid daily (Lev. 19:13). Principles similar to those laid down by Moses are inculcated in the NT, as in Luke 3:11; 14:13; Acts 6:1; Gal. 2:10; James 2:15-16. In later times the practice of begging, which does not appear to have been considered by Moses, became frequent.

BIBLIOGRAPHY: R. de Vaux, *Ancient Israel: Its Life and Institutions* (1961), pp. 68-79, 164-77.

POPLAR. See Vegetable Kingdom.

POR'ATHA (por'a-tha; Old Pers., "liberal, bounteous"). One of the ten sons of Haman slain by the Jews in the palace at Susa (Esther 9:8), about 509 B.C.

PORCH. The rendering of several Heb. and Gk. terms.

1. Heb. *'ûlām* (1 Chron. 28:11). The entrance hall of a building (Ezek. 40:7, 48), a pillar hall (1 Kings 7:6), a throne hall (v. 7), and the veran-

Model of Solomon's Porch at the Temple in Jerusalem

da or "gallery" surrounding a court (Ezek. 41:15). It is especially applied to the vestibule of the Temple (1 Kings 6-7; Joel 2:17). "The porch of the Lord" (2 Chron. 15:8; 29:17) seems to stand for the Temple itself.

2. Heb. *misderôn*. A "vestibule" (so NASB, Judg. 3:23), probably a sort of chamber in the works of Solomon, open in front and at the sides but capable of being enclosed with awnings or curtains. It was perhaps a corridor or colonnade connecting the principal rooms of the house. The NIV renders "porch" here.

3. Gk. *pulōn*. A "gateway" (so NASB and NIV, Matt. 26:71).

4. Gk. *stoa*. A "portico" (so NASB, John 5:2; 10:23; Acts 3:11; 5:12). The NIV translates "colonnade" in the passages.

POR'CIUS (pōr'shi-us; Festus). See Festus.

POR'PHYRY (por'fi-rē). See Mineral Kingdom: Marble.

PORPOISE. See Animal Kingdom.

PORT. See Gate; Refuse Gate.

PORTER. See Gatekeeper.

PORTION.

1. An allowance, as of food, clothing, etc. (1 Sam. 1:5; Ps. 17:14; Prov. 31:15; Isa. 53:12); also called a share (Gen. 14:24) and an allotment (47:22). The command "Go, eat of the fat, drink of the sweet, and send portions to him who has nothing prepared; for this day is holy to our Lord" (Neh. 8:10) has reference to a custom, still existing in the East, of sending a portion of a feast to those who cannot attend it, especially to relatives, or to those in mourning or in a particular time of joy (Esther 9:19).

2. One's lot, destiny, etc. (Job 20:29; 27:13; Ps. 11:6; Isa. 17:14).

3. Part of an estate, one's *inheritance* (which see). It may be that the expression "The Lord is the portion of my inheritance and my cup" (Ps. 16:5; 119:57; Lam. 3:24) includes all the other meanings.

POSTS. See Courier.

POT (Heb. *pārûr, sîr, dûd, masrep, keli;* Gk. *chalkion;* all NASB; cf. Gk. *hudria, xestēs*). The Heb. and Gk. terms translated "pot" in the KJV are not always the same as in the NASB and NIV). A term of wide application, including many sorts of vessels, the most common designation being Heb. *sîr,* a vessel of various sizes and shapes (2 Kings 4:38) and made of different materials, both earthenware and metal. An earthenware vessel for stewing or seething (Heb. *heres*) is mentioned (Ps. 22:15, "potsherd"; Prov. 26:23, "potsherd," KJV; "earthen vessel," NASB; "earthenware," NIV) as well as a culinary vessel (Heb. *dûd,* Job 41:20; Ps. 81:6). Heb. *masrep* refers to a crucible ("refining pot," Prov. 17:3), and Heb. *pārûr* to a cooking pot (Num. 11:8; Judg. 6:19). In the NT a vessel of stone or hard earthenware for holding water is referred to in John 2:6-7 (Gk. *hudria,* "waterpot").

Large pots at Cana

POTENTATE (Gk. *dunastēs*). A term applied to God (1 Tim. 6:15, KJV; cf. Rom. 16:27), expressive of His transcendent power and authority. "Sovereign," NASB; "Ruler," NIV.

POT′IPHAR (pot′i-fer; Egyptian, "whom Re," i.e., the sun-god, "has given," contraction of *Potiphera,* which see). An Egyptian and an officer ("captain of the bodyguard") of Pharaoh. When Joseph was taken to Egypt Potiphar purchased him from the Midianite merchants. Potiphar was so favorably impressed by the ability and fidelity of Joseph that he made him overseer of his house and committed all his possessions to his care. Upon the accusation of his wife, Potiphar cast Joseph into prison (Gen. 39:1-20), c. 1890 B.C. After this we hear no more of Potiphar, unless, which is not likely, he was the chief of the executioners afterward mentioned.

BIBLIOGRAPHY: C. E. Macartney, *Ancient Wives and Modern Husbands* (1934), pp. 71-88; K. A. Kitchen, *Ancient Orient and Old Testament* (1966), pp. 165-66.

POTIPH′ERA, POTIPHERAH (po-tif′er-a). An Egyptian and priest of On (Heliopolis) whose daughter Asenath was married to Joseph (Gen. 41:45, 50; 46:20), about c. 1870 B.C.

POTSHERD (Heb. *ḥeres*). A fragment of an earthen vessel. Scraping the boil (*see* Job 2:8) with a potsherd will not only relieve the intolerable itching but also remove the matter.

Figurative. The potsherd is used as a figure for that which is dry (Ps. 22:15).

POTSHERD GATE. A gate of Jerusalem (Jer. 19:2; "east gate," KJV), not mentioned elsewhere by this name. It is probably identical with the Valley Gate leading to the valley of *Hinnom* (which see), if not with the Refuse Gate (Neh. 2:13; 3:13-14; 12:31), through which one went southward from the city. Potter's works seem to have been located in its vicinity; it is "the 'gate of potsherds,' so called from the many potsherds thrown down before it" (Orelli, *Com.,* ad loc.).

POTS OF MEAT. The pots referred to by this expression in the NASB and NIV are more familiarly known by the KJV term *flesh pots* (Ex. 16:3). They were probably three-legged bronze vessels used for culinary purposes by the Egyptians, such as are represented in the paintings of the tombs.

POTTAGE (*nāzîd,* something "boiled"). A *stew* (so NASB and NIV, Gen. 25:29, 34). *See also* Vegetable Kingdom: Lentils.

POTTER. *See* Handicrafts.

POTTER'S FIELD. A piece of ground that was purchased by the priests with the thirty pieces of silver rejected by Judas. It was converted into a burial place for Jews not belonging to the city (Matt. 27:7). Matthew referred to this disposal of the field as being a fulfillment of an ancient prediction (v. 9). According to Acts 1:18, the purchase is said to have been made by Judas himself, an idiom of Scripture by which an action is sometimes said to be *done* by a person who was the *occasion* of its being done. What that prediction was, and who made it, is not, however, at all clear. Matthew names Jeremiah; but there is no passage in the book of Jeremiah, as we possess it, resembling that which he gives; and that in Zechariah (11:12), which is usually supposed to be alluded to, has only an imperfect likeness to it. Four explanations suggest themselves: (1) That the evangelist unintentionally substituted the name *Jeremiah* for that of Zechariah, at the same time altering the passage to suit his immediate object. (2) That this portion of the book of Zechariah was in the time of Matthew attributed to Jeremiah. (3) That the reference is to some passage of Jeremiah that has been lost from its place in his book and exists only in the evangelist. Some support is afforded to this view by the fact that potters and the localities occupied by them are twice alluded to by Jeremiah. Its partial correspondence with Zech. 11:12-13 is no argument against its having at one time formed a part of the prophecy of Jeremiah; for it is well known to every student of the Bible that similar correspondences are continually found in the Prophets. *See,* for instance, Jer. 48:45; cf. with Num. 21:27, 28; 24:17; Jer. 49:27; cf. with Amos 1:4 (Smith, *Dict.,* s.v.). (4) "That it is to be regarded as a very old copyist's error, of a more ancient date than any of the critical helps that have come down to us" (Luther, *Com.,* on Zech., p. 1528).

Meyer (*Com.,* on Matt. 27:9) says, "According to the historical sense of Zechariah, the prophet, acting in Jehovah's name, resigns his office of shepherd over Ephraim to Ephraim's own ruin; and having requested his wages, consisting of thirty pieces of silver, to be paid him, he casts the money, as being God's property, into the *treasury of the temple.*" Accordingly, Meyer believes "into the treasury" ought to be read *'el* and not *'el hăyōṣēr* "to the potter."

POTTER'S GATE. *See* Potsherd Gate.

POUL'TICE (pōl'tis). A soft medicinal application spread on a cloth and applied to sores or wounds. The only reference in the Bible is to the healing of Hezekiah's boil (2 Kings 20:7; Isa. 38:21) where the Heb. word for "poultice" in the NIV is usually translated "cake," here a cake of figs.

POUND. A weight and a unit of money. *See* Metrology.

POVERTY. *See* Poor.

POWDERS (Heb. *'ăbāqâ,* "dust"). Powdered spices, used for perfume and incense (Song of Sol. 3:6).

POWER. The ability of performing belongs essentially to God, who is all-powerful and omnipotent. In the KJV the term *power* has the sense of *ability, strength* (Gen. 31:6; Ps. 22:20; Isa. 37:27); *right, privilege,* or *dignity* (John 1:12; Acts 5:4; 1 Cor. 7:37; 9:4, Gk. *dunamis*); *absolute authority* (Matt. 28:18, same Gk. as above); the *exertion* or *act* of power, as of the Holy Spirit (Eph. 1:19, Gk. *kratos*), some of which meanings are more directly represented in the NASB and NIV readings.

PRAETO'RIUM (pre-tō'ri-um; Gk. *praitorion,* Matt. 27:27; Mark 15:16; sometimes "judgment hall," KJV).

1. The headquarters in a Roman camp, the tent of the commander in chief.

2. The palace in which the governor or procurator of a province resided (John 18:28, 33; 19:9; Acts 23:35). At Jerusalem the Praetorium was the magnificent palace that Herod the Great built for himself, and that which the Roman procurators seem to have occupied whenever they came from Caesarea to Jerusalem on public business.

Model of Herod the Great's palace, Jerusalem

3. In Rome the Praetorium was probably the quarters built by Tiberius for the imperial bodyguard, the "praetorian guard" (Phil. 1:13). Ramsay (*St. Paul the Traveller,* p. 357) says, "The *pretorium* is the whole body of persons connected with sitting in judgment, the supreme imperial court, doubtless in this case the prefect or both prefects of the Pretorian Guard, representing the emperor in his capacity as the fountain of justice, together with the assessors and high officers of the court."

BIBLIOGRAPHY: C. Kopp, *The Holy Places of the Gospels* (1963), pp. 354, 366-73.

PRAISE. The rendering of a number of Heb. and Gk. words. Praise is an expression of approval or admiration, of gratitude and devotion for blessings received. When directed toward men, it should never descend to flattery; neither should the love of it become so great as to hush the voice of conscience and of duty. Although without it there will be no sense of reproach, when it has gone beyond its proper place it corrupts instead of improving.

Praise of God is the acknowledging of His perfections, works, and benefits. Praise and thanksgiving are generally considered as synonymous, yet some distinguish them thus: praise properly terminates in God, on account of His natural excellencies and perfections, and is that act of devotion by which we confess and admire His several attributes; but *thanksgiving* is a more contracted duty and imports only a grateful sense and acknowledgment of past mercies. We praise God for all His glorious acts of every kind, that regard either us or other men; but we thank Him, properly speaking, for the instances of His goodness alone, and for such only of these as we ourselves are in some way concerned.

BIBLIOGRAPHY: H. H. Rowley, ed., *Old Testament and Modern Study* (1951), pp. 165-209; C. Westermann, *The Praise of God in the Psalms* (1965); R. B. Allen, *Praise! A Matter of Life and Breath* (1980).

PRAYER.

Scriptural Terms. The following Heb. terms are rendered *prayer:* (1) *Tᵉpillâ,* in general, supplication to God (Pss. 65:2; 80:4; Isa. 1:15; Job 16:17; etc.); also intercession, supplication for another (2 Kings 19:4; Isa. 37:4; Jer. 7:16; 11:14). (2) *Pâlal,* to "judge," and then "to interpose as umpire, mediator" (Gen. 20:7; Deut. 9:20; 1 Sam. 7:5; Job 42:8), with the general sense of prayer (Ps. 5:2; 1 Sam. 1:26; 2 Sam. 7:27; etc.). (3) *'Âtar,* "to burn incense," therefore to *pray* to God (Job 33:26), the prayers of the righteous being likened to incense (Rev. 5:8). (4) *Lāhash,* to "whisper a prayer" uttered in a low voice (Isa. 26:16). *Lāhash* is a quiet whispering prayer (like the whispering forms of incantation in 3:3); sorrow renders speechless in the long run; and a consciousness of sin crushes so completely that a man does not dare to address God aloud (cf. 29:4).

The following Gk. terms are rendered *prayer:* (1) *Deēsis,* prayer for particular benefits. (2) *Proseuchē,* prayer in general, not restricted as respects its contents. (3) *Enteuxis* (1 Tim. 4:5), confiding access to God. In combination, *deēsis* gives prominence to the expression of personal need; *proseuchē* to the element of devotion; and *enteuxis* to that of childlike confidence, by representing prayer as the heart's converse with God. (4) *Euchē,* which occurs only once in the NT in the sense of a prayer (James 5:15), but in this noun and its verb, the notion of the vow—of the dedicated thing—is more commonly found than that of prayer. The two other occasions of the word (Acts 18:18; 21:23) bear out this remark (Trench, *Synonyms of the N.T.,* 2:1).

Scriptural History. Prayer, constituting as it does the most direct expression of religious feeling and consciousness, has been, from the beginning, the principal means by which men, created in the image of God, have given expression of their attitude toward Him; and from the earliest times, ever since in the days of Enoch when "men began to call upon the name of the Lord" (Gen. 4:26), it has formed an integral part of the public worship of God. The patriarchs and pious Israelites in all ages have expressed the feelings and dispositions of their hearts by praise, thanksgiving, prayer, and intercession before God (18:22-33; 20:17; 24:12-14; 25:21-22; 32:9-12; Ex. 32:11-13; 1 Sam. 1:10; 2:1-10; 8:6; 12:23; 1 Kings 8:22-53; 17:20-21; 2 Kings 4:33; 19:15-19; Jonah 2:2-9; 4:2-3; Dan. 6:10; 9:3-19; etc.). We find also that wherever the patriarchs erected an altar for worship, they did so with the view of calling upon the name of the Lord (Gen. 12:8; 13:4; 21:33).

The law did not prescribe any prayer for public worship except the confession of sin on the great Day of Atonement (*see* Festivals; also Lev. 16:21), and the thanksgiving on the occasion of the offering of the firstlings and tithes (Deut. 26:3-11), yet it is certain that in Israel no act of worship was unaccompanied by prayer. It was not expressly mentioned in the law because it not only happened that prayer was a regular accompaniment of laying the hand on the victim in sacrifice but also because it was usual for the congregation, or the Levites as representing it (1 Chron. 23:30), to offer up prayer morning and evening while the incense was being burned (Luke 1:10). As early as David's time we hear of private prayer being offered three times a day (Ps. 55:17), which subsequently became an established practice (Dan. 6:10), the hours being at the time of the morning sacrifice, about the third hour (Acts 2:15); at midday, about the sixth hour (10:9); and at the time of the evening sacrifice, about the ninth hour (Dan. 9:21; Acts 3:1).

Grace. Grace before and after meals was an ancient practice, although we find no explicit testimony regarding it earlier than in the NT (Matt. 15:36; John 6:11; Acts 27:35). How earnest and fervent the prayers of pious Israelites were may be seen from the psalms and many other parts of the OT. Prayer degenerated into mere "lip service" at so early a period as to provoke the censure of the older prophets (Isa. 1:15; 29:13). Later, prayer seems to have degenerated into a mere performance, especially among the Pharisees (Matt. 6:5, 7). As a rule the Israelites prayed in a solitary room, especially the upper chamber (Dan. 6:11; Judith 8:5; Tobit 3:12; Acts 1:13), or in elevated places and mountains with the view of being alone (1 Kings 18:42; Matt. 14:23; Mark 6:46; Luke 6:12). If near the sanctuary, they offered their prayers in the court (1 Sam. 2:1; Luke 18:10; Acts 3:1), with faces turned toward the Holy of Holies (1 Kings 8:38), in which direction it was the practice to turn the face during prayer, even when at a distance from the Temple (2 Chron. 6:34; Dan. 6:11).

The Posture. Prayer was generally made standing (1 Sam. 1:26; Dan. 9:20; Matt. 6:5; etc.), but sometimes, as expressive of deeper devotion, the worshiper knelt (1 Kings 8:54; 2 Chron. 6:13; Ezra 9:5; Dan. 6:10; Luke 22:41; etc.), or bowed the head to the ground (Neh. 8:6). In both cases the hands were uplifted and spread toward heaven or in the direction of the Holy of Holies (1 Kings 8:22; Neh. 8:7; Lam. 2:19; 3:41; Ps. 28:2; etc.). In cases of deep, penitential prayer it was usual to strike the breast with the hand (Luke 18:13) and to bend the head toward the bosom (Ps. 35:13; cf. 1 Kings 18:42).

After the sacrificial worship was discontinued prayer came entirely to occupy the place of sacrifice. Minute regulations regarding the order and the different sorts of prayer, as well as the outward posture, are given in the Talmud. The ancient rabbis and their followers regarded the wearing of *phylacteries* (which see) as essential to prayer.

Christian Doctrine. Prayer is the expression of man's dependence upon God for all things. What habitual reverence is to praise, the habitual sense of dependence is to prayer. "Prayer, or communion with God, is not reckoned among the means of grace technically so called. It is regarded rather as the concomitant of the others. But, while it is undeniably true that prayer is a condition of the efficacy of other means, it is itself and alone a means of grace" (Pope, *Systematic Theology*, 3:298). It is a means of grace that has large value, for it affords the privilege of close communion with God, especially when one is alone with Him in its supplications. Although on the one hand there arises a deep sense of need, helplessness, and unworthiness, there also comes an assurance of the divine fullness and love, which enlarges our petitions and brings confidence of answers to our prayers.

Requisites. Prayer requires sincerity, repentance or contrition, purpose of amendment and a good life, the spirit of consecration, faith, and submission to the will of God.

Elements of Power. There are certain elements of power in prayer that have a clear and scriptural ground, such as fervency of mind (James 5:16). In such a prayer the mind is intensely active. The object for which we pray is grasped in all the vigor of thought and feeling. Another element of power lies in the help of the Holy Spirit. There are in Scripture clear promises of His help and statements that mean the same thing (Zech. 12:10; Eph. 6:18). Then we have these explicit words: "And in the same way the Spirit also helps our weakness" (Rom. 8:26). There are many ways in which He may thus help us. He may give us a deeper sense of our spiritual needs and clearer views of the fullness and freeness of the divine grace, and may kindle the fervor of our supplication. We reach a deeper meaning in the words "But the Spirit Himself intercedes for us." He joins us in our prayers, pours His supplications into our own. Nothing less can be the meaning of these deep words. Here is the source of the glowing fervor and the effectual power of prayer. There are instances that cannot be explained otherwise: such as the prayer of Jacob (Gen. 32:24-30), of Moses (Ex. 32:9-14), and of Elijah (James 5:17-18). Another element of this power lies in the intercession of Christ. In His high-priestly office He presents our prayers with the incense of His own blood and the intercession of His own prayers (Rev. 8:3-4).

Objections. The question, "And what would we gain if we entreat Him?" (Job 21:15) is one that continues to be asked. Those who deny the personality of God declare that it is vain to pray, for there is no God to hear our prayers. Such objectors set themselves against the common consciousness of all mankind and may be dismissed with the question, "He who planted the ear, does He not hear?" (Ps. 94:9). Others admit the ability of God to hear but see no use in prayer, since God is so high and His counsels far too firmly established to be ever moved by their poor petitions. We answer, God is "not far from each one of us" (Acts 17:27); and in giving man a strong instinct to pray God has virtually pledged Himself to hear prayer and to answer it (1 John 5:14-15).

Again it is urged that God is immutable. "The idea of a supernatural providence, with answers to prayer, is the idea of a temporal agency of God above the order of nature. The objection is that such an agency is contradictory to the divine immutability. There is no issue respecting the truth of immutability. Is such an agency contradictory to this truth? An affirmative answer must reduce our Christian theism to the baldest deism. Only a false sense of immutability can require the same divine action toward nations and individuals, whatever the changes of moral conduct in them; the same toward Christian believers, whatever the changes of estate with them. A true sense of immutability requires changes of divine action in adjustment to such changes in men. It seems strange that any one who accepts the Scriptures can for a moment give place to this objection.

"Another objection is based on the divine omniscience. This objection is made specially against the efficacy of prayer. God foreknows all things, knows from eternity the state and need of every soul. Hence prayer is not necessary, nor can it have any influence upon the divine mind. These inferences are not warranted. If it were the office of prayer to give information of our wants, it is surely needless and must be useless. Prayer has no such office. It is required as the proper religious movement of a soul in its dependence

Postures in prayer

and need, and thus becomes the means of God's blessings" (*Systematic Theology*, 1:341ff.).

Objection to the need of prayer on the ground of the wisdom and goodness of God—that being wise and good He will give what is good without asking—"admits but of one answer, viz., that it may be agreeable to perfect wisdom to grant that to our prayers which it would not have been agreeable to that same wisdom to have given us without praying for. A favor granted to prayer may be more apt, on that very account, to produce good effects upon the person obliged. It may be consistent with the wisdom of the Deity to withhold his favors till they are asked for, as an expedient to encourage devotion in his rational creation, in order thereby to keep up and circulate a knowledge and sense of their dependency upon him. Prayer has a natural tendency to amend the petitioner himself, and thus to bring him within the rules which the wisdom of the Deity has prescribed to the dispensation of his favors" (Paley, *Moral Philosophy*, book 5, chap. 2).

BIBLIOGRAPHY: O. Hallesby, *Prayer*, (1956); J. G. S. S. Thompson, *The Praying Christ* (1959); H. Thielicke, *Our Heavenly Father* (1960); W. Law, *The Spirit of Prayer* (1969); St. Teresa of Avila, *A Life of Prayer* (1983); A. Murray, *The Believer's Prayer Life* (1984); id., *The Believer's School of Prayer* (1984); id., *Ministry of Intercession* (1984); id., *The Secret of Believing Prayer* (1985); K. Barth, *Prayer* (1985).

PRAYER, LORD'S. See Lord's Prayer.

PREACHER, PREACHING. By preaching is generally understood the delivering of a religious discourse based upon a text of Scripture.

Scripture Terms. The study of the Scripture terms for preaching is interesting, for they show the various characteristics and purposes of preaching:

To Cheer with Good Tidings (Heb. *bāśar,* to "be cheerful, joyful"), as "I have proclaimed glad tidings of righteousness in the great congregation" (Ps. 40:9); "To bring good news to the afflicted," etc. (Isa. 61:1).

To Declare (Heb. *qārā',* to "call" out to) in the sense of proclaiming, as a herald. For example, Sanballat accused Nehemiah of appointing "prophets to proclaim in Jerusalem concerning you" (Neh. 6:7, announce him as king); and the same word is used (8:8) of the Levites *reading* aloud the law and *teaching* the people (v. 9); and Jonah (3:2) was commanded to preach unto Nineveh, i.e., to proclaim judgment and mercy to its people.

To Address a Public Assembly (cf. Heb. *qōhelet,* an "assembler"). Thus Solomon is designated "the Preacher" (Eccles. 1:2; etc.), "the only true signification of which seems to be that given the earliest versions, e.g., Vulgate and Septuagint, i.e., one addressing a public assembly and discoursing of human things; unless one

chooses to derive the signification of preacher or orator from the primary notion of calling and speaking" (Gesenius, *Lex.,* s.v.).

To Announce (Gk. *aggellō*), in several combinations, as: *euaggelizō,* to announce good tidings, "evangelize" (Matt. 11:5; Luke 7:22; Heb. 4:2, 6), especially to instruct men concerning the things pertaining to Christian salvation (Luke 9:6; 20:1; Rom. 15:20; 1 Cor. 1:17; 9:16, 18; etc.); *katangelō,* to "proclaim publicly" (Acts 13:5; 15:36; etc.); *proeuangelizomai,* to announce or promise good tidings "beforehand," i.e., before the event by which the promise is made good (Gal. 3:8).

To Discourse (Gk. *dialegomai,* to "think different things with one's self"), to converse, discourse with anyone (Acts 20:9; cf. 18:4; 19:8; etc.).

To Speak (Gk. *laleō,* to "talk"), to speak to one about a thing, i.e., to *teach* (Acts 2:2; Acts 8:25; 13:42; 14:25; 16:6; etc.). *That which is heard* (Gk. *'akoē,* "hearing"), especially the *preaching* of the gospel (John 12:38; Rom. 10:16).

To Be a Herald (Gk. *kērussō,* to be "a herald"), to officiate as a herald, used of the public declaration of the gospel and matters pertaining to it, by John the Baptist, Jesus, by the apostles and other Christian teachers (Matt. 11:1; Mark 1:4; 3:14; 16:20; Rom. 10:15; etc.).

Freedom of Utterance (Gk. *parrēsia,* "boldness in speaking," Acts 9:27; cf. 2 Cor. 3:12).

Thus it will be seen that to some extent preaching had been recognized in the old dispensation; Noah being "a preacher of righteousness" (2 Pet. 2:5), the psalmist and the prophets delivering their messages of truth in song, and accusation and rebuke, pleading and exhortation, prophecy and promise. The reading and exposition of Scripture was from the beginning the chief object of the synagogue service and is frequently mentioned in the NT (Luke 4:16; Acts 13:15; 15:21). *See* Synagogue.

In the NT times the Lord and His apostles preached wherever the people could be gathered: in the synagogues, on the mountainside, by the shores of seas and rivers, in the public street, at the porch of the Temple. The preaching of the Word of God (the law and the gospel) is the chief means ordained by Christ Himself and is sufficient for all, by which the Holy Spirit brings about the commencement and continuance of saving faith in the heart of the sinner. So the apostle states (Rom. 10:17), "Faith comes from hearing, and hearing by the word of Christ." The history of God's kingdom furnishes a number of instances showing that the operation of the Holy Spirit for conversion and sanctification is inseparably united to the preaching of the word, as, for example, on the Day of Pentecost (Acts 2:37-39; 10:44-47) and in the many remarkable examples of the combined operation of the Word and Spirit in the apostolic age (Acts 9:31; 16:14; Gal. 3:5;

Eph. 1:13; James 1:18). When we consider "what is written in praise of God's testimony under the old covenant (Ps. 19:8-11; 119; Jer. 23:29); and how the Lord himself spoke of the sufficiency of the testimony of Moses and the prophets (Luke 16:27-31); the testimony of Paul (Rom. 1:16) as to the power of God unto salvation; of Peter (1 Pet. 1:23) as to the seed of regeneration; of the epistle to the Hebrews (4:12) as to the sharp and two-edged sword of the word—[and compare] all this with what experience tells us in varied forms of ourselves and others, . . . we shall no longer hesitate with the apostle to call the word of God, as nothing else on earth, 'the sword of the Spirit' (Eph. 6:17)" (Van Oosterzee, 2:736).

BIBLIOGRAPHY: C. H. Dodd, *The Apostolic Preaching and Its Developments* (1936); J. S. Stewart, *Heralds of God* (1946); P. T. Forsyth, *Positive Preaching and the Modern Mind* (1949); J. Knox, *The Integrity of Preaching* (1957); R. H. Mounce, *The Essential Nature of New Testament Preaching* (1960); E. P. Clowney, *Preaching and Biblical Theology* (1961); J. R. W. Stott, *The Preacher's Portrait* (1961); P. C. Mercel, *The Relevance of Preaching* (1963); R. C. Worley, *Preaching and Teaching in the Earliest Church* (1967); R. W. McLaughlin, *The Ethics of Persuasive Preaching* (1979).

PRECIOUS STONES. For discussion of these in detail, *see* Mineral Kingdom.

PREDESTINATION. *See* Election; Sovereignty of God.

PREPARATION (Gk. *paraskeuē*, a "making ready"). In the Jewish sense, the day of preparation (Matt. 27:62; Mark 15:42; Luke 23:54; John 19:31) was the day on which the Jews made the necessary preparation to celebrate a *Sabbath* (which see) or *festival* (which see).

PRESBYTERY (Gk. *presbuterion*). The order or body of elders (1 Tim. 4:14) mentioned in connection with the ordination of Timothy. *See* Elder; Ordination.

PRESENCE (Heb. *pāneh*, "face"). Jehovah's promise to Moses was "My presence shall go with you, and I will give you rest" (Ex. 33:14). "The presence (*face*) of Jehovah is Jehovah in his own personal presence, and is identical with the 'angel' in whom the name of Jehovah was (23:20-21), and who is therefore called in Isa. 63:9 'the angel of his presence' (*face*)" (K. & D., *Com.*).

PRESENCE, BREAD OF THE. *See* Tabernacle: Typology of the Tabernacle and Furniture.

PRESENT. *See* Gift.

PRESIDENT. *See* Commissioner.

PRESS. The equipment used to extract oil or wine from the fruit (*see* Oil, no. 2; Wine Press). The word is also the KJV term for the crowd (so NASB) that surrounded Jesus (Mark 2:4; 5:27, 30; Luke 8:19; 19:3).

PRESSFAT (Heb. *yeqeb;* Hag. 2:16, KJV). A *wine vat* (so NASB and NIV) into which the juice flowed when pressed out of the grapes. *See* Wine Press.

PRESUMPTUOUS, PRESUMPTUOUSLY. Presumption is the act of taking upon one's self more than good sense and propriety warrant; excessive boldness or overconfidence in thought and conduct. In Scripture we have several Heb. words thus rendered:

1. *To act overboldly* (Heb. *zûd,* "to seethe"; figurative, "to be insolent"), spoken mostly of those who knowingly and purposely violate the commands of God and commit sin (Ex. 21:14; Deut. 1:43; 17:13).

2. *Arrogance* (Heb. *zēd,* "arrogant"; *zādôn*), as "presumptuous sins" (Ps. 19:13; NIV, "willful sins"); of resistance to priest or judge through pride. "Resistance to the priest took place when anyone was dissatisfied with his interpretation of the law; to the judge, when anyone was discontented with the sentence that was passed on the basis of the law. Such refractory conduct was to be punished with death, as rebellion against God."

3. *Defiance* (so NASB and NIV, Num. 15:30; "doeth aught presumptuously," KJV) is the synonym for "with a high hand" (from Heb. *yād,* "hand," *rûm,* "be high"); the one who acted in open rebellion against God blasphemed Him and was to be cut off (cf. Gen. 17:14).

4. *Insolence* (Gk. *tolmētēs,* "daring," "bold"), spoken (2 Pet. 2:10) of those who were self-willed, licentious, and contemptuous of authority.

Generally, *presumptuous* sins (Ps. 19:13) are those committed with knowledge (John 15:22), deliberation and contrivance (Prov. 6:14; Ps. 36:4), obstinacy (Jer. 44:16; Deut. 1:43), inattention to the remonstrances of conscience (Acts 7:51), opposition to the dispensations of Providence (2 Chron. 28:22), and repeated commission of the same sin (Ps. 78:17).

PRETENSE (Gk. *prophasis,* "show"). Under color as though they would, etc. (Matt. 23:14; Mark 12:40, "appearance"; Phil. 1:18). The Gk. term is rendered "pretext" in 1 Thess. 2:5, where Paul says that he never "came with flattering speech, . . . nor with a pretext for greed," the meaning being that he had never used his apostolic office in order to disguise or to hide a greedy motive.

PRETOR'IUM. *See* Praetorium.

PREY. *See* Spoil.

PRICE. In the KJV of Zech. 11:12, the meaning of *price* is *wages* (so NASB).

PRICK. The rendering (Num. 33:55) of Heb. *śēk,* a briar or thorn; and so the expression "pricks in your eyes," etc., means to suffer the most painful injuries. The NIV renders "barbs." The term *pricks* in the KJV of Acts 9:5; 26:14 refers to a *goad* (which see; Gk. *kentron*).

PRIEST, PRIESTHOOD. The idea of a priesthood connects itself, in all its forms, pure or corrupted, with the consciousness, always more or less distinct, of sin. Men sense that they have broken a law. The power above them is holier than they are, and they dare not approach it. They crave for the intervention of one whom they can think of as likely to be more acceptable than themselves. He must offer up their prayers, thanksgivings, sacrifices. He becomes their representative in "things pertaining to God." He may become also (though this does not always follow) the representative of God to man. The functions of the priest and prophet may exist in the same person.

In pre-Mosaic times the office of priest was occupied by the father of a family (cf. Job 1:5) or the head of a tribe for his own family or tribe. Abraham, Isaac, and Jacob built altars, offered sacrifices, purified and consecrated themselves and their households (Gen. 12:7; 13:18; 26:25; 33:20; 35:1-3). Melchizedek combined kingship and priesthood in his own person (14:18). Jethro was not merely the spiritual but also the civil head of Midian (Ex. 2:16; 3:1).

In Egypt the Israelites came into contact with a priesthood of another kind, and that contact must have been for a time a close one. The marriage of Joseph with the daughter of the priest of On (a priest, as we may infer by her name, of the goddess Neith [Gen. 41:45]); the special favor Joseph showed to the priestly caste in the years of famine (47:26); the training of Moses in the palace of the pharaohs, probably in the colleges and temples of the priests (Acts 7:22)—all this must have impressed the constitution, the dress, the outward form of life upon the minds of Moses and his contemporaries. There is scarcely any room for doubt that a connection of some kind existed between the Egyptian priesthood and that of Israel. The latter was not indeed an outgrowth or imitation of the former, for the one was "from the earth, earthy," whereas the other was ethical and spiritual.

BIBLIOGRAPHY: E. O. James, *Nature and Function of the Priesthood* (1961); L. Sabourin, *Priesthood: A Comparative Study* (1973).

PRIEST, THE HIGH (Heb. *hakkōhēn,* "the priest," *hakkōhēn haggādōl,* "the great priest"). The high priest formed the culminating point in the Israelite hierarchy. The first to fill this high position was Aaron, who was succeeded by his eldest (surviving) son, Eleazar.

Selection. The high priest was required to satisfy all the necessary conditions of admission to the sacred office. *See* Priesthood, Hebrew.

Support. The source of the high priest's support was the same as that of the other priests; his proportion probably varying according to circumstances. *See* Priesthood, Hebrew.

Dress. As befitted the superior dignity of his office, the high priest wore, in addition to the ordinary priest's attire (namely, the coat, breeches, sash, and cap), an *official dress* entirely peculiar to himself, consisting of four parts: breastpiece, ephod, sash, and turban.

Breastpiece (Heb. *hōshen*). The breastpiece, called also "the breastpiece of judgment" (Ex. 28:15), was a square piece of cloth made of the same material and wrought in the same fashion as the ephod (*see* below). It was doubled so as to form a pocket one span broad. Upon this breastpiece were twelve precious stones set in gold and arranged in four rows, while on the stones were engraved the names of the twelve tribes of Israel. At each of the four corners was a ring of gold. By the two upper rings small chains of wreathed gold were attached, at the other ends of which other chains were fastened for the purpose of attaching them to the ephod on the shoulders. Blue cords (laces) were attached to the two lower rings, the other ends of which were tied to rings that were fastened to the bottom of the front part of the ephod immediately above the sash. Thus the breastpiece was securely bound to the ephod and, at the same time, to the breast, both above and below, so that, held as it was by the chains and cords running obliquely in opposite directions, it could not possibly get displaced (Ex. 28:15-28; 39:8-21).

The breastpiece worn by the high priest

Into the breastpiece were put the Urim and Thummim (Heb. *'ûrîm weṯummîm,* "lights and perfections"), in order that they might be upon Aaron's heart when he went in before the Lord (28:30). Even such early writers as Josephus, Philo, and the rabbis, are unable to furnish any precise information as to what the Urim and Thummim really were. The only Scripture account given of them is in Ex. 28:30; Lev. 8:8, from which it seems evident that they were something of a material nature, which being put into the breastpiece after the latter had been prepared and put on, formed the means through which the high priest was enabled to ascertain the will of Jehovah in regard to any important matter affecting the theocracy (Num. 27:21). That the Urim and Thummim were placed in the pocket is made especially clear from Lev. 8:8, where, in the course of dressing himself, Aaron puts on the breastpiece and then puts the Urim and Thummim inside of it, showing that the things thus put into the breastpiece must be materially distinct from it. They were evidently some sort of small oracular objects. Some scholars connect them with the Babylonian tablets of destiny known as Urtu and Tamitu but this parallel is scarcely valid.

Jewish high priest

Ephod (Heb. *'epôd*). The ephod was woven of blue, purple, scarlet, and fine linen yarn and was embroidered with figures of gold. It consisted of two pieces, the one covering the back, the other the breast and upper part of the body. The two parts were fastened together on the top of each shoulder by a golden clasp or fastening—an onyx set in gold—with the names of six tribes on each stone. Upon this ephod the breastplate was fastened (Ex. 28:6-12; 39:2-7; *see* Ephod in the general listing).

The robe of the ephod was of blue color, woven without any seam. It was worn immediately under the ephod and was longer than it, reaching a little below the knees, so that the priest's coat could be seen under it. The blue robe had no sleeves, but only slits in the sides for the arms to come through. It had a hole for the head to pass through, with a border around it of woven work, to prevent its being torn. The skirt of this robe had a remarkable trimming of pomegranates in blue, red, and crimson, with a bell of gold between each pomegranate alternately.

Sash (Heb. *'abnēṭ,* a "belt"). The sash, or band, was of the same material and manufacture as the ephod and was used to bind the ephod firmly to the body (Ex. 28:8).

Turban (Heb. *miṣnepet,* "wound around"). According to Josephus and Philo the turban of the high priest consisted of an ordinary priest's cap with a turban of dark blue color over it. On the front of this latter was a diadem of pure gold (i.e., a thin gold plate) on which was engraved "Holy to the Lord," fastened with a dark blue cord (Ex. 28:36-38; 39:30-31).

Duties. The functions peculiar to the high priest consisted partly in presenting the sin offering for himself (Lev. 4:3-12) and the congregation (vv. 13-21), as occasion required, and the atoning sacrifice and the burnt offering on the great Day of Atonement (Lev. 16). He also consulted the Lord by means of the Urim and Thummim, in regard to important matters affecting the theocracy, and informing the people thereon (Num. 27:21; 1 Sam. 30:7-8). The high priest had the supervision of the rest of the priests and of the entire worship and was at liberty to exercise all the other priestly functions as well. According to Josephus (*Wars* 5.5.7), he officiated, as a rule, every Sabbath and on new moons or other festivals in the course of the year. In addition to his strictly religious duties, the high priest was the supreme civil head of the people, the supreme head of the state, insofar, that is, as the state was not under the sway of foreign rulers. In the days of national independence the hereditary Hasmonaean high priests were priests and kings at one and the same time; at a later period, the high priests were—at least the presidents of the Sanhedrin, and even in all political matters—the supreme representatives of the people in their relations with the Romans.

Consecration. The consecration of the high priest is discussed in the article Priesthood, Hebrew.

Regulations. The regulations were still more stringent in the case of the high priest than of the ordinary priests. The high priest was not allowed to marry even a widow, but only a virgin of his own people; he was forbidden to approach a corpse or take part in funeral rites, the prohibition being absolute, though exceptions were made in the case of other priests; he was not to go out of the sanctuary to give way to his grief, nor to "profane the sanctuary of his God," i.e., by any defilement of his person that he could and ought to avoid; and he was not to contract a marriage not in keeping with the holiness of his rank (Lev. 21:10-15).

History. In history the high priests naturally arrange themselves into three groups: (1) the Exodus to David's reign, (2) David's reign to the fall of Judah, and (3) following the captivity.

The Exodus to David's Reign. On the death of Aaron the *office* of high priest passed to his eldest son, Eleazar (Num. 20:28), and, according to divine promise (25:13), was vested in his descendants from Phinehas downward (Judg. 20:28). The office continued in Phinehas's family for a certain length of time. Josephus says both that the father of Bukki, Abishua, was the last high priest in Phinehas's line before Zadok (*Ant.* 8.1.3; the name is given as Abiezer in 5.11.5) and that Ozi (Uzzi, KJV, NASB, NIV), Bukki's son, held that position (5.11.5). Then, whenever the date and for whatever reason, the office of high priest passed in the person of Eli into the line of Ithamar, in which it continued till the deposition of Abiathar, Eli's great-great-grandson, by Solomon, who, in appointing Zadok to the office, restored it once more to the exclusive possession of the house of Eleazar (1 Kings 2:26-27, 35).

Only some of the high priests who served before the reign of David are listed in Scripture: *Aaron, Eleazar* (both Num. 20:28), and *Phinehas* (Eleazar's son, Judg. 20:28); and then, from the line of Eleazar's brother Ithamar (1 Chron. 24:3, 6, 31), *Eli* (1 Sam. 1:9-17), *Ahitub* (brother of Ichabod and grandson of Eli, Hofni and Phinehas being killed in battle, 2:34; 4:11; 14:3), *Ahijah* (1 Sam. 14:3; "Ahiah," KJV), or *Ahimelech* (1 Sam. 22:16; 24:3), and *Abiathar* (22:20; 23:6; note that the name *Ahimelech* is given both to the father [1 Sam. 23:6] and the son [2 Sam. 8:17] of Abiathar). (The line of natural descent from Eleazar and his son Phinehas included Abishua, Bukki, Uzzi, Zerahiah, Meraioth, Amariah, Ahitub [not the same, obviously, as Ichabod's brother], and Zadok [1 Chron. 6:3-18, 51-53]).

David's Reign to the Fall of Judah. There were two high priests in the reign of David, apparently of nearly equal authority, Zadok and Abiathar (1 Chron. 15:11; cf. 2 Sam. 8:17; 15:24, 35). It is not unlikely that after the death of Ahimelech and the secession of Abiathar to David, Saul may have made Zadok priest, and that David may have avoided the difficulty of deciding between the claims of his faithful friend Abiathar and his new and important ally Zadok by appointing them to a joint priesthood. The first place, with the ephod and Urim and Thummin, remained with Abiathar, who was in actual possession of them. It appears that Abiathar had special charge of the Ark and the services connected therewith, which agrees exactly with the possession of the ephod by Abiathar and his previous position with David before he became king. Abiathar, however, forfeited his place by taking part with Adonijah against Solomon, and Zadok was made high priest in his place.

The first considerable difficulty that meets us in the historical survey of the high priests of the second group is to ascertain who was high priest at the dedication of Solomon's Temple. Josephus says (*Ant.* 10.8.6) that Zadok was, and the *Seder Olam* makes him the high priest in the reign of Solomon; but 1 Kings 4:2 distinctly asserts that Azariah (grand)son of Zadok was priest under Solomon, and 1 Chron. 6:10 tells us of an Azariah, grandson of the Azariah in v. 9, saying, "it was he who served as the priest in the house which Solomon built in Jerusalem," as if meaning at its first completion. We can hardly be wrong in saying that Azariah the son of Ahimaaz was the first high priest of Solomon's Temple.

Smith thus presents the matter: "In constructing the list of the succession of priests of this group our method must be to compare the genealogical list in 1 Chron. 6:8-15 (KJV) with the notices of high priests in the sacred history and with the list given by Josephus. Now, as regards the genealogy, it is seen at once that there is something defective; for, whereas from David to Jeconiah there are twenty kings, from Zadok to Jehozadak there are but thirteen priests. Then, again, while the pedigree in its six first generations from Zadok, inclusive, exactly suits the history, yet is there a great gap in the middle; for between Amariah, the high priest of Jehoshaphat's reign, and Shallum, the father of Hilkiah, the high priest in Josiah's reign—an interval of about two hundred and forty years—there are but two names, Ahitub and Zadok, and those liable to the utmost suspicion from their reproducing the same sequence which occurs in the earliest part of the same genealogy—Amariah, Ahitub, Zadok. Besides they are not mentioned by Josephus, at least not under the same names. This part, therefore, of the pedigree is useless for our purpose. But the historical books supply us with four and five names for this interval, namely, Jehoiada, Zechariah, Azariah, Urijah, and Azariah in the reign of Hezekiah. If, in the genealogy of 1 Chron. 6, Azariah and Hilkiah have been accidently transposed, as is not impossible, then the Azariah who was high priest in Hezekiah's reign would be the Azariah of 1 Chron. 6:13, 14. Putting the additional historical names at four, and deducting the two suspicious names from the genealogy, we have fifteen high priests indicated in Scripture as contemporary with the twenty kings, with room, however, for one or two more in the history. The high priests of this series ended with Seraiah, who was taken prisoner by Nebuzar-adan and slain at Riblah by Nebuchadnezzar (2 Kings 25:18)."

Following the Captivity. An interval of about fifty-two years elapsed between the high priests of the second and third group, during which there was neither Temple, altar, Ark, nor priest. Jehozadak, who should have succeeded Seraiah, lived and died a captive at Babylon. The pontifical office revived in his son, *Jeshua* (which see, and he stands at the head of this series), honorably distinguished for his zealous cooperation with Zerubbabel in rebuilding the Temple and restoring the dilapidated commonwealth of Israel. His successors, so far as given in the OT, were Joiakim, Eliashib, Joiada, Jonathan, and Jaddua. Jaddua was high priest in the time of Alexander the Great. Jaddua was succeeded by Onias I, his son, and he again by Simon the Just, the last of the men of the great synagogue. Upon Simon's death, his son Onias being under age, Eleazar, Simon's brother, succeeded him. The high priesthood of Eleazar is memorable as being that under which the LXX version of the Scriptures was made at Alexandria.

After the high priesthood had been brought to the lowest degradation by the apostasy and crimes of the last Onias or Menelaus, and after a vacancy of seven years had followed the brief pontificate of Alcimus, his no less infamous successor, a new and glorious succession of high priests arose in the Hasmonaean family. This family was of the division of Jehoiarib (1 Chron. 24:7), whose return from captivity is recorded in 9:10; Neh. 11:10 and lasted from 153 B.C. until the family was destroyed by Herod the Great. Aristobulus, the last high priest of his line, was murdered by order of Herod, his brother-in-law, 35 B.C. (*see* table 24, "The Maccabees [Hasmonaeans]").

"There were no fewer than twenty-eight high priests from the reign of Herod to the destruction of the temple by Titus, a period of one hundred and seven years. The New Testament introduces us to some of these later and oft-changing high priests, viz., Annas, Caiaphas, and Ananias. Theophilus, the son of Ananus, was the high priest from whom Saul received letters to the synagogue at Damascus (Acts 9:1, 14). Phannias, the last high priest, was appointed by lot by the Zealots from the course of priests called by Josephus Eniachim (probably) a corrupt reading for Ja-

chim" (Smith, *Dict.*, s.v.; also Schürer, *History of the Jewish People in the Time of Jesus*).

Typology. Aaron as high priest is a type of Christ. The functions, dress, and ritual connected with the high priest's anointing are minutely instructive of the Person and work of Christ as a Priest. Although Christ is a Priest after the order of Melchizedek (Ps. 110:4; Heb. 5:6; 6:20; 7:17), He executes His priestly office after the *pattern* of Aaron. The order is expounded in Heb. 7, pattern, in Heb. 9. Death often disrupted the Aaronic priesthood; therefore, Christ is a Priest after the order of Melchizedek as "king of righteousness" and "king of peace" (7:2) and in the perpetuity of His priesthood. Melchizedek as a *messianic* type was a king-priest, and the portrayal speaks of the royal authority and unending duration of Christ's high priesthood (7:23-24). The Melchizedek type was needed in addition to the Aaronic type to present a full-orbed typical picture of Christ in His high-priestly work of sacrifice for sin and His present ever-living, all-efficacious, intercessory ministry in behalf of His own (John 17; Heb. 7:24-25).　　M.F.U.

BIBLIOGRAPHY: R. H. Kennett, *Journal of Theological Studies* 6 (1905): 161-86; J. Orr, *The Problem of the Old Testament* (1906), pp. 180-83, 311, 504-5; G. B. Gray, *Sacrifice in the Old Testament* (1925), pp. 179-270; T. W. Manson, ed., *Companion to the Bible* (1939), pp. 418-33; G. C. Aalders, *A Short Introduction to the Pentateuch* (1949), pp. 66-71; G. Milligan, *The Theology of Hebrews* (1978), pp. 101-91.

PRIESTHOOD, HEBREW (Heb. *kōhēn,* one "officiating"; Gk. *hiereus.*) There is no consensus of opinion as to the etymology of the Heb. term *kōhēn,* but the supposition of Bähr (*Symbolik,* 2:15), in connecting it with an Arab. root that is equivalent to the Heb. root *qārab* ("to draw near") answers most nearly to the received usage of the word. In the precise terminology of the law it is used of one who may "draw near" to the divine presence (Ex. 19:22; 30:20), whereas others remain afar off, and it is usually applied to the sons of Aaron. It is, however, used in a wider sense when it is applied to Melchizedek (Gen. 14:18), Potiphera (41:45), Jethro (Ex. 2:16), and to the priests mentioned in 19:22, who exercised priestly functions before the appointment of Aaron and his sons. These last owed their position as priests to natural superiority of rank, either as firstborn or as elders.

In 2 Sam. 8:18 there is a case of great difficulty: the sons of David are described as "chief ministers" (Heb. *kōhănîm*). This conjecture is offered (McClintock and Strong, *Cyclopedia,* s.v.): "David and his sons may have been admitted, not to distinctively priestly acts, such as burning incense (Num. 16:40; 2 Chron. 26:18), but to an honorary, titular priesthood. To wear the ephod in processions (2 Sam. 6:14), at the time when this was the special badge of the order (1 Sam. 22:18), to join the priests and Levites in their songs and dances, might have been conceded, with no deviation from the law, to the members of the royal house."

Keil and Delitzsch (*Com.*, ad loc.) explain as follows: "David's sons were . . . 'confidants'; not priests, domestic priests, court chaplains, or spiritual advisers, . . . but, as the title is explained in the corresponding text of the Chronicles [18:17], when the title had become obsolete, 'the first at the hand (or side) of the king'. The correctness of this explanation is placed beyond the reach of doubt by 1 Kings 4:5, where the *cohen* is called, by way of explanation, 'the king's friend.' . . . These *cohanim,* therefore, were the king's confidential advisers."

Essential Idea of Priesthood. Moses furnishes us with the key to the idea of OT priesthood in Num. 16:5, which consists of three elements—being chosen or set apart for Jehovah as His own, being holy, and being allowed to come or bring near. The *first* expresses the fundamental condition, the *second* the qualification, the *third* the function of the priesthood. According to Ex. 19:5-24, it is upon these three elements that the character of the whole covenant people is based. They were chosen to be God's peculiar people (Deut. 7:6), a kingdom of priests and a holy nation (*see* Ex. 19:4-6). Their sinfulness, however, prevented its realization; and when brought before Jehovah at Sinai they could not endure the immediate presence of God and begged Moses to act as their mediator (20:18-21). The Aaronic priesthood was instituted in order to maintain fellowship between the holy God and the sinful nation, to bring the people's gifts and sacrifices before God, and to convey God's gifts, mercy, salvation, and blessing to the people. By an act of free favor God committed the priesthood to one particular family—that of Aaron (28:1), which priesthood they received as a gift (Num. 18:7, *see* marg.). In like manner the whole tribe of Levi was assigned to the priests as their servants and assistants (*see* Levites). This divine preference was confirmed by the miracle of the budding rod (Num. 17) and the priesthood as a heritage to the descendants of Aaron. The *qualification,* namely, holiness, was represented in outward form by the act of consecration and the robes of office.

The *functions* were shown by the fellowship with Jehovah into which the priests were allowed to enter in the course of the various acts of worship. Holiness is essential to fellowship with God, and Aaron and his sons, no less than the people whom they were to represent before God, were stained by sin. As the sanctity imparted to them by their consecration, their official robes, and other legal requirements, which fitted them to serve at the altar, was only of an outward character, it follows that these could only have had a symbolical meaning. It was doubtless intended that they should symbolize the sinless character of the human priesthood at the same time they served as a type of the perfect priesthood of the true and eternal High Priest.

Priests.

Selection. God selected as priests the sons (descendants) of Aaron (Ex. 6:18, 20; 28:1), but two of his sons, Nadab and Abihu, died without children, having been put to death for burning "strange fire" upon the altar (Lev. 10:1-2). The priesthood was then invested in the descendants of Aaron's two other sons, Eleazar and Ithamar (10:6). The selection went still further, for among these all were disqualified who had any physical defect or infirmity—the blind, lame, disfigured, those with deformed limbs, a broken hand or foot, a hunchback or dwarf, anyone with defects, eczema, scabs, or crushed testicles. Those so disqualified were still supported as the other priests (21:17-23), for no one whose legitimate birth entitled him to admission could be excluded.

In later times the Sanhedrin inquired into the genealogy of the candidate, sitting daily for this purpose in the "Hall of Polished Stones." If he failed to satisfy the court about his perfect legitimacy the candidate was dressed and veiled in black, and permanently removed. If his genealogy was satisfactory, inquiry was next made as to any physical defects, of which Maimonides enumerates 140 that permanently and 22 that temporarily disqualified for the exercise of the priestly office. Those who stood the twofold test were dressed in white raiment, and their names properly inscribed. To this custom pointed allusion is made in Rev. 3:5.

The age for entering the priesthoood is not mentioned, but it was probably from twenty-five (Num. 8:24) to thirty years (4:3, 23, 30, 35, 47).

Support. On their settlement in Canaan the priestly families were assigned thirteen Levitical cities with pasturelands (Josh. 21:13-19). In addition the following were their chief sources of maintenance:

1. One-tenth of the tithes paid to the Levites by the people (Lev. 23:10), partly in the raw state, such as wheat, barley, grapes, fruits (Deut. 18:8), and partly as prepared for consumption, as wine, oil, flour, etc. (Lev. 23:17), and even to the first-fruits of sheep shearing (Deut. 18:4).

2. A special tithe every third year (14:28; 26:12).

3. The redemption money of the firstborn: those of the human race were redeemed for five shekels (Num. 18:16); those of unclean beasts were redeemed by a sum fixed by the priest with a fifth part of the value added (Lev. 27:27); those of clean beasts were not redeemed but offered in sacrifice, the priest receiving the waved breast and the right shoulder (Num. 18:17-18).

4. The redemption money paid for men or things specially dedicated to the Lord (Lev. 27).

5. A percentage of the *spoil* (which see) of war (Num. 31:25-47).

6. The bread of the Presence, the flesh of the offerings (*see* Sacrifices; also Num. 18:8-14; Lev. 6:26, 29; 7:6-10).

The income of the priests must have been moderate, even under the most favorable circumstances, for it depended largely on the varying religious state of the nation; no law existed by which either payment of tithes or any other offering could be enforced. And yet the law obviously was intended to provide against the dangers of a caste of pauper priests.

Dress. When not in actual service neither the priests, nor even the high priest, wore a distinctive dress; but when ministering in the sanctuary the priests were required to wear the following official dress: Linen *breeches,* i.e., short trousers (Ex. 28:42), reaching only from the loins to the thighs, and made of fine twisted linen (39:28); a long *coat* with sleeves, made of finely woven linen (v. 27); a *sash* of fine twisted linen woven of the same colors as were in the veil hung before the Holy Place (v. 29); and a *cap* of linen, probably resembling in shape the inverted calyx of a flower. They had nothing on their feet, as they were not allowed to tread the sanctuary without having their feet bare (*see* Ex. 3:5; Josh. 5:15).

Jewish rabbi

The additional dress of the high priest is given in the article Priest, The High.

Duties. The functions of the priesthood were clearly defined by the Mosaic law and remained substantially the same, whatever changes might be brought about in their social position and organization. The duties prescribed in Exodus and Leviticus are the same as those recognized in Chronicles and Ezekiel. Those functions could be entered upon the eighth day of the service of consecration (Lev. 9:1). They were such as pertained to coming "near to the furnishings of the sanctuary and the altar" (Num. 18:3):

1. In the *Holy Place,* to burn incense on the golden altar, morning and evening; to clean and trim lamps and light them every evening; and to put the bread of the Presence on the table every Sabbath (Ex. 30:7-8; 27:21; Lev. 24:5-8).

2. In the *court,* to keep the fire constantly burning on the altar of burnt offering (Lev. 6:9, 13); to clear away ashes from the altar (vv. 10-11); to offer the morning and evening sacrifices (Ex. 29:38-44); to bless the people after the daily sacrifice (Lev. 9:22; Num. 6:23-27); to wave different portions of the sacrifice; to sprinkle the blood and put various parts of the animal upon the altar and see to their burning; and to blow the silver trumpets and the Jubilee horn at particular festival seasons.

3. Generally, to inspect unclean persons, especially lepers and, when so warranted, to declare them clean (Lev. 13-14); to administer the oath of purgation to the woman accused of adultery (Num. 5:15-30); to appraise things dedicated to the sanctuary (Lev. 27:2-33).

4. Finally, to instruct the people in the law; to act as a high court of appeals in any difficult case (Deut. 17:8-12; 19:17-19; 21:5); and in times of war to address the troops, if deemed necessary, before going into action (20:2-4).

The large number of offerings brought up to the sanctuary at the festival times taxed the strength and endurance of the priests to such an extent that the Levites had to be called in to help them (2 Chron. 29:34; 35:14).

Consecration (Heb. *qādash,* "to be holy," with causative or intensive force, "to make clean"). The ceremony of the consecration of the high priest, as well as of the ordinary priests, to their office is prescribed in Ex. 29:1-34 (cf. 40:12-15); and in the case of Aaron and his sons it was performed by Moses (Lev. 8:1-36). The candidate for consecration was conducted to the door of the Tabernacle and had his body washed with water; was invested with the official dress; was anointed with the holy oil (*see* Oil), which in the case of the high priest, was, according to tradition, poured upon the head, though in the case of the other priests it was merely smeared upon the forehead. In the consecration of Aaron and his sons the fact of anointing is not expressly mentioned, although it had been commanded (Ex. 28:41; 40:15) and the performance of it taken for granted (Lev. 7:36; 10:7; Num. 3:3).

A sacrificial service followed, with Moses officiating as priest. The sacrifice consisted of one young bull for a *sin offering;* one ram for the *burnt offering;* the ram of *consecration;* and a basket containing unleavened bread, unleavened cakes kneaded in oil, and thinner unleavened cakes sprinkled with oil.

The hands of the persons being consecrated (Ex. 29) were laid upon the head of the bull, which was then slaughtered and a portion of its blood sprinkled upon the horns of the altar of burnt offering, the rest being poured upon the ground at the base of the altar. The "fat that [covered] the entrails and the lobe of the liver, and the two kidneys and the fat that [was] on them" were consumed on the altar; while the skin, flesh, and dung were burned outside the camp (vv. 12-13).

The ram for the burnt offering was then brought, and, after the hands of those being consecrated were laid upon its head, it was offered as in the case of other burnt offerings (*see* Sacrifice). Then came the offering of the ram of consecration. The hands of the consecrated were laid upon its head, and it was slaughtered by Moses, who sprinkled some of its blood upon the tip of the right ear of Aaron and his sons, some upon their right thumbs, and some upon the great toes of their right feet, the rest of the blood being sprinkled upon the altar. Then Moses took the fat, the rump, the fat of the entrails, the lobe of the liver, the two kidneys with their fat, the right shoulder of this ram of consecration; and along with these an unleavened cake, a cake of oiled bread, and a thin cake sprinkled with oil, and laid them upon the fat and the right shoulder. Placing these all together on the hands of Aaron, Moses waved them before Jehovah. After this the whole was burned upon the altar.

The breast of the ram—the priest's portion —Moses now waved before Jehovah, afterward sprinkling some of the anointing oil and blood upon the priests and their garments. This concluded the ceremony. The remainder of the flesh was cooked by Aaron and his sons at the door of the Tabernacle and eaten by them. Any portion remaining until the next day was burned. The consecration service lasted seven days (Ex. 29:35; Lev. 8:33-35), the sacrifice being repeated each day. Meantime those being consecrated were not allowed to leave the sanctuary.

After the consecration services, the consecrated, whether high priest or ordinary priest, were required to offer a special grain offering of one-tenth ephah of flour. This was kneaded with oil and baked in separate pieces—one-half being offered in the morning and the other in the evening, wholly burned upon the altar (6:19-23). On the eighth day of consecration, the exercise of the priestly function was begun by the newly consecrated in the offering of a calf for a sin offering, and a ram for a burnt offering, for themselves. This was immediately followed by the offering of sacrifices for the people (chap. 9).

Regulations. Above all Israel, the priests, whom Jehovah had chosen out of the whole nation to be the custodians of His sanctuary and had sanctified to that end, were to prove themselves the consecrated servants of God in their domestic lives and sacred duties. They were not to defile themselves by touching the dead, excepting such as formed part of one's immediate family, such as his mother, father, son, daughter, brother, or sister who was still living with him as a virgin (Lev. 21:1-6); by signs of mourning (vv. 10-12; the wife, though not mentioned, is probably included in the phrase "relatives who are nearest to him"); by marriage with a public prostitute, divorced woman, or a widow in the case of the high priest. Such marriage would be irreconcilable with the holiness of the priesthood (vv. 7-9, 14); but he might marry a virgin (v. 14) or the widow of a priest (Ezek. 44:22). Licentious conduct on the part of any of their own daughters was punished by the offenders' being burned to death (Lev. 21:9). If a priest unwittingly or unavoidably contracted Levitical uncleanness he was required to abstain from the holy things until he had become legally purified (22:2-7); and every transgression of the law of Levitical purity was regarded as a crime punishable by death (22:9).

Before entering the Tabernacle the priests washed their hands and feet (Ex. 30:17-21; 40:30-32); and during the time of their administration they were to drink no wine or strong drink (Lev. 10:9; Ezek. 44:21); they were not to shave their heads.

The priesthood ministering in the Temple was arranged into "ordinary" priests and various officials. Of the latter, besides the high priest were the following: the *Sagan,* or suffragan priest, who officiated for the high priest when he was incapacitated and generally acted as his assistant, taking oversight of the priests, whence he is called "second priest" (2 Kings 25:18; Jer. 52:24); two *Katholikin,* chief treasurers and overseers; seven *Ammarcalin,* subordinate to the *Katholikin,* and who had chief charge of the gates; and three *Gizbarim,* or undertreasurers. These fourteen officers, ranking in the order mentioned, formed the standing "council of the temple," which regulated everything connected with the affairs and services of the sanctuary. Next in rank were the "heads of each division" on duty for a week, and then the "heads of families" of every division. After them followed fifteen overseers, as overseers of gates, guards, lots, etc.

History. The priests, at first, probably exercised their functions according to a definite principle of alternation. But when in the course of time their numbers greatly increased, David divided them into twenty-four divisions, sixteen of them consisting of the descendants of Eleazar and eight of the descendants of Ithamar, with a president of each division (1 Chron. 24:3-18; Matt. 2:4; Josephus *Ant.* 7.14.7). Each division was divided into subdivisions, ranging, according to the Talmud, from five to nine for each main division. Each main division and subdivision was ruled by a *head.* The order in which the divisions took their turn was determined by lot, a new one being appointed each week to conduct the services during that week, beginning and ending on the Sabbath (2 Kings 11:9; 2 Chron. 23:4). These divisions are named in 1 Chron. 24. In like manner the various duties were assigned by lot (Luke 1:9), for which purpose there was a special *profectus sortium* (director of lots) in the Temple. According to rabbinical tradition four divisions returned from captivity, from which twenty-four divisions were chosen by lot.

At the disruption of the kingdom, the priests and Levites remained with the kingdom of Judah, and there alone exercised their functions, occupying themselves with matters of jurisprudence and instructing the people in the law (2 Chron. 17:7-9). King Jehoshaphat created a supreme court in Jerusalem (17:7-9), composed of princes, Levites, and priests; and so long and so far as king and people remained loyal to the law of Moses, the priests were highly esteemed and exercised a healthy influence upon the progress and development of the theocracy. Apostasy sank the priests into immorality, a departure from God, and into idol worship (Hos. 6:9; Mic. 3:11; Zeph. 3:4; Jer. 5:31; 6:13; Ezek. 22:26; Mal. 2). The officiating priests occupied rooms immediately adjoining the Temple, although subsequent to the Exile several priestly families took up their residence in private houses in Jerusalem (Neh. 11:10-18).

A few priests might enter more deeply into the divine life, and so receive, like Jeremiah, Zechariah, and Ezekiel, a special call to the office of a prophet; but others, doubtless, served Jehovah with a divided allegiance, acting also as priests of the high places, sharing in the worship of Baal (Jer. 2:8), the sun and moon, and the host of heaven (8:1-2). Some "ministered . . . before their idols" in the very Temple itself (Ezek. 44:12) and allowed others, "uncircumcised in heart and uncircumcised in flesh," to join them (v. 7). They became sensual, covetous, tyrannical, drunkards, and adulterous (Isa. 28:7-8; 56:10-12), and their corruption was shared by the prophets (Jer. 5:31; Lam. 4:13; Zeph. 3:4).

Although chastened by the captivity, many of the priests disowning their heathen wives (Ezra 10:18-19) and taking part in the instruction of the people (3:2; Neh. 8:9-13), the root evils soon reappeared. The work of the priesthood was made the instrument of covetousness, every ministeri-

al act being performed for a consideration (Mal. 1:10). They "corrupted the covenant of Levi" (2:8) and forgot the idea that the priest was the messenger of the Lord (2:7). They lost their influence and became "despised and abased before all the people" (2:9). This, however, is not to be understood as implying that the priests had now lost all their influence. Politically and socially they still occupied the foremost place quite as much as ever they did; and by virtue of their political standing, in virtue of the powerful resources at their command, and, lastly and above all, in virtue of their sacred prerogative—the priests continued to have an extraordinary significance for the life of the nation.

Symbolical and Typical. The priestly prerogatives and qualifications had an undoubted symbolical and typical meaning, which ought to be recognized but not carried to extremes. The following brief summary is abridged from Keil (*Arch.,* 1:227ff.):

Symbolical. The symbolic aspects of the priesthood included the selection, holiness, and consecration of the priests; the dress of the ordinary priests; and the dress and anointing of the high priest.

1. Selection. In their being chosen to be *Jehovah's peculiar possession,* the priests had no inheritance in Canaan, the Lord Himself being their "portion and . . . inheritance" (Num. 18:20; Deut. 10:9; etc.). Jehovah, as the Lord of the whole earth and owner of Canaan, not only supplied sufficient dwellings for them, but also assigned an adequate allowance in tithes, firstfruits, etc. Thus as belonging to Jehovah and provided for by Him, they were taught to live by faith and to regard their whole good as centering in and coming from the Lord. They were also left free to devote themselves exclusively to the Lord's service, to the ministry of His word and law, and to their sacred duties.

2. Holiness. *Being holy* formed the indispensable condition of approach to God, the Holy One. Hence in the qualifications necessary for the priestly office—bodily defect or infirmity being regarded as the counterpart of spiritual defects and shortcomings—the bodily perfection of the priests was not intended merely to be a reflection in their persons of the sacredness of their functions and ministry and of the place where they officiated, but rather to symbolize the priest's spiritual blamelessness and sanctification of heart. For the same reason every Levitical defilement was to be avoided, and homelife and conjugal relations were to be such as would show consecration to God (Lev. 21).

3. Consecration. This was the outward sign of sanctification. The *washing of the body* symbolized the purifying of the soul from the pollution of sin. This negative preparation was succeeded by the positive impartation of the indispensable

requisites for the holy office, namely, the *dress* and the *anointing*.

4. Dress of the Ordinary Priests. The color of the priest's garments and the individual elements of the clothing he wore were important.

The predominating *color* of the dress was white, symbolical of glory and holiness (Dan. 12:6-7; 10:5; Ezek. 9:3; 10:2, 7; Matt. 28:3; Rev. 7:9; etc.); and the priests wearing garments of that color appeared as holy servants of God.

The *breeches* were intended to "cover their bare flesh," the parts having to do with secretions, and symbolized the native side of holiness.

The *coat* enveloped the whole body and was woven in one piece without a seam, forming the principal article of dress. It indicated spiritual integrity, the blamelessness and righteousness in which the idea of blessedness and life is realized. The four-cornered shape of the cloth of which the coat was made was for a sign that the one wearing it belonged to the kingdom of God.

A priest blowing the shofar

The *cap* resembled in shape the calyx of a flower and pointed to the blooming character, i.e., the fresh vigorous life, of him who wore it. Hence the priest was forbidden to remove this headdress, but was to tie it on, lest it should fall off by accident; for, as the cap represented a flower, its falling off would have a significant resemblance to the falling of a flower (Ps. 103:15; Isa. 40:6-8; James 1:10; 1 Pet. 1:24).

The *sash* put on by an oriental when about to do active work was the priestly sign of service and typical of the towel-girded Christ, who in washing the feet of the disciples proved that He "did not come to be served, but to serve" (Mark

10:45). Consequently it was of the same colors and wrought in the same style as the veils of the sanctuary, in order to show that the wearer was an office bearer and administrator in the kingdom of God.

5. Dress and Anointing of the High Priest. The particular articles of the dress of the high priest had a distinctive symbolical meaning, as did his anointing. *See also* High Priest, Dress of.

Woven of blue yarn and in one piece, the *upper robe* indicated entireness of spiritual integrity, the blue pointing to the heavenly origin and character of the office. As every Israelite was to wear tassels of blue on the hem of his robe to remind him of the law (Num. 15:38-39), we may infer that in the fringe of pomegranates and little bells there lay some reference to the word and testimony of God; and that the tinkling of the bells was to be heard by the high priest to remind him that his calling was to be the representative, guardian, and promulgator of God's commandments.

Wearing the robe, the high priest appeared as the depository and organ of the word, and he could directly approach Jehovah only when clad in the robe of God's word, as the organ of that divine testimony on which covenant fellowship with the Lord was based.

The two parts of which the *ephod* consisted were called shoulders. It was upon the shoulder that the burden of the office rested, upon it the insignia of office was worn (Isa. 22:22). The principal function of the high priest was to appear before God as the reconciling mediator on behalf of the people; to show that this duty devolved upon him, he wore upon the shoulders of the ephod the names of the twelve tribes engraved upon two onyx stones. The *breastpiece*, with the names of the twelve tribes engraved on precious stones, with the Urim and Thummim in its pocket, was the *breastplate of judgment.* By this the high priest was distinguished as the judicial representative of Israel, bearing the people upon his heart, not merely to keep them in mind, but being, as it were, blended together with them by a living sympathy, to intercede with them before Jehovah.

In the *Urim* and *Thummim* (which see, under Urim) the high priest had a means through which God would communicate to him in every case in which the congregation needed divine light in order to know how to act; thus he had a measure of illumination as would enable him to maintain or reestablish the rights of Israel when they were disputed or infringed (Num. 27:21).

The significance of the *headdress* was not so much in its being a turban instead of the cap of the ordinary priests, as in the diadem with its description. The meaning of this diadem lies in its being designated a *crown* (Ex. 29:6; 39:30; Lev. 8:9; also the king's crown, 2 Sam. 1:10;

2 Kings 11:12), indicating that its wearer was the crowned one among his brethren, the supreme spiritual head of the priesthood. This was a holy crown bearing the inscription "Holy to the Lord." He who was thus crowned was consecrated to Jehovah (Ps. 106:10) and was required to wear the badge of his holiness upon his forehead. The high priest, in virtue of the holiness to the Lord conferred upon him, was to have the power to bear or take upon himself, and so to put away the sin that adhered to the people's gifts in consequence of their impurity, in order that those gifts might become acceptable to God, and the people in turn enjoy His favor (Ex. 28:38).

Being *anointed* with oil was symbolical of being endued with the Spirit of God (cf. 1 Sam. 10:1, 6; 16:13; Isa. 61); for the oil, with its power of giving light, furnished a significant symbol of the Spirit of God as the principle of spiritual light and life.

Typical. "All the requirements necessary to qualify for the office of the priest had a typical meaning in the fact that they were insufficient duly to sanctify the priests and to constitute them mediators between the holy God and the sinful people. Freedom from outward defect, cleansing of the body, investing with the official robes, nor the anointing with oil, could be said to purify the inward nature, but only served to represent a state of outward purity, without, however, truly and permanently producing even this. Consequently, the Levitical priests were required to repeat the washing of hands and feet every day before entering upon service at the altar or going into the holy place. On the Day of Atonement the high priest had to offer a sin offering for himself and the rest of the priests before he could perform similar service for the congregation, and make atonement for them before God. If, therefore, a priest who was holy, blameless, undefiled, and separate from sinners was alone qualified to represent sinners before God, and make atonement for them, and if the priests of the Old Testament did not really possess these attributes, but could only be said to be invested with them in a symbolical form in virtue of certain divine prescriptions and promises, it followed that the various regulations as to the qualifications of the priests for the exercise of the functions intrusted to them could have been designed merely as a divine arrangement whereby to foreshadow the nature and character of Him who was to be the true priest and high priest. Accordingly they must have been intended to prepare the way for the realization of the insufficiency of the Levitical priesthood for adequately representing the sinful people before the holy God, and typically to point to the future appearing of the perfect Mediator, who would redeem the people of Israel from all sin, invest them with true sanctification, and make them a genuine kingdom of priests" (Keil, *Arch.*, 2:240).

BIBLIOGRAPHY: A. Edersheim, *The Temple, Its Ministry and Services* (1954); A. Cody, *A History of the Old Testament Priesthood* (1969); J. H. Kurtz, *Sacrificial Worship in the Old Testament* (1980).

PRINCE, PRINCESS. The rendering of a large number of Heb. and Gk. words, although the English terms *prince* and *princess* are more frequent in the KJV, the NASB and NIV sometimes replacing *prince* with *leader* (Num. 1:44; 4:34; 7:42; 31:13), *ruler* (1 Kings 20:14), *official* (1 Kings 4:1-6), or *satrap* (Dan. 6:1).

PRINCIPALITIES (Gk. *archē,* "first," and so "rule, magistracy"). Used by Paul of angels and demons who were invested with power (Rom. 8:38), elsewhere rendered "rulers" (Eph. 1:21; 3:10; 6:12; Col. 1:16; etc.).

PRINCIPLES. The elements, or rudiments, of any art, science, or discipline (Gk. *stoicheion,* Heb. 5:12). In Heb. 6:1 (KJV) "principles" (from Gk. *archē*) refers to the fundamentals of the doctrine of Christ. The NASB reads "elementary teaching," and the NIV, "elementary truths" and "elementary teachings," respectively.

PRIS'CA (pris'ka; Lat. for "old woman"; 2 Tim. 4:19). *See* Priscilla.

PRISCIL'LA (pri-sil'a; Lat. for "little old woman," diminutive of Prisca). The wife of *Aquila* (which see), in connection with whom she is always mentioned (Acts 18:2, 18, 26). She seems to have been in full accord with her husband in sustaining the "church that is in their house" (1 Cor. 16:19), in helping the apostle Paul (Acts 18:18), and in the theological teaching of Apollos (v. 26).

BIBLIOGRAPHY: D. E. Hiebert, *Personalities Around Paul* (1973), pp. 33-45.

PRISON. In Egypt it is plain both that special places were used as prisons and that they were under the custody of a military officer (Gen. 40:3; 42:17). During the wandering in the desert we read on two occasions of confinement "in custody" (Lev. 24:12; Num. 15:34); but as imprisonment was not directed by the law, so we hear of none till the time of the kings, when the prison appears as an appendage to the palace or a special part of it (1 Kings 22:27). Later still it is distinctly described as being in the king's house (Jer. 32:2; 37:21; Neh. 3:25, "court of the guard"). This was the case also at Babylon (2 Kings 25:27). But private houses were sometimes used as places of confinement (Jer. 37:15). Public prisons other than these, though in use by the Canaanite nations (Judg. 16:21, 25), were unknown in Judea previous to the captivity. Under the Herods we hear again of royal prisons attached to the palace, or in royal fortresses (Luke 3:20; Acts 12:4, 10). By the Romans Antonia was used as a prison at Jerusalem (23:10), and at Caesarea the Praetorium of Herod (v. 35). The most ancient prisons were simply water cisterns, out of which, since the sides came nearly together above, one could not easily escape unaided (Gen. 37:20, 22). *See* Punishment.

Figurative. Prison is used as a symbol of deep *affliction* (Ps. 142:7), of *hell* (Rev. 20:7), *bondage* to sin and Satan (Isa. 42:7; 61:1).

Model of the Tower of Antonia, Jerusalem

PRISONER. *See* Punishment.

PRIZE (Gk. *brabeion,* "award"). A reward bestowed on victors (1 Cor. 9:24; Phil. 3:14) in the public *games* (which see) of the Greeks.

PROCH'ORUS (prok'o-rus; Gk. for "leader in a choric dance,") **Procorus** (NIV). The third on the list of deacons following Stephen and Philip (Acts 6:5), A.D. 33. This is the only mention of him made in the NT. There is a tradition that he was consecrated bishop of Nicomedia by the apostle Peter.

PROCLAMATION. The rendering of several Heb. words, denoting to *call,* or *cry aloud,* to express the publishing of the edict of a governing power in a formal manner. The laws of Moses, as well as the temporary edicts of Joshua, were communicated to the people by means of the genealogists, but those of the kings were proclaimed publicly by criers (Jer 34:8, 9; Jonah 3:5-7; cf. Dan. 3:4; 5:29). *See* Preacher, Preaching.

PROC'ORUS. *See* Prochorus.

PROFANE (Heb. from *ḥālal,* to "open, give access to"; Gk. *bebēloō,* "to desecrate"). To profane is to *make common,* to *defile,* since holy things were not open to the people, e.g., a sanctuary

(Lev. 19:8; 21:9), the Sabbath (Ex. 31:14), the name of God (Lev. 19:12), a father's bed by incest (Gen. 49:4). In the NIV, these passages translate as either "defile" or "desecrate." Esau, by despising his birthright, was called a "profane person" (KJV, Heb. 12:16; "godless," NASB and NIV). In Jer. 23:11 (KJV) it is said "both prophet and priest are profane," i.e., *polluted* (so NASB; Heb. *ḥānēp,* "defiled," "polluted"; NIV, "godless"), implying the strongest opposite of holiness.

PROGNOSTICATORS. *See* Magic: Various Forms.

PROMISE. A solemn assertion, by which one pledges his veracity that he will perform, or cause to be performed, that which he mentions (1 Kings 8:56; 2 Chron. 1:9; Ps. 77:8). Promises differ from the commands of God, the former being significations of the divine will concerning a duty to be performed, whereas the latter relate to mercies to be received. Some promises are predictions, as the promise of the Messiah and the blessings of the gospel (Rom. 4:13-14; Gal. 3:14-29). Hence the Hebrews were called the "children of the promise" (Rom. 9:8; Gal. 4:28), as all true believers in Christ are called those "who through faith and patience inherit the promises" (Heb. 6:12); "heirs of the promise" (v. 17). There are four classes of promises mentioned in Scripture: (1) those relating to the Messiah; (2) those relating to the church; (3) those relating to the Gentiles; and (4) those relating to Israel as a nation, now nationally set aside (Rom. 11:1-24), but yet to be restored (Ezek. 37:1-14; Zech. 8:1-12).

PROPERTY. *See* Law of Moses: Civil Division.

PROPHECY. The oral or written message of a prophet.

The Nature of Prophecy. The *predictive* element was a frequent part of the content of the prophet's message. But this is not the only element. The prophets frequently appeared in the role of social and political reformers, stirring preachers of righteousness and religious revivalists in addition to being predictors of judgment or blessing, as the occasion demanded. The prophet's message was ever religious and spiritual, announcing the will of God to men and calling for complete obedience. Often the prophetic element shone out in the prophet's preaching and writing. This element cannot be dispensed with as some modern critics would think. Neither can the opposite extreme of regarding the prophet's message as solely predictive be defended as tenable. Prophetic prognostication was not mere foretelling to appeal to idle curiosity nor even to maintain the integrity of the prophet, although that was occasionally the case (cf. Deut. 18:22). The genius of prophecy was rather a prediction of the future arising from the conditions of the present and was inseparably connected with the profoundly religious and spiritual message the prophet was called to proclaim to his own generation.

Besides being moral and spiritual in its purpose and frequently predictive in content, OT prophecy *was coeval with the beginning of redemptive history.* Critics commonly limit prophecy to the writing prophets and make it a comparatively late development in Israel, confining it to the eighth century or later, but prophecy and written prophetical oracles go back to the most ancient times and are coeval with the beginning of divine revelation (cf. the first prophecy of a divine Redeemer, Gen. 3:15-16). Enoch, the seventh from Adam, was a prophet (Jude 14-15). Noah uttered prophetic oracles (Gen. 9:25-27), Abraham was a prophet (20:7). Moses was a prophet in a very special sense (Num. 12:6-8) and a type of Christ, "the Prophet" par excellence (Deut. 18:18; John 6:14; 7:40). Prophecy occurred in the time of the Judges (Judg. 4:4). There was a dearth of prophetic vision in the time of Samuel (1 Sam. 3:1). Until the close of OT prophecy under Malachi, prophecy was continuously operative in Israel. It rose to great literary heights in Isaiah and Jeremiah. Moreover, prophecy was *of divine origin.* The various titles for the prophets in the original language, such as *rō'eh* (1 Sam. 9:9), *ḥōzeh* (2 Sam. 24:11), and *nābî'* (1 Sam. 9:9), and the manner in which they received their message indisputably pointed to the divine authority and origin of their message.

Biblical Concept of Prophecy. Scripture plainly presents prediction as a manifestation of God's power glorifying His Person, exalting His redemptive work in Christ, and setting forth the divine character of His revealed Word. The words of fulfilled prophecies with regard to the first advent of Christ speak of the wisdom and power of God in interposing for man's need. Scripture not only presents the prophetic word as a demonstration of God's power and wisdom, but it presents His response to man's need. Since man is ignorant of what a day may bring forth, the revelation of God's will for the present and the disclosure of His plans and purposes for the future are of inestimable benefit to the believer. In the light of these facts, widespread neglect of biblical prophecy is not only tragic but inexcusable.

Rules for Interpretation of Prophecy. The prophetic portions of Scripture, constituting about one-fourth of its content, demand careful treatment if one is to avoid excesses and abuses in the study of prophecy.

1. Select a workable system of prophetic interpretation. One ought to investigate thoroughly the available systems, such as premillennialism, amillennialism, and postmillennialism. He must not rest until he is thoroughly persuaded that the system he adopts is the correct one.

2. Fix upon the background of the prophecies.

Many details of the historical background are necessary to see the prophecy in its full sweep and meaning. Neglect of simple matters of history and light from archaeology may result in serious deficiency in interpretation.

3. Observe the context of prophecy. Its immediate setting must be carefully scrutinized and no interpretation permitted that will violate the immediate context. Moreover, the remote text must be handled just as diligently. Each individual prophecy must be related in the widest context to the full sweep of God's purposes from eternity past to eternity future.

4. Pursue normal literal interpretation rather than the mystical. A good rule is as follows: "When the plain sense of Scripture makes common sense, seek no other sense; therefore, take every word at its primary, usual literal meaning unless it is patently a rhetorical figure, or unless the immediate context, studied in the light of related passages and axiomatic and fundamental truths, clearly points otherwise."

5. Determine the correct relationship between the form of prophecy and the ideas conveyed by it. Satisfaction of one's thinking on this line will determine whether the interpreter is attracted to a premillennial, amillennial, or postmillennial interpretation. Whatever system he adopts, he must satisfy himself that his system of interpretation resolves the difficulties and meets the requirements of the specific details and not merely of generalization. Inductive logic must take precedence over inductive reasoning in the interpretation of prophecy and Scripture in general. *See* Prophet.   M.F.U.

BIBLIOGRAPHY: W. G. Scroggie, *Prophecy and History* (n.d.); H. C. von Orelli, *Old Testament Prophecy* (1885); A. B. Davidson, *Old Testament Prophecy* (1904); A. Guillaume, *Prophecy and Divination* (1938); H. H. Rowley, ed., *Studies in Old Testament Prophecy* (1950); id., *The Servant of the Lord* (1952); R. B. Girdlestone, *The Grammar of Prophecy* (1955); J. F. Walvoord, *Israel in Prophecy* (1962); id., *The Church in Prophecy* (1964); R. E. Clements, *Prophecy and Covenant* (1965); J. F. Walvoord, *The Nations in Prophecy* (1967); D. Hill, *New Testament Prophecy* (1979); G. H. Pember, *The Great Prophecies Concerning the Gentiles, the Jews, and the Church of God* (1984); id., *The Great Prophecies of the Centuries Concerning Israel and the Gentiles* (1984); id., *The Church, the Churches, and the Mysteries* (1984); id., *The Great Prophecies of the Centuries Concerning the Church* (1984).

PROPHET. One who is divinely inspired to communicate God's will to His people and to disclose the future to them.

Names. The general Heb. word for prophet is *nābî',* from the verb *nābā';* cf. Akkad. nabū, "to announce, call a declarer, announcer." The primary idea of a prophet, therefore, is a *declarer, announcer,* one who utters a communication. The great majority of biblical critics prefer the active sense of *announcing, pouring forth the* *declarations of God.* Two other Heb. words, *rō'eh* and *ḥōzeh,* are used to designate the prophet, both meaning "one who sees," and sometimes rendered "seer." The three words occur in 1 Chron. 29:29, where they seem to be contrasted with each other: "Now the acts of King David, from first to last, are written in the chronicles of Samuel the *seer* [*rō'eh*], in the chronicles of Nathan the *prophet* [*nābî'*], and in the chronicles of Gad the *seer* [*ḥōzēh*]." *Rō'eh* occurs twelve times (1 Sam. 9:11, 18-19; 2 Sam. 15:27; 1 Chron. 9:22; 26:28; 29:29; 2 Chron. 16:7, 10; Isa. 30:10), and in seven of these it is applied to Samuel. It was superseded in general use by the word nābî, by which Samuel was designated as well as by *rō'eh* (1 Sam. 3:20; 2 Chron. 35:18), and which seems to have been revived after a period of disuse (1 Sam. 10:5, 10-12; 19:20, 24). *Hāzôn* is the word consistently used for the prophetical vision and is found in Samuel, Chronicles, Psalms, Proverbs, and in most of the Prophets. Whether there is any difference in the usage of these words and, if any, what that difference is, has been much debated. On the whole, it would seem that the same persons are designated by the three words. Sometimes the prophets are called *watchmen,* Heb. *ṣōpîm* (Jer. 6:17; Ezek. 3:17; 33:2, 6-7); *shōmēr,* a *watchman* (Isa. 21:11; 62:6); and *rō'eh,* "pastoral," a shepherd (Zech. 11:5, 16). The word is uniformly translated in the LXX by *prophētēs* and in the NASB and NIV by "prophet." In classical Gk. *prophētēs* signifies "one who speaks for another," especially "one who speaks for a god" and so interprets his will to man. Hence its essential meaning is "an interpreter." The use of the word *prophētēs* in its modern sense is postclassical, and is derived from the LXX. From the medieval use of the word *prophēteia* ("prophecy") passed into the English language in the sense of *prediction,* and this sense it has retained as its popular meaning. The larger sense of *interpretation* has not, however, been lost. In fact the English word *prophet,* like the word *inspiration,* has always been used in a larger and in a closer sense.

The Prophetical Order. The prophetical institution was not a temporary expedient, but provision was made for it in the law. That the Israelites might not consult with false prophets, such as diviners, observers of times, and enchanters, Moses gave the promise (Deut. 18:15) "The Lord your God will raise up for you a prophet like me from among you" (cf. vv. 16-22). Although this passage evidently refers to the Messiah, it does not exclude its reference to a succession of prophets, between Moses and Christ, running parallel with the kingdom of Israel. The Scriptures do not represent an unbroken series of prophets, each inducted into office by his predecessor, being silent on this point save in the cases of Joshua and Elisha, who were respectively inducted into office by Moses and Elijah. The

prophets are described as deriving their prophetical office immediately from God, and not to have attached much importance to a series of incumbents, each receiving his commission from another or from others.

From the days of Joshua to Eli "visions were infrequent" (1 Sam. 3:1), for during the time of the Judges the priesthood, which was originally the instrument through which Israel was taught and governed in spiritual things, had sadly degenerated. The people were no longer affected by the acted lessons of the ceremonial service. They needed warnings and exhortations that were less enigmatic. Under these circumstances a new moral power was evoked—the prophetic order. Samuel, himself a Levite, of the family of Kohath (1 Chron. 6:28), and almost certainly a priest, was the instrument used at once for effecting a reform in the priestly order (9:22) and for giving to the prophets a position of importance that they had never before held. Nevertheless, it is not to be supposed that Samuel created the prophetic order as a new thing before unknown. The germs both of the prophetic and regal order are found in the law as given to the Israelites by Moses (Deut. 13:1; 18:18, 20-22), but they were not yet developed because there was not yet the demand for them.

Schools. Samuel took measures to make his work of restoration permanent as well as effective for the moment. For this purpose he instituted companies, or colleges, of prophets. One we find in his lifetime at Ramah (1 Sam. 19:19-20); others afterward at Bethel (2 Kings 2:3), Jericho (2:5), Gilgal (4:38), and elsewhere (6:1). Into them were gathered promising students, and there they were trained for the office that they were afterward destined to fulfill. So successful were these institutions that from the time of Samuel to the closing of the canon of the OT there seems never to have been wanting an adequate supply of men to keep up the line of official prophets. Their chief subject of study was, no doubt, the law and its interpretation—oral, as distinct from symbolical, teaching being henceforward tacitly transferred from the priestly to the prophetical order. Subsidiary subjects of instruction were music and sacred poetry, both of which had been connected with prophecy from the time of Moses (Ex. 15:20) and the Judges (Judg. 4:4; 5).

Manner of Life. The mode of life led by the prophets seems to have been subject to no uniform and rigid law, but, doubtless, changing according to circumstances. It must not be taken for granted that there was any peculiar dress adopted by them because of the instances of Elijah and John the Baptist's wearing hairy garments. Nor from their manner of living are we to conclude that all adopted an ascetic mode of life. Sometimes, perhaps as an example, or because of persecution, they lived in poverty (1 Kings 14:3; 2 Kings 4:1, 38, 42; 6:5). It is probable that the writer of the epistle to the Hebrews (11:37-38) alludes to the sufferings and privation of the prophets, a vivid description of which is given in the accounts of Elijah, Elisha, and Jeremiah (Jer. 20). Their persecution and consequent suffering did not arise from opposition to them as a distinct class, leading an unsociable, ascetic mode of life, but from opposition to their faithful ministry.

Prophetic Function. Robertson observes: "The prophets had a practical office to discharge. It was part of their commission to show the people of God 'their transgressions and the house of Jacob their sins' (Isa. 58:1; Ezek. 22:2; 43:10; Mic. 3:8). They were, therefore, pastors and ministerial monitors of the people of God. It was their duty to admonish and reprove, to denounce prevailing sins, to threaten the people with the terrors of divine judgment, and to call them to repentance. They also brought the message of consolation and pardon (Isa. 40:1-2). They were the watchmen set upon the walls of Zion to blow the trumpet, and timely warning of approaching danger (Ezek. 3:17; 33:7-9; Jer. 6:17; Isa. 62:6). Their function differed from that of the priests, the latter approaching God in behalf of men by means of sacrifice, the former coming to men as ambassadors from God, beseeching them to turn from their evil ways and live. The prophets do not seem to have had any official relation to the government, exerting an influence upon rulers and state affairs, not as officers of the state, but as special messengers from God. Nor must it be inferred that the prophetic and priestly classes were antagonistic. There were times when the priesthood settled down to formality and routine, or exercised their office for gain. At such time the prophetic voice was raised in scathing rebukes, whose terms almost lead one to conclude that in the prophetical estimation the whole priestly order, and all the ceremonies over which they presided, were in the essence wrong. Yet even in the midst of such rebukes there is a tone of respect for the law, and a recognition of the sacred function of the priest. So, also, when we come to any crisis in the history in which a positive advance is made, we perceive that it is not by a conquest of one party over the other, but by the hearty cooperation of both, that the movement of reform or advance succeeds. Moses, the forerunner of the prophets, has Aaron the priest beside him; and Joshua is still surrounded by priests in the carrying out of his work. Samuel is both priest and prophet; David and Solomon, in the same way, are served or admonished by both" (*Early Religion of Israel,* p. 461).

In addition to the declaration of God's will, the denunciation of His judgments, the defense of truth and righteousness, and bearing testimony to the superiority of the moral to the ritual, prophecy had an intimate relation to God's gra-

cious purpose toward Israel (Mic. 5:4; 7:20; Isa. 60:3; 65:25).

Contents and Sphere. The function of the prophet, as already seen, was not merely the disclosure of the future, but included the exposition and application of the law, the declaration of God's will. It thus contained two elements —the *moral,* or *doctrinal,* and the *predictive.* The *doctrinal* element of prophecy teaches "of the existence of an eternal, self-conscious, intelligent, moral, and voluntary Being, who does all things according to the purpose of his will. It ascribes to him all the attributes of such a Being in infinite perfection. It is more or less a commentary upon the doctrine of divine providence, by representing the future even, which it brings to view, as a part of that system of things in which the Creator is present by the direction of his power and the counsels of his wisdom, appointing the issues of futurity, as well as foreseeing the acting with his 'mighty hand and outstretched arm,' seen or unseen, ruling in the kingdom of men, and ordering all things in heaven and earth" (Charles Elliott, *Old Testament Prophecy,* p. 44).

The prophets teach respecting man that he was created by God (Mal. 2:10); has a common origin; has the power of reason (Isa. 1:18); has a capacity for holiness, knowledge, and progress (2:3-5); is ruined and cannot save himself (Hos. 13:9; Jer. 2:22; 13:23); is a subject of God's moral government and owes entire obedience to His law (Dan. 4:34-35; Ezek. 18:4-5, 9; Isa. 1:19-20; 23:11-16); and, lastly, must render worship and homage to God (Isa. 60:6-7; Mal. 1:11; 3:10). All duties arising out of human relations are also clearly stated and enforced. The prophets, moreover, inculcated, with remarkable clearness and decision, the doctrines of faith and repentance (Isa. 26:3-4; 55:7; Ezek. 14:6; 18:30; 36:31).

By the *sphere* of prophecy is meant both the parties to whom it was given and the objects that it more immediately contemplated. Its proper sphere, especially in its stricter sense of containing preintimations of good things to come, is the nation Israel in relation to the coming Messiah and the manner in which this relationship affects both the Jew and Gentile. The church, born on the Day of Pentecost (Acts 2), is not in view in the OT Prophets but was a special mystery revealed to the apostle Paul (Eph. 3:1-10; Rom. 16:25). Future Gentile salvation was clearly revealed in the OT, but not the "mysteries of the kingdom of heaven" (Matt. 13:11) that concern this present age. The bulk of OT prophecy concerns Israel's future national conversion and restoration in the coming millennial kingdom inaugurated at the second advent of Christ (Isa. 35; Zech. 14; etc.).

Prophecy is not intended to open the future to idle curiosity but is for the higher purpose of furnishing light to those whose faith needs confirming. The revelation of future events may be needful in times of discouragement to awaken or sustain hope, to inspire confidence in the midst of general backsliding, and to warn of evil threatening the faithful. The predictions against Babylon, Tyre, Egypt, Nineveh, and other kingdoms were delivered to the people of God to comfort them, by revealing to them the fate of their enemies.

The prophecy of Jonah against Nineveh seems to be exceptional. He was sent to a pagan power to denounce the judgments of God against it. He did not, in his own land and among his own people, preach against Nineveh, but he entered the great city itself and delivered his message there. Thus his was a typical character, and his mission to Nineveh may have been typical of Israel to be "a light to the nations," and was thus intended to remind ancient Israel of the mission that it had neglected and forgotten.

Prophetic Inspiration. The Scriptures teach that the prophets received their communications by the agency of the Spirit of God. When the seventy elders were appointed the Lord said to Moses, "I will take of the Spirit who is upon you, and will put Him upon them" (Num. 11:17, 25). Samuel said to Saul, "Then the Spirit of the Lord will come upon you mightily, and you shall prophesy with them and be changed into another man" (1 Sam. 10:6). "Then Saul sent messengers to take David, but when they saw the company of the prophets prophesying, with Samuel standing and presiding over them, the Spirit of God came upon the messengers of Saul; and they also prophesied" (19:20). According to Peter (2 Pet. 1:21), "no prophecy was ever made by an act of human will, but men moved by the Holy Spirit spoke from God."

The false prophets were those who "speak a vision of their own imagination, not from the mouth of the Lord" (Jer. 23:16); "foolish prophets who are following their own spirit and have seen nothing" (Ezek. 13:3). The true prophet was God's spokesman to man, communicating what he had received from God (Ex. 4:16; 7:1-2).

The modes of communication between God and man are clearly stated on the occasion of the sedition of Aaron and Miriam: "When they had both come forward, He said, 'Hear now My words: If there is a prophet among you, I, the Lord, shall make Myself known to him in a vision. I shall speak with him in a dream. Not so, with My servant Moses, he is faithful in all My household; with him I speak mouth to mouth, even openly, and not in dark sayings, and he beholds the form of the Lord'" (Num. 12:5-8). Three modes are given here: (1) vision, (2) dream, (3) direct communication and manifestation, the highest form being the last, and reserved for Moses. In this he resembled Christ, of whom he was a type. The other two were lower forms, whose comparative rank it is perhaps impossible to determine.

The state of the prophet while under the influence of the Holy Spirit has been a matter of considerable comment. Philo and the Alexandrine school held that the prophet was in a state of entire unconsciousness when under such influence. Athenagoras held that the prophets were entranced and deprived of their natural powers, "the Spirit using them as instruments, as a flute player might blow a flute." Montanus held the same theory: "The Almighty ruled alone in the prophet's soul, whose own self-consciousness retired back. God, therefore, spoke from the soul of the prophet, of which he took entire possession, as if in his own name." But such a theory identifies Jewish prophecy, in all essential points, with heathen divination. When the diviners of the heathen world were under the influence of inspiration, they were supposed to be in a state of mind expressed by the Gk. term *ekstasis,* i.e., a *trance,* their faculties held in complete abeyance. Such a state of mind was regarded as a natural and necessary sign of inspiration, the subject exhibiting the outward signs of violent excitement, resembling insanity.

The Hebrew prophets were not distinguished by such peculiarities. They were not subject to *amentia,* neither were they placed, as Montanus taught, in an altogether passive relation to the divine influence; but they were possessed of intelligent self-consciousness. They did not lose their self-possession but spoke with a full apprehension of existing circumstances. At the same time the mind of the prophet seems to have been raised above its ordinary condition, and he sometimes adopted measures to prepare himself for prophesying (*see* 2 Kings 3:15; 1 Sam. 10:5; 1 Chron. 25:1). The mind of the prophet was passive while he received divine communications in visions and in dreams; but in the announcement of their visions and dreams the prophets were in full possession of intelligent self-consciousness. They were conscious that they had a divine commission, that they were sent by God to communicate His purposes; and, accordingly, they prefaced their prophetic utterances by the formulae "the hand of the Lord was strong on me" (Ezek. 3:14; cf. 1:3; 33:22); "the vision of . . ." (Isa. 1:1; Ezek. 1:1); "declares the Lord" (Jer. 1:8, 19; 2:19; 30:11; Amos 2:11; 4:5); "the word of the Lord came to . . ." (Jonah 1:1; cf. Joel 1:1).

As for the question as to whether or not the prophets had a full knowledge of what they predicted, it would seem that their understandings were not so miraculously enlarged as to grasp the whole of the divine counsels that they were commissioned to enunciate. We have, as Oehler says, the testimony of the prophets themselves to this effect (Dan. 12:8; Zech. 4:5; 1 Pet. 1:10-11).

Prophetic Style. A writer's characteristic manner of expression we call his *style.* The sacred writers form no exception; each one maintains his individuality; and it is therefore perfectly proper to speak of the style of Isaiah, Jeremiah, etc. But apart from the style that is the expression of the mental and moral idiosyncrasies of the prophets there is a style that characterizes them as prophets. This arises from the method of prophetic revelation. When inspired of God their intellectual and emotional nature was quickened. They knew by intuition, and their hearts glowed with seraphic ardor. They were in the region of spirit as contradistinguished from that of sense and time. At the same time they retained their personal characteristics and native susceptibilities. We find that prophecy made large use of the present and past condition of the nation and of the Levitical institutions and ceremonies, as symbols in presenting good things to come: (1) the future was described in terms of the past (Hos. 8:13; 9:3; 11:5; cf. Rev. 2:14, 20); (2) great use was made of the present, and especially of the standpoint and personal circumstances of the one through whom the prophecy was given, to illustrate the future (Ezek. 48:35; cf. Rev. 21:22); (3) frequently the prophetic style received its completion and coloring from the diversified circumstances of the parties addressed and of the prophet himself (Dan. 8-9); and (4) the poetical element arose from the ecstatical condition of the prophet; but, as it was the primary aim of the Hebrew religious teachers to influence the heart and conscience, that poetical element, though never entirely suppressed, was held in restraint to further the ends of spiritual instruction.

BIBLIOGRAPHY: T. H. Robinson, *Prophecy and the Prophets in Ancient Israel* (1923); A. R. Johnson, *The Cultic Prophet in Ancient Israel* (1944); M. Noth, *Bulletin of the John Rylands Library* 32 (1949-50): 194ff.; E. J. Young, *My Servants the Prophets* (1955); C. Kuhl, *The Prophets of Israel* (1960); C. Westermann, *Basic Forms of Prophetic Speech* (1967); H. E. Freeman, *An Introduction to the Old Testament Prophets* (1968); S. J. Schultz, *The Prophets Speak* (1968); F. F. Bruce, *This Is That* (1978), pp. 97-114.

PROPITIATION. The divine side of the work of Christ on the cross. Christ's atoning death for the world's sin altered the whole position of the human race in its relationship to God, for God recognizes what Christ accomplished in behalf of the world whether men enter into the blessings of it or not. The cross has rendered God propitious toward the unsaved as well as toward the erring saint (1 John 2:2). The fact that Christ has borne all sin renders God propitious. The Gk. words dealing with the doctrine of propitiation are *hilasmos,* signifying what our Lord became for the sinner (1 John 2:2; 4:10); *hilastērion,* denoting the place of propitiation (Rom. 3:25; cf. Heb. 9:5); and *hilaskomai,* indicating that God has become gracious, or propitious (Luke 18:13; Heb. 2:17). In this present age since the death of Christ, God does not have to be asked to be propitious, because He has become so through the death of Christ. To ask Him thus to become propitious, in view of Christ's sacrifice, manifests

unbelief. In the OT the Mercy Seat in the Holy of Holies could be made a place of propitiation by sacrifice (Heb. 9:5). Now, however, the blood-sprinkled body of Christ on the cross has become the Mercy Seat for sinners once and for all. The Mercy Seat is thus a continual throne of grace. What otherwise would be an awful judgment throne becomes an altar of infinite mercy. The prayer of the publican (Luke 18:13), "God, be merciful to me, the sinner!" better translated, "God, be Thou propitiated to me, the sinner," was not a request for mercy as though God had to be persuaded to be propitious. Rather, it was expressive of the relationship then existing between God and the OT covenant people of God on the ground of offered sacrifice, when God was requested to be propitious on a special basis. Now the believer can rejoice that God is propitiated. To believe this is to enter into the benefits of it.

M.F.U.

BIBLIOGRAPHY: R. Nicole, *Westminster Theological Journal* 17 (1954-55): 117-57; L. L. Morris, *New Testament Studies* 2 (1955-56): 33-43; id., *Apostolic Preaching of the Cross* (1965), pp. 125-85.

PROSELYTE (Gk. *prosēlutos,* a "newcomer"). The English term is found only in the NT, the Heb. *gēr* being rendered "alien," sometimes "sojourner" and "stranger." From the time of the covenant between Jehovah and Abraham, Israel had been a distinctive people, whose mission it was to proclaim among the nations that Jehovah alone was God. There were at all times strangers living in Israel to whom the Mosaic law did not grant the rights of citizenship, but to whom it did extend toleration and certain privileges, for which it obliged them to comply with certain of the religious enactments prescribed to Israel. They were required not to blaspheme the name of Jehovah (Lev. 24:16), not to indulge in idolatrous worship (20:2), not to commit acts of indecency (18:26), not to work on the Sabbath (Ex. 20:10), not to eat leavened bread during the celebration of the Passover (12:19), and not to eat blood or the flesh of animals that had died a natural death or had been torn by wild beasts (Lev. 17:10, 15).

Naturalization of. Should such strangers wish to become citizens, the law sanctioned their admission on the condition of their being circumcised. They thus bound themselves to observe the whole law and were admitted to the full privileges and blessings of the people of the covenant (Ex. 12:48, 49; cf. Rom. 9:4). The exceptions to strangers thus freely admitted were the Ammonites and Moabites, who were to be strictly excluded to the tenth generation (i.e., forever), and the Edomites, whose sons were not to be admitted until the third generation (Deut. 23:3, 7-8). The reason assigned for these exceptions was that those nations had shown unfriendliness to the Israelites when they left Egypt.

In Canaan. Among the proselytes at the time of the entrance into Canaan, the Kenites were the most conspicuous (Judg. 1:16). The presence of *strangers* was recognized in the solemn declaration of blessings and curses from Ebal and Gerizim (Josh. 8:33). The period after the conquest of Canaan was not favorable to the admission of proselytes, the people having no strong faith, no commanding position. The Gibeonites (9:16-27) furnish the only instance of conversion, and their position was rather that of slaves than of free proselytes.

Under the Monarchy. During the monarchy some foreigners rose to power and fortune, but they were generally treated by David and Solomon as a subject class brought under a system of compulsory labor from which others were exempted (1 Chron. 22:2; 2 Chron. 2:17-18). As some compensation for their sufferings they became the special objects of the care and sympathy of the prophets. During the period of the monarchy, when Israel developed into a powerful state, many foreigners were attracted for the sake of political and commercial relations. Foreign influence increased still more when Israel lost its independence and was made subject to heathen powers, whose yoke the Israelites were never able to remove, except for a somewhat limited period. In such circumstances, in which there was no longer any bond of national unity, the religious fellowship that the law, with its ceremonial regulations, had created among the people developed into an inward bond of union that every day became only more firmly knit. Notwithstanding the stiff formalism of Pharisaic piety, still the spirit that had animated the law and the prophets was able to resist the corrupting influence of an effete heathenism and to attract a considerable number of Gentiles, leading them to seek in the religion of the Jews the salvation that their own gods and idolatrous worship were unable to afford.

Consequently, the Talmud and the rabbinical teachers distinguished two classes of proselytes. *Proselytes of the gate* were Gentile strangers who, while they lived among the Jews, had bound themselves to observe the seven Noachian precepts: six prohibitions—those against idolatry, blasphemy, bloodshed, uncleanness, theft, and eating flesh with the blood; and a seventh, positive command—that of obedience to God. *Proselytes of righteousness* (or proselytes of the covenant) were those who had been formally admitted to participation in the theocratic covenant and had professed their adherence to all the doctrines and precepts of the Mosaic law. The rabbis gave three essentials for admission of males as proselytes to Judaism—circumcision, baptism, and a sacrifice; for females, baptism and sacrifice. Baptism was probably an adaptation of ablution or bathing in water, such as we may well suppose would in every case accompany the circumcision of a Gentile, the law forbidding the unclean to take part in any religious ceremony until they had bathed in water (Ex. 19:10).

"If the baptism of proselytes was of so late an origin, then it is, of course, impossible that the baptism of John and Christian baptism can have been borrowed from it. It is much more likely that the Jews, after the discontinuance of the temple worship, may have taken occasion from Christian baptism to transform the customary bathing with water that was required [for] purification, and which the person to be purified had to perform himself, into a formal act of baptism having the character of a rite of initiation" (Keil, *Arch.,* 1:427).

After the Captivity. The proselytism of the period following the captivity was, for the most part, the conformity, not of a subject race, but of willing adherents. As early as the return from Babylon there is evidence that persons were drawn to a faith they recognized as holier than their own. With the extension of the Roman Empire, the Jews became more widely known and their power to proselytize increased. In most of the large cities of the empire there were men who had been rescued from idolatry and its attendant debasements and had been brought under the power of a higher moral law. The converts who were thus attracted joined, with varying strictness, in the worship of the Jews. In Palestine even Roman centurions learned to love the conquered nation, built synagogues (Luke 7:5), feasted, prayed, and gave alms (Acts 10:2, 30), and became preachers of the new faith to their soldiers (v. 7).

Then to almost every Jewish community there was attached a following of "God-fearing proselytes" (Acts 13:43), Gentiles who adopted the Jewish mode of worship and attended the synagogues but who in the observance of the ceremonial law restricted themselves to certain leading points and so were regarded as outside the fellowship of the Jewish communities.

Proselytism had its dark side; the Jews of Palestine were eager to spread their faith by the same weapons as those with which they had defended it. The Edomites had the alternative of death, exile, or circumcision, and the Ithraeans were converted in the same way. Where force was not used, converts were sought by the most unscrupulous fraud; the vices of the Jew were engrafted on those of the heathen. Their position was pitiable; at Rome and other large cities they were the butt of popular scurrility, bound to make public confession and pay a special tax. Among the Jews proselytes to Judaism gained but little honor, being looked upon with suspicion, as converted Jews often are now. The better rabbis did their best to guard against such evils. Anxious to exclude all unworthy converts, they grouped them, according to their motives, with a somewhat quaint classification. *Love-proselytes* were those who had been drawn to Judaism by the hope of gaining the beloved one. *Man-for-woman*, or *Woman-for-man*, *proselytes* were proselytes who had converted to the religion of a spouse, husband or wife. *Esther-proselytes* were those who conformed to Judaism in order to escape danger, as in the original Purim (Esther 8:17). *King's-table-proselytes* were led to convert by the hope of court favor and promotion, such as must have been the case of many of the converts under David and Solomon. *Lion-proselytes* were those whose conversion originated in a superstitious dread of a divine judgment, as with the Samaritans of 2 Kings 17:26. None of these was regarded as fit for admission within the covenant (Smith, *Bib. Dict.*; Schürer, *History of the Jewish People in the Time of Christ*).

BIBLIOGRAPHY: W. O. E. Oesterley, ed., *Judaism and Christianity* (1937): 1:213-33; T. F. Torrance, *New Testament Studies* 1 (1954): 150-54; T. M. Taylor, *NTS* 2 (1956): 193-98; N. Levison, *Scottish Journal of Theology* 10 (1957): 45-56; J. Neusner, *Journal of Biblical Literature* 83 (1964): 60-66.

PROSTITUTE. See Harlot.

PROVENDER. See Fodder.

PROVERB (Heb. *māshāl*, "to be like"). In the early stages of social intellectual growth, when men begin to observe and generalize on the facts of human life, they clothe the results of observation in the form of short and pithy sentences. Every race not in savage condition has proverbs of this kind. The Heb. word rendered "proverb" has a special significance. The proverb of the Israelites and other people of the East was primarily and essentially a "similitude." It was thus a condensed parable or fable, capable at any time of being expanded, sometimes presented with the lesson clearly taught, sometimes involved in greater or less obscurity, that its very difficulty might stimulate the desire to know and so impress the lesson more deeply on the mind. The proverb might be a "dark saying" requiring—and receiving—an interpretation, as for example is the case in Prov. 17:3, "The refining pot is for silver and the furnace for gold, but the Lord tests hearts," a parable expanded in Mal. 3:3, "And He will sit as a smelter and purifier of silver, and He will purify the sons of Levi and refine them like gold and silver." Other "dark sayings" are deliberately kept obscure, given without any interpretation, and capable of many. Such is the case with Prov. 1:17, "Indeed, it is useless to spread the net in the eyes of any bird."

Individual proverbs are quoted in Scripture before there appears any collection of them. The saying "Out of the wicked comes forth wickedness" was a "proverb of the ancients" in the days of Saul (1 Sam. 24:13). An individual instance of strange inconsistency was generalized as a type of all like anomalies, and the question, "Is Saul also among the prophets?" became a proverb in Israel

(10:11; 19:24). The inclination to transfer to others the guilt that has brought suffering to oneself is expressed in the proverb "The fathers have eaten sour grapes, and the children's teeth are set on edge" (Jer. 31:29; cf. Ezek. 18:2), in both instances being condemned as an error.

The book of Job is full of short, pithy sayings of the proverb type, one of which became the motto of the book of Proverbs: "Behold, the fear of the Lord, that is wisdom; and to depart from evil is understanding" (Job 28:28). When Solomon came into contact with "the sons of the east" (1 Kings 4:30), whose wisdom clothed itself in this form, it was perfectly natural that he should express himself in and become the patron of maxims, precepts, and condensed parables in the shape of proverbs.

The Heb. word *ḥîdâ*, Hab. 2:6, has the meaning of a conundrum, something enigmatical. The passage is thus rendered by Keil and Delitzsch (*Com.*): "Will not all these lift up a proverb upon him, and a song, and a riddle upon him?"

The Lord Jesus employed proverbs in His teaching, such as "Physician, heal yourself " (Luke 4:23; cf. John 16:25, 29, marg.).

BIBLIOGRAPHY: M. Noth and D. W. Thomas, eds., *Wisdom in Israel and the Ancient Near East* (1955); S. G. Champion, *Racial Proverbs* (1963), pp. xxxviii-xciv; G. von Rad, *Wisdom in Israel* (1972), pp. 24-34.

PROVERBS, BOOK OF. "The proverbs of Solomon the son of David, king of Israel" (1:1). The word *proverb* itself means "a sententious brief saying setting forth practical wisdom." In the strictest sense it means a "repetition or comparison." The LXX has "Proverbs or Parables" of Solomon. The Vulg. has *Liber Proverbiorum*. The book is part of the so-called Wisdom Literature of the OT.

Contents. The book consists of sententious sayings of practical wisdom and didactic poems of longer length. Not mere human wisdom is treated but divine wisdom, or God in revelation as Creator and goal of all things, is treated as well (cf. chap. 8).

Outline.
   I. Solomon's proverbs (1:1–9:18)
      A. Wisdom's call (1:1-33)
      B. Wisdom's rewards (2:1–7:27)
      C. Wisdom's praise (8:1–9:18)
  II. Solomon's various sayings (10:1–22:16)
 III. The words to the wise (22:17–24:34)
 IV. Solomon's proverbs set down by Hezekiah's scribes (25:1–29:27)
  V. Agur's words (30:1-33)
 VI. Lemuel's words (31:1-9)
VII. The acrostic poem of the virtuous wife (31:10-31)

Connection with Other Literature. The Proverbs of Amenemope of Egypt, who is dated variously between 1000 and 600 B.C., so closely resemble Prov. 22:17–25:22, usually considered non-Solomonic, that critics commonly see literary dependence of the latter (cf. O. Eissfeldt, *Einleitung*, p. 525). W. F. Albright, for instance, is of the persuasion that the Egyptian proverbs "were taken over, almost certainly through Phoenician intermediation" (*Archaeology and the Religion of Israel* [1942], p. 5). However, it may be said that both the author of this section of Proverbs and the Egyptian author may well have been influenced by a common third source. A much more probable and sounder view is that the biblical work is older, since Prov. 1-24 assuredly was regarded as Solomonic in Hezekiah's time (eighth century B.C.).

Authorship and Date. Critics commonly ascribe little or none of the book to Solomon. Eissfeldt does this on the basis of Aramaisms, but Aram. elements may occur very early in Heb. literature as well as very late. It is now known that the inscription of Zakir, king of Hamath, around 800 B.C., is written in a mixture of Heb. and Aram. Two sections of the book of Proverbs are expressly attributed to Solomon (10:1–22:16; 25:1–29:27). Unless we view the introduction (1:1-6) as a later edition from the fifth or fourth century B.C., there is no reason for denying chaps. 1-9 to Solomon. The third section (22:17–24:34) is similar to the first (chaps. 1-9). This section does not seem to be intended as a separate division on the basis of authorship, for the expression "words of the wise" is not a title to a new section. The fourth section is described as being copied out by Hezekiah's scribes, evidently from an old collection of Solomon's sayings. Certainly this section was not composed by the scribes. Therefore, strong scriptural testimony exists that Solomon was the author of chaps. 1-29; that is, of the entire book except chap. 30 by Agur and chap. 31 by King Lemuel. First Kings 4:32, which attributes "3,000 proverbs" to Solomon, supports such a thesis, as does Solomon's fame for wisdom (1 Kings 3:5-28; 10:1).

BIBLIOGRAPHY: J. H. Greenstone, *Proverbs*, The Holy Scriptures with Commentary (1950); D. Kidner, *Proverbs*, Tyndale Old Testament Commentary (1964); R. K. Harrison, *Introduction to the Old Testament* (1969), pp. 1010-21; W. McKane, *Proverbs*, Old Testament Library (1970); W. Arnot, *Studies in Proverbs* (1978); C. Bridges, *A Modern Study of the Book of Proverbs*, ed. G. F. Santa (1978); R. Wardlaw, *Lectures on the Book of Proverbs*, 3 vols. (1981-82).

PROVIDENCE (Lat. *providentia*, "foreseeing"). A term that in theology designates the continual care that God exercises over the universe He has created. This includes the two facts of preservation and government.

The doctrine of providence is closely connected with that of creation. That God could create the world and then forsake it is inconceivable in view of the perfection of God. Accordingly, in the power and wisdom and goodness of the Creator declared in the Scriptures, we have the pledge of constant divine care over all parts of His creation. That idea finds expression in various places in both the OT and NT (e.g., Ps. 33:13, 15; Isa. 45:7; Acts 17:24-28). Thus there is sufficient explanation of the absence of any mention of providence in the Apostles' Creed. The great truth is implied in the declaration of faith "in God the Father Almighty, Maker of heaven and earth." The faith of believers in revealed religion in all ages has been of the same character; and however often expressed it is still more frequently implied.

Belief in providence, although agreeable with and supported by reason, has its strongest ground in the truth of special divine revelation. It is not surprising that enlightened pagans, such as Cicero and Seneca, argued in its behalf. Even among the opponents of Christianity there have been those who have adhered to a belief in providence. For the idea of providence is not exclusively Christian but is a necessary feature of religion in general. Human history as a whole and the spectacle of the universe in particular furnish abundant illustrations, for broad observation and right reason preclude the idea of a government of the world by chance or blind force; rather, they sustain the belief that "there is a power in the world that makes for righteousness." In addition, the deep necessities of human nature and life are perpetually crying out "for the living God." That facts apparently opposed to faith at this point exist is what should be expected. For universal and perfect providence implies infinite knowledge; and "we know" only "in part." Every mind less than the infinite providence must have its mysteries. Our faith at this point, as at others, must therefore find its chief support and guidance from the Word of God.

The Scriptures bearing upon this subject are numerous and of great variety and force. Space does not admit here the attempt at reference. But aside from the large number of particular passages, the historical parts of the Bible are throughout illustrative of the great reality.

Five principles are of particular note in any discussion of the providence of God as it appears in the Scriptures. First, God's providence is unlimited. It includes all things and all creatures; it has respect to all that takes place in the universe (*see* e.g., Ps. 145:9-17). The distinction between great things and small, often unreasonable in view of the dependence of the great upon the small, is rightly regarded by the care of the infinite God. Things seemingly of only slight importance or accidental are under His overruling power (*see*, for example, 1 Kings 22:34; Esther 6:1; Matt. 6:26; 27:19; Luke 12:6-7; Acts 23:16).

Second, the exercise of God's providence nevertheless has respect to the nature of different objects. All objects cannot be alike precious in His sight. Thus there is ground in Scripture, as in reason, for the distinction between general and particular and special providence. Mankind holds a peculiar relation to God among all the works of His creation; and among mankind, the people of God, the faithful servants of His kingdom, are the objects of His special love and care (*see* Matt. 6:25-32; cf. Pss. 91:11-12; 147:19-20; Acts 14:16-17; Rom. 8:28-39). Thus Scripture clearly reveals God's special love and care of nationally elect Israel in the OT (Mal. 1:2-3) and of the church, the Body of Christ, in the NT (Eph. 1:3-23). Moreover, God's unbroken love to Israel is declared in Israel's future restoration after the period of Gentile visitation (Acts 15:14-16; Rom. 11:1-31). God's providential ways with Jew, Gentile, and the church of God (1 Cor. 10:32) must always be clearly differentiated.

Third, the constant and final aim of God's providence is the fulfillment of His purpose in creation. How broad and wonderful this is may defy our comprehension; but it is declared to be nothing less than the complete establishment of an all-embracing kingdom of God, under the rule of the Lord Jesus Christ (*see* Eph. 1:9-11; Col. 1:19-20).

Fourth, the particular steps in this divine process are often unintelligible to us, but the purpose of God is independent and eternal and is certain of its realization (*see* Ps. 97:2; Rom. 11:33-35; Eph. 1:4-5; etc.).

Fifth, belief in the providence of God, according to the whole purport of Scripture, is of the highest importance because of its connection with a life of trust and gratitude and patience and hope.

Upon the various philosophical speculations as to the methods of God in providence, and His relation to natural causes and to the free agency of man, we cannot here enter. For this we must refer the reader to the works mentioned below.

BIBLIOGRAPHY: A. S. Peake, *The Problem of Pain in the Old Testament* (1904); G. C. Berkouwer, *The Providence of God* (1952); K. Barth, *Church Dogmatics* (1960), 3:3:3-288; W. G. T. Shedd, *Dogmatic Theology* (1979), 1:527-33.

PROVINCE (Heb. *mᵉdînâ*, "district" ruled by a judge; Gk. *eparcheia*).

In the OT the word *province* appears in connection with the wars between Ahab and Ben-hadad (1 Kings 20:14-15, 19), where it is observed that the victory of Ahab was gained chiefly "by the young men of the rulers of the provinces," i.e., probably, of the leaders of tribes in the Gilead country.

More commonly in the OT *province* is used of the divisions of the Chaldean (Dan. 2:49; 3:1, 30) and the Persian (Ezra 2:1; Neh. 7:6; Esther 1:1, 22; 2:3) kingdoms. Several facts as to the administration of the Persian provinces come into view in those passages: Each province has its own governor, who communicates more or less regularly with the central authority for instructions (Ezra 4-5). Each province has its own system of

finance, subject to the king's direction (Herodotus 3.89). The total number of the provinces is given as 127 (Esther 1:1; 8:9). Through the whole extent of the kingdom there is carried something like a postal system. Lastly, the word is used of the smaller sections of a satrapy rather than of the satrapy itself.

The Gk. *eparcheia* (Acts 23:34; 25:1) is used of a region subject to a prefect; a province of the Roman Empire, either a larger province or an appendage to a larger one, as Palestine was to that of Syria. The classification given by Strabo (17, p. 840), recognized in the gospels and Acts, is that of provinces supposed to need military control and therefore placed under the immediate government of the Caesar, and those still belonging theoretically to the Republic and administered by the Senate; and of the latter again proconsular and praetorian. The right of any Roman citizen to appeal from a provincial governor to the emperor was asserted by Paul (Acts 25:1). In the council of 25:12 (Gk. *sumboulion*) we recognize the assessors who were appointed to take part in the judicial functions of the governor.

PROVOCATION. The rendering of several Heb. words and one Gk. word, with the meaning of *bitterness, anger, strife. Provocation* is used to designate the ungrateful, rebellious spirit and consequent conduct of the Israelites (Heb. 3:8, 15, KJV; "day of trial," NASB, marg., "in the provocation"; NIV, "in the rebellion"). The expression in Job 17:2, "my eye gazes on their provocation," means that on the part of his friends Job sees nothing but *disputings.*

PRUDENCE, PRUDENT. The rendering of several Heb. and Gk. words, in all of which there is the underlying meaning of *intelligence, understanding,* and in the good sense of the word when allied with wisdom (Prov. 8:12).

PRUNING HOOK (Heb. *mazmērâ,* Isa. 2:4, 18:5; Joel 3:10; Mic. 4:3). A knife for pruning the vine.

PSALM. *See* Music.

PSALMS. Israel's ancient collection of hymns of praise and worship, widely used in Temple and synagogue worship and particularly cherished by God's people in every age. This collection of devotional material nearly always is found first in the third division of the Heb. canon called the Writings (cf. Luke 24:44, where it represents the entire third part of the Heb. canon).

Name. The ancient Hebrews called this collection *Tehillim,* that is, "songs of praise" or hymns. The fuller designation is *Sefer Tehillim,* that is, "the book of Psalms." The expression *psalms* is from the Gk. term denoting "music on string instruments" or, more generally, "songs adapted to such music."

Authorship. There are 150 psalms arranged in

five books according to an ancient pre-Septuagint scheme. The beginning of each book is marked by Pss. 1, 42, 73, 90, and 107. Seventy-three psalms are ascribed to David in the Heb. titles. This explains the designation "the psalms of David." Although modern critics such as Otto Eissfeldt, Robert Pfeiffer, Julius Bewer, and others customarily deny the Davidic authorship of the Psalms, there is ample internal evidence that David, the great poet and musician of Israel, was the principal author of the Psalter. This position, despite the contention of negative criticism, is indicated by the following reasons: (1) David's name is famous in the OT period for music and song and is closely associated with holy liturgy (2 Sam. 6:5-15; 1 Chron. 16:4; 2 Chron. 7:6; 29:30). (2) David was especially endowed by the Holy Spirit (2 Sam. 23:1-2; Mark 12:36; Acts 2:25-31; 4:25-26). (3) David's music and poetical gifts appear indelibly interwoven on the pages of OT history. He is called "the sweet psalmist of Israel" (2 Sam. 23:1). He was a skilled performer on the harp (1 Sam. 16:16-18). He was the author of the masterful elegy written upon the deaths of Saul and Jonathan (2 Sam. 1:19-27). He is referred to as a model poet-musician by the prophet Amos (Amos 6:5). (4) Much internal evidence in the psalms themselves points to David's authorship. Most of the songs attributed to him reflect some period of his life, such as Pss. 23, 51, and 57. In line with this evidence of Scripture, a number of the psalms indicate Davidic authorship. The common expression *ledavid* is normally construed as indicating Davidic authorship. (5) Certain psalms are cited as Davidic in Scripture in general. Acts 4:25-26 so cites Ps. 2. Acts 2:25-28 so cites Ps. 16; Rom. 4:6-8 cites Ps. 32. Acts 1:16-20 thus refers to Ps. 69, as does Rom. 11:9-10 (cf. Acts 1:20 with Ps. 109:6-20; also Matt. 22:44; Mark 12:36-37; Luke 20:42-44; Acts 2:34 with Ps. 110:1). In addition to the psalms ascribed to David, ancient tradition preserved in the superscription ascribes other psalms to Moses (Ps. 90), Solomon (Pss. 72 and 127), Heman (Ps. 88), Ethan (Ps. 89), Asaph (Pss. 50, 73-80), the sons of Korah (Pss. 42, 44-49, 84, 85, and 87). Forty-nine of the psalms are anonymous according to the Heb. text.

Composition and Date. Close affinity of many of the psalms with the style, forms, and expressions in the Ras Shamra epic poetry from ancient Ugarit, dating from the fourteenth century B.C., demonstrates the antiquity of those odes (cf. J. Patton, *Canaanite Parallels in the Book of Psalms* [1944]). Unless one's thinking is distorted by the unsound presuppositions of the Wellhausen school, it is reasonable to view the bulk of the psalms as preexilic, some dating even from before the Davidic-Solomonic era. Even if one did concede that the book of Psalms in the precise form in which it has come down to us is a postexilic collection, there is not the slightest historical or archaeological reason to suppose with Pfeiffer that the great mass of the psalms was written between 400 and 100 B.C. or that "the real question with regard to the Psalter is not that it contains Maccabaean psalms of the second century, but rather whether any psalms are preexilic psalms" (*Introduction to the O. T.,* p. 629). Fortunately archaeology is silencing such radical, unbelieving criticism. Archaisms and ancient literary forms and expressions closely parallel ancient Canaanite poetic literature and speak eloquently for a preexilic date.

Contents. Although the Psalter is largely composed of devotional hymns, heartfelt praise, and personal testimonies of praise and thanksgiving to the Lord, yet many of these poetic gems give far-reaching predictions and are prophetic as well as devotionally didactic. Psalm 2 is a magnificent prophetic panorama of the Messiah's redemptive career and His return as King of kings. Psalm 22 is an amazingly detailed prophecy of the suffering and death of Christ in His first advent. Psalm 110 is a far-reaching prophecy of Christ as a perpetual Priest. Psalm 16 heralds His future resurrection; Ps. 72 envisions the coming millennial kingdom; Ps. 45 brings into view a vast prophetic perspective. In all the OT there is no more practical, instructive, beautiful, or popular book than the Psalms.   M.F.U.

BIBLIOGRAPHY: J. A. Alexander, *The Psalms: Translated and Explained* (1864); J. Ker, *The Psalms in History and Biography* (1886); E. W. Hengstenberg, *The Psalms* (1896); R. E. Prothero [Ernle], *The Psalms in Human Life* (1914); N. H. Snaith, *Hymns of the Temple* (1951); C. S. Lewis, *Reflections on the Psalms* (1958); H. C. Leupold, *Exposition of the Psalms* (1959); A. Weiser, *The Psalms,* Old Testament Library (1962); C. Westermann, *Praise of God in the Psalms* (1965); R. K. Harrison, *Introduction to the Old Testament* (1969), pp. 976-1003; M. Dahood, *The Psalms,* Anchor Bible, 3 vols. (1965-70); J. J. S. Perowne, *The Book of Psalms,* 2 vols. (1976); A. Maclaren, *The Psalms,* 3 vols. (1981); C. Westermann, *Praise and Lament in the Psalms* (1981).

PSALTERY. *See* Music.

PTOLEMA'IS (tol-e-mā'is). A city originally called Acco and located in Galilee. It was named after Ptolemy when he was in possession of Coele-Syria. Paul was there for one day on his return from his third missionary journey (Acts 21:7). *See* Acco.

PU'AH (pū'a). The name of two men and one woman.

1. Heb. *pû'â,* 1 Chron. 7:1. *See* Puvvah.

2. Heb. *pû'â,* one of the two midwives to whom Pharaoh gave instructions to kill the Hebrew male children at their birth (Ex. 1:15). The two —Shiphrah and Puah—are supposed to have been the chief and representative of their profession.

3. Heb. *pû'â,* the father of Tola, who was of the

The old Testament seaport of Acco, called Ptolemais in Paul's day

tribe of Issachar and a judge of Israel (Judg. 10:1; Num. 26:23).

PUBLICAN. *See* Tax-gatherer.

PUB′LIUS (pub′li-us). The "leading man," and probably governor of Malta, who received and lodged Paul and his companions after their shipwreck. The apostle miraculously healed the father of Publius of a fever and cured others who were brought to him (Acts 28:7-8), A.D. 62 or 59. Roman Catholic martyrologies assert that he was the first bishop of the island and afterward succeeded Dionysius as bishop of Athens. Jerome records a tradition that he was crowned with martyrdom.

PU′DENS (pū′denz; Gk. from Lat. for "modest, bashful"). A Christian at Rome who united with others in sending salutations to their friend Timothy (2 Tim. 4:21). This is the only mention of him in Scripture. He is commemorated in the Byzantine church on April 14 and in the Roman church on May 19. Modern researchers among the Columbaria at Rome, appropriated to members of the imperial household, have brought to light an inscription in which the name of Pudens occurs as that of a servant of Tiberius or Claudius. Although the identity of Paul's Pudens with any legendary or heathen namesake is not proved, yet it is probable that these facts add something to our knowledge of the friend of Paul and Timothy.

PUGNACIOUS (Gk. *plēktēs*). A contentious, quarrelsome person (1 Tim. 3:3; Titus 1:7).

PU′HITE. *See* Puthite.

PU′ITE. *See* Puah, no. 3.

PUL (pul). The name of an Assyrian king mentioned in the OT in several passages (2 Kings 15:19; 1 Chron. 5:26; but *see also* the reference to a nation "Pul" in the KJV of Isa. 66:19, the NASB being *Put* [which see]; cf. NIV marg.). Ac-

cording to those passages Pul received from Menahem, king of Samaria, a tribute of 1,000 talents of silver, in return for which he was, on his part, not to interfere with the exercise of royal authority by Menahem. The passages in Kings and Chronicles have given great trouble to the student of the OT. When the Assyrian inscriptions were first discovered, almost immediately were found in them the names of Sennacherib, Shalmaneser, Tiglath-pileser, and other Assyrian kings, but the name of Pul was found in no inscription. Furthermore, when the Assyrian lists of kings and of eponyms were found, the name of Pul did not appear in them, and at the period to which this king is assigned by the OT there was no gap in any of the lists in which the name of a king (Pul) could be inserted. To add to the difficulty, a king by the name of Phulus is mentioned by Alexander Polyhistor and by Eusebius, both of whom call him king of the Chaldeans, whereas the OT refers to him as an Assyrian king. Numerous efforts on the part of various biblical and Assyrian scholars were made to reconcile the difficulties, but in vain, until the suggestion of Henry Rawlinson, R. Lepsius, and Schrader that Pul was none other than the well-known Assyrian king, Tiglath-pileser III. The theory was that Tiglath-pileser did not belong to the ancient royal house of Assyria; that his name in reality was Pu-lu; that he came, perhaps, from Babylonia into Assyria, and when he had seized the throne called himself by the historical name Tiglath-pileser, a name made famous, about 1110 B.C., by one of the earliest Assyrian conquerors. This theory was supported by Schrader with a masterly array of facts and arguments. At last the Babylonian chronicle was found by Pinches in the British Museum, and on this Babylonian chronicle, at the year 728, stands the name Pul, written Pu-lu; whereas, on the other king lists of the Babylonians at that same year stands the name of Tiglath-pileser. All Assyriologists are now agreed that the Babylonian chronicle has settled the question and that Tiglath-pileser and Pul are one and the same person. It is not, however, certainly known whether the name Pul was the original name of the monarch, or whether it was a name assumed by him when he had become king of Babylon. (For particulars concerning his reign *see* the article Tiglath-pileser.)   R.W.R.

PULSE. *See* Vegetable Kingdom: Vegetables.

PUNISHMENT. The rendering of a considerable variety of Heb. and Gk. words in the Scripture. The principal meanings expressed by these terms are reproof, chastisement, restraint, penalty, full justice, and vengeance. The specific meaning in each case must be determined by the terms employed and the connection.

  Biblical View. The biblical view of punishment differs in the two testaments.

    Old Testament. The punishments most frequently mentioned in the OT, and upon which chief stress is laid, are temporal. They were inflicted directly by God, or were divinely prescribed to be inflicted by persons duly authorized. Instances of the former are found in Gen. 3:16-24; 4:10-13; 6:12, 13; 19:24-25; Num. 16:28-33, and many other places. In early times we find punishment authorized to be inflicted by the hand of man (Gen. 9:5-6), but more and more plainly it appears that this was to be done in accordance with divinely appointed and developed social order. The penalties prescribed under the Jewish economy were of great variety and were related to every kind of crime and breach of civil and ecclesiastical regulations. Among capital offenses were *blasphemy* (Lev. 24:14, 16, 23), *Sabbath-breaking* (Num. 15:32-36), *witchcraft* (Ex. 22:18), *adultery* (Lev. 20:10; cf. 18:20), *rape* (Deut. 22:25), *incest* (Lev. 20:11-12, 14, 17, 19-21; cf. 18:6-18), *kidnapping* (Ex. 21:16), *idolatry* (Lev. 20:1-5; cf. 18:21), and *murder* (Ex. 21:12-14; Lev. 24:17, 21). (*See* further Ex. 21:15, 17; 22:19-24; Lev. 21:9; Deut. 19:16-19; 22:21-24.)

The ordinary mode of capital punishment was stoning, although other forms, such as hanging and burning, are also mentioned. It is believed, however, that these latter were preceded by death in the ordinary way of execution (Ex. 19:13; Lev. 21:9; Num. 25:4; Josh. 7:25).

The meaning of the phrase "cut off from his people" or "cut off from Israel," as descriptive of punishment, is disputed. It is used many times in the OT, sometimes with reference to crimes the penalty for which is death, but frequently also with reference to offenses the penalties for which are not so clear (Ex. 12:15-19; 30:32-33, 38; Lev. 7:25; 17:9; 19:8). Among minor forms of punishment were exemplified the principles of retaliation (Ex. 21:24-25; Lev. 24:19-22) and of compensation (Ex. 21:18-36; 22:2-4, 6-7; Lev. 6:4-5; 24:8-22; Deut. 19:21; 22:18-19). Stripes, stocks, and imprisonment also appear among penalties prescribed or employed (Deut. 25:3; Jer. 20:2).

The severity of the OT dispensation in this respect has often been made a subject of unfavorable criticism. But the character of the people, the condition of the times, and the necessity for impressing the importance of morality and religion and of developing the right national life furnish the sufficient explanation. It is not to be forgotten, moreover, that the doctrine of a future life, as a state of reward and punishment, was not as strongly emphasized in those times as afterward. *See* Immortality.

New Testament. We find in the NT a relaxing of the severity of the OT with respect to temporal penalties; but in connection with this is the bringing into prominence of the motives and influences of the gospel revelation (Matt. 5:19-48; Luke 7:37-50; John 8:3-11).

That capital punishment is discountenanced by the NT is, however, an unwarranted opinion.

The sanctity of human life still has around it its ancient safeguard (cf. Gen. 9:6 with Rom. 13:1-6; Matt. 26:52; Rev. 13:10). The retribution, however, upon which the NT lays chief stress is that of the future. The teachings of Christ and the apostles leave no room for doubt of the fact of future punishment and of the eternal duration of punishment in some form (Matt. 12:32; chap. 25; 26:24; Mark 3:29; 9:43; Rev. 14:11; 20:10). *See* Hell.

Theological and Ethical. The primary ground for the infliction of punishment is not the reformation of offenders. In the divine administration a distinction is clearly made between chastisement and punishments properly so called. In the administration of human government the object of reformation often has a proper recognition, though the reason and warrant for the penal sanctions of law are still deeper than that. The chief end is not the discouragement or prevention of crime or wrongdoing. This is often an important effect, and a proper though still subordinate object. The underlying idea—that most deeply fundamental—is justice.

BIBLIOGRAPHY: H. B. Clark, *Biblical Law* (1944); G. Mendenhall, *Law and Covenant in the Ancient Near East* (1955); R. de Vaux, *Ancient Israel: Its Life and Institutions* (1961), pp. 143-63; S. Mendenhall, *Criminal Jurisprudence of the Ancient Hebrews* (1968).

PUNISHMENT, MOSAIC LAW. The law of retribution seems to underlie punishment in all ages. It is found in the form of *blood revenge* among many ancient peoples as a primitive (Gen. 27:45) custom, going back for its final basis to Gen. 9:5-6 (*see* Redeemer). Very naturally, in acting as redeemer the person would be tempted to inflict greater injury than that which he avenged. According to the Mosaic code, punishment was made to correspond to the heinousness of the offense, that there should fall upon the culprit what he had done to his neighbor, no more, thus giving no authority for personal revenge. It also limited the punishment to the guilty party without extending it to his children (Deut. 24:16). In the case of property, punishment was required only in order for restoration; and by way of restitution, if the guilty man had invaded his neighbor's property or violated the integrity of his house. What is said (19:19-21) in regard to the false witness holds good of all the penal enactments of the Mosaic law: "Then you shall do to him just as he had intended to do to his brother. Thus you shall purge the evil from among you. And the rest will hear and be afraid, and will never again do such an evil thing among you." Thus we see, at the root of all the enactments of the Mosaic penal code there lies the principle of strict but righteous retribution, and its intention is to extirpate evil and produce reverence for the righteousness of the holy God in the heart of the people.

Capital Punishment. That death was regarded as a fit punishment for murder appears plain from the remark of Lamech (Gen. 4:24). In the postdiluvian code, if we may so call it, retribution by the hand of man, even in the case of an offending animal, for bloodshed, is clearly laid down (9:5-6). In the Mosaic law we find the sentence of capital punishment, in the case of murder, clearly laid down. The murderer was to be put to death, even if he should have taken refuge at God's altar or in a city of refuge, and the same principle was to be carried out even in the case of animals (Ex. 21:12, 14, 28, 36; Lev. 24:17, 21; Num. 35:31; Deut. 19:11-13; etc.). The wide range of crimes punishable by death according to the Mosaic law may be accounted for by the peculiar conditions of the Israelites. A nation of newly emancipated slaves, they were probably intractable; and their wanderings and isolation did not permit penal settlements or remedial punishment. They were placed under immediate divine government and surveillance. Willful offenses under such circumstances evinced an incorrigibleness that rendered death the only means of ridding the community of such transgressors, and this was ultimately resorted to in regard to all individuals above a certain age, in order that a better class might enter into Canaan (Num. 14:29, 32, 35).

Capital Crimes. Capital crimes in the OT can be divided into *absolute* and *relative* classes.

Absolute. Capital crimes for which no mitigating factor could alter the severity of the sentence included the following: (1) striking or reviling a parent (Ex. 21:15, 17); (2) blasphemy (Lev. 24:14, 16, 23); (3) Sabbath-breaking (Num. 15:32-36; Ex. 31:14); (4) witchcraft, and false pretension to prophecy (Ex. 22:18; Lev. 20:27; Deut. 13:5; 18:20); (5) adultery (Lev. 20:10; Deut. 22:22); (6) unchastity (Deut. 22:21, 23; Lev. 21:9); (7) rape (Deut. 22:25); (8) incestuous and unnatural connections (Lev. 20:11-17; Ex. 22:19); (9) kidnapping (Ex. 21:16; Deut. 24:7); (10) idolatry, actual or implied, in any shape (Lev. 20:2; Deut. 13:6, 10, 15; 17:2-7; *see* Josh. 7; 22:20; Num. 25:1-8); and (11) false witness, in certain cases (Deut. 19:16, 19).

Relative. There are some thirty-six or thirty-seven cases in the Pentateuch where the penalty named was that of "cutting off from the people." Controversy has arisen concerning the meaning of this expression, and some hold that only excommunication and not the death penalty was the punishment prescribed (*see* discussion below, under *Capital Penalties,* no. 7). The offenses included in this category were those involving a breach—either of *morals,* of the *covenant,* or of the Levitical *ritual.*

1. Breach of morals: willful sin in general (Num. 15:30-31); fifteen cases of incestuous or unclean connection (Lev. 18:23, 29; 20:9-21).

2. Breach of covenant: uncircumcision (Gen. 17:14); neglect of the Passover (Num. 9:13); Sabbath-breaking (Ex. 31:14); neglect of the Day of Atonement (Lev. 23:29); or work done on that day (v. 30); offering children to Molech (20:3); witchcraft (20:6); anointing a stranger with holy oil (Ex. 30:33).

3. Breach of ritual: eating leavened bread during the Passover (12:15, 19); eating the fat of sacrifices (Lev. 7:25); eating blood (7:27; 17:14); eating the sacrifice in an unclean condition (7:20-21; 22:3-4, 9); eating of the sacrifice on the third day after its being offered (19:7-8); making holy ointment for private use (Ex. 30:32-33); making incense for private use (30:34-38); neglect of purification in general (Num. 19:13-20); offering a sacrifice elsewhere than at the Tabernacle (Lev. 17:8-9); slaying an animal elsewhere than at the Tabernacle door (17:3-4); touching holy things illegally (Num. 4:15, 18, 20; cf. 2 Sam. 6:7; 2 Chron. 26:21).

Capital Penalties. Some capital penalties were natively Hebrew; others were borrowed from foreign lands.

Those Properly Hebrew. The Hebrew law prescribed a number of capital penalties.

1. *Crucifixion* (which see).

2. Stoning. Stoning was the ordinary mode of execution (Ex. 17:4; Luke 20:6; John 10:31; Acts 14:5). "So far as can be learned from the Pentateuch *stoning* is enjoined for those cases in which sentence of death was to be executed on individuals judicially; when, on the contrary, either the avenger of blood carried out the punishment, or where many were to be executed, the sword was used, the spear (Num. 25:7), or arrow (Ex. 19:13), to kill from a distance. Thus stoning is enjoined (Lev. 20:27; Deut. 17:3-5) to punish the individual who practiced idolatry and seduced others; on the contrary (13:16), for the punishment of a whole city which was given over to idolatry, it is commanded, 'Thou shalt slay the inhabitants of that city with the sword.' Accordingly it is no doubt stoning is meant when the law merely uses the formulas 'He shall be put to death' or 'his blood be upon him' " (Keil, *Arch.,* 2:357-58). If the crime had been proved by testimony, the witnesses were to cast the first stones at the condemned (Deut. 17:7; John 8:7; Acts 7:58). It was customary to add the raising of a heap of stones over the body or its ashes (Josh. 7:25; 8:29; 2 Sam. 18:17).

3. Hanging. Among the Jews hanging was generally spoken of as following death by some other means (Num. 25:4; Deut. 21:22; 2 Sam. 21:6, 9), as a way of aggravating capital punishment. The law provided that persons hanged should not be allowed to remain suspended overnight, but should be buried the same day, lest —he that was hanged being accursed of God— Jehovah's land should be defiled (Deut. 21:23).

4. Death by the sword, spear, or arrow; death by beheading. Death by the sword or spear was

the mode adopted when either the avenger of blood carried out the punishment or where many were to be executed (Ex. 32:27; Num. 25:7-8); the arrow was used to kill at a distance (Ex. 19:13). Beheading, practiced in Egypt from most ancient times (Gen. 40:19), first appeared among the Jews in the Roman period (Matt. 14:10-12).

5. Burning. In pre-Mosaic times burning was the punishment for unchastity (Gen. 38:24). The Mosaic law enjoined burning for unchastity only in the case of a priest's daughter (Lev. 21:9), or in the case of a man's having carnal intercourse with both a mother and her daughter, all three to be put to death (20:14). Burning is mentioned as following death by other means (Josh. 7:25), and some have thought that it was never used except after death. Certainly this was not the case among other nations (Dan. 3).

6. Strangling. Death by strangulation is said by the rabbis to have been regarded as the most common but least severe of the capital punishments and to have been performed by immersing the convict in clay or mud and then strangling him by a cloth twisted around the neck.

7. "Cutting off." The penalty described by the expression "cutting off from the people" has been variously understood, some thinking that it meant death in all cases, others that in some cases only *excommunication* (which see) must be understood. Jahn (*Arch.*, p. 258) says, "When God is introduced as saying in respect to any person, 'I will cut him off from the people,' the expression means some event in divine providence which shall eventually terminate the life of that person's family" (*see* 1 Kings 14:10; 21:21; 2 Kings 9:8). Saalschütz explains it to be premature death by God's hand. Knobel, Corn, and Ewald held that the death punishment absolutely was meant. Keil observed (*Arch.*, 2:358): "From Lev. 20:2-6, so much only appears, that God himself will cut off the transgressor if the earthly magistrate shuts his eyes to the crime of idolatry and does not cut off the idolater. Certainly in Lev., ch. 20, all the abominations of which it holds in the comprehensive formula (18:29), 'Whosoever shall do any of these abominations, even the souls that do them shall be cut off from among their people,' have not the punishment of death attached to them. For some of the forbidden marriages only childlessness is threatened (20:20, sq.). But from this it merely follows that for certain cases God reserved the cutting off to be otherwise executed; and in these cases the civil magistrate was not to intervene. But in connection with all other offenses, for which the law prescribes cutting off without any such reserve, the civil magistrate was obliged to carry out sentence of death as soon as the guilt was judicially established; even for transgressions of the laws of purification and other matters of ritual, if the sin was proved to have been committed 'with a high hand,' i.e., in presumptuous rebellion against

Jehovah, and not merely in thoughtlessness and haste."

We may, perhaps, conclude that the primary meaning of "cutting off " is a sentence of death to be executed in some cases without remission, but in others avoidable, either (1) by immediate atonement on the offender's part, or (2) by direct interposition of the Almighty, i.e., a sentence of death always "recorded," but not always executed.

Those Coming from Other Lands. Capital punishments borrowed from other lands were the following:

1. Beheading. The Egyptians knew and practiced beheading (Gen. 40:17-19), as did the Hebrews in the time of the early kings (2 Sam. 4:8; 20:21-22; 2 Kings 10:6-8). Herod and his descendants ordered decapitation (Matt. 14:8-12; cf. Acts 12:2).

2. Dichotomy, cutting in pieces (1 Sam. 15:33). Dichotomy was common among the Babylonians, Egyptians, and Persians.

3. Death by torture. Conscious suffering in death was inflicted by burning the offender alive in a furnace (Dan. 3:20-26); roasting him in the fire (Jer. 29:22; 2 Macc. 7:5); putting him to death in hot ashes (2 Macc. 13:5-8); casting him into the lion's den (Dan. 6:7, 16-24); beating him to death on the *tumpanon* (2 Macc. 6:19), probably a circular instrument of torture, on which prisoners were stretched and tortured or beaten to death. In war we find the sawing in pieces of captives (2 Sam. 12:31; 1 Chron. 20:3; cf. Heb. 11:37); the hurling of enemies from precipices (2 Chron. 25:12; cf. Ps. 141:6; Luke 4:29), the latter a frequent punishment among the Romans; the cutting open of the bodies of pregnant women (2 Kings 8:12; 15:16; etc.), and the dashing of children against walls, when hostile cities were taken (Isa. 13:16, 18; Hos. 13:16; etc.). In the NT are incidentally mentioned drowning (Matt. 18:6; Mark 9:42) and fighting with wild beasts (1 Cor. 15:32).

Secondary Punishments. Secondary punishments were of a less severe nature.

Retaliation. The law of retaliation, exacting "eye for eye" (Ex. 21:24-25) is, probably, the most natural of all kinds of punishment, and would be the most just of all, if it could be instantaneously and universally inflicted; but when delayed, it is apt to degenerate into revenge. To prevent this, the law specified the maximum revenge obtainable. It was thus illegal to demand a life when only an eye had been damaged. Moses accordingly adopted the principle, but lodged the application of it in the judge: "If a man injures his neighbor, just as he has done, so it shall be done to him: fracture for fracture, eye for eye, tooth for tooth" (Lev. 24:19-22). This law applied also to the beasts.

But the law of retaliation applied to the free Israelite only, not to slaves. In the case of the latter, if the master struck out an eye and destroyed it, i.e., blinded the slave with the blow, or struck out a tooth, he was to let him go free, as a compensation for the loss of the member. The willful murder of a slave was followed by capital punishment.

Compensation. If compensation was identical, then it was retaliation (*see* above); but it was also analogous, thus a payment for loss of time or power (Ex. 21:18-36; Lev. 24:18-21; Deut. 19:21). A stolen sheep (killed or sold) was to be compensated for by four others, a stolen ox by five others (Ex. 22:1). The thief caught in the act in a dwelling might be killed or sold; if a stolen animal was found alive in his possession, he might be compelled to restore double (22:2-4). Damage done by an animal was to be fully compensated (v. 5); as was damage caused to a neighbor's grain (v. 6). A stolen pledge found in the thief's possession was to be compensated double (v. 7); a pledge lost or damaged was to be compensated (vv. 12-13); whereas a pledge withheld was to be restored with 20 percent of the value (Lev. 6:4-5). All trespass was to pay double (Ex. 22:9). Slander against the woman by her newly married husband was to be compensated for by the payment of one hundred shekels, and the man further punished with stripes (Deut. 22:18-19).

Corporal. Stripes, consisting of forty blows with a rod, were to be applied (Deut. 25:2-3); whence the Jews took care not to exceed thirty-nine (2 Cor. 11:24; Josephus *Ant.* 4.8.21). If a man struck his servant with a rod so that he or she died, he was punishable (Ex. 21:20).

Scourging with thorns is mentioned (Judg. 8:16), as is scourging with "scorpions," i.e., whips with barbed points like the point of a scorpion's sting (1 Kings 12:11). In addition, there is mention of the stocks (Jer. 20:2); passing through fire (2 Sam. 12:31); mutilation (Judg. 1:6; 2 Macc. 7:4); plucking out hair (Isa. 50:6; Neh. 13:25); and later, imprisonment, confiscation, or exile (Ezra 7:26; Jer. 37:15; 38:6; Acts 4:3; 5:18; 12:4; Rev. 1:9).

The Scriptures mention the following corporal punishments inflicted by other nations: putting out the eyes of captives, flaying captives alive, tearing out the tongue. Exposure to wild beasts is mentioned by the apostle Paul (1 Cor. 15:32; 2 Tim. 4:17), but without any particulars.

Imprisonment. Although imprisonment was not unknown to the Israelites from their acquaintance with Egypt (Gen. 39:20; 40:3; 41:10; 42:19), it is not recognized in the Mosaic law as a mode of punishment. "They put him in custody" (Lev. 24:12) means that the offender was secured until a decision concerning his case had been made. Imprisonment is wholly superfluous where bodily punishments prevail and where fines in the case of those without means must be paid by servitude. At the time of the kings imprisonment was introduced, especially as a punishment of too outspoken prophets (2 Chron. 16:10; Jer. 20:2; 32:2). After the Exile imprisonment was quite a common punishment, along with others, in cases of debt (Ezra 7:26; Matt. 18:30). Prisoners were bound with chains (Judg. 16:21; 2 Sam. 3:34; Jer. 40:1); and when the punishment would be made severer, they were placed in stocks (20:2). The Roman *custodia militaris* (military imprisonment) consisted in chaining the prisoner by one or both hands to the soldier who watched him (Acts 12:4; 21:33), or if the offender was in prison, in putting his feet in the stocks (16:24).

BIBLIOGRAPHY: G. Vos, *The Mosaic Origin of the Pentateuchal Codes* (1886), pp. 63f., 65-70, 81-84, 195-98, 200. *See also* Punishment.

Elamites taken prisoner by the Assyrians

PU'NITES (pū'nīts). The descendants of Puvvah or Puvah or Puah, of the tribe of Issachar (Num. 26:33). *See* Puite.

PU'NON (pū'non). A station of the Israelites in their journey to Canaan (Num. 33:42), E of the mountains of Edom, a tribal seat of the Edomite phylarch (Gen. 36:41). It lay next beyond Zalmonah, between it and Oboth. According to Jerome it was "a little village in the desert, where copper was dug up by condemned criminals, between Petra and Zoar." It is identified with present-day Feinan.

PUR (pūr; "lot"). Pur is mentioned only (Esther 3:7; 9:24, 26) in connection with Haman's consulting the astrologers to decide upon the auspicious day for destroying the Hebrews. *See* articles Festivals; Lot.

PU'RAH (pū'ra). The servant of Gideon, who went with him by night when he visited the camp of the Midianites (Judg. 7:10-11; "Phurah," KJV).

PURGE. *See* Uncleanness.

PURIFICATION. *See* Uncleanness.

PURIFIER, OF SILVER. *See* Silver.

PU'RIM (pū'rim). An annual festival of the Jews (Esther 9:26) in commemoration of the wonderful deliverance of the Israelites in Persia. *See* Festivals: Postexilic Festivals.

PURITY (Gk. *hagneia*, "cleanness"). Freedom from foreign mixture, but more particularly the temper directly opposite to criminal sensualities, or the ascendency of irregular passions; chastity (2 Cor. 6:6; 1 Tim. 4:12; 5:2).

PURLOINING. *See* Pilfering.

PURPLE. A type of cloth and a color. *See* article Color.

PURPOSES OF GOD. *See* Election; Sovereignty of God.

PURSE (Heb. *ḥārît,* Isa. 3:22, "money purses," NASB, "crisping pins," KJV; Heb. *kîs,* Prov. 1:14, "purse," NASB, KJV, NIV; Isa. 46:6, "purse," NASB, "bag," KJV and NIV; Heb. *ṣĕrôr,* Hag. 1:6, "purse," NASB and NIV, "bag," KJV; Gk. *balantion,* Luke 10:4; *zōnē,* Mark 6:8, a girdle, and so a "belt"). The Hebrews in journeying were provided with a bag in which they carried their money (Gen. 42:35; Prov. 1:14; 7:20; Isa. 46:6). Ladies wore ornamental purses (Heb. *ḥārît,* 3:22; 2 Kings 5:23, "bags"). The name given to them by Isaiah is supposed to refer to the long, round form of the purse. The "money belt" was also used as a purse (Matt. 10:9; Mark 6:8). *See* Bag.

PUT (put; the KJV frequently reads Phut). The third name in the list of the sons of Ham (Gen. 10:6; 1 Chron. 1:8), elsewhere applied to an African country or people. In the list it follows Cush and Mizraim, and precedes Canaan. We cannot place the tract of Put outside of Africa, and it would thus seem that it was almost parallel to that of the Mizraites, as it could not be farther to the N; the position would well agree with Libya. Latest views of the identification of Put are with Punt, S of African Cush where it is commonly connected with the coast of Somaliland. The few mentions of Put in the Bible clearly indicate a country or people of Africa, and it was, probably, not far from Egypt (Isa. 66:19, KJV, NIV, and NASB marg., "Pul"; cf. Jer. 46:9; Ezek. 27:10; 30:5; 38:5; Nah. 3:9). From these passages we cannot infer anything as to the exact position of this country or people; unless indeed in the book of Nahum the countries of Cush and Put, Mizra-im and Lubim are respectively connected, which might indicate that Put occupied a position S of Egypt. Jeremiah (Jer. 46:9) describes the Egyptian army as consisting of Ethiopians, Putites, and Lydians; and Ezekiel (Ezek. 30:5) prophesies that Ethiopia (NASB marg., Cush) and Put and Lud shall fall by the sword along with the Egyptians.

PUTE'OLI (pū-tē'o-li; "little wells"). A famous watering place of the Romans, located in a sheltered part of the Bay of Naples. Its Gk. name was Dicaearchia. It was the most accessible harbor near to Rome. Paul was brought to this port with other prisoners (Acts 28:13). Vespasian conferred great privileges upon the city. Cicero had a villa here, and Hadrian a tomb. Portions of its famous baths remain to this day, as does a part of the pier at which Paul must have landed on his way to Rome. The present name is Pozzuoli.

PU'THITE (pū'thīt; "Puhites," KJV). According to 1 Chron. 2:53, the "Puthites" were of the "families of Kiriath-jearim," descended from Shobal.

PU'TIEL (pū'ti-el; perhaps, "afflicted of God"). The father of the wife of Eleazar the priest, and mother of Phinehas (Ex. 6:25), before 1210 B.C.

PU'VAH. *See* Puvvah.

PU'VVAH (pū'va). One of the sons of Issachar (Gen. 46:13; NIV, "Puah," but see marg.). The name is given as "Puvah" (Num. 26:23; NIV, "Puah") and "Puah" (1 Chron. 7:1; so NIV). His descendants are called Punites (Num. 26:23; NIV, "Puite").

PYGARG. *See* Animal Kingdom: Ibex.

PYR'RHUS (pir'rus). The father of Sopater of Berea, a companion of Paul on his journey from Philippi to Troas (Acts 20:4). *See* Sopater.

QOPH(ק) (kōf). The nineteenth letter of the Heb. alphabet, corresponding to our English "q." Ps. 119 in its nineteenth section is headed by this letter, in which each verse of the original Heb. begins with *qoph.*

QUAIL. *See* Animal Kingdom.

QUARRIES (Heb. *pāsîl*). *Quarries* in the KJV of Judg. 3:19, 26 may be rendered "idols" (so NASB, NIV). The term is derived from Heb. *pāsal,* "hew," "hew into shape."

QUART (Rev. 6:6, NIV). *See* Metrology: Measures of Capacity: Foreign Measures: Choenix.

QUAR'TUS (kwor'tus; a "fourth"). A Christian of Corinth whose salutations Paul sent to the church at Rome (Rom. 16:23). The usual tradition holds that he was one of the seventy disciples; it is also said that he ultimately became bishop of Berytus.

QUATERNION (Acts 12:4, KJV; Gk. *tedradion,* "a group of four"). Four squads of soldiers (so NASB). The NIV has "four squads of four soldiers each." *See* Squad.

QUEEN. The Hebrews had no equivalent for our word *queen,* in the sense of a female sovereign; neither did the wives of the king have the dignity that the word *queen* now denotes.
1. *Queen regnant or queen consort* (Heb. *malkâ,* the feminine of *melek,* king). It is applied in the sense of queen *regnant* to the queen of Sheba (1 Kings 10:1). It is also applied to the queen *consort,* the chief wife, as distinguished from all other females in the royal harem (Esther 1:9, 11-12; 7:1-3; etc.).
2. *A wife of the first rank* (Heb. *shēgāl*) as distinguished from mere concubines; it is applied to the wives of the first rank in the harems of the Chaldean and Persian monarchs (Neh. 2:6; cf. Dan. 5:2-3).

3. *Mistress* (Heb. *gᵉbîrâ*) is expressive of authority and dominion. *Gebir* ("masculine, lord") is the word that occurs twice with reference to Isaac's blessing of Jacob: "Be master of your brothers," and, "I have made him your master" (Gen. 27:29, 37). It would therefore be applied to the female who exercised the highest authority, and this, in an oriental household, is not the wife but the mother of the master. This is one of the inevitable results of polygamy—the number of wives, their social position before marriage, and their precarious hold upon their husband's affections combine to annihilate their influence. This is transferred to the mother as being the only female who occupies a fixed and dignified position. The extent of the queen mother's influence is well illustrated in the interview between Solomon and Bathsheba (1 Kings 2:19-22). The term *gᵉbîrâ* is applied only twice with reference to the wife of a king—the wife of an Egyptian king (11:19), where the position of royal consort was more queenly than in Palestine; and Jezebel (2 Kings 10:13, "queen mother"), who as the daughter of a powerful king appears to have enjoyed peculiar privileges after marriage.

Where a woman can never become the head of state there can never be a reigning queen; and where polygamy is allowed or practiced there can be no queen consort. By queen, then, we understand the *chief wife* of the king's harem. This rank may be obtained by being the *first* wife of the king or the *first after accession,* especially if she was of high birth and became mother of the firstborn son; otherwise she may be superseded by a woman of higher birth and connections subsequently married or by the one who gave birth to the heir apparent. The king, however, often acted according to his own pleasure, promoting or removing as he willed.

BIBLIOGRAPHY: E. O. James, *The Cult of the Mother God-*

dess (1959); id., *The Ancient Gods* (1960); C. Downing, *The Goddess* (1981), pp. 68-98.

QUEEN OF HEAVEN (Heb. *meleketh hashshāmayim,* Jer. 7:18; 44:17-19, 25). Astarte, an ancient Semitic deity, identical with Babylonian Ishtar (Venus). (*See* Gods, False.) The epithet "of heaven" alludes to her elevated character. Special cakes were baked to this goddess (cf. the "raisin cakes" of Hos. 3:1, with which there may be some connection), which were symbolic representations of the goddess. Her worship belonged chiefly to the women (Jer. 44:17); Astarte represented the female principle of fertility. She was a "mother goddess."

QUICK, QUICKEN. In the Psalms (71:20; 80:18; 119:25, 37, 40, 88; 143:11; and others) the causative form of Heb. *ḥāyâ,* "to live," "to have life," is used, signifying "to make alive," "to comfort, refresh"; the NASB and NIV replace KJV *quicken me* in those passages with the expression *revive me,* or *renew.* When the priest examined one

with leprosy he was commanded, if he saw "quick raw flesh in the rising" ("swelling," NASB and NIV), to pronounce the person unclean (Lev. 13:10, 24). The meaning evidently was that the flesh showed life, i.e., the skin was growing and forming anew.

In the Gk., *zōopoieō* appears in Rom. 8:11; 1 Cor. 15:36; 1 Tim. 6:13; 1 Pet. 3:18; and elsewhere, with the meaning of "to make alive" (cf. NASB and NIV readings). The Gk. term *zōntes* signifies the *living* as opposed to the *dead,* as in the expression "the Judge of the quick ["living," NASB and NIV] and the dead" (Acts 10:42; 2 Tim. 4:1; Heb. 4:12).

QUICKSANDS, THE (Gk. *surtis,* "shoal"; Acts 27:17, KJV). See Syrtis.

QUILT. *See* Pillow.

QUIRIN'IUS (kwi-rin'i-us). *See* Cyrenius.

QUIVER. *See* Armor, Arms.

RA'AMAH (ra'a-ma). The fourth named son (descendant) of Cush and grandson of Ham (Gen. 10:7; 1 Chron. 1:9). The tribe of Raamah afterward became renowned as traders (Ezek. 27:22). Raamah occurs in the inscriptions of Sheba as a place in SW Arabia near Mā'în, referred to as Regma in the LXX and the Vulg.

RAAMI'AH (ra-am'i-a; "Jehovah has thundered"). One of the leaders of the Jews who returned from captivity with Zerubbabel (Neh. 7:7), about 445 B.C. In Ezra 2:2 he is called *Reelaiah* (which see).

RAAM'SES (ram'sēz; Ex. 1:11). *See* Rameses.

RAB'BAH (rab'a; "great," i.e., city). The name of several places:

1. A strong place on the E of the Jordan, which, when its name is first introduced in the sacred records, was the chief city of the Ammonites. In five passages (Deut. 3:11; 2 Sam. 12:26; 17:27; Jer. 49:2; Ezek. 21:20) it is called Rabbah of the sons of Ammon; elsewhere (Josh. 13:25; 2 Sam. 11:1; 12:27, 29; 1 Chron. 20:1; Jer. 49:3; Ezek. 25:5; Amos 1:14) simply Rabbah. It appears in the sacred records as the single city of the Ammonites. When first named it is in the hands of the Ammonites and is mentioned as containing the bed, or sarcophagus, of the giant Og (Deut. 3:11). It was not included in the territory of the tribes E of Jordan; the border of Gad stops at "Aroer which is before Rabbah" (Josh. 13:25). It was probably to Rabbah that Abishai led his forces while holding the Ammonites in check (2 Sam. 10:10, 14), whereas the main army, under Joab, rested at Medeba (1 Chron. 19:7). The next year Rabbah was made the main point of attack, Joab in command (2 Sam. 11:1); and after a siege, probably of two years, it was taken (12:26-29; 1 Chron. 20:1). We are not told whether the city was demolished or whether David was satisfied with the slaughter of its inhabitants. In the time

of Amos, 2½ centuries later, it had again a "wall" and "citadels" and was still the sanctuary of Molech—the "king" (Amos 1:14-15). It was also at the date of the invasion of Nebuchadnezzar (Jer. 49:2-3), when its dependent towns are mentioned, and it is named in terms that imply it was of equal importance with Jerusalem (Ezek. 21:20). At Rabbah, no doubt, Baalis, king of the sons of Ammon (Jer. 40:14), held such court as he could muster; and within its walls was plotted the attack of Ishmael, which cost Gedaliah his life and drove Jeremiah into Egypt. It received the name *Philadelphia* from Ptolemy Philadelphus (285-247 B.C.), and it became one of the important cities of Decapolis; its ancient name, however, still adheres to it. It was once the seat of a bishopric and prosperous, until conquered by the Saracens. Its modern name is Amman, capital of Jordan, about twenty-two miles from the Jordan, in a valley that is a branch or perhaps the main course of the Wadi Zerka, usually identified with the Jabbok. Amman has the longest continuous occupational history of any city in the Near East. Modern Amman covers the ancient city so effectively that excavation is virtually impossible. A Roman theater with seating for 6,000 people stands in the middle of the city. Nearly everything visible on the ancient citadel is Roman, Byzantine, or Umayyad. *See* Rabbath.

2. A city of Judah, named with Kiriath-jearim (Josh. 15:60 only), but its location is entirely unknown. It apparently is mentioned in the el-Amarna Letters as Rubute.

BIBLIOGRAPHY: F.-M. Abel, *Géographie de la Palestine* (1933); G. L. Harding, *The Antiquities of Jordan* (1959).

RAB'BATH OF THE SONS OF AMMON. The full name (Deut. 3:11; Ezek. 21:20; etc.) of *Rabbah,* no. 1 (which see).

RABBI (Heb. *rabbi,* Gk. *hrabbi,* "my teacher"). A respectful term applied by the Jews to their

Amman (ancient Rabbah)

teachers and spiritual instructors (Matt. 23:7-8; John 1:38; 3:26; 6:25). The terms *rabbi* and *rabboni* both mean simply "master" (John 1:38; 20:16). The use of the title *rabbi* cannot be substantiated before the time of Christ. Later Jewish schools had three grades of honor: *rab,* "master," the lowest; *rabbi,* "my master," the second; and *rabboni,* "my lord, my master," the most elevated. M.F.U.

RABBIT. *See* Animal Kingdom.

RAB′BITH (rab′ith; "multitude"). A city in the tribe of Issachar (Josh. 19:20), supposed by Knobel to be Araboneh, NE of Arâneh, at the southern foot of Gilboa. Conder equates it with Râba, eight miles S of Mt. Gilboa.

RABBONI. *See* Rabbi.

RABDOMANCY. *See* Magic: Various Forms.

RAB′-MAG (rab′mag; "chief magician, or priest"). A title ascribed (Jer. 39:3, 13) to *Nergal-sar-ezer* (which see), which title he, with certain other important persons, bears in the Babylonian inscriptions. The NIV translates "high official" in Jer. 39:3, 13 rather than as a title. It probably corresponds to Akkad. *rab mugi* ("great" prince).

RAB′-SARIS (rab′sa-ris; Heb. *rab-saris;* Assyr. *rabu-sha-reshi*). Originally "first eunuch," a title of a high Assyrian official and not a personal name.

1. The title is mentioned in the narrative of Sennacherib's campaign against Judah in the days of Hezekiah (2 Kings 18:17). In the English translation the Assyrian monarch is represented as sending to Jerusalem "Tartan and Rab-saris and Rabshekeh from Lachish." It is now known from the Assyrian monuments that *tartan* (Assyr. *turtannu,* "second in rank"), *rabshakeh* (Assyr. *rabshaqu,* "chief officer") and *rab-saris* were all titles of high Assyrian officials; in fact, they are Assyr. words taken over into Heb. (*See* W. F. Albright, *O. T. Commentary* [1948], p. 161; Millar Burrows, *What Mean These Stones?* [1941], p. 43.)

2. The same title is found in Jer. 39:3 to designate one of the Babylonian princes present at the capture of Jerusalem. The other reference is Jer. 39:13, where the Rab-saris was of the group who set free the prophet Jeremiah from the prison court when he was placed under the custody of Gedaliah. The NIV consistently translates Rab-saris as "chief officer." M.F.U.

RAB′SHAKEH (rab′sha-ki). Assyr. *rab-shaqu,* "chief officer," one of the high Assyrian officials mentioned several times in the narrative of Sennacherib's campaign against Judah during Hezekiah's reign (2 Kings 18:17; Isa. 36:2). The NIV translates "chief officer" in these passages. (*See* Tartan and Rab-saris.) The title is one of high rank, for in the inscriptions of Tiglath-pilesar III an army is mentioned as being sent against Tyre under the command of a *rabshakeh.* M.F.U.

RACA′ (ra-ka′; Gk. from Aram. *rêqā′,* "empty, worthless, good for nothing"). A common term of contempt in the time of Christ (Matt. 5:22), denoting a certain looseness of life and manners. It differs from "fool," which follows in that the latter conveys the idea of *impious, godless,* because such a one neglects and despises what relates to salvation. Thus there would be a greater criminality in calling a man a "fool," since foolishness in Scripture is the opposite of spiritual wisdom.

RA′CAL (ra′kal). A town in the tribe of Judah that David made a depository for spoil taken from the Amalekites (1 Sam. 30:29).

RA′CHEL (rā′chel; "ewe"). The younger daughter of Laban, and one of Jacob's wives.

Meeting with Jacob. When Jacob came to Haran he met some shepherds, who told him, in answer to his inquiries, that they knew Laban and that Rachel was already coming to the well near by to water her father's sheep. He rolled the stone from the well's mouth, watered the sheep, greeted her with a kiss, and told Rachel who he was. Rachel then hastened to her father with the tidings of what had happened (Gen. 29:1-12), about 1960 B.C.

Jacob's Wife. Laban received Jacob as his relative, and, after a month's service, an agreement was entered into between them that Jacob should serve Laban seven years for his daughter Rachel. The motive on the part of Jacob was, doubtless, that his relations with Esau made a protracted stay with Laban advisable, whereas Laban was probably influenced by greed. At the expiration of the period of service Jacob claimed his reward, but he was deceived by Laban, who led his elder daughter, Leah, into the bridechamber. Complaining of the deception, Jacob was told to let Leah's marriage week pass by and then he should have Rachel (Gen. 29:13-30). Mention is made of her jealousy toward her sister on account of Leah's having children, whereas she herself was childless, and of her removing and secreting the household gods of her father. This incident indicates either that she was not altogether free from the superstition and idolatry that prevailed in the land or that she sought by possession of the household gods (teraphim) to gain some special family or inheritance benefits for her husband. She at length became the mother of two sons, Joseph (30:22-24) and Benjamin, and died shortly after the latter's birth (35:16-19). She "was buried on the way to Ephrath (that is, Bethlehem)." The traditional site of her tomb is about one mile N of Bethlehem, but that seems too far S. She died "some distance" from Bethlehem (Gen. 35:16), and probably her tomb was actually

Rachel's tomb, near Bethlehem

located near Jerusalem (the tower of Eder [Migdal-eder], v. 21, was likely on the outskirts of Jerusalem; cf. 1 Sam. 10:2; Jer. 31:15).

Character. "From what is related to us concerning her character there does not seem much to claim any high degree of admiration and esteem. The discontent and fretful impatience shown in her grief at being for a time childless, moved even her fond husband to anger (Gen. 30:1-2). She appears, moreover, to have shared all the duplicity and falsehood of her family. See, for instance, Rachel's stealing her father's images, and the ready dexterity and presence of mind with which she concealed her theft" (chap. 31). In Jer. 31:15-16 the prophet refers to the exile of the ten tribes under Shalmaneser, king of Assyria, and the sorrow caused by their dispersion (2 Kings 17:20), under the symbol of Rachel, the maternal ancestor of the tribes of Ephraim and Manasseh, bewailing the fate of her children. This lamentation was a type of that which was fulfilled in Bethlehem when the infants were slaughtered by order of Herod (Matt. 2:16-18).

H.F.V.

BIBLIOGRAPHY: T. E. Miller, *Portraits of Women of the Bible* (n.d.), pp. 43-54; H. V. Morton, *Women of the Bible* (1964), pp. 39-44.

RAD'DAI (rad'a-ī; "treading down"). The fifth son of Jesse and brother of King David (1 Chron. 2:14), about 1025 B.C.

RAFT. A device used for conveying bulky substances by water. Thus Solomon contracted with Hiram king of Tyre to have cedars cut on the western side of Mt. Lebanon and floated to Joppa (1 Kings 5:9; 2 Chron. 2:16; "floats," KJV).

RAGAU. *See* Reu.

RAGUEL. *See* Reuel, no. 2.

RA'HAB (rā'hab; "broad, wide"). A woman of Jericho at the time of Israel's entrance into Canaan.

Entertains Spies. Just before crossing the Jordan Joshua sent two men to spy out Canaan as far as Jericho. In this city dwelt Rahab, "a harlot," in a house of her own, although she had a father, a mother, brothers, and sisters living in Jericho. From the presence of the flax upon the roof and a scarlet (or crimson) thread in the house, it has been supposed that she was engaged in the manufacture of linen and the art of dyeing. She had heard of the wonderful progress of Israel, the passage of the Red Sea, and the overthrow of their enemies and was convinced that Jehovah purposed to give Canaan to the Israelites. The spies found in her one who was ready to befriend them. Fearful of their being discovered, she hid them among the stalks of flax on the roof and informed the officers sent in to search that they had departed from her house before the closing of the city gates. The officers started in pursuit, and when it was night Rahab informed the spies of what had happened and secured from them a pledge to spare her life and the lives of her kindred, on the condition that she hang out a scarlet "thread" at the window from which they had escaped, and that her family should remain under her roof. She then assisted them to escape by letting them down by a rope from her window, which overlooked the city wall (Josh. 2:1-21), 1440 B.C.

Is Spared. At the taking of Jericho the spies, under the command of Joshua, took Rahab and her relatives out of her house and moved them to a place of safety outside the camp of Israel (Josh. 6:22-23) and thus made good their oath. The narrator adds, "And she has lived in the midst of Israel to this day" (v. 25), not necessarily implying that she was alive at the time he wrote, but that the family of strangers, of which she was reckoned the head, continued to dwell among the children of Israel. Regarding Rahab herself, we learn from Matt. 1:5 that she became the wife of Salmon, the son of Nahshon, and the mother of Boaz, Jesse's grandfather. The suspicion naturally arises that Salmon may have been one of the spies whose life she saved and that gratitude for so great a benefit led in his case to a more tender passion and obliterated the memory of any past disgrace attaching to her name. But however this may be, it is certain, on the authority of Matthew, that Rahab became the mother of the line from which sprang David and, eventually, Christ; that the Rahab (Rachab, KJV) mentioned by Matthew is Rahab the harlot is as certain as that David in the genealogy is the same person as David in the books of Samuel.

Her Character. Both Jewish and Christian writers, for very obvious reasons, have been unwilling to admit the disreputable character of Rahab when introduced into Scripture history and have chosen to interpret the word *zōnâ,* "harlot," as "hostess," as if from *zun,* "to nourish." "Dismissing, as inconsistent with truth, the attempt to clear her character of stain by saying that she was only an innkeeper, and not a harlot, we may yet notice that it is very possible that to a woman of her country and religion such a calling may have implied a far less deviation from the standard of morality than it does with us, and, moreover, that with a purer faith she seems to have entered upon a pure life. As a case of casuistry, her conduct in deceiving the king of Jericho's messengers with a false tale, and, above all, in taking part against her own countrymen, has been much discussed. With regard to the first, strict truth either in Jew or heathen, was a virtue so utterly unknown before the promulgation of the Gospel that, as far as Rahab is concerned, the discussion is quite superfluous. With regard to her taking part against her own countrymen, it can only be justified, but is fully justified, by the circumstance that fidelity to her country would in her case have been infidelity to God, and that

the higher duty to her Maker eclipsed the lower duty to her native land" (Smith, *Dict.,* s.v.). Her faith is commended in the epistle to the Hebrews (11:31) and by James (2:25).

BIBLIOGRAPHY: C. E. Macartney, *Great Women of the Bible* (1942), pp. 43-59; C. J. and A. A. Barber, *Your Marriage Has Real Possibilities* (1984), pp. 135-55.

RA'HAB (Heb. *rāhāb,* "insolence, pride, violence"). A symbolical or poetical name applied to Egypt. It suggests the character of the "sea monster" (Pss. 87:4; 89:10; Isa. 51:9).

RA'HAM (ra'ham; "compassion, pity"). Among the descendants of Caleb, the son of Hezron, Raham is mentioned (1 Chron. 2:44) as the son of Shema and father of Jorkeam. By some Jorkeam is regarded as a place of which Raham was the founder.

RAHEL. *See* Rachel.

RAIL. A KJV expression meaning to upbraid, reproach (2 Chron. 32:17), calumniate (Mark 15:29; Luke 23:39); or to reproach, abuse (1 Cor. 5:11; 1 Tim. 6:4. The NASB and NIV render "insult," "hurling abuse," "reviler," "abusive language."

RAIMENT. Clothing, garments. *See* Dress.

RAIMENT, CHANGES OF. Handsome garments, often given as presents. *See* Dress.

RAIN. The Heb. term for rain generically is *māṭār;* a burst of rain or shower is *geshem;* a poetical word is *rᵉbîbîm,* i.e., "many," from the multitude of drops (Deut. 32:2; Jer. 3:3; 14:22; Mic. 5:7, "showers"; etc.); *zerem* expresses violent rainstorm, tempest, accompanied with hail (Job 24:8). George Adam Smith (*Hist. Geog.,* p. 63) says, "The ruling feature of the climate of Syria is the division of the year into a rainy and a dry season. Toward the end of October heavy rains begin to fall, at intervals, for a day or several days at a time. These are what the Bible calls the *early* or *former* rain (Heb. *yôreh*) literally the *pourer.* It opens the agricultural year. The soil, hardened and cracked by the long summer, is loosened, and the farmer begins plowing. Till the end of November the average rainfall is not large, but it increases through December, January, and February, begins to abate in March, and is practically over by the middle of April. *The latter rains* (Heb. *malqôsh*) of Scripture are the heavy showers of March and April. Coming as they do before the harvest and the long summer drought, they are of far more importance to the country than all the rains of the winter months, and that is why these are passed over in Scripture, and emphasis is laid alone on the *early and the latter rains.* This has given most people to believe that there are only two intervals of rain in the Syrian year, at the vernal and autumnal equinox; but the whole of the winter is the rainy season, as indeed we are told in the well-known lines of the Song of Songs:

'Lo, the winter is past,
The rain is over and gone.'

Hail is common, and is often mingled with rain and with thunderstorms, which happen at intervals through the winter, and are frequent in spring. In May showers are very rare, and from then till October not only is there no rain, but a cloud seldom passes over the sky, and a thunderstorm is a miracle." *See* Dew; Palestine.

Figurative. Rain frequently furnishes the writers of the OT with forcible and appropriate metaphors: (1) Of the word of God (Isa. 55:10); as *rain* and snow return as vapor to the sky, but not without having first of all accomplished the purpose of their descent, so the word of God shall not return to Him without fulfilling its purpose. (2) The wise and refreshing doctrine of faithful ministers (Deut. 32:2; Job 29:23). (3) Of Christ in the communications of His grace (2 Sam. 23:4; Pss. 72:6; 84:6; Ezek. 34:26; Hos. 6:3). (4) Destructive, God's judgments (Job 20:23; Ps. 11:6; Ezek. 38:22), of a poor man oppressing the poor (Prov. 28:3).

BIBLIOGRAPHY: D. Baly, *The Geography of the Bible* (1957), pp. 47-59, 84-86.

RAINBOW (Heb. *qesheth,* "bow in the cloud," Gen. 9:13-16; Ezek. 1:28; Gk. *iris,* Rev. 4:3; 10:1). The token of the covenant that God made with Noah when he came out from the ark, that "never again shall the water become a flood to destroy all flesh." Although some interpreters have concluded that in establishing the rainbow as the sign of His love and the witness of His promise (Eccles. 43:11) God was appropriating something that already existed, we agree with Keil and Delitzsch (*Com.* on Gen. 9:13ff.) that "the establishment of the rainbow as a covenant sign of the promise that there should be no flood again, presupposes that it appears then for the first time in the vault and clouds of heaven. From this it may be inferred, not that it did not rain before the flood (*see* 2:5-6), but that the atmosphere was differently constituted."   M.F.U.

Figurative. Springing as it does from the effect of the sun upon the dark mass of the clouds, it typifies the readiness of the heavenly to pervade the earthly; spread out as it is between heaven and earth, it proclaims peace between God and man; and while spanning the whole horizon, it teaches the all-embracing universality of the Noahic covenant. In the wondrous vision shown to John in the Apocalypse (Rev. 4:3), it is said that "there was a rainbow around the throne, like an emerald in appearance"; amid the awful vision of surpassing glory is seen the symbol of hope, the bright emblem of mercy and of love, looking forward from the awful judgments of the Great Tribulation to the establishment of the millennial kingdom and finally to the sinless eternal state.

BIBLIOGRAPHY: C. J. Bleeker, *The Rainbow* (1975).

RAISINS, RAISIN CAKES. Raisins appear in Scripture either as clusters or bunches of raisins (1 Sam. 25:18; 30:12; 2 Sam. 16:1; 1 Chron. 12:40; all from Heb. *ṣimmûq*), or as raisin cakes (2 Sam. 6:19; 1 Chron. 16:3; Song of Sol. 2:5; Isa. 22:24; Hos. 3:1; all from Heb. *'ǎshîshâ*). NASB "raisin cake" replaces KJV "flagon." *See* Vine.

RA'KEM (ra'kem; "variegated"). A descendant of Machir the son of Manasseh by his wife Maacah (1 Chron. 7:16).

RAK'KATH (rak'ath; Aram. "bank, shore"). A fortified city in the tribe of Naphtali (Josh. 19:35 only). From its relation to Hammath and Chinnereth it would seem to have been located on the western shore of the Sea of Galilee, not far distant from the warm baths of Tiberias, which is on the site of ancient Hammath.

RAK'KON (rak'on; probably "shore"). One of the towns belonging to Dan (Josh. 19:46), apparently near Joppa. Location unknown, but Conder suggests Tell er-Reqqeit, six miles N of Joppa.

RAM. The English rendering of two distinct Heb. words. The first, Heb. *rām,* "high," is the name of three persons:

1. The son of Hezron, a descendant of Perez, of the tribe of Judah, born in Egypt after Jacob's migration, as his name does not appear in Gen. 46:12. He is mentioned first in Ruth (4:19) and appears in the genealogy in 1 Chron. 2:9-10; Matt. 1:3-4; Luke 3:33, after 1875 B.C. In the KJV of Matt. 1:3-4; Luke 3:33, he is called Aram.

2. The firstborn of Jerahmeel and nephew of the preceding (1 Chron. 2:25, 27). The names of his sons were Maz, Jamin, and Eker.

3. A son of Barachel the Buzite is described as "of the family of Ram" (Job 32:2). Ewald identifies Ram with Aram, mentioned in Gen. 22:21, in connection with Uz and Buz, but Aram and Ram are differentiated in Heb., and Aram was not descended from Buz.

The second term, Heb. *'ayil,* refers to the ram, or male sheep. *See* Animal Kingdom: Sheep; and also the article Sacrificial Offerings.

RAM, BATTERING. *See* Armor, Arms.

RA'MA (Matt. 2:18). *See* Ramah, no. 2.

RA'MAH (ra'ma; a "height"; cf. Ezek. 16:24). Many ancient cities and towns of Palestine were located on the tops of hills for safety purposes, and those that were specially conspicuous came to be called *the Height;* and this in time came to be used as a proper name. Several places in Palestine were called by this name. In the NASB we have several forms of the word—Ramath-mizpeh (Josh. 13:26), in Gilead (21:38), Ramoth of the Negev (1 Sam. 30:27), and Ramathaim-zophim (1:1).

1. Ramah of Asher, a town mentioned only

(Josh. 19:29) in the description of the boundaries of Asher. It was evidently near the seacoast. Robinson (*Bibl. Res.*, p. 63) supposes that Ramah was to be found in the village of Rameh, on the SE of Tyre, where several sarcophagi are to be seen. Smith (*Bib. Dict.*) prefers a place of the same name about three miles E of Tyre.

2. Ramah of Benjamin, one of the cities allotted to the tribe of Benjamin, mentioned with Gibeon and Beeroth, and in the same group with Jerusalem (Josh. 18:25). The next reference to it is in Judg. 4:5, where it is said that Deborah dwelt between Ramah and Bethel. Its position is clearly indicated in the story of the Levite (Judg. 19). In the account of his return from Bethlehem to Mt. Ephraim (v. 13) Ramah is mentioned with Gibeah as lying on the N of Jerusalem. Ramah and Gibeah were near the road on the right, about two miles apart. When Israel was divided with Ramah lying between the rival kingdoms, we read of Baasha, king of Israel, going up and fortifying it (1 Kings 15:17). His object was to guard the approach from the N to Jerusalem and thus prevent any of his subjects from going there to worship and so fall away to the king of Judah. The latter was alarmed at the erection of a fortress so near his capital and stopped the work by bribing the Syrians to invade northern Palestine (vv. 18-21), and then carrying off all the building material (v. 22). The position of Ramah is specifically given in the catalog of places (Isa. 10:28-32) disturbed by the gradual approach of the king of Assyria. At Michmash he crossed the ravine; and then successfully dislodged or alarmed Geba, Ramah, and Gibeah of Saul. Each of these may be recognized with almost absolute certainty at the present day. Geba is Jeba, on the S brink of the great valley; and a mile and a half beyond it, directly between it and the main road to the city, is er-Râm (its name the exact equivalent of ha-Râmah), on the elevation that its ancient name implies. Its distance from the city is two hours by foot, i.e., five English or six Roman miles. Nebuchadnezzar established his headquarters on the plain of Hamath, at Riblah (Jer. 39:5), and from thence sent his generals, who took Jerusalem. It was here that the Jewish captives were assembled in chains, among whom was Jeremiah himself (39:8-12; 40:1). Here were probably slaughtered those who, from weakness, age, or poverty, were not believed worthwhile to transport to Babylon, thus fulfilling part of the prophecy: "A voice is heard in Ramah, lamentation and bitter weeping. Rachel is weeping for her children," etc. (31:15 cf. Matt. 2:18). Ramah was rebuilt and reoccupied by the descendants of its former inhabitants after the captivity (Ezra 2:26; Neh. 7:30). The Ramah in 11:33 is believed by some to occupy a different position in the list and may be a distinct place farther W, nearer the plain.

3. Ramah of Gilead (2 Kings 8:29; 2 Chron. 22:6), elsewhere Ramoth-gilead (which see).

4. Ramah of Naphtali, one of the fortified cities of Naphtali (Josh. 19:36), named between Adamah and Hazor. It would appear, in light of the order of the list, to have been in the mountainous country NW of the Sea of Galilee. It is the present Rameh, a large, well-built village, inhabited by Christians and Druses, surrounded by extensive olive groves, and provided with an excellent well. It stands upon the slope of a mountain in a beautiful plain SW of Safed, but without any relics of antiquity.

Aerial view of Ramathaim, ancient Ramah of Benjamin

5. Ramah of Samuel, the birthplace and home of that prophet (1 Sam. 1:19; 2:11; etc.), elsewhere called *Ramathaim-zophim* (which see).

6. Ramah of the Negev. A place on the southern border of Simeon (Josh. 19:8), simply called Baal (1 Chron. 4:33) and probably the same as Bealoth (Josh. 15:24). It cannot be positively identified, though by some the supposition of Van de Velde (*Memoir,* p. 342) appears probable, that it is identical with Ramath-lehi. Some locate it at Khirbet Ghazzah, SE of Arad and on the SE edge of the Negev. *See* Ramoth of the Negev.

7. A place occupied by the Benjamites after their return from captivity (Neh. 11:33), which may be the Ramah of Benjamin (*see* no. 2), or the Ramah of Samuel; but its position in the list (remote from Geba, Michmash, Bethel, v. 31; cf. Ezra 2:26, 28) seems to move it farther W, to the neighborhood of Lod, Hadid, and Ono. The situation of the modern Ramleh agrees with this, a town too important and too well placed not to have existed in ancient times.

BIBLIOGRAPHY: E. Robinson, *Biblical Researches* (1852), 1:576; 3:64, 79, 155; W. F. Albright, *Annual of the American Schools of Oriental Research* 4 (1924): 112, 123, 134-40; H. W. Wiener, *Journal of the Palestine Oriental Society* 7 (1927): 109-11; Y. Aharoni, *The*

Settlement of the Israelite Tribes in Upper Galilee (1957), pp. 2, 76, 78, 81, 86; Z. Kallai-Kleiman, *Vetus Testamentum* 8 (1958): 134-60; M. Avi-Yonah, *The Holy Land* (1966), pp. 133-35; Y. Aharoni, *The Land of the Bible* (1979), pp. 109, 120.

RAMATHA'IM-ZO'PHIM (ra'ma-tha'im-zō'fim; the "double height, watchers"). The birthplace of the prophet Samuel (1 Sam. 1:1), his permanent and official residence (7:17; 8:4), and the place of his burial (25:1). The name in its full form occurs only in 1 Sam. 1:1, everywhere else in the NASB and NIV it is called Ramah. Some locate this place near Gibeah of Saul (10:26; 14:16; 22:6; 26:1), whereas Keil and Delitzsch (*Com.,* on 1 Sam. 1:1) say, "It is identical with Ramah of Benjamin, and was situated upon the site of the present village of er-Ram, two hours NW of Jerusalem." It is not possible to locate the town with certainty.

RA'MATHITE (rā'ma-thīt; "inhabitant of Ramah"). An epithet of Shimei, who was over the vineyards of David (1 Chron. 27:27).

RA'MATH-LE'HI (rā'math-le'hī; "lifting up of the jawbone"). Mentioned in Judg. 15:15-17 as the place where Samson slew a thousand Philistines with the jawbone of a donkey. Then he threw away the jawbone, and as a memorial of the event, and by a characteristic play upon the old name, he called the place Ramath-lehi, i.e., the lifting (or wielding) of the jawbone.

RA'MATH-MIZ'PEH, RA'MATH MIZ'PAH (rā'-math-miz'pe; the "height of the watchtower"). One of the northern landmarks of the territory of Gad (Josh. 13:26). It was probably the same as that early sanctuary at which Jacob and Laban set up their heap of stones (Gen. 31:48-49) and which received the names of Mizpeh, Galeed, and Jegar-sahadutha: and it seems probable that all these are identical with Ramoth-gilead, notorious in the later history of the nation.

RAM'ESES, RAAM'SES, RAM'SES (ram'e-sēz; ram'sēz).

1. A NE Egyptian city of Goshen, first mentioned in Gen. 47:1-11, where it is related that a possession was given to Jacob and his sons "in the land of Rameses," which was in "the land of Goshen." The name *Raamses* occurs in Ex. 1:11 as one of the two store cities built together with Pithom by the enslaved Hebrews. Archaeology has fixed Pithom at Tell el-Retabah and Rameses at Qantir, Hyksos Avaris, and indicates that these cities were (allegedly, at least) built by the famous Rameses II (c. 1290-1224 B.C.). But it seems these towns were merely rebuilt or enlarged by the great pharaoh. The reference in 1:11 must be to the older city Zoan-Tanis, where the oppressed Israelites labored centuries earlier. Accordingly 1:11 does not conflict with 1 Kings 6:1, which places the Exodus about 1441 B.C., and the name *Raamses* is to be construed as a modernization of an archaic place name like Dan for Laish in

Gen. 14:14. Since Zoan-Tanis was a flourishing city during the Hyksos Period (before 1570 B.C.), there was ample time for the enslaved Israelites to have built the earlier city; according to the early date of the Exodus, they entered Egypt c. 1870 B.C. However, many scholars employ this verse and archaeological data to substantiate a 1280 B.C. date for the Exodus, or even later, and do not recognize Raamses as a modernization for Zoan-Tanis.

2. The name of eleven kings who ruled Egypt between about 1300 and 1075 B.C. Two of the Ramessides have special significance for the biblical narrative. Rameses II (1299-1232) is commonly considered to be the pharaoh of the Exodus by those who subscribe to the late date of the Exodus. If one holds to the early date, the Israelites were established on the hills of Palestine while Rameses marched along the Mediterranean coastal plain to do battle with the Hittites and rebuild the Egyptian Empire. Rameses III (1198-1167) repelled the Philistines from the shores of Egypt. They then settled in the plain of Philistia in Canaan and became a continuing threat to the Hebrews.

BIBLIOGRAPHY: K. A. Kitchen, *Ancient Orient and Old Testament* (1966), pp. 58-59, nn. 5, 7-9.

RAMI'AH (ra-mī'a; "Jehovah is lifted up"). An Israelite of the sons of Parosh who put away his Gentile wife after the captivity (Ezra 10:25), 456 B.C.

RA'MOTH (ra'moth; "heights"). One of the four Levitical cities of Issachar (1 Chron. 6:73), although Jarmuth appears (Josh. 21:28-29) in place of Ramoth. *See also* Jeremoth, no. 8; Ramoth-Gilead; and Ramoth of the Negev.

RA'MOTH-GIL'EAD (ra'moth-gil'i-ad; "heights of Gilead," 1 Kings 4:13; 22:3; 2 Kings 8:28; etc.; "Ramoth in Gilead," Deut. 4:43; Josh. 20:8; 21:38; 1 Chron. 6:80; etc.; "Ramah" [NASB, KJV; "Ramoth," NIV] simply, 2 Kings 8:29; 2 Chron. 22:6). One of the chief cities of Gad, on the E of the Jordan. It was allotted to the Levites and appointed a city of refuge (Deut. 4:43; Josh. 20:8), which would indicate that it was a place of importance even at the period of the conquest. In the time of Solomon it was the residence of one of his twelve deputies and was the center of a district that comprised the towns of Jair and the entire region of Argob (1 Kings 4:13). Later it fell into the hands of Ben-hadad, king of Syria, and proved the occasion of Ahab's death, who with Jehoshaphat, king of Judah, endeavored to retake it (22:3-40; 2 Chron. 18:1-34). It appears to have been won back by Israel, for it was in holding it against Hazael that Joram received the wounds that obliged him to return to Jezreel (2 Kings 8:28; 9:14); and it was while Jehu was maintaining possession of Ramoth that he was anointed king of Israel and set out at the head of the army to slay his master (9:1-14). It has been identified by Nelson Glueck with Tell Ramith in N Transjordan, after previous incorrect identifications with Jerash (Gerasa) and es-Salt by former scholars.

BIBLIOGRAPHY: N. Glueck, *Bulletin of the American Schools of Oriental Research* 92 (1943): 10ff.; H. Tadmor, *Israel Exploration Journal* 12 (1962): 114-22; D. Baly, *The Geography of the Bible* (1957), pp. 114, 174, 224, 227.

Rameses II

RA'MOTH OF THE NEGEV (ra'moth of the ne'gev). Mentioned (1 Sam. 30:27, "south Ramoth," KJV) as one of the cities to which David sent portions of the spoils of the Amalekites. It is doubtless the same as *Ramah of the Negev* (which see, Ramah, no. 6).

RAMS' HORNS. *See* Music.

RAMS' SKINS. Dyed red rams' skins formed part of the offering made by the Israelites to the *Tabernacle* (which see).

RANGE. A KJV term used (1) for a cooking *stove* (Heb. *kîr*, Lev. 11:35), (2) a *rank* or row of soldiers (Heb. *s̆edērâ*, 2 Kings 11:8, 15; 2 Chron. 23:14), (3) *planks* of cedar (Heb. *s̆edērâ*, 1 Kings 6:9), or (4) a *range* of mountains (Num. 27:12; Deut. 34:49, NIV).

RANSOM (Heb. from *pādâ*, "release"; *kōper*, "forgiveness"; or *gā'al*). A price paid to recover a person or thing (1 Cor. 6:19-20). A ransom is that

which is substituted for the party (Ex. 21:30). The people of Jehovah are redeemed by wonderful miracles (Isa. 35:10) and are called "the ransomed of the Lord" (51:11; cf. 35:9; 62:12). *See* Redemption; Redeemer.

RA'PHA, or **RA'PHAH** (ra'fa; "He, i.e., God, has healed").

1. The last named of the sons of Benjamin, son of Jacob (1 Chron. 8:2, "Rapha"), after 1900 B.C.

2. The son of Binea and father of Eleasah, the eighth in descent from Jonathan, the son of Saul (1 Chron. 8:37, "Raphah"; Rephaiah in 1 Chron. 9:43), after 1000 B.C.

RA'PHU (ra'fū; "healed, cured"). The father of Palti, which latter represented the tribe of Benjamin among those sent to spy out the Promised Land (Num. 13:9), 1440 B.C.

RAS SHAM'RA (ras sham'ra). Present-day Minet el-Beida, an important archaeological site excavated 1929-37, located on the N Syrian coast about eight miles N of Latakia and opposite the pointed peninsula of Cyprus. The French under C. F. A. Schaeffer began excavation of Ras Shamra (ancient Ugarit) in 1929 and conducted eleven seasons of excavation before the outbreak of World War II. Following the war Schaeffer again assumed leadership of the dig (1948-69). After others had briefly directed the work, Marguerite Yon of the University of Lyons, France, was appointed new director in 1978 and is currently responsible for the excavation of the site. The archaeologists have uncovered a great palace (400 by 270 feet), temple areas, a residential area, an artisans' quarter and especially archives in the palace, the temple of Dagon, and private homes. The total collection is in no less than seven languages written in five scripts, mostly during the fifteenth through the thirteenth centuries B.C. Of special interest and most numerous in the archives were materials written in a new Canaanite alphabetic script of thirty letters. This body of literature is composed in a dialect closely allied to the Heb. of the Mosaic era. The cuneiform material is to be dated in the early fourteenth century B.C. The language is called "Ugaritic," after the ancient city that was known as Ugarit. The great value of these cuneiform texts lies in the remarkable light they shed on the character of Canaanite religion. We now know the Canaanite picture well. El and Baal were the two great gods. Anath, Astarte, and Asherah were the three goddesses that were patronesses of sex and war. The Ugaritic literature has shown the moral depravity and decadence of Canaanite cultures and demonstrates that the divine command to completely destroy Canaanite cults and their devotees was justified (cf. Gen. 15:16). Canaanite religion with its orgiastic nature worship, the cult of fertility in the form of serpent symbols, sensuous nudity, and gross mythology is revealed in its stark reality in these texts. No longer can critics accuse the God of Israel of injustice in ordering the extermination of these debilitating cults. It was a question of Israel's destroying or being destroyed. Ugaritic epic literature is of first-rate importance in understanding OT religion; and these religious texts themselves have shed abundant light on OT poetry, vocabulary, and Heb. etymology and syntax. The discovery at Ras Shamra-Ugarit constitutes one of the major archaeological triumphs of the twentieth century.

M.F.U.

BIBLIOGRAPHY: A. S. Kapelrud, *Ras Shamra Discoveries and the Old Testament* (1963); G. D. Young, ed., *Ugarit in Retrospect* (1981); P. C. Craigie, *Ugarit and the Old Testament* (1983).

RAVEN. See Animal Kingdom.

RAVENOUS, RAVIN. Mentioned in Gen. 49:27, "Benjamin is a ravenous wolf," NASB and NIV; "shall ravin as a wolf," KJV; cf. Nah. 2:12; Ezek. 22:25, 27. In Ps. 22:13 the Heb. in some versions is rendered "ravening": "They open wide their mouth at me, as a ravening and a roaring lion."

RAZOR. See Barber; Hair.

REAI'A, REAI'AH (re-a′ya; "Jehovah has seen").
1. A descendant of Shobal, the son of Judah (1 Chron. 4:2). In 2:52 he is called (apparently) Haroeh (*harō′eh*, "the seer").
2. A Reubenite, son of Micah, and apparently leader of his tribe (1 Chron. 5:5; "Reaia," KJV), before 720 B.C.
3. The children of Reaiah were a family of Temple servants who returned from Babylon with Zerubbabel (Ezra 2:47; Neh. 7:50), before 536 B.C.

REAPING.
Figurative. The relation between *reaping* and *sowing,* recognized among all people, has suggested many illustrations. In the Scripture reaping is frequently used in the figurative sense: (1) The reward of wickedness (Prov. 22:8; Hos. 8:7; 10:13; Gal. 6:8). (2) The reward of righteousness (Hos. 10:12; Gal. 6:8-9); ministers receiving temporal support for spiritual labors (1 Cor. 9:11). (3) The final judgment (Matt. 13:30, 39; Rev. 14:14-16). (4) "The plowman will overtake the reaper" (Amos 9:13) is another form of "Indeed, your threshing will last for you until grape gathering" (Lev. 26:5), the meaning of which is that while one is plowing the land another shall be cutting the ripe grain, so abundant and continuous shall be the harvests. See Agriculture.

RE'BA (re′ba; "fourth"). One of the five Midianite kings slain by the Israelites in Moab (Num. 31:8; Josh. 13:21), about 1200 B.C.

REBEC'CA, REBEK'AH (re-bek′a; a "rope, noose," as of a maiden who ensnares by her beau-

ty). The daughter of Bethuel, Abraham's nephew (Gen. 22:23).
Marriage. In arranging for the marriage of his son Isaac, Abraham entrusted the commission to his servant (generally supposed to be Eliezer) and made him swear not to take a wife for him from the daughters of the Canaanites but to bring one from Abraham's native country and his kindred. He went, therefore, to the city of Nahor, and stopped by the well outside the city at the time when the women came out to draw water. He then prayed to Jehovah, fixing upon a sign by the occurrence of which he might decide upon the maiden whom Jehovah had chosen to be the wife of Isaac. Rebekah did just what had been fixed upon as a token, and Abraham's servant pressed his suit so earnestly that she and her family consented to her marriage, and she started for her future home the following day. Arriving in Canaan, she was received by Isaac and became his wife (Gen. 24).
Mother. For nineteen years after marriage Rebekah remained childless; then, after the prayers of Isaac and her journey to inquire of the Lord, Esau and Jacob were born (Gen. 25:21-26). Jacob was the favorite of his mother (25:28), whereas Esau was a source of grief both to her and Isaac (26:35).
In Philistia. Driven by famine into the country of the Philistines, Isaac was fearful lest the beauty of his wife should be a source of danger to him and therefore declared that she was his sister. Before long the deception was discovered, and Abimelech, the king, commanded that no one should molest her, on punishment of death (Gen. 26:1-11).
Suggests Deception. Some time after that Rebekah suggested the deceit that Jacob practiced upon his father, assisted him in carrying it out, and prevented the consequences of Esau's anger by sending Jacob away to her own kindred (Gen. 27:5-46).
Death and Burial. The Scriptures do not state when or where the death of Rebekah took place, but it has been conjectured that it occurred while Jacob was absent in Paddan-aram, probably before 1950 B.C. The place of her burial, mentioned by Jacob on his deathbed (Gen. 49:31), was in the field of Machpelah. Paul (Rom. 9:10-12) referred to Rebekah as being made acquainted with the purpose of God regarding her children before they were born.

BIBLIOGRAPHY: C. E. Macartney, *Ancient Wives and Modern Husbands* (1934), pp. 29-52.

RE'CAB. See Rechab.

REC'ABITE, REC'ABITES. See Rechabite.

RE'CAH (re′ka). In 1 Chron. 4:12 Beth-rapha, Paseah, and Tehinnah the father of Ir-nahash are said to have been "the men of Recah" ("Rechah," KJV). It is an unidentified place in Judah.

RECEIPT OF CUSTOMS (Matt. 9:9, KJV). The *tax office* (so NASB). *See* Tax-gatherer.

RECEIVER (Heb. *shāqal,* to "weigh," Isa. 33:18, KJV). One who tested the weight of gold and silver. The NASB renders "he who weighs," and the NIV, "the one who took the revenue."

RE'CHAB (re'kab; "charioteer, horseman, rider").

1. One of the two "sons of Rimmon the Beerothite" who slew Ish-bosheth, the son of Saul, in the hope of obtaining favor with David. But when the king heard of their crime he was so filled with abhorrence that he caused them to be put to death (2 Sam. 4:2-12), about 992 B.C.

2. The father of Jehonadab (or Jonadab), who assisted Jehu in destroying the worshipers of Baal (2 Kings 10:15-28), before 842 B.C. He was the ancestor of the Rechabites (Jer. 35:6, 8, 14, 16, 19).

3. The father of Malchijah, which latter was ruler of part of Beth-haccherem and repaired the Refuse Gate of Jerusalem after the captivity (Neh. 3:14), 445 B.C.

RECH'ABITES (rek'a-bīts). Descendants (assuming "father," Jer. 35:8, to be taken literally) of Jonadab the son of Rechab. They appear in sacred history but once, as is fully told in chap. 35, their mode of life being described in vv. 6-11. Their ancestor Jonadab son of Rechab is presumably the same as Jehonadab son of Rechab (2 Kings 10:15, 23). This is all that we know of him, though John of Jerusalem says he was a disciple of Elisha.

In 1 Chron. 2:55 "the house of Rechab" is connected in kinship with the Kenites. Jehonadab's connection with Jehu shows that Jehonadab was at that time in the land of Israel, but the two facts are not definite enough to conflict.

The Rechabite movement, like that of the Nazirites of Amos 2:11, seems to have been the result of an attempt to stem the tide of luxury and license that threatened to sap the strength of the people and the state. A return to the simplicity of nomadic life was required of the Rechabites and was enforced from generation to generation, though the invasion of Nebuchadnezzar drove them to seek other shelter in Jerusalem. It was here that they were tested by Jeremiah under divine command and for their fidelity received the blessing, "Jonadab the son of Rechab shall not lack a man to stand before Me always" (Jer. 35:19). This is sometimes understood in a liturgical sense of ministering before the Lord (Deut. 10:8; 18:5, 7; cf. Gen. 18:22; Judg. 20:28) and is held, not unreasonably, to imply that the Rechabites were adopted into Israel and incorporated with the Levites. R. Judah is cited as having mentioned a Jewish tradition that their daughters married Levites and that their children ministered in the Temple.

The LXX in the title of Ps. 71 mentions the sons of Jonadab. In Neh. 3:14 Malchijah, son of Rechab, repairs a gate of the city. In 1 Chron. 2:55 the "Kenites who came from Hammath, the father of the house of Rechab," are scribes. According to Hegesippus, "one of the priests of the sons of Rechab, the son of Rechabim, who are mentioned by Jeremiah the prophet," cried out protesting against the slaying of James the Just. Followers of the sect still are to be found in Iraq and Yemen.

A parallel has been sought in the Wahabys, followers of Asd-ul-Nahab, during the last and present century. Zealous to protect his countrymen from the vices of Turkish civilization, he forbade the use of opium and tobacco as Muhammad did wine. They have been called the Puritans of Islam; and their rapid and formidable development has been thought to present a strong analogy to the political influence and tenacious vitality of Jehonadab and his descendants.   W.H.; M.F.U.

BIBLIOGRAPHY: F. S. Frick, *Journal of Biblical Literature* 90 (1971): 279-87.

RECHAH. *See* Recah.

RECONCILIATION. The restoration of friendship and fellowship after estrangement. OT reconciliation contains the idea of an "atonement" or covering for sin (Lev. 6:30; 16:20; Ezek. 45:20). In the NT it possesses the idea "to change thoroughly" (Gk. *katallassō,* 2 Cor. 5:18-19), "to change thoroughly from one position to another" (*apokatallattō,* Eph. 2:16; Col. 1:20, 22). Reconciliation, therefore, means that someone or something is completely altered and adjusted to a required standard (cf. Rom. 5:6-11). By the death of Christ the world is changed in its relationship to God. Man is reconciled to God, but God is not said to be reconciled to man. By this change lost humanity is rendered savable. As a result of the changed position of the world through the death of Christ the divine attitude toward the human family can no longer be the same. God is enabled to deal with lost souls in the light of what Christ has accomplished. Although this seems to be a change in God, it is not a reconciliation; it is rather a "propitiation." God places full efficacy in the finished work of Christ and accepts it. Through His acceptance of it He remains righteous and the justifier of any sinner who believes in Jesus as his reconciliation. When an individual sees and trusts in the value of Christ's atoning death, he becomes reconciled to God, hostility is removed, friendship and fellowship eventuate.   M.F.U.

BIBLIOGRAPHY: L. L. Morris, *The Apostolic Preaching of the Cross* (1965); J. Denney, *The Biblical Doctrine of Reconciliation* (1985).

RECORDER (Heb. *mazkîr,* "remember"). A state officer of high rank among the Jews. Among the several new posts created by David when he ascended the throne, was the "recorder" (2 Sam. 8:16; 20:24; 1 Kings 4:3; 2 Kings 18:18, 37; 2 Chron. 34:8; Isa. 36:3, 22). The recorder had to keep the annals of the kingdom; and his office was a different one from that of the *"commander"* (which see). The latter had to draw up the public documents; the recorder had to keep them and incorporate them in the connected history of the nation. Both of these offices are met with throughout the East, and David apparently followed Egyptian models in instituting this office.

RED. See Color.

REDEEM. See Redeemer; Redemption.

REDEEMED. The children of Israel are called "the redeemed of the Lord" (Isa. 62:12; cf. 35:9), as being emancipated from Babylonian captivity and with further reference to spiritual deliverance from the bondage of sin. See Redeemer; Redemption.

REDEEMER (Heb. *gō'ēl*, the "nearest kinsman"). According to the custom of retribution, it fell to the nearest kinsman to avenge the blood of a slain relative; to protect the life and property of a relative. This obligation was called by the Israelites *redeeming*, and the man who was bound to fulfill it *a redeemer*. The law and duty of the *redeemer* are assumed by Moses as a matter of tradition and brought under theocratic principle. Redeemers are reckoned full brothers, next to them the father's brothers, then full cousins, finally the other blood relatives of the clan (Lev. 25:48-49). Since the Hebrews were an agricultural people, the chief function of the redeemer (*gō'ēl*) was to "redeem" the land that had been sold by a brother in distress. When the nation came into bondage it needed a redeemer through the "redemption" of the lands to be secured, and they looked to Jehovah to become their *gō'ēl*. Thus the Exile gave a force and a meaning to the term more striking than it could have had before. Of thirty-three passages in the OT in which *gō'ēl* is applied to God, nineteen occur in Isaiah, and in that part of the complication that deals with conditions existing in the Babylonian Exile (Isa. 48:20; 52:9; 62:12; Ps. 107:2). In spiritualizing the term *gō'ēl*, Isaiah (Isa. 49:26; cf. Ps. 19:14) places it on a par with "savior." See Kinsman; Redemption.

BIBLIOGRAPHY: H. R. Mackintosh, *The Doctrine of the Person of Christ* (1914); B. B. Warfield, *Biblical Doctrines* (1929), pp. 327-72; J. F. Walvoord, *Jesus Christ Our Lord* (1969). For additional information see *The Minister's Library* (1985), pp. 250-53.

REDEMPTION (Heb. *pādâ*, to "deliver," to "sever"). The thoughts constantly impressed upon the Israelites were that they were a people belonging to Jehovah, that He had redeemed them (i.e., severed them from bondage), and that Canaan, with all it might produce, was the gift of God, used by the Israelites as a bounty from

Jehovah. Therefore all Israel owed service to God and were, in spirit at least, to be priests unto the Most High. But because Levi and his descendants were set apart for the service of the sanctuary, all others were to be redeemed in the person of the firstborn both of man and beast. Firstborn sons, so far as the mothers were concerned, were presented to the Lord on the fortieth day after their birth and were redeemed for five shekels (Num. 18:16; cf. Ex. 13:15; Luke 2:27). The firstlings of oxen, sheep, and goats were to be brought to the sanctuary within a year, dating from the eighth day after birth, and sacrificed (Num. 18:17; *see* Sacrifices). The firstborn of a donkey, an unclean animal, was required by the original prescription (Ex. 13:13; 34:20) to be redeemed with a lamb, and if not redeemed, put to death; later, the law provided that it was to be redeemed with money, the amount being according to the priest's valuation, with a fifth part added (Lev. 27:27; Num. 18:15). With regard to the products of the soil, the best of the firstlings were sacred to Jehovah as the Lord of the soil (Ex. 23:19) and were given to the priest to present to Jehovah. In addition to individual offerings, the congregation as a body was required annually to offer to the Lord, by way of thanksgiving for the blessing of the harvest, a firstling sheaf at the *Passover* (which see). These were not to be burned but given to the priests for their use, with the provision that only those who were ceremonially clean could eat thereof. The amount of offerings of this kind was not specified by the law but was left to each individual's discretion. See Tithes.

REDEMPTION (Gk. *apolutrōsis*, a "loosing" away; *lutrōsis*, a "loosing," particularly by paying a price; for other terms, see Strong's *Concordance*). A comprehensive term employed in theology with reference to the special intervention of God for the salvation of mankind. Its meaning centers in the atoning work of Christ as the price paid for human redemption, and on account of which Christ is called the Redeemer. But along with this are other conceptions relating to the necessity for redemption, also the various stages and measures in the redemptive economy and the effects of God's gracious work.

1. Christ is man's Redeemer; but as such He is divinely appointed. The redemption He wrought manifests not only the love of the Son but also that of the Father. The Holy Spirit as well is active in the administration of redemption. The Trinity is a redemptional Trinity (*see* Rom. 5:8; John 3:16; Matt. 28:19). Still, for the reason above named, the Son of God is the Redeemer of mankind (*see* Rom. 3:24; Gal. 3:13; Eph. 1:7; 1 Pet. 1:18-19; 1 Cor. 1:30; cf. Matt. 20:28; 1 Tim. 2:6).

2. Redemption implies antecedent bondage. Thus the word refers primarily to man's subjection to the dominion and curse of sin (*see* Gal.

3:13; 1 Cor. 15:56). Also in a secondary sense to the bondage of Satan as the head of the kingdom of darkness, and to the bondage of death as the penalty of sin (*see* Acts 26:18; Heb. 2:14-15). Redemption from this bondage is represented in the Scriptures as both universal and limited. It is universal in the sense that its advantages are freely offered to all. It is limited in the sense that it is effectual only with respect to those who meet the conditions of salvation announced in the gospel. For such it is effectual in that they receive forgiveness of sins and the power to lead a new and holy life. Satan is no longer their captor, and death has lost its sting and terror. They look forward to the redemption of the body (*see* Heb. 2:9; Acts 3:19; Eph. 1:7; Acts 26:18; 2 Tim. 2:26; 1 Cor. 15:55-57; Rom. 8:15-23). *See* Incarnation; Atonement; Resurrection.   E. MCC.

BIBLIOGRAPHY: B. B. Warfield, *The Person and Work of Christ* (1950), pp. 325-50; L. L. Morris, *The Cross in the New Testament* (1964); id., *The Apostolic Preaching of the Cross* (1965). For additional information see *The Minister's Library* (1985), pp. 253-55.

RED HEIFER. *See* Sacrifices; Uncleanness.

RED SEA (Heb. *yam sûp,* "sea of reeds"). The Reed, or Papyrus, Sea that the Israelites miraculously crossed "may reasonably be supposed to be the Papyrus Lake or Papyrus Marsh, known from the Egyptian documents from the thirteenth century, to be located near Tanis" (W. F. Albright, *O. T. Commentary* [1948], p. 142). The topography of this region has been altered to some degree since the digging of the Suez Canal. Lake Ballah has disappeared. In the fifteenth century B.C. (taking the early date of the Exodus) the vicinity of Lake Timsah between Lake Ballah and the Bitter Lakes may well have been more marshy than it is at the present day. Israel's crossing of the "Reed Sea'" was undoubtedly in the vicinity of Lake Timsah or just N of it (cf. G. E. Wright and F. Filson, *The Westminster Historical Atlas to the Bible* [1945], p. 38). The question of whether the Israelites crossed the Red Sea (the northern tip of the Gulf of Suez) or Sea of Reeds (the Bitter Lakes area to the N of the Gulf of Suez) is much debated and cannot be argued in detail here. It is of some interest to note, however, that in support of the Red Sea the LXX (and Acts 7:36; Heb. 11:29) rendered *yam sûp* in the OT by the Red Sea. Also, if according to Ex. 10:19 a mighty W wind blew the locusts from the entire land of Egypt into the *yam sûp,* it would seem that the body of water large enough and properly placed to drown the locusts would have to be the Red Sea and not Sea of Reeds.

The Red Sea is a 1,350-mile-long body of water extending from the Indian Ocean to the Suez Gulf. It is more than 7,200 feet deep and more than 100 miles wide. The Arabian Peninsula borders on its E coast. Egypt, Cush, and Punt of ancient times border on the W. It has two arms,

one the Gulf of Suez and the other the Gulf of Aqaba. Aqaba figures prominently in the OT (cf. 1 Kings 22:48-49; 2 Chron. 9:21).   M.F.U.; H.F.V.

RED SEA, PASSAGE OF. *See* Exodus.

REED.
   Figurative. "A reed shaken by the wind" (Matt. 11:7; Luke 7:24) is a symbol of a fickle person; "a bruised reed . . . and a dimly burning wick" (Isa. 42:3; Matt. 12:20) represent those who are *spiritually miserable and helpless.* A forceful figure is used by the prophet Ahijah (1 Kings 14:15), "The Lord will strike Israel, as a reed is shaken in the water," meaning that as the reeds are swept by the raging current, so shall Israel be helpless before the judgments of God. A "crushed reed" (Isa. 36:6), or "staff made of reed" (Ezek. 29:6), represents an uncertain support, since it is liable to break when one leans on it and its jagged edges pierce the shoulder of the man who grasps it. *See* Vegetable Kingdom: Reeds, Rushes.

REED. Better, measuring rod or reed, a linear measure in biblical times. *See* Metrology.

REELA'IAH (re-el-a'ya; "Jehovah has caused to tremble"). One of the "people of the province" who returned from Babylon with Zerubbabel (Ezra 2:2), about 536 B.C. In Neh. 7:7 his name is given as Raamiah.

REFINE, REFINER. For refining as an occupation, *see* Handicrafts: Refiner.
   Figurative. The Bible notices of refining are chiefly of a figurative nature: of the corrective judgments of God (Isa. 1:25; 48:10; Jer. 9:7; Zech. 13:9; Mal. 3:2-3); the purity of God's word (Pss. 119:140; 18:30, "tried"); failure of means to effect an end is graphically depicted in Jer. 6:29, "The bellows blow fiercely, the lead is consumed by the fire; in vain the refining goes on, but the wicked are not separated."

REFORMATION (Gk. *diorthōsis,* "a setting right," "a making straight," Heb. 9:10). Refers to the times of perfecting things, by a change of external forms into vital and spiritual worship, referring to the times of the Messiah and the salvation He brought.

REFUGE, CITIES OF. These were six in number (Num. 35): Kadesh, in Naphtali; Shechem, in Mt. Ephraim; Hebron, in Judah (these were W of Jordan); Golan, in Bashan; Ramoth in Gilead, in Gad; Bezer, in Reuben (E of Jordan). *See* Cities of Refuge.

REFUGE, CITY OF. *See* Cities of Refuge.

REFUSE. The rendering of several Heb. and Gk. words.

1. In the case of sacrifices, the refuse ("dung," KJV; "offal," NIV) was burned outside the camp (Ex. 29:14; Lev. 4:11; 8:17; Num. 19:5); hence the extreme disgrace of the threat in Mal. 2:3. Particular directions were laid down in the law to enforce cleanliness with regard to human excrement (Deut. 23:12-13). It was the grossest insult to turn a man's house into a receptacle for it (2 Kings 10:27; Ezra 6:11; Dan. 2:5; 3:29, "dunghill," KJV); public establishments of that nature are still found in the large towns of the East. The use of this substance among the Jews was twofold: as manure and as *fuel* (which see).

2. The "refuse of the wheat" (Heb. *mapāl;* Amos 8:6) was the waste, the chaff, which was sold to the poor by their rich oppressors.

REFUSE GATE (Neh. 2:13; 3:13-14; 12:31; "dung port," or "gate, " KJV and NIV). A gate of ancient Jerusalem located at the SW angle of Mt. Zion. It was doubtless so called because of the piles of sweepings and garbage in the valley of Tophet below.

RE'GEM (re'gem; perhaps from Arab. *ragm,* "a friend"). The first named of the sons of Jahdai, who appears to have been of the family of Caleb (1 Chron. 2:47), after 1440 B.C.

RE'GEMME'LECH (re'gem-me'lek; "friend of the king"). The name of a person sent, with Sharezer, by "the town of Bethel . . . to seek the favor of the Lord" (Zech. 7:2), 518 B.C.

REGENERATION (Gk *paliggenesia,* "a being born again"). The spiritual change wrought in man by the Holy Spirit, by which he becomes the possessor of a new life. It is to be distinguished from justification, because justification is a change in our relation to God, whereas regeneration is a change in our moral and spiritual nature. The necessity, in the one case, is in the fact of guilt; in the other, depravity. They coincide in point of time and are alike instantaneous, and thus are both covered by the general term *conversion,* as that term is popularly and loosely applied (*see* Conversion). Still they are distinct in

that the one is the removal of guilt by divine forgiveness, and the other is the change from the state of depravity, or spiritual death, to that of spiritual life. Regeneration is also to be distinguished from sanctification, inasmuch as the latter is the work of God in developing the new life and bringing it to perfection, whereas the former is the beginning of that life. *See* Sanctification.

Regeneration is represented in the Scriptures principally by such terms as "born again," "born of God," "born of the Spirit" (*see* John 3:3-13; 1 John 3:9; 4:7; 5:1; 1 Pet. 1:23). There are also other forms of expression of deep significance with reference to the same great fact (*see* Ezek. 36:25-26; Eph. 4:22-24; 2 Cor. 5:17; Col. 3:9-10).

The work of regeneration is specially ascribed in the Scriptures to the Holy Spirit (*see* John 3:5-8; Titus 3:5). This is in full accord with the whole tenor of special revelation in representing the agency of the Spirit in the economy of salvation. (*See* Holy Spirit.)

Regeneration by baptism, or baptismal regeneration, has been a widely prevalent error. This is due in part to an improper use of the term. A proselyte from heathenism to the Jewish religion was said to be "born again." A corresponding use of the term crept into the early Christian church. Those who received baptism, the initiatory rite of church membership, were said to be regenerated; but this was probably without any intention of denying the deeper work of the Holy Spirit. It was only a loose and improper way of indicating the change in a man's external relationship. And it is proper to say that some of the advocates of the baptismal regeneration in the Church of England still use the term in this sense and make a distinction between regeneration as effected by baptism and the great work of spiritual renewal. But the error has its broader basis in an unscriptural idea of the character and efficiency of the sacraments. And thus it is held not only by Roman Catholics but also by many Lutherans and many in the Church of England. (*See* Sacraments.)

BIBLIOGRAPHY: A. Kuyper, *The Work of the Holy Spirit* (1941), pp. 293-332; J. F. Walvoord, *The Holy Spirit* (1965), pp. 128-37.

REGISTER. *See* Genealogy.

REHABI'AH (re-ha-bī'a; "Jehovah is enlarged"). The only son of Eliezer, the son of Moses (1 Chron. 23:17; 24:21; 26:24), after 1400 B.C.

RE'HOB (re'hob; "wide street, open space").

1. The father of Hadadezer, king of Zobah, whom David defeated at "the River," i.e., the Euphrates (2 Sam. 8:3, 12), before 986 B.C.

2. A Levite who signed the covenant with Nehemiah (Neh. 10:11), 445 B.C.

3. A city on the northern border of Palestine, marking the limit of the exploration of the spies in that direction (Num. 13:21; 2 Sam. 10:8; "Beth-rehob" in 10:6). It was probably in the

tribe of Naphtali, the modern Tell el-Kadhy (Judg. 18:28).

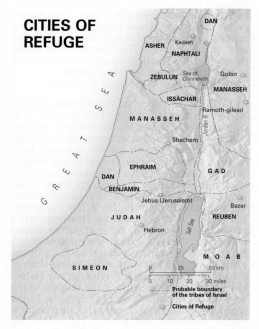

CITIES OF REFUGE

4. A town allotted to Asher (Josh. 19:28), close to Sidon.

5. Another town in Asher (Josh. 19:30). One of these two towns was assigned to the Gershonite Levites (Josh. 21:31; 1 Chron. 6:75) and was not possessed by the Israelites (Judg. 1:31).

REHOBO'AM (rē-ho-bō'am; "enlarger of the people"). The son of Solomon by the Ammonite princess Naamah (1 Kings 14:21, 31). He was born about 972 B.C.

Accession. Rehoboam selected Shechem as the place of his coronation, probably as an act of concession to the Ephraimites, who were always dissatisfied with their inferior position in the confederation of the tribes (1 Kings 12:1; 2 Chron. 10:1), about 931 B.C.

Insurrection. The people demanded a remission of the severe burdens imposed by Solomon, and Rehoboam promised them an answer in three days, during which time he consulted first his father's counselors and then the young men "who grew up with him and served him." Rejecting the advice of his elders to conciliate the people at the beginning of his reign, he returned as his reply the bravado of his contemporaries. Thereupon rose the formidable song of insurrection, heard once before when the tribes quarreled after David's return from the war with Absalom. Rehoboam sent Hadoram to reduce the rebels to reason, but he was stoned to death by them;

whereupon the king and his attendants fled to Jerusalem. He then assembled an army of 180,000 men from the two faithful tribes of Judah and Benjamin, in the hope of reconquering Israel. The expedition, however, was forbidden by the prophet Shemaiah (1 Kings 12:1-24); still, during Rehoboam's lifetime peaceful relations between Israel and Judah were never restored (2 Chron. 12:15; 1 Kings 14:30).

Reign. Rehoboam now strengthened the territories that remained to him by building a number of fortresses (2 Chron. 11:6-10). The pure worship of God was maintained in Judah. But Rehoboam did not check the introduction of pagan abominations into his capital; the worship of Astoreth was allowed to exist, "Asherim" were set up, and the worst immoralities were tolerated (1 Kings 14:22-24; 2 Chron. 12:1).

Egyptian Invasion. In the fifth year of Rehoboam's reign the country was invaded by Egyptians and other African nations under Shishak (Sheshonk I), numbering 1,200 chariots, 60,000 horses, and a vast multitude of infantry. The fortresses about Jerusalem and that city itself were taken, and Rehoboam purchased peace by delivering up the Temple treasures. Shishak left a record of this military venture on the wall of the temple of Amon-Re at Karnak (Luxor), where it may be seen today. After this great humiliation the moral condition of Judah seems to have improved (2 Chron. 12:12) and the rest of Rehoboam's life has been unmarked by any events of importance. He died in 913 B.C., after a reign of seventeen years, having ascended the throne in 931 B.C. at the age of forty-one (1 Kings 14:21; 2 Chron. 12:13). He had eighteen wives, sixty concubines, twenty-eight sons, and sixty daughters. Of all his wives Maacah was his favorite, and to her son Abijah he bequeathed his kingdom (2 Chron. 11:18-22).

BIBLIOGRAPHY: C. E. Macartney, *The Man Who Forgot* (1956), pp. 84-94; K. M. Kenyon, *Archaeology in the Holy Land* (1960), pp. 273ff.; A. Malamat, *Journal of Near Eastern Studies* 22 (1963): 247ff.; Y. Aharoni, *The Land of the Bible* (1979), pp. 330ff.; T. Kirk and G. Rawlinson, *Studies in the Books of Kings* (1983), 2:1-13; E. R. Thiele, *Mysterious Numbers of the Hebrew Kings* (1983), pp. 35-36.

REHO'BOTH (rē-ho'both; "broad places").
1. One of the four cities founded by·Asshur (Gen. 10:11-12), the others being Nineveh, Calah, and Resen. Rehoboth was evidently a part of the great city of Nineveh.

The words "rehoboth ir" are probably to be translated as they are in the Vulg. and in the margin of the KJV, "the streets of the city," i.e., of Nineveh. Rehoboth-Ir is best regarded as a suburb of greater Nineveh, which in course of time came to be included in the city's vast marketplaces.

2. The third of the series of wells dug by Isaac (Gen. 26:22). A Wadi Ruhaibeh, containing the

ruins of a town of the same name, with a large well, is crossed by the road from Khan en-Nukhl to Hebron, by which Palestine is entered on the S. It lies about nineteen miles SW of Beersheba.

3. The city of a certain Shaul, one of the early Edomite kings (Gen. 36:37; 1 Chron. 1:48). Its location is uncertain.

RE'HUM (rē'hum; "compassionate").

1. One of the "people of the province" who returned from the captivity with Zerubbabel (Ezra 2:2), about 536 B.C. In Neh. 7:7 he is called Nehum.

2. An officer of the king of Persia, called the "commander," perhaps lieutenant governor of the province of Samaria, who united with Shimshai in writing a letter to Artaxerxes that influenced him against the Jews (Ezra 4:8-9, 17, 23), 465 B.C.

3. A Levite, son of Bani, who repaired part of the wall of Jerusalem under Nehemiah (Neh. 3:17), 445 B.C.

4. One of the "leaders of the people" who signed with Nehemiah the covenant to serve Jehovah (Neh. 10:25), 445 B.C.

5. One of the priests who accompanied Zerubbabel at the same time as no. 4 (Neh. 12:3).

RE'I (rē'i; "friendly, sociable"). One of David's friends who refused to espouse the cause of Adonijah (1 Kings 1:8), 960 B.C.

REINS. A KJV term used to translate Heb. *kilyâ*, "kidneys," and *ḥălāṣayim*, "loins" (Isa. 11:5); and Gk. *nephros*, "kidneys." In Isa. 11:5, the NASB uses "loins" and "waist." The NIV translates "waist." Elsewhere "reins" is replaced by "kidneys" (Job 16:13); "heart" (Job 19:27, marg., "loins"); "mind," or "heart" (NIV; see Pss. 7:9; 16:7; 26:2; Jer. 12:2; 17:10; 20:12; Rev. 2:23; in all verses in the NASB, marg., "kidneys"); and "pierced within" (Ps. 73:21), or "inward parts" (139:13; Lam. 3:13; both NASB margs., "kidneys"). See Loins; Kidney.

RE'KEM (re'kem; "variegation").

1. One of the five Midianite kings slain by the Israelites along with Balaam (Num. 31:8; Josh. 13:21), c. 1380 B.C.

2. One of the sons of Hebron and father of Shammai, of the tribe of Judah (1 Chron. 2:43-44), after 1380 B.C.

RELEASE A term used in various ways in the KJV, NIV, and NASB. Heb. *sheᵐiṭṭâ*, "a remitting," appears in Deut. 15:1-3; 31:10, with the meaning of *release* or *remission*, and is discussed under the latter term. Another term, Heb. *hănāḥâ*, appears in the KJV of Esther 2:18 as *release*, but in the NASB and NIV as *holiday* (which see).

The Gk. term *apoluō*, "to release," referred to a custom that prevailed of allowing some prominent criminal to go free at the Passover (Matt.

27:15; Luke 23:17; John 18:39). The origin of the custom is unknown, but it is probable that it was common among the Jews before they were subject to the Romans, for Pilate said, "You have a custom." Perhaps it was memorial of the great national deliverance that was celebrated at the feast of the Passover. The Romans, who prided themselves in respecting the usages of conquered people, had fallen in with the custom.

For *release* in the KJV, *see* Remission.

RELIGION. A term, when viewed etymologically, of uncertain derivation. Cicero refers it to *religare*, to read over again, to consider, and thus regards it as meaning attention to divine things. Lactantius and Augustine derive the word from *religare*, to bind back, thus representing religion as the ground of obligation. The word thus translated in the NT, where it occurs but three times, is *thrēskeia*, and it means outward religious service (*see* Acts 26:5; James 1:26-27). In philosophical, as well as in common use, the word has a variety of meanings, e.g., Schleiermacher defines religion as "the feeling of absolute dependence"; Kant, "the observance of moral law as a divine institution"; Fichte, "Faith in the moral order of the universe." In general it refers to any system of faith and worship, such as the religion of the Jews, of pagan nations, or of Christians. In the popular language of believers in Christianity it means especially and almost exclusively the Christian religion. The term calls attention to the all-important fact that man is a religious being. There is that in his nature that prompts him to some sort of faith and worship. With or without special revelation from God, he requires the satisfaction and consolation and guidance that comes from faith in the unseen and the eternal. The limits of this article do not admit of representations of the various forms of religion that have appeared in the history of the race. For these *see* articles under their appropriate heads. Scientific research and comparative study in this direction began in the nineteenth century. The distinction between natural and revealed religion, their relative value and importance, the inadequacy of the one and the completeness of the other properly fall under the head of theology. *See* Theology.

E. MCC.

RELIGIOUS PROSELYTES. *See* Proselytes.

REMALI'AH (rem-a-li'a; perhaps, "Jehovah adorns"). The father of Pekah, king of Israel (2 Kings 15:25, 27, 30, 32, 37; 16:1, 5; 2 Chron. 28:6; Isa. 7:1, 4-5, 9; 8:6), before 735 B.C.

RE'METH (re'meth; "height"). A city of Issachar (Josh. 19:21), called in 1 Chron. 6:73 Ramoth. *See* Ramoth, no. 2.

REMISSION (Heb. *shāmaṭ*, to "let alone"). The Sabbatic year was also called "the year of remission" (Deut. 31:10; "release," KJV; "canceling debts," NIV), because Moses commanded that during that year the poor were not to be oppressed. The specific command was: "Every creditor shall release what he has loaned to his neighbor; he shall not exact it of his neighbor and his brother, because the Lord's remission has been proclaimed" (15:1-3, 9). The Heb. term does not signify a remission of the debt, the relinquishing of all claim for payment, but simply the lengthening of the term, not pressing for payment. Exodus 23:11 says of the land, "But on the seventh year you shall let it rest [Heb. *shāmaṭ*] and lie fallow," etc. This does not mean an entire renunciation of the field or possessions; so in the case of the debt it does not imply an absolute relinquishment of what has been lent, but simply leaving it, i.e., not pressing for it during this year.

REM'PHAN (rem'fan). Better, Rephan. *See* Gods, False: Rompha.

REND (Heb. *qāra'*, and several other terms). The Heb. term *qāra'* is the only one that calls for special notice. It refers to the tearing of one's clothes as a sign of grief, and its figurative use; thus, "Rend your heart and not your garments" (Joel 2:13) signifies contrition of heart and not mere outward signs of grief.

The expression *rentest* (also from *qāra'*) appears in the KJV of Jer. 4:30, "Though thou rentest thy face with painting, in vain shalt thou make thyself fair," but the allusion is not to tearing but rather to the Eastern practice of painting the eyes, as the NASB ("enlarge your eyes with paint") and NIV ("shade your eyes with paint") make clear.

REPENTANCE (Gk. *metanoia,* a "change" of mind). In the theological and ethical sense a fundamental and thorough change in the hearts of men from sin and toward God. Although faith alone is the condition for salvation (Eph. 2:8-10; Acts 16:31), repentance is bound up with faith and inseparable from it, since without some measure of faith no one can truly repent, and repentance never attains to its deepest character till the sinner realizes through saving faith how great is the grace of God against whom he has sinned. On the other hand, there can be no saving faith without true repentance. Repentance contains as essential elements (1) a genuine sorrow toward God on account of sin (2 Cor. 7:9-10; Matt. 5:3-4; Ps. 51); (2) an inward repugnance to sin necessarily followed by the actual forsaking of it (Matt. 3:8; Acts 26:20; Heb. 6:1); and (3) humble self-surrender to the will and service of God (*see* Acts 9:6, as well as Scriptures above referred to). Repentance, it should be observed, has different stages of development. (1) In its lowest and most imperfect form it may arise from fear of the consequences or penalty of sin. If it goes no farther than this it is simply remorse and must end in despair. (2) It deepens in character with the

recognition of the baseness of sin itself. But here again it is merely a burden of soul from which man may seek to free himself in vain till he recognizes the great hope before him in the gospel. (3) It becomes more complete and powerful in those who have experienced the saving grace of God and thus realize more fully the enormity of sin and the depths of the divine compassion that has been operative in their salvation.

Repentance, it is thus to be seen, is the gift of God (Acts 5:31; 11:18; Rom. 2:4). It is so because God has given His word with its revelations concerning sin and salvation; also the Holy Spirit to impress the truth and awaken the consciences of men and lead them to repentance. But as with faith so with repentance—it is left with men to make for themselves the great decision.

E.MCC.; M.F.U.

BIBLIOGRAPHY: G. B. Stevens, *The Christian Doctrine of Salvation* (1905); L. S. Chafer, *Salvation* (1965); J. Colquhoun, *Repentance* (1965); J. Jeremias, *New Testament Theology* (1971), 1:152-58.

REPETITION (Gk. *battologeō,* to "stutter, prate"). Our Lord, in His Sermon on the Mount (Matt. 6:7), cautions us against using "meaningless repetition" in prayer. This injunction is not directed against simple repetition, which may often arise in the fervency of earnest prayer, but against such repetition on the ground of supposed merit. The Gentile nations were accustomed to attach merit to much speaking in their prayers. The Jews adopted this bad practice to such an extent that it was one of their maxims that "he that multiplieth prayer shall be heard."

RE'PHAEL (re'fa-el; "God heals"). A son of the Levite Shemaiah of the house of Obed-edom, appointed one of the gatekeepers of the house of God by David (1 Chron. 26:7), about 960 B.C.

RE'PHAH (re'fa; "wealth, opulence"). A son of Beriah of the tribe of Ephraim (1 Chron. 7:25).

REPHA'IAH (re-fa'ya; "Jehovah heals").

1. The sons of Rephaiah, the sons of Arnan, etc. (1 Chron. 3:21), were, it is supposed, branches of the family of David whose descent or connection with Zerubbabel is for us unascertainable. Rephaiah is probably the same as *Rhesa* (which see), mentioned in Luke 3:27.

2. A son of Ishi, and one of the leaders of Simeon in the time of Hezekiah, who led the expedition of 500 men against the Amalekites of Mt. Seir (1 Chron. 4:42), about 715 B.C.

3. One of the six sons of Tola and head of a family in Issachar (1 Chron. 7:2), before 1440 B.C.

4. The son of Binea and eighth in descent from Jonathan the son of Saul (1 Chron. 9:43), long after 1000 B.C. He is called Raphah in 8:37.

5. The son of Hur and the "official of half the district of Jerusalem." He repaired part of the wall of the city (Neh. 3:9), 445 B.C.

REPH'AIM (ref'a-im; "spirits of the deceased,

giant aborigines"). A race first mentioned in Gen. 14:5 as dwelling in Ashteroth-karnaim (probably not the same as Ashtaroth, the residence of Og, Deut. 1:4; etc.) and being defeated by Chedorlaomer and his allies. In Gen. 15:20 they appear among the nations to be dispossessed by Israel. As they are not mentioned in 10:15-18, they were probably not Canaanites but an older, perhaps aboriginal race. Their few recorded names "have, as Ewald remarks, a Semitic aspect," though, to be sure, they may have been Semitized. They are mentioned in Deut. 2:11, 20; 3:11, 13; Josh. 12:4; 13:12; 17:15, and with the Perizzites (Gen. 15:20). See Giant.

In the Heb. text *repā'îm* is used of the dead in Job 26:5; Ps. 88:10; Prov. 2:18; 9:18; 21:16; Isa. 14:9; 26:14, 19. The translation in the NASB and NIV is "departed spirits," "the dead," or "spirits of the dead."

REPH'AIM, VALLEY OF ("valley of the giants"). First mentioned in Joshua's description of the northern border of Judah (Josh. 15:8). It was the scene of several conflicts between the Philistines and David (2 Sam. 5:17-22; 23:13-17; 1 Chron. 14:9-11). From 11:15-16 it seems clear that Rephaim was not distant from Bethlehem. The valley was proverbial for its crops of grain (Isa. 17:5). It apparently is to be identified with the valley about three miles in length lying SW of Jerusalem and extending halfway to Bethlehem, called Baqa'.

REPH'AITES. *See* Rephaim.

RE'PHAN. *See* Gods, False: Rompha.

REPH'IDIM (ref'i-dim). One of Israel's camping sites on their journey from the wilderness of Sin to Mt. Sinai. At this now-unknown site the episode of the murmuring of the children of Israel occurred because of a lack of water. Accordingly Moses struck the rock in Horeb and obtained an abundance of water (Ex. 17:1-7; 19:2). Moses named the place "Meribah," or strife. At Rephidim also occurred the clash between the Israelites and the Bedouin Amelekites. During this celebrated encounter Aaron and Hur supported Moses' hands in prayer while Joshua secured a great victory (17:8-16).   M.F.U.

REPROACH (Heb. usually *ḥerpâ*; Gk. *oneidos*). A severe expression of censure or blame. It is sometimes directed against God and is then often equivalent to blasphemy (2 Kings 19:4, 16; Isa. 37:4, 17; etc.). It is also the *object* of contempt, scorn, derision, as in "let us rebuild the wall of Jerusalem that we may no longer be a reproach" (Neh. 2:17; cf. Pss. 22:6; 79:4; Jer. 6:10; 24:9; etc.).

REPROBATE. A KJV expression. In the NASB and NIV it is replaced by *rejected* (Jer. 6:30; 2 Tim. 3:8), *depraved* (Rom. 1:28), *fail the test* (2 Cor. 13:5-6), *appear unapproved* (2 Cor. 13:7;

"seem to have failed," NIV), and *worthless for any good deed* (Titus 1:16).

RE'SEN (re'sen). An ancient city of Assyria (Gen. 10:12), one of a number of towns forming the composite city called *Nineveh* (which see). Resen stood midway between Nineveh and Calah.

RESH (ר) (resh). The twentieth letter of the Heb. alphabet, corresponding to English "r." It stands at the beginning of the twentieth section of Ps. 119, in which portion each verse in the Heb. begins with this letter.   M.F.U.

RE'SHEPH (re'shef; "flame"). A son of Beriah, of the tribe of Ephraim (1 Chron. 7:25).

RESPECT OF PERSONS. *See* Partial, Partiality.

RESTITUTION. *See* Punishment: Mosaic Law.

RESURRECTION OF CHRIST. The return of Christ to bodily life on the earth on the third day after His death.

Scripture Doctrine. Only within recent years have rationalistic interpretations of the Scriptures ventured to assert that the phrase "raised from the dead" does not mean an actual bodily resurrection, and that it simply declares that Christ as a spirit did not remain in hell, but was raised to heaven. That this is a most irrational interpretation is seen from the explicit declaration and the whole tenor of the Scriptures upon this point. Likewise the "vision hypothesis," that Christ after His death only appeared to His disciples in a way purely subjective, is contrary to the Scriptures; neither can it be, as we shall see, sustained upon grounds of reason. The resurrection of our Lord is set before us in the NT as the miraculous restoration of His physical life, the reunion of His spirit with His body, and yet in such a way that the material limitations in which He had previously confined His life were set aside. The resurrection was the beginning of the glorification. It occurred on the morning of the third day after His death, counting, according to custom, parts of days as days (cf. Matt. 16:21; Luke 24:1).

The body in which the disciples saw the risen Lord was real, that in which they had seen Him living, and that which had died (*see* Luke 24:39; John 20:24-29). And yet, as is manifest from the gospel accounts of His appearances during the forty days and of His visible ascension, His body was undergoing the mysterious change of that glorification of which the resurrection was the beginning and the ascension into heaven the end (*see* 20:4, 14, 26, 21:4; Luke 24:37). What the change was that adapted the Lord's body to its destined heavenly environment is a question of profitless speculation. But it is evident from the Scriptures that in the resurrection Christ's glorification only began and also that Christ now dwells in heaven in a glorified body (Phil. 3:21;

Col. 3:4). The resurrection of Christ is represented in the Scriptures as wrought by the power of God. Its miraculous power is strongly proclaimed (*see* Acts 13:30; Rom. 1:4; 1 Cor. 15:15); and thus it presents no difficulty for faith to one who really believes in God. Indeed, the Scriptures represent it as in the deepest sense not unnatural but natural that Christ should be raised from the dead (*see* Acts 2:24). The testimony of the Scriptures as to the reality of the resurrection is most ample and without a note of discord as to the essential fact itself. The witnesses were not few, but many (*see,* in addition to accounts in the gospels, 1 Cor. 15:1-8). The declaration of the apostle Paul that he had "seen Jesus our Lord" (1 Cor. 9:1) properly places him among the witnesses to the great reality.

The proclamation of the resurrection lies at the basis of apostolic teaching (*see* Acts 1:22; 4:2, 33; 17:18; 23:6; 1 Cor. 15:14; etc.). It ranks first among the miracles that bear witness to Christ's divine character (Rom. 1:4). It is the divine seal of approval upon Christ's atoning work and thus is in close connection with the justification of sinners (4:25; 5:10; 8:34). It is connected with our spiritual renewal, as the new life of believers comes from the risen Christ (Col. 3:1-3). It is the pledge of the resurrection and glorification of the true followers of Christ (Rom. 8:11; 1 Cor. 15:20-21; Phil. 3:21; 1 Thess. 4:14).

Theological. The denial of this great fact has always come from the enemies of Christianity. This is but natural, as Christianity must stand or fall with the resurrection. That Christ "rose from the dead" has always been a cardinal article of faith in the Christian church. The historic proofs of this fact are most weighty when the relation of the fact to the whole body of saving truth is duly considered. They may fail to convince unbelievers who have no appreciation of the great realities of sin and salvation. But still they are of great value for the defense of the faith and for the comfort of believers. The matter resolves itself mainly into two considerations, namely, the credibility of the witnesses and the difficulties of denial as greater than those of belief. As to the credibility of the witnesses, account is to be taken not only of their number and variety but also of the essential harmony of their reports, the absence of all motive to falsehood, and their self-sacrificing devotion to the gospel that based itself upon the resurrection. The difficulties that beset denial are found (1) in the impossibility of explaining the empty grave except upon the grounds that the resurrection actually took place; (2) the attitude of the enemies of Christ after the resurrection, revealing as it did their helpless confusion; (3) the disciples' sudden transition from hopelessness to triumphant faith, which would be inexplicable except upon the actuality of the resurrection; (4) the founding of Christianity in the world, which can be rationally

accounted for only in view of the fact that Christ actually rose from the dead.   E.MCC.

BIBLIOGRAPHY: W. Milligan, *The Resurrection of Our Lord* (1884); H. Latham, *The Risen Master* (1901); M. L. Loane, *Our Risen Lord* (1965); J. Orr and H. C. G. Moule, *The Resurrection of Christ* (1980). For additional information see *The Minister's Library* (1985), pp. 256-66.

RESURRECTION OF THE BODY (Gk. *anastasis,* "to make to stand," or "rise up"). The reunion of the bodies and souls of men that have been separated by death. This is rightly held to be an important article of Christian belief, though it is left by the revelation of Scripture obscure in many details.

Spiritual. The OT in the earlier parts does not speak explicitly upon this subject. Christ, however, declares the doctrine to be generally presupposed in the old economy (*see* Luke 20:37-38). Allusions to it are to be found in Gen. 22:5, cf. Heb. 11:19; Pss. 16:10-11; 49:14-15; Isa. 26:19; 53:10; Ezek. 37. A clear reference appears in Dan. 12:3. It is plainly taught also in the apocryphal books of the OT (Wisd. 3:1; 4:15; 2 Macc. 7:14, 23, 29). It was a belief held commonly among the Jews in the time of Christ (*see* Matt. 22:30; Luke 20:28-39; John 11:24; Acts 23:6, 8). The Sadducees were the exceptions in their denial of the doctrine. Christ appeared and confirmed this belief, though He was careful to guard against erroneous conceptions held by some in connection with it, as appears in some of the passages to which reference has been made. Naturally it was a marked feature of apostolic doctrine (*see* Acts 4:2; 26:23; 1 Cor. 15; 1 Thess. 4:14; Phil. 3:20-21; Rev. 20:6-14; etc.). The teaching of the Scriptures sums up as follows: (1) The body shall rise again. The integrity of man's being, a creature of soul and body, shall be restored. (2) In some sense the identity of the body shall be preserved. (3) The body is to be changed and refined to fit it for the new surroundings of the future life. For the saints it is to be a "glorified body." (4) The resurrection of the righteous will take place at the coming of Christ (1 Thess. 4:13-18; 1 Cor. 15:53), of the unsaved at the great white throne judgment after the Kingdom age (Rev. 20:11-15). (5) The power is of God in Christ, who said, "I am the resurrection and the life" (John 11:25).

Theological. The article in the Apostles' Creed containing this doctrine was doubtless intended to express the faith of the early church in the teaching of Christ and the apostles. It was also intended to meet the Manichean heresy that there is an essential antagonism between matter and spirit, that matter is by nature evil, and accordingly the soul of man is degraded by union with the body. That this simple but great statement of the dignity of the human body, and that both soul and body are destined to immortality, have been overlaid by many crude speculations is what might have been expected. That in no measure detracts from the great truth of revelation to which the statement points. As to the sense in which the resurrection body shall be identical with the body laid aside in death, that is a matter upon which the Scriptures open the way to no definite conclusion. It may be remarked, however, that the continued identity of the body even in this present life does not depend upon its possession continuously of the same substance, neither is it identity of size or form or appearance. It is identity of relationship and functions. The substance of which the body is composed is constantly changing. Likewise there are changes in respect to other material features. Still the body remains as the vestiture and in some degree the expression of the Spirit in union with it. The coarse representation of bodily resurrection, in which many have indulged, based upon the idea of the literal return of the same fleshly parts laid aside in death, is therefore without warrant in reason. And this is not required nor warranted by Scripture. A careful study of Paul's great chapter upon the subject (1 Cor. 15) must show this. The most that can be affirmed is that God will reinvest the souls of men with bodies, and that these bodies, while changed, shall have in some important sense identity with the bodies that have experienced death and dissolution. It is not strange that this doctrine has been denied by rationalists and materialists and skeptics generally. But it is logically held by Christians because of their faith in Christ and in the teachings that bear His authority. It has great religious and ethical value, inasmuch as it recognizes the dignity of the body and its true relation to the soul in union with it, opening to us the hope of complete glorification.

E.MCC.; M.F.U.

BIBLIOGRAPHY: G. Vos, *Princeton Theological Review* 27 (1929): 1-35, 193-226; K. Barth, *The Resurrection of the Dead* (1933); O. Cullmann, *Immortality of the Soul or Resurrection of the Dead* (1958); J. A. Schep, *The Nature of the Resurrection Body* (1964); R. S. Candlish, *Life in the Risen Saviour* (1977); H. D. F. Salmond, *The Biblical Doctrine of Immortality* (1984), pp. 499-590.

RETINUE (Heb. *ḥayil*, "strength"). A term used respecting the queen of Sheba (1 Kings 10:2, "caravan," NIV; *see* 1 Kings 10:13; 2 Chron. 9:12) and pointing to her great wealth and position. KJV, "train."

RETRIBUTION. *See* Punishment, Future.

RE'U (re'u; "friend"). The son of Peleg and father of Serug, in the ancestry of Abraham (Gen. 11:18-21; 1 Chron. 1:25; Luke 3:35; "Ragau," KJV, Luke 3:35).

REU'BEN (rū'ben; "see a son"). The firstborn son of Jacob and Leah (Gen. 29:32), about 1952 B.C.

His Crime. When Jacob dwelt in Eder, Reuben committed an offense that was too great for Jacob

to forget (Gen. 35:22) and of which he spoke with abhorrence even upon his dying bed.

Befriends Joseph. When his brothers were planning for the destruction of Joseph in Dothan, Reuben, as the eldest son, interfered in his behalf. By his advice Joseph's life was spared—he was merely stripped of his garment and cast into a pit. In Reuben's absence Joseph was sold to the Ishmaelites. When Reuben returned with the intention of rescuing his brother, he found that Joseph was gone (37:21-22, 29).

In Egypt. Reuben accompanied his brothers into Egypt in search of food and accepted Joseph's harsh treatment of himself and his brothers as a proper judgment upon them because of their sin (42:22). He delivered to Jacob Joseph's message demanding Benjamin's presence in Egypt and offered his two sons as pledges for his brother's safe return (v. 37). Upon the removal of Jacob into Egypt, c. 1876 B.C., Reuben had four sons—Hanoch, Pallu, Hezron, and Carmi (46:9).

Character. Reuben seems to have been of an ardent, impetuous, unbalanced, but not ungenerous nature; not crafty and cruel, as were Simeon and Levi, but rather, to use the metaphor of the dying patriarch, "uncontrolled as water," i.e., boiling up like a vessel of water over the wood fire in the nomad tent and as quickly subsiding into apathy when the fuel was spent.

The Tribe of Reuben. At the time of the migration into Egypt Reuben's sons were four, and from them sprang the chief families of the tribe. The census of Mt. Sinai (Num. 1:20-21; 2:11) shows that the numbers of this tribe at the Exodus was 46,500 men above twenty years of age and fit for military service, ranking seventh in population. At the later census, taken thirty-eight years after and just before entering Canaan, its numbers had decreased to 43,730, which made it rank ninth (26:7).

Position. During the journey through the wilderness the position of Reuben was on the S side of the Tabernacle. The "camp" that went under his name was formed of his own tribe, that of Simeon, and of Gad.

Inheritance. The country allotted to this tribe was E of Jordan, extending on the S to the river Arnon, on the E to the desert of Arabia; on the W were the Dead Sea and the Jordan, and the northern border was probably marked by a line running eastward from the Jordan through Wadi Heshbân (Josh. 13:17-21; Num. 32:37-38).

REU'BENITE (rū'ben-īt). A descendant of Reuben (Num. 26:7; etc.).

REU'EL (rū'el; "friend of God's," or "God is a friend").

1. The son of Esau by his wife Basemath (Gen. 36:4, 10). His four sons (36:13; 1 Chron. 1:37) were chiefs of the Edomites (Gen. 36:17).

2. A priest of Midian and a herdsman, who gave a hospitable reception to Moses when he fled

from Egypt, and whose daughter Zipporah became the wife of Moses (Ex. 2:18). Reuel is undoubtedly the same person as *Jethro* (which see), the first being probably his proper name and the latter a title or surname, indicating his rank.

3. In the KJV of Num. 2:14, *Reuel* is given for NASB and NIV *Deuel* (which see).

4. The son of Ibnijah and father of Shephatiah, of the tribe of Benjamin (1 Chron. 9:8).

REU'MAH (rū'ma; "exalted, elevated"). Nahor's concubine, and by him mother of Tebah and others (Gen. 22:24).

REVELATION (Gk. *apokalupsis,* an "uncovering or unveiling"). A term expressive of the fact that God has made known to men truths and realities that men could not discover for themselves.

An important distinction is commonly recognized between general and special revelation.

By general revelation is meant that which is given to all men, in nature and history, and in the nature of man himself. The reality and validity of revelation in this sense is declared in Scripture verses such as Ps. 19:1; Isa. 40:26; Rom. 1:19-20; Ex. 9:16; Acts 14:15-17; Rom. 2:14-15; Matt. 6:22-34. But the actual power of this revelation over men has, in numberless cases, been reduced or nullified by sin (*see* Rom. 1:18-21). And, besides, the coming of sin into the world and the establishment of the economy of redemption has necessitated the making known of truths not made known by general revelation. Therefore God has given the special revelation brought to us in the holy Scriptures. The Scriptures reiterate the truths proclaimed in nature, in history, and in man himself; and, in addition, declare the salvation that God has provided for mankind in Jesus Christ.

It is true that Scripture contains many things not in the nature of revelation—matters of fact, the knowledge of which lay within the reach of unaided human powers. But these are only the framework of the great revelation in connection with them. It is to be observed further that revelation is not to be confounded with inspiration. Revelation refers to the truths or facts that God has made known; inspiration to the process by which the knowledge has come. The proofs of revelation and of inspiration, however closely related and in some measure interwoven, are therefore not identical. *See* Inspiration.

The reality of special revelation is proved by evidence both external and internal. The external proof is found in miracles and prophecy. *See* Miracles; Prophecy.

The internal proofs are the contents of the revelation itself. The greatness of the truths, their adaptation to the necessities of human life, their practical effects when accepted, and above all the personal character of Jesus Christ, who is the center of the whole revelation and the supreme medium thereof, form sufficient proof

that the revelation of the Scriptures has come from God. Thus the revelation is to be recognized as the sun is known, by its own shining. It will not be recognized by those who ignore the reality of sin and the necessity for salvation. But to everyone who truly feels this sad reality, not only will the special revelation of salvation seem possible but also real and indispensable.

They who seek and find the salvation proclaimed by the Scriptures find a peculiar personal evidence of their divine authority. (*See* Assurance.) The term "continuous revelation" has come somewhat prominently into use in recent years. By this is commonly meant that special revelation did not cease with the closing of the Scripture canon.

BIBLIOGRAPHY: J. Orr, *Revelation and Inspiration* (1910); C. H. Dodd, *The Authority of the Bible* (1928); E. F. Scott, *The New Testament Idea of Revelation* (1935); F. W. Camfield, *Revelation and the Holy Spirit;* H. Cunliffe-Jones, *The Authority of the Biblical Revelation* (1945); A. G. Hebert, *The Authority of the Old Testament* (1947); H. W. Robinson, *Inspiration and Revelation in the Old Testament*; E. Brunner, *Revelation and Reason* (1946); K. Barth and E. Brunner, *Natural Theology* (1946); G. C. Berkouwer, *General Revelation,* Studies in Dogmatics (1955); J. Baillie, *The Idea of Revelation in Recent Thought* (1956); J. G. S. S. Thompson, *The Old Testament View of Revelation* (1960); J. I. Packer, *God Speaks to Man* (1965); M. C. Tenney, ed., *The Bible—Living Word of Revelation* (1968); C. F. H. Henry, in W. A. Elwell, ed., *Evangelical Dictionary of Theology* (1984), pp. 944-48.

REVELATION, BOOK OF THE. The last book of the NT and the consummation of biblical prophecy disclosing the future of the Jew, the Gentile, and the church of Christ. This great prophetic unfolding deals mainly with the events preceding the second coming of Christ, the establishment of the millennial kingdom, and, finally, the eternal state.

Name. The name of the book comes from Lat. *revelatio,* "an unveiling"; Gk. *apokalypsis,* "the removing of a veil." It is thus a book written to be understood. The book is not correctly called the Revelation of the apostle John. It is precisely "the Revelation of Jesus Christ" (1:1). That is, it is an unveiling of His future plan for the earth and for His redeemed saints both for time and eternity. It is necessary to view the book as in no sense sealed (22:10; cf. Dan. 12:9). A distinct blessing is vouchsafed to the person that reads and to those who hear the words of this prophecy (Rev. 1:3). It is mere pious chatter to say that God does not intend this book to be understood or that the symbolism and figures of the prophecy are incomprehensible. The figures and symbols of the book, which furnish the basis of its interpretation, are found elsewhere in divine revelation and can only be understood in the light of coherent and connected comparative study of all other lines of prophecy and prophetic type and symbolism. Interpretation of the book demands a thorough acquaintance with all the other great prophecies that merge in this book, which is "like a great Union Station where the trunk lines of prophecy come in from other portions of Scripture" (J. Vernon McGee, *Briefing the Bible* [1949], p. 122).

Great Themes. About a dozen great prophetic themes find their consummation in the book of the Revelation: (1) The Lord Jesus Christ (Gen. 3:15), whose present session (Rev. 3:21), future triumph over evil, redemption of the earth, destruction of the ungodly, and establishment of His earthly kingdom are consummated at His second advent (4:1–19:16). Christ's kingdom rule and His ministry in the eternal state (chaps. 21-22) constitute the grand fulfillment of all prophecy. (2) The church, the Body of Christ (Matt. 16:18; 1 Cor. 12:13; Rev. 2-3). (3) The resurrection and translation of saints (4:1-2). (4) The Great Tribulation (Deut. 4:29-30; Jer. 30:5-8; Rev. 4-19). (5) Satan and demon power (Isa. 14:12-14; Ezek. 28:11-18; Rev. 12:7-12; 16:13; 20:1; etc.). (6) The man of lawlessness (2 Thess. 2:1-8; Rev. 13:1-10). (7) The false prophet (Rev. 13:11-18). (8) Destruction of Gentile world power (Dan. 2:31-45; Rev. 5-19). (9) The redemption of the earth (Rev. 5) with the loosing of the seals, trumpets, and bowls (chaps. 6-19). (10) The second advent of Christ (Rev. 19:1-10). (11) The judgment of sinners (Rev. 20:11-15). (12) The first resurrection and the Kingdom age (Rev. 20:4-6). (13) The new heaven and the new earth (Rev. 21). (14) The eternal state (chap. 22).

Methods of Interpretation. Various interpretations of the book prevail.

The Preterist Interpretation. This views the book as referring chiefly to events contemporary to that day, to comfort the then-persecuted church, written in symbols in a general sense intelligible to the saints of that period.

Continuous Historical Interpretation. This considers the book as forecasting the entire period of church history from the revelator's time to the present, in which the chief phases of the church's struggle to final victory are set forth. This has been a commonly accepted view.

The Spiritualist Interpretation. This separates the symbolism of the book from any historical revelation and regards the book as a pictorial representation of the great principles of divine government for all-time application.

The Futuristic Interpretation. This construes the bulk of the book as future in John's day. It accepts the divinely given key of interpretation in Rev. 1:19 and interprets the "things which you have seen" as embracing 1:9-20; the "things which are," chaps. 2-3, referring to the church period; and the "things which shall be after these things" as referring to the yet future period after the glorification of the church and its removal from the earthly scene, with chaps. 4 to the end concerning chiefly Israel and the Gentile nations

in the still-future period preceding the second coming of Christ.

Background and Destination. The author is John the beloved (1:1). The apostle came to Ephesus around A.D. 70. He seems to have been a circuit minister at Ephesus, Pergamum, Smyrna, Thyatira, Sardis, Philadelphia, and Laodicea. He was put in prison on Patmos Isle in the Aegean in the fifteenth year of Domitian, according to Eusebius (*Ecclesiastical History* 3.18). The Apocalypse was doubtless intended especially for the seven churches of Asia (cf. 1:4 and 10-11 and chaps. 2-3). The book was also evidently intended for other churches in Asia Minor.

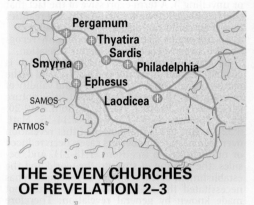

THE SEVEN CHURCHES OF REVELATION 2–3

Occasion and Date. John wrote by express command of Christ (1:10-20). The "angels" of the seven churches of chaps. 2-3 are apparently the "ministers" of those churches, and the apostle wrote to comfort them and their congregations. Quite a few scholars date the book about A.D. 68 or 69 (Westcott, Lightfoot, Hort, and Salmon). The reasons for this, however, are not convincing. The best date seems to be A.D. 95 or 96 (cf. Swete, Milligan, Moffatt, and Zahn). This date accords with evidence from Irenaeus, Clement of Alexandria, and Eusebius to the effect that the banishment to Patmos was in the later reign of Domitian, A.D. 81-96. This view is in agreement with the fact that the Domitian persecution, unlike the Neronic, was the result of the Christians' refusal to worship the emperor (cf. 1:9; 13:9-10, 12).

Authenticity. External witness to the book is sufficiently strong. Traces of the book are found in literature immediately after the apostolic age. Justin Martyr, Irenaeus, Tertullian, Hippolytus, Clement of Alexandria, Origen, the Muratorian Fragment, etc., lend their support to its genuineness. The internal evidence is also adequate. The writer calls himself John four times (1:1, 4, 9; 22:8). He calls himself the "bond-servant" of Christ (1:1) and "brother and fellow partaker in the tribulation and kingdom and perseverance which are in Jesus" (1:9). The fact that he does not call himself an apostle has been urged against authorship by John the apostle, but this argument is invalid to one who believes that the apostle is the author of the fourth gospel where the author's humility is reflected. The early church accepted the fact that it was John who was in exile, and the witness to the fact by Clement of Alexandria, Eusebius, and Irenaeus give this claim good support. The claim that grammatical irregularities of the Apocalypse rule out Johannine authorship are not sustained. Many factors, including the apocalyptic and highly figurative and symbolic meaning of the book, offer sufficient explanation of this phenomenon.

Outline.

I. Introduction and salutation (1:1-8)
II. "The things which you have seen": The glorified Christ (1:9-20)
III. "The things which are": The seven churches (2-3)
  A. The apostolic church: Ephesus (2:1-7)
  B. The persecuted church: Smyrna (2:8-11)
  C. The worldly church: Pergamum (2:12-17)
  D. The pagan church: Thyatira (2:18-29)
  E. The Protestant church: Sardis (3:1-6)
  F. The missionary church: Philadelphia (3:7-13)
  G. The apostate church: Laodicea (3:14-22)
IV. "What must take place after these things": The Great Tribulation and the second coming of Christ (4-22)
  A. The church in heaven with Christ (4)
    1. Loosing of the seven-sealed book (5)
  B. The Great Tribulation (6:1–11:19)
    1. The seven seals (6:1–8:1)
    2. The seven trumpets (8:2–11:19)
  C. The seven performers during the Great Tribulation (12-13)
    1. The woman: Israel (12:1-2)
    2. The red dragon: Satan (12:3-4)
    3. The male child: Christ (12:5-6)
    4. Michael, the archangel, wars with the dragon (12:7-12)
    5. Satan's persecution of the woman, Israel (12:13-16)
    6. The remnant of Israel (12:17)
    7. The Beast out of the sea: political power and a person (13:1-10)
    8. The Beast out of the earth: Antichrist (13:11-18)
  D. The latter part of the Great Tribulation (14)
  E. The seven bowls (15-16)
  F. Judgment of ecclesiastical and commercial Babylon (17-18)
  G. Christ's second advent (19)
  H. The Millennium (20)

I. Eternity unveiled (21-22)
  1. The new earth (21:1)
  2. The New Jerusalem (21:2-27)
  3. The new river (22:1-7)
V. Epilogue, final instructions and invitation (22:8-21)   M.F.U.

BIBLIOGRAPHY: W. Kelly, *Lectures on the Book of Revelation* (n.d.); R. H. Charles, *A Critical and Exegetical Commentary on the Revelation of St. John,* 2 vols., International Critical Commentary (1922); G. H. Lang, *The Revelation of Jesus Christ* (1945); W. Barclay, *The Revelation of John,* 2 vols. (1961); A. C. Gaebelein, *The Revelation* (1961); J. B. Smith, *A Revelation of Jesus Christ* (1961); G. B. Caird, *The Revelation of St. John the Divine,* Harper's New Testament Commentaries (1966); J. F. Walvoord, *The Revelation of Jesus Christ* (1966); F. C. Ottman, *The Unfolding of the Ages in the Revelation of John* (1967); F. A. Tatford, *The Patmos Letters* (1969); G. E. Ladd, *Commentary on the Revelation of John* (1972); G. R. Beasley-Murray, G. Raymond, H. H. Hobbs, and R. F. Robbins, *Revelation: Three Viewpoints* (1977); R. H. Mounce, *The Book of Revelation,* New International Commentary on the New Testament (1977); H. B. Swete, *Commentary on Revelation* (1977); W. M. Ramsay, *The Letters to the Seven Churches* (1978); R. C. Trench, *Commentary on the Epistle to the Seven Churches* (1978); R. Govett, *Govett on Revelation,* 4 vols. in 2 (1981); F. A. Tatford, *The Revelation* (1985).

REVELING. *See* Carousing.

REVENGE, REVENGER. *See* Avenge, Avenger.

REVENUE. *See* King.

REVERENCE. We are taught to reverence God (Pss. 89:7; "and awesome above all," NASB, cf. KJV; 111:9, "fear," KJV) and His sanctuary (Lev. 19:30, "revere," NASB; "have reverence for," NIV). *See* Fear.

Reverence in the sense of paying respect to some distinguished person is mentioned in the KJV in 2 Sam. 9:6; 1 Kings 1:31; Esther 3:2, 5 (where the NASB reads "prostrated" or "paid homage," and the NIV, "bowed down" and "paid honor"); in the parable of the vineyard (Matt. 21:37; Mark 12:6; Luke 20:13; "respect," NASB and NIV); and in Heb. 12:9; Eph. 5:33 of the respect given to fathers and husbands.

REVILE, REVILER, REVILING. The translation of several Gk. and Heb. terms. The Hebrews were warned not to "revile the gods" (KJV), or, more specifically, not to "curse God," as the NASB reads (from Heb. *qālal,* "be slight, trifling," and *'ĕlōhîm,* "gods, God"). Another Heb. term, *giddûpîm,* "vilification," or "reviling words," is used by Isaiah (Isa. 51:7; "insults," NIV) and Zephaniah (Zeph. 2:8) in reference to the revilings of men. Kindred to *giddûpîm* is the Gk. term *loidoreō,* which means to villify, heap reproach on, and is used to represent the treatment of the Lord by His enemies (John 9:28; 1 Pet. 2:23), the question put to Paul by the high priest (Acts 23:4), and the "revilers" (or "slanderers," NIV) in the catalog of evildoers (1 Cor.

6:10). In the expression "they that passed by reviled him" (KJV; "hurling abuse," NASB) the evangelist uses Gk. *blasphēmeō*, a very strong term, signifying to rail at, or calumniate, showing an utter lack of reverence for the divine Sufferer. In Mark 15:32 it is recorded that those who were crucified with Him "reviled him" (KJV), or "were casting the same insult at Him" (NASB; "heaped insults," NIV), both from Gk. *'oneidizō*, meaning that they unjustly reproached Him.

REVIVE (from Heb. *ḥāyâ*, to "live"). In the Psalms (71:20; 80:18; 119:25, 37, 40, 88; 143:11; etc.) the word is used to signify being "made alive," to be "comforted, refreshed." The KJV is *quicken* (which see).

REWARDS (Gk. *misthos*, meaning "hire, wage, reward," Matt. 5:12, 46; 6:1; 10:41; Mark 9:41; 1 Cor. 3:8; etc.). Rewards are offered by God to a believer on the basis of faithful service rendered after salvation. It is clear from Scripture that God offers to the *lost* salvation and for the faithful service of the *saved,* rewards. Often in theological thinking salvation and rewards are confused. However, these two terms must be carefully distinguished. Salvation is a free gift (John 4:10; Rom. 6:23; Eph. 2:8-9, whereas rewards are earned by works (Matt. 10:42; cf. Luke 19:17; 1 Cor. 9:24-25; 2 Tim. 4:7-8). Then, too, salvation is a present possession (Luke 7:50; John 5:24). On the other hand, rewards are future attainment to be dispensed at the second coming of Christ for His own (Matt. 16:27; 2 Tim. 4:8). Rewards will be dispensed at the judgment seat of Christ (2 Cor. 5:10; Rom. 14:10). The doctrine of rewards is inseparably connected with God's grace. A soul is saved on the basis of divine grace; there is no room for the building up of merit on the part of the believer. Yet God recognizes an obligation on His part to reward His saved ones for their service to Him. Nothing can be done to merit salvation, but what the believer has achieved for God's glory, God recognizes with rewards at the judgment seat of Christ. For the central passages on rewards *see* 1 Cor. 3:9-15 and 9:16-27; 2 Cor. 5:10. A principal point of contention between Roman Catholics and Protestants concerns the basis of reward. Roman Catholics hold that reward is based on the actual merit of the good works of believers, whereas Protestants regard rewards as wholly of grace.   M.F.U.

RE'ZEPH (re'zef; "glowing stone or coal"). A stronghold near Haran, taken by the Assyrians (2 Kings 19:12; Isa. 37:12). There were nine cities of this name. This was probably located W of the Euphrates, called now Rusafah, on the route to Palmyra.

REZI'A. *See* Rizia.

REZ'IN (rez'in).

1. A king of Damascus who was contemporary

with Pekah in Israel and with Jotham and Ahaz in Judah. Allying himself with Israel, he carried on constant war against Judah, attacking Jotham toward the close of his reign (2 Kings 15:37), 742 B.C. His chief war was with Ahaz, whose territories he invaded in company with Pekah, about 741 B.C. The combined army laid siege to Jerusalem, where Ahaz was, but "could not overcome him" (2 Kings 16:5; Isa. 7:1). Rezin, however, "recovered Elath for Aram" (2 Kings 16:6). Soon after this he was attacked, defeated, and slain by Tiglath-pileser III, king of Assyria (16:9). Compare Tiglath-pileser's own inscriptions, where the defeat of Rezin and the destruction of Damascus are distinctly mentioned.

2. One of the families of the Temple servants (Ezra 2:48; Neh. 7:50).

RE'ZON (re'zon; "prince"). The son of Eliada, a Syrian in the service of Hadadezer, king of Zobah. When David defeated Hadadezer (2 Sam. 8:3) Rezon forsook his lord and, gathering a band about him, established himself as king of Damascus (1 Kings 11:23-25). The settlement of Rezon at Damascus could not have been till some time after the disastrous battle in which the power of Hadadezer was broken, for we are told that David at the same time defeated the army of Damascene Syrians who came to the relief of Hadadezer and put troops in Damascus, about 984 B.C. From his position at Damascus, Rezon harassed the kingdom of Solomon during the latter part of his reign.

RHE'GIUM (re'ji-um; "broken off," alluding to the abrupt character of the coast). A town on the SW coast of Italy, at the southern entrance of the Strait of Messina, mentioned incidentally (Acts 28:13) in the account of Paul's voyage from Syracuse to Puteoli. It is now called Reggio, a city of about 165,000 inhabitants.

RHE'SA (re'sa). A name given in the genealogy of Christ (Luke 3:27) as the son of Zerubbabel and father of Joanan. He is probably the same as *Rephaiah* (which see).

RHO'DA (rō'da; "rose bush"). Servant girl who announced the arrival of Peter at the door of Mary's house after his release from the prison by the angel (Acts 12:13-14), 44 B.C.

RHODES (rōdz; "a rose"). An island in the Mediterranean Sea, near the coast of Asia Minor. Its capital was also called Rhodes and was an ancient center of commerce, literature, and art. It was built in the fifth century B.C. The Colossus, one of the wonders of the world, was erected at its harbor; the island is about eighteen miles broad and forty-six miles long. In the Middle Ages it was famous as the home of the Knights of St. John. Its population now is about 75,000. Paul touched here (Acts 21:1) on his return voyage to Syria from his third missionary journey, but it is not stated whether or not he landed.

RI'BAI (ri'bī; "my contention"). A Benjamite of Gibeah, whose son Ittai was one of David's mighty men (2 Sam. 23:29; 1 Chron. 11:31), 1000 B.C.

RIBAND (Num. 15:38, KJV). A cord (so NASB, NIV).

RIB'LAH (rib'la; "fertility," cf. Arab. *rabala,* "to increase, multiply").

1. A landmark on the eastern boundary of Israel, as given by Moses (Num. 34:11), the position being given with much precision. It was between Shepham and the Sea of Chinnereth, to the E of Ain (i.e., *the fountain*). This shows that it was different from Riblah of Hamath.

2. Riblah of Hamath (2 Kings 23:33; etc.), the camping ground of the kings of Babylon, from which they directed operations against Palestine and Phoenicia. Pharaoh Neco brought King Jehoahaz here in chains (*see* 25:6, 20, 21; Jer. 39:5-6; 52:9-10, 26-27). Riblah was W of the modern town of Rableh, on the Orontes River just N of the Lebanese border.

RICHES. This term is frequently used in a figurative sense to represent the gifts and graces of God's Holy Spirit, as, "Do you think lightly of the riches of His kindness," etc. (Rom. 2:4; cf. 9:23; Eph. 1:7, 18; 2:7; 3:8; Phil. 4:19).

RIDDLE (Heb. *ḥîdâ,* "tied" in a knot, "twisted"). Elsewhere "dark sentence," "hard question," "dark saying," etc. The Heb. word is derived from an Arab. root meaning "to bend off," "to twist," and is used for a proverb (Prov. 1:6), a song (Ps. 49:4; cf. 78:2), an oracle (cf. Num. 12:8), and a parable (Ezek. 17:2), as well as a riddle in our sense of the word (Judg. 14:12-19). Riddles were generally proposed in verse, like the celebrated riddle of Samson, which, however, was properly no riddle at all, because the Philistines did not possess the only clue on which the solution *could* depend. Keil (*Com.,* 1 Kings 10:1) says that a riddle is "a pointed saying which merely hints at a deeper truth, and leaves it to be guessed." According to Josephus (*Ant.* 8.5.3), Solomon was fond of the riddle. They were also known to the Egyptians and were used at banquets by Greeks and Romans. "Riddle" is used once in the NT (1 Cor. 13:12, marg., NASB; "poor reflection," NIV); being translated "dimly" (Gk. *ainugma,* an "obscure saying"). The gospel revelation is an enigma, "inasmuch as it affords to us no full clearness of light upon God's decrees, ways of salvation, etc., but keeps its contents sometimes in a greater, sometimes in a less degree (Rom. 11:33; 1 Cor. 2:9) concealed, bound up in images, similitudes, types, and the like forms of human limitation and human speech, and, consequently, is for us of a mysterious and *enigmatic nature,*

standing in need of future light, and vouchsafing *faith,* indeed, but not the external figure" (Meyer, *Com.,* ad loc.).

BIBLIOGRAPHY: A. B. Mickelsen, *Interpreting the Bible* (1963), pp. 199-211.

RIDER (Heb. *rōkēb*). It would seem natural that horses should have been used for riding as early as for work; and the book of Job clearly indicates such use in the description of the chase of the ostrich, "She laughs at the horse and his rider" (Job 39:18). The horse and chariot were introduced into the land of the Nile by the Hyksos invaders, c. 1750 B.C. Camels were widely domesticated by the time of Gideon (Judg. 6:5), about 1200 B.C., greatly facilitating desert mobility. By the Egyptians, Babylonians, and early Greeks, war chariots were used instead of cavalry, the drivers of the chariot horses being called "riders" (Ex. 15:1, 21). The Persians discovered the value of cavalry, in which the Hebrews were always deficient. White donkeys were ridden in the time of the Judges, and mules in the age of the kings, horses being generally reserved for chariots. *See* Army; Horses; Chariot.

RIGHTEOUSNESS (Heb. *ṣedeq;* Gk. *dikia*). Purity of heart and rectitude of life; being and doing right. The righteousness or *justice* (which see) of God is the divine holiness applied in moral government and the domain of law. As an attribute of God it is united with His holiness as being essential in His nature; it is legislative or rectoral, as He is the righteous governor of all creatures; and is administrative or judicial, as He is a just dispenser of rewards and punishments. The righteousness of Christ denotes not only His absolute perfection but is taken for His perfect obedience to the law and suffering the penalty thereof in our stead. It is frequently used to designate His holiness, justice, and faithfulness (Gen. 18:25; Deut. 6:25; Pss. 31:1; 119:137, 142; Isa. 45:23; 46:13; 51:5-8). The righteousness of the law is that obedience that the law requires (Rom. 3:10, cf. 19-20; 8:4). The righteousness of faith is the *justification* (which see) that is received by faith (3:21-28; 4:3-25; 5:1-11; 10:6-11; 2 Cor. 5:21; Gal. 2:21). The perfect righteousness of Christ is imputed to the believer when he accepts Christ as his Savior (1 Cor. 1:30; 2 Cor. 5:20-21).

BIBLIOGRAPHY: J. Denney, *The Death of Christ* (1982), pp. 100-102, 117-33.

RIGHT MIND (Gk. *sōphroneō*). The being of a sound mind, as of one who has ceased to be under the power of an evil one (Mark 5:15; Luke 8:35), the opposite of *ekstēnai,* to be beside one's self (2 Cor. 5:13), elsewhere the exercise of self-control, so as to (1) place a moderate estimate upon one's self (Rom. 12:3, "sound judgment") and (2) to curb one's passion (Titus 2:6, "sensible").

RIM'MON (rim'on; "pomegranate").

1. A Benjamite of Beeroth, whose sons, Baanah

and Rechab, murdered Ish-bosheth (2 Sam. 4:2-9), before 988 B.C.

2. A Syrian deity, Akkad. "a thunderer" (2 Kings 5:18), worshiped in Damascus. *See* Gods, False.

3. A town in the S of Judah (Josh. 15:32), allotted to Simeon (19:7; 1 Chron. 4:32); in each passage the name *Rimmon* follows that of Ain, also one of the cities of Judah and Simeon. The two are joined in Neh. 11:29 as *En-rimmon* (which see). The only other notice in the Bible is in Zech. 14:10. It is identified with the village Umm er-Rumāmīn ("mother of pomegranates"), about nine miles N of Beersheba.

4. One of the landmarks of the E boundary of Zebulun (Josh. 19:13) and described as reaching as far as Neah. It is probably identical with *Rimmono* (which see).

BIBLIOGRAPHY: F.-M. Abel, *Géographie de la Palestine* (1938), 2:437; Y. Aharoni, *The Land of the Bible* (1979), pp. 110, 257, 304, 441.

RIMMON'O (rim-on'ō). A city of Zebulun assigned to the Merarite Levites (1 Chron. 6:77). It is thought by some to be identical with the Rimmon "which stretches to Neah" (Josh. 19:13), although others believe that Dimnah (21:35) may have originally been Rimmon, as the D and R in Heb. are easily confused.

RIM'MON-METHO'AR (Josh. 19:13, KJV). *See* Rimmon, no. 4; Rimmono.

RIM'MON-PE'REZ (rim'on-pe'rez; "pomegranate of the breach"). One of the seventeen camping grounds (Num. 33:19) of the Israelites during their thirty-seven years of wandering about in the desert after leaving Kadesh (14:25). Of these seventeen places, Ezion-geber is the only one that can be pointed out with certainty.

RIM'MON, THE ROCK OF. The cliff or mountain pass to which the Benjamites fled when pursued after the slaughter at Gibeah. Six hundred reached it and maintained themselves there for four months, until they were released by the rest of the tribes (Judg. 20:45, 47; 21:13). It is mentioned as being in the wilderness, i.e., no doubt the desert that rises from Jericho to the mountains of Bethel (Josh. 16:1). Rimmon has been preserved in the village of Rammūn, about fifteen miles N of Jerusalem, which stands upon and around the summit of a conical limestone mountain and is visible from all directions.

RIMS. The NASB and NIV rendering in 1 Kings 7:33 of Heb. *gab*, "hollow," or "curved." It replaces KJV *nave*, the center or hub of a wheel. *See* Nave; Hub; Spoke.

RING. The ring was at a very ancient date a symbol of authority and dignity. That it was so among the ancient Egyptians is evident from the fact that Pharaoh gave his ring to Joseph (Gen. 41:42) as a token that he transferred to him the

exercise of royal authority. Such a transfer is twice related of Ahasuerus, once in favor of Haman and again in favor of Mordecai (Esther 3:10-11; 8:2). These were probably signet rings. A probable early instance of a signet ring is to be found in the history of Judah (Gen. 38:18, "seal"); but *ḥātham* signifies a signet ring worn on the hand or suspended by a cord from the neck (Jer. 22:24). In the NT the ring is a symbol of honor and dignity, though no longer of power and authority (Luke 15:22). A man "with a gold ring" (James 2:2, Gk. *chrusodaktulios*, "gold-ringed") was a man of wealth. The ring was generally worn on the fourth finger of the left hand, under the belief that a vein ran from that finger direct to the heart. The wearing of rings on the right hand was a mark of effeminacy, but they were frequently worn in considerable numbers on the left. *See* Jewelry; Tabernacle.

The Jordan River

RINGSTRAKED. The KJV term for the striped rams of Jacob's flock (Gen. 30:35; etc.).

RIN'NAH (rin'a; "a shout"). A son of Simeon, of the tribe of Judah (1 Chron. 4:20).

RIOT. *See* Dissipation; Carouse; Glutton.

RI'PHATH (ri'fath). The second son of Gomer, and grandson of Japheth (Gen. 10:3; 1 Chron. 1:6, in which latter passage the name *Diphath* is given by a clerical error).

RIS'SAH (ri'sa; "a ruin"). One of the stations of Israel in the wilderness (Num. 33:21-22), possibly to be located at el-Kuntilla, about thirty-five miles NW of Ezion-geber.

RITH'MAH (rith'ma; "broom plant"). An encampment of Israel (Num. 33:18-19), probably NE of Hazeroth.

RIVER. The rendering of seven Heb. words. In the case of some of them other terms are employed, such as *canal, stream, channel,* and *flood,* but in certain passages the word *river* stands as an equivalent for every one of them.

A Canal (Heb. *'ūbāl* from *yābal*, to "flow"). This term is used only in Dan. 8:2-3, 6.

Water Channel (Heb. *'āpîq*). This expression is applied to streams or rivers, with a primary respect to the channels, often in Palestine deep rock walls or ravines that contain or bind them; and so *channel* comes usually to be a quite suitable rendering for it (2 Sam. 22:16), though Keil and Delitzsch render it *beds* of the sea (Ps. 18:15; Isa. 8:7).

A River (Heb. *yeʾōr*). A word of Egyptian origin, and frequently used of the Nile, this term appears to have been the common designation for the Nile in Egypt. Subsequent writers, when speaking of the river of Egypt, generally borrow the same word, sometimes using it in the plural for the Nile and its branches (Isa. 7:18; Ezek. 29:3; "streams" in the NIV). The word is sometimes used of rivers or streams generally (2 Kings 19:24; Isa. 37:25; Dan. 12:5-6).

A Flowing Stream (Heb. *yûbal*). This expression, found only in Jer. 17:8, is identical with a Canal, above.

A Stream (Heb. *nāhār*). In a great number of passages, this expression stands for river in the strict and proper sense, being often applied to the Jordan, the Nile, and other rivers. As the Euphrates was the most eminent river in the East, it was often known simply as *hannāhār* ("the river"). Wherever the expression "the river" is used it is to be understood as the Euphrates (Gen. 31:21; Josh. 1:4; 24:2, 14-15; 2 Sam. 10:16; etc.).

A Wadi (Heb. *nahal*, "flowing"). This expression comes nearer to our *torrent* than to the deeper and steadier volume of water that properly bears the name of river; the term was applicable to the many temporary currents in Palestine and surrounding regions, which sometimes flow with great force after heavy rains, but soon become dry channels. The word thus came to mean both a stream and its channel, or *valley;* and sometimes it is applied to a valley or glen, apart altogether from the idea of a stream (Gen. 26:17). In Lev. 11:9-10, it is applied to the stream itself; while we have the "Wadi" and the "brook" Zered (Num. 21:12; Deut. 2:13; the NIV reads "Valley" in both verses), the "stream" and the "river" Jabbok (Gen. 32:23; Deut. 2:37), the "river" and "brook" Kishon (Judg. 4:7; 1 Kings 18:40; in the last references, "Valley," NIV).

A Gushing Fountain Stream (Heb. *peleg,* to "gush," or "flow over"). This expression is used for streams, without respect, apparently, to their size, but to the distribution of their waters through the land. It is used ten times in the Scripture, always in the poetical or prophetical books (Pss. 65:9; 119:136; Job 20:17; 29:6; Prov. 5:16; Isa. 30:25; etc.).

A Channel, Conduit (Heb. *teʿālâ*). The Heb. term is commonly rendered "conduit," or "aqueduct" (2 Kings 18:17; 20:20; Isa. 7:3; 36:2); once "waters" (Job 28:25); also rendered "channels" (Ezek. 31:4). It means simply a *channel,* or *conduit,* for conveying water.

A River, Stream. The Gk. word *potamos,*

"running water," corresponds to a River, and a Stream, above.

Figurative. "Rivers" and "waters" are frequently used in Scripture to symbolize abundance, as of the grace of God (Pss. 36:8; 46:4; Isa. 32:2; 41:18; John 7:38), of peace (Isa. 66:12), of good things of life (Job 20:17; 29:6), of God's providence (Isa. 43:19-20), affliction (Ps. 69:2; Isa. 43:2). The *fruitfulness* of trees planted by rivers is figurative of the permanent prosperity of the righteous (Ps. 1:3; Jer. 17:8). *Drying up* of rivers represents God's judgments (Isa. 19:1-8; Jer. 51:36; Nah. 1:4; Zech. 10:11), as does also their overflowing (Isa. 8:7-8; 28:2, 17; Jer. 47:2).

RIVER OF EGYPT (ē'jipt).
1. The Nile (Gen. 15:18). In the NASB and NIV the word "river" is found, referring especially to the E channel or Pelusiac branch.
2. The great wadi (Heb. *nahal,* called "the brook of Egypt"). The Heb. word *nahal* signifies a stream that flows rapidly in winter or in the rainy season. This is a desert stream, called now Wadi el-'Arish (Num. 34:5; Josh. 15:4, 47; 2 Kings 24:7; Ezek. 47:19). The NIV translates in all these passages "Wadi of Egypt."

RIZI'A (ri-zi'a; "delight"). One of the sons of Ulla, of the tribe of Asher (1 Chron. 7:39; "Rezia," KJV).

RIZ'PAH (riz'pa; "a live coal"). A concubine of King Saul. Rizpah was a foreigner, the daughter (or descendant) of Aiah, a Hivite. She is first mentioned as the subject of an accusation leveled against Abner (2 Sam. 3:7), 997 B.C. We next hear of her in the tragic story narrated in 21:1-11, the particulars of which are as follows: A famine, which lasted three successive years, induced David to seek the face of Jehovah and to ask the cause of the judgment. The Lord replied, "It is for Saul and his bloody house, because he put the Gibeonites to death." David therefore sent for the Gibeonites to inquire of them as to the wrong that had been done them by Saul and how he should make atonement for it. They asked for the crucifixion at Gibeah of seven men of Saul's sons. David granted the request, because, according to the law (Num. 35:33), bloodguiltiness resting upon the land could only be expiated by the blood of the criminal; thus David gave up to the Gibeonites two sons of Rizpah and five sons of Merab, the daughter of Saul. The victims were killed "at the beginning of barley harvest," about the middle of Nisan (our April) and their bodies hung in the full blaze of the summer sun until the fall of rain in October (2 Sam. 21:9-10). During all this time, without any tent to protect her and only a garment of sackcloth to rest upon, Rizpah watched the bodies and "allowed neither the birds of the sky to rest on them by day nor the beasts of the field by night" (v. 10), c. 970 B.C.

ROAD. Not only the trade but the migrations of

races from the most ancient times prove that journeys of great extent were made in early antiquity. Commerce and military expeditions necessitated the making of *roads* and paths, of which the earliest trace is perhaps to be found in the "king's highway" (Num. 20:17; 21:22). At first roads were mere tracks formed by caravans passing from one point to another; afterward regular paths were made by laying earth and stones. These roads were required by law, especially for the approaches to the cities of refuge (Deut. 19:3). In earlier times the roads between different cities were in a miserable condition, hardly passable in winter or in the rainy season, though the hard, rocky ground in the mountainous parts of Palestine made it easy to construct good roads. The king's highway, mentioned above, was the public road—probably constructed at the royal cost and kept up for the king and his armies to travel upon. Perhaps toll was taken for the king from the trading caravans. Regular military roads provided with milestones were first constructed in Palestine by the Romans. Jacob and his family traveled a well-known road from Beersheba to Egypt—the middle, or "Shur road," portions of which have been found. The Hebrews probably became acquainted with road making in Egypt, where, in the Delta especially, the nature of the country would require roads and highways to be thrown up and maintained.

Six roads in Palestine are worthy of mention, three connecting areas outside of Jerusalem, and three leading from Jerusalem: (1) The first road ran from Ptolemais, on the coast of the Mediterranean, to Damascus, which remains to this day. (2) The second passed along the Mediterranean coast southward to Egypt. Beginning at Ptolemais, it ran first to Caesarea, thence to Disopolis, then through Ascalon and Gaza down into Egypt, with a branch through Disopolis to Jerusalem. Down this branch Paul was sent on his way to Felix (Acts 23:23). (3) The third connected Galilee with Judea, running through the intervening Samaria (Luke 17:11; John 4:4). The journey from Galilee to Judea took three days. (4) The fourth, fifth, and sixth were the three chief roads running from Jerusalem: (a) One ran in the NE direction over the Mount of Olives, by Bethany, through openings in hills and winding ways on to Jericho (Matt. 20:29; 21:1; Luke 10:30; 19:1, 28-29, 37), crossing the Jordan into Perea. This was the road taken by the Galilean Jews in coming to and returning from Jerusalem in order to avoid the unfriendly Samaritans. It was the one over which the Israelites came into Canaan, and by which the Syrian and Assyrian armies advanced on Israel (2 Kings 8:28; 9:14; 10:32-33; 1 Chron. 5:26). (b) Another ran from Jerusalem southward to Hebron, between mountains and through pleasant valleys, whence travelers went through the wilderness of Judea to Aila, as the remains of a Roman road still show; or took a

westerly direction on to Gaza, a way still pursued, which is of two days' duration. (c) Still another went from Jerusalem to the Mediterranean at Joppa (Jaffa) and has been used since the time of the Crusades, by pilgrims to the holy city from Europe and Egypt.

The Jericho road

The *highway* (Heb. *mesillâ*, "an embanked highway, a thoroughfare") was frequently prepared for temporary purposes, such as the visit of royalty (Isa. 45; 62:10), and also for permanent use (Num. 20:19; Judg. 20:31; 1 Sam. 6:12; etc.).

BIBLIOGRAPHY: W. W. Mooney, *Travel Among the Ancient Romans* (1920); M. P. Charlesworth, *Trade Routes and Commerce of the Roman Empire* (1924); H. P. Vowles, *Roads and Road Construction* 7 (1929): 85ff.; R. J. Forbes, *Notes on the History of Ancient Roads and Their Construction* (1934); id., *Studies in Ancient Technology* 11 (1955): 126-76; W. F. Leemans, *Foreign Trade in the Old Babylonian Period* (1960); P. Fustier, *The Roads That Led to Rome* (1967).

ROADMARKS (Heb. *ṣiyyûn*, "conspicuous"). Pillars to mark the road for returning exiles (Jer. 31:21). Caravans set up *pillars* or pointed *heaps* of stone to mark the way through the desert against their return.

ROAST. See Food.

ROASTED GRAIN (Heb. *qālî*, "roasted"). Roasted ears or grains of wheat (Lev. 23:14; Ruth 2:14; 1 Sam. 17:17; 25:18; "parched corn," KJV). In 2 Sam. 17:28 the word occurs twice, once as parched grain and once as parched seeds ("parched corn," "parched pulse," KJV).

ROB, ROBBER, ROBBERY. These words are each the rendering of a number of Heb. and Gk. words. Theft and plunder, systematically organized, have ever been principal employments of the nomad tribes of the East since Ishmael the Bedouin became a "wild donkey of a man" and a robber by trade (Gen. 16:12), and robbery has been considered in the highest degree creditable. In the singular history of Abimelech we are told that "the men of Shechem set men in ambush against him on the tops of the mountains, and they robbed all who might pass by them along the road" (Judg. 9:25). Job suffered serious loss from a predatory incursion of the Chaldeans (Job 1:17), as did the people of Keilah, a lowland Judean town, from the Philistines (1 Sam. 23:1). Other instances are recorded of invasions of spoilers (Judg. 2:14; 6:3-4; 1 Sam. 11, 15; 2 Sam. 8, 10; 2 Kings 5:2; 1 Chron. 5:10, 18-22; etc.).

The Mosaic law strictly forbade robbery, as it did other wrongs against others (Lev. 19:13; *see* Law of Moses), and robbery was denounced in the Proverbs (22:22) and by the prophets (Isa. 10:2; 17:14; Ezek. 22:29; 33:15). Hosea (Hos. 6:9) compares the apostate priests to "raiders" who "wait for a man."

In NT times, civilization and Roman power had done much to subdue these predatory hordes; but even then we learn from the parable of the good Samaritan what was to be expected by travelers; and the road from Jerusalem to Jericho was as dangerous a few years ago as in the time of our Lord. Paul mentions "dangers from robbers" (2 Cor. 11:26), and it would appear that he was especially subject to dangers of this kind while passing through Pisidia. These were *plunderers, brigands* (Gk. *lēstēs*), not to be confounded with *thief* (Gk. *kleptēs*), one who takes property by stealth (John 10:8, where both are mentioned).

Luke, in describing the uproar in Ephesus (Acts 19:23-41), says that the clerk of the city, in endeavoring to appease the multitude, told them that Paul and his companions were neither "robbers of temples nor blasphemers of our goddess." The Gk. term used for "robbers of temples" is *hierosulos* (*temple despoiler*), used in its verbal form, "do you rob temples" (Rom. 2:22). The plundering of heathen temples was indirectly forbidden to the Jews (Deut. 7:25).

The apostle Paul, speaking of Christ Jesus (Phil. 2:6), says, "Who, although He existed in the form of God, did not regard equality with God a thing to be grasped" (Gk. *harpagmos,* the act of *seizing,* with the secondary sense of *a thing to be seized;* cf. KJV).

BIBLIOGRAPHY: H. B. Clark, *Biblical Law* (1944); G. Mendenhall, *Law and Covenant in the Ancient Near East* (1955); R. deVaux, *Ancient Israel: Its Life and Institutions* (1961), pp. 143-63; S. Mendelsohn, *Criminal Jurisprudence of the Ancient Hebrews* (1968).

ROBE. *See* Dress; High Priest, Dress of.

ROBO'AM. *See* Rehoboam.

ROCK.

Figurative. A rock is illustrative of God, as the Creator of His people (Deut. 32:18); as the strength of His people (32:4; 2 Sam. 22:2-3; Pss. 18:1-2; 62:7; Isa. 17:10); as their defense and refuge (Pss. 31:2-3; 94:22; etc.), and salvation (Deut. 32:15; Pss. 89:26; 95:1).

ROCK, CHRIST THE. As a Rock, Christ is portrayed as smitten that the Spirit of life may flow from Him to all who will drink (John 4:13-14; 7:27-39; 1 Cor. 10:4; Ex. 17:6). To the church, Christ as the Rock is the foundation (Matt. 16:18) and the chief cornerstone (Eph. 2:20). To the Jews at the first advent, Christ the Rock was a "stumbling stone" (Rom. 9:32; cf. Ps. 118:22; 1 Cor. 1:23). To Israel at the second advent, Christ will be the "top stone" (Zech. 4:7). To the Gentile world governments, Christ the Rock will be the stone "cut out without hands" (Dan. 2:34). As the Rock, Christ will be the stone that will fill the whole earth in the Kingdom age after the destruction of the Gentile world power. To unbelievers, Christ the Rock is a crushing stone of judgment (Matt. 21:44). M.F.U.

ROCK BADGER. *See* Animal Kingdom.

ROCK OF ESCAPE (Heb. *sela'hammaḥleqōt;* "cliff of divisions"). A rock in the wilderness of Maon and the scene of one of David's most remarkable escapes from Saul (1 Sam. 23:28). Not identified with certainty. The KJV and NIV readings for this place are transliterations of the Heb. text.

ROD. The rendering of several Heb. words and one Gk. term.

1. A stick for punishment (Heb. *shēbeṭ,* Ex. 21:20; 2 Sam. 7:14; Job 9:34; Prov. 10:13; Isa. 11:4) and, in a few instances, a shepherd's staff (Ezek. 20:37; Mic. 7:14, "scepter").

Figurative. "He who spares his rod hates his son" (Prov. 13:24) and "the rod and reproof give wisdom" (29:15) are proverbs in which *rod* is used as a figure for *punishment.* "I shall make you pass under the rod" (Ezek. 20:37; "staff," NIV) refers to a custom among shepherds who let the sheep pass under their shepherd's rod for the purpose of counting them and seeing whether they are in good condition or not. The figure is here applied to God, who will cause His flock, the Israelites, to pass under the rod, i.e., to be taken into His special care. Rod is used as a symbol of power and authority (Ps. 2:9), and of afflictions as the means by which God disciplines His people (Job 9:34).

2. A walking staff (Heb. *maṭṭeh,* "branch"; elsewhere "staff," Ex. 4:2; 7:9; 1 Sam. 14:27, 43). In the case of Moses and Aaron the rod was a shepherd's staff, belonging to Moses but sometimes employed by Aaron in performing miracles. It was also called "the staff of God" (Ex. 4:20; 17:9), probably because through it Jehovah wrought wonders. Aaron's priesthood was confirmed by a miracle calculated to silence the murmurings of the people. God commanded Moses to take twelve rods from the tribal princes of Israel and to write upon each the name of the tribe. As only twelve rods were taken for all the tribes of Israel, and Levi was included among them,

Ephraim and Manasseh must have been reckoned as the one tribe of Joseph (*see* Num. 17:1-10). The rods were to be laid in the Tabernacle before the Ark of the Covenant; and there the rod of the man whom Jehovah chose, i.e., entrusted with the priesthood (Num. 16:5), would put forth shoots. On the following morning "the rod of Aaron for the house of Levi had sprouted and put forth buds and produced blossoms, and it bore ripe almonds" (Num. 17:1-9; cf. Heb. 9:4).

Eastern shepherd holding a rod

3. Paul, in recounting his afflictions, writes (2 Cor. 11:25), "Three times I was beaten with rods" (Gk. *hrabdizō*, "to strike with a stick"), i.e., bastinadoed.

Using rods as a means of divination was a common heathen practice. *See* Magic: Rhabdomancy.

ROE, ROEBUCK. *See* Animal Kingdom: Doe; Gazelle; Roebuck.

RO'GELIM (rō'ge-lim; "treaders," i.e., "fullers"). A town in Gilead, the residence of Barzillai (2 Sam. 17:27; 19:31). Nothing further is known respecting it.

ROH'GAH (rō'ga). The second son of Shemer, of the tribe of Asher, and fifth in descent from that patriarch (1 Chron. 7:34), about 1440 B.C.

ROLL, ROLL OF A BOOK. *See* Scroll; Book. The

Heb. term in Isa. 8:1 (KJV) is different from those elsewhere translated *roll* and is given as *tablet* in the NASB and *scroll* in the NIV. The "house of rolls" (Ezra 6:1, KJV) evidently was the royal library and was made up of clay tablets. The NASB and NIV read "archives."

ROLLER (Heb. *hittûl*, "swathed"). A bandage (so NASB; the NIV reads "splint") wrapped around a broken limb (Ezek. 30:21).

ROMAM'TI-E'ZER (rō-mam'ti-e'zer; "I have raised a help"). One of the sons of Heman the seer. In the arrangement of the Temple service by David, Romamti-ezer was appointed head of the twenty-fourth section, consisting of twelve persons of his family (1 Chron. 25:4, 31), a little before 960 B.C.

RO'MAN. A designation referring (1) to a citizen of the Roman Empire (Acts 22:25-29; 23:27; *see* Citizenship, no. 2), (2) to an inhabitant of Rome (cf. Acts 2:10), and (3) to those who represent the Roman government (John 11:48; Acts 28:17).

RO'MAN EMPIRE. The government of the Romans under the emperors, beginning with Augustus, as well as the territory controlled by the Romans.

Its Inauguration. By the victory of Actium (31 B.C.), Octavianus became the undisputed master of the Roman world; but he shrank from taking the name of king or dictator, which were repugnant to the Roman people. But long before he had taken the title of Caesar and now allowed himself to be called Augustus, retaining the old official title of imperator. He was in theory simply the first citizen of the Republic, entrusted with temporary powers to settle the disorders of the state. The empire was nominally elective, but practically it passed by adoption, the emperors officially adopting their political successors. The Julio-Claudian line ruled from 31 B.C. to A.D. 68, the Flavians from 69 to 96, and the "Five Good Emperors" from 96 to 180. And until Nero's time a sort of hereditary right seemed to have been recognized.

Extent. Before the conquests of Pompey and Caesar the Roman Empire was confined to a narrow strip encircling the Mediterranean Sea. Pompey added Asia Minor and Syria; Caesar added Gaul. The generals of Augustus overran the northwestern portion of Spain and the country between the Alps and the Danube. The boundaries were now the Atlantic on the W; the Euphrates on the E; the deserts of Africa, the cataracts of the Nile, and the Arabian deserts on the S; the British Channel, the Rhine, the Danube, and the Black Sea on the N. The only subsequent conquests of importance were those of Britain by Claudius and Dacia by Trajan. The population of the empire at the time of Augustus has been calculated at 85 million.

The Provinces. The usual fate of a country

conquered by Rome was to become a subject province, governed directly from Rome by officers sent out for that purpose. Sometimes, however, petty sovereigns were left in possession of a nominal independence (e.g., Herod in Palestine). There were differences, too, in the political condition of cities within the provinces. Some were free cities, i.e., were governed by their own magistrates and were exempted from occupation by a Roman military post. Other cities were "colonies," i.e., communities of Roman citizens transplanted, like garrisons of the imperial city, into a foreign land. Augustus divided the provinces into two classes: (1) imperial and (2) senatorial, retaining in his own hands, for obvious reasons, those provinces where the presence of a large military force was necessary and committing the peaceful and unarmed provinces to the Senate. The imperial provinces at first were: Gaul, Lusitania, Syria, Phoenicia, Cilicia, Cyprus, and Egypt. The senatorial provinces were: Africa, Numidia, Asia, Achaia, and Epirus, Dalmatia, Macedonia, Sicily, Crete, and Cyrene, Bithynia and Pontus, Sardinia, Baetica. Cyprus and Gallia Narbonensis were subsequently given up by Augustus, who in turn received Dalmatia from the Senate. Many other changes were made afterward. The NT writers invariably designate the governors of senatorial provinces by the correct title of *anthupatoi,* proconsuls (Acts 13:7; 18:12; 19:38). For the governor of an imperial province, properly styled "Legatus Caesaris," the word *hēgemōn* (governor) is used in the NT. The provinces were heavily taxed for the benefit of Rome and her citizens. They are said to have been better governed under the empire than under the Republic, and those of the emperor better than those of the Senate. Two important changes were introduced under the empire. The governors received a fixed pay, and the term of their command was prolonged. The condition of the Roman Empire at the time when Christianity appeared has often been dealt with as affording obvious illustrations of the apostle Paul's expression that the "fulness of time came" (Gal. 4:4). The general peace within the limits of the empire, the formation of military roads, the suppression of piracy, the march of the legions, the voyages of the grain fleets, the general increase of traffic, the spread of the Latin language in the West as Greek had already spread in the East, and the external unity of the empire offered facilities up to this time unknown for the spread of worldwide religion. The tendency, too, of a despotism like that of the Roman Empire to reduce all its subjects to a dead level was a powerful instrument in breaking down the pride of privileged races and national religions and familiarizing men with the truth of "the God who made the world and all things in it" (Acts 17:24, 26). But still more striking than this outward preparation for the diffusion of the gospel was the appearance of a deep and widespread corruption that seemed to defy any human remedy. The chief prophetic notices of the Roman Empire are found in the book of Daniel.

BIBLIOGRAPHY: T. Arnold, *History of Rome,* 3 vols. (1848); id., *History of the Later Roman Commonwealth,* 2 vols. (1849); J. B. Bury, *History of the Roman Empire from Its Foundation to the Death of Marcus Aurelius* (1896); S. Dill, *Roman Society from Nero to Marcus*

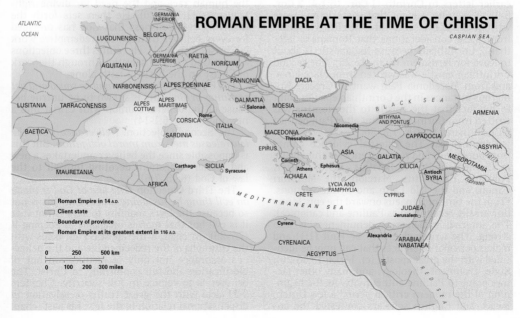

ROMAN EMPIRE AT THE TIME OF CHRIST

Aurelius (1905); G. H. Stevenson, *Roman Provincial Administration to the Age of the Antonines* (1939); J. B. Bury, *The Decline and Fall of the Roman Empire* (1958); R. MacMullen, *Enemies of the Roman Order* (1967); A. N. Sherwin-White, *The Roman Citizenship* (1973).

ROMANS, EPISTLE TO. The greatest of Paul's epistles and considered by many as the greatest book in the NT. Galatians has been called the "Magna Charta" of Christian liberty and the Roman epistle has been called the "constitution" of Christianity. Its subject material, its logical reasoning, its vigor of style, and its relevance to human need give it a foremost place in biblical revelation. It is a book, in one sense, simple and clear, but in another sense so magnificent that it baffles complete comprehension.

Occasion. The epistle appears to have been occasioned by the apostle's interest in the church at Rome. He tells us that he intended to pay a visit in the near future (Acts 19:21; Rom. 1:13; 15:22-29). The fact that Phoebe, a deaconess of the church at Cenchraea, was going to Rome presented an opportunity to send the epistle to the Christians in that city (16:1-2). Paul was all the more compelled to write to this church since it had come into existence apparently without authoritative leadership and needed thorough instruction in the fundamentals of salvation.

Date. The letter was written in Corinth during Paul's three-month visit in Greece (Acts 20:2-3). This fact is made evident by reference to the apostle's journey to Jerusalem with a collection for the poor at the time of writing (Rom. 15:25-27). Since this collection was emphasized in the earlier letters to Corinth (1 Cor. 16:1-4; 2 Cor. 8-9), it is quite evident that these letters were written about the same time. It clearly appears from these considerations that Romans is later than 2 Corinthians because the apostle is about to leave for Jerusalem (Rom. 15:25). The second Corinthian epistle was written from Macedonia, and from Macedonia Paul went to Greece. Numerous instances in the Corinthian epistles point to the fact that the epistle to the Romans was written from Corinth not long after Paul penned 2 Corinthians, that is, A.D. 56.

Genuineness. The external evidence comes from quotations and reminiscences of this epistle in Clement of Rome, Ignatius, Justin Martyr, Polycarp, Hippolytus, Marcion, the Muratori Canon, and the Old Latin and Syriac versions. From the time of Irenaeus onward the epistle was universally recognized as Pauline and canonical. The internal evidence of genuineness is also strong. The writer claims to be Paul (1:1) and makes personal references that can only be identified with the great apostle (cf. 11:13; 15:15-20). Style, argument, theology, and many other factors point to Pauline authenticity. At the beginning of the modern critical period a few Dutch, Swiss, and English scholars contested the au-

thenticity of the book on the ground that the apostle was acquainted with so many individuals by name in a city where he had never been (*see* chap. 16). But this argument has been repeatedly shown to be weak because travel was extensive in Paul's day, and he probably met these individuals elsewhere in the empire before they went to Rome to live.

Background. The origin of Christianity in Rome must be traced to converts scattered throughout the empire who came to visit or live in the imperial city. That Peter was the founder of the church is indefensible since it would be unthinkable that Paul would omit his name if he had been bishop in the city. It is possible that the sojourners at Jerusalem on the Day of Pentecost (Acts 2:10) may also have been instrumental in the founding of the Roman church. Some critics have denied the authenticity of chaps. 15 and 16, but there is no valid internal evidence supporting this, neither is there support for it in the ancient manuscripts. Moreover, his greeting of many persons by name was a studied effort to establish rapport with a church he had never met. Such greetings of individuals would have been unnecessary and unwise in writing Philippians, Corinthians, Ephesians, and others. Furthermore, any omission of members of the church would have incurred the risk of offending someone in the churches with which Paul was familiar. In this case, however, omissions would have hurt no one because he could not possibly have known all the members of the church.

Contents. After introductory matters, the apostle demonstrates the universal sinfulness of the human race and the need for divine righteousness (1:18–3:20). He then sets forth the justifying righteousness that God has provided for every believer through the redemptive work of Christ (3:21–5:11). He refutes three objections against God's way of salvation through the work of Christ on the basis of faith alone.

The First Objection. *Men may be saved and yet continue in sin.* This is shown to be untrue because of the believer's union with Christ into a new moral life (6:1-14).

The Second Objection. *Deliverance from the law releases men from moral obligation.* But this is impossible since the believer undertakes a new and higher obligation, devoting himself to the law of God (6:15–7:6).

The Third Objection. *The law of God is made an evil thing by justifying grace.* But this is not so because the law's inability to save is not that it is evil but that man is incapable of keeping it (7:7-25). In chap. 8 the apostle Paul deals with the triumphs of the redeemed life and the believer's assurance not only of justification but of glorification and full conformity to Christ. The believer is to rejoice in full security. Chapters 9-11 deal with the great truths of salvation in dispensational relation to the Jew: his past (chap.

9), his present (chap. 10), his future (chap. 11). The rest of the epistle consists of exhortations to Christian living (chap. 12), to the doing of civil and social duties (chap. 13), and living according to Christian love and unity (14:1–15:13), ending with personal salutations (15:14–16:27).

Outline.

I. Introduction (1:1-15)
II. Doctrinal exposition (1:16 – 8:39)
   A. The theme (1:16-17)
   B. Justification expounded (1:18 –5:11)
   C. Sanctification expounded (5:12–8:39)
III. Dispensational harmonization (9–11)
   A. Israel's present rejection (9:1-5)
   B. Israel's rejection justified (9:6-29)
   C. Israel's rejection explained (9:30 – 10:21)
   D. Israel's rejection in its extent (11:1-10)
   E. Israel's rejection terminated (11:11-32)
   F. Exultation and praise (11:33-36)
IV. Practical exhortation (12:1–15:13)
   A. The Christian's relation to consecration (12:1-2)
   B. The Christian's relation to God's gifts (12:3-8)
   C. The Christian's relation to fellow Christians (12:9-16)
   D. The Christian's relation to mankind in general (12:17-21)
   E. The Christian's relation to civil government (13:1-14)
   F. The Christian's relation to a weak brother (14:1–15:13)
V. Conclusion (15:14 –16:27)

BIBLIOGRAPHY: C. J. Vaughan, *St. Paul's Epistle to the Romans* (1873); W. Sanday and A. C. Headlam, *A Critical and Exegetical Commentary on the Epistle to the Romans,* International Critical Commentary (1895); C. H. Dodd, *The Epistle of Paul to the Romans,* Moffat New Testament Commentary (1932); K. Barth, *The Epistle to the Romans* (1933); R. C. H. Lenski, *The Interpretation of St. Paul's Epistle to the Romans* (1936); C. Hodge, *Commentary on the Epistle to the Romans* (1950); C. K. Barrett, *A Commentary on the Epistle to the Romans,* Harper's New Testament Commentary (1957); R. Haldane, *Exposition of the Epistle to the Romans* (1959); J. Murray, *The Epistle to the Romans,* 2 vols., New International New Testament Commentary (1959-65); M. Luther, *Lectures on Romans,* trans. W. Pauck (1961); F. F. Bruce, *The Epistle of Paul to the Romans,* Tyndale New Testament Commentaries (1963); M. Black, *Romans,* New Century Bible (1973); M. Luther, *Commentary on the Epistle to the Romans,* trans. J. T. Mueller (1976); E. H. Gifford, *The Epistle of St. Paul to the Romans* (1977); F. L. Godet, *Commentary on Romans* (1977); H. P. Liddon, *Explanatory Analysis of St. Paul's Epistle to the Romans* (1977); H. C. G. Moule, *Studies in Romans* (1977); W. G. T. Shedd, *A Critical Commentary on the Epistle of St. Paul to the Romans* (1978); R. C. Stedman, *From Guilt to Glory,* 2 vols. (1978); E. Käsemann, *Commentary on Romans* (1980); H. C. G. Moule, *The Epistle to the Romans* (1982); H. Olshausen, *Studies in the Epistle to the Romans* (1983).

ROME (Lat. *Roma*). One of the most famous cities of the world. Its name was once a synonym for political power and territorial expansion.

Founding. The story of origin of the city is mythological rather than historical. Romulus, its founder and first king, was according to tradition the son of Mars and was preserved, when cast out by his cruel relatives, through the kind attention of a wolf and a shepherd's wife.

The foundation of Rome traditionally dates from 753 B.C. It takes its name, according to Cicero, from the name of its founder, Romulus. It was located upon marshy ground by the river Tiber, in Italy, about seventeen miles from the Mediterranean Sea, into which the Tiber flows. The Tiber itself is navigable only for small provision boats.

Originally the settlement of Rome was confined to the Palatine hill, but it came to include the Capitoline, Quirinal, Caelian, Aventine, Esquiline, and the Viminal. Servius Tullius was supposed to have enclosed the whole seven hills with a stone wall. Hence it has been called *Urbs Septicollis,* "the city of the seven hills."

Early Monarchy. The monarchical government existed under seven princes according to the early traditional accounts: Romulus, Numa Pompilius, Tullus Hostilius, Ancus Marcius, Tarquinius Priscus, Servius Tullius, and Tarquin the Proud, who was expelled in 509 B.C. Apparently the last three kings were Etruscans, who did more than the Latins would have admitted for the development of the city. They seem to have been responsible for the urbanization process, for draining of swamps, the introduction of various trades, and the development of commerce.

Republic. The abolition of the kingly office and the rule of alien princes were succeeded by a period of government under consuls. Two consuls were elected annually from the patrician families until 367 B.C. when the first plebeian consul was created. The two consuls had equal authority, and together they possessed full authority as the chief executives. Gradually other magistrates were elected as the need arose to create additional departments of government. New assemblies were established also and shared power with the Senate.

Empire. Under the monarchical period and under the Republic the power of Rome steadily increased, and the foundations for the later empire were laid. By 266 Italy was subjugated as far N as the Po Valley. The Punic Wars took place between 264 and 146 B.C., resulting in the destruction of Carthage in 146 and domination of the western basin of the Mediterranean. Between 200 and 146 Rome destroyed Macedonia and worsted the Seleucids, annexing Greece and dominating the eastern basin of the Mediterranean. Gradually she took chunks of territory in the eastern Mediterranean and organized them into provinces. Pompey added Palestine in 63 B.C. For numerous complex reasons Rome endured a period of civil war during much of the first century B.C. Julius Caesar (who had conquered Gaul) fought it out with Pompey and made himself dictator. When Caesar was assassinated in 44 B.C., Brutus and Cassius and others responsible were dispatched by Mark Antony and Octavian, who subsequently fought each other for control of the empire. Octavian won at the battle of Actium in 31 B.C., added Egypt to the territory he controlled, and terminated the Republic and instituted the empire. As Augustus he then ruled until A.D. 14. He was the first of the Julio-Claudian line, which lasted until A.D. 68.

The Arch of Titus, Rome

Jesus was born during the reign of Augustus and the NT era inaugurated. Under Tiberius (14-37) occurred the ministry of John the Baptist and Jesus. Caligula followed (37-41), succeeded by Claudius (41-54). During Claudius's reign Britain was conquered, and Paul conducted his great missionary campaigns. Under Nero (54-68) Rome was burned, the Christians were persecuted, and Paul was martyred. The death of the infamous Nero inaugurated another struggle for power. The result was that Vespasian won and began the Flavian line. Three Flavian emperors ruled: Vespasian (69-79), during whose reign Jerusalem revolted and was destroyed in A.D. 70, Titus (79-81), and Domitian (81-96). Under the latter, persecution of Christians took place, and John evidently was exiled to the Isle of Patmos and wrote the Revelation.

This period was followed by an era of expanding power. Nerva ruled 96-98; Trajan 98-117, conquering Mesopotamia and bringing the empire to its greatest extent; and Hadrian 117-138, when Jerusalem was rebuilt as a pagan city called Aelia Capitolina. Persecution of Christians heightened during the third century. Diocletian (284-305) was the most intense persecutor. After his death there was another clash for power. Constantine the Great became sole ruler from 323 to 337. His conversion made Christianity a legal religion, and persecution ceased.

The City in Paul's Day. When Paul came to Rome, it was a sprawling metropolis of more than 1 million people. It was indeed not only the first city of the empire but the largest and most splendid city of the day. The metropolis was served by many famous roads, including the well-known and ancient Via Appia and Via Latina from the S, the Via Labicana and Via Tiburtina on the E, the Via Salaria, Via Pinciana, and the Via Flaminia from the N, the Via Cornelia and Via Aurelia from the W.

Buildings. Theaters, amphitheaters, baths, circuses, and luxurious private dwellings filled the city. The populace had much leisure. There were no less than 159 holidays in the year. Of these 93 were devoted to games and performances at governmental expense. In the circus the famous chariot races were held. The oldest and largest was the Circus Maximus, which Paul must have passed by after entering the Porta Capena on the Appian Way. This circus at the time of Nero probably seated about 200,000 people. The Circus Flaminius, built in the third century B.C., the Circus of Caligula, and the Circus of Nero were famous for chariot racing and other sports. The famous theaters included the Theater of Pompey, built in 55 B.C., the Theater of Balbus (13 B.C.) seating 7,700, the well-preserved Theater of Marcellus (11 B.C.), seating 14,000. The Flavian Amphitheater, or Colosseum, had not yet been constructed. The Baths of Titus and the Baths of Trijan were not yet built, but there were numerous public baths in the city as early as the beginning of Augustus's reign.

The Forum. In the valley lying between the Capitoline and Palatine hills was the Forum, surrounded by many famous buildings. The Roman emperor resided on the Palatine Hill. In addition to the imperial palace, the Palatine Hill was the site of the famous temple of Apollo and the temple of the Magna Mater, or Cybele.

The city was adorned by many fine parks and gardens, one-eighth of the area being given over to these beauty spots. Amidst this wealth and beauty were scores of temples given over to superstitious idolatry. To such a city came the apostle to the Gentiles with the saving message of the gospel of Christ.   H.F.V.

BIBLIOGRAPHY: A. J. Church, *Roman Life in the Days of Cicero* (1884); W. W. Fowler, *Social Life at Rome in the*

The Forum, Rome

Age of Cicero (1908); E. Hamilton, *The Roman Way* (1932); J. Carcopino, *Daily Life in Ancient Rome* (1966); J. P. V. D. Balsdon, *Life and Leisure in Ancient Rome* (1974).

ROM'PHA. *See* Gods, False.

ROOF. *See* House.

Figurative. To receive one under the shelter of the roof represents hospitality; in the case of Lot this was so greatly estimated that he was willing to sacrifice his duty as a father to maintain it (Gen. 19:8); and by the centurion who considered it too great an honor for him to receive the Lord as a guest (Matt. 8:8).

ROOM. As an apartment (*see* House). The term is sometimes used in the present sense of *entrance, opportunity,* as in the proverb, "A man's gift makes room for him" (Prov. 18:16).

"The place of honor" at a wedding (Luke 14:8; "highest room," KJV) is the rendering of Gk. *prōtoklisia* (the "first reclining place"), the chief place at the table.

ROOT (Heb. *shōresh;* Gk. *hriza,* a common figure often referred to in Scripture).

Figurative. From the important relation that the root bears to the plant we have in Scripture many beautiful and forceful illustrations.

1. The root of a family is the progenitor from whom the race derives its name; thus, "from the serpent's root a viper will come out" (Isa. 14:29), meaning that though the Davidic kingdom was broken down by the Syro-Ephraimitish war, another would arise to be a scourge to Israel's oppressors. The Messiah is called "the root of Jesse" (11:10), as containing its sap and strength in His divine capacity (cf. Rev. 5:5; and 22:16, as "the root and the offspring of David," referring to both His divine and human nature). The progenitor of a race is also called its root (Prov. 12:3).

2. Root means the essential cause of anything, as "the love of money is a root of all sorts of evil"

(1 Tim. 6:10; cf. Heb. 12:15, "that no root of bitterness springing up causes trouble").

3. "Rooted" means firmly established, "being rooted and grounded in love" (Eph. 3:17; cf. Col. 2:7); also "taking root" (Job 5:3; to take "deep root," Ps. 80:9; also Isa. 27:6; 37:31; 40:24).

4. Opposed to this is to "uproot," which has the sense of to destroy, remove (1 Kings 14:15; Job 31:12; Ps. 52:5; Luke 17:6).

5. The roots of a plant being near water is symbolic of prosperity; "my root is spread out to the waters" (Job 29:19); lit., "open to water," and so never lacking. Ezekiel (Ezek. 31:7) says of Assyria, "For its roots extended to many waters," which accounted for "the multitude of its branches" (v. 9). The opposite figure is of a root "dried up" (Hos. 9:16).

6. "Though its roots grow old in the ground" (Job 14:8) denotes loss of vitality; whereas of sinners it is said, "Their root will become like rot and their blossom blow away as dust" (Isa. 5:24).

7. Of our Lord in His humiliation it was said, "He grew up before Him like a tender shoot, and like a root out of parched ground" (Isa. 53:2), "both figures depicting the lowly and unattractive character of the small though vigorous beginning, the miserable character of the external circumstances in the midst of which the birth and growth of the servant had taken place" (Delitzsch, *Com.,* ad loc.).

ROPE, ROPEMAKERS. *See* Handicrafts.

ROSE. *See* Vegetable Kingdom: Crocus; Rose.

ROSH (rōsh; "the head"). In the genealogy of Gen. 46:21, Rosh is reckoned among the sons of Benjamin, but the name does not occur elsewhere, and it is probable that "Ehi and Rosh" (*'ēhî weʾrōsh*) is a corruption of "Ahiram" (cf. Num. 26:38). It is also possible that Rosh is the correct reading, but like Er and Onan of Judah he died childless.

ROT, ROTTEN, ROTTENNESS. The rendering of several Heb. words, used mostly figuratively. Job says (Job 13:28) that he is "decaying like a rotten thing," i.e., a symbol of gradual decay. Bronze and "rotten wood" are contrasted (41:27) as representing strength and weakness. "The name of the wicked will rot" (Prov. 10:7) is illustrative of the speedy oblivion into which they go. "Rottenness ["decay," NIV] in his bones" (12:4; 14:30) means an incurable disease, robbing one of power.

ROUND TIRES. A KJV expression for crescent-shaped ornaments. *See* Dress.

ROW, ROWERS. *See* Ship.

RUBIES. *See* Mineral Kingdom.

RUDDER. *See* Ship.

RUDDY (Heb. *'ādōm,* from *'admōnî,* "to be red"). Applied to David (1 Sam. 16:12; 17:42) and understood by many to mean *red-haired*. It seems rather to refer to the complexion. This view is confirmed by the application of kindred words, as "Her consecrated ones were purer than snow, they were whiter than milk; they were more ruddy in body than corals" (Lam. 4:7); and "My beloved is dazzling and ruddy" (Song of Sol. 5:10), who is immediately described as black-haired (v. 11).

RUDE. Paul writes in 2 Cor. 11:6 (KJV) "But though I be rude in speech, yet not in knowledge." The Gk. term *idiōtes* means properly a *private person*, as opposed to a magistrate, and in this instance in 2 Corinthians it means *unlearned, illiterate*, as opposed to the learned or cultured. The NASB renders "unskilled in speech." A similar use of *idiōtes* appears in Acts 4:13 ("ignorant," KJV; "untrained," NASB; "unschooled," NIV); *idiōtes* in 1 Cor. 14:16, 23, 24 is given as "unlearned" in the KJV and as "ungifted" in the NASB (marg., "unversed in spiritual gifts"). The NIV translates "who do not understand."

RUDIMENTS (Gk. *stoicheion*, "any first thing"). Letters of the alphabet, the "elements" (2 Pet. 3:10), from which all things have come; "primary principles"; *see* Col. 2:8, 20, where reference is made to "the elementary principles of the world" (NASB; "rudiments," KJV; "basic principles," NIV).

RUE. *See* Vegetable Kingdom.

RU'FUS (rū'fus; "red"). Brother of Alexander and son of Simon the Cyrenian, whom the Jews compelled to bear the cross of Jesus when on His way to the crucifixion (Mark 15:21). Rufus is included by the apostle Paul (Rom. 16:13) among those in Rome to whom he sends salutations. It is generally supposed that this Rufus is identical with the one mentioned by Mark, and yet, as this was a common name, they may be different individuals.

RUHA'MAH (rū-ha'ma; "she has received mercy"). A figurative title applied to the daughter of the prophet Hosea, signifying that God would restore Israel to favor (Hos. 2:1) on condition of their repenting and returning to Him. Both Peter (1 Pet. 2:10) and Paul (Rom. 9:25-26) quote this prophecy with evident application to the Gentiles, as well as Jews. Through its apostasy from God, Israel has become like the Gentiles and has fallen from the covenants of promise; consequently the readoption of the Israelites as the children of God will be a practical proof that "the gifts and the calling" of God (Rom. 11:29) with respect to Israel are "irrevocable."

RUIN. The rendering of expressive Heb. terms: Derivatives from Heb. *nāpal* (to "fall"), the ruin of a city by dilapidation, separating all its stones (Isa. 25:2, "Thou hast made . . . a fortified city into a ruin"; 17:1); of a country (Isa. 23:13; Ezek. 31:13; cf. 27:27). Other terms occur in the original, and numerous mounds of ruined cities (*tells*) dot the ancient biblical world. Excavation of the various strata of occupational history of these tells has made possible the modern science of biblical archaeology and immeasurably increased the knowledge of Bible backgrounds.

Figurative. Ruin is a fall or stumbling because of temptation to sin. The "gods of Damascus . . . were the ruin" of King Ahaz (2 Chron. 28:23, KJV; cf. Ezek. 18:30; 21:15, in the KJV, and Prov. 10:29; 18:7, in the NASB). The NIV translates "downfall" in 2 Chron. 28:23; Ezek. 18:30, and "undoing" in Prov. 18:7.

RULER. The rendering of several Heb. and Gk. words, used to designate a large number of officials, although the term *ruler* does not always appear in the same verses in the various translations and versions: the King (1 Sam. 25:30; 2 Sam. 6:21); a *prince* (which see) or other ruler of the people; a prime minister, such as Joseph (Gen. 41:43, KJV), or Daniel (Dan. 2:48; 5:7); a town prefect (Judg. 9:30; 2 Chron. 29:20; Neh. 3:9); a chief adviser (2 Sam. 8:18; 20:26); the steward of a large house (Matt. 24:45, 47; Luke 12:42); a superintendent of workmen, such as herdsmen (Gen. 47:6) or laborers (1 Kings 11:28); an overseer of the king's property (1 Chron. 27:31); the ruler, or governor, of the feast (John 2:8-9); the "ruler of the synagogue" (*see* Synagogue); the chief treasurer (1 Chron. 26:24). The high priest was "chief officer of the house of God" (1 Chron. 9:11; cf. 2 Chron. 35:8), as so was sometimes his assistant (Neh. 11:11). *See* Law, Administration of; Pastor.

RU'MAH (rū'ma; "elevation"). A city named as the home of Pedaiah, the father of Zebidah, Jeboiakim's mother (2 Kings 23:36). Some believe it is the same as Arumah (Judg. 9:41), in the neighborhood of Shechem. Others identify it with Khirbet Rumeh, six miles N of Nazareth.

RUMP. *See* Fat Tail.

RUN, RUNNING. *See* Footman, Games.

RUNNER (Heb. *rāṣ*). Primarily the person who conveyed any message with speed; and subsequently the means of regular communication. Job declares, "Now my days are swifter than a runner" (Job 9:25), showing that at an early time persons possessing swiftness of foot were so commonly employed as couriers as to render such an allusion both intelligent and appropriate. *See* Courier.

RUNNING SORE. *See* Diseases: Wen.

RUSH. *See* Vegetable Kingdom: Reeds, Rushes.

RUST (Gk. *brōsis*, "eating"; *ios*). The first of these Gk. terms is rendered "rust" (Matt. 6:19-20) in the wider sense of *corrosion*. It is, however, generally used, as almost everywhere in Greek writers, of that which is eaten, food (cf. Heb. 12:16; 2 Cor. 9:10). The second term means *poison,* and is so rendered (Rom. 3:13; James 3:8); but in 5:3 is rendered "rust" ("corrosion," NIV) in speaking of the tarnish that spreads over silver. In Ezek. 24:6, 11-12 Jerusalem is likened to a pot with spots of rust (Heb. *hel'â*) that cannot be removed. The uncleanness of the pot is this rust, which is to be burned away by heat.

RUTH (rūth, "a female friend"). A Moabitess, first the wife of Mahlon and then of Boaz, and an ancestress of David and of Christ.

Wife of Mahlon. In the time of the Judges Elimelech, an inhabitant of Bethlehem in Judah, emigrated into the land of Moab with his wife, Naomi, and his two sons, Mahlon and Chilion, because of a famine in the land (Ruth 1:1-2). There he died, and his two sons married Moabite women, named Orpah and Ruth, the latter becoming the wife of Mahlon (4:10), before 1100 B.C.

Return to Bethlehem. After the death of her two sons Naomi resolved to return to her own country and kindred, and Ruth determined to accompany her, notwithstanding her mother-in-law's entreaty that she should follow her sister-in-law and return to her own people and her god. Ruth answered her in beautiful and earnest words: "Do not urge me to leave you or turn back from following you; for where you go, I will go, and where you lodge, I will lodge. Your people shall be my people, and your God, my God. Where you die, I will die, and there I will be buried. Thus may the Lord do to me, and worse, if anything but death parts you and me" (1:16-17). They arrived at Bethlehem just at the beginning of the barley harvest.

Marries Boaz. Ruth went out to glean for the purpose of procuring support for herself and her mother-in-law, and in gleaning came by chance upon Boaz, a relative of Naomi. When he heard that she had come with Naomi from Moab, Boaz spoke kindly to her and gave her permission not only to glean in the field and even among the sheaves but to appease her hunger and thirst with the food and drink of his reapers (2:1-16). His kindness to her induced Naomi to counsel Ruth to seek an opportunity to tell Boaz the claim she had upon him as the nearest kinsman of her deceased husband. Ruth followed this advice, and Boaz promised to fulfill her request provided the nearer redeemer, who was still living, would not perform his duty (3:1-13). As this relative was unwilling to do so, Boaz obtained from him a release, redeemed himself the patrimony of Elimelech, and took Ruth to be his wife (4:1-13). In process of time she became the mother of Obed, the father of Jesse and grandfather of David (vv. 13, 17; Matt. 1:5).

The artifice that Naomi suggested and Ruth adopted to induce Boaz to act as her redeemer (chap. 3) appears, according to our customs, to be objectionable from a moral point of view; judged, however, by the customs of that time it was not. Boaz, who was an honorable man, praised Ruth for having taken refuge with him instead of looking for a husband among younger men and took no offense at the manner in which she had approached him and proposed to become his wife. The anxiety manifested by Ruth is explained by the desire to continue the family name and to have the possessions of her father-in-law redeemed and restored to the family.

BIBLIOGRAPHY: C. E. Macartney, *The Way of a Man with a Maid* (1931), pp. 22-36; id., *Great Women of the Bible* (1942), pp. 9-23; H. H. Rowley, *The Servant of the Lord and Other Old Testament Essays* (1952), pp. 161ff.; C. J. Barber, *Ruth: An Expositional Commentary* (1984), pp. 39-134; C. J. and A. A. Barber, *You Can Have a Happy Marriage* (1984), pp. 17-54.

RUTH, BOOK OF. This book bears as its title its principal character (for plot of book *see* Ruth). Its purpose may be viewed as threefold: (1) to provide part of the lineage of David, (2) to show God's grace in welcoming Gentiles into the family of God, and (3) to demonstrate the function of the kinsman-redeemer as a foregleam of the work of the Messiah.

Date and Authorship. The author of the work is unknown. The Babylonian Talmud ascribes the book to Samuel, and that is a possibility because Samuel anointed David king over Israel. Thus Samuel considered David to be king even though the repudiated Saul was still ruling when Samuel died; and if penned by Samuel, the reference in the book to David as a figure of significance would be quite in order. The historical setting of the book is laid in the time of the Judges (Ruth 1:1), and it seems to have been composed about the same time as the longer work. Some critics argue for a postexilic date of authorship, in part because of alleged Aramaisms in the text. But these Aramaisms have not been proved; Heb. words for the supposed Aram. words are virtually identical. In fact, a strong argument for an early date can be presented by the general character of the Heb. vocabulary, syntax, and classical purity of style. Moreover, after the Exile, and certainly in the days of Ezra and Nehemiah, mixed marriages of the sort indicated here would not have been approved. Therefore the supposed later fabrication of the genealogical note (as suggested by some critics) seems highly unlikely, if not impossible. The book also furnishes a logical historical explanation of David's friendly contacts with the Moabite king, when he fled from Saul and sought asylum in Moab for his parents (1 Sam. 22:3, 4).

Outline.

I. Ruth's decision to return with Naomi (1:1-22)

II. Ruth's service to Naomi and introduction to Boaz (2:1-23)

III. Ruth's invoking of the redemption law (3:1-18)

IV. Ruth's reward (4:1-22)   H.F.V.

BIBLIOGRAPHY: D. Atkinson, *The Wings of Refuge*, 1983; C. J. Barber, *Ruth: An Expositional Commentary*, 1983; E. F. Campbell, Jr., *Ruth*, Anchor Bible, 1975; A. Cundall and L. Morris, *Judges and Ruth*, TOTC, 1968.

RYE. *See* Vegetable Kingdom: Spelt.

---

SABACH'THANI (sa-bak'tha-ni), or **Sabach-tha'ni** (sa-bak-tha'ni; Gk. for Aram. *shabaqtanî;* "thou has left me"), quoted by our Lord upon the cross from Ps. 22 (cf. Matt. 27:46; Mark 15:34). *See* Jesus.

SABAE'ANS (sa-bē'anz). *See* Sabeans.

SAB'AOTH (Gk. *sabaōth,* for Heb. *ṣebā'ôt,* "armies," Rom. 9:29; James 5:4; "Almighty," NIV). In the OT it frequently occurs in the epithet "Jehovah, God of hosts," or simply "Jehovah of hosts." This epithet "Jehovah, God of hosts" designates Him as the supreme head and commander of all the heavenly forces, so that the host of Jehovah and the host of heaven are the same (1 Kings 22:19), that is, the angels, who are the Lord's agents, ever ready to execute His will. It is never applied to God with reference to the army of Israel, although once the companies composing it are called "the hosts of the Lord" (Ex. 12:41), because they were under His guidance and were to fight for His cause.

SABBATH (Heb. *shabbāt,* "repose," i.e., "cessation" from exertion; Gk. *sabbaton*). The name *Sabbath* is applied to various great festivals but principally and usually to the seventh day of the week, the strict observance of which is enforced not merely in the general Mosaic code but also in the Ten Commandments.

Origin. The account of the creation states that God "rested on the seventh day" (Gen. 2:2). The assertion that the Sabbath rest was a Babylonian as well as a Hebrew institution and the inference that the Hebrews may have borrowed the idea from the Babylonians requires some ingenuity to demonstrate. By way of answer the following should be noted: (1) The Babylonians paid special attention to the nineteenth day as well as those that were multiples of seven; they called only the fifteenth day *shabatum*. (2) The Babylonian tablets call the seventh day "an evil day" or "an

unlucky day," whereas Scripture describes it as "a holy day." (3) The Babylonians placed prohibitions only on the "king," "seer," and "the physician," whereas the OT makes the Sabbath binding on all. (4) There was no cessation of business activity on Babylonian special days. (5) Though Babylonians had special regard for days that were multiples of seven, those days rarely ever fell on the seventh day of the week in their lunar calendar and thus were not equivalent to he Hebrew Sabbath.

Jewish Sabbath. The Jewish Sabbath was distinctive and was treated at length in the Bible.

Origin. The Sabbath was of divine institution and is so declared in passages where ceasing to create is called "resting" (Gen. 2:3; Ex. 20:11; 31:17). The blessing and sanctifying of the seventh day have regard, no doubt, to the Sabbath, which Israel, as the people of God, was afterward to keep; but we are not to suppose that the theocratic (Jewish) Sabbath was thus early instituted. The Sabbath was instituted by Moses. It is in Ex. 16:23-29 that we find the first indisputable institution of the day, as one given to and to be kept by the children of Israel. Shortly afterward it was reenacted in the fourth commandment. Many of the rabbis date its first institution from the incident recorded in Ex. 15:25. This, however, seems to lack foundation. We are not on sure ground until we come to the unmistakable institution in chap. 16, in connection with the gathering of manna. The opinion of Grotius is probably correct, that the day was already known, and in some measure observed as holy, but that the rule of abstinence from work was first given then, and shortly afterward more explicitly imposed in the fourth commandment.

Purpose. The Sabbath was a means of binding together more closely the chosen people and keeping them apart from the rest of mankind. Two reasons are given for its observance in Israel—God's resting on the seventh day of creation (Ex. 20:8-11; 31:16-17) and Israel's having been a "slave in the land of Egypt" and having been brought "out of there by a mighty hand and by an outstretched arm" (Deut. 5:15). "These are not the subjects of Sabbath celebration; indeed, the Sabbath has no one event as the subject of its observance, but is only the day which Israel is called to sanctify to the Lord its God, because God blessed and hallowed the day at the creation by resting on it. The completion of creation, the rest of God, is His blessedness in the contemplation of the finished work, the satisfaction of God in His work, which overflows in blessing upon His creatures. This blessedness was lost to the world through the Fall, but not forever, for, through redemption, divine mercy will restore it. The rest of God is the goal which the whole creation is destined to reach. To guide to this goal, the Sabbath was enjoined by way of compensation for the losses which accrue to man under the curse of sin, from that heavy, oppressive labor which draws him from God. Thus the Sabbath was hallowed, i.e., separated from other days of the week to be a holy day for man, by putting the blessing of his rest on the rest of this day. The return of this blessed and hallowed day is to be to him a perpetual reminder and enjoyment of the divine rest. This significance of the Sabbath explains why its keeping through all future generations of Israel is called a perpetual covenant and a sign between Jehovah and the children of Israel forever (Ex. 31:17)" (Keil, *Arch.*, 2:2ff.).

Observance. According to Mosaic law the Sabbath was observed: (1) By cessation from labor (Ex. 20:10). The idea of work is not more precisely defined in the law, except that the kindling of fire for cooking is expressly forbidden (35:3), and the gathering of wood is treated as a transgression (Num. 15:32-36); wherefore it is evident that work, in its widest sense, was to cease. "Accordingly, it was quite in keeping with the law when not only labor, such as burden-bearing (Jer. 17:21-27), but traveling, as forbidden by Ex. 16:29, and trading (Amos 8:5) were to cease on the Sabbath, and when Nehemiah, to prevent marketing on this day, ordered the closing of the gates" (Neh. 10:31; 13:15, 19). (2) By a holy assembly, the doubling of the daily offering by two lambs of the first year, with the corresponding meat and drink offerings (Num. 28:9-10) and the providing of new bread of the Presence in the Holy Place (Lev. 24:8). Thus the Sabbath was to Israel a "day of . . . gladness" (Num. 10:10; cf. Hos. 2:11), "a delight, the holy day of the Lord honorable" (Isa. 58:13). From such passages it will appear that the essence of Sabbath observance is placed in the most unconditional and all-embracing self-denial, the renunciation of the whole natural being and natural desires, the most unconditional dedication to God (*see* Isa. 56:2; Ezek. 20:12, 21). The object of this cessa-

tion from labor and coming together in holy convocation was to give man an opportunity to engage in such mental and spiritual exercises as would tend to the quickening of soul and spirit and the strengthening of spiritual life. In this higher sense it is evident that our Lord meant that "the Sabbath was made for man" (Mark 2:27).

Reward. According to Ezekiel (20:12, 20) the Sabbath was to be a sign between Jehovah and Israel, "that they might know that I am the Lord who sanctifies them." That is, "that Jehovah was sanctifying them—viz., by the Sabbath rest—as a refreshing and elevation of the mind, in which Israel was to have a foretaste of that blessed resting from all works to which the people of God was ultimately to attain" (Keil, *Com.*, ad loc.). The penalty of defiling the Sabbath was death (Ex. 31:15; cf. Num. 15:32-36). But if the law of the Sabbath was broken through ignorance or mistake, pardon was extended after the presentation of a sin offering. At times the Jews dispensed with the extreme severity of the law (Isa. 56:2; Ezek. 20:16; 22:8; Lam. 2:6; Neh. 13:16); indeed, the legal observance of the Sabbath seems never to have been rigorously enforced until after the Exile. *See* Lord's Day; Sunday; Synagogue.

Typology. The Sabbath commemorates God's creation rest. It marks a finished creation. After Sinai it was a day of legal obligation. The Sabbath is mentioned often in the book of Acts in connection with the Jews. In the rest of the NT it occurs but twice (Col. 2:16; Heb. 4:4). In these passages the Sabbath is set forth not as a day to be observed but as typical of the present rest into which the believer entered when he "also rested [ceased] from his works" (v. 10) and trusted Christ.

Contrast to the First Day of the Week. As the Sabbath commemorates God's creation rest, the first day speaks of Christ's resurrection. The seventh day marks God's creative rest. On the first day Christ was unceasingly active. The seventh day commemorates a finished creation, the first day a finished redemption. In the present dispensation of grace Sunday perpetuates the truth that one-seventh of one's time belongs to God. In every other particular there is contrast.

See also Festivals.   M.F.U.

BIBLIOGRAPHY: J. Orr, *The Sabbath Scripturally and Practically Considered* (1886); C. L. Feinberg, *The Sabbath and the Lord's Day* (1952); R. T. Beckwith and W. Stott, *This Is the Day* (1978); N. Turner, *Christian Words* (1980), pp. 388-89.

SABBATH, COVERED WAY FOR THE (Heb. *mûsak hashshabbāt*, 2 Kings 16:18). This was, no doubt, a covered place, stand, or hall in the court of the Temple used by the king whenever he visited the Temple with his attendants on the Sabbath on feast days. In what the removal of it consisted it is impossible to determine from lack of information. Some believe it means to change the name; others believe it to have been a taking down thereof. The motive may have been fear of the king of Assyria or King Ahaz's own idolatry (cf. 2 Chron. 28:24).

SABBATH, DAY AFTER THE (Heb. *māḥărat hashshabbāt*). A term of disputed meaning (Lev. 23:11, 15) occurring in connection with the feast of the Passover. The Sabbath referred to is not the weekly Sabbath but the day of rest, the first day of holy convocation of the Passover, the fifteenth Abib (*Nisan*). As a day of rest on which no laborious work was to be performed (v. 8), the first day of the feast is called "Sabbath," irrespective of the day of the week upon which it fell. Thus "the day after the Sabbath" is equivalent to "the day after the Passover" (Josh. 5:11).

SABBATH, SECOND AFTER THE FIRST (Gk. *sabbaton deuteroprōton*, Luke 6:1, a "certain Sabbath," *see* marg.). This expression has given rise to much discussion, and many views of its meaning are given. Of these we mention only a few. Bleek supposes an interpolation. Wetstein and Storr say that the first Sabbaths of the first, second, and third months of the year were called first, second, and third; the second first-Sabbath would thus be the *first* Sabbath of the *second* month. Louis Cappel suggests the following: The civil year of the Israelites commenced in autumn, in the month Tizri, and the ecclesiastical year in the month Nisan (about mid-March to mid-April), and there were thus every year two first-Sabbaths—one at the commencement of the civil year, of which the name would have been *first-first;* the other at the beginning of the ecclesiastical year, which would be called *second-first.* Edersheim (*Life of Jesus,* 2:54) and Strong (*Concordance,* s.v.) advocate the probable view that the second first-Sabbath was the one following immediately after the Paschal week, the twenty-second Nisan.

SABBATH DAY'S JOURNEY. *See* Metrology: Linear Measures.

SABBATICAL YEAR. *See* Festivals.

SABE'ANS (sa-bē'anz). The inhabitants of a kingdom in SW Arabia, S of Ma'in, N of the kingdom of Qataban in the Yemen-Hadhramaut region of S Arabia. This general region was explored in 1950-51 by the Arabian Expedition of the American Foundation for the Study of Man organized by Wendell Phillips (*see Qataban and Sheba* [1955]). The excavations in S Arabia have helped to outline its general history. The kingdoms of Ma'in, Saba, Qataban, Ausan, and Hadhramaut are now much better known. Before 1200 B.C. there was a southward migration of Sheba and allied tribes. About 1000 B.C. to 700 B.C. there was a great expansion of Sabean influence. From about the ninth century to the middle of the fifth

century B.C. priest-kings of Sheba are known. From c. 400 to 25 B.C. the kingdom of the Minaeans and the kingdom of Qataban flourished. The ruins of Mariaba (Mareb) are a mute evidence of the splendor that the Sabean monarchs possessed. About 950 B.C. the biblically famous Queen of Sheba (Saba) set out on a 1,200-mile trek to visit the rich and powerful king of Israel in the N, taking with her lavish gifts (1 Kings 10:1-13). Although accustomed to wealth and splendor, the queen was so overwhelmed by Solomon's majesty that "she was breathless" (2 Chron. 9:4). In Matt. 12:42 and Luke 11:31 this ruler is designated as "the Queen of the South." The queen's strenuous journey to Jerusalem over inhospitable terrain was almost certainly dictated by commercial reasons. Her conference with Solomon must have involved defining the limits of commercial interests and arranging trade treaties that regulated the equitable exchange of the products of Arabia, including the lucrative incense trade and Palestinian products. Although the Queen of Sheba of Solomon's day has not been attested as yet in S Arabian inscriptions, there is not the slightest reason for denying either her or her visit to the Israelite monarch. The account is definitely not a "romantic tale" as generally used to be supposed (cf. James A. Montgomery, *Arabia and the Bible* [1934], p. 180). Although queens played little part in the later history of southern Arabia, they ruled large tribal confederacies in northern Arabia from the ninth to the seventh centuries B.C., as the cuneiform inscriptions relate. W. F. Albright's researches in S Arabia and the vast quantity of material being studied promise to shed important light on S Arabian history and on the Sabaeans. Much is now known of Sabean religion from excavated tablets. It was of the astral type; their chief deity was Attar, the male counterpart of the goddess of procreation, the Babylonian Ishtar.   M.F.U.

BIBLIOGRAPHY: W. F. Albright, *Bulletin of the American Schools of Oriental Research* 128 (1952): 25-38; G. van Beek, *Biblical Archaeology* 15 (1952): 1-18.

SAB'TA (sab'ta; meaning unknown). The third son of Cush and grandson of Ham (1 Chron. 1:9).

SAB'TAH (sab'ta; Gen. 10:7). *See* Sabta.

SAB'TECA, SAB'TECAH, SAB'TECHCA (sab'-te-ka). The fifth-named son of Cush, the son of Ham (Gen. 10:7; 1 Chron. 1:9; both "Sabtecha," KJV).

SA'CAR. *See* Sharar.

SACHI'A (sa-ki'a). The sixth named of the seven sons of Shaharaim by his wife Hodesh (1 Chron. 8:10). *See* Sakia (NIV).

SACKBUT (*sabka*). *See* Music.

SACKCLOTH (Heb. *śaq;* Gk. *sakkos,* "a mesh," i.e., coarse, loose cloth). A coarse texture of a dark color, made of goat's hair (Isa. 50:3; Rev. 6:12) and resembling the *cilicium* of the Romans. It was used (1) for making sacks (cf. Gen. 42:25; Lev. 11:32; Josh. 9:4) and (2) for making the rough garments used by mourners (Gen. 37:34; Esther 4:1-4), which were in extreme cases worn next to the skin (1 Kings 21:27; 2 Kings 6:30; Job 16:15), and this even by females (Isa. 32:11; Joel 1:8; 2 Macc. 3:19), but at other times were worn over the coat (Jonah 3:6) in place of the outer garment.

Figurative. *Girding with sackcloth* is a figure for heavy afflictions (Ps. 35:13; 69:11; Isa. 3:24; 15:3; 22:12; 32:11). *Putting off,* of joy and gladness (Ps. 30:11; Isa. 20:2). *Covering the heavens,* of severe judgments (Isa. 50:3; Rev. 6:12). Prophets and ascetics wore it over the underclothing to signify the sincerity of their calling (Isa. 20:2).

BIBLIOGRAPHY: H. F. Lutz, *Textiles and Costumes Among the Peoples of the Ancient Near East* (1933), pp. 25-26, 176-77.

Canaanite stone altar of sacrifice

SACRAMENT (Lat. *sacramentum,* a military "oath" of enlistment). The term applied to baptism and the Lord's Supper, which are generally believed to have been instituted for the perpetual observance of the Christian church and placed among its means of grace. As signs they represent in action and by symbols the great blessings of the covenant; as seals they are standing pledges of the divine fidelity in bestowing them on certain conditions, being the Spirit's instrument in aiding and strengthening the faith that they re-

quire and in assuring to that faith the present bestowment of its object.

The Roman Catholic church holds to seven sacraments: baptism, confirmation, the eucharist, penance, extreme unction, orders, and matrimony. It teaches that a sacrament is "a visible sign of invisible grace instituted for our justification" (*The Rom. Catechism,* p. ii, chap. 1, no. 4). The *Catholic Dictionary* (art. "Sacraments") says: "Just as Christ appeared in flesh, just as virtue went forth from that body which he took, just as he saved us by that blood which he willingly shed in love for us, so he continues to make sensible things the channel of that grace by which our lives are elevated and sanctified. In baptism we are born again; in confirmation we grow up to perfect men in Christ," etc.

BIBLIOGRAPHY: J. Jeremias, *The Eucharistic Words of Jesus* (1955); A. M. Stibbs, *Sacrament, Sacrifice and Eucharist* (1961); G. C. Berkouwer, *The Sacraments* (1969); C. K. Barrett, *Church, Ministry, and Sacraments in the New Testament* (1985).

SACRIFICE. The general subject of sacrificial offerings in the Bible is discussed in this article and in two other articles: (1) Sacrifices, Mosaic; and (2) Sacrificial Offerings. There is also an article on the general subject Human Sacrifice.

Scripture Terms. The following terms are used to express the sacrificial act:

1. Something *given;* a *gift* (Gen. 32:13, 18, 20-21; 43:11; etc.); *tribute* (2 Sam. 8:2, 6; 2 Kings 17:4); an *offering* to God (1 Chron. 16:29; Isa. 1:13), spoken especially of a bloodless offering (Heb. *minḥâ; see* Meat Offering, below).

2. Something *brought near,* an offering as a symbol of communion or covenant between man and God (Heb. *qorbān*).

3. A *bloody* sacrifice (Heb. *zebaḥ* from *zābaḥ,* "to stay"), in which the shedding of blood is the essential idea. Thus it is opposed to *minḥâ* (Ps. 40:6) and to *'ōlâ,* the whole burnt offering (Ex. 10:25; 18:12; etc.).

4. *Whole burnt offering* (Heb. *'ōlâ*), that which is completely consumed by fire (Lev. 1:3).

5. Gk. *thusia,* is used both of the sacrifice offered and the act of burning, whether literal or figurative; *prosphora,* "present"; in the NT a *sacrifice* (Acts 21:26; 24:17; Eph. 5:2; Heb. 10:5; etc); *holokautōma,* "wholly consumed" (Lat. *holocaustum*), a whole burnt offering, i.e., a sacrifice the whole of which is burned (Mark 12:33; Heb. 10:6, 8), same as no. 4.

Origin. The beginnings of sacrifice are found in the primitive ages of man and among all the nations of antiquity. Cain and Abel offered sacrifices to God (Gen. 4:3-4)—Cain "of the fruit of the ground" and Abel "of the firstlings of his flock and of their fat portions." Noah expressed his gratitude for deliverance from the Flood by presenting burnt offerings unto the Lord (8:20). The patriarchs were in the habit of building altars and offering sacrifices on them, calling upon God at the places where He had revealed Himself to them (12:7; 13:4; 26:25; 31:54; 33:20; 35:7; 46:1). "Indeed, *to sacrifice* seems as natural to man as to pray; the one indicates what he feels about himself, the other what he feels about God. The one means a felt need of *propitiation,* the other a felt sense of *dependence*" (Edersheim, *The Temple,* p. 81).

Fundamental Idea. The fundamental idea of sacrifices may be gathered partly from their designation, partly from their nature. Sacrifices do not appear to have been instituted at first by divine command; though they must not, on that account, be looked upon as human inventions. They are spontaneous expressions of reverence and gratitude that man feels toward God. But we must not fail to note that with gratitude and reverence there was also the thought of securing a continuance of God's favor and mercy. Neither must we lose sight of their expressing the idea of propitiation and substitution. Nor can we afford to forget that in all ages blood has been the symbol of life and its shedding the symbol of the offering of one's life. Abundant testimony is given of this in *The Blood Covenant,* by H. C. Trumbull. He says that in the earliest recorded sacrifice "the narrative shows Abel lovingly and trustfully reaching out toward God with *substitute* blood, in order to be in covenant oneness with God; while Cain merely proffers a gift from his earthly possessions. Abel so trusts God that he gives *himself* to him. Cain defers to God sufficiently to make a *present* to him. The one shows unbounded faith; the other shows a measure of affectionate reverence" (p. 211).

Again in the sacrifice of Noah we have an expression not only of gratitude and reverence but of a desire for further communications of divine grace. This seems to be implied in the answer given by the Lord to Noah, "I will never again curse the ground on account of man" (Gen. 8:21). In the presentation of the best of his possessions the worshiper symbolized the giving of himself, his life, his aims, to God. "The most direct surrender of himself that a man can make to God is realized in prayer, an act in which the soul merges itself in Him from whom it came, in which the spirit unites itself with its God. Now that which corresponds to this inward surrender, as being an outward, visible, tangible verification of it, is sacrifice, which, on this account, has been called 'embodied prayer.'" In the "burnt offerings" of Job for his children (Job 1:5) and for his three friends (42:8), the idea of expiation is distinctly set forth; for in the first instance the influencing thought with Job was, "Perhaps my sons have sinned"; and in the latter God said to Job's friends, "My servant Job will pray for you. For I will accept him. . . ."

In the Pentateuch the fundamental idea of sacrifice is that of *substitution,* which again seems to imply everything else. In the Levitical sacrifices the firstfruits go for the whole products; the firstlings of the flock, the redemption money for that which cannot be offered, and the life of the sacrifice, which is in its blood, for the life of the sacrificer.

Mosaic Sacrifices. We have seen that in the time of the patriarchs sacrifices were the spontaneous outward expression of grateful reverence and faithfulness toward God. Under the Mosaic law the offering of sacrifices was enjoined as a covenant duty; the material of the sacrifices and the rites to be observed in offering them were minutely described; and the sacrifices thus offered acquired the character of *means of grace.*

The *ground* on which the legal offering of sacrifices is based is the commandment "None shall appear before Me empty-handed" (Ex. 23:15; Deut. 16:16), i.e., "Every man shall give as he is able, according to the blessing of the Lord your God which He has given you" (v. 17). These gifts were not in the nature of tribute, which they were to present to Jehovah as the King of Canaan, but in recognition of their deliverance by Him from Egypt and of their adoption by Him as His peculiar people. Through these gifts they were to enjoy the benefits and blessings of the covenant, forgiveness of sins, sanctification, and true happiness. These gifts were to be accompanied by the consecration of the offerers; and the assurance of God's acceptance of such gifts was to the pious Israelite a divine promise that he would obtain the blessings he sought.

"They thus possessed a *sacramental* virtue and efficacy; and in the OT worship no religious act was regarded as complete unless accompanied with sacrifice. The sacrificial system was framed with the view of awakening a consciousness of sin and uncleanness; of impressing upon the worshipper the possibility of obtaining the forgiveness of sin, and of becoming righteous before God" (Keil, *Arch.,* 1:252).

At the very threshold of the Mosaic dispensation is the sacrifice of the paschal lamb, a *substitute* for Israel's firstborn, and resulting in Israel's redemption. This was commanded to be renewed yearly at the feast of Passover.

But there was one sacrifice that even under the OT required no renewal, offered when Jehovah entered into covenant relationship with Israel, and they became the people of God (*see* Sacrificial Offering: Heifer, The Red). An altar was built at the foot of Mt. Sinai, indicating the presence of Jehovah; it had twelve boundary stones, or pillars, representing the twelve tribes. These were most likely around the altar, and at some distance from it, preparing the soil upon which Jehovah was about to enter into communion with Israel (Ex. 24). The blood of the oxen was divided into two parts, one-half being sprinkled upon the altar, signifying that "the natural life of the people was given up to God, as a life that had passed through death, to be pervaded by his grace; and then through the sprinkling upon the people it was restored to them again, as a life renewed by the grace of God." This covenant was made upon "all the words" that Jehovah had spoken and which the people had promised to observe. Consequently it had for its foundation the divine law and right, as the rule of life for Israel. On the ground of this covenant-sacrifice all others rested.

Symbolical Meaning. The presenting to God as a gift a portion of the results of one's toil implied a surrender of the person of the offerer himself. That God did not require the death of the man, but the surrender of his heart, the Israelites could not fail to learn in the case of Abraham when called upon to offer up Isaac. The presenting of sacrifices under the impression that they embodied the fact of man's surrender of himself to God is insisted upon by Mosaic law as a covenant obligation. But from his being unholy and sinful, man is unable to surrender himself to the holy God. This view was impressed upon the Israelites, and they were reminded of the fundamental principle of the covenant to be holy as Jehovah is holy, by the commandment that the animal offered be free from physical defects.

Leaning the hand upon the head of the animal was a symbol of transferring to the victim the disposition of the offerer in approaching the altar, and to devote it to the object that the sacrifice was intended to secure. It thus took the place of the offerer. Becoming his substitute, its further treatment and disposal were supposed to be fraught with benefit to him. The slaughtering of the animal, as a preliminary to its being offered upon the altar, pointed to the necessity of death in the case of the man inwardly alienated from God by sin, if he ever expected to attain loving fellowship with Him.

When the blood, in which the soul resides, flowed from the animal on its being slaughtered, the soul was understood to be at the same time separated from the body, and it was not till the blood was sprinkled that, in virtue of the divine promise (Lev. 17:11), the soul of the offerer of the sacrifice was brought within the range of the divine favor.

Then, when the flesh of his sacrifice came to be burned upon the altar, the man's own body was understood to be at the same time surrendered to the purifying fire of divine love, so that in this way he was symbolically covered in body and soul from God's wrath and brought within the sphere of the justifying, sanctifying, and saving grace of God.

Typical Meaning. There is a power ascribed (Lev. 17:11) to the blood of the sacrifice, when sprinkled upon the altar, of covering the unholy man from the divine wrath, because the soul was supposed to be in the blood. But that power the blood could not be said to possess, either on

account of its being shed for the man or in virtue of its being shed on the altar. Sacrifices, merely as such, had no virtue to procure for the offerer forgiveness of sin, justification, sanctification, and felicity, all of which the Israelites not only looked for through their sacrifices, but which so far as the OT dispensation admitted of it, they actually received.

The object of the sacrifice is to establish a moral relation between the man as a personal being and God the absolute Spirit, to heal the separation between God and man that had been caused by sin. Now, as free personality is the soil out of which sin has sprung, so must the atonement be a work rooted in free personality as well. Being outside the sphere of moral freedom, the animal may be regarded as innocent and sinless; but for the same reason it cannot possess innocence in the true sense of the word and thus have a righteousness that could form an adequate satisfaction for the sin and guilt of man.

But even a perfect human being, if such could be found, would be unable by laying down his life to offer a sacrifice of such atoning efficacy as would reconcile another to God. The truth is that, in relation to God, everyone must answer for *his own soul* and not for another as well (cf. Ps. 49:7-8). Much less could such a result be effected by means of animal sacrifices and meat offerings; these could not possibly take away sin (Heb. 10:4, 11). If, then, God did invest the animal sacrifice with such significance as is here in question, He can only have done so in view of the true and perfect sacrifice, which in the fullness of time was to be offered through the eternal Spirit (9:14) by Christ, the Son of God and Son of Man.

Although there was no express mention of the typical character thus attaching to the sacrifices prescribed in the law, it was hinted at in the special regulations with regard to the mode of offering them; in time it came to be revealed through prophecy, although it was not till Christ voluntarily offered Himself as a sacrifice at Golgotha that it was completely unveiled. For detailed Typology *see* Sacrificial Offerings.

BIBLIOGRAPHY: W. H. Green, *The Hebrew Feasts* (1885), pp. 165-278; W. O. E. Oesterley, *Sacrifices in Ancient Israel* (1938); V. Taylor, *Jesus and His Sacrifice* (1943); B. B. Warfield, *The Person and Work of Christ* (1950), pp. 391-426; K. W. H. Ringgren, *Sacrifice in the Bible* (1962); R. de Vaux, *Studies in Old Testament Sacrifice* (1964); G. B. Gray, *Sacrifice in the Old Testament, Its Theory and Practice* (1970); E. O. James, *Origins of Sacrifice* (1971); S. H. Kellogg, *The Book of Leviticus* (1978); J. H. Kurtz, *Sacrificial Worship in the Old Testament* (1980).

SACRIFICE, HUMAN. As a supreme test of Abraham's loyalty to Jehovah, he was asked to offer up his son Isaac. From this it has been argued that human sacrifice was customary among the early Israelites. But of this there is no proof. Such sacrifice was in harmony with the fierce ritual of Syria. "The belief in the efficacy of the sacrifice of the firstborn was deeply enrooted in the minds of the people of Canaan. In time of distress and necessity they offered to the gods their best and dearest, 'the fruit of their body for the sin of their soul' (Mic. 6:7). Phoenician mythology related how when war and pestilence afflicted the land, Krones offered up his son Yeoud as a sacrifice, and human sacrifices were prevalent late into historical times. The OT tells us that Ahaz 'made his son to pass through the fire,' a euphemistic expression for those offerings of the firstborn that made the valley of Tophet an abomination (Jer. 7:31)."

The king of Moab, when he saw that "the battle was too fierce for him," "took his oldest son who was to reign in his place, and offered him as a burnt offering upon the wall" (2 Kings 3:26-27).

But there is nothing in Scripture to show that the Israelites practiced human sacrifice, or that it was enjoined by Jehovah. The case is thus put by Robertson (*The Early Religion of Israel*, p. 254): "To Abraham, not unfamiliar with various ways in which among his heathen ancestors the deity was propitiated, the testing question comes, 'Art thou prepared to obey thy God as fully as the people about thee obey their gods?' and in the putting forth of his faith in the act of obedience, he learns that the nature of his God is different. Instead, therefore, of saying that the narrative gives proof of the existence of human sacrifice as an early custom in Israel, it is more reasonable to regard it as giving an explanation why it was that, from early time, this had been a prime distinction of Israel that human sacrifice *was not practiced* as among the heathen."

BIBLIOGRAPHY: E. O. James, *Origins of Sacrifice* (1971); H. L. Strack, *The Jew and Human Sacrifice* (1971).

SACRIFICES, MOSAIC. The sacrifices prescribed by the Mosaic law are included under two classes: those offered *for the sake of* communion with Jehovah; and those offered *in* communion, and may be tabulated as follows: (1) *For* communion, or propitiatory, including sin offerings and trespass offerings. (2) *In* communion (a) burnt offerings; (b) peace offerings, including thank offerings, votive offerings, and freewill offerings; (c) grain and drink offerings.

The propitiatory offerings were intended to lead to the worshiper's being pardoned and brought into communion with God. The others were offered after being admitted to this state of grace. Each of these sacrifices is considered in detail below. It should be carefully borne in mind that, when several sacrifices were offered on the same occasion, those of a propitiatory nature took precedence of the burnt offerings, the latter being followed by the peace offering. The grain and drink offerings were presented alike with the burnt and thank offerings, or simply by themselves.

Material. In this respect the sacrifices were divided into two classes: the *bloody*, those that were slaughtered; and the *bloodless*, i.e., the grain and drink offerings.

The material for altar sacrifices included both animal and vegetable offerings.

Animal. These included oxen, sheep, goats, and fowls (i.e., turtledoves and young pigeons). The pigeons were intended for those who could not afford more costly offerings (Lev. 5:7; 12:8) and to serve as sin offerings of an inferior order. Male and female cattle (both large and small) might be offered (3:1, 6), although among sheep special prominence was given to the ram (Num. 15:5-6; 28:11; etc.) and to the male of goats (7:16, 22; etc.).

The animal intended for sacrifice was required to be (1) of a certain age, eight days at least (Ex. 22:30; Lev. 22:17), although sheep and goats were usually offered when a year old (Ex. 29:38; Lev. 9:3; etc.), oxen when they reached their third year; (2) absolutely free from blemish (Lev. 22:20-24).

Vegetable. These were grain, olive oil, and wine; the incense, partly vegetable and partly mineral; and salt.

The grain was offered (1) roasted in the ear (Lev. 2:14); (2) as *fine flour* (2:1), to both of which incense and oil were added (2:1, 15-16); or (3) as *unleavened bread*, or biscuits. This last was of three kinds—bread baked in the oven, bread baked on a griddle, bread baked in a pan. In each case the flour was mixed with oil (2:1-7).

Every grain offering had to be salted (2:13), as well as the animal sacrifices (Ezek. 43:24; cf. Mark 9:49). Leaven and honey were not allowed in any offering to Jehovah made by fire (Lev. 2:11).

Principle Underlying Selection. The animals, etc., selected for sacrifice were from the ordinary articles of diet among the Hebrews, thus expressing gratitude to God for blessings bestowed and prayer for continuance of His goodness. Further, as those offerings were the fruit of their life and labors, presenting them symbolized consecration to God of their lives with all their energies and endowments.

Presentation of Offerings. The manner of presentation was regulated by the sacrificial ritual and in the case of animal sacrifices was generally as follows:

The animal was brought to the door of the Tabernacle, near which the altar was placed; the person bringing the sacrifice leaned with his hand upon the animal's head, and then slaughtered it at the N side of the altar (Lev. 1:4-5, 11; 3:2, 8; 6:25; 7:2). In the case of sacrifices connected with the regular services of the sanctuary, those offered on festival occasions and in behalf of the whole people, the animals were slaughtered, skinned, and cut up by the priests.

When the animal was slain, the priest caught the flowing blood in a vessel and, according to the nature of the sacrifice, sprinkled some of it either on the side of the altar, its horns, or on the horns of the altar of incense, or upon (i.e., in the direction of) the Ark, emptying what remained at the base of the great altar (Ex. 29:12; Lev. 4:17-18; etc.).

The animal was then skinned by the offerer, cut into pieces (Lev. 1:6; 8:20), and either burned entirely upon the altar or the fat burned on the altar, whereas the remainder of the flesh was burned outside the camp. It was then eaten by the priests or partly by the priests and partly by the one bringing the sacrifice.

If the sacrifice consisted of a pigeon the priest wrung off the pigeon's head and allowed the blood to flow upon the side of the altar. He then took away the viscera and flung it upon the ash heap beside the altar. The head and body were then burned upon the altar (1:15).

In regard to vegetable offerings, if connected with burnt offerings, part of the flour and oil, some of the ears of grain and the cakes, with the incense, were burned upon the altar. The remainder fell to the priests, who had to consume it without leaven in the court of the Tabernacle (2:2-3, 10-11; 6:9-11; 7:9-10; 10:12-13). If, in connection with a thank offering, one cake was presented as a wave offering to Jehovah, that cake fell to the priest who sprinkled the blood (7:14), and the remainder of the offering was to be eaten by those who presented it.

BIBLIOGRAPHY: W. H. Green, *The Hebrew Feasts* (1885), pp. 165-275.

SACRIFICIAL OFFERINGS. The sacrificial offerings were of various types and they were presented according to a regular schedule.

Types of Offering. Seven types of sacrificial offerings were made: sin, guilt (trespass, KJV), burnt, peace, grain (meat, KJV), heave and wave, and the red heifer.

Sin Offering (Heb. *ḥaṭṭā't,* an "offense"). A penalty, or an offering for sin, first directly enjoined in Lev. 4. The Heb. word is not applied to any sacrifice in pre-Mosaic times, and it is therefore peculiarly a sacrifice of the law.

Meaning. In Lev. 4:2 we read that "if a person sins unintentionally in any of these things which the Lord has commanded not to be done, and commits any of them," that conduct would furnish reason for a sin offering. The meaning is that of sinning "in error." This does not mean merely sinning through ignorance, hurry, want of consideration, or carelessness (cf. 5:1, 4, 15) but also sinning unintentionally (Num. 35:11, 15, 22-23); hence such sins as spring from weakness of flesh and blood, as distinguished from those committed "defiantly," i.e., in haughty, defiant rebellion

against God and His commandments. The one sinning presumptuously was to be cut off from among his people (15:30).

The object and effect of the sin offering were declared to be the forgiveness of sin (Lev. 4:20, 26, 31, 35; 5:10) and cleansing (ceremonial purgation) from the pollution of sin (12:8; 14:20; 16:19; etc.). It was thus the offering among the Hebrews in which the ideas of propitiation and of atonement for sin were most distinctly marked. Its presentation presupposed the consciousness of sin on the part of the person presenting it (cf. 4:14, 23, 28; 5:5). The laying on of the hands of the offerer was understood to typify the fact that the sin for which pardon and cleansing were being sought was transferred to the sacrifice, which thereby became sin (4:4, 15). The soul of the offerer, being represented by the blood, was, through the sprinkling of the latter, brought into the fellowship with or within the sphere of operation of the divine grace. When the blood of the sin offering was sprinkled upon the *horns* of the altar, which were symbolic of power and might, the soul was thereby symbolically brought within the efficacy of that divine grace in which it was required to participate in order that its sin might be duly atoned for.

The burning of the fat of the sacrifice upon the altar as an offering made by fire for a soothing aroma unto Jehovah (Lev. 4:31) was symbolic of the handing over of the better part of the man, the part that is susceptible of renewal, to the purifying fire of the divine holiness and love, in order that the inward man might be renewed from day to day by the Spirit of the Lord and at length be changed into the glory of the children of God.

Material. The material for the sin offering was regulated partly by the position of the one in whose behalf it was offered and partly by the nature of the offense for which an atonement was to be made.

1. *A young bull.* Consecration of priests and Levites to their office (Ex. 29:10-14, 35; Num. 8:8-9). For the high priest on the Day of Atonement (Lev. 16:3). Sin of the high priest (4:3), or sin of the whole congregation (4:13).

2. *A male goat.* New moon and annual festivals (Num. 28:15, 22, 30; 29:5, 11, 16, 19; etc.). Dedication of the Tabernacle and Temple (Num. 7:16, 22; Ezra 6:17; cf. 8:35). Sin of a leader (Lev. 4:23).

3. *A female goat.* Sin by one of the common people (Lev. 4:28, 32; 5:6).

4. *A ewe,* of a year old. A Nazirite released from his vow (Num. 6:14). Cleansing of a leper (Lev. 14:10).

5. *A turtledove or young pigeon.* Purifying of a woman after childbirth (Lev. 12:6); a man with a discharge (15:14); a woman who had a protracted discharge of blood (15:29); a Nazirite defiled by contact with a dead body (Num. 6:9-10). A

turtledove or young pigeon, as a substitute for the lamb in case of poverty, on occasion of an ordinary offense (Lev. 5:7); for purification of the leper (14:22).

Turtledove used in sacrificial offering

6. *Tenth of an ephah of flour.* Flour was prescribed as a substitute for the pigeon when poverty prevented the latter, and on the occasion of any ordinary offense (Lev. 5:11).

Occasions. The sin offerings were:

1. *Regular,* offered upon the following occasions: (a) For all the people, at the new moon, Passover, Pentecost, feast of Trumpets, feast of Booths (Num. 28:15–29:38; "Tabernacles," KJV), and the Day of Atonement (Lev. 16). (b) Consecration of priests and Levites (Ex. 29:10-14, 36). (c) The sacrifice of the red heifer, from the ashes of which was made the water of purification (Num. 19:1-10).

2. *Special,* offered on the following occasions: (a) For any *sin of ignorance* against the commandment of the Lord on the part of priest, people, or individual (Lev. 4). (b) For ceremonial defilement (5:2-3), such as of women (12:6-8), leprosy (14:10-11, 31), discharges in men and women (15:15, 30), defilement of a Nazirite, or at expiration of his vow (Num. 6:6-11, 16).

Ritual, or Mode of Presentation. After the animal had been brought forward, and the hand duly laid upon it, it was slaughtered. If the animal was a young bull offered in behalf of the high priest or of the whole congregation, its blood was taken into the Holy Place and there sprinkled seven times toward the inner veil, then upon the horns of the altar of incense; after that the remainder was poured out at the base of the altar of burnt offering (Lev. 4:5-7, 16-18).

If the animal was a ram, a female goat, or a lamb, the blood was merely put upon the horns of the altar of burnt offering, and the remainder was poured out at the base of the altar (4:24-25, 28-30, 32-34). Upon the Day of Atonement the high priest took the blood of the sin offering (the bull) for himself, and the blood of the goat offered in behalf of the people, into the most Holy Place

and sprinkled it upon and before the Mercy Seat (16:14-15).

The next step was, in all cases except pigeons, to separate the fatty portions from the animal, that is, the fat covering the intestines and such as was upon them, the kidneys and their fat, the fat on the loins, the lobe of the liver, and, in the case of a certain kind of sheep, the fat of the tail, and then burn them upon the altar (4:8-10, 19, 26, 31, 35).

In those cases in which the blood was sprinkled in the Holy Place, or the Holy of Holies (and in the case of the bull sacrifice as a sin offering at the consecration of the priests, Ex. 29:14), the flesh, along with the skin, head, bones, intestines, and refuse was carried outside the camp (afterward the city) to a clean place where the ashes of sacrifice were usually emptied, and there consumed by fire (Lev. 4:11-12, 21; 16:27). In the case of the other sin offerings, the blood of which was not applied as above, the flesh was eaten by the priests in the Holy Place (6:26; Num. 18:9-10). The skin probably went, as in the trespass offering, to the officiating priest.

The additional regulations respecting the sin offering were: "whoever touches them shall become consecrated" (Lev. 6:18, 27), i.e., every layman touching the flesh became as holy as the priest and was obliged to guard against defilement in the same manner (cf. 21:1-8); the vessel, in which it was boiled for the priests to eat, was broken if earthenware and scoured if bronze; garments upon which its blood had been sprinkled were to be washed (6:27-28).

Typology. The sin offering as a non-sweet savor presents Christ atoning for the guilt of sin (Heb. 13:11-12). It portrays our Lord as actually burdened with the believer's sin, standing in the sinner's place. It is in contrast to the sweet-savor offering that presents Christ's own perfections. The sin offering tells forth our Lord's death as presented in Isa. 53, Ps. 22, and 1 Pet. 2:24. This offering, however, carefully guards the infinite holiness of Him "who knew no sin to be sin on our behalf" (2 Cor. 5:21; cf. the law of this offering, Lev. 6:24-30). The sin offerings were efficacious and substitutionary and in their expiatory aspect vindicate the law through substitutionary sacrifice.

Guilt Offering (Heb. *'āshăm,* "fault").

Meaning. Although the guilt offering was propitiatory in character, it differed from the sin offering in that the latter made atonement for the *person* of the offender, whereas the former only atoned for one special offense. "In fact, the trespass offering may be regarded as representing ransom for a special wrong, while the sin offering symbolized general redemption" (Edersheim, *Temple,* p. 100).

Material. The guilt offering consisted of a ram, which was valued by a priest according to the shekel of the sanctuary (Lev. 5:15, 18; 6:6;

19:21). The only exception was in the case of a leper and a Nazirite, when the offering consisted of a lamb, without any mention of valuation (14:12; Num. 6:12).

Occasions. The guilt offerings, being prescribed for special sins, are not included in the general festal sacrifices. They were offered for the following offenses:

1. "If a person acts unfaithfully and sins unintentionally against the Lord's holy things" (Lev. 5:15), i.e., to inadvertently take away from Jehovah that which belonged to Him, of sacrifice, firstfruits, tithes, etc. The ram for sacrifice was to be accompanied by compensation for the harm done and the gift of a fifth part of the value to the priest.

2. Ignorant transgression of any definite prohibition of the law (v. 17).

3. Fraud, suppression of the truth, or perjury against a neighbor; with compensation and with the addition of a fifth part of the property in question to the person wronged (6:1-6).

4. Rape of a betrothed slave (19:20-22).

5. At the purification of a leper (14:12) and the polluted Nazirite (Num. 6:12).

Ritual. The sacrifice was slaughtered on the N side of the altar, its blood sprinkled upon the latter, the fat burned upon it, and the flesh eaten by the priests in the Holy Place (as in the sin offering). The skin also belonged to the officiating priest. With reference to the accompanying grain offering, everything baked in the oven and everything prepared in a pan or pot was to belong to the priest officiating; whereas such portions as were mixed with oil or were dry were to belong to "all the sons of Aaron," i.e., divided among all the priests.

Typology. This ritual prefigures Christ's atoning for the damage of sin. It is a non-sweet-savor offering. It has in view not so much the guilt of sin, which is the aspect in the sin offering, but rather the injury. Psalm 51:4 expresses this aspect of the offering: "Against Thee, Thee only, I have sinned, and done what is evil in Thy sight, so that Thou art justified when Thou dost speak, and blameless when Thou dost judge." In other words, that which is due God as an infinitely Holy Being in every sinner is typically signified.

Burnt Offering. The name given this offering (Heb. *ōlâ*, "ascending" as smoke), was given because it was to be wholly consumed and to *rise* in smoke toward heaven. There is also in use the poetical term *kālîl* "complete" (Deut. 33:10; 1 Sam. 7:9; Ps. 51:19; Gk. *holokautōma;* Mark 12:33; Heb. 10:6), alluding to the fact that, with the exception of the skin, it was *wholly* and *entirely* consumed. The victims in the other sacrifices were only partially consumed upon the altar.

Meaning. The burnt offering symbolized the entire surrender to God of the individual or of the congregation. God's acceptance thereof had a view to the renewal and sanctification of the entire man and consecration to a course of life pleasing to God. The law of sacrifice does not teach that the burnt offering had any reference to atonement or forgiveness of sins, provision being made for that by the atoning sacrifices (sin and trespass offerings). The burnt offering was based solely on the assumption that Israel had been admitted into a covenant of grace with Jehovah, and it could only be offered by those Israelites who retained their standing in the covenant. Strangers were permitted, if not guilty of any notorious offense, to offer burnt and thank offerings to Jehovah without being fully (i.e., by circumcision) admitted into covenant with the God of Israel.

Anyone forfeiting his covenant rights by sin or transgression was required to be again reconciled to God by means of a sin offering before he could venture to present a burnt offering. If there was any atoning element in the burnt offering it was only to a limited extent. And yet, inasmuch as sin adheres to all, even in a state of grace, it was necessary that in the burnt offering there should be so much of the element in question as would cover any defects and imperfections.

Expressing as it did the inward religious disposition expected of every true Israelite, the burnt offering was required to be presented in the morning and evening of every day, the Sabbath, the new moons, and festival occasions. At the new moons and festivals the burnt offerings had to be preceded by a sin offering, it being necessary in this way to make atonement for those sins that had been committed in the interval between one festival and another.

Material. The animals prescribed for this sacrifice by the law were a young bull, a ram or male lamb, and a male goat—always a male. In case of poverty, turtledoves or young pigeons might be offered, irrespective of sex (Lev. 1:3, 10, 14). The command for a male was probably to teach that the act of surrender was to be of an active, energetic character.

Occasions. There were regular, special, and freewill burnt offerings.

1. *Regular* burnt offerings were offered as follows: (a) Every morning and evening (Ex. 29:38-42; Num. 28:3-8). (b) Each Sabbath, double that of the daily offering (Num. 28:9-10). (c) At the new moon, the three great festivals, the Day of Atonement, and feast of Trumpets (*see* Num. 28:11–29:39).

2. *Special* burnt offerings were offered as follows: (a) At the consecration of priests (Ex. 29:15; Lev. 8:18; 9:12). (b) At the purification of women (Lev. 12:6-8). (c) At the cleansing of lepers (14:19). (d) Removal of other ceremonial uncleanness (15:15, 30). (e) On any accidental breach of the Nazirite vow, or its conclusion (Num. 6:11, 14).

3. *Freewill* burnt offerings on any solemn oc-

casion, e.g., dedication of the Tabernacle (Num. 7) and of the Temple (1 Kings 8:64).

The burnt offering was the only sacrifice that non-Israelites were allowed to bring. The emperor Augustus had a daily burnt offering brought for him of two lambs and a bull; and ever afterward this sacrifice was regarded as indicating that the Jews recognized him as their ruler. Hence, at the commencement of the Jewish war, Eleazar carried its rejection, which was considered as a mark of rebellion.

Ritual. The victim was led to the altar by the person offering it, duly consecrated by the laying on of hands, and then slain by the offerer. The priest then took the blood and sprinkled it about upon the altar. The animal was flayed, the skin falling to the officiating priest as a perquisite (Lev. 7:8); the flesh was next cut up, the intestines and hind legs washed, and then the several parts, including the head and fat, were laid upon the burning wood, the whole being consumed.

In case the offering was a pigeon the priest wrung off its head and allowed the blood to flow beside the altar; he then took the crop and feathers and flung them on the ash heap beside the altar. He made an incision at the wings and placed the bird upon the altar fire and there

burned it (1:14-17). When the burnt offering consisted of a bull or smaller cattle, the law required it to be followed by a grain and drink offering varying in quantity according to the kind of animal offered—a regulation, however, that did not apply in the case of pigeons.

Typology. This ritual sets forth Christ offering Himself without spot to God in performing the divine will with joy, even to the point of death. In the offering the note of penalty is not conspicuous (Heb. 9:11-14; 10:5-7). The offering is a soothing aroma. These offerings are so-called because they deal with Christ in His own perfections and in His perfect devotion to the Father's will. They are in contrast to the nonsoothing offerings that typify Christ as carrying the sinner's demerit. The whole burnt offering is both atoning and substitutionary: Christ dies in the believer's stead. The sacrificial animals, the bull, the sheep, the goat, and turtledove or pigeon all symbolize Christ in some aspect of His redeeming character. The young ox portrays His patient endurance as a Savior (1 Cor. 9:9-10; Isa. 52:13-15; Phil. 2:5-8). The sheep or ram portrays Christ in unresisting abandonment to death (Isa. 53:7). The goat typifies a sinner and, when used of Christ, as He who was "numbered with trans-

Jewish priest offering a sacrifice on the altar of burnt offering

gressors." The turtledove or pigeon symbolizes mourning innocence (Isa. 38:14; Heb. 7:26). It also portrays poverty (Lev. 5:7). It shows forth Him who became poor that we might become rich (2 Cor. 8:9; Phil. 2:6-8).

Peace Offering (Heb. *zebaḥ shelāmîm*, "sacrifice of peace"), another sacrifice offered *in communion* with God. It was divided into three kinds: the *thank offering* (*zebaḥ hattôdâ*, "sacrifice of thanksgiving," Lev. 7:12; 22:29); the *votive offering* (*zebaḥ neder*, "sacrifice of a vow," Num. 6:2; 15:3, 8); the *freewill offering* (*zebaḥ nedābâ*, Lev. 7:16; 22:18, 21). It always followed all the other sacrifices.

Meaning. The peace offerings have their root in the state of grace with its fellowship with God and find their culminating point in the sacrificial feast. They served to establish the Hebrew more firmly in the fellowhip of the divine grace; to be mindful of God when in possession and enjoyment of His mercies; and when adversity threatened to obscure his feeling and consciousness of God's nearness and mercy, he might be enabled through the peace offering to maintain this feeling and consciousness and quicken them afresh.

In times of prosperity and success he would naturally feel thankful to God and embody his act by means of sacrifice; hence *thank offering*. In case anyone desired to secure a certain blessing, he would endeavor by means of a vow to prevail upon God to bestow it; hence the *votive offering*. The motive impelling the *freewill offering* seems to have centered in the desire to thank God for the enjoyment of His bounties and to be assured of their continuance (*see* Ritual below).

Material. The animals prescribed for these sacrifices were unblemished oxen or smaller cattle of either sex (Lev. 3:1, 6; 9:4, 18; etc.), although deformed animals were allowable in freewill offerings (22:23). These sacrifices were always accompanied by a grain and drink offering (7:11-13; etc.). No mention is found of pigeons being used in the peace offerings.

Occasions. Peace offerings were made on public occasions and on occasions of only private significance.

1. *Public* peace offerings were customary on occasions of festive inauguration (Ex. 24:5; 2 Sam. 6:17-18; 1 Kings 8:63), the election of kings (1 Sam. 11:15), and upon the fortunate result of important enterprises (Deut. 27:7; Josh. 8:31). They were expressly prescribed for the feast of Pentecost (Lev. 23:19). The festivals were observed with peace offerings (Num. 10:10; 2 Chron. 30:22), and Solomon arranged three times a year a sacrificial festival of burnt and peace offerings (1 Kings 9:25).

2. *Private* peace offerings were the result of free impulse, or in fulfillment of a vow (Lev. 7:16; 22:21; Num. 15:8), in recognition of a special favor from Jehovah (Lev. 7:12; 22:29), and regu-

larly at the expiration of a Nazirite vow (Num. 6:14).

Ritual. The offerer led the animal to the altar, laid his hand upon its head, and killed it. The priest caught the blood and sprinkled it upon the altar. At this stage the fat of the intestines—the same parts as in the case of the sin offering—was taken from the animal and burned upon the altar on the burnt offering (Lev. 3:3-5, 9-11, 14-16; 9:18-20). The breast and the right shoulder were then separated from each other, the shoulder being heaved—laid aside—as the portion of the officiating priest, directly from the offerer, whereas the breast was waved, i.e., symbolically presented to the Lord, from whom the priests received it for their use. The priest's part might be eaten by him, either boiled or roasted, in some clean place (7:30-34; 10:13-14). All the flesh of public peace offering (not burned upon the altar) belonged to the priests (23:20).

The rest of the flesh belonged to the offerer, furnishing material for the sacrificial feast. In the case of the thank offering it must be eaten the same day, in other cases no later than the second day. Whatever was not eaten within the prescribed time had to be burned, but not on the altar (7:15-17; 22:30).

One cake of each of the three kinds making up the grain offering was the portion of the officiating priest (7:13-14).

The meaning of the sacrificial proceedings in the case of the peace offering is worthy of study. As stated above, the fat of the peace offering was to be consumed on the top of the burnt offering, "which is on the wood that is on the fire," as an "offering by fire of a soothing aroma to the Lord" (3:5). Thus the peace offering presupposed the previous reconciliation of the offerer with God and the sanctification of his life as the basis of admission into fellowship with God, which was realized in the sacrificial feast. As he partook of this meal, the material food was transformed into a symbol of his being spiritually fed with the mercies of God, of his being satisfied with fullness of joy in the presence of the Lord (Ps. 16:11).

Keil observes: "In consecrated character imparted to the whole victim by assigning the choicest portions of the flesh to the Lord and the officiating priest, the sacrificial feast was transformed into a covenant feast, a feast of love and joy, which symbolized the privilege of dwelling in the house and family of the Lord, and so shadowed forth the rejoicing of his people before him (Deut. 12:12, 18) and the blessedness of eating and drinking in the kingdom of God" (Luke 14:15; 22:30) (*Arch.*, 1:330).

Typology. As a sweet-savor offering this ritual portrays Christ as our peace (Eph. 2:14-18). Christ made peace (Col. 1:20); preached peace (Eph. 2:17). The offering sets forth God as propitiated and the sinner reconciled; God and the sinner brought together in peace, both satisfied with the finished work of Christ. Closely associated with peace is fellowship. With this idea in mind the peace offering afforded food for the priests (Lev. 7:31-34).

Grain and Drink Offerings. "Grain" is the rendering of the Heb. *minḥâ,* "offering," whereas "drink offering" is the rendering of Heb. *nesek,* "libation."

Meaning. One meaning of these offerings, which is analogous to that of the offering of the tithes (firstfruits and the bread of the Presence), appears to be expressed in the words of David: "Everything that is in the heavens and the earth . . . all things come from Thee, and from Thy hand we have given Thee" (1 Chron. 29:10-14). It recognized the sovereignty of Jehovah and His bounty in the bestowal of earthly blessings by dedicating to Him the best of His gifts—flour, as the main support of life; oil, the symbol of richness; wine, as the symbol of vigor and refreshment (*see* Ps. 104:15).

Another meaning is ascribed to these offerings, that of a symbol of the spiritual food that Israel strove after as the fruit of its spiritual labor, or those good works in which true sanctification must necessarily embody itself.

Material. The material of the grain offering consisted either of grain—offered partly unground, in the shape of roasted ears, and partly fine flour; in both instances oil was poured on and incense added—or of cakes, prepared in three different ways with oil but without any leaven (*see* Sacrifices: Classification of). Both kinds of grain offerings were required to be seasoned with salt (Lev. 2:13).

The *drink offering* consisted in every instance of wine.

Occasion. Grain offerings were either *public* or *private,* and were brought either in conjunction with burnt or peace offerings (never with sin or trespass offerings) or by themselves.

The three public grain offerings were the twelve loaves of the bread of the Presence; the omer, or sheaf, of wheat, on the second day of *Passover* (which see); and the two wave loaves at Pentecost.

Four private grain offerings were prescribed by law: (1) the daily grain offering of the high priest, according to the Jewish interpretation of Lev. 6:14-18; (2) that at the consecration of priests (6:20); (3) that in substitution for a sin offering, in case of poverty (5:11-12); and (4) that of jealousy (Num. 5:15).

The following were voluntary: that of fine flour with oil, unbaked (Lev. 2:1); that "baked in an oven," "on the griddle," and the "wafers," which were "made in a pan" (2:4-7).

Ritual. In all baked grain offerings an "omer" was always made into ten cakes—except the high priest's daily grain offering, of which twelve cakes were baked as representative of Israel. In presenting a grain offering the priest first brought it in

the golden or silver dish in which it had been prepared, and then transferred it to a holy vessel, putting oil and frankincense upon it. Standing at the SE corner of the altar, he took the "handful" that was to be burned, put it in another vessel, laid some of the frankincense on it, carried it to the top of the altar, salted it, and then placed it on the fire.

The rest of the offering belonged to the priests (Lev. 6:16-18), except in the grain offering of the high priest and at the consecration of the priests (6:20-23), when it was entirely burned and none allowed to be eaten.

Every grain offering was accompanied by a drink offering of wine; but the law contained no regulation as to the mode in which it was to be presented or how the wine was to be disposed of.

Typology. This offering exhibits Christ in His human perfections tested by suffering. The fine flour represents the sinless humanity of our Lord. The fire is testing by suffering even unto death. Frankincense symbolizes the aroma of His life toward the Father (cf. Ex. 30:34). The absence of leaven, a type of evil, shows forth His character as "the Truth." The oil mingled with the offering speaks of His conception by the Spirit (Matt. 1:18-23). Oil poured upon the offering speaks of His enduement with the Spirit (John 1:32; 6:27).

Heave and Wave Offerings. These offerings took their names from the special ceremonies connected with their presentation.

Heave Offering (Heb. *terûmâ,* "lifted up, raised"). Everything that the Israelites voluntarily (Ex. 25:2-7; 35:24; 36:3, *see* marg.), or in compliance with a legal prescription (Ex. 30:15; Lev. 7:14; Num. 15:19-21; 18:27-30; 31:29-30, *see* marg.), separated from what belonged to them and presented (Ex. 29:28; Num. 18:8, marg.; 5:9, marg.) to Jehovah, not as a sacrifice but as an offering (Isa. 40:20) by way of contribution for religious purposes, such as the erection and maintenance of the sanctuary (Ex. 25:2, 8; 30:13; 35:5, 21, 24; 36:3, 6; Ezra 8:25; etc.) or for the maintenance of the priests.

Those portions of the offerings that were waved were also regarded as gifts to Jehovah, which He was understood to hand over to the priests; every heave offering could likewise be regarded as a wave offering. The heave offerings could only be used by the priests and their children (Num. 18:19; Lev. 22:10).

Wave Offering (Heb. *tenûpâ,* "undulation"). When this offering was presented the offering was placed upon the hands of the offerer and, after putting his hands under those of the offerer, the priest moved the offering backward and forward horizontally. The rabbinical suggestion that there was a distinct rite of "heaving," besides that of "waving," seems to rest on a misunderstanding of such passages as Lev. 2:2, 9; 7:32; 10:15; etc. Some believe that "heaving" applies to an upward movement as well as the horizontal, but there is little ground for that opinion.

The following were the offerings to be *waved* before the Lord—the *breast* of a private thank offering (Lev. 7:30); the fat, breast, and shoulder of the thank offerings at the consecration of the priests, the so-called consecration of offerings (Ex. 29:22-26; Lev. 8:25-29); the firstling sheaf offered on the second day of the Passover (Lev. 23:11); the two lambs as a thank offering at the feast of Pentecost (23:20); the lamb and the log of oil as a trespass offering for the purification of the leper (14:12); the thank offering of the Nazirite (Num. 6:20); the jealousy offering (5:25).

Heifer, The Red. The medium appointed for the purification of such as might be rendered unclean by contact with the dead was composed of running water and the ashes of the "red heifer" (Num. 19:1-5). The ashes were prepared as follows: A heifer, without blemish and that had never been yoked, was slaughtered outside the camp. Eleazar (the son and successor of the high priest) dipped his finger in the blood and sprinkled it seven times toward the sanctuary. Then the heifer, along with the skin, flesh, blood, and refuse, was burned in the presence of the priest, who at the same time took cedar wood, hyssop, and scarlet material and cast them into the flames. A man free from defilement gathered the ashes and carried them to a clean place outside the camp, where they were stored. All persons connected with the ceremony were rendered unclean till evening.

The purifying medium was applied as follows: A man who was himself free from defilement took some of the ashes, put them in a vessel, and poured fresh running water over them. Dipping a bunch of hyssop into the mixture, he sprinkled it upon the person to be purified on the third and seventh days. In like manner the tent in which the corpse had lain and its furniture were all sprinkled with the same water.

The red heifer is called a sin offering (Num. 19:9, 17); and as death is the result of sin, it followed that the removal of the defilement of death would naturally call for a sin offering. The color, condition, and sex of the victim represented a full, fresh, and vigorous life; and possessing this, the animal, as a sin offering, was perfectly adapted to the purpose of bearing the guilt of the sins of the congregation that were imputed to it, as well as of vicariously suffering death as the wages of sin. The heifer was burned outside the camp by way of exhibiting the necessary fruit and consequence of sin.

Typology. The red heifer portrays the sacrifice of Christ as the medium of the believer's cleansing from the pollution contracted in his walk as a pilgrim through the world. The order of cleansing is: (1) The slaying of the sacrifice. (2) The sevenfold sprinkling of the blood, showing forth the completed putting away of the believer's sins

before God (Heb. 9:12-14). (3) The burning of the sacrifice to ashes and their preservation as a memorial of the sacrifice. (4) The cleansing by sprinkling with the ashes mingled with water. The water is typical of the Holy Spirit and the Word (John 7:37-39; Eph. 5:26). The whole ritual portrays the fact that the Holy Spirit employs the Word of God to convict the believer of sin allowed in the life. Thus convicted, the believer is made conscious of the fact that the guilt of sin has been borne in the sacrifice of Christ. Instead of losing hope the convicted believer confesses the unworthy act and is forgiven and cleansed (John 13:3-10; 1 John 1:7-10).

Schedule of Offerings. The offerings prescribed by the Mosaic ritual were presented on a regular schedule—some daily, some on the Sabbath, and some during the various festivals.

Daily (Num. 28:3-8). The daily sacrifice was offered morning and evening, each consisting of a yearling lamb, for a burnt offering; a tenth ephah of flour, for a grain offering; and one-fourth hin of wine, for a drink offering.

Sabbath (Num. 28:9-10; Lev. 24:8). The daily offerings (*see* above); and two yearling lambs, for a burnt offering; two one-tenth ephahs of flour, mingled with oil, for a grain offering; one-half hin of wine, for a drink offering; twelve loaves of the bread of the Presence.

New Moon (Num. 28:11-15). The daily offerings; and two young bulls, one ram, seven lambs, for a burnt offering; flour mingled with oil, three one-tenth ephahs for each bull, two one-tenth ephahs for the ram, and one-tenth an ephah for each lamb; drink offering.

Feast of Trumpets, or Seventh New Moon (Num. 29:1-6). The daily and new moon offerings; and one bull, one ram, seven yearling lambs, for a burnt offering; flour mingled with oil; three one-tenth ephahs for the bull, two one-tenth ephahs for the ram, one-tenth an ephah for each lamb, for a grain offering; one kid of the goats, for a sin offering; drink offerings.

Passover (Ex. 12:1-7). The daily offerings; and a kid (lamb or goat, Ex. 12:5) was selected on the 10th of Abib, slain on the 14th, and its blood sprinkled on the doorposts and lintels.

Unleavened Bread (Num. 28:17-24). The daily offerings; and one goat, for a sin offering; two young bulls, one ram, and seven yearling lambs, burnt offering; flour mingled with oil, three one-tenth ephahs for each bull, two one-tenth ephahs for the ram, one-tenth an ephah for each lamb, grain offering. The above offerings were for each day of the feast (15th to 21st Abib). On the second day of the feast (16th Abib) the first sheaf of the new harvest (barley) was offered by waving, not burning. With this sheaf was offered a male yearling lamb, for a burnt offering; two one-tenth ephahs of flour and oil, for a grain offering; one-fourth hin of wine, for a drink offering.

Pentecost (Feast of Weeks) (Num. 28:26-31;

Lev. 23:16-20). The daily offerings; and a kid of the goats for a sin offering; two young bulls, one ram, seven yearling lambs, for a burnt offering; three one-tenth ephahs of flour and oil for each bull, two one-tenth ephahs for the ram, one-tenth an ephah for each lamb, grain offering; one-half hin of wine for the bull, one-third hin of wine for the ram, one-fourth hin of wine for each lamb, drink offering. After the above was presented, the new grain offering of two wave loaves, made of two one-tenth ephahs of wheat flour, baked with leaven, was offered. With these were offered seven yearling lambs, one young bull, and two rams, for a burnt offering, with the prescribed grain and drink offerings; a male goat, for a sin offering; two yearling lambs for a peace offering.

Day of Atonement (Lev. 16:3; Num. 29:7-11). The daily offerings; and a bull for a sin offering and a ram for a burnt offering, for the priesthood; two goats for a sin offering and a ram for a burnt offering, for the people; followed by one young bull, one ram, seven lambs, for a burnt offering; flour mingled with oil, three one-tenth ephahs for a bull, two one-tenth ephahs for a ram, and one-tenth an ephah for each lamb, grain offering; one-half hin of wine for a bull, one-third hin of wine for a ram, and one-quarter hin of wine for each lamb, drink offering.

Feast of Booths (Tabernacles) (Num. 29:13-38). The daily offerings; and bulls, rams, lambs, and goats according to a prescribed schedule (*see* table 29).

Table 29
Sacrifices Offered
During the Feast of Booths

Day	Bulls	Rams	Lambs	Goats[1]
First	13	2	14	1
Second	12	2	14	1
Third	11	2	14	1
Fourth	10	2	14	1
Fifth	9	2	14	1
Sixth	8	2	14	1
Seventh	7	2	14	1
Total for the seven days	70	14	98	7
Eighth	1	1	7	1

1. The sin offering

The bulls, rams, and lambs together made the burnt offerings, whereas the ram was for a sin offering. Each bull, ram, and lamb was accompanied by its prescribed grain and drink offerings.

Grain Offering. The grain offering consisted of three one-tenth ephahs of flour for a bull, two one-tenth ephahs for a ram, one-tenth an ephah for a lamb; the flour in each case was to be mingled with oil.

Drink Offering. The drink offering consisted of one-half hin of wine for a bullock, one-third hin of wine for a ram, one-fourth hin of wine for a lamb.

M.F.U.

BIBLIOGRAPHY: W. Kelly, *Offerings of Leviticus*, 1-7 (1899); id., *Priesthood, Its Privileges and Its Duties: An Exposition of Leviticus*, 8-15 (1902); id., *The Day of Atonement* (1925); S. H. Kellogg, *The Book of Leviticus* (1978); G. J. Wenham, *The Book of Leviticus*, New International Commentary on the Old Testament (1979); R. K. Harrison, *Leviticus, An Introduction and Commentary*, Tyndale Old Testament Commentaries (1980).

SAD'DUCEE (sad'ū-sē). A member of one of the religious parties that existed among the Jews in the days of our Lord; the others were the Essenes and the Pharisees.

Name. The Heb. word by which they were called is *ṣaddûqîm;* Gk. *Saddoukaios* (Matt. 3:7; 16:1, 6, 11-12; 22:23, 34; Mark 12:18; Luke 20:27; Acts 4:1; 5:17; 23:6-8). The ordinary Jewish statement is that the Sadducees were named from a certain Zadok, a disciple of Antigonus of Socho, who is mentioned in the Mishna as having received the oral law from Simon the Just. Epiphanius states that the Sadducees called themselves such from Heb. *sedeq*, "righteousness," and that there was anciently a Zadok among the priests, but that they did not continue in the doctrines of their chief. Edersheim suggests (*Life of Jesus*, 1:324) "that the linguistic difficulty in the change of the sound *i* into *u—Tsaddiqim* into *Tsadduqim*, may have resulted, not grammatically, but by popular witticism. Some wit may have suggested: Read not *Tsaddiqim*, the 'righteous,' but *Tsadduqim* (from *Tsad-u*), 'desolation,' 'destruction.' Whether or not this suggestion approves itself to critics, the derivation of Sadducees from *Tsaddiqim* is certainly that which offers most probability."

Aristocratic. We gain but a distorted image of the Sadducees if we only look at the points of differences between them and the Pharisees. Still, each party had its strong characteristic, that of the Pharisees being a *rigid realism*, while the Sadducees were *aristocratic*. Josephus repeatedly designates them as those who gain only the rich and have not the people on their side (*Ant.* 13.10.6). "This doctrine is received but by a few, yet by those still of the greatest dignity" (*Ant.* 18.1.4). What Josephus really means is that the Sadducees were the aristocrats, the wealthy *euporoi*, the persons of rank (*prōtoi tois axiōmasin*), i.e., from the *priesthood*. The NT (Acts 5:17) and Josephus (*Ant.* 20.9.1) testify that the high-priestly families belonged to the Sadducean party. The Sadduceans were not, however, merely the priestly party but aristocratic priests.

Tenets. The Sadducees were distinctive in many of the positions they took regarding the law, ritual, and doctrine.

The Law. The Sadducees acknowledged only the written law as binding and rejected the entire traditionary interpretation and further development of the law during the centuries by the scribes. Thus, according to Josephus (*Ant.* 13.10.6), the Sadducees say only what is written is to be esteemed as legal and what has come down from tradition of the fathers need not be observed. Although they rejected the tradition of the elders, they did not, as some of the fathers supposed, reject the Prophets.

In legal matters the Sadducees were, according to Josephus (*Ant.* 20.9.1), "very rigid in judging offenders above all the rest of the Jews," whereas the Pharisees were much milder and more merciful. This may be connected with the fact that the Sadducees strictly adhered to the letter of the law, whereas the Pharisees sought to mitigate its severity by interpretation, although the latter in some instances were the more severe. "They saw in the tradition of the elders an excess of legal strictness which they refused to have imposed upon them, while the advanced religious views were, on the one hand, superfluous to their worldly-mindedness, and on the other, inadmissible by their higher culture and enlightenment" (Schürer, *History of the Jewish People,* div. 2, 1:41).

Levirate marriage. The Sadducees held that the levirate law was obligatory only when marriage was not consummated, i.e., when a woman's betrothed husband died without cohabitating with her, then his surviving brother could perform the duty of *levir* without committing incest, as she was still a virgin. This restriction of the levirate law on the part of the Sadducees imparts additional force to the incident recorded in Matt. 22:23-28; Mark 12:18-23; Luke 20:27-33. According to the understanding of the Sadducees, the marriage would have been consummated only between the woman and the seventh brother; whereas the Pharisees would have made them all cohabit with the woman. The Sadducees would say only the last brother could be her husband, but according to the Pharisaic practice she would have been the real wife of them all.

The ceremony of *taking off the shoe* (Deut. 25:9) was understood literally by the Sadducees, who insisted that the rejected widow should spit into the man's face; the Pharisees held that spitting *before his face* met all the requirements of the case.

The right of retaliation. With the same conservatism and rigor the Sadducees insisted upon the literal carrying out of the law "eye for eye," etc. (Ex. 21:23-25); the Pharisees, with due regard for the interests of the people, maintained that monetary compensation was sufficient.

False witnesses. The Sadducees insisted that false witnesses should be put to death only when the accused had been executed in consequence of their false testimony (Deut. 19:19-21); the Pharisees required that this should take place as soon as sentence had been passed. In this case the Pharisees were the more severe. The Sadducees

required compensation, not only if an ox or a donkey (Ex. 21:32, 35-36), but also if a manservant or a maidservant had injured anyone, arguing that the master is far more answerable for him than his cattle, as he is to watch over his moral conduct. The Pharisees denied this, submitting that the slave was a responsible creature, and that, if the master be held responsible for his conduct, a dissatisfied slave might, out of spite, commit crimes in order to make his master pay.

Inheritance. The law of inheritance formed another distinctive feature of the Sadducees. They maintained that when a son, being heir presumptive and having sisters, died leaving a daughter, that the daughter was not to receive all the property but that the sisters of the deceased were to have an equal share with the daughter. They urged that the daughter was only second degree, whereas the sisters were the first degree. The Pharisees, on the contrary, maintained that the deceased brother's daughter was the rightful and sole heir, inasmuch as she was the descendant of the male heir, whose simple existence disinherited his sisters.

Ritual. Respecting questions of ritual, the Sadducees did not regard as binding Pharisaic decrees with respect, e.g., to clean and unclean. They derided their Pharisaic opponents on account of the oddities and inconsistencies into which their laws of cleanness brought them. But they did not renounce the principle of Levitical uncleanness in itself, for they demanded a higher degree of cleanness for the priest who burned the *red heifer* (which see) than did the Pharisees. They differed somewhat from the Pharisees regarding the festival laws, but the only difference of importance was that the Sadducees did not acknowledge as binding the confused mass of Pharisaic enactments.

In short, "the difference in principle between the two parties is confined, on the whole, to this general rejection of Pharisaic tradition by the Sadducees. All other differences were such as would naturally result from the one party not accepting the other's exegetical tradition. The Sadducee theoretically agreed with Pharisaic tradition in some, perhaps many, particulars—he only denied its *obligation,* and reserved the right of private opinion" (Schürer, div. 2, 2:38).

Doctrine. The Sadducees refused to believe in a resurrection of the body and retribution in a future life or in any personal continuity of the individual (Matt. 22:23; Mark 12:18; Luke 20:27; Josephus *Ant.* 18.1.4.; *Wars* 2.8.14). The Jews "would not consider themselves bound to accept any doctrine as an article of faith, unless it had been proclaimed by Moses, their great lawgiver; . . . and it is certain that in the written law of the Pentateuch there is a total absence of any assertion by Moses of the resurrection of the dead. This fact is presented to Christians in a striking manner by the well-known words of the Pentateuch, which are quoted by Christ in argument with the Sadducees on this subject (Ex. 3:6; Mark 12:26-27; Matt. 22:31-32; Luke 20:37). It cannot be doubted that in such a case Christ would quote to his powerful adversaries the most cogent text in the law; and yet the text actually quoted does not do more than suggest an *inference* on this great doctrine. It is true that in other parts of the OT there are individual passages that express a belief in a resurrection, such as in Isa. 26:19; Dan. 12:2; Job 19:26; and in some of the psalms; and it may at first sight be a subject of surprise that the Sadducees were not convinced by the authority of those passages. But although the Sadducees regarded the books that contained these passages as sacred, it is more than doubtful whether any of the Jews regarded them as sacred in precisely the same sense as the written law." Hence, scarcely any Jew would have believed it necessary to believe in man's resurrection, "unless the doctrine had been proclaimed by Moses; and as the Sadducees disbelieved the transmission of any oral law by Moses, the striking absence of that doctrine from the written law freed them from the necessity of accepting the doctrine as divine" (Smith, *Bib. Dict.*, s.v.).

According to Acts 23:8, the Sadducees denied that there was angel or spirit, i.e., independent spiritual realities besides God. To this category of spirits, denied by them, belonged also the spirits of the departed; for they held the soul to be a refined matter, which perished with the body (Josephus *Ant.* 18.1.4; *Wars* 2.8.14). The two principal explanations that have been suggested as to the belief of the Sadducees on this point are, either they regarded the angels of the OT as transitory unsubstantial representations of Jehovah, or they disbelieved merely the angelical system that was developed among the Jews after the captivity.

Regarding the question of free will and predestination, if we may believe Josephus (*Wars* 2.8.14), the Sadducees, in dissenting from the fantastic, imaginary development of Judaism, came to lay great stress upon human freedom. With a strong insistence upon personal liberty there came a decrease of the religious motive. They insisted that man was placed at his own disposal, and they rejected the belief that a divine cooperation takes place in human action as such. The difference between the Pharisees and the Sadducees seems to have amounted to this—the former accentuated God's preordination, the latter man's free will; and, whereas the Pharisees admitted only a partial influence of the human element on what happened, or the cooperation of the human with the divine, the Sadducees denied all absolute preordination and made man's choice of evil or good to depend entirely on the exercise of free will and self-determination.

The Pharisees accentuated the divine to the verge of fatalism and insisted upon absolute and unalterable preordination of every event in its minutest detail. We can well understand how the Sadducees would oppose notions like these. Neither the NT nor rabbinic writings bring the charge of the denial of God's prevision against the Sadducees.

History. Milligan (*Imperial Bible Dictionary*) says of the party of Sadducees: "Its origin, like that of the Pharisees, is in all probability to be sought in that remarkable period of Jewish history which is embraced between the restoration of Israel to its own land, or rather between the cessation of prophecy after that event, and the Christian era. No traces of Sadduceeism are to be found in Israel previous to the captivity. . . . In the presence of the divinely inspired prophet of Jehovah, the representative of the theocracy in its noblest form and most glorious anticipations, no tendency like that of the Sadducees, so denationalized, so cold, so skeptical, and so worldly, could have taken root. The very nature of the case, therefore, requires us to seek its origin at a more recent date, and naturally carries us to that strange period, of both outward and inward confusion through which, after the death of Alexander the Great, Palestine had to pass." In this Greek period, political interests were combined with Greek culture; and to effect anything in the political world one must of necessity have stood on a more or less friendly footing with Hellenism. In the higher ranks of the priesthood Hellenism gained ground. In the same proportion, it was alienated from the Jewish religious interest. This tendency was checked by the rising of the Maccabees, at which time the religious life was revived and strengthened. It was then that the rigidly legal party of the "Chasidees" gained more and more influence. And therewith their pretensions also increased. Those only were to be acknowledged as true Israelites who observed the law according to the full strictness of the interpretations given to it by the scribes. This made the *aristocratic* party the more strenuous in its opposition, and there resulted a firmer consolidation of parties, the "Chasidees" becoming "Pharisees," and the aristocratic party being called "Sadducees" by their opponents.

Under the earlier Maccabees (Judas, Jonathan, and Simon) this "Zadokite" aristocracy was necessarily in the background. The ancient, high-priestly family, which, at least in some of its members, represented the extreme philo-Hellenistic standpoint, was supplanted. The high-priestly office remained for a time unoccupied. In the year 152 Jonathan was appointed high priest, and thus was founded the new high-priestly dynasty of the Hasmonaeans, whose whole past compelled them at first to support the rigidly legal party. Nevertheless there was not in the times of the first Hasmonaeans (Jonathan, Simon) an entire withdrawal of the Sadducees from the scene. The Hasmonaeans had to come to some kind of understanding with it and to yield to it at least a portion of seats in the "Gerusia." Things remained in this position till the time of John Hyrcanus, when the Sadducees again became the ruling party. John Hyrcanus, Aristobulus I, and Alexander Jannaeus became their followers. The reaction under Alexandra brought the Pharisees back to power. Their *political* supremacy was, however, of no long duration. Although the spiritual power of the Pharisees had increased greatly, the Sadducean aristocracy was able to keep at the helm in politics. The price at which the Sadducees had to secure themselves power at this later period was indeed a high one, for they were obliged in their official actions actually to accommodate themselves to Pharisaic views. With the fall of the Jewish state the Sadducees altogether disappear from history. Their strong point was politics. When deprived of this, their last hour had struck. While the Pharisaic party only gained strength, only obtained more absolute rule over the Jewish people in consequence of the collapse of political affairs, the very ground on which the Sadducees stood was cut away from them. Therefore it is not to be wondered that Jewish scholars soon no longer knew who the Sadducees really were.

BIBLIOGRAPHY: M. H. Segal, *The Expositor* 13 (1917): 81ff.; G. H. Box, *The Expositor* 15 (1918): 19ff., 401ff.; id., 16 (1918): 55ff.; J. W. Lightley, *Jewish Sects and Parties in the Time of Jesus* (1923), pp. 5-178; L. Finkelstein, *Harvard Theological Review* 22 (1929): 185ff.; T. W. Manson, *Bulletin of the John Rylands Library* 22 (1938): 144-59; J. Z. Lauterbach, *Rabbinic Essays* (1951); L. Finkelstein, *The Pharisees*, 2 vols. in 1 (1962); B. I. Reicke, *The New Testament Era* (1968); J. Neusner, ed., *Christianity, Judaism and Other Greco-Roman Cults* (1975), 3:206-17.

SADOC (Matt. 1:14, KJV). *See* Zadok.

SAFFRON. *See* Vegetable Kingdom.

SAIL. The rendering of the Heb. *nēs* (Isa. 33:23; Ezek. 27:7), usually a *standard,* or *flagstaff; and* in the passages cited a *flag* of a ship. In Acts 27:17 it represents the Gk. *skeuos* and seems to be used specially and collectively of the sails and ropes ("sea anchor," NIV) of a *ship* (which see).

SAILOR. The translation of one Gk. and several Heb. terms (1 Kings 9:27; Ezek. 27:9, 27, 29; Jonah 1:5; Acts 27:27, 30; Rev. 18:17). Frequently *shipmen* or *mariners* in the KJV. *See* Ships.

SAINTS. Positionally, every NT believer; experientially, a person eminent for piety and virtue: a consecrated person. Applied to the *pious* Israelites (Pss. 16:3; 34:9), Heb. *qādôsh,* elsewhere "godly ones," "holy ones." Also applied to members of the Body of Christ. *All* the saved of the NT era are saints (*hagioi*) by virtue of their *position* "in Christ" (1 Cor. 1:2; cf. Rom. 6:3-4; 8:1; Eph. 1:3; etc.). The NT refutes the idea of a special class of "saints." Although it is true that *in expe-*

rience some believers are more "holy" than others, yet in their position before God all believers are "sanctified," i.e., saints by virtue of what they are "in Christ." The Christian's perfect *position* (Rom. 6:1-10) is made a comfortable *experience* of Christ by faith (v. 11); "considering" themselves to be what they are in their person before God, they became such in their everyday experience. The more one's experience conforms to one's position, the more practical holiness is manifested in the child of God (saint).

The term *saint* in the NASB and NIV is always the translation of either Heb. *qādôsh* or Gk. *hagios;* both the Heb. and Gk. terms are frequently translated "holy" in those translations. KJV "saint" is sometimes replaced in the NASB by "holy one." The KJV similarly translates *qādôsh* and *hagios,* as well as Heb. *qōdesh* and *ḥāsîd. See* Holiness; Godly Ones.   M.F.U.

SAKI'A. *See* Sachia.

SA'LA (Luke 3:35, KJV). *See* Shelah, no. 3.

SA'LAH (Gen. 10:24, KJV). *See* Shelah, no. 2.

SAL'AMIS (sal'a-mis). A city at the E extremity of the island of Cyprus, and the first place visited by Paul and Barnabas after leaving the mainland at Selucia (Acts 13:5). From the use of "synagogues" in the plural it may be inferred that there were many Jews in the city. And it is probable that from them came some of those early Cypriot Christians mentioned in 11:19-20.

From the eleventh century B.C. until the end of the Roman period, Salamis was the chief city of Cyprus. Unfortunately, because of destructive earthquakes in the region (e.g., 76/77, 332) it may be impossible ever to visualize the city as it was when Paul and Barnabas preached there about A.D. 45. Serious archaeological work was not done at the site until the Cyprus Department of Antiquities began annual campaigns there in 1952. They excavated the Byzantine gymnasium and bath complex N of the city, the large fourth-century basilica of St. Epiphanius, the first-century A.D. theater with seating for more than 15,000, the necropolis, the harbor area, and the city forum. The latter is considered to be the largest in the Roman Empire; it measured 750 feet long and 180 feet wide. At its S end stood a temple of Zeus on a high podium.   H.F.V.

SALA'THIEL. *See* Shealtiel, no. 1.

SAL'CAH, SAL'CHAH. *See* Salecah.

SAL'ECAH (sal'i-ka; KJV, Salcah, Salchal). A city of Bashan, named in the early records of Israel (Deut. 3:10; Josh. 13:11) and apparently one of the capitals of Og's kingdom (12:5). From 1 Chron. 5:11 it would seem that Salecah was on the eastern confines of both Manasseh and Gad. Salecah is the modern Salkhad, a town on the NE border of the mountainous kingdom of Bashan, E of the river Jordan.

SA'LEM (sā'lem, "peaceful"). The name of a place mentioned in connection with Melchizedek as its king (Gen. 14:18; Heb. 7:1-2). It is perhaps the name of Jerusalem (Ps. 76:2). The name appears as Uru-salim ("City of Peace") in the Amarna Letters.

SA'LIM (sā'lim; peaceful). The place W of the Jordan where John was baptizing (John 3:23). It may be identified with Salem, above.

Salim, the place west of the Jordan where John was baptizing

SAL'LAI (sal'a-ī).

1. A leading Benjamite who, with 928 of his tribesmen, settled in Jerusalem on the return from the captivity (Neh. 11:8), 445 B.C.

2. One of the heads of the priests who returned to Jerusalem with Zerubbabel (Neh. 12:20), about 536 B.C. In v. 7 he is called Sallu.

SAL'LU (sal'ū). The name of two Hebrews, spelled differently in the original.

1. A son of Meshullam, a Benjamite dwelling in Jerusalem after the captivity (Neh. 11:7; 1 Chron. 9:7), about 445 B.C.

2. Another form (Neh. 12:7) of the name *Sallai* (which see, no. 2).

SAL'MA (sal'ma).

1. Another form (1 Chron. 2:11) for *Salmon* (which see).

2. The second named of the sons of Caleb, and father (founder) of Bethlehem (1 Chron. 2:51), and of the Netophathites (v. 54), probably about 1400 B.C.

SAL'MON (sa'mon). The son of Nahshon and ancestor of Boaz (Ruth 4:20-21; 1 Chron. 2:11, Salma; Matt. 1:4-5; Luke 3:32), before 1150 B.C.

SALMO'NE (sal-mō'ne). A promontory of E Crete (Acts 27:7); present-day Cape Sidero.

SALO'ME (sa-lō'me; feminine of Solomon).

1. The sister of Herod the Great (*see* article Herod). She is not named in the Bible, but is mentioned in Josephus.

2. The daughter of Herodias by her first husband, Herod Philip (Josephus *Ant.* 18.5.4). She is the "daughter of Herodias," mentioned in Matt. 14:6 as dancing before Herod Antipas and securing, at her mother's instigation, the death of John the Baptist. To do honor to the day and to the company Salome broke through the rule of strict seclusion from the other sex and condescended, though a princess and the daughter of kings, to dance before Antipas and his guests. "The dancing then in vogue in both Rome and the provinces, from its popularity under Augustus, was very like that of our modern ballet. The dancer did not speak, but acted some story by gestures, movements, and attitudes, to the sound of music. Masks were used in all cases to conceal the features, but all other parts of the body, especially the hands and arms, were called into action, and a skillful pantomimist could express feelings, passions, and acts with surprising effect. The dress of the performer was planned to show the beauty of the figure to the greatest advantage, though it varied with the characters represented" (Geikie, *Life of Christ,* p. 300). Salome was married first to Philip, tetrarch of Trachonitis, her paternal uncle, who died childless; and, second, to her cousin Aristobulus, son of Herod, king of Chalcis, by whom she had three sons.

3. The wife of Zebedee, as appears by a comparison of Matt. 27:56 with Mark 15:40. Many modern critics are of the opinion that she was the sister of Mary, the mother of Jesus, alluded to in John 19:25. Others make the expression "His mother's sister" refer to "Mary the wife of Clopas," immediately following. We can hardly regard the point as settled, though the weight of modern criticism is decidedly in favor of the former view. The only events recorded of Salome are that she made a request on behalf of her two sons for seats of honor in the kingdom of heaven (Matt. 20:20), that she attended the crucifixion of Jesus (Mark 15:40), and that she visited His sepulcher (16:1). She is mentioned by name on only the two latter occasions.

BIBLIOGRAPHY: F. Josephus *Ant.* 18.136f.; C. E. Macartney, *The Way of a Man with a Maid* (1931), pp. 153ff.

SALT. Not only did the Hebrews make general use of salt in the food both of man (Job 6:6) and beast (Isa. 30:24), but they used it in their religious services as an accompaniment to the various offerings presented on the altar (Lev. 2:13, "every grain offering of yours, moreover, you shall season with salt"). The salt of the sacrifice is called "the salt of the covenant of your God," because in common life salt was the symbol of a covenant. The meaning that the salt (with its power to strengthen food and preserve it from putrefaction and corruption) imparted to the sacrifice was the unbending truthfulness of that self-surrender to the Lord embodied in the sacrifice, by which all impurity and hypocrisy were repelled. In addition to the uses of salt already specified, the inferior sorts were applied as a manure to the soil or to hasten the decomposition of dung (Matt. 5:13; Luke 14:35). Too large a mixture, however, was held to produce sterility; and hence also arose the custom of sowing with salt the foundations of a destroyed city (Judg. 9:45), as a token of its irretrievable ruin.

See also Mineral Kingdom.

Figurative. As one of the most essential articles of food, salt symbolized hospitality (see Covenant of Salt). Of the ministry of good men, as opposing the spiritual corruption of sinners (Matt. 5:13); of grace in the heart (Mark 9:50); of wisdom or good sense in speech (Col. 4:6); graceless believers as salt without savor (Matt. 5:13; Mark 9:50); from the belief that salt would, by exposure to the air, lose its virtue; salt pits was a figure of desolation (Zeph. 2:9); "salted with fire" (Mark 9:49) refers to the purification of the good and punishment of sinners.

SALT, CITY OF. A city in the wilderness of Judah (Josh. 15:62), probably at the SW extremity of the Dead Sea, where some of the hills are of pure salt, hence its name. Robinson (*Biblical Researchers*, 2:109) believes that it lay near the plain at the S end of the Dead Sea, which he would identify with the *Valley of Salt* (which see).

SALT, COVENANT OF. *See* Covenant of Salt.

SALT, VALLEY OF. A name employed five times in Scripture. The ravine is on the border between Judah and Edom, S of the Dead Sea. It was the scene of several battles (2 Sam. 8:13; 2 Kings 14:7; 1 Chron. 18:12; 2 Chron. 25:11).

SALT SEA. *See* Dead Sea.

SALTWORT. *See* Vegetable Kingdom: Mallows.

SA'LU (sa'lū). The father of Zimri, which latter was slain by Phinehas for bringing a Midianite woman into the camp of Israel (Num. 25:14), about 1400 B.C.

SALUTATION (Heb. *bārak*, in some forms "to bless"; *shālôm*, "well, happy," to be "friendly"; Gk. *aspasmos*, a "greeting"). The friendly greeting that in ancient as in modern times took place when meeting or parting. Salutations may be classed under two heads:

Conversational. The salutation at meeting consisted in early times of various expressions of blessing, such as: "May God be gracious to you" (Gen. 43:29); "May you be blessed of the Lord" (Ruth 3:10; cf. 1 Sam. 15:13); "May the Lord be with you," "May the Lord bless you" (Ruth 2:4); "The blessing of the Lord be upon you; we bless you in the name of the Lord" (Ps. 129:8). Hence the term *bless* received the secondary sense of

"salute." The Heb. term used in these instances (*shālôm*) has no special reference to "peace," but to general well-being, and strictly answers to our "welfare."

The salutation at parting consisted originally of a simple blessing (Gen. 24:60; 28:1; 47:10; Josh. 22:6), but in later times the term *shālôm* was introduced here also in the form "Go in peace," or rather, "Farewell" (1 Sam. 1:17; 20:42; 2 Sam. 15:9). In modern times the ordinary mode of address current in the East resembles the Hebrews': *Es-selám aleykum*, "Peace be on you," and the term *salaam* has been introduced into our own language to describe the oriental salutation. Eastern salutations were often complicated and tedious, taking up much of one's time. Our Lord's injunction "Greet no one on the way" (Luke 10:4) seems to mean that the apostles were to travel like men absorbed in one supreme interest, which would not permit them to lose time in idle ceremonies.

Epistolary. The epistolary salutations in the period subsequent to the OT were framed on the model of the Latin style; the addition of the term *peace* may, however, be regarded as a vestige of the old Hebrew form (2 Macc. 1:1). The writer placed his own name first, and then that of the person whom he saluted; it was only in special cases that this order was reversed (2 Macc. 1:1; 9:19; 1 Esdr. 6:7). A combination of the first and third persons in the terms of the salutation was not unfrequent (Gal. 1:1-2; Philem. 1; 2 Pet. 1:1). A form of prayer for spiritual mercies was also used. The concluding salutation consisted occasionally of a translation of the Lat. *valete* (Acts 15:29; 23:30) but more generally of the term *aspazomai*, "I salute," or the cognate substantive, accompanied by a prayer for peace or grace.

SALVATION. A term that stands for several Heb. and Gk. words, the general idea being safety, deliverance, ease, soundness. In the OT the term refers to various forms of deliverance, both temporal and spiritual. God delivers His people from their enemies and from the snares of the wicked (see Pss. 37:40; 59:2; 106:4). He also saves by granting forgiveness of sins, answers to prayer, joy, and peace (79:9; 69:13; 51:12). The OT prophecies center upon One who was to come as the bringer of salvation (see Messiah).

In the NT salvation is regarded almost exclusively as from the power and dominion of sin. And of this Jesus Christ is the author (see Matt. 1:21; Acts 4:12; Heb. 2:10; 5:9). It is freely offered to all men but is conditioned upon repentance and faith in Christ (see John 3:16; Heb. 2:3). Salvation proceeds from the love of God, is based upon the atonement wrought by Christ, is realized in forgiveness, regeneration, and sanctification, and culminates in the resurrection and glorification of all true believers. *See* Atonement; Forgiveness; Justification; Regeneration; Sanctification; Resurrection.   E. MCC.

BIBLIOGRAPHY: G. C. Berkouwer, *Faith and Justification* (1954); L. S. Chafer, *Salvation* (1965); E. M. B. Green, *The Meaning of Salvation* (1965); N. Turner, *Christian Words* (1980), pp. 390-98. For additional information see *The Minister's Library* (1985), pp. 268-74.

SAMA'RIA, CITY OF (sa-mā'ri-a; "watch" mountain). An important place in central Palestine, noted as the capital of the Northern Kingdom. Its name was given to the surrounding region, and later to a sect.

Geography. Samaria stood upon a hill about three hundred feet high, in a wide basin formed by the valley that runs from Shechem to the coast—the present Wadi esh-Sha'ir, or Barley Vale—and an incoming glen. Surrounded by mountains on three sides, Samaria has a great view to the W. The broad vale is visible for eight miles, then a low range of hills, and over them the sea, about twenty-three miles away.

History. Samaria was purchased from its owner, Shemer, for two talents of silver, by Omri, king of Israel, who "built on the hill, and named the city which he built Samaria, after the name of Shemer, the owner of the hill" (1 Kings 16:24). From that time until the captivity of the ten tribes—about two hundred years—it continued to be the capital.

During all this time it was the seat of idolatry (Isa. 9:9; Jer. 23:13; Ezek. 16:46-55; Amos 6:1; Mic. 1:1). There Ahab built a temple to Baal (1 Kings 16:32-33; cf. 2 Kings 10:35). On the other hand, it was the scene of the ministry of the prophets *Elijah* and *Elisha* (which see). Jehu broke down the temple of Baal but does not appear to have otherwise injured the city (10:18-28). The city was twice besieged by the Syrians, about 863 B.C. (1 Kings 20:1) and about 850 B.C. (2 Kings 6:24–7:20); but on both occasions the siege was ineffectual. It was taken in

Remains of the Roman Temple of Augustus, Samaria

721 B.C. by Shalmaneser's successor, Sargon king of Assyria (18:9-10), and the kingdom of the ten tribes was destroyed. In 331 it yielded to Alexander the Great, who visited it on his way back from Egypt in order to punish the Samaritan murderers of the governor he had appointed over Coele-Syria. Ptolemy Lagos deemed it dangerous enough to have it dismantled before he gave over Coele-Syria to Antigonus; and, being rebuilt, it was again destroyed fifteen years later. It withstood a year's siege by John Hyrcanus, the Maccabee, before being taken by him. It was rebuilt by Gabinius, the successor of Pompey. Augustus gave Samaria to Herod, who fortified and embellished it and named it Sebaste, the Greek for Augustus. Herod built a Greco-Roman theater, a temple to Augustus, and a Roman-style forum and colonnaded road at the site.

In the NT it is recorded (Acts 8:5) that Philip "went down to *the* city of Samaria," which more literally means "into a city of the Samaritans." Still it is likely that the evangelist would resort to the capital city. Thus ends the Bible history of Samaria.

Archaeology. From 1908 to 1910 the site of Samaria was excavated by Harvard University under the direction of G. A. Reisner, D. G. Lyon, and C. S. Fisher (cf. *Harvard Excavations at Samaria* [1908-10], 2 vols. [1924]). From 1931 to 1933 excavation was continued by Harvard University, the Hebrew University of Jerusalem, the British Academy, the British School of Archaeology in

Columns of the Roman forum, Samaria

Jerusalem, and the Palestine Exploration Fund under J. W. Crowfoot's direction. Further work was done in 1935 (cf. J. W. Crowfoot, Kathleen M. Kenyon, and E. L. Sukenik, *The Buildings at Samaria* [1942]). These various excavations have revealed the following periods: (1) The Omri-Ahab Era, Periods I and II. (2) The Jehu Era, Period III. (3) The eighth century, when the city reached its acme of prosperity, Periods IV-VI. Stout walls from the Omri-Ahab Period and other fortifications reveal how Samaria could have held out against the Syrians (2 Kings 6:24-30) and against the powerful Assyrians (17:5). Large numbers of cisterns were also discovered, compensating for the lack of natural water supply. The famous Samarian ostraca are usually placed in the reign of Jeroboam II in the eighth century. These inscribed pieces of pottery were recovered in one of the palace storehouses. They are accounts of royal revenue received in the form of oil and wine. Numerous stewards are mentioned, recalling biblical names such as Nimshi, Ahinoam, and Gomar (Gomer). Also numerous ivories in the form of plaques or furniture inlays were recovered. Portrayed on the ivories are papyrus reeds, lotus, lions, bulls, sphinxes, and Egyptian gods such as Isis and Horus. The high artistic quality and the Egyptian gods indicate strong foreign influence at this period. These ivories recall the "beds of ivory" and "houses of ivory" denounced by Amos (Amos 3:15; 6:4; cf. 1 Kings 22:39). Some of the significant remains at the site today include the palace of Omri and Ahab, the temple to Augustus, the Greco-Roman theater, a gate complex with Hellenistic towers, a basilica adjacent to the forum, and part of the colonnaded street.   M.F.U.

BIBLIOGRAPHY: J. W. Crowfoot, K. M. Kenyon, and E. L. Sukenik, *The Buildings of Samaria* (1924); G. A. Reisner, C. S. Fisher, and D. G. Lyon, *Harvard Excavations at Samaria* (1924); J. W. and G. W. Crowfoot and K. M. Kenyon, *The Objects from Samaria* (1957); J. B. Hennessy, *Levant* 2 (1970): 1-21; P. W. and N. L. Lapp, *Annual of the American Schools of Oriental Research* 41 (1974): 3ff.

SAMA'RIA, REGION OF (Gk. usually *Samareia*). This term includes all the tribes over which Jeroboam made himself king, whether E or W of the Jordan River. The expression "cities of Samaria" (1 Kings 13:32) is used for the kingdom of the ten tribes, which did not receive this name till after the building of the city of Samaria as the capital of the kingdom and the residence of the kings of Israel (16:24). It is used elsewhere in the same sense; thus, by "Ephraim and the inhabitants of Samaria" is meant Israel (Isa. 9:9-12). Israel, Ephraim, and Samaria are equivalent terms in Hosea, who also calls the calf of Bethel "your calf, O Samaria" (Hos. 8:5). In Amos 3:9 the "mountains of Samaria" are spoken of; and we find the expression in Ezekiel (16:53), the "captivity of Samaria and her daughters."

BIBLIOGRAPHY: A. Parrot, *Samaria, the Capital of the Kingdom of Israel* (1958); J. A. Montgomery, *The Samaritans* (1968).

SAMAR'ITANS   (sa-mar'i-tanz;   Heb.

The hills surrounding Samaria

shōmerōnîm). Mentioned in 2 Kings 17:29 as "the people of Samaria." It is customary to refer the Samaritans in this passage to the colonists brought by the king of Assyria in place of the deported Israelites; but the text seems rather to mean that these colonists put their gods into the houses of the high places that the Samaritans, i.e., the former inhabitants of Samaria, had made for their own religious use. But the Samaritans of subsequent history and of the NT are the descendants of the colonists brought in by the king of Assyria.

The Captor and the Captivity. It was Shalmaneser V, who reigned five years, beginning with 727, who laid siege to Samaria; but his successor, Sargon II, claimed to have taken it. At least he did the mopping up at the end of the campaign in 722 B.C. Sargon carried off 27,290 inhabitants as he himself recounts. He took fifty chariots as "the portion of his royalty" and contented himself with the same tribute as "the former king." Thus it is plain that he neither desolated nor depopulated the land. But he put an end to its independence and set over it an Assyrian governor. In 720 we find Samaria, with Arpad, Simyra, and Damascus, joining in the revolt headed by Hamath.

Extent of the Captivity. The captivity must have been confined to Samaria and a small surrounding region. In Hezekiah's time (2 Chron. 30:11), in Josiah's (34:9), and even in Jeremiah's (Jer. 41:5) there were Israelites in the Northern Kingdom who clung to the worship of God at Jerusalem. The 27,290 captives taken away by Sargon may, indeed, have been increased afterward by him or by other monarchs. But all the indications are that the depopulation was not thorough and was limited to the city of Samaria and its vicinity. This would account for the fact that the Galilee of our Lord's day was a Jewish region. The Samaria of Josephus, indeed, embraced what was formerly the territory of Ephraim, but the Cuthaean Samaritans "possessed only a few towns and villages of this large area" and western Manasseh.

Repeopling. The repeopling was not done all at once. In settling the affairs of that unquiet region more than one band of colonists was brought in. Heathen colonists were introduced by Sargon in 721 and again in 715 B.C. (2 Kings 17:24), by Esarhaddon, 680 B.C. (Ezra 4:2), and finally by Osnapper, i.e., Ashurbanipal, the last great Assyrian emperor (669-626 B.C.), who added people from Elam, etc., to the population.

Resultant Population. The Samaritans were a mixed race with a pagan core (Ezra 4:2). Their blood would become more and more Hebraized by the addition of renegade Jews and by the intermarriage with surrounding Israelites, who would find among them the familiar worship of former times.

Worship. Since the priest who was sent to "teach them the custom of the god of the land"

was of the Samaritan captivity, and not from Jerusalem (2 Kings 17:27), their worship must have descended from that of Jeroboam. The schism headed by Jeroboam was not religious, but political (1 Kings 12:4, 16), and his object was to separate Israel not from God but from Jerusalem. His golden calves were designed as images of the God who had brought them up out of the land of Egypt. The notion of plurality is not so clearly marked in Hebrew as in English, "*hinnēh, lo!*" being an interjection ("Behold, your gods!"). There is no sign of plurality, except the verb *he'elûkā*. But *'elōhîm*, even when it refers to the one God, sometimes has a plural verb, and that in cases where we should not expect it (Gen. 20:13; 35:7; 2 Sam. 7:23, in reference to this very deliverance from Egypt; Ps. 58:11, a participle. Thus, Jeroboam's sin may have been a violation not so much of the first commandment as of the second. Indeed, archaeological research suggests that the two golden calves served not as idols but as supports for the invisible presence of Yahweh. This is indicated by popular contemporary Near Eastern iconography, where the gods of the heathen, such as Baal, are pictured enthroned on the back of a bull or some other animal. With all the Jewish horror of Jeroboam's worship, the charge is not usually that he introduced other gods (perhaps only in 1 Kings 14:9, where the reference is possibly to images; and 2 Chron. 11:15), but that it was schismatic (13:9) and irregular (1 Kings 12:31-33). Now, while he decisively separated the people from Jerusalem, it would be altogether for his interest to conciliate them by making the new worship as much like the old as possible (in 1 Kings 12:32 note the phrase "like the feast which is in Judah"). For a few needful changes he might plausibly argue that David and Solomon had taken great liberties; that the Temple with its burdensome cost was far enough from the simple Tabernacle, for whose construction God Himself had given minute directions; that Jerusalem had no special divine sanction; and finally that he himself had just as good a divine call as David and better than Solomon or Rehoboam. Putting all these things together with what is said under the next head of the probability that copies of the Pentateuch would be preserved in the Northern Kingdom, we may be reasonably sure that Jeroboam's ritual would not be very far from that handed down from Moses. This would act as a purge on the imported polytheism of the transplanted peoples but would result in little more than a dual worship — a mixture of paganism and Judaism.

Samaritan Pentateuch. Whether the Northern Kingdom would be likely, in separating from the Levitical worship, to carry the Pentateuch with it is a question that, in the lack of positive evidence, everyone must answer according to his own judgment. The Tabernacle was most of the time in the territory that afterward belonged to the kingdom of Israel. It was in Shiloh till the time of Eli, about 1051 B.C. (1 Sam. 4:3). Shiloh was long remembered as its resting place (Ps. 78:60; Jer. 7:12, 14; 26:6). At the close of David's reign, 960 B.C., it was no farther S than Gibeon (1 Chron. 21:29), a little S of the border. The focus of the old worship thus having been in the Northern Kingdom, of course there would be copies of the ceremonial law there, and it is hardly conceivable that there should not be copies of the whole Pentateuch, if not more of the Bible, at least in the Levitical cities. It is therefore not impossible that the Samaritan Pentateuch came into the hands of the Samaritans as an inheritance from the ten tribes whom they succeeded. However, it is much more probable to conclude that it was introduced by Manasseh (cf. Josephus *Ant.* 11.8. 2, 4) at the time of the foundation of the Samaritan sanctuary on Mt. Gerizim.

Aerial view of Mt. Gerizim, sacred to the Samaritans

First Discord Between Jews and Samaritans. That the Samaritans who wished to join with the Jews are called "enemies" in Ezra 4 may mean either that they were then seen to be enemies in disguise or that they were enemies when the account was written. Perhaps the latter; for in the refusal no charge of hypocrisy was made against them. It was only that the right to build belonged to others and that they could have no part in it. The genealogies were carefully kept (Ezra 8), and it is probable that considerations of birth were so prominent that there was no need of inquiry into anything else.

Were the Jews right? It is not for us to judge. We can only inquire for our own instruction. We must believe that they knew their own business best and presume that they were right. Yet there are some facts that cannot escape our notice.

Their course in regard to aliens and children of mixed marriages, as shown in Ezra 10:3 and indicated in Neh. 13:1, 3 (cf. "ever" of v. 1, with "to the tenth generation" of Deut. 23:3), though natural and probably justifiable under the circumstances, was yet, so far as we know, somewhat in advance of what God had required. Aliens and slaves were allowed to eat the Passover if they were circumcised (Ex. 12:44, 48-49; *see* Moabites).

Subsequent History. The subsequent history of the Samaritans is touched on in the Bible and in extrabiblical literature.

Ancient. The relation between Jew and Samaritan was one of hostility. The expulsion of Manasseh by Nehemiah for an unlawful marriage, and his building of the Samaritan temple on Mt. Gerizim by permission of Darius Nothus, took place about 409 B.C. The inhospitality (Luke 9:52-53) and hostility of the Samaritans induced many pilgrims from the N to Jerusalem to go on the E of the Jordan. The Samaritans sometimes, using rival flames, perplexed the watchers for the signal fires that announced the rising of the paschal moon from Mt. Olivet to the Euphrates. They rejected all the OT except the Pentateuch, concerning which they claimed to have an older copy than the Jews and to observe the precepts better. The Jews repaid hate with hate. They cast suspicion on the Samaritan copy of the law and disallowed the steadfast claim of the Samaritans to Jewish birth (John 4:12). Social and commercial relations, although they could not be broken off (4:8), were reduced to the lowest possible figure. "The Samaritan was publicly cursed in their synagogues—could not be adduced as a witness in the Jewish courts—could not be admitted to any sort of proselytism, and was thus, so far as the Jew could affect his position, excluded from eternal life." It ought to be said, however, that the rabbinic regulations for the relationships of Jews and Samaritans varied greatly at different times and that the older Talmudical authorities inclined to treat the Samaritans more like Jews. In 332 the Samaritans desired Alexander the Great to exempt them from tribute in the sabbatical year, on the ground that, as Israelites, they did not cultivate the land during that year. Becoming satisfied that they were not actually Jews, he deferred granting their request (Josephus *Ant.* 11.8.6, cf. 9.14.3) and on account of their conduct besieged and destroyed Samaria. John Hyrcanus took "Shechem and Gerizzim, and the nation of the Cutheans, who dwelt at that temple which resembled the temple which was at Jerusalem, and which Alexander permitted Sanballat, the general of his army, to build for the sake of Manasseh, who was son-in-law to Jaddua the high priest, as we have formerly related; which temple was now deserted two hundred years after it was built" (Josephus *Ant.* 13.9.1; as for Manasseh, cf. *Ant.* 11.7.1-2). The temple on Gerizim was "deserted," 130 B.C. This gives about 330 for the date of its building. The "Sanballat the Horonite" (*see* Horonite) of the Bible was contemporary with Nehemiah, 445 B.C., and was father-in-law of one of the sons of Joiada the son of Eliashib, the high priest (Neh. 13:28). But the Sanballat of Josephus was a Cuthaean, of the same race as the Samaritans, and was sent to Samaria by Darius Codomanus, the last king of Persia (d. 330). He was father-in-law to Manasseh, the brother of the high priest Jaddua, who was the son of John, the son of Judas, the son of Eliashib (Josephus *Ant.* 11.7.1-2). There must, therefore, have been two Sanballats, unless Josephus has confused the account. In the persecution under Antiochus, 170 B.C., the Samaritans disowned their relation to the Jews and consecrated their temple on Mt. Gerizim to Jupiter.

Later History. After the destruction of Samaria by Alexander the Great, Shechem became more prominent, and there, after the conquest by John Hyrcanus they built a second temple. With lapse of time they reacted from their polytheism into an "ultra Mosaism." In our Lord's time they still preserved their identity after seven centuries; and "though their limits had been gradually contracted, and the rallying place of their religion on Mount Gerizim had been destroyed one hundred and sixty years before by John Hyrcanus (130 B.C.) and though Samaria (the city) had been again and again destroyed, and though their territory had been the battlefield of Syria and Egypt, still preserved their nationality, still worshipped from Shechem and their other impoverished settlements toward their sacred hill; still retained their nationality, and could not coalesce with the Jews." In the first century the Samaritans were numerous enough to excite the fears of Pilate, whose severity toward them cost him his office (Josephus *Ant.* 18.4.1-2), and of Vespasian, under whom more than 10,000 were slaughtered after refusing to surrender (B. J., 3.7.32). They greatly increased in numbers, particularly under Dositheus, about the time of Simon Magus. In the fourth century they were among the chief adversaries of Christianity. They were severely chastised by the emperor Zeno and thereafter were hardly noticed till the latter half of the sixteenth century, when correspondence was opened with them by Joseph Scaliger. Two of their letters to him and one to Job Sudolf are still extant and are full of interest. Shechem is represented by the modern Nâblus, corresponding to Neapolis, which was built by Vespasian, a little W of the old town. Here has been a settlement of about two hundred, who have observed the law and kept the Passover on Mt. Gerizim "with an exactness of minute ceremonial which the Jews have long since intermitted."   W.H.; M.F.U.; H.F.V.

BIBLIOGRAPHY: M. Gaster, *The Samaritans—Their History, Doctrines and Literature* (1925); J. A. Montgomery, *The Samaritans* (1968); J. D. Purvis, *The Samaritan Pentateuch and the Origin of the Samaritan Sect* (1968); R. J. Coggins, *Samaritans and Jews* (1975).

SA'MEKH (ס) (sa'mek). Fifteenth letter of the Heb. alphabet, heading the fifteenth section of Ps. 119.

SAM'GAR-NE'BU (sam'gar-nē'bū; apparently from Akkad. *Shumgir-nabū*, "Nebo, be gracious"; Samgar-nebo, KJV; Samgar, Nebo-Sarsekim, NIV). One of the officers of Nebuchadnezzar's army present at the taking of Jerusalem (Jer. 39:3), 587 B.C.

SAM'LAH (sam'la; "a garment"). One of the kings of Edom before the establishment of the Israelite monarchy (Gen. 36:36-37; 1 Chron. 1:47-48). He was the successor of Hadad (Hadar) and was of the city of Masrekah.

SA'MOS (sa'mos). A noted island in the Aegean Sea, near the coast of Lydia, in Asia Minor, separated by a narrow strait; in its narrowest part not quite a mile wide. When Paul touched there on his voyage from Greece to Syria (Acts 20:15), it was a free city in the province of Asia. It was the seat of the worship of Juno, and her temple, called the Heraeon, was enriched by some of the finest works of art known in Greece. Its chief manufacture was pottery of fine red clay, the Samian ware celebrated all over the civilized world. Its wine ("Levantine") ranks high.

SA'MOTHRACE (sa'mō-thrās). A Greek island in the Aegean Sea that lay on Paul's sea route from Troas to Neapolis in the course of his second missionary journey (Acts 16:11).

SAM'SON (Heb. *shimshôn*, "little sun"). The renowned judge and deliverer of Israel, Samson was the son of Manoah of Zorah, in the tribe of Dan, whose birth was foretold to his parents by an angel, accompanied with the announcement that he was to be a "Nazirite to God from the womb" (Judg. 13:2-5, 24). Samson grew up under special influences of the Spirit of God and at last was impelled to commence the conflict with the Philistines, which only terminated with his death.

Marries a Philistine. When he was about twenty years old Samson saw at Timnath a Philistine girl who pleased him and on his return asked his parents to take her for him as a wife. They were averse to such a marriage, but Samson persisted, perhaps being convinced that it would in some way aid him in visiting vengeance upon the Philistines. On his first visit to his future bride he killed a lion with his hands, and when he went to espouse her he found the skeleton occupied by a swarm of bees. At the wedding feast he proposed a riddle, conforming to the oriental custom of furnishing entertainment for the guests, and promised "thirty changes of clothes" if they could give him an answer. Unable to solve it, they urged his wife to secure the answer from him and inform them. He yielded but, seized with indignation, went to Ashkelon, killed thirty Philistines, and gave the changes of "clothes" to those who had solved the riddle. He returned to his father's house, and his wife was given to his companion (Judg. 14:1-20).

His Revenge. Samson soon after visited his wife but was refused admission to her by her father. He interpreted the treatment that he had received from his father-in-law as the effect of the general attitude of the Philistines toward the Israelites and resolved to avenge his wrong upon the whole nation. He secured 300 foxes (jackals) and, by tying torches to their tails, set fire to the grainfields, vineyards, and olive groves of his enemies (15:1-5). The Philistines retorted by burning Samson's wife and father-in-law; and this provocation so aroused Samson that he "struck them ruthlessly with a great slaughter," after which he went down and dwelt in the "cleft of the rock of Etam" (15:6-8).

Delivered up to the Philistines. The Philistines came to avenge themselves and encamped in Judah. The Judeans, instead of recognizing Samson as a deliverer, went to Etam, to the number of 3,000, for the purpose of binding him and handing him over to their enemies. He consented on condition that they themselves would not kill him. They bound him with two new cords, brought him to Lehi (*lĕḥî,* "a jaw"), and in this apparently helpless condition delivered him to the Philistines. When he heard their shout of joy his extraordinary strength suddenly put itself forth, and, snapping the cords asunder, he seized upon a fresh jawbone of a donkey and killed a thousand men. Casting away his weapon, he called the name of the place Ramath-lehi ("the jawbone height"). Weary and thirsty, Samson, conscious that he was fighting for the cause of Jehovah, prayed unto the Lord, who caused a stream to flow from the rock, which Samson called En-hakkore (i.e., "the well of him that prayed"). Samson drank and was revived (15:9-20).

At Gaza. After this Samson went to the city of Gaza and became intimate with a woman of loose character residing there. The Gazites fastened the city gates, intending to kill him in the morning, when, as they supposed, he would leave the house. But at midnight Samson arose and, breaking away bolts, bars, and hinges, carried the gates to the top of a neighboring hill looking toward Hebron (16:1-3), about 1070 B.C.

Delilah. After this Samson became infatuated with a woman of Sorek, named Delilah, through whom the Philistine lords determined to seize him. They supposed that his supernatural strength arose from an amulet that he wore and offered to Delilah a tempting bribe if she would discover for them his secret. She entered into the agreement and used all her arts and blandishments to persuade Samson to reveal it to her. He

deceived her three times by false statements, but at last, teased into compliance, "he told her all that was in his heart," and said, "If I am shaved, then my strength will leave me and I shall become weak and be like any other man." Delilah, satisfied that Samson had spoken the truth this time, sent word to the Philistines, who came bringing the promised reward. Then she made him sleep, his head upon her lap, cut off his hair, and gave the predetermined signal, "The Philistines are upon you, Samson!" Forsaken by Jehovah, he fell an easy prey to his enemies.

Imprisonment and Death. The Philistines put out Samson's eyes and led him, bound with bronze chains, to Gaza, where he was made to grind grain in the prison. As this was an employment that in the East was usually done by women, to assign it to such a man as Samson was virtually to reduce him to the lowest state of degradation and shame. After a time Samson's hair began to grow, and the Philistines for some reason seemed inattentive to it. With it such a profound repentance seems to have been wrought in his heart as virtually reinvested him with the character and powers he had lost. His captivity was regarded by the Philistines as a great victory, and he seems to have been kept by them, like a wild beast, for show and insult. On the occasion of a sacrificial festival to Dagon, to whom they ascribed the capture of their enemy, they brought Samson from the prison that he might make sport for them. Determined to use his recovered strength against his enemies, a large number of whom crowded the building, Samson persuaded the attendant to place him between the pillars upon which the roof rested. After a brief prayer he grasped the pillars and, leaning forward with resistless force, brought down the building, causing his own death and that of 3,000 Philistines. His relatives came to Gaza, took away his body, and placed it in the burying place of his father, between Zorah and Eshtaol (16:21-31). He judged Israel about 1070 B.C. Though a mournful victory, it was still a victory, and a pledge to Israel that their temporary backslidings and defeats, if sincerely repented of and improved, would lead to ultimate triumph.

Character. The mention of Samson's name in the list (Heb. 11:32) of ancients who "by faith conquered kingdoms, performed acts of righteousness," warrants us a favorable estimate of his character as a whole. And yet the inspired narrative records infirmities that must forever mar the luster of his heroic deeds. In Samson the Nazirite we see a man towering in supernatural strength through his firm faith in, and confident reliance upon, the gift of God committed to him. On the other hand we see in Samson an adventurous, foolhardy, passionate, and willful man, dishonoring and frittering away his God-given power by making it subservient to his own lusts.

Samson's Strength. The superhuman strength of Samson did not really lie in his hair but in the fact of his *relation* to God as a Nazirite, of which his uncut hair was the *mark* or *sign*. As soon as he broke away from his Naziriteship by sacrificing his hair, which he wore in honor of the Lord, Jehovah departed from him, and with Jehovah went his strength.

Overthrow of Dagon's Temple. "So far as the fact itself is concerned, there is no ground for questioning the possibility of Samson's bringing down the whole building by pulling down two middle columns. . . . In all probability we have to picture this temple of Dagon as resembling the modern Turkish kiosks, viz., as consisting of a 'spacious hall, the roof of which rested in front upon four columns, two of them standing at the ends, and two close together in the center. Under this hall the leading men of the Philistines celebrated a sacrificial meal, while the people were assembled upon the top of the roof, which was surrounded by a balustrade' " (K. & D., *Com.*, ad loc.).

BIBLIOGRAPHY: T. Kirk, *Samson: His Life and Work* (1891, reprinted in *Studies in the Book of Judges,* 1983); J. L. Crenshaw, *Samson: A Secret Betrayed, A Vow Ignored* (1979).

SAMUEL. The prophet and judge of Israel (which see, below) and other Bible characters.

1. Son of Ammihud, appointed from the tribe of Simeon to divide the land of Canaan (Num. 34:20), c. 1400 B.C. The NIV reads "Shemuel."

2. A descendant of Tola, and one of the leaders of the tribe of Issachar (1 Chron. 7:2).

SAM'UEL (sam'ū-el; "asked or heard of God"). The son of *Elkanah* (which see), a Levite (1 Chron. 6:27-28, 33-38) of Ramathaim-zophim, on the mountains of Ephraim, and Hannah, to whom he was born in response to her earnest prayer (1 Sam. 1:1-20), probably 1080 B.C.

As a Child. When Hannah prayed for a son she vowed to dedicate him to the Lord as a Nazirite (1 Sam. 1:11) and as soon as he was weaned brought him to Shiloh and gave him over to Eli (1:24-28). Thus Samuel served as a boy before the Lord, clothed with an ephod. He received every year from his mother a robe reaching down to his feet, such as was worn only by high personages, or women, over their other dress (2:11, 18-19).

Call. At the time when Samuel served the Lord before Eli, both as a boy and as a young man, "word from the Lord was rare . . . visions were infrequent." A revelation from God presupposed susceptibility on the part of men. The unbelief and disobedience of the people might restrain the fulfillment of this and all similar promises, and God might even withdraw His word to punish the idolatrous nation. The word of the Lord was then issued to Samuel for the first time. While sleeping in his place, probably in the court of the Tabernacle, where cells were built for the priests and Levites, Samuel heard his name called. Supposing it was Eli who had called him, he hastened to receive his commands, but Eli told him to lie down again, as he had not called. When, however, this was repeated a second and a third time, Eli perceived that the Lord had called Samuel and instructed him how to act should he hear the voice again. The Lord revealed to Samuel the doom of Eli's house, which he reluctantly made known the next morning to the aged priest. Other revelations followed, and their exact fulfillment secured to Samuel a reputation for trustworthiness that made Shiloh an oracle (3:1-21).

Judge. After the disastrous defeat of the Israelites by the Philistines (4:1-11), Samuel does not appear again in history for a period of twenty years. During most of this time the Ark of the Lord rested in Kiriath-jearim, and all the house of Israel lamented after the Lord (7:1-2). Samuel, who had learned that loyalty to Jehovah was necessary to secure to Israel deliverance from its foes, issued a proclamation exposing the sin of idolatry and urging religious amendment. He summoned the tribes to assemble at Mizpah to spend a day in penitence and prayer. At this assembly Samuel seems to have been elected, or in some way recognized, as judge (7:3-6), 1050 B.C.

Ebenezer. When the Philistines heard of the gathering at Mizpah they made war upon the Israelites, who in their fear entreated Samuel not to cease to pray for their deliverance. The Philistines advanced while Samuel was engaged in sacrifice and prayer but were thrown into confusion by a terrific thunderstorm sent by Jehovah. This was an unprecedented phenomenon in that climate at that season of the year. The enemies of Israel were defeated and pursued to a place called Beth-car. As a memorial of the victory, Samuel placed a stone between Mizpah and Shen and named the place Ebenezer ("stone of help"; 7:7-12).

Judicial Labors. Samuel had now the entire government of the nation and visited, in the discharge of his official duties, Bethel, Gilgal, and Mizpah. His own residence was in his native city, Ramah (or Ramathaim), where he judged Israel and also built an altar to conduct the religious affairs of the nation. This was contrary to the letter of the law, but the prophets seem to have had power to dispense with ordinary usage; and, moreover, the Tabernacle at Shiloh had lost what was most essential to it as a sanctuary since it had been despoiled of the Ark by the Philistines (7:15-17).

The Monarchy. Samuel had appointed his sons as judges in his old age, and as they had perverted justice the elders of Israel entreated him to appoint them a king to judge them after the manner of all the nations (8:1-5). The proposed change of government displeased Samuel; nevertheless he laid the matter before Jehovah in prayer and was instructed to consent to their request, although not without setting before them the perils and tyranny of a monarchical government (8:6-19). The people were sent to their homes, and Samuel proceeded to the election of a sovereign. Saul was pointed out by Jehovah as the man whom he was to set apart as king of Israel and was anointed and saluted as monarch (8:19–10:8). After Samuel had privately anointed Saul king, he made provision for his recognition as such by the people. He summoned the people to Mizpah, but before proceeding to the election itself charged the people with their sin in rejecting God by their demand for a king. He then caused the sacred lot to be taken, and the lot fell upon Saul, who was formally introduced to the people (10:17-25).

Renewal of the Monarchy. There were certain "worthless men" who were opposed to Saul's elevation to the throne, but the victory of the Ammonites so influenced the people in his favor that Samuel convened the people at Gilgal to "renew the kingdom." This consisted, probably, of a ratification of the new constitution and the installation of the sovereign. This solemn service was concluded by the farewell address of Samuel, in which he handed over the office of judge to the king. The address was confirmed by the miraculous sign of a thunderstorm in answer to the prayer of Samuel. It was then wheat harvest, which occurs in Palestine between the middle of May and the middle of June, during which time it scarcely ever rains (11:14–12:25).

Reproves Saul. Although Saul had begun his reign, Samuel continued to exercise his functions as prophet and judge. He judged Israel "all the days of his life" (7:15) and from time to time crossed the path of the king. Saul was engaged in war against the Philistines and, having mustered his forces at Gilgal, awaited the coming of Samuel to sacrifice to Jehovah. As Samuel did not appear at the time appointed, Saul, in his anxiety lest the people should lose heart and desert him, resolved to offer the sacrifice himself—a fearful violation of the national law. The offering of the sacrifice was hardly finished when Samuel arrived. Rebuking Saul for his presumption, Samuel made known to him the short continuance of his kingdom. He then left him and went to Gibeah of Benjamin (13:1-15).

Parts with Saul. Later we find Samuel charging Saul with the extermination of the Amalekites, who had attacked, in a most treacherous manner, the Israelites on their journey from Egypt to Sinai. Saul was instructed to put to death man and beast, but he not only left Agag, the king, alive, but spared the best of the cattle, merely executing such as were worthless. Samuel announced to him that his disobedience had secured for him his rejection by Jehovah. Saul entreated Samuel to remain and worship with him but the latter refused and turned to depart. Saul endeavored to retain the prophet by force, and in

the struggle the robe of Samuel was torn. In this event Samuel foresaw the rending away of the kingdom from Saul. Samuel yielded to the renewed entreaty of Saul that he would honor him by his presence before the elders and the people and remained while Saul worshiped. After Saul had prayed, Samuel directed him to bring Agag, king of the Amalekites, whom he killed before the altar of Jehovah, and then returned to his own home at Ramah. From that time they met no more, although Samuel did not cease to grieve for Saul (15:1-35).

Anoints David. Since Saul had been rejected by God, and the government was not to remain in his family, it was necessary, in order to prevent strife and confusion, that his successor should be appointed before the death of the king. Samuel was therefore instructed by the Lord to go to Bethlehem and anoint David, the youngest son of Jesse, as the chosen one. The sacrificial meal over, Samuel returned to Ramah (16:1-13).

Befriends David. Later when Saul, in his insane rage, endeavored to slay David, the latter fled to Samuel, and they both went to and lived in Naioth. The king pursued David, but when he came to Naioth and saw Samuel and the prophets, the Spirit of the Lord came upon him also, and he was obliged to relinquish the attempt to seize him (19:18-24).

Death. In 25:1 we have a brief account of the death of Samuel and the great mourning made for him by the Israelites, who buried him at his own house (about 1017 B.C.). The place long pointed out as his tomb is the height, most conspicuous of all in the neighborhood of Jerusalem, immediately above the town of Gibeon, known to the Crusaders as "Montjoye," as the spot from whence they first saw Jerusalem, now called Neby Samwil, "the prophet Samuel."

Character. In studying the character of Samuel it is impossible not to be impressed with his *piety*. He was dedicated to the service of God by his mother and that service never became an irksome routine. God was the center around which he, as well as heaven, turned. In all his difficulties he turned to God for counsel. In all his acts and decisions he was guided by the word of Jehovah. His advice to the Israelites was the motto of his own life, "Do not turn aside from following the Lord, but serve the Lord with all your heart." Neither was his *patriotism* less apparent. His object was not the possession of power but the welfare of his people. Place, honor, and power were not sought by him, but he by them. And when the people, without respect to his gray hair and long service, called upon him to resign his office there was no cry for pity, neither peevish reproach for their ingratitude. He challenged inspection of his character and official life; remonstrated with Israel on their choice as being an act of disloyalty not against himself, but Jehovah; and warned them of the evils that would result from the establishment of a monarchy. And when Saul was selected as his successor, Samuel received him with the utmost courtesy and treated him with even paternal kindness.

BIBLIOGRAPHY: F. B. Meyer, *Samuel the Prophet* (1902); W. J. Deane and T. Kirk, *Studies in the First Book of Samuel,* 2 vols. in 1 (1983), 1:1-98, 117-28, 114-67, 190-97.

SAMUEL, BOOKS OF. The name of these two books can only find a logical explanation in the fact that Samuel was the principal character in the first part and anointed the other two principal characters. First and Second Samuel were originally a single book. The LXX translators divided them into two books called 1 and 2 Kings. The other books of Kings, which deal with the later historical period, were called 3 and 4 Kings. This designation was carried over into the Old Latin and the Vulg. The same division was transferred to the Heb. Bible in 1448, but with the difference that each book retained the title that it possessed in the Heb. manuscript; 1-4 Kings became 1 and 2 Samuel and 1 and 2 Kings.

Purposes. These two historical books carry on Israelite history from the closing years of the era of the Judges to the establishment of David's kingdom. They also delineate Samuel's personal history. The moral failure of the priesthood and judgeship is recorded in the death of Eli and his sons. The rise of the prophetic office alongside the kingly office is set forth. Samuel, the prophet-judge, is portrayed as the founder of both, as well as of the schools of the prophets (1 Sam. 19:20; 2 Kings 2:3-5). Samuel anointed both Saul and David. The book recounts David's accession to the kingship at Hebron and later at Jerusalem after its conquest (2 Sam. 5:6-12). The great Davidic covenant (7:8-17) is set forth and forms a basis of all subsequent kingdom truth.

Outline.
I. Samuel as judge (1 Sam. 1-7)
  A. His birth and boyhood (1:1–2:10)
  B. Eli's rejection and Samuel's call (2:11–3:21)
  C. Philistine domination (4:1–7:1)
  D. Samuel as judge (7:2-7)
II. Saul as king (1 Sam. 8 – 2 Sam. 1)
  A. Demand for a king (8:1-22)
  B. Choice of Saul (9:1–11:15)
  C. Samuel's farewell address (12:1-25)
  D. Saul's Philistine war (13:1–14:52)
  E. His disobedience and rejection (15:1-35)
  F. David's anointing and call to Saul's court (16:1-23)
  G. David and Goliath (17:1-58)
  H. David's flight from Saul's court (18:1–20:42)
  I. David's wanderings (21:1–30:31)
  J. Saul's death (31:1-13)
  K. David's lament (2 Sam. 1:1-27)

III. David as king (2 Sam. 2-24)
  A. His coronation over Judah (2:1-7)
  B. He establishes national religious unity (2:8 – 6:23)
  C. The Davidic covenant (7:1-29)
  D. David's wars (8:1–10:19)
  E. David's sin and repentance (11:1–12:31)
  F. The crimes of Amnon and Absalom (13:1–14:33)
  G. Absalom's rebellion (15:1–19:8)
  H. David's restoration (19:9–20:26)
  I. The famine (21:1-14)
  J. Roster of heroes (21:15-22)
  K. David's last words (22:1–23:7)
  L. His heroes (23:8-39)
  M. His census and punishment (24:1-25)

Authorship. The book is anonymous. In all probability the author was a prophet in the monarchial period who employed earlier sources left by Samuel, Gad, Nathan (1 Chron. 29:29), and possibly others. This is suggested by the fact that the work possesses unity as well as plan and purpose and is thus to be regarded as the production of a single author or compiler. The date of its composition is likely to be placed not later than David's reign. That the book ends just previous to David's death suggests that it was written at that period. The reference to Judah and Israel (1 Sam. 27:6) need not rule out this date since such a distinction prevailed as early as the Davidic period before the consolidation of the monarchy (18:6; 2 Sam. 2:10; 24:1).

Composition and Date. Otto Eissfeldt (*Einleitung,* pp. 306-7; *Die Komposition der Samuelisbeucher* [1931]) disconnects the text into three sources—L, J, and E—which are regarded as continuations of the sources of the Heptateuch. This theory has not been widely received. It is commonly held that the books of Samuel consist of at least two principal sources, J, the earlier, about the tenth century B.C., and E, the latter, about the eighth century B.C. (R. Pfeiffer, *Intr.,* pp. 341-65). The relationship of these documents is claimed to be similar to J and E in the Pentateuch and the Judges, if not a continuation of these documents, as K. Budde maintained. It is claimed that in the seventh century these two sources were united and allegedly contain contradictions, conflations, differences in style, etc. Later a deuteronomic editor of the sixth century deleted certain portions contrary to his religious convictions, but these were supposedly subsequently restored. The critical theory is to be rejected because it is at variance with the unity of the books, making out the compiler or editor to be a mere blunderer. It is unsound to insist that differences of viewpoint are evidences of variety of authorship. The critical argument that style and diction indicate composite authorship is weak and inconclusive.   M.F.U.

BIBLIOGRAPHY: H. W. Hertzberg, *I and II Samuel: A Commentary* (1964); R. K. Harrison, *Introduction to the*

Old Testament (1969), pp. 695-718; C. J. Barber and J. D. Carter, *Always a Winner* (1977); W. G. Blaikie, *The First Book of Samuel* (1978); id., *The Second Book of Samuel* (1978); P. K. McCarter, Jr., *I Samuel, a New Translation with Introduction,* Anchor Bible (1980); id., *II Samuel, a New Translation with Introduction* (1982); W. J. Deane and T. Kirk, *Studies in First Samuel* (1983); H. Vos, *I, II Samuel* (1983).

SANBAL'LAT (san-bal'at; cf. Akkad. *Sin;* The moon god; "has given life"). He is called "Sanballat the Horonite" (Neh. 2:10, 19; 13:28). This scarcely means that he was from Horonaim in Moab but more likely that he was a resident of Beth-horon in Samaria. All that we know of him from Scripture is that he had apparently some civil or military command in Samaria, in the service of Artaxerxes (4:1-2), and that, from the moment of Nehemiah's arrival in Judea, he set himself to oppose every measure for the welfare of Jerusalem and was a constant adversary to the Tirshatha, the official title of the Persian governor of Judah, borne by Nehemiah (8:9; 10:1). His companions in this hostility were Tobiah the Ammonite and Geshem the Arab (2:19; 4:7), 445 B.C. The only other incident in his life is his alliance with the high priest's family by the marriage of his daughter with one of the grandsons of Eliashib (13:28), which, by the similar connection formed by Tobiah the Ammonite (13:4), appears to have been part of a settled policy concerted between Eliashib and the Samaritan faction. The expulsion from the priesthood of the guilty son of Joiada by Nehemiah must have still further widened the breach between him and Sanballat and between the two parties in the Jewish state. Here, however, the scriptural narrative ends—owing, probably, to Nehemiah's return to Persia—and with it likewise our knowledge of Sanballat.

BIBLIOGRAPHY: C. C. Torrey, *Journal of Biblical Literature* 47 (1928): 384ff.; H. H. Rowley, *Men of God* (1965), pp. 246-76.

SANCTIFICATION (Gk. *hagiasmos,* "separation, a setting apart"). The Heb. term *qōdesh,* rendered "sanctify," has a corresponding meaning. The dominant idea of sanctification, therefore, is separation from the secular and sinful and setting apart for a sacred purpose. As the holiness of God means His separation from all evil (*see* Holiness of God), so sanctification, in the various Scripture applications of the term, has a kindred lofty significance.

In the OT economy, things, places, and times, as well as persons, were sanctified, i.e., consecrated to holy purposes (*see* Gen. 2:3; Ex. 13:2; 40:10-13; etc.). Connected with this were the Mosaic rites of purification (*see,* e.g., Num. 6:11; Lev. 22:16, 32; Heb. 9:13). These rites, however, when applied to persons were efficacious only in a ceremonial and legal sense and did not extend to the purifying of the moral and spiritual nature. They were symbolical and thus were intended not only to remind the Jew of the necessity of spiritual cleansing but also of the gracious purpose of God to actually accomplish the work. So David prayed not only, "Purify me with hyssop, and I shall be clean," but also, "Create in me a clean heart, O God, and renew a steadfast spirit within me" (Ps. 51:7-10).

Although in the OT, as well as in the NT, men are sometimes called upon to sanctify themselves, i.e., to consecrate themselves truly to God (*see* Ex. 19:22; Lev. 11:44; 20:7-8; 1 Pet. 3:15), the thought everywhere prevails that inward cleansing is the work of God. *See* Holy Spirit.

BIBLIOGRAPHY: C. W. Brown, *The Meaning of Sanctification* (1945); G. C. Berkouwer, *Faith and Sanctification* (1952); J. C. Ryle, *Holiness* (1952); W. Marshall, *The Gospel Mystery of Sanctification* (1955); W. E. Sangster, *The Path to Perfection* (1957); S. Neill, *Christian Holiness* (1960); N. Turner, *Christian Words* (1980), pp. 399-402; K. F. W. Prior, *The Way to Holiness* (1982).

SANCTIFICATION, ENTIRE. Is it the privilege of believers to be wholly sanctified in this life? The doctrine of the Roman Catholic church is that baptism, rightly administered, washes away not only guilt but also depravity of every kind; and thus, in its own peculiar way, that church answers the question in the affirmative (*see* Baptism). Among Protestant theologians there is wide difference of belief; and there are undoubtedly greater differences of statement, because of confusion in the use of terms. We have space only to indicate in a most general way the two leading views and to add a few suggestions for guidance.

The Calvinistic View. To the Calvinists, sanctification is imperfect in this life. Corruption of nature remains even in the regenerate so that during this life no man is able to live without sin. For formal expression of this doctrine the reader is referred to the Westminster Confession and to the Larger Catechism of the Presbyterian church.

The Methodist View. The Methodists, on the other hand, despite various shades of opinion and form of statement, see entire sanctification in a true and scriptural sense as being attainable in this life; and accordingly, Christians may arrive at a state of spiritual purity in which they are able to remain free from condemnation. This view is in agreement with the Calvinistic in regarding sanctification as distinct from regeneration (*see* Regeneration). But it is in strongest contrast thereto in regarding the work of spiritual purification as one that may be wrought instantaneously and in the present life. It should be said that the essential features of Methodist doctrine are held by many other denominations.

Summary of New Testament Statement. The NT presents the doctrine of sanctification in three aspects: *positional, experiential,* and *ultimate. Positional* sanctification is the possession of everyone "in Christ." The great doctrinal epistles of the NT first present the marvels of saving grace manifested in the believer's position and then close with an appeal for life consonant with this divinely wrought position (Rom. 12:1; Eph. 4:1; Col. 3:1-2). *Positional* sanctification is just as complete for the weakest and youngest believer as it is for the strongest and oldest. It depends only upon one's union with and position "in Christ." All believers are "saints" and are "sanctified" (Acts 20:32; 1 Cor. 1:2; 6:11; Heb. 10:10, 14; Jude 3). First Corinthians presents proof that imperfect believers are nevertheless positionally sanctified and therefore "saints." The Corinthian Christians were carnal in life (1 Cor. 5:1-2; 6:1-8), but they are twice said to have been "sanctified" (1:2 and 6:11). Thus this positional aspect of sanctification is absolutely essential if the doctrine as a whole is to be clearly understood.

Experiential. The basis of *experiential* sanctification, or actual holiness of life, is positional sanctification, or what one is in Christ. Only those "in Christ," that is, regenerate and thus concomitantly sanctified, are candidates for experiential sanctifications. This phase of sanctification is effected by faith that reckons upon one's position in Christ (Rom. 6:1-10). One's position is true whether or not he reckons or counts it as true. But it becomes *experientially real* only in proportion as one reckons it to be true (6:11).

Ultimate. This is glorification or complete conformity to Christ at His coming (1 John 3:1-3; Rom. 8:29-30; Jude 24, 25).   E. MCC.; M.F.U.

BIBLIOGRAPHY: W. E. R. Sangster, *The Path to Perfection* (1943); J. Wesley, *A Plain Account of Christian Perfection* (1952); R. N. Flew, *The Idea of Perfection in Christian Theology* (1968).

SANCTUARY. A sacred place of resort and worship. Israel's early sanctuary was at Shiloh, which was the center of the nation's religious institutions after the conquest. About this central shrine the twelve tribes were grouped. The close parallel between this institution and the amphictyonies that were found in other Mediterranean lands a few centuries later has been set forth by Martin Noth in *Das System der Zwoelf Staemme Israels* (1930), pp. 39-60. Classical writers report numerous amphictyonies of which a number are explicitly stated to have had twelve tribes. The best known is the famous Delphic amphictyony traceable back at least to the eighth century B.C. Characteristic of these systems was a central sanctuary that formed a bond by which the political structure was cemented together. The Danish excavations at Shiloh have revealed evidences of the destruction of Israel's sanctuary by the Philistines c. 1050 B.C. Shiloh was recognized by the Israelites as their inter-tribal focus from about 1375 B.C. (cf. Judg. 21:19; 1 Sam. 1:3, 7, 9; etc.). Other ancient Near Eastern countries had their great central sanctuary to which pilgrimages were made. Nineveh in Assyria and Nippur in Babylonia were such places of religious resort

during the third quarter of the second millennium. The temple of Sin in Harran and Belit-ekalli in Qatna were popular in the eighteenth century B.C., as shown by the Mari Tablets. The temple of Baaltis in Byblos received votive offerings from Egypt for many centuries. Other shrines in early Israel were at Gibeon, Bethel, Gilgal, Dan, and presumably at Beersheba. Possibly every Israelite town had at least one place where sacrifice might conveniently be offered to the Lord. Such a meeting place was called a *bamah,* a Canaanite word meaning "back" or "ridge." The Conway High Place at Petra, excavated by W. F. Albright in 1934, belongs to the circular processional type and is to be compared to pre-Islamic sanctuaries. The Great High Place of Petra, discovered by George L. Robinson in 1900, and numerous other sites were clearly intended for sacrificial feasts in the open air. Several of them possess rock-cut dining rooms with couches. Rustic *bamoth* were customarily built on hills or under trees, ostensibly for the purpose of catching the cool W wind and obtaining shelter from the sun. At these places of religious resort were held festal gatherings on new moons, Sabbaths, and other occasions. Sacrifices of sheep, goats, and cattle were made as well as offerings of grain, wine, oil, flax, wood, figs, and raisin cakes. Gifts were dispensed to the priest and Levites who had charge of the place, or were consumed in picnic fashion by the worshipers (cf. W. F. Albright, *Archaeology and the Religion of Israel* [1942], pp. 102-7). When the Temple was constructed at Jerusalem by Solomon it became the religious mecca of all the Israelites.   M.F.U.

See Holy Place; Tabernacle; Temple.

BIBLIOGRAPHY: R. de Vaux, *Ancient Israel: Its Life and Institutions* (1961), pp. 274-311.

SAND (Heb. *hôl,* "whirling"). Small loose bits of disintegrating rocks, found abundantly along the southern shores of the Mediterranean and conspicuous in the shifting dunes of the wilderness and desert regions of Arabia, Egypt, and Palestine.

Figurative. The sand of the seashore is often used to express a great multitude; thus God promised Abraham and Jacob to multiply their posterity as the stars of heaven and the sand of the sea (Gen. 22:17; 32:12). Job (Job 6:3) compares the weight of his misfortunes to that of the sand of the sea; and Solomon says (Prov. 27:3), "A stone is heavy and the sand weighty; but the provocation of a fool is heavier than both of them." The omnipotence of God is expressed by His placing the sand as the boundary of the sea (Jer. 5:22). The shifting sand is used as symbolic of instability (Matt. 7:26).

SANDAL (Gk. *sandalion,* representing the Heb. *na'al*). The sandal, apparently the article used by the Hebrews for protecting the feet, consisted simply of a sole attached to the foot by thongs.

The Gk. *hupodēma* properly applies to the sandal exclusively, as it means what is bound *under* the foot.

Material. We learn from the Talmudists that the materials employed in the construction of the sole were either leather, felt, cloth, or wood, and that it was occasionally shod with iron. In Egypt various fibrous substances, such as palm leaves and papyrus stalks, were used in addition to leather, whereas in Assyria wood or leather were employed. In Egypt the sandals were usually turned up at the toe like our skates, though other forms, rounded and pointed, are also exhibited. Royal Egyptian sandals from the Eighteenth Dynasty (the New Kingdom) exist (from about 1546 to 1319 B.C.). In Assyria the heel and the side of the foot were encased, and sometimes the sandal consisted of little less than this. Sandals were worn by all classes of society in Palestine, even by the very poor (Amos 8:6), and both the sandal and the thong were so cheap and common that they passed into a proverb for the most insignificant thing (Gen. 14:23; Ecclus. 46:19).

Sandals

Use. They were not, however, worn at all periods; they were dispensed with indoors and were only put on by persons about to undertake some business away from their homes, such as a military expedition (Isa. 5:27; Eph. 6:15) or a journey (Ex. 12:11; Josh. 9:5, 13; Acts 12:8). On such occasions persons carried an extra pair. During mealtimes the feet were undoubtedly uncovered, as implied in Luke 7:38; John 13:5-6.

Figurative. It was a mark of reverence to take off the shoes in approaching a place or person of eminent sanctity (Ex. 3:5; Josh. 5:15). In Ruth 4:7 (cf. Deut. 25:9-10) it is recorded: "Now this was the custom in former times in Israel concerning the redemption and the exchange of land to confirm any matter: a man removed his sandal and gave it to another; and this was the manner of attestation in Israel." From the expression "former" and from the description of the custom we infer that it had largely gone out of use when the book was written. The custom itself, which existed among the Indians and ancient Germans, arose from the fact that fixed property was taken possession of by treading upon the soil; and hence taking off the shoe and handing it to another was a symbol of the transfer of possession of right of ownership. From this thought we have the expression "Over Edom I shall throw My shoe" (Pss. 60:8; 108:9), i.e., claim it as My own.

It was also an indication of violent emotion or of mourning if a person appeared barefoot in public (2 Sam. 15:30; Isa. 20:2; Song of Sol. 7:1; Ezek. 24:17, 23). To carry or to unloose a person's sandal was a menial office betokening great inferiority on the part of the person performing it (Matt. 3:11; Mark 1:7; John 1:27; Acts 13:25). A sandal thong (or lace), or even sandals themselves (Gen. 14:23; Amos 2:6; 8:6) stand for anything of little value; this is easily understood when one sees a pair of sandals shaped in a few minutes out of a piece of hide, and which would be expensive at a few cents. Sandals with blood on them were figurative of being engaged in war (1 Kings 2:5).

See also Dress.

BIBLIOGRAPHY: R. de Vaux, *Ancient Israel: Its Life and Institutions* (1961), pp. 22, 37, 59, 86, 169.

SAND FLIES. *See* Animal Kingdom: Lice.

SAND LIZARD. *See* Animal Kingdom: Lizard; Snail.

SAN'HEDRIN (san-hē′drin; Aram. form of Gk. *sunedrion,* a "council, assembly session").

History. The rise of this great council of the Hebrews took place in the time of Greek supremacy, though the rabbis endeavor to trace its origin to the college of seventy elders named by Moses. The first occasion on which it is mentioned, and that under the designation of *gerousia* (Gk., the "eldership"), is in the time of Antiochus the Great, 223-187 B.C. From its designation, *gerousia,* it is evident that it was an *aristocratic* body, with the *hereditary high priest* at its head. It continued to exist and exercise its functions under the Asmonaean princes and high priests (2 Macc. 1:10; 4:44; 11:27). When the Roman order of affairs was introduced by Pompey the high priest still retained the position of "governor of the nation" (Josephus *Ant.* 20.10.1), thus making it likely that the *gerousia* still remained. Gabinius, 57-55 B.C., divided the whole Jewish territory into five "conventions" (Josephus *Wars 1.8.5*), or "councils" (Josephus *Ant.* 14.5.4). As things now stood the council of Jerusalem no longer exercised sole jurisdiction. After ten years Caesar reappointed Hyrcanus II to his former position of *ethnarch,* and the jurisdiction of the council of Jerusalem once more extended to Galilee (Josephus *Ant.* 14.8.3-5). Here for the first time the council of Jerusalem was designated by the term *Sanhedrin.* Herod the Great inaugurated his reign by ordering the whole of the Sanhedrin to be put to death (Josephus *Ant.* 14.9.4) and evidently formed a Sanhedrin of those who were disposed to be tractable. After Herod's death Archelaus obtained only a portion of his father's kingdom—Judea and Samaria—and in consequence the jurisdiction was probably restricted to Judea proper. Under the procurators the internal government of the country was to a greater extent in the hands of the Sanhedrin than during the reigns of Herod and Archelaus. In the time of Christ and the apostles the Sanhedrin is frequently mentioned as being the supreme Jewish court of justice (*see* marg., Matt. 5:22; 26:59; Mark 14:55; 15:1; Luke 22:66; Acts 4:15, 21-23; 6:12-15; 22:30; 23:1, 6; 24:20). Sometimes the terms *presbuterion* (Luke 22:66; Acts 22:5) and *gerousia* (Acts 5:21) are substituted for Sanhedrin. The Sanhedrin was undoubtedly abolished, so far as its existing form was concerned, after the destruction of Jerusalem, A.D. 70.

Model of the interior of Sanhedrin court, Jerusalem

Composition. This great council was formed (Matt. 26:3, 57, 59; Mark 14:53; 15:1; Luke 22:66; Acts 4:5-6; 5:21; 22:30) of high priests (i.e., the acting high priest, those who had been high priests, and members of the privileged families from which the high priests were taken), elders (i.e., tribal and family heads of the people and priesthood), and scribes (i.e., legal assessors), Pharisees, and Sadducees alike (cf. Acts 4:1, 5-6; 5:17, 34). According to the Mishna the number of members was seventy, with a president, a vice president, and servants of the court (John 18:22; Mark 14:65; etc.). Josephus and the NT state that the acting high priest, as such, was always head and president. Wherever names are mentioned we find that it is the high priest for the time being that officiates as president—Caiaphas in the time of Christ (Matt. 26:3, 57) and Ananias in the time of Paul (Acts 23:2; 24:1). It is believed that membership was for life and that new members were appointed either by the existing members or by the supreme political authorities. We may well assume that the *one* requirement of legal Judaism, that none but Israelites of pure blood should be eligible for the office of judge in a criminal court, would also be insisted upon in the case of the supreme Sanhedrin. New members were admitted through the ceremony of laying on of hands.

Jurisdiction. The jurisdiction of the Sanhedrin was restricted in the time of Christ to the eleven districts of Judea proper; hence it had no judicial authority over Jesus, so long as He remained in Galilee, but only when He entered Judea. "In a certain sense, no doubt, the Sanhedrin exercised such jurisdiction over *every* Jewish community in the world, and in that sense over Galilee as well. Its orders were regarded as binding throughout the entire dominion of orthodox Judaism. It had power to issue warrants to the congregations (synagogues) in Damascus for the apprehension of Christians in that quarter (Acts 9:2; 22:5; 26:12). At the same time, however, the extent to which the Jewish communities were willing to yield obedience to the orders of the Sanhedrin always depended upon how far they were favorably disposed toward it. It was only within the limits of Judea proper that it exercised any direct authority." It would not be proper to say that the Sanhedrin was the *spiritual* or *theological* in contradistinction to the civil judicatories of the Romans. It was rather that *supreme native* court that here, as almost everywhere else, Rome continued to allow, only imposing certain restrictions with regard to competency. "To this tribunal then belonged all those judicial matters and all those measures of an administrative character which either could not be competently dealt with by inferior local courts, or which the Roman procurator had not specially reserved for himself. The Sanhedrin was, above all, the final court of appeal for questions connected with the Mosaic law, but not in the sense that it was open to anyone to appeal to it against the decision of the inferior courts but rather in so far as it was called upon to intervene in every case in which the lower courts could not agree as to their judgment. And when once it had given a decision in any case the judges of the local court were, on pain of death, bound to acquiesce in it" (Schürer, *History of the Jewish People,* div. 2, 1:185ff.). From the NT, we learn that Jesus appeared before the Sanhedrin on a charge of blasphemy (Matt. 26:65; John 19:7). Peter and John were charged with being false prophets and deceivers of the people (Acts 4-5), Stephen with being a blasphemer (6:9-12), and Paul with being guilty of transgressing the Mosaic law (chap. 23). The Sanhedrin enjoyed a considerable amount of criminal jurisdiction. It had the right of ordering arrests to be made by its own officers (Matt. 26:47; Mark 14:43; Acts 4:3; 5:17-18) and of finally disposing of cases that did not involve the sentence of death (4:5-23; 5:21-40). When it pronounced sentence of death it was required to be ratified by the procurator (John 18:31). Such instances as the stoning of Stephen must be regarded as an excess of jurisdiction or an act of irregular mob justice. Thus the Sanhedrin had a tolerably extensive jurisdiction, the serious restriction being that the Roman authorities could at any time take the initiative and proceed independently, as, for example, when Paul was arrested. Further, the procurator, or even the tribune of the cohorts stationed at Jerusalem, might call the Sanhedrin together for the purpose of submitting to it any matter requiring investigation from the standpoint of Jewish law (Acts 22:30; cf. 23:15, 20, 28).

Time and Place of Meeting. The local courts usually sat on the second and fifth days of the week (Monday and Thursday); but whether this was the practice of the Sanhedrin we have no means of knowing. There were no courts held on *festival* (which see) days, much less on the Sabbath. The *place* in which the Sanhedrin usually met was situated, according to Josephus (*Wars* 5.4.2), close to the so-called Xystos (Xistus), on its E side toward the Temple mount. In cases that did not admit of delay it assembled in the high priest's house (Matt. 26:3, 57; Mark 14:53).

Judicial Procedures. According to the Mishna, the members sat in a semi-circle that they might be able to see one another. In front stood the two clerks of the court, one on the right hand and the other on the left, whose duty it was to record the votes of those who were in favor of acquittal on the one hand and of those who were in favor of condemnation on the other. There also sat in front of them three rows of disciples of the learned men, each of whom had a special seat. The prisoner was required to appear in a humble attitude, dressed in mourning. The following order was observed in *capital* cases: arguments first in favor of *acquittal,* then those in favor of *conviction;* if anyone had spoken in favor of the accused he could not afterward say anything unfavorable, though the converse was allowed; student disciples might speak in favor but not against the accused, although, if the case did not

involve a capital sentence, they could speak for or against the accused; sentence of acquittal might be pronounced on the day of trial, but one of condemnation not until the day following. The voting, each member standing, began with the youngest members of the court, although on some occasions it began with the most distinguished member. For acquittal a simple majority was sufficient; for condemnation a majority of two was required. If twelve of the twenty-three judges necessary to form a quorum voted for acquittal and eleven for conviction the prisoner was discharged; but if twelve were for conviction and eleven for acquittal, then the number of the judges had to be increased by adding two, which was repeated if necessary until either an acquittal was secured or the majority requisite for a conviction was obtained. But, of course, they had to restrict themselves to the maximum number of seventy-one (Keil, *Arch.,* 1:350; Schürer, div. 2, 1:163).

BIBLIOGRAPHY: H. Danby, *Journal of Theological Studies* 21 (1919): 51-76; *The Mishnah,* trans. H. Danby (1933), pp. 382-400; H. Mantel, *Studies in the History of the Sanhedrin* (1961); J. Jeremias, *Jerusalem in the Time of Jesus* (1967), pp. 222-32; A. T. Innes and J. Powell, *The Trial of Christ* (1982).

SANSAN'NAH (san-san'a; "palm branch"). A city in Judah (Josh. 15:31), identified with Khirbet esh-Shamsäniyät about ten miles NE of Beersheba.

SAPH (saf; "a threshold or dish"). A Philistine giant, of the race of Raphah (*see* marg.) slain by Sibbecai the Hushathite (2 Sam. 21:18; 1 Chron. 20:4).

SAPHIR. *See* Shaphir.

SAPPHI'RA (sa-fi'ra; Gk. from Aram., "beautiful"). The wife of Ananias and accomplice in the sin for which he died. About three hours after the death of her husband she entered the place, unconscious of what had happened. Questioned by Peter as to the price obtained for the land they had sold, she repeated the lie of her husband and exposed herself to the fate of Ananias. Peter replied to her: "Why is it that you have agreed together to put the Spirit of the Lord to the test? Behold, the feet of those who have buried your husband are at the door, and they shall carry you out as well." On hearing these words she fell dead (Acts 5:1-2, 7-10).

The offense of Ananias and Sapphira, according to the average standard of human morality, was not a heinous one. They had devoted a large sum to charity; they had defrauded no one but had simply retained their own and then denied the fact. The following considerations are offered in explanation by Whedon (*Com.,* ad loc.): "1. The divine Spirit being present with unparalleled power in the Church, the sin, as Peter says (vers. 3, 4) is *directly against him.* 2. The reason for this selection was to present and record at this *beginning* of the Christian Church a representative and memorial instance of the just doom of the *hypocrite*. This couple were deliberate, positive, conceited, and intentionally *permanent hypocrites*. Their death was God's declaration to all future ages of the true deserts of all deliberate *hypocrites* in the Church of Christ." 3. In addition it may be added that this was evidently a "sin leading to death" (i.e. "physical" death), cf. 1 John 5:16. Similar cases occur in 1 Cor. 5:1-5; 11:30. The deaths of Samson and Saul give typical illustrations of a believer's "sin leading to [*physical*] death" in the OT.

BIBLIOGRAPHY: R. L. Strauss, *Living in Love* (1978), pp. 123-32.

SAPPHIRE. *See* Mineral Kingdom.

SA'RA, SA'RAH (sā'ra; "a princess"; "Sara," KJV, Heb. 11:11). The wife of the patriarch Abraham, although in the KJV only of Num. 26:46 it refers to a daughter of Asher, known in the NASB and NIV as *Serah* (which see). The original name of Abraham's wife Sarah was *Sarai* (which see) and was changed at the same time that Abram's name was changed to Abraham, on the establishment of the covenant of circumcision. The Heb. name of Sarah is *śārâ* ("princess"). Of her birth and parentage we have no certain account in Scripture. In Gen. 20:12 Abraham speaks of her as "my sister, the daughter of my father, but not the daughter of my mother," which would make her his half sister; but the statement of Abraham is held by many to mean no more than that Haran, her father, was his half brother, for the colloquial usage of the Hebrews in this matter makes it easy to understand that he might call a niece a sister. In that case Abraham was really her uncle as well as husband.

As his wife, the history of Sarah is substantially that of Abraham. She came with him from Ur to Haran (Gen. 11:31), from Haran to Canaan (12:5), and accompanied him in all his wanderings.

Taken by Pharaoh. When Abraham went down into Egypt apparently under the powerful and splendid Twelfth Dynasty of the Middle Kingdom (c. 2000-1775), he arranged with Sarah that she should announce herself as his sister, fearing for his life on account of her beauty. Although she was then sixty-five, she was so beautiful to the Egyptians that she was taken by Pharaoh; but, plagued by Jehovah, he returned her to Abraham with a reproof for his untruthfulness (12:10-20).

Hagar. Having no children of her own, Sarah gave to Abraham her Egyptian handmaid, Hagar, who became the mother of Ishmael (chap. 16). Later she demanded that Hagar and Ishmael should be cast out from all rivalry with herself and Isaac (21:9-10), a demand symbolically applied (Gal. 4:22-31) to the displacement of the Old Covenant by the New.

Abimelech. After the destruction of Sodom, Abraham moved to the south country and remained for some time in Gerar. Here Abimelech, the Philistine king, took Sarah, whom Abraham had again announced to be his sister, into his harem, probably to ally himself with Abraham, the rich nomad prince. Warned by God in a dream, Abimelech restored Sarah to her husband (Gen. 20).

Birth of Isaac. Jehovah fulfilled His promise to Sarah, and at the appointed time she gave birth to Isaac (21:1-3). This was recognized at the time, and later by Paul (Rom. 4:19), as a miracle, since both Sarah and Abraham were advanced in years.

Death. Thirty-seven years after the birth of Isaac, and when she had reached the age of 127, Sarah died at Hebron and was buried in the cave of Machpelah (Gen. 21:1-3), c. 1980 B.C. Isaiah is the only prophet who names Sarah (51:2). Paul alludes to her hope of becoming a mother (Rom. 4:19) and afterward cites the promise that she received (9:9), and Peter eulogizes her submission to her husband (1 Pet. 3:6).

BIBLIOGRAPHY: W. H. G. Thomas, *Genesis: A Devotional Commentary* (1946), pp. 118-204; C. J. and A. A. Barber, *Your Marriage Has Real Possibilities* (1984), pp. 69-113.

SA'RAI (sa'rī; perhaps "contentious"). The original name of Sarah, always used in the history from Gen. 11:29 to 17:15.

SA'RAPH (sa'raf; "burning or serpent"). One of the descendants of Shelah, the son of Judah (1 Chron. 4:22), who seems to have lived about the time of the entrance of Israel into Canaan, as he is said to have had dominion in Moab (about 1400 B.C.).

SARDINE, SARDIUS. *See* Mineral Kingdom: Sardine, or Sardius.

SAR'DIS (sar'dis). A city of western Asia Minor about fifty miles E of Symrna, which was the fifth named of the seven churches addressed by John (Rev. 1:11; 3:1, 4). This important city was founded probably as early as the beginning of the Iron Age and located on important commercial routes running E and W through the rich kingdom of Lydia, of which it was the capital. It was also made wealthy by textile manufacturing and jewelry making. Here are said to have been minted the first coins under the opulent Croesus. Cyrus the Great overcame the city in 546 B.C. Antiochus the Great did the same in 218 B.C. Wealthy Sardis citizens took up with mystery cults, notably with that of Cybele.

As a result of extensive archaeological investigation of Sardis the site is gradually becoming better known. Howard C. Butler of Princeton worked there on behalf of the American Society for the Excavation of Sardis from 1910 to 1914. His efforts were chiefly centered on the great temple of Artemis (300 by 160 feet) to the W of the acropolis, and he opened more than one thousand graves in the so-called "Cemetery Hill." In 1958 the Fogg Art Museum of Harvard, Cornell University, and the American Schools of Oriental Research began a joint excavation at Sardis. George M. A. Hanfmann of Harvard was the director for many years. Along the Pactolas River a Roman villa and bath, two Byzantine churches, and the gold-smelting establishment of King Croesus have been found. Along the Izmir-Ankara highway finds have been extensive. On the N side of the road stood more than thirty Byzantine shops. Behind the shops a synagogue was discovered, three times larger than any synagogue preserved in Palestine. Dating to the first half of the third century, it is four hundred feet long and sixty feet wide. This structure has been partially restored. North of the synagogue lay a gymnasium complex consisting of a large court for athletic exercise and a bath establishment. The monumental entrance gate, two stories high, has now been completely restored.   H.F.V.

BIBLIOGRAPHY: E. M. Blaiklock, *Cities of the New Testament* (1965), pp. 112-19; W. M. Ramsay, *Letters to the Seven Churches of Asia* (1978), pp. 354-90.

Gymnasium at Sardis

SARDONYX. *See* Mineral Kingdom.

SAREP'TA (Luke 4:26, KJV). *See* Zarephath.

SAR'GON (sar'gon). The name of an Assyrian king mentioned only once in the Bible (Isa. 20:1),

and then merely to give the date to an important prophecy of Isaiah. The Assyrian form of the name is Sharrukin. Sargon was the successor of Shalmaneser V (*see* Shalmaneser) and the father of Sennacherib (*see* Sennacherib), and he ruled in Assyria 722-705 B.C. Abundant historical materials concerning his reign have come down to us. Remains of the walls that he built, colossal carved bulls covered with inscriptions, tools, palace utensils, and beautifully inscribed prisms have all been found in different parts of Assyria, and all bear their witness to his glory and success.

Lineage. Sargon began to reign in Assyria in the same month in which Shalmaneser V died. This would seem to indicate that there was no doubt or difficulty about the succession. Yet it is clear that he was not the son of Shalmaneser, or apparently any relative of his predecessor. Indeed, he never alludes in any of his known inscriptions to his ancestors. It is therefore, with justice, believed that he was not of royal origin at all. In the reign of his grandson Esarhaddon a genealogical table was made out, by which Sargon's ancestry was traced back to Bel-bani, an early ruler in Assyria. This was evidently only an attempt to gain the honor of noble lineage. Whatever his origin—and it was probably humble, since nothing is said of it—Sargon seems to have been accepted as king without question. He may, therefore, have been adopted by Shalmaneser and designated as his successor.

Exploits. Sargon was one of the greatest soldiers ever produced in Assyria, and his coming upon the scene was at the very time when he was sorely needed by a weakened empire. The reign of Shalmaneser had been brief. His death left the state in confusion. Babylonia was overrun by the Chaldeans and under the leadership of Merodach-baladan was in open revolt. There was a siege in progress at Samaria at the end of Shalmaneser's reign, and the king of Egypt was threatening and ill-tempered. The northern boundary of Assyria was dangerously beset by the tribes of Armenia, and northern Syria again had to be reduced to subjection. With a weak man upon the throne of Assyria, all would have been lost that Tiglath-pileser III had gained and perhaps the empire's very existence would have been in jeopardy. The occasion was great, and Sargon was equal to it.

The first event in the reign of Sargon, according to his own inscription, was the fall of Samaria. He speaks of it in these words: "The city Samaria I besieged, and twenty-seven thousand two hundred and ninety people, inhabitants of it, I took away captive. Fifty chariots in it I seized, but the rest I allowed to retain their possessions. I appointed my governor over them, and the tribute of the late king I imposed upon them." We do not know whether Sargon was actually present at Samaria or not. The city may have been taken by one of his generals, though he says that *he* took it. We know from other clear instances that the Assyrian kings were not careful to distinguish their own from the successes of their generals in the field. Whether he or his representative was the real conqueror, Sargon was proud of the achievement. In his Cylinder Inscription he calls himself "subjugator of the broad land of Beth-Omri," and again elsewhere "the conqueror of the city of Samaria and the whole land of Beth-Omri." In his treatment of Israel Sargon followed the plans first matured by Tiglath-pileser; he "carried Israel away into exile to Assyria, and settled them in Halah and Habor, on the river of Gozan, and in the cities of the Medes" (2 Kings 17:6), and to fill the place thus vacated he brought men from Babylon, Cuthah, Avva, Hamath, and Sephar-vaim, placing them in the cities of Samaria instead of Israel (17:24). This colonization as begun by Tiglath-pileser and extended by Sargon was handed on from people to people till it found its fullest extension in the Roman Empire.

Temple of Artemis, Sardis

After the downfall of Samaria Sargon was speedily confronted by another confederation. A leader in Hamath, Ilu-bi'di by name, had formed a coalition to throw off the Assyrian supremacy. He was aided by several provinces nearby, among them Arpad and Damascus, and was supported by Hanno, king of Gaza. Sargon made haste from Assyria in order to attack Ilu-bi'di before his allies could join him. He met Ilu-bi'di at Qarqar (or Karkar) and completely overcame him. He then

moved southward and found that Hanno was supported by Seveh of Egypt. A battle was fought at Rapichi (modern Refah), and again Sargon was victorious. Seveh and his troops fled in confusion to Egypt, and Hanno was taken prisoner and carried off to Assyria. These victories brought enforced peace in Palestine, and Sargon was free to undertake conquest and pacification elsewhere. In 719 he was carrying on war in the N as far as Lake Urmiah; in the next year he was collecting tribute in Cappadocia. In the year 718 Sargon crossed the Euphrates and attacked Carchemish. The ancient Hittite Empire had fallen about 1200 B.C., but several Hittite city-states continued to maintain themselves in Syria. Carchemish and its provinces alone remained. They were now reduced and the territory completely absorbed into Assyria. The following years were full of abundant labors in the putting down of insurrections in Armenia, Que (eastern Cilicia), and in Arabia, and another attack upon an Egyptian king is recorded. In every case peace was achieved for a season by force, but new disturbances were always breaking forth elsewhere.

In 711 difficulties again attracted Sargon's attention in Syria. Azuri, king of Ashdod, thought that the time was ripe for refusing to pay the Assyrians tribute. Sargon hastily dispatched a Tartan against him (Isa. 20:1), who removed Azuri from the throne and put in his place his brother Achimit, who was an Assyrian sympathizer. The people of Ashdod would not endure a man of such sentiments and deposed him by force. Suddenly Sargon appeared, took Ashdod and Gath, which had joined in the rebellion, carried away the chief inhabitants to Assyria, and filled their places with colonists from the E. This ended the troubles for the present, and Sargon could now turn his attention to Babylonia. The state of this land might well cause alarm. The whole country was in open revolt, under the leadership of Merodach-baladan, who had formed also a confederacy with Elam (*see* Merodach-baladan). Sargon realized that this would be a severe struggle. His plans were carefully laid. He attacked the confederate forces separately, won victories, and soon was in possession of Babylon. In 709 he was again acknowledged as king in Babylon, and the rebellion that had begun with the beginning of his reign was over. The years 709-707 were brilliant indeed. Tribute was sent to him from the island of Dilmun in the Persian Gulf and from Cyprus in the far-away Mediterranean. He was at the zenith of his power, and many lands did him homage.

Last Years. For the last few years of his reign we have no Assyrian documents. Only brief hints show that his armies were engaged till the very last in subduing insurrections here and there over his vast empire. It was indeed impossible that peoples so widely separated and so diverse in all their thoughts and emotions should be speedily welded into a unified and symmetrical empire. Conquests might be made quickly; concourse of feeling must be of slow growth. Sargon died in 705. The broken fragments of the Eponym list seem to say that he was murdered, but they are too badly mutilated to make us perfectly sure. So ended the career of the greatest conqueror who ever ruled in Assyria. He was not so great a pacificator as was Esarhaddon, neither were his works of peace so magnificent as those of Ashurbanipal, but in war he surpassed all who preceded or followed him upon that throne.

Royal City. But he was not only a warrior; he has left at least one magnificent evidence of his skill in the arts of peace. When he began his reign the Assyrian capital was Calah. He determined to erect a new city and place within it a palace that should surpass in magnificence all that had preceded it. The site selected was at the foot of Mt. Musri, N of Nineveh. The city built there he named after himself, Dur-Sharrukin (Sargonsburg), or Khorsabad, and the palace within its square of walls was the first Assyrian ruin explored by moderns. It was first excavated in the years 1842-45 by Botta and was surprising for its magnificence even in ruins. The ruins were further excavated by Victor Place (1851-55) and by Edward Chiera and Henri Frankfort for the Oriental Institute of the University of Chicago (1929-35). Sargon also began the collection of thousands of cuneiform tablets continued by his great

grandson Ashurbanipal. These were recovered in the famous library at Nineveh. But Sargon did not long enjoy his own magnificence. The man of war was not to rest in the results of peace.

BIBLIOGRAPHY: H. W. F. Saggs, *Iraq* 17 (1955): 146-49; H. Tadmor, *Journal of Cuneiform Studies* 12 (1958): 20-40, 77-100; W. W. Hallo, *Biblical Archaeologist* 23 (1960): 50-56; D. D. Luckenbill, *Ancient Records of Assyria and Babylonia* (1968), 2:1-114; J. B. Pritchard, ed., *Ancient Near Eastern Texts* (1969), pp. 119, 165, 265-68, 272, 284, 287, 579, 647; J. P. Lewis, *Historical Backgrounds of Bible History* (1971), pp. 39-43, 56, 74, 94, 107, 176-77.

SA'RID (sa'rid; "survivor"). A place at the center, probably, of the southern boundary of Zebulun (Josh. 19:10), from which the line is traced in a westerly direction (v. 11) and in an easterly direction (v. 12). It is now identified with Tell Shadua, SW of Nazareth and N of the Plain of Esdraelon.

SA'RON (Acts 9:35, KJV). *See* Sharon.

SAR'SECHIM, SAR'SEKIM (sar'se-kim). One of the generals of Nebuchadnezzar's army at the taking of Jerusalem (Jer. 39:3; "Sarsechim," KJV), 587 B.C. Rendered *Nebo-Sarsekim* (which see) in the NIV.

SA'RUCH (Luke 3:35, KJV). *See* Serug.

SA'TAN (sā'tan; Heb. *śāṭān, Gk. Satanas, an*

Relief from the palace of Sargon

"adversary, opponent"). The chief of fallen spirits.

Scripture Names and Titles. Satan is also called the devil, the dragon, the evil one, the angel of the abyss, the ruler of this world, the prince of the power of the air, the god of this world, Apollyon, Abaddon, Belial, and Beelzebub. But Satan and the devil are the names most frequently given. The term *Satan* is used in its generic sense in 1 Kings 11:14, "The Lord raised up an adversary [*śāṭān*] to Solomon, Hadad the Edomite." It is used in the same sense in 1 Kings 11:23; 1 Sam. 29:4; Num. 22:22 (cf. 2 Sam. 19:22; 1 Kings 5:4; 11:25; Ps. 109:6).

Scripture Doctrine. Satan is mentioned first in the book of Job (1:6-12; 2:1-7). He mixes with the sons of God (angels), among whom he no longer has any rightful place; he arbitrarily roams about and seeks his own but is still used as a servant by God, on whom he remains dependent. His independent activity in this passage is mainly that of the spy of evil, the accuser of man to God, especially the accuser of the pious, and he maintains the assertion that even their fear of God stems from personal interest. Job is delivered into the hands of Satan for testing. Satan's intention was to lead Job into apostasy and ruin; but the conduct of Job proves that disinterested fear of God may be a truth. The luster of a fidelity and love that in the loss of all external goods regards God as the highest good is revealed by Job as a triumph over Satan.

Satan is mentioned as a personality in Zech. 3:1, where after the Exile he would hinder the reinstitution of the divine worship, asserting that Israel is rejected by the just judgment of God and is not worthy of the renewal of the priesthood. But the filthy garments are stripped off the high priest, and he receives festal garments instead, with the declaration that his sins are taken away. The vision expresses that the restoration of the priesthood after the Exile is a victory of the gracious God over Satan. It also foreshadows the restoration of the nation Israel as a high-priestly nation in the future Kingdom age. Still in the OT Satan never appears openly as the enemy of God Himself. "Though he has his special purposes and aims, he is yet the servant of God for punishment or trial, the asserter or executor of the negative side of the divine justice" (Dorner, *Christ. Doct.,* 3:79).

In the NT mention is made of a plurality of evil spirits, with Satan as their head (Matt. 8:28; 9:34; 12:26; Luke 11:18-19). They were endowed with high talents, power, and knowledge (Matt. 8:29; Mark 1:24). Although Satan is used in the NT in a figurative sense (Matt. 16:23), Jesus said the enemy is the devil (13:19, 39; Mark 4:15), and the history of the temptation is no misunderstood parable (Matt. 4:10; cf. Luke 22:31). It is declared that Satan was a murderer from the beginning (John 8:44), the enemy and falsifier of God's word

(Matt. 13:19, 39); that he aroused hatred to Jesus and put treason into the heart of Judas (John 13:27, cf. 6:70; Luke 22:53); that the prince of this world is already judged by Christ, or, as Luke puts it, Satan falls "from heaven like lightning" (10:18), i.e., is inwardly and fundamentally vanquished. The whole history of the world subsequent to Christ is a struggle against the empire of Satan. Thus the Apocalypse especially depicts the history of Satan, particularly in the future as he affects the church (Rev. 2:9, 13, 24), the Jew, and the Gentiles (chaps. 4-19).

BIBLIOGRAPHY: F. C. Jennings, *Satan, His Person, Work, Place and Destiny* (n.d.); F. C. Tatford, *The Prince of Darkness* (n.d.); L. S. Chafer, *Systematic Theology* (1947), 2:33-112; id., *Satan: His Motives and Methods* (1964); J. D. Pentecost, *Your Adversary the Devil* (1969); E. M. B. Green, *I Believe in Satan's Downfall* (1981).

SA'TAN, SYNAGOGUE OF (Rev. 2:9, 13; 3:9). Satan's assembly; probably of Jews who persecuted the Christians, because of their misguided zeal for the law of Moses; who, professing to worship God, really served Satan.

SA'TAN, THE DEEP THINGS OF. The false teachings developed in the church of Thyatira (the Roman church of the Dark Ages), preceding the Protestant Reformation (Rev. 2:24). They included every kind of worldliness and demon-inspired corruption of the truth (1 Tim. 4:1-4). These doctrines were called by their advocates "the deep things of God," but the Lord calls them "the deep things of *Satan.*"

SATISFACTION. *See* Atonement; Propitiation.

SATON. A foreign measure of capacity. *See* Metrology.

SATRAP (Aram. *'ăhashdarpᵉnîm*; "lieutenants," KJV). The title of the viceroys who governed the provinces of the Persian Empire (Ezra 8:36; Esther 3:12; 8:9; 9:3; Dan 3:2; 6:1; etc.).

SAT'YR. *See* Gods, False: Shaggy Goat; Animal Kingdom.

SAUL (sawl; "asked for"). In Gen. 36:37, KJV, inaccurately *Saul* for *Shaul* (which see, no. 2); in the NT, the Heb. name of the apostle *Paul* (which see); and in the OT, the name of the first king of Israel. This king was the son of Kish, of the tribe of Benjamin, a powerful and wealthy chief, although the family to which he belonged was of little importance (1 Sam. 9:1, 21). The time and place of Saul's birth are not given. Since Joshua the Israelites had been under the rule of judges raised up by God to meet emergencies that arose through the defection and idolatry of the people. "In those days there was no king in Israel; everyone did what was right in his own eyes" (Judg. 21:25). The corrupt administration of Samuel's sons furnished the Hebrews an occasion for rejecting the theocracy (1 Sam. 8). This, together with an invasion of the Ammonites and a love of novelty, conspired in prompting the demand for a king. Samuel, instructed by God, granted it, but told the people the evils that would follow. They still persisted in their demand, and Saul was introduced into history. The reign of Saul may be divided into two periods: (1) The establishment and vigorous development of his regal supremacy (chaps. 8-15). (2) The decline and overthrow of his monarchy (chaps. 16-31).

Monarchy Established. The establishment of a monarchy is introduced by the negotiations of the elders of Israel with Samuel concerning the appointment of a king (1 Sam. 8).

Meeting of Saul with Samuel. Having been sent by his father after some strayed donkeys, Saul went with his servant through the mountains of Ephraim, through Shalishah and Shaalim, and after that through the land of Benjamin, without finding the donkeys. Arriving at Zuph, he determined to return home, because he was afraid that his father would worry about them (Saul and the servant). But his servant proposed that they should go and consult the man of God who was in the city near at hand, and learn from him what they should do. Samuel, having been forewarned by God, met Saul at the gate of the city, told him he was the one for whom he looked, and invited him to a feast, assuring him that the donkeys were found. He awakened the expectation of Saul by the question, "And for whom is all that is desirable in Israel? Is it not for you and for all your father's household?" (9:20).

Saul Anointed. Early the next day they arose and, after the servant was sent on, Samuel took a flask of oil and poured it upon Saul's head, kissed him, and said, "Has not the Lord anointed you a ruler over His inheritance?" (9:27; 10:1). To confirm the consecration Samuel gave him three signs that should occur on his journey home—*first,* two men at the tomb of Rachel should meet him and tell him of the finding of the donkeys and the anxiety of Saul's father for him; *second,* three men would be met in the plain of Tabor, going with sacrifices to Bethel, and they would give Saul two loaves from their offerings; *third,* at Gibeah he would meet a company of prophets, and he himself would prophesy (10:2-13).

Chosen King. The mysterious interview with Samuel did not seem to suffice for the full acknowledgment of Saul as king. Samuel, therefore, called a national assembly at Mizpah and here instructed the tribes to choose a king by lot. The result of the lot was regarded as a divine decision, and Saul was accredited in the sight of the whole nation as the king appointed by the Lord; also he himself was more fully assured of the certainty of his own election on the part of God. Saul had hidden but was found, brought before the people, introduced to them by Samuel, and received by them with the cry "Long live the

king!" He returned to his home in Gibeah, followed by a band of men "whose hearts God had touched." But he already began to taste the bitterness of royalty, for there were some who said, "How can this one deliver us?" (10:13-27), c. 1025 B.C.

Victory over the Ammonites. Nahash, king of the Ammonites, laid siege to Jabesh in Gilead and consented to save its inhabitants only on the condition that he should put out their right eyes. They asked for seven days in which to send among their brethren for help. They dispatched messengers to Gibeah and, probably unaware of the election of Saul, stated their case to the people. Returning from the field, Saul heard the news, and the Spirit of the Lord came upon him. Deeply angered, he hewed in pieces a yoke of oxen and sent them through all Israel, calling the people to rally about him for the defense of their countrymen. Three hundred thousand came together at Bezek. The next day Saul arranged the army into three divisions, who forced their way into the camp of the foe from three different sides and routed them completely (11:1-11).

Renewal of the Monarchy. After the victory the people were so enthusiastic in favor of Saul that they demanded the death of those who had spoken against him as king. Saul refused to grant them their request, saying, "Not a man shall be put to death this day, for today the Lord has accomplished deliverance in Israel." Samuel called the people to Gilgal, where the election of Saul was confirmed (11:12-15).

Saul's First Transgression. In the second year of his reign Saul set to work systematically to deliver Israel from their enemies. He gathered 3,000 select men (the beginning of a standing army), 2,000 being with himself and the other 1,000 with his son Jonathan. Jonathan struck the garrison of the Philistines in Geba, which became the signal of war; Saul summoned the people to assemble in Gilgal. The Philistines gathered a great army—30,000 chariots, 6,000 horsemen, and foot soldiers "like the sand which is on the seashore"—and encamped in Michmash. Saul waited seven days for Samuel's coming, but as he did not come the people began to disperse and leave Saul, who then resolved that he would offer the sacrifices without the presence of the prophet. Scarcely was the ceremony over when Samuel arrived and asked Saul what he had done. Saul pleaded the danger he was in and his desire to secure the favor of heaven; but the prophet rebuked him and told him that his kingdom should not continue, i.e., to his descendants (13:1-14).

Saul Deserted. Saul did not even accomplish the object of his unreasonable sacrifice, namely, the prevention of the dispersion of the people. When he mustered the people still with him there were only 600 men (13:15). The Philistines overran the country, and the Israelites could not offer a successful resistance, for the Philistines possessed the secret of smelting iron (*see* Iron), and "no blacksmith could be found in all the land of Israel, for the Philistines said, 'Lest the Hebrews make swords or spears' " (v. 19).

Saul's Oath. Jonathan, with a few faithful followers, made an assault upon the Philistine garrison at Michmash, which resulted in a panic in the camp, so that they killed one another. The spies of Saul at Gibeah saw the engagement, and the king called for the Ark and high priest to consult as to what he should do. The tumult in the camp of the Philistines increased, and Saul rushed to the pursuit, driving the foe down the pass of Beth-aven as far as Aijalon. But by a rash denunciation he (1) impeded his success (14:30), (2) involved the people in a violation of the law (vv. 32-33), and (3) unless prevented by the people would have put Jonathan to death for tasting innocently of food. Saul returned from the pursuit of the Philistines (14:1-46).

Other Wars. By this victory over the Philistines Saul first really secured the regal authority over the Israelites. He afterward gained victories over Moab, the Ammonites, Edom, the kings of Zobah, the Philistines again, and the Amalekites (14:47-48). Mention is now made of his family and of his commander in chief, Abner (vv. 49-50), c. 1022 B.C.

Disobedience and Rejection. Samuel, by divine commision, commanded Saul, as the king anointed by Jehovah, to destroy Amalek. He was to utterly destroy everything belonging to it, man and beast (15:3). Saul mustered the people at Telaim 200,000 foot soldiers and 10,000 men of Judah. "So Saul defeated the Amalekites, from Havilah as you go to Shur, which is east of Egypt." But he disobeyed the divine injunction by taking alive Agag, the king, and sparing all the best of the cattle and all that was valuable, destroying only that which was "despised and worthless." Instead of pursuing the campaign and finishing the destruction of the fugitives, he returned to Gilgal. Samuel, informed by God of the king's disobedience, went to Saul, who told him that he had fulfilled the divine command; but the bleating of the sheep and the lowing of the oxen revealed his crime. Saul pleaded that the people wished to offer sacrifice to the Lord in Gilgal. Samuel then reminded the king of the low estate from which God had brought him, of the superiority of *obedience* to sacrifice, and, although Saul acknowledged his sin, repeated the sentence of rejection. As Samuel turned to depart, Saul seized the prophet's robe with such despairing energy that it was torn, whereupon Samuel said that even so had Jehovah torn his kingdom from him and given it to another. Samuel then sent for Agag, hewed him in pieces, and departed in grief from Saul to see him no more (chap. 15).

Saul's Decline and Overthrow. Saul was not immediately deposed, but the consequences of his rejection were speedily brought to light.

David's Introduction to Saul. "The Spirit of the Lord departed from Saul, and an evil spirit from the Lord terrorized him." When his attendants perceived the condition of the king, they advised him to have the evil spirit charmed away by music. They recommended David, who was still residing with his father, although he had been anointed king by Samuel. David was sent for and played upon his harp. "And Saul would be refreshed and be well, and the evil spirit would depart from him" (1 Sam. 16:14-23).

Saul's Conduct Toward David. The overthrow of the Philistine giant (Goliath) by David and his conduct when brought before Saul had won for him the love of Jonathan. The wisdom of his subsequent conduct made him acceptable to the men of war and the people and secured for him the praise of the women who celebrated the overthrow of the Philistines. This aroused the jealousy and rage of Saul, who commenced a series of murderous attempts upon the life of David, whom he seems to have regarded as a rival. He twice attempted to assassinate him with his own hand (18:10-11; 19:10); he sent him on dangerous military expeditions (18:13-17); he gave him Michal, his daughter, to be his wife, hoping that the dowry demanded (a hundred foreskins of the Philistines) would endanger David's life (18:22-27). He seems to have been willing to make any sacrifice in order to effect his purpose against David—sending men even to Samuel at Ramah, where David had fled (19:18-24); attempting, as the text (20:33) would seem to indicate, to take the life of his son Jonathan; slaying Ahimelech, the priest (22:11-19), under pretense of his being a partisan of David, and the eighty-five other priests of the house of Eli, to whom nothing could be imputed, as well as the whole population of Nob. This crime of Saul put David in possession of the sacred lot, which Abiathar, the only surviving member of Eli's priestly family, brought with him and by which he was enabled to obtain divine direction in his critical affairs (22:20, 23; 23:1-2). Having compelled David to assume the position of an outlaw, Saul then took measures to apprehend and destroy him (23:9-24). Although spared by David when in the latter's power at Engedi (chap. 24), Saul took Michal and gave her to Palti as his wife (25:44). After David had again shown his respect for the Lord's anointed by sparing the king while asleep in his camp upon the hill of Hachilah, Saul acknowledged his fault and said to David, "Blessed are you, my son David; you will both accomplish much and surely prevail." And he pursued after David no more (chap. 26).

Saul with the Medium at En-dor. Another invasion of Israel by the Philistines drove King Saul to despair, so that in utter helplessness he had recourse to ungodly means of inquiring into the future. He had "removed from the land those who were mediums and spiritists" (28:3). But now Samuel was dead and, receiving no oracle from God, Saul, in desperation, commanded his servants (v. 7) to seek for a woman who was a medium. They directed him to the woman of En-dor. Assured by Saul that no evil should happen to her, she asked, "Whom shall I bring up for you?" And he said, "Bring up Samuel for me." The woman began her conjuring arts, and when she saw Samuel, she cried aloud. "Why have you deceived me? For you are Saul." The king quieted her fear and then asked her what she had seen. From her description Saul immediately recognized Samuel. Then followed a conversation in which Saul told of his deep distress because of the Philistines. Samuel replied that Jehovah had torn the kingdom out of his hand and given it to David, because he had disobeyed Him in sparing the Amalekites. He foretold his defeat by the Philistines. Samuel added that on the next day Saul and his sons should be with him among the dead. Saul fell prostrate to the earth, faint with terror and exhaustion, for he had fasted all day and night. Urged by the woman and his servants, he partook of food and returned to his camp (28:7-25).

Death and Burial. The two armies arrayed against each other soon came to an engagement in the plain of Jezreel (29:1). The Israelites, obliged to yield, fled up the mountains of Gilboa and were pursued and slain there (31:1). The hottest pursuit was made after Saul and those who rallied around him. His three sons, Jonathan, Abinadab, and Malchi-shua, were slain, and he himself was mortally wounded. He begged his armor bearer to slay him, that he might not fall into the hands of the "uncircumcised." On his refusal Saul fell upon his own sword and died. The day following, when the Philistines stripped the dead, they found Saul and his three sons and, having cut off their heads, sent them as trophies into their own land. They also fastened their bodies to the wall of Beth-shan; but the men of Jabesh-gilead came, took down the bodies, burned them, and buried them under a tree in Jabesh (chap. 31), about 1000 B.C. The news of Saul's death was speedily brought to David at Ziklag. He mourned deeply and slew the Amalekite who claimed to have killed the king (2 Sam. 1:1-15). Besides the children already mentioned Saul left another son, Ish-bosheth, who was shortly afterward proclaimed king by Abner, and two sons, Armoni and Mephibosheth, by his concubine Rizpah (21:8).

Character. There is not in sacred history a character more melancholy to contemplate than that of Saul. He was naturally humble and modest, though of strong passions. His natural rashness was controlled neither by a powerful understanding nor a scrupulous conscience, and the obligations of duty and ties of gratitude, always

felt by him too slightly, were totally disregarded when ambition, envy, and jealousy took possession of his mind. He seems never to have accepted God unconditionally and to have trusted Him implicitly but, as the names of his children would indicate, wavered between the worship of God and pagan superstition. Now he would be under the influence of prophetic inspiration, then the slave of his common pursuits; at one time pleading with the prophet to reveal to him the will of Jehovah, at another disobeying His commands; now driving out of the land all mediums, only to consult afterward the medium of En-dor. In him, also, is seen that moral contradiction that would be incredible did we not so often witness it, of an individual pursuing habitually a course that his better nature pronounces not only sinful but insane (1 Sam. 24:16-22).

Saul and Archaeology. Saul's capital at Gibeah (Tell el-Ful), three miles N of Jerusalem, has been explored and its citadel there excavated. Long ago this was identified with Saul's fortress by the brilliant pioneer Palestine explorer Edward Robinson and was excavated by W. F. Albright in 1922 and 1933 (*see Annual of the Am. Schools* 4 [1922, 1923]; *Bulletin* 52 [1933]: 6-12; *Archaeology of Palestine* [1949], pp. 120f.). Gibeah yielded at the bottom of the mound fortress no. 1, which showed traces of destruction by fire and is probably referred to in Judg. 20:40. Directly above this were the remnants of a second stronghold identified as Saul's. The structure measuring 170 by 155 feet had separately bonded corner towers and casemated walls. The principal building at Gibeah with massive stone construction and deep walls "was like a dungeon rather than a royal residence in comparison with the Canaanite masonry with which Solomon graced Jerusalem" (Madeleine S. and J. Lane Miller, *Ency. of Bible Life* [1944], p. 176). W. F. Albright says, "Saul was only a rustic chieftain as far as architecture and the amenities of life were concerned" (*From the Stone Age to Christianity*, p. 224). What was true of Saul was in a general sense culturally true of all Israel up to the dawn of the Davidic-Solomonic era. Palestinian excavations have fully demonstrated Israel's rusticity of life and poverty in the premonarchial period.

BIBLIOGRAPHY: S. Ridout, *King Saul: The Man After the Flesh* (n.d.); D. M. Gunn, *The Fate of King Saul* (1980); W. J. Deane and T. Kirk, *Studies in the First Book of Samuel* (1983), 1:79-213; 2:3-275; J. A. Sanford, *King Saul, The Tragic Hero* (1985).

SAVIOR. A term applied in Scripture, in its highest sense, to Jesus Christ, but in a subordinate manner to human deliverers.

Names. In the OT Savior is usually some derivative of the verb *yāsha'*, to "save." Beyond this ordinary sense, this term expresses *assistance* and *protection* of every kind—aggressive assistance, "to fight for you against your enemies, to save you" (Deut. 20:4); of *protection* against attack, "He sets up walls and ramparts for security" (Isa. 26:1); of *victory*, "The Lord helped David" (i.e., gave him victory, 2 Sam. 8:6); of *prosperity*, "But you will call your walls salvation" (Isa. 60:18). No better instance of this last sense can be adduced than with the exclamation "Hosannah!" meaning "do save, we beseech Thee," which was uttered as a prayer for God's blessing on any joyous occasion (Ps. 118:25).

The Greek representative of the above is *sōtēr*. The LXX has *sōtēr* where the KJV has "salvation"; and thus the word *Savior* was more familiar to the ear of the reader of the OT in our Lord's age than to us.

Person. The title *Savior* is applied to Jehovah in the OT (2 Sam 22:3; Ps. 106:21; Isa. 43:3, 11; 45:15, 21; 49:26; 60:16; 63:8; Jer. 14:8). The judges were called "saviors," as having rescued their country from oppressors (Judg. 3:9, 15, "deliverer"). Jeroboam II is also called a "deliverer" ("savior"), rescuing Israel from the Syrians (2 Kings 13:5). *See* Atonement; Redeemer; Salvation.

SAVOUR, SAVOURS, SAVOUREST. For the use of the term *savour* in the KJV of Ex. 29:18; Lev. 1:9, 13, 17; Joel 2:20; 2 Cor. 2:14-16; Eph. 5:2. (*See* Aroma.) The expression "thou savourest not" in the KJV of Matt. 16:23; Mark 8:33 has the meaning of "setting one's mind" to something; cf. NASB, NIV. When Jesus speaks of salt's losing its savour in the KJV of Matt. 5:13; Luke 14:34, He refers to its becoming tasteless (NASB), or losing its saltiness (NIV).

SAW (Heb. *mᵉgērâ,* 2 Sam. 12:31; 1 Kings 7:9; 1 Chron. 20:3; *maśśôr,* Isa. 10:15). Egyptian saws, so far as has yet been discovered, were single-handed, although Jerome is believed to allude to circular saws. As is the case in modern oriental saws, the teeth usually incline toward the handle instead of away from it, as ours. They have, in most cases, bronze blades, apparently attached to the handles by leather thongs, but some of those in the British Museum have blades inserted into them like our knives. A double-handed iron saw has been found at Nimrud. No evidence exists of the use of the saw applied to stone in Egypt, neither without the double-handed saw does it seem likely that this should be the case; but we read of sawn stones used in the Temple (1 Kings 7:9). The expression "set them under saws" (2 Sam. 12:31) has been understood to mean hard labor, but "cut them with saws" (1 Chron. 20:3) can hardly be other than torture.

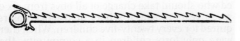

Egyptian saw.

The NIV, however, translates here, "consigning them to labor with saws."

SCAB. *See* Diseases.

SCABBARD (Heb. *ta'ar;* Jer. 47:6, KJV, NIV; also 1 Sam. 17:51; Ezek. 21:3, 5, 30, NIV). A sheath (cf. NASB readings) for a sword, dagger, or bayonet. *See* Armor, Arms.

SCAFFOLD (Heb. *kiyyôr;* 2 Chron. 6:13, KJV only). The platform (so NASB, NIV) upon which Solomon kneeled as he prayed during the dedicatory services of the Temple.

SCALE. For the medical use, *see* Diseases. The term appears also in non-medical connections.

1. Heb. *qaśqeśet:* (a) Of fishes (Lev. 11:9-10, 12; Deut. 14:9-10; Ezek. 29:4); (b) Of the laminae of a coat of mail (1 Sam. 17:5); similarly the Gk. *lepis,* a "flake," incrustation from the eyes (Acts 9:18).

2. *Strong scales* (Heb. *māgēn,* Job 41:15; "shields," NIV), of the scaly armor of the "Leviathan," i.e., crocodile.

3. Of *balances* (Heb. *peles,* Isa. 40:12), or rather a *steelyard. See* Balances.

4. *To scale* the walls of a city, Prov. 21:22 (Heb. *'ālâ*).

SCALL. *See* Diseases: Scale.

SCALP (Heb. *qodqōd*). The *crown* (which see) of the head, the Heb. variously translated in the KJV, NASB, and NIV (Lev. 13:41; Ps. 68:21; Isa. 3:17; Jer. 48:45). Heb. *qorḥâ,* "baldness" (so KJV, NIV, Isa. 3:24) is rendered "plucked-out scalp" in the NASB.

SCAPEGOAT. *See* Azazel; Festivals; Day of Atonement.

SCARLET. A brilliant crimson, the coloring substance for which was obtained from an insect (*Coccus ilicis*) called *qirmiz* in Arab., whence the English word *crimson*. The color-producing insect is found on the holm oak. The female alone produces the coloring matter, feeding on the leaves of the tree and yielding eggs containing a red substance. The Greeks called the insect *kokkos,* meaning "berry," because being pealike it resembles a berry. The Hebrews called the color *shānî,* "brilliance," "crimson"; *shᵉnîtôla'at,* "brightness of (produced by) the worm"; *tôla'atshānî,* "worm of brightness," "crimson-producing worm"; or simply *tôlā',* "worm." In Gk. *kokkinos* was an adjective meaning "pertaining to the coccus worm." The oriental worm is akin to the cochineal insect of Mexico (*Coccus cacti*), but has been supplanted commercially by its New World rival, which yields a much more valuable dye. Scarlet was used in the vestments of the high priest and the hangings of the Tabernacle, in the purification of the leper (Lev. 14:4) and in the water of separation (Num. 19:6; Heb.

9:19).   M.F.U.

SCENT (Heb. *rêaḥ* "odor"). *See* Aroma.

The KJV expression in Jer. 48:11, "his scent is not changed," referring to Moab, has the meaning of retaining one's character ("flavor," NASB; "taste," NIV); "the scent thereof" in the KJV of Hos. 14:7 refers to renown (NASB), or fame (NIV).

SCEPTER (Heb. *shebeṭ*, "rod"; Gk. *hrados,* Heb. 1:8). A staff borne by a ruler as the badge of his authority. Scepters are depicted on many bas-reliefs of Assyrian and Persian kings. Sometimes scepters were short like a mace, sometimes long and garnished with royal insignia. We know that in some cases the scepter was a strong rod (Ezek. 19:11, 14), about the height of a man, which ancient kings and chiefs bore as an insignia of honor. It is believed to originate in the shepherd's staff, since the first kings were mostly nomad princes (Micah 7:14; cf. Lev. 27:32). Diodorus Siculus (*Bibliotheca historica* 3.3) informs us that the scepter of the Egyptian kings bore the shape of a plow; of Osiris a flail and crook; whereas that of the queens, besides the crown, was two loose feathers on the head.

Figurative. The allusions to the scepter are all metaphorical and describe it simply as one of the insignia of supreme power (Gen. 49:10; Num. 24:17; Ps. 45:6; Isa. 14:5; Amos 1:5; Zech. 10:11). The use of the staff as a symbol of authority was not confined to kings; it might be used by any leader (cf. Judg. 5:14, "staff of office").

A Jewish school

SCE'VA (sē'va). A Jew of Ephesus, described as a "chief priest" (Acts 19:14-16), either as having exercised the office at Jerusalem or as being chief of one of the twenty-four divisions. His seven sons attempted to exorcise spirits by using the name of Jesus, and on one occasion severe injury was inflicted by the demoniac on two of them (as implied in the term *amphoterōn,* "both," the true reading in v. 16).

BIBLIOGRAPHY: B. A. Martin, *Journal of Theological Studies* 27 (1976): 405-12.

SCHISM. *See* Heresy, no. 2.

SCHOOL (Gk. *scholē,* Acts 19:9). A place where there is *leisure,* a place of instruction. *See* Tyrannus.

SCHOOLMASTER. *See* Tutor.

SCHOOLS, HEBREW.

Elementary. We have no account of education specifically before the time of Moses. This much is certain, that the mother looked to the training of the children in their earliest years (Prov. 31:1; 2 Tim. 3:15), whereas the boys were trained by their fathers, or in well-to-do families by tutors. This instruction was chiefly in reading and writing, but especially in the law. That reading and writing must have formed part of education from the very settlement of Palestine is evident from the fact that the Israelites were commanded to write the precepts of the law upon the doorposts and gates of their houses (Deut. 6:9; 11:20); and upon their passage over Jordan, to write the law upon great stones (27:2-8), so as to be easily read by every Israelite. These admonitions unquestionably presuppose that the people could read plain *writing* (which see). Arithmetic must have been taught, as the days of the week, the months, the festivals, etc., were not designated by proper names but by numerals. In fact, every art or science that occurs or is alluded to in the OT (and upon the understanding of which depended the understanding of the Scriptures) must have to some extent formed a part of the strictly religious Jewish education. There is, however, no trace of schools for the instruction of youth or of the people in preexilic times. Only in a single instance (2 Chron. 17:7-9) have we any information as to how far and in what way the priests fulfilled their calling to teach the people all the ordinances that God gave through Moses (Lev. 10:11). Although there were no national or elementary schools before the Exile, there were cases in which professional teachers were resorted to—when the position or official duties of the parent rendered his teaching impossible, when the parents were incapacitated; when the child's attainments surpassed the parent's abilities; or when the son was preparing himself for a vocation different from that of his father.

Schools After the Captivity. We possess minute information of the schools after the captivity and at the time of Christ. "The regular instruction of the child commenced with the fifth or sixth year (according to strength), when every child was sent to school. . . . Tradition ascribes to Joshua the son of Gamala the introduction of schools in every town, and the compulsory education in them of all children above the age of six. . . . It was even deemed unlawful to live in a place where there was no school. Such a city deserved to be either destroyed or excommunicated" (Edersheim, *The Life and Times of Jesus the Messiah,* 2:230-31). Joshua arranged that in every province and in every town schoolmasters be appointed who should take charge of all boys from six or seven years of age. A school or teacher was required for every twenty-five children. When there were only forty children in a community, they were allowed to have one master and an assistant.

The father himself, as a rule, saw to it that the child should be in the class at the proper time.

Course of Study. "The grand object of the teacher was moral as well as intellectual training. To keep children from all intercourse with the vicious; to suppress all feelings of bitterness, even though wrong had been done to one's parents; to punish all real wrongdoing; not to prefer one child to another; rather to show sin in its repulsiveness than to predict what punishment would follow, either in this or the next world, so as not to 'discourage' the child—such are some of the rules laid down" (Edersheim, *Sketches of Jewish Life,* pp. 135-36). The teacher was to strictly fulfill all promises made to the child, to avoid bringing up disagreeable or indelicate thoughts, be patient, punish without excessive severity—with a strap but never with a rod. At ten the child began to study the Mishna; at fifteen he had to be ready for the Talmud. In the study of the Scriptures the pupil was to proceed from Leviticus to the rest of the Pentateuch, thence to the Prophets, and lastly to the Hagiographa. Instruction was imparted in questions and answers, or in a catechetical form. After the master had lectured, the pupils asked questions (Luke 2:46), which were frequently answered by parables or counter questions (Matt. 16:13; etc.; 22:17-22; Luke 10:25-26; etc.). Sometimes the teacher introduced the subject by asking a question; the replies of the pupils constituted the discussion, which was concluded by the master pointing out the most appropriate answer. This mode of instruction is strikingly illustrated by the questions put by our Savior to His disciples (Mark 8:27-30).

Theological Schools. The schools of the prophets, called into life by Samuel (1 Sam. 10:5, 10; 19:20) and more firmly organized under Elijah and Elisha in the kingdom of the ten tribes (2 Kings 2:3, 5; 4:38; 6:1), were not theological schools. Not till after the Exile, when prophecy began to fail, did the study of the law become a matter of scholastic learning; and the priest Ezra is first mentioned as one who set his heart to search and do the law of Jehovah and *to teach His statutes and ordinances* in Israel (Ezra 7:10). He is described as "skilled in the law of Moses" (7:6; cf. vv. 12, 21); he must have made the study of the law his chief business. From Ezra onward notable scribes or lawyers are mentioned, who not only applied themselves to the faithful observing and handing down of the letter of the law and of the Scriptures but made the contents of Scripture their special study. They especially applied the law of Moses to the practical duties of life and also gave decisions in doubtful cases (Matt. 2:4; Luke 2:46). Thus a complete system of casuistry, founded on the law, was gradually formed for all the relations of life. This was orally transmitted by the *scribes* (which see) and their associates; and as the "tradition of the elders" (Mark 7:5) was ranked on an equality with, and

eventually above, the written law of Moses. On the institution of these schools we lack more exact information for the period from the Exile to the dissolution of the Jewish state. Students seeking a deeper knowledge of the law turned to eminent scribes for instruction. This was given by the teachers, partly at their homes, partly in the synagogues, partly in the porticoes of the Temple, in the form of conversations or disputations. Instruction was gratuitous, the scribes earning their livelihood by following a trade, unless having means of their own or acquired by marriage. The teachers sat while instructing; the scholars at first stood, but afterward sat at the feet of their teachers (Acts 22:3).

Schools of the Prophets. From 1 Sam. 19:20 we learn that there was a "company" of prophets at Ramah under the superintendency of Samuel, whose members lived in a common building. The origin and history of these schools are involved in obscurity but would seem to have been called into existence by Samuel. We have no direct evidence that there were other such unions besides the one at Ramah, but it is probable that there was one at Gibeah (10:5, 10). The next mention of them is in the times of Elijah and Elisha, called "sons of the prophets" (1 Kings 20:35), living in considerable numbers at Gilgal, Bethel, and Jericho (*see* 2 Kings 4:38; 2:3, 5, 7, 15; 9:1). About one hundred sons of the prophets sat down before Elisha at meals in Gilgal (4:38, 42-43). The number at Jericho may have been as great, for fifty of the sons of the prophets went with Elijah and Elisha to the Jordan (cf. 2:7 with vv. 16-17). From these passages we feel warranted in the belief that the sons of the prophets lived in a common house (*see* also 6:1). Those who were married most likely lived in their own houses (4:1). We must not conclude, from their living together and performing certain duties in common, that these prophets were an OT order of monks. The prophets did not wish to withdraw from active life for the purpose of carrying on a contemplative life of holiness, but their unions were formed for the purpose of mental and spiritual training that they might exert a more powerful influence upon their contemporaries. The name "schools of the prophets" expresses most fully the character of these unions; only we must not think of them as merely educational institutions in which the pupils of the prophets received instruction in prophesying or in theological studies.

"Prophesying could neither be taught nor communicated by instruction, but was a gift of God which he communicated to whomsoever he would. But the communication of this divine gift was by no means an arbitrary thing, but presupposed such a mental and spiritual disposition on the part of the recipient as fitted him to receive it; while the exercise of the gift required a thorough acquaintance with the law and the earlier revelations of God, which the schools of the prophets were well adapted to promote. It is therefore justly and generally assumed that the study of the law and of the history of the divine guidance of Israel formed a leading feature in the occupations of the pupils of the prophets, which also included the cultivation of sacred poetry and music and united exercises for the promotion of the prophetic inspiration" (K. & D., *Com.*, on 1 Sam. 19:18-24). Thus we find that from the time of Samuel the writing of sacred history formed an essential part of the prophet's labor.

The cultivation of sacred music and poetry may be inferred partly from the fact that, according to 1 Sam. 10:5, musicians walked in front of the prophesying prophets, playing as they went along, and partly from the fact that sacred music not only received a fresh impulse from David, who stood in close relation to the association of prophets at Ramah, but was also raised by him into an integral part of public worship. Music was by no means cultivated merely that the sons of the prophets might employ it in connection with their discourses but also as a means of awakening holy susceptibilities and emotions in the soul, of lifting up the spirit to God and so preparing it for the reception of divine revelations (*see* 2 Kings 3:15). Occasion of forming such schools is to be found in the decline of the priesthood under Eli and his sons and the utter absence of the sanctuary in the times of Elijah and Elisha, thus furnishing the faithful with places and means of edification; and in the advantages that would naturally arise from association, in bringing the young men under the influence of their elders, who were under the powerful influence of the Holy Spirit, thus uniting them with their spiritual fathers in fighting for the honor of Jehovah.

BIBLIOGRAPHY: F. H. Swift, *Education in Ancient Israel to A.D. 70* (1919); N. Drazin, *History of Jewish Education from 515 B.C. to 220 C.E.* (1940); W. Barclay, *Educational Ideals in the Ancient World* (1959); W. F. Albright, *Samuel and the Beginnings of the Prophetic Movement* (1961); G. H. Blackburn, *Aims of Education in Ancient Israel* (1966).

SCIENCE (Heb. *maddā'*, Dan. 1:4; Gk. *gnōsis*, 1 Tim. 6:20; both KJV). The two instances are better rendered "knowledge." The NIV of Dan. 1:4 reads "quick to understand."

SCOFFER, SCOFFING. Several terms in the original are so translated. Heb. *lûs*, "to make mouths, deride," refers to a frivolous and impudent person who scoffs at the most sacred precepts and duties of religion, piety, and morals (Ps. 1:1; Prov. 9:7-8; 13:1; 14:6; 15:12; 19:25; 22:10; 24:9; "mocker," or "mocking," in most of these passages, NIV.) In Pss. 44:13; 79:4, Heb. *lā'az*, to "stammer, imitate" in derision, is used to describe Israel as being "a scoffing ["scorn," NIV] and a derision to those around us," whereas in 123:4 "the scoffing ["ridicule," NIV] of those who are at ease" is contrasted with those who

look to God as their master. *See* Mock; Mockers.

SCORCHED LAND (Heb. *shārāb*, "a mirage"). The mirage, especially the appearance of water that is produced as if by magic in the dry, sandy desert (literally perhaps the "desert shine," just as we speak of the "alpine glow"). The sense in which it is used here is figurative. "The [*shārāb*] scorched land will become a pool" (Isa. 35:7; "burning sand," NIV); i.e., the illusive appearance of a lake or pool will become a real pool of refreshing waters.

SCORN (Heb. *sᵉhōq*). Spoken of the wild donkey, having contempt for civilization (Job 39:7). In 39:18 the same word is used of the ostrich who "laughs at the horse and his rider." In Isa. 29:20 the "scorner" ("mocker," NIV) is one who "will be finished" (Heb. *lûs*, "to make mouths, deride," elsewhere "scoffer"). *See* Scoffer; Laugh; Derision; Disdain; Mock.

SCORPION. An instrument of scourging, a whip with barbed points like the point of a scorpion's sting. *See* Animal Kingdom.

Figurative. This instrument was used figuratively by Rehoboam, king of Judea, to represent the harsher measures with which he would deal with the people than had his father (1 Kings 12:11). *See* Scourge.

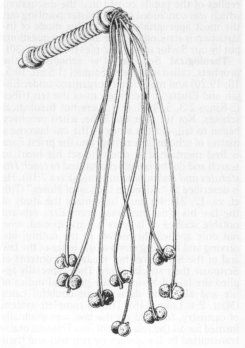

Scourge

SCOURGE. Heb. generally *shûṭ,* to "whip"; noun *shôṭ,* a "whip" (Job 9:23; Isa. 10:26; 28:15, 18); Gk. *mastigoō,* "flog" (Matt. 10:17; 20:19; 23:34; Luke 18:33; John 19:1; Acts 22:24); *phraggelloō,* to *lash,* as a public punishment (Matt. 27:26; Mark 15:15), and its derivative, a *whip* (John 2:15). A common punishment in the East. The instrument of punishment in ancient Egypt, as it is also in modern times generally in the East, was usually the stick, applied to the soles of the feet— bastinado. Under the Roman method the culprit was stripped, stretched with cords or thongs on a frame, and beaten with rods. In case a man was sentenced to stripes the judge was to confine the number to forty, i.e., to forty at most, lest "your brother be degraded in your eyes" (Deut. 25:1-3). There were two ways of scourging—one with thongs or whips made of rope ends or straps of leather, the other with rods or twigs. Scourging is frequently mentioned in the NT (Matt. 10:17; 23:34; Acts 5:40, "flogged"), with thirty-nine stripes as the maximum (2 Cor. 11:24). The *scorpion* (which see) was probably a severer instrument.

Figurative. "The scourge of the tongue" (Job 5:21; "lash of the tongue," NIV) is symbolical of wordy strife (*see* Ps. 31:20). In Heb. 12:6 "scourges" is used of the chastisement sent upon men by God.

SCREECH OWL. *See* Animal Kingdom: Owl.

SCRIBE (Heb. *sōpēr;* Gk. *grammateus*). The *grammateus* of a Greek state was not the mere writer but the keeper and registrar of public documents (Thucydides 4.118; 7.10; so in Acts 19:35, "town clerk"). The name of Kiriath-sepher (Josh. 15:15; Judg. 1:12) may possibly connect itself with some early use of the title. In the song of Deborah (Judg. 5:14) the word in the original Heb. appears to point to military functions of some kind. Thus the NASB replaces KJV "pen of the writer" with "staff of office," marg., "the staff of the scribe," and the NIV reads "commander's staff." The Heb. expression probably refers to the rod or scepter of the commander numbering or marshaling his troops. Three men are mentioned as successively filling the office of "secretary" or scribe under David and Solomon (2 Sam. 8:17; 20:25; 1 Kings 4:3). We may think of them as the king's secretaries, writing his letters, drawing up his decrees, managing his finances (2 Kings 12:10). At a later period the word again connects itself with the act of numbering the military forces of the country (Jer. 52:25, and probably Isa. 33:18). Other associations, however, began to gather around it at about the same period. The zeal of Hezekiah led him to foster the growth of a body of men whose work it was to transcribe old records or to put in writing what had been handed down orally (Prov. 25:1). To this period, accordingly, belongs the new significance of the title. It no longer designates only an officer of the

king's court, but a class, students and interpreters of the law, boasting of their wisdom (Jer. 8:8). *See* Scribes; Writing.

Jewish scribe

SCRIBES, JEWISH. Heb. and Gk. as above; also Gk. *nomikos,* "lawyer," i.e., expert in the Mosaic law (Matt. 22:35; Luke 7:30; 10:25; 11:45, 52; 14:3); *nomodidaskalos,* "teacher of the law" (5:17; Acts 5:34).

Institution. The period of the Sopherim, *scribes,* began with the return of the Jews from captivity. The law read by Ezra (Neh. 8-10) was the Pentateuch in essentially the same form as we have it now; and from that time it was acknowledged by Israel as the binding rule of life, i.e.:

Canonical. Obedience to it was the condition of membership among the chosen people and a share in the promises given to them. The entire Pentateuch came to be regarded as dictated by God, even to the last eight verses, containing the account of Moses' death. From insisting upon divine dictation the next step was to declare that the law had been handed to Moses by God, the only question being whether it was all delivered at once or in volumes. As an addition to the law the writing of the prophets and preexilic history of Israel attained to similar authority. At a still later period there was added to this body of the "prophets" *a third collection* of writings, which gradually entered into the same category of canonical Scriptures. In proportion as the law became comprehensive and complicated there arose the necessity of its scientific study and of a professional acquaintance with it. Its many details and the application of its several enactments to everyday life necessarily involved patient study. In the time of Ezra and long after this was chiefly the concern of *priests,* Ezra himself being both *priest and scribe.* This was naturally the case, as the Pentateuch related largely to priestly functions and privileges. The higher the law rose in the estimation of the people, the more did its study and exposition become an independent business; and an independent class of "biblical scholars or scribes," i.e., of men who made acquaintance with the law a profession, was formed, besides the priests. When under Greek influence the priests, at least those of the higher strata, often applied themselves to pagan culture and more or less neglected the law, the scribes appeared as the zealous guardians of the law. From this time on they were the *teachers* of the people, over whose life they bore complete sway. In NT times the scribes formed a finely compacted class, holding undisputed supremacy over the people. Everywhere they appear as the mouthpiece and representative of the people; the scribe pushes to the front, the crowd respectfully giving way and eagerly hanging on his utterances as those of a recognized authority. The great respect paid them is expressed by the title of honor bestowed upon them, "my master" (Heb. *rabbî;* Gk. *hrabbi,* Matt. 23:7; etc.). From this respectful *address* the *title* rabbi was gradually formed; but its use cannot be proved before the time of Christ.

Respect. The rabbis required from their pupils absolute reverence, surpassing even the honor felt for parents. Thus it was taught that "respect to a teacher should exceed respect for a father, for both father and son owe respect to a teacher" (*Kerithoth* 6.9, fin.). The practical application of this principle was: "If a man's father and teacher have lost anything, the teacher's loss should have the precedence—i.e., he must first be assisted in recovering it—the burden of a teacher is to be born in preference to that of a father, a teacher must be ransomed from captivity before one's own father." The rabbis in general everywhere claimed the first rank (Matt. 23:6-7; Mark 12:38-39; Luke 11:43; 20:46).

Employment. This referred, if not exclusively, yet first and chiefly, to the law and the administration of justice.

As jurists. As such the task of the scribe was threefold: *The theoretic development of the law.* The scribes developed with careful casuistry the general precepts of the law; and where the written law made no direct provision they created a compensation, either by establishing a precedent or by inference from other valid legal decisions. In this way, during the last centuries before Christ, Jewish law became gradually an extensive and complicated science. This law was unwritten and propagated by oral tradition; intense study was necessary to obtain even a general acquaintance with it. In addition to having an acquaintance with the law, the scribes assumed that it was their special province to develop what was already binding into more and more subtle casuistic details. In order to settle a system of law binding upon all, it was necessary to come as near as possible to a general consensus of opinion. Hence the whole process of systematizing the law

was carried on by oral discussion; the acknowledged authorities instructed their pupils in the law and debated legal questions with each other. This made it necessary that the heads at least of the body should dwell in certain central localities, although many would be scattered about the country to give instruction and render legal decisions. The central point till A.D. 70 was Jerusalem; after that at other places, such as Jamnia and Tiberias. Gradually the theories of the scribes became *valid law;* hence, the maxims developed by the scribes were recognized in practice as soon as the schools were agreed about them. The scribes were, in fact, though not by formal appointment, *legislators,* especially after the destruction of the Temple; for since there was then no longer a *civil* court of justice like the Sanhedrin, the judgment of the rabbinical scribes *determined what was valid law.* In case of doubt the matter was brought "before the learned," who pronounced an authoritative decision.

Teaching the Law. This was the second chief task of the scribes. The ideal of legal Judaism was that every Israelite should have a professional acquaintance with the law; if this was impracticable, then the greatest possible number. As a consequence the famous rabbis gathered about them large numbers of pupils. Because the oral law was never committed to writing, constant repetition was necessary in order to fix it in the minds of the students. Thus, in rabbinic diction, "to repeat" means exactly the same as "to teach." Questions were propounded to pupils for their decision, and pupils asked questions of the teachers. As all knowledge of the law was strictly traditional, a pupil had only two duties—to keep everything faithfully in memory and to teach only what had been delivered to him. For such instruction there were special localities, called "houses of teaching," often mentioned in connection with synagogues as places that in legal respects enjoyed certain privileges. In Jerusalem the catechetical lectures were held "in the temple" (Matt. 21:23; 26:55; Mark 14:49; Luke 2:46; 20:1; John 18:20), i.e., in the colonnades or some other space of the outer court.

Judicial. A third duty of the scribes was *passing sentence* in the court of justice; for so far as men were learned in the law they would be called to the office of judge. With respect to the great Sanhedrin it is expressly stated in the NT that *scribes* were among its members. After the fall of the Jewish state, A.D. 70, the scribes, being recognized as independent *legislators,* were also regarded as independent *judges.* Their sentences were voluntarily acquiesced in, whether they gave judgment collectively or as individuals. Being learned in the law and the elaboration of the historical and didactic portions of Scripture, the scribes were specially qualified for *delivering lectures* and *exhortations* in the synagogues. They also had the *care of the text of Scripture* as such.

Literature. In the developing and establishment of the law there was evolved a *law of custom,* besides the written Torah (law), called the Halachah (Heb. *hălākâ,* "that which is current and customary"). The manipulation of the historical and didactic portions of the Holy Scriptures produced an abundant variety of historical and didactic notions, usually comprised under the name of the Haggadah (Heb. *hăggādâ,* "narrative, legend").

The Halachah. The Halachah contained "either simply the laws laid down in Scripture, or else derived from or traced to it by some ingenious and artificial method of exegesis; or added to it, by way of amplification and for safety's sake; or, finally, legalized customs. They provided for every possible and impossible case, entered into every detail of private, family, and public life; and with iron logic, unbending rigor, and most minute analysis pursued and dominated man, turn whither he might, laying on him a yoke which was truly unbearable. The return which it offered was the pleasure and distinction of knowledge, the acquisition of righteousness and the final attainment of rewards" (Edersheim, *Life and Times of Jesus,* 1:98).

The Haggadah. The Haggadah was "an amplification and remodeling of what was originally given, according to the views and necessities of later times. It is true that here also the given text forms the point of departure, and that a similar treatment to that employed in passages from the law takes place in the first instance. The history is worked up by combining the different statements in the text with each other, completing one by another, settling the chronology, etc. Or the religious and ethical parts are manipulated by formulating dogmatic propositions from isolated prophetic utterances, by bringing these into relation to each other, and thus obtaining a kind of dogmatic system. A canonical book of the Old Testament (Book of Chronicles) furnishes a very instructive example of the *historical* Midrash (i.e., exposition, exegesis). A comparison of its narrative with the parallel portions of the older historical books (Kings and Samuel) will strike even the cursory observer with the fact that the chronicler has enlarged the history of the Jewish kings by a whole class of narratives, of which the older documents have as good as nothing" (Schürer, *History of the Jewish People,* div. 2, 1:339ff.).

History. This is properly divided into five periods, indicated by the appellations given to the scribes in successive times:

The *Sopherim* (*see* above), or "scribes," properly so called, lasting from the return from Babylon and ending with the death of Simon the Just, c. 458-300 B.C., about 160 years.

The *Tanaim* ("repeaters," i.e., "teachers" of the law), in NT times, "teachers of the law" (Luke 5:17; Acts 5:34).

The *Amoraim,* or later doctors of the law (Heb., to "expound"), "wise men" and "doctors of the law," who alone constituted the authorized recorders and expositors of the Halachah (A.D. 220 — completion of the Babylonian Talmud, about A.D. 500).

The *Saboraim,* or teachers of the law after the conclusion of the Talmud (Heb. to "think, discern"), who determined the law from a careful examination of all the pros and cons urged by the Amoraim in their controversies on divine, legal, and ritual questions contained in the Talmud, A.D. 500-657.

The *Gaonim,* the last doctors of the law in the rabbinic succession. The period of the Gaonim extends from A.D. 657 to 1034 in Sora, and to 1038 in Pumbaditha (Schürer, *History of the Jewish People;* Edersheim, *Life and Times of Jesus;* McClintock and Strong, *Cyclopedia,* s.v.).

BIBLIOGRAPHY: W. R. Smith, *The Old Testament in the Jewish Church* (1892), pp. 42-72; G. F. Moore, *Judaism in the First Centuries of the Christian Era* (1927), 1:37-47; A. S. Diamond, *The Earliest Hebrew Scribes* (1960); J. W. Bowker, *Jesus and the Pharisees* (1973); A. Finkel, *The Pharisees and the Teacher of Nazareth* (1974); J. Jeremias, *Theological Dictionary of the New Testament, γραμματευς* (1964), 1:740-42; N. Turner, *Christian Words* (1980), pp. 402-4.

SCRIP. (Heb. *yalqûṭ;* Gk. *pēra*). The KJV term *scrip* does not appear in the NASB or the NIV, being replaced in those versions by shepherd's bag (1 Sam. 17:40) or bag (Matt. 10:10; Mark 6:8; Luke 9:3; 10:4; 22:35-36; marg., NASB, is usually *"knapsack"* or *"beggar's bag"*). The scrip of the KJV OT was the bag or wallet in which shepherds carried food or other necessities. The scrip of the KJV NT was the leather bag Galilean peasants used to carry their food when they were on a journey. *See* Bag; Purse.

SCRIPTURE (Heb. *kātûb,* "written"; Gk. *graphē,* "document"). It is not till the return from the captivity that the word meets us with any distinctive force. In the earlier books we read of the law, the book of the law. In Ex. 32:16 the commandments written on the tablets of testimony are said to be "God's writing," but there is no special sense in the word taken by itself. The thought of Scripture as a whole first appears in 2 Chron. 30:5, 18. In the singular it is applied chiefly to this or that passage quoted from the OT (Mark 12:10; John 7:38; 13:18; 19:37; Luke 4:21; Rom. 9:17; Gal. 3:8; etc.). In two difficult passages some have seen the wider, some the narrower sense. (1) *Pasa graphē theopneustos* (2 Tim. 3:16) has been translated in the NASB and NIV, "All Scripture is inspired by God." Others render it, "Every Scripture being inspired, is also profitable. . . ." The RV renders it, "Every Scripture inspired of God is also profitable for teaching," etc. (2) The meaning of the genitive in *pasa prophēteia graphēs* (2 Pet. 1:20) seems at first sight distinctly collective: "No prophecy of [i.e., contained in] Scripture." A closer examination of the passage will perhaps lead to a different conclusion. (3) In the plural, as might be expected, the collective meaning is prominent. In 2 Pet. 3:16 we find an extension of the term to the epistles of Paul; but it remains uncertain whether "the rest of the Scriptures" are the Scriptures of the OT exclusively or include other writings then extant, dealing with the same topics. (4) In one passage, *ta hiera grammata* (2 Tim. 3:15) answers to "the sacred writings," i.e., Scriptures, of the NASB. *See* Bible; Canon.

BIBLIOGRAPHY: R. L. Harris, *The Inspiration and Canonicity of the Bible* (1957); J. K. S. Reid, *The Authority of Scripture* (1957); B. B. Warfield, *The Inspiration and Authority of the Bible* (1958); J. I. Packer, *God Speaks to Man* (1966); M. C. Tenney, ed., *The Bible—Living Word of Revelation* (1968).

SCRIPTURE MANUSCRIPTS, NEW TESTAMENT.

The text of the NT is attested by manuscript testimony more voluminous in quantity and more reliable than that of any of the writings of the same period. Indeed there are no ancient writings whose evidence of a correct text is stronger than the NT. "At present there are 88 catalogued papyri manuscripts, an additional 274 uncial manuscripts in codex format, and 245 lectionaries in uncial script. In addition 2,795 manuscripts and 1,964 lectionaries have been catalogued" (N. L. Geisler and W. E. Nix, *A General Introduction to the Bible* [1986], p. 387, from B. M. Metzger, *Manuscripts of the Greek Bible* [1981], pp. 54-56). This testimony to the NT text is not only remarkable for its bulk but also for its substantial agreement. Although numerous textual variations occur, they are of a relatively minor nature and do not affect any doctrine. Substantial variations affect only about a thousandth part of the entire text, according to the estimation of careful students (cf. Gregory, *Canon and Text of the N.T.* p. 528). Also amazing is the close relationship in point of time between the oldest NT manuscripts and the original texts. Not more than a century and a half intervenes between the oldest copies of the Pauline letters preserved in the Chester Beatty papyri and their original composition, and scarcely three centuries come between the Codex Vaticanus and the Codex Sinaiticus and the period of the composition of the NT. When it is remembered that knowledge of classical authors depends on manuscripts between the ninth and eleventh centuries A.D., or a thousand years removed from their originals, as used to be the case also with the OT, until the discovery of the Dead Sea manuscripts (1947-55), it can be comprehended why the certainty with which the NT text is established surpasses any other book of antiquity.

The Greek manuscripts are the most important materials for textual criticism because the NT books were originally written in Gk. Although the theory that various books of the NT were penned in Aram. and that the respective books of the Gk. NT are merely translations from these originals is held by some scholars, notably C. C. Torrey (all the gospels and the first half of Acts), the discovery of large numbers of papyri has done much to undermine this theory. Supposed mistranslations in the gospels appear in regular idiom in the Gk. papyri of the general period. Manuscripts written in Gk., therefore, incontestably constitute the most important materials for textual criticism. These are made up of papyri, uncial manuscripts, and minuscules or cursive manuscripts.

Papyri. These manuscripts were written on *papyrus* (which see). Since a number of the papyri contain portions of the NT from a century to a century and a half earlier than the oldest uncial manuscripts now available, the importance of the papyri for the study of the NT is inestimable. When Sir Frederic Kenyon first published *Our Bible and the Ancient Manuscripts* in 1895, there existed but one or two papyri that contained a portion of Scripture, but by 1931 the number had increased to fifty-three important ones, and now stands at at least ninety-eight.

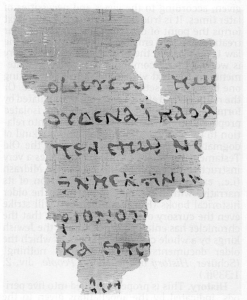

Illustration of the John Rylands fragment, a very early papyrus fragment of a few lines from John's Gospel

By far the most important manuscripts of this class are the Chester Beatty Papyri. These manuscripts, named for the man who purchased the collection, Chester Beatty of London, first became known in 1931. They consist of portions of codices of various books of the OT and the NT; altogether seven manuscripts of the OT and three of the NT, besides some extracanonical books. The material was dated by U. Wilcken to be c. A.D. 200 (*Archiv für Papyrusforschung* 11 [1935]: 112), and thus we have a text 125 to 150 years earlier than that of the Codex Vaticanus. P[45] Chester Beatty Papyrus originally contained all the gospels and Acts, but is extant only in about one-seventh of its original content. P[46] Chester Beatty Papyrus contains most of the Pauline epistles in an aggregate of 86 leaves out of a total of 104; Philemon and the pastoral epistles are not included. P[47] Chester Beatty Papyrus contains a considerable portion of the book of Revelation (9:10–17:2).

Uncial Manuscripts. Uncial manuscripts are written in separated half-capital characters and are early. They are distinguished from the cursives in which the letters are bound together by ligatures. Uncial script looks like letters printed with pen or pencil in contrast to letters written in regular script. At present 274 are known. The most important of these textually are the Codex Vaticanus (B), Codex Sinaiticus (ℵ [Aleph]), Codex Alexandrinus (A), Codex Ephraemi Rescriptus (C), Codex Bezae (D), and Codex Washingtonianus I (W).

Codex Vaticanus (B). Codex Vaticanus has been in the Vatican Library at Rome since 1481. It dates around A.D. 340. The complete codex contains 759 leaves, 142 belonging to the NT.

Codex Sinaiticus (ℵ [Aleph]). Codex Sinaiticus (ℵ [Aleph]), was discovered in St. Catherine's

Illustration of a page from the Codex Sinaiticus

Monastery by Constantin Tischendorf in 1844 and 1859 and apparently dates about A.D. 350. It contains all the NT and a large part of the OT.

Codex Alexandrinus (A). Codex Alexandrinus (A) is in the National Library of the British Museum. It is called Alexandrinus because it was believed to have come from Alexandria, Egypt, and "A" because it was the first important uncial to be used by biblical textual critics. It contains 733 leaves of the original 822, and dates c. A.D. 400 or a little later.

Codex Ephraemi Rescriptus (C). Codex Ephraemi Rescriptus (C) is in the Bibliothèque Nationale in Paris. It is a palimpsest and belongs to the fourth century (c. 345).

Codex Bezae (D [Codex Cantabrigiensis]). Codex Bezae (D) is bilingual—being written in Gk. and Lat. Robert Stephanus (Estienne) used some of the readings in the margin of his Gk. Testament in 1550, and Théodore de Bèze (Beza) employed it in the later editions of his Gk. Testament.

Codex Washingtonianus I (W). Codex Washingtonianus I (W) has 187 leaves containing "the four gospels, portions of all the Pauline epistles except Romans, Hebrews, Deuteronomy, Joshua, and Psalms"; it dates "from the fourth or early fifth century" (Geisler and Nix, p. 400). It was purchased in Egypt in 1906 by C. L. Freer of Detroit and is in the Freer Collection at the Smithsonian Institution.

Codex Claromontanus (D^2 or D^{p2})^{24}. Codex Claromontanus (D^2 or D^{p2})[24] dates from the sixth century and constitutes a leading Western authority for the text of the epistles of Paul. Discovered at Clermont, France, it was taken to Paris in 1656. It is bilingual, containing both Gk. and Lat. texts. At one time it belonged to Beza. *Codex Basilensis (E)* contains the four gospels with some lacunae. It dates from the eighth century and is in Basel, Switzerland.

Codex Laudianus (E^2 or E^a). Codex Laudianus (E^2 or E^a) is in the Bodleian Library at Oxford and is a late sixth or early seventh-century copy of the book of Acts in Gk. and Lat. The *Codex Regius* (L) contains the gospels and is placed in the eighth century. It is now in the Bibliothèque Nationale in Paris.

Codex Borgianus (T). Codex Borgianus (T) contains an Alexandrian text of 179 verses of Luke and John, and dates probably from the fifth century. It is now in Rome.

Codex Koridethianus (Θ [Theta]). Codex Koridethianus (Θ [Theta]) belonged to a monastery at Koridethi and is now in the Library of Tiflis. It contains only the gospels and dates from the ninth century. The manuscript was published in 1913, and its discovery is ranked in importance to that of Codex Sinaiticus.

Minuscule Manuscripts. These are written in the cursive, or flowing, style of script to which the formal and cumbersome uncial style gave way from the eighth century on. The word *minuscule* is taken from the Lat. *minusculus,* "somewhat small," and refers to the small cursive letters connected in script, as differentiated from the capital, or uncial, which were written separately. Thousands of cursives exist. At present 2,795 are known (Metzger, in Geisler and Nix). The importance of the minuscule manuscripts is normally less than the uncials, since they are for the most part later. But there are exceptions, and textual critics often rank certain minuscules higher than certain uncials. The minuscules sometimes run in groups or families and can be traced back to the same uncial. Of the individual minuscules, manuscript 33, from the ninth or possibly tenth century, containing the gospels, Acts, and the epistles, is one of the best. Other important cursives are minuscules 81, 157, and 565.

Lectionaries. These are reading lessons employed in public worship services. Those selected from the gospels are known as *Evangeliaria* or *Evangelistaria.* Those selected from the Acts of the Apostles or the epistles are called *Apostoli* or *Praxapostoli* and are found from the sixth century onward. More than 2,209 Greek lectionaries have been identified and cataloged, and they are more and more being valued for textual criticism (Geisler and Nix, p. 387).   M.F.U.

One of the Dead Sea Scrolls

BIBLIOGRAPHY: B. M. Metzger, *Chapters in the History of New Testament Textual Criticism* (1963); J. H. Greenlee, *Introduction to New Testament Textual Criticism* (1964); F. G. Kenyon, *The Text of the Greek Bible* (1975); B. M. Metzger, *The Early Versions of the New Testament* (1977); H. A. Sturz, *The Byzantine Texttype and New Testament Textual Criticism* (1984); N. L. Geisler and W. E. Nix, *A General Introduction to the Bible,* rev. and exp. (1986).

SCRIPTURE MANUSCRIPTS, OLD TESTAMENT. The word *Scripture* is derived from the Lat. *scriptum,* or *scriptura,* and has for its Gk. equivalent *graphē,* and Heb. *miqrā'* (Neh. 8:8). In its English use in the Bible it means "the writings," as in Ex. 32:16; Dan. 10:21.

The NT employs the plural *graphai,* "writings." The precise writing referred to by the word *Scripture* is not always clear. The word is found thirty-two times in the KJV. The plural, Scriptures, is found twenty-one times, all except one in the NT. In the singular the word refers to passages in the OT, which are quoted or alluded to in the NT. In the plural the reference is to books or collections of books of the OT. The epithet "holy" or "sacred" is applied to the Scriptures in Rom. 1:2 and 2 Tim. 3:15. Their inspiration is distinctly attested in 3:16, "All Scripture is inspired by God." Other translations, "Every Scripture being inspired," or, "Every Scripture is inspired," do not modify the clear declaration of the inspiration of the OT Scriptures. Every separate portion of the holy Book is inspired and forms a living portion of a living and organic whole. Although this expression does not exclude such verbal errors that are the result of transmission of the text over many centuries, it still does certainly assure us that these writings, as we have seen them, are individually pervaded by God's Spirit and warrant our belief that they are (in the words of Clement of Rome, *Epistle to the Corinthians* 1:45) the true utterances of the Holy Spirit and an assertion of the *full* inspiration of the Bible. *See* Canon; Inspiration.

Preservation of the Text. The sacred writings were preserved down to the time of the invention of printing by the process of transcription. Hence there arose at an early period a class of scholars known as scribes (Heb. *sōpᵉrîm*), meaning writers. Their business was to copy the Scriptures (Jer. 8:8). In the reign of Artaxerxes, king of Persia, Ezra was well known as a scribe and went up from Babylon to Jerusalem, "and he was a scribe skilled in the law of Moses" (Ezra 7:6). The scribes became teachers and expounders of the law. In the time of our Lord they were generally hostile to His claims as the Messiah and were among His most bitter persecutors. Through a succession of scribes the Holy Scriptures were transmitted from generation to generation. The ancient Heb. differed in its written character from the Heb. current in our modern Heb. Bibles. It was written in the old Phoenician letters, of which one of the most ancient specimens is found on the Moabite Stone discovered in 1868 at Dibon in Moab and dating about 850 B.C., and also in the Gezer Calendar dating from about 925 B.C. Gradually this early character was displaced, and in the time of Christ the present Heb. characters were in use. It is said in Matt. 5:18, "not the smallest letter or stroke shall pass away from the Law." Hebrew *yodh* is the smallest letter in the Heb. alphabet, but the equivalent letter in the early Phoenician character was not small, showing that the old character had given place at this time to the later Heb. The word *manuscript,* abbreviated MS for singular and MSS for plural, is from the Lat. *codices manuscripti,* i.e., codices written by hand. The word *codex,* from the Lat. *codex,* or *caudex,* the stock of a tree, board covered with wax for writing; hence, book; plural codices, books.

Hebrew manuscripts were originally without accents, vowels, or marks of punctuation. The Heb. vowel points were not introduced until about the sixth century of the Christian era by a body of learned men called the Masoretes, who studied the Heb. Scriptures with great minuteness and made a collection of writings called "the Masora," or the Traditions. By means of their system of vowel points they established the pronunciation and meaning of the original Heb. on a firm foundation.

Until the modern sensational manuscript finds in the Dead Sea area from 1947 to 1956, Heb. manuscripts of the OT were not earlier than the tenth century A.D. Now the Isaiah manuscript of the Dead Sea Scrolls, dating about 150 B.C., together with other fragmentary finds of various OT books, pushes the date of OT manuscripts back about a millennium. But the work of the Masoretes is nevertheless of immense importance, despite recent manuscript discoveries. *See* Dead Sea Scrolls.

The proper task of the Masora was the guarding of the Bible manuscripts against degeneration through carelessness and willfulness on the part of transcribers, and, in consequence, the most painful and minute supervision was exercised upon them; but just in this way the Masora affords a glimpse into the form of the text transmitted from early times, which cannot be too highly valued.

There are two words in our Heb. Bible that served the purpose of modern textual emendations; they are *qere,* "read," and *kethib,* "written." When a word was found in the text that was believed incorrect, instead of substituting the true word, placing it in the text, the Masoretes wrote the correct word in the margin and left the incorrect word in the text, with the vowels of the correct word. The word in the text would be thus shown to be wrong, and by placing these vowels with the word in the margin the true text would be clear. This fear to remove the incorrect word from the text showed a reverence amounting to superstition for the exact wording of their sacred writings. The Heb. manuscripts that have been preserved, except the manuscript finds since 1947, are not nearly so ancient as many of those of the Greek NT, nor are complete manuscripts so numerous, the greater part of the 2,000 extant Heb. manuscripts containing only fragments or portions of the OT.

Some Important Manuscripts. Several manuscripts of particular interest are the following:

The Nash Papyrus. The Nash Papyrus contains "one damaged copy of the Shema (from Deut. 6:4-9) and two fragments of the Decalogue (Ex. 20:2ff.; Deut. 5:6ff.). It is dated between the second century B.C. . . . and the first century A.D." (N. L. Geisler and W. E. Nix, *A General Introduction to the Bible* [1986], p. 358; the early date is advocated by W. F. Albright in "A Biblical Fragment from the Maccabean Age: The Nash Papyrus," *Journal of Biblical Literature* 56 [1937]: 145-76).

Orientales 4445. The manuscript known today as Orientales 4445 "contains Genesis 39:20—Deuteronomy 1:33 (less Numbers 7:47-73 and Numbers 9:12–10:18)" and has been dated as early as the ninth century (A.D. 820 to 850, the Masora notes a century later) and as late as the tenth (*see* Geisler and Nix, p. 358; Christian D. Ginsburg supports the former date; Paul E. Kahle, *The Cairo Geniza,* 2d ed. [1959], the latter, on the basis of the consonantal Heb. text and the pointing).

Codex Cairensis. Codex Cairensis "contains the Former Prophets (Joshua, Judges, 1 and 2 Samuel, 1 and 2 Kings) and the Latter Prophets (Isaiah, Jeremiah, Ezekiel and the Twelve)"; it was "written and vowel-pointed in A.D. 895 by Moses ben Asher in Tiberias in Palestine" (Geisler and Nix, p. 358-59, based on E. Würthwein, *The Text of the O.T.* [1959, 1979]).

The Aleppo Codex. The Aleppo Codex of the Whole Old Testament "was written by Shelomo ben Baya'a [but] pointed (i.e., the vowel marks were added) by Moses ben Asher (c. A.D. 930)" (Geisler and Nix, p. 359, from F. G. Kenyon, *Our Bible and the Ancient Manuscripts,* 4th ed. [1958], p. 359).

The Babylonian Codex (MS Heb. B3). The Babylonian Codex of the Latter Prophets (MS Heb. B3), "sometimes called the Leningrad Codex of the Prophets . . . or the St. Petersburg Codex . . .," is dated A.D. 916" (Geisler and Nix, p. 359; the former name is that used by F. G. Kenyon, *Our Bible and the Ancient Manuscripts,* p. 85; the latter name is used by E. Würthwein, *The Text of the O.T.,* p. 26).

Codex Leningradensis (B19A). A colophon attached to Codex Leningradensis (B19A), "one of the oldest manuscripts of the complete Hebrew Bible that is known," indicates that Samuel ben Jacob copied it in A.D. 1008 from a manuscript written some eight years earlier by Aaron ben Moses ben Asher, although some believe B19A is a copy of the Aleppo Codex (mentioned above; Geisler and Nix, p. 359; Paul E. Kahle, *The Cairo Geniza,* p. 132, holds to the former history; Ginsburg to the latter).

Codex Laudianus. Codex Laudianus is also of the eleventh century. It is in the Bodleian Library in Oxford, England. It agrees quite closely with the Samaritan Pentateuch.

The Reuchlin Codex. The Reuchlin Codex of the Prophets, now at Karlsruhe, is dated A.D. 1105. It "contains a recension of Ben Naphtali, a Tiberian Masorete" (Geisler and Nix, p. 359).

Codex Caesenoe. Codex Caesenoe is in the Maltesta Library in Bologna and is assigned to the end of the eleventh century. It contains the Pentateuch, sections of the Prophets, Song of Solomon, Ruth, Lamentations, Ecclesiastes, and Esther.

Codex Parisiensis. Codex Parisiensis is in the Bibliothèque Nationale in Paris and is assigned to the twelfth century. It contains the entire OT.

Codex 634 of Giovanni de Rossi. Codex 634 of De Rossi contains a small part of the law—Lev. 21:19 and Num. 1:50. It belongs to the eighth century.

Codex Norimbergensis. Codex Norimbergensis, in Nuremberg, contains the Prophets and Hagiographa. It is assigned to the twelfth century.

Agreement in the Manuscripts. The remarkable thing about the Heb. text is the agreement of the old manuscripts that have come down to us. The Heb. text of the OT has been rendered into the Gk. of the LXX version, which many regard as a witness to the true text, even when it varies from our present Heb. text. The exact value of the LXX in determining the original Heb. is yet undetermined, but the question is being illuminated by the Dead Sea manuscript finds.

That the Heb. text has been carefully preserved is evident from the great care taken by Jewish scholars in its preservation. The care of the Masoretes and other scholars in preserving the text indicates care also in ascertaining the true text and serves to assure us of the genuineness of the present Heb. Scriptures.

BIBLIOGRAPHY: B. J. Roberts, *Old Testament Text and Versions* (1951); D. R. Ap Thomas, *A Primer of Old Testament Text Criticism* (1964); E. Würthwein, *The Text of the Old Testament* (1979); N. L. Geisler and W. E. Nix, *A General Introduction to the Bible* (1986).

SCROLL. A book in ancient times consisted of a single long strip of papyrus or parchment, which was usually kept rolled up on a stick and was unrolled when a person wished to read it. Hence arose the term *me̱gillâ* from *gālal,* "to roll," strictly answering to the Lat. *volumen,* whence comes our *volume.* The use of the term *me̱gillâ* implies, of course, the existence of a soft and pliant material, perhaps parchment. The scroll was usually written on one side only, and hence the particular notice of one that was "written on the front and back" (Ezek. 2:10). The writing was arranged in columns.

"Scroll" is sometimes given as the translation of Heb. *sēper,* a "writing," or a "book" (*see* Num. 5:23; Deut. 17:18; Isa. 30:8; 34:4; and also the article Book); or as the translation of the two Heb. terms, *sēper* and *me̱gillâ,* taken together (Jer. 36:2, 4; Ezek. 2:9; for all, see marg.).

In Rev. 6:14 the sky is said to be "split apart like a scroll when it is rolled up" (from Gk. *biblion*).

See also Book; Roll, Roll of a Book.

Law scroll

SCUM. *See* Rust.

SCURVY. *See* Diseases.

SCYTH'IAN (sith'i-an). One of a nomad race, or collection of races, dwelling mostly on the N of the Black Sea and the Caspian, stretching indefinitely into inner Asia. They called themselves Scoloti, and the native traditions traced their origin to Targetaus, son of Zeus, or perhaps son of their corresponding god Papaeus (Hd. 4.59), and a daughter of the river Borysthenes (ibid. 4.5.6). In the name *Targetaus* some have seen the origin of the name *Turk.*

The Scoloti were fierce barbarians who "scalped their enemies, and used their skulls as drinking cups [ibid. 4.64.65], and offered human sacrifices" (Smith). Their "justice," so highly praised by the earlier poets, was probably a rough and ready impartiality, which is easy when there is no regard for human life or suffering. In the only place where Scythians are mentioned (Col. 3:11) they are evidently taken as representatives of the barbarian world. It has been inferred, however, and is by no means impossible, that there were Scythians in the early church.

In the time of Psammetichus, king of Egypt, the contemporary of Josiah, the Scythians invaded Palestine and plundered the temple of Venus Urania in Ashkelon; and they were only prevented from entering Egypt by prayers and presents (Hd. 1.105). Some suppose that their possession of Beth-shean gave it its name Scythopolis (LXX, *Skuthōnpolis,* Judg. 1:27; cf. Judith 3:10; 2 Macc. 12:29; and 1 Macc. 5:52; Josephus, *Skuthopolis*). They took Sardis, 629 B.C.; defeated Cyaxares of

Media, 624; and occupied "Asia" for twenty-eight years, till they were expelled, 596 B.C.

Most moderns, following Josephus (*Ant.* 1.6.1) and Jerome, identify the Magog of Ezek. 38:2; 39:1, 6, the land of which Gog was prince, with the land of the Scythians, who in Ezekiel's time inhabited the region between the Caspian and Black seas. The Scythians of the time of Herodotus and Ezekiel are believed to have been a Japhetic race. They were backward in civilization so that their name became proverbial for wildness or barbarity much as the Greeks used the epithet "barbarian" (cf. Col. 3:11).

W.H.; M.F.U.

BIBIOGRAPHY: Herodotus *History of Herodotus* 3.1-144; T. T. Rice, *The Scythians* (1957); R. P. Vaggione, *Journal of Biblical Literature* 92 (1973): 523-50.

SEA (Heb. *yām,* "roaring"; Gk. *thalassa,* probably "salty"). *Yām* is used in Scripture in the following senses:

1. The "gathering of the waters," i.e., the ocean (Deut. 30:13; 1 Kings 10:22; Ps. 24:2; Job 26:12; 38:8).

2. With the article, of some part of the great encompassing water, namely: (a) Of the Mediterranean Sea, called "eastern" and the "western" sea (Deut. 11:24; 34:2; Joel 2:20); "sea of the Philistines" (Ex. 23:31); "the Great Sea" (Num. 34:6-7; Josh. 15:47); "the sea" (Pss. 80:11; 107:23); "the seashore" (Gen. 49:13; 1 Kings 4:20; etc.). (b) Of the Red Sea (Ex. 15:4; Josh. 24:6), or of one of its gulfs (Num. 11:31; Isa. 11:15), and perhaps the sea (1 Kings 10:22) traversed by Solomon's fleet. The place "where two seas met" (Acts 27:41) is understood by Smith and approved by Ramsay to be "a neck of land projecting toward the island of Samonetta, which shelters St. Paul's Bay on the northwest."

The Mediterranean coast at Ashkelon

3. The term is also applied to the great lakes of Palestine, whether fresh or salt; e.g., (a) The Sea of Chinnereth (Num. 34:11) called in the NT "the Sea of Galilee" (Matt. 4:18), the "Sea of Tiberias" (John 21:1), and the Sea (or lake) of Gennesaret (Matt. 14:34; Mark 6:53; Luke 5:1). (*See* Galilee, Sea of). (b) The Dead Sea, called also the Salt Sea (Gen. 14:3), the sea of the Arabah (Deut. 4:49), and the eastern sea (Joel 2:20; Ezek. 47:18; Zech. 14:8). It is neither named nor alluded to in the NT. (c) The Lake Merom is named only in Josh. 11:5, 7, as the "waters of Merom."

4. *Yām* is also applied to great rivers, as the Nile (Isa. 19:5; Amos 8:8; Nah. 3:8; Ezek. 32:2) and the Euphrates (Jer. 51:36).

Figurative. To enclose "the sea with doors" (Job 38:8) is a symbolical expression for restraining, fixing a bound thereto. "The sea speaks" (Isa. 23:4) is figurative for the rock island upon which new Tyre stood and made her lamentation; the noise of hostile armies is likened to the "roaring of the sea" (5:30; Jer. 6:23); "waves of the sea" represent righteousness (Isa. 48:18), a devastating army (Ezek. 26:3-4), and in their restlessness the wicked (Isa. 57:20) and the unsteady (James 1:6); the diffusion of spiritual truth over the earth is symbolized by the covering waters of the sea (Isa. 11:9; Hab. 2:14); "wild waves of the sea, casting up their own shame like foam" (Jude 13) is a figurative description of false teachers who threw out their obscene teachings like wreckage upon the shore. "The abundance of the sea" (Isa. 60:5) is everything of value that is possessed by islands and coastlands; "the princes of the sea" (Ezek. 26:16) is a figurative term for the merchants of Tyre; "from sea to sea" (Amos 8:12; Mic. 7:12) stands for "from one end of the world to the other."

SEA, BRONZE (1 Kings 7:23-44; 2 Kings 25:2; 2 Chron. 4:2; Jer. 52:17). The great *laver* (which see) in Solomon's Temple. This immense bronze bowl was placed on twelve oxen and orientated toward the four points of the compass. It was a new feature of the sanctuary court (1 Kings 7:23-26). It took the place of the laver of the Tabernacle, was ornately decorated with flowers and high relief, and was for the purpose of ceremonial washings. In the name given to it by Solomon ("sea") and in its construction it demonstrates Syro-Phoenician influence as well as cosmic significance. The sea in the ancient Near East was widely recognized as possessing cosmic import (I. Benzinger, *Hebraeische Archaeologie* [1927], p. 329). Solomon's "bronze sea" can hardly be thought of as completely unconnected with the Mesopotamian "sea" (*apsu*), a term used both as a designation of the subterranean fresh water ocean, the source of life and fertility, and of a basin of holy water set up in the Temple (W. F. Albright, *Archaeology and the Religion of Israel,* pp. 148f, 217, n. 67; G. E. Wright, *The Biblical*

Archaeologist 7 [1944]: 74). Moreover, these various cosmic sources of water were pictured in mythological imagery as dragons, both in Akkad. (Apsu and Tiamat), Canaanite ("sea") *yammu,* and "river," *naharu,* and in biblical Heb. ("sea") *yām,* "rivers," *nehārôt* (Isa. 51:10; Ps. 72:8) for "sea" and for "streams" and "rivers" (Ps. 74:15; Hab. 3:8-9). In Mesopotamia the term *sea* denoted the supposed subterranean source of the great life-giving rivers of that land. Among the Phoenicians and Syrians this expression was used of the Mediterranean as the main source of Canaanite livelihood. The relation of the sea to the portable basins that Solomon made (1 Kings 7:38), which correspond to Phoenician portable basins discovered at Cyprus, was similar to that between the "sea" (*apsu*) and "the portable basins of water" (*egubbe*) in Babylonian temples (W. F. Albright, *Archaeology and the Religion of Israel,* p. 149).

M.F.U.

SEA COWS. *See* Animal Kingdom: Porpoise.

SEA GULL. *See* Animal Kingdom.

SEAH. A dry measure of capacity. *See* Metrology.

SEAL, SIGNET (Heb. *hōtām;* Gk. *sphragis*). A portable instrument used to stamp a document or other article, instead of or with the sign manual. The impression made therewith had the same legal validity as an actual signature, as is still the case in the East. Indeed, the importance attached to this method is so great that without a seal no document is considered authentic. In a similar manner coffers, doors of houses, and tombs were sealed.

Egyptian. The most familiar form of Egyptian jewelry is that of the so-called scaraboid seals; in these an elliptical piece of stone was carved on its upper convex surface into the likeness of a scarabeus, the sacred beetle of the Egyptians; and on the lower flat side bore inscriptions in intaglio. Examples of these seals are known as far back as the Fourth Dynasty, c. 2550 B.C. Sometimes they

Helen and Alice Colburn Fund. Courtesy, Museum of Fine Arts, Boston.

Egyptian scarab, Dynasty XVIII

were made of blue pottery or porcelain and in many cases consisted of a lump of clay, impressed with a seal and attached to the document by strings.

Mesopotamian. At Uruk, biblical Erech (Gen. 10:10), modern Warka, c. 3500 B.C., the cylinder seal was introduced. In the White Temple two small square tablets of gypsum plaster were uncovered that contained impressions of cylinder seals. Such early seals were made in the form of a small engraved cylinder that left its impression by being rolled across soft clay. A jar or package was sealed with moist clay, and the cylinder seal was rolled over it. From their origin somewhere in the fourth millennium B.C., cylinder seals were constantly used until they gave way to the stamp seals of Persian times. They thus have a demonstrable history of more than three millennia. From Mesopotamia their manufacture and employment spread to peripheral regions as widely distant as India and Egypt. The adornment of the seals shows Mesopotamia's original contribution to art. The Uruk seals display amazing vitality and excellence. Henri A. Frankfort, formerly research professor of oriental archaeology at the Oriental Institute of the University of Chicago, made monumental studies in the development of the cylinder seal from the prehistoric period to the dynasties of ancient Sumer and Babylon down to the Persian period. *See* Frankfort's book, *Cylinder Seals,* supplemented by the book *Cylinder Seals from the Diyala Region.* Professor Frankfort dealt with almost 1,000 stratified seals discovered during the course of his direction of work for seven years in Iraq. Leon Legrain of the University of Pennsylvania also published two volumes in the field of cylinder seals. Of special interest is the lapis lazuli seal of Queen Puabi (or Shubad) uncovered by Woolley at Ur. Cylinder seals were incised on various hard surfaces including gold, silver, rock crystal, blue chalcedony, carnelian, marble, ivory, jasper, glazed pottery, and simple baked clay. The well-known seal of Darius the Great displays the king in his two-wheeled chariot between two date palms. Often seals contain both pictures and written material. Jar-handle seals were also common from c. 2500 B.C. These were used not only in signing Babylonian clay documents but in safekeeping jars containing valuable papers or commodities for shipment to distant lands. A cloth was placed over the neck of the container, soft clay smeared on top of the binding cord, and the cylinder rolled over the wet clay. If the seal was undisturbed at its destination, the merchandise was safe.

Hebrew. The use of clay in sealing is noticed in the book of Job (38:14) and the signet ring as an ordinary part of a man's equipment in the case of Judah (Gen. 38:18), who probably, like many modern Arabs, wore it suspended by a string from his neck or arm (Song of Sol. 8:6). The ring or

Mesopotamian cylinder seal (12th to 11th century B.C.)

the seal, as an emblem of authority in Egypt, Persia, and elsewhere is mentioned in the cases of Pharaoh with Joseph (Gen. 41:42), of Ahab (1 Kings 21:8), of Ahasuerus (Esther 3:10, 12; 8:2), of Darius (Dan. 6:17; also 1 Macc. 6:15), and as an evidence of a covenant in Jer. 32:10, 14; Neh. 9:38; 10:1; Hag. 2:23. Engraved signets were in use among the Hebrews in early times, as is evident in the description of the high priest's breastplate (Ex. 28:11, 36; 39:6); and the work of the engraver is mentioned as a distinct occupation (Ecclus. 38:27).

Figurative. "It is changed like clay under the seal," i.e., "it changes like the clay of a signet ring" (Delitzsch, *Com.*, ad loc.), is an allusion to a cylinder seal, revolving like day and night (Job 38:14). In Song of Solomon 8:6 is the prayer "Put me like a seal over your heart," implying the approaching absence of the bridegroom and that the bride wished that her impression might be engraved on his arm and heart, i.e., his *love* and *power*. The meaning of the figurative expression "I will make you [Zerubbabel] like a signet ring" (Hag. 2:23; marg., "seal ring") is evident from the importance of the signet ring in the eyes of an oriental, who is accustomed to carry it continually with him and to take care of it as a valuable possession; also in the same sense when Jehovah says, "Though Coniah [i.e., Jehoiachin] . . . were a signet ring on My right hand, yet I would pull you off" (Jer. 22:24). The term *sealed* is used for that which is *permanent* (Isa. 8:16), *confirmed* (John 6:27; Rom. 4:11), that which is to be *kept secret* (Dan. 12:4, 9), *impenetrable* to men but known to Christ (Rev. 5:2), *approval* (John 3:33). To set "a seal upon the stars" (Job 9:7) means to cover them with clouds so that their light is excluded from men, whereas to seal "the hand of every man" (37:7) is to prevent men from working by reason of the cold. The "seal of the living God," on which is supposed to be engraved the name of Jehovah, impressed upon the foreheads of the faithful, symbolizes safety and deliverance from judgment (Rev. 7:2-8). A seal also denotes the indwelling of the Holy Spirit (Eph. 1:13; 4:30; 2 Cor. 1:22; *see* Mark). The *seals* upon the "foundation of God" (2 Tim. 2:19) are *inscriptions* upon this mystical building, proper to be impressed upon the minds of all professing Chris-

tians, both for *encouragement* and for *warning*.

M.F.U.

BIBLIOGRAPHY: W. H. Ward, *The Seal Cylinders of Western Asia* (1910); W. M. F. Petrie, *Scarabs and Cylinders* (1917); E. Porada, ed., *Corpus of Ancient Near Eastern Seals*, vol. 1 (1948); G. E. Wright, *Biblical Archaeologist* 20 (1957): 159-60, 197-98, 202-3.

SEAM. Our Lord's inner garment, for which the soldiers cast lots (John 19:23), was "seamless," i.e., it was woven entire, from the neck down.

SEA MONSTER. *See* Animal Kingdom: Dragon; Whale.

SEA OF GLASS (Gk. *thalassa hualinē,* "glassy sea," Rev. 4:6; 15:2). The "sea of glass" recalls the typology of the OT, which enters richly into the structure of the Apocalypse. The allusion is evidently to the Tabernacle laver (Ex. 30:18-21) and possibly more directly to the molten sea in the Solomonic Temple (1 Kings 7:23-37); both were used for priestly ablutions. However, the "sea of glass" points to a fixed state of holiness, both inward and outward, and its being "around the throne" would indicate that the purity is in keeping with the holy character of the throne itself. The "sea of glass" is said to be "like crystal." The crystal denotes the splendor and beauty of that scene of holiness spread out before the throne. The two symbols, glass and crystal, are closely allied but are not quite the same. The former is a manufactured article; the latter a native substance. The sea of glass is expressive of smoothness, and this heavenly sea is of crystal, demonstrating that the peace of heaven is not like earthly seas, disturbed by winds, but is crystallized into an eternal peace.

M.F.U.

SEA OF JA'ZER (Jer. 48:32). A lake, now represented by some ponds in the high valley in which the city of *Jazer* (which see) is situated.

SEAR (Gk. *kautēriazō,* "to brand"). The term is used (1 Tim. 4:2) figuratively of the *conscience*. Those of whom the apostle speaks were branded with the marks of sin, i.e., carry about with them the perpetual consciousness of sin. But the meaning seems more precisely to be that their conscience, like cauterized flesh, was deprived of sensation.

SEASHORE, SEACOAST.
1. The shore of a seacoast (Heb. *ḥôp,* "chafed" by waves, Gesenius; or enclosed, Fuerst; cf. English *cove; see* Deut. 1:7; Judg. 5:17; Jer. 47:7; Ezek. 25:16; Josh. 9:1; "coast," NIV).
2. The extremity of the land (Josh. 15:2, KJV, "shore," Heb. *qāṣeh,* "end," "extremity"; several translations for the Heb. term appear in the NASB).
3. The edge, or lip, of the land, in our sense of seashore (Gen. 22:17; Ex. 14:30; etc.; Heb. *śāpâ,* "lip").

4. The beach on which the waves dash (Gk. *algialos;* Matt. 13:2, 48; John 21:4; Acts 21:5; 27:39, 40; "beach," NASB; "shore," KJV; "shore," "beach," NIV).

5. The "lip" of the shore, or the "sea shore" (Heb. 11:12, KJV, from Gk. *thalassa,* "sea," and *cheilos,* "lip"; NASB, NIV, "seashore"), as the place on which or from which the waves pour (cf. Matt. 15:8; Mark 7:6; Rom. 3:13, "lip," from Gk. *cheilos*).

SEASON. See Time.

SEAT. As furniture. See House. Other usages in the Bible are as follows:

1. A throne, as usually rendered, but also any seat occupied by a king (Judg. 3:20) or other distinguished person, as the high priest (1 Sam. 1:9; 4:13, 18; Heb. *kissē'*). In the NT we have Gk. *bēma,* of the "judgment seat" (Matt. 27:19; John 19:13; Acts 18:12, 16-17); of God (Rom. 14:10); of Christ (2 Cor. 5:10); "seat on the tribunal" (Acts 25:6, 10, 17); *kathedra,* in the usual sense of *place* (Matt. 21:12; Mark 11:15); but generally of the exalted seat occupied by men of eminent rank or influence, as teachers and judges; thus "the Pharisees have seated themselves in the chair of Moses," i.e., consider themselves as Moses' successors in explaining and defending the law (Matt. 23:2).

2. An abode (Heb. *môshāb,* "a seat"; 1 Sam. 20:18, 25; Job 29:7); a "sitting," i.e., assembly of persons sitting together (Ps. 1:1); the *site* of an image (Ezek. 8:3).
Figurative. "I sit in the seat of gods" (Ezek. 28:2). The language ascribed to the prince of Tyre is that of pride. "The Tyrian state was the production and seat of its gods. He, the prince of Tyre, presided over this divine creation and divine seat; therefore, he the prince, was himself a god, a manifestation of the deity, having its work and home in the state of Tyre" (Kliefoth). The prophetic meaning sets forth Satan in his connection with the government of this world system (Dan. 10:13, 20; Eph. 6:10).

3. A place, or dwelling (Job 23:3). Heb. *te-kûnâ.*

4. In the KJV seat (Gk. *thronos*) is used figuratively for kingly power (Luke 1:52); of Satan (Rev. 2:13, 13:2; 16:10); of the *elders* (which see; 4:4; 11:16). Translated "throne" in NASB and NIV.

5. "The front seats" (Luke 11:43), "chief seats" (20:46), is the rendering of Gk. *prōtokathedria,* the first or principal seats, and means preeminent in council.

SE'BA (sē'ba).

1. The oldest son of Cush and hence a country and people among the Cushites (Gen. 10:7; 1 Chron. 1:9).

2. The name of a people (Ps. 72:10; Isa. 43:3). See Sabeans.

SE'BAM (sē'bam). Shebam, KJV; one of the

towns in the pastoral district E of Jordan—demanded by, and finally ceded to, the tribes of Reuben and Gad (Num. 32:3 only). It is probably the same that appears in the altered form of *Sibmah* (which see).

SE'BAT (sē'bat) or **She'bat** (shē'bat). The fifth month of the Hebrew civil year. See Calendar; Time.

SECA'CAH (se-ka'ka; "thicket, enclosure"). A town in the wilderness of Judah, near the Dead Sea (Josh. 15:61). Noted for its "great cistern," identified by some with Sikkeh but position uncertain.

SECOND COMING OF CHRIST. The great event that will wind up this present age. Premillennialists believe that Christ will come to establish a visible earthly kingdom over Israel for at least 1,000 years. Amillennialists hold that the second coming of Christ will initiate the eternal state. The amillennialist rejects the future earthly program for Israel and mysticalizes the great OT prophecies concerning Zion and Jerusalem, etc., to refer to the Christian church. The postmillennialist believes that Christ will return to the earth after the Millennium. Premillennialists believe that the return of Christ consists of two events or stages. Pretribulation premillennialists hold that Christ will return for His church (1 Cor. 15:51-55; 1 Thess. 4:13-18), glorify it, and take it to heaven before a seven-year period known as the Great Tribulation (Jer. 30:5; Dan. 9:27; etc.). At the end of this cataclysmic seven-year period Christ will return in power and glory to judge the nations and set up His millennial kingdom. Midtribulationists believe that Christ will return in the middle of Daniel's seventieth week. Posttribulationists reject the idea of a separate appearance of Christ for the church and have the church going through the entire Tribulation. Exhaustive inductive study of Scripture seems to favor the pretribulation-rapture view.   M.F.U.

BIBLIOGRAPHY: J. F. Walvoord, *The Millennial Kingdom* (1959), pp. 263-75; J. D. Pentecost, *Things to Come* (1961), pp. 370-426; R. H. Gundry, *The Church and the Tribulation* (1973); P. Tan, *The Interpretation of Prophecy* (1974); A. A. Hoekema, *The Bible and the Future* (1979); L. Strauss, *Prophetic Mysteries Revealed* (1985). For additional information see *The Minister's Library* (1985), pp. 275-81.

SECOND QUARTER (Heb. *mishneh,* "repetition," 2 Kings 22:14). The residence of the prophetess *Hulda* (which see). The word *mishneh* should be taken as a proper name referring to a district or suburb of the city. The NIV translates "Second District." The same term is used in Zeph. 1:10, where the different quarters of Jerusalem are spoken of.

SECOND SABBATH. (Luke 6:1). See Sabbath, Second After the First.

SECRET. *See* Mystery.

SECT (Gk. *hairesis,* a "choice"). A religious party such as Sadducees (Acts 5:17), Pharisees (15:5), or Nazarenes (24:5; cf. 26:5; 28:22).

SE'CU (se'ku; "a lookout place"). A site of a large well, probably lying on the route between Saul's residence, Gibeah, and that of Samuel, Ramatha-im-zophim (1 Sam. 19:22). The modern Suwei-keh, immediately S of Beeroth, is suggested as its site.

SECUN'DUS (se-kun'dus, "second"). A Thes-salonian Christian and one of the party who went with the apostle Paul from Corinth as far as Asia, probably to Troas or Miletus, on his return from his third missionary visit (Acts 20:4).

SECURITY. The doctrine that maintains the continuation of salvation for those who are saved. It must be distinguished from the doctrine of *assurance* (which see). It must also be clearly remembered that it concerns only the regener-ate. The doctrine of security is based upon twelve undertakings of God for His people, four related to the Father, four to the Son, and four to the Holy Spirit.

The Father's Undertakings. (1) The efficacy of the perpetual prayer of the Son upon the Father (John 17:9-12, 15, 20). (2) Infinite divine power made available to save and keep (John 10:29; Rom. 4:21; 8:31-39; Eph. 1:19-21). (3) God's infi-nite love (Eph. 1:4-5; Rom. 5:7-10). (4) God's sovereign purpose or covenant, which is uncon-ditional (John 3:16; 5:24; 6:37).

The Son's Undertakings. (1) His intercession (John 17:1-26; Rom. 8:34; Heb. 7:23-25). (2) His advocacy (Rom. 8:34; Heb. 9:24; 1 John 2:1-2). (3) His substitutionary death (Rom. 8:1-4; 1 John 2:2). (4) His glorious resurrection (John 3:16; 10:28; Eph. 2:6).

The Spirit's Undertakings. (1) Regeneration, or quickening into eternal life, which is the par-taking of the divine nature and an entrance into that which cannot be removed (John 1:13; 3:3-6; Titus 3:4-6; 1 John 3:9). (2) Baptism, by which the believer is united to Christ so as to partake eternally in the new creation glory and blessing (1 Cor. 6:17; 12:13; Gal. 3:27). (3) Sealing, by which the Holy Spirit stamps and thus secures the Christian as God's child (Eph. 1:13-14; 4:30). (4) Indwelling, by which the Spirit inhabits the redeemed body forever (John 7:37-39; Rom. 5:5; 8:9; 1 Cor. 6:19; 1 John 2:27).

The NT clearly teaches that God offers no sal-vation at the present time that is not eternal. Although this doctrine has been greatly misun-derstood and abused, when rightly understood it offers a powerful boon to a holy life (cf. 1 John 2:1). Arminian doctrines reject security, employ-ing experience as a proof. However, the Scrip-tures commonly so employed, when clearly clas-sified, do not favor insecurity: (1) Passages

concerning false teachers of the last days of the church (1 Tim. 4:1-3; 2 Pet. 2:1-22; Jude 17:19) that concern apostates or those who were never saved. (2) Passages comprehending no more than moral reform: for example, Luke 11:24-26. (3) Passages dispensationally misapplied (Ezek. 21:1-48; 33:7-8; Matt. 18:23-35; 24:13; 25:1-13). (4) Passages relating to loss of rewards and chas-tisement (John 15:2; 1 Cor. 3:15; 9:27; 11:27-32; Col. 1:21-23; 1 John 1:5-9; 5:16). (5) Passages relating to falling from grace, that is, leaving the grace way of life for the legal way of life (Gal. 5:4). (6) Passages containing various admonitions (Heb. 6:4-9; 10:26-31).

The doctrine of security has suffered much confusion and misuse. It is rejected by many theologians and subscribed to by others but abused by antinomian teaching and living. It is nevertheless a clear teaching of Scripture, and when properly understood and faithfully believed it is a doctrine of immense spiritual benefit and blessing.   M.F.U.

BIBLIOGRAPHY: H. Barker, *Secure Forever* (1974); R. G. Gromacki, *Salvation Is Forever* (1974).

SEDITION (Heb. *'eshtaddûr,* "revolt"; Gk. *sta-sis,* a "standing"), **Seditions** (Gk. *dichostasia*). The term *sedition* appears more frequently in the KJV than the NASB or NIV. It has the sense of rebellion (Ezra 4:15, 19; "revolt," NASB), insur-rection (Luke 23:19, 25), or dissension (Acts 15:2; 24:5; "troublemaker," NIV). The Gk. word behind the English term *seditions* (Gal. 5:20, KJV; "dissensions," NASB, NIV) has the meaning of "a standing apart."

SEDUCERS. The term *seducer* in the KJV of 2 Tim. 3:13 (from Gk. *goēs*) has the meaning of "impostors" (so NASB and NIV).

SEED. *See* Agriculture.

Figurative. As the prolific principle of future life, seed in Scripture is taken for the posterity of man (Gen. 3:15; 4:25, marg.; etc.), of beasts (Jer. 31:27), trees (Gen. 1:11-12, 29; etc.). The seed of Abraham denotes not only those who descend from him by natural issue but also those who imitate his character, independent of natural descent (Rom. 4:16, *see* marg.). In this sense the NIV usually translates "offspring." Seed is figurative of God's Word (Luke 8:5, 11; 1 Pet. 1:23), and its preaching is called "sowing" (Luke 8:5; Matt. 13:32; 1 Cor. 9:11). *Sowing* seed is symbolical of scattering or dispersing a people (Zech. 10:9, marg.), of dispensing liberally (Eccles. 11:6; 2 Cor. 9:6), of working evil (Job 4:8), righteous-ness (Hos. 10:12), or deeds in general (Gal. 6:8). Christ compares His death to the sowing of seed with its results (John 12:24); Paul likens the buri-al of the body to the sowing of seed (1 Cor. 15:36-38).

SEEDTIME. *See* Agriculture.

SEER. *See* Prophet.

SEETHE (Heb. *bāshal*), **Seething pot** (Heb. *nā-pah*). The archaic English terms refer to boiling (so NASB and NIV, Ex. 16:23; 23:19; Job 41:20; Jer. 1:13; etc.).

SE'GUB (se'gub; "elevated").

1. The youngest son of Hiel the Bethelite and rebuilder of Jericho. Segub died for his father's sin (1 Kings 16:34), according to Joshua's prediction (cf. Josh. 6:26), between 875 and 854 B.C.

2. The son of Hezron (grandson of Judah) by the daughter of Machir the "father" of Gilead. He was himself the father of Jair (1 Chron. 2:21-22), perhaps about 1900 B.C.

SE'IR (sē'ir; "rough, hairy"). A chief of the *Horites* (which see), the former inhabitants of the country afterward possessed by the Edomites (Gen. 36:20-21; 1 Chron. 1:38). Whether he gave the name to the country or took it from it is uncertain.

SE'IR, LAND OF. The mountainous territory of Edom (Gen. 32:3; 36:30). *See* Seir, Mount.

SE'IR, MOUNT (mownt sē'ir; Gen. 14:6). References to "Seir" in the Bible are to three locations.

Mount Seir. This is the range of mountains running southward from the Dead Sea, E of the valley of Arabah to the Elanitic Gulf. The earliest mention of Mt. Seir is in the Bible account of Chedorlaomer's campaign in the days of Abraham. This was long before the birth of Esau; and it is said that the *Horites* (which see) were then its inhabitants. The Israelites were forbidden to enter this region, as Jehovah had given it to Esau for a possession (Deut. 2:5). The mention of Esau's move to Mt. Seir follows immediately on the mention of Isaac's death and burial (Gen. 35:27–36:8). At the base of this chain of mountains are low hills of limestone or argillaceous rocks, then lofty masses of porphyry, which constitute the body of the mountain; above these is sandstone broken into irregular ridges and grotesque groups of cliffs; and again, farther back and higher than all, are long elevated ridges of limestone without precipices. Beyond all these stretches off indefinitely the high plateau of the great eastern desert. The height of the porphyry cliffs is estimated by Robinson at about two thousand feet above the Arabah (the great valley between the Dead Sea and Elanitic Gulf), whereas the limestone ridges farther back do not fall short of three thousand feet. The whole breadth of the mountainous tract between the Arabah and the eastern desert above is not more than fifteen or twenty miles. These mountains are quite different in character from those that front them on the W side of the Arabah. The latter seem to be not more than two-thirds as high, whereas those on the E appear to enjoy a sufficiency of rain and are covered with tufts of herbs and occasional

trees. The general appearance of the soil resembles that around Hebron, although the face of the country is different. It is, indeed, the region of which Isaac said to his son Esau, "Behold, away from the fertility of the earth shall be your dwelling, and away from the dew of heaven from above" (27:39).

Petra, the probable site of ancient Sela

The Land of Seir. This is the land located to the S and E of Beersheba. Esau married and had children long before he permanently left his old home near Beersheba, and that region over which Esau extended his patriarchal stretch came to be known as "the land of Seir" (or Esau) and the "country [or field] of Edom" (Gen. 32:3). Here Esau was living when Jacob came back from Paddan-aram, for Isaac was not yet dead, and it was not until after his death that Esau moved to Mt. Seir (35:27–36:8). When the brothers had met, Jacob spoke of himself as journeying by easy stages toward the home of Esau, in Seir—Esau's present "Seir," not Esau's prospective "Mount Seir" (cf. 33:13-20; 35:27). Then it was—and even until the very day of Jacob's return—that Esau was a dweller in "the land of Seir, the country of Edom" (32:1-3), not the Mt. Seir, or the Edom that as the equivalent of Mt. Seir. This designation of the land of Esau's occupancy in southern Canaan by the name "Seir," which existed at the time of Jacob's return from Paddan-aram, was never lost to it. It was found there when the Israelites made their unauthorized raid northward from Kadesh-barnea (Deut. 1:44). To the present time there remain traces of the old name of "Seir" in the region SE of Beersheba and yet N of the natural southern boundary line of the land of Canaan. The extensive plain "Es Seer" is there, corresponding with the name and location of "Seir" (1:44) at which, or unto which, the Israelites were chased by the Amorites when they went up in foolhardiness from Kadesh-barnea.

Another Mount Seir. This mountain formed one of the landmarks on the N boundary of Judah

(Josh. 15:10 only). It was to the W of Kiriath-jea-rim and between it and Beth-shemesh. It is a ridge of rock to the SW of Kureyet el Enab, a lofty ridge composed of rugged peaks with a wild and desolate appearance, upon which Saris and Mishir are situated (Robinson, *Biblical Researches,* p. 155).

BIBLIOGRAPHY: N. Glueck, *Hebrew Union College Annual* (1936), pp. 141-57.

SEI'RAH (se-ī'ra; "woody district, shaggy"). A place in the mountains of Ephraim, bordering on Benjamin, to which Ehud went for refuge after killing Eglon at Jericho (Judg. 3:26).

SE'LA (sē'la; "rock"; Judg. 1:36; cf. Obad. 3, marg.). Probably the capital city of the Edomites, later known as Petra. It took its name from its situation and the mode in which it was built, since it was erected in a valley surrounded by rocks and in such a manner that the houses were partly hewn in the natural rock. It was still flourishing in the first centuries of the Christian era, and splendid ruins still exist. The excavations are remarkable, consisting of what appear to be the facades of great temples and immense theaters, hewn in rock of variegated colors. The place seems to have been the center of interest and trade from time immemorial. It was taken by Amaziah, king of Judah, and called by him Joktheel (2 Kings 14:7; cf. 2 Chron. 25:11-12). In about 300 B.C. Sela (Gk. Petra, "rock") passed

View of the road to The Treasury, Petra

from the Edomites to the Nabataean Arabs, whose remarkable kingdom lasted till A.D. 105, when Arabia Petrea became a province of the Roman Empire.

SE'LAH (sē'la). Probably a musical notation indicating an intended pause.

SE'LA-HAMMAH'LEKOTH. *See* Rock of Escape.

SE'LED (se'led; "exultation"). A descendant of Jerahmeel, of the tribe of Judah. He was the elder of two sons of Nadab and died childless (1 Chron. 2:30).

SELEU'CIA (se-lū'shi-a). A town near the mouth of the Orontes and the seaport of *Antioch* (which see) from which Paul sailed forth on his first missionary journey (Acts 13:4). It is almost certain that he landed there on his return (14:26). It was built by Seleucus Nicator, who built so many other cities of the same name that this was one called Seleucia Pieria, being near Mt. Pierus, and also Seleucia ad Mare, being nearer the sea. It retained its importance in Roman times and was a free city in the days of Paul. Now called Magaracik.

SELF-CONTROL (Gk. *egkrateia*); "temperance," KJV. The virtue of one who masters his desires and passions, especially his sensual appetites (Acts 24:25; 1 Cor. 9:25; Gal. 5:23; 2 Pet. 1:6, where it is named as one of the Christian graces).

SELF-WILL (Heb. *rāṣôn,* "pleasure," and, in a wicked sense, "wantonness," Gen. 49:6). In the NT, self-willed is the rendering of Gk. *authadēs,* "self-pleasing, arrogant, overbearing" (Titus 1:7; 2 Pet. 2:10).

SELVEDGE. The edge of a woven or knitted fabric so prepared as not to ravel. The English term, from Heb. *qāṣâ,* "end," "extremity" (*TWOT*), does not appear in the NASB or NIV.

SEMACHI'AH (sem-a-kī'a; "Jehovah his sustained"), **Semaki'ah** (NIV). The last named of the six sons of Shemaiah, the son of Obed-edom (1 Chron. 26:7).

SEMAKI'AH. *See* Semachiah.

SEM'EIN (sem-ine). The son of Josech and father of Mattathias; in our Lord's genealogy (Luke 3:26) probably *Shemaiah* (which see).

SENA'AH (se-na'a). The "sons of Senaah" are enumerated among the "people of Israel" who returned from the captivity with Zerubbabel (Ezra 2:35; Neh. 7:38). In 3:3 the name is given with the article, has-Senaah. (*See* Hassenaah.) The names in these lists are mostly those of towns; but Senaah does not occur elsewhere in the Bible as attached to a town. The Magdal-Senna, or "great Senna," of Eusebius and Jerome, seven miles N of Jericho ("Senna"), however, is not inappropriate in position.

SENATE (Gk. *gerousia,* "eldership"). A deliberative body, and in the NT (Acts 5:21) of not only those elders of the people who were members of the Sanhedrin but *the whole body of elders* generally, the whole council of the representatives of the people (Meyer, *Com.,* ad loc.).

SENATORS (Heb. *zāqēn,* "old"; Ps. 105:22, KJV). Elders (so NASB, NIV).

SE'NEH (se'ne; "thornbush"). The name of one of the two isolated rocks that stood in the passage of Michmash, climbed by Jonathan and his armor-bearer, when he went to examine the Philistine camp (1 Sam. 14:4). It was the southern one of the two (14:5) and the nearest to Geba. The name in Hebrew means a "thorn," or thornbush. Josephus mentions that the last encampment of Titus's army was at a spot "which in the Jews' tongue is called the valley," or perhaps the plain "of thorns, near to a village called Gabath-saoulé," i.e., Gibeah of Saul.

SE'NIR (se'nîr; Deut. 3:9; 1 Chron. 5:23; Song of Sol. 4:8; Ezek. 27:5, "pointed," and so "peak"). The name given by the Amorites to Mt. *Hermon* (which see). The Sidonians called it Sirion, and in Ps. 29:6 Sirion is used poetically for Hermon.

SENNACH'ERIB (se-nak'er-ib; Akkad. "Sin," i.e., the moon god, "has multiplied the brothers"). Sennacherib, one of the kings of Assyria, son of Sargon, ascended the throne on the twelfth day of Ab (July-August), 705 B.C. His father, Sargon, had been a usurper, and having gained his position by the sword, he also lost his life by it at the hands of a murderous soldier. There seems to have been no opposition to Sennacherib's accession, as so often happened in the history of Assyria. He inherited a vast empire from his father, with abundant opportunities for its further extension. He had, however, not inherited his father's boldness or daring, or his resources. All the powers of his mind were employed in holding together that which he had received. It is indeed doubtful whether he left his empire as strong as he had received it.

The records of Sennacherib's reign have not come down to us in as complete a form as those of his predecessor or successor. Of the later years of his reign we have no Assyrian accounts. The earlier years are, however, well covered by the beautiful and well-preserved prism called the Taylor Cylinder, now in the British Museum. Of all Assyrian documents that have come down to us not one is in better preservation than this. It was found by Colonel Taylor in 1830. It is fourteen and one-half inches high and is covered on all of its six sides with fine Assyrian script, which sets forth the annals of the king. Complete translations of the records of Sennacherib can be

found in Daniel D. Luckenbill, *Ancient Records of Assyria and Babylonia,* vol. 2, and in James Pritchard's *Ancient Near Eastern Texts* (1950).

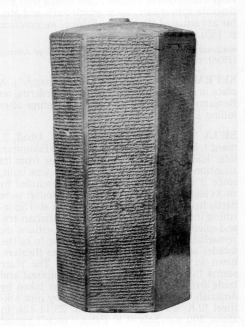

The prism of Sennacherib describing his campaigns and building activities

Against Babylon. Sargon had left a powerful empire, but not all sources of possible difficulty had been blotted out; neither had all peoples within the great territory been reduced to complete submission. Sennacherib was sure to meet with troubles in Babylonia. The people of Babylon had been brought into the Assyrian empire by force. They could not be expected to forget that they had had a magnificent history behind them while the people of Assyria were but laying the foundations of their state. It was hard for a city with so grand a history as Babylon's to yield submission to the upstart power of Assyria. In the confusion that followed the close of Sargon's reign the Babylonians saw the opportunity for another rebellion. The leader of this uprising was Merodach-baladan, who came from the lowland country far S of Babylon, near the Persian Gulf, called, in the texts of that period, the land of Kardunyash. It was probably a national uprising that Merodach-baladan led (*see* Merodach-baladan), but he had allies from the mountain land of Elam, and with their help he had himself crowned king in Babylon. Once more there was national rule in Babylonia, and the Assyrian supremacy was temporarily overthrown. For nine months Merodach-baladan reigned undisputedly.

Then Sennacherib invaded Babylonia with an army that Merodach-baladan could not effectively resist. The contest was fought at Kish, and the defeat of the Babylonians was complete. Merodach-baladan fled alone and escaped with his life. The victorious Sennacherib entered Babylon and plundered everything that had belonged to his unfortunate adversary but seems not to have disturbed the possessions of the citizens. He then marched S into the land of Kaldi, from where the rebels had drawn their supplies. The overthrow was complete in every particular. Seventy-five cities and four hundred smaller towns and hamlets were taken and despoiled. This invasion was carried out with heartless cruelty, as the description of the taking of one city testifies. Sennacherib said, "The men of the city Khirimme, a rebellious enemy, I cast down with arms; I left not one alive; their corpses I bound on stakes and placed them around the city." Over the reduced country an Assyrian named Bel-ibni was made king, subject to Sennacherib. But this was not the end of Sennacherib's difficulties with Babylonia.

Against the Kassites. Sennacherib's next campaign was directed against people called the Kassi, together with the Medes and other races living along and beyond the upper waters of the Tigris. Although he boasted of victory, there seems to have been little result from it. He claimed to have "widened his territory," but we can find no evidence that Assyrian supremacy was actually carried much farther. The chief result of the campaign was probably "a heavy tribute" and the intimidating of some peoples who otherwise might have been troublesome when campaigns against the West were undertaken.

Against Palestine-Syria. The third campaign of Sennacherib was directed against the land of the Hittites, 701 B.C. At this period this term did not mean the same as it did before the days of Sargon, who had destroyed the last of the Hittite city-states in 709 B.C. Land of the Hittites now meant only the land of Phoenicia and Palestine. This western country had often before been invaded by Babylonia and Assyria (*see* articles Assyria; Sargon; Shalmaneser; Tiglath-pileser; and Chedorlaomer), but conquests had temporary effect. Rebellions were frequent. It would be yet a long time before autonomy would die out among the commercial Phoenicians and the patriotic and religious Hebrews. Sennacherib seems to have come suddenly into the W, and his success at first was probably because of the unpreparedness of the native kings and princes. Elulaeus, king of Sidon, offered no resistance but fled from the invader. His cities of Sidon, Sarepta, Acco (now Acre), Ekdippa, and others were quickly subdued and plundered. Ethbaal was made king over them, and a heavy annual tribute was assessed upon the inhabitants. The news of this great Assyrian victory spread southward, and many petty kings sent presents and acknowl-

edged Sennacherib as their suzerain, hoping thereby to save their cities from destruction and their lands from plunder. Among those who thus yielded without a blow for freedom were the rulers of Arvad, Byblos, Moab, and Edom. The king of Ashkelon, Tsidqa, did not send tribute, and his land was therefore next attacked. The resistance seems to have been slight, and Ashkelon was soon taken. The king and all his family were deported to Assyria as captives, and his cities of Beth-dagon, Joppa, Beneberak (Josh. 19:45), and Azuru were plundered. The people of Ekron had also refused to submit to Sennacherib. Their ruler, Padi, who had been set over them by the Assyrians, was chained and delivered over to Hezekiah, king of Judah. This move on their part probably signifies their allegiance to the league of Judah and Egypt, which proposed to resist Sennacherib. When Sennacherib was ready to attack Ekron the Egyptian army appeared accompanied by its allies from Melukhkha. A battle took place at Eltekeh (19:44; 21:23), and once more Sennacherib claimed a victory. Of the fight he says little, except that a few captives were taken. He did not, however, follow up the Egyptians, and it is therefore probable that he respected their prowess and was desirous of avoiding the risk of a second and desperate conflict. He was content rather with taking Eltekeh and Timnah (Gen. 38:12; Josh. 15:10; etc.; modern Tibneh), then falling back to punish Ekron. His own words describe his deeds: "To the city of Ekron I went; the governors (and) princes, who had committed a transgression, I killed and bound their corpses on poles around the city. The inhabitants of the city who had committed sin and evil I counted as spoil; to the rest of them who had committed no sin and wrong, who had no guilt, I spoke peace. Padi, their king, I brought forth from the city of Jerusalem; upon the throne of lordship over them I placed him. The tribute of my lordship I laid upon him."

Invasion of Judah. Immediately upon this victory over Ekron came Sennacherib's invasion of the kingdom of Judah. This is known to us from the biblical account in 2 Kings 18:13–19:36. It fills a large space in Israel's history, and it was a moment of thrilling interest when Sennacherib's own version of the invasion was found. His story is so important for the student of the Bible that it is here translated entire: "As for Hezekiah the Jew, who did not submit to my yoke, forty-six of his strong walled cities, as well as the small cities in their neighborhood, which were without number—by constructing a rampart out of trampled earth and by bringing up battering rams, by the attack of infantry, by tunnels, breaches and *the use of axes*, I besieged and took. Two hundred thousand one hundred and fifty men, young *and* old, male and female, horses, mules, asses, camels, oxen and sheep without number I brought out from them, I counted as spoil. *Hezekiah* himself I shut up like a caged bird in Jerusalem, his royal city; the walls I fortified against him, *and* whosoever came out of the gates of the city, I turned back. His cities, which I had plundered, I divided from his land and gave them to Mitinti, king of Ashdod, to Padi, king of Ekron, and to Sillibel, king of Gaza, and *thus* diminished his territory. To the former tribute, paid yearly, I added the tribute of alliance of my lordship and laid that upon him. Hezekiah himself was overwhelmed by the fear of the brightness of my lordship; the Arabians and his other faithful warriors whom, as a defense for Jerusalem his royal city he had brought in, fell into fear. With thirty talents of gold *and* eight hundred talents of silver, precious stones, rouge dakkasi, lapis lazuli, couches of ivory, thrones of ivory, ivory, *ushu* wood, *ukarinnu* wood, various objects, a heavy treasure, and his daughters, his women of the palace, male and female musicians, to Nineveh, the city of my lordship, I caused to be brought after me; and he sent his ambassadors to give tribute and to pay homage." Sennacherib does not name the place where he received this great tribute from Hezekiah. From the Bible we learn that it was Lachish (18:14). From Sennacherib we also learn that he had besieged and taken the same city of Lachish, present-day Tell ed-Duweir, now well known as a result of archaeological excavation. A splendid wall relief from his palace at Nineveh and now in the British Museum depicts the event. Sennacherib is represented seated upon a throne receiving men bearing presents. In front of the king's head are these words: "Sennacherib, the king of the world, the king of Assyria, sat on his throne, and the spoil of the city of Lachish marched before him." With the words, given above, of tribute and embassies of homage Sennacherib concluded his account of his campaigns to the W. The biblical account

adds one detail more in these words: "Then it happened that night that the angel of the Lord went out, and struck 185,000 in the camp of the Assyrians; and when men rose early in the morning, behold, all of them were dead" (2 Kings 19:35). Of this great destruction there is no hint in Sennacherib's inscriptions. It was indeed not to be expected that such a record would be made under any circumstances. The Assyrians reported only victories. At any rate Sennacherib never invaded Palestine again. The chronological data of the Assyrians locate this famous Judean campaign in the year 701 B.C.

Later Campaigns. After the Judean campaign Sennacherib found opposed to him a powerful coalition of Elamites, Babylonians, Aramaeans, and Medians, with whom he fought at Chalule in the year 691 B.C. The result was a doubtful victory for the Assyrian army. It seems indeed that Sennacherib did little more than ward off destruction and postpone for a time the inevitable ruin of the empire.

Again and again there was trouble and rebellion in Babylonia. Now it is the once-defeated Merodach-baladan, again it is Suzub, the Chaldean. Indeed so numerous were the uprisings in Babylonia that it is now almost impossible to distinguish them and understand their significance. After several invasions and fruitless peacemakings, Sennacherib took Babylon, broke down its walls, and practically ruined the city. This was in 689 B.C. In this year came thus to an end for a time the glory of this once invincible city. The destruction can only be regarded as an act of revengeful folly. It did not quell the turbulent spirits of the Babylonians, who could not be brought into subjection by such means, and it only left a legacy of trouble to Sennacherib's sons and successor. Sennacherib's own opinion of the people of Babylonia was expressed in the phrase "evil devils." He could not understand them, and their patriotic love of the city by the Euphrates was not a sentiment to be admired but passion to be destroyed.

The result of all these wars was only retention of what Sargon had won. Of real expansion there was none.

In spite of wars and dissensions Sennacherib was able also to give attention to the arts of peace. In Nineveh he constructed two magnificent palaces, and the city walls and gates he rebuilt or restored. By constructing the huge so-called Aqueduct of Jerwan, Sennacherib made Nineveh a garden city. This, the first Mesopotamian aqueduct known, brought water from some thirty miles distant. He also introduced the *shadūf* or well sweep from Egypt.

The inscriptions give no hint concerning the manner of Sennacherib's death in the year 681 B.C. The Bible, however, supplies the missing detail by showing that he died at the hands of his

Sennacherib on his throne before Lachish

two sons, Adrammelech and Sharezer, while he was engaged in worship (19:37). These statements agree well with the known facts that Sennacherib had preferred Esarhaddon above his brothers and that there was jealousy among the other members of the family.

BIBLIOGRAPHY: D. D. Luckenbill, *The Annals of Sennacherib* (1924); L. L. Honor, *Sennacherib's Invasion of Judah* (1926); D. W. Thomas, ed., *Documents from Old Testament Times* (1958), pp. 64-73; H. H. Rowley, *Bulletin of the John Rylands Library* 44 (1962): 395-431; D. D. Luckenbill, *Ancient Records of Assyria and Babylonia* (1968), 2:160-98; J. B. Pritchard, ed., *Ancient Near Eastern Texts* (1969), pp. 221, 272-73, 287-89, 291, 301-3, 309, 427-28, 450, 531, 606.

SENSE.
1. (Heb. *šekel* "intelligence"). Thus it is said that Ezra and others "read from the book, from the law of God, translating to give the sense" (Neh. 8:8), i.e., caused the people to understand.
2. Gk. *aisthētērion,* "faculty of the mind" for perceiving, understanding, judging (Heb. 5:14).

SENSUAL. The KJV use of the term in James 3:15; Jude 19 is taken from Gk. *psuchikos,* given as "natural" or "worldly-minded" in the NASB, and "unspiritual," or "natural" in the NIV. It refers to having the nature and characteristics of the *psuchē,* i.e., of the principle of animal life, which men have in common with the beasts (1 Cor. 15:44). It has also the meaning of being governed by the *psuchē,* i.e., by the sensuous nature with its subjection to appetite and passion (Jude 19; cf. 1 Cor. 2:14). So in James 3:15, sensual wisdom is that which is in harmony with the corrupt desires and springing from them.

The term in the NASB is taken from other Gk. and Heb. words in the original and has the meaning of voluptuous (Isa. 47:8), sensual (Ezek. 33:32), physical desire (1 Tim. 5:11), or sensuality (2 Pet. 2:7).

SENSUALITY (Gk. *'aselgeia,* that which "excites disgust"; the term does not appear in the KJV, the Gk. term usually being given there as "lasciviousness"). Unbridled lust, licentiousness, lasciviousness, wantonness. It is included in the list of evil products named by our Lord (Mark 7:22), and is included with drunkenness and carousing (1 Pet. 4:3) and "the deeds of the flesh" such as immorality and impurity (2 Cor. 12:21; Gal. 5:19; Eph. 4:19). In Jude 4 the Gk. is rendered "licentiousness" and is used to describe what ungodly persons turn the grace of God into. The NIV uses the word only in Eph. 4:19.

SENTENCES. The "hard sentences" of Dan. 5:12, KJV, are enigmas (so NASB), or riddles (so NIV); the ability to understand "dark sentences" (Dan. 8:23, KJV) refers to skill in intrigue (so NASB, NIV) or skill in "ambiguous speech," the marginal reading.

SEPARATION. The Levitical law provided that persons contaminated by certain defilements should be excluded for a longer or shorter period from the fellowship of the sanctuary and sometimes even from relations with their fellow countrymen. These defilements comprised the uncleanness of a woman in consequence of childbearing (Lev. 12), leprosy (chaps. 13-14), both natural and diseased secretions from the sexual organs of either male or female (chap. 15), and from a human corpse (Num. 19:11-22). *See* Uncleanness.

SE'PHAR (se'far; "numbering"). "The hill country of the east," mentioned in connection with the Joktanite boundaries (Gen. 10:30). The immigration of the Joktanites was probably from W to E, and they occupied the SW portion of the Arabian peninsula. There is some agreement that Sephar is preserved in the ancient city of Zhafar—now pronounced Isfôr—in the province of Hadramaut, of South Arabia, not far from the seaport Mirbat.

SEPHA'RAD (se-fa'rad). In Obadiah (v. 20) it is said that the exiles of Jerusalem were "in Sepharad." Sepharad may possibly be Sardis in W Asia Minor or a part of Media SW of the Caspian Sea. The name occurs in Assyrian inscriptions and may have a connection with Shaparda mentioned by Sargon as a district of SW Media (cf. 2 Kings 17:6).

SEPHARVAIM (se-far-va'yim). The name of a city under Assyrian rule, from which people were transported and settled in Samaria, in the reign of Sargon, along with other people from Cuthah, Babylon, Avva, and Hamath (2 Kings 17:24). It appears from other biblical allusions that Sepharvaim was in a country that had but a short time before this been conquered by the Assyrians; it was not in a land that formed an integral portion of the Assyrian empire (2 Kings 18:34; 19:13; Isa. 36:19; 37:13). It has been identified commonly with the city Sippar, the ruins of which were found by Hormuzd Rassam, at Abu Habba, SW of Baghdad, and near the Euphrates. This identification is, however, fraught with great difficulty and may indeed be regarded as practically impossible. Sepharvaim has a different form from Sippar; it is mentioned always in connection with Hamath, as though it were located in the vicinity; it was recently conquered by the Assyrians while Sippar was an ancient city in Babylonian territory. For these and other reasons scholars have with practical unanimity ceased to connect Sepharvaim with the ancient Babylonian city of Sippar. Instead of this the identification proposed by Halevy has received common acceptance, namely, that Sepharvaim is the same as the city Sibraim (Ezek. 47:16) and that this is the city mentioned in the Babylonian chronicle under the name of Saberim, which lies in the Hamath district and was conquered by Shalmaneser V in 727

B.C. In these particulars it exactly suits the requirements of the biblical Sepharvaim. The proof is, however, not positive, although the case is at least plausible.

SE'PHARVITE (se'far-vīt). A native of *Sepharvaim* (which see; 2 Kings 17:31).

SEP'TUAGINT. *See* Versions of the Scripture.

SEPULCHER. *See* Tomb.

SE'RAH (se'ra). The daughter of Asher, the son of Jacob (Gen. 46:17; Num. 26:46, "Sarah," KJV; 1 Chron. 7:30). The mention of her name in a list of this kind, in which no others of her sex are named, and contrary to the usual practice of the Jews, seems to indicate something extraordinary in connection with her history or circumstances. The Jews have a tradition that she was remarkable for piety and virtue and was therefore privileged to be the first person to tell Jacob that his son Joseph was still living; on which account she was translated to paradise, where, according to the ancient book Zohar, are four mansions, each presided over by an illustrious woman: Serah, daughter of Asher; the daughter of Pharaoh, who brought up Moses; Jochebed, the mother of Moses; and Deborah, the prophetess.

SERA'IAH (se-ra'ya; "Jehovah has prevailed").
1. The scribe (or "secretary") of David (2 Sam. 8:17), 986 B.C. In other places the name is corrupted into "Sheva" (20:25), "Shisha" (1 Kings 4:3), and "Shavsha" (1 Chron. 18:16).
2. The son of Azariah and high priest in the reign of Zedekiah (2 Kings 25:18; 1 Chron. 6:14; Ezra 7:1). When Jerusalem was captured by the Chaldeans, 587 B.C. he was sent as a prisoner to Nebuchadnezzar at Riblah and there was put to death (Jer. 52:24-27).
3. An Israelite, the son of Tanhumeth the Netophathite, and one of those to whom Gedaliah advised submission to the Chaldeans (2 Kings 25:23; Jer. 40:8), 588 B.C.
4. The second son of Kenaz and father of a Joab, who was the "father of Ge-harashim," i.e., head of a family of the tribe of Judah, in the "valley of craftsmen" (1 Chron. 4:13-14, *see* marg.).
5. Son of Asiel and father of Joshibiah, of the tribe of Simeon (1 Chron. 4:35).
6. A priest who returned from the captivity (Ezra 2:2; Neh. 12:1, 12), 536 B.C. He is, perhaps, the same who is mentioned (Neh. 10:2) as signing the covenant with Nehemiah as "leader of the house of God" (11:11).
7. The son of Azriel and one of the persons commanded by King Jehoiakim to apprehend Jeremiah and Baruch (Jer. 36:26), about 606 B.C.
8. The son of Neriah and brother of Baruch (Jer. 51:59; 61). He went with Zedekiah to Babylon in the fourth year of his reign and is described as *śar-menûhâ*, "quartermaster," a title

that is interpreted by Kimchi as that of the office of chamberlain. Perhaps he was an officer who took charge of the royal caravan on its march and fixed the place where it should halt. Seraiah was sent on an embassy to Babylon about four years before the fall of Jerusalem and was commissioned by the prophet Jeremiah to take with him on his journey the scroll in which he had written the doom of Babylon. He was to sink it in the midst of the Euphrates as a token that Babylon would sink, never to rise again (Jer. 51:60-64), 595 B.C.

SERAPHIM. (Heb. perhaps *śārāp*, "burning, fiery"). The meaning of the word *seraph* is extremely doubtful; the only word that resembles it in the current Hebrew is *śārap*, "to burn," whence the idea of *brilliancy* has been extracted; but it is objected that the Heb. term never bears this secondary sense. Gesenius connects it with an Arab. term *shrafa* signifying "high" or "exalted"; and this may be regarded as the generally received etymology.

Nature. An order of celestial beings, whom Isaiah beheld in vision standing above Jehovah as He sat upon His throne (Isa. 6:2, 6). They are described as each of them having three pairs of wings; with one they covered their faces (a token of humility), with the second they covered their feet (a token of respect), while with the third they flew. They seem to have borne a general resemblance to the human figure, for they are represented as having face, voice, feet, and hands (v. 2).

Occupation. The seraphim that Isaiah saw hovered above on both sides of Him that sat upon the throne, forming two opposite choirs and presenting antiphonal worship. Their occupation was twofold—to celebrate the praises of Jehovah's holiness and power (v. 3) and to act as the medium of communication between heaven and earth (v. 6). They are beings expressive of the divine holiness and demand that the saint shall be cleansed before serving (Isa. 6:6-8). From their antiphonal chant ("one called out to another") we may conceive them to have been ranged in opposite rows on each side of the throne. *See* Cherubim.

BIBLIOGRAPHY: E. J. Young, *The Book of Isaiah* (1965), 1:234-53.

SERAPHS. *See* Seraphim.

SE'RED (se'red; cf. Syr. *serad*, "to be affrighted"). The firstborn of Zebulun (Gen. 46:14) and head of the family of the Seredites (Num. 26:26).

SERGEANTS. *See* Policemen.

SER'GIUS PAUL'US (sur'ji-us-pawl'us). The Roman proconsul of Cyprus at the time when Paul, with Barnabas, visited that island on his first missionary tour. He is described as an intelligent man, and hence entertained Elymas, desiring to learn the truth. On becoming acquainted with Barnabas and Paul he was convinced of the truth and accepted the gospel (Acts 13:7-12).

SERMON ON THE MOUNT. The name usually given to a discourse delivered by Jesus to His disciples and a multitude on a mountain near Capernaum, A.D., perhaps 28 (Matt. 5-7; Luke 6:20-49). The time, however, is no more distinctly given than is the place. Meyer (*Com.,* ad loc.) believes that it was after Jesus had chosen His first four apostles and that "His disciples," in addition to these four, were His disciples generally. Edersheim (*Life and Times of Jesus,* 1:524) locates it immediately after the choice of the twelve, grouping together Luke 6:12-13, 17-19; cf. with Mark 3:13-15 and Matt. 5:1-2.

The Discourse Itself. "It is the same as that found in Luke 6:20-49; for, although differing in respect of its contents, style, and arrangement from that of Matthew, yet, judging from its characteristic introduction and close, its manifold and essential identity as regards the subject-matter, as well as from its mentioning the circumstance that, immediately after, Jesus cured the sick servant in Capernaum (Luke 7:1, ff.), it is clear that Matthew and Luke do not record two different discourses" (Meyer, *Com.*).

The plan, according to Gess, is as follows: the happiness of those who are fit for the kingdom (Matt. 5:3-12); the lofty vocation of Jesus' disciples (5:13-16); the righteousness, superior to that of the Pharisees, after which they must strive who would enter the kingdom (5:17–6:34); the rocks on which they run the risk of striking, and the help against such dangers (7:1-27).

Its Application. This remarkable discourse of Jesus has first of all an all-time moral application, and hence its principles are applicable to the Christian. It is a perennial truth that the pure in spirit, rather than the proud, are blessed and that those who mourn because of their sins, who are meek and hunger and thirst after righteousness are filled. The merciful are always blessed, and the pure in heart "see God." However, in the Jewish slant of Matthew, presenting Christ as King, premillennialists frequently hold the application to be literally the establishment of the future Davidic kingdom. This discourse gives the divine constitution for the righteous government of the earth. It will be the fulfillment of "righteousness" as used by the prophets in describing this kingdom that is to be restored to Israel (cf. Isa. 11:4-5; 32:1; Dan. 9:24). In the time of our Lord the Jews rejected the kingdom because they had made "righteousness" to mean mere ceremonialism and had missed its deeper meaning as a matter of motive and of the heart. The Jews were never rebuked for expecting a visible messianic kingdom. Had they heeded the prophets, however, they would have plainly seen that

only the spiritually poor, the meek, and the pure in heart would have a share in it (Isa. 11:4; Ps. 72). Careful exegesis of the Sermon on the Mount must not confuse it with the era of grace initiated by the death, resurrection, and ascension of Christ. The sermon is commonly construed by expositors as applicable solely to the Christian church. This interpretation, however, can scarcely be reconciled with its scope and purpose, particularly in the gospel of Matthew.

BIBLIOGRAPHY: D. M. Lloyd-Jones, *Studies in the Sermon of the Mount,* 2 vols. (1959); W. D. Davies, *The Setting of the Sermon on the Mount* (1964); J. M. Boice, *The Sermon on the Mount* (1972); W. S. Kissinger, *The Sermon on the Mount: A History of Interpretation and Bibliography* (1975); R. A. Guelich, *The Sermon on the Mount* (1982).

SERPENT. *See* Animal Kingdom; Temptation.

Figurative. The malice of the wicked is compared to the "venom of a serpent" (Ps. 58:4; cf. 140:3); the poisonous bite of the serpent is a figure of the harmful influence of wine (Prov. 23:31-32); unexpected evil is like the bite of a serpent lurking in a wall (Eccles. 10:8), and there is no profit for the charmer of an uncharmed serpent that bites (10:11); enemies who harass and destroy are compared to serpents (Isa. 14:29; Jer. 8:17), whereas the voice of discomfited Egypt is likened to serpents roused from their lair by the woodcutter (46:22). The serpent is a figure for hypocrites (Matt. 23:33), those who are prudent (10:16); and the handling of serpents (Mark 16:18) is mentioned as a proof of supernatural protection (cf. Acts 28:36). *See* Brazen Serpent; Satan.

SERPENT, BRONZE. *See* Bronze Serpent.

SERPENT, FIERY (Heb. *śārāp* "burning," Num. 21:6; Deut. 8:15). As the Israelites traveled around the land of Edom they found food and water scarce and rebelled against Jehovah. In consequence they were afflicted by a plague of fiery serpents (lit., "burning snakes"), so called from their burning, i.e., inflammatory, bite, which filled the victim with heat and poison. The punishment brought the people to reflection and confession of sin. They were pardoned through faith, which they manifested by looking to the *bronze serpent* (which see). The fiery flying serpents (Isa. 30:6) may be so called because of rapid movement, which appears like a flight, or it may refer to a species of serpent, the *Naja tripudians,* which dilates its hood into a kind of shining wing on each side of the neck and is poisonous.

SERPENT CHARMING. The art of taming serpents (Heb. *laḥash,* a "whisper," Jer. 8:17; Eccles. 10:11); those who practiced the art were known as *menaḥashîm.* There can be no question at all of the remarkable power that, from time immemorial, has been exercised by certain people in the East over poisonous serpents. The art is most distinctly mentioned in the Bible and is probably alluded to by James (James 3:7). The usual species operated upon, both in Africa and in India, are the hooded snakes (*Naja tripudians* and *Naja haje*) and the horned *Cerstes*. It is probable that the charmers frequently, and perhaps generally, take the precaution of extracting the poison fangs before the snakes are subjected to their skill, but that this operation is not always attended to is clear from the testimony of Bruce and numerous other writers. Some have supposed that the practice of taking out or breaking off the poison fangs is alluded to in Ps. 58:6, "Shatter their teeth in their mouth." The serpent charmer's usual instrument is a flute.

SE'RUG (se'rug; "shoot, tendril"; "Seruch," KJV, Luke 3:35). The son of Reu, father of Nahor, the grandfather of Abraham (Gen. 11:20; 1 Chron. 1:26; Luke 3:35). When thirty years of age he begat Nahor and lived two hundred years afterward, before 2300 B.C. A city by this name in Mesopotamia near Harn attests the presence of the Hebrew patriarchs in this region.

SERVANT. See Service.

SERVANT OF JEHO'VAH ("My servant," etc.). A term used figuratively in several senses:

1. A *worshiper* of God (Neh. 1:10) and Daniel in particular (Dan. 6:20); pious persons, such as Abraham (Ps. 105:6, 42), Joshua (Josh. 24:29; Judg. 2:8), and many others.

2. A *minister* or ambassador of God on some special service (Isa. 49:6), e.g., Nebuchadnezzar, whom God used to chastise His people (Jer. 27:6; 43:10); but usually some favorite servant, such as the *angels* (Job 4:18); *prophets* (Ezra 9:11; Jer. 7:25; Dan. 9:6; Amos 3:7); and especially *Moses* (Deut. 34:5; Josh. 1:1, 13, 15; Ps. 105:26). Paul and other apostles call themselves the "bond-servant of Christ Jesus" and "of God" (Rom. 1:1; Col. 4:12; Titus 1:1; James 1:1; 2 Pet. 1:1; Jude 1; Rev. 1:1).

3. The *Messiah* is typified as the servant of the Lord for accomplishing the work of redemption (Isa. 42:1; 52:13; cf. Matt. 12:18).

4. The term *servant* is also applied to the relation of men to others occupying high positions: such as Eliezer, who had a position in Abraham's household something similar to that of a prime minister at court (Gen. 15:2; 24:2); Joshua, in relation to Moses (Ex. 33:11); Gehazi, in relation to Elisha (2 Kings 4:12), etc. See Service.

BIBLIOGRAPHY: H. H. Rowley, *The Servant of the Lord* (1952), pp. 1-88; R. D. Culver, *The Sufferings and Glory of the Lord's Righteous Servant* (1958); J. Brown, *The Sufferings and Glories of the Messiah* (1959); O. Cullmann, *The Christology of the New Testament* (1963), pp. 51-82; D. Baron, *The Servant of Jehovah* (1977).

SERVICE. The rendering of several Heb. and Gk. words: Heb. *'ābad*, to "serve, work"; *shārat*, to "attend"; Gk. *diakonia*, "attendance"; *leitourgia*, "public function," as of a priest; *douleuō*, to "be a slave"; *latreuō*, to "minister."

Although there were persons employed for wages (*see* Hireling), the servants of the Israelites, as of other ancient peoples, consisted chiefly of slaves—men and women servants—held as property. These were bought from neighboring nations or from foreign residents in Canaan, were captives taken in war, or were children of slaves born in the house of the master. Insofar as anything like slavery existed, it was a mild and merciful system, as compared to that of other nations. It cannot be said to be a Mosaic institution at all, but, being found by the Jewish lawgiver, it was regulated by statute with the purpose and tendency of mitigating its evils and of restricting its duration. One source of slavery was branded with utter reprobation by Moses; the punishment of death was the penalty for stealing or making merchandise of a human being, whether an Israelite (Deut. 24:7) or foreigner (Ex. 21:61). With regard to the kind of service that might be exacted by Hebrew masters from their servants, a distinction was made between those who were of their own brethren and foreigners.

Hebrew. Because the Israelites were the servants of God they were not to be treated, when they became servants to their brethren, as bond-servants but as hired servants and sojourners, and their masters were to rule over them with kindness (Lev. 25:39). In several ways a Hebrew might become the servant of his brethren:

1. When he, through poverty, became unable to maintain himself as an independent citizen, in which case he might pass by sale under the power of another (Ex. 21:2). "The passage which lays down the law in such a case (Lev. 25:39) does not imply that the sale was compulsory, but is understood by Rosenmüller, Gesenius, Knobel, and others, as meaning that the individual sold himself, or rather the right to his labor, to some one of his brethren, that he might obtain the means of subsistence for himself and family" (Lindsay, in *Imperial Bible Dictionary*.).

2. By the commission of a theft. The law required restitution to the extent at least of double the value of the amount stolen and in some cases even five times more. If the thief could not make the required restitution, then he was to be sold for his theft (Ex. 22:3) and so by his labor make the restitution.

3. The children of a Hebrew servant became, by the condition of their *birth*, servants of the master (Ex. 21:4).

4. Although it is not clearly stated in the law that a man might be claimed personally and with his children sold by his creditors, in fact the person and children of a debtor were claimed (2 Kings 4:1; Neh. 5:5; cf. Isa. 50:1; Job 24:9). From Lev. 25:39, 47, it may be understood that

while the impoverished man might sell himself it was only to work off his debt till the Jubilee year.

5. Every Israelite, male or female, who had become a slave might be redeemed at any time by relatives. If not thus redeemed he was bound to receive his freedom without payment after six years' service, with a present of cattle and food (Ex. 21:2; Deut. 15:12-15). If he brought a wife with him into service, she received her freedom with him; if he received a wife from his master, then she and her children remained in bondage (Ex. 21:3; Jer. 34:8-10).

6. Respecting a female Israelite sold to another Israelite as housekeeper and concubine, these conditions prevailed: (a) She could not "go free as the male slaves do," i.e., she could not leave at the termination of six years or in the year of Jubilee, if her master was willing to fulfill the object for which he had purchased her (Ex. 21:7). (b) If she did not please her lord she was to be immediately redeemed, not sold to a foreign people (v. 8). (c) If he betrothed her to his son, he was bound to make such provision for her as he would for one of his own daughters (v. 9). (d) If either he or his son, having married her, took a second wife, it should not be to the prejudice of the first, either in respect to support, clothing, or cohabitation (v. 10). (e) In failure of these, she was freed without money (v. 11).

7. If a Hebrew servant, from love for master or wife and children, preferred not to accept freedom in the seventh year, but wished to remain in his master's house, he was brought before the elders and had his ear bored against a door or post with an awl in token of lifelong servitude (Ex. 21:6; Deut. 15:17). The boring of the ear is found among many Eastern people as a token of servitude, not only in the case of slaves but also of dervishes and others devoted to a deity. This act was not prescribed in the law as symbolizing anything shameful or despicable; for Moses sought to protect and restore personal freedom and could not therefore approve of anyone's voluntarily devoting himself to perpetual slavery. It was allowed because love and the allegiance of love were prized more highly than loveless personal freedom (Keil, *Biblical Archaeology*). The custom of reducing Hebrews to servitude appears to have fallen into disuse subsequent to the Babylonian captivity. Vast numbers of Hebrews were reduced to slavery as war captives at different periods by the Phoenicians (Joel 3:6), the Philistines (Amos 1:6), the Syrians (1 Macc. 3:41; 2 Macc. 8:11); the Egyptians (Josephus *Ant.* 12.2.2-3), and, above all, by the Romans.

Hebrew Slave and Foreign Master. Should a Hebrew become the servant of a "stranger," meaning a non-Hebrew, the servitude could be terminated only in two ways, by the arrival of the year of Jubilee or by the repayment to the master of the purchase money paid for the servant, after deducting the value of the services already ren-

dered. The estimate was based upon the pay of a hired laborer (Lev. 25:47-55).

Non-Hebrew Slaves. The source of non-Hebrew slaves and their legal standing were treated in the Pentateuch; information concerning the procedures for freeing them comes from extrabiblical sources.

Source. The majority of non-Hebrew slaves were war captives, either of the Canaanites who had survived the general extermination of their race under Joshua, or such as were conquered from the other surrounding nations (Num. 31:26-28). Besides these, many were obtained by purchase from foreign slave dealers (Lev. 25:44-45); and others may have been resident foreigners who were reduced to this state either by poverty or crime. The children of slaves remained slaves, being the class described as "born in the house" (Gen. 14:14; 17:12; Eccles. 2:7), and hence the number was likely to increase as time went on. The average value of a slave appears to have been thirty shekels (Ex. 21:32).

Legal Standing. The slave is described as the "possession" of his master, apparently with a special reference to the power that the latter had of disposing of him to his heirs as he would any other article of personal property (Lev. 25:45-46); the slave is also described as his master's "property" (Ex. 21:21), i.e., as representing a certain money value.

Freeing. That the slave might be set free appears in Ex. 21:26-27. As to the methods by which this might be effected we are told nothing in the Bible; but the rabbinists specify the following four methods: (1) redemption by a money payment, (2) a bill or ticket of freedom, (3) testamentary disposition, or (4) any act that implied freedom, such as making a slave one's heir.

Protection. Both respecting the Israelite and the stranger, provision was made for the protection of his person (Lev. 24:17, 22; Ex. 21:20). A minor personal injury, such as the loss of an eye or a tooth, was to be recompensed by giving the servant his liberty (21:26-27). The position of the slave in regard to religious privileges was favorable. He was to be circumcised (Gen. 17:12) and therefore was entitled to partake of the paschal sacrifice (Ex. 12:44) as well as to participate in the other religious festivals (Deut. 12:12, 18; 16:11, 14) and enjoy the rest of the Sabbath (Ex. 20:11; Deut. 5:14).

BIBLIOGRAPHY: R. H. Barrow, *Slavery in the Roman Empire* (1928); I. Mendelsohn, *Slavery in the Ancient Near East* (1949); W. L. Westermann, *The Slave Systems of Greek and Roman Antiquity* (1955); M. I. Finley, ed., *Slavery in Classical Antiquity* (1960); J. Vogt, *Ancient Slavery and the Idea of Man* (1974); N. Turner, *Christian Words* (1980), pp. 389-90.

SETH (seth). The third son of Adam and father of Enos when he was 105 years old. He died at the age of 912 (Gen. 4:25-26; 5:3-8; 1 Chron. 1:1; Luke 3:38). The significance of his name is "appointed" or "put" in the place of the murdered Abel; but Ewald believes that another signification, which he prefers, is indicated in the text, namely, "seedling," or "germ."

SE'THUR (se'thur; "hidden"). Son of Michael, the representative of the tribe of Asher among the twelve spies sent by Moses to view the Promised Land (Num. 13:13), c. 1440 B.C.

SEVENTH NEW MOON (or feast of Trumpets). *See* Festivals; Sacrifices.

SEVENTY DISCIPLES OF OUR LORD (Luke 10:1, 17). These were, doubtless, persons other than the "twelve," whom our Lord seems to have kept by His side. Considerable speculation has arisen owing to the number seventy; some believe that Jesus had in view the ancient Hebrew analogue of the seventy—originally seventy-two— *elders of the people* (Num. 11:16-25). Godet (*Com.,* on Luke) says, "There is another explanation of the number which seems to us more natural. The Jews held, agreeably to Gen. 10, that the human race was made up of seventy (or seventy-two) peoples—fourteen descended from Japhet, thirty from Ham, and twenty-six from Shem."

SEVENTY WEEKS. These are seventy weeks of years referred to in Daniel's prophecy (Dan. 9:20-27). During these seventy weeks of seven years each Daniel prophesied that Israel's national chastisement would be terminated and the nation reestablished in "everlasting righteousness" (v. 24). In Daniel's vision the weeks are divided into three parts, seven weeks equaling 49 years; sixty-two weeks, totaling 434 years; one week equaling 7 years (vv. 25-27). In the seven weeks, or 49 years, Jerusalem was to be reconstructed in "times of distress." This was brought to pass as recorded in the books of Ezra-Nehemiah. In the sixty-two weeks, or 434 years, the Messiah was to come at His first advent (v. 25), fulfilled in the Messiah's birth and His being "cut off" and having "nothing" at the crucifixion. The date of Christ's crucifixion is evidently not specified except that it is to be after the "sixty-two weeks." The city was to be destroyed by "the people of the prince who is to come." This was fulfilled by the Romans under Titus in A.D. 70. Verse 27, by many commentators, is connected immediately with the events of the first advent. However, many premillennialists place it in the end time and between vv. 26 and 27. In this extended period they place the church age as an era unrevealed in OT prophecy (Matt. 13:11-17; Eph. 3:1-10). During this time it is maintained that the mysteries of the kingdom of heaven (Matt. 13:1-50) and the out-calling of the church are consummated. According to this view, the church age will terminate at an unspecified moment and will usher in Daniel's seventieth week. The personage of v. 27 thus, under their interpre-

tation, is identical with the little horn of Dan. 7, who will make a covenant with the Jews to restore their Judaic ritual for one week—seven years. In the middle of the week he will break the covenant and fulfill 12:11 and 2 Thess. 2:3-11. This interpretation views v. 27 as dealing with the last three-and-one-half years of the Great Tribulation (Matt. 24:15-28). This era is connected with the "time of distress" spoken of by Daniel (Dan. 12:1), with the "abomination of desolation" (Matt. 24:15) and with the "hour of testing" (Rev. 3:10). It is thus apparent that Dan. 9:27 is a battleground between the various millennial schools of eschatological thought. *See* Daniel, Book of; Weeks.   M.F.U.

BIBLIOGRAPHY: R. Anderson, *The Coming Prince* (1957); J. F. Walvoord, *Daniel: Key to Prophetic Revelation* (1967); L. J. Wood, *A Commentary on Daniel* (1972); H. A. Ironside and F. C. Ottman, *Biblical Eschatology* (1983).

SEXTARIUS or **Xestes.** A foreign measure of capacity. *See* Metrology.

SHAALAB'BIN (sha-a-lab'in; Josh. 19:42), or **Shaalbim** (shā-ăl'bĭm; Judg. 1:35; 1 Kings 4:9). A town in Dan named between Ir-shemesh and Aijalon (Josh. 19:42). It is frequently mentioned in the history of David and Solomon under the latter form. It may possibly be the present Selbit, three miles NW of Aijalon.

SHAAL'BONITE (sha-al'bō-nit). Eliahba the Shaalbonite was one of David's thirty-seven mighty men (2 Sam. 23:32; 1 Chron. 11:33). He was a native of a place named Shaalbon, which is not mentioned elsewhere, unless it is identical with Shaalbim or Shaalabbin, of the tribe of Dan.

SHA'ALIM, LAND OF (sha'a-lim; "foxes"). The region through which Saul passed in looking for the donkeys of Kish, which were lost (1 Sam. 9:4). Possibly Shual, near Ophrah (13:17).

SHA'APH (sha'af; Aram. "balsam").

1. The last named of the sons of Jahdai of the tribe of Judah (1 Chron. 2:47).

2. Third named of the four sons of Caleb by Maacah, his concubine. He was the "father" (i.e., founder) of Madmannah (1 Chron. 2:49), after 1380 B.C.

SHAARA'IM (sha-a-ra'im; "two gates").

1. A city near Azekah, in Judah (Josh. 15:36, "Sharaim," KJV; 1 Sam. 17:52).

2. A town in Simeon (1 Chron. 4:31), evidently identical with *Sharuhen* (which see), between Gaza and Beersheba.

SHAASH'GAZ (sha-ash'gaz). The eunuch who had charge of the concubines in the court of Ahasuerus (Esther 2:14), c. 478 B.C.

SHAB'BETHAI (shab'e-thī; perhaps "sabbath-born"). A Levite who assisted in taking account of those who had married Gentile wives (Ezra

10:15), 457 B.C. He is probably the same as the one mentioned (Neh. 8:7) as assisting in the instruction of the people in the law, and as one of the "leaders of the Levites, who were in charge of the outside work of the house of God" (11:16).

SHACHIA. *See* Sachia.

SHAD'DAI (shad'ī). An adjunct used with the Canaanite-Hebrew name for God, *El.* El Shaddai denotes the particular character in which God revealed Himself to the patriarchs (Gen. 17:1; 28:3; 35:11; 43:14; 48:3, *see* marg.). The name is consistently translated in the NIV as God Almighty. Exodus 6:2-3 specifically states that God appeared "to Abraham, Isaac, and Jacob, as God Almighty [*El Shaddai*]" and that He was not known to them by the name *Jehovah,* that is revealed to them under the meaning of that name. Some present-day critics insist that El Shaddai means "God of mountain(s)" and that the Genesis passages inaccurately are translated "God Almighty." This view, however, is unacceptable, and Shaddai is best taken from the root *shādad,* "to be strong or powerful," as in Arab. Thus Shaddai would be an epithet intensifying the thought of power or strength inherent in the word *El* (cf. the Vulg. and the LXX "Omnipotens"). The word *el* is a generic name for god in NW Semitic (Heb. and Ugaritic) and was almost certainly an adjectival formation from the root *'wl,* "to be strong, powerful," and so meaning "the strong or powerful one." In the Ugaritic tablets El is the head of the pantheon, and this is the name by which God is called in the OT (Gen. 33:20). In prose El occurs more often with the adjunct El Elyon, "God Most High" (14:18), El Hai, "the living God" (Josh. 3:10), as well as "El Shaddai." In Hebrew poetry El is much more frequent, where it often stands without an adjunct (Pss. 18:31, 33, 48; 68:21; Job 8:3). M.F.U.

BIBLIOGRAPHY: A. Jukes, *The Names of God* (1967), pp. 59-82. *See also* God.

SHADOW (Heb. *ṣēl;* Gk. *skia*).

Figurative. The English term is used figuratively in a number of ways.

1. "Deep shadow" (Heb. *ṣalmāwet,* "shadow of death," KJV) is taken from the shadow representing darkness, gloom, etc., and so is figurative of the grave (Job 10:21, elsewhere "deep darkness," 12:22; 16:16; Isa. 9:2; Jer. 2:6); also severe trial (Ps. 23:4); state of ignorance (Matt. 4:16).

2. A shadow, swiftly moving, is symbolic of the fleetness of human life (1 Chron. 29:15; Job 8:9; 14:2; Ps. 102:11).

3. Covering and protection from heat; as in "Hide me in the shadow of Thy wings" (Pss. 17:8; cf. 63:7; 91:1; Isa. 49:2).

4. An image cast by an object and representing the form of that object, as opposed to the "body" or thing itself (Col. 2:17); hence *a sketch, outline,* as the Jewish economy (Heb. 8:5; 10:1).

The second Gk. term means "a shadow caused by revolution," as used in James 1:17, "the Father of lights, with whom there is no variation, or shifting shadow." The sun *appears to us* to have changes, from which come summer and winter, day and night, but in reality those changes are caused by the rotation and orbit of the earth. So God, the source of all good, does not change, though He may appear to do so.

SHA'DRACH (sha'drak; apparently Akkad. *Shu-dur,* "command of," and Sumerian *Aku,* the moon god). The name, however, may be simply a corruption of Marduk, the city god of Babylon. It is the Babylonian name given to Hananiah, the chief of the three Hebrew youths.

Captive. He was one of the Jewish captives carried to Babylon by Nebuchadnezzar c. 605 B.C. Being of goodly appearance and of superior understanding, he was selected, with his three companions, for the king's service and was instructed in the language and learning of the Chaldeans as taught in the college of the magicians. Like Daniel he lived on vegetables and water. When the time of his probation was over, he and his three companions, being found superior to all the other magicians, were advanced to stand before the king (Dan. 1:7-19).

Promotion. When Nebuchadnezzar determined to slay the magicians because they could not tell him his forgotten dream, Shadrach united with his companions in prayer to God to reveal the dream to Daniel (Dan. 2:17-18). When Daniel was successful, Shadrach shared in the promotion, being appointed to a high civil office (v. 49).

Fiery Furnace. At the instigation of certain envious Chaldeans an ordinance was published that all persons should worship the golden image to be set up in the plain of Dura, the exact site of which is uncertain as there are several places called Dura in Babylonia. For example, there is a river Dura with Tulūl Dūra nearby. For refusing to comply, Shadrach, with Meshach and Abed-nego, was cast into the fiery furnace, but their faith remained firm, and they escaped unhurt. The king acknowledged Jehovah to be God and promoted His faithful servants (Dan. 3:1-30). After their deliverance from the furnace we hear no more of Shadrach, Meshach, and Abed-nego in the OT; neither are they spoken of in the NT, except in the pointed allusion to them in the epistle to the Hebrews, as having through faith "quenched the power of fire" (Heb. 11:34). But there are repeated allusions to them in the later apocryphal books, and the martyrs of the Maccabean period seem to have been much encouraged by their example (1 Macc. 2:59, 60; 3 Macc. 6:6; 4 Macc. 13:9; 16:3, 21; 18:12).

BIBLIOGRAPHY: J. B. Alexander, *Journal of Biblical Literature* 69 (1950): 375; B. G. Sanders, *Theology* 68 (1955): 340-44.

SHAFT. The translation of various Heb. terms in

the NASB, NIV, and KJV, although the two Heb. terms translated "shaft" in the KJV (*yārēk; ḥēṣ*) are not among those so translated in the NASB. Thus *shaft* in the KJV of Ex. 25:31; 37:17; Num. 8:4 is from Heb. *yārēk,* "thigh," and is replaced in the NASB by the word *base,* in the first two verses and in the NASB and the NIV by *base* in the last verse. (Conversely, the NASB and NIV appearance of *shaft* in Ex. 25:31; 37:17 is from Heb. *qāneh* and replaces KJV *branch,* or *branches.*) The *shaft* of Isa. 49:2 (KJV) is from Heb. *ḥēṣ* and in replaced in the NASB and NIV, by *arrow.*

SHA'GEE (sha'gē; "wandering, erring"). A Hararite, and father of Jonathan, one of David's guard (1 Chron. 11:34). *See* Shammah, no. 5.

SHAGGY GOAT. *See* Gods, False.

SHAHARA'IM (sha-ha-ra'im; "double dawn," i.e., morning and evening twilight). A Benjamite who became the father of several children in the land of Moab (1 Chron. 8:8).

SHAHAZU'MAH (sha-ha-zū'ma, "toward the heights," "Shahazimah," KJV). A place in the tribe of Issachar, between Tabor and the Jordan (Josh. 19:22). Identical with Tell el Mekarkash in the Tabor-Jordan region.

SHA'LIM. *See* Shaalim, Land of.

SHALI'SHAH (sha-li'sha; "triangular"), **Shalisha** (NIV). A district adjoining Mt. Ephraim (1 Sam. 9:4), N of Lydda. Unquestionably the country around Baal-shalishah (2 Kings 4:42). It is mentioned in connection with Saul's search for his father's donkeys.

SHAL'LECHETH, SHALLEKETH, THE GATE OF (shal'e-keth; a "casting down"). One of the gates of the Temple through which refuse was thrown, by the causeway going up out of the Tyropoeon Valley (1 Chron. 26:16). It was the lot of Hosah to act as gatekeeper.

SHAL'LUM (shal'ūm; "recompense, retribution").
1. The sixteenth king of Israel. His father's name was Jabesh. Shallum conspired against Zechariah, son of Jeroboam II, killed him, and thus brought the dynasty of Jehu to a close, as was predicted (2 Kings 10:30), 752 B.C. He reigned only a month, being in turn dethroned and slain by Menahem (15:10-15).
2. The son of Tikvah and husband of the prophetess Huldah (2 Kings 22:14; 2 Chron. 34:22), 626 B.C. He was keeper of the priestly wardrobe and was probably the same as Jeremiah's uncle (Jer. 32:7).
3. Son of Sisamai and father of Jekamiah, and a descendant of Sheshan of Judah (1 Chron. 2:40-41).
4. The third son of Josiah, king of Judah, known in the books of Kings and Chronicles as

Jehoahaz (1 Chron. 3:15; Jer. 22:11). *See* Jehoahaz.
5. Son of Shaul, the son of Simeon (1 Chron. 4:25).
6. A high priest, son of Zadok and father of Hilkiah (1 Chron. 6:12-13), and an ancestor of Ezra (Ezra 7:2), after 950 B.C. He is the Meshullam of 1 Chron. 9:11; Neh. 11:11.
7. The youngest son of Naphtali (1 Chron. 7:13; Shillem, NIV), called Shillem (Gen. 46:24), about 1925 B.C.
8. A descendant of Kore, and chief of the gatekeepers of the sanctuary in the time of David (1 Chron. 9:17, 19, 31), about 980 B.C. He seems to have been the same Shallum whose descendants returned from the Exile (Ezra 2:42; 10:24; Neh. 7:45). With this Shallum we may identify Meshelemiah and Shelemiah (1 Chron. 26:1-2, 9, 14). He is perhaps the "father" of Maaseiah (Jer. 35:4).
9. The father of Jehizkiah, which latter was one of the leaders of Ephraim who took part in returning the prisoners carried away from Judah (2 Chron. 28:12), before 741 B.C.
10. A Jew of the descendants of Bani, who put away his idolatrous wife (Ezra 10:42), 456 B.C.
11. A Levitical porter who did the same as no. 10 (Ezra 10:24), 456 B.C.
12. The son of Hallohesh, the "official of half the district of Jerusalem," who with his daughters assisted in building its walls (Neh. 3:12), 445 B.C.

SHAL'LUN (shal'un; another form of Shallum, "retribution"). The son of Co-hozeh, the official of the district of Beth-haccherem who repaired the Refuse Gate (Neh. 3:15), 445 B.C.

SHAL'MAI (shal'mī). The sons of Shalmai were among the Temple servants who returned with Zerubbabel (Ezra 2:46; Neh. 7:48), about 536 B.C.

SHAL'MAN. An abbreviated form of Shalmaneser, king of Assyria (Hos. 10:14), although some scholars connect the name with a Moabite monarch Salamanu, whose name occurs in an inscription of Tiglath-pileser III (745-727 B.C.) and who was alive in Hosea's day.

SHALMANE'SER (shal-man-ē'zer; Assyr., "the god Shulman is chief"). The Assyrian inscriptions have made known to us five kings with the name Shalmaneser. Of these only one is mentioned by name in the OT, and he is Shalmaneser V, of Assyrian history. But though Shalmaneser III is not named in the OT, the evidence is there of his influence and his work. Without some knowledge of him it is impossible to understand the reign of Ahab, king of Israel, with whom he was contemporary.

Shalmaneser III. The reign of Ashurnasirpal (883-859 B.C.) was one of the most brilliant and daring of all Assyrian history. In him the spirit of the mighty Tiglath-pileser I (about 1110 B.C.)

seemed to live again. The boundaries of the Assyrian empire were carried far beyond their previous limits, and Assyrian influence began to be counted a force far and near. Under his leadership the Assyrians invaded Armenia and ravaged the country S of Lake Van. With the sword went also Assyrian commerce and culture. The Assyrian system of cuneiform writing was introduced into the land where later the kingdom of Van held sway, and so a center of influence was located. Ashurnasirpal also marched victoriously westward, reaching even the Mediterranean and receiving tribute from Tyre and Sidon. But there his work ceased. Would his successor be able to retain what he had won; would he be able to increase it? He was succeeded by his son Shalmaneser III, whose glorious reign (859-824 B.C.) surpassed even his father's.

Of the reign of Shalmaneser III we possess several well-preserved original monuments. The most beautiful of them is the famous Black Obelisk, now in the British Museum. A solid block of basalt, more than six feet high, it is covered on all four sides with inscriptions cut into the stone. Accompanying these are well-executed pictures of the objects that the king had received as gifts or in payment of tribute. A second important text is the Monolith Inscription, a large slab with a nearly life-size portrait of the king, covered with two columns of writing. Besides these, several colossal bulls covered with inscriptions have also

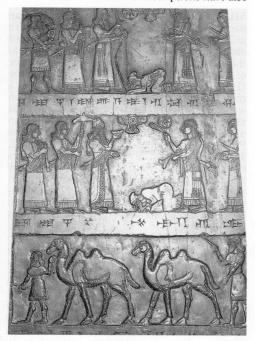

Part of the Black Obelisk of Shalmaneser III

been found. From these original sources of information we can now reconstruct the king's reign.

At the beginning of his reign, Shalmaneser set himself to strengthen the kingdom of his father in Mesopotamia and in Armenia. Five years were devoted to this task. His land was now strong, and he could turn his attention to the outside. In the sixth year of his reign (854 B.C.) he turned westward to take up the work of conquest where his father had left it. Ashurnasirpal II had not disturbed Israel; that was reserved for his son. The fame of the exploits of Shalmaneser had passed through Syria and into Palestine. It was evident to the peoples of all that country that no single nation could successfully oppose so great a warrior as he. The only hope was in a coalition. A union for the general defense was composed of the peoples of Damascus. Hamath, Israel, Phoenicia, Que (eastern Cilicia), and Musri (western Cappadocia). These combined forces Shalmaneser III met in battle at Qarqar (sometimes written Karkar), in 853 B.C., and thus tells the story of the battle: "From *Argana* I departed; to *Qarqar* I approached, *Qarqar,* his royal city, I wasted, destroyed, burned with fire; 1,200 chariots, 1,200 horses, 20,000 men of Adadidri, of Damascus; 700 chariots, 700 horses, 10,000 men of Ithuleni, the Hamathite; 2,000 chariots, 10,000 men of Ahab, the Israelite." Shalmaneser lists eleven kings with their forces and continues thus: "These 12 [there must be a mistake here, for only 11 have been mentioned] kings he took to his assistance; to make battle and war against me they came. With the exalted power which Ashur, the lord, gave me, with the powerful arms which Nergal, who goes before me, had granted me, I fought with them, from *Qarqar* to *Gilzan.* I accomplished their defeat; 14,000 of their warriors I slew with arms; like Ramman I rained a deluge upon them, I strewed hither and yon their bodies." This is a bold claim of an overwhelming victory. It was a victory for the Assyrians beyond a doubt, but it does not appear at this distance that the victory was won without great sacrifices. It is clear, at any rate, that Shalmaneser did not feel it sufficiently great to justify his attempting to seize Hamath or Damascus.

In the year 849 Shalmaneser III again invaded the western land, and again his inscriptions record victory. He was, however, in this campaign not endeavoring to attack Israel, and hence his deeds do not interest students of the Bible. Another expedition followed in 845, and this also was without effect upon Israel. The king was beating down Syria by successive blows, and this time he seems to have dealt a severe blow to the northern confederation, for Damascus was left to stand alone. In 842 Shalmaneser, upon a new invasion, found new rulers to oppose him. *Ben-hadad* (which see) no longer lived, and Hazael was ruler in Damascus. This campaign again excites the interest of biblical students. Jehu was now king of Israel, a man daring enough to usurp a throne but not courageous enough to face the Assyrians. Jehu attempted to buy off the Assyrians by sending costly presents to Shalmaneser. On the Black Obelisk, Shalmaneser has left a picture of Jehu's ambassadors stooping to kiss his feet and bringing him presents. Accompanying the picture are the words "The tribute of Jehu, son of Omri: silver, gold, etc." Jehu was not the son of Omri, but would be so called by the Assyrians, who long spoke of Israel as the "land of Omri." In 839 Shalmaneser received the tribute of Tyre, Sidon, and Byblos, and this was his last expedition to the W. Thereafter he was occupied near home with a rebellion in 827. In 825 he died, and Shamshi-Ramman II, his son, ruled in his stead.

Shalmaneser V, a king of Assyria, who reigned 727-722. He was the successor of Tiglath-pileser III (*see* Tiglath-pileser) and ascended the throne in the month in which his predecessor died. Few historical inscriptions of this king have been found. A weight containing his name and a boundary stone dated in his reign are the monuments of his time that have come into our possession. Our knowledge of his reign begins with the eponym lists. These are lists of the names of Assyrian kings, accompanied in some cases with a brief note mentioning the campaigns conducted by the monarch. In the eponym list for the year 727 B.C. is the record that Shalmaneser ascended the throne. Under the same year is the record of a campaign against a city, the name of which unhappily is broken off. As this record stands before the words recording the king's accession, it may be that the campaign was begun by his predecessor and continued by him. The Babylonian chronicle sets down in this same accession year, during the last three months, the destruction of the city of Shamara'in, or Shaba-ra'in. This city was once thought by some to be the city of Samaria. This view is improbable on philological grounds. With more probability it is now supposed by many to be the biblical Sepharvaim (2 Kings 17:24), but even this view is uncertain. In the year 726 the eponym list says that there was no campaign. For the remaining three years of the king's reign there were campaigns, but the lands against which they were directed are unknown, for the eponym list is broken at this point. It is now known, however, that Shalmaneser V warred against Phoenicia, capturing the mainland of Tyre and taking Sidon and Acre. The next definite information of the events in the reign of Shalmaneser V is found in the OT. Hoshea was king of Israel in Samaria at the time that Shalmaneser was reigning in Assyria. He had paid tribute to the Assyrians but decided to make a bold attempt to throw off the yoke. He therefore sought aid from the Egyptian king So (or Seveh), and this was naturally construed as rebellion by

the Assyrians (17:4). Shalmaneser invaded Palestine and laid siege to Samaria. The siege continued for three years, and at its conclusion many of the inhabitants of Samaria were carried into captivity. Samaria fell in 722 B.C., the year of Shalmaneser's death. The inscriptions of his successor, Sargon, claim that the city was taken by him and not by Shalmaneser (*see* Sargon). This may have been the case. If so, Samaria fell at the beginning of 721 B.C., or it may be merely a boast of Sargon. In any case the historical character of the book of Kings is not impugned.

R.W.R.; M.F.U.

BIBLIOGRAPHY: D. W. Thomas, ed., *Documents from Old Testament Times* (1958), pp. 46-50; D. D. Luckenbill, *Ancient Records of Assyria and Babylonia* (1968), pp. 200-252, 297; J. B. Pritchard, ed., *Ancient Near Eastern Texts* (1969), pp. 277-82.

SHA'MA (sha'ma; "He," i.e., God, "has heard"). The eldest son of Hothan, and, with his brother Jeiel, a member of David's guard (1 Chron. 11:44), about 1000 B.C.

SHAMARI'AH. See Shemariah, no. 2.

SHAMBLES (1 Cor. 10:25, KJV). The Gk. term, *makellon*, refers to a meat market, and it is so translated in the NASB and NIV.

SHA'MED, SHE'MER. See Shemed.

SHAMER. *See* Shemer, no. 2, no. 3; Shomer, no. 1.

SHAM'GAR (sham'gar; apparently a Hurrian name, "Shimigar," i.e., a god, "gave"). The third judge of Israel (Judg. 5:6). Nothing is recorded about the descent of Shamgar, except that he was the son of Anath. He may have been of the tribe of Naphtali, since Beth-anath is in that tribe (1:33). In the days of Shamgar, Israel was in a most depressed condition, and the whole nation was cowed. At this conjuncture Shamgar was raised up to be a deliverer. With nothing but an oxgoad he made a desperate assault upon the Philistines and killed 600 of them (3:31; cf. 1 Sam. 13:21), probably before 1150 B.C. He does not seem to have secured for the Israelites any permanent victory over the Philistines, nor is an account given of the length of his services. Moreover, he is not called a judge but is probably so reckoned because he answered the description as given in Judg. 2:16.

BIBLIOGRAPHY: G. F. Moore, *Journal of the American Oriental Society* 9 (1898): 159ff.; B. Maisler, *Palestine Exploration Quarterly* 66 (1934): 192ff.; E. K. Cox, *Lives That Oft Remind Us* (1940), pp. 85-92; F. C. Fensham, *Journal of Near Eastern Studies* 20 (1961): 197-98.

SHAM'HUTH (sham'huth; "desolation"). The fifth captain for the fifth month in David's arrangement of his army (1 Chron. 27:8), about 1000 B.C. From a comparison of the lists in 1 Chron. 11 and 27, it would seem that Shamhuth is the same as Shammoth the Harorite.

SHA′MIR (sha′mir; "a flint, thorn").

1. A town in the mountains of Judah (Josh. 15:48). It is to be sought in the ruin Sōmerah, thirteen miles SW of Hebron, or at nearby El-Birch.

2. A town upon the mountains of Ephraim, the residence and burial place of judge Tola (Judg. 10:1-2). Its situation is still unknown.

3. A Kohathite Levite, son of Micah, appointed by David to the service of the sanctuary (1 Chron. 24:24).

SHAM′MA (sham′a; "desolation"), the eighth named of the eleven sons of Zophah, an Asherite (1 Chron. 7:37), after 1440 B.C.

SHAM′MAH (sham′a; "desolation").

1. The third named of the sons of Reuel, the son of Esau (Gen. 36:13; 1 Chron. 1:37), and head of one of the families (Gen. 36:17).

2. The third son of Jesse, David's father, and one of the brothers not chosen by Jehovah to be anointed king (1 Sam. 16:9), before 1000 B.C. With his two elder brothers he joined the Hebrew army (17:13). He is elsewhere, by a slight change in the name, called Shimea (1 Chron. 2:13; 20:7) and Shimeah (2 Sam. 13:3, 32).

3. The son of Agee the Hararite, and one of the three captains of David's mighty men, 992 B.C. The exploit by which he obtained this high distinction was the invaluable assistance he rendered to David against the Philistines. By a comparison of the two accounts (2 Sam. 23:11-12; 1 Chron. 11:13-14) it seems that David had joined battle with the Philistines at Pasdammim. Shammah took his stand in the middle of a cultivated field, where the Philistines were in great numbers, and wrested it from the foe. Shammah may also have shared in the dangers of forcing a way through the Philistine host to gratify David's thirst for the waters of Bethlehem (2 Sam. 23:13-17), but Keil and Delitzsch (*Com.*, ad loc.) think that this deed was performed by three of the thirty mighty men whose names are not given.

The scene of Shammah's exploit is said in 2 Samuel to be a field of lentils and in 1 Chronicles a field of barley. It is more likely that it was a field of barley, and that by a slight change and transposition of letters in the original one word was substituted for the other. The reason Shammah is not mentioned in 1 Chronicles is that "three lines have dropped out from the text" in consequence of a copyist's error (K. & D., *Com.*, ad loc.).

4. "Shammah the Harodite" was another of David's mighty men (2 Sam. 23:25). He is called "Shammoth the Harorite" (1 Chron. 11:27) and "Shamhuth the Izrahite" (27:8). In the latter passage he is mentioned as the leader of the fifth division of David's army.

5. In the list of mighty men (2 Sam. 23:32, 33) we find "Jonathan, Shammah the Hararite"; whereas in 1 Chron. 11:34, it is "Jonathan, the son of Shagee the Hararite." Combining the two, Kennicott proposes to read "Jonathan, the son of Shamha, the Hararite" (Smith, *Bib. Dict.*).

SHAM′MAI (sham′i).

1. The elder son of Onam, of the tribe of Judah (1 Chron. 2:28), about 1350 B.C.

2. The son of Rekem, and father of Maon, of the tribe of Judah (1 Chron. 2:44-45), after 1370 B.C.

3. Named, apparently, as the sixth child of Ezrah, of the tribe of Judah (1 Chron. 4:17), after 1190 B.C. Bertheau suggests, however, that the last clause of v. 18 be inserted in v. 17 after the name Jalon. If this suggestion is accepted, then Shammai would be the son of Mered by his wife Bithia.

SHAM′MOTH (sham′ōth; "desolation, ruins"). "The Harorite," one of David's guard (1 Chron. 11:27); apparently the same as "Shammah the Harodite" (2 Sam. 23:25) and "Shamhuth" (1 Chron. 27:8).

SHAMMU′A (sha-mū′a; "renowned, heard-about").

1. The son of Zaccur, and the man who represented the tribe of Reuben among the twelve spies (Num. 13:4), c. 1440 B.C.

2. One of the sons of David (by his wife Bathsheba, cf. 1 Chron. 3:5, where he is called Shimea), born in Jerusalem (2 Sam. 5:14, "Shammuah," KJV; 1 Chron. 14:4), about 989 B.C.

3. A Levite, the father of Abda (Neh. 11:17), before 445 B.C. The same as Shemaiah, the father of Obadiah (1 Chron. 9:16).

4. The representative of the priestly family of Bilgah, or Bilgai, in the days of Joiakim (Neh. 12:18), about 500 B.C.

SHAMMUAH. *See* Shammua.

SHAM′SHERAI (sham′she-rī), or **Shamshera′i** (sham-she-rī). The first named of the six sons of Jeroham, resident at Jerusalem (1 Chron. 8:26), about 1120 B.C.

SHA′PHAM (shā′fam). The chief second in authority among the Gadites in the days of Jotham (1 Chron. 5:12), about 750 B.C.

SHA′PHAN (shā′fan; "hyrax, rock badger"). The scribe or secretary of King Josiah. He was the son of Azaliah (2 Kings 22:3; 2 Chron. 34:8), father of Ahikam (2 Kings 22:12; 2 Chron. 34:20), Elasah (Jer. 29:3), and Gemariah (36:10-12), and grandfather of Gedaliah (39:14; 40:5, 9, 11; 41:2; 43:6), Micaiah (36:11), and probably of Jaazaniah (Ezek. 8:11). There seems to be no sufficient reason for supposing that Shaphan the father of Ahikam, and Shaphan the scribe, were different persons.

The history of Shaphan brings out some points regarding the office of scribe. He appears to be on a level of equality with the governor of the city and the royal recorder, with whom he was sent by the king to Hilkiah to take an account of the money that had been collected by the Levites for the repair of the Temple and to pay the workmen (2 Kings 22:3-4; 2 Chron. 34:8-9; cf. 2 Kings 12:10), about 622 B.C. Ewald calls him minister of finance (*Geschichte*, 3:697). It was on this occasion that Hilkiah communicated his discovery of a copy of the law, which he had probably found while making preparations for the repair of the Temple. Shaphan was entrusted to deliver it to the king, who was so deeply moved upon hearing it read that he sent Shaphan, with the high priest and others, to consult Huldah the prophetess. Shaphan was then apparently an old man, for his son Ahikam must have been in a position of importance, and his grandson Gedaliah was already born. Be this as it may, Shaphan disappears from the scene. He probably died before the fifth year of Jehoiakim, eighteen years later, when we find that Elishama was scribe (Jer. 36:12).

SHA'PHAT (sha'fat; "He, i.e., God, judges").

1. The son of Hori, and the spy chosen from the tribe of Simeon to assist in exploring the Promised Land (Num. 13:5), c. 1440 B.C.

2. The father of the prophet Elisha (1 Kings 19:16, 19; 2 Kings 3:11; 6:31), before 865 B.C.

3. One of the six sons of Shemaiah in the royal line of Judah, after the captivity (1 Chron. 3:22), perhaps about 350 B.C.

4. One of the chiefs of the Gadites in Bashan in the time of Jotham (1 Chron. 5:12), about 738 B.C.

5. The son of Adlai, who was over David's cattle in the valleys (1 Chron. 27:29), after 1000 B.C.

SHA'PHER. *See* Shepher.

SHA'PHIR (sha'fir; "beautiful"). One of the towns in Judah addressed by the prophet Micah (1:11; "Sapir," KJV; the marg. of the NASB gives "pleasantness"), possibly identified with es-Suafir, SE of Ashdad. Robinson found several villages of this name in the vicinity.

SHA'RAI (sha'ri), one of the "sons" of Bani, who put away his Gentile wife (Ezra 10:40), 456 B.C.

SHARA'IM. *See* Shaaraim.

SHA'RAR (sha'rar; Aram. "firm"). An Ararite, the father of Ahiam (2 Sam. 23:33), before 990 B.C. In 1 Chron. 11:35 he is called Sacar, which Kennicott thinks is the true reading.

SHARE'ZER (sha-rē'zer; Akkad. "protect the king").

1. A son of *Sennacherib* (which see), who, with his brother Adrammelech, murdered their father while he was worshiping in the temple of the god Nisroch (2 Kings 19:37; Isa. 37:38), 681 B.C.

2. A messenger sent, with Regem-melech, in the fourth year of Darius, to inquire at the Temple regarding the day of humiliation in the fifth month (Zech. 7:2; "Sherezer," KJV), 518 B.C.

SHAR'ON (shar'un; "a plain"; KJV, Acts 9:35, Saron), a part of the coastal plain of Palestine extending from Joppa to Mt. Carmel, proverbially fertile and noted for its flowery beauty (Isa. 35:2; Song of Sol. 2:1). It has a width of six to twelve miles. The plain was well watered and was a garden spot (1 Chron. 27:29). In modern Palestine it is dotted with citrus farms and numerous settlements. In antiquity it was a favorite caravan route along the sea, connecting Asia Minor, Egypt, and Mesopotamia. The plain furnished a home for very early man, as discovery of cave burial places has indicated. Dor, Lydda, Joppa, Caesarea, Rakkon, and Antipatris were well-known biblical cities located in this plain.

M.F.U.

Plain of Sharon

SHAR'ONITE (shar'un-it). The designation (1 Chron. 27:29) of Shitrai, David's chief herdsman in the plain of Sharon.

SHARU'HEN (sha-rū'hen). A town originally in Judah but afterward allocated to Simeon (Josh. 19:6), hence in the Negev, or S country. It is called Shilhim (15:32) and Shaaraim (1 Chron. 4:31). Its present location is Tell el-Far'ah, a short distance SW of Lachish (Tell ed-Duweir) on the main ancient road between Palestine and Egypt. The site reveals impressive evidence of Hyksos, Egyptian, and Roman fortifications. It rises 150 feet above the surrounding desert terrain and was of immense strategic importance in antiquity. It is NW of Beersheba.

SHA'SHAI (sha'shi; "whitish, or noble"). One of the "sons" of Bani, who put away his Gentile wife after the Exile (Ezra 10:40), 456 B.C.

SHA'SHAK (sha'shak), son of Beriah, a Benjamite (1 Chron. 8:14). He was the father of Ishpan and others (vv. 22-25), after 1360 B.C.

SHA'UL (sha'ul; "asked," i.e., of God).

1. The son of Simeon by a Canaanite woman (Gen. 46:10; Ex. 6:15; Num. 26:13; 1 Chron. 4:24), c. 1900 B.C.

2. An Edomite king, called "Shaul of Rehoboth by the River" (1 Chron. 1:48-49; cf. Gen. 36:37-38).

3. Son of Uzziah, a Kohathite (1 Chron. 6:24).

SHA'ULITES (sha'ul-īts). The family founded by Shaul, no. 1 (Num. 26:13).

SHA'VEH, VALLEY OF (sha've; "valley of the plain"). A valley called also the "King's Valley" or Kidron, on the E of Jerusalem (Gen. 14:17; 2 Sam. 18:18; "king's dale," KJV). Here Absalom had erected a monument to himself; whether in the form of a column, an obelisk, or a monolith cannot be determined. It was situated about two stadia (one-fourth of a mile) E of Jerusalem.

SHA'VEH-KIRIATHA'IM (sha've-kir-ya-tha-im; "plain of Kiriathaim"). A plain near the city of Kiriathaim of Moab (Gen. 14:5). It belonged afterward to Reuben (Num. 32:37; Josh. 13:19). Chedorlaomer defeated the Emim here. "It is probably still to be seen in the ruins of *el Teym,* or *et Tueme,* about a mile to the W of Medabah" (K. & D., *Com.,* on Gen.). *See also* Kiriathaim, no. 2.

SHAVING. *See* Hair.

SHAV'SHA (shav'sha). The secretary of King David (1 Chron. 18:16), and apparently the same as *Seraiah* (which see).

SHEAF. The rendering of three Heb. words:

1. *Bundle of grain* (Heb. *'ălūmmâ,* "bound'; Gen. 37:7; Pss. 126:6; 129:7).

2. *Bunch* (Heb. *'āmîr,* "handful," hence a *sheaf;* Jer. 9:22; Amos 2:13; Mic. 4:12; Zech. 12:6).

3. *A heap* (Heb. *'ōmer*).

The Mosaic law contains the following prescriptions respecting sheaves:

1. One accidentally dropped or left upon the field was not to be taken up but left for the benefit of the poor (Deut. 24:19). *See* Glean.

2. The day after the feast of the Passover the Hebrews brought into the Temple a sheaf of the firstfruits of the harvest, with accompanying ceremonies (Lev. 23:10-12). *See* Festivals.

SHE'AL (shē'al; "asking"), one of the "sons" of Bani, who put away his foreign wife (Ezra 10:29), 456 B.C.

SHEAL'TIEL (shē-al'ti-el; I have "asked God"; in Matt. 1:12; Luke 3:27, LXX, *Salathiel*).

1. Son of Jeconiah, king of Judah, and father of Zerubbabel, according to 1 Chron. 3:17-19 and Matt. 1:12; but son of Neri and father of Zerubbabel, according to Luke 3:27. Upon the incontrovertible principle that no genealogy would assign inferior and private parentage to the true son and heir of a king and, that on the contrary, the son

of a private person would naturally be placed in the royal pedigree on becoming the rightful heir to the throne, we may assert with the utmost confidence that Luke gives us the true state of the case when he informs us that Shealtiel was the son of Neri and a descendant of Nathan the son of David. And from the insertion of Shealtiel in the royal pedigree, both in 1 Chronicles and Matthew's gospel, after the childless Jeconiah, we infer, with no less confidence, that, on the failure of Solomon's line, he was next heir to the throne of David. Keil (*Com.,* ad loc.) supposes that Assir may have left only a daughter, who married a man belonging to a family of her paternal tribe, Neri, and that from this marriage sprang Shealtiel. Coming into the inheritance of his maternal grandfather, he would be legally regarded as his legitimate son.

2. Father of Zerubbabel (Ezra 3:2, 8; 5:2; Neh. 12:1; Hag. 1:1, 12, 14; 2:2, 23).

SHEARI'AH (shē-a-rī'a; "Jehovah esteems"), the fourth of Azel's six sons, and one of the descendants of Saul (1 Chron. 8:38; 9:44), long after 1000 B.C.

SHEARING HOUSE (KJV, 2 Kings 10:12). *See* Beth-eked (Beth Eked) of the Shepherds.

SHE'AR-JA'SHUB (shē'ar-ja'shub; "a remnant shall return"), the son of Isaiah, who accompanied his father when he went to deliver to King Ahaz the prophecy contained in Isa. 7:3, about 735 B.C. The name, like that of Maher-shalal-hash-baz, had a prophetic significance.

SHE ASS. *See* Animal Kingdom: Donkey. *See* Shibah.

SHE'BA (shē'ba).

1. A son of Raamah, son of Cush (Gen. 10:7; 1 Chron. 1:9). He is supposed to have settled somewhere on the shores of the Persian Gulf.

2. A son of Joktan, son of the patriarch Eber (Gen. 10:28; 1 Chron. 1:22). The Joktanites were among the early colonists of southern Arabia and the kingdom that they founded there was for many centuries called the kingdom of Sheba, after one of the sons of Joktan.

3. The elder son of Jokshan, son of Keturah (Gen. 25:3; 1 Chron. 1:32), probably after 2000 B.C. He evidently settled somewhere in Arabia, probably on the eastern shore of the Arabian Gulf, where his posterity appear to have become incorporated with the earlier *Sabeans* (which see) of the Joktanic branch.

4. The son of Bichri, a Benjamite from the mountains of Ephraim (2 Sam. 20:1-22), the last leader of the Absalom insurrection. He is described as a "worthless fellow," but he must have been a person of some consequence from the immense effect produced by his appearance. It was, in fact, all but an anticipation of the revolt of Jeroboam. The occasion seized by Sheba was

the rivalry between the northern and southern tribes on David's return (20:1-2). The king might well say, "Sheba the son of Bichri will do us more harm than Absalom" (v. 6). Sheba traversed the whole of Palestine, apparently rousing the population. Joab followed in full pursuit. It seems to have been his intention to establish himself in the fortress of Abel Beth-maachah, famous for the prudence of its inhabitants (v. 18). That prudence was put to the test on the present occasion. Joab's terms were severe: the head of the insurgent chief. A woman of the place undertook the mission to her city and proposed the execution to her fellow citizens. The head of Sheba was thrown over the wall, and the insurrection ended, about 967 B.C.

5. One of the Gadite leaders residing in Bashan in the reign of Jeroboam II (1 Chron. 5:13), about 784 B.C.

6. The kingdom of Sheba. The kingdom of the *Sabeans* (which see), which, according to some, embraced the greater part of the Yemen, or Arabia Felix. When the fame of Solomon came to the ears of the queen of Sheba (Saba), she undertook a journey to Jerusalem to convince herself of the truth of the report that had reached her. She proposed to test his wisdom by posing "difficult questions" (1 Kings 10:1-13; 2 Chron. 9:1-12). A large number of inscriptions have been found in SW Arabia written in the so-called Sabean characters. They show, among other things, that besides the famous kingdom of Sheba, there was another monarchy called Ma'in, hence the classical and now current term "Minean." The Sabeans were governed by priest-kings (Ps. 72:10). The ruins of their capital city, Mariaba (Mareb), reveal the advancement of their culture. Solomon was able to answer all the queen of Sheba's riddles, and this demonstration of his wisdom, with the wonders of his retinue, his table, and his palace, filled her with amazement. She then said with astonishment to Solomon that of what her eyes now saw she had not heard the half. After an exchange of valuable presents, she returned to her own country. Jesus spoke of her as the "Queen of the South" (Matt. 12:42). Reference is made to the commerce that took the road from Sheba along the western borders of Arabia (Job 6:19; Isa. 60:6; Jer. 6:20; Ezek. 27:22-23).

7. One of the towns allotted to Simeon (Josh. 19:2), between Beersheba and Moladah. Sheba is lacking in the Chronicles, probably omitted through a copyist's error. It is rendered Shema in Josh. 15:26, where it stands before Moladah, just as Sheba does here.

BIBLIOGRAPHY: G. W. van Beek, *The Bible and the Ancient Near East* (1961), pp. 229-48; J. B. Pritchard, ed., *Solomon and Sheba* (1974).

SHE'BAH. *See* Shibah.

SHEBAM. *See* Sebam.

SHEBANI'AH (sheb-a-nī'a; perhaps, "Jehovah has brought back or returned").

1. One of the priests who blew the trumpet before the Ark of the Lord when it was removed from the house of Obed-edom to Jerusalem (1 Chron. 15:24), about 986 B.C.

2. One of the Levites who stood upon the "platform," offered the prayer of confession and thanksgiving (Neh. 9:4-5), and joined in the sacred covenant with Nehemiah (10:10), 445 B.C.

3. Another Levite who signed the covenant (Neh. 10:12).

4. A priest who also signed the covenant (Neh. 10:4). His son is prominently mentioned in 12:14, and he is probably the same as Shecaniah (v. 3).

SHE'BAT. *See* Sebat.

SHE'BER (she'ber; cf. Arab. *sabr,* "lion"). A son of Caleb by his concubine, Maacah (1 Chron. 2:48), about 1365 B.C.

SHEB'NA (sheb'na). A person occupying a high position in Hezekiah's court, officially described as "in charge of the royal household." The office he held included the superintendence of all the domestic affairs of the sovereign (Isa. 22:15), about 719 B.C. He subsequently held the subordinate position of scribe (36:3; 37:2; 2 Kings 19:2), his former post having been given to Eliakim. In his post of eminence Shebna had helped to support a spirit of self-security and forgetfulness of God, and Isaiah was sent to pronounce against him the prophecy of his fall (Isa. 22:15-25).

SHEBU'EL (sheb'u-el; perhaps "Return, O God" or "captive of God,") or **Shubael.**

1. A descendant of Gershom (1 Chron. 23:16; 26:24), who was officer over the treasures of the house of God; called also Shubael (24:20), before 960 B.C. He is the last descendant of Moses of whom there is any trace.

2. One of the fourteen sons of Heman the musician (1 Chron. 25:4), called also Shubael (25:20), before 960 B.C.

SHECANI'AH (shek-a-nī'a; "Jehovah has dwelt").

1. Apparently the son of Obadiah, and presumably a descendant of David (1 Chron. 3:21-22). Keil (*Com.,* ad loc.) thinks that the list from v. 21 to the end of the chapter is a genealogical fragment inserted into the text at some later time.

2. The tenth in order of the priests who were appointed by lot in the reign of David (1 Chron. 24:11), about 960 B.C.

3. One of the priests appointed by Hezekiah to distribute tithes among their brethren (2 Chron. 31:15), 719 B.C.

4. One of the "sons" of Parosh, and ancestor of the Zechariah who, with 150 males, accompanied Ezra from the Exile (Ezra 8:3), before 457 B.C.

5. Another Israelite, and progenitor of Jahaziel, who with 300 males went up with Ezra from Babylon to Jerusalem (Ezra 8:5), before 457 B.C.

6. The son of Jehiel, of the "sons of Elam," and one of the Jews who proposed to Ezra the repudiation of the Gentile wives (Ezra 10:2), 457 B.C.

7. The father of Shemaiah, who was "keeper of the East Gate" and assisted in repairing the wall of Jerusalem under Nehemiah (Neh. 3:29), before 445 B.C.

8. The son of Arah, and father-in-law of Tobiah the Ammonite, who opposed Nehemiah (Neh. 6:18), 445 B.C.

9. One of the "priests and the Levites" (probably the former), who returned with Zerubbabel from Babylon (Neh. 12:3), about 536 B.C.

SHECHANIAH. *See* Shecaniah.

SHE'CHEM (she'kem; a "shoulder, ridge"). The name of an ancient city in Palestine (which see) and of several persons in the Bible.

1. The son of Hamor, the Hivite prince at Shechem (Gen. 33:18). Charmed with the beauty of Dinah, Jacob's daughter, Shechem took her with him and seduced her. This wrong was terribly avenged by the girl's brothers Simeon and Levi (chap. 34; Judg. 9:28; Acts 7:16).

2. A man of Manasseh, of the family of Gilead, and head of the family of Shechemites (Num. 26:31). His family is mentioned in Josh. 17:2.

3. A son of Shemida, a Gileadite (1 Chron. 7:19).

SHECHEM (she'kem; a "shoulder, ridge"). An ancient and important city of Palestine (Gen. 12:6; Acts 7:16), also called Sychar (John 4:5).

Name. It is not known whether the city was named after Shechem (Gen. 33:18; see article above) or whether he received his name from it. The etymology of the Heb. word *shekem* indicates that the place was situated on some mountain or hillside. That presumption agrees with

The hill country near Shechem

Josh. 20:7, which places it "in the hill country of Ephraim" (*see* also 1 Kings 12:25), and with Judg. 9:6-7, which represents it as under the summit of Gerizim, which belonged to the Ephraim range.

Location. After Vespasian destroyed the Samaritan temple on Mt. Gerizim, he built his new city ("Neapolis") farther up the valley, leaving ancient Shechem in ruins. Archaeology has shown that Shechem was Tell Balâtah, not the site of the later Roman city Neapolis or Nablūs, which was considered for a long time to be Shechem, but is NW of it (*see* W. F. Albright, *The Archaeology of Palestine*).

Archaeology. Excavations at Tell Balâtah by the Germans between 1913 and 1934 show that the ancient city of Shechem was a prosperous place between 2000 and 1800 B.C. and later between 1400 and 1200 B.C. Important Bronze Age fortifications were discovered at the site. The ruins include a wall thirty feet high, dated from the seventeenth-sixteenth centuries. A fourteenth-century B.C. temple was also found. Walls evidently dating from the middle of the eleventh century and attributable to the era of Abimelech (Judg. 9) also came to light. Clay tablets inscribed in Akkad. writing were also dug up at the site. A Drew University–McCormick Theological Seminary team began a new excavation at Shechem in 1956, working there again in 1957, 1960, 1962, 1964, 1966, 1968, and 1969. Remains of a fortress-temple fifty-three feet wide and forty-one feet long have been identified as the house of Baal-berith destroyed by Abimelech (c. 1150 B.C.; Judg. 9:3-4, 46).

Bible Allusions. Abraham, on his migration to the land of promise, pitched his tent and built an altar under the oak (or terebinth) of Moreh, at Shechem. "The Canaanite was then in the land"; and it is evident that the region, if not the city, was already in possession of the aboriginal race (*see* Gen. 12:6). At the time of Jacob's arrival here, after his sojourn in Mesopotamia (33:18; chap. 34), Shechem was a Hivite city, of which Hamor, the father of Shechem, was the head. It was at this time that the patriarch purchased "the piece of land" from him that he subsequently bequeathed as a special patrimony to his son Joseph (Gen. 33:19; Josh. 24:32; John 4:5). The field undoubtedly lay on the rich plain of the Mukhna, and its value was greater because of the well Jacob had dug there so that he wouldn't be dependent on his neighbors for a supply of water. The defilement of Dinah, Jacob's daughter, and the capture of Shechem and massacre of all the male inhabitants by Simeon and Levi are events that belong to this period (Gen. 34). In the distribution of the land, Shechem fell to Ephraim (Josh. 20:7) but was assigned to the Levites and became a city of refuge (21:20-21). It was the scene of the promulgation of the law, when its blessings were heard from Gerizim and its curses from Ebal (Deut. 27:11; Josh. 8:33-35). Here Joshua assembled the people shortly before his death and delivered to them his last counsels (24:1, 25). After the death of Gideon, Abimelech, his illegitimate son, induced the Shechemites to revolt and make him king (Judg. 9). After a reign of three years he was expelled from the city. In revenge he destroyed the place and, as an emblem of the fate to which he would consign it, sowed it with salt (vv. 25, 45). It was soon restored, however, for we are told in 1 Kings 12 that all Israel assembled at Shechem, and Rehoboam, Solomon's successor, went there to be inaugurated as king. Here, at this same place, the ten tribes renounced the house of David and transferred their allegiance to Jeroboam (12:16), under whom Shechem became for a time the capital of his kingdom. Most of the people of Shechem were carried into captivity (cf. 2 Kings 17:5-6; 18:9-12), but Shalmaneser sent colonies from Babylon to occupy the place of the exiles (17:24). Another influx of strangers came under Esarhaddon (Ezra 4:2). From the time of the origin of the Samaritans the history of Shechem blends with that of this people and their sacred mount, Gerizim. It was to the Samaritans that Shechem owed the revival of its claims to be considered the religious center of the land, but this was in the interest of a narrow and exclusive sectarianism (John 4:5-40).   H.F.V.

BIBLIOGRAPHY: E. F. Campbell and J. F. Ross, *Biblical Archaeologist* 26 (1963): 2-26; G. E. Wright, *Shechem: The Biography of a Biblical City* (1965); D. W. Thomas, ed., *Archaeology and Old Testament Study* (1967), pp. 355-70; M. Avi-Yonah and E. Stern, eds., *Encyclopedia of Archaeological Excavations in the Holy Land* (1977), 4:1083-94; D. P. Cole, "Shechem I: The Middle Bronze II B Pottery," *Annual of the American Schools of Oriental Research* (1984).

The ruins of ancient Shechem

SHECHI'NAH (shek-ī'na). Another spelling of *Shekinah* (which see).

SHED'EUR (shed'ur; "Shaddai is light"). The father of Elizur, chief of the tribe of Reuben at the time of the Exodus (Num. 1:5; 2:10; 7:30, 35; 10:18), c. 1440 B.C.

SHEEP. The rendering of several words in the original (*see* also Animal Kingdom):

1. A ram just old enough to butt (Ex. 12:5; Job 31:20), Heb. *kebeś*.

2. A *young* sheep, a lamb (Gen. 30:32, 35; Lev. 1:10, etc.; Num. 18:17), Heb. *keseb*.

3. A *flock* of sheep (rendered "flock," Gen. 4:2; 29:10; 31:19; 38:13; etc.), the most frequent word thus rendered, Heb. *ṣōn*.

4. *One* of a flock, a single sheep (Gen. 22:7, 8; Ex. 12:5, "lamb," etc.), though sometimes used collectively (Jer. 50:17), Heb. *śeh*.

5. Any four-footed tame animal accustomed to graze, but always a sheep in the NT (Matt. 7:15; 10:16; 12:11-12, Gk. *probaton*).

Sheep were an important part of the possessions of the ancient Hebrews and of Eastern nations generally. They were used in the sacrificial offerings, both the adult animal (Ex. 20:24; 1 Kings 8:63; 2 Chron. 29:33) and the lamb, i.e., a male from one to three years old, but young lambs of the first year were used more frequently (*see* Ex. 29:38; Lev. 9:3; 12:6; Num. 28:9; etc.). No lamb under eight days old was allowed to be killed (Lev. 22:27). A very young lamb was called *ṭāleh* (1 Sam. 7:9, "suckling lamb"; Isa. 65:25). Sheep and lambs formed an important article of food (1 Sam. 25:18; 1 Kings 1:19; 4:23; Ps. 44:11; etc.). The wool was used for clothing (Lev. 13:47; Deut. 22:11; Prov. 31:13; Job 31:20; etc.). "Rams' skins dyed red" were used as a covering for the Tabernacle (Ex. 25:5). Sheep and lambs were sometimes paid as tribute (2 Kings 3:4). It is striking to notice the immense numbers of sheep that were reared in Palestine in biblical times. Sheep-shearing is alluded to in Gen. 31:19; 38:13; Deut. 15:19; 1 Sam. 25:4; Isa. 53:7; etc. Sheep dogs were employed in biblical times, as is evident from Job 30:1, "the dogs of my flock." Shepherds in Palestine and the East generally go before their flocks, which they induce to follow by calling to them (cf. John 10:4; Pss. 77:20; 80:1), though they also drive them (Gen. 33:13).

Figurative. The nature of sheep and their relation to man have given rise to many beautiful figures. Jehovah was the Shepherd of Israel, and they were His flock (Pss. 23:1; 74:1; 78:52; 79:13; 80:1; Isa. 40:11; Jer. 23:1, 2; etc.). The apostasy of sinners from God is likened to the straying of a lost sheep (Ps. 119:176; Isa. 53:6; Jer. 50:6). Jesus came to earth as the Good Shepherd (Luke 15:4-6; John 10:8-11). As the sheep is an emblem of meekness, patience, and submission, it is expressly mentioned as typifying these qualities in the Person of our blessed Lord (Isa. 53:7; Acts 8:32; etc.).

BIBLIOGRAPHY: E. J. Schochet, *Animal Life in Jewish Tradition* (1984), pp. 13, 15, 36, 60, 152, 192, 251, 282, 295.

A flock of sheep near Bethlehem

SHEEP BREEDER. (Heb. *nōqēd,* "marker," 2 Kings 3:4). A term signifying both a shepherd (Amos 1:1) and also a possessor of flocks. In Arab. it is properly the possessor of a superior kind of sheep or goats.

SHEEPCOTE. A term used once in the KJV for Heb. *gedērâ* (1 Sam. 24:3; the NASB renders "sheepfold" in this verse, and the NIV, "sheep pens") and twice for Heb. *nāweh* (2 Sam. 7:8; 1 Chron. 17:7; both the NASB and NIV of the passages render "pasture"). *See* Sheepfold; Shepherd.

SHEEPFOLD. The rendering of the following Heb. and Gk. terms:

1. Heb. *gedērâ,* an enclosure (1 Sam. 24:3; Num. 32:16, 24, 36; Zeph. 2:6), a built pen, such as joins buildings, and used for cattle as well as sheep.

2. Heb. *miklâ,* a fold or pen (Pss. 78:70; 50:9;

Sheep in the Judean wilderness

Hab. 3:17), probably what we understand by *stalls.*

3. Gk. *aulē,* a court (John 10:1), the roofless enclosure in the open country into which flocks were herded at night.

When sheep are exposed to the depredations of robbers, it is customary in the East to shelter them in well-built enclosures, which are impregnable once the flock is within them. When no danger from this source is feared the flocks are put in folds only when they are to be shorn.

SHEEP GATE (*sha'ar,* "gate"; *haṣṣō'n,* "flock," i.e., "gate of the flock"; NASB and NIV "sheep gate" is KJV "sheep market"). One of the gates of Jerusalem rebuilt by Nehemiah (Neh. 3:1, 32; 12:39). It was located between the Tower of the Hundred ("Tower of Meah," KJV) and the upper room of the corner (3:1, 32), or Gate of the Guard (12:39). It is probably the "sheep gate" mentioned in John 5:2.

SHEEP MARKET. *See* Sheep Gate.

SHEEP MASTER. *See* Sheep Breeder.

SHEEPSHEARER (Heb. from *gāzaz,* to "shear"). What the harvest was to an agricultural people, the sheepshearing was to a pastoral people: celebrated by a festival corresponding to our harvest home, marked often by the same revelry and merrymaking (Gen. 31:19; 1 Sam. 25:4, 8, 36: 2 Sam. 13:23-28; etc.). Sheepshearers are mentioned in Gen. 38:12; 2 Sam. 13:23-24.

SHEEPSKINS (Gk. *mēlōtē*). A simple garment made of the sheep's pelt (*see* Dress, no. 1); used figuratively (Heb. 11:37) to represent a condition of extreme poverty.

SHEE'RAH (shē'ra; "kinswoman"). Daughter of Ephraim (1 Chron. 7:24). She founded the two Beth-horons, "upper and lower," and Uzzen-she-erah, probably about 1169 B.C. This Ephraim was probably a descendant of the patriarch and lived after Israel took possession of Canaan.

SHEET. *See* Fine Linen.

1. Rendered "fine linen" (Prov. 31:24; Isa. 3:23, KJV), and meaning probably a shirt (Judg. 14:12, KJV, Heb. *sādîn*).

2. A "sail" (Gk. *'othonē,* Acts 10:11; 11:5; NIV, "sheet").

SHE GOAT. *See* Animal Kingdom: Goat.

SHEHARI'AH (shē-ha-rī'a; "sought by Jehovah"). The second of the six sons of Jeroham, Benjamites residing in Jerusalem at the captivity (1 Chron. 8:26), 588 B.C.

SHEKEL. A weight and a unit of money. *See* Metrology.

SHEKI'NAH (shek-ī'na; Aram. and late Heb. *shekīnāh,* "residence," i.e., of God). A word not in Scripture but used by later Jews and by Christians to express the visible divine Presence, especially when resting between the cherubim over the Mercy Seat. *See* discussion of the Ark, in the article Tabernacle.

BIBLIOGRAPHY: W. D. Davies, *Paul and Rabbinic Judaism* (1948), pp. 211, 213-15; R. A. Stewart, *Rabbinic Theology* (1961), pp. 40-42.

SHE'LAH (shē'la).

1. The youngest son of Judah by the daughter of Shua (Gen. 38:5, 11, 14, 26; 46:12; Num. 26:20; 1 Chron. 2:3; 4:21), after 1925 B.C. His descendants (1 Chron. 4:21-23) were called Shelanites.

2. The son of Arpachshad (Gen. 10:24; 11:12-15; 1 Chron. 1:18). At 30 years of age he became the father of Eber; he lived to be 433 years old (Gen. 11:14-15). Sometimes "Salah," KJV.

3. The son of Cainan and father of Heber in the genealogy of Christ (Luke 3:35-36).

SHE'LANITE (shē'la-nīt). A descendant of *Shelah* (which see), son of Judah (Num. 26:20).

SHELEMI'AH (shel-e-mi'a; "Jehovah repays").

1. The gatekeeper of the E entrance to the Tabernacle; his son Zechariah had the northern gate (1 Chron. 26:14), about 960 B.C. He is called Meshelemiah (9:21; 26:1-2), Meshullam (Neh. 12:25), and Shallum (1 Chron. 9:17, 31).

2. One of the "sons" of Bani in the time of Ezra (Ezra 10:39), 456 B.C.

3. Another of the "sons" of Bani in the time of Ezra (Ezra 10:41), 456 B.C.

4. The father of Hananiah, who repaired part of the walls of Jerusalem (Neh. 3:30), 445 B.C. He was probably an apothecary, or manufacturer of incense (v. 8).

5. A priest appointed by Nehemiah to serve as a treasurer of the Levitical tithes (Neh. 13:13), 445 B.C.

6. The grandfather of Jehudi, who was sent by the officials to invite Baruch to read Jeremiah's scroll to them (Jer. 36:14), about 606 B.C.

7. Son of Abdeel, one of those who received the orders of Jehoiakim to take Baruch and Jeremiah (Jer. 36:26).

8. The father of Jehucal, or Jucal, in the time of Jedekiah (Jer. 37:3), about 597 B.C.

9. The father of Irijah, the captain of the guard who arrested Jeremiah (Jer. 37:13; 38:1), before 586 B.C.

SHE'LEPH (she'lef; "a drawing forth," but cf. Arab. *salafa,* "to cultivate"). The second of the thirteen sons of Joktan (Gen. 10:26; 1 Chron. 1:20). The tribe that sprang from him has been satisfactorily identified, and is found in the district of Sulaf.

SHE'LESH (she'lesh; "triplet, triad," but cf. Arab. *salis,* "meek, obedient"). A son of Helem, and great-grandson of Asher (1 Chron. 7:35), perhaps about 1290 B.C.

SHELO'MI (shel-ō'mi; "at peace"). The father of Ahihud, who represented the tribe of Asher among those appointed to divide the Promised Land (Num. 34:27), 1171 B.C.

SHEL'OMITH (shel-ō'mith; feminine of Shelomi, "peaceful").

1. The daughter of Dibri, of the tribe of Dan, and mother of the man who was stoned for blasphemy (Lev. 24:11), c. 1439 B.C.

2. The daughter of Zerubbabel (1 Chron. 3:19), perhaps after 536 B.C.

3. First named of the three sons of Shimei, head of the Gershonites in the time of David (1 Chron. 23:9), about 950 B.C. The NIV renders "Shelomoth." In v. 10 his name should probably take that of "Shimei."

4. A Levite, chief of the Izharites in the time of David (1 Chron. 23:18), before 960 B.C. In 24:22 he is called Shelomoth.

5. The last child of Rehoboam by his wife Maacah (2 Chron. 11:20), about 934 B.C.

6. According to the present text, the sons of Shelomith, with the son of Josiphiah at their head, returned from Babylon with Ezra (Ezra 8:10). There appears, however, to be an omission, and the true reading is probably "of the sons of Bani, Shelomith the son of Josiphiah."

SHEL'OMOTH (shel'ō-moth).

1. A Levite and leader of the Izharites (1 Chron. 24:22), elsewhere called Shelomith (23:18).

2. A Levite, and descendant of Eliezer, the son of Moses, who in the reign of David was one of the Temple treasurers (1 Chron. 26:25-26, 28), before 960 B.C. The NIV reads "Shelomith."

SHELU'MIEL (shel'u'mi-el; "peace of God"). The son of Zurishaddai, and leader of the tribe of Simeon at the time of the Exodus (Num. 1:6; 2:12; 7:36, 41; 10:19), c. 1440 B.C.

SHEM (shem; "name"). One of the three sons of Noah, born when his father was 500 years of age (Gen. 5:32), perhaps before 5000 B.C. At the age of 98 years he entered the ark, being married but childless (7:7), and two years after the Flood (i.e., the beginning of the Flood) he became the father of Arpachshad; other children were born still later (11:10-11; 10:22). He assisted Japheth in covering the nakedness of his father when it was made known by Ham. In the prophecy of Noah that is connected with this incident (9:23-27) the first blessing falls on Shem. His death at the age of 600 years is recorded in 11:11. The portion of the earth occupied by the descendants of Shem (10:21-31) intersects the portions of Japheth and Ham and stretches in an uninterrupted line from the Mediterranean Sea to the Indian Ocean. It includes Syria (Aram), Chaldea (Arphachshad), parts of Assyria (Asshur), of Persia (Elam), and of the Arabian peninsula (Joktan). The servitude of Canaan under Shem, predicted by Noah (9:26), was fulfilled primarily in the subjugation of the people of Palestine (Josh. 23:4; 2 Chron. 8:7-8). The eminent spiritual blessings of Shem are fulfilled in the Messiah, who came from the line of Shem (cf. Rom. 9:3-5).

BIBLIOGRAPHY: S. N. Kramer, *Analecta Biblica* 12 (1959): 203-4; id., *The Sumerians* (1963), pp. 297-99; J. J. Davis, *Paradise to Prison* (1975), pp. 143-44.

SHE′MA (she′ma; "report, rumor, fame").

1. The last-named son of Hebron and father of Raham, of the tribe of Judah (1 Chron. 2:43-44).

2. The son of Joel and father of Azaz, of the tribe of Reuben (1 Chron. 5:8). He is probably the same as Shemaiah of v. 4.

3. One of the sons of the Benjamite Elpaal, and one of those who drove out the inhabitants of Gath (1 Chron. 8:13), after 1170 B.C.

4. One of those who stood at Ezra's right hand when he read the law to the people (Neh. 8:4), about 445 B.C.

5. A town in S Judah, between Amam and Moladah (Josh. 15:26). In the parallel list of towns set off from Judah to Simeon (Josh. 19:2) it is given as Sheba, which is perhaps the more nearly correct.

SHEMA′AH (she-ma′a; "report, fame"). A Benjamite of Gibeah, and father of Ahiezer and Joash, who joined David at Ziklag (1 Chron. 12:3), about 1002 B.C.

SHEMA′IAH (she-ma′ya; "Jehovah has heard").

1. A prophet in the reign of Rehoboam. When the king had assembled 180,000 men of Benjamin and Judah to reconquer the Northern Kingdom after its revolt, Shemaiah was commissioned to charge them to return to their homes and not to war against their brethren (1 Kings 12:22-24; 2 Chron. 11:2-4), after 934 B.C. His second and last appearance was upon the occasion of the invasion of Judah and siege of Jerusalem by Shishak, king of Egypt (12:5, 7). He wrote a chronicle containing the events of Rehoboam's reign (v. 15).

2. The son of Shecaniah, among the descendants of Zerubbabel (1 Chron. 3:22). He was keeper of the East Gate of the city and assisted Nehemiah in restoring the wall (Neh. 3:29), 445 B.C. He is probably the same as Semein (Luke 3:26).

3. Father of Shimri and ancestor of Ziza, a leader of the tribe of Simeon (1 Chron. 4:37), before 726 B.C. Perhaps the same as Shimei (vv. 26-27).

4. The son of Joel, a Reubenite, and father of Gog (1 Chron. 5:4). He is probably the same as Shema (v. 8).

5. Son of Hasshub, a Merarite Levite who lived in Jerusalem after the captivity (1 Chron. 9:14). He was one of those who were "very able men for the work of the service of the house of God" (9:13; Neh. 11:15), 445 B.C.

6. The son of Galal and father of the Levite

Obadiah (or Abda), who "lived in the villages of the Netophathites" after the captivity (1 Chron. 9:16), before 445 B.C. In Neh. 11:17 he is called Shammua.

7. Son of Elizaphan, and chief of his house of two hundred men in the reign of David (1 Chron. 15:8, 11). He took part in the removal of the Ark from Obed-edom (15:1-8, 14-15, 25), about 988 B.C.

8. A son of Nethanel the scribe. In the time of David, he registered the division of the priests into twenty-four orders (1 Chron. 24:6), about 960 B.C.

9. The eldest son of Obed-edom the Gittite, and a gatekeeper of the Temple (1 Chron. 26:4, 6-7), before 960 B.C.

10. One of the Levites sent by Jehoshaphat, in his third year, to teach the people of the cities of Judah (2 Chron. 17:8), 872 B.C.

11. A descendant of Jeduthun the singer, who assisted in the purification of the Temple in the reign of Hezekiah (2 Chron. 29:14), 719 B.C. He is perhaps the same as the Shemiah who distributed tithes among his brethren (31:15).

12. A Levite in the reign of Josiah, who, with others, made large contributions of sacrifices for the Passover (2 Chron. 35:9), 621 B.C.

13. One of the sons of Adonikam, who, with his two brothers, brought sixty males from Babylon with Ezra (Ezra 8:13), about 457 B.C.

14. One of the leading men whom Ezra sent for while camped by the river of Ahava for the purpose of obtaining Levites and ministers for the Temple from "the place Casiphia" (Ezra 8:16, 17), about 457 B.C.

15. A priest of the family of Harim, who put away his foreign wife at Ezra's bidding (Ezra 10:21), 456 B.C.

16. A layman of Israel, son of another Harim, who also had married a foreigner (Ezra 10:31), 456 B.C.

17. Son of Delaiah, the son of Mehetabel, a prophet in the time of Nehemiah who, bribed by Tobiah and Sanballat, pretended fear and proposed to Nehemiah that they should seek safety in the Temple (Neh. 6:10), 445 B.C.

18. A head of a priestly house who returned with Zerubbabel from Babylon (Neh. 12:6, 18), 536 B.C. If the same, he lived to sign the covenant with Nehemiah (10:8), 445 B.C. The Shemaiah son of Mattaniah and father of Jonathan mentioned in 12:35 is perhaps the same.

19. One of the leaders of Judah at the time of the dedication of the wall of Jerusalem (Neh. 12:34), 445 B.C.

20. One of the musicians who took part in the dedication of the new wall of Jerusalem (Neh. 12:36), 445 B.C.

21. One of the priestly trumpeters on the same occasion (Neh. 12:42).

22. The father of the prophet *Uriah* (which

see), of Kiriath-jearim (Jer. 26:20), before 609 B.C.

23. Shemaiah the Nehelamite, a false prophet in the time of Jeremiah (Jer. 29:24-32).

24. The father of Delaiah, one of the officials who heard Baruch's scroll (Jer. 36:12), before 607 B.C.

SHEMARI'AH (shem-a-rī'a; "Jehovah keeps or preserves").

1. One of the Benjamite warriors who came to David at Ziklag (1 Chron. 12:5), about 1002 B.C.

2. The second son of Rehoboam by his wife Abihail (2 Chron. 11:19; Shamariah, KJV), about 934 B.C.

3. One of the family of Harim, a layman of Israel, who put away his foreign wife in the time of Ezra (Ezra 10:32), 456 B.C.

4. Another of the family of Bani under the same circumstances (Ezra 10:41).

SHEME'BER (shem-e'ber). King of Zeboiim, and ally of the king of Sodom when he was attacked by the northeastern invaders under Chedorlaomer (Gen. 14:2), about 2065 B.C.

SHE'MED (she'med), properly **She'mer** (shē'mer; "preserved"). The third named son of Elpaal, and builder of Ono and Lod. He was a Benjamite (1 Chron. 8:12), 1380 B.C.

SHE'MER (she'mer; "preserved").

1. The owner of the hill on which the city of Samaria was built (1 Kings 16:24). King Omri bought it for two talents of silver and named it Samaria, after Shemer, about 886 B.C.

2. The son of Mahli and father of Bani, of the tribe of Levi (1 Chron. 6:46), perhaps about 1440 B.C.

3. The second son of Heber, an Asherite (1 Chron. 7:32, where he is called Shomer), and father of Ahi and others (v. 34), perhaps before 1440 B.C.

SHEMI'DA (she-mi'da; "the name," i.e., descendants, "has known"). One of the six sons of Gilead and founder of the family Shemidaites, of the tribe of Manasseh (Num. 26:32; Josh. 17:2). His three sons are mentioned in 1 Chron. 7:19.

SHEMI'DAITES (she-mi'da-its). Descendants (Num. 26:32) of Shemida, who obtained their inheritance among the male posterity of Manasseh (Josh. 17:2).

SHEM'INITH (shem'i-nith). A musical term (1 Chron. 15:21, marg.; titles of Pss. 6, 12), perhaps referring to eight strings or octaves.

SHEMIR'AMOTH (shem-ir'a-moth; possibly "name of the heights" or "name most high").

1. A Levite musician of the second degree in the choir founded by David (1 Chron. 15:18), playing "with harps tuned to alamoth" (v. 20; cf. 16:5), about 986 B.C.

2. One of the Levites sent by Jehoshaphat to teach the law to the inhabitants of Judah (2 Chron. 17:8), after 875 B.C.

SHEMU'EL (she-mū'el; "heard of God"). The same Heb. word commonly translated Samuel, the name of several Bible personages. In the KJV Shemuel appears three times: (1) in Num. 34:20 for the son of Ammihud, appointed from the tribe of Simeon, to divide the land of Canaan, c. B.C. 1400; (2) in 1 Chron. 6:33 for *Samuel* the prophet (which see); and (3) in 1 Chron. 7:2 for descendant of Tola who was one of the chiefs of the tribe of Issachar.

SHEN (shen; Heb. with article *hashshēn*, "the tooth"). Between this place and Mizpah Samuel set up the stone Ebenezer to commemorate the rout of the Philistines (1 Sam. 7:12). The name may indicate a projecting point of rock (14:4) or a place situated upon such a point. Its exact locality is unknown.

SHENAZ'ZAR (shen'a-zar; Akkad., "O Sin," i.e., moon god, "protect"). One of the sons of Jeconiah and brother of Shealtiel (1 Chron. 3:18), after 606 B.C.

SHE'NIR. *See* Senir.

SHE'OL (shē'ol; "Hades," or the world of the dead). A word usually derived from *shā'al*, "to ask or seek," perhaps with the meaning expressed in English, "the insatiable sepulcher." We have no clue to the origin of the word and must seek for its meaning in the several passages in which it occurs. In Gen. 37:35, "And he [Jacob] said, 'I will go down to Sheol in mourning for my son,' " the meaning is obvious. In Num. 16:30 Moses declares that Korah shall go down alive into Sheol (v. 33). In 2 Sam. 22:6 we read, "The cords of Sheol surrounded me." In Job 11:8 there seems to be an allusion to the belief that there is a dark and deep abyss beneath the center of the earth, tenanted by departed spirits, but not necessarily a place of torment. "Sheol from beneath is excited over you," etc. (Isa. 14:9), is thus rendered by Delitzsch (*Com.*, ad loc.), "The kingdom of the dead below is all in uproar on account of thee"; and its meaning thus interpreted, "All Hades is overwhelmed with excitement and wonder, now that the king of Babel . . . is actually approaching."

In the great majority of cases in the OT, Sheol is used to signify the grave; and it can have no other meaning in Gen. 37:35; 42:38; 1 Sam. 2:6; 1 Kings 2:6; Job 14:13; 17:13, 16, and in many passages in the writings of David, Solomon, and the prophets. The darkness and gloom of the grave was such that the word denoting it came to be applied to the abiding place of the miserable. Some passages are doubtful, but concerning others scarcely a question can be entertained (e.g., 11:8; Ps. 139:8; Amos 9:2), in which the word denotes the opposite of heaven. Still more decisive are Ps. 9:17; Prov. 23:14; in which Sheol can only mean the abode of the wicked, as distinguished from and opposed to the righteous. In nearly every instance Sheol is translated as "grave" in the NIV.

In the NT the Gk. *hadēs* is used in much the same sense as Sheol in the OT, except that in fewer cases can it be construed to signify "the grave." It takes this meaning in Acts 2:31, but in general the Hades of the NT appears to be the world of future punishment (e.g., Matt. 11:23; 16:18; Luke 16:23). *See* Hades; Hell; Gehenna.

BIBLIOGRAPHY: J. D. Davis, *Princeton Theological Review* 6 (1908): 246-68; R. H. Charles, *A Critical History of the Doctrine of a Future Life* (1913); E. F. Sutcliffe, *The Old Testament and the Future Life* (1947); N. J. Tromp, *Primitive Conceptions of Death and Nether World in the Old Testament* (1969); S. D. F. Salmond, *The Biblical Doctrine of Immortality* (1984).

SHE'PHAM (she'fam). A place mentioned by Moses in his specification of the eastern boundary of the Promised Land (Num. 34:10-11). Location on NE near Riblah.

SHEPHATI'AH (shef-a-tī'a; "Jehovah judges").
1. The fifth of the six sons born to David in Hebron. His mother's name was Abital (2 Sam. 3:4; 1 Chron. 3:3), about 994 B.C.
2. Son of Reuel and father of Meshullam, a Benjamite leader dwelling in Jerusalem after the captivity (1 Chron. 9:8), before 536 B.C.
3. The Haruphite, or Hariphite, one of the Benjamite warriors who joined David in his retreat at Ziklag (1 Chron. 12:5), about 1002 B.C.
4. Son of Maacah and head of the Simeonites in the time of David (1 Chron. 27:16), before 960 B.C.
5. The last named of the six sons of Jehoshaphat, king of Judah, all of whom were richly endowed by their father (2 Chron. 21:2-3), after 875 B.C.
6. The family of Shephatiah, 372 in number, returned with Zerubbabel (Ezra 2:4; Neh. 7:9). A second detachment of 80, with Zebadiah at their head, came up with Ezra (Ezra 8:8), before 536 B.C.
7. The family of another Shephatiah were among the children of Solomon's servants who came up with Zerubbabel (Ezra 2:57; Neh. 7:59), before 536 B.C.
8. A descendant of Perez, the son of Judah and ancestor of Athaiah (Neh. 11:4), long before 536 B.C.
9. The son of Mattan, one of the officials of Judah, who counseled Zedekiah to put Jeremiah to death (Jer. 38:1, 4), 589 B.C.

SHEPHE'LAH, THE (she-fay'la; "the low," i.e., "land"). The name given to the southern division of the low-lying district between the central highlands of *Palestine* (which see) and the Mediterranean. Though the name may originally have been used to include the maritime plain, the Shephelah proper was the region of low hills between that plain and the high central range. It is about forty miles long, N to S, and eight miles wide, E to W. Its altitude ranges from 500 to 1,000 feet. It contained the strategic defense cities of Lachish, Debir, Libnah, and Beth-shemesh.

BIBLIOGRAPHY: G. F. Owen, *The Holy Land* (1977), pp. 81-89.

THE GREAT SEA — JUDEA — Aphek — Joppa — Jericho — Jordan river — Ashdod — Ekron — Aijalon — Jerusalem — Ashkelon — Gath — PHILISTIA — Gaza — SHEPHELAH — Hebron — WILDERNESS OF JUDEA — Salt Sea — 0 25 50 km — 0 10 20 30 miles — Beersheba — **THE SHEPHELAH** — Tamar — Kadesh-barnea — E D O M

SHE'PHER (Heb. *sheper*, "brightness," Num. 33:23-24; "Shapher," KJV.) A mountain at which the Israelites camped during their wilderness journeying, between Kehelathah and Haradah. Its identification is doubtful.

SHEPHERD (from Heb. *rō'eh*, "one who tends," to "tend"; Gk. *poimēn*).
Duties. The routine of the shepherd's duties appears to have been as follows: In the morning he led forth his flock from the fold (John 10:4), which he did by going before them and calling them, as is still usual in the East. Arriving at the pasturage, he watched the flock with the assistance of dogs (Job 30:1), and, should any sheep stray, he had to search for it until he found it (Ezek. 34:12; Luke 15:4). He supplied them with water, either at a running stream or at troughs attached to wells (Gen. 29:7; 30:38; Ex. 2:16; Ps. 23:2). At evening he brought them back to the fold and checked to see that none was missing by passing them "under the rod" as they entered the door of the enclosure (Lev. 27:32; Ezek. 20:37), checking each sheep as it passed, by a motion of the hand (Jer. 33:13). Finally, he watched the entrance of the fold throughout the night, acting as gatekeeper (John 10:3). The shepherd's office thus required great watchfulness, particularly by night (Luke 2:8; cf. Nah. 3:18). It also required tenderness toward the young and feeble (Isa.

40:11), particularly in driving them to and from the pasturage (Gen. 33:13). In large establishments there were various grades of shepherds; the highest were those "put . . . in charge" (Gen. 47:6), or "chief shepherds" (cf. 1 Pet. 5:4). In a royal household the title *'abbîr,* "chief," was bestowed on the person who held the post (1 Sam. 21:7). Shepherds in Bible lands were of two varieties—those who were nomadic, and migrated to new pastures and sources of water, and those who resided in towns and tended flocks in nearby meadows.

A Bedouin shepherd

Life. The office of the Eastern shepherd, as described in the Bible, involved much hardship and even danger. He was exposed to extremes of heat and cold (Gen. 31:40); his food frequently consisted of the precarious supplies afforded by nature, such as the "sycamore fig" or Egyptian fig (Amos 7:14), the "pods" of the carob tree (Luke 15:16), and perhaps the locusts and wild honey that supported John the Baptist (Matt. 3:4); he had to encounter attacks of wild beasts, occasionally of the larger species, such as lions, wolves, leopards, and bears (1 Sam. 17:34; Isa. 31:4; Jer. 5:6; Amos 3:12); nor was he free from the risk of robbers or predatory hordes (Gen. 31:39). To meet these various foes, the shepherd's equipment consisted of the following articles: a robe, made probably of sheepskin, with the fleece on, which he turned inside out in cold weather, as implied in the comparison in Jer. 43:12 (cf. Juv. 14. 187); a pouch, containing a

small amount of food (1 Sam. 17:40); a sling, which is still the favorite weapon of the Bedouin shepherd (17:40); and, last, a staff, which served the double purpose of a weapon against foes and a crook for the management of the flock (1 Sam. 17:40; Ps. 23:4; Zech. 11:7). If the shepherd was at a distance from his home, he was provided with a light tent (Song of Sol. 1:8; Jer. 35:7), the removal of which was easily effected (Isa. 38:12). In certain localities, moreover, towers were erected for the double purpose of spying on an enemy at a distance and protecting the flock; such towers were erected by Uzziah and Jotham (2 Chron. 26:10; 27:4), whereas their existence in earlier times is testified by the name Migdal-Eder (Gen. 35:21, "tower of Eder"; Mic. 4:8, "tower of the flock"). Shepherds found shelter in caves such as those near Bethlehem or at 'Ain Feshka, where the Dead Sea Scrolls were uncovered, or the Cave of Pan at Banias. Often the shepherd simply slept under the stars or in a light, easily transported tent (Song of Sol. 1:8).

The hatred of the Egyptians toward shepherds (Gen. 46:34) may have been mainly due to their contempt for the sheep itself, which appears to have been valued neither for food nor generally for sacrifice. They were offered for sacrifice only in the district of the Natron lakes.

Figurative. The shepherd is used frequently in Scripture as illustrative:

1. Of God as the Leader of Israel (Pss. 77:20; 80:1).

2. Of Christ as the Good Shepherd (Ezek. 34:23; Zech. 13:7; Isa. 40:11; John 10:14; Heb. 13:20).

3. Of kings as leaders of the people (Isa. 44:28; Jer. 6:3; 49:19).

4. Of ministers (Jer. 23:4), foolish shepherds as bad ministers (Isa. 56:11; Jer. 50:6; Ezek. 34:2, 10; Zech. 11:8, 15-17).

BIBLIOGRAPHY: F. F. Bruce, *New Testament Development of Old Testament Themes* (1969), pp. 100-114.

SHE'PHI (shef'i; "bareness"). The fourth of the five sons of Shobal, the son of Seir of Edom (1 Chron. 1:40), called in the parallel passage (Gen. 36:23) Shepho (Shephi in the NIV).

SHE'PHO (shef'o; Gen. 36:23). *See* Shephi.

SHE'PHUPHAM (she'fū-fam). Mentioned in Num. 26:39 as one of the "sons" of Benjamin and head of the family of Shuphamites. He is doubtless the same person elsewhere (1 Chron. 8:5) called *Shephuphan* (which see). He was, if the same person, a son of Bela the son of Benjamin and was reckoned among Benjamin's sons because, like them, he founded an independent family (K. & D., *Com.,* ad loc.). The NIV reads Shupham.

SHEPHU'PHAN (she-fū'fan). One of the sons of Bela, the firstborn of Benjamin (1 Chron. 8:5). His name is also written Shephupham or Shupham (Num. 26:39) and Muppim (Gen. 46:21).

SHERAH. *See* Sheerah.

SHERD. A piece of broken pottery. The numerous potsherds found in ancient biblical and near-biblical sites are of inestimable value to the archaeologist in dating occupational strata and in determining density of population in any era. Pottery chronology is now a precise science. Perhaps more than any one factor it has lifted modern archaeology out of the category of a treasure hunt and placed it on a solid scientific basis. Sir Flinders Petrie in 1890 worked out sequence dating by types of pottery found in different strata. Petrie's initial methods have been greatly refined. Two basic principles underlying scientific archaeology are (1) *stratigraphy,* or the examination of the kinds of pottery found in occupational levels and (2) *typology,* the study of the relation of the forms of pottery found at a given level. At Ras Shamra in N Syria pottery excavated shows influences as far distant as Turkistan, Susa, and Nineveh. Palestinian pottery gives evidence of great artistic ability, showing Israel's creative skill. *See* Potsherd.   M.F.U.

SHEREBI'AH (sher-e-bī′a; "Jehovah has sent scorching heat"). A Levite of the family of Mahli, the son of Merari, who, with eighteen of his brethren, joined Ezra at the river Ahava (Ezra 8:18, 24). When Ezra read the law to the people, Sherebiah was among the Levites who assisted him (Neh. 8:7), about 445 B.C. He took part in the psalm of confession and thanksgiving that was sung at the solemn fast after the feast of Tabernacles (9:4-5), and signed the covenant with Nehemiah (10:12). He is again mentioned among the chief Levites who belonged to the choir (12:8, 24).

SHE'RESH (she′resh; "root"). Son of Machir the Manassite by his wife Maacah (1 Chron. 7:16).

SHEREZER. *See* Sharezer, no. 2.

SHERIFF. *See* Magistrate.

SHE'SHACH, SHESHAK (she′shak). This is supposed to be a symbolical name for Babel, or Babylon (Jer. 25:26; 51:41). It is thought by some critics to be a cabalistic plan called "Athbash." The letters of the alphabet were numbered both in their correct and reverse orders. When the cypher of a name was devised, its consonants were replaced by the identical numbers in the reverse numbering. Since "B" is the second letter of the Heb. alphabet and "S" or "Sh" the second from the end, and "L" the twelfth from the beginning and "K" the twelfth from the end, the cypher for Babel was Sheshak.

SHE'SHAI (she′shī; "whitish"). One of the three sons of Anak, who dwelt in Hebron (Num. 13:22) and were driven thence and slain by Caleb at the

head of the children of Judah (Josh. 15:14; Judg. 1:10), c. 1364 B.C.

SHE'SHAN (she′shan). A son of Ishi, in the posterity of Jerahmeel, of the tribe of Judah. Having no sons, he gave his daughter, probably Ahlai, to his Egyptian slave, Jarha, through which union the line was perpetuated (1 Chron. 2:31, 34-35), about 1190 B.C.

SHESHBAZ'ZAR (shesh-baz′er; Akkad., apparently "Sun-god, guard the lord or son"). The Chaldean name given, apparently, to Zerubbabel (Ezra 1:8, 11; 5:14, 16). That Sheshbazzar means Zerubbabel is evident from (1) his being called the "prince [*hannāsî′*] of Judah" (1:8), a term marking him as head of the tribe in the Jewish sense; (2) his being characterized as "governor" *pehâ,* appointed by Cyrus, both which Zerubbabel was (5:14); and yet more distinctly by the assertion (5:16) that "Sheshbazzar came and laid the foundations of the house of God in Jerusalem," compared with the promise to Zerubbabel (Zech. 4:9), "The hands of Zerubbabel have laid the foundation of this house, and his hands will finish it."

SHETH (sheth; "a placing, compensation"). In Num. 24:17 (KJV, NASB, NIV) the Heb. term is rendered as a proper name, Sheth, but there is reason to regard it as an appellative and to translate, instead of "the sons of Sheth," "the sons of tumult," or *confusion,* the wild warriors of Moab (cf. Jer. 48:45, "riotous revelers," NASB, with marg., "sons of tumult"). The NIV gives "noisy boasters" as the marginal reading of Num. 24:17 but as the textual reading of Jer. 48:45.

SHE'THAR (she′thar; foreign derivation). One of the seven princes of Persia and Media, who had access to the king's presence and were the first men in the kingdom in the third year of Ahasuerus (Esther 1:14).

SHE'THAR-BOZ'ENAI (she′thar-boz′e-nī). A Persian officer of rank, having a command in the province "beyond the River," under Tattenai, the governor, in the reign of Darius Hystaspes (Ezra 5:3, 6; 6:6, 13). He joined with Tattenai and "his colleagues the officials" in trying to obstruct the progress of the Temple in the time of Zerubbabel and in writing a letter to Darius, of which a copy is preserved in Ezra 5. As for the name Shethar-bozenai, it certainly seems to be Persian. The first element of it appears as the name Shethar, one of the seven Persian princes in Esther 1:14 (Smith).

SHE'THAR-BOZ'NAI. *See* Shethar-bozenai.

SHE'VA (shē′va; "vanity").
1. The scribe or royal secretary of David (2 Sam. 20:25). He is called elsewhere Seraiah (8:17), Shisha (1 Kings 4:3), and Shavsha (1 Chron. 18:16).

2. Son of Caleb the son of Hezron, by his concubine Maacah (1 Chron. 2:49).

SHEWBREAD. *See* Showbread.

SHI'BAH (shē'ba; "seven, an oath"). The famous well that gave its name to the city of Beersheba (Gen. 26:33). According to this version of the occurrence, Shibah ("Shebah," KJV) was the fourth of the series of wells dug by Isaac's people and received its name from him, apparently in allusion to the oaths that had passed between himself and the Philistine chieftains the day before. It should not be overlooked that the well owed its existence and name to Isaac's father (21:32). Some commentators, looking to the fact that there are two large wells at Bir es Sèba, propose to consider the two transactions as distinct, the one belonging to the one well, the other to the other. Others see in the two narratives merely two versions of the circumstances under which this renowned well was first dug.

SHIB'BOLETH (shib'bō-leth; a "stream, as flowing"; or an "ear" of grain, as growing out). This word came into notice in the OT history merely with respect to its proper pronunciation. After the defeat of the Ephraimites by Jephthah and the Gileadites on the farther side of Jordan, the latter seized the fords of the river, with the view of cutting off the return of the Ephraimites. To test whether those who approached the river were really Ephraimites, they asked them to pronounce the word *shibboleth*. If any pronounced it *sibboleth*—the way the Ephraimites did—doing away with the aspirate—he was adjudged an Ephraimite and put to death. Thus 42,000 Ephraimites fell (Judg. 12:5-6).

SHIB'MAH. *See* Sibmah.

SHIC'RON. *See* Shikkeron.

SHIELD. *See* Armor, Arms.

SHIE'RON. *See* Shikkeron.

SHIGGA'ION (shi-ga'yon). Used in the title of Ps. 7, meaning not certain.

SHIGIO'NOTH (shi-gi-o'nōth). Shigionoth, pl. of Shiggaion (Hab. 3:1).

SHI'HON. *See* Shion.

SHI'HOR (shi'hor). One of the Heb. names given to the Nile in Scripture (*see* Isa. 23:3; Jer. 2:18, where *Sihor* is given in the KJV and *Shihor* in the NIV, but *Nile* in the NASB). *Shīhōr* means "black, dark, turbid," suggested by Egyptian *Shi-ḥrw*, "lake or pool of Horus." The name *Sihor* (KJV), or *Shihor* (NASB, NIV) appears also in Josh. 13:3; 1 Chron. 13:5, as the border of a region still to be possessed by the Israelites. Opinions vary as to the identity of this place, but Keil (*Com.*) believes it to be the brook of Egypt, the modern Wadi el-Arish.

SHI'HOR-LIB'NATH (shi'hor-lib'nath; "turbid or muddy stream of Libnath"). It is generally believed to be a river of Carmel, on the borders of Asher, probably the modern Nahr-Zerka, or crocodile brook (Josh. 19:26). Crocodiles are still found in the Zerka.

SHIK'KERON (shik'eron; "drunkenness"; KJV *Shicron*). A town near the western end of the northern boundary of Judah, between Ekron and Mt. Baalah (Josh. 15:11). As it is not named among the cities of Judah (vv. 21-63), it would seem to have been in Dan. It is, perhaps, the present ruined village Beit Shit, about halfway between Ekron and Ashdod.

SHIL'HI (shil'hi; perhaps, "He," i.e., Jehovah, "has sent"). The father of Azubah, the mother of King Jehoshaphat (1 Kings 22:42; 2 Chron. 20:31), before 875 B.C.

SHIL'HIM (shil'him; "missiles"). A place in the S of Judah (Josh. 15:32). It is also called Sharuhen (Josh. 19:6) and Shaaraim (1 Chron. 4:31). *See* Sharuhen.

SHIL'LEM (shil'em; "recompense"). A son of Naphtali (Gen. 46:24; Num. 26:49), elsewhere (1 Chron. 7:13) called *Shallum* (which see). The NIV retains Shillem throughout.

SHIL'LEMITE (shil'e-mīt), a descendant of *Shillem* (which see), mentioned in Num. 26:49.

SHILO'AH (shī-lō'a; Isa. 8:6). *See* Siloam.

SHILOAH, WATERS OF (shī-lō'a). Used (Isa. 8:6) "as a symbol of Davidic monarchy enthroned upon Zion, which had the promise of God, who was enthroned upon Moriah, in contrast with the imperial or world kingdom, which is compared to the overflowing waters of the Euphrates" (Delitzsch, *Com.*, ad loc.). There is no reason to doubt that the "waters" are the same as the *pool of Siloam* (which see).

SHI'LOH (shī'lo). The name, apparently, of a person.

A title of the Messiah (Gen. 49:10), Heb. *shilōh*. Though there has been much discussion as to the grammatical interpretation of the word, Jewish officialdom and the Christian church agree as to the fact that the patriarch is here proclaiming the coming of the Messiah. The NIV renders "until he comes to whom it belongs," thus taking Shiloh as the Heb. phrase *shelōh*; i.e., "that which is to him" or "that which belongs to him." *See* NIV margin. "The objection that the expectation of a personal Messiah was foreign to the patriarchal age, and must have been foreign to the nature of that age" (Kurtz) is not valid. For the expectation of a personal Savior did not arise for the first time with Moses, Joshua, and David, but was contained in the germ of the promise of the seed of the woman and in the blessing of Noah upon Shem, and was still further expanded in the promises of God to the patriarchs. When Jacob had before him the founders of the twelve-tribed nation the question naturally arose, from which of the twelve tribes would the promised Savior proceed? *Reuben* (which see) had forfeited the right of primogeniture by his incest, and it could not pass over to either Simeon or Levi on account of their crime against the Shechemites. Consequently the dying patriarch transferred, both by his blessing and prophecy, the chieftainship and promise to his fourth son, Judah. Judah was to bear the scepter with victorious, lionlike courage, until in the future "Shiloh" was to descend from Judah.

The gradual advance of messianic prophecy places the personal meaning of Shiloh beyond all possible doubt. Balaam's prophecy transfers Jacob's proclamation of the lion nature of Judah to Israel as a nation (Num. 23:24; 24:9) and introduces the figure of the scepter from Gen. 49:9-10. As champion even after the death of Joshua, Judah by divine direction opened the attack upon the Canaanites (Judg. 1:1-10) and also the war against Benjamin (20:18). From Judah was raised up the first judge in the person of Othniel (3:9). The election of David raised Judah to the rank of ruling tribe, and it received the scepter over all the rest (1 Chron. 28:4). The authority of Zerubbabel as "governor of Judah" (Hag. 2:2) would seem to have rested upon a recognition of this traditional supremacy.

Solomon sang of the "king's son" who should have dominion from sea to sea and from the river to the ends of the earth (Ps. 72). The prophets after Solomon prophesied of the Prince of Peace, who should increase government and peace without end upon the throne of David, and of the sprout out of the rod of Jesse, whom the nations should seek (Isa. 9:6-7; 11:1-10; cf. Ezek. 21:27). "Thus did the kingdom of Judah arise from its temporary overthrow to a new and imperishable glory in Jesus Christ (Heb. 7:14), who conquerors all foes as the Lion of the tribe of Judah (Rev. 5:5) and reigns as the true Prince of Peace, as 'our peace' (Eph. 2:14), forever and ever" (K. & D., *Com.,* on Gen.).

SHI'LOH (shī'lo). The site of Israel's early sanctuary in the time of the Judges, is identified with Seilun, thirty miles N of Jerusalem. It was located E of the main road from Jerusalem to Shechem, about nine miles N of Bethel. Considering all factors, Shiloh was a good choice of a sanctuary from the point of view of a central location. It was the focal point of Israel's tribal organization before the establishment of the kingdom. Such a central religious institution of a common shrine around which were grouped the twelve tribes has close parallels in Mediterranean lands (cf. Martin Noth, *Das System der Zwoelf Staemme Israel* [1930], pp. 39-60). Numerous associations such as the Delphic in the eighth century B.C. and the

Etruscan, centering on the temple of the goddess Voltumna, are illustrations. Israel, moreover, was not the only country in the ancient Near East that had its central sanctuary to which pilgrimages were made. Nippur in Babylonia and Nineveh in Assyria in the early second millennium B.C. were such places, as is known from contemporary documents. Other examples are the temple of Sin at Haran and the shrine of Belit-ekalli at Qatna. The sanctuary of Baaltis at Byblos performed a similar function. Excavations by the Danish Expedition (1922, 1926-32, 1969) have uncovered pottery and other evidence demonstrating that Shiloh was destroyed c. 1050 B.C., presumably at the hands of the Philistines when the Ark was carried away (1 Sam. 4). Jeremiah takes this destruction for granted (Jer. 7:12-15; 26:6), and findings at the site offer an interesting instance of archaeology's ability to supplement information contained in the biblical account. When the Philistines brought back the Ark to Israel it was not set up again at Shiloh (1 Sam. 6:21–7:2).

BIBLIOGRAPHY: M. L. Buhl and S. Holm Nielsen, *Shiloh . . . the Pre-Hellenistic Remains* (1969); M. Avi-Yonah and E. Stern, eds., *Encyclopedia of Archaeological Excavations in the Holy Land* (1977), 4:1098-1100.

The area of Shiloh

SHILO'NI (Neh. 11:5, KJV). This word should be rendered "the *Shilonite,*" which see. The NIV reads, "a descendant of Shelah."

SHI'LONITE (shī'lo-nīt).

1. The native or resident of Shiloh—a title ascribed only to the prophet Ahijah (1 Kings 11:29; 12:15; 15:29; 2 Chron. 9:29; 10:15; Neh. 11:5).

2. The Shilonites are mentioned among the descendants of Judah dwelling in Jerusalem at a date difficult to fix (1 Chron. 9:5). They are doubtless the members of the house of Shelah, who in the Pentateuch are more accurately designated Shelanites.

SHIL'SHAH (shil'sha; "triad"). Son of Zophah, of the tribe of Asher (1 Chron. 7:37), before 960 B.C.

SHIM'EA (shim'i-a; "report, rumor, fame").

1. Son of David by Bathsheba (1 Chron. 3:5; Shammua, NIV), called in 2 Sam. 5:14; 1 Chron. 14:4, *Shammua* (which see).

2. A Merarite Levite, son of Uzzah and father of Haggiah (1 Chron. 6:30), before 987 B.C.

3. A Gershonite Levite, ancestor of Asaph the singer (1 Chron. 6:39).

4. The brother of David and father of Jonathan (1 Chron. 2:13; 20:7), elsewhere called Shammah (1 Sam. 16:9) or Shimei (2 Sam. 21:21, NASB; "Shimeah," KJV and NIV).

SHIM'EAH (shim'i-a). A descendant of Jeiel, the father or founder of Gibeon (1 Chron. 8:32), perhaps 536 B.C. He is called Shimeam (9:38).

SHIM'EAM (shim'i-am; "their fame"). The descendant of Jeiel (1 Chron. 9:38), called (8:32) *Shimeah* (which see).

SHIM'EATH (shim'i-ath; fem. of "Shimeah"). An Ammonitess, mother of Jozacar or Zabad, one of the murderers of King Joash (2 Kings 12:21; 2 Chron. 24:26), before 797 B.C.

SHIM'EATHITES (shim'i-a-thīts). One of the families of "scribes" resident at Jabez, in the tribe of Judah (1 Chron. 2:55); descendants, apparently, of a Shimeah not of the Kenites, possibly the brother of David (1 Chron. 2:13; 20:7).

SHIM'EI (shim'ī; perhaps, "a renowned one").

1. Son of Gershon, the son of Levi (Ex. 6:17; Num. 3:18; 1 Chron. 6:17, 29; 23:7, 9-10; Zech. 12:13). In 1 Chron. 6:29, he is called the son of Libni, and both are reckoned as sons of Merari; but there is reason to suppose that there is something omitted in this verse, as he is everywhere else represented to be Libni's *brother*. Strong (*Cyclopoedia*) conjectures that Shelomith should be read instead of Shimei in 1 Chron. 23:10. Keil (*Com.*, ad loc.) thinks the Shimei of vv. 7 and 10 to be another than the one in v. 9. *See* Shimeites.

2. The son of Gera, a Benjamite of the house of Saul, and resident, during David's reign, of Bahurim, on the other side of the Mount of Olives (2 Sam. 16:5).

When David, in his flight from Absalom, had come to Bahurim, Shimei ran out of the place, cursing the king and pelting him and his servants with stones. Abishai wanted to put an end to this cursing and requested permission to "cut off his head," but was forbidden by the king, who said, "Perhaps the Lord will look on my affliction and return good to me instead of his cursing this day." The royal party passed on; Shimei followed them and cast stones and dirt as long as they were in sight (2 Sam. 16:5-13), about 967 B.C.

The next we learn of Shimei is his pleading for pardon at the hands of the king. When David crossed the Jordan in the ferryboat (2 Sam. 19:18), the first person to welcome him was Shimei, who may have seen him approaching from the heights above. He threw himself at David's feet in abject penitence, and, notwithstanding the desire of Abishai that he should be put to death, his life was spared (19:16-23).

But the king's suspicions were not set at rest by this submission, and on his deathbed he recalled the whole scene to his son Solomon. Solomon gave Shimei notice that from henceforth he had to consider himself confined to the walls of Jerusalem on pain of death. He was to build a house in Jerusalem (1 Kings 2:36-37). For three years the agreement was kept. At the end of that time, for the purpose of capturing two slaves who had escaped to Gath, Shimei went out on his donkey and made his journey successfully. On his return the king kept his word, and Shimei was slain by Benaiah (vv. 38-46), around 955 B.C.

3. The brother of David and father of Jonathan (2 Sam. 21:21), elsewhere called Shimea, "Shimma," KJV (1 Chron. 2:13; 20:7), Shimeah, NIV, or *Shammah* (1 Sam. 16:9), which see.

4. An adherent of Solomon at the time of Adonijah's usurpation (1 Kings 1:8), 958 B.C. Unless he is the same as Shimei the son of Ela (4:18), Solomon's deputy, or with Shimea, or Shammah, David's brother, it is impossible to identify him.

5. Son of Ela, and Solomon's deputy in Benjamin (1 Kings 4:18), 954 B.C.

6. Son of Pedaiah and brother of Zerubbabel (1 Chron. 3:19), 536 B.C.

7. A Simeonite, son of Zaccur. Special mention is made of his large family (1 Chron. 4:26-27), perhaps before 1210 B.C.

8. A Reubenite, son of Gog and father of Micah (1 Chron. 5:4).

9. A Gershonite Levite, son of Jahath (1 Chron. 6:42).

10. A Benjamite (1 Chron. 8:21, "Shimhi," KJV), apparently the same as Shema, the son of Elpaal (v. 13).

11. Son of Jeduthun, and head of the tenth division of the singers in David's reign (1 Chron. 25:17), before 960 B.C.

12. The Ramathite who was over David's vineyards (1 Chron. 27:27), before 960 B.C.

13. A Levite of the sons of Heman, who took part in the purification of the Temple under Hezekiah (2 Chron. 29:14), c. 720 B.C.

14. The Levite who, with his brother Conaniah, had charge of the offerings in the reign of Hezekiah (2 Chron. 31:12-13), 719 B.C. Perhaps the same as the preceding.

15. A Levite in the time of Ezra who had married a foreign wife (Ezra 10:23), 456 B.C.

16. One of the family of Hashum who put away his foreign wife at Ezra's command (Ezra 10:33).

17. A son of Bani, who also had married a foreign wife and put her away (Ezra 10:38).

18. Son of Kish, a Benjamite and ancestor of Mordecai (Esther 2:5), before 518 B.C.

SHIM'EITES, SHIMITES (shim'e-īts, shim'īts; "Shimite," KJV). A descendant of Shimei (no. 1), the son of Gershon (Num. 3:21; cf. Zech. 12:13).

SHIM'EON (shim'i-on; "a hearing," i.e., in prayer). A layman of Israel, of the family of Harim, who had married a foreign wife and divorced her in the time of Ezra (Ezra 10:31).

SHIMHI. *See* Shimei, no. 10.

SHIMI. *See* Shimei, no. 1.

SHIMMA. *See* Shimei, no. 3.

SHI'MON (shi'mon). The four sons of Shimon are enumerated in an obscure genealogy of the tribe of Judah (1 Chron. 4:20).

SHIM'RATH (shim'rath; "a guarding, watching"). A Benjamite, the ninth named of the sons of Shimei, no. 10 (1 Chron. 8:21).

SHIM'RI (shim'ri; "vigilant, watchful").

1. Son of Shemaiah, and head of a Simeonite family (1 Chron. 4:37), probably after 1170 B.C.

2. The father of Jediael, one of David's mighty men (1 Chron. 11:45), before 982 B.C.

3. "Simri," KJV. Son of the Merarite Levite Hosah. He was not the firstborn, but for some reason his father made him "first." He was appointed by David to be gatekeeper for the Ark (1 Chron. 26:10), before 960 B.C.

4. The son of Elizaphan, and one of the Levites who aided in the purification of the Temple under Hezekiah (2 Chron. 29:13), c. 720 B.C.

SHIM'RITH (shim'rith; fem. of "Shimri"), a Moabitess, mother of Jehozabad, one of the assassins of King Joash (2 Chron. 24:26; in 2 Kings 12:21, Shomer).

SHIMROM. *See* Shimron.

SHIM'RON (shim'ron; "guardianship").

1. The fourth son of Issachar (Gen. 46:13; Num. 26:24; 1 Chron. 7:1, "Shimrom," KJV), and the head of the family of the Shimronites, about 1910 B.C.

2. A town of Zebulun (Josh. 19:15), one of those that joined the confederacy under Jabin against Joshua (11:1-5), more fully called Shimron-meron (12:20).

SHIM'RONITE (shim'ron-it). A descendant (Num. 26:24) of Shimron, the son of Issachar.

SHIM'RON-ME'RON (shim'ron-mē'ron). A town conquered by Joshua (Josh. 12:20), and probably the same as elsewhere (11:1) called simply *Shimron* (which see).

SHIM'SHAI (shim'shī; "sunny"). The scribe or secretary of Rehum, who was a kind of satrap of

the conquered province of Judea and of the colony of Samaria, supported by the Persian court (Ezra 4:8, 9, 17, 23). He was apparently an Aramean, for the letter that he wrote to Artaxerxes was in Aramaic (4:7), and the form of his name is in favor of this supposition.

SHIN (ש) (shēn). The twenty-first letter of the Heb. alphabet. It is given the English sound "sh," as in "sheen." It heads the twenty-first section of Ps. 119 (which see). The Heb. letter *sin* (ש), pronounced *sēen,* looks exactly like it, except for the placement of the dot above the left arm of the character.

SHI'NAB (shi'nab). The king of Admah in the time of Abraham (Gen. 14:2), c. 1965 B.C.

SHI'NAR (shi'nar). The name of a country (Gen. 10:10; 11:2). In the biblical story, Shinar is the name of the land in which were located the cities of Babel, Erech, Accad, and Calneh. It was, therefore, a part of the land of Babylonia and may be roughly spoken of as southern Babylonia, though some of these cities, perhaps, would more strictly be included in northern Babylonia. Though some in the past have equated Shinar with Sumer (southern Babylonia), scholars do not now consider the two terms to be linguistically equatable. It is best just to identify the plain of Shinar as the plain of southern Mesopotamia. The land to which it is applied in the OT is alluvial and was celebrated in the ancient world not only by the Babylonians but also by the Greeks and Romans as a region of prodigious fertility. Largely because of salinization, this is no longer true.

Before the fourth millennium B.C., a non-Se-

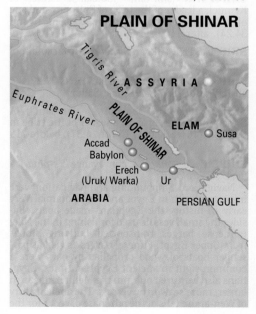

PLAIN OF SHINAR

Tigris River

ASSYRIA

Euphrates River

PLAIN OF SHINAR

ELAM

Susa

Accad

Babylon

Erech
(Uruk/ Warka)

Ur

ARABIA

PERSIAN GULF

mitic people known as the Sumerians entered this fertile region and developed a high degree of civilization and a pictograph cuneiform writing that was the precursor of Semitic cuneiform. Isaiah named Shinar as one of the places from which the Jews would be regathered at the end time (Isa. 11:11). Zechariah 5:11 mentions Shinar in connection with the woman and the ephah, symbolizing the spirit of godless commercialism as originating in Babylon. Nebuchadnezzar carried away Temple treasures taken from Jerusalem to the Shinar area (Dan. 1:2). H.F.V.

BIBLIOGRAPHY: S. N. Kramer, *The Sumerians: Their History, Culture and Character* (1963).

SHINAR, BEAUTIFUL MANTLE FROM. See Beautiful Mantle from Shinar.

SHI'ON (shi'on; "overturning, a ruin"). A city in Issachar (Josh. 19:19), between Hapharaim and Anaharath. A name resembling it at present in that neighborhood is 'Ayunesh-Sh'ian, three miles WNW of Mt. Tabor.

SHIPBUILDER. See Handicrafts.

SHIPHI. See Shipphi.

SHIPH'MITE (shif'mīt). An epithet of Zabdi, officer over David's stores of wine (1 Chron. 27:27); probably as a native of *Shepham* (which see). *See also* Siphmoth.

SHIPH'RAH (shif'ra; "splendor, beauty"). The name of one of the two midwives of the Hebrews who disobeyed the command of Pharaoh to kill the male children (Ex. 1:15-21). See Puah.

SHIPH'TAN (shif'tan; "judicial"). Father of Kemuel, a leader of the tribe of Ephraim, and one of those appointed to divide Canaan (Num. 34:24), after 1400 B.C.

SHIPMASTER (Gk. *kubernētēs*). The captain of a boat (Rev. 18:17; cf. Acts 27:11).

SHIPMEN. Sailors (1 Kings 9:27; Acts 27:27, 30; all KJV and NIV). *See* Ships; Sailor.

SHIP'PHI (shi'fi; "abounding, abundant"). A Simeonite, father of Ziza, a leader of the tribe in the time of Hezekiah (1 Chron. 4:37), before 719 B.C.

SHIPS (Heb. *ŏnîyyâ*, "conveyance"; *sepînâ*, "a boat"; Gk. *ploion*).

Navigation. Shipbuilding and navigation were important both in Egypt and Mesopotamia. Very early in history the Egyptians made boats. Besides the small vessels used for fishing in the Nile, immense barges transported building stones from Upper Egypt. Funeral barges as well as passenger boats of wood propelled by oars were a common sight in ancient Egyptian times. Egyptians also ventured out into the Mediterranean in larger, more seaworthy vessels. The ancient story of Wen-amon tells of the purchase of cedar for the

construction of Egyptian sacred barges. Babylonians built boats that plied the Tigris-Euphrates as well as larger ones that sailed into the Persian Gulf on extended commercial voyages. The Phoenicians were famous boat builders and sailors from early times. Byblos seamen ran a close second to the Egyptians. The famous "Byblos travelers" carried on trade with the Egyptians. This name was given to these vessels because they transported from Phoenicia to Egypt cargoes of wine, papyrus pith, oils, cedar, mummy cases, masts, and flagpoles. In exchange the Phoenicians carried back jewelry, perfumes, gold, metal-work, and luxury wares. By the time of Solomon, Phoenician trading vessels on the Mediterranean went as far as Spain. Skilled Phoenician craftsmen built Solomon's *tarshish* or copper-refining fleet at Ezion-geber, and Tyrian sailors manned them.

Model of an Egyptian funeral boat

Ancient Ships. The types of ships, or boats, used in ancient times varied from region to region.

Egyptian. Long before the time of Menes (c. 2900 B.C.), Egyptians employed ships on the Nile. By the end of the fifth millennium B.C. evidence of ships is found. Amratian vases depict large galleys. Predynastic ships had sharply upturned prows and looked like the gondolas of Venice. During many centuries the Egyptian navy was strong. "Celestial barks" carried deceased pharaohs to their final resting place. James Breasted refers to some of these being 770 cubits long.

Mesopotamian. Round, reed, basketlike barks were calked with bitumen for Mesopotamian river traffic. These common boats were the precursors of later Assyrian craft made of skin and timber rafts supported on inflated skins. Even to the present day the round *guffahs* are still to be seen on the Euphrates. Seafaring vessels came up the Persian Gulf transporting luxury wares to the Tigris-Euphrates region. The Gulf of Suez was also a common water route in antiquity. Caravans picked up the cargoes and followed regular desert routes.

Phoenician. Phoenician ships were not large but were skillfully made and manned. They had masts of cedar, oars of oak, and were often lavishly adorned. They furnished a picturesque sight with varicolored sails. Happily, the Phoenicians had plenty of wood in the forests of Lebanon at their back door. Their famous ships, often no larger than a good-sized coastal fishing boat of the present day, made a brilliant record in ancient history.

Cretan. Early in the second millennium B.C., the island of Crete became famous as a seafaring power. The Minoan sea kings, because of their great commercial wealth, were able to build the famous Minoan culture. From Heracleion near Knossos, Cretan vessels plied trade with such distant places as Troy, Athens, the cities of Asia Minor, and Ugarit in northern Syria. Phaestos on the southern coast of Crete carried on extensive trade with North Africa and Egypt.

Greek. By the seventh century B.C. the Greeks became conspicuous in sea traffic. They improved upon Phoenician boats. The famous Corinthian warships had two decks, one for rowers and one for fighters. The Greeks increased the size of their ships and had to resort to anchors. They also employed slave labor. Corinth was a famous trading center, being situated on a strategic isthmus.

Roman. In antiquity the difference between the long, narrow ship of war and the short-prowed merchant vessel was pronounced (cf. *Odyssey* 5.250; 9.323). Merchant vessels were mostly sailing vessels. Warships were customarily also propelled by oars. Early Roman vessels had from one to three banks of oars. Later vessels were constructed with four, five, or more banks of oars. The rowers were crowded together and faced the stern. The number of rowers in an ancient trireme (that is, a ship with three banks of oars) was 170; that of a Roman quinquereme, five banked, in the Punic wars was 300. Some ships were much larger than this. One eight-banked vessel is said to have had a crew of 1,600. Oars were long, and rhythm was maintained by a stroke of a hammer or the music of a flute.

Phoenician ship from a relief

Bible Reference. The following allusions to seafaring are found in the OT: the prophecy con-

cerning Zebulun (Gen. 49:13); in Balaam's prophecy (Num. 24:24); in one of the warnings of Moses (Deut. 28:68); in Deborah's song (Judg. 5:17); and in the illustrations and descriptions in Job (9:26), the Psalms (48:7; 104:26; 107:23), and Proverbs (23:34; 30:19; 31:14). We have already referred to Solomon's ships (1 Kings 9:26; 2 Chron. 8:18; 9:21) and the disastrous expedition of Jehoshaphat's ships from the same port of Ezion-geber (1 Kings 22:48-49; 2 Chron. 20:36-37). Tyre is depicted allegorically as a splendid ship (Ezek. 27), and Isaiah speaks of the "ships of Tarshish" (Isa. 2:16; 23:1, 14). In the narrative of Jonah (1:3-16), several nautical terms are introduced; and Daniel (11:40) speaks of ships of war.

Frequent mention is made in the NT of vessels on the Sea of Galilee. There Jesus addressed the multitude from on board a boat (Matt., Gk. *ploion*), i.e., a small fishing vessel; and frequent mention is made of His sailing up and down the lake (Matt. 8:23; 9:1; 14:13; John 6:17). Some of His earliest followers were owners of boats that sailed on this inland sea (Matt. 4:21; Luke 5:3; John 21:3). Josephus calls these vessels *skaphē*, "skiff" (cf. Acts 27:16, 30, 32); probably like our modern fishing smack, generally propelled by oars but also employing sails.

Construction and Equipment. Although ancient ships differed from one another, they shared many features of construction and equipment.

The Hull. The hull of ancient vessels presents no special peculiarities; the bow and stern were similar in shape; merchant ships had no hold, the cargo being stowed away upon the deck, the sides of which were protected by an open rail, the stempost and the sternpost rising in a curve, most frequently terminating in an ornament representing a waterfowl bent backward. On the stern projections we sometimes see an awning represented, and on the bow the anchors were stowed. Capstans were evidently used to raise anchors. The personification of ships led to the painting of an eye on each side of the bow, a custom still prevalent in the Mediterranean. Indeed, Western sailors speak of the "eyes" of a ship, and it is said in Acts 27:15 that the ship "could not face the wind." A badge, sign, or emblem was also placed at the prow (28:11).

Masts, Rigging. These, in distinction from the hull or vessel itself, were called *skevē*, "gear" (Acts 27:19, "tackle"). The principal feature was a large mast with one large, square sail fastened to a yard of great length. Other masts were sometimes used, arranged as the mainmast. The sail that was hoisted when the ship of Paul was run aground was a "foresail," or a small sail substituted for the larger sail in stormy weather (Gk. *artemōn*, 27:40). The *mast* or "sail" is mentioned in Isa. 33:23, and from Ezek. 27:5 we learn that Lebanon cedar was sometimes used to make them; "oaks from Bashan" for the oars (v. 6) and "fir trees from Senir" (Anti-Lebanon) for the sheathing of the hull. Ropes and sails were made of byssus linen, the latter being woven in party colors.

Anchors. Although ships rigged and constructed like those of the ancients might, under favorable circumstances, be able to work to windward, it must have been "slowly and with difficulty"; and in the event of a ship's being caught in a gale on a lee shore, the only mode of escape was to anchor. No better proof could be given of the superiority in this branch of seamanship than the successful manner in which Paul's ship was brought to anchor in the face of a lee shore in a gale, and finally run ashore, when it could be done in safety to the lives of all on board (*Imperial Bible Dictionary,* s.v.). The anchors were much like those of modern make, except that in place of the palms, or iron plates attached to the extremities of the arms, the arms themselves were beaten flat, as in Dutch anchors.

Undergirders (Gk. *hupozōmata,* Acts 27:17). The imperfection of the build, and the tendency to strain the seams, led to taking on board "helps" (Gk. *boētheia*), cables or chains, that in case of necessity could be passed around the hull, at right angles to its length and made tight—a process called *frapping* in the English navy.

Steering. Ancient ships were steered by means of two paddle rudders, one on each quarter, acting in a rowlock or through a porthole, as the vessel was large or small. The same thing is true not only of the Mediterranean ships, but of the early vessels of the Northmen. There is nothing out of harmony with this early system of steering in James 3:4, where Gk. *pēdalion,* helm, occurs in the singular; for the pilot (Gk. *euthunōn*) would only use one paddle rudder at a time.

Officers and Crew. Luke mentions (Acts 27:11; cf. Jonah 1:6; Rev. 18:17) two principal officers of the ship: the pilot (Gk. *kubernētēs,* and the *captain* (Gk. *nauklēros*), a shipowner or master of a trading vessel, who took passengers and freight for hire. The "pilot" of James 3:4 (Gk. *euthunōn*) is merely the man at the helm. The "shipmen" (Gk. *nautai*) were common sailors.

Figurative. An industrious housewife is likened to a merchant ship, bringing "her food from afar" (Prov. 31:14). "Shipwreck" is symbolical of one departing from the faith (1 Tim. 1:19).

BIBLIOGRAPHY: L. Casson, *Ancient Mariners* (1959); C. Torr, *Ancient Ships* (1964); L. Casson, *Ships and Seamanship in the Ancient World* (1971); J. Smith, *The Voyage and Shipwreck of Paul* (1977). Interest in ancient sea travel was popularized by T. Heyerdahl, *The Ra Expedition* (1972) and *The Tigris Expedition* (1980).

SHIRTS. *See* Dress.

SHI'SHA (shi'sha). Father of Elihoreph and Ahijah, the royal secretaries in the reign of Solomon (1 Kings 4:3), before 960 B.C. He is apparently the same as Shavsha, who held the same position under David. *See* Shavsha.

SHI'SHAK (shi'shak). Egyptian Sheshonk I (Sheshonq I). Founder of Libyan Dynasty XXII. Shishak is usually dated c. 945-924 B.C. He is the first pharaoh referred to specifically by name in the Bible. He is famous for his plundering expedition in the fifth year of Rehoboam (1 Kings 14:25-28) when he seized Solomon's golden shields and other Temple and royal treasures. Egyptian records do not give the date of Shishak's expedition. The chronology of the early kings of the Davidic line is debated. Albright sets the accession of Rehoboam c. 922 B.C. making the fifth regnal year c. 917 B.C. (*Bulletin of the American Schools of Oriental Research* 87 [1942]: 28; 130 [April 1953]: 7). Thiele put the accession in 931 and the invasion in 925. The gold-masked body of Shishak was uncovered intact in his burial chamber at Tanis (1938-39). In the temple of Karnak (ancient Thebes) his triumphal inscription is recorded. It enumerates his conquests, which include towns in all parts of Judah, extending up the coastal plain and crossing Esdraelon into Gilead indicating that he invaded the Northern Kingdom as well as the Southern Kingdom, in spite of his previous friendship with Jeroboam (11:40; cf. W. F. Albright, *O. T. Commentary* [1948], p. 151). A part of a stela of Shishak has been dug up at Megiddo, evidence that he actually did capture and occupy this important fortress city as recounted in the Karnak inscription. A triumphal Karnak relief displays captives of Shishak taken in his incursions into Palestine.

BIBLIOGRAPHY: J. H. Breasted, *Ancient Records of Egypt* (1962), 4:344-61; id., *A History of Egypt* (1969), pp. 440-46; K. A. Kitchen, *The Third Intermediate Period of Egypt* (1972), pp. 292-302, 432-47.

Shittim

SHIT'RAI (shit'rī). The Sharonite who had charge of David's herds that grazed in Sharon (1 Chron. 27:29), before 970 B.C.

SHITTAH TREE, SHITTIM WOOD. *See* Vegetable Kingdom: Acacia.

SHIT'TIM (shit'im; "acacias").

1. Israel's last camping place E of the Jordan before entering Palestine (Num. 25:1; Josh. 3:1; Mic. 6:5); an abbreviation of Abel-shittim (Num. 33:49). It was the place from which Joshua sent forth spies into Canaan (Josh. 2:1). *See* Abel-shittim.

2. The barren valley of the Jordan above the Dead Sea; it was chosen by the prophet Joel (Joel 3:18; "valley of acacias," NIV) to denote a very dry valley, as the acacia grows in a dry soil. It was probably W of the Jordan. In the prophecy the spring that waters this valley and proceeds from the house of Jehovah, the physical as well as spiritual blessings that will come to Palestine and its inhabitants in the Kingdom age, are portrayed (cf. Zech. 14:8; Ezek. 47:1-12).

SHI'ZA (shi'za). The father of Adina, one of David's Reubenite warriors (1 Chron. 11:42), before 1000 B.C.

SHO'A (sho'a). A people listed with the Babylonians, Chaldeans, and Assyrians (Ezek. 23:23). They may be the Sutu mentioned in the Amarna Letters, Syrian nomads who invaded the E Tigris country and, joining with Aramean peoples, were never conquered by the Assyrians.

SHO'BAB (sho'bab; "backsliding, rebellious").

1. Second named of the sons born to David in Jerusalem (2 Sam. 5:14; 1 Chron. 3:5; 14:4), about 1000 B.C.

2. Apparently the son of Caleb, the son of Hezron, by his wife Azubah (1 Chron. 2:18), about 1390 B.C.

SHO'BACH (sho'bak). The general of Hadadezer, king of the Arameans of Zobah, who was defeated by David in person at Helam. Shobach was wounded and died on the field (2 Sam. 10:15-18). In 1 Chron. 19:16, 18, he is called Shophach, c. 1001 B.C.

SHO'BAI (sho'bī; possibly, "one who takes prisoner"). The sons of Shobai were a family of Temple gatekeepers who returned with Zerubbabel (Ezra 2:42; Neh. 7:45), before 536 B.C.

SHO'BAL (sho'bal).

1. The second son of Seir the Horite (Gen. 36:29-30; 1 Chron. 1:38), and one of the "chiefs," or phylarchs, of the Horites (Gen. 36:29), about 1840 B.C.

2. One of the three sons of Hur, the son of Caleb (1 Chron. 2:50). He became the founder ("father") of Kiriath-jearim, about 1390 B.C. The passage should probably be rendered, "These are the sons [i.e., descendants] of Caleb, through his son Hur," etc. In 1 Chron. 4:1-2, Shobal appears with Hur among the sons of Judah. He is possibly the same as the preceding.

SHO'BEK (sho'bek; cf. Arab. *sabiq*, "victor, one who goes before"). One of the heads of the people who signed the covenant with Nehemiah (Neh. 10:24), 445 B.C.

SHO'BI (sho'bi; possibly, "one who takes captive"). Son of Nahash, of Rabbah, of the sons of Ammon. He was one of the first to meet David at Mahanaim, on his flight from Absalom, and supply him with bedding, cooking utensils, and food (2 Sam. 17:27), about 970 B.C.

SHO'CHO. *See* Soco.

SHO'CHOH. *See* Soco.

SHOCK OF CORN (Heb. *gādîsh*, a "heap"; hence "a tomb," Job 21:32). A "stack" (Ex. 22:6; Job 5:26) of grain reaped (Judg. 15:5).

SHO'CO. *See* Soco.

SHOE. *See* articles Dress; Sandal.

SHOE LATCHET. *See* Latchet.

SHOEMAKER. *See* Handicrafts: Leatherworker.

SHO'HAM (sho'ham; "beryl, onyx"). A Merarite Levite, son of Jaaziah, employed about the Ark by David (1 Chron. 24:27), about 983 B.C.

SHO'MER (sho'mēr; "guard, keeper").

1. Second named of the three sons of Heber, an Asherite (1 Chron. 7:32), called in v. 34 *Shemer* (which see); *Shamer*, KJV.

2. The father of Jehozabad, who killed King Joash (2 Kings 12:21). In the parallel passage in 2 Chron. 24:26, the name is converted into the feminine form Shimrith, who is further described as a Moabitess. This variation may have originated in the dubious gender of the preceding name Shimeath, which is also made feminine by the chronicler. Others suppose that in Kings the father is named and in Chronicles the mother.

SHO'PHACH (sho'fak). The general of Hadadezer (1 Chron. 19:16, 18), called in 2 Sam. 10:16, *Shobach* (which see).

SHOPHAN. *See* Atroph-shophan.

SHORE. *See* Seashore, Seacoast.

SHOULDER. The *neck*, as the place to receive a burden (Gen. 21:14; 24:45; etc.). Twice (Num. 6:19; Deut. 18:3) it represents Heb. word for *arm*, the foreshoulder offered in sacrifice; cf. the right, or "heave" offering, i.e., "shoulder" (Ex. 29:27; Lev. 7:32-34; etc.). The *shoulder,* properly so called, is the spot from which garments are suspended (Ex. 28:12; 39:7), especially of the "shoulder pieces" of the *high priest* (which see). The Gk. term *ōmos* (Matt. 23:4; Luke 15:5) is the common word for shoulder.

Figurative. To *turn a stubborn shoulder* (Neh. 9:29; "turned their backs," NIV), i.e., to refuse an appointed burden, is figurative of disobedience, rebellion; whereas to relieve one's shoulder from his burden (Ps. 81:6) is to deliver him from bondage. Job, in assurance of innocence, exclaims, "Oh . . . the indictment which my adversary has written," i.e., an *indictment* made out in legal form, and adds, "Surely I would carry it on my shoulder" (Job 31:35-36). The meaning doubtless is that he would wear it upon his shoulder as a mark of his dignity. "The staff on their shoulders" (Isa. 9:4) is the staff that strikes the shoulder; or the wood, like a yoke, on the neck of slaves, the badge of servitude. "The government will rest on His shoulders" (9:6), like the expression "Then I will set the key of the house of David on his shoulder" (22:22) refers to the custom of wearing the ensign of office upon the *shoulder,* in token of *sustaining* the government. The same idea is expressed by the epaulets worn in the army and navy. To lay heavy loads on men's shoulders, etc. (Matt. 23:4) is selfishly to burden men with obligations that the scribes and Pharisees would not concern themselves with.

SHOULDER PIECE (Heb. *kātēp,* "clothed"). The side pieces on the upper part of the high priest's ephod, which came over the shoulder, where the front and back flaps were fastened (Ex. 28:7, 12, 25; 39:4).

SHOVEL. The implement used for removing ashes from the altar (Ex. 27:3; etc.). *See* Tabernacle. It is also the rendering of Heb. *raḥat* (Isa. 30:24), a winnowing fork.

SHOWBREAD. A KJV term replaced in the NASB and NIV with bread of the Presence. *See* Tabernacle: Typology of the Tabernacle and Furniture.

SHOWER. *See* Rain.

SHRINE (Gk. *naos,* a "temple," Acts 19:24). A miniature representation of the splendid temple of Artemis, with a statue of the goddess. In the OT the Heb. term *bêth 'ĕlōhîm* ("house of God/gods") is rendered "shrine" by the NIV in Judg. 17:5. *Miqdāsh* appears as "shrine" in the NIV in Isa. 16:12.

SHROUD (Heb. *ḥoresh,* "thicket"; Ezek. 31:3, KJV; "forests," 2 Chron. 27:4, KJV, "wooded areas," NIV; "bough," Isa. 17:9, KJV, "thickets," NIV). Probably a shadowing thicket.

SHRUB (Heb. *sîaḥ,* Gen. 2:5). Elsewhere *bush* (which see; 21:15; Job 30:4, 7).

SHU'A (shū'a).
1. A Canaanite of Adullam, whose daughter was the wife of Judah and the mother of his first three children (Gen. 38:2, 12; "Shuah," KJV), elsewhere called Bath-shua (1 Chron. 2:3).
2. The daughter of Heber, the grandson of Asher (1 Chron. 7:32).

SHU'AH (shū'a).
1. The last named of the six sons of Abraham by Keturah (Gen. 25:2; 1 Chron. 1:32).

2. *See* Shua, no. 1.
3. *See* Shuhah.

SHU'AL (shū'al; "fox, jackal").
1. The third named of the eleven sons of Zophah (1 Chron. 7:36).
2. The "land of Shual" (1 Sam. 13:17) is named as invaded by one of the marauding companies of Philistines; probably five or six miles NE from Bethel in Benjamin. It has not been identified.

SHU'BAEL (shū'ba-el). Two Levites (1 Chron. 24:20; 25:20); called elsewhere *Shebuel* (which see).

SHU'HAH (shū'ha). A brother (although some manuscripts have *son*) of Chelub, among the descendants of Judah (1 Chron. 4:11; "Shuah," KJV).

SHU'HAM (shū'ham). The son of Dan (Num. 26:42); elsewhere (Gen. 46:23), called *Hushim* (which see).

SHU'HAMITE (shū'ham-īt). The descendants of Shuham numbered 4,460 when Israel entered Canaan (Num. 26:42-43).

SHU'HITE (shū'hīt). A term only used as an epithet of Bildad in Job 2:11; 18:1; 25:1; 42:9. It is quite probably a patronymic from Shuah, son of Abraham of Keturah (Gen. 25:2; 1 Chron. 1:32). His descendants formed an Arab tribe, doubtless the Shuhites who resided near the land of Uz (Job 2:11). Assyrian Suhu, on the W of the Euphrates near the mouths of the Balikh and Habur, is a likely identification. In this case the Shuhites would be in the extreme N, toward the Euphrates. This identification would favor a NE, or Aramaic, location for the land of Uz rather than a southern, i.e., an Edomite or Arabian one.
W.H.; M.F.U.

SHU'LAMMITE, SHULAMITE (shū'la-mīt; "peaceful"). The title applied (Song of Sol. 6:13) to the young woman in the Song of Solomon. Since the LXX translates the term *Sounamitis,* i.e., Shunammite, it is evidently derived from the town of Shunam near Mt. Gilboa. The form Shulammite may have been adopted because of its assonance with Solomon (Heb. *Shĕlōmōh*) and, indeed, as a kind of title (not a proper name), it may actually be the feminine of Solomon.

SHU'MATHITES (shū'math-īts). One of the principal families of Kiriath-jearim (1 Chron. 2:53).

SHU'NAMMITE (shū'nam-īt). A native of *Shunem* (which see), as is evident from 2 Kings 4:12, 25, 36; cf. v. 8, where it is applied to the hostess of Elisha. It was also applied to Abishag, the nurse of David in his old age (1 Kings 1:3; 2:17, 21-22).

SHU'NEM (shū'nem). A place belonging to Issachar. Here the Philistines encamped before Saul's last battle (Josh. 19:18; 1 Sam. 28:4). It was the home of Abishag (1 Kings 1:3), also the residence of the woman whose son Elisha restored to life (2 Kings 4:8). Identified with Solem (Sūlam) at the SW foot of Little Hermon, three miles N of Jezreel, and in the midst of a rich country.

The village of Solem, near ancient Shunem, located on the edge of the Plain of Esdraelon, from the Hill of Moreh

SHU'NI (shū'ni). Son of Gad, and founder of the family of the Shunites (Gen. 46:16; Num. 26:15), c. 1910 B.C.

SHU'NITE (shū'nīt). The patronymic given to a descendant of *Shuni* (which see), the son of Gad (Num. 26:15).

SHU'PHAM. *See* Shuphamite.

SHU'PHAMITE (shū'fam-īt). The designation of a descendant of Shephupham (Num. 26:39), or Shephuphan (1 Chron. 8:5). The KJV renders Shupham.

SHUP'PIM (shūp'im).
1. In the genealogy of Benjamin, Shuppim and Huppim, the "sons of Ir," are reckoned (1 Chron. 7:12). Ir is the same as Iri, the son of Bela, the son of Benjamin, so that Shuppim was the great-grandson of Benjamin.
2. A Levite who, together with Hosah, had charge of the Temple gate Shallecheth (1 Chron. 26:16), about 960 B.C. Keil (*Com.,* ad loc.) thinks that the word has come into the text by a repetition of the last two syllables of the preceding word.

SHUP'PITES. *See* Shuppim.

SHUR (shūr; "wall fortification"). Referred to as "east of Egypt, as one goes toward Assyria" (Gen. 25:18); and as "even as far as the land of Egypt" (1 Sam. 27:8); and as "you go to Egypt" (15:7). From its meaning "a wall," as well as from various references to it in the text, it would seem that Shur was a barrier of some kind across the great northeastern highways out of Egypt, near the eastern boundary line of Egypt. This barrier was the great defensive wall built across the eastern frontier—a wall hardly less prominent in the history of ancient Egypt than the Great Wall of China. This fortified barrier is mentioned in records from the Twelfth Dynasty, c. 2000-1775 B.C.

"With the Great Wall standing there across the entrance of Lower Egypt as a barrier and a landmark between the delta and the desert, it follows almost as a matter of course that the region on either side of the wall should bear the *name* of the wall: on the western side was the Land of Mazor, the Land Walled in; on the eastern side was the Wilderness of Shur, the Wilderness Walled out. Hence it comes to pass that the desert country eastward of Lower Egypt is known in the Bible as the Wilderness of Shur" (Trumbull, *Kadesh-Barnea,* pp. 44ff.).

Shur is first mentioned in the narrative of Hagar's flight from Sarah (Gen. 16:7). Abraham afterward "settled between Kadesh and Shur; then he sojourned in Gerar" (20:1). The first clear indication of its position occurs in the account of Ishmael's posterity. "And they settled from Havilah to Shur which is east of Egypt as one goes toward Assyria" (25:18; cf. 1 Sam. 15:7; 27:8). The wilderness of Shur was entered by the Israelites after they had crossed the Red Sea (Ex. 15:22-23). It was called the wilderness of Etham (Num. 33:8).

BIBLIOGRAPHY: C. L. Wooley and T. E. Lawrence, *The Wilderness of Zin* (1936), pp. 57-62; Y. Aharoni, *The Land of the Bible* (1979), pp. 10, 45, 56, 58, 142, 191, 196-97, 287, 291, 345.

SHUSHAN. *See* Susa.

SHUSHAN EDUTH (shū-shan e'dūth; Shushaneduth, KJV; lit., "lily of testimony"). Ps. 60, title. The NIV reads, "To the tune of 'The Lily of the Covenant.' "

SHU'THALHITE. *See* Shuthelahite.

SHU'THELAH (shū'the-la).
1. First named of the three sons of Ephraim (Num. 26:35-36), perhaps about 1850 B.C. His descendants to a second Shuthelah are given in 1 Chron. 7:20-21.
2. The sixth in descent from no. 1, being the son of Zabad and father of Ezer and Elead (1 Chron. 7:21).

SHU'THELAHITE (shū'thel-a-hīt). A designation of a descendant of *Shuthelah* (which see), the son of Ephraim (Num. 26:35).

SHUTTLE (Heb. *'ereg,* a "weaving"). Used in Job 7:6 as a figure of the swiftness of life. His days pass by as swiftly as the little shuttle moves backward and forward in the warp.

SI'A (si-a; "assembly, congregation"). One of the leaders of the Temple servants, whose "sons" returned with Zerubbabel (Neh. 7:47), before 536

B.C. In Ezra 2:44 the name is given as Siaha.

SI'AHA (sia-ha; "congregation"). A leader of the Temple servants (Ezra 2:44). In Neh. 7:47 he is called *Sia* (which see).

SIB'BECAI (sib'e-kī). "The Hushathite," probably so called from his birthplace (1 Chron. 11:29). He belonged to the prominent family of Judah the Zarhites and was captain of the 24,000 men of David's army serving in the eighth month. Sibbecai's great exploit, which gave him a place among the mighty men of David's army, was his combat with Saph, or Sippai, the Philistine giant, in the battle of Gezer, or Gob (2 Sam. 21:18; 1 Chron. 20:4), about 970 B.C.

SIB'BOLETH (sib'o-leth). Another form (Judg. 12:6) of *Shibboleth* (which see).

SIB'MAH (sib'ma; "coolness," cf. Arab. *shabima,* "to be cold"). A town E of Jordan, which was taken possession of and rebuilt by the tribe of Reuben (Josh. 13:19; Num. 32:38). It was probably the same as Sebam (v. 3), and belonged originally to that portion of Moab that was captured by the Amorites under Sihon (21:26). It is mentioned by Isaiah (16:8-9) and Jeremiah (48:32), both making reference to its vintage. The wine of Sibmah was so good that it was placed upon the table of monarchs, and so strong that it struck down, i.e., intoxicated, even those

who were accustomed to good wine. Not positively identified. Some place it at modern Qurn el-Kibsh, about five miles SW of Heshbon.

SIBRA'IM (sib-ra'im; "double hope"). A landmark on the northern boundary of Palestine, between Berothah and Hazer-hatticon (Ezek. 47:16), perhaps the same as Ziphron (Num. 34:9).

SIC'CUTH. *See* Gods, False: Sikkuth.

SI'CHEM. *See* Shechem.

SICK, SICKNESS. *See* Diseases, Treatment of.

SICKLE. The rendering of two Heb. words and one Gk. word:

1. Heb. *ḥermēsh,* a "reaping hook" (Deut. 16:9; 23:25).

2. Heb. *maggāl,* with the same meaning (Jer. 50:16; Joel 3:13).

3. The instrument generally used for cutting grain (Gk. *drepanon*). (*See* Agriculture). The Israelites might pluck and eat the standing grain of a neighbor but were forbidden to "wield a sickle," i.e., reap it (Deut. 23:25).

Figurative. "Puts in the sickle" is a figurative expression for gathering a harvest (Mark 4:29; Rev. 14:14-19).

SID'DIM, VALLEY OF (sid'im; "the valley of the fields"; perhaps so called from the high cultiva-

Salt flats of the southern Dead Sea

Farmworker with sickle

tion in which it was kept before the destruction of Sodom and the other cities). The scene of the battle between Chedorlaomer and his allies, and the five confederate kings (Gen. 14:3). However, it is possible that Siddim may designate "salt flats" from Hittite *siyanta*, "salt." In any case the term denotes the territory S of the peninsula of "The Tongue," which projects into the Dead Sea from the E shore. This region underwent a violent cataclysm about the middle of the twentieth century B.C. when its cities were destroyed and its area became submerged under the waters of the Dead Sea (Gen. 19).

Some writers unwarrantedly contend for the location of Siddim at the N end of the Dead Sea. But archaeological evidence now disfavors this view. The region was full of "tar pits" (14:10), and here the Egyptians got the bitumen with which they embalmed their dead; even to this day "pits" exist.

BIBLIOGRAPHY: J. P. Harland, *Biblical Archaeologist* 5 (1942): 17ff.; id., 6 (1943): 41ff.

SI'DON (sī'don). Sometimes *Zidon*, as in the KJV. This ancient Phoenician city was built on a promontory and small island, which was connected with the mainland by a bridge. The town was some twenty miles N of Tyre, is called Saida at present, and is now located in the republic of Lebanon. It is situated between mountains to its back and the sea to its front. Its people very early took to seafaring commerce. As the oldest capital of the Phoenicians, its antiquity is attested by Gen. 10:15. The city is referred to around 1400 B.C. in the Amarna Letters. It figures prominently in the division of the land after the Hebrew conquest (Josh. 19:28). The Phoenicians were called Sidonians from the eleventh to the eighth centuries B.C. The city's early preeminence is attested

by Homer, who often mentions Sidon but never Tyre, and who employs the name as synonymous with Phoenicia and Phoenicians. Later, however, it was outclassed by Tyre, but Phoenicians generally continued to be known as Sidonians (1 Kings 5:6; 16:31), as if in recollection of Sidon's ancient preeminence. Solomon was influenced by Sidonian cults (11:5-7) and hired expert Sidonian timber cutters. Sidonians worshiped Baal and Ashtoreth. Jezebel of infamy was a daughter of Ethbaal, "king of the Sidonians." Her introduction of the licentious worship of Canaanite cults into Israel brought internal misery (16:31-33; etc.). The Sidonians were skillful in philosophy, art, and astronomy, as is indicated by Strabo, the Greek historian of the first century, B.C. Biblical references include Isa. 23:12; Jer. 27:3; Ezek. 28:21-23; Joel 3:4-7. Shalmaneser of Assyria captured the city in 725 B.C. It was invaded by Sennacherib, dominated by Esarhaddon, overrun by the Babylonians after the fall of Assyria, and made a province by the Persians. It was conquered by Alexander the Great (330 B.C.). It enjoyed importance under the Romans, and Herod embellished it. Our Lord visited the general territory (Mark 7:24, 31) and made reference to the iniquity of its inhabitants (Matt. 11:21-24). Paul visited the place on his way to Rome (Acts 27:3). It figures in early church history, at the time of the Crusades and finally under Muslim rule. M.F.U.

BIBLIOGRAPHY: G. A. Cooke, *A Text Book of North Semitic Inscriptions* (1903), pp. 26-43; F. C. Eiselen, *Sidon: A Study in Oriental History* (1970); P. K. Hitti, *History of Syria* (1951); J. Huxley, *From an Antique Land* (1954), pp. 70-76; D. Baly, *The Geography of the Bible* (1957), pp. 93, 132, 194, 231.

SIDO'NIANS (sī-dō'ni-anz), the inhabitants of Sidon. In Gen. 10:19 Sidon and Gaza are two of the extreme points of Canaan. In 49:13 Jacob makes Sidon the limit of Zebulun. This, perhaps, means that the territory of Sidon, though afterward limited by that of Tyre, originally "extended southward to the tribe of Zebulun and Mount Carmel." In Josh. 19:28, 29, Great Sidon and Tyre are on the border of Asher.

The Sidonians were not dispossessed (Judg. 3:3), and were among the early oppressors of Israel (10:12). In Josh. 13:6 the ASV reads "even all the Sidonians." This would make the inhabitants of the hill country Sidonians, indicating that the Sidonian population had "spread up into the hill country"; and this idea is favored still more by their skill in cutting timber (1 Kings 5:6). So in Judg. 18:7 we find them described as living "quiet and secure," devoted, no doubt, to the cultivation of their lands, and not engaged in trade, having "no dealings with anyone." The language of the text indicates this "careless," "quiet and secure" life was the usual "manner of the Sidonians." The Sidonians adored, as tutelary god and goddess, Baal (whence the name of the king Ethbaal, 1 Kings 16:31) and Ashtoreth (1 Kings 11:5, 33; 2 Kings 23:13).

Jezebel, the wife of Ahab, was the daughter of the king of the Sidonians (1 Kings 16:31), but the example of taking Sidonian women had been set by Solomon (11:1).

In Homer, also, the Sidonians are praised for their skillful workmanship, but never as traders, except as they may have passed under the general name Phoenician (*Iliad* 6.289-95; *Odyssey* 4.614-18; 15.425); and the two are distinguished in the *Iliad* 23.743-44 where Phoenicians convey Sidonian work. The Homeric poems do not mention Tyre, but they mention both Sidon (*Odyssey* 15.425) and the Sidonians (*Iliad* 6.289-90; see also *Odyssey* 4.84 and 618; 15.118; *Iliad* 23.743; and their country Sidonia, *Iliad* 6.291; *Odyssey* 13.285). Strabo the Greek historian (63 B.C.) observes that although the poets glorified Sidon, the Phoenician colonists in Africa gave "more honor" to Tyre.   W.H.; M.F.U.

SIEGE. See Warfare.

SIEVE (Heb. *kebārâ*, "netted," Amos 9:9; *nāpâ*, Isa. 30:28). The ancient Egyptians often made sieves of string, and those for coarser work were constructed of small rushes or reeds.

Figurative. "To shake the nations . . . in a sieve" (Isa. 30:28) refers to a sieve in which everything that does not remain in it as good grain is given up to annihilation. To sift a nation "as grain is shaken in a sieve" (Amos 9:9), or person (Luke 22:31), means to prove, test them.

SIGN. The rendering of several Heb. and Gk. words, which usually denote a miraculous or, at least, divine or extraordinary token of some generally future event. Thus the rainbow was given to Noah as a sign of his covenant (Gen. 9:12-13), and for the same purpose circumcision was appointed to Abraham (17:11; cf. Ex. 3:12; Judg. 6:17). Signs and wonders sometimes denoted those proofs or demonstrations of power and authority furnished by miracles and other tokens of the divine presence (Matt. 12:38; John 4:48; Acts 2:22). The word is used for a miraculous appearance, which would attest the divine authority of a prophet or teacher (*see* Matt. 16:1; 24:30).

BIBLIOGRAPHY: P. Minear, *Eyes of Faith* (1946), pp. 143-45, 183-87.

SIGNET. See Seal.

SI'HON (sī'hon). A king of the Amorites, with capital at Heshbon, near Medeba, in the E Jordanic country not far from Mt. Nebo, who refused to the Israelites permission to pass through his territory when nearing the Promised Land. Shortly before the time of Israel's arrival he had dispossessed the Moabites of a splendid territory, driving them S of the natural bulwark of the Arnon (Num. 21:26-29). When the Israelite host

appeared, he did not hesitate or temporize as Balak, but at once gathered his people together and attacked them (vv. 21-23). But the battle was his last. He and all his host were destroyed, and their district from Arnon to Jabbok became at once the possession of the conqueror, c. 1401 B.C. The kingdom of Sihon is mentioned in Josh. 13:21, 27.

SI'HOR. See Shihor.

SIK'KUTH. See Gods, False.

SI'LAS (sī'las; apparently Gk. from Aram. *Sheilà* [Saul]). This name is evidently a contracted form of Silvanus (sylvan), a prominent member of the church in Jerusalem (Acts 15:22). Of his immediate family no account is given, but his name, derived from the Lat. *silva,* "wood," betokens him a Hellenistic Jew, and he appears to have been a Roman citizen (16:37). He is probably the same as Silvanus, mentioned in Paul's epistles.

Mission to Antioch. Upon the return of Paul and Barnabas to Jerusalem from their missionary tour, a discussion arose respecting circumcision, and the council decided against the extreme Judaizing party. Silas was appointed a delegate to accompany Paul and Barnabas on their return to Antioch with the decree of the Council of Jerusalem (Acts 15:22, 32), A.D. about 50. After accomplishing this mission he remained in Antioch, although granted permission to return (vv. 33-34). The qualification of Silas for speaking to a congregation is stated (v. 32).

Paul's Companion. Upon the separation of Paul and Barnabas, Silas was selected by Paul as the companion of his second missionary journey (Acts 15:40). "The choice of Silas was, of course, due to his special fitness for the work, which had been recognized during his ministration in Antioch. Doubtless he had shown tact and sympathy in managing the questions arising from the relations of the Gentile Christians to the Jews" (Ramsay, *St. Paul,* p. 176). His double character, Hebrew and Roman, was also a qualification for a coadjutor of Paul. In further notices of him we learn that he was scourged and imprisoned with Paul at Philippi (Acts 16). At Berea he was left behind with Timothy, while Paul proceeded to Athens (17:10, 14), and we hear nothing more of his movements until he rejoined the apostle at Corinth (18:5). If the same as Silvanus, his presence at Corinth is several times noticed (2 Cor. 1:19; 1 Thess. 1:1; 2 Thess. 1:1) and he is mentioned (1 Pet. 5:12) as the one who conveyed Peter's first epistle to Asia Minor. The probabilities are in favor of the identity. He probably returned to Jerusalem with Paul, where he remained, ceasing any longer to be his companion. A tradition of very slight authority represents Silas to have become bishop of Corinth.

BIBLIOGRAPHY: D. E. Hiebert, *Personalities Around Paul* (1973), pp. 88-97.

SILENCE.

1. "Stillness, quietness" (Heb. *d^emāmâ*) is used poetically by hendiadys (Job 4:16), *I hear silence and a voice,* i.e., a still voice, a light whisper. The verb is used (29:21), "and kept silent for my counsel," to indicate respectful attention.

2. The state of being dumb (Heb. *ḥārēsh*), which often depends upon deafness and is joined with it. Spoken of God as not listening to and answering the prayers of men (Pss. 28:1; 35:22; 50:3, 21); of men as listening to God without interrupting Him (Isa. 41:1).

3. The act of not speaking (Gk. *sigaō*), of one wishing to speak in a tongue ("unknown"), in which case he is not to speak unless an interpreter is present (1 Cor. 14:28); of women in the churches (v. 34), "an appendix to the regulative section regarding the gifts of the Spirit, vers. 26, 33" (Meyer, Alford, Westcott). Others think that Paul makes an appeal in support of his instruction to the authority or experience of the church.

SILK.

This luxurious material doubtless was introduced into Bible lands from its home in China via India. Phoenician cities imported raw silk, as did Persia and S Europe. Tyre and Berytus were renowned for weaving it. It was a prize material among Medes and Persians, and Greeks knew it by the name "Median garments." In early Christian times silk robes of gorgeous patterns were common in Dura-Europas. Ezekiel refers to silk (16:10, 13) and was so understood by the rabbis (Heb. *meshî*, "drawn"), referring to the fine texture. The NIV translates "costly garments" and "costly fabric" respectively.

The only *undoubted* notice of silk in the Bible occurs in Rev. 18:12, where it is mentioned among the treasures of the typical Babylon (Gk. *sērikos,* from *Sēr,* an Indian tribe from whom silk was procured). It is, however, in the highest degree probable that the texture was known to the Hebrews from the time that their commercial relations were extended by Solomon. The value set upon silk by the Romans, as implied in Rev. 18:12, is noticed by Josephus, as well as by classical writers.

SIL'LA

(sil'a). It is named in 2 Kings 12:20, "the house of Millo as he was going down to Silla." Silla is regarded by many as an abbreviation of *m^esillâ,* "which goes down by the road," and Thenius supposes that the reference is to the road that ran diagonally from the Joppa gate to the Haramarea, corresponding to the present David's road. Some believe it to be a place in the valley below.

SILOAM, POOL OF

(sī'lō-am). The expression "pool of Siloam (which is translated, Sent)" (John 9:7) is found three times in Scripture— Neh. 3:15, "Pool of Shelah"; Isa. 8:6, "waters of Shiloah"; John 9:7, "pool of Siloam." If we compare Neh. 3:15 with 12:37, we find that the Pool of Shelah, the stairs that go down from the city of David (southern portion of the Temple mount), and the king's garden were in close proximity. Josephus frequently mentions Siloam, placing it at the termination of the Valley of the Cheesemongers or the Tyropoeon Valley (*Wars* 5.4.1)—but outside the city wall (*Wars* 5.9.4)—where the old wall bent eastward (*Wars* 5.6.1), and facing the hill upon which was the rock Peristereon, to the E (*Wars* 5.12.2). From these descriptions it is quite evident that Josephus speaks of the same place as the present Birket Silwân, on the other side of the Kidron.

Further, the evangelist's account (John 9:7) of the blind man sent by Jesus to wash *at* the pool of Siloam seems to indicate that it was near the Temple. It was from Siloam that water was brought in a golden vessel to the Temple during the feast of Tabernacles; our Lord probably pointed to it when He stood in the Temple and cried, "If any man is thirsty, let him come to Me and drink" (7:37).

The pool of Siloam is fed by a conduit that is cut for a distance of 1,780 feet through solid rock, and which starts at the so-called Virgin's Spring (*see* En-rogel). The reason for which it was cut is unmistakable. The Virgin's Spring is the only spring of fresh water in the immediate neighborhood of Jerusalem, and in time of siege it was important that, while the enemy should be deprived of access to it, its waters should be made available for those who were within the city. But the spring rose outside the walls, on the sloping cliff that overlooks the valley of Kidron. Accordingly, a long passage was excavated in the rock, by means of which the overflow of the spring was brought into Jerusalem; the spring itself was covered with masonry, so that it could be "sealed" in case of war. That it was so sealed we know from 2 Chron. 32:3-4. The following account of the channel and its inscription is from Major C. R. Conder (*Palestine,* pp. 27ff.). "The course of the channel is serpentine, and the farther end near the pool of Siloam enlarges into a passage of considerable height. Down this channel the waters of the spring rush to the pool whenever the sudden flow takes place. In autumn there is an interval of several days; in winter the sudden flow takes place sometimes twice a day. A natural siphon from an underground basin accounts for this flow, as also for that of the 'Sabbatic river' in North Syria. When it occurs the narrow parts of the passage are filled to the roof with water.

"This passage was explored by Dr. Robinson, Sir Charles Wilson, Sir Charles Warren, and others; but the inscription on the rock close to the mouth of the tunnel was not seen, being then under water. When it was found in 1880 by a boy who entered from the Siloam end of the passage, it was almost obliterated by the deposit of lime crystals on the letters. Professor Sayce, then in

Palestine, made a copy, and was able to find out the general meaning of the letters. In 1881 Dr. Guthe cleaned the text with a weak acid solution, and I was then able, with the aid of Lieutenant Mentell, R.E., to take a proper 'squeeze.' It was a work of labor and requiring patience, for on two occasions we sat for three or four hours cramped up in the water in order to obtain a perfect copy of every letter, and afterward to verify the copies by examining each letter with the candle so placed as to throw the light from right, left, top, bottom. We were rewarded by sending home the first accurate copy published in Europe, and were able to settle many disputed points raised by the imperfect copy of the text before it was cleaned."

The inscription records only the making of the tunnel; that it began at both ends; that the workmen heard the sound of the picks of the other party and were thus guided as they advanced, and that when they broke through they were only a few feet apart. The character of the letters seems to indicate that the scribes of Judah had been accustomed for a long time to write upon papyrus or parchment.

The Siloam Inscription

The pool itself is an oblong tank, partly hewn out of the rock and partly built with masonry, about fifty-three feet long, eighteen feet wide, and nineteen feet deep. The water has a peculiar taste—somewhat brackish—but not disagreeable, though becoming more so with the advance of the hot season.

BIBLIOGRAPHY: H. Vincent and F.-M. Abel, *Jerusalem Nouvelle* (1926), 4:860-64; J. Simons, *Jerusalem in the Old Testament* (1952), pp. 175-94; K. Kenyon, *Jerusalem, Excavating 3000 Years of History* (1967), pp. 69-77, 96-99; D. Ussishkin, *Levant* 8 (1976): 82-95; J. Wilkinson, *Levant* 10 (1978): 116-25.

SILO'AM, TOWER IN. Reference is made by our Lord (Luke 13:4) to this tower as having recently fallen upon and killed eighteen persons. The circumstance itself, and the locality in which it took place, were doubtless quite familiar to His hearers and did not need to be more particularly mentioned. But we are without the means that might enable us more exactly to define either. Some think it to be the village now called Silwân, E of the valley of Kidron and to the NE of the pool. It stands on the W slope of the Mount of Olives. Edersheim (*Life of Jesus,* p. 222) locates the tower at the Siloam Pool, which "had fallen on eighteen persons and killed them," perhaps in connection with that construction of an aqueduct into Jerusalem by Pilate, which called forth, on the part of the Jews, the violent opposition which the Romans so terribly avenged.

SILVA'NUS (sil-vā'nus; "sylvan"). A companion of the apostle Paul, and the one who conveyed Peter's first epistle (1 Pet. 5:12), perhaps the same as *Silas* (which see).

SILVER. *See* Mineral Kingdom.

SILVERLING. A piece of silver. *See* Metrology: Measures of Value, or Money.

SILVERSMITH (Acts 19:24). *See* Handicrafts: Metalworker; Metals.

SIM'EON (sim'ē-un; "hearing"). The second son of Jacob (*see* article immediately below) and the name of others in the Bible.

1. A just and devout Israelite, endowed with the gift of prophecy, and who, having received divine intimation that his death would not take place till he had seen the Messiah, entered the Temple and, there recognizing the Holy Child, took Him in his arms and gave thanks for the privilege of seeing Jesus (Luke 2:25-35), 4 B.C. All attempts to identify him with other Simeons have failed.

2. The son of Judah and father of Levi in the genealogy of our Lord (Luke 3:30). He is perhaps the same as Maaseiah the son of Adaiah (2 Chron. 23:1).

3. The proper name of Niger, one of the teachers and prophets in the church at Antioch (Acts 13:1), the only passage in which he is mentioned. This name shows that he was a Jew by birth, taking that of Niger as more convenient in his dealings with foreigners.

4. A form (Acts 15:14) of the name of Simon Peter.

SIM'EON (sim'ē-un; "hearing"). The name of several NT and OT personages (*see* article immediately above), including the second son of Jacob by Leah (Gen. 29:33), probably c. 1949 B.C. Together with Levi, Simeon undertook to avenge the seduction of their sister *Dinah* (which see) but performed such acts of wanton cruelty and injustice upon the Shechemites that Jacob was fearful of the surrounding people. In obedience, therefore, to his father's command, Simeon moved southward to Bethel (chap. 34; 35:1-4). Joseph selected him as hostage to guarantee the appearance of Benjamin in Egypt (42:24, 36) but he was subsequently released (43:23). Judging from Jacob's dying words (49:5-7) and from Jewish traditions, he was artful, fierce, and cruel.

The Tribe of Simeon. At the migration into Egypt Simeon had six sons. At the Exodus the tribe numbered 59,300 warriors (Num. 1:23), ranking third. When the second census was taken the numbers had decreased to 22,200, and Simeon ranked lowest of the tribes (26:14). The assignment of Simeon in the Promised Land was within the inheritance of the sons of Judah (Josh. 19:1-9; 1 Chron. 4:24-33). This territory, which contained eighteen or nineteen cities with their villages spread around the venerable well of Beersheba, was possessed by the help of Judah (Judg. 1:3, 17).

BIBLIOGRAPHY: C. E. Macartney, *The Man Who Forgot* (1956), pp. 43-52.

SIM'EONITE (sim'ē-on-īt). A patronymic designation of a descendant of *Simeon* (which see) the second son of Jacob by Leah (Num. 25:14; 26:14; 1 Chron. 27:16).

SIMILITUDE. This KJV word is replaced in the NASB and NIV by various terms, among them *form, likeness,* and *image.* The thought is sometimes that of resemblance, as in Dan. 10:16, where KJV "one like the similitude of the sons of men" is replaced in the NASB by "one who resembled a human being." The NIV reads, "one who looked like a man." *See* the article Form, Likeness.

SI'MON (sī'mon; Gk. *Simōn*). Perhaps a contraction of the Heb. *Shimeon*—Simeon.

1. One of the apostles, usually called Simon Peter (*see* Peter).

2. "Simon the Zealot," one of the twelve apostles (Matt. 10:4; Mark 3:18; Luke 6:15; Acts 1:13). The latter term (Gk. *Zēlōtēs*), which is peculiar to Luke, is the Gk. equivalent for the Aram. term *Qanne'ān,* preserved by Matthew and Mark. Each of these equally points out Simon as belonging to the faction of the Zealots, who were conspicuous for their fierce advocacy of the Mosaic ritual. He is not to be identified with Simon the brother of Jesus.

3. A brother of James and Jude, and of Jesus (Matt. 13:55; Mark 6:3). He is believed by many to be the same as Simon the Zealot, but there is no evidence for this. The prevailing opinion is that he is identical with the Simeon who became bishop of Jerusalem after the death of James, but Eusebius said they were two different persons.

4. "Simon the Leper." A resident at Bethany, distinguished as "the leper." It is not improbable that he had been miraculously cured by Jesus. In his house Mary anointed Jesus preparatory to His death and burial (Matt. 26:6-13; Mark 14:3-9; John 12:1-8; etc.).

5. "Simon of Cyrene." A Hellenistic Jew, born at Cyrene, on the N coast of Africa, who was present at Jerusalem at the time of the crucifixion of Jesus, either as an attendant at the feast (cf. Acts 2:10) or as one of the numerous settlers at Jerusalem from that place (6:9). Meeting the procession that conducted Jesus to Golgotha as he was returning from the country, he was pressed into service to bear the cross (Matt. 27:32; Mark 15:21; Luke 23:26) when Jesus Himself was unable to bear it any longer. Mark describes him as

the father of Alexander and Rufus, perhaps because this was the Rufus known to the Roman Christians (Rom. 16:13), for whom he more specifically wrote. The Basilidian Gnostics believed that Simon suffered in the place of Jesus.

6. The Pharisee in whose house a penitent woman washed the feet of Jesus with her tears and anointed them with ointment (Luke 7:40, 43-44).

7. The father of Judas Iscariot (John 6:71; 13:2, 26).

8. The Samaritan magician living in the age of the apostles and usually designated in later history as Simon Magus. According to Justin Martyr (*Apol.* 1.26) he was born at Gitton, a village of Samaria, identified with the modern Kuryet Jît, near Nablus. He probably was educated at Alexandria and there became acquainted with the various tenets of the Gnostic school. Either then or subsequently he was a pupil of Dositheus, who preceded him as a teacher of Gnosticism in Samaria and whom he supplanted with the aid of Cleobius. He is first introduced in the Bible as practicing magical arts in a city of Samaria (perhaps Sychar; Acts 8:5; cf. John 4:5), with such success that he was pronounced to be "the Great Power of God" (Acts 8:10). The preaching and miracles of Philip excited him, and he became one of his disciples and was baptized. Subsequently he witnessed the effect produced by the laying on of hands, practiced by the apostles Peter and John, and, desiring to acquire a similar power, he offered money for it. His object evidently was to apply the power to pursuing magical arts. The motive and the means were equally to be condemned, and his proposition met with a severe denunciation from Peter. It was followed by a petition on the part of Simon, the tenor of which revealed terror but not penitence (v. 24). The word *simony* is derived from his endeavor to obtain spiritual functions by bribe. There are many stories concerning his subsequent career that are, without doubt, fictitious.

9. The Tanner, a Christian convert with whom Peter lodged while at Joppa. His house was by the seaside, as the trade of a tanner was considered unclean by the Jews and not allowed to be carried on inside their towns (Acts 9:43; 10:6, 17, 32).

SIMPLICITY (Heb. *tōm*). Predicted of the 200 followers of Absalom in his conspiracy (2 Sam. 15:11; "innocently," NASB and NIV), who "knew not any thing" (KJV), i.e., of their leader's intention. In Prov. 1:22 simplicity (Heb. *petî*) refers to the naive. Gk. *hoplotēs* stands for an openness of heart that manifests itself in *liberality* (so NASB, Rom. 12:8; cf. KJV) and for single-hearted faith in Christ, the "simplicity that is in Christ" (2 Cor. 11:3, KJV), as opposed to false wisdom in matters pertaining to Christianity. The term also appears in the KJV of 2 Cor. 1:12, referring to the apostle's sincerity (thus NIV).

SIMRI (sim'rī). *See* Shimri, no. 3.

SIN (שׂ) (sēen). A second "s" in the Heb. alphabet (the letter Samekh is the first) and pronounced exactly like it. The Heb. character *Sin* looks like the character *Shin* (which see), except that the dot is placed over the left corner, rather than the right. In transliteration, *sin* is given as "ś" to distinguish it from Samekh ("s"). The character *Sin* does not appear in the NASB as one of the headings for the respective sections of Ps. 119, but it is given, with Shin, in the NIV of the psalm.

SIN (Heb. *ḥaṭṭā'â;* Gk. *hamartia,* a falling away from or missing the right path). Also numerous other Heb. words.

General. The underlying idea of sin is that of law and of a lawgiver. The lawgiver is God. Hence sin is everything in the disposition and purpose and conduct of God's moral creatures that is contrary to the expressed will of God (Rom. 3:20; 4:15; 7:7; James 4:12, 17).

The sinfulness of sin lies in the fact that it is against God, even when the wrong we do is to others or ourselves (Gen. 39:9; Ps. 51:4).

The being and law of God are perfectly harmonious, for "God is love." The sum of all the commandments likewise is love; sin in its nature is egotism and selfishness. Self is put in the place of God (Rom. 15:3; 1 Cor. 13:5; 2 Tim. 3:2, 4; 2 Thess. 2:3-4). Selfishness (not pure self-love, or the exaggeration of it, but in opposition to it) is at the bottom of all disobedience, and it becomes hostility to God when it collides with His law.

All sin therefore has a positive character, and the distinction between sins of commission and those of omission is only on the surface. In both cases sin is actual disobedience (*see* Matt. 23:23).

Original. A term used to denote the effect of Adam's sin upon the moral life of his descendants. It is formally defined as "that whereby man is very far gone from original righteousness, and is of his own nature inclined to evil" (*see* Fall). The fact of sin in this sense is plainly declared in the Scriptures (Rom. 5:12, 19; cf. Gen. 3:5; Eph. 2:1-3; 2 Tim. 2:26; 1 John 3:4). In accord with this is the fact of the universality of sin, also proclaimed in Scripture (Matt. 7:11; 15:19; Rom. 3:9, 23; 1 John 1:8; James 3:2; cf. 1 Kings 8:46; Job 14:4; Prov. 20:9) and borne witness to by history and human self-consciousness.

The nature of the connection between the sin of Adam and the moral condition of his descendants is, however, a matter upon which opinions greatly differ.

The chief forms of doctrine have been as follows:

Calvinists. Calvinists have held that the sin of Adam was immediately imputed to the whole human family, so that not only is the entire race depraved but also guilty on account of the first transgression. To sustain this opinion it is argued that Adam was not only the natural but also the representative, or federal, head of the human race. His fall involved the whole race in guilt (*see* Imputation).

Arminian. The view more generally held is that the effect of Adam's sin upon the moral state of mankind is in accordance with and by virtue of the natural law of heredity. The race inherited proneness to sin. But this proneness to sin does not imply guilt, inasmuch as punishment can justly be inflicted only on account of actual sin, which consists in voluntary transgression. This view is held by many Presbyterians, Congregationalists, Episcopalians, and universally by Methodists.

Pelagianism. The doctrine known as Pelagianism denies any necessary connection between the sin of Adam and the character and actions of his descendants. Every human being is by nature as pure as Adam was before his sin. The prevalence of sin is to be accounted for upon the ground of evil example and surroundings. Accordingly it is possible for men to lead lives of such complete freedom from sin that they may stand in no need of redemption or of regenerating grace. This doctrine is repudiated by all evangelical churches.

The recognition of the reality of sin, not only in the sense of actual disobedience, but also in the sense of innate sinfulness, is essential. For only thus can be seen the necessity for a special revelation, and only thus are men prepared to accept the gospel of salvation in Christ.

Forgiveness of Sin. *See* Justification; Repentance.

The Unpardonable Sin (Matt. 12:31-32; Luke 12:10; Heb. 10:26; 1 John 5:16). The passages referred to undoubtedly point to one particular sin, and that is unpardonable. What this sin is has been a matter of much discussion. The view held by Wesley and others is that it is "the ascribing those miracles to the power of the devil which Christ wrought by the power of the Holy Spirit." This view is by some held to be inadequate. Lange expresses the convictions of some when he says: "We have here to understand fully conscious and stubborn hatred against God and that which is divine as it exists in its highest development." Proponents of this second view hold that this sin is unpardonable not because the grace of God is not sufficient for its forgiveness but because it springs from a state of the soul in which there is left no disposition for repentance and faith in Jesus Christ. Thus they who are in anxiety lest they have committed this sin show in this very fact that such anxiety is groundless. Nevertheless, they who persist in sinning against religious light have great reason to fear lest they become fearfully guilty. But in the above-mentioned Scriptures, it is questionable that Heb. 10:26 and 1 John 5:16 refer to the unpardonable sin. The "sin leading to death" is not spiritual but physical death, resulting from sin in a *believer's* life and consequent chastisement. It has nothing to do with what Jesus called the "unpardonable sin." This is apparently what Wesley described it to be, and, as above-mentioned, it was possible only during the earthly public ministry of the Lord. *See* Holy Spirit, Sin Against.   E. MCC.; M.F.U.

BIBLIOGRAPHY: J. Orr, *Sin as a Problem of Today* (1910); C. R. Smith, *The Bible Doctrine of Sin* (1953); M. Luther, *The Bondage of the Will* (1957); J. Murray, *The Imputation of Adam's Sin* (1959); J. Edwards, *Original Sin* (1970); G. C. Berkouwer, *Sin* (1971); N. Turner, *Christian Words* (1980), pp. 411-16.

SIN (sin; Heb. *sîn*).

1. A city of Egypt, called by the Greeks Pelusium (and thus rendered in Ezek. 30:15-16 in the NIV; see marg.). It lay on the eastern arm of the Nile, about three miles from the sea. This strategic fort had to be captured before any army could penetrate Egypt. Sennacherib failed to take it, but Esarhaddon did in 671 B.C. and overran Egypt. Ezekiel (Ezek. 30:15-16) calls it "the stronghold of Egypt."

2. Wilderness of Sin, a tract or plain lying along the eastern shore of the Red Sea. It is believed to be the present plain of El-Kaa, which commences at the mouth of Wadi Taiyibeh and extends along the whole southwestern side of the peninsula. It was the scene of the murmurings and the miracle of the quail and manna (Ex. 16:1; 17:1; Num. 33:11-12). It is connected also with the Plain El-Markhah on the coast.

SI'NAI (sī'nī). The mountain district reached by the Israelites in the third month after leaving Egypt.

The Mt. Sinai range

Name. The name is ancient and its meaning not definitely fixed. If Semitic it perhaps means "thorny" (i.e., cleft with ravines, from Heb. *sᵉneh,* "thornbush"). It may, however, take its name from the moon god Sin, whose cult had made its way into Arabia.

Bible Notices. When the Israelites left Elim they came to the wilderness of Sin and then to Rephidim, where they encamped (Ex. 16:1; 17:1) and in the third month after the Exodus arrived at the "wilderness of Sinai" (19:1). Moses went up into the mountain and received a preliminary message from Jehovah, declaring His past assistance and promise of future guidance and protection on the condition of obedience (vv. 3-6). The people were commanded to prepare themselves for a direct message from Him, and a boundary line was set around the mountain to prevent any of the people from approaching rashly or inadvertently touching the mountain (v. 12). The top of the mountain was in full view from the camp, so that when the Lord "descended upon it" (v. 18) the thick cloud in which His glory was shrouded was "in the sight of all the people" (vv. 11, 16). The people were brought out of their camp "to meet God, and they stood at the foot of the mountain" (v. 17). "And all the people perceived the thunder and the lightning flashes and the sound of the trumpet and the mountain smoking; and when the people saw it, they trembled and stood at a distance" (20:18).

Moses received the tablets of the law twice (*see* Moses) and was made acquainted with the details of the rites and ceremonies recorded in the Pentateuch (31:18; chap. 34; Lev. 7:37-38; etc.). On the first day of the second month after leaving Egypt the census was taken (Num. 1:1-46); the position was assigned to the various tribes when in camp and on the march (1:47–2:34); the first-born were redeemed (3:40-51); the office and duties of the Levites were enumerated (4:1-49); the Tabernacle was reared and covered with the cloud (9:15-22); and, finally, on the twentieth day of the second month, in the second year, "the sons of Israel set out on their journeys from the wilderness of Sinai" (10:11-12; cf. 33:15-16).

Horeb and Sinai. Concerning these names there has been much difference of opinion. Ewald (*Geschichte,* 2:57) pronounces Sinai the older name and Horeb the name used by the author of Deuteronomy (except 33:2), which book he assigns to a later writer. Hengstenberg (*Pent.,* 2:325-27) agrees with Gesenius that the one name is more general than the other, but he differs in that he makes Horeb the mountain ridge and Sinai the individual summit from which the Ten Commandments were given. The following are his reasons: (1) The name *Sinai* is used at the time that the Israelites were upon the exact spot of the legislation (*see* from Ex. 19:11 to Num. 3:1), whereas Horeb is always used in the recapitulation in Deuteronomy (except 33:2). (2)

The name *Horeb* occurs in the earlier books thrice, all in Exodus, but in circumstances that best suit the general or comprehensive meaning that we attach to it (*see* Ex. 3:1; 17:6; 19:2; cf. 33:6).

"Understanding Horeb to be the more general name, there might still be differences of opinion how wide a circuit should be included under it, though the common opinion seems to be that there is no necessity for taking it wider than that range (some three miles long from north to south) which is called by the modern Arabs *Jebel Tûr* or *Jebel et-Tûr*, sometimes with the addition of Sina, though Robinson says extremely rarely" (McClintock and Strong, *Cyclopedia*, s.v.).

Identification of Sinai. Tradition offers the following sites:

1. Mt. Serbal, on Wadi Feiran. This goes back to the time of Eusebius. The main objection to this identification, however, is that there is no plain or wadi of sufficient size in the neighborhood to offer camping ground for so large a host.

2. Jebel Musa (Mountain of Moses) is the Sinai of later ecclesiastical tradition. Jebel Musa is part of a short ridge extending about two miles. The ridge has two peaks, Ras es-Safsaf, with an altitude of 6,540 feet, and Jebel Musa, 7,363 feet. St. Catherine's Monastery, a monastery of Greek monks, is located at the foot of Jebel Musa.

3. Some scholars reject Jebel Musa because it is near the Serabit copper and turquoise mines, where there were Egyptian soldiers. They select Jebel Hellal, a two-thousand-foot elevation thirty miles S of El-'Arish.

4. Many Jewish scholars identify Mt. Sinai with volcanic Mt. Seir in southern Palestine, a region near enough to Midian for Moses to have led his flocks (Ex. 3:1). George Ernest Wright says (*The 20th Century Encyclopedia of Religious Knowledge* [1955], p. 1023): "A number of scholars today hold that Mount Sinai is to be located in Midian SE of Edom. The chief evidence for this view is a belief that Exodus 19 reflects volcanic activity and that the sacred mountain must be located in a volcanic region." But Wright shows that in a theophany volcanic phenomena are not necessary. Wright thus summarizes the latest evidence: "Consequently, we are left with the traditional location of Mount Sinai as still the most probable." M.F.U.

BIBLIOGRAPHY: E. Robinson, *Biblical Researches* (1841), 1:90-144; B. Rothenberg, *God's Wilderness* (1961); B. Bernstein, *Sinai: The Great and Terrible Wilderness* (1979); J. Buckingham, *A Way Through the Wilderness* (1983); A. Perevolotsky and I. Finkelstein, *Biblical Archaeology Review*, no. 4, 11 (1985): 26ff.; W. H. Stiebing, Jr., *BAR*, 11, no. 4 (1985): 58ff.

SINCERE, SINCERITY (Heb. *tāmîm,* "without blemish"). The acting or speaking without hypocrisy (Josh. 24:14). The Gk. *adolos* means "un-

St. Catherine's monastery at the foot of Mt. Sinai

adulterated." Paul desires the Philippians (1:10) to be pure, their behavior innocent, etc., that thus they may "be *sincere* [Gk. *hagnōs*; "pure," NIV] and blameless until the day of Christ." (See also Eph. 6:24; Titus 2:7 for similar usage in the KJV.) "The sincerity of your love" (2 Cor. 8:8) may properly be rendered that "your love is legitimate" (Gk. *gnēsios*), whereas *eilikrineia* means *found pure* when tested by the sunlight, and so *pure, unsullied* (Phil. 1:10; 1 Cor. 5:8; 2 Cor. 1:12; 2:17).

BIBLIOGRAPHY: N. Turner, *Christian Words* (1980), pp. 416f.

SINEW. The rendering of the Heb. term *gîd hannāsheh*, denoting "the sinew of the hip" (Gen. 32:32; "tendon," NIV), i.e., the *nervus ischiadicus,* the principal nerve in the area of the hip, which is easily injured by any violent strain in wrestling. Because of the dislocation of the thigh of Jacob the Israelites avoid eating this nerve.

SINGING. *See* Music.

SINGLE EYE. Used in the KJV in Matt. 6:22 and Luke 11:34. *See* Simplicity.

SI'NIM (si'nim; Isa. 49:12). The name of a remote people, from whose land men should come to the light of Israel and of the Gentiles. It is, of course, not quite impossible that it may refer to the Lebanon *Sinites* (which see), or with the tribe Sina in the Hindu-Kush (Lacouperie in *Babylonian and Oriental Record*). The LXX gives *Persai,* but the early interpreters looked to the S as to Sin (Pelusium) or Syene.

SI'NITE (sī'nīt; Gen. 10:17; 1 Chron. 1:15). A tribe mentioned only in the phrase "and the Sinite" and in connection with "And Canaan became the father of Sidon, his first-born, and Heth and the Jebusite and the Amorite and the Girgashite and the Hivite and the Arkite and the Sinite and the Arvadite and the Zemarite and the Hamathite" (Gen. 10:15-18). From its position in the list it is inferred that it lay toward the N, perhaps in the northern part of the Lebanon district. In that region were "*Sinna,* a mountain fortress mentioned by Strabo . . . *Sinum,* or *Sini,* the ruins of which existed in the time of Jerome," and others with similar names. The Targums of Onkelos and Jonathan give Orthosia, a maritime town NE of Tripolis. It was a place of importance, as commanding the only road "betwixt Phoenice and the maritime parts of Syria." Delitzsch mentions the cuneiform Sianu, which is mentioned with Semar and Arka.   W.H.

SINLESSNESS OF CHRIST. The perfect freedom of Christ, not only from all outward acts of sin but also from all inward inclination to sin.

Scripture Statement. The OT prophecies relating to Christ, whether symbolically expressed or uttered in words, point to His perfect purity (*see*

Isa. 9:6-7; chap. 53). The NT bears most emphatic testimony to the same fact (*see* Matt. 11:29-30; John 4:34; 6:38; 8:29, 46; 15:10; 17:4; Acts 3:14; Rom. 8:3; 2 Cor. 5:21; Heb. 4:15; 7:26-27; 1 Pet. 1:19; 2:22; 1 John 2:2; 3:5). It is distinctly stated that Christ was tempted, and if so we must admit the abstract possibility of His sinning. Yet His temptations were in no case such as spring from a sinful nature, and the fact remains that He was absolutely without sin (*see* Temptation of Christ).

Theological Suggestions. The sinlessness of Christ is to be looked at with reference to His human nature and is to be distinguished from the holiness that He possessed as an attribute of His divine nature.

The fact of His sinlessness is morally demonstrated, aside from the testimony of the Scriptures, as follows: (1) Christ certainly made upon those around Him the impression that He was a person of at least unusual moral excellence. (2) It is a fact that has the force of a law that the higher imperfect beings rise in moral attainments the more keenly conscious they become of remaining moral defects. (3) Christ manifested no consciousness of moral defect but the opposite. He taught men to confess their sins, but He made no such confession; He taught men to pray for forgiveness but uttered no such prayer for Himself; He declared the necessity of the new birth by the work of the Holy Spirit, but it was for others; He recognized in Himself no such necessity. And thus it follows that in Christ we find a reversal of the law that prevails with respect to all limited measure of human excellence, or He was supremely excellent, absolutely without sin.

The objections of unbelievers are too trivial or too difficult to understand to be discussed here in detail. However, it may be said that the blighting of the barren fig tree cannot be shown to be an interference with the rights of private property. And, moreover, Christ had the right to use this inanimate object for the purpose of symbolically impressing His solemn lesson. The destruction of the swine at Gadara is to be viewed with reference to the deliverance of a human soul as of infinitely higher importance than the loss of the lives of many animals. And, besides, it cannot be shown that Christ willed or directly caused the destruction. We may dismiss this part of the subject in recalling the fact that the unbelieving world has in reality little to say against the moral perfection of Jesus.

The sinlessness of Christ is a fact of many-sided importance. (1) Christ, because He was sinless, is one of the highest (may we not say the highest?) of the credentials of Christianity. He is a moral miracle and is Himself greater than all His miracles. (2) The fact has important relation to the authority of His teaching (*see* Matt. 17:5; John 8:46). (3) Christ in His sinlessness exhibits to us the highest good. He was not free from poverty and persecution and hatred and loneliness and death, but He was free from sin. (4) His sinlessness is related to the value of His atoning sacrifice. His offering of Himself was of unspeakable value because He was spotless (see 1 Pet. 1:19; cf. John 1:29). (5) Likewise, the efficacy of His intercession is based upon the same fact (1 John 2:1; Heb. 4:14-16). (6) This fact also throws light upon His offer of new life to men. He is at the same time our perfect example and the One through whom we receive power to follow in His steps (John 10:10; 1 Pet. 2:21).

The doctrine of Christ's spotless purity is therefore one that has been steadfastly held as of greatest moment by the church in all ages.

E. MCC.

BIBLIOGRAPHY: H. R. Mackintosh, *The Person of Christ* (1914), pp. 35-38, 400-404, 412-15; K. Barth, *Church Dogmatics* (1956-60), 1:2:147f., 163ff.; 2:1:151, 252ff., 316ff.; 3:1:26, 73, 280ff.; J. F. Walvoord, *Jesus Christ Our Lord* (1969), pp. 106-22; J. N. D. Kelly, *Early Christian Doctrines* (1977), pp. 91-96; 146-48, 155-61, 281-93, 296-304.

SIN OFFERING. *See* Sacrificial Offerings.

SI'ON, MOUNT (sī'un).
1. Heb. *har ṣiyyon*, "elevated, lofty." One of the various names of Mt. Hermon, which are fortunately preserved, all not improbably more ancient than "Hermon" itself (Deut. 4:48 only; Siyon, NIV).
2. The Gk. (*Siōn*) of the Heb. name *Zion*, the famous mount of the Temple (1 Macc. 4:37, 60; 5:54; 6:48, 62; 7:33; 10:11; 14:27). *See* Zion.

SIPH'MOTH (sif'moth). One of the places in the S of Judah that David frequented during his wanderings (1 Sam. 30:28). No one yet appears to have suggested an identification of it, but it may be referred to in 1 Chron. 27:27, where Zabdi is called the Shiphmite.

SIP'PAI (sip'ī). One of the descendants of "the giants" slain by Sibbecai at Gezer (1 Chron. 20:4), called in the parallel passage (2 Sam. 21:18) by the equivalent name *Saph* (which see).

SI'RAH (sī'ra). A well about a mile N of Hebron. Abner was recalled here by Joab (2 Sam. 3:26) and treacherously slain. The well is probably the 'Ain Sārah of today.

SIR'ION (sir'i-on; *cuirass*, "coat of mail"). One of the various names of Mt. Hermon, that by which it was known to the Sidonians (Deut. 3:9). The name in Ps. 29:6 is slightly altered in the original (Heb. *shiryōn*).

SISAMAI. *See* Sismai.

SIS'ERA (sis'er-a; uncertain derivation).
1. The "commander" of the army of Jabin king of Canaan. He dwelt in Harosheth-hagoyim, i.e., Harosheth of the Gentiles (present-day Tell 'Amar on the N bank of the Kishon where the stream enters the plain of Acre, about sixteen miles NNW of Megiddo), and for twenty years oppressed the Israelites with a force of 900 chariots of iron (Judg. 4:2-3). When Sisera received tidings of the march of Barak to Mt. Tabor, he mustered his army at the Kishon, where it was thrown into confusion and utterly routed (vv. 10-16). Sisera, to save himself, sprang from his chariot and fled on foot. He took refuge in the tent of Jael, the wife of Heber the Kenite. She received the fugitive in the usual form of oriental hospitality, but when he had fallen asleep Jael took a tent peg and drove it into his temples, so that he died (vv. 17-22), about 1120 B.C. *See* Jael.
2. The name reappears in the lists of the Temple servants, who returned from the captivity with Zerubbabel (Ezra 2:53; Neh. 7:55). It doubtless tells of Canaanite captives devoted to the lowest offices of the Temple.

BIBLIOGRAPHY: J. Simons, *The Geographical and Topographical Texts of the Old Testament* (1959); R. G. Boling and G. E. Wright, *Judges*, Anchor Bible (1975), p. 458; L. J. Wood, *Distressing Days of the Judges* (1975), pp. 16, 102, 106, 113, 184, 194, 198-99; G. Bush, *Notes on Judges* (1976), pp. 42-77; J. Garstang, *Joshua-Judges: The Foundations of Bible History* (1978), pp. 63-64, 109, 247, 292-300, 306.

SIS'MAI (sis'mī; KJV, "Sisamai"). Son of Eleasah and father of Shallum, descendants of Sheshan, in the line of Jerahneel (1 Chron. 2:40).

SISTER (Heb. *'āhôt;* Gk. *adelphē*). A term used by the Hebrews with equal latitude as *brother* (which see). It may denote a relation by the same father and mother, by the same father only, by the same mother only, or merely a near relative (Matt. 13:56; Mark 6:3). Sarah was called the sister of Abraham (Gen. 12:13; 20:12), although only his niece according to some, or, according to others, sister by the father's side. Respecting marrying such relatives, *see* Marriage.

SIS'TRUM (sis'trum). *See* Music.

SIT, SITTING (Heb. *yāshab;* Gk. *kathezomai*). The favorite position of the orientals, who, in the absence of chairs, sit upon the floor with their feet crossed under them. "In Palestine people *sit* at all kinds of work; the carpenter saws, planes, and hews with his hand-adze sitting upon the ground or upon the plank he is planing. The washerwoman sits by the tub; and, in a word, no one stands where it is possible to sit" (Thomson, *Land and Book,* 1:191).

Figurative. Of a *judge* who "sits in judgment" (Isa. 28:6; Joel 3:12; Mal. 3:3, "sit as a smelter and purifier of silver"); hence the "seat of violence," i.e., of unjust judgment (Amos 6:3); mourners, who *sit* upon the ground (Isa. 3:26; 47:1; Job 2:13) or *sit alone* (Lam. 1:1; 3:28); of those who *sit still*, who remain quiet, as opposed to those who go to war (Jer. 8:14).

SITH'RI (sith'ri; "protective"). The son of Uzziel, and grandson of Kohath, of the tribe of Levi (Ex. 6:22). This is the only mention made of him in Scripture.

SIT'NAH (sit'na; strife, "contention, opposition," same root as in Satan). The second of the two wells dug by Isaac, where a contest was had with the Philistines (Gen. 26:21). The modern Shutneh.

SIVAN' (sē-van; Heb. *sīwān* from Akkad. *sīmānu*). The third month of the Hebrew *sacred* year, and ninth of the *civil* year (Esther 8:9). *See* Calendar; Time.

SI'YON. *See* Sion.

SKIN. The term *skin* is used in several ways in Scripture.

1. The rendering generally of the Heb. *'ôr* ("naked"), and meaning the skin of a man, the skin or hide of animals (Lev. 7:8; etc.); also as prepared, i.e., *leather* (11:32; cf. 13:48; Num. 31:20).

2. The human skin as smooth and naked (Job 16:15), Heb. *geled,* "smooth, polished," where Job says, "I have sewed sackcloth over my skin." This is to be attributed doubtless to the hideous distortion of his body by elephantiasis, which will not allow the use of ordinary clothes.

Figurative. "Skin for skin" (Job 2:4) seems to mean "one gives up one's skin to preserve one's skin; one endures pain on a sickly part of the skin, for the sake of saving the whole skin; one holds up the arm to avert the fatal blow from the head." "The skin of my teeth" (19:20) is supposed to be that which surrounds the teeth in the jaw, namely, the periosteum. The disease has destroyed the gums and wasted them away from the teeth, leaving only the periosteum. "Can the Ethiopian change his skin?" (Jer. 13:23) is symbolical of the inability of one to get rid of an evil character that has become second nature.

3. *Flesh* (Heb. *bāśār,* so generally rendered) is translated "skin" in Ps. 102:5, KJV and NIV.

4. *Leather* (Gk. *dermatimos*), that which is made of skin, as in a belt or girdle (Mark 1:6).

SKINK. *See* Animal Kingdom: Snail.

SKIRT (Heb. *shûl).* The flowing *train* of a robe or female dress (Jer. 13:22, 26; Lam. 1:9; Nah. 3:5); more vaguely (*kānāp,* lit., a "wing") the flap of a robe (Deut. 22:30; 27:20).

Figurative. To raise the skirts of a woman's garment is a symbol of insult and disgrace (Jer. 13:22, 26; Nah. 3:5), whereas to cover her with one's skirt was a token of matrimony (cf. Ruth 3:9).

SKULL. *See* Golgotha.

SKY (Heb. *shaḥaq,* "vapor," Deut. 33:26; 2 Sam. 22:12; Job 37:18; etc.). May mean the clouds or the firmament. "And through the skies in His

majesty" (Deut. 33:26) is a figurative expression to denote omnipotence.

SLANDER.

1. The rendering of the Heb. *diblār,* "a defaming, evil report" (Num. 14:36, KJV; Ps. 31:13; Prov. 10:18). In 1 Tim. 3:11 the KJV translators render the Gk. *diabolous* "slanderer" in reference to deacons' wives.

2. The rendering (Ps. 15:3) of Heb. *rāgal,* to "run about" tattling. The NIV translates, "has no slander on his tongue." In the NT the Gk. *katalaleō* is to speak evil of, to malign (Rom. 1:30; 2 Cor. 12:20). This sin is warned against as being destructive and utterly unworthy of a believer. KJV renders "backbite."

SLAVE, SLAVERY. *See* Service.

SLEEP. The rendering of several Heb. and Gk. words, used in the general sense of sleep or rest for the body (Pss. 4:8; 121:4; Jonah 1:5-6). The manner of sleeping in warm Eastern climates is different than that in colder countries. Their beds are generally hard; feather beds are unknown. The poor often sleep on mats or wrapped in their outer garment, for which reason the latter was not allowed to be retained in pledge overnight (Gen. 9:21, 23; Ex. 22:26-27; Deut. 24:12-23). The wealthy sleep on mattresses stuffed with wool or cotton, being often only a thick quilt, used singly or piled upon each other. In winter a similar quilt of finer material forms the cover, whereas a thin blanket suffices in summer; unless, indeed, the convenient outer garment is used (1 Sam. 19:13). *See* Bed.

Figurative. Sleep is employed as a symbol of *death* (Dan. 12:2; John 11:11; etc.; KJV only: Deut. 31:16; 2 Sam. 7:12; Job 7:21); of the *moral slackness,* indolence, or stupid inactivity of the wicked (Rom. 13:11-12; Eph. 5:14; 1 Cor. 11:30).

SLIME. *See* Mineral Kingdom: Pitch; Tar; Bitumen.

SLIME PITS. *See* Siddim.

SLING. *See* Armor, Arms.

Figurative. The proverb "Like one who binds a stone in a sling," etc. (Prov. 26:8), is probably better rendered by Gesenius, "As a bag of gems in a heap of stones," the Heb. (*margēmâ,* "sling") meaning a "heap of stones" (cf. "throw," Matt. 7:6).

SLIP (Heb. *zemōrâ,* "pruned"). The layer of a vine. To "set them with vine slips of a strange god" (Isa. 17:10) is believed to be figurative for making foreign alliances, e.g., with the king of Damascus.

SLOTHFUL. In Prov. 12:27 the expression "a slothful man does not roast his prey" means that such a man does not improve his opportunities. The Heb. *'āṣal* has the usual meaning of to "be slack, indolent" and is most generally used in the

OT (cf. Prov. 12:24, NASB, "slack hand"; "laziness," NIV).

SLOW.

1. *Heavy* (Heb. *kabēd*), as when Moses said, "For I am slow of speech and slow of tongue" (Ex. 4:10); a difficulty in speaking, though not exactly stammering.

2. *Extended* (Heb. *'ārak*, to "make long") is used in the frequent expression "slow to anger" (Ps. 103:8; Prov. 16:32; etc.) and expresses the same state of mind as the term *long-suffering*.

SLUG. *See* Animal Kingdom: Snail.

SMALL COPPER COIN. *See* Metrology.

SMITH. *See* Handicraft; Metals.

SMYR'NA (smur'na; "myrrh"). A rich and prosperous city of Ionia, forty miles N of Ephesus, at the mouth of the small river Meles. Anciently it was one of the finest cities of Asia and was called "the lovely—the crown of Ionia—the ornament of Asia." It is now the chief city of SW Turkey, with a population of more than 1½ million. It is referred to in Rev. 2:8-11 as the seat of one of the seven churches. To its credit the church at Smyrna was still faithful, and against her no word of reproach was uttered. It was Polycarp's field of Christian usefulness, and here he suffered martyrdom, around A.D. 169.

The modern city of Izmir covers NT Smyrna and little archaeological work can be done there. A good part of the Roman marketplace has been excavated, however. Remains unearthed date to

Ruins of the agora at Smyrna

the second century A.D. restoration after a great earthquake. Near the modern city a fairly well preserved Roman aqueduct may be seen. Ancient Smyrna, a few miles away, had its beginnings in the first half of the third millennium B.C. and may have been the residence of Homer. Excavations there under the direction of Ekrem Akurgal are proving to be fruitful.   H.F.V.

BIBLIOGRAPHY: C. J. Cadoux, *Ancient Smyrna* (1938); E. M. Blaiklock, *Cities of the New Testament* (1965), pp. 98-102; W. R. Ramsey, *The Letters to the Seven Churches of Asia* (1978), pp. 251-80.

SNAIL. *See* Animal Kingdom.

SNARE.

1. Usually the rendering of some form of Heb. *yāqash*, to "ensnare"; frequently of *pah*, a "spring net"; Gk. *brochos*, "noose"; *pagis*, "trap."

A net or trap, especially of the fowler (Isa. 8:14; cf. Amos 3:5); also such as seizes man and beast (Job 18:9; Jer. 18:22). Snares were set in the path or hidden in the ground (Ps. 140:5; Prov. 7:23; 22:5; Jer. 18:22). The snare (Heb. *pah*) was formed of two parts that, when set, were spread out upon the ground and slightly fastened with a trapstick, so that as soon as a bird or beast touched the stick the parts flew up and enclosed the bird in the net or caught the foot of the animal (Job 18:9).

2. The rendering of two other Heb. words related to the English *trap:* (a) Heb. *mōqesh*, a noose or *trap* (Pss. 140:5; 141:9; Amos 3:5); and (b) Heb. *pah*, a plate of metal, hence a *trap* (Job 18:9; Isa. 8:14). These terms are rendered "gin" in KJV.

Figurative. Snare is used for anything that may be the cause of *injury* or *destruction*, e.g., the nations about Israel (Josh. 23:13); false gods (Judg. 2:3; Ps. 106:36); false prophets (Hos. 9:8); love of riches (1 Tim. 6:9); death, as a hunter (2 Sam. 22:6; Ps. 18:5; cf. 91:3).

SNIFF (Heb. *nāpah*, to "blow at"). To express contempt, as of God's altar (Mal. 1:13).

SNOUT (Heb. *'ap*, "nostril," hence, "face"). Mentioned in Prov. 11:22: "As a ring of gold in a swine's snout, so is a beautiful woman who lacks discretion." Clark (*Com.*) thus comments: "Beauty in a woman destitute of good breeding and modest carriage is as becoming as a gold ring on the snout of a swine."

SNOW (Heb. *sheleg*, "white"; Gk. *chiōn*). In the historical books of Scripture snow is twice mentioned as actually falling (2 Sam. 23:20; 1 Chron. 11:22; cf. 1 Macc. 13:22). In the poetical books the allusions are so frequent as to make it probable that snow was an ordinary occurrence in Palestine. "During most winters both hail and snow fall on the hills. On the Central Range snow has been known to reach a depth of nearly two feet, and to lie for five days, or even more.... This explains the feat of Benaiah, who *went down* and slew a lion in the midst of a cistern in the day of the snow (2 Sam. 23:20)" (Smith, *Hist. Geog.*, pp. 64ff.). The snow lies deep in the ravines of the highest ridge of Lebanon until the summer is far advanced, and, indeed, never wholly disappears; the summit of Hermon also perpetually glistens with frozen snow. From these sources, probably, the Jews obtained their supplies of ice for the purpose of cooling their beverages in summer (Prov. 25:13).

Figurative. The color of snow is given as an image of brilliancy (Dan. 7:9; Matt. 28:3; Rev. 1:14); of purity (Isa. 1:18; Lam. 4:7, referring to the white robes of the princes); of the blanching effects of leprosy (Ex. 4:6; Num. 12:10; 2 Kings 5:27); of cleansing power (Job 9:30); "snow waters," i.e., melted snow, easily dried up in the burning sand (24:19), is used to express the swift and utter destruction of the godless; snow, fertilizing the earth before it again returns as vapor to the sky, pictures the effective power of God's word (Isa. 55:10). "Does the snow of Lebanon forsake the rock of the open country?" (Jer. 18:14) is thus rendered by Orelli (*Com.*), "Does the snow of Lebanon disappoint on the rock of the fields?" i.e., the Lebanon snow feeds without ceasing, the water flowing therefrom. Phenomena of nature, stable and trustworthy, are contrasted with the fickleness of Israel.

SNUFFERS (KJV, "snuffdishes"). Dishes used to receive the snuff when taken from the lamps of the Holy Place (Ex. 25:38). The NIV translates, "wicktrimmers."

SO (Heb. *Sō'*). A king of Egypt. Hoshea, the last king of Israel, evidently intending to become the vassal of Egypt, sent messengers to So but gave no present, as had been the yearly custom, to the king of Assyria (2 Kings 17:4), 725 B.C. The consequence of this step was the imprisonment of Hoshea, the taking of Samaria, and the carrying captive of the ten tribes (18:10-11).

Identification. As the Hebrew consonants may be rendered Sewe, he is frequently, though incorrectly, identified with Sib'e, commander of Egypt, who, in alliance with king Hanun of Gaza, collided in battle with Sargon of Assyria at Raphia on the Mediterranean about twenty miles S of Gaza (720 B.C.). The allies were defeated, and Hanun was captured. Sib'e fled and was later put under tribute to Assyria. A better identification of So is Osorkon IV.   R.K.H.

SOAP. *See* Mineral Kingdom: Nitre; Soap.

SOBER (Gk. *nēphō* and derivatives). Calm and collected in spirit, temperate, dispassionate (1 Thess. 5:6, 8; 2 Tim. 4:5; 1 Pet. 1:13).

SOCHOCH. *See* Soco.

SOCKET. *See* Tabernacle.

SO'CO (sō'kō; "thorn hedge"; 1 Chron. 4:18;

2 Chron. 11:7; 28:18). KJV sometimes uses Socho. Also called Socoh (1 Sam. 17:1; 1 Kings 4:10; etc.). It was in the low country of Judah (Josh. 15:35) and was settled by the sons of Ezra, of the tribe of Judah. It was one of the cities fortified by Rehoboam after the revolt of the northern tribes (2 Chron. 11:7). Here Goliath was slain, and it was also one of Solomon's food-supply districts. It is probably to be identified with Khirbet Abbad, about two miles S of Azekah.

SO'COH (sō'kō).
1. A city in the low country of Judah (Josh. 15:35). *See* Soco.
2. Another city of Judah, in the mountain district (Josh. 15:48), one of a group of eleven towns. Robinson located it in the Wadi el-Khalîl, about ten miles SW of Hebron; bearing, like the other Soco, the name of Shuweikeh.

SOD, SODDEN. The archaic English terms are replaced in the NASB and NIV by *cooked* (Gen. 25:29; from Heb. *zûd*) or *boiled* (2 Chron. 35:13; Ex. 12:9; Lev. 6:28; and elsewhere; from Heb. *bāshal*).

SODA. *See* Mineral Kingdom: Nitre.

SO'DI (sō'di; "my secret council," i.e., Jehovah). Father of Gaddiel, the spy appointed to represent the tribe of Zebulun (Num. 13:10), c. 1440 B.C.

The Sodom area at the south of the Dead Sea

SODOM. A town of the patriarchal age located in the plain or "valley of the Jordan" (Gen. 13:11-12), together with its sister cities Gomorrah, Admah, Zeboiim, and Zoar. The Bible notes that the district of the Jordan, where these cities were located, was exceedingly fertile and well populated (c. 2065 B.C.) but that not long afterward was abandoned, which is in full accord with archaeological evidence (cf. W. F. Albright, *The Archaeology of Palestine and the Bible*, pp. 133f.). Scholars used to place these cities N of the Dead Sea, but it is now generally agreed that they were situated in "the valley of Siddim" (14:3) and that this was the area at the southern end of the Dead Sea now covered with water. Sometime around the middle of the twenty-first century B.C. this region with its cities was overwhelmed by a great fire (19:23-28). The area is said to have been "full of tar pits" (14:10). Bitumen deposits are still to be found in this locality. The entire valley is on the long fault line that forms the Jordan Valley, the Dead Sea, and the Arabah. An earthquake-ridden region throughout its history, geological activity was doubtless an accompanying factor in the destruction of the cities, although the Bible account records only the miraculous elements. The salt and free sulphur of this area, now a burned-out region of oil and asphalt, were apparently mingled by an earthquake, causing a violent explosion. Carried up into the air red-hot, the exploding salt and sulphur literally caused a rain of fire and brimstone over the whole plain (19:24, 28). The account of Lot's wife being turned into a pillar of salt is frequently connected with the great salt mass in the valley called by the Arabs Jebel Usdum, that is, "Mountain of Sodom." This is a hill some five miles long stretching N and S at the SW end of the Dead Sea. Somewhere under the slowly rising waters of the southern part of the lake in this general locality the "cities of the valley" are probably to be found. In classical and NT times their ruins were still visible, not yet being covered with water (Tacitus *History* 5.7; Josephus *Wars* 4.4). Jesus refers to the destruction of Sodom and Gomorrah (Matt. 10:15). Sodom's wickedness and moral depravity became proverbial (Rom. 9:29; Rev. 11:8). Fresh water irrigation at the southern end of the Dead Sea was sufficient to maintain the five Jordan cities and furnish another evidence of the location of Sodom in this region. *See* Gomorrah.

M.F.U.

BIBLIOGRAPHY: W. F. Albright, *Bulletin of the American Schools of Oriental Research* 14 (1924): 5-7; id., *Annual of the American Schools of Oriental Research* 6 (1924-25): 58-62; M. G. Kyle, *Explorations in Sodom* (1928); F. G. Clapp, *American Journal of Archaeology* 56 (1936): 323-44; G. E. Wright, *BASOR* 71 (1938): 27-34; J. P. Harland, *Biblical Archaeologist* 5 (1942): 17-32; id., *BA* 6 (1943): 41-54.

SODOMA (sodo-ma; Rom 9:29). The Gk. form of *Sodom,* which see.

SOD'OMITE (Heb. *qādēsh,* "consecrated, devoted"). The sodomites were not inhabitants of Sodom, or their descendants, but men *consecrated* to the unnatural vice of Sodom (cf. Gen. 19:4-5; Rom. 1:27) as a religious rite. This dreadful "consecration," or rather desecration, was spread in different forms over Phoenicia, Syria, Phrygia, Assyria, and Babylonia. Ashtaroth, the Greek Astarte, was its chief object. The term was especially applied to the priests of Cybele, called Galli, perhaps from the river Gallus in Bithynia, which was said to make those who drank it mad. In Deut.

23:17 the toleration of a sodomite ("cult prostitute," NASB; "shrine prostitute," NIV) was expressly forbidden, and the pay received by a sodomite was not to be put into the Temple treasury (v. 18). "The wages of a dog" is a figurative expression used to denote the gains of a *qādēsh* (sodomite), who was called *kinaidos* by the Greeks, because of the doglike manner in which he debased himself (*see* Rev. 22:15, where the unclean are called "dogs").

SOLDER (Heb. *debeq,* "joint"). Welding of metal (Isa. 41:7), a metallic substance or mixture used in melted form to hold metals together, as a metal idol.

SOLDIER. *See* Army.

SOL'OMON. Solomon's name (Heb. *Shĕlōmōh*) means "peaceable." He was also called Jedidiah, meaning "beloved of Jehovah." He was a son of King David by Bathsheba (2 Sam. 12:24; 1 Chron. 3:5). He succeeded King David to the throne and ruled c. 965-926 B.C.

Empire. The tendency of scholars in the past has been to give scant credence to the biblical notices of Solomon's power and glory as related in 1 Kings 3-11 (cf. Matt. 6:29; 12:42; Luke 11:31). German scholars Hugo Winckler and Hermann Guthe narrowly restricted the Davidic empire, which Solomon inherited, to Palestine, excluding even Damascus. Zobah, Hadadezer's kingdom conquered by David, was customarily located S of Damascus in Hauran, biblical Bashan. However, analysis of the Assyrian provincial organization, which was constructed on older foundations, shows that Zobah, Assyrian Subatu, lay N of Damascus and not S of it (Emil Forrer, *Die Provinzeinteilung des Assyrischen Reiches* [1921], pp. 62, 69). Egyptian lists and the Amarna Letters also prove that Hadadezer's chief cities, Tibhath and Cun, which David conquered (1 Chron. 18:8), were S of Hums. Thus archaeology has vindicated the wide extent of the Davidic-Solomonic empire as delineated in Kings. The general historical background of the Davidic-Solomonic period has also been authenticated. Solomon's glory used to be commonly dismissed as "Semitic exaggeration" or a romantic tale. It was contended that such a sprawling realm could not have existed between great empires like Egypt, the Hittites, Assyria, and Babylonia. The monuments, however, have shown that during the period from 1100 to 900 B.C. the great empires surrounding Israel were either in decline or temporarily inactive, so that Solomon could rule with the splendor attributed to him in the Bible. After 1150 B.C., the Twentieth Egyptian Dynasty was weak, with a succession of feeble Ramessides. Not until Shishak (Egyptian Sheshonq I, c. 940-920 B.C.) did Egyptian power revive. The Hittite Empire had collapsed c. 1200 B.C., and only small Hittite city-states such as Senjirli, Carchemish, and Hamath existed. Solomon conquered Hamath and made it a store city (2 Chron. 8:3-4). Assyria had no strong rulers from Tiglath-pileser I (c. 1110 B.C.) to the rise of Ashurnasirpal II (c. 880 B.C.). Archaeology has thus authenticated the historical background of the Davidic-Solomonic era.

One of Solomon's pools, located near Bethlehem, which supplies water to Jerusalem

Remarkable Prosperity. Solomon is known as "the first great commercial king of Israel" (Theodore H. Robinson, *The History of Israel,* 1:256). He took full advantage of peculiarly favorable conditions both by land and by sea for trade expansion. The widespread domestication of the Arabian camel from the twelfth century B.C. onward, as Albright has noted (*From the Stone Age to Christianity* [1940], pp. 120f.), effected a remarkable increase in nomadic mobility. It was now possible for desert caravans to venture two or three days' journey from a water supply. Ample archaeological evidence shows that there was extensive caravan trade between the Fertile Crescent and S Arabia in the Solomonic era. Solomon monopolized the entire caravan trade between Arabia and Mesopotamia and from the Red Sea to Palmyra ("Tadmor," 2 Chron. 8:4), an oasis 140 miles NE of Damascus, which he built (1 Kings 9:18). Exercising control over the trade routes both to the E and W of the Jordan, the Israelite monarch was enabled to collect enormous revenue from merchants seeking passage through his territories (1 Kings 10:15). Solomon also exploited the incipient iron industry, as a result of David's breaking the Philistine monopoly on iron (1 Sam. 13:19-20).

Trade in Horses and Chariots. This lucrative business involved Solomon as a middleman in the trading of horses from Egypt and Asia Minor. "Also Solomon's import of horses was from Egypt and Kue, and the king's merchants procured them from Kue for a price" (1 Kings 10:28). As-

syrian records prove that Kue is Cilicia, the country between the Taurus Mountains and the Mediterranean Sea in Asia Minor. According to Herodotus, this region was famous in the Persian period for fine horses (3.90). "A chariot was imported from Egypt for 600 shekels of silver, and a horse for 150" (1 Kings 10:29). Thus, at the rate of four horses to one chariot, Solomon conducted this lucrative business.

Army. Solomon used the horse and chariot trade not only for commercial reasons but to build up a powerful chariot corps (1 Kings 4:26). This army was stationed in a number of chariot cities such as Gezer, Megiddo, Hazor, and Jerusalem (9:15-19). The Israelite monarch is said to have had 1,400 chariots and 1,200 horsemen, which "he stationed . . . in the chariot cities and with the king in Jerusalem" (10:26). Excavations at Megiddo, Hazor, and Gezer have confirmed Solomon's building operations there. Stables capable of housing 450 horses and about 150 chariots have been found at Megiddo, but these have been assigned to the time of Ahab.

Domestic Economy. Solomon divided his realm into twelve districts that ignored old tribal boundaries and were a nucleus of a highly efficient organization (1 Kings 4:7-20). Solomon resorted to heavy direct taxation and free donations of labor (9:20-21) as well as special levies (5:13-18).

Foreign Policy. As a skillful diplomat, Solomon made friendly ties with the important maritime kingdom of Tyre, which was ruled by Hiram I (969-936 B.C.). Hiram, a common Phoenician royal name attested by a royal sarcophagus discovered at Byblos (Gebal), 1924-25, was called "king of the Sidonians." Besides, Solomon cultivated royal marriages. He married a princess of Egypt (1 Kings 3:1-2) and royal women of surrounding smaller kingdoms. The ancient practice of such regal marriages is well illustrated by the Amarna Letters, in which Egyptian pharaohs marry Hittite women and Mitannian princesses.

Voyages to Ophir. Phoenician seamen not only built Solomon's port at Ezion-geber but his navy as well (1 Kings 9:26-28). "Once every three years the ships of Tarshish came bringing gold and silver, ivory and apes and peacocks" (10:22). The word *peacocks* is better rendered as "a kind of monkey" ("baboons," NIV). Ophir was the region of SW Arabia, modern Yemen, on the Red Sea adjacent to Sheba and Havilah (Gen. 10:29). Since the voyage took three years, portions of the African coast must also be meant. The time denoted by "three years" simply means a full year with portions of two others. The navy, accordingly, set sail in November or September of the first year, returning in early spring of the third. Babylonians more than a millennium earlier allowed three years for a voyage to Melukka, approximately in the same general region.

Visit of the Queen of Sheba. Solomon's far-reaching commerce by land and sea must have brought him in competition with the famous queen of Sheba. The account of the visit of this monarch to Jerusalem (1 Kings 10), traversing over 1,200 miles, used to be dismissed as a "romantic tale." Archaeology has shown the plausibility of the account in which the queen must have come seeking delimitations of spheres of commercial interest. Although the queen of Sheba has not been attested epigraphically, researchers in southern Arabia by the American Foundation for the Study of Man (1950-51) have shown the historical reasonableness of the account. This expedition, conducted by Wendell Philips and under the archaeological supervision of F. P. Albright, examined the ruins of four once-flourishing southern Arabian monarchies: Ma'in, Saba (Sheba), Qataban, and Hadhramaut. The famous spice route skirted this region, and the taxes from this trade supported three kingdoms. Large numbers of inscriptions, pottery, and other archaeological finds have been studied, and the historical background of the queen of Sheba has been enriched accordingly.

Solomon's Temple. Solomon's magnificent Temple and the royal buildings at Jerusalem were in striking contrast to Saul's rusticity, exhibited by the excavations of Albright at Gibeah (Tell el Ful). Solomon was greatly indebted to Phoenician architectural ability. The plan of Solomon's Temple was typically Phoenician, as is shown by the discovery of a similar temple at Tell Tainat in northern Syria in 1936 by the University of Chicago. Similar ground plans of sanctuaries from the general period of 1200-900 B.C. show that the specifications of the Solomonic structure are pre-Greek and authentic and are not anachronistically Hellenic. Like Solomon's Temple, the shrine at Tell Tainat was rectangular with three rooms, a portico with two columns, and a shrine with a raised platform. The decorations of the Temple, such as palmettos, cherubim, and lilies, were characteristically Syro-Phoenician. The cherubim (winged lions with human heads) were inherited from the Tabernacle. Three hybrid animals appear in iconography hundreds of times between 1800 and 600 B.C. Many representations are found with a deity or king seated on a cherub-supported throne (cf. 1 Sam. 4:4).

Like the shrine at Tell Tainat, in the northern part of Syria, Solomon's Temple had two columns that stood at the portico. These had dynastically significant names, as is now known (Jachin, Heb. "He will establish," that is, "Yahweh will establish thy throne forever"; Boaz, Heb. "In Him is strength," that is, "In Yahweh is the king's strength," or something similar). These pillars have been thought of as stylized trees or sacred obelisks. W. Robertson Smith explained them as gigantic cressets or fire altars, which identification is followed by Albright (*Archaeology and the Religion of Israel,* pp. 144-48) and is suggested by

the painted tombs of Marisa in southern Palestine, where such incense burners appear, and by the fact that the two pillars are clearly said to be crowned with a *gullah* or oil basin or a lampstand (1 Kings 7:41). Thus Solomon was highly indebted to Syro-Phoenician art.

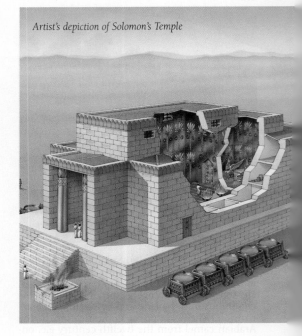

Artist's depiction of Solomon's Temple

Apostasy and Death. By intermarriage with many foreign women, Solomon courted spiritual declension and gross idolatry. Of the numerous deities to which his foreign wives turned his heart, perhaps the best known in the ancient world was Ashtoreth, called "the goddess of the Sidonians" (1 Kings 11:5, 33), since her cult was early established among the Phoenicians. This fertility goddess, known as Astarte among the Greeks and as Ishtar in Babylonia, was the protagonist of sexual love and war in Babylonia and Assyria. Her degraded moral character is revealed by the Ugaritic literature from Ras Shamra. She is pictured on a seal found at Bethel where her name is given in hieroglyphic characters. Solomon thus courted disaster. He died disillusioned and spiritually insensible. The breakup of the monarchy was soon to follow as a result of the folly of his son Rehoboam.

M.F.U.

BIBLIOGRAPHY: A. Malamat, *Biblical Archaeologist* 21 (1958): 96-102; L. J. Wood, *Israel's United Monarchy* (1979), pp. 281-337; T. Kirk and G. Rawlinson, *Studies in the Books of Kings* (1983), 1:1-292; E. R. Thiele, *Mysterious Numbers of the Hebrew Kings* (1983), pp. 51-53.

SOL'OMON, SONG OF. *See* Song of Solomon.

SOL'OMON'S PORCH.

1. The porch of judgment attached to the palace (1 Kings 7:7, KJV; "the hall of the throne," NASB; "the throne hall, the Hall of Justice," NIV). *See* Palace.

2. The "portico" (Gk. *stoa Solomōnos*), the outer corridor of the Temple (John 10:23; Acts 3:11; 5:12). *See* Temple.

SOL'OMON'S SERVANTS (Ezra 2:58; Neh. 7:57, 60). Following as they do in the lists, the priests, Levites, and the Temple servants, they would seem to have some connection with the Temple service. Smith (*Bib. Dict.,* s.v.) suggests: (1) The name as well as the order implies inferiority even to the Temple servants. They are descendants of the *slaves* of Solomon. The servitude of the Temple servants, *"given* to the Lord," was softened by the idea of dedication. (2) The starting point of their history is probably found in 1 Kings 5:13-14; 9:20-21; 2 Chron. 8:7-8. Canaanites, who had been living till then with a certain measure of freedom, were reduced by Solomon to the Helot state and compelled to labor in the king's stone quarries and in building his palaces and cities. To some extent, indeed, the change had been effected under David, but it appears to have been then connected especially with the Temple, and the servitude under his successor was at once harder and more extended (1 Chron. 22:2). (3) The last passage throws some light on their special office. The Temple servants, as in the case of the Gibeonites, were appointed to be cutters of *wood* (Josh. 9:23), and this was enough for the services of the Tabernacle. For the construction and repairs of the Temple another kind of labor was required, and the new slaves were set to the work of shaping and squaring *stones* (1 Kings 5:17-18). Their descendants appear to have formed a distinct order, inheriting, probably, the same functions and the same skill.

BIBLIOGRAPHY: I. Mendelsohn, *Slavery in the Ancient Near East* (1949), pp. 92-106; R. de Vaux, *Ancient Israel: Its Life and Institutions* (1961), pp. 88-90, 141-42; A. F. Rainey, *Israel Exploration Journal* 20 (1970): 191-202.

SOL'OMON'S SONG. *See* Song of Solomon.

SOME DISTANCE. *See* Metrology: Linear Measures.

SON (Heb. *bēn;* Gk. *huios;* the child, *bar,* "son," occurs in the OT and appears in the NT in such words as Barnabas). "Son" is used in a great variety of meanings in both the OT and the NT: (1) the immediate offspring; (2) grandson, as Laban is called "son of Nahor" (Gen. 29:5), though he was his grandson (cf. 24:24, 29); so Mephibosheth is called the "son of Saul," though he was the son of Jonathan, Saul's son (2 Sam. 19:24); (3) remote descendants (Num. 2:14, 18); (4) son by adoption such as Ephraim and Manasseh to Jacob (Gen. 48); (5) son by nation, as "sons of the east" (1 Kings 4:30); (6) son by education, i.e., a disciple, as Eli called Samuel his son (1 Sam. 3:6). Solomon often calls his disciple his son in the Proverbs, and we read of the "sons of the prophets" (1 Kings 20:35; etc.), i.e., those under training for service; similarly a Christian convert (1 Pet. 5:13; cf. 1 Tim. 1:2; Titus 1:4; Philem. 10; 1 Cor. 4:15, 17); (7) son by disposition and conduct, as "sons of Belial" (Judg. 19:22 and 1 Sam. 2:12, marg.), "sons of the mighty," i.e., heroes (Ps. 29:1); "sons of a sorceress," i.e., those who practice sorcery (Isa. 57:3); (8) a production or offspring of any parent, as an arrow is "son of the bow" (Job 41:28, marg.), because the arrow flies from the bow; also "son of His quiver" (Lam. 3:13, marg.); "son of the threshing floor," i.e., threshed grain (Isa. 21:10, marg.); "sons of fresh oil," i.e., branches of the olive (Zech. 4:14, marg.); expressive of deserving, as "a son of beating," i.e., deserving a beating (Deut. 25:2, marg.), so "son of perdition" (John 17:12); (9) "Son of God," by excellence above all, namely, Jesus (Mark 1:1; Luke 1:35; John 1:34; Rom. 1:4; Heb. 4:14); (10) "sons of God," i.e., angels (Job 1:6; 38:7), perhaps so called as possessing power delegated from God, His deputies, vicegerents; (11) "sons of this age" (Luke 16:8), i.e., worldly minded persons, in contrast to the "sons of light"; "sons of disobedience" (Eph. 2:2), those who are unrestrained in evil; "son of hell" (Matt. 23:15); "son of the devil," i.e., under his power (Acts 13:10); "sons of the bridal-chamber" (Matt. 9:15 and Mark 2:19, marg.), the youthful companions of the bridegroom, as in the instance of Samson. Offspring, especially sons, were highly valued among all Eastern nations, and barrenness was regarded as one of the severest afflictions (*see* Gen. 16:2; 29:31; 30:1, 14; etc.). *See* Children; Family.

SONG (Heb. *shîr;* Gk. *ōdē*). Songs were used on occasions of thanksgiving and triumph, such as the song of Moses at the deliverance from Pharaoh (Ex. 15:1); the song of Israel at the well of Beer (Num. 21:17); the song of Moses in Deuteronomy (chap. 32); of Deborah (Judg. 5:12); of David on bringing the Ark to Jerusalem (1 Chron. 13:8); of Hannah (1 Sam. 2); of the virgin Mary (Luke 1:46); the songs in heaven (Rev. 5:9; 14:3; 15:3).

Figurative. Songs (*see* Singing) were indicative of joy, and their absence of sorrow. "You will have songs as in the night" (Isa. 30:29) is a figurative allusion to the joyful singing of the Israelites on the festal night before the Passover. "And behold, you are to them like a sensual song," etc. (Ezek. 33:32), is more correctly rendered, "You are to them like a pleasant singer," etc., i.e., the prophet was like the singer of pleasant songs, to which they listened for pleasure, but without obedience. *See* Music.

SONG OF SOLOMON. This delightful poem,

also called Canticles, stands first in the list of the five Hebrew rolls, or *megilloth*, which were short enough to be publicly read on important anniversaries. Song of Solomon comes first because it was read at the initial and greatest feast of the year, the Passover.

Name. The term Song of Songs (1:1) is a Heb. idiom denoting the superlative degree, that is, the best or most exquisite song. The Gk. *asma asmatōn* and the Lat. *Canticum Canticorum*, like the English "Song of Songs," slavishly transliterates the Heb. idiom. The rendering "The Song of Solomon" is likewise deduced from the data of 1:1 ("the Song of Songs, which is Solomon's") but is not a translation.

Form. Interpretation of the song depends to a large extent on the view taken of its form. Three distinct views are commonly held. The conservative (and we believe the correct view) construes it as a unified lyrical poem with a dramatic form of dialogue. The second view is that it is a drama or melodrama (Origen, Ewald, Koenig, Godet, etc.). Those subscribing to the third view hold it to be an anthology of loosely connected separate love lyrics (Lods, Haupt, Oesterly and Robinson, Pfeiffer, etc.) recited during wedding festivals (Budde, Cheyne, Goodspeed, and Kassuto). That the song is a homogeneous lyric, not an anthology of disconnected love poems without plan, is apparent from the following reasons: (1) Identical imagery and local color predominate in all parts of the song, for example, the bridegroom (beloved) is compared to a young stag in 2:9, 17; 8:14. The bridegroom feeds his flock "among the lilies" in 2:16; 4:5; 6:2-3. The bride is called the "most beautiful among women" in 1:8; 5:9; 6:1. (2) The same persons appear in all parts of the poem: the bride (1:5; 2:16; 3:4; 6:10; 7:10-11; 8:2, 8), the bridegroom (1:7; 2:13; 4:8–5:1; 6:1; 7:11-13) and the daughters of Jerusalem (1:5; 2:7; 3:5, 10; 5:8, 16; 8:4). The view that the poem is a drama is scarcely tenable since it does not have sufficient action, plot, or dramatic sequence. The position that it is a collation of detached erotic lyrics is also unsatisfactory in the light of the unity of the poem. It is scarcely credible that the faithful of antiquity would have persisted in viewing as divinely inspired a poem of mere human love, especially when it was on such a plane often considered unedifying and not allowed to be read by persons under thirty years of age among the Jews.

Interpretation. Literal, allegorical, and typical interpretations are commonly made.

Literal Interpretation. This interpretation construes the poem as a mere representation of human love without any higher or spiritual meaning. Edward J. Young sets forth a species of literal interpretation that is vaguely typical, viewing the poem as didactic and moral and holding that it celebrates the dignity and purity of human love (*Introduction to the O. T.* [1949], p. 327).

Most modern interpreters resort to a shepherd hypothesis in which a third main character is introduced as the shepherd lover of the bride whom Solomon, villainlike, tries to seduce from her lover. The poem is thus made the triumph of pure love over lust, but under an obviously objectionable representation of Solomon. More serious, the shepherd has no tangible existence.

Allegorical Interpretation. This interpretation was common among ancient Jews and popularized among Christians by Origen. The Jewish interpretation represented the poem as setting forth Jehovah's love for Israel. To the Christian, it represented Christ's love for His church. Details were subject to extravagant interpretations. The view has much to be said in its favor. It accords the book a higher spiritual meaning and gives purpose to its canonical recognition. Furthermore, both the OT and the NT set forth the Lord's relation to His people by the figure of marriage. In the OT, however, Israel is presented as the wife of Jehovah (Hos. 2:19-23), in her sin and unbelief now divorced and yet to be restored (Isa. 54:5; Jer. 3:1; Hos. 1-3). On the other hand, in the NT the church is portrayed as a virgin espoused to Christ (2 Cor. 11:2; Eph. 5:23-32; Rom. 7:1-4; Rev. 19:6-8). The allegorical view fails in unnecessarily ruling out the actual historicity of the events and is subject to extravagant, farfetched interpretation.

Typical Interpretation. This interpretation has a mediating view between the two extremes, the literal and the allegorical. It neither denies the historical background nor encourages fantastic interpretations of details, since the typical foreshadows the antitypical in only a few salient points. It avoids the secularity of the literal interpretation and finds an adequate purpose in the book in the typical relation between Solomon, elsewhere a type of Christ, and the Shulamite, a type of the church as the bride of Christ.

Author. The natural indication of 1:1, "the Song of Songs, which is Solomon's," is that Solomon is the author, although the preposition may conceivably be translated "The Song of Songs which is *about* or *concerning* Solomon" (cf. 1:4; 3:7-11; 8:11). Numerous internal arguments also lend support to Solomonic authorship: the place names, evidences of royal luxury, the author's wide acquaintance with plants and animals (cf. 1 Kings 4:33). The presence of one or two Persian and Gk. words need not dispose of the Solomonic authorship. It may simply indicate that the poem in the precise form in which we have it cannot be earlier than the third century B.C. (Eissfeldt). But one may at least inquire if even these features might be original in the light of the incredibly widespread extent of Solomonic commerce and an inevitable influx of foreign words. Likewise the Aramaisms may be the result of the inclusion of Aramaic-speaking countries in Solomon's realm.   M.F.U.

BIBLIOGRAPHY: S. C. Glickman, *A Song for Lovers* (1976); M. H. Pope, *Song of Songs*, Anchor Bible (1977).

SON OF GOD. *See* Sonship of Christ.

SON OF MAN (Gk. *huios tou anthrōpou*). This is a term, like "the Son of God," which is now theologically chiefly associated with Christ and is used in both the OT and the NT. Christ employed this expression to designate Himself some eighty times. It portrays Him as the Representative Man. It designates Him as the "last Adam" in distinction to the "first man, Adam" (1 Cor. 15:45). It sets Him forth as "the second man . . . from heaven" as over against "the first man . . . from the earth" (15:47). "The Son of Man" is thus our Lord's racial name, as the "Son of David" is distinctly His Jewish name and "the Son of God" His divine name. This term is uniformly used of Christ in connection with His mission (cf. Luke 19:10), His death and resurrection (cf. Matt. 12:40; 20:18; 26:2), and His second advent (cf. 24:37-44; Luke 12:40). It transcends purely Jewish limitations and has application to the salvation of the entire race. Thus, when Nathanael owns Christ as "King of Israel" our Lord's reply is, "You shall see greater things than these . . . the angels of God ascending and descending on the Son of Man" (John 1:49-51). It is, for example, in this name that universal judgment is committed to our Lord (5:22,27). The term also implies that in Him the OT prophetic blessings centering in the coming Man are to find their fulfillment (Gen. 3:15; Ps. 8:4; Isa. 7:14; 9:6-7; Zech. 13:7). The term "Son of Man" occurs conspicuously in the book of Ezekiel, being used ninety-two times in addressing the prophet. The thought of going beyond the confines of Judaism is also involved in the phrase when applied to Ezekiel. When Israel was in her captivity, oblivious of her special mission (Jer. 11:10; Ezek. 5:5-8), the Lord reminded her by this term of address to Ezekiel that He would not forsake her but that nevertheless she was only a small portion of the race for whom He was concerned. As used of Ezekiel, the expression "the son of man" suggests what the prophet is to God, not what he is to himself. As "the son of man" the prophet is chosen, spiritually endowed, and delegated by God. These factors are also true of the Messiah as the Representative Man, the new Head of regenerated humanity.   M.F.U.

BIBLIOGRAPHY: G. S. Duncan, *Jesus, Son of Man* (1947); O. Cullmann, *The Christology of the New Testament* (1963), pp. 137-92; F. Hahn, *The Titles of Jesus in Christology* (1969), pp. 15-66; G. H. Dalman, *The Words of Christ* (1981), pp. 234-67.

SONSHIP OF BELIEVERS. *See* Adoption.

SONSHIP OF CHRIST. A matter of doctrine with reference to the divine nature of Christ. It is inwrought with the doctrine of the *Trinity* (which see) and in the very nature of the case

points to a relationship that in its deepest essence cannot be comprehended by the human understanding (*see* Matt. 11:27). And yet the Scriptures throw some rays of light on the subject.

Scriptural. The term Son of God is used in the Scriptures in various senses. In the OT it is sometimes applied to Israel (e.g., Ex. 4:22), also figuratively to heavenly beings (Job 1:6; 38:7). In the NT it is also employed in different applications (Luke 3:38; Matt. 5:9, 45). It is in one instance (Luke 1:35) applied to Christ on account of His miraculous conception. And yet it is plain beyond all question that the Scriptures apply this title to Christ in a sense far deeper than all these. Both Christ Himself and His apostles speak of His sonship in a way that cannot be employed with reference to any, even the highest, of God's creatures (*see* John 3:13, 16; 5:17-31; 6:62; 8:58; 10:30; 14:1, 11; Rom. 1:3-4; 9:5; Col. 2:9; Titus 2:13). *See* Kenosis.

Theological. The doctrine of the Scriptures, universally held by the Christian church, includes the following features:

1. The sonship of Christ involves an antemundane and eternal distinction of personality between the Son and the Father. He is the eternal Son even as the Father is the eternal Father. Thus both Christ and the apostles speak of His preexistent state (John 8:58; 17:5; Rom. 8:3; 2 Cor. 8:9; Phil. 2:5-8). And thus while He teaches men to pray, saying "Our Father," for Himself He simply says "Father," or "My Father" (*see* John 15:8, and many other places).

2. The sonship of Christ implies also that He as the Son "has the ground of his existence in the Father, and as the Father has not in the Son" (*see* Van Oosterzee, 1:276). Christ is the "only begotten God, who is in the bosom of the Father" (John 1:18; cf. v. 15), the "only begotten Son" (3:16), "His own Son" (Rom. 8:3). Upon these and similar Scripture expressions is based the doctrine of the eternal generation. This theological term, however, it is rightly held, is one that is liable to abuse, should never have associated with it anthropomorphistic conceptions, and should exclude all idea of time. The idea to be reverently held is that the Son of God has the ground of His existence eternally in the Father.

3. The Son is in the most complete sense partaker in the same nature with the Father. He possesses the same attributes (John 5:21), performs the same works (Matt. 9:2-6; John 5:24-29), and claims equal honor with the Father (5:23; 14:1). As the Son, having the ground of His existence in the Father, He is in this sense subordinate. Also in His incarnate state He became subordinate in a still deeper sense (*see* Kenosis). And yet before His incarnation He "did not regard equality with God a thing to be grasped"; and in His glorified state "in Him all the fulness of the Deity dwells in bodily form."

The doctrine of the eternal sonship of Christ

has been the ground of many hard-fought battles (*see* particularly Arianism and Sabellianism in works on theology), but the Christian church steadfastly holds to the teachings of the Scriptures. And the truth at this point is most important; for only in the light of this truth can we recognize in Christ the perfect revelation of God and realize the efficacy of His saving ministry.

E. MCC.

BIBLIOGRAPHY: F. Hahn, *The Titles of Jesus in Christology* (1969), pp. 279-333; J. F. Walvoord, *Jesus Christ Our Lord* (1969), pp. 38-42; G. H. Dalman, *The Words of Christ* (1981), pp. 268-88; W. E. Vine, *The Divine Sonship of Christ* (1984).

SOOTHSAYER, SOOTHSAYING. *See* Magic.

SOP. *See* Morsel.

SO'PATER (sō'pa-ter; "savior of his father"). A disciple of Berea, who accompanied Paul from Greece into Asia on his return from his third missionary journey (Acts 20:4). In the *Codex Sinaiticus,* and several other manuscripts, his father's name is given as Pyrrhus. It is a question whether or not he is the same as *Sosipater* (which see).

SOPHE'RETH (so-fe'reth; "secretariat," probably denoting an official position). "The sons of Sophereth" were a family who returned from Babylon with Zerubbabel, among the descendants of Solomon's servants (Neh. 7:57), about 536 B.C. He is called Hassophereth in Ezra 2:55. *See also* Hassophereth.

SORCERER, SORCERY. The term *sorcerer* (Ex. 7:11; Jer. 27:9; etc.), from the Lat. *sors,* "a lot," "one who throws or declares a lot," would assign it initially the more circumscribed sphere of augural prognostication. But the term, as commonly employed, includes one who practices in the whole field of divinatory occultism. As such, it comprehends a necromancer, who may be classified as a certain type of sorcerer. Sorcery is the practice of the occult arts under the power of evil spirits, or demons, and has been common in all ages of the world's history. *See* Magic; Divination.   M.F.U.

BIBLIOGRAPHY: Merrill F. Unger, *Biblical Demonology,* 2d ed. (1953), pp. 143-64.

SO'REK (so'rek; "a choice or excellent vine"). A valley in which was the home of Delilah (Judg. 16:4). Smith (*Hist. Geog.,* p. 218) identifies it with the present Wadi es Surar, through which runs the railroad from Joppa to Jerusalem. It is the way the Philistines used to come up in the days of the Judges and of David; there is no shorter road into Judea from Ekron, Jamnia, and, perhaps, Ashdod. Just before the Wadi es Surar approaches the Judean range its width is increased by the entrance of the Wadi en Najil from the S. It was by the level road up the Sorek Valley that the Ark was taken to Beth-shemesh (1 Sam.

6:10-12). The territory that the book of Joshua assigns to Dan lies down the two parallel valleys that lead through the Shephelah to the sea, Aijalon and Sorek.

SORES. *See* Diseases.

SORROW. The rendering of a number of Heb. and Gk. words, representing mental pain or grief arising from the privation of some good we actually possessed. It is the opposite of joy; contracts the heart, sinks the spirit, and injures the health. Scripture cautions against it (2 Sam. 12:12-23; 1 Thess. 4:13; etc.; cf. Ecclus. 30:24-25). Paul distinguishes two sorts of sorrow: "The sorrow that is according to the will of God produces a repentance without regret, leading to salvation; but the sorrow of the world produces death" (2 Cor. 7:10). The one is that sorrow for sin wrought by God that leads to repentance, whereas the other is a sorrow about worldly objects that, when separated from the fear of God, tends to death, temporal and eternal.

SOSIP'ATER (sō-sip'a-ter; "saver of his father"). A kinsman of Paul mentioned in the salutations of the epistle to the Romans (16:21) as being with the apostle. He is perhaps the same as Sopater.

SOS'THENES (sos'the-nēz; "of safe strength").

1. The leader of the synagogue at Corinth, who was beaten by the Greeks in the presence of Gallio when the latter refused to entertain the charge made to him against Paul (Acts 18:17). Some have thought that he was a Christian and was maltreated thus by his own countrymen, because he was known as a special friend of Paul. A better view is that Sosthenes was one of the bigoted Jews; and that the crowd were Greeks who, taking advantage of the indifference of Gallio and ever ready to show their contempt of the Jews, turned their indignation against Sosthenes. In this case he must have been the successor of Crispus (v. 8).

2. Paul wrote the first epistle to the Corinthians in his own name and that of a certain Sosthenes, whom he terms "our brother" (1 Cor. 1:1). Some have held that he was identical with the Sosthenes mentioned in the Acts. If this be so, he must have been converted at a later period and have been at Ephesus, not at Corinth, when Paul wrote to the Corinthians. The name was a common one, and little stress can be laid on that coincidence. Ramsay (*St. Paul,* p. 259) says: "Probably two persons at Corinth named Sosthenes were brought into relations with Paul, one a Jew, the other a prominent Christian; or, perhaps, the Jew was converted at a later date."

SO'TAI (sō'ti). The "sons" of Sotai were a family of the descendants of Solomon's servants who returned with Zerubbabel (Ezra 2:55; Neh. 7:57), before 536 B.C.

SOUL (generally the rendering of Heb. *nepesh,* a "breathing" creature; Gk. *psuchē,* "breath," etc., the equivalent of *nepesh*). The Heb. term may indicate not only the entire inner nature of man, but also his entire personality, i.e., all that pertains to the person of man; in the sense of person; somebody, everybody (Deut. 26:16; cf. Josh. 11:11, 14). It would thence be wrongly concluded that the soul is what constitutes the person of man; for the brute is also called *nepesh.* In *nepesh* itself is not involved the conception of the personal living, but only of the self-living (the individual). In such cases *nepesh* indicates the person of the man, but not the man as a person. The beast is *nepesh,* as a self-living nature by the power of the spirit that proceeds from God and pervades the entire nature, the individual constitution of which spirit is the soul of the brute; but man is *nepesh* "as a self-living nature by the power of the spirit that proceeds from God, and is in the form of God, and is therefore personal, the operation of which spirit is his endowment with soul" (Delitzsch, *Bib. Psych.,* pp. 181-82).

The Gk. term *psuchē* has the simple meaning of *life* (Matt. 6:25; Luke 12:22); that in which there is life, a *living being* (1 Cor. 15:45); every soul, i.e., *every one* (Acts 3:23). It also has the meaning of the seat of the feelings, desires, affections, aversions (our *soul, heart,* etc.; RV almost uniformly *soul*); the human soul, insofar as it is so constituted that, by the right use of aids offered it by God, it can attain its highest end and secure eternal blessedness; the soul regarded as a moral being designed for everlasting life (3 John 2; Heb. 13:17; James 1:21; 5:20; 1 Pet. 1:9). Another meaning of *psuchē* is the soul as an essence that differs from the body and is not dissolved by death (Matt. 10:28); the soul freed from the body, a disembodied soul (Acts 2:27; Rev. 20:4). *See* Spirit.

BIBLIOGRAPHY: E. D. Burton, *Spirit, Soul, and Flesh* (1918); E. White, *Journal of the Transactions of the Victoria Institute* 83 (1951): 51ff.; id., 87 (1955): 1ff.; J. Laidlaw, *The Biblical Doctrine of Man* (1983), pp. 49-96, 179-220.

SOUR (Heb. *bēser,* "immature"). The proverb quoted in Jer. 31:29-30 and Ezek. 18:2, "The fathers have eaten sour grapes, and the children's teeth are set on edge," is easily understood. The sour grapes that the fathers eat are the sins they commit; the setting of the children's teeth on edge is the consequence thereof, i.e., the suffering that the children have to endure. The teaching of the proverb is that children must atone for their fathers' sin, without any culpability of their own. This fatal error is condemned by both Jeremiah and Ezekiel. Jehovah declares with an oath that this proverb shall not be used anymore, for their iniquity shall be made manifest; and announces that all souls are His, and He will mete out to each his deserts.

SOUTH. The country or quarter of the heavens that the Shemite, standing with his face to the E, supposes to be on his right hand.

1. *Negev* (Heb. *negeb*) means literally the "dry" or "parched" land; and probably took its name from the hot, drying winds that annually blow into Syria from Africa and Arabia. Thus our Lord said (Luke 12:55), "And when you see a south wind blowing, you say, 'It will be a hot day,' and it turns out that way." The word is occasionally applied to a dry tract of land. Caleb's daughter said to her father, "You have given me the land of the Negev, give me also springs of water" (Judg. 1:15). It is also used in the geographical sense in Num. 34:3; Josh. 15:2; 1 Chron. 9:24; 2 Chron. 4:4; Ezek. 40:2; 46:9; etc.

An important use of the word *Negev* (which see) is as the designation of the regions lying S of Judea, consisting of the deserts of Shur, Zin, and Paran, the mountainous country of Edom or Idumea, and part of Arabia Petraea. The Negev at present is a part of the Israeli state. It consists of an area about sixty miles square S of Hebron, extending from N of Beersheba to S of Kadesh-barnea. It drops from the Judean highlands to the Arabian Desert, its ridges criss-crossing in an E and W direction, making it throughout the centuries a barrier against trade routes and marching armies. It formed a natural bulwark against southern Judea. Thus, Israel could not enter the Promised Land from the S because of this formidable obstacle (Deut. 1:42-46). In this rugged terrain David roved as an outlaw (1 Sam. 27:5-10). The Amalekites and the Kenites are especially associated with this part of the country (Num. 13:29; 1 Sam. 27:10). This section later comprised Idumaea or "New Edom." The Negev was suitable for grazing in patriarchal times (Gen. 20:14). Efforts to occupy and cultivate the Negev were successful between the fourth and seventh centuries A.D. Under aggressive control by the Israeli state, the region promises to be developed.   M.F.U.; H.F.V.

2. A bright, sunny region, hence *the south,* the southern quarter (Ezek. 40:24, 27-28; 42:12-13, 18; Eccles. 1:6); poetically for the *south wind* (Job 37:17), Heb. *dērôn.*

3. *Teman* (Heb. *têmān,* what is on the "right" hand), the *south,* the southern quarter (Josh. 12:3; 13:4; Job 9:9; Isa. 43:6); and, perhaps meaning Egypt (Zech. 6:6). It is used poetically for the *south wind* (Ps. 78:26; Song of Sol. 4:16).

4. *Right* (Heb. *yāmîn,* the "right" side), the *south,* as "The north and the south, Thou hast created them" (Ps. 89:12). The word is evidently used here in its widest sense, comprehending not only all the countries lying S, but also the Indian Ocean, etc., the whole hemisphere. In passages where some translations render the word *right,* the meaning would have been clearer had it been rendered (as in the NIV) *south* (2 Sam. 24:5; Job 23:9; cf. 1 Sam. 23:19, 24).

5. *Desert* (Heb. *midbār,* Ps. 75:6), lit., "wilderness," as this lay in the south.

6. The Gk. words are: (1) *lips* (bringing "moisture"), the quarter of the heavens from which the SW wind blows (Acts 27:12); (2) *mesēmbria* ("noon"), but, with respect to locality, *the south* (8:26); (3) *notos,* the southern quarter or wind (Matt. 12:42; Luke 11:31; 13:29; Rev. 21:13).

SOVEREIGNTY OF GOD. A term by which is expressed the supreme rulership of God. This is rightly held to be not an attribute of God but a prerogative based upon the perfections of the divine Being.

The possession of the most complete sovereignty is a necessary part of the proper conception of God and is abundantly declared in the Scriptures (e.g., Pss. 50:1; 66:7; 93:1; Isa. 40:15, 17; 1 Tim. 6:15; Rev. 11:17). The method of the divine rulership is, however, to be judged in the light of special revelation. The term *absolute sovereignty* as used in Calvinism means the sovereign election of a certain number to salvation and the sovereign reprobation of others. There is a sense, indeed, in which the sovereignty of God is absolute. He is under no external restraint whatsoever. He is the Supreme Dispenser of all events. All forms of existence are within the scope of His dominion. And yet this is not to be viewed in any such way as to abridge the reality of the moral freedom of God's responsible creatures or to make men anything else than the arbiters of their own eternal destinies. God has seen fit to create beings with the power of choice between good and evil. He rules over them in justice and wisdom and grace.

This is the whole tenor of the Scriptures and the plain declaration of many passages (e.g., Deut. 10:17; Job 36:5; Acts 10:34-35; Rom. 2:6; Col. 3:25; 1 Pet. 1:17).

Thus understood the sovereignty of God is the great ground of confidence for His people, and the proper basis upon which to urge sinners to repentance. *See* Election.   E.MC.

BIBLIOGRAPHY: J. Orr, *The Christian View of God and the World* (1947); L. S. Chafer, *Systematic Theology* (1948), 1:138-39, 192-223; C. Hodge, *Systematic Theology* (1955) 1:439-41; A. W. Pink, *Sovereignty of God* (1959); C. C. Ryrie, *Biblical Theology of the New Testament* (1959), pp. 108-9, 135-36, 167-74, 232-33, 318-22; J. I. Packer, *Evangelism and the Sovereignty of God* (1961); W. G. T. Shedd, *Dogmatic Theology* (1969), 1:377ff.; H. C. Thiessen, *Lectures in Systematic Theology,* ed. V. Doerksen (1979), pp. 82f., 92, 97, 119.

SOW. *See* Animal Kingdom: Swine.

SOWER, SOWING. *See* Agriculture.

SPADE (Heb. *yātēd,* "peg," a tent pin, Judg. 4:21). Outside the camp of Israel, in their journeying, was a space for the necessities of nature, and among their implements was a spade used for digging a hole before they sat down, and afterward for filling it up. It was a tool for *sticking in,* i.e., for digging (Deut. 23:13). *See also* Paddle.

SPAIN (Gk. *Spania*). The name anciently applied

The region of the Negev

to the peninsula that now comprises Spain and Portugal, the usual Gk. name being Iberia, and the natives being called Iberians. The Carthaginians, during the flourishing times of their republic, established many settlements upon the Spanish coast, such as Carthage (now Cartagena) and Malacca, the royal city (now Malaga). Through the efforts of Hamilcar Barca and Hannibal a considerable part of Spain became a Carthaginian colony and subsequently passed under Roman control. The Hebrews were probably acquainted with the position and mineral wealth of Spain from the time of Solomon.

Paul, in his epistle to the Romans (15:24), tells them of his purpose of visiting Rome whenever he should take his journey into Spain. "Such an intention implies in the plainest way an idea already existent in Paul's mind of Christianity as the religion of the Roman empire." "From" Rome, "the center of the Roman world, Paul would go on to the chief seat of Roman civilization in the west, and would thus complete a first survey" (Ramsay, *St. Paul,* p. 255). Whether the journey was ever made is an open question. *See* Paul.

SPAN. *See* Metrology: Linear Measures.

SPARK. In Job 5:7 Eliphaz declares, "For man is born for trouble, as sparks fly upward," meaning that "misfortune does not grow out of the ground like weeds; it is rather established in the divine order of the world, as it is established in the order of nature that sparks of fire should ascend."

In describing the leviathan, it is said (Job 41:19), "Out of his mouth go burning torches; sparks of fire leap forth." Bartram has observed that as the alligator comes on the land a thick smoke issues from his distended nostrils. This would seem to give the impression of a fire existing beneath and bursting forth.

SPARROW. *See* Animal Kingdom.

Figurative. Our Lord's allusion to God's care for the comparatively worthless sparrow (Matt. 10:29, 31; Luke 12:6-7) is an incentive for man to trust divine Providence.

SPEAR. *See* Armor, Arms.

SPECK (Gk. *karphes,* "dry" twig or straw). Any small, dry particle, such as of chaff, wood, etc. (Matt. 7:3-5; Luke 6:41-42), and figurative of some slight moral defect seen in another. The KJV term is "mote." The self-righteous man is likely to see these, while being unconscious of greater evils in himself. The proverb was a familiar one with the Hebrews.

SPECKLED.
1. (Heb. *nāqōd,* "marked"), spotted, as black goats or sheep, with white spots or vice versa (Gen. 30:32-33, 35, 39; 31:8, 10, 12). Jacob, in order to increase his wages, resorted to the following plan: "In the first place (30:37-39) he took

fresh rods of storax, maple, and walnut trees, all of which have a dazzling white wood under their dark outside, and peeled white strips upon them. These partially peeled and, therefore, mottled rods he placed in the drinking troughs; . . . in order that if copulation took place at the drinking time, it might occur near the mottled sticks, and the young be speckled and mottled in consequence" (K. & D., *Com.*). Jacob was actually indulging in selective breeding.

2. (Heb. *ṣābûa‘,* "dyed"), colored, mottled (Jer. 12:9), elsewhere in modern Heb., the *hyena,* but in the above passage a *many-colored bird of prey.*

SPECKLED BIRD. *See* Animal Kingdom: Hyena.

SPECTACLE (Gk. *theatron*). One to be gazed at and made sport of (1 Cor. 4:9).

SPELT. An inferior kind of wheat (Ex. 9:32). *See* Vegetable Kingdom.

SPICE. The spices mentioned as being used by Nicodemus for the preparation of our Lord's body (John 19:39-40) are "myrrh and aloes." Aloes here must be understood not to be the aloes of medicine (*Aloe*), but the highly scented wood of the *Aquilaria agallochum.* The evangelist John computes the amount at one hundred pounds, referring doubtless to the Roman pound of about twelve ounces. This would make seventy-five pounds. The amount mentioned may seem large, but Josephus (*Ant.* 17.8.3) tells us that there were five hundred spice-bearers at Herod's funeral; and in the Talmud it is said that eighty pounds of opobalsamum were employed at the funeral of a certain rabbi. It must also be remembered that Nicodemus was a rich man. The ancient Bible world enjoyed an extensive trade in spices. Caravan routes by which aromatic vegetable substances were transported from one country to another, particularly across Arabia, became highways for the spread of culture. Spice trade rivaled the modern perfume and cosmetic industry. *See* Vegetable Kingdom.

BIBLIOGRAPHY: M. Zohary, *Plants of the Bible* (1982), pp. 88, 190, 197-206.

SPIDER. *See* Animal Kingdom.
Figurative. Bildad compares the trust of the ungodly and secretly wicked (Heb. *ḥanēp*) to a spider's web (Job 8:14); as easily as a spider's web is cut through by the lightest touch or a breath of wind, so that on which the evil man depends and trusts is cut asunder. In the declaration of Isaiah (Isa. 59:5), they "weave the spider's web," we have a figure to represent the worthlessness and deceptive character of the works of the wicked.

SPIKENARD. *See* Vegetable Kingdom: Nard.

SPIN (Heb. *ṭāwâ;* Gk. *nēthō,* Ex. 35:25-26; Matt. 6:28; cf. Prov. 31:19). The latter passage implies the use of the same instruments that have been in vogue for hand spinning down to the present day, namely, the distaff and spindle. The distaff, however, appears to have been dispensed with, and the term so rendered means the spindle itself, whereas that rendered "spindle" represents the *whirl* of the spindle, a button of circular rim that was affixed to it and gave steadiness to its circular motion. The "whirl" of the Syrian women was made of amber in the time of Pliny. The spindle was held perpendicularly in the one hand, while the other was employed in drawing out the thread.

SPINDLE (Heb. *kîshōr,* "director"). The *twirl* or lower part of the instrument used in giving motion to the whole (Prov. 31:19). In the East it is held in the hand, often perpendicularly, and is twirled with one hand, while the other draws out the thread. The spindle and distaff are the most *ancient* of all the instruments used for *spinning,* or making thread.

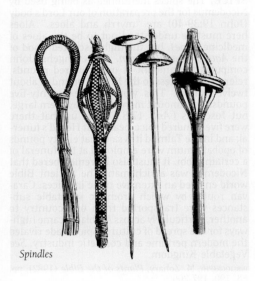

Spindles

SPIRIT (Heb. *rûqh,* "breath, wind"; Gk. *pneuma,* "wind, breath," the "vital principle," etc.). A term used in the Scriptures generally to denote purely spiritual beings; also the spiritual, immortal part in man. Other terms (*nepesh; psuchē*) refer to the animal soul or life of man, though it seems evident that these words are also used frequently in a broader and deeper sense with reference to man's spiritual nature (e.g., Gen. 2:7; Ps. 42:2; Matt. 10:28; 11:29). *See* Soul. There are, however, passages (such as 1 Thess. 5:23; Heb. 4:12) that emphasize a distinction between soul and spirit.

The term *soul* specifies that in the immaterial part of man that concerns life, action, and emo-

tion. *Spirit* is that part related to worship and divine communion. The two terms are often used interchangeably, the same functions being ascribed to each (cf. John 12:27; 1 Cor. 16:18; 2 Cor. 7:13 with Matt. 11:29; 2 Cor. 7:1 with 1 Pet. 2:11; James 5:20 with 1 Cor. 5:5; 1 Pet. 1:9). The deceased are mentioned both as soul and sometimes as spirit (Gen. 35:18; 1 Kings 17:21; Acts 2:27; with Matt. 27:50; John 19:30; Heb. 12:23). However, *soul* and *spirit* are not always employed interchangeably. The soul is said to be lost, for example, but not the spirit. When no technical distinctions are set forth, the Bible is *dichotomous,* but otherwise it is *trichotomous* (cf. Matt. 10:28; Acts 2:31; Rom. 8:10; Eph. 4:4; James 2:26; 1 Pet. 2:11). Theologians have pored over these distinctions ceaselessly. The origin of man's immaterial nature is subject to three theories: (1) The *creational,* maintaining that *soul and spirit* are created at birth. (2) *Traducian. Soul and spirit* are generated the same as the body. (3) The soul is preexistent, embracing the idea of transmigration of souls. M.F.U.

BIBLIOGRAPHY: E. D. Burton, *Spirit, Soul, and Body* (1918); A. R. Johnson, *The Vitality of the Individual in Ancient Israel* (1964); J. Laidlaw, *The Biblical Doctrine of Man* (1983).

SPIRIT, THE HOLY. *See* The Holy Spirit.

SPIRITIST. The spiritist (Heb. *yidd'ōnî*) is properly the "knowing or wise one" as the English word connotes, as well as the LXX "gnostes." Like the "medium" (Heb. *ōb*), it means in the first instance the alleged "spirit of a deceased person" (actually the divining demon). Then it came to mean him or her who divines by such a spirit or demon. Thus both terms mean (1) the divining spirit, (2) the medium through whom the demon divines. The two concepts, "the medium" and "the spiritist," are frequently so closely identified as to be thought of as one, as in Lev. 19:31; 20:6. The same is true of the term "wizard." Implicit in the meaning "spiritist" is the thought of the wise and knowing demon and the clever and cunning medium, who is skillful in oracular science because the intelligent spirit is in him. It is a superhuman knowledge of the spirit inhabiting the human body that makes a spiritistic medium. *See* Magic; Sorcery; Necromancer. M.F.U.

SPIRITS, DISCERNING OF. *See* Discerning of Spirits.

SPIRITUAL GIFTS (Gk. *ta pneumatika,* the spiritual supply; *charismata,* "gifts"). A phrase used to denote the endowments bestowed by the Holy Spirit in the primitive church (1 Cor. 12:1), and the same as "gifts" (v. 4). A *spiritual gift* "means any extraordinary faculty, which operated for the furtherance of the welfare of the Christian community, and which was itself wrought by the grace of God, through the power of the Holy Spirit, in special individuals, in accordance, respectively, with the measure of their individual capacities, whether it were that the Spirit infused entirely new powers, or stimulated those already existing to higher power and activity (Rom. 12:6ff.)" (Meyer, *Com.,* on 1 Cor. 12:1). These gifts included *word of wisdom; knowledge; faith; healing; effecting of miracles; prophecy; distinguishing of spirits; tongues;* and their *interpretation* (vv. 8-10). *See* under various heads.

SPIRITUALITY. The quality of being spiritual, as opposed to material. Thus theology predicates the spirituality of God (*see* Spirit). The spirituality of man refers to the immaterial part of his nature. The term is also used with reference to the disposition or internal condition of men when in such a state as prepares them to recognize and properly appreciate spiritual realities. True spirituality in the last sense is the result of the inworking of the Holy Spirit (*see* 1 Cor. 2:14-15; 3:1, 16, etc.). In an ecclesiastical sense the term is used in the Church of England to denote the whole body of the clergy, with reference to the nature of their office.

SPIT, SPITTLE (Heb. from *rāqaq; yāraq,* Num. 12:14; Deut. 25:9; Gk. *ptusma*). A source of legal defilement, e.g., the spittle of a person having an issue defiled the one upon whom it fell (Lev. 15:8). To spit in one's face was regarded as the grossest insult (Num. 12:14; Deut. 25:9; Isa. 50:6; Matt. 26:67; 27:30); indeed, it was a great indignity to spit toward anyone, so that an oriental never allows himself to spit in the presence of one whom he respects. Spittle was employed by our Lord in the cure of the blind man (John 9:6), and the rabbis cite it as a remedy in like cases, especially the spittle of persons who were fasting.

SPLANCHNOMANCY. *See* Magic.

SPLENDID (Heb. *kebûddâ,* "magnificent"). In speaking of the ungodly alliance between Judah and Chaldea, Judah is said to have sent ambassadors to Chaldea and, for the purpose of receiving the Chaldeans, adorned herself as a woman would do for the reception of her paramours. She seated herself upon a "splendid couch" (Ezek. 23:41), in front of which was a table on which stood the incense and the oil that she ought to have given to Jehovah. KJV renders this word "stately."

SPOIL. The rendering of a number of Heb. and Gk. words. Spoil consisted of captives of both sexes, cattle, and whatever a captured city might contain, especially metallic treasures. Within the limits of Canaan no captives were to be made (Deut. 20:14, 16); beyond those limits, in case of warlike resistance, all the women and children were to be made captives and the men put to death. The law of booty was that it should be divided equally between the army who won it and the people of Israel. But of the former, one head in every 500 was reserved to God and appropriated to the priests; of the latter, one in every 50 was similarly reserved and appropriated to the Levites (Num. 31:26-47; cf. 2 Sam. 8:10-11; 1 Chron. 26:27-28). A portion of the spoil was assigned to the oppressed, the aged, widows, and orphans (2 Macc. 8:28, 30). As regarded the army, David added a regulation that the baggage guard should share equally with the troops engaged (1 Sam. 30:24-25). The division of the spoil was a joyous feast for the people (Isa. 9:3).

SPOKE (Heb. *ḥishshūq,* "conjoined"). In Heb., a rare term referring to the bars in the hub of a wheel supporting the rim (1 Kings 7:33; NASB, NIV). In the KJV, *ḥishshūq* is translated "felloes," the plural of *felly,* an old term referring to the exterior rim of a wheel. Cf. Rims; Hub; Nave.

SPONGE. *See* Animal Kingdom.

SPOONS (Heb. *kap;* KJV, NASB). In the KJV and sometimes the NASB, *containers* for incense. The NASB sometimes uses the term *pans* to refer to these utensils. *See* Tabernacle of Israel: Furniture.

SPORT. *See* Jest; Games.

SPOT.
1. A defect or blemish; used in Job 31:7 (KJV, "blot") to indicate a *moral* weakness (Heb. *mūm*). Compare Lev. 21:17-23; 22:20; 24:19-20; Deut. 32:5; 2 Sam. 14:25; Job 11:15; Prov. 9:7; Song of Sol. 4:7.
2. A *whitish* spot on the skin, the "bright spot" of incipient leprosy (Lev. 13:2-39; 14:56). Heb. *baheret.*
3. Heb. *bōhaq,* to be "pale," "eczema," not to be confused with leprosy (Lev. 13:39).
4. The mark upon the leopard (Heb. *ḥăbarbūrâ,* "a streak"), or, according to Gesenius, the stripes of the tiger (Jer. 13:23), used as an illustration of the inability of men to rid themselves of evil character.
5. Heb. *ṭālā',* to cover with "pieces," spotted, variegated; as "sheep" or "goats" (Gen. 30:32-39; Ezek. 16:16, "various colors").
6. The Gk. (*spilos,* "spot") has also a moral sense of *fault* (Eph. 5:27); compare Jude 12, KJV. Its negative form (*aspilos*) means *spotless,* free from *censure* (1 Tim. 6:14, "stain"), from *vice,* and so *unsullied* (2 Pet. 3:14).

SPOUSE. *See* Marriage.

SPREADING (Heb. *miprāś,* an "expansion"). "Can anyone understand the spreading of the clouds?" (Job 36:29). Here *spreading* does not mean bursting, but an expanding. "It is the growth of the storm clouds, which collect often from a beginning 'small as a man's hand' (1 Kings 18:44), that is intended."

SPRING. A source of water issuing forth from the ground, the same word as "eye" in Heb., *'ayin* (Gen. 16:7; 1 Sam. 29:1; Prov. 8:28), sometimes translated "fountain." Often the Heb. word used denotes a place of a spring or running water (Lev. 11:36; Josh. 15:9; Ps. 74:15; Prov. 25:26), a well-watered place (Heb. *berākâ,* "benediction," and so "prosperity"; "pools," KJV; "blessings," NASB; "springs," NIV; Ps. 84:6). In Isa. 35:7; 49:10 the original word *mabbûa'* has the idea of a gushing source of water. The Gk. *pēgē* occurs in Rev. 7:17; 8:10; 14:7; 21:6. In Gen. 16:7; Lev. 11:36; 1 Sam. 29:1; Rev. 7:17; 8:10; 14:7; 21:6, the NASB and NIV use "spring" to replace KJV *fountain* (which see).

Figurative. The term *spring* is used in the NASB of the source of grace (Ps. 87:7); of the manifestations of divine grace (Isa. 41:8; Joel 3:18); of the church (Song of Sol. 4:12; Isa. 58:11); the KJV and NIV in all these passages except Isa. 41:8 and Isa. 58:11 is *fountain* (which see).

SPRINKLING. Instances of sprinkling are given in the Scriptures, namely, with *blood* (Ex. 29:16, 20-21; Lev. 1:5, 11; etc.); *see* Sacrifice; with *water* (Lev. 14:51; Num. 8:7; 19:13, 20; etc.); with *oil* (Lev. 14:16). *See* Anointing.

Figurative. "Thus He will sprinkle many nations" (Isa. 52:15) would seem to be a figure setting forth the expiation and purifying of many nations; and then the antithesis would be: *Many* were astonished; so *many* (not merely men, but) *nations* shall be sprinkled. They were amazed that such an abject person claimed to be the Messiah; yet it is He that shall justify and cleanse. Many commentators understand the phrase as meaning "He shall cause many nations to leap with astonishment." "The figurative expression, 'to sprinkle with clean water' (Ezek. 36:25), is taken from the illustrations prescribed by the law, more particularly the purifying from defilement by the dead by sprinkling with the water prepared from the ashes of a red heifer" (Num. 19:17-19; cf. Ps. 51:9). "Having our hearts sprinkled clean from an evil conscience" (Heb. 10:22) is in contrast to mere physical cleansing (9:13, 19; cf. Ex. 24:8; Lev. 8:11). As the OT covenant people were sprinkled with the (cleansing) blood of the sacrifice, so are Christians *sprinkled* by the blood of Christ and their consciences delivered from the sense of guilt.

SQUAD. In Acts 12:4 it is stated that "four squads of soldiers" guarded Peter (Gk. *tetradion*; the KJV reads "four quaternions"). It was usual to entrust the custody of captives and prisoners to a guard consisting of four soldiers, two soldiers being confined with the prisoner and two keeping guard outside. In the account in Acts 12:4, one squad at a time stood guard during each of the four successive watches.

STABILITY (Gk. *stereōma*). That upon which a thing can rest; in Col. 2:5 "stability of your faith" ("firm," NIV) refers figuratively, in a military sense, to a *solid front*. *See also* Steadfastness, which is the KJV rendering.

STA'CHYS (sta'kis; an "ear," i.e., of grain). A Christian at Rome to whom Paul sent salutations, calling him "my beloved" (Rom. 16:9). According to an old tradition recorded by Nicephorus Callistus, he was bishop of Byzantium. He is said by Hippolytus and Dorotheus to have been one of the seventy disciples.

STACTE. *See* Vegetable Kingdom.

STADIA. *See* Metrology: Furlong.

STAFF (Heb. *maṭṭeh,* "branch"; Ex. 4:2; 7:9; 1 Sam. 14:27, 43). In the case of Moses and Aaron, the staff, although belonging to Moses, was employed by Aaron in performing miracles. It was also called "the staff of God" (Ex. 4:20; 17:9), probably because through it Jehovah wrought such wonders. *See* Rod.

STAFF (Heb. *maṭṭeh, maqqēl, shēbeṭ;* Gk. *hrabdos;* all meaning a "stick"). Rods and staffs were employed for various purposes by the ancients, as is common with us. They were used by old and infirm persons for support or defense (Ex. 21:19; Zech. 8:4), also by travelers (Gen. 32:10; Ex. 12:11; 2 Kings 4:29; Matt. 10:10). A staff, like a *seal,* was a sign of rank (Gen. 38:18, 25), sometimes inscribed with the owner's name; also a badge of office (Ex. 4:2-4; Num. 20:8-11; etc.). The staff of the shepherd was used to aid in climbing hills, beating bushes and low brush in which

Shepherd with staff

the flock strayed, and where snakes and reptiles abounded.

STAG. The NIV translation of Heb. *'ayyal,* usually rendered "fallow deer." *See* Animal Kingdom: Hart; Fallow Deer.

STAIR (Heb. usually *ma'āleh,* or *ma'ălâ,* an "ascent"; *lûl,* a winding stair, 1 Kings 6:8). See related KJV usages in Song of Sol. 2:14; Ezek. 38:20. The stairs probably ran around the inside of the quadrangle of the house, as they do still, e.g., in the ruin called "the house of Zaccheus" at Jericho. Regarding the meaning of 2 Kings 9:13, *see* Jehu.

STAKE (Heb. *yātēd,* a "peg"). A peg or nail, and often so rendered; especially a *tent pin* (Isa. 33:20). The idea of continuance and permanency is figured by a tent that is not moved or its pegs drawn. The enlargement and strengthening of Zion is illustrated by a tent, the inside space of which is widened, and the tent pins driven deeper into the ground.

STALL. The rendering of Heb. and Gk. words signifying a stable or cattle (Amos 6:4; Mal. 4:2). "Stalls" is used in the sense of *pairs,* as of horses (1 Kings 4:26; 2 Chron. 9:25). The expression "And there be no cattle in the stalls" (Hab. 3:17) is used to denote calamity, disaster. Stables containing stalls for horses have been excavated at Megiddo.

STAMMERER (Heb. *'illēg,* a "stutterer," Isa. 32:4; *lā'ag,* properly, to "speak unintelligibly," 28:11; 33:19). To *mock* or deride.

STANDARD. The rendering of two Heb. words. The standards in use among the Hebrews probably resembled those of the Egyptians and Assyrians—a figure or device of some kind elevated on a pole. (1) The Heb. *nēs* consisted of some well-understood signal that was exhibited on the top of a pole from a bare mountaintop (Isa. 13:2; 18:3; "banner," NIV). What the nature of the signal was, we have no means of knowing. The important point is that the *nēs* was an occasional signal and not a military standard. In Num. 21:8-9 this word is used of the standard ("pole," KJV, NIV) upon which the bronze serpent was placed. (2) The Heb. term *degel* is used to describe the standards that were given to each of the four divisions of the Israelite army at the time of the Exodus (Num. 1:52; 2:2-3, 10, 17-18, 25, 31, 34; 10:14, 18, 22, 25). The character of the Hebrew military standards is a matter of conjecture; they probably resembled the Egyptian, which consisted of a sacred emblem such as an animal, a boat, or the king's name.

Figurative. It was customary to give a defeated party a standard as a token of protection, and that was regarded as the surest pledge of fidelity. God's lifting or setting up a standard (Isa. 11:12) is a most expressive figure and implies a peculiar presence, protection, and aid in leading and directing His people in the execution of His righteous will and giving them comfort and peace in His service.

STAR (Heb. *kôkāb,* "round" or "shining"; Gk. *astēr*).

1. Under the term *stars* the Hebrews included constellations, planets, indeed all the heavenly bodies except the sun and moon. In fact, the ancient Hebrews knew very little of the starry heavens, and no indications are given in Scripture of scientific *astronomy* (which see). We find there only the ordinary observations of landsmen (Job 38:31-33; Amos 5:8), especially shepherds (Ps. 8:3).

Figurative. The patriarchs observed the stars (Gen. 37:9); and metaphors drawn from the starry world, either with reference to the countless number of the stars (22:17; Ex. 32:13; Nah. 3:16; etc.) or to their brightness (Num. 24:17; Isa. 14:12; Rev. 22:16) came into frequent and early use. The psalmist, to exalt the power and omniscience of Jehovah, represents Him as taking a survey of the stars, as a king reviewing his army (Ps. 147:4). Stars were frequently employed as symbols of persons in exalted stations; e.g., "a star shall come forth from Jacob" designates King David (Num. 24:17), applied by some to the Messiah. The patriarchs were called "stars" (Gen. 37:9), and "stars" denote the princes, rulers, and nobles of the earth (Dan. 8:10; Rev. 6:13; 8:10-12; 9:1; 12:4). Christ is called the "morning star," as He introduced the light of gospel day, revealing more fully the truths of God than the ancient prophets (Rev. 22:16). The study of the stars led to their worship (*see* Idolatry) and to calculations of human affairs (*see* Astrology).

2. A star in the east (Matt. 2:2) was seen by the wise men (magi) before their journey to Jerusalem and as they approached Bethlehem. After ascertaining at what time they first observed the star, Herod sent them to Bethlehem, with the request to inform him when they found the child. As they left Jerusalem, the star that had attracted their attention at its "rising" (Gk. *anatolē*), and that, apparently, they had not recently seen, once more appeared. In ancient times such guidance by a star was a matter of belief and expectancy; and "they rejoiced exceedingly with great joy."

This phenomenon has been generally understood to be some supernatural light resembling a star, that appeared in a country far to the E of Jerusalem, to men who were versed in the study of celestial phenomena; and that it conveyed to their minds an impulse to travel to Jerusalem to find a newborn king. However, by some scholars the star has been removed from the category of supernatural events and has been thought to be a conjunction of the planets Jupiter and Saturn. *See* Astronomy.

STARGAZER. *See* Magic.

STATER. *See* Metrology: Measures of Value, or Money.

STATURE (Gk. *hēlikos,* lit., "how much?"). "Stature" in Eph. 4:13 is the *age suitable* for anything; figuratively of an attained state of mind fit for a thing, and so the age in which we are fitted to receive the fullness of Christ.

"Stature" in Matt. 6:27, KJV is more correctly rendered by the NASB "life's span." *See also* Height.

STEADFASTNESS. *Stērigmos* (2 Pet. 3:17), in the usual sense of *stability* (which see).

STEEL. *See* Metals; Mineral Kingdom: Iron.

STENCH. *See* Abomination.

STEPH'ANAS (stef'a-nas; "crown"). A Corinthian disciple whose household Paul baptized (1 Cor. 1:16), being the first converted to Christianity in Achaia, and one of those who "devoted themselves for ministry to the saints" (16:15). About the form that this ministry took, we have no precise information. He appears to have been with Paul when he wrote his first letter to the Corinthians (16:17).

STE'PHEN (stē'ven; Gk. *Stephanos,* a "crown"). Stephen, as his Greek name indicates, was probably of Hellenistic origin. Where or when he was born, however, we have no means of ascertaining.

Deacon. The first authentic account we have of Stephen is in Acts 6:5. In the distribution of the common fund that was entrusted to the apostles for the support of the poorer brethren, the Hellenists complained that partiality was shown to the natives of Palestine and that their own widows were neglected. The apostles took measures immediately to remove the cause of the complaint. Unwilling themselves to be taken from the work of the ministry, they advised the church to select seven men of honest report, full of the Holy Spirit and wisdom, for this business (v. 3). The brethren proceeded immediately to select the prescribed number, among whom Stephen is first mentioned. The newly elected deacons were brought to the apostles, who ordained them to their work (v. 6). From the first Stephen occupied a prominent position. He is described as "a man full of faith and of the Holy Spirit" (v. 5), "full of grace and power" (v. 8), and of irresistible "wisdom and the Spirit" (v. 10). He attracted attention by the great wonders and miracles that he did among the people.

Teaching. From his foreign descent and education, he was naturally led to address himself to the Hellenistic Jews. In these disputations he probably took more advanced grounds than the apostles had respecting the discontinuance and abrogation of the Mosaic system, contending that already it had, as a ritual system, lost all force and binding obligation by its complete fulfillment in

Christ. Certain adherents of several synagogues were leaders in the disputation with Stephen.

Arrest. Unable to withstand his reasoning, they caused his arrest and appeared against him before the Sanhedrin with false witnesses. The charge against him was *blasphemy,* in speaking "against this holy place, and the Law" (v. 13). Stephen doubtless saw that he was to be the victim of a blind and malignant spirit. Yet he stood serene, collected, and undismayed. "All who were sitting in the Council saw his face like the face of an angel" (v. 15), from which we may not unreasonably conclude that it pleased God to manifest His approval of His servant by giving his countenance a supernatural brightness, such as that with which the face of Moses shone when he had been speaking with the Lord.

Defense. The high priest who presided asked the judicial question, "Are these things so?" To this Stephen replied in a speech that has every appearance of being faithfully reported. He began with the call of Abraham and traveled historically in his argument through all the stages of their national existence, evidently designing to prove that the presence and favor of God had not been confined to the Holy Land or the Temple of Jerusalem. He also showed that there was a tendency from the earliest times toward the same ungrateful and narrow spirit that had appeared in this last stage of their political existence. He then suddenly broke away from his narrative and denounced them as "stiff-necked and uncircumcised in heart and ears" and as "always resisting the Holy Spirit" (7:51). The effect upon his hearers was terrible; "they were cut to the quick, and they began gnashing their teeth at him." On the other hand Stephen, filled with the Holy Spirit, was granted a vision of the glory of God, and Jesus at His right hand, risen to welcome his spirit as it should escape his mangled body and to introduce him into the presence of God the Father.

Martyrdom. Enraptured, he exclaimed, "Behold, I see the heavens opened up and the Son of Man standing at the right hand of God." The fate of Stephen was settled, for his judges broke into a loud yell, stopped their ears, ran upon him with one accord, and dragged him out of the city to the place of execution. Saul was present and consented to his death. In striking contrast to the fearful rage of his enemies was the spirit shown by Stephen. First offering a petition for himself, he then prayed, "Lord, do not hold this sin against them," and, in the beautiful language of Scripture, *"fell asleep"* (7:60). "Devout men buried Stephen, and made loud lamentation over him" (8:2), A.D. 34.

Irregularities in the Trial. The trial of Stephen appears to have been irregular, and the judicial act was not completed. There are, indeed, the witnesses and part of the prisoner's defense; and here the legal action stops. The high priest does not, as in our Lord's trial, ask the opinion of the council and then deliver sentence in accordance with their views. The whole proceedings broke up with a tumult at what they deemed blasphemy by Stephen.

Saul Consenting. The witnesses against Stephen acted as his executioners (Deut. 17:7; John 8:7) and laid their outer garments for safety at the feet of Saul. One of the prominent leaders in the transaction was deputed by custom to signify his assent to the act by taking the clothes into his custody.

BIBLIOGRAPHY: R. N. Longenecker, *Paul, Apostle of Liberty* (1964), pp. 271-75; J. Kilgallen, *Analecta Biblica* 67 (1976): 187ff.; F. F. Bruce, *Peter, Stephen, James, and John* (1979).

STEWARD (usually Heb. *śar,* "head" person; Gk. *epitropos,* "manager"; *oikonomos,* "overseer"). A manager or superintendent of another's household, as Eliezer was over the house of Abraham (cf. Gen. 15:2). We read of Joseph's steward (43:19; 44:1, 4) and of Herod's steward (Luke 8:3; "manager," NIV). As great confidence was reposed in these officials, Paul describes Christian ministers as the stewards of God over His church (1 Cor. 4:1-2; "those given a trust," NIV). Believers are also said to be stewards of God, of God's gifts and graces (1 Pet. 4:10).

STICK (Heb. *qeśep,* a "splinter"). The original word is rendered "stick" in Hos. 10:7: "Samaria will be cut off with her king, like a *stick* on the surface of the water." It means a broken branch, a fagot, or splinter. The NIV renders "twig."

STINKWEED. *See* Vegetable Kingdom.

STOCK. The KJV rendering of several Heb. and Gk. words, meaning: the *stump* (Job 14:8); the *trunk* of a tree (Isa. 44:19; "block," NIV); a *tree* or piece of *wood* (Jer. 2:27; 10:8); a *family* or *nation* (Acts 13:26; Phil. 3:5).

STOCKS. The term *stocks* is used frequently in the Bible to refer to confinement of prisoners and once in the KJV to refer to idol worship.

1. Heb. *mahpeket,* "wrench"; Jer. 20:2-3; cf. 2 Chron. 16:10, marg., "the house of the stocks," a wooden frame in which the feet, hands, and neck of a person were so fastened that his body was held in a bent position.

2. The block or log of wood in which the feet of a criminal are fastened and which he must drag about with him when he moves (Job 13:27; 33:11; "shackle," NIV), Heb. *sad.* (Cf. Prov. 7:22, KJV, which NASB renders "fetters," and NIV, "noose" [Heb. *'ekes*].)

3. A *prison;* or, better, *stocks* proper, or some other confinement for the feet (Jer. 29:26), Heb. *sinōq.* Orelli (*Com.,* ad loc.) thinks that the *sinōq* was a kind of *neck iron* (cf. Arab. *zinak,* neck chain).

4. Gk. *xulon,* "wood," a log with holes in which the feet, hands, and neck of prisoners were in-

serted and fastened with thongs (Acts 16:24).

5. In Hos. 4:12, the KJV term *stocks* refers to an object of worship, as the NASB and NIV rendering "wooden idol" shows.

St. Stephen's Gate, Jerusalem, traditional site of his death

STO'ICS (stō'iks). The Stoics and Epicureans, who are mentioned together in Acts 17:18, represent the two opposite schools of practical philosophy that survived the fall of higher speculation in Greece. The Stoic school was founded by Zeno of Citium (about 280 B.C.) and derived its name from the painted "portico" (*stoa*) in which he taught. Zeno was followed by Cleanthes (about 260 B.C.), Cleanthes by Chrysippus (about 240 B.C.), who was regarded as the intellectual founder of the Stoic system. Stoicism soon found an entrance at Rome, and under the empire Stoicism was not unnaturally connected with republican virtue. The ethical system of the Stoics has been commonly supposed to have a close connection with Christian morality. But the morality of Stoicism is essentially based on pride, that of Christianity on humility; the one upholds individual independence, the other absolute faith in another; the one looks for consolation in the issue of fate, the other in Providence; the one is limited by periods of cosmical ruin, the other is consummated in a personal resurrection (Smith, *Dict.*).

BIBLIOGRAPHY: E. Bevan, *Stoics and Skeptics* (1913).

STOMACHER. *See* Dress, garments (the dress of women).

STONE (usually Heb. *'eben;* Gk. *lithos*).

Kinds. The ordinary stones mentioned as found in *Palestine* (which see) are chiefly chalk stone (Isa. 27:9), marble, and sandstone; basalt (Josephus *Ant.* 8.7.4); flint and firestone (2 Macc. 10:3).

Uses. Stones were applied in ancient Palestine to many uses:

1. They were used for the ordinary purposes of building, and in this respect the most noticeable point is the very large size to which they occasionally run (Mark 13:1). Robinson gives the dimensions of one as twenty-four feet long by six feet broad and three feet high. For most public edifices hewn stone was used; an exception was made in regard to altars (Ex. 20:25; Deut. 27:5; Josh. 8:31). The Phoenicians were particularly famous for their skill in hewing stone (2 Sam. 5:11; 1 Kings 5:18). Stones were selected of certain colors in order to form ornamental stringcourses (1 Chron. 29:2). They were also used for pavements (2 Kings 16:17; cf. Esther 1:6).

Stone wall, Jerusalem

2. Large stones were used for closing the entrances of caves (Josh. 10:18; Dan. 6:17), sepulchers (Matt. 27:60; John 11:38; 20:1), and springs (Gen. 29:2).

3. Flint stones (Heb. *ṣûr*, or *ṣôr*), occasionally were used instead of a knife, particularly for circumcision and similar purposes (Ex. 4:25; Josh. 5:2, 3).

4. Stones were further used as ammunition for slings (1 Sam. 17:40, 49), catapults (2 Chron. 26:14), and bows (Wisd. 5:22; cf. 1 Macc. 6:51); and as boundary marks (cf. Deut. 19:14; 27:17; Job 24:2; Prov. 22:28; 23:10); such were probably the stone of Bohan (Josh. 15:6; 18:17), of Abel (1 Sam. 6:15, 18), the stone Ezel (20:19), the great stone by Gibeon (2 Sam. 20:8), and the stone of Zoheleth (1 Kings 1:9); also as weights for scales (Deut. 25:13; Prov. 16:11, *see* marg.), and for mills (2 Sam. 11:21).

5. Large stones were set up to commemorate any remarkable event (Gen. 28:18; 31:45; 35:14; Josh. 4:9; 1 Sam. 7:12). Such stones were occasionally consecrated by anointing (Gen. 28:18).

A similar practice existed in heathen countries, and by a singular coincidence these stones were described in Phoenicia by a name very similar to Bethel, namely, *baetylia*. The only point of resemblance between the two consists in the custom of anointing.

6. That the worship of stones prevailed among the heathen nations surrounding Palestine, and was from them borrowed by apostate Israelites, appears from Isa. 57:6 (cf. Lev. 26:1). "The smooth stones of the ravine" are those that the stream has washed smooth with time and rounded into a pleasing shape. "In Carthage such stones were called *abbadires;* and among the ancient Arabs the *asnâm,* or idols, consisted for the most part of rude blocks of stone of this description. . . . Stone worship of this kind had been practiced by the Israelites before the captivity, and their heathenish practices had been transmitted to the exiles in Babylon" (Delitzsch, *Com.,* ad loc.).

7. Heaps of stones were piled up on various occasions; the making of a treaty (Gen. 31:46); over the grave of a notorious offender (Josh. 7:26; 8:29; 2 Sam. 18:17); such heaps often attained great size from the custom of each passerby's adding a stone.

8. Stones were used for tablets (Ex. 24:12; Josh. 8:32) and guide stones to the *cities of refuge* (which see).

9. "A time to throw stones, and a time to gather stones" (Eccles. 3:5) seems to refer to the custom of spoiling an enemy's field by throwing stones upon it (2 Kings 3:19, 25); and the clearing of a field of stones preparatory to its cultivation (Isa. 5:2).

Figurative. Stones are used figuratively to denote *hardness* or *insensibility* (1 Sam. 25:37; Ezek. 11:19; 36:26), or *firmness, strength* (Gen. 49:24), where "the Stone of Israel" is equivalent to "the Rock of Israel" (2 Sam. 23:3; Isa. 30:29). Christians are called "living stones," i.e., not like the inanimate *things* of the material Temple, but *living men* built up on Christ, the living and chief cornerstone. "I will make Jerusalem a heavy stone for all the peoples" (Zech. 12:3) may be a figure founded upon the labor connected with building, the heavy stones of which hurt those who attempt to carry them away. The "white stone" (Rev. 2:17) has been understood as referring to the pebble of acquittal used in the Greek courts; to the lot cast in elections in Greece; to the white stone given to victors at the Grecian games; and to the stones of hospitality usual in ancient times, a "sort of *carte blanche,* entitling the person who showed it to ask for and receive what he might want." *Precious stones* (which see) are used in Scripture in a figurative sense to signify value, beauty, durability, etc., in those objects with which they are compared (*see* Song of Sol. 5:14; Isa. 54:11-12; Lam. 4:7; Rev. 4:3; 21:11, 21). *See* Stone.

BIBLIOGRAPHY: F. F. Bruce, *Expository Times* 84 (1972-73): 231-35; J. Jeremias, *Theological Dictionary of the New Testament* (1967), 4:268-80.

STONECUTTER. *See* Handicrafts: Stoneworker.

STONEMASON. *See* articles Builder; Handicrafts: Stoneworker; House.

STONEWORKER. *See* Handicrafts.

STONING. *See* Punishment.

STOOL. *See* Birthstool.

STORAGE CITY (Ex. 1:11; 1 Kings 9:19; 2 Chron. 8:4, 6; "store cities," 16:4; 17:12; "storehouse," 32:28), a place of deposit for merchandise and provisions. *See also* City, Storage.

STORAX. *See* Vegetable Kingdom: Myrrh; Poplar; Stacte.

STORE. In Deut. 28:5, 17, the KJV uses this term in place of NASB and NIV "kneading bowl."

STOREHOUSE. The rendering of several original terms, meaning a *treasury* (1 Chron. 27:25; Ps. 33:7; Mal. 3:10, as elsewhere rendered); a *receptacle* for provisions (cf. Deut. 28:8; Prov. 3:10; "barns"), usually underground in the East; a *granary* (Jer. 50:26; cf. Ex. 1:11; Luke 12:24). The Egyptians had storehouses for stuffs and jewels, gold, preserved fruits, grain, liquors, armor, provisions, etc. Their grain storehouses had only two openings, one at the top for pouring in the grain, another on the ground level for drawing it out. For the security and management of these, troops of porters, storekeepers, and accountants were employed to superintend the works, record keepers, and directors. Great nobles coveted the administration of the storehouses, and even the sons of kings did not think it beneath their dignity to be entitled "directors of the granaries" or "directors of the armory."

STORK. *See* Animal Kingdom.

STRAIGHT STREET. One of the ancient thoroughfares of Damascus, on which was located the house of Judas, where Paul was visited by Ananias (Acts 9:11). It still retains the same name in an Arabic form (*Derb el-Mustakim*), running westward from the Bab es-Shurky, or East Gate. Its length was about one English mile, and its breadth about one hundred feet. It is not quite straight now, nor is its architecture imposing.

STRAIN. *See* Gnat, in Animal Kingdom.

STRANGER. *See* Foreigner.

STRANGE WOMAN. *See* Harlot, Whore.

STRANGLE (Heb. *ḥānaq,* to "choke"; Gk. *pnigō*). It was forbidden by Moses, and also by the early Christians, to eat animals put to death by strangulation, i.e., not having the blood properly removed (Gen. 9:4; Acts 15:20).

STRAW (Heb. *teben;* Jer. 23:28; Job 21:18). Both wheat and barley straw were used by the ancient Hebrews, chiefly as fodder for their horses, cattle, and camels (Gen. 24:25; 1 Kings 4:28; Isa. 11:7; 65:25, 1 Cor. 3:12). There is no intimation that straw was used for litter. It was employed by the Egyptians for making bricks (Ex. 5:7, 16), being chopped up and mixed with the clay to make them more compact and to prevent their cracking. This is abundantly illustrated by archaeology. The ancient Egyptians reaped their grain close to the ear, and afterward cut the straw close to the ground and stored it. Pharaoh refused to give this straw to the Israelites. *See* Vegetable Kingdom.

STREAM OF EGYPT. This term occurs once in the KJV (Isa. 27:12) instead of "the river of Egypt" Num. 34:5; Josh. 15:4, 47; etc.; KJV; "brook of Egypt," NASB; "Wadi of Egypt," NIV. *See* Brook; River of Egypt.

STREET (Gk. *hrumē,* Luke 14:21). Often a narrow lane or passage in a town, shut in by buildings on both sides (Matt. 6:2; Acts 9:11; 12:10).

STRIKER. KJV term used in 1 Tim. 3:3; Titus 1:7 of a contentious, quarrelsome person. NASB renders this "pugnacious," and NIV, "violent."

STRINGED INSTRUMENTS. *See* Music.

STRIPES. *See* Punishment.

STROKE (Gk. *keraion,* a "little horn, extremity, point"; KJV, "tittle"), used by Greek grammarians of the accents and diacritical points. In Matt. 5:18; Luke 16:17 it means the little lines or projections by which the Heb. letters, in other respects similar, differ from each other, as ח and ה, ר and ד, ב and כ. The meaning is that not even the minutest part of the law shall perish.

STRONG DRINK. *See* Drink, Strong.

STRONGHOLD ("fortress," as often rendered). A term especially applied to David's hiding places (1 Sam. 22:4-5; 24:22; etc.).

STUBBLE.

1. The dry portion of grain left standing in the fields (Ex. 5:12) and then burned over (Isa. 5:24; Joel 2:5; etc.); or broken up by threshing and separated from the grain (Isa. 40:24; etc.). Heb. *qash.*

2. A KJV rendering (Job 21:18; 1 Cor. 3:12) that is more properly "straw." *See* Vegetable Kingdom: Straw.

STUMBLING, STUMBLING BLOCK or **Stone.**

1. Heb. *mikshôl,* "obstacle," is used as any object over which a person may trip, and hence the cause of ruin or disgust (Jer. 6:21; Ezek. 7:19; etc.), or an *idol* (Zeph. 1:3, *see* marg.), i.e., an incitement to apostasy.

2. Heb. *negep,* "tripping," a cause of stumbling

(Isa. 8:14). Notice the heaping together of synonyms, especially in v. 15.

3. Gk. *proskomma,* an obstacle against which, if one strikes his foot, he necessarily falls; figuratively, that over which the soul stumbles into sin (1 Cor. 8:9). To put a stumbling block in another's way is, figuratively, to furnish an occasion for sinning (Rom. 14:13). "Stumbling stone" is used figuratively of Jesus Christ. It especially annoyed and offended the Jews that His words and deeds, and particularly His ignominious death, failed to correspond to their preconceptions respecting the Messiah (Rom. 9:32-33; 1 Pet. 2:8).

STUMP (Heb. *'iqqar*). The stump of a tree cut down but able to sprout again (Dan. 4:15, 23, 26). Stump is used in KJV text of 1 Sam. 5:4. *See* Trunk.

SU'AH (sū'a; "sweepings"). The first mentioned of eleven sons or descendants of Zophah, one of the "heads" of the house of Asher (1 Chron. 7:36).

SUBURBS. *See* Pasturelands; Levitical Cities.

SU'CATHITE (sū'kath-it). A descendant probably of an unknown Israelite by the name of Sucah, and the last named of the families of scribes living at Jabez (1 Chron. 2:55).

SUC'COTH (suk'oth; "booths").

1. An ancient town in Palestine, and the place where Jacob built booths for his cattle and a house for himself after separating from Esau (Gen. 33:17; Josh. 13:27). The bronze foundries for making the fine work for the Temple were built here (1 Kings 7:46; 2 Chron. 4:17). Here Gideon met with opposition when pursuing the Midianites (Judg. 8:5, 8, 14-16). The place is referred to in Pss. 60:6; 108:7. The site is now located by some at Tell Aḥṣaṣ, a mile or more N of the Jabbok (Nahr ez-Zerḳa), about nine miles NE of Damiyeh.

2. The first encampment of Israel after leaving Rameses (Ex. 12:37). It was the name of a district or region, and not a city. "It is not necessary to suppose that all the Israelites reached Succoth on the day of their hurried start from their homes in Rameses-Goshen. . . . Brugsch argues strongly for the correspondence of the Egyptian Thuku with the Hebrew Succoth. As to the location of the Egyptian Thuku, it is shown by the monuments that Pi-tum (the House of [the god] Tum), the Pithom of the Bible text, was the chief city of the district of Thuku. However, more recently Succoth has been identified with Tell el-Maskhutah."

SUC'COTH-BE'NOTH. *See* Gods, False.

SUK'KIIM (suk'i-im). A race mentioned only in 2 Chron. 12:3 as associated with the *Lubim* (which see) and the Ethiopians in the army with which Shishak invaded Judah in the days of Rehoboam.

Gesenius, connecting the name with *sūkkâ* (a booth or tent), thought them "dwellers in tents," in which case they might be an Arab tribe, like the Scenitae.

According to the LXX they were Troglodytes. This name, from *trōglē,* a hole, and *duō,* to enter, corresponds fairly well with our "cave dwellers." It was given to various races, especially to a race inhabiting both shores of the Red Sea; their territory on the eastern side was SE of Syene and NE of Meroe. Their dwellings have been compared with the catacombs of Naples. Some of these Troglodytes were serpent eaters, but most were herdsmen. Their language seemed to the Greeks a "shriek or whistle" rather than an articulate speech. Their food was principally animal; their drink was a mixture of blood and milk. They were so fleet of foot as to be able to run down the animals that they hunted. They served as light-armed soldiers in the army of Xerxes, 480 B.C. Aristotle "describes the Troglodytae as pygmies who, mounted on their horses, waged incessant war with the cranes in the Ethiopian marshes." The Ababdeh of the Troglodytic region and the Barnagas on the Abyssinian frontier are said to resemble the Troglodytes in manners and customs.

It is said that no hieroglyphic name has been found resembling the name Sukkiim. This would favor the Arabian theory.   W.H.; M.F.U.

SUK'KITES. *See* Sukkiim.

SULPHUR, SULFUR. *See* Gomorrah; Sodom; Mineral Kingdom: Brimstone.

SUMER. *See* Shinar.

SUMMER (Heb. *qayiṣ,* "harvest" of fruits, 2 Sam. 16:1, 2; etc.). *See* Agriculture; Palestine.

SUN (Heb. *shemesh*). Called in the history of the creation the "greater light" in contradistinction to the moon or "lesser light," in conjunction with which it was to serve "for signs, and for seasons, and for days and years"; its special office was "to govern the day" (Gen. 1:14-16). The "signs" referred to were probably such extraordinary phenomena as eclipses, which were regarded as conveying premonitions of coming events (cf. Jer. 10:2; Matt. 24:29, with Luke 21:25).

Sunrise and sunset are the only defined points of time in the absence of artificial contrivances for telling the hour of the day. Between these two points the Jews recognized three periods: when the sun became hot, about 9 A.M. (1 Sam. 11:9; Neh. 7:3); the double light or noon (Gen. 43:16; 2 Sam. 4:5); and "the cool of the day," shortly before sunset (Gen. 3:8). The sun also served to fix the quarters of the hemisphere, E, W, N, and S, which were represented respectively by the rising sun, the setting sun (Isa. 45:6; Ps. 50:1), the dark quarter (Gen. 13:14; Joel 2:20), and the brilliant quarter (Deut. 33:23; Job 37:17; Ezek. 40:24); or otherwise by their position relative to a person facing the rising sun—before, behind, on the left hand, and on the right hand (Job 23:8-9).

The apparent motion of the sun is frequently referred to in terms that would imply its reality (Josh. 10:13; 2 Kings 20:11; Ps. 19:6; Eccles. 1:5; Hab. 3:11).

Figurative. Of God's favor (Ps. 84:11); of the work of God (19:1-6); Christ's coming (Mal. 4:2); of the glory of Christ (Matt. 17:2; Rev. 1:16; 10:1); of supreme rulers (Gen. 37:9; Isa. 13:10); (its clearness) of the purity of the church (Song of Sol. 6:10); (its brightness) of the future glory of saints (cf. Dan. 12:3, with Matt. 13:43); (its power) of the triumph of saints (Judg. 5:31); (darkened) of severe calamities (Ezek. 32:7; Joel 2:10, 31; Matt. 24:29; Rev. 9:2); (going down at noon) of premature destruction (Jer. 15:9; Amos 8:9); (no more going down) of perpetual blessedness (Isa. 60:20); (before or in sight of) of public ignominy (2 Sam. 12:11-12; Jer. 8:2); of the Person of the Savior (John 1:9; Mal. 4:2); and of the glory and purity of heavenly beings (Rev. 1:16; 10:1; 12:1).

SUN, WORSHIP OF. The worship of the sun as the most prominent and powerful agent in the kingdom of nature was widely diffused throughout the countries adjacent to Palestine. The Arabs appear to have paid direct worship to it, without the intervention of any statue or symbol (Job 31:26-27), and this simple style of worship was probably familiar to the ancestors of the Jews in Chaldea and Mesopotamia. The Hebrews must have been well acquainted with the idolatrous worship of the sun during their captivity in Egypt, both from the nearness of On, the chief seat of the worship of the sun, as implied by another name for the city, Heliopolis (Gk. for "sun city," and the equivalent of Heb. *bêt shemesh,* "sun temple," or "house of the sun"; *see* Jer. 43:13, where *bêt shemesh* is given as "Beth-shemesh" in the KJV, as "Heliopolis" in the NASB, and as "temple of the sun" in the NIV), and also from the connection between Joseph and Potiphera ('he who belongs to Re'), the priest of On (Gen. 41:45). After their removal to Canaan the Hebrews came in contact with various forms of idolatry that originated in the worship of the sun, such as the Baal of the Phoenicians, the Molech or Milcom of the Ammonites, and the Hadad of the Syrians. It does not follow that the object symbolized by them was known to the Jews themselves. Hebrews at times became contaminated with the worship of sun images (Lev. 26:30; Isa. 17:8, *see* marg.). The great sun-god of the ancient Middle East was Shamash. Pharaoh Ikhnaton (c. 1380 B.C.) of the Eighteenth Dynasty abolished all images and pictured Aton, the

world-creator and universal ruler, as the sun disc whose rays converged in small hands, dispensing blessings. Ezekiel mentions among many abominations "still greater abomination" (Ezek. 8:15-16). This was the worship of the sun in the portico of the Temple that faced eastward. Says Albright, "It may have been precisely Ezekiel's zeal for pure monotheism which led him to consider this practice as relatively worse than the others."   M.F.U.

BIBLIOGRAPHY: D. W. Thomas, ed., *Documents from Old Testament Times* (1958), pp. 43-45, 142, 145-48.

SUN'DAY, or Lord's Day.

Name and Change of the Day. Sunday is the first day of the week, adopted by the first Christians from the Roman calendar (Lat. *Dies Solis, Day of the Sun*), because it was dedicated to the worship of the sun. The Christians reinterpreted the heathen name as implying the "Sun of Righteousness," with reference to this rising (Mal. 4:2). It was also called *Dies Panis* (*Day of Bread*), because it was an early custom to break bread on that day. In *The Teaching of the Twelve* it is called the "Lord's Day of the Lord" (*Kuriakēn de Kuriou*).

Jewish Christians at first continued to frequent the Temple and synagogue services, but at a very early date "the first day of the week" took the place of the Jewish Sabbath as the chief time of public worship (Acts 20:7; 1 Cor. 16:2) in many of the churches of Jewish Christians. It was the day of the resurrection of Christ, of most of His appearances to the disciples after the resurrection, and on this day the Holy Spirit was poured out at Pentecost. For these reasons, and especially after the destruction of Jerusalem had rendered the sacrificial service of the Temple impossible, Sunday became the recognized day of assembly for fellowship and for the celebration of the Lord's Supper. The Jewish Christians at first observed both the seventh and the first day of the week, but the Gentile Christians kept the "Lord's Day" from the beginning. The relation of the seventh to the first, as understood by the Jewish Christians, may not be easy to determine; yet there seem to be indications that the seventh was regarded as a day of preparation for the first. The idea of Christian worship would attach mainly to the one; the obligation of rest would continue attached to the other; although a certain interchange of characteristics would grow up, as worship necessitated rest, and rest naturally suggested worship.

In his letter to the Magnesians, Ignatius evidently addressed a church of mixed character, since he spoke of some "who were brought up in the ancient order of things," who "have come to the possession of a new hope, no longer observing the Sabbath, but living in the observance of the Lord's Day," etc.

"There is neither in this writer nor in the

Barnabas epistle an intimation that Sunday was regarded as in any way a substitute for the Jewish Sabbath, nor yet a continuation of it; rather it was a new institution. It is, however, impossible to determine the time of its beginning; no impressive enactment, like that in the case of the Decalogue, was needed.... Not until the 4th century do we find a statement intimating that the Jewish Sabbath, with its sanctions and duties, was transferred to the first, or the Lord's Day.... The observance of the Jewish Sabbath in the churches of the Jewish Christians continued for the first five centuries. In the East both days were celebrated with rejoicing; in the West the Jewish Sabbath was observed as a fast.

"The reign of Constantine marks a change in the relations of the people to the Lord's Day. The [decree] of the emperor, commanding the observance of Sunday, seems to have had little regard for its sanctity as a Christian institution; but the day of the sun is to be generally regarded with veneration.... Later enactments made plain the duties of civil and ecclesiastical officers respecting the observance of Sunday, until it takes its place as an institution to be guarded and regulated by the government."

Sanctity and Ground of Observance. "The resurrection of Christ was the one all-sufficient fact which accounts for the rise and growth of the Christian Church. 'Jesus and the resurrection' was the burden of the apostolic preaching. Hence the recollection of the day of the resurrection was so indelibly impressed upon the hearts of the first disciples that on its return they came together to pray and to recall the memory of the Lord by breaking of bread and the celebration of the eucharist. It was the dictate of the glowing love for Christ, whose followers they delighted to be reckoned.... We fail to find the slightest trace of a law or apostolic edict instituting the observance of the 'day of the Lord'; nor is there in the Scriptures an intimation of a substitution of this for the Jewish Sabbath. The primal idea of the Jewish Sabbath was cessation of labor, rest; the transference of this idea to the first day of the week does not appear in the teachings of Christ nor of his apostles. Nor in the Council of Jerusalem, when the most important decisions are reached relative to the ground of union of Jewish and Gentile Christians, is one word found respecting the observance of the Sabbath. Contrariwise, Paul distinctly warns against the imposition of burdens upon the Church respecting days, but declares for a conscientious freedom in these observances. 'Let every man be fully persuaded in his own mind' (Rom. 14:5-6). Still more strongly does he upbraid the Galatian church for putting itself again in bondage to the weak and beggarly elements, as days, months, times, and years; while in his letter to the Colossians (2:16, 17) he speaks of the entire abolition of the Jewish Sabbath."

Justin Martyr, in his dialogue with the Jew Trypho, who taunts the Christians with having no festivals nor Sabbaths, clearly claims that Sunday is to them a new Sabbath and that the entire Mosaic law has been abrogated (*Dialogue with Trypho the Jew,* chaps. 10-11). The new law binding upon Christians regards every day as a Sabbath, instead of passing one day in rest or absolute idleness.

"With respect to the strictness with which the first day of the week was observed during the first three centuries, the following facts are important to notice: Between the death of the apostles and the edict of Milan, the Lord's Day was sanctified by a Church unrecognized by the State and exposed to opposition and sometimes to bitter persecution. The motive for its observance was, therefore, purely moral and religious. The social position of the early Church, drawing its members for the most part from the poorer artisans, traders, and slaves, forbade the strict and general keeping of the Lord's Day, much more of both the Sabbath and Sunday. Thus the universal hallowing of the day of the resurrection was impossible" (Bennett, *Christian Archaeology,* pp. 444ff.).

Legal Observance. In the midst of the corrupt influence of heathenism and the growing indifference of the church, it was thought necessary to bring some stress of authority upon the Christian conscience to hold it to the faithful observance of the first day, as the Jews had known the power of a positive enactment in keeping them steadfast in the hallowing of their Sabbath. "The constant temptation of the Christians to attend upon the heathen spectacles and festivities could, in the case of such whose piety was low, no longer, as at first, be broken by considerations of the high privileges of Christian worship and of the commemoration of the resurrection of Christ, but the restraints coming from a quasi legal enactment were found to be more and more necessary" (ibid., p. 450).

"The obligation to observe the day does not come from the fourth commandment, but from the apostolic institution of the Lord's Day. Nevertheless, from the time of the attempts of the emperors to adjust the civil conditions to the recognition of Sunday as the chief religious holiday, the sense of obligation to keep sacred the first day of the week, coming from legal enactment, more and more supplanted the consideration of the high and holy privilege which had animated the Christian Church during the first years of its activity. From the last part of the 6th century the strict legalistic view becomes more and more prominent, and the rulers in State and Church incline to strengthen the civil and conciliatory enactments respecting the Lord's Day by divine authority, as contained in the fourth commandment" (ibid., p. 451).

BIBLIOGRAPHY: P. K. Jewett, *The Lord's Day* (1971); D. A. Carson, ed., *From Sabbath to Lord's Day* (1982).

SUPERFLUOUS. *See* Blemish.

SUPERSCRIPTION. *See* Inscription.

SUPERSTITION (Gk. *deisidaimonia,* "reverence for the gods"), a word that Festus, in the presence of Agrippa, the Jewish king, employed ambiguously and cautiously (Acts 25:19, "religion," (*see* marg.), so as to leave his own judgment concerning its truth in suspense.

SUPERSTITIOUS. Inaccurate rendering by the KJV in Acts 17:22 of Gk. *deisidaimōn,* "reverencing the gods." NASB and NIV here more appropriately use "religious" (with negative connotation).

SUPH (sōōf; "reeds"), a word (Deut. 1:1) referred to as meaning the *Red Sea;* most probably an abbreviation of Yamsuph, or the Red (Reed) Sea.

SU'PHAH (sōō'fa; Num. 21:14), also used instead of the Red Sea.

SUPPER. *See* Banquet; Food; Lord's Supper.

SUPPLICATION.
1. Heb. *teḥinnâ* has the meaning of a cry for mercy, prayer (1 Kings 8:28; etc.; 2 Chron. 6:19, 24, 29, 35; Ps. 6:9; 55:1; Dan. 9:20; cf. Josh. 11:20; Ezra 9:8).
2. Heb. *ḥānan,* to "incline," to "be favorably disposed"; and then to implore favor, to entreat (1 Kings 8:33; Ps. 30:8; etc.).
3. *Petition* (Gk. *deēsis,* "asking"), in the NT, requests addressed by men to God (James 5:16; 1 Pet. 3:12, "prayer"); joined with *proseuchē,* "prayer," i.e., any pious address to God (Phil. 4:6; cf. 1 Tim. 2:1; 5:5). *Deēsis* is the asking of favor in some special necessity; *proseuchē* is exercised in all presentation of desires and wishes to God. Trench (*Synonyms of the N. T.,* 2d ser., p. 3) makes this important point of distinction, namely, "that *proseuchē* is *res sacra,* a word restricted to sacred uses; it is always prayer to God; *deēsis* has no such restriction."

SUR. One of the gates of the palace area of Jerusalem. It is mentioned only once (2 Kings 11:6).

SURETY (from Heb. *'ārab,* to "braid, intermix"). A deposit or pledge, either in money, goods, or in part payment, which served as security for a bargain (Gk. *egguos*). The earliest form of surety mentioned in Scripture is the pledging of person for person, as when Judah undertook with his father to be surety for Benjamin (Gen. 43:9). And when circumstances seemed to call for a fulfillment of the obligation, he actually offered himself in the place of Benjamin. In this sense the psalmist asks God to be surety for him (Ps. 119:122).

The more common kind of surety spoken of is financial. The Mosaic regulations respecting debts were such that, except in rare cases, the creditor was not likely to suffer any considerable loss; and it may be that this was the reason that the Mosaic law contains no statute on *suretyship.* In later times they were very common, as we learn from Proverbs, where foresight is taught (6:1; 11:15; 17:18) by pointing to the fact that the surety has to stand for the debtor and could not expect any milder treatment than he (20:16; 22:26; cf. Sirach 8:16; 29:20, 24). *See also* Guarantee.

SURFEITING (Gk. *kraipalē*). The Gk. word is translated this way only by the KJV, and only in Luke 21:34. *See also* Carouse; Dissipation.

SU'SA (sū'sa). The Heb. word *shûshan* means "lily," the Gk. form being *susa.* The Persian city of Susa (Shushan, KJV) took its name from the great abundance of lilies that grew in its neighborhood. The famous mound has been excavated, and its early occupational levels go back to c. 4000 B.C, its latest levels to A.D. 1200. It was explored by a French expedition in 1884-86, and the Code of Hammurabi was uncovered there by Jacques de Morgan, 1901. The ancient site lies on the Karkheh about 150 miles N of the Persian Gulf. It is famous in the Bible as one of the capitals of the Persian Empire maintained by Darius the Great (cf. Neh. 1:1; Esther 2:8; 3:15; etc.). The city was a winter residence of the great Persian kings. It was also the place of Daniel's vision (Dan. 8:2) under Belshazzar and the location of Nehemiah's appearances before Artaxerxes (Neh. 1:1; 2:1). Susa colonists were transported to Samaria by Ashurbanipal, that is, "Osnappar," referred to in Ezra 4:9-10. Its present-day name is Shush. Susa became a part of the Achaemenid Empire when Cyrus took Babylon and its provinces. The most splendid monument of Persian Susa is the royal palace, begun by Darius I and enlarged and adorned by later kings (cf. R. de Mecquenem, "A Survey of Persian Art," Art. 1, pp. 321-26). The outline of Darius's splendid palace, which he built of cedar wood from Lebanon, silver from Egypt, gold from Bactria, and ivory from India, can still be traced by some rows of bricks and remains of the pavements. Panels of artistically colored glazed bricks constituted the most remarkable feature in the palace decorations. Many of the designs were executed in relief and show winged bulls and griffins and include the famous "spearmen of the guard."

M.F.U.

BIBLIOGRAPHY: E. M. Yamauchi, *Near Eastern Archaeological Society Bulletin* 8 (1976): 5-14. *See also* Persia.

SU-SANCHITES (Heb., *Shûshanî*). A name found only in the KJV rendering of Ezra 4:9, which the NASB calls "men of Susa" (which see.)

SUSAN'NA (sū-zan'na; Gk. from Heb. "a lily"), one of the women who followed our Lord and His disciples and "were contributing to their support out of their private means" (Luke 8:3), A.D. 28. No particulars of her life are known. The name, apparently of common occurrence, is of the same

Ruins of synagogue at Katzrin, northern Israel

origin and meaning as Sheshan (1 Chron. 2:31, 34-35). The Susanna who figures prominently in the symbolism of the ancient church is the heroine of the apocryphal story of the judgment of Daniel.

SU'SI (sū'si; a "horseman"), the father of Gaddi, who was the representative of the tribe of Manasseh in the first commission sent by Moses to "spy out the land" of Canaan (Num. 13:1, 11), before 1440 B.C.

SWADDLE (Heb. *ṭāpaḥ*, "to bear upon the palm"). An imprecise KJV rendering (Lam. 2:22), which is made clearer by NASB "bore." Elsewhere it is the rendering of *ḥātal*, "to wrap in bandages" (cf. Luke 2:12, "cloths," NASB). *See* Swaddling Band.

SWADDLING BAND. A cloth in which newborn babes were wrapped (cf. Ezek. 16:4; Luke 2:7, 12, KJV), used figuratively in Job 38:9 (KJV, NASB) of a thick darkness or mist. The infant was placed diagonally on a square piece of cloth. Two corners were turned across its body, one across the feet, the other under its head. The whole cloth was fastened by bands wound around the exterior.

SWALLOW. *See* Animal Kingdom.

SWAN. *See* Animal Kingdom.

SWARMING LOCUST. *See* Animal Kingdom: Locust.

SWEAR. *See* Oath.

SWEAT (Heb. *yeza'*, "perspiration"). In setting forth the requisites, obligations, and privileges of the priest's office, Ezekiel (Ezek. 44:18) designates linen as the material for their clothing, assigning as the reason that the priest is not to cause himself to sweat by wearing woolen clothing. Sweat produces uncleanness; and the priest,

by keeping his body clean, is to show even outwardly that he is clean and blameless.

SWEAT, BLOODY. *See* Bloody Sweat.

SWEET CANE. *See* Vegetable Kingdom: Reeds, Rushes.

SWELLING.
1. The KJV phrase "swelling of Jordan" should be rendered "thicket" or "pride" of Jordan. Compare the NASB and NIV of Jer. 12:5; 49:19; 50:44; Zech. 11:3.
2. Gk. *huperogkos*, "a swelling," KJV, is better translated "arrogant words" or "arrogantly," as in the NASB, or "boastful" as in the NIV (2 Pet. 2:18; Jude 16).

SWIFT. *See* Animal Kingdom: Swallow.

SWINE.
Figurative. "As a ring of gold in a swine's snout, so is a beautiful woman who lacks discretion" (Prov. 11:22), and "Like one who offers swine's blood" (Isa. 66:3) is used of those who, without reflection, and merely as an external act, offer sacrifices to God. Even though they offer sacrifices that are prescribed, their state of mind is no more acceptable than if they offered that which was unclean. *See* Animal Kingdom.

SWORD. *See* Armor, Arms.

SYCAMINE, SYCAMORE. *See* Vegetable Kingdom: Mulberry; Sycamore.

SY'CHAR (sī'kar). Sychar has been identified with Shechem. It is now commonly located at the site of the village of 'Askar, on the eastern slope of Ebal, almost two miles ENE from Nablus, about a half mile N of Jacob's well, and a short distance SE of Shechem.

For this the first evidence we get is at the beginning of the fourth century, when two visitors to the land, Eusebius and the Bordeaux Pilgrim (the latter about A.D. 333), both mention a Sychar distinct from Shechem, lying, says the former, before Neapolis, the present Nablus, and the latter adds that it was a Roman mile from Shechem. In medieval times the abbot Daniel (1106-07) spoke of "the hamlet of Jacob called Sichar. Jacob's well is there. Near this place, at half a verst away, is the town of Samaria . . . at present called Neapolis." Fetellus (1130) says: "A mile from Sichem is the town of Sychar; in it is the fountain of Jacob, which, however, is a well." Other travelers mention both Sichem and Sychar. In spite of ecclesiastical tradition, that the name Sychar should have continued to exist all this time in the neighborhood, and solely among the natives, is a strong proof of its having been from the first a native and not an artificial name. *See* Shechem.

BIBLIOGRAPHY: D. Baly, *The Geography of the Bible* (1957), pp. 113-19, 178-80; G. E. Wright, *Shechem, The Biography of a Biblical City* (1965).

SY-CHEM. KJV spelling in Acts 7:16 of *Shechem* (which see.)

SYE'NE (sī-ē'ne; Heb. *Seveneh*). A town of Egypt on the frontier of Cush, or Ethiopia. Ezekiel speaks (Ezek. 29:10) of the desolation of Egypt "from Migdol to Syene and even to the border of Ethiopia," and of its people being slain "from Migdol to Syene" (30:6). Its ancient Egyptian name is *Sun,* preserved in the Coptic *Souan, Senon,* and the Arab. *Aswan* (as in the NIV). It was separated by an arm of the Nile, ninety yards wide, from Elephantine, forming a suburb of that important city. It was a stronghold opposite the island of Elephantine where the famous Elephantine Papyri written in Aramaic were found in 1903. At this place Jews during the Persian Empire had a temple to Jehovah, where they celebrated the religious rites of Judaism.   M.F.U.

SYNAGOGUE (Hellenistic Gk. *sunagōgē,* "gathering *of people,*" "a congregation," "a place of prayer," Acts 16:13).

Object. As only a small proportion of the people could become proficient in the study of the law under the scribes, and as it was desirable that all should have at least an elementary acquaintance therewith, the custom grew up in postexilic times of reading the Scriptures in the synagogue on the Sabbath day. It must be understood that the main object of these Sabbath day assemblages in the synagogues was not public worship in its stricter sense but religious instruction, which to an Israelite was, above all, *instruction in the law.* Thus Josephus says (*Apion* 2.7), "Not once or twice or more frequently did our lawgiver command us to hear the law, but to come together weekly, with the cessation of other work, to hear the law and to learn it accurately." Philo called the synagogues "houses of instruction," in which "the native philosophy" was studied and every kind of virtue taught. In the NT, too, the teaching (Gk. *didaskein*) always figures as the chief function of the synagogue.

Origin. The origin of these Sabbath day meetings in buildings erected for the purpose must be sought for in the postexilic period. The first traces of them are "the meeting places of God" (Ps. 74:8), but their beginning may well be as far back as the time of Ezra. R. H. Pfeiffer and other scholars are of the opinion that the synagogue may have originated in Ezekiel's addresses to the Babylonian exiles (*History of N. T. Times,* p. 50). Such gatherings in the prophet's house (Ezek. 8:1; 20:1) may well have been the forerunners of the synagogue gatherings. In the time of Christ "teaching in the synagogue on the Sabbath day" was already an established custom (Mark 1:21; 6:2; Luke 4:16, 31; 6:6; 13:10; Acts 13:14, 27, 42, 44; 15:21; 16:13; 17:2; 18:4). According to Acts 15:21, "Moses from ancient generations has in every city those who preach him, since he is read in the synagogues every Sabbath." Josephus,

Philo, and, later, Judaism generally, traced back the whole system to Moses, but there is no evidence of a preexilian origin.

Religious Community. The system presupposes a *religious community.* This was an independent organization in towns in which Jews might be excluded from civic rights, or Jews and others had equal rights. In such cases the Jews would be thrown back upon self-organization as a religious community; for whether they cooperated or not in civil affairs, the necessity of independent organization for religious matters was the same. Where only Jews had civic rights, and the local authorities were Jewish, matters relating to the synagogue were probably under their jurisdiction and direction. In the Mishna, for example, it is presumed as quite self-evident that the synagogue, the sacred ark, and the sacred books were quite as much the property of the town as the roads and baths.

Conduct of Synagogues. The general direction of affairs was committed to elders, whereas special officers were appointed for special purposes. But the peculiarity here is that just for the acts proper to public worship—the reading of the Scriptures, preaching, and prayer—no special officials were appointed. These acts were, on the contrary, in the time of Christ still freely performed in turn by members of the congregation.

Officials. Several officials had charge of the regular activity of the synagogue.

The Ruler of the Synagogue (Gk. *'archisunagōgos*) had the care of external order in public worship and the supervision of the concerns of the synagogue in general. This officer was found in the entire sphere of Judaism, not only in Palestine, but also in Egypt, Asia Minor, Greece, Italy, and the Roman Empire in general. The Heb. title *rō'sh hakkeneset* ("the minister of the synagogue") was undoubtedly synonymous with the Gk. term. This office differed from that of an elder of the congregation, although the same person could fill the offices of both. The ruler of the synagogue was so called not as head of the community but as conductor of their assembly for public worship. Among his functions was that of appointing who should read the Scriptures and the prayer, of summoning fit persons to preach, of seeing that nothing improper took place in the synagogue (Luke 13:14); and of taking charge of the synagogue building. Although it was customary to have but one ruler for each synagogue, sometimes more are mentioned (Acts 13:15).

Receiver of Alms (Heb. *gabbā'ê ṣedāqâ*). This official had nothing to do with public worship as such and is to be regarded, therefore, where the civil and religious communities were not separated, rather as a civil official. According to the Mishna, the collection was to be made by two, the distribution by three persons. Not only was money collected, but also natural products.

The Minister (Heb. *ḥazzān hakkᵉneset*; Gk. *huperetēs;* Luke 4:20, "attendant"). His office was to bring forth the Holy Scriptures at public worship and to put them away again. He was in every respect the servant of the congregation, having, for example, to execute the punishment of scourging and also to instruct the children in reading.

The person (Heb. *shᵉlîaḥ ṣibbûr*) who pronounced the prayer in the name of the congregation was also generally regarded as one of the officers of the synagogue. There were also "ten unemployed men," whose business it was, especially in the post-Talmudic period, to be always present for a fee in the synagogue at public worship, for the purpose of making up the number of ten members required for a religious assembly; but they are hardly to be regarded as officials.

Building (Heb. *bêt hakkᵉneset,* "house of assembly"; Gk. *sunagōgē*). Sometimes synagogues were built by preference outside the towns and near rivers or on the seashore for the sake of giving everyone a convenient opportunity for performing such Levitical purification as might be necessary before attending public worship. At other times they were built in the middle of town. The size and architecture varied, of course. Archaeological research has shown that in many towns the synagogue was an important building. This is attested by the gorgeous white limestone structure (dating to the third or fourth century A.D.) uncovered at Capernaum, apparently built on the site of the one where Jesus ministered. Decorational motifs include garland-carrying boys, lions, eagles, stars, vines, and palms. This synagogue measured about seventy by fifty feet and had a balcony for women. At nearby Chorazin was a black basalt synagogue of almost identical size. A marvelous third-century synagogue was excavated at Sardis in Asia Minor. Three times larger than any synagogue preserved in Palestine, it is 400 feet long and 60 feet wide. Among the earliest synagogues known in Palestine are those at Masada and the Herodium (both dating to the second century A.D.). Numerous other synagogues have been found in Palestine. Synagogues also have been uncovered at Chorazin near Capernaum, at Beth Alpha in the Valley of Jezreel, at Bethsaida Julius, and at Kepher Bir'im. At Caesarea, Beth-shan, Lydda, and elsewhere, inscriptional allusions to synagogues have been found. At Corinth an inscription has been recovered reading: "Synagogue of the Jews." This was found on a stone apparently separated from its place in a structure that has disappeared. The synagogue in which Paul preached (Acts 18:4) may have contained this very stone and may have stood on the famous Lechaeum Road. Almost all these synagogues stand N and S, so that the entrance is at the S. As a rule they appear to have

Ruins of the synagogue at Capernaum

had one chief entrance and two smaller side doors.

The fittings of synagogues in NT times were simple. The chief was the *closet* (Heb. *tēbâ*) in which were kept the rolls of the law and the other sacred books. These were wrapped in linen cloths and lay in a case. A representation of an old silver case for the Pentateuch, as well as other types of cases, exists among the modern Samaritans. An elevated place (Gk. *bēma,* "tribune"), upon which stood the reading desk, was erected at least in post-Talmudic times, for the person who read the Scriptures or preached. Lamps were also used; and trombones and trumpets were indispensable instruments in public worship. The former were blown especially on the first day of the year, the latter on the feast days.

Where Located. The value attached to these Sabbath day assemblies leads us to assume that there was in every town of Palestine, and even in smaller places, at least *one* synagogue. In the post-Talmudic period it was required that a synagogue should be built wherever *ten* Israelites were dwelling together. In the larger towns there was a considerable number of synagogues, e.g., in Jerusalem, Alexandria, and Rome. The different synagogues in the same town seem to have been distinguished from each other by special emblems, as a "synagogue of the vine" in Sepphoris and "of the olive tree" in Rome.

Worship. The order of worship in NT times was moderately well developed. The congregation sat in an appointed order, the most distinguished in the front seats, the younger behind; men and women probably apart (*see* Matt. 23:6; Mark 12:39; Luke 11:43; 20:46). In the great synagogue in Alexandria the men are said to have been set apart according to their respective trades. A special division was prepared for lepers. The chief parts of the service were, according to the Mishna, the recitation of the *Shema,* prayer, the reading of the Torah, the reading of the prophets, the blessing of the priest, followed by the *translation* of the Scripture that had been read, and the *discourse.* The Shema, so called from its commencing words, *shᵉma' Yisrā'ēl,* "Hear, O Israel," consists of Deut. 6:4-9; 11:13-21; and Num. 15:37-41, together with benedictions before and after. It is a confession of faith rather than a prayer. The custom of praying the first three and last three benedictions of the Shemoneh Esreh at Sabbath and festival worship goes back to the age of the Mishna. The Shemoneh Esreh was the chief prayer that every Israelite, even women, slaves, and children, had to repeat three times a day—morning, afternoon, and evening. It was the custom to pray standing and with the face turned toward the Holy of Holies, i.e., toward Jerusalem. The prayer was offered by someone named by the ruler of the synagogue, the congregation making only certain responses, especially the amen. He who uttered

the prayer stood in front of the chest in which lay the rolls of the law. Every adult member of the congregation was competent to do this; and might also recite the Shema, read the lesson from the prophets, and, if a priest, pronounce the blessing.

The Scripture lessons, from both the law and the prophets, could be read by any member of the congregation, even by minors, the latter being only excluded from reading the book of Esther at the feast of Purim. If priests and Levites were present, they took precedence in reading the lesson. The reader usually stood (Luke 4:16), but both sitting and standing were allowed at the reading of the book of Esther, and the king was allowed to sit when he read his portion of Scripture at the feast of Tabernacles in the Sabbatic year. The lesson from the Torah was so arranged that the whole Pentateuch was completed in a cycle of three years, for which purpose it was divided into 154 sections.

On Sabbaths several members of the congregation, at the least seven, who were summoned for the purpose by some official (originally, indeed, by the ruler of the synagogue), took part in the reading; each (at the reading of the Torah) to read at least *three* verses, but not to repeat them by heart. The reading of the law was already followed in NT times by a *paragraph from the prophets* (*see* Luke 4:17; Acts 13:15). The prophets not being read in order, a choice of them was open, and they were always read by one person, and that during the chief services of the Sabbath. The Heb. of the Scripture text was no longer the first language of the people, for they spoke Aramaic in daily life; consequently the reading of Scripture was followed by translation into the Aramaic dialect. The reading of the Scripture was followed by a lecture or sermon, explaining and applying the portion read (Matt. 4:23; Mark 1:21; Luke 4:15; 6:6; 13:10; John 6:59; 18:20); the preacher *sat* (Luke 4:20) on an elevated place. The position of preacher was open to any competent member of the congregation.

The service closed with the blessing pronounced by a priestly member of the congregation, to which the whole congregation responded, "Amen." If no priest or Levite was present the blessing was not pronounced but was made into a prayer.   M.F.U.; H.F.V.

BIBLIOGRAPHY: E. L. Sukenik, *Ancient Synagogues in Palestine and Greece* (1932); L. Ginzberg, *Biblical Archaeologist* 7 (1944): 2-20; J. Morgenstern, *Studi orintalistici in onore di G. d. Vida* (1955), 2:192-221; A. E. Guilding, *The Fourth Gospel and Jewish Worship* (1960).

SYN'TYCHE (sin'ti-che; "fortunate"). A Christian woman of Philippi, who seems to have been at variance with another female member named Euodias, or Euodia (Phil. 4:2-3), A.D. 57. Paul entreats them to live in mutual harmony and mentions their names with a respect bordering on fondness, as fellow laborers in the gospel, whose names were written in the book of life. It has been surmised that they were deaconesses, in which case their good fellowship would be of almost vital importance to the infant church.

SYR'ACUSE (sir'a-kūs). A town on the eastern coast of the island of Sicily, once connected with the mainland by a causeway, a fact curiously recorded upon the coinage, which represents dolphins swimming round the head of Arethusa while the island remained, but meeting at the nose of the figure when it was no longer an island. The city was founded about 735 B.C. and was very prosperous. It defeated an Athenian fleet of 200 vessels in 413 B.C. In 212 B.C. it was conquered by the Romans. It was a place of great splendor, the birthplace of Archimedes, and here the apostle Paul remained three days when on his way to Rome (Acts 28:12). It is now called Siracusa and has a population of more than 100,000.

SYR'IA (sir'i-a; Heb. *'ărām;* Gk. *suria*). In Gen. 10:22 *Aram,* the youngest son of Shem, is mentioned as the founder of the Aramaean nation, and thus the country is rightly called "Aram" (Num. 23:7); but the same Heb. word is rendered "Mesopotamia" (Judg. 3:10). The designation *Syria* is an abbreviated form of Assyria and came into common use after the conquests of Alexander the Great.

Territory. Ancient geographers are not agreed

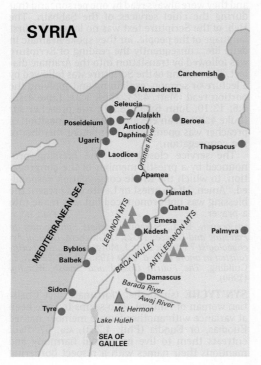

as to the extent of Syria, confounding, as did Herodotus, Syria and Assyria. The Heb. Aram seems to commence on the northern frontier of Palestine and to extend thence northward to the skirts of the Taurus Mts., westward to the Mediterranean and eastward probably to the Habur River. It was subdivided into five principalities: (1) Aram-Dammesek, or Aram of Damascus (cf. 2 Sam. 8:5-6). This was the rich country about Damascus, lying between the Anti-Lebanon Mts. and the desert, and the last with the district about Harran and Orfah, the flat country stretching out from the western extremity of Mons Masius toward the true source of the Khabur (Habor), at Ras-el-Ain. Aram-naharaim seems to be a term including this last tract and extending beyond it, though how far beyond is doubtful. *See* Roger O'Callaghan, *Aram-naharaim,* Pontifical Biblical Institute. (2) Aram-Zobah, or Aram of Zobah (10:6), seems to be the tract between the Euphrates and Coele-Syria. The other divisions were (3) Aram-Maacah (10:6, 8); (4) Aram-Beth-rehob (10:6, 8); and (5) Aram-naharaim (Gen. 24:10), or "Mesopotamia." The exact locations of the last three are difficult to determine. Probably they were portions of the tract intervening between Antilibanus and the desert.

The Greek writers used the term Syria still more vaguely than the Hebrews did Aram. On the one hand they extended it to the Euxine; on the other they carried it to the borders of Egypt. Still they seem always to have had a feeling that Syria proper was a narrower region. The LXX and NT writers distinguish Syria from Phoenicia on the one hand, and from Samaria, Judea, Idumea, etc., on the other. It seems best to take the word in this narrow sense and to regard Syria as bounded by Amanus and Taurus on the N, by the Euphrates and the Arabian Desert on the E, by Palestine on the S, by the Mediterranean near the mouth of the Orontes, and then by Phoenicia upon the W. This tract is about 300 miles long from N to S, and from 50 to 150 miles broad. It contains an area of about 30,000 square miles.

Physical Features. The physical features of Syria are varied.

Mountains. The general character of the tract is mountainous, as the Heb. name Aram (apparently from a root signifying "height") implies. On the W two longitudinal chains, running parallel with the coast at no great distance from one another, extend along two-thirds of the length of Syria, from the latitude of Tyre to that of Antioch. In the latitude of Antioch the longitudinal chains are met by the chain of Amanus, an outlying barrier of the Taurus Mts., having the direction of that range, which in this part is from SW to NE. The most fertile and valuable tract of Syria is the long valley intervening between the Lebanon Mts. and the Anti-Lebanon Mts. The northern mountain region is also fairly productive; but the soil of the plains about Aleppo is poor, and the eastern flank of the Anti-Lebanon, except in one place, is peculiarly sterile. There are four mountain ranges: (1) Lebanon. Extending from the mouth of the Litani to Arka, a distance of nearly one hundred miles, it is composed chiefly of Jura limestone, but varied with sandstone and basalt. (*See* Lebanon.) (2) Anti-Lebanon. This range, as the name implies, stands over against Lebanon, running in the same direction, i.e., nearly N and S, and extending the same length. (3) Bargylus. Mt. Bargylus, now called Jebel Nosairi toward the S and Jebel Kraad toward the N, extends from the mouth of the Nahr-el-Kebir (Eleutherus), nearly opposite Homs, to the vicinity of Antioch, a distance of rather more than one hundred miles. One of the western spurs terminates in a remarkable headland, known to the ancients as Mt. Casius and now called Jebel-el-Akra, or the "Bald Mountain." (4) Amanus, or Nur. North of the mouth of the Orontes River, between its course and the eastern shore of the Gulf of Issus (İskenderun), lies the range of Amanus, which divides Syria from Cilicia. Its average elevation is 5,000 feet, and it terminates abruptly at Ras-el-Khanzir in a high cliff overhanging the sea.

Rivers. The Orontes is the largest river in Syria and has its source about fifteen miles from that of the Litani. Its modern name is the Nahr-el-'Asi, or "Rebel Stream," an appellation given to it on account of its violence in many parts of its course. It is also called el-Maklûb ("The Invert-

ed"), from the fact of its running, as is thought, in a wrong direction. It runs NW across the plain to the foot of Lebanon, where its volume is more than trebled by the great fountain of Ain el-'Asy. From there it winds along the plain of Hamath, passing Riblah, Homs, Hamath, and Armea. At Antioch it sweeps round to the W and falls into the Mediterranean at Seleucia.

The Litani is the next largest river, having its source in a small lake situated in the middle of the Coele-Syrian valley, about six miles to the SW of Baalbek. It enters the sea about five miles N of Tyre.

Other Syrian streams of some consequence are the Barada, or river of Damascus; the Koweik, or river of Aleppo; and the Sajur, a tributary of the Euphrates.

Lakes. The principal lakes of Syria are the Agh-Dengiz, or Lake of Antioch; the Sabakhah, or Salt Lake, between Aleppo and Balis; the Bahr-el-Kades, on the upper Orontes; and the Bahr-el-Merj, or Lake of Damascus.

The Great Valley. By far the most important part of Syria, and on the whole its most striking feature, is the great valley that reaches from the plain of Umk, near Antioch, to the narrow gorge on which the Litani enters about latitude 33° 30'. This valley, which runs nearly parallel with the Syrian coast, extends 230 miles and has a width varying from 6 to 20 miles. The more southern portion of it was known to the ancients as Coele-Syria, or "the Hollow Syria."

The city of Antioch (modern Antakya)

The Eastern Desert. East of the inner mountain chain, and S of the cultivable ground about Aleppo, is the great Syrian Desert, an elevated, dry upland, for the most part of gypsum and marls, producing nothing but a few spare bushes of wormwood and the usual aromatic plants of the wilderness. The region is traversed with difficulty and has never been accurately surveyed. The most remarkable oasis is at Palmyra, where there are several small streams and abundant palm trees.

Principal Towns. These may be arranged, as nearly as possible, in the order of their importance: (1) Antioch; (2) Damascus; (3) Apamea; (4) Seleucia; (5) Tadmor, or Palmyra; (6) Laodicea; (7) Ephiphania (Hamath); (8) Samosata; (9) Hierapolis (Mabug); (10) Chalybon; (11) Emesa; (12) Heliopolis; (13) Laodicea ad Libanum; (14) Cyrrhus; (15) Chalcis; (16) Poseideium; (17) Heraclea; (18) Gindarus; (19) Zeugma; (20) Thapsacus. Of these, Samosata, Zeugma, and Thapsacus are on the Euphrates; Seleucia, Laodicea, Poseideium, and Heraclea on the seashore; Antioch, Apamea, Epiphania, and Emesa (Homs), on the Orontes; Heliopolis and Laodicea ad Libanum, in Coele-Syria; Hierapolis, Chalybon, Cyrrhus, Chalcis, and Gindarus, in the northern highlands; Damascus on the skirt and Palmyra in the center of the eastern desert.

History. Syria has been peopled from of old, and all of the nations of the ancient Near East, as well as Rome in later times, had dealings with the Syrians.

First Occupants. The first occupants appear to have been of Hamitic descent. The Canaanite races, the Hittites, Jebusites, Amorites, etc., are connected in Scripture with Egypt and Ethiopia, Cush and Mizraim (Gen. 10:6, 15-18). These tribes occupied not only Palestine but also lower Syria in very early times, as we may gather from the fact that Hamath is assigned to them in Genesis (10:18). Afterward they seem to have come into possession of upper Syria also. After a while the firstcomers, who were still to a great extent nomads, received a Semitic infusion, which most probably came to them from the SE. The only Syrian town whose existence we find distinctly marked at this time is Damascus (14:15; 15:2), which appears to have been already a place of some importance. Next to Damascus must be placed Hamath (Num. 13:21; 34:8, "Lebo-hamath"). Syria at this time, and for many centuries afterward, seems to have been broken up among a number of petty kingdoms.

Testimony of the Monuments. Egyptian records show that under the powerful Eighteenth and Nineteenth Egyptian Dynasties, when Egypt ruled the East, from the sixteenth to the thirteenth century B.C., Syria as well as Palestine was made a dependency of Egypt. She was forced to relax her hold in consequence of local uprisings, until finally she fully retrieved her position under the Nineteenth Dynasty. Egypt then was met by the Hittites and compelled to call a halt upon the Syrian border (cf. the Amarna Letters, and the Hittite monuments from Boghaz-keui).

Syria and Israel. The Jews came into hostile contact with the Syrians in the time of David. Claiming the frontier of the Euphrates, which God had promised to Abraham (Gen. 15:18), David made war on Hadadezer king of Zobah (2 Sam. 8:3-13). The Damascus Syrians were likewise defeated with great loss (v. 5). Zobah, however, was far from being subdued as yet. When, a few years later, the Ammonites determined on engaging in a war with David and asked the Syrians for aid, Zobah, together with Beth-rehob, sent them 20,000 footmen, and two other Syrian kingdoms furnished 13,000 (10:6). When this army was defeated by Joab, Hadadezer obtained aid from Mesopotamia (v. 16) and tried the chance of a third battle, which likewise went against him and produced the general submission of Syria to the Jewish monarch. The submission thus begun continued under the reign of Solomon (1 Kings 4:21). The only part of Syria that Solomon lost seems to have been Damascus, where an independent kingdom was set up by Rezon, a native of Zobah (11:23-25). On the separation of the ten tribes from Rehoboam, Syria was ripe for revolt. Rezon disappeared from the scene, and Ben-hadad, in the reign of Asa king of Judah, was king of Aram, with Damascus as its capital. (*See* Damascus; Ben-hadad.) He formed an alliance with Asa and subdued the northern part of the kingdom of the ten tribes (15:18-20). Later Ben-hadad laid siege to Samaria, Ahab's capital, but was defeated, meeting with a still greater disaster the following year. In an endeavor to recover Ramoth-gilead, Ahab was defeated and slain. Samaria was again besieged in the days of Jehoram, son of Ahab; but as the result of a panic it was delivered. (*See* Ahab.) War continued to be waged between the Syrian kings (Hazael, Ben-hadad II, Rezin) and kings of Israel (Jehoram, Jehu, Jehoahaz, Joash, Jeroboam II).

In the latter days of Jotham king of Judah, were Rezin king of Aram and Pekah king of Israel confederates against Judah. They invaded the country, threatened the capital, and recovered Elath for Aram, in the reign of Ahaz, who, to protect himself, became a vassal of Tiglath-pileser king of Assyria. The latter accordingly "went up against Damascus and captured it, and carried the people of it away into exile to Kir, and put Rezin to death" (2 Kings 16:9). For a study of the period of Israel's relations with the Aramaeans from Solomon's reign till the fall of Damascus in 732 B.C., *see* Merrill F. Unger, *Israel and the Aramaeans of Damascus* (1957), pp. 47-109.

Relations with Assyria, Babylonia. Syria became attached to the great Assyrian empire, from which it passed to the Babylonians and from them to the Persians. In 333 B.C. it submitted to

Alexander without a struggle. Upon the death of Alexander, Syria became for the first time the head of a great kingdom. On the division of the provinces among his generals, 321 B.C., Seleucus Nicator received Mesopotamia and Syria. Antioch was begun in 300 B.C. and, being finished in a few years, was made the capital of Seleucus's kingdom. The country grew rich with the wealth that now flowed into it on all sides. The most flourishing period was the reign of the founder, Nicator. The empire was then almost as large as that of the Achemenian Persians, for it at one time included Asia Minor and thus reached from the Aegean to India. Beginning with the reign of Nicator's son, Antiochus I, called Soter, Syria progressively declined. It passed under the power of Tigranes king of Armenia, in 83 B.C. and was not made a province of the Roman Empire till after Pompey's complete defeat of Mithridates and his ally Tigranes, 64 B.C.

The Orontes River between Antioch and ancient Seleucia

Under the Romans. As Syria holds an important place in the NT as well as in the OT, some account of its condition under the Romans is in order. That condition was somewhat peculiar. Although the country generally was formed into a Roman province, under governors who were at first propraetors or quaestors, then proconsuls, and finally legates, a number of "free cities" were exempted from the direct rule of the governor. These retained the administration of their own affairs, subject to a tribute levied according to the Roman principles of taxation. Also a number of tracts, assigned to petty princes, commonly natives, were ruled at their pleasure, subject to the same obligations as the free cities as to taxation. The free cities were Antioch, Seleucia, Apamea, Epiphania, Tripolis, Sidon, and Tyre; the principalities were Comagêné, Chalcis ad Belum (near Baalbek), Arethusa, Abila or Abilêné, Palmyra, and Damascus. The principalities were some-

times called kingdoms, sometimes tetrarchies. They were established where it was thought that the natives were so inveterately wedded to their own customs, and so well disposed for revolt, that it was necessary to consult their feelings, to flatter the national vanity, and to give them the semblance without the substance of freedom.

Although previously overrun by the Romans, Syria was not made tributary and governors appointed until 64 B.C. Down to the battle of Pharsalia the country was fairly tranquil; the only trouble was with the Arabs, who occasionally attacked the eastern frontier. The Roman governors, particularly Gabinius, took great pains to restore the ruined cities. After Pharsalia (46 B.C.) the troubles of Syria were renewed. Julius Caesar gave the province to his relative Sextus (47 B.C.), but Pompey's party was still so strong in the East that the next year one of his adherents, Caecilius Bassus, put Sextus to death and established himself in the government so firmly that he was able to resist for three years three proconsuls appointed by the Senate to dispossess him. He only finally yielded upon terms that he himself offered to his antagonists. Bassus had just made his submission when, upon the assassination of Caesar, Syria was disputed between Cassius and Dolabella (43 B.C.). The next year Cassius left his province and went to Philippi, where he committed suicide. Syria then fell to Antony, who appointed as his legate L. Decidius Saxa (41 B.C.). Pacorus, the crown prince of Parthia, overran Syria and Asia Minor, defeating Antony's generals and threatening Rome with the loss of all her Asiatic possessions (40-39 B.C.). Ventidius, however, in 38 B.C., defeated the Parthians, slew Pacorus, and recovered for Rome her former boundary. A quiet time followed. In 27 B.C. a special procurator was therefore appointed to rule it. He was subordinate to the governor of Syria but within his own province had the power of a legatus. Syria continued without serious disturbance from the expulsion of the Parthians (38 B.C.) to the breaking out of the Jewish war (A.D. 66). In 19 B.C. it was visited by Augustus and in A.D. 18-19 by Germanicus, who died at Antioch in the last named year. In A.D. 44-47 it was the scene of a severe famine.

Syria and Christianity. A little earlier than A.D. 47 Christianity had begun to spread into Syria, partly by means of those scattered at the time of Stephen's persecution (Acts 11:19) and partly by the exertions of Paul (Gal. 1:21). As early probably as A.D. 44, Antioch, the capital, became the see of a bishop and was soon recognized as a patriarchate.

BIBLIOGRAPHY: S. Moscati, *Ancient Semitic Civilizations* (1957); M. F. Unger, *Israel and the Aramaeans of Damascus* (1957); A. T. Olmstead, *History of Palestine and Syria to the Macedonian Conquest* (1965).

SYR′IAC (siri-ak). The KJV rendering in Dan. 2:4; compare "Syrian tongue" (Ezra 4:7, KJV) or

"Syrian language" (2 Kings 18:26; Isa. 36:11; both in KJV). A more correct rendering of this Heb. term (*'ărāmît*) is *Aramaic* (which see.)

SYROPHOENI'CIAN (si-rō-pe-ni'shan). A general name (Mark 7:26) of a female inhabitant of the northern portion of Phoenicia, popularly called Syrophoenicia, by reason of its proximity to Syria and its absorption by conquest into that kingdom. The woman of Syrophoenicia appealed to Jesus to heal her daughter, who was possessed with a demon. When she came near to Him and worshiped, saying, "Have mercy on me, O Lord," He replied, "It is not good to take the children's bread and throw it to the dogs" (Math. 15:22). Whether this was to try her faith, or to show that at that time His work and mission were among Israel, is hard to determine. Her faith, however,

was great and met its merited reward in the cure of her daughter. Matthew calls her a "Canaanite woman," referring to her nationality, in common with the Phoenicians, a descendant of Canaan.

SYR'TIS (Gk. *surtis,* "shoal"). A great sandbank in the Mediterranean Sea, especially on the N coast of Africa. Of these the "Syrtis major" was near Cyrenaica, now called the Gulf of Sidra; and the "Syrtis minor," near Byzacene, now the Gulf of Cabes. The ship in which the apostle Paul was sailing was nearer to the former. The ship was caught in a northeasterly gale on the S coast of Crete and was "run aground on the shallows of Syrtis," on the island of Clauda (Acts 27:17). If this line of drift was followed, it would reach the greater Syrtis, hence the natural fear of the sailors.

T

TA'ANACH (ta′a-nak). A royal city of the Canaanites, whose king was among the thirty-one conquered by Joshua (Josh. 12:21). It was apportioned to the western half tribe of Manasseh (17:11; 21:25; 1 Chron. 7:29) and became a city of the Kohathite Levites (Josh. 21:25). In the great struggle of the Canaanites under Sisera against Deborah and Barak it appears to have been the headquarters of their army (Judg. 5:19). They seem to have still occupied the town but to have been compelled to pay tribute (Josh. 17:13; Judg. 1:27-28). Taanach is generally named with Megiddo, and they were evidently the chief cities of that fine, rich district in the western portion of the plain of Esdraelon. Taanach is located some five miles SE of Megiddo, being generally named with Megiddo as an important city of the rich plain of Esdraelon. It is at present a large mound marking the site of an ancient fortress in the militarily strategic Plain of Armageddon. Ernst Sellin conducted three archaeological campaigns there (1902-04) on behalf of the University of Vienna, and Paul Lapp led seasons of

The Jezreel Valley near the site of Taanach, a royal Canaanite city

excavation at the fourteen-acre site in 1963, 1966, and 1968 for the American Schools of Oriental Research and a number of Lutheran schools. The earliest city flourished during the twenty-seventh to the twenty-fifth centuries and thereafter was abandoned for eight centuries. The Hyksos restored it to power during the seventeenth and sixteenth centuries. After 1500 it came under Egyptian control. Hebrews under the leadership of Deborah and Barak destroyed it (c. 1125 according to evidence from the excavations), and it lay in ruins for about one hundred years. The city revived under the united monarchy but was later conquered and destroyed by Shishak of Egypt in about 926 B.C. Though rebuilt, it had little significance thereafter.

M.F.U.; H.F.V.

BIBLIOGRAPHY: M. Avi-Yonah and E. Stern, eds., *Encyclopedia of Archaeological Excavations in the Holy Land* (1978), 4:1138-47.

TA'ANATH-SHI'LOH (ta′a-nath-shī′lō; "approach to Shiloh"). A place mentioned as on the northern boundary of Ephraim (Josh. 16:6), at its eastern end between the Jordan and Janoah. It is Khirbet Ta'na, a heap of ruins SE of Nablus, where there are large cisterns.

TABALI'AH (ta-ba-lī′yah). The third son of Hosah the Merarite who was responsible, with his father and brothers, for keeping the Shalleketh Gate on the W side of the Temple (1 Chron. 26:11, 16). *See* Hosah; Shallecheth; Tebaliah.

TAB'BAOTH (tab′a-oth; "rings, or spots"). One of the Temple servants whose descendants returned from Babylon with Zerubbabel (Ezra 2:43; Neh. 7:46), before 536 B.C.

TAB'BATH (tab′ath). A place mentioned in connection with the flight of the Midianite host (Judg. 7:22). It is identified with Rās Abū Ṭabat.

TA'BEEL (ta′be-el; Aram. "God is good"). Probably the original pronunciation of Tabeal (ta-be-al; "good-not"), evidently a scornful alteration of Tabeel.

1. The father of the man whom Rezin king of Syria and Pekah king of Israel proposed to seat on the throne of Judah instead of Ahaz (Isa. 7:6), c. 735 B.C. In the KJV the name is spelled Tabeal. It has been conjectured that "the son of Tabeel" was identical with Zichri, the "mighty man of Ephraim," whose sanguinary deeds are recorded in 2 Chron. 28:7 and who may have thus promoted the war in hope of receiving the crown. Because of the Aram. form of the name, however, others have supposed him to have been a Syrian warrior, who, in the event of success, might hold the Judaic kingdom in fealty to Rezin, as suzerain. The Targum of Jonathan turns the name into a mere appellative and makes the passage read: "We will make king in the midst of it whoso seems good to us."

2. A Persian official in Samaria, who, together with Bishlam, Mithredath, and others, wrote to King Artaxerxes a letter of bitter hostility regarding the rebuilders of Jerusalem (Ezra 4:7), 522 B.C. The letter was written in Aram., and it has been argued thence, as well as from the form of his name, that he and his companions were Arameans.

TAB'ERAH (tab'e-ra; "burning"). A place in the wilderness of Paran, so called from the fact that the fire of the Lord consumed the discontented of the children of Israel (Num. 11:3; Deut. 9:22).

TABERING (Heb. *tāpap*, to drum). The KJV term used in Nah. 2:7 for beating upon the breast, as an expression of deep mourning; "beating on their breasts," NASB and NIV (cf. Luke 18:13; 23:27).

TABERNACLE. The rendering of several Gk. and Heb. words.

1. Heb. *'ōhel,* "tent" and *mishkān,* "residence" are both used of the Jewish Tabernacle, but the terms are found to be carefully discriminated. *'Ohel* denotes the cloth roof, whereas *mishkān* is used for the wooden walls of the structure.

2. Heb. *sūkkâ,* from *sākak,* to "entwine," is used to denote a hut, booth (Lev. 23:34; Amos 9:11; Zech. 14:16), rendered "tabernacle" in Ps. 76:2 ("tent," NIV).

3. Heb. *sikkût* is used to denote an "idolatrous" booth that the worshipers of idols constructed in their honor, like the Tabernacle of the covenant in honor of Jehovah ("shrine," Amos 5:26, *see* marg.).

4. The Gk. words rendered "tabernacle" are: (1) *Skēnē,* used for any habitation made of green boughs, skin, cloth, etc. (Matt. 17:4; Mark 9:5; Luke 9:33; John 7:2; cf. Heb. 11:9; etc.). The "tabernacle of Moloch" (Acts 7:43; cf. Amos 5:26) was a portable shrine, in which the image of the

god was carried. (2) *Skēnōma,* used of the Tabernacle, etc.

Figurative. "For in the day of trouble He will conceal me in His tabernacle" (Ps. 27:5; cf. 15:1) indicates being on terms of peaceful communion with God, i.e., in the church.

The term *Tabernacle* is transferred to heaven, as the true dwelling place of God (Heb. 9:11; Rev. 13:6). To spread one's tabernacle over others (Rev. 7:15, *skēnōsei 'ep' autous,*) is to afford shelter and protection. The "tabernacle" (hut) of David seems to be employed in contempt of *his house,* i.e., family, reduced to decay and obscurity (Acts 15:16).

TABERNACLE OF IS'RAEL. The fullest, most definite, as well as most reliable source of information respecting the Tabernacle is the Bible, especially the passages in Exodus. Chapters 25-28 minutely prescribe the construction of the edifice and its furniture, while the parallel passage (chaps. 35-40) describes the execution of the task. We are also aided by the specifications of the Temple of Solomon (1 Kings 6; 2 Chron. 3-4), including that seen in vision by Ezekiel (Ezek. 40-43), both of which Temples were modeled, in all essential features, after the plan of the Tabernacle. Outside the Scriptures the principal authority is Josephus, who, in his description of the earliest sacred buildings of the Jews (*Ant.* 3.6.2-8), repeats substantially the statements of Scripture. For a good discussion see "The Tabernacle," by Frank M. Cross, Jr., *The Biblical Archaeologist* 10, no. 3, pp. 45-68.

Names and Synonyms. The Tabernacle of Israel was known by several names.

Dwelling. The name *dwelling* from Heb. *mishkān,* from *shākan,* to "lie down," a "dwelling," connected itself with the Jewish, though not scriptural, word *Shekinah,* as describing the dwelling place of the divine glory. It was not applied in prose to the common dwellings of men but seems to have belonged rather to the speech of poetry (Ps. 76:2; cf. Song of Sol. 1:8). In its application to the Tabernacle it denoted (1) the ten tricolored curtains; (2) the forty-eight boards supporting them; (3) the whole building, including the roof.

Tent. The term *tent* (Heb. *'ōhel*) was connected more with the common life of men, as the *tent* of the patriarchs (Gen. 9:21; etc.). For the most part, as needing something to raise it, it was used, when applied to the sacred tent, with some distinguishing epithet. In one passage only (1 Kings 1:39) does it appear with this meaning by itself. In its application to the Tabernacle the term *'ōhel* meant (1) the tent roof of goat's hair; (2) the whole building.

House. The term *house* (Heb. *bayit*) was applied to the Tabernacle or "house of the Lord" (Ex. 23:19; 34:26; Josh. 6:24; 9:23; Judg. 18:31) as it had been, apparently, to the tents of the patriarchs (Gen. 33:17). So far as it differs from the two preceding words it conveyed the idea of a fixed settled habitation and was, therefore, more fitted to the Tabernacle after the people were settled in Canaan than during their wanderings. Its chief interest to us lies in its having descended from the first word ever applied in the OT to a local sanctuary, Bethel, "the house of God" (Gen. 28:17), keeping its place side by side with other words—tent, Tabernacle, palace, Temple, synagogue—and at last outliving them all; rising in the Christian *Ecclesia* to yet higher uses (1 Tim. 3:15, "house of God," KJV; "household of God," NASB; "God's household," NIV).

Place of Sanctity. The Tabernacle was also referred to as a place of sanctity (Heb. *miqdāsh;* Gk. *hagiasma,* etc.), the *holy,* consecrated place (Ex. 25:8; Lev. 12:4, "sanctuary"). The terms were applied, according to the consecrated scale of holiness of which the Tabernacle bore witness, sometimes to the whole structure (4:6; Num. 4:12, "sanctuary"; 3:38, "tabernacle"), sometimes to the innermost sanctuary, the Holy of Holies (Lev. 16:2).

Temple. The term *temple* (Heb. *hêkāl*), as meaning the stately building or palace of Jehovah (1 Chron. 29:1, 19), was applied more commonly to the Temple (2 Kings 24:13; etc.); but was also used of the Tabernacle at Shiloh (1 Sam. 1:9; 3:3) and Jerusalem (Ps. 5:7).

Tent, or Tabernacle, of Meeting. Two compound phrases were used in Scripture: Heb. *'ōhel mō'ēd,* "the tent of meeting" (Ex. 29:42, 44), lit., the Tabernacle of *meeting,* "where I will meet with you" (v. 42; cf. 30:6, 36; Num. 17:4); and Heb. *'ōhel hā'ēdūt,* "the tent of the testimony" (Num. 9:15; 17:7; 18:2). In the latter case the tent derived its name from that which was the center of its holiness, i.e., the two tables of stone within the Ark, which were emphatically *the* testimony (Ex. 25:16, 21; 31:18).

History. The OT mentions three Tabernacles. The *provisional* Tabernacle was established after the sin of the golden calf. There followed a transitional period, the whole future depending upon the penitence of the people. In this period a tent was pitched, probably that of Moses himself, outside the camp and was called "the tent of meeting." Of this provisional Tabernacle there was no ritual and no priesthood. The people went out to it as to an oracle (Ex. 33:7). The *Sinaitic* Tabernacle was erected in accordance with directions given to Moses by Jehovah (*see* below). The *Davidic* Tabernacle was erected by David in Jerusalem for the reception of the Ark (2 Sam. 6:12, 17), although the old Tabernacle remained until the days of Solomon at Gibeon, together with the bronze altar, as the place where sacrifices were offered (1 Chron. 16:39; 2 Chron. 1:3).

Upon the intercession of Moses, Jehovah renewed His covenant with Israel, gave them another copy of the law, and invited them to make their offerings of material for the construction of the Tabernacle. This they did in excess of what was needed (Ex. 36:5-6), and the work proceeded under the direction of Bezalel and Oholiab (35:30; 36:2). The Tabernacle was completed on the first day of the first month (Nisan) of the second year after the Exodus and the ritual appointed for it begun (40:2). Instead of being placed outside the camp, like the provisional Tabernacle, it stood in its very center. The priests on the E, the other three families of the Levites on the other sides, were closest in attendance, the "bodyguard" of Israel's theocratic King. In the wider square Judah, Zebulum, Issachar were on the E; Ephraim, Manasseh, Benjamin on the W; the less conspicuous tribes, Dan, Asher, Naphtali on the N; Reuben, Simeon, Gad on the S side. When the army put itself in order of march, the position of the Tabernacle, carried by the Levites, was still central, the tribes of the E and S in front, those of the N and W in the rear (Num. 2).

In all special facts connected with the Tabernacle the original thought reappears. It is the place where man *meets* with God.

As long as Canaan remained unconquered and the people were still therefore an army, the Tabernacle was moved from place to place, wherever the host of Israel was for the time being encamped; it was finally placed at Shiloh (Josh. 18:1; 19:51). The reasons for the choice are not given. Partly, perhaps, its central position, partly its belonging to the powerful tribe of Ephraim may have determined the preference.

It remained in Shiloh during the whole period of the Judges; the Ark was taken from the building in the time of Eli (1 Sam. 4:4) and never returned. Excavations by the Danish Expedition at Shiloh indicate that Israel's central sanctuary was destroyed about 1050 b.c., evidently at the hands of the Philistines at the battle of Ebenezer.

Under Samuel's administration worship was transferred to Mizpah (7:6) and elsewhere (9:12; 10:3; 20:6). In David's day the bread of the Presence was kept at Nob (21:1-6), implying the existence there of at least part of the sacred furniture of the Tabernacle; and at the close of his reign "the high place which was at Gibeon" possessed some fragments of the original Tabernacle, with its altar of burnt offering (1 Chron. 16:39; 21:29; cf. 1 Kings 3:4; 2 Chron. 1:3-6). This is the last mention of the edifice itself. Meanwhile David had set up a *tent* on Mt. Zion, to which he finally transported the Ark (1 Chron. 15:1; 16:1; 2 Sam. 6:17), which in turn was superseded by the *Temple* (which see).

A striking Hebrew tradition exists as to the Ark of the Covenant: that it was taken by Jeremiah and secreted in a cavern (2 Macc. 2:4-8) at the time of the Babylonian capture of the city; and that its hiding place has never been found, and never will be, until the Messiah shall set up His kingdom and restore the glory of Israel. There are other rabbinical tales of similar character.

Structure. In Ex. 25:10–27:19 is given the *prescribed order* for the building of the Tabernacle, beginning with the Ark and proceeding outward, whereas in 36:8–38:31 there is a *description* of its construction, pursuing the reverse order, which is followed here. The cubit used here is the Egyptian royal cubit equal to approximately 20.625 inches. The common estimate for the cubit is eighteen inches. Figure 5 gives the plan of the Tabernacle.

The Court. The court was an enclosed space around the Tabernacle 100 cubits long by 50 cubits wide, or, in round numbers, 172 by 86 feet. Enclosing this space was a peculiarly constructed fence. Its framework consisted of pillars of acacia wood, 5 cubits, i.e., a little more than 8½ feet high (Ex. 27:18). They were, doubtless, round and of the same thickness throughout, probably about 5 inches. The bottom was held in place by a "socket," or plate of bronze, evidently laid flat upon the ground. The socket had a mortise, or hole, to receive the tenon that was in the bottom end of the pillar.

The pillars were kept upright by cords (35:18) fastened to pegs of bronze (27:19) driven into the ground, both on the inside and the outside. The "bands" were curtain rods hung upon hooks near the upper end of the pillars and served as the top rail of a fence, to keep the pillars at a proper distance apart. They were of shittim wood, covered with silver; the hooks and the caps that protected the tops of the pillars were of the same metal (38:17, 19). Hooks were also placed at the bottom of the pillars, by which the lower edge of the curtain was fastened. The pillars, when set up and braced by the bands and stay ropes, formed the complete framework of a fence. Upon this was

hung sheets of "fine twisted linen," probably like our *duck,* sewed endwise together so as to form a continuous screen from the doorway all around the corners to the doorway again. This was 5 cubits wide, the same as the height of the pillars. But as the pillars rested upon sockets, the curtain would be kept off the ground.

The "screen" for the gate of the court was in the middle of the eastern end and was "the work of the weaver, of blue and purple and scarlet material, and fine twisted linen" (38:18), i.e., the warp was of bleached linen threads and the woof of alternate bars of wool dyed blue, purple, and scarlet. Its size was five cubits high by twenty cubits long. Entrance into the court was only effected by lifting this curtain at the bottom. In this court was the altar of burnt offering, which probably stood in the center of the front half of the space, about halfway between the entrance and the Tabernacle. Midway between the altar and the Tabernacle (30:18) stood the *laver* (which see). The Tabernacle itself was situated at the front edge of the rear half of the enclosure. Being thirty cubits long and ten cubits wide, it would leave equal spaces (namely, ten cubits) behind it and on either side.

The Tabernacle. The Tabernacle was composed of two parts, the Tabernacle proper (Heb. *mishkān*) and the "tent over the tabernacle" (*'ōhel,* Ex. 26:7). The Tabernacle proper consisted of boards of acacia wood, each ten cubits long by one and a half broad (26:16); their entire surface was plated with sheets of gold. Twenty of these formed each side wall (vv. 18, 20), each board having two tenons at its foot to enter the socket. There were eight rear boards (v. 25), six of which were of the same dimensions as those on the side, thus making nine cubits. As the width of the Tabernacle was probably the same as

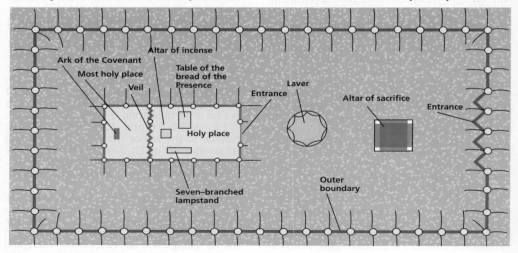

fig 5. The plan of the Tabernacle

its height, ten cubits, thus making the Holy of Holies a perfect cube, this would leave one cubit of space to be filled by the two corner boards. There is nothing in the Heb. to indicate the breadth of these two boards, and we assume that they were only one-half cubit wide. If, now, the rear boards were placed within the side boards, so as to be flush with the end, each corner board would rest on two sockets, and we have the sixteen sockets demanded. This will oblige us to count the rear socket of the sides, as is done with the posts of the courts. The meaning seems to be that as you look at each side, forty sockets are seen; whereas if you look at the rear, sixteen are in view.

In order to keep the boards in line, three series of bars were provided, made of acacia wood overlaid with gold, to pass through rings of gold on the outside of the boards (26:26-29; 36:31-34). Of these, five were on each side and five on the rear, the middle bar reaching from end to end; the upper and lower ones were divided, their ends being fastened (as Josephus suggests) with dowels. They were probably of different lengths, to prevent the break being in the center.

The whole structure was, doubtless, kept in place with cords, one end fastened to the knobs to which the tent cloth was attached, and the other end to pins driven into the ground. The boards were covered on the outside with a double blanket of skins, probably suspended from the knobs mentioned above, thus keeping the wind and dust from entering between the boards and also protecting the gold sheeting. The inner blanket was of "porpoise skins" (26:14; 36:19) but may have been of the Angora goat. This was probably hung with the hair turned inward toward the boards, while the other blanket (of ram skins dyed red) was hung with the hair on the outside, to shed the rain.

The Roof. The roof (Heb. 'ōhel, "tent") of the Tabernacle was made of goats-hair canvas, i.e., camlet, such as is still used by the Arabs, generally looking like a fox skin of black or brownish color (Song of Sol. 1:5). It consisted of an inner covering and a fly. The material was woven in eleven pieces, each thirty cubits long by four wide (Ex. 26:7-9; 36:14); five of these pieces were joined so as to make the inner tent, and six formed the fly. This sixth breadth, being thirty cubits long, would allow itself to be double across the front and single across the rear of the Tabernacle (26:9, 13). The lower edge of each sheet was buttoned over curtain knobs on the boards by means of fifty loops attached to their selvedge. The tent extended one cubit over the sides (vv. 10-13). The roof was sustained by posts, one of them being an extension of the central front doorpost, their heads probably rounded so as not to tear the roof canvas.

The Door of the Tent. The entrance to the Tabernacle was closed with a screen like that of the court, supported by five pillars, covered with gold; their hooks were of gold, and their "bands" (curtain rods) were covered with gold; their sockets were of bronze (Ex. 26:36-37; 36:37-38). If these pillars were arranged so as to leave six spaces, each space would have been a little more than thirty-four inches wide. Evidently the curtain rods had rings in their ends, which slipped down over hooks in the tops of the posts and on the boards.

The Wall Drapery. Each wall drapery consisted of five pieces of cloth woven of the same material as the door screen, four cubits wide and twenty cubits long. These pieces were sewed together at the ends and hung by loops of blue cord to the gold knobs on the inside of the boards (Ex. 26:1-6; 36:8-13). Special dignity was given to these side curtains, compared to that of the door screen, by their embroidery of "cherubim, the work of a skillful workman" (26:1; 36:8), instead of the simple tracery on the latter. As will be seen, the hangings were each twice as wide as the entire circuit of the walls, therefore they must have been gathered into some manner of festoons.

The Veil. The veil (Heb. pārōket, a "separation"), particularly described in Ex. 26:31-33; 36:35-36, was the screen between the Holy Place and the Holy of Holies. It was of the same material as the door screens but was embroidered with cherubim. It is thought that there were two, their extended wings touching each other. The veil, like the other hangings, was suspended upon pillars and, probably, "bands" (curtain rods), though the latter are not mentioned. These pillars (and bands) were covered with gold, the hooks were of gold, and the sockets were of silver. For the veil four pillars were used, and as no one of them ran up to the peak, it did not, therefore, need to be in the center. The upper corners of the veil were fastened to the gold hooks in the boards. If we follow the proportions of the Holy Place and the Most Holy Place in the Temple, we must suppose the latter in the Tabernacle to have been square and the former to have been twice as long as broad. This will fix the dividing line between the two rooms at two-thirds of the width of the seventh board from the rear; the presumption is that the pillars were wholly within the Most Holy Place.

Furniture. There was distinctive furniture in the courtyard and within the sacred structure itself, the Holy Place and the Holy of Holies. Two items were placed in the courtyard, three items were placed in the Holy Place, and one item was placed in the Holy of Holies.

In the Courtyard. An altar and a laver, or basin, were placed in the courtyard.

The Altar of Burnt Offering. The altar of burnt offering (Heb. mizbaḥ hā'ōlâ, Ex. 30:28; "bronze altar," mizbaḥ hanneḥōshet, 39:39; "table of the Lord," Mal. 1:7, 12) was placed between the en-

The Tabernacle

trance and the Tabernacle. It was made strong and light for convenient transportation; a hollow box of acacia wood, five cubits square and three cubits high (Ex. 27:1-8), overlaid with sheets of bronze. At each corner was a "horn," apparently a triangular extension of the sides at their junction. The altar had a grate, or "net" (Heb. *mikbār*, a "netting"), placed halfway between the top and bottom (v. 5). At each corner of the net was a ring, through which were passed the bronze-covered poles by which the altar was carried, like a handbarrow. Of course it was lined both inside and outside with bronze to protect it from the heat. At the end of twenty years 250 censers were flattened out and nailed on its sides, telling their awful story (Num. 16:17, 36-40) to the coming generations. The common censer in Egypt was a small, shallow, platelike vessel, about half a cubit in diameter. As the priests were not allowed to go up the altar by steps (Ex. 20:26) and as it would be too high to reach from the ground, the earth was, probably, raised about the altar so as to approach it by an incline.

The utensils for the altar (27:3) made of bronze were: *ash pails; shovels* for cleaning the altar; *basins* for receiving the blood to be sprinkled on the altar; *flesh hooks,* i.e., large *forks,* to handle the pieces of flesh; *firepans* (38:3; Num. 16:17); *snuffers* (Ex. 25:38). According to Lev. 6:13, the fire on this altar was never allowed to go out.

The Laver. The laver (Heb. *kîyyôr,* "rounded," a "basin") stood about midway between the altar and the Tabernacle. It was the basin used by the officiating priests and was made from the bronze mirrors of the women (Ex. 30:18; 38:8). It was probably round, of considerable size, with another and shallower basin beneath it, into which the water ran after being used, and in which the priests washed their feet. We have no Scripture information as to its size or shape. As no mention is made of a vessel in which were washed the parts of the animals offered in sacrifice, the laver was likely used for this purpose also. As washing in the East was always in running water, the laver was probably supplied with faucets from which the water would flow upon the object to be cleansed, whether the hands or feet of the priests or the parts of the sacrifice (*see* article Laver).

Within the Holy Place. The table of the bread of the Presence (or showbread), the golden lampstand, and the altar of incense were located within the Holy Place.

Table of the Bread of the Presence. The table of the bread of the Presence, or showbread (Heb. *shūlḥān leḥem pānîm,* "table of the face," i.e., of Jehovah) was placed on the N, or right, side, facing the lampstand (Ex. 40:22). It was made of acacia wood, two cubits long, one broad, and one and one-half high. This proportion between the length and the height is accurately maintained in the sculptural form on the Arch of Titus. The surface, or top, of the table, rested on a frame a handbreadth deep; around it ran a rim with a border of gold projecting above the top to keep articles from slipping off the table. The legs were apparently mortised into the sides (as is usual today), with rings near each corner for the carrying staves (25:23-30; 37:10-16).

The bread placed upon the table (Heb. "bread of the Presence") was made of fine wheat flour (unleavened), baked in twelve loaves (cakes), each containing one-fifth of an ephah of flour. These, according to Jewish tradition, as well as the dimensions of the table, would seem to have been placed upon plates in two piles of six each. They were renewed every Sabbath, were to be eaten by the priests exclusively (and that in the sanctuary only), and were then replaced by fresh loaves (1 Sam. 21:6), which had been prepared overnight by the Levites (1 Chron. 9:32). To each pile of loaves incense was added, probably placed in bowls beside the bread, for "a memorial portion for the bread, even an offering made by fire to the Lord" (Lev. 24:5-9).

The utensils belonging to the table were these: the *dishes* for the showbread; *pans* or *spoons* (so KJV and sometimes NASB) for the incense; *jugs* or *jars* (KJV, "covers"), which, as they were used for making libations, were doubtless for wine, with a spout for pouring; and *cups,* all of pure gold.

The Golden Lampstand. The golden lampstand (Heb. *menōrā*) stood on the S, or left, side of the Holy Place, directly opposite the table of showbread (Ex. 40:24). Its construction, except as to size, is minutely described (25:31-40; 37:17-24). The material of which it was made was pure gold, of which an entire talent was used for the lampstand and its vessels. The different parts were of "hammered work," *miqshâ,* hammered out of sheets. It consisted of a pedestal (*yārēk*), elsewhere meaning the *leg* or, rather, the part of the body from which the legs and feet spring; and the shaft (*qāneh,* "reed or stalk"), from which, probably, at equal distances from one another, there projected three branches on each side, rising as high as the central shaft. The central shaft and the six branches terminated in sockets into which the seven lamps were placed. The ornamentation of the lampstand, a beautiful design, consisted of a "cup" (Heb. *gābîa'*), which was almond-shaped (i.e., the nut), tapering from a head. Above this was the "bulb" (Heb. *kaptôr*), like the capital of a column, under the intersection of the branches (25:35). Surmounting all was the "flower" (Heb. *peraḥ,* lit., "blossom"), like a bud just ready to burst into bloom. There were four of these ornamental groupings on the main stem, one being placed at intervals at each of the three points where the branches diverged, the fourth being probably at the upper end, just under the lamp that was placed upon it. There were three of these groups on each branch, one under the lamp, and the two others probably placed equidistant from each other. This was evidently the form of the lampstand, which is known to us chiefly by the passages in Ex. 25:31-40; 37:17-24, the light thrown thereon by the Jewish writers and by the representation on the Arch of Titus at Rome.

The size of the lampstand is not given in the Bible description of it, and we are therefore left to conjecture. Jewish tradition assigns it a height of about five feet and a breadth of about three and one-half feet. On the Arch of Titus it measures two feet nine inches high by two feet broad; but the figures there delineated are not life-size, and the proportion with the table of showbread on the same sculpture, as well as with the men there exhibited, yields a size about the same as the above tradition. We may therefore fix the entire height, including the base, at about three cubits, and the entire breadth at about two cubits. Taking the estimate of a cubit at about eighteen inches, the dimensions would be about fifty-four by thirty-six inches.

Finally came the lamps themselves (Heb. sing. *nēr*), which were of the kind generally used in the East, but here of gold. These were placed, of course, upon the top of the main shaft and the branches in sockets. Opinion generally places them on a horizontal line, although the instructions given in Exodus afford no information. The lamps were supplied with olive oil, *pure* or "clear" (i.e., "prepared from olives which had been cleansed from leaves, twigs, dust, etc., before they were crushed"), *beaten* (i.e., "obtained not by crushing in oil presses, but by beating, when the oil which flows out by itself is of the finest quality and a white color") (K. & D., *Com.*, on Ex. 27:20). It is likely that the plane of the lamps ran from E to W—thus the better lighting of the Holy Place. The lamps were trimmed and lighted at the time of the evening sacrifice (30:8) and trimmed and filled at the time of the morning sacrifice (30:7; 1 Sam. 3:3). They are traditionally believed to have held a "log," i.e., a little more than a half pint.

The utensils belonging to the lampstand were the "snuffers" ("wick trimmers," NIV) and the "trays" (Ex. 25:38), made of the same gold as the lampstand itself. The snuffers were used to pull up the wick and to hold the coal while blowing it to light the lamp. The trays were *coal pans* (27:3; Lev. 16:12), used for bringing the live coals from the great altar.

The Altar of Incense. The altar of incense (Heb. *mizbēaḥ miqṭar qeṭōret*) occupied the middle space near to and in front of the inner veil (Ex. 30:1-6; 37:25-28; 40:5; Lev. 16:18). It was, however, reckoned as belonging to the Most Holy Place (1 Kings 6:22; Heb. 9:4), apparently on account of its great sanctity. In construction it was a simple box of acacia wood, two cubits high, one cubit wide, and one cubit broad, with a top, and horns like the large altar; the whole was covered with gold. It had no grate, because the fire did not come directly in contact with it. It had a molding around the edge, rings to carry it, and staves. No utensils belonged especially to it. Upon this altar neither burnt offerings nor grain offerings were allowed to be offered, nor drink offerings to be poured, but it was used exclusively to burn incense upon morning and evening.

Within the Holy of Holies. The Ark of the Covenant was the only piece of furniture within the Holy of Holies. It was called the "Ark of the Covenant" (Heb. *'ărôn berît*, Num. 10:33), or "Ark of the Testimony" (Heb. *'ărôn hā'ēdūt*, Ex. 25:22; etc.), from the law that was kept therein.

Construction. The Ark was made of acacia wood two and one-half cubits long, one and one-half cubits broad, and one and one-half cubits high (external dimensions) and was plated inside and out with pure gold. Running around each side was a gold border extending above the top of the Ark, so as to keep the lid from moving. This lid was called the "mercy seat" (Ex. 25:20, 22; Heb. *kappōret*, a "covering"), was the same size as the Ark itself, and was made of acacia wood covered with gold. The Ark was transported by means of two gold-covered poles run through two gold rings on each side, from which they were not to be removed (25:15) unless it might be necessary to remove them in order to cover the Ark when the Tabernacle was moved (Num. 4:6).

Upon the lid, or Mercy Seat, or at the ends of the Ark, as in the *Temple* (which see), were placed the *cherubim* (which see), probably figures beaten out of gold as was the lampstand. In shape they were probably human, with the exception of their wings, though some authorities think they were of the same complex form as the cherubim mentioned by Ezekiel (Ezek. 1:5-14). They were no doubt the normal or full height of a man and are always spoken of as maintaining an upright position (2 Chron. 3:13). They stood facing each other, looking down upon the Mercy Seat, with their wings forward in a brooding attitude (Ex. 25:20; cf. Deut. 32:11). The golden censer, with which the high priest once a year entered the Most Holy Place, was doubtless set upon this lid.

Between the cherubim was the *Shekinah* (Heb. *shekinâ*, "residence"), the cloud in which Jehovah appeared above the Mercy Seat (Ex. 25:22; cf. Lev. 16:2). It was not the cloud of incense (16:13), but the manifest appearance of the divine glory. Because Jehovah manifested His essential presence in this cloud, not only could no unclean and sinful man go before the Mercy Seat, i.e., approach the holiness of the all-holy God, but even the anointed high priest, if he went before it at his own pleasure, or without the expiatory blood of sacrifice, would expose himself to certain death.

Contents. The Ark contained the two tables of

stone on which Jehovah wrote the Ten Commandments, or rather those prepared by Moses from the original, broken by him when he heard of Israel's idolatry (Ex. 31:18 –34:29; Deut. 9:10 –10:4); and the copy of the law, written by Moses (31:26), presumed by some to be the Pentateuch in full, and thought to be the same as was afterward discovered in the time of Josiah (2 Kings 22:8). The law must, in the meanwhile, have been removed, together with all the contents, because in the days of Solomon the Ark contained the two tablets only (1 Kings 8:9). The Ark also contained a golden jar of miraculously preserved manna (Ex. 16:33-34) and "Aaron's rod which budded" (Heb. 9:4; cf. Num. 17:10).

Care of the Tabernacle. The following are the directions for the care of the Tabernacle and its furniture (Num. 4:4-33; 7:3-9; 10:17, 21). "The work" (4:4) signifies military service and is used here with special reference to the service of the Levites as the sacred militia of Jehovah. The following were the duties of the Kohathite Levites: When the Tabernacle was to be taken down for removal the priests took down the veil and covered the Ark of Testimony with it; over this they put a covering of "porpoise skin" (so NASB, but more likely the hide of some other creature, the porpoise being ceremonially unclean [see Animal Kingdom: Porpoise]; the KJV and NKJV read "badger skins," and the NIV reads "sea cow") and finally a "cloth of pure blue." Removing the dishes from the table of showbread, they spread over it a cloth of blue, then replaced the dishes and spread upon them a cloth of scarlet and finally a covering of "porpoise skins." The lampstand, with its lamps, snuffers, and trays, was then covered with a cloth of blue, over which was placed a covering of "porpoise skins." The altar of incense was covered with a cloth of blue and "porpoise skins," and then all other "utensils of service" in the sanctuary were wrapped in blue and "porpoise skins" and placed upon "bars," i.e., a bier made of two poles with crosspieces. After this the great altar was cleansed from the ashes, covered with a purple cloth, the altar utensils packed in it, and then covered with "porpoise skins." When all this preparation was completed the Kohathites came forward to bear the furniture away. The only thing not mentioned as prepared by the priests was the laver, probably because it was carried without any covering.

To the care and carrying by the Gershonites were assigned the tapestry of the Tabernacle, namely, the inner covering, the tent of goats' hair, the two outside coverings of the boards, the entrance curtain, the veil, the hangings of the court and its entrance curtain, with all the cords and the various implements used in the said work. Thus their office was to perform whatever was usually done with these portions of the sanctuary, especially in setting up or taking down the Tabernacle (Num. 3:25 –4:33).

The charge of the Merarites was: the boards of the Tabernacle with the bars, the pillars, and their sockets (both of the sacred building and its court), and their pegs and cords. That is, they were to take them down, carry them on the march, and to fix them when the Tabernacle was set up again (3:36-37; 4:31-32). See Levites.

Typology of the Tabernacle and Furniture. The design of the Tabernacle is thus stated: "Let them construct a sanctuary for Me, that I may dwell among them" (Ex. 25:8). This sanctuary was styled "the tent of meeting" (Heb. *'ōhel mô'ēd*) between Jehovah and His people. The Lord said, "I will meet with you, to speak to you there" (29:42); "and I will dwell among the Sons of Israel and will be their God" (v. 45). Thus the Tabernacle and all that pertained to it were typical of the presence of God with His people. In accordance with this promise, the glory of Jehovah filled the Tabernacle, but His presence was manifested to the people in the pillar of cloud and fire above the sacred structure (40:34-38; Num. 9:15-23). The fiery cloud by day moved at God's direction and thus prefigured His guidance. The entire divine institution portrayed the approach of God's redeemed people to His presence. Following is a discussion of the Tabernacle typology as presented by many Bible teachers.

General Typology. The Tabernacle in comprehensive terms is set forth in the NT as typical in three ways: (1) of the church, as "a dwelling of God in the Spirit" (Ex. 25:8; Eph. 2:19-22), (2) of the believer who is "a temple of the Holy Spirit" (1 Cor. 6:19; cf. 2 Cor. 6:16), (3) as a portrayal of heavenly reality (Heb. 9:23-24). In its minute details the Tabernacle speaks of Christ. This is true of the high priest, the furniture, the ritual, and the worship.

As a Type of Christ. The furniture of the Tabernacle typified Christ and His ministry.

The Bronze Altar. The bronze altar (Ex. 27:1-8) was a type of Christ's cross, on which our Lord as a whole burnt offering offered Himself without spot unto God.

Laver. The laver, in which the priests washed before entering the Holy Place or approaching the altar to minister, was a type of Christ cleansing the believer from the defilement of sin (John 13:2-10) and from every "spot or wrinkle or any such thing" (Eph. 5:25-27).

The Golden Lampstand. The lampstand typified Christ as the light of the world, bringing to us the full radiance of divine life. It is noteworthy that natural light was shut out from the Tabernacle. Only the Spirit of God can show us the things of Christ (1 Cor. 2:14-15). The divine Spirit takes the things of Christ and reveals them to us, as Jesus announced in His Upper Room discourse (John 16:14-15).

The Table of the Bread of the Presence. The table of the bread of the Presence, or showbread, was a type of Christ as the Bread of Life, the

Sustainer of each individual believer-priest (1 Pet. 2:9; Rev. 1:6). The manna portrayed the life-giving Christ; the showbread of the Presence the life-sustaining Christ. Christ is the Bread that came down from heaven (John 6:33-58). The bread prefigured the "grain of wheat" (12:24) pulverized in the mill of suffering (cf. v. 27) and subjected to the fire of divine judgment for sin (vv. 31-33).

The Altar of Incense. The altar of incense (Ex. 30:1-10) portrayed Christ our Intercessor (John 17:1-26; Heb. 7:25) through whom our prayers and petitions ascend to God (13:15; Rev. 8:3-4). It also spoke of the Christian as a believer-priest offering the sacrifice of praise and worship (Heb. 13:15).

The Veil. The veil (Ex. 26:31-35) was a type of Christ's human body (Matt. 26:26; 27:50; Heb. 10:20). Accordingly, the veil was supernaturally torn in two when Christ died (Matt. 27:51), granting instant access to God to everyone who approaches on the ground of faith in Him. The death of Christ portrayed by the veil also marked the termination of all legality. The unobstructed way to God was now open. The officiating priesthood at the death of Christ must have repaired the veil that had been rent. Antitypically these pictures attempt to put the believer or sinner back under the law.

The Ark of the Covenant. The materials, contents, and employment of the Ark of the Covenant (Ex. 25:10-22) were significant. In its materials, acacia wood and gold, the Ark was a type of the humanity and deity of Christ. Acacia wood grew in the desert and fittingly portrayed Christ's humanity in His lowliness as a "root out of parched ground" (Isa. 53:2). The fact that the Ark was overlaid with pure gold (Ex. 25:11) suggested deity in manifestation. In its contents the Ark typified Christ as having God's law in His heart (25:16, 21) and portrayed Christ in resurrection inasmuch as it contained Aaron's rod that budded (Num. 17:10). The employment of the Ark, particularly the Mercy Seat, typified the divine throne. It was transformed from a throne of judgment to a throne of grace as far as the erring Israelite was concerned by the blood of atonement that was sprinkled upon it. The cherubim with outstretched wings guarded the holiness of the Mercy Seat. The Ark was the commencement of everything in the Tabernacle symbolism. It was placed in the Holy of Holies, showing that God begins from Himself in His outreach toward man in revelation. On the other hand, in the human approach the worship begins from without, moving toward God in the very center of the holiest place. Man begins at the bronze altar, that is, at the cross, where atonement is made in the light of the fire of God's judgment.   M.F.U.

BIBLIOGRAPHY: J. Strong, *The Tabernacle of Israel in the Desert* (1888); W. S. Caldecott, *The Tabernacle: Its History and Structure* (1904); S. Ridout, *Lectures on the Tabernacle* (1952); R. H. Mount, Jr., *The Law Prophesied* (1963); A. H. Hillyard, *The Tabernacle in the Wilderness* (1965); M. L. G. Guillebaud, *Evangelical Quarterly* 31 (1959): 90-96; J. Blenkinsopp, *Journal of Biblical Literature* 88 (1969): 143-56; H. W. Soltau, *The Holy Vessels and Furniture of the Tabernacle* (1970); S. F. Olford, *The Tabernacle* (1971); L. T. Talbot, *Christ in the Tabernacle* (1978); G. H. Dolman and M. Rainsford, *The Tabernacle* (1982); H. W. Soltau, *The Tabernacle, the Priesthood, and the Offerings* (1985).

TABERNACLES, FEAST OF. Often called the feast of Booths (so NASB). It is one of the yearly festivals. *See* the articles Festivals; Sacrifices.

TAB'ITHA (tab'i-tha; Gk. from Aram. *ṭebitā'*, "gazelle"). A benevolent Christian widow of Joppa whom Peter restored to life (Acts 9:36-42). She was probably a Hellenistic Jewess, known to the Greeks by the name *Dorcas* (which see) and to the Hebrews by the Aram. equivalent. It is not certain, however, that Tabitha bore both names; Luke may have translated the name for the benefit of his Gentile readers and used its definition thereafter for their convenience. The Greeks used Dorcas, i.e., "female gazelle," as a term of endearment for their women. Soon after Peter had miraculously cured the palsied Aeneas in Lydda, the church at Joppa was bereaved by the death of Tabitha. They at once sent for the apostle, whether merely to receive his Christian consolation or in the hope that he could restore their friend to life, is not evident. A touching picture is given of the widows who stood "weeping, and showing all

St. Peter's church, Jaffa, near the traditional site of Tabitha's tomb

the tunics and garments that Dorcas used to make." Peter "sent them all out and knelt down and prayed," then commanded the lifeless woman to arise. She opened her eyes, arose, and by the apostle was presented to her friends. The facts, which became widely known, produced a profound impression in Joppa and occasioned many conversions (9:42).

TABLE. *See also* Tablet.

1. A *divan*, i.e., a company of persons seated round about a room (Song of Sol. 1:12), Heb. *mēsab*.

2. A table as spread with food, viands (Judg. 1:7; 1 Sam. 20:29, 34; 1 Kings 2:7; etc.), Heb. *shūlḥān*, "spread out, extended." As to the form of tables among the Hebrews, little is known; but, as among other orientals, they were probably not high. They were doubtless similar to those of modern Arabs, a piece of skin or leather, a mat, or a linen cloth spread upon the ground. Hence the fitness of the name *something spread,* and the figurative expression "May their table before them become a snare" (Ps. 69:22), i.e., let their feet become entangled in it, as it is spread on the ground.

3. Gk. *anakeimai*, to lie or recline at table (John 13:28) on the divan. The Romans often arranged reclining divans on three sides of a low table, the fourth side being open for serving the food. This arrangement was called *triclinium*.

Reclining at table

4. Gk. *trapeza*, a table on which food is placed (Matt. 15:27; Mark 7:28; Luke 16:21; 22:21, 30); the table of the bread of the Presence (Heb. 9:2); the table or stand of a money changer, where he sits, exchanging different kinds of money for a fee and paying back with interest loans or deposits (Matt. 21:12; Mark 11:15; John 2:15).

Figurative. "The table of the Lord is to be despised" (Mal. 1:7; cf. v. 12) is what the prophets charge the priests with representing. The table of Jehovah is the altar, and they made it contemptible by offering upon it bad, blemished animals, which were unfit for sacrifices. "They will speak lies to each other at the same table" (Dan. 11:27) is a figure of feigned friendship. Eating, especially in the presence of enemies (Ps. 23:5; cf. Isa.

21:5), denotes a sense of security. In 1 Cor. 10:21, "You cannot partake of the table of the Lord and the table of demons" brings into sharp contrast the Holy Communion and the sacrifices offered to heathen deities. Paul makes the real existences answering to the heathen conception of these gods to be *demons.*

TABLE OF SHOWBREAD. *See* Tabernacle.

TABLE OF THE LORD. A phrase used to designate the Table of the Christian church, and evidently taken from 1 Cor. 10:21. In the OT the words *table* (which see) and altar appear to have been applied to the same thing (Ezek. 41:22).

TABLET.

1. Heb. *lûaḥ* ("glistening"), a board of polished stone or wood used for writing on (Prov. 3:3; Isa. 30:8; Hab. 2:2).

2. Gk. *pinakidion* (Luke 1:63) and Gk. *plax,* "flat," the former being a small writing tablet, the latter meaning the same as no. 1 (2 Cor. 3:3).

3. The inaccurate KJV rendering of (a) Heb. *kûmāz,* "jewel," probably gold *drops,* or beads, worn around the neck or arm by the Israelites in the desert (Ex. 35:22; Num. 31:50; "ornaments" and "necklaces," NIV), or (b) Heb. *bāttê hannepesh* ("houses of the breath," i.e., perfume boxes, Isa. 3:20).

TABLETS OF THE LAW (Heb. *lūḥōt hā'eben,* "stone tablets," Ex. 24:12), also called "tablets of the covenant" (Deut. 9:9, 15), or "of the testimony" (Ex. 31:18). These were given to Moses on Mt. Sinai, having the Ten Commandments written on them "by the finger of God."

TA'BOR (ta'bor).

The Mount. Now called Jebel et Tur, this is a conical and quite symmetrical mound of limestone on the northeastern part of the plain of Esdraelon. It is about six miles E of Nazareth. The northern slope is covered with oak trees and syringa. It rises to the height of 1,350 feet above the plain, which itself is 400 feet above the Mediterranean Sea. The ascent is usually made on the W side, near the little village of Debûrieh, probably the ancient Daberath (Josh. 19:12). Tabor is named (19:22) as a boundary between Issachar and Zebulun. Barak, at the command of Deborah, gathered his forces on Tabor and descended thence with "ten thousand men" into the plain, conquering Sisera on the banks of the Kishon (Judg. 4:6-15). Here the brothers of Gideon were slain by Zebah and Zalmunna (8:18-19); and some think Tabor is intended when it is said (Deut. 33:19) of Issachar and Zebulun that "they shall call peoples to the mountain; there they shall offer righteous sacrifices." In the time of Christ the summit is said to have been crowned by a fortified town, the ruins of which are there now (1 Chron. 6:77). It is difficult to see how such a scene as that of Christ's transfiguration could have taken place there, and the NT clearly points to some part of Hermon as the place.

The City. Tabor is mentioned in the lists of 1 Chron. 6 as a city of the Merarite Levites, in the tribe of Zebulun (v. 77). The list of the towns of Zebulun (Josh. 19) contains the name of Chisloth-tabor (v. 12). It is therefore possible either that Chisloth-tabor was abbreviated to Tabor by the chronicler, or that by the time these later lists were compiled the Merarites had established themselves on the sacred mountain and that Tabor is Mt. Tabor.

The Oak or Terebinth. Mentioned (1 Sam. 10:3) as one of the points in the homeward journey of Saul after his anointing by Samuel. The place is nowhere else mentioned, and nothing further can be determined concerning it than that it stood by the road leading from Rachel's tomb to Gibeah.

BIBLIOGRAPHY: E. Robinson, *Biblical Researches* (1856), 2:351-60; 3:340; D. Baly, *The Geography of the Bible* (1957), pp. 38, 151, 173-74, 195-96.

TABRET. *See* Music.

TAB'RIMMON (tab'rim-on; Aram. "Rimmon is good"). Rimmon was the god of thunder, a weather god, of Damascus, Akkad. "thunderer"), the father of Ben-hadad I, king of Syria in the reign of Asa (1 Kings 15:18), before 900 B.C.

TACH'MONITE, THE. *See* Jashobeam; Tahchemonite, The.

TACKLE (Heb. *hebel,* Isa. 33:23; Gk. *skeue,* Acts 27:19) represents the spars, ropes, chains, etc., of a *ship* (which see).

TAD'MOR (tad'mōr; cf. Heb. *tamar,* "a palm tree"). A city built by Solomon in the wilderness (2 Chron. 8:4); the parallel passage (1 Kings 9:18, "Tamar") adds "in the land of Judah," indicating the land on the southern border of Palestine (Ezek. 47:19; 48:28). The Greeks and Romans called the city Palmyra. It was 145 miles from Damascus and the center of vast commercial traffic as well as a military station. Its grandeur is attested by its magnificent ruins. Presuming that Tadmor is the same as Palmyra, the following facts may be mentioned. The first author of antiquity who mentions Palmyra is Pliny the Elder. Later, Appian writes of it in connection with Mark Antony's design to allow his cavalry to plunder it. In the second century A.D. it seems to have been beautified by the emperor Hadrian. It became a Roman colony under Caracalla (A.D. 211-17). In the reign of Gallienus the Roman Senate invested Odenathus, a senator of Palmyra, with the regal dignity on account of his services in defeating Sapor king of Persia. Upon his assassination his widow, Zenobia, wished to make of Palmyra an independent monarchy and for a while successfully resisted the Roman arms; but she was defeated and taken prisoner by the emperor Aurelian (A.D. 273), who left a Roman garrison in Palmyra. This garrison was massacred in a revolt, for which Aurelian punished the city so severely that it never recovered from the blow. Today a living town of more than five thousand named Palmyra or Tadmor is an important station on the Iraq-Tripoli oil pipeline about one-half mile from the ruins of ancient Palmyra.

Systematic archaeological work at Palmyra be-

Mt. Tabor

gan in 1900 with efforts of the Russian Archaeological Institute of Constantinople. A German team under the leadership of Theodor Wiegand excavated there from 1902 to 1917. French expeditions attacked the site between the wars. A Swiss archaeological mission worked there from 1954 to 1956, and a Polish team under the leadership of K. Michalowski began excavating in 1957. Excavators found that the main street extended across the S central part of the western half of the city a distance of about 1,100 meters. Lined with Corinthian columns and shops, it was eleven meters wide and had six-meter-wide lanes on both sides running under covered porticoes. From this thoroughfare side streets opened at right angles. South of the street stood most of the city's chief structures, including the temple of Nebo, a well-preserved theater, and the debating hall of the senate. The Sanctuary of Bel stood in the eastern part of the city. At the W end sprawled the great camp of Diocletian.   H.F.V.

BIBLIOGRAPHY: J. Stercky, *Palmyra* (1952).

TA'HAN (ta'han).
1. The head of one of the families of the tribe of Ephraim at the end of the Exodus (Num. 26:35), c. 1440 B.C.
2. Apparently the son of Telah and the father of Ladan, in the genealogy of Ephraim (1 Chron. 7:25), after 1440 B.C.

TA'HANITES (ta'ha-nīts), the descendants (Num. 26:35) of Tahan, no. 1.

TAHAP'ANES (ta-hap'a-nēz). *See* Tahpanhes.

TA'HASH (ta'hash; "dugong"; Thahash, KJV). A son of Nahor (Gen. 22:24).

TA'HATH (ta'hath; "that which is beneath").
1. A Kohathite Levite, son of Assir and father of Uriel, or Zephaniah, in the ancestry of Samuel and Heman (1 Chron. 6:24, 37).
2. An Ephraimite, son of Bered and father of Eleadah (1 Chron. 7:20). Perhaps identical with Tahan, no. 1.
3. Apparently the grandson of the foregoing, being registered as a son of Eleadah and the father of Zabad (1 Chron. 7:20).
4. The name of a desert station between Makheloth and Terah (Num. 33:26); not identified.

TAHCH'EMONITE, THE (tak'e-mo-nīt; Tachmonite, KJV; Tahkemonite, NIV). "A Tahchemonite, chief of the captains," among David's men (2 Sam. 23:8), is in 1 Chron. 11:11 called "Jashobeam, the son of a Hachmonite." Kennicott has concluded that "the Tahchemonite" is a corruption of the "son of Hachmoni," which was the family or local name of Jashobeam; thus, he concludes "Jashobeam the Hachmonite" to have been the true reading.

TAH'PANHES (ta'pan-hēz; Jer. 2:16; 43:7-9; 44:1; 46:14), **Tahap'anes**, ta-hap'-a-nēz; Jer.

2:16, KJV, or **Tehaph'nehes** (te-haf'ne-hēz; Ezek. 30:18). An important city in the time of Jeremiah and Ezekiel. Jeremiah (Jer. 39) and Josephus (*Ant.* 10.9.1) say that Nebuchadnezzar (Nebuzaradan) had taken Jerusalem, made Zedekiah captive, burned the city, and carried away most of the inhabitants to Babylon. A feeble remnant of Judah gathered under Johanan and fled to Tahpanhes, in Egypt. In this party were the king's daughters, Jeremiah the prophet, and Baruch, his scribe (compare other passages above). Here stood a house of Pharaoh, respecting which the command came to Jeremiah, "Take some large stones in your hands and hide them in the mortar in the brick terrace which is at the entrance of Pharaoh's palace in Tahpanhes, in the sight of some of the Jews; and say to them, 'Thus says the Lord of hosts, the God of Israel, "Behold, I am going to send and get Nebuchadnezzar the king of Babylon, My servant, and I am going to set his throne right over these stones that I have hidden; and he will spread his canopy over them," ' " (Jer. 43:8-10). That this prediction became history, and that the Babylonian king did twice invade Egypt and conquered it, is no longer doubted.

The site of Tahpanhes was found by Sir Flinders Petrie and identified with modern Tell Defenneh, an Egyptian frontier town at the easternmost mouth of the Nile River in the Delta. Petrie excavated at the site in 1883 and 1884 and found a pavement thought to be the one referred to in Jer. 43. It was a platform that served as part of the complex of fortifications. Petrie also discovered a small fort dating back to Rameses I and II (thirteenth century B.C.), although the city itself was built during the reign of Psamtik (663-609).   H.F.V.

BIBLIOGRAPHY: W. M. F. Petrie, *Tanis II:* . . . (1888), pp. 47-96.

TAH'PENES (ta'pen-ēz). An Egyptian wife of the pharaoh who received Hadad, the Edomite prince, when he fled from his father's desolated capital (1 Kings 11:18-20), about 940 B.C. The sister of Tahpenes was given to Hadad in marriage, and their son, Genubath, was "weaned" by the queen herself and brought up "in Pharaoh's house among the sons of Pharaoh." At that time Egypt was divided into perhaps three monarchies. Psusennes, of the Tanitic line, has been conjectured to have been the husband of this Tahpenes, and the brother-in-law of Hadad, and the father-in-law of Solomon; but there has been no name found among those of that period bearing any resemblance to Tahpenes.

TA'HREA (ta'rē-a). A great-grandson of Jonathan, and one of the four sons of Micah (1 Chron. 9:41), after 1037 B.C. In the parallel passage (8:35) he is called *Tarea* (which see).

TAH'TIM-HOD'SHI (ta-tim-hod'shi). One of

the places visited by Joab during his census of the land of Israel. It occurs between Gilead and Dan-jaan (2 Sam. 24:6). The name has puzzled all the interpreters but is thought by some to mean "the Hittites of Kadesh." *See* Kadesh.

TAIL. *See* Fat Tail.

TAILOR. *See* Dress.

TAKEN UP (Gk. *metatethē*, "placed over into another sphere"). The term is used in Heb. 11:5 of Enoch who was "taken up [KJV, 'translated'] so that he should not see death . . . for he obtained the witness that before his being taken up he was pleasing to God." Genesis 5:24 records that he was changed without seeing death from an unglorified earthly state to one of glory and heavenly immortality.

TALENT. A weight and a unit of money. *See* Metrology.

TAL'ITHA KUM (tal'i-tha koom). Two Aram. words (Mark 5:41), signifying "Little girl, arise."

TAL'MAI (tal'mī; "pertaining to furrows, plowman," but cf. Hurrian *talma*, "big").

1. One of the gigantic sons of Anak who dwelt in Hebron (Num. 13:22). They were expelled from their stronghold by Caleb (Josh. 15:14) and killed by the men of Judah (Judg. 1:10), about 1380 B.C. There is a tall race, of light complexion, figured on the Egyptian monuments and called in the hieroglyphic inscriptions Tanmahu, who have been supposed to represent the descendants of this man. The interchange of the sound *l* for *n*, so constant in all languages, makes plausible the conjecture that this is the Egyptian rendering of Talmai.

2. The son of Ammihud, and king of Geshur, a small Aramaean kingdom in the NE of Bashan (2 Sam. 3:3; 13:37; 1 Chron. 3:2). His daughter Maacah was one of David's wives and mother of Absalom, before 1000 B.C.

TAL'MON (tal'mon). The head of a family of gatekeepers in the Temple, "the gatekeepers for the camp of the sons of Levi" (1 Chron. 9:17-18; Neh. 11:19). Some of his descendants returned with Zerubbabel (Ezra 2:42; Neh. 7:45) and were employed in their hereditary office in the days of Nehemiah and Ezra (12:25).

TA'MAH (ta'ma). *See* Temah.

TA'MAR (ta'mer; "a palm tree").

1. The wife of Er, the son of Judah and, after his death, of his brother Onan. The sudden death of his two sons so soon after their marriage with Tamar made Judah hesitate to give her the third also, thinking, very likely, according to a superstition (Tobit 2:7ff.), that either she herself or marriage with her had been the cause of their deaths. He therefore sent her to her father, with the promise that he would give her his youngest son as soon as he was grown up, though he never

intended to do so. Desirous of retaining the family inheritance and name through children, Tamar waited until satisfied that Shelah was not to be given to her as a husband and then determined to procure children from Judah himself, who had become a widower. She ensnared him by pretending to be a prostitute consecrated to the impure rites of Canaanite worship. He gave her pledges, which she produced some three months later, when she was accused of unchastity and sentenced to death by Judah. He acknowledged his own guilt and the provocation he had furnished her to do wrong. Tamar's life was spared, and she became the mother of the twins Perez and Zerah (Gen. 38:6-30; Matt. 1:3), about 1925 B.C.

2. A daughter of David by Maacah, as is evident from her being the full sister of Absalom (2 Sam. 13:1; cf. 3:3). Amnon, the eldest son of David by Ahinoam (3:2), desired Tamar because of her beauty, and, being unable to gratify that desire, he "made himself ill." Jonadab noticed his condition and, learning its cause, suggested to him the means of accomplishing his purpose. Amnon feigned illness and begged his father, who visited him, to allow his sister to come to his house and prepare food for which he had a fancy. She came and prepared some cakes, probably in an outer room; but Amnon refused to eat, and, ordering all his attendants to retire, he called her into his chamber and there raped her. Amnon's love gave way to brutal hatred, and he ordered her to leave his apartments. Tamar remonstrated, telling him that this wrong would be greater than that already done her. The meaning of this seems to be that by being thus sent away it would inevitably be supposed that she had been guilty of some shameful conduct herself. Her brother would not listen to her but ordered one of the attendants to put her out and bolt the door. Despite the fact that she wore the dress of a princess, a "long-sleeved garment," Amnon's servant treated her as a common woman and turned her out of the house. Then Tamar put ashes upon her head, rent her royal dress, laid her hand upon her head, and ran crying through the streets. She shortly encountered Absalom, who took her to his house, where she remained in a state of widowhood. David failed to punish the crime of his firstborn, but Tamar was avenged two years afterward by Absalom (13:1-32; 1 Chron. 3:9), about 980 B.C.

3. Daughter of Absalom (2 Sam. 14:27). She ultimately, by her marriage with Uriel of Gibeah, became the mother of Maacah, the future queen of Judah, or wife of Abijah (1 Kings 15:2).

4. A place on the southern border of Palestine, supposed to be Thamara, on the road from Hebron to Elath (Ezek. 47:19; 48:28).

BIBLIOGRAPHY: For *Wife of Er*, see: R. S. Candlish, *Studies in Genesis* (1979), pp. 598-607.

For *Daughter of David*, see: J. Kitto, *Daily Bible*

Illustrations (1981), 1:769-72; F. W. Krummacher, *David, The King of Israel* (1983), pp. 397-400.

TAMARISK TREE (Gen. 21:33; 1 Sam. 22:6; 31:13). A tree planted by Abraham at Beersheba when he "called on the name of the Lord, the Everlasting God." With its long life, hard wood, and evergreen leaves, this tree was a type of the ever-enduring grace of the faithful, covenant-keeping God. *See also* Vegetable Kingdom.

TAMBOURINE. *See* Music.

TAM'MUZ (tam'uz). The name of the fourth Babylonian month and of an ancient Akkadian deity. *See* Gods, False.

TA'NACH (ta'nak; Josh. 21:25, KJV). *See* Taanach.

TANHU'METH (tan-hu'meth; "consolation"). The father of *Seraiah* (which see), in the time of Gedaliah (2 Kings 25:23), 588 B.C. In this passage he appears as a Netophathite by the clerical omission of another name, as is evident from the parallel passage (Jer. 40:8).

TANIS. *See* Zoan-Tanis.

TANNER. A dresser of hides (Acts 9:43). *See* Handicrafts: Leatherworker.

TA'PHATH (ta'fath). The daughter of Solomon, who married Ben-abinadab, who was deputy for the region of Dor (1 Kings 4:11), after 960 B.C.

TAPPU'AH (tap-pū'a; an "apple").
1. The second named of the four sons of Hebron, of the lineage of Caleb (1 Chron. 2:43), before 1370 B.C.
2. A city of Judah in the Shephelah, or lowland (Josh. 15:34), probably Beit-Nettif (Beth-letepha, a corruption of Beth-el-Taphua).
3. A town in the tribe of Ephraim (Josh. 16:8), near Manasseh, in which latter territory probably lay the "land of Tappuah" (17:8). It probably contained a fine spring, hence En-tappuah, and is commonly identified with Sheik Abu Zarad, near present-day Jāsūf, about eight miles S of Shechem.

TAR. *See* Mineral Kingdom.

TA'RAH (ta'ra). *See* Terah.

TAR'ALAH (tar'a-la). A town in the western section of the territory of Benjamin (Josh. 18:27), perhaps identical with the modern village of Beit-Tirza in Wadi Ahmed, N of Beit-Jala.

TA'REA (ta're-a). Son of Micah, in the lineage of King Saul (1 Chron. 8:35; "Tahrea" in 9:41).

TARES. *See* Vegetable Kingdom.

TARGET (Heb. *kîdôn*), a javelin (1 Sam. 17:6, KJV); or *ṣinnâ*, a large shield (1 Kings 10:16; 2 Chron. 9:15; 14:8, KJV). The NIV renders Heb. *maṭṭār* (1 Sam. 20:20; Job 16:12), *maṭṭārā'* (Lam. 3:12), and *mipgā'* (Job 7:20) as "target."

TAR'PELITES (tar'pel-its; only Ezra 4:9, KJV). Some conjecture that the word has no ethnic connotation but is a special title of Persian officials at Samaria. *See* Tripolis.

TAR'SHISH (tar'shish).
1. This is a Phoenician word from the Akkad. meaning smelting plant or refinery. The term *tarshish* is employed in the OT in connection with ships, merchants, and trade (1 Kings 10:22; 22:48; "trading ships," NIV). The "navy," or "fleet of Tarshish" (Heb. *'onî tarshîsh*) that Solomon's ally Hiram I of Tyre built for the Hebrew monarch at Ezion-geber on the Persian Gulf has been illuminated from ancient oriental sources. A better rendering of Solomon's merchant marine in the light of increased knowledge of early Phoenician trading activities in the Mediterranean would be "smeltery" or "refining fleet," which brought smelted metal home from the colonial mines. Phoenician boats used to ply the sea regularly, transporting smelted ores from the mining towns in Sardinia and Spain. A Phoenician inscription from Nora in Sardinia from the ninth century B.C. refers to a *tarshish*, or smelting site, on this island. Smeltery fleets or *tarshish* ships hauled material from this and other mining stations in the western Mediterranean. Ships of *tarshish* were built by Jehoshaphat in imitation of Solomon. His venture, however, came to grief (22:49; 2 Chron. 20:36-37). Tarshish ships developed from the original idea of material-carrying boats to all ships of first-rate magnitude to whatever place the voyage may have taken them (Ps. 48:7; Isa. 23:1; 60:9; Ezek. 27:25).
2. Second son of Javan, the grandson of Japheth (Gen. 10:4; 1 Chron. 1:7).
3. A man, the son of Bilhan, the Benjaminite (1 Chron. 7:10).
4. A high Persian official at Susa (Shushan, KJV; Esther 1:14).   M.F.U.
BIBLIOGRAPHY: W. F. Albright, *Bulletin of the American Schools of Oriental Research* 83 (1941): 14ff.; id., *Studies in the History of Culture* (1942), pp. 11-50.

TAR'SUS (tar'sus). The capital of Cilicia, and the birthplace and early residence of the apostle Paul (Acts 9:11; 21:39; 22:3). The passages 9:30 and 11:25 give the limits of his residence in his native town, which succeeded the first visit to Jerusalem and preceded his active ministry at Antioch and elsewhere (cf. 22:21; Gal. 1:21). It was during this period, probably, that he planted the gospel there, and it has never since entirely died out. It would seem that Paul was there also at the beginning of his second and third missionary journeys (Acts 15:41; 18:23).

Tarsus was situated in a wide and fertile plain on the banks of the Cydnus, which flowed through it; hence it is sometimes called Tarsoi in the plural. The founding of Tarsus is legendary. The Assyrians entered Cilicia c. 850 B.C., and

Shalmaneser III's Black Obelisk mentions the taking of the city. It appears in history in Xenophon's time, when it was a city of considerable importance. It was occupied by Cyrus and his troops for twenty days and plundered.

Cleopatra's Arch at Tarsus

After Alexander's conquests had swept this way and the Seleucid kingdom was established at Antioch, Tarsus usually belonged to that kingdom, though for a time it was under the Ptolemies. In the civil wars of Rome it took Caesar's side, and on the occasion of a visit from him had its name changed to Juliopolis. Augustus made it a "free city." It was renowned as a place of education under the early Roman emperors. Strabo compares it in this respect to Athens and Alexandria. Tarsus also was a place of much commerce.

"It is probable, but not certain, that Paul's family had been planted in Tarsus with full rights as part of a colony settled there by one of the Seleucid kings in order to strengthen their hold on the city. . . . The Seleucid kings seem to have had a preference for Jewish colonists in their foundations in Asia Minor" (Ramsay, *Paul the Traveller*, p. 32). Both land and sea highways made Tarsus a famed ancient emporium. The famous Cilician Gates, one of antiquity's most famous mountain passes, is not far distant, and access by water to the Mediterranean made Tarsus a famous trading center.

BIBLIOGRAPHY: E. M. Blaiklock, *The Cities of the New Testament* (1965), pp. 18-21; W. M. Ramsay, *The Cities of St. Paul* (1965), pp. 85-245.

TAR′TAK. *See* Gods, False.

TAR′TAN (tar′tan; Assyr. *tartanu* and *turtanu*). The title or official designation of the commander in chief of the Assyrian army (2 Kings 18:17; the NIV translates the term as "supreme commander"). Archaeology has shown conclusively that the expression "tartan" is not a proper name.   M.F.U.

TASKMASTERS (Heb. *śārê missîm*, "masters of burdens," Ex. 1:11; *nāgaś*, to "drive," 3:7; 5:6-

14). Persons appointed by order of Pharaoh to see that the Hebrews were assigned hard, wearing toil. It was his hope, by such oppression, to break down the physical strength of Israel and thus lessen their offspring; and also to crush their spirit so as to banish the very wish for liberty. So Israel was compelled to build provision cities, i.e., cities for storing the harvests.

TASSEL (Heb. *gᵉdîl*, "twisted" thread, Deut. 22:12; *ṣiṣit*, "flowery, bloomlike," as in Num. 15:38-39). In both references, the KJV renders the word "fringe." Tassels were to be sewn upon the hem of the outside garment to remind the Israelites of the commandments of God, that they might have them constantly before their eyes and follow them. These tassels were made of twisted blue thread and fastened upon each corner of the garment. The color blue was used to remind the Jews of the heavenly origin of the law. Fringed garments, elaborately wrought, were common among the ancient Egyptians and Babylonians.

TAT′TENAI (tat′en-ī). A Persian governor of Samaria when Zerubbabel began to rebuild Jerusalem. He seems to have been appealed to by the Samaritans to oppose that undertaking and, accompanied by another high official, Shethar-bozenai, went to Jerusalem. They sent a fair and temperate report of what they saw and heard to the supreme government, suggesting that search be instituted to learn whether the building was going on in accordance with a royal decree (Ezra 5:3, 6). The statement of the work of the Jews was verified by the discovery of the original decree of Cyrus, and Tattenai and his colleagues applied themselves with vigor to the execution of the royal commands (6:6, 13), 536-519 B.C.

TATTLER (Gr. *phluaros*, from *phluō*, "to throw up bubbles," 1 Tim. 5:13, KJV). A gossip.

TAU. *See* Tav.

TAV (ת) (tou). Written tau in the KJV, the twenty-second and last letter of the Heb. alphabet, pronounced "t," or "th" when preceded by a vowel. This letter (Heb. *taw*) heads the twenty-second section of Ps. 119, in which portion every verse of the original Heb. commences with this letter.   M.F.U.

TAVERN. *See* Inn.

TAW. *See* Tav.

TAX′ES.
  In Early Times. From the very beginning of the Mosaic polity provision was made for a national income. Taxes, like all other things in that polity, had a religious origin and import. While Israel was in the migratory state, only such incidental taxes were levied, or, rather, such voluntary contributions were received as need required. Only when the nation became settled in

Palestine did taxation assume a regular and organized form.

Under the Judges. Under the theocratic government, provided for by the law, the only payments obligatory upon the people as being of permanent obligation were: the *tithes* (which see), the *firstfruits* (which see), the redemption money of the *firstborn* (which see), and such other offerings as belonged to special occasions.

Under the Monarchy. The kingdom, with its centralized government and greater magnificence, involved, of course, a larger expenditure and, therefore, a heavier taxation. The chief burdens appear to have been: (1) A tithe of the produce both of the soil and of livestock (1 Sam. 8:15, 17); (2) forced military service for a month every year (1 Sam. 8:12; 1 Kings 9:22; 1 Chron. 27:1); (3) gifts to the king (1 Sam. 10:27; 16:20; 17:18); (4) import duties (1 Kings 10:15); (5) the monopoly of certain branches of commerce (1 Kings 9:28; 10:28-29); (6) the appropriation to the king's use of the early crop of hay (Amos 7:1). At times, too, in the history of both kingdoms there were special burdens. A tribute of fifty shekels a head had to be paid by Menahem to the Assyrian king (2 Kings 15:20), and under his successor, Hoshea, this assumed the form of an annual tribute (17:4).

Under the Persians. The financial system of Darius Hystaspes provided for the payment by each satrap of a fixed sum as the tribute due from his province. In Judea, as in other provinces, the inhabitants had to provide in kind for the maintenance of the governor's household, besides a money payment of forty shekels a day (Neh. 5:14-15). A formal enumeration is given in Ezra 4:13 and 7:24 of the three great branches of the revenue: (1) the fixed, *measured* payments (Heb. *middâ*), probably direct taxation; (2) the excise or *octroi,* on articles of consumption (Heb. *bᵉlō*); (3) probably toll payable at bridges, forts, or certain stations on the highway, Heb. *hēlek.* The influence of Ezra secured for the whole ecclesiastical order, from the priests down to the Temple servants, an immunity from all three (Ezra 7:24);

Milestone, Capernaum—an important frontier town for taxes.

but the burden pressed heavily upon the people in general.

Under Egypt and Syria. The taxes imposed upon the Jews became still heavier, the "farming" system of finance being adopted in the worst form. The taxes were put up at auction; and the contract sum for those of Phoenicia, Judea, and Samaria has been estimated at about 8,000 talents. A man would bid double that sum and would then force from the province a handsome profit for himself.

Roman Taxation. "The Roman taxation, which bore upon Israel with such crushing weight, was systematic, cruel, relentless, and utterly regardless. In general, the provinces of the Roman empire, and what of Palestine belonged to them, were subject to two great taxes—poll tax (or, rather, income tax) and ground tax. All property and income that fell not under the ground tax was subject to poll tax, which amounted for Syria and Cilicia to one per cent. The poll tax was really twofold, consisting of income tax and head money, the latter, of course, the same in all cases, and levied on all persons (bond or free) up to the age of sixty-five—women being liable from the age of twelve, and men from that of fourteen. Landed property was subject to a tax of one tenth of all grain and one fifth of the wine and fruit grown, partly in product and partly commuted into money. Besides these, there was tax and duty on all imports and exports, levied on the great public highways and in the seaports. Then there was bridge money and road money, and duty on all that was bought and sold in the towns. . . . The Romans had a peculiar way of levying these taxes—not directly, but indirectly—which kept the treasury quite safe, whatever harm it might inflict upon the taxpayer, while at the same time it threw upon him the whole cost of the collection. Senators and magistrates were prohibited from engaging in business or trade; but the highest order, the equestrian, was largely composed of great capitalists. These Roman knights formed joint stock companies which bought at public auction the revenues of a province at a fixed price, generally for five years. The board had its chairman, or *magister,* and its offices at Rome. These were the real publicans, who underlet certain of the taxes" (Edersheim, *Sketches of Jewish Social Life,* pp. 53ff.). See Tribute.

BIBLIOGRAPHY: A. Edersheim, *Sketches of Jewish Social Life in the Days of Christ* (1961), pp. 45f., 52-56; H. Daniel-Rops, *Daily Life in Palestine at the Time of Christ* (1962), pp. 161-65; A. N. Sherwin-White, *Roman Society and Roman Law in the New Testament* (1963), pp. 125-27.

TAX-GATHERER (Gk. *telōnēs;* KJV "publican"). A collector of the Roman revenue. The Roman Senate had found it convenient, at a period as early as—if not earlier than—the second Punic war, to farm the *vectigalia* (direct taxes) and the portoria (customs) to capitalists, who undertook to pay a given sum into the treasury (in publicum) and so received the name of publicani. Contracts of this kind fell naturally into the hands of the equites, who were the commercial and financial class of Romans. Not infrequently they went beyond the means of any individual capitalist, and a joint-stock company (societas) was formed, with one of the partners, or an agent appointed by them, acting as managing director (magister). Under this officer, who resided commonly at Rome, transacting the business of the company, paying profits to the partners and the like, were the submagistri, living in the provinces. Under them, in like manner, were the portitores, the actual customhouse officers, who examined each bale of goods exported or imported, assessed its value more or less arbitrarily, wrote out the ticket, and enforced payment. The latter were commonly natives of the province in which they were stationed, being brought daily into contact with all classes of the population. It is this class (portitores) to which the term tax-gatherer refers exclusively in the NT. These tax-gatherers were encouraged by their superior in vexatious and even fraudulent exactions, and remedy was almost impossible. They overcharged (Luke 3:13) and brought false charges of smuggling in the hope of extorting hush money (19:8). The strong feeling of many Jews as to the unlawfulness of paying tribute made matters worse. The scribes (Matt. 22:16-21) for the most part were not against it and thus were considered traitors. The publicans were also regarded as traitors and apostates, defiled by their frequent contacts with the heathen and being willing tools of the oppressor. Practically excommunicated, this class furnished some of the earliest disciples of John the Baptist and Jesus. The position of Zaccheus as a "chief tax-gatherer" (Luke 19:2, Gk. architelōnēs) implies a gradation of some kind among the publicans; perhaps he was one of the submagistri. In Augustus's day (27 B.C.-A.D. 14) the practice of selling tax-collection contracts to joint-stock companies ceased, and tax collectors were put on the public payroll. Thus a kind of Internal Revenue Service was established and continued through the rest of the NT period.

"The Talmud distinguishes two classes of publicans—the tax-gatherer in general (Gabbai) and the Mokhes or Mokhsa, who was specially the douanier, or customhouse official. Although both classes fell under the rabbinic ban, the douanier—such as Matthew was—was the object of chief execration. And this because his exactions were more vexatious and gave more scope to rapacity. The Gabbai, or tax-gatherer, collected the regular dues, which consisted of ground, income, and poll tax. . . . If this offered many opportunities for vexatious exactions and rapacious injustice, the Mokhes might inflict much greater hardship upon the poor people. There

was a tax and duty upon all imports and exports; on all that was bought and sold; bridge money, road money, harbor dues, town dues, etc. The classical reader knows the ingenuity which could invent a tax and find a name for every kind of exaction, such as on axles, wheels, pack animals, pedestrians, roads, highways; on admission to markets; on carriers, bridges, ships, and quays; on crossing rivers, on dams, on licenses—in short, on such a variety of objects that even the research of modern scholars has not been able to identify all the names. But even this was as nothing compared to the vexation of being constantly stopped on the journey, having to unload all one's pack animals, when every bale and package was opened, and the contents tumbled about, private letters opened, and the Mokhes ruled supreme in his insolence and rapacity" (Edersheim, Life and Times of Jesus, 1:515ff.). See Taxes.

BIBLIOGRAPHY: E. Schürer, A History of the Jewish People in the Time of Jesus Christ, ed. G. Vermes and F. Millar (1973), 1.2.71f.; I. Abrahams, Studies in Pharisaism and the Gospels (1967), pp. 54-61.

TAXING. See Census: New Testament.

TEACH (Heb. properly lāmad, but many other words also; Gk. didaskō, and other terms). Inasmuch as men are delivered from the bondage of sin and built up in righteousness through the agency of the truth, teaching becomes essential. Moses and Aaron were teachers of Israel in the statutes of Jehovah (Ex. 18:20; Lev. 10:11; 14:57), having been first taught of God (Ex. 4:12). Moses commanded fathers to teach their children the commandments of God with persistency and care (Deut. 4:9-10, 14; 11:19). The priests were to instruct the people, especially by reading the law to them at the feast of Tabernacles, in the seventh year (24:8; 31:9-13). It is frequently recorded of Jesus that He taught the people (Matt. 5:2; Mark 1:21; 4:2; Luke 4:15, 31; etc.).

Teaching is an important branch of the commission that Christ gave to His apostles before His ascension. "Go," said He, "and make disciples of all the nations, . . . teaching them" (Matt. 28:19-20); as recorded by Mark, another evangelist, "Preach the gospel to all creation" (Mark 16:15). In this way they were to make disciples, as the Gk. mathēteusate states. It is one of the precious promises of the new covenant that all its subjects shall be "taught of the Lord" (Isa. 54:13; quoted by Jesus, John 6:45).

"Teachers" are mentioned as among those receiving divine gifts (Eph. 4:11), i.e., those who taught in the religious assemblies of Christians, with the special assistance of the Holy Spirit (cf. 1 Cor. 12:28-30; Acts 13:1; James 3:1). If anyone was accepted as a teacher in this sense, he was the more dangerous, as he would seem to be inspired in his utterances (2:1).

BIBLIOGRAPHY: A. Edersheim, Sketches of Jewish Social Life in the Days of Christ (1961), pp. 133-37; R. de

Vaux, *Ancient Israel: Its Life and Institutions* (1961), pp. 48-50.

TEACHER (Gk. *didaskalos,* Luke 2:46; 5:17; Acts 5:34). Jewish teachers, at least some of them, had private lecture rooms but also taught in public. Their method was the same as prevailed among the Greeks, that is, any disciple was allowed to ask questions to which the teacher replied. They did not have any official position and received no salary other than voluntary gifts from their disciples. They were chiefly of the sect of the Pharisees. *See* Lawyer; Rabbi.

TEARS. *See* Mourn.

TE'BAH (te'ba; "slaughter"). The first named of the four sons of Nahor by his concubine Reumah (Gen. 22:24). *See* Betah.

TEBALI'AH (teb-a-lī'a; "Jehovah has immersed," i.e., "dipped or immersed"). The third named of the sons of Hosah, "of the sons of Merari" (1 Chron. 26:10, 11). *See* Tabaliah.

TE'BETH (te'beth; Akkad. *ṭebetu,* "the month of sinking in," i.e., wet, muddy month). The tenth month of the second year of the Hebrews (Esther 2:16), corresponding in the main to January.

TEHAPH'NEHES (te-haf'ne-hēz; Ezek. 30:18). *See* Tahpanhes.

TEHIN'NAH (te-hin'na; "graciousness"). A name occurring in the genealogy of the men of Recah, of the tribe of Judah. He is mentioned as a son of Eshton and founder of the city of Ir-na-hash (1 Chron. 4:12).

TEIL TREE. *See* Vegetable Kingdom.

TE'KEL (te'kel; Aram. *tᵉḳal,* "weighed"). The second word in the sentence of the Babylonian king (Dan. 5:25, 27). The interpretation presents the double meaning "You have been weighed on the scales and found deficient," i.e., in moral worth.

TEKO'A (te-kō'a; perhaps "trumpet clang"). A town in Judah, about six miles S of Bethlehem and on the range of hills that rise near Hebron and stretch toward the Dead Sea. By the "wilderness of Tekoa" (2 Chron. 20:20) must be understood the adjacent region E of the town. Tekoa is now called Tequa and is a ruined site, showing many Hebrew traces. Tekoa is first mentioned in the account (2 Sam. 14:2, 4, 9) of Joab's employing a "wise woman" residing there to effect a reconciliation between David and Absalom. Here also Ira the son of Ikkesh, one of David's thirty "mighty men," was born, and therefore was called "the Tekoite" (23:26). Tekoa was one of the places fortified by Rehoboam at the beginning of his reign to prevent an invasion from the S (2 Chron. 11:6). People from Tekoa took part in building the walls of Jerusalem after the captivity (Neh. 3:5, 27). Jeremiah exclaims (Jer. 6:1),

"Now blow a trumpet in Tekoa, and raise a signal over Beth-haccerem," both signals warning of an enemy's approach. Tekoa was also the birthplace of Amos (Amos 1:1), and here he was called to be a prophet of God.

BIBLIOGRAPHY: M. H. Heicksen, *Grace Journal* 10 (1969): 3-10; J. J. Davis, *Bulletin of the Near Eastern Archaeological Society* 4 (1974): 27-49.

Tell Lachish

TEKO'ITE (te-kō'īt). An inhabitant of *Tekoah* (which see).

TEL-A'BIB (tel-a'bib; "mound or hill of ears of grain"). The residence of Ezekiel on the river Chebar (Ezek. 3:15). The Chebar was a great canal (called a river, *Nāru* in Babylonia) SE of Babylon. Tel-abib doubtless derives its name from the fertility of the valley, rich in grain, by which it was surrounded. The NIV renders it Tel Aviv.

TE'LAH (te'la; "fracture, breach, break"). The son of Rephah (or Resheph), and father of Tahan, in the lineage between Ephraim and Joshua (1 Chron. 7:25), before 1440 B.C.

TELA'IM (te-la'im; "young lambs"). Probably the same as *Telem* (which see), the place where Saul gathered his army to fight Amalek (1 Sam. 15:4).

TELAS'SAR (te-las'er; "the hill of Asshur"). A city that lay in the hill country of the upper Mesopotamian plain identified by some as Tel Afer. It is mentioned in 2 Kings 19:12 and in Isa. 37:12 as a city inhabited by "the sons of Eden," which had been conquered and was held in the time of Sennacherib by the Assyrians. It was apparently a city of Bit Adini, a small kingdom on the upper Euphrates.

TEL A'VIV. *See* Tel Abib.

TE'LEM (te'lem).
1. One of the Temple gatekeepers who put away his Gentile wife (Ezra 10:24), 456 b.c.
2. A town on the southern border of Judah

(Josh. 15:24), between Ziph and Bealoth. It is very probably the same as *Telaim* (which see).

TEL-HAR'ESHA (tel-har'e-sha; Neh. 7:61, KJV). *See* Tel-harsha.

TEL-HAR'SHA (tel-har'sha; "mound of workmanship"), **Tel Harsha** (NIV), **Tel-harsa** (KJV). One of the Babylonian towns from which some Jews, who "could not show their fathers' houses, or their descendants, whether they were of Israel," returned to Judea with Zerubbabel (Neh. 7:61; cf. Ezra 2:59). It was probably in the low country near the sea, in the neighborhood of Tel-melah and Cherub.

TELL. An Arab. word denoting a truncated artificial mound built up by successive layers of ancient civilization. The word occurs in Heb. in Josh. 11:13: "Israel did not burn any cities that stood on their mounds [Heb. *'al tillam*], except Hazor alone, which Joshua burned." The word *tell* is now widely used in place names in Arab countries in the Near Middle East and in Egypt and, as correctly translated in the biblical passage, denotes a mound. Examples of place names incorporating *tell* are numerous in Palestine: Tell en Nasbeh, Tell el Ful (Gibeah), Tell Jezer (Gezer), Tell ed-Duweir (Lachish), etc. In Egypt the well-known Tell Amarna is found. In Mesopotamia examples are Tell Abib, Tell Melah, and many others. When a site had been occupied for many centuries, the occupational levels formed one upon another "in such a way as to suggest a giant layer cake" (Millar Burrows, *What Mean These Stones?* [1941], p. 12). Digging in such a way as to keep the superimposed occupational levels distinct is the modern scientific means of excavation. The remains found in each layer, particularly pottery, may be carefully studied and clearly dated as the result of the now-developed science of stratigraphy. When a city was destroyed by a catastrophe such as war, fire, or earthquake, new settlers simply leveled the ruins and built upon them. Thus the ground level of the new city was raised several feet higher than the old one and the remnants of the old lay under the new. This process kept repeating as time went on until the occupational site rose higher and higher. When the site was finally abandoned, the winds and rains of many years leveled off the top and eroded the sides, except where the process was arrested by a city wall. This is the explanation of the flat tops of the mounds. The fact that ancient oriental cities followed this pattern has been one of the greatest boons to modern scientific archaeology and the precise dating of ancient cultures. Tell Beisan (*see* figure 6), the ancient fortress city of Beth-shan (1 Sam. 31:10), which guarded the eastern approaches of the valley of Esdraelon, has been excavated and shows eighteen levels from the top, running from A.D. 600 (Level 1) to c. 3500 B.C. (Level 18). When the archaeologist strikes virgin soil, he knows he has reached the time when the site was first occupied. M.F.U.

The tell on which the ancient city of Beersheba stood

BIBLIOGRAPHY: J. A. Thompson, *The Bible and Archaeology* (1982), pp. 3-13.

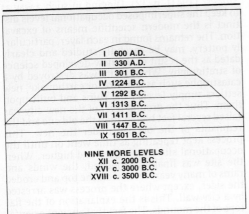

Level	Date
I	600 A.D.
II	330 A.D.
III	301 B.C.
IV	1224 B.C.
V	1292 B.C.
VI	1313 B.C.
VII	1411 B.C.
VIII	1447 B.C.
IX	1501 B.C.

NINE MORE LEVELS

XII	c. 2000 B.C.
XVI	c. 3000 B.C.
XVIII	c. 3500 B.C.

Fig. 6. Illustration of the occupational levels (strata) of a mound (tell). This is Tell Beisan, ancient fortress city of Bethshan, which guarded the eastern approaches to the Valley of Esdraelon.

TELL EL-AMAR'NA (tel el-a-mar'na; "mound of the city of the horizon"). The frequent name for the Amarna site, though there has never been a mound there. It is the ancient Akhetaton, the capital city of Amenhotep IV (Akhnaton) who reigned c. 1387-1366 B.C. *See* Amarna, el-.

TEL-ME'LAH (tel-me'la; "hill of salt," called in 1 Esd. 5:36 "Thermeleth"). A place probably near the Persian Gulf, from which the Jews returned (Ezra 2:59; Neh. 7:61).

TE'MA (tē'ma). The ninth son of Ishmael (Gen. 25:15; 1 Chron. 1:30); from whom came the tribe called after him, mentioned in Job 6:19; Jer. 25:23; also the land occupied by this tribe (Isa. 21:14). It denotes Taima in Arabia midway between Damascus and Mecca.

TE'MAH (tē'ma). The sons of Temah were among the Temple servants who returned with Zerubbabel (Ezra 2:53; Neh. 7:55), before 536 B.C.

TE'MAN (tē'man; the "south," or "right").

1. The eldest son of Eliphaz, the son of Esau (Gen. 36:11; 1 Chron. 1:36). He was a chief of the Edomites (Gen. 36:15, 42; 1 Chron. 1:36, 53) and gave his name to the region in which the tribe he founded settled (Gen. 36:34), after 1900 B.C.

2. The country of the Temanites, the southern portion of Edom. In after ages it was the chief stronghold of Edom; hence when the Lord, by the prophet Ezekiel, pronounced the doom of Edom, He said, "I will lay it waste; from Teman even to Dedan they will fall by the sword" (Ezek. 25:13). The Temanites were celebrated for their courage and wisdom (Jer. 49:7); hence the force and point of Obadiah's judgment "Your mighty men will be dismayed, O Teman" (Obad. 9). In Hab. 3:3 Teman is used for Edom in general.

TEMPERANCE. *See* Self-control; Temperate.

TEMPERATE (Gk. *sōphrōn*). Has the meaning of a *sound mind* (Titus 2:2).

TEMPLE. A building set apart for the worship of a deity. Here attention is especially called to the three buildings at Jerusalem that successively bore the name of Temple. As these were all built upon the same site and after the same general pattern, they were in nature and design the same, namely, that of the one built by Solomon. This latter was, in its essential features, a reproduction of the Tabernacle, in more lasting material and having the necessary adjuncts of a permanent building.

Name. The usual and appropriate Heb. term for temple is *hêkāl*, an old Akkad. word signifying "palace, a large building," frequently joined with *Jehovah*, and denoting "the palace of deity." Occasionally it is also qualified by *qōdesh* ("sanctuary"), to designate its sacredness. Sometimes the simpler phrase "house of Jehovah" (Heb. *beth yhwh*) is used.

The Gk. terms employed are *naos* ("shrine"), and *hieron* (a "sacred" place).

The Temple of Solomon. The idea that the Tabernacle, a temporary building, should be supplanted by a permanent one of stone, seems to have been suggested to David by the Spirit (1 Chron. 28:12, 19), especially after he had secured peace by conquest of his enemies (2 Sam. 7:1-13; 1 Chron. 17:1-14; 28:1-19); but he was forbidden to build for the reason that he stated to Solomon, "But the word of the Lord came to me, saying, 'You have shed much blood, and have waged great wars; you shall not build a house to My name, because you have shed so much blood on the earth before Me' " (1 Chron. 22:8). He, however, collected much material for the building and made arrangements to have the task completed by his son Solomon. The latter was a man of peace, and his reign a period of peace and prosperity (2 Sam. 7:9-13; 1 Kings 5:3-4; 1 Chron. 22:7-10).

Preparation. Solomon, as soon as he was securely seated upon the throne, made arrangements for beginning to build the Temple (1 Chron. 22, 28-29). He entered into a treaty with Hiram king of Tyre, stipulating that this monarch should permit him to get cedar and cypress wood and blocks of stone from Lebanon, and that he would allow workmen sent by Solomon to fell the wood and quarry and hew the stones, under the direction of skilled workmen, subjects of Hiram. In return Solomon was to send supplies of wheat, oil, and wine. It was also arranged that Solomon was to have the services of a skillful artist by the name of Huram-abi to take charge of the castings and of the manufacare of the more valuable furnishings of the Temple (1 Kings 5; 2 Chron. 2). So, in the fourth year of his reign, c. 960 B.C., Solomon began the erection of the sacred edifice, which was built on Mt. Moriah to the E of Zion, an eminence that David himself had selected for the purpose when he built an altar upon it after the plague had ceased (1 Chron. 21:18, 26; 22:1). To secure an adequate site for the Temple and its courts, an area of at least 600 by 300 feet was required. The summit of the hill had to be leveled and slightly enlarged by means of fill and retaining walls built on the sides. The edifice was completed in the eleventh year of Solomon's reign, i.e., in seven and a half years (c. 953 B.C.).

The Structure. The Temple proper was a building formed of hewn stones, 60 cubits long, 20 wide, and 30 in height (measuring from the inside), and covered with a flat roof composed of rafters and boards of cedar, overlaid with marble (*see* figure 7 for a plan of the Temple). Josephus (*Ant.* 8.3.2) says, "[The height of the temple] was sixty cubits, and the length was the same, and its breadth twenty. There was another [story of equal dimensions]; so that the entire [height] of the temple was a hundred and twenty cubits." Josephus probably gave the external dimensions, whereas in the book of Kings the internal measurements are given. Inside, the building was divided by means of a partition of cedar wood into the Holy Place and the Most Holy Place, so that the former was 40 cubits long, 20 wide, and 30 high, and the latter was a cube measuring 20 cubits in each direction. The other 10 cubits formed "upper rooms" (2 Chron. 3:9). On the inside the walls were lined with wood, so as to cover the stones; the walls and roof were covered with cedar and the floor with planks of cypress wood. The side walls were covered over with carved work, representing cherubim, palms, garlands, and opening flowers (1 Kings 6:18; 2 Chron. 3:5), so that all was overlaid with thin plates of gold. The floor as well as the walls and ceilings were covered with gold (1 Kings 6:30).

The entrance to the Holy of Holies consisted of a folding door in the partition wall, four cubits wide, made of olive wood and ornamented with overlaid carvings of cherubim, palms, and opening flowers. These doors, as well as those at the entrance of the Holy Place, were hung on hinges of gold (7:50). These doors stood open, but a veil, similar in material and ornamentation to the veil in the Tabernacle, hung over them. The entrance to the Holy Place consisted of a folding door of cypress wood with doorposts of olive wood, each one being divided into an upper and lower section (like Dutch doors), and ornamented in the same manner as the door of the Holy of Holies.

In the front of the building was a porch 20 cubits wide and 10 cubits deep (6:3; 2 Chron. 3:4). There would seem to be an error in the text (cf. 2 Chron. 3:4) as to the height of the "porch";

because a front 120 cubits high to a house only 30 cubits high could not properly be called *'ulām* (a "porch"); it could only have been a *migdāl* (a "tower"). Two bronze pillars, Jachin and Boaz (*see* below), stood at the entrance of the Temple. On the sides and rear of the building, wings were added, each three stories high, containing rooms for storing furniture and provisions required for the Temple service. These wings were so constructed that the rafters of the different stories rested upon projections on the outside of the walls of the main building, so as to avoid inserting them in the walls themselves (1 Kings 6:5-6). Each story was 5 cubits high, and 5, 6, and 7 cubits wide, respectively; they were connected by passages and stairs (6:8).

The Courts. There was an inner court (1 Kings 6:36) running around the Temple and reserved exclusively for the priests. It was formed by an outer or boundary wall, composed of three layers of hewn stone and a "row of cedar beams," probably laid upon the stones to protect the masonry. Outside of this was the "great court" (2 Chron. 4:9), intended for the use of the people and probably enclosed with masonry. Access to it was by doors of bronze. From the fact that the (inner) court of the priests is called "the upper court" (Jer. 36:10), it is likely that it was on a higher level than the outer court; and it is not unlikely that the Temple itself was higher than the inner court, so that the whole would have a terracelike aspect. So far as can be gathered from subsequent statements of an incidental nature (2 Kings 23:11; Jer. 35:4; 36:10; Ezek. 8; etc.), it would appear that there were vestibules and porticoes at the gates of the outer court, and that, if we may judge from the pattern of the Temple, at all four sides, probably in the corners and on both sides of the gate, as the Temple of Ezekiel's vision would seem to show. The measurement of the courts is not given, but following the analogy of the Tabernacle (cf. Ezek. 40:27), we may venture to assume that the court of the priests was 100 cubits, and the same in breadth, measuring it on the E, or front, side of the Temple. This would make the entire measurement 100 cubits wide by 200 in length. We will then have for the outer court an area of at least 400 cubits long and 200 cubits wide.

The Furniture. In the Holy of Holies was placed the Ark, with its Mercy Seat, which was taken from the Tabernacle. It stood between two cherubim, which were 10 cubits high, made of olive wood and overlaid with gold. Their wings were outstretched and were about 5 cubits long, touching each other over the Ark, while the outer wings touched the side walls of the room (1 Kings 6:23-28; 2 Chron. 3:10-13). They stood upon their feet and faced "the main room," i.e., toward the Holy Place (3:13).

In the Holy Place were the altar of incense, or

"golden altar" (1 Kings 7:48; cf. 6:22; 2 Chron. 4:19), made of cedar wood and overlaid with gold; ten golden lampstands with seven lamps to each (these were placed in front of the Holy of Holies, five of them being on the right side and five on the left; 1 Kings 7:49; 2 Chron. 4:7); and ten tables for the bread of the Presence, five being on each side (4:8). The form and construction of these objects have not been minutely described, as they were clearly modeled after those in the Tabernacle, only made on a larger scale to correspond with the greater dimensions of the Temple rooms. Of course the several articles of furniture were accompanied by their utensils—cups and snuffers for the lampstand and bowls, spoons, firepans, etc. for the tables (1 Kings 7:50; 2 Chron. 4:22; etc.).

In the inner court was the altar of burnt offering (1 Kings 8:64), which according to 2 Chron. 4:1 was 20 cubits square and 10 cubits high, and patterned after the one in the Tabernacle. The following utensils for this altar are mentioned: basins, shovels, bowls, pails, and forks (1 Kings 7:40, 45; 2 Chron. 4:11, 16). (See Altar.) A little to the S, but between the altar and the porch, stood the bronze sea, a huge round basin. There were also on each side of the altar, at the right and left wings of the Temple, ten bronze lesser lavers on wheels (1 Kings 7:27-39; 2 Chron. 4:6). See the article Laver.

Archaeology. Archaeology has shown that the plan of Solomon's Temple was characteristically Phoenician, as would be expected, since it was constructed by a Tyrian architect (1 Kings 7:13-15). Similar plans of sanctuaries of the general period, 1200-900 B.C., have been excavated in northern Syria. The temple at Tell Tainat, excavated in 1936 by the University of Chicago, is smaller but similar to Solomon's structure. At Tell Tainat the shrine gives evidence that Solomon's Temple was pre-Greek and authentic as 1 Kings 6-7 would indicate. Archaeology has also shown that the proto-Aeolian pilaster capital, extensively used in Solomon's Temple, also used at Megiddo, Samaria, and Shechem from the period 1000 to 700 B.C. The Temple decorations such as lilies, palmettes, and cherubim were likewise characteristically Syro-Phoenician. The cherubim or winged sphinxes appear hundreds of times in the iconography of western Asia between 1800 and 600 B.C. The two columns, Jachin and Boaz, are also illustrated at Tell Tainat and elsewhere in the ancient Near East. Such pillars flanked the main entrance of the Temple and were common in the first millennium B.C. in Syria, Phoenicia, and Cyprus. They spread to Assyria, where they are found in Sargon's temple at Khorsabad and to the Phoenician colonies in the Mediterranean. For archaeological light see the article Jachin and Boaz.

History. After the completion of the building, Solomon had the Ark placed in the Holy of Holies, and dedicated the Temple with solemn thanksgiving and prayer, accompanied with liberal thank offerings. This service, participated in by the heads of the tribes as well as by men from all parts of Israel, lasted seven days. So large was the number of animals offered that it was necessary for a time to convert the inner court in front of the porch into a place of sacrifice, as the altar of burnt offering was not capable of holding the multitude of sacrifices (1 Kings 8:1-6; 2 Chron. 5-6; 7:7). Immediately after the consecration prayer, which Solomon offered while kneeling upon the bronze platform that was erected in the inner court in front of the altar (2 Chron. 6:13),

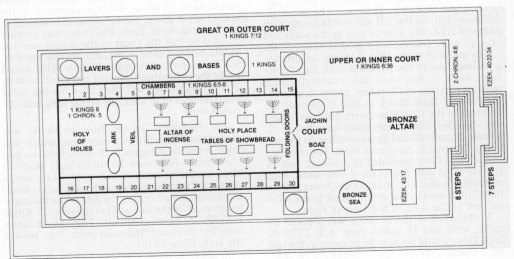

Fig. 7. The plan of Solomon's Temple

fire fell from heaven and consumed the burnt offering (7:1).

At the disruption of the kingdom, the Temple ceased to be the sanctuary of all the Israelite people; Jeroboam erected special places of worship at Bethel and Dan for the use of the revolting ten tribes; but the Temple continued to be the authorized center of worship for the kingdom of Judah. As early as the days of Rehoboam, the Temple treasures were plundered by Shishak king of Egypt (1 Kings 14:26), and gold and silver from there were subsequently sent to Ben-hadad, king of Syria, to purchase an alliance against Baasha, king of Israel (15:18-21).

Under Jehoshaphat the outer court was renewed (2 Chron. 20:5), and under Jehoash considerable repairs were made upon the Temple itself (2 Kings 12:5-12), necessitated by the havoc wrought by the wicked Athaliah (2 Chron. 24:7). During the reign of Amaziah all the gold and silver (as well as the utensils that had gold or silver about them) that were in the Temple were plundered by Jehoash king of Israel (2 Kings 14:14). After this Jotham "built the upper gate" of the Temple (15:35; 2 Chron. 27:3), probably at the entrance to the inner court. Ahaz, on the other hand, had the altar of burnt offering taken away and another put in its place, designed after one he had seen in Damascus; he also had the

decorations removed from the laver stands, the basins themselves taken out, the oxen removed from under the bronze sea, and the latter placed upon a "pavement of stone" (2 Kings 16:10-17). This was done to secure for the king of Assyria those artistic objects, as he had already given him silver and gold from the Temple and palace (v. 8). King Hezekiah was also compelled to pay tribute to Sennacherib. He took silver from the Temple and stripped the gold from the Temple doors and posts (18:15-16). Worst of all was the desecration of the Temple by Manasseh. He caused altars for "all the host of heaven" to be erected in both courts, set up an image of Asherah in the sanctuary (21:4-5, 7), and erected in the Temple court "houses of the male cult prostitutes" (23:7), probably tents or huts, for the paramours to dwell in, and in which there were also women who wove tent-temples for Asherah. He kept horses consecrated to the sun in a place set apart for them in the inner court toward the back of the Temple (v. 11). Josiah purged the sacred place of these abominations (vv. 4-8); but soon afterward Nebuchadnezzar captured Jerusalem and gathered together all the treasures of the Temple, including the golden utensils, and carried off (24:13). Eleven years later Jerusalem was destroyed by the Chaldeans, who burned the Temple to the ground after pillaging it of its remaining valuables, which they took to Babylon (25:9, 13-17; Jer. 52:13, 17-23).

The Temple of Zerubbabel. "We have very few particulars regarding the temple which the Jews erected after their return from the captivity (about 520 B.C.), and no description that would enable us to realize its appearance. But there are some dimensions given in the Bible and elsewhere which are extremely interesting as affording points of comparison between it and the temples which preceded it, or were erected after it. The first and most authentic are those given in the Book of Ezra (6:3), when quoting the decree of Cyrus, wherein it is said, 'Let the house be builded, the place where they offered sacrifices, and let the foundations thereof be strongly laid; the height thereof threescore cubits; and the breadth thereof threescore cubits; with three rows of great stones, and a row of new timber.' Josephus quotes this passage almost literally, but in doing so enables us with certainty to translate the word here called *row* as 'story'—as indeed the sense would lead us to infer. The other dimension of sixty cubits in breadth is twenty cubits in excess of that of Solomon's temple, but there is no reason to doubt its correctness, for we find from Josephus and the Talmud that it was the dimension adopted for the temple when rebuilt, or rather repaired, by Herod. We are left, therefore, with the alternative of assuming that the porch and the chambers all around were twenty cubits in width, including the thickness of the walls, instead of ten cubits, as in the earlier build-

The Dome of the Rock

ing. This alteration in the width of the pteromata made the temple one hundred cubits in length by sixty in breadth, with a height, it is said, of sixty cubits, including the upper room, or Talar, though we cannot help suspecting that this last dimension is somewhat in excess of the truth. The only other description of this temple is found in Hecataeus the Abderite, who wrote shortly after the death of Alexander the Great. As quoted by Josephus (*Against Apion* 1.22), he says that 'There is [in Jerusalem] about the middle of the city, a wall of stone, the length of which is five hundred feet, and the breadth a hundred cubits, with double [gates],' in which he describes the temple as being situated. Hecataeus also mentions that the altar was twenty cubits square and ten high. And although he mentions the temple itself, he unfortunately does not supply us with any dimensions. From these dimensions we gather that if 'the priests and Levites and elders of families were disconsolate at seeing how much more sumptuous the old temple was than the one which on account of their poverty they had just been able to erect' (Ezra 3:12), it certainly was not because it was smaller, as almost every dimension had been increased one third" (Smith, *Bib. Dict.*).

According to the Talmud this Temple lacked five things that were in Solomon's Temple, namely, the Ark, the sacred fire, the Shekinah, the Holy Spirit, and the Urim and Thummim. The Holy of Holies was empty, and on the spot where the Ark should have stood, a stone was set upon which the high priest placed the censer on the great Day of Atonement. In the Holy Place there was only one golden lampstand, one table of the bread of the Presence, and the altar of incense (1 Macc. 1:21; 4:49); in the court was an altar of burnt offering built of stone (4:45-47).

History. This Temple was plundered by Antiochus Epiphanes, who also defiled it with idolatrous worship (1 Macc. 1:21-25, 37-39; 46-51; 4:38; 2 Macc. 6:2-5), but was restored by Judas Maccabeus (1 Macc. 4:36-51). He also fortified the outside against future attacks (6:7). It was taken by Pompey on the Day of Atonement after a three months' siege, and later by Herod the Great (Josephus *Ant.* 14.4.2-4; 16.2).

Ezekiel's Temple. The vision of a temple that the prophet Ezekiel saw while residing on the banks of the Chebar in Babylonia in the twenty-fifth year of the captivity does not add much to our knowledge of the subject. It is not a description of a temple that ever was built but of one that is to be built in Jerusalem during the ideal spiritual and political conditions to prevail during the Kingdom age (cf. Isa. 11; 35; 60; Zech. 14:8-20). The temple itself is quite similar to that built by Solomon. There can be little doubt that the arrangements of Herod's Temple were in a great measure influenced by the description here given (*see* Ezek. 41:1–43:17).

Herod's Temple. The Temple as it existed after the captivity was not such as would satisfy a man as vain and fond of display as Herod the Great; and he accordingly undertook the task of rebuilding it on a grander scale. Although the reconstruction was practically equivalent to an entire rebuilding, still this Temple cannot be spoken of as a third one, for Herod himself said, in so many words, that it was only intended to be regarded as an enlarging and further beautifying of that of Zerubbabel. After the necessary preparation the work of building was begun in the eighteenth year of Herod's reign (20 or 21 B.C.). The Temple proper, in which priests and Levites were employed, was finished in a year and a half, and the courts in the course of eight years. Subsidiary buildings were gradually erected, added to through the reigns of his successors, so that the entire undertaking was not completed till the time of Agrippa II and the procurator Albinus (A.D. 64).

For our knowledge of the last and greatest of the Jewish Temples we are indebted almost wholly to the works of Josephus, with an occasional hint from the Talmud. The Bible unfortunately contains nothing to assist in this respect.

The Temple and its courts occupied an area of 1 stadium (Josephus), or 500 cubits (Talmud). They were arranged in terrace form, one court being higher than another, and the Temple highest of all, so as to be easily seen from any part of the city or vicinity, thus presenting an imposing appearance (Mark 13:2-3).

The Outer Court. The outer court was surrounded with a high wall having several gates on its W side. It had porticoes running all around it, those on three of the sides having double and that on the S side having triple piazzas. These porticoes were covered with roofs of cedar supported on marble pillars, 25 cubits high, and were paved with mosaic work. This outer court, which could be frequented by Gentiles and unclean persons, had on its inner side and extending all around a rampart surrounded with a stone parapet, i.e., a mound 10 cubits broad, the top of which was reached by a flight of fourteen steps. This constituted the outer boundary of the *inner Temple area* (*to deuteron hieron,* Josephus *Wars* 5.5.2). Some distance back from the rampart was the wall by which the Temple and its inner courts were surrounded. On the outside this was 40 cubits high, while on the inside it was only 25, the level of the inner space being so much higher.

Women's Court. Entering by the E gate one came to the *court of the women,* a square of 135 cubits, separated from the *court of the Israelites* by a wall on the W side and having gates on the N and S sides for the women to enter by. These gates, as well as those on the E and W sides of this court, had rooms built over them to a height of 40 cubits, each room being ornamented with two pillars 12 cubits in circumference, and provided with double doors 30 cubits high and 40 wide, overlaid with gold and silver. According to *Middoth* 2.3, the gates, with the exception of the eastern one, were only 20 cubits high and 10 wide.

The eastern gate, called in the Talmud *Nicanor's,* or the *great* gate, was made of Corinthian brass and was regarded as the principal gate on account of its greater height (being 50 cubits) and width (40 cubits) and from its being more richly decorated with precious metals. It is undoubtedly the "gate of the temple which is called Beautiful" (Acts 3:2). Around the walls of the court, except the W side, ran porticoes (porches), the roof of which rested on lofty and highly finished pillars. In each corner was a room, used, respectively, for storing the wood deemed unfit to be burned on the altar; for those affected with leprosy to wash themselves; for storing sacrificial wine and oil; and that one in which the Nazirites shaved their hair and cooked the flesh of the consecration sacrifices. According to Josephus it was in some of the pillars of this court that the thirteen alms boxes were placed.

The Inner Court. The entrance to the court of the Israelites was the western gate of the outer court and was reached by a stair of fifteen steps. This inner court measured 187 cubits long (from E to W) and 135 wide (from S to N), and surrounded the Temple. Against its walls were

chambers for storing the utensils required for the services. It had three gates on both the S and N sides, making seven entrances in all. Eleven cubits of the eastern end were partitioned off by a stone balustrade 1 cubit high, for the men (the *court of the Israelites*), separating it from the rest of the space that went to form the court of the priests. In this latter court stood the *altar of burnt offering,* made of unwrought stone, 30 cubits in length and breadth, and 15 high. West of this was the Temple, and between it and the altar stood the laver.

The Temple Proper. The Temple stood so much higher than the court of the priests that it was approached by a flight of twelve steps. It stood in the western end of the inner court on the NW part of the Temple mount and was built, according to Josephus (*Ant.* 15.11.3), upon new foundations of massive blocks of white marble, richly ornamented with gold both inside and out. Some of these stones were 45 cubits long, 6 broad, and 5 high. Its length and height, including the porch, were 100 cubits; on each side of the vestibule there was a wing 20 cubits wide, making the total width of this part of the building 100 cubits. The porch was 10 cubits deep, measuring from E to W, 50 wide, 90 in height, and had an open gateway 70 cubits high and 25 in width.

The interior of the Temple was divided into the

Model of Herod's Temple, Jerusalem

Holy Place and the Holy of Holies. "The temple had doors also at the entrance, and lintels over them, of the same height with the temple itself. They were adorned with embroidered veils, with their flowers of purple, and pillars interwoven: and over these, but under the crown-work, was spread out a golden vine, with its branches hanging down from a great height" (Josephus *Ant.* 15.11.3). The holy place was 40 cubits long, 20 wide, and 60 in height. It contained one golden lampstand, a single table of the bread of the Presence, and one altar of incense. Separated from it by a wooden partition was the Holy of Holies, 20 cubits long and 60 high, which was empty. The rabbinical writers maintain that there were two veils over its entrance. It was this veil that was rent on the occasion of our Lord's crucifixion. As in the case of Solomon's Temple, side rooms three stories high were built on the sides of the main structure. For a discussion of recent excavation on the Temple mount, *see* Jerusalem.

BIBLIOGRAPHY: G. A. Cooke, *Zeitschrift für die alttestamentliche Wissenschaft* (1924), pp. 105-15; F. J. Hollis, *The Archaeology of Herod's Temple* (1934); G. E. Wright, *Biblical Archaeologist* 3 (1941): 17-31; L. Waterman, *Journal of Near Eastern Studies* 2 (1943): 284-94; H. K. Eversull, *The Temple in Jerusalem* (1946); L. Waterman, *JNES* 6 (1947): 161-63; id., *JNES* 7 (1948): 54-55; G. E. Wright, *JNES* 7 (1948): 53; C. G. Howie, *Bulletin of the American Schools of Oriental Research* 107 (1950): 13-19; P. L. Garber, *BA* 14 (1951): 2-24; A. Edersheim, *The Temple, Its Ministry and Services* (1954); A. Parrot, *Le Temple de Jerusalem* (1954); G. E. Wright, *BA* 18 (1955): 43-45; P. L. Garber, *Journal of Biblical Literature* 77 (1958): 123-27; G. E. Wright and W. F. Albright, *JBL* 77 (1958): 129-32; G. Schrenk, *Theological Dictionary of the New Testament* (1965), 3:230-47; O. Michel, *TDNT* (1967), 4:880-90.

TEMPLE SERVANTS (Heb. *netînîm*, those "given," i.e., to the Temple; "Nethinim," KJV). The name applied to those who were set apart to do the menial work of the sanctuary.

Origin and Duties. As early as the time of Joshua, the Gibeonites had been appointed to act as "hewers of wood and drawers of water" for the sanctuary (Josh. 9:21) and thus became the original Temple servants. As these Gibeonites were greatly decreased in numbers by the persecutions of Saul and in the massacre at Nob (1 Sam. 22:1-19), and as the service as arranged by David required an increase of menial servants, "David and the princes" gave the Temple servants for "the service of the Levites" (Ezra 8:20). These were probably prisoners of war who had become proselytes and were called Temple servants in postexilian times (1 Chron. 9:2; Ezra 2:43; 7:7; Neh. 7:46). Being given to the Levites, their duty was to relieve the latter of every menial and laborious work connected with the Temple, such as drawing water, carrying wood, etc. No prescribed list of duties is given in the Scriptures, as these servants were entirely at the disposal of the Levites.

Number, Revenue, Position, etc. The first

Temple servants, it must be remembered, were the Levites, who were *given* to Aaron and his sons (Num. 3:9; 8:19). These were, as already mentioned, relieved by the Gibeonites. For convenience they most probably lived near the Temple, and were supported by contributions of the people. Only 612 Temple servants returned from Babylon—392 with Zerubbabel (Ezra 2:58; Neh. 7:60), and 220 with Ezra (Ezra 8:20), under the leadership of Ziha and Gishpa (Neh. 11:21), who, as their foreign names indicate, were a separate people. Some of the Temple servants lived in Ophel, which they helped to rebuild (3:26; 11:21), because of its proximity to the Temple; others, as before the Exile, dwelt in the Levitical cities (Ezra 2:70). They were governed by a leader of their own people (2:43; Neh. 7:46). Like other sacred ministers, they were exempted from taxation by the Persian satrap (Ezra 7:24) and were supported from the Temple treasury and the second tithes. Though they conformed to the Jewish religion (Ex. 12:48; Deut. 29:11; Josh. 9:21; Neh. 10:28), they occupied a very low position, being reckoned below the *Mamzer,* or illegal offspring (Mishna *Kiddushin* 3.12; 4.1; *Jebamoth* 2.4). According to Jewish authorities, they were restricted to intermarriage among themselves, and if a Jew or Jewess married one of them, the offspring shared in all the disqualifications of the Temple servants; and they were not exempted from military service when newly married. If a woman had an illegitimate child, it was ascribed to a *Nethin,* and the offspring took the degraded position of the *Nethin,* unless the mother could supply proof of other fatherhood. The decision of a court of justice was invalid if one of the members was a *Nethin,* as he was not considered a member of the congregation specified in Lev. 4:13; Num. 35:24. Eventually they apparently merged with the Jewish population, as no allusion to them occurs either in the Apocrypha or the NT.

BIBLIOGRAPHY: B. A. Levine, *Journal of Biblical Literature* 89 (1963): 207-12; G. F. Oehler, *Theology of the Old Testament* (1978), p. 376.

TEMPT, TEST (Heb. *nāsâ;* Gk. *peirazō,* both meaning to "test or try"). The word is used in different senses; it does not always involve an evil purpose, as an inducement to sin.

1. "God tested Abraham" (Gen. 22:1) in commanding him to offer up his son Isaac, intending to prove his obedience and faith, to confirm and strengthen him by this trial, and to furnish in him an example of perfect obedience for all succeeding ages. When it is recorded that God tested His people, whether they would walk in His way or not (Ex. 16:4), and that He permitted false prophets to arise among them, who prophesied vain things to try them whether they would seek the Lord with their whole hearts, we should interpret these expressions by that of James 1:13-14, "Let no one say when he is tempted, 'I am

being tempted by God'; for God cannot be tempted by evil, and He Himself does not tempt anyone."

2. Satan tempts us to every kind of evil and lays snares for us, even in our best actions. He lays inducements before our minds to solicit us to sin (1 Cor. 7:5; 1 Thess. 3:5; James 1:13, 14). Hence Satan is called "the serpent of old," "the devil," and "the tempter" (Rev. 12:9; Matt. 4:3). He tempted our first parents (*see* Temptation); our Savior (*see* Temptation of Christ); he tempted Ananias and Sapphira to lie to the Holy Spirit (Acts 5:3).

3. Men are said to tempt God when they unreasonably require proofs of the divine presence, power, or goodness. It is proper for us to seek divine assistance and to pray to Him to give us what we need, but we are not to tempt Him or expose ourselves to dangers from which we cannot escape without miraculous interposition. God is not obliged to work miracles in our favor; He requires of us only such actions as are within the ordinary measure of our strength. The Israelites frequently tempted God in the desert, as if they had reason to doubt His presence, His goodness, or His power, after all His appearances in their behalf (Ex. 16:2, 7, 12; Num. 20:12; Ps. 78:18, 41; etc.).

4. Men tempt or try one another when they would know whether things or men are really what they seem or are desired; also when they wish them to depart from the right. The queen of Sheba came to prove the wisdom of Solomon by giving him riddles to explain (1 Kings 10:1; 2 Chron. 9:1). The scribes and Pharisees often tested our Lord and endeavored to catch Him in their snares (Matt. 16:1; 19:3; 22:18).

TEMPTATION (Heb. *massâ;* Gk. *peirasmos,* a "testing"). Generally understood as the enticement of a person to commit sin by offering some seeming advantage. The sources of temptation are Satan, the world, and the flesh. We are exposed to them in every state, in every place, and in every time. The nearest approach to a definition of the process of temptation from within is given us by James, "But each one is tempted when he is carried away and enticed by his own lust" (James 1:14). "Temptation proper in the case of a fallen creature is, strictly speaking, within. It craves the gratification that is offered from without: 'then when it hath conceived, it bringeth forth sin' (1:15). The contest in the regenerate man is this lust of the flesh opposing the Spirit of the new nature; and the Spirit continually moving the renewed spirit to oppose its desires. In this sense our first parents were not tempted, though in their case the temptation from without assailed a will capable of falling, and was the means of engendering the concupiscence that then engendered all sin. In this sense the glorified in heaven, after a probation ended,

will be incapable of temptation. In this sense our sinless Redeemer was absolutely untemptable and impeccable. 'He was in all points tempted like as we are, yet without sin' (Heb. 4:15). . . . He had no mother lust which could conceive and bring forth sin. . . . But there is another aspect of temptation which brings him still nearer to us, and that is, the trial of the spirit from without. This he underwent to the utmost; indeed, as much beyond the possibility of his servants' temptation as their internal temptation was impossible to him" (Pope, *Christ. Theol.,* 3:205). *See* Tempt; Temptation of Christ.

BIBLIOGRAPHY: D. Bonhoeffer, *Temptation* (1953); W. E. Hulme, *The Dynamics of Sanctification* (1966), pp. 14-35, 111-34; Donald MacDonald, *The Biblical Doctrine of Creation and the Fall* (1984).

TEMPTATION OF CHRIST. An experience in the life of our Lord recorded in Matt. 4:1-11; Mark 1:12-13; Luke 4:1-13. That Christ was tempted on other occasions in other ways than here indicated would seem evident from Luke 22:28 and Heb. 4:15. This temptation, however, through which He passed immediately after His baptism and before beginning His ministry, was an event of so much importance as to be regarded as preeminently His temptation. And to this temptation, exclusive reference is commonly made.

Character of the Narration. Much labor and ingenuity are often expended in seeking to determine to what extent the narrative of the gospels is to be taken literally. How much of it is to be understood as descriptive of actual outward occurrences, and how much was internal, subjective? Did Satan actually bear Christ away to a "pinnacle of the temple" at Jerusalem? Did he also take our Lord to "a very high mountain" from the summit of which he showed Him "all the kingdoms of the world"? Did such changes in the scene of the temptation actually take place in an outward, material sense, or did they simply take place in the mind of Jesus? Is the gospel narrative in these respects marked by the figurative manner common among orientals? Upon these questions the opinions of commentators are greatly divided. There has been no end of discussion, and with little profit. The popular interpretation has been literal. And not a few scholars have attempted to defend this interpretation. But, on the other hand, even as orthodox a scholar as Calvin has held the account to be that of a vision or allegory. But it should be observed that whichever view is taken, the reality of the temptation is in no measure lessened, nor is the fact disguised that the real agent of the temptation was Satan.

The Temptation as Related to the Character of Christ. How could He, the sinless One, be tempted? Did the temptation imply in any sense the possibility of His falling into sin? As to the first question, it should be remembered that temptation does not necessarily imply a sinful nature on the part of the one tempted. The first man, Adam, though created in the image and after the likeness of God, was tempted and fell into sin. And does not the passage Heb. 4:15 teach that not only did Jesus successfully resist temptation, but also that His temptation was not such as springs up within a sinful nature? Christ was "without sin" in both these senses. His temptation was wholly from without, from the evil one, though appealing to desires within Him that were wholly innocent. As to the possibility of His yielding to temptation, these views have been held: (1) The Calvinistic view, that Christ had no volitional power to yield to temptation. Edwards strongly advocated this view in his work on the will. (2) The Arminian view, that the man Jesus had such volitional power. (3) The view that "the eternal Logos had the volitional power to sin, having concentrated and reduced himself to finite and human conditions." Van Osterzee appropriately says, "The sinlessness of the Lord is to be regarded as an attribute of his true humanity, and thus to be clearly distinguished from the absolute holiness of him who cannot even be tempted of evil. The moral purity of the Lord did not in itself exclude even the least possibility of sinning. Had such possibility been absolutely wanting, the for-

mer would, even in the Son of man, have lost all moral worth." The great thing here is precisely this, that He who was exposed to the severest temptation ever so maintained the dominion over Himself that it could be said of Him, He was able not to sin, *"potuit non peccare."* As the result of a sustained conflict, He so perfectly vanquished the power of evil that sinning became for Him morally an absolute impossibility; in other words, the *"potuit non peccare"* was evermore raised to a *"non potuit peccare."* He could not sin. And yet discussion upon this theme, as Edersheim says, "sounds, after all, like the stammering of divine words by a babe." It is a subject for reverent faith rather than exact dogmatizing.

The Nature of the Threefold Temptation. According to Mark, the temptation was protracted throughout the "forty days." The temptations described by Matthew and Luke are therefore regarded as the culminating features of the long struggle. The order of the temptations varies in the two gospels named, a matter of little or no consequence. The long fast, once a favorite matter for infidel objections, no longer presents any difficulty whatever. The significance of the separate assaults of evil has been variously interpreted, a fact due in considerable measure to the comprehensiveness of the whole great event. Says Smith: "The three temptations are ad-

The Mount of Temptation, traditional site of Jesus' temptation by Satan

dressed to the three forms in which the disease of sin makes its appearance in the soul—to the solace of sense, and the love of praise and the desire of gain (1 John 2:16). But there is one element common to them all, they are attempts to call up a willful and wayward spirit in contrast to a patient and self-denying one." The subject, however, can hardly be summed up thus briefly.

1. The temptation to change the stones into bread by a miracle was an appeal to Christ to step out of His divinely appointed path for the sake of satisfying His hunger. He had accepted the conditions of a human life, and it was for Him to do His duty and trust in God for sustenance. His power to work miracles was not for Himself but for others (see Kenosis). Had He obeyed the temptation He would have become unlike men who must put their trust in divine Providence. "He would have become his own providence."

2. The second temptation was to prove His sonship, to exhibit His faith in His sonship, by casting Himself down from a pinnacle of the Temple. This temptation was at the opposite extreme from the preceding. The first was a temptation to distrust, the second that of extravagant, unwarranted confidence, or presumption. Again was the call to step out of the path divinely appointed, but by presumptuously plunging Himself into needless peril. The Scripture quoted by the adversary was quoted in a mutilated form. "He will give His angels charge concerning you." "To guard you in all your ways" was left out. As in the former instance all temptation to give unlawful prominence to temporal, material good is illustrated, so in the present instance all attempts to build up Christ's kingdom by means of display, rather than by the patient, divinely appointed processes, find their rebuke; likewise all forms of fanatical presumption.

3. The temptation to win power by an act of homage to the devil.

Inconceivable as this may seem at first, nevertheless this was the bold form in which was embodied the idea of winning power for good and holy ends by a compromise with evil at the outset. It was an appeal to holy ambition, but upon the ground of doing evil that good might come. The kingdom was to be won, but in the way suggested it would have been at the expense of ruining the King. At this point also the great temptation of Christ has its most practical lessons.

The manner and complete success of Christ's resistance appear upon the surface of the narrative and call here for no comment.   E.MCC.

BIBLIOGRAPHY: C. E. Macartney, *Great Interviews of Jesus* (1944), pp. 9-24; id., *Trials of Great Men of the Bible* (1946), pp. 127-39; G. C. Morgan, *The Crises of the Christ* (1963), pp. 109-54; F. W. Farrar, *The Life of Christ* (1982), pp. 54-64.

TEN. *See* Number.

TEN COMMANDMENTS (Gk. *deka*, "ten," *logos*, "word").

Name. Decalogue is the name by which the Greek Fathers designated "the Ten Commandments," which were written by God on tablets of stone and given to Moses on Mt. Sinai. In Heb. the name is "ten commandments" (*'aseret haddᵉbārîm*, Ex. 34:28; Deut. 4:13; 10:4). It is also called "the moral law," "the two tablets of the testimony" (Ex. 34:29), "the tablets of the covenant" (Deut. 9:9), and "His covenant" (Deut. 4:13). In the NT it is called "the commandments" (*'entolai*, Matt. 19:17; Rom. 13:9) and "the Law" (1 Tim. 1:7-10).

Versions. There are two versions of the Ten Commandments given in the Pentateuch. The first is contained in Ex. 20, the second in Deut. 5. These are substantially and almost verbally identical, except that the reasons given for the observance of the fourth commandment are not the same. In Exodus the reason is based on one's obligations to God as the Creator (Gen. 2:3). In Deuteronomy the reason is one's duty to others and the memory of the bondage in Egypt. This variation has led many to the belief that the original law was simply "Remember the Sabbath day, to keep it holy." It may, however, be the fact that the form as it stands in Exodus is the divine original, but that Moses in reviewing the law just before his farewell to his people added a fresh and fuller significance that the history of Israel suggested.

Nature. The Ten Commandments are a statement of the terms of the covenant God made with His chosen people; and in this respect they are to be distinguished from the elaborate system of law known as the Mosaic. The vast legal system of Israel, civil, criminal, judicial, and ecclesiastical, was framed after the covenant law, not with a view of expanding it, but to enforce it. As Fairbairn suggests, its chief object was to secure through the instrumentality of the magistrate, that if the proper love should fail to influence the hearts and lives of the people, still right should be maintained. The elaborate system was designed as an educator, to lead the people into the great principles of life embodied in the Ten Commandments and afterward exhibited in Christ. The Mosaic system was only a temporary expedient to achieve a given end, whereas the Ten Commandments are a statement of principles to continue for all time.

This unique place of the Ten Commandments is seen in the circumstance of their delivery. The rest of the law was given by God through the lips of Moses, but these were spoken by God Himself and with an awful display of splendor and solemnity never before witnessed (Ex. 19). It appears also that angels were active in the promulgation of the law ("holy ones," Deut. 33:2-3; "angels," Acts 7:53; Gal. 3:19; Heb. 2:2). In addition, these laws were written by God's own finger and on durable tablets of stone (Deut. 9:11). In the symbolism of the East, the stone signified the perpetuity of the law written upon it. Written on both sides, it meant the completeness of the code.

Still another fact marks the unique place of the Ten Commandments. The tablets of stone were put in the most sacred place in the world—in the Tabernacle, in the "holy of holies," in the Ark of the Covenant. Thus they were plainly recognized as containing in themselves the sum and substance of what was held to be strictly required by the covenant.

Contents. That the Ten Commandments contain the essential principles of the moral law, and are therefore of permanent obligation, is affirmed in the NT. Jesus held the Ten Commandments up as the perfect code. When the young man asked Him the way of attaining eternal life, Jesus quoted from the Ten Commandments and told him to obey them and live (Mark 10:19; Luke 18:18-20). And again, after assenting to the two features of the Ten Commandments as the very essence of the law, He said, "Do this, and you will live" (Luke 10:28; cf. Matt. 19:17).

In His dispute with the Pharisees the chief point at issue was this: They exalted the minor law, the ceremonial observance, and threw the duties inculcated in the Ten Commandments in the background; He brought the Ten Commandments forward and gave them their true place. So did the apostles (Rom 13:9). In the protracted discussion concerning the law, all Paul's examples are taken from these tablets or from what they clearly forbade or required.

Source. The foundation and source of the moral law is God's character. "I am the Lord your God, who brought you out of the land of Egypt, out of the house of slavery" is the way the Ten Commandments are introduced. The Heb. name here used (Everlasting Eternal Almighty) intimates that the principles of law have their standing in the character of God. "I am . . . you shall." That is the connection. And that is what makes the moral law so awful in its unchangeable majesty. It is law because God is. It cannot be changed without changing the character of Jehovah Himself. Right is what it is, because God is what He is, and therefore it is as unchangeable as God.

The fact that God has placed the law of His own character on man is proof that man is capable of the divine. Expressing as it does man's true nature, to vary from its requirements is to fall below the dignity of true manhood. In this sense the Ten Commandments are, as the Reformers taught, identical with the "eternal law of nature."

Prohibitory. The Ten Commandments are a series of prohibitions. The negative form is due to the shocking depravity of those to whom it was addressed. A prohibition means a disposition to do the thing prohibited. If men were not inclined to worship something other than God the first commandment would not be needed. If there were no murder in men's hearts the sixth commandment would not be required. And this is true of all the laws. Paul says, "[The law] was added because of transgressions" (Gal. 3:19). The law is put in the negative form for another reason: the law can only restrain the act. It cannot implant the positive virtue. Statutory law may restrain and regulate actions. It cannot transform the sinful heart. It is of necessity negative.

Divisions. The Ten Commandments are not numbered in the sacred text, and the church has been divided as to how the division should be made. There are three general modes of division attempted: (1) That which the Reformed churches have adopted, and which is called the Philonic division. It makes Ex. 20:2-3 the first commandment, vv. 4-6 the second, and v. 7 the third. This division is supported by the following reasons: (a) It is made on the principle that polytheism and idolatry are identical. (b) There are three ways of dishonoring God—in denying His unity, His spirituality, and His deity. (c) It divides the two tablets into three and seven laws, three having a mystical reference to God, and seven to the church. (d) It obviates the need of making the unnatural division of the commandment against covetousness into two. (2) The second division is called the Augustinian and unites vv. 3-6 into one commandment. It divides the commandment concerning covetousness into two. By this method the Roman church supported the legitimacy of sacred images that were not worshiped. (3) The third, or Talmudic division, makes v. 2 the first commandment, and vv. 3-6 the second.

Order. The order in which these laws were written on the two tablets of stone is not a matter of grave consideration. If the division were equal, as many think, then the law concerning honor to parents is exalted to a high rank, associated as it is with our duty to honor God. But even without a numerical equality of the two tablets the division is philosophical. Our duties to God come first —His being, His worship, His name, and His day. Then come our duties to our fellowmen. They have their beginning in the home. Then they reach out beyond the home circle to all mankind, having regard, first, for our neighbor's life; second, to his wife; third, to his property; fourth, to his position. Finally, the tenth commandment touches the spring of all moral completeness, the desire of the heart. It is really the intent of the heart that determines the moral character of the act. It cannot be reached by human legislation. It exposes to the conscience the utter failure of an act that might otherwise be blameless. It was this law that brought Paul with all his righteousness under sentence of condemnation (Rom. 7:7).

The two tablets are summarized in the two

great laws "You shall love the Lord your God with all your heart and with all your soul and with all your mind; and your neighbor as yourself."

A.H.T.

BIBLIOGRAPHY: E. Hopkins, *An Exposition of the Ten Commandments* (n.d.); G. E. Mendenhall, *Law and Covenant in Israel and the Ancient Near East* (1955); F. A. Tatford, *The Message of Sinai* (1957); T. Watson, *The Ten Commandments* (1962); H. H. Rowley, *Men of God* (1963), pp. 1-36; R. S. Wallace, *The Ten Commandments* (1965).

TENDERHEARTED.

1. Gk. *eusplagchos*, "having strong bowels," in biblical and ecclesiastical language, compassionate, kindhearted (Eph. 4:32; cf. 1 Pet. 3:8).

2. Heb. *rak lēbāb*, "timid" (2 Chron. 13:7, KJV).

TENONS (Ex. 26:17, 19; 36:22, 24; "projections," NIV). Probably dowel pins at the end of the planks of the *Tabernacle* (which see).

TENT (Heb. usually *'ōhel;* Gk. *skēnē*). A movable habitation made of curtains extended upon poles. The patriarchs of the Israelites, whose fathers and kindred already possessed fixed houses in Mesopotamia, dwelled in tents because they lived in Canaan only as pilgrims. The Israelites did not dwell in houses until their return from Egypt. Their tents, in material, form, and furniture, no doubt resembled the tents of the present Bedouin, consisting sometimes of plaited mats, but generally of cloth coverings, either coarser, of goat hair (black, Song of Sol. 1:5), or finer, woven from yarn. The goat-hair cloth is sufficient to resist the heaviest rain. The tent poles, called *amud,* or columns, are usually nine in number, placed in three groups, but many tents have only one pole, others two or three. The ropes that hold the tent in its place are fastened not to the tent cover itself but to loops consisting of a leather thong tied to the ends of a stick, around which is twisted a piece of old cloth, which is itself sewed to the tent cover. The ends of the tent ropes are fastened to short sticks, or pins, called *wed* or *aoutad,* which are driven into the ground with a mallet (cf. Judg. 4:21). Around the back and sides of the tent runs a piece of stuff removable at pleasure to admit air. The tent is divided into two rooms, separated by a carpet partition drawn across the middle of the tent and fastened to the three middle posts. The furniture deemed necessary is a carpet, cushions, a low table (sometimes replaced by a round skin), eating and cooking utensils, and a lamp. When the pasture near an encampment is exhausted, the tents are taken down, packed on camels, and moved (Isa. 38:12; Gen. 26:17, 22, 25). The larger tents of the well-to-do are divided into three rooms; the first, at the entrance, in the case of common people, is reserved for the young and tender of the flock or herd, the second for the men, and the innermost for the women. The manufacture of tents

formed a regular trade, at which Paul occasionally labored, especially in connection with Aquila (Acts 18:3).

Bedouin tent

Figurative. So prominent a feature of oriental life could hardly fail to suggest many striking metaphors. "The light in his tent is darkened" (Job 18:6) is a symbol of misfortune. When Job said, "The friendship of God was over my tent" (29:4), he admitted that the blessed fellowship of God's confiding, unreserved communion ruled over his tent. The heavens are compared to a tent (Isa. 40:22). The prosperity of Israel restored is referred to as an enlargement of a tent (54:2; *see* also 33:20). The setting up of a tent, especially a large one, was a work needing the help of others, and one bereft of friends is referred to as having no helpers in erecting his tent (Jer. 10:20). The tent being rapidly taken down and removed became a symbol of the frailty of life (Isa. 38:12; 2 Cor. 5:1) and in 5:4 *tent* is used figuratively for the *human body* in which the soul dwells and which is taken down to death.

TENTH DEAL. KJV term replaced in the NASB and NIV by "one-tenth of an ephah." *See* Metrology: Dry Measures of Capacity: *Ephah.*

TE'RAH (tē'ra; cf. Akkad. *turahu,* "ibex").

1. The son of Nahor born in Ur of the Chaldees; the father of Abram, Nahor, and Haran, and through them the ancestor of the great families of the Israelites, Ishmaelites, Midianites, Moabites, and Ammonites (Gen. 11:24-32). Scripture reveals that Terah was an idolater (Josh. 24:2), that he took part in the family migration toward Canaan, and that he died in Haran at the age of 205 years, c. 2100 B.C.

2. A camping place of Israel in the desert, located between Tahath and Mithkah (Num. 33:27-28).

TERAPHIM. The teraphim were figurines or images in human form also called "household idols." Rachel's theft of Laban's teraphim (Gen. 31:34, *see* marg.) is much better understood in the light of the documents from Nuzi, not far from modern Kirkuk, excavated 1925-34. The possession of these household gods may have implied leadership of the family and, in the case of a married daughter, assured her husband the right to the property of her father (Cyrus H. Gordon, *Revue Biblique* 44 [1945]: 35ff). Since Laban evidently had sons of his own when Jacob left for Canaan, they alone had the right to their father's gods, and the theft of these household idols by Rachel was a serious offense (Gen. 31:19, 30, 35) aimed at preserving for her husband the first title to her father's estate. Albright construes the teraphim as meaning "vile things," but the images were not necessarily cultic or lewd, as frequently the depictions of Astarte were. Micah's teraphim (Judg. 17:5) were used for purposes of securing an oracle (cf. 1 Sam. 15:23; Hos. 3:4; Zech. 10:2). Babylonian kings oracularly consulted the teraphim (Ezek. 21:21). Josiah abolished the teraphim (2 Kings 23:24), but these images had a strange hold on the Hebrew people even until after the exilic period. The NIV usually translates "teraphim" as "gods" or "idols."

M.F.U.

BIBLIOGRAPHY: M. Greenberg, *Journal of Biblical Literature* 81 (1962): 239-48; C. Labuschagne, *Vetus Testamentum* 16 (1966): 115-17; J. B. Pritchard, ed., *Ancient Near Eastern Texts* (1969), pp. 129-35.

Roman theater at Ephesus

TEREBINTH. *See* Vegetable Kingdom: Oak.

TE'RESH (te'resh; cf. Avestan *tarshav*, "firm, solid"). One of the two eunuchs whose plot to assassinate Ahasuerus was discovered by Mordecai (Esther 2:21; 6:2). He was hanged about 478 B.C.

TERRACE. (Heb. *mesillâ*, "thoroughfare," 2 Chron. 9:11, KJV) staircase, steps.

TERROR. The rendering of several Heb. words and one Gk. word denoting great fear, that which agitates both body and mind. Some of these words have as their primary meaning the *cause* of fear, others the *result*. Thus *'êmâ* (Josh. 2:9; Job 20:25; Pss. 55:4; 88:15) is that which inspires dread, as a king (Job 33:7); idols (Jer. 50:38), from the "fear" with which they fill their worshipers; *mehittâ* (Isa. 54:14) is a breaking in pieces, and so consternation, from *hātat*, to "be broken, confounded" (Gen. 35:5; Ezek. 26:17; 32:23-32); *bālâ* denotes the falling away of a person in sickness, a garment through age, etc., and so the mind consumed with anxiety and care. Other words simply express fear, as the Gk. word *phobos*. Death is called the "king of terrors" (Job 18:14; cf. 24:17), in distinction to the terrible disease that is called its "first-born" (18:13). Death is also personified elsewhere (Ps. 49:15; Isa. 28:15).

TER'TIUS (tur'shi-us, from Lat. *tertius*, "third"). Probably a Roman, he was the scribe for Paul in writing the epistle to the Romans (Rom. 16:22). Some have proposed without reason to identify him with Silas. Nothing certain is known of him.

TERTUL'LUS (ter-tul'us, diminutive form of Tertius). "A certain attorney" retained by the high priest and Sanhedrin to accuse the apostle Paul at Caesarea before the procurator Felix (Acts 24:1, 2). He evidently belonged to the class of professional attorneys who were to be found not only in Rome but in other parts of the empire, where they went with the expectation of finding occupation at the tribunals of the provincial magistrates. We may infer that Tertullus was of Roman, or, at all events, of Italian, origin; the Sanhedrin would naturally desire his services on account of their own ignorance of the Latin language and of the ordinary procedure of a Roman law court. The historian probably gave only an abstract of the speech, giving in full, however, the most salient points and those which had the most forcibly impressed themselves upon him, such as the introduction and the character ascribed to Paul (v. 5).

TESTAMENT. *See* Covenant.

TETH (ט) (tāth). The ninth letter of the Heb. alphabet. It stands at the beginning of the ninth section of Ps. 119, in which section each verse begins with that letter.

TETRARCH (Gk. *tetrarchēs*). Properly the sovereign or governor of the fourth part of a country.

1. Herod Antipas (Matt. 14:1; Luke 3:1, 19; 9:7; Acts 13:1), who is commonly distinguished as "Herod the tetrarch," although the title of "king" is also assigned to him both by Matthew (14:9) and by Mark (6:14, 22-28).

2. Herod Philip, who is said by Luke (Luke 3:1)

to have been "tetrarch of the region of Ituraea and Trachonitis."

3. Lysanias, who is said (Luke 3:1) to have been "tetrarch of Abilene." The title of tetrarch was at this time probably applied to petty tributary princes without any such determinate meaning. But it appears from Josephus that the tetrarchies of Antipas and Philip were regarded as each constituting a fourth part of their father's kingdom (*Ant.* 17.11.4). We conclude that in these two cases, at least, the title was used in its strict and literal sense.

BIBLIOGRAPHY: S. Perowne, *The Later Herods* (1958).

THADDAE'US (tha-di'us). A name in Mark's catalog of the twelve apostles (Mark 3:18) in the great majority of manuscripts. From a comparison with the catalog of Luke (Luke 6:16; Acts 1:13) it seems scarcely possible to doubt that the names of Judas and Thaddaeus were borne by one and the same person. Edersheim (*Life of Jesus,* 1:522) derives the term Thaddaeus from *thodah,* praise. KJV (Matt. 10:3) lists him as "Lebbaeus, whose surname was Thaddaeus."

THA'HASH (tha'hash). *See* Tahash.

THA'MAH (tha'ma). *See* Temah.

THA'MAR (tha'mar). *See* Tamar.

THANK OFFERING. *See* Sacrificial Offerings.

THANKSGIVING (Heb. *tôdâ;* Gk. *eucharistia*). A duty of which gratitude is the grace. This obligation of godliness is acknowledged by the universal sentiment of mankind; but as a Christian grace it has some blessed peculiarities. It is gratitude for all the benefits of divine Providence, especially for the general and personal gifts of redemption. The very term most in use shows this; it is *charis,* which is the grace of God in Christ, operating in the soul of the believer as a principle and going back to Him in gratitude: "Thanks be to God for His indescribable gift!" (2 Cor. 9:15). The ethical gratitude of Christianity connects every good gift and every perfect gift with the gift of Christ. Moreover, it is a thanksgiving that in the Christian economy, and in it alone, redounds to God for all things: *in everything give thanks.* This characteristic flows from the former. The rejoicing that we have in the Lord, and the everlasting consolation we possess in Him, makes every possible variety of divine dispensation a token for good. The Christian privilege is to find reason for gratitude in all things: "for this is God's will for you in Christ Jesus" (1 Thess. 5:18).

THANKWORTHY. KJV rendering of the Gk. *charis* (grace) in 1 Pet. 2:19, "suffering unjustly" wins God's favor.

THA'RA (tha'ra). *See* Terah.

THAR'SHISH (thar'shish). *See* Tarshish.

THEATER (Gk. *theatron,* "place for seeing"). (1) A place in which dramatic spectacles were exhibited and public assemblies held (Acts 19:29, 31). (2) A public show and, figuratively, a man who is exhibited to be gazed at and made sport of (1 Cor. 4:9, "a spectacle"). The writer of the epistle to the Hebrews speaks (12:1) of "so great a cloud of witnesses," having in mind, no doubt, the scene in which Christians are viewed as running a race, and not the theater or stage, where the eyes of the spectators are fixed on them.

The Greek Theater. Theater in Greece was originally intended for the performance of dithyrambic choruses at the feast of Dionysus. The hymn celebrated the sufferings and actions of the god in a style corresponding to the passionate character of his worship; and it was sung to the accompaniment of a flute and a dance around the altar. From the first it consisted of two principal parts: (1) the circular dancing place (*orchestra*), with the altar of the god in the center, and (2) the place for the spectators, or the theater (*theatron*) proper. The *theatron* was in the form of a semicircle, with the seats rising one above another in concentric tiers. The seats were almost always cut in the slope of a hill. When the dithyrambic choruses had developed into the drama, a structure called the *skēnē* (Lat. *scena*) was added, with a stage for dramatic representations. It was erected on the side of the *orchēstra* away from the spectators and at such a height and distance as to allow the stage to be in full view from every part of the theater. The first stone theater was that built at Athens, the home of Greek drama; and the theaters in every part of the Hellenic world were constructed on the same general principles. It is estimated that the theater in Athens had room for 14,000 persons. The tickets of admission discovered in Attica are of two kinds: (1) ordinary lead tokens or (2) counters of bone or ivory.

Roman theater at Bethshan

The Roman Theater. "In Rome, where dramatic representations, in the strict sense of the term, were not given until 240 B.C., a wooden stage was erected in the circus for each performance, and taken down again. . . . Those who wanted seats had to bring their own chairs; sometimes, by order of the senate, sitting was forbidden. In 154 B.C. an attempt was made to build a permanent theater with fixed seats, but it had to be pulled down by order of the senate. In 145 B.C., on the conquest of Greece, theaters were provided with seats after the Greek models were erected; these, however, were only of wood, and served for one representation alone. The first stone theater was built by Pompey in 55 B.C., a second one by Cornelius Balbus (13 B.C.), and in the same year the one dedicated by Augustus to his nephew Marcellus, and called by his name, the ruins of which still exist. Besides these there were no other stone theaters in Rome. The Roman theater differed from the Greek. In the first place the *auditorium* formed a semicircle only, with the front wall of the stage building as its diameter, while in the Greek it was larger than a semicircle. Again a covered colonnade ran round the highest story of the Roman theater, the roof of which was of the same height as the highest part of the stage. The orchestra, moreover, which was inclosed by the *cavea,* contained places for spectators; these were, at the first, reserved exclusively for senators; foreign ambassadors whom it was wished to honor were afterward admitted to them. . . . Places of dignity were also assigned to magistrates and priests, probably on the *podium,* or the space in front of the lowest row of seats, where there was room for a few rows of chairs. The first fourteen rows of the ordinary seats were (68 B.C.) appropriated to the *equites;* after them came the general body of citizens, who were probably arranged in the order of their tribes; in the upper part of the *cavea* were the women, who sat apart, in accordance with a decree of Augustus; the lowest class were relegated to the highest tier. Even children were admitted, only slaves being excluded. Admission was free, as was the case with all entertainments intended for the people. The tickets of admission did not indicate any particular seat, but only the block of seats and the row in which it would be found" (Seyffert, *Dict. of Class Antiq.,* s.v.). At Athens, Corinth, Antioch, Amman, Jerash, Pompeii, and Italian Ostia can be seen the ruins of theaters that were in use during the biblical period. Amphitheaters for gladiatorial and athletic contests were as popular as theaters (cf. 1 Cor. 9:24-27; 2 Tim. 4:7).

BIBLIOGRAPHY: M. Bieber, *The History of the Greek and Roman Theater* (1961).

THEBES (thēbz). The Greek name of a city of Egypt, and its capital during the brilliant Eighteenth Dynasty (Jer. 46:25; Ezek. 30:14-15). It was also called No or No-Amon (the home of Amon, portion of Amon) as in the KJV of the preceding texts. Amon was the Egyptian god whose residence in the area accounts for this alternate name of Thebes. Thebes is referred to by classical writers as being ancient and large. The city spread itself on both banks of the Nile, just as London and Paris extend over both banks of the Thames and Seine. On the right, or E, bank are the temples of Karnak and of Luxor. On the left, or W, bank, going from N to S, was a series of mortuary temples: of Qurna, of Deir-el-Bahri, the Rameseum, the Colossi of Memmon (Amenhotep III), the temple of Deir-el-Medineh, and of Medinet-Habu. In the vicinity of the west bank temples are the Valley of the Kings, the Valley of the Queens, and the Valley of the Nobles. Karnak is an especially great marvel, its architecture a wonder of construction skill. Its great hall contains 134 columns, the loftiest 70 feet in height and 12 feet in diameter; the hall itself is 340 feet wide by 277 feet long, every stone a book and every column a library in itself. The temple of Luxor is also notable. It is a compound 858 feet long, built primarily by Amenhotep III, with additions by Rameses II and Alexander the Great.

Roman theater at Caesarea

Of all these the most wonderful was Karnak, with its great hall, its impressive obelisks (the tallest 97 feet high), and Shishak's inscription recording his invasion of Judah in Rehoboam's reign.

Thebes was the metropolis of Upper Egypt. When Strabo visited the place in 24 B.C., he said the extent of its ruins was about nine miles. Population estimates of the city at its height range as high as 1 million. It became famous in the Eleventh Dynasty, and suffered in the Thirteenth because of the invasion of the Hyksos. In the sixteenth century B.C. Amosis liberated the country and it reached its height of magnificence. The splendor of the city departed with the removal of the residence of the pharaohs to the Delta. Thebes declined after Assyrian attacks under Esarhaddon and Ashurbanipal in the seventh century B.C. It was crushed by Rome 30-29 B.C.

Frederick L. Norden, sponsored by King Christian IV of Denmark, made the first survey of Thebes in the winter of 1737 and 1738. The first large collection of copies of inscriptional material was made by Champollion and his colleague Rosellini in 1828 and 1829. Georges Legrain worked at the temple of Karnak for the Service des Antiquités from 1895 until his death in 1917. He was followed by Henri Chevrier, who was in charge of work at Thebes from 1926 to 1956. The story of Howard Carter's work in the Valley of the Kings and his discovery of the tomb of Tutankhamen in 1922 has often been told. The Oriental Institute of the University of Chicago has been working on a massive architectural and epigraphic survey of the site since 1919.

BIBLIOGRAPHY: C. F. Nims, *Thebes of the Pharaohs* (1965).

THE'BEZ (thē'bez). The scene of the death of the usurper Abimelech (Judg. 9:50). He had suffocated a thousand Shechemites in the stronghold of Baal-berith by the smoke of green wood and then besieged and took Thebez. This town possessed a strong tower, to which the men, women, and children fled. When Abimelech advanced toward the tower and drew near to set the door on fire, a woman threw a millstone down upon him from the roof of the tower, smashing his skull. Whereupon he called to his armorbearer to give him a deathblow with his sword, that men might not say of him, "A woman slew him." Thebez is preserved in the large village of Tubâs, NE of Shechem, a still important town. It is situated on the slope and summit of a hill whose sides are pierced with numerous cisterns, some in use. Hundreds of people even now live underground in caves cut in the rock.

THEFT. *See* Law.

THEOCRACY (Gk. *theokratia,* "rule of God"). The form of government among the early Israelites in which Jehovah was recognized as their supreme civil ruler, and His laws were taken as the statute book of the kingdom. Moses, Joshua, and the Judges were the appointees and agents of Jehovah. The kings were each specifically anointed in His name, and the prophets were commissioned to inform them of His will. They did not hesitate to rebuke and even veto the kings' actions if contrary to the divine will. The later history of Israel is a rehearsal of the conflict and intercourse between the great Head of the kingdom and the refractory functionaries.

According to the amillennial view, the theocratic idea passed over, in its spiritual import, to the Messiah as the heir of David's perpetual dynasty, Christ becoming the Ruler of His church in the hearts of its members. According to premillennial eschatology, Christ was rejected as king by the Jews. His death, burial, and resurrection brought in an entirely new entity, the church, begun at Pentecost (Acts 2) and to be completed at the coming of Christ for His own (1 Thess. 4:13-18; 1 Cor. 15:53-54). According to pretribulation rapturists, the church will be removed preceding Daniel's seventieth week when the Lord will again deal with Israel (Dan. 9:27). After the apocalyptic judgments of this seven-year period and the destruction of godless Gentiles and wicked Jews, the remnant of Israel will be the nucleus of the theocratic kingdom established over Israel at the second coming of Christ (cf. Acts 1:6). This mediatorial Davidic kingdom, in which Jews will be reinstated to full divine favor as head over the nations, will last at least 1,000 years (Rev. 20), after which there will be a Satanic revolt and judgment. After this the eternal state will be brought in (Rev. 21-22). Thus, amillennialists and premillennialists differ as to the state of Israel and the nation's theocratic future.   M.F.U.

BIBLIOGRAPHY: A. J. McClain, *The Greatness of the Kingdom* (1959); J. D. Pentecost, *Things to Come* (1964), pp. 433-75; D. H. Dalman, *The Words of Christ* (1981), pp. 234-88, 316-23.

THEOPH'ILUS (the-of'i-lus; "friend of God"). The person to whom Luke inscribes his gospel and the Acts of the apostles (Luke 1:3; Acts 1:1). There is a considerable number and variety of theories concerning him. The traditional connection of Luke with Antioch has disposed some to look upon Antioch as the residence of Theophilus and possibly as the seat of his government. We may safely reject the patristic notion that Theophilus was either a fictitious person or a mere personification of Christian love. The epithet *kratiste* ("most excellent") is sufficient evidence of his historical existence. It does not, indeed, prove that he was a governor, but it makes most probable that he was a person of high rank. All that can be conjectured with any degree of safety concerning him comes to this, that he was a Gentile of rank and consideration who came under the influence of Luke, or under that of Paul at Rome, and was converted to the Christian faith.

"The only traditional information we possess about this person is that found in the 'Clementine Recognitions' (10.71), about the middle of the 2nd century: 'So that Theophilus, who was at the head of all the men in power at the city [of Antioch], consecrated, under the name of a church, the great basilica [the palace] in which he resided.' According to this, Theophilus was a great lord residing in the capital of Syria" (Godet, *Com.,* on Luke).

THESSALO'NIAN (thes-a-lō'ni-an). The designation (Acts 20:4; 1 Thess. 1:1; 2 Thess. 1:1) "of Thessalonica" (Acts 27:2) of an inhabitant of *Thessalonica* (which see).

THESSALONIANS, FIRST EPISTLE TO. This, perhaps the earliest Pauline epistle, was written by the apostle in conjunction with Silvanus (Silas) and Timothy.

Occasion. Paul had established the Thessalonian church on his second missionary journey and was expelled from Thessalonica. From this city he went to Berea and to Athens. The epistle alludes to Paul's life at Thessalonica (chap. 2). At Athens he had sent Timothy back to Thessalonica to help the Christians amid their persecutions (3:1-3). Acts 18:5 records that Silas and Timothy rejoined the apostle at Corinth. It is clear, therefore, that the epistle was written from that city in A.D. 52 or 53. Three special needs existed among the Thessalonians, calling for apostolic instruction: (1) They were careless about their daily work, evidently under the impression that the second advent would very shortly take place. (2) There was concern among them lest their Christian friends who had died would suffer loss at the coming of Christ for His own. (3) Friction existed between church officers and those who possessed miraculous spiritual endowments.

Purpose. The letter was written to urge the Thessalonians to worthwhile conduct and work in the light of the return of Christ; to comfort them concerning those who had died in the Lord; and to instruct them in the elementary truths of the Christian gospel.

Outline.

   I. Salutation (1:1)

  II. The exemplary church (1:1-10)

     A. Gratitude for the Thessalonians (1:2-4)

     B. Operation of the gospel among them (1:5-10)

 III. The exemplary minister (2:1-20)

     A. Paul's ministry at Thessalonica (2:1-12)

     B. The Thessalonians' response (2:13-16)

     C. The apostle's subsequent relations with the Thessalonians (2:17-20)

 IV. The exemplary brother (3:1-13)

     A. Apostolic concern and their welfare (3:1-8)

     B. The apostolic intercession (3:9-13)

  V. Exemplary walk (4:1-18)

     A. The walk described (4:1-12)

     B. The coming of Christ, the dynamic of a holy walk (4:13-18)

 VI. Exemplary watchfulness and the Day of the Lord (5:1-24)

     A. The Day of the Lord and the need for watchfulness (5:1-11)

     B. Duties of church and private life (5:12-22)

     C. Prayer for sanctification (5:23-24)

 VII. Conclusion (5:25-28)

Attestation and Authorship. The epistle claims to be written by Paul (1:1; 2:18). Paul's character shines out from this epistle. Note his anxiety for the believers' welfare (3:1-2), his earnest desire for their spiritual edification (3:8-11), his compassion toward them (2:7), and his sympathy with those in distress (4:13, 18). External evidence is found in Marcion, who accepted it into his canon. It is found also in the Old Syriac and the Old Latin versions. The Muratorian Canon catalogs it sixth in the list of Pauline epistles. Irenaeus first refers to it by name in *Against Heresies* 5.6.1. Tertullian also quotes it as "written by the Apostle." Clement of Alexandria seems to be the first to ascribe it to Paul in *Instructor* 1.5. Thenceforth references to it are numerous.

M.F.U.

BIBLIOGRAPHY: E. H. Askwith, *An Introduction to the Thessalonian Epistles* (1902); G. G. Findlay, *The Epistles of Paul the Apostle to the Thessalonians.* Cambridge Greek Testament (1911); L. L. Morris, *The First and Second Epistles to the Thessalonians,* New International Commentary on the New Testament (1959); id., *The Epistles of Paul to the Thessalonians,* Tyndale New Testament Commentaries (1960); J. E. Frame, *A Critical and Exegetical Commentary on the Epistles of St. Paul to the Thessalonians,* International Critical Commentary (1960); W. Hendriksen, *Exposition of I and II Thessalonians* (1964); D. E. Hiebert, *The Thessalonian Epistles* (1971); E. Best, *A Commentary on the First and Second Epistles to the Thessalonians,* Harper's New Testament Commentaries (1972); J. Eadie, *A Commentary on the Greek Text of the Epistles of Paul to the Thessalonians* (1976); G. Milligan, *St. Paul's Epistles to the Thessalonians* (1980).

THESSALONIANS, SECOND EPISTLE TO. The second epistle of Paul to the Thessalonians was written to correct the erroneous notion among the Christians at Thessalonica that the persecutions from which they were suffering were those of "the great and awesome day of the Lord" (Joel 2:31) from which they had been taught to expect deliverance by "the coming of our Lord Jesus Christ, and our gathering together to Him" (2 Thess. 2:1). The theme of this epistle, obscured by the mistranslation of the KJV in 2:2, "the day of Christ is at hand," is correctly rendered in NASB "The day of the Lord has come."

Purpose. Second Thessalonians was written to instruct the Thessalonians concerning the day of Christ "and our gathering together to Him" (2 Thess. 2:1) and to settle them in their conviction that in the day of Christ the Lord would appear to translate the living saints and to raise the deceased ones, so that actually the apostle Paul in 2 Thess. 2:1 is arguing for a pretribulation out-taking of the church as the Body of Christ. In 2:1-12 he outlines the events of the Day of the Lord that will occur after the out-taking of the church.

Plan. (1) The apostle comforts the Thessalonians in their sufferings (1:4-10). He argues for the imminency of the coming of Christ for His own (2:1). (2) He stresses the fact that the Day of the Lord, so voluminously prophesied in the OT, will not arrive until *the apostasy* has set in and the "man of lawlessness" has been made manifest (2:2-10). (3) He urges the Thessalonians to faithfulness in view of the coming of Christ for His own (2:13–3:5). (4) He warns the idle and the disorderly to be properly adjusted to the doctrine taught (3:6-15). (5) He shows them how to distinguish his epistles from those of forgers (3:17).

Outline.

I. Salutation (1:1-4)
II. Comfort in their sufferings (1:5-12)
III. The Day of the Lord and the man of sin (2:1-12)
   A. Argument for pretribulation rapture (2:1-2)
   B. Signs of the Day of the Lord (2:3-12)
IV. Exhortations and instructions (2:13 –3:15)
   A. Exhortations to steadfastness and faithfulness (2:13 –3:5)
   B. Admonition against disorderliness and idleness (3:6-15)
V. Benediction (3:16-18)

Attestation and Authorship. The essential evidence for this epistle is earlier and more extensive than that of the first epistle. Justin Martyr refers to 2:3-4 in his *Dialogue with Trypho,* chap. 110. Irenaeus mentions it by name, ascribing it to Paul. Tertullian quotes it as by the "apostle," manifestly Paul, as seen by the context. Clement of Alexandria makes reference to 3:1-2 in *Stromata* (5.3). The Muratorian Canon, Old Syriac, Old Latin, and Marcion's Canon include it. The epistle is of immense importance eschatologically.
M.F.U.

BIBLIOGRAPHY: *See* Thessalonians, First Epistle.

THESSALONICA (thes-a-lo-ni′ka). Called anciently Therma. It was named after the wife of Cassander, who rebuilt the city. Under the Romans it was one of four divisions of Macedonia. Paul and Silas organized a church there (Acts 17:1-4; 1 Thess. 1:9). In Acts 20:1-3, Paul's visit is named; see also Phil. 4:16; 2 Tim. 4:10. In Acts 17:6, 8, the rulers of the city are called, in the original, *politarchai.* This title of a political magistrate is otherwise unknown in extant Gk. literature. At the western entrance to the city there remained standing until 1876 a Roman arch. This contained an inscription on its gate mentioning certain city officials called "politarchs." Other inscriptions also contained the same word. The politarchs were elected by "the people," which refers to the assembly of the *demos.* Thus one of the assertions of historical inaccuracy in Scripture has been answered. The modern city Salonika is a strategic Balkan metropolis having a population of more than 400,000. Because of its position it played a vital role in the First and Second World Wars. Located on the great road (*Via Egnatia*) that connected Rome with the whole region N of the Aegean Sea, Thessalonica was an invaluable center for the spread of the gospel. In fact it was nearly, if not quite, on a level with Corinth and Ephesus in its share of the commerce of the Levant. The circumstance

noted in 17:1, that here was the synagogue of the Jews in this part of Macedonia, evidently had much to do with the apostle's plans and also doubtless with his success. The first scene of the apostle's work at Thessalonica was the synagogue (17:2-3). As a result of German occupation during World War II, the city lost about all its Jewish population. Because the modern city covers the site of the ancient city, little can be seen of NT Thessalonica. Remains of the ancient agora are visible in the center of modern Thessalonica, however. The apostle Paul's ministry in Thessalonica fit his urban strategy—his effort to reach the empire through its cities.

BIBLIOGRAPHY: E. M. Blaiklock, *Cities of the New Testament* (1965), pp. 45-49.

Ruins of ancient agora at Thessalonica

THEU′DAS (thū′das). An insurgent mentioned by Gamaliel in his speech before the Sanhedrin, at the time of the arraignment of the apostles (Acts 5:35-39). He seems to have been a religious impostor and to have had about 400 adherents, who were all slain or scattered. Josephus (*Ant.* 20.5.1) informs us "that a certain magician, whose name was Theudas, persuaded a great part of the people to take their effects with them, and follow him to the river Jordan; for he told them he was a prophet, and that he would, by his own command, divide the river, and afford them an easy passage over it; and many were deluded by his words. Fadus ... sent a troop of horsemen out against them; who falling upon them unexpectedly, slew many of them, and took many of them alive. They also took Theudas alive, and cut off his head, and carried it to Jerusalem."

THICKET (Heb. *gā'ôn,* "pride"). "The thicket of the Jordan" (Jer. 12:5; 49:19; 50:44; "swelling," KJV) is a phrase that could also be rendered "pride of the Jordan," as in Zech. 11:3. Orelli renders it "jungles of Jordan," where lions lurk. *See also* Vegetable Kingdom: Forest.

THIEF. *See* Law.

THIEVES. The prophet Isaiah (Isa. 1:23) says of

the Israelite rulers that they were "companions of thieves," meaning that they allowed themselves to be bribed by presents of stolen goods so they would overlook acts of injustice. The men who under this name appear in the crucifixion account were robbers rather than thieves, belonging to the lawless bands by which Palestine was at that time and afterward infested. Against these brigands every Roman procurator had to wage continual war. It was necessary to use armed police to counter them (cf. Luke 22:52). Of the previous history of the two who suffered on Golgotha we know nothing. They had been tried and condemned and were waiting their execution before our Lord was accused. It is probable enough, as the death of Barabbas was clearly expected at the same time, that they had taken part in his insurrection. At first the thieves reviled our Lord, but afterward one of them in penitence prayed to be remembered when Jesus should come to His kingdom (Matt. 27:38, 44; Mark 15:27).

THIGH (Heb. *yārēk*; Gk. *mēros*). The part of the body from the legs to the trunk.

1. In taking an oath it was an ancient custom to put the hand under the thigh. Abraham required it of his servant when he made him swear that he would not take a wife for Isaac of the daughters of the Canaanites (Gen. 24:2-9). Jacob required it of Joseph when he bound him by oath to bury him in Canaan (47:29-31). This custom, the so-called bodily oath, was, no doubt, connected with the significance of the hip as the part from which the posterity issued (46:26, marg.) and the seat of vital power. The early Jewish commentators supposed it to be especially connected with the rite of circumcision.

2. It is stated (Gen. 32:25-32) that the angel touched the hollow of Jacob's thigh and put it out of joint. By the dislocation of his hip the carnal nature of his previous wrestling was declared to be powerless and wrong. By his wrestling with God, Jacob entered upon a new stage in his life. Because of the dislocation of Jacob's thigh the custom began among his descendants of refraining from eating the *nervus ischiadicus*, the principal nerve in the area of the hip, which is easily injured by any violent strain in wrestling.

3. If the wife accused by her husband of infidelity was guilty, a part of the curse pronounced upon her was that her thigh should waste away (Num. 5:21). It is impossible to determine precisely the nature of this disease. Michaelis supposes it to have been dropsy of the ovary.

Figurative. "Hip and thigh" involved cruel, unsparing slaughter. *To uncover the leg* (Isa. 47:2) was to lay aside all feminine modesty. *Striking the thigh* signified deepest shame (Jer. 31:19) or sorrow (Ezek. 21:12).

THIM'NATHAH (thim'na-tha). *See* Timnah.

THINGS SACRIFICED TO IDOLS (1 Cor. 8:1, 4, 7, 10; cf. Acts 15:20; "Meats offered to idols," 15:29, KJV). This consisted of those parts of the animals offered in heathen sacrifices that remained after the priests had received their share, and that were either eaten in the temple or at home in connection with sacrificial feasts, or else purchased by poor or miserly persons in the meat markets. This was a very practical matter, as the Christian might easily come to eat such meat, either through being invited to a feast by heathen acquaintances (10:27) or by buying it in the market (10:25), and thereby offense would be given to scrupulous consciences. On the other hand, those of freer spirit, and with more of Paul's own mode of thinking, might be apt to make light of the matter and forget how a Christian ought to spare the weak. *See* Expediency.

THIRD OF A SHEKEL. A unit of money. *See* Metrology.

THIRST (Heb. *ṣāmē'*; Gk. *dipsos*). A painful sensation occasioned by the absence of liquids from the stomach. This sensation is sometimes accompanied by vehement desire, and the term is therefore used figuratively in the Scripture in the moral sense of a longing after God (Pss. 42:2; 63:1; cf. 143:6; etc.). A longing after criminal indulgence is also called thirst (Jer. 2:25). A state of continued satisfaction is expressed by the phrase "They shall hunger no more, neither thirst anymore" (Rev. 7:16).

THISTLES, THORNS. *See* articles Thorn; Vegetable Kingdom.

THOM'AS (tom'as; from Aram. *te'ômā'*, "twin"). One of the twelve apostles, he was also called Didymus, its Gk. equivalent. Because of the meaning of Thomas's name, *twin*, several in the early Christian era attempted to identify his twin brother or sister. But, it is likely that the twin is not even mentioned in the NT, making such identification impossible. He is said to have been born in Antioch, but is also considered by some a native of Galilee, like most of the other apostles (John 21:2).

In the first three gospels there is an account of his call to the apostleship (Matt. 10:3; Mark 3:18; Luke 6:15). The rest that we know of him is derived from the gospel of John. When Jesus declared His intention of going to Bethany after Lazarus's death, Thomas, apprehensive of danger, said to the other disciples, "Let us also go, that we may die with Him" (John 11:16). At the Last Supper, when Jesus was speaking of His departure, Thomas said to Him, "Lord, we do not know where You are going, how do we know the way?" (14:5). When Jesus appeared to the first assembly after His resurrection, Thomas, for some reason, was absent. The others told him, "We have seen the Lord!" Thomas broke forth into an exclamation that conveys to us at once the vehemence of his doubt and the vivid picture that his mind retained of his Master's form as he had seen Him lifeless on the cross (20:25). "And after eight days again His disciples were inside, and Thomas with them. Jesus came, the doors having been shut, and stood in their midst, and said, 'Peace be with you.'" Turning to Thomas, He uttered the words that convey as strongly the sense of condemnation and tender reproof as those of Thomas had shown hesitation and doubt. "Then He said to Thomas, 'Reach here your finger, and see My hands; and reach here your hand, and put it into My side; and be not unbelieving, but believing.'" The effect upon Thomas was immediate. Doubt was removed, and faith asserted itself strongly. The words in which he expressed his belief contain a high assertion of his Master's divine nature: "Thomas answered and said to Him, 'My Lord and my God!'" The answer of our Lord sums up the moral of the whole narrative: "Because you have seen Me, have you believed? Blessed are they who did not see, and yet believed" (20:26-29). From this incident came the title of "Doubting Thomas," and he has been characterized as "slow to believe, subject to despondency, seeing all the difficulties of a case, viewing things on the darker side." It may be that he was of a critical tendency of mind, in which he did not recognize the statement of eyewitnesses as a sufficient ground of faith. After the above-mentioned incident, we hear of Thomas only twice again, once on the Sea of Galilee, with six other disciples (21:2), and again in the assembly of the apostles after the ascension (Acts 1:13). Early traditions, as believed in the fourth century, represent him as preaching in Parthia, or Persia, and as finally being buried in Edessa. Later traditions carry him farther E. His martyrdom is said to have been occasioned by a lance.

BIBLIOGRAPHY: F. W. Robertson, Sermons on Bible Subjects (1910), pp. 320-23; C. E. Macartney, The Wisest Fool (1949), pp. 142-52; C. J. Barber, Searching for Identity (1975), pp. 133-44; J. D. Jones, The Apostles of Christ (1982), pp. 172-94.

THORN. The rendering of several Heb. and Gk. words. *See also* Vegetable Kingdom.

Figurative. "A painful thorn" (Ezek. 28:24) should be rendered a smarting sting, figurative of the hurts of paganism. "The most upright like a thorn hedge" (Mic. 7:4) refers to the corruption of the nation, which was so great that even the most upright injured all who came in contact with him. In Job 5:5, "and take it to a place of thorns" means that even a thorny hedge does not prevent them from taking the food of the orphan. From want of energy "the way of the sluggard is as a hedge of thorns" (Prov. 15:19), i.e., full of almost insurmountable obstacles (cf. 22:5). To be overgrown with thorns is a figure of desolation (cf. 24:31). "The crackling of thorn bushes under a pot" (Eccles. 7:6) is that to which the laughter

of fools is compared. The wicked are often compared to thorns (2 Sam. 23:6; Nah. 1:10). Dried cow dung was the common fuel in Palestine; its slowness in burning makes the quickness of a fire of thorns most graphic as an image of the sudden end of fools (cf. Ps. 118:12). Thorns and thistles are symbolic of the false prophets (Matt. 7:16).

THORN IN THE FLESH. *See* Paul.

THREE TAVERNS. *See* Appii Forum.

THRESHING. *See* Agriculture.

Figurative. Threshing is used in Scripture as a figure of providential chastisement (Isa. 21:10); crushing oppression (41:15; Mic. 4:12-13); judicial visitation (Jer. 51:33); the labors of ministers (1 Cor. 9:9-10). Dust made by threshing is a figure of complete destruction (2 Kings 13:7).

THRESHING FLOOR (Heb. *gōren*, "even"). A level and hard-beaten plot in the open air (Judg. 6:37; 2 Sam. 6:6), on which sheaves of grain were threshed (Isa. 21:10; Jer. 51:33; Mic. 4:12; Matt. 3:12). The top of a rock was a favorite spot for this purpose; on this the sheaves were spread out and sometimes beaten with flails—a method practiced especially with the lighter grains, such as fitches or cummin (Isa. 28:27)—but more commonly by oxen. The oxen were either yoked side by side and driven around over the grain, or were yoked to a drag (Lat. *tribulum* or *trahea*), consisting of a board or a block of wood, with stones or pieces of iron fastened to the lower surface to make it rough. This was dragged over the grain, beating out the kernels.

The threshing floors were watched all night to guard against theft of the grain (Ruth 3:3-6, 14); they were often of considerable value, and frequently named in connection with a winepress (Deut. 16:13; 2 Kings 6:27; Hos. 9:2; Joel 2:24), since grain, wine, and oil were the more important products of the soil. They were sometimes given specific names, such as that of Nacon (2 Sam. 6:6) or Chidon (1 Chron. 13:9), Atad

Winnowing on a threshing floor

Tiberias from the seashore

(Gen. 50:10), Ornan or Araunah (2 Sam. 24:18, 20; 1 Chron. 21:15).

THRESHOLD. The rendering of:

1. Heb. *săph,* a sill or bottom of a doorway (Judg. 19:27; 1 Kings 14:17; Ezek. 40:6-7; Zeph. 2:14).

2. Heb. *miptān,* a "stretcher," probably the bottom beam or sill of a door (1 Sam. 5:4-5; Ezek. 9:3; 10:4, 18; 46:2; 47:1).

BIBLIOGRAPHY: H. C. Trumbull, *The Threshold Covenant* (1896).

THRONE (Heb. *kisse';* Gk. *thronos; bēma*). The Heb. term *kĭssē'* applies to any elevated seat occupied by a person in authority, whether a judge (Ps. 122:5) or a military chief (Jer. 1:15). The use of a chair in a country where the usual postures were squatting and reclining was at all times regarded as a symbol of dignity (2 Kings 4:10; Prov. 9:14). In order to specify a throne in our sense of the term it was necessary to add to *kĭssē'* the notion of royalty; hence the frequent occurrence of such expressions as "the throne of his kingdom" (Deut. 17:18; 1 Kings 1:46; cf. 2 Chron. 7:18). The characteristic feature of the royal throne was its elevation: Solomon's throne was approached by six steps (1 Kings 10:19; 2 Chron. 9:18); and Jehovah's throne is described as "lofty and exalted" (Isa. 6:1). The materials and workmanship were costly. It was furnished with

Roman bath, Tiberias

arms or "stays." The steps were also lined with pairs of lions. As to the form of the chair, we are only informed in 1 Kings 10:19 that there was "a round top to the throne at its rear." The king sat on his throne on state occasions. At such times he appeared in his royal robes.

Figurative. The throne was the symbol of supreme power and dignity (Gen. 41:40). To "sit on the throne" implied the exercise of regal power (Deut. 17:18; 1 Kings 16:11); to sit on the throne of another (1 Kings 1:13) meant to succeed him as king. "Thrones" also designate earthly potentates and celestial beings, archangels (Col. 1:16).

BIBLIOGRAPHY: A. R. Johnson, *Sacral Kingship in Ancient Israel* (1955).

THUM'MIM (thum'im). *See* Urim and Thummim.

THUNDER (Heb. *qôl*, a "voice," i.e., of Jehovah; *rā'am*, a "peal"; Gk. *brontē*). From a physical point of view the most noticeable feature in connection with thunder is the extreme rarity of its occurrence during the summer months in Palestine and adjacent countries. From the middle of April to the middle of September it is hardly ever heard. Hence it was selected by Samuel as a striking expression of the divine displeasure toward the Israelites (1 Sam. 12:17). Rain in harvest was deemed as extraordinary as snow in summer (Prov. 26:1), and Jerome asserts that he had never witnessed it in the latter part of June or in July (*Com.*, on Amos 4:7). The plague of hail in Egypt is naturally represented as accompanied with thunder (Ex. 9:22-29, 33-34). It accompanied the lightning at the giving of the law (19:16; 20:18). It is referred to as a natural phenomenon subject to laws of the Creator ("thunderbolt," Job 28:26; 38:25).

In John 12:28 it is related that there came "a voice out of heaven" in response to the prayer of Jesus. "It is a voice which came miraculously from God; yet, as regards its intelligibility conditioned by the subjective disposition and receptivity of the hearers, which sounded with a *tone as of thunder,* so that the definite words which resounded in this form of sound remained unintelligible to the unsusceptible, who simply heard that majestic kind of sound, but not its contents, and said, *brontēn gegonenai* ('It is thunder')" (Meyer, *Com.*, ad loc.). Mark (Mark 3:17) says that our Lord surnamed James and John "Boanerges, which means, 'Sons of Thunder.'" Some have thought that this applied to them because of their eloquence; others to their courage and energy. It seems more likely that it referred to their impetuous, ardent temperament.

Figurative. In the imaginative philosophy of the Hebrews thunder was regarded as the voice of Jehovah (Job 37:2, 4-5; 40:9; Pss. 18:13; 29:3), who dwelt behind the thunder (Ps. 81:7). Thunder was, to the mind of the Jew, the symbol of

divine power (29:3; etc.) and vengeance (1 Sam. 2:10; 2 Sam. 22:14).

THUNDERBOLT. In the KJV of Ps. 78:48, the translation of Heb. *reshep*, "flame," "fire," "spark" ("bolts of lightning," NASB, NIV); another Heb. expression, *hăzîz qōlôth,* is translated "thunderbolt" in the NASB of Job 28:26; 38:25 ("thunderstorm," NIV).

THYATI'RA (thī-a-tī'ra). A city in Asia Minor, the seat of one of the seven apocalyptic churches (Rev. 1:11; 2:18). It was situated in the confines of Mysia and Ionia, a little S of the river Lycus and at the northern extremity of the valley between Mt. Tmolus and the southern ridge of Temnus. It was one of the many Macedonian colonies established in Asia Minor in the sequel of the destruction of the Persian Empire by Alexander. The waters of Thyatira are said to be so well adapted for dyeing that in no place can the scarlet cloth out of which fezes are made be so brilliantly or so permanently dyed as here. So in the Acts (16:14) Lydia, the first convert of Paul at Philippi, is mentioned as "a seller of purple fabrics" from Thyatira. The principal deity of the city was Apollo, worshiped as the sun-god under the surname Tyrimnas. He was no doubt introduced by the Macedonian colonists, for the name is Macedonian. A priestess of Artemis is also mentioned in the inscriptions. The modern city of Akhisar, about 50,000 in population, marks the site of the ancient city in the territory that is now Anatolian Turkey. Nothing of the ancient city can be seen. Remains of a Byzantine church remind one that the gospel once came to this place.

BIBLIOGRAPHY: E. B. Blaiklock, *Cities of the New Testament* (1965), pp. 107-11; W. M. Ramsay, *The Letters to the Seven Churches of Asia* (1978), pp. 316-53.

THYINE WOOD. *See* Vegetable Kingdom: Citron Wood.

TIBE'RIAS (tī-bē'ri-as). A city in the time of Christ, on the Sea of Galilee; first mentioned in

Synagogue ruins, Tiberias

the NT (John 6:1, 23; 21:1, "Sea of Tiberias"), and then by Josephus, who states that it was built by Herod Antipas and was named by him in honor of the emperor Tiberius, A.D. 14-37. It was one of nine towns around the sea, each one having not less than 15,000 inhabitants. Because Tiberias was situated on the edge of the ancient walled town Rakkath (Josh. 19:35), or Hammath, whose cemetery lies beneath it, in Jesus' time it was avoided by strict Jews. Our Lord apparently did not visit the city, noted for its laxness as a hot-water bath resort. Tiberias was the capital of Galilee from the time of its origin until the reign of Herod Agrippa II, who changed the seat of power back again to Sepphoris, where it had been before the founding of the new city. Many of the inhabitants were Greeks and Romans, and foreign custom prevailed there to such an extent as to give offense to stricter Jews. After the destruction of Jerusalem in A.D. 70, Tiberias became a Jewish metropolis and center of rabbinic learning. After A.D. 150, it was well known as the seat of the Sanhedrin and the rabbinical schools from which came the Talmud and the Masorah. The city lies about twelve miles S of the entrance of the Jordan into the Lake of Galilee and six miles N of the river's exit from the sea. The vicinity is rich in archaeological possibilities, especially the area between the city and the famous hot springs. Masonry of various dates survives, including a synagogue.

BIBLIOGRAPHY: M. Avi-Yonah and E. Stern, eds., *Encyclopedia of Archaeological Excavations in the Holy Land* (1978), pp. 1171-76.

TIBE'RIAS, THE SEA OF. Another name (John 21:1 only) for the Sea of Galilee (cf. 6:1). It is thought that the evangelist used this name because it was more familiar to nonresidents in Palestine than the indigenous names of the "Sea of Galilee" or "Sea of Gennesaret."

TIBE'RIUS (ti-bē'ri-us; "pertaining to the Tiber"; in full, Tiberius Claudius Nero Caesar). The second Roman emperor, successor of Augustus, who began to reign A.D. 14 and reigned until A.D. 37. He was the son of Tiberius Claudius Nero and Livia, and hence a stepson of Augustus. He was born at Rome on November 16, 42 B.C. He became emperor in his fifty-fifth year, after having distinguished himself as a commander in various wars and having displayed notable talents as an orator and an administrator of civil affairs. He even gained the reputation of possessing the sterner virtues of the Roman character and was regarded as entirely worthy of the imperial honors to which his birth and supposed personal merits opened the way. Yet, on being raised to supreme power, he suddenly became, or showed himself to be, a very different man. The historian Tacitus's vilification of his character is now known to be overdrawn, and Tiberius has been rehabilitated in recent years. Tiberius died at the age of seventy-

eight, after a reign of twenty-three years. He is mentioned in Scripture only in Luke 3:1, where he is termed Tiberius Caesar. John the Baptist, it is said in vv. 2-3, began his ministry in the fifteenth year of his reign, an important chronological statement, helping to determine the year of Christ's birth and entrance on His public life.

BIBLIOGRAPHY: F. B. Marsh, *The Reign of Tiberius* (1931); R. Seager, *Tiberius* (1972); B. M. Levick, *Tiberius the Politician* (1976).

Head of Emperor Tiberius

TIB'HATH (tib'hath; "slaughter"). A city of Hadadezer, king of Zobah (1 Chron. 18:8), called *Betah* (which see) in 2 Sam. 8:8, probably an accidental transposition of the first two letters. *See* Tebah.

TIB'NI (tib'ni; "straw"). The sixth king of Israel, and son of Ginath. After the tragic death of Zimri there was a division among the people. "Half of the people followed Tibni . . . the other half followed Omri." After a struggle lasting four years Omri's party prevailed, and, according to the brief account of the historian, "Tibni died and Omri became king" (1 Kings 16:21-22), about 880 B.C.

TI'DAL (tī'dal). The name of a king (Gen. 14:1) who accompanied Chedorlaomer in his raid into Palestine about 1960 B.C. Of the personality of this king nothing is known. The country ruled by Tidal was Goiim, often translated "nations" or "Gentiles." It is not yet certainly located. Hommel believed it to be Goi, in northeastern Babylonia. *See* articles on Chedorlaomer; Arioch; and Amraphel.

TIG'LATH-PILE'SER (tig'lath-pī-lē'zer). The name of an Assyrian king (*see* also Pul). The name of Tiglath-pileser fills a large place in the history of the Hebrew people before the fall of

Samaria. It was in the reign of Tiglath-pileser III, known also as Pul, that they first felt the menace of complete overthrow by the Assyrians.

Name and Origin. The name Tiglath-pileser appears in Assyr. under the form of *Tukulti-apil-esharra*, meaning "my trust is the son of Esharra," i.e., the god Ninib, but this was abbreviated even by the Assyrians themselves. It was a famous name in the annals of Assyria, for one of the greatest Assyrian conquerors, Tiglath-pileser I (about 1120 b.c.), had borne it. Tiglath-pileser III was, however, a far greater man than his earlier namesake. He was not of royal origin. Of his origin, indeed, nothing is known. It is probable that he was an Assyrian general. He may have been also an administrator or governor of one of the vast provinces of the Assyrian empire. He appears suddenly upon the scene of historical action. He says nothing in his inscriptions of his father or mother. His inscriptions were mutilated long after his death by Esarhaddon, an indignity offered to no other king, and these facts lead irresistibly to the conclusion that he was not a member of the royal family. The king who preceded him upon the throne was Asshur-nirari III, who reigned weakly from 754 to 745 b.c. In the year 746 there was a rebellion against his rule. Whether Tiglath-pileser, then perhaps a general, started this rebellion, participated in it, or merely reaped its results, we have no means of knowing; but immediately upon the death of Asshur-nirari III he was acknowledged king of Assyria.

Reign. The first years of his reign showed him a masterful man. In other instances in Assyrian history such an usurpation would have been followed by petty wars and insurrections all over the kingdom, but no audible murmur was heard at the beginning of his reign. He was evidently known everywhere as a man with whom it would be dangerous to trifle. His reign was not long (745-727 b.c.), and he may have come to the throne comparatively late in life. Whatever his name was, he assumed at once the royal style of Tiglath-pileser, adopting the royal name as his own. Were it not for the abuse of his inscriptions at the hands of Esarhaddon, we should know all the events of his reign in great detail. He had restored the palace of Shalmaneser in Calah. Upon the walls of its great rooms he placed stone slabs with beautifully engraved inscriptions recounting the campaigns of his reign. Besides these he left inscriptions written upon clay, giving accounts of his campaigns grouped in geographical order and supplemented these by other inscriptions on clay containing lists of the countries conquered, but without any details of the campaigns. The first matter that claimed the attention of the new king was an invasion of Babylonia, rendered necessary to drive out nomadic Aramaeans who had invaded and settled in the country and threatened to destroy its civilization.

The march of the new Assyrian king southward was a triumphal progress. He was heralded as a deliverer and soon reestablished an orderly government in the kingdom of Babylonia. After this he turned NW and E, where he collected heavy tribute from peoples who had refused to pay it during the weak reign of his predecessor. At the very beginning he introduced an entirely new method of dealing with conquered peoples. Before his reign the Assyrian kings had for the most part contented themselves with predatory raids by which they enormously increased the wealth of Assyria, but contributed little to the upbuilding of stable government in the conquered lands. Peoples thus conquered paid tribute while the conqueror was at hand and refused when they thought he was far enough away to place them out of danger. Some of the previous kings had tried colonization and deportation in a very slight fashion but without conspicuous success. Tiglath-pileser III made these his chief methods. He first conquered a people and then deported the best of them to another part of his dominion, bringing from that place enough people to colonize the land thus vacated. For many peoples this was punishment worse than death. From his point of view it contributed to stability by making successful rebellion almost an impossibility. Further, he set Assyrian governors over conquered provinces and endeavored not only to collect tribute annually but also to administer all the affairs of the land as a part of the Assyrian empire that he was building. Campaign followed campaign, N, E, and S, with lesser invasions also in the west. All these things little affected the Hebrew people. They were, however, a threat of what might occur when once he was free to attend to the conquest of Palestine.

Relation with Israel. Nominally some of the states of Syria and Palestine were already Assyrian tributaries, but Assyrian influence had been little felt for a long time. If it had been possible to unite all the petty kingdoms of Syria, Palestine, and their neighboring countries into one great confederation for mutual defense, it would probably have been possible to prevent the reconquest of the west by the Assyrians, even under so great a master as Tiglath-pileser III. But the weakness of the west lay in its utter inability to put aside selfish and petty concerns to work for united interests. Some of these states determined again, about 739 b.c., to throw off the Assyrian yoke. At the head of the coalition thus formed was Azariah, or Uzziah, king of Judah. To support him, Hamath, Damascus, Tyre, Que, Melid, Samaria, and others to the number of nineteen had banded together. It was indeed a promising confederation. If all these states had put their full quota of men into the field under competent military direction, they would, no doubt, have been able to resist the Assyrians and to prevent or at least postpone the engulfing of Syria into

Tiglath-pileser

the now rapidly growing Assyrian empire. But before any combination of their forces could be brought about, Tiglath-pileser came W and entered Palestine, apparently determined to attack the ringleader, Uzziah, in his own territory, before his allies could come to his aid. As soon as he entered the Northern Kingdom, Menahem threw down his arms and paid the Assyrians 1,000 talents of silver as a token of subjection. Here was practically an end of the entire confederation. Tiglath-pileser was apparently satisfied with this collapse; and as the others were willing to pay tribute, he did not pursue the advantage that he had gained but went back to Assyria laden with heavy booty, to which Rezin of Damascus and Hiram of Tyre had also contributed. In 734 B.C. he was again on the Mediterranean coast. In this year he seems to have crossed the plain of Syria, near Damascus, and to have gone straight to the coast, which he followed toward the S. He had no fear of Tyre or of Sidon, for they were busy with commerce, and he needed but to strike but a few light blows before Gaza was reached. Here, if ever, Egypt and Syria and all the west ought to have made a stand against the Assyrians; but no stand was made, and Gaza was overwhelmed. In the reign of Ahaz, king of Judah, there was another opportunity for him to form a coalition with Pekah of Samaria and Rezin of Damascus against Assyria. But Pekah and Rezin thought they saw in the youth of Ahaz a chance for the enrichment of their own kingdoms. They united forces and invaded Judah. So began the Syro-Ephraimitic war. Ahaz was likely to be overwhelmed. To whom should he turn for help? No help was to be

had in Egypt, and in the madness of the hour he sent an embassy to meet Tiglath-pileser and ask for help against Damascus and Samaria. Tiglath-pileser accepted a bribe from Ahaz, for it suited his own purposes to do so, and at once threatened Damascus. This drew off from Judah the armies of Damascus and Samaria. Tiglath-pileser then passed by Damascus, came down the seacoast past his tributary states of Tyre and Sidon, and turned into the plain of Esdraelon above Carmel. His own accounts fail us at this point, but the biblical narrative fills the gap by stating that he took a number of cities and overran the land (2 Kings 15:29). He might then have attacked Samaria itself, but a party of assassins made that unnecessary, for they slew Samaria's king, and in his place Tiglath-pileser set up Hoshea as the nominal king of Samaria, but as his personal representative (15:30). Damascus was next besieged and captured (732 B.C.) and the entire country about it given over to desolation. Tiglath-pileser boasts that he destroyed at this time 591 cities, whose inhabitants were carried away with all their possessions to Assyria. Ahaz of Judah came to pay honor in Damascus to this foreign conqueror, who was now practically master over the whole country. He it was who had prepared the way for the destruction of Samaria by Shalmaneser V and Sargon II (722-721 B.C.). His later career has but little bearing upon the OT story. In 728 B.C., on New Year's Day, he was solemnly anointed king of Babylon, and in 727 he died. Upon any basis of estimate whatever he ranks as one of the greatest conquerors and one of the greatest executives among all the great rulers who made Assyria a dreaded name in Asia. He made the Assyrian empire out of a kingdom and a few dependencies. He made it a world power, binding province to province, and transforming local centers into general centers by deportation and colonization.   R.W.R.; M.F.U.

BIBLIOGRAPHY: D. J. Wiseman, *Iraq* 13 (1951): 21-24; id., 18 (1956): 117-29; H. W. F. Saggs, *Iraq* 19 (1957): 114-54; D. D. Luckenbill, *Ancient Records of Assyria and Babylonia* (1968), 1:72-104, 269-96; R. D. Barnett and M. Falkner, *The Sculptures of Tiglath-pileser III* (1962); H. Tadmor, *Inscriptions of Tiglath-pileser III* (1978).

TI'GRIS (tī'gris). Used in the LXX as the equivalent of the Heb. *Hiddeqel* ("Hiddekel," Gen. 2:14, marg.), one of the rivers of Eden. The name of Hiddekel, or Tigris, was also Akkad. In the old language of Babylonia it was termed *Idiglat, Digla,* "the encircling." From *Idliglat* the Persians formed their Tigra with a play upon a word in their own language that signified an "arrow." The Tigris, we are told, flowed to the "east of Ashur." But the Ashur meant is not the land of Assyria but the city of Ashur, the primitive capital of the country, now represented by the mound of Kalah Sherghat. The land of Assyria lay to the E as well as to the W of the Tigris. Daniel (Dan.

10:4) calls it "the great river, that is, the Tigris." It rises in the mountains of Armenia, about thirty miles NW of Diarbekir, at no great distance from the sources of the Euphrates, and pursues a meandering course of upward of eleven hundred miles, when at last the Tigris and Euphrates unite and flow as one stream into the Persian Gulf. *See* Hiddekel.

TIK'VAH (tik'va; "hope, expectation").

1. The son of Harhas, and father of Shallum, the husband of Huldah the prophetess (2 Kings 22:14), before 624 B.C. He is called Tokhath in 2 Chron. 34:22; Tikvah, KJV.

2. The father of Jahzeiah, which latter was one of the rulers appointed by Ezra to superintend the divorcement of the Gentile wives after the captivity (Ezra 10:15), before 437 B.C.

TIK'VATH (tik'vath). *See* Tikvah.

TILE (Heb. *lebēnâ* from *lāban*, "to be white," so called from whitish clay), a brick (Ezek. 4:1, KJV; "tablet," NIV, NKJV) used to write upon.

TILES (Gk. *keramos*, "pottery ware"). The rendering of Luke 5:19, "through the tiles" (*dia tōn keramōn*), has been the cause of considerable difficulty. Some have understood the tiles to be the layer of sticks, brush, and hard-rolled clay that constitutes the ordinary flat roof of an oriental house. Of course, the breaking up of this might be readily repaired, but would cause intolerable dust at the time. Edersheim (*Life of Jesus*, 1:503) says: "The roof itself, which had hard-beaten earth or rubble underneath it, was paved with brick, stone, or any other hard substance, and surrounded by a balustrade which, according to Jewish law, was at least three feet high. It is scarcely possible to imagine that the bearers of the paralytic would have attempted to dig through this into a room below, not to speak of the interruption and inconvenience caused to those below by such an operation. But no such objection attaches if we regard it not as the main roof of the house, but as that of the covered gallery under which we are supposing the Lord to have stood. . . . In such case it would have been comparatively easy to 'unroof' the covering of 'tiles,' and then 'having dug out' an opening through the lighter framework which supported the tiles, to let down their burden 'into the midst before Jesus.' "

TIL'GATH-PILNE'SER (til'gath-pil-ne'zer). A variation (1 Chron. 5:6, 26; 2 Chron. 28:20) of *Tiglath-pileser* (which see).

TILLAGE. A KJV term that appears as the translation of two different Heb. words.

1. Heb. *nîr* is translated "tillage" in the KJV of Prov. 13:23 ("fallow ground," NASB, NKJV; "field," NIV). The Heb. term appears elsewhere; see Jer. 4:3; Hos. 10:12, where *nîr* appears as both a noun ("fallow ground") and a verb ("break up").

2. Heb. *'abôdâ* is not always translated "tillage." It refers to labor or service, either as servile labor (Lev. 25:39); work, or business (1 Chron. 9:19); or work of the field, agriculture (Neh. 10:37; 1 Chron. 27:26; both "tillage," KJV; the NKJV reads "farming communities" and "work of the field," respectively; NIV, "towns where we work" and "who farmed the land," respectively).

TI'LON (ti'lon). The last named of the four "sons" of Shimon, of the tribe of Judah (1 Chron. 4:20).

TIMAE'US (ti-mē'us), father of the blind beggar cured by Christ (Mark 10:46), the son being thence called *Bartimaeus* (which see).

TIMBREL. *See* Music.

TIME. The rendering of several Heb. and Gk. terms, of which the following are most important:

1. *Day* (Heb. *yôm*), used both in the particular sense of a natural day (*see* below), and in the general sense of a set time or period of time.

2. *An appointed time* (Heb. *zeman*); thus "there is an appointed time for everything" (Eccles. 3:1), i.e., everything remains but for a time; all things are frail and fleeting. In Dan. 2:16 (*see* marg.) it is an appointed season.

3. *Set or appointed time* (Heb. *mô'ēd*, an "appointment"), a space of time, appointed and definite (Ex. 34:18; 1 Sam. 13:8; cf. Jer. 8:7; etc.).

4. *Time to come* (Heb. *māḥār*, "tomorrow"; Ex. 13:14; Josh. 4:6, 21; cf. 1 Sam. 20:12).

5. *A set time* (Aram. *'iddān*) is used in the book of Daniel in a sense that has been much disputed. In Dan. 4:16, cf. vv. 23, 25, 32, the prophet writes of Nebuchadnezzar, "Let his mind be changed from that of a man, and let a beast's mind be given to him, and let seven periods of time pass over him." Gesenius (*Lexicon*) gives its meaning as prophetic language for a year. "Following the example of the LXX and of Josephus, many ancient and recent interpreters understood by the word *'iddānîn, years,* because the *times* in 7:25; 12:7 are also years, and because in 4:29 mention is made of twelve months, and thereby the *time* is defined as one year. But from 4:29 the duration of the *'iddānîn* cannot at all be concluded, and in 7:25 and 12:7 the *times* are not years. *'Iddān* designates generally a definite period of time, whose length or duration may be very different" (Keil, *Com.*, on Dan. 4:16).

6. Heb. *'ēt* is a general term for *time*; e.g., the *time of evening* (Josh. 8:29); *time of bearing* (Job 39:1-2); *at* or *about* a time (Dan. 9:21); *time* or *season* of love (Ezek. 16:8), i.e., of young women at marriageable age, etc.

7. Heb. *pa'am*, a "stroke," a tread of the foot, step (Ps. 119:126); one time (Gen. 18:32, "this once"; Ex. 9:27; Prov. 7:12, "now").

8. *Hidden time*, i.e., obscure and long, of which the beginning or end is indefinite, *dura-*

tion, everlasting, eternity (Josh. 24:2; Deut. 32:7, "days of old"; Prov. 8:23, "everlasting"; Heb. *'ôlām,* "concealed").

9. An *occasion, set* time (Gk. *kairos*). A *space* of time, opportunity, etc. (Gk. *chronos*).

BIBLIOGRAPHY: J. Barr, *Biblical Words for Time* (1962).

TIME, DIVISIONS OF. The following are mentioned in Scripture:

Year (Heb. *shānâ,* as a "revolution" of time). So called from the *change* of the seasons. The years of the Hebrews in the preexilic period were *lunar,* of 354 days 8 hours 38 seconds, and consisted of 12 unequal lunar months. As this falls short of the true year (an astronomical month having 29 days 12 hours 44 minutes 2.84 seconds), they were compelled, in order to preserve the regularity of harvest and vintage (Ex. 23:16), to add a month occasionally, thus making it on the average to coincide with the solar year (containing 365 days 5 hours 48 minutes 45 seconds). The method of doing this among the very ancient Hebrews is unknown. Among the later Jews an intercalary month was inserted after Adar and was called Ve-dar, or second Adar. The intercalation was regularly decreed by the Sanhedrin, which observed the rule never to add a month to the sabbatical year.

The Hebrew year began, as the usual enumeration of the months shows (Lev. 23:34; 25:9; Num. 9:11; 2 Kings 25:8; Jer. 39:2; cf. 1 Macc. 4:52; 10:21), with Abib or Nisan (Esther 3:7), subsequent to and in accordance with the Mosaic arrangement. As we constantly find this arrangement spoken of as a *festal* calendar, most rabbinical and many Christian scholars understand that the *civil* year began, as with modern Jews, with Tisri (October), but the *ecclesiastical* year with Nisan.

A well-defined and universal era was unknown among the ancient Hebrews. National events were sometimes dated from the Exodus from Egypt (Ex. 19:1; Num. 33:38; 1 Kings 6:1), usually from the accession of the kings (as in Kings, Chronicles, and Jeremiah) or the erection of Solomon's Temple (1 Kings 8:1-2; 9:10). Later events were dated from the beginning of the Exile (Ezek. 33:21; 40:1), but this system was not used in Ezek. 1:1. For special purposes, such as the tithing of cattle and the planting of trees, the Jewish year began at distinct times. The regnal year began with Nisan. The first year of each king's reign began on the first day of Nisan after his accession, the preceding days being counted to his predecessor. This accounts for the precise specification of the time of three months as exceptional in the case of the reigns of Jehoahaz and Jeconiah. The postexilian books date according to the reigning years of the Persian masters of Palestine (Ezra 4:24; 6:15; 7:7-9; Neh. 2:1; 13:6; Hag. 1:1-2; etc.).

As Syrian vassals the Jews adopted the Greek (1 Macc. 1:10) or Seleucid era, which dated from the overthrow of Babylon by Seleucus Nicator I. Still another national reckoning is given (1 Macc. 13:41-42), namely, from the year of the deliverance of the Jews from the Syrian yoke, i.e., the seventeenth year of the Seleucian era, or from the autumn of 143 B.C.

Month (Heb. *ḥōdesh,* the "new" moon). The Hebrew months were lunar and began from when the new moon was seen; at least this is the case from the postexilian period. In this period the length of the lunar month depended upon the day when the appearance of the new moon was announced by the Sanhedrin, which thus made the month either twenty-nine days or thirty days, according to how the day was included in the following or the preceding month. The general rule was that in one year not less than four nor more than eight full months should occur. The final adjustment of the lunar to the solar year was by intercalation; so that whenever in the last month, Adar, it became evident that the Passover, which must be held in the following month, Nisan, would occur before harvest, an entire month was interjected between Adar and Nisan, constituting an intercalary year. This, however, according to the Gemara, did not take place in a sabbatic year but always in that which preceded it; nor in two successive years, nor yet more than three years apart.

Before the Exile the individual months were usually designated by numbers (the twelfth month occurs in 2 Kings 25:27; Jer. 52:31); yet we find also the following names: "Ear month" (Heb. *ḥōdesh hā'ābîb;* Ex. 13:4; 23:15; Deut. 16:1), corresponding to the later Nisan; "Bloom month" (*ḥōdesh ziw;* 1 Kings 6:1, 37), the second month; "Rain month" (*yeraḥ bûl;* 6:38), the eighth month; "Freshet month" (*yeraḥ hā'ētānîm;* 8:2), the seventh month; all of which seem to be mere appellatives. Occasionally the months were newly numbered after the postexilian period.

After the Exile the months received the following names: (1) *Nisan* (Neh. 2:1; Esther 3:7), the first month, in which the Passover was held and in which the vernal equinox fell; (2) *Iyâr* (Targum on 2 Chron. 30:2); (3) *Sivân* (Esther 8:9); (4) *Tammûz;* (5) *Ab;* (6) *Elul* (Neh. 6:15), the last month of the civil year in the postexilian age; (7) *Tishrî,* in which the festivals of the Day of Atonement and Tabernacles fell; (8) *Marcheśvân* (Josephus *Ant.* 1.3.3); (9) *Chislêu* (Neh. 1:1; Zech. 7:1); (10) *Tebêth* (Esther 2:16); (11) *Shebât* (Zech. 1:7); (12) *Adâr* (Esther 3:7; 8:12).

Week (Heb. *shābûa',* "sevened"; Gk. *sabbaton,* "rest," by extension "sennight," i.e., the interval between two sabbaths). The division of time into weeks occurs as early as Gen. 2:2-3; and in the narrative of the Deluge more than one allusion occurs to this mode of computing time (7:4, 10; 8:10, 12). Later, weeks appear to have been known among the Syrians of Mesopotamia (29:27-28), and still later they attached a certain sacredness to the number *seven,* if we may judge from the procedure of Balaam (Num. 23:1, 4, 14, 29). Weeks appear to have been known in Egypt in the time of Joseph (Gen. 50:10-11). Weekly institutions constituted a prominent feature of the Mosaic law (Num. 19:11; 28:17; Ex. 13:6-7; 34:18; Lev. 14:38; 23:42; Deut. 16:8, 13). Ordinarily, however, days rather than weeks (as among the Greeks and Romans) constituted the conventional mode of computing time (*see* Lev. 12:5; Dan. 10:2-3).

In the postexilic period reckoning by weeks became more customary, and at length special names for particular weekdays came into use (Mark 16:2, 9; Luke 24:1; Acts 20:7; 1 Cor. 16:2). The astronomical derivation of the week naturally grows out of the obvious fact that the moon changes about every seven—properly, 7⅜—days, so that the lunar month divides itself into four quarters. The days of the week were named long before the Christian era on regular astronomical principles from the seven planets, which was an Egyptian invention. They began with Saturn's day (Saturday), inasmuch as Saturn was the outermost planet; but among the Jews this day (the Sabbath) was the last of the week, and so the Jewish and Christian week commences with Sunday. These pagan names were never in general use among the Jews. Weeks (or heptads) of years belong, among the Jews, to prophetical poetry, but in one instance they occur in a literal sense in prose (Dan. 9:24-27).

Day (Heb. *yôm;* Gk. *hēmera*). One of the commonest and most ancient of the divisions of time. As used in Gen. 1:5; etc., *day* marks an entire revolution of time, as of natural day and night —not day as distinguished from night, but day and night together. "If the days of creation are regulated by the recurring interchange of light and darkness, they must be regarded not as periods of time of incalculable duration, of years or thousands of years, but as simple earthly days. It is true the morning and evening of the first three days were not produced by the rising and setting of the sun, since the sun was not yet created; but the constantly recurring interchange of light and darkness, which produced day and night upon the earth, cannot for a moment be understood as denoting that the light called forth from the darkness of chaos returned to that darkness again, and thus periodically burst forth and disappeared. The only way in which we can represent it to ourselves is by supposing that the light called forth by the creative mandate was separated from the dark mass of the earth, and concentrated outside or above the globe, so that the interchange of light and darkness took place as soon as the dark chaotic mass began to rotate, and to assume in the process of creation the form of a spherical body. The time occupied in the first rotations of the earth upon its axis cannot, indeed, be measured by our hourglass; but even if they were slower at first, and did not attain their present velocity till the completion of our solar system, this would make no essential difference between the first three days and the last three, which were regulated by the rising and setting of the sun" (K. & D., *Com.,* on Gen. 1:5).

From an early period the time of reckoning the day was from sunset to sunset, and this became the Jewish method (Lev. 23:32; cf. Ex. 12:18). The Phoenicians, Numidians, and other nations of the East are said to have followed the same custom, if it was not indeed the custom generally followed in remote antiquity. "The ancient Germans (Tacitus, ch. xi) compute not the number of days, but of nights; the night appears to draw on the day." And Caesar says (*Bell. Gal.* 6.18) of the Gauls, "They measure time not by the number of days, but of nights; and accordingly ob-

Table 30
The Jewish Division of the Day

English Hour	Jewish Designation	Scripture	Name in the Talmud
6:00 p.m.	Sunset	Gen. 28:11; Ex. 17:12; Josh. 8:29	
6:20 "	Stars appear		Twilight (Arab. *'Ahra*)
10:00 "	First watch ends	Lam 2:19	Evening Shema, or prayer
12:00 "	Midnight	Ex. 11:4; Ruth 3:8; Ps. 119:62; Matt. 25:6; Luke 11:5	The donkey brays
2:00 a.m.	Second watch ends	Judg. 7:19	
3:00 "	Rooster crow	Mark 13:35; cf. Matt. 26:75	The dog barks
4:30 "	Second rooster crow	Matt. 26:75; Mark 14:30	
5:40 "	Column of dawn		Twilight (Arab. *Subah*)
6:00 "	Sunrise (third watch ends)	Gen. 19:23; Ex. 14:24; Josh. 1:15, 1 Sam. 11:11	Three blasts of the trumpet (Arab. *Doher*); morning sacrifice
9:00 "	First hour of prayer	Acts 2:15	
12:00 m.	Noon	Gen. 43:16; 1 Kings 18:26; Job 5:14	
1:30 p.m.	Great vesper		
3:30 "	Small vesper		First Mincha
5:40 "			Second Mincha (Arab. *'Aser*); Arab. *Mogoreb,* before sunset
6:00 "	Sunset	Gen 15:12; Ex. 17:12; Luke 4:40	Evening sacrifice at the NE of the altar; nine blasts of the trumpet Six blasts of the trumpet, on the eve of the Sabbath

serve their birthdays, and the beginning, of months and years, so as to make the day follow the night." Of this custom we have a memorial in our "sennight," "fortnight," to express the period of seven and fourteen days respectively.

Figurative. Day is often used by sacred writers, in a general sense, for a definite period of time —an era or season, when something remarkable has taken place or is destined to do so (Gen. 2:4; Isa. 22:5; Joel 2:2; etc.). And it accorded with Hebrew usage to designate by the term day or night what probably formed only a part of these; thus by three days and three nights might be understood only a portion of three (Matt. 12:40; 27:63-64; cf. 1 Kings 12:5, 12). As it is also by day that the more active portion of man's life is spent, so day is used to express the whole term of life considered as a season of active labor (John 9:4).

Hour (Aram. *shā'â*, properly a "look"; Gk. *hōra*). It would appear that the Babylonians were among the first to adopt the division of twelve equal parts for the day, as Herodotus testifies (2.109) that the Greeks derived this custom from the Babylonians. The Hebrews also adopted it; and in the NT we read of the third, sixth, and ninth hours of the day, which were the more marked divisions of the twelve. The night was divided into the same number of parts. From the variations in sunrise and sunset this division, which had these natural phenomena for its two terminations, could never be exact and was therefore unsuited to nations that had reached a high degree of civilization. Such nations accordingly adopted midnight as the fixed point from which the whole daily cycle might be reckoned, divided into twice twelve, or twenty-four hours.

Table 30, "The Jewish Division of the Day," gives the divisions of the day according to natural phenomena and religious observances.

BIBLIOGRAPHY: *See* Calendar; Time.

TIMES, OBSERVER OF. KJV phrase replaced in the NASB and NKJV with reference to those "who practice witchcraft," and in the NIV with those "who practice divination or sorcery" (Deut. 18:10, 14; Lev. 19:26; 2 Kings 21:6; 2 Chron. 33:6). *See* Magic: Various Forms.

TIM'NA (tim'na; Heb. *timnâ*; cf. the same name in S. Arabia; the capital of Qataban, some fifty miles SE of Marib).

1. A concubine of Eliphaz son of Esau, and mother of Amalek (Gen. 36:12). In 1 Chron. 1:36 she is named (by an ellipsis) as a *son* of Eliphaz. She is probably the same as the sister of Lotan and daughter of Seir the Horite (Gen. 36:22; 1 Chron. 1:39).

2. A chief of Edom (Gen. 36:40; 1 Chron. 1:51; "Timnah," KJV).

TIM'NAH (tim'na; Heb. *timnâ*, "an allotted portion"). A name that occurs, simple and compounded, and with slight variations of form, sev-

eral times in the topography of the Holy Land.

1. A place that formed one of the landmarks on the N boundary of the allotment of Judah (Josh. 15:10), and belonging to Dan (19:43), also mentioned in connection with Samson (Judg. 14:1, 5; "Timnath," KJV). The modern representative of this name is probably *Tibnah*, a village about two miles W of Ain Shems (Beth-shemesh), among the broken undulating country by which the central mountains of this part of Palestine descend to the maritime plain. In the later history of the Jews, Timnah must have been a conspicuous place. It was fortified by Bacchides as one of the most important military posts of Judea (1 Macc. 9:50), and it became the head of a district, or toparchy.

2. A town in the mountain district of Judah (Josh. 15:57). It was the place near which Tamar entrapped Judah into intercourse with her (Gen. 38:12-14; "Timnath," KJV). A distinct place from no. 1.

3. The KJV spelling of the name of a chief ("duke," KJV) of Edom (Gen. 36:40; 1 Chron. 1:51).

BIBLIOGRAPHY: M. Avi-Yonah and E. Stern, eds., *Encyclopedia of Archaeological Excavations in the Holy Land* (1978), 4:1184-1203.

TIM'NATH. *See* Timnah.

TIM'NATH-HE'RES (tim'nath-he'res; "portion of the sun"; Judg. 2:9). *See* Timnath-Serah.

TIM'NATH-SE'RAH (tim'nath-se'ra; "double portion," Josh. 19:50; 24:30). The name of the city that was presented to Joshua after the partition of the country (19:50); and in "the territory of his inheritance," where he was buried (24:30). It is specified as being "in the hill country of Ephraim, on the north of Mount Gaash." In Judg. 2:9, the name is altered to Timnath-heres. The latter form is that adopted by the Jewish writers. Accordingly, they identify the place with Kefar Cheres, which is said by Rabbi Jacob, hap-Parchi, and other Jewish travelers, to be about five miles S ("nine miles," G. A. Smith) of Shechem (*Nablûs*). No place with that name appears on the maps. Another and more promising identification is Tibnah, 12 miles NE of Lydda and 8½ miles SW of Kefr Haris, where the Samaritans locate the sepulchers of Joshua and Caleb. "Heres" is probably "Serah" inadvertently written backward.

TIM'NITE (tim'nīt). A designation of Samson's father-in-law, from his residence in Timnah (Judg. 15:6).

TI'MON (ti'mon; Gk. "reckoning, worthy"). The fifth named of the seven "deacons" appointed to serve as distributors of food on the occasion of complaints of partiality being made by the Hellenistic Jews at Jerusalem (Acts 6:5). Nothing further is known of him.

TIMO'THEUS (ti-mo'the-us), the Gk. form of *Timothy* (which see).

TIM'OTHY (tim'o-thi; "venerating God"). The convert and friend of Paul. Timothy was the son of one of those mixed marriages that, though unlawful, were frequent in the later periods of Jewish history. His mother was a Jewess, whereas his father (name unknown) was a Greek (Acts 16:1-3).

Early Life. The picture of Timothy's early life, as described by the apostle Paul, portrays a mother and grandmother, full of tenderness and faith, piously instructing him in the Scriptures and training him to hope for the Messiah of Israel (2 Tim. 1:5; 3:15). Thus, though far removed from the larger colonies of Israelite families, he was brought up in a thoroughly Jewish atmosphere; however he could hardly be called a Jewish boy, having never been admitted by circumcision within the pale of God's ancient covenant.

Conversion. Timothy was probably living at Lystra when Paul made his first visit to that city (Acts 16:1), and he appears to have been converted at that time (14:6; cf. 2 Tim. 1:5). No mention is made of Timothy until the time of Paul's second visit, but it is safe to assume that his spiritual life and education were under the care of the elders of the church (Acts 14:23).

Circumcision. Those who had the deepest insight into character and spoke with a prophetic utterance pointed to Timothy (1 Tim. 1:18; 4:14) as specially fit for missionary work; and Paul desired to have him as a companion. The apostle circumcised him (Acts 16:3), and Timothy was set apart as an evangelist by the laying on of hands (1 Tim. 4:14; 2 Tim. 4:5).

"He took him and circumcised him" (Acts 16:1, 3). Paul's conduct in circumcising Timothy has been considered inconsistent with his principle and conduct in refusing to circumcise Titus (Gal. 2:3-4). "The two cases are, however, entirely different. In the latter there was an attempt to enforce circumcision as necessary to salvation; in the former it was performed as a voluntary act, and simply on prudential grounds" (Haley, *Alleged Discrepancies*, p. 260).

Paul's Companion. Henceforth Timothy was one of Paul's most constant companions. They and Silvanus, and probably Luke also, journeyed to Philippi (Acts 16:12), and there the young evangelist was already conspicuous for his filial devotion and zeal (Phil. 2:19-22). He seems to have been left behind at Philippi to watch over the infant church. He appeared at Berea, where he remained with Silas after Paul's departure (Acts 17:14), joining Paul at Athens. From Athens he was sent back to Thessalonica (1 Thess. 3:2), since he had special gifts for comforting and teaching. He left Thessalonica, not for Athens, but for Corinth, and his name is united with Paul's in the opening words of both letters writ-

ten from that city to the Thessalonians (1:1; 2 Thess. 1:1). Of the five following years of his life we have no record. He is next mentioned as being sent on in advance when the apostle was contemplating the long journey that was to include Macedonia, Achaia, Jerusalem, and Rome (Acts 19:22). It is probable that he returned by the same route and met Paul according to a previous arrangement (1 Cor. 16:10) and was thus with him when the second epistle was written to the church of Corinth (2 Cor. 1:1). He returned with the apostle to that city and joined in messages of greeting to the disciples whom he had known personally at Corinth and who had since gone to Rome (Rom. 16:21). He formed one of the company of friends who went with Paul to Philippi and then sailed by themselves, waiting for his arrival by a different ship (Acts 20:3-6). No further mention is made of him until he rejoined the apostle, probably soon after his arrival in Rome. He was with Paul when the epistles to the Philippians, the Colossians, and Philemon were written (Phil. 1:1; 2:19; Col. 1:1; Philem. 1). It follows from 1 Tim. 1:3 that he and Paul, after the release of the latter from his imprisonment, revisited proconsular Asia, that the apostle then continued his journey to Macedonia, while Timothy remained, half-reluctantly, even weeping at the separation (2 Tim. 1:4), at Ephesus to check if possible the outgrowth of heresy and licentiousness that had sprung up there. He had to exercise rule over presbyters, some older than himself (1 Tim. 4:12); to render judgments (5:1, 19-20); to regulate the almsgiving and sisterhood of the church (vv. 3-10); and to ordain overseers and deacons (3:1-13). These duties, together with the danger of being entangled in the disputes of rival sects, made Paul anxious for the steadfastness of his disciple. Among his last recorded words Paul expressed his desire to see him again (2 Tim. 4:9, 21). It is uncertain whether Timothy was able to fulfill these last requests of the apostle, or that he reached Rome before Paul's death, although some have seen in Heb. 13:23 an indication that he shared Paul's imprisonment.

Legends. According to an old tradition, Timothy continued to act as bishop of Ephesus and suffered martyrdom under Domitian or Nerva.

BIBLIOGRAPHY: D. E. Hiebert, *Personalities Around Paul* (1973), pp. 98-113.

TIMOTHY, FIRST EPISTLE. The first of three pastoral letters written by Paul to two of his young converts (1 Tim. 1:2; cf. Titus 1:4) who had accompanied him on many of his missionary journeys. They had been established as pastors of churches, and these epistles were directed to them to give them instructions for the orderly management of the organized congregations. These letters thus have a special message to youthful ministers. Although the letters are directed to young pastors and not to churches, their messages are peculiarly applicable to the churches.

Date. Apparently Paul was released from prison at Rome between A.D. 63 and 67. If this is true, it was during this interval that he composed this epistle. He also sent Titus an epistle at this time. If Paul endured only one Roman imprisonment, 1 Timothy was written just before his last visit to Jerusalem.

Theme. The golden text of the epistle may be said to be 3:15, "That you may know how one ought to conduct himself in the household of God, which is the church of the living God, the pillar and support of the truth." The approaching end of the apostolic period witnessed the increase of the number of the local churches and the consequent need of definite revelation concerning questions of order, creed, and discipline. At first these problems had been solved by the apostles themselves. But now definite instructions applicable to all occasions and periods were necessary.

Purpose. The apostle had four main goals in penning this letter to Timothy: (1) to encourage him to oppose false teaching (1:3-7, 18-20; 6:3-5, 20-21), (2) to furnish Timothy with written credentials authorized by himself (1:3-4), (3) to instruct him in the management of ecclesiastical affairs (3:14-15), (4) to exhort him to diligence in the performance of his pastoral duties (4:6–6:2).

Outline.
  I. Salutation (1:1-2)
 II. Defense of the church's faith (1:3-20)
III. Regulations for church conduct (2:1–3:16)
    A. Concerning prayer (2:1-8)
    B. Place of women (2:9-15)
    C. Qualifications of elders and deacons (3:1-16)
 IV. Warning against apostasy and false doctrine (4:1-5)
  V. Prescriptions for ministerial conduct, private and public (4:6–6:2)
 VI. False and true teachers contrasted (6:3-19)
VII. Closing appeal to faithfulness (6:20-21)

Attestation and Authenticity. Three classifications of objections—(1) chronological, (2) linguistic, and (3) ecclesiastical—have been commonly urged against the pastoral epistles (1 and 2 Timothy and Titus). Some assume Paul was in prison in Rome only once and that the pastorals cannot be fitted into the events of his ministry. But the third group of Paul's epistles distinctly favors the idea that Paul was released after two years (Acts 28:30-31). The linguistic peculiarities hinge on the numerous *hapax legomena* in the pastorals—ninety-six in 1 Timothy; sixty in 2 Timothy; forty-three in Titus, this being about twice as many as in the other Pauline epistles. This argument, however, has never been conclusive, since Paul was writing on a distinct subject that required a different vocabulary. Ecclesiastical objection maintains that the pastorals imply

too finished a stage of church organization for so early a period as the Pauline age. This, however, is hardly a tenable objection since the apostle had already ordained elders in every city on his first missionary journey; and the churches that he addressed, as at Philippi (Phil. 1:1), were well organized with "overseers and deacons." There is no evidence in these epistles of "a second-century sacerdotalism." All the pastorals are to be taken as genuinely Pauline since their internal evidence manifestly reflects the character and temperament of the great apostle.   M.F.U.

BIBLIOGRAPHY: J. H. Bernard, *The Pastoral Epistles*, Cambridge Greek Testament (1922); D. Guthrie, *The Pastoral Epistles*, Tyndale New Testament Commentary (1957); D. E. Hiebert, *First Timothy* (1957); H. A. Kent, Jr., *The Pastoral Epistles* (1958); C. K. Barrett, *The Pastoral Epistles* (1963); J. N. D. Kelly, *The Pastoral Epistles* (1963); P. N. Harrison, *Paulines and Pastorals* (1964); W. Hendriksen, *Exposition of the Pastoral Epistles* (1968); H. P. Liddon, *Explanatory Analysis of St. Paul's Epistle to Timothy* (1978); P. Fairbairn, *The Pastoral Epistles* (1980).

TIMOTHY, SECOND EPISTLE. This pastoral letter has been called the "swan song" of Paul. It is the final message of the apostle. There is a deep solemnity in the epistle bordering on a note of sadness. But above it there is a tone of triumph. "I have fought the good fight, I have finished the course, I have kept the faith" (4:6-8).

Date. The following is a probable calendar of Paul's life during the closing years of his career: A.D. 58 he was arrested in Jerusalem; A.D. 61 he arrived in Rome; A.D. 61-63 mark his first Roman imprisonment; A.D. 64-67 he was released, during which interval he wrote 1 Timothy and Titus from Macedonia; A.D. 67, 2 Timothy was penned from Rome; A.D. 67-68 Paul was arrested and put to death.

Purpose. Second Timothy, like 2 Peter, Jude, and 2 and 3 John, concerns the personal walk and testimony of a true servant-soldier of Christ in a day of apostasy. After the salutation, 1:1-3, Paul (1) appeals for loyalty to the gospel, 1:3-18, and for soldierly endurance in Timothy's ministry, 2:1-13. (2) He gives important direction concerning Timothy's ministerial conduct, 2:14-26. (3) He warns against perilous times that are to come, 3:1-9. (4) He urges Timothy to follow his example, 3:10-13. (5) He alludes to Timothy's early training as a basis for his present faithfulness, 3:14-17. (6) He urges faithful proclamation of the word of truth in view of approaching apostasy and his own martyrdom, 4:1-8. (7) He expresses longing for fellowship, 4:9-18. (8) He dispatches greetings, 4:19-22.

Outline.
  I. Salutation (1:1-3)
 II. Appeal to faithfulness and endurance (1:4-18)
III. Appeal to activity in service (2:1-26)
    A. As a good soldier (2:1-14)

B. As a good student (2:15-26)
IV. Warning of apostasy (3:1–4:5)
    A. Prophetic foreview of the last days (3:1-9)
    B. Authority of the Scriptures in the last days (3:10-17)
    C. Instructions for the last day (4:1-5)
V. Allegiance to the Lord (4:6-22)
    A. Paul's final testimony (4:6-8)
    B. His last words (4:9-22)   <small>M.F.U.</small>

BIBLIOGRAPHY: D. E. Hiebert, *Second Timothy* (1958); J. R. W. Stott, *Guard the Gospel* (1973). See also Timothy, First Epistle.

TIN. *See* Mineral Kingdom.

TINKLE, TINKLING ORNAMENTS (Heb. *'akas*). Mentioned as a characteristic of the manner in which the Jewish women carried themselves (Isa. 3:16). They could take only short steps because of the chains by which the costly foot rings worn above their ankles were joined together. These chains were probably ornamented with bells, as is sometimes the case now in the East, which tinkled as they walked. *See also* Dress.

TIPH'SAH (tif'sa; "a ford, passage"). The limit of Solomon's dominion toward the Euphrates (1 Kings 4:24) and said to have been attacked by Menahem king of Israel (2 Kings 15:16). It is generally admitted that this town is the same as the one known to Greeks and Romans as Thapsacus, a strong fortress on the western bank of the Euphrates above the confluence of the Balikh. Situated at the termination of the great trade road from Egypt, Phoenicia, and Syria to Mesopotamia and the kingdoms of inner Asia, its possession was of great importance.

TI'RAS (ti'ras). The youngest son of Japheth, the son of Noah (Gen. 10:2; 1 Chron. 1:5). Several efforts have been made to identify his descendants; ancient authorities generally fixed on the Thracians. But the matter is still enveloped in obscurity. Probably best equated with the Tyrsenoi, an ancient Pelasgic people of the Aegean coastland.

TI'RATHITE (ti'ra-thīt). The designation of one of the three families of scribes residing at Jabez (1 Chron. 2:55); the others were the Shimeathites and Sucathites.

TIRE, TIRES. A KJV term. *See* articles Dress; Turban.

TIR'HAKAH (tir'ha-ka). An Ethiopian prince mentioned in 2 Kings 19:9 as coming against Sennacherib in the Assyrian invasion of Judah (701 B.C.). His name appears as Taharka in the Egyptian records. At the time an Ethiopian dynasty was ruling Egypt in the person of Shabaka, not Tirhakah, who did not ascend the throne until c. 691 b.c., some dozen years later. The explanation is that Tirhakah, mentioned as king

(2 Kings 19:9; Isa. 37:9) actually opposed Sennacherib in 701 B.C. as a high military commander under his uncle, Shabaka, who was the ruling pharaoh. Whether the nephew had the status of a regent at the time, or whether the Judean analyst wrote proleptically, is not known. Tirhakah became the third king in the Twenty-fifth Egyptian Dynasty. Against Esarhaddon he was initially victorious, but three years later (670 B.C.) he was defeated, expelled from Memphis, and never returned. He maintained himself in Upper Egypt until his death in 663 B.C., when the Twenty-sixth Dynasty took over under Psamtik I.   <small>M.F.U.</small>

BIBLIOGRAPHY: A. Gardiner, *Egypt of the Pharaohs* (1961), pp. 335-51; K. A. Kitchen, *The Third Intermediate Period in Egypt* (1972), pp. 154-56, 164-68, 383-86.

TIR'HANAH (tir'ha-na; derivation uncertain). The second son of Caleb the Hezronite by his concubine Maacah (1 Chron. 2:48).

TIR'IA (tir'i-a; "fear"). The third named of the four sons of Jehallelel of the tribe of Judah (1 Chron. 4:16).

TIR'ZAH (tur'za; "delightfulness, pleasantness").

1. The youngest of the five daughters of Zelophehad (Num. 26:33; 27:1; 36:11; Josh. 17:3), c. 1370 B.C. This was the case that gave rise to the Levirate provision that in the event of a man's dying without male children his property should pass to his daughters.

2. An ancient Canaanite city, whose king was among the thirty-one overcome by Joshua W of the Jordan (Josh. 12:24). It was the capital of the kings of Israel down to the time of Omri (1 Kings 14:17; 15:21, 33; 16:6; etc.), who besieged Zimri there. The latter perished in the flames of his palace (16:18). Once, and once only, does Tirzah reappear, as the seat of the conspiracy of Menahem (son of Gadi) against Shallum (2 Kings 15:14, 16). Its beauty was well known (Song of Sol. 6:4).

Tell el-Far'ah, "mound of the elevated ridge," was identified by W. F. Albright in 1931 as Tirzah. This is a spacious mound located some six miles NE of Nablus. Roland de Vaux, on behalf of the French School of Archaeology in Jerusalem, excavated at Far'ah for nine seasons between 1946 and 1960. Building remains go back to about 3000 B.C. when the town was comparatively well planned and surrounded by a wall strengthened by towers. Abandoned about 2500 B.C., it was effectively occupied once more in the eighteenth century B.C. A Canaanite-type temple of the early ninth century gives an indication of the syncretistic character of Yahweh worship in the Northern Kingdom. In the ninth century the site was temporarily abandoned, tallying with Omri's action of moving the capital to Samaria. During the eighth century B.C. the town was reoccupied and again a reused Canaanite temple served as a wor-

ship center. This city was destroyed, apparently by the Assyrians when they laid siege to Samaria in 725 B.C.
M.F.U.; H.F.V.

BIBLIOGRAHY: A. M. Steve, *Palestine Exploration Quarterly* 88 (1956): 125-40.

TISHBE. *See* Tishbite.

TISHBITE. A term applied in the OT to Elijah (1 Kings 17:1; 21:17; 2 Kings 1:3, 8; 9:36). The term Tishbite refers to a native of a certain town by the name of Tishbeh, Tishbe, or something similar. Since a site of this name is unknown (although a Thisbe is mentioned as being on the right of Kydios [Kadesh] of Naphtali in Galilee above Asher), scholars such as Nelson Glueck render 1 Kings 17:1 as "Elijah, the Jabeshite, from Jabesh-Gilead." Jabesh-Gilead was a few miles W of Abel-Meholah. Under this view the brook Cherith, where Elijah sojourned, would be a small branch of the Jabesh, which empties into the Jordan.
M.F.U.

BIBLIOGRAPHY: N. Glueck, *Annual of the American Schools of Oriental Research* 25-28 (1951), Part 1: 218, 225-27; D. Baly, *The Geography of the Bible* (1957), pp. 115, 118-19, 220, 222, 224-31, 234, 237; id., *Geographical Companion to the Bible* (1963), pp. 44, 48, 51-53, 72-76, 82-86.

TITHE (Heb. *ma'ăśēr;* Gk. *dekatē,* a "tenth"). The use of tithes is frequently referred to in both secular and biblical history.

In Early Times. The two prominent instances in Genesis are: (1) Abram presenting the tenth of the spoils of his victory to Melchizedek (Gen. 14:20; Heb. 7:2, 6). (2) Jacob, after his vision at Luz, devoting a tenth of all his property to God provided that he should return home in safety (Gen. 28:22).

Mosaic Law. The tenth of all produce, flocks, and cattle was declared to be sacred to Jehovah by way, so to speak, of rent to Him who was, strictly speaking, the Owner of the land, and in return for the produce of the ground; though, if so disposed, a man was at liberty to redeem the tithes of the fruits of his field and his trees by paying the value of them with a fifth part added (Lev. 27:30-33). The law did not specify the various fruits of the field and of the trees that were to be tithed. The Mishna (*Maaseroth* 1.1) includes everything eatable, everything that was stored up or that grew out of the earth. The Pharisees, as early as the time of Jesus, made the law to include the minutest kitchen herbs, such as mint and cummin (Matt. 23:23; Luke 11:42). With regard to animal tithes, the law prescribed that every tenth beast that passed under the staff, i.e., under which the shepherd made them pass when he counted his flock, was to be sacred to the Lord, good and bad alike. It forbade any attempt to substitute one beast for another on pain of both animals—the tenth as well as the one ex-

Site of Tirzah, an ancient Canaanite city

changed for it—being required to be redeemed (Lev. 27:32-33). This tenth, called *Terumoth*, was ordered to be assigned to the Levites as the reward of their service, and it was ordered further that they were themselves to dedicate to the Lord a tenth of these receipts, which were to be devoted to the maintenance of the high priest (Num. 18:21-28).

This legislation is modified or extended in the book of Deuteronomy, i.e., from thirty-eight to forty years later. Commands are given to the people: (1) They were to bring their tithes, together with their votive and other offerings and firstfruits, to the chosen center of worship, there to be eaten in celebration in company with their children, their servants, and the Levites (Deut. 12:5-18). (2) All the produce of the soil was to be tithed every year, and these tithes with the firstlings of the flock and herd were to be eaten in the metropolis. (3) But in case of distance, permission was given to convert the produce into money, which was to be taken to the appointed place and there spent for food for a festal celebration, in which the Levite was to be included (14:22-27). (4) Then follows the direction that at the end of three years all the tithe of that year was to be gathered and laid up within the "gates" and that a festival was to be held in which the stranger, the fatherless, and the widow, together with the Levite, were to partake (vv. 28-29, *see* marg.). (5) Last, it was ordered that after taking the tithe in each third year, "the year of tithing," every Israelite had to declare that he had done his best to fulfill the divine command (26:12-14).

From all this we gather (1) that one-tenth of the whole produce of the soil was to be assigned for the maintenance of the Levites; (2) that out of this the Levites were to dedicate a tenth to God for the use of the high priest; (3) that a tithe, in all probability a *second* tithe, was to be applied to festival purposes; and (4) that in every third year either this festival tithe or a *third* tenth was to be eaten in company with the poor and the Levites. The question arises, Were there *three* tithes taken in this third year; or is the third tithe only the second under a different description? It must be allowed that the *third* tithe is not without support. Josephus distinctly says that one-tenth was to be given to the priests and Levites, one-tenth was to be applied to feasts in the metropolis, and that a tenth besides these was every third year to be given to the poor (cf. Tob. 1:7-8). On the other hand, Maimonides says that the third and sixth years' *second* tithe was shared between the poor and the Levites, i.e., that there was no third tithe. Of these opinions, that which maintains three separate and complete tithings seems improbable. It is plain that under the kings the tithe system partook of the general neglect into which the observance of the law declined, and that Hezekiah, among his other reforms, took effectual means to revive its use (2 Chron. 31:5, 12, 19).

Similar measures were taken after the captivity by Nehemiah (Neh. 12:44), and in both these cases special officers were appointed to take charge of the stores and storehouses for the purpose. Yet, notwithstanding partial evasion or omission, the system itself was continued to a late period in Jewish history (Heb. 7:5-8; Matt. 23:23; Luke 18:12).

The firstborn, the firstlings, and of the tenth of the flocks and herds and produce of the soil were offered to Jehovah as being sacred to Him. Tithes and offerings, along with the firstborn, were intended, therefore, to represent the entire produce of the land and the whole of property generally. Being paid over as they were to Jehovah, they constituted a practical confession and acknowledgment that the whole land and all possessions in general belonged to Him and that it was He alone who conferred them upon those who enjoyed them.

BIBLIOGRAPHY: C. M. Carmichael, *The Laws of Deuteronomy* (1974), pp. 40, 80, 82-86, 91, 253; J. A. Thompson, *Deuteronomy*, Tyndale Old Testament Commentaries (1975), pp. 166-71, 180-85; P. C. Craigie, *The Book of Deuteronomy* (1976), pp. 216-19, 233-34; S. H. Kellogg, *The Book of Leviticus* (1978), pp. 559-66; G. Bush, *Notes on Numbers* (1981), pp 267-70.

TITIUS JUSTUS. *See* Justus, no. 2.

TITTLE. *See* Stroke.

TI'TUS (tī'tus; a common Lat. name, Grecized Titos). A fellow laborer of Paul. We find no mention of Titus in the Acts and must draw materials for a biography of him from 2 Corinthians, Galatians, and Titus, combined with 2 Timothy. If, as seems probable, the journey mentioned in Gal. 2:1, 3 is the same as that recorded in Acts 15, then Titus was closely associated with Paul at Antioch and accompanied him and Barnabas from there to Jerusalem. At Troas the apostle was disappointed in not meeting Titus (2 Cor. 2:13), who had been sent on a mission to Corinth; but in Macedonia Titus joined him (7:6-7, 13-15). He was sent back to Corinth in company with two other trustworthy Christians, bearing the second epistle to the Corinthians and with the earnest request that he would attend to the collection being taken for the poor Christians of Judea (8:6, 17). The "brethren" who took the first epistle to Corinth (1 Cor. 16:11-12) were doubtless Titus and his companion, whoever he may have been. In the interval between the first and second imprisonment of Paul at Rome, he and Titus visited Crete (Titus 1:5). Here Titus remained and received a letter written to him by the apostle. From this letter we learn that Titus was originally converted through Paul's instrumentality (v. 4). Next we learn the various particulars of the responsible duties that he had to discharge in Crete. He was to complete what Paul had been obliged to leave unfinished (v. 5) and to organize the church throughout the island by appointing presbyters in every city. Next he was to control and silence (v. 11) the restless and mischievous Judaizers, and he was to be peremptory in so doing (v. 13). He was to urge the duties of a decorous and Christian life upon the women (2:3-5), some of whom, possibly, had something of an official character (vv. 3-4). The notices that remain are more strictly personal. Titus was to look for the arrival in Crete of Artemas and Tychicus (3:12), and then he was to hasten to join Paul at Nicopolis, where the apostle was proposing to pass the winter. Zenas and Apollos were in Crete, or expected there, for Titus was to send them on their journey and supply them with whatever they needed for it (v. 13). Whether Titus did join the apostle at Nicopolis we cannot tell. But we naturally connect the mention of this place with what Paul wrote shortly afterward (2 Tim. 4:10); for Dalmatia lay not far N of Nicopolis. From the form of the whole sentence it seems probable that this disciple had been with Paul in Rome during his final imprisonment.

Tradition. The traditional connection of Titus with Crete is much more specific and constant, though here again we cannot be certain of the facts. He is said to have been permanent bishop on the island and to have died there at an advanced age. The modern capital, Candia, appears to claim the honor of being his burial place. In the fragment by the lawyer Zenas, Titus is called bishop of Gortyna. Last, the name of Titus was the watchword of the Cretans when they were invaded by the Venetians (Smith, *Dict.,* s.v.).

BIBLIOGRAPHY: D. E. Hiebert, *Personalities Around Paul* (1973), pp. 114-24.

TITUS. An epistle of Paul written to his trusted companion Titus, who had been left as superintendent of the churches on the island of Crete. Like the first epistle to Timothy, this letter had as its purpose to give the young pastor instructions to aid him in his work.

Occasion and Date. Paul was led to pen this epistle because of the condition of Christian work on the island of Crete, the need of Titus for help, and the fact that Zenas and Apollos were going to the island. The apostle himself had begun to organize the work in this field but had to leave before the task was finished. The entrance of false teaching in the form of legalism necessitated a strong stand for the truth. In his task Titus needed clear instruction as well as encouragement. When Zenas and Apollos planned a journey through Crete, Paul sent Titus this letter to help and encourage him (Titus 3:13). The thought and style of this epistle resemble 1 Timothy more than 2 Timothy. The date of its composition was, therefore, around A.D. 65.

Purpose. (1) After an extended greeting, 1:1-4, Paul urges Titus to complete the organization of the work in Crete, 1:5. (2) Paul reviews the requirements of elders, 1:6-9. (3) He urges a strong position against false teachers, 1:10-16. (4) He gives instruction concerning the various classes in home relations, 2:1-10. (5) He elucidates how a holy and godly life is made possible, 2:11-15. (6) He enjoins good citizenship, 3:1-2. (7) He reviews the reasons for godly living, 3:3-8. (8) He issues a warning against false teaching, 3:9-11. (9) He outlines his future plans, 3:12-14. (10) He dispatches greetings, 3:15.

Outline.

   I. Salutation (1:1-4)
  II. The problems of the church as an organization (1:5-16)
     A. Qualifications of elders (1:5-9)
     B. Necessity for a strong stand against false teachers (1:10-16)
 III. The problems of pastoral teaching and preaching (2:1–3:11)
     A. Inculcating duties and domestic relations (2:1-10)
     B. Motivating true Christian living (2:11-15)
     C. Teaching concerning Christian citizenship (3:1-2)
     D. Inspiring godly living (3:3-8)
     E. Dealing with heretics (3:9-11)
 IV. Conclusion (3:12-15)   M.F.U.

BIBLIOGRAPHY: D. E. Hiebert, *Titus and Philemon* (1957). See also Timothy, First Epistle, for commentaries on three "Pastoral Epistles."

TI'ZITE (tī'zīt). The designation of *Joha* (which see), the brother of Jediael and son of Shimri, a hero in David's army (1 Chron. 11:45).

TO'AH (tō'a; cf. Akkad. *tahu,* "child"). Son of Zuph and father of Eliel, ancestor of Samuel and Heman (1 Chron. 6:34), called Tohu (1 Sam. 1:1) and Nahath (1 Chron. 6:26).

TOB (tōb; "good"). The land of Tob was, according to 2 Sam. 10:6, 8, a district in the NE of Perea, on the border of Syria, or between Syria and Ammonitis, called Tōbion (1 Macc. 5:13), or more correctly Toubin (2 Macc. 12:17). There Jephthah took refuge when expelled from home by his half-brothers (Judg. 11:3), and there he remained, at the head of a band of plunderers, till he was brought back by the "elders of Gilead" (v. 5). The "men of Tob" ("Ishtob," KJV) are mentioned in 2 Sam. 10:6, 8, and after a long interval Tob appears again, in the Maccabean history (1 Macc. 5:13), in the names Tobie and Tubieni (2 Macc. 12:17). G. A. Smith (*Hist. Geog.,* p. 587) says: "The name of the land of Tob, which was north of Mizpeh, may survive in that of the wady and village of Taiyibeh, east of Pella."

TOBADONI'JAH (tob-ad-o-nī'ja; "good is the Lord Jehovah"). One of the Levites sent by Jehoshaphat through the cities of Judah to teach the law to the people (2 Chron. 17:8), after 875 B.C.

TOBI'AH (to-bî'a; "good is Jehovah").

1. "The sons of Tobiah" were one of the families returning with Zerubbabel who were unable to prove their kinship with Israel (Ezra 2:60; Neh. 7:62), before 536 B.C.

2. One of the leading opponents to the rebuilding of Jerusalem under Nehemiah. Tobiah was formerly a slave at the Persian court and had probably, as a favorite, been appointed governor of the Ammonites (Neh. 2:10, 19). Tobiah, though a slave and an Ammonite, found means to ally himself with a priestly family, and his son Jehohanan married the daughter of Meshullam the son of Berechiah. He himself was the son-in-law of Shecaniah the son of Arah (6:18), and these family relations created for him a strong faction among the Jews. He and *Sanballat* (which see), on receiving news of the expected arrival of Nehemiah, were greatly exasperated and endeavored to terrify him by asking whether he intended to rebel against the king. Nehemiah replied that they had no authority of any kind in Jerusalem and did not allow himself to be intimidated (2:19-20). When he heard that the building of the walls had actually commenced, Tobiah, in unmingled scorn, declared, "Even what they are building—if a fox should jump on it, he would break their stone wall down!' (4:3). Then followed the league against the Jews entered into by Sanballat and Tobiah with the surrounding nations (vv. 7-8). After that an unsuccessful attempt was made to inveigle Nehemiah into a conference in the valley of Ono (6:1-3). Still later we find Tobiah carrying on a secret correspondence with the Jewish nobles hostile to Nehemiah (vv. 17-19). During Nehemiah's absence from Jerusalem, Eliashib the high priest installed Tobiah in "a large room," i.e., one of the very large buildings in the forecourts of the Temple, from which he was ejected by Nehemiah upon his return (13:4-9).

BIBLIOGRAPHY: C. C. McCown, *Biblical Archaeologist* 20 (1957): 63-76; B. Mazar, *Israel Exploration Journal* 7 (1957): 137-45, 229-38; P. W. Lapp, *Bulletin of the American Schools of Oriental Research* 171 (1963): 8-39. *See also* Nehemiah, Book of.

TOBI'JAH (to-bî'ja; Heb. same as *Tobiah* [which see]).

1. One of the Levites sent by Jehoshaphat to teach the law in the cities of Judah (2 Chron. 17:8), after 875 B.C.

2. One of the Israelites living during the captivity in the time of Zechariah, in whose presence the prophet was commanded to take crowns of silver and gold and put them on the head of Joshua the high priest (Zech. 6:10, 14), 519 B.C.

TO'CHEN, or **Token** (tō'ken; "a weight, measure"). One of the towns of Simeon (1 Chron. 4:32); probably the same as Telem (Josh. 15:24) or Telaim (1 Sam. 15:4).

TOGAR'MAH (to-gar'ma). A son of Gomer, and brother of Ashkenaz and Riphath (Gen. 10:3;

1 Chron. 1:6). The descendants of Togarmah (Beth Togarmah, NIV) are mentioned among the merchants who trafficked with Tyre in "horses and war horses and mules" (Ezek. 27:14). They are also named with Persia, Ethiopia, and Put as followers of Gog, the chief prince of Meshech and Tubal (38:5, 6). The name may be preserved in the E. Cappadocian city of Til-garimmu, listed in the Assyrian records.

TO'HU (tō'hu; cf. Akkad. *tahu*, "child"; 1 Sam. 1:1), the same as Toah (1 Chron. 6:34), or Nahath (v. 26).

TO'I (tō'i), or **Tou.** The king of Hamath on the Orontes, in the time of David. When the latter defeated the Syrian king Hadadezer, Toi's powerful enemy, Toi sent his son Joram (Hadoram) to congratulate him upon his victory and to offer presents of silver, gold, and bronze (2 Sam. 8:9-10), about 984 B.C. The name is apparently Hittite.

TOKEN (Heb. *'ôt*, a sign). KJV term replaced in the NASB with *sign* (which see). *See,* as a place name, Tochen.

TOK'HATH (tok'hath). The father of Shallum (2 Chron. 34:22. *See* Tikvah, no. 1.

TO'LA (tō'la; "a worm").

1. The eldest son of Issachar (Gen. 46:13; 1 Chron. 7:1). His six sons (7:2) became progenitors of the Tolaites (Num. 26:23), which numbered in David's time 22,600 fighting men (1 Chron. 7:2).

2. A judge of Israel. He was the son of Puah, of the tribe of Issachar. He succeeded Abimelech in the judgeship and ruled Israel twenty-three years in Shamir, Mt. Ephraim, where he died and was buried (Judg. 10:1-2). The date is uncertain, as Tola doubtless ruled contemporaneously with some other judge.

TO'LAD (tō'lad; "posterity"). A town in Simeon in David's time (1 Chron. 4:29); given in the fuller form Eltolad (Josh. 15:30). Possibly Khirbet Erka Sakra, thirteen miles SE of Beersheba.

TO'LAITES (tō'la-īts). The general name of the descendants of *Tola* (which see), the son of Issachar (Num. 26:23).

TOLL. *See* Tax; Tribute; Publican.

TOMB (Heb. *gādîsh*, "heaped" up, a "tumulus"; Gk. *mnēmeion*, a "remembrance"). A natural cave enlarged and adapted by excavation, or an artificial imitation of one, was the standard type of sepulcher. This was what the structure of the Jewish soil supplied or suggested.

"The caves, or rock-hewn sepulchers, consisted of an antechamber in which the bier was deposited, and an inner or rather lower cave in which the bodies were deposited, in a recumbent position, in niches. According to the Talmud these abodes of the dead were usually six feet long, nine feet wide, and ten feet high. Here there were niches for eight bodies—three on each side of the entrance and two opposite. Larger sepulchers held thirteen bodies. The entrance to the sepulcher was guarded by a large stone or by a door (Matt. 27:65; Mark 15:46; John 11:38-39). This structure of the tombs will explain some of the particulars connected with the burial of our Lord, how the women coming early to the grave had been astonished in finding the 'very great stone' 'rolled away from the door of the sepulcher,' and then, when they entered the outer cave, were affrighted to see what seemed 'a young man sitting on the right side, clothed in a long white garment' (Mark 16:4, 5)" (Edersheim, *Sketches of Jewish Social Life*, p. 171).

Early tomb in Jerusalem, sealed with a rolling stone

Of the twenty-two kings of Judah who reigned at Jerusalem from c. 1000 to 590 B.C., eleven, or exactly one-half, were buried in one burial chamber in the "city of David." Of all these it is merely said that they were buried in the tombs of their fathers or "of the kings" in the city of David, except of two—Asa and Hezekiah. Two more of these kings (Jehoram and Joash) were buried also in the city of David, "but not in the tombs of the kings." The passages in Neh. 3:16 and in Ezek. 43:7, 9, together with the reiterated assertion of Kings and Chronicles, that these tombs were situated in the city of David, leave no doubt but that

they were on Zion, or the Eastern Hill, and in immediate proximity to the Temple. They were in fact certainly within that enclosure now known as the "Haram Area"; but those royal tombs have evidently not survived to modern times. *See* Dead; Grave.

BIBLIOGRAPHY: N. Avigad, *Ancient Monuments in the Kidron Valley* (1954), pp. 144-46.

TONGS (Heb. *melqāh*, 1 Kings 7:49; 2 Chron. 4:21; Isa. 6:6). Pincers either for holding coals or for trimming a lamp, from Heb. *lāqah*, "to take," or *malqāh* (Ex. 25:38; Num. 4:9, KJV), rendered "snuffers" in NASB and in Ex. 37:32, KJV. The NIV and NKJV translate "wick trimmers."

TONGUE (Heb. *lāshôn;* Gk. *glōssa*) is variously used in Scripture.

1. Literally for the human tongue (Judg. 7:5; Job 27:4; Ps. 35:28; Prov. 15:2; Zech. 14:12; Mark 7:33, 35; etc.); the tongue of the dog (Ps. 68:23); of the viper (Job 20:16; "fangs," NIV).

2. A particular language or dialect spoken by any particular people, e.g., they "began to speak with other tongues" (Acts 2:4, 11; 1 Cor. 12:10).

3. For the people speaking a language (Isa. 66:18; Dan. 3:4, 7, marg.; Rev. 5:9; 7:9; 10:11; etc.).

4. Personified. "Every tongue will swear allegiance" (Isa. 45:23; 54:17; Rom. 14:11; Phil. 2:11). Such expressions as the following are used: the tongue is said to devise (Ps. 52:2), to hate (Prov. 26:28), to rejoice (Acts 2:26), to be bridled (James 1:26), to be tamed (3:8).

5. Figuratively for speech generally. "Let us not love with word or with tongue" (1 John 3:18); "a soft tongue," i.e., *soothing language* (Prov. 25:15). "Insolence of their tongue" (Hos. 7:16)—i.e., verbal abuse—"strife of tongues" (Ps. 31:20), and "scourge of the tongue" (Job 5:21) mean contention and execration. "They bend their tongue like their bow" (Jer. 9:3) is to tell determined and malicious falsehoods. To "sharpen their tongues" (Ps. 140:3) is to prepare cutting speeches (cf. 57:4); whereas to "strike" with the tongue (Jer. 18:18) is to traduce. To mock is figuratively expressed by to "stick out your tongue" (Isa. 57:4). To hide "under his tongue" (Job 20:12) is to enjoy wickedness; while "honey and milk are under your tongue" is figurative for delicious language (Song of Sol. 4:11). To divide the tongues of the wicked to bring about dissension among them (Ps. 55:9). The sticking of the tongue to the palate may mean profound attention (Job 29:10), excessive thirst (Lam. 4:4; Ps. 22:15), or dumbness (Ezek. 3:26; Ps. 137:6). To gnaw one's tongue is a sign of fury, despair, or torment (Rev. 16:10).

6. Vicious uses of the tongue are expressed by the following phrases: flattery (Ps. 5:9; Prov. 28:23), backbiting (Ps. 15:3; Prov. 25:23), deceit (Ps. 50:19), unrestrained speech (73:9), lying (109:2); etc. *Virtuous* uses are specified: keeping

the tongue (34:13; 1 Pet. 3:10; Prov. 21:23), bridling the tongue (James 1:26); etc.

TONGUES, CONFUSION OF. See Languages, Confusion of.

TONGUES, GIFT OF. The promise and the fulfillment of the gift of tongues are referred to in NT passages.

Promise of. The promise of a new power coming from the divine Spirit, giving not only comfort and insight into truth but fresh powers of utterance of some kind, appears often in our Lord's teaching. The disciples were to take no thought of what they should speak, for the Spirit of their Father would speak in them (Matt. 10:19-20; Mark 13:11). The lips of Galilean peasants were to speak freely and boldly before kings. In Mark 16:17 we have a more definite term employed: "They will speak with new tongues." It can hardly be questioned that the obvious meaning of the promise is that the disciples should speak in new languages that they had not learned as other men learn them.

Fulfillment. After our Lord's ascension, while the disciples were gathered together in one place, "suddenly there came from heaven a noise like a violent, rushing wind, and it filled the whole house where they were sitting. And there appeared to them tongues as of fire distributing themselves, and they rested on each one of them" (Acts 2:2-3). After this *external* phenomenon there ensued the *internal* filling with the Holy Spirit of all who were assembled. The *immediate result* was that they began to speak "with other tongues." For the sure determination of what Luke meant by this, it is decisive that *heterais glossais* "other tongues," on the part of the speakers was, in point of fact, the same thing that the congregated Parthians, Medes, Elamites, etc., designated as "our own tongue" or "language" cf. v. 8. The "other tongues," therefore, are, according to the text, to be considered as absolutely nothing else than *languages, which were different from the native language of the speakers.* "They, the Galileans, spoke, one Parthian, another Median, etc., consequently languages of *another sort*, i.e., *foreign* (1 Cor. 14:21); and these indeed—the point wherein precisely appeared the *miraculous* operation of the Spirit—*not acquired by study* (Mark 16:17)" (Meyer, *Com.*, ad loc.). When the event is admitted to be distinctly miraculous, and the power a special gift of God, it need not be considered either impossible or inconceivable; and incapacity of conceiving the *modus operandi* should not lead to a refusal of the credibility and certainty of the fact.

In the list of spiritual endowments mentioned in 1 Cor. 12:8-10 are "various kinds of tongues," and "the interpretation of tongues" (cf. vv. 28-30; 14:4-5, 13-14). Speaking with tongues is understood by many to be a miraculous gift by which a person is able to speak a foreign tongue without learning it. On the other hand there are those who, with Meyer, understand by *glossais lalein* an outburst of prayer in petition, praise, and thanksgiving, that was "so ecstatic that in connection with it the speaker's own conscious intellectual activity was suspended, while the tongue did not serve as the instrument of the utterance of self-active reflection, but, independently of it, was involuntarily set in motion by the Holy Spirit, by whom the man in his deepest nature was seized and borne away" (*Com.*, ad loc.). The spiritual gifts are classified and compared, arranged, apparently, according to their worth, placed under regulation. The facts that may be gathered are briefly these: (1) The phenomena of the gift of tongues were not confined to one church or section of a church. (2) The comparison of gifts, in both the lists given by Paul (1 Cor. 12:8-10, 28-30), places that of tongues and the interpretation of tongues lowest in the scale. (3) The main characteristic of the "tongue" is that it is unintelligible. The man "speaks mysteries" (v. 2), prays, blesses, gives thanks, in the tongue (14:15-16), but no one understands him. He can hardly be said, indeed, to understand himself. (4) The peculiar nature of the gift leads the apostle into what appears at first a contradiction. "Tongues are for a sign" (v. 22), not to believers, but to those who do not believe; yet the effect on unbelievers is not that of attracting but repelling. They involve of necessity a disturbance of the equilibrium between the understanding and the feelings. Therefore, for those who believe already, prophecy is the greater gift.

BIBLIOGRAPHY: R. G. Gromacki, *The Modern Tongues Movement* (1967); K. Koch, *The Strife of Tongues* (1969); D. L. Gelpi, *Pentecostalism: A Theological Viewpoint* (1970); J. P. Kildahl, *The Psychology of Speaking in Tongues* (1972); M. F. Unger, *The Baptism and Gifts of the Holy Spirit* (1974); R. Quebedeaux, *The New Charismatics* (1976); C. R. Smith, *Tongues in Biblical Perspective* (1976); J. F. MacArthur, Jr., *The Charismatics* (1978); R. L. Thomas, *Understanding Spiritual Gifts* (1978); N. Babcox, *A Search for Charismatic Reality* (1985).

TONGUES OF FIRE. In the account of the descent of the Holy Spirit upon the disciples at Pentecost it is said (Acts 2:3): "And there appeared to them tongues as of fire [Gk. *glōssai hōsei puros*] distributing themselves, and they rested on each one of them." The words mean that there were seen by them tongues that looked like little flames of fire, luminous but not burning; not really consisting of fire, but only "as of fire." As only *similar* to fire, they bore an analogy to *electric* phenomena; their tongue-shape referred as a sign to that miraculous speaking that ensued immediately after and the *fire*like form of the *divine* Presence (cf. Ex. 3:2), which was here operative in a manner so entirely peculiar. The whole phenomenon is to be understood as a miraculous operation of God manifesting Himself in the Spirit, by which, as by the preceding sound from heaven, the effusion of the Spirit was made known as *divine,* and His efficacy on the minds of those who were to receive Him was enhanced (Meyer, *Com.,* ad loc.).

TOOLS. *See* Handicrafts.

TOOTH (Heb. *shēn; leḥî,* in Ps. 58:6; Prov. 30:14; Joel 1:6; Gk. *odous*).

Literal Use. In this sense the term is used with reference to the loss of the member by violence, in illustration of the law of retaliation (Ex. 21:24; Lev. 24:20; Deut. 19:21). Such loss admitted of a pecuniary compensation, under private arrangement unless the injured party became exorbitant in his demand, when the case was referred to a judge. Our Lord's comment upon the law (Matt. 5:38) prohibits private revenge. *Leḥî* is used for the human jawbone (Ps. 3:7), for that of a donkey (Judg. 15:15-17), and for that of a leviathan (Job 41:14). Although *shinnayîm* is the general word for teeth, the Hebrews had a distinct term for molars or jaw teeth, especially of the larger animals; thus *metalleʻ ôt* (29:17; Ps. 57:4; Prov. 30:14; Joel 1:6) and, by transposition, Heb. *malleteʻ ôt* (Ps. 58:6).

Figurative. "His teeth white from milk" (Gen. 49:12) seems to denote an abundance of milk, as "his eyes are dull from wine" denotes plenty thereof. "The teeth of beasts I will send upon them" (Deut. 32:24) expresses devastation by wild animals. "The teeth of . . . lions" (Job 4:10) is a symbol of the cruelty and rapacity of the wicked. To "take my flesh in my teeth" (13:14) is thought by some to mean to gnaw it with anguish (cf. Rev. 16:10), while others interpret it "to be intent upon the maintenance of life, as a wild beast upon the preservation of his prey, by holding it between its teeth and carrying it away" (Delitzsch, *Com.,* ad loc.). *Gnashing of teeth* means grinding the teeth with rage or despair (Job 16:9; Pss. 35:16; 37:12; 112:10; Lam. 2:16; Matt. 8:12; etc.). By "the skin of my teeth" (Job 19:20) is generally understood the gums; Delitzsch, however, thinks it to be the periosteum, a skin in the jaw. Job's disease was such that the gums especially were destroyed and wasted away about the teeth; only the periosteum around the teeth was still left to him, and single remnants of the covering of his loose and projecting teeth. To "smite on the cheek" and to shatter "the teeth" mean to disgrace and disable (Ps. 3:7; cf. Mic. 6:13; 1 Kings 20:35; Lam. 3:30). The teeth of calumniators, etc., are compared to "spears and arrows" (Ps. 57:4); and to shatter the teeth of such persons is to disable them (58:6). To escape from being "torn by their teeth" of one's enemies is to avoid their malice (124:6; Zech. 9:7). Oppression is compared to "jaw teeth like knives" (Prov. 30:14). Beautiful teeth are compared to "a flock of newly shorn ewes . . . and not one among

them has lost her young" (Song of Sol. 4:2; 6:6). To break the "teeth with gravel" is a forcible figure (Lam. 3:16; cf. Prov. 20:17), referring to the *grit* that often mixes with bread baked in ashes, as the custom in the East, and figurative of harsh disappointment. "Teeth of iron" (Dan. 7:19) is the symbol of destructive power. Hypocritical and greedy prophets are represented as those who "bite with their teeth, they cry, 'Peace' " (Mic. 3:5). "I will . . . remove their detestable things from between their teeth" (Zech. 9:7) refers to idolaters keeping a feast, which is interrupted by Jehovah and idolatry abolished. "Cleanness of teeth" (Amos 4:6) is the figure of hunger, famine. The action of acid setting teeth "on edge" is referred to in Jer. 31:30; Ezek. 18:2.

TOPAZ. *See* Mineral Kingdom.

TO'PHEL (tō'fel). Apparently a boundary of the great Sinaitic desert of Paran (Deut. 1:1). It is supposed by Hengstenberg and Robinson, and many of the more modern writers, to be the large village of Tâfîlĕh, the chief place in Jebal, W of the Edomite mountains. The suggestion of Schultz that Tophel may have been the place where the Israelites purchased food and drink of the Edomites (2:28-29) has much to be said in its favor; for the situation of Tophel warrants the supposition that it was here that they passed for the first time from the wilderness to an inhabited land. Its identification remains uncertain.

TO'PHETH (tō'feth; KJV, Tophet). Topheth is commonly supposed to be derived from *tōp,* or drum, from the drums used to drown the cries of children who were made to pass through the fire to Molech. Gesenius connects the root idea with *tût,* "to spit," and rendered the place-name to be "spit" upon, to "be abhorred" (Job 17:6). Others regard Topheth as from *topteh* ("contempt"), "the place of burning" dead bodies.

Topheth lay somewhere E or SE of Jerusalem, for Jeremiah went out by the potsherd gate, or E gate, to go to it (Jer. 19:2). It was in "the valley of the son of Hinnom" (7:31), which is "by the entrance of the potsherd gate" (19:2). Thus it was not identical with Hinnom. It was in Hinnom and was, perhaps, one of its chief groves or gardens, watered by Siloam, perhaps a little to the S of the present Birket el-Hamra. The name Topheth occurs only in the OT (2 Kings 23:10; Isa. 30:33; Jer. 7:31-32; 19:6, 11-14). The NT does not refer to it, nor the Apocrypha.

In Topheth the deity (Baal, Jer. 19:5; Molech, 32:35) was worshiped by sacrifices in pagan fashion, first by the ancient Canaanites and afterward by apostate Israelites (cf. Ps. 106:38; Jer. 7:31). This was done first by Ahaz (2 Kings 16:3), then especially by Manasseh (21:6). Thus it became the place of abomination, the very gate or pit of hell. The pious kings defiled it (23:10) and threw down its altars and high places, pouring into it all the filth of the city, till it became the abhorrence of Jerusalem. Every vestige of Topheth, name and grove, is gone, and we can only guess at the spot.

TORAH (Heb. instruction, "law"). The name of the first of the three divisions of the Hebrew canon—Torah (Law), Nebiim (Prophets), and Kethubim (Writings). The Torah, or Law, comprises the five books of Moses, which were the mainstay of Judaism. The Torah, however, came to have a wider meaning among Jews and embraced the whole body of religious literature of Judaism inherited from their prophets, priests, and wise men. In addition to the written Torah the Pharisees and rabbis recognized an oral Torah, composed of specific applications of the general principles of the written Torah. In the time of our Lord the oral traditions had become so minute and devoid of spiritual meaning as to set aside the Law of God and in some cases completely nullify it (cf. Matt. 15:2; Mark 7:9, 18; Col. 2:8). In the period of the rise of the synagogue (c. 400-168 B.C.), the Law was divided into sections for systematic public reading. The Pentateuch came to be divided into 290 "open" and 379 "closed" *parashiyoth*. The "open" marked by a *pe* (p) are paragraphs beginning a new line. The "closed" are shorter and are marked by a *samekh* (s) and preceded by a blank space in the line. The Mishnah (c. A.D. 200) mentions these divisions, which existed earlier. The Talmud (c. A.D. 500) distinguishes between the *open* and *closed parashiyoth*. By the time of Christ, the Prophets had been added to the Torah lessons for weekly public reading (Luke 4:16-21).   M.F.U.

BIBLIOGRAPHY: H. Danby, trans., *The Mishnah* (1933), pp. 446-61; E. K. J. Rosenthal, ed., *Law and Religion* (1938), 3:50-53, 62.

TORCH. The Heb. *lappîd* (Zech. 12:6) and the Gk. *lampas* (John 18:3) usually signify a lamp or light.

Figurative. A flaming torch is used by the prophet (Zech. 12:6) as a symbol of great anger and destruction. In Nah. 2:3, KJV, "flaming torches" is an incorrect rendering of Heb. *peladah* ("steel"), which NASB translates "flashing steel."

TOR'MAH (tor'ma; "fraud, deceit") occurs only in the margin of Judg. 9:31. A few commentators have conjectured that the word was originally the same as Arumah (v. 41). The LXX and Aram. take the word as an appellative— *en kruphē*, "secretly"; so also do Rashi and most of the earlier commentators (NIV, "secretly"), while R. Kimchi the elder has decided in favor of the second rendering as a proper name. As the word only occurs here it is impossible to determine in favor of either view.

TORTOISE. See Animal Kingdom: Great Lizard.

TORTURER (Gk. *basanistēs*, Matt. 18:34; KJV, "tormentor"). One who elicits the truth by means of the rack; an inquisitor; used in this passage of a jailor, probably because the business of torturing was assigned to him. Torture was usually employed to extort confession or evidence, as when Claudius Lysias, the chief captain, commanded Paul to be brought into the castle and "examined by scourging" (Acts 22:24).

TOU (too; 1 Chron. 18:9-10). See Toi.

TOW (tō). Better, *flax* (which see, Vegetable Kingdom). The coarse and broken part of flax hemp or jute, separated by the hatchel or swingle and ready for spinning. Heb. *ne'ōret*, Judg. 16:9. It is extremely inflammable.

TOWEL (Gk. *lention*). A linen cloth or apron, which servants put on when about to work (John 13:4-5). Girding one's self with a towel was the common mark of a slave, by whom the service of foot washing was ordinarily performed.

TOWER.

1. A siege tower (Isa. 23:13; Heb. *bāḥûn*, "strong").

2. *Migdāl* is from a root meaning "to become great." *See* Migdol.

3. *Pinnôt*, the corners and battlements of the walls of the fortifications (Zeph. 1:16; 3:6; 2 Chron. 26:15).

4. *Mispeh*. See Mizpeh.

5. Gk. *Purgos*, a "tower," a fortified structure rising to a considerable height to repel a hostile attack or to enable a watchman to see in every direction. The "tower in Siloam" seems to designate a tower in the walls of Jerusalem, near the fountain of Siloam (Luke 13:4). Watchtowers or fortified posts in frontier or exposed situations are mentioned in Scripture, such as the tower of Eder, etc. (Gen. 35:21; Mic. 4:8; Isa. 21:8; etc.), the tower of Lebanon (Song of Sol. 7:4). Remains of such fortifications may still be seen, which probably have followed more ancient structures built in the same places for like purposes. Besides these military structures, we read in Scripture of towers built in vineyards as an almost necessary appendage to them (Isa. 5:2; Matt. 21:33; Mark 12:1). Such towers are still in use in Palestine in vineyards, especially near Hebron, and are used as lodges for the keepers of the vineyards.

TOWN. Not always carefully distinguished from city and is sometimes the rendering of Heb. *'îr*, a place guarded by watchmen; generally rendered "city"; *qîr* or *qîrâ*, "wall." In the Gk. we have *kōmē*, "hamlet." Neither in the OT nor in the NT is the distinction between cities and towns carefully observed. "Palestine had at all times a far larger number of towns and villages than might have been expected from its size, or from the general agricultural pursuits of its inhabitants. Even at the time of its first occupation under

Joshua we find . . . about six hundred towns . . . with probably an average population of from two to three thousand. But the number of towns and villages, as well as their populousness, greatly increased in later times. . . . Alike the New Testament, Josephus, and the rabbis give us three names, which may be rendered villages, township, or towns—the latter being surrounded by walls, and again distinguished into those fortified already at the time of Joshua, and those of later date. A township might be either 'great,' if it had its synagogue, or small if it wanted such; this being dependent on the residence of at least ten men [see Synagogue]. The villages had no synagogue; but their inhabitants were supposed to go to the nearest township for market on the Monday and Thursday of every week, when service was held for them, and the local Sanhedrin also sat (Megill., i, 1-3). . . . Approaching one of the ancient fortified towns, one would come to a low wall that protected a ditch. Crossing this moat, one would be at the city wall proper, and enter through a massive gate, often covered with iron, and secured by strong bars and bolts. Above the gate rose the watchtower. 'Within the gate' was the shady or sheltered retreat where 'the elders' sat. . . . The gates opened upon large squares, on which the various streets converged. . . . These streets are all named, mostly after the trades or guilds which have there their bazaars. In these bazaars many of the workmen sat outside their shops, and in the interval of labor exchanged greetings or banter with the passers-by. . . . The rule of these towns and villages was exceedingly strict. The representatives of Rome were chiefly either military men or else fiscal or political agents. Then every town had its Sanhedrin, consisting of twenty-three members if the place numbered at least one hundred and twenty men, or of three members if the population were smaller. . . . Of course all ecclesiastical and, so to speak, strictly Jewish causes, and all religious questions, were within their special cognizance. Lastly, there were also in every place what may be called municipal authorities, under the presidency of a mayor—the representative of the elders—an institution so frequently mentioned in Scripture, and deeply rooted in Jewish society. Perhaps these may be referred to (Luke 7:3) as sent by the centurion of Capernaum to intercede for him with the Lord.

"What may be called the police and sanitary regulations were of the strictest character. Of Caesarea, e.g., we know that there was a regular system of drainage into the sea. . . . (Josephus, Ant., xv, 9, 6). But in every town and village sanitary rules were strictly attended to. Cemeteries, tanneries, and whatever also might be prejudicial to health had to be removed at least fifty cubits outside a town. Bakers' and dyers'

Watchtower near Shiloh

1298

shops, or stables, were not allowed under the dwelling of another person. Again, in building, the line of each street had to be strictly kept, nor was even a projection beyond it allowed. In general the streets were wider than those of modern Eastern cities. The nature of the soil, and the circumstance that so many towns were built on hills (at least in Judea), would, of course, be advantageous in a sanitary point of view. It would also render the paving of the streets less requisite. But we know that certain towns *were* paved—Jerusalem with white stones (Josephus, *Ant.*, xx, 9, 7). To obviate occasions of dispute, neighbors were not allowed to have windows looking into the courts or rooms of others, nor might the principal entrance to a shop be through a court common to two or three dwellings" (Edersheim, *Sketches of Jewish Social Life,* pp. 87-93).

BIBLIOGRAPHY: S. F. Frick, *The City in Ancient Israel* (1977).

TOWN CLERK (Gk. *grammateus*). The city secretary, recorder, to whose office belonged the superintendence of the archives, the drawing up of official decrees, and the reading of them in public assemblies of the people. This official appeased the mob in Ephesus when Demetrius and his fellow craftsmen raised a tumult (Acts 19:35). The speech delivered by him may be analyzed thus: He argued that such excitement as the Ephesians evinced was undignified, inasmuch as they stood above all suspicion in religious matters (vv. 35-36); that it was unjustifiable, since they could establish nothing against the men whom they accused (v. 37); that it was unnecessary, since other means of redress were open to them (vv. 38-39); and, finally, if neither pride nor a sense of justice availed anything, fear of the Roman power should restrain them from such illegal proceedings (v. 40).

TRACHONI′TIS or **Traconitis** (trak-o-nī′tis; Gk. "rough or hilly region," only in Luke 3:1). "Trachonitis was the territory which contained the Trachon or Trachons. These are described by Strabo (xvi, 2, 20) as 'the two so-called Trachones' lying 'behind Damascus.' The name . . . corresponds exactly to the two great stretches of lava, 'the tempests in stone,' which lie to the southeast of Damascus—the Lejá and the Safá. Each of these is called by the Arabs a *wa'ar,* a word meaning rough, stony tract, and thus equivalent to Trachon. The latter, beyond the reach of civilization, was little regarded, and the Lejá became known as the Trachon *par excellence,* as is proved by the two inscriptions at either end of it—in Musmireh, the ancient Phaenä, and the Bereke, each of which is called a chief town of the Trachon. . . . Now the Trachonitis was obviously the Trachon *plus* some territory round it. In the north it extended westward from the borders of the Lejá to the districts of Ulatha

and Paneas in the northern Jaulan; and in the south it bordered with Batanea, but also touched Mons Alsadamus, the present Jebel Hauran. Philo uses the name Trachonitis for the whole territory of Philip" (Smith, *Hist. Geog.,* p. 543).

The portion of Philip's tetrarchy most difficult to define is the Ituraean, and it is uncertain whether it covered or overlapped Trachonitis. Luke's reference is ambiguous, and we have no modern echo of the name to guide us.

TRADE. In the sense of traffic, commerce (*nātan,* to "give," i.e., to pay), something as an equivalent for the sale (Ezek. 27:12-14); (*sāhar,* to "go about, travel"), to traverse the country as a merchant, to trade, traffic (Gen. 34:10); Gk. *'ergazomai,* to "work," to make gains by trading, or "do business" (cf. Matt. 25:16).

Trade is the rendering of Heb. *kᵉna'an* (lit., *Canaan*). The expression "a city of traders" (Ezek. 17:4; thus NIV) should read "a city or land of Canaan" (cf. 16:29); the sentence will then read, "He plucked off the topmost of its young twigs, and carried it into a land of Canaan," an epithet applied to Babylonia as being a land whose trading spirit had turned it into a Canaan. In Gen. 42:34 "trade" is the rendering of *sāhar,* and in 1 Kings 10:15, "trader," the Heb. is *mishār,* from the same root, signifying to travel about for the purpose of trade. Similar in meaning is the Heb. word in Ezek. 28:5, 18. "Traders" (Isa. 23:8) is from the Heb. signifying Canaanite.

TRADITION (Gk. *paradosis,* a "giving over"). A giving over either by *word of mouth* or in *writing;* objectively, *what is delivered,* as Paul's teaching (2 Thess. 2:15; 3:6; 1 Cor. 11:2). It is also used of the body of precepts, especially ritual, which, in the opinion of the later Jews, were orally delivered by Moses and orally transmitted in unbroken succession to subsequent generations. These precepts, both illustrating and expanding the written law, as they did, were to be obeyed with equal reverence (Matt. 15:2-3, 6; Mark 7:3, 5, 9, 13; Col. 2:8). "My ancestral traditions" (Gal. 1:14) are precepts received from the fathers, whether handed down in the OT books or orally. Meyer, in his *Com.* on Matt. 15:2, says: "The Jews, founding upon Deut. 4:14; 17:10, for the most part attached greater importance to this tradition than to the written law. They laid special stress upon the traditional precept, founded on Lev. 15:11, which required that the hands should be washed before every meal. Jesus and his disciples ignored this tradition as such, which had been handed down from the men of olden time."

TRAIN.

1. "Train up a child," etc. (Prov. 22:6), has the sense in Heb. *ḥānak* of "to imbue one with anything," to initiate; and so to train up a child

according to his way, according to his disposition and habits.

2. Isaiah 6:1 says that the Lord's train (Heb. *shûl*) filled the Temple. "The heavenly temple is that superterrestrial place, which Jehovah transforms into heaven and a temple, by manifesting himself there to angels and saints. But while he manifests his glory there he is obliged also to veil it, because created beings are unable to bear it. But that which veils his glory is no less splendid than that portion of it which is revealed. And this was the truth embodied for Isaiah in the long robe and train. He saw the Lord, and what more he saw was the all-filling robe of the indescribable One" (Delitzsch, *Com.*, ad loc.).

3. First Kings 10:2, KJV, uses train in reference to the queen of Sheba's wealth. *See* Retinue.

TRANCE. In the NT the word occurs three times (Acts 10:10; 11:5; 22:17; Gk. *'ekstasis*). "The word may be defined as the "throwing of the mind out of its normal state, of the man who by some sudden emotion is transported out of himself, so that in this rapt condition, although he is awake, his mind is so drawn off from all surrounding objects and wholly fixed on things divine that he sees nothing but the forms and images lying within, and perceives with his bodily eyes and ears realities shown him by God."

TRANSFER. In both its Heb. and Gk. originals, *transfer* has the sense of the removal of a person or thing from one state or condition to another. In 2 Sam. 3:10 it refers to transferring a kingdom from Saul to David. In like manner, the Christian is transferred from the domain of darkness into the kingdom of God's beloved Son by regeneration (Col. 1:13).

TRANSFIGURATION (Gk. *metamorphoō*, to "change into another form"). It is recorded (Matt. 17:2; Mark 9:2) that our Lord "was transfigured" before His disciples Peter, James, and John; and this is explained (Luke 9:29): "And while He was praying, the appearance of His face became different, and His clothing became white and gleaming." Each of the evangelists represents it as taking place about eight days after the first distinct intimation our Lord made to them of His approaching sufferings, death, and resurrection. The location is merely given as a high mountain, which is traditionally thought to have been Mt. Tabor; but as Jesus was at this time sojourning in the neighborhood of Caesarea Philippi, it seems likely that it was one of the ridges of Hermon. While our Lord was praying He was "transfigured," i.e., His external aspect was changed, His face gleaming like the sun, and His clothing being so white that it shone like light. The cause of this appearance was that His divine glory shone out through His human form and was not, as in the case of Moses, caused by God's having appeared to Him.

The disciples seem to have been asleep when this divine radiance began to shine forth; but when they woke up they were filled with wonder and fear, beholding also two men, Moses and Elijah, in glory, conversing with Him. Peter recovered himself and, in the rapture of the moment, suggested that three tents or "tabernacles" should be pitched to secure the continued presence and fellowship of such glorious company. He had scarcely given expression to his thought when a bright cloud overshadowed them, out of which came a voice saying, "This is My Son, My Chosen One; listen to Him!" (Luke 9:35). The theme of conversation is not given by Matthew or Mark, but Luke records that they spoke concerning His death.

Premillennialists see in the transfiguration scene all the essential features of the future millennial kingdom in manifestation: (1) The Lord appears, not in humiliation, but in glory (Matt. 17:2). (2) Moses is present in a glorified state, representative of the redeemed who have passed via death into the kingdom (Matt. 13:43; Luke 9:30-31). (3) Elijah is also seen glorified, representative of the redeemed who have come into the kingdom by translation (1 Thess. 4:13-18; 1 Cor. 15:50-53). (4) The unglorified disciples, Peter, James, and John, represent in the vision and for the time being Israel in the flesh in the future kingdom (Acts 1:6; Ezek. 37:21-27). (5) The crowd at the foot of the mountain (Matt. 17:14) represents the nations who are to enter the kingdom after it is established over Israel (Isa. 11:10-12). The scene as a whole represents the second coming of Christ in glory to establish His kingdom, or in the words interpreting the scene: "the Son of Man coming in His kingdom" (Matt. 16:28). Agreeable with this interpretation of the transfiguration episode is Peter's comment in 2 Pet. 1:16-18. As the preaching of the kingdom was fast approaching its end in the rejection and imminent death of the King, it became necessary to encourage the disciples in the expectation of the messianic kingdom promised to Israel in the OT. The transfiguration bore out this assurance.   M.F.U.

BIBLIOGRAPHY: A. M. Ramsey, *The Glory of God and the Transfiguration of Christ* (1949), pp. 101-51; A. Edersheim, *The Life and Times of Jesus the Messiah* (1962), 2:91-101; G. C. Morgan, *The Crises of the Christ* (1965), pp. 155-97; J. D. Pentecost, *The Glory of God* (1978), pp. 57-68; F. W. Farrar, *The Life of Christ* (1982), pp. 241-44.

TRANSFORMED (Gk. *metamorphoō*). Used of the change of the moral character for the better (Rom. 12:2), through the *renewal of the thinking power*. "The apostle considers it as a peculiar operation of the Christian faith, that believers are seriously concerned to prove in everything what is the will of God (Eph. 5:10); whereas man, in his natural state, looks more to the point of how he may please men" (Tholuck, *Com.*). The apostle (2 Cor. 3:18) speaks of the Christian's being "transformed into the same image from glory to glory," etc. In this passage the gospel is spoken of as a *mirror,* in which the glory of Christ gives itself to be seen; the Christian, studying the gospel, becomes so transformed that the same image which he sees in the "mirror"—the image of the glory of Christ—presents itself on him, i.e., he is so transformed that he becomes like the glorified Christ. *See* Disguise.

TRANSGRESSION (Heb. mostly *pesha',* "revolt"; Gk. *parabasis,* "violation"). Sometimes used synonymously with sin, but sometimes used in a distinctive sense as indicating a violation of the law through ignorance, e.g., Ex. 34:7; Rom. 4:25. All sin is transgression, but all transgression is not sin in the sense of incurring guilt. *See* Sin.

TRANSLATE. This term, used in the KJV of 2 Sam. 3:10; Col. 1:13; and Heb. 11:5, has the sense of removal of a person or thing from one state or condition to another, and in the NASB is rendered "transfer," "take up," or "go up." This word is applied to Elijah's ascension (2 Kings 2:11) and the change of saints at the coming of the Lord (John 14:3; 1 Cor. 15:50-53; 1 Thess. 4:13-18; 1 John 3:1-3). The NIV limits it to the sense of rendering one language into another (Ezra 4:18; John 1:42; Acts 9:36). *See* Taken Up; Transfer.

TRANSLATIONS, ENGLISH BIBLE.

Early Versions. There were portions of the Bible, and possibly the entire work, rendered into the English vernacular very early in the history of the language. Gildas states that "when the English martyrs gave up their lives in the 4th century all the copies of the Holy Scriptures which could be found were burned in the streets." Cranmer, Thomas More, and Foxe, with many others, bore testimony to the existence of "divers copies of the Holy Bible in the English tongue." The following are fragments of translations that are clearly traced: Caedmon's versification of an English translation (689); St. Cuthbert's *Evangelistarium,* which is a Latin translation with an interlinear English (689); St. Aldhelm's translation; Eadfurth's translation (720); King Alfred's (901); Aelfric's (995). These, however, were all made from the Lat. and not from the original Heb. After the Norman Conquest the language underwent a great change; the old English Bibles fell into disuse, until they were practically unknown; only a few fragments remained.

Wycliffe's Version. In the fourteenth century there was a growing demand for an English version. This need was met by two translations, made respectively by John Wycliffe and John Purvey. Each carried on his work without the knowl-

A page from the Wycliffe Bible

edge of the other. Wycliffe's was completed in 1384 and Purvey's in 1388. The latter, however, was thought to be only a correction of the former and at one time was even published in the name of Wycliffe. The Wycliffe version is distinctive in several ways. (1) It is written in the everyday speech of the common people. In many instances the word *children* is rendered "brat"; *father* is "dad"; *chariot* is "cart." (2) It gives the exact rendering of the English idiom for the ancient. Thus, *raca* is "Fy" or "Pugh"; *mammon* is "richesse." (3) It is highly literal in its translation. The following is a specimen: "The disciplis scien to hym, Maister now the Jewis soughten for to stoone thee, and est goist thou thidir? Jheus answered whether ther ben not twelue ouris of the dai? If ony man wandre in the night he stomblish, for light is not in him. He seith these thingis and aftir these thingis he seith to hem Lazarus oure freend slepith but Y go to reise hym fro sleep. Therfor hise disciplis seiden: Lord if he slepith he schal be saaf."

Tyndale's Version. In 1526 William Tyndale made a translation of the NT from the original Gk. He afterward made a translation of the Pentateuch and other portions of the OT. The whole was printed in Germany and imported into England. Tyndale's introduction and comments awakened intense opposition; and many copies of the work were publicly burned by the order of the

Bishop of London. As in Wyclif's version, the language was the common speech of the people. Many of his words have lost their old-time meaning, as is seen in the following rendering of Titus 1:1: "Paul, the rascal of God and the villein of Jesus Christ." The aim of the translator was to render the simple sense of the original uninfluenced by theological thought. Thus, instead of "grace" he used the word "favor," "love" instead of "charity," "acknowledging" instead of "confessing," "elders" instead of "priests," "repentance" instead of "penance," "congregation" instead of "church."

Coverdale's Version. In 1535 Miles Coverdale completed and printed an English translation of the entire Bible. It was probably done under the influence of Cromwell and with the aid of many assistants. It was not with Coverdale, as it was with Tyndale, a work of love. He undertook it as a task imposed upon him and did it perfunctorily and mechanically. Nor was it a translation from the original, but mainly from the German and Lat. It shows a strong royal and ecclesiastical influence. It uses a variety of English equivalents for the same original. It bears the marks of haste and carelessness.

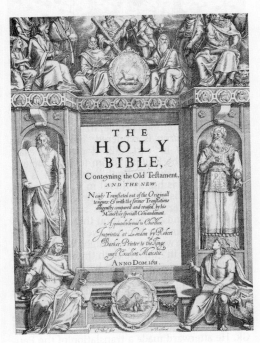

Title page of the King James Version, first printed 1611

Matthew's Bible. This is the first "Authorized Version" of the Holy Bible in English. It is a fusion of the Tyndale and the Coverdale versions and was printed in London by the king's license in 1537, by publishers Grafton and Whitchurch. It bears the name of Thomas Matthew, which is undoubtedly a pseudonym. The real editor was John Rogers. His notes and comments were far in advance of his time and soon evoked a strong ecclesiastical opposition to this version.

Taverner's Version. This version appeared in 1539 and was made necessary by ecclesiastical opposition to the Matthew's Bible. It, however, is but an expurgated edition of this version.

Cranmer's Version. This version was printed in 1539 with the sanction of Cranmer's name. The translation was made by a corps of scholars under the direction of the archbishop and his assistants. It was a large folio and illustrated with a picture supposed to be the work of Holbein. It had the license of the king and was called "The Great Bible."

The Geneva Bible. This was a popular revision of "The Great Bible" made by Heb. and Gk. scholars who were refugees in Geneva. The cost of the latter (about $30) made it inaccessible to the people. The purpose of the Geneva version was to give to England a household edition of the Word of God. It was a small book with marginal notes and was divided into chapters and verses. It at once became popular, and more than two hundred editions were published.

The Bishop's Bible. This work appeared in 1568 and was made on the suggestion of Archbishop Parker. He was assisted in his work by eight of his bishops and some of the scholars of the church. It was elegantly printed, profusely illustrated, and ornamented with elaborate initial letters. From one of these, introducing the epistle to the Hebrews, this version was popularly called "The Leda Bible." It never received the approval of the scholars, and its cost kept it from the possession of the people.

The Rheims and Douay Version. A translation was made by Martin, Allen, and Bristow, refugees in Rheims, where in 1582 they published the NT. The work was completed by the publication in 1609 of the OT. This was done in Douay, which fact gives the name to the version. Altogether aside from its Roman Catholic viewpoint, it is the poorest rendering into English of any of the versions. The following are given as fair specimens of its literary style: "Purge the old leaven that you may be a new paste, as you are asymes." "You are evacuated from Christ." In Gal. 5:21-22 this version substitutes "ebrieties" for "drunkenness" "comessations" for "carousing," and "longanimity" for "patience." In Heb. 9:23, for "the copies of the things in the heavens," the Douay has "the exemplars of the celestials." In Heb. 13:16, "and do not neglect doing good and sharing; for with such sacrifices God is pleased," the Douay reads, "Beneficence and communication do not forget, for with such hosts God is promerited."

The Authorized Version. It is also known as the King James Bible, from James I, by whose authority and support it was undertaken and completed. It was begun in 1604 and finished in seven years. Forty-seven of the ablest scholars were selected to do the work, each taking a portion and finally reviewing the whole. It was to correspond with the Bishop's Bible, except where the original Heb. and Gk. made this impossible. The excellence of the work done is attested by the simple fact that this version has held the heart of the English-speaking world for nearly three centuries and that no subsequent version has been able to supplant it.

The Revised Version. There have been a number of attempts at revision of the KJV, but nothing of importance was done until 1870 when the convocation of Canterbury formally originated an inquiry that resulted in a new version completed in 1885. This version was felt to be needed because of the change that two centuries had made in the meaning of many English words; because of the fuller knowledge then possessed of the Heb. and the Gk. text; because of the confessed inaccuracy of many of the renderings in the KJV; and because of the obscurities occasioned by the form of the English text where there is no distinction made between prose and poetry, and where the divisions into chapters and verses make unnatural and abrupt breaks in the inspired thought. The aim of the translators was to introduce as few alterations into the text of the KJV as faithfulness to the truth would allow and to make the language of such alterations conform to that of the rest of the book. The new version has not won the heart of the English-speaking world but is accepted as an able commentary on the text that since 1611 has been a sacred classic.

The American Standard Version. The RV with such alterations as were recommended by the American branch of revisers, and that was not published until 1901.

The Polychrome Version. An entirely new translation made from the original text, under the direction of Professor Haupt of Johns Hopkins University, and which aims to give the rendering on the basis of the most recent school of higher criticism. This translation has had only slight acceptance.

The Twentieth Century New Testament. This version, by a group of some twenty scholars representing various segments of the Christian church, used the Westcott and Hort Gk. text. It came out in London (1898-1901), with a revised edition appearing in 1904. One of its distinctive features, besides modern language and idiom, was its chronological placement of the various books, Mark's gospel appearing first instead of Matthew's in the traditional order.

Historical New Testament. This was translated by James Moffatt in polished modern idiom and appeared in Edinburgh in 1901. It reflects the higher-critical scholarship current at the beginning of the century. Moffatt's second translation appeared in Edinburgh in 1913. This contained several transpositions of chapters, paragraphs, and verses based upon Von Soden's edition of the Gk. NT. Moffatt published a translation of the OT in 1924, rendering the divine name Jehovah as "The Eternal." This translation, lucid in many places, followed higher-critical hypotheses and conclusions, which are seen throughout. In 1935 a revised and final edition of the Moffatt Bible was published. This too reflects higher-critical views, especially the documentary partition theories of the Pentateuch.

The Westminster Version of the Sacred Scriptures. This was a Roman Catholic translation. Heading the general editorship was Cuthbert Lattey of the Society of Jesus. The work dates from 1913, with a freely translated NT published in New York in 1937, containing footnotes indicating variation in Gk. and Vulg. readings. The OT books follow the Heb. original.

The Holy Scriptures According to the Masoretic Text, A New Translation. This was a Jewish rendering that appeared in 1917. It was prepared by a committee of Jewish scholars headed by Max L. Margolis as editor-in-chief. It closely follows the Masoretic Heb. text, reflecting a curious mixture of Jewish traditional readings and the results of modern biblical scholarship. Cf. Alexander Sperber, "A New Bible Translation," *Alexander Marx Jubilee Volume*, English Section (1950), pp. 547-80.

The New Testament in Modern Speech. This was produced in 1903 by Richard F. Weymouth, D. Litt. It was edited and partly revised by E. Hampden-Cook. It is a serviceable translation and effects careful rendering of the aorist and perfect tenses in Gk. The first American edition, revised by J. A. Robertson, appeared at Boston in 1943.

The New Testament, An American Translation. Based on the Westcott and Hort Gk. text, this version was prepared by Edgar J. Goodspeed (Chicago, 1923). In 1927 *The Old Testament, An American Translation* was prepared by Theophile J. Meek of the University of Toronto, Leroy Waterman of the University of Michigan, J. M. Powis Smith of the University of Chicago, and A. R. Gordon of the University of Montreal. Ninety-one pages of appendix in this edition list emendations of the Heb. preferred over the Masoretic text. In 1939 *The Complete Bible, An American Translation* appeared. This consisted of Theophile J. Meek's literary revision of the OT, Goodspeed's rendering of the Apocrypha, and Goodspeed's NT, which had appeared in 1931, as *The Bible, An American Translation.*

The Riverside New Testament. This translation leans heavily upon several previous translations and was executed by William G. Ballantine from the 1934 revised Nestle's Gk. text.

Books of the Old Testament in Colloquial Speech. The rendition of numerous scholars and published by the National Adult School Union (London, 1923 and later).

The Centenary Translation of the New Testament. This translation appeared in two volumes, Philadelphia, 1924. It was put out by Helen B. Montgomery of Rochester, N.Y. to mark the centenary of the American Baptist Publication Society. It strives after too modern and almost flippant (at times) renderings and popular headings that tend to cheapen the dignity of Scripture idiom.

The New Testament, A Translation in the Language of the People. Published in Boston in 1937 and reprinted in Chicago, 1950, this was founded on Westcott and Hort's Gk. text. Charles B. Williams, a professor of Gk. at Union University, Tennessee, was the author. Williams aimed at exact translation of the Gk. tenses.

The New Testament in Basic English (Cambridge, 1941). The *Old Testament in Basic English* appeared in 1950. This translation aimed to couch the Bible message in less than a thousand common English words supplemented of necessity by as few special biblical words as possible. Simplicity was the aim at the sacrifice of beauty and attractiveness of diction.

The Holy Bible. This was a Roman Catholic venture and aimed at revising the Challoner-Rheims version, and of course adhering closely to the Lat. Vulg. It was prepared by a group of twenty-seven Roman Catholic scholars and published by the Episcopal Committee of the Confraternity of Christian Doctrine (Paterson, N.J., 1941). The same committee is publishing the various books of the OT translated from the Heb. The book of Genesis appeared in 1948, the Psalms and Song of Solomon in 1950, and the books from Genesis to Ruth, 1952. The Sapiential books, Job to Serach (Ecclesiasticus), appeared in 1955. Beautifully printed with helpful critical notes, the translations are often fresh and challenging.

The Berkeley Version of the New Testament. This chiefly used Tischendorf's eighth edition of the Gk. text (1869-1872) and appeared in Berkeley, Calif., in 1945. It is the work of Gerrit Verkuyl, who for many years was associated with the board of Christian education of the Presbyterian Church in the U.S.A. After considerable ministry of the NT alone, the OT (done by various scholars) was added to it in 1959, to form the *Holy Bible, The Berkeley Version in Modern English* (which see, below).

The New Testament Letters. This helpful translation with harder passages expanded by clear paraphrase was done by J. W. C. Wand, Bishop of London (Oxford, 1946).

The New World Translation of the Christian Greek Scriptures. This is a vernacular translation published by the Jehovah's Witnesses. It appeared in Brooklyn in 1950. It aims to render the Westcott and Hort Gk. text into vernacular English. Bruce M. Metzger has given a critique of its Unitarianism in *Theology Today* 10 (1952): 65-85. The first of three projected renderings of the Heb. OT by the Jehovah's Witnesses appeared in 1953. It displays ignorance of some basic Heb. grammatical forms, including the *waw consecutive.*

Revised Standard Version. The *Revised Standard Version* is an authorized revision of the *American Standard Version* of 1901. The OT section was copyrighted in 1952, the NT section in 1946. This translation of the entire Bible was launched with great fanfare and at great expense. Its reception, however, has been mixed. Hailed by liberals, it has been unfavorably received by many conservatives. Its translators were almost completely of the liberal school. Although possessing the results of the latest scholarship, the translators have departed from the KJV, RV, and ASV in their high veneration for the Heb. Masoretic text of the OT, and in many instances the translation contains renderings of pivotal passages that are doctrinally weak and unreliable. It appears it will not supplant the KJV, RV, or ASV, at least among conservative Christians.

Letters to the Young Churches. This was done by J. B. Phillips (New York, 1948) of the Anglican church and is characterized by appealing English idiom. Phillips also published *The Gospels Translated into Modern English* (New York, 1953). He completed the translation of the NT, published under the title *The New Testament in Modern English* (New York, 1958).

The New Testament, A New Translation in Plain English (London, 1952). This was done by Charles Kingsley Williams at the invitation, in 1937, of the Society for the Promotion of Christian Knowledge. Its aim was to translate the Scriptures in about 2,000 common words listed by a group of educators in the *Interim Report on Vocabulary Selection,* 1936.

The Holy Bible, The Berkeley Version in Modern English. This appeared in Grand Rapids, Mich., 1959. The NT section is that of the Berkeley Version of the NT, by Gerrit Verkuyl, that appeared in 1945. The OT is the work of some twenty biblical scholars assisted by others under the editorship of Gerrit Verkuyl. This is translated from the original languages with numerous helpful nondoctrinal notes to aid the reader. It is designated as *The Holy Bible, The Berkeley Version in Modern English* and aims to avoid the archaisms and other expressions that are out-of-date in the KJV.

The Jerusalem Bible. After World War II, Roman Catholic scholars produced the *Jerusalem Bible,* which was published between 1956 and

1966. It was actually based on a French Bible translated by the Dominican School in Jerusalem but was revised and rendered into good idiomatic English, which in numerous places exhibits striking lyrical and dramatic qualities. The underlying scholarship is liberal in nature, but the translation has been done carefully in the Roman Catholic tradition and resists attempts at paraphrasing quite successfully. Although some liberties have been taken in the rearranging of the Heb. text, the *Jerusalem Bible* lends itself well to liturgical and devotional use.

The New American Standard Bible. This is basically a revision of the *American Standard Version* (1901) and was produced by the Lockman Foundation of La Habra, Calif. It is a highly respected literal translation by a committee of conservative scholars and was published in this sequence: the gospel of John (1960), the four gospels (1962), the New Testament (1963), the whole Bible (1967). The three stated objectives of the translators were clarity of English, accuracy of translation, and adequacy of notes. The NT translators followed the twenty-third edition of the Nestle Gk. text, even though they sometimes preferred the text underlying the ASV (e.g., the long ending of Mark 16:9-20 is adopted). Although the English style is not always smooth, many students and teachers choose the NASB because it avoids paraphrasing that often obscures or even misrepresents the statements and meaning of the original text.

The New English Bible. The *New English Bible* emerged from an ecumenical resolve to produce a fresh translation that would convey the sense of the original in contemporary English. Fourteen years after the initial resolution, the NT was published in 1961, and the OT and Apocrypha nine years later. The finished product was marked predominantly by liberal scholarship, and though it exhibited some creditable phraseology it encountered heavy criticism on literary grounds generally. The translators were accused of manipulating the OT text in some areas, allowing liberal theological presuppositions to influence their translation, using unnecessary paraphrasing, limiting the usefulness of the book by including British provincial idioms, and permitting sentences that were either vulgar in meaning or rough in syntax. The attempt to blend scholarship and the popular idiom failed to produce a version that could match the King James Version or the *Revised Standard Version* liturgically, making the translation more suitable for private use.

The New International Version. An interdenominational enterprise by evangelical scholars resulted in a widely acclaimed translation known as the *New International Version*. Underwritten by the New York Bible Society, the NT was issued in 1973 and the OT some five years later. Though the version was not marked by the

textual dislocations of earlier liberal translations, it employed the concept of dynamic equivalence in a manner that resulted in a great deal of paraphrasing. On occasions this tendency not only obscured the meaning of the original, but actually misrepresented it. As with many modern translations, the *New Internatinal Version* supplied footnotes that furnished textual information or gave alternative translations. Despite attempts to accommodate the version to liturgical needs, the literary style does not always lend itself to public worship, although the version has been recognized by many evangelical churches because of its conservative theological approach.

The New King James Bible. Published by Thomas Nelson, the NT of the *New King James Version* was issued in 1979 and the complete Bible in 1982. As with other versions, archaic literary and syntactical forms were replaced with modern equivalents, but an attempt was made to retain familiar passages in their traditional form as far as possible. The *New King James Version* has been praised widely for the way in which the revisers managed to capture the flavor and ethos of the King James Version, and the OT has been declared by some scholars to be the best and most accurate rendering of the Hebrew in the past century.

The New Living Translation. Tyndale's *New Living Translation* began as a revision of Ken Taylor's *The Living Bible*, but the ninety evangelical scholars commissioned to this task decided instead to complete a new translation that was accurate to the original language and yet lively and dynamic. The NLT accomplishes this goal by translating entire thoughts into everyday English rather than by translating just words.

The English Standard Version. The *English Standard Version* (ESV), published by Crossway, J.I. Packer, gen. ed., is a revision of the *Revised Standard Version* by a team of evangelical scholars. Using the elegance and accuracy of the RSV as their base, the translators reviewed the Hebrew and Greek text to arrive at the most accurate and understandable Bible translation possible. Where word choice in the RSV has become archaic, more current phraseology was chosen.   R.K.H.

BIBLIOGRAPHY: C. Goulson, *The English Bible* (1961); *The Cambridge History of the Bible*, ed. P. R. Ackroyd et al., 3 vols. (1963-70); J. G. MacGregor, *A Literary History of the Bible* (1968); H. W. Robinson, ed., *The Bible in Its Ancient and English Versions* (1970); F. F. Bruce, *The History of the English Bible* (1978).

TRAPPER (from Heb. *yāqōsh*, to "lay snares"; Pss. 91:3; 124:7 ["fowler," NIV]; also rendered "fowler," Prov. 6:5; Jer. 5:26; "bird catcher," Hos. 9:8). One who took birds by means of nets, snares, decoys, etc. Among the Egyptians "fowling was one of the great amusements of all classes. Those who followed this sport for their livelihood used nets and traps, but the amateur sportsman pursued his game in the thickets, and felled them with the throw-stick. . . . The throw-stick was made of heavy wood, and flat, so as to offer little resistance to the air in its flight, and the distance to which an expert could throw it was considerable. It was about one foot and a quarter to two feet in length, and about one and a half inches in breadth, slightly curved at the upper end. They frequently took with them a decoy bird, and in order to keep it to its post, a female was selected, whose nest, containing eggs, was deposited in the boat" (Wilkinson, *Ancient Egyptians,* 1: 234ff.). According to the Mosaic law anyone finding a bird's nest was forbidden to take the mother with the eggs or young (Deut. 22:6-7), lest the species be extinguished; or, perhaps, to impress upon men the sacredness of the relation between parent and young.

TREAD, TREADERS. *See* Winepress.

TREATY. *See* Alliance; Covenant.

TREE (Heb. *'ēs;* Gk. *dendron*). Trees in Palestine, as elsewhere, were objects of beauty and utility (Ps. 1:3).

Mosaic Regulations. When the Israelites planted fruit trees in Palestine they were to treat the fruit of every tree as uncircumcised, i.e., not to eat it. "The reason for this command is not to be sought for in the fact that in the first three years fruit trees bear only a little fruit, and that somewhat insipid, and that if the blossom or fruit is broken off the first year the trees will bear all the more plentifully afterward, though this end would no doubt be thereby attained; but it rests rather upon ethical grounds. Israel was to treat the fruits of horticulture with the most careful regard as a gift of God, and sanctify the enjoyment of them by a thank offering. In the fourth year the whole of the fruit was to be a holiness of praise for Jehovah, i.e., to be offered to the Lord as a holy sacrificial gift, in praise and thanksgiving for the blessing which he had bestowed upon the fruit trees" (K & D., *Com.*). The Hebrews were forbidden to destroy the fruit trees of their enemies in time of war, for the tree of the field is man's life (Deut. 20:19-20).

Noted Trees. There are in Scripture many memorable trees, e.g., Allon-bacuth (Gen. 35:8), the tamarisk in Gibeah (1 Sam. 22:6), the oak in Shechem (Josh. 24:26), under which the law was set up; the palm tree of Deborah (Judg. 4:5), the diviner's oak (9:37), the oak in Zaanannim (4:11), and others (1 Sam. 10:3; 14:2). Among the pagans this observation of particular trees was ex-

tended to a regular worship of them. *See* Vegetable Kingdom.

Worship of Trees. Among the Canaanites and other Eastern peoples, worship was carried on in *holy groves* (which see). In the absence of groves they chose green trees with thick foliage (Ezek. 6:13; 20:28), such as the vigorous oak, the evergreen terebinth (Isa. 1:29-30; 57:5, *see* marg.), and the poplar or osier, which remains green even in the heat of summer (Hos. 4:13). To explain how this worship came about, Stade (*Geschicte,* 1:451) says that at such places were graves of patriarchs or other heroes—as Hebron, the burying place of Abraham, etc.; but Robertson (*Early Religion of Israel,* p. 248) says: "I believe the prophet, who reproved the worship under green trees, came nearer to a true explanation of the origin of the worship in the hint, 'because the shadow thereof is good' (Hos. 4:13), than modern critics, with their learned disquisition as to the tree suggesting life and being the abode of 'a spirit or a divinity.' "

TREE SNAKE. *See* Animal Kingdom: Owl; Snake.

TRESPASS OFFERING. *See* Sacrificial Offerings.

TRIAL. *See* Law, Administration of; Temptation.

TRIBE. *See* Israel, Constitution of.

TRIBULATION, THE GREAT. This is the period of unparalleled suffering that, according to premillennial eschatology, will precede the establishment of the future kingdom of Israel (Acts 1:6). The trouble will embrace the entire earth (Rev. 3:10). Yet in a distinctive sense it will center upon Jerusalem and Palestine, being called by Jeremiah specifically "the time of Jacob's distress" (Jer. 30:7). It will involve the Jewish people who will have gone back to Palestine in unbelief. It will also be connected with catastrophic judgments upon the Gentile nations because of their wickedness and anti-Semitism. The colossal scenes of the Revelation, beginning with chap. 5 and the opening of the seven-sealed book, through chap. 10, form a prelude to worldwide commotion prior to the Great Tribulation itself described in chaps. 11-18. The Great Tribulation is identical with the last three and one-half years of Daniel's seventieth week of years (Dan. 9:24-27; Rev. 11:2-3). The gigantic wars, cataclysms, pestilences, etc., that befall the earth are actually the manifestation of the risen, victorious Christ taking an open hand to claim His redeemed rights to the earth in preparation for the divine program involving His people on the earth. Psalm 2, in giving the order of the establishment of the kingdom in the ousting of Christ's enemies, closely interweaves the first advent and the Messiah's death in shame with His second advent in glory to receive the rewards of His conquest over sin and death. The Tribulation will see the nations raging (Ps. 2:1) and the derision of Jehovah (v. 4) that men should vainly imagine to set aside His covenant (2 Sam. 7:8-16) and His plan for the earth (Ps. 89:34-37). The Great Tribulation foreseen in Ps. 2 is described in Matt 24:15-51. It eventuates in the establishment of the rejected King in Zion (Ps. 2:6) and the subjugation of the earth to the King's millennial rule (vv. 7-9), with a present appeal to Gentile world powers to be warned by the certainty of the establishment of Christ's kingdom (vv. 10-12). According to Rev. 13-19, there will be the cruel reign of the "beast coming up out of the sea" (13:1) who, breaking his covenant with the Jews (2 Thess. 2:4), will demand divine worship. This earth ruler, the Beast, is empowered by Satan, and the entire terrific episode of fighting God is made possible by the unprecedented activity of demons (Rev. 9:1-11; 16:13-16). The terrific bowl judgments of chap. 16 are the "Lamb's" final demonstration of power. He destroys His enemies and frees His redeemed earth from the domination of wicked men at His visible, glorious return, and sets up the kingdom. Those who are not premillennialists hold that the Tribulation of Revelation was fulfilled in the Roman persecutions of the church or in great catastrophes occurring over the last nineteen centuries.   M.F.U.

BIBLIOGRAPHY: J. D. Pentecost, *Things to Come* (1958), pp. 156, 164, 179, 182, 184, 193, 195, 210, 237, 239, 251, 275, 314; J. B. Payne, *The Imminent Appearing of Christ* (1962); J. F. Walvoord, *Israel in Prophecy* (1962); id., *The Nations in Prophecy* (1967); L. J. Wood, *The Bible and Future Events* (1973), pp. 54-158; W. K. Price, *The Coming Antichrist* (1974); L. Strauss, *Prophetic Mysteries Revealed* (1980); W. R. Kimball, *What the Bible Says About the Great Tribulation* (1983); H. A. Ironside and F. C. Ottman, *Biblical Eschatology* (1985).

TRIBUTE. Several Heb. and Gk. terms are translated "tribute" in the KJV, NIV, and NASB: Heb. *missâ,* number, is used for that which an Israelite gave to the Lord according to his ability (Deut. 16:10); and Aram. *belô,* something consumed, or excise, refers to a tax on things consumed (Ezra 4:13; 7:24). Several other terms, translated "tribute" in the KJV and NIV are rendered "taxes" in the NASB: Heb. *mekes,* is a portion paid to the Lord (Num. 31:28); Heb. *middat,* is a fine imposed (Ezra 6:8 ["revenues," NIV]; Neh. 5:4 ["tax," NIV]); Gk. *didrachon,* a double drachma is a Temple tax levied on all Jews (Matt. 17:24); and Gk. *phoros,* a burden, was the annual tax upon houses, lands, and persons (Luke 20:22; 23:2). "Tribute money," KJV, was the coin with which the tax was paid (Matt. 22:19). *See* Forced Labor; Fine; Poll Tax.

BIBLIOGRAPHY: J. N. Postgate, *Neo-Assyrian Royal Grants and Decrees* (1969), pp. 9-16.

TRIBUTE MONEY. *See* Tribute.

Assyrians weighing tribute on scales

TRIGON. *See* Music.

TRINITY. The term by which is expressed the unity of three Persons in the one God. The Christian doctrine is: (1) That there is only one God, one divine nature and being. (2) This one divine Being is tripersonal, involving the distinctions of the Father, the Son, and the Holy Spirit. (3) These three are joint partakers of the same nature and majesty of God. This doctrine is preeminently one of revelation. And although it brings before us one of the great mysteries of revelation and transcends finite comprehension, it is essential to the understanding of the Scriptures, and, as we shall see, has its great value and uses.

Scripture Doctrine. Although the doctrine of the Trinity is implicit rather than explicit in the OT, at the same time it is properly held that with the accompanying light of the NT this truth can be found in the OT (e.g., Num. 6:24-26; Isa. 6:3; 63:9-10, the sanctity of the symbolical number three—the plural form of Elohim, also places in which the Deity is spoken of as conversing with Himself). This is in accord with the gradual development of revealed truth in other particulars. The religion of the OT is emphatically monotheistic. The almost exclusive proclamation of the unity of God was essential as a safeguard against polytheism.

The NT teaching upon this subject is not given in the way of formal statement. The formal statement, however, is legitimately and necessarily deduced from the Scriptures of the NT, and these, as has been suggested, cast a light backward upon the intimations of the OT. Reliance, it is held by many competent critics, is not to be placed upon the passages in Acts 20:28 and

1 Tim. 3:16; and 1 John 5:7 is commonly regarded as spurious. Aside from these, however, it is plain that both Christ and the apostles ascribe distinct personality to the Father, the Son, and the Holy Spirit (*see* articles, Father, God the; Sonship of Christ; Holy Spirit, the). And these utterances are such as to admit legitimately of no other conception than that of the unity of these three Persons in the ontological oneness of the whole divine nature (*see,* e.g., Matt. 28:19; John 14:16-17; 1 Cor. 12:4-6; 2 Cor. 13:14; Eph. 4:4-6; 1 Pet. 1:2; Rev. 1:4-6). The same worship is paid and the same works are ascribed to each of these three Persons, and in such a way as to indicate that these three are united in the fullness of the one living God. The monotheism of the OT is maintained, while glimpses are nevertheless afforded into the tripersonal mode of the divine existence.

Theological Suggestions. The Christian faith at this period does not ground itself upon philosophy, for it here extends to a matter far above the reach of philosophical reflection. Also, little stress, if any, is to be laid upon apparent resemblances between pagan religions and Christianity at this point—resemblances more apparent than real. The doctrine is to be accepted by faith in the divine revelation; and although it is above reason and cannot be comprehended in its depth and fullness, it does not follow that it is opposed to reason.

The question as to whether the Trinity is merely one of manifestation or that of essential nature has been raised again and again in the history of the church (*see* Sabellianism in the article Doctrine). Undoubtedly the history of revelation shows progress in the unfolding of truth concerning God. And in that sense the Trinity is dispensational. But it is also emphatically to be borne in mind that if God reveals Himself, He must reveal Himself as He is, and the Trinity of revelation must therefore rest upon a Trinity of nature. The attempt to remove difficulty by any sort of Sabellian interpretation only raises difficulty of a deeper character. Can God on the whole reveal Himself other than He actually is?

On the other hand Christianity has reason to guard itself, as it has generally sought to do, against tritheistic conceptions. Both the unity and the tripersonal nature of God are to be maintained. And thus the proper baptismal formula is not "In the name of God the Father, God the Son, and God the Holy Spirit," but the words as our Lord gave them (Matt. 28:19).

It is admitted by all who thoughtfully deal with this subject that the Scripture revelation here leads us into the presence of a deep mystery and that all human attempts at expression are of necessity imperfect. The word *person,* it may be, is inadequate and is doubtless used often in a way that is misleading. "That God is alike one Person, and in the same sense three Persons, is what Christianity has never professed" (Van Oosterzee). Said Augustine, "Three persons, if they are to be so called, for the unspeakable exaltedness of the object cannot be set forth by this term." And yet the long-standing and prevailing doctrine of the church expresses more nearly than any other the truth concerning God as it comes to us in the Holy Scriptures. And it is further to be borne in mind that this teaching of the church has been called forth for the purpose of combating various forms of error. It has not been held as a complete or perfect expression of the truth concerning the unfathomable being of God, but rather as a protest against the denials of the personality and supreme deity of the Son and of the Holy Spirit.

Accordingly, the doctrine has a large measure of importance. It has been called "a bulwark for Christian theism." Unitarianism is very apt to degenerate into deism or pantheism. Also this doctrine affords us a glimpse into the wonderful being of God, while at the same time it constantly proclaims the impossibility of comprehending God. Thus while it is a stumbling block to rationalism, it is for those who accept it a safeguard against all tendency to rationalism or intellectual pride. And, further, in the Trinity we should behold not only a God who is exalted far above us, but also Christ with us and the Holy Spirit who will dwell in us. Thus in a proper way is harmonized the divine transcendence with the divine immanence.

The glory of the gospel depends upon this truth; for Christ is most clearly seen to be God's unspeakable gift, the Bringer of the most perfect revelation and the Author of eternal salvation, when we recognize His essential oneness with the Father. Likewise the Holy Spirit is thus seen to be, in His relation to a sinful world and to the church, as well as to individual believers, the infinite source of hope and new and holy life.

Historical. Briefly, it may be said that the faith of the early Christians at this point, as at many others, was without attempt at scientific form. The elements of the doctrine, however, were embraced by their simple reliance upon the teaching of Christ and His apostles. It was only gradually, and after a considerable period in conflict with Judaism and paganism, that the thought of the church arrived at something of a formal statement. The word *Trinity* (*Trinitas*) was first employed by Tertullian (2d century), though his word was only the Lat. translation of the Gk. *trias,* employed by Theophilus of Antioch. The word *Person* was also first employed by Tertullian, though he used it in the inadmissible sense of individual.

The Council of Nicaea (A.D. 325) was an epoch in Christian history. The heresy of Sabellius and Paul of Samosata, that refused to recognize the Father as in any personal sense distinct from the Son and the Holy Spirit, had been previously condemned. But Arius, who began with the Sabellian idea that the Trinity is only one of manifestation, changed his position and declared that there were three Persons in God, but that these three were unequal in glory. In short, the Son and the Holy Spirit owed their existence to the divine will and, accordingly, were creatures of God (see Arianism in books on doctrine). The Council of Nicea, in opposition to Arianism and various other theories, adopted the formal statement of the consubstantiality of the Father, the Son, and the Holy Spirit, while maintaining the distinction of personality. The doctrine of the Nicene Council was reaffirmed at various succeeding councils and is the generally recognized doctrine of the Christian church. E.MCC.; M.F.U.

BIBLIOGRAPHY: K. Barth, *Church Dogmatics* (1936), 1:1-339ff.; H. Bavinck, *The Doctrine of God* (1951), pp. 225-334; R. S. Franks, *The Doctrine of the Trinity* (1953); E. H. Bickersteth, *The Trinity* (1965); J. M. Boice, *The Sovereign God,* Foundations of the Christian Faith (1978), pp. 137-47, 210.

TRIPOLIS. The NIV rendering of Tarpela (Ezra 4:9). *See* Tarpelites.

TRI'UMPH (Heb. *'ālaz,* to "exult"; *'ālaṣ,* to "jump" for joy; Gk. *thriambeuō,* a "noisy song"). The nations of antiquity generally celebrated success in war by a triumph, which usually included a splendid procession, a display of captives and spoil, and a solemn thanksgiving to the gods.

The Egyptians. The return of a king in triumph from war was a grand solemnity celebrated with all the pomp that the wealth of the nation could command. The inhabitants flocked to meet him and with welcome acclamations greeted his arrival and the success of his arms. The priests and chief people of each place advanced with garlands and bouquets of flowers; the principal person present addressed him in an appropriate speech; and as the troops filed through the streets or passed outside the walls, the people followed with acclamations, uttering earnest thanksgiving to the gods, the protectors of Egypt, and praying them forever to continue the same marks of favor to their monarch and their nation. The Assyrian sculptures abound with similar representations.

After the battle

The Romans. Among the Romans the highest honor that could be bestowed on a citizen or magistrate was the triumph or solemn procession in which a victorious general passed from the gate of the city to the capitol. He set out from the Campus Martius along the Via Triumphalis, and from thence through the most public places of the city. The streets were strewn with flowers, and the altars smoked with incense. The procession was formed as follows: First, a band of musicians, singing and playing triumphal songs; the oxen to be sacrificed, their horns gilded and heads adorned with headbands and garlands; the spoils, and captives in chains; the lictors (officers who attended chief magistrates appearing in public), carrying fasces (the officers' insignia of office; it consisted of a bundle of rods bound with an ax with its blade projecting and was carried before magistrates as a badge of authority) adorned with laurel; a great company of musicians and dancers; a long train of persons carrying perfumes; the general dressed in purple embroidered with gold, wearing a crown of laurel and carrying in his right hand a laurel branch and a scepter in his left, his face painted with vermilion, and a golden ball suspended from his neck. He stood erect in his chariot; a public slave was by his side to remind him of the vicissitudes of fortune and of his mortality. Behind him came the consuls, senators, and other magistrates, on foot; the whole procession closed with the victorious army.

The Hebrews. They celebrated their victories by triumphal processions. The women and children danced to the accompaniment of musical instruments (Judg. 11:34), singing hymns of triumph to Jehovah. The hymns that were sung by Miriam (Ex. 15:1-21) and Deborah (Judg. 5:1-31) are notable examples. Triumphal songs were uttered for the living (1 Sam. 18:6-8; 2 Chron. 20:21-28), and elegies for the dead (2 Sam. 1:17-27; 2 Chron. 35:25). Great demonstrations of joy were made, and the shout of victory resounded from mountain to mountain (Isa. 42:11; 52:7-8; 63:1-4; Jer. 50:2; Ezek. 7:7; Nah. 1:15). Monuments in honor of victory were erected, and the arms of the enemy were hung up as trophies in the Temples (1 Sam. 21:9; 31:10; 2 Sam. 8:11, 12; 2 Kings 11:10).

Indignities to prisoners, such as maiming, blinding, and killing, formed a leading feature among ancient nations. Many representations appear upon the monuments of putting the foot upon the head or neck of a conquered foe (Josh. 10:24), and that forms the ground of many figurative representations in the Scriptures (Ps. 110:1; Isa. 60:14; 1 Cor. 15:26).

TRO'AS (trō'az; Gk. the Troad, region about Troy). A city on the coast of Mysia, opposite the SE extremity of the island of Tenedos, and near Troy. It was formerly called Antigonia Troas, having been built by Antigonus; but it was embellished by Lysimachus and named Alexandria Troas in honor of Alexander the Great. It flourished under the Romans and, with its environs, was raised by Augustus to be a *colonia*. It was while in Troas that Paul received the divine intimation that he was to carry the gospel into Europe (Acts 16:8-11); where he rested for a short time on the northward road from Ephesus (during the next missionary journey), in the expectation of meeting Titus (2 Cor. 2:12-13); where on his return southward he met those who had preceded him from Philippi (Acts 20:5-6), and remained a week; and where, years after, he left a cloak, some books, and parchments in the house of Carpus (2 Tim. 4:13).

BIBLIOGRAPHY: E. M. Blaiklock, *Cities of the New Testament* (1965), pp. 35-38.

Site of Troas, a harbor city on the shore of Asia Minor

TROGYL'LIUM (tro-jil'i-um). A town and promontory on the Ionian coast, directly opposite Samos; the channel here was about one mile in width. Paul sailed through this channel on his way to Jerusalem at the close of his third missionary journey; the marg. of Acts 20:15 states that he spent the night in Trogyllium. "St. Paul's Port" is the name still given to the harbor here.

TROPH'IMUS (trof'i-mus; Gk. "nourishing"). A companion of the apostle Paul. He was a native of Ephesus in Asia Minor and, together with Tychicus, accompanied Paul on his third missionary journey when returning from Macedonia toward Syria (Acts 20:4). Trophimus went to Jerusalem, where he was the innocent cause of the tumult in which the apostle was apprehended. Certain Jews from the district of Asia saw the two missionaries together and *supposed* that Paul had taken Trophimus into the Temple (21:27-29). In 2 Tim. 4:20 Paul writes that he had left Trophimus in ill health in Miletus.

BIBLIOGRAPHY: C. E. Macartney, *The Man Who Forgot Paul* (1973), pp. 208-12.

(1956), pp. 105-16; D. E. Hiebert, *Personalities Around Paul* (1973), pp. 208-12.

TROW. A KJV rendering, using this archaic English word, for the Gk. *dokeō* in Luke 17:9. It means "to be of the opinion, to think."

TRUCEBREAKER The KJV rendering of Gk. *'aspondos*, "without a treaty," in 2 Tim. 3:3 ("irreconcilable," NASB; "unforgiving," NIV).

TRUMP, TRUMPET. *See* Music.

TRUMPETS, FEAST OF. Called also Seventh New Moon. *See* Festivals; Sacrifices.

TRUNK (Heb. *'iqqēr*). In 1 Sam. 5:4 it is recorded that the image of Dagon was miraculously overthrown, his hands and head cut off, and only the trunk ("body" NIV) left. This was to prove to the Philistines the utter helplessness of their god.

TRYPHAE'NA (tri-fay'na), or **Tryphe'na** (KJV and NIV only; "delicate, luxurious, dainty"). A Christian woman of Rome to whom, in connection with Tryphosa, Paul sent a special salutation (Rom. 16:12). What other relation the two women had is not known, but it is more than likely that they were fellow deaconesses.

TRYPHO'SA (tri-fō'sa; Gk. "delicate, luxurious"). *See* Tryphaena.

TSADHE' (צ) (tsa-di'). The eighteenth letter of the Heb. alphabet, corresponding to no single letter in English. It is anglicized by *ts* or *tz*. It heads the eighteenth section of Ps. 119, in which section each verse of the Heb. commences with this letter.   M.F.U.

TU'BAL (tū'bal; meaning uncertain). One of the seven sons of Japheth (Gen. 10:2; 1 Chron. 1:5). He is thought to have been the founder of the Tiberani, said by the scholiasts to have been a Scythian tribe. Tubal and Meshech, the Tabali and Mushki of the Assyrian monuments, were the representatives of eastern Asia Minor. Their territory originally extended far to the S. In the time of Sargon and Sennacherib, the territory of the Tabali adjoined Cilicia, while the Mushki inhabited the highlands to the E of them, where they were in contact with the Hittites. In later days, however, Meschech had retreated to the N, and the classical geographers place the Tibarêni and the Mushki not far from the Black Sea.

TU'BAL-CAIN (tū'bal-kān; Tubal, "the smith"). The son of Lamech by his wife Zillah. He is described (Gen. 4:22) as "the forger of all instruments of bronze and iron."

TUNIC. *See* Dress.

TURBAN. A piece of cloth wrapped several times around the head and the rendering in the NASB of four Heb. words. *See also* Dress; and the discussion of the high priest in the articles Priesthood, Hebrew; Priest, High.

1. Heb. *miṣnepet* (Ex. 28:4, 37, 39; 29:6; etc.), the headdress of the high priest. The KJV renders "miter" or "diadem" (Ezek. 21:26).

2. Heb. *ṣānîp* (Zech. 3:5; Job 29:14; Isa. 3:23 ["tiara," NIV]), a headdress composed of twisted clothes of various colors. In the KJV this term is translated "miter" (Zech. 3:5), "hood" (Isa. 3:23), and "diadem" (Isa. 62:3; Job 29:14). In the NASB and NIV of Isa. 62:3 the Heb. term is rendered "diadem."

3. Heb. *ṭebûlîm* (Ezek. 23:15 only), another term for turban; in the KJV the rendering is "dyed attire."

4 Heb. *pe'ēr*, a turban (Ezek. 24:17; "tire," KJV) or headdress (Isa. 3:20; "bonnet," KJV).

TURPENTINE. *See* Vegetable Kingdom.

TURQUOISE. *See* Mineral Kingdom.

TURTLE, TURTLEDOVE. *See* Animal Kingdom.

TUTOR (Gk. *paidagōgos*). A guide and guardian for boys. Among the Greeks and Romans the name was applied to trustworthy slaves who were charged with the duty of supervising the life and morals of boys of the better class. The name carries with it the idea of severity (as of a stern censor and enforcer of morals) in 1 Cor. 4:15, where the father is distinguished from the tutor as one whose discipline is usually milder. The NIV, however, translates it as "guardian." In Gal. 3:24-25, the Mosaic law is likened to a tutor because it arouses the consciousness of sin, and is called *paidagōgos* ("our tutor to lead us to Christ"), i.e., as preparing the soul for Christ, because those who have learned by experience with the law that they are not sinless and cannot be commended to God by their works, welcome the more eagerly the hope of salvation offered them through the death and resurrection of Christ, the Son of God. The term is sometimes translated "schoolmaster," but that is misleading because the *paidagōgos* had the responsibility of taking a boy to the schoolmaster in the morning and leaving him there. Likewise the law as a *paidagōgos* leads a person to Christ as schoolmaster and leaves him there.   H.F.V.

TWELVE. *See* Number.

TWILIGHT. *See* Time.

TWINKLING. The apostle Paul, in speaking of those who shall be alive when Christ comes in judgment, says (1 Cor. 15:51-52), "We shall all be changed, *in a moment* [Gk. *en atomō*, "that which cannot be divided"], in the *twinkling of an eye* [*en hripē 'ophthalmou*, the "jerk" of the eyelash]." Both these were common expressions to denote the shortest conceivable time.

TYCH'ICUS (tik'i-kus; "fortuitous"). One of Paul's fellow laborers. He is first mentioned as a companion of the apostle during a portion of Paul's return journey from the third missionary tour (Acts 20:4). He is there expressly called (with Trophimus) a native of Asia Minor; but while Trophimus went with Paul to Jerusalem (21:29), Tychicus was left behind in Asia, probably at Miletus (20:15, 38). In Paul's first imprisonment he was with the apostle again (Col. 4:7-8; Eph. 6:21-22). The next reference to him is in Titus 3:12. Here Paul (writing possibly from Ephesus) says that it is probable he may send Tychicus to Crete, about the time when he himself goes to Nicopolis. In 2 Tim. 4:12 (written at Rome during the second imprisonment), he says, "Tychicus I have sent to Ephesus." There is much probability in the conjecture that Tychicus was one of the two "brethren" (Trophimus being the other) who were associated with Titus (2 Cor. 8:16-24) in conducting the business of the collection for the poor Christians in Judea.

BIBLIOGRAPHY: D. E. Hiebert, *Personalities Around Paul* (1973), pp. 213-22.

TYRAN'NUS (ti-ran'us; Lat. from Gk. "a tyrant, an absolute sovereign"). The man in whose school Paul taught for two years during his sojourn at Ephesus (Acts 19:9). The fact that Paul taught in his school after leaving the synagogue favors the opinion that Tyrannus was a Greek, but whether he was a convert is uncertain. Paul taught every day in the lecture room of Tyrannus. "Public life in the Ionian cities ended regularly at the fifth hour (11 A.M.); . . . thus Paul himself would be free, and the lecture room would be disengaged after the fifth hour; and the time, which was devoted generally to home life and rest, was applied by him to mission work" (Ramsay, *St. Paul*, p. 271).

TYRE (tīr; Heb. *ṣûr*, "a rock"; Gk. *Turos*). An ancient Phoenician city, located on the shore of the Mediterranean Sea, twenty miles from Sidon and twenty-three miles from Acre. It once consisted of two parts—a rocky coast defense of great strength on the mainland, and a city upon a small but well-protected island, about half a mile from the shore. Tyre was already a city on an island in the fourteenth century B.C., as we learn from an Egyptian papyrus of that date. At the time that Alexander the Great besieged Tyre for seven months, a road was built from the mainland to the island; thereafter the island was merely the tip of a peninsula, formed as sand drifted against the roadway. The configuration of the locality was changed, for with the causeway being built, the island no longer existed. The city was spoken of as "the bestower of crowns, whose merchants were princes, whose traders were the honored of the earth" (Isa. 23:8). The Tyrian merchants sailed to all ports and colonized almost everywhere. David early formed an alliance with them for trading purposes (2 Sam. 5:11; 1 Kings 5:1;

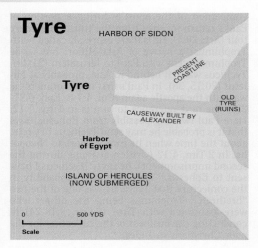

Tyre   HARBOR OF SIDON

PRESENT COASTLINE

Tyre

OLD TYRE (RUINS)

CAUSEWAY BUILT BY ALEXANDER

Harbor of Egypt

ISLAND OF HERCULES (NOW SUBMERGED)

0   500 YDS

Scale

2 Chron. 2:3). *See* Hiram; Solomon; Tarshish; Ezion-geber.

These friendly relations survived for a time the disastrous secession of the ten tribes, and a century later Ahab married a daughter of Ethbaal, king of the Sidonians (1 Kings 16:31). According to Menander, she was the daughter of Ithobal, king of Tyre. When mercantile cupidity induced the Tyrians and the neighboring Phoenicians to buy Hebrew captives from their enemies and to sell them as slaves to the Greeks and Edomites, there commenced denunciations and, at first, threats of retaliation (Joel 3:4-8; Amos 1:9-10). But the likelihood of the denunciations being fulfilled first arose from the progressive conquests of the Assyrian monarchs.

Our knowledge of its condition from then until the siege by Nebuchadnezzar depends entirely on mention of it by the Hebrew prophets, who denounced the idolatry and wickedness of the city (Isa. 23:1; Jer. 25:22; Ezek. 26-28; Amos 1:9-10; Zech. 9:2-4). Some of these writings are quite extensive, and Ezek. 27 is especially detailed. One point that particularly arrests the attention is that Tyre, like its splendid daughter Carthage, employed mercenary soldiers (Ezek. 27:8-9). Independently, however, of this fact respecting Tyrian mercenary soldiers, Ezekiel gives interesting details respecting the trade of Tyre. It appears that its gold came from Arabia by the Persian Gulf (v. 22), just as in the time of Solomon it came from Arabia by the Red Sea.

Only thirty-four years before the destruction of Jerusalem the celebrated reformation of Josiah occurred (622 B.C.). This momentous religious revolution (2 Kings 22-23) fully explains the exultation and malevolence of the Tyrians. In that reformation Josiah had heaped insults on the gods who were the objects of Tyrian veneration and love. Indeed, he seemed to have endeavored to exterminate their religion (23:20). These acts

must have been regarded by the Tyrians as a series of sacrilegious and abominable outrages; we can scarcely doubt that the death in battle of Josiah at Megiddo and the subsequent destruction of the city and Temple of Jerusalem were hailed by them as instances of divine retribution in human affairs. Their joy, however, must soon have given way to other feelings when Nebuchadnezzar invaded Phoenicia and laid siege to Tyre. That siege lasted thirteen years (585-572 B.C.), and it is still a disputed point whether Tyre was actually taken by Nebuchadnezzar on this occasion. Alexander the Great took the island city in 332 B.C., after a seven-month siege. Victory came only after he built a half-mile causeway out to the island. At the time our Lord visited Tyre (Matt. 15:21; Mark 7:24) it was perhaps more populous than Jerusalem. Paul spent seven days there (Acts 21:3-7). Tyre suffered violent destruction in the thirteenth century when the Muslims took it from the Crusaders. After the death of Stephen the Martyr, a church was formed here, and it was early the seat of a Christian bishopric.

The most celebrated product of Tyre, and a source of very great wealth, was the famous purple dye made from mollusks (*murex*) found on the nearby shores. Sidon was the older city (cf. Gen. 10:15; Isa. 23:12). In later centuries, however, Tyre far outstripped Sidon. Canaanite cults, which we now know from the Ras Shamra literature of the fourteenth century B.C. to be effete and morally debasing, helped to make Tyre a profligate, self-centered, opulent, and worldly wise city. The cult of Melcarth was firmly established for many centuries. Ezekiel denounced the wicked city (Ezek. 28:1-19).

Systematic excavations at Tyre began in 1947 under the leadership of Maurice Chehab, director-general of the Lebanese Department of Antiquities, and they continued until the outbreak of hostilities in 1975. Much of Roman and Byzantine Tyre has been laid bare. Chehab focused his attention primarily on three sections: (1) the area where the E-W Roman road intersected the N-S road; (2) a nearby Crusader church; and (3) the island city. Along the road the Lebanese excavated scores of marble sarcophagi, many beautifully executed; a monumental arch of the second century A.D.; and a marvelous hippodrome 500 meters long. Nearby, the Crusader cathedral of the twelfth century has been excavated. In the area of the island city, Chehab uncovered the main thoroughfare of the Byzantine period, a rectangular arena, a massive bath complex, and a marketplace or a palestra. Tyre was becoming one of the archaeological showplaces of the Mediterranean world when the Lebanese troubles began.

H.F.V.

BIBLIOGRAPHY: N. Jidejian, *Tyre Through the Ages* (1969); H. J. Katzenstein, *The History of Tyre* (1973).

TY'RUS. The KJV uses this Gk. form of Tyre in a number of OT verses (Jer. 25:22; 27:3; 47:4; Ezek. 26:2-4, 7, 15; 27:2, 3, 8, 32; Hos. 9:13; Amos 1:9, 10; Zech. 9:2, 3).

U

U

U'CAL (ū'kal; "I am strong" or, possibly, "consumed"). A word that occurs as a proper name in Prov. 30:1: "The man declares to Ithiel, to Ithiel and Ucal." Most authorities endorse this translation and regard these two persons as disciples of "Agur the son of Jakeh," a Hebrew teacher, whose authorship of this unique chapter has rescued his name from obscurity; but the passage is very obscure. By slightly varying the punctuation it has been translated, "I have labored for God, and have obtained" (Cocceius); "I have wearied myself for God, and have given up the investigation" (J. D. Michaelis); "I have wearied myself for God, and have fainted" (Bertheau); "I have wearied myself for God, and I became dull" (Hitzig). If any of these views is correct, the repetition of the first clause of the sentence is merely for poetical effect. Bunsen, however, supposes the speaker to have given himself a symbolical name, somewhat in the manner of the English Puritans, and translates, "The saying of the man 'I-have-wearied-myself-for-God:' I have wearied myself for God, and have fainted away." Davidson, with greater accuracy, reads: "I am weary, O God, I am weary, O God, and am become weak." Ewald combines the two names into one, which he renders, "God-be-with-me-and-I-am-strong," and bestows it upon a character whom he supposes to engage in a dialogue with Agur. Keil follows Ewald's translation of the names but disjoins them and regards the first as typifying the reverential believers in God among Agur's disciples, and the second the self-righteous freethinkers "who thought themselves superior to the revealed law, and in practical atheism indulged the lusts of the flesh."

U'EL (ū'el; "will of God"). One of the sons of Bani. He is mentioned in Ezra 10:34 as one of those who put away their Gentile wives after the captivity, 456 B.C.

UK'NAZ. *See* Kenaz.

U'LAI (ū'lī). A river that flowed S from central Iran through the old Persian imperial city of Susa. It was there in vision that Daniel saw the revelation of the ram and goat (Dan. 8:2, 16).

E.H.M.

U'LAM (ū'lam; perhaps, "leader, first"; cf. Arab. *'awwal,* "first").

1. A son of Sheresh, and father of Bedan, of the tribe of Manasseh. Mentioned only in the genealogical record (1 Chron. 7:16-17).

2. The firstborn of Eshek, a direct descendant from Mephibosheth, the grandson of King Saul; he lived about 588 B.C. His sons and grandsons, numbering 150, were famous as archers and "mighty men of valor" (1 Chron. 8:39-40).

UL'LA (ūl'a; 1 Chron. 7:39-40). A descendant of Asher, and father of three of the "choice and mighty men of valor" of the tribe.

UM'MAH (um'ma). One of the towns allotted to the tribe of Asher, probably near the Mediterranean coast (Josh. 19:30). E.H.M.

UNCIAL LETTERS. *See* Scripture Manuscripts: Old Testament; Scripture Manuscripts: New Testament.

UNCIRCUMCISED (Heb. *'ārēl,* "exposed"; Gk. *'akrobustia*). Used figuratively for a *pagan* (Gen. 34:14; Judg. 14:3; 15:18; 1 Sam. 14:6; Jer. 9:26; Rom. 4:9; 1 Cor. 7:18; etc.); "of uncircumcised lips" (Ex. 6:12, 30, *see* marg.) means one whose lips are, as it were, covered with a foreskin, so that he cannot easily bring out his words, "slow of tongue" (4:10); of "uncircumcised . . . ears" (Acts 7:51; cf. Jer. 6:10, marg.) are those whose ears are closed with a foreskin, i.e., closed to the prophet's testimony by their impure heart; "uncircumcised in heart" (Ezek. 44:9; Acts 7:51; cf. Lev. 26:41; James 1:21; Col. 2:13) are those who are in an impure, God-offending state of nature (Jer. 4:4, "remove the foreskins of your hearts"). The "uncircumcised" tree was the one under three years of age, whose fruit by the law was treated as unclean (Lev. 19:23, see marg.).

UNCLEAN, UNCLEANNESS. Although sin has its origin and its seat in the soul, it pervades the whole body as the soul's organ, bringing about the body's dissolution in death and decomposition. Its effects have spread from man to the whole of the earthly creation, because, having dominion over nature, he has brought nature with him into the service of sin. God has also made the irrational creature subject to "futility" and "corruption" on account of man's sin (Rom. 8:20-21). "It is in this penetration of sin into the material creation that we may find the explanation of the fact that from the very earliest times men have neither used every kind of herb nor every kind of animal as food; but that, while they have, as it were, instinctively avoided certain plants as injurious to health or destructive to life, they have also had a *horror naturalis* (i.e., an inexplicable disgust) at many of the animals, and have avoided their flesh as unclean. A similar horror must have been produced upon man from the very first, before his heart was altogether hardened by death as the wages of sin, or rather by the effects of death, viz., the decomposition of the body; and different diseases and states of the body, that were connected with symptoms of corruption and decomposition, may also have been regarded as rendering unclean. Hence, in all nations and all the religion of antiquity, we find that contrast between clean and unclean, which was developed in a dualistic form, it is true, in many of the religious systems, but had its primary root in the corruption that had entered the world through sin" (K. & D., *Com.*, on Lev. 11).

This contrast between *clean* and *unclean* was limited by Moses to three particulars: (1) food; (2) contact with dead bodies, human and animal; (3) bodily conditions and diseases. The law pointed out most minutely the unclean objects and various defilements within these spheres, and prescribed the means for avoiding or removing them. Here the subject will be treated as follows: (1) causes of uncleanness; (2) disabilities of uncleanness; (3) purification from uncleanness.

Causes of Uncleanness. Certain foods, contact with a dead body, and certain bodily conditions and diseases rendered a person ceremonially unclean.

Food. Certain articles of diet were prohibited as causing uncleanness. These were things strangled or dead of themselves or through beasts or birds of prey; whatever beast did not both divide the hoof and chew the cud; and certain other smaller animals rated as "swarming things"; certain classes of birds mentioned in Lev. 11, and

Deut. 14, twenty or twenty-one in all; whatever in the waters had not both fins and scales; whatever winged insect had not also four legs, the two hind legs for leaping; in addition to things offered in sacrifice to idols; and all blood, or whatever contained it (except, perhaps, the blood of fish, as would appear from that only of beast and bird being forbidden, Lev. 7:26) and, therefore, flesh cut from a live animal; as also all fat, at any rate that about the intestines, and probably wherever discernible and separable among the flesh (3:13-17; 7:23). The eating of blood was prohibited even to "the aliens" (17:10). Besides these, there was the prohibition against boiling a kid in its mother's milk (Ex. 23:19; 34:26; Deut. 14:21). Thus it will be seen that all animals are unclean that bear the image of sin, of death, and corruption, e.g., all larger land animals, all ravenous beasts that lie in wait for life or tear and devour the living; all winged creatures, not only birds of prey, but all marsh birds and others, which live on worms, carrion, and all sorts of impurities; all serpentlike fish and slimy shellfish, and small "swarming things," except some kinds of locusts, "because, partly, they recall the old serpent, partly they seek their food in all sorts of impurities, partly they crawl in the dust and represent corruption in the slimy character of their bodies" (Keil, *Bib. Arch.*, 2:117-18).

Defilement by Death. The dead body of a human being, no matter whether he had been killed (Num. 19:16, 18; 31:19) or had died a natural death, had the effect of rendering unclean for seven days the tent (or house) in which the man had died, and any open vessels that were in it, as well as the persons who lived in it or happened to enter it. It was equally defiling to touch the body of anyone who had died in the open air or even to touch a dead man's bones or a grave. When one was thus defiled the uncleanness was not confined to himself but extended to everything he touched and everyone who touched him, and all were unclean till evening (19:22).

The carcass of any animal, clean or unclean, defiled until the evening everyone who touched, carried, or ate it, so that he was required to bathe himself in water and wash his clothes before he became clean again (Lev. 11:24-28, 31, 36, 39-40; 17:15). But it was just as defiling to touch clean animals slaughtered by men, and unclean animals that had been killed by them, as it was to touch unclean animals while still alive. Eight kinds of the smaller animals (Heb. *sheres*, a "swarm") are mentioned that communicated their defiling influence to inanimate objects, such as earthen pots for cooking. Such defilement occurred if they or any part of their carcasses happened to fall on or in the pots. Also, food prepared with water that had been in the pots was contaminated. So was any seed that water was put on and then it was touched by a carcass (11:32-37).

Defilement by Bodily Conditions and Diseases.
(1) *Leprosy* (which see), either in connection with persons, dwellings, or fabrics (Lev. 13-14). (2) The discharge of seminal fluid, whether of an involuntary character (as during sleep) or such as occurred during sexual intercourse. Both alike made the man, and in the latter case the woman also, unclean till evening (15:16-18). (3) A discharge, whether the menstrual discharge of the woman, the morbid issue of blood in a woman, or a discharge in men, i.e., the discharge of mucus from the urethra (Num. 5:2). (4) Childbirth. Contact with persons in the above states or even with clothing or furniture that had been used by them while in those states involved uncleanness in a minor degree (Lev. 15:5-11, 21-24).

Disabilities of Uncleanness. Defilement by contact with a dead human body rendered the person or object unclean for seven days. Defilement from the carcass of an animal made the person or object unclean until evening. The leper was required to rend his clothes, to bare his head, to put a covering upon his upper lip, and then to cry to everyone he met, "Unclean; unclean"; besides this, he had to isolate himself by living outside the camp (or city) (Lev. 13:45-46; Num. 5:2-3; 12:10, 14-15). Houses affected with leprosy were examined by the priest, who, before entering, had all of the contents of the house removed in order to prevent everything within from becoming unclean. If symptoms of leprosy were discovered, the house was closed for seven days. After seven days the house was again examined, and if indications of leprosy were evident, the affected stones were removed, with the scrapings of the walls, and carefully replastered. If the evil broke out anew, the house was pronounced unclean, pulled down, and moved to an unclean place outside the city. Leprosy in clothes or fabrics made of linen, wool, or leather required that the article should be shut up for seven days, and if still affected it was burned (Lev. 13:47-59). Persons or objects defiled by the discharge of seminal fluid were unclean until evening; persons defiled by a discharge were removed from the camp (Num. 5:2); the menstruous woman was considered unclean for seven days, as well as the man who might have intercourse with her at this time; everything on which she lay or sat was unclean until evening (Lev. 15:19-24). A man or woman with an issue was unclean as long as the disorder lasted. They also rendered unclean anything upon which they sat or lay, or the person whom they might touch, and in the case of the man anyone upon whom his spittle might come (15:25-29). The woman at childbirth became unclean for seven days at the birth of a boy, and fourteen if it was a girl, besides being obliged to remain at home in the blood of her purifying for thirty-three days more in the former case and sixty-six in the latter. She was debarred from touching anything holy and from coming to the sanctuary (12:2-8).

Purification from Uncleanness. The regulations with respect to defilements and their corresponding purifications were not prescriptions framed with a view to the cultivation of cleanliness, tidiness, and decency—not merely sanitary regulations—but they were of a religious nature, having as their object the cultivation of holiness and spiritual life. It was owing to the well-understood connection between defilements on the one hand and sin and its consequence *death* on the other that the Levitical purification rites ranked side by side with the sacrifices and that they formed, quite as much as the latter, an integral part of the Mosaic ritual. The term "purification," in its legal and technical sense, is applied to the ritual observances whereby an Israelite was formally absolved from the taint of uncleanness, whether evidenced by any overt act or state or whether connected with man's natural depravity.

The following regulations respecting purification are given in the law:

Of Those Defiled by Contact with the Dead. The medium appointed in such cases was a kind of sprinkling water, composed of running water and the ashes of a sin offering specially suited to the occasion (Num. 19). A heifer, without blemish, and that had never been yoked, was slaughtered outside the camp. Eleazar was to dip his finger in the blood and sprinkle it seven times toward the sanctuary. The entire heifer was then burned in the presence of the priest, who cast cedar wood, hyssop, and scarlet wool into the flames. The ashes were then carried by a man free from defilement to a clean place outside the camp, where they were stored for use as occasion might require. A man free from defilement took some of these ashes, put them into a vessel, and then poured some fresh running water over them. Dipping a bunch of hyssop into the mixture, he sprinkled it upon the person to be purified, both on the third and the seventh day. On the latter day, after atonement had been made, the person being purified was required to wash his clothes and bathe himself in water, after which he became clean on the evening of that day. The tent in which the corpse had lain, as well as the furniture that it contained, were all sprinkled with this same water and were thus purified (vv. 12, 17-19).

Of Those Recovered from Leprosy. The ceremonial for the purifications is based upon the idea that his malady is the bodily symbol not so much of sin as of death. "As being a decomposing of the juices of the body, as a putrefying and dropping off of its members, as being the presence of corruption in the living body, leprosy forms the counterpart of death. . . . Consequently the person affected with this disease was required to display the tokens of his intimate association with death in the kind of dress he wore, in his shaved head, and in his rent garments; and hence it was, too, that he was excluded not merely from the pale of the sanctuary, but was even debarred from all intercourse whatever with the covenant people, called as it was to a holy nation" (Keil, *Bib. Arch.*, 1:393).

The rites are described in Lev. 14:4-32. The two stages of the proceedings indicated were these: the first, which took place outside the camp, the readmission of the leper to the community of men; the second, before the sanctuary, his readmission to communion with God. In the first stage the slaughter of the one bird and the dismissal of the other symbolized the punishment of death deserved and fully remitted. In the second, the use of oil and its application to the same parts of the body as in the consecration of priests (8:23-24) symbolized the rededication of the leper to the service of Jehovah. The ceremonies to be observed in the purification of a house or a garment infected with leprosy were identical with the first stage of the proceedings used for the leper (14:33-53).

Of Those Defiled by Sexual Discharges. Such purification was, in every instance, effected by bathing the body and washing the objects defiled in running water, the purifying medium of nature's own providing. If, however, the state of defilement lasted longer than seven days, as in the case of those suffering from an issue of blood, a discharge of mucus from the urethra, or childbirth, then a sin offering and a burnt offering were added to the washing with water. These were offered at a certain period after the healing and the washing—those suffering from an issue of blood or a mucus discharge, and the leper after his first cleansing, at seven days; in the case of childbirth it was thirty-three or sixty-six days. In those cases where the defilement lasted more than a week, communion with the Lord could only be secured by the offering of a sin offering (of a pigeon) and a burnt offering (a lamb).

The necessity of purification was extended in the post-Babylonian period to a variety of unauthorized cases. Cups and pots, bronze vessels, and couches were washed as a matter of ritual observance (Mark 7:4). The washing of the hands before meals was conducted in a formal manner (v. 3), and minute regulations were laid down on this subject in a treatise of the Mishna entitled *Yadaim.* What may have been the specific causes of uncleanness in those who came up to purify themselves before the Passover (John 11:55), or in those who had taken upon themselves the Nazirite's vow (Acts 21:24, 26), we are not informed; in either case it may have been contact with a corpse, though in the latter it would rather appear to have been a general purification preparatory to the accomplishment of the vow. In conclusion it may be observed that the distinctive feature in the Mosaic rites of purification is their expiatory character. The idea of uncleanness was not peculiar to the Jew. But with all other nations simple ablution sufficed—no sacrifices were demanded. The Jew alone was taught, by the use of expiatory offerings, to discern to its full extent the connection between the outward sign and the inward fount of impurity.

BIBLIOGRAPHY: R. de Vaux, *Ancient Israel: Its Life and Institutions* (1961), pp. 56, 60, 460; J. Neusner, *The Idea of Purity in Ancient Israel* (1973).

UNCTION. See Anointing.

UNDEFILED. In the NT "undefiled" is the rendering of the Gk. *amiantos*, "not defiled," i.e., free from that by which the nature of a thing is deformed or its force and vigor impaired. Thus Jesus was undefiled (Heb 7:26; "blameless," NIV), i.e., pure from sin. The undefiled bed (13:4; "pure," NIV) is one free from adultery. A religion that is sincere and undefiled (James 1:27) and the inheritance that is imperishable and undefiled (1 Pet. 1:4) are also mentioned. In the OT the KJV uses this term to speak of the morally sound man in Ps. 119:1 and of the pure bride in Song of Sol. 5:2 and 6:9 (NASB and NIV call the man "blameless," and the bride "perfect one" and "flawless one" and "perfect one" respectively).

UNDERGIRDING. See Ship.

UNDERSETTERS (Heb. *kātēp*, a "shoulder," usually so rendered). These were part of the laver in Solomon's Temple as described in 1 Kings 7:30, 34, KJV. The NIV renders "supports" and "handles."

UNEDUCATED (Gk. *agrammatos*, "unlettered"). Illiterate, without learning (Acts 4:13).

UNGIFTED (Gk. *idiōtēs*), a "private" person, i.e., an "unlearned, illiterate" man (1 Cor. 14:16, 23-24), as opposed to the educated.

UNICORN. See Animal Kingdom: Wild Ox.

UNITY (Heb. *yaḥad*, adverb "unitedly"). Used to signify a oneness of sentiment, affection, or behavior, such as should exist among the people of God (Ps. 133:1). The "unity of the faith" (Eph. 4:13; Gk. *henotēs*, "oneness") is the unanimity of belief in the same great truths of God, and the possession of the grace of faith in a similar form and degree.

UNKNOWN GOD (Gk. *agnōstos theos*, "unknown god"). The inscription observed by Paul upon an altar in Athens (Acts 17:23), which he ingeniously noted in his speech before the people as an instance of their religiousness. This was not addressed to the philosophers; they did not dedicate altars to unknown gods but regarded all such proceedings as the mere superstition of the vulgar. Pausanius (1.1.4) and Philostratus (*Vit. Appolon.* 6.2) both mention "unknown gods," and it is evident from both passages that at Athens there were *several* altars so inscribed. "It is related that Epimenides put an end to a plague in

Athens by causing black and white sheep, which he had let loose on the Areopagus, to be sacrificed on the spots where they lay down, *to the god concerned,* yet not known by name, viz., who was the author of the plague; and that therefore one may find in Athens *altars without the designation of a god by name.* From this particular instance the general view may be derived, *that on important occasions,* when the reference to a god known by name was wanting, as in public calamities of which no definite god could be assigned as the author, in order to honor or propitiate the god concerned by sacrifice, without lighting upon a wrong one, altars were erected which were destined and designated *'agnōsto theō* (unknown god)" (Meyer, *Com.*).

UNKNOWN TONGUE (1 Cor. 14:2, 4, 13, 14, 19, 27). This is a gloss by the KJV, because the Gk. has simply *glōssa* ("tongue"). It was obviously a different language from the speaker's native one (Mark 16:17; Acts 2:4). *See* Tongues, gift of.

UNLEARNED. *See* Uneducated.

UNLEAVENED BREAD (Heb. *maṣṣâ,* "sweet"; Gk. *'azumos*). Bread baked from unfermented dough, or (NIV) without yeast (Gen. 19:3; Judg. 6:19; 1 Sam. 28:24). This was formally presented for the Paschal (Passover) cakes (Ex. 12:8, 15, 20; 13:3, 6-7) and thus became a symbol of the festival popularly called "the feast of unleavened bread." *See* Leaven; Festivals; Sacrifices.

UN'NI (ū'ni; "afflicted" or perhaps "answered").

1. A relative of Heman the singer, who with other Levites was appointed, by order of King David, to perform in the Tabernacle service (1 Chron. 15:18, 20), about 986 B.C.

2. A Levite employed in the musical service of the Temple after the return from captivity (Neh. 12:9), 535 B.C. This name should be written Unno.

UNTEMPERED MORTAR. *See* Mineral Kingdom: Mortar.

UPHAR'SIN (ū-far'sin). *See* Mene.

U'PHAZ (ū'făz). The name of a famous gold region (Jer. 10:9; Dan. 10:5), it is thought by many to be a corruption of *Ophir* (which see); but Orelli (*Com.,* on Jer. 10:9) says: "It is inconceivable that the word arose by error from this well-known name. Assyria and Babylon might have other gold mines. Still the views respecting the site of this Uphaz remain mere conjectures."

UPPER CHAMBER or **ROOM** (Heb. *'ăliyâ,* "lofty"; 1 Kings 17:19, 23; 2 Kings 1:2; 23:12; 1 Chron. 28:11; 2 Chron. 3:9; Judg. 3:23, "roof chamber"; 2 Sam. 18:33, "chamber over the gate"; Gk. *anōgeon;* Mark 14:15; Luke 22:12; *huperoon,* "upper," Acts 1:13; 9:37, 39; 20:8). A room in the upper part of the house, used to receive company, hold feasts, and retire for medi-

tation and prayer (Mark 14:15; Luke 22:12). Among the Hebrews it seems to have been on or connected with the flat roofs of their dwellings; in Greek houses it occupied the upper story (1 Kings 17:19, 23; 2 Kings 4:10; Acts 1:13; 9:37, 39; 10:9; 20:8). Rich, luxury-loving men were charged with sinfully multiplying chambers of this sort (Jer. 22:13-14). They were used as a "cool roof chamber" (Judg. 3:20; cf. 2 Kings 1:2; 23:12). In Scripture the lower portion was the winter house, the upper room was the summer house; or, if on the same story, the outer apartment is the summer house, the inner is the winter house.

The Chapel of the Last Supper, Mt. Zion

UR (*ūr;* "light"). Mentioned in 1 Chron. 11:35 as the father of Eliphal, one of David's "mighty men," before 1000 B.C. There is evident confusion at this point in the genealogical list, both here and in the parallel passage (2 Sam. 23:34). Hepher must either be regarded as another name for Ur or else omitted as an error in copying. The phrase "the son of" should be erased from 2 Sam. 23:34, and Ahasbai and Ur might then be identified.

For the city, *see* Ur of the Chaldees.

UR'BANUS (ūr-ba'nus; Gk. *Urbanon* from Lat. *Urbanus;* "urbane, polite, of the city"; KJV, "Urbane"). A Christian at Rome to whom Paul sent salutations, as having been his associate in labor, "our fellow worker in Christ" (Rom. 16:9).

U'RI (ū'ri; an abbreviation of Urijah).

1. The father of Bezalel, one of the architects of the Tabernacle. He was of the tribe of Judah, and son of Hur (Ex. 31:2; 35:30; 38:22; 1 Chron. 2:20; 2 Chron. 1:5), before 1440 b.c.

2. The father of Geber, Solomon's deputy in Gilead (1 Kings 4:19), before 960 b.c.

3. One of the Temple gatekeepers who put away his Gentile wife after the Exile (Ezra 10:24), 456 b.c.

URI'AH (ū-rī'a; "Jehovah is light").

1. One of David's heroes (1 Chron. 11:41; 2 Sam. 23:39, and husband of Bathsheba. He was a Hittite. His name, however, and his manner of speech (2 Sam. 11:11) indicate that he had adopted the Jewish religion. He married Bathsheba, a woman of extraordinary beauty, the daughter of Eliam. During the time of the illicit relationship between David and his wife, Uriah was in camp with Joab. But when the king was informed by Bathsheba that she was with child by him, he ordered Uriah to come to Jerusalem on the pretext of asking news of the war—really in the hope that Uriah's return to his wife might cover his own crime. The king met with an unexpected obstacle in the austere, loyal spirit that guided Uriah's conduct and that gives a good picture of the high character and discipline of David's officers. On the morning of the third day David sent him back to the camp with a letter containing the command to Joab to cause his death in the battle. Joab was to observe the part of the wall of Rabbah-Ammon where the greatest force of the besieged was congregated and there to send Uriah. A sally took place. Uriah and the officers with him advanced as far as the gate of the city and were there shot down by the archers on the wall. Joab forewarned the messenger that if the king broke into a furious passion on hearing of the loss, the messenger should end the story with the words "Your servant Uriah the Hittite is also dead" (2 Sam. 11:24), about 980 b.c.

2. A priest in the reign of Ahaz, who is introduced in Scripture history as a witness to Isaiah's prophecy concerning Maher-shalal-hash-baz (Isa. 8:2), about 735 b.c. He is perhaps the same as Urijah, the priest who built the idolatrous altar for King Ahaz (2 Kings 16:10-16). He was probably high priest at the time, succeeding Azariah, who was high priest in the reign of Uzziah and was succeeded by that Azariah who was high priest in the reign of Hezekiah. Hence it is likely that he was a son of the former and the father of the latter.

3. A priest of the family of Hakkoz (KJV, "Koz") who supported Ezra while reading the law to the people (Neh. 8:4; KJV, "Urijah"), 457 b.c. He is

probably the same as the father of Meremoth (Ezra 8:33; Neh. 3:4, 21).

4. The son of Shemaiah of Kiriath-jearim, who prophesied in the days of Jehoiakim. When the king sought his death he fled to Egypt, but his retreat was soon discovered. Elnathan brought him to Jehoiakim, who put him to death and cast his body among the graves of the common people (Jer. 26:20-23), about 609 b.c.

URIAS (ū-rī-as). The Gk. form of *Uriah*, used in Matt. 1:6, KJV. *See* Uriah, no. 1.

U'RIEL (ū'ri-el; "God is light").

1. A Levite of the family of Kohath. His father's name was Uzziah (1 Chron. 6:24).

2. Chief of the Kohathites, who assisted, with 120 of his brethren, in bringing the Ark from the house of Obed-edom (1 Chron. 15:5, 11), about 992 b.c.

3. Uriel of Gibeah was the father of Maacah, or Micaiah, wife of Rehoboam, and mother of Abijah (2 Chron. 13:2), before 930 b.c. In 11:20 she is called the daughter (granddaughter) of Absalom.

URI'JAH (ū-rī'ja; 2 Kings 16:10; etc.). *See* Uriah, no. 2.

U'RIM AND THUM'MIM (ū'rim, thum'im; "lights and perfections"). Into the breastplate of the *high priest* (which see) were placed "the Urim and the Thummim, and they shall be over Aaron's heart when he goes in before the Lord" (Ex. 28:30). These formed the medium through which the high priest ascertained the will of Jehovah in regard to any important matter affecting the theocracy (Num. 27:21). Even such early writers as Josephus, Philo, and the rabbis do not furnish any precise information as to what the Urim and Thummim really were. On every side we meet confessions of ignorance.

Meaning of the Words. In *Urim*, Hebrew scholars, with hardly an exception, have seen the plural of *ur* (light or fire). The LXX translators, however, appear to have had reasons that led them to another rendering. The literal English equivalent would of course be "lights"; but the renderings in the LXX and Vulg. indicate, at least, a traditional belief among the Jews that the plural form did not involve numerical plurality.

In *Thummim* there also is almost a consensus as to the derivation from *tōm* (perfection, completeness). What has been said as to the plural of Urim applies here also. "Light and Perfection" would probably be the best English equivalent. The mere phrase, as such, leaves it therefore uncertain whether each word by itself denoted many things of a given kind, or whether the two taken together might have referred to two distinct objects or to one and the same object. In Deut. 33:8 they are named separately, "Thy Thummim and Thy Urim," the first order being inverted. Urim is found alone in Num. 27:21;

1 Sam. 28:6; Thummim is never used by itself, unless it is in Ps. 16:5.

Scripture References. The first reference (Ex. 28:30) to these objects would seem to indicate that they needed no explanation. Inside the breastplate, as the tablets of the covenant were placed inside the Ark (25:16; 28:30), were to be placed "the Urim and the Thummim," the Light and the Perfection; and they, too, were to be on Aaron's heart when he went in before the Lord (28:15-30). Not a word describes them. They are mentioned as things already familiar both to Moses and the people, connected naturally with the functions of the high priest, as mediating between Jehovah and His people. The command was fulfilled (Lev. 8:8). They passed from Aaron to Eleazar with the sacred ephod and other *pontificalia* (Num. 20:28). They were mentioned again (27:21; Deut. 33:8-9). Once, and once only, were they mentioned by name in the history of the Judges and the monarchy (1 Sam. 28:6). There was no longer a priest with Urim and Thummim (Ezra 2:63; Neh. 7:65) to answer hard questions.

Theories. Some think the Urim and Thummim to have been identical with the twelve stones on the breastplate. Josephus (*Ant.* 3.8.9) identifies them with the sardonyxes on the shoulders of the ephod and says that they were bright before a victory or when the sacrifice was acceptable, dark when any disaster was impending. "Another theory is that in the middle of the ephod, or within its folds, there was a stone or plate of gold, on which was engraved the sacred name of Jehovah; and that by virtue of this, fixing his gaze on it, or reading an invocation which was also engraved with the name, or standing in his ephod before the mercy seat, or at least before the veil of the sanctuary, he became capable of prophesying, hearing the divine voice within, or listening to it as it proceeded in articulate sounds from the glory of the Shekinah."

Michaelis (*Laws of Moses,* 5:52) gives his opinion that the Urim and Thummim were three stones, on one of which was written Yes, on another No, whereas the third was left neutral or blank. These were used as lots, and the high priest decided according as the one or the other was drawn out. Kalisch (on Ex. 28:31) identifies the Urim and the Thummim with the twelve tribal gems. He looks on the name as one to be explained by an hendiadys (light and perfection —perfect illumination) and believes the high priest, by concentrating his thoughts on the attributes they represented, to have divested himself of all selfishness and prejudice and so to have passed into a true prophetic state. The process of consulting Jehovah by Urim and Thummim is not given in Scripture.

BIBLIOGRAPHY: E. Robertson, *Vetus Testamentum* 14 (1964): 67ff.

UR OF THE CHALDEES. Abraham's native city customarily is located in southern Babylonia, not very far from the ancient city of Uruk to the NE and about 150 miles from the head of the Persian Gulf. Eridu is to the SW. Modern excavation of the site of Ur began in 1854 with J. E. Taylor. The city was then only a ruined site named the Mound of Bitumen (Arab. al muqayyar). In 1918 H. R. Hall resumed excavations. Sir Leonard Woolley conducted excavations from 1922 to 1934. The famous royal cemeteries, dating c. 2500 B.C., yielded jewelry and art treasures of unbelievable beauty, particularly gorgeous head attire, personal jewels, and a golden tumbler and cup of Queen Puabi (formerly rendered Shubad). Several musical instruments and other beautifully crafted objects demonstrate that this city had achieved a high level of civilization 500 years before Abraham. The Heb. Bible is quite clear in its statements that Abraham's home was originally in Lower Mesopotamia in the city of Ur and that he emigrated to Haran and Upper Mesopotamia on his way to Canaan (Gen. 11:28-31; 12:1-4; 15:7; Neh. 9:7). Interestingly enough, Ur in connection with Abraham is referred to as "Ur of the Chaldeans." The qualifying phrase "of the Chaldeans" is not an anachronism, as many critics contend (cf. Jack Finegan, *Light from the Ancient East,* p. 57, n. 28). It is rather an instance of numerous archaic place names being defined by a later scribal gloss to make clear to a subsequent age where and what these places were when their history and locality had been forgotten. The Chaldeans came into southern Babylonia after 1000 B.C. It was, of course, quite natural for the Hebrew scribe to define the then incomprehensible foreign name by a term intelligible to his own day. As a result of archaeological excavation, the city of Ur is now one of the best-known sites of southern Babylonia. Woolley in his *Abra-*

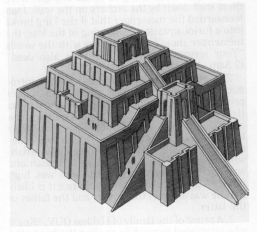

Artist's impression of the Ziggurat at Ur

ham: Recent Discoveries and Hebrew Origins (1936), pp. 72-117, gives a description of the worship of the city god of Ur, the moon god Nannar and his consort Ningal. Woolley describes in minute detail the sacred *temenos* of the city in which were the famous ziggurat and the various buildings erected to the moon god and his consort, with a description of the moon god ritual. It is now possible to have a far clearer idea of Abraham's surroundings when "the God of glory appeared to our father Abraham when he was in Mesopotamia, before he lived in Haran" (Acts 7:2). Archaeology has revealed that in Abraham's day Ur was a great and prosperous city, with perhaps 360,000 people living in the city and its suburbs. The biblical chronology as preserved in the MT would place the life of Abraham, at least in part, under the new Sumero-Akkadian Empire of Ur-Nammu, the founder of the strong Third Dynasty of Ur (c. 2070-1960 B.C.).

It should be noted, however, that other scholarship points to a *northern* location for the Ur from which Abraham came. Mesopotamian literature mentions this "northern Ur," as attested in the archival materials at Alalakh, Ugarit, Hattusha, and Ebla, although its precise location is unknown. (*See* Abraham.) Third Dynasty kings took the new title "king of Sumer and Akkad." The greatest work of Ur-Nammu was the erection of the great ziggurat at Ur, upon which Abraham gazed, as did Joseph upon the pyramids in Egypt. Happily, the ziggurat at Ur is the best-preserved type of this characteristic architectural feature of early Babylonia. The resurrection of Ur offers a

Near biblical Ur

fine example of archaeology's increasing ability to illustrate ancient biblical history.

BIBLIOGRAPHY: C. L. Woolley, *Excavations at Ur* (1954); M. E. L. Mallowan and D. J. Wiseman, *Ur in Retrospect* (1960); C. J. Gadd, *Archaeology and Old Testament Study* (1967), pp. 87-101; C. L. Woolley, *Ur 'of the Chaldees,'* rev. P. R. S. Moorey (1982).

USURY (Heb. *neshek*, a "biting," i.e., "extortion"; Gk. *tokos*, a "yield"). Used in the sense of *interest* for money and does not necessarily imply the demand for exorbitant increase. According to the Mosaic law, the Israelites were forbidden to take usury from their brethren upon the loan of money, food, or anything else, i.e., they were not upon the return of the loan to demand anything more (Lev. 25:36-37; Deut. 23:19-20; etc.), although interest might be taken from foreigners (v. 20). Because the Israelites were not a commercial people, money was not often loaned for the purpose of business, but rather to aid the struggling poor. This last is the only kind of usury forbidden in the law, and the avoiding of this is sometimes given among the characteristics of the godly man (Ps. 15:5; Jer. 15:10; cf. Prov. 28:8).

The practice of mortgaging lands, sometimes at exorbitant interest, grew up among the Jews during the captivity, in direct violation of the law (Lev. 25:36; Ezek. 18:8, 13, 17); and Nehemiah exacted an oath to insure its discontinuance (Neh. 5:3-13). Jesus denounced all extortion, and proclaimed a new law of love and forbearance (Luke 6:30, 35). The taking of usury in the sense of a reasonable rate of interest for the use of money employed in trade is different and is nowhere forbidden; it is referred to in the NT as a perfectly understood and allowable practice (Matt. 25:27; Luke 19:23).

U'THAI (ū'thī).

1. The son of Ammihud, of the sons of Perez, the son of Judah. He resided at Jerusalem after the return from Babylon (1 Chron. 9:4).

2. One of the sons of Bigvai, who returned with seventy males in the second caravan with Ezra (Ezra 8:14), about 457 B.C.

UZ (ūz).

1. A son of Aram (Gen. 10:23; 1 Chron. 1:17), and a grandson of Shem.

2. A son of Nahor, by Milcah (Gen. 22:21; KJV, "Huz").

3. A son of Dishan, and grandson of Seir (Gen. 36:28).

4. The land of Uz was the country in which Job lived (Job 1:1). The LXX renders it *en chōra tē 'Ausitidi,* and Ptolemy (5.19.2) says that the Aisitai, i.e., the Uzzites, dwelt in the Arabian Desert, W from Babylon, under the Caucabenes and adjacent to the Edomites of Mt. Seir, who at one period occupied Uz, probably as conquerors

(Lam. 4:21). The position of the country may further be deduced from the native lands of Job's friends—Eliphaz, the Temanite, being an Edomite; Elihu, the Buzite, probably a neighbor of the Chaldeans; and Bildad, the Shuhite, being one of the Bene-Kedem. "The land of Uz" is mentioned in only two other passages of Scripture; it is grouped by Jeremiah (Jer. 25:20) with Egypt, Philistia, Edom, and Moab, but in Lam. 4:21 he identifies it with a portion of Edom or affirms that some of the Edomites in his day inhabited Uz.

U'ZAI (ū′zī). The father of Palal, one of those who assisted in rebuilding the walls of Jerusalem (Neh. 3:25), before 447 B.C.

U'ZAL (ū′zal; derivation uncertain). The sixth of the thirteen sons of Joktan, a descendant of Shem (Gen. 10:27; 1 Chron. 1:21). Authorities quite generally agree that Sanaa, the metropolis of Yemen, is the modern name of Uzal founded by this person.

UZ'ZA (ūz′a; "strength").
1. Apparently the proprietor of (or the person after whom was named) the garden in which Manasseh and Amon were buried (2 Kings 21:18, 26), before 643 B.C.
2. The son of Shimei (1 Chron. 6:29, KJV; Uzzah, NASB, NIV). See Uzzah, no. 2.
3. The older of the two sons of Ehud the Benjamite, born to him after the removal of his former children (1 Chron. 8:7).
4. The "sons of Uzza" were a family of Temple servants who returned with Zerubbabel (Ezra 2:49; Neh. 7:51), before 536 B.C.

UZ'ZAH (ūz′a; "strength").
1. One of the sons of Abinadab of Kiriath-jearim. He, with his brother Ahio, accompanied the Ark when David sought to move it to Jerusalem. When the procession had reached the threshing floor of Nacon, the oxen drawing the cart upon which the Ark was placed stumbled. Uzzah, who was walking beside it, put out his hand to prevent its falling. He died immediately, being struck by God on account of his offense. The event caused a profound reaction, and David, fearing to carry the Ark any farther, had it placed in the house of Obed-edom (2 Sam. 6:3-10; 1 Chron. 13:7, 9-11), about 988 B.C.
Why was Uzzah so severely punished? This is a question variously answered. We think the following answer correct: "According to Num., ch. 4, the ark was not only to be moved by none but Levites, but it was to be carried on the shoulders; and in v. 15 even the Levites were expressly forbidden to touch it on pain of death. But instead of taking these instructions as their rule, they had followed the example of the Philistines when they sent back the ark (1 Sam. 6:7, sq.), and had placed it upon a new cart and directed Uzzah to drive it, while, as his conduct on the occasion

clearly shows, he had no idea of the unapproachable holiness of the ark of God, and had to expiate his offense with his life, as a warning to all the Israelites" (K. & D., *Com.*, ad loc.).
2. A Levite of the sons of Merari, the son of Shimei, and father of Shimea (1 Chron. 6:29).

UZ'ZEN-SHEE'RAH (ūz′en-shē′ra; Uzzensherah, KJV). A place near Beth-horon, founded or rebuilt by Sheerah, an Ephraimitess (1 Chron. 7:24) and probably an heiress who had received these places as her inheritance. The place Uzzensheerah is not elsewhere referred to.

UZ'ZI (ūz′i; "strong").
1. Son of Bukki, and father of Zerahiah, in the line of the high priests (1 Chron. 6:5, 51; Ezra 7:4). Josephus relates that after high priesthood was removed from the family of Eleazar and given to Eli, of the family of Ithamar, either after the service of Bukki's father, Abishua (*Ant.* 8.1.3), or after the service of Bukki's son, Ozi (5.11.5; "Uzzi," KJV, NASB, NIV; in this passage Josephus gives the name of Bukki's father as Abiezar).
2. Son of Tola, the son of Issachar (1 Chron. 7:2-3).
3. Son of Bela, of the tribe of Benjamin (1 Chron. 7:7).
4. The son of Michri and father of Elah, among the ancestors of a Benjamite house that settled at Jerusalem after the return from captivity (1 Chron. 9:8), before 536 B.C.
5. A Levite, son of Bani, and overseer of the Levites dwelling at Jerusalem in the time of Nehemiah (Neh. 11:22), 536 B.C.
6. A priest, chief of the division of Jedaiah, in the time of Joiakim the high priest (Neh. 12:19). He is probably the same as one of the priests who assisted Ezra in the dedication of the wall of Jerusalem (12:42), about 500 B.C.

UZZI'A (ū-zī′a; probably for "Uzziah"), the "Ashterathite" (i.e., from Ashtaroth, beyond Jordan), who was one of David's warriors (1 Chron. 11:44), after 1000 B.C.

UZZI'AH (ū-zī′a; "Jehovah is strength").
1. The tenth king of Judah. In some passages his name appears in the lengthened form Azariah, which Gesenius attributes to an error of the copyists. This is possible, but there are other instances of the princes of Judah changing their names on succeeding to the throne. His father was Amaziah, who was slain by conspirators.
After the murder of Amaziah, his son Uzziah, who had been coregent since the age of sixteen, occupied the throne alone (2 Kings 14:21; 2 Chron. 26:1), 767 B.C. He began his reign by a successful expedition against his father's enemies the Edomites who had revolted from Judah in Jehoram's time, eighty years before, and penetrated as far as the head of the Gulf of Aqaba, where he took the important place of Elath (2 Kings 14:22). Uzziah waged other victorious

wars in the S, especially against the Mehunim, or people of Maân, and the Arabs of Gurbaal. Toward the W Uzziah fought with equal success against the Philistines, leveled to the ground the walls of Gath, Jabneh, and Ashdod, and founded new fortified cities in the Philistine territory.

Uzziah strengthened the walls of Jerusalem and was a great patron of agriculture. He never deserted the worship of the true God and was much influenced by Zechariah, a prophet who is only mentioned in connection with him (2 Chron. 26:5). So the Southern Kingdom was raised to a condition of prosperity that it had not known since the death of Solomon. During his reign an earthquake occurred that was apparently very serious in its consequences, for it is alluded to as a chronological epoch by Amos (Amos 1:1) and by Zechariah (Zech. 14:5) as a natural disaster from which the people "fled."

The end of Uzziah was less prosperous than his beginning. Elated with his splendid career, he determined to burn incense on the altar of God but was opposed by the high priest Azariah and eighty others (*see* Ex. 30:7-8; Num. 16:40; 18:7). The king was enraged at their resistance. As he pressed forward with his censer, he was suddenly struck with leprosy; "and king Uzziah was a leper to the day of his death." Uzziah was buried "with his fathers," but apparently not actually in the royal sepulchers (2 Chron. 26:21, 23), about 740 B.C.

The great Assyrian conqueror Tiglath-pileser's westward advance in 743 B.C. called for a new Syrian-Palestinian coalition to resist the Assyrian danger. The natural leader of such an alliance was Judah under Uzziah (Azariah). This king headed by far the strongest and most influential state in Syria-Palestine at the time (2 Kings 14:21-22; 2 Chron. 26; Stanley Cook, *The Cambridge Ancient History,* 3:378). He was far more powerful than Menahem of Israel and Rezin of Damascus, both of whom evidently had to pay tribute to the Assyrians. It is not surprising, therefore, that Tiglath-pileser should make clear reference in his annals to *Azriyau* of *Yaudu* in connection with what is obviously a reference to an anti-Syrian coalition (D. D. Luckenbill, *Ancient Records of Assyria and Babylonia,* 1, sect. 7: 70; Edwin R. Thiele, *The Mysterious Numbers*

of the Hebrew Kings [1951], p. 78). Azariah's disappearance from the Assyrian records with no hint of his fate except that the far-reaching coalition he headed was broken up by the military power of Tiglath-pileser III would point to the conclusion that shortly thereafter he died, probably not later than 742 B.C., in any case before the Assyrians could take punitive action against him.

M.F.U.

2. A Kohathite Levite, and ancestor of Samuel (1 Chron. 6:24), perhaps 1300 B.C.

3. Father of Jonathan, one of David's overseers (1 Chron. 27:25), before 1000 B.C.

4. Father of Athaiah, or Uthai, a resident in Jerusalem after the Exile (Neh. 11:4), before 536 B.C.

5. A priest of the sons of Harim, who had taken a foreign wife in the days of Ezra (Ezra 10:21), 456 B.C.

M.F.U.

BIBLIOGRAPHY: C. E. Macartney, *The Man Who Forgot* (1956), pp. 64-71; T. Kirk and G. Rawlinson, *Studies in the Books of Kings* (1983), 2:149-55; E. R. Thiele, *Mysterious Numbers of the Hebrew Kings* (1983), pp. 63, 108-9, 119-20, 139-62.

UZZI'EL (ū-zi'el; "God is strength").

1. Fourth son of Kohath, father of Mishael, Elzaphan, or Elizaphan, and Zithri, and uncle to Aaron (Ex. 6:18, 22; Lev. 10:4), before 1440 B.C.

2. A Simeonite leader, son of Ishi, in the days of Hezekiah (1 Chron. 4:42), about 712 B.C.

3. Head of a Benjamite house, of the sons of Bela (1 Chron. 7:7).

4. A musician of the sons of Heman, in David's reign (1 Chron. 25:4).

5. A Levite of the sons of Jeduthun, who took an active part in purifying the Temple in the days of Hezekiah (2 Chron. 29:14-19), 719 B.C.

6. Son of Harhaiah, probably a priest in the days of Nehemiah, who took part in repairing the wall (Neh. 3:8). He is described as being "of the goldsmiths," i.e., of those priests whose hereditary office was to repair or make the sacred vessels, about 445 B.C.

UZZI'ELITE (ū-zi'e-līt). A descendant of Uzziel the Levite. In David's time the Uzzielites numbered 112 adult males (Num. 3:27; 1 Chron. 15:10; 26:23).

V

VAIN, VANITY.

1. Something vain, empty, fruitless, worthless (Job 9:29; 21:34; Jer. 10:3, 8, *see* marg.; Zech. 10:2), Heb. *hebel*, "a breath"; specifically of idols (2 Kings 17:15; Ps. 31:6; Jonah 2:8). The NIV usually translates this Heb. word as "worthless." A nothingness, an empty thing (Prov. 22:8; Heb. *'awen*, "a panting"; "trouble," NIV).

2. Heb. *shāw'* has the meaning of "desolation"; so "months of vanity" (Job 7:3; "futility," NIV) are those of calamity.

3. Gk. *mataiotēs* corresponds to *shāw'* and means that which is devoid of truth and appropriateness (2 Pet. 2:18; "empty," NIV); elsewhere "futility," or "frustration" (Rom. 8:20; Eph. 4:17).

VAIZA'THA (vī-za'tha; from Old Pers., "son of the atmosphere"). One of the ten sons of Haman, whom the Jews slew in Susa (Esther 9:9), after 480 B.C.

VALLEY. The rendering of the following Heb. and Gk. words:

1. Rather a plain than a valley, wider than the latter, but, like it, surrounded by mountains (Heb. *biq'â*, "a split"). It denotes a wide alluvial bottom, and its levelness is referred to in Isa. 40:4; usually rendered "valley" (Deut. 8:7; 11:11; 34:3; Josh. 11:8, 17; 12:7; Ps. 104:8; Amos 1:5; etc.), but also "plain" (Gen. 11:2; 2 Chron. 35:22; Neh. 6:2; Ezek. 3:22-23; 8:4). This Heb. term is applied to the following places: The *plain of Shinar* (Gen. 11:2); *valley of Jericho* (Deut. 34:3); *valley of Lebanon* (Josh. 11:17); *plain of Megiddo* (2 Chron. 35:22; Zech. 12:11); *valley of Mizpeh* (Josh. 11:8); *plain of Ono* (Neh. 6:2); *valley of Aven* (Amos 1:5).

2. A long, broad sweep between parallel ranges of hills of less extent than no. 1, corresponding quite closely to our idea in general of a *valley* in its usual sense (Heb. *'ēmeq*, "a deep place"). It is applied to the following localities: *valley of Achor* (Josh. 7:24, 26; 15:7; Isa. 65:10; Hos. 2:15); *valley of Aijalon* (Josh. 10:12); *valley of Hebron* (Gen. 37:14); *valley of Jehoshaphat* (Joel 3:2, 12), called (v. 14) figuratively *the valley of decision; valley of Jezreel* (Josh. 17:16; Judg. 6:33; Hos. 1:5). This term is sometimes used as an appellative for certain well-known localities, e.g., *the valley of weeping* (Ps. 84:6, "valley of Baca," see marg.); *the valley of blessing* (2 Chron. 20:26, "valley of Beracah," see marg.); *valley of the oak* (1 Sam. 17:2, 19; 21:9, "valley of Elah"); *valley of giants* (Josh. 15:8; 18:16; 2 Sam. 5:18, 22; etc., "valley of Rephaim"); *valley of Shaveh* (Gen. 14:17), or *the King's Valley* (14:17; 2 Sam. 18:18); *valley of the slime pits* (Gen. 14:3, 8, 10, "valley of Siddim"); *the valley of booths* (Pss. 60:6; 108:7, "valley of Succoth"); etc.

3. A deep, narrow *ravine* with a stream in the bottom, either between hills or through an open plain (Heb. *gê*, or *gê'*, "a gorge"): *the valley of Hinnom* (Josh. 15:8; 18:16; Neh. 11:30), or *of the son of Hinnom* (Josh. 15:8; 18:16; 2 Kings 23:10; etc., KJV; Ben-hinnom, NASB; Ben Hinnom, NIV), the ravine on the southwestern side of Jerusalem, whence the term *Gehenna; the valley of Iphtahel*, a ravine between Zebulun and Asher (Josh. 19:14, 27); *the valley of Zephathah*, a ravine in the tribe of Simeon (2 Chron. 14:10); *the valley of Gedor*, another ravine in Simeon (1 Chron. 4:39); *the valley of Hamon-gog* (Ezek. 39:11, 15), or *of the passers-by* (v. 11), a ravine on the E of the Sea of Galilee; *the valley of the craftsmen* (1 Chron. 4:14, marg.), a ravine in a ravine near Jerusalem; *the valley of salt* (2 Sam. 8:13; 2 Kings 14:7; 1 Chron. 18:12; 2 Chron. 25:11; Ps. 60, title), a ravine on the southwestern shore of the Dead Sea; *the valley of Zeboim* (1 Sam. 13:18), in the tribe of Benjamin. Others, such as *the valley of vision* (Isa. 22:1, 5), *of the Slaughter* (Jer. 7:32; 19:6), are fanciful names;

and still more poetical is *the valley of the shadow of death* (Ps. 23:4).

4. *Wadi* (Heb. *naḥal*, "receiving"; sometimes "brook," "river," "stream"). Wadi expresses as no English word can the bed of a stream (often wide and shelving, and like a "valley" in character, which in the rainy season may be nearly filled by a foaming torrent, though for the greater part of the year dry) and the stream itself that after the subsidence of the rains has shrunk to insignificant dimensions. Many of the wadis of Syria, owing to the demolition of the trees that formerly shaded the country and prevented too rapid evaporation after rain, are now entirely and constantly dry. As Palestine is emphatically a land of wadis, so this Heb. term frequently occurs in the Bible. Stanley enumerated these water courses or torrent beds—those of Gerar, of Eshcol, of Zered, of Arnon, of Jabbok, of Kanah, of Kishon, of Besor, of Sorek, of Kidron, of Gaash, of Cherith, of Gad. This last could not be distinguished by a mere English reader from the "river of Egypt," the Nile, although in the original an entirely different word is used.

VALLEY, THE KING'S. *See* Shaveh, Valley of.

VALLEY GATE (Heb. *sha'ar haggay'*). An entrance at the northwestern end of Jerusalem (Neh. 2:13; 3:13; cf. 2 Chron. 26:9; 33:14), probably corresponding to the present Jaffa gate.

VANIAH (va-nī'a). One of the sons of Bani, and an Israelite who divorced his Gentile wife after the captivity (Ezra 10:36), 456 B.C.

VASH'TI (vash'tē). The wife of Xerxes (or, KJV, *Ahasuerus* [which see]), king of Persia. She refused to humiliate herself before the king's courtiers and was therefore deposed in favor of Esther (Esther 1:3-22).   E.H.M.

VAULT (Heb. *ḥûg*). "It is He who sits above the vault of the earth" (Isa. 40:22; NIV, "circle"). The same word is applied in Job 22:14 to the heavens, which the ancients supposed to be a hollow sphere. The figure then is of Jehovah sitting or walking above the heavens, which were thought to arch over the earth. The KJV renders the Heb. word "circle" and "circuit."

VAV (ו) (vav). The Heb. letter *waw*, sixth in the alphabet. It stands at the beginning of each verse in the original of Ps. 119:41-48.

VEGETABLE KINGDOM. The flora of Syria and Palestine is very rich. The phaenogamous plants and higher cryptogams are distributed through 124 orders, 850 genera, and about 3,500 species, with many well-characterized varieties. Only one hundred names of plants are given in the Bible. Of these thirty-six cannot be determined with certainty. Of the sixty-four that are determinable, thirty-five are cultivated. Of the identity of most of these, as *wheat, barley, flax, olives, vines, figs,* etc., there can be no doubt. Of the wild plants mentioned, some, as *algum, lign aloes,* etc., are exotics, of which it is impossible to determine with certainty the species. Others, as *chestnut, juniper, hemlock, mulberry, poplar, rose of Sharon,* are mistranslations. Others, as *reed,*

The Jezreel Valley

thistle, thorn, refer to plants agreeing in mode of growth rather than ordinal or generic relationships, and are the equivalent of a number of Heb. words, the generic or specific signification of which has been lost. Others still, as the *lily,* are ordinal for all plants of a given type. The effort, therefore, to construct a scriptural flora, accurate and precise in its details, must be abandoned, and each name of a plant treated on its own merits.

Acacia (Heb. *shiṭṭâ; shiṭṭîm*). A tree, of which two species, *Acacia seyal,* Del., and *A. tortilis,* Hayne, grow in the deserts of Sinai and et-Tih, and around the Dead Sea. The wood is hard, very heavy, indestructible by insects, of a fine and beautiful grain, and thus suitable in every way for the construction of the framework and furniture of the Tabernacle. It also yields the officinal gum arabic. Shittim, Abel-shittim, and the valley of Shittim were named from this tree. Acacia (*seyal*) is remarkably luxuriant in dry places, sometimes attaining a height of twenty feet. It is adorned with lovely yellow flowers. Its insect-resisting wood was used also for tanning leather, for fuel, and for parts of mummy cases.   M.F.U.

Acacia Tree

Al'gum (al'gum), or **Almug Trees.** There is no reason to doubt the identity of the *algum* and the *almug,* as is proved by a comparison of 1 Kings 10:11 and 2 Chron. 9:10. As to the algum trees "from Lebanon" (2:8), they may have been the same as those that were imported from Ophir. In this case they may have then been indigenous, or cultivated, and have since become extinct; or they may have been another sort of tree called by the same name, as in the case with many other trees. There is no necessity for supposing an interpolation, nor even for inferring, as some have

done, that "from Lebanon" refers to *cedar trees* and *cypress trees* only, and not to *algums.* We have no means of determining with certainty what tree was intended. The weight of authority is in favor of the *red sandalwood,* but not a particle of evidence exists. As now seen in commerce, it is not suitable either for steps (9:11) or for "supports" (1 Kings 10:12), more properly *balustrades,* or for *lyres and harps.* Since Josephus says algum wood resembles the wood of the fig tree, but is whiter and has a brighter sheen, it may be the *Sabtalum album,* a native of India and used in India and China as an odiferous substance to perfume temples and houses of Sanskrit *valgu, valgum.*

Al'mond (al'mond; Heb. *shāqēd,* "the awakening one," probably from its early blossoming). A tree very much resembling the peach in form and blossom; it is only another species of the same genus. Its flowers appear as early as February, or even January. The almond is diffused by culture from China to Spain, on both sides of the Mediterranean, in the S of England, and in southern portions of the United States. There is no region, however, where it thrives better than in Syria.

The almond tree blossoms toward the end of January or the beginning of February, before the coming of the leaves, so that the appearance of a tree in full bloom is striking. Although the blossoms are tinged with pink, the general effect is white. The fruit is eaten in two stages, the first the tender, acidulous, unripe, crisp pod, and the other the ripe almonds, so familiar everywhere. There are four species of wild almonds in the Bible lands. The Heb. name of the almond is the "waker," in allusion to its being the first of the fruit trees to awake in the winter and put forth its luxuriant blossoms. This tree is referred to by Jacob when he tells his sons to take into Egypt "some of the best products of the land . . . and almonds" (Gen. 43:11). In Eccles. (12:5), "the almond tree blossoms," doubtless refers to the profuse flowering and white appearance of the tree when in full bloom and before the leaves appear (Jer. 1:11-12). In Num. 17:8 the rod of Aaron is described as having "sprouted and put forth buds and produced blossoms, and it bore ripe almonds." With its oblong oval shape sharpened at one end and rounded at the other, the almond nut is remarkably graceful. This naturally led to its selection for ornamental carved work; and it was the pattern selected for the bowls of the golden lampstand (Ex. 25:33-34; 37:19), "symbolizing the speedy and powerful result of light" (Keil, *Arch.,* 1:146). *See also* Almond Blossoms in the general listing.

Figurative. In Jer. 1:11-12 there is an allusion to another of the meanings of the Heb. root, which is to *hasten.* In the first of the two verses the almond tree is mentioned by its name *shāqēd,* and in the second it is said "for I am watching My word," *watching* being from the

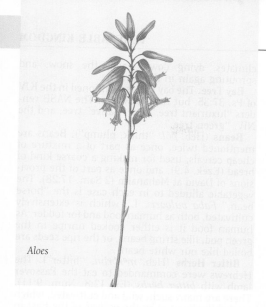

Aloes

same root as *almond*. The almond was chosen to symbolize God's haste in fulfilling His promises.

There can be no reasonable doubt that the allusion in Eccles. 12:5 is to the white hair of the aged.

Al'oes, Lign Aloes (al'ōs; Heb. *'ăhālîm;* Gk. *aloē*). This is doubtless the *lignum aloes* of the ancients, the product of *Aquilaria agallocha,* Roxb., and other trees of the same genus, growing in India and China. It was well known to the Greeks and also to the Arabians. The species grows in Sylhet, in the E of Bengal, being a large tree with lanceolate (shaped like a lance head) leaves, the wood containing a resin and an essential oil, constituting the perfume prized in antiquity. It is mentioned in four places in the OT and once in the NT (Num. 24:6; Ps. 45:8; Prov. 7:17; Song of Sol. 4:14; John 19:39). A question has been raised as to the identity of the tree mentioned in Num. 24:6 with the other trees of the same name. This question may safely be answered in the affirmative. Although the lign aloes is a native of India and China, it is easy to suppose that it was cultivated in the tropical valley of the Jordan, which is well known to have produced in ancient times certain trees of which all traces have now disappeared. But even if it were to be supposed that it was not cultivated in Palestine, it might have been alluded to as a well-known tree of foreign growth, of which the luxuriance was proverbial, in this respect resembling the *cedar,* in the same passage, which, if it indicated the *cedar of Lebanon,* was to the Israelites of that day also a foreign tree, mentioned as an emblem of prosperity.

Amo'mum (a-mō'mŭm; Gk. *amōmum*). This word occurs only in Rev. 18:13 and is rendered "spice." Amomum is a fragrant plant of India. It belongs to a genus of plants, natural order *Scita-*

mineoe, belonging to tropical regions of the Old World and allied to the ginger plant. They are herbaceous, with creeping rootstocks and large sheathing leaves, and are remarkable for the pungency and aromatic properties of their seeds. Several specimens yield the spices cardamom and grains of paradise. The one mentioned in Revelation had seeds like grapes, from which an ointment was made.

An'ise. *See* Dill.

Apple. The Heb. word *tappûaḥ* for apple is nearly the same as the Arab. *tuffâh;* and wherever the name of the tree has been preserved in the name of a place, as in Beth Tappuah, the Arab. has preserved it in the modified form, in this *tuffâh,* showing that the reference to the familiar fruit is recognized. The apple is a favorite fruit of the natives of this land; and although they do not now possess any very fine varieties, they are particularly fond of the smell of an apple (Song of Sol. 7:8). They habitually smell an apple to revive themselves when faint (2:5). Most of the apples cultivated here are sweet (v. 3). The allusions to the size of the apple tree (2:3; 8:5) are borne out by fact. There is no need, then, to seek for any other tree, as some have done, to meet the Scripture requirements.

Aspala'thus (as-pa-la'thus). The name of one or more aromatic substances mentioned only once in the Apocrypha (Ecclus. 24:15). The substance and plant producing it are indeterminable.

Balm (Heb. *ṣŏrî*), an aromatic gum, or resin (Gen. 37:25). Probably produced in Gilead, or a prime article of commerce there (Jer. 8:22; 46:11; 51:8), well known to Jacob (Gen. 43:11) and dealt in by Judah and Israel in the latter days of their monarchies (Ezek. 27:17). No tree now growing in Gilead produces the traditional balm, now known as *Mecca balsam.* This substance is

Balm

the gum of *Balsamodendron gileadense* and *B. opobalsamum,* which grow in southern Arabia. But there can be no doubt that in Roman times these trees were cultivated in the lower Jordan Valley. This would bring a part of its area of cultivation within the limits of Gilead. In any case it was to such an extent an article of commerce in that district that it went by the name of *balm of Gilead.* Dioscorides erroneously says that the tree grew "only in the country of the Jews, which is Palestine, in the Ghor." Balm of Gilead was once an important element in the *materia medica,* but it has now fallen into disuse. Some have supposed that *mastich* is the balm of Gilead. Avicenna, however, clearly distinguishes it from that well-known gum. The so-called balm of Gilead, prepared by the monks of Jericho from the fruits of the *zaqqûm, Balanites aegyptiaca,* Del., has no claim except their authority. It is said, however, to have healing properties.

Balsam Tree. The rendering in the NASB of two Heb. words. In 2 Sam. 5:23-24; 1 Chron. 14:14-15, Heb. *bākā',* "weeping, distilling," is given as "balsam trees" in the NASB and NIV; the KJV reads "mulberry trees." "Balsam" is also the marginal reading in the NASB of Ps. 84:6, as an alternate to "Baca." In Song of Sol. 5:1, 13; 6:2, Heb. *bāśām* is given as "balsam" in the NASB and as "spice" and "spices" in the KJV and NIV.

Barley (Heb. *śe'ôrâ;* Gk. *krithinos*). A well-known grain, cultivated from the remotest antiquity, and frequently mentioned in the Bible. A wild species, found in Galilee and northeastward to the Syrian Desert, *Hordeum ithaburense,* Boiss. (*H. spontaneum,* Koch), may be the original stock from which the cultivated varieties were derived. It is conspicuous by its very long awns, which are sometimes a foot in length. Barley is the universal feed for horses, mules, and, to a certain extent, for donkeys (1 Kings 4:28), taking the place of oats with us. It is still used for bread among the very poor (2 Kings 4:42). It was sometimes mixed with other cheap grains for making bread (Ezek. 4:9). Because of its cheapness it was the jealousy offering (Num. 5:15); and part of the price of an adulteress (Hos. 3:2) and of lewd women (Ezek. 13:19). Barley bread showed the low rank and poverty of Gideon (Judg. 7:13).

The barley harvest is earlier than the wheat harvest (Ex. 9:31-32). It begins in April in the Jordan Valley and continues to be later as the altitude increases, until, at a height of six thousand feet above the sea, it takes place in July and August. Barley is sown in October and November, after the "early rain." It is never sown in the spring, for the simple reason that it would not have rain, and so could not mature any grain, even if there were moisture enough in the soil to cause it to germinate. That which is sown on the higher levels behaves like winter wheat in cold climates, dying down under the snow, and sprouting again in the spring.

Bay Tree. The bay tree is mentioned in the KJV of Ps. 37:35, but not elsewhere. The NASB renders "luxuriant tree," lit., "native" tree, and the NIV, "green tree."

Beans (Heb. *pôl,* "thick, plump"). Beans are mentioned twice, once as part of a mixture of cheap cereals, used for making a coarse kind of bread (Ezek. 4:9), and once as part of the provisions of David at Mahanaim (2 Sam. 17:28). The vegetable alluded to in each case is the "horse bean," *Faba vulgaris,* L., which is extensively cultivated, both as human food and for fodder. As human food it is either cooked unripe in the green pod, like string beans, or the ripe seeds are boiled like our white beans.

Bitter Herbs (Heb. *merôrîm,* "bitter"). The Hebrews were commanded to eat the Passover lamb with *bitter herbs* (Ex. 12:8; Num. 9:11). There are many such, wild and cultivated, which are habitually used by the natives of the East in salads; among them are *lettuce, watercress, pepper grass,* and *endive.* The object of the ordinance was both to remind the Israelites of their "bitter" bondage (Ex. 1:14) and of the *haste* with which they made their exit from Egypt. Unleavened bread, a roasted lamb, and a few bitter herbs constituted a meal the elements of which were always at hand and could be got together with the least possible delay. These herbs are not distasteful to the orientals, who are very fond of them.

Box Tree (Heb. *tidhār,* NASB, except for Ezek. 27:6, where "boxwood" is the rendering of Heb. *'āshûr; te'ashshûr,* KJV). Reference to the box tree appears in the NASB and KJV of Isa. 41:19; 60:13, though a different Heb. word is behind the English of the NASB and KJV. (The NIV renders "cypress" in both places.) In the NASB "box tree" is rendered for *tidhār,* whereas "cypress" is rendered for *te'ashshûr.* In the KJV *te'ashshûr* is rendered "box tree," and *tidhār* is rendered "pine." The NIV translates *tidhār* as "fir."

The box tree is mentioned in Isa. 41:19; 60:13 in connection with the cedar, acacia, myrtle, olive, juniper, and cypress (NASB; cedar, shittah, myrtle, oil tree, fir, and pine, KJV; cedar, acacia, myrtle, olive, fir, and cypress, NIV). It seems unlikely that a shrub, known only in far northern Syria, should be associated with these familiar trees. The Syrian box, *Buxus longi folia,* Boiss., is only two to three feet high, and must have been unfamiliar to the readers of the Bible in the time of Isaiah. The old Arab. version gives *sherbîn,* which is either the wild cypress or the *lizzâb, Juniperus excelsa,* M. B. Possibly the acacia is implied here.

Bramble. *See* Thistles, Thorns.

Briers. *See* Thistles, Thorns.

Broom Tree (Heb. *rôtem;* Job 30:4; Ps. 120:4; 1 Kings 19:4, marg., all NASB and NIV). The plant intended is doubtless the *retem* of the

Arabs, *Retama roetam,* L., a desert, almost leafless, shrub, furnishing a poor refuge from the sun's rays. Its roots make good fuel and charcoal (Ps. 120:4).

Bulrush. *See* Reed.

Burning Bush (Heb. *s*ᵉ*neh,* "bramble"; Ex. 3:2-5; Deut. 33:16). One of the many thorny shrubs growing in Sinai. The monks of the Convent of St. Catherine point out a blackberry bush (*Rubus tomentosus,* Borck, var. *collinus,* Boiss.), growing behind the chapel of the convent, as the bush in question. This is improbable, as Rubus is not indigenous there. The burning bush might be one of the *seyal* trees, *Acacia tortilis,* Hayne, or *A. seyal,* Del., or the *nebk, Zizyphus spina christi,* L., or some other thornbush.

Calamus. *See* Reed.

Cane. *See* Reed.

Caperberry (Eccles. 12:5; Heb. *'abîyônâ,* "provocative of desire"). The immature fruit of *Capparis spinosa,* L., a plant growing everywhere in clefts of rocks and walls. It is a stimulant and is supposed to be an aphrodisiac. If *caperberry* is the correct rendering of *'abîyônâ* in Eccles. 12:5, "the caperberry is ineffective" (NASB), the meaning of the passage is that even the caperberry shall fail to excite desire; it will be "ineffective." The KJV reads, "desire shall fade"; the NIV, "desire is no longer stirred."

Cassia (kash'i-a; Heb. *qiddâ;* Ex. 30:24; Ezek. 27:19; *q*ᵉ*ṣî'â,* "peeled"; Ps. 45:8). Probably *Cassia lignea* of commerce, which consists of strips of the bark of *Cinnamomum Cassia,* Blume, a plant growing in China and Malaysia. Cassia buds are the immature flowers of the same. Both have the flavor and aroma of cinnamon.

Castor Oil Plant. A swift-growing plant designated by the Heb. *qîqāyôn* (Jonah 4:6-10). The LXX renders the Heb. by the Gk. *kolokynthē,* meaning the pumpkin *Cucurbita pepo,* which is in reality a type of the gourd family (cf. KJV rendering of Jonah 4:6-10). The NIV translates "vine." On the other hand, the Heb. *qîqāyôn* is similar to Greco-European *kiki,* designating the castor oil plant. This plant attains a height from eight to ten feet, sometimes growing rapidly. If this was the plant that shaded Jonah, its rapid growth was miraculous.   M.F.U.

Cedar (Heb. *'erez*). By far the greater number of references to the cedar in the Scriptures are to be understood of the famous "cedar of Lebanon." This is a tree of wide distribution and fulfills well the conditions demanded, with the following exceptions: (1) The *cedar wood used in purification,* in connection with scarlet and hyssop. This would seem to have been a tree found in the Sinaitic desert and in use long before the Israelites could have easily obtained the cedar of Lebanon. It might well have been *Juniperus phoenicia,* L., which is found in Mt. Hor and its neighborhood, and could also have grown on the mountains of Sinai. (2) The "cedars in God's

garden" (Ezek. 31:8). The comparison to Assyria, called "a cedar in Lebanon" (v. 3, KJV), with these trees would seem to indicate some other tree. We have no means of determining what it was. (3) The "cedars beside the waters" (Num. 24:6) can hardly be cedars of Lebanon, because this tree never grows in such a location. True, in poetry, even in the Scriptures, it is not to be expected that all the congruities of time and place shall be rigidly observed. But unless we suppose such poetic license, we must infer that the trees here referred to were some water-loving species then known as *cedars,* now no longer determinable.

Coriander

It is likely that the subalpine regions of Lebanon and Antilebanon were clothed with these trees. At Besherreh in the Republic of Lebanon about one hundred miles N of Beirut there was a fine group of the ancient cedars of Lebanon. Cedars are abundant in the Taurus Mts. in southern Turkey, including the Nur Mts., anciently called the Amanus Mts. Their range is from the Himalayas to the Atlas, and from central Asia Minor to Lebanon. They also existed in Cyprus.

The ancient trees had reddish-brown bark and sturdy trunks as much as forty feet in girth. Their branch spread was wide, they bore cones some five inches long, and they had bright green needles about one-half inch long. They grew slowly, and their wood was a fine prize for architectural uses. The cedar was a tall tree (Isa. 2:13; etc.) "with beautiful branches and forest shade" (Ezek. 31:3); its wood was suitable for masts of ships (27:5); for beams, pillars, and boards (1 Kings 6:9; 7:2); and for carved work (Isa. 44:14). Of this noble tree much of the Temple was built, as well as Solomon's house and other important public edifices in Jerusalem. It was used for roofing the temple of Artemis (Diana) at Ephesus and that of Apollo at Utica, the palace of the Persian kings at

Susa, and other famous buildings. Its claim to be the "king of trees" is not to be considered with reference to the whole forest world, but only in comparison with the trees found in Bible lands. This claim was never disputed in the period of the Hebrew nationality in this land, and the sacred grove at Besherreh, on Lebanon, still bears the ancient name of "the cedars of the Lord." *See* Cypress. M.F.U.

Chaff. The husks that surround the seeds of the cereals. *Chaff* is the correct rendering for the Heb. *mōṣ* ("winnowed"). *Chaff,* after the threshing is over, is mingled with the *cut* and *split straw* (*teben*). Winnowing separates the product of threshing into four heaps—*grain, cut straw, chaff,* and finally the *dust,* caused by the comminution of a part of the straw and chaff and its commingling with the dust of the earthen floor. This, which is *'ûr* in Heb., is erroneously translated "chaff " (Dan. 2:35).

Chestnut Tree (Heb. *'armôn*). As this tree is not found in the Holy Land, some other must be sought that will fill the conditions required. The *plane tree* (which see), as the Heb. is elsewhere rendered, is of a stature and imposing appearance sufficient to make it suitable for comparison in the group with which the cedar of Lebanon is compared (Ezek. 31:8). This tree often attains a height of a hundred feet and a diameter at its base of from six to ten feet. It is abundant along all water courses in Syria and Mesopotamia.

Cinnamon (Heb. *qinnāmôn*). No one can doubt the substance intended, as the Heb. name is the same as the English. It was used by that race as a perfume for the holy oil (Ex. 30:23) and for beds (Prov. 7:17). It seems to have been cultivated by Solomon (Song of Sol. 4:14). It is a part of the wares of Babylon the Great (Rev. 18:13).

Cinnamon

Citron Wood. A prize ornamental wood obtained from a large tree of the cypress family (*Collistris quadrivalius*). This luxury commodity was marketed in the emporia of mystic Babylon (Rev. 18:12). The wood was reddish brown, extremely hard, and fragrant. The Romans prized it greatly, and it was expensive. M.F.U.

Corian'der (cor-i-an'der). The aromatic seed of *Coriandrum sativum,* L. It is somewhat larger than a hemp seed and only spoken of to illustrate the size and color of the grains of manna (Ex. 16:31; Num. 11:7).

Corn. The generic name in the KJV for the cereal grains. Those cultivated in Bible lands are *wheat, barley, vetch, fitches* (*Nigella sativa,* L.), *millet, beans, pulse* (edible seeds in general), *lentils,* and *maize. See* Harvest; Fan; Threshing Floor; Agriculture.

Cotton (Heb. *karpas,* from Sanskrit *karpāsa,* "cotton"). Indian cotton was cultivated in Persia. There is no evidence, however, that the ancient Hebrews knew cotton, although it has been cultivated from time immemorial in India and other parts of the East.

Crocus (Heb. *ḥăbaṣelet*). Mentioned in Isa. 35:1, it is probably the *narcissus* that is referred to. *See also* Rose.

Crown of Thorns. *See* Thistles, Thorns.

Cucumber. There are two kinds of cucumbers cultivated in the East, both of which were probably known to the ancient Egyptians and the Hebrews. One is identical with our ordinary kind, but more delicate in flavor and more wholesome. The other is tougher, drier, and less delicate in flavor. The former kind grows only in irrigated ground, while the latter flourishes during the hot, rainless months of summer, without a drop of water, except what it can extract from the parched soil or absorb from the atmosphere during the night. It was doubtless the custom in Egypt to water both kinds, and hence the succulent character of the vegetable so keenly missed by the Israelites during their thirsty journey in the wilderness (Num. 11:5; Heb. *qishshū',* "hard").

The field of cucumbers (Isa. 1:8; Heb. *miqshâ;* "melons," NIV) is still a feature of oriental landscapes, some of these found on rolling ground, exposed to the blazing sun of August, without water, and others being among the irrigated orchards of orange and other fruit trees, but all supplied with a *hut,* where the watchman keeps guard over the tempting vegetable, none of which would reach its lawful owner but for this precaution. This hut is a frail structure of poles and leaves, adapted only to protect the watchman from the sun by day and the dew by night, during the rainless summer of Syria and Palestine. As soon as the last of the cucumbers is gathered, the hut is "left," a useless reminder of past plenty and prosperity.

Cum'min (kum'in; Heb. *kammôn,* "preserving"; Gk. *kuminon*). One of the aromatic seeds, subject to tithe by the Jewish law (Matt. 23:23).

It is still known by its ancient name (*kammûn*) throughout the Arab world. It is an aromatic and carminative, used in cooking and in domestic medicine. It is still threshed with a rod (Isa. 28:25-27). It has been superseded in modern times by caraway seeds, which are more nutritious and tasty.

Cummin

Cypress, Cypresses. The rendering of three Heb. words referring to a tree found in Bible lands.

1. The Heb. word *berôsh* is given as "cypress" in the NASB, "pine" in the NIV, and "fir" in the KJV (1 Kings 5:8, 10; 6:15, 34; 9:11; 2 Kings 19:23; 2 Chron. 2:8; 3:5; Song of Sol. 1:17; Isa. 14:8; 37:24; 55:13; Hos. 14:8; Nah. 2:3; Zech. 11:2; and Ezek. 31:8) with only the exceptions of Isa. 41:19 and 60:13, where it is rendered juniper in the NASB and fir in the KJV.

2. The Heb. word *te'ashshûr* is rendered "cypress" in the NASB and NIV and "box tree" in the KJV of Isa. 41:19; 60:13.

3. The Heb. word *tirzâ* is rendered "cypress" in

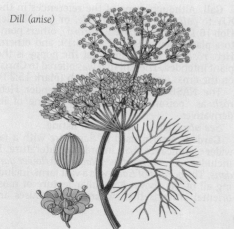

Dill (anise)

the NASB, the NIV, and the KJV of Isa. 44:14. The marginal reading in the NASB is "holm oak."

Dill (Heb. *qesah;* Isa. 28:25; Gk. *anēthon*). The Gk. *anēthon* is the exact equivalent of the Lat. *anethum,* which is *dill.* The NIV translates "caraway." It is the aromatic, carminative seed of *Anethum graveolens,* L., an umbelliferae, cultivated widely in the East and used both in cooking and domestic medicine. It was subject to a tithe among the Hebrews (Matt. 23:23).

Ebony (Heb. *hobnî*). The hard, close-grained, black heart wood of *Diospyros ebenum,* L., which grows in the East Indies. It has been an article of commerce from ancient times, having been brought to Palestine from Dedan, on the Persian Gulf (Ezek. 27:15). It is used for cabinet work, rulers, etc. Ebony was brought in ancient times from Ethiopia, but there is no certainty as to the tree that produced it. Virgil (*Georgics* 2.116) says that "India also produces the black ebony."

Fig (Heb. *te'ēnâ;* Gk. *sukon*). The fruit of the well-known tree. It is one of the favorite kinds of food in the East and, in the dried state, a considerable article of commerce. The failure of the fig trees was a national calamity. Their productiveness was a token of peace and the divine favor. They are associated with the *vine,* the *palm,* and the *pomegranate.* The *fig tree* differs from most other fruit trees in that its fruit is green and inconspicuous, concealed among leaves until near the time of ripening. If the promise given from a distance by the leaves is not fulfilled on approaching (Mark 11:13), the tree is a *hypocrite.* Such a one our Savior cursed.

Fir (Heb. *berôsh;* Ps. 104:17; Ezek. 27:5; *'ōren;* Isa. 44:14). The Heb. term *berôsh* is more frequently translated "cypress" in the NASB (and is twice translated "juniper," Isa. 41:19; 60:13; but "pine" in the NIV); it is also translated "fir." In Isa. 44:14 *'ōren* is rendered "fir" in the NASB, "pine" in the NIV, but "ash" in the KJV. The tall trunk of the fir is well adapted for masts.

Fitches. A KJV term, replaced in the NASB by cummin (Heb. *qesah;* Isa. 28:25, 27) and spelt (Heb. *kûssemet;* Ezek. 4:9). The NIV translates by "caraway" and "spelt" respectively. *See* Cummin; Spelt.

Flag. A KJV term replaced in the NASB and NIV by rushes (Heb. *'ahû;* Job 8:11; Heb. *sûp;* Isa. 19:6) or reeds (Heb. *sûp;* Ex. 2:3, 5). *See* Reeds, Rushes.

Flax (Heb. *pishtâ*). A well-known plant, *Linum sativum,* L. The fibers of the bark, when separated, twisted, bleached, and woven, are *linen.* In the raw state they are "tow" (Judg. 16:9). Somewhat twisted, tow constitutes a "wick" (Isa. 42:3; 43:17).

Flowers. The flowers of the Holy Land are renowned for their beauty. The most showy and widely diffused are the *scarlet* and *blue anemones,* the *scarlet ranunculi* and *poppies,* the

Spring flowers in the Holy Land

numerous *silenes*, the purple *pea blossom*, a number of showy *roses*, the scarlet *pomegranate*, a host of *composites,* the *styrax,* a number of *crocuses, colchicums, irises, tulips,* and *ixiolirions,* etc. In many places they are so abundant as to impart a rich and varied coloring to the landscape.

For the flower as part of the ornamentation of the Temple furniture, *see* Flower, Flowers in the general listing.

Forest (Heb. *Ya'ar,* a "thicket"). Although the Holy Land was never a wooded country in historic times, it was doubtless more so at the time of the Hebrew conquest than it has been ever since. Numerous woods and forests are mentioned by name. According to Albright, in the Middle Bronze Age (2000–1500B.C.) the mountains of Palestine were heavily forested on the watershed ridge and the western slope so that there was little arable land (cf. Albright, *Archaeology of Palestine and the Bible,* pp. 130-33). Since the cistern had not come into use, the general situation favors the biblical representation of the patriarchs being free to roam over wide areas of sparsely populated central highland range and to be free to feed flocks on the lower ranges. Israel has had a program to reforest the land.

Frankincense (Heb. *l^ebōnâ). See* Galbanum.

Fruit. The Holy Land is not only a land of *flowers* but also of *fruits.* Owing to the great diversity of level, from the tropical valley of the Jordan, 1,300 feet below the sea, to subalpine Lebanon, the fruits of the country present a cosmopolitan variety. The most characteristic are the banana, orange, and other citrus fruits, dates, most of the rosaceous fruits, the persimmon, and the jujube, grapes, figs, olives, and pomegranates. The orange is in season for six months, the grape nearly as long. Figs ripen during four months. Almost all garden vegetables thrive, and many of them are in season for months.

Gal'banum (gal'ba-num; Heb. *l^ebōnâ,* "whiteness"). A gum resin with a pungent balsamic odor (Ex. 30:34). It was one of the constituents of the sacred incense. Two ferulas, *F. galbaniflua,* Boiss, et Buhse, and *F. rubricaulis,* Boiss., both growing in Persia, are believed to be the sources of the gum. It is used in medicine as an *antispasmodic.* It is a greasy, sticky, granulated resin, presenting a whitish appearance at first, but afterward changing to yellow, having a pungent odor and taste, and which, when mixed with fragrant substances, has the effect of increasing the odor and fixing it longer.

The garden of Gethsemane

Gall. Although some of the references in the KJV to *gall* clearly point to *bile,* or gall bladder (Job 16:13; 24:14, 25; Heb. *m^erōrâ),* others point to a plant (Deut. 29:18; Lam. 3:19; and others; Heb. *rôsh).* It is probable that the poppy is the plant intended. The gall that was offered to Christ on the cross was doubtless myrrh (Mark 15:23).

The NASB and NIV frequently render Heb. *rôsh* as "poison" (or "venom"), or one of its derivatives.

See also Gall in the general listing.

Garden. A term used in Scripture with a far wider significance than in ordinary literature. It includes *park, orchard, vegetable* and *flower gardens.* The *garden of Eden* was a vast farm, including all of the above. A peculiar feature of most oriental cities is that, whereas the houses are crowded together and few gardens are found among them, the environs are mostly composed of fruit and vegetable gardens and trees of various sorts, planted for utilitarian purposes. The effect of these gardens, surrounding the towns as in the case of Jaffa, Sidon, Beirut, Damascus, and Homs, is extremely beautiful.

Garlic (Heb. *shūm*). A well-known vegetable, more agreeable to the oriental than to most European palates. It is mentioned only once (Num. 11:5).

Gopher Wood (Heb. *gōpher*). An unknown wood, used in the construction of the Ark (Gen. 6:14). The NIV translates by "cypress" with hesitation.

Gourds, Wild (Heb. *paqqū'â*, "splitting" open; 2 Kings 4:39). Probably *colocynths*, which grew abundantly in the locality alluded to and suit the requirements of the passage.

Grapes. *See* Vine.

Grass. A term used in Scripture in an indefinite sense, referring to *green herbage* in general. All the four Heb. words, *yereq, ḥāṣîr, deshe',* and *'ēśeb,* translated "grass," have this wide meaning. The idea conveyed to us by the term *grasses,* as plants with hollow columns, strap-shaped leaves, and an inflorescence of glumes and pales, is a strictly modern creation of descriptive botany.

Green Herbs, Green Grass, Green Thing. *See* Grass.

Hedge. Hedges are more commonly used to separate gardens and orchards in the East than are walls. Many thorny plants are set out for this purpose. Also some of the giant grasses, as *Arundo Donax,* L., and *Saccharum Aegyptiacum,* L.

Henna (Heb. *kōper,* from Malay *Kapur*). This plant, *Lawsonia alba,* L., is cultivated everywhere in the Holy Land. Its clusters of cream-colored flowers are much admired by the orientals and form a part of almost every nosegay during the flowering season. The scriptural allusions (Song of Sol. 1:14; 4:13) show that it was equally esteemed in ancient times. Its leaves are also used for dyeing fingernails and toenails a reddish orange color. There is, however, no allusion to this use of the plant in Scripture.

Hyssop (Heb. *'ezôb;* Gk. *hussōpos*); a labiate plant, probably *Origanum Maru,* L. It was used in sprinkling (Ex. 12:22; Lev. 14; Heb. 9:19), and in quenching the thirst of a victim on the cross (John 19:29). It grew out of walls (1 Kings 4:33), probably those of terraces. There is no reason to believe that the "reed" (Matt. 27:48; Mark 15:36) on which the sponge soaked in vinegar was raised to Christ's mouth was the same as the "hyssop" upon which the sponge was put (John 19:29). Even were it so, the stem of the *caper plant,* which has been proposed as the *hyssop,* would not suit the requirements of the term *reed,* which suggests a *straight,* not a *zigzag,* stem. For fur-

Hyssop

ther discussion of hyssop, *see* the article in the general listing.

Ivy (2 Macc. 6:7) grows everywhere over rocky walls in the Holy Land.

Juniper. The juniper appears in the KJV and the NASB but not always as the rendering of the same Heb. words. It never appears in the NIV. Heb. *rōtem* is rendered "juniper" in both translations of 1 Kings 19:4-5 (NIV has "broom tree") but as "juniper" in the KJV and "broom" tree in the NASB and NIV of Job 30:4; Ps. 120:4. Heb. *berôsh,* which is most frequently rendered "cypress" in the NASB, is given as "fir" in the KJV, "pine" in the NIV, and "juniper" in the NASB of Isa. 41:19; 60:13. Heb. *'ăro'ēr* is given as "juniper" in the NASB of Jer. 48:6 but as "heath" in the KJV and "bush" in the NIV of that verse. *See* Broom Tree; Cypress; Fir.

Leeks (Heb. *ḥaṣîr*), a kind of onion, *Allium Porrum,* L., cultivated extensively in the East. It is mentioned once with onions and garlic (Num. 11:5).

Lentils (Heb. *'ădāshâ;* Gen. 25:34; 2 Sam. 17:28; 23:11; Ezek. 4:9). The seed of *Ervum Lens,* L., a cereal cultivated everywhere in the East. A soup or "stew" made of it is as much used now for food as it was in Jacob's time.

Lign Aloes. *See* Aloes.

Lily (Heb. *shûshan*). In a special sense the word for *iris* is as broad in its application as its rendering in our versions, *lily.* The expression "lily of the valleys" (Song of Sol. 2:1) does not refer to the flower understood by this designation in ordinary speech, as it is not found in Palestine. The lily of other passages in the Song of Solomon was evidently a garden flower (2:16; 4:5; 6:3). The

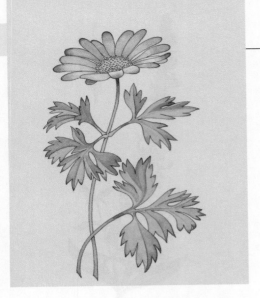

Some scholars believe the "lily of the field" is the anemone

Poppy, another possible "lily of the field"

allusion (5:13) may be to its rosy color, or fragrance, or both. From earliest times the lily has been imitated in stone and bronze, as an architectural ornament (1 Kings 7:19; 2 Chron. 4:5). The expression "lilies of the field" (*ta krina tou agrou,* Matt. 6:28-30) is well translated. Fortunately we only have to go to the grain fields of Palestine to find precisely what fulfills the conditions of the allusion. They are as follows: A plant that would naturally be called a *lily* (not a *ranunculus,* or an *anemone,* or a *poppy,* plants having names of their own in both Gk. and English, and never confounded with lilies in either ancient or modern speech), growing among the wheat, adorned with regal colors, and having stems, which, when dried, were used as fuel for the oriental oven. There are three species of the *sword lily, Gladiolus segetum,* Gawl, *G. Illyricus,* Koch, and *G. atroviolaceus,* Boiss., with pink to purple and blackish violet flowers, which grow everywhere among standing corn, and have stems suitable for light fuel. As they are the only plants that fulfill all the conditions, we cannot but believe that they were the very plants to which our Savior pointed to illustrate the heavenly Father's care of His children.

See also Lily Blossom in the general listing.

Mallows (Heb. *mallûaḥ,* "salt plant"). A term used only once in the Bible (Job 30:4, marg., "plant of the salt marshes"; "salt herbs," NIV). The Arab. equivalent of the Heb. *mallûaḥ* refers to the *sea orache, Atriplex Halimus,* L., a plant growing in just such regions as the one referred to by Job. Dioscorides says that they were cooked as vegetables. The leaves are sour and furnish little nourishment.

Mandrake (Heb. *dûday;* Gen. 30:14; Song of Sol. 7:13). A narcotic plant of the order *Solanaceae, Mandragora officinarum,* L., esteemed by the ancients as a love medicine and evidently so referred to in both the above-cited passages. Taken in considerable quantities, it is an acrid narcotic poison. It is not used in modern medicine.

Manna (Heb. *mān,* "what?"). Many have sought to identify manna with some substance naturally produced in the desert, answering to the conditions of the food rained down on the Israelites in the wilderness, during a period of forty years. There is a substance called *mann* by the Arabs, and having some nutrient properties, that exudes from *Tamarix mannifera,* Ehr., and certain oaks, and *Alhagi Maurorum,* D.C., and *A. Camelorum,* Fisch. But this substance corresponds in no way with the properties of the scriptural *manna.* The latter was clearly a miraculous production and ceased as soon as the necessity for it passed away (Ex. 16:14, 31; Num. 11:7-9; Josh. 5:12). Among its most remarkable characteristics was the double supply on Friday and the total lack on the Sabbath.

Mas'tich (mas'tik). A fragrant, terebinthine gum, exuding from *Pistacia Lentiscus,* L., a small tree, growing abundantly in Palestine and Syria, mentioned only in the Apocrypha (Sus. 54). It is the common chewing gum of the East. A preserve is also made of it.

Melons (Heb. *'ăbaṭṭîaḥ;* Num. 11:5). Doubtless generic for *watermelons* and *cantaloupes,* of which there are several luscious varieties in the Holy Land. Being inexpensive, and serving to quench the thirst engendered by the hot climate of Bible lands, melons would naturally be lamented by the Israelites in the desert. The NIV translates Heb. *miqshâ* as "melons" in Isa. 1:8.

Mildew (Heb. *yērāqôn,* "paleness"). Various sorts of parasitic fungi on plants, the growth of which is promoted by moisture. It is the opposite of "blasting" (*shiddāpôn,* which is the drying up of plants by the hot sirocco, or khamsîn winds (*see* Deut. 28:22; 1 Kings 8:37; etc.).

Millet (Heb. *dōḥan;* Ezek. 4:9). The seed of *Panicum miliaceum,* L., and of *Setaria Italica,* Kth. It is about as large as a mustard seed. In the single passage where it occurs, it formed part of the basis of a complex bread. Some have supposed that *Sorghum vulgare,* L., is the plant intended by the Heb. original *dōḥan.*

Mint. A tithable herb. The most common species of mint is *Mentha sativa,* L., which is commonly cultivated and used as a flavoring in salads and in cooking. *Hēduosmon* (Matt. 23:23; Luke 11:42) was probably generic for other kinds of mint, as well as the above.

Mint

Mulberry (Gk. *sukaminos*). The Gk. term meant also the sycamore, but the English term has come to mean only the black mulberry, *Morus nigra,* L. The fruit of it resembles in shape and external appearance the larger sorts of blackberries, but it has a decidedly different, though pleasant, acid flavor. It is mentioned only once in the NT (Luke 17:6). Wherever *sukaminos* occurs in the LXX it refers to the sycamore.

In the KJV the mulberry appears as the rendering of Heb. *bākā'* in 2 Sam. 5:23-34; 1 Chron. 14:14-15, but the NASB and NIV more correctly give "balsam."

Mustard (Gk. *sinapi*). A well-known plant of which two species, *Sinapsis arvensis,* L., and *S. alba,* L., flourish in the Holy Land. Besides these

S. nigra, L., the *black mustard* is cultivated as a condiment. All produce minute seeds (Matt. 17:20; Luke 17:6). All, in favorable soil in this warm climate, attain a size quite sufficient for the requirements of the passages (Matt. 13:31-32; Mark 4:31-32; Luke 13:19). The birds in the latter passage, it will be observed, *nest* in the branches. The term *tree* is to be taken only as an exaggerated contrast with the minute seed and to be explained by the parallel "but when it is full grown, it is larger than the garden plants, and becomes a tree" (Matt. 13:32). Palestinian mustard trees sometimes grow to a height of ten to fifteen feet or more.

Myrrh (Heb. *mōr,* "distilling"; Arab. *murr;* Gk. *smyrna,* "myrrha"). It is the well-known gum resin extracted from the Arabian *Balsamodendron Myrrha,* Nees. It was used as a perfume, for embalming, and as an ingredient of the holy anointing oil. It was one of the gifts of the magi. Another Heb. word, *lōṭ,* is translated *myrrh* (Gen. 37:25; 43:11). It should be translated *ladanum* (Gen. 37:25, marg.). This is a gummy exudation from *Cistus villosus,* L., a plant growing in great abundance in the Holy Land.

H.F.V.

Mustard

Myrtle. A well-known and beautiful evergreen shrub, *Myrtus communis,* L., with white flowers, and berries that are at first white, and then turn bluish black. They are edible, although rather too astringent for Western palates. The Heb. name of Esther, *Hadasseh,* is derived from the name of this plant (Heb. *ḥādas*). The translation "myrtle trees" (Zech. 1:8, 10-11) is an error, as the original has only *ḥădassîm,* "myrtles," with no hint as to whether they were *trees* or *shrubs.*

Nard (nard; Heb. *nērd;* Gk. *nardos*). An aromatic oil extracted from an East Indian plant,

Nardostachys jatamansi, D.C. (Song of Sol. 4:13; Mark 14:3; John 12:3).

Nettle. The Heb. *hārûl,* which occurs thrice (Job 30:7; Prov. 24:31; Zeph. 2:9) and is translated in some versions "nettle," probably signifies *thorn, scrub,* or *brush.* The Holy Land is preeminently a land of such scrubs, and the sense of the above passages is well met by the term. The Heb. word *qimmôsh (qimôsh),* "nettles" (Isa. 34:13), from a root signifying *to sting,* doubtless refers to the true *nettles,* of the genera *Urtica* and *Forskahlea,* of the order *Urticaceae,* of which there are a number of species in this land. This rendering perfectly suits the passages cited.

Nuts. The nuts of Gen. 43:11 (Heb. *botneh*) are without doubt *pistachios,* as so rendered. They are, and always have been, luxuries in the East. The nut trees of the Song of Sol. 6:11 (*ĕgōz*), are *walnuts.* They are commonly cultivated and greatly esteemed in Bible lands.

Oak. Several kinds of oak are found in Palestine and adjoining countries. *Quercus sessiliflora* flourishes on lofty Lebanon slopes and in the Hauran. The prickly evergreen oak is found in four varieties. These varieties of oak are found in Carmel, Bashan, and Gilead and often attain considerable size. The deciduous Valonia oak is found in Galilee and Gilead. The Heb. word *'allôn* is apparently the correct Heb. term, for it was a characteristic tree of Bashan (Gen. 35:8; Isa. 2:13; Ezek. 27:6; Zech. 11:2). Another Heb. term for oak is *'ēlâ.* In two passages it is associated with *'allôn* and is translated "terebinth," a rendering frequently used in preference to "oak" (Isa. 6:13; Hos. 4:13). Heb. *'ayil; 'allâ;* and *'ēlôn* are also rendered "oak." The marginal reading of Heb. *tirzâ* in the NASB of Isa. 44:14 is "holm oak," although both the NASB and KJV render "cypress" in the text proper. The NIV translates simply "oak."

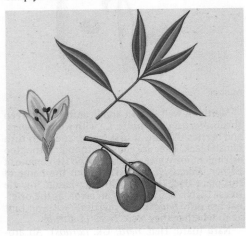

Olive

Olive Tree

Olive (Heb. *zayit;* Gk. from *elaia*). A tree, with leaves of the characteristic dull green at their upper surface and a silvery sheen at their lower, cultivated in all Bible countries. It is alluded to many times in the Bible, often as an emblem of peace, prosperity, and wealth. Much is said of its beauty, fruitfulness, and usefulness to mankind. Its berries and oil are now, as always, leading articles of commerce. Disasters to olive trees are national afflictions, and the failure of the crop is a cause of ruin and considered a sign of divine wrath. The olive berry (Isa. 17:6; James 3:12) is a small drupe, of an oblong ovoid shape, green when young, becoming dark purple, then black, and containing a large amount of oil and a bitter element. The bitter, appetizing taste and the nutritive properties of the berry cause it to be a prime food in all Eastern lands. It is eaten after pickling in brine or preserved in olive oil. Only the fully ripe berries are preserved in the latter way. But the chief value of the olive tree consists in the rich and abundant oil that is expressed from the berry. Large groves of olive trees grow in the neighborhoods of most of the cities of the coast of Syria and Palestine, throughout Lebanon and the hill country of Palestine, Asia Minor, Greece, and Italy. The oil produced from them was one of the chief articles of commerce in ancient eastern Mediterranean lands. Oil forms a large element in the diet of the people, being used for salads, which are an accompaniment to most of their meals, and for frying, in place of butter. It is also much used in the manufacture of soap. It is boiled with crude carbonate of soda, making an excellent grade of hard soap. Considerable quantities are exported to Europe, and the remainder is consumed in the country.

The Heb. expression *'ēṣ shemen* is of uncertain meaning. It occurs only in three connections (1 Kings 6:23, 31-33, "olive"; Neh. 8:15, "wild olive"; Isa. 41:19, marg., "oleaster"). From its name, it evidently denotes some tree rich in oleaginous or resinous matter, the presence of which is a sign of fertility. It is of a size and hardness sufficient to furnish material for a carved image ten cubits high. It grows in the mountains and has foliage suited for booths. But it is not the olive, which is mentioned by name in the same connection (Neh. 8:15); it is some *fatwood* tree, for example, any of the *pines*. It is useless to seek to identify it.

Onions (Heb. *beṣel*). Much as the onion is cultivated and used as an article of food and commerce, it is only mentioned once in the Bible, in connection with the longing of the Israelites in the desert for the good things of Egypt (Num. 11:5). Those familiar with the delicately flavored onions of the East prefer them to the ranker product of the West.

Palm Tree (Heb. *tāmār;* Gk. *phoinix*). The palm tree in Scripture commonly designates the date palm, *Phoenix dactylifera*. Israel encountered seventy palm trees at Elim (Ex. 15:27; Num. 33:9), and the palm was a welcome sight to weary travelers, for it signified rest, shade, and refreshment.

The palm often is eighty feet in height. Its stem ends in a picturesque bunch of leaves. The tree is highly ornamental as well as useful. Its sap yields sugar from which a strong drink called *arrack* is made; and wax, oil, tannin, and dye stuffs are also derived from the palm. Its fruit is highly edible and nourishing and is widely used as food. Even the seeds are ground as food for camels. The leaves are used to cover roofs and for fences, baskets, mats, and other household articles. In the Bible the palms are characterized as "beautiful trees" and were used to celebrate the feast of Booths, or Tabernacles (Lev. 23:40). In

Palm grove in the Jordan valley

Hebrew-Phoenician art they formed a characteristic motif for the Solomonic Temple (1 Kings 6:29; 2 Chron. 3:5; cf. Ezekiel's Temple, Ezek. 40:16; 41:18). The beauty and utility of the palm furnished a lovely figure for the psalmist of the prosperity of the godly (Ps. 92:12). By Christian times the palm came to denote victory (Rev. 7:9). The finest and best palm trees were found around Jericho (sometimes called the "city of palm trees"), Engedi, and along the banks of the Jordan. Normally they live a century and a half to two centuries. The palm tree has a long tap root that goes down to sources of water. The fact that it grows in perennial freshness in almost desert-like conditions makes it a fitting symbol of constancy, patience, uprightness, and prosperity.

Figurative. For the figurative use of *palm, see* the article in the general listing. M.F.U.

Pan'nag (Heb. *pannag;* Ezek. 27:17, marg.), a substance, perhaps the one known by the Arabs as *halâwa*. It is made of a decoction of soapwort root, to which is added syrup of dibs and sesame oil. The mixture is stirred over the fire until the elements are fully incorporated and set aside to crystallize. *Pannag* was, as *halâwa* is now, an article of internal commerce in Palestine and Syria, and exported to other lands. In Akkad. *pannigu* is a kind of cake. The NIV translates in Ezek. 27:17 "confections."

Papyrus. The papyrus is a water plant that grew luxuriantly in ancient times in Egypt and certain sections of Palestine. In ancient times papyrus writing material was made by cutting the pith of the papyrus plant into thin strips, crisscrossing them, and pressing them into sheets. These pale yellow sheets were frequently combined to form rolls from ten to thirty feet long and about nine and one-half inches high. Egyptians sometimes had huge papyrus rolls, such as the 123-foot-long Papyrus Harris. Use of papyrus for writing materials goes back to the Old Kingdom in Egypt, probably before 2700 B.C. The dry Egyptian climate was favorable to the preservation of papyri and some extant copies go back to the third millennium. In antiquity Egypt was a source of supply for ancient paper. Gebal on the Mediterranean coast received papyrus from Egypt, and this center of the paper trade was later called Byblos, meaning "papyrus" or "book" by the Greeks. Our modern word *Bible* through Gk. and Lat. goes back to this source. Leather was used early, and parchment also came into use later. Papyrus reeds tied together to form boats were used in ancient Egypt. Isaiah refers to Ethiopians dispatching messengers by the sea "in papyrus vessels" (18:2). In Egyptian art the papyrus growing in the marshes of the Delta symbolized Lower Egypt. The lotus, on the other hand, stood for Upper Egypt. For further discussion, *see also* Papyrus in the general listing.

M.F.U.; H.F.V.

Papyrus plant

Pine Tree. *See* Box Tree.

Plane Tree (Heb. *'armôn,* "naked"; Gen. 30:37; Ezek. 31:8; the KJV incorrectly renders "chestnut tree"). The plane tree is frequently found in Palestine, on the coast and in the N. Shedding its outward bark, it came by its Heb. name, "smooth," or "naked." Similarly, a scratch in the bark of this tree would at once show a *white streak* (Gen. 30:37). The oriental plane tree (*Plantus orientalis*) grows to a height of some eighty-five feet and has palmately lobed leaves like the sycamore maple. The oriental plane is found in southern Europe and in western Asia. It

Papyrus swamp, Lake Huleh

grows well on hillsides beside streams and is planted artificially in many places.

Pods (Heb. *hiryônîm,* "seed pods," 2 Kings 6:25; Gk. *keration,* "horned"; Luke 15:16). The pods of *Ceratonia siliqua,* L., the *carob tree.* This tree is an evergreen, cultivated everywhere in the Holy Land. The pods are eaten by the people, and a concoction known as *dibs kharrûb,* i.e., *carob honey,* is made from them.

Pome'granate (pom'gran'it), a well-known tree, *Punica granatum,* L., cultivated everywhere in the East. The fruit is spherical, often four inches or more in diameter, green when young, turning red in ripening, with a woody, astringent rind, enclosing a large number of luscious pulpy seeds of a pinkish color. The pomegranate is frequently mentioned in company with the vine, fig, and palm. The rind contains much tannin, and a decoction of it is a remedy against the tapeworm (*see* 1 Sam. 14:2; Song of Sol. 4:13; etc.).

Poplar. The translation of Heb. (*libneh*), Arab. *lubna,* "white tree" (Gen. 30:37; Hos. 4:13). There can be little doubt that *storax* is the correct rendering of the Heb. *Storav officinale,* L., although usually a shrub attains a height of twenty feet, which would answer the requirements of the passage in Hosea. The lower surface of its leaves is white, and it bears a wealth of large white blossoms, which well entitle it to the name of the *white tree.* Its effect on the landscape is similar to that of *Cornus florida,* L., the *flowering dogwood* of the northern woods in the United States.

Raisin. *See* Vine.

Reeds, Rushes. Six Heb. words are used for marsh plants. Two, *'āhû* and *sûp,* are rendered "marsh grass" (Gen. 41:2, 18; both "reeds" in the NIV), "rushes" (Job 8:11; "reeds," NIV), and "reeds" (Ex. 2:3, 5). (The KJV renders "flag" in Job 8:11 for *'āhû* and "flags" in Ex. 2:3, 5; Isa. 19:6 for *sûp.*) Of the remaining four:

1. Heb. *'agmôn* is rendered "reed," "rope," "rush," and "bulrush." It doubtless refers in a general way to swamp plants of the orders *Cyperaceae* and *Gramineae,* and the like.

2. Heb. *gōme'* probably includes the *papyrus, bulrushes, club rushes,* and *twig rush,* i.e., plants of the orders *Juncaceae* and *Cyperaceae.*

3. Heb. *qāneh,* which is cognate with *cane,* may be considered as the equivalent of the English *reed,* taken as that term is in a broad sense. It includes the tall grasses with woody stems, such as *Arundo Donax,* L., the *Persian reed, Saccharum Aegyptiacum,* Willd., and the Arab. *ghazzâr* (both of which may be considered as included under the expression "a reed shaken by the wind," Matt. 11:7). *Phragmites communis,* L., the *true reed. Qāneh* is variously translated "reed," "stalk," "cane," "calamus."

4. Heb. *'ārôt,* translated "bulrushes" (Isa. 19:7; "plants," NIV).

Rose (Heb. *hăbaṣṣelet*). The word occurs in

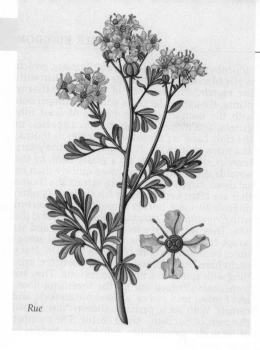

Rue

Song of Sol. 2:1. In Isa. 35:1 it is rendered "crocus." It is probable that *narcissus* is the correct rendering. Two species, *Narcissus Tazetta*, L., and *N. serotinas*, L., grow in the Holy Land. The rose is mentioned in the Apocrypha (Ecclus. 24:14; 39:13). There are seven species of rose that grow in the Holy Land. The most widely distributed of these is *Rosa Phoenicia*, Boiss., which grows on the coast and in the mountains. A pink rose with fragrant petals is cultivated in Damascus for the sake of its essential oil, the famous *attar of roses*. Rose water and syrup of rose leaves are also extensively manufactured throughout the country.

Rue (Gk. *pēganon*). A plant with a penetrating, and to most persons disagreeable, odor. It was tithable (Luke 11:42). The officinal species, *Ruta graveolens*, L., is cultivated. The allied wild species, *R. Chalepensis*, L., is widely diffused throughout the country.

Rush. See Reed.

Rye. See Spelt.

Saffron (Heb. *karkōm;* Song of Sol. 4:14). An aromatic, composed of the styles of several species of crocus, principally *C. cancellatus*, Herb. Bot. They are of an orange color and are principally used to impart an agreeable odor and flavor to boiled rice. The flowerets of *Carthamus tinctorius*, L., known as *safflower*, or *bastard saffron*, are used for a similar purpose.

Saltwort. See Mallows.

Shittah Tree, Shittim Wood. See Acacia.

Spelt. An inferior kind of wheat, the chaff clinging to the grain. The Egyptians used it for bread (Herodotus 2.36). In Egypt it came up after barley. It is the rendering (Ex. 9:32; Ezek. 4:9) of the Heb. *küssmet*. In Isa. 28:25 the rendering is sometimes "rye." The RV and NIV render it in all three passages "spelt." We believe it to be the *kirsenneh*, which is the cognate Arab. for the leguminous plant *Vicia ervilia*, L., a cereal cultivated throughout the East. Rye is unknown in those lands. It would be better to translate *küssemet* by *vetch*, with a marginal note, "the kirsenneh of the Arabs."

Spice, Spicery. Two generic Heb. words for aromatics occur in the OT, *sam* and *besem*. Several of the individual aromatics included under these words are given, such as *frankincense, stacte, onycha, galbanum, myrrh, cinnamon, calamus,* and *cassia* (Ex. 30:23-24, 34). These and numerous other aromatics, among them *nard* and *lign aloes*, were used as perfumes, anointing oils, and incense, and for embalming bodies. *Nekō't* (Gen. 37:25) has been supposed by some to be *gum tragacanth*. We are inclined, however, to regard it as a generic term, translated "spicery," or better, *aromatics*.

Stac'te (stak'ti; Heb. *nāṭāp;* Ex. 30:34). An aromatic; RV marg. "opobalsamum" is not probable. The NIV renders it "gum resin." Nor is it likely that it is *storax*, which we believe to be a product of the plant designated as *libneh* (see Poplar). *Stacte* is in fact *myrrh*, and its Heb. original in the above passage, *nāṭāp*, signifying *drops*, probably refers to *myrrh in tears*. The same word (Job 36:27) is used for *drops of water*.

Stinkweed (Heb. *bo'shâ;* cf. "to be bad" in Heb.; "to have a stench" in Aram.). Mentioned along with briars (Job 31:40; "weeds," NIV), there are multitudes of these in the fields of Palestine and Syria, such as the goose weed, arum, henbane, and mandrake.

Storax. See Myrrh, Poplar, Stacte.

Straw. During the process of oriental threshing, the straw is cut into bits half an inch to two inches in length, and more or less crushed, shredded, pulverized, and mixed with the chaff. This product is known in Arab. as *tibn*, the cognate of the Heb. *teben*, which is usually translated "straw," sometimes incorrectly "chaff" and "stubble." As hay is unknown, this cut straw is its substitute.

Sweet Cane. See Reed.

Sycamore. A fig tree; the rendering in the OT of *shāqām* and *shiqmâ* in the Heb.; Gk. *sukaminos* in the LXX. It is a spreading tree, *Ficus Sysomorus*, L., of the order Urticaceae, often planted by roadsides where it provides a pleasant view for sightseers. It also grows wild and reaches a large size. Its wood is light but durable, and is much used for house carpentry and fuel. It was once abundant in the Holy Land (1 Kings 10:27; etc.) and in Egypt (Ps. 78:47). Its fruit is a small edible fig.

Tamarisk. The tamarisk is a bush tree, highly ornamental, which yields pink and white flowers

Thistle

in spring. A number of species occur in Palestine. It is the correct rendering of Heb. *'ēshel* (Gen. 21:33; 1 Sam. 22:6; 31:13).   M.F.U.

Tares (Gk. *zizanion*); RV *darnel.* Tares are numerous in the grainfields, along with a large number of other species of plants not suitable for human food. They are left until the stalks are well grown, and then, not long before the harvest (Matt. 13:30), women and children, and sometimes men, go carefully among the grain and pull up all but the wheat and barley. Today these weeds are not burned but fed to cattle. If any tares remain unnoticed until the grain is harvested and threshed out, the seeds are separated from the wheat and barley and set aside for poultry. There are four kinds of tares in the Holy Land, by far the most common of which in the grainfields is *Lolium temulentum,* L., or the bearded darnel. It is a poisonous grass, almost indistinguishable from wheat while the two are growing into blade. But when they come into ear, they can be separated without difficulty.

Teil Tree. The better rendering of this KJV term in Isa. 6:13 is "terebinth." *See* Oak.

Terebinth. *See* Oak.

Thicket. *See* Forest.

Thistles, Thorns (including *Bramble, Brier*). Seventeen Heb. words are used for plants with prickles and thorns. Probably most of them once referred to definite species, which we have no means of determining now. It is clear that translators, both ancient and modern, have given up in despair all hope of unraveling the intricacies of the tangle. Thus they have translated these numerous terms to suit their conviction of the needs of the context of the various passages in which they occur. One of them, *sirpād* (Isa. 55:13), is probably not a thorn (but see NIV

"thornbush"), but rather the *elecampane,* which is placed in the above passage in parallelism with the *myrtle.* The number of names for thorny plants, though so large, is small in comparison with the number of such plants. At least fifty genera, and more than two hundred species, in the Holy Land are armed with prickles or thorns, and many more with stinging hairs. If the weary traveler sits confidingly on a grassy bank by the wayside, he is sure to rise more quickly than he sat down, happy if he is able to extract the thorns that are often broken off in his flesh. It is often difficult to force horses through fields overrun with *Eryngiums, Cirsiums, Onopordons,* and the like. They will swerve from side to side, and attempt to leap over their tormentors and sometimes become almost frantic from the pain. Many herbs have heads several inches in diameter, bristling with spines two to six inches long. They are sometimes dragged out on the threshing floors and broken into pieces, as food for donkeys and camels. With such, perhaps, Gideon "disciplined the men of Succoth" (Judg. 8:16). The number of intricate thornbushes suitable for hedges is large (Job 5:5).

The *"crown of thorns"* that was plaited for our Savior's head (Mark 15:17; etc.); Gk. *akanthinos,* may have been composed of *Calycotome villosa,* L., or *Poterium spinosum,* L. *Zizyphus spina-Christi,* L., the traditional Christ thorn, would not have been easy to procure in Jerusalem.

Tow. *See* Flax.

Trees. Trees are valued in this land, mainly for yielding fruit or timber. Systematic planting of shade trees is almost unknown, except in cemeteries and around the tombs of saints. The forests have been greatly reduced in number and contain few large trees (*see* Forest). Some efforts have been made from time to time to acclimatize foreign trees. Solomon appears to have had botanical gardens, and they are mentioned by Josephus as existing in his day. Pliny mentions the palm groves of Jericho. Trees have important symbolical meanings in Scripture. Man fell because of eating the fruit of the "tree of the knowledge of good and evil" and was driven off in the attempt to attain the "tree of life." This tree, in restored paradise, supplies food and medicine for all.

Turpentine. A tree mentioned only in the Apocrypha (Ecclus. 24:16), the turpentine is the *terebinth (butm* of the Arabs), *Pistacia terebinthus,* L., and its variety Palestina (*P. palaestina,* Boiss.). It is generally diffused, the trees being usually solitary, seldom in groves or forests. Another species, *Pistacia muticia,* Fisch et Meyer, is more common E of the Jordan and in Jebel Bil'âs, of the Syrian Desert. Several of the words translated "oak" in the KJV may refer to this tree. *See also* Oak.

Vegetables (Dan. 1:12, 16). A word of far more restricted meaning than the Heb. *zēre'onîm,* or *zērā'ôm,* something "sown," which signifies pri-

Spiny burnet, possibly used to make the "crown of thorns"

marily *vegetables* in general and more particularly *edible seeds that are cooked*, such as *lentils, horse beans, beans, chick-peas,* and the like. Daniel and his companions were pleading for a simple vegetable diet in place of the rich, unwholesome dishes of the king's table.

Vine. A plant mentioned early and frequently in Scripture. It was and is one of the most important sources of livelihood and wealth to the people of the East. It is associated with the *fig, palm,* and *pomegranate* in the enumeration of the products of the land. *Gepen* is generic for *vine, śōrēq* (Jer. 2:21), a "choice vine," and *nāzîr* ("unpruned vine").

Vinegar. Vinegar of excellent quality is made from the light wines of the country. It is uncertain whether the vinegar presented to our Savior on the cross was acid wine or true vinegar.

Vine of Sodom (Deut. 32:32). It is impossible to identify any plant growing near the site of Sodom that corresponds with this poetical allusion. Various plants have been suggested, but none of them fulfills the necessary conditions. The *colocynth* is a vine, but it does not produce clusters or grapelike fruit. The *'ushr, Calotropis procera,* Willd., also bears neither clusters or grapes. *Solanum nigrum,* L., and its allied species, called in Arab. *'inab-edh-dhîb,* "wolf's grapes," have fruits too small to be called grapes, are not vines, and are not peculiar to this region. *Solanum coagulans,* Forsk., is not a vine, and bears fruits like small tomatoes, not grapes. *Cucumis prophetarum,* L., produces no clusters or grapes. In our view it is better to regard the *vine of Sodom* as a poetic creation, similar to the wine in the same passage. The poet, filled with the idea of bitterness suggested by the waters of the Dead Sea, pictures an ideal vine, nourished by this bitter sea, producing bitter clusters,

grapes of gall, the wine of which is dragon's poison and the cruel venom of asps. Such imagery is in strict accord with Heb. poetical license.

Vineyards. Vineyards are often hedged about, but as often not. They are provided with towers or booths for watchmen. The vines must be regularly pruned. *Grapes* are of many kinds in the Holy Land and of superior excellence. The *vintage* takes place in September and October, a season of great rejoicing. The grapes are either eaten as such, or dried into raisins, or the juice expressed in the wine vat and fermented into wine, or boiled down in great caldrons into dibs, i.e., grape honey. Neither the unfermented juice (*mistār*) of the grapes nor the inspissated syrup is known as wine. The latter is never diluted as a beverage.

Weeds (Heb. *sûp;* Jonah 2:5). These are *sea weeds* (Gk. *chortos;* Ecclus. 40:16), *worthless land plants.*

Wheat. Wheat was cultivated in Palestine and adjacent lands at an early period. Palestinian wheat was sown in November or December after the early rains. The harvest was in April, May, or June. Wheat flour constituted the ordinary ingredient of the bread of the Hebrews (Ex. 29:2). The grains were also roasted and eaten. The fertile, well-watered Nile Valley was the granary of the ancient world, particularly in times of famine (Gen. 41:22). Grains of wheat have been found in Egyptian tombs and elsewhere.

Willow. Several species of willows are found in the Holy Land. There are two Heb. words for willow—*ṣapṣāpâ,* the equivalent of the Arab. *sifsâf,* and *'ārāb.* Tradition says that the willow on which the Israelites hung their harps was the *weeping willow,* called from that circumstance *Salix Babylonica,* L. Many places mentioned in Scripture are named from willows.

Wormwood (Heb. *la'ănâ;* Gk. *apsinthos*). Bitter plants growing in waste, usually desert, places. They are an emblem of calamity and injustice. They belong to the genus *Artemisia,* of which there are five species in the tablelands and deserts of Palestine and Syria.   G.F.P.

BIBLIOGRAPHY: M. Zohary, *Plants of the Bible* (1982).

VEIL (Heb. *pārōket*). The screen separating the Holy Place and Most Holy Place in the *Tabernacle* (which see) and *Temple* (which see). It was this piece of tapestry that was rent by the earthquake at Christ's crucifixion (Matt. 27:51; etc.).

VENGEANCE. Punishment inflicted in return for an injury or offense suffered; retribution; often passionate or unrestrained revenge.

1. Heb. *nāqam,* to "grudge," is to punish. In a bad sense, as of an injured person, it is to take vengeance, to avenge oneself (1 Sam. 18:25; Ezek. 25:15), and is the manifestation of *vindictiveness* (Lam. 3:60). When vengeance is predicted of the Lord, it must be taken in the better

sense of righteous punishment (Ps. 94:1; Jer. 11:20; 20:12; etc.)

2. Gk. *'ekdikesis,* "punishment." This word expresses the idea of vindicating one from wrongs (Luke 21:22), avenging an injured person (Acts 7:24).

VENISON. See Game.

VENOM. See Poison; Gall.

VERSIONS OF THE SCRIPTURES. A general name for translations of the Scriptures into other languages than the original. After the Heb. tongue became a dead language in the second century before Christ, and still more after the spread of Christianity, translations of the Heb. Scriptures into the prevailing languages became a necessity. Accordingly, almost every language then current had at least one version, which received ecclesiastical authority, and was used instead of the original Heb. text.

In the case of the NT, there did not for a long time exist any occasion for a translation, since the Gk. language, in which it was written, was universally prevalent in the civilized world at the time of the promulgation of the gospel. In certain provinces of the Roman Empire, however, the Lat. soon came into common use, especially in North Africa, and hence the Old Lat. and afterward the Vulgate (Vulg.) arose. Still later the Syr. version was made for the use of the oriental Christians, to whom that language was vernacular.

This article will deal principally with the Gk. LXX, the Aram. Targums, the Syr. Peshitta and the Lat. Vulg. These ancient versions were made directly from the Heb. The Samaritan Pentateuch (although not strictly a version) will also be discussed, as will also other ancient as well as modern versions.

The Greek Septuagint (LXX). The Heb. OT enjoys the unique distinction of being the first book or rather library of books, for such it is, known to be translated into another language. This translation is called the Septuagint (LXX) and was made in the third and second centuries B.C. During this period the entire Heb. Bible was put into the Gk. language. It was in the reign of Ptolemy Philadelphus (285-246 B.C.) that the Pentateuch was put into the Gk. tongue. Originally the term LXX was applied to the Gk. Pentateuch. Uncertainty is attached to the origin of the LXX, and its beginning is enshrouded in legend. Its alleged seventy-two translators (six from each of the twelve tribes) is traditional, the number seventy apparently being an approximation for seventy-two; or the number seventy may have developed in the course of tradition. Note that Ex. 24:1, 9 refers to the seventy elders of Israel, and the membership of the Sanhedrin was composed of that number (cf. M. Hadas, *Aristeas to Philocrates,* 1951). Certainly by the middle of the

second century B.C. the OT was completely rendered in Gk. The name *Septuagint* was eventually applied to the entire Gk. OT.

Representing a pre-Masoretic Heb. text, the LXX is accordingly of basic textual and exegetical value. However, in evaluating the LXX as a translation, many factors must be kept in mind, such as the general purpose and character of the work, the peculiar difficulties facing translators, and the general principles guiding them in the performance of their task. Surveying the translation in its entirety, it may be said that it varies in its standard of excellence. The Pentateuch is on the whole a close and serviceable translation. The Psalms, on the other hand, and the book of Isaiah show obvious signs of incompetence (cf. H. B. Swete, *Introduction to the O. T. in Greek,* pp. 315ff.). In the latter part of Jeremiah, the Gk., according to R. R. Ottley (*A Handbook to the Septuagint,* p. 110), is "unintelligibly literal." The book of Daniel is mere Midrashic paraphrase.

Use of the Septuagint in Textual Criticism. Scholars readily admit that the LXX cannot be used in a merely mechanical manner to emend the Masoretic text. Although it is indispensable in the textual criticism of the Heb. OT, the varying quality of its translation necessitates great caution. Frequently extreme literalism and freedom of rendering occur in the same verse or in close contact. The translators also employ peculiar exegetical principles. Often expressions concerning God, which were looked upon as crude or offensive, were toned down, and anthropomorphisms were frequently deleted. The translators did not mean to change the original, but their exegetical principles display a theological tendency, which, however, was not consistently carried out. In the past the Septuagint has suffered by comparison with the MT in instances where the two differed. That is to say, readings in the MT were preferred. However, as a result of studies in the Dead Sea Scrolls, the LXX has gained greater favor. For further study of the LXX in textual criticism, *see* C. T. Fritsch, *The Anti-Anthropomorphisms of the Greek Pentateuch* (1943); D. H. Gard, "The Exegetical Method of the Greek Translator of the Book of Job," *Journal of Biblical Literature,* Monograph Series, vol. 8 (1952); J. W. Wevers, "Principles of Interpretation Guiding the Fourth Translator of the Book of the Kingdoms" (3 Kings 22:1-4 Kings 25:30) in *Catholic Biblical Quarterly* 14 (1952): 40-56; "A Study in the Exegetical Principles Underlying the Greek Text of 2 Samuel 11:2 through 1 Kings 2:11," *Catholic Biblical Quarterly* 15 (1953): 30-45; *Text History of the Greek Genesis* (1974); H. F. Gehman, "The Theological Approach of the Greek Translator of Job 1-15," *Journal of Biblical Literature* 68 (1949): 231-40; P. Walters, *The Text of the Septuagint* (1973); D. W. Gooding, *Relics of Ancient Exegesis* (1975); J. G. Janzen, *Studies in the Text of Jeremiah* (1973).

Linguistic Studies of the Septuagint. Important studies on the LXX are included in J. H. Moulton, *Grammar of N. T. Greek,* vol. 1, 3d ed. (1908); and J. H. Moulton and W. F. Howard, *Grammar of N. T. Greek,* vol. 2 (1929). The latter also contains an appendix on Semitisms in the NT. H. St. J. Thackeray, a *Grammar of the O. T. in Greek According to the Septuagint* (1909), is an important volume on Septuagintal studies. Henry Snyder Gehman has a valuable article, "The Hebraic Character of Septuagint Greek," in *Vetus Testamentum* 1 (1951): 81-90; also *Hebraisms of the Old Greek Version of Genesis,* 3 (1953): 141-48; L. C. Allen, *The Greek Chronicles* (1974); J. Reider's *Prolegomena to a Greek-Hebrew and Hebrew-Greek Index to Aquila* (1916), is also an important linguistic study of the LXX.

Handbooks of the Septuagint. H. B. Swete, *An Introduction to the O. T. in Greek,* revised by R. R. Ottley (1914), is an important handbook. R. R. Ottley's *A Handbook to the Septuagint* (1920), is a general work. F. G. Kenyon's *The Text of the Greek Bible* (1937), his *Our Bible and the Ancient Manuscripts,* 5th ed. (1958), and S. Jellicoe's, *The Septuagint and Modern Study* (1968), offer significant studies of the LXX.

Editions of the Septuagint. A. Rahlfs' *Septuaginta,* 2 vols. (1949), and H. B. Swete, *The O. T. in Greek According to the Septuagint,* vol. 1 (1925); vol. 2 (1922), vol. 3 (1912), are standard. Hatch and Redpath have compiled a concordance to the LXX, two volumes and supplement (1897). Very important is the large Cambridge Edition of *The O. T. in Greek* begun under the editorship of A. E. Brooke and N. McLean. Volume 1, *The Octateuch,* appeared in 1906-17. H. St. J. Thackeray edited vol. 2 in conjunction with Brooke and McLean. This was entitled *The Later Historical Books* (Samuel, Kings, Chronicles, Esdras, and Ezra-Nehemiah) (1927-35). Volume 3 appeared in 1940 and contained Esther, Judith, and Tobit by the same three scholars.

Another scholarly edition of the LXX, with copious critical helps, is the *Septuaginta, Vetus Testamentum Graecum (Auctoritate Societatis Litterarum Gottingensis editum).* Volume 9, consisting of *1 Maccabees,* edited by W. Kappler, appeared in 1936. Volume 10, *The Psalms with the Odes,* edited by A. Rahlfs, was published in 1931. Volume 13, *The Twelve Minor Prophets,* came out in 1943. There appeared also vol. 14, *Isaiah* (1939); vol. 16, *Ezekiel* (1952); and *Susannah, Daniel, Bel and the Dragon* (1954).

Early Recensions of the Septuagint. From the place of its origin in Egypt, the LXX spread to all parts of the Hellenistic-Jewish world. Centers such as Antioch, Alexandria, and Caesarea developed different textual traditions. Since the LXX became the OT of the Christians, who employed it in their arguments with the Jews, a need arose for a new rendering of the OT in Gk. that would be true to the Heb. This was accomplished in Aquila's rival Jewish version made around A.D. 130. The work is a slavishly literal Gk. translation of the early second-century Heb. text.

Possibly somewhat earlier than Aquila, Theodotion revised the LXX. His version won wide popularity among Christians. Theodotion's rendering of Daniel prevails in all extant Gk. manuscripts except one. Probably toward the end of the second century Symmachus revised Aquila. By the time of Origen, A.D. 185-254, the text of the LXX had become woefully corrupt. Origen's *Hexapla* was a colossal undertaking to revise the text. It contained five columns in Gk. The first column consisted of the text then current consonantal Heb. The second was composed of the Heb. text rendered in Gk. letters; the third, Aquila's version; the fourth, Symmachus's version; the fifth, the LXX revised by Origen; and the sixth, Theodotion's version.

According to Harry M. Orlinsky, the so-called *Tetrapla* was not a separate form of Origen's critical apparatus, with two columns of the six columns left out. Rather, the designation simply refers to the work as a whole, with the four Gk. columns emphasized instead of all six in the *Hexapla.* Cf. "Origen's Tetrapla—a Scholarly Fiction?" in *World Congress of Jewish Studies* (summer 1947, 1952), pp. 173-82.

Lucian, a scholar at Antioch (d. 311), made a revision of the LXX. The occurrence of Lucianic readings in Old Lat. texts preceding Lucian precipitated grave problems, and an old-Lucian or a pre-Lucianic recension from Antioch in Syria has been postulated by such scholars as James A. Montgomery and Paul Kahle. Kahle has done extensive work in the LXX and does not believe that there was one original old Gk. version and that consequently the manuscripts of the LXX cannot actually be traced back to one archetype. He takes the position that there were earlier renderings of the Pentateuch before the revision made in the time of Ptolomy and that this revision became the standard Gk. Torah. Thus when the church needed a canonical text of the Gk. OT, it took one form of the various texts with revisions and adapted it for Christian use. Cf. *Theologische Studien und Kritiken* (1915), 88:410-26; *The Cairo Geniza* (Schweich Lectures, 1947).

P. de Lagarde, however, saw the problems involved and undertook a correct procedure for recovering the pristine text of the LXX. He was followed by A. Rahlfs, whose *Septuaginta Studien* (3 Heft) appeared in 1911. M. L. Margolis labored to establish the text of the LXX on Lagarde's principles in his *The Book of Joshua in Greek* (1931), parts 1-4 (1–19:38). Cf. Harry M. Orlinsky, "On the Present State of Proto-Septuagint Studies," *Journal of the American Oriental Society* 61 (1941): 81-91. Cf. also "Current Progress in Septuagint Research" in H. R. Willoughby, ed., *The Study of the Bible Today and Tomorrow*

(1947). P. Katz ("Das Problem des Urtextes der Septuaginta," in *Theologische Zeitung* [1949]: 1-24) espouses Lagarde's principles and vindicates Rahlfs's research.

Importance of the Septuagint. The importance of the LXX from every angle can scarcely be over-estimated. This can be asserted despite its deficiencies and limitations. Religiously and spiritually the LXX gave the great revealed truths concerning creation, redemption, sin, and salvation to the world. It released these from the narrow isolation of the Heb. language and people and gave them to the Greco-Roman world through the divinely prepared instrument of the Gk. language, the lingua franca of the Greco-Roman age (300 B.C. to A.D. 300). The LXX was a definite factor in the preparation for the coming of Christianity and the NT revelation. In making the OT available in the same universal language in which the NT was destined to appear, it foreshadowed the giving of the Holy Scriptures in one international and universal language of the period.

The LXX was the Bible of early Christianity before the NT was written. After the NT Scriptures came on the scene, they were added to the LXX to form the completed Scriptures of Christianity.

Besides this momentous ministry, the LXX met the religious and liturgical requirements of Jews living in Alexandria, Egypt. This was the center of culture and learning of ancient Judaism. It also met the needs of Jewish proselytes in the Greco-Roman world in the pre-Christian era, and it was a vital force in both Alexandrian Judaism and philosophy and in the philosophy of the Jewish Diaspora.

Historically as well as religiously and spiritually, the LXX is of immense importance. As the first translation of the Heb. OT into a foreign language, the LXX gained great fame. The very fact that it was put into the language of culture and education of the day made its use wide. Philo of Alexandria used the LXX extensively. Josephus depended upon it. Jesus and the NT writers quoted from it as well as from the Heb. The Jews of the Diaspora used it. However, the schools and synagogues of Palestine venerated the sacred Heb. With the dawn of Christianity the LXX became the Scripture of Christians. It was venerated and quoted and used in controversy. The Old Lat., Egyptian, Ethiopic, Gothic, Slavonic, and other versions were made from it, and it was used in early missionary activity.

The Septuagint and Later Greek Versions. By the beginning of the second century A.D., reaction against the LXX took place in Jewish circles. By this time Christians had come to venerate the LXX as inspired and authoritative and used it in controversy with Jews to prove the messiahship of Jesus. By this time many mistakes had crept into the LXX, and the Jews were particularly annoyed by the use made of it by Christians.

Resulting hostility by Jewish scholars toward the LXX led to Aquila's rival Jewish version. This extremely literal Gk. translation of the second-century Heb. text, made about A.D. 130, became a substitute for the LXX for Jews who spoke Gk. (*see* above). Aquila was trained under Rabbi Akiba and perfected in Jewish tradition. He stuck closely to the literal Heb. text, and for that reason his version is of critical importance.

Theodotion's revision of the LXX was another attempt to bring the LXX into harmony with the current Heb. text. Theodotion was not a disciple of the Jewish rabbis or a slavish literalist. He was enabled to make a version attaining wide acceptance among Christians. Particularly striking was his rendering of Daniel (*see* above). He executed his translation possibly before Aquila. (Cf. H. M. Orlinsky, *Jewish Quarterly Review* N. S. 27 [1936]: 143.)

Another revision of the LXX was made by Symmachus. It was executed toward the end of the second century and was a strong reaction against Aquila's extremely literal rendering. It was revised with the aid of the LXX and Theodotion and aimed at the meaning rather than the mere letter.

Another important milestone in the revision of the LXX was Origen's *Hexapla*. It was an attempt to correct the woefully corrupt Septuagintal text. Origen's labors took place in the first half of the third century A.D. This great scholar went back to the Heb. text to recover the correct text of the Gk. Bible. Precisely, Origen's *Hexapla* consisted of six columns, hexapla meaning sixfold. The first column was in Heb., the consonantal text. The other five columns were in Gk. The second column consisted of the Heb. text given in Gk. letters, the third Aquila's version, the fourth Symmachus's version, the fifth the LXX revised by Origen, the important column, and the sixth, Theodotion's version.

The priceless fifth column was a major critical achievement. The library at Caesarea housed the *Hexapla* until the seventh century A.D. when the city was burned by the Muslims. The sixth column, which had many symbols, was copied and recopied many times. It became separated from the rest of the work. The critical symbols were more or less incomprehensible. Happily, a Syr. translation of part of the fifth column with critical symbols is in existence, containing the poetic and prophetic books. It is in the Ambrosian Library at Milan. The first volume, containing the Pentateuch and the historical books, was in existence in 1574. Subsequently, however, it has disappeared. Fragments of the so-called Syro-Hexaplaric version exist in the British Museum.

Other revisions of the LXX include that of Lucian, a scholar at Antioch in the fourth century. This recension was used at Antioch and Constantinople. In Egypt, Hesychius made another revision, but little is known of this.

Manuscripts of the Septuagint. The oldest and most important of the LXX manuscripts are the following:

Codex Vaticanus (B). This valuable vellum manuscript is the property of the Roman Catholic church. Dating from the second quarter of the fourth century A.D., it came to light in 1481 when it first appeared in the Vatican Library catalog. Vaticanus offers the best text of the LXX as a whole for the OT. It contains Theodotion's translation of Daniel. In 1828-38, Cardinal A. Mai edited this great codex, but it was not made accessible to the scholarly world at large until 1889-90, when the Vatican issued a photographic facsimile of the entire contents.

Codex Alexandrinus (A). Its fame derives from the fact that in 1078 it was presented to the Patriarch of Alexandria. The National Library of the British nation came into possession of the famous manuscript in the seventeenth century, and it is now in the British Museum. It dates from the middle of the fifth century A.D. and is Egyptian in origin. This uncial codex gives the OT and the NT. Notable lacunae are Genesis, 1 Samuel, and Psalms. Apparently it generally follows Origen's Hexaplaric edition of the LXX, but contains earlier readings.

St. Catherine's monastery, where the Codex Sinaiticus was discovered in the nineteenth century

Codex Sinaiticus (Aleph [א]). This dates from the fourth century. It was discovered by Constantine Tischendorf in the famous monastery of St. Catherine's on Mt. Sinai in the middle of the nineteenth century. Codex Sinaiticus is one of the prized possessions of the British Museum, having been purchased from the Soviet Union in 1933 for more than half a million dollars. The fragments were published at various periods by the discoverer. E. Nestle collected them in a supplement to the sixth and seventh editions of Tischendorf's *Vetus Testamentum Graece* (1880-87).

Codex Ephraemi Rescriptus (C). This codex is in the Bibliothèque Nationale in Paris and dates around the fifth century A.D. The biblical text on its sixty-four OT leaves has been erased to make room for a treatise for St. Ephraim of Syria in the twelfth century. It is thus a palimpsest, and the underlying biblical text can be deciphered only with great difficulty.

Codex Cottonianus (D) and the Bodleian Genesis (E). These contain large portions of Genesis and are to be listed with the more important uncials.

Scripts Used in Septuagint Manuscripts. Septuagint manuscripts are fortunately quite numerous in the world's libraries. The earliest are called uncials and the later, cursives. The former are written in separate capital letters and the latter in small flowing script. There are about 240 uncial manuscripts now in existence. Many cursives exist. Collations of large numbers of LXX manuscripts are given in the still indispensable edition of R. Holmes and J. Parson, *Vetus Testamentum Graece cum Variis lectionibus*, 5 vols. (1798-1827). The "Larger Cambridge Septuagint," ed. A. E. Brooke and N. McLean, vol. 1 (1906, etc.), also contains fragmentary manuscripts. Rahlfs's *Septuaginta* (1935), is based principally on the three great uncial codices, Aleph (א), A, and B, with selective variants of other sources collated in the small critical apparatus. It is of primary critical importance.

The Aramaic Targums. These are free paraphrastic renderings of the Heb. Scriptures into Aram. The word itself comes from an Aram. quadri-literal verb *trgm* meaning "to translate from one language to another" or "to interpret." When Aram. supplanted Heb., an interpreter was needed after each verse of the Heb. Bible was read in order to render the passage freely in the language of the people. For a long time oral, the Targums were finally written down. The original Palestinian Targums of the Law and the Prophets (those of the Writings are later) date from the second century A.D. They were edited in Babylonia during the third century and are extant in the form of late recensions.

The Targum of Onkelos. The oldest and best Targum on the Pentateuch is the one designated Onkelos. Five good-sized pieces, placed by scholars about A.D. 700-900, of a Palestinian Pentateuchal Targum differing from Onkelos were discovered in a genizah (storeroom or repository) of an ancient synagogue in Old Cairo. Freely paraphrastic with Haggadic addition, it displays an underlying Heb. consonantal text differing from the Masoretic. Paul Kahle describes the Aram. as stemming from the first century, representing, he claims, a much earlier stage in the history of the Targums than that of the other Targums.

The Targum of Jonathan. The Targum of Jonathan on the Prophets is the oldest and the official Targum on the Prophets (Joshua, Kings, Isaiah, and the minor prophets). It is much more paraphrastic than Onkelos and often becomes a running commentary. It was revised in Palestine, rewritten in Babylon in the fourth and fifth centuries, and survives in a different recension in the Codex Reuchlinianus, edited by P. de Lagarde in 1872. The Targums on the Hagiographa are several in number; one on the Psalms, Job, and Proverbs is in existence and another on the Rolls (Song of Solomon, Ruth, Lamentations, Ecclesiastes, and Esther). Another is extant on Chronicles. The Targum on Esther appeared in three recensions, attesting its wide popularity. The Targums on the Megilloth (rolls) and on Chronicles seemingly belong to an ancient Jerusalem Targum on the *Kethubim.*

Targum of Jonathan-ben-Uzziel and Jerushalmi-Targum on the Pentateuch. Onkelos and Jonathan on the Pentateuch and Prophets, whatever be their exact date, place, authorship, and editorship, are the oldest of existing Targums and belong, in their present shape, to Babylon and the Babylonian academies flourishing between the third and fourth centuries A.D. The one extending from the first verse of Genesis to the last of Deuteronomy is known by the name of Targum Jonathan (ben Uzziel), or Pseudo-Jonathan, on the Pentateuch. The other, interpreting single verses, often single words only, is extant in the following proportions: a third on Genesis, a fourth on Deuteronomy, a fifth on Numbers, three-twentieths on Exodus, and approximately one-fourteenth on Leviticus. The latter is generally called *Targum Jerushalmi,* or, down to the eleventh century (Hai Gaon, Chananel), *Targum Erets Israel,* Targum of Jerusalem, or of the Land of Israel. Not before the first half of this century did the fact become fully and incontestably established that both Targums were in reality one —that both were known down to the fourteenth century under no other name than Targum Jerushalmi—and that some forgetful scribe, about that time, must have taken the abbreviation *"y, " "j"* (T. J.) over one of the two documents, and instead of dissolving it into Targum-Jerushalmi, dissolved it erroneously into what he must until then have been engaged in copying, namely, Targum-Jonathan, scribe ben Uzziel (on the Prophets).

Targums of Joseph the Blind on the Hagiographa. The Targums on the Hagiographa that we now possess have been attributed vaguely to different authors, it being assumed in the first instance that they were the work of one man. Popular belief fastened upon Joseph the Blind. Yet, if ever he did translate the Hagiographa, it is certain that those we possess are not by his or his disciples' hands, i.e., of the time of the fourth century. Between him and our hagiographical Targums, many centuries must have elapsed.

Targum on the Book of Chronicles. This Targum was unknown up to a recent period. In 1680 it was edited for the first time from an Erfurt manuscript by M. F. Beck, and in 1715 from a more complete as well as correct manuscript at Cambridge, by D. Wilkins. The name of Hungary occurring in it and its frequent use of the Jerusalem-Targum to the Pentateuch, amounting sometimes to simple copying, show sufficiently that its author is neither "Jonathan B. Uzziel" nor "Joseph the Blind," as has been suggested. But the language, style, and the Haggadah, with which it abounds, point to a late period and to Palestine as the place where it was written. Its use must be limited to philological, historical, and geographical studies.

The Targum to Daniel. Munk found it, not indeed in the original Aram., but in what appears to him to be an extract of it written in Persian.

Apocryphal Pieces of Esther. There is also an Aram. translation extant of the apocryphal pieces of Esther.

The Syriac Peshitta. The spread of Christianity into Syria necessitated the translation of the Bible into the Syr. language. Syriac belongs to the Aram. branch of the Semitic languages and might be termed "Christian Aramaic."

The Old Syriac. Although no manuscript of the Old Syr. version has survived, nevertheless such a translation existed and preceded the later Peshitta Syr. version. This is proved from quotations in St. Ephraem's Commentaries on the Acts and Pauline epistles preserved in the Armenian tongue. Cf. Conybeare in J. H. Ropes, *The Text of Acts* (1926), pp. 373-453. Old Syr. variants persist in church writers down to the twelfth century, as Vööbus's researches have demonstrated. This Old Syr. version probably stems from Edessa. C. C. Torrey, however, maintains that Palestine was the place of its origin (*Documents of the Primitive Church* [1941], pp. 345-70).

The Peshitta Syriac Version. The common Syr. Bible, corresponding to the Vulg. of the Lat., after the ninth century A.D. came to be known as the Peshitta. This expression denotes "simple," presumably to differentiate it from the symbols and complexities of the Syro-Hexaplaric version, based on the LXX as found in Origen's *Hexapla.* A number of scholars are of the opinion that the Peshitta of the OT, particularly of the Pentateuch, is of Jewish or Christian-Jewish origin. R. H. Pfeiffer, *Introduction to the O. T.* (1941), p. 120; A. Baumstark, *Geschichte der syrischen Literatur* (1922), p. 18; J. Block, *American Journal of Semitic Languages* 35 (1919): 215-22.

Books such as Genesis, 2 Samuel, and Psalms display influence from the Septuagint. Proverbs is a free translation but faithful to the original as a whole. Chronicles is quite paraphrastic, like the Targums. Esther is a good translation of the Heb. Ezra and Lamentations stick close to the MT.

The Palestinian Syriac. The Pentateuch of this version, scholars commonly maintain, was made from the LXX. However, some authorities are of the opinion that it refers back to a Jewish-Palestinian Pentateuch Targum. Cf. Baumstark, *Oriens Christianus*, 3d series, vol. 10, pp. 201-24.

The Philoxenian Syriac. The difficulty here is whether the Philoxenian Syr. version was reissued by Thomas of Heraclea (Harclean Syr.) or whether the second was an entirely new version. Be this as it may, in the Acts of the Apostles the textual variants of the Harclean Syr. are of such weight that they are second only to Codex Bezae in significance for the Western text. Cf. Guenther Zuntz, *The Ancestry of the Harklean N. T.* (1945).

Vulgate. The term *Vulgate* is the popular name given to the common Lat. version of the Bible, usually attributed to Jerome. This version should be of a deep interest to all the Western churches. For many centuries it was the only Bible generally used; and, directly or indirectly, it is the real parent of all the vernacular versions of western Europe. The Gothic version of Ulphilas alone is independent of it. In the age of the Reformation the Vulg. was the guide rather than the source of the popular versions. That of Luther (NT, in 1523) was the most important, and in this the Vulg. had great weight. From Luther the influence of the Lat. passed to our own King James Version. But the claims of the Vulg. to the attention of the scholars rest on wider grounds. It is not only the source of our current theological terminology, but it is, in one shape or other, the most important early witness to the text and interpretation of the whole Bible.

Name. The name *Vulgate,* which is equivalent to *Vulgata editio* (the *current* text of Holy Scripture), has necessarily been used differently in various ages of the church. There can be no doubt that the phrase originally answered to the *koinē ekdosis* of the Gk. Scriptures. In this sense it is used constantly by Jerome in his commentaries.

The Old Latin Versions. The history of the earliest Lat. version of the Bible is lost in obscurity. All that can be affirmed with certainty is that it was made in Africa. During the first two centuries the church of Rome was essentially Greek-speaking. The same condition was true of Gaul; but the church of North Africa seems to have been Latin-speaking from the first. At what date this church was founded is uncertain. It is from Tertullian that we must seek the earliest testimony to the existence and character of the *Old Latin* (*Vetus Latina*). On the first point the evidence of Tertullian, if candidly examined, is decisive. He

distinctly recognizes the general currency of a Lat. version of the NT, although not necessarily of every book at present included in the canon. This was characterized by a "rudeness" and "simplicity" that seem to point to the nature of its origin. The version of the NT appears to have arisen from individual and successive efforts; and the work of private hands would necessarily be subject to revision for ecclesiastical use. The separate books would be united in a volume, and thus a standard text of the whole collection would be established. With regard to the OT the case is less clear. It is probable that the Jews who were settled in North Africa were confined to the Greek towns; otherwise it might be supposed that the Lat. version of the OT is in part anterior to the Christian era, and that (as in the case of Gk.) a preparation for a Christian Lat. dialect was already made when the gospel was introduced into Africa. However this may have been, the substantial similarity of the different parts of the OT and the NT establishes a connection between them and justifies the belief that there was one popular Lat. version of the Bible current in Africa in the last quarter of the second century.

With regard to the African canon of the NT, the old version offers important evidence. From considerations of style and language, it seems certain that the epistle to the Hebrews, James, and 2 Peter did not form part of the original African version. In the OT, on the other hand, the Old Lat. erred by excess and not by defect.

The Labors of Jerome. At the close of the fourth century the Lat. texts of the Bible current in the Western church had fallen into the greatest corruption. The evil was yet greater in prospect than at the time, for the separation of the East and West was growing imminent. But in the crisis of danger the great scholar was raised up who probably alone, for 1,500 years, possessed the qualifications necessary for producing an original version of the Scriptures for the use of the Lat. churches. Jerome (Eusebius Hieronymus) was born in A.D. 329, at Stridon, in Dalmatia, and died at Bethlehem A.D. 420. After long and self-denying studies in the East and West, Jerome went to Rome in A.D. 382, probably at the request of Damasus, the pope, to assist in an important synod. His active biblical labors date from this epoch. In examining them it will be convenient to follow the order of time, noticing (1) the revision of the Old Lat. version of the NT; (2) the revision of the Old Lat. version (from the Gk.) of the OT; (3) the new version of the OT from the Heb.

Jerome had not been long in Rome (A.D. 383) when Damasus asked him to make a revision of the current Lat. version of the NT with the help of the Gk. original. "There were," he says, "almost as many forms of text as copies." The gospels had naturally suffered most. Jerome therefore applied himself to these first. But his aim was to revise the Old Lat. and not to make a new version. Yet, although he had this limited objective, the various forms of corruption that had been introduced were, as he describes them, so numerous that the difference of the old and revised (Hieronymian) text is clear and striking throughout. Some of the changes Jerome introduced were made purely on linguistic grounds, but it is impossible to ascertain on what principle he proceeded in this respect. Others involved questions of interpretation. But the greater number consisted in the removal of the interpolations by which especially the synoptic gospels were disfigured. This revision, however, was hasty.

Jerome next undertook the revision of the OT from the LXX. About the same time (about A.D. 383) at which he was engaged on the revision of the NT, Jerome undertook also a first revision of the Psalter. This he made with the help of the Gk., but the work was not complete or careful. This revision was called the *Roman* Psalter, probably because it was made for the use of the Roman church at the request of Damasus. In a short time "the old error prevailed over the new correction." Therefore, at the urgent request of Paula and Eustochium, Jerome commenced a new and more thorough revision (Gallican Psalter). The exact date at which this was made is not known. But it may be fixed with great probability very shortly after A.D. 387, when he retired to Bethlehem, and certainly before 391, when he had begun his new translations from the Heb. In the new revision Jerome attempted to represent as far as possible, by the help of the Gk. version, the real reading of the Heb. This new edition soon obtained wide popularity. Gregory of Tours is said to have introduced it from Rome into the public services in France, and from this it obtained the name of the *Gallican* Psalter. Numerous manuscripts remain containing the Lat. Psalter in two or more forms. From the second (Gallican) revision of the Psalms, Jerome appears to have proceeded to a revision of the other books of the OT, restoring all, with the help of the Gk., to generally conform with the Heb. The revised texts of the Psalter and Job have alone been preserved, but there is no reason to doubt that Jerome carried out his design of revising all the "canonical Scriptures." He speaks of this work as a whole in several places and distinctly represents it as a Lat. version of Origen's Hexaplar text (although the reference may be confined to the Psalter, which was the immediate subject of discussion). But though it seems certain that the revision was made, there is great difficulty in tracing its history.

The next work of Jerome was the translation of the OT from the Heb. This version was not undertaken with any ecclesiastical sanction, as the revision of the gospels was, but at the urgent request of private friends. Or it was from his own sense of the imperious necessity of the work. Its

history is told in the main in the prefaces to the several installments that were successively published. The books of Samuel and Kings were issued first, and to these he prefixed the famous *Prologus galeatus*, addressed to Paula and Eustochium, in which he gave an account of the Heb. canon. At the time when this was published (about A.D. 391-92), other books seem to have been already translated. In 393 the sixteen prophets were in circulation, and Job had recently been put into the hands of Jerome's most intimate friends. Indeed, it would appear that already in 392 he had in some sense completed a version of the OT; but many books were not completed and published until some years afterward. The next books he put into circulation, but with the provision that they should be confined to friends, were Ezra and Nehemiah. He translated them at the request of Dominica and Rogatianus, who had urged him to carry out the task for three years. This was probably in the year 394, for in the preface he alludes to his intention of discussing a question he treats in *Epistle* 57, written in 395. In the preface to the Chronicles he alludes to the same epistle as "lately written," and these books may therefore be set down for that year. The three books of Solomon followed (A.D. 398), having been "the work of three days," when he had just recovered from the effects of a severe illness. The *Octateuch* (i.e., Pentateuch, Joshua, Judges, Ruth, and Esther) was probably issued after A.D. 400. The remaining books were completed at the request of Eustochius, shortly after the death of Paula (A.D. 404).

Thus the present Vulg. contains elements belonging to every period and form of the Lat. version: (1) Unrevised Old Latin: Wisdom, Ecclus., 1 and 2 Macc., Baruch; (2) Old Latin revised from the LXX: Psalter; (3) Jerome's free translation from the original text: Judith, Tobit; (4) Jerome's translation from the original: OT except Psalter; (5) Old Latin revised from manuscripts: Gospels; (6) Old Latin cursorily revised: the remainder of NT.

Revision of Alcuin. Meanwhile the text of the different parts of the Lat. Bible were rapidly deteriorating, the simultaneous use of the old and new versions necessarily leading to great corruptions of both texts. Mixed texts were formed according to the taste or judgment of scribes, and the confusion was furthur increased by changes introduced by those having some knowledge of the Gk. The growing corruption, which could not be checked by private labor, attracted the attention of Charlemagne, who entrusted to Alcuin (about A.D. 802) the task of revising the Lat. text for public use. This Alcuin appears to have done simply by the use of manuscripts of the Vulg. and not by reference to the original texts. Alcuin's revision probably contributed much toward preserving a good Vulg. text. The best manuscripts of his recension do not differ widely from the pure Hieronymian text, and his authority must have done much to check the spread of the interpolations that reappear afterward and that were derived from the inter-mixture of the old and new versions. But the new revision was gradually deformed, though later attempts at correction were made by Lanfranc of Canterbury (A.D. 1089), Cardinal Nicolaus (A.D. 1150), and the Cistercian abbot Stephanus (about A.D. 1150).

Page from the Lindisfarne Gospels, A.D. 700

History of the Printed Text. It was a noble omen for the future of printing that the first book issued from the press was the Bible; and the splendid pages of the *Mazarin Vulgate* (Mainz: Gutenberg and Fust) stand yet unsurpassed by the latest efforts of typography. This work is referred to about the year 1455 and presents the common text of the fifteenth century. Other editions followed in rapid succession. The first collection of various readings appears in a Paris edition of 1504, and others followed at Venice and Lyons in 1511, 1513; but Cardinal Ximenes (1502-17) was the first who seriously revised the Lat. text, to which he assigned the middle place of honor in his polyglot between the Heb. and Gk. texts. This was followed in 1528 (2d edition, 1532) by an edition of R. Stephens. About the same time various attempts were made to correct the Lat. from the original texts (Erasmus, 1516; Pagninus, 1518-28; Cardinal Cajetanus; Steuchius, 1529; Clarius, 1542), or even to make a new Lat. version (Jo. Campensis, 1533). A more important edition of R. Stephens followed in 1540, in which he made use of twenty manuscripts and introduced considerable alterations into his for-

mer text. In 1541 another edition was published by Jo. Benedictus at Paris, which was based on the collation of manuscripts and editions, and was often reprinted afterward. Vercellone speaks much more highly of the *Biblia Ordinaria*, with glosses, etc., published at Lyons, 1545, as giving readings in accordance with the oldest manuscripts, though the sources from which they are derived are not given.

The Sixtine and Clementine Vulgates. The first session of the Council of Trent was held on December 13, 1545. After some preliminary arrangements the Nicene Creed was formally declared as the foundation of the Christian faith on February 4, 1546, and then the council proceeded to the question of the authority, text, and interpretation of Holy Scripture. A committee was appointed to report upon the subject; it held private meetings from February 20 to March 17. Considerable varieties of opinion existed as to the relative value of the original and Lat. texts, and the final decree was intended to serve as a compromise. In affirming the authority of the "old Vulgate" it contains no estimate of the value of the original texts. A papal board was engaged upon the work of revision, but it was currently reported that the difficulties of publishing an authoritative edition were insurmountable. Nothing further was done toward the revision of the Vulg. under Gregory XIII, but preparations were made for an edition of the LXX. This appeared in 1587, in the second year of the pontificate of Sixtus V, who had been one of the chief promoters of the work. After the publication of the LXX, Sixtus immediately devoted himself to the production of an edition of the Vulg. He himself revised the text, and when the work was printed he examined the sheets with the utmost care and corrected the errors with his own hand. The edition appeared in 1590, with the famous constitution *Aeternus ille* (dated March 1, 1589) prefixed, in which Sixtus affirmed with characteristic decision the plenary authority of the edition for all future time. He further expressly forbade the publication of various readings in copies of the Vulg. Upon the accession of Gregory XIV, a commission was appointed to revise the Sixtine text, under the presidency of the Cardinal Colonna (Columna). At first the commissioners made but slow progress, and it seemed likely that a year would elapse before the revision was completed. The mode of proceeding was therefore changed, and the commission moved to Zagorolo, the country seat of Colonna. If we may believe the inscription that still commemorates the event, and the current report of the time, the work was completed in *nineteen days.* The task was hardly finished when Gregory died (October 1591), and the publication of the revised text was again delayed. His successor, Innocent IX, died within the same year, and at the beginning of 1592 Clement VIII was raised to the papacy.

Clement entrusted the final revision of the text to Toletus, and the whole was printed before the end of 1592.

Revision of the Vulgate. Revision of the Lat. Vulg. was undertaken by the Roman Catholic church in 1907. Pope Pius X delegated Abbot Gasquet, leader of the English Benedictines, as head of a commission to revise the Vulg. text. Nine volumes have appeared: Genesis (1926); Exodus, Leviticus (1929); Numbers, Deuteronomy (1936); Joshua, Judges, Ruth (1939); Samuel (1944); Kings (1945); Chronicles (1948); Ezra, Tobias, Judith (1950); Esther, Job (1951). However, the rule for evaluating variant readings for the revised Vulg. has been subject to serious challenge by many critics, namely, E. K. Rand, Stummer, and Chapman.

In 1941 the Roman church began a new translation of the Psalms directly from the Heb. This work appeared in 1944. In 1945 a second edition came from the press with the seventeen canticles in the OT and NT that are used in the Roman Breviary. *See* Augustinus Bea, *Il Nuova salterio latino* (2d ed., 1946), in French (1948) and in German (1949).

Augustinus Bea put out his Lat. rendering of the book of Ecclesiastes in 1950. Faithfulness to the original Heb. was aimed at, but the Lat. Vulg., as well as other versions, exerted strong influence.

The Samaritan Pentateuch. Actually, the Samaritan Pentateuch is not a version of a portion of the Heb. OT, but is a part of the text itself. It is an independent text of the Pentateuch that has had its own distinct transmission by scribes from the fifth century B.C. without any known contacts with the numerous Heb. texts.

Origin. After the return of the Jews from the Babylonian captivity in 530 B.C., the Samaritans offered their aid in rebuilding the Jewish Temple. They became persistent enemies of the Jews when their offer was refused and did all in their power to hinder the work of building (Ezra 4). At the time of Nehemiah they continued their opposition. They did their best to stop the building of the walls of Jerusalem. Under Nehemiah's regime the grandson of the high priest Eliashib was discovered to have married the daughter of Sanballat, the governor of Samaria and a bitter foe of the Jews. Nehemiah expelled the offender along with others who would not commit themselves to the general reformation (Neh. 13:28-30). This incident, which took place around 432 B.C., has been widely regarded as furnishing the historical background of the Samaritan split.

Josephus, the historian of the first century A.D., misplaces the story a century later in the time of Alexander the Great. He actually names the expelled priest as Manasseh and declares that he took with him a copy of the law when he fled to Samaria and established the rival cult in the Mt. Gerizim temple. This, undoubtedly, is the tradi-

tional basis of the Jewish-Samaritan hostility, with a rival temple and priesthood on Mt. Gerizim at Shechem, and a rival torah as the sacred book of the new religious system.

Critical Value. The first appearance of the Samaritan Pentateuch to the modern scholarly world in 1616 aroused great hopes of its high textual value. It has, however, failed to fulfill these expectations. Gesenius, the celebrated Hebraist, in 1815 attributed little critical help to the Samaritan Pentateuch, holding that in scarcely a single instance was it superior to the Masoretic reading. The sweeping character of Gesenius's conclusions has not been accepted in recent years by all scholars. The tendency is to give more consideration to Samaritan readings. However, there are several considerations tending to decrease the critical importance of the Samaritan Pentateuch. First, it covers the best-preserved part of the OT. The law of Moses is not only the best-preserved portion of the Heb. Bible but the best-translated part. It is, accordingly, the section needing least correction and benefiting least from an independent textual tradition.

Second, the bulk of the variations from the Heb. text are unimportant. It varies from the traditional MT in some 6,000 cases, agreeing with the Septuagint in about 1,900 instances. A large proportion of those are quite insignificant as affecting the meaning of the passage. Only a few are actually important. Cf. Paul Kahle in *Theologische Studien und Kritiken* 88 (1915): 399-429.

A. Sperber is of the opinion that the grammatical variations are to some degree explainable on the thesis that the Samaritan text retains North Israelite dialectal peculiarities, whereas the MT preserves a southern or Judean dialectal tradition (*Hebrew Union College Annual* 12-13 [1937-38]: 151ff.). H. M. Wiener, *The Expositor,* 8th series, 2 (1911): 200-219, demonstrates that when the Gk. version diverges most from the MT, the Samaritans followed the latter with great closeness.

From about fifty quotations preserved on the notes in Origen's *Hexapla,* it is now known that there was a Gk. translation of the Samaritan Pentateuch known as the Samariticon. Discovery of fragments of the version (Gen. 37; Deut. 24-29; ed. P. Glaue and A. Rahlfs, *Mitteilungen des Septuaginta-Unternehmens,* vol. 2 [1911]) point to the conclusion that it was executed from the Samaritan Pentateuch by translators who knew the Septuagint.

Paul Kahle's research has shown that several Arab. versions of the Samaritan Pentateuch were made from the eleventh to the thirteenth century (cf. *The Cairo Geniza,* pp. 36-39).

In the third place, the manuscripts of the Samaritan Pentateuch are of a late date. The eighteenth-century textual critic Kennicott collected sixteen Samaritan manuscripts, none of those being as old as the oldest Heb. manuscripts. The one in the New York Library dates from A.D. 1232 and is the oldest. The first copy of the Samaritan Pentateuch to reach Europe, after a millennium of oblivion, was taken there by the Italian traveler Pietro della Valle from the Samaritan community in Damascus. It appeared in the *Paris Polyglot* (1645) and the *London Polyglot* (1657). The Samaritan Pentateuch was known to Origen, Eusebius of Caesarea, Ephiphanius, etc., a millennium before, but subsequently was lost to scholarship.

History. The Samaritan Pentateuch is found vaguely quoted by some of the early Fathers of the church, under the name of "the old Hebrew according to the Samaritans." Eusebius of Caesarea observes that the LXX and the Samaritan Pentateuch agree against the received text in the number of years from the Deluge to Abraham. Cyril of Alexandria speaks of certain words (Gen. 4:8) not present in the Heb., but found in the Samaritan. The Talmud, on the other hand, mentions the Samaritan Pentateuch distinctly and contemptuously as a clumsily forged record. Down to within the last 250 years, however, no copy of this divergent code of laws had reached Europe, and it began to be pronounced a fiction, and the plain words of the church Fathers—the better-known authorities—who quoted it, were subjected to subtle interpretations. Suddenly, in 1616, Pietro della Valle, one of the first discoverers also of the cuneiform inscriptions, acquired a complete codex from the Samaritans in Damascus. In 1623 it was presented by Achille Harley de Saucy to the Library of the Oratory in Paris, and in 1628 there appeared a brief description of it by J. Morinus in his preface to the Roman text of the LXX. It was published in the Paris Polyglot, whence it was copied, with few emendations from other codices, by Walton. The number of manuscripts in Europe gradually grew to sixteen. During the present century another fragmentary copy was acquired by the Gotha Library. A copy of the Pentateuch with Targum (? Samaritan version) in parallel columns, quarto, on parchment, was taken from Nâblus by Grove in 1861 for the Comte de Paris.

Perhaps the main contribution of the Samaritan Pentateuch to modern criticism is its striking attestation to the substantial accuracy of the MT. It is, as we have seen, in striking agreement with the text except in mostly unimportant variations.

Other Ancient Versions. As Christianity spread, new Scripture versions began to appear.

The Coptic Version. The conversion to Christianity of the native Egyptians unfamiliar with Gk., beginning in the third century, resulted in the formation of a Coptic, or Egyptian, church and created a need for a translation of the Bible into Coptic dialects. The earliest version, completed about 350, is the Sahidic, the dialect of Upper Egypt. Translations were also made into Akhmimic, also Upper Egypt; Fayumic, Middle Egypt; and Bohairic, around Alexandria. All of these versions were made from fourth-century LXX texts but contained occasional earlier readings (cf. Henry Snyder Gehman, *Journal of Biblical Literature* 46 [1927]:279-330; Coptic biblical manuscripts are available in the *Bibliothecae Pierpont Morgan codices coptici photographice expressi* . . . [1922], 56 vols.). Winifred Kammerer, *A Coptic Bibliography* (1950), describes the contents of these volumes.

Gehman's textual researches on Daniel demonstrate that the Sahidic version reflects a blending of Origen's Hexaplaric text, Theodotion, and Hesychius. He found, moreover, that the Bohairic was made from the Hexaplaric text affected by Hesychius. Sahidic Acts shows close connection with Codex Vaticanus.

The Ethiopic Version. Christianity was introduced into Abyssinia by Christian missionaries in the fourth century. Between the fifth and eighth centuries the Bible was translated into Ethiopic. Scholars say that outside of Abyssinia there exist about twelve hundred manuscripts of various parts of the Ethiopic Bible, most of them dating late (from the sixteenth to the eighteenth century). Most of these, it is shown, were revised with the aid of Arab. translations. The Ethiopic Bible does not show signs of a single unified text influenced throughout by the same Gk. source. Gleave's studies uphold Charles's thesis that the Ethiopic reflects Symmachus's Gk. and shows signs of Origen's *Hexapla*. Montgomery believes translators followed the Gk. text in the NT slavishly at times and in other instances they paraphrased loosely where the passage was too difficult for them (cf. James A. Montgomery, "The Ethiopic Text of Acts of the Apostles," *Harvard Theological Review* 27 [1934]:169-205).

The Arabic Versions. The rapid expansion of Islam after the death of Mohammed (632) disseminated the Arab. language and created a need for an Arab. translation. The first recorded version is that of John, Bishop of Seville, made in 724, a dozen years after the Muslims overran Spain. Saadia Gaon's version made from the Heb. (tenth century) was the first and most important Arab. version among the Jews. Two Arab. versions were current in Egypt, one from the Bohairic dialect and the other from the Sahidic. Both were influenced by the Heb. and Samaritan texts.

Bucking traditional scholarly opinion, a number of investigators have favored a pre-Islamic date for the early Arab. versions (cf. Curt Peters, *Acta orientalia* 18 [1940]: 124-37; Anton Baumstark, *Islamica* 4 [1931]:562-75). The Arab. text of the prophetic books in the Paris Polyglot was translated at Alexandria, Egypt, from a Gk. text, according to Vaccari, which was close to Codex Alexandrinus (*Biblica* 2 [1921]: 401-23; 3 [1922]: 401-23; 4 [1923]: 312-14).

The Armenian and Georgian Versions. The Armenian Bible came into existence as a nationalistic and religious reaction against the use of Syr. in public worship, a language incomprehensible to the common people. According to Moses of Chorene, Mesrop, the inventor of the Armenian alphabet, at the beginning of the fifth century began a translation of the Bible from the Syr. According to Lazar of Pharphi, the translation was made not from the Syr. but from the Gk. Modern critics argue the point. J. A. Robinson, Conybeare, Merk, Blake, and Baumstark hold that it was translated from the Syr. Macler, Colwell, and Lyonnet hold that it was translated directly from the Gk. Recently Lyonnet has explored the possibility that there existed an Armenian Diatessaron and that this is reflected in the Armenian gospels (St. Lyonnet, *Les origines de la version armenienne et le Diatessaron* [1950]).

The Georgian church separated from the Armenian at the end of the sixth century. Thus the Georgian version of the Scriptures is closely akin to the Armenian. The original translation shows an Armenian-Syriac foundation that indicates some septuagintal influence. R. P. Blake holds that the manuscript tradition of the various parts of the Georgian OT is not uniform. According to him, Armenian and LXX Gk. were the languages of the original translation and later revision, which were made at different times and from different archetypes.

The edition printed in Moscow in 1743 is presumably a revision of a direct translation from the Armenian. Recent scholarship has shown that it is much closer to the Armenian text than had been previously imagined. The earliest known manuscripts for the gospels are the Adysh manuscript (A.D. 897), Opiza manuscript (A.D. 913), and Tbet (A.D. 995). These hand down two strata of the Old Georgian text, and both are connected with the Caesarean family.

Gothic and Slavonic Versions. Both of these translations are based on the Lucianic recension of the LXX. The Gothic Bible was prepared about 350 by Ulfilas, called "the apostle to the Goths," a warlike Teutonic race living in Dacia N of the Danube River and W of the Black Sea. Wilhelm Streitberg edited existing fragments of both the OT and NT and reconstructed the Gk. *Vorlage* (*Die gotische Bibel* [1908]; 3d ed. [1950]). Cf. Hans Lietzmann, "Die Vorlage der gotischen Bibel," *Zeitschrift fuer deutsches Altertum und deutsche Literatur* 56 (1919); W. S. Friederichsen, *The Gothic Version of the Gospels, A Study of Its Style and Textual History* (1926); id., *The Gothic Version of the Epistles, A Study of Style and Textual History* (1939).

In the ninth century the Slavonic version was made by Cyril and Methodius, two missionaries who were converted Slavs, a people from Asia who had settled in central and eastern Europe. The oldest copy of the entire Slavonic Bible is dated 1499. Whether influence from the Lat. Vulg. can be detected in the Old Slavonic has been argued against by Meillet (*Revue des études slaves* 6 [1926]: 39-41).

The Anglo-Saxon Version. Researchers have shown that underlying the Anglo-Saxon version are various recensions of the Vulg., notably the Irish recension and that of Alcuin. Alongside of this are strains of Old Latin texts. Peters believes that a Tatianic element has been transmitted by means of the Old Latin. Cf. Allison Drake, *The Authorship of the West Saxon Gospels* (1894); L. M. Harris, *Studies in the Anglo-Saxon Version of the Gospels* (1901); James W. Bright, *The Gospel of Saint John in West Saxon* (1904-6); Curt Peters, in *Biblica* 23 (1942): 323-32, who discusses the Diatessaron text of Matt. 2:9 and the West Saxon version of the gospels. M.F.U.

Modern Versions. *See* Translations: English Bible.

BIBLIOGRAPHY: F. H. A. Scriver, *Introduction to the Criticism of the New Testament* (1894); C. D. Ginsburg, *Introduction to the Massoretico-Critical Edition of the Hebrew Bible* (1897); P. Kahle, *The Cairo Geniza* (1947), pp. 129ff.; M. Burrows, *Dead Sea Scrolls of St. Mark's Monastery* (1950); B. J. Roberts, *The Old Testament Text and Versions* (1951); G. Kuntz, *The Text of the Epistles* (1953); F. M. Cross, *The Ancient Library of Qumran* (1958); F. G. Kenyon, *Our Bible and the Ancient Manuscripts* (1958); M. Black, *An Aramaic Approach to the Gospels and Acts* (1967); B. M. Metzger, *The Text of the New Testament* (1968); T. H. Robinson, *Ancient and English Versions of the Bible* (1970); G. M. Lamsa, trans., *The Holy Bible from Ancient Eastern Manuscripts* (1971); S. P. Brock, ed., *A Classified Bibliography of the Septuagint* (1973); L. H. Brockington, *The Hebrew Text of the Old Testament* (1973); P. Walters, *TheText of the Septuagint* (1973); F. M. Cross and S. Talmon, *Qumran and the History of the Biblical Text* (1975); J. A. Fitzmyer, *The Dead Sea Scrolls: Major Publications and Tools for Study* (1975); D. W. Gooding, *Relics of Ancient Exegesis* (1975); B. M. Metzger, *The Early Versions of the New Testament* (1977); E. Würthwein, *The Text of the Old Testament* (1979); F. F. Bruce, *The Books and the Parchments* (1984); H. A. Sturz, *The Byzantine Text-type and New Testament Textual Criticism* (1984).

VESTRY. *See* Wardrobe.

VIAL. *See* Flask.

VILLAGE. A collection of houses less regular and important than a *town* (which see) or *city* (which see). "Village" is the rendering of several Heb. and Gk. words.

1. Heb. *kāpār*, "protected" (1 Chron. 27:25; Song of Sol. 7:11) is the proper term for village. It appears also in the forms *kepîr* ("covered" as by walls; Neh. 6:2, *see* marg.), and *kōper* (1 Sam. 6:18); and is represented by the Arab. *kefr*, still so much used. In the Heb. the prefix *kāpar* implied a regular village, such as Capernaum, which had in later times, however, outgrown the limits implied by its original designation.

2. Heb. *ḥāṣer*, "enclosed," is properly an *enclo-*

Probable site of the New Testament village of Bethphage

sure, as of farm buildings enclosing a court (Josh. 13:23, 28), the encampment of nomads (Gen. 25:16; Deut. 2:23), and of hamlets near towns (Josh. 15:32-62; 1 Chron. 4:33; Neh. 11:25), especially unwalled pastures of walled towns (Lev. 25:31; cf. v. 34).

3. Gk. *kōmē* is applied to Bethphage (Matt. 21:1), Bethany (Luke 10:38; John 11: 1), Emmaus (Luke 24:13), and Bethlehem (John 7:42). A distinction between city or town (*polis*) and village (*kōmē*) is pointed out in Luke 8:1.

VINE.

Names. The following Heb. and Gk. names denote the vine:

1. Heb. *gepen*, "twining," or more definitely, *gepen hayyayin*, "the vine of the wine" (Gen. 40:9 and fifty-two other places).

2. Heb. *śôrēq* is a term denoting some choice kind of wine (Jer. 2:21; Isa. 5:2; Gen. 49:11), thought to be the same as that now called in Morocco *serki*, and in Persia *kishmish*, with small, round, dark berries and soft stones.

3. Heb. *nāzîr*, "unpruned," is an "untrimmed vine" (Lev. 25:5, 11), i.e., one that every seventh and every fiftieth year was *not pruned*.

4. Gk. *ampelos*, a generic word for vine.

Culture. The grapevine (*Vitus vinifera*) is supposed to be a native of the shores of the Caspian. Its culture extends from about the twenty-first to the fiftieth degree of N latitude and reaches from Portugal on the W to the confines of India on the E. It is, however, only along the center of this zone that the finest wines are made. Although Egypt is not now noted for its grapes, they are mentioned early in Scripture (Gen. 40:9-11;

Num. 20:5; Ps. 78:47), and the monuments amply confirm the culture of grapes in ancient Egypt.

Palestine, even before Israel took possession of it, was a land of vineyards (Deut. 6:11; 28:30; cf. Num. 13:23). Moses enacted rules and regulations for the culture of the vines while their prospective owners still wandered in the desert (Ex. 22:5; 23:11; Lev. 25:5, 11; Num. 6:3; Deut. 22:9; 23:24; 24:21). For this culture the portion of Judah was especially adapted. When the tribe of Judah obtained for their inheritance the hilly slopes of the S, the prophecy of their ancestor was fulfilled, "He washes his garments in wine, and his robes in the blood of grapes" (Gen. 49:11). Here, more than elsewhere, are to be seen on the sides of the hills the vineyards, marked by their watchtowers (*see* Towers) and walls, placed on their ancient terraces—the earliest and latest symbol of Judah. The elevation of the hills and tablelands of Judah is the true climate of the vine, and at Hebron, according to the Jewish tradition, was its primeval seat. It was from the Judean valley of Eshcol—"the torrent of the cluster" —that the spies cut down the gigantic cluster of grapes. Although from many of its most famous haunts the vine has disappeared—e.g., from Engedi—both in southern Palestine and on the slopes of Lebanon there are specimens sufficient to vindicate the old renown of this "land of vineyards." The grapes of Hebron are still considered the finest in the Holy Land. Bunches weighing from six to seven pounds are said to be by no means uncommon.

Grapevine

Vineyard (Heb. *kerem*, "garden"; Gk. *ampelōn*). The preparation of a vineyard is the most costly and troublesome of all the operations of that primitive husbandry in Eastern lands, the methods of which have remained unchanged and unimproved from the earliest records. It is, in fact, the only branch of agriculture practiced there that demands any considerable outlay. In the first place, the vineyard must be carefully enclosed by a permanent fence, which is required for no other crop. The pasturelands outside the villages are all unfenced, and the boundaries only marked by well-known stones or landmarks. The grainfields are equally open, or only protected by thorn branches strewn on the ground, whereas the olive yards nearer the town or village are equally unprotected. When the vineyard has been thus hedged, the next operation is to gather out the stones; not the small stones that strew all the hillsides and are indispensable for the retention of moisture in the soil but the larger boulders, which are heaped in long rows like a ruined stone wall. On these rows the vines are trailed to preserve the fruit from dampness. Next there must be a *wine press* (which see) hewn out of the native rock; for the grapes are always pressed on the spot, lest they should be bruised and injured by conveying them a distance. These wine presses, or vats, are the most imperishable records of the past in the deserted land. They are simply two parallel troughs, one above the other, with a perforated channel between them. The bunches of grapes are thrown into the upper vat, where they are trodden, and the juice flows into the lower one. These "wine vats," found in abundance through the whole land and even far into the southern desert, are silent witnesses to its former fertility. Then, unless the vineyard adjoins the village, there must be a temporary lodge, or booth, erected on poles. But, more generally, a permanent tower, of which many traces may still be seen, was built for the watchman to use during the season, to guard the vintage from thieves or jackals (cf. Isa. 5:1-7).

Mosaic Regulations. It was forbidden by the law to eat the fruit of a vineyard during the first three years after its planting. The fourth year all the fruit was holy to the Lord, "to praise the Lord." Only in the fifth year did the produce of the vines fall entirely to the owner's disposal (Lev. 19:23-25; cf. Mark 12:2). In later times, however, although it was still considered wrong to eat the fruit during the first three years, the rule was greatly relaxed regarding the fourth year. Various markings were adopted whereby the passerby might distinguish the three-year from the four-year vineyard, and so escape the peril of eating from the former. The proper "season" for claiming produce would therefore not come until the fifth year.

The vine in the Mosaic ritual was subject to the usual restrictions of the "seventh year" (Ex. 23:11) and the Jubilee of the fiftieth year (Lev. 25:11). The gleanings were to be left for the poor and the stranger (Jer. 49:9; Deut. 24:21). The vineyard was not to be sown "with two kinds of seed" (Deut. 22:9), but fig trees were sometimes planted in vineyards (Luke 13:6; cf. 1 Kings 4:25:

"Every man under his vine and his fig tree"). Persons passing through a vineyard were allowed to eat grapes therein but not to carry any away (Deut. 23:24).

Vintage (Heb. *bāṣîr*, "clipped"). The vintage began in September and was a time of general festivity. The towns were deserted, and the people lived in the vineyards—in lodges and tents (Judg. 9:27; Jer. 25:30; Isa. 16:10). The grapes were gathered with shouts of joy by the grape gatherers (6:9; 25:30), put into baskets, and then carried to the wine press.

In Palestine the finest grapes, even today, are dried as raisins, and the juice of the remainder, after having been trodden and pressed, is boiled down to a syrup, called *dibs* (Heb. *debash*). It is used by all classes, wherever vineyards are found, as a condiment with their food. Even the leaves and the stocks of the vine are useful. The cuttings of the vine and the leaves are used as fertilizer for the vineyards. The leaves are also used as a vegetable. Chopped meat and rice are rolled up together in single leaves and then boiled for the table, making a delicious dish. The leaves are also used for fodder, whereas the wood serves as fuel (Ezek. 15:2-4; cf. John 15:5-6).

Figurative. The vine is a symbol of the nation Israel; thus Israel was a vine brought from Egypt (Ps. 80:8; cf. Isa. 5). To dwell under one's vine and fig tree is an emblem of domestic happiness and peace (1 Kings 4:25; Ps. 128:3; Mic. 4:4) and a prophetic figure of future millennial blessing. The rebellious people of Israel are compared to "worthless" grapes, "vine," "the degenerate shoots of a foreign vine" (Isa. 5:2, 4; Jer. 2:21; Hos. 10:1, marg.). By the vine our Lord symbolizes the spiritual union existing between Himself and believers (John 15:1-6), unfruitful branches being mere professors. The quick growth of the vine is a symbol of the growth of saints in grace (Hos. 14:7); its rich clusters, of the graces of the saints (Song of Sol. 7:8); the worthlessness of its wood, of the unprofitableness of the wicked (Ezek. 15:2-3, 6); a vine putting forth fruit but not bringing it to maturity is representative of Israel not answering the rightful expectations of Jehovah (Hos. 10:1, marg.). The vineyard is used as a figure of Israel's chastisement for her sin (Isa. 5:7; 27:2; Jer. 12:10; cf. Matt. 21:33); whereas the failure of the vineyard is a symbol of severe calamities (Isa. 32:10); to plant vineyards and eat the fruit thereof is a figure of peaceful prosperity (Neh. 9:25; Isa. 65:21; Ezek. 28:26). *See* Vegetable Kingdom.

VINEGAR. *See* Wine.

VINE OF SODOM. *See* Vegetable Kingdom.

VINEYARD. *See* Vine.

VIOLENCE. Vehement, forcible, or destructive action, often involving infringement, outrage, or assault. The rendering of two Heb. words and one Gk. word:

1. Heb. *ḥāmās* has the sense of using violence, especially with evil intent (Gen. 6:11, 13; 49:5; Ps. 18:48, "violent man," KJV).

2. Heb. *gāzal*, to "strip off," means to *rob* (cf. Lev. 6:2; Job 20:19; 24:2). In these passages the sense is that of seizing another's property by fraud or injustice, especially by the rich and powerful who seize the possessions of the poor by fraud and force.

3. Gk. *bia*, vital, "activity," strength in violent action, force (Acts 5:26; 24:7). In Matt. 11:12, "the kingdom of heaven suffers violence" (*biazetai*), carried by storm, i.e., a share in the heavenly kingdom is sought for with the most ardent zeal and the most intense exertion. The NIV reads, "the kingdom of heaven has been forcefully advancing, and forceful men lay hold of it."

VIPER. See Animal Kingdom.

VIRGIN. The KJV and NASB render two Heb. words and one Gk. word in this way.

1. Heb. *beṯûlâ*, a woman of marriageable age would usually, but not necessarily, be chaste. Rebekah was described explicitly as a virgin (Gen. 24:16), and the intended wife of a priest was also required to be unsullied. But the lamenting widow of Joel 1:8 was obviously not a virgin. It is unfortunate that the NASB and NIV have not normally rendered the term by something less specific than "virgin," which in some contexts is inappropriate.

2. Heb. *'almâ*, a girl or young woman, whether of marriageable age or not, who is a virgin (Ex. 2:8; Ps. 68:25, NASB; KJV, "damsel"; NIV, "girl"; Prov. 30:19; etc.). There is no technical Heb. term for *virgo intacta*, but *'almâ* supplies an appropriate word. Thus there can be no doubt that *'almâ* in Isa. 7:14 does mean specifically a virgin, which is emphasized further by Matt. 11:23. The Holy Spirit through Isaiah did not use *beṯûlâ*, which in any event would have been incorrect technically, because of the need to meet the immediate historical situation and also to proclaim to and from the house of David of the coming of a virgin-born Messiah.

3. Gk. *parthenos*, a "virgin" (Matt. 1:23; 25:1, 33), i.e., either a marriageable maiden or a young married woman, a pure virgin (2 Cor. 11:2). In Rev. 14:4 it is used in the sense of a man who has abstained from all uncleanness and whoredom attendant upon idolatry, and so has kept his chastity.

Respecting the virginity of Mary, the mother of our Lord, *see* Mary.   R.K.H.

BIBLIOGRAPHY: J. G. Machen, *The Virgin Birth of Christ* (1932), pp. 122-23, 127, 244-45, 263-68, 335-36, 341, 347.

VISION (some derivative of Heb. *ḥāzâ*, to "perceive"; Gk. *haraō*; or of *rā'â*, to "see"; *optomai*).

A supernatural presentation of certain scenery or circumstances to the mind of a person while awake (Num. 12:6-8). Balaam speaks of himself as having seen "the vision of the Almighty" (24:16). In the time of Eli it is said, "And word from the Lord was rare in those days, visions were infrequent" (1 Sam. 3:1), i.e., there was no public and recognized revelation of the divine will (cf. Prov. 29:18, "Where there is no vision, the people are unrestrained"). *See* Dream.

VOCATION (Gk. *klēsis*, an "invitation"). A theological term signifying calling (Rom. 11:29; 1 Cor. 1:26; Eph. 1:18; 4:4; Phil. 3:14; 2 Thess. 1:11; 2 Tim. 1:9; Heb. 3:1; 2 Pet. 1:10).

The dominant idea is that God in His grace calls men to forsake a sinful life and to enter into the kingdom and service of the Lord Jesus Christ.

The long-standing point of controversy between Calvinistic and Arminian theologians relates to the character of this call. The former hold that there is an "external call" addressed indiscriminately to all men, whereas the "effectual call" is given only to those who by the divine decree are predestined to everlasting life. The latter refuse to recognize any such distinction.

Methodists and Arminians generally regard the divine call, under whatever external conditions it is made, as always being a call of thoroughly gracious reality. It is so effective that if it is heeded, the person is certain of salvation. *See* Election; Atonement; Holy Spirit.

VOPH'SI (vof-si). The father of Nahbi, one of the explorers of Canaan (Num. 13:14).

VOW (Heb. from *nādar*, to "promise"; Gk. *euchē*, a "prayer"). Defined as a religious undertaking, either positive, to do something, or negative, to abstain from doing a certain thing. Under the Old Covenant the principle of vowing was recognized as in itself a suitable expression of the religious sentiment, and as such was placed under certain regulations. It was not, except in a few special cases, imposed as an obligation on the individual conscience. The Lord never said, "You shall vow so and so"; but, "If you should make a vow, or when you do so, then let such and such conditions be observed." The conditions specified in the law related almost exclusively to the faithful performance of what had been freely undertaken by the worshiper—what he had pledged himself before God to render in active service or dedicated gifts. He was on no account to draw back from his plighted word but conscientiously to carry it out. Otherwise a slight would be put upon God and a stain left upon the conscience of the worshiper (Deut. 23:21-23; Eccles. 5:5; Ps. 50:14; Nah. 1:15).

Mosaic Regulations. These were several.

1. A man could not devote to sacred uses the firstborn of man or beast that was devoted already

(Lev. 27:26); if he vowed land, he might redeem it or not (vv. 16, 20). *See* Redemption.

2. Animals fit for sacrifice, if devoted, were not to be redeemed or changed. If a man attempted to do so, he was required to bring both the devotee and the substitute (27:9-10, 33). They were to be free from blemish (Mal. 1:14). An animal unfit for sacrifice might be redeemed, with the addition of a fifth to the priest's valuation, or it became the property of the priests (Lev. 27:12-13).

3. The case of *persons* was: A man might devote either himself, his child (not the firstborn), or his slave. If no redemption took place, the devoted person became a slave of the sanctuary (2 Sam. 15:8). (*See* Nazirite.) Otherwise he might be redeemed at a valuation according to age and sex (Lev. 27:1-7).

General Regulations. Vows were entirely voluntary but once made were regarded as compulsory, and evasion of performance of them was held to be contrary to true religion (Num. 30:2;

Deut. 23:21; Eccles. 5:4). If persons in a dependent condition made vows—such as an unmarried daughter living in her father's home, or a wife, even if she afterward became a widow—the vow, if in the first case her father, or in the second her husband, heard and disallowed it, was void. But if they heard without disallowance, it was to remain good (Num. 30:3-16). Votive offerings arising from the profit on any impure traffic were wholly forbidden (Deut. 23:18).

Vows in general and their binding force as a test of religion are mentioned (Job 22:27; Pss. 22:25; 50:14; 66:13; 116:14; Prov. 7:14; Isa. 19:21; Nah. 1:15). *See also* Oath.

BIBLIOGRAPHY: J. Pedersen, *Israel: Its Life and Culture* (1959), 3-4:265-67, 324-30; R. de Vaux, *Ancient Israel: Its Life and Institutions* (1961), pp. 39-40, 260, 291, 417, 465-66.

VULGATE. *See* Versions of the Scriptures.

VULTURE. *See* Animal Kingdom.

WA'DI (wa'dē). *See* River.

WAGES.

1. Usually some form of Heb. *śākār* (Gen. 31:8; Ex. 2:9; Ezek. 29:18-19); elsewhere "hire," "reward," etc.

2. Heb. *maskōret* (Gen. 29:15; 31:41; Ruth 2:12).

3. Heb. *pe'ullâ* (Lev. 19:13; Ps. 109:20, "reward").

4. Two Gk. words are thus rendered: *misthos*, John 4:36; elsewhere "reward," or "hire"; *opsōnion*, Luke 3:14; 2 Cor. 11:8; Luke 6:23, "reward."

Wages, according to the earliest uses of mankind, are a return for something of value, specifically for work performed. Thus labor is recognized as property, and wages as the price paid or obtained in exchange for such property. The earliest mention of wages is of a recompense not in money, but in kind. This was given to Jacob by Laban (Gen. 29:15, 20; 31:7-8, 41). Such payment was natural among a pastoral and changing population like that of the tent-dwellers of Syria. In Egypt money payments by way of wages were in use, but the terms cannot now be ascertained.

Among the Hebrews wages in general, whether of soldiers or laborers, are mentioned (Hag. 1:6; Ezek. 29:18-19; John 4:36). The *rate* of wages is only mentioned in the parable of the householder and vineyard (Matt. 20:2), where the laborer's wages are given as one denarius per day (about sixteen cents), a rate that agrees with Tob. 5:14, where a drachma is mentioned as the rate per day, a sum that may be taken as fairly equivalent to the denarius and to the usual pay of a soldier in the latter days of the Roman republic. In earlier times it is probable that the rate was lower. But it is likely that laborers, and also soldiers, were supplied with provisions. The Mosaic law was strict in requiring daily payment of wages (Lev. 19:13; Deut. 15:14-15). The employer who re-

fused to give his laborers sufficient provisions was censured (Job 24:9-11), and the iniquity of withholding wages was denounced (Jer. 22:13; Mal. 3:5; James 5:4). *See* Service.

WAGON (Heb. *'ăgālâ*, that which "rolls" or "turns" around; Gen. 45:19, 21, 27; 46:5; elsewhere "cart"; Ezek. 23:24, Heb. *galgal*, lit., a "wheel," *see* marg.). The oriental wagon, or *'ăgālâ*, is a vehicle composed of two or three planks, fixed on two solid circular blocks of wood, from two to five feet in diameter, which serve as wheels. To the floor are sometimes attached wings, which splay outward like the sides of a wheelbarrow. For the conveyance of passengers, mattresses or clothes are laid in the bottom, and the vehicle is drawn by bulls or oxen. The covered wagons for conveying the materials for the Tabernacle were probably constructed on Egyptian models. Others of a lighter description, and more nearly approaching the modern cart, occur in the Assyrian monuments. Some of these have eight, others as many as twelve, spokes in their wheels.

An Assyrian wagon or ox-cart

WAIL. *See* Mourning.

WALK.

Figurative. *Walk* is often used in Scripture for conduct in life, general demeanor, and deportment. Thus it is said that Enoch and Noah "walked with God," i.e., they maintained a course of action conformed to God's will and acceptable in His sight. In the OT and NT we find God promising to walk with His people, and His people, on the other hand, desiring the influence of the Holy Spirit that they may walk in His statutes. To "walk in the darkness" (1 John 1:6) is to be involved in unbelief and misled by error; to "walk in the light" (v. 7) is to be well informed, holy, and happy; to "walk by faith" (2 Cor. 5:7) may be rendered "through faith we walk," i.e., faith is the sphere through which we walk. To "walk according to the flesh" (Rom. 8:4; cf. 2 Pet. 2:10) is to gratify the carnal desires, to yield to fleshly appetites, and to be obedient to the lusts of the flesh; while to "walk by the Spirit" (Gal. 5:16) is to be guided and aided by the Holy Spirit, the active and animating principle of the Christian life.

WALL (Heb. properly *qîr*, as a "defense"; or *hômâ*, as a "barrier"; sometimes *shūr*, perhaps from its "rocky" character; Gk. *teichos*). In ancient times the walls of cities and houses were usually built of earth or of *bricks* (which see) of clay, mixed with reeds and hardened in the sun. When any breach took place in such a mass of earth, by heavy rains or a defect in the foundation, the consequences were serious (Ps. 62:3; Isa. 30:13); and we can easily understand how such walls could be readily destroyed by fire (Amos 1:7, 10, 14). The extensive mounds on the plains of Mesopotamia and Assyria, marking the sites of ancient cites, show that the walls were principally constructed of earth or clay. The wall surrounding the palace of Khorsabad is fixed by Botta at 48 feet 9 inches; probably about the same as that of Nineveh, upon which three chariots

Walls of Jerusalem

could be driven abreast. The wall of Babylon was 87 feet broad, and six chariots could be driven together upon it. Not infrequently stone walls, with towers and a moat, surrounded fortified cities (Isa. 2:15; 9:10; Neh. 4:3; Zeph. 1:16).

Figurative. In Scripture language a wall is a symbol of *salvation* (Isa. 26:1; 60:18); of *protection*—by God (Zech. 2:5); by those who provide protection (1 Sam. 25:16; Isa. 2:15; 5:5); by the *wealth of the rich* in his own conceit (Prov. 18:11). A "wall of bronze" is symbolical of prophets in their testimony against the wicked (Jer. 15:20); the "dividing wall" (Eph. 2:14), of the separation of Jews and Gentiles; "whitewashed walls" (Acts 23:3), of hypocrites.

WANDERING IN THE WILDERNESS. *See* Wilderness of Wandering.

WAR. Warfare and bloodshed are described realistically in the Bible from the time of the entrance of sin into the human race (Gen. 3). The first great messianic prophecy (3:15) announces hostility between the seed of the woman and the seed of the serpent. The great drama is consummated by the seed of the woman's conquering the seed of the serpent, ousting his control of the earth (Rev. 6-19), and ruling as King of kings and Lord of lords at His second advent. Throughout the millennial earth, peace will be supreme; but the peace of eternity will only eventuate as the final revolt of Satan is put down and he and all his followers are placed in the eternal lake of fire (20:1-3, 7-10). In the light of this biblical description of the struggle of good against evil, Christ against Antichrist, it is not surprising that war should be prominent in Bible history, not only among the Israelites but among surrounding nations.

Sumerians. The Sumerians, the pre-Semitic inhabitants of the fertile plains of the Euphrates in southern Babylonia before 3000 B.C., excelled in the arts of war. They employed the four-wheeled war chariot and the battle bow and developed military equipment. A striking example is a solid gold helmet of incredible workmanship, fashioned before 2500 B.C. This superb piece of armor was unearthed by Sir Leonard Woolley. Extant from this early period also is a gold sheath dagger with a lapis lazuli handle, flint arrows, electrum double ax heads, and copper spear heads. The Standard of Ur portrays infantrymen with copper helmets and heavy cloaks. These soldiers carry short spears or axes, and charioteers are armed with spears and javelins. The Sumerian armies used chariots and phalanxes before 3000 B.C.

Egyptians. Egyptians were not especially militarily minded. They preferred to hire the warlike Nubians to man their foreign expeditions. In the Old Kingdom the common Egyptian soldier was equipped with a leather shield, a long bow with arrows of flint, a mace, a long spear, a curved dagger, and occasionally a battleax. He wore a simple uniform. The New Empire, from 1550 B.C. on, used horse, chariot, and composite bow. These formidable weapons enabled Egypt to conquer and rule the East. During this period fine javelins, spears, daggers, and arrows with points of ivory, glass, or wood were employed. The collection of Tutankhamen in the Cairo Museum illustrates the high development of New Kingdom weapons. Egyptians excelled in fort building. The forts were erected along the cataracts of Upper Egypt to restrain the invasion of the war-loving Nubians. A series of similar forts guarded the Delta area from Asiatic invaders, especially on the NE. The famous turquoise and copper mines of the Sinai Peninsula were also protected by well-manned fortresses. Only occasionally would Egypt build up any considerable navy, since she was protected by her isolated inland position. However, at certain periods the Egyptians conducted successful naval engagements. One striking example is Rameses III, who used his fleet against an invasion of sea peoples (including Philistines), a Lybian confederacy in the twelfth century B.C.

Assyrian. The Assyrians were the "giants of the Semites" at the beginning of the ninth century B.C. under Ashurnasirpal II, Shalmaneser III, and later under great militarists and conquerors like Tiglath-pileser III, Sargon II, Sennacherib, and Esarhaddon. The cruel and relentless Assyrian armies made Israel and surrounding countries tremble. With powerful bows and arrows shot from chariots, their irresistible cavalry attacks, and their employment of all of the weapons of their Sumerian and Babylonian precursors, they were a terrifying scourge.

Chaldean. Even more fearful than the Assyrians were the superb Chaldean fighters and horsemen. They employed all the military art and weapons of the Assyrians. Habakkuk outlines the terror the Chaldeans caused the Hebrews (Hab. 1:6-9). Ezekiel enumerates the military equip-

ment of the common Chaldean soldier. He speaks of warriors clothed in full armor and of horsemen riding on horses; of "weapons, chariots, and wagons, and with a company of peoples. They will set themselves against you on every side with buckler and shield and helmet" (Ezek. 23:24).

The Hebrews. Religious elements were a part of Hebrew warfare, and were evident in the preliminary steps, the conduct of the battle, and the treatment of the conquered people.

Preliminary Steps. Before beginning an aggressive warfare, the Hebrews sought for the divine sanction by consulting either the Urim and Thummim (Judg. 1:1; 20:2, 27-28; 1 Sam. 14:37; 23:2; 28:6; 30:8) or some acknowledged prophet (1 Kings 22:6; 2 Chron. 18:5). Divine aid was further sought in actual warfare by bringing into the field the Ark of the Covenant, which was the symbol of Jehovah Himself (1 Sam. 4:4, 18; 14:18). Formal proclamations of war were not interchanged between the belligerents. Before entering the enemy's district, spies were sent to ascertain the character of the country and the preparations of its inhabitants for resistance (Num. 13:17; Josh. 2:1; Judg. 7:10-11; 1 Sam. 26:4).

Actual Warfare. When an engagement was imminent, a sacrifice was offered (1 Sam. 7:9; 13:9) and an encouraging address delivered either by the commander (2 Chron. 20:20) or by a priest (Deut. 20:2). Then followed the battle signal (1 Sam. 17:52; Isa. 42:13; Jer. 50:42; Ezek. 21:22; Amos 1:14). The combat assumed the form of a number of hand-to-hand contests. Hence the high value attached to the fleetness of foot and strength of arm (2 Sam. 1:23; 2:18; 1 Chron. 12:8). At the same time various strategic devices were practiced, such as the ambush (Josh. 8:2, 12; Judg. 20:36), surprise (Judg. 7:16), or circumvention (2 Sam. 5:23). Another mode of settling the dispute was by the selection of champions (1 Sam. 17; 2 Sam. 2:14), who were spurred on to exertion by the offer of high reward (1 Sam. 17:25; 18:25; 2 Sam. 18:11; 1 Chron. 11:6). The

Representation of an Assyrian siege and capture of a town

contest having been decided, the conquerors were recalled from the pursuit by the sound of a trumpet (2 Sam. 2:28; 18:16; 20:22).

Siege of a Town. The siege of a town or fortress was conducted in the following manner: a kind of embankment was thrown up around the place (Ezek. 4:2; Mic. 5:1), constructed out of the trees found in the neighborhood (Deut. 20:20) together with earth and any other materials at hand. This line not only cut off the besieged from the surrounding country, but also served as a base of operations for the besiegers. The next step was to throw out from this line one or more "mounds," or "banks," in the direction of the city (2 Sam. 20:15; 2 Kings 19:32; Isa. 37:33). These were gradually increased in height until they were about half as high as the city wall. On these mounds or "siege walls," towers were erected (2 Kings 25:1; Jer. 52:4; Ezek. 4:2; 17:17; 21:22; 26:8), from where the slingers and archers might attack effectively. Battering rams (Ezek. 4:2; 21:22) were brought up to the walls by means of the siege wall, and scaling ladders might also be placed on it.

Roman ballista, or mechanical sling

Treatment of Conquered. The treatment of the conquered was extremely severe in ancient times. The bodies of the soldiers killed in action were plundered (1 Sam. 31:8-9; 2 Macc. 8:27); survivors were either killed in some savage manner (Judg. 9:45; 2 Sam. 12:31; 2 Chron. 25:12), were mutilated (Judg. 1:6; 1 Sam. 11:2), or were carried into captivity (Num. 31:26; Deut. 20:14). Sometimes the bulk of the population of the conquered country was moved to a distant locality. The Mosaic law mitigated to a certain extent the severity of the ancient treatment of the conquered. The conquerors celebrated their success by the erection of monuments (1 Sam. 7:12; 2 Sam. 8:13), by hanging up trophies in their public buildings (1 Sam. 21:9; 31:10; 2 Kings 11:10), and by triumphal songs and dances in which the whole population took part (Ex. 15:1-21; Judg. 5; 1 Sam. 18:6-8; 2 Sam. 22; Judith 16:2-17; 1 Macc. 4:24).

Roman. Roman armor was unequaled in the ancient world. A superb example of this is shown in the Hadrian marble torso in the Athenian agora. Our Lord came into close contact with Roman legions and military might. The long Roman sword appears in the prophecy of Calvary uttered by Simeon to Mary, the mother of Jesus: "A sword will pierce even your own soul" (Luke 2:35). Jesus refers to the sword (Matt. 26:55), and His side was pierced by the long Roman spear, while the soldiers gambled at the foot of the cross. Widely traveled, the apostle Paul on numerous occasions came into close contact with Roman military power. In all the cities in which he preached, Roman soldiers or legions were present. When he was ordered by Claudius Lysias to go to Caesarea for government trial, 200 soldiers, 200 spearmen, and 70 horsemen formed his personal escort. Paul's graphic description of the panoplied Roman warrior in Eph. 6:10-20 is thus perfectly natural. In this remarkable illustration of the Spirit-filled believer's conflict in prayer are outlined the main items in the equipment of a Roman warrior.

Figurative. War is a figure of our contest with death (Eccles. 8:8). In the song of Moses, Jehovah is declared to be "a warrior" (Ex. 15:3), One who knows how to make war and possesses the power to destroy His foes. War illustrates the malignity of the wicked (Ps. 55:21), the contest of saints with the enemies of their salvation (Rom. 7:23; 2 Cor. 10:3; Eph. 6:12; 1 Tim. 1:18), and between Antichrist and the saints (Rev. 11:7; 13:4, 7).

M.F.U.

BIBLIOGRAPHY: G. von Rad, *Der heilige Krieg im alten Israel* (1951); R. de Vaux, *Ancient Israel: Its Life and Institutions* (1961), pp. 247-67; Y. Yadin, *The Scroll of the War of the Sons of Light Against the Sons of Darkness* (1962); id., *The Art of Warfare in Bible Lands* (1963).

WARDROBE (Heb. *meltâhâ,* apparently from an old root meaning "to spread" out). Mentioned in connection with the temple of Baal (2 Kings 10:22). The priests of Baal, like those of almost all religions, had their sacred garments that were worn at the time of worship and were kept in the wardrobe in the temple.

WARES (Ezek. 27:12-27). The essential meaning of the Heb. seems to be an *exchange,* or *equivalent,* alluding to the frequency of *barter* in ancient trade. KJV incorrectly renders it "fairs."

WASHING. *See* Ablution.

WASP. *See* Animal Kingdom.

WATCH.

1. The rendering of some form of the Heb. *shâmar* (to "protect") and may mean a day or night watch; thus there was a guard of the king's house (2 Kings 11:5-7) and in Jerusalem under Nehemiah (Neh. 4:9; 7:3). The Jews, like the Greeks and Romans, divided the night into mili-

tary watches instead of hours, each watch representing the period for which sentinels or pickets remained on duty. Thus we read of "a watch in the night" (Ps. 90:4). The proper Jewish reckoning recognized only three such watches, entitled the first or "beginning of the night watches" (Lam. 2:19), the middle watch (Judg. 7:19), and the morning watch (Ex. 14:24; 1 Sam. 11:11). Those would last respectively from sunset to 10:00 P.M.; from 10:00 P.M. to 2:00 A.M.; and from 2:00 A.M. to sunrise. Subsequent to the establishment of the Roman supremacy, the number of watches was increased to four, which were described either according to their numerical order, as in the case of the "fourth watch" (Matt. 14:25), Gk. *phulakē*, or by the terms "evening," "midnight," "cockcrowing," and "morning" (Mark 13:35). These terminated respectively at 9:00 P.M., midnight, 3:00 A.M., and 6:00 A.M.

2. Heb. *shāqad* (to "be alert") is to be wakeful, and so watchful, either for good (Jer. 31:28; 51:12, see marg.) or evil (Isa. 29:20, see marg.).

3. Gk. *grēgoreō* means to "keep awake, to watch," and so to take heed, lest through remissiveness and indolence one be led to forsake Christ (Matt. 26:41; Mark 14:38).

4. A Roman sentry, one of the soldiers who guarded the tomb of the Lord (Matt. 27:65-66). Gk. *koustōdia*; "Watch," KJV.

5. Gk. *nēphō* (to "abstain from wine, be sober") is used in the NT figuratively, to "be calm and collected in spirit; to be temperate, dispassionate, circumspect" (1 Thess. 5:6; 2 Tim. 4:5).

WATCHMAN'S HUT. *See* Cottage.

WATCHTOWER. *See* Tower.

WATER (Heb. *mayim;* Gk. *hudōr*). Frequently mentioned in Scripture both as an element in fertility and as a drink.

Supply. The long rainy season in Palestine means a considerable rainfall, and while it lasts the land gets a thorough soaking. But the land is limestone and very porous. The heavy rains are quickly drained away, the wadis are left dry, the lakes become marshes or dwindle to dirty ponds. On the W of Jordan there remain only a few short perennial streams, of which but one or two, and these mere rills, are found in the hill country. Hence the water of running streams and fountains, as opposed to that of stagnant cisterns, pools, or marshes, is called *living water* (Gen. 26:19, marg.; Zech. 14:8; John 4:10-11; 7:38; Rev. 7:17). In the hot countries of the East the assuaging of thirst is one of the most delightful sensations that can be experienced (Ps. 143:6; Prov. 25:25), and every attention that humanity and hospitality can suggest is paid to furnish travelers with water. Public reservoirs or pools are opened in several parts of Egypt and Arabia. Sometimes water is so scarce that it must be paid for (Num. 20:17, 19; Lam. 5:4).

Peculiar Usages. Among the optical illusions that the deserts of the East have furnished is the *mirage*. This phenomenon of "waters that fail," was called by the Hebrews *shārāb*, i.e., "heat," and is rendered "the scorched land" (Isa. 35:7); properly, "And the mirage shall become a pool," i.e., the desert that presents the appearance of a lake shall be changed into real water.

Figurative. Water occasionally is used for *tears* (Jer. 9:1); hence, figuratively, *trouble* (Ps. 66:12) and *misfortune* (Lam. 3:54; Pss. 69:1; 119:136; 124:4-5); *persecution* (88:17); *hostile* armies (Isa. 8:7; 17:13). Water is used for *children* or *posterity* (Num. 24:7; Isa. 48:1, see marg.); for *clouds* (Ps. 104:3); for the refreshing power of the Holy Spirit (Isa. 12:3; 35:6-7; 55:1; John 7:37-38); divine *support* (Isa. 8:6); the gifts and graces of the Holy Spirit (41:17-18; 44:3; Ezek. 36:25); water *poured out*, the *wrath of God* (Hos. 5:10); and of *faintness* by terror (Ps. 22:14). *Deep* water is used of the counsel in the heart (Prov. 20:5) and of the words of the wise (18:4). Water "spilled on the ground" is a figure of death (2 Sam. 14:14), its *instability* figures a wavering disposition (Gen. 49:4). "*Stolen* water" (Prov. 9:17) denotes unlawful pleasures with strange women. The difficulty of stopping water (17:14) is a symbol of strife and contention, while its rapid flowing away represents the career of the wicked (Job 24:18, see marg.; Ps. 58:7). *See* Fountain; Well.

WATERFALL (Heb. *ṣinnôr*, "hollow"). This was

View of well at Beersheba

a cataract, waterspout (Ps. 42:7), rendered in 2 Sam. 5:8, "water tunnel."

WATER OF JEALOUSY. *See* Jealousy Offering.

WATERPOT (Gk. *hudria*). A large vessel of stone in which water was kept standing (John 2:6-7) for the sake of *cleansing,* which the Jews practiced before and after meals. The "firkin" (Gk. *metrētēs*) was a measure containing about 8 ⅞ gallons. The "waterpot" mentioned in 4:28 was a jar of earthenware in which water was carried.

WATER TUNNEL (Heb. *ṣinnôr*). The term occurs in the proposal of David that someone should "strike the Jebusites . . . through the water tunnel" (2 Sam. 5:8). KJV renders it "gutter," and RSV and NIV render it "the water shaft," but more recent evidence points to "a grappling hook" used by besiegers in scaling ramparts. The word is now known to be typically Canaanite, and the sense "hook" has been handed down through Aram. to modern Arab. *See* W. F. Albright in *O.T. Commentary* (1948), p. 149.

WAVE OFFERING. *See* Sacrificial Offerings.

WAW (ו). The sixth letter of the Heb. alphabet, often given as *Vav* (which see).

WEAKNESS (Heb. *mōrek*, NASB, Lev. 26:36 only; Gk. *asthenia, asthēma, asthenēs*). Frequently this term is used in the NASB and NIV as the replacement for KJV "infirmity" or "infirmities," but in some verses the expression appears in the KJV, NIV, and NASB (1 Cor. 1:25; 2:3; 15:43; 2 Cor. 12:9; 13:4; Heb. 7:18; 11:34). In the NASB of Lev. 26:36 the term replaces KJV "faintness."

Romans 6:19, "weakness of your flesh" means the weakness of human nature in respect to understanding. Paul says in 1 Cor. 2:3, "I was with you in weakness," meaning the inability to do great things, want of skill in speaking, or of human wisdom. In Heb. 5:2 and 7:28 the high priest is spoken of as "beset with weakness," which means a tendency to sin, unlike our great High Priest. In Heb. 4:15, "we do not have a high priest who cannot sympathize with our weakness" denotes all human disabilities, as well as in Rom. 8:26 and 2 Cor. 12:5, 9.

WEAN, WEANING. *See* Children.

WEAPON. *See* Armor, Arms.

WEASEL. *See* Animal Kingdom: Mole.

WEAVER, WEAVING. *See* Handicrafts.

WEB. *See* Animal Kingdom: Spider.

WEDDING. *See* Marriage.

WEEDS. *See* Vegetable Kingdom.

WEEK. A measure of *time* (which see).

WEEKLY SABBATH. *See* Festivals.

WEEKS, FEAST OF. *See* Festivals: Pentecost.

WEEPING. *See* Mourning.

WEIGHT. For measures of weight, *see* Metrology.

1. Heb. *'eben,* a "stone." A weight of balance, even when not made of stone, since anciently, as at the present day, the orientals often made use of stones for weights (Lev. 19:36; Deut. 25:15; etc.).

2. Heb. *mishqāl* or *mishqôl* may mean either the *weight* numerically estimated (Gen. 24:22; Lev. 19:35; Num. 7:13; etc.) or the act of *weighing* (Ezra 8:34).

3. Heb. *peles* (Prov. 16:11; "balance," Isa. 40:12).

4. In the NT "weight" is mentioned only once in its literal sense and is the rendering of Gk. *talantiaios,* "talentlike" in weight (Rev. 16:21, *see* marg.). The Israelites were commanded to have "just weights" (Lev. 19:36; Deut. 25:15; Prov. 20:10, 23), and the prophet Micah (Mic. 6:11) denounced the "bag of deceptive weights," referring to the stone weights that were carried in a bag.

Entrance to Hezekiah's water tunnel

Figuratively. Job, in speaking of the fixed laws ordained by Jehovah for the duration of the world, particularizes by examples: "He imparted weight to the wind" (28:25), i.e., the measure of its force of feebleness. To "eat bread by weight" (Ezek. 4:16, cf. v. 10) denotes extreme poverty or scarcity of food. The NIV renders "rationed food." The "weight of glory" (2 Cor. 4:17) is a figurative expression to denote the intensity of the celestial splendor, especially as contrasted with the transitoriness of present afflictions. The writer of Hebrews (12:1) urges his readers to "lay aside every weight," KJV; "encumbrance," NASB; "everything that hinders," NIV (Gk. *ogkos*). This word means anything "prominent, an encumbrance," thus anything that hinders a person in running his spiritual race.

WELL. The rendering of the following Heb. and Gk. words:

1. Heb. *be'ēr* (a "pit"), something *dug*, and having the meaning of our word *cistern* (Gen. 16:14; 21:19; 26:19-22, 25; 2 Sam. 17:18; etc.).
2. Heb. *bôr* (from no. 1) is found in 1 Sam. 19:22; 2 Sam. 3:26; 23:15-16; 1 Chron. 11:17-18.
3. Heb. *ma'yān* (from no. 4), a *spring*, as in Ps. 84:6.
4. Heb. *'ayin* (an "eye"), a fountain; whether so called from its resemblance to the eye, or, vice versa the eye, from its resemblance to a fountain, is doubtful (Neh. 2:13 "well," NIV); a living *spring*.
5. Gk. *pēgē* ("gushing"), a fountain spread by a spring (John 4:6, 14).
6. Gk. *phrear* ("hole," John 4:11-12), a pit *dug*, and thus distinguished from a living spring.

Importance. The heat and the large flocks and herds have made a supply of water a special necessity (Judg. 1:15) in a hot climate. Among Eastern nations it has always involved questions of property of the highest importance, sometimes giving rise to serious contention. Thus Abraham opened the well Beersheba, and its possession was attested with special formality (Gen. 21:30-31). The Koran notices abandoned wells as signs of desertion (Sur. 22). To acquire wells that they had not dug themselves was one of the marks of favor foretold to the Hebrews on their entrance

Eastern well

into Canaan (Deut. 6:11). To possess a well was considered a mark of independence (Prov. 5:15); and to abstain from the use of wells belonging to others, a disclaimer of interference with their property (Num. 20:17, 19; 21:22). Similar rights of possession, actual and hereditary, exist among the Arabs of the present day.

Construction. Wells in Palestine are usually excavated from the solid limestone rock, sometimes with steps to descend into them (Gen. 24:16). The brims are furnished with a curb or low wall of stone, bearing ancient furrows worn by the ropes used in drawing water. It was on a curb of this sort that our Lord sat when He conversed with the woman of Samaria (John 4:6), and it was its usual stone cover that the woman placed on the mouth of the well at Bahurim (2 Sam. 17:19), which was dry at times.

Raising the Water. The usual methods for raising water are as follows: (1) The rope and bucket, or waterskin (Gen. 24:14-20; John 4:11). (2) The *sakiyeh,* or Persian wheel. This consists of a vertical wheel furnished with a set of buckets or earthen jars, attached to a cord passing over the wheel. These descend empty and return full as the wheel revolves. (3) A modification of the last method, by which a man, sitting opposite a wheel furnished with buckets, turns it by drawing with his hands one set of spokes prolonged beyond its circumference and pushing another set from him with his feet. (4) A method very common, both in ancient and modern Egypt, is the *shaduf,* a simple contrivance consisting of a lever moving on a pivot, which is loaded at one end with a lump of clay or some other weight and has at the other a bowl or bucket. Wells are usually furnished with troughs of wood or stone, into which the water is emptied for the use of persons or animals coming to the wells. Unless machinery is used, which is commonly worked by men, women are usually the water carriers.

Figurative. Wells are figurative of: God as the source of salvation (John 4:10; cf. Isa. 12:3; Jer. 2:13; Song of Sol. 4:15); "drinking from one's own," domestic happiness (cf. Prov. 5:15).

WEN. *See* Diseases.

WEST. The oriental, in speaking of the quarters of the heavens, supposes that his face is turned to the E. So the E is *before* him, the W *behind,* the S at his *right* hand, and the N at his *left.* The "going down of the sun" (*bo' hashshemesh*) also denoted the W, as did the "sea" (*yām*), which was westward from Palestine.

WHALE. *See* Animal Kingdom.

WHEAT. *See* Vegetable Kingdom.

Figurative. On account of its excellence as a food, wheat is a figure of good men, as tares are of evil (Matt. 3:12; 13:25, 29-30; Luke 3:17).

WHEEL. Wheels were well known in the ancient

biblical world. Water buckets were manipulated by ropes pulled over wheels set up at wells and cisterns (Eccles. 12:6). The potter's wheel referred to in Jer. 18:3 and other places was ancient. Solomon's Temple was equipped with wheeled basins (1 Kings 7:30-33). Nahum refers to the noise of the chariot wheels of the Assyrians (Nah. 3:2). Ezekiel saw wheels in his apocalyptic vision (Ezek. 1:15-21). Chariot wheels go back to about 3000 B.C. or earlier and were wooden discs manufactured of two half-circle pieces fastened with metal around a central core. Sumerian chariots were four- or two-wheeled. Common Egyptian chariots had wheels of six spokes that, however, were larger than the eight-spoked wheels of Etruscan chariots.   M.F.U.

Dusk in the Judean wilderness

WHELP (Heb. *bēn*, "son or offspring," Job 4:11 ("cub," NIV); elsewhere *gûr*, or *gôr*, Gen. 49:9; Deut. 33:22; both "cub" in the NIV).

WHIRLWIND. This term is taken from Heb. *sûpâ* from the root meaning to "snatch away," signifying a sweeping desolating blast (Hos. 8:7), and *sā'ār*, from a root, to *toss,* indicating the same thing, but more with reference to its vehement agitating motion (2 Kings 2:1, 11). Both words are elsewhere rendered "storm."

Figurative. In a large proportion of the passages the terms are used in a figurative sense, as with reference to the resistless and sweeping destruction sure to overtake the wicked (Ps. 58:9; Prov. 1:27; 10:25; Isa. 41:16; etc.).

WHISTLE (Heb. *shāraq*). Used in the sense of "to allure or entice," as a beekeeper who by whistling induces the bees to come out of their hives and settle on the ground (Isa. 5:26; 7:18). KJV renders the word "hiss" in these verses.

WHITE. *See* Colors.

WHITE OWL. *See* Animal Kingdom: Owl.

WHITEWASH. *See* Mineral Kingdom: Mortar.

WHORE. *See* Harlot, Whore.

WIDOW (Heb. *'almānâ*, "bereaved"; Gk. *chēra*, "deficient," as of a husband).

Mosaic Regulations. In the Mosaic legislation special regard was paid to widows. It is true that no legal provision was made for their maintenance. But they were left dependent partly on the affection of relatives, especially the oldest son, whose birthright, or extra share of the property, imposed this duty upon him. They also were dependent on the privileges provided for other distressed classes, such as participation in the triennial third tithe (Deut. 14:29; 26:12), in gleaning (24:19-21), and in religious feasts (16:11, 14). God Himself claimed a special interest in the widows, even calling Himself their Husband (Pss. 68:5; 146:9), uttering the severest denunciations against those who defrauded and oppressed them (94:6; Ezek. 22:7; Mal. 3:5). With regard to the remarriage of widows, the only restriction imposed by the Mosaic law referred to the widow who was left childless, in which case the brother of the deceased husband had a right to marry her (Deut. 25:5-6; Matt. 22:23-30). *See also* the article Marriage, Levirate.

New Testament Usage. In the apostolic church the widows were sustained at the church's expense, relief being daily administered under the superintendence of officers appointed for this special purpose (Acts 6:1-6). Particular directions are given by Paul regarding those persons entitled to such maintenance (1 Tim. 5:3-16). From all the widows only a certain number were to be enrolled; the qualifications for enrollment were (1) that they were not under sixty years of age; (2) that they had been the wife of one man, probably meaning *only once married,* and (3) that they had led useful and charitable lives (vv. 9-10). Some have thought this implies a receiving of the more elderly and approved widows into a kind of ecclesiastical order (v. 9), either as deaconesses or as overseers for those of their own sex. But the language is indefinite.

BIBLIOGRAPHY: R. de Vaux, *Ancient Israel: Its Life and Institutions* (1961), pp. 39-40, 54-55; C. J. Barber, *Ruth: An Expositional Commentary* (1983), see notes, pp. 135-71.

WIFE. *See* Marriage.

WILD ASS. *See* Animal Kingdom: Donkey.

WILD BEASTS. *See* Animal Kingdom.

WILD DONKEY. *See* Animal Kingdom: Donkey.

WILDERNESS. A wild, uninhabited region suitable only for pasturage (Heb. *midbār*, Ps. 107:4) or sparse human occupation. A sterile tract of country not supporting human life (Heb. *'arābâ,* Job 24:5), and hence a place of desolation (Heb. *yeshîmôn,* Deut. 32:10). The Gk. term *erēmia,* "solitude," is used in the NT. *See* Desert.

WILDERNESS OF WANDERING. The land in which the Israelites sojourned and wandered for forty years on their way from Egypt to Canaan. It lay within the peninsula of Sinai, or that peninsula extended, i.e., within the angle or fork formed by the two branches of the Red Sea—the Gulf of Suez and the Gulf of Aqaba—or the lines that those branches produced, having the Holy Land to the N of it. It is that portion of Arabia called Arabia Petraea (or rocky Arabia), from its rocky and rugged character. It consisted of several districts: (1) the wilderness of Shur, or Etham, i.e., the great wall of Egypt, extending from Suez to the Mediterranean; (2) the wilderness of Paran, occupying the center of the peninsula; (3) the wilderness of Sin, in the lower part of the peninsula; (4) the wilderness of Zin to the NE. It was in the plain or wilderness of Paran (Gen. 14:6; 21:21; Num. 13:26), still called the Wilderness of Wandering, and in the neighboring mountains, that the children of Israel chiefly wandered after their retreat from Kadesh. But their wandering was not altogether confined to this region, for it seems to have extended to the region of Sinai, or the district of the *Tawarah* Arabs, and then, toward the close of the thirty-eight years, to the plain of the Arabah and to the wilderness of Zin. All of this region was deficient in water. Hence the occasion for the miraculous stream of water that "followed" the Israelites for so many years. It was deficient also in food for *man* but apparently not in food for *cattle*. There is little doubt that the wilderness once afforded greater resources than at present, although there seems to have been no city or village (Ps. 107:4). The *wandering* of Israel, properly speaking, commenced on their retreat from Kadesh (Num. 14:33; 32:13), for up to that time their journey had been direct, first to Sinai and then to Kadesh.

The Direct Journey. The first part, namely, to Sinai, has been discussed in the article on *Exodus* (which see). Having rested there for about one year, the Israelites moved northward to the wilderness of Paran (Num. 10:12); Taberah (11:3;

Deut. 9:22); Kibroth-hattaavah (Num. 11:34; 33:16); Hazeroth (11:35; 33:17); desert of Arabah by the way of Mt. Seir (Deut. 1:1-2, 19); Rithmah (Num. 33:18); Kadesh in the desert of Paran (Num. 12:16; 13:26; Deut. 1:1, 19).

Wanderings. In consequence of their unbelief and rebellion, the Lord swore that they should *wander* in the wilderness until all who were above twenty years of age should perish (Num. 14:29). Their *wandering*, therefore, began on their retreat from Kadesh. They camped in the following stations until their return to Kadesh: Rimmon-perez (33:19); Libnah (v. 20); Rissah (v. 21); Kehelathah (v. 22); Mt. Shepher (v. 23); Haradah (v. 24); Makheloth (v. 25); Tahath (v. 26); Terah (v. 27); Mithkah (v. 28); Hashmonah (v. 29); Moseroth (v. 30); Bene-jaakan (v. 31); Hor-haggidgad (v. 32); Jotbathah (v. 33); Abronah (v. 34); Ezion-geber (v. 35), by the way of the Red Sea (Deut. 2:1); Kadesh, in the wilderness of Zin (Num. 20:1), by the way of Mt. Seir (Deut. 2:1).

From Kadesh to Jordan. To Beeroth Bene-jaakan (Deut. 10:6); Mt. Hor (Num. 20:22; 33:37), or Moserah (Deut. 10:6), where Aaron died; Gudgodah (v. 7); Jotbathah (v. 7); by way of the Red Sea (Num. 21:4); by Ezion-geber (Deut. 2:8); Elath (v. 8); Zalmonah (Num. 33:41); Punon (v. 42); Oboth (21:10; 33:43); Iyeabarim (21:11; 33:44), or Iyim (33:45); Wadi Zered (21:12; Deut. 2:13-14); Arnon (Num. 21:13; Deut. 2:24); Dibon-gad (Num. 33:45); Almon-diblathaim (v. 46); Beer (well) in the desert (21:16, 18); Mattanah (21:18); Nahaliel (v. 19); Bamoth (v. 19); Pisgah (v. 20), or mountains of Abarim, near Nebo (33:47); by way of Bashan to the plains of Moab by Jordan (21:33; 22:1; 33:48).

BIBLIOGRAPHY: E. Robinson, *Biblical Researches* (1841), 1:98-100, 129, 131, 179; A. P. Stanley, *Sinai and Palestine* (1905), pp. 16-19, 22, 24-27; W. M. F. Petrie and C. T. Currelly, *Researches in Sinai* (1906), pp. 12, 247-56, 269; A. E. Lucas, *The Route of the Exodus* (1938), pp. 44-45, 68; B. Rothenberg, *God's Wilderness* (1961); J. Buckingham, *Way Through the Wilderness* (1983).

WILD GOAT. *See* Animal Kingdom: Satyr; Wild Goat.

WILD OX. *See* Animal Kingdom.

WILD VINE or **Grape.** *See* Vegetable Kingdom.

WILLOW. *See* Vegetable Kingdom.

WILLS. Under a system of close inheritance like that of the Jews, the scope for bequest in respect of land was limited by the right of redemption and general reentry in the Jubilee year. Keil says (*Bib. Arch.*, pp. 309, 311, n. 5), "Of wills there is not a trace to be found in the Mosaic law or throughout the whole of the Old Testament. . . . Neither the expression 'command his house' (put his house in order), II Sam. 17:23; II Kings 20:1; Isa. 38:1, nor the writing mentioned in Tob. 7:14,

A possible site of the Israelite campground at Sinai

indicates a testamentary disposition. Not till the time of the later Jews do testaments occur; comp. Gal. 3:15; Heb. 9:17, and among princely families (Josephus, *Ant.*, xiii, 16, 1; xvii, 3, 2; *War*, ii, 2, 3), as well as in Talmudic law, after the Greek and Roman fashion."

WIMPLE. *See* Dress.

WINDOW. *See* House.

WINDS. That the Hebrews recognized the existence of four prevailing winds as issuing, broadly speaking, from the four cardinal points—N, S, E, and W—may be inferred from their custom of using the expression "four winds" as being equivalent to the "four quarters" of the hemisphere (Ezek. 37:9; Dan. 8:8; Zech. 2:6; Matt. 24:31).

1. The N wind or, as it was usually called, "the north," was naturally the coldest of the four (Ecclus. 43:20), and its presence is hence invoked as favorable to vegetation in Song of Sol. 4:16. It blows chiefly in October and brings dry cold (Job 37:9). It is described in Prov. 25:23 as bringing rain; in this case we must understand the NW wind. The NW wind prevails from the autumn equinox to the beginning of November and the N wind from June to the equinox.

2. The E wind crosses the sandy wastes of the Arabian Desert before reaching Palestine and was hence termed the wind "from across the wilderness" (Job 1:19; Jer. 13:24). It blows with violence and is hence supposed to be used generally for any violent wind (Job 27:21; 38:24; Ps. 48:7; Isa. 27:8; Ezek. 27:26). It is probably in this sense that it is used in Ex. 14:21. In Palestine the E wind prevails from February to June.

3. The name *sheriqôt*, our *sirocco* (lit., "the east"), is used of all winds blowing in from the desert, E, SE, S, and even S-SW. They are hot winds. "When you see a south wind blowing, you say, 'It will be a hot day,' and it turns out that way" (Luke 12:55; cf. Job 37:17; Jer. 4:11; Ezek. 17:10; 19:12; Hos. 13:15). They blow chiefly in the spring, and for a day at a time; and they readily pass over into rain by a slight change in the direction, from S-SW to full SW.

4. The W and SW winds reach Palestine loaded with moisture gathered from the Mediterranean and are hence expressively termed by the Arabs "the fathers of the rain." Westerly winds prevail in Palestine from November to February and, damp from the sea, drop their moisture and cause the winter rains. "In summer the winds blow chiefly out of the drier northwest, and, meeting only warmth, do not cause showers, but greatly mitigate the daily heat. This latter function is fulfilled morning by morning with almost perfect punctuality. . . . He strikes the coast soon after sunrise; in Hauran, in June and July, he used to reach us between ten and twelve o'clock, and blew so well that the hours previous to that were generally the hottest of our day. The peas-ants do all their winnowing against this steady wind" (Smith, *Hist. Geog.*, pp. 66-67).

In addition to the four regular winds, the Bible mentions local squalls (Mark 4:37; Luke 8:23), to which the Sea of Gennesaret was liable. In the narrative of Paul's voyage the Gk. term *lips* is used to describe the SW wind; the Lat. *carus* or *caurus* (*chôros*), the NW wind (Acts 27:12); and *euroclydon*, a wind of a very violent character coming from E-NE (v. 14).

WINE. The product of the wine press was described in Heb. by a variety of terms, indicative either of the quality or of the use of the liquid.

1. Heb. *yayin* ("effervescing") is rendered invariably "wine," except in Judg. 13:14, "vine"; Song of Sol. 2:4, "banquet hall." This term corresponds to the Gk. *oinos*, and our *wine*. In most of the passages in the Bible where *yayin* is used (83 out of 138), it certainly means *fermented grape juice*; and in the remainder it may fairly be presumed to do so. The intoxicating character of *yayin* in general is plain from Scripture. To it are attributed the dull eyes (Gen. 49:12), the mocking and brawling (Prov. 20:1; Isa. 28:7), the excitement of the spirit (Prov. 31:7; Isa. 5:11; Zech. 9:15; 10:7), the enchained affections of its addicts (Hos. 4:11), the perverted judgment (Prov. 31:5; Isa. 28:7), the indecent exposure (Hab. 2:15-16), and the sickness resulting from the "heat [*hēmâ*] of wine" (Hos. 7:5).

In actual instances: Noah planted a vineyard and drank of the wine, *yayin*, and was *drunk* (Gen. 9:21); Nabal drank wine, *yayin*, and was *very drunk* (1 Sam. 25:36-37); the "drunkards of Ephraim" were "overcome with wine [*yayin*]" (Isa. 28:1). Jeremiah says, "I have become like a drunken man, even like a man overcome with wine [*yayin*]" (Jer. 23:9). The intoxicating quality of *yayin* is confirmed by rabbinical testimony. The Mishna, in the treatise on the Passover, says that four cups of wine were poured out and blessed and drunk by each of the company at the eating of the Paschal lamb, and that water was also mixed with wine, because it was considered too strong to be drunk alone. The Gemara adds, "The cup of blessing is not to be blessed, *until it is mixed* with water." To meet the objection, How can intoxication be hindered? the rabbis replied, "Because wine between eating does not intoxicate a man." But although usually intoxicating, it was not only permitted to be imbibed, but was also used for sacred purposes and was spoken of as a blessing (Gen. 49:11-12; Deut. 14:24-26; Ex. 29:40; Lev. 23:13; Num. 15:5). Some, indeed, have argued from these passages that *yayin* could not always have been alcoholic. But this is begging the question and that in defiance of the facts. Although invariably fermented, it was not always inebriating, and in most instances, doubtless, was but slightly alcoholic, like the *vin ordinaire* of France.

2. Heb. *tîrôsh*, properly signifies "must," the freshly pressed juice of the grape (the *gleuchos* of the Greeks, or sweet wine). It is rendered "wine" or "new wine" in Neh. 10:39; 13:5, 12; Prov. 3:10; Isa. 24:7; 65:8; Hos. 4:11; 9:2; Joel 1:10; Mic. 6:15; Hag. 1:11; Zech. 9:17. The question as to whether either of the above terms ordinarily signified a solid substance can be settled at once by a reference to the manner in which they were consumed. With regard to *yayin*, we are not aware of a single passage that couples it with the act of *eating*. In the only passage where the act of consuming *tîrôsh* alone is mentioned (Isa. 62:8-9), the verb is *shāthâ*, which constantly indicates the act of *drinking*. There are, moreover, passages that seem to imply the actual manufacture of *tîrôsh* by the same process by which wine was ordinarily made (Mic. 6:15; Prov. 3:10; Joel 2:24). As to the intoxicating character of this drink, the allusions to its effects are confined to a single passage, "Harlotry, wine [*yayin*], and new wine [*tîrôsh*] take away the understanding" (Hos. 4:11), where *tîrôsh* appears as the climax of engrossing influences, in immediate connection with *yayin*.

3. Heb. *shēkār* (an "intoxicant"), an inebriating drink, whether the wine prepared or distilled is from barley, honey, or dates, *yayin* referring more particularly to wine made from grapes. *Shēkār* is usually rendered "strong drink" (Num. 28:7; cf. Ps. 69:12). The liquors included under *shēkār* might therefore be pomegranate wine, palm wine, apple wine, honey wine, or perhaps even beer, for some have identified it with the liquor obtained from barley by the Egyptians. The word is used in the following passages in such a manner as to show decisively that it denotes an intoxicating drink: Lev. 10:9, where the priests are forbidden to drink wine, or *shēkār*, when they go into the Tabernacle; 1 Sam. 1:15, where Hannah, charged with drunkenness by Eli, replies it was not so —"I have drunk neither wine nor strong drink [*shēkār*]"; Ps. 69:12, where the psalmist complains, "I am the song of the drunkard"; Prov. 31:4-5, "It is not for kings to drink wine, or for rulers to desire strong drink [*shēkār*], lest they drink and forget what is decreed"; Isa. 5:22, "Woe to those who are heroes in drinking wine, and valiant men in mixing strong drink [*shēkār*]" (cf. 28:7; 29:9).

4. Heb. *'āsîs* (Song of Sol. 8:2; Isa. 49:26; Joel 1:5; 3:18; Amos 9:13) is derived from a word signifying "to tread" and therefore refers to the method by which the juice was expressed from the fruit. It refers to *new* wine as being recently trodden out, but not necessarily to unfermented wine.

5. Heb. *Sōbe'*, "potation," occurs only three times (Isa. 1:22; Hos. 4:18; Nah. 1:10, "drunken"), but the verb and participle are used often—the latter to denote drunk, a drunkard.

6. Heb. *mesek*, a "mixture," is wine mixed with water or aromatics (Ps. 75:8, "well mixed"). But the noun appears to have been restricted in usage to a bad sense, to denote wine mingled with stupefying or excitement-producing drugs, so that the wine might produce more powerful effects than were possible otherwise, at a time when distillation had not been discovered.

7. In the NT are the following Gk. words: *oinos*, including every sort of wine. *Gleuchos* ("must"), "sweet wine," which seems to have been of an intoxicating nature. It is used in Acts 2:13, where the charge is made, "They are full of sweet wine," to which Peter replies (v. 15), "These men are not drunk, as you suppose." If the wine was not intoxicating, the accusation could only have been ironical. From the explanations of the ancient lexicographers we may infer that the luscious qualities of this wine were due not to its being recently made but to its being produced from the purest juice of the grape. *Genēma tēs ampelou*, "fruit of the vine" (Luke 22:18). *Oinos akratos*, "pure wine" (Rev. 14:10). *Oxos*, "sour wine or vinegar" (Matt. 27:48; Mark 15:36; etc.). *Sikera* (Luke 1:15, "liquor"), an intoxicating beverage made of a mixture of sweet ingredients, whether from grain or vegetables, the juice of fruits, or a decoction of honey. It corresponds to no. 3.

Biblical History of Wine. Wine is first mentioned in the case of Noah, who "planted a vineyard. And he drank of the wine [*yayin*] and became drunk" (Gen. 9:20-21). The next mentions are made in 19:32-35, where it is said that the daughters of Lot made their father drink wine (*yayin*) so that he became intoxicated. It is mentioned in the blessing pronounced by Isaac upon Jacob (27:28), in connection with Egypt (40:11), when the chief butler says, "I took the grapes and squeezed them into Pharaoh's cup." With regard to the uses of wine in private life, there is little to say. It was produced on occasions of ordinary hospitality (14:18) and at festivals, such as marriages (John 2:3-10). The monuments of ancient Egypt furnish abundant evidence that the people of that country, both male and female, indulged liberally in the use of wine. Under the Mosaic law wine formed the usual drink offering that accompanied the daily sacrifice (Ex. 29:40), the presentation of the firstfruits (Lev. 23:13), and other offerings (Num. 15:5). Tithe was to be paid of wine as of other products. The priest was also to receive firstfruits of wine, as of other articles (Deut. 18:4; cf. Ex. 22:29). The use of wine at the Paschal feast was not commanded by the law but had become an established custom at all events in the post-Babylonian period. The wine was mixed with warm water on these occasions, as implied in mention of the warming kettle. Hence in the early Christian church it was usual to mix the sacramental wine with water.

Figurative. Wine is figurative of the blood of Christ (Matt. 26:27-29); of the blessings of the gospel (Prov. 9:2, 5; Isa. 25:6; 55:1); of the exhilarating effect of the Holy Spirit's fullness (Eph. 5:18); of the wrath and judgments of God (Pss. 60:3; 75:8; Jer. 13:12-14; 25:15-18); of the abominations of the apostasy (Rev. 17:2; 18:3); of violence (Prov. 4:17). *See* Drink, Strong.

WINE PRESS. Each vineyard had its wine press; it was the practice to extract the juice from the grape in the field. These presses were generally hewn out of the solid rock (Isa. 5:2; Matt. 21:33), and a large number of them remain today. From the scanty notices contained in the Bible we gather that the wine presses of the Jews consisted of two receptacles or vats placed at different elevations. In the upper one, the grapes were trodden, while the lower one received the juice. The two vats are mentioned together only in Joel 3:13: "The wine press [*gat*] is full; the vats ['troughs,' *yekeb*] overflow." *Gat* is also strictly applied to the upper vat in Neh. 13:15; Lam. 1:15; and Isa. 63:2. Heb. *pûrâ*, "crushing," is used in a parallel sense in Hag. 2:16, probably referring to the contents of a wine vat rather than to the press or vat itself (Isa. 5:2; Matt. 21:33).

Vintage scene on Roman lamp

Figurative. The forceful use of the wine press as a figure is found in Isa. 63:3-6, where Jehovah is pictured taking vengeance upon the ungodly nations. The nations are the grapes, which are cut off and put into the wine press (Joel 3:13); and the red upon His garments is the life blood of these nations. This work of wrath had been executed by Jehovah because He had in His heart a day of vengeance, which could not be delayed, and because the year of His promised redemption had arrived. The NT counterpart of this passage is the destruction of Antichrist and his army (Rev. 19:11-15). He who effects this destruction is the Faithful and True, the Logos of God. The vision of John is evidently based upon that of Isaiah. Merciless oppression is forcibly illustrated in Job 24:9-12, where men are said to "tread wine presses but thirst."

BIBLIOGRAPHY: C. Seltman, *Wine in the Ancient World* (1957); J. P. Free, *Archaeology and Bible History* (1962), pp. 43-44.

WING (Heb. generally *kānāp*, "extremity"; Gk. *pterux*, "feather"). The Heb. word conveys the meaning not only of the wings of birds, but also the skirt, or flap, of a garment (Ruth 3:9; Jer. 2:34), or the extremity of a country (Job 38:13; Isa. 24:16).

Figurative. God said that He had borne His people on eagles' wings (Ex. 19:4; Deut. 32:11), i.e., He had brought them out of Egypt with strong and loving care. The eagle watches over its young in the most careful manner, flying under them when it leads them from the nest, lest they should fall upon the rocks. To "mount up with wings like eagles" (Isa. 40:31), i.e., their course of life, which has Jehovah for its object, is, as it were, possessed of wings. The *wings* of the sun (Mal. 4:2) are the rays by which it is surrounded. As the rays of the sun spread light and warmth over the earth for the benefit of plants and living creatures, so will the sun of righteousness bring healing for all the hurts inflicted by sin. "The wings of the wind" (2 Sam. 22:11; Ps. 18:10) and "of the dawn" (139:9) are expressive of the swiftness with which the winds and the morning move onward. The idea of protection and defense is given by such expressions as "Hide me in the shadow of Thy wings" (17:8; cf. 36:7; 57:1; 61:4; 63:7; 91:4; Matt. 23:37; Luke 13:34).

WINNOW (Heb. *zārâ*, to "toss" about). The process of separating the chaff from the grain by throwing it against the wind (Isa. 30:24). *See* Agriculture.

Figurative. To winnow is used in the sense of to *scatter*, as enemies (Isa. 41:16); to "winnow them with a winnowing fork at the gates" (Jer. 15:7) is to cause defeat and dispersion on the border of the land; also the winnowing of Babylon (51:2) speaks of her devastation. "And His winnowing fork is in His hand" (Matt. 3:12) refers to Christ as the judge, separating evil from good.

WINNOWING FORK (Heb. *mizreh;* Gk. *ptuon*). A sort of long-handled wooden shovel used in the process of winnowing (Jer. 15:7; Matt. 3:12; Luke 3:17; cf. Isa. 30:24). At the present day in Syria a large wooden fork is used.

WINTER (Heb. usually *hōrep*, strictly "autumn"; Gk. *cheimōn*, the "rainy" season). In Palestine winter includes part of autumn and the seasons of seedtime and cold, extending from the beginning of September to the beginning of March (Gen. 8:22; Ps. 74:17; Zech. 14:8; Matt. 24:20). The cold of winter is not usually very severe, though the N winds are very penetrating from the middle of December to the middle of February. Snow and hail during most winters fall on the hills. On the central range snow has been known to reach a depth of nearly two feet and to lie for five days or even more, and the pools at Jerusalem have sometimes been covered with ice. But this is rare. On the central range the ground seldom freezes, and the snow usually disappears in a day. On the plateaus E of Jordan snow lies regularly for some days every winter, and on the top of Hermon there are fields of it during the summer. *See also* Calendar.

WINTER HOUSE (Heb. *ḥōrep*). In Scripture the lower portion of the house was called the "winter house," as was also the inner apartment, while the outer and upper ones were called the summer house (Jer. 36:22).

WISDOM. The rendering of several Heb. terms.

1. Heb. *ḥokmâ* has the special meaning of "dexterity, skill" in an art (cf. Ex. 28:3; 31:6; 36:1-2). It also and more generally means intelligent, sensible, judicious, endued with reason and using it (Deut. 4:6; 34:9; Prov. 10:1; etc.); skillful to judge (1 Kings 2:9). Thus the wisdom of Solomon is manifested in his acute judgment (3:26-28; 10:1-8), in the verses and sentences he composed or retained in his memory (5:12; Prov. 1:2). Wisdom includes skill in civil matters (Isa. 19:11), the faculty of interpreting dreams and prophesying (Dan. 5:11), as well as the art of enchantment and magic (Ex. 7:11). A higher and more enlightened wisdom is ascribed to angels (2 Sam. 14:20) and to God (Job 9:4).

2. Heb. *śākal* (to "be prudent, circumspect," 1 Sam. 18:30; Job 22:2; cf. Pss. 2:10; 94:8; etc.).

3. Heb. *tûshîyâ* (properly "uprightness"), counsel, understanding (Job 11:6; 12:16; 26:3; Prov. 3:21; etc.).

4. Heb. *bînâ* ("understanding"), the faculty of insight, intelligence (Prov. 4:5, 7; 17:10, "understanding").

Occasional Uses. Wisdom is used for (1) ingenuity, mechanical dexterity (Ex. 28:3; 31:3); (2) craftiness, sublety, whether good or bad (Ex. 1:10; Prov. 14:8); (3) the skill or arts of magicians, etc. (Gen. 41:8; Ex. 7:11; Eccles. 9:17-18); (4) sagacity, learning, experience (Job 12:2, 12; 38:37; Ps. 105:22); (5) the current pagan philosophy of the apostolic age (1 Cor. 1:20; 2:5; 3:19; 2 Cor. 1:12).

Dominant Uses. An attribute of God, wisdom is intimately related to the divine knowledge, manifesting itself in the selection of proper ends with the proper means for their accomplishment. Thus not only the world of nature but especially the economy of redemption is a manifestation of divine wisdom (*see* Ps. 104:24; Rom. 11:33; 1 Cor. 1:24; Rev. 7:12). Thus the OT appeal of wisdom to men is the appeal of the only wise God (*see* Proverbs and Psalms).

In men wisdom is not only practical understanding of matters relating to this life (1 Kings 3:12), but in the highest sense it is the theoretical and practical acceptance of divine revelation. Wisdom is in the deepest sense a divine gift (*see* Acts 6:10; 1 Cor. 2:6; 12:8; Eph. 1:17; Col. 1:9; 3:16; James 1:5; 3:15-17).

WITCH, WITCHCRAFT. *See* Magic; Saul; Sorcery.

WITHERED. *See* Diseases.

WITNESS (Heb. *ēd;* Gk. *martureō,* to "testify").

A Memorial. Among people with whom writing is not common, the evidence of a transaction is given by some tangible memorial or significant ceremony. Abraham gave seven ewe lambs to Abimelech as evidence of his ownership of the well of Beersheba. Jacob raised a heap of stones to be "a witness," a boundary mark between himself and Laban (Gen. 21:30; 31:48, 52). The tribes of Reuben and Gad raised an "altar" as a witness to the covenant between themselves and the rest of the nation; Joshua set up a stone as evidence of the allegiance promised by Israel to God (Josh. 22:10, 26, 34; 24:26-27).

Legal Usages. Thus also symbolical usages, in ratification of contracts or completed arrangements, as the ceremony of shoe-loosing (cf. Deut. 25:9-10; Ruth 4:7-8), the ordeal prescribed in the case of a suspected wife (Num. 5:17-31), with which may be compared the ordeal of the Styx. But written evidence was by no means unknown to the Jews. Divorce was to be proved by a written document (Deut. 24:1, 3). In civil contracts, at least in later times, documentary evidence was required and carefully preserved (Isa. 8:16; Jer. 32:10-16).

Evidence in Law. On the whole the law was careful to provide and enforce evidence for all its infractions and all transactions bearing on them. Among special provisions with respect to evidence are the following: (1) Two witnesses at least were required to establish any charge (Num. 35:30; Deut. 17:6; John 8:17; 2 Cor. 13:1; cf. 1 Tim. 5:19). (2) In the case of the suspected wife, evidence besides the husband's was required (Num. 5:13). (3) The witness who withheld the truth was censured (Lev. 5:1). (4) False witness was punished with the punishment due to the offense that it sought to establish. (5) Slanderous reports and officious witness were discouraged (Ex. 20:16; 23:1; Lev. 19:16; etc.). (6) The witnesses were the first executioners (Deut. 13:9; Acts 7:58-59). (7) In case of an animal left in charge of someone else and torn by wild beasts, the keeper was to bring the carcass in proof of the fact and disproof of his own criminality (Ex. 22:13). (8) According to Josephus, women and slaves could not bear testimony (*Ant.* 4.8.15).

New Testament Use of Word. In the NT the original notion of a witness is exhibited in the special form of one who attests his belief in the gospel by personal suffering. Hence it is that the use of the ecclesiastical term "martyr" has arisen.

BIBLIOGRAPHY: H. Danby, trans., *The Mishnah* (1933), pp. 246, 341, 369-70, 386-90, 399-403; S. Mendenhall, *The Criminal Jurisprudence of the Ancient Hebrews* (1968), pp. 13, 31, 70, 76-79, 82, 94-98, 103, 121, 130; A. A.

Trites, *The New Testament Concept of Witness* (1977).

WITNESS OF THE SPIRIT. The direct testimony of the Holy Spirit to true believers as to their acceptance with God and their adoption into the divine household.

Scriptural. The two classic passages upon which this doctrine is especially based are Rom. 8:16; Gal. 4:6. It is, however, argued that just as Christ in His visible ministry not only forgave sins but also announced to penitent sinners their forgiveness, so it is one of the offices of the Holy Spirit still to proclaim directly to those who are pardoned the fact of their pardon. Also this view is confirmed by other representations than those named in the Scriptures of the presence and activity of the Holy Spirit (*see* Rom. 8:1-2; 2 Cor. 1:22; Eph. 1:13; 4:30). The Holy Spirit is "the spirit of adoption." It is because He speaks within us that we are able to cry, "Abba! Father," are consciously free from condemnation, and are "sealed" in Him with the Holy Spirit of promise (Rom. 8:15; Eph. 1:13).

Theological Suggestions. The fact to which the witness of the Spirit particularly relates is that of the gracious change in the relation of the pardoned sinner to God. He is no longer guilty and "an alien" but forgiven, and by adoption a child of God. The one point upon which the Scriptures lay emphasis is that the Spirit's witness is to the fact of adoption, connected, of course, with justification and regeneration.

The witness of our own spirit is to be distinguished from the witness of the Holy Spirit. In Rom. 8:16 the word used is *summartureō*, which means two or more witnesses jointly, yet distinctly, giving testimony to the same fact. And two witnesses are mentioned here, the spirit of the man himself and the Spirit of God. The witness of our own spirit is indirect in the sense that it is based upon a comparison of the facts of our spiritual life and experiences with the representations and requirements of the Scriptures. We know whether or not we have truly repented and believed in Christ and whether we have peace and joy and love and the spirit of obedience (*see* 5:1; 8:1-14; 1 John 2:29; 3:14, 19, 21; 4:7). But the witness of the Spirit is beyond this, though associated with it. As Wesley says, "The testimony of the Spirit is an inward impression on the souls of believers, whereby the Spirit of God directly testifies to their spirit that they are 'children of God,'" and further, "There is in every believer both the testimony of God's Spirit and the testimony of his own that he is a child of God." This direct and distinct witness of the Spirit is frequently merged into and confused with the witness of our own spirit, as notably by Chalmers (*Lectures on Rom.,* p. 202), where he reduces the work of the Spirit to the engraving upon us the lineaments of a living epistle of Jesus Christ, and tells us in the epistle of a written revelation what these lineaments are. But this is in opposition to a fair exegesis of Rom. 8:16, where the idea of two joint yet distinct testimonies appear.

The witness of the Spirit is to be regarded as a sequence to or reward of saving faith and not the basis of such faith or a necessary element therein. Wesleyan writers, and Wesley himself, have not always been sufficiently clear upon this point. At times Wesley distinguishes most clearly between "justifying faith and a sense of pardon," and adds, "How can a sense of pardon be the condition of our receiving it?" (*Works,* 12:109-10). But elsewhere (*Sermons,* 10:8-9) he argues that "we cannot love God till we know he loves us; and we cannot know his pardoning love to us till his Spirit witnesses to our spirit." He is seeking to prove here that the witness of the Spirit must precede the witness of our own spirit. But in seeking this he goes too far, making the witness of the Spirit the basis of our faith and an essential element therein. It is of the greatest importance to understand that saving faith is simply complete reliance of the penitent soul upon the grace of God in Jesus Christ, as offered in His Word, and that the witness of the Spirit comes in God's own time and way to those who do thus truly repent and believe. The Spirit's witness is a great boon offered to all believers, and none should rest without it. But there are ways of directly seeking it that involve not faith but unbelief and disparagement of the sure promises of God as contained in His Holy Word.

BIBLIOGRAPHY: C. W. Hodge, *Princeton Theological Review* 11 (1913): 41-84; B. L. Ramm, *The Witness of the Spirit* (1960).

WIZARD. See Magic: Spiritist.

WOLF. The following allusions are made to the wolf in the Scriptures: Its ferocity is mentioned in Gen. 49:27; Ezek. 22:27; Hab. 1:8; Matt. 7:15; its nocturnal habits in Jer. 5:6; Zeph. 3:3; Hab. 1:8; its attacking sheep in Ecclus. 13:17; John 10:12; Matt. 10:16; Luke 10:3.

Figurative. Of the wicked (Matt. 10:16; Luke 10:3); of wicked rulers (Ezek. 22:27; Zeph. 3:3); of false teachers (Matt. 7:15; Acts 20:29); of the devil (John 10:12); of the tribe of Benjamin (Gen. 49:27); of fierce enemies (Jer. 5:6; Hab. 1:8); of the peaceful reign of the Messiah, under the metaphor of a wolf dwelling with a lamb (Isa. 11:6; 65:25). See Animal Kingdom: Jackal; Wolf.

WONDERS (Heb. *pālā',* to "separate," to "distinguish"). Something great, unaccountable, a miracle or marvel (Job 5:9; 10:16, "power"; Pss. 9:1; 17:7; etc.); "wonderful deeds" (1 Chron. 16:12, 24).

WOODWORKER. See Handicrafts.

WOOL. See Dress.

WORD. See Logos.

WORM. See Animal Kingdom.

WORMS. *See* Diseases.

WORMWOOD. *See* Vegetable Kingdom.

WORSHIP. The act of paying honor to a deity; religious reverence and homage. The rendering of the following Heb. and Gk. words:

1. Heb. *shāḥâ* (to "bow down"), to prostrate oneself before another in order to do him honor and reverence (Gen. 22:5; etc.). This mode of salutation consisted in falling upon the knees and then touching the forehead to the ground (19:1; 42:6; 48:12; 1 Sam. 25:41; etc., often rendered "bowed"). It is, however, used specifically to bow down before God; spoken of worship rendered to God, and also to false gods (Gen. 22:5; Ex. 24:1; 33:10; Judg. 7:15; Job 1:20; Pss. 22:27; 86:9).

2. Aram. *sᵉgîd* (to "fall down"), spoken of in connection with idol worship; to fall down in adoration of idols (Dan. 3:5-6, 10-12, 14-15, 28); in honor of a man, as of Daniel (2:46).

3. Heb. *'āṣab* (to "carve, labor"), to *serve* an idol, as in Jer. 44:19; or according to others, to *fashion her,* i.e., the image (*see* Orelli, *Com.,* ad loc.).

4. The Gk. words thus rendered are: *proskuneō*, properly to "kiss the hand to (toward) one," in token of reverence; also by kneeling or prostration to do homage—the word most frequently used in the NT; *sebomai,* to "revere" a deity (Matt. 15:9; Mark 7:7; Acts 18:13; 19:27). Proselytes of the gate are called worshipers of God (*sebomenē tōn theon,* 16:14; 18:7), or simply "devout persons" (*tois sebomenois,* 17:17, "God-fearing"). *Latreuō* (to "serve") in the NT means to render religious service or honor and in the *strict* sense to perform sacred services, to offer gifts, to worship God in the observance of the rites instituted for His worship (Heb. 10:2; 9:9). *Ethelothrēskeia* ("voluntary worship"), i.e., worship that one devises and prescribes for himself, contrary to the contents and nature of the faith that ought to be directed to Christ; used for the misdirected zeal and practices of ascetics (Col. 2:23). *Therapeuō* to "do service," as in Acts 17:25.

General Observations. It is as natural to worship as it is to live. The feeling and expression of high adoration, reverence, trust, love, loyalty, and dependence upon a higher power, human or divine, is a necessity to man. These sentiments, toward something or somebody, and whether real or imaginary, appeal to a greater or less degree to every man. And that something determines his worship. "Worship is as old as humanity. It has its root in a necessity of the human soul as native to it as the consciousness of God itself, which impels it to testify by word and act its love and gratitude to the Author of life and the Giver of all good" (Keil, *Bib. Arch.,* p. 55).

Primitive Worship. We are not informed as to the nature of the worship rendered by our first parents. But we learn from earliest records that

their sons were moved to present a portion of the product of their labor in sacrifice to God. Men as early as Enosh, the grandson of Adam (Gen. 4:26), called upon the name of the Lord. In other words, the regular and solemn worship of God as Jehovah (i.e., as the God of salvation) was celebrated in word and act—with prayer and sacrifice. Max Müller says: "That feeling of sonship which distinguishes man from every other creature, and not only exalts him above the brute, but completely secures him against sinking into a purely physical state of being, that original intuition of God, and that consciousness of his being dependent upon a higher power, can only be the result of a primitive revelation in the most literal sense of the word." This view is held by Schelling. The other view is that worship cannot be traced to a divine source; that the original condition of the human family was of an extremely rude and imperfect character; and that fetishism, being the lowest form of religion, was also the earliest and that for this reason we ought to regard religion, even in its most advanced forms, as springing originally from a barbarous fetishism. But the grounds upon which this opinion is based are weak in the extreme. "It would be nearer the truth to say that they are as divine as they are human in their origin, seeing that they are based upon the relation of man to God involved in his creation, and are evoked by a sense of the divine training and guidance under which he finds himself after his creation" (Keil, *Bib. Arch.,* p. 56).

In primitive times the form of worship that Enosh introduced was still maintained, for Enoch "walked with God" (Gen. 5:24). Noah was righteous before Him, expressing his gratitude by presenting burnt offerings (6:9; 8:20-21).

In a subsequent age God chose for Himself a faithful servant in the person of Abraham. He made him the depository of His revelation and the father and founder of His chosen people, who were destined to preserve the knowledge and worship of His name until the time when the Savior would come from their midst. While other nations multiplied their modes of worship according to the political constitution that they adopted and to suit the number and variety of their duties, they devised a corresponding variety of ritual, with a large priesthood and a multitude of sacred observances. But Abraham and the posterity born to him preserved a simple form of worship, as became shepherds and in keeping with the revelation imparted to them. Wherever they pitched their tents for any length of time they built *altars* in order that, in compliance with ancient usage, they might call upon the name of the Lord (12:7-8; 13:4, 18; etc.). Those altars were, doubtless, simple mounds (Heb. *bāmôt*) composed of earth and stone, and the animals sacrificed upon them consisted of those that were edible (i.e., clean), taken from the fold.

We have no information regarding the particular ceremonies observed in connection with these sacrifices. But it is probable that prayer was offered by the patriarchs in person, who were in the habit of discharging the priestly functions. The offerings were for the most part burnt offerings, i.e., offerings that were entirely consumed upon the altar, although instances are given of a portion of the sacrifice being reserved for use in the sacrificial feasts. In the selection of animals for sacrifices the patriarchs were probably guided by the directions given to Abraham (15:9); the way in which the sacrifice of Isaac terminated (22:12-13) must have shown that the animal sacrificed was to be regarded merely as a symbol of the heart's devotion to God. Whether these sacrifices were offered at regular intervals or on special occasions (*see* Job 1:5), we cannot say.

Besides altars, *memorial stones* (Heb. *maṣṣēbôt*) were erected by the patriarchs on spots where God had favored them with special revelations. Drink offerings were poured upon them (Gen. 28:18, 22; 35:14). The narrative of Jacob's vow (2:20-22) tells of his promise that, if God would watch over him, supply his wants, and bring him back in safety, he would acknowledge Jehovah as his God, consecrate the pillar he had set up and make it a house of God, and render to Jehovah a tenth of all his income. He excluded strange gods from his house (35:1-4). After due preparation on the part of his household, he built an altar at Bethel.

To the above-mentioned forms of worship, the rite of circumcision was added. In obedience to a divine order, and as a token of the covenant that Jehovah made with him, Abraham performed this rite upon himself and the male members of his household, commanding his posterity that it was an inviolable obligation (17:1-14, 23-27). Nothing further is known regarding the forms of worship that prevailed among the patriarchs.

Mosaic. When Israel became a nation with an organized civil government, in order to fulfill its divine mission it was necessary that its religious affairs should also be remodeled and that the character and style of its worship should be fixed and regulated by positive divine enactments. This did not necessitate an entirely new system of worship, since they were to serve and honor the God of their fathers. Therefore the worship introduced by Moses was grafted on that of Israel's ancestors. It was improved and perfected only as the circumstances of the Israelites as a confederacy of tribes or a monarchy seemed to require, with such forms and ceremonies as would further Israel's divinely appointed mission. This object was further secured by the Mosaic ritual, inasmuch as it embraced all the essential elements of a complete system of worship. It gave precise directions as to the *place* of worship, with its structure and arrangements, instituting a distinct order of sacred functions, prescribing the religious ceremonies, fixing the sacred seasons and the manner in which they were to be observed.

This system bore the stamp of genuine worship. It was framed by Moses in accordance with revelation and recognized Jehovah as the true God. Nor is it a vital objection to its being true worship on the grounds that it had a material and sensuous character and that many of its forms and ceremonies were similar to the rituals of pagan religions. These facts have been variously misconstrued and have been taken advantage of for the purpose of disparaging the origin and character of the Mosaic worship. It is true that the Mosaic worship embodies itself, for the most part, in outward forms and ceremonies, for one can only give expression to his relation to his Creator through *corporeal media*. Religious thought and feeling can express themselves only in word and act, and therefore forms are necessary in every kind of worship. And being copies or impressions of religious ideas, they must have an allegorical or symbolical character.

Further, the religion of the OT is monotheism, in contradiction to the polytheism of heathen nations. Jehovah is represented not only as the only true God, not merely as the almighty Creator, Preserver, and Governor of the world and every creature; not simply as the eternal, absolute Spirit, the good and merciful One who has destined man to enjoy the felicity of life that springs from personal fellowship with Himself. But He is also pictured as the omnipresent and near One watching over all His creatures, to keep the weak and distressed. He seeks to conduct those who have wandered from Him back to the fountain of life. He selected for Himself, from degenerate humanity, a race to be in a special sense His people and to whom He, in a special sense, would be God, with the purpose of saving the world. This is accompanied with such directions for the regulations of their life, that, if accepted and complied with, Israel would become to Jehovah "My own possession among all the peoples" (Ex. 19:5-6), "a kingdom of priests and a holy nation."

Christian. The church of Christ is not only His representative body on earth, it is also the temple of divine service continuing and perfecting the worship of the past. This service includes offerings presented to God and blessings received from Him. The former embraces the entire ordinance of worship, with its nature, reasons, and observances; the latter embraces the means of grace, common prayer, the Word, and the sacraments. These, however, are really one, and their relations to each other as one are of great importance. Both require for their realization the institution of the evangelical ministry. The worship of the Christian church may be regarded in its divine principles and in its human arrangements. As to the former, its object is the revealed Trinity; its form is mediatorial, through the incarnate

Son, by the Holy Spirit; its attributes are spirituality, simplicity, purity, and reverent decorum; its seasons are preeminently the Lord's Day and all times of holy assembly. As to the latter, it is left to the congregation itself to determine the minor details, according to the pattern shown in the Scripture.

As an institute of worship the church of Christ has its ordinary channels for the communication of the influences of the Holy Spirit to the souls of men, namely, the means of grace; the supreme means are the Word and prayer. Special attention is also called to the *sacraments* (which see) of baptism and the Lord's Supper.

BIBLIOGRAPHY: W. D. Maxwell, *A History of Christian Worship* (1936); O. Cullmann, *Early Christian Worship* (1953); R. P. Martin, *Worship in the Early Church* (1974); R. B. Allen, *Praise! A Matter of Life and Breath* (1980); R. G. Rayburn, *O Come Let Us Worship* (1980); R. B. Allen and G. L. Borror, *Worship: Rediscovering the Missing Jewel* (1982).

WORTHLESS MEN, WORTHLESS FELLOWS. NASB and NIV rendering of KJV "Belial," in OT references. *See* Belial.

WOUNDS. *See* Diseases.

WRATH (Gk. *orgē*). A term found several times in the NT (Rom. 2:8; Eph. 4:31; Col. 3:8; Rev. 19:15). The NIV translates "anger" in Eph. 4:31; Col. 3:8. "The general opinion of scholars is that . . . orgē, represents more of an abiding and settled habit of the mind (*'ira inveterata'*), with the purpose of revenge" (Trench, 1:178-79).

BIBLIOGRAPHY: R. V. G. Tasker, *The Biblical Doctrine of the Wrath of God* (1951); G. H. C. MacGregor, *New Testament Studies* 7 (1960-61): 101-9.

WRINKLE. Paul speaks (Eph. 5:27) of the church as a bride "having no spot or wrinkle" (Gk. *hrutis*), probably meaning the tokens of approaching age. If so, it reminds us of the continued youth and attractiveness of the church. Job complained (Job 16:8),"Thou hast filled me with wrinkles" KJV; "shriveled me up," NASB; "bound me," NIV (Heb. *qamōṭ*), a figurative expression meaning to be shriveled up.

WRITING. The art of reducing human thought to a permanent form in readable characters or signs upon an impressionable substance or material.

Antiquity. About 3400 B.C. writing entered the arena of history. The Sumerians used a pictograph script employing innumerable small pictures to stand for words. This was the oldest written language. At Uruk in southern Babylonia, where the first cylinder seals were discovered, writing emerged. In the Red temple at Uruk a number of flat clay tablets were written in a crude pictograph script. This gave way to Sumerian cuneiform (from the Lat. *cuneus*, meaning "wedge," referring to the wedge-shaped form of the letters made with the imprint of a stylus upon wet clay). The Semitic Babylonians, who came into Lower Babylonia and inherited the culture of the Sumerians, adopted cuneiform writing. This type of script spread to Assyria, and the mounds of Mesopotamia have yielded innumerable clay tablets inscribed in this style of writing. The Amarna Letters (c. 1400-1350 B.C.), consisting of some three hundred clay tablets written in an Akkadianized language, illustrate the wide use of cuneiform writing even in the foreign office in Egypt. Of special importance in the history of writing was the discovery of the Ras Shamra epic religious literature at Ugarit in N Syria (1929-37). Although this was written in cuneiform, it turned out to be the simple alphabetic, easily read variety, closely allied to alphabetic Heb. It offers innumerable parallels to OT vocabulary, syntax, and poetic style. Since 1923, a number of important Canaanite inscriptions have been unearthed at the ancient city of Byblos, biblical Gebal, including that written on the sarcophagus of Ahiram, belonging probably to the eleventh century B.C. Phoenician inscriptions from Cyprus, Sardinia, Carthage, and other colonies in the western Mediterranean date from after 900 B.C. The Gezer Calendar, written in perfect classical Heb., dates about 925 B.C.; the Moabite Stone, c. 850 B.C. The Samaritan Ostraca date from the reign of Jeroboam II, c. 776 B.C.; the Siloam Inscription, 701 B.C.; and the Lachish Letters, 589 B.C. As far as the OT is concerned, the important thing is that a simple alphabetic language was divinely prepared to record the history of redemption instead of the unwieldy and cumbersome syllabic cuneiform scripts of Babylonia-Assyria or the complex hieroglyphic writing of Egypt. Hebrew takes its origin from the old Phoenician alphabet, from which all alphabets in current use, Semitic and non-Semitic, have been derived. The origin of the proto-Semitic alphabet is still obscure. Sir Flinders Petrie uncovered early samples of this script at Serabit el Khadem in the Sinaitic Peninsula (1904-5). This discovery pushed alphabetic writing back before the time of Moses. Albright has precisely dated these documents in the early fifteenth century B.C. (*Bulletin of the American Schools of Oriental Research* 110 [April 1958]: 22). It is of unusual significance that this early "Sinai-Hebrew script" was found in the very region where Moses was instructed to write (Ex. 17:8-14). Earlier samples of alphabetic script have been found in the Syro-Palestine area; these date 1800-1500 B.C. In Egypt writing on papyrus goes back at least to the Old Kingdom (c. 2800-2500 B.C.). At Boghaz-keui, the Hittite capital, large numbers of tablets written in cuneiform characters in the Hittite language and a half dozen other languages were found in 1906 and later.

Scripture Mention. Writing is first mentioned in Ex. 17:14, and the connection clearly implies that it was not then employed for the first time but was so familiar that it was used for historic

Account of the fall of Nineveh inscribed on a clay tablet

not. It seems a natural inference that the accomplishments of reading and writing were not widely spread among the people, when we find that they are universally attributed to those of high rank or education—kings, priests, prophets, and professional scribes.

Materials. These were of several types.

Clay Tablets. Writing on soft, wet clay with a stylus and cuneiform script was the oldest medium of inscription in the Tigris-Euphrates Valley, the so-called "cradle of civilization."

Skins of Animals. Skins were used at an early date in Egypt, at least by the time of the Fourth Dynasty (2550-2450 B.C.), and their use was widespread. Carefully prepared skins of sheep or goats were sewn together to make rolls that varied from a foot or 2 to perhaps 100 feet, according to the number of books written on one roll. The skin was either wound in a single roll with a stick or wound around two sticks, one at each end. Not until the second or third century A.D. did the roll give way to the codex, or book form with leaves sewn together.

Papyrus Rolls. These were prepared for writing in Egypt during the Old Kingdom (c. 2800 B.C.), perhaps earlier. Egyptian papyrus rolls are still in existence from the end of the third millennium B.C. The story of Wen-Amon tells of the exportation of papyrus rolls from Egypt to Gebal in Phoenicia. Ordinary papyrus rolls were about 30 feet long, but sometimes, as in the case of Papyrus Harris and the Book of the Dead, 123 to 133 feet in length. But among the Jews the common use of the standard-size papyrus rolls necessitated the splitting up of certain books like the law of Moses into five books. The reed, or calamus, made from the hollow stem of coarse grass or rush, was cut diagonally with a knife to form a flexible point. To keep the pen point in good writing order, the scribe carried a knife with him, hence the term "scribe's knife" (Jer. 36:23). Ink was made of soot, lamp black, and gum diluted with water. *See also* Ink; Inkhorn; Pen; Roll.

M.F.U.

BIBLIOGRAPHY: G. A. Barton, *The Origin and Development of Babylonian Writing*, 2 vols. (1913); A. H. Gardiner, *Journal of Egyptian Archaeology* 2 (1915): 61ff.; F. G. Kenyon, *Ancient Books and Modern Discoveries* (1927); F. R. Blake, *Journal of the American Oriental Society* 60 (1940): 391ff.; M. Burrows, *What Mean These Stones?* (1941); E. A. Speiser, *Introduction to Hurrian* (1941); I. J. Gelb, *Old Akkadian Writing and Grammar*, M.A.D. 2 (1952); W. L. Morgan, *The Bible and the Ancient Near East* (1961), pp. 57ff.; I. J. Gelb, *A Study of Writing* (1963); S. Moscati, ed., *An Introduction to the Comparative Grammar of the Semitic Languages* (1964); T. A. Caldwell et al., *An Akkadian Grammar* (1974), pp. i-iv, 1-19; G. R. Driver, *Semitic Writing* (1976); A. H. Gardiner, *Egyptian Grammar* (1984), pp. 1-15; S. Segert; *A Basic Grammar of the Ugaritic Language* (1984), pp. 3-106.

records. Moses is commanded to preserve the memory of Amalek's onslaught in the desert by committing it to writing. The tables of the testimony are said to be "written by the finger of God" (Ex. 31:18) on both sides, and the writing was the writing of God (32:16). The curses against the adulteress were written by the priest "on a scroll," and blotted out with water (Num. 5:23). This proceeding, though principally distinguished by its symbolical character, involved the use of some kind of ink and of a material on which the curses were written that would not be destroyed by water. Hitherto, however, nothing had been said of the application of writing to the purposes of ordinary life or of the knowledge of the art among the common people. Up to this point such knowledge was attributed only to Moses and the priests. From Deut. 24:1, 3, however, it would appear that it was extended to others. It is not absolutely necessary to infer from this that the art of writing was an accomplishment possessed by every Hebrew citizen. It is more than probable that these certificates of divorce, though apparently informal, were the work of professional scribes. One of the duties of the king (17:18) was that he should transcribe the book of the law for his own private study. In Isa. 29:11-12 there is clearly a distinction drawn between the man who was able to read and the man who was

XYZ

XER′XES (zurk′sēz). The Gk. name of *Ahasuerus* (which see), husband of Esther. He ruled the Persian Empire from 485 to 465 B.C. According to Esther 1:3, the banquet that led to the deposition of Queen Vashti took place in Xerxes' third year (483) and the selection of Esther as a new queen in his seventh year (479; Esther 2:16). Between these two events occurred Xerxes' disastrous campaign in Greece, which resulted in the termination of Persian military actions against Greece.

H.F.V.

Relief of Xerxes from the treasury room of the palace at Persepolis

XESTES. The sextarius, or xestes, was a foreign measure of capacity (*see* Metrology). *See also* Pitcher.

YAH. A contraction (Ps. 68:4, marg.) for *Jehovah* (*see* [The] LORD; Yahweh). Yah also enters into the composition of many Heb. names, such as Adonijah, Isaiah, etc. The KJV renders it Jah.

YAHWEH (ya′way). The Heb. tetragrammaton (YHWH) traditionally pronounced Jehovah (*see*

discussion in the articles Lord; [The] LORD) is now known to be correctly vocalized *yahwê*. New inscriptional evidence from the second and first millennia B.C. point toward this fact. The old view of Le Clerc, later propounded by Paul Haupt and developed by W. F. Albright, has commended itself in the light of the phonetic development and grammatical evidence of increased knowledge of Northwest Semitic and kindred tongues. This thesis holds *Yahweh* to be originally a finite causative verb from the Northwest Semitic root *hwy*, "to be, to come into being," so that the divine name would mean "He causes to be, or exist," i.e., "He creates." Amorite personal names after 2,000 B.C. lend support to the Haupt-Albright view, demonstrating that the employment of the causative stem *yahweh*, "he creates," was in vogue in the linguistic background of early Heb. Another recent etymology is that of Sigmund Mowinckel and James Montgomery. This suggests that *Yahu* (an abbreviated form of *Yahweh* current in personal names) is a compound formation *ya* (O!) and *hu* or *huwa* (he), "O He!" The name *Yahweh* has been found to be unique to Israel and has not been verified as the name of any deity outside Israel. *See* Jehovah; Elohim.

BIBLIOGRAPHY: Julian Obermann, "The Divine Name YHWH in the Light of Recent Discoveries," *Journal of Biblical Literature* 68 (1949): 301-23; B. Alfrink, *Theologische Zeitschrift* 5 (1949), pp. 72ff; B. Alfrink, B. D. Eerdmans and G. J. Thierry, *Oudtestamentische Studien* 5 (1948): 1-62; W. Zimmerli, *I Am Yahweh* (1982).

YEAR. *See* Time.

YEAST. *See* Leaven.

YELLOW. *See* Colors.

YI′RON (yi′ron). One of the "fortified cities" of Naphtali (Josh. 19:38; "Iron," KJV, NIV), probably the present village of Jarûn, SE of Bint-Jebeil.

YODH, YOD (') (Heb. yōd). The tenth letter of the Heb. alphabet, standing at the head of the tenth section of Ps. 119, in which section each verse begins with this letter. M.F.U.

YOKE. A bar or frame of wood by which two draft animals, especially oxen, are joined at the necks or heads for working together, for drawing a load or pulling a plow. The rendering of a number of Heb. and Gk. words.

Yoked oxen plowing

ZA'ANAN (za'a-nan). A place named by Micah (Mic. 1:11) in his address to the towns of the Shephelah. Keil objects to its identification with Zenan, "as Zenan was in the plain, and Zaanan was most probably to the north of Jerusalem."

ZAANAN'NIM (za-a-na'nim). "The oak in Zaanannim." Probably a sacred tree marking the spot near which Heber the Kenite was encamped when Sisera took refuge in his tent (Judg. 4:11). It is said to be near Kedesh, NW of Lake Huleh. Probably the same tree mentioned in Josh. 19:33, it is identified with Khan et-Tujjar, about three miles NE of Mt. Tabor and about five miles W of the Sea of Galilee.

ZA'AVAN (za'a-van). The second son of Ezer, son of Seir the Horite (Gen. 36:27; 1 Chron. 1:42). *See* Horite.

ZA'BAD (za'bad; Arab. "He, i.e., God, has given").

1. Son of Nathan, who was the son of Attai. The mother of Attai was Ahlai, Sheshan's daughter (1 Chron. 2:31-37), and hence Zabad was called the son of Ahlai (11:41), about 992 B.C. He was one of David's mighty men, but none of his deeds has been recorded.

2. An Ephraimite, son of Tahath, and father of Shuthelah, no. 2 (1 Chron. 7:21).

3. Son of Shimeath, an Ammonitess; an assassin who, with Jehozabad, killed King Joash (2 Chron. 24:26), 797 B.C. The assassins were both put to death by Amaziah, but their children were spared (25:3-4) in obedience to the law of Moses (Deut. 24:16). In 2 Kings 12:21 his name is written, probably more correctly, Jozacar.

4, 5, 6. Three Israelites, "sons" respectively of Zattu (Ezra 10:27), Hashum (10:33), and Nebo

(10:43), who divorced their Gentile wives after the captivity, 456 B.C.

ZAB'BAI (zab'ī).

1. One of the "sons" of Bebai, who divorced his Gentile wife (Ezra 10:28), 456 B.C.

2. Father of the Baruch who assisted in repairing the walls of Jerusalem after the Exile (Neh. 3:20), 445 B.C.

ZAB'BUD (zab'ud; "given"). A "son" of Bigvai, who returned from Babylon with Ezra (Ezra 8:14), 459 B.C. The NIV reads Zaccur; *see* NASB margin.

ZAB'DI (zab'di; "giving").

1. The son of Zerah and grandfather of Achan, of the tribe of Judah (Josh. 7:1, 17-18), before 1395 B.C. The NIV reads Zimri (cf. 1 Chron. 2:6).

2. The third of the nine sons of Shimei the Benjamite (1 Chron. 8:19).

3. The Shiphmite (i.e., inhabitant of Shepham), and in charge of David's wine cellars (1 Chron. 27:27), about 960 B.C.

4. Son of Asaph the singer, and grandfather of Mattaniah, a prominent Levite in the time of Nehemiah (Neh. 11:17), 445 B.C.

ZAB'DIEL (zab'di-el; cf. Arab. "El has given").

1. The father of Jashobeam the commander of the first division of David's army (1 Chron. 27:2), about 960 B.C.

2. The "son of Haggedolim" (i.e., "valiant warriors"; KJV, "mighty men of valour"), who was overseer of 128 of the captives returned from the captivity (Neh. 11:14, *see* marg.), 445 B.C.

ZA'BUD (za'bud; "given"). The son of Nathan (1 Kings 4:5). He is described as a priest, and as holding at the court of Solomon the confidential post of "king's friend," which had been occupied by Hushai the Archite during the reign of David (2 Sam. 15:37; 16:16; 1 Chron. 27:33).

ZABULON. *See* Zebulun.

ZAC'CAI (zak'ī; probably shortened form of Zechariah). The sons of Zaccai to the number of 760 returned with Zerubbabel (Ezra 2:9; Neh. 7:14), before 536 B.C.

ZACCHE'US (zak-ē'us); more properly **Zacchaeus** (Gk. for Heb. *Zaccai*). A chief tax-gatherer (*architelōnēs*), or publican, residing at Jericho, who, being a short man, climbed into a sycamore tree in order that he might see Jesus as He passed through that town. When Jesus came to the tree, He paused, looked up, and called Zaccheus by name. He told him to hasten and come down, because He intended to be a guest at his house. With undisguised joy Zaccheus hastened down and welcomed the Master. The people murmured, saying that He had "gone to be the guest of a man who is a sinner." Zaccheus was especially odious as being a Jew and occupying an official rank among the tax-gatherers, which would indicate unusual activity in the service of the Roman oppressors. He seems to have been deeply moved by the consideration shown him by Jesus and, before all the people, made the vow that attested his penitence: "Behold, Lord, half of my possessions I will give to the poor, and if I have defrauded anyone of anything, I will give back four times as much," greater restitution than the law required (Num. 5:7). Jesus thereupon made the declaration "Today salvation has come to this house, because he, too, is [in the true spiritual sense] a son of Abraham" (Luke 19:1-10). *See also* Tax-gatherer.

BIBLIOGRAPHY: C. E. Macartney, *Great Interviews of Jesus* (1944), pp. 52-62; G. C. Morgan, *The Great Physician* (1963), pp. 253-60; J. D. M. Derrett, *Law in the New Testament* (1970), pp. 278-85.

ZAC'CUR, ZACCHUR (zak'ur; "remembered").
1. The father of Shammua, the Reubenite spy (Num. 13:4), before 1440 B.C.
2. Son of Hammuel, and father of Shimei (1 Chron. 4:26; KJV, "Zacchur").
3. A Levite, and third named of the four sons of Merari by Jaaziah (1 Chron. 24:27).
4. Son of Asaph the singer, and leader of the third division of Levitical musicians (1 Chron. 25:2, 10; Neh. 12:35).
5. The son of Imri, and one who assisted Nehemiah in rebuilding the city wall (Neh. 3:2), 445 B.C.
6. A Levite, or family of Levites, who signed the covenant with Nehemiah (Neh. 10:12), 445 B.C.
7. A Levite whose son or descendant Hanan was one of the treasurers appointed by Nehemiah over the storehouses (Neh. 13:13), 434 B.C.

ZACHARIAH (zak-a-rī'a). Another form of *Zechariah*, used in KJV, 2 Kings 14:29; 15:8-10. *See* Zechariah, no. 1.

ZACHARI'AS (zak-a-rī'as).
1. The father of John the Baptist (Luke 1:5-23, 59-79).
2. Gk. form of Heb. *Zechariah. See* Zechariah, no. 13.

ZA'DOK (za'dok; "just, righteous").
1. Son of Ahitub, and, with Abiathar, high priest in the time of David. He was of the house of Eleazar, the son of Aaron (1 Chron. 24:3), and eleventh in descent from Aaron.
First Chron. 12:28 says he joined David at Hebron, after Saul's death, with 22 captains of his father's house and, apparently, with 900 men (4,600 Levites came to David; Jehoiada was the leader of 3,700, and Zadok probably was in charge of the remaining men, vv. 26-27), 1000 B.C.
From this time Zadok was unwavering in his loyalty to David. When Absalom revolted and David fled from Jerusalem, Zadok and all the Levites bearing the Ark accompanied him. It was only at the king's express command that they returned to Jerusalem and became the medium of com-

munication between the king and Hushai the Archite (2 Sam. 15; 17:15). After Absalom's death Zadok and Abiathar were the persons who persuaded the elders of Judah to invite David to return (19:11). When Adonijah, in David's old age, maneuvered to attain the throne and had persuaded Joab and Abiathar the priest to join his party, Zadok was unmoved. He was employed by David to anoint Solomon to be king in his place (1 Kings 1).
For this fidelity he was rewarded by Solomon who "dismissed Abiathar from being priest to the Lord" and appointed Zadok as priest in his place (2:27, 35). From this time, however, we hear little of him. It is said in general terms in the enumeration of Solomon's officers of state that Zadok was the priest (4:4; 1 Chron. 29:22), but no single act of his is mentioned. Zadok and Abiathar were *kōhǎnim*, i.e., officiating high priests (2 Sam. 15:35-36; 19:11). The duties of the office were divided. Zadok ministered before the Tabernacle at Gibeon (1 Chron. 16:39); Abiathar had the care of the Ark at Jerusalem, although not exclusively (15:11; 2 Sam. 15:24-25, 29).
2. In the genealogy of the high priests in 1 Chron. 6:12 there is a second Zadok, son of a second Ahitub, and father of Shallum. It is supposed by some that the name was inserted by error of a copyist, while others identify him with Odeas, mentioned by Josephus (*Ant*. 10.8.6). He is perhaps the same person as the one mentioned in 1 Chron. 9:11; Neh. 11:11.
3. Father of Jerusha, the wife of Uzziah, and mother of King Jotham (2 Kings 15:33; 2 Chron. 27:1), before 738 B.C.
4. Son of Baana, who repaired a portion of the wall in the time of Nehemiah (Neh. 3:4). He is probably the same as the one in the list of those that signed the covenant in 10:21, for in both cases his name follows that of Meshezabel, 445 B.C.
5. Son of Immer, a priest who repaired a portion of the wall opposite his house (Neh. 3:29), 445 B.C.
6. The scribe whom Nehemiah appointed one of the three principal treasurers of the Temple (Neh. 13:13), 445 B.C.

BIBLIOGRAPHY: H. H. Rowley, *Journal of Biblical Literature* 58 (1959): 113ff.; R. de Vaux, *Ancient Israel: Its Life and Institutions* (1961), pp. 372-405.

ZA'HAM (za'ham; "loathsome fool"). The last of the three sons of Rehoboam by Abihail (2 Chron. 11:19), about 930 B.C. Keil (*Com.*, ad loc.) holds that Mahalath was the wife of Rehoboam and that Abihail, the daughter of Eliab, was Mahalath's mother.

ZA'HAR (zā'har). A place mentioned only once in the NIV (Ezek. 27:18) and otherwise unknown. The KJV, NKJV, and NASB translate "white wool" where the NIV has "wool from Zabar." E.H.M.

ZA'IR (za'ir; "little"). A place E of the Dead Sea, in Edom, where Israel defeated the Edomites (2 Kings 8:21). Its identification is uncertain.

ZA'LAPH (za'laf; perhaps "caper plant"). The father of Hanun, who assisted in repairing the wall of Jerusalem after the captivity (Neh. 3:30), 445 B.C.

ZAL'MON (zal'mon; "dark," cf. Arab. *zalima* and Ethiopic *ṣalma,* "to be dark").

1. An Ahohite (i.e., sprung from the Benjamite family of Ahoah), and one of David's warriors (2 Sam. 23:28). In the parallel passage (1 Chron. 11:29), he is called *Ilai* (which see).

2. A wood near Shechem (Judg. 9:48), a kind of "black forest," as rendered by Luther. David (Ps. 68:14, "it was snowing in Zalmon") uses language symbolical of the presence of light in darkness, or brightness in calamity.

ZALMO'NAH (zal-mō'na; "dark, shades," cf. Arab. *Zalmyn*). A station of Israel in the wilderness (Num. 33:41-42). It lay SE of Edom, perhaps in the Wadi el-Amrân, which runs into the Wadi Ithm, close to where Elath anciently stood.

ZALMUN'NA (zal'-mū'na; probably "shade denied," i.e., "deprived of protection"). One of the two kings of Midian who were captured and killed by Gideon (Judg. 8:5-21; Ps. 83:11), about 1100 B.C. *See* Zebah.

ZAMZUM'MIN (zam-zum'in; "noisemakers, murmurers," cf. Arab. *zamzama,* "to mumble, to hum"). Only in Deut. 2:20, the name given by the Ammonites to the people called by others *Rephaim* (which see). They were "a people as great, numerous and tall as the Anakim" (v. 21). From a slight similarity between the two names, and from the mention of both in connection with the Emim, it is usually assumed that the Zamzummin were identical with the *Zuzim* (which see). *See also* Giant: Rephaim.

ZAMZUM'MITES. *See* Zamzummin.

ZANO'AH (zȧ-nō'ȧ).

1. A town in the low country of Judah (Josh. 15:34) inhabited by Judeans after the captivity (Neh. 11:30). The inhabitants of Zanoah assisted in repairing the walls of Jerusalem (3:13). The site is marked now by Khirbet Zanū' or Zanuḥ in the Wadi Ismail, some ten miles W of Jerusalem.

2. A town in the hill country of Judah, ten miles SW of Hebron (Josh. 15:56), perhaps to be identified with Zenuta. In 1 Chron. 4:18 Jekuthiel is said to have been the father (i.e., founder or rebuilder) of Zanoah.

BIBLIOGRAPHY: W. F. Albright, *Bulletin of the American Schools of Oriental Research* 18 (1925): 10-11.

ZAPH'ENATH-PANE'AH (zaf'e-nath-pa-ne'a; Egyptian, "sustenance of the land is the living one"). The name given to Joseph by the reigning pharaoh (Gen. 41:45). Some modern Egyptolo-

gists maintain that the designation represents Egyptian "jed-pa-Neter-ef-'onekh," which would be construed: "says the god: He will live," "he" referring to the newborn child having the name. However, the name apparently refers to Joseph as sustainer of life with reference to his divine call as a savior during famine. M.F.U.

ZA'PHON (za'fōn; "north"). A place mentioned, in connection with Beth-haram, Beth-nimrah, and Succoth, as part of the inheritance of Gad (Josh. 13:27). It was in "the valley" (i.e., of Jordan), probably not far from the southern extremity of the Sea of Galilee. Located by Nelson Glueck at Tell el Kos in modern Jordan.

ZARED. *See* Zered.

ZAR'EPHATH (zar'e-fath). A town that derives its claim to notice from having been the residence of the prophet Elijah during the latter part of the drought (1 Kings 17:9-10). Beyond stating that it was near to, or dependent on, Sidon, the Bible gives no clue to its position. Josephus (*Ant.* 8.13.2) says that it was "not far from Sidon and Tyre, for it lay between them." It is on the seashore, N of Tyre. To this Jerome adds (*Onom.,* "Sarefta") that it "lay on the public road," i.e., the coast road. Both conditions are implied in the mention of the town in the itinerary of Paula by Jerome, and both are fulfilled in the situation of the modern village of *Ṣarafend.* Of the old town considerable indications remain. One group of foundations is on a headland called *'Ain el-Kantarah;* but the chief remains are S of this and extend for a mile or more, having many fragments of columns, slabs, and other architectural features. Zarephath is mentioned in the NT in Luke 4:26 ("Sarepta," KJV). James B. Pritchard of the University of Pennsylvania led an excavation at the site from 1969 to 1974. He was able to document the history of the town from its founding in about 1600 B.C. to Roman and Byzantine times. Evidence revealed production of purple dye, olive oil, metal goods, and pottery. A shrine dedicated to two goddesses of fertility, Tanit and Astart, helped to throw light on the religion of the seventh through the fifth centuries. *See also* James B. Pritchard, *Recovering Sarepta, A Phoenician City* (1978). H.F.V.

ZAR'ETHAN (zar'e-than), **Zaretan, Zartanah.**

1. A place named in the account of the passage of the Jordan by the Israelites: "The waters which were flowing down from above stood and rose up in one heap, a great distance away at Adam, the city that is beside Zarethan" (Josh. 3:16; "Zaretan," KJV). "Near Beisan is an unusually large mound called Tell es Sârem. A good deal of clay is found here, and a mile to the south is a stream the Arabic of which means 'red river.' . . . It has been suggested that the waters of the Jordan were suddenly dammed up by a landslip or similar convulsion. The appearance of the banks, and the

curious bends of the river near this place, would seem to support the idea. . . . It is clear from the Bible statement that the waters were arrested a long way off, above Jericho" (Harper, *Bib. and Mod. Disc.*, p. 148). Nelson Glueck, however, identified Zarethan as Tell es-Sa'idiyeh, about one mile W of the Jordan and overlooking the Wadi Kufringi on the N.

2. A place named (1 Kings 4:12; "Zartanah," KJV) to define the position of Beth-Shean.

3. A place in the plain of the Jordan, mentioned in connection with Succoth (1 Kings 7:46), near which the bronze vessels for the Temple were cast. It is given as Zeredah (Zeredthah, KJV) in 2 Chron. 4:17.

BIBLIOGRAPHY: J. B. Pritchard, *Sarepta* (1975).

ZAR'HITES. *See* Zerahites.

ZAT'TU (zat'u), **Zatthu.** An Israelite whose "sons" to the number of 945 (Ezra 2:8) or 845 (Neh. 7:13) returned with Zerubbabel (before 536 B.C.). Seven of his descendants renounced their Gentile wives (Ezra 10:27), and a person (or family) was among those who signed the covenant made by Nehemiah (Neh. 10:14; KJV, "Zatthu").

ZA'YIN (ז) (za'yin). The seventh letter of the Heb. alphabet. It stands at the head of the seventh section of Ps. 119, in which each verse begins with this letter in the Heb.

ZA'ZA (za'za). The second son of Jonathan, a descendant of Jerahmeel, of the tribe of Judah (1 Chron. 2:33).

ZEA'LOT (ze'lot; Gk. "a zealous one"). KJV uses "Zelotes" (zē-lō'tez). Gk. for Aram. *Cananaean;* a member of a Jewish patriotic party, the surname of the apostle Simon (Matt. 10:4; Mark 3:18; Luke 6:15; Acts 1:13), to distinguish him from Simon Peter. In the first two verses the KJV uses the name "Simon the Canaanite," perhaps a transliteration of the Heb. Aram. *qānā'nā,* "zealot." Meyer (*Com.*, on Matt. 10:4) says: *"Zealots were a class of men who, like Phinehas (Num. 25:7), were fanatical defenders of the theocracy; and who, while taking vengeance on those who wronged it, were themselves guilty of great excesses. But the ho Kananaios is not to be explained in this way, inasmuch as this form of the epithet is derived from the name of some place or other."*

ZEBADI'AH (zeb-a-dī'a; "Jehovah has given").

1. A Benjamite of the sons of Beriah (1 Chron. 8:15).

2. A Benjamite of the sons of Elpaal (1 Chron. 8:17).

3. One of the two sons of Jeroham of Gedor, who joined David at Ziklag (1 Chron. 12:7), before 1000 B.C.

4. Third son of Meshelemiah the Korahite (1 Chron. 26:2).

5. Son of Asahel the brother of Joab, of the fourth division of David's army (1 Chron. 27:7), before 960 B.C.

6. A Levite in the reign of Jehoshaphat, sent to teach the law in the cities of Judah (2 Chron. 17:8), 872 B.C.

7. The son of Ishmael, and ruler of the house of Judah in the reign of Jehoshaphat (2 Chron. 19:11), about 853 B.C.

8. Son of Michael, of the "sons" of Shephatiah, who returned with Ezra from captivity with eighty males (Ezra 8:8), about 457 B.C.

9. A priest of the sons of Immer, who had married a foreign wife after the return from Babylon (Ezra 10:20), 456 B.C.

ZE'BAH (zē'ba; "sacrifice"). One of the two Midianite kings overthrown by Gideon. He is mentioned in Judg. 8:5-21; Ps. 83:11, and always in connection with Zalmunna. They seem to have commanded the invasion of Palestine, leading their hordes with the cry "Let us possess for ourselves the pastures of God" (v. 12). Although Oreb and Zeeb, two of the minor leaders of the incursion, had been slain, with a vast number of their people, by the Ephraimites at the central fords of the Jordan, the two kings had succeeded in making their escape by a passage farther to the N (probably the ford near Beth-shean), and thence by the Wadi Yabïs, through Gilead to Karkor, a place that is not fixed, but that doubtlessly lay high up on the Hauran. Here they were resting with 15,000 men, a mere remnant of their huge horde, when Gideon overtook them. The name of Gideon still caused terror, and the Bedouin were entirely unprepared for his attack. They fled in dismay, and the two kings were taken. They were taken to Ophrah, the native village of their captor, and then Gideon asked them, "What kind of men were they whom you killed at Tabor?" Up to this time the sheikhs may have believed that they were reserved for ransom. But once these words were spoken, there could not have been any doubt what their fate was to be. They met it like noble children of the desert, simply requesting that the blow should be struck by their captor himself; and Gideon arose and killed them.

BIBLIOGRAPHY: G. A. Cooke, *A Textbook of North Semitic Inscriptions* (1903), pp. 195-99; L. J. Wood, *The Distressing Days of the Judges* (1975), pp. 105, 222-25, 232.

ZEBAIM. *See* Pochereth-hazzebaim.

ZEB'EDEE (zeb'e-dē; the Gk. form, probably, of Zabdi or Zebediah). The father of James and John (Matt. 4:21), and the husband of Salome (27:56; Mark 15:40). He was a Galilean fisherman, living probably either at or near Bethsaida. From the mention of his "hired servants" (Mark 1:20) and the acquaintance between John and Annas the high priest, it has been inferred that the family was in good circumstances. He appears only once in the gospel narrative, namely, in Matt. 4:21-22; Mark 1:19-20, where he is in his boat with his two sons, mending their nets.

ZEBI'DAH (ze-bi'da; "given"). A daughter of Pedaiah, of Rumah, wife of Josiah and mother of King Jehoiakim (2 Kings 23:36), before 608 B.C.

ZEBI'NA (ze-bi'na; Aram. "bought, purchased"). One of the "sons" of Nebo, who put away his Gentile wife after the captivity (Ezra 10:43), 456 B.C.

ZEBOI'IM (ze-boy'im; Gen. 14:2, 8). The rendering of *ṣebōyim* ("gazelles"), one of the five cities in the valley of Siddim destroyed by Jehovah (Gen. 10:19; Deut. 29:23; Hos. 11:8). It was ruled over by a separate king, Shemeber (Gen. 14:2, 8). *See* Sodom.

ZEBO'IM (ze-bō'im; Heb. *ṣebō'im,* "hyenas"). The name of a valley, i.e., the ravine or gorge, apparently E of Michmash (1 Sam. 13:18), near to which one of the columns of the Philistines came. "The wilderness" is no doubt the district of uncultivated mountain tops and sides lying between the central portion of Benjamin and the Jordan Valley. In that very district there is a wild gorge known as Shuk ed-Duba, "ravine of the hyena."

ZE'BUL (ze'bul; "habitation, dwelling"). Ruler of the city of Shechem under Abimelech. He advised Abimelech of the defection of the Shechemites, counseling him to advance upon the city. When Gaal and his men went out to fight against Abimelech, Zebul closed the gates of the city against them and thus assisted in their overthrow (Judg. 9:28-41), about 1100 B.C.

ZEB'ULUN (zeb'ū-lun; "dwelling, habitation"; Gk. form "Zabulon" appears in KJV in Matt. 4:13, 15; Rev. 7:8).

1. The tenth son of Jacob, and the sixth and last of Leah (Gen. 30:19-20). We have nothing recorded concerning Zebulun personally. In the genealogical list (chap. 46) he is mentioned as having, at the time of the migration into Egypt, three sons, founders of the chief families of the tribe (cf. Num. 26:26).

Tribe. During the desert journey Zebulun, with Judah and Issachar, formed the first camp. The tribe then numbered 57,400 (Num. 1:31). At Sinai the head of the tribe was Eliab, son of Helon (7:24); and at Shiloh, it was Elizaphan, son of Parnach (34:25). Its representative among the spies was Gaddiel, son of Sodi (13:10). The territory of Zebulun in Canaan lay between the Sea of Galilee and the Mediterranean. Nazareth and Cana were in it; and it embraced a section of the shore of the former sea, where Christ performed so many of His miracles, thus fulfilling the prophecy of Isaiah (Isa. 9:1-2; cf. Matt. 4:12-16). In the visions of Ezekiel (Ezek. 48:26-33) and of John (Rev. 7:8) this tribe finds due mention.

2. A place on the eastern border of the tribe of Asher, between Beth-dagon and the valley of Iphtahel (Josh. 19:27).

BIBLIOGRAPHY: D. Baly, *The Geography of the Bible* (1957), pp. 130, 154, 172-74, 186, 188, 190; id., *Geographical Companion to the Bible* (1963), pp. 17, 75.

ZEB'ULUNITE (zeb'ū-lun-īt). A member of the tribe of Zebulun (Num. 26:27; Judg. 12:11-12).

ZECHARI'AH (zek-a-rī'a; "Jehovah remembers").

1. The son of Jeroboam II, the last of the house of Jehu, and fourteenth king of Israel. He ascended the throne upon the death of his father (2 Kings 14:29), about 753 B.C. He reigned only six months, being put to death by Shallum (15:8-10).

2. A chief of the Reubenites at the time of the captivity by Tiglath-pileser (1 Chron. 5:7), about 740 B.C.

3. Son of Meshelemiah, or Shelemiah, a Korahite and keeper of the N gate of the Tabernacle of the congregation (1 Chron. 9:21). In 26:2, 14, he is described as "a counselor with insight."

4. One of the sons of Jeiel (1 Chron. 9:37).

5. A Levite of the second order in the Temple band as arranged by David, appointed to play "with harps tuned to alamoth" (1 Chron. 15:18, 20; 16:5), about 975 B.C.

6. One of the priests who, with trumpets, accompanied the Ark from the house of Obededom (1 Chron. 15:24), about 988 B.C.

7. Son of Isshiah, or Jesiah, a Kohathite Levite, descended from Uzziel (1 Chron. 24:25).

8. Fourth son of Hosah, of the sons of Merari (1 Chron. 26:11).

9. The father of Iddo, who was chief of his tribe, Manasseh in Gilead, in the reign of David (1 Chron. 27:21), about 1000 B.C.

10. One of the officials of Judah sent to teach the people the law in the reign of Jehoshaphat (2 Chron. 17:7), c. 885 B.C.

11. The son of Benaiah and father of Jahaziel; the latter was the Gershonite Levite who encouraged the army of Jehoshaphat against the Moabites (2 Chron. 20:14), before 875 B.C.

12. One of the sons of King Jehoshaphat (2 Chron. 21:2), c. 880 B.C.

13. Son of the high priest Jehoiada in the reign of Joash, king of Judah (2 Chron. 24:20), and therefore the king's cousin. After the death of Jehoiada, Zechariah probably succeeded to his office. In attempting to check the reaction in favor of idolatry that immediately followed, he fell a victim to a conspiracy formed against him by the king and was stoned in the court of the Temple, 836 B.C. It is probable that "Zechariah, the son of Berechiah," who was slain between the Temple and the altar (Matt. 23:35; Luke 11:51), is the same as Zechariah the son of Jehoiada. The name of Berechiah as his father may have crept into the text from a marginal gloss, the writer

confusing this Zechariah either with Zechariah the prophet, who was the son of Berechiah, or with another Zechariah, the son of Jeberechiah (Isa. 8:2).

14. A prophet in the reign of Uzziah, who appears to have acted as the king's counselor, but of whom nothing is known (2 Chron. 26:5), after 780 B.C.

15. The father of Abijah, or Abi, Hezekiah's mother (2 Chron. 29:1), before 719 B.C.

16. A Levite who, in the reign of Hezekiah, assisted in the purification of the Temple (2 Chron. 29:13), 719 B.C.

17. A Kohathite Levite and an overseer of the Temple restoration in the reign of Josiah (2 Chron. 34:12), 621 B.C.

18. One of the rulers of the Temple in the reign of Josiah (2 Chron. 35:8), about 621 B.C.

19. The leader of the "sons" of Parosh, who, with 150 others, returned with Ezra (Ezra 8:3), about 457 B.C.

20. The leader of the twenty-eight "sons" of Bebai, who returned from captivity with Ezra (Ezra 8:11), 457 B.C.

21. One of the leaders of the people whom Ezra summoned in council at the river Ahava (Ezra 8:16). He stood at Ezra's left hand when he expounded the law to the people (Neh. 8:4), 457 B.C.

22. One of the family of Elam who divorced a foreign wife after the captivity (Ezra 10:26), 456 B.C.

23. One of the ancestors of Athaiah, of the tribe of Judah (Neh. 11:4), before 536 B.C.

24. The son of "the Shilonite" and father of Joiarib, of the family of Perez (Neh. 11:5).

25. A priest and ancestor of Adaiah; the latter was prominent in Jerusalem after the captivity (Neh. 11:12), before 445 B.C.

26. The representative of the priestly family of Iddo in the days of Joiakim the son of Jeshua (Neh. 12:16). Probably the same as Zechariah the prophet, the son of Iddo, about 536 B.C.

27. One of the priests, son of Jonathan, who blew trumpets at the dedication of the city wall by Ezra and Nehemiah (Neh. 12:35, 41), 445 B.C.

28. The son of Jeberechiah, who was taken by the prophet Isaiah as one of the "faithful witnesses for testimony," when he wrote concerning Maher-shalal-hash-baz (Isa. 8:2), about 742 B.C.

29. The eleventh of the twelve minor prophets. Zechariah was of priestly descent, a son of Berechiah and grandson of Iddo (Zech. 1:1, 7), the chief of one of the priestly families that returned from exile along with Zerubbabel (Neh. 12:4). His mention in Ezra 5:1; 6:14 as the son of Iddo is explained by the hypothesis that owing to some unexplained cause—perhaps the death of his father—Zechariah followed his grandfather in the priestly office, and so the historian dropped the father's name. Zechariah commenced his prophetic labors in the eighth month of the second

year of Darius, 520 B.C. In the fourth year of Darius a deputation of Jews came to the Temple to inquire whether the day on which Jerusalem and the Temple were reduced to ashes by the Chaldeans was still to be kept as a day of mourning and fasting. Zechariah replied that, in the sight of Jehovah, obedience is better than fasting. Two other oracles delivered by Zechariah are recorded in his book of prophecies (Zech. 9-11 and 12-14).

ZECHARIAH, BOOK OF. One of the postexilic books of the minor prophets. The prophet's name means in Heb. "Yahweh remembers." He was a "son of Berechiah, the son of Iddo . . ." (Zech. 1:1; Ezra 5:1; 6:14; Neh. 12:16). The prophet began his ministry two months after his contemporary Haggai, in October-November 520 B.C. The combined prophecies or preaching of the two eventuated in the finished Temple in the latter part of 516 B.C. The total prophetic ministry of Zechariah (at this period) lasted about two years, in contrast to Haggai, whose total recorded ministry occupied only four months. Zechariah's last dated prophecy was marked November-December 518 B.C. Chapters 9-14, constituting the last part of Zechariah's prophecy, are undated and must be put much later, probably after 480 B.C., in the light of the allusion to Javan, or Greece. No serious impediment exists for denying a half-century ministry to the prophet. Doubtless he outlived Darius I the Great (522-486 B.C.), whose exploits in saving the Persian Empire are recorded on the famous Rock of Behistun, which proved the key to unlocking Babylonian-Assyrian cuneiform toward the end of the first half of the nineteenth century. Zechariah prophesied during the high priesthood of Joshua and the governorship of Zerubbabel.

Character of the Book. George L. Robinson aptly terms the book "the most Messianic, the most truly apocalyptic and eschatological of all the writings of the OT" (*Int'l. Stand. Bible Ency.*, p. 3136). Zechariah contains more allusions to the coming Messiah, both in His first and second advents and future millennial glory, than all the other minor prophets combined. His series of eight night visions extending from 1:7 to 6:8 gives a remarkably detailed depiction of the future messianic kingdom over Israel. Even more striking is the symbolical crowning of the high priest (6:9-15). This portrays the union of the kingly and priestly office in the Messiah during the Kingdom age. Chapter 8 gives one of the clearest descriptions of the future restoration of Jerusalem (vv. 1-5) and the return of Israel to the land (vv. 6-8), with a remarkable setting forth of the future prosperity of the land and people Israel during the reign of Christ subsequent to His second advent (vv. 9-23). In the last section of the prophecies (chaps. 9-14) two prophetic burdens, or oracles, are given, outlining the great messianic future of Israel. The first prophetic burden presents Christ in His first advent when rejected (9:1–11:17). This constitutes one of the most amazing and detailed prophecies of Christ's rejection and crucifixion. The second prophetic burden delineates the second advent in glory and the acceptance of the Messiah-King by a delivered remnant that will form the nucleus of the nation in the Kingdom age (12:1–14:21). Chapters 12 and 13 describe the future deliverance and national conversion of Israel (cf. Rom. 11:25-26). Chapter 14 portrays the second coming of Christ in glory to set up His earthly kingdom (14:1-21; cf. Rev. 19:11-16).

Messianic Designations. Important messianic predictions in Zechariah include the Branch (chaps. 3 and 6; cf. Isa. 4:2; Jer. 23:5); Christ as King-Priest (Zech. 6:13); Christ's triumphal entry into Jerusalem and coming glory (9:9-10); Christ portrayed as Shepherd (11:12-13); Christ crucified (12:10); the sufferings of Christ (13:7); the second coming of Christ (chap. 14).

Outline.

I. Call to repentance (1:1-6)
II. Foregleams of the future messianic kingdom (1:7–8:23)
   A. A series of eight night visions (1:7–6:8)
      1. The man among the myrtle trees (1:7-17)
      2. The four horns and craftsmen (1:18-21)
      3. The man with the measuring line (2:1-13)
      4. The cleansing of the high priest (3:1-10)
      5. The lampstand and the two olive branches (4:1-14)
      6. The flying scroll (5:1-4)
      7. The woman and the ephah (5:5-11)
      8. The four chariots (6:1-8)
   B. The symbolical crowning of the high priest (6:9-15)
   C. The answer to the question of the feasts (7:1– 8:23)
      1. The question and divine reply (7:1-14)
      2. Future restoration of Jerusalem (8:1-5)
      3. Future return to Palestine (8:6-8)
      4. Kingdom prosperity of land and people (8:9-23)
III. Two prophetic burdens: Israel's great messianic future (9:1–14:21)
   A. The first burden: The first advent and rejection of the Messiah-King (9:1–11:17)
      1. The advent (9:1–10:12)
      2. The rejection (11:1-17)
   B. The second burden: Second advent and acceptance of the Messiah-King (12:1–14:21)

1. Future deliverance and national conversion of Israel (12:1–13:9)
2. The Messiah-King's return in glory (14:1-21)

Authorship. The Zecharian authenticity of chaps. 1-8 is practically uncontested. Chapters 9-14, however, are commonly denied Zecharian authorship, but great confusion exists among scholars who hold that another than Zechariah was the writer. Some scholars make all of chaps. 9-14 preexilic; others assert a postexilic authorship; others confidently assign chaps. 9-11 to one or more preexilic authors, and chaps. 12-14 to one or more postexilic authors. Zecharian authorship is favored by the voice of tradition that was practically uncontested until Joseph Mede in 1653 denied that chaps. 9-11 were the work of Zechariah. The external point of view of chaps. 9-14 is postexilic. No reigning king of Judah or Israel is mentioned. The kingship of the Messiah alone is recognized. The reference to the sons of Greece (9:13) is postexilic but not necessarily post-Zecharian. Similar rare expressions are found in both sections of the book (cf. 7:14, marg., "from passing and returning," with 9:8, "passes by and returns"). The expression "declares the Lord" appears prominently in both parts, some fourteen times in chaps. 1-8 and in 10:12; 12:1, 4; 13:2, 7-8 in the later section. "Lord of hosts" appears characteristically in both sections. The poetic style of chaps. 9-14 in contrast to the prosaic form of chaps. 1-8 does not necessitate a different author. Undoubtedly Zechariah penned chaps. 9-14 considerably later than chaps. 1-8, probably when he was an aged man.

BIBLIOGRAPHY: D. Baron, *The Visions and Prophecies of Zechariah* (1962); M. F. Unger, *Unger's Bible Commentary: Zechariah* (1963); R. K. Harrison, *Introduction to the Old Testament* (1968), pp. 949-57; J. G. Baldwin, *Haggai, Zechariah, Malachi*, Tyndale Old Testament Commentaries (1972); C. H. H. Wright, *Zechariah and His Prophecies* (1980); F. E. Gaebelein, ed., *Expositor's Bible Commentary*, vol. 7 (1985), pp. 595-696.

ZE′CHER or **Zeker** (ze′ker; "memorial"). One of the sons of Jeiel and his wife Maacah; Jeiel was the father or founder of Gibeon (1 Chron. 8:29, 31; 9:37, "Zechariah").

ZE′DAD (zē′dad). A city on the northern boundary of Palestine, mentioned by Moses (Num. 34:8) and Ezekiel (Ezek. 47:15). It is identified with Sadad, SE of Homs on the road from Riblah to Palmyra.

ZEDEKI′AH (zed-e-kī′a; "Jehovah is just or righteous").

1. Son of Chenaanah, and the person who acted as spokesman of the prophets when consulted by Ahab as to the result of his proposed expedition to Ramoth-gilead (875 B.C.). Preparing himself with a pair of iron horns (the horns of the *re′ēm*, or wild buffalo, the recognized emblem of the tribe of Ephraim), Zedekiah illustrated the

manner in which Ahab would drive the Syrians before him. When Micaiah delivered his prophecy, Zedekiah came near and struck him upon the cheek. For this he was threatened by Micaiah in terms that evidently alluded to some personal danger. The probability that Zedekiah and his followers were false prophets is strengthened by the question of the king, "Is there not yet a prophet of the Lord here that we may inquire of him?" (1 Kings 22:11; 2 Chron. 18:10).

2. The last king of Judah. Zedekiah was the son of Josiah by his wife Hamutal, and therefore a brother of Jehoahaz (2 Kings 24:18; cf. 23:31; 1 Chron. 3:15). His original name of Mattaniah was changed to Zedekiah by Nebuchadnezzar when he carried off his nephew Jehoiachin to Babylon and left him on the throne at Jerusalem.

Zedekiah was twenty-one years of age when he was made king (2 Kings 24:17-18; 2 Chron. 36:11), 597 B.C. The earlier portion of his reign was marked by agitation throughout the whole of Syria against the Babylonian yoke. In this movement Jerusalem seems to have taken the lead, since in the fourth year of Zedekiah's reign ambassadors from all the neighboring kingdoms —Tyre, Sidon, Edom, and Moab —were at his court to consult regarding steps to be taken. This happened either during the king's absence or immediately after his return from Babylon, where he went, perhaps, to deceive Nebuchadnezzar about his contemplated revolt (Jer. 51:59). The first act of overt rebellion of which any record survives was the formation of an alliance with Egypt, of itself equivalent to a declaration of enmity with Babylon. As a natural consequence it brought on Jerusalem an immediate invasion of the Chaldeans. The mention of this event in the Bible is slight, occurring only in Jer. 37:5-11; 34:21; and Ezek. 17:15-20. But Josephus (Ant. 10.7.3) relates it more fully and gives the date of its occurrence, namely, the eighth year of Zedekiah. Nebuchadnezzar, aware of Zedekiah's defection, sent an army and reduced the whole country of Judea, except for Jerusalem, Lachish, and Azekah (Jer. 34:7). Pharaoh marched to the assistance of Zedekiah, and the Chaldeans at once raised the siege and advanced to meet him. The nobles seized this opportunity to reenslave those whom they had so recently freed (chap. 34). Shortly after this, Jeremiah was put in prison and would probably have lost his life but for the interference of Zedekiah (37:15-21). On the tenth day of the tenth month of Zedekiah's ninth year the Chaldeans were again before the walls (52:4). From this time forward the siege progressed slowly but surely to its consummation, accompanied by both famine and pestilence. Zedekiah again interfered to preserve the life of Jeremiah from the vengeance of the officials (38:7-13). While the king was hesitating, the end was rapidly coming nearer. The city was indeed reduced to the last extremity. The fire of the besiegers had been destructive throughout the siege, but it was now aided by severe famine. The bread had long since been consumed (38:9), and all the terrible expedients had been tried to which the wretched inhabitants of a besieged town are forced to resort in such cases. At last, after sixteen dreadful months, the catastrophe occurred. It was on the ninth day of the fourth month, about the middle of July, at midnight, as Josephus writes with careful minuteness, (Ant. 10.8.2) that the breach was made in those stout and venerable walls. Entering through the breach, the Chaldeans made their way, as their custom was, to the center of the city, and for the first time the Temple was entered by a hostile force. Zedekiah fled but was betrayed by some Jews who had deserted to the enemy. After his capture he and his sons were sent to Nebuchadnezzar at Riblah, while his daughters were kept at Jerusalem. Nebuchadnezzar reproached Zedekiah for breaking his oath of allegiance. He ordered his sons to be slain before him and then his own eyes to be put out. He was loaded with chains and taken to Babylon, where he died.

At first sight there seems a discrepancy between Jer. 34:3; 2 Kings 25:7; and Ezek. 12:13. The first passage, however, does not assert that he should see the king and go there. The above facts verify the predictions. Zedekiah saw the *king* of Babylon but not the *city* itself, having lost his sight before being taken there.

3. A son of Jeconiah and grandson of Jehoiakim, king of Judah (1 Chron. 3:16), 598 B.C. or later. Some identify him with the person mentioned in v. 15, but Keil (*Com.*, ad loc.) conjectures that he was a literal son, not simply a successor of Jeconiah, and that he died before the Exile.

4. The son of Maaseiah, and a false prophet among the captives in Babylon. He was denounced by Jeremiah (Jer. 29:21) for having, with Ahab, uttered false prophecies, and for immoral conduct. Their names were to become a byword and their terrible fate—death by burning—a warning, about 586 B.C.

5. The son of Hananiah, and one of the officials of Judah who received the announcement that Baruch had delivered the words of Jeremiah to the people (Jer. 36:12), 607 B.C.

BIBLIOGRAPHY: T. Kirk and G. Rawlinson, *Studies in the Book of Kings* (1983), 2:230-38; E. R. Thiele, *Mysterious Numbers of the Hebrew Kings* (1983), pp. 187, 190, 206.

ZE'EB (zē'eb; "a wolf"). One of the leaders of Midian who were defeated by Gideon, probably near the Jordan. Zeeb was slain in a wine press, which in later times bore his name (Judg. 7:24-25; 8:3; Ps. 83:11).

ZE'KER. *See* Zecher.

ZE'LA. *See* Zelah.

ZE'LAH (zē'la; "slope, side"). A town in Benjamin that was the family burying place of Kish, the father of Saul (2 Sam. 21:14; cf. Josh. 18:28), probably the native place of Saul, the first king of Israel. It has not been identified. Probably Khirbet Ṣalaḥ, NW of Jerusalem.

ZE'LEK (zē'lek; "cleft, fissure"). An Ammonite and one of David's valiant men (2 Sam. 23:37; 1 Chron. 11:39).

ZELO'PHEHAD (ze-lo'fe-had; "shadow of the fear," i.e., "protection against fear"). The son of Hepher and descendant of Manasseh through Gilead (Josh. 17:3), before 1170 B.C. He died without male heirs, and his five daughters claimed his inheritance. The claim was admitted by divine direction, and a law was issued, to be of general application, that if a man died without sons, his inheritance should pass to his daughters (Num. 26:33; 27:1-11). A still further enactment (chap. 36) provided that such heiresses should not marry out of their own tribes—a regulation that the five daughters of Zelophehad complied with; all married Manassites.

BIBLIOGRAPHY: T. Pedersen, *Israel, Its Life and Culture* (1926), 1-2:94-96; N. H. Snaith, *Vetus Testamentum* 16 (1966): 124-27; J. Weingreen, *Vetus Testamentum* 16 (1966): 518-22.

ZEL'ZAH (zel'za). A place in the border of Benjamin, mentioned by Samuel when leaving Saul at Ramah (1 Sam. 10:2). Among the signs that the prophet said would confirm his anointing of Saul was the latter's meeting with two men at Rachel's tomb. This was on the way from Bethel to Bethlehem, and to the W in full view is the village of Beit Jala, which may be identical with Zelzah.

ZEMARA'IM (zem-a-ra'im; "double fleece").

1. One of the ancient towns assigned to Benjamin (Josh. 18:22), in the eastern section of its territory and grouped with Beth-arabah and Bethel. It is probably to be identified with the ruins of Khirbet es-Samrah, on the road from Jerusalem to Jericho.

2. The mountain from which Abijah, king of Judah, addressed Jeroboam and the army of Israel (2 Chron. 13:4). It is described as being "in the hill country of Ephraim," i.e., within the general highland district of that tribe.

ZEM'ARITES (zem'a-rīts; only found in Gen. 10:18 and 1 Chron. 1:16). The name of a people reckoned among the sons of Canaan, "the Arvadites, the Zemarites, and the Hamathites," thus it is naturally assumed that the Zemarites lived between Arvad and Hamath. The old interpreters, such as the Jerusalem Targum, the Arab. version, etc., locate them at Emessa, the modern Hums. Michaelis placed them at Sumra, the classical Simyra. It is possible that the names Zemaraim (Josh. 18:22) and Mt. Zemaraim (2 Chron. 13:4) represent southern migrations of Zemarites; or, as the list in Gen. 10:15-18 is not altogether in

strict geographical order, the Zemarites as a whole may have lived in the vicinity of Zemaraim and Mt. Zemaraim.

ZEMI'RAH (ze-mī'ra; "music"). One of the nine sons of Becher, the son of Benjamin (1 Chron. 7:8).

ZE'NAN (ze'nan; "point," or perhaps, "place of flocks"). A town in the lowland district of Judah (Josh. 15:37), supposed to be the same as Zaanan (Mic. 1:11).

ZE'NAS (zē'nas; shortened from Zenadorus, "gift of Zeus"). A Christian lawyer of Crete mentioned in Titus 3:13 in connection with Apollos. It is impossible to determine whether Zenas was a Roman jurisconsult or a Jewish doctor. Grotius thinks that he was a Greek who had studied Roman law. The NT usage of *nomikos*, "lawyer," leads rather to the other inference.

ZEPHANI'AH (zef-a-nī'a; "Jehovah conceals or treasures").

1. A Kohathite Levite, ancestor of Samuel and Heman (1 Chron. 6:36).

2. The son of Maaseiah (Jer. 21:1); he was *sāgān*, or second priest, in the reign of Zedekiah. He succeeded Jehoiada (29:25-26) and was probably a ruler of the Temple, whose office it was, among others, to punish pretenders to the gift of prophecy. In this capacity he was appealed to by Shemaiah the Nehelamite to punish Jeremiah (29:27). Twice he was sent from Zedekiah to inquire of Jeremiah about the city's siege by the Chaldeans (21:1) and to implore him to intercede for the people (37:3). On the capture of Jerusalem he was taken to Riblah and slain (52:24, 27; 2 Kings 25:18, 21), about 587 B.C.

3. The prophet, son of Cushi, who prophesied against Judah and Jerusalem in the days of King Josiah (Zeph. 1:1), about 630 B.C.

4. Father of Josiah (Zech. 6:10) and of Hen, according to the Textus Receptus, Zech. 6:14, 520 B.C.

ZEPHANIAH, BOOK OF. One of the minor prophets, whose name in Heb. means "Jehovah hides, or protects." He was likely a great-grandson of Hezekiah (Zeph. 1:1). The allusion to "king" has caused some critics such as Aage Bentzen (*Introduction* [1949], 2:154) to deny this. If he was not related to Hezekiah, however, there is no adequate explanation of the prophet's abandonment of the usual custom of referring only to the father in the superscription.

Date. The prophet exercised his ministry in the early reign of Josiah (640-608 B.C.), doubtless prior to the great reformation of 621 B.C. This is confirmed by the allusion to the presence of foreign cults (1:4) and to Assyria (2:13). It is certainly possible that Zephaniah had access to the court and perhaps, like his contemporaries Nahum and Jeremiah exerted much influence in bringing about the revival under Hezekiah. Zephaniah deals with the coming invasion of Nebuchadnezzar as a figure of the Day of the Lord (1:1–2:3). He utters stern predictions of judgment on certain peoples (2:4-15). He outlines the moral state of Israel for which the captivity was to come as a punishment (3:1-7). He prophesies that the judgment of the nations is to be followed by kingdom blessing under the Messiah (3:8-20).

Outline.
I. The Day of the Lord prefigured (1:1–3:7)
   A. In judgment upon Judah and Jerusalem (1:1–2:3)
   B. In judgment upon surrounding nations (2:4-15)
   C. In Jehovah's manifestation to sinful Jerusalem (3:1-7)
II. The kingdom prophesied (3:8-20)
   A. The judgment of the nations (3:8-13)
   B. The Messiah revealed as King (3:14-20)

Composition. On subjective and insufficient grounds the authenticity of various parts of chaps. 2 and 3 have been contested by such critics as Stade, Kuenen, Wellhausen, Budde, and Eissfeldt. Oesterley and Robinson acknowledge that the general authenticity of the book has not been seriously doubted, although they note that different editors have discovered reason to support considerable interpolations (*Intr.* [1934]). However, from a strictly objective view, there is no valid reason to deny any of the prophecies to Zephaniah.

BIBLIOGRAPHY: H. C. von Orelli, *The Twelve Minor Prophets* (1977), pp. 260-80; R. K. Harrison, *Introduction to the Old Testament* (1969), pp. 939-43; C. J. Barber, *Habakkuk and Zephaniah* (1985); F. E. Gaebelein, ed., *Expositor's Bible Commentary* (1985), 7:537-65.

ZE'PHATH (ze'fath; "beacon, watchtower"). The earlier name (Judg. 1:17) of a Canaanite town destroyed by Judah and Simeon and renamed Hormah. Two identifications have been proposed for Zephath: that of Robinson with the well-known pass es-Sufâ; and that of other scholars with a site three miles E of Beersheba called Tell es-Saba'.

ZEPH'ATHAH (zef'a-tha; "watchtower"). A valley near Mareshah (2 Chron. 14:10) where Asa and his troops fought against Zerah the Ethiopian's army. A deep valley is found near the site of Mareshah, running down to Beit Jibrin (Eleutheropolis) and thence into the plain of Philistia. This may be the valley of Zephathah.

ZE'PHI (ze'fi; 1 Chron. 1:36). *See* Zepho.

ZE'PHO (ze'fo), or **Ze'phi** (ze'fi; "watch"). A son of Eliphaz son of Esau (Gen. 36:11); one of the "chiefs" of the Edomites (v. 15). In 1 Chron. 1:36 he is called Zephi.

ZE'PHON (ze'fon; "watching, expectation"). The first of the seven sons of Gad (Num. 26:15); progenitor of the Zephonites.

ZEPH'ONITES (ze'fon-īts; Num. 26:15). *See* Zephon.

ZER (zur). A fortified town in the territory assigned to Naphtali (Josh. 19:35). It has not been identified.

ZE'RAH (ze'ra; "dawning, rising, shining").
1. Son of Reuel the son of Esau (Gen. 36:13; 1 Chron. 1:37), and one of the "chiefs" of the Edomites (Gen. 36:17). Jobab, an early king of Edom, perhaps belonged to his family (36:33; 1 Chron. 1:44).
2. Twin son with his brother Perez of Judah and Tamar (Gen. 38:30 ["Zarah" in KJV]; 1 Chron. 2:6; Matt. 1:3 [KJV uses Gk. form *Zara* here]). His descendants were called Zerahites, Ezrahites, and Izrahites (Num. 26:20; 1 Kings 4:31; 1 Chron. 27:8).
3. A son of Simeon (1 Chron. 4:24; "Zohar," Gen. 46:10).
4. A Gershonite Levite, son of Iddo, or Adaiah (1 Chron. 6:21, 41).
5. The Ethiopian (or Cushite) king defeated by Asa. After a period of ten years' peace, Asa's reign was disturbed by war. Zerah, with a million men and three hundred chariots, invaded the kingdom and pressed forward to Mareshah. There Asa marched to meet him and drew up his army for battle in the valley of Zephathah. After commending his cause to Jehovah, Asa made the attack, which was eminently successful. Asa pursued the fleeing Ethiopians as far as Gerar, crippling them so that they could not recover and again make a stand (2 Chron. 14:9-13). Some scholars identify Zerah with one of the Osorkons of the Twenty-second or Bubastite Dynasty, particularly with Osorkon I (924-895 B.C.), successor of Shishak. However, the reference may simply be to an Arab invasion, since the name Zerah occurs in Arab. inscriptions.

ZERAHI'AH (zer-a-hī'a; "Jehovah has risen").
1. A priest, son of Uzzi and ancestor of Ezra the scribe (1 Chron. 6:6, 51; Ezra 7:4), about 457 B.C.
2. Father of Eliehoenai, of the sons of Pahath-Moab (Ezra 8:4), about 457 B.C.

ZER'AHITES (zer'a-hīts). "Zarhites" in KJV. A branch of the tribe of Judah, descended from Zerah, the son of Judah (Num. 26:13, 20; Josh. 7:17; 1 Chron. 27:11, 13).

ZE'RED (ze'red). A brook separating Moab from Edom (Deut. 2:13-14), where the Israelites encamped before crossing the Arnon (Num. 21:12; "Zared," KJV). It seems to be the same as the Wâdi el-Hesā, a watercourse entering the Dead Sea at the SE corner, forming one of the last obstacles overcome by Israel on their way from Egypt to the Promised Land.

ZEREDAH (zer'e-da).
1. A town in Mt. Ephraim given as the birthplace of Jeroboam, the son of Nebat the Ephrath-

ite, and servant (i.e., officer) of Solomon (1 Kings 11:26). By some it is identified with *Zarethan* (which see); others, because of its connection with Mt. Ephraim, think that it cannot be the same. Conder identified it with Surdah, a village a little more than a mile S of Jufua. 'Ain Seredah, the fountain of Khirbet Balâtah in Mt. Ephraim fifteen miles SW of Shechem at the bend of the Wadi Deir Ballut, offers an exact equivalent of name (Albright).

2. Another name (2 Chron. 4:17; here KJV has "Zaredathah") for *Zarethan* (which see), the place of Solomon's brass foundry.

ZEREDATH. See Zarethan, no. 2; Zeredah, no. 2.

ZER'ERAH (zer'e-ra). A place mentioned (Judg. 7:22) in describing the route of the Midianites before Gideon. Keil and Delitzsch (*Com.*) identify it with *Zarethan* (which see).

ZE'RESH (ze'resh; evidently from the Avestan root *zarsh*, "the joyful one"). The wife of Haman the Agagite, who advised the hanging of Mordecai (Esther 5:10, 14; 6:13), about 478 B.C.

ZE'RETH (ze'reth; perhaps, "splendor"). Son of Ashhur, the founder of Tekoa, by his wife Helah (1 Chron. 4:7), perhaps 1370 B.C.

ZE'RETH-SHA'HAR (ze'reth-sha'har; "the splendor of dawn"). "Zareth-shahar" in KJV. A city in Reuben "on the hill of the valley" (Josh. 13:19), and near the eastern shore of the Dead Sea. Identified with the ruins of Zara in Wadi Zurka Main.

ZE'RI (ze'ri). One of the sons of Jeduthun, and a Levitical harpist in the reign of David (1 Chron. 25:3). He is probably the Izri mentioned in v. 11.

ZE'ROR (ze'ror; a "particle"). A Benjamite ancestor of Kish, the father of Saul (1 Sam. 9:1), before 1095 B.C.

ZERU'AH (ze-rū'a; "smitten, leprous"). The mother of Jeroboam the son of Nebat (1 Kings 11:26), before 934 B.C.

ZERUB'BABEL (ze-rub'a-bel; Heb. from Akkad. *zēru Bābili,* "seed [progeny] of Babylon"). In the NT, the KJV uses the Gk. form *Zorobabel.* The head of the tribe of Judah at the time of the return from the Babylonian captivity.

Family. Zerubbabel is called the son of Shealtiel (Ezra 3:2, 8; 5:2; Neh. 12:1; Hag. 1:1, 12, 14; 2:2), and in the genealogies (Matt. 1:12; Luke 3:27). In 1 Chron. 3:19 he is called the son of Pedaiah, the brother of Shealtiel (*see* note below). Josephus (*Ant.* 11.3.10) speaks of him as "the son of Salathiel, of the posterity of David, and of the tribe of Judah."

History. In the first year of Cyrus, Zerubbabel was living in Babylon and was recognized as a prince of Judah in the captivity. He was probably in the king's service, as he had received an Aram.

name (Sheshbazzar) and had been entrusted by Cyrus with the office of governor of Judea.

Goes to Jerusalem. Zerubbabel led the first colony of captives to Jerusalem, accompanied by Jeshua the high priest, a considerable number of priests, Levites, and heads of houses of Judah and Benjamin. Arriving at Jerusalem, their first task was to build the altar on its old site and to restore the daily sacrifice (Ezra 2; 3:1-3), about 536 B.C.

Rebuilding the Temple. The great work of Zerubbabel was the rebuilding of the Temple. Aided by a grant of material and money, Zerubbabel was enabled to lay the foundation in the second month of the second year of their return. This was done with the utmost solemnity, amid the trumpet blasts of the priests, the music of the Levites, and the loud songs of thanksgiving of the people (vv. 8-13).

Hindrances. The work had not advanced far before the mixed settlers in Samaria put in a claim to take part in it. When Zerubbabel and his companions declined the offer, they endeavored to hinder its completion. They "frightened them from building" and hired counselors to misrepresent them at the court. The result was that no further progress was made during the remaining years of the reign of Cyrus and the eight years of Cambyses and Smerdis (4:1-24). Zerubbabel does not appear completely blameless for this long delay. The difficulties in the way of building the Temple were not such as needed to have stopped the work. And during this long suspension of sixteen years Zerubbabel and the rest of the people had been busy in building costly houses for themselves (Hag. 1:2-4).

Building Resumed. Moved by the exhortations of the prophets Haggai and Zechariah, Zerubbabel threw himself heartily into the work. He was zealously seconded by Jeshua and all the people. This was in the second year of the reign of Darius Hystaspes (520 B.C.), who commanded Tattenai and Shetharbozenai to assist the Jews at the king's expense with whatever they needed. The work advanced so rapidly that on the third day of the month Adar, in the sixth year of Darius, the Temple was finished. It was then dedicated with much pomp and rejoicing (Ezra 5:1–6:22), 516 B.C. The only other works of Zerubbabel mentioned in Scripture are the restoration of the divisions of priests and Levites, and of the provision for their maintenance, according to the method instituted by David (6:18; Neh. 12:47); the registration of the returned captives according to their genealogies (Neh. 7:5); and the keeping of the Passover in the seventh year of Darius. In the genealogies of Jesus (Matt. 1:12; Luke 3:27), Matthew follows his line from Jechoniah and Solomon, whereas Luke follows it through Neri and Nathan. Zerubbabel was legal successor and heir of Jeconiah's royal estate, the grandson of Neri, and the lineal descendant of Nathan, the son of David.

The discrepancy between 1 Chron. 3:19 and other passages as to the parentage of Zerubbabel is explained by Keil (*Com.*, ad loc.) by the supposition that "Shealtiel died without any male descendants, leaving his wife a widow. . . . After Shealtiel's death his second brother, Pedaiah, fulfilled the Levirate duty, and begat, in his marriage with his sister-in-law, Zerubbabel, who was now regarded, in all that related to laws of heritage, as Shealtiel's son."

BIBLIOGRAPHY: L. E. Browne, *Early Judaism* (1929); A. C. Welch, *Post-Exilic Judaism* (1935); J. S. Wright, *The Building of the Second Temple* (1958); P. R. Ackroyd, *Exile and Restoration* (1968).

ZERUI'AH (zer-ū-ī'a). The mother of David's three great generals, Abishai, Joab, and Asahel. She and Abigail are specified (1 Chron. 2:16) as sisters of the son of Jesse (David), but it is stated in 2 Sam. 17:25, that Abigail was the daughter of Nahash. Some early commentators have concluded that Abigail and Zeruiah were only stepsisters of David, i.e., daughters of his mother by Nahash, and not by Jesse. Of Zeruiah's husband there is no mention in the Bible.

ZE'THAM (zē'tham; "olive tree"). The son of Ladan, a Gershonite Levite (1 Chron. 23:8); he was, with his brother, a keeper of the Temple treasury (26:22), about 960 B.C.

ZE'THAN (zē'than; "olive tree"). A Benjamite, of the sons of Bilhan (1 Chron. 7:10), probably about 960 B.C.

ZE'THAR (zē'thar; Old Persian, Avestan [jantar] "smiter, slayer"). One of the seven eunuchs of Ahasuerus (Esther 1:10), about 480 B.C.

ZEUS. The supreme god of the Greeks. The Rom. and KJV rendering is Jupiter. *See* Gods, False: Zeus.

ZI'A (zī'a; "trembling motion"). One of the Gadites who lived in Bashan (1 Chron. 5:13).

ZI'BA (zī'ba; probably from Aram. "branch, twig"). A former servant of Saul who was called after David asked, "Is there yet anyone left of the house of Saul, that I may show him kindness for Jonathan's sake?" Consequently, Mephibosheth was found, and Ziba was commanded to cultivate the land that was restored to King Saul's grandson (2 Sam. 9:2-12). At this first mention of Ziba he had fifteen sons and twenty servants (v. 10). When David, in his flight from Jerusalem, had gone a little over the summit (Mt. of Olives), Ziba met him with a present of donkeys, food, and wine. To the king's inquiry, "Where is your master's son?" Ziba replied, "Behold, he is staying in Jerusalem, for he said, 'Today the house of Israel will restore the kingdom of my father to me.'" This improbable tale was believed by David in the excited state in which he then was, and he gave to Ziba all the property of Mephibosheth (16:1-4). On David's return Mephibosheth accused Ziba of

having slandered him, and David commanded that the land should be divided between them (19:29).

ZIB'EON (zib'e-un). Father of Anah, whose daughter Oholibamah was Esau's wife (Gen. 36:2). Although called a Hivite, he is probably the same as Zibeon, the son of Seir, the Horite (36:20, 24, 29; 1 Chron. 1:38, 40).

ZIB'IA (zib'i-a; "gazelle"). A Benjamite, the son of Shaharaim by his wife Hodesh (1 Chron. 8:9).

ZIB'IAH (zib'i-a; "gazelle"). A native of Beersheba and mother of King Jehoash (2 Kings 12:1; 2 Chron. 24:1).

ZICH'RI (zik'ri; "mindful"), **Zicri** (NIV).
1. Son of Izhar, the son of Kohath (Ex. 6:21).
2. A Benjamite, of the sons of Shimei (1 Chron. 8:19).
3. A Benjamite, of the sons of Shashak (1 Chron. 8:23).
4. A Benjamite, of the sons of Jeroham (1 Chron. 8:27).
5. Son of Asaph (1 Chron. 9:15); elsewhere called Zabdi (Neh. 11:17) and Zaccur (12:35).
6. A descendant of Eliezer, the son of Joram and father of the treasurer Shelomoth (1 Chron. 26:25), before 960 B.C.
7. The father of Eliezer the chief officer of the Reubenites in the reign of David (1 Chron. 27:16).
8. Of the tribe of Judah. His son Amasiah volunteered at the head of 200,000 men in Jehoshaphat's army (2 Chron. 17:16), after 875 B.C.
9. Father of Elishaphat, one of the conspirators with Jehoiada to make Joash king (2 Chron. 23:1), about 799 B.C.
10. A mighty man of Ephraim who slew Maaseiah the son of King Ahaz, the governor of the palace, and the prime minister (2 Chron. 28:7), about 735 B.C.
11. The father of Joel. The son was overseer of the Benjamites after their return to Jerusalem from captivity (Neh. 11:9), before 536 B.C.
12. A priest of the family of Abijah in the days of Joiakim (Neh. 12:17), about 445 B.C.

ZID'DIM (zid'im; "sides"). A place in Naphtali (Josh. 19:35). Evidently Kefar Hattya, mentioned in the Talmud, less than a mile N of the well-known Horns of Hattin.

ZIDON. *See* Sidon.

ZIDONIANS. *See* Sidonians.

ZIF (zīf). The early name of the second Hebrew month. *See* table 1, "the Jewish Calendar," in article Calendar.

ZI'HA (zi'ha).
1. One of the Temple servants whose descendants returned from the captivity (Ezra 2:43; Neh. 7:46), before 536 B.C.

2. A leader of the Temple servants after the return from Babylon (Neh. 11:21), 536 B.C.

ZIK'LAG (zik'lag). A town in the Negev, or S country of Judah (Josh. 15:31). The next mention is of its assignment, with other places in Judah, to Simeon (19:5). Ziklag was David's residence for a year and four months by the appointment of Achish king of Gath (1 Sam. 27:6). It was destroyed once by the Amalekites, who in turn were routed utterly by David (chap. 30). It was at Ziklag that David received the news of Saul's death (2 Sam. 1:1; 4:10). It was inhabited in the post-captivity period (Neh. 11:28).

It is now believed that Ziklag is to be identified with Tell esh-Sharia, about twenty miles SE of Gaza and about halfway between Gaza and Beersheba. Eliezer Oren excavated there for six seasons between 1972 and 1978. The area on the summit of the tell is approximately four acres. The site was found to be inhabited from the seventeenth century B.C. to the sixth century A.D. The earliest cities were Canaanite. Stratum 9 was thought to have been destroyed by the Philistines early in the twelfth century B.C. Thereafter they occupied the place in the twelfth and eleventh centuries B.C. (Stratum 8). Stratum 7 dated to the tenth-ninth century B.C. At that time there were well-planned public and private structures that may date from the building activities of Solomon or Rehoboam. And the destruction at the end of the period may have been perpetrated by Shishak in 926 B.C. (1 Kings 14:25-28).   H.F.V.

ZIL'LAH (zil'a; "shadow," i.e., protection). One of the two wives of Lamech the Cainite, to whom he addressed his song (Gen. 4:19, 22-23). She was the mother of Tubal-cain and Naamah.

ZILL'E'THAI (zil'e-thī; "shadow, protection").

1. A Benjamite, of the sons of Shimei (1 Chron. 8:20), after 1170 B.C.

2. One of the captains of thousands of Manasseh who deserted to David at Ziklag (1 Chron. 12:20), about 1000 B.C.

ZIL'PAH (zil'pa; cf. Arab. *zulfah,* "dignity"). The female servant given by Laban to his daughter Leah as an attendant (Gen. 29:24), and by Leah to Jacob as a concubine. She was the mother of Gad and Asher (30:9-13; 35:26; 37:2; 46:18), about 1925 B.C.

ZIM'MAH (zim'a; "purpose").

1. A Gershonite Levite, son of Jahath, the grandson of Gershom (1 Chron. 6:20), after 1210 B.C. He is probably the same as the son of Shimei in v. 42.

2. Father or ancestor of Joah, a Gershonite in the reign of Hezekiah (2 Chron. 29:12), before 726 B.C. At a much earlier period we find Zimmah and Joah as father and son (1 Chron. 6:20-21), for in the various families the same name often repeats itself.

ZIM'RAN (zim'ran; probably "antelope"). The eldest son of Keturah and Abraham (Gen. 25:2; 1 Chron. 1:32). His descendants have not been positively identified.

ZIM'RI (zim'ri; "pertaining to an antelope").

1. The son of Salu, a Simeonite leader slain by Phinehas with the Midianite woman Cozbi (Num. 25:14), c. 1400 B.C. When the Israelites at Shittim were suffering for their impure worship of Baal-peor, Zimri brought this woman into his tent to commit adultery with her. This shameless wickedness so inflamed Phinehas, the high priest, that he seized a spear and pierced both of them through.

2. The fifth king of Israel, who reigned only seven days. He is first mentioned as commander of half the chariots of the royal army and as chief conspirator against King Elah, who was murdered while indulging in a drunken revel in the house of his steward in Tirzah. His first act as king was the slaying of all the house of Baasha. The army at that time was besieging the Philistine town of Gibbethon. When they heard of Elah's murder, they proclaimed their general, Omri, king. He immediately marched against Tirzah and took the city. Zimri retreated into the innermost part of the late king's palace, set it on fire, and perished in the flames (1 Kings 16:9-20), about 885 B.C.

3. The oldest of the five sons of Zerah, the son of Judah (1 Chron. 2:6).

4. Son of Jehoaddah and descendant of Saul (1 Chron. 8:36; 9:42).

ZIN (zin). A wilderness or open, uncultivated region lying S of Palestine (Num. 13:21; 20:1; 27:14; 33:36; 34:3-4; Deut. 32:51; Josh. 15:1). By some it is supposed to be a portion of the desert tract between the Dead Sea and the Gulf of Aqaba. But it must have been W of this tract (called Arabah), as is clearly indicated in Num. 34:4. Directly W of the Arabah is a wild mountain region, rising in successive slopes or terraces from the Arabah in one direction and from the Desert et-Tīh in another. It now bears the name of the Arabs who inhabit it, and is commonly known as the Azâzimeh mountains, or the Azâzimat. This is a distinct and well-defined local wilderness, fully meeting the conditions of the various references to the wilderness of Zin in the Bible. It may fairly be identified as that wilderness and also as a portion of the wilderness of Paran in its larger sense. Yet its northeastern portion was probably in Edom. It is possible that only the remainder was known as Zin. The wilderness of Zin is not to be confused with the *wilderness of Sin* (which see), the original words being quite different.

ZI'NA (zi'na; 1 Chron. 23:10). *See* Zizah.

ZION. Originally the rock escarpment on the ridge between the Kidron and the Tyropeoean valleys of Jerusalem. Subsequently the term was widened to include the entire western ridge of early Jerusalem. Centuries later the term was applied to the entire city (Ps. 126:1; Isa. 1:26-27). By the fourth century the name of Zion was adapted to the southern portion of the western hill.

Archaeological Location. Zion constituted a formidable natural fortress that the Jebusites inhabited before Jerusalem was taken by David (2 Sam. 5:7). The Gihon Spring (the Virgin Fountain), below the eastern rock escarpment, and En-rogel (Job's Well), at the junction of the Kidron and Hinnom valleys, were factors in the early choice of the site. Jerusalem's water system has been explored, showing that the inhabitants of Jerusalem (c. 2000 B.C.) had made a rock-cut passage similar to the one at Gezer and Megiddo (Chester C. McCown, *The Ladder of Progress in Palestine* [1943], p. 230). Evidence brought to light as the result of excavations of Sir Charles Warren, Clermont-Ganneau, Hermann Guthe, Frederick Bliss, Captain Raymond Weill, John Garstang, and J. W. Crowfoot show that the city that David captured was like a huge human footprint about 1,250 feet long by 400 feet wide. This became the City of David, or Zion. In Zion David constructed his palace (5:11). David acquired the threshing floor of Araunah farther up the ridge. There he erected an altar (24:18-25), and there

Solomon built his palatial Temple. *See also* Jerusalem.

Theological Use. Zion has a threefold significance in the Bible apart from its original historical significance.

David's City. In the OT Zion refers to Jerusalem, the city that David conquered and made a capital of the united kingdom of Israel (1 Chron. 11:5; Ps. 2:6; Isa. 2:3).

The Millennial City. In a prophetic sense, Zion has reference to Jerusalem as the future capital city of the nation Israel in the Kingdom age (Isa. 1:27; 2:3; 4:1-6; Joel 3:16; Zech. 1:16-17; 8:3-8; Rom. 11:26). Amillennial theologians spiritualize, rather "mysticalize," the term to mean the Christian church of this age.

The Heavenly City. The NT also refers to Zion as the New Jerusalem (Heb. 12:22-24), the eternal city into which the church will be received (cf. Rev. 21-22).   M.F.U.

BIBLIOGRAPHY: G. N. H. Peters, *The Theocratic Kingdom* (1957), 3:32-63; B. Mazar, *The Mountain of the Lord* (1975); G. Oehler, *Theology of the Old Testament* (1978), pp. 509-21.

ZI'OR (zi'or; "smallness"). A town in the mountain district of Judah (Josh. 15:54), mentioned in the group of towns around Hebron to the S. It has been identified with Ṣa'ir (Ṣi'īr), five miles NNE of Hebron.

Mt. Zion, Jerusalem

ZIPH (zif).

1. The oldest of the four sons of Jehallelel (1 Chron. 4:16).

2. A town apparently in the S, or Simeonite, part of Judah (Josh. 15:24), mentioned with Ithnan and Telem. Identified with ez-Zeifeh, SW of Kurnūb.

3. A town in the desert ("wilderness") of Ziph, to which David fled from Saul (1 Sam. 23:14-15; 26:2-3); it was fortified by Rehoboam (2 Chron. 11:8), having been originally built by Mesha the son of Caleb (1 Chron. 2:42). It has been preserved in the ruins of Tell Zīf, four miles SE of Hebron. The "wilderness of Ziph" was that portion of the desert of Judah that was near to and surrounded the town of Ziph.

ZI'PHAH (zi'fa; fem. of "Ziph"). The second son of Jehallelel; brother of Ziph (1 Chron. 4:16).

ZIPH'ION (zif'i-on; Gen. 46:16). *See* Zephon.

ZIPH'ITES (zif'īts; 1 Sam. 23:19; 26:1; Ps. 54 *title*). The inhabitants of Ziph, who twice revealed to Saul the hiding place of David in their vicinity. The interesting events that happened at the place, including the farewell interview between David and Jonathan, the sparing of Saul's life by David, and the temporary relenting of Saul, belong to the geography or to the biographies of Saul and David. This Ziph was in the highland district in Judah, located between Carmel and Juttah (Josh. 15:55). The Ziph of v. 24 is a different place.

ZIPH'RON (zif'ron). A place on the northern boundary of the Promised Land, and, consequently of Naphtali (Num. 34:9), where it is mentioned between Zedad and Hazar-enan. It is thought by Knobel and Wetstein to be preserved in the ruins of Zifran, NE of Damascus, near the road from Palmyra. In the parallel passage (Ezek. 47:16) Hazer-hatticon occurs in a similar connection.

ZIP'POR (zip'ōr; "bird, sparrow"). Father of Balak, king of Moab. His name occurs only in the expression "son of Zippor" (Num. 22:2, 4, 10, 16; 23:18; Josh. 24:9; Judg. 11:25), c. 1400 B.C. No mention is made as to whether he was the "former king of Moab" alluded to in Num. 21:26, or if he himself ever reigned.

ZIPPO'RAH (zi-pō'ra; fem. of Zippor, "sparrow"). Daughter of Reuel, or Jethro, the priest of Midian; wife of Moses and mother of his two sons, Gershom and Eliezer (Ex. 2:21; 4:25; 18:2; cf. v. 6), c. 1440 B.C. The only incident recorded of her actions is the circumcision of Gershom (4:24-26). *See also* Moses.

ZITHER. A musical instrument (Dan. 3:5, 7, 10, 15) identified by the KJV as a harp and by the NASB as a lyre (marg. "zither"). *See* Music.

ZITH'RI. *See* Sithri.

ZIV (ziv). The second Jewish month, approximating our May (1 Kings 6:1, 34).

ZIZ (ziz; "a flower, a bright, shining thing"). An ascent or cleft leading up from the Dead Sea toward Tekoa (2 Chron. 20:16; cf. v. 20), by which the band of Moabites, Ammonites, and Meunites who attacked Jehoshaphat made their way. There can be very little doubt that the pass was that of 'Ain Jidy, "the very same route which is taken by the Arabs in their marauding expeditions at the present day; along the shore as far as to *Ain Jidy,* and then up the pass, and so northward below Tekûa" (Robinson, *Bib. Res.,* 1: 508, 530). The name "ascent, or height of Hazziz" has perhaps remained attached to the Wadi el Haṣaṣah, which leads from the W shore of the Dead Sea N of Engedi to the tableland of Judea.

ZI'ZA (zi'za).

1. Son of Shiphi, a leader of the Simeonites in the reign of Hezekiah (1 Chron. 4:37), about 719 B.C.

2. Son of Rehoboam by Maacah, the granddaughter of Absalom (2 Chron. 11:20), after 934 B.C.

ZI'ZAH (zi'za), a Gershonite Levite, second son of Shimei (2 Chron. 23:11; called Zina in v. 10). It is spelled Ziza in the NIV.

ZO'AN-TANIS (zō'an). A Delta city located on the E bank of the Tanitic branch of the Nile (Ps. 78:12, 43). This important royal store city was built seven years after Hebron in Palestine (Num. 13:22). Rameses II later rebuilt the location probably at Qantir and called it Rameses. The oppressed Israelites built the earlier site before it was named Rameses, according to the date of the Exodus as preserved in the Masoretic Text. (*See* Rameses.) It is, therefore, clear that Zoan and Tanis are names referring to the same site, or one contiguous. Zoan continued in importance until the time of Alexander the Great, whose brilliant city Alexandria stripped Tanis of its commercial importance. The modern village of San marks the ancient site. Excavations by Pierre Montet since 1930 have uncovered extensive buildings evidently erected by Hebrew slave labor. (*See* Exodus.)

The Bible reveals that Zoan was one of the oldest cities in Egypt, having been built seven years after Hebron, which already existed in the time of Abraham (Num. 13:22), about 2000 B.C.; that it was one of the principal capitals of the pharaohs (Isa. 19:11, 13); and that "the field of Zoan" was the scene of the marvelous works that God wrought at the hand of Moses (Ps. 78:12, 43). To Tanis came ambassadors either of Hoshea or Ahaz, or else possibly of Hezekiah: "For their princes are at Zoan, and their ambassadors arrive at Hanes" (Isa. 30:4). Tanis was not necessarily the capital. But the same prophet, perhaps, points distinctly to a Tanite line (19:13, *see* marg.). The doom of Zoan is foretold by Ezekiel, "I will . . . set a fire in Zoan" (Ezek. 30:14), where it occurs among the cities to be taken by Nebuchadnezzar.

BIBLIOGRAPHY: A. H. Gardiner, *Ancient Egyptian Onomastica* (1942), 2:199-201; H. Kees, *Tanis* (1964); J. van Seters, *The Hyksos* (1966), pp. 128ff., 140ff.

ZO'AR (zō'er; 'littleness, smallness"). One of the five cities that lay on the floor of the Jordan Valley. They were called Cities of the Kikkar, or Circle. It was one of the most ancient cities of the land of Canaan. Its original name was Bela (Gen. 14:2, 8). In the general destruction of the cities of the plain, Zoar was spared to afford shelter to Lot (19:22-23, 30). It is mentioned in the account of the death of Moses as one of the landmarks that bounded his view from Pisgah (Deut. 34:3), and it appears to have been known in the time both of Isaiah (Isa. 15:5) and Jeremiah (Jer. 48:34). These are all the mentions of Zoar contained in the Bible. The narrative of Gen. 19 implies that it was very near to Sodom (vv. 15, 22-23). The position of Sodom is now believed to be at the S extremity of the Dead Sea, and the five cities of the plain are thought to be under the waters of the shallow S part of that sea. *See* Sodom; Gomorrah.

Zoar area, at the southern end of the Dead Sea

ZOBA. The archaeological location of Zoba to the N of Damascus instead of S of it has been an element in authenticating the historicity of 1 Kings 3-11, which delineates Solomon's great power and glory. German scholars such as Hugo Winckler and Hermann Guthe showed a tendency to restrict the Davidic-Solomonic empire to Palestine proper, locating Hadadezer's conquered kingdom in Hauran, biblical Bashan. Analysis of the Assyrian provincial organization, however, which was constructed on older foundations, shows that Zoba (Assyr. Subatu) lay N, not S, of Damascus (E. Forrer, *Die Provinzeinteilung des Assyrischen Reiches* [1921], pp. 62, 69). Egyptian lists and the Amarna Letters prove also that Hadadezer's chief cities, Tibhath and

Cun, which David took in this region (1 Chron. 18:8), were in this territory S of Hums. Scientific research has thus substantiated the sprawling extent of Davidic-Solomonic territorial control and illustrated the reasonableness of the biblical representations of Solomon's prosperity and splendor.   M.F.U.

ZO'BAH (zō'ba). A portion of northern Syria lying between Hamath and the Euphrates, so closely connected with Hamath that the great city was sometimes called Hamath-zobah. Saul, David, and Solomon all had trouble with the people of Zobah (1 Sam. 14:47; 1 Kings 11:23-25; 2 Sam. 8:3, 5, 12; 23:36; 1 Chron. 18:3, 5, 9; 19:6; 2 Chron. 8:3; Ps. 60).

ZOBE'BAH (zō-bē'ba). The second child (probably daughter, as the word is feminine) of Koz (Hakkoz) of the tribe of Judah (1 Chron. 4:8). The NIV renders *Hazzobebah* (which see).

ZO'HAR (zō'har; "whiteness").
1. A Hittite, and father of Ephron. From Ephron Abraham bought the grave of Machpelah (Gen. 23:8; 25:9).
2. Fifth named of the six sons of Simeon (Gen. 46:10; Ex. 6:15); elsewhere (1 Chron. 4:24) called Zerah.

ZO'HELETH (zō'he-leth; "serpent, slippery"). A rocky and dangerous ledge or plateau "beside En-rogel" upon which Adonijah slew oxen and sheep (1 Kings 1:9). It overhangs the Kidron Valley. This has been most satisfactorily identified by M. Clermont Ganneau with the present Arab name Zaḥweilah, a cliff on which the village of Silwân, or Silvam, stands. To this the women of the village resort to draw water at the "Virgin's Fount."

ZO'HETH (zō'heth). Son of Ishi, of the tribe of Judah (1 Chron. 4:20).

ZO'PHAH (zō'fa; "bellied jug," cf. Arab. *ṣuffaḥa,* "to make wide"). Son of Helem, or Hotham, the son of Heber, an Asherite (1 Chron. 7:35-36).

ZO'PHAI (zō'fī). A Kohathite Levite, son of Elkanah and ancestor of Samuel (1 Chron. 6:26), before 1050 B.C. In v. 35 he is called Zuph.

ZO'PHAR (zō'fer; perhaps "chirper," cf. Arab. *ṣafara,* "to whistle"). One of the three friends of Job (Job 2:11; 11:1; 20:1; 42:9). He is called a Naamathite, or inhabitant of Naamah, whose location is probably in N Arabia. In the LXX, Zophar, the friend of Job, is called "king of the Minaeans."

ZO'PHIM (zō'fim; "watchers, field of watchers"). The "field of Zophim" was on the top of Pisgah (Num. 23:14), one of the high places to which Balak brought Balaam, that he might see Israel. It is the modern Tail'at eṣ Ṣufa.

ZO'RAH (zō'ra; "stroke, scourge, hornet"). A

town of Dan, really within the limits of Judah (Josh. 19:41; Judg. 18:2). It was both the birthplace and burial place of Samson (13:2, 24-25; 16:31) and was afterward fortified by Rehoboam (2 Chron. 11:10). It was on the hillside overlooking Sorek.

Valley of Sorek, ancient Zorah

ZO'RATHITES (zō'ra-thīts). People of Zorah, from a town in the lowland of Judah (Josh. 15:33) but assigned to Dan (19:41). In 1 Chron. 4:1-2 the "families of the Zorathites" are descended from Ahumai and Lahad, sons of Jahath the son of Reaiah, the son of Shobal, the son of Judah. Their home *ṣor'â*, Zorah, is mentioned in Josh. 15:33; 19:41; Judg. 13:2, 25; 18:2, 8, 11; 2 Chron. 11:10; Neh. 11:29 ("Zareah," KJV). The Zorathites of 1 Chron. 4:2 and Zareathites of 2:53 (KJV) are alike. They refer to one people. It is better to read 2:50, "These were the sons of Caleb. The sons of Hur, the first-born of Ephrathah, were Shobal the father of Kiriath-jearim" (NASB). The list of Judah's "sons" (4:1) will then be successive descendants. The "Zorites" of 2:54 will belong to a separate branch.   w.h.; m.f.u.

ZO'RITES, THE (zō'rīts). These are named in the genealogies of Judah (1 Chron. 2:54), apparently among the descendants of Salma and near connections of Joab. They are hence classed with the "Zorathites and the Eshtaolites" (v. 53).

ZOROBABEL. *See* Zerubbabel.

ZU'AR (zū'er; "small, little"). The father of Nethanel, of the tribe of Issachar. Nethanel was head of his tribe at the time of the Exodus (Num. 1:8; 2:5; 7:18, 23; 10:15), before 1440 B.C.

ZUPH (zuf; "honeycomb").
1. A Levite of the family of Kohath, and father of Tohu, in the ancestry of Samuel (1 Sam. 1:1; 1 Chron. 6:35; "Zophai," v. 26).
2. A district at which Saul and his servant arrived after passing through those of Shalishah, of Shaalim; a Benjaminite district (1 Sam. 9:5 only). It evidently contained the city in which they encountered Samuel (v. 6), and that again was certainly not far from the tomb of Rachel. The district apparently lay S of Benjamin. It has not been identified with certainty.

ZUR (zur; "a rock").
1. Father of Cozbi (Num. 25:15); he was one of the five princes of Midian who were slain by the Israelites when Balaam fell (31:8; Josh. 13:21), about 1380 B.C.
2. Son of Jeiel, the founder of Gibeon (1 Chron. 8:30; 9:36).

ZU'RIEL (zur'i-el; "my rock is God"). Son of Abihail, and leader of the Merarite Levites at the time of the Exodus (Num. 3:35), 1440 B.C.

ZURISHAD'DAI (zu-ri-shad'ī; "my rock is the Almighty"). Father of Shelumiel, the head of the tribe of Simeon at the time of the Exodus (Num. 1:6; 2:12; 7:36, 41; 10:19), 1440 B.C.

ZU'ZIM (zu'zim; only Gen. 14:5). The name of an ancient people dwelling in Ham, who were smitten by Chedorlaomer. The LXX (both manuscripts) has *'ethnē ischura;* the Targum of Onkelos and the Samaritan version also translate the name "strong people." This rendering depends upon some different Heb. reading, possibly *'azzûzîm.* Sayce thinks it originated in a transcription of a cuneiform rendering of Zamzummin. It is quite generally suspected to be an abridgment of *Zamzummin* (which see).

ZU'ZITES. *See* Zuzim.

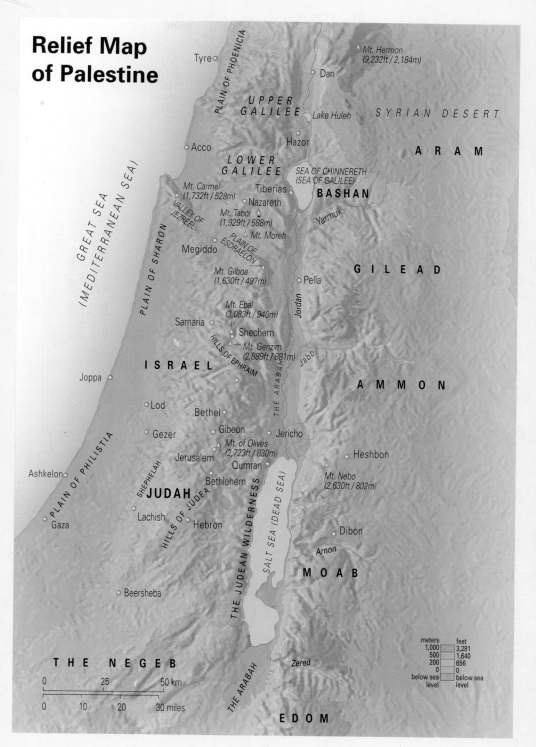

Relief Map
of Palestine

Tyre

PLAIN OF PHOENICIA

Dan

△ Mt. Hermon
(9,232ft / 2,184m)

UPPER
GALILEE

Lake Huleh

SYRIAN DESERT

Acco

Hazor

LOWER
GALILEE

SEA OF CHINNERETH
(SEA OF GALILEE)

ARAM

GREAT SEA
(MEDITERRANEAN SEA)

Mt. Carmel
(1,732ft / 528m) △

Tiberias

BASHAN

VALLEY OF
JEZREEL

Nazareth

Yarmuk

Mt. Tabor
(1,929ft / 588m) △

PLAIN OF SHARON

△ Mt. Moreh

PLAIN OF
ESDRAELON

Megiddo

GILEAD

Mt. Gilboa
(1,630ft / 497m)

Pella

Jordan

Mt. Ebal
(3,083ft / 940m)

Samaria

Shechem

ISRAEL

Mt. Gerizim
(2,889ft / 881m)

HILLS OF EPHRAIM

Jabb

THE ARABAH

AMMON

Joppa

Lod

Bethel

Gezer

Gibeon

Jericho

Mt. of Olives
(2,723ft / 830m)

PLAIN OF PHILISTIA

Jerusalem

Qumran

Heshbon

Ashkelon

Bethlehem

Mt. Nebo
(2,630ft / 802m)

SHEPHELAH

JUDAH

HILLS OF JUDEA

Gaza

Lachish

Hebron

THE JUDEAN WILDERNESS

SALT SEA (DEAD SEA)

Dibon

Arnon

MOAB

Beersheba

THE NEGEB

THE ARABAH

Zered

meters | feet
1,000 | 3,281
500 | 1,640
200 | 656
0 | 0
below sea level | below sea level

0   25   50 km

0   10   20   30 miles

EDOM

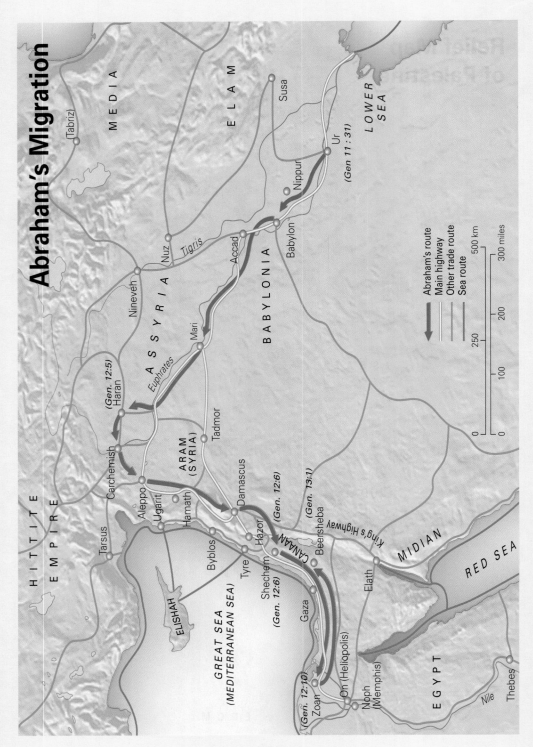

Abraham's Migration

MEDIA

[Tabriz]

ELAM

Susa

LOWER SEA

Nineveh

Nuz

Tigris

Accad

Babylon

Nippur

Ur
(Gen 11:31)

ASSYRIA

BABYLONIA

Mari

Euphrates

(Gen. 12:5)
Haran

Carchemish

Tadmor

ARAM
(SYRIA)

Aleppo

Ugarit

Hamath

Damascus

(Gen. 12:6)

(Gen. 13:1)

Beersheba

King's Highway

MIDIAN

HITTITE EMPIRE

Tarsus

Byblos

Tyre

Hazor

CANAAN

Elath

RED SEA

ELISHAH

GREAT SEA
(MEDITERRANEAN SEA)

Shechem

(Gen. 12:6)

Gaza

(Gen. 12:10)

Zoan

On (Heliopolis)

Noph
(Memphis)

EGYPT

Nile

Thebes

Abraham's route
Main highway
Other trade route
Sea route

500 km

300 miles

250

0   100   200

0

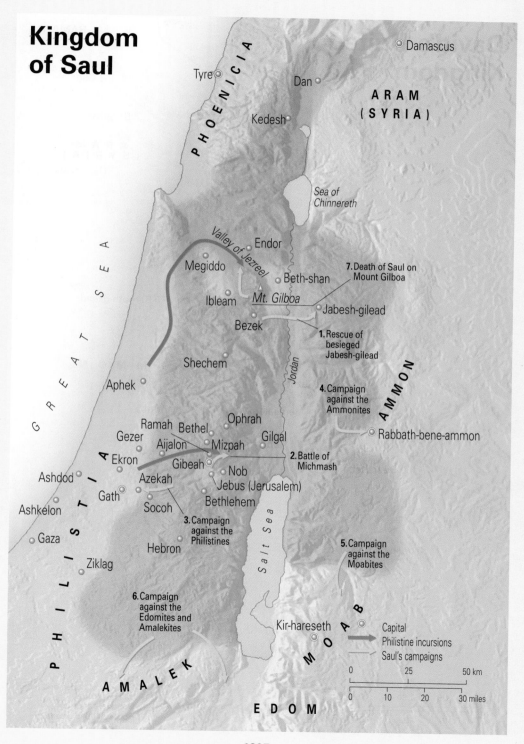

Kingdom
of Saul

Damascus

Tyre

PHOENICIA

Dan

Kedesh

ARAM
(SYRIA)

Sea of
Chinnereth

Valley of Jezreel

Endor

Megiddo

Beth-shan

7. Death of Saul on
Mount Gilboa

Ibleam

Mt. Gilboa

Jabesh-gilead

Bezek

1. Rescue of
besieged
Jabesh-gilead

GREAT SEA

Shechem

Jordan

4. Campaign
against the
Ammonites

AMMON

Aphek

Ramah   Bethel

Ophrah

Gezer

Gilgal

Rabbath-bene-ammon

Aijalon

Mizpah

Ekron

Gibeah

2. Battle of
Michmash

Ashdod

Azekah

Nob

Jebus (Jerusalem)

Gath

Socoh

Bethlehem

PHILISTIA

Ashkelon

3. Campaign
against the
Philistines

Salt Sea

5. Campaign
against the
Moabites

Gaza

Hebron

Ziklag

6. Campaign
against the
Edomites and
Amalekites

Kir-hareseth

MOAB

Capital
Philistine incursions
Saul's campaigns

AMALEK

EDOM

0		25		50 km
0	10	20		30 miles

1397

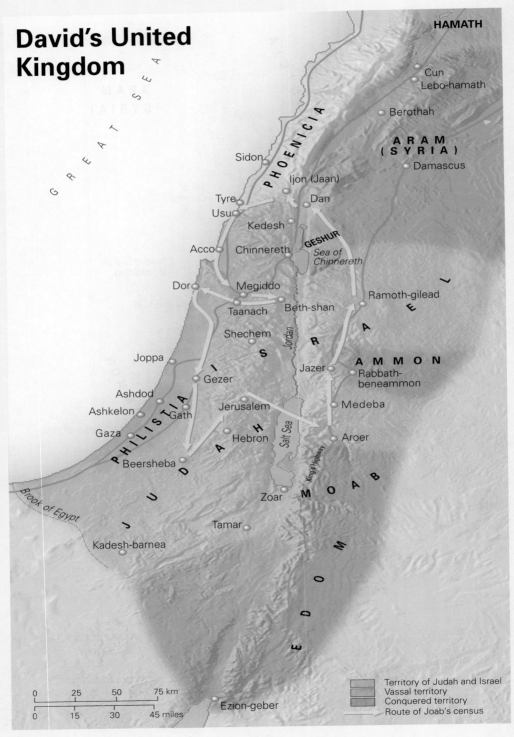

David's United Kingdom

HAMATH

Cun
Lebo-hamath

Berothah

**A R A M
(S Y R I A)**
Damascus

GREAT SEA

PHOENICIA

Sidon

Ijon (Jaan)

Tyre
Usu

Dan

Kedesh

GESHUR
*Sea of
Chinnereth*

Acco

Chinnereth

Dor

Megiddo

Taanach

Beth-shan

Ramoth-gilead

Shechem

I S R A E L

Jordan

Joppa

Gezer

Jazer

AMMON

Rabbath-
beneammon

Ashdod

Ashkelon

Gath

Jerusalem

Medeba

Gaza

PHILISTIA

J U D A H

Hebron

Salt Sea

Aroer

Beersheba

King's Highway

M O A B

Zoar

Brook of Egypt

J

Tamar

Kadesh-barnea

E D O M

	Territory of Judah and Israel
	Vassal territory
	Conquered territory
	Route of Joab's census

0   25   50   75 km

0   15   30   45 miles

Ezion-geber

1398

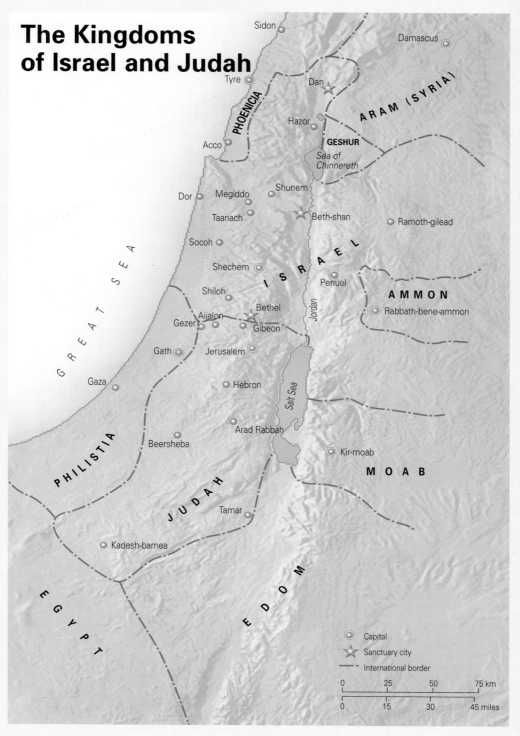

The Kingdoms of Israel and Judah

Sidon

Damascus

Tyre

Dan

PHOENICIA

ARAM (SYRIA)

Hazor

GESHUR

Acco

Sea of Chinnereth

Dor

Megiddo

Shunem

Taanach

Beth-shan

Ramoth-gilead

Socoh

Shechem

I S R A E L

Shiloh

Penuel

AMMON

Aijalon

Bethel

Gezer

Gibeon

Jordan

Rabbath-bene-ammon

Gath

Jerusalem

G R E A T   S E A

Gaza

Hebron

Salt Sea

Arad Rabbah

Beersheba

Kir-moab

M O A B

PHILISTIA

J U D A H

Tamar

Kadesh-barnea

E G Y P T

E D O M

	Capital
	Sanctuary city
	International border

| 0 | 25 | 50 | 75 km |

| 0 | 15 | 30 | 45 miles |

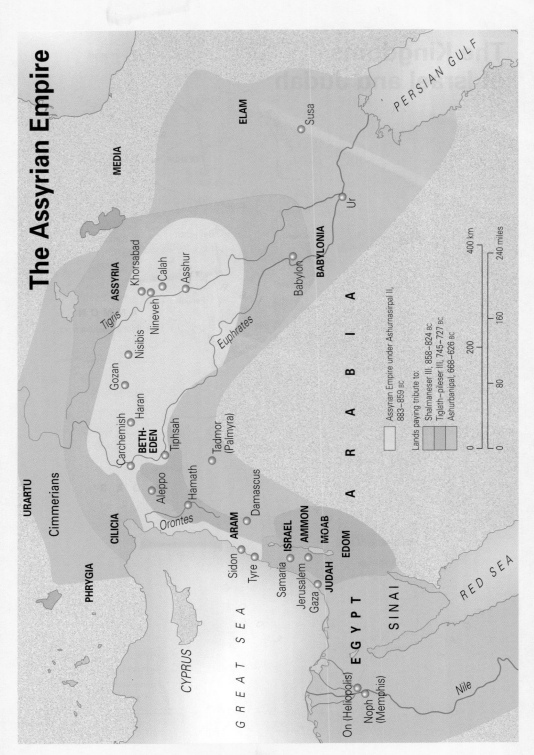

The Assyrian Empire

PERSIAN GULF

ELAM

MEDIA

Susa

ASSYRIA

Khorsabad
Calah
Asshur

Ur

Nineveh
Nisibis

BABYLONIA

Gozan

Babylon

Tigris

Euphrates

Haran

Carchemish

BETH-
EDEN

Tiphsah

Tadmor
(Palmyra)

URARTU

Cimmerians

Aleppo
Hamath

Damascus

A R A B I A

CILICIA

Orontes

ARAM

PHRYGIA

Sidon

ISRAEL
AMMON

Tyre

MOAB

Samaria

EDOM

Jerusalem
Gaza

JUDAH

E G Y P T

SINAI

CYPRUS

G R E A T   S E A

RED SEA

On (Heliopolis)

Noph
(Memphis)

Nile

Assyrian Empire under Ashurnasirpal II,
883–859 BC

Lands paying tribute to:

Shalmaneser III, 853–824 BC
Tiglath–pileser III, 745–727 BC
Ashurbanipal, 668–626 BC

0   80   160   200   400 km
0   80   160   240 miles

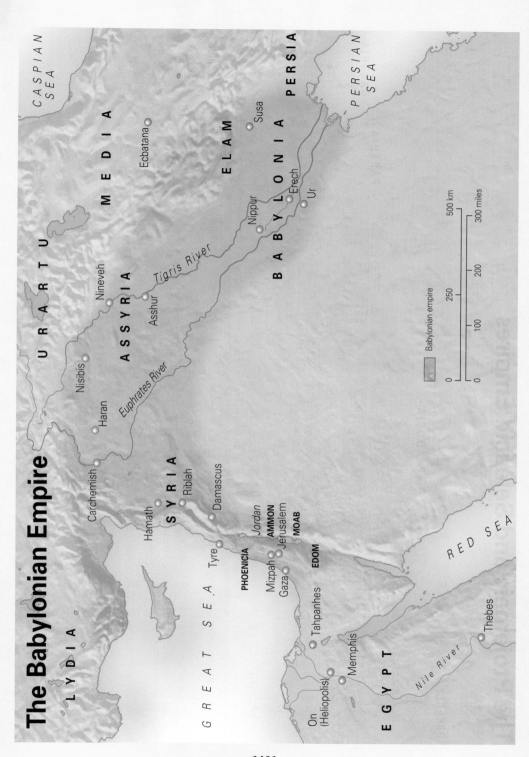

The Babylonian Empire

CASPIAN SEA

LYDIA

U R A R T U

M E D I A

Ecbatana

PERSIAN SEA

E L A M

Susa

P E R S I A

Nisibis

Nineveh

A S S Y R I A

Asshur

Tigris River

Nippur

B A B Y L O N I A

Erech

Ur

Haran

Euphrates River

Carchemish

S Y R I A

Riblah

Hamath

Damascus

Jordan

AMMON

Tyre

PHOENICIA

Mizpah

Jerusalem

MOAB

Gaza

EDOM

G R E A T   S E A

Tahpanhes

On
(Heliopolis)

Memphis

E G Y P T

Nile River

Thebes

RED SEA

Babylonian empire

500 km

300 miles

250

200

100

0

0

The Ptolemaic and Seleucid Empires

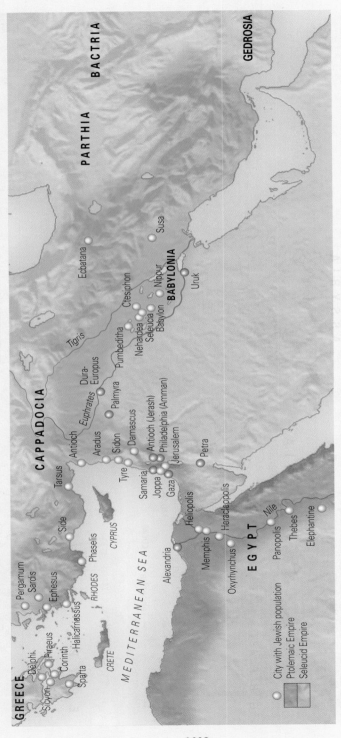

The Hasmonean Kingdom

M E D I T E R R A N E A N   S E A

Tyre

Antiochia

PHOENICIA

Gischala

Seleucia

Ptolemais

Sea of Galilee

Gabara

Hippos

Geba

Sepphoris

Abila

Dium

Mount Tabor△

Philoteria

Dora

GALILEE

Gadara

GILEAD

Strato's Tower

Scythopolis

Pella

SAMARIA

Gerasa

Apollonia

Samaria

Jordan

Mount Gerizim△

Shechem

Joppa

Arimathea

PEREA

Lydda

Philadelphia

Jamnia

JUDEA

Jericho

Emmaus

Azotus

Jerusalem

Samaga

Ascalon

Medeba

Anthedon

Marisa

Beth-zur

Dead Sea

Gaza

Hebron

Orda

Gerar

IDUMEA

En-gedi

MOAB

Raphia

Beersheba

Malatha

Rhinocorura

NABATAEA

Zoar

Independent Judea after Jonathan's campaigns, 142 BC
Land conquered by Simon, 142-135 BC
John Hyrcanus I, 128-104 BC
Aristobulus I, 104-103 BC
Alexander Jannaeus, 103-76 BC
Boundary of Hasmonean kingdom, 76 BC
Hellenistic city

0   25   50 km

0   10   20   30 miles

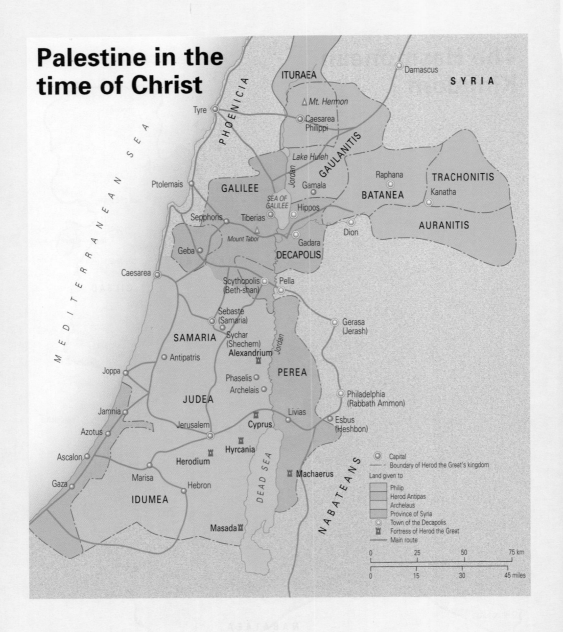

Palestine in the time of Christ

MEDITERRANEAN SEA

PHOENICIA

Tyre

Ptolemais

GALILEE

Sepphoris
Tiberias

SEA OF
GALILEE

Mount Tabor

Geba

Caesarea

Scythopolis
(Beth-shan)

Sebaste
(Samaria)

SAMARIA

Sychar
(Shechem)

Antipatris

Alexandrium

Joppa

Phaselis
Archelais

PEREA

JUDEA

Jamnia

Livias

Azotus

Jerusalem

Cyprus

Ascalon

Hyrcania

Herodium

Marisa

Gaza

Hebron

IDUMEA

Masada

DEAD SEA

ITURAEA

△ Mt. Hermon

Caesarea
Philippi

Lake Huleh

Jordan

GAULANITIS

Gamala

Hippos

Gadara

DECAPOLIS

Pella

Jordan

Gerasa
(Jerash)

Philadelphia
(Rabbath Ammon)

Esbus
(Heshbon)

Machaerus

NABATEANS

Damascus

SYRIA

Raphana

TRACHONITIS

Kanatha

BATANEA

Dion

AURANITIS

Capital

Boundary of Herod the Great's kingdom

Land given to
Philip
Herod Antipas
Archelaus
Province of Syria

Town of the Decapolis

Fortress of Herod the Great

Main route

0	25	50	75 km

0	15	30	45 miles

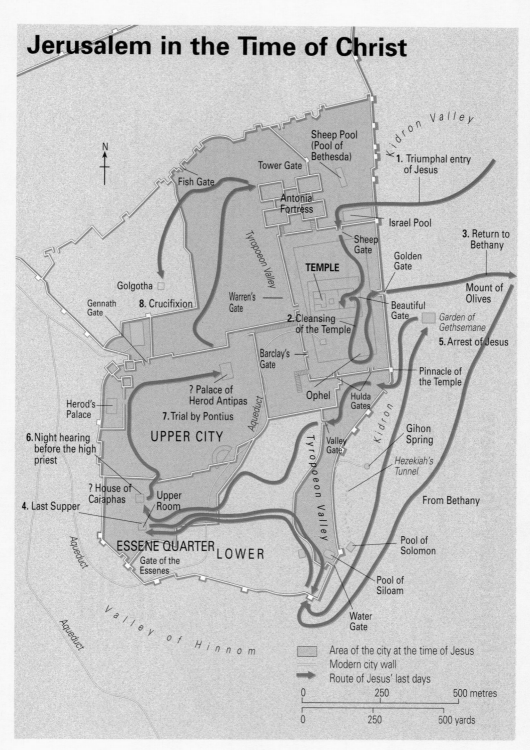

Jerusalem in the Time of Christ

N

Fish Gate

Tower Gate

Sheep Pool
(Pool of
Bethesda)

Antonia
Fortress

1. Triumphal entry
of Jesus

Kidron Valley

Israel Pool

3. Return to
Bethany

Sheep
Gate

Golden
Gate

Tyropoeon Valley

TEMPLE

Golgotha

Warren's
Gate

Mount of
Olives

Gennath
Gate

8. Crucifixion

Beautiful
Gate

2. Cleansing
of the Temple

Garden of
Gethsemane

5. Arrest of Jesus

Barclay's
Gate

Ophel

Hulda
Gates

Pinnacle of
the Temple

? Palace of
Herod Antipas

Herod's
Palace

7. Trial by Pontius

Aqueduct

Kidron

Gihon
Spring

6. Night hearing
before the high
priest

UPPER CITY

Valley
Gate

Hezekiah's
Tunnel

Tyropoeon Valley

? House of
Caiaphas

Upper
Room

From Bethany

4. Last Supper

Aqueduct

ESSENE QUARTER LOWER

Gate of the
Essenes

Pool of
Solomon

Valley of Hinnom

Pool of
Siloam

Aqueduct

Water
Gate

Aqueduct

	Area of the city at the time of Jesus
	Modern city wall
→	Route of Jesus' last days

0   250   500 metres

0   250   500 yards

Paul's Missionary Journeys

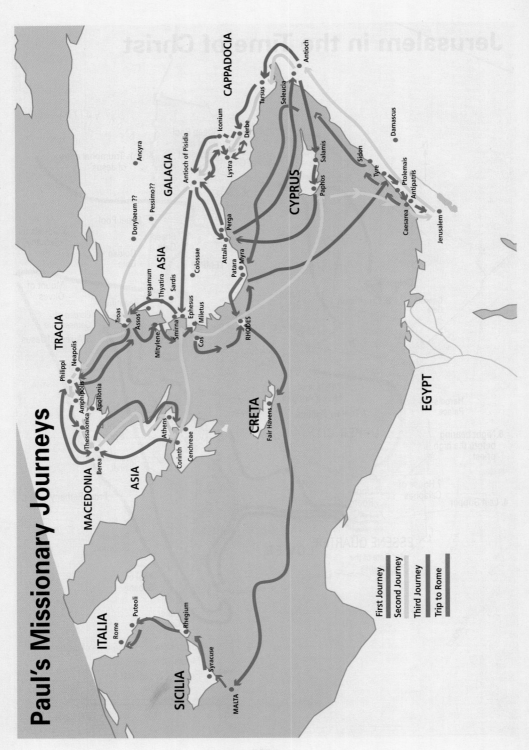

ITALIA
Rome
Puteoli
Rhegium
SICILIA
Syracuse
MALTA

MACEDONIA
Berea
Thessalonica
Amphipolis
Apollonia
Philippi
Neapolis
TRACIA
Athens
Corinth
Cenchreae
ASIA

CRETA
Fair Havens

Troas
Assos
Mitylene
Pergamum
Thyatira
Sardis
Smirna
Ephesus
Miletus
Cos
RHODES
ASIA
Colossae
Attalia
Patara
Myra
Perga

GALACIA
Antioch of Pisidia
Iconium
Lystra
Derbe
Dorylaeum ??
Pessimo??
Ancyra

CAPPADOCIA
Tarsus
Seleucia
Antioch

CYPRUS
Salamis
Paphos

Damascus
Sidon
Tyre
Ptolemais
Antipatris
Caesarea
Jerusalem

EGYPT

Legend:
First Journey
Second Journey
Third Journey
Trip to Rome

The Spread of Christianity

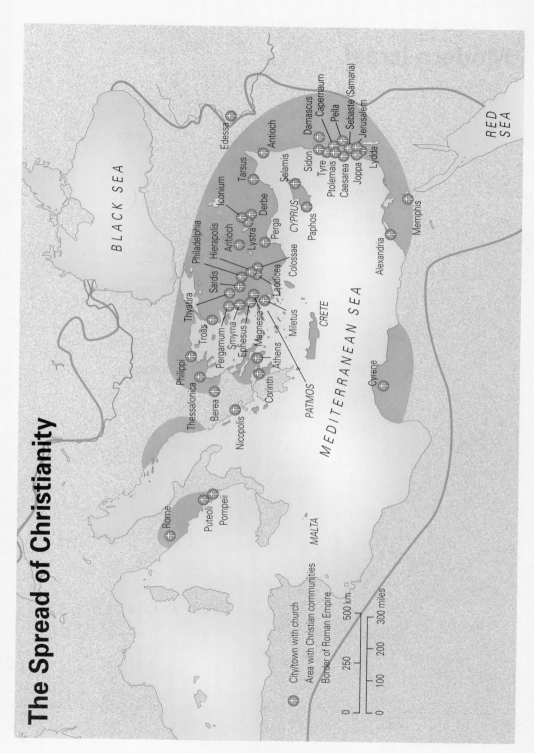

BLACK SEA

RED SEA

MEDITERRANEAN SEA

Edessa
Antioch
Tarsus
Iconium
Antioch
Derbe
Lystra
Perga
Hierapolis
Philadelphia
Sardis
Laodicea
Colossae
Thyatira
Pergamum
Smyrna
Magnesia
Troas
Ephesus
Miletus
Athens
Corinth
Philippi
Thessalonica
Berea
Nicopolis

Damascus
Capernaum
Pella
Sebaste (Samaria)
Jerusalem
Sidon
Tyre
Ptolemais
Caesarea
Joppa
Lydda

Salamis
CYPRUS
Paphos

Memphis
Alexandria
Cyrene

CRETE
PATMOS
MALTA

Rome
Puteoli
Pompeii

⊕ City/town with church
Area with Christian communities
Border of Roman Empire

500 km
250
0

300 miles
200
100
0

1407

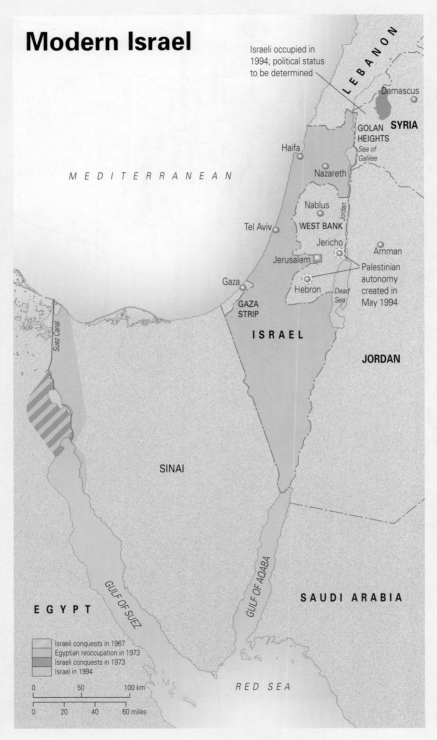

Modern Israel

Israeli occupied in 1994; political status to be determined

LEBANON

Damascus

SYRIA

GOLAN
HEIGHTS

*Sea of
Galilee*

Haifa

M E D I T E R R A N E A N

Nazareth

Nablus

Jordan

WEST BANK

Tel Aviv

Jericho

Amman

Jerusalem

Palestinian
autonomy
created in
May 1994

Gaza

Hebron

*Dead
Sea*

GAZA
STRIP

I S R A E L

JORDAN

SINAI

Suez Canal

GULF OF SUEZ

GULF OF AQABA

SAUDI ARABIA

EGYPT

Israeli conquests in 1967
Egyptian reoccupation in 1973
Israeli conquests in 1973
Israel in 1994

| 0 | 50 | 100 km |
| 0 | 20 | 40 | 60 miles |

RED SEA